CONTENTS

CONTACT TELEPHONE NUMBERS

Nationwide Rail Times
TELEPHONE
Traveline

03457 48 49 50
24 Hours Daily

Nationwide Bus Times
TELEPHONE
Traveline
0871 200 22 33

Timetable and fares available at:
www.nationalrail.co.uk

National Rail Enquiries provides up-to-the-minute advice on all aspects of journey planning, fares and buying tickets, live train running updates and other useful information.

WEEKENDS

Normal services are shown herein, but some dates are missing. These are days on which engineering work demands a timetable revision. For details telephone: 03457 484950 or go to *www.nationalrail.co.uk/engineering*

Cover picture: Ex-LNER class B1 2-6-0 no. 61264 climbs west away from Retford and crosses over the Retford to Worksop line, with the 'Lincolnshire Poacher' railtour on 1st April 2006. The train ran from Kings Cross to Cleethorpes. It will shortly start to descend and join the Worksop line at Thrumpton West Junction, formerly known as Whisker Hill Junction. This is reproduced from one of the latest Middleton Press albums, Gainsborough to Sheffield. *(R.J.Stewart-Smith)*

Published by

MP Middleton Press

Easebourne Lane
Midhurst, West Sussex, GU29 9AZ
Tel: 01730 813169
info@middletonpress.co.uk www.middletonpress.co.uk

ISBN 978 1 910356-20-3

Printed and bound by CPI Group (UK) Ltd, Croydon, CR0 4YY

References and Symbols used in this Timetable

Date and Time Symbols

- **a** Arrival time
- **d** Departure time
- **p** Previous night
- **s** Stops to set down only
- **u** Stops to pick up only
- **x** Stops on request.

- **M** Monday
- **T** Tuesday
- **W** Wednesday
- **Th** Thursday
- **F** Friday
- **S** Saturday
- **Su** Sunday
- Adding **'O'** to the abbreviation for the day or days (eg **WO**) means the train runs **only** on the day or days preceding the **'O'**
- Adding **'X'** to the abbreviation for the day or days (eg **FX**) means the train runs on all the days in this section of the Timetable **except** the day or days preceding the **'X'**

⟆ Wavy Line between train times indicates that this train does **not** run during the full period of the Timetable on which the train is shown

BHX Does not run on designated Bank Holidays

↳ Train continued in a later column

↤ Train continued from an earlier column

Station Symbols

⊖ Stations having interchange with London Underground services

10 Figure in box indicates the minimum Interchange Time in minutes to allow between trains at this station; example shows 10 minutes—see also **Connections** page

✈ Airport Link – station for interchange. See also Airport Links pages

Tram/Metro Interchange

Train Numbers

On certain tables, route codes are shown as part of the column heading information. These codes correspond with numbers that will be displayed on trains which are equipped to display such information.

Train Symbols

Catering Symbols

Services are available for First and Standard Class ticket holders, for all or part of the journey, unless otherwise shown.

Alterations may apply at Bank Holiday periods. See the directory of Train Operators for further information and availability of complimentary refreshments.

⊠ Complimentary restaurant or full meal service where available, consisting of breakfast, light lunch or evening meal served at seat for First Class ticket holders only. Also a counter buffet service of hot and cold snacks, sandwiches, hot/cold drinks is available to all passengers for the sale of refreshments, for all or part of the journey, unless otherwise shown.

✕ A Restaurant (table) service (for First Class ticket holders, also Standard Class ticket holders if accommodation is available), and a buffet service of hot and cold snacks, sandwiches, hot/cold drinks is available for the sale of refreshments, for all or part of the journey, unless otherwise shown.

⊘ A service of hot light meals to order and also a buffet service of snacks, sandwiches, hot/cold drinks is available for the sale of refreshments, for all or part of the journey, unless otherwise shown.

☕ A counter buffet service of hot and cold snacks, sandwiches, hot/cold drinks is available to all passengers for the sale of refreshments, for all or part of the journey, unless otherwise shown.

An at-seat trolley service of cold snacks, sandwiches and hot and cold drinks is available for the sale of refreshments, for all or part of the journey, unless otherwise shown.

Other Symbols

R Seat Reservations recommended.

R Seat Reservations compulsory.

◇ Seat Reservations available.

1 First Class accommodation.

Train Operator Codes

AR	Alliance Rail
AW	Arriva Trains Wales
CC	c2c
CH	Chiltern Railways
CS	Serco Caledonian Sleeper
EM	East Midlands
GC	Grand Central
GN	Govia Thameslink Railway (Great Northern)
GR	Virgin Trains East Coast
GW	Great Western Railway

GX	Gatwick Express
HT	Hull Trains
HX	Heathrow Express
IL	Island Line
LE	Abellio Greater Anglia
LM	West Midlands Trains (run both the London North Western and the West Midlands Railway franchises)
LO	Transport for London
ME	Merseyrail
NT	Northern Rail

NY	North Yorkshire Moors Railway
SE	South Eastern Trains
SN	Southern
SR	Scotrail
SW	South Western Railway
TL	Govia Thameslink Railway
TP	First TransPennine Express
VT	Virgin West Coast
WR	West Coast Railway
XC	Cross Country
XR	Crossrail

FOREWORD

Notable in this issue is the introduction of some electric trains to and from Blackpool. Also, Maghull North is due to open on 18th June 2018 and Kenilworth station opened on 30th April 2018.

The May 2018 timetable contains the most significant changes to take place in recent years. Notable alterations are included below:

-The introduction of 18 trains per hour on the Thameslink Core, regularly linking stations to Cambridge and Peterborough to the Thameslink network for the first time. Major changes to Southeastern services to accommodate this. Also, changes to East Midlands Trains' Midland Main Line services to accommodate this.

-A completely new timetable for Southern, with every train changing times. Associated changes will also be made to Gatwick Express services.

-Improvements to journey times and the introduction of six trains per hour between Leeds and Manchester on the TransPennine Express services.

Please also note, Network Rail have stated that further updates to the following tables are possible during the validity period: 026, 071, 115, 131, 165, 172, 175, 176, 179, 180, 196, 200 and 201.

The Swanage Railway is receiving three through trains from Southwestern Railway each Saturday from 26th May to 8th September, all terminating at Corfe Castle; the first regular through service for 46 years. Timings were too late for inclusion herein.

A large (A1) *National Rail Passenger Network Diagram* is available from us (please see page 21). We apologise, again, for the late delivery of the *Rail Times*, due to delays in the data supply chain. The fortnightly journal *RAIL* contains the most detailed study of timetable issues and Barry Doe is its specialist contributor. We must all be grateful to him for his efforts.

Owing to the number of emergency cancellations and diversions, we always recommend confirming train times by visiting *www.nationalrail.co.uk* or telephoning **03457 484950**.

Vic Bradshaw-Mitchell
Middleton Press

Feedback or complaint about National Rail Enquiries?
Email: customer.relations@nationalrail.co.uk
Phone: 0800 022 3720 (Open Monday to Friday 09:00 to 17:00 except Christmas Day)
Customer Relations Team, Suite 410, 1 Northumberland Avenue,
Trafalgar Square, London WC2N 5BW

These contact details are only for those wishing to comment on National Rail Enquiries. Comments, complaints and feedback about delays, refunds and claims, train journeys, stations or ticket offices should be sent to the appropriate Train Operating Company or station operator.

TIMETABLES COMPILED BY NETWORK RAIL:

YOUR FEEDBACK IS VALUABLE

If you have any comments on these timetables or feedback on how you feel they could be improved, please contact the Network Rail Publications Manager by writing to:
Planning Publication, Network Rail, The Quadrant: MK, Elder Gate, Milton Keynes, MK9 1EN
Or e-mail: NRT-WTT@networkrail.co.uk

Heritage Railways

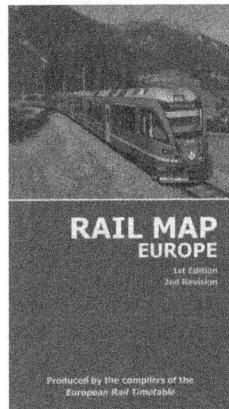

EUROSTAR

LONDON - LILLE - PARIS and BRUSSELS *by Eurostar*

Minimum check-in time is 30 minutes, but passengers are advised to allow longer due to immigration procedures. Not available for London - Ebbsfleet - Ashford or v.v. Special fares payable that include three classes of service: business premier, standard premier and standard. All times shown are local times (France and Belgium are one hour ahead of Great Britain). All Eurostar services are Ⓡ, non-smoking and convey ✕ in Business Premier and Standard Premier, 🍸 in Standard.

Service May 27 - July 28

km	km	*train number*	9080	9108	9002	9110	9110	9004	9006	9008	9008	9010	9114	9116	9116	9116	9014	9018	9018	9128	9020	9022	9060	9024	9132	9028	
		notes	①–⑤	①⑤	⑥	②③④	⑥	①–⑤	①–⑥	⑥	①–⑤	⑦	①–⑥	②③④	①⑤	⑥⑦			⑧		⑥		①				
		notes	j	j				j	j				A		j	g		B	e		C	b					
0	0	**London** St Pancras......... d.	0540	0613	0618	0647	0657	0701	0731	0752	0755	0819	0831	0854	0854	0858	0922	1014	1024	1058	1101	1131	1201	1224	1258	1331	...
35	35	Ebbsfleet International ..... d.	0558	0630		0707				0812	0812	0838		0912	0912	0915		1034	1042	1115				1242	1315		...
90	90	Ashford International........ d.	0624	0652	0655	0728	0728										0955e										...
166	166	Calais Fréthun................ a.				0859									1056	1059									1459		...
267	267	Lille Europe..................... a.				0930	0926							1123	1127	1130				1326					1530		...
	373	**Brussels** Midi/Zuid ..... a.		0922		1007	1005						1119	1202	1205	1208				1405					1607		...
492		**Paris** Nord .... a.	0917	...	0947	...	...	1017	1047	1117	1117	1147	...	...	...	...	1247	1347	1347	...	1417	1447	1517	1547	...	1647	...

train number	9030	9136	9032	9140	9036	9038	9040	9042	9150	9044	9148	9152	9046	9152	9048	9050	9158	9054	9056	
notes	⑤⑦	⑦				①⑤⑦		⑧	⑥	⑥	⑧	⑦	①–⑤	①–⑤	⑧	⑤⑥⑦			⑦	
notes	g	g									A	g	j	j	k	bg				
London St Pancras.......... d.	1401	1404	1422	1504	1531	1601	1631	1701	1704	1731	1731	1755	1801	1804	1831	1901	1934	2001	2031	...
Ebbsfleet International ...... d.																				...
Ashford International......... d.			1455e									1828e								...
Calais Fréthun.................. a.																	2129			...
Lille Europe...................... a.		1626		1726				298|	1926			2026		2026			2200			...
Brussels Midi/Zuid....... a.		1705		1805					2005		2019	2105		2105			2238			...
Paris Nord....................... a.	1717	...	1747	...	1847	1917	1947	2020	...	2047	...	...	2117	...	2147	2217	...	2317	2347	...

train number	9109	9005	9007	9113	9009	9011	9117	9013	9015	9019	9121	9021	9023	9131	9025	9027	9133	9031	9033	9035	9037	9141	9141	9039	9145	9043	
notes	①	①	①–⑥	①–⑥	①–⑤	⑥⑦					①–⑥	⑤⑦	①–⑥	⑦	⑦		①–⑥		⑦	⑥	①⑤⑦	⑦	①–⑥		⑦		
notes	j	j	j	j	j	g		j				g	j			b	j					g	j		g		
Paris Nord....................... d.	...	0643	0713	...	0743	0813	...	0843	0913	1013	...	1043	1113	...	1139	1213	...	1313	1340	1413	1443	...	...	1513	...	1613	...
Brussels Midi/Zuid....... d.	0656			0756			0852				1056			1156			1252					1452	1456		1556		...
Lille Europe...................... d.	0735			0835			0930							1235			1330					1530	1535		1635		...
Calais Fréthun.................. d.							1001										1401					1601					...
Ashford International......... a.													1207		1237e									1607e			...
Ebbsfleet International ...... a.									1018			1148					1345	1418		1518		1545	1545			1718	...
London St Pancras.......... a.	0759	0802	0832	0857	0900	0930	0957	1000	1039	1130	1157	1209	1239	1257	1309	1330	1405	1439	1500	1539	1602	1605	1605	1640	1657	1739	...

train number	9045	9149	9047	9153	9049	9051	9159	9157	9053	9055	9161	9163	9067	9059	9165	9061	9063	
notes	⑦		①–⑥	⑧	⑦	⑧	⑦	①–⑤	①–⑤		⑦	①⑤	⑦	①–⑥	②③④	⑦	⑧	
notes	h g		j e		h				j				g	j		w		
Paris Nord....................... d.	1643	...	1713	...	1740	1813	...	...	1843	1913	...	...	1943	2013	...	2043	2113	...
Brussels Midi/Zuid....... d.		1656		1756			1852	1856			1952	1952			2022			...
Lille Europe...................... d.		1736		1835			1930					2030			2100			...
Calais Fréthun.................. d.							2001					2101			2131			...
Ashford International......... a.		1734e											2037e	2107e				...
Ebbsfleet International ...... a.				1845		1918	1945			2018		2045			2115		2218	...
London St Pancras.......... a.	1800	1806	1832	1903	1906	1939	2003	1957	2004	2039	2057	2103	2109	2139	2139	2200	2239	...

A – To Amsterdam, see Table **18**.
B – June 17.
C – July 21.
b – Not July 21.
e – Not June 17.
g – Also May 28.
h – Not May 27.
j – Not May 28.
k – Also July 21.
w – Also May 28; not May 27.

Service July 29 - Sept. 1. For service May 27 - July 28 see above. For service from Sept. 2 see next page.

km	km	*train number*	9108	9002	9110	9110	9004	9006	9008	9008	9010	9114	9116	9116	9116	9014	9018	9128	9022	9024	9132	9028	9030	9136	9032	9140	
		notes	①⑤	⑥	②③④	⑥	①–⑤	①–⑥	⑥	①–⑤	⑦	①–⑥	②③④	①⑤	⑥⑦		⑧		①⑤				⑤	⑦			
		notes	j				t	j	k	j		A		j	k				⑥⑦				k	k			
0	0	**London** St Pancras......... d.	0613	0618	0647	0657	0701	0728	0752	0755	0819	0831	0854	0854	0854	0922	1024	1058	1131	1224	1258	1331	1401	1404	1422	1504	...
35	35	Ebbsfleet International ..... d.	0630		0704				0812	0812	0838		0912	0912	0915		1042	1115		1242	1315						...
90	90	Ashford International........ d.	0652	0655	0728	0728										0955									1455		...
166	166	Calais Fréthun................ a.			0859									1056	1059						1459						...
267	267	Lille Europe..................... a.			0930	0926							1123	1127	1130			1326			1530			1626		1726	...
	373	**Brussels** Midi/Zuid ..... a.	0922		1007	1005						1119	1202	1205	1208			1405			1608			1705		1805	...
492		**Paris** Nord .... a.	...	0947	...	...	1017	1056	1117	1117	1147	...	...	...	...	1247	1347	...	1447	1547	...	1647	1717	...	1747	...	...

train number	9036	9038	9040	9042	9150	9044	9148	9152	9046	9152	9048	9050	9158	9054	9056	
notes		⑤⑦		⑧	⑥	⑥	⑧	⑦	①–⑤	①–⑤	①⑤⑦				⑦	
notes		k					A	k	j	j	k				k	
London St Pancras.......... d.	1531	1601	1631	1701	1704	1731	1731	1755	1801	1804	1831	1901	1934	2001	2031	...
Ebbsfleet International ...... d.																...
Ashford International......... d.								1828								...
Calais Fréthun.................. a.													2129			...
Lille Europe...................... a.					1926			2026		2026			2200			...
Brussels Midi/Zuid....... a.					2005		2019	2105		2105			2238			...
Paris Nord....................... a.	1847	1917	1947	2020	...	2047	...	...	2117	...	2147	2217	...	2317	2347	...

train number	9109	9007	9113	9009	9011	9117	9013	9015	9019	9021	9023	9131	9025	9027	9133	9031	9033	9035	9037	9141	9141	9039	9145	9043	9045	9149	
notes	①	①–⑥	①–⑥	①–⑤	⑥⑦		①			⑤	①–⑥	⑦	⑦	①⑤	①–⑥		⑦	⑥	①⑤⑦	⑦	①–⑥		⑦		⑦		
notes	j	t	j	j	k		j			k	j		k	⑥⑦	j					k	j		k		h		
Paris Nord....................... d.	...	0708	...	0737	0808	...	0838	0910	1010	1040	1110	...	1139	1211	...	1309	1337	1411	1440	...	...	1510	...	1610	1640	...	...
Brussels Midi/Zuid....... d.	0656		0756			0852						1156			1252					1452	1456		1556			1656	...
Lille Europe...................... d.	0735		0835			0930						1235			1330					1530	1535		1635			1736	...
Calais Fréthun.................. d.						1001									1401					1601							...
Ashford International......... a.											1207		1238									1607				1734	...
Ebbsfleet International ...... a.								1018		1148					1345	1418		1518		1545	1545			1718			...
London St Pancras.......... a.	0759	0832	0857	0900	0930	0957	1000	1040	1130	1209	1239	1257	1309	1330	1405	1439	1500	1539	1602	1605	1605	1640	1657	1739	1800	1806	...

train number	9047	9153	9049	9051	9159	9157	9053	9055	9161	9163	9067	9059	9165	9061	9063	
notes	①–⑥	⑧	⑦	⑧	⑦	①–⑤	②③		⑦	①⑤⑥	⑦	①–⑥	②③④	⑦	⑧	
notes	j		k				④⑤				k	j		h		
Paris Nord....................... d.	1708	...	1740	1806	...	...	1838	1913	...	...	1941	2010	...	2041	2111	...
Brussels Midi/Zuid....... d.		1756			1852	1856			1952	1952			2022			...
Lille Europe...................... d.		1835			1930					2030			2100			...
Calais Fréthun.................. d.					2000					2101						...
Ashford International......... a.											2037	2107				...
Ebbsfleet International ...... a.		1845		1918	1945			2018		2045			2115		2218	...
London St Pancras.......... a	1832	1903	1906	1939	2003	1957	2002	2039	2057	2103	2109	2139	2133	2200	2239	...

A – To Amsterdam, see Table **18**.
h – Also Aug. 27; not Aug. 26.
j – Not Aug. 27.
k – Also Aug. 27.
t – Not Aug. 15, 27.

LONDON - LILLE - PARIS and BRUSSELS *by Eurostar*

Minimum check-in time is 30 minutes, but passengers are advised to allow longer due to immigration procedures. Not available for London - Ebbsfleet - Ashford or v.v. Special fares payable that include three classes of service: business premier, standard premier and standard. All times shown are local times (France and Belgium are one hour ahead of Great Britain). All Eurostar services are 🅁, non-smoking and convey ✕ in Business Premier and Standard Premier, 🍸 in Standard.

Service Sept. 2 - Nov. 3. For service until Sept. 1 see previous page. For service from Nov. 4 see below.

km	km	*train number*	**9080**	**9108**	**9002**	**9110**	**9110**	**9004**	**9006**	**9008**	**9008**	**9010**	**9114**	**9116**	**9116**	**9116**	**9014**	**9018**	**9128**	**9020**	**9022**	**9024**	**9132**	**9028**	**9032**	**9140**
		notes	①–⑤		⑥	①–⑤	⑥	①–⑤	①⑤⑥	⑥	①–⑤	⑦	①–⑥	①–⑤		⑥⑦					⑤⑥⑦					
		notes	**h**	**B**		**E**							**A**	**G**	**B**			**b**		**C**	**b**					
0	*0*	**London** St Pancras .... d.	0540	0613	0618	0647	0657	0701	0728	0752	0755	0819	0831	0854	0854	0858	0922	1024	1058	1101	1131	1224	1258	1331	1422	1504
35	*35*	Ebbsfleet International ..... d.	0558	0630	|	0704	|	|	|	0812	0812	0838	|	0912	0915	0915	|	1042	1115	|	|	1242	1315	|	|	|
90	*90*	Ashford International .... d.	0624	0655	0655	0728	0728	|	|	|	|	|	|	|	|	|	0955	|	|	|	|	|	|	|	1455	|
166	*166*	Calais Fréthun .... a.	|	|	|	0859	|	|	|	|	|	|	|	|	1056	1059	|	|	|	|	|	|	1459	|	|	|
267	*267*	Lille Europe .... a.	|	0849	|	0930	0926	|	|	|	|	|	|	1123	1127	1130	|	|	1326	|	|	|	1530	|	|	1726
	373	**Brussels** Midi / Zuid ..... a.	|	0922	|	1007	1005	|	|	|	|	|	1119	1202	1205	1208	|	|	1405	|	|	|	1607	|	|	1805
492		**Paris** Nord .... a.	0917	...	0947	...	...	1017	1056	1117	1117	1147	...	...	...	...	1247	1347	...	1417	1447	1547	...	1647	1747	...

train number	**9036**	**9038**	**9040**	**9042**	**9150**	**9044**	**9148**	**9152**	**9046**	**9152**	**9048**	**9050**	**9158**	**9054**	**9056**
notes		⑤⑦		Ⓑ	⑥	⑥	Ⓑ	⑦	①–⑤	①–⑤	⑤⑦				⑦
notes							**A**				**k**	**b**			
London St Pancras .... d.	1531	1601	1631	1701	1704	1731	1731	1755	1801	1804	1831	1901	1934	2001	2031
Ebbsfleet International ...... d.	|	|	|	|	|	|	|	|	|	|	|	|	|	|	|
Ashford International .... d.	|	|	|	|	|	|	|	1828	|	|	|	|	|	|	|
Calais Fréthun .... a.	|	|	|	|	|	|	|	|	|	|	|	|	2129	|	|
Lille Europe .... a.	|	|	|	|	1926	|	|	2026	|	2026	|	|	2200	|	|
Brussels Midi / Zuid .... a.	|	|	|	|	2005	|	2019	2105	|	2105	|	|	2238	|	|
Paris Nord .... a.	1847	1917	1947	2020	...	2047	...	...	2117	...	2147	2217	...	2317	2347

train number	**9109**	**9005**	**9007**	**9113**	**9009**	**9011**	**9117**	**9013**	**9015**	**9019**	**9121**	**9023**	**9131**	**9027**	**9133**	**9031**	**9035**	**9037**	**9141**	**9141**	**9039**	**9043**	**9045**	**9149**	**9047**	**9153**
notes	①	①	①–⑥	①–⑥	①–⑤	⑥⑦		①–⑤			①–⑥		⑦	⑤⑥⑦	①–⑥		⑥⑦	⑤	⑦	①–⑥			⑦			Ⓑ
notes			**h**	**h**										**b**												
Paris Nord .... d.	...	0643	0713	...	0743	0813	...	0843	0913	1013	...	1113	...	1213	...	1313	1413	1443	...	...	1513	1613	1643	...	1713	...
Brussels Midi / Zuid .... d.	0656	|	|	0756	|	|	0852	|	|	|	1056	|	1156	|	1252	|	|	|	1452	1456	|	|	|	1656	|	1756
Lille Europe .... d.	0735	|	|	0835	|	|	0930	|	|	|	|	|	1235	|	1330	|	|	|	1530	1535	|	|	|	1735	|	1835
Calais Fréthun .... d.	|	|	|	|	|	|	1001	|	|	|	|	|	|	|	1401	|	|	|	1601	|	|	|	|	|	|	|
Ashford International .... a.	|	|	|	|	|	|	|	|	|	|	|	1207	|	|	|	|	|	|	|	|	1607	|	|	1734	|	|
Ebbsfleet International ...... a.	|	|	|	|	|	|	|	|	1018	|	|	|	|	|	1345	1418	1518	|	1545	1545	|	1718	|	|	|	1845
London St Pancras .... a.	0759	0802	0832	0857	0900	0930	0957	1000	1039	1130	1157	1239	1257	1330	1405	1439	1539	1602	1605	1605	1640	1739	1800	1806	1832	1903

train number	**9051**	**9159**	**9157**	**9053**	**9055**	**9163**	**9161**	**9059**	**9165**	**9061**	**9063**
notes	Ⓑ	⑦	①–⑤	⑤⑦		①⑤⑥	⑦		②③④	⑦	Ⓑ
notes											
Paris Nord .... d.	1813	...	...	1843	1913	...	...	2013	...	2043	2113
Brussels Midi / Zuid .... d.	|	1852	1856	|	|	1952	1956	|	2022	|	|
Lille Europe .... d.	|	1930	1935	|	|	2030	2035	|	2100	|	|
Calais Fréthun .... d.	|	2001	|	|	|	2101	|	|	2131	|	|
Ashford International .... a.	|	|	|	|	|	|	|	2107	|	|	|
Ebbsfleet International ...... a.	1918	1945	|	|	2018	2045	|	|	2115	|	2218
London St Pancras .... a.	1939	2003	1957	2004	2039	2103	2057	2139	2133	2200	2239

A – To Amsterdam, see Table **18**.
B – Sept. 3, 7, 10, 14, 17.
C – Oct. 20.
E – ①–⑤ (not Sept. 3, 7, 10, 14, 17, Nov. 1, 2).
G – ①–⑤ (not Sept. 3, 7, 10, 14, 17).
b – Not Oct. 20.
h – Not Nov. 1, 2.
j – Not Nov. 1.
k – Also Oct. 20.

Service Nov. 4 - Dec 8. For service Sept. 2 - Nov. 3 see table above. For service until Sept. 1 see previous page.

km	km	*train number*	**9080**	**9002**	**9110**	**9110**	**9004**	**9006**	**9008**	**9008**	**9010**	**9114**	**9116**	**9116**	**9014**	**9018**	**9018**	**9128**	**9022**	**9024**	**9132**	**9028**	**9032**	**9140**	**9036**	**9038**
		notes	①–⑤	⑥	①–⑤	⑥	①–⑤	①⑤⑥	⑥	①–⑤	⑦	①–⑥	①–⑤	⑥⑦					⑤⑥⑦							⑤⑦
		notes										**A**				**w**	**e**									
0	*0*	**London** St Pancras .... d.	0540	0618	0647	0657	0701	0728	0752	0755	0819	0831	0854	0858	0924	1014	1024	1058	1131	1224	1258	1331	1422	1504	1531	1601
35	*35*	Ebbsfleet International ..... d.	0558	|	0704	|	|	|	0812	0812	0838	|	0912	0915	|	1034	1042	1115	|	1242	1315	|	|	|	|	|
90	*90*	Ashford International .... d.	0624	0655	0728	0728	|	|	|	|	|	|	|	|	0955**e**	|	|	|	|	|	|	|	1455**e**	|	|	|
166	*166*	Calais Fréthun .... a.	|	|	0859	|	|	|	|	|	|	|	|	1059	|	|	|	|	|	|	1459	|	|	|	|	|
267	*267*	Lille Europe .... a.	|	|	0930	0926	|	|	|	|	|	|	1123	1130	|	|	|	1326	|	|	1530	|	|	1726	|	|
	373	**Brussels** Midi / Zuid ..... a.	|	|	1007	1005	|	|	|	|	|	1119	1202	1208	|	|	|	1405	|	|	1607	|	|	1805	|	|
492		**Paris** Nord .... a.	0917	0947	...	...	1017	1056	1117	1117	1147	...	...	...	1247	1347	1347	...	1447	1547	...	1647	1747	...	1847	1917

train number	**9040**	**9042**	**9150**	**9044**	**9148**	**9152**	**9046**	**9152**	**9048**	**9050**	**9158**	**9054**	**9056**
notes		Ⓑ	⑥	⑥	Ⓑ	⑦	①–⑤	①–⑤	⑦	Ⓑ			⑦
notes					**A**								
London St Pancras .... d.	1631	1701	1704	1731	1731	1755	1801	1804	1831	1901	1934	2001	2031
Ebbsfleet International ...... d.	|	|	|	|	|	|	|	|	|	|	|	|	|
Ashford International .... d.	|	|	|	|	|	1828**e**	|	|	|	|	|	|	|
Calais Fréthun .... a.	|	|	|	|	|	|	|	|	|	|	2129	|	|
Lille Europe .... a.	|	|	1926	|	|	2026	|	2026	|	|	2200	|	|
Brussels Midi / Zuid .... a.	|	|	2005	|	2019	2105	|	2105	|	|	2238	|	|
Paris Nord .... a.	1947	2020	...	2047	...	...	2117	...	2147	2217	...	2317	2347

train number	**9109**	**9005**	**9007**	**9113**	**9009**	**9011**	**9117**	**9013**	**9015**	**9019**	**9121**	**9023**	**9131**	**9027**	**9133**	**9031**	**9035**	**9141**	**9141**	**9039**	**9043**	**9045**	**9149**	**9047**	**9153**	**9051**
notes	①	①	①–⑥	①–⑥	①–⑤	⑥⑦		①–⑤		⑤	①–⑥		⑦	⑤⑥⑦	①–⑥		⑥⑦	⑦	①–⑥		Ⓑ	⑦			Ⓑ	Ⓑ
notes																										
Paris Nord .... d.	...	0643	0713	...	0743	0813	...	0843	0913	1013	...	1113	...	1213	...	1313	1413	...	...	1513	1613	1643	...	1713	...	1813
Brussels Midi / Zuid .... d.	0656	|	|	0756	|	|	0852	|	|	|	1056	|	1156	|	1252	|	|	1452	1456	|	|	|	1656	|	1756	|
Lille Europe .... d.	0735	|	|	0835	|	|	0930	|	|	|	|	|	1235	|	1330	|	|	1530	1535	|	|	|	1735	|	1835	|
Calais Fréthun .... d.	|	|	|	|	|	|	1001	|	|	|	|	|	|	|	1401	|	|	1601	|	|	|	|	|	|	|	|
Ashford International .... a.	|	|	|	|	|	|	|	|	|	|	|	1207**e**	|	|	|	|	|	|	|	1607**e**	|	|	1734**e**	|	|	|
Ebbsfleet International ...... a.	|	|	|	|	|	|	|	|	1018	|	|	|	|	|	1345	1418	1518	1545	1545	|	1718	|	|	|	1845	1918
London St Pancras .... a.	0759	0802	0832	0857	0900	0930	0957	1000	1039	1130	1157	1239	1257	1330	1405	1439	1539	1605	1605	1640	1739	1800	1806	1832	1903	1939

train number	**9159**	**9157**	**9053**	**9055**	**9163**	**9161**	**9059**	**9165**	**9061**	**9063**
notes	⑦	①–⑤	⑤⑦		①⑤⑥	⑦		②③④	⑦	Ⓑ
notes										
Paris Nord .... d.	...	...	1843	1913	...	...	2013	...	2043	2113
Brussels Midi / Zuid .... d.	1852	1856	|	|	1952	1956	|	2022	|	|
Lille Europe .... d.	1930	1935	|	|	2030	2035	|	2100	|	|
Calais Fréthun .... d.	2001	|	|	|	2101	|	|	2131	|	|
Ashford International .... a.	|	|	|	|	|	|	2107**e**	|	|	|
Ebbsfleet International ...... a.	1945	|	|	2018	2045	|	|	2115	|	2218
London St Pancras .... a.	2003	1957	2004	2039	2103	2057	2139	2133	2200	2239

A – To Amsterdam, see Table **18**.
e – Not Nov. 25.
w – Nov. 25.

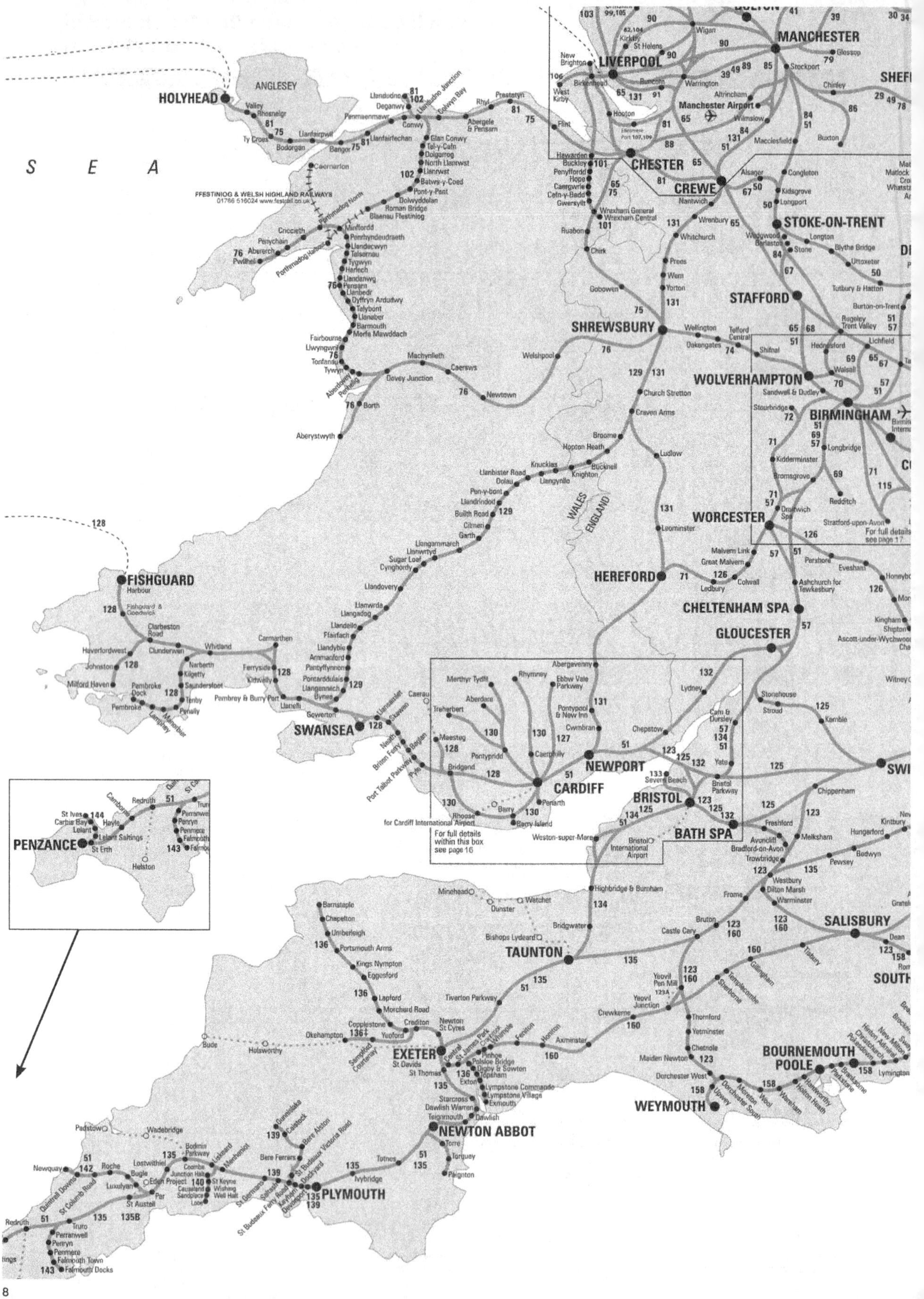

S E A
ANGLESEY
HOLYHEAD
Valley
Rhosneigr
Ty Croes
Bodorgan
Llanfairpwll
Bangor
Llanfairfechan
Penmaenmawr
Conwy
Llandudno
Deganwy
Llandudno Junction
Colwyn Bay
Abergele & Pensarn
Rhyl
Prestatyn
Flint
Glan Conwy
Tal-y-Cafn
Dolgarrog
North Llanrwst
Llanrwst
Betws-y-Coed
Pont-y-Pant
Dolwyddelan
Roman Bridge
Blaenau Ffestiniog
Caernarfon
FFESTINIOG & WELSH HIGHLAND RAILWAYS
01766 516024 www.festrail.co.uk
Porthmadog North
Porthmadog Harbour
Criccieth
Penychain
Abererch
Pwllheli
Minffordd
Penrhyndeudraeth
Llandecwyn
Talsarnau
Tygwyn
Harlech
Llandanwg
Pensarn
Llanbedr
Dyffryn Ardudwy
Talybont
Llanaber
Barmouth
Morfa Mawddach
Fairbourne
Llwyngwril
Tonfanau
Tywyn
Aberdovey
Penhelig
Dovey Junction
Machynlleth
Caersws
Newtown
Borth
Aberystwyth
Welshpool
SHREWSBURY
Wellington
Oakengates
Telford Central
Shifnal
Church Stretton
Craven Arms
Broome
Hopton Heath
Bucknell
Knucklas
Knighton
Llangynllo
Llanbister Road
Dolau
Pen-y-bont
Llandrindod
Builth Road
Cilmeri
Garth
Llangammarch
Llanwrtyd
Sugar Loaf
Cynghordy
Llandovery
Llanwrda
Llangadog
Llandeilo
Ffairfach
Llandybie
Ammanford
Pantyffynnon
Pontarddulais
Llangennech
Bynea
Llanelli
Pembrey & Burry Port
Kidwelly
Ferryside
Carmarthen
Whitland
Narberth
Kilgetty
Saundersfoot
Tenby
Penally
Manorbier
Lamphey
Pembroke
Pembroke Dock
Milford Haven
Johnston
Haverfordwest
Clunderwen
Clarbeston Road
Fishguard & Goodwick
FISHGUARD
Harbour
Ludlow
Leominster
HEREFORD
WALES
ENGLAND
LIVERPOOL
New Brighton
Birkenhead
West Kirby
Hooton
Ellesmere Port
Runcorn
Warrington
Wigan
St Helens
Kirkby
Bolton
MANCHESTER
Manchester Airport
Altrincham
Wilmslow
Stockport
Glossop
Chinley
Buxton
Macclesfield
Congleton
Kidsgrove
Longport
STOKE-ON-TRENT
Alsager
CREWE
CHESTER
Hawarden
Buckley
Penyffordd
Hope
Caergwrle
Cefn-y-Bedd
Gwersyllt
Wrexham General
Wrexham Central
Ruabon
Chirk
Gobowen
Nantwich
Wrenbury
Whitchurch
Prees
Wem
Yorton
Wedgwood
Barlaston
Stone
Longton
Blythe Bridge
Uttoxeter
Tutbury & Hatton
Burton-on-Trent
STAFFORD
Rugeley Trent Valley
Lichfield
Hednesford
Walsall
WOLVERHAMPTON
Sandwell & Dudley
BIRMINGHAM
Stourbridge
Kidderminster
Longbridge
Bromsgrove
Redditch
Droitwich Spa
Stratford-upon-Avon
For full details see page 17
WORCESTER
Malvern Link
Great Malvern
Colwall
Ledbury
Pershore
Evesham
Ashchurch for Tewkesbury
CHELTENHAM SPA
GLOUCESTER
Kingham
Shipton
Ascott-under-Wychwood
Stonehouse
Stroud
Kemble
Cam & Dursley
Yate
Lydney
Chepstow
Abergavenny
Merthyr Tydfil
Rhymney
Ebbw Vale Parkway
Aberdare
Treherbert
Pontypool & New Inn
Cwmbran
Maesteg
Pontypridd
Caerphilly
NEWPORT
Bridgend
CARDIFF
Penarth
Barry
Barry Island
Rhoose
for Cardiff International Airport
For full details within this box see page 16
SWANSEA
Gowerton
Llansamlet
Skewen
Neath
Briton Ferry
Baglan
Port Talbot Parkway
Pyle
Severn Beach
Bristol Parkway
BRISTOL
BATH SPA
Weston-super-Mare
Bristol International Airport
Chippenham
Freshford
Avoncliff
Bradford-on-Avon
Trowbridge
Melksham
Westbury
Dilton Marsh
Warminster
Frome
Hungerford
Kintbury
Bedwyn
Pewsey
SALISBURY
Dean
Highbridge & Burnham
Bridgwater
Minehead
Dunster
Watchet
Bishops Lydeard
TAUNTON
Tiverton Parkway
Castle Cary
Bruton
Yeovil Pen Mill
Yeovil Junction
Templecombe
Gillingham
Tisbury
Sherborne
Crewkerne
Thornford
Yetminster
Chetnole
Maiden Newton
Dorchester West
Dorchester South
Upwey
WEYMOUTH
Moreton
Wool
Wareham
Holton Heath
Hamworthy
Parkstone
BOURNEMOUTH
POOLE
Branksome
Lymington
Barnstaple
Chapelton
Umberleigh
Portsmouth Arms
Kings Nympton
Eggesford
Lapford
Morchard Road
Copplestone
Yeoford
Crediton
Newton St Cyres
Okehampton
Sampford Courtenay
Bude
Holsworthy
EXETER
St Davids
Central
St James Park
Polsloe Bridge
Pinhoe
Whimple
Feniton
Honiton
Axminster
Digby & Sowton
Topsham
Exton
St Thomas
Lympstone Commando
Lympstone Village
Exmouth
Starcross
Dawlish Warren
Dawlish
Teignmouth
NEWTON ABBOT
Torre
Torquay
Paignton
Totnes
Ivybridge
PLYMOUTH
Dockyard
Devonport
Keyham
St Budeaux Ferry Road
St Budeaux Victoria Road
Saltash
St Germans
Bere Ferrers
Bere Alston
Calstock
Gunnislake
Menheniot
Liskeard
St Keyne Wishing Well Halt
Causeland
Sandplace
Looe
Coombe Junction Halt
Bodmin Parkway
Lostwithiel
Par
St Austell
Luxulyan
Bugle
Roche
Eden Project
Padstow
Wadebridge
Newquay
Quintrell Downs
St Columb Road
Truro
Redruth
Perranwell
Penryn
Penmere
Falmouth Town
Falmouth Docks
PENZANCE
St Ives
Carbis Bay
Lelant
Lelant Saltings
St Erth
Hayle
Camborne
Helston
SWINDON
SOUTHAMPTON

DONCASTER
Robin Hood Airport
GRIMSBY
Scunthorpe
Brigg
Barnsley
Kirton Lindsey
Gainsborough Central
Gainsborough Lea Road
Market Rasen
Rotherham
SHEFFIELD
Worksop
RETFORD
Chesterfield
Creswell
Whitwell
Shirebrook
Langwith-Whaley Thorns
Mansfield
Mansfield Woodhouse
Saxilby
LINCOLN
Hykeham
Swinderby
Collingham
Metheringham
Ruskington
Sutton Parkway
Kirkby-in-Ashfield
Newstead
Hucknall
Bulwell
Alfreton
Matlock
Matlock Bath
Cromford
Whatstandwell
Ambergate
Langley Mill
Ilkeston
Belper
Duffield
NEWARK
North Gate
Rauceby
Sleaford
Ancaster
Skegness
Havenhouse
Wainfleet
Thorpe Culvert
Boston
NOTTINGHAM
DERBY
Beeston
Attenborough
Peartree
Spondon
Long Eaton
Loughborough
Barrow-on-Soar
East Midlands Parkway
Willington
GRANTHAM
Heckington
Swineshead
Hubberts Bridge
Spalding
Sileby
Syston
Melton Mowbray
Oakham
Stamford
LEICESTER
South Wigston
Narborough
Hinckley
Nuneaton
Tamworth
Birmingham International
COVENTRY
RUGBY
Leamington Spa
Market Harborough
Corby
Oundle
KETTERING
Wellingborough
PETERBOROUGH
Whittlesea
March
Manea
Wisbech
KINGS LYNN
Watlington
Downham Market
Littleport
Ely
Waterbeach
Hunstanton
Sandringham
Swaffham
Dereham
Sheringham
West Runton
Cromer
Roughton Road
Gunton
North Walsham
Worstead
Hoveton & Wroxham
Salhouse
NORWICH
Great Yarmouth
Berney Arms
Haddiscoe
Somerleyton
Oulton Broad North
Oulton Broad South
Lowestoft
Beccles
Brampton
Halesworth
Darsham
Saxmundham
Wymondham
Spooner Row
Attleborough
Eccles Road
Harling Road
Thetford
Brandon
Lakenheath
Shippea Hill
Diss
Long Buckby
NORTHAMPTON
Huntingdon
Cambridge North
CAMBRIDGE
Newmarket
Bury St Edmunds
Stowmarket
Westerfield
IPSWICH
Felixstowe
HARWICH
Manningtree
Walton-on-the-Naze
Clacton-on-Sea
Marks Tey
COLCHESTER
Sudbury
Braintree
Witham
Chelmsford
STANSTED Airport
Bishops Stortford
Harlow
Royston
St Neots
Bedford
MILTON KEYNES
Bletchley
Letchworth
Hitchin
Stevenage
Luton
Dunstable
Welwyn Garden City
Hertford
St Albans
Hemel Hempstead
Watford
Amersham
High Wycombe
Aylesbury
Aylesbury Parkway
Princes Risborough
Chinnor
Banbury
Buckingham
Bicester
Honeybourne
Moreton-in-Marsh
Kingham
Shipton
Chipping Norton
Charlbury
Finstock
Combe
Hanborough
Witney
Abingdon
OXFORD
Didcot Parkway
SWINDON
Henley-on-Thames
Marlow
Maidenhead
Twyford
READING
Slough
Windsor
Heathrow Airport
Staines
Richmond
Ascot
Surbiton
Woking
Basingstoke
Aldershot
Guildford
Dorking
Redhill
GATWICK Airport
Crawley
Horsham
Haywards Heath
East Croydon
Oxted
East Grinstead
Uckfield
LEWES
BRIGHTON
Hove
WORTHING
Littlehampton
Bognor Regis
CHICHESTER
Havant
PORTSMOUTH
Fareham
Southampton Airport Parkway
SOUTHAMPTON
Totton
Eastleigh
Winchester
Micheldever
Shawford
Romsey
Chandlers Ford
Mottisfont & Dunbridge
Dean
Grateley
Andover
Whitchurch
Overton
Alton
Haslemere
Newbury
Thatcham
Midgham
Theale
Aldermaston
Kintbury
Newbury Racecourse
Lymington Town
Lymington Pier
Brockenhurst
Sway
New Milton
Beaulieu Road
Ashurst New Forest
LONDON
Chingford
Shenfield
Romford
Barking
Upminster
Basildon
Wickford
Southminster
Southend Airport
SOUTHEND
Shoeburyness
Tilbury
Dartford
Ebbsfleet International
Sheerness-on-Sea
Chatham
Gillingham
Sittingbourne
Faversham
Herne Bay
MARGATE
RAMSGATE
CANTERBURY
Maidstone
Sevenoaks
Tonbridge
Tunbridge Wells
ASHFORD
FOLKESTONE
DOVER
Deal
Rye
HASTINGS
Bexhill
EASTBOURNE
Newhaven
Seaford
CHANNEL TUNNEL
Fréthun-Calais
BOULOGNE
Etaples
Pier Head
Ryde
Esplanade
St Johns Road
Brading
Sandown
Lake
Shanklin
Ventnor
ISLE OF WIGHT
For full details within this box see pages 14-15
For full details within this box see pages 12-15
full details within this box page 17
ENGLISH CHANNEL
FR

PERTH
Leuchars
St Andrews
Gleneagles
Cupar
Springfield
Ladybank
Markinch
Dunblane
Alloa
Cardenden
Kirkcaldy
Dunfermline
Inverkeithing
North Berwick
Falkirk
EDINBURGH
Drem
Dunbar
Longniddry
Prestonpans
Bathgate
Gorebridge
Shotts
Motherwell
Carstairs
Lanark
BERWICK-UPON-TWEED
Duns
Stow
Earlston
Galashiels
Melrose
Tweedbank
Selkirk
Hawick
For full details within this box see pages 20-21
Chathill
Alnmouth for Alnwick
Acklington
Widdrington
Pegswood
Morpeth
SCOTLAND
ENGLAND
Langholm
Lockerbie
Dumfries
Annan
Gretna Green
For full details within this box see schematic map on p20
Cramlington
Manors
NEWCASTLE
Heworth
CARLISLE
Brampton
Haltwhistle
Bardon Mill
Haydon Bridge
Hexham
Corbridge
Riding Mill
Stocksfield
Prudhoe
Wylam
Blaydon
Wetheral
Dalston
Wigton
Aspatria
Maryport
Flimby
Workington
Harrington
Parton
Whitehaven
Corkickle
St Bees
Nethertown
Braystones
Sellafield
Seascale
Drigg
Ravenglass for Eskdale
Bootle
Silecroft
Millom
Green Road
Foxfield
Kirkby-in-Furness
Askam
BARROW
Roose
Dalton
Ulverston
Cark
Kents Bank
Grange-over-Sands
Arnside
Silverdale
Carnforth
Morecambe
Bare Lane
Heysham Port
Lancaster
WINDERMERE
Windermere
Staveley
Burneside
Kendal
Oxenholme Lake District
Armathwaite
Lazonby & Kirkoswald
Langwathby
Penrith North Lakes
Appleby
Kirkby Stephen
Garsdale
Dent
Ribblehead
Horton-in-Ribblesdale
Settle
Wennington
Bentham
Clapham
Giggleswick
Long Preston
Hellifield
SUNDERLAND
Chester-le-Street
Durham
Seaham
HARTLEPOOL
Seaton Carew
Billingham
Stockton
Thornaby
South Bank
British Steel Redcar
Redcar Central
Redcar East
Longbeck
Marske
Saltburn
MIDDLESBROUGH
Bishop Auckland
Shildon
Newton Aycliffe
Heighington
North Road
DARLINGTON
Eaglescliffe
Marton
Gypsy Lane
Nunthorpe
Great Ayton
Battersby
Castleton Moor
Danby
Lealholm
Commondale
Kildale
Glaisdale
Egton
Grosmont
Whitby
Ruswarp
Sleights
Goathland
Levisham
Pickering
Richmond
Catterick Camp Centre
Dinsdale
Allens West
Yarm
Northallerton
Thirsk
SCARBOROUGH
Seamer
Filey
Hunmanby
Bempton
Bridlington
Nafferton
Driffield
Hutton Cranswick
Arram
Beverley
Cottingham
HULL
Malton
HARROGATE
Knaresborough
YORK
For full details within this box see pages 18-19
Ilkley
Skipton
Keighley
Clitheroe
Colne
Burnley
Blackburn
BLACKPOOL
Kirkham
Lytham
PRESTON
LEEDS
BRADFORD
HALIFAX
WAKEFIELD
HUDDERSFIELD
Selby
Gilberdyke
Broomfleet
Brough
Ferriby
Hessle
Goole
Barton-on-Humber
Barrow Haven
New Holland
Goxhill
Thornton Abbey
Ulceby
Barnetby
Habrough
Stallingborough
Healing
Great Coates
GRIMSBY
Town
Docks
New Clee
Cleethorpes
Southport
Ormskirk
BOLTON
Rochdale
Barnsley
Scunthorpe
Brigg
Kirton Lindsey
DONCASTER
Robin Hood Airport
Wigan
Kirkby
St Helens
MANCHESTER
Glossop
New Brighton
LIVERPOOL
West Kirby
Birkenhead
Runcorn
Warrington
Stockport
Altrincham
Manchester Airport
Wilmslow
Chinley
Rotherham
SHEFFIELD
Gainsborough Central
Gainsborough Lea Road
Market Rasen
Llandudno Junction
Colwyn Bay
Rhyl
Prestatyn
Abergele & Pensarn
Glan Conwy
Tal-y-Cafn
Dolgarrog
North Llanrwst
Llanrwst
Betws-y-Coed
Pont-y-Pant
Flint
Hooton
Ellesmere Port
Hawarden
Buckley
Penyffordd
Hope
Caergwrle
Cefn-y-Bedd
Gwersyllt
CHESTER
CREWE
Nantwich
Macclesfield
Buxton
Alsager
Congleton
Kidsgrove
Longport
Chesterfield
Worksop
Whitwell
Creswell
Shirebrook
Langwith-Whaley Thorns
Mansfield
Mansfield Woodhouse
RETFORD
Saxilby
LINCOLN
Matlock
Matlock Bath
Cromford
Whatstandwell
Ambergate
Alfreton
Sutton Parkway
Kirkby-in-Ashfield
Newstead
Hucknall
Newark Castle
Rolleston
Fiskerton
Bleasby
Thurgarton
Hykeham
Swinderby
Collingham
Metheringham
Ruskington
NEWARK
Thorpe Culvert

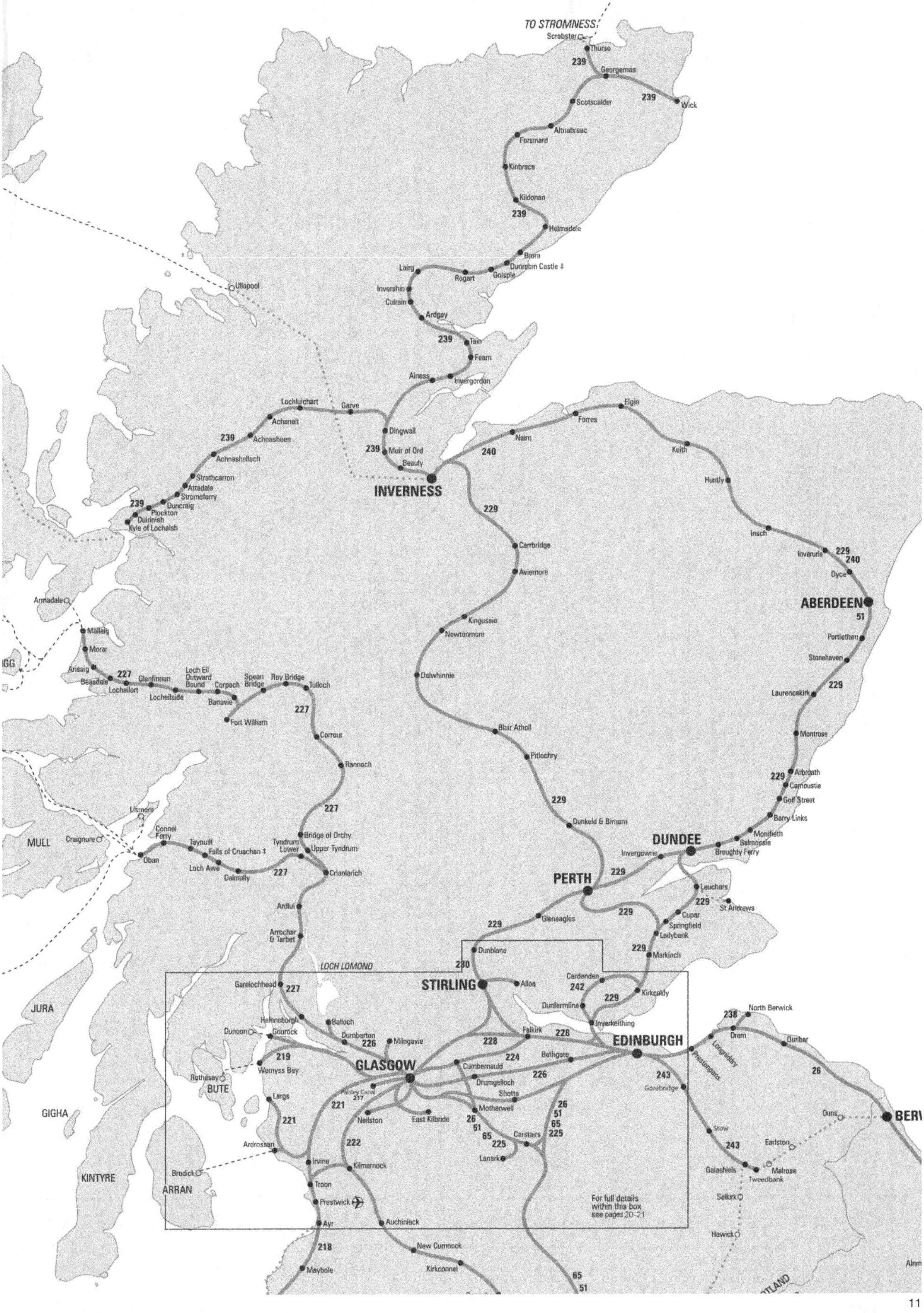

TO STROMNESS
Scrabster
Thurso
Georgemas
Wick
Scotscalder
Altnabreac
Forsinard
Kinbrace
Kildonan
Helmsdale
Brora
Dunrobin Castle ‡
Golspie
Rogart
Lairg
Invershin
Culrain
Ardgay
Tain
Fearn
Alness
Invergordon
Ullapool
Lochluichart
Garve
Achanalt
Achnasheen
Achnashellach
Strathcarron
Attadale
Stromeferry
Duncraig
Plockton
Duirinish
Kyle of Lochalsh
Dingwall
Muir of Ord
Beauty
INVERNESS
Nairn
Forres
Elgin
Keith
Huntly
Insch
Inverurie
Dyce
ABERDEEN
Portlethen
Stonehaven
Laurencekirk
Montrose
Arbroath
Carnoustie
Golf Street
Barry Links
Monifieth
Balmossie
Broughty Ferry
DUNDEE
Invergowrie
Carrbridge
Aviemore
Kingussie
Newtonmore
Dalwhinnie
Blair Atholl
Pitlochry
Dunkeld & Birnam
PERTH
Gleneagles
Leuchars
St Andrews
Cupar
Springfield
Ladybank
Markinch
Cardenden
Kirkcaldy
Dunfermline
Inverkeithing
Armadale
Mallaig
Morar
Arisaig
Beasdale
Lochailort
Glenfinnan
Locheilside
Loch Eil Outward Bound
Corpach
Banavie
Fort William
Spean Bridge
Roy Bridge
Tulloch
Corrour
Rannoch
Bridge of Orchy
Tyndrum Lower
Upper Tyndrum
Crianlarich
Lismore
MULL
Craignure
Oban
Connel Ferry
Taynuilt
Falls of Cruachan ‡
Loch Awe
Dalmally
Ardlui
Arrochar & Tarbet
LOCH LOMOND
Dunblane
STIRLING
Alloa
Garelochhead
Helensburgh
Balloch
Dumbarton
Milngavie
Dunoon
Gourock
Wemyss Bay
Rothesay
BUTE
JURA
GIGHA
KINTYRE
ARRAN
Brodick
GLASGOW
Paisley Canal
Largs
Ardrossan
Irvine
Troon
Prestwick
Ayr
Maybole
Kilmarnock
Auchinleck
New Cumnock
Kirkconnel
Neilston
East Kilbride
Cumbernauld
Drumgelloch
Shotts
Motherwell
Carstairs
Lanark
Falkirk
Bathgate
EDINBURGH
Prestonpans
Longniddry
Drem
North Berwick
Dunbar
Gorebridge
Stow
Galashiels
Tweedbank
Melrose
Earlston
Duns
Selkirk
Hawick
BERW
Alnm
For full details within this box see pages 20-21
239
240
229
227
228
226
224
225
222
221
219
218
217
230
242
243
238
26
51
65

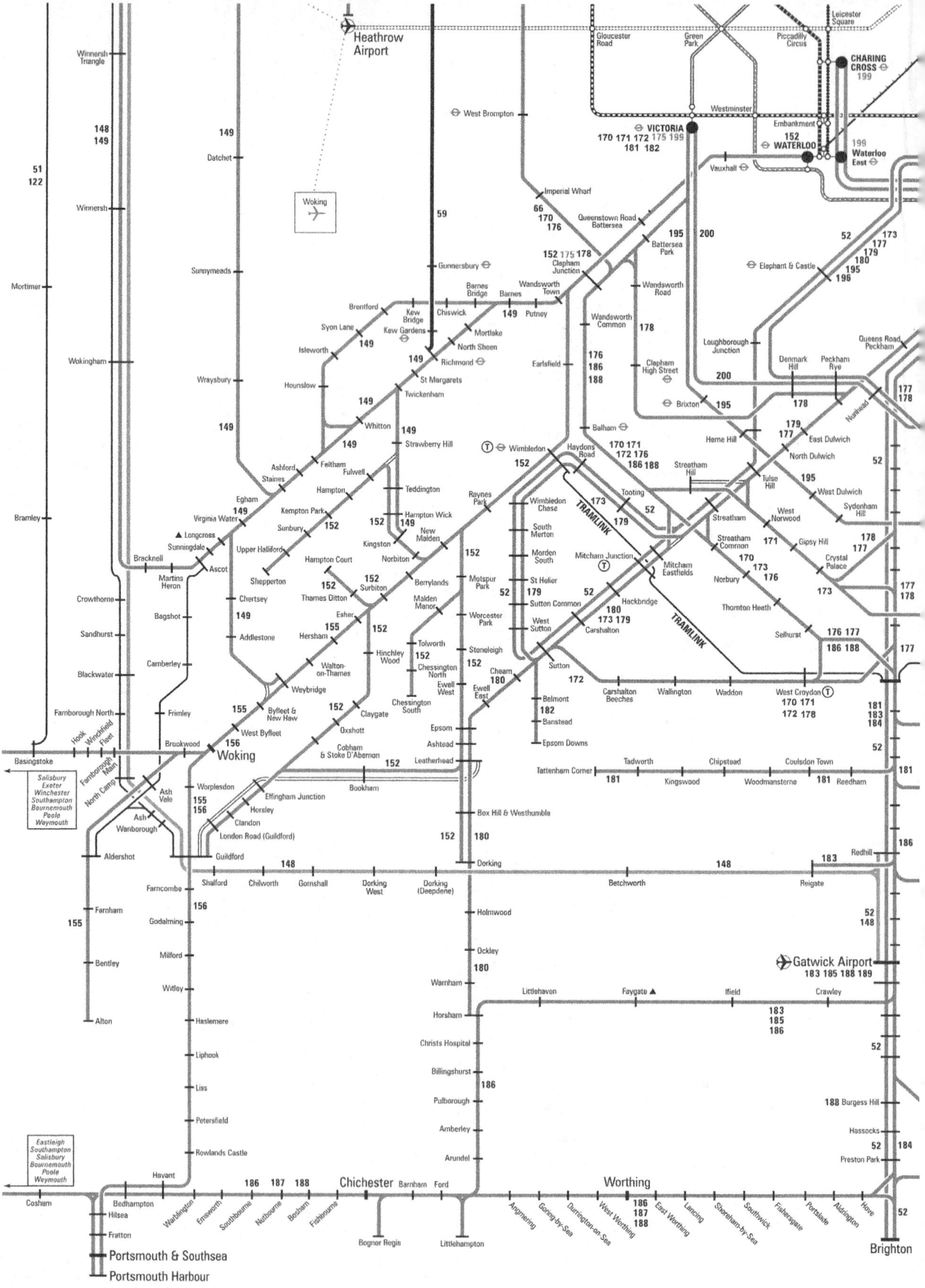

Heathrow Airport
Woking
Leicester Square
Gloucester Road
Green Park
Piccadilly Circus
CHARING CROSS
199
West Brompton
Westminster
Embankment
VICTORIA
170 171 172 175 199
181 182
152
WATERLOO
199
Waterloo East
Vauxhall
Imperial Wharf
66
170
176
Queenstown Road Battersea
195
200
Battersea Park
52
173
177
179
180
195
196
Elephant & Castle
152 175 178
Clapham Junction
Wandsworth Town
Wandsworth Road
Gunnersbury
59
Barnes Bridge
Barnes
149
Putney
Brentford
Kew Bridge
Chiswick
Kew Gardens
Mortlake
North Sheen
Richmond
St Margarets
Twickenham
Syon Lane
Isleworth
Hounslow
Whitton
Strawberry Hill
Wandsworth Common
178
Earlsfield
176
186
188
Clapham High Street
Loughborough Junction
Queens Road Peckham
Denmark Hill
Peckham Rye
200
Brixton
195
Nunhead
177
178
Balham
Wimbledon
Haydons Road
170 171
172 176
186 188
Streatham Hill
Herne Hill
179
177
East Dulwich
North Dulwich
Tulse Hill
West Dulwich
Sydenham Hill
Tooting
173
179
TRAMLINK
Streatham
West Norwood
Streatham Common
171
Gipsy Hill
Crystal Palace
Norbury
Thornton Heath
Selhurst
176 177
186 188
Mitcham Junction
Mitcham Eastfields
Hackbridge
Carshalton
Wimbledon Chase
South Merton
Morden South
St Helier
Sutton Common
West Sutton
Sutton
Cheam
Belmont
Banstead
Epsom Downs
Carshalton Beeches
Wallington
Waddon
West Croydon
170 171
172 178
181
183
184
Raynes Park
Motspur Park
Worcester Park
Stoneleigh
Ewell West
Ewell East
New Malden
Norbiton
Kingston
Hampton Wick
Teddington
Fulwell
Hampton
Kempton Park
Sunbury
Upper Halliford
Shepperton
Hampton Court
Thames Ditton
Surbiton
Berrylands
Malden Manor
Tolworth
Chessington North
Chessington South
Hinchley Wood
Esher
Hersham
Walton-on-Thames
Weybridge
Byfleet & New Haw
West Byfleet
Claygate
Oxshott
Cobham & Stoke D'Abernon
Epsom
Ashtead
Leatherhead
Bookham
Effingham Junction
Horsley
Clandon
London Road (Guildford)
Guildford
Box Hill & Westhumble
Dorking
Feltham
Ashford
Staines
Egham
Virginia Water
Longcross
Sunningdale
Ascot
Bracknell
Martins Heron
Chertsey
Addlestone
Bagshot
Camberley
Frimley
Brookwood
Woking
Worplesdon
Datchet
Sunnymeads
Wraysbury
Winnersh Triangle
Winnersh
Wokingham
Crowthorne
Sandhurst
Blackwater
Farnborough North
Mortimer
Bramley
51
122
148
149
Basingstoke
Hook
Winchfield
Fleet
Farnborough Main
North Camp
Ash Vale
Ash
Wanborough
Aldershot
155
156
Salisbury
Exeter
Winchester
Southampton
Bournemouth
Poole
Weymouth
Shalford
Chilworth
Gomshall
Dorking West
Dorking (Deepdene)
Betchworth
Reigate
Redhill
Farncombe
Godalming
Milford
Witley
Haslemere
Liphook
Liss
Petersfield
Rowlands Castle
Havant
Farnham
Bentley
Alton
Holmwood
Ockley
Warnham
Horsham
Christs Hospital
Billingshurst
Pulborough
Amberley
Arundel
Tattenham Corner
Tadworth
Kingswood
Chipstead
Woodmansterne
Coulsdon Town
Reedham
Gatwick Airport
183 185 188 189
Littlehaven
Faygate
Ifield
Crawley
183
185
186
188 Burgess Hill
Hassocks
Preston Park
Brighton
Eastleigh
Southampton
Salisbury
Bournemouth
Poole
Weymouth
Cosham
Bedhampton
Hilsea
Fratton
Portsmouth & Southsea
Portsmouth Harbour
Warblington
Emsworth
Southbourne
Nutbourne
Bosham
Fishbourne
Chichester
Barnham
Ford
Bognor Regis
Littlehampton
Worthing
186
187
188
Angmering
Goring-by-Sea
Durrington-on-Sea
West Worthing
East Worthing
Lancing
Shoreham-by-Sea
Southwick
Fishersgate
Portslade
Aldrington
Hove

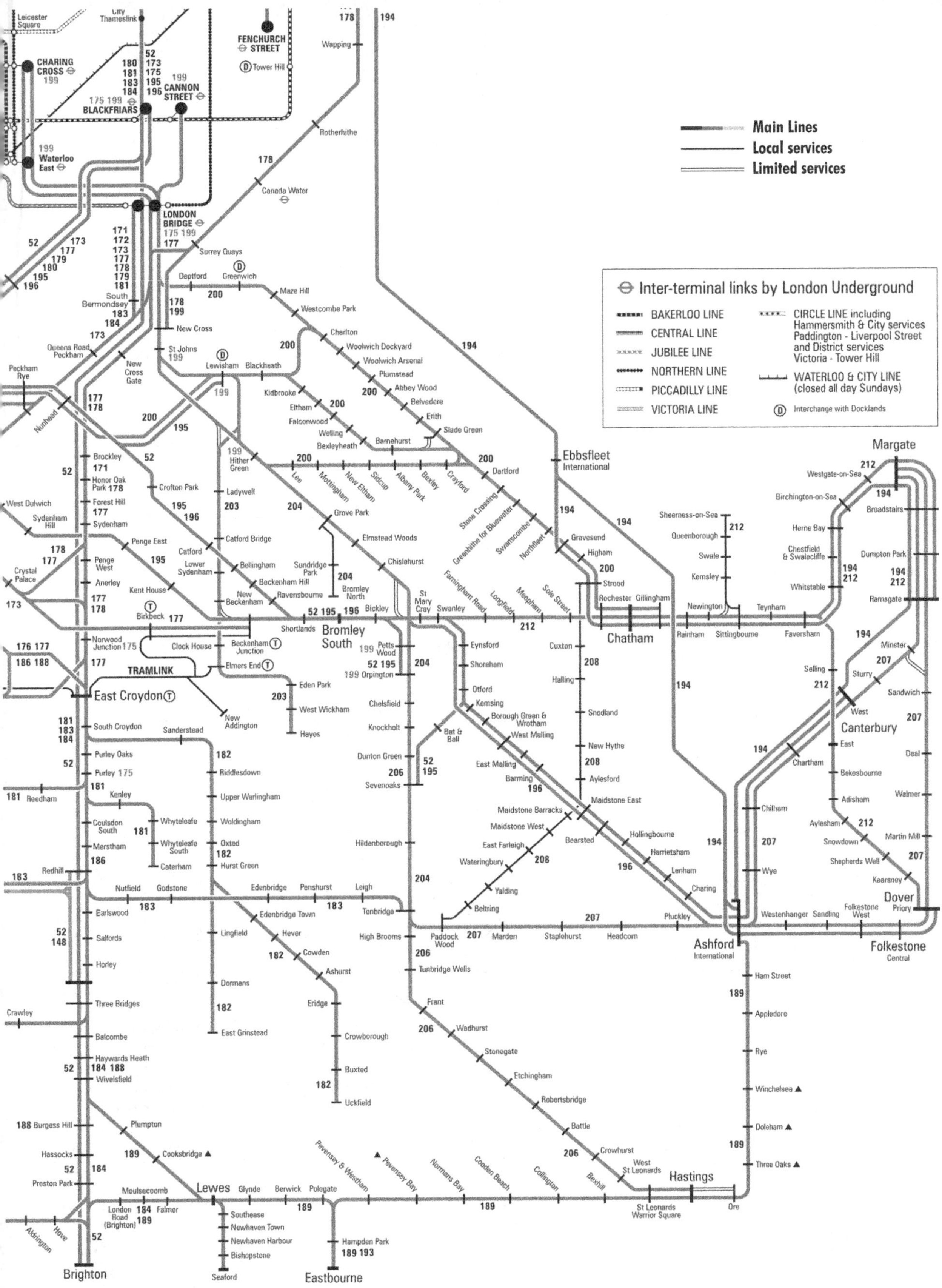
Main Lines
Local services
Limited services
⊖ Inter-terminal links by London Underground
BAKERLOO LINE
CENTRAL LINE
JUBILEE LINE
NORTHERN LINE
PICCADILLY LINE
VICTORIA LINE
CIRCLE LINE including Hammersmith & City services Paddington - Liverpool Street and District services Victoria - Tower Hill
WATERLOO & CITY LINE (closed all day Sundays)
Interchange with Docklands
Leicester Square
City Thameslink
FENCHURCH STREET
Tower Hill
CHARING CROSS
CANNON STREET
BLACKFRIARS
Waterloo East
LONDON BRIDGE
Wapping
Rotherhithe
Canada Water
Surrey Quays
Deptford
Greenwich
Maze Hill
Westcombe Park
Charlton
Woolwich Dockyard
Woolwich Arsenal
Plumstead
Abbey Wood
Belvedere
Erith
Slade Green
South Bermondsey
Queens Road Peckham
New Cross
New Cross Gate
St Johns
Lewisham
Blackheath
Kidbrooke
Eltham
Falconwood
Welling
Bexleyheath
Barnehurst
Peckham Rye
Nunhead
Brockley
Honor Oak Park
Crofton Park
Hither Green
Lee
Mottingham
New Eltham
Sidcup
Albany Park
Bexley
Crayford
Dartford
Ebbsfleet International
West Dulwich
Sydenham Hill
Forest Hill
Sydenham
Ladywell
Grove Park
Stone Crossing
Greenhithe for Bluewater
Swanscombe
Northfleet
Gravesend
Higham
Strood
Rochester
Gillingham
Chatham
Penge East
Penge West
Catford
Catford Bridge
Lower Sydenham
Elmstead Woods
Chislehurst
Crystal Palace
Anerley
Kent House
Bellingham
Beckenham Hill
Ravensbourne
Sundridge Park
Bromley North
Birkbeck
New Beckenham
Shortlands
Bromley South
Bickley
St Mary Cray
Swanley
Farningham Road
Longfield
Meopham
Sole Street
Norwood Junction
Clock House
Beckenham Junction
Elmers End
TRAMLINK
East Croydon
New Addington
Petts Wood
Orpington
Eden Park
West Wickham
Hayes
Chelsfield
Knockholt
Eynsford
Shoreham
Otford
Kemsing
Borough Green & Wrotham
West Malling
East Malling
Barming
Bat & Ball
Dunton Green
Sevenoaks
Cuxton
Halling
Snodland
New Hythe
Aylesford
Maidstone East
Maidstone Barracks
Maidstone West
East Farleigh
Wateringbury
Yalding
Beltring
Bearsted
Hollingbourne
Harrietsham
Lenham
Charing
Pluckley
Sheerness-on-Sea
Queenborough
Swale
Kemsley
Newington
Rainham
Sittingbourne
Teynham
Faversham
Margate
Westgate-on-Sea
Birchington-on-Sea
Broadstairs
Herne Bay
Chestfield & Swalecliffe
Whitstable
Dumpton Park
Ramsgate
Minster
Sturry
Selling
Sandwich
Canterbury West
Canterbury East
Chartham
Chilham
Wye
Bekesbourne
Adisham
Aylesham
Snowdown
Shepherds Well
Kearsney
Deal
Walmer
Martin Mill
Dover Priory
Folkestone West
Folkestone Central
Sandling
Westenhanger
Ashford International
South Croydon
Sanderstead
Purley Oaks
Purley
Riddlesdown
Upper Warlingham
Woldingham
Kenley
Reedham
Coulsdon South
Whyteleafe
Whyteleafe South
Caterham
Merstham
Oxted
Hurst Green
Redhill
Nutfield
Godstone
Edenbridge
Penshurst
Leigh
Tonbridge
Hildenborough
Earlswood
Salfords
Horley
Lingfield
Dormans
East Grinstead
Edenbridge Town
Hever
Cowden
Ashurst
Eridge
Crowborough
Buxted
Uckfield
High Brooms
Tunbridge Wells
Paddock Wood
Marden
Staplehurst
Headcorn
Frant
Wadhurst
Stonegate
Etchingham
Robertsbridge
Battle
Crowhurst
West St Leonards
Hastings
St Leonards Warrior Square
Ore
Ham Street
Appledore
Rye
Winchelsea
Doleham
Three Oaks
Crawley
Three Bridges
Balcombe
Haywards Heath
Wivelsfield
Burgess Hill
Hassocks
Preston Park
Plumpton
Cooksbridge
Lewes
Moulsecoomb
London Road (Brighton)
Falmer
Glynde
Berwick
Polegate
Pevensey & Westham
Pevensey Bay
Normans Bay
Cooden Beach
Collington
Bexhill
Southease
Newhaven Town
Newhaven Harbour
Bishopstone
Seaford
Hampden Park
Eastbourne
Brighton
Hove
Aldrington

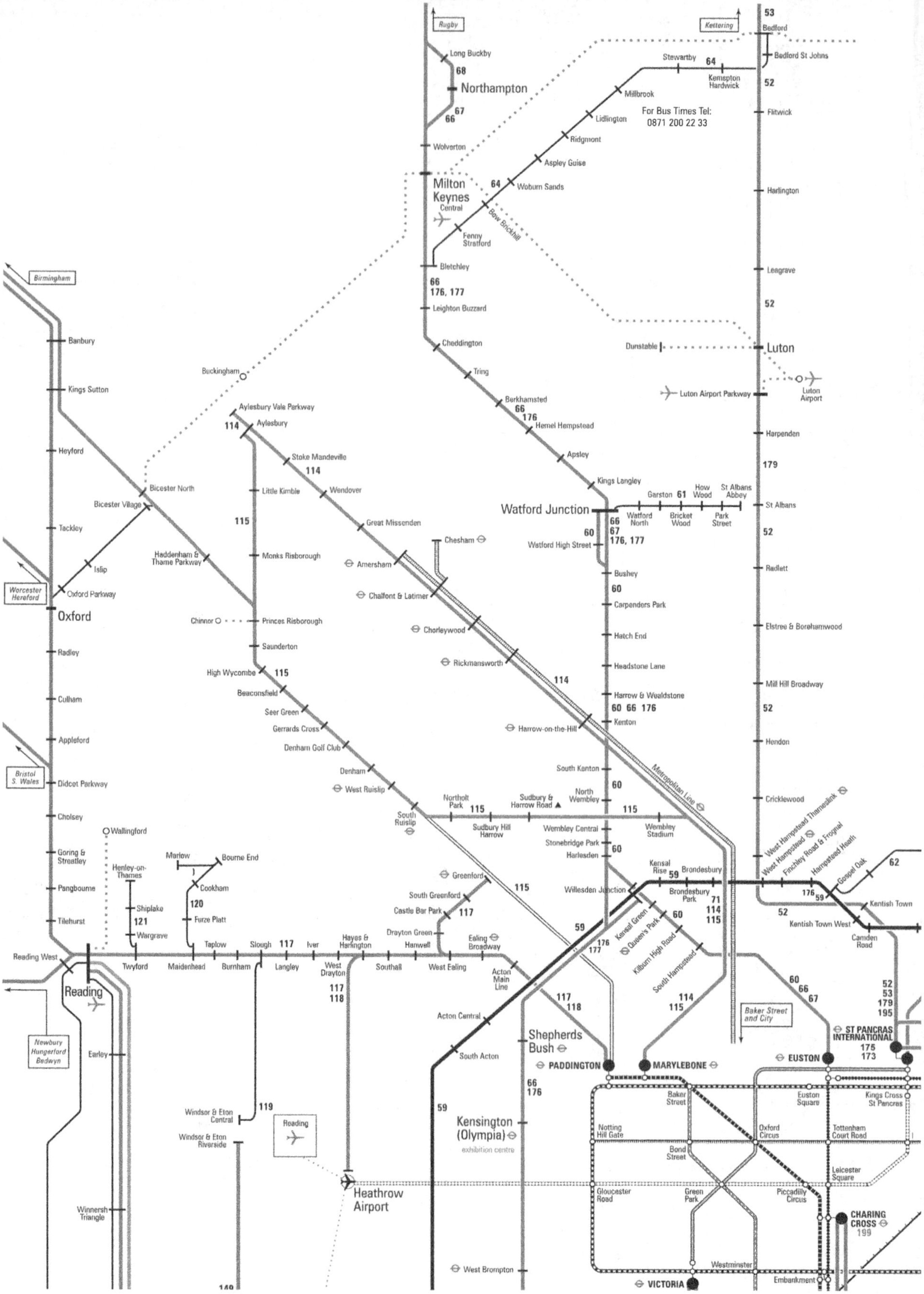

Rugby
Kettering
53
Bedford
Bedford St Johns
Long Buckby
68
Northampton
67
66
Stewartby
64
Kempston Hardwick
52
Millbrook
For Bus Times Tel:
0871 200 22 33
Lidlington
Flitwick
Ridgmont
Wolverton
Aspley Guise
Milton Keynes Central
64
Woburn Sands
Harlington
Bow Brickhill
Fenny Stratford
Bletchley
66
176, 177
Leighton Buzzard
Leagrave
52
Birmingham
Banbury
Cheddington
Dunstable
Luton
Tring
Luton Airport
Luton Airport Parkway
Buckingham
Kings Sutton
Berkhamsted
66
176
Hemel Hempstead
Aylesbury Vale Parkway
114
Aylesbury
Harpenden
Heyford
Stoke Mandeville
114
Apsley
179
Kings Langley
Bicester North
Little Kimble
Wendover
Garston
61
How Wood
St Albans Abbey
Bicester Village
Watford Junction
St Albans
Watford North
Bricket Wood
Park Street
66
67
176, 177
115
Great Missenden
60
Tackley
Chesham
Watford High Street
52
Haddenham & Thame Parkway
Monks Risborough
Amersham
Islip
Bushey
Radlett
Worcester Hereford
Oxford Parkway
Chalfont & Latimer
60
Oxford
Carpenders Park
Chinnor
Princes Risborough
Chorleywood
Elstree & Borehamwood
Hatch End
Radley
Saunderton
Rickmansworth
Headstone Lane
High Wycombe
115
114
Mill Hill Broadway
Beaconsfield
Culham
Harrow & Wealdstone
60 66 176
Seer Green
52
Gerrards Cross
Kenton
Harrow-on-the-Hill
Appleford
Hendon
Denham Golf Club
Metropolitan Line
Bristol S. Wales
South Kenton
Denham
60
Didcot Parkway
West Ruislip
Northolt Park
115
Sudbury & Harrow Road
North Wembley
Cricklewood
115
South Ruislip
Cholsey
Sudbury Hill Harrow
Wembley Central
Wembley Stadium
Wallingford
West Hampstead Thameslink
Stonebridge Park
West Hampstead
Goring & Streatley
Marlow
Bourne End
Harlesden
60
Finchley Road & Frognal
Henley-on-Thames
Kensal Rise
59
Brondesbury
Hampstead Heath
62
Greenford
Gospel Oak
Pangbourne
Cookham
115
Willesden Junction
Brondesbury Park
71
114
115
176
59
120
South Greenford
Shiplake
Kentish Town
Castle Bar Park
117
52
121
60
Tilehurst
Furze Platt
Kentish Town West
Wargrave
Drayton Green
59
Kensal Green
Queen's Park
Camden Road
Taplow
Slough
117
Iver
Hayes & Harlington
Hanwell
Ealing Broadway
176
177
Kilburn High Road
Reading West
South Hampstead
Twyford
Maidenhead
Burnham
Langley
West Drayton
Southall
West Ealing
Acton Main Line
60
66
67
117
118
Reading
117
118
52
53
179
195
114
115
Baker Street and City
Acton Central
Shepherds Bush
ST PANCRAS INTERNATIONAL
175
173
Newbury Hungerford Bedwyn
Earley
South Acton
PADDINGTON
MARYLEBONE
EUSTON
66
176
Baker Street
Euston Square
Kings Cross St Pancras
Windsor & Eton Central
119
59
Reading
Kensington (Olympia)
exhibition centre
Notting Hill Gate
Oxford Circus
Tottenham Court Road
Windsor & Eton Riverside
Bond Street
Leicester Square
Heathrow Airport
Gloucester Road
Green Park
Piccadilly Circus
Winnersh Triangle
CHARING CROSS
199
West Brompton
Westminster
149
Embankment
VICTORIA

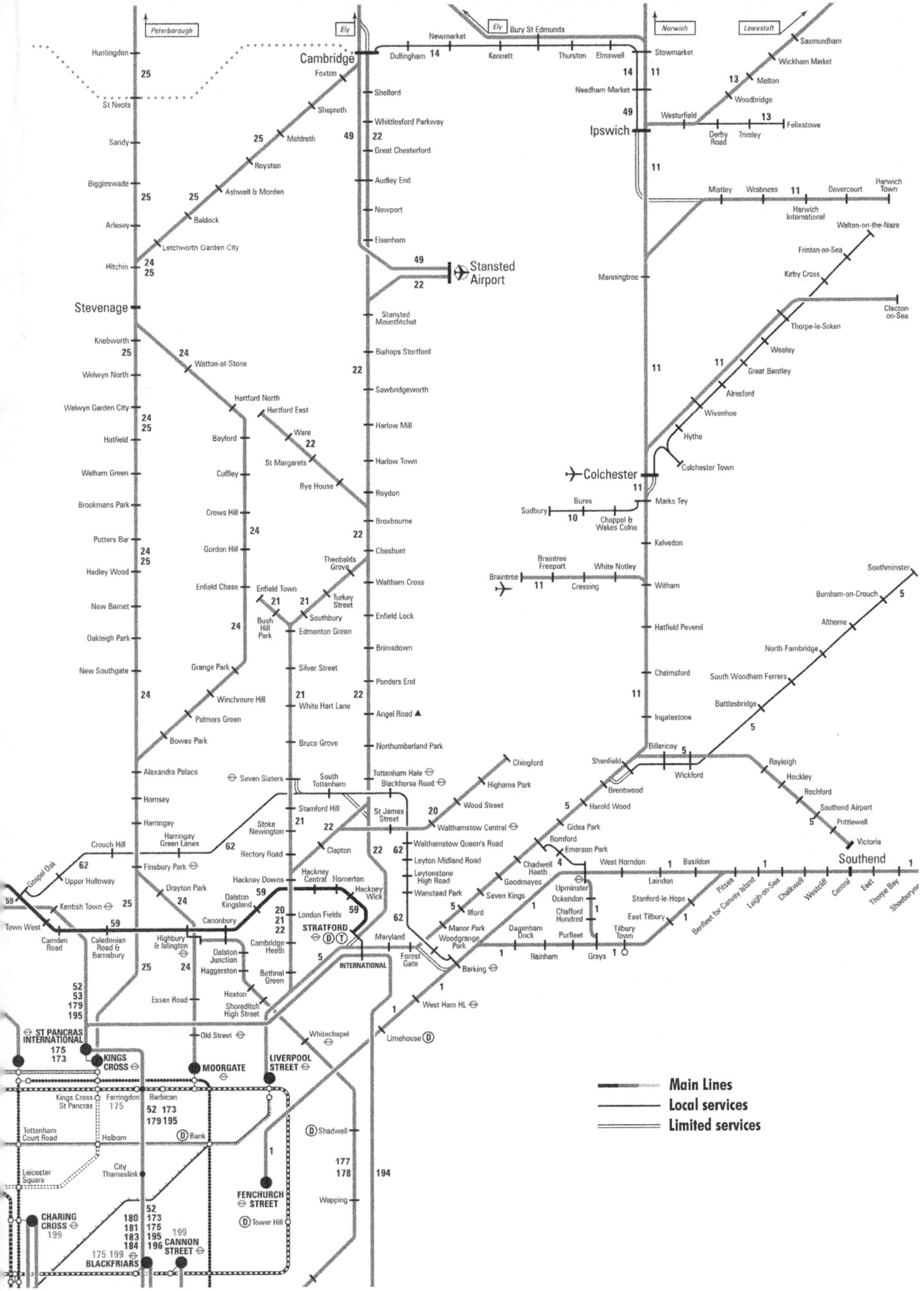
Peterborough
Ely
Ely
Bury St Edmunds
Norwich
Lowestoft
Huntingdon
St Neots
Sandy
Biggleswade
Arlesey
Hitchin
Stevenage
Knebworth
Welwyn North
Welwyn Garden City
Hatfield
Welham Green
Brookmans Park
Potters Bar
Hadley Wood
New Barnet
Oakleigh Park
New Southgate
Alexandra Palace
Hornsey
Harringay
Finsbury Park
Drayton Park
Highbury & Islington
Essex Road
Old Street
Cambridge
Foxton
Shepreth
Meldreth
Royston
Ashwell & Morden
Baldock
Letchworth Garden City
Watton-at-Stone
Hertford North
Bayford
Cuffley
Crews Hill
Gordon Hill
Enfield Chase
Grange Park
Winchmore Hill
Palmers Green
Bowes Park
Hertford East
Ware
St Margarets
Rye House
Newmarket
Dullingham
Kennett
Thurston
Elmswell
Stowmarket
Needham Market
Ipswich
Shelford
Whittlesford Parkway
Great Chesterford
Audley End
Newport
Elsenham
Stansted Airport
Stansted Mountfitchet
Bishops Stortford
Sawbridgeworth
Harlow Mill
Harlow Town
Roydon
Broxbourne
Cheshunt
Theobalds Grove
Waltham Cross
Enfield Lock
Brimsdown
Ponders End
Angel Road
Northumberland Park
Tottenham Hale
Blackhorse Road
Enfield Town
Bush Hill Park
Turkey Street
Southbury
Edmonton Green
Silver Street
White Hart Lane
Bruce Grove
Seven Sisters
South Tottenham
Stamford Hill
Stoke Newington
Rectory Road
Hackney Downs
Clapton
St James Street
Walthamstow Central
Wood Street
Highams Park
Chingford
Walthamstow Queen's Road
Leyton Midland Road
Leytonstone High Road
Wanstead Park
Woodgrange Park
Crouch Hill
Harringay Green Lanes
Gospel Oak
Upper Holloway
Kentish Town
Town West
Camden Road
Caledonian Road & Barnsbury
Canonbury
Dalston Kingsland
Dalston Junction
Haggerston
Hoxton
Shoreditch High Street
Hackney Central
Homerton
Hackney Wick
London Fields
Cambridge Heath
Bethnal Green
STRATFORD
INTERNATIONAL
Maryland
Forest Gate
Manor Park
Ilford
Seven Kings
Goodmayes
Chadwell Heath
Romford
Gidea Park
Harold Wood
Brentwood
Shenfield
Emerson Park
Upminster
Barking
West Ham HL
Limehouse
Whitechapel
Shadwell
Wapping
ST PANCRAS INTERNATIONAL
KINGS CROSS
MOORGATE
LIVERPOOL STREET
Kings Cross St Pancras
Farringdon
Barbican
Tottenham Court Road
Holborn
Bank
Leicester Square
City Thameslink
FENCHURCH STREET
Tower Hill
CHARING CROSS
BLACKFRIARS
CANNON STREET
Westerfield
Derby Road
Trimley
Felixstowe
Woodbridge
Melton
Wickham Market
Saxmundham
Mistley
Wrabness
Harwich International
Dovercourt
Harwich Town
Manningtree
Walton-on-the-Naze
Frinton-on-Sea
Kirby Cross
Clacton-on-Sea
Thorpe-le-Soken
Weeley
Great Bentley
Alresford
Wivenhoe
Hythe
Colchester Town
Colchester
Marks Tey
Sudbury
Bures
Chappel & Wakes Colne
Kelvedon
Braintree
Braintree Freeport
Cressing
White Notley
Witham
Hatfield Peverel
Chelmsford
Ingatestone
Billericay
Wickford
Southminster
Burnham-on-Crouch
Althorne
North Fambridge
South Woodham Ferrers
Battlesbridge
Rayleigh
Hockley
Rochford
Southend Airport
Prittlewell
Victoria
Southend
West Horndon
Laindon
Basildon
Pitsea
Benfleet for Canvey Island
Leigh-on-Sea
Chalkwell
Westcliff
Central
East
Thorpe Bay
Shoeburyness
Stanford-le-Hope
East Tilbury
Tilbury Town
Ockendon
Chafford Hundred
Purfleet
Grays
Rainham
Dagenham Dock
Main Lines
Local services
Limited services

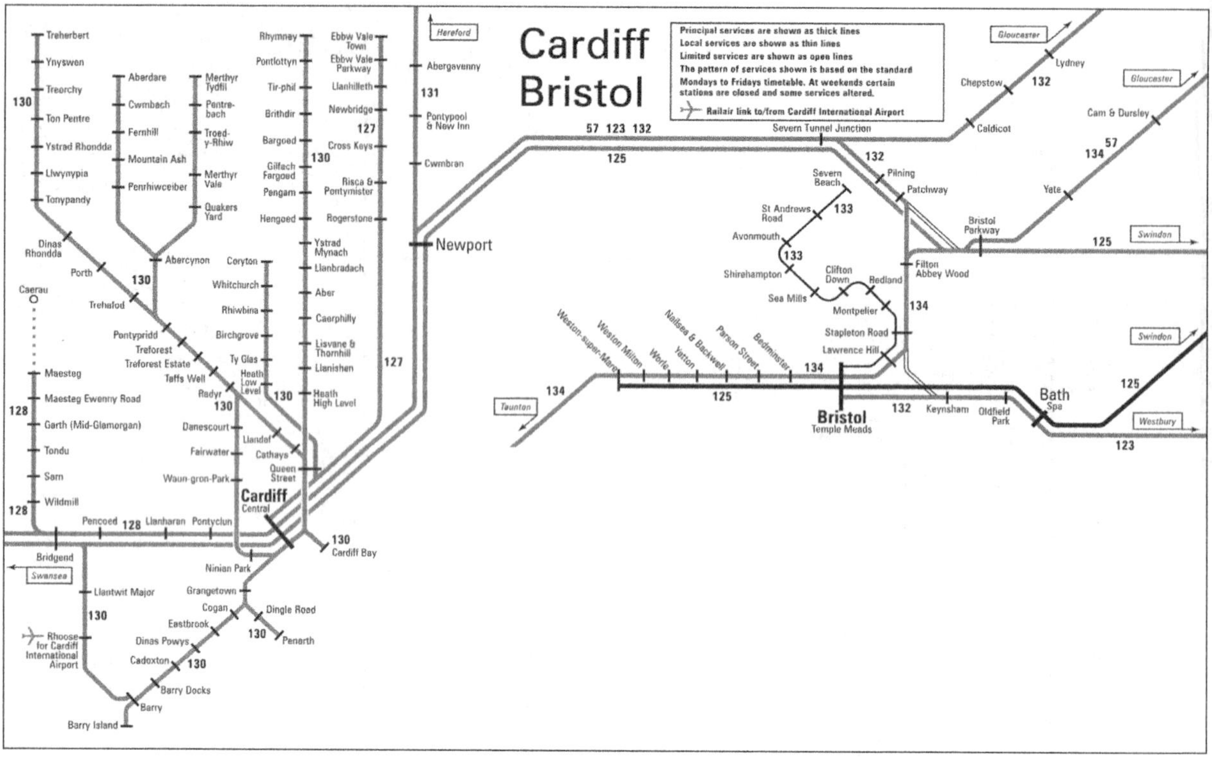
Cardiff
Bristol
Principal services are shown as thick lines
Local services are shown as thin lines
Limited services are shown as open lines
The pattern of services shown is based on the standard Mondays to Fridays timetable. At weekends certain stations are closed and some services altered.
Railair link to/from Cardiff International Airport
Treherbert
Ynyswen
Treorchy
Ton Pentre
Ystrad Rhondda
Llwynypia
Tonypandy
Dinas Rhondda
Porth
Trehafod
Aberdare
Cwmbach
Fernhill
Mountain Ash
Penrhiwceiber
Merthyr Tydfil
Pentre-bach
Troed-y-Rhiw
Merthyr Vale
Quakers Yard
Abercynon
Pontypridd
Treforest
Treforest Estate
Taffs Well
Radyr
Danescourt
Fairwater
Waun-gron Park
Rhymney
Pontlottyn
Tir-phil
Brithdir
Bargoed
Gilfach Fargoed
Pengam
Hengoed
Ystrad Mynach
Llanbradach
Aber
Caerphilly
Lisvane & Thornhill
Llanishen
Heath High Level
Heath Low Level
Ty Glas
Birchgrove
Rhiwbina
Whitchurch
Coryton
Llandaf
Cathays
Queen Street
Cardiff Central
Ebbw Vale Town
Ebbw Vale Parkway
Llanhilleth
Newbridge
Cross Keys
Risca & Pontymister
Rogerstone
Hereford
Abergavenny
Pontypool & New Inn
Cwmbran
Newport
Caerau
Maesteg
Maesteg Ewenny Road
Garth (Mid-Glamorgan)
Tondu
Sarn
Wildmill
Bridgend
Swansea
Pencoed
Llanharan
Pontyclun
Ninian Park
Grangetown
Cogan
Dingle Road
Penarth
Eastbrook
Dinas Powys
Cadoxton
Barry Docks
Barry
Barry Island
Llantwit Major
Rhoose for Cardiff International Airport
Cardiff Bay
Gloucester
Lydney
Chepstow
Caldicot
Severn Tunnel Junction
Cam & Dursley
Yate
Bristol Parkway
Swindon
Severn Beach
Pilning
Patchway
St Andrews Road
Avonmouth
Shirehampton
Sea Mills
Clifton Down
Redland
Montpelier
Stapleton Road
Lawrence Hill
Filton Abbey Wood
Weston-super-Mare
Weston Milton
Worle
Yatton
Nailsea & Backwell
Parson Street
Bedminster
Bristol Temple Meads
Keynsham
Oldfield Park
Bath Spa
Westbury
Taunton
57 123 132
125
130
127
128
131
132
133
134
57
123

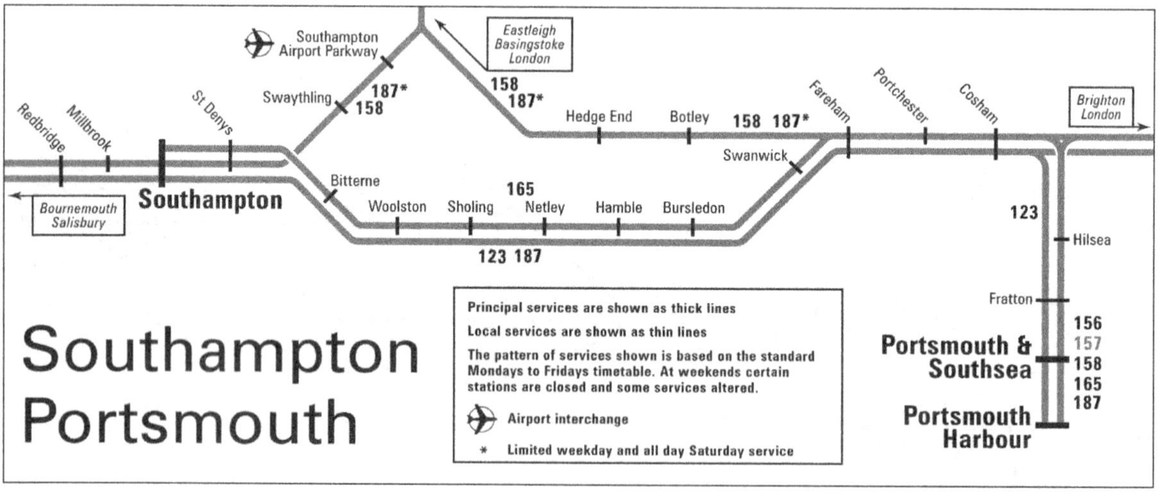
Southampton
Portsmouth
Principal services are shown as thick lines
Local services are shown as thin lines
The pattern of services shown is based on the standard Mondays to Fridays timetable. At weekends certain stations are closed and some services altered.
Airport interchange
* Limited weekday and all day Saturday service
Southampton Airport Parkway
Eastleigh Basingstoke London
Swaythling
187*
158
158
187*
Hedge End
Botley
158 187*
Fareham
Portchester
Cosham
Brighton London
Redbridge
Millbrook
St Denys
Southampton
Bournemouth Salisbury
Bitterne
Woolston
Sholing
165
Netley
Hamble
Bursledon
Swanwick
123 187
123
Hilsea
Fratton
Portsmouth & Southsea
Portsmouth Harbour
156
157
158
165
187

CENTRAL LONDON UNDERGROUND

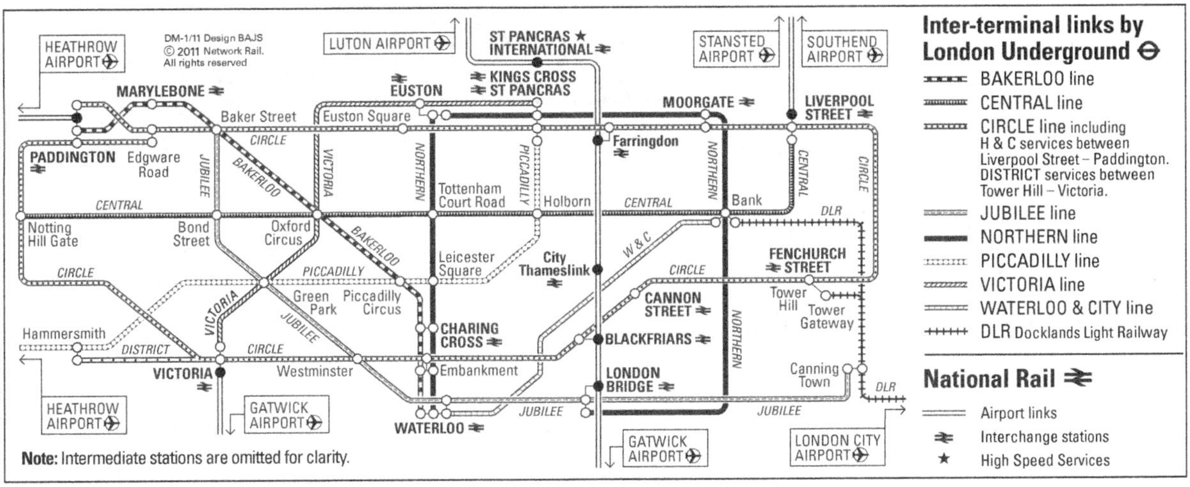

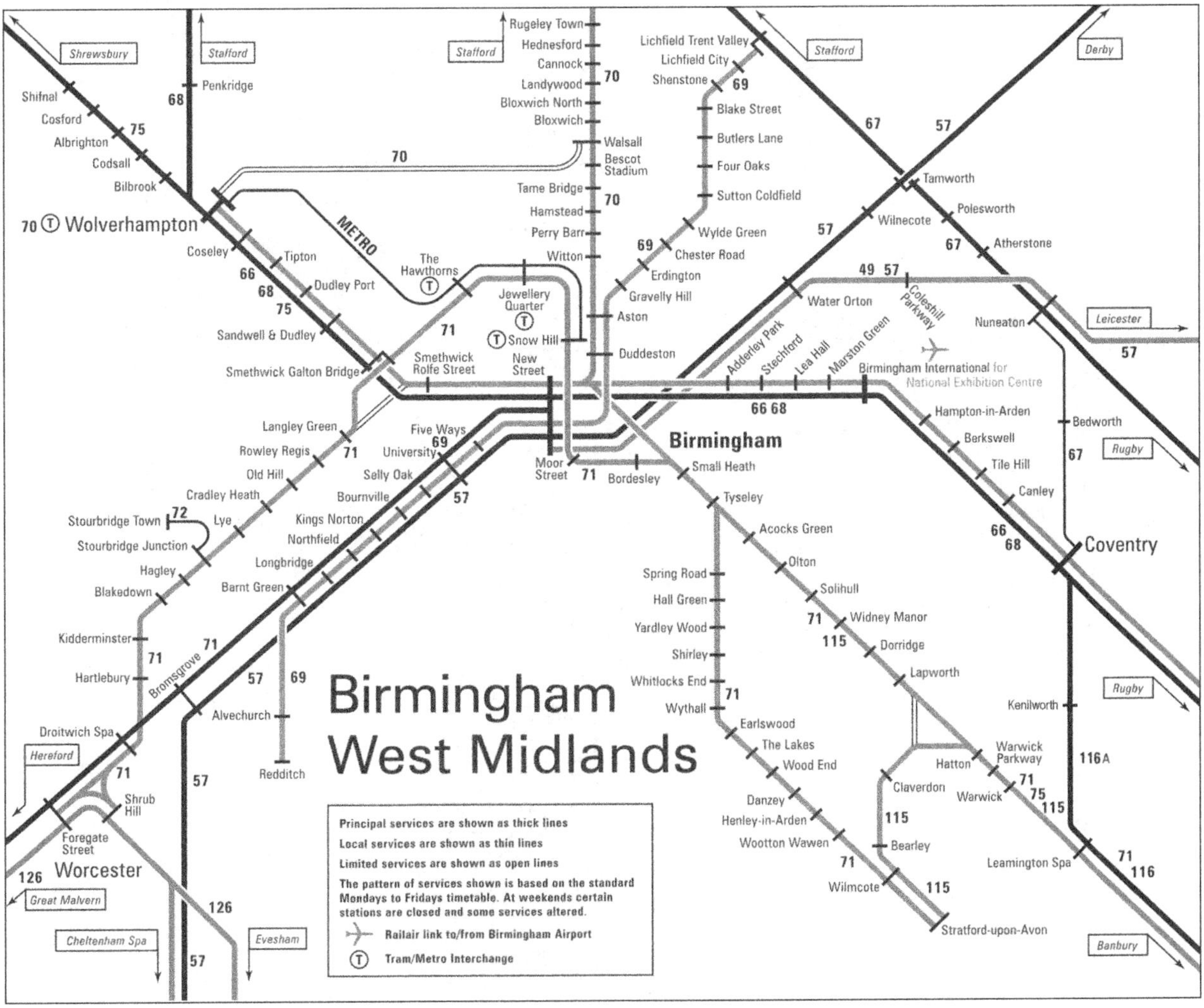

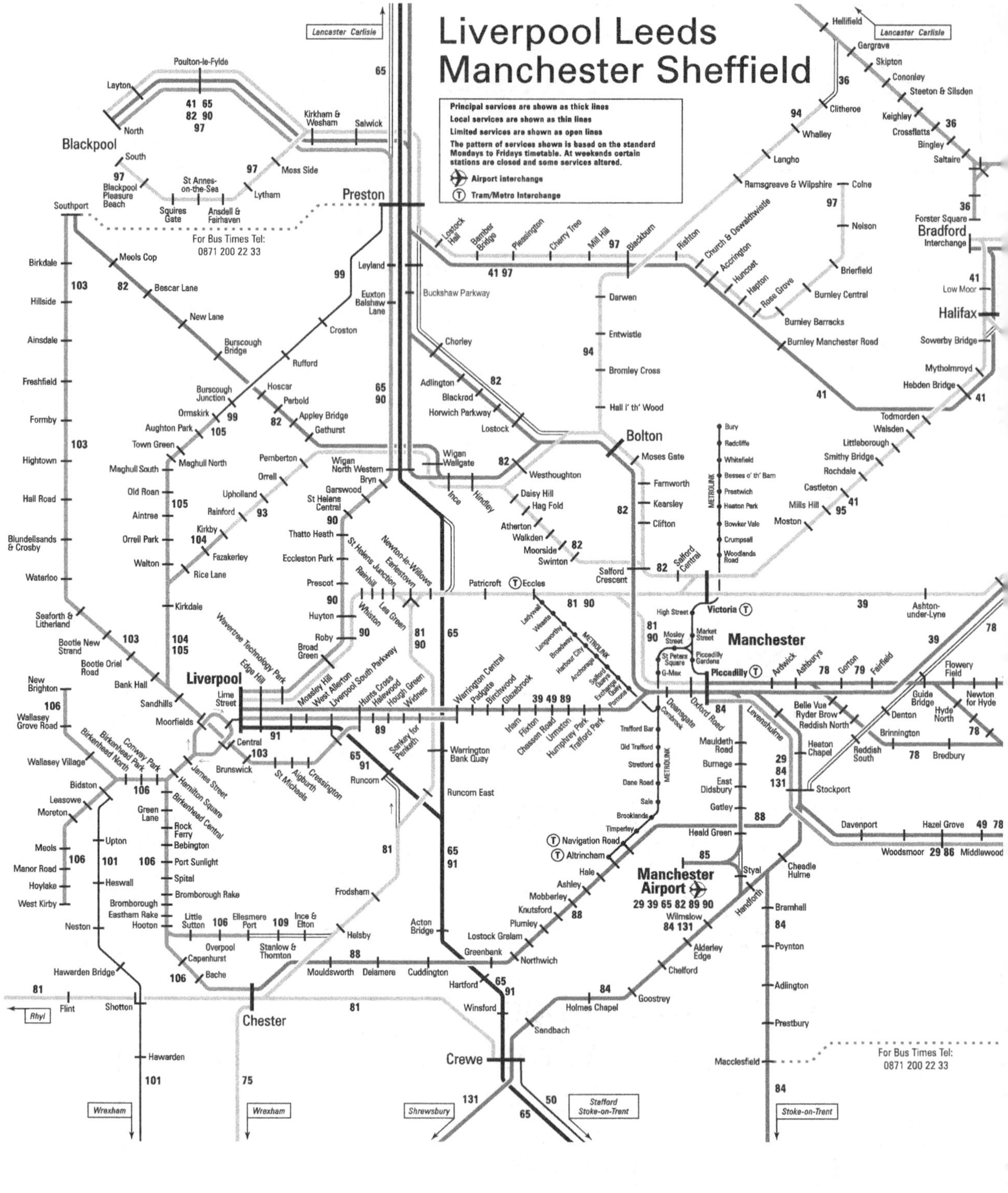
Liverpool Leeds
Manchester Sheffield
Principal services are shown as thick lines
Local services are shown as thin lines
Limited services are shown as open lines
The pattern of services shown is based on the standard Mondays to Fridays timetable. At weekends certain stations are closed and some services altered.
Airport interchange
Tram/Metro Interchange
Lancaster Carlisle
Lancaster Carlisle
Poulton-le-Fylde
Layton
North
Blackpool
South
Blackpool Pleasure Beach
St Annes-on-the-Sea
Squires Gate
Ansdell & Fairhaven
Lytham
Moss Side
Kirkham & Wesham
Salwick
Preston
Southport
For Bus Times Tel:
0871 200 22 33
Birkdale
Hillside
Ainsdale
Freshfield
Formby
Hightown
Hall Road
Blundellsands & Crosby
Waterloo
Seaforth & Litherland
Bootle New Strand
Bootle Oriel Road
Bank Hall
Sandhills
Moorfields
New Brighton
Wallasey Grove Road
Wallasey Village
Bidston
Leasowe
Moreton
Meols
Manor Road
Hoylake
West Kirby
Meols Cop
Bescar Lane
New Lane
Burscough Bridge
Hoscar
Parbold
Appley Bridge
Gathurst
Burscough Junction
Ormskirk
Aughton Park
Town Green
Maghull South
Maghull North
Old Roan
Aintree
Orrell Park
Walton
Rice Lane
Fazakerley
Kirkby
Rainford
Upholland
Orrell
Pemberton
Kirkdale
Croston
Rufford
Leyland
Euxton Balshaw Lane
Buckshaw Parkway
Chorley
Adlington
Blackrod
Horwich Parkway
Lostock
Wigan North Western
Wigan Wallgate
Bryn
Garswood
St Helens Central
Thatto Heath
Eccleston Park
Prescot
Huyton
Roby
Broad Green
Wavertree Technology Park
Edge Hill
Liverpool
Lime Street
Central
Brunswick
St Michaels
Aigburth
Cressington
Mossley Hill
West Allerton
Liverpool South Parkway
Hunts Cross
Halewood
Hough Green
Widnes
Sankey for Penketh
Runcorn
Runcorn East
Warrington Bank Quay
Warrington Central
Padgate
Birchwood
Glazebrook
Irlam
Flixton
Chassen Road
Urmston
Humphrey Park
Trafford Park
Patricroft
Eccles
St Helens Junction
Rainhill
Whiston
Lea Green
Earlestown
Newton-le-Willows
Conway Park
Birkenhead Park
Birkenhead North
Hamilton Square
James Street
Birkenhead Central
Green Lane
Rock Ferry
Bebington
Port Sunlight
Spital
Bromborough Rake
Bromborough
Eastham Rake
Hooton
Upton
Heswall
Neston
Little Sutton
Ellesmere Port
Ince & Elton
Helsby
Overpool
Capenhurst
Stanlow & Thornton
Bache
Chester
Hawarden Bridge
Flint
Shotton
Rhyl
Hawarden
Wrexham
Wrexham
Frodsham
Acton Bridge
Mouldsworth
Delamere
Cuddington
Greenbank
Hartford
Winsford
Crewe
Shrewsbury
Stafford Stoke-on-Trent
Lostock Gralam
Northwich
Plumley
Knutsford
Mobberley
Ashley
Hale
Altrincham
Navigation Road
Sandbach
Holmes Chapel
Goostrey
Chelford
Alderley Edge
Wilmslow
Manchester Airport
Styal
Handforth
Heald Green
Gatley
East Didsbury
Burnage
Mauldeth Road
Levenshulme
Stockport
Cheadle Hulme
Bramhall
Poynton
Adlington
Prestbury
Macclesfield
For Bus Times Tel:
0871 200 22 33
Stoke-on-Trent
Davenport
Woodsmoor
Hazel Grove
Middlewood
Heaton Chapel
Reddish South
Reddish North
Ryder Brow
Belle Vue
Denton
Brinnington
Bredbury
Hyde North
Newton for Hyde
Guide Bridge
Flowery Field
Ashton-under-Lyne
Ardwick
Ashburys
Gorton
Fairfield
Manchester
Piccadilly
Oxford Road
Deansgate
Victoria
Salford Central
Salford Crescent
High Street
Market Street
Mosley Street
St Peters Square
Piccadilly Gardens
G-Mex
Cornbrook
Trafford Bar
Old Trafford
Stretford
Dane Road
Sale
Brooklands
Timperley
METROLINK
Ladywell
Weaste
Langworthy
Broadway
Harbour City
Anchorage
Salford Quays
Exchange Quay
Pomona
Swinton
Moorside
Walkden
Atherton
Hag Fold
Daisy Hill
Hindley
Ince
Westhoughton
Bolton
Moses Gate
Farnworth
Kearsley
Clifton
Hall i' th' Wood
Bromley Cross
Entwistle
Darwen
Bury
Radcliffe
Whitefield
Besses o' th' Barn
Prestwich
Heaton Park
Bowker Vale
Crumpsall
Woodlands Road
Lostock Hall
Bamber Bridge
Pleasington
Cherry Tree
Mill Hill
Blackburn
Rishton
Church & Oswaldtwistle
Accrington
Huncoat
Hapton
Rose Grove
Burnley Barracks
Burnley Manchester Road
Burnley Central
Brierfield
Nelson
Colne
Ramsgreave & Wilpshire
Langho
Whalley
Clitheroe
Hellifield
Gargrave
Skipton
Cononley
Steeton & Silsden
Keighley
Crossflatts
Bingley
Saltaire
Forster Square
Bradford
Interchange
Low Moor
Halifax
Sowerby Bridge
Mytholmroyd
Hebden Bridge
Todmorden
Walsden
Littleborough
Smithy Bridge
Rochdale
Castleton
Mills Hill
Moston
29 39 65 82 89 90
84 131

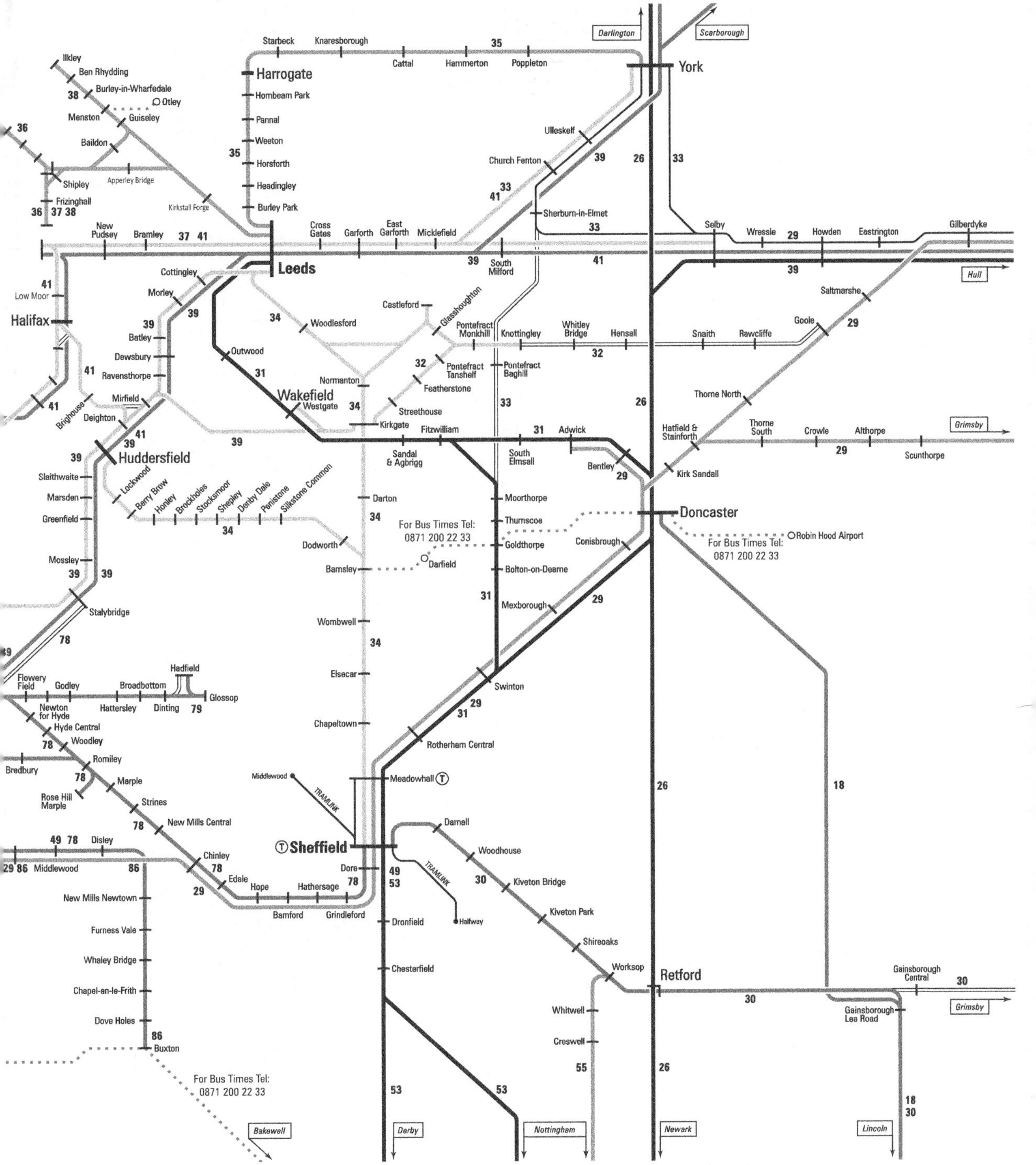
Darlington
Scarborough
York
Starbeck
Knaresborough
35
Cattal
Hammerton
Poppleton
Harrogate
Hornbeam Park
Pannal
Weeton
Horsforth
Headingley
Burley Park
Ilkley
Ben Rhydding
Burley-in-Wharfedale
Otley
Menston
Guiseley
Baildon
Shipley
Apperley Bridge
Frizinghall
Kirkstall Forge
New Pudsey
Bramley
Leeds
Cross Gates
Garforth
East Garforth
Micklefield
Ulleskelf
Church Fenton
Sherburn-in-Elmet
South Milford
Selby
Wressle
Howden
Eastrington
Gilberdyke
Hull
Saltmarshe
Goole
Low Moor
Halifax
Cottingley
Morley
Batley
Dewsbury
Ravensthorpe
Mirfield
Brighouse
Deighton
Castleford
Glasshoughton
Woodlesford
Outwood
Pontefract Monkhill
Knottingley
Whitley Bridge
Hensall
Snaith
Rawcliffe
Pontefract Tanshelf
Pontefract Baghill
Normanton
Featherstone
Wakefield Westgate
Streethouse
Kirkgate
Fitzwilliam
Adwick
Thorne North
Hatfield & Stainforth
Thorne South
Crowle
Althorpe
Grimsby
Scunthorpe
Huddersfield
Slaithwaite
Marsden
Greenfield
Mossley
Stalybridge
Lockwood
Berry Brow
Honley
Brockholes
Stocksmoor
Shepley
Denby Dale
Penistone
Silkstone Common
Sandal & Agbrigg
South Elmsall
Bentley
Kirk Sandall
Darton
Moorthorpe
Thurnscoe
Goldthorpe
Bolton-on-Dearne
Doncaster
For Bus Times Tel: 0871 200 22 33
Robin Hood Airport
Dodworth
Barnsley
Darfield
Conisbrough
Mexborough
Wombwell
Elsecar
Chapeltown
Swinton
Rotherham Central
Meadowhall
Middlewood
TRAMLINK
Sheffield
Flowery Field
Godley
Hadfield
Broadbottom
Glossop
Newton for Hyde
Hattersley
Dinting
Hyde Central
Woodley
Romiley
Bredbury
Marple
Rose Hill Marple
Strines
New Mills Central
Disley
Middlewood
Chinley
Edale
Hope
Hathersage
Bamford
Grindleford
Dore
Darnall
Woodhouse
Kiveton Bridge
Kiveton Park
Shireoaks
Worksop
Retford
Gainsborough Central
Gainsborough Lea Road
Dronfield
Halfway
Chesterfield
New Mills Newtown
Furness Vale
Whaley Bridge
Chapel-en-le-Frith
Dove Holes
Buxton
Whitwell
Creswell
Bakewell
Derby
Nottingham
Newark
Lincoln

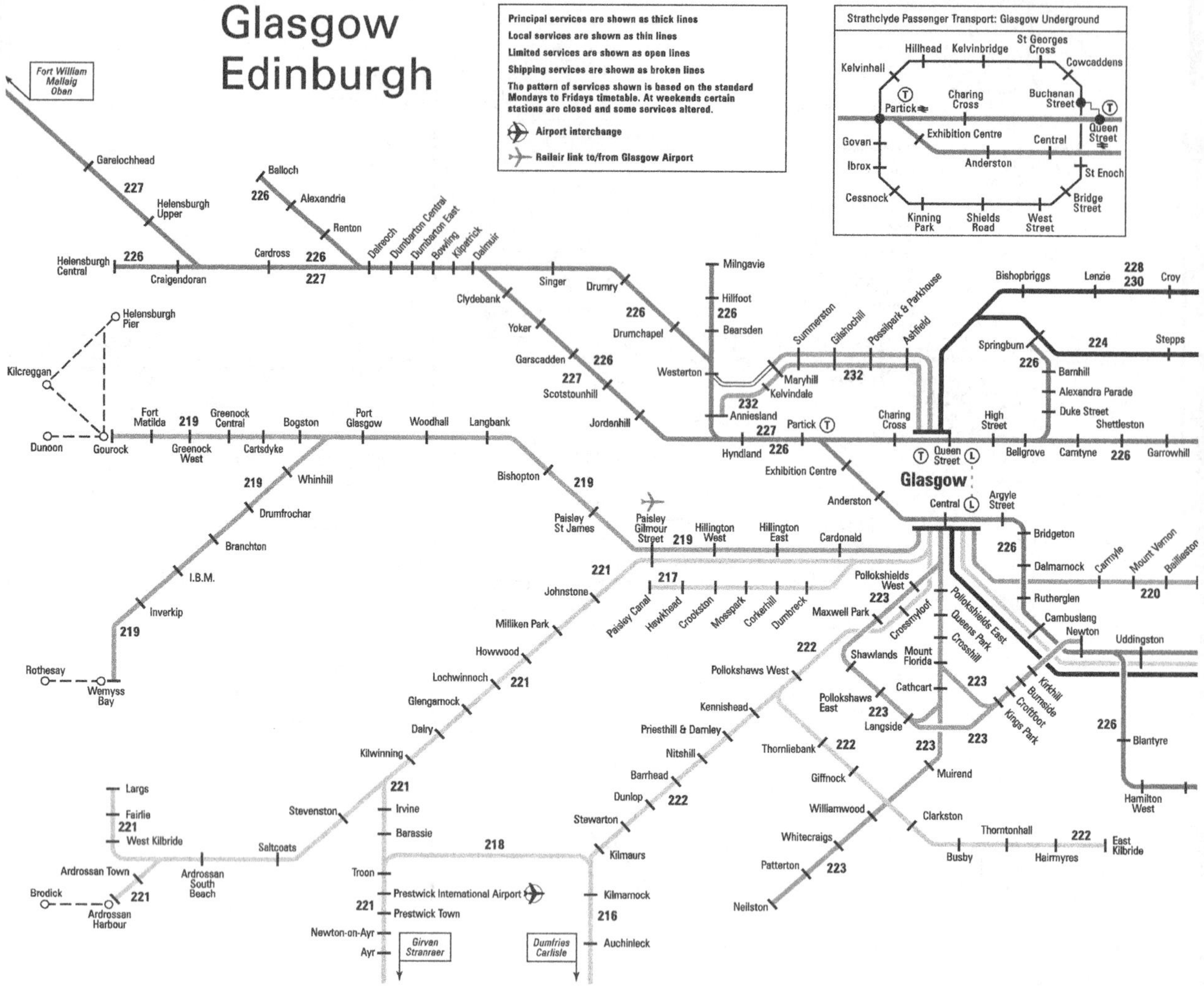
Glasgow
Edinburgh
Principal services are shown as thick lines
Local services are shown as thin lines
Limited services are shown as open lines
Shipping services are shown as broken lines
The pattern of services shown is based on the standard Mondays to Fridays timetable. At weekends certain stations are closed and some services altered.
Airport interchange
Railair link to/from Glasgow Airport
Strathclyde Passenger Transport: Glasgow Underground
Hillhead
Kelvinbridge
St Georges Cross
Cowcaddens
Kelvinhall
Partick
Charing Cross
Buchanan Street
Queen Street
Exhibition Centre
Central
Govan
Ibrox
Anderston
St Enoch
Cessnock
Bridge Street
Kinning Park
Shields Road
West Street
Fort William Mallaig Oban
Garelochhead
227
Helensburgh Upper
Balloch
226
Alexandria
Renton
Helensburgh Central
226
Craigendoran
Cardross
226
227
Dalreoch
Dumbarton Central
Dumbarton East
Bowling
Kilpatrick
Dalmuir
Singer
Drumry
Clydebank
Yoker
226
Drumchapel
Garscadden
226
227
Scotstounhill
Jordanhill
Westerton
Milngavie
Hillfoot
226
Bearsden
Summerston
Gilshochill
Possilpark & Parkhouse
Ashfield
Maryhill
232
Kelvindale
232
Anniesland
227
Partick
Hyndland
226
Charing Cross
Queen Street
Exhibition Centre
Glasgow
Anderston
Central
Argyle Street
Bishopbriggs
Lenzie
228
230
Croy
Springburn
224
Stepps
226
Barnhill
Alexandra Parade
Duke Street
High Street
Shettleston
Bellgrove
Carntyne
226
Garrowhill
Helensburgh Pier
Kilcreggan
Dunoon
Gourock
Fort Matilda
219
Greenock Central
Greenock West
Cartsdyke
Bogston
Port Glasgow
Woodhall
Langbank
219
Whinhill
Drumfrochar
Branchton
I.B.M.
Inverkip
219
Rothesay
Wemyss Bay
Bishopton
219
Paisley St James
Paisley Gilmour Street
219
Hillington West
Hillington East
Cardonald
221
Johnstone
217
Paisley Canal
Hawkhead
Crookston
Mosspark
Corkerhill
Dumbreck
Pollokshields West
223
Maxwell Park
Crossmyloof
Pollokshields East
Queens Park
Crosshill
Bridgeton
226
Dalmarnock
Carmyle
Mount Vernon
Baillieston
220
Rutherglen
Cambuslang
Newton
Uddingston
Milliken Park
Howwood
Lochwinnoch
221
Glengarnock
Dalry
Kilwinning
222
Shawlands
Mount Florida
Pollokshaws West
223
Cathcart
Kirkhill
Burnside
Croftfoot
Kings Park
Kennishead
Pollokshaws East
223
Langside
226
Blantyre
Priesthill & Darnley
Nitshill
Thornliebank
222
223
223
Muirend
Barrhead
Giffnock
Dunlop
222
Stewarton
Williamwood
Clarkston
Thorntonhall
222
East Kilbride
Hamilton West
Busby
Hairmyres
Whitecraigs
Patterton
223
Neilston
Largs
Fairlie
221
West Kilbride
Stevenston
221
Irvine
Barassie
Saltcoats
Ardrossan Town
Ardrossan South Beach
Brodick
221
Ardrossan Harbour
218
Kilmaurs
Troon
Prestwick International Airport
221
Prestwick Town
Kilmarnock
216
Newton-on-Ayr
Ayr
Girvan Stranraer
Dumfries Carlisle
Auchinleck

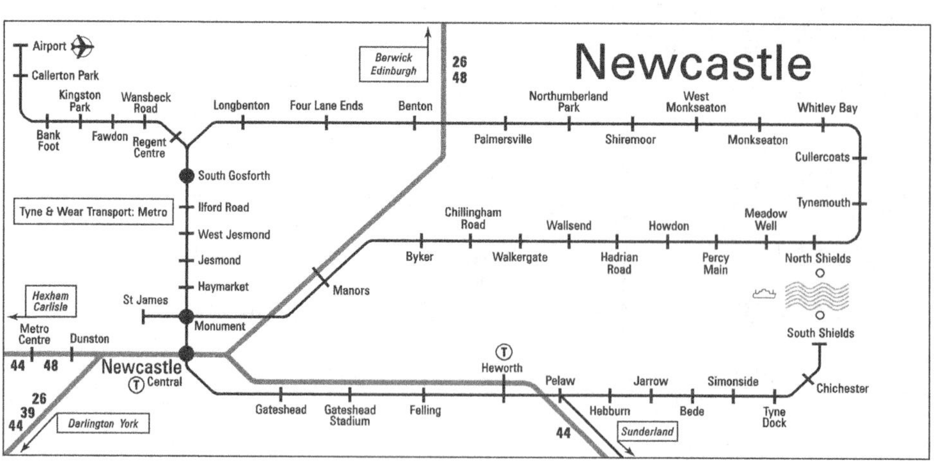
Newcastle
Airport
Callerton Park
Kingston Park
Wansbeck Road
Bank Foot
Fawdon
Regent Centre
Longbenton
Four Lane Ends
Benton
Berwick Edinburgh
26
48
Northumberland Park
West Monkseaton
Whitley Bay
Palmersville
Shiremoor
Monkseaton
Cullercoats
South Gosforth
Tyne & Wear Transport: Metro
Ilford Road
West Jesmond
Jesmond
Haymarket
Chillingham Road
Wallsend
Howdon
Meadow Well
Tynemouth
Byker
Walkergate
Hadrian Road
Percy Main
North Shields
Manors
Hexham Carlisle
St James
Monument
South Shields
Metro Centre
Dunston
44
48
Newcastle
Central
Heworth
Pelaw
Jarrow
Simonside
Chichester
26
39
44
Darlington York
Gateshead
Gateshead Stadium
Felling
Hebburn
Bede
Tyne Dock
44
Sunderland

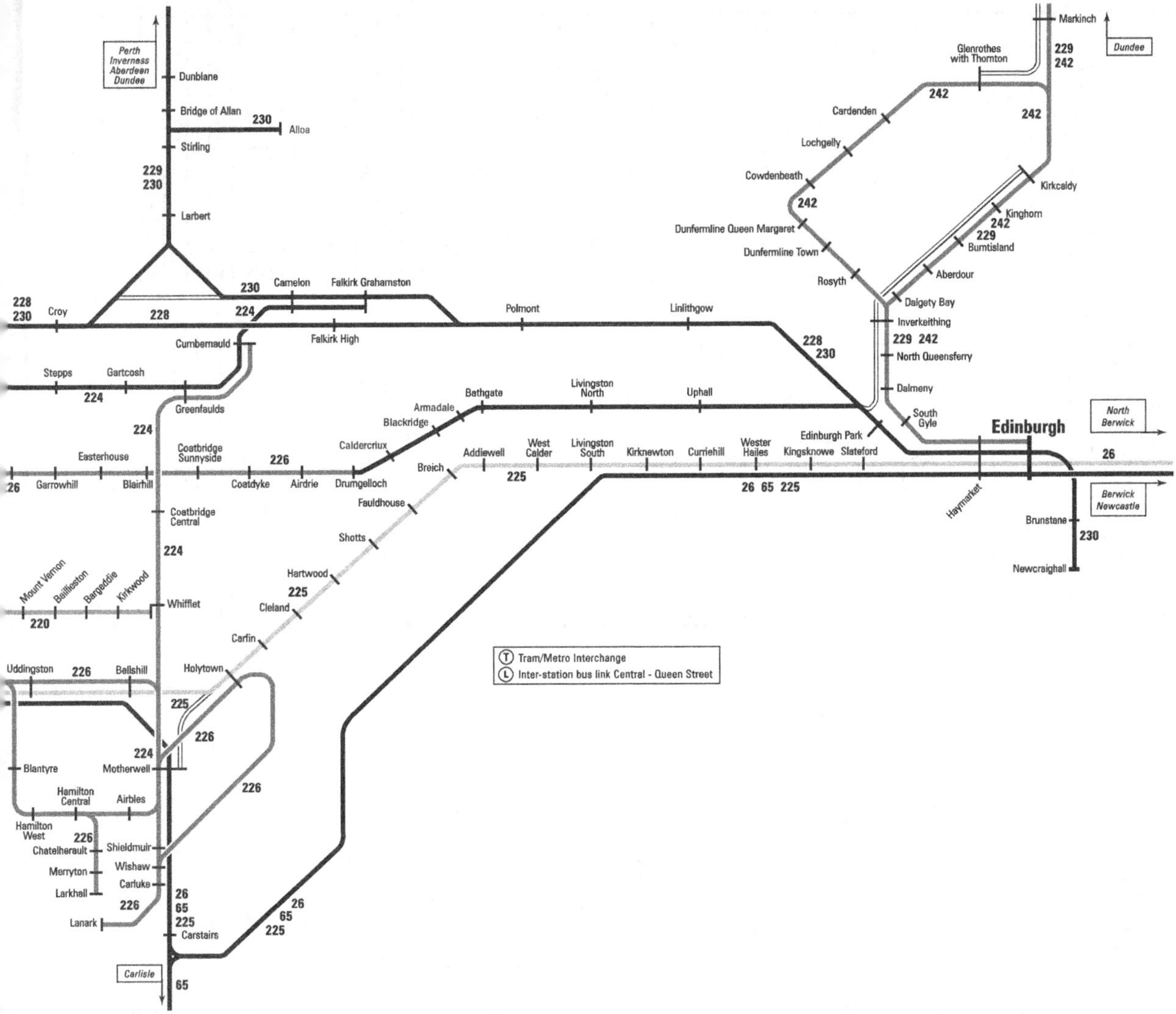

National Rail Passenger Network Diagram 2018

FULL COLOUR A1 Map (folded to A4 size) to accompany the COMPREHENSIVE RAIL TIMES FOR GREAT BRITAIN

For easy journey planning. £9.95 plus £1.35 P&P (UK)

MAIL ORDER from **MP** Middleton Press only

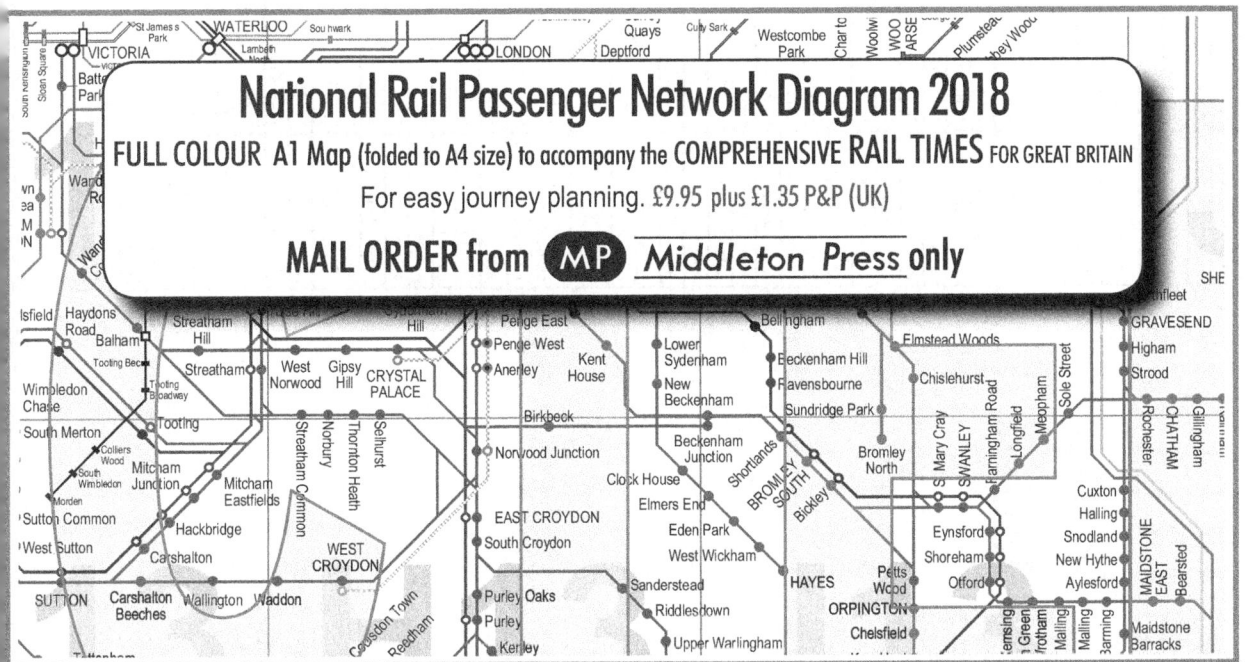

Station Index

A

B

Beaconsfield	T115
Bearley	T115
Bearsden	T226
Bearsted	T196, T197
Beasdale	T227
Beaulieu Road	T158
Beauly	T239
Bebington	T107
Beccles	T013
Beckenham Hill	T195, T196
Beckenham Junction	T173, T195
Bedford	T052, T052MML, T053, T064
Bedford St Johns	T064
Bedhampton	T156, T157, T186
Bedminster	T134
Bedworth	T063
Bedwyn	T116
Beeston	T053, T056, T057
Bekesbourne	T212
Belle Vue	T078
Bellgrove	T226
Bellingham	T195, T196
Bellshill	T224, T225
Belmont	T172, T180
Belper	T056
Beltring	T208
Belvedere	T200, T201
Bempton	T043
Ben Rhydding	T038
Benfleet	T001
Bentham	T042
Bentley	T155
Bentley (S.Yorks)	T029, T031
Bere Alston	T139
Bere Ferrers	T139
Berkhamsted	T066, T176
Berkswell	T068
Bermuda Park	T063
Berney Arms	T015
Berry Brow	T034
Berrylands	T152
Berwick	T190
Berwick-Upon-Tweed	T026, T051
Bescar Lane	T082
Bescot Stadium	T070
Betchworth	T148
Bethnal Green	T020, T021, T022

Betws-Y-Coed	T102
Beverley	T043
Bexhill	T190, T192
Bexley	T200
Bexleyheath	T200
Bicester North	T115
Bicester Village	T115
Bickley	T195, T196
Bidston	T101, T106
Biggleswade	T025
Bilbrook	T074
Billericay	T006
Billingham	T044
Billingshurst	T186
Bingham	T019
Bingley	T036, T042
Birchgrove	T130
Birchington-on-Sea	T194, T212
Birchwood	T089
Birkbeck	T173
Birkdale	T103
Birkenhead Central	T107
Birkenhead North	T106
Birkenhead Park	T106
Birmingham International	T051, T065, T066, T068, T071, T074, T075, T076, T116
Birmingham Moor Street	T071, T115
Birmingham New Street	T047, T051, T057, T065, T066, T068, T069, T070, T071, T074, T075, T076, T081, T084, T091, T116, T135
Birmingham Snow Hill	T071, T115
Bishop Auckland	T044
Bishopbriggs	T228, T230
Bishops Stortford	T022
Bishopstone	T189
Bishopton	T219
Bitterne	T165
Blackburn	T041, T042, T094, T097
Blackheath	T200
Blackhorse Road	T062
Blackpool North	T041, T042, T065, T082, T090, T094, T097

Blackpool Pleasure Beach	T097
Blackpool South	T097
Blackridge	T226
Blackrod	T082
Blackwater	T148
Blaenau Ffestiniog	T102
Blair Atholl	T229
Blairhill	T226
Blake Street	T069
Blakedown	T071
Blantyre	T225
Blaydon	T048
Bleasby	T027
Bletchley	T064, T066, T176
Bloxwich	T070
Bloxwich North	T070
Blundellsands & Crosby	T103
Blythe Bridge	T050
Bodmin Parkway	T051, T135
Bodorgan	T081
Bognor Regis	T186, T188
Bogston	T219
Bolton	T065, T082, T094
Bolton-Upon-Dearne	T031
Bookham	T152
Bootle	T100
Bootle New Strand	T103
Bootle Oriel Road	T103
Bordesley	T071
Borough Green & Wrotham	T196, T197
Borth	T076
Bosham	T186
Boston	T019
Botley	T158
Bottesford	T019
Bourne End	T120
Bournemouth	T051, T158
Bournville	T069
Bow Brickhill	T064
Bowes Park	T024
Bowling	T226
Box Hill & Westhumble	T152, T180
Bracknell	T149
Bradford Forster Square	T026, T036, T037, T038

Bradford Interchange	T026, T032, T037, T040, T041
Bradford-On-Avon	T123, T160
Brading	T167
Braintree	T011
Braintree Freeport	T011
Bramhall	T084
Bramley	T037, T041
Bramley (Hants)	T122
Brampton (Cumbria)	T048
Brampton (Suffolk)	T013
Branchton	T219
Brandon	T017
Branksome	T158
Braystones	T100
Bredbury	T078
Breich	T224
Brentford	T149
Brentwood	T005
Bricket Wood	T061
Bridge Of Allan	T229, T230
Bridge Of Orchy	T227
Bridgend	T125, T128, T130
Bridgeton	T225
Bridgwater	T134, T135
Bridlington	T043
Brierfield	T097
Brigg	T028
Brighouse	T026, T032, T041
Brighton	T025, T052, T123, T184, T186, T188, T189, T190, T192
Brimsdown	T022
Brinnington	T078
Bristol Parkway	T051, T057, T058, T123, T125, T128, T132, T134, T135
Bristol Temple Meads	T051, T057, T058, T123, T125, T132, T133, T134, T135, T160
Brithdir	T130
British Steel Redcar	T044
Briton Ferry	T128
Brixton	T195
Broad Green	T090
Broadbottom	T079
Broadstairs	T194, T207, T212
Brockenhurst	T051, T158, T159

Brockholes	T034
Brockley	T171, T177, T178
Bromborough	T107
Bromborough Rake	T107
Bromley Cross	T094
Bromley North	T204
Bromley South	T052, T195, T196, T197, T212
Bromsgrove	T057, T069, T071
Brondesbury	T059
Brondesbury Park	T059
Brookmans Park	T024
Brookwood	T155
Broome	T129
Broomfleet	T029
Brora	T239
Brough	T029, T039
Broughty Ferry	T229
Broxbourne	T022
Bruce Grove	T021
Brundall	T015
Brundall Gardens	T015
Brunstane	T243
Brunswick	T103
Bruton	T123, T160
Bryn	T090
Buckenham	T015
Buckley	T101
Bucknell	T129
Buckshaw Parkway	T082
Bugle	T142
Builth Road	T129
Bulwell	T055
Bures	T010
Burgess Hill	T184
Burley Park	T035
Burley-In-Wharfedale	T038
Burnage	T085
Burneside	T083
Burnham	T117
Burnham-On-Crouch	T006
Burnley Barracks	T097
Burnley Central	T097
Burnley Manchester Road	T041, T097
Burnside	T223
Burntisland	T242
Burscough Bridge	T082

C

Burscough Junction	T099
Bursledon	T165
Burton Joyce	T027
Burton-On-Trent	T051, T057
Bury St Edmunds	T014
Busby	T222
Bush Hill Park	T021
Bushey	T066
Bushey	T060
Butlers Lane	T069
Buxted	T182
Buxton	T082, T086
Byfleet & New Haw	T155
Bynea	T129
Cadoxton	T130
Caergwrle	T101
Caerphilly	T130
Caersws	T076
Caldercruix	T226
Caledonian Rd & Barnsbury	T059
Calstock	T139
Cam & Dursley	T123, T134
Camberley	T149
Camborne	T051, T135
Cambridge	T014, T017, T022, T025, T047, T052, T196
Cambridge Heath	T021
Cambridge North	T017, T022, T025
Cambuslang	T224, T225
Camden Road	T059
Camelon	T230, T231
Canada Water	T177, T178
Canley	T068
Cannock	T070
Canonbury	T059, T177, T178
Canterbury East	T212
Canterbury West	T194, T197, T207
Cantley	T015
Capenhurst	T107
Carbis Bay	T144
Cardenden	T242
Cardiff Bay	T124
Cardiff Central	T051, T057, T058, T075, T081, T123, T125, T127, T128, T130, T131, T132, T134, T135

Cardiff Queen Street	T124, T130
Cardonald	T219
Cardross	T226
Carfin	T224
Cark	T082
Carlisle	T042, T048, T051, T065, T100, T216
Carlton	T027
Carluke	T224, T225
Carmarthen	T128
Carmyle	T225
Carnforth	T042, T082
Carnoustie	T229
Carntyne	T226
Carpenders Park	T060
Carrbridge	T229
Carshalton	T173, T179, T180
Carshalton Beeches	T172
Carstairs	T065, T224, T225
Cartsdyke	T219
Castle Bar Park	T117
Castle Cary	T123, T135, T160
Castleford	T032, T034
Castleton	T041
Castleton Moor	T045
Caterham	T181
Catford	T052, T195, T196
Catford Bridge	T203
Cathays	T130
Cathcart	T223
Cattal	T035
Causeland	T140
Cefn-Y-Bedd	T101
Chadwell Heath	T005
Chafford Hundred Lakeside	T001
Chalfont & Latimer	T114
Chalkwell	T001
Chandlers Ford	T158
Chapel-en-le-Frith	T086
Chapelton	T136
Chapeltown	T034
Chappel & Wakes Colne	T010
Charing	T196, T197
Charing Cross	T226
Charlbury	T126
Charlton	T200, T201

Chartham	T197, T207
Chassen Road	T089
Chatelherault	T225
Chatham	T194, T200, T201, T212
Chathill	T048
Cheadle Hulme	T084
Cheam	T180
Cheddington	T066
Chelford	T084
Chelmsford	T011
Chelsfield	T204, T206
Cheltenham Spa	T051, T057, T058, T123, T125
Cherry Tree	T097
Chertsey	T149
Cheshunt	T021, T022
Chessington North	T152
Chessington South	T152
Chester	T065, T075, T081, T088, T107, T131
Chester Road	T069
Chester-le-Street	T026, T039, T044, T051
Chesterfield	T034, T049, T051, T053
Chestfield & Swa-lecliffe	T212
Chetnole	T123
Chichester	T123, T165, T186, T188
Chilham	T197, T207
Chilworth	T148
Chingford	T020
Chinley	T078
Chippenham	T123, T125
Chipstead	T181
Chirk	T075, T131
Chislehurst	T204
Chiswick	T149
Cholsey	T116
Chorley	T082
Chorleywood	T114
Christchurch	T158
Christs Hospital	T186
Church & Os-waldtwistle	T097
Church Fenton	T033, T040
Church Stretton	T129, T131
Cilmeri	T129

City Thameslink	T024, T025, T052, T052MML, T173, T175, T179, T180, T181, T182, T183, T184, T185, T188, T195, T196, T197, T201
Clacton-on-Sea	T011
Clandon	T152
Clapham (Nth Yorkshire)	T042
Clapham High Street	T178
Clapham Junction	T059, T066, T149, T152, T155, T156, T158, T160, T170, T171, T172, T175, T176, T178, T180, T181, T182, T183, T184, T185, T186, T188, T189, T190
Clapton	T020
Clarbeston Road	T128
Clarkston	T222
Claverdon	T115
Claygate	T152
Cleethorpes	T027, T028, T029
Cleland	T224
Clifton	T082
Clifton Down	T133
Clitheroe	T042, T094, T097
Clock House	T203
Clunderwen	T128
Clydebank	T226
Coatbridge Central	T225, T231
Coatbridge Sun-nyside	T226
Coatdyke	T226
Cobham & Stoke D'Abernon	T152
Codsall	T074
Cogan	T130
Colchester	T010, T011, T014
Colchester Town	T011
Coleshill Parkway	T047
Collingham	T027
Collington	T190, T192
Colne	T097
Colwall	T071, T126
Colwyn Bay	T075, T081

Combe	T126
Commondale	T045
Congleton	T051, T084
Conisbrough	T029
Connel Ferry	T227
Conon Bridge	T239
Cononley	T036
Conway Park	T106
Conwy	T081
Cooden Beach	T190, T192
Cookham	T120
Cooksbridge	T190
Coombe Junction Halt	T140
Copplestone	T136
Corbridge	T048
Corby	T053
Corkerhill	T217
Corkickle	T100
Corpach	T227
Corrour	T227
Coryton	T130
Coseley	T068
Cosford	T074
Cosham	T123, T158, T165, T186
Cottingham	T043
Cottingley	T039
Coulsdon South	T183
Coulsdon Town	T181
Coventry	T051, T063, T065, T066, T068, T071, T116A, T116
Coventry Arena	T063
Cowden	T182
Cowdenbeath	T242
Cradley Heath	T071, T115
Craigendoran	T226
Cramlington	T048
Cranbrook	T160
Craven Arms	T129, T131
Crawley	T183, T185, T186
Crayford	T200
Crediton	T136
Cressing	T011
Cressington	T103
Creswell (derbys)	T055

Crewe	T050, T051, T065, T067, T081, T084, T085, T091, T131
Crewkerne	T160
Crews Hill	T024
Crianlarich	T227
Criccieth	T076
Cricklewood	T052
Croftfoot	T223
Crofton Park	T195, T196
Cromer	T016
Cromford	T056
Crookston	T217
Cross Gates	T040
Crossflatts	T036
Crosshill	T223
CrossKeys	T127
Crossmyloof	T222
Croston	T099
Crouch Hill	T062
Crowborough	T182
Crowhurst	T206
Crowle	T029
Crowthorne	T148
Croy	T228, T230
Crystal Palace	T171, T173, T177, T178
Cuddington	T088
Cuffley	T024
Culham	T116
Culrain	T239
Cumbernauld	T225, T226, T231
Cupar	T051, T229
Curriehill	T224
Cuxton	T208
Cwmbach	T130
Cwmbran	T131
Cynghordy	T129

D

Dagenham Dock	T001
Daisy Hill	T082
Dalgety Bay	T242
Dalmally	T227
Dalmarnock	T225
Dalmeny	T242
Dalmuir	T226, T227
Dalreoch	T226
Dalry	T221
Dalston	T100
Dalston Junction	T177, T178
Dalston Kingsland	T059
Dalton	T082
Dalwhinnie	T229
Danby	T045
Danescourt	T130
Danzey	T071
Darlington	T026, T039, T044, T051
Darnall	T030
Darsham	T013
Dartford	T052, T200, T201, T212
Darton	T034
Darwen	T094
Datchet	T149
Davenport	T086
Dawlish	T051, T135
Dawlish Warren	T135
Deal	T194, T207
Dean	T158
Deansgate	T082, T084, T085, T086, T089
Deganwy	T081, T102
Deighton	T039
Delamere	T088
Denby Dale	T034
Denham	T115
Denham Golf Club	T115
Denmark Hill	T052, T178, T195, T196, T200
Dent	T042
Denton	T078A
Deptford	T200, T201
Derby	T050, T051, T053, T056, T057
Derby Road	T013
Devonport	T135, T139
Dewsbury	T039, T041
Didcot Parkway	T116, T125, T126
Digby & Sowton	T136
Dilton Marsh	T123
Dinas Powys	T130
Dinas Rhondda	T130
Dingle Road	T130
Dingwall	T239
Dinsdale	T044
Dinting	T079
Disley	T086
Diss	T011
Dockyard	T135, T139
Dodworth	T034
Dolau	T129
Doleham	T192
Dolgarrog	T102
Dolwyddelan	T102
Doncaster	T018, T026, T029, T031, T051, T053
Dorchester South	T158
Dorchester West	T123, T158
Dore & Totley	T078
Dorking	T152, T180
Dorking Deepdene	T148
Dorking West	T148
Dormans	T182
Dorridge	T071, T115
Dove Holes	T086
Dover Priory	T194, T207, T212
Dovercourt	T011
Dovey Junction	T076
Downham Market	T017, T025
Drayton Green	T117
Drayton Park	T024
Drem	T238
Driffield	T043
Drigg	T100
Droitwich Spa	T071
Dronfield	T034
Drumchapel	T226
Drumfrochar	T219
Drumgelloch	T226
Drumry	T226
Duddeston	T069, T070
Dudley Port	T068
Duffield	T056
Duirinish	T239
Duke Street	T226
Dullingham	T014
Dumbarton Central	T226, T227
Dumbarton East	T226
Dumbreck	T217
Dumfries	T216
Dumpton Park	T212
Dunbar	T026, T051, T238
Dunblane	T229, T230
Duncraig	T239
Dundee	T026, T051, T065, T229
Dunfermline Queen Margaret	T242
Dunfermline Town	T242
Dunkeld & Birnam	T229
Dunlop	T222
Dunrobin Castle	T239
Dunston	T048
Dunton Green	T204
Durham	T026, T039, T044, T051
Durrington-on-Sea	T186, T188
Dyce	T229, T240
Dyffryn Ardudwy	T076

E

Eaglescliffe	T026, T044
Ealing Broadway	T116, T117
Earlestown	T081, T090
Earley	T149
Earlsfield	T152, T155
Earlswood (Surrey)	T183
Earlswood (west Midlands)	T071
East Croydon	T025, T052, T066, T170, T173, T175, T176, T177, T181, T182, T183, T184, T185, T186, T188, T189, T190
East Didsbury	T085
East Dulwich	T173
East Farleigh	T208
East Garforth	T040
East Grinstead	T182
East Kilbride	T222
East Malling	T196, T197
East Midlands Parkway	T049, T053
East Tilbury	T001
East Worthing	T188
Eastbourne	T190, T192
Eastbrook	T130
Easterhouse	T226
Eastham Rake	T107
Eastleigh	T158
Eastrington	T029
Ebbsfleet Interna-tional	T192, T194, T200, T207, T212
Ebbw Vale Parkway	T127
Ebbw Vale Town	T127
Eccles	T090
Eccles Road	T017
Eccleston Park	T090
Edale	T078
Eden Park	T203
Edenbridge	T183
Edenbridge Town	T182
Edge Hill	T089, T090, T091
Edinburgh	T026, T042, T051, T065, T224, T225, T226, T227, T228, T229, T230, T238, T242, T243
Edinburgh Gateway	T229, T242
Edinburgh Park	T226, T230
Edmonton Green	T021
Effingham Junction	T152
Eggesford	T136
Egham	T149
Egton	T045
Elephant & Castle	T052, T052MML, T173, T179, T180, T195, T196, T212
Elgin	T240
Ellesmere Port	T107, T109
Elmers End	T203
Elmstead Woods	T204
Elmswell	T014
Elsecar	T034
Elsenham	T022
Elstree & Boreham-wood	T052, T052MML
Eltham	T200
Elton & Orston	T019
Ely	T014, T017, T025, T047, T049
Emerson Park	T004
Emsworth	T186
Energlyn & Churchill Park	T130
Enfield Chase	T024
Enfield Lock	T022
Enfield Town	T021
Entwistle	T094
Epsom	T152, T180
Epsom Downs	T172, T180
Erdington	T069
Eridge	T182
Erith	T200, T201
Esher	T155
Eskbank	T243
Essex Road	T024
Etchingham	T206

F

Euxton Balshaw Lane	T090
Evesham	T126
Ewell East	T180
Ewell West	T152
Exeter Central	T135, T136, T160
Exeter St Davids	T051, T135, T136, T160
Exeter St Thomas	T135
Exhibition Centre	T225, T226
Exmouth	T135, T136
Exton	T136
Eynsford	T195, T196
Fairbourne	T076
Fairfield	T078
Fairlie	T221
Fairwater	T130
Falconwood	T200
Falkirk Grahamston	T228, T230, T231
Falkirk High	T228
Falls Of Cruachan	T227
Falmer	T189, T190
Falmouth Docks	T143
Falmouth Town	T143
Fareham	T123, T158, T165, T186, T188
Farnborough (Main)	T155, T158
Farnborough North	T148
Farncombe	T156
Farnham	T155
Farningham Road	T212
Farnworth	T082
Farringdon	T024, T025, T052, T052MML, T173, T175, T179, T180, T181, T182, T183, T184, T185, T188, T195, T196, T197, T201
Fauldhouse	T224
Faversham	T194, T212
Faygate	T183
Fazakerley	T104
Fearn	T239
Featherstone	T032
Felixstowe	T013
Feltham	T149
Feniton	T160
Fenny Stratford	T064
Fernhill	T130

Ferriby	T029
Ferryside	T128
Ffairfach	T129
Filey	T043
Filton Abbey Wood	T123, T132, T134, T135
Finchley Road & Frognal	T059
Finsbury Park	T024, T025, T052, T196
Finstock	T126
Fishbourne (Sussex)	T186
Fishersgate	T188
Fishguard & Goodwick	T128
Fishguard Harbour	T128
Fiskerton	T027
Fitzwilliam	T031
Five Ways	T069
Fleet	T155, T158
Flimby	T100
Flint	T075, T081
Flitwick	T052MML
Flixton	T089
Flowery Field	T079
Folkestone Central	T194, T207
Folkestone West	T194, T207
Ford	T186
Forest Gate	T005
Forest Hill	T171, T177, T178
Formby	T103
Forres	T240
Forsinard	T239
Fort Matilda	T219
Fort William	T065, T227
Four Oaks	T069
Foxfield	T100
Foxton	T025
Frant	T206
Fratton	T123, T156, T157, T158, T165, T186
Freshfield	T103
Freshford	T123
Frimley	T149
Frinton-on-Sea	T011
Frizinghall	T036, T037, T038
Frodsham	T081

G

Frome	T123, T135, T160
Fulwell	T149, T152
Furness Vale	T086
Furze Platt	T120
Gainsborough Central	T028
Gainsborough Lea Road	T018, T030
Galashiels	T243
Garelochhead	T227
Garforth	T039, T040
Gargrave	T042
Garrowhill	T226
Garscadden	T226
Garsdale	T042
Garston (Hertfordshire)	T061
Garswood	T090
Gartcosh	T231
Garth (Mid Glamorgan)	T128
Garth (Powys)	T129
Garve	T239
Gathurst	T082
Gatley	T085
Gatwick Airport	T025, T052, T052MML, T148, T183, T184, T185, T186, T188, T189, T190
Georgemas Junction	T239
Gerrards Cross	T115
Gidea Park	T005
Giffnock	T222
Giggleswick	T042
Gilberdyke	T029
Gilfach Fargoed	T130
Gillingham (Dorset)	T160
Gillingham (Kent)	T194, T200, T201, T212
Gilshochill	T232
Gipsy Hill	T171, T173
Girvan	T218
Glaisdale	T045
Glan Conwy	T102
Glasgow Central	T026, T042, T051, T065, T216, T217, T218, T219, T221, T222, T223, T224, T225
Glasgow Central L. Level	T225, T226

Glasgow Queen St	T227, T228, T229, T230, T231, T232
Glasgow Queen St L. Level	T226
Glasshoughton	T032
Glazebrook	T089
Gleneagles	T229
Glenfinnan	T227
Glengarnock	T221
Glenrothes with Thornton	T242
Glossop	T079
Gloucester	T051, T057, T058, T123, T125, T128, T134
Glynde	T190
Goathland	T045
Gobowen	T075, T131
Godalming	T156
Godley	T079
Godstone	T183
Goldthorpe	T031
Golf Street	T229
Golspie	T239
Gomshall	T148
Goodmayes	T005
Goole	T029, T032
Goostrey	T084
Gordon Hill	T024
Gorebridge	T243
Goring & Streatley	T116
Goring-by-Sea	T186, T188
Gorton	T078, T079
Gospel Oak	T059, T062, T176
Gourock	T219
Gowerton	T128, T129
Goxhill	T028
Grange Park	T024
Grange-over-Sands	T082
Grangetown	T130
Grantham	T019, T026, T049
Grateley	T160
Gravelly Hill	T069
Gravesend	T194, T200, T201, T212
Grays	T001
Great Ayton	T045
Great Bentley	T011
Great Chesterford	T022
Great Coates	T028

Great Malvern	T071, T123, T126
Great Missenden	T114
Great Yarmouth	T015
Green Lane	T107
Green Road	T100
Greenbank	T088
Greenfaulds	T225, T226, T231
Greenfield	T039
Greenford	T117
Greenhithe For Bluewater	T200, T201, T212
Greenock Central	T219
Greenock West	T219
Greenwich	T052, T200, T201
Gretna Green	T216
Grimsby Docks	T028
Grimsby Town	T027, T028, T029
Grindleford	T078
Grosmont	T045
Grosmont North Yorks Moors	T045
Grove Park	T204
Guide Bridge	T078A, T078, T079
Guildford	T051, T148, T149, T152, T155, T156
Guiseley	T038
Gunnersbury	T059
Gunnislake	T139
Gunton	T016
Gwersyllt	T101
Gypsy Lane	T045

H

Habrough	T027, T028, T029
Hackbridge	T173, T179, T180
Hackney Central	T059
Hackney Downs	T020, T021, T022
Hackney Wick	T059
Haddenham & Thame Parkway	T115
Haddiscoe	T015
Hadfield	T079
Hadley Wood	T024
Hag Fold	T082
Haggerston	T177, T178
Hagley	T071
Hairmyres	T222
Hale	T088
Halesworth	T013
Halewood	T089

Halifax	T026, T032, T041
Hall Green	T071
Hall I' Th' Wood	T094
Hall Road	T103
Halling	T208
Haltwhistle	T048
Ham Street	T192
Hamble	T165
Hamilton Central	T225
Hamilton Square	T106, T107
Hamilton West	T225
Hammerton	T035
Hampden Park	T190, T192
Hampstead Heath	T059
Hampton	T152
Hampton Court	T152
Hampton Wick	T149, T152
Hampton-in-Arden	T068
Hamstead	T070
Hamworthy	T158
Hanborough	T126
Handforth	T084
Hanley Bus Station	T067
Hanwell	T117
Hapton	T097
Harlech	T076
Harlesden	T060
Harling Road	T017
Harlington	T052MML
Harlow Mill	T022
Harlow Town	T022
Harold Wood	T005
Harpenden	T052, T052MML
Harrietsham	T196, T197
Harringay	T024
Harringay Green Lanes	T062
Harrington	T100
Harrogate	T026, T035
Harrow & Weald-stone	T066, T176
Harrow & Weald-stone	T060
Harrow-on-the-Hill	T114
Hartford	T091
Hartlebury	T071
Hartlepool	T026, T044
Hartwood	T224
Harwich International	T011, T013, T014

Harwich Town	T011
Haslemere	T156
Hassocks	T184
Hastings	T190, T192, T206
Hatch End	T060
Hatfield	T024, T025
Hatfield & Stainforth	T029
Hatfield Peverel	T011
Hathersage	T078
Hattersley	T079
Hatton	T071, T115
Havant	T123, T156, T157, T165, T186, T188
Havenhouse	T019
Haverfordwest	T128
Hawarden	T101
Hawarden Bridge	T101
Hawkhead	T217
Haydon Bridge	T048
Haydons Road	T173, T179
Hayes	T203
Hayes & Harlington	T117
Hayle	T051, T135
Haymarket	T026, T051, T065, T224, T225, T226, T228, T229, T230, T238, T242
Haywards Heath	T184, T188, T189, T190
Hazel Grove	T078, T082, T086
Headcorn	T207
Headingley	T035
Headstone Lane	T060
Heald Green	T082, T085
Healing	T028
Heath High Level	T130
Heath Low Level	T130
Heathrow Terminal 4	T117, T118
Heathrow Terminal 5	T117, T118
Heathrow Terminals 2 & 3	T117, T118
Heaton Chapel	T084, T086
Hebden Bridge	T041
Heckington	T019
Hedge End	T158
Hednesford	T070
Heighington	T044

Helensburgh Central	T226
Helensburgh Upper	T226, T227
Hellifield	T042
Helmsdale	T239
Helsby	T081, T109
Hemel Hempstead	T066, T176
Hendon	T052MML
Hengoed	T130
Henley-in-Arden	T071
Henley-on-Thames	T121
Hensall	T032
Hereford	T071, T075, T126, T131
Herne Bay	T194, T212
Herne Hill	T052, T173, T179, T180, T195
Hersham	T155
Hertford East	T022
Hertford North	T024
Hessle	T029
Heswall	T101
Hever	T182
Heworth	T044
Hexham	T044, T048
Heyford	T116
Heysham Port	T042, T098
High Brooms	T206
High Street	T226
High Wycombe	T115
Higham	T200, T201
Highams Park	T020
Highbridge & Burnham	T134
Highbury & Islington	T024
Highbury & Islington-1	T059, T176, T177, T178
Highbury And Islington Ell	T177, T178
Hightown	T103
Hildenborough	T204, T206, T207
Hillfoot	T226
Hillington East	T219
Hillington West	T219
Hillside	T103
Hilsea	T156, T157, T158, T165, T186
Hinchley Wood	T152
Hinckley	T047
Hindley	T082
Hinton Admiral	T158

Hitchin	T025, T052
Hither Green	T199, T200, T204
Hockley	T006
Hollingbourne	T196, T197
Holmes Chapel	T084
Holmwood	T180
Holton Heath	T158
Holyhead	T065, T075, T081, T131
Holytown	T224, T225
Homerton	T059
Honeybourne	T126
Honiton	T160
Honley	T034
Honor Oak Park	T171, T177, T178
Hook	T155
Hooton	T107
Hope (Derbyshire)	T078
Hope (Flintshire)	T101
Hopton Heath	T129
Horley	T183
Hornbeam Park	T035
Hornsey	T024
Horsforth	T035
Horsham	T052, T180, T183, T185, T186
Horsley	T152
Horton-in-Ribbles-dale	T042
Horwich Parkway	T082
Hoscar	T082
Hough Green	T089
Hounslow	T149
Hove	T123, T184, T186, T188
Hoveton & Wrox-ham	T016
How Wood	T061
Howden	T029, T039
Howwood	T221
Hoxton	T177, T178
Hoylake	T106
Hubberts Bridge	T019
Hucknall	T055
Huddersfield	T031, T034, T039, T041
Hull	T026, T029, T033, T039, T043
Hull Paragon Interchange	T028
Humphrey Park	T089

Huncoat	T097
Hungerford	T116, T135
Hunmanby	T043
Huntingdon	T025, T052
Huntly	T240
Hunts Cross	T089, T103
Hurst Green	T182
Hutton Cranswick	T043
Huyton	T090
Hyde Central	T078
Hyde North	T078
Hykeham	T027
Hyndland	T225, T226
Hythe	T011

I

I.B.M.	T219
Ifield	T183
Ilford	T005
Ilkeston	T034, T049
Ilkley	T038
Imperial Wharf	T059, T066, T170, T176
Ince	T082
Ince & Elton	T109
Ingatestone	T011
Insch	T240
Invergordon	T239
Invergowrie	T229
Inverkeithing	T026, T051, T229, T242
Inverkip	T219
Inverness	T026, T065, T229, T239, T240
Invershin	T239
Inverurie	T229, T240
Ipswich	T011, T013, T014, T017
Irlam	T089
Irvine	T221
Isleworth	T149
Islip	T115
Iver	T117
Ivybridge	T135

J

James Cook	T045
James Street	T106, T107
Jewellery Quarter	T071
Johnston	T128
Johnstone	T221
Jordanhill	T226

K

Kearsley	T082
Kearsney	T212
Keighley	T026, T036, T042
Keith	T240
Kelvedon	T011
Kelvindale	T232
Kemble	T125
Kempston Hardwick	T064
Kempton Park	T152
Kemsing	T196, T197
Kemsley	T212
Kendal	T083
Kenilworth	T116A
Kenley	T181
Kennett	T014
Kennishead	T222
Kensal Green	T060
Kensal Rise	T059
Kensington (Olympia)	T059, T066, T170, T176
Kent House	T195
Kentish Town	T052, T052MML, T195, T196
Kentish Town West	T059
Kenton	T060
Kents Bank	T082
Kettering	T053
Kew Bridge	T149
Kew Gardens	T059
Keyham	T135, T139
Keynsham	T123, T132
Kidbrooke	T200
Kidderminster	T071, T115
Kidsgrove	T050, T067, T084
Kidwelly	T128
Kilburn High Road	T060
Kildale	T045
Kildonan	T239
Kilgetty	T128
Kilmarnock	T216, T218, T222
Kilmaurs	T222
Kilpatrick	T226
Kilwinning	T218, T221
Kinbrace	T239
Kingham	T126
Kinghorn	T242
Kings Langley	T066
Kings Lynn	T017, T025
Kings Norton	T069
Kings Nympton	T136
Kings Park	T223
Kings Sutton	T115, T116
Kingsknowe	T224
Kingston	T149, T152
Kingswood	T181
Kingussie	T229
Kintbury	T116
Kirby Cross	T011
Kirk Sandall	T029
Kirkby	T082, T104
Kirkby In Ashfield	T055
Kirkby Stephen	T042
Kirkby-in-Furness	T100
Kirkcaldy	T026, T051, T229, T242
Kirkconnel	T216
Kirkdale	T104, T105
Kirkham & Wesham	T082, T097
Kirkhill	T223
Kirknewton	T224
Kirkstall Forge	T036, T037, T038
Kirkwood	T225
Kirton Lindsey	T028
Kiveton Bridge	T030
Kiveton Park	T030
Knaresborough	T035
Knebworth	T024, T025
Knighton	T129
Knockholt	T204
Knottingley	T032
Knucklas	T129
Knutsford	T088
Kyle Of Lochalsh	T239

L

Ladybank	T051, T229
Ladywell	T203
Laindon	T001
Lairg	T239
Lake	T167
Lakenheath	T017
Lamphey	T128
Lanark	T225
Lancaster	T042, T051, T065, T082, T098, T100
Lancing	T186, T188
Landywood	T070
Langbank	T219
Langho	T094
Langley	T117
Langley Green	T071
Langley Mill	T034, T049, T053
Langside	T223
Langwathby	T042
Langwith -Whaley Thorns	T055
Lapford	T136
Lapworth	T071, T115
Larbert	T229, T230
Largs	T221
Larkhall	T225
Laurencekirk	T229
Lawrence Hill	T133, T134
Layton	T082, T097
Lazonby & Kirko-swald	T042
Lea Bridge	T022
Lea Green	T039, T090
Lea Hall	T068
Leagrave	T052MML
Lealholm	T045
Leamington Spa	T051, T071, T115, T116A, T116
Leasowe	T106
Leatherhead	T152, T180
Ledbury	T071, T126
Lee	T200
Leeds	T026, T031, T032, T034, T035, T036, T037, T038, T039, T040, T041, T042, T051, T053, T097
Leicester	T047, T053
Leigh (Kent)	T183
Leigh-on-Sea	T001
Leighton Buzzard	T066, T176
Lelant	T144
Lelant Saltings	T144
Lenham	T196, T197
Lenzie	T228, T230
Leominster	T131
Letchworth Garden City	T025, T052
Leuchars	T026, T051, T229
Levenshulme	T084, T086
Levisham	T045
Lewes	T184, T189, T190, T192
Lewisham	T195, T199, T200, T203, T204
Leyland	T082, T090
Leyton Midland Road	T062
Leytonstone High Road	T062
Lichfield City	T069
Lichfield Trent Valley	T065, T067, T069
Lidlington	T064
Limehouse	T001
Lincoln	T018, T026, T027, T030, T053
Lingfield	T182
Lingwood	T015
Linlithgow	T228, T230
Liphook	T156
Liskeard	T051, T135, T140
Liss	T156
Lisvane & Thornhill	T130
Little Kimble	T115
Little Sutton	T107
Littleborough	T041
Littlehampton	T186, T188
Littlehaven	T183
Littleport	T017, T025
Liverpool Central	T103, T104, T105, T106, T107
Liverpool Lime Street	T039, T049, T065, T089, T090, T091, T106, T107
Liverpool South Parkway	T049, T065, T089, T091
Liverpool Sth Parkway	T103
Livingston North	T226
Livingston South	T224
Llanaber	T076
Llanbedr	T076
Llanbister Road	T129
Llanbradach	T130
Llandaf	T130
Llandanwg	T076
Llandecwyn	T076
Llandeilo	T129
Llandovery	T129
Llandrindod	T129
Llandudno	T075, T081, T102
Llandudno Junction	T065, T075, T081, T102, T131
Llandybie	T129
Llanelli	T128, T129
Llanfairfechan	T081
Llanfairpwll	T081
Llangadog	T129
Llangammarch	T129
Llangennech	T129
Llangynllo	T129
Llanharan	T128
Llanhilleth	T127
Llanishen	T130
Llanrwst	T102
Llansamlet	T128
Llantwit Major	T130
Llanwrda	T129
Llanwrtyd	T129
Llwyngwril	T076
Llwynypia	T130
Loch Awe	T227
Loch Eil Outward Bound	T227
Lochailort	T227
Locheilside	T227
Lochgelly	T242
Lochluichart	T239
Lochwinnoch	T221
Lockerbie	T051, T065
Lockwood	T034
London Blackfriars	T024, T025, T052, T052MML, T173, T175, T179, T180, T181, T182, T183, T184, T185, T188, T195, T196, T197, T199, T201, T212
London Bridge	T024, T025, T052, T052MML, T170, T171, T172, T173, T175, T177, T179, T180, T181, T182, T183, T184, T185, T186, T188, T189, T190, T196, T196, T197, T199, T200, T201, T203, T204, T206, T207, T212
London Cannon Street	T199, T200, T201, T203, T204, T206, T207, T212

London Charing Cross	T199, T200, T201, T203, T204, T206, T207, T212
London Euston	T060, T065, T066, T067, T068, T081, T084, T091
London Fenchurch St	T001
London Fields	T021
London Kings Cross	T017, T024, T025, T026, T029, T032, T041, T044
London Liverpool St	T001, T005, T006, T011, T015, T017, T020, T021, T022
London Marylebone	T071, T114, T115
London Paddington	T115, T116, T117, T118, T123, T125, T126, T128, T135
London Road (Brighton)	T189, T190
London Road (Guildford)	T152
London Victoria	T170, T171, T172, T175, T180, T181, T182, T183, T184, T185, T186, T188, T189, T190, T195,T196, T197, T199, T200, T201, T212
London Waterloo	T149, T152, T155, T156, T158, T160, T180
London Waterloo (East)	T199, T200, T201, T203, T204, T206, T207, T212
Long Buckby	T066, T068
Long Eaton	T053, T056, T057
Long Preston	T042
Longbeck	T044
Longbridge	T069
Longcross	T149
Longfield	T212
Longniddry	T238
Longport	T050, T084
Longton	T050
Looe	T140
Lostock	T082
Lostock Gralam	T088
Lostock Hall	T097
Lostwithiel	T051, T135
Loughborough	T053
Loughborough Jn	T052, T173, T179, T180, T195
Low Moor	T041
Lowdham	T027
Lower Sydenham	T203
Lowestoft	T013, T015
Ludlow	T131
Luton	T052, T052MML, T053, T201
Luton Airport Parkway	T052, T052MML, T053, T201
Luxulyan	T142
Lye	T071
Lymington Pier	T159
Lymington Town	T159
Lympstone Commando	T136
Lympstone Village	T136
Lytham	T097

M

Macclesfield	T051, T065, T084
Machynlleth	T076
Maesteg	T128
Maesteg (Ewenny Road)	T128
Maghull	T105
Maghull North	T105
Maiden Newton	T123
Maidenhead	T116, T117, T120
Maidstone Barracks	T208
Maidstone East	T025, T052, T196, T197
Maidstone West	T207, T208
Malden Manor	T152
Mallaig	T227
Malton	T039
Malvern Link	T071, T123, T126
Manchester Airport	T029, T039, T065, T078, T081, T082, T084, T085, T089, T090
Manchester Oxford Road	T039, T049, T081, T082, T084, T085, T086, T089, T090
Manchester Piccadilly	T029, T039, T049, T051, T053, T065, T078, T079, T081, T082, T084, T085, T086, T088, T089, T090, T094, T128, T131
Manchester Victoria	T039, T041, T082, T090, T094, T097
Manea	T014, T017
Manningtree	T011, T014
Manor Park	T005
Manor Road	T106
Manorbier	T128
Manors	T048
Mansfield	T055
Mansfield Woodhouse	T055
March	T014, T017, T047, T049
Marden	T207
Margate	T194, T207, T212
Market Harborough	T053
Market Rasen	T027
Markinch	T051, T229
Marks Tey	T010, T011
Marlow	T120
Marple	T078
Marsden	T039
Marske	T044
Marston Green	T068
Martin Mill	T207
Martins Heron	T149
Marton	T045
Maryhill	T232
Maryland	T005
Maryport	T100
Matlock	T056
Matlock Bath	T056
Mauldeth Road	T085
Maxwell Park	T223
Maybole	T218
Maze Hill	T200, T201
Meadowhall	T029, T030, T031, T033, T034
Meldreth	T025
Melksham	T123
Melton	T013
Melton Mowbray	T047, T053
Menheniot	T135
Menston	T038
Meols	T106
Meols Cop	T082
Meopham	T212
Merryton	T225
Merstham	T183
Merthyr Tydfil	T130
Merthyr Vale	T130
Metheringham	T018
Metrocentre	T044, T048
Mexborough	T029
Micheldever	T158
Micklefield	T040
Middlesbrough	T026, T039, T044, T045
Middlewood	T086
Midgham	T116
Milford (Surrey)	T156
Milford Haven	T128
Mill Hill (Lancashire)	T097
Mill Hill Broadway	T052MML
Millbrook (Bedfordshire)	T064
Millbrook (Hants)	T158
Milliken Park	T221
Millom	T100
Mills Hill	T041
Milngavie	T226
Milton Keynes Central	T065, T066, T067, T176
Minffordd	T076
Minster	T207
Mirfield	T026, T032, T039, T041
Mistley	T011
Mitcham Eastfields	T173, T179, T180
Mitcham Junction	T173, T179, T180
Mobberley	T088
Monifieth	T229
Monks Risborough	T115
Montpelier	T133
Montrose	T026, T051, T229
Moorfields	T103, T104, T105, T106, T107
Moorgate	T024
Moorside	T082
Moorthorpe	T031, T033
Morar	T227
Morchard Road	T136
Morden South	T179
Morecambe	T042, T098
Moreton	T106
Moreton (Dorset)	T158
Moreton-in-Marsh	T126
Morfa Mawddach	T076
Morley	T039
Morpeth	T026, T048, T051
Mortimer	T122
Mortlake	T149
Moses Gate	T082
Moss Side	T097
Mossley (Grtr Manchester)	T039
Mossley Hill	T089, T091
Mosspark	T217
Moston	T041
Motherwell	T026, T051, T065, T224, T225, T231
Motspur Park	T152
Mottingham	T200
Mottisfont & Dunbridge	T158
Mouldsworth	T088
Moulsecoomb	T189, T190
Mount Florida	T223
Mount Vernon	T225
Mountain Ash	T130
Muir Of Ord	T239
Muirend	T223
Musselburgh	T238
Mytholmroyd	T041

N

Nafferton	T043
Nailsea & Backwell	T134
Nairn	T240
Nantwich	T131
Narberth	T128
Narborough	T047
Navigation Road	T088
Neath	T125, T128
Needham Market	T011, T014
Neilston	T223
Nelson	T097
Neston	T101
Netherfield	T019
Nethertown	T100
Netley	T165
New Barnet	T024
New Beckenham	T203

New Brighton	T106
New Clee	T028
New Cross	T178, T199, T200, T203, T204
New Cross Gate	T171, T177, T178, T181
New Cumnock	T216
New Eltham	T200
New Holland	T028
New Hythe	T208
New Lane	T082
New Malden	T152
New Mills Central	T078
New Mills Newtown	T086
New Milton	T158
New Pudsey	T037, T041
New Southgate	T024
Newark Castle	T027, T053
Newark North Gate	T026, T027
Newbridge (Ebbw Vale)	T127
Newbury	T116, T135
Newbury Race-course	T116
Newcastle	T026, T039, T044, T045, T048, T051, T216
Newcourt	T136
Newcraighall	T243
Newhaven Harbour	T189
Newhaven Town	T189
Newington	T212
Newmarket	T014
Newport (Essex)	T022
Newport (South Wales)	T051, T057, T075, T123, T125, T128, T131, T132, T135
Newquay	T135, T142
Newstead	T055
Newton	T223, T225
Newton Abbot	T051, T135
Newton Aycliffe	T044
Newton For Hyde	T079
Newton St Cyres	T136
Newton-le-Willows	T039, T081, T090
Newton-on-Ayr	T221
Newtongrange	T243
Newtonmore	T229
Newtown (Powys)	T076
Ninian Park	T130
Nitshill	T222
Norbiton	T152
Norbury	T170, T173, T176
Normans Bay	T190, T192
Normanton	T034
North Berwick	T238
North Camp	T148
North Dulwich	T173
North Fambridge	T006
North Llanrwst	T102
North Queensferry	T242
North Road	T044
North Sheen	T149
North Walsham	T016
North Wembley	T060
Northallerton	T026, T039
Northampton	T066, T067, T068
Northfield	T069
Northfleet	T200, T201
Northolt Park	T115
Northumberland Park	T022
Northwich	T088
Norton Bridge Sta-tion Drv	T067
Norwich	T011, T015, T016, T017, T026, T049
Norwood Junction	T171, T172, T175, T177, T178, T180, T181, T183
Nottingham	T019, T027, T034, T049, T051, T053, T055, T056, T057
Nuneaton	T047, T063, T065, T066, T067
Nunhead	T195, T196, T200
Nunthorpe	T045
Nutbourne	T186
Nutfield	T183

O

Oakengates	T074
Oakham	T047, T053
Oakleigh Park	T024
Oban	T227
Ockendon	T001
Ockley	T180
Okehampton	T136
Old Hill	T071
Old Roan	T105
Old Street	T024
Oldfield Park	T123, T132
Olton	T071
Ore	T190, T192, T206
Ormskirk	T099, T105
Orpington	T052, T195, T196, T199, T204, T206, T207
Orrell	T082
Orrell Park	T105
Otford	T195, T196, T197
Oulton Broad North	T015
Oulton Broad South	T013
Outwood	T031
Overpool	T107
Overton	T160
Oxenholme Lake District	T051, T065, T082, T083
Oxford	T051, T115, T116, T117, T126
Oxford Parkway	T115
Oxshott	T152
Oxted	T182

P

Paddock Wood	T207, T208
Padgate	T089
Paignton	T051, T135
Paisley Canal	T217
Paisley Gilmour St.	T218, T219, T221
Paisley St James	T219
Palmers Green	T024
Pangbourne	T116
Pannal	T035
Pantyffynnon	T129
Par	T051, T135, T142
Parbold	T082
Park Street	T061
Parkstone (Dorset)	T158
Parson Street	T134
Partick	T225, T226
Parton	T100
Patchway	T132
Patricroft	T090
Patterton	T223
Peartree	T050
Peckham Rye	T052, T173, T178, T195, T196, T200
Pegswood	T048
Pemberton	T082
Pembrey & Burry Port	T128
Pembroke	T128
Pembroke Dock	T128
Pen-y-bont	T129
Penally	T128
Penarth	T130
Pencoed	T128
Pengam	T130
Penge East	T195
Penge West	T177, T178
Penhelig	T076
Penistone	T034
Penkridge	T065, T068
Penmaenmawr	T081
Penmere	T143
Penrhiwceiber	T130
Penrhyndeudraeth	T076
Penrith North Lakes	T051, T065
Penryn	T143
Pensarn	T076
Penshurst	T183
Pentre-bach	T130
Penychain	T076
Penyffordd	T101
Penzance	T051, T135, T144
Perranwell	T143
Perry Barr	T070
Pershore	T126
Perth	T026, T065, T229
Peterborough	T014, T017, T018, T025, T026, T047, T049, T052
Petersfield	T156
Petts Wood	T195, T196, T199, T204
Pevensey & Westham	T190, T192
Pevensey Bay	T190, T192
Pewsey	T135
Pickering	T045
Pilning	T132
Pinhoe	T160
Pitlochry	T229
Pitsea	T001
Pleasington	T097
Plockton	T239
Pluckley	T207
Plumley	T088
Plumpton	T190
Plumstead	T200, T201
Plymouth	T051, T135, T139
Pokesdown	T158
Polegate	T190
Polesworth	T067
Pollokshaws East	T223
Pollokshaws West	T222
Pollokshields East	T223
Pollokshields West	T223
Polmont	T228, T230
Polsloe Bridge	T136
Ponders End	T022
Pont-y-pant	T102
Pontarddulais	T129
Pontefract Baghill	T033
Pontefract Monkhill	T026, T031, T032
Pontefract Tanshelf	T032
Pontlottyn	T130
Pontyclun	T128
Pontypool and New Inn	T131
Pontypridd	T130
Poole	T158
Poppleton	T035
Port Glasgow	T219
Port Sunlight	T107
Port Talbot Parkway	T125, T128
Portchester	T158, T165, T186
Porth	T130
Porthmadog	T076
Portlethen	T229
Portslade	T186, T188
Portsmouth & Southsea	T123, T156, T157, T158, T165, T186, T188
Portsmouth Arms	T136
Portsmouth Harbour	T123, T156, T157, T158, T165, T186, T188
Possilpark & Parkhouse	T232
Potters Bar	T024, T025
Poulton-le-Fylde	T041, T082, T097
Poynton	T084
Prees	T131
Prescot	T090
Prestatyn	T075, T081
Prestbury	T084
Preston	T041, T042, T051, T065, T082, T090, T094, T097, T099
Preston Park	T184, T188

Prestonpans	T238
Prestwick Int. Airport	T218, T221
Prestwick Town	T218, T221
Priesthill & Darnley	T222
Princes Risborough	T115
Prittlewell	T006
Prudhoe	T048
Pulborough	T186
Purfleet	T001
Purley	T170, T177, T181, T183
Purley Oaks	T181
Putney	T149
Pwllheli	T076
Pye Corner	T127
Pyle	T128

Q

Quakers Yard	T130
Queen's Park (London)	T060
Queenborough	T212
Queens Park	T223
Queens Rd Peckham	T173, T178
Queenstown Rd.(Battersea)	T149
Quintrell Downs	T142

R

Radcliffe (Notts)	T019
Radlett	T052MML
Radley	T116
Radyr	T130
Rainford	T082
Rainham	T001, T052
Rainham (Kent)	T194, T200, T201, T212
Rainhill	T090
Ramsgate	T194, T207, T212
Ramsgreave & Wilpshire	T094
Rannoch	T227
Rauceby	T019
Ravenglass For Eskdale	T100
Ravensbourne	T195, T196
Ravensthorpe	T039
Rawcliffe	T032
Rayleigh	T006
Raynes Park	T152
Reading	T051, T116, T117, T122, T125, T126, T128, T135, T148, T149, T158
Reading West	T116, T122
Rectory Road	T021
Redbridge	T158
Redcar Central	T044
Redcar East	T044
Reddish North	T078
Reddish South	T078A
Redditch	T069
Redhill	T148, T183
Redland	T133
Redruth	T051, T135
Reedham	T181
Reedham (Norfolk)	T015
Reigate	T148, T183
Renton	T226
Retford	T026, T028, T030
Rhiwbina	T130
Rhoose Cardiff Int Airport	T130
Rhosneigr	T081
Rhyl	T075, T081
Rhymney	T130
Ribblehead	T042
Rice Lane	T104
Richmond	T059, T149
Rickmansworth	T114
Riddlesdown	T182
Ridgmont	T064
Riding Mill	T048
Risca & Pontymister	T127
Rishton	T097
Robertsbridge	T206
Roby	T090
Rochdale	T041, T082, T097
Roche	T142
Rochester	T194, T200, T201, T212
Rochford	T006
Rock Ferry	T107
Rogart	T239
Rogerstone	T127
Rolleston	T027
Roman Bridge	T102
Romford	T004, T005, T006, T011
Romiley	T078
Romsey	T123, T158
Roose	T082
Rose Grove	T097
Rose Hill Marple	T078
Rosslare Harbour	T128
Rosyth	T242
Rotherham Central	T029, T031, T033
Rotherhithe	T177, T178
Roughton Road	T016
Rowlands Castle	T156
Rowley Regis	T071, T115
Roy Bridge	T227
Roydon	T022
Royston	T025, T052
Ruabon	T075, T131
Rufford	T099
Rugby	T065, T066, T067, T068
Rugeley Town	T070
Rugeley Trent Valley	T067, T070
Runcorn	T065, T091
Runcorn East	T081
Ruskington	T018
Ruswarp	T045
Rutherglen	T225
Ryde Esplanade	T167
Ryde Pier Head	T167
Ryde St Johns Road	T167
Ryder Brow	T078
Rye	T190, T192
Rye House	T022

S

Salford Central	T082, T094
Salford Crescent	T082, T094
Salfords	T183
Salhouse	T016
Salisbury	T123, T158, T160
Saltaire	T036
Saltash	T135
Saltburn	T044
Saltcoats	T221
Saltmarshe	T029
Salwick	T097
Sampford Courtenay	T136
Sandal & Agbrigg	T031
Sandbach	T084
Sanderstead	T181, T182
Sandhills	T103, T104, T105
Sandhurst	T148
Sandling	T207
Sandown	T167
Sandplace	T140
Sandwell & Dudley	T066, T068, T074
Sandwich	T194, T207
Sandy	T025
Sankey For Penketh	T089
Sanquhar	T216
Sarn	T128
Saundersfoot	T128
Saunderton	T115
Sawbridgeworth	T022
Saxilby	T018, T030
Saxmundham	T013
Scarborough	T026, T039, T043
Scotscalder	T239
Scotstounhill	T226
Scunthorpe	T029
Sea Mills	T133
Seaford	T189
Seaforth & Litherland	T103
Seaham	T044
Seamer	T039, T043
Seascale	T100
Seaton Carew	T044
Seer Green	T115
Selby	T026, T029, T033, T039, T040, T041
Selhurst	T170, T173, T176
Sellafield	T100
Selling	T212
Selly Oak	T069
Settle	T042
Seven Kings	T005
Seven Sisters	T021, T022
Sevenoaks	T052, T195, T196, T204, T206, T207
Severn Beach	T133
Severn Tunnel Jn	T123, T132
Shadwell	T177, T178
Shalford	T148
Shanklin	T167
Shawfair	T243
Shawford	T158
Shawlands	T223
Sheerness-on-Sea	T212
Sheffield	T018, T026, T029, T030, T031, T033, T034, T049, T051, T053, T078, T089
Shelford	T022
Shenfield	T005, T006, T011
Shenstone	T069
Shepherd's Bush	T059, T066, T170, T176
Shepherds Well	T212
Shepley	T034
Shepperton	T152
Shepreth	T025
Sherborne	T160
Sherburn-in-Elmet	T033
Sheringham	T016
Shettleston	T226
Shieldmuir	T225
Shifnal	T074
Shildon	T044
Shiplake	T121
Shipley	T026, T036, T037, T038, T042
Shippea Hill	T017
Shipton	T126
Shirebrook	T055
Shirehampton	T133
Shireoaks	T030
Shirley	T071
Shoeburyness	T001
Sholing	T165
Shoreditch High Street	T177, T178
Shoreham (Kent)	T195, T196
Shoreham-by-Sea	T123, T186, T188
Shortlands	T195, T196
Shotton	T081, T101
Shotts	T224
Shrewsbury	T074, T075, T076, T129, T131
Sidcup	T200
Sileby	T053
Silecroft	T100
Silkstone Common	T034
Silver Street	T021
Silverdale	T082
Singer	T226
Sittingbourne	T194, T212

Skegness	T019
Skewen	T128
Skipton	T026, T036, T042
Slade Green	T200, T201
Slaithwaite	T039
Slateford	T224
Sleaford	T018, T019
Sleights	T045
Slough	T116, T117, T119, T125, T126, T135
Small Heath	T071
Smallbrook Junction	T167
Smethwick Galton Bridge	T068, T071, T074, T075, T076
Smethwick Rolfe Street	T068
Smithy Bridge	T041
Snaith	T032
Snodland	T208
Snowdown	T212
Sole Street	T212
Solihull	T071, T115
Somerleyton	T015
South Acton	T059
South Bank	T044
South Bermondsey	T173
South Croydon	T181, T182
South Elmsall	T031
South Greenford	T117
South Gyle	T242
South Hampstead	T060
South Kenton	T060
South Merton	T179
South Milford	T040
South Ruislip	T115
South Tottenham	T062
South Wigston	T047
South Woodham Ferrers	T006
Southall	T117
Southampton Airport Pkway	T051, T158
Southampton Central	T051, T123, T158, T165, T186, T188
Southbourne	T186
Southbury	T021
Southease	T189
Southend Airport	T006
Southend Central	T001

Southend East	T001
Southend Victoria	T006
Southminster	T006
Southport	T082, T103
Southwick	T186, T188
Sowerby Bridge	T041
Spalding	T018
Spean Bridge	T227
Spital	T107
Spondon	T056
Spooner Row	T017
Spring Road	T071
Springburn	T226, T231
Springfield	T229
Squires Gate	T097
St Albans Abbey	T061
St Albans City	T052, T052MML, T179, T201
St Andrews Bus Station	T229
St Andrews Road	T133
St Annes-on-the-Sea	T097
St Austell	T051, T135
St Bees	T100
St Budeaux Ferry Road	T135, T139
St Budeaux Victoria Road	T139
St Columb Road	T142
St Denys	T158, T165
St Erth	T051, T135, T144
St Germans	T135
St Helens Central	T090
St Helens Junction	T090
St Helier	T179
St Ives	T144
St James Street	T020
St James' Park	T136
St Johns	T199, T200, T203, T204
St Keyne Wishing Well Halt	T140
St Leonards Warrior Sq	T190, T192, T206
St Margarets	T149
St Margarets (Herts)	T022
St Mary Cray	T052, T195, T196, T197, T212
St Michaels	T103
St Neots	T025

St Pancras International	T024, T025, T052, T052MML, T053, T173, T175, T179, T180, T181, T182, T183, T184, T185, T188, T192, T194, T195, T196, T197, T200, T201, T207, T212
Stafford	T051, T065, T067, T068, T084
Staines	T149
Stallingborough	T028
Stalybridge	T039, T078A
Stamford	T047
Stamford Hill	T021
Stanford-le-Hope	T001
Stanlow & Thornton	T109
Stansted Airport	T017, T022, T047
Stansted Mountfitchet	T022
Staplehurst	T207
Stapleton Road	T133, T134
Starbeck	T035
Starcross	T135
Staveley	T083
Stechford	T068
Steeton & Silsden	T036
Stepps	T231
Stevenage	T024, T025, T026, T052, T196
Stevenston	T221
Stewartby	T064
Stewarton	T222
Stirling	T026, T229, T230
Stockport	T029, T049, T051, T065, T078A, T078, T082, T084, T086, T088, T089, T131
Stocksfield	T048
Stocksmoor	T034
Stockton	T044
Stoke Mandeville	T114
Stoke Newington	T021
Stoke-on-trent	T050, T051, T065, T067, T084
Stone	T067
Stone Crossing	T200, T201
Stone Crown Street	T067

Stone Granville Square	T067
Stonebridge Park	T060
Stonegate	T206
Stonehaven	T026, T051, T229
Stonehouse	T125
Stoneleigh	T152
Stourbridge Junction	T071, T072, T115
Stourbridge Town	T072
Stow	T243
Stowmarket	T011, T014
Stranraer	T218
Stratford	T001, T005, T006, T011, T022, T059, T176
Stratford International	T192, T194, T200, T207, T212
Stratford-upon-Avon	T071, T115
Stratford-upon-Avon Parkway	T071, T115, T175, T181
Strathcarron	T239
Strawberry Hill	T149, T152
Streatham	T052, T173, T179, T180
Streatham Common	T170, T173, T176
Streatham Hill	T171
Streethouse	T032
Strines	T078
Stromeferry	T239
Strood	T194, T200, T201, T208, T212
Stroud	T125
Sturry	T207
Styal	T084
Sudbury	T010
Sudbury & Harrow Road	T115
Sudbury Hill Harrow	T115
Sugar Loaf	T129
Summerston	T232
Sunbury	T152
Sunderland	T026, T044, T048
Sundridge Park	T204
Sunningdale	T149
Sunnymeads	T149
Surbiton	T152, T155
Surrey Quays	T177, T178
Sutton	T052, T170, T171, T172, T173, T179, T180

T

Sutton Coldfield	T069
Sutton Common	T179
Sutton Parkway	T055
Swale	T212
Swanley	T052, T195, T196, T197, T212
Swanscombe	T200, T201
Swansea	T125, T128, T129, T131
Swanwick	T165, T186
Sway	T158
Swaythling	T158
Swinderby	T027
Swindon	T123, T125, T135
Swineshead	T019
Swinton	T082
Swinton (S.Yorks)	T029, T031, T033
Sydenham	T171, T177, T178
Sydenham Hill	T195
Syon Lane	T149
Syston	T053
Tackley	T116
Tadworth	T181
Taffs Well	T130
Tain	T239
Tal-y-Cafn	T102
Talsarnau	T076
Talybont	T076
Tame Bridge Parkway	T070
Tamworth	T051, T057
Tamworth Low Level	T065, T067
Taplow	T117
Tattenham Corner	T181
Taunton	T051, T125, T134, T135
Taynuilt	T227
Teddington	T149, T152
Tees-side Airport	T044
Teignmouth	T051, T135
Telford Central	T074, T075, T076
Templecombe	T160
Tenby	T128
Teynham	T212
Thames Ditton	T152
Thatcham	T116, T135
Thatto Heath	T090
The Hawthorns	T071
The Lakes	T071

Theale	T116, T135
Theobalds Grove	T021
Thetford	T017, T049
Thirsk	T026, T039
Thornaby	T039, T044
Thorne North	T029
Thorne South	T029
Thornford	T123
Thornliebank	T222
Thornton Abbey	T028
Thornton Heath	T170, T173, T176
Thorntonhall	T222
Thorpe Bay	T001
Thorpe Culvert	T019
Thorpe-le-Soken	T011
Three Bridges	T183, T184, T185, T186
Three Oaks	T192
Thurgarton	T027
Thurnscoe	T031
Thurso	T239
Thurston	T014
Tilbury Town	T001
Tile Hill	T068
Tilehurst	T116
Tipton	T068
Tir-Phil	T130
Tisbury	T160
Tiverton Parkway	T051, T135
Todmorden	T041, T097
Tolworth	T152
Ton Pentre	T130
Tonbridge	T183, T204, T206, T207, T208
Tondu	T128
Tonfanau	T076
Tonypandy	T130
Tooting	T173, T179
Topsham	T136
Torquay	T051, T135
Torre	T135
Totnes	T051, T135
Tottenham Hale	T022
Totton	T158
Town Green	T105
Trafford Park	T089
Trefforest	T130
Trefforest Estate	T130
Trehafod	T130
Treherbert	T130
Treorchy	T130
Trimley	T013
Tring	T066, T176
Troed y Rhiw	T130
Troon	T218, T221
Trowbridge	T123, T160
Truro	T051, T135, T143
Tulloch	T227
Tulse Hill	T052, T173, T179, T180
Tunbridge Wells	T206
Turkey Street	T021
Tutbury & Hatton	T050
Tweedbank	T243
Twickenham	T149
Twyford	T116, T117, T121
Ty Croes	T081
Ty Glas	T130
Tygwyn	T076
Tyndrum Lower	T227
Tyseley	T071
Tywyn	T076

U

Uckfield	T182
Uddingston	T224, T225
Ulceby	T028
Ulleskelf	T033, T040
Ulverston	T082
Umberleigh	T136
University	T057, T069, T071
Uphall	T226
Upholland	T082
Upminster	T001, T004
Upper Halliford	T152
Upper Holloway	T062
Upper Tyndrum	T227
Upper Warlingham	T181, T182
Upton	T101
Upwey	T123, T158
Urmston	T089
Uttoxeter	T050

V

Valley	T081
Vauxhall	T149, T152, T155
Virginia Water	T149

W

Waddon	T172
Wadhurst	T206
Wainfleet	T019
Wakefield Kirkgate	T026, T031, T032, T034, T039, T053
Wakefield Westgate	T026, T031, T032, T051, T053
Walkden	T082
Wallasey Grove Road	T106
Wallasey Village	T106
Wallington	T172
Wallyford	T238
Walmer	T207
Walsall	T070
Walsden	T041
Waltham Cross	T022
Walthamstow Central	T020
Walthamstow Queen's Road	T062
Walton	T105
Walton-on-Thames	T155
Walton-on-the-Naze	T011
Wanborough	T148, T149
Wandsworth Common	T170, T171, T176
Wandsworth Road	T178
Wandsworth Town	T149
Wanstead Park	T062
Wapping	T177, T178
Warblington	T186
Ware	T022
Wareham	T158
Wargrave	T121
Warminster	T123, T160
Warnham	T180
Warrington Bank Quay	T051, T065, T081, T090, T109
Warrington Central	T049, T089
Warwick	T071, T115
Warwick Parkway	T071, T115
Water Orton	T047, T057
Waterbeach	T017, T025
Wateringbury	T208
Waterloo	T103
Watford High Street	T060
Watford Junction	T060, T061, T065, T066, T067, T176
Watford North	T061
Watlington	T017, T025
Watton-at-stone	T024
Waun-gron Park	T130
Wavertree Technology Park	T090
Wedgwood Old Road Bridge	T067
Weeley	T011
Weeton	T035
Welham Green	T024
Welling	T200
Wellingborough	T053
Wellington (Shropshire)	T074, T075, T076
Welshpool	T076
Welwyn Garden City	T024, T025, T052, T196
Welwyn North	T024, T025
Wem	T131
Wembley Central	T060, T066, T176
Wembley Stadium	T115
Wemyss Bay	T219
Wendover	T114
Wennington	T042
West Allerton	T089, T091
West Brompton	T059, T066, T170, T176
West Byfleet	T155
West Calder	T224
West Croydon	T170, T171, T172, T177, T178, T180
West Drayton	T117
West Dulwich	T195
West Ealing	T117
West Ham	T001
West Hampstead	T059, T176
West Hampstead Thameslink	T052, T052MML, T179, T201
West Horndon	T001
West Kilbride	T221
West Kirby	T106
West Malling	T196, T197
West Norwood	T171, T173
West Ruislip	T115
West Runton	T016
West St Leonards	T206
West Sutton	T179
West Wickham	T203
West Worthing	T186, T188
Westbury	T123, T135, T160
Westcliff	T001
Westcombe Park	T200, T201
Westenhanger	T207
Wester Hailes	T224
Westerfield	T013
Westerton	T226
Westgate-on-Sea	T212
Westhoughton	T082
Weston Milton	T134
Weston-super-Mare	T051, T125, T134, T135
Wetheral	T048
Weybridge	T149, T155
Weymouth	T123, T158
Whaley Bridge	T086
Whalley	T094
Whatstandwell	T056
Whifflet	T225, T231
Whimple	T160
Whinhill	T219
Whiston	T090
Whitby	T045
Whitchurch (Cardiff)	T130
Whitchurch (Hants)	T160
Whitchurch (Shrops)	T131
White Hart Lane	T021
White Notley	T011
Whitechapel	T177, T178
Whitecraigs	T223
Whitehaven	T100
Whitland	T128
Whitley Bridge	T032
Whitlocks End	T071
Whitstable	T194, T212
Whittlesea	T014, T017
Whittlesford Parkway	T022
Whitton	T149
Whitwell	T055
Whyteleafe	T181
Whyteleafe South	T181
Wick	T239
Wickford	T006
Wickham Market	T013
Widdrington	T048
Widnes	T049, T089
Widney Manor	T071
Wigan North Western	T051, T065, T082, T090
Wigan Wallgate	T082
Wigton	T100
Wildmill	T128

Table T001-F

Mondays to Fridays

21 May to 7 December

London - Southend Central and Shoeburyness

Miles	Miles	Miles	Miles			CC MX A	CC MO B	CC MX A	CC MO A	CC MX A	CC MO A	CC MX A	CC MX A	CC MX A		CC MX C	CC MO	CC MX	CC MX A	CC MX	CC MX	CC	CC	CC	
0	0	0	—	**London Fenchurch St**	d											00 11	00 11	00 19		00 25	00 34		05 00		
1¾	1¾	1¾	—	Limehouse	d											00 15	00 15	00 23		00 29	00 38		05 04		
4	4	4	—	West Ham	d									00 04		00 20	00 20	00 28		00 34	00 43		05 09		
—	—	—	0	**London Liverpool St**	d																				
—	—	—	4	Stratford	d																				
7½	7½	7½	8	Barking	d							00 03		00 09		00 25	00 26	00 33		00 39	00 49	04 53	05 14	05 20	
15¼	—	15¼	—	Upminster	d						00 04	00 11	00 04			00 33	00 34	00 41			00 57	05 01	05 22		
—	—	18½	—	Ockendon	d								00 09			00 39						05 06			
—	—	21	—	Chafford Hundred Lakeside	d								00 13			00 42						05 10			
—	10½	—	—	Dagenham Dock	d									00 14						00 44				05 24	
—	12¾	—	—	Rainham	d									00 17						00 47				05 28	
—	16	—	—	Purfleet	d									00 22						00 52				05 33	
—	19¾	23	—	Grays	d								00 18	00a30		00 46				00a58		05 14		05a40	
—	21½	24¾	—	Tilbury Town	d								00 21			00 49						05 17			
—	25¼	28¼	—	East Tilbury	d								00 27			00 55						05 23			
—	27¼	30½	—	Stanford-le-Hope	d				00 02				00 30			00 59						05 27			
19¾	—	—	—	West Horndon	d						00 09	00 16					00 39	00 46			01 02		05 27		
22¾	—	—	—	Laindon	d			00 01			00 14	00 21					00 44	00 51			01 07		05 32		
24¼	—	—	—	Basildon	d		00 02	00 04			00 17	00 24					00 47	00 54	←		01 10		05 35		
26½	32½	35¾	—	Pitsea	d		00 06	00 08	00 11	00 12	00 21	00 28	00 39			01 07	00 51	00 58	01 07		01 14	05 35	05 39		
29¼	35¼	38½	—	Benfleet	d		00 09	00 11	00 14	00 16	00 24	00 31	00 42			→	00 54	01 01	01 11		01 17	05 38	05 42		
32½	38½	41¾	—	Leigh-on-Sea	d		00 14	00 16	00 19	00 20	00 29	00 36	00 47				00 59	01 06	01 15		01 22	05 43	05 47		
33¾	39¾	43	—	Chalkwell	d		00 16	00 18	00 21	00 23	00 31	00 38	00 49				01 01	01 08	01 18		01 24	05 45	05 49		
34¾	40¾	44	—	Westcliff	d		00 18	00 20	00 23	00 25	00 33	00 40	00 51				01 03	01 10	01 20		01 26	05 47	05 51		
35¾	41¾	45	—	Southend Central	a		00 21	00 23	00 26	00 27	00 36	00 43	00 54				01 06	01 13	01 22		01 29	05 50	05 54		
—	—	—	—		d		00 21	00 23	00 26	00 27	00 36	00 43	00 54				01 06	01 13	01 22		01 29		05 54		
36½	42½	45¾	—	Southend East	d		00 23	00 25	00 28	00 29	00 38	00 45	00 56				01 08	01 15	01 24		01 31		05 56		
38	44	47¼	—	Thorpe Bay	d	00 03	00 26	00 28	00 31	00 32	00 41	00 48	00 58				01 11	01 18	01 27		01 34		05 59		
39½	45½	48¾	—	**Shoeburyness**	a	00 07	00 32	00 32	00 37	00 36	00 47	00 52	01 02				01 17	01 22	01 31		01 38		06 03		

		CC	CC	CC	CC	CC	CC	CC	CC	CC		CC	CC	CC	CC	CC	CC	CC	CC	CC		CC	CC	CC	CC
London Fenchurch St	d	05 07	05 24	05 30	05 40		06 00	06 04	06 08	06 19		06 26	06 35	06 39	06 42	06 46	06 49	06 56	06 59	07 02		07 07	07 13	07 17	07 20
Limehouse	d	05 11	05 28	05 34	05 44		06 05	06 08	06 13	06 23		06 31	06 40	06 44	06 46	06 50	06 53		07 03	07 06		07 12		07 21	07 25
West Ham	d	05 16	05 33	05 39	05 49		06 10	06 13	06 18	06 28		06 36	06 45	06 49	06 51	06 55	06 59		07 08	07 11		07 17		07 27	07 30
London Liverpool St	d																								
Stratford	d																								
Barking	d	05 22	05 39	05 44	05 54	06 01	06 16	06 18	06 24	06 34		06 42	06 50	06 54	06 57	07 01	07 04	07 09	07 14	07 17		07 23	07 27	07 34	07 36
Upminster	d	05 30		05 53	06 02			06 26	06 32	06 42			06 59	07 03		07 09	07 13		07 23			07 33			07 44
Ockendon	d	05 36			06 08				06 40					07 10								07 40			
Chafford Hundred Lakeside	d	05 39			06 11				06 43					07 14								07 44			
Dagenham Dock	d		05 43			06 05	06 20					06 46			07 01					07 21				07 38	
Rainham	d		05 47			06 09	06 24					06 50			07 05					07 25				07 42	
Purfleet	d		05 52			06 14	06 29					06 55			07 10					07 30				07 47	
Grays	d	05 44	05a59		06 16	06a21	06a36		06 48			07a04		07a21	07 16					07a37		07 48		07a54	
Tilbury Town	d	05 47			06 19				06 51						07 19							07 51			
East Tilbury	d	05 53			06 25				06 57						07 25							07 57			
Stanford-le-Hope	d	05 56			06 28				07 00						07 29							08 01			
West Horndon	d			05 58				06 31					07 04						07 28						
Laindon	d			06 03				06 36		06 50			07 09			07 18	07 21	07a24	07 34						07 52
Basildon	d			06 06				06 39		06 54			07 12			07 21	07 25		07 38				07 45		07 56
Pitsea	d	06 04		06 10	06 39			06 43	07a08				07 16		07a38	07 25	07 28		07 42			08a09			07 59
Benfleet	d	06 08		06 13	06 42			06 46		06 59			07 20			07 28	07 32		07 45						08 03
Leigh-on-Sea	d	06 13		06 18	06 47			06 51		07 04			07 25			07 33	07 37		07 50				07a54		08 07
Chalkwell	d	06 15		06 20	06 49			06 53		07 06			07 27			07 36	07 40		07 53						08 10
Westcliff	d	06 17		06 22	06 51			06 55		07 08			07 29			07 38	07 42		07 55						08 12
Southend Central	a	06 20		06 25	06 55			06 58		07 11			07 32			07 42	07 45		07 58						08 14
	d			06 25				06 58		07 11			07 32				07 46		07 58						08 15
Southend East	d			06 27				07 00		07 13			07 34				07 48		08 00						08 17
Thorpe Bay	d			06 29				07 03		07 16			07 37				07 50		08 03						08 19
Shoeburyness	a			06 33				07 08		07 23			07 43				07 54		08 07						08 23

		CC	CC	CC	CC	CC		CC	CC	CC	CC	CC	CC	CC	CC	CC		CC	CC	CC	CC	CC	CC D	CC	CC
London Fenchurch St	d	07 26	07 29	07 32	07 35	07 37		07 44	07 47	07 50	07 52	07 56	07 59	08 02	08 05	08 08		08 11	08 14	08 20	08 26	08 32	08 35	08 41	08 47
Limehouse	d	07 30	07 33	07 36	07 39	07 42		07 48	07 51	07 54	07 57		08 03	08 06	08 09				08 18	08 24	08 30		08 40		08 51
West Ham	d	07 35	07 38	07 41	07 44	07 47		07 53	07 56	07 59	08 02	08 05	08 08	08 11	08 14			08 19	08 24	08 30	08 35	08 40	08 45	08 51	08 56
London Liverpool St	d																								
Stratford	d																								
Barking	d	07 40	07 43	07 47	07 49	07 53		07 58	08 02	08 05	08 07	08 10	08 13	08 17	08 19			08 24	08 30	08 35	08 42	08 46	08 52	08 57	09 01
Upminster	d				07 57	08 02							08 22		08 27			08 33		08 43		08 54	09 03		09 09
Ockendon	d					08 10												08 40					09 10		
Chafford Hundred Lakeside	d					08 13												08 44					09 14		
Dagenham Dock	d			07 51						08 10				08 22					08 35		08 46				
Rainham	d			07 55						08 13				08 26					08 39		08 50				
Purfleet	d			08 00						08 18				08 31					08 45		08 57				
Grays	d			08 06		08 19				08a25				08a37				08 48	08a52		09a05		09 18		
Tilbury Town	d			08 09		08 22												08 51					09 21		
East Tilbury	d			08 15		08 28												08 57					09 27		
Stanford-le-Hope	d			08 18		08 31												09 00					09 31		
West Horndon	d				08 02								08 27							08 48		08 59			09 14
Laindon	d	07a55	08 00		08 07				08 17		08a22	08 26	08 32		08 35	08 40				08 52		09 03		09 13	09 19
Basildon	d		08 03		08 10			08 14	08 20			08 29	08 35		08 39	08 43				08 56		09 07		09 17	09 22
Pitsea	d		08 06	08a26	08 14	08a39			08 23			08 33	08 39		08 42			09a08		08 59		09 10	09 41		09 26
Benfleet	d		08 10		08 17				08 27			08 36	08 42		08 46	08 50				09 03		09 14	→	09 23	09 29
Leigh-on-Sea	d		08 14		08 22			08a26	08 32			08 41	08 47		08 50	08 55				09 07		09 18		09 27	09 34
Chalkwell	d		08 17		08 24				08 34			08 43	08 49		08 53	08 58				09 10		09 21		09 30	09 36
Westcliff	d		08 19		08 26				08 36			08 45	08 51		08 55	09 00				09 12		09 23		09 32	09 38
Southend Central	a		08 22		08 29				08 39			08 48	08 54		08 58	09 02				09 15		09 25		09 34	09 41
	d				08 29							08 48				09 03				09 16		09 26		09 35	09 41
Southend East	d				08 31							08 50				09 05				09 18		09 28		09 37	09 43
Thorpe Bay	d				08 34							08 53				09 07				09 20		09 30		09 39	09 46
Shoeburyness	a				08 39							08 57				09 15				09 24		09 34		09 44	09 50

A From London Fenchurch Street
B From London Liverpool Street
C To Shoeburyness
D To Southend Central

For services between London Liverpool Street and Southend Victoria refer to Table T006

Table T001-F

Mondays to Fridays

21 May to 7 December

London - Southend Central and Shoeburyness

		CC		CC	CC A	CC	CC B	CC	CC	CC A	CC	CC		CC C	CC	CC A	CC	CC	CC C	CC	CC A	CC		CC	CC C
London Fenchurch St	d	08 50		08 59		09 05	09 11	09 17	09 20		09 26	09 34		09 41	09 51		09 55	10 04	10 11	10 19		10 25		10 34	10 41
Limehouse	d			09 03		09 09	09 16	09 21	09 24		09 30	09 39		09 45	09 55		09 59	10 08	10 15	10 23		10 29		10 38	10 45
West Ham	d	08 59		09 08		09 14	09 21	09 26	09 29		09 36	09 44		09 50	10 00		10 04	10 13	10 20	10 28		10 34		10 43	10 50
London Liverpool St	d																								
Stratford	d																								
Barking	d	09 09		09 15		09 20	09 26	09 31	09 34		09 41	09 49		09 55	10 05		10 09	10 18	10 25	10 33		10 39		10 48	10 55
Upminster	d					09 28	09 36		09 42			09 57		10 03	10 13			10 26	10 33	10 41				10 56	11 03
Ockendon	d						09 41							10 09					10 39						11 09
Chafford Hundred Lakeside	d						09 45							10 13					10 43						11 13
Dagenham Dock	d	09 14									09 46						10 14					10 44			
Rainham	d	09 17									09 49						10 17					10 47			
Purfleet	d	09 22									09 54						10 22					10 52			
Grays	d	09a29					09 49				10a01			10 17			10a29		10 47			10a59			11 17
Tilbury Town	d						09 52							10 20					10 50						11 20
East Tilbury	d						09 58							10 26					10 56						11 26
Stanford-le-Hope	d						10 01							10 30					11 00						11 30
West Horndon	d					09 33						10 02						10 31						11 01	
Laindon	d			09 29		09 38		09 46	09 50			10 07			10 21			10 36		10 49				11 06	
Basildon	d			09 33	←	09 41		09 49	09 54	←		10 10			10 25			10 39		10 53				11 09	
Pitsea	d				09 41	09 45	10 09		09 57	10 09		10 14		10 38		←		10 43	11 09		←			11 13	11 38
Benfleet	d			09 39	09 45	09 48	→	09 55	10 01	10 13		10 17		10 42	10 30	10 42		10 46	11 13	10 58	11 13			11 16	11 42
Leigh-on-Sea	d			09 43	09 50	09 53		10 00	10 05	10 17		10 22		→	10 35	10 46		10 51	→	11 03	11 17			11 21	→
Chalkwell	d			09 46	09 52	09 56		10 02	10 08	10 20		10 24			10 37	10 49		10 53		11 05	11 20			11 23	
Westcliff	d			09 48	09 54	09 58		10 04	10 10	10 22		10 26			10 39	10 51		10 55		11 07	11 22			11 25	
Southend Central	a			09 50	09 57	10 00		10 07	10 12	10 24		10 29			10 42	10 54		10 58		11 10	11 25			11 28	
	d			09 51		10 00		10 07	10 13	10 25		10 29			10 42			10 58		11 10				11 28	
Southend East	d			09 53		10 02		10 09	10 15	10 27		10 31			10 44			11 00		11 12				11 30	
Thorpe Bay	d			09 55		10 05		10 12	10 17	10 29		10 34			10 47			11 03		11 15				11 33	
Shoeburyness	a			10 01		10 09		10 16	10 21	10 33		10 38			10 51			11 07		11 19				11 37	

		CC	CC A	CC	CC	CC C	CC	CC A		CC	CC	CC C	CC	CC A	CC	CC	CC C	CC		CC A	CC	CC	CC C	CC	CC A
London Fenchurch St	d	10 49		10 55	11 04	11 11	11 19			11 25	11 34	11 39	11 49		11 45	12 04	12 11	12 19			12 25	12 34	12 41	12 49	
Limehouse	d	10 53		10 59	11 08	11 15	11 23			11 29	11 38	11 43	11 53		11 59	12 08	12 15	12 23			12 29	12 38	12 45	12 53	
West Ham	d	10 58		11 04	11 13	11 20	11 28			11 34	11 43	11 48	11 58		12 04	12 13	12 20	12 28			12 34	12 43	12 50	12 58	
London Liverpool St	d																								
Stratford	d																								
Barking	d	11 03		11 09	11 18	11 25	11 33			11 39	11 48	11 53	12 03		12 09	12 18	12 25	12 33			12 39	12 48	12 55	13 03	
Upminster	d	11 11			11 26	11 33	11 41				11 56	12 02	12 11			12 26	12 33	12 41				12 56	13 03	13 11	
Ockendon	d					11 39						12 07					12 39						13 09		
Chafford Hundred Lakeside	d					11 43						12 11					12 43						13 13		
Dagenham Dock	d			11 14						11 44					12 14						12 44				
Rainham	d			11 17						11 47					12 17						12 47				
Purfleet	d			11 22						11 52					12 22						12 52				
Grays	d			11a29		11 47				11a59		12 17			12a29		12 47				12a59		13 17		
Tilbury Town	d					11 50						12 20					12 50						13 20		
East Tilbury	d					11 56						12 26					12 56						13 26		
Stanford-le-Hope	d					12 00						12 30					13 00						13 30		
West Horndon	d				11 31						12 01					12 31						13 01			
Laindon	d	11 19			11 36		11 49				12 06		12 19			12 36		12 49				13 06		13 19	
Basildon	d	11 23			11 39		11 53				12 09		12 23			12 39		12 53				13 09		13 23	
Pitsea	d		←		11 43	12 08		←			12 13	12 38		←		12 43	13 08			←		13 13	13 38		←
Benfleet	d	11 28	11 42		11 46	12 12	11 58	12 12			12 16	12 42	12 28	12 42		12 46	13 12	12 58		13 12		13 16	13 42	13 28	13 42
Leigh-on-Sea	d	11 33	11 46		11 51	→	12 03	12 16			12 21	→	12 33	12 46		12 51	→	13 03		13 16		13 21	→	13 33	13 46
Chalkwell	d	11 35	11 49		11 53		12 05	12 19			12 23		12 35	12 49		12 53		13 05		13 19		13 23		13 35	13 49
Westcliff	d	11 37	11 51		11 55		12 07	12 21			12 25		12 37	12 51		12 55		13 07		13 21		13 25		13 37	13 51
Southend Central	a	11 40	11 54		11 58		12 10	12 24			12 28		12 40	12 54		12 58		13 10		13 24		13 28		13 40	13 54
	d	11 40			11 58		12 10				12 28		12 40			12 58		13 10				13 28		13 40	
Southend East	d	11 42			12 00		12 12				12 30		12 42			13 00		13 12				13 30		13 42	
Thorpe Bay	d	11 45			12 03		12 15				12 33		12 45			13 03		13 15				13 33		13 45	
Shoeburyness	a	11 49			12 07		12 19				12 37		12 49			13 07		13 19				13 38		13 49	

		CC	CC	CC C		CC	CC A	CC	CC	CC C	CC	CC A	CC	CC		CC C	CC	CC A	CC	CC	CC C	CC	CC A	CC	
London Fenchurch St	d	12 55	13 04	13 11		13 19		13 25	13 34	13 41	13 49		13 55	14 04		14 11	14 19		14 25	14 34	14 41	14 49		14 55	
Limehouse	d	12 59	13 08	13 16		13 23		13 29	13 38	13 45	13 53		13 59	14 08		14 15	14 23		14 29	14 38	14 45	14 53		14 59	
West Ham	d	13 04	13 13	13 21		13 28		13 34	13 43	13 50	13 58		14 04	14 13		14 20	14 28		14 34	14 43	14 50	14 58		15 04	
London Liverpool St	d																								
Stratford	d																								
Barking	d	13 09	13 18	13 26		13 33		13 39	13 48	13 55	14 03		14 09	14 18		14 25	14 33		14 39	14 48	14 55	15 03		15 09	
Upminster	d		13 26	13 34		13 41			13 56	14 03	14 11			14 26		14 33	14 41			14 56	15 03	15 11			
Ockendon	d			13 39						14 09						14 39					15 09				
Chafford Hundred Lakeside	d			13 43						14 13						14 43					15 13				
Dagenham Dock	d	13 14						13 44					14 14						14 44					15 14	
Rainham	d	13 17						13 47					14 17						14 47					15 17	
Purfleet	d	13 22						13 52					14 22						14 52					15 22	
Grays	d	13a29		13 47				13a59		14 17			14a29			14 47			14a59		15 17			15a29	
Tilbury Town	d			13 50						14 20						14 50					15 20				
East Tilbury	d			13 56						14 26						14 56					15 26				
Stanford-le-Hope	d			14 00						14 30						15 00					15 30				
West Horndon	d		13 31						14 01					14 31						15 01					
Laindon	d		13 36			13 49			14 06		14 19			14 36			14 49			15 06		15 19			
Basildon	d		13 39			13 53			14 09		14 23			14 39			14 53			15 09		15 23			
Pitsea	d		13 43	14 08			←		14 13	14 38		←		14 43		15 08		←		15 13	15 38		←		
Benfleet	d		13 46	14 12		13 58	14 12		14 16	14 42	14 28	14 42		14 46		15 12	14 58	15 12		15 16	15 42	15 28	15 42		
Leigh-on-Sea	d		13 51	→		14 03	14 16		14 21	→	14 33	14 46		14 51		→	15 03	15 16		15 21	→	15 33	15 46		
Chalkwell	d		13 53			14 05	14 19		14 23		14 35	14 49		14 53			15 05	15 19		15 23		15 35	15 49		
Westcliff	d		13 55			14 07	14 21		14 25		14 37	14 51		14 55			15 07	15 21		15 25		15 37	15 51		
Southend Central	a		13 58			14 10	14 25		14 28		14 40	14 54		14 58			15 10	15 24		15 28		15 40	15 54		
	d		13 58			14 10			14 28		14 40			14 58			15 10			15 28		15 40			
Southend East	d		14 00			14 12			14 30		14 42			15 00			15 12			15 30		15 42			
Thorpe Bay	d		14 03			14 15			14 33		14 45			15 03			15 15			15 33		15 45			
Shoeburyness	a		14 07			14 19			14 37		14 49			15 07			15 19			15 38		15 49			

A From London Fenchurch Street
B To Shoeburyness
C To Southend Central

For services between London Liverpool Street and Southend Victoria refer to Table T006

London - Southend Central and Shoeburyness

Station		CC	CC A	CC	CC B	CC	CC	CC	CC	CC		CC	CC	CC	CC	CC	CC	CC	CC	CC		CC	CC	CC C	CC
London Fenchurch St	d	15 04	15 11	15 19		15 25	15 34	15 41	15 49	15 55		16 00	16 04	16 07	16 10	16 16	16 19	16 22	16 25	16 28		16 31	16 34	16 37	16 40
Limehouse	d	15 08	15 15	15 23		15 29	15 38	15 45	15 53	15 59		16 05	16 09	16 12	16 15	16 21	16 24	16 27	16 30	16 33		16 36	16 39	16 42	16 45
West Ham	d	15 13	15 20	15 28		15 35	15 44	15 50	15 59	16 05		16 10	16 14	16 17	16 21	16 26	16 29	16 32	16 35	16 38		16 41	16 44	16 47	16 50
London Liverpool St	d																								
Stratford	d																								
Barking	d	15 18	15 25	15 33		15 40	15 49	15 56	16 04	16 11		16 16	16 20	16 23	16 26	16 32	16 35	16 38	16 41	16 44				16 53	16 56
Upminster	d	15 26	15 33	15 41			15 57	16 04	16 13			16 24	16 29		16 35	16 40	16 44		16 49	16 53			16 59		17 04
Ockendon	d		15 39					16 10							16 40				16 57						17 10
Chafford Hundred Lakeside	d		15 43					16 14							16 44				17 01						17 14
Dagenham Dock	d					15 45				16 16				16 28				16 42						16 57	
Rainham	d					15 49				16 20				16 31				16 46						17 01	
Purfleet	d					15 55				16 25				16 36				16 52						17 07	
Grays	d		15 47			16a01		16 19		16a31				16a44	16 49			16 58	17a08					17 13	17a22
Tilbury Town	d		15 50					16 22							16 52			17 01						17 16	
East Tilbury	d		15 56					16 28							16 58			17 07						17 22	
Stanford-le-Hope	d		16 00					16 32							17 01			17 11						17 26	
West Horndon	d	15 31					16 02						16 34				16 49						17 04		
Laindon	d	15 36		15 49			16 07		16 21				16 39			16 49	16 54					17 04	17 09		
Basildon	d	15 39		15 53			16 10		16 24			16 34	16 42				16 57			17 02			17 13		
Pitsea	d	15 43	16 08		←		16 13	16a40					16 46		17a11		17 01	17a21					17 16	17 41	
Benfleet	d	15 46	16 11	15 58	16 11		16 17		16 30			16 40	16 50				17 05			17 09			17 20	→	
Leigh-on-Sea	d	15 51	→	16 03	16 16		16 21		16 34			16 45	16 55				17 10			17a16			17 25		
Chalkwell	d	15 53		16 05	16 18		16 24		16 37			16 47	16 57			17 01	17 12					17 19	17 28		
Westcliff	d	15 55		16 09	16 20		16 26		16 39			16 49	16 59			17 03	17 14					17 21	17 30		
Southend Central	a	15 58		16 12	16 24		16 28		16 41			16 52	17 04			17 05	17 19					17 23	17 35		
	d	15 58		16 12			16 29		16 42			16 52				17 06						17 24			
Southend East	d	16 00		16 14			16 31		16 44			16 54				17 08						17 26			
Thorpe Bay	d	16 03		16 17			16 33		16 46			16 57				17 10						17 28			
Shoeburyness	a	16 07		16 21			16 37		16 50			17 03				17 16						17 34			

Station		CC	CC D	CC	CC	CC		CC	CC B	CC	CC	CC	CC	CC	CC	CC		CC	CC	CC	CC	CC	CC	CC	CC
London Fenchurch St	d	16 45		16 51	16 54	16 57		17 01		17 04	17 07	17 10	17 13	17 16	17 19	17 22		17 25	17 28	17 31	17 34	17 37	17 40	17 43	17 46
Limehouse	d	16 50		16 56	16 59	17 02		17 06		17 09	17 12	17 15	17 18	17 21	17 24	17 27		17 30	17 33	17 36	17 39	17 42	17 45	17 48	17 51
West Ham	d	16 55		17 01	17 04	17 07				17 14	17 17		17 23	17 26	17 29	17 32		17 35		17 41	17 44	17 47	17 50	17 53	
London Liverpool St	d																								
Stratford	d																								
Barking	d	17 01		17 07	17 10	17 13		17 16		17 20	17 24	17 26				17 39		17 41	17 44		17 50	17 54			18 01
Upminster	d	17 09			17 18	17 22				17 29		17 34	17 38		17 44			17 49		17 55	17 59		18 04		18 11
Ockendon	d				17 26							17 40						17 57					18 10		
Chafford Hundred Lakeside	d				17 30							17 44						18 01					18 14		
Dagenham Dock	d			17 12							17 29					17 44						17 59			
Rainham	d			17 16							17 33					17 48						18 03			
Purfleet	d			17 21							17 38					17 53						18 08			
Grays	d			17 27	17a37						17 44	17a50				17 59		18a07				18 14	18a21		
Tilbury Town	d			17 30							17 47					18 02						18 17			
East Tilbury	d			17 36							17 53					18 08						18 23			
Stanford-le-Hope	d			17 40							17 57					18 12						18 27			
West Horndon	d	17 14								17 34					17 49						18 04				
Laindon	d	17 19				17 30				17 39			17 46	17 50	17 54				18 00		18 09				18 19
Basildon	d	17 23	←					17 35		17 43				17 54	17 58					18 06	18 12				18 23
Pitsea	d	17 26	17 41	17a50					←	17 46	18a07				18 01	18a22					18 16	18a37			
Benfleet	d	17 30	17 45			17 37		17 41	17 45	17 50			17 54		18 05				18 09	18 12	18 20			18 24	18 29
Leigh-on-Sea	d	17 35	→			17a44		17 46	17 50	17 55			18a01		18 10				18a16		18 25			18 29	18a35
Chalkwell	d	17 38						17 49	17 52	17 58				18 04	18 13					18 18	18 27			18 31	
Westcliff	d	17 40						17 51	17 54	18 00				18 07	18 15					18 20	18 29			18 33	
Southend Central	a	17 42						17 53	17 57	18 02				18 09	18 17					18 23	18 32			18 36	
	d	17 43						17 54	17 57	18 03				18 10	18 18					18 23	18 32			18 36	
Southend East	d	17 45						17 56	17 59	18 05				18 12	18 20					18 25	18 34			18 38	
Thorpe Bay	d	17 47						17 58	18 02	18 07				18 15	18 22					18 28	18 37			18 41	
Shoeburyness	a	17 54						18 03	18 07	18 14				18 19	18 28					18 33	18 43			18 46	

Station		CC		CC	CC	CC	CC	CC	CC	CC	CC	CC		CC	CC	CC A	CC	CC	CC	CC A	CC	CC B		CC	CC E
London Fenchurch St	d	17 49		17 52	17 55	17 58	18 01	18 04	18 07	18 10	18 13	18 16		18 19	18 22	18 25	18 31	18 34	18 37	18 40	18 46			18 52	
Limehouse	d	17 54		17 57	18 00	18 03	18 06	18 09	18 12	18 15	18 18	18 21		18 24	18 27	18 30	18 36	18 39	18 42	18 45	18 51			18 57	
West Ham	d	17 59		18 02		18 08	18 11	18 14		18 20	18 23	18 26		18 29	18 32	18 35	18 41		18 47	18 50	18 56			19 02	
London Liverpool St	d																								
Stratford	d																								
Barking	d			18 09	18 11		18 17	18 20	18 23	18 26				18 35	18 38			18 50	18 53	18 56				19 08	
Upminster	d	18 14			18 19		18 26	18 29		18 34				18 44		18 48	18 54	18 59		19 04				19 16	
Ockendon	d				18 27					18 40						18 57				19 10					
Chafford Hundred Lakeside	d				18 31					18 44						19 01				19 14					
Dagenham Dock	d			18 13					18 27						18 43				18 57						
Rainham	d			18 17					18 31						18 47				19 01						
Purfleet	d			18 23					18 37						18 52				19 07						
Grays	d			18 29	18a38				18 43	18a50					18 58	19 05			19a15	19 18					
Tilbury Town	d			18 32					18 46						19 01	19 08				19 21					
East Tilbury	d			18 38					18 52						19 07	19 14				19 27					
Stanford-le-Hope	d			18 42					18 56						19 10	19 18				19 31					
West Horndon	d	18 19						18 34						18 49				19 04						19 21	
Laindon	d	18 24				18 31		18 39				18 48		18 54				19 09			19 15			19 26	
Basildon	d	18 28					18 36	18 43						18 58			19 04	19 13			19 19	←		19 30	←
Pitsea	d	18 31		18a52				18 46	19a06					19 01	19a20	19 28		19 16		19 42		19 28		19 33	19 42
Benfleet	d	18 35				18 39	18 43	18 50			18 54			19 05		→	19 10	19 20		→	19 25	19 31		19 37	19 46
Leigh-on-Sea	d	18 40				18 44	18 50	18 55			19a01			19 10			19 15	19 25			19 30	19 36		19 42	→
Chalkwell	d	18 43				18 47		18 58				19 04		19 13			19 17	19 27			19 32	19 38		19 45	
Westcliff	d	18 45				18 49		19 00				19 06		19 15			19 19	19 29			19 34	19 40		19 47	
Southend Central	a	18 48				18 52	18 58	19 02				19 08		19 17			19 22	19 34			19 37	19 44		19 49	
	d	18 48				18 52		19 03				19 09		19 18			19 22				19 37			19 50	
Southend East	d	18 50				18 54		19 05				19 11		19 20			19 24				19 39			19 52	
Thorpe Bay	d	18 53				18 57		19 07				19 13		19 22			19 27				19 42			19 54	
Shoeburyness	a	18 58				19 02		19 13				19 19		19 28			19 33				19 48			20 00	

A To Southend Central
B From London Fenchurch Street
C To Shoeburyness
D From London Fenchurch Street to Shoeburyness
E From London Fenchurch Street to Southend Central

For services between London Liverpool Street and Southend Victoria refer to Table T006

Please check the 'Additional Notes to Individual Tables' section for any other general notes that apply to this Table

Table T001-F

Mondays to Fridays

21 May to 7 December

London - Southend Central and Shoeburyness

Station		CC	CC	CC A	CC B	CC C	CC B	CC A		CC	CC	CC D	CC	CC A	CC	CC	CC D	CC		CC A	CC	CC	CC D	CC	CC A
London Fenchurch St	d	18 55	19 03		19 06	19 11	19 20			19 25	19 34	19 41	19 49		19 55	20 05	20 11	20 19			20 25	20 34	20 41	20 49	
Limehouse	d	19 00	19 08		19 11	19 15	19 25			19 29	19 38	19 45	19 53		19 59	20 09	20 15	20 23			20 29	20 38	20 45	20 53	
West Ham	d	19 05	19 13		19 16	19 20	19 30			19 34	19 43	19 50	19 58		20 04	20 14	20 20	20 28			20 34	20 43	20 50	20 58	
London Liverpool St	d																								
Stratford	d																								
Barking	d	19 11			19 22	19 25	19 36			19 40	19 49	19 55	20 04		20 10	20 19	20 25	20 33			20 40	20 48	20 55	21 03	
Upminster	d				19 30	19 33	19 44				19 57	20 03	20 12			20 27	20 33	20 41				20 56	21 03	21 11	
Ockendon	d					19 39						20 09					20 39						21 09		
Chafford Hundred Lakeside	d					19 43						20 13					20 43						21 13		
Dagenham Dock	d	19 15								19 44					20 14						20 44				
Rainham	d	19 19								19 48					20 18						20 48				
Purfleet	d	19 25								19 54					20 24						20 55				
Grays	d	19 31				19 47				20a01		20 17			20a31		20 47				21a01		21 17		
Tilbury Town	d	19 34				19 50						20 20					20 50						21 20		
East Tilbury	d	19 40				19 56						20 26					20 56						21 26		
Stanford-le-Hope	d	19 44				20 00						20 30					21 00						21 30		
West Horndon	d				19 35						20 02					20 32						21 01			
Laindon	d		19 32		19 40		19 53				20 06		20 20			20 37		20 49				21 06		21 19	
Basildon	d		19 36		19 44		19 56	←			20 10		20 23			20 40		20 53				21 09		21 23	
Pitsea	d	19a54		←	19 48	20 08	20 00	20 08			20 13	20 38		←		20 44	21 08			←		21 13	21 38		←
Benfleet	d		19 42	19 46	19 52	→	20 03	20 12			20 17	20 42	20 29	20 42		20 47	21 12	20 58		21 12		21 16	21 42	21 28	21 42
Leigh-on-Sea	d		19 47	19 51	19 57		20 08	20 16			20 22	→	20 33	20 46		20 52	→	21 03		21 16		21 21	→	21 33	21 46
Chalkwell	d		19 49	19 53	19 59		20 10	20 19			20 25		20 36	20 49		20 54		21 05		21 19		21 23		21 35	21 49
Westcliff	d		19 51	19 55	20 01		20 12	20 21			20 27		20 38	20 51		20 56		21 07		21 21		21 25		21 37	21 51
Southend Central	a		19 54	19 59	20 04		20 15	20 23			20 29		20 40	20 55		20 59		21 10		21 25		21 28		21 40	21 55
	d		19 54		20 04		20 15	20 24			20 30		20 41			20 59		21 10				21 28		21 40	
Southend East	d		19 56		20 06		20 17	20 26			20 32		20 43			21 01		21 12				21 30		21 42	
Thorpe Bay	d		19 59		20 09		20 20	20 28			20 34		20 45			21 04		21 15				21 33		21 45	
Shoeburyness	a		20 03		20 13		20 24	20 32			20 39		20 49			21 08		21 19				21 37		21 49	

Station		CC	CC	CC D		CC	CC A	CC	CC	CC D	CC	CC A	CC	CC		CC C	CC	CC	CC A	CC C	CC	CC A	CC	CC	
London Fenchurch St	d	20 55	21 04	21 11		21 19		21 25	21 34	21 41	21 49		21 55	22 04		22 11	22 25	22 29		22 41	22 49		22 55	23 04	
Limehouse	d	20 59	21 08	21 15		21 23		21 29	21 38	21 45	21 53		21 59	22 08		22 15	22 29	22 33		22 45	22 53		22 59	23 08	
West Ham	d	21 04	21 13	21 20		21 28		21 34	21 43	21 50	21 58		22 04	22 13		22 20	22 34	22 38		22 50	22 58		23 04	23 13	
London Liverpool St	d																								
Stratford	d																								
Barking	d	21 09	21 18	21 25		21 33		21 39	21 49	21 55	22 03		22 09	22 18		22 25	22 39	22 43		22 55	23 03		23 09	23 18	
Upminster	d		21 26	21 33		21 41			21 57	22 03	22 11			22 26		22 33		22 51		23 03	23 11			23 26	
Ockendon	d			21 39						22 09						22 39				23 09					
Chafford Hundred Lakeside	d			21 43						22 13						22 43				23 13					
Dagenham Dock	d	21 14						21 44					22 14				22 44						23 14		
Rainham	d	21 17						21 47					22 17				22 47						23 17		
Purfleet	d	21 22						21 52					22 22				22 52						23 22		
Grays	d	21a29		21 47				21a59		22 17			22a29			22 47	22a59			23 17			23a29		
Tilbury Town	d			21 50						22 20						22 50				23 20					
East Tilbury	d			21 56						22 26						22 56				23 26					
Stanford-le-Hope	d			22 00						22 30						23 00				23 30					
West Horndon	d		21 31						22 02					22 31				22 56			23 16			23 31	
Laindon	d		21 36			21 49			22 07		22 19			22 36				23 01			23 21			23 36	
Basildon	d		21 39			21 53			22 10		22 23			22 39				23 04	←		23 24	←		23 39	
Pitsea	d		21 43	22 08			←		22 14	22 38		←		22 43		23 12		23 08	23 12	23 38	23 28	23 38		23 43	
Benfleet	d		21 46	22 12		21 58	22 12		22 18	22 42	22 28	22 42		22 46		→		23 11	23 16	→	23 31	23 42		23 46	
Leigh-on-Sea	d		21 51	→		22 03	22 16		22 23	→	22 33	22 46		22 51				23 16	23 20		23 36	23 46		23 51	
Chalkwell	d		21 53			22 05	22 19		22 25		22 35	22 49		22 53				23 18	23 23		23 38	23 49		23 53	
Westcliff	d		21 55			22 07	22 21		22 27		22 37	22 51		22 55				23 20	23 25		23 40	23 51		23 55	
Southend Central	a		21 58			22 10	22 25		22 30		22 40	22 55		22 58				23 23	23 27		23 43	23 54		23 58	
	d		21 58			22 10			22 30		22 40			22 58				23 23	23 28		23 43	23 54		23 58	
Southend East	d		22 00			22 12			22 32		22 42			23 00				23 25	23 30		23 45	23 56		23 59	
Thorpe Bay	d		22 03			22 15			22 35		22 45			23 03				23 28	23 32		23 48	23 58		00 03	
Shoeburyness	a		22 07			22 19			22 39		22 49			23 07				23 32	23 36		23 52	00 03		00 07	

A From London Fenchurch Street
B not 28 May
C To Shoeburyness
D To Southend Central

For services between London Liverpool Street and Southend Victoria refer to Table T006

Table T001-F

Mondays to Fridays

21 May to 7 December

London - Southend Central and Shoeburyness

Station		CC A	CC	CC	CC B	CC A	CC	CC B	CC
London Fenchurch St ⊖	d	23 11	23 25	23 29		23 41	23 49		23 55
Limehouse	d	23 15	23 29	23 33		23 45	23 53		23 59
West Ham ⊖	d	23 20	23 34	23 38		23 50	23 58		00 04
London Liverpool St ⊖	d								
Stratford ⊖	d								
Barking ⊖	d	23 25	23 39	23 43		23 55	00 03		00 09
Upminster ⊖	d	23 33		23 51		00 04	00 11		
Ockendon	d	23 39				00 09			
Chafford Hundred Lakeside	d	23 43				00 13			
Dagenham Dock	d		23 44						00 14
Rainham	d		23 47						00 17
Purfleet	d		23 52						00 22
Grays	d	23 47	23a59			00 18			00a30
Tilbury Town	d	23 50				00 21			
East Tilbury	d	23 56				00 27			
Stanford-le-Hope	d	23 59				00 30			
West Horndon	d			23 56			00 16		
Laindon	d			00 01			00 21		
Basildon	d			00 04	←		00 24	←	
Pitsea	d	00 12		00 08	00 12	00 39	00 28	00 39	
Benfleet	d	↪		00 11	00 16	↪	00 31	00 42	
Leigh-on-Sea	d			00 16	00 20		00 36	00 47	
Chalkwell	d			00 18	00 23		00 38	00 49	
Westcliff	d			00 20	00 25		00 40	00 51	
Southend Central	a			00 23	00 27		00 43	00 54	
	d			00 23	00 27		00 43	00 54	
Southend East	d			00 25	00 29		00 45	00 56	
Thorpe Bay	d			00 28	00 32		00 48	00 58	
Shoeburyness	a			00 32	00 36		00 52	01 02	

Saturdays

26 May to 8 December

Station		CC B	CC B	CC B	CC B	CC B	CC B	CC A	CC	CC B
London Fenchurch St ⊖	d							00 11	00 19	
Limehouse	d							00 15	00 23	
West Ham ⊖	d						00 04	00 20	00 28	
London Liverpool St ⊖	d									
Stratford ⊖	d									
Barking ⊖	d				00 03		00 09	00 25	00 33	
Upminster ⊖	d				00 11	00 04		00 33	00 41	
Ockendon	d					00 09		00 39		
Chafford Hundred Lakeside	d					00 13		00 42		
Dagenham Dock	d						00 14			
Rainham	d						00 17			
Purfleet	d						00 22			
Grays	d					00 18	00a30	00 46		
Tilbury Town	d					00 21		00 49		
East Tilbury	d					00 27		00 55		
Stanford-le-Hope	d					00 30		00 59		
West Horndon	d				00 16				00 46	
Laindon	d		00 01		00 21				00 51	
Basildon	d		00 04		00 24				00 54	←
Pitsea	d		00 08	00 12	00 28	00 39		01 07	00 58	01 07
Benfleet	d		00 11	00 16	00 31	00 42		↪	01 01	01 11
Leigh-on-Sea	d		00 16	00 20	00 36	00 47			01 06	01 15
Chalkwell	d		00 18	00 23	00 38	00 49			01 08	01 18
Westcliff	d		00 20	00 25	00 40	00 51			01 10	01 20
Southend Central	a		00 23	00 27	00 43	00 54			01 13	01 22
	d		00 23	00 27	00 43	00 54			01 13	01 22
Southend East	d		00 25	00 29	00 45	00 56			01 15	01 24
Thorpe Bay	d	00 03	00 28	00 32	00 48	00 58			01 18	01 27
Shoeburyness	a	00 07	00 32	00 36	00 52	01 02			01 22	01 31

Station		CC	CC	CC	CC	CC	CC	CC	CC C	CC	CC B	CC	CC C	CC
London Fenchurch St ⊖	d	00 25	00 34	05 03		05 10	05 33	05 40	05 54	06 05		06 10	06 24	06 32
Limehouse	d	00 29	00 38	05 07		05 14	05 37	05 44	05 58	06 09		06 14	06 28	06 36
West Ham ⊖	d	00 34	00 43	05 12		05 19	05 42	05 49	06 03	06 14		06 19	06 33	06 41
London Liverpool St ⊖	d													
Stratford ⊖	d													
Barking ⊖	d	00 39	00 49	05 17	05 23	05 25	05 47	05 55	06 09	06 19		06 25	06 39	06 46
Upminster ⊖	d		00 57	05 26	05 31		05 56		06 17	06 28			06 47	06 55
Ockendon	d				05 39				06 22				06 52	
Chafford Hundred Lakeside	d				05 43				06 26				06 56	
Dagenham Dock	d	00 44				05 29		05 59				06 29		
Rainham	d	00 47				05 33		06 03				06 33		
Purfleet	d	00 52				05 38		06 08				06 38		
Grays	d	00a58			05 47	05a45		06a15	06 30			06a45	07 00	
Tilbury Town	d				05 50				06 33				07 03	
East Tilbury	d				05 56				06 39				07 09	
Stanford-le-Hope	d				06 00				06 43				07 13	
West Horndon	d		01 02	05 31			06 01			06 33				07 00
Laindon	d		01 07	05 35			06 05			06 37				07 04
Basildon	d		01 10	05 39			06 09			06 41	←			07 08
Pitsea	d		01 14	05 42	06 08		06 12		06 51	06 44	06 51		07 21	07 11
Benfleet	d		01 17	05 46	06 12		06 16		↪	06 48	06 55		↪	07 15
Leigh-on-Sea	d		01 22	05 50	06 16		06 20			06 52	06 59			07 19
Chalkwell	d		01 24	05 53	06 19		06 23			06 55	07 02			07 22
Westcliff	d		01 26	05 55	06 21		06 25			06 57	07 04			07 24
Southend Central	a		01 29	05 57	06 25		06 27			06 59	07 09			07 26
	d		01 29	05 58			06 28			07 00				07 27
Southend East	d		01 31	06 00			06 30			07 02				07 29
Thorpe Bay	d		01 34	06 02			06 32			07 04				07 31
Shoeburyness	a		01 38	06 08			06 38			07 10				07 37

A To Shoeburyness B From London Fenchurch Street C To Southend Central

For services between London Liverpool Street and Southend Victoria refer to Table T006

Table T001-F

Saturdays

26 May to 8 December

London - Southend Central and Shoeburyness

Station		CC A	CC	CC B	CC	CC A	CC	CC B	CC	CC A
London Fenchurch St ⊖	d		06 40	06 54	07 02		07 10	07 24	07 32	
Limehouse	d		06 44	06 58	07 06		07 14	07 28	07 36	
West Ham ⊖	d		06 49	07 03	07 11		07 19	07 33	07 41	
London Liverpool St ⊖	d									
Stratford ⊖	d									
Barking ⊖	d		06 55	07 09	07 16		07 25	07 39	07 46	
Upminster ⊖	d			07 17	07 25			07 47	07 55	
Ockendon	d			07 22				07 52		
Chafford Hundred Lakeside	d			07 26				07 56		
Dagenham Dock	d		06 59				07 29			
Rainham	d		07 03				07 33			
Purfleet	d		07 08				07 38			
Grays	d		07a15	07 30			07a45	08 00		
Tilbury Town	d			07 33				08 03		
East Tilbury	d			07 39				08 09		
Stanford-le-Hope	d			07 43				08 13		
West Horndon	d				07 30				08 00	
Laindon	d				07 34				08 04	
Basildon	d	←			07 38	←			08 08	←
Pitsea	d	07 21		07 51	07 41	07 51		08 21	08 11	08 21
Benfleet	d	07 25		→	07 45	07 55		→	08 15	08 25
Leigh-on-Sea	d	07 29			07 49	07 59			08 19	08 29
Chalkwell	d	07 32			07 52	08 02			08 22	08 32
Westcliff	d	07 34			07 54	08 04			08 24	08 34
Southend Central	a	07 39			07 56	08 09			08 26	08 39
	d				07 57				08 27	
Southend East	d				07 59				08 29	
Thorpe Bay	d				08 01				08 31	
Shoeburyness	a				08 07				08 37	

Station		CC	CC B	CC	CC A	CC	CC B	CC	CC A	CC	CC	CC B	CC	CC A
London Fenchurch St ⊖	d	07 40	07 54	08 02		08 10	08 24	08 32		08 40		08 54	09 02	
Limehouse	d	07 44	07 58	08 06		08 14	08 28	08 36		08 44		08 58	09 06	
West Ham ⊖	d	07 49	08 03	08 11		08 19	08 33	08 41		08 49		09 03	09 11	
London Liverpool St ⊖	d										08 43			
Stratford ⊖	d										08 51			
Barking ⊖	d	07 55	08 09	08 16		08 25	08 39	08 46		08 55	09 02	09 09	09 16	
Upminster ⊖	d		08 17	08 25			08 47	08 55			09 11	09 17	09 25	
Ockendon	d		08 22				08 52					09 22		
Chafford Hundred Lakeside	d		08 26				08 56					09 26		
Dagenham Dock	d	07 59				08 29				08 59				
Rainham	d	08 03				08 33				09 03				
Purfleet	d	08 08				08 38				09 08				
Grays	d	08a15	08 30			08a45	09 00			09a15		09 30		
Tilbury Town	d		08 33				09 03					09 33		
East Tilbury	d		08 39				09 09					09 39		
Stanford-le-Hope	d		08 43				09 13					09 43		
West Horndon	d			08 30				09 00			09 16		09 30	
Laindon	d			08 34				09 04			09 20		09 34	
Basildon	d			08 38	←			09 08	←		09 24		09 38	←
Pitsea	d		08 51	08 41	08 51		09 21	09 11	09 21		09 27	09 51	09 41	09 51
Benfleet	d		→	08 45	08 55		→	09 15	09 25		09 31	→	09 45	09 55
Leigh-on-Sea	d			08 49	08 59			09 19	09 29		09 35		09 49	09 59
Chalkwell	d			08 52	09 02			09 22	09 32		09 38		09 52	10 02
Westcliff	d			08 54	09 04			09 24	09 34		09 40		09 54	10 04
Southend Central	a			08 56	09 09			09 26	09 39		09 42		09 56	10 09
	d			08 57				09 27			09 43		09 57	
Southend East	d			08 59				09 29			09 45		09 59	
Thorpe Bay	d			09 01				09 31			09 47		10 01	
Shoeburyness	a			09 07				09 37			09 53		10 07	

Station		CC	CC		CC B	CC	CC A	CC	CC	CC B	CC	CC A	CC	CC
London Fenchurch St ⊖	d	09 10			13 24	13 32		13 40		13 54	14 02		14 10	
Limehouse	d	09 14			13 28	13 36		13 44		13 58	14 06		14 14	
West Ham ⊖	d	09 19			13 33	13 41		13 49		14 03	14 11		14 19	
London Liverpool St ⊖	d		09 13						13 43					14 13
Stratford ⊖	d		09 21						13 51					14 21
Barking ⊖	d	09 25	09 31		13 39	13 46		13 55	14 02	14 09	14 16		14 25	14 31
Upminster ⊖	d		09 40		13 47	13 55			14 11	14 17	14 25			14 40
Ockendon	d				13 52					14 22				
Chafford Hundred Lakeside	d				13 56					14 26				
Dagenham Dock	d	09 29						13 59					14 29	
Rainham	d	09 33		and at				14 03					14 33	
Purfleet	d	09 38		the same				14 08					14 38	
Grays	d	09a45		minutes	14 00			14a15		14 30			14a45	
Tilbury Town	d			past	14 03					14 33				
East Tilbury	d			each	14 09					14 39				
Stanford-le-Hope	d			hour until	14 13					14 43				
West Horndon	d		09 45			14 00			14 16		14 30			14 45
Laindon	d		09 49			14 04			14 20		14 34			14 49
Basildon	d		09 53			14 08	←		14 24		14 38	←		14 53
Pitsea	d		09 56		14 21	14 11	14 21		14 27	14 51	14 41	14 51		14 56
Benfleet	d		10 00		→	14 15	14 25		14 31	→	14 45	14 55		15 00
Leigh-on-Sea	d		10 04			14 19	14 29		14 35		14 49	14 59		15 04
Chalkwell	d		10 07			14 22	14 32		14 38		14 52	15 02		15 07
Westcliff	d		10 09			14 24	14 34		14 40		14 54	15 04		15 09
Southend Central	a		10 11			14 26	14 39		14 42		14 56	15 09		15 11
	d		10 12			14 27			14 43		14 57			15 12
Southend East	d		10 14			14 29			14 45		14 59			15 14
Thorpe Bay	d		10 16			14 31			14 47		15 01			15 16
Shoeburyness	a		10 22			14 37			14 53		15 07			15 22

Station		CC B	CC	CC A	CC	CC	CC B	CC	CC A	CC
London Fenchurch St ⊖	d	14 24	14 32		14 40		14 54	15 02		15 10
Limehouse	d	14 28	14 36		14 44		14 58	15 06		15 14
West Ham ⊖	d	14 33	14 41		14 49		15 03	15 11		15 19
London Liverpool St ⊖	d					14 43				
Stratford ⊖	d					14 51				
Barking ⊖	d	14 39	14 46		14 55	15 02	15 09	15 16		15 25
Upminster ⊖	d	14 47	14 55			15 11	15 17	15 25		
Ockendon	d	14 52					15 22			
Chafford Hundred Lakeside	d	14 56					15 26			
Dagenham Dock	d				14 59					15 29
Rainham	d				15 03					15 33
Purfleet	d				15 08					15 38
Grays	d	15 00			15a15		15 30			15a46
Tilbury Town	d	15 03					15 33			
East Tilbury	d	15 09					15 39			
Stanford-le-Hope	d	15 13					15 43			
West Horndon	d		15 00			15 16		15 30		
Laindon	d		15 04			15 20		15 34		
Basildon	d		15 08	←		15 24		15 38	←	
Pitsea	d	15 21	15 11	15 21		15 27	15 51	15 41	15 51	
Benfleet	d	→	15 15	15 25		15 31	→	15 45	15 55	
Leigh-on-Sea	d		15 19	15 29		15 35		15 49	15 59	
Chalkwell	d		15 22	15 32		15 38		15 52	16 02	
Westcliff	d		15 24	15 34		15 40		15 54	16 04	
Southend Central	a		15 26	15 39		15 42		15 56	16 09	
	d		15 27			15 43		15 57		
Southend East	d		15 29			15 45		15 59		
Thorpe Bay	d		15 31			15 47		16 01		
Shoeburyness	a		15 37			15 53		16 07		

Station		CC	CC B	CC	CC A	CC	CC	CC B	CC	CC A	CC	
London Fenchurch St ⊖	d		15 24	15 32		15 40		15 54	16 02		16 10	
Limehouse	d		15 28	15 36		15 44		15 58	16 06		16 14	
West Ham ⊖	d		15 33	15 41		15 49		16 03	16 11		16 19	
London Liverpool St ⊖	d	15 13					15 43					
Stratford ⊖	d	15 21					15 51					
Barking ⊖	d	15 31	15 39	15 46		15 55	16 02	16 09	16 16		16 25	
Upminster ⊖	d	15 40	15 47	15 55			16 11	16 17	16 25			
Ockendon	d		15 52					16 22				
Chafford Hundred Lakeside	d		15 56					16 26				
Dagenham Dock	d					15 59					16 29	
Rainham	d					16 03					16 33	and at
Purfleet	d					16 08					16 38	the same
Grays	d		16 00			16a15		16 30			16a45	minutes
Tilbury Town	d		16 03					16 33				past
East Tilbury	d		16 09					16 39				each
Stanford-le-Hope	d		16 13					16 43				hour until
West Horndon	d	15 45		16 00			16 16		16 30			
Laindon	d	15 49		16 04			16 20		16 34			
Basildon	d	15 53		16 08	←		16 24		16 38	←		
Pitsea	d	15 56	16 21	16 11	16 21		16 27	16 51	16 41	16 51		
Benfleet	d	16 00	→	16 15	16 25		16 31	→	16 45	16 55		
Leigh-on-Sea	d	16 04		16 19	16 29		16 35		16 49	16 59		
Chalkwell	d	16 07		16 22	16 32		16 38		16 52	17 02		
Westcliff	d	16 09		16 24	16 34		16 40		16 54	17 04		
Southend Central	a	16 11		16 26	16 39		16 42		16 56	17 09		
	d	16 12		16 27			16 43		16 57			
Southend East	d	16 14		16 29			16 45		16 59			
Thorpe Bay	d	16 16		16 31			16 47		17 01			
Shoeburyness	a	16 22		16 37			16 53		17 07			

Station		CC	CC B	CC	CC A	CC	CC	CC B	CC	CC A	CC	CC
London Fenchurch St ⊖	d		20 24	20 32		20 40		20 54	21 02		21 10	
Limehouse	d		20 28	20 36		20 44		20 58	21 06		21 14	
West Ham ⊖	d		20 33	20 41		20 49		21 03	21 11		21 19	
London Liverpool St ⊖	d	20 13					20 43					21 13
Stratford ⊖	d	20 21					20 51					21 21
Barking ⊖	d	20 31	20 39	20 46		20 55	21 02	21 09	21 16		21 25	21 31
Upminster ⊖	d	20 40	20 47	20 55			21 11	21 17	21 25			21 40
Ockendon	d		20 52					21 22				
Chafford Hundred Lakeside	d		20 56					21 26				
Dagenham Dock	d					20 59					21 29	
Rainham	d					21 03					21 33	
Purfleet	d					21 08					21 38	
Grays	d		21 00			21a15		21 30			21a45	
Tilbury Town	d		21 03					21 33				
East Tilbury	d		21 09					21 39				
Stanford-le-Hope	d		21 13					21 43				
West Horndon	d	20 45		21 00			21 16		21 30			21 45
Laindon	d	20 49		21 04			21 20		21 34			21 49
Basildon	d	20 53		21 08	←		21 24		21 38	←		21 53
Pitsea	d	20 56	21 21	21 11	21 21		21 27	21 51	21 41	21 51		21 56
Benfleet	d	21 00	→	21 15	21 25		21 31	→	21 45	21 55		22 00
Leigh-on-Sea	d	21 04		21 19	21 29		21 35		21 49	21 59		22 04
Chalkwell	d	21 07		21 22	21 32		21 38		21 52	22 02		22 07
Westcliff	d	21 09		21 24	21 34		21 40		21 54	22 04		22 09
Southend Central	a	21 11		21 26	21 39		21 42		21 56	22 09		22 11
	d	21 12		21 27			21 43		21 57			22 12
Southend East	d	21 14		21 29			21 45		21 59			22 14
Thorpe Bay	d	21 16		21 31			21 47		22 01			22 16
Shoeburyness	a	21 22		21 37			21 53		22 07			22 22

A From London Fenchurch Street B To Southend Central

For services between London Liverpool Street and Southend Victoria refer to Table T006

Table T001-F

London - Southend Central and Shoeburyness

Saturdays
26 May to 8 December

Station		CC	CC	CC	CC	CC	CC	CC A	CC	CC B	CC	CC	CC A	CC	CC B	CC	CC	CC	CC	CC
London Fenchurch St	d	21 24	21 40		21 54	22 10		22 24	22 32		22 40		22 54	23 05			23 20	23 24	23 41	23 58
Limehouse	d	21 28	21 44		21 58	22 14		22 28	22 36		22 44		22 58	23 09			23 24	23 28	23 45	00 04
West Ham	d	21 33	21 49		22 03	22 19		22 33	22 41		22 49		23 03	23 14			23 29	23 33	23 51	00 09
London Liverpool St	d			21 43			22 07					22 43				23 27				
Stratford	d			21 51			22 15					22 51				23 35				
Barking	d	21 39	21 55	22 02	22 09	22 25	22 32	22 39	22 46		22 55	23 03	23 09	23 19		23 43	23 35	23 39	23 57	00 15
Upminster	d	21 47		22 11	22 17		22 41	22 47	22 55			23 12	23 17	23 28		23 52		23 47	00 05	
Ockendon	d	21 52			22 22			22 52					23 22					23 52	00 10	
Chafford Hundred Lakeside	d	21 56			22 26			22 56					23 26					23 56	00 14	
Dagenham Dock	d		21 59			22 29					22 59						23 39			00 19
Rainham	d		22 03			22 33					23 03						23 43			00 23
Purfleet	d		22 08			22 38					23 08						23 48			00 28
Grays	d	22 00	22a15		22 30	22a45		23 00			23a15		23 30				23 54	00 02	00 18	00 34
Tilbury Town	d	22 03			22 33			23 03					23 33				23 57	00 05	00 21	00 37
East Tilbury	d	22 09			22 39			23 09					23 39				00 03	00 11	00 27	00 43
Stanford-le-Hope	d	22 13			22 43			23 13					23 43				00 06	00 14	00 31	00 46
West Horndon	d			22 16			22 46		23 00			23 17		23 33		23 57				
Laindon	d			22 20			22 50		23 04			23 21		23 38		00 02				
Basildon	d			22 24			22 54		23 08	←		23 25		23 41	←	00 06				
Pitsea	d	22 21		22 27	22 51		22 57	23 21	23 11	23 21		23 28	23 54	23 45	23 54	00 09	00 15	00 23	00 39	00 54
Benfleet	d	22 25		22 31	22 55		23 01	→	23 15	23 25		23 32	→	23 49	23 57	00 13	00 18	00 26	00 42	00 58
Leigh-on-Sea	d	22 29		22 35	22 59		23 05		23 19	23 29		23 36		23 54	00 02	00 17	00 23	00 31	00 47	01 02
Chalkwell	d	22 32		22 38	23 02		23 08		23 22	23 32		23 39		23 56	00 04	00 20	00 25	00 33	00 49	01 05
Westcliff	d	22 34		22 40	23 04		23 10		23 24	23 34		23 41		23 58	00 06	00 22	00 27	00 35	00 51	01 07
Southend Central	a	22 39		22 42	23 09		23 12		23 26	23 36		23 43		00 01	00 09	00 24	00 30	00 38	00 54	01 09
	d			22 43			23 13		23 27	23 37		23 44		00 02	00 09	00 25	00 30	00 38	00 54	01 10
Southend East	d			22 45			23 15		23 29	23 39		23 46		00 04	00 11	00 27	00 32	00 40	00 56	01 12
Thorpe Bay	d			22 47			23 17		23 31	23 41		23 48		00 06	00 14	00 29	00 35	00 43	00 59	01 14
Shoeburyness	a			22 53			23 23		23 37	23 47		23 54		00 12	00 20	00 35	00 41	00 49	01 05	01 20

Sundays
20 May to 2 December

Station		CC C	CC C	CC D	CC C	CC C	CC C	CC	CC C	CC	CC	CC	CC	CC	CC	CC	CC	CC	CC	CC	CC	CC	CC
London Fenchurch St	d									00 11	00 41	06 34		07 04	07 25		07 34	07 49	07 55		08 19	08 25	08 34
Limehouse	d								00 04	00 16	00 45	06 38		07 08	07 29		07 38	07 53	07 59		08 23	08 29	08 38
West Ham	d								00 09	00 21	00 50	06 43		07 13	07 34		07 43	07 58	08 04		08 28	08 34	08 43
London Liverpool St	d							00 06															
Stratford	d							00 14															
Barking	d							00 21	00 15	00 27	00 56	06 49	06 56	07 19	07 40	07 43	07 49	08 04	08 10	08 19	08 34	08 40	08 49
Upminster	d						00 05	00 30		00 36	01 04	06 58	07 04	07 28	07 49		07 57		08 19	08 27		08 49	08 57
Ockendon	d						00 10			00 41			07 10				08 03			08 33			09 03
Chafford Hundred Lakeside	d						00 14			00 45			07 13				08 06			08 36			09 06
Dagenham Dock	d								00 19							07 47		08 08			08 38		
Rainham	d								00 23							07 51		08 12			08 42		
Purfleet	d								00 28							07 56		08 17			08 47		
Grays	d					00 02	00 18		00 34	00 49			07 18			08a03	08 10	08a24		08 40	08a54		09 10
Tilbury Town	d					00 05	00 21		00 37	00 52			07 21				08 13			08 43			09 13
East Tilbury	d				00 03	00 11	00 27		00 43	00 58			07 27				08 19			08 49			09 19
Stanford-le-Hope	d				00 06	00 14	00 31		00 46	01 01			07 30				08 23			08 53			09 23
West Horndon	d							00 35			01 09	07 03		07 33	07 54				08 24			08 54	
Laindon	d			00 02				00 40			01 14	07 08		07 38	07 59				08 29			08 59	
Basildon	d			00 06				00 44			01 17	07 11		07 41	08 02				08 32			09 02	
Pitsea	d			00 09	00 15	00 23	00 39	00 47	00 54	01 10	01 21	07 15	07 39	07 45	08 06		08 31		08 36	09 01		09 06	09 31
Benfleet	d			00 13	00 18	00 26	00 42	00 51	00 58	01 13	01 24	07 18	07 42	07 48	08 09		08 34		08 39	09 04		09 09	09 34
Leigh-on-Sea	d		00 02	00 17	00 23	00 31	00 47	00 55	01 02	01 18	01 29	07 23	07 47	07 53	08 14		08 39		08 44	09 09		09 14	09 39
Chalkwell	d		00 04	00 20	00 25	00 33	00 49	00 58	01 05	01 20	01 31	07 25	07 49	07 55	08 16		08 41		08 46	09 11		09 16	09 41
Westcliff	d		00 06	00 22	00 27	00 35	00 51	01 00	01 07	01 22	01 33	07 27	07 51	07 57	08 18		08 43		08 48	09 13		09 18	09 43
Southend Central	a		00 09	00 24	00 30	00 38	00 54	01 02	01 09	01 25	01 36	07 30	07 56	08 00	08 21		08 48		08 51	09 18		09 21	09 48
	d	00 02	00 09	00 25	00 30	00 38	00 54	01 03	01 10	01 25	01 36	07 30		08 00	08 21				08 51			09 21	
Southend East	d	00 04	00 11	00 27	00 32	00 40	00 56	01 05	01 12	01 27	01 38	07 32		08 02	08 23				08 53			09 23	
Thorpe Bay	d	00 06	00 14	00 29	00 35	00 43	00 59	01 07	01 14	01 30	01 41	07 35		08 05	08 26				08 56			09 26	
Shoeburyness	a	00 12	00 20	00 35	00 41	00 49	01 05	01 13	01 20	01 36	01 47	07 41		08 11	08 32				09 02			09 32	

A To Shoeburyness
B From London Fenchurch Street
C From London Fenchurch Street
D From London Liverpool Street

For services between London Liverpool Street and Southend Victoria refer to Table T006

Table T001-F

London - Southend Central and Shoeburyness

Sundays
20 May to 2 December

Station		CC	CC	CC	CC	CC	CC	CC	CC	CC	CC	CC		CC	CC	CC	CC	CC	CC	CC	CC	CC	CC
London Fenchurch St	d	08 49	08 55	09 04	09 19	09 25	09 34	09 49		10 04	10 19			19 34	19 49		20 04	20 19		20 34	20 49		21 04
Limehouse	d	08 53	08 59	09 08	09 23	09 29	09 38	09 53		10 08	10 23			19 38	19 53		20 08	20 23		20 38	20 53		21 08
West Ham	d	08 58	09 04	09 13	09 28	09 34	09 43	09 58		10 13	10 28			19 43	19 58		20 13	20 28		20 43	20 58		21 13
London Liverpool St	d								09 53			10 23				19 53			20 23			20 53	
Stratford	d								10 00			10 30				20 00			20 30			21 00	
Barking	d	09 04	09 10	09 19	09 34	09 40	09 49	10 04	10 09	10 19	10 34	10 39		19 49	20 04	20 09	20 19	20 34	20 39	20 49	21 04	21 09	21 19
Upminster	d		09 19	09 27		09 49	09 57		10 19	10 27		10 49		19 57		20 19	20 27		20 49	20 57		21 19	21 27
Ockendon	d			09 33			10 03			10 33				20 03			20 33			21 03			21 33
Chafford Hundred Lakeside	d			09 36			10 06			10 36				20 06			20 36			21 06			21 36
Dagenham Dock	d	09 08			09 38			10 08			10 38				20 08			20 38			21 08		
Rainham	d	09 12			09 42			10 12			10 42		and at		20 12			20 42			21 12		
Purfleet	d	09 17			09 47			10 17			10 47		the same		20 17			20 47			21 17		
Grays	d	09a24		09 40	09a54		10 10	10a24		10 40	10a54		minutes	20 10	20a24		20 40	20a54		21 10	21a24		21 40
Tilbury Town	d			09 43			10 13			10 43			past	20 13			20 43			21 13			21 43
East Tilbury	d			09 49			10 19			10 49			each	20 19			20 49			21 19			21 49
Stanford-le-Hope	d			09 53			10 23			10 53			hour until	20 23			20 53			21 23			21 53
West Horndon	d		09 24			09 54			10 24			10 54				20 24			20 54			21 24	
Laindon	d		09 29			09 59			10 29			10 59				20 29			20 59			21 29	
Basildon	d		09 32			10 02			10 32			11 02				20 32			21 02			21 32	
Pitsea	d		09 36	10 01		10 06	10 31		10 36	11 01		11 06		20 31		20 36	21 01		21 06	21 31		21 36	22 01
Benfleet	d		09 39	10 04		10 09	10 34		10 39	11 04		11 09		20 34		20 39	21 04		21 09	21 34		21 39	22 04
Leigh-on-Sea	d		09 44	10 09		10 14	10 39		10 44	11 09		11 14		20 39		20 44	21 09		21 14	21 39		21 44	22 09
Chalkwell	d		09 46	10 11		10 16	10 41		10 46	11 11		11 16		20 41		20 46	21 11		21 16	21 41		21 46	22 11
Westcliff	d		09 48	10 13		10 18	10 43		10 48	11 13		11 18		20 43		20 48	21 13		21 18	21 43		21 48	22 13
Southend Central	a		09 51	10 18		10 21	10 48		10 51	11 18		11 21		20 48		20 51	21 18		21 21	21 46		21 51	22 18
	d		09 51			10 21			10 51			11 21				20 51			21 21	21 46		21 51	
Southend East	d		09 53			10 23			10 53			11 23				20 53			21 23	21 48		21 53	
Thorpe Bay	d		09 56			10 26			10 56			11 26				20 56			21 26	21 51		21 56	
Shoeburyness	a		10 02			10 32			11 02			11 32				21 02			21 32	21 57		22 02	

Station		CC	CC	CC	CC	CC	CC	CC	CC	CC	CC	CC
London Fenchurch St	d	21 19		21 34	21 49			22 11			23 11	23 41
Limehouse	d	21 23		21 38	21 53			22 15			23 15	23 45
West Ham	d	21 28		21 43	21 58			22 20			23 20	23 50
London Liverpool St	d		21 23			21 53	22 23		22 53	23 23		
Stratford	d		21 30			22 00	22 30		23 00	23 30		
Barking	d	21 34	21 39	21 49	22 04	22 09	22 39	22 26	23 09	23 39	23 26	23 56
Upminster	d		21 49	21 57		22 19	22 49	22 34	23 19	23 49	23 34	00 04
Ockendon	d			22 03				22 40			23 40	
Chafford Hundred Lakeside	d			22 06				22 43			23 43	
Dagenham Dock	d	21 38			22 08							
Rainham	d	21 42			22 12							
Purfleet	d	21 47			22 17							
Grays	d	21a54		22 10	22a24			22 48			23 48	
Tilbury Town	d			22 13				22 51			23 51	
East Tilbury	d			22 19				22 57			23 57	
Stanford-le-Hope	d			22 23				23 01			00 02	
West Horndon	d		21 54			22 24	22 54		23 24	23 54		00 09
Laindon	d		21 59			22 29	22 59		23 29	23 59		00 14
Basildon	d		22 02			22 32	23 02		23 32	00 02		00 17
Pitsea	d		22 06	22 31		22 36	23 06	23 11	23 36	00 06	00 11	00 21
Benfleet	d		22 09	22 34		22 39	23 09	23 14	23 39	00 09	00 14	00 24
Leigh-on-Sea	d		22 14	22 39		22 44	23 14	23 19	23 44	00 14	00 19	00 29
Chalkwell	d		22 16	22 41		22 46	23 16	23 21	23 46	00 16	00 21	00 31
Westcliff	d		22 18	22 43		22 48	23 18	23 23	23 48	00 18	00 23	00 33
Southend Central	a		22 21	22 46		22 51	23 21	23 26	23 51	00 21	00 26	00 36
	d		22 21	22 46		22 51	23 21	23 26	23 51	00 21	00 26	00 36
Southend East	d		22 23	22 48		22 53	23 23	23 28	23 53	00 23	00 28	00 38
Thorpe Bay	d		22 26	22 51		22 56	23 26	23 31	23 56	00 26	00 31	00 41
Shoeburyness	a		22 32	22 57		23 02	23 32	23 37	00 02	00 32	00 37	00 47

For services between London Liverpool Street and Southend Victoria refer to Table T006

Table T001-R

Mondays to Fridays

21 May to 7 December

Shoeburyness and Southend Central - London

Miles	Miles	Miles	Miles			CC MX A	CC MX B	CC MX C	CC D	CC	CC E	CC	CC	CC	CC	CC D	CC	CC E	CC	CC D	CC	CC D	CC D
0	0	0	—	**Shoeburyness**	d					04 15					04 59		05 13				05 28		05 34
1½	1½	1½	—	Thorpe Bay	d				04 06	04 18			04 35		05 03	05 07	05 17				05 32		05 38
3	3	3	—	Southend East	d				04 08	04 21			04 37		05 05	05 09	05 19				05 34		05 40
3¾	3¾	3¾	—	**Southend Central**	a				04 11	04 23			04 40		05 08	05 12	05 22				05 37		05 43
—	—	—	—		d				04 11	04 24			04 40		05 08	05 12	05 22				05 37		05 43
4¾	4¾	4¾	—	Westcliff	d				04 14	04 26			04 42		05 10	05 14	05 24				05 39		05 45
5¾	5¾	5¾	—	Chalkwell	d				04 16	04 28			04 44		05 13	05 16	05 27				05 42		05 48
7	7	7	—	Leigh-on-Sea	d				04 19	04 31			04 47		05 15	05 19	05 30				05 44		05 50
10¼	10¼	10¼	—	Benfleet	d				04 23	04 36			04 51		05 20	05 23	05 35				05 49		05 55
13	13	13	—	Pitsea	d				04 28	04 40			04 56		05 23	05 28	05 38			05 48	05 52		06 04
15¾	—	—	—	Basildon	d					04 43					05 27		05 42				05 56		
16¾	—	—	—	Laindon	d					04 46					05 31		05 46				06 00		
20¼	—	—	—	West Horndon	d			00 03		04 51					05 35		05 50				06 04		
—	18¼	18¼	—	Stanford-le-Hope	d				04 34				05 02			05 34				05 54			06 10
—	20½	20½	—	East Tilbury	d				04 37				05 06			05 37				05 58			06 14
—	24	24	—	**Tilbury Town**	d				04 43				05 12			05 43				06 04			06 20
—	25¾	25¾	—	Grays	d				04 46			04 53	05 15	05 25		05 46			05 53	06 07		06 14	06 23
—	29½	—	—	Purfleet	d							04 59		05 31					05 59	06 13			06 29
—	32¾	—	—	Rainham	d							05 04		05 36					06 04	06 18			06 34
—	35	—	—	Dagenham Dock	d						←	05 07		05 39				←	06 08	06 22			06 38
—	—	27¾	—	Chafford Hundred Lakeside	d				04 50		04 50		05 19			05 50		05 50				06 18	
—	—	30¼	—	Ockendon	d				→		04 54		05 23			→		05 54				→	
24¼	—	33½	—	Upminster ⊖	d		00 01	00 08		04 56	05 00		05 30		05 41		05 56	06 01			06 10		
32	38	41¼	0	Barking ⊖	d		00 09	00 16		05 05	05 08	05 13	05 38	05 45	05 49		06 04	06 09	06 14	06 28	06 18		06 44
—	—	—	4	Stratford ⊖	a															→			→
—	—	—	8	**London Liverpool St** ⊖	a																		
34¾	40¾	44	—	West Ham ⊖	d	00 05	00 14	00 21		05 10	05 13	05 18	05 43	05 50	05 55		06 10	06 15	06 19		06 23		
35½	41½	44¾	—	Limehouse	d	00 10	00 19	00 26		05 15	05 18	05 23	05 48	05 55	06 00		06 15	06 20	06 24		06 28		
39¼	45½	48¾	—	**London Fenchurch St** ⊖	a	00 15	00 24	00 32		05 20	05 23	05 28	05 53	06 00	06 04		06 19	06 25	06 29		06 33		

		CC	CC F	CC	CC A	CC C	CC D	CC D	CC	CC D	CC	CC A	CC E	CC	CC	CC B	CC	CC D	CC D	CC	CC	CC	CC F
Shoeburyness	d	05 38		05 44					05 57		06 07			06 11						06 25			
Thorpe Bay	d	05 42		05 48				05 56	06 01		06 11			06 15						06 29	06 38		
Southend East	d	05 44		05 50				05 58	06 03		06 13			06 17						06 31	06 40		
Southend Central	a	05 47		05 53				06 01	06 06					06 20						06 34			
	d	05 47		05 53				06 01	06 06	06 11				06 20						06 34			
Westcliff	d	05 49		05 55				06 03	06 08	06 13				06 22						06 36			
Chalkwell	d	05 52		05 57				06 06	06 11	06 16				06 25						06 39			
Leigh-on-Sea	d	05 54		06 00				06 08	06 14	06 18	06 22			06 28	06 35					06 42	06 47		
Benfleet	d	05 59		06 05				06 13	06 19	06 23	06 27			06 33	06 40					06 47	06 53		
Pitsea	d			06 08				06 19	06 23	06 28	06 31			06 37					06 45	06 51			
Basildon	d			06 12					06 27		06 35			06 41	06 46					06 55	06 59		
Laindon	d	06 06		06 16					06 30		06 39			06 44	06 49					06 58		07 04	
West Horndon	d			06 20					06 35						06 54							07 09	
Stanford-le-Hope	d							06 25		06 34									06 51				
East Tilbury	d							06 29		06 37									06 54				
Tilbury Town	d							06 35		06 43									07 00				
Grays	d						06 31	06 38		06 47							06 52	07 01	07 04				
Purfleet	d							06 44									06 58		07 09				
Rainham	d							06 49									07 03		07 15				
Dagenham Dock	d				←			06 53				←				←	07 07		07 18				
Chafford Hundred Lakeside	d				06 18		06 35			06 51		06 35				06 51		07 06					
Ockendon	d				06 23		→			→		06 40				06 56		→					
Upminster ⊖	d	06 15	←	06 26	06 30	←			06 40			06 49	←	06 54	06 59	07 03				07 08		07 14	←
Barking ⊖	d		06 28		06 38	06 44		07 00			06 54		07 00	07 03	07 08	07 11	07 14		07 25			07 23	07 25
Stratford ⊖	a							→											→				
London Liverpool St ⊖	a																						
West Ham ⊖	d	06 27	06 33	06 39	06 43	06 49			06 53		06 59	07 02	07 05	07 09	07 13	07 17	07 20			07 23	07 26	07 29	07 32
Limehouse	d	06 33	06 39	06 44	06 48	06 55			06 59		07 05	07 08	07 11	07 14	07 19	07 22	07 25			07 28	07 31	07 34	07 37
London Fenchurch St ⊖	a	06 37	06 44	06 49	06 53	07 00			07 06		07 11	07 14	07 17	07 21	07 25	07 29	07 32			07 35	07 38	07 41	07 44

A From Grays
B From Southend Central
C From Shoeburyness
D To London Fenchurch Street
E From Thorpe Bay
F From Pitsea

For services between Southend Victoria and London Liverpool Street refer to Table 6

Table T001-R

Mondays to Fridays

21 May to 7 December

Shoeburyness and Southend Central - London

		CC A	CC B	CC B	CC	CC	CC	CC A	CC C	CC	CC	CC	CC	CC	CC	CC	CC	CC	CC	CC	CC	CC
Shoeburyness	d				06 41	06 48							07 02			07 18					07 31	
Thorpe Bay	d				06 45	06 52							07 06		07 12	07 22				07 29	07 35	
Southend East	d				06 47	06 54							07 08		07 14	07 24				07 31	07 37	
Southend Central	a				06 50	06 57							07 11		07 17	07 27				07 34	07 40	
	d			06 46	06 50	06 57						07 04	07 11		07 17	07 27				07 34	07 40	
Westcliff	d			06 49	06 52	06 59						07 06	07 13		07 19	07 29				07 36	07 42	
Chalkwell	d			06 51	06 55	07 02						07 09	07 16		07 22	07 32				07 39	07 45	
Leigh-on-Sea	d			06 54	06 58	07 05	07 08					07 11		07 21	07 25		07 37			07 42	07 48	
Benfleet	d			06 58	07 03	07 10	07 13					07 17		07 26	07 30		07 42			07 47	07 53	
Pitsea	d			07 05	07 06		07 17					07 22		07 30	07 34				07 35	07 51		
Basildon	d				07 10		07 21							07 34	07 38	07 42	07 48				07 59	
Laindon	d				07 14	07 18				07 31					07 45		07 52					08 04
West Horndon	d				07 18					07 36					07 51							08 09
Stanford-le-Hope	d			07 12								07 28							07 42			
East Tilbury	d			07 15								07 31							07 45			
Tilbury Town	d			07 22								07 37							07 51			
Grays	d		07 17	07 25							07 31	07 41						07 47	07 56			
Purfleet	d			07 31								07 46							08 02			
Rainham	d			07 36								07 52							08 07			
Dagenham Dock	d	←		07 40								07 55							08 11			
Chafford Hundred Lakeside	d	07 06	07 21								07 35							07 51				
Ockendon	d	07 11	07 26								07 41							07 56				
Upminster ⊖	d	07 19	07 33					←	←	07 41	07 48				07 57			08 03		08 06		08 14
Barking ⊖	d	07 28	07 41	07 46	07 35			07 41	07 46	07 50	07 56	08 02						08 11	08 19			08 23
Stratford ⊖	a		→	→																		
London Liverpool St ⊖	a																					
West Ham ⊖	d	07 35			07 41		07 44	07 47	07 53	07 56	08 02	08 08	07 50	07 59	08 11	08 05	08 14	08 17	08 26	08 20	08 23	08 29
Limehouse	d	07 40			07 46		07 49	07 52	07 58	08 01	08 07	08 13	07 55	08 04	08 16		08 19	08 22	08 31	08 25	08 28	08 34
London Fenchurch St ⊖	a	07 47			07 53	07 48	07 56	07 59	08 05	08 08	08 14	08 20	08 02	08 11	08 23	08 16	08 26	08 29	08 38	08 32	08 35	08 41

		CC	CC	CC B	CC B	CC	CC	CC	CC A	CC C	CC	CC	CC	CC	CC	CC B	CC B	CC	CC	CC A	CC D	CC B	CC B
Shoeburyness	d					07 39	07 45					08 00						08 15					
Thorpe Bay	d					07 43	07 49					08 04						08 19					
Southend East	d					07 45	07 51					08 06						08 21					
Southend Central	a					07 48	07 54					08 09						08 24					
	d				07 44	07 48	07 54				08 04	08 09						08 24					
Westcliff	d				07 46	07 50	07 56				08 06	08 11						08 26					
Chalkwell	d				07 49	07 53	07 59				08 09	08 14						08 29					
Leigh-on-Sea	d				07 52	07 56		08 04			08 12	08 17						08 32	08 36				
Benfleet	d				07 56	08 01		08 09			08 17	08 22						08 37	08 41				
Pitsea	d		07 52		08 03	08 04		08 13							08 19		08 34	08 40					08 49
Basildon	d					08 08	08 13	08 17				08 29						08 44					
Laindon	d					08 12		08 22					08 34						08 50				
West Horndon	d						08 21						08 39										
Stanford-le-Hope	d		07 58		08 10										08 25		08 40						08 55
East Tilbury	d		08 02		08 13										08 29		08 44						08 59
Tilbury Town	d		08 08		08 19										08 35		08 50						09 05
Grays	d	08 01	08 11	08 18	08 23									08 31	08 38	08 47	08 53					09 02	09 08
Purfleet	d		08 17		08 28										08 44		08 59						09 14
Rainham	d		08 22		08 34										08 49		09 04						09 19
Dagenham Dock	d		08 26		08 37				←						08 53		09 08			←			09 23
Chafford Hundred Lakeside	d	08 05		08 22					08 22					08 35		08 51				08 51		09 06	
Ockendon	d	08 10		→					08 26					08 41		→				08 56		→	
Upminster ⊖	d	08 18				08 21	08 26		08 33	←			08 44	08 48				08 54		09 03	←		
Barking ⊖	d	08 26	08 32		08 44			08 38	08 41	08 44		08 49	08 53	08 56	08 59		09 14	09 03		09 11	09 14		09 29
Stratford ⊖	a				→												→						→
London Liverpool St ⊖	a																						
West Ham ⊖	d	08 32	08 38			08 35	08 41	08 44	08 47	08 50	08 53	08 56	08 59	09 02	09 05			09 08	09 13	09 17	09 20		
Limehouse	d	08 37	08 43			08 40	08 46	08 49	08 52	08 55	08 58	09 01	09 04	09 07	09 10			09 14	09 18	09 22	09 25		
London Fenchurch St ⊖	a	08 44	08 50			08 47	08 53	08 56	08 59	09 02	09 05	09 08	09 11	09 14	09 17			09 20	09 25	09 28	09 32		

		CC	CC	CC A	CC D	CC	CC	CC	CC B	CC	CC D	CC B	CC B	CC B	CC	CC A	CC C	CC	CC B	CC B	CC	CC A
Shoeburyness	d		08 34				08 49								09 11			09 27			09 41	
Thorpe Bay	d		08 38				08 53								09 15			09 31			09 45	
Southend East	d		08 40				08 55								09 17			09 33			09 47	
Southend Central	a		08 43				08 58								09 20			09 36			09 50	
	d	08 34	08 43			08 50	08 58			09 02			09 12		09 20			09 36	09 42		09 50	
Westcliff	d	08 36	08 45			08 52	09 00			09 05			09 15		09 22			09 38	09 45		09 52	
Chalkwell	d	08 39	08 48			08 55	09 03			09 07			09 17		09 25			09 41	09 47		09 55	
Leigh-on-Sea	d	08 42	08 51			08 58	09 05			09 10			09 20		09 27			09 43	09 50		09 57	
Benfleet	d	08 47	08 56			09 03	09 10			09 15			09 24		09 32			09 48	09 54		10 02	
Pitsea	d	08 50				09 06			09 15	09 19			09 29					09 51	09 59			
Basildon	d	08 54	09 02			09 10	09 16			09 23					09 38			09 55			10 08	
Laindon	d	08 58	09 05			09 14	09 20			09 26					09 41			09 58			10 11	
West Horndon	d	09 02				09 18				09 31								10 03				
Stanford-le-Hope	d								09 21				09 35						10 05			
East Tilbury	d								09 25				09 38						10 08			
Tilbury Town	d								09 31				09 44						10 14			
Grays	d							09 17	09 34			09 41	09 48	10 10					10 17	10 40		
Purfleet	d								09 40			09 47		10 16						10 46		
Rainham	d								09 45			09 52		10 21						10 52		
Dagenham Dock	d			←					09 48			09 55		10 24			←			10 56		
Chafford Hundred Lakeside	d			09 06				09 21					09 52				09 52		10 21			
Ockendon	d			09 11				09 25					→				09 56		→			
Upminster ⊖	d	09 08	09 14	09 18	←	09 24	09 28	09 32		09 36	←				09 49	←	10 03	10 08			10 19	←
Barking ⊖	d	09 17	09 22	09 26	09 29	09 32	09 36	09 40	09 54	09 45	09 54	10 02		10 30	09 58	10 02	10 11	10 17		11 04	10 27	10 30
Stratford ⊖	a								→			→		→						→		
London Liverpool St ⊖	a																					
West Ham ⊖	d	09 23	09 28	09 32	09 35	09 38	09 42	09 46		09 50	09 59				10 03	10 07	10 16	10 22			10 32	10 35
Limehouse	d	09 28	09 33	09 37	09 40	09 43	09 47	09 51		09 56	10 05				10 08	10 12	10 21	10 28			10 37	10 40
London Fenchurch St ⊖	a	09 35	09 40	09 44	09 47	09 50	09 54	09 58		10 00	10 10				10 13	10 17	10 26	10 32			10 41	10 45

A From Grays
B To London Fenchurch Street
C From Southend Central
D From Pitsea

For services between Southend Victoria and London Liverpool Street refer to Table 6

Shoeburyness and Southend Central - London

		CC A	CC	CC B	CC B	CC	CC C	CC A	CC	CC B		CC B	CC	CC C	CC A	CC	CC B	CC B	CC	CC C		CC A	CC	CC B	CC B
Shoeburyness	d		09 57			10 11			10 27				10 41			10 57			11 11				11 27		
Thorpe Bay	d		10 01			10 15			10 31				10 45			11 01			11 15				11 31		
Southend East	d		10 03			10 17			10 33				10 47			11 03			11 17				11 33		
Southend Central	a		10 06			10 20			10 36				10 50			11 06			11 20				11 36		
	d		10 06	10 12		10 20			10 36	10 42			10 50			11 06	11 12		11 20				11 36	11 39	
Westcliff	d		10 08	10 15		10 22			10 38	10 45			10 52			11 08	11 15		11 22				11 38	11 42	
Chalkwell	d		10 11	10 17		10 25			10 41	10 47			10 55			11 11	11 17		11 25				11 41	11 44	
Leigh-on-Sea	d		10 13	10 20		10 28			10 43	10 50			10 57			11 13	11 20		11 27				11 43	11 47	
Benfleet	d		10 18	10 24		10 33			10 48	10 54			11 02			11 18	11 24		11 32				11 48	11 51	
Pitsea	d		10 21	10 29					10 51	10 59						11 21	11 29						11 51	11 56	
Basildon	d		10 25			10 39			10 55				11 08			11 25			11 38				11 55		
Laindon	d		10 28			10 42			10 58				11 11			11 28			11 41				11 58		
West Horndon	d		10 33						11 03							11 33							12 03		
Stanford-le-Hope	d			10 35						11 05							11 35							12 02	
East Tilbury	d			10 38						11 08							11 38							12 05	
Tilbury Town	d			10 44						11 14							11 44							12 11	
Grays	d			10 47	11 10					11 17		11 40					11 47	12 10						12 14	12 40
Purfleet	d				11 16							11 46						12 16							12 46
Rainham	d				11 21							11 51						12 21							12 51
Dagenham Dock	d	←			11 24			←				11 54			←			12 24				←			12 54
Chafford Hundred Lakeside	d	10 21		10 51				10 51		11 21					11 21		11 51					11 51		12 18	
Ockendon	d	10 25		→				10 55		→					11 25		→					11 55		→	
Upminster ⊖	d	10 31	10 39			10 50	←	11 01	11 08				11 19	←	11 31	11 38			11 49	←		12 01	12 08		
Barking ⊖	d	10 39	10 47		11 30	10 58	11 04	11 09	11 17			12 00	11 27	11 30	11 39	11 47		12 30	11 57	12 00		12 09	12 16		13 00
Stratford ⊖	a				→							→						→							→
London Liverpool St ⊖	a																								
West Ham ⊖	d	10 44	10 52			11 03	11 09	11 14	11 22				11 32	11 35	11 44	11 52			12 02	12 05		12 14	12 21		
Limehouse	d	10 49	10 57			11 08	11 14	11 19	11 27				11 37	11 40	11 49	11 57			12 07	12 10		12 19	12 26		
London Fenchurch St ⊖	a	10 54	11 01			11 12	11 18	11 24	11 31				11 41	11 45	11 54	12 01			12 11	12 15		12 24	12 30		

		CC	CC C	CC A	CC	CC B		CC B	CC	CC C	CC A	CC	CC B	CC B	CC	CC C		CC A	CC	CC B	CC B	CC	CC C	CC A	CC
Shoeburyness	d	11 41			11 57				12 11			12 27			12 41				12 57			13 11			13 27
Thorpe Bay	d	11 45			12 01				12 15			12 31			12 45				13 01			13 15			13 31
Southend East	d	11 47			12 03				12 17			12 33			12 47				13 03			13 17			13 33
Southend Central	a	11 50			12 06				12 20			12 36			12 50				13 06			13 20			13 36
	d	11 50			12 06	12 12			12 20			12 36	12 42		12 50				13 06	13 11		13 20			13 36
Westcliff	d	11 52			12 08	12 15			12 22			12 38	12 45		12 52				13 08	13 14		13 22			13 38
Chalkwell	d	11 55			12 11	12 17			12 25			12 41	12 47		12 55				13 11	13 16		13 25			13 41
Leigh-on-Sea	d	11 57			12 13	12 20			12 27			12 43	12 50		12 57				13 13	13 19		13 27			13 43
Benfleet	d	12 02			12 18	12 24			12 32			12 48	12 54		13 02				13 18	13 23		13 32			13 48
Pitsea	d				12 21	12 29						12 51	12 59						13 21	13 28					13 51
Basildon	d	12 08			12 25				12 38			12 55			13 08				13 25			13 38			13 55
Laindon	d	12 11			12 28				12 41			12 58			13 11				13 28			13 41			13 58
West Horndon	d				12 33							13 03							13 33						14 03
Stanford-le-Hope	d					12 35							13 05							13 34					
East Tilbury	d					12 38							13 08							13 37					
Tilbury Town	d					12 44							13 14							13 43					
Grays	d					12 47		13 10					13 17	13 40						13 46	14 10				
Purfleet	d							13 16						13 46							14 16				
Rainham	d							13 21						13 51							14 21				
Dagenham Dock	d			←				13 24			←			13 54				←			14 24			←	
Chafford Hundred Lakeside	d			12 18		12 51					12 51		13 21					13 21		13 50				13 50	
Ockendon	d			12 22		→					12 55		→					13 25		→				13 54	
Upminster ⊖	d	12 19	←	12 28	12 38				12 49	←	13 01	13 08			13 19	←		13 31	13 38			13 49	←	14 01	14 08
Barking ⊖	d	12 27	12 30	12 36	12 46			13 30	12 57	13 00	13 09	13 16		14 00	13 27	13 30		13 39	13 46		14 30	13 57	14 00	14 09	14 16
Stratford ⊖	a							→						→							→				
London Liverpool St ⊖	a																								
West Ham ⊖	d	12 32	12 35	12 42	12 51				13 02	13 05	13 14	13 21			13 32	13 35		13 44	13 51			14 02	14 05	14 14	14 21
Limehouse	d	12 37	12 40	12 47	12 56				13 07	13 10	13 19	13 26			13 37	13 40		13 49	13 56			14 07	14 10	14 19	14 26
London Fenchurch St ⊖	a	12 41	12 45	12 52	13 00				13 11	13 16	13 24	13 31			13 41	13 45		13 55	14 01			14 11	14 15	14 24	14 31

		CC B		CC B	CC	CC C	CC A	CC	CC B	CC B	CC	CC C		CC A	CC	CC B	CC B	CC	CC C	CC A	CC	CC B		CC B	CC
Shoeburyness	d				13 41			13 57			14 11				14 27			14 41			14 57				15 10
Thorpe Bay	d				13 45			14 01			14 15				14 31			14 45			15 01				15 14
Southend East	d				13 47			14 03			14 17				14 33			14 47			15 03				15 16
Southend Central	a				13 50			14 06			14 20				14 36			14 50			15 06				15 19
	d	13 42			13 50			14 06	14 12		14 20				14 36	14 42		14 50			15 06	15 11			15 19
Westcliff	d	13 45			13 52			14 08	14 15		14 22				14 38	14 45		14 52			15 08	15 14			15 21
Chalkwell	d	13 47			13 55			14 11	14 17		14 25				14 41	14 47		14 55			15 11	15 16			15 24
Leigh-on-Sea	d	13 50			13 57			14 13	14 20		14 27				14 43	14 50		14 57			15 13	15 19			15 26
Benfleet	d	13 54			14 02			14 18	14 24		14 32				14 48	14 54		15 02			15 18	15 23			15 31
Pitsea	d	13 59						14 21	14 29						14 51	14 59					15 21	15 28			
Basildon	d				14 08			14 25			14 38				14 55			15 08			15 25				15 37
Laindon	d				14 11			14 28			14 41				14 58			15 11			15 28				15 40
West Horndon	d							14 33							15 03						15 33				
Stanford-le-Hope	d	14 05							14 35							15 05						15 34			
East Tilbury	d	14 08							14 38							15 08						15 37			
Tilbury Town	d	14 14							14 44							15 14						15 43			
Grays	d	14 17		14 40					14 47	15 10						15 17	15 40					15 46		16 09	
Purfleet	d			14 46						15 16							15 46							16 15	
Rainham	d			14 51						15 21							15 51							16 20	
Dagenham Dock	d			14 54			←			15 24				←			15 54			←				16 24	
Chafford Hundred Lakeside	d	14 21					14 21		14 51					14 51		15 21				15 21		15 50			
Ockendon	d	→					14 25		→					14 55		→				15 25		→			
Upminster ⊖	d				14 19	←	14 31	14 38			14 49	←		15 01	15 08			15 19	←	15 31	15 38				15 48
Barking ⊖	d			15 00	14 27	14 30	14 39	14 46		15 30	14 57	15 00		15 09	15 16		16 00	15 27	15 30	15 39	15 46			16 31	15 57
Stratford ⊖	a			→						→							→							→	
London Liverpool St ⊖	a																								
West Ham ⊖	d				14 32	14 35	14 44	14 51			15 02	15 05		15 14	15 21			15 32	15 35	15 44	15 51				16 02
Limehouse	d				14 37	14 40	14 49	14 56			15 07	15 10		15 19	15 27			15 37	15 40	15 49	15 56				16 07
London Fenchurch St ⊖	a				14 41	14 45	14 54	15 00			15 11	15 15		15 25	15 31			15 42	15 45	15 54	16 00				16 12

A From Southend Central
B To London Fenchurch Street
C From Grays

For services between Southend Victoria and London Liverpool Street refer to Table 6

Table T001-R

Mondays to Fridays

21 May to 7 December

Shoeburyness and Southend Central - London

		CC A	CC B	CC	CC C	CC	CC A	CC		CC B	CC	CC	CC	CC C	CC C	CC	CC	CC B		CC A	CC C	CC	CC	CC D	CC
Shoeburyness	d			15 27		15 41					15 55	16 00				16 12	16 18								16 40
Thorpe Bay	d			15 31		15 45					15 59	16 04				16 16	16 22						16 38		16 44
Southend East	d			15 33		15 47					16 01	16 06				16 18	16 24						16 40		16 46
Southend Central	a			15 36		15 50					16 04	16 09				16 21	16 27						16 43		16 49
	d			15 36	15 42	15 50					16 04	16 09			16 13	16 21	16 27					16 35	16 43		16 49
Westcliff	d			15 38	15 44	15 52					16 06	16 11			16 15	16 23	16 29					16 37	16 45		16 51
Chalkwell	d			15 41	15 47	15 55					16 09	16 14			16 17	16 26	16 32					16 40	16 48		16 54
Leigh-on-Sea	d			15 43	15 50	15 57					16 12	16 16			16 20	16 29	16 34					16 42	16 51		16 57
Benfleet	d			15 48	15 54	16 02					16 17	16 21			16 24	16 34	16 39					16 47	16 56		17 02
Pitsea	d			15 51	15 59	16 05						16 25			16 29		16 43				16 49	16 51			17 06
Basildon	d			15 55		16 09					16 23	16 29				16 40	16 47					16 55	17 02		17 10
Laindon	d			15 59		16 12		16 18			16 26	16 32				16 43	16 51					16 58	17 05		17 13
West Horndon	d			16 03				16 23			16 31					16 48						17 03			17 18
Stanford-le-Hope	d				16 05										16 36						16 55				
East Tilbury	d				16 08										16 39						16 59				
Tilbury Town	d				16 15										16 45						17 05				
Grays	d				16 19								16 38	16 48	16 49						17 08				
Purfleet	d												16 44		16 55						17 13				
Rainham	d												16 49		17 01						17 18				
Dagenham Dock	d		←							←			16 53		17 04					←	17 22				
Chafford Hundred Lakeside	d		15 50		16 22					16 22				16 52						16 52					
Ockendon	d		15 54		→					16 26				→						16 57					
Upminster ⊖	d	←	16 01	16 09		16 21	←	16 28		16 33		16 41				16 53	16 59	←		17 04		17 08	17 14	←	17 25
Barking ⊖	d	16 00	16 11	16 17		16 29	16 31	16 37		16 41		16 49	16 59		17 10	17 01	17 07	17 10		17 13	17 28	17 17	17 22	17 28	17 34
Stratford ⊖	a														→						→				
London Liverpool St ⊖	a																								
West Ham ⊖	d	16 06	16 16	16 22		16 34	16 37	16 42		16 46	16 50	16 55	17 04			17 07	17 13	17 16		17 18		17 22	17 29	17 34	17 40
Limehouse	d	16 11	16 21	16 27		16 39	16 42	16 47		16 51	16 55	17 00	17 09			17 12		17 21		17 24		17 27		17 39	
London Fenchurch St ⊖	a	16 16	16 26	16 32		16 44	16 48	16 52		16 56	16 59	17 04	17 14			17 17	17 23	17 26		17 29		17 32	17 38	17 44	17 50

		CC	CC	CC		CC	CC C	CC	CC	CC	CC D	CC	CC	CC		CC	CC	CC	CC C	CC	CC D	CC	CC	CC	
Shoeburyness	d	16 49		16 57				17 05		17 15				17 27						17 43				17 59	
Thorpe Bay	d	16 53		17 01				17 09		17 19				17 31						17 47				18 03	
Southend East	d	16 55		17 03				17 11		17 21				17 33						17 49				18 05	
Southend Central	a	16 58		17 06				17 14		17 24				17 36						17 52				18 08	
	d	16 58		17 06				17 14		17 24		17 28		17 36				17 46		17 52				18 08	
Westcliff	d	17 00		17 08				17 16		17 26		17 31		17 38				17 48		17 54				18 10	
Chalkwell	d	17 03		17 11				17 19		17 29		17 33		17 40				17 51		17 57				18 13	
Leigh-on-Sea	d	17 05		17 13				17 21	17 24	17 31		17 36		17 43			17 50	17 53		17 59		18 06		18 15	
Benfleet	d	17 10		17 18				17 26	17 30	17 36		17 41		17 47				17 58		18 04		18 12		18 20	
Pitsea	d	17 14		17 21			17 25	17 29				17 44		17 51					17 54	18 07				18 23	
Basildon	d	17 18		17 25				17 33	17 37	17 43		17 48		17 55			17 59	18 04		18 11		18 18		18 27	
Laindon	d	17 21		17 28				17 36		17 46		17 51		17 58				18 08		18 14		18 22		18 30	
West Horndon	d			17 33										18 03						18 19				18 35	
Stanford-le-Hope	d						17 31												18 00						
East Tilbury	d						17 35												18 04						
Tilbury Town	d						17 41												18 10						
Grays	d		17 17			17 28	17 44						17 47			17 55			18 13				18 17		
Purfleet	d					17 34	17 49									18 01			18 19						
Rainham	d					17 40	17 54									18 07			18 24						
Dagenham Dock	d					17 43	17 58									18 10			18 28						
Chafford Hundred Lakeside	d		17 21										17 51										18 21		
Ockendon	d		17 27										17 57										18 28		
Upminster ⊖	d		17 34	17 38				17 45			←	17 59	18 05	18 08			18 12	18 16		18 24	←	18 30	18 35	18 40	
Barking ⊖	d	17 37	17 43	17 47		17 50	18 05	17 53			18 05	18 07	18 13	18 16		18 18		18 25	18 35	18 32	18 35	18 39	18 43	18 48	
Stratford ⊖	a						→												→						
London Liverpool St ⊖	a																								
West Ham ⊖	d	17 43	17 49	17 52		17 55		17 58		18 06	18 10	18 13	18 19	18 22		18 24		18 30		18 37	18 40	18 44	18 48	18 53	
Limehouse	d		17 54	17 57		18 00		18 03				18 18	18 24	18 27		18 30		18 35		18 42	18 45	18 50	18 53	18 58	
London Fenchurch St ⊖	a	17 53	17 59	18 02		18 05		18 08	18 10	18 15	18 19	18 23	18 29	18 31		18 34	18 37	18 40		18 47	18 50	18 54	18 58	19 03	

		CC	CC C	CC C	CC	CC A	CC D	CC C	CC	CC D		CC	CC	CC	CC	CC C	CC C	CC C	CC	CC A		CC B	CC	CC C	CC
Shoeburyness	d				18 14				18 28			18 44			18 59				19 14				19 27		19 41
Thorpe Bay	d				18 18				18 32			18 48			19 03				19 18				19 31		19 45
Southend East	d				18 20				18 34			18 50			19 05				19 20				19 33		19 47
Southend Central	a				18 23				18 37			18 53			19 08				19 23				19 36		19 50
	d				18 23				18 37			18 53			19 08		19 12		19 23				19 36	19 42	19 50
Westcliff	d				18 25				18 39			18 55			19 10		19 15		19 25				19 38	19 45	19 52
Chalkwell	d				18 28				18 42			18 58			19 13		19 17		19 28				19 41	19 47	19 55
Leigh-on-Sea	d				18 30				18 44			19 00			19 15		19 20		19 30				19 43	19 50	19 57
Benfleet	d				18 35				18 49			19 05			19 20		19 24		19 35				19 48	19 54	20 02
Pitsea	d			18 27	18 38			18 42	18 53				18 59		19 23		19 29						19 51	19 59	
Basildon	d				18 42				18 57			19 11			19 27				19 41				19 55		20 08
Laindon	d				18 45				19 00			19 14			19 30				19 44				19 58		20 11
West Horndon	d				18 50				19 04						19 35								20 03		
Stanford-le-Hope	d			18 34				18 49					19 05				19 35							20 05	
East Tilbury	d			18 37				18 52					19 09				19 38							20 08	
Tilbury Town	d			18 43				18 58					19 15				19 44							20 14	
Grays	d	18 31	18 44	18 47				19 02					19 19	19 23		19 42	19 47	20 10						20 17	
Purfleet	d	18 37	18 50					19 07						19 29		19 48		20 16							
Rainham	d	18 42	18 56					19 12						19 34		19 53		20 21							
Dagenham Dock	d	18 46	19 00				←	19 16						19 37		19 56		20 24				←			
Chafford Hundred Lakeside	d			18 51			18 51						19 22				19 51					19 51		20 21	
Ockendon	d			→			18 57						19 26				→					19 55		→	
Upminster ⊖	d				18 55	←	19 04		19 09	←		19 22	19 33		19 40				19 52	←		20 01	20 08		20 19
Barking ⊖	d	18 52	19 07		19 03	19 07	19 12	19 22	19 17	19 22		19 30	19 41	19 43	19 48	20 03		20 30	20 00	20 03		20 09	20 16		20 27
Stratford ⊖	a		→					→								→		→							
London Liverpool St ⊖	a																								
West Ham ⊖	d	18 58			19 08	19 12	19 17		19 22	19 27		19 35	19 46	19 49	19 53				20 05	20 08		20 14	20 21		20 32
Limehouse	d	19 04			19 13	19 18	19 22		19 27	19 32			19 51	19 54	19 58				20 10	20 13		20 19	20 26		20 37
London Fenchurch St ⊖	a	19 08			19 18	19 24	19 27		19 32	19 38		19 45	19 56	19 59	20 04				20 14	20 19		20 24	20 30		20 41

A From Grays
B From Southend Central
C To London Fenchurch Street
D From Pitsea

For services between Southend Victoria and London Liverpool Street refer to

Table T001-R

Shoeburyness and Southend Central - London

Mondays to Fridays
21 May to 7 December

		CC A	CC B	CC	CC	CC		CC C	CC	CC C	CC	CC A	CC B	CC	CC	CC		CC C	CC	CC C	CC	CC A	CC B	CC	CC
Shoeburyness	d			19 57					20 27		20 41			20 57					21 27		21 41			21 57	
Thorpe Bay	d			20 01					20 31		20 45			21 01					21 31		21 45			22 01	
Southend East	d			20 03					20 33		20 47			21 03					21 33		21 47			22 03	
Southend Central	a			20 06					20 36		20 50			21 06					21 36		21 50			22 06	
	d			20 06		20 12			20 36	20 42	20 50			21 06		21 12			21 36	21 42	21 50			22 06	
Westcliff	d			20 08		20 15			20 38	20 45	20 52			21 08		21 15			21 38	21 45	21 52			22 08	
Chalkwell	d			20 11		20 17			20 41	20 47	20 55			21 11		21 17			21 41	21 47	21 55			22 11	
Leigh-on-Sea	d			20 13		20 20			20 43	20 50	20 57			21 13		21 20			21 43	21 50	21 57			22 13	
Benfleet	d			20 18		20 24			20 48	20 54	21 02			21 18		21 24			21 48	21 54	22 02			22 18	
Pitsea	d			20 21		20 29			20 51	20 59				21 21		21 29			21 51	21 59				22 21	
Basildon	d			20 25					20 55		21 08			21 25					21 55		22 08			22 25	
Laindon	d			20 28					20 58		21 11			21 28					21 58		22 11			22 28	
West Horndon	d			20 33					21 03					21 33					22 03					22 33	
Stanford-le-Hope	d					20 35				21 05						21 35				22 05					
East Tilbury	d					20 38				21 08						21 38				22 08					
Tilbury Town	d					20 44				21 14						21 44				22 14					
Grays	d				20 40	20 47		21 10		21 17					21 43	21 47		22 10		22 17					22 40
Purfleet	d				20 46			21 16							21 49			22 16							22 46
Rainham	d				20 51			21 21							21 54			22 21							22 51
Dagenham Dock	d		←		20 54			21 24					←		21 58			22 24					←		22 54
Chafford Hundred Lakeside	d		20 21			20 51				21 21			21 21			21 51				22 21			22 21		
Ockendon	d		20 25			20 55				→			21 25			21 55				→			22 25		
Upminster	⊖ d	←	20 31	20 38		21 01			21 08		21 19	←	21 31	21 38		22 01			22 08		22 19	←	22 31	22 38	
Barking	⊖ d	20 30	20 39	20 46	21 00	21 09		21 30	21 16		21 27	21 30	21 39	21 46	22 05	22 09		22 30	22 16		22 27	22 30	22 39	22 46	23 00
Stratford 7	⊖ ⛴ a							→										→							
London Liverpool St 15	⊖ a																								
West Ham	⊖ d	20 35	20 44	20 51	21 05	21 14			21 21		21 32	21 35	21 44	21 51	22 10	22 14			22 21		22 32	22 35	22 44	22 51	23 05
Limehouse	⛴ d	20 40	20 49	20 56	21 10	21 19			21 26		21 37	21 40	21 49	21 56	22 15	22 19			22 26		22 37	22 40	22 49	22 56	23 10
London Fenchurch St 7	⊖ a	20 44	20 54	21 00	21 14	21 24			21 30		21 41	21 45	21 54	22 00	22 19	22 24			22 31		22 41	22 45	22 54	23 00	23 14

		CC		CC	CC	CC	CC	CC	CC	CC
Shoeburyness	d			22 27			22 57			23 27
Thorpe Bay	d			22 31			23 01			23 31
Southend East	d			22 33			23 03			23 33
Southend Central	a			22 36			23 06			23 36
	d	22 12		22 36		22 42	23 06		23 12	23 36
Westcliff	d	22 15		22 38		22 45	23 08		23 15	23 38
Chalkwell	d	22 17		22 41		22 47	23 11		23 17	23 41
Leigh-on-Sea	d	22 20		22 43		22 50	23 13		23 20	23 43
Benfleet	d	22 24		22 48		22 54	23 18		23 24	23 48
Pitsea	d	22 29		22 51		22 59	23 21		23 29	23 51
Basildon	d			22 55			23 25			23 55
Laindon	d			22 58			23 28			23 58
West Horndon	d			23 03			23 33			00 03
Stanford-le-Hope	d	22 35				23 05			23 35	
East Tilbury	d	22 38				23 08			23 38	
Tilbury Town	d	22 44				23 14			23 44	
Grays	d	22 47			23 10	23 17		23 39	23 47	
Purfleet	d				23 16			23 45		
Rainham	d				23 21			23 50		
Dagenham Dock	d				23 24			23 54		
Chafford Hundred Lakeside	d	22 51				23 21			23 51	
Ockendon	d	22 55				23 25			23 55	
Upminster	⊖ d	23 01		23 08		23 31	23 38		00 01	00 08
Barking	⊖ d	23 09		23 16	23 30	23 39	23 46	23 59	00 09	00 16
Stratford 7	⊖ ⛴ a									
London Liverpool St 15	⊖ a									
West Ham	⊖ d	23 14		23 21	23 35	23 44	23 51	00 05	00 14	00 21
Limehouse	⛴ d	23 19		23 26	23 40	23 49	23 56	00 10	00 19	00 26
London Fenchurch St 7	⊖ a	23 24		23 30	23 45	23 54	00 01	00 15	00 24	00 32

A From Grays
B From Southend Central
C To London Fenchurch Street

For services between Southend Victoria and London Liverpool Street refer to Table 6

Table T001-R

Shoeburyness and Southend Central - London

Saturdays
26 May to 8 December

			CC A	CC B	CC C	CC	CC	CC	CC	CC	CC		CC	CC	CC	CC	CC	CC	CC	CC	CC	CC	CC	CC D	CC
Shoeburyness	d						04 25		05 09				05 39			06 09			06 39			07 09			07 24
Thorpe Bay	d						04 29		05 13				05 43			06 13			06 43			07 13			07 28
Southend East	d						04 31		05 15				05 45			06 15			06 45			07 15			07 30
Southend Central	a						04 34		05 18				05 48			06 18			06 48			07 18			07 33
	d					04 13	04 34	04 55	05 18		05 25		05 48		05 55	06 18		06 25	06 48		06 55	07 18		07 25	07 33
Westcliff	d					04 16	04 36	04 58	05 20		05 28		05 50		05 58	06 20		06 28	06 50		06 58	07 20		07 28	07 35
Chalkwell	d					04 18	04 39	05 00	05 23		05 30		05 53		06 00	06 23		06 30	06 53		07 00	07 23		07 30	07 38
Leigh-on-Sea	d					04 21	04 41	05 03	05 25		05 33		05 55		06 03	06 25		06 33	06 55		07 03	07 25		07 33	07 40
Benfleet	d					04 25	04 46	05 07	05 30		05 37		06 00		06 07	06 30		06 37	07 00		07 07	07 30		07 37	07 45
Pitsea	d					04 30	04 49	05 12	05 33		05 42		06 03		06 12	06 33		06 42	07 03		07 12	07 33		07 42	07 48
Basildon	d						04 53		05 37				06 07			06 37			07 07			07 37			07 52
Laindon	d						04 56		05 40				06 10			06 40			07 10			07 40			07 55
West Horndon	d				00 03		05 01		05 45				06 15			06 45			07 15			07 45			08 00
Stanford-le-Hope	d					04 36		05 18			05 48				06 18			06 48			07 18			07 48	
East Tilbury	d					04 39		05 21			05 51				06 21			06 51			07 21			07 51	
Tilbury Town	d					04 45		05 27			05 57				06 27			06 57			07 27			07 57	
Grays	d					04 49		05 31		05 50	06 01			06 20	06 31		06 50	07 01		07 20	07 31		07 50	08 01	
Purfleet	d									05 56				06 26			06 56			07 26			07 56		
Rainham	d									06 01				06 31			07 01			07 31			08 01		
Dagenham Dock	d									06 04				06 34			07 04			07 34			08 04		
Chafford Hundred Lakeside	d					04 52		05 35			06 05				06 35			07 05			07 35			08 05	
Ockendon	d					04 56		05 39			06 09				06 39			07 09			07 39			→	
Upminster	⊖ d			00 01	00 08	05 03	05 06	05 45	05 51		06 15		06 21		06 45	06 51		07 15	07 21		07 45	07 51			08 05
Barking	⊖ d			00 09	00 16	05 11	05 14	05 54	06 00	06 10	06 24		06 29	06 40	06 54	06 59	07 10	07 24	07 29	07 40	07 54	07 59	08 10		08 14
Stratford 7	⊖ ⛴ a																								08 22
London Liverpool St 15	⊖ a																								08 32
West Ham	⊖ d		00 05	00 14	00 21	05 16	05 19	05 59	06 05	06 15	06 29		06 34	06 45	06 59	07 04	07 15	07 29	07 34	07 45	07 59	08 04	08 15		
Limehouse	⛴ d		00 10	00 19	00 26	05 21	05 24	06 04	06 10	06 20	06 34		06 39	06 50	07 04	07 09	07 20	07 34	07 39	07 50	08 04	08 09	08 20		
London Fenchurch St 7	⊖ a		00 15	00 24	00 32	05 28	05 30	06 10	06 16	06 26	06 40		06 46	06 56	07 10	07 16	07 26	07 40	07 46	07 56	08 10	08 16	08 26		

		CC B	CC	CC	CC D	CC	CC B		CC	CC	CC D	CC	CC B	CC	CC	CC D	CC	CC B		CC	CC	CC D	CC	
Shoeburyness	d		07 39			07 54			12 09			12 24		12 39			12 54			13 09			13 24	
Thorpe Bay	d		07 43			07 58			12 13			12 28		12 43			12 58			13 13			13 28	
Southend East	d		07 45			08 00			12 15			12 30		12 45			13 00			13 15			13 30	
Southend Central	a		07 48			08 03			12 18			12 33		12 48			13 03			13 18			13 33	
	d		07 48		07 55	08 03			12 18		12 25	12 33		12 48		12 55	13 03			13 18		13 25	13 33	
Westcliff	d		07 50		07 58	08 05			12 20		12 28	12 35		12 50		12 58	13 05			13 20		13 28	13 35	
Chalkwell	d		07 53		08 00	08 08			12 23		12 30	12 38		12 53		13 00	13 08			13 23		13 30	13 38	
Leigh-on-Sea	d		07 55		08 03	08 10			12 25		12 33	12 40		12 55		13 03	13 10			13 25		13 33	13 40	
Benfleet	d		08 00		08 07	08 15			12 30		12 37	12 45		13 00		13 07	13 15			13 30		13 37	13 45	
Pitsea	d		08 03		08 12	08 18			12 33		12 42	12 48		13 03		13 12	13 18			13 33		13 42	13 48	
Basildon	d		08 07			08 22		and at the same minutes past each hour until	12 37			12 52		13 07			13 22			13 37			13 52	
Laindon	d		08 10			08 25			12 40			12 55		13 10			13 25			13 40			13 55	
West Horndon	d		08 15			08 30			12 45			13 00		13 15			13 30			13 45			14 00	
Stanford-le-Hope	d				08 18						12 48					13 18						13 48		
East Tilbury	d				08 21						12 51					13 21						13 51		
Tilbury Town	d				08 27						12 57					13 27						13 57		
Grays	d			08 20	08 31					12 50	13 01				13 20	13 31					13 50	14 01		
Purfleet	d			08 26						12 56					13 26						13 56			
Rainham	d			08 31						13 01					13 31						14 01			
Dagenham Dock	d	←		08 34			←			13 04			←		13 34			←			14 04			
Chafford Hundred Lakeside	d	08 05			08 35		08 35				13 05		13 05			13 35		13 35				14 05		
Ockendon	d	08 09			→		08 39				→		13 09			→		13 39				→		
Upminster	⊖ d	08 15	08 21			08 35	08 45		12 51			13 05	13 15	13 21			13 35	13 45		13 51			14 05	
Barking	⊖ d	08 24	08 29	08 40		08 44	08 54		12 59	13 10		13 14	13 24	13 29	13 40		13 44	13 54		13 59	14 10		14 14	
Stratford 7	⊖ ⛴ a					08 52						13 22					13 52						14 21	
London Liverpool St 15	⊖ a					09 02						13 32					14 02						14 32	
West Ham	⊖ d	08 29	08 34	08 45			08 59		13 04	13 15			13 29	13 34	13 45			13 59		14 04	14 15			
Limehouse	⛴ d	08 34	08 39	08 50			09 04		13 09	13 20			13 34	13 39	13 50			14 04		14 09	14 20			
London Fenchurch St 7	⊖ a	08 40	08 46	08 56			09 10		13 16	13 26			13 40	13 46	13 56			14 10		14 16	14 26			

		CC B	CC	CC	CC D	CC	CC B	CC	CC	CC D	CC		CC B	CC	CC	CC D	CC	CC B	CC	CC	CC D	CC		CC B
Shoeburyness	d		13 39			13 54		14 09			14 24			18 39			18 54		19 09			19 24		
Thorpe Bay	d		13 43			13 58		14 13			14 28			18 43			18 58		19 13			19 28		
Southend East	d		13 45			14 00		14 15			14 30			18 45			19 00		19 15			19 30		
Southend Central	a		13 48			14 03		14 18			14 33			18 48			19 03		19 18			19 33		
	d		13 48		13 55	14 03		14 18		14 25	14 33			18 48		18 55	19 03		19 18		19 25	19 33		
Westcliff	d		13 50		13 58	14 05		14 20		14 28	14 35			18 50		18 58	19 05		19 20		19 28	19 35		
Chalkwell	d		13 53		14 00	14 08		14 23		14 30	14 38			18 53		19 00	19 08		19 23		19 30	19 38		
Leigh-on-Sea	d		13 55		14 03	14 10		14 25		14 33	14 40			18 55		19 03	19 10		19 25		19 33	19 40		
Benfleet	d		14 00		14 07	14 15		14 30		14 37	14 45			19 00		19 07	19 15		19 30		19 37	19 45		
Pitsea	d		14 03		14 12	14 18		14 33		14 42	14 48			19 03		19 12	19 18		19 33		19 42	19 48		
Basildon	d		14 07			14 22		14 37			14 52	and at the same minutes past each hour until		19 07			19 22		19 37			19 52		
Laindon	d		14 10			14 25		14 40			14 55			19 10			19 25		19 40			19 55		
West Horndon	d		14 15			14 30		14 45			15 00			19 15			19 30		19 45			20 00		
Stanford-le-Hope	d				14 18					14 48						19 18					19 48			
East Tilbury	d				14 21					14 51						19 21					19 51			
Tilbury Town	d				14 27					14 57						19 27					19 57			
Grays	d			14 20	14 31				14 50	15 01					19 20	19 31				19 50	20 01			
Purfleet	d			14 26					14 56						19 26					19 56				
Rainham	d			14 31					15 01						19 31					20 01				
Dagenham Dock	d	←		14 34			←		15 04				←		19 34			←		20 04				←
Chafford Hundred Lakeside	d	14 05			14 35		14 35			15 05			19 05			19 35		19 35			20 05			20 05
Ockendon	d	14 09			→		14 39			→			19 09			→		19 39			→			20 09
Upminster	⊖ d	14 15	14 21			14 35	14 45	14 51			15 05		19 15	19 21			19 35	19 45	19 51			20 05		20 15
Barking	⊖ d	14 24	14 29	14 40		14 44	14 54	14 59	15 10		15 14		19 24	19 29	19 40		19 44	19 54	19 59	20 10		20 14		20 24
Stratford 7	⊖ ⛴ a					14 52					15 22						19 52					20 22		
London Liverpool St 15	⊖ a					15 02					15 32						20 02					20 32		
West Ham	⊖ d	14 29	14 34	14 45			14 59	15 04	15 15				19 29	19 34	19 45			19 59	20 04	20 15				20 29
Limehouse	⛴ d	14 34	14 39	14 50			15 04	15 09	15 20				19 34	19 39	19 50			20 04	20 09	20 20				20 34
London Fenchurch St 7	⊖ a	14 40	14 46	14 56			15 10	15 16	15 26				19 40	19 46	19 56			20 10	20 16	20 26				20 40

A From Grays
B From Southend Central
C From Shoeburyness
D To London Fenchurch Street

Table T001-R

Shoeburyness and Southend Central - London

Saturdays

26 May to 8 December

		CC	CC	CC A	CC	CC B	CC	CC	CC A		CC	CC B	CC	CC A	CC	CC B	CC	CC A	CC		CC B	CC	CC	CC A	CC
Shoeburyness	d	19 39			19 54		20 09				20 24				20 54				21 24			21 39			21 54
Thorpe Bay	d	19 43			19 58		20 13				20 28				20 58				21 28			21 43			21 58
Southend East	d	19 45			20 00		20 15				20 30				21 00				21 30			21 45			22 00
Southend Central	a	19 48			20 03		20 18				20 33				21 03				21 33			21 48			22 03
	d	19 48		19 55	20 03		20 18		20 25		20 33			20 55	21 03			21 25	21 33			21 48		21 55	22 03
Westcliff	d	19 50		19 58	20 05		20 20		20 28		20 35			20 58	21 05			21 28	21 35			21 50		21 58	22 05
Chalkwell	d	19 53		20 00	20 08		20 23		20 30		20 38			21 00	21 08			21 30	21 38			21 53		22 00	22 08
Leigh-on-Sea	d	19 55		20 03	20 10		20 25		20 33		20 40			21 03	21 10			21 33	21 40			21 55		22 03	22 10
Benfleet	d	20 00		20 07	20 15		20 30		20 37		20 45			21 07	21 15			21 37	21 45			22 00		22 07	22 15
Pitsea	d	20 03		20 12	20 18		20 33		20 42		20 48			21 12	21 18			21 42	21 48			22 03		22 12	22 18
Basildon	d	20 07			20 22		20 37				20 52				21 22				21 52			22 07			22 22
Laindon	d	20 10			20 25		20 40				20 55				21 25				21 55			22 10			22 25
West Horndon	d	20 15			20 30		20 45				21 00				21 30				22 00			22 15			22 30
Stanford-le-Hope	d			20 18					20 48					21 18				21 48						22 18	
East Tilbury	d			20 21					20 51					21 21				21 51						22 21	
Tilbury Town 3	d			20 27					20 57					21 27				21 57						22 27	
Grays	d		20 20	20 31				20 50	21 01				21 20	21 31			21 50	22 01					22 20	22 31	
Purfleet	d		20 26					20 56					21 26				21 56						22 26		
Rainham	d		20 31					21 01					21 31				22 01						22 31		
Dagenham Dock	d		20 34			←		21 04				←	21 34			←	22 04				←		22 34		
Chafford Hundred Lakeside	d			20 35		20 35			21 05			21 05		21 35		21 35		22 05			22 05			22 35	
Ockendon	d			→		20 39			→			21 09		→		21 39		→			22 09			→	
Upminster ⊖	d	20 21			20 35	20 45	20 51				21 05	21 15			21 35	21 45			22 05		22 15	22 21			22 35
Barking ⊖	d	20 29	20 40		20 44	20 54	20 59	21 10			21 14	21 24	21 40		21 44	21 54	22 10		22 14		22 24	22 29	22 40		22 44
Stratford 7 ⊖	a				20 52						21 21				21 51				22 22						22 52
London Liverpool St 15 ⊖	a				21 02						21 31				22 01				22 32						23 02
West Ham ⊖	d	20 34	20 45			20 59	21 04	21 15				21 29	21 45			21 59	22 15				22 29	22 34	22 45		
Limehouse	d	20 39	20 50			21 04		21 20				21 34	21 50			22 04	22 20				22 34		22 50		
London Fenchurch St 7 ⊖	a	20 46	20 56			21 10	21 16	21 26				21 40	21 56			22 10	22 26				22 40	22 46	22 56		

		CC B	CC	CC A	CC		CC B	CC	CC A	CC	CC B	CC	CC
Shoeburyness	d				22 24					22 58		23 28	
Thorpe Bay	d				22 28					23 02		23 32	
Southend East	d				22 30					23 04		23 34	
Southend Central	a				22 33					23 07		23 37	
	d			22 25	22 33				22 55	23 07		23 37	23 45
Westcliff	d			22 28	22 35				22 58	23 09		23 39	23 47
Chalkwell	d			22 30	22 38				23 00	23 12		23 42	23 50
Leigh-on-Sea	d			22 33	22 40				23 03	23 14		23 44	23 52
Benfleet	d			22 37	22 45				23 07	23 19		23 49	23 57
Pitsea	d			22 42	22 48				23 12	23 25		23 52	00 01
Basildon	d				22 52					23 28		23 56	
Laindon	d				22 55					23 31		23 59	
West Horndon	d				23 00					23 36		00 04	
Stanford-le-Hope	d			22 48					23 18				00 07
East Tilbury	d			22 51					23 21				00 11
Tilbury Town 3	d			22 57					23 27				00 17
Grays	d		22 50	23 01				23 20	23 31				00 20
Purfleet	d		22 56					23 26					
Rainham	d		23 01					23 31					
Dagenham Dock	d	←	23 04				←	23 34			←		
Chafford Hundred Lakeside	d	22 35		23 05			23 05		23 35		23 35		00 23
Ockendon	d	22 39		→			23 09		→		23 39		00 27
Upminster ⊖	d	22 45			23 05		23 15			23 41	23 45	00 09	00 34
Barking ⊖	d	22 54	23 10		23 16		23 24	23 40		23 49	23 54	00 18	00a44
Stratford 7 ⊖	a				23 24								
London Liverpool St 15 ⊖	a				23 34								
West Ham ⊖	d	22 59	23 15				23 29	23 45		23 54	23 59	00 23	
Limehouse	d	23 04	23 20				23 34	23 50		23 59	00 04	00 28	
London Fenchurch St 7 ⊖	a	23 10	23 26				23 40	23 56		00 06	00 10	00 34	

A To London Fenchurch Street

B From Southend Central

For services between Southend Victoria and London Liverpool Street refer to Table 6

Table T001-R

Shoeburyness and Southend Central - London

Sundays

20 May to 2 December

		CC A	CC B	CC A	CC	CC C		CC	CC D	CC	CC	CC C	CC	CC D	CC	CC		CC	CC C	CC	CC E	CC	CC C	CC	CC D
Shoeburyness	d				05 40	06 04		06 10		06 40		06 57	07 10			07 40				08 10			08 27	08 40	
Thorpe Bay	d				05 44	06 08		06 14		06 44		07 01	07 14			07 44				08 14			08 31	08 44	
Southend East	d				05 46	06 10		06 16		06 46		07 03	07 16			07 46				08 16			08 33	08 46	
Southend Central	a				05 49	06 13		06 19		06 49		07 06	07 19			07 49				08 19			08 36	08 49	
	d				05 49	06 13		06 19		06 49		07 06	07 19			07 49			08 05	08 19			08 36	08 49	
Westcliff	d				05 51	06 15		06 21		06 51		07 08	07 21			07 51			08 08	08 21			08 38	08 51	
Chalkwell	d				05 54	06 17		06 24		06 54		07 10	07 24			07 54			08 10	08 24			08 40	08 54	
Leigh-on-Sea	d				05 56	06 20		06 26		06 56		07 13	07 26			07 56			08 13	08 26			08 43	08 56	
Benfleet	d				06 01	06 24		06 31		07 01		07 17	07 31			08 01			08 17	08 31			08 47	09 01	
Pitsea	d			00 01	06 04	06 29		06 34		07 04		07 22	07 34			08 04			08 22	08 34			08 52	09 04	
Basildon	d				06 08			06 38		07 08			07 38			08 08				08 38				09 08	
Laindon	d				06 11			06 41		07 11			07 41			08 11				08 41				09 11	
West Horndon	d		00 04		06 16			06 46		07 16			07 46			08 16				08 46				09 16	
Stanford-le-Hope	d			00 07		06 35						07 28							08 28				08 58		
East Tilbury	d			00 11		06 38						07 31							08 31				09 01		
Tilbury Town 3	d			00 17		06 44						07 37							08 37				09 07		
Grays	d			00 20		06 48					07 37	07 41			08 07			08 30	08 41			09 00	09 11		
Purfleet	d										07 43				08 13			08 36				09 06			
Rainham	d										07 48				08 18			08 41				09 11			
Dagenham Dock	d								←		07 51			←	08 21			08 44			←	09 14			←
Chafford Hundred Lakeside	d			00 23		06 51			06 51			07 44		07 44					08 44		08 44		09 14		09 14
Ockendon	d			00 27		→			06 55			→		07 48					→		08 48		→		09 18
Upminster ⊖	d		00 09	00 34	06 21			06 51	07 02	07 21			07 51	07 55		08 21				08 51	08 55			09 21	09 25
Barking ⊖	d		00 18	00a44	06 29			06 59	07 10	07 29	07 57		07 59	08 04	08 27	08 29		08 50		08 59	09 04	09 20		09 31	09 34
Stratford 7 ⊖	a																							09 38	
London Liverpool St 15 ⊖	a																							09 49	
West Ham ⊖	d		00 23		06 34			07 04	07 15	07 34	08 02		08 04	08 09	08 32	08 34		08 55		09 04	09 09	09 25			09 39
Limehouse	d	00 04	00 28		06 39			07 09	07 20	07 39	08 07		08 09	08 14	08 37	08 39		09 00		09 09	09 14	09 30			09 44
London Fenchurch St 7 ⊖	a	00 10	00 34		06 45			07 16	07 27	07 46	08 13		08 16	08 20	08 43	08 46		09 06		09 16	09 20	09 36			09 50

		CC		CC C	CC	CC E	CC	CC C	CC	CC E	CC	CC C	CC	CC D	CC	CC C	CC	CC E	CC	CC C	
Shoeburyness	d				09 10				09 40			09 57	10 10				10 40				
Thorpe Bay	d				09 14				09 44			10 01	10 14				10 44				
Southend East	d				09 16				09 46			10 03	10 16				10 46				
Southend Central	a				09 19				09 49			10 06	10 19				10 49				
	d			09 05	09 19			09 35	09 49			10 06	10 19			10 35	10 49			11 05	
Westcliff	d			09 08	09 21			09 38	09 51			10 08	10 21			10 38	10 51			11 08	
Chalkwell	d			09 10	09 24			09 40	09 54			10 10	10 24			10 40	10 54			11 10	
Leigh-on-Sea	d			09 13	09 26			09 43	09 56			10 13	10 26			10 43	10 56			11 13	
Benfleet	d			09 17	09 31			09 47	10 01			10 17	10 31			10 47	11 01			11 17	
Pitsea	d			09 22	09 34			09 52	10 04			10 22	10 34			10 52	11 04			11 22	
Basildon	d				09 38				10 08				10 38				11 08				and at the same minutes past each hour until
Laindon	d				09 41				10 11				10 41				11 11				
West Horndon	d				09 46				10 16				10 46				11 16				
Stanford-le-Hope	d			09 28				09 58				10 28				10 58				11 28	
East Tilbury	d			09 31				10 01				10 31				11 01				11 31	
Tilbury Town 3	d			09 37				10 07				10 37				11 07				11 37	
Grays	d	09 30		09 41			10 00	10 11			10 30	10 41			11 00	11 11			11 30	11 41	
Purfleet	d	09 36					10 06				10 36				11 06				11 36		
Rainham	d	09 41					10 11				10 41				11 11				11 41		
Dagenham Dock	d	09 44				←	10 14			←	10 44			←	11 14			←	11 44		
Chafford Hundred Lakeside	d			09 44		09 44		10 14		10 14		10 44		10 44		11 14		11 14		11 44	
Ockendon	d			→		09 48		→		10 18		→		10 48		→		11 18		→	
Upminster ⊖	d				09 51	09 55			10 21	10 25			10 51	10 55			11 21	11 25			
Barking ⊖	d	09 50			10 01	10 04	10 20		10 31	10 34	10 50		11 01	11 04	11 20		11 31	11 34	11 50		
Stratford 7 ⊖	a				10 08				10 38				11 08				11 38				
London Liverpool St 15 ⊖	a				10 19				10 49				11 19				11 49				
West Ham ⊖	d	09 55				10 09	10 25			10 39	10 55			11 09	11 25			11 39	11 55		
Limehouse	d	10 00				10 14	10 30			10 44	11 00			11 14	11 30			11 44	12 00		
London Fenchurch St 7 ⊖	a	10 06				10 20	10 36			10 50	11 06			11 20	11 36			11 50	12 06		

		CC	CC E	CC	CC C	CC	CC E	CC	CC C		CC	CC E	CC	CC C	CC	CC E	CC	CC C	CC		CC E	CC	CC C	CC	CC E
Shoeburyness	d	19 10				19 40					20 10				20 40				21 10					21 40	
Thorpe Bay	d	19 14				19 44					20 14				20 44				21 14					21 44	
Southend East	d	19 16				19 46					20 16				20 46				21 16					21 46	
Southend Central	a	19 19				19 49					20 19				20 49				21 19					21 49	
	d	19 19			19 35	19 49			20 05		20 19			20 35	20 49			21 05	21 19				21 35	21 49	
Westcliff	d	19 21			19 38	19 51			20 08		20 21			20 38	20 51			21 08	21 21				21 38	21 51	
Chalkwell	d	19 24			19 40	19 54			20 10		20 24			20 40	20 54			21 10	21 24				21 40	21 54	
Leigh-on-Sea	d	19 26			19 43	19 56			20 13		20 26			20 43	20 56			21 13	21 26				21 43	21 56	
Benfleet	d	19 31			19 47	20 01			20 17		20 31			20 47	21 01			21 17	21 31				21 47	22 01	
Pitsea	d	19 34			19 52	20 04			20 22		20 34			20 52	21 04			21 22	21 34				21 52	22 04	
Basildon	d	19 38				20 08					20 38				21 08				21 38					22 08	
Laindon	d	19 41				20 11					20 41				21 11				21 41					22 11	
West Horndon	d	19 46				20 16					20 46				21 16				21 46					22 16	
Stanford-le-Hope	d				19 58				20 28					20 58				21 28					21 58		
East Tilbury	d				20 01				20 31					21 01				21 31					22 01		
Tilbury Town 3	d				20 07				20 37					21 07				21 37					22 07		
Grays	d			20 00	20 11			20 30	20 41				21 00	21 11			21 30	21 41				22 00	22 11		
Purfleet	d			20 06				20 36					21 06				21 36					22 06			
Rainham	d			20 11				20 41					21 11				21 41					22 11			
Dagenham Dock	d		←	20 14			←	20 44				←	21 14			←	21 44				←	22 14			←
Chafford Hundred Lakeside	d		19 44		20 14		20 14		20 44			20 44		21 14		21 14		21 44			21 44		22 14		22 14
Ockendon	d		19 48		→		20 18		→			20 48		→		21 18		→			21 48		→		22 18
Upminster ⊖	d	19 51	19 55			20 21	20 25				20 51	20 55			21 21	21 25			21 51		21 55			22 21	22 25
Barking ⊖	d	20 01	20 04	20 20		20 31	20 34	20 50			21 01	21 04	21 20		21 31	21 34	21 50		22 01		22 04	22 20		22 31	22 34
Stratford 7 ⊖	a	20 08				20 38					21 09				21 38				22 08					22 38	
London Liverpool St 15 ⊖	a	20 19				20 49					21 19				21 49				22 19					22 49	
West Ham ⊖	d		20 09	20 25			20 39	20 55				21 09	21 25			21 39	21 55				22 09	22 25			22 39
Limehouse	d		20 14	20 30			20 44	21 00				21 14	21 30			21 44	22 00				22 14	22 30			22 44
London Fenchurch St 7 ⊖	a		20 20	20 36			20 50	21 06				21 20	21 36			21 50	22 06				22 20	22 36			22 50

A From Southend Central

B From Shoeburyness

C To London Fenchurch Street

D From Shoeburyness

E From Southend Central

Table T001-R

Sundays
20 May to 2 December

Shoeburyness and Southend Central - London

		CC	CC	CC A	CC		CC B
Shoeburyness	d		22 10		22 40		
Thorpe Bay	d		22 14		22 44		
Southend East	d		22 16		22 46		
Southend Central	a		22 19		22 49		
	d		22 19	22 35	22 49		
Westcliff	d		22 21	22 38	22 51		
Chalkwell	d		22 24	22 40	22 54		
Leigh-on-Sea	d		22 26	22 43	22 56		
Benfleet	d		22 31	22 47	23 01		
Pitsea	d		22 34	22 52	23 04		
Basildon	d		22 38		23 08		
Laindon	d		22 41		23 11		
West Horndon	d		22 46		23 16		
Stanford-le-Hope	d			22 58			
East Tilbury	d			23 01			
Tilbury Town	d			23 07			
Grays	d	22 30		23 11			
Purfleet	d	22 36					
Rainham	d	22 41					
Dagenham Dock	d	22 44					←
Chafford Hundred Lakeside	d			23 15			23 15
Ockendon	d			→			23 19
Upminster ⊖	d		22 51		23 21		23 26
Barking ⊖	d	22 50	23 01		23 30		23 35
Stratford ⊖	a		23 08				
London Liverpool St ⊖	a		23 19				
West Ham ⊖	d	22 55			23 35		23 40
Limehouse	d	23 00			23 40		23 45
London Fenchurch St ⊖	a	23 06			23 46		23 51

A To London Fenchurch Street **B** From Southend Central

For services between Southend Victoria and London Liverpool Street refer to Table 6

Table T004-F

Mondays to Saturdays
21 May to 8 December

Romford - Upminster

Miles			LO	LO	LO	LO	LO	LO	LO	LO	LO		LO	LO	LO	LO	LO	LO	LO	LO	LO		LO	LO	LO
0	**Romford**	d	06 11	06 41	07 11	07 41	08 11	08 41	09 11	09 41	10 11		10 41	11 11	11 41	12 11	12 41	13 11	13 41	14 11	14 41		15 11	15 41	16 11
2	Emerson Park	d	06 15	06 45	07 15	07 45	08 15	08 45	09 15	09 45	10 15		10 45	11 15	11 45	12 15	12 45	13 15	13 45	14 15	14 45		15 15	15 45	16 15
3½	**Upminster** ⊖	a	06 20	06 50	07 20	07 50	08 20	08 50	09 20	09 50	10 20		10 50	11 20	11 50	12 20	12 50	13 20	13 50	14 20	14 50		15 20	15 50	16 20

		LO	LO	LO	LO	LO	LO		LO	LO	LO	LO	LO
Romford	d	16 41	17 11	17 41	18 11	18 41	19 11		19 41	20 11	20 41	21 11	21 41
Emerson Park	d	16 45	17 15	17 45	18 15	18 45	19 15		19 45	20 15	20 45	21 15	21 45
Upminster ⊖	a	16 50	17 20	17 50	18 20	18 50	19 20		19 50	20 20	20 50	21 20	21 50

Sundays
20 May to 2 December

		LO	LO	LO	LO	LO	LO	LO	LO	LO		LO	LO	LO	LO	LO	LO	LO	LO	LO		LO	LO	LO	LO
Romford	d	08 41	09 11	09 41	10 11	10 41	11 11	11 41	12 11	12 41		13 11	13 41	14 11	14 41	15 11	15 41	16 11	16 41	17 11		17 41	18 11	18 41	19 11
Emerson Park	d	08 45	09 15	09 45	10 15	10 45	11 15	11 45	12 15	12 45		13 15	13 45	14 15	14 45	15 15	15 45	16 15	16 45	17 15		17 45	18 15	18 45	19 15
Upminster ⊖	a	08 50	09 20	09 50	10 20	10 50	11 20	11 50	12 20	12 50		13 20	13 50	14 20	14 50	15 20	15 50	16 20	16 50	17 20		17 50	18 20	18 50	19 20

		LO
Romford	d	19 41
Emerson Park	d	19 45
Upminster ⊖	a	19 50

Table T004-R

Mondays to Saturdays
21 May to 8 December

Upminster - Romford

Miles			LO	LO	LO	LO	LO	LO		LO	LO	LO	LO	LO	LO	LO	LO	LO		LO	LO	LO	LO	LO	LO
0	**Upminster** ⊖	d	06 24	06 54	07 24	07 54	08 24	08 54		09 24	09 54	10 24	10 54	11 24	11 54	12 24	12 54	13 24		13 54	14 24	14 54	15 24	15 54	16 24
1½	Emerson Park	d	06 28	06 58	07 28	07 58	08 28	08 58		09 28	09 58	10 28	10 58	11 28	11 58	12 28	12 58	13 28		13 58	14 28	14 58	15 28	15 58	16 28
3½	**Romford**	a	06 33	07 03	07 33	08 03	08 33	09 03		09 33	10 03	10 33	11 03	11 33	12 03	12 33	13 03	13 33		14 03	14 33	15 03	15 33	16 03	16 33

		LO	LO	LO		LO	LO	LO	LO	LO	LO	LO	LO
Upminster ⊖	d	16 54	17 24	17 54		18 24	18 54	19 24	19 54	20 24	20 54	21 24	21 54
Emerson Park	d	16 58	17 28	17 58		18 28	18 58	19 28	19 58	20 28	20 58	21 28	21 58
Romford	a	17 03	17 33	18 03		18 33	19 03	19 33	20 03	20 33	21 03	21 33	22 03

Sundays
20 May to 2 December

		LO	LO	LO	LO	LO	LO	LO	LO	LO		LO	LO	LO	LO	LO	LO	LO	LO	LO		LO	LO	LO	LO
Upminster ⊖	d	08 54	09 24	09 54	10 24	10 54	11 24	11 54	12 24	12 54		13 24	13 54	14 24	14 54	15 24	15 54	16 24	16 54	17 24		17 54	18 24	18 54	19 24
Emerson Park	d	08 58	09 28	09 58	10 28	10 58	11 28	11 58	12 28	12 58		13 28	13 58	14 28	14 58	15 28	15 58	16 28	16 58	17 28		17 58	18 28	18 58	19 28
Romford	a	09 03	09 33	10 03	10 33	11 03	11 33	12 03	12 33	13 03		13 33	14 03	14 33	15 03	15 33	16 03	16 33	17 03	17 33		18 03	18 33	19 03	19 33

		LO
Upminster ⊖	d	19 54
Emerson Park	d	19 58
Romford	a	20 03

Table T005-F

Mondays to Fridays

21 May to 7 December

London Liverpool Street - Ilford - Shenfield

Miles	Station		XR MX	XR MO	LE MO A	LE MX A	XR MX	XR MX	XR MO	LE MO A	LE MX B	LE MX A	XR	LE ◇ C	XR	XR	XR	XR	XR	XR	XR	XR	XR
0	**London Liverpool Street** ⊖	d	00 01	00 05	00 14	00 15	00 20	00 32	00 35	00 44	00 46	00 50	00 55	05 23	05 24	05 40	06 00	06 10	06 20	06 30	06 40	06 50	06 57
4	Stratford ⊖	d	00 08	00 12	00 21	00 22	00 27	00 39	00 42	00 51	00 53	00 57	01 02	05 30	05 31	05 47	06 07	06 17	06 27	06 37	06 47	06 57	07 04
4½	Maryland	d	00 10	00 14			00 29	00 41	00 44				01 04		05 33	05 49	06 09	06 19	06 29	06 39	06 49	06 59	
5¼	Forest Gate	d	00 12	00 16			00 31	00 43	00 46				01 06		05 35	05 51	06 11	06 21	06 31	06 41	06 51	07 01	
6¼	Manor Park	d	00 14	00 18			00 33	00 45	00 48				01 08		05 37	05 53	06 13	06 23	06 33	06 43	06 53	07 03	
7¼	Ilford	d	00 17	00 21			00 36	00 48	00 51				01 11		05 40	05 56	06 16	06 26	06 36	06 46	06 56	07 06	07 11
8½	Seven Kings	d	00 19	00 23			00 38	00 50	00 53				01 13		05 42	05 58	06 18	06 28	06 38	06 48	06 58	07 08	07 13
9¼	Goodmayes	d	00 21	00 25			00 40	00 52	00 55				01 15		05 44	06 00	06 20	06 30	06 40	06 50	07 00	07 10	07 15
10	Chadwell Heath	d	00 23	00 27			00 42	00 54	00 57				01 17		05 46	06 02	06 22	06 32	06 42	06 52	07 02	07 12	07 17
12½	Romford	d	00 27	00 31	00 34	00 32	00 46	00 58	01 01	01 04		01 08	01 21	05 38	05 50	06 06	06 26	06 36	06 46	06 56	07 06	07 16	07 21
13½	Gidea Park	a	00 33	00 37	00 39		00 50	01 04	01 07	01 09	01 07		01 25		05 54	06 10	06 30	06 40	06 50	07 00	07 10	07 20	07 27
—		d			00 39		00 50			01 09	01 07		01 25		05 54	06 10	06 30	06 40	06 50	07 00	07 10	07 20	
15	Harold Wood	d			00 42		00 53			01 12			01 28		05 57	06 13	06 33	06 43	06 53	07 03	07 13	07 23	
18¼	Brentwood	d			00 46		00 57			01 16			01 32		06 01	06 17	06 37	06 47	06 57	07 07	07 17	07 27	
20¼	**Shenfield**	a			00 51	00 44	01 05			01 21	01 17	01 20	01 40	05 47	06 07	06 23	06 43	06 53	07 04	07 13	07 23	07 33	

Station		XR	XR	LE D	XR	XR	XR	XR	XR	XR	XR	XR	XR	XR	XR	XR	XR	XR	XR	XR	XR	XR	XR
London Liverpool Street ⊖	d	07 00	07 07	07 08	07 10	07 17	07 20	07 27	07 30	07 37	07 40	07 47	07 50	07 57	08 00	08 07	08 10	08 17	08 20	08 27	08 30	08 37	08 40
Stratford ⊖	d	07 07	07 14	07 15	07 17	07 24	07 27	07 34	07 37	07 44	07 47	07 54	07 57	08 04	08 07	08 14	08 17	08 24	08 27	08 34	08 37	08 44	08 47
Maryland	d	07 09			07 19		07 29		07 39		07 49		07 59		08 09		08 19		08 29		08 39		08 49
Forest Gate	d	07 11			07 21		07 31		07 41		07 51		08 01		08 11		08 21		08 31		08 41		08 51
Manor Park	d	07 13			07 23		07 33		07 43		07 53		08 03		08 13		08 23		08 33		08 43		08 53
Ilford	d	07 16	07 21		07 26	07 31	07 36	07 41	07 46	07 51	07 56	08 01	08 06	08 11	08 16	08 21	08 26	08 31	08 36	08 41	08 46	08 51	08 56
Seven Kings	d	07 18	07 23		07 28	07 33	07 38	07 43	07 48	07 53	07 58	08 03	08 08		08 18	08 23	08 28		08 38	08 43	08 48		08 58
Goodmayes	d	07 20	07 25		07 30	07 35	07 40	07 45	07 50	07 55	08 00	08 05	08 10		08 20	08 25	08 30		08 40	08 45	08 50		09 00
Chadwell Heath	d	07 22	07 27		07 32	07 37	07 42	07 47	07 52	07 57	08 02	08 07	08 12		08 22	08 27	08 32		08 42	08 47	08 52		09 02
Romford	d	07 26	07 31	07 23	07 36	07 41	07 46	07 51	07 56	08 01	08 06	08 11	08 16	08 21	08 26	08 31	08 36	08 41	08 46	08 51	08 56	09 01	09 06
Gidea Park	a	07 30	07 37		07 40	07 47	07 50	07 57	08 00	08 07	08 10	08 17	08 20	08 27	08 30	08 37	08 40	08 47	08 50	08 57	09 00	09 07	09 10
	d	07 30			07 40		07 50		08 00		08 10		08 20		08 30		08 40		08 50		09 00		09 10
Harold Wood	d	07 33			07 43		07 53		08 03		08 13		08 23		08 33		08 43		08 53		09 03		09 13
Brentwood	d	07 37			07 47		07 57		08 07		08 17		08 27		08 37		08 47		08 57		09 07		09 17
Shenfield	a	07 43		07 32	07 53		08 05		08 13		08 25		08 33		08 45		08 53		09 05		09 13		09 23

Station		XR	XR	XR	XR	XR	LE E	XR	XR	XR	XR	LE ◇ A	XR	XR	LE E	XR	XR	XR	XR	LE ◇ A	XR	XR
London Liverpool Street ⊖	d	08 50	09 00	09 10	09 20	09 30	09 38	09 40	09 50	10 00	10 10	10 13	10 20	10 30	10 38	10 40	10 50	11 00	11 10	11 13	11 20	11 30
Stratford ⊖	d	08 57	09 07	09 17	09 27	09 37	09 45	09 47	09 57	10 07	10 17	10 20	10 27	10 37	10 45	10 47	10 57	11 07	11 17	11 20	11 27	11 37
Maryland	d	08 59	09 09	09 19	09 29	09 39		09 49	09 59	10 09	10 19		10 29	10 39		10 49	10 59	11 09	11 19		11 29	11 39
Forest Gate	d	09 01	09 11	09 21	09 31	09 41		09 51	10 01	10 11	10 21		10 31	10 41		10 51	11 01	11 11	11 21		11 31	11 41
Manor Park	d	09 03	09 13	09 23	09 33	09 43		09 53	10 03	10 13	10 23		10 33	10 43		10 53	11 03	11 13	11 23		11 33	11 43
Ilford	d	09 06	09 16	09 26	09 36	09 46		09 56	10 06	10 16	10 26		10 36	10 46		10 56	11 06	11 16	11 26		11 36	11 46
Seven Kings	d	09 08	09 18	09 28	09 38	09 48		09 58	10 08	10 18	10 28		10 38	10 48		10 58	11 08	11 18	11 28		11 38	11 48
Goodmayes	d	09 10	09 20	09 30	09 40	09 50		10 00	10 10	10 20	10 30		10 40	10 50		11 00	11 10	11 20	11 30		11 40	11 50
Chadwell Heath	d	09 12	09 22	09 32	09 42	09 52		10 02	10 12	10 22	10 32		10 42	10 52		11 02	11 12	11 22	11 32		11 42	11 52
Romford	d	09 16	09 26	09 36	09 46	09 56	09 53	10 06	10 16	10 26	10 36	10 28	10 46	10 56	10 53	11 06	11 16	11 26	11 36	11 28	11 46	11 56
Gidea Park	a	09 20	09 30	09 40	09 50	10 00		10 10	10 20	10 30	10 40		10 50	11 00		11 10	11 20	11 30	11 40		11 50	12 00
	d	09 20	09 30	09 40	09 50	10 00		10 10	10 20	10 30	10 40		10 50	11 00		11 10	11 20	11 30	11 40		11 50	12 00
Harold Wood	d	09 23	09 33	09 43	09 53	10 03		10 13	10 23	10 33	10 43		10 53	11 03		11 13	11 23	11 33	11 43		11 53	12 03
Brentwood	d	09 27	09 37	09 47	09 57	10 07		10 17	10 27	10 37	10 47		10 57	11 07		11 17	11 27	11 37	11 47		11 57	12 07
Shenfield	a	09 33	09 43	09 53	10 03	10 13	10 02	10 23	10 33	10 43	10 53	10 37	11 03	11 13	11 02	11 23	11 33	11 43	11 53	11 37	12 03	12 13

Station		LE E	XR	XR	XR	XR	LE ◇ A	XR	XR	LE E	XR	XR		XR	XR	LE A	XR	XR	LE E	XR	XR	XR	XR
London Liverpool Street ⊖	d	11 38	11 40	11 50	12 00	12 10	12 13	12 20	12 30	12 38	12 40	12 50		15 00	15 10	15 13	15 20	15 30	15 38	15 40	15 50	16 00	16 08
Stratford ⊖	d	11 45	11 47	11 58	12 07	12 17	12 20	12 27	12 37	12 45	12 47	12 57		15 07	15 17	15 20	15 27	15 37	15 45	15 47	15 57	16 07	16 15
Maryland	d		11 49	12 00	12 09	12 19		12 29	12 39		12 49	12 59	and at	15 09	15 19		15 29	15 39		15 49	15 59	16 09	16 17
Forest Gate	d		11 51	12 02	12 11	12 21		12 31	12 41		12 51	13 01	the same	15 11	15 21		15 31	15 41		15 51	16 01	16 11	16 19
Manor Park	d		11 53	12 04	12 13	12 23		12 33	12 43		12 53	13 03	minutes	15 13	15 23		15 33	15 43		15 53	16 03	16 13	16 21
Ilford	d		11 56	12 07	12 16	12 26		12 36	12 46		12 56	13 06	past	15 16	15 26		15 36	15 46		15 56	16 06	16 16	16 24
Seven Kings	d		11 58	12 09	12 18	12 28		12 38	12 48		12 58	13 08	each	15 18	15 28		15 38	15 48		15 58	16 08	16 18	16 26
Goodmayes	d		12 00	12 11	12 20	12 30		12 40	12 50		13 00	13 10	hour until	15 20	15 30		15 40	15 50		16 00	16 10	16 20	16 28
Chadwell Heath	d		12 02	12 13	12 22	12 32		12 42	12 52		13 02	13 12		15 22	15 32		15 42	15 52		16 02	16 12	16 22	16 30
Romford	d	11 53	12 06	12 17	12 26	12 36	12 28	12 46	12 56	12 53	13 06	13 16		15 26	15 36	15 28	15 46	15 56	15 53	16 06	16 16	16 26	16 34
Gidea Park	a		12 10	12 21	12 30	12 40		12 50	13 00		13 10	13 20		15 30	15 40		15 50	16 00		16 10	16 20	16 30	16 38
	d		12 10	12 21	12 30	12 40		12 50	13 00		13 10	13 20		15 30	15 40		15 50	16 00		16 10	16 20	16 30	16 38
Harold Wood	d		12 13	12 24	12 33	12 43		12 53	13 03		13 13	13 23		15 33	15 43		15 53	16 03		16 13	16 23	16 33	16 41
Brentwood	d		12 17	12 28	12 37	12 47		12 57	13 07		13 17	13 27		15 37	15 47		15 57	16 07		16 17	16 27	16 37	16 45
Shenfield	a	12 02	12 23	12 34	12 43	12 53	12 37	13 03	13 13	13 02	13 23	13 33		15 43	15 53	15 37	16 03	16 13	16 02	16 23	16 33	16 45	16 53

Station		XR	XR	XR	XR	XR	XR	XR	XR	XR	XR	XR	XR	XR	XR	XR	XR	XR	XR	XR	XR	XR	XR
London Liverpool Street ⊖	d	16 15	16 22	16 29	16 36	16 40	16 47	16 50	16 57	17 00	17 07	17 10	17 17	17 20	17 27	17 30	17 36	17 39	17 42	17 46	17 49	17 52	17 56
Stratford ⊖	d	16 22	16 29	16 36	16 43	16 47	16 54	16 57	17 04	17 07	17 14	17 17	17 24	17 27	17 34	17 37	17 43	17 46	17 49	17 53	17 56	17 59	18 03
Maryland	d	16 24	16 31	16 38		16 49		16 59		17 09		17 19		17 29		17 39	17 45			17 55			18 05
Forest Gate	d	16 26	16 33	16 40		16 51		17 01		17 11		17 21		17 31		17 41			17 52			18 02	
Manor Park	d	16 28	16 35	16 42		16 53		17 03		17 13		17 23		17 33		17 43		17 50			18 00		18 08
Ilford	d	16 31	16 38	16 45	16 50	16 56	17 00	17 06	17 10	17 16	17 20	17 26	17 30	17 36	17 40	17 46	17 50	17 53	17 56	18 00	18 03	18 06	18 11
Seven Kings	d	16 34	16 40	16 48	16 52		17 02		17 12		17 22		17 32		17 42		17 52	17 56	17 59	18 02	18 06	18 09	18 14
Goodmayes	d	16 36	16 42	16 50	16 54		17 04		17 14		17 24		17 34		17 44		17 54	17 58	18 01	18 04	18 08	18 11	18 16
Chadwell Heath	d	16 38	16 44	16 52	16 56	17 00	17 06	17 10	17 16	17 20	17 26	17 30	17 36	17 40	17 46	17 50	17 56	18 00	18 03	18 06	18 10	18 13	18 18
Romford	d	16 42	16 48	16 56	17 00	17 04	17 10	17 14	17 20	17 24	17 30	17 34	17 40	17 44	17 50	17 54	18 00	18 04	18 07	18 10	18 14	18 17	18 22
Gidea Park	a	16 47	16 53	17 01	17 04	17 10	17 14	17 20	17 24	17 30	17 34	17 40	17 44	17 50	17 54	18 00	18 04	18 07	18 13	18 14	18 17	18 23	18 25
	d		16 53		17 04		17 14		17 24		17 34		17 44		17 54		18 04	18 07		18 14	18 17		18 25
Harold Wood	d		16 56		17 07		17 17		17 27		17 37		17 47		17 57		18 07	18 10		18 17	18 20		18 28
Brentwood	d		17 00		17 11		17 21		17 31		17 41		17 51		18 01		18 11	18 15		18 21	18 25		18 33
Shenfield	a		17 09		17 19		17 29		17 39		17 49		17 59		18 09		18 19	18 23		18 29	18 33		18 41

A To Southend Victoria
B To Colchester
C To Clacton-on-Sea
D To Ipswich
E To Colchester Town

Table T005-F

Mondays to Fridays

21 May to 7 December

London Liverpool Street - Ilford - Shenfield

Station		XR	XR	XR	XR	XR	XR	XR	XR	XR	XR	XR	XR	XR	XR	XR	XR	XR	XR	XR	XR	XR	XR
London Liverpool Street ⊖	d	18 00	18 04	18 08	18 12	18 16	18 20	18 24	18 28	18 32	18 37	18 42	18 47	18 52	18 57	19 02	19 08	19 15	19 22	19 30	19 38	19 45	19 52
Stratford ⊖	d	18 07	18 11	18 15	18 19	18 24	18 27	18 31	18 35	18 39	18 44	18 49	18 54	18 59	19 04	19 09	19 15	19 22	19 29	19 37	19 45	19 52	19 59
Maryland	d		18 13		18 21		18 29		18 37		18 46		18 56		19 06		19 17	19 24	19 31	19 39	19 47	19 54	20 01
Forest Gate	d	18 10		18 18		18 27		18 34		18 42		18 52		19 02		19 12	19 19	19 26	19 33	19 41	19 49	19 56	20 03
Manor Park	d		18 16		18 24		18 32		18 40		18 49		18 59		19 09		19 21	19 28	19 35	19 43	19 51	19 58	20 05
Ilford	d	18 14	18 19	18 22	18 27	18 31	18 35	18 38	18 43	18 46	18 52	18 56	19 02	19 06	19 12	19 16	19 24	19 31	19 38	19 46	19 54	20 01	20 08
Seven Kings	d	18 17	18 22	18 25	18 30	18 34	18 38	18 41	18 46	18 49	18 55	18 59	19 05	19 09	19 15	19 19	19 26	19 33	19 40	19 48	19 56	20 03	20 10
Goodmayes	d	18 19	18 24	18 27	18 32	18 36	18 40	18 43	18 48	18 51	18 57	19 01	19 07	19 11	19 17	19 21	19 28	19 35	19 42	19 50	19 58	20 05	20 12
Chadwell Heath	d	18 21	18 26	18 29	18 34	18 38	18 42	18 45	18 50	18 53	18 59	19 03	19 09	19 13	19 19	19 23	19 30	19 37	19 44	19 52	20 00	20 07	20 14
Romford	d	18 25	18 30	18 33	18 38	18 42	18 46	18 49	18 54	18 57	19 03	19 07	19 13	19 17	19 23	19 27	19 34	19 41	19 48	19 56	20 04	20 11	20 18
Gidea Park	a	18 31	18 33	18 39	18 41	18 48	18 49	18 54	18 57	19 02	19 06	19 12	19 16	19 22	19 26	19 30	19 38	19 45	19 52	20 00	20 08	20 15	20 22
	d		18 33		18 41		18 49		18 57		19 06		19 16		19 26	19 30	19 38	19 45	19 53	20 00	20 08		20 22
Harold Wood	d		18 36		18 44		18 52		19 00		19 09		19 19		19 29	19 33	19 41	19 48	19 56	20 03	20 11		20 25
Brentwood	d		18 41		18 49		18 57		19 05		19 14		19 24		19 34	19 38	19 45	19 52	20 00	20 07	20 15		20 29
Shenfield	a		18 49		18 57		19 05		19 13		19 22		19 32		19 42	19 45	19 51	19 58	20 07	20 13	20 21		20 35

Station		XR	XR	LE ◇ A	XR	XR	LE B	XR	XR	XR	XR	LE ◇ A	XR	XR	LE B	XR	XR	XR	XR	LE ◇ A	XR
London Liverpool Street ⊖	d	20 00	20 10	20 13	20 20	20 30	20 38	20 40	20 50	21 00	21 10	21 13	21 20	21 30	21 38	21 40	21 50	22 00	22 10	22 13	22 20
Stratford ⊖	d	20 07	20 17	20 20	20 27	20 37	20 45	20 47	20 57	21 07	21 17	21 20	21 27	21 37	21 45	21 47	21 57	22 07	22 17	22 20	22 27
Maryland	d	20 09	20 19		20 29	20 39		20 49	20 59	21 09	21 19		21 29	21 39		21 49	21 59	22 09	22 19		22 29
Forest Gate	d	20 11	20 21		20 31	20 41		20 51	21 01	21 11	21 21		21 31	21 41		21 51	22 01	22 11	22 21		22 31
Manor Park	d	20 13	20 23		20 33	20 43		20 53	21 03	21 13	21 23		21 33	21 43		21 53	22 03	22 13	22 23		22 33
Ilford	d	20 16	20 26		20 36	20 46		20 56	21 06	21 16	21 26		21 36	21 46		21 56	22 06	22 16	22 26		22 36
Seven Kings	d	20 18	20 28		20 38	20 48		20 58	21 08	21 18	21 28		21 38	21 48		21 58	22 08	22 18	22 28		22 38
Goodmayes	d	20 20	20 30		20 40	20 50		21 00	21 10	21 20	21 30		21 40	21 50		22 00	22 10	22 20	22 30		22 40
Chadwell Heath	d	20 22	20 32		20 42	20 52		21 02	21 12	21 22	21 32		21 42	21 52		22 02	22 12	22 22	22 32		22 42
Romford	d	20 26	20 36	20 28	20 46	20 56	20 53	21 06	21 16	21 26	21 36	21 28	21 46	21 56	21 53	22 06	22 16	22 26	22 36	22 28	22 46
Gidea Park	a	20 30	20 40		20 50	21 00		21 10	21 20	21 30	21 40		21 50	22 00		22 10	22 20	22 30	22 40		22 50
	d	20 30	20 40		20 50	21 00		21 10	21 20	21 30	21 40		21 50	22 00		22 10	22 20	22 30	22 40		22 50
Harold Wood	d	20 33	20 43		20 53	21 03		21 13	21 23	21 33	21 43		21 53	22 03		22 13	22 23	22 33	22 43		22 53
Brentwood	d	20 37	20 47		20 57	21 07		21 17	21 27	21 37	21 47		21 57	22 07		22 17	22 27	22 37	22 47		22 57
Shenfield	a	20 43	20 53	20 37	21 03	21 13	21 02	21 23	21 33	21 43	21 53	21 37	22 03	22 13	22 02	22 23	22 33	22 43	22 53	22 37	23 03

Station		XR		XR
London Liverpool Street ⊖	d	22 35		23 50
Stratford ⊖	d	22 42		23 57
Maryland	d	22 44		23 59
Forest Gate	d	22 46		00 01
Manor Park	d	22 48	and	00 03
Ilford	d	22 51	every 15	00 06
Seven Kings	d	22 53	minutes	00 08
Goodmayes	d	22 55	until	00 10
Chadwell Heath	d	22 57		00 12
Romford	d	23 01		00 16
Gidea Park	a	23 05		00 20
	d	23 05		00 20
Harold Wood	d	23 08		00 23
Brentwood	d	23 12		00 27
Shenfield	a	23 20		00 35

Saturdays

26 May to 8 December

Station		XR	LE A	XR	XR	LE C	LE A	XR	XR	LE D	XR	XR	XR	XR	LE E	XR	XR	XR	LE A	XR	XR	LE B	XR
London Liverpool Street ⊖	d	00 01	00 15	00 20	00 32	00 46	00 50	00 55	05 20	05 34		05 50	06 10	06 30	06 38	06 45	07 00	07 10	07 13	07 20	07 30	07 38	07 40
Stratford ⊖	d	00 08	00 22	00 27	00 39	00 53	00 57	01 02	05 27	05 41		05 57	06 17	06 37	06 45	06 52	07 07	07 17	07 20	07 27	07 37	07 45	07 47
Maryland	d	00 10		00 29	00 41			01 04	05 29			05 59	06 19	06 39		06 54	07 09	07 19		07 29	07 39		07 49
Forest Gate	d	00 12		00 31	00 43			01 06	05 31			06 01	06 21	06 41		06 56	07 11	07 21		07 31	07 41		07 51
Manor Park	d	00 14		00 33	00 45			01 08	05 33			06 03	06 23	06 43		06 58	07 13	07 23		07 33	07 43		07 53
Ilford	d	00 17		00 36	00 48			01 11	05 36			06 06	06 26	06 46		07 01	07 16	07 26		07 36	07 46		07 56
Seven Kings	d	00 19		00 38	00 50			01 13	05 38		05 53	06 08	06 28	06 48		07 03	07 18	07 28		07 38	07 48		07 58
Goodmayes	d	00 21		00 40	00 52			01 15	05 40		05 55	06 10	06 30	06 50		07 05	07 20	07 30		07 40	07 50		08 00
Chadwell Heath	d	00 23		00 42	00 54			01 17	05 42		05 57	06 12	06 32	06 52		07 07	07 22	07 32		07 42	07 52		08 02
Romford	d	00 27	00 32	00 46	00 58		01 08	01 21	05 46	05 49	06 01	06 16	06 36	06 56	06 53	07 11	07 26	07 36	07 28	07 46	07 56	07 53	08 06
Gidea Park	a	00 33		00 50	01 04	01 07		01 25	05 50		06 05	06 20	06 40	07 00		07 15	07 30	07 40		07 50	08 00		08 10
	d			00 50		01 07		01 25	05 50		06 05	06 20	06 40	07 00		07 15	07 30	07 40		07 50	08 00		08 10
Harold Wood	d			00 53				01 28	05 53		06 08	06 23	06 43	07 03		07 18	07 33	07 43		07 53	08 03		08 13
Brentwood	d			00 57				01 32	05 57		06 12	06 27	06 47	07 07		07 22	07 37	07 47		07 57	08 07		08 17
Shenfield	a		00 45	01 05		01 17	01 20	01 40	06 03	05 58	06 18	06 33	06 53	07 13	07 02	07 28	07 43	07 53	07 37	08 03	08 13	08 02	08 23

Station		XR		XR	XR	LE A	XR	XR	LE B	XR	XR	XR	XR	LE ◇ A	XR	XR	LE B	XR	XR	XR	XR	LE ◇ A
London Liverpool Street ⊖	d	07 50		18 00	18 10	18 13	18 20	18 30	18 38	18 40	18 50	19 00	19 10	19 13	19 20	19 30	19 38	19 40	19 50	20 00	20 10	20 13
Stratford ⊖	d	07 57		18 07	18 17	18 20	18 27	18 37	18 45	18 47	18 57	19 07	19 17	19 20	19 27	19 37	19 46	19 47	19 57	20 07	20 17	20 20
Maryland	d	07 59	and at	18 09	18 19		18 29	18 39		18 49	18 59	19 09	19 19		19 29	19 39		19 49	19 59	20 09	20 19	
Forest Gate	d	08 01	the same	18 11	18 21		18 31	18 41		18 51	19 01	19 11	19 21		19 31	19 41		19 51	20 01	20 11	20 21	
Manor Park	d	08 03	minutes	18 13	18 23		18 33	18 43		18 53	19 03	19 13	19 23		19 33	19 43		19 53	20 03	20 13	20 23	
Ilford	d	08 06	past	18 16	18 26		18 36	18 46		18 56	19 06	19 16	19 26		19 36	19 46		19 56	20 06	20 16	20 26	
Seven Kings	d	08 08	each	18 18	18 28		18 38	18 48		18 58	19 08	19 18	19 28		19 38	19 48		19 58	20 08	20 18	20 28	
Goodmayes	d	08 10	hour until	18 20	18 30		18 40	18 50		19 00	19 10	19 20	19 30		19 40	19 50		20 00	20 10	20 20	20 30	
Chadwell Heath	d	08 12		18 22	18 32		18 42	18 52		19 02	19 12	19 22	19 32		19 42	19 52		20 02	20 12	20 22	20 32	
Romford	d	08 16		18 26	18 36	18 28	18 46	18 56	18 53	19 06	19 16	19 26	19 36	19 28	19 46	19 56	19 54	20 06	20 16	20 26	20 36	20 28
Gidea Park	a	08 20		18 30	18 40		18 50	19 00		19 10	19 20	19 30	19 40		19 50	20 00		20 10	20 20	20 30	20 40	
	d	08 20		18 30	18 40		18 50	19 00		19 10	19 20	19 30	19 40		19 50	20 00		20 10	20 20	20 30	20 40	
Harold Wood	d	08 23		18 33	18 43		18 53	19 03		19 13	19 23	19 33	19 43		19 53	20 03		20 13	20 23	20 33	20 43	
Brentwood	d	08 27		18 37	18 47		18 57	19 07		19 17	19 27	19 37	19 47		19 57	20 07		20 17	20 27	20 37	20 47	
Shenfield	a	08 33		18 43	18 53	18 37	19 03	19 13	19 02	19 23	19 33	19 43	19 53	19 37	20 03	20 13	20 03	20 23	20 33	20 43	20 53	20 37

A To Southend Victoria
B To Colchester Town
C To Colchester
D To Ipswich
E To Harwich International

Table T005-F

Saturdays

26 May to 8 December

London Liverpool Street - Ilford - Shenfield

		XR	XR	LE ■ A	XR	XR	XR	XR	LE ◇■ B	XR	XR	LE ■ A	XR	XR	LE ◇■ B	XR	LE ■ C	XR	LE ◇■ B	XR	XR	LE ■ B
London Liverpool Street ■ ⊖	d	20 20	20 30	20 38	20 40	20 50	21 00	21 10	21 13	21 20	21 35	21 38	21 50	22 05	22 13	22 20	22 32	22 35	22 44	22 47	23 05	23 14
Stratford ■ ⊖	d	20 27	20 37	20 45	20 47	20 57	21 07	21 17	21 20	21 27	21 42	21 45	21 57	22 12	22 20	22 27	22 41	22 42	22 51	22 54	23 12	23 21
Maryland	d	20 29	20 39		20 49	20 59	21 09	21 19		21 29	21 44		21 59	22 14		22 29		22 44			23 14	
Forest Gate	d	20 31	20 41		20 51	21 01	21 11	21 21		21 31	21 46		22 01	22 16		22 31		22 46		22 57	23 16	
Manor Park	d	20 33	20 43		20 53	21 03	21 13	21 23		21 33	21 48		22 03	22 18		22 33		22 48		22 59	23 18	
Ilford ■	d	20 36	20 46		20 56	21 06	21 16	21 26		21 36	21 51		22 06	22 21		22 36		22 51		23 02	23 21	
Seven Kings	d	20 38	20 48		20 58	21 08	21 18	21 28		21 38	21 53		22 08	22 23		22 38		22 53		23 04	23 23	
Goodmayes	d	20 40	20 50		21 00	21 10	21 20	21 30		21 40	21 55		22 10	22 25		22 40		22 55		23 06	23 25	
Chadwell Heath	d	20 42	20 52		21 02	21 12	21 22	21 32		21 42	21 57		22 12	22 27		22 42		22 57		23 08	23 27	
Romford	d	20 46	20 56	20 53	21 06	21 16	21 26	21 36	21 28	21 46	22 01	21 53	22 16	22 31	22 28	22 46	22 49	23 01	23 04	23 12	23 31	23 34
Gidea Park ■	a	20 50	21 00		21 10	21 20	21 30	21 40		21 50	22 05		22 20	22 35		22 50		23 05	23 08	23 16	23 35	23 38
	d	20 50	21 00		21 10	21 20	21 30	21 40		21 50	22 05		22 20	22 35		22 50		23 05	23 08	23 16	23 35	23 38
Harold Wood	d	20 53	21 03		21 13	21 23	21 33	21 43		21 53	22 08		22 23	22 38		22 53		23 08	23 11	23 19	23 38	23 41
Brentwood	d	20 57	21 07		21 17	21 27	21 37	21 47		21 57	22 12		22 27	22 42		22 57		23 12	23 16	23 23	23 42	23 46
Shenfield ■	a	21 03	21 13	21 02	21 23	21 33	21 43	21 53	21 37	22 03	22 18	22 02	22 33	22 48	22 37	23 05	22 58	23 20	23 21	23 31	23 50	23 51

		XR	XR	LE ■ B	XR
London Liverpool Street ■ ⊖	d	23 17	23 35	23 44	23 47
Stratford ■ ⊖	d	23 24	23 42	23 51	23 54
Maryland	d		23 44		
Forest Gate	d	23 27	23 46		23 57
Manor Park	d	23 29	23 48		23 59
Ilford ■	d	23 32	23 51		00 02
Seven Kings	d	23 34	23 53		00 04
Goodmayes	d	23 36	23 55		00 06
Chadwell Heath	d	23 38	23 57		00 08
Romford	d	23 42	00 01	00 04	00 12
Gidea Park ■	a	23 46	00 05	00 08	00 16
	d	23 46	00 05	00 08	00 16
Harold Wood	d		00 08	00 11	
Brentwood	d		00 12	00 16	
Shenfield ■	a	23 58	00 20	00 21	00 28

Sundays

20 May to 2 December

		XR D	XR	LE ■ B	XR	XR	LE ■ B	XR	XR	XR	LE ■ B	XR	LE ■ B	LE ■ E	XR	LE ■ B	XR	XR	LE ■ B	XR	
London Liverpool Street ■ ⊖	d		00 01	00 15	00 20	00 35	00 50	00 55	06 35	07 05	07 14	07 35	07 44	07 55	08 05	08 14	08 17	08 35	08 44	08 47	and at the same minutes past each hour until
Stratford ■ ⊖	d		00 08	00 22	00 27	00 42	00 57	01 02	06 42	07 12	07 21	07 42	07 51	08 02	08 12	08 21	08 24	08 42	08 51	08 54	
Maryland	d		00 10		00 29	00 44		01 04	06 44	07 14		07 44			08 14			08 44			
Forest Gate	d		00 12		00 31	00 46		01 06	06 46	07 16		07 46			08 16		08 27	08 46		08 57	
Manor Park	d		00 14		00 33	00 48		01 08	06 48	07 18		07 48			08 18		08 29	08 48		08 59	
Ilford ■	d	00 02	00 17		00 36	00 51		01 11	06 51	07 21		07 51			08 21		08 32	08 51		09 02	
Seven Kings	d	00 04	00 19		00 38	00 53		01 13	06 53	07 23		07 53			08 23		08 34	08 53		09 04	
Goodmayes	d	00 06	00 21		00 40	00 55		01 15	06 55	07 25		07 55			08 25		08 36	08 55		09 06	
Chadwell Heath	d	00 08	00 23		00 42	00 57		01 17	06 57	07 27		07 57			08 27		08 38	08 57		09 08	
Romford	d	00 12	00 27	00 32	00 46	01 01	01 08	01 21	07 01	07 31	07 34	08 01	08 04	08 13	08 31	08 34	08 42	09 01	09 04	09 12	
Gidea Park ■	a	00 16	00 33		00 50	01 07		01 25	07 05	07 35	07 38	08 05	08 08		08 35	08 38	08 48	09 05	09 08	09 18	
	d	00 16			00 50			01 25	07 05	07 35	07 38	08 05	08 08		08 35	08 38		09 05	09 08		
Harold Wood	d				00 53			01 28	07 08	07 38	07 41	08 08	08 11		08 38	08 41		09 08	09 11		
Brentwood	d				00 57			01 32	07 12	07 42	07 46	08 12	08 16		08 42	08 46		09 12	09 16		
Shenfield ■	a	00 28		00 44	01 05		01 20	01 40	07 20	07 50	07 51	08 20	08 21	08 26	08 50	08 51		09 20	09 21		

		XR	LE ■ B	XR	XR	LE ■ B	XR	XR	LE ■ B	XR	XR	LE ■ B	XR	LE ■ B	XR	LE ■ B
London Liverpool Street ■ ⊖	d	21 05	21 14	21 17	21 35	21 44	21 47	22 05	22 14	22 17	22 35	22 44	23 05	23 14	23 35	23 44
Stratford ■ ⊖	d	21 12	21 21	21 24	21 42	21 51	21 54	22 12	22 21	22 24	22 42	22 51	23 12	23 21	23 42	23 51
Maryland	d	21 14			21 44			22 14			22 44		23 14		23 44	
Forest Gate	d	21 16		21 27	21 46		21 57	22 16		22 27	22 46		23 16		23 46	
Manor Park	d	21 18		21 29	21 48		21 59	22 18		22 29	22 48		23 18		23 48	
Ilford ■	d	21 21		21 32	21 51		22 02	22 21		22 32	22 51		23 21		23 51	
Seven Kings	d	21 23		21 34	21 53		22 04	22 23		22 34	22 53		23 23		23 53	
Goodmayes	d	21 25		21 36	21 55		22 06	22 25		22 36	22 55		23 25		23 55	
Chadwell Heath	d	21 27		21 38	21 57		22 08	22 27		22 38	22 57		23 27		23 57	
Romford	d	21 31	21 34	21 42	22 01	22 04	22 12	22 31	22 34	22 42	23 01	23 04	23 31	23 34	00 01	00 04
Gidea Park ■	a	21 35	21 38	21 48	22 05	22 08	22 18	22 35	22 38	22 48	23 05	23 08	23 35	23 38	00 05	00 08
	d	21 35	21 38		22 05	22 08		22 35	22 38		23 05	23 08	23 35	23 38	00 05	00 08
Harold Wood	d	21 38	21 41		22 08	22 11		22 38	22 41		23 08	23 11	23 38	23 41	00 08	00 11
Brentwood	d	21 42	21 46		22 12	22 16		22 42	22 46		23 12	23 16	23 42	23 46	00 12	00 16
Shenfield ■	a	21 50	21 51		22 20	22 21		22 50	22 51		23 20	23 21	23 50	23 51	00 20	00 21

A To Colchester Town
B To Southend Victoria
C To Colchester
D From London Liverpool Street
E To Harwich International

Table T005-R

Mondays to Fridays

21 May to 7 December

Shenfield - Ilford - London Liverpool Street

Miles			XR MX A	XR MO A	XR MX A	XR	XR	XR	LE ■ B	XR	XR	XR	XR	XR	XR	XR	XR	XR	XR	XR	XR	XR	XR
0	Shenfield ■	d				04 44		05 12	05 24	05 29		05 44		05 59		06 14	06 24		06 34		06 44		06 54
2	Brentwood	d				04 47		05 15		05 32		05 47		06 02		06 17	06 27		06 37		06 47		06 57
5¼	Harold Wood	d				04 52		05 20		05 37		05 52		06 07		06 22	06 32		06 42		06 52		07 02
6¾	Gidea Park ■	d				04 56	05 11	05 24		05 41	05 49	05 56	06 04	06 11	06 19	06 26	06 35	06 39	06 45	06 49	06 55	06 59	07 05
7¾	Romford	d				04 58	05 13	05 26	05 32	05 43	05 51	05 58	06 06	06 13	06 21	06 28	06 38	06 41	06 48	06 51	06 58	07 01	07 08
10¼	Chadwell Heath	d		00 01	00 02	05 02	05 17	05 30		05 47	05 55	06 02	06 10	06 17	06 25	06 32	06 42	06 45	06 52	06 55	07 02	07 05	07 12
11	Goodmayes	d		00 03	00 04	05 04	05 19	05 32		05 49	05 57	06 04	06 12	06 19	06 27	06 34	06 44	06 47		06 57		07 07	
11¾	Seven Kings	d		00 05	00 06	05 06	05 21	05 34	05 37	05 51	05 59	06 06	06 14	06 21	06 29	06 36	06 46	06 49		06 59		07 09	
12¾	Ilford ■	d		00 08	00 09	05 09	05 24	05 37		05 54	06 03	06 09	06 17	06 26	06 32	06 39	06 49	06 52	06 57	07 02	07 07	07 12	07 17
14	Manor Park	d		00 10	00 12	05 12	05 27	05 40		05 57	06 05	06 12	06 20	06 30	06 35	06 42		06 55		07 05		07 15	
15	Forest Gate	d		00 13	00 14	05 14	05 29	05 42		05 59	06 08	06 14	06 22	06 32	06 37	06 44		06 57		07 07		07 17	
15¾	Maryland	d	00 01	00 15	00 16	05 16	05 31	05 44		06 01	06 10	06 16	06 24	06 34	06 39	06 46		06 59		07 09		07 19	
16¾	Stratford ■ ⊖	d	00 04	00 17	00 19	05 19	05 34	05 47	05 42	06 04	06 12	06 19	06 27	06 37	06 42	06 49	06 55	07 02	07 05	07 12	07 15	07 22	07 25
20¼	London Liverpool Street ■ ⊖	a	00 15	00 28	00 30	05 27	05 43	05 55	05 51	06 12	06 20	06 27	06 35	06 45	06 50	06 57	07 05	07 12	07 15	07 22	07 25	07 33	07 36

		XR	XR	XR	XR	XR	XR	XR	XR	XR	XR	XR	XR	XR	XR	XR	XR	XR	XR	XR	XR	XR
Shenfield ■	d		07 01		07 10		07 19		07 28		07 37	07 42		07 49		07 56		08 02		08 12		08 22
Brentwood	d		07 04		07 13		07 22		07 31		07 40	07 45		07 52		07 59		08 05		08 15		08 25
Harold Wood	d		07 09		07 18		07 27		07 36		07 45	07 50		07 57		08 04		08 10		08 20		08 30
Gidea Park ■	d	07 09	07 13	07 18	07 22	07 27	07 31	07 36	07 40	07 45	07 49	07 54	07 58	08 01	08 05	08 08	08 12	08 15	08 19	08 24	08 29	08 33
Romford	d	07 11	07 16	07 20	07 25	07 29	07 34	07 38	07 43	07 47	07 52	07 56	08 00	08 03	08 07	08 10	08 14	08 17	08 21	08 26	08 31	08 36
Chadwell Heath	d	07 15	07 20	07 24	07 29	07 33	07 38	07 42	07 47	07 51	07 56	08 00	08 04	08 07	08 11	08 14	08 18	08 21	08 25	08 30	08 35	08 40
Goodmayes	d	07 17	07 22	07 26	07 31	07 35	07 40	07 44	07 49	07 53	07 58	08 02	08 06	08 09	08 13	08 16	08 20	08 23	08 27	08 32		08 42
Seven Kings	d	07 19	07 24	07 28	07 33	07 37	07 42	07 46	07 51	07 55	08 00	08 04	08 08	08 11	08 15	08 18	08 22	08 25	08 29	08 34		08 44
Ilford ■	d	07 22	07 27	07 31	07 36	07 40	07 45	07 49	07 54	07 58	08 03	08 07	08 11	08 14	08 18	08 21	08 25	08 28	08 32	08 37	08 40	08 47
Manor Park	d	07 25		07 34		07 43		07 52		08 01		08 10		08 17			08 28			08 40	08 43	
Forest Gate	d	07 27	07 31		07 40		07 49		07 58		08 07		08 15			08 25			08 36		08 45	
Maryland	d	07 29		07 37		07 46		07 55		08 04		08 13			08 23			08 33			08 47	
Stratford ■ ⊖	d	07 32	07 35	07 39	07 43	07 48	07 52	07 57	08 01	08 06	08 10	08 15	08 19	08 22	08 25	08 29	08 32	08 36	08 40	08 44	08 50	08 53
London Liverpool Street ■ ⊖	a	07 42	07 45	07 49	07 53	07 58	08 02	08 08	08 11	08 17	08 21	08 26	08 30	08 33	08 37	08 41	08 44	08 47	08 51	08 55	09 01	09 05

		XR	XR	XR	XR	LE ■ C	XR	XR	XR	XR	XR	XR	XR	XR	XR	LE ■ C	XR	XR	XR	LE ■ D	XR	XR	XR
Shenfield ■	d		08 32		08 42	08 46		08 52		09 02		09 14	09 24	09 34	09 44	09 46	09 54	10 04	10 14	10 18	10 24	10 34	10 44
Brentwood	d		08 35		08 45			08 55		09 05		09 17	09 27	09 37	09 47		09 57	10 07	10 17		10 27	10 37	10 47
Harold Wood	d		08 40		08 50			09 00		09 10		09 22	09 32	09 42	09 52		10 02	10 12	10 22		10 32	10 42	10 52
Gidea Park ■	d	08 37	08 44	08 49	08 53		08 57	09 04	09 09	09 13	09 17	09 26	09 36	09 46	09 56		10 06	10 16	10 26		10 36	10 46	10 56
Romford	d	08 39	08 46	08 51	08 56	08 55	08 59	09 06	09 11	09 16	09 19	09 28	09 38	09 48	09 58	09 55	10 08	10 18	10 28	10 26	10 38	10 48	10 58
Chadwell Heath	d	08 43	08 50	08 55	09 00		09 03	09 10	09 15	09 20	09 23	09 32	09 42	09 52	10 02		10 12	10 22	10 32		10 42	10 52	11 02
Goodmayes	d	08 45	08 52		09 02		09 05	09 12		09 22	09 25	09 34	09 44	09 54	10 04		10 14	10 24	10 34		10 44	10 54	11 04
Seven Kings	d	08 47	08 54		09 04		09 07	09 14		09 24	09 27	09 36	09 46	09 56	10 06		10 16	10 26	10 36		10 46	10 56	11 06
Ilford ■	d	08 50	08 57	09 00	09 07		09 10	09 17	09 20	09 27	09 30	09 39	09 49	09 59	10 09		10 19	10 29	10 39		10 49	10 59	11 09
Manor Park	d	08 53		09 03			09 13		09 23		09 33	09 42	09 52	10 02	10 12		10 22	10 32	10 42		10 52	11 02	11 12
Forest Gate	d	08 55		09 05			09 15		09 25		09 35	09 44	09 54	10 04	10 14		10 24	10 34	10 44		10 54	11 04	11 14
Maryland	d	08 57		09 07			09 17		09 27		09 37	09 46	09 56	10 06	10 16		10 26	10 36	10 46		10 56	11 06	11 16
Stratford ■ ⊖	d	09 00	09 03	09 10	09 13	09s05	09 20	09 23	09 30	09 33	09 40	09 49	09 59	10 09	10 19	10 03	10 29	10 39	10 49	10 34	10 59	11 09	11 19
London Liverpool Street ■ ⊖	a	09 11	09 15	09 21	09 25	09 16	09 31	09 35	09 41	09 45	09 51	09 59	10 07	10 17	10 27	10 12	10 37	10 47	10 59	10 43	11 09	11 19	11 29

		LE ■ C	XR	XR	XR	LE ■ D	XR	XR	XR	LE ■ C	XR	XR	XR	LE ■ D	XR	XR	XR	LE ◇■ C	XR	XR	XR	LE ■ D	XR
Shenfield ■	d	10 45	10 54	11 04	11 14	11 20	11 24	11 34	11 44	11 45	11 54	12 04	12 14	12 20	12 24	12 34	12 44	12 45	12 54	13 04	13 14	13 20	13 24
Brentwood	d		10 57	11 07	11 17		11 27	11 37	11 47		11 57	12 07	12 17		12 27	12 37	12 47		12 57	13 07	13 17		13 27
Harold Wood	d		11 02	11 12	11 22		11 32	11 42	11 52		12 02	12 12	12 22		12 32	12 42	12 52		13 02	13 12	13 22		13 32
Gidea Park ■	d		11 06	11 16	11 26		11 36	11 46	11 56		12 06	12 16	12 26		12 36	12 46	12 56		13 06	13 16	13 26		13 36
Romford	d	10 53	11 08	11 18	11 28	11 28	11 38	11 48	11 58	11 53	12 08	12 18	12 28	12 28	12 38	12 48	12 58	12 53	13 08	13 18	13 28	13 28	13 38
Chadwell Heath	d		11 12	11 22	11 32		11 42	11 52	12 02		12 12	12 22	12 32		12 42	12 52	13 02		13 12	13 22	13 32		13 42
Goodmayes	d		11 14	11 24	11 34		11 44	11 54	12 04		12 14	12 24	12 34		12 44	12 54	13 04		13 14	13 24	13 34		13 44
Seven Kings	d		11 16	11 26	11 36		11 46	11 56	12 06		12 16	12 26	12 36		12 46	12 56	13 06		13 16	13 26	13 36		13 46
Ilford ■	d		11 19	11 29	11 39		11 49	11 59	12 09		12 19	12 29	12 39		12 49	12 59	13 09		13 19	13 29	13 39		13 49
Manor Park	d		11 22	11 32	11 42		11 52	12 02	12 12		12 22	12 32	12 42		12 52	13 02	13 12		13 22	13 32	13 42		13 52
Forest Gate	d		11 24	11 34	11 44		11 54	12 04	12 14		12 24	12 34	12 44		12 54	13 04	13 14		13 24	13 34	13 44		13 54
Maryland	d		11 26	11 36	11 46		11 56	12 06	12 16		12 26	12 36	12 46		12 56	13 06	13 16		13 26	13 36	13 46		13 56
Stratford ■ ⊖	d	11 01	11 29	11 39	11 49	11 36	11 59	12 09	12 19	12 02	12 29	12 39	12 49	12 36	12 59	13 09	13 19	13 01	13 29	13 39	13 49	13 36	13 59
London Liverpool Street ■ ⊖	a	11 10	11 39	11 47	11 57	11 45	12 07	12 17	12 27	12 10	12 37	12 47	12 57	12 45	13 07	13 17	13 27	13 10	13 37	13 47	13 57	13 45	14 07

		XR	XR	LE ◇■ C	XR	XR	XR	LE ■ D	XR	XR	XR	LE ◇■ C	XR	XR	XR	LE ■ D	XR	XR	XR	LE ◇■ C	XR	XR
Shenfield ■	d	13 34	13 44	13 45	13 54	14 04	14 14	14 20	14 24	14 34	14 44	14 45	14 54	15 04	15 14	15 20	15 24	15 34	15 44	15 45	15 54	16 04
Brentwood	d	13 37	13 47		13 57	14 07	14 17		14 27	14 37	14 47		14 57	15 07	15 17		15 27	15 37	15 47		15 57	16 07
Harold Wood	d	13 42	13 52		14 02	14 12	14 22		14 32	14 42	14 52		15 02	15 12	15 22		15 32	15 42	15 52		16 02	16 12
Gidea Park ■	d	13 46	13 56		14 06	14 16	14 26		14 36	14 46	14 56		15 06	15 16	15 26		15 36	15 46	15 56		16 06	16 16
Romford	d	13 48	13 58	13 53	14 08	14 18	14 28	14 28	14 38	14 48	14 58	14 53	15 08	15 18	15 28	15 28	15 38	15 48	15 58	15 53	16 08	16 18
Chadwell Heath	d	13 52	14 02		14 12	14 22	14 32		14 42	14 52	15 02		15 12	15 22	15 32		15 42	15 52	16 02		16 12	16 22
Goodmayes	d	13 54	14 04		14 14	14 24	14 34		14 44	14 54	15 04		15 14	15 24	15 34		15 44	15 54	16 04		16 14	16 24
Seven Kings	d	13 56	14 06		14 16	14 26	14 36		14 46	14 56	15 06		15 16	15 26	15 36		15 46	15 56	16 06		16 16	16 26
Ilford ■	d	13 59	14 09		14 19	14 29	14 39		14 49	14 59	15 09		15 19	15 29	15 39		15 49	15 59	16 09		16 19	16 29
Manor Park	d	14 02	14 12		14 22	14 32	14 42		14 52	15 02	15 12		15 22	15 32	15 42		15 52	16 02	16 12		16 22	16 32
Forest Gate	d	14 04	14 14		14 24	14 34	14 44		14 54	15 04	15 14		15 24	15 34	15 44		15 54	16 04	16 14		16 24	16 34
Maryland	d	14 06	14 16		14 26	14 36	14 46		14 56	15 06	15 16		15 26	15 36	15 46		15 56	16 06	16 16		16 26	16 36
Stratford ■ ⊖	d	14 09	14 19	14 01	14 29	14 39	14 49	14 36	14 59	15 09	15 19	15 01	15 29	15 39	15 49	15 36	15 59	16 09	16 19	16 01	16 29	16 39
London Liverpool Street ■ ⊖	a	14 17	14 27	14 10	14 37	14 47	14 57	14 47	15 07	15 17	15 27	15 10	15 37	15 47	15 57	15 45	16 07	16 17	16 27	16 11	16 37	16 47

A From Shenfield
B From Colchester
C From Southend Victoria
D From Colchester Town

Table T005-R

Shenfield - Ilford - London Liverpool Street

Mondays to Fridays
21 May to 7 December

	XR	XR	XR	XR	XR	XR	XR	XR	XR	XR	XR	XR	XR	XR	XR	XR	XR	XR	XR	XR	XR
Shenfield d	16 14	16 24	16 34	16 44		16 54		17 04		17 14		17 24		17 34		17 44		17 54		18 04	
Brentwood d	16 17	16 27	16 37	16 47		16 57		17 07		17 17		17 27		17 37		17 47		17 57		18 07	
Harold Wood d	16 22	16 32	16 42	16 52		17 02		17 12		17 22		17 32		17 42		17 52		18 02		18 12	
Gidea Park d	16 26	16 36	16 46	16 56	17 02	17 06	17 12	17 16	17 22	17 26	17 32	17 37	17 42	17 46	17 52	17 56	18 02	18 06	18 12	18 16	18 22
Romford d	16 28	16 38	16 48	16 58	17 04	17 08	17 14	17 18	17 24	17 28	17 34	17 39	17 44	17 48	17 54	17 58	18 04	18 08	18 14	18 18	18 24
Chadwell Heath d	16 32	16 42	16 52	17 02		17 12		17 22		17 32		17 43		17 52		18 02		18 12		18 22	
Goodmayes d	16 34	16 44	16 54	17 04		17 14		17 24		17 34		17 45		17 54		18 04		18 14		18 24	
Seven Kings d	16 36	16 46	16 56	17 06		17 16		17 26		17 36		17 47		17 56		18 06		18 16		18 26	
Ilford d	16 39	16 49	16 59	17 09	17 12	17 19	17 22	17 29	17 32	17 39	17 42	17 50	17 52	17 59	18 02	18 09	18 12	18 19	18 22	18 29	18 32
Manor Park d	16 42	16 52	17 02	17 12	17 15		17 25		17 35		17 45		17 55		18 05		18 15		18 25		18 35
Forest Gate d	16 44	16 54	17 04	17 14	17 17		17 27		17 37		17 47		17 57		18 07		18 17		18 27		18 37
Maryland d	16 46	16 56	17 06	17 16	17 19		17 29		17 39		17 49		17 59		18 09		18 19		18 29		18 39
Stratford ⊖ d	16 49	16 59	17 09	17 19	17 22	17 27	17 32	17 37	17 42	17 45	17 52	17 57	18 02	18 06	18 12	18 16	18 22	18 25	18 32	18 35	18 42
London Liverpool Street ⊖ a	16 57	17 07	17 17	17 27	17 30	17 35	17 40	17 45	17 50	17 53	18 00	18 05	18 11	18 15	18 21	18 24	18 30	18 33	18 40	18 43	18 50

	XR	LE A	XR	XR	XR	XR	XR	XR	XR	XR	LE B	XR	XR	XR	LE ◇ C	XR	XR	XR	LE D	XR	XR	XR
Shenfield d	18 14	18 20		18 24		18 34	18 44	18 54	19 04	19 14	19 20	19 24	19 34	19 44	19 45	19 54	20 04	20 14	20 20	20 24	20 34	20 44
Brentwood d	18 17			18 27		18 37	18 47	18 57	19 07	19 17		19 27	19 37	19 47		19 57	20 07	20 17		20 27	20 37	20 47
Harold Wood d	18 22			18 32		18 42	18 52	19 02	19 12	19 22		19 32	19 42	19 52		20 02	20 12	20 22		20 32	20 42	20 52
Gidea Park d	18 26		18 32	18 36	18 42	18 46	18 56	19 06	19 16	19 26		19 36	19 46	19 56		20 06	20 16	20 26		20 36	20 46	20 56
Romford d	18 28	18 28	18 34	18 38	18 44	18 48	18 58	19 08	19 18	19 28	19 28	19 38	19 48	19 58	19 53	20 08	20 18	20 28	20 28	20 38	20 48	20 58
Chadwell Heath d	18 32			18 42		18 52	19 02	19 12	19 22	19 32		19 42	19 52	20 02		20 12	20 22	20 32		20 42	20 52	21 02
Goodmayes d	18 34			18 44		18 54	19 04	19 14	19 24	19 34		19 44	19 54	20 04		20 14	20 24	20 34		20 44	20 54	21 04
Seven Kings d	18 36			18 46		18 56	19 06	19 16	19 26	19 36		19 46	19 56	20 06		20 16	20 26	20 36		20 46	20 56	21 06
Ilford d	18 39		18 42	18 49	18 52	18 59	19 09	19 19	19 29	19 39		19 49	19 59	20 09		20 19	20 29	20 39		20 49	20 59	21 09
Manor Park d			18 45		18 55	19 02	19 12	19 22	19 32	19 42		19 52	20 02	20 12		20 22	20 32	20 42		20 52	21 02	21 12
Forest Gate d			18 47		18 57	19 04	19 14	19 24	19 34	19 44		19 54	20 04	20 14		20 24	20 34	20 44		20 55	21 04	21 14
Maryland d			18 49		18 59	19 06	19 16	19 26	19 36	19 46		19 56	20 06	20 16		20 26	20 36	20 46		20 57	21 06	21 16
Stratford ⊖ d	18 45	18 36	18 52	18 55	19 02	19 09	19 19	19 29	19 39	19 49	19 36	19 59	20 09	20 19	20 01	20 29	20 39	20 49	20 36	20 59	21 09	21 19
London Liverpool Street ⊖ a	18 53	18 45	19 00	19 05	19 10	19 18	19 27	19 37	19 47	19 57	19 45	20 07	20 17	20 27	20 10	20 37	20 47	20 57	20 45	21 07	21 17	21 27

	LE C	XR	XR	XR	XR	XR	XR	LE C	XR	XR	LE D	XR	XR	XR	XR	LE B	XR	LE E	XR
Shenfield d	20 45	20 54	21 04	21 14	21 24	21 34	21 44	21 45	21 59	22 14	22 20	22 29	22 44	22 59	23 14	23 20	23 29	23 39	23 44
Brentwood d		20 57	21 07	21 17	21 27	21 37	21 47		22 02	22 17		22 32	22 47	23 02	23 17		23 32		23 47
Harold Wood d		21 02	21 12	21 22	21 32	21 42	21 52		22 07	22 22		22 37	22 52	23 07	23 22		23 37		23 52
Gidea Park d		21 06	21 16	21 26	21 36	21 46	21 56		22 11	22 26		22 41	22 56	23 11	23 26		23 41		23 56
Romford d	20 53	21 08	21 18	21 28	21 38	21 48	21 58	21 53	22 13	22 28	22 28	22 43	22 58	23 13	23 28	23 28	23 43	23 47	23 58
Chadwell Heath d		21 12	21 22	21 32	21 42	21 52	22 02		22 17	22 32		22 47	23 02	23 17	23 32		23 47		00 02
Goodmayes d		21 14	21 24	21 34	21 44	21 54	22 04		22 19	22 34		22 49	23 04	23 19	23 34		23 49		00 04
Seven Kings d		21 16	21 26	21 36	21 46	21 56	22 06		22 21	22 36		22 51	23 06	23 21	23 36		23 51		00 06
Ilford d		21 19	21 29	21 39	21 49	21 59	22 09		22 24	22 39		22 54	23 09	23 24	23 39		23 54		00 09
Manor Park d		21 22	21 32	21 42	21 52	22 02	22 12		22 27	22 42		22 57	23 12	23 27	23 42		23 57		00 12
Forest Gate d		21 24	21 34	21 44	21 54	22 04	22 14		22 30	22 44		22 59	23 14	23 31	23 44		23 59		00 14
Maryland d		21 26	21 36	21 46	21 56	22 06	22 16		22 32	22 46		23 01	23 16	23 33	23 46		00 01		00 16
Stratford ⊖ d	21 01	21 29	21 39	21 49	21 59	22 09	22 19	22 01	22 35	22 49	22 36	23 04	23 19	23 35	23 49	23 36	00 04	23 56	00 19
London Liverpool Street ⊖ a	21 10	21 37	21 47	21 57	22 07	22 17	22 27	22 10	22 43	22 57	22 45	23 12	23 27	23 46	00 01	23 48	00 15	00 06	00 30

Saturdays
26 May to 8 December

	XR F	XR F	XR	XR	LE G	XR	LE C	XR	XR	XR	XR	XR	LE C	XR	LE G	XR	XR	XR	LE D	XR	XR	XR
Shenfield d			04 44	05 14	05 24	05 29	05 35	05 44	05 59	06 14	06 24	06 34	06 35	06 44	06 46	06 54	07 04	07 14	07 20	07 24	07 34	07 44
Brentwood d			04 47	05 17		05 32		05 47	06 02	06 17	06 27	06 37		06 47		06 57	07 07	07 17		07 27	07 37	07 47
Harold Wood d			04 52	05 22		05 37		05 52	06 07	06 22	06 32	06 42		06 52		07 02	07 12	07 22		07 32	07 42	07 52
Gidea Park d			04 56	05 26		05 41		05 56	06 11	06 26	06 36	06 46		06 56		07 06	07 16	07 26		07 36	07 46	07 56
Romford d			04 58	05 28	05 32	05 43	05 43	05 58	06 13	06 28	06 38	06 48	06 43	06 58	06 54	07 08	07 18	07 28	07 28	07 38	07 48	07 58
Chadwell Heath d		00 02	05 02	05 32		05 47		06 02	06 17	06 32	06 42	06 52		07 02		07 12	07 22	07 32		07 42	07 52	08 02
Goodmayes d		00 04	05 04	05 34		05 49		06 04	06 19	06 34	06 44	06 54		07 04		07 14	07 24	07 34		07 44	07 54	08 04
Seven Kings d		00 06	05 06	05 36	05 37	05 51		06 06	06 21	06 36	06 46	06 56		07 06		07 16	07 26	07 36		07 46	07 56	08 06
Ilford d		00 09	05 09	05 39		05 54		06 09	06 24	06 39	06 49	06 59		07 09		07 19	07 29	07 39		07 49	07 59	08 09
Manor Park d		00 12	05 12	05 42		05 57		06 12	06 27	06 42	06 52	07 02		07 12		07 22	07 32	07 42		07 52	08 02	08 12
Forest Gate d		00 14	05 14	05 44		05 59		06 14	06 29	06 44	06 54	07 04		07 14		07 24	07 34	07 44		07 54	08 04	08 14
Maryland d	00 01	00 16	05 16	05 46		06 01		06 16	06 31	06 46	06 56	07 06		07 16		07 26	07 36	07 46		07 56	08 06	08 16
Stratford ⊖ d	00 04	00 19	05 19	05 49	05 42	06 04	05 51	06 19	06 34	06 49	06 59	07 09	06 51	07 19	07 02	07 29	07 39	07 49	07 36	07 59	08 09	08 19
London Liverpool Street ⊖ a	00 15	00 30	05 27	05 57	05 51	06 13	06 00	06 27	06 42	06 57	07 07	07 17	07 00	07 27	07 11	07 37	07 47	07 57	07 46	08 07	08 17	08 27

	LE C		XR	XR	XR	LE D	XR	XR	XR	LE ◇ C	XR	XR	LE D	XR	XR	LE ◇ C	XR	XR	LE D	XR	XR
Shenfield d	07 45	and at the same minutes past each hour until	19 54	20 04	20 14	20 20	20 24	20 34	20 44	20 45	20 59	21 14	21 20	21 29	21 44	21 45	21 59	22 14	22 20	22 29	22 41
Brentwood d			19 57	20 07	20 17		20 27	20 37	20 47		21 02	21 17		21 32	21 47		22 02	22 17		22 32	22 44
Harold Wood d			20 02	20 12	20 22		20 32	20 42	20 52		21 07	21 22		21 37	21 52		22 07	22 22		22 37	22 49
Gidea Park d			20 06	20 16	20 26		20 36	20 46	20 56		21 11	21 26		21 41	21 56		22 11	22 26		22 41	22 53
Romford d	07 53		20 08	20 18	20 28	20 28	20 38	20 48	20 58	20 53	21 13	21 28	21 28	21 43	21 58	21 53	22 13	22 28	22 28	22 43	22 55
Chadwell Heath d			20 12	20 22	20 32		20 42	20 52	21 02		21 17	21 32		21 47	22 02		22 17	22 32		22 47	22 59
Goodmayes d			20 14	20 24	20 34		20 44	20 54	21 04		21 19	21 34		21 49	22 04		22 19	22 34		22 49	23 01
Seven Kings d			20 16	20 26	20 36		20 46	20 56	21 06		21 21	21 36		21 51	22 06		22 21	22 36		22 51	23 03
Ilford d			20 19	20 29	20 39		20 49	20 59	21 09		21 24	21 39		21 54	22 09		22 24	22 39		22 54	23 06
Manor Park d			20 22	20 32	20 42		20 52	21 02	21 12		21 27	21 42		21 57	22 12		22 27	22 42		22 57	23 08
Forest Gate d			20 24	20 34	20 44		20 54	21 04	21 14		21 29	21 44		21 59	22 14		22 29	22 44		22 59	23 11
Maryland d			20 26	20 36	20 46		20 56	21 06	21 16		21 31	21 46		22 01	22 16		22 31	22 46		23 01	23 13
Stratford ⊖ d	08 01		20 29	20 39	20 49	20 36	20 59	21 09	21 19	21 01	21 34	21 49	21 36	22 04	22 19	22 01	22 34	22 49	22 36	23 04	23 15
London Liverpool Street ⊖ a	08 10		20 37	20 47	20 57	20 46	21 07	21 17	21 27	21 10	21 42	21 57	21 46	22 12	22 27	22 10	22 42	22 57	22 46	23 12	23 27

A From Braintree
B From Ipswich
C From Southend Victoria
D From Colchester Town; except the 08:20 Shenfield departure which comes from Harwich International
E From Southminster
F From Shenfield
G From Colchester

Table T005-R

Shenfield - Ilford - London Liverpool Street

Saturdays
26 May to 8 December

	XR	XR	LE A	XR	LE B	XR
Shenfield d	22 56	23 11	23 20	23 26	23 41	23 44
Brentwood d	22 59	23 14		23 29		23 47
Harold Wood d	23 04	23 19		23 34		23 52
Gidea Park d	23 08	23 23		23 38		23 56
Romford d	23 10	23 25	23 28	23 40	23 49	23 58
Chadwell Heath d	23 14	23 29		23 44		00 02
Goodmayes d	23 16	23 31		23 46		00 04
Seven Kings d	23 18	23 33		23 48		00 06
Ilford d	23 21	23 36		23 51		00 09
Manor Park d	23 23	23 38		23 53		00 12
Forest Gate d	23 26	23 41		23 56		00 14
Maryland d	23 28	23 43		23 58		00 16
Stratford ⊖ d	23 30	23 45	23s41	23 59	00s03	00 19
London Liverpool Street ⊖ a	23 42	23 57	23 50	00 12	00 12	00 30

Sundays
20 May to 2 December

	XR C	XR	XR	XR	LE D	XR	LE E	XR	LE D	XR	LE F	XR	LE D	XR	XR	LE D	XR	XR	LE D	XR	XR	LE D
Shenfield d				06 43	06 53		07 11	07 13	07 23		07 41	07 43	07 53		08 13	08 23		08 43	08 53		09 13	09 23
Brentwood d				06 46	06 56			07 16	07 26			07 46	07 56		08 16	08 26		08 46	08 56		09 16	09 26
Harold Wood d				06 51	07 01			07 21	07 31			07 51	08 01		08 21	08 31		08 51	09 01		09 21	09 31
Gidea Park d		05 55	06 25	06 55	07 05	07 11		07 25	07 35	07 41		07 55	08 05	08 11	08 25	08 35	08 41	08 55	09 05	09 11	09 25	09 35
Romford d		05 57	06 27	06 57	07 07	07 13	07 21	07 27	07 37	07 43	07 51	07 57	08 07	08 13	08 27	08 37	08 43	08 57	09 07	09 13	09 27	09 37
Chadwell Heath d	00 02	06 01	06 31	07 01		07 17		07 31		07 47		08 01		08 17	08 31		08 47	09 01		09 17	09 31	
Goodmayes d	00 04	06 03	06 33	07 03		07 19		07 33		07 49		08 03		08 19	08 33		08 49	09 03		09 19	09 33	
Seven Kings d	00 06	06 05	06 35	07 05		07 21		07 35		07 51		08 05		08 21	08 35		08 51	09 05		09 21	09 35	
Ilford d	00 09	06 08	06 38	07 08		07 24		07 38		07 54		08 08		08 24	08 38		08 54	09 08		09 24	09 38	
Manor Park d	00 12	06 10	06 40	07 10		07 26		07 40		07 56		08 10		08 26	08 40		08 56	09 10		09 26	09 40	
Forest Gate d	00 14	06 13	06 43	07 13		07 29		07 43		07 59		08 13		08 29	08 43		08 59	09 13		09 29	09 43	
Maryland d	00 16	06 15	06 45	07 15				07 45				08 15			08 45			09 15			09 45	
Stratford ⊖ d	00 19	06 17	06 47	07 17	07 20	07 32	07s35	07 47	07 50	08 02	08s05	08 17	08 20	08 32	08 47	08 50	09 02	09 17	09 20	09 32	09 47	09 50
London Liverpool Street ⊖ a	00 30	06 28	06 58	07 28	07 29	07 43	07 44	07 58	07 59	08 13	08 14	08 28	08 29	08 43	08 58	09 02	09 13	09 28	09 29	09 43	09 58	09 59

	XR	XR	LE D	XR	XR	LE D	XR	XR	LE D		XR	XR	LE D	XR	XR	LE D	XR	XR	LE D	XR	XR	LE D
Shenfield d		09 43	09 53		10 13	10 23		10 43	10 53	and at the same minutes past each hour until		15 13	15 23		15 43	15 53		16 13	16 23		16 43	16 53
Brentwood d		09 46	09 56		10 16	10 26		10 46	10 56			15 16	15 26		15 46	15 56		16 16	16 26		16 46	16 56
Harold Wood d		09 51	10 01		10 21	10 31		10 51	11 01			15 21	15 31		15 51	16 01		16 21	16 31		16 51	17 01
Gidea Park d	09 41	09 55	10 05	10 11	10 25	10 35	10 41	10 55	11 05		15 11	15 25	15 35	15 41	15 55	16 05	16 11	16 25	16 35	16 41	16 55	17 05
Romford d	09 43	09 57	10 07	10 13	10 27	10 37	10 43	10 57	11 07		15 13	15 27	15 37	15 43	15 57	16 07	16 13	16 27	16 37	16 43	16 57	17 07
Chadwell Heath d	09 47	10 01		10 17	10 31		10 47	11 01			15 17	15 31		15 47	16 01		16 17	16 31		16 47	17 01	
Goodmayes d	09 49	10 03		10 19	10 33		10 49	11 03			15 19	15 33		15 49	16 03		16 19	16 33		16 49	17 03	
Seven Kings d	09 51	10 05		10 21	10 35		10 51	11 05			15 21	15 35		15 51	16 05		16 21	16 35		16 51	17 05	
Ilford d	09 54	10 08		10 24	10 38		10 54	11 08			15 24	15 38		15 54	16 08		16 24	16 38		16 54	17 08	
Manor Park d	09 56	10 10		10 26	10 40		10 56	11 10			15 26	15 40		15 56	16 10		16 26	16 40		16 56	17 10	
Forest Gate d	09 59	10 13		10 29	10 43		10 59	11 13			15 29	15 43		15 59	16 13		16 29	16 43		16 59	17 13	
Maryland d		10 15			10 45			11 15				15 45			16 15			16 45			17 15	
Stratford ⊖ d	10 02	10 17	10 20	10 32	10 47	10 50	11 02	11 17	11 20		15 32	15 47	15 50	16 02	16 17	16 20	16 32	16 47	16 50	17 02	17 17	17 20
London Liverpool Street ⊖ a	10 13	10 28	10 31	10 43	10 58	10 59	11 13	11 28	11 29		15 43	15 58	15 59	16 13	16 28	16 29	16 43	16 58	16 59	17 13	17 28	17 31

	XR	XR	LE D	XR	XR	LE D	XR	XR	LE D	XR	XR	LE D	XR	XR	LE D	XR	XR	LE D	XR	XR	LE D
Shenfield d		17 13	17 23		17 43	17 53		18 13	18 23		18 43	18 53		19 13	19 23		19 43	19 53		20 13	20 23
Brentwood d		17 16	17 26		17 46	17 56		18 16	18 26		18 46	18 56		19 16	19 26		19 46	19 56		20 16	20 26
Harold Wood d		17 21	17 31		17 51	18 01		18 21	18 31		18 51	19 01		19 21	19 31		19 51	20 01		20 21	20 31
Gidea Park d	17 11	17 25	17 35	17 41	17 55	18 05	18 11	18 25	18 35	18 41	18 55	19 05	19 11	19 25	19 35	19 41	19 55	20 05	20 11	20 25	20 35
Romford d	17 13	17 27	17 37	17 43	17 57	18 07	18 13	18 27	18 37	18 43	18 57	19 07	19 13	19 27	19 37	19 43	19 57	20 07	20 13	20 27	20 37
Chadwell Heath d	17 17	17 31		17 47	18 01		18 17	18 31		18 47	19 01		19 17	19 31		19 47	20 01		20 17	20 31	
Goodmayes d	17 19	17 33		17 49	18 03		18 19	18 33		18 49	19 03		19 19	19 33		19 49	20 03		20 19	20 33	
Seven Kings d	17 21	17 35		17 51	18 05		18 21	18 35		18 51	19 05		19 21	19 35		19 51	20 05		20 21	20 35	
Ilford d	17 24	17 38		17 54	18 08		18 24	18 38		18 54	19 08		19 24	19 38		19 54	20 08		20 24	20 38	
Manor Park d	17 26	17 40		17 56	18 10		18 26	18 40		18 56	19 10		19 26	19 40		19 56	20 10		20 26	20 40	
Forest Gate d	17 29	17 43		17 59	18 13		18 29	18 43		18 59	19 13		19 29	19 43		19 59	20 13		20 29	20 43	
Maryland d		17 45			18 15			18 45			19 15			19 45			20 15			20 45	
Stratford ⊖ d	17 32	17 47	17 50	18 02	18 17	18 20	18 32	18 47	18 50	19 02	19 17	19 20	19 32	19 47	19 50	20 02	20 17	20 20	20 32	20 47	20 50
London Liverpool Street ⊖ a	17 43	17 58	17 59	18 13	18 28	18 31	18 43	18 58	18 59	19 13	19 28	19 29	19 43	19 58	19 59	20 13	20 28	20 29	20 43	20 58	20 59

	XR	XR	LE D	XR	XR	LE D	XR	LE D	XR	LE D	XR	LE D	XR	LE D	XR
Shenfield d		20 43	20 53		21 13	21 23	21 43	21 53	22 13	22 23	22 43	22 53	23 13	23 23	23 43
Brentwood d		20 46	20 56		21 16	21 26	21 46	21 56	22 16	22 26	22 46	22 56	23 16	23 26	23 46
Harold Wood d		20 51	21 01		21 21	21 31	21 51	22 01	22 21	22 31	22 51	23 01	23 21	23 31	23 51
Gidea Park d	20 41	20 55	21 05	21 11	21 25	21 35	21 55	22 05	22 25	22 35	22 55	23 05	23 25	23 35	23 55
Romford d	20 43	20 57	21 07	21 13	21 27	21 37	21 57	22 07	22 27	22 37	22 57	23 07	23 27	23 37	23 57
Chadwell Heath d	20 47	21 01		21 17	21 31		22 01		22 31		23 01		23 31		00 01
Goodmayes d	20 49	21 03		21 19	21 33		22 03		22 33		23 03		23 33		00 03
Seven Kings d	20 51	21 05		21 21	21 35		22 05		22 35		23 05		23 35		00 05
Ilford d	20 54	21 08		21 24	21 38		22 08		22 38		23 08		23 38		00 08
Manor Park d	20 56	21 10		21 26	21 40		22 10		22 40		23 10		23 40		00 10
Forest Gate d	20 59	21 13		21 29	21 43		22 13		22 43		23 13		23 43		00 13
Maryland d		21 15			21 45		22 15		22 45		23 15		23 45		00 15
Stratford ⊖ d	21 02	21 17	21 20	21 32	21 47	21 50	22 17	22 20	22 47	22 50	23 17	23 20	23 47	23 50	00 17
London Liverpool Street ⊖ a	21 13	21 28	21 29	21 43	21 58	21 59	22 28	22 29	22 58	22 59	23 28	23 31	23 58	23 59	00 28

A From Ipswich
B From Southminster
C From Shenfield
D From Southend Victoria
E From Chelmsford
F From Colchester

Table T006-F

Mondays to Fridays

21 May to 7 December

London Liverpool Street - Shenfield - Wickford - Southminster and Southend

Miles	Miles	Station		LE	LE	LE	LE	LE	LE	LE	LE	LE	LE	LE	LE	LE	LE	LE	LE	LE	LE	LE	LE
				MX	MO	MX	MO	MO	MO	MX	MX	MO	MO	MX	MX	MO							
				■	■	■	■	■	■	■	■	■	■	■	■	■	■	◇■	■	■	■	◇■	■
				A	A	A	A	B	C		B	A	C	B		A		D				D	
0	0	**London Liverpool Street** ⊖	d					00 02	00 14	00 15	00 18		00 44	00 46	00 50			05 23		05 35	05 55	06 02	
4	4	Stratford ⊖	d					00 09	00 21	00 22	00 25		00 51	00 53	00 57			05 30		05 42	06 02	06 09	
12½	12½	Romford	d				00 04		00 34	00 32		←	01 04		01 08	←		05 38					
20¼	20¼	**Shenfield**	a				00 21	00 31	00 51	00 44	00 47	00 51	01 21	01 17	01 20	01 21		05 47		06 01	06 18	06 24	
—	—		d			00 09	00 21		00 51	00 45		00 51	01 21		01 20	01 21			05 55	06 03	06 19		06 30
24¼	24¼	Billericay	d			00 15	00 27		→	00 51		00 57	→		01 26	01 27			06 01	06 09	06 25		06 36
29	29	**Wickford**	d		00 03	00 21	00 33			00 56		01 03			01 31	01 33	05 16		06 09	06 15	06 31		06 45
—	31½	Battlesbridge	d														05 20		06 13				06 49
—	34	South Woodham Ferrers	d														05 24		06 17				06 53
—	37¼	North Fambridge	d														05 41		06 24				07 03
—	40¼	Althorne	d														05 46		06 29				07 08
—	43¼	Burnham-on-Crouch	d														05 51		06 34				07 13
—	45½	**Southminster**	a														05 57		06 40				07 19
33¼	—	Rayleigh	d		00 08	00 26	00 38			01 01		01 08			01 36	01 38				06 20	06 36		
36¼	—	Hockley	d	00 01	00 12	00 31	00 42			01 06		01 12			01 41	01 42				06 25	06 41		
38¾	—	Rochford	d	00 04	00 16	00 34	00 46			01 09		01 16			01 44	01 46				06 28	06 44		
39¾	—	Southend Airport ✈	d	00 07	00 18	00 37	00 48			01 12		01 18			01 47	01 48				06 31	06 47		
40¾	—	Prittlewell	d	00 10		00 40				01 16					01 50					06 35	06 50		
41½	—	**Southend Victoria**	a	00 18	00 28	00 48	00 58			01 23		01 29			01 58	01 59				06 38	06 54		

Station		LE	LE	LE	LE	LE	LE	LE	LE	LE	LE	LE	LE	LE	LE	LE	LE	LE	LE	LE	LE	LE	LE
		■	■	■	■	■	■	■	■	■	■	◇■	■	■	■	■	■	■	■	■	■	■	◇■
		E			F	G			E		H	D			G		E		H	H			D
London Liverpool Street ⊖	d	06 12	06 15	06 35	06 38	06 48	06 50		07 02	07 05	07 08	07 17	07 20	07 33	07 36	07 40	07 46	07 57	08 00	08 06	08 13		08 16
Stratford ⊖	d	06 20	06 22	06 42	06 45	06 55	06 57		07 09	07 12	07 15	07 24	07 27	07 42	07 45		07 54	08 05	08 08	08 14	08 21		08 24
Romford	d										07 23												
Shenfield	a	06 36	06 38	06 57	07 00	07 11	07 13		07 24	07 27	07 32	07 39	07 42	07 58	08 01		08 10	08 21	08 25	08 30	08 37		08 40
	d		06 39	06 59			07 14			07 29			07 43	07 58				08 22			08 39		
Billericay	d		06 45	07 05			07 20			07 35			07 49	08 04				08 28			08 45		
Wickford	d		06 51	07 11			07 26	07 36		07 41			07 55	08 10		08 18		08 34			08 51	08 56	
Battlesbridge	d							07 40								08 22						09 00	
South Woodham Ferrers	d							07 44								08 26						09 04	
North Fambridge	d							07 53								08 32						09 11	
Althorne	d							07 58								08 37						09 16	
Burnham-on-Crouch	d							08 03								08 42						09 21	
Southminster	a							08 09								08 48						09 27	
Rayleigh	d		06 56	07 16			07 31			07 46			08 00	08 15				08 39			08 56		
Hockley	d		07 01	07 21			07 36			07 51			08 05	08 20				08 44			09 01		
Rochford	d		07 04	07 24			07 39			07 54			08 08	08 23				08 47			09 04		
Southend Airport ✈	d		07 07	07 27			07 42			07 57			08 11	08 26				08 50			09 07		
Prittlewell	d		07 10	07 30			07 45			08 01			08 14	08 29				08 53			09 10		
Southend Victoria	a		07 14	07 34			07 50			08 04			08 18	08 34				08 57			09 14		

Station		LE	LE	LE	LE	LE	LE	LE	LE	LE	LE	LE	LE	LE	LE	LE	LE	LE	LE	LE	LE	LE
		■	■	■	■	■	■	◇■	◇■	◇■	■	■	■	◇■	■	◇■	■	◇■	◇■	■	■	◇■
			G	E			H		D			G	E		H			D		G	E	
London Liverpool Street ⊖	d	08 32	08 36	08 48	08 55		09 02	09 13	09 18	09 34		09 38	09 48	09 55	10 02	10 13		10 18	10 35	10 38	10 48	10 55
Stratford ⊖	d	08 42	08 45	08 55	09 02		09 09	09 21	09 25	09 42		09 45	09 55	10 02	10 09	10 20		10 25	10 42	10 45	10 55	11 02
Romford	d											09 53				10 28				10 53		
Shenfield	a	08 58	09 02	09 11	09 17		09 24	09 37	09 40	09 57		10 02	10 11	10 18	10 24	10 37		10 40	10 57	11 02	11 11	11 17
	d	08 59			09 19			09 39		09 59				10 19		10 39			10 59			11 19
Billericay	d	09 05			09 25			09 45		10 05				10 25		10 45			11 05			11 25
Wickford	d	09 11			09 31	09 36		09 51		10 11	10 16			10 31		10 51	10 56		11 11			11 31
Battlesbridge	d					09 40					10 20						11 00					
South Woodham Ferrers	d					09 44					10 24						11 04					
North Fambridge	d					09 51					10 31						11 11					
Althorne	d					09 56					10 36						11 16					
Burnham-on-Crouch	d					10 01					10 41						11 21					
Southminster	a					10 07					10 47						11 27					
Rayleigh	d	09 16			09 36			09 56		10 16				10 36		10 56			11 16			11 36
Hockley	d	09 21			09 41			10 01		10 21				10 41		11 01			11 21			11 41
Rochford	d	09 24			09 44			10 04		10 24				10 44		11 04			11 24			11 44
Southend Airport ✈	d	09 27			09 47			10 07		10 27				10 47		11 07			11 27			11 47
Prittlewell	d	09 30			09 50			10 10		10 30				10 50		11 10			11 30			11 50
Southend Victoria	a	09 34			09 54			10 14		10 34				10 54		11 14			11 34			11 54

Station		LE	LE	LE	LE	LE	LE	LE	LE	LE	LE	LE	LE	LE	LE	LE	LE	LE	LE	LE	LE	LE	LE
		■	■	◇■	◇■	◇■	■	■	■	◇■	■	◇■	■	◇■	◇■	■	■	◇■	■	■	◇■	◇■	◇■
			H		D			G	E		H			D		G	E			H		D	
London Liverpool Street ⊖	d		11 02	11 13	11 18	11 35		11 38	11 48	11 55	12 02	12 13		12 18	12 35	12 38	12 48	12 55		13 02	13 13	13 18	13 35
Stratford ⊖	d		11 09	11 20	11 25	11 42		11 45	11 55	12 02	12 09	12 20		12 25	12 42	12 45	12 55	13 02		13 09	13 20	13 25	13 42
Romford	d			11 28				11 53				12 28				12 53					13 28		
Shenfield	a		11 24	11 37	11 41	11 57		12 02	12 11	12 17	12 24	12 37		12 40	12 57	13 02	13 11	13 18		13 24	13 37	13 40	13 57
	d			11 39		11 59				12 19		12 39			12 59			13 19			13 39		13 59
Billericay	d			11 45		12 05				12 25		12 45			13 05			13 25			13 45		14 05
Wickford	d	11 36		11 51		12 11	12 16			12 31		12 51	12 56		13 11			13 31	13 36		13 51		14 11
Battlesbridge	d	11 40					12 20						13 00						13 40				
South Woodham Ferrers	d	11 44					12 24						13 04						13 44				
North Fambridge	d	11 51					12 31						13 11						13 51				
Althorne	d	11 56					12 36						13 16						13 56				
Burnham-on-Crouch	d	12 01					12 41						13 21						14 01				
Southminster	a	12 07					12 47						13 27						14 07				
Rayleigh	d			11 56		12 16				12 36		12 56			13 16			13 36			13 56		14 16
Hockley	d			12 01		12 21				12 41		13 01			13 21			13 41			14 01		14 21
Rochford	d			12 04		12 24				12 44		13 04			13 24			13 44			14 04		14 24
Southend Airport ✈	d			12 07		12 27				12 47		13 07			13 27			13 47			14 07		14 27
Prittlewell	d			12 10		12 30				12 50		13 10			13 30			13 51			14 10		14 30
Southend Victoria	a			12 14		12 34				12 54		13 14			13 34			13 54			14 14		14 34

A From London Liverpool Street
B To Colchester
C To Southend Victoria
D To Clacton-on-Sea
E To Braintree
F To Harwich Town
G To Colchester Town
H To Ipswich

NRT MAY 2018 EDITION

Table T006-F

Mondays to Fridays

21 May to 7 December

London Liverpool Street - Shenfield - Wickford - Southminster and Southend

Station		LE	LE	LE	LE	LE	LE	LE	LE	LE	LE	LE	LE	LE	LE	LE	LE	LE	LE	LE	LE	LE	LE
		■	■	■	◇■	■	■	■	◇■	■	■	■	■	■	■	■	◇■	■	■	■	■	■	◇■
			A	B		C			D		A	B			C		D			A	B		C
London Liverpool Street ⊖	d		13 38	13 48	13 55	14 02	14 13		14 18	14 35	14 38	14 48	14 55		15 02	15 13	15 18	15 35		15 38	15 48	15 55	16 02
Stratford ⊖	d		13 45	13 55	14 02	14 09	14 20		14 25	14 42	14 45	14 55	15 02		15 09	15 20	15 25	15 42		15 45	15 55	16 02	16 09
Romford	d		13 53				14 28				14 53					15 28				15 53			
Shenfield	a		14 02	14 11	14 18	14 24	14 37		14 40	14 57	15 02	15 11	15 17		15 24	15 37	15 40	15 57		16 02	16 11	16 17	16 25
	d				14 19		14 39			14 59			15 19			15 39		15 59				16 19	
Billericay	d				14 25		14 45			15 05			15 25			15 45		16 05				16 25	
Wickford	d	14 16			14 31		14 51	14 56		15 11			15 31	15 36		15 51		16 11	16 14			16 31	
Battlesbridge	d	14 20						15 00						15 40					16 18				
South Woodham Ferrers	d	14 24						15 04						15 44					16 22				
North Fambridge	d	14 31						15 11						15 51					16 29				
Althorne	d	14 36						15 16						15 56					16 34				
Burnham-on-Crouch	d	14 41						15 21						16 01					16 39				
Southminster	a	14 47						15 27						16 07					16 45				
Rayleigh	d				14 36		14 56			15 16			15 36			15 56		16 16				16 36	
Hockley	d				14 41		15 01			15 21			15 41			16 01		16 21				16 41	
Rochford	d				14 44		15 04			15 24			15 44			16 04		16 24				16 44	
Southend Airport ✈	d				14 47		15 07			15 27			15 47			16 07		16 27				16 47	
Prittlewell	d				14 50		15 10			15 30			15 50			16 10		16 31				16 50	
Southend Victoria	a				14 54		15 14			15 34			15 54			16 14		16 34				16 54	

Station		LE	LE	LE	LE	LE	LE	LE	LE	LE	LE	LE	LE	LE	LE	LE	LE	LE	LE	LE	LE	LE
		■	◇■	■	■	■	◇■	■	■	■	■	◇■	■	■	■	■	■	■	■	■	■	■
			D	E			C	B		E		F			B				A			B
London Liverpool Street ⊖	d	16 10	16 14	16 17	16 24		16 32	16 34	16 40	16 47	16 54	17 02	17 04	17 15	17 20	17 22	17 25	17 34	17 40	17 45	17 54	18 00
Stratford ⊖	d	16 18	16 22	16 25	16 32			16 42	16 48	16 55	17 02	17 10	17 13	17 23	17 29	17 32	17 34	17 43		17 53	18 03	18 09
Romford	d																					
Shenfield	a	16 34	16 38	16 41	16 48		16 54	16 58	17 04	17 11	17 18	17 26	17 29	17 39	17 45		17 50	17 59	18 05	18 09	18 19	18 25
	d	16 34			16 48				17 04		17 19		17 30	17 39			17 52	18 00		18 09	18 20	
Billericay	d	16 41			16 55				17 11		17 26		17 37	17 46			17 58	18 06		18 16	18 26	
Wickford	d	16 48			17 02	17 06			17 18		17 33		17 44	17 53		18 00	18 05	18 13		18 23	18 33	
Battlesbridge	d					17 10										18 04						
South Woodham Ferrers	d					17 14										18 08						
North Fambridge	d					17 21										18 14						
Althorne	d					17 26										18 19						
Burnham-on-Crouch	d					17 31										18 24						
Southminster	a					17 37										18 32						
Rayleigh	d	16 53			17 07				17 23		17 38		17 49	17 58			18 10	18 18		18 28	18 38	
Hockley	d	16 57			17 11				17 27		17 42		17 53	18 02			18 15	18 23		18 32	18 43	
Rochford	d	17 01			17 15				17 31		17 46		17 57	18 06			18 18	18 26		18 36	18 46	
Southend Airport ✈	d	17 03			17 17				17 33		17 48		17 59	18 08			18 21	18 29		18 38	18 49	
Prittlewell	d	17 06			17 20				17 36		17 51		18 02	18 11			18 24	18 32		18 41	18 52	
Southend Victoria	a	17 15			17 26				17 42		17 57		18 08	18 17			18 30	18 38		18 47	18 58	

Station		LE	LE	LE	LE	LE	LE	LE	LE	LE	LE	LE	LE	LE	LE	LE	LE	LE	LE	LE	LE	LE	LE
		■	■	■	■	■	■	◇■	■	■	■	■	■	◇■	◇■	■	■	■	◇■	◇■	◇■	■	◇■
					G			C				B		D			A	B		C			D
London Liverpool Street ⊖	d	18 02	18 05	18 14	18 20	18 25	18 35	18 38	18 41	18 45	18 55	19 02	19 15	19 18	19 35		19 38	19 48	19 55	20 02	20 13		20 18
Stratford ⊖	d	18 12	18 14	18 23	18 29	18 33	18 43	18 46	18 49	18 53	19 03	19 09	19 22	19 25	19 42		19 45	19 55	20 03	20 09	20 20		20 25
Romford	d																				20 28		
Shenfield	a		18 31	18 39	18 45	18 49	18 59	19 02		19 09	19 19	19 24	19 38	19 40	19 57		20 00	20 11	20 18	20 24	20 37		20 40
	d		18 31	18 41		18 50	18 59			19 10	19 20		19 39		19 58				20 19		20 39		
Billericay	d		18 38	18 47		18 57	19 06			19 17	19 27		19 45		20 04				20 25		20 45		
Wickford	d	18 41	18 45	18 54		19 04	19 13		19 19	19 24	19 34		19 51		20 10	20 16			20 31		20 51	20 56	
Battlesbridge	d	18 45							19 23							20 20						21 00	
South Woodham Ferrers	d	18 49							19 27							20 24						21 04	
North Fambridge	d	18 55							19 34							20 31						21 11	
Althorne	d	19 00							19 39							20 36						21 16	
Burnham-on-Crouch	d	19 05							19 44							20 41						21 21	
Southminster	a	19 13							19 52							20 47						21 27	
Rayleigh	d		18 50	18 59		19 09	19 18			19 29	19 39		19 56		20 15				20 36		20 56		
Hockley	d		18 55	19 04		19 13	19 22			19 33	19 43		20 01		20 20				20 41		21 01		
Rochford	d		18 58	19 07		19 17	19 26			19 37	19 47		20 04		20 23				20 44		21 04		
Southend Airport ✈	d		19 01	19 10		19 19	19 28			19 39	19 49		20 07		20 26				20 47		21 07		
Prittlewell	d		19 04	19 13		19 22	19 31			19 42	19 52		20 10		20 29				20 50		21 10		
Southend Victoria	a		19 10	19 19		19 28	19 37			19 47	19 58		20 14		20 34				20 54		21 14		

Station		LE	LE	LE	LE	LE	LE	LE	LE	LE	LE	LE	LE	LE	LE	LE	LE	LE	LE	LE	LE	LE
		◇■	■	■	◇■	■	■	◇■	◇■	◇■	■	■	■	◇■	■	◇■	■	◇■	■	◇■	■	■
			A	B			G		D			A	B		H			D	H		C	
London Liverpool Street ⊖	d	20 35	20 38	20 48	20 55		21 02	21 13	21 18	21 35		21 38	21 48	21 55	22 02	22 13		22 18	22 38	22 45	23 02	23 15
Stratford ⊖	d	20 42	20 45	20 55	21 02		21 09	21 20	21 25	21 42		21 45	21 55	22 02	22 09	22 20		22 25	22 45	22 52	23 09	23 22
Romford	d		20 53					21 28				21 53				22 28						
Shenfield	a	20 57	21 02	21 11	21 17		21 24	21 37	21 40	21 57		22 02	22 11	22 17	22 24	22 37		22 40	23 00	23 07	23 25	23 37
	d	20 59			21 19			21 39		21 59				22 19		22 39				23 09		23 39
Billericay	d	21 05			21 25			21 45		22 05				22 25		22 45				23 15		23 45
Wickford	d	21 11			21 31	21 36		21 51		22 11	22 16			22 31		22 51	22 56			23 21		23 51
Battlesbridge	d					21 40					22 20						23 00					
South Woodham Ferrers	d					21 44					22 24						23 04					
North Fambridge	d					21 51					22 31						23 11					
Althorne	d					21 56					22 36						23 16					
Burnham-on-Crouch	d					22 01					22 41						23 21					
Southminster	a					22 07					22 47						23 27					
Rayleigh	d	21 16			21 36			21 56		22 16				22 36		22 56				23 26		23 56
Hockley	d	21 21			21 41			22 01		22 21				22 41		23 01				23 31		00 01
Rochford	d	21 24			21 44			22 04		22 24				22 44		23 04				23 34		00 04
Southend Airport ✈	d	21 27			21 47			22 07		22 27				22 47		23 07				23 37		00 07
Prittlewell	d	21 30			21 50			22 10		22 30				22 50		23 10				23 40		00 10
Southend Victoria	a	21 34			21 54			22 14		22 34				22 54		23 14				23 48		00 18

A To Colchester Town
B To Braintree
C To Ipswich
D To Clacton-on-Sea
E To Witham
F To Norwich
G To Harwich International
H To Colchester

Table T006-F

London Liverpool Street - Shenfield - Wickford - Southminster and Southend

Mondays to Fridays
21 May to 7 December

	LE ◇ A	LE	LE B
London Liverpool Street d	23 18	23 45	23 48
Stratford d	23 25	23 52	23 55
Romford d			
Shenfield a	23 40	00 07	00 10
Shenfield d		00 09	
Billericay d		00 15	
Wickford d		00 21	
Battlesbridge d			
South Woodham Ferrers d			
North Fambridge d			
Althorne d			
Burnham-on-Crouch d			
Southminster a			
Rayleigh d		00 26	
Hockley d		00 31	
Rochford d		00 34	
Southend Airport d		00 37	
Prittlewell d		00 40	
Southend Victoria a		00 48	

Saturdays
26 May to 8 December

	LE C	LE C	LE	LE B	LE B	LE	LE	LE D	LE	LE	LE D	LE	LE	LE ◇ A	LE	LE E	LE F	LE	LE	LE D	LE	LE ◇ A
London Liverpool Street d			00 15	00 18	00 46	00 50		05 34		05 35	06 02	06 05		06 18	06 35	06 38	06 48	06 55		07 02	07 13	07 18
Stratford d			00 22	00 25	00 53	00 57		05 41		05 43	06 09	06 12		06 25	06 42	06 45	06 55	07 02		07 09	07 20	07 25
Romford d			00 32			01 08		05 49								06 53					07 28	
Shenfield a			00 45	00 47	01 17	01 20		05 58		06 01	06 24	06 27		06 40	06 57	07 02	07 11	07 17		07 24	07 37	07 41
Shenfield d		00 09	00 45			01 20				06 03		06 29			06 59			07 19			07 39	
Billericay d		00 15	00 51			01 26				06 09		06 35			07 05			07 25			07 45	
Wickford d		00 21	00 56			01 31	05 36		06 12	06 15		06 41	06 56		07 11			07 31	07 36		07 51	
Battlesbridge d							05 40		06 16				07 00						07 40			
South Woodham Ferrers d							05 44		06 20				07 04						07 44			
North Fambridge d							05 51		06 31				07 11						07 51			
Althorne d							05 56		06 36				07 16						07 56			
Burnham-on-Crouch d							06 01		06 41				07 21						08 01			
Southminster a							06 07		06 47				07 27						08 07			
Rayleigh d		00 26	01 01			01 36				06 20		06 46			07 16			07 36			07 56	
Hockley d	00 01	00 31	01 06			01 41				06 25		06 51			07 21			07 41			08 01	
Rochford d	00 04	00 34	01 09			01 44				06 28		06 54			07 24			07 44			08 04	
Southend Airport d	00 07	00 37	01 12			01 47				06 31		06 57			07 27			07 47			08 07	
Prittlewell d	00 10	00 40	01 16			01 50				06 34		07 00			07 30			07 50			08 10	
Southend Victoria a	00 18	00 48	01 23			01 58				06 38		07 04			07 34			07 54			08 14	

	LE	LE	LE G	LE F	LE	LE D	LE	LE	LE ◇ A	LE	LE G	LE F	LE	LE	LE D	LE ◇	LE ◇ A	LE ◇	LE	LE G	LE F	LE ◇
London Liverpool Street d	07 35		07 38	07 48	07 55	08 02	08 13		08 18	08 35	08 38	08 48	08 55		09 02	09 13	09 18	09 35		09 38	09 48	09 55
Stratford d	07 42		07 45	07 55	08 02	08 09	08 20		08 25	08 42	08 45	08 55	09 02		09 09	09 20	09 25	09 42		09 45	09 55	10 02
Romford d			07 53				08 28				08 53					09 28				09 53		
Shenfield a	07 57		08 02	08 11	08 17	08 24	08 37		08 41	08 57	09 02	09 11	09 17		09 24	09 37	09 41	09 57		10 02	10 11	10 17
Shenfield d	07 59				08 19		08 39			08 59			09 19			09 39		09 59				10 19
Billericay d	08 05				08 25		08 45			09 05			09 25			09 45		10 05				10 25
Wickford d	08 11	08 16			08 31		08 51	08 56		09 11			09 31	09 36		09 51		10 11	10 16			10 31
Battlesbridge d		08 20						09 00						09 40					10 20			
South Woodham Ferrers d		08 24						09 04						09 44					10 24			
North Fambridge d		08 31						09 11						09 51					10 31			
Althorne d		08 36						09 16						09 56					10 36			
Burnham-on-Crouch d		08 41						09 21						10 01					10 41			
Southminster a		08 47						09 27						10 07					10 47			
Rayleigh d	08 16				08 36		08 56			09 16			09 36			09 56		10 16				10 36
Hockley d	08 21				08 41		09 01			09 21			09 41			10 01		10 21				10 41
Rochford d	08 24				08 44		09 04			09 24			09 44			10 04		10 24				10 44
Southend Airport d	08 27				08 47		09 07			09 27			09 47			10 07		10 27				10 47
Prittlewell d	08 30				08 50		09 10			09 30			09 50			10 10		10 30				10 50
Southend Victoria a	08 34				08 54		09 14			09 34			09 54			10 14		10 34				10 54

A To Clacton-on-Sea
B To Colchester
C From London Liverpool Street
D To Ipswich
E To Harwich International
F To Braintree
G To Colchester Town

Table T006-F

London Liverpool Street - Shenfield - Wickford - Southminster and Southend

Saturdays
26 May to 8 December

	LE A	LE ◇	LE	LE ◇ B	LE ◇	LE C	LE D	LE ◇	LE	LE A	LE ◇	LE ◇ B	LE ◇	LE	LE C	LE D	LE ◇	LE A	LE ◇	LE	LE ◇ B	LE ◇
London Liverpool Street d	10 02	10 13		10 18	10 35	10 38	10 48	10 55		11 02	11 13	11 18	11 35		11 38	11 48	11 55	12 02	12 13		12 18	12 35
Stratford d	10 09	10 20		10 25	10 42	10 45	10 55	11 02		11 09	11 20	11 25	11 42		11 45	11 55	12 02	12 09	12 20		12 25	12 42
Romford d		10 28				10 53					11 28				11 53				12 28			
Shenfield a	10 24	10 37		10 41	10 57	11 02	11 11	11 17		11 24	11 37	11 41	11 57		12 02	12 11	12 17	12 24	12 37		12 41	12 57
Shenfield d		10 39			10 59			11 19			11 39		11 59				12 19		12 39			12 59
Billericay d		10 45			11 05			11 25			11 45		12 05				12 25		12 45			13 05
Wickford d		10 51	10 56		11 11			11 31	11 36		11 51		12 11	12 16			12 31		12 51	12 56		13 11
Battlesbridge d			11 00						11 40					12 20						13 00		
South Woodham Ferrers d			11 04						11 44					12 24						13 04		
North Fambridge d			11 11						11 51					12 31						13 11		
Althorne d			11 16						11 56					12 36						13 16		
Burnham-on-Crouch d			11 21						12 01					12 41						13 21		
Southminster a			11 27						12 07					12 47						13 27		
Rayleigh d		10 56			11 16			11 36			11 56		12 16				12 36		12 56			13 16
Hockley d		11 01			11 21			11 41			12 01		12 21				12 41		13 01			13 21
Rochford d		11 04			11 24			11 44			12 04		12 24				12 44		13 04			13 24
Southend Airport d		11 07			11 27			11 47			12 07		12 27				12 47		13 07			13 27
Prittlewell d		11 10			11 30			11 50			12 10		12 30				12 50		13 10			13 30
Southend Victoria a		11 14			11 34			11 54			12 14		12 34				12 54		13 14			13 34

	LE C	LE D	LE ◇	LE	LE A	LE ◇	LE ◇ B	LE ◇	LE	LE C	LE D	LE ◇	LE A	LE	LE	LE ◇ B	LE	LE C	LE D	LE	LE
London Liverpool Street d	12 38	12 48	12 55		13 02	13 13	13 18	13 35		13 38	13 48	13 55	14 02	14 13		14 18	14 35	14 38	14 48	14 55	
Stratford d	12 45	12 55	13 02		13 09	13 20	13 25	13 42		13 45	13 55	14 02	14 09	14 20		14 25	14 42	14 45	14 55	15 02	
Romford d	12 53					13 28				13 53				14 28				14 53			
Shenfield a	13 02	13 11	13 17		13 24	13 37	13 41	13 57		14 02	14 11	14 17	14 24	14 37		14 41	14 58	15 02	15 11	15 17	
Shenfield d			13 19			13 39		13 59				14 19		14 39			14 59			15 19	
Billericay d			13 25			13 45		14 05				14 25		14 45			15 05			15 25	
Wickford d			13 31	13 36		13 51		14 11	14 16			14 31		14 51	14 56		15 11			15 31	15 36
Battlesbridge d				13 40					14 20						15 00						15 40
South Woodham Ferrers d				13 44					14 24						15 04						15 44
North Fambridge d				13 51					14 31						15 11						15 51
Althorne d				13 56					14 36						15 16						15 56
Burnham-on-Crouch d				14 01					14 41						15 21						16 01
Southminster a				14 07					14 47						15 27						16 07
Rayleigh d			13 36			13 56		14 16				14 36		14 56			15 16			15 36	
Hockley d			13 41			14 01		14 21				14 41		15 01			15 21			15 41	
Rochford d			13 44			14 04		14 24				14 44		15 04			15 24			15 44	
Southend Airport d			13 47			14 07		14 27				14 47		15 07			15 27			15 47	
Prittlewell d			13 50			14 10		14 30				14 50		15 10			15 30			15 50	
Southend Victoria a			13 54			14 14		14 34				14 54		15 14			15 34			15 54	

	LE A	LE	LE ◇ B	LE	LE	LE C	LE D	LE	LE A	LE	LE	LE ◇ B	LE	LE C	LE D	LE	LE	LE ◇ A	LE	LE ◇ B	LE	LE
London Liverpool Street d	15 02	15 13	15 18	15 35		15 38	15 48	15 55	16 02	16 13		16 18	16 35	16 38	16 48	16 55		17 02	17 13	17 18	17 35	
Stratford d	15 09	15 20	15 25	15 42		15 45	15 55	16 02	16 09	16 20		16 25	16 42	16 45	16 55	17 02		17 09	17 20	17 25	17 42	
Romford d		15 28				15 53				16 28				16 53					17 28			
Shenfield a	15 24	15 37	15 41	15 57		16 02	16 11	16 17	16 24	16 37		16 41	16 57	17 02	17 11	17 17		17 24	17 37	17 41	17 57	
Shenfield d		15 39		15 59				16 19		16 39			16 59			17 19			17 39		17 59	
Billericay d		15 45		16 05				16 25		16 45			17 05			17 25			17 45		18 05	
Wickford d		15 51		16 11	16 16			16 31		16 51	16 56		17 11			17 31	17 36		17 51		18 11	18 16
Battlesbridge d					16 20						17 00						17 40					18 20
South Woodham Ferrers d					16 24						17 04						17 44					18 24
North Fambridge d					16 31						17 11						17 51					18 31
Althorne d					16 36						17 16						17 56					18 36
Burnham-on-Crouch d					16 41						17 21						18 01					18 41
Southminster a					16 47						17 27						18 07					18 47
Rayleigh d		15 56		16 16				16 36		16 56			17 16			17 36			17 56		18 16	
Hockley d		16 01		16 21				16 41		17 01			17 21			17 41			18 01		18 21	
Rochford d		16 04		16 24				16 44		17 04			17 24			17 44			18 04		18 24	
Southend Airport d		16 07		16 27				16 47		17 07			17 27			17 47			18 07		18 27	
Prittlewell d		16 10		16 30				16 50		17 10			17 30			17 50			18 10		18 30	
Southend Victoria a		16 14		16 34				16 54		17 14			17 34			17 54			18 14		18 34	

	LE C	LE D	LE	LE ◇ A	LE	LE	LE ◇ B	LE	LE C	LE D	LE	LE	LE ◇ A	LE ◇	LE ◇ B	LE E	LE ◇	LE	LE C	LE D	LE ◇	LE A
London Liverpool Street d	17 38	17 48	17 55	18 02	18 13		18 18	18 35	18 38	18 48	18 55		19 02	19 13	19 18	19 32	19 35		19 38	19 48	19 55	20 02
Stratford d	17 45	17 55	18 02	18 09	18 20		18 25	18 42	18 45	18 55	19 02		19 09	19 20	19 25	19 39	19 43		19 46	19 55	20 02	20 09
Romford d	17 53				18 28				18 53					19 28					19 54			
Shenfield a	18 02	18 11	18 17	18 24	18 37		18 41	18 57	19 02	19 11	19 17		19 24	19 37	19 41	19 56	19 59		20 03	20 11	20 17	20 24
Shenfield d			18 19		18 39			18 59			19 19			19 39			19 59				20 19	
Billericay d			18 25		18 45			19 05			19 25			19 45			20 05				20 25	
Wickford d			18 31		18 51	18 56		19 11			19 31	19 36		19 51			20 12	20 16			20 31	
Battlesbridge d						19 00						19 40						20 20				
South Woodham Ferrers d						19 04						19 44						20 24				
North Fambridge d						19 11						19 51						20 31				
Althorne d						19 16						19 56						20 36				
Burnham-on-Crouch d						19 21						20 01						20 41				
Southminster a						19 27						20 07						20 47				
Rayleigh d			18 36		18 56			19 16			19 36			19 56			20 17				20 36	
Hockley d			18 41		19 01			19 21			19 41			20 01			20 21				20 41	
Rochford d			18 44		19 04			19 24			19 44			20 04			20 25				20 44	
Southend Airport d			18 47		19 07			19 27			19 47			20 07			20 28				20 47	
Prittlewell d			18 50		19 10			19 30			19 50			20 10			20 31				20 50	
Southend Victoria a			18 54		19 14			19 34			19 54			20 14			20 35				20 54	

A To Ipswich
B To Clacton-on-Sea
C To Colchester Town
D To Braintree
E To Harwich International

Table T006-F

Saturdays

26 May to 8 December

London Liverpool Street - Shenfield - Wickford - Southminster and Southend

		LE	LE	LE	LE	LE	LE	LE	LE	LE	LE	LE	LE	LE	LE	LE	LE	LE	LE	LE	LE	LE
		◇1	1	◇1	◇1	1	1	◇1	1	1	◇1	◇1	◇1	1	1	1	◇1	1	◇1	1	◇1	1
				A		B	C			D		A			B	C		E			A	E
London Liverpool Street 15 ⊖	d	20 13		20 18	20 35	20 38	20 48	20 55		21 02	21 13	21 18	21 35		21 38	21 48	21 55	22 02	22 13		22 18	22 32
Stratford 7 ⊖ ⛴	d	20 20		20 25	20 42	20 45	20 55	21 02		21 09	21 20	21 25	21 42		21 45	21 55	22 02	22 09	22 20		22 25	22 41
Romford	d	20 28				20 53					21 28				21 53				22 28			22 49
Shenfield 3	a	20 37		20 41	20 58	21 02	21 11	21 17		21 24	21 37	21 41	21 57		22 02	22 11	22 17	22 24	22 37		22 41	22 58
	d	20 39			20 59			21 19			21 39		21 59				22 19		22 39			
Billericay	d	20 45			21 05			21 25			21 45		22 05				22 25		22 45			
Wickford 2	d	20 51	20 56		21 11			21 31	21 36		21 51		22 11	22 16			22 31		22 51	22 56		
Battlesbridge	d		21 00						21 40					22 20						23 00		
South Woodham Ferrers	d		21 04						21 44					22 24						23 04		
North Fambridge	d		21 11						21 51					22 31						23 11		
Althorne	d		21 16						21 56					22 36						23 16		
Burnham-on-Crouch	d		21 21						22 01					22 41						23 21		
Southminster	a		21 27						22 07					22 47						23 27		
Rayleigh	d	20 56			21 16			21 36			21 56		22 16				22 36		22 56			
Hockley	d	21 01			21 21			21 41			22 01		22 21				22 41		23 01			
Rochford	d	21 04			21 24			21 44			22 04		22 24				22 44		23 04			
Southend Airport ✈	d	21 07			21 27			21 47			22 07		22 27				22 47		23 07			
Prittlewell	d	21 10			21 30			21 50			22 10		22 30				22 50		23 10			
Southend Victoria	a	21 14			21 34			21 54			22 14		22 34				22 54		23 14			

		LE	LE	LE	LE	LE	LE
		◇1	1	1	1	1	1
			F		E		E
London Liverpool Street 15 ⊖	d	22 44	23 02	23 14	23 32	23 44	23 58
Stratford 7 ⊖ ⛴	d	22 51	23 09	23 21	23 41	23 51	00 05
Romford	d	23 04		23 34		00 04	
Shenfield 3	a	23 21	23 32	23 51	00 03	00 21	00 29
	d	23 21		23 51		00 21	
Billericay	d	23 27		23 57		00 27	
Wickford 2	d	23 33		00 03		00 33	
Battlesbridge	d						
South Woodham Ferrers	d						
North Fambridge	d						
Althorne	d						
Burnham-on-Crouch	d						
Southminster	a						
Rayleigh	d	23 38		00 08		00 38	
Hockley	d	23 42		00 12		00 42	
Rochford	d	23 46		00 16		00 46	
Southend Airport ✈	d	23 48		00 18		00 48	
Prittlewell	d	23 51		00 21		00 51	
Southend Victoria	a	23 59		00 29		00 59	

Sundays

20 May to 2 December

		LE	LE	LE	LE	LE	LE	LE	LE	LE	LE	LE
		1	1	1	1	1	1	1	1	1	1	1
		G	G	H		E						D
London Liverpool Street 15 ⊖	d				00 15	00 18	00 50		07 14		07 44	07 55
Stratford 7 ⊖ ⛴	d			00 05	00 22	00 25	00 57		07 21		07 51	08 02
Romford	d		00 04		00 32		01 08		07 34		08 04	08 13
Shenfield 3	a		00 21	00 29	00 44	00 47	01 20		07 51		08 21	08 26
	d		00 21		00 45		01 20		07 51		08 21	
Billericay	d		00 27		00 51		01 26		07 57		08 27	
Wickford 2	d	00 03	00 33		00 56		01 31	07 30	08 03	08 06	08 33	
Battlesbridge	d							07 34		08 10		
South Woodham Ferrers	d							07 38		08 14		
North Fambridge	d							07 44		08 21		
Althorne	d							07 49		08 26		
Burnham-on-Crouch	d							07 54		08 31		
Southminster	a							08 00		08 38		
Rayleigh	d	00 08	00 38		01 01		01 36		08 08		08 38	
Hockley	d	00 12	00 42		01 06		01 41		08 12		08 42	
Rochford	d	00 16	00 46		01 09		01 44		08 16		08 46	
Southend Airport ✈	d	00 18	00 48		01 12		01 47		08 18		08 48	
Prittlewell	d	00 21	00 51		01 15		01 50					
Southend Victoria	a	00 29	00 59		01 23		01 58		08 25		08 55	

		LE	LE	LE	LE	LE		LE	LE	LE	LE	LE
		1	1	1	1	1		1	1	1	◇1	1
		F			A			F			A	
London Liverpool Street 15 ⊖	d	08 02	08 14		08 32	08 44		21 02	21 14		21 32	21 44
Stratford 7 ⊖ ⛴	d	08 09	08 21		08 39	08 51		21 09	21 21		21 39	21 51
Romford	d		08 34			09 04			21 34			22 04
Shenfield 3	a	08 31	08 51		09 01	09 21		21 31	21 51		22 01	22 21
	d		08 51			09 21	and at		21 51			22 21
Billericay	d		08 57			09 27	the same		21 57			22 27
Wickford 2	d		09 03	09 06		09 33	minutes		22 03	22 06		22 33
Battlesbridge	d			09 10			past			22 10		
South Woodham Ferrers	d			09 14			each			22 14		
North Fambridge	d			09 21			hour until			22 21		
Althorne	d			09 26						22 26		
Burnham-on-Crouch	d			09 31						22 31		
Southminster	a			09 37						22 37		
Rayleigh	d		09 08			09 38			22 08			22 38
Hockley	d		09 12			09 42			22 12			22 42
Rochford	d		09 16			09 46			22 16			22 46
Southend Airport ✈	d		09 18			09 48			22 18			22 48
Prittlewell	d											
Southend Victoria	a		09 25			09 55			22 25			22 55

A To Clacton-on-Sea
B To Colchester Town
C To Braintree
D To Harwich International
E To Colchester
F To Ipswich
G From London Liverpool Street
H From London Liverpool Street to Colchester

Table T006-F

Sundays

20 May to 2 December

London Liverpool Street - Shenfield - Wickford - Southminster and Southend

		LE	LE	LE	LE	LE	LE	LE	LE
		1	1	◇1	1	1	1	1	1
		A		B		A		C	
London Liverpool Street 15 ⊖	d	22 02	22 14	22 32	22 44	23 02	23 14	23 32	23 44
Stratford 7 ⊖ ⛴	d	22 09	22 21	22 39	22 51	23 09	23 21	23 39	23 51
Romford	d		22 34		23 04		23 34		00 04
Shenfield 3	a	22 31	22 51	23 01	23 21	23 31	23 51	00 01	00 21
	d		22 51		23 21		23 51		00 21
Billericay	d		22 57		23 27		23 57		00 27
Wickford 2	d		23 03		23 33		00 03		00 33
Battlesbridge	d								
South Woodham Ferrers	d								
North Fambridge	d								
Althorne	d								
Burnham-on-Crouch	d								
Southminster	a								
Rayleigh	d		23 08		23 38		00 08		00 38
Hockley	d		23 12		23 42		00 12		00 42
Rochford	d		23 16		23 46		00 16		00 46
Southend Airport ✈	d		23 18		23 48		00 18		00 48
Prittlewell	d								
Southend Victoria	a		23 28		23 58		00 28		00 58

A To Ipswich
B To Clacton-on-Sea
C To Colchester

Southend and Southminster - Wickford - Shenfield - London Liverpool Street

Miles	Miles			LE	LE	LE A	LE	LE A	LE	LE	LE	LE ◇ B	LE	LE C	LE	LE ◇ B	LE	LE	LE D	LE	LE E	LE	LE
0	—	**Southend Victoria**	d	04 00	04 30		05 00		05 20		05 40		06 00		06 11			06 26		06 40		06 50	
0¾	—	Prittlewell	d	04 02	04 32		05 02		05 22		05 42		06 02		06 13			06 28		06 42		06 52	
1¾	—	Southend Airport ✈	d	04 05	04 35		05 05		05 25		05 45		06 05		06 16			06 31		06 45		06 55	
2¾	—	Rochford	d	04 08	04 38		05 08		05 28		05 48		06 08		06 19			06 34		06 48		06 58	
5¼	—	Hockley	d	04 12	04 42		05 12		05 32		05 52		06 12		06 23			06 38		06 52		07 02	
8½	—	Rayleigh	d	04 16	04 46		05 16		05 36		05 56		06 16		06 27			06 42		06 56		07 06	
—	0	**Southminster**	d							05 26							06 09						06 48
—	2¾	Burnham-on-Crouch	d							05 30							06 13						06 52
—	5¾	Althorne	d							05 35							06 18						06 57
—	8¾	North Fambridge	d							05 41							06 24						07 03
—	11½	South Woodham Ferrers	d							05 46							06 30						07 10
—	14	Battlesbridge	d							05 50							06 34						07 14
12½	16½	**Wickford**	d	04 21	04 51		05 21		05 41	05a56	06 01		06 21		06 32		06 40	06 47		07 01		07 11	07 19
17¼	21¼	Billericay	d	04 27	04 57		05 27		05 47		06 07		06 27		06 39		06 46	06 53		07 08		07 18	07 26
—	—	**Shenfield**	a	04 38	05 08		05 35		05 55		06 15		06 35		06 45		06 53	07 01		07 14		07 24	07 32
21¼	25¼	**Shenfield**	d	04 38	05 08	05 24	05 35	05 53	05 55		06 15	06 25	06 35	06 42	06 45	06 50	06 53	07 01	07 08	07 14	07 19	07 24	07 32
29	33	Romford	d			05 32																	
37½	41½	Stratford ⊖	d	04 58	05 28	05 42	05 49	06 07	06 10		06 31	06 39	06 49	06s58	07s02	07s06	07s09	07s19	07s23	07s31	07s35	07s41	07s49
41½	45½	**London Liverpool Street** ⊖	a	05 06	05 37	05 51	05 58	06 16	06 19		06 40	06 48	06 58	07 09	07 14	07 18	07 21	07 30	07 35	07 42	07 46	07 52	08 01

		LE	LE C	LE ◇ B	LE	LE C	LE	LE F	LE	LE ◇ B	LE	LE	LE F	LE G	LE	LE B	LE	LE F	LE	LE E	LE B	LE	LE
Southend Victoria	d	07 03			07 13		07 23		07 32		07 42				07 52		08 03		08 12				08 30
Prittlewell	d	07 05			07 15		07 25		07 34		07 44				07 54		08 05		08 14				08 32
Southend Airport ✈	d	07 08			07 18		07 28		07 37		07 47				07 57		08 08		08 17				08 35
Rochford	d	07 11			07 21		07 31		07 40		07 50				08 00		08 11		08 20				08 38
Hockley	d	07 15			07 25		07 35		07 44		07 54				08 04		08 15		08 24				08 42
Rayleigh	d	07 19			07 29		07 39		07 48		07 58				08 08		08 19		08 28				08 46
Southminster	d											07 37										08 16	
Burnham-on-Crouch	d											07 41										08 20	
Althorne	d											07 46										08 25	
North Fambridge	d											07 52										08 32	
South Woodham Ferrers	d											07 59										08 38	
Battlesbridge	d																					08 42	
Wickford	d	07 24			07 34		07 44		07 53		08 03	08 07			08 13		08 24		08 33			08 47	08 51
Billericay	d	07 31			07 41		07 51		08 00		08 10	08 14			08 20		08 31		08 40			08 54	08 58
Shenfield	a				07 47		07 57		08 06		08 16				08 26		08 37		08 46			09 00	09 04
Shenfield	d		07 39	07 41	07 47	07 50	07 57	08 01	08 06	08 09	08 16		08 21	08 24	08 26	08 29	08 37	08 42	08 46	08 51	08 55	09 00	09 04
Romford	d																		08 55				
Stratford ⊖	d	07s52	07s55	07s58	08s04	08s07	08s15	08s18	08s23	08s25	08s33	08s35	08s38	08s40	08s43	08s45	08s56	08s59	09s05	09s08		09s17	09s21
London Liverpool Street ⊖	a	08 03	08 07	08 09	08 15	08 19	08 26	08 30	08 36	08 38	08 46	08 48	08 50	08 54	08 56	08 58	09 08	09 11	09 16	09 19	09 21	09 28	09 33

		LE H	LE C	LE ◇ I	LE	LE	LE E	LE	LE D	LE	LE	LE ◇ B	LE D	LE	LE E	LE	LE	LE J	LE	LE ◇ B	LE D	LE
Southend Victoria	d				08 52			09 10		09 30				09 50		10 10			10 30			10 50
Prittlewell	d				08 54			09 12		09 32				09 52		10 12			10 32			10 52
Southend Airport ✈	d				08 57			09 15		09 35				09 55		10 15			10 35			10 55
Rochford	d				09 00			09 18		09 38				09 58		10 18			10 38			10 58
Hockley	d				09 04			09 22		09 42				10 02		10 22			10 42			11 02
Rayleigh	d				09 08			09 26		09 46				10 06		10 26			10 46			11 06
Southminster	d					08 56					09 36						10 16					
Burnham-on-Crouch	d					09 00					09 40						10 20					
Althorne	d					09 05					09 45						10 25					
North Fambridge	d					09 11					09 51						10 31					
South Woodham Ferrers	d					09 16					09 56						10 36					
Battlesbridge	d					09 20					10 00						10 40					
Wickford	d				09 13	09a26		09 31		09 51	10a06			10 11		10 31	10a46		10 51			11 11
Billericay	d				09 20			09 37		09 57				10 17		10 37			10 57			11 17
Shenfield	a				09 27			09 45		10 05				10 25		10 45			11 05			11 25
Shenfield	d	09 09	09 21	09 25	09 27		09 38	09 46	09 51	10 05		10 08	10 18	10 25	10 38	10 45		10 51	11 05	11 08	11 20	11 25
Romford	d							09 55					10 26			10 53					11 28	
Stratford ⊖	d	09s25	09s37	09s41	09s43		09 52	10 03	10 06	10 19		10 22	10 34	10 39	10 52	11 01		11 05	11 19	11 22	11 36	11 39
London Liverpool Street ⊖	a	09 36	09 50	09 54	09 55		10 01	10 12	10 15	10 28		10 31	10 43	10 48	11 01	11 10		11 14	11 28	11 31	11 45	11 48

		LE	LE E	LE	LE J	LE	LE	LE ◇ B	LE D	LE	LE E	LE ◇	LE	LE J	LE ◇	LE ◇ B	LE D	LE ◇	LE	LE E	LE ◇	LE J	LE ◇
Southend Victoria	d			11 10		11 30				11 50		12 10			12 30			12 50			13 10		13 30
Prittlewell	d			11 12		11 32				11 52		12 12			12 32			12 52			13 12		13 32
Southend Airport ✈	d			11 15		11 35				11 55		12 15			12 35			12 55			13 15		13 35
Rochford	d			11 18		11 38				11 58		12 18			12 38			12 58			13 18		13 38
Hockley	d			11 22		11 42				12 02		12 22			12 42			13 02			13 22		13 42
Rayleigh	d			11 26		11 46				12 06		12 26			12 46			13 06			13 26		13 46
Southminster	d	10 56					11 36						12 16						12 56				
Burnham-on-Crouch	d	11 00					11 40						12 20						13 00				
Althorne	d	11 05					11 45						12 25						13 05				
North Fambridge	d	11 11					11 51						12 31						13 11				
South Woodham Ferrers	d	11 16					11 56						12 36						13 16				
Battlesbridge	d	11 20					12 00						12 40						13 20				
Wickford	d	11a26		11 31		11 51	12a06			12 11		12 31	12a46		12 51			13 11	13a26		13 31		13 51
Billericay	d			11 37		11 57				12 17		12 37			12 57			13 17			13 37		13 57
Shenfield	a			11 45		12 05				12 25		12 45			13 05			13 25			13 45		14 05
Shenfield	d		11 38	11 45	11 51	12 05		12 08	12 20	12 25	12 38	12 45		12 51	13 05	13 08	13 20	13 25		13 38	13 45	13 51	14 05
Romford	d			11 53					12 28			12 53					13 28				13 53		
Stratford ⊖	d		11 52	12 02	12 05	12 19		12 22	12 36	12 39	12 52	13 01		13 05	13 19	13 22	13 36	13 39		13 52	14 01	14 05	14 19
London Liverpool Street ⊖	a		12 01	12 10	12 14	12 28		12 31	12 45	12 48	13 01	13 10		13 14	13 28	13 31	13 45	13 48		14 03	14 10	14 14	14 28

A From Colchester
B From Colchester Town
C From Witham
D From Colchester Town
E From Braintree
F From Chelmsford
G From Harwich International
H From Harwich Town
I From Clacton-on-Sea
J From Ipswich

Table T006-R

Mondays to Fridays

21 May to 7 December

Southend and Southminster - Wickford - Shenfield - London Liverpool Street

		LE	LE ◇ A	LE B	LE ◇	LE C	LE ◇	LE	LE D	LE ◇	LE ◇ A	LE B	LE ◇	LE	LE C	LE ◇	LE D	LE ◇	LE	LE ◇ A	LE B	LE ◇
Southend Victoria	d				13 50		14 10			14 30			14 50			15 10		15 30				15 50
Prittlewell	d				13 52		14 12			14 32			14 52			15 12		15 32				15 52
Southend Airport ✈	d				13 55		14 15			14 35			14 55			15 15		15 35				15 55
Rochford	d				13 58		14 18			14 38			14 58			15 18		15 38				15 58
Hockley	d				14 02		14 22			14 42			15 02			15 22		15 42				16 02
Rayleigh	d				14 06		14 26			14 46			15 06			15 26		15 46				16 06
Southminster	d	13 36						14 16						14 56					15 36			
Burnham-on-Crouch	d	13 40						14 20						15 00					15 40			
Althorne	d	13 45						14 25						15 05					15 45			
North Fambridge	d	13 51						14 31						15 11					15 51			
South Woodham Ferrers	d	13 56						14 36						15 16					15 56			
Battlesbridge	d	14 00						14 40						15 20					16 00			
Wickford	d	14a06			14 11		14 31	14a46		14 51			15 11	15a26		15 31		15 51	16a06			16 11
Billericay	d				14 17		14 37			14 57			15 17			15 37		15 57				16 17
Shenfield	a				14 25		14 45			15 05			15 25			15 45		16 05				16 25
Shenfield	d		14 08	14 20	14 25	14 38	14 45		14 51	15 05	15 08	15 20	15 25		15 38	15 45	15 51	16 05		16 08	16 20	16 25
Romford	d			14 28			14 53					15 28				15 53						
Stratford ⊖	d		14 22	14 36	14 39	14 52	15 01		15 05	15 19	15 22	15 36	15 39		15 52	16 01	16 05	16 19		16 22	16 35	16 39
London Liverpool Street ⊖	a		14 31	14 47	14 50	15 01	15 10		15 15	15 28	15 33	15 45	15 48		16 01	16 11	16 14	16 28		16 31	16 44	16 48

		LE C	LE ◇	LE	LE D	LE ◇	LE ◇ A	LE B	LE ◇	LE E	LE C	LE ◇	LE	LE D	LE ◇	LE ◇ A	LE ◇	LE C	LE ◇	LE B	LE F	LE ◇	LE
Southend Victoria	d		16 10			16 30			16 50			17 10			17 25		17 35		17 50			18 05	
Prittlewell	d		16 12			16 32			16 52			17 12			17 27		17 37		17 52			18 07	
Southend Airport ✈	d		16 15			16 35			16 55			17 15			17 30		17 40		17 55			18 10	
Rochford	d		16 18			16 38			16 58			17 18			17 33		17 43		17 58			18 13	
Hockley	d		16 22			16 42			17 02			17 22			17 37		17 47		18 02			18 17	
Rayleigh	d		16 26			16 46			17 06			17 26			17 41		17 51		18 06			18 21	
Southminster	d			16 14									17 06										17 56
Burnham-on-Crouch	d			16 18									17 10										18 00
Althorne	d			16 23									17 15										18 05
North Fambridge	d			16 29									17 21										18 14
South Woodham Ferrers	d			16 34									17 26										18 19
Battlesbridge	d			16 38									17 30										18 23
Wickford	d		16 31	16a44		16 51			17 11			17 31	17 37		17 46		17 56		18 11			18 26	18a29
Billericay	d		16 37			16 57			17 17			17 37			17 52		18 02		18 17			18 32	
Shenfield	a		16 45			17 05			17 25			17 45	17 48		18 00		18 10		18 25			18 40	
Shenfield	d	16 40	16 45		16 51	17 05	17 08	17 22	17 25	17 28	17 38	17 45	17 49	17 51	18 00	18 08	18 10	18 20	18 25	18 27	18 38	18 40	
Romford	d																	18 28					
Stratford ⊖	d	16 54	16 59		17 06	17 19	17 22	17 36	17 39	17 42	17 52	17 59	18 08	18 06	18 14	18 22	18 25	18 36	18 39	18 42	18 52	18 55	
London Liverpool Street ⊖	a	17 03	17 13		17 16	17 29	17 34	17 46	17 49	17 53	18 01	18 11	18 17	18 15	18 24	18 31	18 35	18 45	18 48	18 51	19 01	19 06	

		LE E	LE ◇	LE ◇	LE ◇ A	LE C	LE D	LE ◇	LE	LE E	LE ◇	LE D	LE ◇	LE	LE ◇ A	LE B	LE ◇	LE D	LE	LE	LE C	LE D	LE
Southend Victoria	d		18 20	18 30				18 50			19 10		19 30				19 50		20 10				20 30
Prittlewell	d		18 22	18 32				18 52			19 12		19 32				19 52		20 12				20 32
Southend Airport ✈	d		18 25	18 35				18 55			19 15		19 35				19 55		20 15				20 35
Rochford	d		18 28	18 38				18 58			19 18		19 38				19 58		20 18				20 38
Hockley	d		18 32	18 42				19 02			19 22		19 42				20 02		20 22				20 42
Rayleigh	d		18 36	18 46				19 06			19 26		19 46				20 06		20 26				20 46
Southminster	d								18 36					19 19						20 16			
Burnham-on-Crouch	d								18 40					19 23						20 20			
Althorne	d								18 45					19 28						20 25			
North Fambridge	d								19 01					19 39						20 31			
South Woodham Ferrers	d								19 06					19 44						20 36			
Battlesbridge	d								19 10					19 48						20 40			
Wickford	d		18 41	18 51				19 11	19 17		19 31		19 51	19 55			20 11		20 31	20a46			20 51
Billericay	d		18 47	18 57				19 17	19 23		19 37		19 57				20 17		20 37				20 57
Shenfield	a		18 55	19 05				19 25	19 36		19 45		20 05	20 08			20 25		20 45				21 05
Shenfield	d	18 51	18 57	19 05	19 08	19 13	19 20	19 25		19 38	19 45	19 51	20 05		20 08	20 20	20 25	20 38	20 45		20 47	20 53	21 05
Romford	d						19 28				19 53					20 28			20 53				
Stratford ⊖	d	19 05	19 11	19 19	19 22	19 27	19 36	19 39		19 52	20 01	20 05	20 19		20 22	20 36	20 39	20 52	21 01			21 07	21 19
London Liverpool Street ⊖	a	19 14	19 20	19 28	19 33	19 36	19 45	19 48		20 01	20 10	20 14	20 28		20 31	20 45	20 48	21 01	21 10		21 12	21 16	21 28

		LE ◇ A	LE	LE	LE B	LE C	LE	LE G	LE	LE	LE ◇ A	LE B	LE	LE	LE C	LE B	LE	LE ◇ A	LE D	LE	LE ◇ H	LE
Southend Victoria	d		20 50				21 10		21 30				22 00				22 30			23 00		
Prittlewell	d		20 52				21 12		21 32				22 02				22 32			23 02		
Southend Airport ✈	d		20 55				21 15		21 35				22 05				22 35			23 05		
Rochford	d		20 58				21 18		21 38				22 08				22 38			23 08		
Hockley	d		21 02				21 22		21 42				22 12				22 42			23 12		
Rayleigh	d		21 06				21 26		21 46				22 16				22 46			23 16		
Southminster	d			20 56						21 36				22 16								22 56
Burnham-on-Crouch	d			21 00						21 40				22 20								23 00
Althorne	d			21 05						21 45				22 25								23 05
North Fambridge	d			21 11						21 51				22 31								23 11
South Woodham Ferrers	d			21 16						21 56				22 36								23 16
Battlesbridge	d			21 20						22 00				22 40								23 20
Wickford	d		21 11	21a26			21 31		21 51	22a07			22 21	22a46			22 51			23 21		23 26
Billericay	d		21 17				21 37		21 57				22 27				22 57			23 27		23 32
Shenfield	a		21 25				21 45		22 05				22 35				23 05			23 35		23 39
Shenfield	d	21 08	21 25		21 27	21 38	21 45	21 51	22 05		22 08	22 20	22 35		22 38	22 51	23 05	23 08	23 20	23 35	23 37	23 39
Romford	d						21 53					22 28							23 28			23 47
Stratford ⊖	d	21 22	21 39		21 42	21 52	22 01	22 05	22 19		22 22	22 36	22 49		22 52	23s05	23 19	23 22	23 36	23 49	23s52	23 56
London Liverpool Street ⊖	a	21 31	21 48		21 51	22 01	22 10	22 14	22 28		22 31	22 45	22 58		23 01	23 14	23 28	23 31	23 48	00 01	00 03	00 06

A From Clacton-on-Sea
B From Colchester Town
C From Braintree
D From Ipswich
E From Colchester
F From Witham
G From Harwich International
H From Norwich

Southend and Southminster - Wickford - Shenfield - London Liverpool Street

		LE	LE	LE A	LE	LE A	LE	LE A	LE	LE	LE A	LE	LE ◇ B	LE C	LE	LE	LE D	LE	LE E	LE	LE	LE ◇ B	LE F
Southend Victoria	d	04 00	04 30		05 00		05 30		06 00			06 30			06 50			07 10		07 30			
Prittlewell	d	04 02	04 32		05 02		05 32		06 02			06 32			06 52			07 12		07 32			
Southend Airport ✈	d	04 05	04 35		05 05		05 35		06 05			06 35			06 55			07 15		07 35			
Rochford	d	04 08	04 38		05 08		05 38		06 08			06 38			06 58			07 18		07 38			
Hockley	d	04 12	04 42		05 12		05 42		06 12			06 42			07 02			07 22		07 42			
Rayleigh	d	04 16	04 46		05 16		05 46		06 16			06 46			07 06			07 26		07 46			
Southminster	d									06 16						06 56					07 36		
Burnham-on-Crouch	d									06 20						07 00					07 40		
Althorne	d									06 25						07 05					07 45		
North Fambridge	d									06 31						07 11					07 51		
South Woodham Ferrers	d									06 36						07 16					07 56		
Battlesbridge	d									06 40						07 20					08 00		
Wickford 2	d	04 21	04 51		05 21		05 51		06 21	06a46		06 51			07 11	07a26		07 31		07 51	08a06		
Billericay	d	04 27	04 57		05 27		05 57		06 27			06 57			07 17			07 37		07 57			
Shenfield	a	04 38	05 08		05 35		06 05		06 35			07 05			07 25			07 45		08 05			
Shenfield 3	d	04 38	05 08	05 24	05 35	05 53	06 05	06 24	06 35		06 46	07 05	07 08	07 20	07 25		07 38	07 45	07 51	08 05		08 08	08 20
Romford	d			05 32	05 43				06 43		06 54			07 28				07 53					08 28
Stratford 7 ⊖	d	04 58	05 28	05 42	05 51	06 07	06 19	06 38	06 51		07 02	07 19	07 22	07 36	07 39		07 52	08 01	08 05	08 19		08 22	08 36
London Liverpool Street 15 ⊖	a	05 06	05 36	05 51	06 00	06 16	06 28	06 47	07 00		07 11	07 28	07 31	07 46	07 49		08 01	08 10	08 14	08 28		08 31	08 46

		LE	LE D	LE	LE	LE E	LE	LE ◇ B	LE C	LE	LE	LE D	LE	LE ◇ E	LE	LE	LE ◇ B	LE C	LE	LE D	LE	LE	LE ◇ E
Southend Victoria	d	07 50		08 10			08 30			08 50			09 10		09 30				09 50		10 10		
Prittlewell	d	07 52		08 12			08 32			08 52			09 12		09 32				09 52		10 12		
Southend Airport ✈	d	07 55		08 15			08 35			08 55			09 15		09 35				09 55		10 15		
Rochford	d	07 58		08 18			08 38			08 58			09 18		09 38				09 58		10 18		
Hockley	d	08 02		08 22			08 42			09 02			09 22		09 42				10 02		10 22		
Rayleigh	d	08 06		08 26			08 46			09 06			09 26		09 46				10 06		10 26		
Southminster	d				08 16						08 56					09 36						10 16	
Burnham-on-Crouch	d				08 20						09 00					09 40						10 20	
Althorne	d				08 25						09 05					09 45						10 25	
North Fambridge	d				08 31						09 11					09 51						10 31	
South Woodham Ferrers	d				08 36						09 16					09 56						10 36	
Battlesbridge	d				08 40						09 20					10 00						10 40	
Wickford 2	d	08 11		08 31	08a46		08 51			09 11	09a26		09 31		09 51	10a06			10 11		10 31	10a46	
Billericay	d	08 17		08 37			08 57			09 17			09 37		09 57				10 17		10 37		
Shenfield	a	08 25		08 45			09 05			09 25			09 45		10 05				10 25		10 45		
Shenfield 3	d	08 25	08 38	08 45		08 51	09 05	09 08	09 20	09 25		09 38	09 45	09 51	10 05		10 08	10 20	10 25	10 38	10 45		10 51
Romford	d			08 53					09 28				09 53					10 28			10 53		
Stratford 7 ⊖	d	08 39	08 52	09 01		09 05	09 19	09 22	09 36	09 39		09 52	10 01	10 05	10 19		10 22	10 36	10 39	10 52	11 01		11 05
London Liverpool Street 15 ⊖	a	08 49	09 01	09 10		09 14	09 28	09 31	09 46	09 49		10 01	10 10	10 14	10 28		10 31	10 46	10 49	11 01	11 10		11 14

		LE	LE ◇ B	LE C	LE	LE	LE D	LE ◇	LE ◇ E	LE ◇	LE	LE ◇ B	LE C	LE ◇	LE D	LE ◇	LE	LE E	LE ◇	LE ◇ B	LE C	LE ◇
Southend Victoria	d	10 30			10 50			11 10		11 30				11 50		12 10			12 30			12 50
Prittlewell	d	10 32			10 52			11 12		11 32				11 52		12 12			12 32			12 52
Southend Airport ✈	d	10 35			10 55			11 15		11 35				11 55		12 15			12 35			12 55
Rochford	d	10 38			10 58			11 18		11 38				11 58		12 18			12 38			12 58
Hockley	d	10 42			11 02			11 22		11 42				12 02		12 22			12 42			13 02
Rayleigh	d	10 46			11 06			11 26		11 46				12 06		12 26			12 46			13 06
Southminster	d					10 56					11 36						12 16					
Burnham-on-Crouch	d					11 00					11 40						12 20					
Althorne	d					11 05					11 45						12 25					
North Fambridge	d					11 11					11 51						12 31					
South Woodham Ferrers	d					11 16					11 56						12 36					
Battlesbridge	d					11 20					12 00						12 40					
Wickford 2	d	10 51			11 11	11a26		11 31		11 51	12a06			12 11		12 31	12a46		12 51			13 11
Billericay	d	10 57			11 17			11 37		11 57				12 17		12 37			12 57			13 17
Shenfield	a	11 05			11 25			11 45		12 05				12 25		12 45			13 05			13 25
Shenfield 3	d	11 05	11 08	11 20	11 25		11 38	11 45	11 51	12 05		12 08	12 20	12 25	12 38	12 45		12 51	13 05	13 08	13 20	13 25
Romford	d			11 28				11 53					12 28			12 53					13 28	
Stratford 7 ⊖	d	11 19	11 22	11 36	11 39		11 52	12 01	12 05	12 19		12 22	12 36	12 39	12 52	13 01		13 05	13 19	13 22	13 36	13 39
London Liverpool Street 15 ⊖	a	11 28	11 31	11 46	11 49		12 01	12 10	12 14	12 28		12 31	12 46	12 49	13 01	13 10		13 14	13 28	13 31	13 46	13 49

		LE	LE D	LE ◇	LE E	LE ◇	LE	LE ◇ B	LE C	LE ◇	LE D	LE ◇	LE	LE E	LE ◇	LE ◇ B	LE C	LE ◇	LE	LE D	LE ◇	LE E	LE ◇
Southend Victoria	d			13 10		13 30				13 50		14 10			14 30			14 50			15 10		15 30
Prittlewell	d			13 12		13 32				13 52		14 12			14 32			14 52			15 12		15 32
Southend Airport ✈	d			13 15		13 35				13 55		14 15			14 35			14 55			15 15		15 35
Rochford	d			13 18		13 38				13 58		14 18			14 38			14 58			15 18		15 38
Hockley	d			13 22		13 42				14 02		14 22			14 42			15 02			15 22		15 42
Rayleigh	d			13 26		13 46				14 06		14 26			14 46			15 06			15 26		15 46
Southminster	d	12 56					13 36						14 16						14 56				
Burnham-on-Crouch	d	13 00					13 40						14 20						15 00				
Althorne	d	13 05					13 45						14 25						15 05				
North Fambridge	d	13 11					13 51						14 31						15 11				
South Woodham Ferrers	d	13 16					13 56						14 36						15 16				
Battlesbridge	d	13 20					14 00						14 40						15 20				
Wickford 2	d	13a26		13 31		13 51	14a06			14 11		14 31	14a46		14 51			15 11	15a26		15 31		15 51
Billericay	d			13 37		13 57				14 17		14 37			14 57			15 17			15 37		15 57
Shenfield	a			13 45		14 05				14 25		14 45			15 05			15 25			15 45		16 05
Shenfield 3	d		13 38	13 45	13 51	14 05		14 08	14 20	14 25	14 38	14 45		14 51	15 05	15 08	15 20	15 25		15 38	15 45	15 51	16 05
Romford	d			13 53					14 28			14 53					15 28				15 53		
Stratford 7 ⊖	d		13 52	14 01	14 05	14 19		14 22	14 36	14 39	14 52	15 01		15 05	15 19	15 22	15 36	15 39		15 52	16 01	16 05	16 19
London Liverpool Street 15 ⊖	a		14 01	14 10	14 14	14 28		14 31	14 46	14 50	15 01	15 10		15 14	15 28	15 31	15 46	15 49		16 01	16 10	16 14	16 28

A From Colchester
B From Clacton-on-Sea
C From Colchester Town
D From Braintree
E From Ipswich
F From Harwich International

Table T006-R

Saturdays
26 May to 8 December

Southend and Southminster - Wickford - Shenfield - London Liverpool Street

		LE	LE ◇ A	LE B	LE ◇	LE C	LE	LE	LE D	LE	LE ◇ A	LE B	LE	LE	LE C	LE	LE D	LE	LE	LE ◇ A	LE B	LE
Southend Victoria	d				15 50		16 10			16 30			16 50			17 10		17 30				17 50
Prittlewell	d				15 52		16 12			16 32			16 52			17 12		17 32				17 52
Southend Airport ✈	d				15 55		16 15			16 35			16 55			17 15		17 35				17 55
Rochford	d				15 58		16 18			16 38			16 58			17 18		17 38				17 58
Hockley	d				16 02		16 22			16 42			17 02			17 22		17 42				18 02
Rayleigh	d				16 06		16 26			16 46			17 06			17 26		17 46				18 06
Southminster	d	15 36						16 16						16 56					17 36			
Burnham-on-Crouch	d	15 40						16 20						17 00					17 40			
Althorne	d	15 45						16 25						17 05					17 45			
North Fambridge	d	15 51						16 31						17 11					17 51			
South Woodham Ferrers	d	15 56						16 36						17 16					17 56			
Battlesbridge	d	16 00						16 40						17 20					18 00			
Wickford 2	d	16a06			16 11		16 31	16a46		16 51			17 11	17a26		17 31		17 51	18a06			18 11
Billericay	d				16 17		16 37			16 57			17 17			17 37		17 57				18 17
Shenfield	a				16 25		16 45			17 05			17 25			17 44		18 05				18 25
Shenfield 3	d		16 08	16 20	16 25	16 38	16 45		16 51	17 05	17 08	17 20	17 25		17 38	17 45	17 51	18 05		18 08	18 20	18 25
Romford	d			16 28			16 53					17 28				17 53					18 28	
Stratford 7 ⊖	d		16 22	16 36	16 39	16 52	17 01		17 05	17 19	17 22	17 36	17 39		17 52	18 01	18 05	18 19		18 22	18 36	18 39
London Liverpool Street 15 ⊖	a		16 31	16 46	16 49	17 01	17 10		17 14	17 28	17 31	17 46	17 49		18 03	18 10	18 14	18 28		18 31	18 46	18 49

		LE C	LE	LE	LE D	LE	LE ◇ A	LE B	LE	LE	LE C	LE ◇	LE D	LE ◇	LE	LE ◇ A	LE B	LE ◇	LE C	LE ◇	LE	LE D	LE ◇
Southend Victoria	d		18 10			18 30			18 50			19 10		19 30				19 50		20 10			20 30
Prittlewell	d		18 12			18 32			18 52			19 12		19 32				19 52		20 12			20 32
Southend Airport ✈	d		18 15			18 35			18 55			19 15		19 35				19 55		20 15			20 35
Rochford	d		18 18			18 38			18 58			19 18		19 38				19 58		20 18			20 38
Hockley	d		18 22			18 42			19 02			19 22		19 42				20 02		20 22			20 42
Rayleigh	d		18 26			18 46			19 06			19 26		19 46				20 06		20 26			20 46
Southminster	d			18 16						18 56					19 36						20 16		
Burnham-on-Crouch	d			18 20						19 00					19 40						20 20		
Althorne	d			18 25						19 05					19 45						20 25		
North Fambridge	d			18 31						19 11					19 51						20 31		
South Woodham Ferrers	d			18 36						19 16					19 56						20 36		
Battlesbridge	d			18 40						19 20					20 00						20 40		
Wickford 2	d		18 31	18a46		18 51			19 11	19a26		19 31		19 51	20a06			20 11		20 31	20a46		20 51
Billericay	d		18 37			18 57			19 17			19 37		19 57				20 17		20 37			20 57
Shenfield	a		18 45			19 05			19 25			19 45		20 05				20 25		20 45			21 05
Shenfield 3	d	18 38	18 45		18 51	19 05	19 08	19 20	19 25		19 38	19 45	19 51	20 05		20 08	20 20	20 25	20 38	20 45		20 51	21 05
Romford	d		18 53					19 28				19 53					20 28			20 53			
Stratford 7 ⊖	d	18 52	19 01		19 05	19 19	19 22	19 36	19 39		19 52	20 01	20 05	20 19		20 22	20 36	20 39	20 52	21 01		21 05	21 19
London Liverpool Street 15 ⊖	a	19 01	19 10		19 14	19 28	19 31	19 46	19 49		20 01	20 10	20 14	20 28		20 31	20 46	20 49	21 01	21 10		21 14	21 28

		LE ◇ A	LE B	LE ◇	LE	LE C	LE ◇	LE E	LE ◇	LE	LE ◇ A	LE B	LE ◇	LE	LE C	LE D	LE ◇	LE ◇ A	LE D	LE	LE ◇ F	LE
Southend Victoria	d			20 50			21 10		21 30				22 00				22 30			23 00		
Prittlewell	d			20 52			21 12		21 32				22 02				22 32			23 02		
Southend Airport ✈	d			20 55			21 15		21 35				22 05				22 35			23 05		
Rochford	d			20 58			21 18		21 38				22 08				22 38			23 08		
Hockley	d			21 02			21 22		21 42				22 12				22 42			23 12		
Rayleigh	d			21 06			21 26		21 46				22 16				22 46			23 16		
Southminster	d				20 56					21 36				22 16								22 56
Burnham-on-Crouch	d				21 00					21 40				22 20								23 00
Althorne	d				21 05					21 45				22 25								23 05
North Fambridge	d				21 11					21 51				22 31								23 11
South Woodham Ferrers	d				21 16					21 56				22 36								23 16
Battlesbridge	d				21 20					22 00				22 40								23 20
Wickford 2	d			21 11	21a26		21 31		21 51	22a06			22 21	22a46			22 51			23 21		23 26
Billericay	d			21 17			21 37		21 57				22 27				22 57			23 27		23 32
Shenfield	a			21 25			21 45		22 05				22 35				23 05			23 35		23 40
Shenfield 3	d	21 08	21 20	21 25		21 38	21 45	21 51	22 05		22 08	22 20	22 35		22 38	22 51	23 05	23 08	23 20	23 35	23 37	23 41
Romford	d		21 28				21 53					22 28							23 28			23 49
Stratford 7 ⊖	d	21 22	21 36	21 39		21 52	22 01	22 05	22 19		22 22	22 36	22 49		22 52	23s12	23s26	23s29	23s41	23s56	23s59	00s03
London Liverpool Street 15 ⊖	a	21 34	21 46	21 49		22 01	22 10	22 14	22 28		22 31	22 46	22 58		23 01	23 21	23 35	23 38	23 50	00 05	00 10	00 12

A From Clacton-on-Sea
B From Colchester Town
C From Braintree
D From Ipswich
E From Harwich International
F From Norwich

Table T006-R

Sundays

20 May to 2 December

Southend and Southminster - Wickford - Shenfield - London Liverpool Street

		LE	LE A	LE	LE B	LE	LE B	LE C	LE	LE	LE D	LE	LE E	LE	LE	LE D	LE	LE E	LE	LE	LE D
Southend Victoria	d	06 15		06 45		07 15			07 49			08 19		08 49			09 19		09 49		
Prittlewell	d																				
Southend Airport	d	06 19		06 49		07 19			07 53			08 23		08 53			09 23		09 53		
Rochford	d	06 22		06 52		07 22			07 56			08 26		08 56			09 26		09 56		
Hockley	d	06 26		06 56		07 26			08 00			08 30		09 00			09 30		10 00		
Rayleigh	d	06 30		07 00		07 30			08 04			08 34		09 04			09 34		10 04		
Southminster	d									08 06					09 06					10 06	
Burnham-on-Crouch	d									08 10					09 10					10 10	
Althorne	d									08 15					09 15					10 15	
North Fambridge	d									08 21					09 21					10 21	
South Woodham Ferrers	d									08 26					09 26					10 26	
Battlesbridge	d									08 30					09 30					10 30	
Wickford	d	06 35		07 05		07 35			08 10	08a37		08 40		09 10	09a37		09 40		10 10	10a37	
Billericay	d	06 41		07 11		07 41			08 16			08 46		09 16			09 46		10 16		
Shenfield	a	06 52		07 22		07 52			08 23			08 53		09 23			09 53		10 23		
Shenfield	d	06 53	07 11	07 23	07 41	07 53	08 11	08 20	08 23		08 41	08 53	09 11	09 23		09 41	09 53	10 11	10 23		10 41
Romford	d	07 07	07 21	07 37	07 51	08 07			08 37			09 07		09 37			10 07		10 37		
Stratford	d	07 20	07s35	07 50	08s05	08 20	08s35	08s50	08 50		09s05	09 20	09s35	09 50		10s05	10 20	10s35	10 50		11s05
London Liverpool Street	a	07 29	07 44	07 59	08 14	08 29	08 44	08 59	09 02		09 14	09 29	09 44	09 59		10 14	10 31	10 44	10 59		11 14

		LE		LE E	LE	LE	LE D	LE	LE E	LE	LE	LE D	LE	LE E	LE	LE	LE D	LE	LE E	LE	LE	LE D
Southend Victoria	d	10 19			14 49			15 19		15 49			16 19		16 49			17 19		17 49		
Prittlewell	d																					
Southend Airport	d	10 23			14 53			15 23		15 53			16 23		16 53			17 23		17 53		
Rochford	d	10 26			14 56			15 26		15 56			16 26		16 56			17 26		17 56		
Hockley	d	10 30	and at		15 00			15 30		16 00			16 30		17 00			17 30		18 00		
Rayleigh	d	10 34	the same		15 04			15 34		16 04			16 34		17 04			17 34		18 04		
Southminster	d		minutes			15 06					16 06					17 06					18 06	
Burnham-on-Crouch	d		past			15 10					16 10					17 10					18 10	
Althorne	d		each			15 15					16 15					17 15					18 15	
North Fambridge	d		hour until			15 21					16 21					17 21					18 21	
South Woodham Ferrers	d					15 26					16 26					17 26					18 26	
Battlesbridge	d					15 30					16 30					17 30					18 30	
Wickford	d	10 40			15 10	15a37		15 40		16 10	16a37		16 40		17 10	17a37		17 40		18 10	18a37	
Billericay	d	10 46			15 16			15 46		16 16			16 46		17 16			17 46		18 16		
Shenfield	a	10 53			15 23			15 53		16 23			16 53		17 23			17 53		18 23		
Shenfield	d	10 53		15 11	15 23		15 41	15 53	16 11	16 23		16 41	16 53	17 11	17 23		17 41	17 53	18 11	18 23		18 41
Romford	d	11 07			15 37			16 07		16 37			17 07		17 37			18 07		18 37		
Stratford	d	11 20		15s35	15 50		16s05	16 20	16s35	16 50		17s05	17 20	17s35	17 50		18s05	18 20	18s35	18 50		19s05
London Liverpool Street	a	11 29		15 44	15 59		16 14	16 29	16 44	16 59		17 14	17 31	17 44	17 59		18 14	18 31	18 44	18 59		19 14

		LE	LE E	LE	LE	LE D	LE	LE E	LE	LE	LE D	LE	LE E	LE	LE	LE C	LE D	LE	LE E	LE	LE D	LE	LE
Southend Victoria	d	18 19		18 49			19 19		19 49			20 19		20 49				21 19		21 49			22 19
Prittlewell	d																						
Southend Airport	d	18 23		18 53			19 23		19 53			20 23		20 53				21 23		21 53			22 23
Rochford	d	18 26		18 56			19 26		19 56			20 26		20 56				21 26		21 56			22 26
Hockley	d	18 30		19 00			19 30		20 00			20 30		21 00				21 30		22 00			22 30
Rayleigh	d	18 34		19 04			19 34		20 04			20 34		21 04				21 34		22 04			22 34
Southminster	d				19 06					20 06					21 06							22 06	
Burnham-on-Crouch	d				19 10					20 10					21 10							22 10	
Althorne	d				19 15					20 15					21 15							22 15	
North Fambridge	d				19 21					20 21					21 21							22 21	
South Woodham Ferrers	d				19 26					20 26					21 26							22 26	
Battlesbridge	d				19 30					20 30					21 30							22 30	
Wickford	d	18 40		19 10	19a37		19 40		20 10	20a37		20 40		21 10	21a37			21 40		22 10		22 36	22 40
Billericay	d	18 46		19 16			19 46		20 16			20 46		21 16				21 46		22 16			22 46
Shenfield	a	18 53		19 23			19 53		20 23			20 53		21 23				21 53		22 23		22 47	22 53
Shenfield	d	18 53	19 11	19 23		19 41	19 53	20 11	20 23		20 41	20 53	21 11	21 23		21 26	21 41	21 53	22 11	22 23	22 41		22 53
Romford	d	19 07		19 37			20 07		20 37			21 07		21 37				22 07		22 37			23 07
Stratford	d	19 20	19s35	19 50		20s05	20 20	20s35	20 50		21s05	21 20	21s35	21 50		21s53	22s00	22 20	22s30	22 50	23s00		23 20
London Liverpool Street	a	19 29	19 44	19 59		20 14	20 29	20 44	20 59		21 14	21 29	21 44	21 59		22 02	22 10	22 29	22 40	22 59	23 10		23 31

		LE E	LE	LE	LE F
Southend Victoria	d		22 49		
Prittlewell	d				
Southend Airport	d		22 53		
Rochford	d		22 56		
Hockley	d		23 00		
Rayleigh	d		23 04		
Southminster	d			22 45	
Burnham-on-Crouch	d			22 49	
Althorne	d			22 54	
North Fambridge	d			23 00	
South Woodham Ferrers	d			23 05	
Battlesbridge	d			23 09	
Wickford	d		23 10	23 15	
Billericay	d		23 16		
Shenfield	a		23 23	23 26	
Shenfield	d	23 11	23 23		23 37
Romford	d		23 37		
Stratford	d	23s30	23 50		23s57
London Liverpool Street	a	23 40	23 59		00 07

A From Chelmsford
B From Colchester
C From Harwich International
D From Clacton-on-Sea
E From Ipswich
F From Norwich

Table T010-F

Marks Tey - Sudbury

Mondays to Fridays

21 May to 7 December

Miles			LE	LE	LE	LE	LE	LE	LE	LE	LE	LE	LE	LE	LE	LE	LE	LE	LE	LE	LE
0	Colchester	d																			
5	Marks Tey	d	06 01	06 52	07 39	08 22	09 09	10 01	11 01	12 01	13 01	14 01	15 01	16 01	17 08	18 05	19 14	20 05	21 01	22 01	23 01
8½	Chappel & Wakes Colne	d	06 07	06 58		08 28	09 15	10 07	11 07	12 07	13 07	14 07	15 07	16 07	17 14	18 11	19 20	20 11	21 07	22 07	23 07
11¾	Bures	d	06 13	07 04		08 34	09 21	10x13	11x13	12x13	13x13	14x13	15x13	16x13	17x20	18x17	19x26	20x17	21x13	22x13	23x13
16¾	Sudbury	a	06 21	07 12	07 55	08 42	09 29	10 21	11 21	12 21	13 21	14 21	15 21	16 21	17 28	18 25	19 34	20 25	21 21	22 21	23 21

Saturdays

26 May to 8 December

		LE	LE	LE	LE	LE	LE	LE	LE	LE	LE	LE	LE	LE	LE	LE	LE	LE	LE
Colchester	d	05 50																	
Marks Tey	d	06 01	07 01	08 01	09 01	10 01	11 01	12 01	13 01	14 01	15 01	16 01	17 01	18 01	19 01	20 01	21 01	22 01	23 01
Chappel & Wakes Colne	d	06 07	07 07	08 07	09 07	10 07	11 07	12 07	13 07	14 07	15 07	16 07	17 07	18 07	19 07	20 07	21 07	22 07	23 07
Bures	d	06x13	07x13	08x13	09x13	10x13	11x13	12x13	13x13	14x13	15x13	16x13	17x13	18x13	19x13	20x13	21x13	22x13	23x13
Sudbury	a	06 21	07 21	08 21	09 21	10 21	11 21	12 21	13 21	14 21	15 21	16 21	17 21	18 21	19 21	20 21	21 21	22 21	23 21

Sundays

20 May to 2 December

		LE	LE	LE	LE	LE	LE	LE	LE	LE	LE	LE	LE	LE	LE	LE	LE
Colchester	d	07 01															
Marks Tey	d	07 15	08 15	09 15	10 15	11 15	12 15	13 15	14 15	15 15	16 15	17 15	18 15	19 15	20 15	21 15	22 15
Chappel & Wakes Colne	d	07 21	08 21	09 21	10 21	11 21	12 21	13 21	14 21	15 21	16 21	17 21	18 21	19 21	20 21	21 21	22 21
Bures	d	07x27	08x27	09x27	10x27	11x27	12x27	13x27	14x27	15x27	16x27	17x27	18x27	19x27	20x27	21x27	22x27
Sudbury	a	07 35	08 35	09 35	10 35	11 35	12 35	13 35	14 35	15 35	16 35	17 35	18 35	19 35	20 35	21 35	22 35

Table T010-R

Sudbury - Marks Tey

Mondays to Fridays

21 May to 7 December

Miles			LE	LE	LE	LE	LE	LE	LE	LE	LE	LE	LE	LE	LE	LE	LE	LE	LE	LE	LE	LE
0	Sudbury	d	05 30	06 29	07 16	07 59	08 46	09 33	10 26	11 26	12 26	13 26	14 26	15 26	16 32	17 32	18 37	19 38	20 32	21 26	22 26	23 26
5	Bures	d	05 37	06 36	07 23	08 06	08 53	09 40	10x33	11x33	12x33	13x33	14x33	15x33	16x39	17x39	18x44	19x45	20x39	21x33	22x33	23x33
8¼	Chappel & Wakes Colne	d	05 43	06 42	07 29	08 12	08 59	09 46	10 39	11 39	12 39	13 39	14 39	15 39	16 45	17 45	18 50	19 51	20 45	21 39	22 39	23 39
11¾	Marks Tey	a	05 49	06 48	07 35	08 18	09 05	09 52	10 45	11 45	12 45	13 45	14 45	15 45	16 51	17 51	18 56	19 57	20 51	21 45	22 45	23 45
16¾	Colchester	a																				00 01

Saturdays

26 May to 8 December

		LE	LE	LE	LE	LE	LE	LE	LE	LE	LE	LE	LE	LE	LE	LE	LE	LE	LE
Sudbury	d	06 26	07 26	08 26	09 26	10 26	11 26	12 26	13 26	14 26	15 26	16 26	17 26	18 26	19 26	20 26	21 26	22 26	23 26
Bures	d	06x33	07x33	08x33	09x33	10x33	11x33	12x33	13x33	14x33	15x33	16x33	17x33	18x33	19x33	20x33	21x33	22x33	23x33
Chappel & Wakes Colne	d	06 39	07 39	08 39	09 39	10 39	11 39	12 39	13 39	14 39	15 39	16 39	17 39	18 39	19 39	20 39	21 39	22 39	23 39
Marks Tey	a	06 45	07 45	08 45	09 45	10 45	11 45	12 45	13 45	14 45	15 45	16 45	17 45	18 45	19 45	20 45	21 45	22 45	23 45
Colchester	a																		00 01

Sundays

20 May to 2 December

		LE	LE	LE	LE	LE	LE	LE	LE	LE	LE	LE	LE	LE	LE	LE	LE
Sudbury	d	07 42	08 42	09 42	10 42	11 42	12 42	13 42	14 42	15 42	16 42	17 42	18 42	19 42	20 42	21 42	22 42
Bures	d	07x49	08x49	09x49	10x49	11x49	12x49	13x49	14x49	15x49	16x49	17x49	18x49	19x49	20x49	21x49	22x49
Chappel & Wakes Colne	d	07 55	08 55	09 55	10 55	11 55	12 55	13 55	14 55	15 55	16 55	17 55	18 55	19 55	20 55	21 55	22 55
Marks Tey	a	08 01	09 01	10 01	11 01	12 01	13 01	14 01	15 01	16 01	17 01	18 01	19 01	20 01	21 01	22 01	23 01
Colchester	a																23 10

Table T011-F

Mondays to Fridays
21 May to 7 December

London - Chelmsford, Colchester, Walton-on-Naze, Clacton, Harwich, Ipswich and Norwich

Miles	Miles	Miles	Miles	Miles			LE MX ■ A	LE B	LE MX ■	LE MO ■	LE MX ■	LE MX ■	LE ■ C	LE ■ B	LE ■	LE ■	LE ■	LE ■	LE ■	LE ■	LE ■	LE ■	LE ◇■	LE ■
0	—	—	—	—	**London Liverpool Street** ■ ⊖	d				00 02	00 18	00 46											05 23	
4	—	—	—	—	Stratford ■ ⊖	d				00 09	00 25	00 53											05 30	
12¼	—	—	—	—	Romford	d																	05 38	
20¼	—	—	—	—	Shenfield ■	d				00 32	00 47	01 17											05 48	
23½	—	—	—	—	Ingatestone	d				00 36	00 52	01 21											05 52	
29¾	—	—	—	—	**Chelmsford**	d				00 43	00 59	01 28											05 59	
36	—	—	—	—	Hatfield Peverel	d				00 49	01 05												06 05	
38½	0	—	—	—	**Witham** ■	d			00 07	00 56	01 11	01 39			05 21								06 12	06 16
—	3	—	—	—	White Notley	d			00 14						05 28									06 23
—	4¼	—	—	—	Cressing	d			00 16						05 30									06 25
—	5½	—	—	—	Braintree Freeport	d			00 19						05 33									06 28
—	6¼	—	—	—	**Braintree**	a			00 23						05 37									06 32
42¼	—	—	—	—	Kelvedon	d				01 00	01 16												06 16	
46¾	—	—	—	—	Marks Tey ■	d				01 06	01 21												06 22	
51¾	0	0	—	—	**Colchester** ■	a				01 20	01 35	01 58											06 29	
—	—	—	—	—		d	00 04						05 40					06 10	06 15		06 20		06 30	
—	—	2¼	—	—	Colchester Town	a															06 27			
—	—	—	—	—		d																		
—	2¾	3¼	—	—	Hythe	d																		
—	—	5¾	—	—	Wivenhoe	d																	06 37	
—	—	7½	—	—	Alresford (Essex)	d																		
—	—	9¾	—	—	Great Bentley	d																		
—	—	12½	—	—	Weeley	d																		
—	—	14¾	0	—	Thorpe-le-Soken ■	a																	06 50	
—	—	—	—	—		d											06 02					06 30	06 50	
—	—	—	4¾	—	**Clacton-on-Sea**	a																	06 59	
—	—	17¼	—	—	Kirby Cross	d											06 10					06 38		
—	—	18½	—	—	Frinton-on-Sea	d											06 13					06 41		
—	—	19¾	—	—	**Walton-on-the-Naze**	a											06 17					06 45		
59½	—	—	—	0	Manningtree ■	d	00 12						05 49			05 58		06 18	06 23					
—	0	—	—	1¾	Mistley	d										06 02		06 22						
—	—	—	—	5¾	Wrabness	d										06 07		06 27						
—	—	—	—	9½	Harwich International	d										06 15		06 36						
—	—	—	—	10¾	Dovercourt	d										06 18		06 39						
—	—	—	—	11¼	**Harwich Town**	a										06 20		06 41						
68¾	10½	—	—	—	**Ipswich**	a	00 30						05 59						06 34					
—	—	—	—	—		d		05 10					06 00	06 16						06 39				
77	—	—	—	—	Needham Market	d		05 20						06 25										
80¾	—	—	—	—	Stowmarket	d		05a26					06a11	06a30						06 50				
95	—	—	—	—	Diss	d														07 03				
115	—	—	—	—	**Norwich**	a														07 24				

		LE ■ B	LE ◇■	LE ■	LE ◇■	LE ■	LE ■	LE ■	LE ◇■	LE ■	LE ■	LE ■	LE ■	LE ■ C	LE ◇■	LE ■ D	LE ■	LE ■ E	LE ■	LE ◇■	LE ■ F	LE ◇■
London Liverpool Street ■ ⊖	d		06 00		06 02	06 12			06 25			06 38	06 48		07 00		07 02		07 08	07 17		07 30
Stratford ■ ⊖	d				06 09	06 20			06u33			06 45	06 55				07 09		07 15	07 24		
Romford	d																		07 23			
Shenfield ■	d				06 25	06 36						07 01	07 11		07u22		07 25		07 33	07 40		
Ingatestone	d					06 40							07 15							07 44		
Chelmsford	d		06 30		06 34	06 47			06 58			07 10	07 22				07 34		07 42	07 52		08 02
Hatfield Peverel	d					06 53											07 40					
Witham ■	d				06 45	07 03			07 09			07 21	07 33				07 48		07 53	08 03		
White Notley	d					07 10											07 55					
Cressing	d					07 12											07 57					
Braintree Freeport	d					07 15											08 00					
Braintree	a					07 19											08 04					
Kelvedon	d				06 49							07 25							07 57			
Marks Tey ■	d				06 55							07 31	07 40						08 03	08 11		
Colchester ■	a		06 49		07 02				07 22			07 38	07 47		07 50				08 10	08 18		08 21
	d		06 50		07 02		07 10		07 23		07 26	07 43	07 48		07 51	07 56			08 10	08 19		08 23
Colchester Town	a										07 34		07 56			08 03						
	d										07 38					08 07						
Hythe	d				07 07						07 42					08 11				08 23		
Wivenhoe	d				07 11						07 46					08 15				08 27		
Alresford (Essex)	d				07 14											08 19						
Great Bentley	d				07 18											08 23						
Weeley	d				07 22											08 26					←	
Thorpe-le-Soken ■	a				07 28						07 57					08 31				08 38	08 31	
	d			06 57	07 28					07 37	07 57					08 40				08 38	08 40	
Clacton-on-Sea	a				07 37						08 06					→				08 47		
Kirby Cross	d			07 05						07 45											08 45	
Frinton-on-Sea	d			07 08						07 48											08 48	
Walton-on-the-Naze	a			07 12						07 52											08 52	
Manningtree ■	d		06 58				07 18	07 24	07 31			07 51			07 59				08 18			08 31
Mistley	d							07 28				07 55										
Wrabness	d							07 33				08 01										
Harwich International	d							07 41				08 10						07 50				
Dovercourt	d							07 44				08 13										
Harwich Town	a							07 46				08 15										
Ipswich	a		07 10				07 30		07 42						08 11			08 17	08 31			08 43
	d	06 54	07 12						07 44					08 03	08 12			08 20				08 44
Needham Market	d	07 03																08 29				
Stowmarket	d	07a08	07 23						07 55					08a15	08 23			08a34				08 55
Diss	d		07 35						08 08						08 36							09 08
Norwich	a		07 55						08 27						08 55							09 27

A From London Liverpool Street
B To Cambridge
C To Peterborough
D To Walton-on-the-Naze
E To Cambridge
F From Colchester

NRT MAY 2018 EDITION

Table T011-F

Mondays to Fridays
21 May to 7 December

London - Chelmsford, Colchester, Walton-on-Naze, Clacton, Harwich, Ipswich and Norwich

		LE ■	LE ■		LE ◇■	LE ■ A	LE ■	LE ■ B	LE ■	LE ■	LE ■	LE ◇■	LE ■ C	LE ◇■	LE ■	LE ■	LE ■ D	LE ◇■	LE ■ B	LE ■	LE ■ E	LE ■	LE ◇■
London Liverpool Street ■ ⊖	d	07 36	07 46		07 55				08 00	08 06		08 16		08 30	08 36	08 48		09 00				09 02	09 18
Stratford ■ ⊖	d	07 45	07 54						08 08	08 14		08 24		08u38	08 45	08 55						09 09	09 25
Romford	d																						
Shenfield ■	d	08 01	08 11						08 25	08 30		08 41			09 03	09 11						09 25	09 41
Ingatestone	d	08 05								08 34		08 45				09 15							09 45
Chelmsford	d	08 12	08 20						08 34	08 41		08 52		09 03	09 12	09 22						09 34	09 52
Hatfield Peverel	d	08 19				←				08 47												09 40	
Witham ■	d	08 25	08 35	08 38		08 38			08 45	08 54		09 03			09 23	09 35						09 47	10 03
White Notley	d		08 42	→												09 42							
Cressing	d		08 44													09 44							
Braintree Freeport	d		08 47													09 47							
Braintree	a		08 51													09 51							
Kelvedon	d	08 29							08 49						09 27							09 51	
Marks Tey ■	d	08 35							08 55			09 10			09 33							09 57	
Colchester ■	a	08 42			08 45	08 53			09 02	09 06		09 17		09 23	09 40			09 46				10 04	10 15
	d	08 43			08 47	08 56			09 02	09 06	09 14	09 18		09 23	09 41			09 47			09 56	10 04	10 16
Colchester Town	a	08 51				09 03					09 21				09 49						10 03		
	d					09 07															10 07		
Hythe	d					09 11															10 11		
Wivenhoe	d					09 15						09 25									10 15		10 23
Alresford (Essex)	d					09 19															10 19		
Great Bentley	d					09 23															10 23		
Weeley	d					09 26							←								10 26		
Thorpe-le-Soken ■	a					09 31						09 36	09 31								10 31		10 35
	d					09 38						09 36	09 38								10 37		10 35
Clacton-on-Sea	a					→						09 45									→		10 44
Kirby Cross	d												09 43										
Frinton-on-Sea	d												09 46										
Walton-on-the-Naze	a												09 50										
Manningtree ■	d				08 55		09 00			09 14				09 31				09 55		10 00		10 12	
Mistley	d						09 04													10 04			
Wrabness	d						09 09													10 09			
Harwich International	d						09 17													10 17			
Dovercourt	d						09 20													10 20			
Harwich Town	a						09 22													10 22			
Ipswich	a				09 07				09 21	09 26				09 43				10 07				10 25	
	d				09 08			09 20						09 44			10 00	10 08	10 20				
Needham Market	d							09 29											10 29				
Stowmarket	d							09a34						09 55			10a11		10a34				
Diss	d				09 29									10 08				10 29					
Norwich	a				09 48									10 27				10 50					

		LE ■ F	LE ■ G	LE ◇■	LE ■	LE ■	LE ◇■	LE ■ B	LE ■	LE ■ E	LE ■	LE ◇■	LE ■ F	LE ■	LE ◇■	LE ■	LE ■	LE ■ D	LE ◇■	LE ■ B	LE ■	LE ■ E
London Liverpool Street ■ ⊖	d			09 30	09 38	09 48	10 00				10 02	10 18			10 30	10 38	10 48		11 00			
Stratford ■ ⊖	d			09u38	09 45	09 55					10 09	10 25			10u38	10 45	10 55					
Romford	d				09 53											10 53						
Shenfield ■	d				10 03	10 11					10 25	10 41				11 03	11 11					
Ingatestone	d					10 15						10 45					11 15					
Chelmsford	d			10 03	10 12	10 22					10 34	10 52			11 03	11 12	11 22					
Hatfield Peverel	d										10 40											
Witham ■	d				10 23	10 34					10 47	11 03				11 23	11 34					
White Notley	d					10 41											11 41					
Cressing	d					10 43											11 43					
Braintree Freeport	d					10 46											11 46					
Braintree	a					10 50											11 50					
Kelvedon	d				10 27						10 51					11 27						
Marks Tey ■	d				10 33						10 57					11 33						
Colchester ■	a			10 22	10 40		10 46				11 04	11 15			11 22	11 40			11 46			
	d		10 20	10 23	10 41		10 47			10 56	11 04	11 16		11 20	11 23	11 41			11 47			11 56
Colchester Town	a		10 27		10 49					11 03				11 27		11 49						12 03
	d									11 07												12 07
Hythe	d									11 11												12 11
Wivenhoe	d									11 15		11 23										12 15
Alresford (Essex)	d									11 19												12 19
Great Bentley	d									11 23												12 23
Weeley	d	←								11 26			←									12 26
Thorpe-le-Soken ■	a	10 31								11 31		11 35	11 31									12 31
	d	10 37								11 37		11 35	11 37									12 37
Clacton-on-Sea	a									→		11 44										→
Kirby Cross	d	10 42											11 42									
Frinton-on-Sea	d	10 45											11 45									
Walton-on-the-Naze	a	10 49											11 49									
Manningtree ■	d			10 31			10 55		11 00		11 12				11 31				11 55		12 00	
Mistley	d								11 04												12 04	
Wrabness	d								11 09												12 09	
Harwich International	d								11 17												12 17	
Dovercourt	d								11 20												12 20	
Harwich Town	a								11 22												12 22	
Ipswich	a			10 43			11 07				11 25				11 43				12 07			
	d			10 44			11 08	11 20							11 44			11 58	12 08	12 20		
Needham Market	d							11 29												12 29		
Stowmarket	d			10 55				11a34							11 55			12a09		12a34		
Diss	d			11 08			11 29								12 08				12 29			
Norwich	a			11 27			11 50								12 27				12 50			

A From London Liverpool Street to Walton-on-the-Naze
B To Cambridge
C From London Liverpool Street
D To Peterborough
E To Walton-on-the-Naze
F From Colchester
G From Colchester Town

Table T011-F

Mondays to Fridays

21 May to 7 December

London - Chelmsford, Colchester, Walton-on-Naze, Clacton, Harwich, Ipswich and Norwich

Station		LE 1	LE ◇1	LE 1 A	LE 1	LE ◇1 ☕	LE 1	LE 1	LE ◇1 ☕	LE 1 B	LE 1	LE 1 C	LE 1	LE ◇1	LE 1 A	LE 1	LE ◇1 ☕	LE 1	LE 1	LE 1 D	LE ◇1 ☕	LE 1 B	LE 1
London Liverpool Street 15 ⊖	d	11 02	11 18			11 30	11 38	11 48	12 00				12 02	12 18			12 30	12 38	12 48		13 00		
Stratford 7 ⊖	d	11 09	11 25			11u38	11 45	11 55					12 09	12 25			12u38	12 45	12 55				
Romford	d						11 53											12 53					
Shenfield 3	d	11 25	11 41				12 03	12 11					12 25	12 41				13 03	13 11				
Ingatestone	d		11 45					12 15						12 45					13 15				
Chelmsford	d	11 34	11 52			12 03	12 12	12 22					12 34	12 52			13 03	13 12	13 22				
Hatfield Peverel	d	11 40											12 40										
Witham 2	d	11 47	12 03				12 23	12 34					12 47	13 03				13 23	13 34				
White Notley	d							12 41											13 41				
Cressing	d							12 43											13 43				
Braintree Freeport	d							12 46											13 46				
Braintree	a							12 50											13 50				
Kelvedon	d	11 51					12 27						12 51					13 27					
Marks Tey 2	d	11 57					12 33						12 57					13 33					
Colchester 4	a	12 04	12 15			12 22	12 40		12 46				13 04	13 15			13 22	13 40			13 46		
	d	12 04	12 16		12 20	12 23	12 41		12 47			12 56	13 04	13 16		13 20	13 23	13 41			13 47		
Colchester Town	a				12 27		12 49					13 03				13 27		13 49					
	d											13 07											
Hythe	d											13 11											
Wivenhoe	d		12 23									13 15		13 23									
Alresford (Essex)	d											13 19											
Great Bentley	d											13 23											
Weeley	d			←								13 26			←								
Thorpe-le-Soken 1	a		12 35	12 31								13 31		13 35	13 31								
	d		12 35	12 37								13 37		13 35	13 37								
Clacton-on-Sea	a		12 44									→		13 44									
Kirby Cross	d			12 42											13 42								
Frinton-on-Sea	d			12 45											13 45								
Walton-on-the-Naze	a			12 49											13 49								
Manningtree 5	d	12 12				12 31			12 55		13 00		13 12				13 31				13 55		14 00
Mistley	d										13 04												14 04
Wrabness	d										13 09												14 09
Harwich International	d										13 17												14 17
Dovercourt	d										13 20												14 20
Harwich Town	a										13 22												14 22
Ipswich	a	12 25				12 43			13 07				13 25				13 43				14 07		
	d					12 44			13 08	13 20							13 44			13 58	14 08	14 20	
Needham Market	d									13 29												14 29	
Stowmarket	d					12 55				13a34							13 55			14a09		14a34	
Diss	d					13 08			13 29								14 08				14 29		
Norwich	a					13 27			13 50								14 27				14 50		

Station		LE 1 C	LE 1	LE ◇1	LE 1 A	LE 1	LE ◇1 ☕	LE 1	LE 1	LE ◇1 ☕	LE 1 B	LE 1	LE 1 C	LE 1	LE ◇1	LE 1 A	LE 1	LE ◇1 ☕	LE 1	LE 1	LE 1 D	LE ◇1 ☕	LE 1 B
London Liverpool Street 15 ⊖	d		13 02	13 18			13 30	13 38	13 48	14 00				14 02	14 18			14 30	14 38	14 48		15 00	
Stratford 7 ⊖	d		13 09	13 25			13u38	13 45	13 55					14 09	14 25			14u38	14 45	14 55			
Romford	d							13 53											14 53				
Shenfield 3	d		13 25	13 41				14 03	14 11					14 25	14 41				15 03	15 11			
Ingatestone	d			13 45					14 15						14 45					15 15			
Chelmsford	d		13 34	13 52			14 03	14 12	14 22					14 34	14 52			15 03	15 12	15 22			
Hatfield Peverel	d		13 40											14 40									
Witham 2	d		13 47	14 03				14 23	14 34					14 47	15 03				15 23	15 35			
White Notley	d								14 41											15 42			
Cressing	d								14 43											15 44			
Braintree Freeport	d								14 46											15 47			
Braintree	a								14 50											15 51			
Kelvedon	d		13 51					14 27						14 51					15 27				
Marks Tey 2	d		13 57					14 33						14 57					15 33				
Colchester 4	a		14 04	14 15			14 22	14 40		14 46				15 04	15 15			15 22	15 40			15 46	
	d	13 56	14 04	14 16		14 20	14 23	14 41		14 47			14 56	15 04	15 16		15 20	15 23	15 41			15 47	
Colchester Town	a	14 03				14 27		14 49					15 03				15 27		15 49				
	d	14 07											15 07										
Hythe	d	14 11											15 11										
Wivenhoe	d	14 15		14 23									15 15		15 23								
Alresford (Essex)	d	14 19											15 19										
Great Bentley	d	14 23											15 23										
Weeley	d	14 26			←								15 26			←							
Thorpe-le-Soken 1	a	14 31		14 35	14 31								15 31		15 35	15 31							
	d	14 37		14 35	14 37								15 37		15 35	15 37							
Clacton-on-Sea	a	→		14 44									→		15 44								
Kirby Cross	d				14 42											15 42							
Frinton-on-Sea	d				14 45											15 45							
Walton-on-the-Naze	a				14 49											15 49							
Manningtree 5	d		14 12				14 31			14 55		15 00		15 12				15 31				15 55	
Mistley	d											15 04											
Wrabness	d											15 09											
Harwich International	d											15 17											
Dovercourt	d											15 20											
Harwich Town	a											15 22											
Ipswich	a		14 25				14 43			15 07				15 25				15 43				16 07	
	d						14 44			15 08	15 20							15 44			16 00	16 08	16 20
Needham Market	d										15 29												16 29
Stowmarket	d						14 55				15a34							15 55			16a12		16a34
Diss	d						15 08			15 29								16 08				16 30	
Norwich	a						15 27			15 48								16 27				16 50	

A From Colchester
B To Cambridge
C To Walton-on-the-Naze
D To Peterborough

Table T011-F

Mondays to Fridays

21 May to 7 December

London - Chelmsford, Colchester, Walton-on-Naze, Clacton, Harwich, Ipswich and Norwich

Station		LE 1	LE 1 A	LE 1	LE 1	LE ◇1	LE 1 B	LE 1	LE ■ 1 ☕	LE 1	LE 1	LE 1	LE ■ 1 ☕	LE 1 C	LE 1	LE 1 A	LE ◇1	LE 1	LE 1	LE ◇1	LE 1 B	LE 1
London Liverpool Street 15 ⊖	d			15 02		15 18			15 30		15 38	15 48	16 00				16 02			16 14		16 17
Stratford 7 ⊖	d			15 09		15 25					15 45	15 55					16 09			16 22		16 25
Romford	d										15 53											
Shenfield 3	d			15 25		15 41					16 03	16 11					16 25			16 38		16 41
Ingatestone	d					15 45				15 58		16 15										16 46
Chelmsford	d			15 34		15 52			16 00	16 05	16 12	16 22					16 35			16 48		16 53
Hatfield Peverel	d			15 40						16 11							16 41					
Witham 2	d			15 47		16 03				16 18	16 23	16 35					16 47					17a06
White Notley	d											16 42										
Cressing	d											16 44										
Braintree Freeport	d											16 47										
Braintree	a											16 51										
Kelvedon	d			15 51						16 22	16 27						16 52			16 59		
Marks Tey 2	d			15 57						16 28	16 33						16 57			17 05		
Colchester 4	a			16 04		16 15			16 21	16 36	16 40		16 46				17 04			17 12		
	d		15 56	16 04	16 14	16 16		16 20	16 21		16 41		16 47			16 56	17 05		17 09	17 13		
Colchester Town	a		16 03					16 27			16 49					17 03			17 16			
	d		16 07													17 07						
Hythe	d		16 11													17 11				17 17		
Wivenhoe	d		16 15			16 23										17 15				17 21		
Alresford (Essex)	d		16 19													17 19						
Great Bentley	d		16 23													17 23						
Weeley	d		16 26				←									17 26					←	
Thorpe-le-Soken 1	a		16 31			16 35	16 31									17 31				17 35	17 31	
	d		16 37			16 35	16 37									17 37				17 35	17 37	
Clacton-on-Sea	a		→			16 44										→				17 46		
Kirby Cross	d						16 42														17 42	
Frinton-on-Sea	d						16 45														17 45	
Walton-on-the-Naze	a						16 49														17 49	
Manningtree 5	d	16 00		16 12	16 23				16 29				16 55		17 00		17 13	17 24				
Mistley	d	16 04			16 27										17 04			17 28				
Wrabness	d	16 09			16 32										17 09			17 33				
Harwich International	d	16 17			16 41										17 17			17 41				
Dovercourt	d	16 20			16 44										17 20			17 44				
Harwich Town	a	16 22			16 46										17 22			17 46				
Ipswich	a			16 25					16 40				17 07				17 27					
	d								16 41				17 08	17 20								
Needham Market	d													17 29								
Stowmarket	d								16 52				17 19	17a34								
Diss	d								17 05				17 32									
Norwich	a								17 24				17 53									

Station		LE ■ 1 ☕	LE 1 D	LE 1 A	LE ◇1	LE 1	LE 1 B	LE ◇1	(LE ◇1)	LE 1 A	LE 1	LE ■ 1 E ☕	LE 1 C	LE ◇1	LE 1 B	LE ◇1	(LE ◇1)	LE 1	LE 1	LE 1 F	LE 1	LE ■ 1 ☕	LE 1
London Liverpool Street 15 ⊖	d	16 30			16 32	16 34		16 44			16 47	17 00		17 02		17 08		17 12	17 18		17 20	17 30	
Stratford 7 ⊖	d					16 42		16 52			16 55			17 10		17 16		17 20	17 26		17 29		
Romford	d																						
Shenfield 3	d				16 54	16 58					17 11			17 26							17 45		
Ingatestone	d										17 16										17 49		
Chelmsford	d				17 04	17 08		17 15			17 23			17 36		17 40		17 44	17 50		17 57		
Hatfield Peverel	d					17 14												17 50					
Witham 2	d				17 14	17 21					17a36			17 46		17 50		17a59			18 10		
White Notley	d					17 28															18 17		
Cressing	d					17 30															18 19		
Braintree Freeport	d					17 33															18 22		
Braintree	a					17 39															18 28		
Kelvedon	d							17 27								17 55			18 02				
Marks Tey 2	d							17 32						17 54		18 00				←			
Colchester 4	a	17 16			17 26			17 40						18 01		18 08			18 12	18 08			
	d	17 17		17 24	17 27			17 44	17 47	17 56				18 01		18 11	18 16		18 12	18 16			
Colchester Town	a			17 33						18 03							→			18 26			
	d			17 37						18 07													
Hythe	d			17 41						18 11						18 16							
Wivenhoe	d			17 45				17 51		18 15						18 20							
Alresford (Essex)	d			17 49				17 55		18 19						18 24							
Great Bentley	d			17 53				17 59		18 23						18 28							
Weeley	d			17 56			←			18 26					←								
Thorpe-le-Soken 1	a			18 01			18 01	18 06		18 31					18 31	18 35							
	d			18 10			18 10	18 06		18 38					18 38	18 35							
Clacton-on-Sea	a			→				18 17		→						18 46							
Kirby Cross	d						18 15								18 43								
Frinton-on-Sea	d						18 18								18 46								
Walton-on-the-Naze	a						18 22								18 50								
Manningtree 5	d				17 35				17 57					18 09					18 20			18 27	18 35
Mistley	d								18 01														18 39
Wrabness	d								18 06														18 44
Harwich International	d								18 15														18 52
Dovercourt	d								18 18														18 55
Harwich Town	a								18 22														18 57
Ipswich	a	17 34			17 50							17 59		18 20					18 35			18 37	
	d	17 36	17 48									18 00	18 17	18 25								18 39	
Needham Market	d		17 57										18 26										
Stowmarket	d	17 47	18a02										18a31	18 36								18 50	
Diss	d	18 00										18 21		18 48								19 04	
Norwich	a	18 22										18 42		19 09								19 25	

A To Walton-on-the-Naze
C To Cambridge
E The East Anglian

Table T011-F

Mondays to Fridays

21 May to 7 December

London - Chelmsford, Colchester, Walton-on-Naze, Clacton, Harwich, Ipswich and Norwich

		LE ◇1	LE 1	LE 1	LE 1	LE 1 A	LE 1 ☕	LE 1 B	LE ◇1	LE 1	LE 1 C	LE 1	LE 1 D	LE 1 ☕	LE 1 E	LE ◇1	LE 1 B	LE 1	LE 1	LE 1	LE 1 F	LE 1 G
London Liverpool Street 15 ⊖	d	17 32	17 38			17 40	17 50		17 52			17 58	18 00	18 10		18 12		18 18				18 20
Stratford 7 ⊖	d	17 40	17 46						18 00			18 06	18 09			18 20		18 26				18 29
Romford	d																					
Shenfield 3	d					18 05							18 25									18 45
Ingatestone	d					18 09							18 29									18 49
Chelmsford	d	18 05	18 12			18 17			18 25				18 37			18 47		18 52				18 57
Hatfield Peverel	d		18 18					←				18 35					←	18 58				
Witham 2	d	18 15				18 31		18 31	18 36			18 41	19 01			18 58	19 01					19 11
White Notley	d					↳							↳				19 08					↳
Cressing	d																19 10					
Braintree Freeport	d																19 13					
Braintree	a																19 19					
Kelvedon	d		18 25					18 37				18 46						19 07				
Marks Tey 2	d	18 23							18 46							19 05						
Colchester 4	a	18 30	18 36				18 42	18 48	18 53			18 56		19 00		19 13		19 17				
	d	18 30	18 36		18 41		18 43	18 49	18 54			18 57		19 02	19 06	19 13		19 18	19 20			
Colchester Town	a							18 59							19 13				19 27		←	
	d														19 18							
Hythe	d				18 45				18 58						19 22	19 18					19 22	
Wivenhoe	d	18 38			18 49				19 02						→	19 22					19 26	
Alresford (Essex)	d				18 53																19 30	
Great Bentley	d				18 57																19 34	
Weeley	d				19 00																19 37	
Thorpe-le-Soken 1	a	18 51			19 05				19 13							19 33					19 42	
	d	18 51		18 56	19 05				19 13							19 33				19 37	19 42	
Clacton-on-Sea	a	19 02			19 14				19 24							19 44					19 51	
Kirby Cross	d			19 04																19 42		
Frinton-on-Sea	d			19 07																19 45		
Walton-on-the-Naze	a			19 11																19 49		
Manningtree 5	d		18 44				18 52			19 02		19 05		19 11				19 26				
Mistley	d									19 06												
Wrabness	d									19 11												
Harwich International	d									19 19												
Dovercourt	d									19 22												
Harwich Town	a									19 24												
Ipswich	a		18 59				19 03					19 19		19 21				19 41				
	d						19 04				19 13			19 23								
Needham Market	d										19 22											
Stowmarket	d						19 16				19a27			19 34								
Diss	d						19 29							19 47								
Norwich	a						19 50							20 09								

		LE 1 ☕	LE 1	LE 1 B	LE 1 H	LE 1 I		LE ◇1	LE ◇1	LE 1 B	LE 1 ☕	LE 1 C	LE 1	LE 1	LE 1 I	LE ◇1	LE ◇1	LE 1 F	LE 1 ☕	LE 1	LE 1	LE 1	LE 1
London Liverpool Street 15 ⊖	d	18 30				18 32		18 38	18 48		19 00		19 02			19 08	19 18		19 30		19 32		19 38
Stratford 7 ⊖	d					18 40		18 46	18 56				19 09			19 15	19 25				19 39		19 45
Romford	d																						
Shenfield 3	d							19 02					19 25				19 41						20 01
Ingatestone	d							19 07									19 45						
Chelmsford	d					19 05		19 14	19 20				19 34			19 39	19 52				20 02		20 10
Hatfield Peverel	d			←		19 11							19 40										20 16
Witham 2	d			19 11		19 17		19 24	19 30				19 49			19 50	20 03				20 13		20 23
White Notley	d												19 56										
Cressing	d												19 58										
Braintree Freeport	d												20 01										
Braintree	a												20 05										
Kelvedon	d			19 17		19 22										19 55							20 27
Marks Tey 2	d			19 23				19 32								20 00							20 33
Colchester 4	a	19 21		19 30		19 33		19 39	19 43		19 47					20 07	20 15		20 19		20 25		20 40
	d	19 23		19 30		19 37	19 39	19 39	19 44		19 47				19 56	20 08	20 16		20 20	20 20	20 25		20 41
Colchester Town	a						19 50								20 03					20 27			20 49
	d														20 07								
Hythe	d								19 48						20 11								
Wivenhoe	d					19 44			19 52						20 15		20 23						
Alresford (Essex)	d					19 48									20 19								
Great Bentley	d					19 52									20 23								
Weeley	d					19 55				←					20 26			←					
Thorpe-le-Soken 1	a					20 00			20 04	20 00					20 31		20 35	20 31					
	d					20 09			20 04	20 09					20 37		20 35	20 37					
Clacton-on-Sea	a					↳			20 15						↳		20 44						
Kirby Cross	d									20 14								20 42					
Frinton-on-Sea	d									20 17								20 45					
Walton-on-the-Naze	a									20 23								20 49					
Manningtree 5	d	19 32	19 38	19 40				19 47			19 55			20 00		20 16			20 28		20 34	20 38	
Mistley	d		19 42											20 04								20 42	
Wrabness	d		19 47											20 09								20 47	
Harwich International	d		19 55	20a02										20 17							20a54	20 55	
Dovercourt	d		19 58											20 20								20 58	
Harwich Town	a		20 00											20 22								21 00	
Ipswich	a	19 42						20 03			20 07					20 30			20 40				
	d	19 44			20 00						20 08	20 18							20 41				
Needham Market	d											20 28											
Stowmarket	d	19 55			20a11						20 19	20a34							20 52				
Diss	d	20 08									20 32								21 05				
Norwich	a	20 30									20 51								21 24				

A To Colchester Town
B From London Liverpool Street
C To Cambridge
D To Braintree
E To Clacton-on-Sea
F From Colchester
G To Harwich International
H To Peterborough
I To Walton-on-the-Naze

Table T011-F

Mondays to Fridays

21 May to 7 December

London - Chelmsford, Colchester, Walton-on-Naze, Clacton, Harwich, Ipswich and Norwich

		LE 1	LE ◇1 ☕	LE A	LE 1 B	LE 1	LE 1 C	LE ◇1	LE ◇1	LE 1 D	LE 1	LE ◇1 ☕	LE 1	LE 1	LE 1 E	LE ◇1 ☕	LE F	LE 1	LE 1 C	LE 1	LE ◇1	LE 1 D	LE ◇1 ☕
London Liverpool Street 15 ⊖	d	19 48	20 00					20 02	20 18			20 30	20 38	20 48		21 00				21 02	21 18		21 30
Stratford 7 ⊖	d	19 55						20 09	20 25			20u38	20 45	20 55						21 09	21 25		21u38
Romford	d												20 53										
Shenfield 3	d	20 11						20 25	20 41				21 03	21 11						21 25	21 41		
Ingatestone	d	20 15							20 45					21 15							21 45		
Chelmsford	d	20 22						20 34	20 52			21 03	21 12	21 22						21 34	21 52		22 03
Hatfield Peverel	d							20 40												21 40			
Witham 2	d	20 34						20 47	21 03				21 23	21 34						21 47	22 03		
White Notley	d	20 41												21 41									
Cressing	d	20 43												21 43									
Braintree Freeport	d	20 46												21 46									
Braintree	a	20 50												21 50									
Kelvedon	d							20 51					21 27							21 51			
Marks Tey 2	d							20 57					21 33							21 57			
Colchester 4	a		20 46					21 04	21 15			21 22	21 40			21 46				22 04	22 15		22 22
	d		20 47				20 56	21 04	21 16		21 20	21 23	21 41			21 47			21 56	22 04	22 16		22 23
Colchester Town	a						21 03				21 27		21 49						22 03				
	d						21 07												22 07				
Hythe	d						21 11												22 11				
Wivenhoe	d						21 15		21 23										22 15		22 23		
Alresford (Essex)	d						21 19												22 19				
Great Bentley	d						21 23												22 23				
Weeley	d						21 26			←									22 26			←	
Thorpe-le-Soken 1	a						21 31		21 35	21 31									22 31		22 35	22 31	
	d				20 54		21 37		21 35	21 37									22 37		22 35	22 37	
Clacton-on-Sea	a				21 03		↳		21 44										↳		22 44		
Kirby Cross	d									21 42												22 42	
Frinton-on-Sea	d									21 45												22 45	
Walton-on-the-Naze	a									21 49												22 49	
Manningtree 5	d		20 55			21 00		21 12				21 32				21 56		22 00		22 12			22 32
Mistley	d					21 04												22 04					
Wrabness	d					21 09												22 09					
Harwich International	d					21 17									21 38			22 17		22a28			
Dovercourt	d					21 20												22 20					
Harwich Town	a					21 22												22 22					
Ipswich	a		21 07					21 25				21 43			22 04	22 07							22 44
	d		21 08	21 17								21 45				22 09	22 19						22 45
Needham Market	d			21 27													22 29						
Stowmarket	d		21 19	21a33								21 56				22 20	22a35						22 57
Diss	d		21 32									22 09				22 33							23 11
Norwich	a		21 51									22 29				22 53							23 30

		LE 1	LE 1	LE 1	LE 1	LE 1 B	LE 1 C	LE 1	LE ◇1	LE 1 D	LE ◇1 ☕	LE 1	LE 1	LE 1	LE 1 G	LE 1	LE ◇1	LE ◇1 ☕	LE 1
London Liverpool Street 15 ⊖	d	21 38	21 48	22 00				22 02	22 18		22 30		22 38			23 02	23 18	23 30	23 48
Stratford 7 ⊖	d	21 45	21 55					22 09	22 25		22u38		22 45			23 09	23 25	23u38	23 55
Romford	d	21 53																	
Shenfield 3	d	22 03	22 11					22 25	22 41				23 01			23 25	23 41		00 11
Ingatestone	d		22 15						22 45				23 05				23 45		00 15
Chelmsford	d	22 12	22 22	22 28				22 34	22 52		23 03		23 12			23 34	23 52	00 03	00 22
Hatfield Peverel	d							22 40								23 40			00 28
Witham 2	d	22 23	22 34					22 47	23 03				23 23	23 25		23 47	00 03		00 35
White Notley	d		22 41											23 32					
Cressing	d		22 43											23 34					
Braintree Freeport	d		22 46											23 37					
Braintree	a		22 50											23 41					
Kelvedon	d	22 27						22 51					23 27			23 51			00 39
Marks Tey 2	d	22 33						22 57					23 33		23 46	23 57			00 45
Colchester 4	a	22 40		22 47				23 05	23 15		23 22		23 47		00 01	00 04	00 15	00 22	00 59
	d	22 41		22 47			22 56		23 16		23 23					00 04	00 16	00 23	
Colchester Town	a	22 49					23 03												
	d						23 07												
Hythe	d						23 11												
Wivenhoe	d						23 15		23 23								00 23		
Alresford (Essex)	d						23 19										00 27		
Great Bentley	d						23 23										00 31		
Weeley	d						23 26			←									
Thorpe-le-Soken 1	a						23 31		23 35	23 31							00 38		
	d					23 16	23 37		23 35	23 37							00 38		
Clacton-on-Sea	a					23 25	↳		23 44								00 53		
Kirby Cross	d									23 42									
Frinton-on-Sea	d									23 45									
Walton-on-the-Naze	a									23 49									
Manningtree 5	d			22 55	23 00						23 32	23 36				00 12		00 32	
Mistley	d				23 04							23 40							
Wrabness	d				23 09							23 45							
Harwich International	d				23 17							23 53							
Dovercourt	d				23 20							23 56							
Harwich Town	a				23 22							23 58							
Ipswich	a			23 08							23 44					00 30		00 44	
	d										23 45							00 45	
Needham Market	d																		
Stowmarket	d										23 57							00 57	
Diss	d										00 11							01 11	
Norwich	a										00 30							01 36	

A To Cambridge
B From Walton-on-the-Naze
C To Walton-on-the-Naze
D From Colchester
E To Lowestoft
F To Bury St Edmunds
G 23:26 from Sudbury

Table T011-F

Saturdays
26 May to 8 December

London - Chelmsford, Colchester, Walton-on-Naze, Clacton, Harwich, Ipswich and Norwich

Station		LE A	LE B	LE	LE	LE	LE C	LE B	LE	LE	LE	LE	LE	LE ◇	LE	LE D	LE	LE B	LE E	LE	LE ◇	LE F	LE ◇
London Liverpool Street	d				00 18	00 46							05 34							06 02	06 18		06 30
Stratford	d				00 25	00 53							05 41							06 09	06 25		06u38
Romford	d												05 49										
Shenfield	d				00 47	01 17							05 59							06 25	06 41		
Ingatestone	d				00 52	01 21							06 03								06 45		
Chelmsford	d				00 59	01 28							06 10							06 34	06 52		07 03
Hatfield Peverel	d				01 05								06 16							06 40			
Witham	d			00 07	01 11	01 39			05 34				06 23		06 34					06 47	07 03		
White Notley	d			00 14					05 41						06 41								
Cressing	d			00 16					05 43						06 43								
Braintree Freeport	d			00 19					05 46						06 46								
Braintree	a			00 23					05 50						06 50								
Kelvedon	d				01 16								06 27							06 51			
Marks Tey	d				01 21								06 33							06 57			
Colchester	a				01 35	01 58							06 40							07 04	07 15		07 22
	d	00 04					05 40			05 53	06 20	06 24	06 40						06 56	07 04	07 16		07 23
Colchester Town	a										06 27								07 03				
	d																		07 07				
Hythe	d																		07 11				
Wivenhoe	d																		07 15		07 23		
Alresford (Essex)	d																		07 19				
Great Bentley	d																		07 23				
Weeley	d																		07 26			←	
Thorpe-le-Soken	a																		07 31		07 35	07 31	
	d															06 37			07 37		07 35	07 37	
Clacton-on-Sea	a																		→		07 44		
Kirby Cross	d															06 42						07 42	
Frinton-on-Sea	d															06 45						07 45	
Walton-on-the-Naze	a															06 49						07 49	
Manningtree	d	00 12					05 49			06 01		06 32	06 48				07 00			07 12			07 31
Mistley	d									06 05							07 04						
Wrabness	d									06 10							07 09						
Harwich International	d									06 18							07 17						
Dovercourt	d									06 21							07 20						
Harwich Town	a									06 23							07 22						
Ipswich	a	00 30					05 59					06 44	07 00							07 25			07 43
	d		05 10				06 00	06 16						07 10				07 20					07 44
Needham Market	d		05 20					06 25										07 29					
Stowmarket	d		05a26				06a11	06a30						07 21				07a34					07 55
Diss	d													07 34									08 08
Norwich	a													07 53									08 27

Station		LE	LE	LE	LE C	LE ◇	LE E	LE G	LE	LE	LE ◇	LE F	LE	LE ◇	LE	LE	LE ◇	LE B	LE	LE E	LE	LE ◇	LE F
London Liverpool Street	d	06 38		06 48		07 00				07 02	07 18			07 30	07 38	07 48	08 00				08 02	08 18	
Stratford	d	06 45		06 55						07 09	07 25			07u38	07 45	07 55					08 09	08 25	
Romford	d	06 53													07 53								
Shenfield	d	07 03		07 11						07 25	07 41				08 03	08 11					08 25	08 41	
Ingatestone	d			07 15							07 45					08 15						08 45	
Chelmsford	d	07 12		07 22						07 34	07 52			08 03	08 12	08 22					08 34	08 52	
Hatfield Peverel	d									07 40											08 40		
Witham	d	07 23		07 34						07 47	08 03				08 23	08 34					08 47	09 03	
White Notley	d			07 41												08 41							
Cressing	d			07 43												08 43							
Braintree Freeport	d			07 46												08 46							
Braintree	a			07 50												08 50							
Kelvedon	d	07 27								07 51					08 27						08 51		
Marks Tey	d	07 33								07 57					08 33						08 57		
Colchester	a	07 40				07 47				08 04	08 15			08 22	08 40		08 46				09 04	09 15	
	d	07 40	07 44			07 47	07 56			08 04	08 16		08 20	08 23	08 41		08 47			08 56	09 04	09 16	
Colchester Town	a		07 51				08 03						08 27		08 49					09 03			
	d						08 07													09 07			
Hythe	d						08 11													09 11			
Wivenhoe	d						08 15				08 23									09 15		09 23	
Alresford (Essex)	d						08 19													09 19			
Great Bentley	d						08 23													09 23			
Weeley	d						08 26					←								09 26			←
Thorpe-le-Soken	a						08 31				08 35	08 31								09 31		09 35	09 31
	d						08 37				08 35	08 37								09 37		09 35	09 37
Clacton-on-Sea	a						→				08 44									→		09 44	
Kirby Cross	d											08 42											09 42
Frinton-on-Sea	d											08 45											09 45
Walton-on-the-Naze	a											08 49											09 49
Manningtree	d	07 48				07 55			08 00	08 12				08 31			08 55		09 00		09 12		
Mistley	d								08 04										09 04				
Wrabness	d								08 09										09 09				
Harwich International	d	08a09						07 50	08 17										09 17				
Dovercourt	d								08 20										09 20				
Harwich Town	a								08 22										09 22				
Ipswich	a					08 07		08 17		08 25				08 43			09 07				09 25		
	d				08 00	08 08		08 20						08 44			09 08	09 20					
Needham Market	d							08 29										09 29					
Stowmarket	d				08a11			08a34						08 55				09a34					
Diss	d					08 29								09 08			09 29						
Norwich	a					08 50								09 27			09 50						

A From London Liverpool Street
B To Cambridge
C To Peterborough
D From Clacton-on-Sea
E To Walton-on-the-Naze
F From Colchester
G To Cambridge

Table T011-F

Saturdays
26 May to 8 December

London - Chelmsford, Colchester, Walton-on-Naze, Clacton, Harwich, Ipswich and Norwich

Station		LE	LE ◇	LE	LE	LE A	LE ◇	LE B	LE	LE C	LE	LE ◇	LE D	LE	LE ◇	LE	LE	LE ◇	LE B	LE	LE C	LE
London Liverpool Street	d		08 30	08 38	08 48		09 00				09 02	09 18			09 30	09 38	09 48	10 00				10 02
Stratford	d		08u38	08 45	08 55						09 09	09 25			09u38	09 45	09 55					10 09
Romford	d			08 53												09 53						
Shenfield	d			09 03	09 11						09 25	09 41				10 03	10 11					10 25
Ingatestone	d				09 15							09 45					10 15					
Chelmsford	d		09 03	09 12	09 22						09 34	09 52			10 03	10 12	10 22					10 34
Hatfield Peverel	d										09 40											10 40
Witham	d			09 23	09 34						09 47	10 03				10 23	10 34					10 47
White Notley	d				09 41												10 41					
Cressing	d				09 43												10 43					
Braintree Freeport	d				09 46												10 46					
Braintree	a				09 50												10 50					
Kelvedon	d			09 27							09 51					10 27						10 51
Marks Tey	d			09 33							09 57					10 33						10 57
Colchester	a		09 22	09 40			09 46				10 04	10 15			10 22	10 40		10 46				11 04
	d	09 20	09 23	09 41			09 47			09 56	10 04	10 16		10 20	10 23	10 41		10 47			10 56	11 04
Colchester Town	a	09 27		09 49						10 03				10 27		10 49					11 03	
	d									10 07											11 07	
Hythe	d									10 11											11 11	
Wivenhoe	d									10 15		10 23									11 15	
Alresford (Essex)	d									10 19											11 19	
Great Bentley	d									10 23											11 23	
Weeley	d									10 26			←								11 26	
Thorpe-le-Soken	a									10 31		10 35	10 31								11 31	
	d									10 37		10 35	10 37								11 37	
Clacton-on-Sea	a									→		10 44									→	
Kirby Cross	d												10 42									
Frinton-on-Sea	d												10 45									
Walton-on-the-Naze	a												10 49									
Manningtree	d		09 31				09 55		10 00		10 12				10 31			10 55		11 00		11 12
Mistley	d								10 04											11 04		
Wrabness	d								10 09											11 09		
Harwich International	d								10 17											11 17		
Dovercourt	d								10 20											11 20		
Harwich Town	a								10 22											11 22		
Ipswich	a		09 43				10 07				10 25				10 43			11 07				11 25
	d		09 44			09 58	10 08	10 20							10 44			11 08	11 20			
Needham Market	d							10 29											11 29			
Stowmarket	d		09 55			10a09		10a34							10 55				11a34			
Diss	d		10 08				10 29								11 08			11 29				
Norwich	a		10 27				10 50								11 27			11 50				

Station		LE ◇	LE D	LE	LE ◇	LE	LE	LE A	LE ◇	LE B	LE	LE C	LE	LE ◇	LE D	LE	LE ◇	LE	LE	LE ◇	LE B	LE	LE C
London Liverpool Street	d	10 18			10 30	10 38	10 48		11 00				11 02	11 18			11 30	11 38	11 48	12 00			
Stratford	d	10 25			10u38	10 45	10 55						11 09	11 25			11u38	11 45	11 55				
Romford	d					10 53												11 53					
Shenfield	d	10 41				11 03	11 11						11 25	11 41				12 03	12 11				
Ingatestone	d	10 45					11 15							11 45					12 15				
Chelmsford	d	10 52			11 03	11 12	11 22						11 34	11 52			12 03	12 12	12 22				
Hatfield Peverel	d												11 40										
Witham	d	11 03				11 23	11 34						11 47	12 03				12 23	12 34				
White Notley	d						11 41												12 41				
Cressing	d						11 43												12 43				
Braintree Freeport	d						11 46												12 46				
Braintree	a						11 50												12 50				
Kelvedon	d					11 27							11 51					12 27					
Marks Tey	d					11 33							11 57					12 33					
Colchester	a	11 15			11 22	11 40			11 46				12 04	12 15			12 22	12 40		12 46			
	d	11 16		11 20	11 23	11 41			11 47			11 56	12 04	12 16		12 20	12 23	12 41		12 47			12 56
Colchester Town	a			11 27		11 49						12 03				12 27		12 49					13 03
	d											12 07											13 07
Hythe	d											12 11											13 11
Wivenhoe	d	11 23										12 15		12 23									13 15
Alresford (Essex)	d											12 19											13 19
Great Bentley	d											12 23											13 23
Weeley	d		←									12 26			←								13 26
Thorpe-le-Soken	a	11 35	11 31									12 31		12 35	12 31								13 31
	d	11 35	11 37									12 37		12 35	12 37								13 37
Clacton-on-Sea	a	11 44										→		12 44									→
Kirby Cross	d		11 42												12 42								
Frinton-on-Sea	d		11 45												12 45								
Walton-on-the-Naze	a		11 49												12 49								
Manningtree	d				11 31				11 55		12 00		12 12				12 31			12 55		13 00	
Mistley	d										12 04											13 04	
Wrabness	d										12 09											13 09	
Harwich International	d										12 17											13 17	
Dovercourt	d										12 20											13 20	
Harwich Town	a										12 22											13 22	
Ipswich	a				11 43				12 07				12 25				12 43			13 07			
	d				11 44			11 58	12 08	12 20							12 44			13 08	13 20		
Needham Market	d									12 29											13 29		
Stowmarket	d				11 55			12a09		12a34							12 55				13a34		
Diss	d				12 08				12 29								13 08			13 29			
Norwich	a				12 27				12 50								13 27			13 50			

A To Peterborough
B To Cambridge
C To Walton-on-the-Naze
D From Colchester

Table T011-F

Saturdays
26 May to 8 December

London - Chelmsford, Colchester, Walton-on-Naze, Clacton, Harwich, Ipswich and Norwich

Station		LE 1	LE ◇1	LE 1 A	LE 1	LE ◇1 ☕	LE 1	LE 1	LE 1 B	LE ◇1 ☕	LE 1 C	LE 1	LE 1 D	LE 1	LE ◇1	LE 1 A	LE 1	LE ◇1 ☕	LE 1	LE 1	LE ◇1 ☕	LE 1 C
London Liverpool Street 15 ⊖	d	12 02	12 18			12 30	12 38	12 48		13 00				13 02	13 18			13 30	13 38	13 48	14 00	
Stratford 7 ⊖	d	12 09	12 25			12u38	12 45	12 55						13 09	13 25			13u38	13 45	13 55		
Romford	d						12 53												13 53			
Shenfield 3	d	12 25	12 41				13 03	13 11						13 25	13 41				14 03	14 11		
Ingatestone	d		12 45					13 15							13 45					14 15		
Chelmsford	d	12 34	12 52			13 03	13 12	13 22						13 34	13 52			14 03	14 12	14 22		
Hatfield Peverel	d	12 40												13 40								
Witham 2	d	12 47	13 03				13 23	13 34						13 47	14 03				14 23	14 34		
White Notley	d							13 41												14 41		
Cressing	d							13 43												14 43		
Braintree Freeport	d							13 46												14 46		
Braintree	a							13 50												14 50		
Kelvedon	d	12 51					13 27							13 51					14 27			
Marks Tey 2	d	12 57					13 33							13 57					14 33			
Colchester 4	a	13 04	13 15			13 22	13 40			13 46				14 04	14 15			14 22	14 40		14 46	
	d	13 04	13 16		13 20	13 23	13 41			13 47			13 56	14 04	14 16		14 20	14 23	14 41		14 47	
Colchester Town	a				13 27		13 49						14 03				14 27		14 49			
	d												14 07									
Hythe	d												14 11									
Wivenhoe	d		13 23										14 15		14 23							
Alresford (Essex)	d												14 19									
Great Bentley	d												14 23									
Weeley	d			←									14 26			←						
Thorpe-le-Soken 1	a		13 35	13 31									14 31		14 35	14 31						
	d		13 35	13 37									14 37		14 35	14 37						
Clacton-on-Sea	a		13 44										→		14 44							
Kirby Cross	d			13 42												14 42						
Frinton-on-Sea	d			13 45												14 45						
Walton-on-the-Naze	a			13 49												14 49						
Manningtree 5	d	13 12				13 31				13 55		14 00		14 12				14 31			14 55	
Mistley	d											14 04										
Wrabness	d											14 09										
Harwich International	d											14 17										
Dovercourt	d											14 20										
Harwich Town	a											14 22										
Ipswich	a	13 25				13 43				14 07				14 25				14 43			15 07	
	d					13 44			13 58	14 08	14 20							14 44			15 08	15 20
Needham Market	d										14 29											15 29
Stowmarket	d					13 55			14a09		14a34							14 55				15a34
Diss	d					14 08				14 29								15 08			15 29	
Norwich	a					14 27				14 50								15 27			15 48	

Station		LE 1	LE 1 D	LE 1	LE ◇1	LE 1 A	LE 1	LE ◇1 ☕	LE 1	LE 1	LE 1 B	LE ◇1 ☕	LE 1 C	LE 1	LE 1 D	LE 1	LE ◇1	LE 1 A	LE 1	LE ◇1 ☕	LE 1	LE 1	LE ◇1 ☕
London Liverpool Street 15 ⊖	d			14 02	14 18			14 30	14 38	14 48		15 00				15 02	15 18			15 30	15 38	15 48	16 00
Stratford 7 ⊖	d			14 09	14 25			14u38	14 45	14 55						15 09	15 25			15u38	15 45	15 55	
Romford	d								14 53												15 53		
Shenfield 3	d			14 25	14 41				15 03	15 11						15 25	15 41				16 03	16 11	
Ingatestone	d				14 45					15 15							15 45					16 15	
Chelmsford	d			14 34	14 52			15 03	15 12	15 22						15 34	15 52			16 03	16 12	16 22	
Hatfield Peverel	d			14 40												15 40							
Witham 2	d			14 47	15 03				15 23	15 34						15 47	16 03				16 23	16 34	
White Notley	d									15 41												16 41	
Cressing	d									15 43												16 43	
Braintree Freeport	d									15 46												16 46	
Braintree	a									15 50												16 50	
Kelvedon	d			14 51					15 27							15 51					16 27		
Marks Tey 2	d			14 57					15 33							15 57					16 33		
Colchester 4	a			15 04	15 15			15 23	15 40			15 46				16 04	16 15			16 22	16 40		16 46
	d		14 56	15 04	15 16		15 20	15 23	15 41			15 47			15 56	16 04	16 16		16 20	16 23	16 41		16 47
Colchester Town	a		15 03				15 27		15 49						16 03				16 27		16 49		
	d		15 07												16 07								
Hythe	d		15 11												16 11								
Wivenhoe	d		15 15		15 23										16 15		16 23						
Alresford (Essex)	d		15 19												16 19								
Great Bentley	d		15 23												16 23								
Weeley	d		15 26			←									16 26			←					
Thorpe-le-Soken 1	a		15 31		15 35	15 31									16 31		16 35	16 31					
	d		15 37		15 35	15 37									16 37		16 35	16 37					
Clacton-on-Sea	a		→		15 44										→		16 44						
Kirby Cross	d					15 42												16 42					
Frinton-on-Sea	d					15 45												16 45					
Walton-on-the-Naze	a					15 49												16 49					
Manningtree 5	d	15 00		15 12				15 31				15 55		16 00		16 12				16 31			16 55
Mistley	d	15 04												16 04									
Wrabness	d	15 09												16 09									
Harwich International	d	15 17												16 17									
Dovercourt	d	15 20												16 20									
Harwich Town	a	15 22												16 22									
Ipswich	a			15 25				15 43				16 07				16 25				16 43			17 07
	d							15 44			15 58	16 08	16 20							16 44			17 08
Needham Market	d												16 29										
Stowmarket	d							15 55			16a09		16a34							16 55			17 19
Diss	d							16 08				16 29								17 08			17 32
Norwich	a							16 27				16 50								17 27			17 51

A From Colchester
B To Peterborough
C To Cambridge
D To Walton-on-the-Naze

Table T011-F

Saturdays
26 May to 8 December

London - Chelmsford, Colchester, Walton-on-Naze, Clacton, Harwich, Ipswich and Norwich

Station		LE 1 A	LE 1	LE 1 B	LE 1	LE ◇1	LE 1 C	LE 1	LE ◇1 ☕	LE 1	LE 1	LE 1 D	LE ◇1 ☕	LE 1 A	LE 1	LE 1 B	LE ◇1	LE ◇1	LE 1 C	LE 1	LE ◇1 ☕	LE 1	LE 1
London Liverpool Street 15 ⊖	d				16 02	16 18			16 30	16 38	16 48		17 00				17 02	17 18			17 30	17 38	17 48
Stratford 7 ⊖	d				16 09	16 25			16u38	16 45	16 55						17 09	17 25			17u38	17 45	17 55
Romford	d									16 53												17 53	
Shenfield 3	d				16 25	16 41				17 03	17 11						17 25	17 41				18 03	18 11
Ingatestone	d					16 45					17 15							17 45					18 15
Chelmsford	d				16 34	16 52			17 03	17 12	17 22						17 34	17 52			18 03	18 12	18 22
Hatfield Peverel	d				16 40												17 40						
Witham 2	d				16 47	17 03				17 23	17 34						17 47	18 03				18 23	18 34
White Notley	d										17 41												18 41
Cressing	d										17 43												18 43
Braintree Freeport	d										17 46												18 46
Braintree	a										17 50												18 50
Kelvedon	d				16 51					17 27							17 51					18 27	
Marks Tey 2	d				16 57					17 33							17 57					18 33	
Colchester 4	a				17 04	17 15			17 22	17 40			17 46				18 04	18 15			18 22	18 40	
	d			16 56	17 04	17 16		17 20	17 23	17 41			17 47			17 56	18 04	18 16		18 20	18 23	18 41	
Colchester Town	a			17 03				17 27		17 49						18 03				18 27		18 49	
	d			17 07												18 07							
Hythe	d			17 11												18 11							
Wivenhoe	d			17 15		17 23										18 15		18 23					
Alresford (Essex)	d			17 19												18 19							
Great Bentley	d			17 23												18 23							
Weeley	d			17 26			←									18 26			←				
Thorpe-le-Soken 1	a			17 31		17 35	17 31									18 31		18 35	18 31				
	d			17 37		17 35	17 37									18 37		18 35	18 37				
Clacton-on-Sea	a			→		17 44										→		18 44					
Kirby Cross	d						17 42												18 42				
Frinton-on-Sea	d						17 45												18 45				
Walton-on-the-Naze	a						17 49												18 49				
Manningtree 5	d		17 00		17 12				17 31				17 55		18 00		18 12				18 31		
Mistley	d		17 04												18 04								
Wrabness	d		17 09												18 09								
Harwich International	d		17 17												18 17								
Dovercourt	d		17 20												18 20								
Harwich Town	a		17 22												18 22								
Ipswich	a				17 25				17 43				18 07				18 25				18 43		
	d	17 20							17 44			17 58	18 08	18 20							18 44		
Needham Market	d	17 29												18 29									
Stowmarket	d	17a34							17 55			18a09		18a34							18 55		
Diss	d								18 08				18 29								19 08		
Norwich	a								18 27				18 50								19 27		

Station		LE ◇1 ☕	LE 1 A	LE 1	LE 1 B	LE ◇1	LE ◇1	LE 1 C	LE 1	LE ◇1 ☕	LE 1	LE 1	LE 1 D	LE ◇1 ☕	LE 1 A	LE 1	LE 1 B	LE ◇1	LE ◇1	LE 1 C	LE 1	LE ◇1 ☕
London Liverpool Street 15 ⊖	d	18 00				18 02	18 18			18 30	18 38	18 48		19 00				19 02	19 18			19 30
Stratford 7 ⊖	d					18 09	18 25			18u38	18 45	18 55						19 09	19 25			19u38
Romford	d										18 53											
Shenfield 3	d					18 25	18 41				19 03	19 11						19 25	19 41			
Ingatestone	d						18 45					19 15							19 45			
Chelmsford	d					18 34	18 52			19 03	19 12	19 22						19 34	19 52			20 03
Hatfield Peverel	d					18 40												19 40				
Witham 2	d					18 47	19 03				19 23	19 34						19 47	20 03			
White Notley	d											19 41										
Cressing	d											19 43										
Braintree Freeport	d											19 46										
Braintree	a											19 50										
Kelvedon	d					18 51					19 27							19 51				
Marks Tey 2	d					18 57					19 33							19 57				
Colchester 4	a	18 46				19 04	19 15			19 22	19 40			19 46				20 04	20 15			20 22
	d	18 47			18 56	19 04	19 16		19 20	19 23	19 41			19 47			19 56	20 04	20 16		20 20	20 23
Colchester Town	a				19 03				19 27		19 49						20 03				20 27	
	d				19 07												20 07					
Hythe	d				19 11												20 11					
Wivenhoe	d				19 15		19 23										20 15		20 23			
Alresford (Essex)	d				19 19												20 19					
Great Bentley	d				19 23												20 23					
Weeley	d				19 26			←									20 26			←		
Thorpe-le-Soken 1	a				19 31		19 35	19 31									20 31		20 35	20 31		
	d				19 37		19 35	19 37									20 37		20 35	20 37		
Clacton-on-Sea	a				→		19 44										→		20 44			
Kirby Cross	d							19 42												20 42		
Frinton-on-Sea	d							19 45												20 45		
Walton-on-the-Naze	a							19 49												20 49		
Manningtree 5	d	18 55		19 00		19 12				19 31				19 55		20 00		20 12				20 31
Mistley	d			19 04												20 04						
Wrabness	d			19 09												20 09						
Harwich International	d			19 17												20 17						
Dovercourt	d			19 20												20 20						
Harwich Town	a			19 22												20 22						
Ipswich	a	19 07				19 25				19 43				20 07				20 25				20 43
	d	19 08	19 20							19 44			19 58	20 08	20 20							20 44
Needham Market	d		19 29												20 29							
Stowmarket	d		19a34							19 55			20a09		20a34							20 55
Diss	d	19 29								20 08				20 29								21 08
Norwich	a	19 50								20 27				20 50								21 27

A To Cambridge
B To Walton-on-the-Naze
C From Colchester
D To Peterborough

Table T011-F

Saturdays
26 May to 8 December

London - Chelmsford, Colchester, Walton-on-Naze, Clacton, Harwich, Ipswich and Norwich

		LE ■	LE ■	LE ■	LE ◇■ ☕	LE A	LE ■	LE ■ B	LE ■	LE ◇■	LE ■ C	LE ■	LE ◇■ ☕	LE ■	LE ■	LE ■ D	LE ◇■	LE ■ E	LE ■	LE ■ B	LE ■	LE ◇■	LE ■ C
London Liverpool Street 15 ⊖	d	19 32	19 38	19 48	20 00				20 02	20 18			20 30	20 38	20 48		21 00				21 02	21 18	
Stratford 7 ⊖	d	19 39	19 46	19 55					20 09	20 25			20u38	20 45	20 55						21 09	21 25	
Romford	d		19 54											20 53									
Shenfield 3	d	19 57	20 04	20 11					20 25	20 41				21 03	21 11						21 25	21 41	
Ingatestone	d			20 15						20 45					21 15							21 45	
Chelmsford	d	20 07	20 13	20 22					20 34	20 52			21 03	21 12	21 22						21 34	21 52	
Hatfield Peverel	d								20 40												21 40		
Witham 2	d	20 20	20 24	20 34					20 47	21 03				21 23	21 34						21 47	22 03	
White Notley	d			20 41											21 41								
Cressing	d			20 43											21 43								
Braintree Freeport	d			20 46											21 46								
Braintree	a			20 50											21 50								
Kelvedon	d		20 28						20 51					21 27							21 51		
Marks Tey 2	d		20 34						20 57					21 33							21 57		
Colchester 4	a	20 32	20 41		20 46				21 04	21 15			21 22	21 40			21 46				22 04	22 15	
	d	20 32	20 42		20 47			20 56	21 04	21 16		21 20	21 23	21 41			21 48			21 56	22 04	22 16	
Colchester Town	a		20 50					21 03				21 27		21 49						22 03			
	d							21 07												22 07			
Hythe	d							21 11												22 11			
Wivenhoe	d							21 15		21 23										22 15		22 23	
Alresford (Essex)	d							21 19												22 19			
Great Bentley	d							21 23												22 23			
Weeley	d							21 26			←									22 26			←
Thorpe-le-Soken 1	a							21 31		21 35	21 31									22 31		22 35	22 31
	d							21 37		21 35	21 37									22 37		22 35	22 37
Clacton-on-Sea	a							→		21 44										→		22 44	
Kirby Cross	d										21 42												22 42
Frinton-on-Sea	d										21 45												22 45
Walton-on-the-Naze	a										21 49												22 49
Manningtree 5	d	20 40			20 55		21 00		21 12				21 32				21 56		22 00		22 12		
Mistley	d						21 04												22 04				
Wrabness	d						21 09												22 09				
Harwich International	d	20a56					21 17									21 38			22 17		22a28		
Dovercourt	d						21 20												22 20				
Harwich Town	a						21 22												22 22				
Ipswich	a				21 07				21 25				21 43			22 03	22 08						
	d				21 08	21 17							21 45					22 19					
Needham Market	d					21 27												22 29					
Stowmarket	d					21a33							21 56					22a35					
Diss	d				21 29								22 09										
Norwich	a				21 50								22 29										

		LE ◇■ ☕	LE ■	LE ■	LE ■	LE ■	LE ■ F	LE ■ B	LE ■	LE ◇■	LE ■ C	LE ◇■ ☕	LE ■	LE ■	LE ■	LE ■ G	LE ■	XR	LE ◇■ ☕	LE ■	XR	LE ■
London Liverpool Street 15 ⊖	d	21 30	21 38	21 48	22 00				22 02	22 18		22 30		22 32			23 02	23 17	23 30	23 32	23 47	23 58
Stratford 7 ⊖	d	21u38	21 45	21 55					22 09	22 25		22u38		22 41			23 09	23 24	23u38	23 41	23 54	00 05
Romford	d		21 53											22 49				23 42			00 12	
Shenfield 3	d		22 03	22 11					22 25	22 41				22 59			23 33	23a58		00 04	00a28	00 30
Ingatestone	d			22 15						22 45				23 03						00 08		
Chelmsford	d	22 03	22 12	22 22	22 28				22 34	22 52		23 03		23 10			23 42			00 15		00 39
Hatfield Peverel	d								22 40					23 16						00 21		
Witham 2	d		22 23	22 34					22 47	23 03				23 23	23 25		23 53			00 28		00 50
White Notley	d			22 41											23 32							
Cressing	d			22 43											23 34							
Braintree Freeport	d			22 46											23 37							
Braintree	a			22 50											23 41							
Kelvedon	d		22 27						22 51					23 27			23 57			00 32		
Marks Tey 2	d		22 33						22 57					23 33		23 46	00 03			00 38		
Colchester 4	a	22 22	22 40		22 47				23 05	23 15		23 22		23 47		00 01	00 10		00 26	00 52		01 11
	d	22 23	22 41		22 48			22 56		23 16		23 23					00 10		00 26			
Colchester Town	a		22 49					23 03														
	d							23 07														
Hythe	d							23 11														
Wivenhoe	d							23 15		23 23												
Alresford (Essex)	d							23 19														
Great Bentley	d							23 23														
Weeley	d							23 26			←											
Thorpe-le-Soken 1	a							23 31		23 35	23 31											
	d						23 16	23 37		23 35	23 37											
Clacton-on-Sea	a						23 25	→		23 44												
Kirby Cross	d										23 42											
Frinton-on-Sea	d										23 45											
Walton-on-the-Naze	a										23 49											
Manningtree 5	d	22 32			22 56	23 00						23 32	23 36				00 18		00 36			
Mistley	d					23 04							23 40									
Wrabness	d					23 09							23 45									
Harwich International	d					23 17							23 53									
Dovercourt	d					23 20							23 56									
Harwich Town	a					23 22							23 58									
Ipswich	a	22 44			23 08							23 44					00 36		00 47			
	d	22 45										23 45							00 49			
Needham Market	d																					
Stowmarket	d	22 57										23 57							01 01			
Diss	d	23 11										00 11							01 14			
Norwich	a	23 30										00 36							01 40			

A To Cambridge
B To Walton-on-the-Naze
C From Colchester
D To Lowestoft
E To Bury St Edmunds
F From Walton-on-the-Naze
G 23:26 from Sudbury

Table T011-F

Sundays
20 May to 2 December

London - Chelmsford, Colchester, Walton-on-Naze, Clacton, Harwich, Ipswich and Norwich

		LE ■	LE ■	LE ■	LE ■	LE A	LE ■	LE ■ B	LE ■	LE ■	LE ■ A	LE ■	LE ■	LE ■	LE ■	LE ■	LE ◇■	LE ■	LE ■ C	LE ■	LE ■	LE ■
London Liverpool Street 15 ⊖	d			00 18										07 55	08 02		08 30			08 32		09 02
Stratford 7 ⊖	d			00 25										08 02	08 09					08 39		09 09
Romford	d													08 13								
Shenfield 3	d			00 47										08 27	08 32					09 02		09 32
Ingatestone	d			00 52											08 36							09 36
Chelmsford	d			00 59										08 36	08 43					09 11		09 43
Hatfield Peverel	d			01 05											08 49							09 49
Witham 2	d	00 05		01 11	07 35					08 25				08 47	08 56					09 22	09 25	09 56
White Notley	d	00 12			07 42					08 32											09 32	
Cressing	d	00 14			07 44					08 34											09 34	
Braintree Freeport	d	00 17			07 47					08 37											09 37	
Braintree	a	00 21			07 51					08 41											09 41	
Kelvedon	d			01 16											09 00							10 00
Marks Tey 2	d			01 21											09 06					09 29		10 06
Colchester 4	a			01 35										08 59	09 13		09 25			09 37		10 13
	d		00 30				07 30		08 13			08 18	08 37	08 59	09 13		09 25		09 32	09 37		10 13
Colchester Town	a																					
	d																					
Hythe	d												08 42							09 42		
Wivenhoe	d		00 37										08 46							09 46		
Alresford (Essex)	d		00 41										08 49							09 49		
Great Bentley	d		00 45										08 53							09 53		
Weeley	d																					
Thorpe-le-Soken 1	a		00 52										09 00							10 00		
	d		00 52										09 00					09 02		10 00		
Clacton-on-Sea	a		01 01										09 09							10 09		
Kirby Cross	d																	09 07				
Frinton-on-Sea	d																	09 10				
Walton-on-the-Naze	a																	09 14				
Manningtree 5	d						07 38		08 21			08 26		09 07	09 21	09 26	09 33		09 40			10 21
Mistley	d											08 30				09 30						
Wrabness	d											08 35				09 35						
Harwich International	d										08 30	08 43		09a25		09 43						
Dovercourt	d											08 46				09 46						
Harwich Town	a											08 48				09 48						
Ipswich	a						07 50		08 33		08 53				09 35		09 45		09 51			10 33
	d					07 32		07 55			09 02						09 46		09 55			
Needham Market	d					07 42					09 12											
Stowmarket	d					07a48		08a06			09a17						09 57		10a06			
Diss	d																10 10					
Norwich	a																10 31					

		LE ■	LE ◇■ ☕	LE ■ A	LE ■	LE ◇■	LE ■	LE ■	LE ■	LE ◇■ ☕	LE ■	LE ◇■	LE ■	LE ■ C	LE ◇■ D ☕	LE ■	LE ■	LE ◇■ ☕	LE ■ A	LE ■	LE ◇■	LE ■	LE ■
London Liverpool Street 15 ⊖	d		09 30			09 32		10 02		10 30		10 32			11 00	11 02		11 30			11 32		12 02
Stratford 7 ⊖	d					09 39		10 09				10 39				11 09					11 39		12 09
Romford	d																						
Shenfield 3	d					10 02		10 32				11 02				11 32					12 02		12 32
Ingatestone	d							10 36								11 36							12 36
Chelmsford	d					10 11		10 43				11 11				11 43					12 11		12 43
Hatfield Peverel	d							10 49								11 49							12 49
Witham 2	d					10 22	10 25	10 56				11 22	11 25			11 56					12 22	12 25	12 56
White Notley	d						10 32						11 32									12 32	
Cressing	d						10 34						11 34									12 34	
Braintree Freeport	d						10 37						11 37									12 37	
Braintree	a						10 41						11 41									12 41	
Kelvedon	d							11 00								12 00							13 00
Marks Tey 2	d					10 29		11 06				11 29				12 06					12 29		13 06
Colchester 4	a		10 25			10 37		11 13		11 25		11 37			11 56	12 13		12 25			12 37		13 13
	d		10 25			10 37		11 13		11 25		11 37			11 56	12 13		12 25			12 37		13 13
Colchester Town	a																						
	d																						
Hythe	d					10 42						11 42									12 42		
Wivenhoe	d					10 46						11 46									12 46		
Alresford (Essex)	d					10 49						11 49									12 49		
Great Bentley	d					10 53						11 53									12 53		
Weeley	d																						
Thorpe-le-Soken 1	a					11 00						12 00									13 00		
	d				10 02	11 00					11 02	12 00								12 02	13 00		
Clacton-on-Sea	a					11 09						12 09									13 09		
Kirby Cross	d				10 07						11 07									12 07			
Frinton-on-Sea	d				10 10						11 10									12 10			
Walton-on-the-Naze	a				10 14						11 14									12 14			
Manningtree 5	d	10 26	10 33					11 21	11 26	11 33						12 21	12 26	12 33					13 21
Mistley	d	10 30							11 30								12 30						
Wrabness	d	10 35							11 35								12 35						
Harwich International	d	10 43							11 43								12 43						
Dovercourt	d	10 46							11 46								12 46						
Harwich Town	a	10 48							11 48								12 48						
Ipswich	a		10 45					11 33		11 45					12 13	12 34		12 45					13 33
	d		10 46	11 02						11 46				11 55	12 15			12 46	13 02				
Needham Market	d			11 12															13 12				
Stowmarket	d		10 57	11a18						11 57				12a06	12 26			12 57	13a18				
Diss	d		11 10							12 10					12 38			13 10					
Norwich	a		11 31							12 31					13 00			13 31					

A To Cambridge
B until 9 September. To Peterborough
C To Peterborough
D until 9 September

Table T011-F

Sundays
20 May to 2 December

London - Chelmsford, Colchester, Walton-on-Naze, Clacton, Harwich, Ipswich and Norwich

		LE 1	LE ◇1 ☕	LE 1	LE ◇1	LE 1	LE 1 A	LE 1	LE 1	LE ◇1 ☕	LE 1 B	LE 1	LE ◇1	LE 1	LE 1	LE 1	LE ◇1 ☕	LE 1	LE ◇1	LE 1	LE 1 A	LE 1
London Liverpool Street 15 ⊖	d		12 30		12 32			13 02		13 30			13 32		14 02		14 30		14 32			15 02
Stratford 7 ⊖	d				12 39			13 09					13 39		14 09				14 39			15 09
Romford	d																					
Shenfield 3	d				13 02			13 32					14 02		14 32				15 02			15 32
Ingatestone	d							13 36							14 36							15 36
Chelmsford	d				13 11			13 43					14 11		14 43				15 11			15 43
Hatfield Peverel	d							13 49							14 49							15 49
Witham 2	d				13 22	13 25		13 56					14 22	14 25	14 56				15 22	15 25		15 56
White Notley	d					13 32								14 32						15 32		
Cressing	d					13 34								14 34						15 34		
Braintree Freeport	d					13 37								14 37						15 37		
Braintree	a					13 41								14 41						15 41		
Kelvedon	d							14 00							15 00							16 00
Marks Tey 2	d				13 29			14 06					14 29		15 06				15 29			16 06
Colchester 4	a		13 25		13 37			14 13		14 25			14 37		15 13		15 25		15 37			16 13
	d		13 25		13 37			14 13		14 25			14 37		15 13		15 25		15 37			16 13
Colchester Town	a																					
	d																					
Hythe	d				13 42								14 42						15 42			
Wivenhoe	d				13 46								14 46						15 46			
Alresford (Essex)	d				13 49								14 49						15 49			
Great Bentley	d				13 53								14 53						15 53			
Weeley	d																					
Thorpe-le-Soken 1	a				14 00								15 00						16 00			
	d			13 02	14 00							14 02	15 00					15 02	16 00			
Clacton-on-Sea	a				14 09								15 09						16 09			
Kirby Cross	d			13 07								14 07						15 07				
Frinton-on-Sea	d			13 10								14 10						15 10				
Walton-on-the-Naze	a			13 14								14 14						15 14				
Manningtree 5	d	13 26	13 33					14 21	14 26	14 33					15 21	15 26	15 33					16 21
Mistley	d	13 30							14 30							15 30						
Wrabness	d	13 35							14 35							15 35						
Harwich International	d	13 43							14 43							15 43						
Dovercourt	d	13 46							14 46							15 46						
Harwich Town	a	13 48							14 48							15 48						
Ipswich	a		13 45					14 33		14 45					15 35		15 45					16 33
	d		13 46				13 55			14 46	15 02						15 46				15 55	
Needham Market	d										15 12											
Stowmarket	d		13 57				14a06			14 57	15a18						15 57				16a06	
Diss	d		14 10							15 10							16 10					
Norwich	a		14 31							15 31							16 31					

		LE 1	LE ◇1 ☕	LE 1 B	LE 1	LE ◇1	LE 1	LE 1	LE 1	LE ◇1 ☕	LE 1	LE ◇1	LE 1	LE 1 A	LE 1	LE 1	LE ◇1 ☕	LE 1 B	LE 1	LE ◇1	LE 1	LE ◇1 C ☕	LE 1
London Liverpool Street 15 ⊖	d		15 30			15 32		16 02		16 30		16 32			17 02		17 30			17 32		18 00	18 02
Stratford 7 ⊖	d					15 39		16 09				16 39			17 09					17 39			18 09
Romford	d																						
Shenfield 3	d					16 02		16 32				17 02			17 32					18 02			18 32
Ingatestone	d							16 36							17 36								18 36
Chelmsford	d					16 11		16 43				17 11			17 43					18 11			18 43
Hatfield Peverel	d							16 49							17 49								18 49
Witham 2	d					16 22	16 25	16 56				17 22	17 25		17 56					18 22	18 25		18 56
White Notley	d						16 32						17 32								18 32		
Cressing	d						16 34						17 34								18 34		
Braintree Freeport	d						16 37						17 37								18 37		
Braintree	a						16 41						17 41								18 41		
Kelvedon	d							17 00							18 00								19 00
Marks Tey 2	d					16 29		17 06				17 29			18 06					18 29			19 06
Colchester 4	a		16 25			16 37		17 13		17 25		17 37			18 13		18 25			18 37		18 56	19 13
	d		16 25			16 37		17 13		17 25		17 37			18 13		18 25			18 37		18 56	19 13
Colchester Town	a																						
	d																						
Hythe	d					16 42						17 42								18 42			
Wivenhoe	d					16 46						17 46								18 46			
Alresford (Essex)	d					16 49						17 49								18 49			
Great Bentley	d					16 53						17 53								18 53			
Weeley	d																						
Thorpe-le-Soken 1	a					17 00						18 00								19 00			
	d				16 02	17 00					17 02	18 00							18 02	19 00			
Clacton-on-Sea	a					17 09						18 09								19 09			
Kirby Cross	d				16 07						17 07								18 07				
Frinton-on-Sea	d				16 10						17 10								18 10				
Walton-on-the-Naze	a				16 14						17 14								18 14				
Manningtree 5	d	16 26	16 33					17 21	17 26	17 33					18 21	18 26	18 33						19 21
Mistley	d	16 30							17 30							18 30							
Wrabness	d	16 35							17 35							18 35							
Harwich International	d	16 43							17 43							18 43							
Dovercourt	d	16 46							17 46							18 46							
Harwich Town	a	16 48							17 48							18 48							
Ipswich	a		16 45					17 33		17 45					18 33		18 45					19 13	19 34
	d		16 46	17 02						17 46				17 55			18 46	19 02				19 15	
Needham Market	d			17 12														19 12					
Stowmarket	d		16 57	17a18						17 57				18a06			18 57	19a18				19 26	
Diss	d		17 10							18 10							19 10					19 38	
Norwich	a		17 31							18 31							19 31					20 00	

A To Peterborough
B To Cambridge
C until 9 September

NRT MAY 2018 EDITION

Table T011-F

Sundays
20 May to 2 December

London - Chelmsford, Colchester, Walton-on-Naze, Clacton, Harwich, Ipswich and Norwich

		LE 1	LE ◇1 ☕	LE 1	LE ◇1	LE 1	LE ◇1 ☕	LE 1	LE 1	LE ◇1 ☕	LE A	LE 1	LE ◇1		LE 1	LE 1	LE 1	LE 1	LE 1	LE ◇1 ☕	LE ◇1	LE 1	LE 1
London Liverpool Street 15 ⊖	d		18 30		18 32		19 00	19 02		19 30			19 32			20 02				20 30	20 32		21 02
Stratford 7 ⊖	d				18 39			19 09					19 39			20 09					20 39		21 09
Romford	d																						
Shenfield 3	d				19 02			19 32					20 02			20 32					21 02		21 32
Ingatestone	d							19 36								20 36							21 36
Chelmsford	d				19 11			19 43					20 11			20 43					21 11		21 43
Hatfield Peverel	d							19 49								20 49							21 49
Witham 2	d				19 22	19 25		19 56					20 22		20 25	20 56					21 22	21 25	21 56
White Notley	d					19 32									20 32							21 32	
Cressing	d					19 34									20 34							21 34	
Braintree Freeport	d					19 37									20 37							21 37	
Braintree	a					19 41									20 41							21 41	
Kelvedon	d							20 00								21 00							22 00
Marks Tey 2	d				19 29			20 06					20 29			21 06					21 29		22 06
Colchester 4	a		19 25		19 37		19 55	20 13		20 25			20 37			21 13				21 25	21 37		22 13
	d		19 25		19 37		19 55	20 13		20 25			20 40	20 46		21 13				21 25	21 37		22 13
Colchester Town	a																						
	d																						
Hythe	d				19 42								20 45								21 42		
Wivenhoe	d				19 46								20 49								21 46		
Alresford (Essex)	d				19 49								20 52								21 49		
Great Bentley	d				19 53								20 56								21 53		
Weeley	d																						
Thorpe-le-Soken 1	a				20 00								21 03								22 00		
	d			19 02	20 00							20 02	21 03				21 05				22 00		
Clacton-on-Sea	a				20 09								21 12								22 09		
Kirby Cross	d			19 07								20 07					21 10						
Frinton-on-Sea	d			19 10								20 10					21 13						
Walton-on-the-Naze	a			19 14								20 14					21 17						
Manningtree 5	d	19 26	19 33				20 03	20 21	20 26	20 33				20 55		21 21			21 26	21 34			22 21
Mistley	d	19 30							20 30										21 30				
Wrabness	d	19 35							20 35										21 35				
Harwich International	d	19 43							20 43					21a14				21 10	21 43				
Dovercourt	d	19 46							20 46										21 46				
Harwich Town	a	19 48							20 48										21 48				
Ipswich	a		19 45				20 15	20 33		20 45						21 33		21 37		21 45			22 33
	d		19 46				20 16			20 46	21 02									21 47			
Needham Market	d										21 12												
Stowmarket	d		19 57				20 27			20 57	21a18									21 58			
Diss	d		20 10				20 40			21 10										22 11			
Norwich	a		20 31				21 01			21 31										22 31			

		LE 1	LE ◇1 ☕	LE 1	LE ◇1	LE 1	LE 1 B	LE 1	LE ◇1 ☕	LE 1	LE ◇1	LE 1	LE 1	LE ◇1	LE 1
London Liverpool Street 15 ⊖	d		21 30		21 32			22 02	22 30		22 32		23 02	23 30	23 32
Stratford 7 ⊖	d				21 39			22 09			22 39		23 09		23 39
Romford	d														
Shenfield 3	d				22 02			22 32			23 02		23 32		00 02
Ingatestone	d							22 36					23 36		
Chelmsford	d				22 11			22 43			23 11		23 43		00 11
Hatfield Peverel	d							22 49					23 49		
Witham 2	d				22 22	22 25		22 56			23 22	23 25	23 56		00 22
White Notley	d					22 32						23 32			
Cressing	d					22 34						23 34			
Braintree Freeport	d					22 37						23 37			
Braintree	a					22 41						23 41			
Kelvedon	d							23 00					23 59		
Marks Tey 2	d				22 29		23 02	23 06			23 29		00 06		00 29
Colchester 4	a		22 25		22 37		23 10	23 13	23 25		23 37		00 13	00 25	00 43
	d		22 25		22 37			23 13	23 25		23 37		00 13	00 25	
Colchester Town	a														
	d														
Hythe	d				22 42						23 42				
Wivenhoe	d				22 46						23 46				
Alresford (Essex)	d				22 49						23 49				
Great Bentley	d				22 53						23 53				
Weeley	d														
Thorpe-le-Soken 1	a				23 00						23 59				
	d			22 02	23 00					23 02	23 59				
Clacton-on-Sea	a				23 09						00 15				
Kirby Cross	d			22 07						23 07					
Frinton-on-Sea	d			22 10						23 10					
Walton-on-the-Naze	a			22 14						23 14					
Manningtree 5	d	22 26	22 34					23 21	23 34				00 21	00 34	
Mistley	d	22 30													
Wrabness	d	22 35													
Harwich International	d	22 43													
Dovercourt	d	22 46													
Harwich Town	a	22 48													
Ipswich	a		22 46					23 33	23 46				00 39	00 46	
	d		22 47						23 47					00 47	
Needham Market	d														
Stowmarket	d		22 59						23 59					00 59	
Diss	d		23 13						00 13					01 13	
Norwich	a		23 32						00 32					01 37	

A To Cambridge
B 22:42 from Sudbury

Norwich, Ipswich, Harwich, Clacton, Walton-on-Naze, Colchester and Chelmsford - London

Miles	Miles	Miles	Miles	Miles			LE MX	LE	LE	LE	LE	LE	LE	LE	LE	LE	LE	LE	LE	LE	LE	LE
							■	■	■	◇■	■	■	◇■	◇■ ☕	■	■	◇■	■	■ A	■	■	■■ ☕
0	—	—	—	—	**Norwich**	d								05 00								05 30
20	—	—	—	—	Diss	d								05 18								05 48
34¼	—	—	—	—	Stowmarket	d								05 30					05 52			06 00
38	—	—	—	—	Needham Market	d													05 57			
46¼	—	—	0	—	**Ipswich**	a								05 42					06 07			06 12
—	—	—	—	—		d				05 12				05 44				06 00				06 14
—	0	—	—	—	**Harwich Town**	d					05 24											
—	0½	—	—	—	Dovercourt	d					05 26											
—	1¾	—	—	—	Harwich International	d					05 29											
—	5½	—	—	—	Wrabness	d					05 35											
—	9½	—	10½	—	Mistley	d					05 41											
55½	11¼	—	—	—	Manningtree ■	d				05 24	05a46			05 54				06 11				06 24
—	—	0	—	—	**Walton-on-the-Naze**	d									05 33					06 03		
—	—	1¼	—	—	Frinton-on-Sea	d									05 36					06 06		
—	—	2½	—	—	Kirby Cross	d									05 39					06 09		
—	—	—	0	—	**Clacton-on-Sea**	d							05 20				05 40					
—	—	5	4¾	—	Thorpe-le-Soken ■	a							05 28		05 45		05 48			06 15		
—	—	—	—	—		d							05 28				05 48					
—	—	7¼	—	—	Weeley	d											05 52					
—	—	10	—	—	Great Bentley	d											05 56					
—	—	12¼	—	—	Alresford (Essex)	d											06 00					
—	—	14	—	—	Wivenhoe	d							05 38				06 04					
—	—	16½	—	—	Hythe	d											06 08					
—	—	18	—	—	Colchester Town	a																
—	—	—	—	—		d															06 19	
63¼	—	19¾	—	—	**Colchester** ■	a				05 33			05 46	06 03			06 14	06 20			06 26	06 33
—	—	—	—	—		d		04 43	05 12	05 34			05 47	06 05			06 15	06 20			06 27	06 35
68¼	—	—	—	—	Marks Tey ■	d		04 49	05 18				05 53					06 26			06 33	
72¾	—	—	—	—	Kelvedon	d		04 54	05 23				05 59				06 25	06 32				
—	—	—	—	0	**Braintree**	d	00 27					05 43										
—	—	—	—	0¾	Braintree Freeport	d	00 29					05 45										
—	—	—	—	2	Cressing	d	00 32					05 48										
—	—	—	—	3¼	White Notley	d	00 35					05 51										
76½	—	—	—	6¼	**Witham** ■	d	00a43	05 00	05 29	05 48		06a00	06 05			06 18	06 31	06 38			06 47	
79	—	—	—	—	Hatfield Peverel	d		05 04	05 33							06 22						
85¼	—	—	—	—	**Chelmsford**	d		05 11	05 40	05 58			06 14			06 29	06 40	06 47			06 56	
91½	—	—	—	—	Ingatestone	d		05 18	05 47							06 36					07 03	
94¾	—	—	—	—	Shenfield ■	a		05 23	05 52				06 24			06 42	06 50				07 08	
102¾	—	—	—	—	Romford	a		05 32														
111	—	—	—	—	Stratford ■ ⊖ ⛴	a		05 42	06 07	06s23			06 39	06s44		06s58	07s06				07s23	07s15
115	—	—	—	—	**London Liverpool Street** ■ ⊖	a		05 51	06 16	06 34			06 48	06 54		07 09	07 18	07 23			07 35	07 27

A From Bury St Edmunds

Table T011-R

Mondays to Fridays

21 May to 7 December

Norwich, Ipswich, Harwich, Clacton, Walton-on-Naze, Colchester and Chelmsford - London

		LE	LE	LE	LE	LE	LE	LE	LE	LE	LE	LE	LE	LE	LE	LE	LE	LE	LE	LE	LE
		◇■	■	■	■	■	■■ ☕	■	■	■	◇■	◇■	■	■ A	B	■	◇■	■■ ☕	■	■	■
Norwich	d						06 00											06 24			
Diss	d						06 18											06 42			
Stowmarket	d						06 30								06 42			06 54			
Needham Market	d														06 47						
Ipswich	a						06 42								07 00			07 06			
	d			06 29			06 44					06 52		06 59				07 08			
Harwich Town	d				06 24								06 52								
Dovercourt	d				06 26								06 54								
Harwich International	d				06 29								06 57	07a27							
Wrabness	d				06 35								07 03								
Mistley	d				06 41								07 09								
Manningtree ■	d			06 39	06a46		06 54					07 02	07a14					07 18			
Walton-on-the-Naze	d								06 31											06 58	
Frinton-on-Sea	d								06 34											07 01	
Kirby Cross	d								06 37											07 04	
Clacton-on-Sea	d	06 10						06 28			06 38						06 47		06 51		
Thorpe-le-Soken ■	a	06 18						06 36	06 43		06 46						06 55		06 59	07 10	
	d	06 18						06 36			06 46						06 55		06 59		
Weeley	d							06 40											07 03		
Great Bentley	d							06 43											07 06		
Alresford (Essex)	d							06 47											07 10		
Wivenhoe	d	06 29						06 51			06 57						07 06		07 14		
Hythe	d	06 33						06 55			07 01						07 10		07 18		
Colchester Town	a							06 59											07 22		
	d					06 47		07 03											07 27		
Colchester ■	a	06 39		06 48		06 54	07 03	07 13			07 07	07 12					07 16	07 28	07 36		
	d	06 40		06 49		06 55	07 05				07 08	07 13					07 17	07 30			
Marks Tey ■	d			06 55		07 01						07 19					07 23				
Kelvedon	d	06 50		07 00							07 18						07 29				
Braintree	d		06 40																		
Braintree Freeport	d		06 42																		
Cressing	d		06 45																		
White Notley	d		06 48																		
Witham ■	d		06 57	07 06		07 10				07 17						07 29	07 35				
Hatfield Peverel	d		07 02													07 33					
Chelmsford	d	07 03	07 09			07 19				07 27	07 31	07 35				07 40					07 49
Ingatestone	d									07 33		07 42									07 56
Shenfield ■	a		07 19							07 39	07 41					07 50					08 01
Romford	a																				
Stratford ■ ⊖ ⛴	a	07s27	07s35	07s38		07s44				07s55	07s58	08s01				08s07	08s09				08s18
London Liverpool Street ■ ⊖	a	07 38	07 46	07 50		07 56	07 58			08 07	08 09	08 13				08 19	08 22	08 24			08 30

A From Lowestoft

B From Bury St Edmunds

Table T011-R

Mondays to Fridays
21 May to 7 December

Norwich, Ipswich, Harwich, Clacton, Walton-on-Naze, Colchester and Chelmsford - London

		LE	LE	LE	LE	LE	LE	LE	LE	LE	LE	LE	LE	LE	LE	LE	LE	LE	LE	LE	LE	LE
		■	◇■	◇■	■	■	■ ■ ⊏P	■	■	E	◇■	■ ■ ⊏P	A	■	■	■ B	■	■	■ ■ C ⊏P	■ D	■	■
Norwich	d						06 48					07 05							07 40			
Diss	d						07 06					07 23							07 58			
Stowmarket	d			07 03			07 18					07 35	07 45									
Needham Market	d												07 50									
Ipswich	a			07 16			07 30					07 47	08 02						08 18			
	d			07 17			07 32				07 38	07 49							08 20			
Harwich Town	d							07 16													07 58	
Dovercourt	d							07 18													08 00	
Harwich International	d					07 15		07 21		07 50											08 03	
Wrabness	d							07 27		07 56											08 09	
Mistley	d							07 33		08 02											08 15	
Manningtree ■	d			07 27		07 31	07 43	07 38			07 49	07 59									08 20	
Walton-on-the-Naze	d															07 38						08 00
Frinton-on-Sea	d															07 41						08 03
Kirby Cross	d															07 44						08 06
Clacton-on-Sea	d		07 05						07 16									07 45		←		
Thorpe-le-Soken ■	a		07 13						07 24							07 50		07 53		07 50		08 11
	d		07 13						07 24							07 58		07 53		07 58		08 12
Weeley	d								07 28							→				08 02		
Great Bentley	d								07 31											08 05		
Alresford (Essex)	d								07 35											08 09		
Wivenhoe	d		07 24						07 39									08 03		08 13		08 22
Hythe	d								07 43											08 17		08 26
Colchester Town	a																			08 21		
	d																08 00			08 32		
Colchester ■	a		07 32	07 37		07 41		07 47	07 50		07 58	08 08					08 09	08 16		08 40	08 29	08 35
	d		07 33	07 38		07 42		07 54			07 59	08 10					08 18			08 48	08 37	
Marks Tey ■	d			07 44		07 48					08 05						08 24			→		
Kelvedon	d		07 43	07 49				08 04			08 10						08 30					
Braintree	d	07 26													08 12							
Braintree Freeport	d	07 28													08 14							
Cressing	d	07 31													08 17							
White Notley	d	07 34													08 20							
Witham ■	d	07 43	07 50	07 55		08 03		08 10			08 16				08 28		08 36				08 50	
Hatfield Peverel	d	07 48				08 07									08 32							
Chelmsford	d	07 55	07 59		08 09	08 14		08 19						08 30	08 39		08 45				08 59	
Ingatestone	d				08 16									08 37	08 46							
Shenfield ■	a		08 09		08 21	08 24		08 29						08 42	08 51		08 55				09 09	
Romford	a																					
Stratford ■ ⊖ ⛴	a	08s20	08s25	08s28	08s38	08s40		08s45			08s48	08s52		08s59	09s08						09s25	
London Liverpool Street ■ ⊖	a	08 32	08 38	08 40	08 50	08 54	08 42	08 58			09 01	09 04		09 11	09 19		09 21		09 24		09 36	

A From Cambridge
B To London Liverpool Street
C The East Anglian
D From Walton-on-the-Naze to London Liverpool Street
E To Cambridge

Table T011-R

Mondays to Fridays
21 May to 7 December

Norwich, Ipswich, Harwich, Clacton, Walton-on-Naze, Colchester and Chelmsford - London

		LE	LE	LE	LE	LE	LE	LE	LE	LE	LE	LE	LE	LE	LE	LE	LE	LE	LE	LE	LE	LE
		◇■	■	■	◇■ A	◇■	■ ■ ⊏P	■	■	◇■	■ B	■ ■ ⊏P	■ C	■ D	◇■	■	◇■	■ A	■	■ ■ ⊏P	■	■
Norwich	d						08 00					08 30								09 00		
Diss	d						08 17					08 47								09 17		
Stowmarket	d	08 10					08 29				08 45		09 12							09 29		
Needham Market	d										08 50											
Ipswich	a	08 24					08 41				09 02	09 08	09 26							09 41		
	d	08 26					08 43			08 58		09 09					09 30			09 43		
Harwich Town	d		08 28																09 28			
Dovercourt	d		08 30																09 30			
Harwich International	d		08 33																09 33			
Wrabness	d		08 39																09 39			
Mistley	d		08 45																09 45			
Manningtree ■	d	08 36	08a50				08 53			09 08		09 19					09 40		09a50	09 53		
Walton-on-the-Naze	d													09 00								
Frinton-on-Sea	d													09 03								
Kirby Cross	d													09 06								
Clacton-on-Sea	d					08 11									09 05			←				
Thorpe-le-Soken ■	a					08 19								09 12	09 13			09 12				
	d					08 19								09 17	09 13			09 17				
Weeley	d					08 23								→				09 21				
Great Bentley	d					08 26												09 24				
Alresford (Essex)	d					08 30												09 28				
Wivenhoe	d					08 34									09 23			09 32				
Hythe	d					08 38												09 36				
Colchester Town	a				←													09 40				
	d								08 58							09 35		09 44			10 00	
Colchester ■	a	08 45			08 40	08 46	09 02		09 05	09 17		09 28			09 31	09 42	09 49	09 52		10 02	10 07	
	d	08 45			08 48		09 03		09 07	09 17		09 30			09 33	09 43	09 50			10 03		
Marks Tey ■	d				08 54				09 13								09 56					
Kelvedon	d				09 00				09 19							09 52						
Braintree	d							09 00														10 00
Braintree Freeport	d							09 02														10 02
Cressing	d							09 05														10 05
White Notley	d							09 08														10 08
Witham ■	d			08 58	09 06			09 16	09 29						09 46	09 58	10 05					10 16
Hatfield Peverel	d			09 02					09 33													
Chelmsford	d	09 04		09 09	09 15		09 21	09 26	09 40						09 56	10 07	10 14			10 21		10 26
Ingatestone	d			09 16				09 32							10 02							10 32
Shenfield ■	a			09 21	09 25			09 38	09 50						10 08	10 17						10 38
Romford	a															10 26						
Stratford ■ ⊖ ⛴	a	09s28		09s37	09s41		09s46	09 52	10 06	10 01					10 22	10 34				10s45		10 52
London Liverpool Street ■ ⊖	a	09 39		09 50	09 54		09 58	10 01	10 15	10 10		10 19			10 31	10 43	10 44			10 55		11 01

		LE	LE	LE	LE	LE	LE	LE	LE	LE	LE	LE	LE	LE	LE	LE	LE	LE	LE	LE	LE	LE	LE
		■	■ B	◇■ ⊏P	■	■ D	◇■	■	■ A	◇■ ⊏P	■	■	■	■ B	◇■ ⊏P	■ C	■	■ D	◇■	■	■ A	◇■ ⊏P	■
Norwich	d			09 30						10 00					10 30							11 00	
Diss	d			09 47						10 17					10 47							11 17	
Stowmarket	d		09 47							10 29				10 47		11 14						11 29	
Needham Market	d		09 52											10 52									
Ipswich	a		10 02	10 08						10 41				11 04	11 08	11 28						11 41	
	d	09 52		10 09						10 43			10 52		11 09							11 43	
Harwich Town	d				10 28												11 28						
Dovercourt	d				10 30												11 30						
Harwich International	d				10 33												11 33						
Wrabness	d				10 39												11 39						
Mistley	d				10 45												11 45						
Manningtree ■	d	10 02		10 19	10a50					10 53			11 02		11 19		11a50					11 53	
Walton-on-the-Naze	d					10 00												11 00					
Frinton-on-Sea	d					10 03												11 03					
Kirby Cross	d					10 06												11 06					
Clacton-on-Sea	d						10 05		←										11 05		←		
Thorpe-le-Soken ■	a					10 12	10 13		10 12									11 12	11 13		11 12		
	d					10 17	10 13		10 17									11 17	11 13		11 17		
Weeley	d					→			10 21									→			11 21		
Great Bentley	d								10 24												11 24		
Alresford (Essex)	d								10 28												11 28		
Wivenhoe	d						10 23		10 32										11 23		11 32		
Hythe	d								10 36												11 36		
Colchester Town	a								10 40												11 40		
	d							10 35	10 44		11 00									11 35	11 44		12 00
Colchester ■	a	10 12		10 28			10 31	10 42	10 52	11 02	11 07		11 12		11 28				11 31	11 42	11 52	12 02	12 07
	d	10 12		10 30			10 33	10 43		11 03			11 12		11 30				11 33	11 43		12 03	
Marks Tey ■	d	10 18						10 49					11 18							11 49			
Kelvedon	d	10 23						10 54					11 23							11 54			
Braintree	d											11 00											
Braintree Freeport	d											11 02											
Cressing	d											11 05											
White Notley	d											11 08											
Witham ■	d	10 29					10 46	11 00				11 16	11 29						11 46	12 00			
Hatfield Peverel	d	10 33											11 33										
Chelmsford	d	10 40					10 56	11 09		11 21		11 26	11 40						11 56	12 09		12 21	
Ingatestone	d						11 02					11 32							12 02				
Shenfield ■	a	10 51					11 08	11 19				11 38	11 51						12 08	12 19			
Romford	a							11 28												12 28			
Stratford ■ ⊖ ⛴	a	11 05					11 22	11 36		11s45		11 52	12 05						12 22	12 36		12s45	
London Liverpool Street ■ ⊖	a	11 14		11 19			11 31	11 45		11 55		12 01	12 14		12 19				12 31	12 45		12 55	

A From Walton-on-the-Naze
B From Cambridge
C From Peterborough
D To Colchester

Table T011-R

Mondays to Fridays
21 May to 7 December

Norwich, Ipswich, Harwich, Clacton, Walton-on-Naze, Colchester and Chelmsford - London

		LE ■	LE ■	LE ■ A	LE ◇■ ⊡	LE ■	LE ■ B	LE ◇■	LE ■	LE ■ C	LE ◇■ ⊡	LE ■	LE ■	LE ■	LE ■ A	LE ◇■ ⊡	LE ■ D	LE ■	LE ■ B	LE ◇■	LE ■	LE ■ C
Norwich	d				11 30						12 00					12 30						
Diss	d				11 47						12 17					12 47						
Stowmarket	d			11 47							12 29				12 47		13 14					
Needham Market	d			11 52											12 52							
Ipswich	a			12 02	12 08						12 41				13 04	13 08	13 28					
	d		11 52		12 09						12 43			12 52		13 09						
Harwich Town	d					12 28												13 28				
Dovercourt	d					12 30												13 30				
Harwich International	d					12 33												13 33				
Wrabness	d					12 39												13 39				
Mistley	d					12 45												13 45				
Manningtree ■	d		12 02		12 19	12a50					12 53			13 02		13 19		13a50				
Walton-on-the-Naze	d						12 00												13 00			
Frinton-on-Sea	d						12 03												13 03			
Kirby Cross	d						12 06												13 06			
Clacton-on-Sea	d							12 05		←										13 05		←
Thorpe-le-Soken ■	a						12 12	12 13		12 12									13 12	13 13		13 12
	d						12 17	12 13		12 17									13 17	13 13		13 17
Weeley	d						→			12 21									→			13 21
Great Bentley	d									12 24												13 24
Alresford (Essex)	d									12 28												13 28
Wivenhoe	d							12 23		12 32										13 23		13 32
Hythe	d									12 36												13 36
Colchester Town	a									12 40												13 40
	d								12 35	12 44		13 00									13 35	13 44
Colchester ■	a		12 11		12 28			12 31	12 42	12 52	13 02	13 07		13 12		13 28				13 31	13 42	13 52
	d		12 12		12 30			12 33	12 43		13 03			13 12		13 30				13 33	13 43	
Marks Tey ■	d		12 18						12 49					13 18							13 49	
Kelvedon	d		12 23						12 54					13 23							13 54	
Braintree	d	12 00											13 00									
Braintree Freeport	d	12 02											13 02									
Cressing	d	12 05											13 05									
White Notley	d	12 08											13 08									
Witham ■	d	12 16	12 29					12 46	13 00				13 16	13 29						13 46	14 00	
Hatfield Peverel	d		12 33											13 33								
Chelmsford	d	12 26	12 40					12 56	13 09		13 21		13 26	13 40						13 56	14 09	
Ingatestone	d	12 32						13 02					13 32							14 02		
Shenfield ■	a	12 38	12 50					13 08	13 19				13 38	13 51						14 08	14 19	
Romford	a								13 28												14 28	
Stratford ■ ⊖	a	12 52	13 05					13 22	13 36		13s45		13 52	14 05						14 22	14 36	
London Liverpool Street ■ ⊖	a	13 01	13 14		13 19			13 31	13 45		13 55		14 03	14 14		14 19				14 31	14 47	

		LE ◇■ ⊡	LE ■	LE ■	LE ■	LE ■ A	LE ◇■ ⊡	LE ■	LE ■ B	LE ◇■	LE ■	LE ■ C	LE ◇■ ⊡	LE ■	LE ■	LE ■	LE ■ A	LE ◇■ ⊡	LE ■ D	LE ■	LE ■ B	LE ◇■	LE ■
Norwich	d	13 00					13 30						14 00					14 30					
Diss	d	13 17					13 47						14 17					14 47					
Stowmarket	d	13 29				13 47							14 29				14 47		15 14				
Needham Market	d					13 52											14 52						
Ipswich	a	13 41				14 02	14 08						14 41				15 04	15 08	15 28				
	d	13 43			13 52		14 09						14 43			14 52		15 09					
Harwich Town	d							14 28												15 28			
Dovercourt	d							14 30												15 30			
Harwich International	d							14 33												15 33			
Wrabness	d							14 39												15 39			
Mistley	d							14 45												15 45			
Manningtree ■	d	13 53			14 02		14 19	14a50					14 53			15 02		15 19		15a50			
Walton-on-the-Naze	d								14 00												15 00		
Frinton-on-Sea	d								14 03												15 03		
Kirby Cross	d								14 06												15 06		
Clacton-on-Sea	d									14 05		←										15 05	
Thorpe-le-Soken ■	a								14 12	14 13		14 12									15 12	15 13	
	d								14 17	14 13		14 17									15 17	15 13	
Weeley	d								→			14 21									→		
Great Bentley	d											14 24											
Alresford (Essex)	d											14 28											
Wivenhoe	d									14 23		14 32										15 23	
Hythe	d											14 36											
Colchester Town	a											14 40											
	d		14 00								14 35	14 44		15 00									15 35
Colchester ■	a	14 02	14 07		14 12		14 28			14 31	14 42	14 52	15 02	15 07		15 11		15 28				15 31	15 42
	d	14 03			14 12		14 30			14 33	14 43		15 03			15 12		15 30				15 33	15 43
Marks Tey ■	d				14 18						14 49					15 18							15 49
Kelvedon	d				14 23						14 54					15 23							15 54
Braintree	d			14 00											15 00								
Braintree Freeport	d			14 02											15 02								
Cressing	d			14 05											15 05								
White Notley	d			14 08											15 08								
Witham ■	d			14 16	14 29					14 46	15 00				15 16	15 29						15 46	16 00
Hatfield Peverel	d				14 33											15 33							
Chelmsford	d	14 21		14 26	14 40					14 56	15 09		15 21		15 26	15 40						15 55	16 09
Ingatestone	d			14 32						15 02					15 32							16 02	
Shenfield ■	a			14 38	14 51					15 08	15 19				15 38	15 50						16 07	16 19
Romford	a										15 28												
Stratford ■ ⊖	a	14s45		14 52	15 05					15 22	15 36		15s45		15 52	16 05						16 22	16 35
London Liverpool Street ■ ⊖	a	14 55		15 01	15 15		15 19			15 33	15 45		15 55		16 01	16 14		16 17				16 31	16 44

A From Cambridge
B To Colchester
C From Walton-on-the-Naze
D From Peterborough

Table T011-R

Mondays to Fridays
21 May to 7 December

Norwich, Ipswich, Harwich, Clacton, Walton-on-Naze, Colchester and Chelmsford - London

		LE ■ A	LE ◇■ ⊡	LE ■	LE ■	LE ■	LE ■ B	LE ◇■ ⊡	LE ■	LE ■ C	LE ◇■	LE ■	LE ■	LE ■ A	LE ◇■ ⊡	LE ■	LE ■	LE ■	LE ■ B	LE ■	LE ◇■ ⊡	LE ■ D	LE ■ C
Norwich	d		15 00					15 30							16 00						16 30		
Diss	d		15 17					15 47							16 17						16 47		
Stowmarket	d		15 29				15 47								16 29				16 47			17 14	
Needham Market	d						15 52												16 52				
Ipswich	a		15 41				16 06	16 08							16 41				17 04		17 08	17 28	
	d		15 43			15 52		16 09							16 43			16 52			17 09		
Harwich Town	d								16 28											16 53			
Dovercourt	d								16 30											16 55			
Harwich International	d								16 33											16 58			
Wrabness	d								16 39											17 04			
Mistley	d								16 45											17 10			
Manningtree ■	d		15 53			16 02		16 19	16a50						16 53			17 02		17a15	17 19		
Walton-on-the-Naze	d									16 00													17 00
Frinton-on-Sea	d									16 03													17 03
Kirby Cross	d									16 06													17 06
Clacton-on-Sea	d	←									16 05			←									
Thorpe-le-Soken ■	a	15 12								16 12	16 13			16 12									17 12
	d	15 17								16 17	16 13			16 17									17 17
Weeley	d	15 21								→				16 21									→
Great Bentley	d	15 24												16 24									
Alresford (Essex)	d	15 28												16 28									
Wivenhoe	d	15 32									16 23			16 32									
Hythe	d	15 36												16 36									
Colchester Town	a	15 40												16 40									
	d	15 44		16 00								16 35		16 44		16 56							
Colchester ■	a	15 52	16 02	16 07		16 11		16 28			16 31	16 42		16 54	17 02	17 05		17 11			17 28		
	d		16 03			16 12		16 30			16 33	16 43	16 53		17 03			17 12			17 30		
Marks Tey ■	d					16 18							16 59					17 18					
Kelvedon	d					16 23						16 52						17 23					
Braintree	d				16 00												17 00						
Braintree Freeport	d				16 02												17 02						
Cressing	d				16 05												17 05						
White Notley	d				16 08												17 08						
Witham ■	d				16 17	16 29					16 46	16 58	17 08				17 16	17 29					
Hatfield Peverel	d					16 33						17 02						17 33					
Chelmsford	d		16 21		16 27	16 40					16 56	17 09	17 17		17 21		17 26	17 40					
Ingatestone	d				16 34						17 02						17 32						
Shenfield ■	a				16 39	16 51					17 08	17 19	17 27				17 38	17 50					
Romford	a																						
Stratford ■ ⊖	a		16s45		16 54	17 06					17 22	17 36	17 42		17s45		17 52	18 06					
London Liverpool Street ■ ⊖	a		16 57		17 03	17 16		17 19			17 34	17 46	17 53		17 58		18 01	18 15			18 19		

		LE ◇■	LE ■	LE ■	LE ■ A	LE ■	LE ■	LE ◇■ ⊡	LE ■ B	LE ■	LE ■	LE ■	LE ◇■ ⊡	LE ■ C	LE ◇■	LE ■	LE ■	LE ■	LE ■ A	LE ■ E	LE ■	LE ■
Norwich	d							17 00					17 30									
Diss	d							17 17					17 47									
Stowmarket	d							17 29	17 48				17 59									
Needham Market	d								17 53													
Ipswich	a							17 41	18 04				18 11									
	d					17 33		17 43					18 13					18 22				
Harwich Town	d						17 28			18 00												18 26
Dovercourt	d						17 30			18 02												18 28
Harwich International	d						17 33			18 05												18 31
Wrabness	d						17 39			18 11												18 37
Mistley	d						17 45			18 17												18 43
Manningtree ■	d					17 43	17a50	17 53		18a22								18 33				18a48
Walton-on-the-Naze	d													17 57								
Frinton-on-Sea	d													18 00								
Kirby Cross	d													18 03								
Clacton-on-Sea	d	17 05			←										18 05				←		18 22	
Thorpe-le-Soken ■	a	17 13			17 12									18 09	18 13				18 09		18 30	
	d	17 13			17 17									18 17	18 13				18 17		18 30	
Weeley	d				17 21									→					18 21			
Great Bentley	d				17 24														18 24			
Alresford (Essex)	d				17 28														18 28			
Wivenhoe	d	17 23			17 32										18 23				18 32		18 40	
Hythe	d				17 36														18 36		18 44	
Colchester Town	a				17 40														18 40		18 48	
	d			17 30	17 44											18 32			18 44		18 52	
Colchester ■	a	17 31		17 37	17 52	17 52		18 02					18 28		18 33	18 39		18 42	18 52		19 00	
	d	17 33		17 48				18 03				18 12	18 30		18 33			18 43		18 55		
Marks Tey ■	d			17 55								18 18						18 49		19 01		
Kelvedon	d			18 00								18 23						18 54				
Braintree	d		17 44														18 33					
Braintree Freeport	d		17 46														18 36					
Cressing	d		17 49														18 39					
White Notley	d		17 52														18 42					
Witham ■	d	17 46	18 00	18 06							18 16	18 29			18 46		18 51	19 00		19 16		
Hatfield Peverel	d			18 10								18 33					18 55					
Chelmsford	d	17 56	18 09	18 17				18 21			18 26	18 40			18 56		19 02	19 09		19 26		
Ingatestone	d	18 02									18 32				19 02					→		
Shenfield ■	a	18 08	18 19	18 27							18 38	18 50			19 08		19 12	19 19				
Romford	a		18 28															19 28				
Stratford ■ ⊖	a	18 22	18 36	18 42				18s45			18 52	19 05			19 22		19 27	19 36				
London Liverpool Street ■ ⊖	a	18 31	18 45	18 51				18 55			19 01	19 14	19 17		19 33		19 36	19 45				

A From Walton-on-the-Naze
B From Cambridge
C To Colchester
D From Peterborough
E To London Liverpool Street

Table T011-R

Saturdays
26 May to 8 December

Norwich, Ipswich, Harwich, Clacton, Walton-on-Naze, Colchester and Chelmsford - London

		LE	LE	LE	LE	LE	LE	LE	LE	LE	LE	LE	LE	LE	LE	LE	LE	LE	LE	LE	LE	LE	LE
		■	■	■	■		■	◇■	■	■	◇■	■	■	◇■	■	■	■	◇■	■	■	■		◇■
						A							B		C		D					E	
								⊡			⊡							⊡					⊡
Norwich	d							05 00			05 30							06 00					06 30
Diss	d							05 17			05 47							06 17					06 47
Stowmarket	d							05 29										06 29				06 44	
Needham Market	d																					06 49	
Ipswich	a							05 41			06 08							06 41				07 02	07 08
	d							05 43			06 09							06 43		06 52	06 59		07 09
Harwich Town	d											06 28											
Dovercourt	d											06 30											
Harwich International	d											06 33									07a27		
Wrabness	d											06 39											
Mistley	d											06 45											
Manningtree ■	d							05 53			06 19	06a50						06 53		07 02			07 19
Walton-on-the-Naze	d												06 00										
Frinton-on-Sea	d												06 03										
Kirby Cross	d												06 06										
Clacton-on-Sea	d						05 30							06 05	06 24		←						
Thorpe-le-Soken ■	a						05 38						06 12	06 13	06 32		06 12						
	d						05 38						06 17	06 13			06 17						
Weeley	d												→				06 21						
Great Bentley	d																06 24						
Alresford (Essex)	d																06 28						
Wivenhoe	d						05 48							06 23			06 32						
Hythe	d																06 36						
Colchester Town	a																06 40						
	d															06 35	06 44						
Colchester ■	a						05 57	06 02			06 28			06 31		06 42	06 52	07 02		07 11			07 28
	d		04 43	05 12	05 43	05 50		06 03		06 07	06 30			06 33		06 43		07 03		07 12			07 30
Marks Tey ■	d		04 49	05 18	05 49	05a57				06 13						06 49				07 18			
Kelvedon	d		04 54	05 23	05 54					06 18						06 54				07 23			
Braintree	d	00 27							06 00										07 00				
Braintree Freeport	d	00 29							06 02										07 02				
Cressing	d	00 32							06 05										07 05				
White Notley	d	00 35							06 08										07 08				
Witham ■	d	00a43	05 00	05 29	06 00				06a16	06 24				06 46		07 00			07 16	07 29			
Hatfield Peverel	d		05 04	05 33	06 04					06 28										07 33			
Chelmsford	d		05 11	05 40	06 11			06 21		06 35				06 56		07 09		07 21	07 26	07 40			
Ingatestone	d		05 18	05 47	06 18									07 02					07 32				
Shenfield ■	a		05 23	05 52	06 23					06 45				07 08		07 19			07 38	07 50			
Romford	a		05 32							06 54						07 28							
Stratford ■ ⊖ ⛴	a		05 42	06 07	06 38			06s45		07 02				07 22		07 36		07s45	07 52	08 05			
London Liverpool Street ■ ⊖	a		05 51	06 16	06 47			06 55		07 11	07 19			07 31		07 46		07 55	08 01	08 14			08 19

		LE	LE	LE	LE	LE	LE	LE	LE	LE	LE	LE	LE	LE	LE	LE	LE	LE	LE	LE	LE	LE	LE	LE
		■	◇■	■	■	■	◇■	■	■	■	■		◇■	■	■	◇■	■	■	▪ ■	■	■	■	◇■	■
		B			D				G			F			B			D						F
							⊡						⊡						⊡					
Norwich	d						07 00						07 30						08 00					
Diss	d						07 17						07 47						08 17					
Stowmarket	d						07 29					07 45							08 29					08 47
Needham Market	d											07 50												08 52
Ipswich	a						07 41					08 02	08 08						08 41					09 02
	d						07 43				07 52		08 09						08 43				08 52	
Harwich Town	d					07 28								08 28										
Dovercourt	d					07 30								08 30										
Harwich International	d			07 20		07 33			07 50					08 33										
Wrabness	d					07 39			07 56					08 39										
Mistley	d					07 45			08 02					08 45										
Manningtree ■	d			07 33		07a50	07 53				08 02		08 19	08a50					08 53				09 02	
Walton-on-the-Naze	d	07 00													08 00									
Frinton-on-Sea	d	07 03													08 03									
Kirby Cross	d	07 06													08 06									
Clacton-on-Sea	d		07 05		←											08 05		←						
Thorpe-le-Soken ■	a	07 12	07 13		07 12										08 12	08 13		08 12						
	d	07 17	07 13		07 17										08 17	08 13		08 17						
Weeley	d	→			07 21										→			08 21						
Great Bentley	d				07 24													08 24						
Alresford (Essex)	d				07 28													08 28						
Wivenhoe	d		07 23		07 32											08 23		08 32						
Hythe	d				07 36													08 36						
Colchester Town	a				07 40													08 40						
	d				07 44			08 00									08 35	08 44			09 00			
Colchester ■	a		07 31	07 42	07 52		08 02	08 07			08 11		08 28			08 31	08 42	08 52			09 07		09 11	
	d		07 33	07 43			08 03				08 12		08 30			08 33	08 43			09 03			09 12	
Marks Tey ■	d			07 49							08 18						08 49						09 18	
Kelvedon	d			07 54							08 23						08 54						09 23	
Braintree	d									08 00												09 00		
Braintree Freeport	d									08 02												09 02		
Cressing	d									08 05												09 05		
White Notley	d									08 08												09 08		
Witham ■	d		07 46	08 00						08 16	08 29					08 46	09 00					09 16	09 29	
Hatfield Peverel	d										08 33												09 33	
Chelmsford	d		07 56	08 09			08 21			08 26	08 40					08 56	09 09			09 20		09 26	09 40	
Ingatestone	d		08 02							08 32						09 02						09 32		
Shenfield ■	a		08 08	08 19						08 38	08 50					09 08	09 19					09 38	09 50	
Romford	a			08 28													09 28							
Stratford ■ ⊖ ⛴	a		08 22	08 36			08s45			08 52	09 05					09 22	09 36		09s42	09 45		09 52	10 05	
London Liverpool Street ■ ⊖	a		08 31	08 46			08 55			09 01	09 14		09 19			09 31	09 46		09 52	09 55		10 01	10 14	

A To Sudbury
B To Colchester
C To Walton-on-the-Naze
D From Walton-on-the-Naze
E From Bury St Edmunds
F From Cambridge
G To Cambridge

Table T011-R

Saturdays
26 May to 8 December

Norwich, Ipswich, Harwich, Clacton, Walton-on-Naze, Colchester and Chelmsford - London

		LE	LE	LE	LE	LE	LE	LE	LE	LE	LE	LE	LE	LE	LE	LE	LE	LE	LE	LE	LE	LE
		◇■	■	■	■	◇■	■	■	◇■	■	■	■	◇■	■	▪ ■	■	■	◇■	■	■	▪ ■	■
			A		B			C						D			B			C		
		⊡							⊡						⊡						⊡	
Norwich	d	08 30							09 00						09 30						10 00	
Diss	d	08 47							09 17						09 47						10 17	
Stowmarket	d		09 14						09 29					09 47							10 29	
Needham Market	d													09 52								
Ipswich	a	09 08	09 28						09 41					10 02	10 08						10 41	
	d	09 09							09 43				09 52		10 09						10 43	
Harwich Town	d			09 28												10 28						
Dovercourt	d			09 30												10 30						
Harwich International	d			09 33												10 33						
Wrabness	d			09 39												10 39						
Mistley	d			09 45												10 45						
Manningtree ■	d	09 19		09a50					09 53				10 02		10 19	10a50					10 53	
Walton-on-the-Naze	d				09 00												10 00					
Frinton-on-Sea	d				09 03												10 03					
Kirby Cross	d				09 06												10 06					
Clacton-on-Sea	d					09 05		←										10 05		←		
Thorpe-le-Soken ■	a				09 12	09 13		09 12									10 12	10 13		10 12		
	d				09 17	09 13		09 17									10 17	10 13		10 17		
Weeley	d				→			09 21									→			10 21		
Great Bentley	d							09 24												10 24		
Alresford (Essex)	d							09 28												10 28		
Wivenhoe	d					09 23		09 32										10 23		10 32		
Hythe	d							09 36												10 36		
Colchester Town	a							09 40												10 40		
	d						09 35	09 44			10 00								10 35	10 44		
Colchester ■	a	09 28				09 31	09 42	09 52			10 07		10 11		10 28			10 31	10 42	10 52		
	d	09 30				09 33	09 43			10 03			10 12		10 30			10 33	10 43			11 03
Marks Tey ■	d						09 49						10 18						10 49			
Kelvedon	d						09 54						10 23						10 54			
Braintree	d											10 00										
Braintree Freeport	d											10 02										
Cressing	d											10 05										
White Notley	d											10 08										
Witham ■	d					09 46	10 00					10 16	10 29					10 46	11 00			
Hatfield Peverel	d												10 33									
Chelmsford	d					09 56	10 09			10 20		10 26	10 40					10 56	11 09			11 20
Ingatestone	d					10 02						10 32						11 02				
Shenfield ■	a					10 08	10 19					10 38	10 50					11 08	11 19			
Romford	a						10 28												11 28			
Stratford ■ ⊖ ⛴	a					10 22	10 36		10s42	10 45		10 52	11 05					11 22	11 36		11s42	11 45
London Liverpool Street ■ ⊖	a	10 19				10 31	10 46		10 52	10 54		11 01	11 14		11 19			11 31	11 46		11 52	11 55

		LE	LE	LE	LE	LE	LE	LE	LE	LE	LE	LE	LE	LE	LE	LE	LE	LE	LE	LE	LE	LE	LE
		■	■	◇■	■	◇■	■	■	■	◇■	■	■	◇■	■	■	■	■	◇■	■	■	◇■	■	■
					D		A		B			C					D			B			C
						⊡							⊡					⊡					
Norwich	d					10 30							11 00					11 30					
Diss	d					10 47							11 17					11 47					
Stowmarket	d				10 47		11 14						11 29				11 47						
Needham Market	d				10 52												11 52						
Ipswich	a				11 02	11 08	11 28						11 41				12 02	12 08					
	d			10 52		11 09							11 43			11 52		12 09					
Harwich Town	d							11 28											12 28				
Dovercourt	d							11 30											12 30				
Harwich International	d							11 33											12 33				
Wrabness	d							11 39											12 39				
Mistley	d							11 45											12 45				
Manningtree ■	d			11 02		11 19		11a50					11 53			12 02		12 19	12a50				
Walton-on-the-Naze	d								11 00											12 00			
Frinton-on-Sea	d								11 03											12 03			
Kirby Cross	d								11 06											12 06			
Clacton-on-Sea	d									11 05		←									12 05		←
Thorpe-le-Soken ■	a								11 12	11 13		11 12								12 12	12 13		12 12
	d								11 17	11 13		11 17								12 17	12 13		12 17
Weeley	d								→			11 21								→			12 21
Great Bentley	d											11 24											12 24
Alresford (Essex)	d											11 28											12 28
Wivenhoe	d									11 23		11 32									12 23		12 32
Hythe	d											11 36											12 36
Colchester Town	a											11 40											12 40
	d	11 00									11 35	11 44		12 00								12 35	12 44
Colchester ■	a	11 07		11 12		11 28				11 31	11 42	11 52	12 02	12 07		12 12		12 28			12 31	12 42	12 52
	d			11 12		11 30				11 33	11 43		12 03			12 12		12 30			12 33	12 43	
Marks Tey ■	d			11 18							11 49					12 18						12 49	
Kelvedon	d			11 23							11 54					12 23						12 54	
Braintree	d		11 00												12 00								
Braintree Freeport	d		11 02												12 02								
Cressing	d		11 05												12 05								
White Notley	d		11 08												12 08								
Witham ■	d		11 16	11 29						11 46	12 00				12 16	12 29					12 46	13 00	
Hatfield Peverel	d			11 33												12 33							
Chelmsford	d		11 26	11 40						11 56	12 09		12 21		12 26	12 40					12 56	13 09	
Ingatestone	d		11 32							12 02					12 32						13 02		
Shenfield ■	a		11 38	11 51						12 08	12 19				12 38	12 51					13 08	13 19	
Romford	a										12 28											13 28	
Stratford ■ ⊖ ⛴	a		11 52	12 05						12 22	12 36		12s45		12 52	13 05					13 22	13 36	
London Liverpool Street ■ ⊖	a		12 01	12 14		12 19				12 31	12 46		12 55		13 01	13 14		13 19			13 31	13 46	

A From Peterborough
B To Colchester
C From Walton-on-the-Naze
D From Cambridge

Norwich, Ipswich, Harwich, Clacton, Walton-on-Naze, Colchester and Chelmsford - London

		LE ◇1	LE 1 A	LE 1	LE 1	LE 1 B	LE 1	LE ◇1		LE 1	LE 1	LE 1 C	LE ◇1	LE 1	LE 1	LE 1	LE 1 D	LE 1 E		LE 1 F	LE 1	LE ◇1	LE 1 G	LE 1	LE 1
Norwich	d	18 00						18 30														19 00			
Diss	d	18 17						18 47														19 17			
Stowmarket	d	18 29				18 48												19 14				19 29			
Needham Market	d					18 53																			
Ipswich	a	18 41				19 03		19 08										19 28				19 41			
	d	18 43			18 49			19 09								19 25				19 35		19 43			
Harwich Town	d									19 05											19 28				
Dovercourt	d									19 07											19 30				
Harwich International	d									19 10											19 33				
Wrabness	d									19 16											19 39				
Mistley	d									19 22											19 45				
Manningtree 5	d	18 53			18 59			19 19		19a27						19 35				19 45	19a50	19 53			
Walton-on-the-Naze	d			18 34								18 57		19 18											
Frinton-on-Sea	d			18 37								19 00		19 21											
Kirby Cross	d			18 43								19 03		19 24											
Clacton-on-Sea	d												19 02				←								
Thorpe-le-Soken 1	a			18 49								19 09	19 10	19 30			19 09								
	d											19 17	19 10				19 17								
Weeley	d											→					19 21								
Great Bentley	d																19 24								
Alresford (Essex)	d																19 28								
Wivenhoe	d												19 23				19 32								
Hythe	d																19 36								
Colchester Town	a																19 40								
	d						19 08								19 35		19 44							20 00	
Colchester 4	a	19 02			19 08		19 15	19 28					19 31		19 42	19 46	19 52			19 54		20 02		20 07	
	d	19 03			19 12			19 30					19 33		19 43					19 55		20 03			
Marks Tey 2	d				19 18										19 49					20 01					
Kelvedon	d				19 23										19 54										
Braintree	d										19 25														20 11
Braintree Freeport	d										19 27														20 13
Cressing	d										19 30														20 16
White Notley	d										19 33														20 19
Witham 2	d				19 29						19 42		19 46		20 00					20 16					20 27
Hatfield Peverel	d		←		19 33																		←		
Chelmsford	d	19 21	19 26		19 40						19 51		19 56		20 09					20 26		20 21	20 26		20 36
Ingatestone	d		19 32										20 02							→			20 32		
Shenfield 3	a		19 38		19 50								20 08		20 19								20 38		20 46
Romford	a														20 28										
Stratford 7 ⊖	a	19s45	19 52		20 05						20 14		20 22		20 36							20s45	20 52		
London Liverpool Street 15 ⊖	a	19 55	20 01		20 14			20 20			20 23		20 31		20 45							20 55	21 01		21 12

		LE 1	LE 1 B	LE ◇1		LE 1	LE 1 C	LE ◇1	LE 1 H	LE 1	LE 1	LE 1 D	LE 1	LE ◇1		LE 1	LE 1	LE 1	LE 1 B	LE ◇1	LE 1 C	LE ◇1	LE 1	LE 1	
Norwich	d			19 30										20 00						20 30					
Diss	d			19 47										20 17						20 47					
Stowmarket	d		19 48											20 29					20 47						
Needham Market	d		19 53																20 52						
Ipswich	a		20 04	20 10										20 41					21 01	21 08					
	d	19 52		20 10							20 22			20 43					21 03	21 09					
Harwich Town	d					20 05							20 28										21 04		
Dovercourt	d					20 07							20 30										21 06		
Harwich International	d					20 10							20 33					20 45	21a29				21 09		
Wrabness	d					20 16							20 39										21 15		
Mistley	d					20 22							20 45										21 21		
Manningtree 5	d	20 02		20 20		20a27					20 32		20a50	20 53				20 58		21 19			21 26		
Walton-on-the-Naze	d						19 56		20 33												21 00				
Frinton-on-Sea	d						19 59		20 36												21 03				
Kirby Cross	d						20 02		20 42												21 06				
Clacton-on-Sea	d							20 05				←										21 05			
Thorpe-le-Soken 1	a						20 08	20 13	20 48			20 08									21 12	21 13			
	d						20 17	20 13				20 17									21 17	21 13			
Weeley	d						→					20 21									→				
Great Bentley	d											20 24													
Alresford (Essex)	d											20 28													
Wivenhoe	d							20 23				20 32										21 23			
Hythe	d											20 36													
Colchester Town	a											20 40													
	d									20 35		20 44				21 00								21 35	
Colchester 4	a	20 12		20 29				20 31		20 42	20 45	20 52		21 02		21 07		21 07		21 28		21 31	21 35	21 42	
	d	20 12		20 30				20 33		20 50				21 03				21 12		21 30		21 33		21 43	
Marks Tey 2	d	20 18								20 56								21 18						21 49	
Kelvedon	d	20 23								21 01								21 23						21 54	
Braintree	d																21 00								
Braintree Freeport	d																21 02								
Cressing	d																21 05								
White Notley	d																21 08								
Witham 2	d	20 31						20 46		21 07							21 16	21 29				21 46		22 00	
Hatfield Peverel	d	20 35																21 33							
Chelmsford	d	20 42						20 56		21 16				21 21			21 26	21 40				21 56		22 09	
Ingatestone	d							21 02									21 32					22 02			
Shenfield 3	a	20 52						21 08		21 26							21 38	21 50				22 08		22 19	
Romford	a																							22 28	
Stratford 7 ⊖	a	21 07						21 22		21 42				21s45			21 52	22 05				22 22		22 36	
London Liverpool Street 15 ⊖	a	21 16		21 19				21 31		21 51				21 55			22 01	22 14		22 19		22 31		22 45	

A From Colchester
B From Cambridge
C To Colchester
D From Walton-on-the-Naze
E From Peterborough
F To London Liverpool Street
G From Ipswich
H To Clacton-on-Sea

Table T011-R

Mondays to Fridays

21 May to 7 December

Norwich, Ipswich, Harwich, Clacton, Walton-on-Naze, Colchester and Chelmsford - London

		LE 1 A	LE 1 B	LE 1	LE ◇1	LE 1 C	LE 1	LE 1	LE 1 D	LE ◇1		LE 1	LE 1 B	LE 1	LE 1	LE ◇1	LE 1 C	LE 1	LE 1 E	LE 1		LE 1 A	LE 1	LE C	LE 1
Norwich	d				21 00											22 00							23 05		
Diss	d				21 17											22 17							23 23		
Stowmarket	d	21 14			21 29	21 47										22 29	22 47					23 08	23 36	23 51	
Needham Market	d					21 52											22 53							23 56	
Ipswich	a	21 28			21 41	22 04										22 41	23 03					23 21	23 49	00 07	
	d	21 28			21 43							22 23				22 43						23 22			
Harwich Town	d			21 28										22 28											23 28
Dovercourt	d			21 30										22 30											23 30
Harwich International	d			21 33										22 33											23 33
Wrabness	d			21 39										22 39											23 39
Mistley	d			21 45										22 45											23 45
Manningtree 5	d	21 38		21a50	21 53							22 33		22a50		22 53						23 32			23 50
Walton-on-the-Naze	d								22 00										23 00						
Frinton-on-Sea	d								22 03										23 03						
Kirby Cross	d								22 06										23 06						
Clacton-on-Sea	d		←							22 05			←							23 05					
Thorpe-le-Soken 1	a		21 12						22 12	22 13			22 12						23 12	23 13					
	d		21 17						22 17	22 13			22 17							23 13					
Weeley	d		21 21						→				22 21							23 17					
Great Bentley	d		21 24										22 24							23 20					
Alresford (Essex)	d		21 28										22 28							23 24					
Wivenhoe	d		21 32							22 23			22 32							23 28					
Hythe	d		21 36										22 36							23 32					
Colchester Town	a		21 40										22 40												
	d		21 44					22 00					22 44					23 00							
Colchester 4	a	21 51	21 52		22 02			22 07		22 31		22 42	22 52			23 02		23 07		23 38		23 43			23 59
	d				22 03			22 12		22 33		22 43				23 03									
Marks Tey 2	d							22 18				22 49													
Kelvedon	d							22 23				22 54													
Braintree	d						22 00								22 56										
Braintree Freeport	d						22 02								22 58										
Cressing	d						22 05								23 01										
White Notley	d						22 08								23 04										
Witham 2	d						22 16	22 29		22 46		23 00			23a12	23 16									
Hatfield Peverel	d							22 33																	
Chelmsford	d				22 21		22 26	22 40		22 56		23 09				23 25									
Ingatestone	d						22 32			23 02															
Shenfield 3	a						22 38	22 50		23 08		23 19				23 36									
Romford	a											23 28													
Stratford 7 ⊖	a				22s45		22 52	23s05		23 22		23 36				23s52									
London Liverpool Street 15 ⊖	a				22 55		23 01	23 14		23 31		23 48				00 03									

		LE 1
Norwich	d	
Diss	d	
Stowmarket	d	
Needham Market	d	
Ipswich	a	
	d	
Harwich Town	d	
Dovercourt	d	
Harwich International	d	
Wrabness	d	
Mistley	d	
Manningtree 5	d	
Walton-on-the-Naze	d	
Frinton-on-Sea	d	
Kirby Cross	d	
Clacton-on-Sea	d	
Thorpe-le-Soken 1	a	
	d	
Weeley	d	
Great Bentley	d	
Alresford (Essex)	d	
Wivenhoe	d	
Hythe	d	
Colchester Town	a	
	d	
Colchester 4	a	
	d	
Marks Tey 2	d	
Kelvedon	d	
Braintree	d	23 45
Braintree Freeport	d	23 47
Cressing	d	23 50
White Notley	d	23 53
Witham 2	d	00a01
Hatfield Peverel	d	
Chelmsford	d	
Ingatestone	d	
Shenfield 3	a	
Romford	a	
Stratford 7 ⊖	a	
London Liverpool Street 15 ⊖	a	

A From Peterborough
B From Walton-on-the-Naze
C From Cambridge
D To Colchester
E To Clacton-on-Sea

Table T011-R

Saturdays
26 May to 8 December

Norwich, Ipswich, Harwich, Clacton, Walton-on-Naze, Colchester and Chelmsford - London

Station		LE ◇1 ☕	LE 1	LE 1	LE 1	LE 1 A	LE ◇1 ☕	LE 1 B	LE 1	LE 1 C	LE ◇1	LE 1	LE 1 D	LE ◇1 ☕	LE 1	LE 1	LE 1	LE 1 A	LE ◇1 ☕	LE 1	LE 1 C	LE ◇1
Norwich	d	12 00					12 30							13 00					13 30			
Diss	d	12 17					12 47							13 17					13 47			
Stowmarket	d	12 29				12 47		13 14						13 29				13 47				
Needham Market	d					12 52												13 52				
Ipswich	a	12 41				13 02	13 08	13 28						13 41				14 02	14 08			
	d	12 43			12 52		13 09							13 43			13 52		14 09			
Harwich Town	d								13 28											14 28		
Dovercourt	d								13 30											14 30		
Harwich International	d								13 33											14 33		
Wrabness	d								13 39											14 39		
Mistley	d								13 45											14 45		
Manningtree	d	12 53			13 02		13 19		13a50					13 53			14 02		14 19	14a50		
Walton-on-the-Naze	d									13 00											14 00	
Frinton-on-Sea	d									13 03											14 03	
Kirby Cross	d									13 06											14 06	
Clacton-on-Sea	d										13 05		←									14 05
Thorpe-le-Soken	a									13 12	13 13		13 12								14 12	14 13
	d									13 17	13 13		13 17								14 17	14 13
Weeley	d									→			13 21								→	
Great Bentley	d												13 24									
Alresford (Essex)	d												13 28									
Wivenhoe	d										13 23		13 32									14 23
Hythe	d												13 36									
Colchester Town	a												13 40									
	d		13 00									13 35	13 44		14 00							
Colchester	a	13 02	13 07		13 11		13 28				13 31	13 42	13 52	14 02	14 07		14 11		14 28			14 31
	d	13 03			13 12		13 30				13 33	13 43		14 03			14 12		14 30			14 33
Marks Tey	d				13 18							13 49					14 18					
Kelvedon	d				13 23							13 54					14 23					
Braintree	d			13 00												14 00						
Braintree Freeport	d			13 02												14 02						
Cressing	d			13 05												14 05						
White Notley	d			13 08												14 08						
Witham	d			13 16	13 29						13 46	14 00				14 16	14 29					14 46
Hatfield Peverel	d				13 33												14 33					
Chelmsford	d	13 21		13 26	13 40						13 56	14 09		14 21		14 26	14 40					14 56
Ingatestone	d			13 32							14 02					14 32						15 02
Shenfield	a			13 38	13 50						14 08	14 19				14 38	14 50					15 08
Romford	a											14 28										
Stratford	a	13s45		13 52	14 05						14 22	14 36		14s45		14 52	15 05					15 22
London Liverpool Street	a	13 55		14 01	14 14		14 19				14 31	14 46		14 55		15 01	15 14		15 19			15 31

Station		LE 1	LE 1 D	LE ◇1 ☕	LE 1	LE 1	LE 1	LE 1 A	LE ◇1 ☕	LE 1 B	LE 1	LE 1 C	LE ◇1	LE 1	LE 1 D	LE ◇1 ☕	LE 1	LE 1	LE 1	LE 1 A	LE ◇1 ☕	LE 1	LE 1 C
Norwich	d			14 00					14 30							15 00					15 30		
Diss	d			14 17					14 47							15 17					15 47		
Stowmarket	d			14 29				14 47		15 14						15 29				15 47			
Needham Market	d							14 52												15 52			
Ipswich	a			14 41				15 02	15 08	15 28						15 41				16 02	16 08		
	d			14 43			14 52		15 09							15 43			15 52		16 09		
Harwich Town	d										15 28											16 28	
Dovercourt	d										15 30											16 30	
Harwich International	d										15 33											16 33	
Wrabness	d										15 39											16 39	
Mistley	d										15 45											16 45	
Manningtree	d			14 53			15 02		15 19		15a50					15 53			16 02		16 19	16a50	
Walton-on-the-Naze	d											15 00											16 00
Frinton-on-Sea	d											15 03											16 03
Kirby Cross	d											15 06											16 06
Clacton-on-Sea	d		←										15 05		←								
Thorpe-le-Soken	a		14 12									15 12	15 13		15 12								16 12
	d		14 17									15 17	15 13		15 17								16 17
Weeley	d		14 21									→			15 21								→
Great Bentley	d		14 24												15 24								
Alresford (Essex)	d		14 28												15 28								
Wivenhoe	d		14 32										15 23		15 32								
Hythe	d		14 36												15 36								
Colchester Town	a		14 40												15 40								
	d	14 35	14 44		15 00									15 35	15 44		16 00						
Colchester	a	14 42	14 52	15 02	15 07		15 11		15 28				15 31	15 42	15 52	16 02	16 07		16 11		16 28		
	d	14 43		15 03			15 12		15 30				15 33	15 43		16 03			16 12		16 30		
Marks Tey	d	14 49					15 18							15 49					16 18				
Kelvedon	d	14 54					15 23							15 54					16 23				
Braintree	d					15 00												16 00					
Braintree Freeport	d					15 02												16 02					
Cressing	d					15 05												16 05					
White Notley	d					15 08												16 08					
Witham	d	15 00				15 16	15 29						15 46	16 00				16 16	16 29				
Hatfield Peverel	d						15 33												16 33				
Chelmsford	d	15 09		15 21		15 26	15 40						15 56	16 09		16 21		16 26	16 40				
Ingatestone	d					15 32							16 02					16 32					
Shenfield	a	15 19				15 38	15 50						16 08	16 19				16 38	16 50				
Romford	a	15 28												16 28									
Stratford	a	15 36		15s45		15 52	16 05						16 22	16 36		16s45		16 52	17 05				
London Liverpool Street	a	15 46		15 55		16 01	16 14		16 19				16 31	16 46		16 55		17 01	17 14		17 19		

A From Cambridge
B From Peterborough
C To Colchester
D From Walton-on-the-Naze

Table T011-R

Saturdays
26 May to 8 December

Norwich, Ipswich, Harwich, Clacton, Walton-on-Naze, Colchester and Chelmsford - London

Station		LE ◇1	LE 1	LE 1 A	LE ◇1 ☕	LE 1	LE 1	LE 1	LE 1 B	LE ◇1 ☕	LE 1 C	LE 1	LE 1 D	LE ◇1	LE 1	LE 1 A	LE ◇1 ☕	LE 1	LE 1	LE 1	LE 1 B	LE ◇1 ☕	LE 1
Norwich	d				16 00					16 30							17 00					17 30	
Diss	d				16 17					16 47							17 17					17 47	
Stowmarket	d				16 29				16 47		17 14						17 29				17 49	17 59	
Needham Market	d								16 52												17 54		
Ipswich	a				16 41				17 02	17 08	17 28						17 41				18 03	18 11	
	d				16 43			16 52		17 09							17 43			17 52		18 13	
Harwich Town	d											17 28											18 28
Dovercourt	d											17 30											18 30
Harwich International	d											17 33											18 33
Wrabness	d											17 39											18 39
Mistley	d											17 45											18 45
Manningtree	d				16 53			17 02		17 19		17a50					17 53			18 02			18a50
Walton-on-the-Naze	d												17 00										
Frinton-on-Sea	d												17 03										
Kirby Cross	d												17 06										
Clacton-on-Sea	d	16 05		←										17 05		←							
Thorpe-le-Soken	a	16 13		16 12									17 12	17 13		17 12							
	d	16 13		16 17									17 17	17 13		17 17							
Weeley	d			16 21									→			17 21							
Great Bentley	d			16 24												17 24							
Alresford (Essex)	d			16 28												17 28							
Wivenhoe	d	16 23		16 32										17 23		17 32							
Hythe	d			16 36												17 36							
Colchester Town	a			16 40												17 40							
	d		16 35	16 44		17 00									17 35	17 44		18 00					
Colchester	a	16 31	16 42	16 52	17 02	17 07		17 11		17 28				17 31	17 42	17 52	18 02	18 07		18 11		18 28	
	d	16 33	16 43		17 03			17 12		17 30				17 33	17 43		18 03			18 12		18 30	
Marks Tey	d		16 49					17 18							17 49					18 18			
Kelvedon	d		16 54					17 23							17 54					18 23			
Braintree	d						17 00												18 00				
Braintree Freeport	d						17 02												18 02				
Cressing	d						17 05												18 05				
White Notley	d						17 08												18 08				
Witham	d	16 46	17 00				17 16	17 29						17 46	18 00				18 16	18 29			
Hatfield Peverel	d							17 33												18 33			
Chelmsford	d	16 56	17 09		17 21		17 26	17 40						17 56	18 09		18 21		18 26	18 40			
Ingatestone	d	17 02					17 32							18 02					18 32				
Shenfield	a	17 08	17 19				17 38	17 50						18 08	18 19				18 38	18 50			
Romford	a		17 28												18 28								
Stratford	a	17 22	17 36		17s45		17 52	18 05						18 22	18 36		18s45		18 52	19 05			
London Liverpool Street	a	17 31	17 46		17 55		18 03	18 14		18 19				18 31	18 46		18 55		19 01	19 14		19 19	

Station		LE 1 D	LE ◇1	LE 1	LE 1 A	LE ◇1 ☕	LE 1	LE 1	LE 1	LE 1 B	LE ◇1 ☕	LE 1 C	LE 1	LE 1 D	LE ◇1	LE 1	LE 1 A	LE ◇1 ☕	LE 1	LE 1	LE 1	LE 1 B
Norwich	d					18 00					18 30							19 00				
Diss	d					18 17					18 47							19 17				
Stowmarket	d					18 29				18 49		19 14						19 29				19 47
Needham Market	d									18 54												19 52
Ipswich	a					18 41				19 03	19 08	19 28						19 41				20 02
	d					18 43			18 52		19 09							19 43			19 52	
Harwich Town	d												19 28									
Dovercourt	d												19 30									
Harwich International	d												19 33									
Wrabness	d												19 39									
Mistley	d												19 45									
Manningtree	d					18 53			19 02		19 19		19a50					19 53			20 02	
Walton-on-the-Naze	d	18 00												19 00								
Frinton-on-Sea	d	18 03												19 03								
Kirby Cross	d	18 06												19 06								
Clacton-on-Sea	d		18 05		←										19 05		←					
Thorpe-le-Soken	a	18 12	18 13		18 12									19 12	19 13		19 12					
	d	18 17	18 13		18 17									19 17	19 13		19 17					
Weeley	d	→			18 21									→			19 21					
Great Bentley	d				18 24												19 24					
Alresford (Essex)	d				18 28												19 28					
Wivenhoe	d		18 23		18 32										19 23		19 32					
Hythe	d				18 36												19 36					
Colchester Town	a				18 40												19 40					
	d			18 35	18 44		19 00									19 35	19 44		20 00			
Colchester	a		18 31	18 42	18 52	19 02	19 07		19 11		19 28				19 31	19 42	19 52	20 02	20 07		20 11	
	d		18 33	18 43		19 03			19 12		19 30				19 33	19 43		20 03			20 12	
Marks Tey	d			18 49					19 18							19 49					20 18	
Kelvedon	d			18 54					19 23							19 54					20 23	
Braintree	d							19 00												20 00		
Braintree Freeport	d							19 02												20 02		
Cressing	d							19 05												20 05		
White Notley	d							19 08												20 08		
Witham	d		18 46	19 00				19 16	19 29						19 46	20 00				20 16	20 29	
Hatfield Peverel	d								19 33												20 33	
Chelmsford	d		18 56	19 09		19 21		19 26	19 40						19 56	20 09		20 21		20 26	20 40	
Ingatestone	d		19 02					19 32							20 02					20 32		
Shenfield	a		19 08	19 19				19 38	19 50						20 08	20 19				20 38	20 50	
Romford	a			19 28												20 28						
Stratford	a		19 22	19 36		19s45		19 52	20 05						20 22	20 36		20s45		20 52	21 05	
London Liverpool Street	a		19 31	19 46		19 55		20 01	20 14		20 19				20 31	20 46		20 55		21 01	21 14	

A From Walton-on-the-Naze
B From Cambridge
C From Peterborough
D To Colchester

Table T011-R

Saturdays
26 May to 8 December

Norwich, Ipswich, Harwich, Clacton, Walton-on-Naze, Colchester and Chelmsford - London

		LE 1	LE 1	LE 1 A	LE ◇1	LE 1	LE 1 B	LE ◇1 ☕		LE 1	LE 1	LE 1	LE 1 C	LE 1	LE 1 A	LE ◇1	LE 1	LE ◇1 D		LE 1 B	LE 1	LE ◇1 ☕	LE 1	LE 1	LE 1
Norwich	d							20 00														21 00			
Diss	d							20 17														21 17			
Stowmarket	d							20 29					20 46					21 14				21 29			
Needham Market	d												20 51												
Ipswich	a							20 41					21 01					21 28				21 41			
	d	20 09						20 43					21 01	21 09				21 28				21 43			21 52
Harwich Town	d		20 28																		21 28				
Dovercourt	d		20 30																		21 30				
Harwich International	d		20 33									20 45	21a29								21 33				
Wrabness	d		20 39																		21 39				
Mistley	d		20 45																		21 45				
Manningtree 5	d	20 19	20a50					20 53				20 58		21 19				21 38			21a50	21 53			22 02
Walton-on-the-Naze	d			20 00											21 00										
Frinton-on-Sea	d			20 03											21 03										
Kirby Cross	d			20 06											21 06										
Clacton-on-Sea	d				20 05		←									21 05				←					
Thorpe-le-Soken 1	a			20 12	20 13		20 12								21 12	21 13				21 12					
	d			20 17	20 13		20 17								21 17	21 13				21 17					
Weeley	d			→			20 21								→					21 21					
Great Bentley	d						20 24													21 24					
Alresford (Essex)	d						20 28													21 28					
Wivenhoe	d				20 23		20 32									21 23				21 32					
Hythe	d						20 36													21 36					
Colchester Town	a						20 40													21 40					
	d					20 35	20 44			21 00							21 35			21 44			22 00		
Colchester 4	a	20 28			20 31	20 42	20 52	21 02		21 07		21 07		21 28		21 31	21 42	21 49		21 52		22 02	22 07		22 11
	d	20 30			20 33	20 43		21 03				21 12		21 30		21 33	21 43					22 03			22 12
Marks Tey 2	d					20 49						21 18					21 49								22 18
Kelvedon	d					20 54						21 23					21 54								22 23
Braintree	d										21 00													22 00	
Braintree Freeport	d										21 02													22 02	
Cressing	d										21 05													22 05	
White Notley	d										21 08													22 08	
Witham 2	d				20 46	21 00					21 16	21 29				21 46	22 00							22 16	22 29
Hatfield Peverel	d											21 33													22 33
Chelmsford	d				20 56	21 09		21 21			21 26	21 40				21 56	22 09					22 21		22 26	22 40
Ingatestone	d				21 02						21 32					22 02								22 32	
Shenfield 3	a				21 08	21 19					21 38	21 50				22 08	22 19							22 38	22 50
Romford	a					21 28											22 28								
Stratford 7 ⊖ ⛴	a				21 22	21 36		21s45			21 52	22 05				22 22	22 36					22s45		22 52	23s12
London Liverpool Street 15 ⊖	a	21 17			21 34	21 46		21 55			22 01	22 14		22 17		22 31	22 46					22 55		23 01	23 21

		LE 1 C	LE 1 A	LE ◇1		LE 1	LE 1 B	LE 1	LE 1	LE ◇1	LE 1 C	LE 1	LE 1 E	LE 1		LE 1	LE 1 F	LE 1	LE C	LE 1	LE 1
Norwich	d									22 00								23 05			
Diss	d									22 17								23 22			
Stowmarket	d	21 47								22 29	22 46						23 08	23 36	23 51		
Needham Market	d	21 52									22 51								23 56		
Ipswich	a	22 02								22 41	23 03						23 22	23 49	00 08		
	d					22 23				22 43				23 15			23 22				
Harwich Town	d							22 28												23 28	
Dovercourt	d							22 30												23 30	
Harwich International	d							22 33												23 33	
Wrabness	d							22 39												23 39	
Mistley	d							22 45												23 45	
Manningtree 5	d					22 33		22a50		22 53				23 25			23 32			23 50	
Walton-on-the-Naze	d		22 00										23 00								
Frinton-on-Sea	d		22 03										23 03								
Kirby Cross	d		22 06										23 06								
Clacton-on-Sea	d			22 05			←									23 05					
Thorpe-le-Soken 1	a		22 12	22 13			22 12						23 12			23 13					
	d		22 17	22 13			22 17									23 13					
Weeley	d		→				22 21									23 17					
Great Bentley	d						22 24									23 20					
Alresford (Essex)	d						22 28									23 24					
Wivenhoe	d			22 23			22 32									23 28					
Hythe	d						22 36									23 32					
Colchester Town	a						22 40														
	d						22 44					23 00									
Colchester 4	a			22 31		22 42	22 52			23 02		23 07		23 35		23 38	23 43			23 59	
	d			22 33		22 43				23 03											
Marks Tey 2	d					22 49															
Kelvedon	d					22 54															
Braintree	d								22 56												23 45
Braintree Freeport	d								22 58												23 47
Cressing	d								23 01												23 50
White Notley	d								23 04												23 53
Witham 2	d			22 46		23 00			23a12	23 16											00a01
Hatfield Peverel	d																				
Chelmsford	d			22 56		23 09				23 25											
Ingatestone	d			23 02																	
Shenfield 3	a			23 08		23 19				23 37											
Romford	a					23 28															
Stratford 7 ⊖ ⛴	a			23s29		23s41				23s59											
London Liverpool Street 15 ⊖	a			23 38		23 50				00 10											

A To Colchester
B From Walton-on-the-Naze
C From Cambridge
D From Peterborough. ◇ from Ipswich
E To Clacton-on-Sea
F From Peterborough

Table T011-R

Sundays
20 May to 2 December

Norwich, Ipswich, Harwich, Clacton, Walton-on-Naze, Colchester and Chelmsford - London

		LE 1	LE 1	LE 1	LE A	LE 1	LE 1	LE ◇1 ☕	LE 1	LE 1		LE ◇1	LE 1	LE ◇1 ☕	LE 1	LE 1	LE 1	LE ◇1	LE ◇1 B ☕	LE 1		LE ◇1 ☕	LE 1	LE 1	LE 1
Norwich	d							07 00						08 00					08 20			09 00			
Diss	d							07 17						08 17					08 38			09 17			
Stowmarket	d							07 29						08 29					08 50			09 29			
Needham Market	d																								
Ipswich	a							07 41						08 41					09 02			09 41			
	d							07 43	07 51				08 09	08 43					09 05	09 09		09 43			
Harwich Town	d															08 53								09 53	
Dovercourt	d															08 55								09 55	
Harwich International	d						07 20		08a16							08 58								09 58	
Wrabness	d															09 04								10 04	
Mistley	d															09 10								10 10	
Manningtree 5	d						07 34	07 53					08 19	08 53		09a15				09 19		09 53		10a15	
Walton-on-the-Naze	d														08 29								09 29		
Frinton-on-Sea	d														08 32								09 32		
Kirby Cross	d														08 35								09 35		
Clacton-on-Sea	d											07 35						08 35							
Thorpe-le-Soken 1	a											07 43			08 41			08 43					09 41		
	d											07 43						08 43							
Weeley	d																								
Great Bentley	d											07 48						08 48							
Alresford (Essex)	d											07 52						08 52							
Wivenhoe	d											07 56						08 56							
Hythe	d											08 00						09 00							
Colchester Town	a																								
	d																								
Colchester 4	a						07 43	08 02				08 06	08 29	09 02				09 06	09 20	09 29		10 02			
	d			06 54	07 01	07 24	07 48	08 03				08 06	08 30	09 03				09 06	09 23	09 30		10 03			
Marks Tey 2	d			07 00	07a14	07 30						08 12	08 36					09 12		09 36					
Kelvedon	d			07 05		07 35							08 41							09 41					
Braintree	d	00 25								08 00							09 00								10 00
Braintree Freeport	d	00 27								08 02							09 02								10 02
Cressing	d	00 30								08 05							09 05								10 05
White Notley	d	00 33								08 08							09 08								10 08
Witham 2	d	00a41		07 11		07 41	08 01			08a16		08 21	08 47				09a16	09 21		09 47					10a16
Hatfield Peverel	d			07 15		07 45							08 51							09 51					
Chelmsford	d		06 58	07 22		07 52	08 10					08 30	08 58					09 30		09 58					
Ingatestone	d		07 05	07 29		07 59							09 05							10 05					
Shenfield 3	a		07 10	07 40		08 10	08 20					08 40	09 10					09 40		10 10					
Romford	a		07 21	07 51																					
Stratford 7 ⊖ ⛴	a		07s35	08s05		08s35	08s50					09s05	09s35					10s05		10s35					
London Liverpool Street 15 ⊖	a		07 44	08 14		08 44	08 59	09 04				09 14	09 44	10 03				10 14	10 30	10 44		11 03			

		LE ◇1	LE 1	LE C	LE ◇1 ☕	LE 1		LE 1	LE 1	LE ◇1	LE 1	LE 1 D	LE ◇1 ☕	LE 1	LE 1	LE 1		LE ◇1	LE 1	LE 1 C	LE ◇1 ☕	LE 1	LE 1	LE 1	LE ◇1
Norwich	d				10 00								11 00								12 00				
Diss	d				10 17								11 17								12 17				
Stowmarket	d			10 20	10 29							11 14	11 29							12 20	12 29				
Needham Market	d			10 25																12 25					
Ipswich	a			10 38	10 41							11 28	11 41							12 36	12 41				
	d		10 09		10 43						11 09		11 43						12 09		12 43				
Harwich Town	d							10 53							11 53								12 53		
Dovercourt	d							10 55							11 55								12 55		
Harwich International	d							10 58							11 58								12 58		
Wrabness	d							11 04							12 04								13 04		
Mistley	d							11 10							12 10								13 10		
Manningtree 5	d		10 19		10 53			11a15			11 19		11 53		12a15				12 19		12 53		13a15		
Walton-on-the-Naze	d					10 29								11 29								12 29			
Frinton-on-Sea	d					10 32								11 32								12 32			
Kirby Cross	d					10 35								11 35								12 35			
Clacton-on-Sea	d	09 35								10 35								11 35							12 35
Thorpe-le-Soken 1	a	09 43				10 41				10 43				11 41				11 43				12 41			12 43
	d	09 43								10 43								11 43							12 43
Weeley	d																								
Great Bentley	d	09 48								10 48								11 48							12 48
Alresford (Essex)	d	09 52								10 52								11 52							12 52
Wivenhoe	d	09 56								10 56								11 56							12 56
Hythe	d	10 00								11 00								12 00							13 00
Colchester Town	a																								
	d																								
Colchester 4	a	10 06	10 29		11 02					11 06	11 29		12 02					12 06	12 29		13 02				13 06
	d	10 06	10 30		11 03					11 06	11 30		12 03					12 06	12 30		13 03				13 06
Marks Tey 2	d	10 12	10 36							11 12	11 36							12 12	12 36						13 12
Kelvedon	d		10 41								11 41								12 41						
Braintree	d								11 00							12 00								13 00	
Braintree Freeport	d								11 02							12 02								13 02	
Cressing	d								11 05							12 05								13 05	
White Notley	d								11 08							12 08								13 08	
Witham 2	d	10 21	10 47						11a16	11 21	11 47					12a16		12 21	12 47					13a16	13 21
Hatfield Peverel	d		10 51								11 51								12 51						
Chelmsford	d	10 30	10 58							11 30	11 58							12 30	12 58						13 30
Ingatestone	d		11 05								12 05								13 05						
Shenfield 3	a	10 40	11 10							11 40	12 10							12 40	13 10						13 40
Romford	a																								
Stratford 7 ⊖ ⛴	a	11s05	11s35							12s05	12s35							13s05	13s35						14s05
London Liverpool Street 15 ⊖	a	11 14	11 44		12 03					12 14	12 44		13 03					13 14	13 44		14 03				14 14

A To Sudbury
B until 9 September
C From Cambridge
D until 9 September. From Peterborough

Table T011-R

Sundays

20 May to 2 December

Norwich, Ipswich, Harwich, Clacton, Walton-on-Naze, Colchester and Chelmsford - London

	LE 1	LE 1 A	LE ◇1 ☕	LE 1	LE 1	LE 1	LE ◇1	LE 1	LE 1 B	LE ◇1 ☕	LE 1	LE 1	LE 1	LE ◇1	LE 1	LE 1 A	LE ◇1 ☕	LE 1	LE 1	LE 1	LE ◇1
Norwich d			13 00							14 00							15 00				
Diss d			13 17							14 17							15 17				
Stowmarket d		13 14	13 29						14 20	14 29						15 14	15 29				
Needham Market d									14 25												
Ipswich a		13 28	13 41						14 36	14 41						15 28	15 41				
d	13 09		13 43					14 09		14 43					15 09		15 43				
Harwich Town d					13 53							14 53							15 53		
Dovercourt d					13 55							14 55							15 55		
Harwich International d					13 58							14 58							15 58		
Wrabness d					14 04							15 04							16 04		
Mistley d					14 10							15 10							16 10		
Manningtree 5 d	13 19		13 53		14a15			14 19		14 53		15a15			15 19		15 53		16a15		
Walton-on-the-Naze d				13 29							14 29							15 29			
Frinton-on-Sea d				13 32							14 32							15 32			
Kirby Cross d				13 35							14 35							15 35			
Clacton-on-Sea d							13 35							14 35							15 35
Thorpe-le-Soken 1 a				13 41			13 43				14 41			14 43				15 41			15 43
d							13 43							14 43							15 43
Weeley d																					
Great Bentley d							13 48							14 48							15 48
Alresford (Essex) d							13 52							14 52							15 52
Wivenhoe d							13 56							14 56							15 56
Hythe d							14 00							15 00							16 00
Colchester Town a																					
d																					
Colchester 4 a	13 29		14 02				14 06	14 29		15 02				15 06	15 29		16 02				16 06
d	13 30		14 03				14 06	14 30		15 03				15 06	15 30		16 03				16 06
Marks Tey 2 d	13 36						14 12	14 36						15 12	15 36						16 12
Kelvedon d	13 41							14 41							15 41						
Braintree d						14 00							15 00							16 00	
Braintree Freeport d						14 02							15 02							16 02	
Cressing d						14 05							15 05							16 05	
White Notley d						14 08							15 08							16 08	
Witham 2 d	13 47					14a16	14 21	14 47					15a16	15 21	15 47					16a16	16 21
Hatfield Peverel d	13 51							14 51							15 51						
Chelmsford d	13 58						14 30	14 58						15 30	15 58						16 30
Ingatestone d	14 05							15 05							16 05						
Shenfield 3 a	14 10						14 40	15 10						15 40	16 10						16 40
Romford a																					
Stratford 7 ⊖ a	14s35						15s05	15s35						16s05	16s35						17s05
London Liverpool Street 15 ⊖ a	14 44		15 03				15 14	15 44		16 03				16 14	16 44		17 03				17 14

	LE ◇1 C ☕	LE 1	LE 1 B	LE 1 ☕	LE 1	LE 1	LE 1	LE ◇1	LE ◇1 ☕	LE 1	LE 1 A	LE ◇1 ☕	LE 1	LE 1	LE 1	LE ◇1	LE 1	LE 1 B	LE ◇1 ☕	LE 1	LE 1	LE 1
Norwich d	15 23			16 00					16 20			17 00							18 00			
Diss d	15 40			16 17					16 38			17 17							18 17			
Stowmarket d	15 52		16 20	16 29					16 50		17 11	17 29						18 20	18 29			
Needham Market d			16 25															18 25				
Ipswich a	16 04		16 36	16 41					17 02		17 25	17 41						18 36	18 41			
d	16 06	16 09		16 43					17 05	17 09		17 43					18 09		18 43			
Harwich Town d						16 53								17 53							18 53	
Dovercourt d						16 55								17 55							18 55	
Harwich International d						16 58								17 58							18 58	
Wrabness d						17 04								18 04							19 04	
Mistley d						17 10								18 10							19 10	
Manningtree 5 d		16 19		16 53		17a15				17 19		17 53		18a15			18 19		18 53		19a15	
Walton-on-the-Naze d					16 29								17 29							18 29		
Frinton-on-Sea d					16 32								17 32							18 32		
Kirby Cross d					16 35								17 35							18 35		
Clacton-on-Sea d								16 35								17 35						
Thorpe-le-Soken 1 a					16 41			16 43					17 41			17 43				18 41		
d								16 43								17 43						
Weeley d																						
Great Bentley d								16 48								17 48						
Alresford (Essex) d								16 52								17 52						
Wivenhoe d								16 56								17 56						
Hythe d								17 00								18 00						
Colchester Town a																						
d																						
Colchester 4 a	16 21	16 29		17 02				17 06	17 20	17 29		18 02				18 06	18 29		19 02			
d	16 23	16 30		17 03				17 06	17 23	17 30		18 03				18 06	18 30		19 03			
Marks Tey 2 d		16 36						17 12		17 36						18 12	18 36					
Kelvedon d		16 41								17 41							18 41					
Braintree d							17 00								18 00							19 00
Braintree Freeport d							17 02								18 02							19 02
Cressing d							17 05								18 05							19 05
White Notley d							17 08								18 08							19 08
Witham 2 d		16 47					17a16	17 21		17 47					18a16	18 21	18 47					19a16
Hatfield Peverel d		16 51								17 51							18 51					
Chelmsford d		16 58						17 30		17 58						18 30	18 58					
Ingatestone d		17 05								18 05							19 05					
Shenfield 3 a		17 10						17 40		18 10						18 40	19 10					
Romford a																						
Stratford 7 ⊖ a		17s35						18s05		18s35						19s05	19s35					
London Liverpool Street 15 ⊖ a	17 30	17 44		18 03				18 14	18 31	18 44		19 03				19 14	19 44		20 03			

A From Peterborough
B From Cambridge
C until 9 September

Table T011-R

Sundays

20 May to 2 December

Norwich, Ipswich, Harwich, Clacton, Walton-on-Naze, Colchester and Chelmsford - London

	LE ◇1	LE 1	LE 1 A	LE ◇1 ☕	LE 1	LE 1	LE 1	LE ◇1	LE 1	LE 1	LE 1	LE 1 B	LE ◇1 ☕	LE 1	LE 1	LE ◇1	LE 1	LE 1 A	LE ◇1	LE 1	LE 1
Norwich d				19 00									20 00						21 00		
Diss d				19 17									20 17						21 17		
Stowmarket d			19 11	19 29								20 20	20 29					21 11	21 29		
Needham Market d												20 25									
Ipswich a			19 25	19 41								20 36	20 41					21 25	21 41		
d		19 09	19 25	19 43					20 09			20 37	20 43				21 09	21 25	21 43		
Harwich Town d						19 53								20 53							21 53
Dovercourt d						19 55								20 55							21 55
Harwich International d						19 58					20 35	21a05		20 58							21 58
Wrabness d						20 04								21 04							22 04
Mistley d						20 10								21 10							22 10
Manningtree 5 d		19 19	19 35	19 53		20a15			20 19		20 48		20 53	21a15			21 19	21 35	21 53		22a15
Walton-on-the-Naze d					19 29					20 29										21 29	
Frinton-on-Sea d					19 32					20 32										21 32	
Kirby Cross d					19 35					20 35										21 35	
Clacton-on-Sea d	18 35							19 35								20 35					
Thorpe-le-Soken 1 a	18 43				19 41			19 43		20 41						20 43				21 41	
d	18 43							19 43								20 43					
Weeley d																					
Great Bentley d	18 48							19 48								20 48					
Alresford (Essex) d	18 52							19 52								20 52					
Wivenhoe d	18 56							19 56								20 56					
Hythe d	19 00							20 00								21 00					
Colchester Town a																					
d																					
Colchester 4 a	19 06	19 29	19 46	20 02				20 06	20 29		20 57		21 02			21 06	21 29	21 46	22 02		
d	19 06	19 30		20 03				20 06	20 30		20 57		21 03			21 06	21 30		22 03		
Marks Tey 2 d	19 12	19 36						20 12	20 36							21 12	21 36				
Kelvedon d		19 41							20 41								21 41				
Braintree d							20 00								21 00						
Braintree Freeport d							20 02								21 02						
Cressing d							20 05								21 05						
White Notley d							20 08								21 08						
Witham 2 d	19 21	19 47					20a16	20 21	20 47						21a16	21 21	21 47				
Hatfield Peverel d		19 51							20 51								21 51				
Chelmsford d	19 30	19 58						20 30	20 58		21 15					21 30	21 58				
Ingatestone d		20 05							21 05								22 05				
Shenfield 3 a	19 40	20 10						20 40	21 10		21 25					21 40	22 10				
Romford a																					
Stratford 7 ⊖ a	20s05	20s35						21s05	21s35		21s53					22s00	22s30				
London Liverpool Street 15 ⊖ a	20 14	20 44		21 03				21 14	21 44		22 02		22 04			22 10	22 40		23 03		

	LE 1	LE ◇1	LE 1	LE 1	LE 1 B	LE 1	LE 1	LE ◇1	LE 1	LE 1	LE B
Norwich d								22 00		23 05	
Diss d								22 17		23 23	
Stowmarket d					22 20			22 29		23 36	23 55
Needham Market d					22 25						23 59
Ipswich a					22 38			22 41		23 51	00 11
d			22 09					22 43			
Harwich Town d									22 53		
Dovercourt d									22 55		
Harwich International d									22 58		
Wrabness d									23 04		
Mistley d									23 10		
Manningtree 5 d			22 19					22 53	23 15		
Walton-on-the-Naze d				22 18							
Frinton-on-Sea d				22 21							
Kirby Cross d				22 24							
Clacton-on-Sea d		21 35				22 23					
Thorpe-le-Soken 1 a		21 43		22 30		22 31					
d		21 43				22 31					
Weeley d											
Great Bentley d		21 48									
Alresford (Essex) d		21 52									
Wivenhoe d		21 56				22 41					
Hythe d		22 00				22 45					
Colchester Town a											
d											
Colchester 4 a		22 06	22 29			22 51		23 02	23 24		
d		22 06	22 30					23 03			
Marks Tey 2 d		22 12	22 36								
Kelvedon d			22 41								
Braintree d	22 00						22 56				
Braintree Freeport d	22 02						22 58				
Cressing d	22 05						23 01				
White Notley d	22 08						23 04				
Witham 2 d	22a16	22 21	22 47				23a12	23 16			
Hatfield Peverel d			22 51								
Chelmsford d		22 30	22 58					23 25			
Ingatestone d			23 05								
Shenfield 3 a		22 40	23 10					23 36			
Romford a											
Stratford 7 ⊖ a		23s00	23s30					23s57			
London Liverpool Street 15 ⊖ a		23 10	23 40					00 07			

A From Peterborough
B From Cambridge

Table T013-F

Ipswich - Felixstowe and Lowestoft

Mondays to Fridays
21 May to 7 December

Miles	Miles			LE	LE	LE	LE	LE	LE	LE	LE	LE	LE	LE	LE	LE	LE	LE	LE	LE	LE	LE	LE
																■							
—	—	Harwich International	d																				
0	—	**Ipswich**	d	05 04	06 04	06 20		07 14	07 35	08 25	08 57	09 17	09 58	10 17	10 58	11 17	11 58	12 17	12 58	13 17	13 58	14 17	14 58
3½	0	Westerfield	d	05 10	06 10	06 26		07 20	07 41	08 31	09 03		10 04		11 04		12 04		13 04		14 04		15 04
—	2½	Derby Road	d	05 15	06 15			07 25		08 36	09 08		10 09		11 09		12 09		13 09		14 09		15 09
—	10½	Trimley	d	05 24	06 24			07 34		08 45	09 17		10 18		11 18		12 18		13 18		14 18		15 18
—	12¼	**Felixstowe**	a	05 30	06 30			07 40		08 51	09 23		10 24		11 24		12 24		13 24		14 24		15 24
10¼	—	Woodbridge	d			06 37			07 53			09 32		10 32		11 32		12 32		13 32		14 32	
11½	—	Melton	d			06 41			07 57			09 36		10 36		11 36		12 36		13 36		14 36	
15¾	—	Wickham Market	d			06 48			08 04			09 43		10 43		11 43		12 43		13 43		14 43	
22½	—	Saxmundham	d			06a58	07 44		08 15			09 54		10 54		11 54		12 54		13 54		14 54	
26¾	—	Darsham	d				07 51		08 21			10 00		11 00		12 00		13 00		14 00		15 00	
32	—	Halesworth	d				08 00		08 31			10 10		11 10		12 10		13 10		14 10		15 10	
36	—	Brampton (Suffolk)	d				08x07		08x37			10x16		11x16		12x16		13x16		14x16		15x16	
40¼	—	Beccles	d				08 16		08 46			10 25		11 25		12 25		13 25		14 25		15 25	
46¾	—	Oulton Broad South	d				08 25		08 56			10 35		11 35		12 35		13 35		14 35		15 35	
49	—	**Lowestoft**	a				08 33		09 06			10 43		11 43		12 43		13 43		14 43		15 44	

		LE	LE	LE	LE	LE	LE	LE	LE	LE	LE	LE	LE	LE	LE	LE
		■								■					■	
Harwich International	d														21 38	
Ipswich	d	15 17	15 54	15 58	16 58	17 17	17 58	18 13	18 58	19 17	19 58	20 17	20 58	21 17	22 17	22 28
Westerfield	d		16 00	16 04	17 04		18 04	18 19	19 04		20 04		21 04			22 34
Derby Road	d			16 09	17 09		18 09		19 09		20 09		21 09			22 39
Trimley	d			16 18	17 18		18 18		19 18		20 18		21 18			22 48
Felixstowe	a			16 24	17 24		18 24		19 24		20 24		21 24			22 57
Woodbridge	d	15 32	16 18			17 32		18 30		19 32		20 32		21 32	22 32	
Melton	d	15 36	16 22			17 36		18 34		19 36		20 36		21 36	22 36	
Wickham Market	d	15 43	16 29			17 43		18 40		19 43		20 43		21 43	22 43	
Saxmundham	d	15 54	16 40			17 54		18 51		19 54		20 54		21 54	22 54	
Darsham	d	16 00	16 47			18 00		18 58		20 00		21 00		22 00	23 00	
Halesworth	d	16 10	16 56			18 10		19 07		20 10		21 10		22 10	23 10	
Brampton (Suffolk)	d	16x16	17x03			18x16		19x14		20x16		21x16		22x16	23x16	
Beccles	d	16 25	17 19			18 25		19 25		20 25		21 25		22 25	23 25	
Oulton Broad South	d	16 35	17 28			18 35		19 35		20 35		21 35		22 35	23 35	
Lowestoft	a	16 43	17 36			18 43		19 43		20 43		21 43		22 43	23 43	

Saturdays
26 May to 8 December

		LE	LE	LE	LE	LE	LE	LE	LE	LE	LE	LE	LE	LE	LE	LE	LE	LE	LE	LE	LE	LE	LE
								■								■							
Harwich International	d																						
Ipswich	d	05 58	06 58	07 17	07 58	08 17	08 58	09 17	09 58	10 17	10 58	11 17	11 58	12 17	12 58	13 17	13 58	14 17	14 58	15 17	15 58	16 17	16 58
Westerfield	d	06 04	07 04		08 04		09 04		10 04		11 04		12 04		13 04		14 04		15 04		16 04		17 04
Derby Road	d	06 09	07 09		08 09		09 09		10 09		11 09		12 09		13 09		14 09		15 09		16 09		17 09
Trimley	d	06 18	07 18		08 18		09 18		10 18		11 18		12 18		13 18		14 18		15 18		16 18		17 18
Felixstowe	a	06 24	07 24		08 24		09 24		10 24		11 24		12 24		13 24		14 24		15 24		16 24		17 24
Woodbridge	d			07 32		08 32		09 32		10 32		11 32		12 32		13 32		14 32		15 32		16 32	
Melton	d			07 36		08 36		09 36		10 36		11 36		12 36		13 36		14 36		15 36		16 36	
Wickham Market	d			07 43		08 43		09 43		10 43		11 43		12 43		13 43		14 43		15 43		16 43	
Saxmundham	d			07 54		08 54		09 54		10 54		11 54		12 54		13 54		14 54		15 54		16 54	
Darsham	d			08 00		09 00		10 00		11 00		12 00		13 00		14 00		15 00		16 00		17 00	
Halesworth	d			08 10		09 10		10 10		11 10		12 10		13 10		14 10		15 10		16 10		17 10	
Brampton (Suffolk)	d			08x16		09x16		10x16		11x16		12x16		13x16		14x16		15x16		16x16		17x16	
Beccles	d			08 25		09 25		10 25		11 25		12 25		13 25		14 25		15 25		16 25		17 25	
Oulton Broad South	d			08 35		09 35		10 35		11 35		12 35		13 35		14 35		15 35		16 35		17 41	
Lowestoft	a			08 43		09 43		10 43		11 43		12 43		13 43		14 43		15 43		16 43		17 51	

		LE	LE	LE	LE	LE	LE	LE	LE	LE	LE	LE
		■								■	■	
					(bus)		(bus)		(bus)			(bus)
Harwich International	d										21 38	
Ipswich	d	17 17	17 58	18 17	19 00	19 17	20 00	20 17	21 00	21 17	22 17	22 30
Westerfield	d		18 04									
Derby Road	d		18 09		19 10		20 10		21 10			22 40
Trimley	d		18 18		19 30		20 30		21 30			23 00
Felixstowe	a		18 24		19 40		20 40		21 40			23 10
Woodbridge	d	17 32		18 32		19 32		20 32		21 32	22 32	
Melton	d	17 36		18 36		19 36		20 36		21 36	22 36	
Wickham Market	d	17 43		18 43		19 43		20 43		21 43	22 43	
Saxmundham	d	17 54		18 54		19 54		20 54		21 54	22 54	
Darsham	d	18 00		19 00		20 00		21 00		22 00	23 00	
Halesworth	d	18 10		19 10		20 10		21 10		22 10	23 10	
Brampton (Suffolk)	d	18x16		19x16		20x16		21x16		22x16	23x16	
Beccles	d	18 25		19 25		20 25		21 25		22 25	23 25	
Oulton Broad South	d	18 35		19 35		20 35		21 35		22 35	23 35	
Lowestoft	a	18 43		19 43		20 43		21 43		22 43	23 43	

Table T013-F

Ipswich - Felixstowe and Lowestoft

Sundays
20 May to 2 December

		LE	LE	LE	LE	LE	LE	LE	LE	LE	LE	LE	LE	LE
			■									■		
		(bus)		(bus)	(bus)		(bus)			(bus)	(bus)		(bus)	(bus)
Harwich International	d													
Ipswich	d	09 55	10 02	10 55	11 55	12 02	12 55	13 55	14 02	14 55	15 55	16 02	16 55	17 55
Westerfield	d		10 08			12 08		14 01	14 08			16 08		
Derby Road	d	10 05		11 05	12 05		13 05	14 06		15 05	16 05		17 05	18 05
Trimley	d	10 25		11 25	12 25		13 25	14 15		15 25	16 25		17 25	18 25
Felixstowe	a	10 35		11 35	12 35		13 35	14 21		15 35	16 35		17 35	18 35
Woodbridge	d		10 19			12 19			14 19			16 19		
Melton	d		10 23			12 23			14 23			16 23		
Wickham Market	d		10 29			12 29			14 29			16 29		
Saxmundham	d		10 40			12 40			14 40			16 40		
Darsham	d		10 47			12 47			14 47			16 47		
Halesworth	d		10 56			12 56			14 56			16 56		
Brampton (Suffolk)	d		11x03			13x03			15x03			17x03		
Beccles	d		11 12			13 12			15 12			17 21		
Oulton Broad South	d		11 21			13 21			15 21			17 30		
Lowestoft	a		11 30			13 30			15 30			17 39		

		LE	LE	LE	LE	LE	LE
							■
			(bus)		(bus)		
Harwich International	d						
Ipswich	d	18 02	18 55	19 07	19 55	20 02	22 02
Westerfield	d	18 08		19 13		20 08	22 08
Derby Road	d		19 05		20 05		
Trimley	d		19 25		20 25		
Felixstowe	a		19 35		20 35		
Woodbridge	d	18 19		19 24		20 19	22 19
Melton	d	18 23		19 28		20 23	22 23
Wickham Market	d	18 29		19 34		20 29	22 29
Saxmundham	d	18 40		19 45		20 40	22 40
Darsham	d	18 47		19 52		20 47	22 47
Halesworth	d	18 56		20 01		20 56	22 56
Brampton (Suffolk)	d	19x03		20x08		21x03	23x03
Beccles	d	19 12		20 21		21 12	23 12
Oulton Broad South	d	19 21		20 30		21 21	23 21
Lowestoft	a	19 30		20 39		21 30	23 30

Table T013-R

Lowestoft and Felixstowe - Ipswich

Mondays to Fridays

21 May to 7 December

Miles	Miles			LE	LE ■	LE	LE ■	LE	LE	LE		LE	LE	LE ■	LE	LE	LE	LE	LE	LE		LE	LE ■	LE	LE
0	—	**Lowestoft**	d		05 25		06 14	06 41		07 27				09 07		10 07		11 07		12 07			13 07		14 07
2¼	—	Oulton Broad South	d		05 31		06 20	06 47		07 33				09 13		10 13		11 13		12 13			13 13		14 13
8½	—	Beccles	d		05 41		06 30	06 57		07 43				09 25		10 25		11 25		12 25			13 25		14 25
13	—	Brampton (Suffolk)	d		05x49		06x38	07x05		07x51				09x33		10x33		11x33		12x33			13x33		14x33
17	—	Halesworth	d		05 56		06 45	07 12		07 58				09 41		10 41		11 41		12 41			13 41		14 41
22¼	—	Darsham	d		06 05		06 54	07 21		08 07				09 49		10 49		11 49		12 49			13 49		14 49
26½	—	Saxmundham	d		06 13		07 03	07 29		08 16				09 57		10 57		11 57		12 57			13 57		14 57
33¼	—	Wickham Market	d		06 23		07 13	07 39		08 26				10 07		11 07		12 07		13 07			14 07		15 07
37¼	—	Melton	d		06 30		07 20	07 46		08 33				10 13		11 13		12 13		13 13			14 13		15 13
38¾	—	Woodbridge	d		06 35		07 25	07 51		08 38				10 18		11 18		12 18		13 18			14 18		15 18
—	0	**Felixstowe**	d	05 34		06 36			07 47			08 54	09 28		10 28		11 28		12 28			13 28		14 28	
—	1¾	Trimley	d	05 37		06 39			07 50			08 57	09 31		10 31		11 31		12 31			13 31		14 31	
—	9¾	Derby Road	d	05 47		06 49			08 00			09 09	09 41		10 41		11 41		12 41			13 41		14 41	
45½	12¼	Westerfield	d	05 52		06 54	07 35	08 01	08 05	08 49		09 14	09 46		10 46		11 46		12 46			13 46		14 46	
49	—	**Ipswich**	a	06 01	06 53	07 02	07 44	08 09	08 14	08 56		09 24	09 54	10 36	10 54	11 36	11 54	12 36	12 54	13 36		13 54	14 36	14 54	15 36
—	—	Harwich International	a		07 27																				

		LE	LE	LE	LE	LE		LE ■	LE	LE	LE	LE	LE	LE	LE	LE		LE
Lowestoft	d		15 07		16 07			17 02		18 07		19 07		20 07		21 07		
Oulton Broad South	d		15 13		16 13			17 08		18 13		19 13		20 13		21 13		
Beccles	d		15 25		16 25			17 25		18 25		19 25		20 25		21 25		
Brampton (Suffolk)	d		15x33		16x33			17x33		18x33		19x33		20x33		21x33		
Halesworth	d		15 41		16 41			17 41		18 41		19 41		20 41		21 41		
Darsham	d		15 49		16 49			17 49		18 49		19 49		20 49		21 49		
Saxmundham	d		15 57		17 07			17 57		18 57		19 57		20 57		21 57		
Wickham Market	d		16 07		17 17			18 07		19 07		20 07		21 07		22 07		
Melton	d		16 13		17 23			18 13		19 13		20 13		21 13		22 13		
Woodbridge	d		16 18		17 28			18 18		19 18		20 18		21 18		22 18		
Felixstowe	d	15 28		16 28		17 28			18 28		19 28		20 28		21 28			23 01
Trimley	d	15 31		16 31		17 31			18 31		19 31		20 31		21 31			23 04
Derby Road	d	15 41		16 41		17 41			18 41		19 41		20 41		21 41			23 14
Westerfield	d	15 46		16 46		17 46			18 46		19 46		20 46		21 46	22 29		23 19
Ipswich	a	15 54	16 36	16 54	17 46	17 54		18 36	18 54	19 36	19 54	20 37	20 54	21 36	21 54	22 36		23 27
Harwich International	a																	

Saturdays

26 May to 8 December

		LE	LE ■	LE	LE ■	LE	LE	LE	LE	LE		LE	LE	LE ■	LE	LE	LE	LE	LE	LE		LE	LE ■	LE	LE
Lowestoft	d		06 07		07 07		08 07		09 07			10 07		11 07		12 07		13 07		14 07			15 07		16 07
Oulton Broad South	d		06 13		07 13		08 13		09 13			10 13		11 13		12 13		13 13		14 13			15 13		16 13
Beccles	d		06 25		07 25		08 25		09 25			10 25		11 25		12 25		13 25		14 25			15 25		16 25
Brampton (Suffolk)	d		06x33		07x33		08x33		09x33			10x33		11x33		12x33		13x33		14x33			15x33		16x33
Halesworth	d		06 41		07 41		08 41		09 41			10 41		11 41		12 41		13 41		14 41			15 41		16 41
Darsham	d		06 49		07 49		08 49		09 49			10 49		11 49		12 49		13 49		14 49			15 49		16 49
Saxmundham	d		06 57		07 57		08 57		09 57			10 57		11 57		12 57		13 57		14 57			15 57		16 57
Wickham Market	d		07 07		08 07		09 07		10 07			11 07		12 07		13 07		14 07		15 07			16 07		17 07
Melton	d		07 13		08 13		09 13		10 13			11 13		12 13		13 13		14 13		15 13			16 13		17 13
Woodbridge	d		07 18		08 18		09 18		10 18			11 18		12 18		13 18		14 18		15 18			16 18		17 18
Felixstowe	d	06 28		07 28		08 28		09 28		10 28			11 28		12 28		13 28		14 28			15 28		16 28	
Trimley	d	06 31		07 31		08 31		09 31		10 31			11 31		12 31		13 31		14 31			15 31		16 31	
Derby Road	d	06 41		07 41		08 41		09 41		10 41			11 41		12 41		13 41		14 41			15 41		16 41	
Westerfield	d	06 46		07 46		08 46		09 46		10 46			11 46		12 46		13 46		14 46			15 46		16 46	
Ipswich	a	06 54	07 36	07 54	08 36	08 54	09 36	09 54	10 36	10 54		11 36	11 54	12 36	12 54	13 36	13 54	14 36	14 54	15 36		15 54	16 36	16 54	17 36
Harwich International	a																								

		LE	LE	LE	LE 🚌	LE			LE 🚌	LE ■		LE 🚌	LE		LE 🚌	LE			LE 🚌
Lowestoft	d		17 07			18 07				19 07			20 07			21 07			
Oulton Broad South	d		17 13			18 13				19 13			20 13			21 13			
Beccles	d		17 25			18 25				19 25			20 25			21 25			
Brampton (Suffolk)	d		17x33			18x33				19x33			20x33			21x33			
Halesworth	d		17 41			18 41				19 41			20 41			21 41			
Darsham	d		17 49			18 49				19 49			20 49			21 49			
Saxmundham	d		17 57			18 57				19 57			20 57			21 57			
Wickham Market	d		18 07			19 07				20 07			21 07			22 07			
Melton	d		18 13			19 13				20 13			21 13			22 13			
Woodbridge	d		18 18			19 18				20 18			21 18			22 18			
Felixstowe	d	17 28		18 28	18 50				19 50			20 50			21 50				23 15
Trimley	d	17 31		18 31	18 55				19 55			20 55			21 55				23 20
Derby Road	d	17 41		18 41	19 15				20 15			21 15			22 15				23 40
Westerfield	d	17 46		18 46												22 29			
Ipswich	a	17 54	18 36	18 54	19 30	19 36			20 30	20 36		21 30	21 36		22 30	22 36			23 55
Harwich International	a																		

Table T013-R

Lowestoft and Felixstowe - Ipswich

Sundays

20 May to 2 December

		LE ■	LE 🚌		LE 🚌	LE			LE 🚌		LE 🚌	LE		LE 🚌		LE 🚌		LE ■		LE 🚌		LE 🚌	LE		LE 🚌
Lowestoft	d	08 05				10 05						12 05						14 05					16 05		
Oulton Broad South	d	08 11				10 11						12 11						14 11					16 11		
Beccles	d	08 21				10 21						12 21						14 21					16 21		
Brampton (Suffolk)	d	08x29				10x29						12x29						14x29					16x29		
Halesworth	d	08 36				10 36						12 36						14 36					16 36		
Darsham	d	08 44				10 44						12 44						14 44					16 44		
Saxmundham	d	08 53				10 53						12 53						14 53					16 53		
Wickham Market	d	09 02				11 02						13 02						15 02					17 02		
Melton	d	09 09				11 09						13 09						15 09					17 09		
Woodbridge	d	09 14				11 14						13 14						15 14					17 14		
Felixstowe	d		09 50		10 50				11 50		12 50			13 50		14 50				15 50		16 50			17 50
Trimley	d		09 55		10 55				11 55		12 55			13 55		14 55				15 55		16 55			17 55
Derby Road	d		10 15		11 15				12 15		13 15			14 15		15 15				16 15		17 15			18 15
Westerfield	d	09 24				11 24						13 24						15 24					17 24		
Ipswich	a	09 32	10 30		11 30	11 32			12 30		13 30	13 32		14 30		15 30		15 32		16 30		17 30	17 32		18 30
Harwich International	a																								

		LE			LE 🚌	LE		LE 🚌		LE 🚌	LE ■
Lowestoft	d	17 05				18 05					20 05
Oulton Broad South	d	17 11				18 11					20 11
Beccles	d	17 21				18 21					20 21
Brampton (Suffolk)	d	17x29				18x29					20x29
Halesworth	d	17 36				18 36					20 36
Darsham	d	17 44				18 44					20 44
Saxmundham	d	17 53				18 53					20 53
Wickham Market	d	18 02				19 02					21 02
Melton	d	18 09				19 09					21 09
Woodbridge	d	18 14				19 14					21 14
Felixstowe	d				18 50			19 50		20 50	
Trimley	d				18 55			19 55		20 55	
Derby Road	d				19 15			20 15		21 15	
Westerfield	d	18 24				19 24					21 24
Ipswich	a	18 32			19 30	19 32		20 30		21 30	21 32
Harwich International	a										

Table T014-F

Mondays to Fridays
21 May to 7 December

Ipswich - Bury St. Edmunds, Cambridge, Ely and Peterborough

Miles	Miles	Miles			LE	LE ■	LE ■	LE ■	LE ■	LE ■	LE ■	LE ■	LE ■
—	—	—	Colchester	d		05 40							
—	—	—	Manningtree	d		05 49							
—	—	0	Harwich International	d						07 50			
0	0	18	**Ipswich**	d	05 10	06 00	06 16	06 54	08 03	08 20	09 20	10 00	10 20
8¼	—	—	Needham Market	d	05 20		06 25	07 03		08 29	09 29		10 29
12	12	—	Stowmarket	d	05 26	06 12	06 31	07 09	08 16	08 35	09 35	10 12	10 35
17¾	—	—	Elmswell	d	05 35		06 39	07 17		08 44	09 43		10 43
22¼	—	—	Thurston	d	05 41		06 45	07 23		08 50	09 49		10 49
26½	26½	—	**Bury St Edmunds**	a	05 48	06 28	06 51	07 29	08 32	08 56	09 55	10 28	10 55
—	—	—	**Bury St Edmunds**	d	05 49	06 29	06 54	07 33	08 33	08 58	09 57	10 29	10 57
36	—	—	Kennett	d	06 00		07 04	07 43			10 07		
41	—	—	Newmarket	d	06 09		07 15	07 52		09 18	10 19		11 18
44¼	—	—	Dullingham	d	06 14		07 20	08 00		09 23			11 23
55½	—	—	**Cambridge**	a	06 33		07 41	08 19		09 42	10 41		11 41
—	51	—	**Ely** ■	a		06 56			08 59			10 58	
—	—	—		d		06 57			08 59			10 58	
—	60¾	—	Manea	a		07 07			09 10			11 09	
—	66½	—	March	a		07 15			09 17			11 16	
—	74¼	—	Whittlesea	a		07 26			09 29			11 28	
—	81¼	—	**Peterborough** ■	a		07 38			09 40			11 39	

		LE ■	LE ■	LE ■	LE ■	LE ■	LE ■	LE ■	LE ■	LE ■	LE ■
Colchester	d										
Manningtree	d										
Harwich International	d										
Ipswich	d	11 20	11 58	12 20	13 20	13 58	14 20	15 20	16 00	16 20	17 20
Needham Market	d	11 29		12 29	13 29		14 29	15 29		16 29	17 29
Stowmarket	d	11 35	12 11	12 35	13 35	14 11	14 35	15 35	16 12	16 35	17 35
Elmswell	d	11 43		12 43	13 43		14 43	15 43		16 43	17 43
Thurston	d	11 49		12 49	13 49		14 49	15 49		16 49	17 49
Bury St Edmunds	a	11 55	12 27	12 55	13 55	14 27	14 55	15 55	16 29	16 55	17 55
Bury St Edmunds	d	11 57	12 29	12 57	13 57	14 29	14 57	15 57	16 29	16 57	17 57
Kennett	d	12 07			14 07			16 07		17 07	18 07
Newmarket	d	12 19		13 18	14 19		15 18	16 19		17 19	18 19
Dullingham	d			13 23			15 23				
Cambridge	a	12 41		13 41	14 41		15 41	16 41		17 44	18 41
Ely ■	a		12 58			14 58			16 58		
	d		12 58			14 58			16 59		
Manea	a		13 09			15 09			17 10		
March	a		13 16			15 16			17 17		
Whittlesea	a		13 28			15 28			17 29		
Peterborough ■	a		13 39			15 39			17 40		

		LE ■	LE ■	LE ■	LE ■	LE ■	LE	LE
Colchester	d							
Manningtree	d							
Harwich International	d							
Ipswich	d	17 48	18 17	19 13	20 00	20 18	21 17	22 19
Needham Market	d	17 57	18 26	19 22		20 28	21 27	22 29
Stowmarket	d	18 03	18 32	19 28	20 12	20 35	21 33	22 35
Elmswell	d	18 11	18 40	19 36		20 44	21 42	22 44
Thurston	d	18 17	18 46	19 42		20 50	21 48	22 50
Bury St Edmunds	a	18 23	18 52	19 48	20 28	20 56	21 55	22 57
Bury St Edmunds	d	18 30	18 57	19 57	20 29	20 57	21 56	
Kennett	d			20 07			22 07	
Newmarket	d		19 18	20 19		21 18	22 20	
Dullingham	d		19 23			21 23	22 25	
Cambridge	a		19 41	20 41		21 42	22 43	
Ely ■	a	18 57			20 59			
	d	18 58			21 01			
Manea	a	19 09			21 10			
March	a	19 16			21 18			
Whittlesea	a	19 28			21 30			
Peterborough ■	a	19 39			21 40			

Saturdays
26 May to 8 December

		LE	LE ■	LE ■	LE ■	LE ■	LE ■	LE ■	LE ■	LE ■
Colchester	d		05 40							
Manningtree	d		05 49							
Harwich International	d						07 50			
Ipswich	d	05 10	06 00	06 16	07 20	08 00	08 20	09 20	09 58	10 20
Needham Market	d	05 20		06 25	07 29		08 29	09 29		10 29
Stowmarket	d	05 26	06 12	06 31	07 35	08 12	08 35	09 35	10 11	10 35
Elmswell	d	05 35		06 39	07 43		08 44	09 43		10 43
Thurston	d	05 41		06 45	07 49		08 50	09 49		10 49
Bury St Edmunds	a	05 48	06 28	06 52	07 55	08 28	08 56	09 55	10 27	10 55
Bury St Edmunds	d	05 49	06 29	06 54	07 57	08 29	08 57	09 57	10 29	10 57
Kennett	d	06 00		07 06	08 07			10 07		
Newmarket	d	06 09		07 16	08 19		09 18	10 19		11 18
Dullingham	d	06 14		07 21	08 24		09 23			11 23
Cambridge	a	06 32		07 40	08 40		09 40	10 40		11 40
Ely ■	a		06 57			08 58			10 57	
	d		06 58			08 58			10 58	
Manea	a		07 09			09 09			11 09	
March	a		07 16			09 16			11 16	
Whittlesea	a		07 28			09 28			11 28	
Peterborough ■	a		07 39			09 39			11 39	

		LE ■	LE ■	LE ■	LE ■	LE ■	LE ■	LE ■	LE ■	LE ■	LE ■	LE ■	LE ■	LE ■
Colchester	d													
Manningtree	d													
Harwich International	d													
Ipswich	d	11 20	11 58	12 20	13 20	13 58	14 20	15 20	15 58	16 20	17 20	17 58	18 20	19 20
Needham Market	d	11 29		12 29	13 29		14 29	15 29		16 29	17 29		18 29	19 29
Stowmarket	d	11 35	12 11	12 35	13 35	14 11	14 35	15 35	16 11	16 35	17 35	18 11	18 35	19 35
Elmswell	d	11 43		12 43	13 43		14 43	15 43		16 43	17 43		18 43	19 43
Thurston	d	11 49		12 49	13 49		14 49	15 49		16 49	17 49		18 49	19 49
Bury St Edmunds	a	11 55	12 27	12 55	13 55	14 27	14 55	15 55	16 27	16 55	17 55	18 27	18 55	19 55
Bury St Edmunds	d	11 57	12 29	12 57	13 57	14 29	14 57	15 57	16 29	16 57	17 57	18 29	18 57	19 57
Kennett	d	12 08			14 07			16 07		17 09	18 07			20 07
Newmarket	d	12 19		13 18	14 19		15 18	16 19		17 19	18 19		19 18	20 19
Dullingham	d			13 23			15 23						19 23	
Cambridge	a	12 40		13 40	14 40		15 40	16 40		17 40	18 40		19 40	20 40
Ely ■	a		12 58			14 58			16 58			18 58		
	d		12 58			14 58			16 58			18 58		
Manea	a		13 09			15 09			17 09			19 09		
March	a		13 16			15 16			17 16			19 16		
Whittlesea	a		13 28			15 28			17 28			19 28		
Peterborough ■	a		13 39			15 39			17 39			19 39		

For complete service between Ely and Peterborough refer to Table T017

For complete service between Colchester and Stowmarket refer to Table T011

Table T014-F

Saturdays
26 May to 8 December

Ipswich - Bury St. Edmunds, Cambridge, Ely and Peterborough

		LE ■	LE ■	LE	LE ■
Colchester	d				
Manningtree	d				
Harwich International	d				
Ipswich	d	19 58	20 20	21 17	22 19
Needham Market	d		20 29	21 27	22 29
Stowmarket	d	20 11	20 35	21 33	22 35
Elmswell	d		20 43	21 42	22 44
Thurston	d		20 49	21 48	22 50
Bury St Edmunds	a	20 27	20 55	21 55	22 57
Bury St Edmunds	d	20 29	20 57	21 56	
Kennett	d			22 07	
Newmarket	d		21 18	22 19	
Dullingham	d		21 23	22 25	
Cambridge	a		21 40	22 42	
Ely ■	a	20 58			
	d	20 58			
Manea	a	21 09			
March	a	21 16			
Whittlesea	a	21 28			
Peterborough ■	a	21 39			

Sundays
20 May to 2 December

		LE	LE ■ A	LE ■	LE ■	LE ■	LE ■	LE ■	LE ■	LE ■	LE ■	LE ■	LE ■	LE ■	LE
Colchester	d				09 32										
Manningtree	d				09 40										
Harwich International	d			08 30											
Ipswich	d	07 32	07 55	09 02	09 55	11 02	11 55	13 02	13 55	15 02	15 55	17 02	17 55	19 02	21 02
Needham Market	d	07 42		09 12		11 12		13 12		15 12		17 12		19 12	21 12
Stowmarket	d	07 48	08 07	09 18	10 07	11 18	12 07	13 18	14 07	15 18	16 07	17 18	18 07	19 18	21 18
Elmswell	d	07 57		09 27		11 27		13 27		15 27		17 27		19 27	21 27
Thurston	d	08 03		09 33		11 33		13 33		15 33		17 33		19 33	21 33
Bury St Edmunds	a	08 10	08 23	09 40	10 23	11 40	12 23	13 40	14 23	15 40	16 23	17 40	18 23	19 40	21 40
Bury St Edmunds	d	08 11	08 24	09 41	10 24	11 41	12 24	13 41	14 24	15 41	16 24	17 41	18 24	19 41	21 41
Kennett	d	08 22		09 52		11 52		13 52		15 52		17 52		19 52	21 52
Newmarket	d	08 31		10 01		12 01		14 01		16 01		18 01		20 01	22 01
Dullingham	d	08 36		10 06		12 06		14 06		16 06		18 06		20 06	22 06
Cambridge	a	08 57		10 25		12 25		14 25		16 25		18 25		20 24	22 24
Ely ■	a		08 51		10 51		12 51		14 51		16 51		18 51		
	d		08 52		10 52		12 52		14 52		16 52		18 52		
Manea	a														
March	a		09 08		11 08		13 08		15 08		17 08		19 08		
Whittlesea	a		09 20		11 20		13 20		15 20		17 20		19 20		
Peterborough ■	a		09 31		11 31		13 31		15 31		17 31		19 31		

A until 9 September

For complete service between Ely and Peterborough refer to Table T017

For complete service between Colchester and Stowmarket refer to Table T011

Table T014-R

Mondays to Fridays

21 May to 7 December

Peterborough, Ely, Cambridge and Bury St. Edmunds - Ipswich

Miles	Miles	Miles			LE ■	LE	LE	LE ■	LE ■	LE ■	LE ■	LE ■	LE ■	LE ■	LE ■	LE ■	LE ■	LE ■	LE ■	LE ■	LE ■	LE ■	LE ■
0	—	—	**Peterborough** ■	d					07 49			09 50			11 50			13 50			15 50		
7	—	—	Whittlesea	d					07 57			09 58			11 58			13 58			15 58		
14¾	—	—	March	d					08 08			10 09			12 09			14 09			16 09		
20½	—	—	Manea	d					08 16			10 17			12 17			14 17			16 17		
30¼	—	—	**Ely** ■	a					08 29			10 31			12 31			14 31			16 31		
—	—	—		d					08 30			10 32			12 32			14 32			16 32		
—	0	—	**Cambridge**	d			06 42	07 44		08 48	09 47		10 47	11 47		12 47	13 47		14 47	15 47		16 47	17 47
—	11¼	—	Dullingham	d				08 00			10 03			12 03			14 03			16 03		17 03	18 03
—	14½	—	Newmarket	d			07 02	08 05		09 07	10 08		11 07	12 08		13 07	14 08		15 07	16 08		17 08	18 08
—	19½	—	Kennett	d			07 10			09 15			11 15			13 15			15 15			17 16	18 16
54¾	29¼	—	**Bury St Edmunds**	a			07 23	08 23	08 56	09 26	10 26	10 58	11 26	12 26	12 58	13 26	14 26	14 58	15 26	16 26	16 58	17 27	18 27
—	—	—	**Bury St Edmunds**	d	05 31	06 21	07 23	08 24	08 56	09 27	10 26	10 58	11 26	12 26	12 58	13 26	14 26	14 58	15 26	16 26	16 58	17 28	18 28
—	33¼	—	Thurston	d	05 37	06 27	07 30	08 30		09 33	10 32		11 32	12 32		13 32	14 32		15 32	16 32		17 34	18 34
—	37¾	—	Elmswell	d	05 43	06 34	07 36	08 36		09 39	10 38		11 38	12 38		13 38	14 38		15 38	16 38		17 40	18 40
69¼	43¾	—	Stowmarket	d	05 52	06 42	07 45	08 45	09 12	09 47	10 47	11 14	11 47	12 47	13 14	13 47	14 47	15 14	15 47	16 47	17 14	17 48	18 48
—	47¼	—	Needham Market	d	05 57	06 47	07 50	08 50		09 52	10 52		11 52	12 52		13 52	14 52		15 52	16 52		17 53	18 53
81¼	55¾	0	**Ipswich**	a	06 07	07 00	08 02	09 02	09 26	10 02	11 04	11 28	12 02	13 04	13 28	14 02	15 04	15 28	16 06	17 04	17 28	18 04	19 03
—	—	18	Harwich International	a																			
—	—	—	Manningtree	a																			
—	—	—	Colchester	a																			

		LE ■	LE ■	LE ■	LE ■	LE ■	LE ■	LE ■	LE
Peterborough ■	d	17 50			19 50			21 45	
Whittlesea	d	17 58			19 58			21 53	
March	d	18 09			20 09			22 04	
Manea	d	18 17			20 17			22 12	
Ely ■	a	18 31			20 31			22 25	
	d	18 32			20 32			22 26	
Cambridge	d		18 47	19 47		20 47	21 47		22 47
Dullingham	d			20 03			22 03		23 03
Newmarket	d		19 07	20 08		21 07	22 09		23 08
Kennett	d		19 15			21 15			23 16
Bury St Edmunds	a	18 58	19 26	20 26	20 58	21 26	22 26	22 52	23 29
Bury St Edmunds	d	18 58	19 27	20 26	20 58	21 26	22 27	22 52	23 29
Thurston	d		19 33	20 32		21 32	22 33		23 35
Elmswell	d		19 39	20 38		21 38	22 40		23 42
Stowmarket	d	19 14	19 48	20 47	21 14	21 47	22 47	23 08	23 51
Needham Market	d		19 53	20 52		21 52	22 53		23 56
Ipswich	a	19 28	20 04	21 01	21 28	22 04	23 03	23 21	00 07
Harwich International	a			21 29					
Manningtree	a				21 38			23 32	
Colchester	a				21 51			23 43	

Saturdays

26 May to 8 December

		LE	LE	LE ■	LE ■	LE ■	LE ■	LE ■	LE ■	LE ■	LE ■	LE ■	LE ■	LE ■	LE ■	LE ■	LE ■	LE ■	LE ■	LE ■	LE ■	LE ■	LE ■
Peterborough ■	d				07 50			09 50			11 50			13 50			15 50			17 50			19 50
Whittlesea	d				07 58			09 58			11 58			13 58			15 58			17 58			19 58
March	d				08 09			10 09			12 09			14 09			16 09			18 09			20 09
Manea	d				08 17			10 17			12 17			14 17			16 17			18 17			20 17
Ely ■	a				08 31			10 31			12 31			14 31			16 31			18 31			20 32
	d				08 32			10 32			12 32			14 32			16 32			18 32			20 32
Cambridge	d		06 42	07 47		08 47	09 47		10 47	11 47		12 47	13 47		14 47	15 47		16 47	17 47		18 47	19 47	
Dullingham	d			08 03			10 03			12 03			14 03			16 03		17 03	18 03			20 03	
Newmarket	d		07 02	08 08		09 07	10 08		11 07	12 08		13 07	14 08		15 07	16 08		17 08	18 08		19 07	20 08	
Kennett	d		07 10			09 15			11 15			13 15			15 15			17 16	18 16		19 15		
Bury St Edmunds	a		07 23	08 25	08 58	09 26	10 25	10 58	11 26	12 25	12 58	13 26	14 25	14 58	15 26	16 25	16 58	17 27	18 27	18 58	19 26	20 25	20 58
Bury St Edmunds	d	06 23	07 23	08 26	08 58	09 26	10 26	10 58	11 26	12 26	12 58	13 26	14 26	14 58	15 26	16 26	16 58	17 28	18 28	18 58	19 26	20 26	20 58
Thurston	d	06 29	07 30	08 32		09 32	10 32		11 32	12 32		13 32	14 32		15 32	16 32		17 34	18 34		19 32	20 32	
Elmswell	d	06 36	07 36	08 38		09 38	10 38		11 38	12 38		13 38	14 38		15 38	16 38		17 40	18 40		19 38	20 38	
Stowmarket	d	06 44	07 45	08 47	09 14	09 47	10 47	11 14	11 47	12 47	13 14	13 47	14 47	15 14	15 47	16 47	17 14	17 49	18 49	19 14	19 47	20 46	21 14
Needham Market	d	06 49	07 50	08 52		09 52	10 52		11 52	12 52		13 52	14 52		15 52	16 52		17 54	18 54		19 52	20 51	
Ipswich	a	07 02	08 02	09 02	09 28	10 02	11 02	11 28	12 02	13 02	13 28	14 02	15 02	15 28	16 02	17 02	17 28	18 03	19 03	19 28	20 02	21 01	21 28
Harwich International	a																					21 29	
Manningtree	a																						21 38
Colchester	a																						21 49

For complete service between Ely and Peterborough refer to Table T017

For complete service between Colchester and Stowmarket refer to Table T011

Table T014-R

Saturdays

26 May to 8 December

Peterborough, Ely, Cambridge and Bury St. Edmunds - Ipswich

		LE ■	LE ■	LE ■	LE
Peterborough ■	d			21 45	
Whittlesea	d			21 53	
March	d			22 04	
Manea	d			22 12	
Ely ■	a			22 25	
	d			22 26	
Cambridge	d	20 47	21 47		22 47
Dullingham	d		22 03		23 03
Newmarket	d	21 07	22 08		23 08
Kennett	d	21 15			23 16
Bury St Edmunds	a	21 26	22 25	22 52	23 29
Bury St Edmunds	d	21 26	22 26	22 52	23 29
Thurston	d	21 32	22 32		23 35
Elmswell	d	21 38	22 38		23 42
Stowmarket	d	21 47	22 46	23 08	23 51
Needham Market	d	21 52	22 51		23 56
Ipswich	a	22 02	23 03	23 22	00 08
Harwich International	a				
Manningtree	a			23 32	
Colchester	a			23 43	

Sundays

20 May to 2 December

		LE	LE ■ A	LE ■	LE ■	LE ■	LE ■	LE ■	LE ■	LE ■	LE ■	LE ■	LE ■	LE ■	LE
Peterborough ■	d		09 50		11 50		13 50		15 47		17 45		19 47		
Whittlesea	d		09 58		11 58		13 58		15 55		17 53		19 55		
March	d		10 09		12 09		14 09		16 06		18 04		20 06		
Manea	d														
Ely ■	a		10 31		12 31		14 31		16 25		18 23		20 25		
	d		10 32		12 32		14 32		16 29		18 29		20 28		
Cambridge	d	09 14		11 14		13 14		15 14		17 14		19 14		21 14	22 50
Dullingham	d	09 30		11 30		13 30		15 30		17 30		19 30		21 30	23 06
Newmarket	d	09 36		11 36		13 36		15 36		17 36		19 36		21 36	23 12
Kennett	d	09 44		11 44		13 44		15 44		17 44		19 44		21 44	23 20
Bury St Edmunds	a	09 56	10 58	11 56	12 58	13 56	14 58	15 56	16 55	17 56	18 55	19 56	20 55	21 56	23 32
Bury St Edmunds	d	09 57	10 58	11 57	12 58	13 57	14 58	15 57	16 55	17 57	18 55	19 57	20 55	21 57	23 33
Thurston	d	10 03		12 03		14 03		16 03		18 03		20 03		22 03	23 39
Elmswell	d	10 09		12 09		14 09		16 09		18 09		20 09		22 09	23 45
Stowmarket	d	10 20	11 14	12 20	13 14	14 20	15 14	16 20	17 11	18 20	19 11	20 20	21 11	22 20	23 55
Needham Market	d	10 25		12 25		14 25		16 25		18 25		20 25		22 25	23 59
Ipswich	a	10 38	11 28	12 36	13 28	14 36	15 28	16 36	17 25	18 36	19 25	20 36	21 25	22 38	00 11
Harwich International	a											21 05			
Manningtree	a										19 35		21 35		
Colchester	a										19 46		21 46		

A until 9 September

For complete service between Ely and Peterborough refer to Table T017

For complete service between Colchester and Stowmarket refer to Table T011

Table T015-F

Norwich - Great Yarmouth and Lowestoft

Mondays to Fridays

21 May to 7 December

Miles	Miles	Miles			LE	LE	LE	LE	LE	LE	LE	LE	LE		LE	LE	LE MFO A	LE	LE	LE MFO A	LE	LE	LE		LE
—	—	—	London Liverpool Street 15 ⊖	d																					
0	0	0	**Norwich**	d	05 06	05 36	06 11	06 27	06 45	06 52	07 36	07 55	08 09		08 36	08 55	09 06	09 36	10 05	10 25	10 36	10 58	11 36		12 05
4¾	4¾	4¾	Brundall Gardens	d		05 43	06 18			06 59		08 02			08 43			09 43			10 43		11 43		
5¾	5¾	5¾	Brundall	d	05 15	05 46	06 21	06 36	06 54	07 02	07 45	08 05			08 46			09 46	10 14		10 46		11 46		12 14
8	—	—	Lingwood	d			06 26			07 07			08 21		08 51			09 51			10 51				
10½	—	—	Acle	d			06 35			07 12			08 28		08 59			09 56			10 56				
—	7¾	7¾	Buckenham	d																					
—	10	10	Cantley	d		05 52			07 00		07 51	08 11							10 20				11 52		12 20
—	12¼	12¼	Reedham (Norfolk)	d		05 56		06 44	07 04		07 55	08 16							10 24				11 57		12 24
—	16	—	Berney Arms	d							08x01												12x03		
18¼	20½	—	**Great Yarmouth**	a	05 40		06 48			07 26	08 12		08 42		09 12		09 35	10 09		10 54	11 11		12 13		
—	—	16¼	Haddiscoe	d		06 05			07 13			08 24							10 33						12 33
—	—	18	Somerleyton	d		06 09			07 17			08 28							10 37						12 37
—	—	22	Oulton Broad North	d		06 15		07 00	07 23			08 35				09 25			10 43			11 28			12 43
—	—	23½	**Lowestoft**	a		06 22		07 07	07 30			08 41				09 32			10 52			11 35			12 50

		LE	LE	LE MFO A	LE	LE	LE MFO A	LE	LE		LE	LE	LE	LE	LE	LE	LE	LE	LE		LE	LE	LE	LE	LE
London Liverpool Street 15 ⊖	d																								
Norwich	d	12 36	12 58	13 18	13 36	14 05	14 25	14 40	14 55		15 36	15 50	16 38	16 58	17 06	17 36	17 50	18 04	18 40		19 02	19 40	20 05	20 38	21 05
Brundall Gardens	d	12 43			13 43			14 47			15 43		16 45		17 13	17 43		18 11	18 47			19 47		20 45	
Brundall	d	12 46			13 46	14 14		14 50			15 46	15 59	16 48	17 07	17 16	17 46	17 59	18 14	18 50		19 11	19 50	20 14	20 48	21 14
Lingwood	d	12 51			13 51			14 55			15 51		16 53		17 21	17 51		18 19	18 55			19 55		20 53	
Acle	d	12 56			13 56			15 00			15 56		16 58		17 28	17 56		18 28	19 00			20 00		20 58	
Buckenham	d																								
Cantley	d					14 20			15 07			16 05		17 13			18 05				19 17		20 20		21 20
Reedham (Norfolk)	d					14 24			15 12			16 09		17 17			18 09				19 21		20 24		21 24
Berney Arms	d																								
Great Yarmouth	a	13 11		13 47	14 09		14 54	15 13			16 09		17 13		17 41	18 11		18 41	19 13			20 13		21 13	
Haddiscoe	d					14 33						16 18		17 26			18 18				19 30		20 33		21 33
Somerleyton	d					14 37						16 22		17 30			18 22				19 34		20 37		21 37
Oulton Broad North	d		13 28			14 43			15 28			16 28		17 36			18 28				19 43		20 43		21 43
Lowestoft	a		13 35			14 50			15 37			16 35		17 43			18 35				19 50		20 50		21 50

		LE	LE	LE	LE
London Liverpool Street 15 ⊖	d				
Norwich	d	21 40	22 05	22 40	23 00
Brundall Gardens	d	21 47			
Brundall	d	21 50	22 14	22 49	23 09
Lingwood	d	21 55			23 14
Acle	d	22 00			23 18
Buckenham	d				
Cantley	d		22 20	22 55	
Reedham (Norfolk)	d		22 24	22 59	
Berney Arms	d				
Great Yarmouth	a	22 13			23 31
Haddiscoe	d		22 33	23 08	
Somerleyton	d		22 37	23 12	
Oulton Broad North	d		22 43	23 18	
Lowestoft	a		22 52	23 25	

Saturdays

26 May to 8 September

		LE	LE	LE	LE	LE	LE	LE	LE	LE		LE	LE	LE	LE	LE	LE	LE	LE	LE		LE	LE	LE	LE
London Liverpool Street 15 ⊖	d																								
Norwich	d	05 30	05 40	06 36	06 50	07 06	07 36	07 50	08 09	08 36		08 55	09 06	09 36	09 55	10 05	10 25	10 36	10 58	11 20		11 36	12 05	12 18	12 36
Brundall Gardens	d		05 47	06 43		07 13		07 57		08 43				09 43				10 43				11 43			12 43
Brundall	d	05 39	05 50	06 46	06 59	07 16	07 45	08 00		08 46				09 46		10 14		10 46				11 46	12 14		12 46
Lingwood	d			06 51		07 21			08 21	08 51				09 51				10 51							12 51
Acle	d			06 56		07 28			08 28	08 58				09 56				10 56							12 56
Buckenham	d															10x18									
Cantley	d		05 56		07 05		07 51	08 06								10 22						11 52	12 20		
Reedham (Norfolk)	d	05 47	06 01		07 09		07 55	08 11								10 26						11 57	12 24		
Berney Arms	d						08x01															12x03			
Great Yarmouth	a	06 02		07 09		07 41	08 12		08 41	09 11			09 35	10 09	10 26		10 54	11 09		11 51		12 13		12 47	13 09
Haddiscoe	d		06 09		07 18			08 19								10 35							12 33		
Somerleyton	d		06 13		07 22			08 23								10 39							12 37		
Oulton Broad North	d		06 20		07 28			08 30				09 25				10 45			11 28				12 43		
Lowestoft	a		06 26		07 35			08 36				09 32				10 52			11 35				12 50		

		LE	LE	LE	LE	LE		LE	LE	LE	LE	LE	LE	LE	LE	LE		LE	LE	LE	LE	LE	LE	LE	LE
London Liverpool Street 15 ⊖	d																								
Norwich	d	12 58	13 18	13 36	14 05	14 18		14 36	14 58	15 18	15 36	15 50	16 40	16 58	17 06	17 36		17 50	18 06	18 40	19 05	19 33	20 05	20 40	21 05
Brundall Gardens	d			13 43				14 43			15 43		16 47		17 13	17 43			18 13	18 47		19 40		20 47	
Brundall	d			13 46	14 14			14 46			15 46	15 59	16 50	17 07	17 16	17 46		17 59	18 16	18 50	19 14	19 43	20 14	20 50	21 14
Lingwood	d			13 51				14 51			15 51		16 55		17 21	17 51			18 21	18 55		19 48		20 55	
Acle	d			13 56				14 56			15 56		17 00		17 28	17 56			18 28	19 00		19 53		21 00	
Buckenham	d																								
Cantley	d				14 20				15 10			16 05		17 13				18 05			19 20		20 20		21 20
Reedham (Norfolk)	d				14 24				15 15			16 09		17 17				18 09			19 24		20 24		21 24
Berney Arms	d																								
Great Yarmouth	a		13 49	14 09		14 47		15 09		15 45	16 09		17 13		17 41	18 09			18 41	19 13		20 06		21 13	
Haddiscoe	d				14 33							16 18		17 26				18 18			19 33		20 33		21 33
Somerleyton	d				14 37							16 22		17 30				18 22			19 37		20 37		21 37
Oulton Broad North	d	13 28			14 43				15 31			16 28		17 36				18 28			19 43		20 43		21 43
Lowestoft	a	13 35			14 50				15 37			16 35		17 43				18 35			19 50		20 50		21 50

A from 23 July until 7 September

Table T015-F

Norwich - Great Yarmouth and Lowestoft

Saturdays

26 May to 8 September

		LE	LE	LE	LE
London Liverpool Street 15 ⊖	d				
Norwich	d	21 40	22 05	22 40	23 00
Brundall Gardens	d	21 47			
Brundall	d	21 50	22 14	22 49	23 09
Lingwood	d	21 55			23 14
Acle	d	22 00			23 18
Buckenham	d				
Cantley	d		22 20	22 55	
Reedham (Norfolk)	d		22 24	22 59	
Berney Arms	d				
Great Yarmouth	a	22 13			23 31
Haddiscoe	d		22 33	23 08	
Somerleyton	d		22 37	23 12	
Oulton Broad North	d		22 43	23 18	
Lowestoft	a		22 50	23 25	

Saturdays

15 September to 8 December

		LE	LE	LE	LE	LE	LE	LE	LE	LE		LE	LE	LE	LE	LE	LE	LE	LE	LE		LE	LE	LE	LE
London Liverpool Street 15 ⊖	d																								
Norwich	d	05 30	05 40	06 36	06 50	07 06	07 36	07 50	08 09	08 36		08 55	09 36	10 05	10 36	10 58	11 36	12 05	12 36	12 58		13 36	14 05	14 36	14 58
Brundall Gardens	d		05 47	06 43		07 13		07 57		08 43			09 43		10 43		11 43		12 43			13 43		14 43	
Brundall	d	05 39	05 50	06 46	06 59	07 16	07 45	08 00		08 46			09 46	10 14	10 46		11 46	12 14	12 46			13 46	14 14	14 46	
Lingwood	d			06 51		07 21			08 21	08 51			09 51		10 51				12 51			13 51		14 51	
Acle	d			06 56		07 28			08 28	08 58			09 56		10 56				12 56			13 56		14 56	
Buckenham	d													10x18											
Cantley	d		05 56		07 05		07 51	08 06						10 22			11 52	12 20					14 20		15 10
Reedham (Norfolk)	d	05 47	06 01		07 09		07 55	08 11						10 26			11 57	12 24					14 24		15 15
Berney Arms	d						08x01										12x03								
Great Yarmouth	a	06 02		07 09		07 41	08 12		08 41	09 11			10 09		11 09		12 13		13 09			14 09		15 09	
Haddiscoe	d		06 09		07 18			08 19						10 35				12 33					14 33		
Somerleyton	d		06 13		07 22			08 23						10 39				12 37					14 37		
Oulton Broad North	d		06 20		07 28			08 30				09 25		10 45		11 28		12 43		13 28			14 43		15 31
Lowestoft	a		06 26		07 35			08 36				09 32		10 52		11 35		12 50		13 35			14 50		15 37

		LE	LE	LE	LE	LE		LE	LE	LE	LE	LE	LE	LE	LE	LE		LE	LE	LE	LE
London Liverpool Street 15 ⊖	d																				
Norwich	d	15 36	15 50	16 40	16 58	17 06		17 36	17 50	18 06	18 40	19 05	19 33	20 05	20 40	21 05		21 40	22 05	22 40	23 00
Brundall Gardens	d	15 43		16 47		17 13		17 43		18 13	18 47		19 40		20 47			21 47			
Brundall	d	15 46	15 59	16 50	17 07	17 16		17 46	17 59	18 16	18 50	19 14	19 43	20 14	20 50	21 14		21 50	22 14	22 49	23 09
Lingwood	d	15 51		16 55		17 21		17 51		18 21	18 55		19 48		20 55			21 55			23 14
Acle	d	15 56		17 00		17 28		17 56		18 28	19 00		19 53		21 00			22 00			23 18
Buckenham	d																				
Cantley	d		16 05		17 13				18 05			19 20		20 20		21 20			22 20	22 55	
Reedham (Norfolk)	d		16 09		17 17				18 09			19 24		20 24		21 24			22 24	22 59	
Berney Arms	d																				
Great Yarmouth	a	16 09		17 13		17 41		18 09		18 41	19 13		20 06		21 13			22 13			23 31
Haddiscoe	d		16 18		17 26				18 18			19 33		20 33		21 33			22 33	23 08	
Somerleyton	d		16 22		17 30				18 22			19 37		20 37		21 37			22 37	23 12	
Oulton Broad North	d		16 28		17 36				18 28			19 43		20 43		21 43			22 43	23 18	
Lowestoft	a		16 35		17 43				18 35			19 50		20 50		21 50			22 50	23 25	

Sundays

20 May to 9 September

		LE	LE	LE	LE	LE	LE	LE	LE	LE		LE	LE	LE	LE	LE	LE	LE	LE	LE		LE	LE	LE	LE
London Liverpool Street 15 ⊖	d																								
Norwich	d	07 25	07 36	08 05	08 45	08 58	09 36	10 05	10 45	10 58		11 36	12 05	12 45	12 58	13 36	14 05	14 45	14 58	15 36		16 05	16 45	16 58	17 36
Brundall Gardens	d				08 52				10 52					12 52				14 52					16 52		
Brundall	d		07 45	08 14	08 55	09 07	09 45	10 14	10 55	11 07		11 45	12 14	12 55	13 07	13 45	14 14	14 55	15 07	15 45		16 14	16 55	17 07	17 45
Lingwood	d				09 00				11 00					13 00				15 00					17 00		
Acle	d				09 05				11 05					13 05				15 05					17 05		
Buckenham	d						09x49					11x49								15x49				17x11	
Cantley	d		07 51	08 20		09 13	09 53	10 20		11 13		11 53	12 20		13 13	13 51	14 20		15 13	15 53		16 20		17 15	17 51
Reedham (Norfolk)	d		07 55	08 24		09 17	09 57	10 24		11 17		11 57	12 24		13 17	13 55	14 24		15 17	15 57		16 24		17 19	17 55
Berney Arms	d		08x01				10x03					12x03				14x01				16x03					
Great Yarmouth	a		08 12		09 18		10 14		11 18			12 14		13 18		14 12		15 18		16 14			17 18		18 10
Haddiscoe	d			08 33		09 26		10 33		11 26			12 33		13 26		14 33		15 26			16 33		17 28	
Somerleyton	d			08 37		09 30		10 37		11 30			12 37		13 30		14 37		15 30			16 37		17 32	
Oulton Broad North	d	07 55		08 43		09 36		10 43		11 36			12 43		13 36		14 43		15 36			16 43		17 38	
Lowestoft	a	08 01		08 50		09 43		10 50		11 43			12 50		13 43		14 50		15 43			16 50		17 45	

		LE	LE	LE	LE	LE		LE	LE	LE	LE
London Liverpool Street 15 ⊖	d										
Norwich	d	18 05	18 45	18 58	19 36	20 05		20 45	20 58	21 36	22 36
Brundall Gardens	d		18 52					20 52			22 43
Brundall	d	18 14	18 55	19 07	19 45	20 14		20 55	21 07	21 45	22 46
Lingwood	d		19 00					21 00			22 51
Acle	d		19 05					21 05			22 56
Buckenham	d										
Cantley	d	18 20		19 13	19 51	20 20			21 13	21 51	
Reedham (Norfolk)	d	18 24		19 17	19 55	20 24			21 17	21 55	
Berney Arms	d										
Great Yarmouth	a		19 18		20 10			21 18		22 10	23 09
Haddiscoe	d	18 33		19 26		20 33			21 26		
Somerleyton	d	18 37		19 30		20 37			21 30		
Oulton Broad North	d	18 43		19 36		20 43			21 36		
Lowestoft	a	18 50		19 43		20 50			21 43		

Table T015-F

Sundays

16 September to 2 December

Norwich - Great Yarmouth and Lowestoft

		LE	LE	LE	LE	LE	LE	LE	LE	LE	LE	LE	LE	LE	LE	LE	LE	LE	LE	LE	LE	LE	LE
London Liverpool Street ⊖	d																						
Norwich	d	07 25	07 36	08 45	08 58	09 36	10 45	10 58	11 36	12 45	12 58	13 36	14 45	14 58	15 36	16 45	16 58	17 36	18 45	18 58	19 36	20 45	20 58
Brundall Gardens	d			08 52			10 52			12 52			14 52			16 52			18 52			20 52	
Brundall	d		07 45	08 55	09 07	09 45	10 55	11 07	11 45	12 55	13 07	13 45	14 55	15 07	15 45	16 55	17 07	17 45	18 55	19 07	19 45	20 55	21 07
Lingwood	d			09 00			11 00			13 00			15 00			17 00			19 00			21 00	
Acle	d			09 05			11 05			13 05			15 05			17 05			19 05			21 05	
Buckenham	d					09x49			11x49						15x49		17x11						
Cantley	d		07 51		09 13	09 53		11 13	11 53		13 13	13 51		15 13	15 53		17 15	17 51		19 13	19 51		21 13
Reedham (Norfolk)	d		07 55		09 17	09 57		11 17	11 57		13 17	13 55		15 17	15 57		17 19	17 55		19 17	19 55		21 17
Berney Arms	d		08x01			10x03			12x03			14x01											
Great Yarmouth	a		08 12	09 18		10 14	11 18		12 14	13 18		14 12	15 18		16 14	17 18		18 10	19 18		20 10	21 18	
Haddiscoe	d				09 26			11 26			13 26			15 26			17 28			19 26			21 26
Somerleyton	d				09 30			11 30			13 30			15 30			17 32			19 30			21 30
Oulton Broad North	d	07 55			09 36			11 36			13 36			15 36			17 38			19 36			21 36
Lowestoft	a	08 01			09 43			11 43			13 43			15 43			17 45			19 43			21 43

		LE	LE
London Liverpool Street ⊖	d		
Norwich	d	21 36	22 36
Brundall Gardens	d		22 43
Brundall	d	21 45	22 46
Lingwood	d		22 51
Acle	d		22 56
Buckenham	d		
Cantley	d	21 51	
Reedham (Norfolk)	d	21 55	
Berney Arms	d		
Great Yarmouth	a	22 10	23 09
Haddiscoe	d		
Somerleyton	d		
Oulton Broad North	d		
Lowestoft	a		

Table T015-R

Mondays to Fridays

21 May to 7 December

Lowestoft and Great Yarmouth - Norwich

Miles	Miles	Miles			LE	LE	LE	LE	LE	LE	LE	LE	LE	LE	LE	LE	LE MFO A	LE	LE	LE	LE MFO A	LE	LE
0	—	—	**Lowestoft**	d		05 42		06 35			07 35	07 47			08 50			09 48		10 57			11 48
1½	—	—	Oulton Broad North	d		05 47		06 39			07 40	07 53			08 55			09 53		11 02			11 53
5½	—	—	Somerleyton	d		05 53		06 45			07 46				09 01			09 59					11 59
7¼	—	—	Haddiscoe	d		05 57		06 49			07 50				09 05			10 03					12 03
—	0	0	**Great Yarmouth**	d	05 43		06 24		06 58	07 30			08 17	08 46		09 17	09 52		10 17		11 13	11 17	
—	—	4½	Berney Arms	d																			
11¼	—	8¼	Reedham (Norfolk)	d		06 06		06 58			07 59	08 10			09 14			10 12					12 12
13½	—	10½	Cantley	d		06 10		07 02			08 03	08 14			09 18			10 16					12 16
15¾	—	12¾	Buckenham	d																			
—	8	—	Acle	d	05 54		06 35		07 13	07 41			08 28	08 59		09 28			10 28			11 28	
—	10½	—	Lingwood	d	05 59		06 40		07 17	07 46			08 33	09 03		09 33			10 33			11 33	
17¾	12¾	14¾	Brundall	d	06 03	06 17	06 44	07 09	07 22	07 50	08 10		08 37		09 25	09 37		10 23	10 37			11 37	12 23
18¾	13¾	15¾	Brundall Gardens	d	06 06		06 47		07 24	07 53			08 40			09 40			10 40			11 40	
23½	18½	20½	**Norwich**	a	06 15	06 27	06 57	07 20	07 35	08 05	08 20	08 31	08 50	09 19	09 35	09 52	10 20	10 33	10 50	11 35	11 45	11 52	12 33
—	—	—	London Liverpool Street ⊖	a																			

		LE	LE	LE	LE MFO A	LE	LE	LE	LE	LE MFO A	LE	LE	LE	LE	LE B	LE C	LE	LE	LE	LE	LE	LE	LE
Lowestoft	d		12 57			13 48		14 57			15 48		16 48				17 48			18 48		19 55	
Oulton Broad North	d		13 02			13 53		15 02			15 53		16 53				17 53			18 53		20 00	
Somerleyton	d					13 59					15 59		16 59				17 59			18 59		20 06	
Haddiscoe	d					14 03					16 03		17 03				18 03			19 03		20 10	
Great Yarmouth	d	12 17		13 17	13 52		14 17		15 17	15 42		16 17		17 17	17 47	17 47		18 17	18 47		19 17		20 17
Berney Arms	d								15x24							17x54							
Reedham (Norfolk)	d					14 12			15 32		16 12		17 12		18 01	18 01	18 12		19 01	19 12		20 19	
Cantley	d					14 16			15 36		16 17		17 16		18 05	18 05	18 16		19 05	19 16		20 23	
Buckenham	d																						
Acle	d	12 28		13 28			14 28					16 28		17 28				18 28			19 28		20 28
Lingwood	d	12 33		13 33			14 33					16 33		17 33				18 33			19 33		20 33
Brundall	d	12 37		13 37		14 23	14 37		15 42		16 23	16 37	17 23	17 37	18 12	18 12	18 23	18 37	19 12	19 23	19 37	20 30	20 37
Brundall Gardens	d	12 40		13 40			14 40		15 45			16 40		17 40				18 40			19 40		20 40
Norwich	a	12 50	13 33	13 52	14 20	14 33	14 50	15 33	15 55	16 10	16 39	16 50	17 33	17 55	18 23	18 23	18 33	18 52	19 25	19 33	19 50	20 43	20 50
London Liverpool Street ⊖	a																						

		LE	LE	LE	LE	LE	LE	LE
Lowestoft	d	20 57		21 48		22 48		23 30
Oulton Broad North	d	21 02		21 53		22 53		23 35
Somerleyton	d			21 59		22 59		
Haddiscoe	d			22 03		23 03		
Great Yarmouth	d		21 17		22 17		23 34	
Berney Arms	d							
Reedham (Norfolk)	d			22 12		23 12	23 47	23 52
Cantley	d			22 16		23 16		23 56
Buckenham	d							
Acle	d		21 28		22 28			
Lingwood	d		21 33		22 33			
Brundall	d		21 37	22 23	22 37	23 23	23 55	00 03
Brundall Gardens	d		21 40		22 40			
Norwich	a	21 33	21 52	22 32	22 50	23 33	00 07	00 16
London Liverpool Street ⊖	a							

Saturdays

26 May to 8 September

		LE	LE	LE	LE	LE	LE	LE	LE	LE	LE	LE	LE	LE	LE	LE	LE	LE	LE	LE	LE	LE	LE
Lowestoft	d		06 38			07 40			08 48			09 48			10 57				11 48			12 57	
Oulton Broad North	d		06 43			07 45			08 53			09 53			11 02				11 53			13 02	
Somerleyton	d		06 49			07 51			08 59			09 59							11 59				
Haddiscoe	d		06 53			07 55			09 03			10 03							12 03				
Great Yarmouth	d	06 15		07 17	07 45		08 17	08 47		09 17	09 47		10 17	10 41		11 15	11 17	11 57		12 17	12 55		13 17
Berney Arms	d																						
Reedham (Norfolk)	d		07 02			08 04			09 12			10 12							12 12				
Cantley	d		07 06			08 08			09 16			10 16							12 16				
Buckenham	d																						
Acle	d	06 26		07 28	07 56		08 28	08 58		09 28			10 28				11 28			12 28			13 28
Lingwood	d	06 31		07 33	08 01		08 33	09 03		09 33			10 33				11 33			12 33			13 33
Brundall	d	06 35	07 13	07 37	08 05	08 15	08 37		09 23	09 37		10 23	10 37				11 37		12 23	12 37			13 37
Brundall Gardens	d	06 38		07 40	08 08		08 40			09 40			10 40				11 40			12 40			13 40
Norwich	a	06 48	07 24	07 50	08 18	08 25	08 50	09 17	09 33	09 50	10 16	10 33	10 50	11 14	11 33	11 45	11 52	12 25	12 33	12 50	13 25	13 33	13 50
London Liverpool Street ⊖	a																						

		LE	LE	LE	LE	LE	LE	LE	LE	LE	LE	LE	LE	LE	LE	LE	LE	LE	LE	LE	LE	LE	LE
Lowestoft	d		13 48			14 57			15 48		16 48			17 48			18 48		19 55		20 57		21 48
Oulton Broad North	d		13 53			15 02			15 53		16 53			17 53			18 53		20 00		21 02		21 53
Somerleyton	d		13 59						15 59		16 59			17 59			18 59		20 06				21 59
Haddiscoe	d		14 03						16 03		17 03			18 03			19 03		20 10				22 03
Great Yarmouth	d	13 55		14 17	14 55		15 12	15 55		16 17		17 17	17 47		18 17	18 47		19 17		20 17		21 17	
Berney Arms	d						15x19						17x54										
Reedham (Norfolk)	d		14 12				15 27		16 12		17 12		18 01	18 12		19 01	19 12		20 19				22 12
Cantley	d		14 16				15 31		16 16		17 16		18 05	18 16		19 05	19 16		20 23				22 16
Buckenham	d								16x20														
Acle	d			14 28						16 28		17 28			18 28			19 28		20 28		21 28	
Lingwood	d			14 33						16 33		17 33			18 33			19 33		20 33		21 33	
Brundall	d		14 23	14 37			15 37		16 23	16 37	17 23	17 37	18 12	18 23	18 37	19 12	19 23	19 37	20 30	20 37		21 37	22 23
Brundall Gardens	d			14 40			15 40			16 40		17 40			18 40			19 40		20 40		21 40	
Norwich	a	14 25	14 33	14 50	15 25	15 33	15 50	16 25	16 33	16 50	17 33	17 50	18 23	18 33	18 50	19 23	19 33	19 50	20 40	20 50	21 33	21 50	22 35
London Liverpool Street ⊖	a																						

A from 23 July until 7 September **B** from 10 September **C** until 7 September

Table T015-R

Lowestoft and Great Yarmouth - Norwich

Saturdays
26 May to 8 September

		LE	LE	LE	LE
Lowestoft	d		22 48		23 30
Oulton Broad North	d		22 53		23 35
Somerleyton	d		22 59		
Haddiscoe	d		23 03		
Great Yarmouth	d	22 17		23 34	
Berney Arms	d				
Reedham (Norfolk)	d		23 12	23 47	23 52
Cantley	d		23 16		23 56
Buckenham	d				
Acle	d	22 28			
Lingwood	d	22 33			
Brundall	d	22 37	23 23	23 55	00 03
Brundall Gardens	d	22 40			
Norwich	a	22 50	23 33	00 07	00 14
London Liverpool Street 15 ⊖	a				

Saturdays
15 September to 8 December

		LE	LE	LE	LE	LE	LE	LE	LE	LE	LE	LE	LE	LE	LE	LE	LE	LE	LE	LE	LE	LE	LE
Lowestoft	d		06 38			07 40			08 48		09 48		10 57		11 48		12 57		13 48		14 57		15 48
Oulton Broad North	d		06 43			07 45			08 53		09 53		11 02		11 53		13 02		13 53		15 02		15 53
Somerleyton	d		06 49			07 51			08 59		09 59				11 59				13 59				15 59
Haddiscoe	d		06 53			07 55			09 03		10 03				12 03				14 03				16 03
Great Yarmouth	d	06 15		07 17	07 45		08 17	08 47		09 17		10 17		11 17		12 17		13 17		14 17		15 12	
Berney Arms	d																					15x19	
Reedham (Norfolk)	d		07 02			08 04			09 12		10 12				12 12				14 12			15 27	16 12
Cantley	d		07 06			08 08			09 16		10 16				12 16				14 16			15 31	16 16
Buckenham	d																						16x20
Acle	d	06 26		07 28	07 56		08 28	08 58		09 28		10 28		11 28		12 28		13 28		14 28			
Lingwood	d	06 31		07 33	08 01		08 33	09 03		09 33		10 33		11 33		12 33		13 33		14 33			
Brundall	d	06 35	07 13	07 37	08 05	08 15	08 37		09 23	09 37	10 23	10 37		11 37	12 23	12 37		13 37	14 23	14 37		15 37	16 23
Brundall Gardens	d	06 38		07 40	08 08		08 40			09 40		10 40		11 40		12 40		13 40		14 40		15 40	
Norwich	a	06 48	07 24	07 50	08 18	08 25	08 50	09 17	09 33	09 50	10 33	10 50	11 33	11 52	12 33	12 50	13 33	13 50	14 33	14 50	15 33	15 50	16 33
London Liverpool Street 15 ⊖	a																						

		LE	LE	LE	LE	LE	LE	LE	LE	LE	LE	LE	LE	LE	LE	LE	LE	LE	LE
Lowestoft	d		16 48			17 48			18 48		19 55		20 57		21 48		22 48		23 30
Oulton Broad North	d		16 53			17 53			18 53		20 00		21 02		21 53		22 53		23 35
Somerleyton	d		16 59			17 59			18 59		20 06				21 59		22 59		
Haddiscoe	d		17 03			18 03			19 03		20 10				22 03		23 03		
Great Yarmouth	d	16 17		17 17	17 47		18 17	18 47		19 17		20 17		21 17		22 17		23 34	
Berney Arms	d																		
Reedham (Norfolk)	d		17 12		18 01	18 12		19 01	19 12		20 19				22 12		23 12	23 47	23 52
Cantley	d		17 16		18 05	18 16		19 05	19 16		20 23				22 16		23 16		23 56
Buckenham	d																		
Acle	d	16 28		17 28			18 28			19 28		20 28		21 28		22 28			
Lingwood	d	16 33		17 33			18 33			19 33		20 33		21 33		22 33			
Brundall	d	16 37	17 23	17 37	18 12	18 23	18 37	19 12	19 23	19 37	20 30	20 37		21 37	22 23	22 37	23 23	23 55	00 03
Brundall Gardens	d	16 40		17 40			18 40			19 40		20 40		21 40		22 40			
Norwich	a	16 50	17 33	17 50	18 23	18 33	18 50	19 23	19 33	19 50	20 40	20 50	21 33	21 50	22 35	22 50	23 33	00 07	00 14
London Liverpool Street 15 ⊖	a																		

Sundays
20 May to 9 September

		LE	LE	LE	LE	LE	LE	LE	LE	LE	LE	LE	LE	LE	LE	LE	LE	LE	LE	LE	LE	LE	LE
Lowestoft	d		08 56		09 46		10 56		11 46		12 56		13 46		14 56		15 46		16 56		17 46		18 56
Oulton Broad North	d		09 01		09 51		11 01		11 51		13 01		13 51		15 01		15 51		17 01		17 51		19 01
Somerleyton	d		09 07		09 57		11 07		11 57		13 07		13 57		15 07		15 57		17 07		17 57		19 07
Haddiscoe	d		09 11		10 01		11 11		12 01		13 11		14 01		15 11		16 01		17 11		18 01		19 11
Great Yarmouth	d	08 17		09 22		10 17		11 22		12 17		13 22		14 17		15 22		16 17		17 22		18 17	
Berney Arms	d	08x24				10x24				12x24				14x24				16x24					
Reedham (Norfolk)	d	08 31	09 20		10 10	10 31	11 20		12 10	12 31	13 20		14 10	14 31	15 20		16 10	16 31	17 20		18 10	18 30	19 20
Cantley	d	08 35	09 24		10 14	10 35	11 24		12 14	12 35	13 24		14 14	14 35	15 24		16 14	16 35	17 24		18 14	18 34	19 24
Buckenham	d				10x18	10x39				12x39								16x39					
Acle	d			09 33				11 33				13 33				15 33				17 33			
Lingwood	d			09 38				11 38				13 38				15 38				17 38			
Brundall	d	08 42	09 31	09 42	10 21	10 43	11 31	11 42	12 21	12 43	13 31	13 42	14 21	14 42	15 31	15 42	16 21	16 43	17 31	17 42	18 21	18 40	19 31
Brundall Gardens	d			09 45				11 45				13 45				15 45				17 45			
Norwich	a	08 53	09 43	09 55	10 31	10 54	11 40	11 55	12 31	12 54	13 40	13 55	14 31	14 53	15 40	15 55	16 31	16 55	17 40	17 55	18 31	18 51	19 40
London Liverpool Street 15 ⊖	a																						

		LE	LE	LE	LE	LE	LE	LE	LE	LE
Lowestoft	d		19 46		20 56		21 46			23 35
Oulton Broad North	d		19 51		21 01		21 51			23 40
Somerleyton	d		19 57		21 07		21 57			
Haddiscoe	d		20 01		21 11		22 01			
Great Yarmouth	d	19 22		20 17		21 22		22 17	23 17	
Berney Arms	d									
Reedham (Norfolk)	d		20 10	20 30	21 20		22 10	22 30	23 30	23 55
Cantley	d		20 14	20 34	21 24		22 14	22 34	23 34	
Buckenham	d									
Acle	d	19 33				21 33				
Lingwood	d	19 38				21 38				
Brundall	d	19 42	20 21	20 40	21 31	21 42	22 21	22 40	23 40	00 04
Brundall Gardens	d	19 45				21 45			23 43	
Norwich	a	19 55	20 31	20 53	21 40	21 55	22 31	22 52	23 53	00 13
London Liverpool Street 15 ⊖	a									

Table T015-R

Lowestoft and Great Yarmouth - Norwich

Sundays
16 September to 2 December

		LE	LE	LE	LE	LE	LE	LE	LE	LE	LE	LE	LE	LE	LE	LE	LE	LE	LE	LE	LE	LE	LE
Lowestoft	d			09 46			11 46			13 46			15 46			17 46			19 46			21 46	
Oulton Broad North	d			09 51			11 51			13 51			15 51			17 51			19 51			21 51	
Somerleyton	d			09 57			11 57			13 57			15 57			17 57			19 57			21 57	
Haddiscoe	d			10 01			12 01			14 01			16 01			18 01			20 01			22 01	
Great Yarmouth	d	08 17	09 22		10 17	11 22		12 17	13 22		14 17	15 22		16 17	17 22		18 17	19 22		20 17	21 22		22 17
Berney Arms	d	08x24			10x24			12x24			14x24												
Reedham (Norfolk)	d	08 31		10 10	10 31		12 10	12 31		14 10	14 31		16 10	16 31		18 10	18 30		20 10	20 30		22 10	22 30
Cantley	d	08 35		10 14	10 35		12 14	12 35		14 14	14 35		16 14	16 35		18 14	18 34		20 14	20 34		22 14	22 34
Buckenham	d			10x18	10x39			12x39						16x39									
Acle	d		09 33			11 33			13 33			15 33			17 33			19 33			21 33		
Lingwood	d		09 38			11 38			13 38			15 38			17 38			19 38			21 38		
Brundall	d	08 42	09 42	10 21	10 43	11 42	12 21	12 43	13 42	14 21	14 42	15 42	16 21	16 43	17 42	18 21	18 40	19 42	20 21	20 40	21 42	22 21	22 40
Brundall Gardens	d		09 45			11 45			13 45			15 45			17 45			19 45			21 45		
Norwich	a	08 53	09 55	10 31	10 54	11 55	12 31	12 54	13 55	14 31	14 53	15 55	16 31	16 55	17 55	18 31	18 51	19 55	20 31	20 53	21 55	22 31	22 52
London Liverpool Street 15 ⊖	a																						

		LE	LE
Lowestoft	d		23 35
Oulton Broad North	d		23 40
Somerleyton	d		
Haddiscoe	d		
Great Yarmouth	d	23 17	
Berney Arms	d		
Reedham (Norfolk)	d	23 30	23 55
Cantley	d	23 34	
Buckenham	d		
Acle	d		
Lingwood	d		
Brundall	d	23 40	00 04
Brundall Gardens	d	23 43	
Norwich	a	23 53	00 13
London Liverpool Street 15 ⊖	a		

Table T016-F

Mondays to Fridays

21 May to 7 December

Norwich - Cromer and Sheringham

Miles			LE	LE	LE	LE	LE	LE	LE	LE	LE	LE	LE	LE	LE	LE	LE	LE	LE FX	LE FO
0	**Norwich**	d	05 10	05 40	07 15	08 21	09 45	10 45	11 45	12 45	13 45	14 45	15 45	16 45	17 45	18 55	19 55	21 15	22 45	23 05
6	Salhouse	d		05 50	07 25	08 31	09 55		11 55		13 55		15 55	16 55	17 55		20 05	21 25	22 55	23 15
8¾	Hoveton & Wroxham	d	05 24	05 55	07 30	08 36	10 00	10 59	12 00	12 59	14 00	14 59	16 00	17 00	18 00	19 09	20 10	21 30	23 00	23 20
13	Worstead	d		06 02	07 37	08 43		11 05		13 05		15 05	16 07	17 07	18 07	19 15	20 17	21 37	23 07	23 27
—	**North Walsham**	a	05 34	06 07	07 42	08 48	10 10	11 11	12 10	13 11	14 10	15 11	16 12	17 12	18 12	19 21	20 22	21 42	23 12	23 32
16	**North Walsham**	d	05 34	06 10	07 45	08 51	10 13	11 13	12 13	13 13	14 13	15 14	16 15	17 15	18 18	19 21	20 25	21 43	23 13	23 33
19¾	Gunton	d		06 16	07 51	08 57	10 19		12 19		14 19		16 21	17 21	18 24	19 27	20 31	21 49	23 19	23 39
23½	Roughton Road	d		06 23	07 57	09 03	10 25		12 25		14 25		16 27	17 27	18 30	19 34	20 37	21 55	23 25	23 45
—	**Cromer**	a	05 49	06 28	08 03	09 09	10 31	11 28	12 31	13 28	14 31	15 29	16 33	17 33	18 36	19 40	20 43	22 01	23 31	23 51
26½	**Cromer**	d	05 56	06 39	08 06	09 12	10 34	11 31	12 34	13 31	14 34	15 32	16 36	17 36	18 39	19 43	20 46	22 04	23 34	23 54
28¾	West Runton	d	06 00	06 44	08 11	09 17	10 39	11 36	12 39	13 36	14 39	15 37	16 41	17 41	18 44	19 48	20 51	22 09	23 39	23 59
30½	**Sheringham**	a	06 07	06 49	08 16	09 22	10 44	11 41	12 44	13 41	14 44	15 42	16 46	17 46	18 49	19 53	20 56	22 14	23 44	00 04

Saturdays

26 May to 8 December

		LE	LE	LE	LE	LE	LE	LE	LE	LE	LE	LE	LE	LE	LE	LE	LE	LE
Norwich	d	05 20	05 45	07 15	08 21	09 45	10 45	11 45	12 45	13 45	14 45	15 45	16 45	17 45	18 55	19 55	21 15	23 05
Salhouse	d		05 55	07 25	08 31	09 55		11 55		13 55		15 55	16 55	17 55		20 05	21 25	23 15
Hoveton & Wroxham	d	05 34	06 00	07 30	08 36	10 00	10 59	12 00	12 59	14 00	14 59	16 00	17 00	18 00	19 09	20 10	21 30	23 20
Worstead	d		06 07	07 37	08 43		11 05		13 05		15 05	16 07	17 07	18 07	19 15	20 17	21 37	23 27
North Walsham	a	05 44	06 12	07 42	08 48	10 10	11 11	12 10	13 11	14 10	15 11	16 12	17 12	18 12	19 21	20 22	21 42	23 32
North Walsham	d	05 44	06 13	07 45	08 51	10 13	11 13	12 13	13 13	14 13	15 14	16 15	17 15	18 18	19 21	20 25	21 43	23 33
Gunton	d		06 19	07 51	08 57	10 19		12 19		14 19		16 21	17 21	18 24	19 27	20 31	21 49	23 39
Roughton Road	d		06 25	07 57	09 03	10 25		12 25		14 25		16 27	17 27	18 30	19 34	20 37	21 55	23 45
Cromer	a	05 59	06 31	08 03	09 09	10 31	11 28	12 31	13 28	14 31	15 29	16 33	17 33	18 36	19 40	20 43	22 01	23 51
Cromer	d	06 02	06 36	08 06	09 12	10 34	11 31	12 34	13 31	14 34	15 32	16 36	17 36	18 39	19 43	20 46	22 04	23 54
West Runton	d	06 07	06 40	08 11	09 17	10 39	11 36	12 39	13 36	14 39	15 37	16 41	17 41	18 44	19 48	20 51	22 09	23 59
Sheringham	a	06 12	06 46	08 16	09 22	10 44	11 41	12 44	13 41	14 44	15 42	16 46	17 46	18 49	19 53	20 56	22 14	00 04

Sundays

20 May to 2 December

		LE	LE	LE	LE	LE	LE	LE	LE	LE	LE	LE	LE	LE
Norwich	d	08 36	09 45	10 36	11 45	12 36	13 45	14 36	15 45	16 36	17 45	18 36	19 45	20 36
Salhouse	d	08 46		10 46		12 46		14 46		16 46		18 46		20 46
Hoveton & Wroxham	d	08 51	09 59	10 51	11 59	12 51	13 59	14 51	15 59	16 51	17 59	18 51	19 59	20 51
Worstead	d	08 58		10 58		12 58		14 58		16 58		18 58		20 58
North Walsham	a	09 03	10 09	11 03	12 09	13 03	14 09	15 03	16 09	17 03	18 09	19 03	20 09	21 03
North Walsham	d	09 04	10 11	11 06	12 11	13 06	14 11	15 06	16 11	17 06	18 11	19 06	20 11	21 06
Gunton	d	09 10		11 12		13 12		15 12		17 12		19 12		21 12
Roughton Road	d	09 16		11 18		13 18		15 18		17 18		19 18		21 18
Cromer	a	09 22	10 26	11 24	12 26	13 24	14 26	15 24	16 26	17 24	18 26	19 24	20 26	21 24
Cromer	d	09 25	10 29	11 27	12 29	13 27	14 29	15 27	16 29	17 27	18 29	19 27	20 29	21 27
West Runton	d	09 30		11 32		13 32		15 32		17 32		19 32		21 32
Sheringham	a	09 36	10 38	11 38	12 38	13 38	14 38	15 38	16 38	17 38	18 38	19 38	20 38	21 38

Table T016-R

Mondays to Fridays

21 May to 7 December

Sheringham and Cromer - Norwich

Miles			LE	LE	LE	LE	LE	LE	LE	LE	LE	LE	LE	LE	LE	LE	LE	LE	LE	LE FX
0	**Sheringham**	d		06 31	07 16	08 22	09 44	10 47	11 44	12 47	13 44	14 47	15 46	16 49	17 49	18 52	19 56	21 10	22 17	23 47
1¾	West Runton	d		06 35	07 20	08 26	09 48	10 51	11 48	12 51	13 48	14 51	15 50	16 53	17 53	18 56	20 00	21 14	22 21	23 51
—	**Cromer**	a		06 39	07 24	08 30	09 52	10 55	11 52	12 55	13 52	14 55	15 54	16 57	17 57	19 00	20 04	21 18	22 25	23 55
4	**Cromer**	d	05 53	06 42	07 27	08 33	09 55	10 58	11 55	12 58	13 55	14 58	15 57	17 00	18 00	19 03	20 07	21 21	22 28	23 58
7	Roughton Road	d	05 59	06 48	07 33	08 39	10 01		12 01		14 01	15 04	16 03		18 06		20 13	21 27	22 34	
10¾	Gunton	d	06 05	06 54	07 39	08 45	10 07		12 07		14 07		16 09		18 12		20 19	21 33	22 40	
—	**North Walsham**	a	06 10	07 00	07 45	08 51	10 13	11 13	12 13	13 13	14 13	15 14	16 15	17 15	18 18	19 18	20 25	21 39	22 46	00 13
14½	**North Walsham**	d	06 11	07 00	07 45	08 51	10 13	11 14	12 13	13 14	14 13	15 14	16 15	17 15	18 18	19 21	20 25	21 43	22 46	00 13
17½	Worstead	d	06 16	07 05	07 50	08 56	10 18		12 18		14 18		16 20		18 23		20 30	21 48	22 51	
21¾	Hoveton & Wroxham	d	06 23	07 12	07 57	09 03	10 25	11 24	12 25	13 24	14 25	15 24	16 27	17 25	18 30	19 31	20 37	21 55	22 58	00 22
24½	Salhouse	d	06 27	07 17	08 02	09 08		11 28		13 28		15 29	16 32		18 34		20 42	21 59	23 03	
30½	**Norwich**	a	06 40	07 29	08 14	09 23	10 41	11 41	12 41	13 41	14 41	15 41	16 44	17 41	18 47	19 46	20 55	22 12	23 15	00 37

Saturdays

26 May to 8 December

		LE	LE	LE	LE	LE	LE	LE	LE	LE	LE	LE	LE	LE	LE	LE	LE	LE
Sheringham	d	00 07	06 21	07 16	08 22	09 44	10 47	11 44	12 47	13 44	14 47	15 46	16 49	17 49	18 52	19 56	21 10	22 17
West Runton	d	00 11	06 25	07 20	08 26	09 48	10 51	11 48	12 51	13 48	14 51	15 50	16 53	17 53	18 56	20 00	21 14	22 21
Cromer	a	00 15	06 29	07 24	08 30	09 52	10 55	11 52	12 55	13 52	14 55	15 54	16 57	17 57	19 00	20 04	21 18	22 25
Cromer	d	00 18	06 32	07 27	08 33	09 55	10 58	11 55	12 58	13 55	14 58	15 57	17 00	18 00	19 03	20 07	21 21	22 28
Roughton Road	d		06 38	07 33	08 39	10 01		12 01		14 01	15 04	16 03		18 06		20 13	21 27	22 34
Gunton	d		06 44	07 39	08 45	10 07		12 07		14 07		16 09		18 12		20 19	21 33	22 40
North Walsham	a	00 33	06 50	07 45	08 51	10 13	11 13	12 13	13 13	14 13	15 14	16 15	17 15	18 18	19 18	20 25	21 39	22 46
North Walsham	d	00 33	06 50	07 45	08 51	10 13	11 14	12 13	13 14	14 13	15 14	16 15	17 15	18 18	19 21	20 25	21 43	22 46
Worstead	d		06 55	07 50	08 56	10 18		12 18		14 18		16 20		18 23		20 30	21 48	22 51
Hoveton & Wroxham	d	00 42	07 02	07 57	09 03	10 25	11 24	12 25	13 24	14 25	15 24	16 27	17 25	18 30	19 31	20 37	21 55	22 58
Salhouse	d		07 07	08 02	09 08		11 28		13 28		15 29	16 32		18 35		20 42	21 59	23 03
Norwich	a	00 57	07 20	08 14	09 21	10 41	11 41	12 41	13 41	14 41	15 41	16 44	17 41	18 47	19 46	20 55	22 12	23 15

Sundays

20 May to 2 December

		LE	LE	LE	LE	LE	LE	LE	LE	LE	LE	LE	LE	LE	LE
Sheringham	d	00 07	09 42	10 41	11 42	12 41	13 42	14 41	15 42	16 41	17 42	18 41	19 42	20 41	21 42
West Runton	d	00 11	09 46		11 46		13 46		15 46		17 46		19 46		21 46
Cromer	a	00 15	09 50	10 47	11 50	12 47	13 50	14 47	15 50	16 47	17 50	18 47	19 50	20 47	21 50
Cromer	d	00 18	09 53	10 51	11 53	12 51	13 53	14 51	15 53	16 51	17 53	18 51	19 53	20 51	21 53
Roughton Road	d		09 59		11 59		13 59		15 59		17 59		19 59		21 59
Gunton	d		10 05		12 05		14 05		16 05		18 05		20 05		22 05
North Walsham	a	00 33	10 11	11 06	12 11	13 06	14 11	15 06	16 11	17 06	18 11	19 06	20 11	21 06	22 11
North Walsham	d	00 33	10 12	11 06	12 12	13 06	14 12	15 06	16 12	17 06	18 12	19 06	20 12	21 06	22 12
Worstead	d		10 17		12 17		14 17		16 17		18 17		20 17		22 17
Hoveton & Wroxham	d	00 42	10 24	11 16	12 24	13 16	14 24	15 16	16 24	17 16	18 24	19 16	20 24	21 16	22 24
Salhouse	d		10 28		12 28		14 28		16 28		18 28		20 28		22 28
Norwich	a	00 57	10 40	11 31	12 40	13 31	14 40	15 31	16 40	17 31	18 40	19 31	20 40	21 31	22 40

Table T017-F

Mondays to Fridays

21 May to 7 December

London and Cambridge - Ely, Kings Lynn, Peterborough and Norwich

Miles	Miles	Miles			LE MX ■	GN MX	GN MO ■	GN MX	TL MX ■	XC ◇■	XC ◇■	LE ■	GN		EM ◇	GN	LE ■	EM ◇	XC ◇■	LE ■	GN	LE ■	EM ◇		TL ■
—	—	—	**London Liverpool Street** ⊖	d																					
—	—	0	**London Kings Cross** ⊖	d					00 01							05 42									05 55
—	—	—	Ipswich	d													06 00								
—	0	—	Stansted Airport ✈	d							05 16								06 12						
0	24½	58	**Cambridge**	d			00 04	00 08	01a25	05 15	05 55	06 02	06 14			06 35			06 56	07 00	07 10	07 21			07 24
2¼	26¾	60¼	Cambridge North	d			00 08	00 13				06 06	06 18			06 39				07 04	07 14	07 25			07a29
5¼	—	63¼	Waterbeach	d			00 12	00 17					06 22			06 44					07 18				
14¾	39¼	72¾	**Ely**	a			00 22	00 26		05 29	06 09	06 19	06 33			06 53	06 56		07 11	07 17	07 28	07 38			
—	—	—		d			00 22	00 27		05 30	06 10	06 19	06 33		06 51	06 54	06 57	07 08	07 12	07 17	07 28		07 44		
—	—	78¼	Littleport	d		00 06	00 29	00 34					06 41			07 01					07 36				
—	—	88½	Downham Market	d		00 15	00 38	00 43					06 50			07 13					07 49				
—	—	93¼	Watlington	d		00 21	00 44	00 49					06 56			07 25					07 55				
—	—	99¼	**Kings Lynn**	a		00 29	00 52	00 57					07 04			07 34					08 03				
—	49	—	Manea	d							06 20						07 08								
—	54¾	—	March	d						05 46	06 28				07 07		07 15		07 29				08 00		
—	62½	—	Whittlesea	d						05 58	06 39						07 27		07 40				08 12		
—	69¾	—	**Peterborough**	d						06a08	06a50				07a25		07a38		07a50				08a22		
21½	—	—	Shippea Hill	d																07x27					
26¾	—	—	Lakenheath	d																					
30¾	—	—	Brandon	d								06 35						07 25		07 37					
38	—	—	Thetford	d								06 44						07 33		07 46					
45¾	—	—	Harling Road	d								06 52								07 54					
48¾	—	—	Eccles Road	d								06 57								07 59					
52¼	—	—	Attleborough	d								07 03						07 47		08 05					
55¾	—	—	Spooner Row	d																08x10					
58¼	—	—	Wymondham	d	00 01							07 11						07 54		08 15					
68¼	—	—	**Norwich**	a	00 14							07 25						08 13		08 30					

		GN	EM ◇	TL ■	XC ◇■	TL	GN	LE ■	TL		GN	EM ◇	GN	LE ■	TL ■	LE ◇■	XC ◇■	TL ■	GN		LE ■	TL ■	EM ◇	EM ◇ A	GN
London Liverpool Street ⊖	d															07 28									
London Kings Cross ⊖	d	06 42		06 42		06 51	07 12						07 42		07 42			07 51	08 12						08 42
Ipswich	d													08 03											
Stansted Airport ✈	d				07 21				←								08 21					←			
Cambridge	d	07 35		07a39	08 01	08 22	08 05	08 10	08 22				08 35		08a39	08 55	09 01	09 22	09 06		09 09	09 22			09 35
Cambridge North	d	07 39				→	08 09	08 15	08a28				08 39			08a59		→	09 10		09 14	09a28			09 39
Waterbeach	d	07 44					08 14				←		08 44												09 44
Ely	a	07 54			08 14		08 23	08 27			08 23		08 54	08 59			09 14		09 23		09 26				09 54
	d	07 55	08 16		08 16		08 32	08 28			08 32	08 51	08 55	08 59			09 15				09 27		09 48	09 50	09 55
Littleport	d	08 04					→				08 39		09 04												10 04
Downham Market	d	08 17									08 48		09 17												10 17
Watlington	d	08 23									08 54		09 26												10 23
Kings Lynn	a	08 31									09 02		09 34												10 31
Manea	d													09 10											
March	d				08 33							09 07		09 18			09 33								
Whittlesea	d													09 29											
Peterborough	d				08a50							09a25		09a40			09a50							10a26	
Shippea Hill	d																								
Lakenheath	d																								
Brandon	d							08 44													09 43				
Thetford	d		08 38					08 53													09 52		10 09		
Harling Road	d																								
Eccles Road	d																								
Attleborough	d		08 52					09 08													10 07				
Spooner Row	d																				10x12				
Wymondham	d		09 00					09 15													10 16				
Norwich	a		09 15					09 30													10 30		10 44		

		TL ■	LE ◇■	XC ◇■	EM ◇		TL ■	GN	LE ■	TL ■	EM ◇	GN	LE ■	TL ■	LE ◇■		XC ◇■	EM ◇	TL ■	GN	LE ■	TL ■	EM ◇	GN	TL ■
London Liverpool Street ⊖	d		08 28												09 28										
London Kings Cross ⊖	d	08 42					08 51	09 12				09 42		09 42					09 51	10 12				10 42	10 42
Ipswich	d												10 00												
Stansted Airport ✈	d			09 21						←							10 27					←			
Cambridge	d	09a42	09 56	10 00			10 22	10 05	10 11	10 22		10 35		10a40	10 52		11 01		11 22	11 04	11 09	11 22		11 35	11a40
Cambridge North	d		10a00				→	10 09	10 15	10a28		10 39			10a56				→	11 08	11 13	11a28		11 39	
Waterbeach	d											10 44												11 44	
Ely	a			10 13				10 22	10 28			10 54	10 58				11 14			11 22	11 26			11 54	
	d			10 15	10 19				10 29		10 51	10 55	10 58				11 15	11 22			11 28		11 51	11 55	
Littleport	d											11 04												12 04	
Downham Market	d											11 17												12 17	
Watlington	d											11 23												12 23	
Kings Lynn	a											11 31												12 31	
Manea	d												11 09												
March	d			10 32									11 17				11 32						12 08		
Whittlesea	d												11 28												
Peterborough	d			10a50							11a27		11a39				11a50						12a24		
Shippea Hill	d																								
Lakenheath	d																								
Brandon	d								10 45												11 44				
Thetford	d				10 40				10 53									11 43			11 53				
Harling Road	d																								
Eccles Road	d																								
Attleborough	d								11 08												12 08				
Spooner Row	d																								
Wymondham	d								11 16												12 15				
Norwich	a				11 12				11 30									12 15			12 30				

A until 31 August, from 8 October

Table T017-F

Mondays to Fridays

21 May to 7 December

London and Cambridge - Ely, Kings Lynn, Peterborough and Norwich

			LE ◇■	XC ◇■	EM ◇	TL ■	GN	LE ■	TL ■	EM ◇	GN		LE ■	TL ■	LE ◇■	XC ◇■	EM ◇	TL ■	GN	LE ■	TL ■		EM ◇	GN	TL ■
London Liverpool Street ⊖	d		10 28												11 28										
London Kings Cross ⊖	d					10 51	11 12				11 42			11 42				11 51	12 12					12 42	12 42
Ipswich	d												11 58												
Stansted Airport ✈	d			11 27					←							12 27					←				
Cambridge	d		11 52	12 01		12 22	12 04	12 09	12 22		12 35			12a40	12 52	13 01		13 22	13 04	13 09	13 22			13 35	13a40
Cambridge North	d		11a56			→	12 08	12 13	12a28		12 40				12a56			→	13 08	13 13	13a28			13 39	
Waterbeach	d										12 44													13 44	
Ely	a			12 14			12 23	12 26			12 54		12 58			13 14			13 23	13 26				13 54	
	d			12 15	12 16			12 28		12 50	12 55		12 58			13 15	13 18			13 28			13 50	13 55	
Littleport	d										13 04													14 04	
Downham Market	d										13 17													14 17	
Watlington	d										13 23													14 23	
Kings Lynn	a										13 31													14 31	
Manea	d												13 09												
March	d			12 32									13 17			13 32									
Whittlesea	d												13 28												
Peterborough	d			12a50						13a23			13a39			13a50							14a25		
Shippea Hill	d																								
Lakenheath	d																								
Brandon	d							12 44												13 44					
Thetford	d				12 38			12 53									13 40			13 53					
Harling Road	d																								
Eccles Road	d																								
Attleborough	d							13 08												14 08					
Spooner Row	d																								
Wymondham	d							13 15												14 15					
Norwich	a				13 13			13 30									14 13			14 30					

		LE ◇■	XC ◇■	EM ◇	TL ■	GN	LE ■		TL ■	EM ◇	GN	LE ■	TL ■	LE ◇■	XC ◇■	EM ◇	TL ■		GN	LE ■	TL ■	GN	EM ◇	GN	TL ■
London Liverpool Street ⊖	d	12 28												13 28											
London Kings Cross ⊖	d				12 51	13 12					13 42		13 42				13 51		14 12					14 42	14 42
Ipswich	d											13 58													
Stansted Airport ✈	d		13 27						←						14 27						←				
Cambridge	d	13 52	14 01		14 22	14 04	14 09		14 22		14 35		14a40	14 52	15 01		15 22		15 04	15 09	15 22	15 30		15 35	15a40
Cambridge North	d	13a56			→	14 08	14 13		14a28		14 39			14a56			→		15 08	15 13	15a28	15 34		15 39	
Waterbeach	d										14 44											15 39		15 44	
Ely	a		14 14			14 23	14 26				14 54	14 58			15 14				15 23	15 26		15 50		15 54	
	d		14 15	14 16			14 28			14 48	14 55	14 58			15 15	15 19				15 28			15 50	15 55	
Littleport	d										15 04													16 04	
Downham Market	d										15 17													16 17	
Watlington	d										15 23													16 23	
Kings Lynn	a										15 31													16 31	
Manea	d											15 09													
March	d		14 32									15 17			15 32										
Whittlesea	d											15 28													
Peterborough	d		14a50							15a27		15a39			15a50								16a25		
Shippea Hill	d																								
Lakenheath	d																								
Brandon	d						14 44													15 44					
Thetford	d			14 38			14 53									15 40				15 53					
Harling Road	d																								
Eccles Road	d																								
Attleborough	d						15 08													16 08					
Spooner Row	d																								
Wymondham	d						15 15													16 15					
Norwich	a			15 11			15 30									16 13				16 30					

		LE ■	LE ◇■		XC ◇■	EM ◇	TL ■	GN	LE ■	GN	TL ■	EM ◇	GN		LE ■	TL ■	LE ◇■	XC ◇■	EM ◇	TL ■	GN	LE ■	LE ◇■		TL ■
London Liverpool Street ⊖	d		14 28														15 28						15 58		
London Kings Cross ⊖	d						14 51	15 12					15 42			15 42				15 51	16 12				
Ipswich	d														16 00										
Stansted Airport ✈	d	15 10			15 27						←							16 27							←
Cambridge	d	15 44	15 52		16 01		16 24	16 04	16 09	16 20	16 24		16 35			16a40	16 52	17 01		17 26	17 04	17 09	17 21		17 26
Cambridge North	d	15 48	15a56				→	16 08	16 13		16a29		16 39				16a56			→	17 08	17 13	17 26		17a31
Waterbeach	d	15 53								16 27			16 44										17 30		
Ely	a	16 03			16 14			16 23	16 26	16 36			16 54		16 58			17 14			17 22	17 26	17 42		
	d				16 15	16 19			16 28	16 37		16 49	16 55		16 59			17 15	17 18			17 28			
Littleport	d									16 44			17 04												
Downham Market	d									16 53			17 17												
Watlington	d									16 59			17 23												
Kings Lynn	a									17 07			17 31												
Manea	d														17 10										
March	d				16 32										17 18			17 32							
Whittlesea	d														17 29										
Peterborough	d				16a50							17a22			17a40			17a50							
Shippea Hill	d																								
Lakenheath	d																								
Brandon	d								16 44													17 44			
Thetford	d					16 40			16 53										17 40			17 53			
Harling Road	d																								
Eccles Road	d																								
Attleborough	d								17 08													18 08			
Spooner Row	d																								
Wymondham	d								17 15													18 15			
Norwich	a					17 13			17 29										18 13			18 29			

Table T017-F

Mondays to Fridays
21 May to 7 December

London and Cambridge - Ely, Kings Lynn, Peterborough and Norwich

		EM ◇	GN	TL ■	GN	XC ◇■	EM ◇	TL ■	GN		LE ■	LE ◇■ A	LE ■	TL ■	EM ◇	LE ■	GN	TL ■	LE ◇■		XC ◇■	EM ◇	TL ■	GN	LE ◇■
London Liverpool Street ⊖	d											17 07							17 37						18 07
London Kings Cross ⊖	d		16 42	16 42				16 51	17 12								17 42	17 42					17 51	18 12	
Ipswich	d															17 48									
Stansted Airport	d					17 27								←							18 21				
Cambridge	d		17 39	17a40	17 44	18 01		18 26	18 07		18 11	18 19	18 22	18 26			18 41	18a43	18 51		19 00		19 25	19 09	19 19
Cambridge North	d		17 44		17 48			→	18 11		18 15		18 26	18a32			18 45		18a55				→	19 14	
Waterbeach	d		17 49		17 53							18 25	18 30				18 50								19 25
Ely	a		17 58		18 03	18 14			18 24		18 28	18 34	18 41			18 57	18 59				19 15			19 25	19 35
	d	17 52	17 59			18 15	18 22				18 28	18 35			18 52	18 58	19 02				19 15	19 24		19 30	19 35
Littleport	d		18 08									18 42					19 09								19 47
Downham Market	d		18 17									18 52					19 18							19 47	19 57
Watlington	d		18 23									18 58					19 24							19 53	20 03
Kings Lynn	a		18 31									19 09					19 32							20 01	20 14
Manea	d					18 26										19 09									
March	d					18 34									19 08	19 17					19 33				
Whittlesea	d															19 28									
Peterborough	d	18a25				18a50									19a26	19a39					19a50				
Shippea Hill	d																								
Lakenheath	d																								
Brandon	d										18 44														
Thetford	d						18 43				18 53											19 45			
Harling Road	d																								
Eccles Road	d																								
Attleborough	d										19 08														
Spooner Row	d																								
Wymondham	d										19 15														
Norwich	a						19 16				19 29											20 19			

		LE ■	TL ■	EM ◇	GN		TL ■	LE ■	XC ◇■	EM ◇	TL ■	GN	LE ◇■	LE ■	TL ■		GN	LE ■	TL ■	LE ◇■	XC ◇■	TL ■	GN	LE	TL ■
London Liverpool Street ⊖	d							18 37					19 07							19 28					
London Kings Cross ⊖	d				18 42		18 42				18 51	19 12					19 42		19 42			19 51	20 12		
Ipswich	d																	20 00							
Stansted Airport	d		←						19 21						←						20 21				←
Cambridge	d	19 22	19 25		19 41		19a42	19 52	20 01		20 24	20 06	20 16	20 19	20 24		20 38		20a43	20 57	21 01	21 22	21 08	21 15	21 22
Cambridge North	d	19 26	19a30		19 45			19a56			→	20 11		20 23	20a29		20 42			21a01		→	21 12	21 20	21a27
Waterbeach	d				19 50								20 22				20 47						21 17		
Ely	a	19 39			20 00				20 14			20 23	20 32	20 36			20 57	20 59			21 15		21 27	21 32	
	d	19 39		19 52	20 02				20 15	20 18			20 33	20 37			20 58	21 01			21 16		21 29	21 33	
Littleport	d				20 10								20 41				21 06						21 36		
Downham Market	d				20 19								20 51				21 18						21 47		
Watlington	d				20 25								20 57				21 23						21 53		
Kings Lynn	a				20 33								21 08				21 32						22 01		
Manea	d																	21 10							
March	d								20 32									21 19			21 34				
Whittlesea	d																	21 30							
Peterborough	d			20a25					20a50									21a40			21a51				
Shippea Hill	d																								
Lakenheath	d																								
Brandon	d	19 56												20 53										21 49	
Thetford	d	20 04								20 38				21 01										21 57	
Harling Road	d																								
Eccles Road	d																								
Attleborough	d	20 19												21 16										22 12	
Spooner Row	d																								
Wymondham	d	20 27												21 24										22 20	
Norwich	a	20 41								21 13				21 38										22 35	

			GN	EM ◇	TL ■	LE ◇■	TL ■	GN	TL ■	GN	TL ■		LE ■	LE ◇■	GN	GN	TL ■	LE ◇■	GN	TL ■
London Liverpool Street ⊖	d					20 28								21 28				22 28		
London Kings Cross ⊖	d		20 42		20 42		20 51	21 12		21 42	21 42				22 12	22 42	22 42		23 12	23 42
Ipswich	d																			
Stansted Airport	d								←											
Cambridge	d		21 37		21a40	21 52	22 22	22 08	22 22	22 38	22a40		22 55	22 58	23 09	23 38	23a41	23 52	00 08	00a40
Cambridge North	d		21 41			21a56	→	22 12	22a28	22 42			22 59	23a03	23 13	23 42		23a56	00 13	
Waterbeach	d		21 46					22 17		22 47					23 17	23 47			00 17	
Ely	a		21 56					22 27		22 57			23 12		23 28	23 57			00 26	
	d		21 57	22 18						22 58			23 13			23 58			00 27	
Littleport	d		22 05							23 06						00 06			00 34	
Downham Market	d		22 17							23 17						00 15			00 43	
Watlington	d		22 23							23 23						00 21			00 49	
Kings Lynn	a		22 31							23 31						00 29			00 57	
Manea	d																			
March	d																			
Whittlesea	d																			
Peterborough	d																			
Shippea Hill	d																			
Lakenheath	d																			
Brandon	d												23 29							
Thetford	d			22 39									23 38							
Harling Road	d																			
Eccles Road	d																			
Attleborough	d			22 53									23 53							
Spooner Row	d																			
Wymondham	d			23 00									00 01							
Norwich	a			23 18									00 14							

A The Fenman

Table T017-F

Saturdays
26 May to 8 December

London and Cambridge - Ely, Kings Lynn, Peterborough and Norwich

		LE ■	GN	GN	LE ■	TL ■	XC ◇■	XC ◇■	LE ■	EM ◇		GN	LE ◇■	LE ■	EM ◇	XC ◇■	LE ■	GN	EM ◇	TL ■		GN	TL ■	LE ◇■	XC ◇■
London Liverpool Street ⊖	d				00 10								05 20											06 28	
London Kings Cross ⊖	d					00 01						05 42								05 51		06 42	06 42		
Ipswich	d													06 00											
Stansted Airport	d							05 25								06 27									07 27
Cambridge	d			00 08	01a19	01a25	05 15	05 55	06 05			06 35	06 52			06 57	07 00	07 10		07 25		07 37	07a39	07 52	08 01
Cambridge North	d			00 13					06 09			06 38	06a57				07 05	07 14		07a30		07 41		07a57	
Waterbeach	d			00 17								06 44										07 46			
Ely	a			00 26			05 29	06 09	06 22			06 53		06 57		07 12	07 18	07 27				07 57			08 14
	d			00 27			05 30	06 10	06 22	06 51		06 54		06 58	07 06	07 12	07 18		07 48			07 57			08 15
Littleport	d		00 06	00 34								07 04										08 05			
Downham Market	d		00 15	00 43								07 17										08 17			
Watlington	d		00 21	00 49								07 23										08 23			
Kings Lynn	a		00 29	00 57								07 31										08 31			
Manea	d							06 20						07 09											
March	d						05 46	06 28		07 07				07 17		07 29			08 04						08 32
Whittlesea	d						05 58	06 39						07 28		07 40			08 14						
Peterborough	d						06a08	06a50		07a25				07a39		07a49			08a27						08a50
Shippea Hill	d																07x27								
Lakenheath	d																								
Brandon	d								06 38						07 22		07 37								
Thetford	d								06 47						07 30		07 46								
Harling Road	d								06 55								07 54								
Eccles Road	d								07 00								07 59								
Attleborough	d								07 06						07 44		08 05								
Spooner Row	d																08x10								
Wymondham	d	00 01							07 14						07 51		08 15								
Norwich	a	00 14							07 28						08 13		08 30								

		EM ◇	TL ■	GN	LE ■	TL ■		EM ◇	GN	LE ■	TL ■	LE ◇■	XC ◇■	TL ■	GN	LE ■		TL ■	EM ◇	EM ◇	GN	TL ■	LE ◇■	XC ◇■	EM ◇
London Liverpool Street ⊖	d											07 28											08 28		
London Kings Cross ⊖	d		06 51	07 12					07 42		07 42			07 51	08 12						08 42	08 42			
Ipswich	d									08 00															
Stansted Airport	d					←							08 27					←						09 27	
Cambridge	d		08 23	08 04	08 09	08 23			08 35		08a40	08 52	09 01	09 22	09 04	09 09		09 22			09 35	09a40	09 52	10 01	
Cambridge North	d		→	08 08	08 13	08a29			08 38			08a57		→	09 08	09 13		09a28			09 38		09a57		
Waterbeach	d								08 44												09 44				
Ely	a			08 23	08 26				08 54	08 58			09 14		09 23	09 26					09 54			10 14	
	d	08 16			08 28			08 48	08 55	08 58			09 15			09 28			09 45	09 46	09 55			10 15	10 22
Littleport	d								09 04												10 04				
Downham Market	d								09 17												10 17				
Watlington	d								09 23												10 23				
Kings Lynn	a								09 31												10 31				
Manea	d									09 09															
March	d							09 05		09 17			09 32											10 32	
Whittlesea	d									09 28															
Peterborough	d							09a22		09a39			09a50							10a21				10a50	
Shippea Hill	d																								
Lakenheath	d																								
Brandon	d				08 44											09 44									
Thetford	d	08 37			08 53											09 53			10 07						10 43
Harling Road	d																								
Eccles Road	d																								
Attleborough	d	08 51			09 08											10 08									
Spooner Row	d																								
Wymondham	d	08 58			09 15											10 15									
Norwich	a	09 15			09 30											10 30			10 43						11 15

		TL ■		GN	LE ■	TL ■	EM ◇	GN	LE ■	TL ■	LE ◇■	XC ◇■		EM ◇	TL ■	GN	LE ■	TL ■	EM ◇	GN	TL ■	LE ◇■		XC ◇■	EM ◇
London Liverpool Street ⊖	d										09 28											10 28			
London Kings Cross ⊖	d	08 51		09 12				09 42		09 42					09 51	10 12				10 42	10 42				
Ipswich	d								09 58																
Stansted Airport	d					←						10 27						←						11 27	
Cambridge	d	10 24		10 04	10 09	10 24		10 35		10a40	10 52	11 01			11 22	11 04	11 09	11 22		11 35	11a40	11 52		12 01	
Cambridge North	d	→		10 08	10 13	10a29		10 38			10a57				→	11 08	11 13	11a28		11 38		11a57			
Waterbeach	d							10 44												11 44					
Ely	a			10 23	10 26			10 54	10 57			11 14				11 23	11 26			11 54				12 14	
	d				10 28		10 48	10 55	10 58			11 15		11 16			11 28		11 48	11 55				12 15	12 16
Littleport	d							11 04												12 04					
Downham Market	d							11 17												12 17					
Watlington	d							11 23												12 23					
Kings Lynn	a							11 31												12 31					
Manea	d								11 09																
March	d								11 17			11 32							12 05					12 32	
Whittlesea	d								11 28																
Peterborough	d						11a19		11a39			11a49							12a21					12a49	
Shippea Hill	d																								
Lakenheath	d																								
Brandon	d				10 44												11 44								
Thetford	d				10 53									11 37			11 53								12 38
Harling Road	d																								
Eccles Road	d																								
Attleborough	d				11 08												12 08								
Spooner Row	d																								
Wymondham	d				11 15												12 15								
Norwich	a				11 30									12 13			12 30								13 13

Table T017-F

Saturdays

26 May to 8 December

London and Cambridge - Ely, Kings Lynn, Peterborough and Norwich

		TL ■	GN	LE ■	TL ■	EM ◇	GN	LE ■		TL ■	LE ◇■	XC ◇■	EM ◇	TL ■	GN	LE ■	TL ■	EM ◇		GN	TL ■	LE ◇■	XC ◇■	EM ◇	TL ■
London Liverpool Street ⊖	d										11 28											12 28			
London Kings Cross ⊖	d	10 51	11 12				11 42			11 42				11 51	12 12					12 42	12 42				12 51
Ipswich	d							11 58																	
Stansted Airport ✈	d				←							12 27					←						13 27		
Cambridge	d	12 22	12 04	12 09	12 22		12 35			12a40	12 52	13 01		13 22	13 04	13 09	13 22			13 35	13a40	13 52	14 01		14 22
Cambridge North	d	→	12 08	12 13	12a28		12 38				12a57			→	13 08	13 13	13a28			13 38		13a57			→
Waterbeach	d						12 44													13 44					
Ely	a		12 23	12 26			12 54	12 58				13 14			13 23	13 26				13 54			14 14		
	d			12 28		12 51	12 55	12 58				13 15	13 22			13 28		13 48		13 55			14 15	14 16	
Littleport	d						13 04													14 04					
Downham Market	d						13 17													14 17					
Watlington	d						13 23													14 23					
Kings Lynn	a						13 31													14 31					
Manea	d							13 09																	
March	d							13 17				13 32											14 32		
Whittlesea	d							13 28																	
Peterborough	d					13a26		13a39				13a49						14a25					14a50		
Shippea Hill	d																								
Lakenheath	d																								
Brandon	d			12 44												13 44									
Thetford	d			12 53									13 43			13 53								14 37	
Harling Road	d																								
Eccles Road	d																								
Attleborough	d			13 08												14 08									
Spooner Row	d																								
Wymondham	d			13 15												14 15									
Norwich	a			13 30									14 12			14 30								15 13	

		GN	LE ■	TL ■		EM ◇	GN	LE ■	TL ■	LE ◇■	XC ◇■	EM ◇	TL ■	GN		LE ■	TL ■	EM ◇	GN	TL ■	LE ◇■	XC ◇■	EM ◇	TL ■	
London Liverpool Street ⊖	d									13 28											14 28				
London Kings Cross ⊖	d	13 12					13 42		13 42				13 51	14 12					14 42	14 42				14 51	
Ipswich	d							13 58																	
Stansted Airport ✈	d			←							14 27						←					15 27			
Cambridge	d	14 04	14 09	14 22			14 35		14a40	14 52	15 01		15 22	15 04		15 09	15 22		15 35	15a40	15 52	16 01		16 22	
Cambridge North	d	14 08	14 13	14a28			14 38			14a57			→	15 08		15 13	15a28		15 38		15a57			→	
Waterbeach	d						14 44												15 44						
Ely	a	14 23	14 26				14 54	14 58			15 14			15 23		15 26			15 54			16 14			
	d		14 28			14 48	14 55	14 58			15 15	15 19				15 27		15 47	15 55			16 15	16 22		
Littleport	d						15 04												16 04						
Downham Market	d						15 17												16 17						
Watlington	d						15 23												16 23						
Kings Lynn	a						15 31												16 31						
Manea	d							15 09																	
March	d							15 17			15 32											16 32			
Whittlesea	d							15 28																	
Peterborough	d					15a23		15a39			15a49							16a25				16a50			
Shippea Hill	d																								
Lakenheath	d															15x40									
Brandon	d		14 44													15 46									
Thetford	d		14 53									15 40				15 54							16 44		
Harling Road	d																								
Eccles Road	d																								
Attleborough	d		15 08													16 09									
Spooner Row	d																								
Wymondham	d		15 15													16 17									
Norwich	a		15 30									16 12				16 31							17 12		

		GN	LE ■	TL ■	EM ◇	GN	LE ■	TL ■	LE ◇■	XC ◇■		EM ◇	TL ■	GN	LE ■	TL ■	EM ◇	GN	TL ■	LE ◇■		XC ◇■	EM ◇	TL ■	GN
London Liverpool Street ⊖	d								15 28											16 28					
London Kings Cross ⊖	d	15 12				15 42		15 42					15 51	16 12				16 42	16 42					16 51	17 12
Ipswich	d						15 58																		
Stansted Airport ✈	d			←						16 27						←						17 27			
Cambridge	d	16 04	16 09	16 22		16 35		16a40	16 52	17 01			17 22	17 04	17 09	17 22		17 35	17a40	17 52		18 01		18 22	18 04
Cambridge North	d	16 08	16 13	16a28		16 38			16a57				→	17 08	17 13	17a28		17 38		17a57				→	18 08
Waterbeach	d					16 44												17 44							
Ely	a	16 23	16 26			16 54	16 58			17 14				17 23	17 26			17 54				18 14			18 23
	d		16 28		16 47	16 55	16 58			17 15		17 17			17 28		17 47	17 55				18 15	18 16		
Littleport	d					17 04												18 04							
Downham Market	d					17 17												18 17							
Watlington	d					17 23												18 23							
Kings Lynn	a					17 31												18 31							
Manea	d						17 09															18 25			
March	d						17 17			17 32												18 34			
Whittlesea	d						17 28																		
Peterborough	d				17a23		17a39			17a49							18a23					18a51			
Shippea Hill	d																								
Lakenheath	d																								
Brandon	d		16 44												17 44										
Thetford	d		16 53									17 38			17 53								18 37		
Harling Road	d																								
Eccles Road	d																								
Attleborough	d		17 08												18 08										
Spooner Row	d																								
Wymondham	d		17 15												18 15										
Norwich	a		17 30									18 13			18 30								19 13		

Table T017-F

Saturdays

26 May to 8 December

London and Cambridge - Ely, Kings Lynn, Peterborough and Norwich

		LE ■	TL ■	EM ◇	GN	LE ■		TL ■	LE ◇■	XC ◇■	EM ◇	TL ■	GN	LE ■	TL ■	EM ◇		GN	EM ◇	TL ■	LE ◇■	XC ◇■	TL ■	GN	LE ■
London Liverpool Street ⊖	d								17 28												18 28				
London Kings Cross ⊖	d				17 42			17 42				17 51	18 12					18 42		18 42			18 51	19 12	
Ipswich	d					17 58																			
Stansted Airport ✈	d		←							18 27					←							19 27			
Cambridge	d	18 09	18 22		18 35			18a40	18 52	19 01		19 22	19 04	19 09	19 22			19 35		19a40	19 52	20 01	20 22	20 04	20 09
Cambridge North	d	18 13	18a28		18 38				18a57			→	19 08	19 13	19a28			19 38			19a57		→	20 08	20 13
Waterbeach	d				18 44													19 44							
Ely	a	18 26			18 54	18 58				19 14			19 20	19 27				19 54				20 15		20 21	20 26
	d	18 28		18 48	18 55	18 58				19 15	19 22		19 25	19 29		19 48		19 55	20 16			20 16		20 23	20 28
Littleport	d				19 04								19 34					20 04							
Downham Market	d				19 17								19 44					20 17						20 42	
Watlington	d				19 23								19 52					20 23							
Kings Lynn	a				19 31								20 00					20 31						21 00	
Manea	d					19 09																			
March	d			19 05		19 17				19 32												20 32			
Whittlesea	d					19 28																			
Peterborough	d			19a24		19a39				19a50						20a23						20a50			
Shippea Hill	d																								
Lakenheath	d																								
Brandon	d	18 44												19 45											20 44
Thetford	d	18 53									19 43			19 54					20 38						20 53
Harling Road	d																								
Eccles Road	d																								
Attleborough	d	19 08												20 09											21 08
Spooner Row	d																								
Wymondham	d	19 15												20 16											21 15
Norwich	a	19 30									20 16			20 30					21 13						21 30

		TL ■		GN	LE ■	TL ■	LE ◇■	TL ■	GN	LE ■	TL ■	GN		EM ◇	TL ■	LE ◇■	TL ■	GN	TL ■	GN	TL ■	LE ■		LE ◇■	GN
London Liverpool Street ⊖	d						19 28									20 28								21 28	
London Kings Cross ⊖	d			19 42		19 42		19 51	20 12			20 42			20 42		20 51	21 12		21 42	21 42				22 12
Ipswich	d				19 58																				
Stansted Airport ✈	d	←									←								←						
Cambridge	d	20 22		20 35		20a40	20 52	21 22	21 05	21 09	21 22	21 35			21a40	21 52	22 22	22 05	22 22	22 35	22a40	22 55		22 59	23 05
Cambridge North	d	20a28		20 38			20a57	→	21 09	21 13	21a28	21 38				21a57	→	22 09	22a28	22 38		22 59		23a04	23 09
Waterbeach	d			20 44								21 44								22 44					
Ely	a			20 54	20 58				21 21	21 26		21 54						22 23		22 54		23 12			23 23
	d			20 55	20 58				21 25	21 28		21 55		22 17						22 55		23 12			
Littleport	d			21 04					21 33			22 04								23 02					
Downham Market	d			21 17					21 42			22 17								23 11					
Watlington	d			21 23					21 52			22 23								23 17					
Kings Lynn	a			21 31					22 00			22 31								23 25					
Manea	d				21 09																				
March	d				21 17																				
Whittlesea	d				21 28																				
Peterborough	d				21a39																				
Shippea Hill	d																								
Lakenheath	d																								
Brandon	d									21 44												23 28			
Thetford	d									21 53				22 38								23 37			
Harling Road	d																								
Eccles Road	d																								
Attleborough	d									22 08				22 52								23 52			
Spooner Row	d																								
Wymondham	d									22 15				22 59								23 59			
Norwich	a									22 32				23 19								00 13			

		GN	TL ■	LE ◇■	GN	TL ■
London Liverpool Street ⊖	d			22 28		
London Kings Cross ⊖	d	22 42	22 42		23 12	23 38
Ipswich	d					
Stansted Airport ✈	d					
Cambridge	d	23 35	23a40	23 52	00 08	00a41
Cambridge North	d	23 38		23a57	00 13	
Waterbeach	d	23 44			00 17	
Ely	a	23 54			00 26	
	d	23 55			00 27	
Littleport	d	00 03			00 34	
Downham Market	d	00 12			00 43	
Watlington	d	00 18			00 49	
Kings Lynn	a	00 26			00 57	
Manea	d					
March	d					
Whittlesea	d					
Peterborough	d					
Shippea Hill	d					
Lakenheath	d					
Brandon	d					
Thetford	d					
Harling Road	d					
Eccles Road	d					
Attleborough	d					
Spooner Row	d					
Wymondham	d					
Norwich	a					

Table T017-F

Sundays
20 May to 2 December

London and Cambridge - Ely, Kings Lynn, Peterborough and Norwich

		GN	GN	LE A	LE	TL	LE	GN	LE ◇	GN		LE ◇	EM ◇ A	LE	TL	LE	XC ◇	GN	LE ◇	EM ◇		EM ◇ A	TL	LE	XC ◇
London Liverpool Street ⊖	d				00 10							08 57							09 57						
London Kings Cross ⊖	d					00 01		07 52		09 11					09 46			10 11					10 46		
Ipswich	d			07 55										09 55											
Stansted Airport ✈	d																10 25								11 25
Cambridge	d		00 08		01a19	01a25	08 50	09 04	09 25	10 04		10 27			10a48	10 50	11 00	11 04	11 27				11a48	11 50	12 00
Cambridge North	d		00 13				08 54	09 08	09a30	10 08		10a32				10 54		11 08	11a32					11 54	
Waterbeach	d		00 17					09 12		10 12								11 12							
Ely	a		00 26	08 51			09 07	09 22		10 22				10 51		11 07	11 14	11 22						12 07	12 14
	d		00 27	08 52			09 07	09 22		10 22			10 41	10 52		11 07	11 15	11 22		11 39		11 48		12 07	12 15
Littleport	d	00 03	00 34					09 29		10 29								11 29							
Downham Market	d	00 12	00 43					09 38		10 38								11 38							
Watlington	d	00 18	00 49					09 44		10 44								11 44							
Kings Lynn	a	00 26	00 57					09 52		10 52								11 52							
Manea	d																								
March	d			09 09										11 09			11 32								12 32
Whittlesea	d			09 20										11 20											
Peterborough	d			09a31									11a13	11a31			11a51			12a11					12a51
Shippea Hill	d																								
Lakenheath	d						09x20									11x20									
Brandon	d						09 26									11 26						12 04		12 23	
Thetford	d						09 34									11 34						12 12		12 32	
Harling Road	d																								
Eccles Road	d																								
Attleborough	d						09 49									11 49						12 26		12 47	
Spooner Row	d																								
Wymondham	d						09 57									11 57						12 33		12 54	
Norwich	a						10 13									12 13						12 52		13 12	

		GN	LE ◇	LE	TL	LE		XC ◇	GN	LE ◇	EM ◇ B	TL	LE	XC ◇	EM ◇	GN		LE ◇	EM ◇	LE	TL	LE	XC ◇	GN	LE ◇
London Liverpool Street ⊖	d		10 57							11 57								12 57							13 57
London Kings Cross ⊖	d	11 11			11 46				12 11			12 46				13 11					13 46			14 11	
Ipswich	d			11 55																13 55					
Stansted Airport ✈	d							12 25						13 25									14 25		
Cambridge	d	12 04	12 27		12a48	12 50		13 00	13 04	13 27		13a48	13 50	14 00		14 04		14 27			14a48	14 50	15 00	15 04	15 27
Cambridge North	d	12 08	12a32			12 54			13 08	13a31			13 54			14 08		14a32				14 54		15 08	15a32
Waterbeach	d	12 12							13 12							14 12								15 12	
Ely	a	12 22		12 51		13 07		13 14	13 22				14 07	14 14		14 22				14 51		15 07	15 14	15 22	
	d	12 22		12 52		13 07		13 15	13 22		13 34		14 07	14 15	14 19	14 22			14 40	14 52		15 07	15 15	15 22	
Littleport	d	12 29							13 29							14 29								15 29	
Downham Market	d	12 38							13 38							14 38								15 38	
Watlington	d	12 44							13 44							14 44								15 44	
Kings Lynn	a	12 52							13 52							14 52								15 52	
Manea	d																								
March	d			13 09				13 32						14 32						15 09			15 32		
Whittlesea	d			13 20																15 20					
Peterborough	d			13a31				13a51						14a51					15a13	15a31			15a51		
Shippea Hill	d																								
Lakenheath	d					13x20																			
Brandon	d					13 26							14 23		14 35							15 23			
Thetford	d					13 34					13 55		14 32		14 43							15 32			
Harling Road	d																								
Eccles Road	d																								
Attleborough	d					13 49							14 47		14 57							15 47			
Spooner Row	d																								
Wymondham	d					13 57							14 54		15 08							15 54			
Norwich	a					14 13					14 28		15 13		15 24							16 13			

		EM ◇		EM ◇	TL	LE	XC ◇	GN	LE ◇	EM ◇	LE	TL		LE	XC ◇	GN	LE ◇	EM ◇	EM ◇	TL	LE	XC ◇		GN	LE ◇
London Liverpool Street ⊖	d								14 57								15 57								16 57
London Kings Cross ⊖	d				14 46			15 11				15 46				16 11				16 46				17 11	
Ipswich	d										15 55														
Stansted Airport ✈	d						15 25								16 25							17 25			
Cambridge	d				15a48	15 50	16 00	16 04	16 27			16a48		16 50	17 00	17 04	17 27			17a48	17 50	18 00		18 04	18 27
Cambridge North	d					15 54		16 08	16a32					16 54		17 08	17a32				17 54			18 08	18a32
Waterbeach	d							16 12								17 12								18 12	
Ely	a					16 07	16 14	16 22			16 51			17 07	17 14	17 22					18 07	18 14		18 22	
	d	15 40		15 46		16 07	16 15	16 22		16 34	16 52			17 07	17 15	17 22		17 36	17 49		18 07	18 15		18 22	
Littleport	d							16 29								17 29								18 30	
Downham Market	d							16 38								17 38								18 39	
Watlington	d							16 44								17 44								18 44	
Kings Lynn	a							16 52								17 52								18 53	
Manea	d																								
March	d			16 03			16 32				17 09				17 32							18 32			
Whittlesea	d										17 20														
Peterborough	d			16a20			16a51				17a31				17a51				18a20			18a51			
Shippea Hill	d																								
Lakenheath	d					16x20																			
Brandon	d					16 26								17 23							18 23				
Thetford	d	16 01				16 34				16 55				17 32				17 57			18 32				
Harling Road	d																								
Eccles Road	d																								
Attleborough	d					16 49								17 47							18 47				
Spooner Row	d																								
Wymondham	d					16 57								17 54							18 54				
Norwich	a	16 35				17 13				17 26				18 13				18 30			19 10				

A until 9 September

Table T017-F

Sundays
20 May to 2 December

London and Cambridge - Ely, Kings Lynn, Peterborough and Norwich

		EM ◇	EM ◇	LE	TL	LE	XC ◇	GN		LE ◇	EM ◇	EM ◇	TL	LE	XC ◇	GN	LE ◇	EM ◇		TL	GN	LE ◇	EM ◇	TL	LE
London Liverpool Street ⊖	d									17 57							18 57					19 57			
London Kings Cross ⊖	d				17 46			18 11					18 46			19 11				19 46	20 11			20 46	
Ipswich	d			17 55																					
Stansted Airport ✈	d						18 25								19 25										
Cambridge	d				18a48	18 50	19 00	19 04		19 27			19a48	19 50	20 00	20 05	20 27			20a48	21 04	21 27		21a45	21 50
Cambridge North	d					18 54		19 08		19a32				19 54		20 09	20a32				21 08	21a32			21 54
Waterbeach	d							19 12								20 13					21 12				
Ely	a			18 51		19 07	19 14	19 22						20 07	20 14	20 23					21 22				22 07
	d	18 35	18 47	18 52		19 07	19 15	19 22			19 30	19 49		20 07	20 15	20 23		20 35			21 22		21 44		22 07
Littleport	d							19 29								20 30					21 29				
Downham Market	d							19 38								20 39					21 38				
Watlington	d							19 44								20 45					21 44				
Kings Lynn	a							19 52								20 53					21 52				
Manea	d																								
March	d			19 09			19 32								20 32										
Whittlesea	d			19 20																					
Peterborough	d		19a20	19a31			19a51					20a23			20a51								22a16		
Shippea Hill	d																								
Lakenheath	d																								
Brandon	d					19 23								20 23											22 23
Thetford	d	18 56				19 32					19 52			20 32				20 56							22 32
Harling Road	d																								
Eccles Road	d																								
Attleborough	d					19 47								20 47				21 10							22 47
Spooner Row	d																								
Wymondham	d					19 54								20 54				21 17							22 54
Norwich	a	19 28				20 13					20 26			21 10				21 35							23 13

		GN	LE ◇	EM ◇		TL	GN	LE ◇	TL	GN
London Liverpool Street ⊖	d		20 57					21 57		
London Kings Cross ⊖	d	21 11				21 46	22 11		22 46	23 11
Ipswich	d									
Stansted Airport ✈	d									
Cambridge	d	22 04	22 27			22a48	23 04	23 27	23a45	00 04
Cambridge North	d	22 08	22a32				23 08	23a32		00 08
Waterbeach	d	22 12					23 12			00 12
Ely	a	22 22					23 22			00 22
	d	22 22		22 30			23 22			00 22
Littleport	d	22 29					23 29			00 29
Downham Market	d	22 38					23 38			00 38
Watlington	d	22 44					23 44			00 44
Kings Lynn	a	22 52					23 52			00 52
Manea	d									
March	d									
Whittlesea	d									
Peterborough	d									
Shippea Hill	d									
Lakenheath	d									
Brandon	d									
Thetford	d			22 51						
Harling Road	d									
Eccles Road	d									
Attleborough	d			23 05						
Spooner Row	d									
Wymondham	d			23 12						
Norwich	a			23 25						

Norwich, Peterborough, Kings Lynn and Ely - Cambridge and London

Miles	Miles	Miles			TL MX ■	TL MX ■	TL MX ■	GN MO ■	TL ■	TL ■	GN	TL ■	TL ■	GN	TL ■	LE ◇■	GN	TL ■	GN	LE ■	GN
0	—	—	**Norwich**	d																05 33	
10	—	—	Wymondham	d																05 45	
12¾	—	—	Spooner Row	d																	
16	—	—	Attleborough	d																05 52	
19½	—	—	Eccles Road	d																	
22¾	—	—	Harling Road	d																	
30½	—	—	Thetford	d																06 06	
37½	—	—	Brandon	d																06 14	
41½	—	—	Lakenheath	d																	
46¾	—	—	Shippea Hill	d																	
—	0	—	**Peterborough ■**	d					03 24	04 20		04 54	05 24	05 42	05 54		06 05	06 24			06 36
—	7	—	Whittlesea	d																	
—	15	—	March	d																	
—	20¾	—	Manea	d																	
—	—	0	**Kings Lynn**	d							04 43					05 17			05 40		
—	—	6	Watlington	d							04 50					05 24			05 47		
—	—	10¾	Downham Market	d							04 57					05 31			05 54		
—	—	21	Littleport	d							05 07					05 40			06 04		
53½	30½	26½	**Ely ■**	a							05 15					05 49			06 12	06 31	
—	—	—		d							05 15					05 50			06 12	06 31	
—	—	36	Waterbeach	d							05 25					05 59			06 22		
66	43	39	Cambridge North	d							05 30					06 04			06 27	06 44	
68¾	45¾	41¾	**Cambridge**	a							05 34					06 10			06 34	06 52	
—	69¾	—	Stansted Airport ✈	a																	
—	—	—	Ipswich	a	00d10	00d15	00d39	00d40	04d45	05 35		06 07	06 37		07 07			07 37			
—	—	99¼	**London Kings Cross ■ ⊖**	a	00 18	00 21	00 45	00 49	04 51		06 32			06 44			07 14		07 33		07 44
—	—	—	**London Liverpool Street ■ ⊖**	a												07 25					

		TL ■	GN	GN	EM ◇	LE ◇■ A	EM ◇	TL ■	GN	GN	GN	GN	GN	LE ◇■	LE ■	EM ◇	TL ■	GN	GN
Norwich	d				05 50										06 33	06 51			
Wymondham	d				06 03										06 45				
Spooner Row	d																		
Attleborough	d				06 10										06 52				
Eccles Road	d																		
Harling Road	d																		
Thetford	d				06 24										07 06	07 19			
Brandon	d														07 14				
Lakenheath	d																		
Shippea Hill	d																		
Peterborough ■	d						06 27	06 54	07 05	07 14			07 35						
Whittlesea	d																		
March	d						06 43												
Manea	d																		
Kings Lynn	d		06 10			06 17					06 40							07 07	07 18
Watlington	d		06 17			06 24					06 47							07 14	
Downham Market	d		06 24			06 31					06 54							07 21	07 30
Littleport	d					06 40					07 04							07 31	
Ely ■	a		06 42		06 46	06 49	07 02				07 12				07 31	07 40		07 43	07 46
	d		06 42	06 45		06 50					07 12	07 15		07 30	07 33			07 43	07 47
Waterbeach	d			06 56		06 59					07 22							07 53	
Cambridge North	d	06 48	06 55			07 04						07 29		07 42	07 46		07 50		08 00
Cambridge	a	06 54	07 00	07 03		07 10					07 30	07 34		07 47	07 53		07 56	08 01	08 04
Stansted Airport ✈	a																		
Ipswich	a	08d14						08 07									09d18		
London Kings Cross ■ ⊖	a	08 20	08 02						08 14	08 17	08 34		08 46				09 25		09 04
London Liverpool Street ■ ⊖	a					08 25								09 20					

A The Fenman

Table T017-R

Mondays to Fridays

21 May to 7 December

Norwich, Peterborough, Kings Lynn and Ely - Cambridge and London

		XC ◇■	LE ◇■	TL ■	EM ◇	GN	GN	LE ■	LE ■	TL ■	TL ■	GN	EM ◇	XC ◇■	TL ■	TL ■	GN	LE ◇■	GN
Norwich	d								07 34				07 57						
Wymondham	d								07 46										
Spooner Row	d																		
Attleborough	d								07 53										
Eccles Road	d																		
Harling Road	d																		
Thetford	d								08 07				08 24						
Brandon	d								08 15										
Lakenheath	d																		
Shippea Hill	d																		
Peterborough ■	d	07 12		07 24	07 38	08 04		07 49		07 54				08 18	08 23	08 57	09 17		
Whittlesea	d	07 20						07 57											
March	d	07 31			07 54			08 08						08 34					
Manea	d	07 38						08 16											
Kings Lynn	d						07 42					08 12							08 44
Watlington	d						07 49					08 19							08 51
Downham Market	d						07 56					08 26							08 58
Littleport	d						08 06					08 36							09 08
Ely ■	a	07 51			08 12		08 15	08 29	08 32			08 44	08 47	08 52					09 16
	d	07 52	08 00				08 15	08 30	08 33			08 45		08 54					09 17
Waterbeach	d		08 09				08 25					08 55							09 26
Cambridge North	d		08 14				08 30		08 45		08 50	09 00						09 14	09 31
Cambridge	a	08 08	08 20				08 35		08 52		08 56	09 04		09 13				09 19	09 36
Stansted Airport ✈	a	08 39												09 43					
Ipswich	a			08 37				09 26		09 07	10d17				09 33	10 07			
London Kings Cross ■ ⊖	a					09 18	09 43				10 25	10 05					10 20		10 34
London Liverpool Street ■ ⊖	a		09 50															10 44	

		TL ■	LE ■	EM ◇	EM ◇ A	GN	XC ◇■	TL ■	EM ◇	LE ◇■	GN	LE ■	TL ■	TL ■	LE ■	EM ◇	GN	XC ◇■	TL ■
Norwich	d		08 40		08 57										09 40	09 57			
Wymondham	d		08 52												09 52				
Spooner Row	d																		
Attleborough	d		08 59												09 59				
Eccles Road	d																		
Harling Road	d																		
Thetford	d		09 13		09 24										10 13	10 24			
Brandon	d		09 21												10 21				
Lakenheath	d																		
Shippea Hill	d																		
Peterborough ■	d			09 03			09 18	09 26	09 40			09 50	09 54					10 19	10 24
Whittlesea	d											09 58							
March	d						09 34					10 09						10 35	
Manea	d											10 17							
Kings Lynn	d					09 10					09 44								
Watlington	d					09 17					09 51								
Downham Market	d					09 28					09 58								
Littleport	d					09 38					10 08								
Ely ■	a		09 38	09 42	09 45	09 48	09 49		10 13		10 16	10 31			10 38	10 45		10 53	
	d		09 38			09 48	09 52				10 17	10 32			10 38		10 47	10 53	
Waterbeach	d					09 58					10 26								
Cambridge North	d	09 44	09 51			10 03				10 14	10 31			10 44	10 51		11 01		
Cambridge	a	09 50	09 59			10 07	10 08			10 20	10 36			10 50	10 59		11 06	11 09	
Stansted Airport ✈	a						10 40											11 40	
Ipswich	a	11d14						10 37				11 28	11 07	12d14					11 37
London Kings Cross ■ ⊖	a	11 20				11 04					11 34			12 20			12 02		
London Liverpool Street ■ ⊖	a									11 44									

A until 31 August, from 8 October

Table T017-R

Mondays to Fridays

21 May to 7 December

Norwich, Peterborough, Kings Lynn and Ely - Cambridge and London

			LE ◇■	GN	EM ◇	TL ■				TL ■	LE ■	EM ◇	GN	XC ◇■	TL ■	EM ◇		LE ◇■		GN	LE ■	TL ■			TL ■
Norwich	d										10 40	10 57													
Wymondham	d										10 52														
Spooner Row	d																								
Attleborough	d										10 59														
Eccles Road	d																								
Harling Road	d																								
Thetford	d										11 13	11 24													
Brandon	d										11 21														
Lakenheath	d																								
Shippea Hill	d																								
Peterborough ■	d				10 45	10 54								11 18	11 23	11 41					11 50	11 54			
Whittlesea	d																				11 58				
March	d													11 34							12 09				
Manea	d																				12 17				
Kings Lynn	d			10 44																11 44					
Watlington	d			10 51																11 51					
Downham Market	d			10 58																11 58					
Littleport	d			11 08																12 08					
Ely ■	a			11 16	11 19						11 38	11 47		11 52		12 13				12 17	12 31				
	d			11 17							11 38		11 47	11 53						12 17	12 32				
Waterbeach	d			11 26																12 26					
Cambridge North	d		11 14	11 31						11 44	11 51		12 01					12 14		12 31					12 44
Cambridge	a		11 20	11 36						11 50	11 59		12 06	12 09				12 20		12 37					12 50
Stansted Airport ✈	a													12 40											
Ipswich	a					12 06				13d14					12 37						13 28	13 07			14d14
London Kings Cross ■ ⊖	a			12 35						13 20			13 03							13 33					14 20
London Liverpool Street ■ ⊖	a		12 45															13 44							

		LE ■	EM ◇	GN		XC ◇■	TL ■	EM ◇	TL ■		LE ◇■	GN				TL ■	LE ■	EM ◇	GN	XC ◇■	TL ■	EM ◇		LE ◇■	
Norwich	d	11 40	11 57														12 40	12 57							
Wymondham	d	11 52															12 52								
Spooner Row	d																								
Attleborough	d	11 59															12 59								
Eccles Road	d																								
Harling Road	d																								
Thetford	d	12 13	12 24														13 13	13 24							
Brandon	d	12 21															13 21								
Lakenheath	d																								
Shippea Hill	d																								
Peterborough ■	d					12 19	12 24	12 42	12 54											13 19	13 24	13 41			
Whittlesea	d																								
March	d					12 35														13 35					
Manea	d																								
Kings Lynn	d											12 44													
Watlington	d											12 51													
Downham Market	d											12 58													
Littleport	d											13 08													
Ely ■	a	12 38	12 45			12 53		13 14				13 17					13 38	13 45		13 53		14 13			
	d	12 38		12 47		12 53						13 17					13 38		13 47	13 53					
Waterbeach	d											13 26													
Cambridge North	d	12 51		13 01							13 14	13 31				13 44	13 51		14 01					14 14	
Cambridge	a	12 59		13 06		13 09					13 20	13 37				13 50	13 59		14 06	14 09				14 20	
Stansted Airport ✈	a					13 40														14 40					
Ipswich	a						13 37		14 07							15d14					14 37				
London Kings Cross ■ ⊖	a			14 03								14 33				15 20			15 02						
London Liverpool Street ■ ⊖	a										14 45													15 45	

		GN	LE ■	TL ■			TL ■	LE ■	EM ◇	GN		XC ◇■	TL ■	EM ◇	TL ■		LE ◇■	GN				TL ■	LE ■	EM ◇	GN
Norwich	d							13 40	13 57														14 40	14 57	
Wymondham	d							13 52															14 52		
Spooner Row	d																								
Attleborough	d							13 59															14 59		
Eccles Road	d																								
Harling Road	d																								
Thetford	d							14 13	14 24														15 13	15 24	
Brandon	d							14 21															15 21		
Lakenheath	d																								
Shippea Hill	d																								
Peterborough ■	d		13 50	13 54								14 19	14 24	14 41	14 54										
Whittlesea	d		13 58																						
March	d		14 09									14 35													
Manea	d		14 17																						
Kings Lynn	d	13 44																14 44							
Watlington	d	13 51																14 51							
Downham Market	d	13 58																14 58							
Littleport	d	14 07																15 08							
Ely ■	a	14 16	14 31					14 38	14 45			14 53		15 14				15 17					15 38	15 45	
	d	14 17	14 32					14 38		14 47		14 53						15 17					15 38		15 45
Waterbeach	d	14 25																15 26							
Cambridge North	d	14 30					14 44	14 51		15 01							15 14	15 31				15 44	15 51		16 00
Cambridge	a	14 36					14 50	15 00		15 06		15 09					15 20	15 37				15 50	15 59		16 05
Stansted Airport ✈	a											15 40													
Ipswich	a		15 28	15 07			16d14						15 37		16 07							17d14			
London Kings Cross ■ ⊖	a	15 33					16 20			16 04								16 33				17 20			17 03
London Liverpool Street ■ ⊖	a																16 44								

Table T017-R

Mondays to Fridays

21 May to 7 December

Norwich, Peterborough, Kings Lynn and Ely - Cambridge and London

		XC ◇■	TL ■	EM ◇		LE ◇■		GN	LE ■	TL ■			TL ■	LE ■	EM ◇	GN		XC ◇■	TL ■	EM ◇	TL ■		LE ◇■	GN	
Norwich	d													15 40	15 48										
Wymondham	d													15 52											
Spooner Row	d																								
Attleborough	d													15 59	16 05										
Eccles Road	d														16 10										
Harling Road	d														16 14										
Thetford	d													16 13	16 23										
Brandon	d													16 21											
Lakenheath	d																								
Shippea Hill	d																								
Peterborough ■	d	15 19	15 24	15 40					15 50	15 54								16 19	16 24	16 41	16 54				
Whittlesea	d								15 58																
March	d	15 35							16 09									16 35							
Manea	d								16 17																
Kings Lynn	d							15 44																16 44	
Watlington	d							15 51																16 51	
Downham Market	d							15 58																16 58	
Littleport	d							16 08																17 08	
Ely ■	a	15 53		16 13				16 17	16 31					16 38	16 45			16 52		17 13				17 17	
	d	15 53						16 17	16 32					16 38		16 47		16 53						17 17	
Waterbeach	d							16 26																17 26	
Cambridge North	d					16 14		16 31					16 44	16 51		17 02							17 14	17 31	
Cambridge	a	16 08				16 20		16 37					16 50	16 59		17 06		17 09					17 20	17 37	
Stansted Airport ✈	a	16 40																17 40							
Ipswich	a		16 37						17 28	17 07			18d14						17 37		18 07				
London Kings Cross ■ ⊖	a							17 33					18 20			18 03								18 33	
London Liverpool Street ■ ⊖	a					17 44																	18 45		

				TL ■	LE ■	GN	GN	EM ◇	XC ◇■	TL ■		GN		EM ◇	LE ■	TL ■		GN		TL ■	LE ■	EM ◇		XC ◇■	GN
Norwich	d				16 38			16 57													17 35	17 54			
Wymondham	d				16 50			17 09													17 47	18 06			
Spooner Row	d				16x54																				
Attleborough	d				16 59																17 54	18 13			
Eccles Road	d																				17 59				
Harling Road	d																				18 03				
Thetford	d				17 13			17 27													18 13	18 27			
Brandon	d				17 21																18 21				
Lakenheath	d																								
Shippea Hill	d																								
Peterborough ■	d								17 18	17 24				17 44	17 50	17 54		18 32						18 18	
Whittlesea	d								17 26						17 58										
March	d								17 37						18 09									18 34	
Manea	d								17 45						18 17										
Kings Lynn	d						17 16					17 44													
Watlington	d											17 51													
Downham Market	d						17 29					17 58													
Littleport	d											18 08													
Ely ■	a				17 38		17 45	17 48	17 58			18 16		18 19	18 31						18 37	18 48		18 52	
	d				17 38	17 47	17 50		17 59			18 17			18 32						18 38			18 52	18 57
Waterbeach	d						17 59					18 27													
Cambridge North	d			17 44	17 51	17 59						18 32								18 50	18 54				19 09
Cambridge	a			17 50	17 59	18 04	18 07		18 16			18 36								18 55	19 00			19 08	19 13
Stansted Airport ✈	a								18 54															19 40	
Ipswich	a			19d14						18 36					19 28	19 07				20d16					
London Kings Cross ■ ⊖	a			19 20			19 04					19 35						19 50		20 25					20 12
London Liverpool Street ■ ⊖	a																								

		TL ■		LE ◇■	GN	EM ◇	TL ■	XC ◇■			GN		TL ■	LE ■	GN	EM ◇	XC ◇■	TL ■		EM ◇	GN	LE ◇■	GN	LE ■	TL ■
Norwich	d													18 40		18 57									
Wymondham	d													18 52											
Spooner Row	d																								
Attleborough	d													18 59											
Eccles Road	d																								
Harling Road	d																								
Thetford	d													19 13		19 24									
Brandon	d													19 21											
Lakenheath	d																								
Shippea Hill	d																								
Peterborough ■	d	18 24				18 45	18 52	18 59			19 42						19 19	19 24		19 42	20 19			19 50	19 54
Whittlesea	d																							19 58	
March	d					19 00		19 15									19 35							20 09	
Manea	d																							20 17	
Kings Lynn	d				18 44																		19 44		
Watlington	d				18 51																		19 51		
Downham Market	d				18 58																		19 58		
Littleport	d				19 08																		20 08		
Ely ■	a				19 16	19 19		19 33						19 37		19 48	19 53			20 15			20 18	20 31	
	d				19 17			19 34						19 38	19 47		19 53						20 18	20 32	
Waterbeach	d				19 26																		20 28		
Cambridge North	d			19 14	19 31								19 48	19 52	20 01							20 11	20 33		
Cambridge	a			19 19	19 36			19 50					19 55	20 01	20 06		20 09					20 16	20 38		
Stansted Airport ✈	a																20 39								
Ipswich	a	19 37					20 05						21d14					20 36						21 28	21 07
London Kings Cross ■ ⊖	a				20 33						20 47		21 20		21 02						21 23		21 33		
London Liverpool Street ■ ⊖	a			20 45																		21 44			

Table T017-R

Mondays to Fridays
21 May to 7 December

Norwich, Peterborough, Kings Lynn and Ely - Cambridge and London

		TL	LE	GN	XC	TL	TL	LE	GN	GN	TL	GN	XC	TL	EM	LE	LE
		■			◇■	■	■	◇■			■		◇■	■	◇	◇■	■
Norwich	d		19 35														21 15
Wymondham	d		19 48														21 27
Spooner Row	d																
Attleborough	d		19 55														21 34
Eccles Road	d																
Harling Road	d																
Thetford	d		20 10														21 48
Brandon	d		20 18														21 56
Lakenheath	d																
Shippea Hill	d																
Peterborough ■	d				20 19	20 24	20 54			21 41			21 16	21 24	21 39		
Whittlesea	d																
March	d				20 35								21 32				
Manea	d																
Kings Lynn	d								20 44								
Watlington	d								20 51								
Downham Market	d								20 59								
Littleport	d								21 08								
Ely ■	a		20 36		20 53				21 16				21 50		22 13		22 13
	d		20 37	20 47	20 53				21 17			21 47	21 52				22 13
Waterbeach	d								21 26								
Cambridge North	d	20 44	20 49	20 59				21 15	21 31		21 44	22 00				22 14	22 26
Cambridge	a	20 50	20 57	21 06	21 09			21 20	21 36		21 50	22 05	22 06			22 20	22 32
Stansted Airport ✈	a				21 40								22 52				
Ipswich	a	22d14				21 36	22 06				23d14			22 36			
London Kings Cross ■ ⊖	a	22 20		22 03					22 32	22 46	23 20	23 03					
London Liverpool Street ■ ⊖	a							22 45								23 48	

		GN	LE	TL	TL	TL	GN	XC	GN	LE	TL	TL
			■	■	■	■		◇■		■	■	■
Norwich	d									22 40		
Wymondham	d									22 52		
Spooner Row	d											
Attleborough	d									22 59		
Eccles Road	d											
Harling Road	d											
Thetford	d									23 13		
Brandon	d									23 21		
Lakenheath	d											
Shippea Hill	d											
Peterborough ■	d		21 45	21 54	22 24			22 18			22 54	23 20
Whittlesea	d		21 53									
March	d		22 04					22 36				
Manea	d		22 12									
Kings Lynn	d	21 44							22 44			
Watlington	d	21 51							22 51			
Downham Market	d	21 58							22 58			
Littleport	d	22 08							23 08			
Ely ■	a	22 16	22 25					22 54	23 16	23 38		
	d	22 17	22 26				22 46	22 54	23 17	23 38		
Waterbeach	d	22 26							23 26			
Cambridge North	d	22 31				22 44	23 02		23 31	23 51		
Cambridge	a	22 36				22 50	23 07	23 10	23 37	23 59		
Stansted Airport ✈	a											
Ipswich	a		23 21	23 06	23d37	00d15					00d10	00d39
London Kings Cross ■ ⊖	a	23 34			23 43	00 21	00 08				00 18	00 45
London Liverpool Street ■ ⊖	a											

Table T017-R

Saturdays
26 May to 8 December

Norwich, Peterborough, Kings Lynn and Ely - Cambridge and London

		TL	TL	TL	TL	TL	TL	GN	TL	TL	GN	TL	GR	LE	GN	TL	LE	EM	GN	EM	TL
		■	■	■	■	■	■		■	■		■	■	◇■		■	■	◇		◇	■
Norwich	d																05 37	05 50			
Wymondham	d																05 49	06 02			
Spooner Row	d																				
Attleborough	d																05 56	06 09			
Eccles Road	d																				
Harling Road	d																				
Thetford	d																06 10	06 23			
Brandon	d																06 18				
Lakenheath	d																				
Shippea Hill	d																				
Peterborough ■	d				03 24	04 18	04 54		05 24	05 54		06 24	06 39							06 27	06 54
Whittlesea	d																				
March	d																			06 43	
Manea	d																				
Kings Lynn	d														05 44						
Watlington	d														05 51						
Downham Market	d														05 58						
Littleport	d														06 08						
Ely ■	a														06 16		06 35	06 44		07 03	
	d							05 17			05 47				06 17		06 35		06 47		
Waterbeach	d							05 27							06 27						
Cambridge North	d							05 32			06 01			06 14	06 32	06 44	06 48		07 01		
Cambridge	a							05 37			06 06			06 20	06 37	06 50	06 56		07 06		
Stansted Airport ✈	a																				
Ipswich	a	00d10	00d15	00d39	04d45	05 34	06 06		06 36	07 06		07 36				08d14					08 07
London Kings Cross ■ ⊖	a	00 18	00 21	00 45	04 51			06 33			07 03		07 28		07 33	08 20			08 03		
London Liverpool Street ■ ⊖	a													07 44							

		LE	GN	TL	LE	EM	GN	XC	TL	EM	GN	LE	GN	LE	TL
		◇■		■	■	◇		◇■	■	◇		◇■		■	■
Norwich	d				06 40	06 53									
Wymondham	d				06 52										
Spooner Row	d														
Attleborough	d				06 59										
Eccles Road	d														
Harling Road	d														
Thetford	d				07 13	07 22									
Brandon	d				07 21										
Lakenheath	d														
Shippea Hill	d														
Peterborough ■	d							07 13	07 24	07 35	08 04			07 50	07 54
Whittlesea	d							07 21						07 58	
March	d							07 32		07 53				08 09	
Manea	d							07 39						08 17	
Kings Lynn	d		06 44										07 44		
Watlington	d		06 51										07 51		
Downham Market	d		06 58										07 58		
Littleport	d		07 08										08 08		
Ely ■	a		07 16		07 38	07 45		07 53		08 13			08 16	08 31	
	d		07 17		07 38		07 47	07 53					08 17	08 32	
Waterbeach	d		07 27										08 27		
Cambridge North	d	07 14	07 32	07 44	07 51		08 01					08 14	08 32		
Cambridge	a	07 20	07 36	07 50	07 59		08 06	08 09				08 20	08 37		
Stansted Airport ✈	a							08 39							
Ipswich	a			09d14					08 37					09 28	09 07
London Kings Cross ■ ⊖	a		08 33	09 20			09 03				09 16		09 33		
London Liverpool Street ■ ⊖	a	08 44										09 44			

		TL	LE	EM	GN	XC	TL	TL	GN	LE	GN	EM	TL	LE	GN	EM	XC	TL	GN	LE
		■	■	◇		◇■	■	■		◇■		◇	■	■		◇	◇■	■		◇■
Norwich	d		07 40	07 57										08 40		08 57				
Wymondham	d		07 52											08 52						
Spooner Row	d																			
Attleborough	d		07 59											08 59						
Eccles Road	d																			
Harling Road	d																			
Thetford	d		08 13	08 24										09 13		09 24				
Brandon	d		08 21											09 21						
Lakenheath	d																			
Shippea Hill	d																			
Peterborough ■	d					08 19	08 24	08 54	09 04			09 00					09 18	09 24	10 04	
Whittlesea	d																			
March	d					08 35											09 34			
Manea	d																			
Kings Lynn	d										08 44				09 13					
Watlington	d										08 51									
Downham Market	d										08 58				09 25					
Littleport	d										09 08									
Ely ■	a		08 38	08 45		08 53					09 16	09 34		09 38	09 42	09 45	09 53			
	d		08 38		08 47	08 53					09 17			09 38	09 47		09 55			
Waterbeach	d										09 27									
Cambridge North	d	08 44	08 51		09 01					09 14	09 32		09 44	09 51	10 01					10 14
Cambridge	a	08 50	08 59		09 06	09 09				09 20	09 37		09 50	09 59	10 05		10 11			10 20
Stansted Airport ✈	a					09 40											10 40			
Ipswich	a	10d14					09 37	10 07					11d14					10 37		
London Kings Cross ■ ⊖	a	10 20			10 03				10 16		10 35		11 20		11 04				11 13	

Table T017-R

Saturdays

26 May to 8 December

Norwich, Peterborough, Kings Lynn and Ely - Cambridge and London

		GN	GN	EM	LE	TL	TL	LE	GN	EM	XC	TL	LE	GN	EM	TL	GN
				◇	■	■	■	■		◇	◇■	■	◇■		◇	■	
Norwich	d							09 38		09 57							
Wymondham	d							09 50									
Spooner Row	d																
Attleborough	d							09 57									
Eccles Road	d																
Harling Road	d																
Thetford	d							10 11		10 24							
Brandon	d							10 19									
Lakenheath	d							10x24									
Shippea Hill	d																
Peterborough ■	d			09 45	09 50	09 54					10 18	10 24			10 40	10 53	
Whittlesea	d				09 58												
March	d				10 09						10 34						
Manea	d				10 17												
Kings Lynn	d		09 44						10 13								10 44
Watlington	d		09 51														10 51
Downham Market	d		09 58						10 25								10 58
Littleport	d		10 08														11 08
Ely ■	a		10 16	10 19	10 31			10 38	10 42	10 45	10 51				11 13		11 16
	d	10 12	10 17		10 32			10 38	10 47		10 52			11 12			11 17
Waterbeach	d		10 27														11 27
Cambridge North	d	10 24	10 32				10 44	10 51	11 02				11 14	11 24			11 32
Cambridge	a	10 30	10 37				10 50	10 59	11 06		11 09		11 20	11 30			11 37
Stansted Airport ✈	a										11 40						
Ipswich	a				11 28	11 07	12d14					11 37				12 07	
London Kings Cross ■ ⊖	a		11 33				12 20		12 05								12 34
London Liverpool Street ■ ⊖	a												12 44				

		TL	LE	EM	GN	XC	TL	EM	LE	GN	LE	TL	TL	LE	EM	GN	XC	TL	LE
		■	■	◇		◇■	■	◇	◇■		■	■	■	■	◇		◇■	■	◇■
Norwich	d		10 40	10 57										11 40	11 57				
Wymondham	d		10 52											11 52					
Spooner Row	d																		
Attleborough	d		10 59											11 59					
Eccles Road	d																		
Harling Road	d																		
Thetford	d		11 13	11 24										12 13	12 24				
Brandon	d		11 21											12 21					
Lakenheath	d																		
Shippea Hill	d																		
Peterborough ■	d					11 19	11 24	11 41			11 50	11 54					12 19	12 24	
Whittlesea	d										11 58								
March	d					11 35					12 09						12 35		
Manea	d										12 17								
Kings Lynn	d									11 44									
Watlington	d									11 51									
Downham Market	d									11 58									
Littleport	d									12 08									
Ely ■	a		11 38	11 46		11 52		12 13		12 16	12 31			12 38	12 45		12 53		
	d		11 38		11 47	11 53				12 17	12 32			12 38		12 47	12 53		
Waterbeach	d									12 27									
Cambridge North	d	11 44	11 51		12 01				12 14	12 32			12 44	12 51		13 01			13 14
Cambridge	a	11 50	11 59		12 06	12 09			12 20	12 37			12 50	12 59		13 06	13 09		13 20
Stansted Airport ✈	a					12 40											13 40		
Ipswich	a	13d14					12 36				13 28	13 07	14d14					13 37	
London Kings Cross ■ ⊖	a	13 20			13 03					13 33			14 20			14 03			
London Liverpool Street ■ ⊖	a								13 44										14 44

		GN	EM	TL	TL	LE	EM	GN	XC	TL	EM	LE	GN	LE	TL	TL	LE	EM
			◇	■	■	■	◇		◇■	■	◇	◇■		■	■	■	■	◇
Norwich	d					12 40	12 57										13 40	13 57
Wymondham	d					12 52											13 52	
Spooner Row	d																	
Attleborough	d					12 59											13 59	
Eccles Road	d																	
Harling Road	d																	
Thetford	d					13 13	13 24										14 13	14 24
Brandon	d					13 21											14 21	
Lakenheath	d																	
Shippea Hill	d																	
Peterborough ■	d		12 44	12 54					13 19	13 24	13 40			13 50	13 54			
Whittlesea	d													13 58				
March	d								13 35					14 09				
Manea	d													14 17				
Kings Lynn	d	12 44											13 44					
Watlington	d	12 51											13 51					
Downham Market	d	12 58											13 58					
Littleport	d	13 08											14 08					
Ely ■	a	13 16	13 19			13 38	13 45		13 53		14 13		14 16	14 31			14 38	14 45
	d	13 17				13 38		13 47	13 53				14 17	14 32			14 38	
Waterbeach	d	13 27											14 27					
Cambridge North	d	13 32			13 44	13 51		14 01				14 14	14 32			14 44	14 51	
Cambridge	a	13 37			13 50	13 59		14 06	14 09			14 20	14 37			14 50	14 59	
Stansted Airport ✈	a								14 40									
Ipswich	a			14 06	15d14					14 37				15 28	15 06	16d14		
London Kings Cross ■ ⊖	a	14 33			15 20			15 03					15 33			16 20		
London Liverpool Street ■ ⊖	a											15 44						

Table T017-R

Saturdays

26 May to 8 December

Norwich, Peterborough, Kings Lynn and Ely - Cambridge and London

		GN	XC	TL	EM	TL	LE	GN	TL	LE	EM	GN	XC	TL	LE	GN	EM	LE
			◇■	■	◇	■	◇■		■	■	◇		◇■	■	◇■		◇	■
Norwich	d									14 40	14 57							
Wymondham	d									14 52								
Spooner Row	d																	
Attleborough	d									14 59								
Eccles Road	d																	
Harling Road	d																	
Thetford	d									15 13	15 24							
Brandon	d									15 21								
Lakenheath	d																	
Shippea Hill	d																	
Peterborough ■	d		14 19	14 24	14 41	14 54							15 19	15 24			15 45	15 50
Whittlesea	d																	15 58
March	d		14 35										15 35					16 09
Manea	d																	16 17
Kings Lynn	d							14 44								15 44		
Watlington	d							14 51								15 51		
Downham Market	d							14 58								15 58		
Littleport	d							15 08								16 08		
Ely ■	a		14 53		15 14			15 17		15 38	15 45		15 53			16 16	16 19	16 31
	d	14 47	14 53					15 17		15 38		15 47	15 53			16 17		16 32
Waterbeach	d							15 27								16 27		
Cambridge North	d	15 01					15 14	15 32	15 44	15 51		16 01			16 14	16 32		
Cambridge	a	15 06	15 09				15 20	15 37	15 50	15 59		16 06	16 09		16 20	16 37		
Stansted Airport ✈	a		15 40										16 40					
Ipswich	a			15 37		16 07			17d14					16 36				17 28
London Kings Cross ■ ⊖	a	16 03						16 35	17 20			17 04				17 33		
London Liverpool Street ■ ⊖	a						16 44								17 44			

		TL	TL	LE	EM	GN	XC	TL	EM	TL	LE	GN	TL	LE	EM	GN	XC	TL
		■	■	■	◇		◇■	■	◇	■	◇■		■	■	◇		◇■ 🚲	■
Norwich	d			15 35	15 52									16 38	16 54			
Wymondham	d			15 47										16 50	17 06			
Spooner Row	d													16x54				
Attleborough	d			15 54	16 09									16 59				
Eccles Road	d			15 59														
Harling Road	d			16 03														
Thetford	d			16 13	16 23									17 13	17 24			
Brandon	d			16 21										17 21				
Lakenheath	d																	
Shippea Hill	d																	
Peterborough ■	d	15 54					16 19	16 24	16 39	16 54							17 18	17 24
Whittlesea	d																17 26	
March	d						16 35										17 37	
Manea	d																17 45	
Kings Lynn	d											16 44						
Watlington	d											16 51						
Downham Market	d											16 58						
Littleport	d											17 08						
Ely ■	a			16 38	16 45		16 53		17 13			17 16		17 38	17 45		17 58	
	d			16 38		16 47	16 53					17 17		17 38		17 47	18 00	
Waterbeach	d											17 27						
Cambridge North	d		16 44	16 51		17 01					17 14	17 32	17 44	17 51		18 01		
Cambridge	a		16 50	16 59		17 06	17 09				17 20	17 37	17 50	17 59		18 06	18 15	
Stansted Airport ✈	a						17 40										18 53	
Ipswich	a	17 06	18d14					17 37		18 07			19d14					18 36
London Kings Cross ■ ⊖	a		18 20			18 03						18 34	19 20			19 03		
London Liverpool Street ■ ⊖	a										18 44							

		EM	LE	GN	LE	TL	TL	LE	EM	GN	XC	TL	LE	GN	EM	TL	TL
		◇	◇■		■	■	■	■	◇		◇■	■	◇■		◇	■	■
Norwich	d							17 35	17 50								
Wymondham	d							17 47	18 02								
Spooner Row	d																
Attleborough	d							17 54	18 09								
Eccles Road	d							17 59									
Harling Road	d							18 03									
Thetford	d							18 13	18 23								
Brandon	d							18 21									
Lakenheath	d																
Shippea Hill	d																
Peterborough ■	d	17 40			17 50	17 56					18 19	18 24			18 44	18 54	
Whittlesea	d				17 58												
March	d				18 09						18 35				19 01		
Manea	d				18 17												
Kings Lynn	d			17 44										18 44			
Watlington	d			17 51										18 51			
Downham Market	d			17 58										18 58			
Littleport	d			18 08										19 08			
Ely ■	a	18 13		18 16	18 31			18 38	18 45		18 53			19 16	19 19		
	d			18 17	18 32			18 38		18 47	18 53			19 17			
Waterbeach	d			18 27										19 27			
Cambridge North	d		18 14	18 32			18 44	18 51		19 01			19 14	19 32			19 44
Cambridge	a		18 20	18 37			18 50	18 59		19 06	19 09		19 20	19 37			19 50
Stansted Airport ✈	a										19 40						
Ipswich	a				19 28	19 07	20d14					19 36				20 06	21d14
London Kings Cross ■ ⊖	a			19 35			20 20			20 03				20 33			21 20
London Liverpool Street ■ ⊖	a		19 44										20 44				

Table T017-R

Saturdays
26 May to 8 December

Norwich, Peterborough, Kings Lynn and Ely - Cambridge and London

		LE	EM	GN	XC	TL	EM		LE	GN		LE	TL			TL	LE	GN	XC	TL		TL		LE	GN
		1	◇		◇1	1	◇		◇1			1	1			1	1		◇1	1		1		◇1	
Norwich	d	18 38	18 57														19 40								
Wymondham	d	18 50															19 52								
Spooner Row	d																								
Attleborough	d	18 57															19 59								
Eccles Road	d																								
Harling Road	d																								
Thetford	d	19 11	19 24														20 13								
Brandon	d	19 19															20 21								
Lakenheath	d																								
Shippea Hill	d	19x27																							
Peterborough 8	d				19 19	19 24	19 41					19 50	19 54						20 19	20 24		20 54			
Whittlesea	d											19 58													
March	d				19 35							20 09							20 35						
Manea	d											20 17													
Kings Lynn	d									19 44															20 44
Watlington	d									19 51															20 51
Downham Market	d									19 58															20 58
Littleport	d									20 08															21 08
Ely 8	a	19 38	19 45		19 53		20 14			20 17		20 32					20 38		20 53						21 16
	d	19 38		19 47	19 54					20 17		20 32					20 38	20 47	20 53						21 17
Waterbeach	d									20 27															21 27
Cambridge North	d	19 51		20 01					20 14	20 32						20 44	20 51	21 01						21 14	21 32
Cambridge	a	19 59		20 06	20 09				20 20	20 37						20 50	20 59	21 06	21 09					21 20	21 37
Stansted Airport ✈	a				20 40														21 40						
Ipswich	a					20 36						21 28	21 07			22d14				21 36		22 06			
London Kings Cross 15 ⊖	a			21 03						21 33						22 20		22 03							22 33
London Liverpool Street 15 ⊖	a								21 44															22 44	

			TL	GN	XC	TL		LE	LE	EM	GN	LE	TL	TL	TL	XC		GN	TL	GN	LE	TL			
			1		◇1	1		◇1	1	◇		1	1	1	1	◇1			1		1	1			
Norwich	d								21 10												22 40				
Wymondham	d								21 22												22 52				
Spooner Row	d																								
Attleborough	d								21 29												22 59				
Eccles Road	d																								
Harling Road	d																								
Thetford	d								21 43												23 13				
Brandon	d								21 51												23 21				
Lakenheath	d																								
Shippea Hill	d																								
Peterborough 8	d				21 19	21 24				21 40		21 45	21 54	22 24		22 14			22 54			23 20			
Whittlesea	d											21 53													
March	d				21 35							22 04				22 29									
Manea	d											22 12													
Kings Lynn	d										21 44									22 57					
Watlington	d										21 51									23 04					
Downham Market	d										21 58									23 11					
Littleport	d										22 08									23 20					
Ely 8	a				21 53				22 10	22 13	22 16	22 25				22 47				23 28	23 38				
	d			21 47	21 53				22 10		22 17	22 26				22 48		22 51		23 29	23 38				
Waterbeach	d										22 27									23 38					
Cambridge North	d		21 44	22 01				22 14	22 23		22 32				22 44			23 04		23 43	23 51				
Cambridge	a		21 50	22 06	22 09			22 20	22 31		22 37				22 50	23 03		23 08		23 47	23 59				
Stansted Airport ✈	a				22 40																				
Ipswich	a		23d14			22 36						23 22	23 06	23d37	00d16				00d12			00d39			
London Kings Cross 15 ⊖	a		23 20	23 03							23 33			23 43	00 24			00 08	00 21			00 45			
London Liverpool Street 15 ⊖	a							23 44																	

Table T017-R

Sundays
20 May to 2 December

Norwich, Peterborough, Kings Lynn and Ely - Cambridge and London

		TL	TL	TL	GN	GN		TL	TL		GN	GN		TL		LE			GN	LE	LE	EM	GN		TL
		1	1	1	1	1		1	1		1	1		1		◇1			1	1	1	◇	1		1
					A	A															A	A			
Norwich	d																			09 03		09 47			
Wymondham	d																			09 15					
Spooner Row	d																								
Attleborough	d																			09 22					
Eccles Road	d																								
Harling Road	d																								
Thetford	d																			09 36		10 15			
Brandon	d																			09 44					
Lakenheath	d																			09x49					
Shippea Hill	d																								
Peterborough 8	d				05 45	06 42		07 45	08 45			09 15		09 45							09 50		10 15		10 45
Whittlesea	d																				09 58				
March	d																				10 09				
Manea	d																								
Kings Lynn	d										08 26								09 26						
Watlington	d										08 33								09 33						
Downham Market	d										08 40								09 40						
Littleport	d										08 49								09 49						
Ely 8	a										08 57								09 57	10 03	10 31	10 37			
	d										08 57								09 57	10 03	10 32				
Waterbeach	d										09 07								10 07						
Cambridge North	d										09 12					09 44			10 12	10 16					
Cambridge	a										09 16					09 49			10 16	10 22					
Stansted Airport ✈	a																								
Ipswich	a	00d12	00d16	00d39	07d14	08d00		08d56	09 56					10 56							11 28				11 56
London Kings Cross 15 ⊖	a	00 21	00 24	00 45	07 23	08 09		09 02			10 10	10 17							11 10				11 17		
London Liverpool Street 15 ⊖	a															11 14									

					LE	GN	LE	EM	EM	GN		TL				LE	GN	LE	LE		TL			LE	GN
					◇1	1	1	◇	◇	1		1				◇1	1	1	1		1			◇1	1
									A																
Norwich	d						10 03	10 47										11 03							
Wymondham	d						10 15											11 15							
Spooner Row	d																								
Attleborough	d						10 22											11 22							
Eccles Road	d																								
Harling Road	d																								
Thetford	d						10 36	11 14										11 36							
Brandon	d						10 44											11 44							
Lakenheath	d																	11x49							
Shippea Hill	d																								
Peterborough 8	d								11 09	11 15		11 45							11 50		12 45				
Whittlesea	d																		11 58						
March	d								11 25										12 09						
Manea	d																								
Kings Lynn	d					10 26											11 26								12 26
Watlington	d					10 33											11 33								12 33
Downham Market	d					10 40											11 40								12 40
Littleport	d					10 49											11 49								12 49
Ely 8	a					10 57	11 01	11 35	11 43								11 57	12 03	12 31						12 57
	d					10 57	11 03										11 57	12 03	12 32						12 57
Waterbeach	d					11 07											12 07								13 07
Cambridge North	d				10 44	11 12	11 16									11 44	12 12	12 16						12 44	13 12
Cambridge	a				10 49	11 16	11 22									11 49	12 16	12 22						12 49	13 16
Stansted Airport ✈	a																								
Ipswich	a											12 56							13 28		13 56				
London Kings Cross 15 ⊖	a					12 10				12 17							13 10								14 10
London Liverpool Street 15 ⊖	a				12 14											13 14								14 14	

A until 9 September

Table T017-R

Sundays
20 May to 2 December

Norwich, Peterborough, Kings Lynn and Ely - Cambridge and London

		LE	EM	LE	XC	GN	LE	EM	TL	LE	EM	LE	XC	TL	GN	LE	EM	EM
		■	◇ A	◇■	◇■	■	■	◇	■	■	◇	◇■	◇■	■	■	■	◇	◇
Norwich	d	12 03					13 03				13 47					14 03		14 53
Wymondham	d	12 15					13 15									14 15		
Spooner Row	d																	
Attleborough	d	12 22					13 22									14 22		
Eccles Road	d																	
Harling Road	d																	
Thetford	d	12 36					13 36				14 14					14 36		15 20
Brandon	d	12 44					13 44									14 44		
Lakenheath	d																	
Shippea Hill	d																	
Peterborough ■	d		12 56		13 18			13 43	13 45	13 50			14 18	14 45			14 58	
Whittlesea	d									13 58								
March	d				13 34					14 09			14 34					
Manea	d																	
Kings Lynn	d					13 26									14 26			
Watlington	d					13 33									14 33			
Downham Market	d					13 40									14 40			
Littleport	d					13 49									14 49			
Ely ■	a	13 01	13 31		13 51	13 57	14 01	14 16		14 31	14 35		14 52		14 57	15 01	15 31	15 41
	d	13 03			13 52	13 57	14 03			14 32			14 52		14 57	15 03		
Waterbeach	d					14 07									15 07			
Cambridge North	d	13 16		13 44		14 12	14 16					14 44			15 12	15 16		
Cambridge	a	13 22		13 49	14 08	14 16	14 22					14 49	15 08		15 16	15 22		
Stansted Airport ✈	a				14 45								15 45					
Ipswich	a								14 56	15 28				15 56				
London Kings Cross ■ ⊖	a					15 10									16 10			
London Liverpool Street ■ ⊖	a			15 14								16 14						

		LE	XC	TL	GN	LE	LE	EM	LE	XC	TL	EM	GN	LE	EM	EM	LE
		◇■	◇■	■	■	■	■	◇	◇■	◇■	■	◇	■	■	◇	◇	◇■
Norwich	d					15 03						15 54		16 03		16 54	
Wymondham	d					15 15								16 15			
Spooner Row	d																
Attleborough	d					15 22								16 22			
Eccles Road	d																
Harling Road	d																
Thetford	d					15 36						16 21		16 36		17 21	
Brandon	d					15 44								16 44			
Lakenheath	d					15x49											
Shippea Hill	d																
Peterborough ■	d		15 18	15 45			15 47	15 58		16 18	16 45	17a12			16 59		
Whittlesea	d						15 55										
March	d		15 34				16 06			16 34							
Manea	d																
Kings Lynn	d				15 26								16 26				
Watlington	d				15 33								16 33				
Downham Market	d				15 40								16 40				
Littleport	d				15 49								16 49				
Ely ■	a		15 52		15 57	16 03	16 25	16 31		16 52			16 57	17 01	17 32	17 44	
	d		15 52		15 57	16 03	16 29			16 52			16 57	17 03			
Waterbeach	d				16 07								17 07				
Cambridge North	d	15 44			16 12	16 16			16 44				17 12	17 16			17 44
Cambridge	a	15 49	16 08		16 16	16 22			16 49	17 08			17 16	17 22			17 49
Stansted Airport ✈	a		16 45							17 45							
Ipswich	a			16 56			17 25				17 56						
London Kings Cross ■ ⊖	a				17 11								18 10				
London Liverpool Street ■ ⊖	a	17 14							18 14								19 14

A until 9 September

Table T017-R

Sundays
20 May to 2 December

Norwich, Peterborough, Kings Lynn and Ely - Cambridge and London

		XC	TL	GN	LE	LE	GN	LE	EM	EM	LE	XC	TL	GN	LE	EM	EM
		◇■	■	■	■	■	■	■	◇	◇	◇■	◇■	■	■	■	◇	◇
Norwich	d				17 03					17 54					18 03		18 56
Wymondham	d				17 15										18 15		
Spooner Row	d																
Attleborough	d				17 22										18 22		
Eccles Road	d																
Harling Road	d																
Thetford	d				17 36					18 21					18 36		19 23
Brandon	d				17 44										18 44		
Lakenheath	d																
Shippea Hill	d																
Peterborough ■	d	17 18	17 45			17 45			17 57			18 18	18 45			18 49	
Whittlesea	d					17 53											
March	d	17 34				18 04			18 13			18 34					
Manea	d																
Kings Lynn	d			17 26			17 54							18 26			
Watlington	d			17 33			18 01							18 33			
Downham Market	d			17 40			18 08							18 40			
Littleport	d			17 49			18 17	←						18 49			
Ely ■	a	17 52		17 57	18 01	18 23	18 25	18 23	18 31	18 43		18 52		18 57	19 01	19 22	19 45
	d	17 52		17 57	18 03	18 29	18 26	18 29				18 52		18 57	19 03		
Waterbeach	d			18 07		→								19 07			
Cambridge North	d			18 12	18 16		18 38				18 44			19 12	19 16		
Cambridge	a	18 08		18 16	18 22		18 42				18 49	19 08		19 16	19 22		
Stansted Airport ✈	a	18 45										19 45					
Ipswich	a		18 56					19 25					19 55				
London Kings Cross ■ ⊖	a			19 13			19 36							20 10			
London Liverpool Street ■ ⊖	a										20 14						

		LE	XC	TL	GN	LE	EM	LE	XC	TL	GN	LE	EM	LE	XC	TL
		◇■	◇■	■	■	■	◇	◇■	◇■	■	■	■	◇	■	◇■	■
Norwich	d											20 03	20 52			
Wymondham	d											20 15				
Spooner Row	d															
Attleborough	d											20 22				
Eccles Road	d															
Harling Road	d															
Thetford	d											20 36	21 19			
Brandon	d											20 44				
Lakenheath	d															
Shippea Hill	d															
Peterborough ■	d		19 18	19 45		19 47	19 57		20 18	20 45					21 18	21 45
Whittlesea	d					19 55										
March	d		19 34			20 06			20 34						21 34	
Manea	d															
Kings Lynn	d				19 26						20 26					
Watlington	d				19 33						20 33					
Downham Market	d				19 40						20 40					
Littleport	d				19 49						20 49					
Ely ■	a		19 52		19 57	20 25	20 32		20 52		20 57	21 01	21 40		21 52	
	d		19 52		19 57	20 28			20 52		20 57	21 03			21 52	
Waterbeach	d				20 07						21 07					
Cambridge North	d	19 44			20 12			20 44			21 12	21 16		21 44		
Cambridge	a	19 49	20 07		20 16			20 49	21 07		21 16	21 22		21 49	22 07	
Stansted Airport ✈	a		20 45						21 45						22 45	
Ipswich	a			20 56		21 25				21 57						22d57
London Kings Cross ■ ⊖	a				21 10						22 10			23 00		23 03
London Liverpool Street ■ ⊖	a	21 14						22 14								

		GN	EM	LE	XC	TL	GN	LE
		■	◇	■	◇■	■	■	■
Norwich	d							22 03
Wymondham	d							22 15
Spooner Row	d							
Attleborough	d							22 22
Eccles Road	d							
Harling Road	d							
Thetford	d							22 36
Brandon	d							22 44
Lakenheath	d							
Shippea Hill	d							
Peterborough ■	d		21 54		22 16	22 45		
Whittlesea	d							
March	d				22 32			
Manea	d							
Kings Lynn	d	21 26					22 26	
Watlington	d	21 33					22 33	
Downham Market	d	21 40					22 40	
Littleport	d	21 49					22 49	
Ely ■	a	21 57	22 27		22 51		22 57	23 01
	d	21 57			22 51		22 57	23 03
Waterbeach	d	22 07					23 07	
Cambridge North	d	22 12		22 44			23 12	23 16
Cambridge	a	22 16		22 49	23 06		23 16	23 22
Stansted Airport ✈	a							
Ipswich	a					23d57	00d40	
London Kings Cross ■ ⊖	a	23 13				00 03	00 49	
London Liverpool Street ■ ⊖	a							

Table T018-F

Mondays to Fridays
21 May to 7 December

Peterborough - Sleaford, Lincoln and Doncaster

Miles	Miles			EM A	NT	NT B	EM C	EM	EM	NT B	EM	NT B	EM	NT B	EM	NT B	EM	EM	NT B	EM	NT B	EM	NT B
0	—	**Peterborough 8**	d	06 30				07 30					08 33		09 35			10 40		11 50		12 41	
16½	—	Spalding	d	06a53				07a51					08 54		09 56			11 01		12 13		13 02	
35½	—	Sleaford	a										09 18		10 20			11 25		12 38		13 26	
—	—		d				06 53		07 43		08 40		09 18		10 21			11 25		12 42		13 26	
40	—	Ruskington	d				07 02		07 51		08 49		09 28		10 29			11 34		12 50		13 35	
47½	—	Metheringham	d				07 12		08 01		08 59		09 37		10 38			11 43		12 59		13 44	
56¾	—	**Lincoln**	a				07 26		08 15		09 13		09 53		10 53			11 57		13 14		14 03	
—	—		d		07 02	07 22				08 22	09 15	09 19		10 20		11 20	11 54		12 20	13 15	13 20		14 20
62¾	—	Saxilby	d		07 10	07 31				08 32	09 23	09 29		10 29		11 29	12 02		12 30	13 23	13 30		14 29
72¼	0	Gainsborough Lea Road	d		07 23	07 44				08 44	09 35	09 41		10 42		11 42	12 15		12 42	13 35	13 42		14 41
—	32¾	Sheffield 7	d		08a20	08a41				09a42		10a38		11a42		12a42			13a42		14a42		15a42
93½	51½	**Doncaster 7**	a								10 02						12 45			14 04			

		EM	NT B	NT B	EM ◇	NT B	EM	NT B	EM	EM	EM	NT B	EM	NT	EM	NT	EM	NT
Peterborough 8	d	13 41			15 11		16 25		17 32		18 36						20 30	
Spalding	d	14 04			15 32		16 46		17a55		18a59						20a51	
Sleaford	a	14 29			15 56		17 15											
	d	14 29			16 14		17 16			17 56			19 00		20 05			
Ruskington	d	14 37			16 22		17 24			18 04			19 08		20 13			
Metheringham	d	14 46			16 32		17 34			18 14			19 17		20 22			
Lincoln	a	15 00			16 45		17 48			18 29			19 32		20 39			
	d		15 20	16 20		17 22		18 22		18 31		19 23	19 32	20 19		21 29		22 42
Saxilby	d		15 30	16 29		17 31		18 31		18 39		19 32	19 40	20 28		21 37		22 50
Gainsborough Lea Road	d		15 42	16 42		17 44		18 44		18 55		19 45	19 51	20 40		21 50		23 05
Sheffield 7	d		16a42	17a42		18a41		19a41				20a41		21a38		22a48		00a03
Doncaster 7	a									19 25			20 21					

Saturdays
26 May to 8 December

		EM A	NT	EM C	NT B	EM	EM	NT B	EM	NT B	EM	NT B	EM	NT B	EM	NT B	EM	NT B	EM	EM	NT B	EM	NT B
Peterborough 8	d	06 30				07 30					08 33		09 32				11 52		12 42				
Spalding	d	06a52				07a52					08 54		09 53				12 13		13 03				
Sleaford	a										09 17		10 20				12 39		13 27				
	d			06 50			07 43				09 19		10 20				12 41		13 27				
Ruskington	d			06 59			07 51				09 28		10 28				12 49		13 36				
Metheringham	d			07 09			08 01				09 37		10 37				12 58		13 46				
Lincoln	a			07 22			08 15				09 56		10 53				13 14		14 03				
	d		06 42		07 22			08 22	09 15	09 19		10 20		11 20	11 54	12 20		13 20		14 10	14 20	15 10	15 20
Saxilby	d		06 50		07 31			08 32	09 23	09 29		10 29		11 29	12 02	12 30		13 30		14 18	14 29	15 18	15 30
Gainsborough Lea Road	d		07 03		07 44			08 44	09 35	09 41		10 42		11 42	12 15	12 42		13 42		14 30	14 41	15 30	15 42
Sheffield 7	d		08a00		08a41			09a42		10a38		11a42		12a42		13a42		14a42			15a42		16a42
Doncaster 7	a								10 05						12 43					14 58		16 00	

		NT B	EM ◇	NT B	EM	NT B	EM	EM	NT B	EM	EM	NT	EM	NT	EM	NT
Peterborough 8	d		15 11		16 25		17 32			18 36					20 30	
Spalding	d		15 32		16 47		17a55			18a58					20a52	
Sleaford	a		16 00		17 17											
	d		16 14		17 19			17 54			19 00		20 10			
Ruskington	d		16 22		17 27			18 02			19 08		20 18			
Metheringham	d		16 32		17 37			18 12			19 17		20 27			
Lincoln	a		16 47		17 51			18 27			19 32		20 44			
	d	16 20		17 22		18 22			19 23		19 32	20 19		21 29		22 44
Saxilby	d	16 29		17 31		18 31			19 32		19 40	20 28		21 37		22 52
Gainsborough Lea Road	d	16 42		17 44		18 44			19 45		19 52	20 40		21 50		23 05
Sheffield 7	d	17a42		18a41		19a41			20a41			21a38		22a48		00a03
Doncaster 7	a										20 21					

Sundays
20 May to 2 December

		NT D	NT D	NT D	NT D	NT D	NT	NT	NT	NT	NT	NT	NT	NT
Peterborough 8	d													
Spalding	d													
Sleaford	a													
	d													
Ruskington	d													
Metheringham	d													
Lincoln	a													
	d	10 14	11 14	12 14	13 14	14 14	15 12	16 09	17 14	18 21	19 20	20 17	21 20	21 51
Saxilby	d	10 23	11 23	12 23	13 23	14 23	15 21	16 19	17 23	18 30	19 29	20 26	21 29	22 00
Gainsborough Lea Road	d	10 35	11 35	12 35	13 35	14 35	15 33	16 32	17 35	18 42	19 41	20 39	21 41	22 12
Sheffield 7	d	11a34	12a34	13a34	14a36	15a36	16a33	17a32	18a36	19a37	20a41	21a34	22a42	23a12
Doncaster 7	a													

A From Nottingham
B To Leeds
C To Leicester
D To Huddersfield

For connections from London Kings Cross refer to Table T025

Table T018-R

Mondays to Fridays
21 May to 7 December

Doncaster, Lincoln and Sleaford - Peterborough

Miles	Miles			EM	EM	EM	NT	EM	EM A	NT	NT B	EM	NT B	EM	NT B	EM	EM	NT B	EM	NT B	EM C	EM	NT B
0	0	**Doncaster 7**	d							06 03							10 24					13 01	
—	18¾	Sheffield 7	d				05 45			06 38	07 39		08 38		09 38			10 39		11 37			12 38
21¼	51½	Gainsborough Lea Road	d				06 39			07 36	08 34		09 32		10 35		10 53	11 34		12 32		13 29	13 34
30¾	—	Saxilby	d				06 51			07 50	08 46		09 44		10 47		11 04	11 46		12 43		13 42	13 49
36¾	—	**Lincoln**	a				07 07			08 05	08 56		09 56		10 59		11 16	11 58		12 55		13 53	14 01
—	—		d	06 17		07 05			08 00			09 11		10 18		11 10			12 10		13 30		
46¼	—	Metheringham	d			07 18			08 12			09 23		10 31		11 23			12 22		13 43		
53½	—	Ruskington	d			07 27			08 21			09 32		10 41		11 32			12 31		13 52		
58	—	Sleaford	a	06 46		07 37			08 31			09 42		10 50		11 42			12 41		14 02		
—	—		d						08 34			09 43		10 51		11 42			12 42		14 03		
77	—	Spalding	d		07 00			08 00	09 00			10 07		11 13		12 04			13 07		14 25		
93½	—	**Peterborough 8**	a		07 22			08 20	09 23			10 31		11 34		12 26			13 28		14 46		

		EM	NT B	EM	EM	EM ◇ C	NT B	NT B	EM D	EM E	NT B	EM	NT B	EM	EM	NT B	EM	EM F	NT	EM	EM	NT	EM G
Doncaster 7	d				14 27												19 39				20 36		
Sheffield 7	d		13 37				14 38	15 38			16 38		17 37			18 42			19 48			20 59	
Gainsborough Lea Road	d		14 32		14 52		15 36	16 35			17 32		18 39			19 41	20 02		20 47		21 00	21 55	
Saxilby	d		14 43		15 05		15 48	16 47			17 44		18 53			19 55	20 14		20 58		21 12	22 06	
Lincoln	a		14 55		15 15		16 00	16 59			17 56		19 05			20 07	20 24		21 10		21 25	22 17	
	d	14 41		15 12		16 00			17 18	17 18		18 10		19 15				20 48					
Metheringham	d	14 54		15 25		16 13			17 32	17 32		18 23		19 28				21 01					
Ruskington	d	15 03		15 34		16 22			17 42	17 42		18 32		19 37				21 10					
Sleaford	a	15 13		15 44		16 33			17 51	17 53		18 42		19 47				21 19					
	d	15 16				16 34																	
Spalding	d	15 38				16 56									18 08					19 59			21 05
Peterborough 8	a	15 59				17 18									18 28					20 22			21 27

Saturdays
26 May to 8 December

		EM	EM	NT	EM	EM A	NT	NT B	NT B	EM	NT B	EM	EM	NT B	NT B	EM C	EM	NT B	EM	NT B	EM	NT B	EM ◇ C
Doncaster 7	d						06 02						10 24				13 05				15 07		
Sheffield 7	d			05 45			06 38	07 39	08 38		09 38			10 39	11 37			12 38		13 37		14 38	
Gainsborough Lea Road	d			06 39			07 36	08 34	09 32		10 35		10 48	11 34	12 32		13 29	13 34		14 32	15 31	15 36	
Saxilby	d			06 51			07 47	08 46	09 44		10 47		10 59	11 46	12 43		13 42	13 49		14 43	15 43	15 48	
Lincoln	a			07 07			08 02	08 56	09 56		10 59		11 10	11 58	12 55		13 54	14 01		14 55	15 58	16 00	
	d		07 05			08 01				10 18		11 10				13 33			14 41				16 01
Metheringham	d		07 18			08 14				10 31		11 23				13 46			14 54				16 14
Ruskington	d		07 27			08 23				10 41		11 32				13 55			15 03				16 23
Sleaford	a		07 37			08 32				10 50		11 42				14 05			15 13				16 34
	d					08 35				10 51		11 42				14 06			15 16				16 34
Spalding	d	07 00			08 05	09 00				11 19		12 04				14 29			15 38				16 57
Peterborough 8	a	07 22			08 27	09 24				11 43		12 28				14 51			16 02				17 23

		NT B	EM	EM	NT B	EM	NT B	EM	EM	NT B	EM F	NT	EM	EM	NT	EM G
Doncaster 7	d			16 27										20 33		
Sheffield 7	d	15 38			16 38		17 37			18 42		19 48			20 59	
Gainsborough Lea Road	d	16 35		16 52	17 32		18 39			19 41		20 47		20 56	21 55	
Saxilby	d	16 47		17 03	17 44		18 53			19 55		20 58		21 09	22 06	
Lincoln	a	16 59		17 19	17 56		19 05			20 07		21 10		21 24	22 17	
	d		17 15			18 10		19 05			20 49					
Metheringham	d		17 28			18 23		19 18			21 02					
Ruskington	d		17 37			18 32		19 27			21 11					
Sleaford	a		17 47			18 42		19 37			21 20					
	d															
Spalding	d								18 08				19 59			21 03
Peterborough 8	a								18 31				20 22			21 25

Sundays
20 May to 2 December

		NT	NT	NT	NT	NT H	NT H	NT H	NT H	NT H	NT H	NT	NT	NT	NT
Doncaster 7	d														
Sheffield 7	d	08 45	09 41	10 41	11 41	12 44	13 36	14 41	15 41	16 37	17 35	18 43	19 24	20 24	21 24
Gainsborough Lea Road	d	09 33	10 36	11 32	12 36	13 35	14 31	15 32	16 32	17 33	18 27	19 39	20 15	21 19	22 20
Saxilby	d	09 45	10 48	11 44	12 48	13 47	14 43	15 44	16 44	17 46	18 40	19 51	20 27	21 31	22 32
Lincoln	a	09 57	11 00	11 56	13 00	13 58	14 55	15 57	16 57	17 58	18 52	20 07	20 39	21 44	22 45
	d														
Metheringham	d														
Ruskington	d														
Sleaford	a														
	d														
Spalding	d														
Peterborough 8	a														

A From Nottingham
B From Leeds
C From Newark North Gate
D until 21 September. From Leicester
E from 24 September. From Leicester
F To Boston
G To Nottingham
H From Huddersfield

For connections to London Kings Cross refer to Table T025

Table T019-F

Nottingham and Grantham - Skegness

Mondays to Fridays
21 May to 7 December

Miles	Miles			EM A	EM	EM	EM	EM	EM ◇ B	EM ◇ C	EM	EM ◇ D	EM	EM ◇ D	EM	EM ◇ D	EM	EM ◇ D	EM	EM ◇ D	EM	EM ◇ D	EM
0	—	**Nottingham 8**	d	05 07		05 50	06 41	07 35	07 52	08 35	08 45	09 34	09 55	10 34	10 45	11 34	11 45	12 34	12 45	13 34	13 45	14 34	14 45
4½	—	Netherfield	d								08 51												
5	—	Radcliffe (Notts)	d				06 51				08 56								12 55				14 55
8½	—	Bingham	d	05 21		06 04	06 57	07 49			09 02		10 09		10 59		11 59		13 01		13 59		15 01
10¾	—	Aslockton	d	05 25				07 53			09 06				11 03						14 03		
14½	—	Elton & Orston	d																				
15	0	Bottesford	d	05 32		06 13	07 05	07 59			09 12				11 10				13 09				15 09
22¼	—	**Grantham 7**	a	05 46		06 27	07 19	08 12	08 23	09 06	09 26	10 06		11 07	11 23	12 10	12 19	13 07	13 23	14 05	14 23	15 07	15 22
—	—		d			06 31	07 23	08 16			09 32				11 27		12 25		13 27		14 27		15 26
34	12¾	Ancaster	d					08 34											13 45				
37¾	—	Rauceby	d				07 46	08 40															
40	—	**Sleaford**	d			06 57	07 51	08 45			10 03		10 44		11 53		12 50		13 55		14 52		15 52
44½	—	Heckington	d			07 04	07 58	08 52			10 10		10 51		12 00		12 57		14 02		14 59		15 59
49½	—	Swineshead	d				08 04																16 05
52¾	—	Hubberts Bridge	d				08 09																16 10
56½	—	**Boston**	d		06 25	07 25	08 18	09 12			10 26		11 11		12 19		13 15		14 21		15 17		16 20
73¾	—	Thorpe Culvert	d			07 47																	
75¾	—	Wainfleet	d		06 49	07 51	08 43	09 36			10 50		11 35		12 44		13 40		14 47		15 42		16 45
77	—	Havenhouse	d			07 55																	
80¾	—	**Skegness**	a		07 03	08 05	08 56	09 49			11 02		11 50		12 58		13 54		15 00		15 56		16 59

		EM ◇ D	EM	EM ◇ D	EM	EM ◇ D	EM	EM ◇ D	EM	EM ◇ D	EM E	EM
Nottingham 8	d	15 34	15 45	16 35	16 45	17 34	17 44	18 37	18 44	20 34		20 51
Netherfield	d		15 51		16 51		17 50					
Radcliffe (Notts)	d		15 56		16 56		17 55					21 01
Bingham	d		16 02		17 02	17 48	18 01		18 58			21 07
Aslockton	d		16 06		17 06	17 52	18 05		19 03			21 11
Elton & Orston	d				17 10							
Bottesford	d		16 12		17 14		18 12		19 10			21 17
Grantham 7	a	16 08	16 25	17 06	17 28	18 09	18 25	19 07	19 23	21 07		21 32
	d		16 29		17 32		18 29		19 26			21 38
Ancaster	d				17 50				19 44			
Rauceby	d				17 56				19 50			
Sleaford	d		16 55		18 01		18 55		19 55		21 20	22 03
Heckington	d		17 02		18 08		19 02		20 02		21 28	22 10
Swineshead	d											
Hubberts Bridge	d											
Boston	d		17 21		18 26		19 21		20 19		21a53	22a29
Thorpe Culvert	d		17 43									
Wainfleet	d		17 48		18 51		19 46		20 44			
Havenhouse	d		17 51									
Skegness	a		18 00		19 05		19 59		20 57			

Saturdays
26 May to 8 December

		EM A	EM	EM	EM	EM	EM ◇ C	EM F	EM ◇ C	EM	EM ◇ D	EM	EM G	EM ◇ D	EM	EM ◇ D	EM	EM ◇ D	EM	EM ◇ D	EM	EM ◇ D	EM
Nottingham 8	d	05 07		05 50	06 41	07 31	07 45	08 24	08 35	08 40	09 34	09 55	09 43	10 34	10 45	11 34	11 45	12 34	12 45	13 34	13 45	14 34	14 45
Netherfield	d									08 48													
Radcliffe (Notts)	d									08 52									12 55				
Bingham	d	05 21		06 04	06 55	07 45				08 58		10 09			10 59		11 59		13 01		13 59		14 59
Aslockton	d	05 25				07 49				09 02					11 03						14 03		
Elton & Orston	d																						
Bottesford	d	05 32		06 13	07 04	07 56				09 09					11 09				13 09				15 08
Grantham 7	a	05 46		06 27	07 18	08 09	08 15		09 06	09 23	10 06		10 15	11 05	11 23	12 05	12 19	13 06	13 25	14 05	14 23	15 07	15 22
	d			06 31	07 24	08 17				09 30			10 21		11 27		12 25		13 29		14 27		15 26
Ancaster	d					08 35																	
Rauceby	d					08 41																	
Sleaford	d			06 57	07 51	08 46		09 17		09 56		10 44	10 57		11 53		12 50		13 55		14 52		15 52
Heckington	d			07 04	07 58	08 53				10 03		10 51			12 00		12 57		14 02		14 59		15 59
Swineshead	d				08 04																		16 05
Hubberts Bridge	d				08 09																		16 10
Boston	d		06 25	07 25	08 18	09 12		09 50		10 22		11 11	11 27		12 19		13 15		14 21		15 17		16 20
Thorpe Culvert	d			07 47																			
Wainfleet	d		06 49	07 51	08 43	09 36				10 47		11 35			12 44		13 40		14 46		15 42		16 45
Havenhouse	d			07 55																			
Skegness	a		07 03	08 05	08 56	09 48		10 31		11 00		11 50	12 07		12 58		13 54		15 00		15 56		16 59

A To Spalding
B From Mansfield Woodhouse to Norwich
C To Norwich
D From Liverpool Lime Street to Norwich
E From Lincoln
F from 21 July until 8 September. From Derby
G from 21 July until 8 September

For connections from London Kings Cross refer to Table T026

Table T019-F

Nottingham and Grantham - Skegness

Saturdays
26 May to 8 December

		EM ◇ A	EM	EM ◇ A	EM	EM ◇ A	EM	EM ◇ A	EM	EM ◇ A	EM B	EM
Nottingham 8	d	15 34	15 45	16 34	16 45	17 34	17 44	18 37	18 45	20 34		20 51
Netherfield	d		15 51		16 51		17 50					
Radcliffe (Notts)	d		15 56		16 56		17 55					21 01
Bingham	d		16 02		17 02	17 48	18 01		18 59			21 07
Aslockton	d		16 06		17 06	17 52	18 05		19 03			21 11
Elton & Orston	d				17 10							
Bottesford	d		16 12		17 14		18 12		19 10			21 17
Grantham 7	a	16 06	16 25	17 04	17 28	18 09	18 25	19 08	19 23	21 06		21 31
	d		16 29		17 32		18 29		19 26			21 36
Ancaster	d				17 50				19 44			
Rauceby	d				17 56				19 50			
Sleaford	d		16 55		18 01		18 55		19 55		21 21	22 01
Heckington	d		17 02		18 08		19 02		20 02		21 29	22 08
Swineshead	d											
Hubberts Bridge	d											
Boston	d		17 21		18 26		19 21		20 19		21a53	22a29
Thorpe Culvert	d		17 43									
Wainfleet	d		17 48		18 51		19 46		20 43			
Havenhouse	d		17 51									
Skegness	a		18 00		19 05		19 59		20 57			

Sundays
20 May to 9 September

		EM	EM ◇	EM	EM C	EM ◇ D	EM	EM	EM ◇ E	EM	EM ◇ D	EM ◇ E	EM	EM ◇ F	EM	EM ◇ A	EM	EM ◇ A	EM ◇ A	EM	EM ◇ A	EM	EM ◇ A
Nottingham 8	d	08 15		09 00	09 41	09 52	10 00	11 09	11 39	11 57	12 40	13 47	13 57	14 45	14 56	15 50	16 23	16 45	17 36	18 16	18 46	19 48	20 45
Netherfield	d																16 29		17 42				
Radcliffe (Notts)	d																16 34		17 46				
Bingham	d	08 29		09 14	09 55		10 14	11 23		12 11	12 54		14 11		15 10		16 40		17 52	18 30	19 00	20 02	20 59
Aslockton	d																16 44		17 56				
Elton & Orston	d																						
Bottesford	d																16 50		18 03				
Grantham 7	a	08 49			10 15	10 27	10 35	11 44	12 13	12 29	13 13	14 20	14 31	15 16	15 31	16 20	17 03	17 15	18 16	18 50	19 21	20 22	21 18
	d				10 20			11 50		12 33			14 35		15 36		17 07			18 54		20 27	
Ancaster	d																						
Rauceby	d																						
Sleaford	d			09 49	10 46			12 15		12 59			15 08		16 02		17 36			19 20		20 53	
Heckington	d			09 56	10 53			12 22		13 06			15 15		16 09		17 43			19 27		21 00	
Swineshead	d																						
Hubberts Bridge	d																						
Boston	d		09 31	10 16	11 11			12 41		13 24			15 32		16 29		18 02			19 50		21a17	
Thorpe Culvert	d																						
Wainfleet	d		09 55	10 40	11 36			13 06		13 49			15 57		16 53		18 27			20 14			
Havenhouse	d																						
Skegness	a		10 08	10 54	11 50			13 20		14 00			16 11		17 08		18 38			20 26			

Sundays
16 September to 2 December

		EM	EM	EM	EM	EM ◇	EM ◇ D	EM ◇	EM ◇ E	EM ◇ F	EM	EM ◇ A	EM	EM ◇ A	EM ◇ A	EM	EM ◇ A	EM ◇ A
Nottingham 8	d	08 15	09 15	10 00	11 15	11 57	12 40		13 47	14 45	14 56	15 50	16 23	16 45	17 36	18 31	18 46	20 45
Netherfield	d												16 29		17 42			
Radcliffe (Notts)	d												16 34		17 46			
Bingham	d	08 29	09 29	10 14	11 29	12 11	12 54				15 10		16 40		17 52	18 45	19 00	20 59
Aslockton	d												16 44		17 56			
Elton & Orston	d																	
Bottesford	d												16 50		18 03			
Grantham 7	a	08 49	09 50	10 35	11 50	12 29	13 13		14 20	15 16	15 31	16 20	17 03	17 15	18 16	19 08	19 21	21 18
	d					12 33		13 50			15 36		17 07			19 13		
Ancaster	d																	
Rauceby	d																	
Sleaford	d					12 59		14 16			16 02		17 36			19 41		
Heckington	d					13 06		14 23			16 09		17 43			19 48		
Swineshead	d																	
Hubberts Bridge	d																	
Boston	d					13 24		14 45			16 29		18 02			20a10		
Thorpe Culvert	d																	
Wainfleet	d					13 49		15 09			16 53		18 27					
Havenhouse	d																	
Skegness	a					14 00		15 24			17 08		18 38					

A From Liverpool Lime Street to Norwich
B From Lincoln
C From Mansfield Woodhouse
D To Norwich
E From Sheffield to Norwich
F From Manchester Piccadilly to Norwich

For connections from London Kings Cross refer to Table T026

Table T019-R

Skegness - Grantham and Nottingham

Mondays to Fridays

21 May to 7 December

Miles	Miles			EM ◇	EM ◇	EM ◇ A	EM ◇	EM ◇ A	EM ◇	EM ◇ A	EM ◇	EM ◇ B	EM ◇
0	—	**Skegness**	d				07 09		08 10		09 06		10 15
3¼	—	Havenhouse	d				07 15						
5	—	Wainfleet	d				07 19		08 18		09 14		10 23
7	—	Thorpe Culvert	d				07 23						
23¾	—	**Boston**	d		06 13		07 46		08 45		09 41		10 50
27½	—	Hubberts Bridge	d				07 52						
30¾	—	Swineshead	d				07 57						
35¾	—	Heckington	d		06 27		08 02		08 59		09 55		11 04
40¼	—	**Sleaford**	d		06 35		08 11		09 07		10 03		11 12
42½	—	Rauceby	d		06 39		08 15						
46¼	0	Ancaster	d		06 45		08 21						11 21
57¾	—	**Grantham** 7	a		07 04		08 42		09 39		10 31		11 41
—	—		d	06 10	07 10	07 58	08 45	08 56	09 45	09 58	10 36	11 00	11 45
65¾	12¾	Bottesford	d	06 21	07 21	08 11			09 56				11 56
67¾	—	Elton & Orston	d	06 25									
69½	—	Aslockton	d	06 29	07 27	08 18	09 00				10 52		
71¾	—	Bingham	d	06 33	07 31	08 22	09 05		10 04		10 57		12 04
75¼	—	Radcliffe (Notts)	d	06 39	07 37	08 28			10 09				12 09
77	—	Netherfield	d		07 42	08 33							
80¼	—	**Nottingham** 8	a	06 54	07 53	08 40	09 20	09 27	10 21	10 35	11 14	11 34	12 22

		EM ◇ A	EM ◇	EM ◇ A	EM ◇	EM ◇ A	EM ◇	EM ◇ A	EM ◇	EM ◇ A	EM ◇
Skegness	d		11 15		12 15		13 15		14 15		15 09
Havenhouse	d										
Wainfleet	d		11 23		12 23		13 23		14 23		15 17
Thorpe Culvert	d										
Boston	d		11 50		12 50		13 50		14 50		15 44
Hubberts Bridge	d										15 50
Swineshead	d										15 55
Heckington	d		12 04		13 04		14 04		15 04		16 01
Sleaford	d		12 12		13 13		14 13		15 12		16 10
Rauceby	d										16 14
Ancaster	d										16 20
Grantham 7	a		12 41		13 42		14 42		15 41		16 41
	d	12 02	12 45	12 59	13 48	13 58	14 45	14 58	15 45	16 01	16 45
Bottesford	d				13 56				15 56		
Elton & Orston	d										
Aslockton	d		13 00				15 00		16 02		
Bingham	d		13 04		14 07		15 05		16 07		17 02
Radcliffe (Notts)	d						15 10				
Netherfield	d										
Nottingham 8	a	12 35	13 23	13 36	14 22	14 35	15 23	15 34	16 25	16 35	17 20

		EM ◇ A	EM ◇	EM ◇ A	EM ◇	EM ◇ C	EM ◇ D	EM ◇	EM ◇ E	EM ◇	EM ◇ E	EM ◇ F	EM ◇ G	EM ◇
Skegness	d		16 11		17 30			18 14		19 14		20 15	20 15	21 02
Havenhouse	d		16 17											
Wainfleet	d		16 21		17 38			18 22		19 22		20 23	20 23	21 10
Thorpe Culvert	d		16 25											
Boston	d		16 48		18 05			18 48		19 49		20 50	20 50	21 37
Hubberts Bridge	d													
Swineshead	d													
Heckington	d		17 04		18 19			19 04		20 05		21 04	21 04	21 51
Sleaford	d		17 13		18 27			19 13		20 13		21 18	21 18	22 00
Rauceby	d													
Ancaster	d													
Grantham 7	a		17 42					19 41		20 40		21 45	21 45	
	d	16 58	17 45	17 57		18 55	18 57	19 45	19 59	20 44	21 00	21 49	21 49	
Bottesford	d		17 56					19 56				22 00	22 00	
Elton & Orston	d													
Aslockton	d		18 02					20 02				22 06	22 06	
Bingham	d		18 07		19 03	19 12	19 17	20 06		21 01		22 10	22 10	22 35
Radcliffe (Notts)	d							20 12		21 07				
Netherfield	d							20 16						
Nottingham 8	a	17 35	18 22	18 35	19 21	19 28	19 35	20 25	20 31	21 20	21 36	22 26	22 29	22 53

Saturdays

26 May to 8 December

		EM	EM	EM ◇ A	EM ◇	EM ◇ A	EM ◇	EM ◇ A	EM ◇	EM ◇ A
Skegness	d				07 09		08 15		09 15	
Havenhouse	d				07 15					
Wainfleet	d				07 19		08 23		09 23	
Thorpe Culvert	d				07 23					
Boston	d		06 13		07 46		08 50		09 50	
Hubberts Bridge	d				07 52					
Swineshead	d				07 57					
Heckington	d		06 27		08 02		09 04		10 05	
Sleaford	d		06 35		08 11		09 12		10 14	
Rauceby	d		06 39		08 15					
Ancaster	d		06 45		08 21					
Grantham 7	a		07 07		08 42		09 41		10 43	
	d	06 10	07 10	07 58	08 45	08 59	09 45	09 56	10 46	10 55
Bottesford	d	06 21	07 21	08 11			09 56			
Elton & Orston	d	06 25								
Aslockton	d	06 29	07 27	08 17	09 00				11 01	
Bingham	d	06 33	07 32	08 22	09 05		10 04		11 06	
Radcliffe (Notts)	d	06 39	07 37	08 27						
Netherfield	d		07 42	08 32						
Nottingham 8	a	06 54	07 52	08 39	09 20	09 35	10 21	10 35	11 23	11 36

		EM ◇	EM ◇ A	EM ◇	EM ◇ A	EM H	EM ◇	EM ◇ A	EM I	EM ◇	EM ◇ A	EM ◇	EM ◇ A	EM ◇
Skegness	d	10 15		11 15		11 40	12 15		12 35	13 15		14 15		15 09
Havenhouse	d													
Wainfleet	d	10 23		11 23			12 23			13 23		14 23		15 17
Thorpe Culvert	d													
Boston	d	10 50		11 50		12 25	12 50		13 15	13 50		14 50		15 44
Hubberts Bridge	d													15 50
Swineshead	d													15 55
Heckington	d	11 04		12 04			13 04			14 04		15 04		16 01
Sleaford	d	11 12		12 12		12 47	13 12		13 39	14 13		15 12		16 10
Rauceby	d													16 14
Ancaster	d	11 21												16 20
Grantham 7	a	11 41		12 41			13 41			14 42		15 41		16 41
	d	11 45	11 56	12 45	12 57		13 46	13 58		14 45	14 59	15 45	15 57	16 45
Bottesford	d	11 56					13 56					15 56		
Elton & Orston	d													
Aslockton	d			13 00						15 00				
Bingham	d	12 04		13 04			14 05			15 05		16 04		17 02
Radcliffe (Notts)	d	12 09												
Netherfield	d													
Nottingham 8	a	12 22	12 35	13 23	13 35	13 44	14 24	14 33	14 38	15 23	15 35	16 22	16 35	17 20

A From Norwich to Liverpool Lime Street
B until 31 August, from 8 October. From Norwich to Liverpool Lime Street
C from 23 July until 5 October. From Norwich to Manchester Piccadilly
D until 20 July, from 8 October. From Norwich to Manchester Piccadilly
E From Norwich
F until 5 October
G from 8 October
H from 21 July until 8 September. To Derby
I from 21 July until 8 September

For connections to London Kings Cross refer to Table T026

Table T019-R

Skegness - Grantham and Nottingham

Saturdays

26 May to 8 December

		EM ◇ A	EM ◇	EM ◇ A	EM ◇	EM ◇ B	EM ◇	EM ◇ C	EM ◇	EM ◇ C	EM ◇	EM D	EM ◇
Skegness	d		16 11		17 24		18 14		19 19		20 15		21 02
Havenhouse	d		16 17										
Wainfleet	d		16 21		17 32		18 22		19 27		20 23		21 10
Thorpe Culvert	d		16 25										
Boston	d		16 48		17 59		18 49		19 54		20 50		21 37
Hubberts Bridge	d												
Swineshead	d												
Heckington	d		17 04		18 13		19 04		20 10		21 04		21 51
Sleaford	d		17 13		18 21		19 13		20 18		21 12		22 00
Rauceby	d												
Ancaster	d												
Grantham 7	a		17 42				19 41		20 45		21 43		
	d	16 58	17 45	17 59		18 58	19 45	20 03	20 48	20 58	21 47	22 02	
Bottesford	d		17 56				19 56				21 58		
Elton & Orston	d												
Aslockton	d		18 02				20 02				22 04		
Bingham	d		18 07		19 00	19 15	20 06		21 05		22 08		22 35
Radcliffe (Notts)	d						20 12						
Netherfield	d						20 16						
Nottingham 8	a	17 35	18 22	18 34	19 22	19 31	20 24	20 36	21 25	21 32	22 25	22 32	22 54

Sundays

20 May to 9 September

		EM	EM	EM	EM ◇	EM ◇ A	EM	EM ◇ A	EM	EM ◇ E
Skegness	d				10 14		11 15		12 27	
Havenhouse	d									
Wainfleet	d				10 22		11 23		12 35	
Thorpe Culvert	d									
Boston	d		09 06		10 49		11 49		13 02	
Hubberts Bridge	d									
Swineshead	d									
Heckington	d		09 20		11 03		12 03		13 16	
Sleaford	d		09 28		11 11		12 11		13 24	
Rauceby	d									
Ancaster	d									
Grantham 7	a		09 57		11 40		12 41			
	d	09 00	10 01	10 45	11 46	11 56	12 45	12 52		15 09
Bottesford	d				11 57			13 03		
Elton & Orston	d									
Aslockton	d				12 03			13 09		
Bingham	d	09 17	10 18	11 02	12 07		13 02	13 13	14 00	
Radcliffe (Notts)	d				12 13			13 19		
Netherfield	d				12 18			13 23		
Nottingham 8	a	09 33	10 38	11 20	12 26	12 30	13 21	13 30	14 16	15 39

		EM ◇	EM ◇ A	EM ◇	EM ◇ A	EM	EM ◇ B	EM ◇ B	EM F	EM ◇ C	EM ◇	EM ◇ C	EM	EM ◇ C
Skegness	d	14 10		15 15		16 22			18 07		19 15		20 43	
Havenhouse	d													
Wainfleet	d	14 18		15 23		16 30			18 15		19 23		20 51	
Thorpe Culvert	d													
Boston	d	14 45		15 52		16 57			18 42		19 50		21 18	
Hubberts Bridge	d													
Swineshead	d													
Heckington	d	14 59		16 12		17 11			18 56		20 04		21 32	
Sleaford	d	15 07		16 20		17 19			19 04		20 12		21 42	
Rauceby	d													
Ancaster	d													
Grantham 7	a	15 35		16 46					19 33		20 41		22 10	
	d	15 40	15 55	16 50	16 56		17 55	18 58	19 37	19 57	20 45	21 02	22 13	22 55
Bottesford	d													
Elton & Orston	d													
Aslockton	d													
Bingham	d	15 57		17 07		17 55	18 12		19 54		21 02		22 30	
Radcliffe (Notts)	d													
Netherfield	d													
Nottingham 8	a	16 17	16 24	17 22	17 31	18 11	18 27	19 33	20 12	20 31	21 20	21 34	22 49	23 28

Sundays

16 September to 2 December

		EM	EM	EM G	EM	EM ◇ A	EM	EM ◇ E	EM ◇	EM ◇ A
Skegness	d								14 10	
Havenhouse	d									
Wainfleet	d								14 18	
Thorpe Culvert	d									
Boston	d						12 13		14 45	
Hubberts Bridge	d									
Swineshead	d									
Heckington	d						12 27		14 59	
Sleaford	d						12 35		15 07	
Rauceby	d									
Ancaster	d									
Grantham 7	a						13 04		15 35	
	d	09 00	10 01	10 45	12 01	12 52		15 09	15 40	15 55
Bottesford	d					13 03				
Elton & Orston	d									
Aslockton	d					13 09				
Bingham	d	09 17	10 18	11 02	12 18	13 13			15 57	
Radcliffe (Notts)	d					13 19				
Netherfield	d					13 23				
Nottingham 8	a	09 33	10 37	11 19	12 36	13 30		15 39	16 17	16 24

		EM ◇ A	EM	EM ◇ B	EM ◇ B	EM	EM ◇ C	EM ◇	EM ◇ C	EM ◇ C
Skegness	d		16 10			18 07		19 15		
Havenhouse	d									
Wainfleet	d		16 18			18 15		19 23		
Thorpe Culvert	d									
Boston	d		16 45			18 42		19 50		
Hubberts Bridge	d									
Swineshead	d									
Heckington	d		16 59			18 56		20 04		
Sleaford	d		17 07			19 04		20 12		
Rauceby	d									
Ancaster	d									
Grantham 7	a		17 41			19 33		20 41		
	d	16 56	17 45	17 55	18 58	19 37	19 57	20 45	21 02	22 55
Bottesford	d									
Elton & Orston	d									
Aslockton	d									
Bingham	d		18 02	18 12		19 54		21 02		
Radcliffe (Notts)	d									
Netherfield	d									
Nottingham 8	a	17 31	18 20	18 27	19 33	20 12	20 31	21 20	21 34	23 28

A From Norwich to Liverpool Lime Street
B From Norwich to Manchester Piccadilly
C From Norwich
D From Spalding
E From Peterborough to Liverpool Lime Street
F To Mansfield Woodhouse
G To Derby

For connections to London Kings Cross refer to Table T026

Table T020-F

London - Chingford

Mondays to Fridays
21 May to 7 December

Miles			LO MO	LO MX	LO MO	LO MX	LO MO	LO WO	LO TTh FO	LO MX	LO MO	LO MX	LO	LO	LO	LO	LO	LO	LO	LO	LO	LO	LO
0	**London Liverpool Street** 15 ⊖	d	00 03	00 03	00 18	00 18	00 33	00 33	00 33	00 48	01 03	01 03	06 03	06 33	06 48	07 03	07 18	07 33	07 48	08 05	08 18	08 35	08 48
1¼	Bethnal Green	d	00 06	00 06	00 21	00 21	00 36	00 36	00 37				06 06	06 36	06 51	07 06	07 21	07 36	07 51		08 21		08 51
3	Hackney Downs	d	00 10	00 10	00 25	00 25	00 40	00 40	00 41	00 55	01 10	01 10	06 10	06 40	06 55	07 10	07 25	07 40	07 55	08 12	08 25	08 42	08 55
4	Clapton	d	00 13	00 13	00 28	00 28	00 43	00 43	00 44	00 58	01 13	01 13	06 13	06 43	06 58	07 13	07 28	07 43	07 58	08 15	08 28	08 45	08 58
5¾	St James Street	d	00 16	00 16	00 32	00 32	00 47	00 47	00 48	01 02	01 17	01 17	06 16	06 46	07 01	07 17	07 32	07 47	08 02	08 18	08 31	08 48	09 01
6¼	Walthamstow Central ⊖	d	00 18	00 18	00 34	00 34	00 49	00 49	00 50	01 04	01 19	01 19	06 18	06 48	07 03	07 19	07 34	07 49	08 04	08 20	08 33	08 50	09 03
7	Wood Street	d	00 20	00 20	00 36	00 36	00 51	00 51	00 52	01 06	01 21	01 21	06 20	06 50	07 05	07 21	07 36	07 51	08 06	08 22	08 35	08 52	09 05
8½	Highams Park	d	00 23	00 23	00 39	00 39	00 54	00 54	00 55	01 09	01 24	01 24	06 23	06 53	07 08	07 24	07 39	07 54	08 09	08 25	08 38	08 55	09 08
10½	**Chingford**	a	00 29	00 30	00 44	00 45	00 59	01 00	01 01	01 15	01 29	01 30	06 30	07 00	07 17	07 30	07 45	08 02	08 15	08 32	08 45	09 02	09 17

		LO	LO	LO	LO		LO	LO	LO	LO	LO	LO	LO	LO	LO	LO	LO	LO	LO	LO	LO	LO
London Liverpool Street 15 ⊖	d	09 03	09 18	09 33	09 48	and at the same minutes past each hour until	15 03	15 18	15 33	15 48	16 03	16 18	16 33	16 48	17 03	17 18	17 33	17 48	18 03	18 18	18 33	18 48
Bethnal Green	d	09 06	09 21	09 36	09 51		15 06	15 21	15 36	15 51	16 06	16 21	16 36	16 51		17 21		17 51		18 21		18 51
Hackney Downs	d	09 10	09 25	09 40	09 55		15 10	15 25	15 40	15 55	16 10	16 25	16 40	16 55	17 10	17 25	17 40	17 55	18 10	18 25	18 40	18 55
Clapton	d	09 13	09 28	09 43	09 58		15 13	15 28	15 43	15 58	16 13	16 28	16 43	16 58	17 12	17 28	17 42	17 58	18 12	18 28	18 42	18 58
St James Street	d	09 16	09 31	09 46	10 01		15 16	15 31	15 46	16 01	16 16	16 31	16 46	17 01	17 16	17 31	17 46	18 01	18 16	18 31	18 46	19 01
Walthamstow Central ⊖	d	09 18	09 33	09 48	10 03		15 18	15 33	15 48	16 03	16 19	16 34	16 49	17 04	17 18	17 34	17 48	18 04	18 18	18 34	18 48	19 04
Wood Street	d	09 20	09 35	09 50	10 05		15 20	15 35	15 50	16 05	16 21	16 36	16 51	17 06	17 20	17 36	17 50	18 06	18 20	18 36	18 50	19 06
Highams Park	d	09 23	09 38	09 53	10 08		15 23	15 38	15 53	16 08	16 24	16 39	16 54	17 09	17 23	17 39	17 53	18 09	18 23	18 39	18 53	19 09
Chingford	a	09 30	09 45	10 00	10 15		15 30	15 45	16 00	16 15	16 32	16 47	17 02	17 17	17 32	17 47	18 02	18 17	18 32	18 47	19 02	19 17

		LO	LO	LO	LO	LO		LO	LO	LO	LO	LO	LO	LO
London Liverpool Street 15 ⊖	d	19 03	19 18	19 33	19 48	20 03	and at the same minutes past each hour until	22 18	22 33	22 48	23 03	23 18	23 33	23 48
Bethnal Green	d		19 21	19 36	19 51	20 06		22 21	22 36	22 51	23 06	23 21	23 36	23 51
Hackney Downs	d	19 10	19 25	19 40	19 55	20 10		22 25	22 40	22 55	23 10	23 25	23 40	23 55
Clapton	d	19 12	19 28	19 43	19 58	20 13		22 28	22 43	22 58	23 13	23 28	23 43	23 58
St James Street	d	19 16	19 31	19 46	20 01	20 16		22 31	22 46	23 01	23 16	23 31	23 46	00 01
Walthamstow Central ⊖	d	19 18	19 33	19 48	20 03	20 18		22 33	22 48	23 03	23 18	23 33	23 48	00 03
Wood Street	d	19 20	19 35	19 50	20 05	20 20		22 35	22 50	23 05	23 20	23 35	23 50	00 05
Highams Park	d	19 23	19 38	19 53	20 08	20 23		22 38	22 53	23 08	23 23	23 38	23 53	00 08
Chingford	a	19 30	19 45	20 00	20 15	20 30		22 45	23 00	23 15	23 30	23 45	00 01	00 15

Saturdays
26 May to 8 December

		LO	LO	LO	LO	LO	LO	LO	LO	LO	LO		LO	LO	LO	LO	LO	LO
London Liverpool Street 15 ⊖	d	00 03	00 18	00 33	00 48	01 03	06 03	06 33	06 48	07 03	07 18	and at the same minutes past each hour until	22 33	22 48	23 03	23 18	23 33	23 48
Bethnal Green	d	00 06	00 21	00 37			06 06	06 36	06 51	07 06	07 21		22 36	22 51	23 06	23 21	23 36	23 51
Hackney Downs	d	00 10	00 25	00 41	00 55	01 10	06 10	06 40	06 55	07 10	07 25		22 40	22 55	23 10	23 25	23 40	23 55
Clapton	d	00 13	00 28	00 44	00 58	01 13	06 13	06 43	06 58	07 13	07 28		22 43	22 58	23 13	23 28	23 43	23 58
St James Street	d	00 16	00 32	00 48	01 02	01 17	06 16	06 46	07 01	07 16	07 31		22 46	23 01	23 16	23 31	23 46	00 01
Walthamstow Central ⊖	d	00 18	00 34	00 50	01 04	01 19	06 18	06 48	07 03	07 18	07 33		22 48	23 03	23 18	23 33	23 48	00 03
Wood Street	d	00 20	00 36	00 52	01 06	01 21	06 20	06 50	07 05	07 20	07 35		22 50	23 05	23 20	23 35	23 50	00 05
Highams Park	d	00 23	00 39	00 55	01 09	01 24	06 23	06 53	07 08	07 23	07 38		22 53	23 08	23 23	23 38	23 53	00 08
Chingford	a	00 30	00 45	01 01	01 15	01 30	06 30	07 00	07 15	07 30	07 45		23 00	23 15	23 30	23 45	23 59	00 15

Sundays
20 May to 2 December

		LO	LO	LO	LO	LO	LO	LO	LO	LO	LO	LO	LO	LO	LO	LO		LO	LO	LO	LO	LO
London Liverpool Street 15 ⊖	d	00 03	00 18	00 33	00 48	01 03	07 33	08 03	08 18	08 33	08 48	09 03	09 18	09 33	09 48	10 03	and at the same minutes past each hour until	22 18	22 33	22 48	23 03	23 18
Bethnal Green	d	00 06	00 21	00 36									09 21	09 36	09 51	10 06		22 21	22 36	22 51	23 06	23 21
Hackney Downs	d	00 10	00 25	00 40	00 55	01 10	07 40	08 10	08 25	08 40	08 55	09 10	09 25	09 40	09 55	10 10		22 25	22 40	22 55	23 10	23 25
Clapton	d	00 13	00 28	00 43	00 58	01 13	07 43	08 13	08 28	08 43	08 58	09 13	09 28	09 43	09 58	10 13		22 28	22 43	22 58	23 13	23 28
St James Street	d	00 16	00 32	00 47	01 02	01 17	07 46	08 16	08 31	08 46	09 01	09 16	09 31	09 46	10 01	10 16		22 31	22 46	23 01	23 16	23 31
Walthamstow Central ⊖	d	00 18	00 34	00 49	01 04	01 19	07 48	08 18	08 33	08 48	09 03	09 18	09 33	09 48	10 03	10 18		22 33	22 48	23 03	23 18	23 33
Wood Street	d	00 20	00 36	00 51	01 06	01 21	07 50	08 20	08 35	08 50	09 05	09 20	09 35	09 50	10 05	10 20		22 35	22 50	23 05	23 20	23 35
Highams Park	d	00 23	00 39	00 54	01 09	01 24	07 53	08 23	08 38	08 53	09 08	09 23	09 38	09 53	10 08	10 23		22 38	22 53	23 08	23 23	23 38
Chingford	a	00 30	00 45	01 00	01 15	01 30	07 59	08 29	08 44	08 59	09 14	09 29	09 44	09 59	10 14	10 29		22 44	22 59	23 14	23 29	23 44

		LO	LO
London Liverpool Street 15 ⊖	d	23 33	23 48
Bethnal Green	d	23 36	23 51
Hackney Downs	d	23 40	23 55
Clapton	d	23 43	23 58
St James Street	d	23 46	00 01
Walthamstow Central ⊖	d	23 48	00 03
Wood Street	d	23 50	00 05
Highams Park	d	23 53	00 08
Chingford	a	23 59	00 14

Table T020-R

Chingford - London

Mondays to Fridays
21 May to 7 December

Miles			LO	LO	LO	LO	LO	LO	LO	LO	LO	LO	LO	LO	LO	LO	LO	LO	LO	LO	LO	LO	LO
0	**Chingford**	d	05 10	05 25	05 40	05 55	06 10	06 29	06 44	06 59	07 14	07 29	07 44	07 59	08 14	08 29	08 44	08 57	09 12	09 27	09 40	09 55	10 10
2	Highams Park	d	05 14	05 29	05 44	05 59	06 14	06 33	06 48	07 03	07 18	07 33	07 48	08 03	08 18	08 33	08 48	09 01	09 16	09 31	09 44	09 59	10 14
3½	Wood Street	d	05 17	05 32	05 47	06 02	06 17	06 36	06 51	07 06	07 21	07 36	07 51	08 06	08 21	08 36	08 51	09 04	09 19	09 34	09 47	10 02	10 17
4¼	Walthamstow Central ⊖	d	05 19	05 34	05 49	06 04	06 19	06 39	06 54	07 09	07 24	07 39	07 54	08 09	08 24	08 39	08 54	09 07	09 22	09 37	09 49	10 04	10 19
4¾	St James Street	d	05 21	05 36	05 51	06 06	06 21	06 42	06 56	07 12	07 26	07 42	07 56	08 12	08 26	08 42	08 56	09 10	09 25	09 40	09 51	10 06	10 21
6½	Clapton	d	05 24	05 39	05 54	06 09	06 24	06 45	07 00	07 15	07 30	07 45	08 00	08 15	08 30	08 45	09 00	09 13	09 28	09 43	09 54	10 09	10 24
7½	Hackney Downs	d	05 28	05 43	05 58	06 13	06 28	06 49	07 03	07 18	07 33	07 48	08 03	08 18	08 33	08 48	09 03	09 17	09 32	09 47	09 58	10 13	10 28
9¼	Bethnal Green	d	05 32	05 47	06 02	06 17	06 32	06 53	07 07		07 37		08 07		08 37		09 07	09 21	09 36	09 51	10 02	10 17	10 32
10½	**London Liverpool Street** 15 ⊖	a	05 37	05 52	06 07	06 22	06 37	06 59	07 11	07 26	07 44	07 56	08 14	08 29	08 44	08 59	09 14	09 27	09 42	09 57	10 07	10 22	10 37

		LO	LO	LO	LO MTh FO	LO TWO	LO	LO	LO	LO		LO	LO	LO	LO	LO	LO	LO	LO	LO	LO	LO
Chingford	d	10 25	10 40	10 55	11 10	11 10	11 25	11 40	11 55	12 10	and at the same minutes past each hour until	16 25	16 40	16 55	17 10	17 25	17 39	17 55	18 09	18 25	18 39	18 55
Highams Park	d	10 29	10 44	10 59	11 14	11 14	11 29	11 44	11 59	12 14		16 29	16 44	16 59	17 14	17 29	17 43	17 59	18 13	18 29	18 43	18 59
Wood Street	d	10 32	10 47	11 02	11 17	11 17	11 32	11 47	12 02	12 17		16 32	16 47	17 02	17 17	17 32	17 46	18 02	18 16	18 32	18 46	19 02
Walthamstow Central ⊖	d	10 34	10 49	11 04	11 19	11 19	11 34	11 49	12 04	12 19		16 34	16 49	17 04	17 19	17 34	17 48	18 04	18 18	18 34	18 48	19 04
St James Street	d	10 36	10 51	11 06	11 21	11 21	11 36	11 51	12 06	12 21		16 36	16 51	17 06	17 21	17 36	17 50	18 06	18 20	18 36	18 50	19 06
Clapton	d	10 39	10 54	11 09	11 24	11 25	11 39	11 54	12 09	12 24		16 39	16 54	17 09	17 24	17 39	17 55	18 09	18 24	18 39	18 54	19 09
Hackney Downs	d	10 43	10 58	11 13	11 28	11 28	11 43	11 58	12 13	12 28		16 43	16 58	17 13	17 28	17 43	17 58	18 13	18 27	18 43	18 57	19 13
Bethnal Green	d	10 47	11 02	11 17	11 32	11 32	11 47	12 02	12 17	12 32		16 47	17 02	17 17	17 32	17 47	18 02	18 17	18 31	18 47	19 01	19 17
London Liverpool Street 15 ⊖	a	10 52	11 07	11 22	11 37	11 37	11 52	12 07	12 22	12 37		16 52	17 07	17 22	17 37	17 55	18 06	18 25	18 36	18 52	19 06	19 25

		LO	LO	LO	LO	LO	LO		LO	LO	LO	LO
Chingford	d	19 09	19 25	19 40	19 55	20 10	20 25	and at the same minutes past each hour until	22 40	22 55	23 10	23 25
Highams Park	d	19 13	19 29	19 44	19 59	20 14	20 29		22 44	22 59	23 14	23 29
Wood Street	d	19 16	19 32	19 47	20 02	20 17	20 32		22 47	23 02	23 17	23 32
Walthamstow Central ⊖	d	19 18	19 34	19 49	20 04	20 19	20 34		22 49	23 04	23 19	23 34
St James Street	d	19 20	19 36	19 51	20 06	20 21	20 36		22 51	23 06	23 21	23 36
Clapton	d	19 24	19 39	19 54	20 09	20 24	20 39		22 54	23 09	23 24	23 39
Hackney Downs	d	19 27	19 43	19 58	20 13	20 28	20 43		22 58	23 13	23 28	23 43
Bethnal Green	d	19 31	19 47	20 02	20 17	20 32	20 47		23 02	23 17	23 32	23 47
London Liverpool Street 15 ⊖	a	19 36	19 55	20 07	20 22	20 37	20 52		23 07	23 22	23 37	23 52

Saturdays
26 May to 8 December

		LO	LO	LO	LO		LO	LO	LO	LO	LO	LO
Chingford	d	05 10	05 25	05 40	05 55	and at the same minutes past each hour until	22 10	22 25	22 40	22 55	23 10	23 25
Highams Park	d	05 14	05 29	05 44	05 59		22 14	22 29	22 44	22 59	23 14	23 29
Wood Street	d	05 17	05 32	05 47	06 02		22 17	22 32	22 47	23 02	23 17	23 32
Walthamstow Central ⊖	d	05 19	05 34	05 49	06 04		22 19	22 34	22 49	23 04	23 19	23 34
St James Street	d	05 21	05 36	05 51	06 06		22 21	22 36	22 51	23 06	23 21	23 36
Clapton	d	05 24	05 39	05 54	06 09		22 24	22 39	22 54	23 09	23 24	23 39
Hackney Downs	d	05 28	05 43	05 58	06 13		22 28	22 43	22 58	23 13	23 28	23 43
Bethnal Green	d	05 32	05 47	06 02	06 17		22 32	22 47	23 02	23 17	23 32	23 47
London Liverpool Street 15 ⊖	a	05 36	05 51	06 06	06 21		22 36	22 51	23 06	23 21	23 36	23 51

Sundays
20 May to 2 December

		LO	LO	LO	LO	LO	LO	LO	LO	LO	LO	LO	LO	LO		LO	LO	LO	LO	LO	LO
Chingford	d	06 40	06 55	07 10	07 25	07 40	07 55	08 10	08 25	08 40	08 55	09 10	09 25	09 40	and at the same minutes past each hour until	21 55	22 10	22 25	22 40	22 55	23 10
Highams Park	d	06 44	06 59	07 14	07 29	07 44	07 59	08 14	08 29	08 44	08 59	09 14	09 29	09 44		21 59	22 14	22 29	22 44	22 59	23 14
Wood Street	d	06 47	07 02	07 17	07 32	07 47	08 02	08 17	08 32	08 47	09 02	09 17	09 32	09 47		22 02	22 17	22 32	22 47	23 02	23 17
Walthamstow Central ⊖	d	06 49	07 04	07 19	07 34	07 49	08 04	08 19	08 34	08 49	09 04	09 19	09 34	09 49		22 04	22 19	22 34	22 49	23 04	23 19
St James Street	d	06 51	07 06	07 21	07 36	07 51	08 06	08 21	08 36	08 51	09 06	09 21	09 36	09 51		22 06	22 21	22 36	22 51	23 06	23 21
Clapton	d	06 54	07 09	07 24	07 39	07 54	08 09	08 24	08 39	08 54	09 09	09 24	09 39	09 54		22 09	22 24	22 39	22 54	23 09	23 24
Hackney Downs	d	06 58	07 13	07 28	07 43	07 58	08 13	08 28	08 43	08 58	09 13	09 28	09 43	09 58		22 13	22 28	22 43	22 58	23 13	23 28
Bethnal Green	d										09 17	09 32	09 47	10 02		22 17	22 32	22 47	23 02	23 17	23 32
London Liverpool Street 15 ⊖	a	07 06	07 21	07 36	07 51	08 06	08 21	08 36	08 51	09 06	09 21	09 36	09 51	10 06		22 21	22 36	22 51	23 06	23 21	23 36

Table T021-F

London - Cheshunt (via Seven Sisters) and Enfield Town

Mondays to Fridays

21 May to 7 December

Miles	Miles			LO MX	LO	LO	LO	LO	LO	LO	LO	LO	LO	LO	LO	LO	LO	LO	LO	LO	LO	LO	LO
0	0	**London Liverpool Street** 15 ⊖	d	00 01	05 45	06 00	06 15	06 21	06 36	06 45	06 51	07 07	07 15	07 21	07 36	07 45	07 51	08 00	08 07	08 15	08 30	08 38	08 45
1¼	1¼	Bethnal Green	d	00 03	05 48	06 03		06 24	06 39		06 54	07 10		07 24	07 39		07 54		08 10	08 18	08 33		08 48
1¾	1¾	Cambridge Heath	d	00 05	05 50	06 05		06 26	06 41		06 56	07 12		07 26	07 41		07 56		08 12	08 20	08 35	08 43	08 50
2½	2½	London Fields	d	00 07	05 52	06 07		06 28	06 43		06 58	07 14		07 28	07 43		07 58		08 14	08 22	08 37	08 45	08 52
3	3	Hackney Downs	d	00 09	05 54	06 09	06 22	06 30	06 45	06 52	07 00	07 16	07 22	07 30	07 45	07 52	08 00	08 07	08 16	08 24	08 39	08 47	08 54
3¾	3¾	Rectory Road	d	00 12	05 57	06 12		06 33	06 48	06 55	07 03	07 19	07 25	07 33	07 48	07 55	08 03		08 19	08 27	08 42	08 49	08 57
4¼	4¼	Stoke Newington	d	00 13	05 58	06 13		06 34	06 49	06 56	07 04	07 20	07 26	07 34	07 49	07 56	08 04		08 20	08 28	08 43	08 51	08 58
5	5	Stamford Hill	d	00 15	06 00	06 15		06 36	06 51	06 58	07 06	07 22	07 28	07 36	07 51	07 58	08 06		08 22	08 30	08 45	08 53	09 00
5½	5½	Seven Sisters ⊖	d	00 17	06 03	06 18	06 27	06 39	06 54	07 01	07 09	07 25	07 31	07 39	07 54	08 01	08 09	08 16	08 25	08 33	08 48	08 55	09 03
6¼	6¼	Bruce Grove	d	00 19	06 05	06 20		06 41	06 56	07 03	07 11	07 27	07 33	07 41	07 56	08 03	08 11		08 27	08 35	08 50	08 57	09 05
7¼	7¼	White Hart Lane	d	00 21	06 07	06 22		06 43	06 58	07 05	07 13	07 29	07 35	07 43	07 58	08 05	08 13		08 29	08 37	08 52	08 59	09 07
8	8	Silver Street	d	00 23	06 09	06 24		06 45	07 00	07 07	07 15	07 31	07 37	07 45	08 00	08 07	08 15		08 31	08 39	08 54	09 01	09 09
8½	8½	Edmonton Green	d	00 25	06 11	06 26	06 32	06 47	07 02	07 09	07 17	07 33	07 39	07 47	08 02	08 09	08 17	08 21	08 33	08 43	08 56	09 03	09 11
—	9¾	Bush Hill Park	d	00 28		06 29		06 50		07 12	07 20		07 42	07 50		08 12	08 20		08 36		08 59		09 14
—	10¾	**Enfield Town**	a	00 34		06 33		06 54		07 18	07 24		07 48	07 54		08 18	08 24		08 42		09 05		09 20
10½	—	Southbury	d		06 14		06 36		07 05			07 36			08 05			08 24		08 47		09 07	
12¼	—	Turkey Street	d		06 17		06 39		07 08			07 39			08 08			08 27		08 50		09 10	
13½	—	Theobalds Grove	d		06 20		06 41		07 11			07 42			08 11			08 30		08 52		09 12	
14½	—	**Cheshunt**	a		06 24		06 50		07 15			07 50			08 19			08 39		08 58		09 17	

		LO	LO	LO	LO	LO		LO	LO	LO	LO	LO	LO	LO	LE A	LO	LO	LO	LE A	LO	LO	LO
London Liverpool Street 15 ⊖	d	09 00	09 15	09 30	09 45	10 00		15 15	15 30	15 45	16 00	16 15	16 21	16 30	16 41	16 45	16 52	17 00	17 11	17 15	17 22	17 30
Bethnal Green	d	09 03	09 18	09 33	09 48	10 03		15 18	15 33	15 48	16 03	16 18		16 33		16 48		17 03		17 18		17 33
Cambridge Heath	d	09 05	09 20	09 35	09 50	10 05		15 20	15 35	15 50	16 05	16 20	16 26	16 35		16 50	16 57	17 05		17 20	17 27	17 35
London Fields	d	09 07	09 22	09 37	09 52	10 07		15 22	15 37	15 52	16 07	16 22	16 28	16 37		16 52	16 59	17 07		17 22	17 29	17 37
Hackney Downs	d	09 09	09 24	09 39	09 54	10 09		15 24	15 39	15 54	16 09	16 24	16 30	16 39	16 48	16 54	17 01	17 09	17 18	17 24	17 31	17 39
Rectory Road	d	09 12	09 27	09 42	09 57	10 12	and at	15 27	15 42	15 57	16 12	16 27	16 32	16 42		16 57	17 03	17 12		17 27	17 33	17 42
Stoke Newington	d	09 13	09 28	09 43	09 58	10 13	the same	15 28	15 43	15 58	16 13	16 28	16 34	16 43		16 58	17 05	17 13		17 28	17 35	17 43
Stamford Hill	d	09 15	09 30	09 45	10 00	10 15	minutes	15 30	15 45	16 00	16 15	16 30		16 45		17 00		17 15		17 30		17 45
Seven Sisters ⊖	d	09 18	09 33	09 48	10 03	10 18	past	15 33	15 48	16 03	16 18	16 33	16 37	16 48	16 54	17 03	17 09	17 18	17 24	17 33	17 39	17 48
Bruce Grove	d	09 20	09 35	09 50	10 05	10 20	each	15 35	15 50	16 05	16 20	16 35	16 39	16 50		17 05	17 11	17 20		17 35	17 41	17 50
White Hart Lane	d	09 22	09 37	09 52	10 07	10 22	hour until	15 37	15 52	16 07	16 22	16 37	16 41	16 52		17 07	17 13	17 22		17 37	17 43	17 52
Silver Street	d	09 24	09 39	09 54	10 09	10 24		15 39	15 54	16 09	16 24	16 39	16 43	16 54		17 09	17 15	17 24		17 39	17 45	17 54
Edmonton Green	d	09 26	09 41	09 56	10 11	10 26		15 41	15 56	16 11	16 26	16 41	16 46	16 56	17 00	17 11	17 17	17 26	17 30	17 41	17 47	17 56
Bush Hill Park	d	09 29		09 59		10 29			15 59		16 29	16 44		16 59		17 14		17 29		17 44		17 59
Enfield Town	a	09 35		10 03		10 33			16 03		16 33	16 50		17 05		17 20		17 33		17 50		18 05
Southbury	d		09 44		10 14			15 44		16 14			16 49				17 21				17 51	
Turkey Street	d		09 47		10 17			15 47		16 17			16 52				17 24				17 54	
Theobalds Grove	d		09 50		10 20			15 50		16 20			16 55				17 26				17 56	
Cheshunt	a		09 54		10 24			15 54		16 24			17 00		17 09		17 31		17 39		18 05	

		LE A	LO	LO	LO	LE A	LO	LO	LO	LE A	LO	LO	LO	LO	LO	LO	LO	LO	LO	LO	LO	LO	LO
London Liverpool Street 15 ⊖	d	17 41	17 45	17 52	18 00	18 11	18 15	18 22	18 30	18 41	18 45	19 00	19 15	19 22	19 30	19 45	20 00	20 15	20 30	20 45	21 00	21 15	21 30
Bethnal Green	d		17 48		18 03		18 18		18 33		18 48	19 03	19 18		19 33	19 48	20 03	20 18	20 33	20 48	21 03	21 18	21 33
Cambridge Heath	d		17 50	17 57	18 05		18 20	18 27	18 35		18 50	19 05	19 20		19 35	19 50	20 05	20 20	20 35	20 50	21 05	21 20	21 35
London Fields	d		17 52	17 59	18 07		18 22	18 29	18 37		18 52	19 07	19 22	19 28	19 37	19 52	20 07	20 22	20 37	20 52	21 07	21 22	21 37
Hackney Downs	d	17 48	17 54	18 01	18 09	18 18	18 24	18 31	18 39	18 48	18 54	19 09	19 24	19 30	19 39	19 54	20 09	20 24	20 39	20 54	21 09	21 24	21 39
Rectory Road	d		17 57	18 03	18 12		18 27	18 33	18 42		18 57	19 12	19 27	19 32	19 42	19 57	20 12	20 27	20 42	20 57	21 12	21 27	21 42
Stoke Newington	d		17 58	18 05	18 13		18 28	18 35	18 43		18 58	19 13	19 28	19 34	19 43	19 58	20 13	20 28	20 43	20 58	21 13	21 28	21 43
Stamford Hill	d		18 00		18 15		18 30		18 45		19 00	19 15	19 30		19 45	20 00	20 15	20 30	20 45	21 00	21 15	21 30	21 45
Seven Sisters ⊖	d	17 54	18 03	18 09	18 18	18 24	18 33	18 39	18 48	18 54	19 03	19 18	19 33	19 37	19 48	20 03	20 18	20 33	20 48	21 03	21 18	21 33	21 48
Bruce Grove	d		18 05	18 11	18 20		18 35	18 41	18 50		19 05	19 20	19 35	19 39	19 50	20 05	20 20	20 35	20 50	21 05	21 20	21 35	21 50
White Hart Lane	d		18 07	18 13	18 22		18 37	18 43	18 52		19 07	19 22	19 37	19 41	19 52	20 07	20 22	20 37	20 52	21 07	21 22	21 37	21 52
Silver Street	d		18 09	18 15	18 24		18 39	18 45	18 54		19 09	19 24	19 39	19 43	19 54	20 09	20 24	20 39	20 54	21 09	21 24	21 39	21 54
Edmonton Green	d	18 00	18 11	18 17	18 26	18 30	18 41	18 47	18 56	19 00	19 11	19 26	19 41	19 45	19 56	20 11	20 26	20 41	20 56	21 11	21 26	21 41	21 56
Bush Hill Park	d		18 14		18 29		18 44		18 59			19 29		19 48	19 59		20 29		20 59		21 29		21 59
Enfield Town	a		18 20		18 35		18 50		19 05			19 35		19 55	20 03		20 33		21 03		21 33		22 03
Southbury	d			18 21				18 51			19 15		19 44			20 14		20 44		21 14		21 44	
Turkey Street	d			18 24				18 54			19 18		19 47			20 17		20 47		21 17		21 47	
Theobalds Grove	d			18 26				18 56			19 20		19 50			20 20		20 50		21 20		21 50	
Cheshunt	a	18 09		18 31		18 39		19 01		19 09	19 28		19 58			20 28		20 54		21 24		21 54	

		LO	LO	LO	LO	LO	LO	LO	LO	LO
London Liverpool Street 15 ⊖	d	21 45	22 00	22 15	22 30	22 45	23 00	23 15	23 30	23 45
Bethnal Green	d	21 48	22 03	22 18	22 33	22 48	23 03	23 18	23 33	23 48
Cambridge Heath	d	21 50	22 05	22 20	22 35	22 50	23 05	23 20	23 35	23 50
London Fields	d	21 52	22 07	22 22	22 37	22 52	23 07	23 22	23 37	23 52
Hackney Downs	d	21 54	22 09	22 24	22 39	22 54	23 09	23 24	23 39	23 54
Rectory Road	d	21 57	22 12	22 27	22 42	22 57	23 12	23 27	23 42	23 57
Stoke Newington	d	21 58	22 13	22 28	22 43	22 58	23 13	23 28	23 43	23 58
Stamford Hill	d	22 00	22 15	22 30	22 45	23 00	23 15	23 30	23 45	23 59
Seven Sisters ⊖	d	22 03	22 18	22 33	22 48	23 03	23 18	23 33	23 48	00 03
Bruce Grove	d	22 05	22 20	22 35	22 50	23 05	23 20	23 35	23 50	00 05
White Hart Lane	d	22 07	22 22	22 37	22 52	23 07	23 22	23 37	23 52	00 07
Silver Street	d	22 09	22 24	22 39	22 54	23 09	23 24	23 39	23 54	00 09
Edmonton Green	d	22 11	22 26	22 41	22 56	23 11	23 26	23 41	23 56	00 11
Bush Hill Park	d		22 29		22 59		23 29		23 59	
Enfield Town	a		22 33		23 03		23 33		00 03	
Southbury	d	22 14		22 44		23 14		23 44		00 14
Turkey Street	d	22 17		22 47		23 17		23 47		00 17
Theobalds Grove	d	22 20		22 50		23 20		23 50		00 20
Cheshunt	a	22 24		22 54		23 24		23 54		00 24

A To Hertford East

Table T021-F

London - Cheshunt (via Seven Sisters) and Enfield Town

Saturdays

26 May to 8 December

		LO	LO	LO	LO	LO	LO	LO		LO	LO	LO	LO	LO
London Liverpool Street 15 ⊖	d	00 01	05 15	05 30	05 45	06 00	06 15	06 30		22 45	23 00	23 15	23 30	23 45
Bethnal Green	d	00 03	05 18		05 48	06 03	06 18	06 33		22 48	23 03	23 18	23 33	23 48
Cambridge Heath	d	00 05	05 20		05 50	06 05	06 20	06 35		22 50	23 05	23 20	23 35	23 50
London Fields	d	00 07	05 22		05 52	06 07	06 22	06 37		22 52	23 07	23 22	23 37	23 52
Hackney Downs	d	00 09	05 24	05 38	05 54	06 09	06 24	06 39		22 54	23 09	23 24	23 39	23 54
Rectory Road	d	00 12	05 27		05 57	06 12	06 27	06 42	and at	22 57	23 12	23 27	23 42	23 57
Stoke Newington	d	00 13	05 28		05 58	06 13	06 28	06 43	the same	22 58	23 13	23 28	23 43	23 58
Stamford Hill	d	00 15	05 30		06 00	06 15	06 30	06 45	minutes	23 00	23 15	23 30	23 45	23 59
Seven Sisters ⊖	d	00 17	05 33	05 48	06 03	06 18	06 33	06 48	past	23 03	23 18	23 33	23 48	00 03
Bruce Grove	d	00 19	05 35	05 50	06 05	06 20	06 35	06 50	each	23 05	23 20	23 35	23 50	00 05
White Hart Lane	d	00 21	05 37	05 52	06 07	06 22	06 37	06 52	hour until	23 07	23 22	23 37	23 52	00 07
Silver Street	d	00 23	05 39	05 54	06 09	06 24	06 39	06 54		23 09	23 24	23 39	23 54	00 09
Edmonton Green	d	00 25	05 41	05 56	06 11	06 26	06 41	06 56		23 11	23 26	23 41	23 56	00 11
Bush Hill Park	d	00 28		05 59		06 29		06 59			23 29		23 59	
Enfield Town	a	00 34		06 03		06 33		07 03			23 33		00 03	
Southbury	d		05 44		06 14		06 44			23 14		23 44		00 14
Turkey Street	d		05 47		06 17		06 47			23 17		23 47		00 17
Theobalds Grove	d		05 50		06 20		06 50			23 20		23 50		00 20
Cheshunt	a		05 54		06 24		06 54			23 24		23 54		00 24

Sundays

20 May to 2 December

		LO	LO	LO	LO	LO	LO	LO	LO	LO	LO	LO	LO		LO	LO	LO	LO	LO	LO
London Liverpool Street 15 ⊖	d	00 01	07 30	07 45	08 00	08 15	08 30	08 45	09 00	09 15	09 30	09 45	10 00		22 15	22 30	22 45	23 00	23 15	23 30
Bethnal Green	d	00 03								09 18	09 33	09 48	10 03		22 18	22 33	22 48	23 03	23 18	23 33
Cambridge Heath	d	00 05								09 20	09 35	09 50	10 05		22 20	22 35	22 50	23 05	23 20	23 35
London Fields	d	00 07								09 22	09 37	09 52	10 07		22 22	22 37	22 52	23 07	23 22	23 37
Hackney Downs	d	00 09	07 39	07 54	08 09	08 24	08 39	08 54	09 09	09 24	09 39	09 54	10 09		22 24	22 39	22 54	23 09	23 24	23 39
Rectory Road	d	00 12	07 42	07 57	08 12	08 27	08 42	08 57	09 12	09 27	09 42	09 57	10 12	and at	22 27	22 42	22 57	23 12	23 27	23 42
Stoke Newington	d	00 13	07 43	07 58	08 13	08 28	08 43	08 58	09 13	09 28	09 43	09 58	10 13	the same	22 28	22 43	22 58	23 13	23 28	23 43
Stamford Hill	d	00 15	07 45	08 00	08 15	08 30	08 45	09 00	09 15	09 30	09 45	10 00	10 15	minutes	22 30	22 45	23 00	23 15	23 30	23 45
Seven Sisters ⊖	d	00 18	07 48	08 03	08 18	08 33	08 48	09 03	09 18	09 33	09 48	10 03	10 18	past	22 33	22 48	23 03	23 18	23 33	23 48
Bruce Grove	d	00 20	07 50	08 05	08 20	08 35	08 50	09 05	09 20	09 35	09 50	10 05	10 20	each	22 35	22 50	23 05	23 20	23 35	23 50
White Hart Lane	d	00 22	07 52	08 07	08 22	08 37	08 52	09 07	09 22	09 37	09 52	10 07	10 22	hour until	22 37	22 52	23 07	23 22	23 37	23 52
Silver Street	d	00 24	07 54	08 09	08 24	08 39	08 54	09 09	09 24	09 39	09 54	10 09	10 24		22 39	22 54	23 09	23 24	23 39	23 54
Edmonton Green	d	00 26	07 56	08 11	08 26	08 41	08 56	09 11	09 26	09 41	09 56	10 11	10 26		22 41	22 56	23 11	23 26	23 41	23 56
Bush Hill Park	d	00 29	07 59		08 29		08 59		09 29		09 59		10 29			22 59		23 29		23 59
Enfield Town	a	00 33	08 03		08 33		09 03		09 33		10 03		10 33			23 03		23 33		00 03
Southbury	d			08 14		08 44		09 14		09 44		10 14			22 44		23 14		23 44	
Turkey Street	d			08 17		08 47		09 17		09 47		10 17			22 47		23 17		23 47	
Theobalds Grove	d			08 20		08 50		09 20		09 50		10 20			22 50		23 20		23 50	
Cheshunt	a			08 24		08 54		09 24		09 54		10 24			22 54		23 24		23 54	

Table T021-R

Cheshunt (via Seven Sisters) and Enfield Town - London

Mondays to Fridays

21 May to 7 December

Miles	Miles			LO	LO	LO	LO	LO	LO	LE A		LO	LO	LO	LE A	LO	LO	LO	LE A	LO		LO	LO	LE A	LO
0	—	**Cheshunt**	d	05 16		06 01			06 33	06 47			06 52		07 17		07 22		07 47			07 52		08 17	
1	—	Theobalds Grove	d	05 19		06 04			06 36				06 55				07 25					07 55			
2¼	—	Turkey Street	d	05 21		06 06			06 38				06 57				07 27					07 57			
4	—	Southbury	d	05 24		06 09			06 41				07 00				07 30					08 00			
—	0	**Enfield Town**	d		05 52		06 18	06 33				06 53		07 08		07 23		07 38		07 53			08 08		08 23
—	1	Bush Hill Park	d		05 55		06 21	06 36				06 56		07 11		07 26		07 41		07 56			08 11		08 26
6	2¼	Edmonton Green	d	05 28	05 58	06 13	06 24	06 39	06 45	06 55		06 59	07 04	07 14	07 25	07 29	07 34	07 44	07 55	07 59		08 04	08 14	08 25	08 29
6½	2¾	Silver Street	d	05 30	06 00	06 15	06 26	06 41	06 47			07 01	07 06	07 16		07 31	07 36	07 46		08 01		08 06	08 16		08 31
7¼	3½	White Hart Lane	d	05 32	06 02	06 17	06 28	06 43	06 49			07 03	07 08	07 18		07 33	07 38	07 48		08 03		08 08	08 18		08 33
8¼	4½	Bruce Grove	d	05 34	06 04	06 19	06 30	06 45	06 51			07 05	07 10	07 20		07 35	07 40	07 50		08 05		08 10	08 20		08 35
9	5¼	Seven Sisters ⊖	d	05 36	06 06	06 21	06 33	06 48	06 54	07 02		07 08	07 13	07 23	07 32	07 38	07 43	07 53	08 02	08 08		08 13	08 23	08 32	08 38
9½	5¾	Stamford Hill	d	05 38	06 08	06 23	06 35	06 50	06 56			07 10		07 25		07 40		07 55		08 10			08 25		08 40
10¼	6½	Stoke Newington	d	05 40	06 10	06 25	06 37	06 52	06 58			07 12	07 16	07 27		07 42	07 46	07 57		08 12		08 16	08 27		08 42
10¾	7	Rectory Road	d	05 42	06 12	06 27	06 39	06 54	07 00			07 14	07 18	07 29		07 44	07 48	07 59		08 14		08 18	08 29		08 43
11½	7¾	Hackney Downs	d	05 45	06 15	06 30	06 43	06 58	07 04	07 08		07 18	07 22	07 33	07 38	07 48	07 52	08 03	08 08	08 18		08 22	08 33	08 38	08 48
12	8¼	London Fields	d	05 47	06 17	06 32	06 45	07 00	07 06			07 20	07 24	07 35		07 50	07 54	08 05		08 20		08 24	08 35		08 50
12¾	9	Cambridge Heath	d	05 49	06 19	06 34	06 47	07 02	07 08			07 22		07 37		07 52		08 07		08 22			08 37		08 52
13¼	9½	Bethnal Green	d	05 51	06 21	06 36	06 49		07 10			07 24		07 39		07 54		08 09		08 24			08 39		08 54
14½	10¾	**London Liverpool Street** 15 ⊖	a	05 55	06 26	06 40	06 56	07 11	07 16	07 18		07 31	07 31	07 46	07 48	08 01	08 05	08 16	08 18	08 31		08 35	08 46	08 48	09 01

		LO	LO	LO	LO	LO		LO	LO	LO	LO	LO	LO	LO	LO	LO		LO	LO	LO	LO	LO	LO	LO	LO
Cheshunt	d	08 22		08 43				09 07		09 31		10 01		10 31		11 01			11 31		12 01		12 31		13 01
Theobalds Grove	d	08 25		08 46				09 10		09 34		10 04		10 34		11 04			11 34		12 04		12 34		13 04
Turkey Street	d	08 27		08 48				09 12		09 36		10 06		10 36		11 06			11 36		12 06		12 36		13 06
Southbury	d	08 30		08 51				09 15		09 39		10 09		10 39		11 09			11 39		12 09		12 39		13 09
Enfield Town	d		08 38		08 53	09 08			09 23		09 52		10 22		10 52			11 22		11 52		12 22		12 52	
Bush Hill Park	d		08 41		08 56	09 11			09 26		09 55		10 25		10 55			11 25		11 55		12 25		12 55	
Edmonton Green	d	08 34	08 44	08 55	08 59	09 14		09 19	09 29	09 43	09 58	10 13	10 28	10 43	10 58	11 13		11 28	11 43	11 58	12 13	12 28	12 43	12 58	13 13
Silver Street	d	08 36	08 46		09 01	09 16		09 21	09 31	09 45	10 00	10 15	10 30	10 45	11 00	11 15		11 30	11 45	12 00	12 15	12 30	12 45	13 00	13 15
White Hart Lane	d	08 38	08 48		09 03	09 18		09 23	09 33	09 47	10 02	10 17	10 32	10 47	11 02	11 17		11 32	11 47	12 02	12 17	12 32	12 47	13 02	13 17
Bruce Grove	d	08 40	08 50		09 05	09 20		09 25	09 35	09 49	10 04	10 19	10 34	10 49	11 04	11 19		11 34	11 49	12 04	12 19	12 34	12 49	13 04	13 19
Seven Sisters ⊖	d	08 43	08 53	09 02	09 08	09 23		09 28	09 38	09 51	10 06	10 21	10 36	10 51	11 06	11 21		11 36	11 51	12 06	12 21	12 36	12 51	13 06	13 21
Stamford Hill	d		08 55		09 10	09 25			09 40	09 53	10 08	10 23	10 38	10 53	11 08	11 23		11 38	11 53	12 08	12 23	12 38	12 53	13 08	13 23
Stoke Newington	d	08 46	08 57		09 12	09 27		09 31	09 42	09 55	10 10	10 25	10 40	10 55	11 10	11 25		11 40	11 55	12 10	12 25	12 40	12 55	13 10	13 25
Rectory Road	d	08 48	08 59		09 14	09 29		09 33	09 44	09 57	10 12	10 27	10 42	10 57	11 12	11 27		11 42	11 57	12 12	12 27	12 42	12 57	13 12	13 27
Hackney Downs	d	08 52	09 03	09 08	09 18	09 33		09 37	09 48	10 00	10 15	10 30	10 45	11 00	11 15	11 30		11 45	12 00	12 15	12 30	12 45	13 00	13 15	13 30
London Fields	d	08 54	09 05		09 20	09 35		09 39	09 50	10 02	10 17	10 32	10 47	11 02	11 17	11 32		11 47	12 02	12 17	12 32	12 47	13 02	13 17	13 32
Cambridge Heath	d		09 07		09 22	09 37			09 52	10 04	10 19	10 34	10 49	11 04	11 19	11 34		11 49	12 04	12 19	12 34	12 49	13 04	13 19	13 34
Bethnal Green	d		09 09		09 24	09 39			09 54	10 06	10 21	10 36	10 51	11 06	11 21	11 36		11 51	12 06	12 21	12 36	12 51	13 06	13 21	13 36
London Liverpool Street 15 ⊖	a	09 05	09 16	09 22	09 31	09 46		09 46	10 01	10 10	10 26	10 40	10 56	11 14	11 26	11 40		11 56	12 10	12 26	12 40	12 56	13 10	13 26	13 40

		LO		LO	LO	LO	LO	LO	LO	LO	LO	LO		LO	LO	LO	LO	LO	LO	LO	LO	LO		LO	LO
Cheshunt	d			13 31		14 01		14 31		15 01		15 31			16 01		16 31			17 06				17 40	
Theobalds Grove	d			13 34		14 04		14 34		15 04		15 34			16 04		16 34			17 09				17 43	
Turkey Street	d			13 36		14 06		14 36		15 06		15 36			16 06		16 36			17 11				17 45	
Southbury	d			13 39		14 09		14 39		15 09		15 39			16 09		16 39			17 14				17 48	
Enfield Town	d	13 22			13 52		14 22		14 52		15 22			15 52		16 22		16 51	17 06		17 21	17 36			17 51
Bush Hill Park	d	13 25			13 55		14 25		14 55		15 25			15 55		16 25		16 54	17 09		17 24	17 39			17 54
Edmonton Green	d	13 28		13 43	13 58	14 13	14 28	14 43	14 58	15 13	15 28	15 43		15 58	16 13	16 28	16 43	16 57	17 12	17 18	17 27	17 42		17 52	17 57
Silver Street	d	13 30		13 45	14 00	14 15	14 30	14 45	15 00	15 15	15 30	15 45		16 00	16 15	16 30	16 45	16 59	17 14	17 20	17 29	17 44			17 59
White Hart Lane	d	13 32		13 47	14 02	14 17	14 32	14 47	15 02	15 17	15 32	15 47		16 02	16 17	16 32	16 47	17 01	17 16	17 22	17 31	17 46			18 01
Bruce Grove	d	13 34		13 49	14 04	14 19	14 34	14 49	15 04	15 19	15 34	15 49		16 04	16 19	16 34	16 49	17 03	17 18	17 24	17 33	17 48			18 03
Seven Sisters ⊖	d	13 36		13 51	14 06	14 21	14 36	14 51	15 06	15 21	15 36	15 51		16 06	16 21	16 36	16 51	17 05	17 20	17 27	17 35	17 50		17 58	18 05
Stamford Hill	d	13 38		13 53	14 08	14 23	14 38	14 53	15 08	15 23	15 38	15 53		16 08	16 23	16 38	16 53	17 07	17 22		17 37	17 52			18 07
Stoke Newington	d	13 40		13 55	14 10	14 25	14 40	14 55	15 10	15 25	15 40	15 55		16 10	16 25	16 40	16 55	17 09	17 24	17 30	17 39	17 54		18 01	18 09
Rectory Road	d	13 42		13 57	14 12	14 27	14 42	14 57	15 12	15 27	15 42	15 56		16 12	16 27	16 42	16 57	17 11	17 26		17 41	17 56			18 11
Hackney Downs	d	13 45		14 00	14 15	14 30	14 45	15 00	15 15	15 30	15 45	15 59		16 15	16 30	16 45	17 00	17 14	17 29	17 33	17 44	17 59		18 04	18 14
London Fields	d	13 47		14 02	14 17	14 32	14 47	15 02	15 17	15 32	15 47	16 01		16 17	16 32	16 47	17 02	17 16	17 31		17 46	18 01			18 16
Cambridge Heath	d	13 49		14 04	14 19	14 34	14 49	15 04	15 19	15 34	15 49	16 03		16 19	16 34	16 49	17 04	17 18	17 33		17 48	18 03			18 18
Bethnal Green	d	13 51		14 06	14 21	14 36	14 51	15 06	15 21	15 36	15 51	16 05		16 21	16 36	16 51	17 06	17 20	17 35		17 50	18 05			18 20
London Liverpool Street 15 ⊖	a	13 56		14 10	14 26	14 44	14 56	15 10	15 26	15 40	15 56	16 14		16 26	16 40	16 56	17 10	17 25	17 44	17 46	17 55	18 11		18 19	18 25

		LO	LO	LO	LO	LO	LO	LO		LO	LO	LO	LO	LO		LO	LO	LO	LO		LO	LO	LE ◇1 B	LE A
Cheshunt	d		18 10			18 40				19 10		19 31		20 01			22 31		23 01			23 31	23 52	23 59
Theobalds Grove	d		18 13			18 43				19 13		19 34		20 04			22 34		23 04			23 34		
Turkey Street	d		18 15			18 45				19 15		19 36		20 06			22 36		23 06			23 36		
Southbury	d		18 18			18 48				19 18		19 39		20 09			22 39		23 09			23 39		
Enfield Town	d	18 06		18 21	18 36		18 51	19 06			19 22		19 52		and at	22 22		22 52			23 22			
Bush Hill Park	d	18 09		18 24	18 39		18 54	19 09			19 25		19 55		the same	22 25		22 55			23 25			
Edmonton Green	d	18 12	18 22	18 27	18 42	18 52	18 57	19 12		19 22	19 28	19 43	19 58	20 13	minutes	22 28	22 43	22 58	23 13		23 28	23 43		
Silver Street	d	18 14		18 29	18 44		18 59	19 14			19 30	19 45	20 00	20 15	past	22 30	22 45	23 00	23 15		23 30	23 45		
White Hart Lane	d	18 16		18 31	18 46		19 01	19 16			19 32	19 47	20 02	20 17	each	22 32	22 47	23 02	23 17		23 32	23 47		
Bruce Grove	d	18 18		18 33	18 48		19 03	19 18			19 34	19 49	20 04	20 19	hour until	22 34	22 49	23 04	23 19		23 34	23 49		
Seven Sisters ⊖	d	18 20	18 28	18 35	18 50	18 58	19 05	19 20		19 28	19 36	19 51	20 06	20 21		22 36	22 51	23 06	23 21		23 36	23 51	00 04	00 12
Stamford Hill	d	18 22		18 37	18 52		19 07	19 22			19 38	19 53	20 08	20 23		22 38	22 53	23 08	23 23		23 38	23 53		
Stoke Newington	d	18 24	18 31	18 39	18 54	19 01	19 09	19 24		19 31	19 40	19 55	20 10	20 25		22 40	22 55	23 10	23 25		23 40	23 55		
Rectory Road	d	18 26		18 41	18 56		19 11	19 26			19 42	19 57	20 12	20 27		22 42	22 57	23 12	23 27		23 42	23 57		
Hackney Downs	d	18 29	18 34	18 44	18 59	19 04	19 14	19 29		19 34	19 45	20 00	20 15	20 30		22 45	23 00	23 15	23 30		23 45	23 59		00 17
London Fields	d	18 31		18 46	19 01		19 16	19 31			19 47	20 02	20 17	20 32		22 47	23 02	23 17	23 32		23 47	00 02		
Cambridge Heath	d	18 33		18 48	19 03		19 18	19 33			19 49	20 04	20 19	20 34		22 49	23 04	23 19	23 34		23 49	00 04		
Bethnal Green	d	18 35		18 50	19 05		19 20	19 35			19 51	20 06	20 21	20 36		22 51	23 06	23 21	23 36		23 51	00 06		
London Liverpool Street 15 ⊖	a	18 40	18 49	18 59	19 10	19 19	19 25	19 40		19 49	19 56	20 10	20 26	20 40		22 56	23 10	23 26	23 40		23 56	00 10	00 18	00 26

A From Hertford East

B From Cambridge

Table T021-R

Cheshunt (via Seven Sisters) and Enfield Town - London

Saturdays

26 May to 8 December

		LO	LE ◇1 A	LO	LO	LO	LO		LO	LO	LO	LO		LO	LO	LO	LO
Cheshunt	d	05 16	05 30	06 01		06 31			22 01		22 31			23 01		23 31	
Theobalds Grove	d	05 19		06 04		06 34			22 04		22 34			23 04		23 34	
Turkey Street	d	05 21		06 06		06 36			22 06		22 36			23 06		23 36	
Southbury	d	05 24		06 09		06 39			22 09		22 39			23 09		23 39	
Enfield Town	d				06 22		06 52	and at		22 22		22 52			23 22		23 52
Bush Hill Park	d				06 25		06 55	the same		22 25		22 55			23 25		23 55
Edmonton Green	d	05 28		06 13	06 28	06 43	06 58	minutes	22 13	22 28	22 43	22 58		23 13	23 28	23 43	23 58
Silver Street	d	05 30		06 15	06 30	06 45	07 00	past	22 15	22 30	22 45	23 00		23 15	23 30	23 45	23 59
White Hart Lane	d	05 32		06 17	06 32	06 47	07 02	each	22 17	22 32	22 47	23 02		23 17	23 32	23 47	00 02
Bruce Grove	d	05 34		06 19	06 34	06 49	07 04	hour until	22 19	22 34	22 49	23 04		23 19	23 34	23 49	00 04
Seven Sisters ⊖	d	05 36	05 42	06 21	06 36	06 51	07 06		22 21	22 36	22 51	23 06		23 21	23 36	23 51	00 06
Stamford Hill	d	05 38		06 23	06 38	06 53	07 08		22 23	22 38	22 53	23 08		23 23	23 38	23 53	00 08
Stoke Newington	d	05 40		06 25	06 40	06 55	07 10		22 25	22 40	22 55	23 10		23 25	23 40	23 55	00 10
Rectory Road	d	05 42		06 27	06 42	06 57	07 12		22 27	22 42	22 57	23 12		23 27	23 42	23 57	00 12
Hackney Downs	d	05 45		06 30	06 45	07 00	07 15		22 30	22 45	23 00	23 15		23 30	23 45	23 59	00 15
London Fields	d	05 47		06 32	06 47	07 02	07 17		22 32	22 47	23 02	23 17		23 32	23 47	00 02	00 17
Cambridge Heath	d	05 49		06 34	06 49	07 04	07 19		22 34	22 49	23 04	23 19		23 34	23 49	00 04	00 19
Bethnal Green	d	05 51		06 36	06 51	07 06	07 21		22 36	22 51	23 06	23 21		23 36	23 51	00 06	00 21
London Liverpool Street 15 ⊖	a	05 55	05 57	06 40	06 55	07 10	07 25		22 40	22 55	23 10	23 25		23 40	23 55	00 10	00 25

Sundays

20 May to 2 December

		LO	LO	LO	LO	LO	LO	LO	LO	LO	LO		LO	LO	LO	LO		LO	LO	LO
Cheshunt	d	07 31		08 01		08 31		09 01		09 31			22 01		22 31			23 01		23 31
Theobalds Grove	d	07 34		08 04		08 34		09 04		09 34			22 04		22 34			23 04		23 34
Turkey Street	d	07 36		08 06		08 36		09 06		09 36			22 06		22 36			23 06		23 36
Southbury	d	07 39		08 09		08 39		09 09		09 39			22 09		22 39			23 09		23 39
Enfield Town	d		07 52		08 22		08 52		09 22		09 52			22 22		22 52			23 22	
Bush Hill Park	d		07 55		08 25		08 55		09 25		09 55	and at		22 25		22 55			23 25	
Edmonton Green	d	07 43	07 58	08 13	08 28	08 43	08 58	09 13	09 28	09 43	09 58	the same	22 13	22 28	22 43	22 58		23 13	23 28	23 43
Silver Street	d	07 45	08 00	08 15	08 30	08 45	09 00	09 15	09 30	09 45	10 00	minutes	22 15	22 30	22 45	23 00		23 15	23 30	23 45
White Hart Lane	d	07 47	08 02	08 17	08 32	08 47	09 02	09 17	09 32	09 47	10 02	past	22 17	22 32	22 47	23 02		23 17	23 32	23 47
Bruce Grove	d	07 49	08 04	08 19	08 34	08 49	09 04	09 19	09 34	09 49	10 04	each	22 19	22 34	22 49	23 04		23 19	23 34	23 49
Seven Sisters ⊖	d	07 51	08 06	08 21	08 36	08 51	09 06	09 21	09 36	09 51	10 06	hour until	22 21	22 36	22 51	23 06		23 21	23 36	23 51
Stamford Hill	d	07 53	08 08	08 23	08 38	08 53	09 08	09 23	09 38	09 53	10 08		22 23	22 38	22 53	23 08		23 23	23 38	23 53
Stoke Newington	d	07 55	08 10	08 25	08 40	08 55	09 10	09 25	09 40	09 55	10 10		22 25	22 40	22 55	23 10		23 25	23 40	23 55
Rectory Road	d	07 57	08 12	08 27	08 42	08 57	09 12	09 27	09 42	09 57	10 12		22 27	22 42	22 57	23 12		23 27	23 42	23 57
Hackney Downs	d	08 00	08 15	08 30	08 45	09 00	09 15	09 30	09 45	10 00	10 15		22 30	22 45	23 00	23 15		23 30	23 45	23 59
London Fields	d							09 32	09 47	10 02	10 17		22 32	22 47	23 02	23 17		23 32	23 47	00 02
Cambridge Heath	d							09 34	09 49	10 04	10 19		22 34	22 49	23 04	23 19		23 34	23 49	00 04
Bethnal Green	d							09 36	09 51	10 06	10 21		22 36	22 51	23 06	23 21		23 36	23 51	00 06
London Liverpool Street 15 ⊖	a	08 10	08 25	08 40	08 55	09 10	09 25	09 40	09 55	10 10	10 25		22 40	22 55	23 10	23 25		23 40	23 55	00 10

A From Cambridge

Table T022-F

Mondays to Fridays

21 May to 7 December

London - Broxbourne, Hertford East, Bishops Stortford, Stansted Airport, Cambridge and Cambridge North

Miles	Miles	Miles			LE MO	LE MO	LE MX	LE MX	LE MO	LE MO	LE MX	LE	LE MFO	LE MFO	XC	LE MTh FO	LE TWO	LE	LE	XC	LE	LE	LE
					■			■	■	◇■	◇■	■	■	■	◇■	■	■		■	◇■	■	◇■	■
					A	B	A	A	A	A	A	A			C					C			
0	—	—	**London Liverpool Street** ⊖	d									03 40	04 10		04 40	04 40		05 10		05 25	05 28	05 40
3	—	—	Hackney Downs	d																			
—	0	0	Stratford ⊖	d																			
—	—	2¼	Lea Bridge	d																			
—	6¾	—	Seven Sisters ⊖	d																			
6	—	4¼	Tottenham Hale ⊖	d								00 10				04 52	04 59		05 22		05 37	05 40	05 52
7	—	5¾	Northumberland Park	d																			
7¾	—	6	Angel Road	d																			
10	—	—	Ponders End	d			00 01																
10¾	—	—	Brimsdown	d			00 03																
11¾	—	—	Enfield Lock	d			00 06																
12¾	—	—	Waltham Cross	d			00 08																
14	—	12¼	Cheshunt	d			00 11					00 18				05 00	05 07					05 48	
17¼	—	15½	**Broxbourne**	a			00 16					00 23				05 05	05 12					05 53	
—	0	—	**Broxbourne**	d		00 03	00 16					00 23				05 05	05 12	05 40				05 53	
—	1¾	—	Rye House	d		00 06	00 20											05 43					
—	3	—	St Margarets (Herts)	d		00 09	00 23											05 46					
—	5	—	Ware	d		00 13	00 27											05 50					
—	7	—	**Hertford East**	a		00 19	00 32											05 56					
20	—	18½	Roydon	d								00 27										05 57	
22¾	—	21	Harlow Town	d							00 01	00 31				05 11	05 18		05 38		05 53	06 01	
24½	—	22¾	Harlow Mill	d							00 04	00 34										06 04	
26¾	—	25	Sawbridgeworth	d					00 04		00 08	00 38							05 43			06 08	
30¼	—	28½	**Bishops Stortford**	a					00 11		00 14	00 44				05 20	05 27		05 49		06 02	06 14	06 17
30¼	—	28½	**Bishops Stortford**	d	00 03			00 04			00 14					05 20	05 27		05 50		06 03	06 14	06 18
33¾	0	—	Stansted Mountfitchet	d							00 18					05 24	05 31					06 18	06 23
—	—	—	**Stansted Airport** ✈	a	00 12			00 13					04 30	04 57		05 39	05 39		06 00		06 12		06 30
—	3¾	—	**Stansted Airport** ✈	d											05 16					06 12			
35½	8¼	—	Elsenham	d							00 22											06 22	
40	—	—	Newport (Essex)	d							00 27											06 27	
41¾	—	—	Audley End	d							00 30				05 37					06 24		06 30	
45¾	—	—	Great Chesterford	d						00 05	00 35											06 35	
49	—	—	Whittlesford Parkway	d						00 10	00 40											06 40	
52½	—	—	Shelford	d						00 14	00 44											06 44	
55¾	—	—	**Cambridge**	a						00 20	00 51				05 51					06 43		06 55	
—	—	—		d																			
58	—	—	**Cambridge North**	a																			

		LE	LE	LE	LE	LE	LE	LE	LE	XC	LE	LE	LE	LE	LE	LE	LE	LE	LE	LE	LE	LE	LE
				■	◇■		■		■	◇■	◇■	■	■	◇■			■	◇■	■		■	■	◇■
			D			A				C	E			A									
London Liverpool Street ⊖	d	05 42	05 52	05 55	05 58		06 10	06 12	06 25		06 28		06 40		06 42		06 55	06 58	07 10	07 12	07 23	07 25	07 28
Hackney Downs	d	05 48						06 18							06 48					07 18			
Stratford ⊖	d		06 03									06 35				06 49							
Lea Bridge	d		06 09													06 55							
Seven Sisters ⊖	d					←																	
Tottenham Hale ⊖	d	05 55	06 15	06 07	06 10	06 15	06 22	06 25	06 37		06 40	06 44	06 52		06 55	07 00	07 07	07 10	07 22	07 25		07 37	07 41
Northumberland Park	d		→			06 17						06 47											
Angel Road	d					06 19																	
Ponders End	d	05 59						06 29								07 04				07 29			
Brimsdown	d	06 02						06 32								07 07				07 32			
Enfield Lock	d	06 04				06 24		06 34							07 01					07 34			
Waltham Cross	d	06 07						06 37							07 04					07 37			
Cheshunt	d	06 09			06 18	06 28		06 39			06 51	06 54			07 06	07 11		07 21		07 39			07 51
Broxbourne	a	06 15			06 23	06 33		06 45			06 55	06 59			07 12	07 17		07 26		07 45	07 48		07 56
Broxbourne	d	06 15			06 25	06 37		06 45			06 55	06 59			07 15			07 26		07 45			07 56
Rye House	d	06 18				06 40		06 48							07 18					07 48			
St Margarets (Herts)	d	06 21				06 43		06 51							07 21					07 51			
Ware	d	06 25				06 47		06 55							07 25					07 55			
Hertford East	a	06 31				06 53		07 01							07 31					08 02			
Roydon	d				06 29						07 00							07 30					08 00
Harlow Town	d			06 26	06 33				06 55		07 11						07 25	07 34				07 56	08 04
Harlow Mill	d				06 36						07 15							07 37					08 07
Sawbridgeworth	d				06 39						07 18			←				07 41					08 11
Bishops Stortford	a			06 35	06 45		06 49				07 24	07 14	07 17	07 24				07 47	07 50				08 17
Bishops Stortford	d			06 35	06 46		06 50				07 28		07 18	07 28				07 47	07 51				08 17
Stansted Mountfitchet	d				06 50						→			07 32			07 36	07 51					08 21
Stansted Airport ✈	a			06 44			06 59		07 12				07 30				07 43		08 00			08 13	
Stansted Airport ✈	d									07 21													
Elsenham	d				06 54									07 36				07 55					08 25
Newport (Essex)	d				06 59									07 41				08 00					08 30
Audley End	d				07 02					07 37				07 44				08 03					08 33
Great Chesterford	d				07 07									07 49				08 08					08 38
Whittlesford Parkway	d				07 12									07 54				08 13					08 43
Shelford	d				07 16									07 58				08 17					08 47
Cambridge	a				07 24					07 56				08 05				08 26					08 54
	d																						08 55
Cambridge North	a																						08 59

A From London Liverpool Street
B From Stratford
C To Birmingham New Street
D To Hertford East
E To Cambridge

Table T022-F

Mondays to Fridays

21 May to 7 December

London - Broxbourne, Hertford East, Bishops Stortford, Stansted Airport, Cambridge and Cambridge North

		LE	XC	LE	LE	LE	LE	LE	LE	LE	LE	LE	LE	LE	LE	LE	LE	XC	LE	LE	LE	LE	LE
		■	◇■	■		■	■	◇■	◇■	■	■		■	◇■	◇■	◇■	■	◇■	■		■	◇■	■
			A											B		C		A					
London Liverpool Street ⊖	d			07 40	07 42	07 53	07 55	07 58	08 03		08 10	08 12	08 25	08 28	08 33				08 40	08 42	08 55	08 58	
Hackney Downs	d				07 48							08 18								08 48			
Stratford ⊖	d	07 34								08 04							08 34						09 00
Lea Bridge	d	07 40								08 10							08 40						09 06
Seven Sisters ⊖	d																						
Tottenham Hale ⊖	d	07 47		07 52	07 55		08 07	08 11	08 15	08 18	08 22	08 25	08 37	08 40	08 45		08 48		08 52	08 55	09 07	09 10	09 14
Northumberland Park	d	07 49								08 20							08 50						09 16
Angel Road	d	07 51															08 52						
Ponders End	d				07 59							08 29								08 59			
Brimsdown	d				08 02							08 32								09 02			
Enfield Lock	d				08 04					08 26		08 34								09 04			09 22
Waltham Cross	d				08 07							08 37								09 07			
Cheshunt	d	07 58			08 09			08 21		08 29		08 39		08 48			08 59			09 09		09 18	09 25
Broxbourne	a	08 04			08 15	08 18		08 25		08 35		08 45		08 53			09 05			09 15		09 23	09 31
Broxbourne	d	08 10			08 15			08 25		08 39		08 45		08 53			09 09			09 15		09 23	09 34
Rye House	d				08 18							08 48								09 18			
St Margarets (Herts)	d				08 21							08 51								09 21			
Ware	d				08 25							08 55								09 25			
Hertford East	a				08 32							09 02								09 32			
Roydon	d	08 14								08 43				08 57			09 13						09 39
Harlow Town	d	08 18					08 26	08 36		08 47			08 55	09 05			09 17				09 25	09 29	09 43
Harlow Mill	d	08 21								08 50							09 20						09 46
Sawbridgeworth	d	08 25						08 42		08 54				09 11		←	09 24						09 49
Bishops Stortford	a	08 32		08 20				08 47		09 02	08 51			09 17		09 17	09 32		09 20			09 38	09 56
Bishops Stortford	d			08 21				08 47			08 51			09 17		09 17			09 21			09 39	
Stansted Mountfitchet	d						08 37	08 51						→		09 21					09 37		
Stansted Airport ✈	a			08 30			08 45				09 01		09 14						09 31		09 47		
Stansted Airport ✈	d		08 21															09 21					
Elsenham	d							08 55								09 25							
Newport (Essex)	d							09 00								09 30							
Audley End	d		08 38					09 03							09 23	09 33		09 39				09 51	
Great Chesterford	d							09 08								09 38							
Whittlesford Parkway	d							09 13								09 43						09 58	
Shelford	d							09 17								09 47							
Cambridge	a		08 58					09 26	09 07						09 39	09 54		09 57				10 09	
	d															09 56							
Cambridge North	a															10 00							

		LE	LE	LE	LE	LE	LE	LE	XC	LE	LE	LE	LE	LE	LE	LE	LE	LE	LE	LE	XC	LE
		■	■		■	◇■	■	■	◇■		■	◇■	■	■	■		■	◇■	■	■	◇■	
									A												A	
London Liverpool Street ⊖	d	09 10		09 12	09 25	09 28		09 40		09 42	09 55	09 58		10 10		10 12	10 25	10 28		10 40		10 42
Hackney Downs	d			09 18						09 48						10 18						10 48
Stratford ⊖	d						09 30						10 00						10 30			
Lea Bridge	d						09 36						10 06						10 36			
Seven Sisters ⊖	d																					
Tottenham Hale ⊖	d	09 22		09 25	09 37	09 40	09 44	09 52		09 55	10 07	10 10	10 13	10 22		10 25	10 37	10 40	10 43	10 52		10 55
Northumberland Park	d						09 46						10 15									
Angel Road	d						09 48															
Ponders End	d			09 29						09 59						10 29						10 59
Brimsdown	d			09 32						10 02						10 32						11 02
Enfield Lock	d			09 34						10 04			10 21			10 34						11 04
Waltham Cross	d			09 37			09 54			10 07						10 37			10 50			11 07
Cheshunt	d			09 39		09 48	09 56			10 09		10 18	10 25			10 39		10 48	10 52			11 09
Broxbourne	a			09 45		09 53	10 02			10 15		10 23	10 30			10 45		10 53	10 58			11 15
Broxbourne	d			09 45		09 53	10 05			10 15		10 23	10 34			10 45		10 53	10 58			11 15
Rye House	d			09 48						10 18						10 48						11 18
St Margarets (Herts)	d			09 51						10 21						10 51						11 21
Ware	d			09 55						10 25						10 55						11 25
Hertford East	a			10 01						10 31						11 01						11 31
Roydon	d					09 57							10 39					10 57				
Harlow Town	d				09 55	10 01	10 12				10 25	10 29	10 43				10 55	11 01	11 11			
Harlow Mill	d					10 04							10 46					11 04				
Sawbridgeworth	d					10 08	10 17						10 49					11 08	11 17			
Bishops Stortford	a	09 45				10 14	10 23	10 17				10 38	10 56	10 45				11 14	11 23	11 17		
Bishops Stortford	d	09 45				10 14		10 18				10 39		10 45				11 14		11 18		
Stansted Mountfitchet	d					10 18					10 36							11 18				
Stansted Airport ✈	a	09 55			10 12			10 27			10 44			10 55			11 13			11 27		
Stansted Airport ✈	d		10 10						10 27						11 10						11 27	
Elsenham	d					10 22												11 22				
Newport (Essex)	d					10 27												11 27				
Audley End	d		10 24			10 30			10 40			10 51			11 24			11 30			11 40	
Great Chesterford	d					10 35												11 35				
Whittlesford Parkway	d		10 31			10 40						10 58			11 31			11 40				
Shelford	d					10 44												11 44				
Cambridge	a		10 43			10 51			10 59			11 09			11 43			11 51			11 59	
	d					10 52												11 52				
Cambridge North	a					10 56												11 56				

A To Birmingham New Street
B To Cambridge North
C From London Liverpool Street

Table T022-F

Mondays to Fridays

21 May to 7 December

London - Broxbourne, Hertford East, Bishops Stortford, Stansted Airport, Cambridge and Cambridge North

		LE	LE	LE	LE	LE	LE		LE	LE	LE	LE	XC	LE	LE	LE	LE		LE	LE	LE	LE	LE	LE	LE
		■	◇■	■	■	■			■	◇■	■	■	◇■		■	◇■	■		■	■		■	◇■	■	■
													A												
London Liverpool Street 15 ⊖	d	10 55	10 58		11 10		11 12		11 25	11 28		11 40		11 42	11 55	11 58			12 10		12 12	12 25	12 28		12 40
Hackney Downs	d						11 18							11 48							12 18				
Stratford 7 ⊖	d			11 00							11 30						12 00							12 30	
Lea Bridge	d			11 06							11 36						12 06							12 36	
Seven Sisters ⊖	d																								
Tottenham Hale ⊖	d	11 07	11 10	11 13	11 22		11 25		11 37	11 40	11 43	11 52		11 55	12 07	12 10	12 13		12 22		12 25	12 37	12 40	12 43	12 52
Northumberland Park	d			11 15													12 15								
Angel Road	d																								
Ponders End	d						11 29							11 59							12 29				
Brimsdown	d						11 32							12 02							12 32				
Enfield Lock	d			11 21			11 34							12 04			12 21				12 34				
Waltham Cross	d						11 37				11 50			12 07							12 37			12 50	
Cheshunt	d		11 18	11 25			11 39			11 48	11 52			12 09		12 18	12 25				12 39		12 48	12 52	
Broxbourne 3	a		11 23	11 30			11 45			11 53	11 58			12 15		12 23	12 30				12 45		12 53	12 58	
Broxbourne 3	d		11 23	11 34			11 45			11 53	11 58			12 15		12 23	12 34				12 45		12 53	12 58	
Rye House	d						11 48							12 18							12 48				
St Margarets (Herts)	d						11 51							12 21							12 51				
Ware	d						11 55							12 25							12 55				
Hertford East	a						12 01							12 31							13 01				
Roydon	d			11 39						11 57							12 39						12 57		
Harlow Town	d	11 25	11 29	11 43					11 55	12 01	12 11				12 25	12 29	12 43					12 55	13 01	13 11	
Harlow Mill	d			11 46						12 04							12 46						13 04		
Sawbridgeworth	d			11 49						12 08	12 17						12 49						13 08	13 17	
Bishops Stortford	a		11 38	11 56	11 45					12 14	12 23	12 17				12 38	12 56		12 45				13 14	13 23	13 17
Bishops Stortford	d		11 39		11 45					12 14		12 18				12 39			12 45				13 14		13 18
Stansted Mountfitchet	d	11 36								12 18					12 36								13 18		
Stansted Airport ✈	a	11 44			11 55				12 12			12 27			12 44				12 55			13 12			13 27
Stansted Airport ✈	d					12 10							12 27							13 10					
Elsenham	d									12 22													13 22		
Newport (Essex)	d									12 27													13 27		
Audley End	d		11 51			12 24				12 30			12 40			12 51				13 24			13 30		
Great Chesterford	d									12 35													13 35		
Whittlesford Parkway	d		11 58			12 31				12 40						12 58				13 31			13 40		
Shelford	d									12 44													13 44		
Cambridge	a		12 09			12 43				12 51			12 59			13 09				13 43			13 51		
	d									12 52													13 52		
Cambridge North	a									12 56													13 56		

		XC	LE		LE	LE	LE	LE	LE	LE	LE	LE	LE		LE	XC	LE	LE	LE	LE	LE	LE	LE		LE
		◇■			■	◇■	■	■	■		■	◇■	■		■	◇■		■	◇■	■	■	■			■
		A														A						B			
London Liverpool Street 15 ⊖	d		12 42		12 55	12 58		13 10		13 12	13 25	13 28			13 40		13 42	13 55	13 58		14 10		14 12		14 25
Hackney Downs	d		12 48							13 18							13 48						14 18		
Stratford 7 ⊖	d						13 00						13 30							14 00					
Lea Bridge	d						13 06						13 36							14 06					
Seven Sisters ⊖	d																								
Tottenham Hale ⊖	d		12 55		13 07	13 10	13 13	13 22		13 25	13 37	13 40	13 43		13 52		13 55	14 07	14 10	14 13	14 22		14 25		14 37
Northumberland Park	d						13 15													14 15					
Angel Road	d																								
Ponders End	d		12 59							13 29							13 59						14 29		
Brimsdown	d		13 02							13 32							14 02						14 32		
Enfield Lock	d		13 04				13 21			13 34							14 04			14 21			14 34		
Waltham Cross	d		13 07							13 37			13 50				14 07						14 37		
Cheshunt	d		13 09			13 18	13 25			13 39		13 48	13 52				14 09		14 18	14 25			14 39		
Broxbourne 3	a		13 15			13 23	13 30			13 45		13 53	13 58				14 15		14 23	14 30			14 45		
Broxbourne 3	d		13 15			13 23	13 34			13 45		13 53	13 58				14 15		14 23	14 34			14 45		
Rye House	d		13 18							13 48							14 18						14 48		
St Margarets (Herts)	d		13 21							13 51							14 21						14 51		
Ware	d		13 25							13 55							14 25						14 55		
Hertford East	a		13 31							14 01							14 31						15 01		
Roydon	d						13 39					13 57								14 39					
Harlow Town	d				13 25	13 29	13 43				13 55	14 01	14 11					14 25	14 29	14 43					14 55
Harlow Mill	d						13 46					14 04								14 46					
Sawbridgeworth	d						13 49					14 08	14 17							14 49					
Bishops Stortford	a					13 38	13 56	13 45				14 14	14 23		14 17				14 38	14 56	14 45				
Bishops Stortford	d					13 39		13 45				14 14			14 18				14 39		14 45				
Stansted Mountfitchet	d				13 36							14 18						14 36							
Stansted Airport ✈	a				13 44			13 55			14 12				14 27			14 44			14 55				15 13
Stansted Airport ✈	d	13 27							14 10							14 27						15 10			
Elsenham	d											14 22													
Newport (Essex)	d											14 27													
Audley End	d	13 40				13 51			14 24			14 30				14 40			14 51			15 24			
Great Chesterford	d											14 35													
Whittlesford Parkway	d					13 58			14 31			14 40							14 58			15 31			
Shelford	d											14 44													
Cambridge	a	13 59				14 09			14 43			14 51				14 59			15 09			15 43			
	d											14 52										15 44			
Cambridge North	a											14 56										15 48			

A To Birmingham New Street

B To Ely

Table T022-F

Mondays to Fridays

21 May to 7 December

London - Broxbourne, Hertford East, Bishops Stortford, Stansted Airport, Cambridge and Cambridge North

		LE	LE	LE	XC	LE	LE	LE	LE		LE	LE	LE	LE	LE	LE	LE	XC	LE		LE	LE	LE	LE	LE
		◇■	■	■	◇■		■	◇■	■		■	■		■	◇■	■	■	◇■			■	◇■	■	■	
					A													A				B			
London Liverpool Street 15 ⊖	d	14 28		14 40		14 42	14 55	14 58			15 10		15 12	15 25	15 28		15 40		15 42		15 55	15 58		16 10	16 12
Hackney Downs	d					14 48							15 18						15 48						16 19
Stratford 7 ⊖	d		14 30						15 00							15 30							16 00		
Lea Bridge	d		14 36						15 06							15 36							16 06		
Seven Sisters ⊖	d																								
Tottenham Hale ⊖	d	14 40	14 43	14 52		14 55	15 07	15 10	15 13		15 22		15 25	15 37	15 40	15 43	15 52		15 55		16 07	16 10	16 13	16 22	16 25
Northumberland Park	d								15 15														16 15		
Angel Road	d																						16 17		
Ponders End	d					14 59							15 29						15 59						16 30
Brimsdown	d					15 02							15 32						16 02						16 32
Enfield Lock	d					15 04			15 21				15 34						16 04				16 22		16 35
Waltham Cross	d		14 50			15 07							15 37			15 50			16 07						16 37
Cheshunt	d	14 48	14 52			15 09		15 18	15 25				15 39		15 48	15 52			16 09			16 18	16 26		16 40
Broxbourne 3	a	14 53	14 58			15 15		15 23	15 30				15 45		15 53	15 58			16 15			16 23	16 31		16 45
Broxbourne 3	d	14 53	14 58			15 15		15 23	15 34				15 45		15 53	15 58			16 15			16 23	16 35		16 46
Rye House	d					15 18							15 48						16 18						16 49
St Margarets (Herts)	d					15 21							15 51						16 21						16 52
Ware	d					15 25							15 55						16 25						16 56
Hertford East	a					15 31							16 01						16 31						17 04
Roydon	d	14 57							15 39						15 57							16 27	16 39		
Harlow Town	d	15 01	15 11				15 25	15 29	15 43					15 55	16 01	16 11					16 25	16 31	16 43		
Harlow Mill	d	15 04							15 46						16 04							16 34	16 46		
Sawbridgeworth	d	15 08	15 17						15 49						16 08	16 17						16 38	16 50		
Bishops Stortford	a	15 14	15 23	15 17				15 38	15 56		15 45				16 14	16 23	16 17					16 44	16 58	16 47	
Bishops Stortford	d	15 14		15 18				15 41			15 45				16 14		16 18					16 44		16 48	
Stansted Mountfitchet	d	15 18					15 36	15 45							16 18						16 36	16 48			
Stansted Airport ✈	a			15 27			15 44				15 55			16 12			16 27				16 44			17 01	
Stansted Airport ✈	d				15 27							16 10						16 27							
Elsenham	d	15 22						15 49							16 22							16 52			
Newport (Essex)	d	15 27						15 55							16 27							16 57			
Audley End	d	15 30			15 40			15 58				16 24			16 30			16 40				17 00			
Great Chesterford	d	15 35						16 03							16 35							17 05			
Whittlesford Parkway	d	15 40						16 08				16 31			16 40							17 10			
Shelford	d	15 44						16 12							16 44							17 14			
Cambridge	a	15 51			15 59			16 20				16 43			16 51			16 59				17 20			
	d	15 52													16 52							17 21			
Cambridge North	a	15 56													16 56							17 25			

		LE	LE	LE	XC		LE	LE	LE	LE	LE	LE	LE	LE	LE		LE	LE	LE	LE	LE	LE	LE	LE	XC
		■	■	■	◇■		■		◇■		■	■		◇■	■		■		◇■			■		◇■	◇■
					A			C		D	E			F			G	C		D					A
London Liverpool Street 15 ⊖	d	16 25	16 28				16 39	16 41	16 43			16 54	16 56	17 07	17 09			17 11	17 13			17 24	17 26	17 37	
Hackney Downs	d							16 48					17 03					17 18					17 33		
Stratford 7 ⊖	d			16 30							16 47										17 17				
Lea Bridge	d			16 36							16 53										17 23				
Seven Sisters ⊖	d							16 54										17 24							
Tottenham Hale ⊖	d	16 37	16 40	16 43			16 52		16 55		16 58	17 06	17 09	17 19	17 22				17 25		17 28	17 36	17 39	17 49	
Northumberland Park	d										17 01										17 31				
Angel Road	d										17 03										17 33				
Ponders End	d			16 48									17 14										17 44		
Brimsdown	d			16 50									17 16										17 46		
Enfield Lock	d			16 53							17 08		17 19								17 38		17 49		
Waltham Cross	d			16 55						←	17 10		17 21							←	17 40		17 51		
Cheshunt	d			16 58				17 09	17 04	17 09	17 13		17 24					17 39	17 34	17 39	17 43		17 54		
Broxbourne 3	a		16 53	17 03				→	17 10	17 15	17 18		17 31					→	17 39	17 45	17 48		18 01		
Broxbourne 3	d		16 53	17 04					17 10	17 15	17 23								17 40	17 45	17 52				
Rye House	d									17 19										17 49	17 55				
St Margarets (Herts)	d									17 22										17 52	17 58				
Ware	d									17 26										17 56	18 02				
Hertford East	a									17 33										18 03	18 10				
Roydon	d								17 14		17 28						←		17 44						
Harlow Town	d	16 56	17 00	17 13					17 18		17 43	17 26			17 40		17 43		17 48			17 56			
Harlow Mill	d								17 21		→						17 46		17 51						
Sawbridgeworth	d		17 05						17 25								17 50		17 55						
Bishops Stortford	a	17 05	17 11	17 25			17 17		17 31			17 35		17 43			17 58		18 01			18 05		18 13	
Bishops Stortford	d	17 05	17 12				17 18		17 31			17 35		17 44					18 01			18 05		18 14	
Stansted Mountfitchet	d		17 16						17 36						17 52				18 06						
Stansted Airport ✈	a	17 17					17 29					17 47			18 01							18 17			
Stansted Airport ✈	d				17 27																				18 21
Elsenham	d								17 39										18 09						
Newport (Essex)	d								17 45										18 15						
Audley End	d		17 26		17 40				17 48					17 56					18 18					18 26	18 38
Great Chesterford	d								17 53										18 23						
Whittlesford Parkway	d		17 33						17 58					18 04					18 28					18 34	
Shelford	d								18 02										18 32						
Cambridge	a		17 45		17 59				18 11					18 17					18 41					18 48	18 57
	d																							18 51	
Cambridge North	a																							18 55	

A To Birmingham New Street

B To Ely

C To Hertford East

D From London Liverpool Street

E To Bishops Stortford

F To Kings Lynn. The Fenman

G From Stratford

Table T022-F

Mondays to Fridays
21 May to 7 December

London - Broxbourne, Hertford East, Bishops Stortford, Stansted Airport, Cambridge and Cambridge North

		LE	LE	LE	LE	LE	LE	LE	LE	LE	LE	LE	LE	LE	LE	LE	LE	LE	XC	LE	LE	LE
		■		◇■		■	■		◇■	■	■		◇■			■		■	◇■	■		◇■
			A		B	C			D		E	A		B					F		A	
London Liverpool Street 15 ⊖	d	17 39	17 41	17 43			17 54	17 56	18 07	18 09		18 11	18 13			18 24	18 26	18 37		18 39	18 41	18 43
Hackney Downs	d		17 48					18 03				18 18					18 33				18 48	
Stratford 7 ⊖	d					17 47									18 17							
Lea Bridge	d					17 53									18 23							
Seven Sisters ⊖	d		17 54									18 24									18 54	
Tottenham Hale ⊖	d	17 52		17 55		17 58	18 06	18 09	18 19	18 22			18 25		18 28	18 36	18 39	18 49		18 52		18 55
Northumberland Park	d					18 01									18 31							
Angel Road	d					18 03									18 33							
Ponders End	d							18 14									18 44					
Brimsdown	d							18 16									18 46					
Enfield Lock	d					18 08		18 19							18 38		18 49					
Waltham Cross	d				←	18 10		18 21						←	18 40		18 51					
Cheshunt	d		18 09	18 04	18 09	18 13		18 24				18 39	18 34	18 39	18 43		18 54				19 09	19 04
Broxbourne 3	a		→	18 09	18 15	18 18		18 31				→	18 39	18 45	18 48		19 01				→	19 09
Broxbourne 3	d			18 10	18 15	18 23							18 40	18 45	18 52							19 10
Rye House	d				18 19									18 49	18 55							
St Margarets (Herts)	d				18 22									18 52	18 58							
Ware	d				18 26									18 56	19 02							
Hertford East	a				18 33									19 03	19 10							
Roydon	d			18 14		18 28					←		18 44									19 14
Harlow Town	d	18 10		18 18		18 43	18 26			18 40	18 43		18 48			18 56				19 10		19 18
Harlow Mill	d			18 21		→					18 46		18 51									19 21
Sawbridgeworth	d	18 15		18 25							18 50		18 55							19 15		19 25
Bishops Stortford	a			18 31			18 35		18 43		18 58		19 01			19 05		19 13				19 31
Bishops Stortford	d			18 31			18 35		18 44				19 01			19 05		19 14				19 31
Stansted Mountfitchet	d			18 36						18 52			19 06									19 36
Stansted Airport ✈	a	18 32					18 47			19 01						19 17				19 32		
Stansted Airport ✈	d																		19 21			
Elsenham	d			18 39									19 09									19 39
Newport (Essex)	d			18 45									19 15									19 45
Audley End	d			18 48					18 56				19 18					19 26	19 38			19 48
Great Chesterford	d			18 53									19 23									19 53
Whittlesford Parkway	d			18 58					19 04				19 28					19 34				19 58
Shelford	d			19 02									19 32									20 02
Cambridge	a			19 14					19 17				19 41					19 49	19 56			20 12
	d																	19 52				
Cambridge North	a																	19 56				

		LE	LE	LE	LE	LE	LE	LE	LE	LE	LE	LE	LE	XC	LE	LE	LE	LE	LE	LE	LE	LE	LE
			■	■		◇■	■	■	◇■		■	◇■	■	◇■	■		■	◇■	■	■		■	◇■
		B	C			D		E						F									
London Liverpool Street 15 ⊖	d			18 54	18 56	19 07	19 09		19 11	19 13	19 25	19 28			19 40	19 42	19 55	19 58		20 10	20 12	20 25	20 28
Hackney Downs	d				19 03					19 19						19 48					20 18		
Stratford 7 ⊖	d		18 47										19 30						20 00				
Lea Bridge	d		18 53										19 36						20 06				
Seven Sisters ⊖	d																						
Tottenham Hale ⊖	d		18 58	19 06	19 09	19 19	19 22		19 25	19 28	19 37	19 40	19 43		19 52	19 55	20 07	20 10	20 13	20 22	20 25	20 37	20 40
Northumberland Park	d		19 01										19 45						20 15				
Angel Road	d		19 03										19 47										
Ponders End	d				19 14					19 32						19 59					20 29		
Brimsdown	d				19 16					19 35						20 02					20 32		
Enfield Lock	d		19 08		19 19					19 37						20 04			20 21		20 34		
Waltham Cross	d	←	19 10		19 21					19 40			19 53			20 07					20 37		
Cheshunt	d	19 09	19 13		19 24				19 34	19 42		19 49	19 55			20 09		20 18	20 25		20 39		20 48
Broxbourne 3	a	19 15	19 18		19 31				19 39	19 48		19 55	20 01			20 15		20 23	20 30		20 45		20 53
Broxbourne 3	d	19 15	19 23		19 36				19 40	19 48		19 55	20 04			20 15		20 23	20 34		20 45		20 53
Rye House	d	19 19			19 39					19 51						20 18					20 48		
St Margarets (Herts)	d	19 22			19 42					19 54						20 21					20 51		
Ware	d	19 26			19 47					19 58						20 25					20 55		
Hertford East	a	19 33			19 54					20 04						20 31					21 01		
Roydon	d		19 28					←	19 44			20 00	20 09						20 39				20 57
Harlow Town	d		19 43	19 26			19 40	19 43	19 48		19 58	20 04	20 13				20 25	20 29	20 43			20 55	21 01
Harlow Mill	d		→					19 46	19 51			20 07	20 16						20 46				21 04
Sawbridgeworth	d							19 50	19 55			20 10	20 19					20 34	20 49				21 08
Bishops Stortford	a			19 35			19 49	19 56	20 01			20 16	20 28		20 20			20 40	20 56	20 45			21 14
Bishops Stortford	d			19 35			19 49		20 01			20 17			20 21			20 40		20 45			21 14
Stansted Mountfitchet	d						19 53		20 06			20 21					20 36						21 18
Stansted Airport ✈	a			19 47			20 00				20 15				20 30		20 43			20 55		21 12	
Stansted Airport ✈	d													20 21									
Elsenham	d								20 09			20 25											21 22
Newport (Essex)	d								20 15			20 30											21 27
Audley End	d					19 56			20 18			20 33		20 39				20 52					21 30
Great Chesterford	d								20 23			20 38											21 35
Whittlesford Parkway	d					20 03			20 28			20 43						21 00					21 40
Shelford	d								20 32			20 47											21 44
Cambridge	a					20 15			20 39			20 55		21 00				21 09					21 51
	d											20 57											21 52
Cambridge North	a											21 01											21 56

A To Hertford East
B From London Liverpool Street
C To Bishops Stortford
D To Kings Lynn
E From Stratford
F To Birmingham New Street

Table T022-F

Mondays to Fridays
21 May to 7 December

London - Broxbourne, Hertford East, Bishops Stortford, Stansted Airport, Cambridge and Cambridge North

		LE	LE	XC	LE	LE	LE	LE	LE	LE	LE	LE	LE	LE	LE	XC	LE	LE	LE	LE	LE	XC
		■	■	■		■	◇■	■	■	■		■	◇■	■	■	■		■	◇■	■	■	■
London Liverpool Street 15 ⊖	d		20 40		20 42	20 55	20 58		21 10		21 12	21 25	21 28		21 40		21 42	21 55	21 58		22 10	
Hackney Downs	d				20 48						21 18						21 48					
Stratford 7 ⊖	d	20 30						21 00						21 30						22 00		
Lea Bridge	d	20 36						21 06						21 36						22 06		
Seven Sisters ⊖	d																					
Tottenham Hale ⊖	d	20 43	20 52		20 55	21 07	21 10	21 13	21 22		21 25	21 37	21 40	21 43	21 52		21 55	22 07	22 10	22 13	22 22	
Northumberland Park	d							21 15												22 15		
Angel Road	d																					
Ponders End	d				20 59						21 29						21 59					
Brimsdown	d				21 02						21 32						22 02					
Enfield Lock	d				21 04			21 21			21 34						22 04			22 21		
Waltham Cross	d	20 50			21 07						21 37			21 50			22 07					
Cheshunt	d	20 52			21 09		21 18	21 25			21 39		21 48	21 52			22 09		22 18	22 25		
Broxbourne 3	a	20 58			21 15		21 23	21 30			21 45		21 53	21 58			22 15		22 23	22 30		
Broxbourne 3	d	20 58			21 15		21 23	21 34			21 45		21 53	21 58			22 15		22 23	22 34		
Rye House	d				21 18						21 48						22 18					
St Margarets (Herts)	d				21 21						21 51						22 21					
Ware	d				21 25						21 55						22 25					
Hertford East	a				21 31						22 01						22 31					
Roydon	d							21 39					21 57							22 39		
Harlow Town	d	21 11				21 25	21 29	21 43				21 55	22 01	22 11				22 25	22 29	22 43		
Harlow Mill	d							21 46					22 04							22 46		
Sawbridgeworth	d	21 17					21 34	21 49					22 08	22 17					22 34	22 49		
Bishops Stortford	a	21 23	21 17				21 40	21 56	21 45				22 14	22 23	22 17				22 40	22 56	22 45	
Bishops Stortford	d		21 18				21 40		21 45				22 14		22 18				22 40		22 45	
Stansted Mountfitchet	d					21 36							22 18					22 36				
Stansted Airport ✈	a		21 27			21 44			21 55		22 12				22 27			22 43			22 57	
Stansted Airport ✈	d			21 27						22 10						22 27						22 57
Elsenham	d												22 22									
Newport (Essex)	d												22 27									
Audley End	d			21 40			21 52			22 24			22 30			22 40			22 52			23 10
Great Chesterford	d												22 35									
Whittlesford Parkway	d						22 00			22 31			22 40						23 00			
Shelford	d												22 44									
Cambridge	a			21 56			22 09			22 44			22 51			22 56			23 09			23 26
	d												22 58									
Cambridge North	a												23 03									

		LE	LE	LE	LE	LE	LE	LE	LE	LE	LE	LE	LE	LE	LE	LE
															FX	FO
			■	◇■	■	■		■	◇■	■		■	◇■		■	■
London Liverpool Street 15 ⊖	d	22 12	22 25	22 28		22 40	22 42	22 55	22 58		23 12	23 25	23 28	23 42	23 58	23 58
Hackney Downs	d	22 18					22 48				23 18			23 48		
Stratford 7 ⊖	d				22 30					23 00						
Lea Bridge	d				22 36					23 06						
Seven Sisters ⊖	d															
Tottenham Hale ⊖	d	22 25	22 37	22 40	22 43	22 52	22 55	23 07	23 10	23 13	23 25	23 37	23 40	23 54	00 10	00 10
Northumberland Park	d									23 15				23 57		
Angel Road	d															
Ponders End	d	22 29					22 59				23 29			00 01		
Brimsdown	d	22 32					23 02				23 32			00 03		
Enfield Lock	d	22 34					23 04			23 21	23 34			00 06		
Waltham Cross	d	22 37			22 50		23 07				23 37			00 08		
Cheshunt	d	22 39		22 48	22 52		23 09		23 18	23 25	23 39		23 48	00 11	00 18	00 18
Broxbourne 3	a	22 45		22 53	22 58		23 15		23 23	23 30	23 45		23 53	00 16	00 23	00 23
Broxbourne 3	d	22 45		22 53	22 59		23 15		23 23	23 30	23 45		23 53	00 16	00 23	00 23
Rye House	d	22 48					23 18				23 48			00 20		
St Margarets (Herts)	d	22 51					23 21				23 51			00 23		
Ware	d	22 55					23 25				23 55			00 27		
Hertford East	a	23 01					23 31				00 01			00 32		
Roydon	d			22 57						23 34			23 57		00 27	00 27
Harlow Town	d		22 55	23 01	23 11			23 25	23 29	23 38		23 55	00 01		00 31	00 31
Harlow Mill	d			23 04						23 41			00 04		00 34	00 34
Sawbridgeworth	d			23 08	23 17				23 34	23 45			00 08		00 38	00 38
Bishops Stortford	a			23 14	23 23	23 17			23 40	23 51		00 04	00 14		00 44	00 44
Bishops Stortford	d			23 14		23 18			23 40			00 04	00 14			00 44
Stansted Mountfitchet	d			23 18				23 37					00 18			00 48
Stansted Airport ✈	a		23 12			23 30		23 44				00 13				
Stansted Airport ✈	d															
Elsenham	d			23 22									00 22			00 52
Newport (Essex)	d			23 27									00 27			00 57
Audley End	d			23 30					23 52				00 30			01 00
Great Chesterford	d			23 35									00 35			01 05
Whittlesford Parkway	d			23 40					23 59				00 40			01 10
Shelford	d			23 44									00 44			
Cambridge	a			23 51					00 09				00 51			01 19
	d			23 52												
Cambridge North	a			23 56												

Table T022-F

Saturdays

26 May to 8 December

London - Broxbourne, Hertford East, Bishops Stortford, Stansted Airport, Cambridge and Cambridge North

		LE A	LE ■ A	LE ◇■ A	LE ■ A	LE ■	LE ■	XC ◇■ B	LE ■	LE ■	LE ◇■ C	LE ■	LE ◇■ A	LE ■	XC ◇■ B	LE	LE ■ D	LE ■	LE ◇■	LE ■ A	LE ■	LE ■	LE
London Liverpool Street ⊖	d					03 40	04 10		04 40	05 10	05 20	05 25		05 40		05 42	05 51	05 55	05 58			06 10	06 12
Hackney Downs	d															05 48							06 18
Stratford ⊖	d										05 29						06 00						
Lea Bridge	d										05 35						06 06						
Seven Sisters ⊖	d												←							←			
Tottenham Hale ⊖	d				00 10				04 52	05 22	05 40	05 37	05 40	05 52		05 55	06 13	06 07	06 10	06 13		06 22	06 25
Northumberland Park	d										→						→			06 15			
Angel Road	d																						
Ponders End	d	00 01														05 59							06 29
Brimsdown	d	00 03														06 02							06 32
Enfield Lock	d	00 06														06 04				06 21			06 34
Waltham Cross	d	00 08														06 07							06 37
Cheshunt	d	00 11			00 18				05 00				05 48			06 09			06 18	06 25			06 39
Broxbourne	a	00 16			00 23				05 05				05 53			06 15			06 23	06 30			06 45
Broxbourne	d	00 16			00 23				05 05				05 53			06 15			06 23	06 34			06 45
Rye House	d	00 20														06 18							06 48
St Margarets (Herts)	d	00 23														06 21							06 51
Ware	d	00 27														06 25							06 55
Hertford East	a	00 32														06 31							07 01
Roydon	d				00 27								05 57							06 39			
Harlow Town	d			00 01	00 31				05 11	05 38		05 53	06 01					06 24	06 29	06 43			
Harlow Mill	d			00 04	00 34								06 04							06 46			
Sawbridgeworth	d			00 08	00 38					05 43			06 08							06 49			
Bishops Stortford	a			00 14	00 44				05 20	05 49		06 02	06 14	06 17				06 33	06 38	06 56		06 45	
Bishops Stortford	d		00 04	00 14	00 44				05 20	05 50		06 02	06 14	06 18				06 33	06 39			06 45	
Stansted Mountfitchet	d			00 18	00 48				05 24			06 06	06 18					06 37					
Stansted Airport ✈	a		00 13			04 30	05 00		05 39	05 59		06 13		06 27				06 44				06 57	
Stansted Airport ✈	d							05 25							06 27						06 48		
Elsenham	d			00 22	00 52								06 22										
Newport (Essex)	d			00 27	00 57								06 27										
Audley End	d			00 30	01 00			05 37					06 30		06 40				06 51		07 02		
Great Chesterford	d			00 35	01 05								06 35										
Whittlesford Parkway	d			00 40	01 10								06 40						06 58		07 09		
Shelford	d			00 44									06 44										
Cambridge	a			00 51	01 19			05 51					06 51		06 56				07 09		07 20		
	d												06 52										
Cambridge North	a												06 57										

		LE ■ D	LE ■	LE ◇■	LE ■ A	LE ■	XC ◇■ B	LE	LE ■	LE ◇■	LE ■	LE ■	LE ■	LE	LE ■	LE ◇■	LE ■	LE ■	XC ◇■ B	LE	LE ■	LE ◇■	LE ■
London Liverpool Street ⊖	d	06 21	06 25	06 28		06 40		06 42	06 55	06 58			07 10	07 12	07 25	07 28		07 40		07 42	07 55	07 58	
Hackney Downs	d							06 48						07 18						07 48			
Stratford ⊖	d	06 30									07 00						07 30						08 00
Lea Bridge	d	06 36									07 06						07 36						08 06
Seven Sisters ⊖	d				←																		
Tottenham Hale ⊖	d	06 43	06 37	06 40	06 43	06 52		06 55	07 07	07 10	07 13		07 22	07 25	07 37	07 40	07 43	07 52		07 55	08 07	08 10	08 13
Northumberland Park	d	→									07 15												08 15
Angel Road	d																						
Ponders End	d							06 59						07 29						07 59			
Brimsdown	d							07 02						07 32						08 02			
Enfield Lock	d							07 04			07 21			07 34						08 04			08 21
Waltham Cross	d				06 50			07 07						07 37			07 50			08 07			
Cheshunt	d			06 48	06 52			07 09		07 18	07 25			07 39		07 48	07 52			08 09		08 18	08 25
Broxbourne	a			06 53	06 58			07 15		07 23	07 30			07 45		07 53	07 58			08 15		08 23	08 30
Broxbourne	d			06 53	06 58			07 15		07 23	07 34			07 45		07 53	07 58			08 15		08 23	08 34
Rye House	d							07 18						07 48						08 18			
St Margarets (Herts)	d							07 21						07 51						08 21			
Ware	d							07 25						07 55						08 25			
Hertford East	a							07 31						08 01						08 31			
Roydon	d			06 57							07 39					07 57							08 39
Harlow Town	d		06 55	07 01	07 11				07 25	07 29	07 43				07 55	08 01	08 11				08 25	08 29	08 43
Harlow Mill	d			07 04							07 46					08 04							08 46
Sawbridgeworth	d			07 08	07 17						07 49					08 08	08 17						08 49
Bishops Stortford	a			07 14	07 23	07 17				07 38	07 56		07 45			08 14	08 23	08 17				08 38	08 56
Bishops Stortford	d			07 14		07 18				07 39			07 45			08 14		08 18				08 39	
Stansted Mountfitchet	d			07 18					07 36							08 18					08 36		
Stansted Airport ✈	a		07 12			07 27			07 44				07 57		08 12			08 27			08 44		
Stansted Airport ✈	d						07 27					07 48							08 27				
Elsenham	d			07 22												08 22							
Newport (Essex)	d			07 27												08 27							
Audley End	d			07 30			07 40			07 51		08 02				08 30			08 40			08 51	
Great Chesterford	d			07 35												08 35							
Whittlesford Parkway	d			07 40						07 58		08 09				08 40						08 58	
Shelford	d			07 44												08 44							
Cambridge	a			07 51			07 59			08 09		08 19				08 51			08 59			09 09	
	d			07 52												08 52							
Cambridge North	a			07 57												08 57							

A From London Liverpool Street
B To Birmingham New Street
C To Cambridge North
D To Bishops Stortford

Table T022-F

Saturdays

26 May to 8 December

London - Broxbourne, Hertford East, Bishops Stortford, Stansted Airport, Cambridge and Cambridge North

		LE ■	LE ■	LE	LE ■	LE ◇■	LE ■	LE ■	XC ◇■ A	LE	LE ■	LE ◇■	LE ■	LE ■	LE ■	LE	LE ■	LE ◇■	LE ■	LE ■	XC ◇■ A	LE
London Liverpool Street ⊖	d	08 10		08 12	08 25	08 28		08 40		08 42	08 55	08 58		09 10		09 12	09 25	09 28		09 40		09 42
Hackney Downs	d			08 18						08 48						09 18						09 48
Stratford ⊖	d						08 30						09 00						09 30			
Lea Bridge	d						08 36						09 06						09 36			
Seven Sisters ⊖	d																					
Tottenham Hale ⊖	d	08 22		08 25	08 37	08 40	08 43	08 52		08 55	09 07	09 10	09 13	09 22		09 25	09 37	09 40	09 43	09 52		09 55
Northumberland Park	d												09 15									
Angel Road	d																					
Ponders End	d			08 29						08 59						09 29						09 59
Brimsdown	d			08 32						09 02						09 32						10 02
Enfield Lock	d			08 34						09 04			09 21			09 34						10 04
Waltham Cross	d			08 37			08 50			09 07						09 37			09 50			10 07
Cheshunt	d			08 39		08 48	08 52			09 09		09 18	09 25			09 39		09 48	09 52			10 09
Broxbourne	a			08 45		08 53	08 58			09 15		09 23	09 30			09 45		09 53	09 58			10 15
Broxbourne	d			08 45		08 53	08 58			09 15		09 23	09 34			09 45		09 53	09 58			10 15
Rye House	d			08 48						09 18						09 48						10 18
St Margarets (Herts)	d			08 51						09 21						09 51						10 21
Ware	d			08 55						09 25						09 55						10 25
Hertford East	a			09 01						09 31						10 01						10 31
Roydon	d					08 57							09 39					09 57				
Harlow Town	d				08 55	09 01	09 11				09 25	09 29	09 43				09 55	10 01	10 11			
Harlow Mill	d					09 04							09 46					10 04				
Sawbridgeworth	d					09 08	09 17						09 49					10 08	10 17			
Bishops Stortford	a	08 45				09 14	09 23	09 17				09 38	09 56	09 45				10 14	10 23	10 17		
Bishops Stortford	d	08 45				09 14		09 18				09 39		09 45				10 14		10 18		
Stansted Mountfitchet	d					09 18					09 36							10 18				
Stansted Airport ✈	a	08 55			09 12			09 27			09 44			09 55			10 12			10 27		
Stansted Airport ✈	d		09 10						09 27						10 10						10 27	
Elsenham	d					09 22												10 22				
Newport (Essex)	d					09 27												10 27				
Audley End	d		09 24			09 30			09 40			09 51			10 24			10 30			10 40	
Great Chesterford	d					09 35												10 35				
Whittlesford Parkway	d		09 31			09 40						09 58			10 31			10 40				
Shelford	d					09 44												10 44				
Cambridge	a		09 44			09 51			09 59			10 09			10 43			10 51			10 59	
	d					09 52												10 52				
Cambridge North	a					09 57												10 57				

		LE ■	LE ◇■	LE ■	LE ■	LE ■	LE	LE ■	LE ◇■	LE ■	LE ■	XC ◇■ A	LE	LE ■	LE ◇■	LE ■	LE ■	LE ■	LE	LE ■	LE ◇■	LE ■	LE ■
London Liverpool Street ⊖	d	09 55	09 58		10 10		10 12	10 25	10 28		10 40		10 42	10 55	10 58		11 10		11 12	11 25	11 28		11 40
Hackney Downs	d						10 18						10 48						11 18				
Stratford ⊖	d			10 00						10 30						11 00						11 30	
Lea Bridge	d			10 06						10 36						11 06						11 36	
Seven Sisters ⊖	d																						
Tottenham Hale ⊖	d	10 07	10 10	10 13	10 22		10 25	10 37	10 40	10 43	10 52		10 55	11 07	11 10	11 13	11 22		11 25	11 37	11 40	11 43	11 52
Northumberland Park	d			10 15												11 15							
Angel Road	d																						
Ponders End	d						10 29						10 59						11 29				
Brimsdown	d						10 32						11 02						11 32				
Enfield Lock	d			10 21			10 34						11 04			11 21			11 34				
Waltham Cross	d						10 37			10 50			11 07						11 37			11 50	
Cheshunt	d		10 18	10 25			10 39		10 48	10 52			11 09		11 18	11 25			11 39		11 48	11 52	
Broxbourne	a		10 23	10 30			10 45		10 53	10 58			11 15		11 23	11 30			11 45		11 53	11 58	
Broxbourne	d		10 23	10 34			10 45		10 53	10 58			11 15		11 23	11 34			11 45		11 53	11 58	
Rye House	d						10 48						11 18						11 48				
St Margarets (Herts)	d						10 51						11 21						11 51				
Ware	d						10 55						11 25						11 55				
Hertford East	a						11 01						11 31						12 01				
Roydon	d			10 39					10 57							11 39					11 57		
Harlow Town	d	10 25	10 29	10 43				10 55	11 01	11 11				11 25	11 29	11 43				11 55	12 01	12 11	
Harlow Mill	d			10 46					11 04							11 46					12 04		
Sawbridgeworth	d			10 49					11 08	11 17						11 49					12 08	12 17	
Bishops Stortford	a		10 38	10 56	10 45				11 14	11 23	11 17				11 38	11 56	11 45				12 14	12 23	12 17
Bishops Stortford	d		10 39		10 45				11 14		11 18				11 39		11 45				12 14		12 18
Stansted Mountfitchet	d	10 36							11 18					11 36							12 18		
Stansted Airport ✈	a	10 44			10 55			11 13			11 27			11 44			11 55			12 12			12 27
Stansted Airport ✈	d					11 10						11 27						12 10					
Elsenham	d								11 22												12 22		
Newport (Essex)	d								11 27												12 27		
Audley End	d		10 51			11 23			11 30			11 40			11 51			12 24			12 30		
Great Chesterford	d								11 35												12 35		
Whittlesford Parkway	d		10 58			11 29			11 40						11 58			12 31			12 40		
Shelford	d								11 44												12 44		
Cambridge	a		11 09			11 43			11 51			11 59			12 09			12 43			12 51		
	d								11 52												12 52		
Cambridge North	a								11 57												12 57		

A To Birmingham New Street

Table T022-F

Saturdays

26 May to 8 December

London - Broxbourne, Hertford East, Bishops Stortford, Stansted Airport, Cambridge and Cambridge North

		XC ◇■ A	LE	LE ■		LE ◇■	LE ■	LE ■	LE ■	LE	LE ■	LE ◇■	LE ■	LE ■		XC ◇■ A	LE	LE ■	LE ◇■	LE ■	LE ■	LE ■	LE	LE ■
London Liverpool Street ■ ⊖	d		11 42	11 55		11 58		12 10		12 12	12 25	12 28		12 40			12 42	12 55	12 58		13 10		13 12	13 25
Hackney Downs	d		11 48							12 18							12 48						13 18	
Stratford ■ ⊖	d						12 00						12 30							13 00				
Lea Bridge	d						12 06						12 36							13 06				
Seven Sisters ⊖	d																							
Tottenham Hale ⊖	d		11 55	12 07		12 10	12 13	12 22		12 25	12 37	12 40	12 43	12 52			12 55	13 07	13 10	13 13	13 22		13 25	13 37
Northumberland Park	d						12 15													13 15				
Angel Road	d																							
Ponders End	d		11 59							12 29							12 59						13 29	
Brimsdown	d		12 02							12 32							13 02						13 32	
Enfield Lock	d		12 04				12 21			12 34							13 04			13 21			13 34	
Waltham Cross	d		12 07							12 37			12 50				13 07						13 37	
Cheshunt	d		12 09			12 18	12 25			12 39		12 48	12 52				13 09		13 18	13 25			13 39	
Broxbourne ■	a		12 15			12 23	12 30			12 45		12 53	12 58				13 15		13 23	13 30			13 45	
Broxbourne ■	d		12 15			12 23	12 34			12 45		12 53	12 58				13 15		13 23	13 34			13 45	
Rye House	d		12 18							12 48							13 18						13 48	
St Margarets (Herts)	d		12 21							12 51							13 21						13 51	
Ware	d		12 25							12 55							13 25						13 55	
Hertford East	a		12 31							13 01							13 31						14 01	
Roydon	d						12 39					12 57								13 39				
Harlow Town	d			12 25		12 29	12 43				12 55	13 01	13 11					13 25	13 29	13 43				13 55
Harlow Mill	d						12 46					13 04								13 46				
Sawbridgeworth	d						12 49					13 08	13 17							13 49				
Bishops Stortford	a					12 38	12 56	12 45				13 14	13 23	13 17					13 38	13 56	13 45			
Bishops Stortford	d					12 39		12 45				13 14		13 18					13 39		13 45			
Stansted Mountfitchet	d			12 36								13 18						13 36						
Stansted Airport ✈	a			12 44				12 55			13 12			13 27				13 44			13 55			14 12
Stansted Airport ✈	d	12 27							13 10							13 27						14 10		
Elsenham	d											13 22												
Newport (Essex)	d											13 27												
Audley End	d	12 40				12 51			13 24			13 30				13 40			13 51			14 24		
Great Chesterford	d											13 35												
Whittlesford Parkway	d					12 58			13 31			13 40							13 58			14 31		
Shelford	d											13 44												
Cambridge	a	12 59				13 09			13 43			13 51				13 59			14 09			14 43		
	d											13 52												
Cambridge North	a											13 57												

		LE ◇■	LE ■	LE ■	XC ◇■ A	LE	LE ■	LE ◇■	LE ■	LE ■		LE ■	LE	LE ■	LE ◇■	LE ■	LE ■	XC ◇■ A	LE	LE ■		LE ◇■	LE ■	LE ■	LE ■
London Liverpool Street ■ ⊖	d	13 28		13 40		13 42	13 55	13 58		14 10			14 12	14 25	14 28		14 40		14 42	14 55		14 58		15 10	
Hackney Downs	d					13 48							14 18						14 48						
Stratford ■ ⊖	d		13 30						14 00							14 30							15 00		
Lea Bridge	d		13 36						14 06							14 36							15 06		
Seven Sisters ⊖	d																								
Tottenham Hale ⊖	d	13 40	13 43	13 52		13 55	14 07	14 10	14 13	14 22			14 25	14 37	14 40	14 43	14 52		14 55	15 07		15 10	15 13	15 22	
Northumberland Park	d								14 15														15 15		
Angel Road	d																								
Ponders End	d					13 59							14 29						14 59						
Brimsdown	d					14 02							14 32						15 02						
Enfield Lock	d					14 04			14 21				14 34						15 04				15 21		
Waltham Cross	d		13 50			14 07							14 37			14 50			15 07						
Cheshunt	d	13 48	13 52			14 09		14 18	14 25				14 39		14 48	14 52			15 09			15 18	15 25		
Broxbourne ■	a	13 53	13 58			14 15		14 23	14 30				14 45		14 53	14 58			15 15			15 23	15 30		
Broxbourne ■	d	13 53	13 58			14 15		14 23	14 34				14 45		14 53	14 58			15 15			15 23	15 34		
Rye House	d					14 18							14 48						15 18						
St Margarets (Herts)	d					14 21							14 51						15 21						
Ware	d					14 25							14 55						15 25						
Hertford East	a					14 31							15 01						15 31						
Roydon	d	13 57							14 39						14 57								15 39		
Harlow Town	d	14 01	14 11				14 25	14 29	14 43					14 55	15 01	15 11				15 25		15 29	15 43		
Harlow Mill	d	14 04							14 46						15 04								15 46		
Sawbridgeworth	d	14 08	14 17						14 49						15 08	15 17							15 49		
Bishops Stortford	a	14 14	14 23	14 17				14 38	14 56	14 45					15 14	15 23	15 17					15 38	15 56	15 45	
Bishops Stortford	d	14 14		14 18				14 39		14 45					15 14		15 18					15 39		15 45	
Stansted Mountfitchet	d	14 18					14 36								15 18					15 36					
Stansted Airport ✈	a			14 27			14 44			14 55				15 12			15 27			15 44				15 55	
Stansted Airport ✈	d				14 27							15 10						15 27							16 10
Elsenham	d	14 22													15 22										
Newport (Essex)	d	14 27													15 27										
Audley End	d	14 30			14 40			14 51				15 24			15 30			15 40				15 51			16 24
Great Chesterford	d	14 35													15 35										
Whittlesford Parkway	d	14 40						14 58				15 31			15 40							15 58			16 31
Shelford	d	14 44													15 44										
Cambridge	a	14 51			14 59			15 09				15 43			15 51			15 58				16 09			16 43
	d	14 52													15 52										
Cambridge North	a	14 57													15 57										

A To Birmingham New Street

Table T022-F

Saturdays

26 May to 8 December

London - Broxbourne, Hertford East, Bishops Stortford, Stansted Airport, Cambridge and Cambridge North

		LE	LE ■	LE ◇■	LE ■	LE ■		XC ◇■ A	LE	LE ■	LE ◇■	LE ■	LE ■	LE ■	LE	LE ■		LE ◇■	LE ■	LE ■	XC ◇■ A	LE	LE ■	LE ◇■	LE ■
London Liverpool Street ■ ⊖	d	15 12	15 25	15 28		15 40			15 42	15 55	15 58		16 10		16 12	16 25		16 28		16 40		16 42	16 55	16 58	
Hackney Downs	d	15 18							15 48						16 18							16 48			
Stratford ■ ⊖	d				15 30							16 00							16 30						17 00
Lea Bridge	d				15 36							16 06							16 36						17 06
Seven Sisters ⊖	d																								
Tottenham Hale ⊖	d	15 25	15 37	15 40	15 43	15 52			15 55	16 07	16 10	16 13	16 22		16 25	16 37		16 40	16 43	16 52		16 55	17 07	17 10	17 13
Northumberland Park	d											16 15													17 15
Angel Road	d																								
Ponders End	d	15 29							15 59						16 29							16 59			
Brimsdown	d	15 32							16 02						16 32							17 02			
Enfield Lock	d	15 34							16 04			16 21			16 34							17 04			17 21
Waltham Cross	d	15 37			15 50				16 07						16 37				16 50			17 07			
Cheshunt	d	15 39		15 48	15 52				16 09		16 18	16 25			16 39			16 48	16 52			17 09		17 18	17 25
Broxbourne ■	a	15 45		15 53	15 58				16 15		16 23	16 30			16 45			16 53	16 58			17 15		17 23	17 30
Broxbourne ■	d	15 45		15 53	15 58				16 15		16 23	16 34			16 45			16 53	16 58			17 15		17 23	17 34
Rye House	d	15 48							16 18						16 48							17 18			
St Margarets (Herts)	d	15 51							16 21						16 51							17 21			
Ware	d	15 55							16 25						16 55							17 25			
Hertford East	a	16 01							16 31						17 01							17 31			
Roydon	d			15 57								16 39						16 57							17 39
Harlow Town	d		15 55	16 01	16 11					16 25	16 29	16 43				16 55		17 01	17 11				17 25	17 29	17 43
Harlow Mill	d			16 04								16 46						17 04							17 46
Sawbridgeworth	d			16 08	16 17							16 49						17 08	17 17						17 49
Bishops Stortford	a			16 14	16 23	16 17					16 38	16 56	16 45					17 14	17 23	17 17				17 38	17 56
Bishops Stortford	d			16 14		16 18					16 39		16 45					17 14		17 18				17 39	
Stansted Mountfitchet	d			16 18						16 36								17 18					17 36		
Stansted Airport ✈	a		16 12			16 27				16 44			16 55			17 12				17 27			17 44		
Stansted Airport ✈	d							16 27						17 10							17 27				
Elsenham	d			16 22														17 22							
Newport (Essex)	d			16 27														17 27							
Audley End	d			16 30				16 40			16 51			17 24				17 30			17 40			17 51	
Great Chesterford	d			16 35														17 35							
Whittlesford Parkway	d			16 40							16 58			17 31				17 40						17 58	
Shelford	d			16 44														17 44							
Cambridge	a			16 51				16 59			17 09			17 43				17 51			17 59			18 09	
	d			16 52														17 52							
Cambridge North	a			16 57														17 57							

		LE ■		LE ■	LE	LE ■	LE ◇■	LE ■	LE ■	XC ◇■ A	LE	LE ■		LE ◇■	LE ■	LE ■	LE ■	LE	LE ■	LE ◇■	LE ■	LE ■		XC ◇■ A	LE
London Liverpool Street ■ ⊖	d	17 10			17 12	17 25	17 28		17 40		17 42	17 55		17 58		18 10		18 12	18 25	18 28		18 40			18 42
Hackney Downs	d				17 18						17 48							18 18							18 48
Stratford ■ ⊖	d							17 30							18 00						18 30				
Lea Bridge	d							17 36							18 06						18 36				
Seven Sisters ⊖	d																								
Tottenham Hale ⊖	d	17 22			17 25	17 37	17 40	17 43	17 52		17 55	18 07		18 10	18 13	18 22		18 25	18 37	18 40	18 43	18 52			18 55
Northumberland Park	d														18 15										
Angel Road	d																								
Ponders End	d				17 29						17 59							18 29							18 59
Brimsdown	d				17 32						18 02							18 32							19 02
Enfield Lock	d				17 34						18 04				18 21			18 34							19 04
Waltham Cross	d				17 37			17 50			18 07							18 37			18 50				19 07
Cheshunt	d				17 39		17 48	17 52			18 09			18 18	18 25			18 39		18 48	18 52				19 09
Broxbourne ■	a				17 45		17 53	17 58			18 15			18 23	18 30			18 45		18 53	18 58				19 15
Broxbourne ■	d				17 45		17 53	17 58			18 15			18 23	18 34			18 45		18 53	18 58				19 15
Rye House	d				17 48						18 18							18 48							19 18
St Margarets (Herts)	d				17 51						18 21							18 51							19 21
Ware	d				17 55						18 25							18 55							19 25
Hertford East	a				18 01						18 31							19 01							19 31
Roydon	d						17 57								18 39					18 57					
Harlow Town	d					17 55	18 01	18 11				18 25		18 29	18 43				18 55	19 01	19 11				
Harlow Mill	d						18 04								18 46					19 04					
Sawbridgeworth	d						18 08	18 17							18 49					19 08	19 17				
Bishops Stortford	a	17 45					18 14	18 23	18 17					18 38	18 56	18 45				19 14	19 23	19 17			
Bishops Stortford	d	17 45					18 14		18 18					18 39		18 45				19 14		19 18			
Stansted Mountfitchet	d						18 18					18 36								19 18					
Stansted Airport ✈	a	17 55				18 12			18 27			18 43				18 57			19 12			19 27			
Stansted Airport ✈	d			18 10						18 27							19 10							19 27	
Elsenham	d						18 22													19 22					
Newport (Essex)	d						18 27													19 27					
Audley End	d			18 24			18 30			18 40				18 51			19 24			19 30				19 40	
Great Chesterford	d						18 35													19 35					
Whittlesford Parkway	d			18 31			18 40							18 58			19 31			19 40					
Shelford	d						18 44													19 44					
Cambridge	a			18 43			18 51			18 59				19 09			19 43			19 51				19 59	
	d						18 52													19 52					
Cambridge North	a						18 57													19 57					

A To Birmingham New Street

Table T022-F

Saturdays

26 May to 8 December

London - Broxbourne, Hertford East, Bishops Stortford, Stansted Airport, Cambridge and Cambridge North

		LE 1	LE ◇1	LE 1	LE 1	LE 1	LE	LE 1		LE ◇1	LE 1	LE 1	XC 1	LE	LE 1	LE ◇1	LE 1	LE 1		LE 1	LE	LE 1	LE ◇1	LE 1	LE 1
London Liverpool Street 15 ⊖	d	18 55	18 58		19 10		19 12	19 25		19 28		19 40		19 42	19 55	19 58		20 10			20 12	20 25	20 28		20 40
Hackney Downs	d						19 18							19 48							20 18				
Stratford 7 ⊖	d			19 00							19 30						20 00							20 30	
Lea Bridge	d			19 06							19 36						20 06							20 36	
Seven Sisters ⊖	d																								
Tottenham Hale ⊖	d	19 07	19 10	19 13	19 22		19 25	19 37		19 40	19 43	19 52		19 55	20 07	20 10	20 13	20 22			20 25	20 37	20 40	20 43	20 52
Northumberland Park	d			19 15													20 15								
Angel Road	d																								
Ponders End	d						19 29							19 59							20 29				
Brimsdown	d						19 32							20 02							20 32				
Enfield Lock	d			19 21			19 34							20 04			20 21				20 34				
Waltham Cross	d						19 37				19 50			20 07							20 37			20 50	
Cheshunt	d		19 18	19 25			19 39			19 48	19 52			20 09		20 18	20 25				20 39		20 48	20 52	
Broxbourne 3	a		19 23	19 30			19 45			19 53	19 58			20 15		20 23	20 30				20 45		20 53	20 58	
Broxbourne 3	d		19 23	19 34			19 45			19 53	19 58			20 15		20 23	20 34				20 45		20 53	20 58	
Rye House	d						19 48							20 18							20 48				
St Margarets (Herts)	d						19 51							20 21							20 51				
Ware	d						19 55							20 25							20 55				
Hertford East	a						20 01							20 31							21 01				
Roydon	d			19 39						19 57							20 39						20 57		
Harlow Town	d	19 25	19 29	19 43				19 55		20 01	20 11				20 25	20 29	20 43					20 55	21 01	21 11	
Harlow Mill	d			19 46						20 04							20 46						21 04		
Sawbridgeworth	d			19 49						20 08	20 17						20 49						21 08	21 17	
Bishops Stortford	a		19 38	19 56	19 45					20 14	20 23	20 17				20 38	20 56	20 45					21 14	21 23	21 17
Bishops Stortford	d		19 39		19 45					20 14		20 18				20 39		20 45					21 14		21 18
Stansted Mountfitchet	d	19 36								20 18					20 36								21 18		
Stansted Airport ✈	a	19 44			19 55			20 12				20 27			20 44			20 55				21 12			21 27
Stansted Airport ✈	d					20 10							20 27							21 10					
Elsenham	d									20 22													21 22		
Newport (Essex)	d									20 27													21 27		
Audley End	d		19 51			20 24				20 30			20 40			20 51				21 24			21 30		
Great Chesterford	d									20 35													21 35		
Whittlesford Parkway	d		19 58			20 31				20 40						20 58				21 31			21 40		
Shelford	d									20 44													21 44		
Cambridge	a		20 09			20 43				20 51			20 57			21 09				21 43			21 51		
	d									20 52													21 52		
Cambridge North	a									20 57													21 57		

		XC 1	LE	LE 1		LE ◇1	LE 1	LE 1	LE 1	LE	LE 1	LE ◇1	LE 1	LE 1		XC 1	LE	LE 1	LE ◇1	LE 1	LE 1	LE	LE 1	LE ◇1	
London Liverpool Street 15 ⊖	d		20 42	20 55		20 58		21 10		21 12	21 25	21 28		21 40			21 42	21 55	21 58		22 10	22 12	22 25	22 28	
Hackney Downs	d		20 48							21 18							21 48					22 18			
Stratford 7 ⊖	d						21 00						21 30							22 00					
Lea Bridge	d						21 06						21 36							22 06					
Seven Sisters ⊖	d																								
Tottenham Hale ⊖	d		20 55	21 07		21 10	21 13	21 22		21 25	21 37	21 40	21 43	21 52			21 55	22 07	22 10	22 13	22 22	22 25	22 37	22 40	
Northumberland Park	d						21 15													22 15					
Angel Road	d																								
Ponders End	d		20 59							21 29							21 59					22 29			
Brimsdown	d		21 02							21 32							22 02					22 32			
Enfield Lock	d		21 04				21 21			21 34							22 04			22 21		22 34			
Waltham Cross	d		21 07							21 37			21 50				22 07					22 37			
Cheshunt	d		21 09			21 18	21 25			21 39		21 48	21 52				22 09		22 18	22 25		22 39		22 48	
Broxbourne 3	a		21 15			21 23	21 30			21 45		21 53	21 58				22 15		22 23	22 30		22 45		22 53	
Broxbourne 3	d		21 15			21 23	21 34			21 45		21 53	21 58				22 15		22 23	22 34		22 45		22 53	
Rye House	d		21 18							21 48							22 18					22 48			
St Margarets (Herts)	d		21 21							21 51							22 21					22 51			
Ware	d		21 25							21 55							22 25					22 55			
Hertford East	a		21 31							22 01							22 31					23 01			
Roydon	d						21 39					21 57								22 39				22 57	
Harlow Town	d			21 25		21 29	21 43				21 55	22 01	22 11					22 25	22 29	22 43			22 55	23 01	
Harlow Mill	d						21 46					22 04								22 46				23 04	
Sawbridgeworth	d						21 49					22 08	22 17							22 49				23 08	
Bishops Stortford	a					21 38	21 56	21 45				22 14	22 23	22 17					22 38	22 56	22 45			23 14	
Bishops Stortford	d					21 39		21 45				22 14		22 18					22 39		22 45			23 14	
Stansted Mountfitchet	d			21 36								22 18						22 36						23 18	
Stansted Airport ✈	a			21 44				21 55			22 12			22 27				22 44			22 55		23 12		
Stansted Airport ✈	d	21 27							22 10							22 27									
Elsenham	d											22 22												23 22	
Newport (Essex)	d											22 27												23 27	
Audley End	d	21 40				21 51			22 24			22 30				22 40			22 51					23 30	
Great Chesterford	d											22 35												23 35	
Whittlesford Parkway	d					21 58			22 31			22 40							22 58					23 40	
Shelford	d											22 44												23 44	
Cambridge	a	21 58				22 09			22 43			22 51				22 57			23 08					23 51	
	d											22 59												23 52	
Cambridge North	a											23 04												23 57	

Table T022-F

Saturdays

26 May to 8 December

London - Broxbourne, Hertford East, Bishops Stortford, Stansted Airport, Cambridge and Cambridge North

		LE 1	LE 1	XC 1	LE	LE 1	LE ◇1	LE 1	LE	LE 1		LE ◇1	LE	LE 1
London Liverpool Street 15 ⊖	d		22 40		22 42	22 55	22 58		23 12	23 25		23 28	23 42	23 58
Hackney Downs	d				22 48				23 18				23 48	
Stratford 7 ⊖	d	22 30						23 00						
Lea Bridge	d	22 36						23 06						
Seven Sisters ⊖	d													
Tottenham Hale ⊖	d	22 43	22 52		22 55	23 07	23 10	23 13	23 25	23 37		23 40	23 54	00 10
Northumberland Park	d							23 15					23 57	
Angel Road	d													
Ponders End	d				22 59				23 29				00 01	
Brimsdown	d				23 02				23 32				00 03	
Enfield Lock	d				23 04			23 21	23 34				00 06	
Waltham Cross	d	22 50			23 07				23 37				00 08	
Cheshunt	d	22 52			23 09		23 18	23 25	23 39			23 48	00 11	00 18
Broxbourne 3	a	22 58			23 15		23 23	23 30	23 45			23 53	00 16	00 23
Broxbourne 3	d	22 58			23 15		23 23	23 30	23 45			23 53	00 16	00 23
Rye House	d				23 18				23 48				00 20	
St Margarets (Herts)	d				23 21				23 51				00 23	
Ware	d				23 25				23 55				00 27	
Hertford East	a				23 31				00 01				00 32	
Roydon	d							23 34				23 57		00 27
Harlow Town	d	23 11				23 25	23 29	23 38		23 55		00 01		00 31
Harlow Mill	d							23 41				00 04		00 34
Sawbridgeworth	d	23 17						23 45				00 08		00 38
Bishops Stortford	a	23 23	23 17				23 38	23 51		00 04		00 14		00 44
Bishops Stortford	d		23 18				23 39			00 04		00 14		00 44
Stansted Mountfitchet	d					23 36						00 18		00 48
Stansted Airport ✈	a		23 27			23 43				00 13				
Stansted Airport ✈	d			23 27										
Elsenham	d											00 22		00 52
Newport (Essex)	d											00 27		00 57
Audley End	d			23 40			23 51					00 30		01 00
Great Chesterford	d											00 35		01 05
Whittlesford Parkway	d						23 58					00 40		01 10
Shelford	d											00 44		
Cambridge	a			23 58			00 08					00 51		01 19
	d													
Cambridge North	a													

Sundays

20 May to 2 December

		LE A	LE 1 A	LE ◇1 A	LE 1 A	LE 1	LE 1	LE 1	LE 1	LE		LE 1	LE 1	LE 1	LE 1	LE 1	LE 1	LE 1	LE 1	LE ◇1 B		LE 1	LE ◇1 C	LE 1	LE 1 B
London Liverpool Street 15 ⊖	d					04 10	04 40	05 10	05 40			06 10	06 25	06 40	06 55	07 10	07 25	07 40		07 42		07 55		08 10	
Hackney Downs	d																			07 48					
Stratford 7 ⊖	d																								
Lea Bridge	d																								
Seven Sisters ⊖	d																								
Tottenham Hale ⊖	d				00 10		04 52	05 22	05 52			06 22	06 37	06 52	07 07	07 22	07 37	07 52		07 55		08 07		08 22	
Northumberland Park	d																								
Angel Road	d																								
Ponders End	d	00 01																		07 59					
Brimsdown	d	00 03																		08 02					
Enfield Lock	d	00 06																		08 04					
Waltham Cross	d	00 08																		08 07					
Cheshunt	d	00 11			00 18				06 00											08 09					
Broxbourne 3	a	00 16			00 23				06 05											08 15					
Broxbourne 3	d	00 16			00 23				06 05	08 10										08 23					
Rye House	d	00 20								08 13															
St Margarets (Herts)	d	00 23								08 16															
Ware	d	00 27								08 20															
Hertford East	a	00 32								08 27															
Roydon	d				00 27															08 27			←		
Harlow Town	d			00 01	00 31		05 08	05 38	06 11				06 53		07 23		07 53			08 31		08 23	08 31		
Harlow Mill	d			00 04	00 34															→			08 34		
Sawbridgeworth	d			00 08	00 38																		08 38		
Bishops Stortford	a			00 14	00 44		05 17	05 47	06 20			06 45		07 15		07 45		08 15					08 44	08 47	
Bishops Stortford	d		00 04	00 14	00 44		05 18	05 48	06 21			06 46		07 16		07 46		08 16					08 44	08 48	
Stansted Mountfitchet	d			00 18	00 48		05 22						07 04				08 04						08 48		
Stansted Airport ✈	a		00 13			04 58	05 29	05 57	06 30			06 55	07 12	07 25	07 40	07 55	08 12	08 25				08 40		08 57	
Stansted Airport ✈	d																		08 40						09 09
Elsenham	d			00 22	00 52																		08 52		→
Newport (Essex)	d			00 27	00 57																		08 57		
Audley End	d			00 30	01 00														08 53				09 00		
Great Chesterford	d			00 35	01 05																		09 05		
Whittlesford Parkway	d			00 40	01 10														09 01				09 10		
Shelford	d			00 44																					
Cambridge	a			00 51	01 19														09 10				09 19		
	d																								
Cambridge North	a																								

A not 20 May. From London Liverpool Street

B To Cambridge

C From London Liverpool Street

Table T022-F

Sundays
20 May to 2 December

London - Broxbourne, Hertford East, Bishops Stortford, Stansted Airport, Cambridge and Cambridge North

		LE	LE ■	LE ◇■	LE ■	LE ■	LE	LE ■	LE ◇■	LE ■	LE ■ A	LE	LE ■	LE ◇■	LE ■	LE ■	XC ◇■ B	LE	LE ■	LE ◇■	LE ■	LE ■ A	LE
London Liverpool Street ⊖	d		08 25	08 28		08 40		08 55	08 57	09 10			09 25	09 28		09 40			09 55	09 57	10 10		
Hackney Downs	d								09 03											10 03			
Stratford ⊖	d	08 14					08 44					09 14						09 44					10 14
Lea Bridge	d	08 20					08 50					09 20						09 50					10 20
Seven Sisters ⊖	d																						
Tottenham Hale ⊖	d	08 25	08 37	08 40		08 52	08 55	09 07	09 10	09 22		09 25	09 37	09 40		09 52		09 55	10 07	10 10	10 22		10 25
Northumberland Park	d																						
Angel Road	d																						
Ponders End	d	08 29					08 59					09 29						09 59					10 29
Brimsdown	d	08 32					09 02					09 32						10 02					10 32
Enfield Lock	d	08 34					09 04					09 34						10 04					10 34
Waltham Cross	d	08 37					09 07					09 37						10 07					10 37
Cheshunt	d	08 39		08 48			09 09		09 18			09 39		09 48				10 09		10 18			10 39
Broxbourne ■	a	08 45		08 53			09 15		09 23			09 45		09 53				10 15		10 23			10 45
Broxbourne ■	d	08 45		08 53			09 15		09 23			09 45		09 53				10 15		10 23			10 45
Rye House	d	08 48					09 18					09 48						10 18					10 48
St Margarets (Herts)	d	08 51					09 21					09 51						10 21					10 51
Ware	d	08 55					09 25					09 55						10 25					10 55
Hertford East	a	09 01					09 31					10 01						10 31					11 01
Roydon	d								09 27											10 27			
Harlow Town	d		08 55	08 59				09 25	09 31				09 55	09 59					10 25	10 31			
Harlow Mill	d								09 34											10 34			
Sawbridgeworth	d			09 04					09 38					10 04						10 38			
Bishops Stortford	a			09 10		09 15			09 44	09 47				10 10		10 15				10 44	10 47		
Bishops Stortford	d			09 10		09 16			09 44	09 48				10 10		10 15				10 44	10 48		
Stansted Mountfitchet	d		09 06						09 48				10 06							10 48			
Stansted Airport ✈	a		09 13		←	09 25		09 42		09 57			10 13		←	10 25			10 42		10 57		
Stansted Airport ✈	d				09 09						10 09				10 09		10 25					11 09	
Elsenham	d								09 52		→									10 52		→	
Newport (Essex)	d								09 57											10 57			
Audley End	d			09 22	09 26				10 00					10 22	10 26		10 39			11 00			
Great Chesterford	d								10 05											11 05			
Whittlesford Parkway	d			09 30	09 34				10 10					10 30	10 34					11 10			
Shelford	d			09 34										10 34									
Cambridge	a			09 41	09 44				10 19					10 41	10 44		10 54			11 19			
	d								10 27											11 27			
Cambridge North	a								10 32											11 32			

		LE ■	LE ◇■	LE ■	LE ■	XC ◇■ B	LE	LE ■	LE ◇■	LE ■	LE ■ A	LE	LE ■	LE ◇■	LE ■	LE ■	XC ◇■ B	LE	LE ■	LE ◇■
London Liverpool Street ⊖	d	10 25	10 28		10 40			10 55	10 57	11 10			11 25	11 28		11 40			11 55	11 57
Hackney Downs	d								11 03											12 03
Stratford ⊖	d						10 44					11 14						11 44		
Lea Bridge	d						10 50					11 20						11 50		
Seven Sisters ⊖	d																			
Tottenham Hale ⊖	d	10 37	10 40		10 52		10 55	11 07	11 10	11 22		11 25	11 37	11 40		11 52		11 55	12 07	12 10
Northumberland Park	d																			
Angel Road	d																			
Ponders End	d						10 59					11 29						11 59		
Brimsdown	d						11 02					11 32						12 02		
Enfield Lock	d						11 04					11 34						12 04		
Waltham Cross	d						11 07					11 37						12 07		
Cheshunt	d		10 48				11 09		11 18			11 39		11 48				12 09		12 18
Broxbourne ■	a		10 53				11 15		11 23			11 45		11 53				12 15		12 23
Broxbourne ■	d		10 53				11 15		11 23			11 45		11 53				12 15		12 23
Rye House	d						11 18					11 48						12 18		
St Margarets (Herts)	d						11 21					11 51						12 21		
Ware	d						11 25					11 55						12 25		
Hertford East	a						11 31					12 01						12 31		
Roydon	d								11 27											12 27
Harlow Town	d	10 55	10 59					11 25	11 31				11 55	11 59					12 25	12 31
Harlow Mill	d								11 34											12 34
Sawbridgeworth	d		11 04						11 38					12 04						12 38
Bishops Stortford	a		11 10		11 15				11 44	11 47				12 10		12 15				12 44
Bishops Stortford	d		11 10		11 15				11 44	11 48				12 10		12 15				12 44
Stansted Mountfitchet	d	11 06							11 48				12 06							12 48
Stansted Airport ✈	a	11 13		←	11 25			11 42		11 57			12 13		←	12 25			12 42	
Stansted Airport ✈	d			11 09		11 25					12 09				12 09		12 25			
Elsenham	d								11 52		→									12 52
Newport (Essex)	d								11 57											12 57
Audley End	d		11 22	11 26		11 39			12 00					12 22	12 26		12 39			13 00
Great Chesterford	d								12 05											13 05
Whittlesford Parkway	d		11 30	11 34					12 10					12 30	12 34					13 10
Shelford	d		11 34											12 34						
Cambridge	a		11 41	11 44		11 54			12 19					12 41	12 44		12 54			13 19
	d								12 27											13 27
Cambridge North	a								12 32											13 31

A To Cambridge
B To Birmingham New Street

Table T022-F

Sundays
20 May to 2 December

London - Broxbourne, Hertford East, Bishops Stortford, Stansted Airport, Cambridge and Cambridge North

		LE ■	LE ■ A	LE	LE ■	LE ◇■	LE ■	LE ■	XC ◇■ B	LE	LE ■	LE ◇■		LE ■	LE ■ A	LE	LE ■	LE ◇■	LE ■	LE ■	XC ◇■ B	LE	LE ■	LE ◇■
London Liverpool Street ⊖	d	12 10			12 25	12 28		12 40			12 55	12 57		17 10			17 25	17 28		17 40			17 55	17 57
Hackney Downs	d											13 03												18 03
Stratford ⊖	d			12 14						12 44						17 14						17 44		
Lea Bridge	d			12 20						12 50						17 20						17 50		
Seven Sisters ⊖	d																							
Tottenham Hale ⊖	d	12 22		12 25	12 37	12 40		12 52		12 55	13 07	13 10		17 22		17 25	17 37	17 40		17 52		17 55	18 07	18 10
Northumberland Park	d																							
Angel Road	d																							
Ponders End	d			12 29						12 59						17 29						17 59		
Brimsdown	d			12 32						13 02						17 32						18 02		
Enfield Lock	d			12 34						13 04						17 34						18 04		
Waltham Cross	d			12 37						13 07						17 37						18 07		
Cheshunt	d			12 39		12 48				13 09		13 18				17 39		17 48				18 09		18 18
Broxbourne ■	a			12 45		12 53				13 15		13 23	and at the same minutes past each hour until			17 45		17 53				18 15		18 23
Broxbourne ■	d			12 45		12 53				13 15		13 23				17 45		17 53				18 15		18 23
Rye House	d			12 48						13 18						17 48						18 18		
St Margarets (Herts)	d			12 51						13 21						17 51						18 21		
Ware	d			12 55						13 25						17 55						18 25		
Hertford East	a			13 01						13 31						18 01						18 31		
Roydon	d											13 27												18 27
Harlow Town	d				12 55	12 59					13 25	13 31					17 55	17 59					18 25	18 31
Harlow Mill	d											13 34												18 34
Sawbridgeworth	d					13 04						13 38						18 04						18 38
Bishops Stortford	a	12 47				13 10		13 15				13 44		17 47				18 10		18 15				18 44
Bishops Stortford	d	12 48				13 10		13 15				13 44		17 48				18 10		18 15				18 44
Stansted Mountfitchet	d				13 06							13 48					18 06							18 48
Stansted Airport ✈	a	12 57			13 13		←	13 25			13 42			17 57			18 13		←	18 25			18 42	
Stansted Airport ✈	d		13 09				13 09		13 25						18 09				18 09		18 25			
Elsenham	d		→									13 52			→									18 52
Newport (Essex)	d											13 57												18 57
Audley End	d					13 22	13 26		13 39			14 00						18 22	18 26		18 39			19 00
Great Chesterford	d											14 05												19 05
Whittlesford Parkway	d					13 30	13 34					14 10						18 30	18 34					19 10
Shelford	d					13 34												18 34						
Cambridge	a					13 41	13 44		13 54			14 19						18 41	18 44		18 54			19 19
	d											14 27												19 27
Cambridge North	a											14 32												19 32

		LE ■	LE ■ A	LE	LE ■	LE ◇■	LE ■	LE ■	XC ◇■ B	LE	LE ■	LE ◇■	LE ■	LE ■ A	LE	LE ■	LE ◇■	LE ■	LE ■	XC ■	LE	LE ■
London Liverpool Street ⊖	d	18 10			18 25	18 28		18 40			18 55	18 57	19 10			19 25	19 28		19 40			19 55
Hackney Downs	d											19 03										
Stratford ⊖	d			18 14						18 44					19 14						19 44	
Lea Bridge	d			18 20						18 50					19 20						19 50	
Seven Sisters ⊖	d																					
Tottenham Hale ⊖	d	18 22		18 25	18 37	18 40		18 52		18 55	19 07	19 10	19 22		19 25	19 37	19 40		19 52		19 55	20 07
Northumberland Park	d																					
Angel Road	d																					
Ponders End	d			18 29						18 59					19 29						19 59	
Brimsdown	d			18 32						19 02					19 32						20 02	
Enfield Lock	d			18 34						19 04					19 34						20 04	
Waltham Cross	d			18 37						19 07					19 37						20 07	
Cheshunt	d			18 39		18 48				19 09		19 18			19 39		19 48				20 09	
Broxbourne ■	a			18 45		18 53				19 15		19 23			19 45		19 53				20 15	
Broxbourne ■	d			18 45		18 53				19 15		19 23			19 45		19 53				20 15	
Rye House	d			18 48						19 18					19 48						20 18	
St Margarets (Herts)	d			18 51						19 21					19 51						20 21	
Ware	d			18 55						19 25					19 55						20 25	
Hertford East	a			19 01						19 31					20 01						20 31	
Roydon	d											19 27										
Harlow Town	d				18 55	18 59					19 25	19 31				19 55	19 59					20 25
Harlow Mill	d											19 34										
Sawbridgeworth	d					19 04						19 38					20 04					
Bishops Stortford	a	18 47				19 10		19 15				19 44	19 47				20 10		20 15			
Bishops Stortford	d	18 48				19 10		19 15				19 44	19 48				20 10		20 15			
Stansted Mountfitchet	d				19 06							19 48				20 06						
Stansted Airport ✈	a	18 57			19 13		←	19 25			19 42		19 57			20 13		←	20 25			20 42
Stansted Airport ✈	d		19 09				19 09		19 25					20 09				20 09		20 25		
Elsenham	d		→									19 52		→								
Newport (Essex)	d											19 57										
Audley End	d					19 22	19 26		19 39			20 00					20 22	20 26		20 39		
Great Chesterford	d											20 05										
Whittlesford Parkway	d					19 30	19 34					20 10					20 30	20 34				
Shelford	d					19 34											20 34					
Cambridge	a					19 41	19 44		19 56			20 19					20 41	20 45		20 54		
	d											20 27										
Cambridge North	a											20 32										

A To Cambridge
B To Birmingham New Street

Table T022-F

Sundays

20 May to 2 December

London - Broxbourne, Hertford East, Bishops Stortford, Stansted Airport, Cambridge and Cambridge North

		LE ◇1	LE 1	XC 1	LE	LE 1	LE ◇1	LE 1	LE 1	LE	LE 1	LE ◇1	LE 1	LE 1 A	LE	LE 1	LE ◇1	LE 1	LE 1	XC 1	LE	LE 1	LE ◇1
London Liverpool Street 15 ⊖	d	19 57	20 10			20 25	20 28		20 40		20 55	20 57	21 10			21 25	21 28		21 40			21 55	21 57
Hackney Downs	d	20 03										21 03											22 03
Stratford 7 ⊖	d				20 14					20 44					21 14						21 44		
Lea Bridge	d				20 20					20 50					21 20						21 50		
Seven Sisters ⊖	d																						
Tottenham Hale ⊖	d	20 10	20 22		20 25	20 37	20 40		20 52	20 55	21 07	21 10	21 22		21 25	21 37	21 40		21 52		21 55	22 07	22 10
Northumberland Park	d																						
Angel Road	d																						
Ponders End	d				20 29					20 59					21 29						21 59		
Brimsdown	d				20 32					21 02					21 32						22 02		
Enfield Lock	d				20 34					21 04					21 34						22 04		
Waltham Cross	d				20 37					21 07					21 37						22 07		
Cheshunt	d	20 18			20 39		20 48			21 09		21 18			21 39		21 48				22 09		22 18
Broxbourne 3	a	20 23			20 45		20 53			21 15		21 23			21 45		21 53				22 15		22 23
Broxbourne 3	d	20 23			20 45		20 53			21 15		21 23			21 45		21 53				22 15		22 23
Rye House	d				20 48					21 18					21 48						22 18		
St Margarets (Herts)	d				20 51					21 21					21 51						22 21		
Ware	d				20 55					21 25					21 55						22 25		
Hertford East	a				21 01					21 31					22 01						22 31		
Roydon	d	20 27										21 27											22 27
Harlow Town	d	20 31				20 55	20 59				21 25	21 31				21 55	21 59					22 25	22 31
Harlow Mill	d	20 34										21 34											22 34
Sawbridgeworth	d	20 38					21 04					21 38					22 04						22 38
Bishops Stortford	a	20 44	20 47				21 10		21 15			21 44	21 47				22 10		22 15				22 44
Bishops Stortford	d	20 44	20 48				21 10		21 15			21 44	21 48				22 10		22 15				22 44
Stansted Mountfitchet	d	20 48				21 06						21 48				22 06							22 48
Stansted Airport ✈	a		20 58			21 15			21 27		21 42		21 57			22 13		←	22 25			22 42	
Stansted Airport ✈	d			21 04				21 18						22 09				22 09		22 25			
Elsenham	d	20 52										21 52		→									22 52
Newport (Essex)	d	20 57										21 57											22 57
Audley End	d	21 00		21 16			21 22	21 32				22 00					22 22	22 26		22 40			23 00
Great Chesterford	d	21 05										22 05											23 05
Whittlesford Parkway	d	21 10					21 30	21 40				22 10					22 30	22 34					23 10
Shelford	d						21 34										22 34						
Cambridge	a	21 19		21 34			21 41	21 49				22 19					22 41	22 44		22 55			23 19
	d	21 27										22 27											23 27
Cambridge North	a	21 32										22 32											23 32

		LE 1	XC 1	LE	LE 1	LE ◇1	LE 1	LE	LE 1	LE ◇1	LE 1	LE 1	LE	LE 1
London Liverpool Street 15 ⊖	d	22 10			22 25	22 28	22 40		22 55	22 57	23 25	23 28		23 58
Hackney Downs	d									23 03				
Stratford 7 ⊖	d			22 14				22 44					23 32	
Lea Bridge	d			22 20				22 50					23 38	
Seven Sisters ⊖	d													
Tottenham Hale ⊖	d	22 22		22 25	22 37	22 40	22 52	22 55	23 07	23 10	23 37	23 40	23 43	00 10
Northumberland Park	d													
Angel Road	d													
Ponders End	d			22 29				22 59					23 47	
Brimsdown	d			22 32				23 02					23 50	
Enfield Lock	d			22 34				23 04					23 52	
Waltham Cross	d			22 37				23 07					23 55	
Cheshunt	d			22 39		22 48		23 09		23 18		23 48	23 57	00 18
Broxbourne 3	a			22 45		22 53		23 15		23 23		23 53	00 03	00 23
Broxbourne 3	d			22 45		22 53		23 15		23 23		23 53	00 03	00 23
Rye House	d			22 48				23 18					00 06	
St Margarets (Herts)	d			22 51				23 21					00 09	
Ware	d			22 55				23 25					00 13	
Hertford East	a			23 01				23 31					00 19	
Roydon	d									23 27				00 27
Harlow Town	d				22 55	22 59			23 25	23 31	23 53	23 59		00 31
Harlow Mill	d									23 34				00 34
Sawbridgeworth	d					23 04				23 38		00 04		00 38
Bishops Stortford	a	22 47				23 10	23 15			23 44	00 02	00 11		00 44
Bishops Stortford	d	22 48				23 10	23 15			23 44	00 03			
Stansted Mountfitchet	d				23 06					23 48				
Stansted Airport ✈	a	22 57			23 13		23 25		23 42		00 12			
Stansted Airport ✈	d		23 04											
Elsenham	d									23 52				
Newport (Essex)	d									23 57				
Audley End	d		23 18			23 22				23 59				
Great Chesterford	d									00 05				
Whittlesford Parkway	d					23 30				00 10				
Shelford	d					23 34				00 14				
Cambridge	a		23 35			23 41				00 20				
	d													
Cambridge North	a													

A To Cambridge

Table T022-R

Mondays to Fridays

21 May to 7 December

Cambridge North, Cambridge, Stansted Airport, Bishops Stortford, Hertford East and Broxbourne - London

Miles	Miles	Miles			LE MX ◇1 A	LE 1 B	LE MX C	LE MO 1 B	LE MX 1 B	LE MX 1	LE 1 B	LE 1	XC 1	LE ◇1	LE	LE 1 D	LE MFO 1	LE TW ThO 1	LE 1 E	XC 1	LE ◇1	LE 1	LE 1
0	—	—	**Cambridge North**	d																			
2¼	—	—	**Cambridge**	a																			
—	—	—		d									04 44	04 48						05 17	05 20	05 31	
5½	—	—	Shelford	d																		05 36	
9	—	—	Whittlesford Parkway	d										04 55							05 28	05 41	
12¾	—	—	Great Chesterford	d																	05 32		
16¼	—	—	Audley End	d									04 58	05 03						05 34	05 38	05 49	
18	—	—	Newport (Essex)	d																	05 41		
22½	0	—	Elsenham	d																	05 46		
—	—	—	**Stansted Airport** ✈	a									05 12							05 48			
—	4½	—	**Stansted Airport** ✈	d								00 30					05 30						06 00
24¾	8¼	—	Stansted Mountfitchet	d																	05 50		06 06
27¾	—	0	**Bishops Stortford**	a								00 39		05 16			05 39				05 56	06 02	06 10
27¾	—	0	**Bishops Stortford**	d							00 08	00 39		05 16		05 30	05 39	05 39			05 56	06 02	06 10
31¼	—	3¾	Sawbridgeworth	d										05 21		05 35					06 01	06 07	
33½	—	5¾	Harlow Mill	d										05 24		05 38						06 10	
35¼	—	7½	Harlow Town	d					00 01		00 16	00 47		05 27		05 41	05 47	05 47			06 06	06 13	06 17
38	—	10¼	Roydon	d										05 31		05 45					06 10		
—	0	—	**Hertford East**	d						00 07					05 25								
—	2	—	Ware	d											05 29								
—	4	—	St Margarets (Herts)	d											05 33								
—	5¼	—	Rye House	d											05 36				←				
40¾	—	13¼	**Broxbourne** 3	a						00 19				05 36	05 40	05 50	05 53	05 53	05 50		06 14	06 20	
—	7	—	**Broxbourne** 3	d						00 19				05 36	05 40	05 56	05 53	05 53	05 56		06 15	06 20	
44	—	16¼	Cheshunt	d										05 41	05 44	→	05 57	05 57	06 01		06 19		
45¼	—	—	Waltham Cross	d											05 47				06 03				
46¼	—	—	Enfield Lock	d											05 49				06 06				
47¼	—	—	Brimsdown	d											05 52				06 08				
48	—	—	Ponders End	d											05 54				06 10				
50¼	—	22¾	Angel Road	d											05 57				06 14				
51	—	23½	Northumberland Park	d											05 59				06 16				
52	—	24¼	Tottenham Hale ⊖	d										05 49	06 03		06 07	06 07	06 19		06 28	06 31	06 34
—	0	—	Seven Sisters ⊖	d	00 04	00 08	00 12	00 21	00 21														
—	—	26¼	Lea Bridge	d															06 23				
—	6¾	28½	Stratford 7 ⊖	a															06 32			06 45	
55	—	—	Hackney Downs	d			00 17								06 08								
58	—	—	**London Liverpool Street** 15 ⊖	a	00 18	00 22	00 26	00 35	00 36	00 49	00 51	01 21		06 03	06 18		06 23	06 23			06 43		06 49

		LE	LE ◇1	LE 1	LE	LE	LE ◇1	LE F	LE 1 D	LE 1	LE ◇1 G	LE H	LE 1	LE 1 E	LE	LE ◇1	LE 1	XC 1	LE ◇1	LE	LE 1	LE	LE
Cambridge North	d										06 04												
Cambridge	a										06 10												
	d		05 48				05 51				06 18					06 21		06 35	06 47				
Shelford	d						05 56									06 26							
Whittlesford Parkway	d		05 55				06 00				06 25					06 30			06 55				
Great Chesterford	d						06 04									06 34							
Audley End	d		06 04				06 10				06 34					06 40		06 51	07 04				
Newport (Essex)	d						06 13									06 43							
Elsenham	d						06 19									06 49							
Stansted Airport ✈	a																	07 09					
Stansted Airport ✈	d			06 15						06 30			06 45				07 00				07 15		
Stansted Mountfitchet	d						06 22			06 36						06 52							
Bishops Stortford	a		06 17	06 24			06 28			06 40	06 47		06 54			06 58	07 09		07 17		07 24		
Bishops Stortford	d		06 18	06 24			06 29		06 34	06 41	06 47		06 54			06 58	07 09		07 17		07 24		
Sawbridgeworth	d						06 33		06 39							07 03	07 14						
Harlow Mill	d						06 37		06 42							07 06							
Harlow Town	d		06 27	06 32			06 40		06 56	06 49			07 02			07 10	07 19				07 32		
Roydon	d						06 44		07 00							07 14							
Hertford East	d	06 06				06 27									06 57							07 17	07 27
Ware	d	06 10				06 31									07 01							07 21	07 31
St Margarets (Herts)	d	06 14				06 35									07 05							07 25	07 35
Rye House	d	06 17				06 38									07 08							07 28	07 38
Broxbourne 3	a	06 22	06 34			06 43	06 48		07 05						07 13	07 18						07 33	07 43
Broxbourne 3	d	06 26	06 34		06 39	06 43	06 49	07 00	07 09						07 13	07 18				07 30		07 39	07 43
Cheshunt	d	06 30			06 44	06 47	06 53	07 05	07 14						07 17	07 23				07 35		07 44	07 47
Waltham Cross	d	06 33			06 46			07 07	07 16				07 12							07 37		07 46	
Enfield Lock	d	06 35			06 49			07 10	07 19											07 40	07 43	07 49	
Brimsdown	d	06 38			06 51			07 12					07 17							07 42	07 47	07 51	
Ponders End	d	06 40						07 14												07 44			
Angel Road	d								07 24														
Northumberland Park	d				06 56				07 26			←		←								07 56	
Tottenham Hale ⊖	d	06 45	06 49	06 51	06 59		07 02	07 20	07 29	07 05	07 08	07 20	07 23	07 29		07 32	07 35		07 38	07 50	07 53	07 59	
Seven Sisters ⊖	d					07 02		→	→						07 32								08 02
Lea Bridge	d				07 03									07 33								08 03	
Stratford 7 ⊖	a				07 13									07 43								08 13	
Hackney Downs	d	06 52				07 08						07 26			07 38					07 56			08 08
London Liverpool Street 15 ⊖	a	07 02	07 05	07 08		07 18	07 20			07 23	07 25	07 38	07 41		07 48	07 50	07 53		07 55	08 08	08 10		08 18

A From Cambridge
B From Stansted Airport
C From Hertford East
D To Stratford
E From Bishops Stortford
F To London Liverpool Street
G From Kings Lynn
H From Broxbourne

Table T022-R

Mondays to Fridays

21 May to 7 December

Cambridge North, Cambridge, Stansted Airport, Bishops Stortford, Hertford East and Broxbourne - London

	LE ◇1	LE A	LE 1 B	LE 1	LE ◇1 C	LE D	LE 1	LE 1 E	LE	LE ◇1	LE 1	XC 1	LE ◇1	LE	LE 1	LE	LE ◇1 F	LE 1	XC ◇1 G	LE	LE 1 B	LE ◇1
Cambridge North d					07 04												07 42					
Cambridge a					07 10												07 47					
d	06 51				07 17					07 21		07 35	07 47				07 51		08 13			08 18
Shelford d	06 56									07 26							07 56					
Whittlesford Parkway d	07 00				07 25					07 30			07 55				08 00					08 25
Great Chesterford d	07 04									07 34							08 04					
Audley End d	07 10				07 34					07 40		07 51	08 04				08 10		08 27			08 34
Newport (Essex) d	07 13									07 43							08 13					
Elsenham d	07 19									07 49							08 19					
Stansted Airport ✈ a												08 09							08 39			
Stansted Airport ✈ d				07 30			07 43				08 00				08 15			08 30				
Stansted Mountfitchet d	07 22						07 49			07 52							08 22					
Bishops Stortford a	07 28			07 39	07 47		07 53			07 58	08 09		08 17		08 24		08 28	08 39				08 48
Bishops Stortford d	07 28		07 33	07 40	07 47		07 54			07 58	08 09		08 17		08 24		08 28	08 39			08 43	08 49
Sawbridgeworth d	07 33		07 38							08 03	08 14						08 33				08 48	
Harlow Mill d	07 36		07 41							08 06							08 36					
Harlow Town d	07 40		07 56	07 48			08 02			08 10	08 19				08 32		08 40				08 53	08 57
Roydon d	07 44		08 00							08 14							08 44					
Hertford East d									07 57							08 17				08 39		
Ware d									08 01							08 21				08 43		
St Margarets (Herts) d									08 05							08 25				08 47		
Rye House d									08 08							08 28				08 50		
Broxbourne ■ a	07 48		08 05						08 13	08 18						08 36	08 48			08 55	09 00	09 03
Broxbourne ■ d	07 48	08 00	08 09			←		←	08 13	08 18				08 30		08 39	08 48			08 55	09 09	09 04
Cheshunt d	07 53	08 05	08 14	07 57		08 05		08 14	08 17	08 23				08 35		08 44	08 53			09 00	→	
Waltham Cross d		→	→			08 07	08 12	08 16						08 37		08 46				09 02		
Enfield Lock d						08 10		08 19						08 40		08 49				09 05		
Brimsdown d						08 12	08 17							08 42		08 51				09 07		
Ponders End d						08 14								08 44						09 09		
Angel Road d								08 24														
Northumberland Park d								08 26								08 56						
Tottenham Hale ⊖ d	08 02			08 05	08 08	08 20	08 23	08 29		08 32	08 35		08 38	08 50	08 53	08 59	09 02	09 05		09 15		09 19
Seven Sisters ⊖ d									08 32													
Lea Bridge d								08 33								09 03						
Stratford ■ ⊖ a								08 43								09 13						
Hackney Downs d						08 26			08 38					08 56						09 21		
London Liverpool Street ■ ⊖ a	08 20			08 23	08 25	08 37	08 40		08 48	08 50	08 53		08 55	09 07	09 09		09 20	09 23		09 33		09 35

	LE 1	LE 1 E	LE ◇1 F	LE 1	LE	LE 1	LE 1	LE ◇1	LE 1	XC ◇1 G	LE	LE 1	LE 1	LE ◇1	LE 1	LE 1	LE	LE 1	LE 1	LE ◇1	LE 1
Cambridge North d			08 14											09 14							
Cambridge a			08 20											09 19							
d			08 21					08 48		09 15				09 20	09 31					10 04	
Shelford d			08 26					08 53						09 25							
Whittlesford Parkway d			08 31					09 00						09 30	09 38					10 11	
Great Chesterford d			08 35					09 04						09 34							
Audley End d			08 40					09 10		09 29				09 40	09 46					10 19	
Newport (Essex) d			08 43					09 13						09 43							
Elsenham d			08 49					09 19						09 49							
Stansted Airport ✈ a										09 43					10 00						
Stansted Airport ✈ d	08 45			09 00		09 15			09 30			09 45				10 00		10 15			10 30
Stansted Mountfitchet d	08 51		08 53			09 21		09 24						09 52				10 21			
Bishops Stortford a			08 58	09 09				09 29	09 39					09 58		10 09				10 32	10 39
Bishops Stortford d			08 58	09 09			09 13	09 29	09 39				09 47	09 58		10 09			10 15	10 32	10 39
Sawbridgeworth d			09 03				09 18	09 33					09 52	10 03					10 20		
Harlow Mill d			09 06				09 21	09 37						10 06					10 23		
Harlow Town d	09 02		09 10			09 32	09 24	09 40				10 01	10 05	10 09				10 32	10 26	10 40	
Roydon d			09 14				09 28							10 13					10 30		
Hertford East d					09 09						09 39						10 09				
Ware d					09 13						09 43						10 13				
St Margarets (Herts) d					09 17						09 47						10 17				
Rye House d		←			09 20						09 50						10 20				
Broxbourne ■ a		09 00	09 18		09 25		09 33	09 46			09 55		10 11	10 17			10 25		10 35	10 46	
Broxbourne ■ d		09 09	09 18		09 25		09 39	09 46			09 55		10 12	10 17			10 25		10 39	10 46	
Cheshunt d		09 14	09 23		09 30		09 43	09 50			09 59		10 16	10 21			10 29		10 44	10 50	
Waltham Cross d		09 16			09 32						10 01		10 19				10 31				
Enfield Lock d		09 19			09 35		09 47				10 04						10 34		10 47		
Brimsdown d					09 37						10 06						10 36				
Ponders End d					09 39						10 08						10 38				
Angel Road d		09 24					09 52														
Northumberland Park d		09 26					09 54												10 53		
Tottenham Hale ⊖ d	09 21	09 29	09 32	09 35	09 45	09 48	09 57	10 00	10 03		10 14	10 17	10 27	10 30		10 33	10 44	10 48	10 56	11 00	11 03
Seven Sisters ⊖ d																					
Lea Bridge d		09 33					10 01						10 31						11 00		
Stratford ■ ⊖ a		09 43					10 08						10 40						11 10		
Hackney Downs d					09 51						10 20						10 50				
London Liverpool Street ■ ⊖ a	09 38		09 50	09 53	10 01	10 03		10 15	10 17		10 28	10 31		10 44		10 47	10 58	11 02		11 14	11 17

A To London Liverpool Street
B To Stratford
C From Kings Lynn. The Fenman
D From Broxbourne
E From Bishops Stortford
F From Ely
G From Birmingham New Street

Table T022-R

Mondays to Fridays

21 May to 7 December

Cambridge North, Cambridge, Stansted Airport, Bishops Stortford, Hertford East and Broxbourne - London

	XC ◇1 A	LE	LE 1	LE 1	LE ◇1	LE 1	LE 1	LE	LE 1	LE 1	LE ◇1	LE 1	XC ◇1 B	LE	LE 1	LE 1	LE ◇1	LE 1	LE 1	LE	LE 1	LE 1
Cambridge North d					10 14												11 14					
Cambridge a					10 20												11 20					
d	10 10				10 21	10 30					11 04		11 11				11 21	11 30				
Shelford d					10 26												11 26					
Whittlesford Parkway d					10 30	10 38					11 11						11 30	11 38				
Great Chesterford d					10 34												11 34					
Audley End d	10 25				10 40	10 46					11 19		11 25				11 40	11 46				
Newport (Essex) d					10 43												11 43					
Elsenham d					10 49												11 49					
Stansted Airport ✈ a	10 40					11 00							11 40					12 00				
Stansted Airport ✈ d			10 45				11 00		11 15			11 30			11 45				12 00		12 15	
Stansted Mountfitchet d					10 52				11 21								11 52				12 21	
Bishops Stortford a					10 58		11 09				11 32	11 39					11 58		12 09			
Bishops Stortford d				10 47	10 58		11 09			11 15	11 32	11 39				11 47	11 58		12 09			12 15
Sawbridgeworth d				10 52	11 03					11 20						11 52	12 03					12 20
Harlow Mill d					11 06					11 23							12 06					12 23
Harlow Town d			11 00	11 05	11 09				11 32	11 26	11 40				12 00	12 05	12 09				12 32	12 26
Roydon d					11 13					11 30							12 13					12 30
Hertford East d		10 39						11 09						11 39						12 09		
Ware d		10 43						11 13						11 43						12 13		
St Margarets (Herts) d		10 47						11 17						11 47						12 17		
Rye House d		10 50						11 20						11 50						12 20		
Broxbourne ■ a		10 55		11 11	11 17			11 25		11 35	11 46			11 55		12 11	12 17			12 25		12 35
Broxbourne ■ d		10 55		11 12	11 17			11 25		11 39	11 46			11 55		12 12	12 17			12 25		12 39
Cheshunt d		10 59		11 16	11 21			11 29		11 44	11 50			11 59		12 16	12 21			12 29		12 44
Waltham Cross d		11 01		11 19				11 31						12 01		12 19				12 31		
Enfield Lock d		11 04						11 34		11 47				12 04						12 34		12 47
Brimsdown d		11 06						11 36						12 06						12 36		
Ponders End d		11 08						11 38						12 08						12 38		
Angel Road d																						
Northumberland Park d										11 53												12 53
Tottenham Hale ⊖ d		11 14	11 17	11 27	11 31		11 33	11 44	11 48	11 56	12 01	12 03		12 14	12 17	12 27	12 31		12 33	12 44	12 48	12 56
Seven Sisters ⊖ d																						
Lea Bridge d				11 31						12 00						12 31						13 00
Stratford ■ ⊖ a				11 40						12 10						12 40						13 10
Hackney Downs d		11 20						11 50						12 20						12 50		
London Liverpool Street ■ ⊖ a		11 31	11 33		11 44		11 47	12 01	12 03		12 14	12 17		12 31	12 33		12 45		12 47	13 01	13 03	

	LE ◇1	LE 1	XC ◇1 A	LE	LE 1	LE 1	LE ◇1	LE 1	LE 1	LE	LE 1	LE 1	LE ◇1	LE 1	XC ◇1 A	LE	LE 1	LE 1	LE ◇1	LE 1	LE 1
Cambridge North d							12 14												13 14		
Cambridge a							12 20												13 20		
d	12 04		12 11				12 21	12 30					13 04		13 11				13 21	13 30	
Shelford d							12 26												13 26		
Whittlesford Parkway d	12 11						12 30	12 38					13 11						13 30	13 38	
Great Chesterford d							12 34												13 34		
Audley End d	12 19		12 25				12 40	12 46					13 19		13 25				13 40	13 46	
Newport (Essex) d							12 43												13 43		
Elsenham d							12 49												13 49		
Stansted Airport ✈ a			12 40					13 00							13 40					14 00	
Stansted Airport ✈ d		12 30			12 45				13 00		13 15			13 30			13 45				14 00
Stansted Mountfitchet d							12 52				13 21								13 52		
Bishops Stortford a	12 32	12 39					12 58		13 09				13 32	13 39					13 58		14 09
Bishops Stortford d	12 32	12 39				12 47	12 58		13 09			13 15	13 32	13 39				13 47	13 58		14 09
Sawbridgeworth d						12 52	13 03					13 20						13 52	14 03		
Harlow Mill d							13 06					13 23							14 06		
Harlow Town d	12 40				13 00	13 05	13 09				13 32	13 26	13 40				14 00	14 05	14 09		
Roydon d							13 13					13 30							14 13		
Hertford East d				12 39						13 09						13 39					
Ware d				12 43						13 13						13 43					
St Margarets (Herts) d				12 47						13 17						13 47					
Rye House d				12 50						13 20						13 50					
Broxbourne ■ a	12 46			12 55		13 11	13 17			13 25		13 35	13 46			13 55		14 11	14 17		
Broxbourne ■ d	12 46			12 55		13 12	13 17			13 25		13 39	13 46			13 55		14 12	14 17		
Cheshunt d	12 50			12 59		13 16	13 21			13 29		13 44	13 50			13 59		14 16	14 21		
Waltham Cross d				13 01		13 19				13 31						14 01		14 19			
Enfield Lock d				13 04						13 34		13 47				14 04					
Brimsdown d				13 06						13 36						14 06					
Ponders End d				13 08						13 38						14 08					
Angel Road d																					
Northumberland Park d												13 53									
Tottenham Hale ⊖ d	13 01	13 03		13 14	13 17	13 27	13 30		13 33	13 44	13 48	13 56	14 00	14 03		14 14	14 17	14 27	14 30		14 33
Seven Sisters ⊖ d																					
Lea Bridge d						13 31						14 00						14 31			
Stratford ■ ⊖ a						13 40						14 10						14 40			
Hackney Downs d				13 20						13 50						14 20					
London Liverpool Street ■ ⊖ a	13 14	13 17		13 28	13 31		13 44		13 47	13 58	14 02		14 14	14 17		14 28	14 31		14 45		14 47

A From Birmingham New Street
B From Gloucester

Table T022-R

Mondays to Fridays
21 May to 7 December

Cambridge North, Cambridge, Stansted Airport, Bishops Stortford, Hertford East and Broxbourne - London

		LE	LE ■	LE ■	LE ◇■	LE ■	XC ◇■ A	LE	LE ■	LE ■	LE ◇■	LE ■	LE ■	LE	LE ■	LE ■	LE ◇■	LE ■	XC ◇■ A	LE	LE ■	LE ■	LE ◇■
Cambridge North	d										14 14												15 14
Cambridge	a										14 20												15 20
	d				14 04		14 11				14 21	14 30					15 04		15 11				15 21
Shelford	d										14 26												15 26
Whittlesford Parkway	d				14 11						14 30	14 38					15 11						15 30
Great Chesterford	d										14 34												15 34
Audley End	d				14 19		14 25				14 40	14 46					15 19		15 25				15 40
Newport (Essex)	d										14 43												15 43
Elsenham	d										14 49												15 49
Stansted Airport ✈	a						14 40					15 00							15 40				
Stansted Airport ✈	d		14 15			14 30			14 45				15 00		15 15			15 30			15 45		
Stansted Mountfitchet	d		14 21								14 52				15 21								15 52
Bishops Stortford	a				14 32	14 39					14 58		15 09				15 32	15 39					15 58
Bishops Stortford	d			14 15	14 32	14 39				14 47	14 58		15 09			15 15	15 32	15 39				15 47	15 58
Sawbridgeworth	d			14 20						14 52	15 03					15 20						15 52	16 03
Harlow Mill	d			14 23							15 06					15 23							16 06
Harlow Town	d		14 32	14 26	14 40				15 00	15 05	15 09				15 32	15 26	15 40				16 00	16 03	16 09
Roydon	d			14 30							15 13					15 30							16 13
Hertford East	d	14 09						14 39						15 09						15 39			
Ware	d	14 13						14 43						15 13						15 43			
St Margarets (Herts)	d	14 17						14 47						15 17						15 47			
Rye House	d	14 20						14 50						15 20						15 50			
Broxbourne ■	a	14 25		14 35	14 46			14 55		15 11	15 17			15 25		15 35	15 46			15 55		16 10	16 17
Broxbourne ■	d	14 25		14 39	14 46			14 55		15 12	15 17			15 25		15 39	15 46			15 55		16 10	16 17
Cheshunt	d	14 29		14 44	14 50			14 59		15 16	15 21			15 29		15 44	15 50			15 59		16 14	16 21
Waltham Cross	d	14 31						15 01		15 19				15 31						16 01		16 16	
Enfield Lock	d	14 34		14 47				15 04						15 34		15 47				16 04			
Brimsdown	d	14 36						15 06						15 36						16 06			
Ponders End	d	14 38						15 08						15 38						16 08			
Angel Road	d															15 52							
Northumberland Park	d			14 53												15 54						16 23	
Tottenham Hale ⊖	d	14 44	14 48	14 56	15 01	15 03		15 14	15 17	15 27	15 31		15 33	15 44	15 48	15 58	16 01	16 04		16 14	16 17	16 27	16 30
Seven Sisters ⊖	d																						
Lea Bridge	d			15 00						15 31						16 02						16 31	
Stratford ■ ⊖	a			15 10						15 40						16 10						16 38	
Hackney Downs	d	14 50						15 20						15 50						16 20			
London Liverpool Street ■ ⊖	a	14 58	15 02		15 15	15 17		15 28	15 31		15 45		15 48	15 59	16 03		16 15	16 18		16 31	16 33		16 44

		LE ■	LE ■	LE	LE ■	LE ■	LE ◇■	LE ■	XC ◇■ A	LE	LE ■	LE ■	LE ◇■	LE ◇■	LE ■	LE	LE ■	LE ■	LE ■	LE ◇■	LE ■	XC ◇■ A	LE
Cambridge North	d												16 14										
Cambridge	a												16 20										
	d	15 30					15 51		16 11				16 21	16 36						16 51		17 11	
Shelford	d						15 56						16 26							16 56			
Whittlesford Parkway	d	15 38					16 00						16 30	16 43						17 00			
Great Chesterford	d						16 04						16 34							17 04			
Audley End	d	15 46					16 10		16 25				16 40	16 52						17 10		17 25	
Newport (Essex)	d						16 13						16 43							17 13			
Elsenham	d						16 19						16 49							17 19			
Stansted Airport ✈	a	16 00							16 40													17 40	
Stansted Airport ✈	d		16 00		16 15			16 30			16 45				17 00			17 15			17 30		
Stansted Mountfitchet	d				16 21		16 24						16 52					17 21		17 24			
Bishops Stortford	a		16 09				16 30	16 39					16 58	17 05	17 09					17 30	17 39		
Bishops Stortford	d		16 09			16 15	16 30	16 39				16 43	16 58	17 05	17 09				17 15	17 30	17 39		
Sawbridgeworth	d					16 20						16 48	17 03						17 20	17 35			
Harlow Mill	d					16 23						16 51							17 23	17 38			
Harlow Town	d				16 32	16 26	16 38				17 00	16 54	17 08					17 32	17 26	17 41			
Roydon	d					16 30						16 58							17 30				
Hertford East	d			16 09						16 39						17 09							17 39
Ware	d			16 13						16 43						17 13							17 43
St Margarets (Herts)	d			16 17						16 47						17 17							17 47
Rye House	d			16 20						16 50						17 20							17 50
Broxbourne ■	a			16 25		16 35	16 44			16 56		17 03	17 14			17 26			17 35	17 47			17 56
Broxbourne ■	d			16 25		16 39	16 44			16 56		17 07	17 14			17 26	17 35		17 40	17 47			17 56
Cheshunt	d			16 29		16 44	16 48			17 00		17 12	17 18			17 30			17 44	17 51			18 00
Waltham Cross	d			16 31						17 02		17 14				17 33							18 02
Enfield Lock	d			16 34		16 47				17 05						17 35			17 48				18 05
Brimsdown	d			16 36						17 07						17 38							18 07
Ponders End	d			16 38						17 09						17 40							18 09
Angel Road	d					16 52													17 53				
Northumberland Park	d					16 54						17 21							17 55				
Tottenham Hale ⊖	d		16 33	16 44	16 48	16 58	17 01	17 04		17 15	17 18	17 24	17 27	17 30	17 33	17 46		17 51	17 58	18 01	18 04		18 15
Seven Sisters ⊖	d																						
Lea Bridge	d					17 02						17 28							18 02				
Stratford ■ ⊖	a					17 09						17 36							18 09				
Hackney Downs	d			16 50						17 21						17 51							18 21
London Liverpool Street ■ ⊖	a		16 47	16 59	17 02		17 16	17 18		17 30	17 32		17 44	17 46	17 48	18 00	18 02	18 08		18 16	18 18		18 29

A From Birmingham New Street

Table T022-R

Mondays to Fridays
21 May to 7 December

Cambridge North, Cambridge, Stansted Airport, Bishops Stortford, Hertford East and Broxbourne - London

		LE ■	LE ■	LE ■	LE ◇■	LE ■	LE	LE ■	LE ■	LE ■	LE	LE ◇■	LE ■	LE	LE ■	LE ■	XC ◇■ A	LE	LE ◇■	LE ■	LE	LE ■
Cambridge North	d				17 14																	
Cambridge	a				17 20																	
	d				17 21							17 51					18 18		18 21			
Shelford	d				17 26							17 56							18 26			
Whittlesford Parkway	d				17 30							18 00							18 30			
Great Chesterford	d				17 34							18 04							18 34			
Audley End	d				17 40							18 10					18 32		18 40			
Newport (Essex)	d				17 43							18 13							18 43			
Elsenham	d				17 49							18 19							18 49			
Stansted Airport ✈	a																18 54					
Stansted Airport ✈	d		17 45			18 00			18 15				18 30			18 45				19 00		19 15
Stansted Mountfitchet	d				17 52				18 21			18 24							18 52			19 21
Bishops Stortford	a				17 58	18 09						18 29	18 39						18 58	19 09		
Bishops Stortford	d			17 47	17 58	18 09				18 15		18 30	18 39						18 58	19 09		
Sawbridgeworth	d			17 52	18 03					18 20		18 35							19 03			
Harlow Mill	d				18 06					18 23									19 06			
Harlow Town	d		18 00	17 57	18 09				18 32	18 26		18 40				19 00			19 09			19 32
Roydon	d				18 13					18 30									19 13			
Hertford East	d						18 09				18 25			18 39							19 09	
Ware	d						18 13				18 29			18 43							19 13	
St Margarets (Herts)	d						18 17				18 33			18 47							19 17	
Rye House	d						18 20				18 36			18 50							19 20	
Broxbourne ■	a			18 04	18 17		18 26			18 35	18 43	18 46		18 56					19 17		19 26	
Broxbourne ■	d	18 05		18 10	18 17		18 26	18 35		18 40		18 46		18 56	19 05			19 10	19 17		19 26	
Cheshunt	d			18 14	18 21		18 30			18 44		18 50		19 00				19 14	19 21		19 30	
Waltham Cross	d			18 17			18 32							19 02				19 17			19 32	
Enfield Lock	d						18 35			18 48				19 05							19 35	
Brimsdown	d						18 37							19 07							19 37	
Ponders End	d						18 39							19 09							19 39	
Angel Road	d									18 53												
Northumberland Park	d			18 23						18 55								19 23				
Tottenham Hale ⊖	d		18 21	18 27	18 30	18 33	18 45		18 51	18 58		19 01	19 04	19 15		19 21		19 27	19 30	19 33	19 45	19 48
Seven Sisters ⊖	d																					
Lea Bridge	d			18 31						19 02								19 31				
Stratford ■ ⊖	a			18 38						19 09								19 38				
Hackney Downs	d						18 51							19 21							19 51	
London Liverpool Street ■ ⊖	a	18 31	18 38		18 45	18 47	18 59	19 01	19 08			19 16	19 18	19 29	19 31	19 38			19 45	19 48	19 59	20 03

		LE ■	LE	LE ◇■	LE ■	XC ◇■ A	LE	LE ■	LE	LE ◇■	LE ■	LE	LE ■	LE ■	LE ◇■	LE ■	XC ◇■ A	LE	LE ■	LE ■	LE ◇■	LE ■	LE
Cambridge North	d									19 14											20 11		
Cambridge	a									19 19											20 16		
	d			18 51		19 10				19 20					20 04		20 11				20 21		
Shelford	d			18 56						19 26											20 26		
Whittlesford Parkway	d			19 00						19 30					20 11						20 30		
Great Chesterford	d			19 04						19 34											20 34		
Audley End	d			19 10		19 25				19 40					20 19		20 25				20 40		
Newport (Essex)	d			19 13						19 43											20 43		
Elsenham	d			19 19						19 49											20 49		
Stansted Airport ✈	a					19 40											20 39						
Stansted Airport ✈	d				19 30			19 45			20 00		20 15			20 30			20 45			21 00	
Stansted Mountfitchet	d			19 24						19 52			20 21								20 52		
Bishops Stortford	a			19 29	19 39					19 58	20 09				20 32	20 39					20 58	21 09	
Bishops Stortford	d	19 15		19 30	19 39					19 58	20 09			20 15	20 32	20 39				20 47	20 58	21 09	
Sawbridgeworth	d	19 20		19 35						20 03				20 20						20 52	21 03		
Harlow Mill	d	19 23								20 06				20 23							21 06		
Harlow Town	d	19 26		19 40				20 00		20 09			20 32	20 26	20 40				21 00	20 57	21 09		
Roydon	d	19 30								20 13				20 30							21 13		
Hertford East	d		19 25				19 39					20 10						20 39					21 09
Ware	d		19 29				19 43					20 14						20 43					21 13
St Margarets (Herts)	d		19 33				19 47					20 18						20 47					21 17
Rye House	d		19 36				19 50					20 21						20 50					21 20
Broxbourne ■	a	19 35	19 42	19 46			19 55			20 17		20 25		20 35	20 46			20 55		21 04	21 17		21 25
Broxbourne ■	d	19 39		19 46			19 55		20 12	20 17		20 25		20 39	20 46			20 55		21 07	21 17		21 25
Cheshunt	d	19 43		19 50			19 59		20 16	20 21		20 29		20 44	20 50			20 59		21 12	21 21		21 29
Waltham Cross	d						20 01		20 19			20 32						21 01		21 14			21 31
Enfield Lock	d	19 47					20 04					20 34		20 47				21 04					21 34
Brimsdown	d						20 06					20 37						21 06					21 36
Ponders End	d						20 08					20 39						21 08					21 38
Angel Road	d	19 52																					
Northumberland Park	d	19 54												20 53									
Tottenham Hale ⊖	d	19 57		20 00	20 03		20 14	20 17	20 27	20 30	20 33	20 44	20 48	20 56	21 01	21 03		21 14	21 17	21 23	21 30	21 33	21 44
Seven Sisters ⊖	d																						
Lea Bridge	d	20 01							20 31					21 00						21 27			
Stratford ■ ⊖	a	20 10							20 38					21 10						21 40			
Hackney Downs	d						20 20					20 50						21 20					21 50
London Liverpool Street ■ ⊖	a			20 15	20 17		20 31	20 33		20 45	20 47	20 59	21 03		21 14	21 17		21 28	21 31		21 44	21 47	21 58

A From Birmingham New Street

Table T022-R

Mondays to Fridays

21 May to 7 December

Cambridge North, Cambridge, Stansted Airport, Bishops Stortford, Hertford East and Broxbourne - London

Station		LE ■	LE ■	LE ◇■	LE ■	XC ◇■ A	LE	LE ■	LE ■	LE ◇■	LE ■
Cambridge North	d									21 15	
Cambridge	a									21 20	
	d			21 04		21 11				21 21	21 30
Shelford	d									21 26	
Whittlesford Parkway	d			21 11						21 30	21 38
Great Chesterford	d									21 34	
Audley End	d			21 19		21 25				21 40	21 46
Newport (Essex)	d									21 43	
Elsenham	d									21 49	
Stansted Airport ✈	a					21 40					22 00
Stansted Airport ✈	d	21 15			21 30			21 45			
Stansted Mountfitchet	d	21 21								21 52	
Bishops Stortford	a			21 32	21 39					21 58	
Bishops Stortford	d		21 15	21 32	21 39				21 47	21 58	
Sawbridgeworth	d		21 20						21 52	22 03	
Harlow Mill	d		21 23							22 06	
Harlow Town	d	21 32	21 26	21 40				22 00	22 05	22 09	
Roydon	d		21 30							22 13	
Hertford East	d						21 39				
Ware	d						21 43				
St Margarets (Herts)	d						21 47				
Rye House	d						21 50				
Broxbourne ■	a		21 35	21 46			21 55		22 11	22 17	
Broxbourne ■	d		21 39	21 46			21 55		22 12	22 17	
Cheshunt	d		21 44	21 50			21 59		22 16	22 21	
Waltham Cross	d						22 01		22 19		
Enfield Lock	d		21 47				22 04				
Brimsdown	d						22 06				
Ponders End	d						22 08				
Angel Road	d										
Northumberland Park	d		21 53								
Tottenham Hale ⊖	d	21 48	21 56	22 01	22 03		22 14	22 17	22 27	22 31	
Seven Sisters ⊖	d										
Lea Bridge	d		22 00						22 31		
Stratford ■ ⊖	a		22 10						22 40		
Hackney Downs	d						22 20				
London Liverpool Street ■ ⊖	a	22 02		22 14	22 17		22 28	22 31		22 45	

Station		LE ■	LE	LE ■	LE ■	LE ◇■	LE ■	LE	LE ■	XC ◇■ A	LE ◇■	LE ■
Cambridge North	d										22 14	
Cambridge	a										22 20	
	d					22 04				22 10	22 21	
Shelford	d										22 26	
Whittlesford Parkway	d					22 11					22 30	
Great Chesterford	d										22 34	
Audley End	d					22 19				22 25	22 40	
Newport (Essex)	d										22 43	
Elsenham	d										22 49	
Stansted Airport ✈	a									22 52		
Stansted Airport ✈	d	22 00		22 15			22 30		22 45			23 00
Stansted Mountfitchet	d			22 21							22 52	
Bishops Stortford	a	22 09				22 32	22 39				22 58	23 09
Bishops Stortford	d	22 09			22 15	22 32	22 39				22 58	23 09
Sawbridgeworth	d				22 20						23 03	
Harlow Mill	d				22 23						23 06	
Harlow Town	d			22 32	22 26	22 40			23 00		23 09	
Roydon	d				22 30						23 13	
Hertford East	d		22 09					22 39				
Ware	d		22 13					22 43				
St Margarets (Herts)	d		22 17					22 47				
Rye House	d		22 20					22 50				
Broxbourne ■	a		22 25		22 35	22 46		22 55			23 17	
Broxbourne ■	d		22 25		22 39	22 46		22 55			23 17	
Cheshunt	d		22 29		22 44	22 50		22 59			23 21	
Waltham Cross	d		22 31					23 01				
Enfield Lock	d		22 34		22 47			23 04				
Brimsdown	d		22 36					23 06				
Ponders End	d		22 38					23 08				
Angel Road	d											
Northumberland Park	d				22 53							
Tottenham Hale ⊖	d	22 33	22 44	22 48	22 56	23 01	23 03	23 14	23 17		23 30	23 33
Seven Sisters ⊖	d											
Lea Bridge	d				23 00							
Stratford ■ ⊖	a				23 09							
Hackney Downs	d		22 50					23 20				
London Liverpool Street ■ ⊖	a	22 47	22 58	23 02	23 18	23 15	23 17	23 28	23 33		23 48	23 50

Station		LE	LE ■	LE ◇■	LE ■	LE FO ■	LE	LE ■	LE ■
Cambridge North	d								
Cambridge	a								
	d			22 51		23 27			
Shelford	d			22 56		23 32			
Whittlesford Parkway	d			23 00		23 36			
Great Chesterford	d			23 04		23 40			
Audley End	d			23 10		23 46			
Newport (Essex)	d			23 13		23 49			
Elsenham	d			23 19		23 54			
Stansted Airport ✈	a								
Stansted Airport ✈	d		23 15		23 30			23 45	23 59
Stansted Mountfitchet	d		23 21	23 24		23 59			
Bishops Stortford	a			23 29	23 39	00 03			00 08
Bishops Stortford	d			23 29	23 39				00 08
Sawbridgeworth	d			23 33					
Harlow Mill	d			23 37					
Harlow Town	d		23 33	23 40				00 01	00 16
Roydon	d			23 44					
Hertford East	d	23 09					23 39		
Ware	d	23 13					23 43		
St Margarets (Herts)	d	23 17					23 47		
Rye House	d	23 20					23 50		
Broxbourne ■	a	23 25		23 48			23 55		
Broxbourne ■	d	23 25		23 48			23 55		
Cheshunt	d	23 29		23 52			23 59		
Waltham Cross	d	23 31							
Enfield Lock	d	23 34							
Brimsdown	d	23 36							
Ponders End	d	23 38							
Angel Road	d								
Northumberland Park	d								
Tottenham Hale ⊖	d	23 44	23 48						
Seven Sisters ⊖	d			00 04	00 08		00 12	00 21	
Lea Bridge	d								
Stratford ■ ⊖	a								
Hackney Downs	d	23 50					00 17		
London Liverpool Street ■ ⊖	a	23 58	00 02	00 18	00 22		00 26	00 36	00 51

A From Birmingham New Street

Table T022-R

Saturdays

26 May to 8 December

Cambridge North, Cambridge, Stansted Airport, Bishops Stortford, Hertford East and Broxbourne - London

Station		LE ◇■ A	LE ■ B	LE C	LE ■ B	LE ■	LE ■ B	LE ■	LE ◇■	XC ■
Cambridge North	d									
Cambridge	a									
	d								04 38	04 56
Shelford	d									
Whittlesford Parkway	d								04 45	
Great Chesterford	d									
Audley End	d								04 53	
Newport (Essex)	d									
Elsenham	d									
Stansted Airport ✈	a									05 20
Stansted Airport ✈	d							00 30		
Stansted Mountfitchet	d									
Bishops Stortford	a							00 39	05 06	
Bishops Stortford	d						00 08	00 39	05 07	
Sawbridgeworth	d								05 11	
Harlow Mill	d								05 15	
Harlow Town	d				00 01		00 16	00 47	05 18	
Roydon	d								05 22	
Hertford East	d					00 07				
Ware	d									
St Margarets (Herts)	d									
Rye House	d									
Broxbourne ■	a					00 19			05 26	
Broxbourne ■	d					00 19			05 26	
Cheshunt	d								05 30	
Waltham Cross	d									
Enfield Lock	d									
Brimsdown	d									
Ponders End	d									
Angel Road	d									
Northumberland Park	d									
Tottenham Hale ⊖	d									
Seven Sisters ⊖	d	00 04	00 08	00 12	00 21				05 42	
Lea Bridge	d									
Stratford ■ ⊖	a									
Hackney Downs	d			00 17						
London Liverpool Street ■ ⊖	a	00 18	00 22	00 26	00 36	00 49	00 51	01 21	05 57	

Station		LE ■	LE ■	LE	LE ■	LE ◇■	LE ■	XC ■	LE	LE ■	LE ■	LE ◇■	LE ■	LE ■
Cambridge North	d													
Cambridge	a													
	d					05 21		05 41				06 04		06 10
Shelford	d					05 26								
Whittlesford Parkway	d					05 30						06 11		06 18
Great Chesterford	d					05 34								
Audley End	d					05 40		05 56				06 19		06 26
Newport (Essex)	d					05 43								
Elsenham	d					05 49								
Stansted Airport ✈	a							06 08						06 41
Stansted Airport ✈	d		05 30				06 00			06 15			06 30	
Stansted Mountfitchet	d					05 52				06 21				
Bishops Stortford	a		05 39			05 58	06 09					06 32	06 39	
Bishops Stortford	d	05 14	05 39		05 47	05 58	06 09				06 15	06 32	06 39	
Sawbridgeworth	d	05 19			05 52	06 03					06 20			
Harlow Mill	d	05 22				06 06					06 23			
Harlow Town	d	05 25			06 05	06 09				06 32	06 26	06 40		
Roydon	d	05 29				06 13					06 30			
Hertford East	d								06 09					
Ware	d								06 13					
St Margarets (Herts)	d								06 17					
Rye House	d								06 20					
Broxbourne ■	a	05 33			06 11	06 17			06 25		06 35	06 46		
Broxbourne ■	d	05 33		05 55	06 12	06 17			06 25		06 39	06 46		
Cheshunt	d	05 37		05 59	06 16	06 21			06 29		06 44	06 50		
Waltham Cross	d	05 40		06 01	06 19				06 31					
Enfield Lock	d	05 42		06 04					06 34		06 47			
Brimsdown	d	05 45		06 06					06 36					
Ponders End	d	05 47		06 08					06 38					
Angel Road	d													
Northumberland Park	d	05 51									06 53			
Tottenham Hale ⊖	d	05 55	06 01	06 14	06 27	06 30	06 33		06 44	06 48	06 56	07 00	07 03	
Seven Sisters ⊖	d													
Lea Bridge	d	05 59			06 31						07 00			
Stratford ■ ⊖	a	06 05			06 40						07 10			
Hackney Downs	d			06 20					06 50					
London Liverpool Street ■ ⊖	a	06 14	06 15	06 28		06 44	06 47		06 58	07 01		07 14	07 17	

Station		LE	LE ■	LE ■	LE ◇■	LE ■	XC ■	LE	LE ■	LE ■	LE ◇■	LE ■
Cambridge North	d				06 14							
Cambridge	a				06 20							
	d				06 21		06 40				07 04	
Shelford	d				06 26							
Whittlesford Parkway	d				06 30						07 11	
Great Chesterford	d				06 34							
Audley End	d				06 40		06 54				07 19	
Newport (Essex)	d				06 43							
Elsenham	d				06 49							
Stansted Airport ✈	a						07 08					
Stansted Airport ✈	d		06 45			07 00			07 15			07 30
Stansted Mountfitchet	d				06 52				07 21			
Bishops Stortford	a				06 58	07 09					07 32	07 39
Bishops Stortford	d			06 47	06 58	07 09				07 15	07 32	07 39
Sawbridgeworth	d			06 52	07 03					07 20		
Harlow Mill	d				07 06					07 23		
Harlow Town	d		07 00	07 03	07 09				07 32	07 26	07 40	
Roydon	d				07 13					07 30		
Hertford East	d	06 39						07 09				
Ware	d	06 43						07 13				
St Margarets (Herts)	d	06 47						07 17				
Rye House	d	06 50						07 20				
Broxbourne ■	a	06 55		07 09	07 17			07 25		07 35	07 46	
Broxbourne ■	d	06 55		07 12	07 17			07 25		07 39	07 46	
Cheshunt	d	06 59		07 16	07 21			07 29		07 44	07 50	
Waltham Cross	d	07 01		07 19				07 31				
Enfield Lock	d	07 04						07 34		07 47		
Brimsdown	d	07 06						07 36				
Ponders End	d	07 08						07 38				
Angel Road	d											
Northumberland Park	d									07 53		
Tottenham Hale ⊖	d	07 14	07 17	07 27	07 30	07 33		07 44	07 48	07 56	08 00	08 03
Seven Sisters ⊖	d											
Lea Bridge	d			07 31						08 00		
Stratford ■ ⊖	a			07 40						08 10		
Hackney Downs	d	07 20						07 50				
London Liverpool Street ■ ⊖	a	07 28	07 31		07 44	07 47		07 58	08 02		08 14	08 17

Station		LE ■	LE	LE ■	LE ■	LE ◇■	LE ■	XC ■	LE	LE ■	LE ■	LE ◇■
Cambridge North	d					07 14						
Cambridge	a					07 20						
	d	07 10				07 21		07 40				08 04
Shelford	d					07 26						
Whittlesford Parkway	d	07 18				07 30						08 11
Great Chesterford	d					07 34						
Audley End	d	07 26				07 40		07 54				08 19
Newport (Essex)	d					07 43						
Elsenham	d					07 49						
Stansted Airport ✈	a	07 41						08 08				
Stansted Airport ✈	d			07 45			08 00			08 15		
Stansted Mountfitchet	d					07 52				08 21		
Bishops Stortford	a					07 58	08 09					08 32
Bishops Stortford	d				07 47	07 58	08 09				08 15	08 32
Sawbridgeworth	d				07 52	08 03					08 20	
Harlow Mill	d					08 06					08 23	
Harlow Town	d			08 02	08 05	08 09				08 32	08 26	08 40
Roydon	d					08 13					08 30	
Hertford East	d		07 39						08 09			
Ware	d		07 43						08 13			
St Margarets (Herts)	d		07 47						08 17			
Rye House	d		07 50						08 20			
Broxbourne ■	a		07 55		08 11	08 17			08 25		08 35	08 46
Broxbourne ■	d		07 55		08 12	08 17			08 25		08 39	08 46
Cheshunt	d		07 59		08 16	08 21			08 29		08 44	08 50
Waltham Cross	d		08 01		08 19				08 31			
Enfield Lock	d		08 04						08 34		08 47	
Brimsdown	d		08 06						08 36			
Ponders End	d		08 08						08 38			
Angel Road	d											
Northumberland Park	d										08 53	
Tottenham Hale ⊖	d		08 14	08 17	08 27	08 30	08 33		08 44	08 48	08 56	09 00
Seven Sisters ⊖	d											
Lea Bridge	d				08 31						09 00	
Stratford ■ ⊖	a				08 40						09 10	
Hackney Downs	d		08 20						08 50			
London Liverpool Street ■ ⊖	a		08 28	08 31		08 44	08 47		08 58	09 02		09 14

A From Cambridge **B** From Stansted Airport **C** From Hertford East

Table T022-R

Saturdays
26 May to 8 December

Cambridge North, Cambridge, Stansted Airport, Bishops Stortford, Hertford East and Broxbourne - London

		LE 1	XC ◇1 A	LE	LE 1	LE 1	LE ◇1	LE 1	LE 1	LE	LE 1	LE 1
Cambridge North	d						08 14					
Cambridge	a						08 20					
	d		08 10				08 21	08 30				
Shelford	d						08 26					
Whittlesford Parkway	d						08 30	08 38				
Great Chesterford	d						08 34					
Audley End	d		08 25				08 40	08 46				
Newport (Essex)	d						08 43					
Elsenham	d						08 49					
Stansted Airport ✈	a		08 39					09 00				
Stansted Airport ✈	d	08 30			08 45				09 00		09 15	
Stansted Mountfitchet	d						08 52				09 21	
Bishops Stortford	a	08 39					08 58		09 09			
Bishops Stortford	d	08 39				08 47	08 58		09 09			09 15
Sawbridgeworth	d					08 52	09 03					09 20
Harlow Mill	d						09 06					09 23
Harlow Town	d				09 00	09 05	09 09				09 32	09 26
Roydon	d						09 13					09 30
Hertford East	d			08 39						09 09		
Ware	d			08 43						09 13		
St Margarets (Herts)	d			08 47						09 17		
Rye House	d			08 50						09 20		
Broxbourne 8	a			08 55		09 11	09 17			09 25		09 35
Broxbourne 8	d			08 55		09 12	09 17			09 25		09 39
Cheshunt	d			08 59		09 16	09 21			09 29		09 44
Waltham Cross	d			09 01		09 19				09 31		
Enfield Lock	d			09 04						09 34		09 47
Brimsdown	d			09 06						09 36		
Ponders End	d			09 08						09 38		
Angel Road	d											
Northumberland Park	d											09 53
Tottenham Hale ⊖	d	09 03		09 14	09 17	09 27	09 30		09 33	09 44	09 48	09 56
Seven Sisters ⊖	d											
Lea Bridge	d					09 31						10 00
Stratford 7 ⊖	a					09 40						10 10
Hackney Downs	d			09 20						09 50		
London Liverpool Street 15 ⊖	a	09 17		09 28	09 31		09 44		09 47	09 58	10 02	

		LE ◇1	LE 1	XC ◇1 A	LE	LE 1	LE 1	LE ◇1	LE 1	LE 1	LE
Cambridge North	d							09 14			
Cambridge	a							09 20			
	d	09 04		09 11				09 21	09 30		
Shelford	d							09 26			
Whittlesford Parkway	d	09 11						09 31	09 38		
Great Chesterford	d							09 35			
Audley End	d	09 19		09 25				09 40	09 46		
Newport (Essex)	d							09 43			
Elsenham	d							09 49			
Stansted Airport ✈	a			09 40					10 00		
Stansted Airport ✈	d		09 30			09 45				10 00	
Stansted Mountfitchet	d							09 52			
Bishops Stortford	a	09 32	09 39					09 58		10 09	
Bishops Stortford	d	09 32	09 39				09 47	09 58		10 09	
Sawbridgeworth	d						09 52	10 03			
Harlow Mill	d							10 06			
Harlow Town	d	09 40				10 00	10 05	10 09			
Roydon	d							10 13			
Hertford East	d				09 39						10 09
Ware	d				09 43						10 13
St Margarets (Herts)	d				09 47						10 17
Rye House	d				09 50						10 20
Broxbourne 8	a	09 46			09 55		10 11	10 17			10 25
Broxbourne 8	d	09 46			09 55		10 12	10 17			10 25
Cheshunt	d	09 50			09 59		10 16	10 21			10 29
Waltham Cross	d				10 01		10 19				10 31
Enfield Lock	d				10 04						10 34
Brimsdown	d				10 06						10 36
Ponders End	d				10 08						10 38
Angel Road	d										
Northumberland Park	d										
Tottenham Hale ⊖	d	10 00	10 03		10 14	10 17	10 27	10 30		10 33	10 44
Seven Sisters ⊖	d										
Lea Bridge	d						10 31				
Stratford 7 ⊖	a						10 40				
Hackney Downs	d				10 20						10 50
London Liverpool Street 15 ⊖	a	10 14	10 17		10 28	10 31		10 44		10 47	10 58

		LE 1	LE 1	LE ◇1	LE 1	XC ◇1 A	LE	LE 1	LE 1	LE ◇1	LE 1	LE 1
Cambridge North	d									10 14		
Cambridge	a									10 20		
	d			10 04		10 11				10 21	10 30	
Shelford	d									10 26		
Whittlesford Parkway	d			10 11						10 30	10 38	
Great Chesterford	d									10 34		
Audley End	d			10 19		10 26				10 40	10 46	
Newport (Essex)	d									10 43		
Elsenham	d									10 49		
Stansted Airport ✈	a					10 40					11 00	
Stansted Airport ✈	d	10 15			10 30			10 45				11 00
Stansted Mountfitchet	d	10 21								10 52		
Bishops Stortford	a			10 32	10 39					10 58		11 09
Bishops Stortford	d		10 15	10 32	10 39				10 47	10 58		11 09
Sawbridgeworth	d		10 20						10 52	11 03		
Harlow Mill	d		10 23							11 06		
Harlow Town	d	10 32	10 26	10 40				11 00	11 05	11 09		
Roydon	d		10 30							11 13		
Hertford East	d						10 39					
Ware	d						10 43					
St Margarets (Herts)	d						10 47					
Rye House	d						10 50					
Broxbourne 8	a		10 35	10 46			10 55		11 11	11 17		
Broxbourne 8	d		10 39	10 46			10 55		11 12	11 17		
Cheshunt	d		10 44	10 50			10 59		11 16	11 21		
Waltham Cross	d						11 01		11 19			
Enfield Lock	d		10 47				11 04					
Brimsdown	d						11 06					
Ponders End	d						11 08					
Angel Road	d											
Northumberland Park	d		10 53									
Tottenham Hale ⊖	d	10 48	10 56	11 00	11 03		11 14	11 17	11 27	11 31		11 33
Seven Sisters ⊖	d											
Lea Bridge	d		11 00						11 31			
Stratford 7 ⊖	a		11 10						11 40			
Hackney Downs	d						11 20					
London Liverpool Street 15 ⊖	a	11 02		11 14	11 17		11 28	11 31		11 44		11 47

		LE	LE 1	LE 1	LE ◇1	LE 1	XC ◇1 B	LE	LE 1	LE 1	LE ◇1	LE 1
Cambridge North	d										11 14	
Cambridge	a										11 20	
	d				11 04		11 11				11 21	11 30
Shelford	d										11 26	
Whittlesford Parkway	d				11 11						11 30	11 38
Great Chesterford	d										11 34	
Audley End	d				11 19		11 26				11 40	11 46
Newport (Essex)	d										11 43	
Elsenham	d										11 49	
Stansted Airport ✈	a						11 40					12 00
Stansted Airport ✈	d		11 15			11 30			11 45			
Stansted Mountfitchet	d		11 21								11 52	
Bishops Stortford	a				11 32	11 39					11 58	
Bishops Stortford	d			11 15	11 32	11 39				11 47	11 58	
Sawbridgeworth	d			11 20						11 52	12 03	
Harlow Mill	d			11 23							12 06	
Harlow Town	d		11 32	11 26	11 40				12 00	12 05	12 09	
Roydon	d			11 30							12 13	
Hertford East	d	11 09						11 39				
Ware	d	11 13						11 43				
St Margarets (Herts)	d	11 17						11 47				
Rye House	d	11 20						11 50				
Broxbourne 8	a	11 25		11 35	11 46			11 55		12 11	12 17	
Broxbourne 8	d	11 25		11 39	11 46			11 55		12 12	12 17	
Cheshunt	d	11 29		11 44	11 50			11 59		12 16	12 21	
Waltham Cross	d	11 31						12 01		12 19		
Enfield Lock	d	11 34		11 47				12 04				
Brimsdown	d	11 36						12 06				
Ponders End	d	11 38						12 08				
Angel Road	d											
Northumberland Park	d			11 53								
Tottenham Hale ⊖	d	11 44	11 48	11 56	12 00	12 03		12 14	12 17	12 27	12 31	
Seven Sisters ⊖	d											
Lea Bridge	d			12 00						12 31		
Stratford 7 ⊖	a			12 10						12 40		
Hackney Downs	d	11 50						12 20				
London Liverpool Street 15 ⊖	a	11 58	12 02		12 14	12 17		12 28	12 31		12 44	

A From Birmingham New Street

B From Gloucester

Table T022-R

Saturdays
26 May to 8 December

Cambridge North, Cambridge, Stansted Airport, Bishops Stortford, Hertford East and Broxbourne - London

		LE 1	LE	LE 1	LE 1	LE ◇1	LE 1	XC ◇1 A	LE	LE 1	LE 1	LE ◇1
Cambridge North	d											12 14
Cambridge	a											12 20
	d					12 04		12 11				12 21
Shelford	d											12 26
Whittlesford Parkway	d					12 11						12 30
Great Chesterford	d											12 34
Audley End	d					12 19		12 25				12 40
Newport (Essex)	d											12 43
Elsenham	d											12 49
Stansted Airport ✈	a							12 40				
Stansted Airport ✈	d	12 00		12 15			12 30			12 45		
Stansted Mountfitchet	d			12 21								12 52
Bishops Stortford	a	12 09				12 32	12 39					12 58
Bishops Stortford	d	12 09			12 15	12 32	12 39				12 47	12 58
Sawbridgeworth	d				12 20						12 52	13 03
Harlow Mill	d				12 23							13 06
Harlow Town	d			12 32	12 26	12 40				13 00	13 05	13 09
Roydon	d				12 30							13 13
Hertford East	d		12 09						12 39			
Ware	d		12 13						12 43			
St Margarets (Herts)	d		12 17						12 47			
Rye House	d		12 20						12 50			
Broxbourne 8	a		12 25		12 35	12 46			12 55		13 11	13 17
Broxbourne 8	d		12 25		12 39	12 46			12 55		13 12	13 17
Cheshunt	d		12 29		12 44	12 50			12 59		13 16	13 21
Waltham Cross	d		12 31						13 01		13 19	
Enfield Lock	d		12 34		12 47				13 04			
Brimsdown	d		12 36						13 06			
Ponders End	d		12 38						13 08			
Angel Road	d											
Northumberland Park	d				12 53							
Tottenham Hale ⊖	d	12 33	12 44	12 48	12 56	13 00	13 03		13 14	13 17	13 27	13 31
Seven Sisters ⊖	d											
Lea Bridge	d				13 00						13 31	
Stratford 7 ⊖	a				13 10						13 40	
Hackney Downs	d		12 50						13 20			
London Liverpool Street 15 ⊖	a	12 47	12 58	13 02		13 14	13 17		13 28	13 31		13 44

		LE 1	LE 1	LE	LE 1	LE 1	LE ◇1	LE 1	XC ◇1 A	LE	LE 1
Cambridge North	d										
Cambridge	a										
	d	12 30					13 04		13 11		
Shelford	d										
Whittlesford Parkway	d	12 38					13 11				
Great Chesterford	d										
Audley End	d	12 46					13 19		13 25		
Newport (Essex)	d										
Elsenham	d										
Stansted Airport ✈	a	13 00							13 40		
Stansted Airport ✈	d		13 00		13 15			13 30			13 45
Stansted Mountfitchet	d				13 21						
Bishops Stortford	a		13 09				13 32	13 39			
Bishops Stortford	d		13 09			13 15	13 32	13 39			
Sawbridgeworth	d					13 20					
Harlow Mill	d					13 23					
Harlow Town	d				13 32	13 26	13 40				14 00
Roydon	d					13 30					
Hertford East	d			13 09						13 39	
Ware	d			13 13						13 43	
St Margarets (Herts)	d			13 17						13 47	
Rye House	d			13 20						13 50	
Broxbourne 8	a			13 25		13 35	13 46			13 55	
Broxbourne 8	d			13 25		13 39	13 46			13 55	
Cheshunt	d			13 29		13 44	13 50			13 59	
Waltham Cross	d			13 31						14 01	
Enfield Lock	d			13 34		13 47				14 04	
Brimsdown	d			13 36						14 06	
Ponders End	d			13 38						14 08	
Angel Road	d										
Northumberland Park	d					13 53					
Tottenham Hale ⊖	d		13 33	13 44	13 48	13 56	14 00	14 03		14 14	14 17
Seven Sisters ⊖	d										
Lea Bridge	d					14 00					
Stratford 7 ⊖	a					14 10					
Hackney Downs	d			13 50						14 20	
London Liverpool Street 15 ⊖	a		13 47	13 58	14 02		14 14	14 17		14 28	14 31

		LE 1	LE ◇1	LE 1	LE 1	LE	LE 1	LE 1	LE ◇1	LE 1	XC ◇1 A	LE
Cambridge North	d		13 14									
Cambridge	a		13 20									
	d		13 21	13 30					14 04		14 11	
Shelford	d		13 26									
Whittlesford Parkway	d		13 30	13 38					14 11			
Great Chesterford	d		13 34									
Audley End	d		13 40	13 46					14 19		14 25	
Newport (Essex)	d		13 43									
Elsenham	d		13 49									
Stansted Airport ✈	a			14 00							14 40	
Stansted Airport ✈	d				14 00		14 15			14 30		
Stansted Mountfitchet	d		13 52				14 21					
Bishops Stortford	a		13 58		14 09				14 32	14 39		
Bishops Stortford	d	13 47	13 58		14 09			14 15	14 32	14 39		
Sawbridgeworth	d	13 52	14 03					14 20				
Harlow Mill	d		14 06					14 23				
Harlow Town	d	14 05	14 09				14 32	14 26	14 40			
Roydon	d		14 13					14 30				
Hertford East	d					14 09						14 39
Ware	d					14 13						14 43
St Margarets (Herts)	d					14 17						14 47
Rye House	d					14 20						14 50
Broxbourne 8	a	14 11	14 17			14 25		14 35	14 46			14 55
Broxbourne 8	d	14 12	14 17			14 25		14 39	14 46			14 55
Cheshunt	d	14 16	14 21			14 29		14 44	14 50			14 59
Waltham Cross	d	14 19				14 31						15 01
Enfield Lock	d					14 34		14 47				15 04
Brimsdown	d					14 36						15 06
Ponders End	d					14 38						15 08
Angel Road	d											
Northumberland Park	d							14 53				
Tottenham Hale ⊖	d	14 27	14 30		14 33	14 44	14 48	14 56	15 01	15 03		15 14
Seven Sisters ⊖	d											
Lea Bridge	d	14 31						15 00				
Stratford 7 ⊖	a	14 40						15 10				
Hackney Downs	d					14 50						15 20
London Liverpool Street 15 ⊖	a		14 44		14 47	14 58	15 02		15 14	15 17		15 28

		LE 1	LE 1	LE ◇1	LE 1	LE 1	LE	LE 1	LE 1	LE ◇1	LE 1	XC ◇1 A
Cambridge North	d			14 14								
Cambridge	a			14 20								
	d			14 21	14 30					15 04		15 11
Shelford	d			14 26								
Whittlesford Parkway	d			14 30	14 38					15 11		
Great Chesterford	d			14 34								
Audley End	d			14 40	14 46					15 19		15 25
Newport (Essex)	d			14 43								
Elsenham	d			14 49								
Stansted Airport ✈	a				15 00							15 40
Stansted Airport ✈	d	14 45				15 00		15 15			15 30	
Stansted Mountfitchet	d			14 52				15 21				
Bishops Stortford	a			14 58		15 09				15 32	15 39	
Bishops Stortford	d		14 47	14 58		15 09			15 15	15 32	15 39	
Sawbridgeworth	d		14 52	15 03					15 20			
Harlow Mill	d			15 06					15 23			
Harlow Town	d	15 00	15 05	15 09				15 32	15 26	15 40		
Roydon	d			15 13					15 30			
Hertford East	d						15 09					
Ware	d						15 13					
St Margarets (Herts)	d						15 17					
Rye House	d						15 20					
Broxbourne 8	a		15 11	15 17			15 25		15 35	15 46		
Broxbourne 8	d		15 12	15 17			15 25		15 39	15 46		
Cheshunt	d		15 16	15 21			15 29		15 44	15 50		
Waltham Cross	d		15 19				15 31					
Enfield Lock	d						15 34		15 47			
Brimsdown	d						15 36					
Ponders End	d						15 38					
Angel Road	d											
Northumberland Park	d								15 53			
Tottenham Hale ⊖	d	15 17	15 27	15 30		15 33	15 44	15 48	15 56	16 01	16 03	
Seven Sisters ⊖	d											
Lea Bridge	d		15 31						16 00			
Stratford 7 ⊖	a		15 40						16 10			
Hackney Downs	d						15 50					
London Liverpool Street 15 ⊖	a	15 31		15 44		15 47	15 58	16 02		16 14	16 17	

A From Birmingham New Street

Table T022-R

Saturdays

26 May to 8 December

Cambridge North, Cambridge, Stansted Airport, Bishops Stortford, Hertford East and Broxbourne - London

		LE	LE ■	LE ■	LE ◇■	LE ■	LE ■	LE	LE ■	LE ■	LE ◇■	LE ■	XC ◇■ A	LE	LE ■	LE ■	LE ◇■	LE ■	LE ■	LE	LE ■	LE ■	LE ◇■
Cambridge North	d				15 14												16 14						
Cambridge	a				15 20												16 20						
	d				15 21	15 30					16 04		16 11				16 21	16 30					17 04
Shelford	d				15 26												16 26						
Whittlesford Parkway	d				15 30	15 38					16 11						16 30	16 38					17 11
Great Chesterford	d				15 34												16 34						
Audley End	d				15 40	15 46					16 19		16 25				16 40	16 46					17 19
Newport (Essex)	d				15 43												16 43						
Elsenham	d				15 49												16 49						
Stansted Airport ✈	a					16 00							16 40					17 00					
Stansted Airport ✈	d		15 45				16 00		16 15			16 30			16 45				17 00		17 15		
Stansted Mountfitchet	d				15 52				16 21								16 52				17 21		
Bishops Stortford	a				15 58		16 09				16 32	16 39					16 58		17 09				17 32
Bishops Stortford	d			15 47	15 58		16 09			16 15	16 32	16 39				16 47	16 58		17 09			17 15	17 32
Sawbridgeworth	d			15 52	16 03					16 20						16 52	17 03					17 20	
Harlow Mill	d				16 06					16 23							17 06					17 23	
Harlow Town	d		16 00	16 05	16 09				16 32	16 26	16 40				17 00	17 05	17 09				17 32	17 26	17 40
Roydon	d				16 13					16 30							17 13					17 30	
Hertford East	d	15 39						16 09						16 39						17 09			
Ware	d	15 43						16 13						16 43						17 13			
St Margarets (Herts)	d	15 47						16 17						16 47						17 17			
Rye House	d	15 50						16 20						16 50						17 20			
Broxbourne	a	15 55		16 11	16 17			16 25		16 35	16 46			16 55		17 11	17 17			17 25		17 35	17 46
Broxbourne	d	15 55		16 12	16 17			16 25		16 39	16 46			16 55		17 12	17 17			17 25		17 39	17 46
Cheshunt	d	15 59		16 16	16 21			16 29		16 44	16 50			16 59		17 16	17 21			17 29		17 44	17 50
Waltham Cross	d	16 01		16 19				16 31						17 01		17 19				17 31			
Enfield Lock	d	16 04						16 34		16 47				17 04						17 34		17 47	
Brimsdown	d	16 06						16 36						17 06						17 36			
Ponders End	d	16 08						16 38						17 08						17 38			
Angel Road	d																						
Northumberland Park	d									16 53												17 53	
Tottenham Hale ⊖	d	16 14	16 17	16 27	16 30		16 33	16 44	16 48	16 56	17 01	17 03		17 14	17 17	17 27	17 30		17 33	17 44	17 48	17 56	18 01
Seven Sisters ⊖	d																						
Lea Bridge	d			16 31						17 00						17 31						18 00	
Stratford ⊖	a			16 40						17 10						17 40						18 10	
Hackney Downs	d	16 20						16 50						17 20						17 50			
London Liverpool Street ⊖	a	16 28	16 31		16 44		16 47	16 58	17 02		17 14	17 17		17 28	17 31		17 44		17 47	17 58	18 02		18 14

		LE ■	XC ◇■ A	LE	LE ■	LE ■	LE ◇■	LE ■	LE ■	LE	LE ■	LE ■	LE ◇■	LE ■	LE	LE ■	XC ◇■ A	LE ■	LE ◇■	LE ■	LE ■	LE
Cambridge North	d						17 14												18 14			
Cambridge	a						17 20												18 20			
	d		17 11				17 21	17 30					18 04				18 17		18 21	18 30		
Shelford	d						17 26												18 26			
Whittlesford Parkway	d						17 30	17 38					18 11						18 29	18 38		
Great Chesterford	d						17 34												18 33			
Audley End	d		17 25				17 40	17 46					18 19				18 33		18 40	18 46		
Newport (Essex)	d						17 43												18 43			
Elsenham	d						17 49												18 49			
Stansted Airport ✈	a		17 40					18 00									18 53			19 00		
Stansted Airport ✈	d	17 30			17 45				18 00		18 15			18 30		18 45					19 00	
Stansted Mountfitchet	d						17 52				18 21								18 52			
Bishops Stortford	a	17 39					17 58		18 09				18 32	18 39					18 58		19 09	
Bishops Stortford	d	17 39				17 47	17 58		18 09			18 15	18 32	18 39				18 47	18 58		19 09	
Sawbridgeworth	d					17 52	18 03					18 20						18 52	19 03			
Harlow Mill	d						18 06					18 23							19 06			
Harlow Town	d				18 00	18 05	18 09				18 32	18 26	18 40			19 00		19 05	19 09			
Roydon	d						18 13					18 30							19 13			
Hertford East	d			17 39						18 09					18 39							19 09
Ware	d			17 43						18 13					18 43							19 13
St Margarets (Herts)	d			17 47						18 17					18 47							19 17
Rye House	d			17 50						18 20					18 50							19 20
Broxbourne	a			17 55		18 11	18 17			18 25		18 35	18 46		18 55			19 11	19 17			19 25
Broxbourne	d			17 55		18 12	18 17			18 25		18 39	18 46		18 55			19 12	19 17			19 25
Cheshunt	d			17 59		18 16	18 21			18 29		18 44	18 50		18 59			19 16	19 21			19 29
Waltham Cross	d			18 01		18 19				18 31					19 01			19 19				19 31
Enfield Lock	d			18 04						18 34		18 47			19 04							19 34
Brimsdown	d			18 06						18 36					19 06							19 36
Ponders End	d			18 08						18 38					19 08							19 38
Angel Road	d																					
Northumberland Park	d											18 53										
Tottenham Hale ⊖	d	18 03		18 14	18 17	18 27	18 30		18 33	18 44	18 48	18 56	19 00	19 03	19 14	19 17		19 27	19 30		19 33	19 44
Seven Sisters ⊖	d																					
Lea Bridge	d					18 31						19 00						19 31				
Stratford ⊖	a					18 40						19 10						19 40				
Hackney Downs	d			18 20						18 50					19 20							19 50
London Liverpool Street ⊖	a	18 17		18 28	18 31		18 44		18 47	18 58	19 02		19 14	19 17	19 28	19 31			19 44		19 47	19 58

A From Birmingham New Street

Table T022-R

Saturdays

26 May to 8 December

Cambridge North, Cambridge, Stansted Airport, Bishops Stortford, Hertford East and Broxbourne - London

		LE ■	LE ■	LE ◇■	LE ■	XC ◇■ A	LE	LE ■	LE ■	LE ◇■	LE ■	LE ■	LE	LE ■	LE ■	LE ◇■	LE ■	XC ◇■ A	LE	LE ■	LE ■	LE ◇■	LE ■
Cambridge North	d									19 14												20 14	
Cambridge	a									19 20												20 20	
	d			19 04		19 11				19 21	19 30					20 04		20 11				20 21	20 30
Shelford	d									19 26												20 26	
Whittlesford Parkway	d			19 11						19 30	19 38					20 11						20 30	20 38
Great Chesterford	d									19 34												20 34	
Audley End	d			19 19		19 25				19 40	19 46					20 19		20 25				20 40	20 46
Newport (Essex)	d									19 43												20 43	
Elsenham	d									19 49												20 49	
Stansted Airport ✈	a					19 40					20 00							20 40					21 00
Stansted Airport ✈	d	19 15			19 30			19 45				20 00		20 15			20 30			20 45			
Stansted Mountfitchet	d	19 21								19 52				20 21								20 52	
Bishops Stortford	a			19 32	19 39					19 58		20 09				20 32	20 39					20 58	
Bishops Stortford	d		19 15	19 32	19 39				19 47	19 58		20 09			20 15	20 32	20 39				20 47	20 58	
Sawbridgeworth	d		19 20						19 52	20 03					20 20						20 52	21 03	
Harlow Mill	d		19 23							20 06					20 23							21 06	
Harlow Town	d	19 32	19 26	19 40				20 00	20 05	20 09				20 32	20 26	20 40				21 00	21 05	21 09	
Roydon	d		19 30							20 13					20 30							21 13	
Hertford East	d						19 39						20 09						20 39				
Ware	d						19 43						20 13						20 43				
St Margarets (Herts)	d						19 47						20 17						20 47				
Rye House	d						19 50						20 20						20 50				
Broxbourne	a		19 35	19 46			19 55		20 11	20 17			20 25		20 35	20 46			20 55		21 11	21 17	
Broxbourne	d		19 39	19 46			19 55		20 12	20 17			20 25		20 39	20 46			20 55		21 12	21 17	
Cheshunt	d		19 44	19 50			19 59		20 16	20 21			20 29		20 44	20 50			20 59		21 16	21 21	
Waltham Cross	d						20 01		20 19				20 31						21 01		21 19		
Enfield Lock	d		19 47				20 04						20 34		20 47				21 04				
Brimsdown	d						20 06						20 36						21 06				
Ponders End	d						20 08						20 38						21 08				
Angel Road	d																						
Northumberland Park	d		19 53												20 53								
Tottenham Hale ⊖	d	19 48	19 56	20 00	20 03		20 14	20 17	20 27	20 30		20 33	20 44	20 48	20 56	21 00	21 03		21 14	21 17	21 27	21 30	
Seven Sisters ⊖	d																						
Lea Bridge	d		20 00						20 31						21 00						21 31		
Stratford ⊖	a		20 10						20 40						21 10						21 40		
Hackney Downs	d						20 20						20 50						21 20				
London Liverpool Street ⊖	a	20 02		20 14	20 17		20 28	20 31		20 44		20 47	20 58	21 02		21 14	21 17		21 28	21 31		21 44	

		LE ■	LE	LE ■	LE ■	LE ◇■	LE ■	XC ◇■ A	LE	LE ■	LE ■	LE ◇■	LE ■	LE ■	LE	LE ■	LE ■	LE ◇■	LE ■	XC ◇■ A	LE	LE ■
Cambridge North	d											21 14										
Cambridge	a											21 20										
	d					21 04		21 11				21 21	21 30					22 04		22 11		
Shelford	d											21 26										
Whittlesford Parkway	d					21 11						21 30	21 38					22 11				
Great Chesterford	d											21 34										
Audley End	d					21 19		21 25				21 40	21 46					22 19		22 25		
Newport (Essex)	d											21 43										
Elsenham	d											21 49										
Stansted Airport ✈	a							21 40					22 00							22 40		
Stansted Airport ✈	d	21 00		21 15			21 30			21 45				22 00		22 15			22 30			22 45
Stansted Mountfitchet	d			21 21								21 52				22 21						
Bishops Stortford	a	21 09				21 32	21 39					21 58		22 09				22 32	22 39			
Bishops Stortford	d	21 09			21 15	21 32	21 39				21 47	21 58		22 09			22 15	22 32	22 39			
Sawbridgeworth	d				21 20						21 52	22 03					22 20					
Harlow Mill	d				21 23							22 06					22 23					
Harlow Town	d			21 32	21 26	21 40				22 00	22 05	22 09				22 32	22 26	22 40				23 00
Roydon	d				21 30							22 13					22 30					
Hertford East	d		21 09						21 39						22 09						22 39	
Ware	d		21 13						21 43						22 13						22 43	
St Margarets (Herts)	d		21 17						21 47						22 17						22 47	
Rye House	d		21 20						21 50						22 20						22 50	
Broxbourne	a		21 25		21 35	21 46			21 55		22 11	22 17			22 25		22 35	22 46			22 55	
Broxbourne	d		21 25		21 39	21 46			21 55		22 12	22 17			22 25		22 39	22 46			22 55	
Cheshunt	d		21 29		21 44	21 50			21 59		22 16	22 21			22 29		22 44	22 50			22 59	
Waltham Cross	d		21 31						22 01		22 19				22 31						23 01	
Enfield Lock	d		21 34		21 47				22 04						22 34		22 47				23 04	
Brimsdown	d		21 36						22 06						22 36						23 06	
Ponders End	d		21 38						22 08						22 38						23 08	
Angel Road	d																					
Northumberland Park	d				21 53												22 53					
Tottenham Hale ⊖	d	21 33	21 44	21 48	21 56	22 00	22 03		22 14	22 17	22 27	22 30		22 33	22 44	22 48	22 56	23 00	23 03		23 14	23 17
Seven Sisters ⊖	d																					
Lea Bridge	d				22 00						22 31						23 00					
Stratford ⊖	a				22 10						22 40						23 10					
Hackney Downs	d		21 50						22 20						22 50						23 20	
London Liverpool Street ⊖	a	21 47	21 58	22 02		22 14	22 17		22 28	22 31		22 44		22 47	22 58	23 02	23 19	23 14	23 17		23 28	23 31

A From Birmingham New Street

Saturdays
26 May to 8 December

Cambridge North, Cambridge, Stansted Airport, Bishops Stortford, Hertford East and Broxbourne - London

Station		LE ◇1	LE 1	LE	LE 1	LE ◇1	LE 1	LE 1	LE	LE 1	LE 1
Cambridge North	d	22 14									
Cambridge	a	22 20									
	d	22 21				22 51		23 25			
Shelford	d	22 26				22 56		23 30			
Whittlesford Parkway	d	22 30				23 00		23 34			
Great Chesterford	d	22 34				23 04		23 38			
Audley End	d	22 40				23 10		23 44			
Newport (Essex)	d	22 43				23 13		23 47			
Elsenham	d	22 49				23 19		23 53			
Stansted Airport ✈	a										
Stansted Airport ✈	d		23 00		23 15		23 30			23 45	23 59
Stansted Mountfitchet	d	22 52			23 21	23 24		23 57			
Bishops Stortford	a	22 58	23 09			23 29	23 39	00 02			00 08
Bishops Stortford	d	22 58	23 09			23 29	23 39				00 08
Sawbridgeworth	d	23 03				23 33					
Harlow Mill	d	23 06				23 37					
Harlow Town	d	23 09			23 32	23 40				23 59	00 16
Roydon	d	23 13				23 44					
Hertford East	d			23 09					23 39		
Ware	d			23 13					23 43		
St Margarets (Herts)	d			23 17					23 47		
Rye House	d			23 20					23 50		
Broxbourne 3	a	23 17		23 25		23 48			23 55		
Broxbourne 3	d	23 17		23 25		23 48			23 55		
Cheshunt	d	23 21		23 29		23 52			23 59		
Waltham Cross	d			23 31					00 01		
Enfield Lock	d			23 34					00 04		
Brimsdown	d			23 36					00 06		
Ponders End	d			23 38					00 08		
Angel Road	d										
Northumberland Park	d										
Tottenham Hale ⊖	d	23 30	23 33	23 44	23 48	00 01	00 04		00 14	00 17	
Seven Sisters ⊖	d										
Lea Bridge	d										
Stratford 7 ⊖	a										
Hackney Downs	d			23 50					00 20		
London Liverpool Street 15 ⊖	a	23 44	23 47	23 58	00 02	00 14	00 17		00 28	00 31	00 51

Sundays
20 May to 2 December

Station		LE ◇1	LE 1	LE	LE	LE 1	LE 1	LE 1	LE 1	LE 1	LE 1	LE 1	LE 1	LE 1	LE 1	LE 1	LE	LE 1	LE ◇1	LE 1	LE 1	LE	LE 1
		A	B	C		B	B																
Cambridge North	d																						
Cambridge	a																						
	d																		07 32		07 39		
Shelford	d																						
Whittlesford Parkway	d																		07 39		07 46		
Great Chesterford	d																						
Audley End	d																		07 47		07 55		
Newport (Essex)	d																						
Elsenham	d																						
Stansted Airport ✈	a																				08 09		
Stansted Airport ✈	d							00 30	05 30	06 00	06 30		07 00	07 15		07 30		07 45		08 00			08 15
Stansted Mountfitchet	d																	07 51					
Bishops Stortford	a							00 39	05 39	06 09	06 39		07 09			07 39			08 00	08 09			
Bishops Stortford	d						00 08	00 39	05 39	06 09	06 39	06 42	07 09		07 26	07 39			08 00	08 09			
Sawbridgeworth	d											06 46			07 30				08 05				
Harlow Mill	d														07 34								
Harlow Town	d						00 16	00 47	05 47	06 17	06 47	06 51	07 17	07 30	07 37			08 02	08 10				08 30
Roydon	d														07 41								
Hertford East	d				00 07												07 39					08 09	
Ware	d																07 43					08 13	
St Margarets (Herts)	d																07 47					08 17	
Rye House	d																07 50					08 20	
Broxbourne 3	a				00 19							06 57			07 45		07 55		08 16			08 25	
Broxbourne 3	d											06 57			07 45		07 55		08 16			08 25	
Cheshunt	d											07 01			07 49		07 59		08 20			08 29	
Waltham Cross	d			00 01								07 04					08 01					08 31	
Enfield Lock	d			00 04								07 06					08 04					08 34	
Brimsdown	d			00 06								07 09					08 06					08 36	
Ponders End	d			00 08								07 11					08 08					08 38	
Angel Road	d																						
Northumberland Park	d																						
Tottenham Hale ⊖	d	00 01	00 04	00 14		00 17			06 04	06 33	07 03	07 17	07 33	07 46	07 58	08 01	08 14	08 17	08 29	08 32		08 44	08 47
Seven Sisters ⊖	d																						
Lea Bridge	d																08 18					08 48	
Stratford 7 ⊖	a														08 08		08 25					08 55	
Hackney Downs	d			00 20								07 22											
London Liverpool Street 15 ⊖	a	00 14	00 17	00 28		00 31	00 51	01 21	06 18	06 46	07 16	07 31	07 46	08 00		08 14		08 31	08 43	08 46			09 01

A not 20 May. From Cambridge
B not 20 May. From Stansted Airport
C not 20 May. From Hertford East

Table T022-R

Sundays
20 May to 2 December

Cambridge North, Cambridge, Stansted Airport, Bishops Stortford, Hertford East and Broxbourne - London

Station		LE ◇1	LE 1	LE	LE 1	LE 1	LE ◇1	LE 1	LE	LE 1	LE ◇1	LE 1	XC 1	LE	LE 1	LE 1	LE ◇1	LE 1	LE	LE 1	LE ◇1	
Cambridge North	d																				09 44	
Cambridge	a																				09 49	
	d	07 51				08 24	08 32				08 51		09 15			09 25	09 32				09 51	
Shelford	d	07 56									08 56										09 56	
Whittlesford Parkway	d	08 00				08 32	08 39				09 00					09 33	09 39				10 00	
Great Chesterford	d	08 04									09 04										10 04	
Audley End	d	08 10				08 40	08 47				09 10		09 29			09 43	09 47				10 10	
Newport (Essex)	d	08 13									09 13										10 13	
Elsenham	d	08 19									09 19										10 19	
Stansted Airport ✈	a					08 54							09 45			10 00						
Stansted Airport ✈	d		08 30		08 45			09 00		09 15		09 30			09 45			10 00		10 15		
Stansted Mountfitchet	d	08 22			08 51						09 22				09 51						10 22	
Bishops Stortford	a	08 28	08 39				09 00	09 09			09 28	09 39					10 00	10 09			10 28	
Bishops Stortford	d	08 28	08 39				09 00	09 09			09 28	09 39					10 00	10 09			10 28	and at the same minutes past each hour until
Sawbridgeworth	d	08 32					09 05				09 32						10 05				10 32	
Harlow Mill	d	08 36									09 36										10 36	
Harlow Town	d	08 39			09 02		09 10			09 30	09 39				10 02		10 10			10 30	10 39	
Roydon	d	08 43									09 43										10 43	
Hertford East	d			08 39					09 09					09 39					10 09			
Ware	d			08 43					09 13					09 43					10 13			
St Margarets (Herts)	d			08 47					09 17					09 47					10 17			
Rye House	d			08 50					09 20					09 50					10 20			
Broxbourne 3	a	08 47		08 55			09 16		09 25		09 47			09 55			10 16		10 25		10 47	
Broxbourne 3	d	08 47		08 55			09 16		09 25		09 47			09 55			10 16		10 25		10 47	
Cheshunt	d	08 51		08 59			09 20		09 29		09 51			09 59			10 20		10 29		10 51	
Waltham Cross	d			09 01					09 31					10 01					10 31			
Enfield Lock	d			09 04					09 34					10 04					10 34			
Brimsdown	d			09 06					09 36					10 06					10 36			
Ponders End	d			09 08					09 38					10 08					10 38			
Angel Road	d																					
Northumberland Park	d																					
Tottenham Hale ⊖	d	09 00	09 03	09 14	09 17		09 29	09 32	09 44	09 47	10 00	10 03		10 14	10 17		10 29	10 32	10 44	10 47	11 00	
Seven Sisters ⊖	d																					
Lea Bridge	d			09 18					09 48					10 18					10 48			
Stratford 7 ⊖	a			09 25					09 55					10 25					10 55			
Hackney Downs	d	09 05									10 05										11 05	
London Liverpool Street 15 ⊖	a	09 14	09 16		09 31		09 43	09 46		10 01	10 14	10 16			10 31		10 43	10 46		11 01	11 14	

Station		LE 1	XC 1	LE	LE 1	LE 1	LE ◇1	LE 1	LE	LE 1	LE ◇1	LE 1	XC ◇1	LE	LE 1	LE 1	LE ◇1	LE 1	LE	LE 1	LE ◇1	
													A									
Cambridge North	d										13 44										14 44	
Cambridge	a										13 49										14 49	
	d		13 15			13 25	13 32				13 51		14 10			14 25	14 32				14 51	
Shelford	d										13 56										14 56	
Whittlesford Parkway	d					13 33	13 39				14 00					14 33	14 39				15 00	
Great Chesterford	d										14 04										15 04	
Audley End	d		13 29			13 43	13 47				14 10		14 25			14 43	14 47				15 10	
Newport (Essex)	d										14 13										15 13	
Elsenham	d										14 19										15 19	
Stansted Airport ✈	a		13 45			14 00							14 45			15 00						
Stansted Airport ✈	d	13 30			13 45			14 00		14 15		14 30			14 45			15 00		15 15		
Stansted Mountfitchet	d				13 51						14 22				14 51						15 22	
Bishops Stortford	a	13 39					14 00	14 09			14 28	14 39					15 00	15 09			15 28	
Bishops Stortford	d	13 39					14 00	14 09			14 28	14 39					15 00	15 09			15 28	and at the same minutes past each hour until
Sawbridgeworth	d						14 05				14 32						15 05				15 32	
Harlow Mill	d										14 36										15 36	
Harlow Town	d				14 02		14 10			14 30	14 39				15 02		15 10			15 30	15 39	
Roydon	d										14 43										15 43	
Hertford East	d			13 39					14 09					14 39					15 09			
Ware	d			13 43					14 13					14 43					15 13			
St Margarets (Herts)	d			13 47					14 17					14 47					15 17			
Rye House	d			13 50					14 20					14 50					15 20			
Broxbourne 3	a			13 55			14 16		14 25		14 47			14 55			15 16		15 25		15 47	
Broxbourne 3	d			13 55			14 16		14 25		14 47			14 55			15 16		15 25		15 47	
Cheshunt	d			13 59			14 20		14 29		14 51			14 59			15 20		15 29		15 51	
Waltham Cross	d			14 01					14 31					15 01					15 31			
Enfield Lock	d			14 04					14 34					15 04					15 34			
Brimsdown	d			14 06					14 36					15 06					15 36			
Ponders End	d			14 08					14 38					15 08					15 38			
Angel Road	d																					
Northumberland Park	d																					
Tottenham Hale ⊖	d	14 03		14 14	14 17		14 29	14 32	14 44	14 47	15 00	15 03		15 14	15 17		15 29	15 32	15 44	15 47	16 00	
Seven Sisters ⊖	d																					
Lea Bridge	d			14 18					14 48					15 18					15 48			
Stratford 7 ⊖	a			14 25					14 55					15 25					15 55			
Hackney Downs	d										15 05										16 05	
London Liverpool Street 15 ⊖	a	14 16			14 31		14 43	14 46		15 01	15 14	15 16			15 31		15 43	15 46		16 01	16 14	

A From Birmingham New Street

Table T022-R

Sundays

20 May to 2 December

Cambridge North, Cambridge, Stansted Airport, Bishops Stortford, Hertford East and Broxbourne - London

Station		LE ■	XC ◇■ A	LE	LE ■	LE ■	LE ◇■	LE ■	LE	LE ■	LE ◇■	LE ■	XC ◇■ A	LE	LE ■	LE ■	LE ◇■	LE ■	LE	LE ■	LE ◇■	LE ■	XC ◇■ A
Cambridge North	d										19 44										20 44		
Cambridge	a										19 49										20 49		
	d		19 10			19 25	19 32				19 51		20 10			20 25	20 32				20 51		21 10
Shelford	d										19 56										20 56		
Whittlesford Parkway	d					19 33	19 39				20 00					20 33	20 39				21 00		
Great Chesterford	d										20 04										21 04		
Audley End	d		19 25			19 43	19 47				20 10		20 25			20 41	20 47				21 10		21 25
Newport (Essex)	d										20 13										21 13		
Elsenham	d										20 19										21 19		
Stansted Airport ✈	a		19 45			20 00							20 45			20 55							21 45
Stansted Airport ✈	d	19 30			19 45			20 00		20 15		20 30			20 45			21 00		21 15		21 30	
Stansted Mountfitchet	d				19 51						20 22				20 51						21 22		
Bishops Stortford	a	19 39					20 00	20 09			20 28	20 39					21 00	21 09			21 28	21 39	
Bishops Stortford	d	19 39					20 00	20 09			20 28	20 39					21 00	21 09			21 28	21 39	
Sawbridgeworth	d						20 05				20 32						21 05				21 32		
Harlow Mill	d										20 36										21 36		
Harlow Town	d				20 02		20 10			20 30	20 39				21 02		21 10			21 30	21 39		
Roydon	d										20 43										21 43		
Hertford East	d			19 39					20 09					20 39					21 09				
Ware	d			19 43					20 13					20 43					21 13				
St Margarets (Herts)	d			19 47					20 17					20 47					21 17				
Rye House	d			19 50					20 20					20 50					21 20				
Broxbourne ■	a			19 55			20 16		20 25		20 47			20 55			21 16		21 25		21 47		
Broxbourne ■	d			19 55			20 16		20 25		20 47			20 55			21 16		21 25		21 47		
Cheshunt	d			19 59			20 20		20 29		20 51			20 59			21 20		21 29		21 51		
Waltham Cross	d			20 01					20 31					21 01					21 31				
Enfield Lock	d			20 04					20 34					21 04					21 34				
Brimsdown	d			20 06					20 36					21 06					21 36				
Ponders End	d			20 08					20 38					21 08					21 38				
Angel Road	d																						
Northumberland Park	d																						
Tottenham Hale ⊖	d	20 03		20 14	20 17		20 29	20 32	20 44	20 47	21 00	21 03		21 14	21 17		21 29	21 32	21 44	21 47	22 00	22 03	
Seven Sisters ⊖	d																						
Lea Bridge	d			20 18					20 48					21 18					21 48				
Stratford ■ ⊖	a			20 25					20 55					21 25					21 55				
Hackney Downs	d										21 05										22 05		
London Liverpool Street ■ ⊖	a	20 16			20 31		20 43	20 46		21 01	21 14	21 16			21 31		21 43	21 46		22 01	22 14	22 16	

Station		LE	LE ■	LE ■	LE ◇■	LE ■	LE	LE ■	LE ■	LE ■	XC ◇■ A	LE	LE ■	LE ◇■	LE ■	LE ■	LE ■	LE ■	LE ■	LE ■
Cambridge North	d								21 44							22 44				
Cambridge	a								21 49							22 49				
	d			21 24	21 32				21 51		22 10			22 32		22 51				
Shelford	d								21 56							22 56				
Whittlesford Parkway	d			21 33	21 39				22 00					22 39		23 00				
Great Chesterford	d								22 04							23 04				
Audley End	d			21 43	21 47				22 10		22 25			22 47		23 10				
Newport (Essex)	d								22 13							23 13				
Elsenham	d								22 19							23 19				
Stansted Airport ✈	a			22 00							22 45									
Stansted Airport ✈	d		21 45			22 00		22 15		22 30			22 45		23 00		23 15	23 30	23 45	23 59
Stansted Mountfitchet	d		21 51						22 22				22 51			23 22				
Bishops Stortford	a				22 00	22 09			22 28	22 39				23 00	23 09	23 28		23 39		00 08
Bishops Stortford	d				22 00	22 09			22 28	22 39				23 00	23 09			23 39		00 08
Sawbridgeworth	d				22 05				22 32					23 05						
Harlow Mill	d								22 36											
Harlow Town	d		22 02		22 10			22 30	22 39				23 02	23 10			23 30	23 47	23 59	00 16
Roydon	d								22 43											
Hertford East	d	21 39					22 09					22 39								
Ware	d	21 43					22 13					22 43								
St Margarets (Herts)	d	21 47					22 17					22 47								
Rye House	d	21 50					22 20					22 50								
Broxbourne ■	a	21 55			22 16		22 25		22 47			22 55		23 16						
Broxbourne ■	d	21 55			22 16		22 25		22 47			22 55		23 16						
Cheshunt	d	21 59			22 20		22 29		22 51			22 59		23 20						
Waltham Cross	d	22 01					22 31					23 01								
Enfield Lock	d	22 04					22 34					23 04								
Brimsdown	d	22 06					22 36					23 06								
Ponders End	d	22 08					22 38					23 08								
Angel Road	d																			
Northumberland Park	d																			
Tottenham Hale ⊖	d	22 14	22 17		22 29	22 32	22 44	22 47	23 00	23 03		23 14	23 17	23 29	23 32		23 46			
Seven Sisters ⊖	d																	00 08	00 21	
Lea Bridge	d	22 18							23 04			23 18								
Stratford ■ ⊖	a	22 25							23 11			23 25								
Hackney Downs	d						22 50													
London Liverpool Street ■ ⊖	a		22 31		22 43	22 46	22 58	23 01		23 16			23 31	23 43	23 46		23 59	00 22	00 35	00 51

A From Birmingham New Street

Table T024-F

Mondays to Fridays

21 May to 7 December

London - Welwyn Garden City and Hertford North

Miles	Miles	Station		TL MX ■	GN MO A 🚌	GN MO A 🚌	GN MO B	GN MO A 🚌	GN MO A	GN MX	GN MO A 🚌	GN MO ■	GN MO A 🚌	GN MO	GN MX	GN MX	GN MO A 🚌	TL MX ■	GN MO A	GN MO B	GN MX	GN MO ■	GN MX
—	—	London Bridge	d																				
—	—	London Blackfriars	d																				
—	—	City Thameslink	d																				
—	—	Farringdon	d																				
—	—	St Pancras International	d																				
0	—	London Kings Cross ■ ⊖	d									00 02						00 23				00 32	
—	—	Finsbury Park	a									00 08						00 28				00 38	
—	0	Moorgate ⊖	d													00 07			00 17	00 17	00 17		00 27
—	0½	Old Street ⊖	d													00 09			00 19	00 19	00 19		00 29
—	1¾	Essex Road	d											00 02	00 02	00 12			00 22	00 22	00 22		00 32
—	2¼	Highbury & Islington ⊖	d											00 05	00 05	00 15			00 25	00 25	00 25		00 35
—	2¾	Drayton Park	d											00 07	00 07	00 17			00 27	00 27	00 27		00 37
2½	3½	Finsbury Park ⊖	a											00 09	00 10	00 20			00 29	00 29	00 30		00 40
—	—	Finsbury Park	d	00 01			00 01		00 01	00 03		00 09		00 10	00 11	00 23		00 29	00 30	00 30	00 32	00 39	00 41
3½	4½	Harringay	d				00 03		00 03	00 06				00 13	00 14	00 26			00 33	00 33	00 34		
4	5	Hornsey	d				00 05		00 05	00 08				00 15	00 16	00 28			00 35	00 35	00 36		
5	6	Alexandra Palace	d				00 08		00a09	00 11				00 18	00 19	00 31			00a38	00 38	00 40		00 45
6½	—	New Southgate	d											00 21	00 22								
8½	—	Oakleigh Park	d											00 24	00 25								
9¼	—	New Barnet	d											00 27	00 28								00 51
10½	—	Hadley Wood	d											00 30	00 31								00 54
12¾	—	Potters Bar	d	00 13								00 20		00 34	00 35			00 42				00 50	00 58
14½	—	Brookmans Park	d											00 37	00 38								
15½	—	Welham Green	d											00 39	00 41								
17¾	—	Hatfield	d	00 18								00 26		00 43	00 44			00 48				00 56	01 04
20¼	—	Welwyn Garden City ■	d	00 28								00 31		00a51	00a49			00 58				01 01	01a09
22	—	Welwyn North	d	00 31								00 34						01 01				01s04	
25	—	Knebworth	d	00 35								00 38						01 05				01s08	
—	6¾	Bowes Park	d				00 10			00 14						00 34				00 40	00 42		
—	7¾	Palmers Green	d		00 01		00 13			00 16						00 36				00 43	00 45		
—	8¾	Winchmore Hill	d		00 08		00 16			00 19						00 39				00 46	00 48		
—	9½	Grange Park	d		00 14		00 18			00 21						00 41				00 48	00 50		
—	10¼	Enfield Chase	d		00 19		00 20	←		00 23						00 43				00 50	00 52		
—	11	Gordon Hill	d		00 25		00 23	00 25		00 26	←					00 46				00 53	00 55		
—	12½	Crews Hill	d		→	00 05	00 26	00 35		00 29	00 35					00 49				00 56	00 58		
—	14¼	Cuffley	d			00 13	00 29	→		00 32	00 43					00 52	←			00 59	01 01		
—	17¼	Bayford	d			00 28	00 33			00 36	00 58		←			00 56	00 58			01 03	01 06		
—	20¼	Hertford North	a			00 43	00 38			00 42	→		00 43			01 02	01 13			01 09	01 10		
—	25	Watton-at-Stone	a			→	00 44						00 57				→				01 18		
27½	30	Stevenage ■	a	00 39			00 52					00 43	01 14					01 09			01 25	01 13	

Station		GN MO	TL MX ■	GN MO A 🚌	GN MO	GN MO ■ B	GN MO ■ A	TL MX ■	GN MX	GN MO ■	GN MX	GN	GN	TL ■	GN	TL ■	GN	GN	TL ■	GN	TL	GN	GN
London Bridge	d																						
London Blackfriars	d		00 37																				
City Thameslink	d																						
Farringdon	d		00 41																				
St Pancras International	d		00 46																				
London Kings Cross ■ ⊖	d					01 02	01 02	01 05	01 09	01 32	01 40	05 06	05 21	05 25		05 55			06 21		06 30		
Finsbury Park	a		00 52			01 08	01 08	01 10	01 14	01 38	01 47	05 12	05 27	05 30		06 00			06 26		06 36		
Moorgate ⊖	d	00 27			00 48										05 37		05 57	06 07		06 17		06 27	06 37
Old Street ⊖	d	00 29			00 50										05 39		05 59	06 09		06 19		06 29	06 39
Essex Road	d	00 32			00 53										05 42		06 02	06 12		06 22		06 32	06 42
Highbury & Islington ⊖	d	00 35			00 56										05 45		06 05	06 15		06 25		06 35	06 45
Drayton Park	d	00 37			00 58										05 47		06 07	06 17		06 27		06 37	06 47
Finsbury Park ⊖	a	00 39			01 00										05 50		06 10	06 20		06 30		06 40	06 50
Finsbury Park	d	00 41	00 54			01 09	01 09	01 11	01 16	01 39	01 48	05 13	05 27	05 33	05 53	06 01	06 13	06 23	06 31	06 34	06 37	06 43	06 53
Harringay	d	00 43							01 18			05 16	05 30		05 56		06 16	06 26				06 46	06 56
Hornsey	d	00 45							01 20			05 18	05 32		05 58		06 18	06 28				06 48	06 58
Alexandra Palace	d	00 48				01 13	01 14		01 24	01 43	01 53	05 21	05 35		06 01		06 21	06 31		06 38		06 51	07 01
New Southgate	d	00 51								01 46	01 56						06 24				06 45	06 54	
Oakleigh Park	d	00 54								01 49	01 59						06 28				06 48	06 58	
New Barnet	d	00 57								01 51	02 02						06 30			06 44	06 51	07 00	
Hadley Wood	d	01 00								01 54	02 04						06 33					07 03	
Potters Bar	d	01 04						01 22		01 58	02 08			05 45		06 13	06 37		06 43	06 49	06 56	07 07	
Brookmans Park	d	01 07																		06 52			
Welham Green	d	01 09																		06 55			
Hatfield	d	01 13						01 28		02 04	02 14			05 51		06 18	06 43		06 48	06 58	07 02	07 13	
Welwyn Garden City ■	d	01a21	01 13				01s31	01 34		02 09	02a20			05 56		06 26	06a48		06 56	07a03	07a06	07a18	
Welwyn North	d							01 37		02s12				06 00		06 30			07 00				
Knebworth	d							01 41		02s16				06 04		06 34			07 04				
Bowes Park	d								01 26				05 38		06 04			06 34					07 04
Palmers Green	d					01 16			01 29			05 25	05 40		06 06			06 36					07 06
Winchmore Hill	d					01 19			01 32			05 27	05 43		06 09			06 39					07 09
Grange Park	d								01 34				05 45		06 11			06 41					07 11
Enfield Chase	d					01 21			01 36			05 30	05 48		06 13			06 43					07 13
Gordon Hill	d					01 23			01 38			05 33	05 51		06 16			06 46					07 16
Crews Hill	d											05 36	05 54		06 19			06 49					07 19
Cuffley	d					01 28			01 43			05 39	05 57		06 22			06 52					07 22
Bayford	d			←								05 43	06 01		06 27			06 57					07 26
Hertford North	a			01 13		01 34			01 52			05 49	06 06		06 31			07 01					07 31
Watton-at-Stone	a			01 27									06 12		06 39			07 14					07 39
Stevenage ■	a		01 21	01 44		01 45	01 41	01 45		02 21			06 20	06 08		06 38		07 22	07 08				

A from 29 October

B until 22 October

See Table 025 for fast trains between London and Stevenage

Table T024-F

Mondays to Fridays

21 May to 7 December

London - Welwyn Garden City and Hertford North

	TL	GN	GN	GN	GN	GN	GN	TL ■	GN	GN	GN	GN	GN	GN	GN	TL ■	GN	GN	GN	GN	GN
London Bridge d																					
London Blackfriars d																					
City Thameslink d																					
Farringdon d																					
St Pancras International d																					
London Kings Cross ⊖ d	06 51			07 06				07 21				07 36				07 51			08 06		
Finsbury Park a	06 57			07 15				07 27				07 45				07 57			08 12		
Moorgate ⊖ d		06 45	06 52		07 00	07 05	07 10		07 15	07 20	07 25		07 30	07 35	07 40		07 50	07 55		08 00	08 05
Old Street ⊖ d		06 47	06 54		07 02	07 07	07 12		07 17	07 22	07 27		07 32	07 37	07 42		07 52	07 57		08 02	08 07
Essex Road d		06 50	06 57		07 05	07 10	07 15		07 20	07 25	07 30		07 35	07 40	07 45		07 55	08 00		08 05	08 10
Highbury & Islington ⊖ d		06 53	07 00		07 08	07 13	07 18		07 23	07 28	07 33		07 38	07 43	07 48		07 58	08 03		08 08	08 13
Drayton Park d		06 55	07 02		07 10	07 15	07 20		07 25	07 30	07 35		07 40	07 45	07 50		08 00	08 05		08 10	08 15
Finsbury Park ⊖ a		06 58	07 05		07 12	07 18	07 23		07 28	07 33	07 38		07 42	07 48	07 53		08 03	08 08		08 12	08 18
Finsbury Park d	07 01	07 00	07 05	07 15	07 15	07 18	07 23	07 31	07 30	07 33	07 38	07 45	07 45	07 48	07 53	08 01	08 03	08 08	08 15	08 15	08 18
Harringay d			07 08				07 26			07 36	07 41				07 56			08 11			
Hornsey d			07 10				07 28			07 38	07 43				07 58			08 13			
Alexandra Palace d		07 07	07 13		07 21	07 23	07 31		07 37	07 41	07 47		07 51	07 54	08 01		08 07	08 17		08 21	08 24
New Southgate d				07 21	07 24							07 51	07 54						08 21	08 24	
Oakleigh Park d				07 24	07 28							07 54	07 58						08 24	08 28	
New Barnet d		07 13		07 27	07 30				07 43			07 57	08 00				08 13		08 27	08 30	
Hadley Wood d					07 33								08 03							08 33	
Potters Bar d	07 13	07 19		07 32	07 37			07 43	07 49			08 02	08 07			08 13	08 19		08 32	08 37	
Brookmans Park d		07 22							07 52								08 22				
Welham Green d		07 24							07 54								08 24				
Hatfield d	07 18	07 28		07 38	07 43			07 48	07 58			08 08	08 13			08 18	08 28		08 38	08 43	
Welwyn Garden City ■ d	07 26	07a33		07a42	07a48			07 56	08a03			08a12	08a18			08 26	08a33		08a42	08a48	
Welwyn North d	07 30							08 00								08 30					
Knebworth d	07 34							08 04								08 34					
Bowes Park d						07 26					07 50							08 20			
Palmers Green d			07 17			07 28	07 35			07 45	07 52			07 58	08 05			08 22			08 28
Winchmore Hill d			07 20			07 31	07 38			07 48	07 55			08 01	08 08			08 25			08 31
Grange Park d						07 33					07 57							08 27			
Enfield Chase d			07 23			07 35	07 41			07 51	08 00			08 04	08 11			08 30			08 34
Gordon Hill d			07a27			07 38	07a44			07 54	08a03			08 07	08 15			08a33			08 37
Crews Hill d						07 41								08 10							08 40
Cuffley d						07 44				07 58				08 13	08 19						08 43
Bayford d						07 48								08 17							08 47
Hertford North a						07 54				08 06				08 23	08 28						08 53
Watton-at-Stone a										08 14					08 35						
Stevenage ■ a	07 38							08 08		08 22						08 38					

	GN	TL ■	GN	GN	GN	GN	GN	GN	GN	TL ■	GN	GN	GN	GN	GN	TL ■	GN	GN	GN	GN	TL ■	GN
London Bridge d																						
London Blackfriars d																						
City Thameslink d																						
Farringdon d																						
St Pancras International d																						
London Kings Cross ⊖ d		08 21				08 36				08 51			09 06			09 21					09 51	
Finsbury Park a		08 28				08 45				08 57			09 11			09 27					09 56	
Moorgate ⊖ d	08 10		08 15	08 20	08 25		08 30	08 35	08 40		08 45	08 55		09 00	09 10		09 20	09 25	09 30	09 40		09 50
Old Street ⊖ d	08 12		08 17	08 22	08 27		08 32	08 37	08 42		08 47	08 57		09 02	09 12		09 22	09 27	09 32	09 42		09 52
Essex Road d	08 15		08 20	08 25	08 30		08 35	08 40	08 45		08 50	09 00		09 05	09 15		09 25	09 30	09 35	09 45		09 55
Highbury & Islington ⊖ d	08 18		08 23	08 28	08 33		08 38	08 43	08 48		08 53	09 03		09 08	09 18		09 28	09 33	09 38	09 48		09 58
Drayton Park d	08 20		08 25	08 30	08 35		08 40	08 45	08 50		08 55	09 05		09 10	09 20		09 30	09 35	09 40	09 50		10 00
Finsbury Park ⊖ a	08 23		08 28	08 33	08 38		08 42	08 48	08 53		08 58	09 08		09 12	09 23		09 33	09 38	09 43	09 53		10 03
Finsbury Park d	08 23	08 31	08 30	08 33	08 38	08 45	08 45	08 48	08 53	09 01	09 00	09 09	09 15	09 15	09 24	09 31	09 33	09 39	09 44	09 54	10 00	10 03
Harringay d	08 26			08 36	08 41				08 56			09 11			09 26			09 41	09 46	09 56		
Hornsey d	08 28			08 38	08 43				08 58			09 13			09 28			09 43	09 48	09 58		
Alexandra Palace d	08 31		08 37	08 41	08 47		08 51	08 53	09 01		09 07	09 17		09 21	09 32		09 38	09 47	09 51	10 02		10 07
New Southgate d						08 51	08 54						09 21	09 24			09 41		09 54			10 10
Oakleigh Park d						08 54	08 58						09 24	09 28			09 44		09 58			10 14
New Barnet d			08 43			08 57	09 00				09 13		09 27	09 30			09 46		10 00			10 16
Hadley Wood d							09 03							09 33			09 49		10 03			10 19
Potters Bar d		08 43	08 49			09 02	09 07			09 13	09 19		09 32	09 37		09 43	09 53		10 07		10 13	10 23
Brookmans Park d			08 52								09 22						09 56					10 26
Welham Green d			08 54								09 24						09 59					10 28
Hatfield d		08 48	08 58			09 08	09 13			09 18	09 28		09 38	09 43		09 48	10 02		10 13		10 18	10 32
Welwyn Garden City ■ d		08 56	09a03			09a13	09a18			09 26	09a33		09a42	09a48		09 56	10a07		10a18		10 26	10a37
Welwyn North d		09 00								09 30						10 00					10 30	
Knebworth d		09 04								09 34						10 04					10 34	
Bowes Park d					08 50							09 19			09 34			09 49		10 04		
Palmers Green d	08 35			08 45	08 52			08 57	09 05			09 22			09 37			09 52		10 07		
Winchmore Hill d	08 38			08 48	08 55			09 00	09 08			09 25			09 40			09 55		10 10		
Grange Park d					08 57							09 27			09 42			09 57		10 12		
Enfield Chase d	08 41			08 51	09 00			09 04	09 11			09 29			09 44			09 59		10 14		
Gordon Hill d	08a44			08 54	09a03			09 07	09 15			09 32			09 47			10 02		10 17		
Crews Hill d								09 10				09 35						10 05				
Cuffley d				08 58				09 13	09 19			09 38			09 52			10 08		10 22		
Bayford d								09 17				09 42						10 12				
Hertford North a				09 06				09 23	09 28			09 48			09 59			10 18		10 29		
Watton-at-Stone a				09 14					09 35						10 10					10 41		
Stevenage ■ a		09 08		09 22						09 38					10 18	10 08					10 38	

See Table 025 for fast trains between London and Stevenage

Table T024-F

Mondays to Fridays

21 May to 7 December

London - Welwyn Garden City and Hertford North

	GN	GN	GN	TL ■	GN	GN	GN	GN	TL ■	GN	GN	GN	GN	TL ■	GN	GN	GN	GN	TL ■	GN	GN	GN
London Bridge d																						
London Blackfriars d																						
City Thameslink d																						
Farringdon d																						
St Pancras International d																						
London Kings Cross ⊖ d				10 21					10 51					11 21					11 51			
Finsbury Park a				10 27					10 57					11 27					11 57			
Moorgate ⊖ d	09 55	10 00	10 10		10 20	10 25	10 30	10 40		10 50	10 55	11 00	11 10		11 20	11 25	11 30	11 40		11 50	11 55	12 00
Old Street ⊖ d	09 57	10 02	10 12		10 22	10 27	10 32	10 42		10 52	10 57	11 02	11 12		11 22	11 27	11 32	11 42		11 52	11 57	12 02
Essex Road d	10 00	10 05	10 15		10 25	10 30	10 35	10 45		10 55	11 00	11 05	11 15		11 25	11 30	11 35	11 45		11 55	12 00	12 05
Highbury & Islington ⊖ d	10 03	10 08	10 18		10 28	10 33	10 38	10 48		10 58	11 03	11 08	11 18		11 28	11 33	11 38	11 48		11 58	12 03	12 08
Drayton Park d	10 05	10 10	10 20		10 30	10 35	10 40	10 50		11 00	11 05	11 10	11 20		11 30	11 35	11 40	11 50		12 00	12 05	12 10
Finsbury Park ⊖ a	10 08	10 13	10 23		10 33	10 38	10 43	10 53		11 03	11 08	11 13	11 23		11 33	11 38	11 43	11 53		12 03	12 08	12 13
Finsbury Park d	10 09	10 14	10 24	10 31	10 33	10 39	10 44	10 54	11 01	11 03	11 09	11 14	11 24	11 31	11 33	11 39	11 44	11 54	12 01	12 03	12 09	12 14
Harringay d	10 11	10 16	10 26			10 41	10 46	10 56			11 11	11 16	11 26			11 41	11 46	11 56			12 11	12 16
Hornsey d	10 13	10 18	10 28			10 43	10 48	10 58			11 13	11 18	11 28			11 43	11 48	11 58			12 13	12 18
Alexandra Palace d	10 17	10 21	10 32		10 38	10 47	10 51	11 02		11 08	11 17	11 21	11 32		11 38	11 47	11 51	12 02		12 08	12 17	12 21
New Southgate d		10 24			10 41		10 54			11 11		11 24			11 41		11 54			12 11		12 24
Oakleigh Park d		10 28			10 44		10 58			11 14		11 28			11 44		11 58			12 14		12 28
New Barnet d		10 30			10 46		11 00			11 16		11 30			11 46		12 00			12 16		12 30
Hadley Wood d		10 33			10 49		11 03			11 19		11 33			11 49		12 03			12 19		12 33
Potters Bar d		10 37		10 43	10 53		11 07		11 13	11 23		11 37		11 43	11 53		12 07		12 13	12 23		12 37
Brookmans Park d					10 56					11 26					11 56					12 26		
Welham Green d					10 59					11 29					11 59					12 29		
Hatfield d		10 43		10 48	11 02		11 13		11 18	11 32		11 43		11 48	12 02		12 13		12 18	12 32		12 43
Welwyn Garden City ■ d		10a48		10 56	11a07		11a18		11 26	11a37		11a48		11 56	12a07		12a18		12 26	12a37		12a48
Welwyn North d				11 00					11 30					12 00					12 30			
Knebworth d				11 04					11 34					12 04					12 34			
Bowes Park d	10 19		10 34			10 49		11 04			11 19		11 34			11 49		12 04			12 19	
Palmers Green d	10 22		10 37			10 52		11 07			11 22		11 37			11 52		12 07			12 22	
Winchmore Hill d	10 25		10 40			10 55		11 10			11 25		11 40			11 55		12 10			12 25	
Grange Park d	10 27		10 42			10 57		11 12			11 27		11 42			11 57		12 12			12 27	
Enfield Chase d	10 29		10 44			10 59		11 14			11 29		11 44			11 59		12 14			12 29	
Gordon Hill d	10 32		10 47			11 02		11 17			11 32		11 47			12 02		12 17			12 32	
Crews Hill d	10 35					11 05					11 35					12 05					12 35	
Cuffley d	10 38		10 52			11 08		11 22			11 38		11 52			12 08		12 22			12 38	
Bayford d	10 42					11 12					11 42					12 12					12 42	
Hertford North a	10 48		10 59			11 18		11 29			11 48		11 59			12 18		12 29			12 48	
Watton-at-Stone a			11 10					11 41					12 10					12 41				
Stevenage ■ a			11 18	11 09					11 38				12 18	12 08					12 38			

	GN	TL ■	GN	GN	GN	GN	TL ■	GN	GN	GN	GN	TL ■	GN	GN	GN	GN	TL ■	GN	GN	GN	GN
London Bridge d																					
London Blackfriars d																					
City Thameslink d																					
Farringdon d																					
St Pancras International d																					
London Kings Cross ⊖ d		12 21					12 51					13 21					13 51				
Finsbury Park a		12 27					12 57					13 27					13 57				
Moorgate ⊖ d	12 10		12 20	12 25	12 30	12 40		12 50	12 55	13 00	13 10		13 20	13 25	13 30	13 40		13 50	13 55	14 00	14 10
Old Street ⊖ d	12 12		12 22	12 27	12 32	12 42		12 52	12 57	13 02	13 12		13 22	13 27	13 32	13 42		13 52	13 57	14 02	14 12
Essex Road d	12 15		12 25	12 30	12 35	12 45		12 55	13 00	13 05	13 15		13 25	13 30	13 35	13 45		13 55	14 00	14 05	14 15
Highbury & Islington ⊖ d	12 18		12 28	12 33	12 38	12 48		12 58	13 03	13 08	13 18		13 28	13 33	13 38	13 48		13 58	14 03	14 08	14 18
Drayton Park d	12 20		12 30	12 35	12 40	12 50		13 00	13 05	13 10	13 20		13 30	13 35	13 40	13 50		14 00	14 05	14 10	14 20
Finsbury Park ⊖ a	12 23		12 33	12 38	12 43	12 53		13 03	13 08	13 13	13 23		13 33	13 38	13 43	13 53		14 03	14 08	14 13	14 23
Finsbury Park d	12 24	12 31	12 33	12 39	12 44	12 54	13 01	13 03	13 09	13 14	13 24	13 31	13 33	13 39	13 44	13 54	14 01	14 03	14 09	14 14	14 24
Harringay d	12 26			12 41	12 46	12 56			13 11	13 16	13 26			13 41	13 46	13 56			14 11	14 16	14 26
Hornsey d	12 28			12 43	12 48	12 58			13 13	13 18	13 28			13 43	13 48	13 58			14 13	14 18	14 28
Alexandra Palace d	12 32		12 38	12 47	12 51	13 02		13 08	13 17	13 21	13 32		13 38	13 47	13 51	14 02		14 08	14 17	14 21	14 32
New Southgate d			12 41		12 54			13 11		13 24			13 41		13 54			14 11		14 24	
Oakleigh Park d			12 44		12 58			13 14		13 28			13 44		13 58			14 14		14 28	
New Barnet d			12 46		13 00			13 16		13 30			13 46		14 00			14 16		14 30	
Hadley Wood d			12 49		13 03			13 19		13 33			13 49		14 03			14 19		14 33	
Potters Bar d		12 43	12 53		13 07		13 13	13 23		13 37		13 43	13 53		14 07		14 13	14 23		14 37	
Brookmans Park d			12 56					13 26					13 56					14 26			
Welham Green d			12 59					13 29					13 59					14 29			
Hatfield d		12 48	13 02		13 13		13 18	13 32		13 43		13 48	14 02		14 13		14 18	14 32		14 43	
Welwyn Garden City ■ d		12 56	13a07		13a18		13 26	13a37		13a48		13 56	14a07		14a18		14 26	14a37		14a48	
Welwyn North d		13 00					13 30					14 00					14 30				
Knebworth d		13 04					13 34					14 04					14 34				
Bowes Park d	12 34			12 49		13 04			13 19		13 34			13 49		14 04			14 19		14 34
Palmers Green d	12 37			12 52		13 07			13 22		13 37			13 52		14 07			14 22		14 37
Winchmore Hill d	12 40			12 55		13 10			13 25		13 40			13 55		14 10			14 25		14 40
Grange Park d	12 42			12 57		13 12			13 27		13 42			13 57		14 12			14 27		14 42
Enfield Chase d	12 44			12 59		13 14			13 29		13 44			13 59		14 14			14 29		14 44
Gordon Hill d	12 47			13 02		13 17			13 32		13 47			14 02		14 17			14 32		14 47
Crews Hill d				13 05					13 35					14 05					14 35		
Cuffley d	12 52			13 08		13 22			13 38		13 52			14 08		14 22			14 38		14 52
Bayford d				13 12					13 42					14 12					14 42		
Hertford North a	12 59			13 18		13 29			13 48		13 59			14 18		14 29			14 48		14 59
Watton-at-Stone a	13 10					13 41					14 10					14 41					15 10
Stevenage ■ a	13 18	13 08					13 38				14 22	14 08					14 38				15 20

See Table 025 for fast trains between London and Stevenage

Table T024-F

Mondays to Fridays

21 May to 7 December

London - Welwyn Garden City and Hertford North

		TL ■	GN	GN	GN	GN	TL ■	GN		GN	GN	GN	TL ■	GN	GN	GN	GN	TL ■		GN	GN	GN	GN	TL ■	GN
London Bridge	d																								
London Blackfriars	d																								
City Thameslink	d																								
Farringdon	d																								
St Pancras International	d																								
London Kings Cross ■ ⊖	d	14 21					14 51						15 19					15 51						16 21	
Finsbury Park	a	14 27					14 57						15 25					15 57						16 27	
Moorgate ⊖	d		14 20	14 25	14 30	14 40		14 50		14 55	15 00	15 10		15 20	15 25	15 30	15 40			15 50	15 55	16 00	16 10		16 15
Old Street ⊖	d		14 22	14 27	14 32	14 42		14 52		14 57	15 02	15 12		15 22	15 27	15 32	15 42			15 52	15 57	16 03	16 13		16 18
Essex Road	d		14 25	14 30	14 35	14 45		14 55		15 00	15 05	15 15		15 25	15 30	15 35	15 45			15 55	16 00	16 06	16 16		16 21
Highbury & Islington ⊖	d		14 28	14 33	14 38	14 48		14 58		15 03	15 08	15 18		15 28	15 33	15 38	15 48			15 58	16 03	16 08	16 18		16 23
Drayton Park	d		14 30	14 35	14 40	14 50		15 00		15 05	15 10	15 20		15 30	15 35	15 40	15 50			16 00	16 05	16 11	16 21		16 26
Finsbury Park ⊖	a		14 33	14 38	14 43	14 53		15 03		15 08	15 13	15 23		15 33	15 38	15 43	15 53			16 03	16 08	16 13	16 23		16 28
Finsbury Park	d	14 31	14 33	14 39	14 44	14 54	15 01	15 03		15 09	15 14	15 24	15 29	15 33	15 39	15 44	15 54	16 01		16 03	16 09	16 15	16 24	16 31	16 30
Harringay	d			14 41	14 46	14 56				15 11	15 16	15 26			15 41	15 46	15 56				16 11	16 17	16 26		
Hornsey	d			14 43	14 48	14 58				15 13	15 18	15 28			15 43	15 48	15 58				16 13	16 19	16 28		
Alexandra Palace	d		14 38	14 47	14 51	15 02		15 08		15 17	15 21	15 32		15 38	15 47	15 51	16 02			16 08	16 17	16 22	16 32		16 37
New Southgate	d		14 41		14 54			15 11			15 24			15 41		15 54				16 11		16 25			16 40
Oakleigh Park	d		14 44		14 58			15 14			15 28			15 44		15 58				16 14		16 29			16 44
New Barnet	d		14 46		15 00			15 16			15 30			15 46		16 00				16 16		16 31			16 46
Hadley Wood	d		14 49		15 03			15 19			15 33			15 49		16 03				16 19		16 34			16 49
Potters Bar	d	14 43	14 53		15 07		15 13	15 23			15 37		15 42	15 53		16 07		16 13		16 23		16 38		16 43	16 53
Brookmans Park	d		14 56					15 26						15 56						16 26		16 41			16 56
Welham Green	d		14 59					15 29						15 59						16 29		16 44			16 59
Hatfield	d	14 48	15 02		15 13		15 18	15 32			15 43		15 48	16 02		16 13		16 18		16 32		16 47		16 51	17 02
Welwyn Garden City ■	d	14 56	15a07		15a18		15 26	15a37			15a48		15 56	16a07		16a18		16 26		16a37		16a52		16 56	17a07
Welwyn North	d	15 00					15 30						16 00					16 30						17 00	
Knebworth	d	15 04					15 34						16 04					16 34						17 04	
Bowes Park	d			14 49		15 04				15 19		15 34			15 49		16 04				16 19		16 34		
Palmers Green	d			14 52		15 07				15 22		15 37			15 52		16 07				16 22		16 37		
Winchmore Hill	d			14 55		15 10				15 25		15 40			15 55		16 10				16 25		16 40		
Grange Park	d			14 57		15 12				15 27		15 42			15 57		16 12				16 27		16 42		
Enfield Chase	d			14 59		15 14				15 29		15 44			15 59		16 14				16 29		16 45		
Gordon Hill	d			15 02		15 17				15 32		15 47			16 02		16 17				16 32		16 47		
Crews Hill	d			15 05						15 35					16 05						16 35				
Cuffley	d			15 08		15 22				15 38		15 52			16 08		16 22				16 38		16 52		
Bayford	d			15 12						15 42					16 12						16 42				
Hertford North	a			15 18		15 29				15 48		15 59			16 18		16 29				16 48		17 01		
Watton-at-Stone	a					15 41						16 10					16 37								
Stevenage ■	a	15 08					15 38					16 18	16 08					16 38						17 08	

		GN	GN	GN		GN	GN	GN ■	TL ■	GN	GN	GN	GN	GN		GN	GN	GN ■	TL ■	GN	GN	GN	GN	GN
London Bridge	d																							
London Blackfriars	d																							
City Thameslink	d																							
Farringdon	d																							
St Pancras International	d																							
London Kings Cross ■ ⊖	d			16 36				16 54	16 51				17 06					17 24	17 21				17 36	
Finsbury Park	a			16 45					16 57				17 15						17 27				17 45	
Moorgate ⊖	d	16 20	16 25			16 30	16 40			16 45	16 50	16 55		17 00		17 05	17 09			17 15	17 20	17 25		17 30
Old Street ⊖	d	16 23	16 28			16 33	16 43			16 48	16 53	16 58		17 03		17 08	17 12			17 18	17 23	17 28		17 33
Essex Road	d	16 26	16 31			16 36	16 46			16 51	16 56	17 01		17 06		17 11	17 15			17 21	17 26	17 31		17 36
Highbury & Islington ⊖	d	16 28	16 33			16 38	16 48			16 53	16 58	17 03		17 08		17 13	17 17			17 23	17 28	17 33		17 38
Drayton Park	d	16 31	16 36			16 41	16 51			16 56	17 01	17 06		17 11		17 16	17 20			17 26	17 31	17 36		17 41
Finsbury Park ⊖	a	16 33	16 38			16 43	16 53			16 58	17 03	17 08		17 13		17 18	17 22			17 28	17 33	17 38		17 43
Finsbury Park	d	16 34	16 39	16 45		16 45	16 54		17 01	17 00	17 04	17 09	17 15	17 15		17 19	17 23		17 31	17 30	17 34	17 39	17 45	17 45
Harringay	d	16 36	16 41				16 56				17 06	17 11					17 25				17 36	17 41		
Hornsey	d	16 38	16 43				16 58				17 08	17 13					17 27				17 38	17 43		
Alexandra Palace	d	16 42	16 47			16 52	17 02			17 07	17 12	17 17		17 22		17 24	17 31			17 37	17 42	17 47		17 52
New Southgate	d			16 52		16 55				17 10			17 22	17 25						17 40			17 52	17 55
Oakleigh Park	d			16 55		16 59				17 14			17 25	17 29						17 44			17 55	17 59
New Barnet	d			16 57		17 01				17 16			17 27	17 31						17 46			17 57	18 01
Hadley Wood	d					17 04				17 19				17 34						17 49				18 04
Potters Bar	d			17 02		17 08			17 13	17 23			17 32	17 38					17 43	17 53			18 02	18 08
Brookmans Park	d					17 11				17 26				17 41						17 56				18 11
Welham Green	d					17 14				17 29				17 44						17 59				18 14
Hatfield	d			17 08		17 17			17 21	17 32			17 38	17 47					17 51	18 02			18 08	18 17
Welwyn Garden City ■	d			17a12		17a22			17 26	17a37			17a42	17a52					17 56	18a07			18a12	18a22
Welwyn North	d							17 11	17 30									17 41	18 00					
Knebworth	d							17a15	17 34									17a45	18 04					
Bowes Park	d		16 49				17 04					17 19					17 33					17 49		
Palmers Green	d	16 46	16 52				17 07				17 16	17 22				17 28	17 36				17 46	17 52		
Winchmore Hill	d	16 49	16 55				17 10				17 19	17 25				17 31	17 39				17 49	17 55		
Grange Park	d		16 57				17 12					17 27					17 41					17 57		
Enfield Chase	d	16 52	17 00				17 15				17 22	17 30				17 34	17 44				17 52	18 00		
Gordon Hill	d	16 55	17a03				17 17				17 25	17a33				17 37	17a47				17 55	18a03		
Crews Hill	d	16 58									17 28										17 58			
Cuffley	d	17 01					17 22				17 31					17 42					18 01			
Bayford	d	17 05									17 35										18 05			
Hertford North	a	17 10					17 31				17 40					17 51					18 10			
Watton-at-Stone	a	17 16									17 47										18 16			
Stevenage ■	a	17 24							17 38										18 08		18 24			

See Table 025 for fast trains between London and Stevenage

Table T024-F

Mondays to Fridays

21 May to 7 December

London - Welwyn Garden City and Hertford North

		GN	GN	GN ■	TL ■	GN	GN	GN	GN	GN		GN	GN	GN ■	TL ■	GN	GN	GN	GN	GN		GN	GN ■	TL ■	GN
London Bridge	d																								
London Blackfriars	d																								
City Thameslink	d																								
Farringdon	d																								
St Pancras International	d																								
London Kings Cross ■ ⊖	d			17 54	17 51				18 06					18 24	18 21				18 36				18 54	18 51	
Finsbury Park	a				17 57				18 15						18 27				18 45					18 57	
Moorgate ⊖	d	17 35	17 40			17 45	17 50	17 55		18 00		18 05	18 10			18 15	18 20	18 25		18 32		18 40			18 45
Old Street ⊖	d	17 38	17 43			17 48	17 53	17 58		18 03		18 08	18 13			18 18	18 23	18 28		18 35		18 43			18 48
Essex Road	d	17 41	17 46			17 51	17 56	18 01		18 06		18 11	18 16			18 21	18 26	18 31		18 38		18 46			18 51
Highbury & Islington ⊖	d	17 43	17 48			17 53	17 58	18 03		18 08		18 13	18 18			18 23	18 28	18 33		18 40		18 48			18 53
Drayton Park	d	17 46	17 51			17 56	18 01	18 06		18 11		18 16	18 21			18 26	18 31	18 36		18 43		18 51			18 56
Finsbury Park ⊖	a	17 48	17 53			17 58	18 03	18 08		18 13		18 18	18 23			18 28	18 33	18 38		18 45		18 53			18 58
Finsbury Park	d	17 49	17 54		18 01	18 00	18 04	18 09	18 15	18 15		18 19	18 24		18 31	18 30	18 34	18 39	18 45	18 46		18 54		19 01	19 00
Harringay	d		17 56				18 06	18 11					18 26				18 36	18 41				18 56			
Hornsey	d		17 58				18 08	18 13					18 28				18 38	18 43				18 58			
Alexandra Palace	d	17 55	18 02			18 07	18 12	18 17		18 22		18 25	18 32			18 37	18 42	18 47		18 52		19 02			19 07
New Southgate	d					18 10			18 22	18 25						18 40			18 52	18 55					19 10
Oakleigh Park	d					18 14			18 25	18 29						18 44			18 55	18 59					19 14
New Barnet	d					18 16			18 27	18 31						18 46			18 57	19 01					19 16
Hadley Wood	d					18 19				18 34						18 49				19 04					19 19
Potters Bar	d				18 13	18 23			18 32	18 38					18 43	18 53			19 02	19 08				19 13	19 23
Brookmans Park	d					18 26				18 41						18 56				19 11					19 26
Welham Green	d					18 29				18 44						18 59				19 14					19 29
Hatfield	d				18 21	18 32			18 38	18 47					18 51	19 02			19 08	19 17				19 21	19 32
Welwyn Garden City ■	d				18 26	18a37			18a42	18a52					18 56	19a07			19a12	19a22				19 26	19a37
Welwyn North	d			18 11	18 30									18 41	19 00								19 11	19 30	
Knebworth	d			18a15	18 34									18a45	19 04								19a15	19 34	
Bowes Park	d		18 04					18 19					18 34					18 49				19 04			
Palmers Green	d	17 59	18 07				18 16	18 22				18 29	18 37				18 46	18 52				19 07			
Winchmore Hill	d	18 02	18 10				18 19	18 25				18 32	18 40				18 49	18 55				19 10			
Grange Park	d		18 12					18 27					18 42					18 57				19 12			
Enfield Chase	d	18 05	18 15				18 22	18 30				18 35	18 45				18 52	19 00				19 15			
Gordon Hill	d	18 08	18 17				18 25	18a33				18 38	18 47				18 55	19 03				19 17			
Crews Hill	d						18 28										18 58	19 06							
Cuffley	d	18 13	18 22				18 31					18 43	18 52				19 01	19 09				19 22			
Bayford	d						18 35										19 05	19 13							
Hertford North	a	18 22	18 31				18 40					18 52	19 01				19 10	19 19				19 31			
Watton-at-Stone	a						18 47										19 16								
Stevenage ■	a				18 38										19 08		19 24							19 38	

		GN	GN	GN	GN	GN		TL ■	GN	GN	GN	GN	TL ■	GN	GN	GN		GN	TL ■	GN	GN	GN	GN	TL ■	GN
London Bridge	d																								
London Blackfriars	d																								
City Thameslink	d																								
Farringdon	d																								
St Pancras International	d																								
London Kings Cross ■ ⊖	d			19 06				19 23					19 51						20 21					20 51	
Finsbury Park	a			19 15				19 29					19 57						20 27					20 57	
Moorgate ⊖	d	18 50	18 55		19 00	19 10			19 15	19 25	19 30	19 40		19 50	19 55	20 00		20 10		20 20	20 25	20 30	20 40		20 50
Old Street ⊖	d	18 53	18 58		19 03	19 12			19 17	19 27	19 33	19 42		19 52	19 57	20 02		20 12		20 22	20 27	20 32	20 42		20 52
Essex Road	d	18 56	19 01		19 06	19 15			19 20	19 30	19 36	19 45		19 55	20 00	20 05		20 15		20 25	20 30	20 35	20 45		20 55
Highbury & Islington ⊖	d	18 58	19 03		19 08	19 18			19 23	19 33	19 38	19 48		19 58	20 03	20 08		20 18		20 28	20 33	20 38	20 48		20 58
Drayton Park	d	19 01	19 06		19 11	19 20			19 25	19 35	19 41	19 50		20 00	20 05	20 10		20 20		20 30	20 35	20 40	20 50		21 00
Finsbury Park ⊖	a	19 03	19 08		19 13	19 23			19 28	19 38	19 43	19 53		20 03	20 08	20 13		20 23		20 33	20 38	20 43	20 53		21 03
Finsbury Park	d	19 04	19 09	19 15	19 14	19 24		19 32	19 30	19 39	19 44	19 54	20 01	20 03	20 09	20 14		20 24	20 31	20 33	20 39	20 44	20 54	21 01	21 03
Harringay	d	19 06	19 11			19 26				19 41	19 46	19 56			20 11	20 16		20 26			20 41	20 46	20 56		
Hornsey	d	19 08	19 13			19 28				19 43	19 48	19 58			20 13	20 18		20 28			20 43	20 48	20 58		
Alexandra Palace	d	19 12	19 17		19 22	19 32			19 37	19 47	19 51	20 02		20 08	20 17	20 21		20 32		20 38	20 47	20 51	21 02		21 08
New Southgate	d			19 22	19 25				19 40		19 54			20 11		20 24				20 41		20 54			21 11
Oakleigh Park	d			19 25	19 29				19 44		19 58			20 14		20 28				20 44		20 58			21 14
New Barnet	d			19 27	19 31				19 46		20 00			20 16		20 30				20 46		21 00			21 16
Hadley Wood	d				19 34				19 49		20 03			20 19		20 33				20 49		21 03			21 19
Potters Bar	d			19 32	19 38			19 45	19 53		20 07		20 13	20 23		20 37			20 43	20 53		21 07		21 13	21 23
Brookmans Park	d								19 56					20 26						20 56					21 26
Welham Green	d								19 59					20 29						20 59					21 29
Hatfield	d			19 38	19 44			19 50	20 02		20 13		20 18	20 32		20 43			20 48	21 02		21 13		21 18	21 32
Welwyn Garden City ■	d			19a42	19a49			19 56	20a07		20a18		20 26	20a37		20a48			20 56	21a07		21a18		21 26	21a37
Welwyn North	d							20 00					20 30						21 00					21 30	
Knebworth	d							20 04					20 34						21 04					21 34	
Bowes Park	d		19 19			19 34				19 49		20 04			20 19			20 34			20 49		21 04		
Palmers Green	d	19 16	19 22			19 37				19 52		20 07			20 22			20 37			20 52		21 07		
Winchmore Hill	d	19 19	19 25			19 40				19 55		20 10			20 25			20 40			20 55		21 10		
Grange Park	d		19 27			19 42				19 57		20 12			20 27			20 42			20 57		21 12		
Enfield Chase	d	19 22	19 30			19 44				19 59		20 14			20 29			20 44			20 59		21 14		
Gordon Hill	d	19 25	19a33			19 47				20 02		20 17			20 32			20 47			21 01		21 16		
Crews Hill	d	19 28								20 05					20 35						21 04				
Cuffley	d	19 31				19 52				20 08		20 22			20 38			20 52			21 08		21 21		
Bayford	d	19 35								20 12					20 42						21 12				
Hertford North	a	19 40				19 59				20 18		20 29			20 48			20 59			21 18		21 29		
Watton-at-Stone	a	19 47				20 10						20 37						21 10							
Stevenage ■	a					20 21		20 08					20 38					21 21	21 08					21 38	

See Table 025 for fast trains between London and Stevenage

NRT MAY 2018 EDITION

Table T024-F

Mondays to Fridays

21 May to 7 December

London - Welwyn Garden City and Hertford North

		GN	GN	GN	TL 1	GN	GN	GN	GN	TL 1	GN	GN	GN	GN	TL 1	GN	GN	GN	GN	TL 1	GN	GN
London Bridge	d																					
London Blackfriars	d																					
City Thameslink	d																					
Farringdon	d																					
St Pancras International	d																					
London Kings Cross 15 ⊖	d				21 21					21 51					22 21					22 51		
Finsbury Park	a				21 27					21 57					22 27					22 57		
Moorgate ⊖	d	20 55	21 00	21 10		21 20	21 25	21 30	21 40		21 50	21 55	22 00	22 10		22 20	22 25	22 30	22 40		22 50	22 55
Old Street ⊖	d	20 57	21 02	21 12		21 22	21 27	21 32	21 42		21 52	21 57	22 02	22 12		22 22	22 27	22 32	22 42		22 52	22 57
Essex Road	d	21 00	21 05	21 15		21 25	21 30	21 35	21 45		21 55	22 00	22 05	22 15		22 25	22 30	22 35	22 45		22 55	23 00
Highbury & Islington ⊖	d	21 03	21 08	21 18		21 28	21 33	21 38	21 48		21 58	22 03	22 08	22 18		22 28	22 33	22 38	22 48		22 58	23 03
Drayton Park	d	21 05	21 10	21 20		21 30	21 35	21 40	21 50		22 00	22 05	22 10	22 20		22 30	22 35	22 40	22 50		23 00	23 05
Finsbury Park ⊖	a	21 08	21 13	21 23		21 33	21 38	21 43	21 53		22 03	22 08	22 13	22 23		22 33	22 38	22 43	22 53		23 03	23 08
Finsbury Park	d	21 09	21 14	21 24	21 31	21 33	21 39	21 44	21 54	22 01	22 03	22 09	22 14	22 24	22 31	22 33	22 39	22 44	22 54	23 01	23 03	23 09
Harringay	d	21 11	21 16	21 26			21 41	21 46	21 56			22 11	22 16	22 26			22 41	22 46	22 56			23 11
Hornsey	d	21 13	21 18	21 28			21 43	21 48	21 58			22 13	22 18	22 28			22 43	22 48	22 58			23 13
Alexandra Palace	d	21 17	21 21	21 32		21 38	21 47	21 51	22 02		22 08	22 17	22 21	22 32		22 38	22 47	22 51	23 02		23 08	23 17
New Southgate	d		21 24			21 41		21 54			22 11		22 24			22 41		22 54			23 11	
Oakleigh Park	d		21 28			21 44		21 58			22 14		22 28			22 44		22 58			23 14	
New Barnet	d		21 30			21 46		22 00			22 16		22 30			22 46		23 00			23 16	
Hadley Wood	d		21 33			21 49		22 03			22 19		22 33			22 49		23 03			23 19	
Potters Bar	d		21 37		21 43	21 53		22 07		22 13	22 23		22 37		22 43	22 53		23 07		23 13	23 23	
Brookmans Park	d					21 56					22 26					22 56					23 26	
Welham Green	d					21 59					22 29					22 59					23 29	
Hatfield	d		21 43		21 48	22 02		22 13		22 18	22 32		22 43		22 48	23 02		23 13		23 18	23 32	
Welwyn Garden City 4	d		21a48		21 56	22a07		22a18		22 26	22a37		22a48		22 56	23a07		23a18		23 26	23a37	
Welwyn North	d				22 00					22 30					23 00					23 30		
Knebworth	d				22 04					22 34					23 04					23 34		
Bowes Park	d	21 19		21 34			21 49		22 04			22 19		22 34			22 49		23 04			23 19
Palmers Green	d	21 22		21 37			21 52		22 07			22 22		22 37			22 52		23 07			23 22
Winchmore Hill	d	21 25		21 40			21 55		22 10			22 25		22 40			22 55		23 10			23 25
Grange Park	d	21 27		21 42			21 57		22 12			22 27		22 42			22 57		23 12			23 27
Enfield Chase	d	21 29		21 44			21 59		22 14			22 29		22 44			22 59		23 14			23 29
Gordon Hill	d	21 31		21 47			22 01		22 17			22 31		22 47			23 01		23 17			23 31
Crews Hill	d	21 34					22 04					22 34					23 04					23 34
Cuffley	d	21 38		21 52			22 08		22 22			22 38		22 52			23 08		23 22			23 38
Bayford	d	21 42					22 12					22 42					23 12					23 42
Hertford North	a	21 48		21 59			22 20		22 29			22 48		22 59			23 18		23 29			23 48
Watton-at-Stone	a			22 10					22 41					23 10					23 37			
Stevenage 4	a			22 21	22 08					22 38				23 18	23 10					23 37		

		GN	GN	TL 1	GN	GN	GN	TL 1	GN	GN
London Bridge	d									
London Blackfriars	d									
City Thameslink	d									
Farringdon	d									
St Pancras International	d									
London Kings Cross 15 ⊖	d			23 24				23 51		
Finsbury Park	a			23 29				23 57		
Moorgate ⊖	d	23 00	23 10		23 20	23 27	23 37		23 47	23 57
Old Street ⊖	d	23 02	23 12		23 22	23 29	23 39		23 49	23 59
Essex Road	d	23 05	23 15		23 25	23 32	23 42		23 52	00 02
Highbury & Islington ⊖	d	23 08	23 18		23 28	23 35	23 45		23 55	00 05
Drayton Park	d	23 10	23 20		23 30	23 37	23 47		23 57	00 07
Finsbury Park ⊖	a	23 13	23 23		23 33	23 40	23 50		00 01	00 10
Finsbury Park	d	23 14	23 24	23 31	23 33	23 41	23 53	00 01	00 03	00 11
Harringay	d	23 16	23 26		23 36	23 44	23 56		00 06	00 14
Hornsey	d	23 18	23 28		23 38	23 46	23 58		00 08	00 16
Alexandra Palace	d	23 21	23 32		23 41	23 49	00 01		00 11	00 19
New Southgate	d	23 24				23 52				00 22
Oakleigh Park	d	23 28				23 55				00 25
New Barnet	d	23 30				23 58				00 28
Hadley Wood	d	23 33				00 01				00 31
Potters Bar	d	23 37		23 43		00 05		00 13		00 35
Brookmans Park	d	23 40				00 08				00 38
Welham Green	d	23 43				00 11				00 41
Hatfield	d	23 46		23 50		00 14		00 18		00 44
Welwyn Garden City 4	d	23a51		23 56		00a19		00 28		00a49
Welwyn North	d			00 01				00 31		
Knebworth	d			00 05				00 35		
Bowes Park	d		23 34		23 44		00 04		00 14	
Palmers Green	d		23 37		23 46		00 06		00 16	
Winchmore Hill	d		23 40		23 49		00 09		00 19	
Grange Park	d		23 42		23 51		00 11		00 21	
Enfield Chase	d		23 44		23 53		00 13		00 23	
Gordon Hill	d		23 47		23 56		00 16		00 26	
Crews Hill	d				23 59		00 19		00 29	
Cuffley	d		23 52		00 02		00 22		00 32	
Bayford	d				00 06		00 26		00 36	
Hertford North	a		00 01		00 11		00 31		00 42	
Watton-at-Stone	a				00 17		00 37			
Stevenage 4	a			00 08	00 25		00 45	00 39		

See Table 025 for fast trains between London and Stevenage

Table T024-F

Saturdays

26 May to 8 December

London - Welwyn Garden City and Hertford North

		TL 1	GN	GN	GN	TL 1	GN	GN	TL 1	TL 1	GN	GN	GN	GN	TL 1	GN	TL 1	GN	GN	TL 1	GN	GN	GN
London Bridge	d																						
London Blackfriars	d								00 37														
City Thameslink	d																						
Farringdon	d								00 41														
St Pancras International	d								00 46														
London Kings Cross 15 ⊖	d					00 23				01 05	01 09	01 40	05 06	05 21	05 25		05 51			06 21			
Finsbury Park	a					00 28			00 52	01 10	01 14	01 47	05 12	05 27	05 30		05 57			06 26			
Moorgate ⊖	d				00 07		00 17	00 27								05 37		05 57	06 07		06 17	06 27	06 37
Old Street ⊖	d				00 09		00 19	00 29								05 39		05 59	06 09		06 19	06 29	06 39
Essex Road	d			00 02	00 12		00 22	00 32								05 42		06 02	06 12		06 22	06 32	06 42
Highbury & Islington ⊖	d			00 05	00 15		00 25	00 35								05 45		06 05	06 15		06 25	06 35	06 45
Drayton Park	d			00 07	00 17		00 27	00 37								05 47		06 07	06 17		06 27	06 37	06 47
Finsbury Park ⊖	a			00 10	00 20		00 30	00 40								05 50		06 10	06 20		06 30	06 40	06 50
Finsbury Park	d	00 01	00 03	00 11	00 23	00 29	00 32	00 41	00 54	01 11	01 16	01 48	05 13	05 27	05 31	05 53	06 01	06 12	06 23	06 31	06 33	06 43	06 53
Harringay	d		00 06	00 14	00 26		00 34				01 18		05 16	05 30		05 56		06 14	06 26			06 46	06 56
Hornsey	d		00 08	00 16	00 28		00 36				01 20		05 18	05 32		05 58		06 16	06 28			06 48	06 58
Alexandra Palace	d		00 11	00 19	00 31		00 40	00 45			01 24	01 53	05 21	05 35		06 01		06 20	06 31		06 38	06 51	07 01
New Southgate	d			00 22								01 56						06 23			06 41	06 54	
Oakleigh Park	d			00 25								01 59						06 26			06 44	06 58	
New Barnet	d			00 28				00 51				02 02						06 29			06 46	07 00	
Hadley Wood	d			00 31				00 54				02 04						06 32			06 49	07 03	
Potters Bar	d	00 13		00 35		00 42		00 58		01 22		02 08			05 42		06 13	06 36		06 43	06 53	07 07	
Brookmans Park	d			00 38														06 39			06 56		
Welham Green	d			00 41														06 41			06 59		
Hatfield	d	00 18		00 44		00 48		01 04		01 28		02 14			05 48		06 18	06 45		06 48	07 02	07 13	
Welwyn Garden City 4	d	00 28		00a49		00 58		01a09	01 13	01 34		02a20			05 56		06 26	06a50		06 56	07a07	07a18	
Welwyn North	d	00 31				01 01				01 37					06 00		06 30			07 00			
Knebworth	d	00 35				01 05				01 41					06 04		06 34			07 04			
Bowes Park	d		00 14		00 34		00 42				01 26			05 38		06 04			06 34				07 04
Palmers Green	d		00 16		00 36		00 45				01 29		05 25	05 40		06 06			06 36				07 06
Winchmore Hill	d		00 19		00 39		00 48				01 32		05 27	05 43		06 09			06 39				07 09
Grange Park	d		00 21		00 41		00 50				01 34			05 45		06 11			06 41				07 11
Enfield Chase	d		00 23		00 43		00 52				01 36		05 30	05 48		06 13			06 43				07 13
Gordon Hill	d		00 26		00 46		00 55				01 38		05 33	05 51		06 16			06 46				07 16
Crews Hill	d		00 29		00 49		00 58						05 36	05 54		06 19			06 49				07 19
Cuffley	d		00 32		00 52		01 01				01 43		05 39	05 57		06 22			06 52				07 22
Bayford	d		00 36		00 56		01 06						05 43	06 01		06 27			06 57				07 27
Hertford North	a		00 42		01 02		01 10				01 52		05 49	06 06		06 31			07 04				07 34
Watton-at-Stone	a						01 18							06 12		06 39			07 11				07 41
Stevenage 4	a	00 39				01 09	01 25		01 21	01 45				06 20	06 08		06 38		07 18	07 08			

		TL 1	GN	GN	GN	GN	TL 1	GN	GN	GN	GN	TL 1	GN	GN	GN	GN	TL 1	GN	GN	GN	GN	TL 1	GN
London Bridge	d																						
London Blackfriars	d																						
City Thameslink	d																						
Farringdon	d																						
St Pancras International	d																						
London Kings Cross 15 ⊖	d	06 51					07 21					07 51					08 21					08 51	
Finsbury Park	a	06 56					07 26					07 56					08 26					08 57	
Moorgate ⊖	d		06 47	06 55	07 00	07 10		07 20	07 25	07 30	07 40		07 50	07 55	08 00	08 10		08 20	08 25	08 30	08 40		08 50
Old Street ⊖	d		06 49	06 57	07 02	07 12		07 22	07 27	07 32	07 42		07 52	07 57	08 02	08 12		08 22	08 27	08 32	08 42		08 52
Essex Road	d		06 52	07 00	07 05	07 15		07 25	07 30	07 35	07 45		07 55	08 00	08 05	08 15		08 25	08 30	08 35	08 45		08 55
Highbury & Islington ⊖	d		06 55	07 03	07 08	07 18		07 28	07 33	07 38	07 48		07 58	08 03	08 08	08 18		08 28	08 33	08 38	08 48		08 58
Drayton Park	d		06 57	07 05	07 10	07 20		07 30	07 35	07 40	07 50		08 00	08 05	08 10	08 20		08 30	08 35	08 40	08 50		09 00
Finsbury Park ⊖	a		07 00	07 08	07 13	07 23		07 33	07 38	07 43	07 53		08 03	08 08	08 13	08 23		08 33	08 38	08 43	08 53		09 03
Finsbury Park	d	07 01	07 03	07 09	07 14	07 24	07 31	07 33	07 39	07 44	07 54	08 01	08 03	08 09	08 14	08 24	08 31	08 33	08 39	08 44	08 54	09 01	09 03
Harringay	d			07 11	07 16	07 26			07 41	07 46	07 56			08 11	08 16	08 26			08 41	08 46	08 56		
Hornsey	d			07 13	07 18	07 28			07 43	07 48	07 58			08 13	08 18	08 28			08 43	08 48	08 58		
Alexandra Palace	d		07 08	07 17	07 21	07 32		07 38	07 47	07 51	08 02		08 08	08 17	08 21	08 32		08 38	08 47	08 51	09 02		09 08
New Southgate	d		07 11		07 24			07 41		07 54			08 11		08 24			08 41		08 54			09 11
Oakleigh Park	d		07 14		07 28			07 44		07 58			08 14		08 28			08 44		08 58			09 14
New Barnet	d		07 16		07 30			07 46		08 00			08 16		08 30			08 46		09 00			09 16
Hadley Wood	d		07 19		07 33			07 49		08 03			08 19		08 33			08 49		09 03			09 19
Potters Bar	d	07 13	07 23		07 37		07 43	07 53		08 07		08 13	08 23		08 37		08 43	08 53		09 07		09 13	09 23
Brookmans Park	d		07 26					07 56					08 26					08 56					09 26
Welham Green	d		07 29					07 59					08 29					08 59					09 29
Hatfield	d	07 18	07 32		07 43		07 48	08 02		08 13		08 18	08 32		08 43		08 48	09 02		09 13		09 18	09 32
Welwyn Garden City 4	d	07 26	07a37		07a48		07 56	08a07		08a18		08 26	08a37		08a48		08 56	09a07		09a18		09 26	09a37
Welwyn North	d	07 30					08 00					08 30					09 00					09 30	
Knebworth	d	07 34					08 04					08 34					09 04					09 34	
Bowes Park	d			07 19		07 34			07 49		08 04			08 19		08 34			08 49		09 04		
Palmers Green	d			07 22		07 37			07 52		08 07			08 22		08 37			08 52		09 07		
Winchmore Hill	d			07 25		07 40			07 55		08 10			08 25		08 40			08 55		09 10		
Grange Park	d			07 27		07 42			07 57		08 12			08 27		08 42			08 57		09 12		
Enfield Chase	d			07 29		07 44			07 59		08 14			08 29		08 44			08 59		09 14		
Gordon Hill	d			07 32		07 47			08 02		08 17			08 32		08 47			09 02		09 17		
Crews Hill	d			07 35					08 05					08 35					09 05				
Cuffley	d			07 38		07 52			08 08		08 22			08 38		08 52			09 08		09 22		
Bayford	d			07 42					08 12					08 42					09 12				
Hertford North	a			07 48		07 59			08 18		08 29			08 48		08 59			09 18		09 29		
Watton-at-Stone	a					08 10					08 41					09 10					09 41		
Stevenage 4	a	07 38				08 18	08 08					08 38				09 18	09 08					09 38	

See Table 025 for fast trains between London and Stevenage

London - Welwyn Garden City and Hertford North

		GN	GN	GN	TL	GN	GN	GN	GN	TL	GN	GN	GN	GN	TL	GN	GN	GN	GN	TL	GN	GN
London Bridge	d																					
London Blackfriars	d																					
City Thameslink	d																					
Farringdon	d																					
St Pancras International	d																					
London Kings Cross ⊖	d				09 21					09 51					10 21					10 51		
Finsbury Park	a				09 27					09 57					10 27					10 57		
Moorgate ⊖	d	08 55	09 00	09 10		09 20	09 25	09 30	09 40		09 50	09 55	10 00	10 10		10 20	10 25	10 30	10 40		10 50	10 55
Old Street ⊖	d	08 57	09 02	09 12		09 22	09 27	09 32	09 42		09 52	09 57	10 02	10 12		10 22	10 27	10 32	10 42		10 52	10 57
Essex Road	d	09 00	09 05	09 15		09 25	09 30	09 35	09 45		09 55	10 00	10 05	10 15		10 25	10 30	10 35	10 45		10 55	11 00
Highbury & Islington ⊖	d	09 03	09 08	09 18		09 28	09 33	09 38	09 48		09 58	10 03	10 08	10 18		10 28	10 33	10 38	10 48		10 58	11 03
Drayton Park	d	09 05	09 10	09 20		09 30	09 35	09 40	09 50		10 00	10 05	10 10	10 20		10 30	10 35	10 40	10 50		11 00	11 05
Finsbury Park ⊖	a	09 08	09 13	09 23		09 33	09 38	09 43	09 53		10 03	10 08	10 13	10 23		10 33	10 38	10 43	10 53		11 03	11 08
Finsbury Park	d	09 09	09 14	09 24	09 31	09 33	09 39	09 44	09 54	10 01	10 03	10 09	10 14	10 24	10 31	10 33	10 39	10 44	10 54	11 01	11 03	11 09
Harringay	d	09 11	09 16	09 26			09 41	09 46	09 56			10 11	10 16	10 26			10 41	10 46	10 56			11 11
Hornsey	d	09 13	09 18	09 28			09 43	09 48	09 58			10 13	10 18	10 28			10 43	10 48	10 58			11 13
Alexandra Palace	d	09 17	09 21	09 32		09 38	09 47	09 51	10 02		10 08	10 17	10 21	10 32		10 38	10 47	10 51	11 02		11 08	11 17
New Southgate	d		09 24			09 41		09 54			10 11		10 24			10 41		10 54			11 11	
Oakleigh Park	d		09 28			09 44		09 58			10 14		10 28			10 44		10 58			11 14	
New Barnet	d		09 30			09 46		10 00			10 16		10 30			10 46		11 00			11 16	
Hadley Wood	d		09 33			09 49		10 03			10 19		10 33			10 49		11 03			11 19	
Potters Bar	d		09 37		09 42	09 53		10 07		10 13	10 23		10 37		10 42	10 53		11 07		11 13	11 23	
Brookmans Park	d					09 56					10 26					10 56					11 26	
Welham Green	d					09 59					10 29					10 59					11 29	
Hatfield	d		09 43		09 48	10 02		10 13		10 18	10 32		10 43		10 48	11 02		11 13		11 18	11 32	
Welwyn Garden City	d		09a48		09 56	10a07		10a18		10 26	10a37		10a48		10 56	11a07		11a18		11 26	11a37	
Welwyn North	d				10 00					10 30					11 00					11 30		
Knebworth	d				10 04					10 34					11 04					11 34		
Bowes Park	d	09 19		09 34			09 49		10 04			10 19		10 34			10 49		11 04			11 19
Palmers Green	d	09 22		09 37			09 52		10 07			10 22		10 37			10 52		11 07			11 22
Winchmore Hill	d	09 25		09 40			09 55		10 10			10 25		10 40			10 55		11 10			11 25
Grange Park	d	09 27		09 42			09 57		10 12			10 27		10 42			10 57		11 12			11 27
Enfield Chase	d	09 29		09 44			09 59		10 14			10 29		10 44			10 59		11 14			11 29
Gordon Hill	d	09 32		09 47			10 02		10 17			10 32		10 47			11 02		11 17			11 32
Crews Hill	d	09 35					10 05					10 35					11 05					11 35
Cuffley	d	09 38		09 52			10 08		10 22			10 38		10 52			11 08		11 22			11 38
Bayford	d	09 42					10 12					10 42					11 12					11 42
Hertford North	a	09 48		09 59			10 18		10 29			10 48		10 59			11 18		11 29			11 48
Watton-at-Stone	a			10 10					10 41					11 10					11 41			
Stevenage	a			10 18	10 08					10 38				11 18	11 08					11 38		

		GN	GN	TL	GN	GN	GN	GN	TL	GN	GN	GN	GN	TL	GN	GN	GN	GN	TL	GN	GN	GN	GN
London Bridge	d																						
London Blackfriars	d																						
City Thameslink	d																						
Farringdon	d																						
St Pancras International	d																						
London Kings Cross ⊖	d			11 21					11 51					12 21					12 51				
Finsbury Park	a			11 27					11 57					12 28					12 57				
Moorgate ⊖	d	11 00	11 10		11 20	11 25	11 30	11 40		11 50	11 55	12 00	12 10		12 20	12 25	12 30	12 40		12 50	12 55	13 00	13 10
Old Street ⊖	d	11 02	11 12		11 22	11 27	11 32	11 42		11 52	11 57	12 02	12 12		12 22	12 27	12 32	12 42		12 52	12 57	13 02	13 12
Essex Road	d	11 05	11 15		11 25	11 30	11 35	11 45		11 55	12 00	12 05	12 15		12 25	12 30	12 35	12 45		12 55	13 00	13 05	13 15
Highbury & Islington ⊖	d	11 08	11 18		11 28	11 33	11 38	11 48		11 58	12 03	12 08	12 18		12 28	12 33	12 38	12 48		12 58	13 03	13 08	13 18
Drayton Park	d	11 10	11 20		11 30	11 35	11 40	11 50		12 00	12 05	12 10	12 20		12 30	12 35	12 40	12 50		13 00	13 05	13 10	13 20
Finsbury Park ⊖	a	11 13	11 23		11 33	11 38	11 43	11 53		12 03	12 08	12 13	12 23		12 33	12 38	12 43	12 53		13 03	13 08	13 13	13 23
Finsbury Park	d	11 14	11 24	11 31	11 33	11 39	11 44	11 54	12 01	12 03	12 09	12 14	12 24	12 31	12 33	12 39	12 44	12 54	13 01	13 03	13 09	13 14	13 24
Harringay	d	11 16	11 26			11 41	11 46	11 56			12 11	12 16	12 26			12 41	12 46	12 56			13 11	13 16	13 26
Hornsey	d	11 18	11 28			11 43	11 48	11 58			12 13	12 18	12 28			12 43	12 48	12 58			13 13	13 18	13 28
Alexandra Palace	d	11 21	11 32		11 38	11 47	11 51	12 02		12 08	12 17	12 21	12 32		12 38	12 47	12 51	13 02		13 08	13 17	13 21	13 32
New Southgate	d	11 24			11 41		11 54			12 11		12 24			12 41		12 54			13 11		13 24	
Oakleigh Park	d	11 28			11 44		11 58			12 14		12 28			12 44		12 58			13 14		13 28	
New Barnet	d	11 30			11 46		12 00			12 16		12 30			12 46		13 00			13 16		13 30	
Hadley Wood	d	11 33			11 49		12 03			12 19		12 33			12 49		13 03			13 19		13 33	
Potters Bar	d	11 37		11 42	11 53		12 07		12 13	12 23		12 37		12 43	12 53		13 07		13 13	13 23		13 37	
Brookmans Park	d				11 56					12 26					12 56					13 26			
Welham Green	d				11 59					12 29					12 59					13 29			
Hatfield	d	11 43		11 48	12 02		12 13		12 18	12 32		12 43		12 48	13 02		13 13		13 18	13 32		13 43	
Welwyn Garden City	d	11a48		11 56	12a07		12a18		12 26	12a37		12a48		12 56	13a07		13a18		13 26	13a37		13a48	
Welwyn North	d			12 00					12 30					13 00					13 30				
Knebworth	d			12 04					12 34					13 04					13 34				
Bowes Park	d		11 34			11 49		12 04			12 19		12 34			12 49		13 04			13 19		13 34
Palmers Green	d		11 37			11 52		12 07			12 22		12 37			12 52		13 07			13 22		13 37
Winchmore Hill	d		11 40			11 55		12 10			12 25		12 40			12 55		13 10			13 25		13 40
Grange Park	d		11 42			11 57		12 12			12 27		12 42			12 57		13 12			13 27		13 42
Enfield Chase	d		11 44			11 59		12 14			12 29		12 44			12 59		13 14			13 29		13 44
Gordon Hill	d		11 47			12 02		12 17			12 32		12 47			13 02		13 17			13 32		13 47
Crews Hill	d					12 05					12 35					13 05					13 35		
Cuffley	d		11 52			12 08		12 22			12 38		12 52			13 08		13 22			13 38		13 52
Bayford	d					12 12					12 42					13 12					13 42		
Hertford North	a		11 59			12 18		12 29			12 48		12 59			13 18		13 29			13 48		13 59
Watton-at-Stone	a		12 10					12 41					13 14					13 41					14 10
Stevenage	a		12 18	12 08					12 38				13 22	13 08					13 38				14 18

See Table 025 for fast trains between London and Stevenage

Table T024-F

Saturdays

26 May to 8 December

London - Welwyn Garden City and Hertford North

		TL	GN	GN	GN	GN	TL	GN	GN	GN	GN	TL	GN	GN	GN	GN	TL	GN	GN	GN	GN	TL
London Bridge	d																					
London Blackfriars	d																					
City Thameslink	d																					
Farringdon	d																					
St Pancras International	d																					
London Kings Cross ⊖	d	13 21					13 51					14 21					14 51					15 21
Finsbury Park	a	13 27					13 57					14 27					14 57					15 27
Moorgate ⊖	d		13 20	13 25	13 30	13 40		13 50	13 55	14 00	14 10		14 20	14 25	14 30	14 40		14 50	14 55	15 00	15 10	
Old Street ⊖	d		13 22	13 27	13 32	13 42		13 52	13 57	14 02	14 12		14 22	14 27	14 32	14 42		14 52	14 57	15 02	15 12	
Essex Road	d		13 25	13 30	13 35	13 45		13 55	14 00	14 05	14 15		14 25	14 30	14 35	14 45		14 55	15 00	15 05	15 15	
Highbury & Islington ⊖	d		13 28	13 33	13 38	13 48		13 58	14 03	14 08	14 18		14 28	14 33	14 38	14 48		14 58	15 03	15 08	15 18	
Drayton Park	d		13 30	13 35	13 40	13 50		14 00	14 05	14 10	14 20		14 30	14 35	14 40	14 50		15 00	15 05	15 10	15 20	
Finsbury Park ⊖	a		13 33	13 38	13 43	13 53		14 03	14 08	14 13	14 23		14 33	14 38	14 43	14 53		15 03	15 08	15 13	15 23	
Finsbury Park	d	13 31	13 33	13 39	13 44	13 54	14 01	14 03	14 09	14 14	14 24	14 31	14 33	14 39	14 44	14 54	15 01	15 03	15 09	15 14	15 24	15 31
Harringay	d			13 41	13 46	13 56			14 11	14 16	14 26			14 41	14 46	14 56			15 11	15 16	15 26	
Hornsey	d			13 43	13 48	13 58			14 13	14 18	14 28			14 43	14 48	14 58			15 13	15 18	15 28	
Alexandra Palace	d		13 38	13 47	13 51	14 02		14 08	14 17	14 21	14 32		14 38	14 47	14 51	15 02		15 08	15 17	15 21	15 32	
New Southgate	d		13 41		13 54			14 11		14 24			14 41		14 54			15 11		15 24		
Oakleigh Park	d		13 44		13 58			14 14		14 28			14 44		14 58			15 14		15 28		
New Barnet	d		13 46		14 00			14 16		14 30			14 46		15 00			15 16		15 30		
Hadley Wood	d		13 49		14 03			14 19		14 33			14 49		15 03			15 19		15 33		
Potters Bar	d	13 43	13 53		14 07		14 13	14 23		14 37		14 43	14 53		15 07		15 13	15 23		15 37		15 43
Brookmans Park	d		13 56					14 26					14 56					15 26				
Welham Green	d		13 59					14 29					14 59					15 29				
Hatfield	d	13 48	14 02		14 13		14 18	14 32		14 43		14 48	15 02		15 13		15 18	15 32		15 43		15 48
Welwyn Garden City	d	13 56	14a07		14a18		14 26	14a37		14a48		14 56	15a07		15a18		15 26	15a37		15a48		15 56
Welwyn North	d	14 00					14 30					15 00					15 30					16 00
Knebworth	d	14 04					14 34					15 04					15 34					16 04
Bowes Park	d			13 49		14 04			14 19		14 34			14 49		15 04			15 19		15 34	
Palmers Green	d			13 52		14 07			14 22		14 37			14 52		15 07			15 22		15 37	
Winchmore Hill	d			13 55		14 10			14 25		14 40			14 55		15 10			15 25		15 40	
Grange Park	d			13 57		14 12			14 27		14 42			14 57		15 12			15 27		15 42	
Enfield Chase	d			13 59		14 14			14 29		14 44			14 59		15 14			15 29		15 44	
Gordon Hill	d			14 02		14 17			14 32		14 47			15 02		15 17			15 32		15 47	
Crews Hill	d			14 05					14 35					15 05					15 35			
Cuffley	d			14 08		14 22			14 38		14 52			15 08		15 22			15 38		15 52	
Bayford	d			14 12					14 42					15 12					15 42			
Hertford North	a			14 18		14 29			14 48		14 59			15 18		15 29			15 48		15 59	
Watton-at-Stone	a					14 41					15 13					15 41					16 10	
Stevenage	a	14 08					14 38				15 21	15 08					15 38				16 18	16 08

		GN	GN	GN	GN	TL	GN	GN	GN	GN	TL	GN	GN		GN	GN	TL	GN	GN	GN	GN	TL	GN	GN
London Bridge	d																							
London Blackfriars	d																							
City Thameslink	d																							
Farringdon	d																							
St Pancras International	d																							
London Kings Cross ⊖	d					15 51					16 21						21 51					22 21		
Finsbury Park	a					15 57					16 27						21 57					22 27		
Moorgate ⊖	d	15 20	15 25	15 30	15 40		15 50	15 55	16 00	16 10		16 20	16 25		21 30	21 40		21 50	21 55	22 00	22 10		22 20	22 25
Old Street ⊖	d	15 22	15 27	15 32	15 42		15 52	15 57	16 02	16 12		16 22	16 27		21 32	21 42		21 52	21 57	22 02	22 12		22 22	22 27
Essex Road	d	15 25	15 30	15 35	15 45		15 55	16 00	16 05	16 15		16 25	16 30		21 35	21 45		21 55	22 00	22 05	22 15		22 25	22 30
Highbury & Islington ⊖	d	15 28	15 33	15 38	15 48		15 58	16 03	16 08	16 18		16 28	16 33		21 38	21 48		21 58	22 03	22 08	22 18		22 28	22 33
Drayton Park	d	15 30	15 35	15 40	15 50		16 00	16 05	16 10	16 20		16 30	16 35		21 40	21 50		22 00	22 05	22 10	22 20		22 30	22 35
Finsbury Park ⊖	a	15 33	15 38	15 43	15 53		16 03	16 08	16 13	16 23		16 33	16 38		21 43	21 53		22 03	22 08	22 13	22 23		22 33	22 38
Finsbury Park	d	15 33	15 39	15 44	15 54	16 01	16 03	16 09	16 14	16 24	16 31	16 33	16 39		21 44	21 54	22 01	22 03	22 09	22 14	22 24	22 31	22 33	22 39
Harringay	d		15 41	15 46	15 56			16 11	16 16	16 26			16 41		21 46	21 56			22 11	22 16	22 26			22 41
Hornsey	d		15 43	15 48	15 58			16 13	16 18	16 28			16 43		21 48	21 58			22 13	22 18	22 28			22 43
Alexandra Palace	d	15 38	15 47	15 51	16 02		16 08	16 17	16 21	16 32		16 38	16 47	and at the same minutes past each hour until	21 51	22 02		22 08	22 17	22 21	22 32		22 38	22 47
New Southgate	d	15 41		15 54			16 11		16 24			16 41			21 54			22 11		22 24			22 41	
Oakleigh Park	d	15 44		15 58			16 14		16 28			16 44			21 58			22 14		22 28			22 44	
New Barnet	d	15 46		16 00			16 16		16 30			16 46			22 00			22 16		22 30			22 46	
Hadley Wood	d	15 49		16 03			16 19		16 33			16 49			22 03			22 19		22 33			22 49	
Potters Bar	d	15 53		16 07		16 13	16 23		16 37		16 43	16 53			22 07		22 13	22 23		22 37		22 43	22 53	
Brookmans Park	d	15 56					16 26					16 56						22 26					22 56	
Welham Green	d	15 59					16 29					16 59						22 29					22 59	
Hatfield	d	16 02		16 13		16 18	16 32		16 43		16 48	17 02			22 13		22 18	22 32		22 43		22 48	23 02	
Welwyn Garden City	d	16a07		16a18		16 26	16a37		16a48		16 56	17a07			22a18		22 26	22a37		22a48		22 56	23a07	
Welwyn North	d					16 30					17 00						22 30					23 00		
Knebworth	d					16 34					17 04						22 34					23 04		
Bowes Park	d		15 49		16 04			16 19		16 34			16 49			22 04			22 19		22 34			22 49
Palmers Green	d		15 52		16 07			16 22		16 37			16 52			22 07			22 22		22 37			22 52
Winchmore Hill	d		15 55		16 10			16 25		16 40			16 55			22 10			22 25		22 40			22 55
Grange Park	d		15 57		16 12			16 27		16 42			16 57			22 12			22 27		22 42			22 57
Enfield Chase	d		15 59		16 14			16 29		16 44			16 59			22 14			22 29		22 44			22 59
Gordon Hill	d		16 01		16 17			16 32		16 47			17 02			22 17			22 32		22 47			23 02
Crews Hill	d		16 04					16 35					17 05						22 35					23 05
Cuffley	d		16 08		16 22			16 38		16 52			17 08			22 22			22 38		22 52			23 08
Bayford	d		16 12					16 42					17 12						22 42					23 12
Hertford North	a		16 18		16 29			16 48		16 59			17 18			22 29			22 48		22 59			23 18
Watton-at-Stone	a				16 41					17 10						22 41					23 10			
Stevenage	a					16 38				17 18	17 08						22 38				23 18	23 08		

See Table 025 for fast trains between London and Stevenage

Table T024-F

London - Welwyn Garden City and Hertford North

Saturdays
26 May to 8 December

Station		GN	GN	TL ■	GN	GN	GN	GN	TL ■	GN	GN	GN	TL ■	GN	GN
London Bridge	d														
London Blackfriars	d														
City Thameslink	d														
Farringdon	d														
St Pancras International	d														
London Kings Cross ⊖	d			22 51					23 21				23 51		
Finsbury Park	a			22 57					23 27				23 57		
Moorgate ⊖	d	22 30	22 40		22 50	22 55	23 00	23 10		23 20	23 27	23 37		23 47	23 57
Old Street ⊖	d	22 32	22 42		22 52	22 57	23 02	23 12		23 22	23 29	23 39		23 49	23 59
Essex Road	d	22 35	22 45		22 55	23 00	23 05	23 15		23 25	23 32	23 42		23 52	00 02
Highbury & Islington ⊖	d	22 38	22 48		22 58	23 03	23 08	23 18		23 28	23 35	23 45		23 55	00 05
Drayton Park	d	22 40	22 50		23 00	23 05	23 10	23 20		23 30	23 37	23 47		23 57	00 07
Finsbury Park ⊖	a	22 43	22 53		23 03	23 08	23 13	23 23		23 33	23 40	23 50		23 59	00 10
Finsbury Park	d	22 44	22 54	23 01	23 03	23 08	23 14	23 24	23 31	23 33	23 41	23 53	00 01	00 03	00 11
Harringay	d	22 46	22 56			23 11	23 16	23 26		23 36	23 44	23 56		00 06	00 14
Hornsey	d	22 48	22 58			23 13	23 18	23 28		23 38	23 46	23 58		00 08	00 16
Alexandra Palace	d	22 51	23 02		23 08	23 16	23 21	23 32		23 41	23 49	00 01		00 11	00 19
New Southgate	d	22 54			23 11		23 24				23 52				00 22
Oakleigh Park	d	22 58			23 14		23 28				23 55				00 25
New Barnet	d	23 00			23 16		23 30				23 58				00 28
Hadley Wood	d	23 03			23 19		23 33				00 01				00 31
Potters Bar	d	23 07		23 13	23 23		23 37		23 43		00 05		00 13		00 35
Brookmans Park	d				23 26		23 40				00 08				00 38
Welham Green	d				23 29		23 43				00 11				00 41
Hatfield	d	23 13		23 18	23 32		23 46		23 50		00 14		00 18		00 44
Welwyn Garden City	d	23a18		23 26	23a37		23a51		23 57		00a19		00 28		00a49
Welwyn North	d			23 30					00 01				00 31		
Knebworth	d			23 34					00 05				00 35		
Bowes Park	d		23 04			23 18		23 34		23 44		00 04		00 14	
Palmers Green	d		23 07			23 21		23 37		23 46		00 06		00 16	
Winchmore Hill	d		23 10			23 24		23 40		23 49		00 09		00 19	
Grange Park	d		23 12			23 26		23 42		23 51		00 11		00 21	
Enfield Chase	d		23 14			23 28		23 44		23 53		00 13		00 23	
Gordon Hill	d		23 17			23 31		23 47		23 56		00 16		00 26	
Crews Hill	d					23 34				23 59		00 19			
Cuffley	d		23 22			23 37		23 52		00 02		00 22		00 30	
Bayford	d					23 41				00 06		00 26			
Hertford North	a		23 29			23 47		00 01		00 11		00 31		00 39	
Watton-at-Stone	a		23 37							00 17		00 37			
Stevenage	a			23 38					00 09	00 25		00 45	00 39		

Sundays
20 May to 2 December

Station		TL ■ A	GN A	GN A	GN	TL ■	GN	GN	TL ■ A	TL ■	GN	GN	GN B	GN C	GN B	GN C	GN	GN B	GN C	GN ■	GN	GN B	GN C
London Bridge	d																						
London Blackfriars	d								00 37														
City Thameslink	d																						
Farringdon	d								00 41														
St Pancras International	d								00 46														
London Kings Cross ⊖	d					00 23				01 05	01 09	01 40	05 54	05 54	06 24	06 24	06 36	06 54	06 54	07 02			
Finsbury Park	a					00 28			00 52	01 10	01 14	01 46	05 59	05 59	06 29	06 29	06 41	06 59	06 59	07 08			
Moorgate ⊖	d				00 07		00 17	00 27													07 01	07 18	07 18
Old Street ⊖	d				00 09		00 19	00 29													07 03	07 20	07 20
Essex Road	d			00 02	00 12		00 22	00 32													07 06	07 23	07 23
Highbury & Islington ⊖	d			00 05	00 15		00 25	00 35													07 09	07 26	07 26
Drayton Park	d			00 07	00 17		00 27	00 37													07 11	07 28	07 28
Finsbury Park ⊖	a			00 10	00 20		00 30	00 40													07 13	07 30	07 30
Finsbury Park	d	00 01	00 03	00 11	00 23	00 29	00 32	00 41	00 54	01 11	01 16	01 47	06 00	06 00	06 30	06 30	06 42	07 00	07 00	07 09	07 14	07 31	07 31
Harringay	d		00 06	00 14	00 26		00 34				01 18		06 03	06 03	06 33	06 33	06 45	07 03	07 03		07 17	07 34	07 34
Hornsey	d		00 08	00 16	00 28		00 36				01 20		06 05	06 05	06 35	06 35	06 47	07 05	07 05		07 19	07 36	07 36
Alexandra Palace	d		00 11	00 19	00 31		00 40	00 45			01 24	01 51	06a08	06 08	06a38	06 38	06 50	07a08	07 08		07 22	07a39	07 39
New Southgate	d			00 22								01 54					06 53				07 25		
Oakleigh Park	d			00 25								01 57					06 56				07 28		
New Barnet	d			00 28				00 51				02 00					06 58				07 31		
Hadley Wood	d			00 31				00 54				02 02					07 01				07 34		
Potters Bar	d	00 13		00 35		00 42		00 58		01 22		02 06					07 05			07 20	07 38		
Brookmans Park	d			00 38													07 08				07 41		
Welham Green	d			00 41													07 11				07 43		
Hatfield	d	00 18		00 44		00 48		01 04		01 28		02 12					07 14			07 26	07 47		
Welwyn Garden City	d	00 28		00a49		00 58		01a09	01 13	01 34		02a18					07a22			07 31	07a55		
Welwyn North	d	00 31				01 01				01 37										07 34			
Knebworth	d	00 35				01 05				01 41										07 38			
Bowes Park	d		00 14		00 34		00 43				01 26			06 10		06 40			07 10				07 41
Palmers Green	d		00 16		00 36		00 45				01 29			06 13		06 43			07 13				07 44
Winchmore Hill	d		00 19		00 39		00 48				01 32			06 16		06 46			07 16				07 47
Grange Park	d		00 21		00 41		00 50				01 34			06 18		06 48			07 18				07 49
Enfield Chase	d		00 23		00 43		00 52				01 36			06 20		06 50			07 20				07 51
Gordon Hill	d		00 26		00 46		00 55				01 38			06 23		06 53			07 23				07 54
Crews Hill	d				00 49		00 58							06 26		06 56			07 26				07 57
Cuffley	d		00 30		00 52		01 01				01 43			06 29		06 59			07 29				08 00
Bayford	d				00 56		01 06							06 33		07 03			07 33				08 04
Hertford North	a		00 39		01 02		01 10				01 52			06 39		07 08			07 38				08 09
Watton-at-Stone	a						01 18									07 14			07 44				08 15
Stevenage	a	00 39				01 09	01 25		01 21	01 45						07 22			07 52	07 43			08 23

A not 20 May
B from 28 October
C until 21 October

See Table 025 for fast trains between London and Stevenage

Table T024-F

London - Welwyn Garden City and Hertford North

Sundays
20 May to 2 December

Station		GN	GN A	GN B	GN ■	GN	GN A	GN B	GN	GN A	GN B	GN ■	GN	GN	GN B	GN	GN		GN B	GN ■	GN	GN	GN B
London Bridge	d																						
London Blackfriars	d																						
City Thameslink	d																						
Farringdon	d																						
St Pancras International	d																						
London Kings Cross ⊖	d				08 02							09 02								15 02			
Finsbury Park	a				08 08							09 08								15 08			
Moorgate ⊖	d	07 31	07 48	07 48		08 01	08 17	08 17	08 31	08 47	08 47		08 57	09 07	09 17	09 27	09 37		14 47		14 57	15 07	15 17
Old Street ⊖	d	07 33	07 50	07 50		08 03	08 19	08 19	08 33	08 49	08 49		08 59	09 09	09 19	09 29	09 39		14 49		14 59	15 09	15 19
Essex Road	d	07 36	07 53	07 53		08 06	08 22	08 22	08 36	08 52	08 52		09 02	09 12	09 22	09 32	09 42		14 52		15 02	15 12	15 22
Highbury & Islington ⊖	d	07 39	07 56	07 56		08 09	08 25	08 25	08 39	08 55	08 55		09 05	09 15	09 25	09 35	09 45		14 55		15 05	15 15	15 25
Drayton Park	d	07 41	07 58	07 58		08 11	08 27	08 27	08 41	08 57	08 57		09 07	09 17	09 27	09 37	09 47		14 57		15 07	15 17	15 27
Finsbury Park ⊖	a	07 43	08 00	08 00		08 13	08 29	08 29	08 43	08 59	08 59		09 09	09 19	09 29	09 39	09 49		14 59		15 09	15 19	15 29
Finsbury Park	d	07 44	08 01	08 01	08 09	08 14	08 30	08 30	08 44	09 00	09 00	09 09	09 10	09 20	09 30	09 40	09 50		15 00	15 09	15 10	15 20	15 30
Harringay	d	07 47	08 04	08 04		08 17	08 33	08 33	08 47	09 03	09 03		09 13	09 23	09 33	09 43	09 53		15 03		15 13	15 23	15 33
Hornsey	d	07 49	08 06	08 06		08 19	08 35	08 35	08 49	09 05	09 05		09 15	09 25	09 35	09 45	09 55	and at	15 05		15 15	15 25	15 35
Alexandra Palace	d	07 52	08a09	08 09		08 22	08a38	08 38	08 52	09a08	09 08		09 18	09 28	09 38	09 48	09 58	the same	15 08		15 18	15 28	15 38
New Southgate	d	07 55				08 25			08 55				09 21	09 31		09 51	10 01	minutes			15 21	15 31	
Oakleigh Park	d	07 58				08 28			08 58				09 24	09 34		09 54	10 04	past			15 24	15 34	
New Barnet	d	08 01				08 31			09 01				09 27	09 37		09 57	10 07	each			15 27	15 37	
Hadley Wood	d	08 04				08 34			09 04				09 30	09 40		10 00	10 10	hour until			15 30	15 40	
Potters Bar	d	08 08			08 20	08 38			09 08			09 20	09 34	09 44		10 04	10 14			15 20	15 34	15 44	
Brookmans Park	d	08 11				08 41			09 11				09 37			10 07					15 37		
Welham Green	d	08 13				08 43			09 13				09 39			10 09					15 39		
Hatfield	d	08 17			08 26	08 47			09 17			09 26	09 43	09 50		10 13	10 20			15 26	15 43	15 50	
Welwyn Garden City	d	08a25			08 31	08a52			09a22			09 31	09a48	09a55		10a18	10a25			15 31	15a48	15a55	
Welwyn North	d				08 34							09 34								15 34			
Knebworth	d				08 38							09 38								15 38			
Bowes Park	d			08 11				08 40			09 10				09 40				15 10				15 40
Palmers Green	d			08 14				08 43			09 13				09 43				15 13				15 43
Winchmore Hill	d			08 16				08 46			09 16				09 46				15 16				15 46
Grange Park	d			08 18				08 48			09 18				09 48				15 18				15 48
Enfield Chase	d			08 21				08 50			09 20				09 50				15 20				15 50
Gordon Hill	d			08 23				08 53			09 23				09 53				15 23				15 53
Crews Hill	d			08 26				08 56			09 26				09 56				15 26				15 56
Cuffley	d			08 29				08 59			09 29				09 59				15 29				15 59
Bayford	d			08 34				09 03			09 33				10 03				15 33				16 03
Hertford North	a			08 38				09 08			09 38				10 08				15 38				16 08
Watton-at-Stone	a			08 45				09 14			09 44				10 14				15 44				16 14
Stevenage	a			08 52	08 43			09 22			09 52	09 43			10 22				15 52	15 43			16 22

Station		GN	GN	GN B	GN ■	GN	GN	GN B	GN ■	GN	GN	GN B	GN ■	GN	GN	GN B	GN ■	GN	GN	GN B	GN ■	GN
London Bridge	d																					
London Blackfriars	d																					
City Thameslink	d																					
Farringdon	d																					
St Pancras International	d																					
London Kings Cross ⊖	d				16 02				16 32				17 02				17 32				18 02	
Finsbury Park	a				16 08				16 38				17 08				17 38				18 08	
Moorgate ⊖	d	15 27	15 37	15 47		15 57	16 07	16 17		16 27	16 37	16 47		16 57	17 07	17 17		17 27	17 37	17 47		17 57
Old Street ⊖	d	15 29	15 39	15 49		15 59	16 09	16 19		16 29	16 39	16 49		16 59	17 09	17 19		17 29	17 39	17 49		17 59
Essex Road	d	15 32	15 42	15 52		16 02	16 12	16 22		16 32	16 42	16 52		17 02	17 12	17 22		17 32	17 42	17 52		18 02
Highbury & Islington ⊖	d	15 35	15 45	15 55		16 05	16 15	16 25		16 35	16 45	16 55		17 05	17 15	17 25		17 35	17 45	17 55		18 05
Drayton Park	d	15 37	15 47	15 57		16 07	16 17	16 27		16 37	16 47	16 57		17 07	17 17	17 27		17 37	17 47	17 57		18 07
Finsbury Park ⊖	a	15 39	15 49	15 59		16 09	16 19	16 29		16 39	16 49	16 59		17 09	17 19	17 29		17 39	17 49	17 59		18 09
Finsbury Park	d	15 40	15 50	16 00	16 09	16 10	16 20	16 30	16 39	16 40	16 50	17 00	17 09	17 10	17 20	17 30	17 39	17 40	17 50	18 00	18 09	18 10
Harringay	d	15 43	15 53	16 03		16 13	16 23	16 33		16 43	16 53	17 03		17 13	17 23	17 33		17 43	17 53	18 03		18 13
Hornsey	d	15 45	15 55	16 05		16 15	16 25	16 35		16 45	16 55	17 05		17 15	17 25	17 35		17 45	17 55	18 05		18 15
Alexandra Palace	d	15 48	15 58	16 08		16 18	16 28	16 38		16 48	16 58	17 08		17 18	17 28	17 38		17 48	17 58	18 08		18 18
New Southgate	d	15 51	16 01			16 21	16 31			16 51	17 01			17 21	17 31			17 51	18 01			18 21
Oakleigh Park	d	15 54	16 04			16 24	16 34			16 54	17 04			17 24	17 34			17 54	18 04			18 24
New Barnet	d	15 57	16 07			16 27	16 37			16 57	17 07			17 27	17 37			17 57	18 07			18 27
Hadley Wood	d	16 00	16 10			16 30	16 40			17 00	17 10			17 30	17 40			18 00	18 10			18 30
Potters Bar	d	16 04	16 14		16 20	16 34	16 44		16 50	17 04	17 14		17 20	17 34	17 44		17 50	18 04	18 14		18 20	18 34
Brookmans Park	d	16 07				16 37				17 07				17 37				18 07				18 37
Welham Green	d	16 09				16 39				17 09				17 39				18 09				18 39
Hatfield	d	16 13	16 20		16 26	16 43	16 50		16 56	17 13	17 20		17 26	17 43	17 50		17 56	18 13	18 20		18 26	18 43
Welwyn Garden City	d	16a18	16a25		16 31	16a48	16a55		17 01	17a18	17a25		17 31	17a48	17a55		18 01	18a18	18a25		18 31	18a48
Welwyn North	d				16 34				17 04				17 34				18 05				18 34	
Knebworth	d				16 38				17 08				17 38				18 09				18 38	
Bowes Park	d			16 10				16 40				17 10				17 40				18 10		
Palmers Green	d			16 13				16 43				17 13				17 43				18 13		
Winchmore Hill	d			16 16				16 46				17 16				17 46				18 16		
Grange Park	d			16 18				16 48				17 18				17 48				18 18		
Enfield Chase	d			16 20				16 50				17 20				17 50				18 20		
Gordon Hill	d			16 23				16 53				17 23				17 53				18 23		
Crews Hill	d			16 26				16 56				17 26				17 56				18 26		
Cuffley	d			16 29				16 59				17 29				17 59				18 29		
Bayford	d			16 33				17 03				17 33				18 03				18 33		
Hertford North	a			16 38				17 08				17 38				18 08				18 38		
Watton-at-Stone	a			16 44				17 14				17 44				18 14				18 44		
Stevenage	a			16 52	16 43			17 22	17 13			17 52	17 43			18 22	18 14			18 52	18 43	

A from 28 October
B until 21 October

See Table 025 for fast trains between London and Stevenage

Table T024-F

Sundays
20 May to 2 December

London - Welwyn Garden City and Hertford North

	GN	GN A	GN ■	GN	GN	GN A	GN ■	GN	GN	GN A	GN	GN	GN A	GN ■	GN	GN	GN A	GN	GN	GN A	GN ■	GN
London Bridge d																						
London Blackfriars d																						
City Thameslink d																						
Farringdon d																						
St Pancras International d																						
London Kings Cross ⊖ d			18 32				19 02							20 02							21 02	
Finsbury Park a			18 38				19 08							20 08							21 08	
Moorgate ⊖ d	18 07	18 17		18 27	18 37	18 47		18 57	19 07	19 17	19 27	19 37	19 47		19 57	20 07	20 17	20 27	20 37	20 47		20 57
Old Street ⊖ d	18 09	18 19		18 29	18 39	18 49		18 59	19 09	19 19	19 29	19 39	19 49		19 59	20 09	20 19	20 29	20 39	20 49		20 59
Essex Road d	18 12	18 22		18 32	18 42	18 52		19 02	19 12	19 22	19 32	19 42	19 52		20 02	20 12	20 22	20 32	20 42	20 52		21 02
Highbury & Islington ⊖ d	18 15	18 25		18 35	18 45	18 55		19 05	19 15	19 25	19 35	19 45	19 55		20 05	20 15	20 25	20 35	20 45	20 55		21 05
Drayton Park d	18 17	18 27		18 37	18 47	18 57		19 07	19 17	19 27	19 37	19 47	19 57		20 07	20 17	20 27	20 37	20 47	20 57		21 07
Finsbury Park ⊖ a	18 19	18 29		18 39	18 49	18 59		19 09	19 19	19 29	19 39	19 49	19 59		20 09	20 19	20 29	20 39	20 49	20 59		21 09
Finsbury Park d	18 20	18 30	18 39	18 40	18 50	19 00	19 09	19 10	19 20	19 30	19 40	19 50	20 00	20 09	20 10	20 20	20 30	20 40	20 50	21 00	21 09	21 10
Harringay d	18 23	18 33		18 43	18 53	19 03		19 13	19 23	19 33	19 43	19 53	20 03		20 13	20 23	20 33	20 43	20 53	21 03		21 13
Hornsey d	18 25	18 35		18 45	18 55	19 05		19 15	19 25	19 35	19 45	19 55	20 05		20 15	20 25	20 35	20 45	20 55	21 05		21 15
Alexandra Palace d	18 28	18 38		18 48	18 58	19 08		19 18	19 28	19 38	19 48	19 58	20 08		20 18	20 28	20 38	20 48	20 58	21 08		21 18
New Southgate d	18 31			18 51	19 01			19 21	19 31		19 51	20 01			20 21	20 31		20 51	21 01			21 21
Oakleigh Park d	18 34			18 54	19 04			19 24	19 34		19 54	20 04			20 24	20 34		20 54	21 04			21 24
New Barnet d	18 37			18 57	19 07			19 27	19 37		19 57	20 07			20 27	20 37		20 57	21 07			21 27
Hadley Wood d	18 40			19 00	19 10			19 30	19 40		20 00	20 10			20 30	20 40		21 00	21 10			21 30
Potters Bar d	18 44		18 50	19 04	19 14		19 20	19 34	19 44		20 04	20 14		20 20	20 34	20 44		21 04	21 14		21 20	21 34
Brookmans Park d				19 07				19 37			20 07				20 37			21 07				21 37
Welham Green d				19 09				19 39			20 09				20 39			21 09				21 39
Hatfield d	18 50		18 56	19 13	19 20		19 26	19 43	19 50		20 13	20 20		20 26	20 43	20 50		21 13	21 20		21 26	21 43
Welwyn Garden City ■ d	18a55		19 01	19a18	19a25		19 31	19a48	19a55		20a18	20a25		20 31	20a48	20a55		21a18	21a25		21 31	21a48
Welwyn North d			19 04				19 34							20 34							21 34	
Knebworth d			19 08				19 38							20 38							21 38	
Bowes Park d		18 40				19 10				19 40			20 10				20 40			21 10		
Palmers Green d		18 43				19 13				19 43			20 13				20 43			21 13		
Winchmore Hill d		18 46				19 16				19 46			20 16				20 46			21 16		
Grange Park d		18 48				19 18				19 48			20 18				20 48			21 18		
Enfield Chase d		18 50				19 20				19 50			20 20				20 50			21 20		
Gordon Hill d		18 53				19 23				19 53			20 23				20 53			21 23		
Crews Hill d		18 56				19 26				19 56			20 26				20 56			21 26		
Cuffley d		18 59				19 29				19 59			20 29				20 59			21 29		
Bayford d		19 03				19 33				20 03			20 33				21 03			21 33		
Hertford North a		19 08				19 38				20 08			20 38				21 08			21 38		
Watton-at-Stone a		19 14				19 44				20 14			20 44				21 14			21 44		
Stevenage ■ a		19 22	19 13			19 52	19 43			20 22			20 52	20 43			21 22			21 52	21 43	

	GN	GN A	GN	GN	GN A	GN ■	GN	GN B	GN A	GN	GN B	GN A	GN ■	GN	GN A	GN B	GN	GN A	GN B	GN
London Bridge d																				
London Blackfriars d																				
City Thameslink d																				
Farringdon d																				
St Pancras International d																				
London Kings Cross ⊖ d						22 02							23 02							
Finsbury Park a						22 08							23 08							
Moorgate ⊖ d	21 07	21 17	21 27	21 37	21 47		21 57	22 17	22 17	22 27	22 47	22 47		22 57	23 17	23 17	23 27	23 47	23 47	23 57
Old Street ⊖ d	21 09	21 19	21 29	21 39	21 49		21 59	22 19	22 19	22 29	22 49	22 49		22 59	23 19	23 19	23 29	23 49	23 49	23 59
Essex Road d	21 12	21 22	21 32	21 42	21 52		22 02	22 22	22 22	22 32	22 52	22 52		23 02	23 22	23 22	23 32	23 52	23 52	00 02
Highbury & Islington ⊖ d	21 15	21 25	21 35	21 45	21 55		22 05	22 25	22 25	22 35	22 55	22 55		23 05	23 25	23 25	23 35	23 55	23 55	00 05
Drayton Park d	21 17	21 27	21 37	21 47	21 57		22 07	22 27	22 27	22 37	22 57	22 57		23 07	23 27	23 27	23 37	23 57	23 57	00 07
Finsbury Park ⊖ a	21 19	21 29	21 39	21 49	21 59		22 09	22 29	22 29	22 39	22 59	22 59		23 09	23 29	23 29	23 39	23 59	23 59	00 09
Finsbury Park d	21 20	21 30	21 40	21 50	22 00	22 09	22 10	22 30	22 30	22 40	23 00	23 00	23 09	23 10	23 30	23 30	23 40	00 01	00 01	00 10
Harringay d	21 23	21 33	21 43	21 53	22 03		22 13	22 33	22 33	22 43	23 03	23 03		23 13	23 33	23 33	23 43	00 03	00 03	00 13
Hornsey d	21 25	21 35	21 45	21 55	22 05		22 15	22 35	22 35	22 45	23 05	23 05		23 15	23 35	23 35	23 45	00 05	00 05	00 15
Alexandra Palace d	21 28	21 38	21 48	21 58	22 08		22 18	22a38	22 38	22 48	23a08	23 08		23 18	23 38	23a38	23 48	00 08	00a09	00 18
New Southgate d	21 31		21 51	22 01			22 21			22 51				23 21			23 51			00 21
Oakleigh Park d	21 34		21 54	22 04			22 24			22 54				23 24			23 54			00 24
New Barnet d	21 37		21 57	22 07			22 27			22 57				23 27			23 56			00 27
Hadley Wood d	21 40		22 00	22 10			22 30			23 00				23 30			23 59			00 30
Potters Bar d	21 44		22 04	22 14		22 20	22 34			23 04			23 20	23 34			00 04			00 34
Brookmans Park d			22 07				22 37			23 07				23 37			00 07			00 37
Welham Green d			22 09				22 39			23 09				23 39			00 09			00 39
Hatfield d	21 50		22 13	22 20		22 26	22 43			23 13			23 26	23 43			00 13			00 43
Welwyn Garden City ■ d	21a55		22a18	22a25		22 31	22a48			23a18			23 31	23a48			00a21			00a51
Welwyn North d						22 34							23 34							
Knebworth d						22 38							23 38							
Bowes Park d		21 40			22 10				22 40			23 10			23 40			00 10		
Palmers Green d		21 43			22 13				22 43			23 13			23 43			00 13		
Winchmore Hill d		21 46			22 16				22 46			23 16			23 46			00 16		
Grange Park d		21 48			22 18				22 48			23 18			23 48			00 18		
Enfield Chase d		21 50			22 20				22 50			23 20			23 50			00 20		
Gordon Hill d		21 53			22 23				22 53			23 23			23 53			00 23		
Crews Hill d		21 56			22 26				22 56			23 26			23 56			00 26		
Cuffley d		21 59			22 29				22 59			23 29			23 59			00 29		
Bayford d		22 03			22 33				23 03			23 33			00 03			00 33		
Hertford North a		22 08			22 38				23 08			23 38			00 09			00 38		
Watton-at-Stone a		22 14			22 44				23 14			23 44						00 44		
Stevenage ■ a		22 22			22 52	22 42			23 22			23 52	23 43					00 52		

A until 21 October **B** from 28 October

See Table 025 for fast trains between London and Stevenage

Table T024-R

Mondays to Fridays
21 May to 7 December

Hertford North and Welwyn Garden City - London

Miles	Miles		GN MO	GN MX	GN MX	GN	GN MX	TL MX ■	GN MX	GN MO A	GN MO B	GN MX	GN MO A	GN MO B	GN MO A 🚌	GN	GN MO ■	GN	GN MO A	GN MO A 🚌	TL MX ■	GN MO
—	—	Stevenage d															00 07				00 16	
—	12¾	**Watton-at-Stone** d																				
16½	—	**Hertford North** d																				
—	19½	**Bayford** d																				
—	23	**Cuffley** d																		00 09		
—	24¾	**Crews Hill** d																		00 17		
—	26¼	**Gordon Hill** d																		00 27		
—	27	**Enfield Chase** d									00 01	00 01			00 03					00s33		
—	27¾	**Grange Park** d									00 03	00 03			00 08					00s38		
—	28½	**Winchmore Hill** d									00 05	00 05			00 14					00s44		
—	29½	**Palmers Green** d									00 07	00 08		←	00 22					00s52		
—	30½	**Bowes Park** a									00 10	00 10		00 10	00 32					01s02		
9¾	—	**Knebworth** d									→						00 10				00 19	
12¾	—	**Welwyn North** d															00 14				00 23	
14½	—	**Welwyn Garden City** ■ d															00 19				00 28	
17	—	**Hatfield** d															00 23				00 31	
19¼	—	**Welham Green** d																				
20¼	—	**Brookmans Park** d																				
22	—	**Potters Bar** d						00 02									00 29				00 38	
24¼	—	**Hadley Wood** d																				
25½	—	**New Barnet** d																				
26¼	—	**Oakleigh Park** d																				
28¼	—	**New Southgate** a																				
29¾	31¼	**Alexandra Palace** d					00 04			00 13		00 13		00 14	00a37				00 43	01a07		
30¾	32¼	**Hornsey** d					00 06			00 15		00 16		00 16					00s45			
31¼	32¾	**Harringay** d					00 08			00 17		00 18	←	00 18					00s47			
32¼	33¾	Finsbury Park ⊖ a					00 11	00 15		00 23		00 20	00 23	00 24			00 39		00s50		00 51	
—	—	Finsbury Park d			00 01		00 11			00 24		00 21	00 24	00 25								
—	34½	**Drayton Park** d			00 04	00 07	00 14		00 17	→		00 24	00 26	00 27		00 27		00 37				00 58
—	35	**Highbury & Islington** ⊖ d			00 07		00 17					00 27	00 29	00 30								
—	35½	**Essex Road** d			00 09		00 19					00 29	00 31	00 32								
—	36¾	**Old Street** ⊖ d	00 01	00 02	00 12		00 22					00 32	00 34	00 35								
—	37¼	**Moorgate** ⊖ a	00 05	00 06	00 16		00 26					00 36	00 38	00 39								
—	—	Finsbury Park d				00a10		00 15	00a20							00a29	00 40	00a40			00 51	01a00
34¾	—	London Kings Cross ⊖ a						00 21									00 49		01 00		00 57	
—	—	St Pancras International d																				
—	—	Farringdon d																				
—	—	City Thameslink d																				
—	—	London Blackfriars a																				
—	—	London Bridge a																				

	GN MO A	GN MO A 🚌	GN MO A	GN	GN	GN	GN	GN	GN	TL ■	TL ■	GN	GN	GN	GN	GN	GN	GN	GN	TL ■	GN	GN
Stevenage d					04 22				05 02	05 06	05 13								05 32	05 40		
Watton-at-Stone d									05 09										05 39			
Hertford North d		00 09			04 33				05 15						05 33				05 48			
Bayford d		00s24							05 20						05 38				05 52			
Cuffley d		00s39			04 40				05 24						05 42				05 57			
Crews Hill d		00s47							05 27						05 45				06 00			
Gordon Hill d		00s57			04 45				05 31						05 49				06 03			
Enfield Chase d		01s03			04 47				05 33						05 51				06 05			
Grange Park d		01s08							05 35						05 53				06 07			
Winchmore Hill d		01s14			04 50				05 37						05 55				06 10			
Palmers Green d		01s22			04 53				05 40						05 58				06 12			
Bowes Park a		01s32							05 42						06 00				06 15			
Knebworth d										05 09										05 43		
Welwyn North d										05 13										05 47		
Welwyn Garden City ■ d				04 00		05 00				05 18	05 22	05 24	05 32				05 38			05 52	06 02	
Hatfield d				04 04		05 05				05 21		05 29	05 37				05 43			05 55	06 07	
Welham Green d				04 08								05 32					05 47					
Brookmans Park d				04 10								05 35					05 49					
Potters Bar d				04 14		05 11				05 28		05 38	05 43				05 53			06 02	06 13	
Hadley Wood d				04 17								05 42					05 56					
New Barnet d				04 20		05 16						05 45	05 48				05 59				06 18	
Oakleigh Park d				04 22		05 18						05 47	05 50				06 01				06 20	
New Southgate a				04 25		05 21						05 50	05 53				06 04				06 23	
Alexandra Palace d	01 13	01a37	01 43	04 30	04 57				05 45			05 53			06 03		06 10		06 18			
Hornsey d	01s15		01s45	04 32	04 59				05 48			05 56			06 06				06 20			
Harringay d	01s17		01s47	04 34	05 01				05 50			05 58			06 08				06 22			
Finsbury Park ⊖ a	01s20		01s50	04 39	05 04	05 29			05 52	05 41	05 35	06 00	05 59		06 10		06 14		06 25	06 13	06 28	
Finsbury Park d							05 41		05 55			06 01			06 11		06 16		06 26			
Drayton Park d							05 44	05 47	05 58			06 04		06 07	06 14	06 17	06 19	06 27	06 29			06 37
Highbury & Islington ⊖ d							05 46		06 01			06 07			06 17		06 22		06 31			
Essex Road d							05 48		06 03			06 09			06 19		06 24		06 33			
Old Street ⊖ d							05 52		06 06			06 12			06 22		06 27		06 37			
Moorgate ⊖ a							05 56		06 10			06 16			06 26		06 31		06 41			
Finsbury Park d				04 40	05 05	05 30		05a50		05 41	05 37		06 00	06a10		06a20		06a30		06 14	06 29	06a40
London Kings Cross ⊖ a	01 30		02 00	04 46	05 13	05 36				05 47			06 06							06 20	06 35	
St Pancras International d											05 45											
Farringdon d											05 49											
City Thameslink d											05 51											
London Blackfriars a											05 53											
London Bridge a																						

A from 29 October **B** until 22 October

See Table 025 for fast trains between London and Stevenage

Table T024-R

Mondays to Fridays

21 May to 7 December

Hertford North and Welwyn Garden City - London

		GN	GN	GN	GN	GN	GN	TL ■	GN	GN ■	GN	GN	GN	GN	GN	GN	GN	GN	GN	TL ■	GN ■	GN
Stevenage	d						06 06	06 10											06 28	06 40		
Watton-at-Stone	d						06 13												06 35			
Hertford North	d	06 00			06 10		06 20						06 28		06 32				06 42			
Bayford	d				06 15										06 37							
Cuffley	d	06 07			06 19		06 27						06 36		06 41				06 49			
Crews Hill	d				06 22										06 44							
Gordon Hill	d	06 14			06 26		06 33						06 41		06 48				06 55			
Enfield Chase	d	06 16			06 28		06 35						06 43		06 50				06 57			
Grange Park	d	06 18			06 30								06 45						06 59			
Winchmore Hill	d	06 20			06 33		06 39						06 48		06 54				07 02			
Palmers Green	d	06 23			06 36		06 42						06 51		06 57				07 05			
Bowes Park	a	06 25			06 38								06 53						07 07			
Knebworth	d							06 13		06 28										06 43	07 01	
Welwyn North	d							06 17		06 32										06 47	07 04	
Welwyn Garden City ■	d		06 08					06 22	06 24		06 32						06 38			06 52		
Hatfield	d		06 13					06 25	06 29		06 37						06 43			06 55		
Welham Green	d		06 17						06 33								06 47					
Brookmans Park	d		06 19						06 35								06 49					
Potters Bar	d		06 23					06 32	06 39		06 43						06 53			07 02		
Hadley Wood	d		06 26								06 46						06 56					
New Barnet	d		06 29						06 44		06 49						06 59					
Oakleigh Park	d		06 31								06 51						07 01					
New Southgate	a		06 34								06 54						07 04					
Alexandra Palace	d	06 28	06 38		06 41		06 46		06 50				06 57		07 01		07 08		07 11			
Hornsey	d	06 31			06 44		06 49		06 53						07 04				07 14			
Harringay	d	06 33			06 46		06 51		06 56						07 06				07 16			
Finsbury Park ⊖	a	06 35	06 42		06 48		06 53	06 43	06 58		07 01		07 02		07 08		07 12		07 18	07 13		
Finsbury Park	d	06 36	06 43		06 49		06 54		06 59				07 04		07 09		07 14		07 19			
Drayton Park	d	06 39	06 46	06 47	06 52	06 55	06 57		07 02			07 02	07 07	07 10	07 12	07 15	07 17	07 20	07 22			07 25
Highbury & Islington ⊖	d	06 42	06 49		06 54		06 59		07 04				07 09		07 14		07 19		07 24			
Essex Road	d	06 44	06 51		06 56		07 01		07 06				07 11		07 16		07 21		07 26			
Old Street ⊖	d	06 47	06 54		07 00		07 05		07 10				07 15		07 20		07 25		07 30			
Moorgate ⊖	a	06 51	06 58		07 04		07 09		07 14				07 19		07 24		07 29		07 34			
Finsbury Park	d			06a50		06a58		06 44			07 01	07a05		07a12		07a18		07a23		07 14		07a28
London Kings Cross ■ ⊖	a							06 50		06 51	07 07									07 20	07 25	
St Pancras International	d																					
Farringdon	d																					
City Thameslink	d																					
London Blackfriars	a																					
London Bridge	a																					

		GN	GN	GN	GN	GN	GN	GN	GN	GN	TL ■	GN ■	GN	GN	GN	GN	GN	GN	GN	GN	GN	GN	GN
Stevenage	d										07 10												
Watton-at-Stone	d													07 05									
Hertford North	d							07 02						07 11	07 15							07 32	
Bayford	d							07 07							07 20							07 37	
Cuffley	d							07 11						07 18	07 24							07 41	
Crews Hill	d							07 14							07 27							07 44	
Gordon Hill	d					07 11		07 18						07 24	07 31					07 41		07 48	
Enfield Chase	d					07 13		07 20						07 27	07 33					07 43		07 50	
Grange Park	d					07 15								07 29	07 35					07 45			
Winchmore Hill	d					07 18		07 24						07 32	07 38					07 48		07 54	
Palmers Green	d					07 21		07 27						07 35	07 41					07 51		07 57	
Bowes Park	a					07 23								07 37	07 43					07 53			
Knebworth	d										07 13	07 28											
Welwyn North	d										07 17	07 32											
Welwyn Garden City ■	d		06 54	07 02						07 08	07 22						07 24	07 32					
Hatfield	d		06 59	07 07						07 13	07 25						07 29	07 37					
Welham Green	d		07 03							07 17							07 33						
Brookmans Park	d		07 05							07 19							07 35						
Potters Bar	d		07 09	07 13						07 23	07 32						07 39	07 43					
Hadley Wood	d			07 16						07 26								07 46					
New Barnet	d		07 14	07 19						07 29							07 44	07 49					
Oakleigh Park	d			07 21						07 31								07 51					
New Southgate	a			07 24						07 34								07 54					
Alexandra Palace	d		07 20			07 27		07 31		07 38				07 41	07 46		07 50			07 57		08 01	
Hornsey	d		07 23					07 34						07 44	07 49		07 53					08 04	
Harringay	d		07 25					07 36						07 46	07 51		07 55					08 06	
Finsbury Park ⊖	a		07 27	07 31		07 32		07 38		07 42	07 43			07 48	07 53		07 57	08 01		08 02		08 08	
Finsbury Park	d		07 29			07 34		07 39		07 44				07 49	07 54		07 59			08 04		08 09	
Drayton Park	d	07 30	07 32		07 35	07 37	07 40	07 42	07 45	07 47			07 50	07 52	07 57	08 00	08 02		08 05	08 07	08 10	08 12	08 15
Highbury & Islington ⊖	d		07 34			07 39		07 44		07 49				07 54	07 59		08 04			08 09		08 14	
Essex Road	d		07 36			07 41		07 46		07 51				07 56	08 01		08 06			08 11		08 16	
Old Street ⊖	d		07 40			07 45		07 50		07 55				08 00	08 05		08 10			08 15		08 20	
Moorgate ⊖	a		07 44			07 49		07 54		07 59				08 04	08 09		08 14			08 19		08 24	
Finsbury Park	d	07a33		07 31	07a38		07a42		07a48		07 44		07a53			08a03		08 01	08a08		08a12		08a18
London Kings Cross ■ ⊖	a			07 38							07 50	07 51						08 08					
St Pancras International	d																						
Farringdon	d																						
City Thameslink	d																						
London Blackfriars	a																						
London Bridge	a																						

See Table 025 for fast trains between London and Stevenage

Table T024-R

Mondays to Fridays

21 May to 7 December

Hertford North and Welwyn Garden City - London

		GN	GN	GN	GN	GN	TL ■	GN ■	GN	GN	GN	GN	GN	GN	GN	GN	GN	TL ■	GN ■	GN	GN	GN	GN
Stevenage	d					07 28	07 40											08 10					
Watton-at-Stone	d					07 35															08 05		
Hertford North	d					07 44									08 02						08 12		
Bayford	d					07 48									08 07								
Cuffley	d					07 53									08 11						08 19		
Crews Hill	d					07 56									08 14								
Gordon Hill	d			07 55		08 00							08 11		08 18						08 25		
Enfield Chase	d			07 57		08 02							08 13		08 20						08 27		
Grange Park	d			07 59		08 04							08 15								08 29		
Winchmore Hill	d			08 02		08 07							08 18		08 24						08 32		
Palmers Green	d			08 05		08 10							08 21		08 27						08 35		
Bowes Park	a			08 07		08 12							08 23								08 37		
Knebworth	d						07 43	08 02										08 13	08 28				
Welwyn North	d						07 47	08 06										08 17	08 33				
Welwyn Garden City ■	d	07 38					07 52			07 54	08 02						08 08	08 22					08 24
Hatfield	d	07 43					07 55			07 59	08 07						08 13	08 25					08 29
Welham Green	d	07 47								08 03							08 17						08 33
Brookmans Park	d	07 49								08 05							08 19						08 35
Potters Bar	d	07 53					08 02			08 09	08 13						08 23	08 32					08 39
Hadley Wood	d	07 56									08 16						08 26						
New Barnet	d	07 59								08 14	08 19						08 29						08 44
Oakleigh Park	d	08 01									08 21						08 31						
New Southgate	a	08 04									08 24						08 34						
Alexandra Palace	d	08 08		08 11		08 16				08 20			08 27		08 31		08 38				08 41		08 50
Hornsey	d			08 14		08 19				08 23					08 34						08 44		08 53
Harringay	d			08 16		08 21				08 25					08 36						08 46		08 55
Finsbury Park ⊖	a	08 12		08 18		08 23	08 13			08 27	08 31		08 32		08 38		08 42	08 43			08 48		08 57
Finsbury Park	d	08 14		08 19		08 24				08 29			08 34		08 39		08 44				08 49		08 59
Drayton Park	d	08 17	08 20	08 22	08 25	08 27			08 30	08 32		08 35	08 37	08 40	08 42	08 45	08 47			08 50	08 52	08 55	09 02
Highbury & Islington ⊖	d	08 19		08 24		08 29				08 34			08 39		08 44		08 49				08 54		09 04
Essex Road	d	08 21		08 26		08 31				08 36			08 41		08 46		08 51				08 56		09 06
Old Street ⊖	d	08 25		08 30		08 35				08 40			08 45		08 50		08 55				09 00		09 10
Moorgate ⊖	a	08 29		08 34		08 39				08 44			08 49		08 54		08 59				09 04		09 14
Finsbury Park	d		08a23		08a28		08 14		08a33		08 31	08a38		08a42		08a48		08 44		08a53		08a58	
London Kings Cross ■ ⊖	a						08 20	08 25			08 38							08 50	08 52				
St Pancras International	d																						
Farringdon	d																						
City Thameslink	d																						
London Blackfriars	a																						
London Bridge	a																						

		GN	GN	GN	GN	GN	GN	GN	GN	GN	TL ■	GN ■	GN	GN	GN	GN	GN	GN	GN	GN	TL ■	GN
Stevenage	d									08 28	08 40										09 06	
Watton-at-Stone	d									08 35												
Hertford North	d					08 32				08 44									09 02			
Bayford	d					08 37				08 49									09 07			
Cuffley	d					08 41				08 53									09 11			
Crews Hill	d					08 44				08 56									09 14			
Gordon Hill	d			08 41		08 48			08 55	09 00							09 11		09 18			
Enfield Chase	d			08 43		08 50			08 57	09 02							09 13		09 20			
Grange Park	d			08 45					08 59	09 04							09 15					
Winchmore Hill	d			08 48		08 54			09 02	09 07							09 18		09 24			
Palmers Green	d			08 51		08 57			09 05	09 10							09 21		09 27			
Bowes Park	a			08 53					09 07	09 12							09 23					
Knebworth	d										08 43	08 58									09 09	
Welwyn North	d										08 47										09 13	
Welwyn Garden City ■	d	08 32					08 38				08 52			08 54	09 02					09 08	09 22	
Hatfield	d	08 37					08 43				08 55			08 59	09 07					09 13	09 25	
Welham Green	d						08 47							09 03						09 17		
Brookmans Park	d						08 49							09 05						09 19		
Potters Bar	d	08 43					08 53				09 02			09 09	09 13					09 23	09 32	
Hadley Wood	d	08 46					08 56								09 16					09 26		
New Barnet	d	08 49					08 59							09 14	09 19					09 29		
Oakleigh Park	d	08 51					09 01								09 21					09 31		
New Southgate	a	08 54					09 04								09 24					09 34		
Alexandra Palace	d			08 57		09 01	09 08		09 11	09 16				09 20			09 27		09 31	09 38		
Hornsey	d					09 04			09 14	09 19				09 23					09 34			
Harringay	d					09 06			09 16	09 21				09 25					09 36			
Finsbury Park ⊖	a	09 01		09 02		09 08	09 12		09 18	09 23	09 13			09 27	09 30		09 32		09 38	09 42	09 43	
Finsbury Park	d			09 04		09 09	09 14		09 19	09 24				09 29			09 34		09 39	09 44		
Drayton Park	d		09 05	09 07	09 10	09 12	09 17	09 20	09 22	09 27			09 30	09 32		09 35	09 37	09 40	09 42	09 47		09 50
Highbury & Islington ⊖	d			09 09		09 14	09 19		09 24	09 29				09 34			09 39		09 44	09 49		
Essex Road	d			09 11		09 16	09 21		09 26	09 31				09 36			09 41		09 46	09 51		
Old Street ⊖	d			09 15		09 20	09 25		09 30	09 35				09 40			09 45		09 50	09 55		
Moorgate ⊖	a			09 19		09 24	09 29		09 34	09 39				09 44			09 49		09 54	09 59		
Finsbury Park	d	09 01	09a08		09a12			09a23			09 18		09a33		09 31	09a38		09a43			09 44	09a53
London Kings Cross ■ ⊖	a	09 08									09 25	09 21			09 38						09 50	
St Pancras International	d																					
Farringdon	d																					
City Thameslink	d																					
London Blackfriars	a																					
London Bridge	a																					

See Table 025 for fast trains between London and Stevenage

Table T024-R

Mondays to Fridays

21 May to 7 December

Hertford North and Welwyn Garden City - London

		GN	GN	GN	GN	GN	GN	GN	GN	GN	TL ■	GN
Stevenage	d									09 28	09 40	
Watton-at-Stone	d	09 07								09 35		
Hertford North	d	09 17					09 30			09 47		
Bayford	d						09 35					
Cuffley	d	09 25					09 39			09 55		
Crews Hill	d						09 42					
Gordon Hill	d	09 31					09 46			10 01		
Enfield Chase	d	09 33					09 48			10 03		
Grange Park	d	09 35					09 50			10 05		
Winchmore Hill	d	09 37					09 52			10 07		
Palmers Green	d	09 40					09 55			10 10		
Bowes Park	a	09 42					09 57			10 12		
Knebworth	d										09 43	
Welwyn North	d										09 47	
Welwyn Garden City ■	d				09 24			09 38			09 52	
Hatfield	d				09 29			09 43			09 55	
Welham Green	d				09 33			09 47				
Brookmans Park	d				09 36			09 49				
Potters Bar	d				09 40			09 53			10 02	
Hadley Wood	d				09 44			09 56				
New Barnet	d				09 47			09 59				
Oakleigh Park	d				09 49			10 01				
New Southgate	a				09 52			10 04				
Alexandra Palace	d	09 45			09 55		10 00	10 08		10 15		
Hornsey	d	09 48			09 58		10 03			10 18		
Harringay	d	09 50			10 00		10 05			10 20		
Finsbury Park ⊖	a	09 52			10 02		10 07	10 12		10 22	10 13	
Finsbury Park	d	09 53			10 03		10 08	10 13		10 23		
Drayton Park	d	09 56	10 00	10 05	10 06	10 10	10 11	10 16	10 20	10 26		10 30
Highbury & Islington ⊖	d	09 59			10 09		10 14	10 19		10 29		
Essex Road	d	10 01			10 11		10 16	10 21		10 31		
Old Street ⊖	d	10 04			10 14		10 19	10 24		10 34		
Moorgate ⊖	a	10 08			10 18		10 23	10 28		10 38		
Finsbury Park	d		10a03	10a08		10a13			10a23		10 17	10a33
London Kings Cross ■ ⊖	a										10 25	
St Pancras International	d											
Farringdon	d											
City Thameslink	d											
London Blackfriars	a											
London Bridge	a											

		GN	GN	GN	GN	GN	TL ■	GN	GN	GN	GN	GN
Stevenage	d						10 10					
Watton-at-Stone	d								10 07			
Hertford North	d				10 00				10 17			
Bayford	d				10 05							
Cuffley	d				10 09				10 25			
Crews Hill	d				10 12							
Gordon Hill	d				10 16				10 31			
Enfield Chase	d				10 18				10 33			
Grange Park	d				10 20				10 35			
Winchmore Hill	d				10 22				10 37			
Palmers Green	d				10 25				10 40			
Bowes Park	a				10 27				10 42			
Knebworth	d						10 13					
Welwyn North	d						10 17					
Welwyn Garden City ■	d		09 58			10 09	10 22					10 28
Hatfield	d		10 03			10 13	10 25					10 33
Welham Green	d					10 17						
Brookmans Park	d					10 19						
Potters Bar	d		10 10			10 23	10 32					10 40
Hadley Wood	d		10 14			10 26						10 44
New Barnet	d		10 17			10 29						10 47
Oakleigh Park	d		10 19			10 31						10 49
New Southgate	a		10 22			10 34						10 52
Alexandra Palace	d		10 25		10 30	10 38			10 45			10 55
Hornsey	d		10 28		10 33				10 48			10 58
Harringay	d		10 30		10 35				10 50			11 00
Finsbury Park ⊖	a		10 32		10 37	10 42	10 43		10 52			11 02
Finsbury Park	d		10 33		10 38	10 43			10 53			11 03
Drayton Park	d	10 35	10 36	10 40	10 41	10 46		10 50	10 56	11 00	11 05	11 06
Highbury & Islington ⊖	d		10 39		10 44	10 49			10 59			11 09
Essex Road	d		10 41		10 46	10 51			11 01			11 11
Old Street ⊖	d		10 44		10 49	10 54			11 04			11 14
Moorgate ⊖	a		10 48		10 53	10 58			11 08			11 18
Finsbury Park	d	10a38		10a43			10 44	10a53		11a03	11a08	
London Kings Cross ■ ⊖	a						10 50					
St Pancras International	d											
Farringdon	d											
City Thameslink	d											
London Blackfriars	a											
London Bridge	a											

		GN	GN	GN	GN	GN	TL ■	GN	GN	GN	GN	GN
Stevenage	d					10 28	10 40					
Watton-at-Stone	d					10 35						
Hertford North	d		10 30			10 47						11 00
Bayford	d		10 35									11 05
Cuffley	d		10 39			10 55						11 09
Crews Hill	d		10 42									11 12
Gordon Hill	d		10 46			11 01						11 16
Enfield Chase	d		10 48			11 03						11 18
Grange Park	d		10 50			11 05						11 20
Winchmore Hill	d		10 52			11 07						11 22
Palmers Green	d		10 55			11 10						11 25
Bowes Park	a		10 57			11 12						11 27
Knebworth	d						10 43					
Welwyn North	d						10 47					
Welwyn Garden City ■	d			10 39			10 52			10 58		
Hatfield	d			10 43			10 55			11 03		
Welham Green	d			10 47								
Brookmans Park	d			10 49								
Potters Bar	d			10 53			11 02			11 10		
Hadley Wood	d			10 56						11 14		
New Barnet	d			10 59						11 17		
Oakleigh Park	d			11 01						11 19		
New Southgate	a			11 04						11 22		
Alexandra Palace	d		11 00	11 08		11 15				11 25		11 31
Hornsey	d		11 03			11 18				11 28		11 34
Harringay	d		11 05			11 20				11 30		11 36
Finsbury Park ⊖	a		11 07	11 12		11 22	11 13			11 32		11 38
Finsbury Park	d		11 08	11 13		11 23				11 33		11 39
Drayton Park	d	11 10	11 11	11 16	11 20	11 26		11 30	11 35	11 36	11 40	11 42
Highbury & Islington ⊖	d		11 14	11 19		11 29				11 39		11 45
Essex Road	d		11 16	11 21		11 31				11 41		11 47
Old Street ⊖	d		11 19	11 24		11 34				11 44		11 50
Moorgate ⊖	a		11 23	11 28		11 38				11 48		11 54
Finsbury Park	d	11a13			11a23		11 14	11a33	11a38		11a43	
London Kings Cross ■ ⊖	a						11 20					
St Pancras International	d											
Farringdon	d											
City Thameslink	d											
London Blackfriars	a											
London Bridge	a											

		GN	TL ■	GN	GN	GN	GN	GN	GN	GN	GN
Stevenage	d		11 10								
Watton-at-Stone	d				11 07						
Hertford North	d				11 17					11 30	
Bayford	d									11 35	
Cuffley	d				11 25					11 39	
Crews Hill	d									11 42	
Gordon Hill	d				11 31					11 46	
Enfield Chase	d				11 33					11 48	
Grange Park	d				11 35					11 50	
Winchmore Hill	d				11 37					11 52	
Palmers Green	d				11 40					11 55	
Bowes Park	a				11 42					11 57	
Knebworth	d		11 13								
Welwyn North	d		11 17								
Welwyn Garden City ■	d	11 09	11 22					11 28			11 39
Hatfield	d	11 13	11 25					11 33			11 43
Welham Green	d	11 17									11 47
Brookmans Park	d	11 19									11 49
Potters Bar	d	11 23	11 32					11 40			11 53
Hadley Wood	d	11 26						11 44			11 56
New Barnet	d	11 29						11 47			11 59
Oakleigh Park	d	11 31						11 49			12 01
New Southgate	a	11 34						11 52			12 04
Alexandra Palace	d	11 38			11 45			11 55		12 00	12 08
Hornsey	d				11 48			11 58		12 03	
Harringay	d				11 50			12 00		12 05	
Finsbury Park ⊖	a	11 42	11 43		11 52			12 02		12 07	12 12
Finsbury Park	d	11 43			11 53			12 03		12 08	12 13
Drayton Park	d	11 46		11 50	11 56	12 00	12 05	12 06	12 10	12 11	12 16
Highbury & Islington ⊖	d	11 49			11 59			12 09		12 14	12 19
Essex Road	d	11 51			12 01			12 11		12 16	12 21
Old Street ⊖	d	11 54			12 04			12 14		12 19	12 24
Moorgate ⊖	a	11 58			12 08			12 18		12 23	12 28
Finsbury Park	d		11 44	11a53		12a03	12a08		12a13		
London Kings Cross ■ ⊖	a		11 50								
St Pancras International	d										
Farringdon	d										
City Thameslink	d										
London Blackfriars	a										
London Bridge	a										

See Table 025 for fast trains between London and Stevenage

Table T024-R

Mondays to Fridays

21 May to 7 December

Hertford North and Welwyn Garden City - London

		GN	GN	TL ■	GN	GN	GN	GN	GN	GN	TL ■	GN
Stevenage	d		11 28	11 40							12 10	
Watton-at-Stone	d		11 35									
Hertford North	d		11 47						12 00			
Bayford	d								12 05			
Cuffley	d		11 55						12 09			
Crews Hill	d								12 12			
Gordon Hill	d		12 01						12 16			
Enfield Chase	d		12 03						12 18			
Grange Park	d		12 05						12 20			
Winchmore Hill	d		12 07						12 22			
Palmers Green	d		12 10						12 25			
Bowes Park	a		12 12						12 27			
Knebworth	d			11 43							12 13	
Welwyn North	d			11 47							12 17	
Welwyn Garden City ■	d			11 52			11 58			12 09	12 22	
Hatfield	d			11 55			12 03			12 13	12 25	
Welham Green	d									12 17		
Brookmans Park	d									12 19		
Potters Bar	d			12 02			12 10			12 23	12 32	
Hadley Wood	d						12 14			12 26		
New Barnet	d						12 17			12 29		
Oakleigh Park	d						12 19			12 31		
New Southgate	a						12 22			12 34		
Alexandra Palace	d		12 15				12 25		12 30	12 38		
Hornsey	d		12 18				12 28		12 33			
Harringay	d		12 20				12 30		12 35			
Finsbury Park ⊖	a		12 22	12 13			12 32		12 37	12 42	12 43	
Finsbury Park	d		12 23				12 33		12 38	12 43		
Drayton Park	d	12 20	12 26		12 30	12 35	12 36	12 40	12 41	12 46		12 50
Highbury & Islington ⊖	d		12 29				12 39		12 44	12 49		
Essex Road	d		12 31				12 41		12 46	12 51		
Old Street ⊖	d		12 34				12 44		12 49	12 54		
Moorgate ⊖	a		12 38				12 48		12 53	12 58		
Finsbury Park	d	12a23		12 14	12a33	12a38		12a43			12 44	12a53
London Kings Cross ■ ⊖	a			12 20							12 50	
St Pancras International	d											
Farringdon	d											
City Thameslink	d											
London Blackfriars	a											
London Bridge	a											

		GN	GN	GN	GN	GN	GN	GN	GN	GN	TL ■	GN
Stevenage	d									12 28	12 40	
Watton-at-Stone	d	12 11								12 35		
Hertford North	d	12 17					12 30			12 47		
Bayford	d						12 35					
Cuffley	d	12 25					12 39			12 55		
Crews Hill	d						12 42					
Gordon Hill	d	12 31					12 46			13 01		
Enfield Chase	d	12 33					12 48			13 03		
Grange Park	d	12 35					12 50			13 05		
Winchmore Hill	d	12 37					12 52			13 07		
Palmers Green	d	12 40					12 55			13 10		
Bowes Park	a	12 42					12 57			13 12		
Knebworth	d										12 43	
Welwyn North	d										12 47	
Welwyn Garden City ■	d				12 28			12 39			12 52	
Hatfield	d				12 33			12 43			12 55	
Welham Green	d							12 47				
Brookmans Park	d							12 49				
Potters Bar	d				12 40			12 53			13 02	
Hadley Wood	d				12 44			12 56				
New Barnet	d				12 47			12 59				
Oakleigh Park	d				12 49			13 01				
New Southgate	a				12 52			13 04				
Alexandra Palace	d	12 45			12 55		13 00	13 08		13 15		
Hornsey	d	12 48			12 58		13 03			13 18		
Harringay	d	12 50			13 00		13 05			13 20		
Finsbury Park ⊖	a	12 52			13 02		13 07	13 12		13 22	13 13	
Finsbury Park	d	12 53			13 03		13 08	13 13		13 23		
Drayton Park	d	12 56	13 00	13 05	13 06	13 10	13 11	13 16	13 20	13 26		13 30
Highbury & Islington ⊖	d	12 59			13 09		13 14	13 19		13 29		
Essex Road	d	13 01			13 11		13 16	13 21		13 31		
Old Street ⊖	d	13 04			13 14		13 19	13 24		13 34		
Moorgate ⊖	a	13 08			13 18		13 23	13 28		13 38		
Finsbury Park	d		13a03	13a08		13a13			13a23		13 14	13a33
London Kings Cross ■ ⊖	a										13 20	
St Pancras International	d											
Farringdon	d											
City Thameslink	d											
London Blackfriars	a											
London Bridge	a											

		GN	GN	GN	GN	GN	TL ■	GN	GN	GN	GN	GN
Stevenage	d						13 08					
Watton-at-Stone	d								13 07			
Hertford North	d				13 00				13 17			
Bayford	d				13 05							
Cuffley	d				13 09				13 25			
Crews Hill	d				13 12							
Gordon Hill	d				13 16				13 31			
Enfield Chase	d				13 18				13 33			
Grange Park	d				13 20				13 35			
Winchmore Hill	d				13 22				13 37			
Palmers Green	d				13 25				13 40			
Bowes Park	a				13 27				13 42			
Knebworth	d						13 13					
Welwyn North	d						13 17					
Welwyn Garden City ■	d		12 58			13 09	13 22					13 28
Hatfield	d		13 03			13 13	13 25					13 33
Welham Green	d					13 17						
Brookmans Park	d					13 19						
Potters Bar	d		13 10			13 23	13 32					13 40
Hadley Wood	d		13 14			13 26						13 44
New Barnet	d		13 17			13 29						13 47
Oakleigh Park	d		13 19			13 31						13 49
New Southgate	a		13 22			13 34						13 52
Alexandra Palace	d		13 25		13 30	13 38			13 45			13 55
Hornsey	d		13 28		13 33				13 48			13 58
Harringay	d		13 30		13 35				13 50			14 00
Finsbury Park ⊖	a		13 32		13 37	13 42	13 43		13 52			14 02
Finsbury Park	d		13 33		13 38	13 43			13 53			14 03
Drayton Park	d	13 35	13 36	13 40	13 41	13 46		13 50	13 56	14 00	14 05	14 06
Highbury & Islington ⊖	d		13 39		13 44	13 49			13 59			14 09
Essex Road	d		13 41		13 46	13 51			14 01			14 11
Old Street ⊖	d		13 44		13 49	13 54			14 04			14 14
Moorgate ⊖	a		13 48		13 53	13 58			14 08			14 18
Finsbury Park	d	13a38		13a43			13 44	13a53		14a03	14a08	
London Kings Cross ■ ⊖	a						13 50					
St Pancras International	d											
Farringdon	d											
City Thameslink	d											
London Blackfriars	a											
London Bridge	a											

		GN	GN	GN	GN	GN	TL ■	GN	GN	GN	GN	GN
Stevenage	d					13 28	13 40					
Watton-at-Stone	d					13 35						
Hertford North	d		13 30			13 47						14 00
Bayford	d		13 35									14 05
Cuffley	d		13 39			13 55						14 09
Crews Hill	d		13 42									14 12
Gordon Hill	d		13 46			14 01						14 16
Enfield Chase	d		13 48			14 03						14 18
Grange Park	d		13 50			14 05						14 20
Winchmore Hill	d		13 52			14 07						14 22
Palmers Green	d		13 55			14 10						14 25
Bowes Park	a		13 57			14 12						14 27
Knebworth	d						13 43					
Welwyn North	d						13 47					
Welwyn Garden City ■	d			13 39			13 52			13 58		
Hatfield	d			13 43			13 55			14 03		
Welham Green	d			13 47								
Brookmans Park	d			13 49								
Potters Bar	d			13 53			14 02			14 10		
Hadley Wood	d			13 56						14 14		
New Barnet	d			13 59						14 17		
Oakleigh Park	d			14 01						14 19		
New Southgate	a			14 04						14 22		
Alexandra Palace	d		14 00	14 08		14 15				14 25		14 30
Hornsey	d		14 03			14 18				14 28		14 33
Harringay	d		14 05			14 20				14 30		14 35
Finsbury Park ⊖	a		14 07	14 13		14 22	14 13			14 32		14 37
Finsbury Park	d		14 08	14 13		14 23				14 33		14 38
Drayton Park	d	14 10	14 11	14 16	14 20	14 26		14 30	14 35	14 36	14 40	14 41
Highbury & Islington ⊖	d		14 14	14 19		14 29				14 39		14 44
Essex Road	d		14 16	14 21		14 31				14 41		14 46
Old Street ⊖	d		14 19	14 24		14 34				14 44		14 49
Moorgate ⊖	a		14 23	14 28		14 38				14 48		14 53
Finsbury Park	d	14a13			14a23		14 14	14a33	14a38		14a43	
London Kings Cross ■ ⊖	a						14 20					
St Pancras International	d											
Farringdon	d											
City Thameslink	d											
London Blackfriars	a											
London Bridge	a											

See Table 025 for fast trains between London and Stevenage

Hertford North and Welwyn Garden City - London

		GN		TL 1	GN	GN	GN	GN	GN	GN	GN	GN		GN	GN	TL 1	GN	GN	GN	GN	GN	GN		TL 1	GN
Stevenage	d			14 10											14 28	14 40								15 10	
Watton-at-Stone	d					14 11									14 35										
Hertford North	d					14 17					14 30				14 47						15 00				
Bayford	d										14 35										15 05				
Cuffley	d					14 25					14 39				14 55						15 09				
Crews Hill	d										14 42										15 12				
Gordon Hill	d					14 31					14 46				15 01						15 16				
Enfield Chase	d					14 33					14 48				15 03						15 18				
Grange Park	d					14 35					14 50				15 05						15 20				
Winchmore Hill	d					14 37					14 52				15 07						15 22				
Palmers Green	d					14 40					14 55				15 10						15 25				
Bowes Park	a					14 42					14 57				15 12						15 27				
Knebworth	d			14 13												14 43								15 13	
Welwyn North	d			14 17												14 47								15 17	
Welwyn Garden City 4	d	14 09		14 22					14 28			14 39				14 52			14 58			15 09		15 22	
Hatfield	d	14 13		14 25					14 33			14 43				14 55			15 03			15 13		15 25	
Welham Green	d	14 17										14 47										15 17			
Brookmans Park	d	14 19										14 49										15 19			
Potters Bar	d	14 23		14 32					14 40			14 53				15 02			15 10			15 23		15 32	
Hadley Wood	d	14 26							14 44			14 56							15 14			15 26			
New Barnet	d	14 29							14 47			14 59							15 17			15 29			
Oakleigh Park	d	14 31							14 49			15 01							15 19			15 31			
New Southgate	a	14 34							14 52			15 04							15 22			15 34			
Alexandra Palace	d	14 38				14 45			14 55		15 00	15 08			15 15				15 25		15 30	15 38			
Hornsey	d					14 48			14 58		15 03				15 18				15 28		15 33				
Harringay	d					14 50			15 00		15 05				15 20				15 30		15 35				
Finsbury Park ⊖	a	14 42		14 43		14 52			15 02		15 07	15 12			15 22	15 13			15 32		15 37	15 42		15 43	
Finsbury Park	d	14 43				14 53			15 03		15 08	15 13			15 23				15 33		15 38	15 43			
Drayton Park	d	14 46			14 50	14 56	15 00	15 05	15 06	15 10	15 11	15 16		15 20	15 26		15 30	15 35	15 36	15 40	15 41	15 46			15 50
Highbury & Islington ⊖	d	14 49				14 59			15 09		15 14	15 19			15 29				15 39		15 44	15 49			
Essex Road	d	14 51				15 01			15 11		15 16	15 21			15 31				15 41		15 46	15 51			
Old Street ⊖	d	14 54				15 04			15 14		15 19	15 24			15 34				15 44		15 49	15 54			
Moorgate ⊖	a	14 58				15 08			15 18		15 23	15 28			15 38				15 48		15 53	15 58			
Finsbury Park	d			14 44	14a53		15a03	15a08		15a13				15a23		15 14	15a33	15a38		15a43				15 44	15a53
London Kings Cross 15 ⊖	a			14 50												15 20								15 50	
St Pancras International	d																								
Farringdon	d																								
City Thameslink	d																								
London Blackfriars	a																								
London Bridge	a																								

		GN	GN	GN	GN	GN	GN	GN		GN	GN	GN	TL 1	GN	GN	GN	GN	GN		GN	GN	GN	TL 1	GN	GN
Stevenage	d											15 28	15 40										16 10		
Watton-at-Stone	d	15 07										15 35													
Hertford North	d	15 17					15 30					15 47								16 00					
Bayford	d						15 35													16 05					
Cuffley	d	15 25					15 39					15 55								16 09					
Crews Hill	d						15 42													16 12					
Gordon Hill	d	15 31					15 46					16 01								16 16					
Enfield Chase	d	15 33					15 48					16 03								16 18					
Grange Park	d	15 35					15 50					16 05								16 20					
Winchmore Hill	d	15 37					15 52					16 07								16 22					
Palmers Green	d	15 40					15 55					16 10								16 25					
Bowes Park	a	15 42					15 57					16 12								16 27					
Knebworth	d												15 43										16 13		
Welwyn North	d												15 47										16 17		
Welwyn Garden City 4	d					15 28				15 39			15 52				15 58					16 09	16 22		
Hatfield	d					15 33				15 43			15 55				16 03					16 13	16 25		
Welham Green	d									15 47												16 17			
Brookmans Park	d									15 49												16 19			
Potters Bar	d					15 40				15 53			16 02				16 10					16 23	16 32		
Hadley Wood	d					15 44				15 56							16 14					16 26			
New Barnet	d					15 47				15 59							16 17					16 29			
Oakleigh Park	d					15 49				16 01							16 19					16 31			
New Southgate	a					15 52				16 04							16 22					16 34			
Alexandra Palace	d	15 45				15 55	16 00			16 08		16 15					16 25			16 30		16 38			
Hornsey	d	15 48				15 58	16 03					16 18					16 28			16 33					
Harringay	d	15 50				16 00	16 05					16 20					16 30			16 35					
Finsbury Park ⊖	a	15 52				16 02	16 07			16 12		16 22	16 13				16 32			16 37		16 42	16 43		
Finsbury Park	d	15 53		15 58		16 03	16 08			16 13		16 23			16 28		16 33			16 38		16 43		16 48	
Drayton Park	d	15 56	16 00	16 01	16 05	16 06	16 11	16 11		16 16	16 21	16 26		16 26	16 31	16 31	16 36	16 36		16 41	16 41	16 46		16 51	16 51
Highbury & Islington ⊖	d	15 59		16 03		16 09	16 14			16 19		16 29			16 33		16 39			16 44		16 49		16 53	
Essex Road	d	16 01		16 05		16 11	16 16			16 21		16 31			16 35		16 41			16 46		16 51		16 55	
Old Street ⊖	d	16 04		16 09		16 14	16 19			16 24		16 34			16 39		16 44			16 49		16 54		16 59	
Moorgate ⊖	a	16 08		16 13		16 18	16 23			16 28		16 38			16 43		16 48			16 53		16 58		17 03	
Finsbury Park	d		16a03		16a08			16a13			16a23		16 14	16a28		16a33		16a38			16a43		16 44		16a53
London Kings Cross 15 ⊖	a												16 20										16 50		
St Pancras International	d																								
Farringdon	d																								
City Thameslink	d																								
London Blackfriars	a																								
London Bridge	a																								

See Table 025 for fast trains between London and Stevenage

Hertford North and Welwyn Garden City - London

		GN	GN	GN		GN	GN	GN	GN	GN	GN	GN	GN	GN		TL 1	GN	GN	GN	GN	GN	GN	GN	GN	
Stevenage	d													16 26		16 40									
Watton-at-Stone	d	16 07												16 33											
Hertford North	d	16 14				16 28								16 40				16 56							
Bayford	d	16 19												16 44											
Cuffley	d	16 23				16 35								16 49				17 03							
Crews Hill	d	16 26												16 52											
Gordon Hill	d	16 30				16 40								16 56				17 08					17 12		
Enfield Chase	d	16 32				16 42								16 58				17 10					17 14		
Grange Park	d	16 34				16 44								17 00									17 16		
Winchmore Hill	d	16 37				16 47								17 02				17 13					17 19		
Palmers Green	d	16 39				16 49								17 05				17 16					17 21		
Bowes Park	a	16 42				16 52								17 07									17 24		
Knebworth	d															16 43									
Welwyn North	d															16 47									
Welwyn Garden City 4	d						16 28		16 32		16 43					16 52			16 58	17 02					
Hatfield	d						16 33		16 36		16 48					16 55				17 07					
Welham Green	d								16 40		16 51														
Brookmans Park	d								16 42		16 54														
Potters Bar	d						16 40		16 46		16 57					17 02			17 08	17 13					
Hadley Wood	d						16 44		16 49										17 11						
New Barnet	d						16 47		16 52		17 02								17 14	17 18					
Oakleigh Park	d						16 49		16 54										17 16	17 20					
New Southgate	a						16 52		16 57										17 19	17 23					
Alexandra Palace	d	16 45				16 55	16 55		17 01		17 08			17 12				17 20	17 23				17 27		
Hornsey	d	16 48					16 58		17 03					17 14									17 29		
Harringay	d	16 50					17 00		17 05					17 16									17 31		
Finsbury Park ⊖	a	16 52				16 59	17 02		17 08		17 12			17 19		17 14		17 24	17 27	17 29			17 34		
Finsbury Park	d	16 53				16 59	17 03		17 08		17 13			17 19				17 24	17 28				17 34		
Drayton Park	d	16 56	16 56	17 01		17 02	17 06	17 06	17 11	17 11	17 16	17 16	17 20	17 22			17 26	17 27	17 31		17 31	17 36	17 37	17 41	
Highbury & Islington ⊖	d	16 59				17 05	17 09		17 14		17 19			17 25				17 30	17 34				17 40		
Essex Road	d	17 01				17 07	17 11		17 16		17 21			17 27				17 32	17 36				17 42		
Old Street ⊖	d	17 04				17 10	17 14		17 19		17 24			17 30				17 35	17 39				17 45		
Moorgate ⊖	a	17 08				17 14	17 18		17 23		17 28			17 34				17 39	17 43				17 49		
Finsbury Park	d		16a58	17a03				17a08		17a13		17a18	17a22			17 14	17a28			17 29	17a33	17a38		17a43	
London Kings Cross 15 ⊖	a															17 20				17 35					
St Pancras International	d																								
Farringdon	d																								
City Thameslink	d																								
London Blackfriars	a																								
London Bridge	a																								

		GN	GN	TL 1	GN	GN	GN	GN	GN	GN		GN	GN	GN	GN	GN	GN	GN	GN	GN		GN	TL 1	GN	GN
Stevenage	d			17 10																		17 30	17 40		
Watton-at-Stone	d	16 59																				17 37			
Hertford North	d	17 06					17 11								17 37							17 43			
Bayford	d						17 15															17 47			
Cuffley	d	17 13					17 20								17 44							17 52			
Crews Hill	d						17 23															17 55			
Gordon Hill	d	17 20					17 26		17 39						17 50		17 54					17 58			
Enfield Chase	d	17 22					17 28		17 41								17 56					18 00			
Grange Park	d						17 30															18 02			
Winchmore Hill	d	17 25					17 33		17 44								17 59					18 04			
Palmers Green	d	17 28					17 35		17 46								18 01					18 07			
Bowes Park	a						17 38															18 09			
Knebworth	d			17 13																			17 43		
Welwyn North	d			17 17																			17 47		
Welwyn Garden City 4	d		17 13	17 22						17 28		17 32						17 43					17 52		17 58
Hatfield	d		17 18	17 25								17 37						17 48					17 55		
Welham Green	d		17 21															17 51							
Brookmans Park	d		17 24															17 54							
Potters Bar	d		17 27	17 32						17 38		17 43						17 57					18 02		18 08
Hadley Wood	d									17 41															18 11
New Barnet	d		17 32							17 44		17 48						18 02							18 14
Oakleigh Park	d									17 46		17 50													18 16
New Southgate	a									17 49		17 53													18 19
Alexandra Palace	d	17 32	17 38				17 42		17 50	17 53					17 57		18 05	18 09				18 12			18 23
Hornsey	d	17 34					17 44								17 59							18 15			
Harringay	d	17 36					17 46								18 01							18 17			
Finsbury Park ⊖	a	17 39	17 42	17 44			17 49		17 54	17 57		17 59			18 04		18 09	18 13				18 19	18 14		18 27
Finsbury Park	d	17 39	17 43				17 49		17 54	17 58					18 04		18 09	18 13				18 20			18 28
Drayton Park	d	17 42	17 46		17 46	17 51	17 52	17 56	17 57	18 01			18 01	18 06	18 07	18 11	18 12	18 16	18 16	18 21		18 23		18 26	18 31
Highbury & Islington ⊖	d	17 45	17 49				17 55		18 00	18 04					18 10		18 15	18 19				18 26			18 34
Essex Road	d	17 47	17 51				17 57		18 02	18 06					18 12		18 17	18 21				18 28			18 36
Old Street ⊖	d	17 50	17 54				18 00		18 05	18 09					18 15		18 20	18 24				18 31			18 39
Moorgate ⊖	a	17 54	17 58				18 04		18 09	18 13					18 19		18 24	18 28				18 35			18 43
Finsbury Park	d			17 44	17a48	17a53		17a58				17 59	18a03	18a08		18a13			18a18	18a23			18 14	18a28	
London Kings Cross 15 ⊖	a			17 50								18 06											18 20		
St Pancras International	d																								
Farringdon	d																								
City Thameslink	d																								
London Blackfriars	a																								
London Bridge	a																								

See Table 025 for fast trains between London and Stevenage

Table T024-R

Mondays to Fridays

21 May to 7 December

Hertford North and Welwyn Garden City - London

Station		GN	GN	GN	GN	GN		GN	GN	TL ■	GN	GN	GN	GN	GN	GN		GN	GN	GN	GN	GN	GN	GN	TL ■
Stevenage	d									18 10														18 30	18 40
Watton-at-Stone	d											18 09												18 37	
Hertford North	d					18 03						18 17							18 30					18 47	
Bayford	d					18 07													18 35						
Cuffley	d					18 12						18 25							18 39					18 55	
Crews Hill	d					18 15													18 42						
Gordon Hill	d				18 12	18 20						18 30							18 46					19 00	
Enfield Chase	d				18 14	18 22						18 32							18 48					19 02	
Grange Park	d				18 16							18 34							18 50					19 04	
Winchmore Hill	d				18 18	18 25						18 36							18 52					19 06	
Palmers Green	d				18 21	18 28						18 39							18 55					19 09	
Bowes Park	a				18 23							18 41							18 57					19 11	
Knebworth	d									18 13															18 43
Welwyn North	d									18 17															18 47
Welwyn Garden City ■	d	18 02							18 13	18 22				18 28	18 32						18 43				18 52
Hatfield	d	18 07							18 18	18 25					18 37						18 48				18 55
Welham Green	d								18 21												18 51				
Brookmans Park	d								18 24												18 54				
Potters Bar	d	18 13							18 27	18 32				18 38	18 43						18 57				19 02
Hadley Wood	d													18 41											
New Barnet	d	18 18							18 32					18 44	18 48						19 02				
Oakleigh Park	d	18 20												18 46	18 50										
New Southgate	a	18 23												18 49	18 53										
Alexandra Palace	d				18 27	18 32			18 38			18 46		18 53					19 00		19 08			19 15	
Hornsey	d				18 29	18 34						18 48							19 03					19 18	
Harringay	d				18 31	18 36						18 50							19 05					19 20	
Finsbury Park ⊖	a	18 29			18 34	18 39			18 42	18 44		18 53		18 57	18 59				19 07		19 12			19 22	19 14
Finsbury Park	d				18 34	18 39			18 43			18 53		18 58					19 08		19 13			19 23	
Drayton Park	d		18 31	18 36	18 37	18 42		18 43	18 46		18 51	18 56	18 56	19 01		19 01		19 06	19 11	19 11	19 16	19 20	19 25	19 26	
Highbury & Islington ⊖	d				18 40	18 45			18 49			18 59		19 04					19 14		19 19			19 29	
Essex Road	d				18 42	18 47			18 51			19 01		19 06					19 16		19 21			19 31	
Old Street ⊖	d				18 45	18 50			18 54			19 04		19 09					19 19		19 24			19 34	
Moorgate ⊖	a				18 49	18 54			18 58			19 08		19 13					19 23		19 28			19 38	
Finsbury Park	d	18 31	18a33	18a38				18a45		18 44	18a53		18a58		19 02	19a03		19a08		19a13		19a23	19a28		19 14
London Kings Cross ■ ⊖	a	18 38								18 50					19 11										19 20
St Pancras International	d																								
Farringdon	d																								
City Thameslink	d																								
London Blackfriars	a																								
London Bridge	a																								

Station		GN		GN	GN	GN	GN	TL ■	GN	GN	GN	GN		GN	GN	GN	GN	GN	GN	TL ■	GN	GN		GN	GN
Stevenage	d							19 10											19 30	19 40					
Watton-at-Stone	d									19 09									19 37						
Hertford North	d				19 00					19 15						19 30			19 47						
Bayford	d				19 05											19 35									
Cuffley	d				19 09					19 23						19 39			19 55						
Crews Hill	d				19 12											19 42									
Gordon Hill	d				19 16					19 30						19 46			20 01						
Enfield Chase	d				19 18					19 32						19 48			20 03						
Grange Park	d				19 20					19 34						19 50			20 05						
Winchmore Hill	d				19 22					19 36						19 52			20 07						
Palmers Green	d				19 25					19 39						19 55			20 10						
Bowes Park	a				19 27					19 41						19 57			20 12						
Knebworth	d							19 13												19 43					
Welwyn North	d							19 17												19 47					
Welwyn Garden City ■	d	18 58					19 13	19 22				19 28					19 43			19 52				19 58	
Hatfield	d						19 18	19 25									19 48			19 55				20 03	
Welham Green	d						19 21										19 51								
Brookmans Park	d						19 24										19 54								
Potters Bar	d	19 08					19 27	19 32				19 38					19 57			20 02				20 10	
Hadley Wood	d	19 11										19 41												20 14	
New Barnet	d	19 14					19 32					19 44					20 02							20 17	
Oakleigh Park	d	19 16										19 46												20 19	
New Southgate	a	19 19										19 49												20 22	
Alexandra Palace	d	19 23			19 30		19 38			19 45		19 53				20 00	20 08		20 15					20 25	
Hornsey	d				19 33					19 48						20 03			20 18					20 28	
Harringay	d				19 35					19 50						20 05			20 20					20 30	
Finsbury Park ⊖	a	19 27			19 37		19 42	19 44		19 52		19 57				20 07	20 12		20 22	20 14				20 32	
Finsbury Park	d	19 28			19 38		19 43			19 53		19 58				20 08	20 13		20 23					20 33	
Drayton Park	d	19 31		19 35	19 41	19 41	19 46		19 50	19 56	20 00	20 01		20 05	20 10	20 11	20 16	20 20	20 26		20 30	20 35		20 36	20 40
Highbury & Islington ⊖	d	19 34			19 44		19 49			19 59		20 04				20 14	20 19		20 29					20 39	
Essex Road	d	19 36			19 46		19 51			20 01		20 06				20 16	20 21		20 31					20 41	
Old Street ⊖	d	19 39			19 49		19 54			20 04		20 09				20 19	20 24		20 34					20 44	
Moorgate ⊖	a	19 43			19 53		19 58			20 08		20 13				20 23	20 28		20 38					20 48	
Finsbury Park	d			19a38		19a43		19 44	19a53		20a03			20a08	20a13			20a23		20 16	20a33	20a38			20a43
London Kings Cross ■ ⊖	a							19 50												20 25					
St Pancras International	d																								
Farringdon	d																								
City Thameslink	d																								
London Blackfriars	a																								
London Bridge	a																								

See Table 025 for fast trains between London and Stevenage

Table T024-R

Mondays to Fridays

21 May to 7 December

Hertford North and Welwyn Garden City - London

Station		GN	GN	TL ■	GN	GN	GN	GN		GN	GN	GN	GN	GN	GN	TL ■	GN	GN		GN	GN	GN	GN	TL ■	GN
Stevenage	d			20 10											20 28	20 40								21 10	
Watton-at-Stone	d					20 09									20 35										
Hertford North	d	20 00				20 17						20 30			20 47							21 00			
Bayford	d	20 05										20 35										21 05			
Cuffley	d	20 09				20 25						20 39			20 55							21 09			
Crews Hill	d	20 12										20 42										21 12			
Gordon Hill	d	20 16				20 31						20 46			21 01							21 16			
Enfield Chase	d	20 18				20 33						20 48			21 03							21 18			
Grange Park	d	20 20				20 35						20 50			21 05							21 20			
Winchmore Hill	d	20 22				20 37						20 52			21 07							21 22			
Palmers Green	d	20 25				20 40						20 55			21 10							21 25			
Bowes Park	a	20 27				20 42						20 57			21 12							21 27			
Knebworth	d			20 13												20 43								21 13	
Welwyn North	d			20 17												20 47								21 17	
Welwyn Garden City ■	d		20 08	20 22						20 28			20 39			20 52				20 58			21 09	21 22	
Hatfield	d		20 13	20 25						20 33			20 43			20 55				21 03			21 13	21 25	
Welham Green	d		20 17										20 47										21 17		
Brookmans Park	d		20 19										20 49										21 19		
Potters Bar	d		20 23	20 32						20 40			20 53			21 02				21 10			21 23	21 32	
Hadley Wood	d		20 26							20 44			20 56							21 14			21 26		
New Barnet	d		20 29							20 47			20 59							21 17			21 29		
Oakleigh Park	d		20 31							20 49			21 01							21 19			21 31		
New Southgate	a		20 34							20 52			21 04							21 22			21 34		
Alexandra Palace	d	20 30	20 38			20 45				20 55		21 00	21 08		21 15					21 25		21 30	21 38		
Hornsey	d	20 33				20 48				20 58		21 03			21 18					21 28		21 33			
Harringay	d	20 35				20 50				21 00		21 05			21 20					21 30		21 35			
Finsbury Park ⊖	a	20 37	20 42	20 43		20 52				21 02		21 07	21 12		21 22	21 13				21 32		21 37	21 42	21 43	
Finsbury Park	d	20 38	20 43			20 53				21 03		21 08	21 13		21 23					21 33		21 38	21 43		
Drayton Park	d	20 41	20 46		20 50	20 56	21 00	21 05		21 06	21 10	21 11	21 16	21 20	21 26		21 30	21 35		21 36	21 40	21 41	21 46		21 50
Highbury & Islington ⊖	d	20 44	20 49			20 59				21 09		21 14	21 19		21 29					21 39		21 44	21 49		
Essex Road	d	20 46	20 51			21 01				21 11		21 16	21 21		21 31					21 41		21 46	21 51		
Old Street ⊖	d	20 49	20 54			21 04				21 14		21 19	21 24		21 34					21 44		21 49	21 54		
Moorgate ⊖	a	20 53	20 58			21 08				21 18		21 23	21 28		21 38					21 48		21 53	21 58		
Finsbury Park	d			20 44	20a53		21a03	21a08			21a13			21a23		21 14	21a33	21a38			21a43			21 44	21a53
London Kings Cross ■ ⊖	a			20 50												21 20								21 50	
St Pancras International	d																								
Farringdon	d																								
City Thameslink	d																								
London Blackfriars	a																								
London Bridge	a																								

Station		GN	GN	GN		GN	GN	GN	GN	GN	GN	TL ■	GN	GN		GN	GN	GN	GN	TL ■	GN	GN	GN	GN	
Stevenage	d										21 28	21 40								22 10					
Watton-at-Stone	d	21 01									21 35														
Hertford North	d	21 17						21 30			21 47							22 00				22 16			
Bayford	d							21 35										22 05							
Cuffley	d	21 25						21 39			21 55							22 09				22 24			
Crews Hill	d							21 42										22 12							
Gordon Hill	d	21 31						21 46			22 01							22 16				22 31			
Enfield Chase	d	21 33						21 48			22 03							22 18				22 33			
Grange Park	d	21 35						21 50			22 05							22 20				22 35			
Winchmore Hill	d	21 37						21 52			22 07							22 22				22 37			
Palmers Green	d	21 40						21 55			22 10							22 25				22 40			
Bowes Park	a	21 42						21 57			22 12							22 27				22 42			
Knebworth	d											21 43								22 13					
Welwyn North	d											21 47								22 17					
Welwyn Garden City ■	d					21 28			21 39			21 52				21 58			22 09	22 22					
Hatfield	d					21 33			21 43			21 55				22 03			22 13	22 25					
Welham Green	d								21 47										22 17						
Brookmans Park	d								21 49										22 19						
Potters Bar	d					21 40			21 53			22 02				22 10			22 23	22 32					
Hadley Wood	d					21 44			21 56							22 14			22 26						
New Barnet	d					21 47			21 59							22 17			22 29						
Oakleigh Park	d					21 49			22 01							22 19			22 31						
New Southgate	a					21 52			22 04							22 22			22 34						
Alexandra Palace	d	21 45				21 55		22 00	22 08		22 15					22 25		22 30	22 38			22 45			
Hornsey	d	21 48				21 58		22 03			22 18					22 28		22 33				22 48			
Harringay	d	21 50				22 00		22 05			22 20					22 30		22 35				22 50			
Finsbury Park ⊖	a	21 52				22 02		22 07	22 12		22 22	22 13				22 32		22 37	22 42	22 43		22 52			
Finsbury Park	d	21 53				22 03		22 08	22 13		22 23					22 33		22 38	22 43			22 53			
Drayton Park	d	21 56	22 00	22 05		22 06	22 10	22 11	22 16	22 20	22 26		22 30	22 35		22 36	22 40	22 41	22 46		22 50	22 56	23 00	23 05	
Highbury & Islington ⊖	d	21 59				22 09		22 14	22 19		22 29					22 39		22 44	22 49			22 59			
Essex Road	d	22 01				22 11		22 16	22 21		22 31					22 41		22 46	22 51			23 01			
Old Street ⊖	d	22 04				22 14		22 19	22 24		22 34					22 44		22 49	22 54			23 04			
Moorgate ⊖	a	22 08				22 18		22 23	22 28		22 38					22 48		22 53	22 58			23 08			
Finsbury Park	d		22a03	22a08			22a13			22a23		22 14	22a33	22a38			22a43			22 44	22a53		23a03	23a08	
London Kings Cross ■ ⊖	a											22 20								22 50					
St Pancras International	d																								
Farringdon	d																								
City Thameslink	d																								
London Blackfriars	a																								
London Bridge	a																								

See Table 025 for fast trains between London and Stevenage

Table T024-R

Mondays to Fridays

21 May to 7 December

Hertford North and Welwyn Garden City - London

		GN	GN	GN	GN	GN	TL ■	GN	GN	GN		GN	TL ■	GN	GN	GN	GN	GN	GN	TL ■
Stevenage	d					22 28	22 40						23 10						23 28	23 40
Watton-at-Stone	d					22 35									23 07				23 35	
Hertford North	d			22 33		22 45						23 03			23 15			23 33	23 43	
Bayford	d			22 38								23 08						23 38	23 47	
Cuffley	d			22 42		22 53						23 12			23 23			23 42	23 52	
Crews Hill	d			22 45								23 15						23 45	23 55	
Gordon Hill	d			22 49		22 59						23 19			23 29			23 49	23 59	
Enfield Chase	d			22 51		23 01						23 21			23 31			23 51	00 01	
Grange Park	d			22 53		23 03						23 23			23 33			23 53	00 03	
Winchmore Hill	d			22 55		23 05						23 25			23 35			23 55	00 05	
Palmers Green	d			22 58		23 08						23 28			23 38			23 58	00 08	
Bowes Park	a			23 00		23 10						23 30			23 40			00 01	00 10	
Knebworth	d						22 43						23 14							23 43
Welwyn North	d						22 47						23 18							23 47
Welwyn Garden City ■	d	22 22					22 52		22 52				23 22				23 24			23 52
Hatfield	d	22 29					22 55		22 59				23 26				23 29			23 55
Welham Green	d	22 32							23 02								23 33			
Brookmans Park	d	22 35							23 05								23 35			
Potters Bar	d	22 38					23 02		23 08				23 32				23 39			00 02
Hadley Wood	d	22 42							23 12								23 42			
New Barnet	d	22 45							23 15								23 45			
Oakleigh Park	d	22 47							23 17								23 47			
New Southgate	a	22 50							23 20								23 50			
Alexandra Palace	d	22 53		23 03		23 13			23 23			23 33			23 43		23 53	00 04	00 13	
Hornsey	d	22 56		23 06		23 16			23 26			23 36			23 46		23 55	00 06	00 16	
Harringay	d	22 58		23 08		23 18			23 28			23 38			23 48		23 57	00 08	00 18	
Finsbury Park ⊖	a	23 00		23 10		23 20	23 13		23 30			23 40	23 43		23 50		00 01	00 11	00 20	00 15
Finsbury Park	d	23 03		23 11		23 21			23 31			23 41			23 51		00 01	00 11	00 21	
Drayton Park	d	23 06	23 10	23 14	23 20	23 24		23 30	23 34	23 37		23 44		23 47	23 54	23 57	00 04	00 14	00 24	
Highbury & Islington ⊖	d	23 09		23 17		23 27			23 37			23 47			23 57		00 07	00 17	00 27	
Essex Road	d	23 11		23 19		23 29			23 39			23 49			23 59		00 09	00 19	00 29	
Old Street ⊖	d	23 14		23 22		23 32			23 42			23 52			00 02		00 12	00 22	00 32	
Moorgate ⊖	a	23 18		23 26		23 36			23 46			23 56			00 06		00 16	00 26	00 36	
Finsbury Park	d		23a13		23a23		23 14	23a33		23a40			23 44	23a50		00a01				00 15
London Kings Cross ■ ⊖	a						23 20						23 50							00 21
St Pancras International	d																			
Farringdon	d																			
City Thameslink	d																			
London Blackfriars	a																			
London Bridge	a																			

Saturdays

26 May to 8 December

		GN	GN	GN	GN	TL ■	GN	GN	GN	GN		TL ■	GN	GN	GN	GN	GN	GN	TL ■	TL ■		GN	GN	GN	GN
Stevenage	d											00 16		04 22				05 00	05 04	05 11					
Watton-at-Stone	d																	05 07							
Hertford North	d													04 33				05 15						05 33	
Bayford	d																	05 20						05 38	
Cuffley	d													04 40				05 24						05 42	
Crews Hill	d																	05 27						05 45	
Gordon Hill	d													04 45				05 31						05 49	
Enfield Chase	d							00 01						04 47				05 33						05 51	
Grange Park	d							00 03										05 35						05 53	
Winchmore Hill	d							00 05						04 50				05 37						05 55	
Palmers Green	d							00 08						04 53				05 40						05 58	
Bowes Park	a							00 10										05 42						06 00	
Knebworth	d											00 19							05 07						
Welwyn North	d											00 23							05 11						
Welwyn Garden City ■	d											00 28	04 00		05 00				05 16	05 20		05 24			
Hatfield	d											00 31	04 04		05 05				05 19			05 29			
Welham Green	d												04 08									05 32			
Brookmans Park	d												04 10									05 35			
Potters Bar	d					00 02						00 38	04 14		05 11				05 26			05 38			
Hadley Wood	d												04 17									05 42			
New Barnet	d												04 20		05 16							05 45			
Oakleigh Park	d												04 22		05 18							05 47			
New Southgate	a												04 25		05 21							05 50			
Alexandra Palace	d				00 04			00 13					04 30	04 57				05 45				05 53		06 03	
Hornsey	d				00 06			00 16					04 32	04 59				05 48				05 56		06 06	
Harringay	d				00 08			00 18					04 34	05 01				05 50				05 58		06 08	
Finsbury Park ⊖	a				00 11	00 15		00 20				00 51	04 39	05 04	05 29			05 52	05 39	05 34		06 00		06 10	
Finsbury Park	d		00 01		00 11			00 21								05 41		05 53				06 01		06 11	
Drayton Park	d		00 04	00 07	00 14		00 17	00 24	00 27	00 37						05 44	05 47	05 58				06 04	06 07	06 14	06 17
Highbury & Islington ⊖	d		00 07		00 17			00 27								05 46		06 01				06 07		06 17	
Essex Road	d		00 09		00 19			00 29								05 48		06 03				06 09		06 19	
Old Street ⊖	d	00 02	00 12		00 22			00 32								05 52		06 06				06 12		06 22	
Moorgate ⊖	a	00 06	00 16		00 26			00 36								05 56		06 10				06 16		06 26	
Finsbury Park	d			00a10		00 15	00a20		00a30	00a40		00 51	04 40	05 05	05 30		05a50		05 39	05 35			06a10		06a20
London Kings Cross ■ ⊖	a					00 21						00 57	04 46	05 13	05 36				05 46						
St Pancras International	d																			05 45					
Farringdon	d																			05 49					
City Thameslink	d																								
London Blackfriars	a																			05 53					
London Bridge	a																								

See Table 025 for fast trains between London and Stevenage

Table T024-R

Saturdays

26 May to 8 December

Hertford North and Welwyn Garden City - London

		GN	GN	GN	TL ■	GN		GN	GN	GN	GN	TL ■	GN	GN	GN	GN		GN	GN	GN	GN	TL ■	GN	GN	GN
Stevenage	d			05 32	05 40						06 06	06 10									06 28	06 40			
Watton-at-Stone	d			05 39							06 13										06 35				
Hertford North	d			05 48				06 00			06 19							06 30			06 47				
Bayford	d			05 52				06 05										06 35							
Cuffley	d			05 57				06 09			06 26							06 39			06 55				
Crews Hill	d			06 00				06 12										06 42							
Gordon Hill	d			06 04				06 16			06 31							06 46			07 01				
Enfield Chase	d			06 06				06 18			06 33							06 48			07 03				
Grange Park	d			06 08				06 20			06 35							06 50			07 05				
Winchmore Hill	d			06 10				06 22			06 38							06 52			07 07				
Palmers Green	d			06 13				06 25			06 40							06 55			07 10				
Bowes Park	a			06 15				06 27			06 43							06 57			07 12				
Knebworth	d				05 44							06 13										06 43			
Welwyn North	d				05 47							06 17										06 47			
Welwyn Garden City ■	d	05 38			05 52				06 08			06 22			06 28				06 38			06 52			06 58
Hatfield	d	05 43			05 56				06 13			06 25			06 33				06 43			06 55			07 03
Welham Green	d	05 47							06 17										06 47						
Brookmans Park	d	05 49							06 19										06 49						
Potters Bar	d	05 53			06 03				06 23			06 32			06 40				06 53			07 02			07 10
Hadley Wood	d	05 56							06 26						06 44				06 56						07 14
New Barnet	d	05 59							06 29						06 47				06 59						07 17
Oakleigh Park	d	06 01							06 31						06 49				07 01						07 19
New Southgate	a	06 04							06 34						06 52				07 04						07 22
Alexandra Palace	d	06 10		06 18				06 30	06 38		06 46				06 55			07 00	07 08		07 15				07 25
Hornsey	d			06 21				06 33			06 49				06 58			07 03			07 18				07 28
Harringay	d			06 23				06 35			06 51				07 00			07 05			07 20				07 30
Finsbury Park ⊖	a	06 14		06 25	06 14			06 37	06 42		06 53	06 43			07 02			07 07	07 12		07 22	07 13			07 32
Finsbury Park	d	06 16		06 26				06 38	06 43		06 54				07 03			07 08	07 13		07 23				07 33
Drayton Park	d	06 19	06 27	06 29		06 37		06 41	06 46	06 47	06 57		06 57	07 05	07 06	07 10		07 11	07 16	07 20	07 26		07 30	07 35	07 36
Highbury & Islington ⊖	d	06 22		06 32				06 44	06 49		07 00				07 09			07 14	07 19		07 29				07 39
Essex Road	d	06 24		06 34				06 46	06 51		07 02				07 11			07 16	07 21		07 31				07 41
Old Street ⊖	d	06 27		06 37				06 49	06 54		07 05				07 14			07 19	07 24		07 34				07 44
Moorgate ⊖	a	06 31		06 41				06 53	06 58		07 09				07 18			07 23	07 28		07 38				07 48
Finsbury Park	d		06a30		06 15	06a40				06a50		06 44	07a00	07a08		07a13				07a23		07 14	07a33	07a38	
London Kings Cross ■ ⊖	a				06 21							06 50										07 20			
St Pancras International	d																								
Farringdon	d																								
City Thameslink	d																								
London Blackfriars	a																								
London Bridge	a																								

		GN		GN	GN	TL ■	GN	GN	GN	GN	GN	GN		GN	GN	GN	GN	TL ■	GN	GN	GN	GN		GN	GN
Stevenage	d					07 10											07 28	07 40							
Watton-at-Stone	d							07 07									07 35								
Hertford North	d			07 00				07 17						07 30			07 47							08 00	
Bayford	d			07 05										07 35										08 05	
Cuffley	d			07 09				07 25						07 39			07 55							08 09	
Crews Hill	d			07 12										07 42										08 12	
Gordon Hill	d			07 16				07 31						07 46			08 01							08 16	
Enfield Chase	d			07 18				07 33						07 48			08 03							08 18	
Grange Park	d			07 20				07 35						07 50			08 05							08 20	
Winchmore Hill	d			07 22				07 37						07 52			08 07							08 22	
Palmers Green	d			07 25				07 40						07 55			08 10							08 25	
Bowes Park	a			07 27				07 42						07 57			08 12							08 27	
Knebworth	d					07 13												07 43							
Welwyn North	d					07 17												07 47							
Welwyn Garden City ■	d				07 08	07 22					07 28				07 39			07 52			07 58				08 09
Hatfield	d				07 13	07 25					07 33				07 43			07 55			08 03				08 13
Welham Green	d				07 17										07 47										08 17
Brookmans Park	d				07 19										07 49										08 19
Potters Bar	d				07 23	07 32					07 40				07 53			08 02			08 10				08 23
Hadley Wood	d				07 26						07 44				07 56						08 14				08 26
New Barnet	d				07 29						07 47				07 59						08 17				08 29
Oakleigh Park	d				07 31						07 49				08 01						08 19				08 31
New Southgate	a				07 34						07 52				08 04						08 22				08 34
Alexandra Palace	d			07 30	07 38			07 45			07 55			08 00	08 08		08 15				08 25			08 30	08 38
Hornsey	d			07 33				07 48			07 58			08 03			08 18				08 28			08 33	
Harringay	d			07 35				07 50			08 00			08 05			08 20				08 30			08 35	
Finsbury Park ⊖	a			07 37	07 42	07 43		07 52			08 02			08 07	08 12		08 22	08 13			08 32			08 37	08 42
Finsbury Park	d			07 38	07 43			07 53			08 03			08 08	08 13		08 23				08 33			08 38	08 43
Drayton Park	d	07 40		07 41	07 46		07 50	07 56	08 00	08 05	08 06	08 10		08 11	08 16	08 20	08 26		08 30	08 35	08 36	08 40		08 41	08 46
Highbury & Islington ⊖	d			07 44	07 49			07 59			08 09			08 14	08 19		08 29				08 39			08 44	08 49
Essex Road	d			07 46	07 51			08 01			08 11			08 16	08 21		08 31				08 41			08 46	08 51
Old Street ⊖	d			07 49	07 54			08 04			08 14			08 19	08 24		08 34				08 44			08 49	08 54
Moorgate ⊖	a			07 53	07 58			08 08			08 18			08 23	08 28		08 38				08 48			08 53	08 58
Finsbury Park	d	07a43				07 44	07a53		08a03	08a08		08a13				08a23		08 14	08a33	08a38		08a43			
London Kings Cross ■ ⊖	a					07 50												08 20							
St Pancras International	d																								
Farringdon	d																								
City Thameslink	d																								
London Blackfriars	a																								
London Bridge	a																								

See Table 025 for fast trains between London and Stevenage

Table T024-R

Saturdays

26 May to 8 December

Hertford North and Welwyn Garden City - London

Station		TL 1	GN	GN	GN	GN	GN	GN	GN	GN	GN	GN	TL 1	GN	GN	GN	GN	GN	GN	TL 1	GN	GN	GN
Stevenage	d	08 10										08 28	08 40							09 10			
Watton-at-Stone	d			08 07								08 35										09 07	
Hertford North	d			08 17					08 30			08 47						09 00				09 17	
Bayford	d								08 35									09 05					
Cuffley	d			08 25					08 39			08 55						09 09				09 25	
Crews Hill	d								08 42									09 12					
Gordon Hill	d			08 31					08 46			09 01						09 16				09 31	
Enfield Chase	d			08 33					08 48			09 03						09 18				09 33	
Grange Park	d			08 35					08 50			09 05						09 20				09 35	
Winchmore Hill	d			08 37					08 52			09 07						09 22				09 37	
Palmers Green	d			08 40					08 55			09 10						09 25				09 40	
Bowes Park	a			08 42					08 57			09 12						09 27				09 42	
Knebworth	d	08 13											08 43							09 13			
Welwyn North	d	08 17											08 47							09 17			
Welwyn Garden City 4	d	08 22					08 28			08 39			08 52			08 58			09 09	09 22			
Hatfield	d	08 25					08 33			08 43			08 55			09 03			09 13	09 25			
Welham Green	d									08 47									09 17				
Brookmans Park	d									08 49									09 19				
Potters Bar	d	08 32					08 40			08 53			09 02			09 10			09 23	09 32			
Hadley Wood	d						08 44			08 56						09 14			09 26				
New Barnet	d						08 47			08 59						09 17			09 29				
Oakleigh Park	d						08 49			09 01						09 19			09 31				
New Southgate	a						08 52			09 04						09 22			09 34				
Alexandra Palace	d			08 45			08 55		09 00	09 08		09 15				09 25		09 30	09 38			09 45	
Hornsey	d			08 48			08 58		09 03			09 18				09 28		09 33				09 48	
Harringay	d			08 50			09 00		09 05			09 20				09 30		09 35				09 50	
Finsbury Park ⊖	a	08 43		08 52			09 02		09 07	09 12		09 22	09 13			09 32		09 37	09 42	09 43		09 52	
Finsbury Park	d			08 53			09 03		09 08	09 13		09 23				09 33		09 38	09 43			09 53	
Drayton Park	d		08 50	08 56	09 00	09 05	09 06	09 10	09 11	09 16	09 20	09 26		09 30	09 35	09 36	09 40	09 41	09 46		09 50	09 56	10 00
Highbury & Islington ⊖	d			08 59			09 09		09 14	09 19		09 29				09 39		09 44	09 49			09 59	
Essex Road	d			09 01			09 11		09 16	09 21		09 31				09 41		09 46	09 51			10 01	
Old Street ⊖	d			09 04			09 14		09 19	09 24		09 34				09 44		09 49	09 54			10 04	
Moorgate ⊖	a			09 08			09 18		09 23	09 28		09 38				09 48		09 53	09 58			10 08	
Finsbury Park	d	08 44	08a53		09a03	09a08		09a13			09a23		09 14	09a33	09a38		09a43			09 44	09a53		10a03
London Kings Cross 15 ⊖	a	08 50											09 20							09 50			
St Pancras International	d																						
Farringdon	d																						
City Thameslink	d																						
London Blackfriars	a																						
London Bridge	a																						

Station		GN	GN	GN	GN	GN	GN	GN	TL 1	GN	GN	GN	GN	GN	GN	TL 1	GN	GN	GN	GN	GN	GN
Stevenage	d							09 28	09 40							10 10						
Watton-at-Stone	d							09 35										10 07				
Hertford North	d				09 30			09 47						10 00				10 17				
Bayford	d				09 35									10 05								
Cuffley	d				09 39			09 55						10 09				10 25				
Crews Hill	d				09 42									10 12								
Gordon Hill	d				09 46			10 01						10 16				10 31				
Enfield Chase	d				09 48			10 03						10 18				10 33				
Grange Park	d				09 50			10 05						10 20				10 35				
Winchmore Hill	d				09 52			10 07						10 22				10 37				
Palmers Green	d				09 55			10 10						10 25				10 40				
Bowes Park	a				09 57			10 12						10 27				10 42				
Knebworth	d								09 43							10 13						
Welwyn North	d								09 47							10 17						
Welwyn Garden City 4	d		09 28			09 39			09 52			09 58			10 09	10 22					10 28	
Hatfield	d		09 33			09 43			09 55			10 03			10 13	10 25					10 33	
Welham Green	d					09 47									10 17							
Brookmans Park	d					09 49									10 19							
Potters Bar	d		09 40			09 53			10 02			10 10			10 23	10 32					10 40	
Hadley Wood	d		09 44			09 56						10 14			10 26						10 44	
New Barnet	d		09 47			09 59						10 17			10 29						10 47	
Oakleigh Park	d		09 49			10 01						10 19			10 31						10 49	
New Southgate	a		09 52			10 04						10 22			10 34						10 52	
Alexandra Palace	d		09 55		10 00	10 08		10 15				10 25		10 30	10 38			10 45			10 55	
Hornsey	d		09 58		10 03			10 18				10 28		10 33				10 48			10 58	
Harringay	d		10 00		10 05			10 20				10 30		10 35				10 50			11 00	
Finsbury Park ⊖	a		10 02		10 07	10 12		10 22	10 13			10 32		10 37	10 42	10 43		10 52			11 02	
Finsbury Park	d		10 03		10 08	10 13		10 23				10 33		10 38	10 43			10 53			11 03	
Drayton Park	d	10 05	10 06	10 10	10 11	10 16	10 20	10 26		10 30	10 35	10 36	10 40	10 41	10 46		10 50	10 56	11 00	11 05	11 06	11 10
Highbury & Islington ⊖	d		10 09		10 14	10 19		10 29				10 39		10 44	10 49			10 59			11 09	
Essex Road	d		10 11		10 16	10 21		10 31				10 41		10 46	10 51			11 01			11 11	
Old Street ⊖	d		10 14		10 19	10 24		10 34				10 44		10 49	10 54			11 04			11 14	
Moorgate ⊖	a		10 18		10 23	10 28		10 38				10 48		10 53	10 58			11 08			11 18	
Finsbury Park	d	10a08		10a13			10a23		10 14	10a33	10a38		10a43			10 44	10a53		11a03	11a08		11a13
London Kings Cross 15 ⊖	a								10 20							10 50						
St Pancras International	d																					
Farringdon	d																					
City Thameslink	d																					
London Blackfriars	a																					
London Bridge	a																					

See Table 025 for fast trains between London and Stevenage

Table T024-R

Saturdays

26 May to 8 December

Hertford North and Welwyn Garden City - London

Station		GN	GN	GN	GN	TL 1	GN	GN	GN	GN	GN	GN	TL 1	GN	GN	GN	GN	GN	GN	GN	GN	GN	GN
Stevenage	d				10 28	10 40							11 10										11 28
Watton-at-Stone	d				10 35										11 07								11 35
Hertford North	d	10 30			10 47						11 00				11 17					11 30			11 47
Bayford	d	10 35									11 05									11 35			
Cuffley	d	10 39			10 55						11 09				11 25					11 39			11 55
Crews Hill	d	10 42									11 12									11 42			
Gordon Hill	d	10 46			11 01						11 16				11 31					11 46			12 01
Enfield Chase	d	10 48			11 03						11 18				11 33					11 48			12 03
Grange Park	d	10 50			11 05						11 20				11 35					11 50			12 05
Winchmore Hill	d	10 52			11 07						11 22				11 37					11 52			12 07
Palmers Green	d	10 55			11 10						11 25				11 40					11 55			12 10
Bowes Park	a	10 57			11 12						11 27				11 42					11 57			12 12
Knebworth	d					10 44							11 13										
Welwyn North	d					10 47							11 17										
Welwyn Garden City 4	d		10 39			10 52			10 58			11 09	11 22					11 28			11 39		
Hatfield	d		10 43			10 56			11 03			11 13	11 25					11 33			11 43		
Welham Green	d		10 47									11 17									11 47		
Brookmans Park	d		10 49									11 19									11 49		
Potters Bar	d		10 53			11 03			11 10			11 23	11 32					11 40			11 53		
Hadley Wood	d		10 56						11 14			11 26						11 44			11 56		
New Barnet	d		10 59						11 17			11 29						11 47			11 59		
Oakleigh Park	d		11 01						11 19			11 31						11 49			12 01		
New Southgate	a		11 04						11 22			11 34						11 52			12 04		
Alexandra Palace	d	11 00	11 08		11 15				11 25		11 30	11 38			11 45			11 55		12 00	12 08		12 15
Hornsey	d	11 03			11 18				11 28		11 33				11 48			11 58		12 03			12 18
Harringay	d	11 05			11 20				11 30		11 35				11 50			12 00		12 05			12 20
Finsbury Park ⊖	a	11 07	11 12		11 22	11 13			11 32		11 37	11 42	11 43		11 52			12 02		12 07	12 12		12 22
Finsbury Park	d	11 08	11 13		11 23				11 33		11 38	11 43			11 53			12 03		12 08	12 13		12 23
Drayton Park	d	11 11	11 16	11 20	11 26		11 30	11 35	11 36	11 40	11 41	11 46		11 50	11 56	12 00	12 05	12 06	12 10	12 11	12 16	12 20	12 26
Highbury & Islington ⊖	d	11 14	11 19		11 29				11 39		11 44	11 49			11 59			12 09		12 14	12 19		12 29
Essex Road	d	11 16	11 21		11 31				11 41		11 46	11 51			12 01			12 11		12 16	12 21		12 31
Old Street ⊖	d	11 19	11 24		11 34				11 44		11 49	11 54			12 04			12 14		12 19	12 24		12 34
Moorgate ⊖	a	11 23	11 28		11 38				11 48		11 53	11 58			12 08			12 18		12 23	12 28		12 38
Finsbury Park	d			11a23		11 14	11a33	11a38		11a43			11 44	11a53		12a03	12a08		12a13			12a23	
London Kings Cross 15 ⊖	a					11 20							11 50										
St Pancras International	d																						
Farringdon	d																						
City Thameslink	d																						
London Blackfriars	a																						
London Bridge	a																						

Station		TL 1	GN	GN	GN	GN	GN	GN	TL 1	GN	GN	GN	GN	GN	GN	GN	GN	GN	GN	TL 1	GN	GN	GN
Stevenage	d	11 40							12 10										12 28	12 40			
Watton-at-Stone	d										12 07								12 35				
Hertford North	d						12 00				12 17					12 30			12 47				
Bayford	d						12 05									12 35							
Cuffley	d						12 09				12 25					12 39			12 55				
Crews Hill	d						12 12									12 42							
Gordon Hill	d						12 16				12 31					12 46			13 01				
Enfield Chase	d						12 18				12 33					12 48			13 03				
Grange Park	d						12 20				12 35					12 50			13 05				
Winchmore Hill	d						12 22				12 37					12 52			13 07				
Palmers Green	d						12 25				12 40					12 55			13 10				
Bowes Park	a						12 27				12 42					12 57			13 12				
Knebworth	d	11 43							12 13											12 43			
Welwyn North	d	11 47							12 18											12 47			
Welwyn Garden City 4	d	11 52			11 58			12 09	12 22					12 28			12 39			12 52			12 58
Hatfield	d	11 55			12 03			12 13	12 26					12 33			12 43			12 55			13 03
Welham Green	d							12 17									12 47						
Brookmans Park	d							12 19									12 49						
Potters Bar	d	12 02			12 10			12 23	12 32					12 40			12 53			13 02			13 10
Hadley Wood	d				12 14			12 26						12 44			12 56						13 14
New Barnet	d				12 17			12 29						12 47			12 59						13 17
Oakleigh Park	d				12 19			12 31						12 49			13 01						13 19
New Southgate	a				12 22			12 34						12 52			13 04						13 22
Alexandra Palace	d				12 25		12 30	12 38			12 45			12 55		13 00	13 08		13 15				13 25
Hornsey	d				12 28		12 33				12 48			12 58		13 03			13 18				13 28
Harringay	d				12 30		12 35				12 50			13 00		13 05			13 20				13 30
Finsbury Park ⊖	a	12 13			12 32		12 37	12 42	12 43		12 52			13 02		13 07	13 12		13 22	13 13			13 32
Finsbury Park	d				12 33		12 38	12 43			12 53			13 03		13 08	13 13		13 23				13 33
Drayton Park	d		12 30	12 35	12 36	12 40	12 41	12 46		12 50	12 56	13 00	13 05	13 06	13 10	13 11	13 16	13 20	13 26		13 30	13 35	13 36
Highbury & Islington ⊖	d				12 39		12 44	12 49			12 59			13 09		13 14	13 19		13 29				13 39
Essex Road	d				12 41		12 46	12 51			13 01			13 11		13 16	13 21		13 31				13 41
Old Street ⊖	d				12 44		12 49	12 54			13 04			13 14		13 19	13 24		13 34				13 44
Moorgate ⊖	a				12 48		12 53	12 58			13 08			13 18		13 23	13 28		13 38				13 48
Finsbury Park	d	12 14	12a33	12a38		12a43			12 44	12a53		13a03	13a08		13a13			13a23		13 14	13a33	13a38	
London Kings Cross 15 ⊖	a	12 20							12 50											13 20			
St Pancras International	d																						
Farringdon	d																						
City Thameslink	d																						
London Blackfriars	a																						
London Bridge	a																						

See Table 025 for fast trains between London and Stevenage

Table T024-R

Saturdays

26 May to 8 December

Hertford North and Welwyn Garden City - London

		GN		GN	GN	TL ■	GN	GN	GN	GN	GN	GN		GN	GN	GN	GN	TL ■	GN	GN	GN	GN		GN	GN
Stevenage	d					13 10											13 28	13 40							
Watton-at-Stone	d							13 07									13 35								
Hertford North	d			13 00				13 17						13 30			13 47							14 00	
Bayford	d			13 05										13 35										14 05	
Cuffley	d			13 09				13 25						13 39			13 55							14 09	
Crews Hill	d			13 12										13 42										14 12	
Gordon Hill	d			13 16				13 31						13 46			14 01							14 16	
Enfield Chase	d			13 18				13 33						13 48			14 03							14 18	
Grange Park	d			13 20				13 35						13 50			14 05							14 20	
Winchmore Hill	d			13 22				13 37						13 52			14 07							14 22	
Palmers Green	d			13 25				13 40						13 55			14 10							14 25	
Bowes Park	a			13 27				13 42						13 57			14 12							14 27	
Knebworth	d					13 14												13 43							
Welwyn North	d					13 17												13 47							
Welwyn Garden City ■	d				13 09	13 22					13 28				13 39			13 52			13 58				14 09
Hatfield	d				13 13	13 26					13 33				13 43			13 55			14 03				14 13
Welham Green	d				13 17										13 47										14 17
Brookmans Park	d				13 19										13 49										14 19
Potters Bar	d				13 23	13 33					13 40				13 53			14 02			14 10				14 23
Hadley Wood	d				13 26						13 44				13 56						14 14				14 26
New Barnet	d				13 29						13 47				13 59						14 17				14 29
Oakleigh Park	d				13 31						13 49				14 01						14 19				14 31
New Southgate	a				13 34						13 52				14 04						14 22				14 34
Alexandra Palace	d			13 30	13 38			13 45			13 55			14 00	14 08		14 15				14 25			14 30	14 38
Hornsey	d			13 33				13 48			13 58			14 03			14 18				14 28			14 33	
Harringay	d			13 35				13 50			14 00			14 05			14 20				14 30			14 35	
Finsbury Park ⊖	a			13 37	13 42	13 44		13 52			14 02			14 07	14 12		14 22	14 13			14 32			14 37	14 42
Finsbury Park	d			13 38	13 43			13 53			14 03			14 08	14 13		14 23				14 33			14 38	14 43
Drayton Park	d	13 40		13 41	13 46		13 50	13 56	14 00	14 05	14 06	14 10		14 11	14 16	14 20	14 26		14 30	14 35	14 36	14 40		14 41	14 46
Highbury & Islington ⊖	d			13 44	13 49			13 59			14 09			14 14	14 19		14 29				14 39			14 44	14 49
Essex Road	d			13 46	13 51			14 01			14 11			14 16	14 21		14 31				14 41			14 46	14 51
Old Street ⊖	d			13 49	13 54			14 04			14 14			14 19	14 24		14 34				14 44			14 49	14 54
Moorgate ⊖	a			13 53	13 58			14 08			14 18			14 23	14 28		14 38				14 48			14 53	14 58
Finsbury Park	d	13a43				13 45	13a53		14a03	14a08		14a13				14a23		14 14	14a33	14a38		14a43			
London Kings Cross ■■ ⊖	a					13 51												14 20							
St Pancras International	d																								
Farringdon	d																								
City Thameslink	d																								
London Blackfriars	a																								
London Bridge	a																								

		TL ■	GN	GN	GN	GN	GN	GN		GN	GN	GN	GN	TL ■	GN	GN	GN	GN		GN	GN	TL ■	GN	GN	GN
Stevenage	d	14 10											14 28	14 40								15 10			
Watton-at-Stone	d			14 07									14 35											15 07	
Hertford North	d			14 17						14 30			14 47							15 00				15 17	
Bayford	d									14 35										15 05					
Cuffley	d			14 25						14 39			14 55							15 09				15 25	
Crews Hill	d									14 42										15 12					
Gordon Hill	d			14 31						14 46			15 01							15 16				15 31	
Enfield Chase	d			14 33						14 48			15 03							15 18				15 33	
Grange Park	d			14 35						14 50			15 05							15 20				15 35	
Winchmore Hill	d			14 37						14 52			15 07							15 22				15 37	
Palmers Green	d			14 40						14 55			15 10							15 25				15 40	
Bowes Park	a			14 42						14 57			15 12							15 27				15 42	
Knebworth	d	14 13												14 43								15 13			
Welwyn North	d	14 17												14 47								15 17			
Welwyn Garden City ■	d	14 22					14 28				14 39			14 52			14 58				15 09	15 22			
Hatfield	d	14 25					14 33				14 43			14 55			15 03				15 13	15 25			
Welham Green	d										14 47										15 17				
Brookmans Park	d										14 49										15 19				
Potters Bar	d	14 32					14 40				14 53			15 02			15 10				15 23	15 32			
Hadley Wood	d						14 44				14 56						15 14				15 26				
New Barnet	d						14 47				14 59						15 17				15 29				
Oakleigh Park	d						14 49				15 01						15 19				15 31				
New Southgate	a						14 52				15 04						15 22				15 34				
Alexandra Palace	d			14 45			14 55			15 00	15 08		15 15				15 25			15 30	15 38			15 45	
Hornsey	d			14 48			14 58			15 03			15 18				15 28			15 33				15 48	
Harringay	d			14 50			15 00			15 05			15 20				15 30			15 35				15 50	
Finsbury Park ⊖	a	14 43		14 52			15 02			15 07	15 12		15 22	15 13			15 32			15 37	15 42	15 43		15 52	
Finsbury Park	d			14 53			15 03			15 08	15 13		15 23				15 33			15 38	15 43			15 53	
Drayton Park	d		14 50	14 56	15 00	15 05	15 06	15 10		15 11	15 16	15 20	15 26		15 30	15 35	15 36	15 40		15 41	15 46		15 50	15 56	16 00
Highbury & Islington ⊖	d			14 59			15 09			15 14	15 19		15 29				15 39			15 44	15 49			15 59	
Essex Road	d			15 01			15 11			15 16	15 21		15 31				15 41			15 46	15 51			16 01	
Old Street ⊖	d			15 04			15 14			15 19	15 24		15 34				15 44			15 49	15 54			16 04	
Moorgate ⊖	a			15 08			15 18			15 23	15 28		15 38				15 48			15 53	15 58			16 08	
Finsbury Park	d	14 44	14a53		15a03	15a08		15a13				15a23		15 14	15a33	15a38		15a43				15 44	15a53		16a03
London Kings Cross ■■ ⊖	a	14 50												15 20								15 50			
St Pancras International	d																								
Farringdon	d																								
City Thameslink	d																								
London Blackfriars	a																								
London Bridge	a																								

See Table 025 for fast trains between London and Stevenage

Table T024-R

Saturdays

26 May to 8 December

Hertford North and Welwyn Garden City - London

		GN	GN	GN		GN	GN	GN	GN	TL ■	GN	GN	GN	GN		GN	GN	TL ■	GN	GN	GN	GN	GN	GN	
Stevenage	d								15 28	15 40								16 10							
Watton-at-Stone	d								15 35											16 07					
Hertford North	d					15 30			15 47							16 00				16 17					
Bayford	d					15 35										16 05									
Cuffley	d					15 39			15 55							16 09				16 25					
Crews Hill	d					15 42										16 12									
Gordon Hill	d					15 46			16 01							16 16				16 31					
Enfield Chase	d					15 48			16 03							16 18				16 33					
Grange Park	d					15 50			16 05							16 20				16 35					
Winchmore Hill	d					15 52			16 07							16 22				16 37					
Palmers Green	d					15 55			16 10							16 25				16 40					
Bowes Park	a					15 57			16 12							16 27				16 42					
Knebworth	d									15 43								16 13							
Welwyn North	d									15 47								16 17							
Welwyn Garden City ■	d		15 28				15 39			15 52			15 58				16 09	16 22					16 28		
Hatfield	d		15 33				15 43			15 55			16 03				16 13	16 26					16 33		
Welham Green	d						15 47										16 17								
Brookmans Park	d						15 49										16 19								
Potters Bar	d		15 40				15 53			16 02			16 10				16 23	16 33					16 40		
Hadley Wood	d		15 44				15 56						16 14				16 26						16 44		
New Barnet	d		15 47				15 59						16 17				16 29						16 47		
Oakleigh Park	d		15 49				16 01						16 19				16 31						16 49		
New Southgate	a		15 52				16 04						16 22				16 34						16 52		
Alexandra Palace	d		15 55			16 00	16 08		16 15				16 25			16 30	16 38			16 45			16 55		
Hornsey	d		15 58			16 03			16 18				16 28			16 33				16 48			16 58		
Harringay	d		16 00			16 05			16 20				16 30			16 35				16 50			17 00		
Finsbury Park ⊖	a		16 02			16 07	16 12		16 22	16 13			16 32			16 37	16 42	16 43		16 52			17 02		
Finsbury Park	d		16 03			16 08	16 13		16 23				16 33			16 38	16 43			16 53			17 03		
Drayton Park	d	16 05	16 06	16 10		16 11	16 16	16 20	16 26		16 30	16 35	16 36	16 40		16 41	16 46		16 50	16 56	17 00	17 05	17 06	17 10	
Highbury & Islington ⊖	d		16 09			16 14	16 19		16 29				16 39			16 44	16 49			16 59			17 09		
Essex Road	d		16 11			16 16	16 21		16 31				16 41			16 46	16 51			17 01			17 11		
Old Street ⊖	d		16 14			16 19	16 24		16 34				16 44			16 49	16 54			17 04			17 14		
Moorgate ⊖	a		16 18			16 23	16 28		16 38				16 48			16 53	16 58			17 08			17 18		
Finsbury Park	d	16a08		16a13				16a23		16 14	16a33	16a38		16a43				16 44	16a53		17a03	17a08		17a13	
London Kings Cross ■■ ⊖	a									16 20								16 50							
St Pancras International	d																								
Farringdon	d																								
City Thameslink	d																								
London Blackfriars	a																								
London Bridge	a																								

		GN	GN	GN	GN	TL ■	GN	GN	GN	GN		GN	GN	TL ■	GN	GN	GN	GN	GN	GN		GN	GN	GN	GN
Stevenage	d				16 28	16 40								17 10											17 28
Watton-at-Stone	d				16 35											17 07									17 35
Hertford North	d	16 30			16 47							17 00				17 17						17 30			17 47
Bayford	d	16 35										17 05										17 35			
Cuffley	d	16 39			16 55							17 09				17 25						17 39			17 55
Crews Hill	d	16 42										17 12										17 42			
Gordon Hill	d	16 46			17 01							17 16				17 31						17 46			18 01
Enfield Chase	d	16 48			17 03							17 18				17 33						17 48			18 03
Grange Park	d	16 50			17 05							17 20				17 35						17 50			18 05
Winchmore Hill	d	16 52			17 07							17 22				17 37						17 52			18 07
Palmers Green	d	16 55			17 10							17 25				17 40						17 55			18 10
Bowes Park	a	16 57			17 12							17 27				17 42						17 57			18 12
Knebworth	d					16 43								17 13											
Welwyn North	d					16 48								17 17											
Welwyn Garden City ■	d		16 39			16 53			16 58				17 09	17 22					17 28				17 39		
Hatfield	d		16 43			16 56			17 03				17 13	17 25					17 33				17 43		
Welham Green	d		16 47										17 17										17 47		
Brookmans Park	d		16 49										17 19										17 49		
Potters Bar	d		16 53			17 03			17 10				17 23	17 32					17 40				17 53		
Hadley Wood	d		16 56						17 14				17 26						17 44				17 56		
New Barnet	d		16 59						17 17				17 29						17 47				17 59		
Oakleigh Park	d		17 01						17 19				17 31						17 49				18 01		
New Southgate	a		17 04						17 22				17 34						17 52				18 04		
Alexandra Palace	d	17 00	17 08		17 15				17 25			17 30	17 38			17 45			17 55			18 00	18 08		18 15
Hornsey	d	17 03			17 18				17 28			17 33				17 48			17 58			18 03			18 18
Harringay	d	17 05			17 20				17 30			17 35				17 50			18 00			18 05			18 20
Finsbury Park ⊖	a	17 07	17 12		17 22	17 13			17 32			17 37	17 42	17 43		17 52			18 02			18 07	18 12		18 22
Finsbury Park	d	17 08	17 13		17 23				17 33			17 38	17 43			17 53			18 03			18 08	18 13		18 23
Drayton Park	d	17 11	17 16	17 20	17 26		17 30	17 35	17 36	17 40		17 41	17 46		17 50	17 56	18 00	18 05	18 06	18 10		18 11	18 16	18 20	18 26
Highbury & Islington ⊖	d	17 14	17 19		17 29				17 39			17 44	17 49			17 59			18 09			18 14	18 19		18 29
Essex Road	d	17 16	17 21		17 31				17 41			17 46	17 51			18 01			18 11			18 16	18 21		18 31
Old Street ⊖	d	17 19	17 24		17 34				17 44			17 49	17 54			18 04			18 14			18 19	18 24		18 34
Moorgate ⊖	a	17 23	17 28		17 38				17 48			17 53	17 58			18 08			18 18			18 23	18 28		18 38
Finsbury Park	d			17a23		17 14	17a33	17a38		17a43				17 44	17a53		18a03	18a08		18a13				18a23	
London Kings Cross ■■ ⊖	a					17 20								17 50											
St Pancras International	d																								
Farringdon	d																								
City Thameslink	d																								
London Blackfriars	a																								
London Bridge	a																								

See Table 025 for fast trains between London and Stevenage

Table T024-R

Saturdays

26 May to 8 December

Hertford North and Welwyn Garden City - London

		TL 1	GN	GN	GN	GN		GN	GN	TL 1	GN	GN	GN	GN	GN	GN		GN	GN	GN	GN	TL 1	GN	GN	GN
Stevenage	d	17 40								18 10											18 28	18 40			
Watton-at-Stone	d											18 07									18 35				
Hertford North	d							18 00				18 17						18 30			18 47				
Bayford	d							18 05										18 35							
Cuffley	d							18 09				18 25						18 39			18 55				
Crews Hill	d							18 12										18 42							
Gordon Hill	d							18 16				18 31						18 46			19 01				
Enfield Chase	d							18 18				18 33						18 48			19 03				
Grange Park	d							18 20				18 35						18 50			19 05				
Winchmore Hill	d							18 22				18 37						18 52			19 07				
Palmers Green	d							18 25				18 40						18 55			19 10				
Bowes Park	a							18 27				18 42						18 57			19 12				
Knebworth	d	17 43								18 13												18 43			
Welwyn North	d	17 47								18 18												18 47			
Welwyn Garden City	d	17 52			17 58				18 09	18 23					18 28				18 39			18 52			18 58
Hatfield	d	17 55			18 03				18 13	18 26					18 33				18 43			18 55			19 03
Welham Green	d								18 17										18 47						
Brookmans Park	d								18 19										18 49						
Potters Bar	d	18 02			18 10				18 23	18 32					18 40				18 53			19 02			19 10
Hadley Wood	d				18 14				18 26						18 44				18 56						19 14
New Barnet	d				18 17				18 29						18 47				18 59						19 17
Oakleigh Park	d				18 19				18 31						18 49				19 01						19 19
New Southgate	a				18 22				18 34						18 52				19 04						19 22
Alexandra Palace	d				18 25			18 30	18 38			18 45			18 55			19 00	19 08		19 15				19 25
Hornsey	d				18 28			18 33				18 48			18 58			19 03			19 18				19 28
Harringay	d				18 30			18 35				18 50			19 00			19 05			19 20				19 30
Finsbury Park ⊖	a	18 13			18 32			18 37	18 42	18 43		18 52			19 02			19 07	19 12		19 22	19 13			19 32
Finsbury Park	d				18 33			18 38	18 43			18 53			19 03			19 08	19 13		19 23				19 33
Drayton Park	d		18 30	18 35	18 36	18 40		18 41	18 46		18 50	18 56	19 00	19 05	19 06	19 10		19 11	19 16	19 20	19 26		19 30	19 35	19 36
Highbury & Islington ⊖	d				18 39			18 44	18 49			18 59			19 09			19 14	19 19		19 29				19 39
Essex Road	d				18 41			18 46	18 51			19 01			19 11			19 16	19 21		19 31				19 41
Old Street ⊖	d				18 44			18 49	18 54			19 04			19 14			19 19	19 24		19 34				19 44
Moorgate ⊖	a				18 48			18 53	18 58			19 08			19 18			19 23	19 28		19 38				19 48
Finsbury Park	d	18 14	18a33	18a38		18a43				18 44	18a53		19a03	19a08		19a13				19a23		19 14	19a33	19a38	
London Kings Cross ⊖	a	18 20								18 50												19 20			
St Pancras International	d																								
Farringdon	d																								
City Thameslink	d																								
London Blackfriars	a																								
London Bridge	a																								

		GN		GN	GN	TL 1	GN	GN	GN	GN	GN	GN		GN	GN	GN	GN	TL 1	GN	GN	GN	GN		GN	GN
Stevenage	d					19 10											19 28	19 40							
Watton-at-Stone	d							19 07									19 35								
Hertford North	d			19 00				19 17						19 30			19 47							20 00	
Bayford	d			19 05										19 35										20 05	
Cuffley	d			19 09				19 25						19 39			19 55							20 09	
Crews Hill	d			19 12										19 42										20 12	
Gordon Hill	d			19 16				19 31						19 46			20 01							20 16	
Enfield Chase	d			19 18				19 33						19 48			20 03							20 18	
Grange Park	d			19 20				19 35						19 50			20 05							20 20	
Winchmore Hill	d			19 22				19 37						19 52			20 07							20 22	
Palmers Green	d			19 25				19 40						19 55			20 10							20 25	
Bowes Park	a			19 27				19 42						19 57			20 12							20 27	
Knebworth	d					19 13												19 43							
Welwyn North	d					19 19												19 47							
Welwyn Garden City	d				19 09	19 24					19 28				19 39			19 52			19 58				20 09
Hatfield	d				19 13	19 27					19 33				19 43			19 55			20 03				20 13
Welham Green	d				19 17										19 47										20 17
Brookmans Park	d				19 19										19 49										20 19
Potters Bar	d				19 23	19 34					19 40				19 53			20 02			20 10				20 23
Hadley Wood	d				19 26						19 44				19 56						20 14				20 26
New Barnet	d				19 29						19 47				19 59						20 17				20 29
Oakleigh Park	d				19 31						19 49				20 01						20 19				20 31
New Southgate	a				19 34						19 52				20 04						20 22				20 34
Alexandra Palace	d			19 30	19 38			19 45			19 55			20 00	20 08		20 15				20 25			20 30	20 38
Hornsey	d			19 33				19 48			19 58			20 03			20 18				20 28			20 33	
Harringay	d			19 35				19 50			20 00			20 05			20 20				20 30			20 35	
Finsbury Park ⊖	a			19 37	19 42	19 44		19 52			20 02			20 07	20 12		20 22	20 13			20 32			20 37	20 42
Finsbury Park	d			19 38	19 43			19 53			20 03			20 08	20 13		20 23				20 33			20 38	20 43
Drayton Park	d	19 40		19 41	19 46		19 50	19 56	20 00	20 05	20 06	20 10		20 11	20 16	20 20	20 26		20 30	20 35	20 36	20 40		20 41	20 46
Highbury & Islington ⊖	d			19 44	19 49			19 59			20 09			20 14	20 19		20 29				20 39			20 44	20 49
Essex Road	d			19 46	19 51			20 01			20 11			20 16	20 21		20 31				20 41			20 46	20 51
Old Street ⊖	d			19 49	19 54			20 04			20 14			20 19	20 24		20 34				20 44			20 49	20 54
Moorgate ⊖	a			19 53	19 58			20 08			20 18			20 23	20 28		20 38				20 48			20 53	20 58
Finsbury Park	d	19a43				19 45	19a53		20a03	20a08		20a13				20a23		20 14	20a33	20a38		20a43			
London Kings Cross ⊖	a					19 51												20 20							
St Pancras International	d																								
Farringdon	d																								
City Thameslink	d																								
London Blackfriars	a																								
London Bridge	a																								

See Table 025 for fast trains between London and Stevenage

Table T024-R

Saturdays

26 May to 8 December

Hertford North and Welwyn Garden City - London

		TL 1	GN	GN	GN	GN	GN	GN		GN	GN	GN	GN	TL 1	GN	GN	GN	GN		GN	GN	TL 1	GN	GN	GN
Stevenage	d	20 10											20 28	20 40								21 10			
Watton-at-Stone	d			20 07									20 35											21 07	
Hertford North	d			20 17						20 30			20 47							21 00				21 17	
Bayford	d									20 35										21 05					
Cuffley	d			20 25						20 39			20 55							21 09				21 25	
Crews Hill	d									20 42										21 12					
Gordon Hill	d			20 31						20 46			21 01							21 16				21 31	
Enfield Chase	d			20 33						20 48			21 03							21 18				21 33	
Grange Park	d			20 35						20 50			21 05							21 20				21 35	
Winchmore Hill	d			20 37						20 52			21 07							21 22				21 37	
Palmers Green	d			20 40						20 55			21 10							21 25				21 40	
Bowes Park	a			20 42						20 57			21 12							21 27				21 42	
Knebworth	d	20 13												20 43								21 13			
Welwyn North	d	20 17												20 47								21 17			
Welwyn Garden City	d	20 22					20 28				20 39			20 52			20 58				21 09	21 22			
Hatfield	d	20 25					20 33				20 43			20 55			21 03				21 13	21 25			
Welham Green	d										20 47										21 17				
Brookmans Park	d										20 49										21 19				
Potters Bar	d	20 32					20 40				20 53			21 02			21 10				21 23	21 32			
Hadley Wood	d						20 44				20 56						21 14				21 26				
New Barnet	d						20 47				20 59						21 17				21 29				
Oakleigh Park	d						20 49				21 01						21 19				21 31				
New Southgate	a						20 52				21 04						21 22				21 34				
Alexandra Palace	d			20 45			20 55			21 00	21 08		21 15				21 25			21 30	21 38			21 45	
Hornsey	d			20 48			20 58			21 03			21 18				21 28			21 33				21 48	
Harringay	d			20 50			21 00			21 05			21 20				21 30			21 35				21 50	
Finsbury Park ⊖	a	20 43		20 52			21 02			21 07	21 12		21 22	21 13			21 32			21 37	21 42	21 43		21 52	
Finsbury Park	d			20 53			21 03			21 08	21 13		21 23				21 33			21 38	21 43			21 53	
Drayton Park	d		20 50	20 56	21 00	21 05	21 06	21 10		21 11	21 16	21 20	21 26		21 30	21 35	21 36	21 40		21 41	21 46		21 50	21 56	22 00
Highbury & Islington ⊖	d			20 59			21 09			21 14	21 19		21 29				21 39			21 44	21 49			21 59	
Essex Road	d			21 01			21 11			21 16	21 21		21 31				21 41			21 46	21 51			22 01	
Old Street ⊖	d			21 04			21 14			21 19	21 24		21 34				21 44			21 49	21 54			22 04	
Moorgate ⊖	a			21 08			21 18			21 23	21 28		21 38				21 48			21 53	21 58			22 08	
Finsbury Park	d	20 44	20a53		21a03	21a08		21a13				21a23		21 14	21a33	21a38		21a43				21 44	21a53		22a03
London Kings Cross ⊖	a	20 50												21 20								21 50			
St Pancras International	d																								
Farringdon	d																								
City Thameslink	d																								
London Blackfriars	a																								
London Bridge	a																								

		GN	GN	GN		GN	GN	GN	GN	TL 1	GN	GN	GN	GN		GN	GN	TL 1	GN	GN	GN	GN	GN	GN	
Stevenage	d								21 28	21 40								22 10							
Watton-at-Stone	d								21 35											22 07					
Hertford North	d					21 30			21 47							22 00				22 17					
Bayford	d					21 35										22 05									
Cuffley	d					21 39			21 55							22 09				22 25					
Crews Hill	d					21 42										22 12									
Gordon Hill	d					21 46			22 01							22 16				22 31					
Enfield Chase	d					21 48			22 03							22 18				22 33					
Grange Park	d					21 50			22 05							22 20				22 35					
Winchmore Hill	d					21 52			22 07							22 22				22 37					
Palmers Green	d					21 55			22 10							22 25				22 40					
Bowes Park	a					21 57			22 12							22 27				22 42					
Knebworth	d									21 43								22 13							
Welwyn North	d									21 47								22 17							
Welwyn Garden City	d		21 28				21 39			21 52			21 58				22 09	22 22					22 22		
Hatfield	d		21 33				21 43			21 55			22 03				22 13	22 25					22 29		
Welham Green	d						21 47										22 17						22 32		
Brookmans Park	d						21 49										22 19						22 35		
Potters Bar	d		21 40				21 53			22 02			22 10				22 23	22 32					22 38		
Hadley Wood	d		21 44				21 56						22 14				22 26						22 42		
New Barnet	d		21 47				21 59						22 17				22 29						22 45		
Oakleigh Park	d		21 49				22 01						22 19				22 31						22 47		
New Southgate	a		21 52				22 04						22 22				22 34						22 50		
Alexandra Palace	d		21 55			22 00	22 08		22 15				22 25			22 30	22 38			22 45			22 53		
Hornsey	d		21 58			22 03			22 18				22 28			22 33				22 48			22 56		
Harringay	d		22 00			22 05			22 20				22 30			22 35				22 50			22 58		
Finsbury Park ⊖	a		22 02			22 07	22 12		22 22	22 13			22 32			22 37	22 42	22 43		22 52			23 00		
Finsbury Park	d		22 03			22 08	22 13		22 23				22 33			22 38	22 43			22 53			23 03		
Drayton Park	d	22 05	22 06	22 10		22 11	22 16	22 20	22 26		22 30	22 35	22 36	22 40		22 41	22 46		22 50	22 56	23 00	23 05	23 06	23 10	
Highbury & Islington ⊖	d		22 09			22 14	22 19		22 29				22 39			22 44	22 49			22 59			23 09		
Essex Road	d		22 11			22 16	22 21		22 31				22 41			22 46	22 51			23 01			23 11		
Old Street ⊖	d		22 14			22 19	22 24		22 34				22 44			22 49	22 54			23 04			23 14		
Moorgate ⊖	a		22 18			22 23	22 28		22 38				22 48			22 53	22 58			23 08			23 18		
Finsbury Park	d	22a08		22a13				22a23		22 14	22a33	22a38		22a43				22 44	22a53		23a03	23a08		23a13	
London Kings Cross ⊖	a									22 20								22 50							
St Pancras International	d																								
Farringdon	d																								
City Thameslink	d																								
London Blackfriars	a																								
London Bridge	a																								

See Table 025 for fast trains between London and Stevenage

Table T024-R

Saturdays
26 May to 8 December

Hertford North and Welwyn Garden City - London

		GN	GN	GN	TL ■	GN	GN	GN	GN	TL ■		GN	GN	GN	GN	GN	GN	TL ■
Stevenage	d			22 28	22 40					23 10							23 28	23 40
Watton-at-Stone	d			22 35									23 07				23 35	
Hertford North	d	22 33		22 45					23 03				23 15			23 33	23 43	
Bayford	d	22 38							23 08							23 38	23 47	
Cuffley	d	22 42		22 53					23 12				23 23			23 42	23 52	
Crews Hill	d	22 45							23 15							23 45	23 55	
Gordon Hill	d	22 49		22 59					23 19				23 29			23 49	23 59	
Enfield Chase	d	22 51		23 01					23 21				23 31			23 51	00 01	
Grange Park	d	22 53		23 03					23 23				23 33			23 53	00 03	
Winchmore Hill	d	22 55		23 05					23 25				23 35			23 55	00 05	
Palmers Green	d	22 58		23 08					23 28				23 38			23 58	00 08	
Bowes Park	a	23 00		23 10					23 30				23 40			00 01	00 10	
Knebworth	d				22 43					23 13								23 43
Welwyn North	d				22 47					23 17								23 47
Welwyn Garden City ■	d				22 52		22 52			23 22					23 22			23 52
Hatfield	d				22 55		22 59			23 25					23 29			23 55
Welham Green	d						23 02								23 32			
Brookmans Park	d						23 05								23 35			
Potters Bar	d				23 02		23 08			23 32					23 38			00 02
Hadley Wood	d						23 12								23 42			
New Barnet	d						23 15								23 45			
Oakleigh Park	d						23 17								23 47			
New Southgate	a						23 20								23 50			
Alexandra Palace	d	23 03		23 13			23 23		23 33				23 43		23 53	00 04	00 13	
Hornsey	d	23 06		23 16			23 26		23 36				23 46		23 55	00 06	00 16	
Harringay	d	23 08		23 18			23 28		23 38				23 48		23 57	00 08	00 18	
Finsbury Park ⊖	a	23 10		23 20	23 13		23 30		23 40	23 43			23 50		23 59	00 11	00 20	00 15
Finsbury Park	d	23 11		23 21			23 31		23 41				23 51		00 01	00 11	00 21	
Drayton Park	d	23 14	23 20	23 24		23 30	23 34	23 37	23 44			23 47	23 54	23 57	00 04	00 14	00 24	
Highbury & Islington ⊖	d	23 17		23 27			23 37		23 47				23 57		00 07	00 17	00 27	
Essex Road	d	23 19		23 29			23 39		23 49				23 59		00 09	00 19	00 29	
Old Street ⊖	d	23 22		23 32			23 42		23 52				00 02		00 12	00 22	00 32	
Moorgate ⊖	a	23 26		23 36			23 46		23 56				00 06		00 16	00 26	00 36	
Finsbury Park	d		23a23		23 14	23a33		23a40		23 44		23a50		23a59				00 16
London Kings Cross ■ ⊖	a				23 20					23 50								00 24
St Pancras International	d																	
Farringdon	d																	
City Thameslink	d																	
London Blackfriars	a																	
London Bridge	a																	

Sundays
20 May to 2 December

		GN A	GN A	GN A	GN A	TL ■ A	GN	GN A	GN	GN		TL ■ A	GN B	GN C	GN	GN	GN ■ D	GN ■ E	GN	GN B		GN C	GN	GN	GN B
Stevenage	d											00 16					06 39	06 39							06 59
Watton-at-Stone	d																								07 06
Hertford North	d												06 17							06 47					07 12
Bayford	d												06 21							06 51					07 17
Cuffley	d												06 26							06 56					07 21
Crews Hill	d												06 29							06 59					07 24
Gordon Hill	d												06 32							07 02					07 28
Enfield Chase	d							00 01					06 35							07 05					07 30
Grange Park	d							00 03					06 37							07 07					07 32
Winchmore Hill	d							00 05					06 39							07 09					07 35
Palmers Green	d							00 08					06 41							07 11					07 37
Bowes Park	a							00 10					06 44							07 14					07 40
Knebworth	d											00 19					06 43	06 43							
Welwyn North	d											00 23					06 47	06 47							
Welwyn Garden City ■	d											00 28				06 29	06 52	06 53						06 59	
Hatfield	d											00 31				06 34	06 56	06 57						07 04	
Welham Green	d															06 38								07 08	
Brookmans Park	d															06 40								07 10	
Potters Bar	d					00 02						00 38				06 44	07 03	07 03						07 14	
Hadley Wood	d															06 47								07 17	
New Barnet	d															06 50								07 20	
Oakleigh Park	d															06 52								07 22	
New Southgate	a															06 55								07 25	
Alexandra Palace	d				00 04			00 13					06 47	06 47		06 59				07 17		07 17		07 29	07 43
Hornsey	d				00 06			00 16					06 49	06 49		07 01				07 19		07 19		07 31	07 45
Harringay	d				00 08			00 18					06 51	06 51		07 03				07 21		07 21		07 33	07 47
Finsbury Park ⊖	a				00 11	00 15		00 20				00 51	06 57	06 57		07 09	07 13	07 13		07 27		07 27		07 39	07 53
Finsbury Park	d		00 01		00 11			00 21					06 58	06 58		07 10				07 28		07 28		07 40	07 54
Drayton Park	d		00 04	00 07	00 14		00 17	00 24	00 27	00 37			07 00	07 00	07 11	07 12			07 28	07 30		07 30	07 41	07 42	07 56
Highbury & Islington ⊖	d		00 07		00 17			00 27					07 03	07 03		07 15				07 33		07 33		07 45	07 59
Essex Road	d		00 09		00 19			00 29					07 05	07 05		07 17				07 35		07 35		07 47	08 01
Old Street ⊖	d	00 02	00 12		00 22			00 32					07 08	07 08		07 20				07 38		07 38		07 50	08 04
Moorgate ⊖	a	00 06	00 16		00 26			00 36					07 12	07 12		07 24				07 42		07 42		07 54	08 08
Finsbury Park	d			00a10		00 16	00a20		00a30	00a40		00 51			07a13		07 14	07 14	07a30				07a43		
London Kings Cross ■ ⊖	a					00 24						00 58					07 23	07 23							
St Pancras International	d																								
Farringdon	d																								
City Thameslink	d																								
London Blackfriars	a																								
London Bridge	a																								

A not 20 May
B until 21 October
C from 28 October
D from 16 September
E until 9 September

See Table 025 for fast trains between London and Stevenage

Table T024-R

Sundays
20 May to 2 December

Hertford North and Welwyn Garden City - London

		GN A	GN	GN	GN	GN B		GN ■	GN A	GN	GN	GN	GN	GN B	GN	GN		GN	GN	GN	GN B	GN ■	GN B	GN	GN
Stevenage	d					07 29		07 40						07 59							08 29	08 40			
Watton-at-Stone	d					07 36								08 06							08 36				
Hertford North	d					07 42								08 12							08 42				
Bayford	d					07 47								08 17							08 47				
Cuffley	d					07 51								08 21							08 51				
Crews Hill	d					07 54								08 24							08 54				
Gordon Hill	d					07 58								08 28							08 58				
Enfield Chase	d					08 00								08 30							09 00				
Grange Park	d					08 02								08 32							09 02				
Winchmore Hill	d					08 05								08 35							09 05				
Palmers Green	d					08 07								08 37							09 07				
Bowes Park	a					08 10								08 40							09 10				
Knebworth	d							07 44														08 44			
Welwyn North	d							07 48														08 48			
Welwyn Garden City ■	d				07 29			07 53			07 56		08 03			08 26			08 33			08 53		08 56	
Hatfield	d				07 34			07 57			08 01		08 08			08 31			08 38			08 57		09 01	
Welham Green	d				07 38								08 12						08 42						
Brookmans Park	d				07 40								08 14						08 44						
Potters Bar	d				07 44			08 04			08 08		08 18			08 38			08 48			09 04		09 08	
Hadley Wood	d				07 47						08 11		08 21			08 41			08 51					09 11	
New Barnet	d				07 50						08 14		08 24			08 44			08 54					09 14	
Oakleigh Park	d				07 52						08 16		08 26			08 46			08 56					09 16	
New Southgate	a				07 55						08 19		08 29			08 49			08 59					09 19	
Alexandra Palace	d	07 43			07 59	08 13			08 13		08 23		08 33	08 43		08 53			09 03		09 13			09 23	
Hornsey	d	07 45			08 01	08 15			08 15		08 25		08 35	08 45		08 55			09 05		09 15			09 25	
Harringay	d	07 47			08 03	08 17			08 17		08 27		08 37	08 47		08 57			09 07		09 17			09 27	
Finsbury Park ⊖	a	07 53			08 09	08 23		08 14	08 23		08 30		08 40	08 50		09 00			09 10		09 20	09 14		09 30	
Finsbury Park	d	07 54			08 10	08 24			08 24		08 31		08 41	08 51		09 01			09 11		09 21			09 31	
Drayton Park	d	07 56	07 58	08 11	08 12	08 26			08 26	08 27	08 33	08 41	08 43	08 53	08 57	09 03		09 07	09 13	09 17	09 23		09 27	09 33	09 37
Highbury & Islington ⊖	d	07 59			08 15	08 29			08 29		08 36		08 46	08 56		09 06			09 16		09 26			09 36	
Essex Road	d	08 01			08 17	08 31			08 31		08 38		08 48	08 58		09 08			09 18		09 28			09 38	
Old Street ⊖	d	08 04			08 20	08 34			08 34		08 41		08 51	09 01		09 11			09 21		09 31			09 41	
Moorgate ⊖	a	08 08			08 24	08 38			08 38		08 45		08 55	09 05		09 15			09 25		09 35			09 45	
Finsbury Park	d		08a00	08a13				08 15		08a29		08a43			08a59			09a09		09a19		09 15	09a29		09a39
London Kings Cross ■ ⊖	a							08 24														09 21			
St Pancras International	d																								
Farringdon	d																								
City Thameslink	d																								
London Blackfriars	a																								
London Bridge	a																								

		GN		GN	GN B	GN ■	GN B	GN	GN	GN	GN	GN B		GN ■	GN B	GN	GN	GN	GN	GN B	GN ■	GN B		GN	GN
Stevenage	d				08 59	09 11						09 29		09 40						09 59	10 11				
Watton-at-Stone	d				09 06							09 36								10 06					
Hertford North	d				09 12							09 42								10 12					
Bayford	d				09 17							09 47								10 17					
Cuffley	d				09 21							09 51								10 21					
Crews Hill	d				09 24							09 54								10 24					
Gordon Hill	d				09 28							09 58								10 28					
Enfield Chase	d				09 30							10 00								10 30					
Grange Park	d				09 32							10 02								10 32					
Winchmore Hill	d				09 35							10 05								10 35					
Palmers Green	d				09 37							10 07								10 37					
Bowes Park	a				09 40							10 10								10 40					
Knebworth	d					09 15								09 44							10 15				
Welwyn North	d					09 19								09 47							10 19				
Welwyn Garden City ■	d	09 03				09 24		09 28		09 33				09 53		09 56		10 03			10 24			10 26	
Hatfield	d	09 08				09 28		09 32		09 38				09 57		10 01		10 08			10 28			10 31	
Welham Green	d	09 12								09 42								10 12							
Brookmans Park	d	09 14								09 44								10 14							
Potters Bar	d	09 18				09 34		09 39		09 48				10 04		10 08		10 18			10 34			10 38	
Hadley Wood	d	09 21						09 42		09 51						10 11		10 21						10 41	
New Barnet	d	09 24						09 45		09 54						10 14		10 24						10 44	
Oakleigh Park	d	09 26						09 47		09 56						10 16		10 26						10 46	
New Southgate	a	09 29						09 50		09 59						10 19		10 29						10 49	
Alexandra Palace	d	09 33			09 43			09 54		10 03		10 13				10 23		10 33		10 43				10 53	
Hornsey	d	09 35			09 45			09 56		10 05		10 15				10 25		10 35		10 45				10 55	
Harringay	d	09 37			09 47			09 58		10 07		10 17				10 27		10 37		10 47				10 57	
Finsbury Park ⊖	a	09 40			09 50	09 45		10 01		10 10		10 20		10 14		10 30		10 40		10 50	10 45			11 00	
Finsbury Park	d	09 41			09 51			10 02		10 11		10 21				10 31		10 41		10 51				11 01	
Drayton Park	d	09 43		09 47	09 53		09 57	10 04	10 07	10 13	10 17	10 23			10 27	10 33	10 37	10 43	10 47	10 53		10 57		11 03	11 07
Highbury & Islington ⊖	d	09 46			09 56			10 07		10 16		10 26				10 36		10 46		10 56				11 06	
Essex Road	d	09 48			09 58			10 09		10 18		10 28				10 38		10 48		10 58				11 08	
Old Street ⊖	d	09 51			10 01			10 12		10 21		10 31				10 41		10 51		11 01				11 11	
Moorgate ⊖	a	09 55			10 05			10 16		10 25		10 35				10 45		10 55		11 05				11 15	
Finsbury Park	d			09a49		09 46	09a59		10a09		10a19			10 15	10a29		10a39		10a49		10 46	10a59			11a09
London Kings Cross ■ ⊖	a					09 52								10 21							10 52				
St Pancras International	d																								
Farringdon	d																								
City Thameslink	d																								
London Blackfriars	a																								
London Bridge	a																								

A from 28 October
B until 21 October

See Table 025 for fast trains between London and Stevenage

Table T024-R

Sundays

20 May to 2 December

Hertford North and Welwyn Garden City - London

		GN	GN	GN	GN	GN	GN	GN		GN	GN	GN	GN	GN	GN	GN	GN	GN		GN	GN	GN	GN	GN	GN
					■								■								■				
				A		A						A		A						A		A			
Stevenage	d			10 29	10 40							10 59	11 11							11 29	11 40				
Watton-at-Stone	d			10 36								11 06								11 36					
Hertford North	d			10 42								11 12								11 42					
Bayford	d			10 47								11 17								11 47					
Cuffley	d			10 51								11 21								11 51					
Crews Hill	d			10 54								11 24								11 54					
Gordon Hill	d			10 58								11 28								11 58					
Enfield Chase	d			11 00								11 30								12 00					
Grange Park	d			11 02								11 32								12 02					
Winchmore Hill	d			11 05								11 35								12 05					
Palmers Green	d			11 07								11 37								12 07					
Bowes Park	a			11 10								11 40								12 10					
Knebworth	d				10 44								11 15								11 44				
Welwyn North	d				10 48								11 19								11 48				
Welwyn Garden City 4	d	10 33			10 53		10 56			11 03			11 24		11 26		11 33				11 53		11 56		12 03
Hatfield	d	10 38			10 57		11 01			11 08			11 28		11 31		11 38				11 57		12 01		12 08
Welham Green	d	10 42								11 12							11 42								12 12
Brookmans Park	d	10 44								11 14							11 44								12 14
Potters Bar	d	10 48			11 04		11 08			11 18			11 34		11 38		11 48				12 04		12 08		12 18
Hadley Wood	d	10 51					11 11			11 21					11 41		11 51						12 11		12 21
New Barnet	d	10 54					11 14			11 24					11 44		11 54						12 14		12 24
Oakleigh Park	d	10 56					11 16			11 26					11 46		11 56						12 16		12 26
New Southgate	a	10 59					11 19			11 29					11 49		11 59						12 19		12 29
Alexandra Palace	d	11 03		11 13			11 23			11 33		11 43			11 53		12 03			12 13			12 23		12 33
Hornsey	d	11 05		11 15			11 25			11 35		11 45			11 55		12 05			12 15			12 25		12 35
Harringay	d	11 07		11 17			11 27			11 37		11 47			11 57		12 07			12 17			12 27		12 37
Finsbury Park ⊖	a	11 10		11 20	11 14		11 30			11 40		11 50	11 45		12 00		12 10			12 20	12 14		12 30		12 40
Finsbury Park	d	11 11		11 21			11 31			11 41		11 51			12 01		12 11			12 21			12 31		12 41
Drayton Park	d	11 13	11 17	11 23		11 27	11 33	11 37		11 43	11 47	11 53		11 57	12 03	12 07	12 13	12 17		12 23		12 27	12 33	12 37	12 43
Highbury & Islington ⊖	d	11 16		11 26			11 36			11 46		11 56			12 06		12 16			12 26			12 36		12 46
Essex Road	d	11 18		11 28			11 38			11 48		11 58			12 08		12 18			12 28			12 38		12 48
Old Street ⊖	d	11 21		11 31			11 41			11 51		12 01			12 11		12 21			12 31			12 41		12 51
Moorgate ⊖	a	11 25		11 35			11 45			11 55		12 05			12 15		12 25			12 35			12 45		12 55
Finsbury Park	d		11a19		11 15	11a29		11a39			11a49		11 46	11a59		12a09		12a19			12 15	12a29		12a39	
London Kings Cross 15 ⊖	a				11 21								11 52								12 21				
St Pancras International	d																								
Farringdon	d																								
City Thameslink	d																								
London Blackfriars	a																								
London Bridge	a																								

		GN	GN	GN		GN	GN	GN	GN	GN	GN	GN	GN	GN		GN	GN	GN	GN	GN	GN	GN	GN	GN	
											■														
			A	A						A		A						A	A					A	
Stevenage	d		11 59							12 29	12 40							12 59						13 29	
Watton-at-Stone	d		12 06							12 36								13 06						13 36	
Hertford North	d		12 12							12 42								13 12						13 42	
Bayford	d		12 17							12 47								13 17						13 47	
Cuffley	d		12 21							12 51								13 21						13 51	
Crews Hill	d		12 24							12 54								13 24						13 54	
Gordon Hill	d		12 28							12 58								13 28						13 58	
Enfield Chase	d		12 30							13 00								13 30						14 00	
Grange Park	d		12 32							13 02								13 32						14 02	
Winchmore Hill	d		12 35							13 05								13 35						14 05	
Palmers Green	d		12 37							13 07								13 37						14 07	
Bowes Park	a		12 40							13 10								13 40						14 10	
Knebworth	d										12 44														
Welwyn North	d										12 48														
Welwyn Garden City 4	d					12 26		12 33			12 53		12 56			13 03				13 26		13 33			
Hatfield	d					12 31		12 38			12 57		13 01			13 08				13 31		13 38			
Welham Green	d							12 42								13 12						13 42			
Brookmans Park	d							12 44								13 14						13 44			
Potters Bar	d					12 38		12 48			13 04		13 08			13 18				13 38		13 48			
Hadley Wood	d					12 41		12 51					13 11			13 21				13 41		13 51			
New Barnet	d					12 44		12 54					13 14			13 24				13 44		13 54			
Oakleigh Park	d					12 46		12 56					13 16			13 26				13 46		13 56			
New Southgate	a					12 49		12 59					13 19			13 29				13 49		13 59			
Alexandra Palace	d		12 43			12 53		13 03		13 13			13 23			13 33		13 43		13 53		14 03		14 13	
Hornsey	d		12 45			12 55		13 05		13 15			13 25			13 35		13 45		13 55		14 05		14 15	
Harringay	d		12 47			12 57		13 07		13 17			13 27			13 37		13 47		13 57		14 07		14 17	
Finsbury Park ⊖	a		12 50			13 00		13 10		13 20	13 14		13 30			13 40		13 50		14 00		14 10		14 20	
Finsbury Park	d		12 51			13 01		13 11		13 21			13 31			13 41		13 51		14 01		14 11		14 21	
Drayton Park	d	12 47	12 53	12 57		13 03	13 07	13 13	13 17	13 23		13 27	13 33	13 37		13 43	13 47	13 53	13 57	14 03	14 07	14 13	14 17	14 23	
Highbury & Islington ⊖	d		12 56			13 06		13 16		13 26			13 36			13 46		13 56		14 06		14 16		14 26	
Essex Road	d		12 58			13 08		13 18		13 28			13 38			13 48		13 58		14 08		14 18		14 28	
Old Street ⊖	d		13 01			13 11		13 21		13 31			13 41			13 51		14 01		14 11		14 21		14 31	
Moorgate ⊖	a		13 05			13 15		13 25		13 35			13 45			13 55		14 05		14 15		14 25		14 35	
Finsbury Park	d	12a49		12a59			13a09		13a19		13 15	13a29		13a39			13a49		13a59		14a09		14a19		
London Kings Cross 15 ⊖	a										13 21														
St Pancras International	d																								
Farringdon	d																								
City Thameslink	d																								
London Blackfriars	a																								
London Bridge	a																								

A until 21 October

See Table 025 for fast trains between London and Stevenage

Table T024-R

Sundays

20 May to 2 December

Hertford North and Welwyn Garden City - London

		GN	GN	GN	GN	GN	GN	GN	GN	GN		GN	GN	GN	GN	GN	GN	GN	GN	GN		GN	GN	GN	GN
		■														■									
			A					A	A						A		A						A	A	
Stevenage	d	13 40						13 59							14 29	14 40							14 59		
Watton-at-Stone	d							14 06							14 36								15 06		
Hertford North	d							14 12							14 42								15 12		
Bayford	d							14 17							14 47								15 17		
Cuffley	d							14 21							14 51								15 21		
Crews Hill	d							14 24							14 54								15 24		
Gordon Hill	d							14 28							14 58								15 28		
Enfield Chase	d							14 30							15 00								15 30		
Grange Park	d							14 32							15 02								15 32		
Winchmore Hill	d							14 35							15 05								15 35		
Palmers Green	d							14 37							15 07								15 37		
Bowes Park	a							14 40							15 10								15 40		
Knebworth	d	13 44														14 44									
Welwyn North	d	13 48														14 48									
Welwyn Garden City 4	d	13 53		13 56		14 03				14 26			14 33			14 53		14 56		15 03					15 26
Hatfield	d	13 57		14 01		14 08				14 31			14 38			14 57		15 01		15 08					15 31
Welham Green	d					14 12							14 42							15 12					
Brookmans Park	d					14 14							14 44							15 14					
Potters Bar	d	14 04		14 08		14 18				14 38			14 48			15 04		15 08		15 18					15 38
Hadley Wood	d			14 11		14 21				14 41			14 51					15 11		15 21					15 41
New Barnet	d			14 14		14 24				14 44			14 54					15 14		15 24					15 44
Oakleigh Park	d			14 16		14 26				14 46			14 56					15 16		15 26					15 46
New Southgate	a			14 19		14 29				14 49			14 59					15 19		15 29					15 49
Alexandra Palace	d			14 23		14 33		14 43		14 53			15 03		15 13			15 23		15 33			15 43		15 53
Hornsey	d			14 25		14 35		14 45		14 55			15 05		15 15			15 25		15 35			15 45		15 55
Harringay	d			14 27		14 37		14 47		14 57			15 07		15 17			15 27		15 37			15 47		15 57
Finsbury Park ⊖	a	14 14		14 30		14 40		14 50		15 00			15 10		15 20	15 14		15 30		15 40			15 50		16 00
Finsbury Park	d			14 31		14 41		14 51		15 01			15 11		15 21			15 31		15 41			15 51		16 01
Drayton Park	d		14 27	14 33	14 37	14 43	14 47	14 53	14 57	15 03		15 07	15 13	15 17	15 23		15 27	15 33	15 37	15 43		15 47	15 53	15 57	16 03
Highbury & Islington ⊖	d			14 36		14 46		14 56		15 06			15 16		15 26			15 36		15 46			15 56		16 06
Essex Road	d			14 38		14 48		14 58		15 08			15 18		15 28			15 38		15 48			15 58		16 08
Old Street ⊖	d			14 41		14 51		15 01		15 11			15 21		15 31			15 41		15 51			16 01		16 11
Moorgate ⊖	a			14 45		14 55		15 05		15 15			15 25		15 35			15 45		15 55			16 05		16 15
Finsbury Park	d	14 15	14a29		14a39		14a49		14a59			15a09		15a19		15 15	15a29		15a39			15a49		15a59	
London Kings Cross 15 ⊖	a	14 21														15 21									
St Pancras International	d																								
Farringdon	d																								
City Thameslink	d																								
London Blackfriars	a																								
London Bridge	a																								

		GN	GN	GN	GN	GN		GN	GN	GN	GN	GN	GN	GN	GN	GN		GN	GN	GN	GN	GN	GN	GN	GN
						■															■				
					A			A					A	A						A		A			
Stevenage	d				15 29	15 40							15 59							16 29	16 41				
Watton-at-Stone	d				15 36								16 06							16 36					
Hertford North	d				15 42								16 12							16 42					
Bayford	d				15 47								16 17							16 47					
Cuffley	d				15 51								16 21							16 51					
Crews Hill	d				15 54								16 24							16 54					
Gordon Hill	d				15 58								16 28							16 58					
Enfield Chase	d				16 00								16 30							17 00					
Grange Park	d				16 02								16 32							17 02					
Winchmore Hill	d				16 05								16 35							17 05					
Palmers Green	d				16 07								16 37							17 07					
Bowes Park	a				16 10								16 40							17 10					
Knebworth	d					15 44															16 44				
Welwyn North	d					15 48															16 48				
Welwyn Garden City 4	d		15 33			15 53			15 56		16 03				16 26			16 33			16 53		16 56		17 03
Hatfield	d		15 38			15 57			16 01		16 08				16 31			16 38			16 57		17 01		17 08
Welham Green	d		15 42								16 12							16 42							17 12
Brookmans Park	d		15 44								16 14							16 44							17 14
Potters Bar	d		15 48			16 04			16 08		16 18				16 38			16 48			17 04		17 08		17 18
Hadley Wood	d		15 51						16 11		16 21				16 41			16 51					17 11		17 21
New Barnet	d		15 54						16 14		16 24				16 44			16 54					17 14		17 24
Oakleigh Park	d		15 56						16 16		16 26				16 46			16 56					17 16		17 26
New Southgate	a		15 59						16 19		16 29				16 49			16 59					17 19		17 29
Alexandra Palace	d		16 03		16 13				16 23		16 33		16 43		16 53			17 03		17 13			17 23		17 33
Hornsey	d		16 05		16 15				16 25		16 35		16 45		16 55			17 05		17 15			17 25		17 35
Harringay	d		16 07		16 17				16 27		16 37		16 47		16 57			17 07		17 17			17 27		17 37
Finsbury Park ⊖	a		16 10		16 20	16 14			16 30		16 40		16 50		17 00			17 10		17 20	17 14		17 30		17 40
Finsbury Park	d		16 11		16 21				16 31		16 41		16 51		17 01			17 11		17 21			17 31		17 41
Drayton Park	d	16 07	16 13	16 17	16 23			16 27	16 33	16 37	16 43	16 47	16 53	16 57	17 03	17 07		17 13	17 17	17 23		17 27	17 33	17 37	17 43
Highbury & Islington ⊖	d		16 16		16 26				16 36		16 46		16 56		17 06			17 16		17 26			17 36		17 46
Essex Road	d		16 18		16 28				16 38		16 48		16 58		17 08			17 18		17 28			17 38		17 48
Old Street ⊖	d		16 21		16 31				16 41		16 51		17 01		17 11			17 21		17 31			17 41		17 51
Moorgate ⊖	a		16 25		16 35				16 45		16 55		17 05		17 15			17 25		17 35			17 45		17 55
Finsbury Park	d	16a09		16a19		16 15		16a29		16a39		16a49		16a59		17a09			17a19		17 15	17a29		17a39	
London Kings Cross 15 ⊖	a					16 21															17 21				
St Pancras International	d																								
Farringdon	d																								
City Thameslink	d																								
London Blackfriars	a																								
London Bridge	a																								

A until 21 October

See Table 025 for fast trains between London and Stevenage

Table T024-R

Sundays

20 May to 2 December

Hertford North and Welwyn Garden City - London

		GN	GN A	GN A	GN	GN	GN	GN	GN A	GN ■	GN A	GN	GN	GN	GN	GN A	GN A	GN	GN	GN	GN	GN A
Stevenage	d		16 59						17 29	17 40						17 59						18 29
Watton-at-Stone	d		17 06						17 36							18 06						18 36
Hertford North	d		17 12						17 42							18 12						18 42
Bayford	d		17 17						17 47							18 17						18 47
Cuffley	d		17 21						17 51							18 21						18 51
Crews Hill	d		17 24						17 54							18 24						18 54
Gordon Hill	d		17 28						17 58							18 28						18 58
Enfield Chase	d		17 30						18 00							18 30						19 00
Grange Park	d		17 32						18 02							18 32						19 02
Winchmore Hill	d		17 35						18 05							18 35						19 05
Palmers Green	d		17 37						18 07							18 37						19 07
Bowes Park	a		17 40						18 10							18 40						19 10
Knebworth	d									17 44												
Welwyn North	d									17 48												
Welwyn Garden City ■	d				17 26		17 33			17 53		17 56		18 03				18 26		18 33		
Hatfield	d				17 31		17 38			17 57		18 01		18 08				18 31		18 38		
Welham Green	d						17 42							18 12						18 42		
Brookmans Park	d						17 44							18 14						18 44		
Potters Bar	d				17 38		17 48			18 04		18 08		18 18				18 38		18 48		
Hadley Wood	d				17 41		17 51					18 11		18 21				18 41		18 51		
New Barnet	d				17 44		17 54					18 14		18 24				18 44		18 54		
Oakleigh Park	d				17 46		17 56					18 16		18 26				18 46		18 56		
New Southgate	a				17 49		17 59					18 19		18 29				18 49		18 59		
Alexandra Palace	d		17 43		17 53		18 03		18 13			18 23		18 33		18 43		18 53		19 03		19 13
Hornsey	d		17 45		17 55		18 05		18 15			18 25		18 35		18 45		18 55		19 05		19 15
Harringay	d		17 47		17 57		18 07		18 17			18 27		18 37		18 47		18 57		19 07		19 17
Finsbury Park ⊖	a		17 50		18 00		18 10		18 20	18 14		18 30		18 40		18 50		19 00		19 10		19 20
Finsbury Park	d		17 51		18 01		18 11		18 21			18 31		18 41		18 51		19 01		19 11		19 21
Drayton Park	d	17 47	17 53	17 57	18 03	18 07	18 13	18 17	18 23		18 27	18 33	18 37	18 43	18 47	18 53	18 57	19 03	19 07	19 13	19 17	19 23
Highbury & Islington ⊖	d		17 56		18 06		18 16		18 26			18 36		18 46		18 56		19 06		19 16		19 26
Essex Road	d		17 58		18 08		18 18		18 28			18 38		18 48		18 58		19 08		19 18		19 28
Old Street ⊖	d		18 01		18 11		18 21		18 31			18 41		18 51		19 01		19 11		19 21		19 31
Moorgate ⊖	a		18 05		18 15		18 25		18 35			18 45		18 55		19 05		19 15		19 25		19 35
Finsbury Park	d	17a49		17a59		18a09		18a19		18 15	18a29		18a39		18a49		18a59		19a09		19a19	
London Kings Cross ■ ⊖	a									18 21												
St Pancras International	d																					
Farringdon	d																					
City Thameslink	d																					
London Blackfriars	a																					
London Bridge	a																					

		GN ■	GN A	GN	GN	GN	GN	GN A	GN A	GN	GN	GN	GN	GN A	GN ■	GN A	GN	GN	GN	GN	GN A	GN A	GN
Stevenage	d	18 40						18 59						19 29	19 40						19 59		
Watton-at-Stone	d							19 06						19 36							20 06		
Hertford North	d							19 12						19 42							20 12		
Bayford	d							19 17						19 47							20 17		
Cuffley	d							19 21						19 51							20 21		
Crews Hill	d							19 24						19 54							20 24		
Gordon Hill	d							19 28						19 58							20 28		
Enfield Chase	d							19 30						20 00							20 30		
Grange Park	d							19 32						20 02							20 32		
Winchmore Hill	d							19 35						20 05							20 35		
Palmers Green	d							19 37						20 07							20 37		
Bowes Park	a							19 40						20 10							20 40		
Knebworth	d	18 44													19 44								
Welwyn North	d	18 48													19 48								
Welwyn Garden City ■	d	18 53		18 56		19 03				19 26		19 33			19 53		19 56		20 03				20 26
Hatfield	d	18 57		19 01		19 08				19 31		19 38			19 57		20 01		20 08				20 31
Welham Green	d					19 12						19 42							20 12				
Brookmans Park	d					19 14						19 44							20 14				
Potters Bar	d	19 04		19 08		19 18				19 38		19 48			20 04		20 08		20 18				20 38
Hadley Wood	d			19 11		19 21				19 41		19 51					20 11		20 21				20 41
New Barnet	d			19 14		19 24				19 44		19 54					20 14		20 24				20 44
Oakleigh Park	d			19 16		19 26				19 46		19 56					20 16		20 26				20 46
New Southgate	a			19 19		19 29				19 49		19 59					20 19		20 29				20 49
Alexandra Palace	d			19 23		19 33		19 43		19 53		20 03		20 13			20 23		20 33		20 43		20 53
Hornsey	d			19 25		19 35		19 45		19 55		20 05		20 15			20 25		20 35		20 45		20 55
Harringay	d			19 27		19 37		19 47		19 57		20 07		20 17			20 27		20 37		20 47		20 57
Finsbury Park ⊖	a	19 14		19 30		19 40		19 50		20 00		20 10		20 20	20 14		20 30		20 40		20 50		21 00
Finsbury Park	d			19 31		19 41		19 51		20 01		20 11		20 21			20 31		20 41		20 51		21 01
Drayton Park	d		19 27	19 33	19 37	19 43	19 47	19 53	19 57	20 03	20 07	20 13	20 17	20 23		20 27	20 33	20 37	20 43	20 47	20 53	20 57	21 03
Highbury & Islington ⊖	d			19 36		19 46		19 56		20 06		20 16		20 26			20 36		20 46		20 56		21 06
Essex Road	d			19 38		19 48		19 58		20 08		20 18		20 28			20 38		20 48		20 58		21 08
Old Street ⊖	d			19 41		19 51		20 01		20 11		20 21		20 31			20 41		20 51		21 01		21 11
Moorgate ⊖	a			19 45		19 55		20 05		20 15		20 25		20 35			20 45		20 55		21 05		21 15
Finsbury Park	d	19 15	19a29		19a39		19a49		19a59		20a09		20a19		20 15	20a29		20a39		20a49		20a59	
London Kings Cross ■ ⊖	a	19 21													20 21								
St Pancras International	d																						
Farringdon	d																						
City Thameslink	d																						
London Blackfriars	a																						
London Bridge	a																						

A until 21 October

See Table 025 for fast trains between London and Stevenage

Table T024-R

Sundays

20 May to 2 December

Hertford North and Welwyn Garden City - London

		GN	GN	GN	GN A	GN ■	GN A	GN	GN	GN	GN	GN A	GN B	GN A	GN	GN	GN A	GN ■	GN B	GN	GN	GN
Stevenage	d				20 29	20 40						20 59					21 29	21 40				
Watton-at-Stone	d				20 36							21 06					21 36					
Hertford North	d				20 42							21 12					21 42					
Bayford	d				20 47							21 17					21 47					
Cuffley	d				20 51							21 21					21 51					
Crews Hill	d				20 54							21 24					21 54					
Gordon Hill	d				20 58							21 28					21 58					
Enfield Chase	d				21 00							21 30					22 00					
Grange Park	d				21 02							21 32					22 02					
Winchmore Hill	d				21 05							21 35					22 05					
Palmers Green	d				21 07							21 37					22 07					
Bowes Park	a				21 10							21 40					22 10					
Knebworth	d					20 44												21 44				
Welwyn North	d					20 48												21 47				
Welwyn Garden City ■	d		20 33			20 53		20 56		21 03						21 33		21 53				22 03
Hatfield	d		20 38			20 57		21 01		21 08						21 38		21 57				22 08
Welham Green	d		20 42							21 12						21 42						22 12
Brookmans Park	d		20 44							21 14						21 44						22 14
Potters Bar	d		20 48			21 04		21 08		21 18						21 48		22 03				22 18
Hadley Wood	d		20 51					21 11		21 21						21 51						22 21
New Barnet	d		20 54					21 14		21 24						21 54						22 24
Oakleigh Park	d		20 56					21 16		21 26						21 56						22 26
New Southgate	a		20 59					21 19		21 29						21 59						22 29
Alexandra Palace	d		21 03		21 13			21 23		21 33		21 43	21 43			22 03	22 13		22 13			22 33
Hornsey	d		21 05		21 15			21 25		21 35		21 45	21 45			22 05	22 15		22 15			22 35
Harringay	d		21 07		21 17			21 27		21 37		21 47	21 47			22 07	22 17		22 17			22 37
Finsbury Park ⊖	a		21 10		21 20	21 14		21 30		21 40		21 50	21 50			22 10	22 20	22 14	22 20			22 40
Finsbury Park	d		21 11		21 21			21 31		21 41		21 51	21 51			22 11	22 21		22 21			22 41
Drayton Park	d	21 07	21 13	21 17	21 23		21 27	21 33	21 37	21 43	21 47	21 53	21 53	21 57	22 07	22 13	22 23		22 23	22 27	22 37	22 43
Highbury & Islington ⊖	d		21 16		21 26			21 36		21 46		21 56	21 56			22 16	22 26		22 26			22 46
Essex Road	d		21 18		21 28			21 38		21 48		21 58	21 58			22 18	22 28		22 28			22 48
Old Street ⊖	d		21 21		21 31			21 41		21 51		22 01	22 01			22 21	22 31		22 31			22 51
Moorgate ⊖	a		21 25		21 35			21 45		21 55		22 05	22 05			22 25	22 35		22 35			22 55
Finsbury Park	d	21a09		21a19		21 15	21a29		21a39		21a49			21a59	22a09			22 14		22a29	22a39	
London Kings Cross ■ ⊖	a					21 21												22 21				
St Pancras International	d																					
Farringdon	d																					
City Thameslink	d																					
London Blackfriars	a																					
London Bridge	a																					

		GN A	GN B	GN	GN	GN	GN A	GN ■	GN B	GN	GN	GN	GN A	GN B	GN	GN A
Stevenage	d	21 59					22 29	22 40					22 59			23 29
Watton-at-Stone	d	22 06					22 36						23 06			23 36
Hertford North	d	22 12					22 42						23 12			23 42
Bayford	d	22 17					22 47						23 17			23 47
Cuffley	d	22 21					22 51						23 21			23 51
Crews Hill	d	22 24					22 54						23 24			23 54
Gordon Hill	d	22 28					22 58						23 28			23 57
Enfield Chase	d	22 30					23 00						23 30			00 01
Grange Park	d	22 32					23 02						23 32			00 03
Winchmore Hill	d	22 35					23 05						23 35			00 05
Palmers Green	d	22 37					23 07						23 37			00 07
Bowes Park	a	22 40					23 10						23 40			00 10
Knebworth	d							22 44								
Welwyn North	d							22 48								
Welwyn Garden City ■	d					22 33		22 53				23 03				
Hatfield	d					22 38		22 57				23 08				
Welham Green	d					22 42						23 12				
Brookmans Park	d					22 44						23 14				
Potters Bar	d					22 48		23 03				23 18				
Hadley Wood	d					22 51						23 21				
New Barnet	d					22 54						23 24				
Oakleigh Park	d					22 56						23 26				
New Southgate	a					22 59						23 29				
Alexandra Palace	d	22 43	22 43			23 03	23 13		23 13			23 33	23 43	23 43		00 14
Hornsey	d	22 45	22 45			23 05	23 15		23 15			23 35	23 45	23 45		00 16
Harringay	d	22 47	22 47			23 07	23 17		23 17			23 37	23 47	23 47		00 18
Finsbury Park ⊖	a	22 50	22 50			23 10	23 20	23 14	23 20			23 40	23 50	23 50		00 24
Finsbury Park	d	22 51	22 51			23 11	23 21		23 21			23 41	23 51	23 51		00 25
Drayton Park	d	22 53	22 53	22 57	23 07	23 13	23 23		23 23	23 27	23 37	23 43	23 53	23 53	23 57	00 27
Highbury & Islington ⊖	d	22 56	22 56			23 16	23 26		23 26			23 46	23 56	23 56		00 30
Essex Road	d	22 58	22 58			23 18	23 28		23 28			23 48	23 58	23 58		00 32
Old Street ⊖	d	23 01	23 01			23 21	23 31		23 31			23 51	00 01	00 01		00 35
Moorgate ⊖	a	23 05	23 05			23 25	23 35		23 35			23 55	00 05	00 05		00 39
Finsbury Park	d			22a59	23a09			23 14		23a29	23a39				23a59	
London Kings Cross ■ ⊖	a							23 21								
St Pancras International	d															
Farringdon	d															
City Thameslink	d															
London Blackfriars	a															
London Bridge	a															

A until 21 October

B from 28 October

See Table 025 for fast trains between London and Stevenage

Brighton, Gatwick Airport, Maidstone East and London - Stevenage, Cambridge, Kings Lynn and Peterborough

Miles	Miles			TL MX ■	TL MO ■	GN MX	GN MO ■	GN MX	GN MO ■	GN MX	TL MX ■	TL MX ■		TL MX ■	TL MX ■	GN MO ■	GN MX	GN	TL MX ■	GN MO ■	TL MX ■	TL MX ■		GN MO ■ A	GN MO ■ B
—	—	Brighton	d																						
—	—	Gatwick Airport	d																						
—	—	East Croydon	d																		00 10				
—	—	Maidstone East	d																						
—	—	London Bridge	d																						
—	—	London Blackfriars	d																		00 37				
—	—	City Thameslink	d																						
—	—	Farringdon	d																		00 41				
—	—	St Pancras International	d																						
—	—	St Pancras International	d																						
—	—	St Pancras International	d																		00 46				
0	0	London Kings Cross ■ ⊖	d													00 02	00 32		00 23	00 32		01 05		01 02	01 02
2½	2½	Finsbury Park ⊖	d												00 01	00 09	00 39		00 29	00 39	00 54	01 11		01 09	01 09
12¾	12¾	Potters Bar	d												00 13	00 20			00 42	00 50		01 22			
17¾	17¾	Hatfield	d												00 18	00 26			00 48	00 56		01 28			
20¼	20¼	Welwyn Garden City ■	d												00 28	00 31			00 58	01 01	01 13	01 34		01s31	
22	22	**Welwyn North**	d									00 01			00 31	00 34			01 01	01s04		01 37			
25	25	**Knebworth**	d									00 05			00 35	00 38			01 05	01s08		01 41			
27½	27½	**Stevenage ■**	d								00 03	00 09		00 14	00 40	00 44	01 04		01 10	01 14	01 22	01 46		01 46	01 46
31¾	31¾	**Hitchin ■**	d								00 09	00 14		00 22	00 48	00 53	01 13		01 18	01 23	01 30	01 54		01 56	01 56
34¾	—	**Letchworth Garden City**	d							00 10	00 14	00 19			00 54	00 58	01s18		01 24			02 00		02s01	02s01
36¾	—	**Baldock**	d								00 17	00 23			00 57	01 02	01s21		01 27			02 03		02s04	02s04
41	—	**Ashwell & Morden**	d						00 04			00 27			01 01	01 07			01 31			02 07		02s09	02s09
45	—	**Royston**	d						00 09	00 19	00 25	00 32			01 06	01 12	01s29		01a37			02a13		02a15	02a15
48	—	**Meldreth**	d						00 13			00 36			01 10	01 16									
50	—	**Shepreth**	d						00 16			00 39			01 13	01 20									
51	—	**Foxton**	d						00 19			00 41			01 15	01 22									
58	—	Cambridge	a						00 30	00 35	00 40	00 54			01 25	01 33	01 44								
—	—	Cambridge	d				00 04	00 08										06 14							
60¼	—	Cambridge North	d				00 08	00 13										06 18							
—	—	Waterbeach	d				00 12	00 17										06 22							
—	—	Ely	d				00 22	00 27										06 33							
—	—	**Littleport**	d			00 06	00 29	00 34										06 41							
—	—	**Downham Market**	d			00 15	00 38	00 43										06 50							
—	—	**Watlington**	d			00 21	00 44	00 49										06 56							
—	—	**Kings Lynn**	a			00 29	00 52	00 57										07 04							
—	37	**Arlesey**	d											00 27						01s28	01 35				
—	41	**Biggleswade**	d	00 01	00 04									00 32						01s33	01 41				
—	44	**Sandy**	d	00 04	00 07									00 36						01s37	01 44				
—	51½	**St Neots**	d	00 11	00 15									00 43						01s45	01 52				
—	58¾	**Huntingdon**	d	00 19	00 22									00 51						01s56	01 59				
—	76¼	Peterborough ■	a	00 37	00 41									01 09						02 12	02 17				

A from 29 October B until 22 October

Please refer to Table T024 for the full service between Hertford North and Letchworth via Stevenage

Brighton, Gatwick Airport, Maidstone East and London - Stevenage, Cambridge, Kings Lynn and Peterborough

		TL MX ■	GN MO ■	TL ■		TL ■	TL ■	TL ■	GN	TL ■	GR ■ ■ ■	GR ■ ■ ■	GN	TL ■		TL ■	GR ■ ■ ■	TL ■	TL ■	TL ■	GN	GR ■ ■ ■	TL	TL ■
Brighton	d																	05 06						
Gatwick Airport	d																	05 46		05 49				06 13
East Croydon	d																	06 01		06 16				06 46
Maidstone East	d																							
London Bridge	d																							
London Blackfriars	d																	06 22		06 37				07 07
City Thameslink	d																	06 24		06 39				07 09
Farringdon	d																	06 26		06 41				07 11
St Pancras International	d																							
St Pancras International	d																							
St Pancras International	d																	06 31		06 46				07 16
London Kings Cross ■ ⊖	d	01 36	01 32	05 03		05 18	05 33	05 25	05 42	05 48	05 55	06 12		05 55		06 18	06 33		06 21		06 42	07 06	06 51	
Finsbury Park ⊖	d	01 44	01 39	05 09		05 24	05 42	05 33		05 54				06 01		06 24		06 42	06 31	06 54			07 01	07 24
Potters Bar	d		01 58					05 45						06 13					06 43				07 13	
Hatfield	d		02 04					05 51						06 18					06 48				07 18	
Welwyn Garden City ■	d		02 09					05 56						06 26					06 56				07 26	
Welwyn North	d		02s12					06 00						06 30					07 00				07 30	
Knebworth	d		02s16					06 04						06 34					07 04				07 34	
Stevenage ■	d	02 12	02 22	05 34		05 49	06 02	06 08		06 14	06 17	06 34		06 38		06 44	06 55	07 03	07 08	07 14		07 28	07 38	07 44
Hitchin ■	d	02 20	02 31	05 42		05 58	06 08	06 14		06 20				06 44		06 50		07 08	07 16	07 20			07 44	07 50
Letchworth Garden City	d			05 48			06 13	06 19						06 49				07 13	07 25				07 49	
Baldock	d			05 51			06 16	06 23						06 53				07 16	07 28				07 53	
Ashwell & Morden	d							06 27						06 57					07 32				07 57	
Royston	d			05 59			06 24	06 32						07 02				07 24	07 37				08 02	
Meldreth	d							06 36						07 06					07 41				08 06	
Shepreth	d							06 39						07 09					07 44				08 09	
Foxton	d							06 41						07 11					07 46				08 11	
Cambridge	a			06 14			06 39	06 51	06 30					07 21				07 39	07 56		07 30		08 21	
Cambridge	d								06 35				07 10	07 24							07 35		08 22	
Cambridge North	d								06 39				07 14	07a29							07 39		08a28	
Waterbeach	d								06 44				07 18								07 44			
Ely	d								06 54				07 28								07 55			
Littleport	d								07 01				07 36								08 04			
Downham Market	d								07 13				07 49								08 17			
Watlington	d								07 25				07 55								08 23			
Kings Lynn	a								07 34				08 03								08 31			
Arlesey	d	02 25				06 03				06 25						06 55				07 25				07 55
Biggleswade	d	02 31	02s39			06 08				06 30						07 00				07 30				08 00
Sandy	d	02 34				06 12				06 34						07 04				07 34				08 04
St Neots	d	02 42	02s50			06 19				06 41						07 12				07 41				08 11
Huntingdon	d	02 49	03s01			06 27				06 49						07 19				07 49				08 19
Peterborough ■	a	03 07	03 17			06 42				07 07	06 46	07 03				07 35	07 24			08 06		07 57		08 40

Please refer to Table T024 for the full service between Hertford North and Letchworth via Stevenage

Table T025-F

Mondays to Fridays

21 May to 7 December

Brighton, Gatwick Airport, Maidstone East and London - Stevenage, Cambridge, Kings Lynn and Peterborough

		GN	TL	TL	TL	GN	TL	TL	TL	TL	TL	GN	GR	TL	TL	TL	TL	TL	GN	GR	TL	TL	TL
Brighton	d		06 05						07 07							08 07							09 08
Gatwick Airport	d		06 46		06 43			07 13	07 46		07 43				08 13	08 46		08 43				09 19	09 46
East Croydon	d		07 01		07 16			07 46	08 01		08 16				08 46	09 01		09 16				09 45	10 01
Maidstone East	d																						
London Bridge	d																						
London Blackfriars	d		07 22		07 37			08 07	08 22		08 37				09 07	09 22		09 37				10 07	10 22
City Thameslink	d		07 24		07 39			08 09	08 24		08 39				09 09	09 24		09 39				10 09	10 24
Farringdon	d		07 26		07 41			08 11	08 26		08 41				09 11	09 26		09 41				10 11	10 26
St Pancras International	d																						
St Pancras International	d																						
St Pancras International	d		07 31		07 46			08 16	08 31		08 46				09 16	09 31		09 46				10 16	10 31
London Kings Cross ⊖	d	07 12		07 21		07 42	07 51			08 21		08 42	09 06	08 51			09 21		09 42	10 06	09 51		
Finsbury Park ⊖	d		07 42	07 31	07 54		08 01	08 24	08 42	08 31	08 54			09 01	09 24	09 42	09 31	09 54			10 00	10 24	10 42
Potters Bar	d			07 43			08 13			08 43				09 13			09 43				10 13		
Hatfield	d			07 48			08 18			08 48				09 18			09 48				10 18		
Welwyn Garden City	d			07 56			08 26			08 56				09 26			09 56				10 26		
Welwyn North	d			08 00			08 30			09 00				09 30			10 00				10 30		
Knebworth	d			08 04			08 34			09 04				09 34			10 04				10 34		
Stevenage	d		08 03	08 08	08 14		08 38	08 44	09 03	09 08	09 14		09 28	09 38	09 44	10 03	10 08	10 14		10 28	10 38	10 44	11 03
Hitchin	d		08 08	08 14	08 20		08 44	08 50	09 09	09 14	09 20			09 44	09 50	10 09	10 14	10 20			10 44	10 50	11 09
Letchworth Garden City	d		08 13	08 19			08 49		09 14	09 19				09 49		10 14	10 19				10 49		11 14
Baldock	d		08 16	08 23			08 53		09 17	09 23				09 53		10 17	10 23				10 53		11 17
Ashwell & Morden	d			08 27			08 57			09 27				09 57			10 27				10 57		
Royston	d		08 24	08 32			09 02		09 25	09 32				10 02		10 25	10 32				11 02		11 25
Meldreth	d			08 36			09 06			09 36				10 06			10 36				11 06		
Shepreth	d			08 39			09 09			09 39				10 09			10 39				11 09		
Foxton	d			08 41			09 11			09 41				10 11			10 41				11 11		
Cambridge	a	08 00	08 39	08 51		08 30	09 21		09 42	09 51		09 30		10 21		10 40	10 54		10 30		11 21		11 40
Cambridge	d	08 05				08 35	09 22					09 35		10 22					10 35		11 22		
Cambridge North	d	08 09				08 39	09a28					09 39		10a28					10 39		11a28		
Waterbeach	d	08 14				08 44						09 44							10 44				
Ely	d	08 32				08 55						09 55							10 55				
Littleport	d	08 39				09 04						10 04							11 04				
Downham Market	d	08 48				09 17						10 17							11 17				
Watlington	d	08 54				09 26						10 23							11 23				
Kings Lynn	a	09 02				09 34						10 31							11 31				
Arlesey	d				08 25			08 55			09 25				09 55			10 25				10 55	
Biggleswade	d				08 30			09 00			09 30				10 00			10 30				11 00	
Sandy	d				08 34			09 04			09 34				10 04			10 34				11 04	
St Neots	d				08 41			09 11			09 41				10 11			10 41				11 11	
Huntingdon	d				08 49			09 19			09 49				10 19			10 49				11 19	
Peterborough	a				09 05			09 35			10 05		09 57		10 40			11 05		10 57		11 39	

		TL	TL	GN	GR	TL	TL	TL	TL	TL	GN	GR	TL	TL	TL	TL	TL	GN	GR	TL	TL	TL
Brighton	d							10 08							11 08							12 08
Gatwick Airport	d		09 49				10 19	10 46		10 49				11 19	11 46		11 49				12 19	12 46
East Croydon	d		10 15				10 45	11 01		11 15				11 45	12 01		12 15				12 45	13 01
Maidstone East	d																					
London Bridge	d																					
London Blackfriars	d		10 37				11 07	11 22		11 37				12 07	12 22		12 37				13 07	13 22
City Thameslink	d		10 39				11 09	11 24		11 39				12 09	12 24		12 39				13 09	13 24
Farringdon	d		10 41				11 11	11 26		11 41				12 11	12 26		12 41				13 11	13 26
St Pancras International	d																					
St Pancras International	d																					
St Pancras International	d		10 46				11 16	11 31		11 46				12 16	12 31		12 46				13 16	13 31
London Kings Cross ⊖	d	10 21		10 42	11 06	10 51			11 21		11 42	12 06	11 51			12 21		12 42	13 06	12 51		
Finsbury Park ⊖	d	10 31	10 54			11 01	11 24	11 42	11 31	11 54			12 01	12 24	12 42	12 31	12 54			13 01	13 24	13 42
Potters Bar	d	10 43				11 13			11 43				12 13			12 43				13 13		
Hatfield	d	10 48				11 18			11 48				12 18			12 48				13 18		
Welwyn Garden City	d	10 56				11 26			11 56				12 26			12 56				13 26		
Welwyn North	d	11 00				11 30			12 00				12 30			13 00				13 30		
Knebworth	d	11 04				11 34			12 04				12 34			13 04				13 34		
Stevenage	d	11 10	11 14		11 28	11 38	11 44	12 03	12 08	12 14		12 28	12 38	12 44	13 03	13 08	13 14		13 28	13 38	13 44	14 03
Hitchin	d	11 18	11 20			11 44	11 50	12 09	12 14	12 20			12 44	12 50	13 09	13 14	13 20			13 44	13 50	14 09
Letchworth Garden City	d	11a24				11 50		12 14	12 19				12 49		13 14	13 19				13 49		14 14
Baldock	d					11 53		12 17	12 23				12 53		13 17	13 23				13 53		14 17
Ashwell & Morden	d					11 57			12 27				12 57			13 27				13 57		
Royston	d					12 02		12 25	12 32				13 02		13 25	13 32				14 02		14 25
Meldreth	d					12 06			12 36				13 06			13 36				14 06		
Shepreth	d					12 09			12 39				13 09			13 39				14 09		
Foxton	d					12 11			12 41				13 11			13 41				14 11		
Cambridge	a			11 31		12 21		12 40	12 54		12 31		13 21		13 40	13 54		13 30		14 21		14 40
Cambridge	d			11 35		12 22					12 35		13 22					13 35		14 22		
Cambridge North	d			11 39		12a28					12 40		13a28					13 39		14a28		
Waterbeach	d			11 44							12 44							13 44				
Ely	d			11 55							12 55							13 55				
Littleport	d			12 04							13 04							14 04				
Downham Market	d			12 17							13 17							14 17				
Watlington	d			12 23							13 23							14 23				
Kings Lynn	a			12 31							13 31							14 31				
Arlesey	d		11 25				11 55			12 25				12 55			13 25				13 55	
Biggleswade	d		11 30				12 00			12 30				13 00			13 30				14 00	
Sandy	d		11 34				12 04			12 34				13 04			13 34				14 04	
St Neots	d		11 41				12 11			12 41				13 11			13 41				14 11	
Huntingdon	d		11 49				12 19			12 49				13 19			13 49				14 19	
Peterborough	a		12 05		11 57		12 39			13 05		12 57		13 39			14 05		13 58		14 39	

Please refer to Table T024 for the full service between Hertford North and Letchworth via Stevenage

Table T025-F

Mondays to Fridays

21 May to 7 December

Brighton, Gatwick Airport, Maidstone East and London - Stevenage, Cambridge, Kings Lynn and Peterborough

		TL	TL	GN	GR	TL	TL	TL	TL	TL	GN	GR	GN	TL	TL	TL	TL	TL	GN	GR	GN	TL	TL
Brighton	d							13 08								14 08							
Gatwick Airport	d		12 49				13 19	13 46		13 49					14 19	14 46		14 49					15 19
East Croydon	d		13 15				13 45	14 01		14 15					14 45	15 01		15 15					15 45
Maidstone East	d																						
London Bridge	d																						
London Blackfriars	d		13 37				14 07	14 22		14 37					15 07	15 22		15 37					16 07
City Thameslink	d		13 39				14 09	14 24		14 39					15 09	15 24		15 39					16 09
Farringdon	d		13 41				14 11	14 26		14 41					15 11	15 26		15 41					16 11
St Pancras International	d																						
St Pancras International	d																						
St Pancras International	d		13 46				14 16	14 31		14 46					15 16	15 31		15 46					16 16
London Kings Cross ⊖	d	13 21		13 42	14 06	13 51			14 21		14 42	15 06		14 51			15 19		15 42	16 06	16 12	15 51	
Finsbury Park ⊖	d	13 31	13 54			14 01	14 24	14 42	14 31	14 54				15 01	15 24	15 42	15 29	15 54				16 01	16 24
Potters Bar	d	13 43				14 13			14 43					15 13			15 42					16 13	
Hatfield	d	13 48				14 18			14 48					15 18			15 48					16 18	
Welwyn Garden City	d	13 56				14 26			14 56					15 26			15 56					16 26	
Welwyn North	d	14 00				14 30			15 00					15 30			16 00					16 30	
Knebworth	d	14 04				14 34			15 04					15 34			16 04					16 34	
Stevenage	d	14 08	14 14		14 28	14 38	14 44	15 03	15 08	15 14		15 28		15 38	15 44	16 03	16 08	16 14		16 28		16 38	16 44
Hitchin	d	14 14	14 20			14 44	14 50	15 09	15 14	15 20				15 44	15 50	16 09	16 14	16 20				16 44	16 50
Letchworth Garden City	d	14 19				14 49		15 14	15 19					15 49		16 14	16 19					16 49	
Baldock	d	14 23				14 53		15 17	15 23					15 53		16 17	16 23					16 53	
Ashwell & Morden	d	14 27				14 57			15 27					15 57			16 27				16 45	16 57	
Royston	d	14 32				15 02		15 25	15 32					16 02		16 25	16 32					17 02	
Meldreth	d	14 36				15 06			15 36					16 06			16 36					17 06	
Shepreth	d	14 39				15 09			15 39					16 09			16 39					17 09	
Foxton	d	14 41				15 11			15 41					16 11			16 41					17 11	
Cambridge	a	14 54		14 30		15 21		15 40	15 54		15 30			16 23		16 40	16 54		16 30		17 02	17 24	
Cambridge	d			14 35		15 22					15 35		16 20	16 24					16 35		17 04	17 26	
Cambridge North	d			14 39		15a28					15 39			16a29					16 39		17 08	17a31	
Waterbeach	d			14 44							15 44		16 27						16 44				
Ely	d			14 55							15 55		16 37						16 55		17a22		
Littleport	d			15 04							16 04		16 44						17 04				
Downham Market	d			15 17							16 17		16 53						17 17				
Watlington	d			15 23							16 23		16 59						17 23				
Kings Lynn	a			15 31							16 31		17 07						17 31				
Arlesey	d		14 25				14 55			15 25					15 55			16 25					16 55
Biggleswade	d		14 30				15 00			15 30					16 00			16 30					17 00
Sandy	d		14 34				15 04			15 34					16 04			16 34					17 04
St Neots	d		14 41				15 11			15 41					16 11			16 41					17 11
Huntingdon	d		14 49				15 19			15 49					16 19			16 49					17 19
Peterborough	a		15 05		14 57		15 39			16 05		15 57			16 39			17 05		16 57			17 35

		GN	TL	TL	GN	TL	GN	GN	GN	TL	TL	GN	GN	GN	TL	TL	TL	GN	GN	GN	TL	TL
Brighton	d		15 08												16 08							
Gatwick Airport	d		15 46			15 49					16 19				16 46		16 49					17 19
East Croydon	d		16 01			16 15					16 45				17 01		17 15					17 45
Maidstone East	d																					
London Bridge	d																					
London Blackfriars	d		16 22			16 37					17 07				17 22		17 37					18 07
City Thameslink	d		16 24			16 39					17 09				17 24		17 39					18 09
Farringdon	d		16 26			16 41					17 11				17 26		17 41					18 11
St Pancras International	d																					
St Pancras International	d																					
St Pancras International	d		16 31			16 46					17 16				17 31		17 46					18 16
London Kings Cross ⊖	d	16 42		16 21	16 36		16 54	17 06	17 12	16 51		17 24	17 36	17 42		17 21		17 54	18 06	18 12	17 51	
Finsbury Park ⊖	d		16 42	16 31		16 54				17 01	17 24				17 42	17 31	17 54				18 01	18 24
Potters Bar	d			16 43						17 13						17 43					18 13	
Hatfield	d			16 51						17 21						17 51					18 21	
Welwyn Garden City	d			16 56						17 26						17 56					18 26	
Welwyn North	d			17 00			17 11			17 30		17 41				18 00		18 11			18 30	
Knebworth	d			17 04			17 16			17 34		17 46				18 04		18 16			18 34	
Stevenage	d		17 03	17 08		17 14		17 28		17 38	17 44		17 59		18 03	18 08	18 14		18 28		18 38	18 44
Hitchin	d		17 09	17 14		17 20	17 25			17 44	17 50	17 54			18 09	18 14	18 20	18 25			18 44	18 50
Letchworth Garden City	d		17 14	17 19			17 31			17 49		18 00			18 14	18 19		18 31			18 49	
Baldock	d		17 17	17 23			17a35			17 53		18 03			18 17	18 23		18a35			18 53	
Ashwell & Morden	d	17 14		17 27					17 44	17 57				18 15		18 27				18 44	18 57	
Royston	d	17 19	17 25	17 32					17 51	18 02		18a12		18 21	18 25	18 32				18 50	19 02	
Meldreth	d			17 36						18 06						18 36					19 06	
Shepreth	d			17 39						18 09						18 39					19 09	
Foxton	d			17 41						18 11						18 41					19 11	
Cambridge	a	17 34	17 40	17 54					18 06	18 25				18 36	18 43	18 54				19 05	19 21	
Cambridge	d	17 39							18 07	18 26				18 41						19 09	19 25	
Cambridge North	d	17 44							18 11	18a32				18 45						19 14	19a30	
Waterbeach	d	17 49												18 50								
Ely	d	17 59							18a24					19 02						19 30		
Littleport	d	18 08												19 09								
Downham Market	d	18 17												19 18						19 47		
Watlington	d	18 23												19 24						19 53		
Kings Lynn	a	18 31												19 32						20 01		
Arlesey	d					17 25					17 55						18 25					18 55
Biggleswade	d				17 09	17 30		17 40			18 00		18 11				18 30		18 40			19 00
Sandy	d					17 34					18 03						18 34					19 04
St Neots	d				17 19	17 41		17 50			18 11		18 21				18 41		18 50			19 11
Huntingdon	d				17 27	17 49		17 58			18 18		18 29				18 49		18 58			19 19
Peterborough	a				17 43	18 05		18 14			18 34		18 53				19 05		19 18			19 41

Please refer to Table T024 for the full service between Hertford North and Letchworth via Stevenage

Table T025-F

Mondays to Fridays
21 May to 7 December

Brighton, Gatwick Airport, Maidstone East and London - Stevenage, Cambridge, Kings Lynn and Peterborough

		GN	GN	GN	TL	TL	TL	GN	GR	GN		TL	TL	GN	TL	TL	GN	TL	GN	GN		GN	TL	TL	GR
		■	■		■	■	■	■	■			■	■		■	■	■	■	■	■			■	■	■
Brighton	d				17 08										18 08										
Gatwick Airport	d				17 46		17 49						18 19		18 46			18 49						19 19	
East Croydon	d				18 01		18 15						18 45		19 01			19 15						19 45	
Maidstone East	d																								
London Bridge	d																								
London Blackfriars	d				18 22		18 37						19 07		19 22			19 37						20 07	
City Thameslink	d				18 24		18 39						19 09		19 24			19 39						20 09	
Farringdon	d				18 26		18 41						19 11		19 26			19 41						20 11	
St Pancras International	d																								
St Pancras International	d																								
St Pancras International	d				18 31		18 46						19 16		19 31			19 46						20 16	
London Kings Cross ⊖	d	18 24	18 36	18 42		18 21		18 54	19 06	19 12		18 51		19 42		19 23	19 36		19 57	20 06		20 12	19 51		20 33
Finsbury Park ⊖	d				18 42	18 31	18 54					19 01	19 24		19 42	19 32		19 53					20 01	20 24	
Potters Bar	d					18 43						19 13				19 45							20 13		
Hatfield	d					18 51						19 21				19 50							20 18		
Welwyn Garden City	d					18 56						19 26				19 56							20 26		
Welwyn North	d	18 41				19 00		19 11				19 30				20 00							20 30		
Knebworth	d	18 46				19 04		19 16				19 34				20 04							20 34		
Stevenage	d		18 58		19 03	19 08	19 14		19 28			19 38	19 44		20 03	20 08		20 14		20 28			20 38	20 44	20 55
Hitchin	d	18 55			19 09	19 14	19 20	19 25				19 44	19 50		20 09	20 14		20 20	20 25				20 44	20 50	
Letchworth Garden City	d	19 01			19 14	19 19		19 32				19 49			20 14	20 19			20 31				20 49		
Baldock	d	19 04			19 17	19 23		19a35				19 53			20 17	20 23			20a35				20 53		
Ashwell & Morden	d			19 14		19 27				19 44		19 57				20 27							20 57		
Royston	d	19a14		19 21	19 25	19 32				19 50		20 02		20 18	20 25	20 32						20 48	21 02		
Meldreth	d					19 36						20 06				20 36							21 06		
Shepreth	d					19 39						20 09				20 39							21 09		
Foxton	d					19 41						20 11				20 41							21 11		
Cambridge	a			19 36	19 42	19 51				20 05		20 22		20 33	20 43	20 51						21 03	21 21		
Cambridge	d			19 41						20 06		20 24		20 38								21 08	21 22		
Cambridge North	d			19 45						20 11		20a29		20 42								21 12	21a27		
Waterbeach	d			19 50										20 47								21 17			
Ely	d			20 02						20a23				20 58								21 29			
Littleport	d			20 10										21 06								21 36			
Downham Market	d			20 19										21 18								21 47			
Watlington	d			20 25										21 23								21 53			
Kings Lynn	a			20 33										21 32								22 01			
Arlesey	d						19 25						19 55					20 25						20 55	
Biggleswade	d		19 10				19 30						20 00				20 09	20 30		20 39				21 00	
Sandy	d						19 34						20 04					20 34						21 04	
St Neots	d		19 20				19 41						20 11				20 18	20 41		20 48				21 11	
Huntingdon	d		19 28				19 49						20 19				20 26	20 49		20 56				21 19	
Peterborough	a		19 43				20 05		19 58				20 35				20 43	21 05		21 12				21 35	21 24

		GN	TL	TL	TL	GN		GR	GN	GN	TL	TL	GR	GN	TL	TL		TL	GN	GN	GN	TL	TL	GN	TL
			■	■	■	■		■	■		■	■	■		■	■		■	■	■		■	■		■
Brighton	d		19 08												20 08										21 08
Gatwick Airport	d		19 46		19 49							20 19			20 46			20 49					21 19		21 46
East Croydon	d		20 01		20 15							20 46			21 01			21 15					21 45		22 01
Maidstone East	d																								
London Bridge	d																								
London Blackfriars	d		20 22		20 37							21 07			21 22			21 37					22 07		22 22
City Thameslink	d		20 24		20 39							21 09			21 24			21 39					22 09		22 24
Farringdon	d		20 26		20 41							21 11			21 26			21 41					22 11		22 26
St Pancras International	d																								
St Pancras International	d																								
St Pancras International	d		20 31		20 46							21 16			21 31			21 46					22 16		22 31
London Kings Cross ⊖	d	20 42		20 21		20 54		21 00	21 06	21 12	20 51		21 33	21 42		21 21			21 54	22 06	22 12	21 51		22 42	
Finsbury Park ⊖	d		20 42	20 31	20 54						21 01	21 24			21 42	21 31		21 54				22 01	22 24		22 42
Potters Bar	d			20 43							21 13					21 43						22 13			
Hatfield	d			20 48							21 18					21 48						22 18			
Welwyn Garden City	d			20 56							21 26					21 56						22 26			
Welwyn North	d			21 00							21 30					22 00						22 30			
Knebworth	d			21 04		21 14					21 34					22 04			22 14			22 34			
Stevenage	d		21 03	21 08	21 14			21 22	21 28		21 38	21 44	21 56		22 03	22 08		22 14		22 28		22 38	22 44		23 03
Hitchin	d		21 09	21 14	21 20	21 25					21 44	21 50			22 09	22 14		22 20	22 24			22 44	22 50		23 09
Letchworth Garden City	d	21 10	21 14	21 19		21 31					21 49				22 14	22 19			22a30			22 49			23 14
Baldock	d		21 17	21 23		21a35					21 53				22 17	22 23						22 53			23 17
Ashwell & Morden	d			21 27							21 57					22 27						22 57			
Royston	d		21 25	21 32						21 48	22 02			22 18	22 25	22 32					22 48	23 02		23 18	23 25
Meldreth	d			21 36							22 06					22 36						23 06			
Shepreth	d			21 39							22 09					22 39						23 09			
Foxton	d			21 41							22 11					22 41						23 11			
Cambridge	a	21 32	21 40	21 54						22 03	22 21			22 33	22 40	22 54					23 04	23 21		23 33	23 41
Cambridge	d	21 37								22 08	22 22			22 38							23 09			23 38	
Cambridge North	d	21 41								22 12	22a28			22 42							23 13			23 42	
Waterbeach	d	21 46								22 17				22 47							23 17			23 47	
Ely	d	21 57								22a27				22 58							23a28			23 58	
Littleport	d	22 05												23 06										00 06	
Downham Market	d	22 17												23 17										00 15	
Watlington	d	22 23												23 23										00 21	
Kings Lynn	a	22 31												23 31										00 29	
Arlesey	d				21 25							21 55						22 25					22 55		
Biggleswade	d				21 30				21 39			22 00						22 30		22 39			23 00		
Sandy	d				21 34							22 04						22 34					23 04		
St Neots	d				21 41				21 48			22 11						22 41		22 48			23 11		
Huntingdon	d				21 49				21 56			22 19						22 49		22 56			23 19		
Peterborough	a				22 05			21 51	22 12			22 35	22 25					23 05		23 12			23 37		

Please refer to Table T024 for the full service between Hertford North and Letchworth via Stevenage

Table T025-F

Mondays to Fridays
21 May to 7 December

Brighton, Gatwick Airport, Maidstone East and London - Stevenage, Cambridge, Kings Lynn and Peterborough

		TL		TL	GN	TL	TL	GN	GN	TL	TL	TL		TL	TL
		■		■	■	■	■			■	■	■		■	■
Brighton	d									22 08					
Gatwick Airport	d			21 49			22 19			22 46		22 49			23 35
East Croydon	d			22 15			22 45			23 01		23 15			00 10
Maidstone East	d														
London Bridge	d														
London Blackfriars	d			22 37			23 07			23 22		23 37			00 37
City Thameslink	d			22 39											
Farringdon	d			22 41			23 11			23 26		23 41			00 41
St Pancras International	d														
St Pancras International	d														
St Pancras International	d			22 46			23 16			23 31		23 46			00 46
London Kings Cross ⊖	d	22 21			23 06	22 51		23 12	23 42		23 24			23 51	
Finsbury Park ⊖	d	22 31		22 54		23 01	23 24			23 42	23 31	23 54		00 01	00 54
Potters Bar	d	22 43				23 13					23 43			00 13	
Hatfield	d	22 48				23 18					23 50			00 18	
Welwyn Garden City	d	22 56				23 26					23 56			00 28	01 13
Welwyn North	d	23 00				23 30					00 01			00 31	
Knebworth	d	23 04				23 34					00 05			00 35	
Stevenage	d	23 10		23 14	23 29	23 38	23 44			00 03	00 09	00 14		00 40	01 22
Hitchin	d	23 16		23 20		23 44	23 50			00 09	00 14	00 22		00 48	01 30
Letchworth Garden City	d	23 21				23 49			00 10	00 14	00 19			00 54	
Baldock	d	23 24				23 53				00 17	00 23			00 57	
Ashwell & Morden	d	23 29				23 57					00 27			01 01	
Royston	d	23 34				00a03		23 49	00 19	00 25	00 32			01 06	
Meldreth	d	23 37									00 36			01 10	
Shepreth	d	23 40									00 39			01 13	
Foxton	d	23 42									00 41			01 15	
Cambridge	a	23 54						00 04	00 35	00 40	00 54			01 25	
Cambridge	d							00 08							
Cambridge North	d							00 13							
Waterbeach	d							00 17							
Ely	d							00 27							
Littleport	d							00 34							
Downham Market	d							00 43							
Watlington	d							00 49							
Kings Lynn	a							00 57							
Arlesey	d			23 25			23 55					00 27			01 35
Biggleswade	d			23 30	23 40		00 01					00 32			01 41
Sandy	d			23 34			00 04					00 36			01 44
St Neots	d			23 41	23 49		00 11					00 43			01 52
Huntingdon	d			23 49	23 57		00 19					00 51			01 59
Peterborough	a			00 07	00 15		00 37					01 09			02 17

Saturdays
26 May to 8 December

		TL	GN	GN	GN	TL	TL	TL	TL	GN		TL	TL	TL	TL	TL	TL	TL	TL	GN		TL	GR	GR	TL
		■				■	■	■	■			■	■	■	■	■	■	■	■			■	■	■	■
Brighton	d																								
Gatwick Airport	d																								
East Croydon	d												00 10												
Maidstone East	d																								
London Bridge	d																								
London Blackfriars	d												00 37												
City Thameslink	d																								
Farringdon	d												00 41												
St Pancras International	d																								
St Pancras International	d																								
St Pancras International	d												00 46												
London Kings Cross ⊖	d									00 32		00 23		01 05	01 36	05 03	05 18	05 33	05 25	05 42		05 48	05 55	06 12	05 51
Finsbury Park ⊖	d								00 01	00 39		00 29	00 54	01 11	01 44	05 09	05 24	05 42	05 31			05 54			06 01
Potters Bar	d								00 13			00 42		01 22					05 42						06 13
Hatfield	d								00 18			00 48		01 28					05 48						06 18
Welwyn Garden City	d								00 28			00 58	01 13	01 34					05 56						06 26
Welwyn North	d						00 01		00 31			01 01		01 37					06 00						06 30
Knebworth	d						00 05		00 35			01 05		01 41					06 04						06 34
Stevenage	d					00 03	00 09	00 14	00 40	01 04		01 10	01 22	01 46	02 12	05 34	05 49	06 02	06 08			06 14	06 17	06 34	06 38
Hitchin	d					00 09	00 14	00 22	00 48	01 13		01 18	01 30	01 54	02 20	05 42	05 58	06 08	06 14			06 20			06 44
Letchworth Garden City	d				00 10	00 14	00 19		00 54	01s18		01 24		02 00		05 48		06 13	06 19						06 49
Baldock	d					00 17	00 23		00 57	01s21		01 27		02 03		05 51		06 16	06 23						06 53
Ashwell & Morden	d						00 27		01 01			01 31		02 07					06 27						06 57
Royston	d				00 19	00 25	00 32		01 06	01s29		01a37		02a13		05 59		06 24	06 32						07 02
Meldreth	d						00 36		01 10										06 36						07 06
Shepreth	d						00 39		01 13										06 39						07 09
Foxton	d						00 41		01 15										06 41						07 11
Cambridge	a				00 35	00 40	00 54		01 25	01 44						06 14		06 39	06 54	06 30					07 23
Cambridge	d			00 08																06 35					07 25
Cambridge North	d			00 13																06 38					07a30
Waterbeach	d			00 17																06 44					
Ely	d			00 27																06 54					
Littleport	d		00 06	00 34																07 04					
Downham Market	d		00 15	00 43																07 17					
Watlington	d		00 21	00 49																07 23					
Kings Lynn	a		00 29	00 57																07 31					
Arlesey	d							00 27					01 35		02 25		06 03					06 25			
Biggleswade	d	00 01						00 32					01 41		02 31		06 08					06 30			
Sandy	d	00 04						00 36					01 44		02 34		06 12					06 34			
St Neots	d	00 11						00 43					01 52		02 42		06 19					06 41			
Huntingdon	d	00 19						00 51					01 59		02 49		06 27					06 49			
Peterborough	a	00 37						01 09					02 17		03 07		06 42					07 07	06 46	07 03	

Please refer to Table T024 for the full service between Hertford North and Letchworth via Stevenage

Brighton, Gatwick Airport, Maidstone East and London - Stevenage, Cambridge, Kings Lynn and Peterborough

		TL	GR	TL	TL	TL		GN	GR	TL	TL	TL	TL	TL	GN	TL		TL	TL	TL	TL	GN	GR	TL	TL
Brighton	d			05 06								06 08							07 08						
Gatwick Airport	d			05 46		05 49					06 19	06 46		06 49				07 19	07 46		07 49				08 19
East Croydon	d			06 01		06 15					06 45	07 01		07 15				07 45	08 01		08 15				08 45
Maidstone East	d																								
London Bridge	d																								
London Blackfriars	d			06 22		06 37					07 07	07 22		07 37				08 07	08 22		08 37				09 07
City Thameslink	d																								09 09
Farringdon	d			06 26		06 41					07 11	07 26		07 41				08 11	08 26		08 41				09 11
St Pancras International	d																								
St Pancras International	d																								
St Pancras International	d			06 31		06 46					07 16	07 31		07 46				08 16	08 31		08 46				09 16
London Kings Cross	d	06 18	06 30		06 21			06 42	07 06	06 51			07 21		07 42	07 51				08 21		08 42	09 06	08 51	
Finsbury Park	d	06 24		06 42	06 31	06 54				07 01	07 24	07 42	07 31	07 54		08 01		08 24	08 42	08 31	08 54			09 01	09 24
Potters Bar	d				06 43					07 13			07 43			08 13				08 43				09 13	
Hatfield	d				06 48					07 18			07 48			08 18				08 48				09 18	
Welwyn Garden City	d				06 56					07 26			07 56			08 26				08 56				09 26	
Welwyn North	d				07 00					07 30			08 00			08 30				09 00				09 30	
Knebworth	d				07 04					07 34			08 04			08 34				09 04				09 34	
Stevenage	d	06 44	06 52	07 03	07 08	07 14			07 28	07 38	07 44	08 03	08 08	08 14		08 38		08 44	09 03	09 08	09 14		09 29	09 38	09 44
Hitchin	d	06 50		07 08	07 14	07 20				07 44	07 50	08 09	08 14	08 20		08 44		08 50	09 09	09 14	09 20			09 44	09 50
Letchworth Garden City	d			07 13	07 19					07 49		08 14	08 19			08 49			09 14	09 19				09 49	
Baldock	d			07 16	07 23					07 53		08 17	08 23			08 53			09 17	09 23				09 53	
Ashwell & Morden	d				07 27					07 57			08 27			08 57				09 27				09 57	
Royston	d			07 24	07 32					08 02		08 25	08 32			09 02			09 25	09 32				10 02	
Meldreth	d				07 36					08 06			08 36			09 06				09 36				10 07	
Shepreth	d				07 39					08 09			08 39			09 09				09 39				10 10	
Foxton	d				07 41					08 11			08 41			09 11				09 41				10 12	
Cambridge	a			07 39	07 54			07 30		08 22		08 40	08 54		08 30	09 21			09 40	09 54		09 30		10 23	
Cambridge	d							07 37		08 23					08 35	09 22						09 35		10 24	
Cambridge North	d							07 41		08a29					08 38	09a28						09 38		10a29	
Waterbeach	d							07 46							08 44							09 44			
Ely	d							07 57							08 55							09 55			
Littleport	d							08 05							09 04							10 04			
Downham Market	d							08 17							09 17							10 17			
Watlington	d							08 23							09 23							10 23			
Kings Lynn	a							08 31							09 31							10 31			
Arlesey	d	06 55				07 25					07 55			08 25				08 55			09 25				09 55
Biggleswade	d	07 00				07 30					08 00			08 30				09 00			09 30				10 00
Sandy	d	07 04				07 34					08 04			08 34				09 04			09 34				10 04
St Neots	d	07 11				07 41					08 11			08 41				09 11			09 41				10 11
Huntingdon	d	07 19				07 49					08 19			08 49				09 19			09 49				10 19
Peterborough	a	07 35	07 21			08 05			07 57		08 39			09 05				09 36			10 05		09 58		10 40

		TL		TL	TL	GN	GR	TL	TL	TL	TL	TL		GN	GR	TL	TL	TL	TL	TL	GN	GR		TL	TL
Brighton	d	08 08								09 08								10 08							
Gatwick Airport	d	08 46			08 49				09 19	09 46		09 49					10 19	10 46		10 49					11 19
East Croydon	d	09 01			09 15				09 45	10 01		10 15					10 45	11 01		11 15					11 45
Maidstone East	d																								
London Bridge	d																								
London Blackfriars	d	09 22			09 37				10 07	10 22		10 37					11 07	11 22		11 37					12 07
City Thameslink	d	09 24			09 39				10 09	10 24		10 39					11 09	11 24		11 39					12 09
Farringdon	d	09 26			09 41				10 11	10 26		10 41					11 11	11 26		11 41					12 11
St Pancras International	d																								
St Pancras International	d																								
St Pancras International	d	09 31			09 46				10 16	10 31		10 46					11 16	11 31		11 46					12 16
London Kings Cross	d			09 21		09 42	10 06	09 51			10 21			10 42	11 06	10 51			11 21		11 42	12 06		11 51	
Finsbury Park	d	09 42		09 31	09 54			10 01	10 24	10 42	10 31	10 54				11 01	11 24	11 42	11 31	11 54				12 01	12 24
Potters Bar	d			09 42				10 13			10 42					11 13			11 42					12 13	
Hatfield	d			09 48				10 18			10 48					11 18			11 48					12 18	
Welwyn Garden City	d			09 56				10 26			10 56					11 26			11 56					12 26	
Welwyn North	d			10 00				10 30			11 00					11 30			12 00					12 30	
Knebworth	d			10 04				10 34			11 04					11 34			12 04					12 34	
Stevenage	d	10 03		10 08	10 14		10 29	10 38	10 44	11 03	11 08	11 14			11 28	11 38	11 44	12 03	12 08	12 14		12 28		12 38	12 44
Hitchin	d	10 09		10 14	10 20			10 44	10 50	11 09	11 14	11 20				11 44	11 50	12 09	12 14	12 20				12 44	12 50
Letchworth Garden City	d	10 14		10 19				10 49		11 14	11 19					11 49		12 14	12 19					12 49	
Baldock	d	10 17		10 23				10 53		11 17	11 23					11 53		12 17	12 23					12 53	
Ashwell & Morden	d			10 27				10 57			11 27					11 57			12 27					12 57	
Royston	d	10 25		10 32				11 02		11 25	11 32					12 02		12 25	12 32					13 02	
Meldreth	d			10 36				11 06			11 36					12 06			12 36					13 06	
Shepreth	d			10 39				11 09			11 39					12 09			12 39					13 09	
Foxton	d			10 41				11 11			11 41					12 11			12 41					13 11	
Cambridge	a	10 40		10 54		10 30		11 21		11 40	11 54			11 30		12 21		12 40	12 54		12 30			13 21	
Cambridge	d					10 35		11 22						11 35		12 22					12 35			13 22	
Cambridge North	d					10 38		11a28						11 38		12a28					12 38			13a28	
Waterbeach	d					10 44								11 44							12 44				
Ely	d					10 55								11 55							12 55				
Littleport	d					11 04								12 04							13 04				
Downham Market	d					11 17								12 17							13 17				
Watlington	d					11 23								12 23							13 23				
Kings Lynn	a					11 31								12 31							13 31				
Arlesey	d				10 25				10 55			11 25					11 55			12 25					12 55
Biggleswade	d				10 30				11 00			11 30					12 00			12 30					13 00
Sandy	d				10 34				11 04			11 34					12 04			12 34					13 04
St Neots	d				10 41				11 11			11 41					12 11			12 41					13 11
Huntingdon	d				10 49				11 19			11 49					12 19			12 49					13 19
Peterborough	a				11 05		10 58		11 39			12 05			11 57		12 39			13 05		12 57			13 39

Please refer to Table T024 for the full service between Hertford North and Letchworth via Stevenage

Table T025-F

Saturdays

26 May to 8 December

Brighton, Gatwick Airport, Maidstone East and London - Stevenage, Cambridge, Kings Lynn and Peterborough

		TL	TL	TL	GN	TL	TL	TL		TL	TL	GN	GR	TL	TL	TL	TL	TL		GN	GR	TL	TL	TL	TL
Brighton	d	11 08						12 08								13 08								14 08	
Gatwick Airport	d	11 46		11 49			12 19	12 46			12 49				13 19	13 46		13 49					14 19	14 46	
East Croydon	d	12 01		12 15			12 45	13 01			13 15				13 45	14 01		14 15					14 45	15 01	
Maidstone East	d																								
London Bridge	d																								
London Blackfriars	d	12 22		12 37			13 07	13 22			13 37				14 07	14 22		14 37					15 07	15 22	
City Thameslink	d	12 24		12 39			13 09	13 24			13 39				14 09	14 24		14 39					15 09	15 24	
Farringdon	d	12 26		12 41			13 11	13 26			13 41				14 11	14 26		14 41					15 11	15 26	
St Pancras International	d																								
St Pancras International	d																								
St Pancras International	d	12 31		12 46			13 16	13 31			13 46				14 16	14 31		14 46					15 16	15 31	
London Kings Cross	d		12 21		12 42	12 51				13 21		13 42	14 06	13 51			14 21			14 42	15 06	14 51			15 21
Finsbury Park	d	12 42	12 31	12 54		13 01	13 24	13 42		13 31	13 54			14 01	14 24	14 42	14 31	14 54				15 01	15 24	15 42	15 31
Potters Bar	d		12 43			13 13				13 43				14 13			14 43					15 13			15 43
Hatfield	d		12 48			13 18				13 48				14 18			14 48					15 18			15 48
Welwyn Garden City	d		12 56			13 26				13 56				14 26			14 56					15 26			15 56
Welwyn North	d		13 00			13 30				14 00				14 30			15 00					15 30			16 00
Knebworth	d		13 04			13 34				14 04				14 34			15 04					15 34			16 04
Stevenage	d	13 03	13 08	13 15		13 38	13 44	14 03		14 08	14 14		14 29	14 38	14 44	15 03	15 08	15 14			15 28	15 38	15 44	16 03	16 08
Hitchin	d	13 09	13 14	13 20		13 44	13 50	14 09		14 14	14 20			14 44	14 50	15 09	15 14	15 20				15 44	15 50	16 09	16 14
Letchworth Garden City	d	13 14	13 19			13 49		14 14		14 19				14 49		15 14	15 19					15 49		16 14	16 19
Baldock	d	13 17	13 23			13 53		14 17		14 23				14 53		15 17	15 23					15 53		16 17	16 23
Ashwell & Morden	d		13 27			13 57				14 27				14 57			15 27					15 57			16 27
Royston	d	13 25	13 32			14 02		14 25		14 32				15 02		15 25	15 32					16 02		16 25	16 32
Meldreth	d		13 36			14 06				14 36				15 06			15 36					16 06			16 36
Shepreth	d		13 39			14 09				14 39				15 09			15 39					16 09			16 39
Foxton	d		13 41			14 11				14 41				15 11			15 41					16 11			16 41
Cambridge	a	13 40	13 54		13 30	14 21		14 40		14 54		14 30		15 21		15 40	15 54			15 30		16 21		16 40	16 54
Cambridge	d				13 35	14 22						14 35		15 22						15 35		16 22			
Cambridge North	d				13 38	14a28						14 38		15a28						15 38		16a28			
Waterbeach	d				13 44							14 44								15 44					
Ely	d				13 55							14 55								15 55					
Littleport	d				14 04							15 04								16 04					
Downham Market	d				14 17							15 17								16 17					
Watlington	d				14 23							15 23								16 23					
Kings Lynn	a				14 31							15 31								16 31					
Arlesey	d			13 25			13 55				14 25				14 55			15 25					15 55		
Biggleswade	d			13 31			14 00				14 30				15 00			15 30					16 00		
Sandy	d			13 34			14 04				14 34				15 04			15 34					16 04		
St Neots	d			13 42			14 11				14 41				15 11			15 41					16 11		
Huntingdon	d			13 49			14 19				14 49				15 19			15 49					16 19		
Peterborough	a			14 05			14 40				15 05		14 58		15 39			16 07			15 57		16 40		

		TL	GN	GR		TL	TL	TL	TL	GN	TL	GN	TL	TL		TL	TL	GN	TL	GN	TL	TL	GN	TL	
Brighton	d							15 08								16 08								17 08	
Gatwick Airport	d	14 49					15 19	15 46			15 49			16 19		16 46			16 49			17 19		17 46	
East Croydon	d	15 15					15 45	16 01			16 15			16 45		17 01			17 15			17 45		18 01	
Maidstone East	d																								
London Bridge	d																								
London Blackfriars	d	15 37					16 07	16 22			16 37			17 07		17 22			17 37			18 07		18 22	
City Thameslink	d	15 39					16 09	16 24			16 39			17 09		17 24			17 39			18 09		18 24	
Farringdon	d	15 41					16 11	16 26			16 41			17 11		17 26			17 41			18 11		18 26	
St Pancras International	d																								
St Pancras International	d																								
St Pancras International	d	15 46					16 16	16 31			16 46			17 16		17 31			17 46			18 16		18 31	
London Kings Cross	d		15 42	16 06		15 51			16 21	16 36		16 42	16 51				17 21	17 36		17 42	17 51		18 12		
Finsbury Park	d	15 54				16 01	16 23	16 42	16 31		16 54		17 01	17 24		17 42	17 31		17 54		18 01	18 24		18 42	
Potters Bar	d					16 13			16 43				17 13				17 43				18 13				
Hatfield	d					16 18			16 48				17 18				17 48				18 18				
Welwyn Garden City	d					16 26			16 56				17 26				17 56				18 26				
Welwyn North	d					16 30			17 00				17 30				18 00				18 30				
Knebworth	d					16 34			17 04				17 34				18 04				18 34				
Stevenage	d	16 14		16 29		16 38	16 43	17 03	17 08		17 14		17 38	17 44		18 03	18 08		18 14		18 38	18 44		19 03	
Hitchin	d	16 20				16 44	16 49	17 09	17 14		17 20		17 44	17 50		18 09	18 14		18 20		18 44	18 50		19 09	
Letchworth Garden City	d					16 49		17 14	17 19				17 49			18 14	18 19				18 49			19 14	
Baldock	d					16 53		17 17	17 23				17 53			18 17	18 23				18 53			19 17	
Ashwell & Morden	d					16 57			17 27				17 57				18 27				18 57				
Royston	d					17 02		17 25	17 32				18 02			18 25	18 32				19 02			19 25	
Meldreth	d					17 06			17 36				18 06				18 36				19 06				
Shepreth	d					17 09			17 39				18 09				18 39				19 09				
Foxton	d					17 11			17 41				18 11				18 41				19 11				
Cambridge	a		16 30			17 21		17 40	17 54			17 30	18 21			18 40	18 54			18 30	19 21		19 02	19 40	
Cambridge	d		16 35			17 22						17 35	18 22							18 35	19 22		19 04		
Cambridge North	d		16 38			17a28						17 38	18a28							18 38	19a28		19 08		
Waterbeach	d		16 44									17 44								18 44					
Ely	d		16 55									17 55								18 55			19 25		
Littleport	d		17 04									18 04								19 04			19 34		
Downham Market	d		17 17									18 17								19 17			19 44		
Watlington	d		17 23									18 23								19 23			19 52		
Kings Lynn	a		17 31									18 31								19 31			20 00		
Arlesey	d	16 25					16 54				17 25			17 55					18 25			18 55			
Biggleswade	d	16 30					16 59			17 09	17 30			18 00				18 09	18 30			19 00			
Sandy	d	16 34					17 03				17 34			18 04					18 34			19 04			
St Neots	d	16 41					17 10			17 19	17 41			18 11				18 21	18 41			19 11			
Huntingdon	d	16 49					17 18			17 27	17 49			18 19				18 29	18 49			19 19			
Peterborough	a	17 05		17 00			17 33			17 44	18 04			18 37				18 45	19 05			19 34			

Please refer to Table T024 for the full service between Hertford North and Letchworth via Stevenage

Table T025-F

Saturdays
26 May to 8 December

Brighton, Gatwick Airport, Maidstone East and London - Stevenage, Cambridge, Kings Lynn and Peterborough

Station		TL	GN	TL	GN	GR	TL	TL	GN	TL	TL	TL
Brighton	d									18 08		
Gatwick Airport	d			17 49				18 19		18 46		18 49
East Croydon	d			18 15				18 45		19 01		19 15
Maidstone East	d											
London Bridge	d											
London Blackfriars	d			18 37				19 07		19 22		19 37
City Thameslink	d			18 39				19 09		19 24		19 39
Farringdon	d			18 41				19 11		19 26		19 41
St Pancras International	d											
St Pancras International	d											
St Pancras International	d			18 46				19 16		19 31		19 46
London Kings Cross	d	18 21	18 36		18 42	19 06	18 51		19 12		19 21	
Finsbury Park	d	18 31		18 54			19 01	19 23		19 42	19 31	19 54
Potters Bar	d	18 43					19 13				19 43	
Hatfield	d	18 48					19 18				19 48	
Welwyn Garden City	d	18 56					19 26				19 56	
Welwyn North	d	19 00					19 30				20 00	
Knebworth	d	19 04					19 34				20 04	
Stevenage	d	19 08		19 14		19 28	19 38	19 43		20 03	20 08	20 14
Hitchin	d	19 14		19 20			19 44	19 49		20 09	20 14	20 20
Letchworth Garden City	d	19 19					19 49			20 14	20 19	
Baldock	d	19 23					19 53			20 17	20 23	
Ashwell & Morden	d	19 27					19 57				20 27	
Royston	d	19 32					20 02			20 25	20 32	
Meldreth	d	19 36					20 06				20 36	
Shepreth	d	19 39					20 09				20 39	
Foxton	d	19 41					20 11				20 41	
Cambridge	a	19 54			19 30		20 21		20 02	20 40	20 54	
Cambridge	d				19 35		20 22		20 04			
Cambridge North	d				19 38		20a28		20 08			
Waterbeach	d				19 44							
Ely	d				19 55				20 23			
Littleport	d				20 04							
Downham Market	d				20 17				20 42			
Watlington	d				20 23							
Kings Lynn	a				20 31				21 00			
Arlesey	d			19 25				19 54				20 25
Biggleswade	d		19 09	19 30				19 59				20 30
Sandy	d			19 34				20 03				20 34
St Neots	d		19 19	19 41				20 10				20 41
Huntingdon	d		19 27	19 49				20 18				20 49
Peterborough	a		19 43	20 04		19 57		20 33				21 04

Station		GN	GN	TL	TL	TL	TL	TL	GN	GN	TL	TL
Brighton	d					19 08						
Gatwick Airport	d				19 19	19 46		19 49				20 19
East Croydon	d				19 45	20 01		20 15				20 45
Maidstone East	d											
London Bridge	d											
London Blackfriars	d				20 07	20 22		20 37				21 07
City Thameslink	d				20 09	20 24		20 39				
Farringdon	d				20 11	20 26		20 41				21 11
St Pancras International	d											
St Pancras International	d											
St Pancras International	d				20 16	20 31		20 46				21 16
London Kings Cross	d	19 42	20 12	19 51			20 21		20 42	21 12	20 51	
Finsbury Park	d			20 01	20 24	20 42	20 31	20 54			21 01	21 24
Potters Bar	d			20 13			20 43				21 13	
Hatfield	d			20 18			20 48				21 18	
Welwyn Garden City	d			20 26			20 56				21 26	
Welwyn North	d			20 30			21 00				21 30	
Knebworth	d			20 34			21 04				21 34	
Stevenage	d			20 38	20 44	21 03	21 08	21 14			21 38	21 44
Hitchin	d			20 44	20 50	21 09	21 14	21 20			21 44	21 50
Letchworth Garden City	d		20 40	20 49		21 14	21 19			21 40	21 49	
Baldock	d			20 53		21 17	21 23				21 53	
Ashwell & Morden	d			20 57			21 27				21 57	
Royston	d		20 49	21 02		21 25	21 32			21 49	22 02	
Meldreth	d			21 06			21 36				22 06	
Shepreth	d			21 09			21 39				22 09	
Foxton	d			21 11			21 41				22 11	
Cambridge	a	20 30	21 04	21 21		21 40	21 54		21 30	22 04	22 21	
Cambridge	d	20 35	21 05	21 22					21 35	22 05	22 22	
Cambridge North	d	20 38	21 09	21a28					21 38	22 09	22a28	
Waterbeach	d	20 44							21 44			
Ely	d	20 55	21 25						21 55	22a23		
Littleport	d	21 04	21 33						22 04			
Downham Market	d	21 17	21 42						22 17			
Watlington	d	21 23	21 52						22 23			
Kings Lynn	a	21 31	22 00						22 31			
Arlesey	d				20 55			21 25				21 55
Biggleswade	d				21 00			21 30				22 00
Sandy	d				21 04			21 34				22 04
St Neots	d				21 11			21 41				22 11
Huntingdon	d				21 19			21 49				22 19
Peterborough	a				21 34			22 05				22 39

Please refer to Table T024 for the full service between Hertford North and Letchworth via Stevenage

Table T025-F

Saturdays
26 May to 8 December

Brighton, Gatwick Airport, Maidstone East and London - Stevenage, Cambridge, Kings Lynn and Peterborough

Station		TL	TL	TL	GN	GN	TL	TL	TL	TL	TL	GN
Brighton	d	20 08							21 08			
Gatwick Airport	d	20 46		20 49				21 19	21 46		21 49	
East Croydon	d	21 01		21 15				21 45	22 01		22 15	
Maidstone East	d											
London Bridge	d											
London Blackfriars	d	21 22		21 37				22 07	22 22		22 37	
City Thameslink	d											
Farringdon	d	21 26		21 41				22 11	22 26		22 41	
St Pancras International	d											
St Pancras International	d											
St Pancras International	d	21 31		21 46				22 16	22 31		22 46	
London Kings Cross	d		21 21		21 42	22 12	21 51			22 21		22 42
Finsbury Park	d	21 42	21 31	21 54			22 01	22 24	22 42	22 31	22 54	
Potters Bar	d		21 43				22 13			22 43		
Hatfield	d		21 48				22 18			22 48		
Welwyn Garden City	d		21 56				22 26			22 56		
Welwyn North	d		22 00				22 30			23 00		
Knebworth	d		22 04				22 34			23 04		
Stevenage	d	22 03	22 08	22 14			22 38	22 44	23 03	23 08	23 14	
Hitchin	d	22 09	22 14	22 20			22 44	22 50	23 09	23 14	23 20	
Letchworth Garden City	d	22 14	22 19			22 40	22 49		23 14	23 19		
Baldock	d	22 17	22 23				22 53		23 17	23 23		
Ashwell & Morden	d		22 27				22 57			23 27		
Royston	d	22 25	22 32			22 49	23 02		23 25	23 32		
Meldreth	d		22 36				23 06			23 36		
Shepreth	d		22 39				23 09			23 39		
Foxton	d		22 41				23 11			23 41		
Cambridge	a	22 40	22 54		22 30	23 04	23 22		23 40	23 54		23 30
Cambridge	d				22 35	23 05						23 35
Cambridge North	d				22 38	23 09						23 38
Waterbeach	d				22 44							23 44
Ely	d				22 55	23a23						23 55
Littleport	d				23 02							00 03
Downham Market	d				23 11							00 12
Watlington	d				23 17							00 18
Kings Lynn	a				23 25							00 26
Arlesey	d			22 25				22 55			23 25	
Biggleswade	d			22 30				23 00			23 30	
Sandy	d			22 34				23 04			23 34	
St Neots	d			22 41				23 11			23 41	
Huntingdon	d			22 51				23 19			23 49	
Peterborough	a			23 07				23 39			00 07	

Station		GN	TL	TL	GN	TL	TL	TL	TL	TL A	TL B
Brighton	d					22 08					
Gatwick Airport	d			22 19		22 46		22 49		23 35	23 35
East Croydon	d			22 45		23 01		23 15		00 10	00 10
Maidstone East	d										
London Bridge	d										
London Blackfriars	d			23 07		23 22		23 37		00 37	00 37
City Thameslink	d										
Farringdon	d			23 11		23 26		23 41		00 41	00 41
St Pancras International	d										
St Pancras International	d										
St Pancras International	d			23 16		23 31		23 46		00 46	00 46
London Kings Cross	d	23 12	22 51		23 42		23 21		23 51		
Finsbury Park	d		23 01	23 24		23 38	23 31	23 54	00 01	00 54	00 54
Potters Bar	d		23 13				23 43		00 13		
Hatfield	d		23 18				23 50		00 18		
Welwyn Garden City	d		23 26				23 57		00 28	01 13	01 13
Welwyn North	d		23 30				00 01		00 31		
Knebworth	d		23 34				00 05		00 35		
Stevenage	d		23 38	23 44		23 59	00 09	00 14	00 40	01 22	01 22
Hitchin	d		23 44	23 50		00 09	00 18	00 23	00 48	01a30	01 30
Letchworth Garden City	d	23 40	23 49		00 10	00 14	00 23		00 54		
Baldock	d		23 53			00 17	00 27		00 57		
Ashwell & Morden	d		23 57				00 31		01 01		
Royston	d	23 49	00a03		00 19	00 26	00 36		01 06		
Meldreth	d						00 40		01 10		
Shepreth	d						00 43		01 13		
Foxton	d						00 45		01 15		
Cambridge	a	00 04			00 34	00 41	00 55		01 25		
Cambridge	d	00 08									
Cambridge North	d	00 13									
Waterbeach	d	00 17									
Ely	d	00 27									
Littleport	d	00 34									
Downham Market	d	00 43									
Watlington	d	00 49									
Kings Lynn	a	00 57									
Arlesey	d			23 55				00 28			01 35
Biggleswade	d			00 01				00 33			01 41
Sandy	d			00 04				00 37			01 44
St Neots	d			00 12				00 44			01 52
Huntingdon	d			00 19				00 52			01 59
Peterborough	a			00 37				01 10			02 17

A from 15 September

B until 8 September

Please refer to Table T024 for the full service between Hertford North and Letchworth via Stevenage

Table T025-F

Sundays
20 May to 2 December

Brighton, Gatwick Airport, Maidstone East and London - Stevenage, Cambridge, Kings Lynn and Peterborough

		TL	GN	GN	GN	TL	TL	TL	TL	TL	GN	TL	TL	TL	TL	GN	GN	GN	GN	GN	GN	TL	GR
													A	B									
Brighton	d																						
Gatwick Airport	d																						
East Croydon	d												00 10	00 10									
Maidstone East	d																						
London Bridge	d																						
London Blackfriars	d												00 37	00 37									
City Thameslink	d																						
Farringdon	d												00 41	00 41									
St Pancras International	d																						
St Pancras International	d																						
St Pancras International	d												00 46	00 46									
London Kings Cross ⊖	d									00 12	00 32	00 23			01 05	06 31	07 02	07 35	07 52	08 11	08 02	08 39	09 03
Finsbury Park ⊖	d								00 01	00 20	00 39	00 29	00 54	00 54	01 11	06 38	07 09	07 42	07 59	08 17	08 09	08 46	
Potters Bar	d								00 13			00 42			01 22		07 20				08 20		
Hatfield	d								00 18			00 48			01 28		07 26				08 26		
Welwyn Garden City	d								00 28			00 58	01 13	01 13	01 34		07 31				08 31		
Welwyn North	d						00 01		00 31			01 01			01 37		07 34				08 34		
Knebworth	d						00 05		00 35			01 05			01 41		07 38				08 38		
Stevenage	d						00 09	00 14	00 40	00 53	01 04	01 10	01 22	01 22	01 46	07 03	07 44	08 08	08 20	08 38	08 44	09 06	09 25
Hitchin	d					00 09	00 18	00 23	00 48	01 02	01 13	01 18	01a30	01 30	01 54	07 13	07 53	08 18	08 26	08 44	08 50	09 12	
Letchworth Garden City	d				00 10	00 14	00 23		00 54		01s18	01a23			02a00	07 18	07 58		08 32		08 55	09 18	
Baldock	d					00 17	00 27		00 57		01s21					07 22	08 01		08 35		08 59	09 22	
Ashwell & Morden	d						00 31		01 01								08 06				09 04		
Royston	d				00 19	00 26	00 36		01 06		01s29					07 30	08 12		08 44		09 09	09 30	
Meldreth	d						00 40		01 10								08 16				09 13		
Shepreth	d						00 43		01 13								08 19				09 17		
Foxton	d						00 45		01 15								08 22				09 19		
Cambridge	a				00 34	00 41	00 55		01 25		01 44					07 45	08 35		08 58		09 31	09 48	
Cambridge	d			00 08															09 04				
Cambridge North	d			00 13															09 08				
Waterbeach	d			00 17															09 12				
Ely	d			00 27															09 22				
Littleport	d		00 03	00 34															09 29				
Downham Market	d		00 12	00 43															09 38				
Watlington	d		00 18	00 49															09 44				
Kings Lynn	a		00 26	00 57															09 52				
Arlesey	d							00 28		01 07				01 35				08 23		08 49			
Biggleswade	d	00 01						00 33		01 12				01 41				08 29		08 54			
Sandy	d	00 04						00 37		01 16				01 44				08 33		08 57			
St Neots	d	00 12						00 44		01 23				01 52				08 41		09 05			
Huntingdon	d	00 19						00 52		01 31				01 59				08 49		09 12			
Peterborough	a	00 37						01 10		01 49				02 17				09 05		09 28			09 54

A from 16 September

B from 27 May until 9 September

Please refer to Table T024 for the full service between Hertford North and Letchworth via Stevenage

Table T025-F

Sundays
20 May to 2 December

Brighton, Gatwick Airport, Maidstone East and London - Stevenage, Cambridge, Kings Lynn and Peterborough

		GN	GN	GN	TL	TL	GN	GN	TL	GR	TL	GN	GN	TL	TL	GN	GN	TL	GR	TL	GN	GN	GR
Brighton	d																						
Gatwick Airport	d				08 46	09 11			09 46		10 11			10 46	11 11			11 46		12 11			
East Croydon	d				09 07	09 37			10 07		10 37			11 07	11 37			12 07		12 37			
Maidstone East	d																						
London Bridge	d																						
London Blackfriars	d				09 31	10 01			10 31		11 01			11 31	12 01			12 31		13 01			
City Thameslink	d																						
Farringdon	d				09 35	10 05			10 35		11 05			11 35	12 05			12 35		13 05			
St Pancras International	d																						
St Pancras International	d																						
St Pancras International	d				09 40	10 10			10 40		11 10			11 40	12 10			12 40		13 10			
London Kings Cross ⊖	d	09 12	09 02	09 11			10 02	10 11		11 03		11 02	11 11			12 02	12 11		13 03		13 02	13 11	13 33
Finsbury Park ⊖	d	09 18	09 09		09 47	10 17	10 09		10 46		11 17	11 09		11 46	12 17	12 09		12 46		13 17	13 09		
Potters Bar	d		09 20				10 20					11 20				12 20					13 20		
Hatfield	d		09 26				10 26					11 26				12 26					13 26		
Welwyn Garden City	d		09 31				10 31					11 31				12 31					13 31		
Welwyn North	d		09 34				10 34					11 34				12 34					13 34		
Knebworth	d		09 38				10 38					11 38				12 38					13 38		
Stevenage	d	09 39	09 44		10 07	10 37	10 44		11 07	11 25	11 37	11 44		12 06	12 37	12 44		13 06	13 25	13 37	13 44		13 55
Hitchin	d	09 45	09 50		10 13	10 43	10 50		11 13		11 43	11 50		12 12	12 43	12 50		13 12		13 43	13 50		
Letchworth Garden City	d		09 56		10 18		10 55		11 18			11 55		12 18		12 55		13 18			13 55		
Baldock	d		09 59		10 22		10 59		11 22			11 59		12 22		12 59		13 22			13 59		
Ashwell & Morden	d		10 04				11 04					12 04				13 04					14 04		
Royston	d		10 10		10 30		11 09		11 30			12 09		12 30		13 09		13 30			14 09		
Meldreth	d		10 14				11 13					12 13				13 13					14 13		
Shepreth	d		10 17				11 17					12 17				13 17					14 17		
Foxton	d		10 19				11 19					12 19				13 19					14 19		
Cambridge	a		10 32	09 58	10 48		11 30	10 58	11 48			12 32	11 58	12 48		13 32	12 58	13 48			14 32	13 58	
Cambridge	d			10 04				11 04					12 04				13 04					14 04	
Cambridge North	d			10 08				11 08					12 08				13 08					14 08	
Waterbeach	d			10 12				11 12					12 12				13 12					14 12	
Ely	d			10 22				11 22					12 22				13 22					14 22	
Littleport	d			10 29				11 29					12 29				13 29					14 29	
Downham Market	d			10 38				11 38					12 38				13 38					14 38	
Watlington	d			10 44				11 44					12 44				13 44					14 44	
Kings Lynn	a			10 52				11 52					12 52				13 52					14 52	
Arlesey	d	09 50				10 48					11 48				12 48					13 48			
Biggleswade	d	09 55				10 54					11 54				12 54					13 54			
Sandy	d	09 58				10 57					11 57				12 57					13 57			
St Neots	d	10 06				11 05					12 05				13 05					14 05			
Huntingdon	d	10 13				11 12					12 12				13 12					14 12			
Peterborough	a	10 29				11 28				11 54	12 28				13 28				13 54	14 28			14 24

		TL	TL	GN	GN	TL	GR	TL	GN	GN	TL	TL	GN	GN	TL	GN	GN	TL	GN	GN	TL	GN
Brighton	d																					
Gatwick Airport	d	12 46	13 11			13 46		14 11			14 46	15 11			15 46			16 11			16 46	
East Croydon	d	13 07	13 37			14 07		14 37			15 07	15 37			16 07			16 37			17 07	
Maidstone East	d																					
London Bridge	d																					
London Blackfriars	d	13 31	14 01			14 31		15 01			15 31	16 01			16 31			17 01			17 31	
City Thameslink	d																					
Farringdon	d	13 35	14 05			14 35		15 05			15 35	16 05			16 35			17 05			17 35	
St Pancras International	d																					
St Pancras International	d																					
St Pancras International	d	13 40	14 10			14 40		15 10			15 40	16 10			16 40			17 10			17 40	
London Kings Cross ⊖	d			14 02	14 11		15 03		15 02	15 11			16 02	16 11		16 32	16 56		17 02	17 11		17 32
Finsbury Park ⊖	d	13 46	14 17	14 09		14 46		15 17	15 09		15 46	16 17	16 09		16 46	16 39		17 17	17 09		17 46	17 39
Potters Bar	d			14 20					15 20				16 20			16 50			17 20			17 50
Hatfield	d			14 26					15 26				16 26			16 56			17 26			17 56
Welwyn Garden City	d			14 31					15 31				16 31			17 01			17 31			18 01
Welwyn North	d			14 34					15 34				16 34			17 04			17 34			18 05
Knebworth	d			14 38					15 38				16 38			17 08			17 38			18 09
Stevenage	d	14 06	14 37	14 44		15 06	15 25	15 37	15 44		16 06	16 37	16 44		17 06	17 14		17 37	17 44		18 06	18 14
Hitchin	d	14 12	14 43	14 50		15 12		15 43	15 50		16 12	16 43	16 50		17 12	17 20		17 43	17 50		18 12	18 20
Letchworth Garden City	d	14 18		14 55		15 18			15 55		16 18		16 55		17 18	17a26			17 55		18 18	18a27
Baldock	d	14 22		14 59		15 22			15 59		16 22		16 59		17 22				17 59		18 22	
Ashwell & Morden	d			15 04					16 04				17 04						18 04			
Royston	d	14 30		15 09		15 30			16 09		16 30		17 09		17 30				18 09		18 30	
Meldreth	d			15 13					16 13				17 13						18 13			
Shepreth	d			15 17					16 17				17 17						18 17			
Foxton	d			15 19					16 19				17 19						18 19			
Cambridge	a	14 48		15 32	14 58	15 48			16 32	15 58	16 48		17 32	16 58	17 48				18 31	17 58	18 48	
Cambridge	d				15 04					16 04				17 04						18 04		
Cambridge North	d				15 08					16 08				17 08						18 08		
Waterbeach	d				15 12					16 12				17 12						18 12		
Ely	d				15 22					16 22				17 22						18 22		
Littleport	d				15 29					16 29				17 29						18 30		
Downham Market	d				15 38					16 38				17 38						18 39		
Watlington	d				15 44					16 44				17 44						18 44		
Kings Lynn	a				15 52					16 52				17 52						18 53		
Arlesey	d		14 48					15 48				16 48						17 48				
Biggleswade	d		14 54					15 54				16 54					17 31	17 54				
Sandy	d		14 57					15 57				16 57						17 57				
St Neots	d		15 05					16 05				17 05					17 42	18 05				
Huntingdon	d		15 12					16 12				17 12					17 50	18 12				
Peterborough	a		15 28				15 54	16 28				17 29					18 06	18 29				

Please refer to Table T024 for the full service between Hertford North and Letchworth via Stevenage

Table T025-F

Sundays

20 May to 2 December

Brighton, Gatwick Airport, Maidstone East and London - Stevenage, Cambridge, Kings Lynn and Peterborough

		GN	TL	GN	GN	TL	GN	GN	GR	TL	GN	GN	GR	TL	TL	GN	GN	GR	TL	TL	GN	GN	GR
Brighton	d																						
Gatwick Airport	d		17 11			17 46				18 11				18 46	19 11				19 46	20 11			
East Croydon	d		17 37			18 07				18 37				19 07	19 37				20 07	20 37			
Maidstone East	d																						
London Bridge	d																						
London Blackfriars	d		18 01			18 31				19 01				19 31	20 01				20 31	21 01			
City Thameslink	d																						
Farringdon	d		18 05			18 35				19 05				19 35	20 05				20 35	21 05			
St Pancras International	d																						
St Pancras International	d																						
St Pancras International	d		18 10			18 40				19 10				19 40	20 10				20 40	21 10			
London Kings Cross 15 ⊖	d	17 56		18 02	18 11		18 32	18 56	19 06		19 02	19 11	19 35			20 02	20 11	20 35			21 02	21 11	21 35
Finsbury Park ⊖	d		18 17	18 09		18 46	18 39			19 17	19 09			19 46	20 17	20 09			20 46	21 17	21 09		
Potters Bar	d			18 20			18 50				19 20					20 20					21 20		
Hatfield	d			18 26			18 56				19 26					20 26					21 26		
Welwyn Garden City 4	d			18 31			19 01				19 31					20 31					21 31		
Welwyn North	d			18 34			19 04				19 34					20 34					21 34		
Knebworth	d			18 38			19 08				19 38					20 38					21 38		
Stevenage 4	d		18 37	18 44		19 06	19 14		19 28	19 37	19 44		19 57	20 06	20 37	20 44		20 57	21 06	21 37	21 44		21 57
Hitchin 4	d		18 43	18 50		19 12	19 20			19 43	19 50			20 12	20 43	20 50			21 12	21 43	21 50		
Letchworth Garden City	d			18 55		19 18	19a26				19 55			20 18		20 55			21 18		21 55		
Baldock	d			18 59		19 22					19 59			20 22		20 59			21 22		21 59		
Ashwell & Morden	d			19 04							20 04					21 04					22 04		
Royston	d			19 09		19 30					20 09			20 30		21 09			21 30		22 09		
Meldreth	d			19 13							20 13					21 13					22 13		
Shepreth	d			19 17							20 17					21 17					22 17		
Foxton	d			19 19							20 19					21 19					22 19		
Cambridge	a			19 32	18 58	19 48					20 31	20 00		20 48		21 31	20 58		21 45		22 30	21 58	
Cambridge	d				19 04							20 05					21 04					22 04	
Cambridge North	d				19 08							20 09					21 08					22 08	
Waterbeach	d				19 12							20 13					21 12					22 12	
Ely	d				19 22							20 23					21 22					22 22	
Littleport	d				19 29							20 30					21 29					22 29	
Downham Market	d				19 38							20 39					21 38					22 38	
Watlington	d				19 44							20 45					21 44					22 44	
Kings Lynn	a				19 52							20 53					21 52					22 52	
Arlesey	d		18 48							19 48					20 48					21 48			
Biggleswade	d	18 31	18 54					19 31		19 54					20 54					21 54			
Sandy	d		18 57							19 57					20 57					21 57			
St Neots	d	18 41	19 05					19 42		20 05					21 05					22 05			
Huntingdon	d	18 49	19 12					19 50		20 12					21 12					22 12			
Peterborough 8	a	19 05	19 29					20 06	19 57	20 29			20 26		21 29			21 26		22 29			22 26

		TL	TL	GN	GN	TL	GN	GN	TL
Brighton	d								
Gatwick Airport	d	20 46	21 11			21 46			22 11
East Croydon	d	21 07	21 37			22 07			22 47
Maidstone East	d								
London Bridge	d								
London Blackfriars	d	21 31	22 01			22 31			23 12
City Thameslink	d								
Farringdon	d	21 35	22 05			22 35			23 16
St Pancras International	d								
St Pancras International	d								
St Pancras International	d	21 40	22 10			22 40			23 21
London Kings Cross 15 ⊖	d			22 02	22 11		23 11	23 02	
Finsbury Park ⊖	d	21 46	22 17	22 09		22 46		23 09	23 28
Potters Bar	d			22 20				23 20	
Hatfield	d			22 26				23 26	
Welwyn Garden City 4	d			22 31				23 31	
Welwyn North	d			22 34				23 34	
Knebworth	d			22 38				23 38	
Stevenage 4	d	22 06	22 37	22 43		23 06		23 44	23 48
Hitchin 4	d	22 12	22 43	22 50		23 12		23 50	23 53
Letchworth Garden City	d	22 18		22 55		23 18	23 38	23 55	
Baldock	d	22 22		22 59		23 22		23 59	
Ashwell & Morden	d			23 04				00 04	
Royston	d	22 30		23 09		23 30	23 48	00 09	
Meldreth	d			23 13				00 13	
Shepreth	d			23 17				00 16	
Foxton	d			23 19				00 19	
Cambridge	a	22 48		23 30	22 58	23 45	00 02	00 30	
Cambridge	d				23 04		00 04		
Cambridge North	d				23 08		00 08		
Waterbeach	d				23 12		00 12		
Ely	d				23 22		00 22		
Littleport	d				23 29		00 29		
Downham Market	d				23 38		00 38		
Watlington	d				23 44		00 44		
Kings Lynn	a				23 52		00 52		
Arlesey	d		22 48						23 58
Biggleswade	d		22 54						00 04
Sandy	d		22 57						00 07
St Neots	d		23 05						00 15
Huntingdon	d		23 15						00 22
Peterborough 8	a		23 30						00 41

Please refer to Table T024 for the full service between Hertford North and Letchworth via Stevenage

Table T025-R

Mondays to Fridays

21 May to 7 December

Peterborough, Kings Lynn, Cambridge and Stevenage - London, Maidstone East, Gatwick Airport and Brighton

Miles	Miles			TL MX	GN MO	TL MX	TL MX	TL MX	TL	GN	GN	TL	TL	TL	GN	TL	TL	GN	TL	GN	TL	GN	GN
0	—	Peterborough 8	d						03 24				04 20				04 54				05 24	05 42	
17½	—	**Huntingdon**	d						03 39				04 35				05 11				05 41	05 56	
24¾	—	**St Neots**	d						03 46				04 42				05 18				05 48	06 04	
32¼	—	**Sandy**	d						03 54				04 50				05 26				05 56		
35¼	—	**Biggleswade**	d						03 58				04 54				05 30				06 00	06 14	
39¼	—	**Arlesey**	a						04 02				04 58				05 34				06 04		
—	—	**Kings Lynn**	d																	04 43			
—	—	**Watlington**	d																	04 50			
—	—	**Downham Market**	d																	04 57			
—	—	**Littleport**	d																	05 07			
—	—	Ely	d																	05 15			
—	—	Waterbeach	d																	05 25			
—	—	Cambridge North	d																	05 30			
—	2¼	Cambridge	a																	05 34			
—	—	Cambridge	d											04 54					05 27	05 40			
—	7	**Foxton**	d																05 36				
—	8	**Shepreth**	d																05 38				
—	10	**Meldreth**	d																05 41				
—	13	**Royston**	d					00 09						05 09		05 18			05 48	05 54			
—	17	**Ashwell & Morden**	d													05 22			05 52				
—	21¼	**Baldock**	d				00 03	00 17						05 17		05 27			05 57				06 12
—	23¼	**Letchworth Garden City**	a				00 06	00 20						05 20		05 30			06 00	06 04			06 15
44½	26	**Hitchin 4**	d		00 01	00 06	00 10	00 28	04 11			05 00	05 07	05 26		05 34	05 41		06 04		06 11		06 20
48¾	30¼	**Stevenage 4**	d		00 07	00 12	00 16	00 34	04 17	04 22	05 02	05 06	05 13	05 32	05 32	05 40	05 47	06 06	06 10		06 17		
51¼	33	**Knebworth**	d		00 10		00 19					05 09				05 43			06 13				06 28
54¼	36	**Welwyn North**	d		00 14		00 23					05 13				05 47			06 17				06 32
56	37¾	Welwyn Garden City 4	d		00 19		00 28					05 18	05 22			05 52			06 22				
58½	40¼	Hatfield	d		00 23		00 31					05 21				05 55			06 25				
63½	45¼	Potters Bar	d	00 02	00 29		00 38					05 28				06 02			06 32				
73¾	55½	Finsbury Park ⊖	a	00 15	00 39	00 38	00 51	00 59	04 45	05 04	05 52	05 41	05 35	05 51	06 25	06 13	06 07	06 53	06 43		06 37		
76¼	58	London Kings Cross 15 ⊖	d	00a21	00a49	00a45	00a57	01a06	04a51	05a13		05a47				06a20			06a50	06a32		06a44	06a51
—	—	St Pancras International	d										05 45	06 00			06 15				06 45		
—	—	Farringdon	d										05 49	06 04			06 19				06 49		
—	—	City Thameslink	d										05 51	06 06			06 21				06 51		
—	—	London Blackfriars	d										05 54	06 09			06 24				06 54		
—	—	London Bridge	a																				
—	—	Maidstone East	d																				
—	—	East Croydon	d										06 16	06 29			06 46				07 16		
—	—	Gatwick Airport	d										06a50	06 45			07a19				07a46		
—	—	Brighton	a											07 22									

		GN	TL	TL	TL	GN	GN	GN	TL	GN	TL	GN	GN	GN	TL	TL	GN	TL	GN	GN	GN	TL	GN
Peterborough 8	d				05 54		06 05				06 24	06 36						06 54	07 05	07 14			
Huntingdon	d				06 11		06 20				06 41	06 50						07 11	07 20	07 30			
St Neots	d				06 18		06 28				06 48	06 59						07 18	07 28	07 39			
Sandy	d				06 26						06 56							07 26					
Biggleswade	d				06 30		06 38				07 00	07 08						07 30	07 38				
Arlesey	a				06 34						07 04							07 34					
Kings Lynn	d									05 40							06 10						06 40
Watlington	d									05 47							06 17						06 47
Downham Market	d									05 54							06 24						06 54
Littleport	d									06 04													07 04
Ely	d									06 12							06 42						07 12
Waterbeach	d									06 22													07 22
Cambridge North	d									06 27						06 48	06 55						
Cambridge	a									06 34						06 54	07 00						07 30
Cambridge	d		05 54	05 59		06 10			06 28	06 40					06 54	06 57	07 10					07 27	07 40
Foxton	d			06 08					06 38							07 06						07 36	
Shepreth	d			06 10					06 40							07 08						07 38	
Meldreth	d			06 13					06 43							07 11						07 41	
Royston	d		06 09	06 18		06 24		06 36	06 48	06 54					07 09	07 18	07 24				07 38	07 48	07 54
Ashwell & Morden	d			06 22		06 29			06 52	06 59						07 22	07 29					07 52	07 59
Baldock	d		06 17	06 27				06 45	06 57					07 12	07 17	07 27					07 46	07 57	
Letchworth Garden City	a		06 20	06 30				06 48	07 00					07 15	07 20	07 30					07 49	08 00	
Hitchin 4	d		06 26	06 34	06 41			06 53	07 04		07 11			07 20	07 26	07 34		07 41			07 55	08 04	
Stevenage 4	d	06 28	06 32	06 40	06 47		06 49		07 10		07 17	07 20	07 28		07 32	07 40		07 47	07 51			08 10	
Knebworth	d			06 43				07 01	07 13					07 28		07 43					08 02	08 13	
Welwyn North	d			06 47				07 04	07 17					07 32		07 47					08 06	08 17	
Welwyn Garden City 4	d			06 52					07 22							07 52						08 22	
Hatfield	d			06 55					07 25							07 55						08 25	
Potters Bar	d			07 02					07 32							08 02						08 32	
Finsbury Park ⊖	a	07 18	06 51	07 13	07 07				07 43		07 37		08 23		07 51	08 13		08 07				08 43	
London Kings Cross 15 ⊖	d			07a20		07a02	07a14	07a25	07a50	07a33		07a44		07a51		08a20	08a02		08a14	08a17	08a25	08a50	08a34
St Pancras International	d		07 00		07 15						07 45				08 00			08 15					
Farringdon	d		07 04		07 19						07 49				08 04			08 19					
City Thameslink	d		07 06		07 21						07 51				08 06			08 21					
London Blackfriars	d		07 09		07 24						07 54				08 09			08 24					
London Bridge	a																						
Maidstone East	d																						
East Croydon	d		07 30		07 46						08 16				08 30			08 46					
Gatwick Airport	d		07 45		08a15						08a45				08 46			09a15					
Brighton	a		08 19												09 20								

Please refer to Table T024 for the full service between Hertford North and Letchworth via Stevenage

Table T025-R

Mondays to Fridays
21 May to 7 December

Peterborough, Kings Lynn, Cambridge and Stevenage - London, Maidstone East, Gatwick Airport and Brighton

		TL	GN	GN	GN	TL	TL	GN	GN	TL	GN	GN	GR	GR	TL	GN	TL	GN	TL	TL	GN	TL
Peterborough	d	07 24	07 35							07 54	08 04		08 29				08 23					08 57
Huntingdon	d	07 41	07 49							08 11	08 20						08 38					09 12
St Neots	d	07 48	07 57							08 18	08 28						08 45					09 20
Sandy	d	07 56								08 26							08 53					09 27
Biggleswade	d	08 00	08 08							08 30	08 39						08 57					09 31
Arlesey	a	08 04								08 34							09 01					09 35
Kings Lynn	d							07 07	07 18							07 42					08 12	
Watlington	d							07 14								07 49					08 19	
Downham Market	d							07 21	07 30							07 56					08 26	
Littleport	d							07 31								08 06					08 36	
Ely	d							07 43	07 47							08 15					08 45	
Waterbeach	d							07 53								08 25					08 55	
Cambridge North	d						07 50		08 00							08 30				08 50	09 00	
Cambridge	a						07 56	08 01	08 04							08 35				08 56	09 04	
Cambridge	d					07 54	07 57	08 10							08 25	08 40			08 54	08 57	09 10	
Foxton	d						08 07								08 34					09 06		
Shepreth	d						08 10								08 36					09 08		
Meldreth	d						08 13								08 39					09 11		
Royston	d					08 08	08 18	08 24							08 44	08 55			09 09	09 18	09 24	
Ashwell & Morden	d					08 13	08 22								08 48	09 00				09 22		
Baldock	d				08 12	08 18	08 27					08 42			08 53				09 16	09 27		
Letchworth Garden City	a				08 15	08 21	08 30	08 34				08 45			08 56	09 07			09 19	09 30		
Hitchin	d	08 11			08 20	08 26	08 34			08 41		08 50			09 00		09 07		09 24	09 34		09 41
Stevenage	d	08 17	08 21	08 28		08 32	08 40			08 47	08 53		08 59	09 04	09 06		09 13	09 28	09 30	09 40		09 47
Knebworth	d				08 28		08 43					08 58			09 09					09 43		
Welwyn North	d				08 33		08 47								09 13					09 47		
Welwyn Garden City	d						08 52								09 22					09 52		
Hatfield	d						08 55								09 25					09 55		
Potters Bar	d						09 02								09 32					10 02		
Finsbury Park ⊖	a	08 37		09 23		08 51	09 13			09 07					09 43		09 33	10 22	09 50	10 13		10 07
London Kings Cross ⊖	d		08a46		08a52		09a25	09a04			09a18	09a21	09a24	09a31	09a50	09a43				10a25	10a05	
St Pancras International	d	08 45				09 00				09 15							09 45		10 00			10 15
Farringdon	d	08 49				09 04				09 19							09 49		10 04			10 19
City Thameslink	d	08 51				09 06				09 21							09 51		10 06			10 21
London Blackfriars	d	08 54				09 09				09 24							09 54		10 09			10 24
London Bridge	a																					
Maidstone East	d																					
East Croydon	d	09 16				09 29				09 46							10 16		10 29			10 46
Gatwick Airport	d	09a42				09 45				10a12							10a42		10 45			11a12
Brighton	a					10 20													11 19			

		GN	GR	TL	GN	TL	GN	TL	TL	GN	TL	GR	TL	GN	TL	GN	TL	TL	TL	GR	GR	TL	GN
Peterborough	d	09 17				09 26					09 54				10 24				10 54	11 28			
Huntingdon	d	09 32				09 41					10 11				10 41				11 11				
St Neots	d	09 40				09 48					10 18				10 48				11 18				
Sandy	d					09 56					10 26				10 56				11 26				
Biggleswade	d	09 49				10 00					10 30				11 00				11 30				
Arlesey	a					10 04					10 34				11 04				11 34				
Kings Lynn	d				08 44					09 10				09 44									10 44
Watlington	d				08 51					09 17				09 51									10 51
Downham Market	d				08 58					09 28				09 58									10 58
Littleport	d				09 08					09 38				10 08									11 08
Ely	d				09 17					09 48				10 17									11 17
Waterbeach	d				09 26					09 58				10 26									11 26
Cambridge North	d				09 31				09 44	10 03				10 31				10 44					11 31
Cambridge	a				09 36				09 50	10 07				10 36				10 50					11 36
Cambridge	d			09 27	09 42			09 54	09 57	10 14			10 27	10 44			10 54	10 57				11 27	11 44
Foxton	d			09 36					10 06				10 36					11 06				11 36	
Shepreth	d			09 38					10 08				10 38					11 08				11 38	
Meldreth	d			09 41					10 11				10 41					11 11				11 41	
Royston	d			09 48				10 09	10 18				10 48				11 09	11 18				11 48	
Ashwell & Morden	d			09 52					10 22				10 52					11 22				11 52	
Baldock	d			09 57				10 17	10 27				10 57				11 17	11 27				11 57	
Letchworth Garden City	a			10 00				10 20	10 30				11 00				11 20	11 30				12 00	
Hitchin	d			10 04		10 11		10 26	10 34		10 41		11 04		11 11		11 26	11 34	11 41			12 04	
Stevenage	d		10 06	10 10		10 17	10 28	10 32	10 40		10 47	11 04	11 10		11 17	11 28	11 32	11 40	11 47	11 58	12 03	12 10	
Knebworth	d			10 13					10 43				11 13					11 43				12 13	
Welwyn North	d			10 17					10 47				11 17					11 47				12 17	
Welwyn Garden City	d			10 22					10 52				11 22					11 52				12 22	
Hatfield	d			10 25					10 55				11 25					11 55				12 25	
Potters Bar	d			10 32					11 02				11 32					12 02				12 32	
Finsbury Park ⊖	a			10 43		10 37	11 22	10 51	11 13		11 07		11 43		11 37	12 22	11 51	12 13	12 06			12 43	
London Kings Cross ⊖	d	10a20	10a31	10a50	10a34				11a20	11a04		11a31	11a50	11a34				12a20		12a22	12a30	12a50	12a35
St Pancras International	d					10 45		11 00			11 15				11 45		12 00		12 15				
Farringdon	d					10 49		11 04			11 19				11 49		12 04		12 19				
City Thameslink	d					10 51		11 06			11 21				11 51		12 06		12 21				
London Blackfriars	d					10 54		11 09			11 24				11 54		12 09		12 24				
London Bridge	a																						
Maidstone East	d																						
East Croydon	d					11 16		11 29			11 46				12 16		12 29		12 46				
Gatwick Airport	d					11a42		11 45			12a12				12a42		12 45		13a12				
Brighton	a							12 19									13 19						

Please refer to Table T024 for the full service between Hertford North and Letchworth via Stevenage

Table T025-R

Mondays to Fridays
21 May to 7 December

Peterborough, Kings Lynn, Cambridge and Stevenage - London, Maidstone East, Gatwick Airport and Brighton

		TL	GN	TL	TL	TL	GR	GR	GN	TL	TL	GN	TL	TL	TL	GR	GR	TL	GN	TL	GN	TL	TL
Peterborough	d	11 23				11 54	12 30				12 24				12 54	13 30				13 24			
Huntingdon	d	11 41				12 11					12 41				13 11					13 41			
St Neots	d	11 48				12 18					12 48				13 18					13 48			
Sandy	d	11 56				12 26					12 56				13 26					13 56			
Biggleswade	d	12 00				12 30					13 00				13 30					14 00			
Arlesey	a	12 04				12 34					13 04				13 34					14 04			
Kings Lynn	d								11 44										12 44				
Watlington	d								11 51										12 51				
Downham Market	d								11 58										12 58				
Littleport	d								12 08										13 08				
Ely	d								12 17										13 17				
Waterbeach	d								12 26										13 26				
Cambridge North	d				11 44				12 31					12 44					13 31				13 44
Cambridge	a				11 50				12 37					12 50					13 37				13 50
Cambridge	d			11 54	11 57				12 44				12 54	12 57				13 27	13 44			13 54	13 57
Foxton	d				12 06									13 06				13 36					14 06
Shepreth	d				12 08									13 08				13 38					14 08
Meldreth	d				12 11									13 11				13 41					14 11
Royston	d			12 09	12 18								13 09	13 18				13 48				14 09	14 18
Ashwell & Morden	d				12 22									13 22				13 52					14 22
Baldock	d			12 17	12 27								13 17	13 27				13 57				14 17	14 27
Letchworth Garden City	a			12 20	12 30								13 20	13 30				14 00				14 20	14 30
Hitchin	d	12 11		12 26	12 34	12 41				13 00	13 11		13 26	13 34	13 41			14 04		14 11		14 26	14 34
Stevenage	d	12 17	12 28	12 32	12 40	12 47	12 59	13 04		13 08	13 17	13 28	13 32	13 40	13 47	13 59	14 04	14 10		14 17	14 28	14 32	14 40
Knebworth	d				12 43					13 13				13 43				14 13					14 43
Welwyn North	d				12 47					13 17				13 47				14 17					14 47
Welwyn Garden City	d				12 52					13 22				13 52				14 22					14 52
Hatfield	d				12 55					13 25				13 55				14 25					14 55
Potters Bar	d				13 02					13 32				14 02				14 32					15 02
Finsbury Park ⊖	a	12 37	13 22	12 51	13 13	13 07				13 43	13 37	14 22	13 51	14 13	14 07			14 43		14 37	15 22	14 51	15 13
London Kings Cross ⊖	d				13a20		13a23	13a31	13a33	13a50				14a20		14a23	14a31	14a50	14a33				15a20
St Pancras International	d	12 45		13 00		13 15					13 45		14 00		14 15					14 45		15 00	
Farringdon	d	12 49		13 04		13 19					13 49		14 04		14 19					14 49		15 04	
City Thameslink	d	12 51		13 06		13 21					13 51		14 06		14 21					14 51		15 06	
London Blackfriars	d	12 54		13 09		13 24					13 54		14 09		14 24					14 54		15 09	
London Bridge	a																						
Maidstone East	d																						
East Croydon	d	13 16		13 29		13 46					14 16		14 29		14 46					15 16		15 29	
Gatwick Airport	d	13a42		13 45		14a12					14a42		14 45		15a12					15a42		15 45	
Brighton	a			14 19									15 19									16 19	

		TL	GR	GR	TL	GN	TL	GN	TL	TL	TL	GR	GR	TL	GN	TL	GN	TL	TL	TL	GR	GR
Peterborough	d	13 54	14 30				14 24				14 54	15 30				15 24				15 54	16 29	
Huntingdon	d	14 11					14 41				15 11					15 41				16 11		
St Neots	d	14 18					14 48				15 18					15 48				16 18		
Sandy	d	14 26					14 56				15 26					15 56				16 26		
Biggleswade	d	14 30					15 00				15 30					16 00				16 30		
Arlesey	a	14 34					15 04				15 34					16 04				16 34		
Kings Lynn	d					13 44									14 44							
Watlington	d					13 51									14 51							
Downham Market	d					13 58									14 58							
Littleport	d					14 07									15 08							
Ely	d					14 17									15 17							
Waterbeach	d					14 25									15 26							
Cambridge North	d					14 30				14 44					15 31				15 44			
Cambridge	a					14 36				14 50					15 37				15 50			
Cambridge	d				14 27	14 44			14 54	14 57				15 27	15 44			15 54	15 57			
Foxton	d				14 36					15 06				15 36					16 06			
Shepreth	d				14 38					15 08				15 38					16 08			
Meldreth	d				14 41					15 11				15 41					16 11			
Royston	d				14 48				15 09	15 18				15 48				16 09	16 18			
Ashwell & Morden	d				14 52					15 22				15 52					16 22			
Baldock	d				14 57				15 17	15 27				15 57				16 17	16 27			
Letchworth Garden City	a				15 00				15 20	15 30				16 00				16 20	16 30			
Hitchin	d	14 41			15 04		15 11		15 26	15 34	15 41			16 04		16 11		16 26	16 34	16 41		
Stevenage	d	14 47	14 59	15 04	15 10		15 17	15 28	15 32	15 40	15 47	15 59	16 04	16 10		16 17	16 26	16 32	16 40	16 47	16 59	17 04
Knebworth	d				15 13					15 43				16 13					16 43			
Welwyn North	d				15 17					15 47				16 17					16 47			
Welwyn Garden City	d				15 22					15 52				16 22					16 52			
Hatfield	d				15 25					15 55				16 25					16 55			
Potters Bar	d				15 32					16 02				16 32					17 02			
Finsbury Park ⊖	a	15 07			15 43		15 37	16 22	15 51	16 13	16 07			16 43		16 37	17 19	16 51	17 14	17 07		
London Kings Cross ⊖	d		15a23	15a31	15a50	15a33				16a20		16a23	16a33	16a50	16a33				17a20		17a23	17a31
St Pancras International	d	15 15					15 45		16 00		16 15					16 45		17 00		17 15		
Farringdon	d	15 19					15 49		16 04		16 19					16 49		17 04		17 19		
City Thameslink	d	15 21					15 51		16 06		16 21					16 51		17 06		17 21		
London Blackfriars	d	15 24					15 54		16 09		16 24					16 54		17 09		17 24		
London Bridge	a																					
Maidstone East	d																					
East Croydon	d	15 46					16 16		16 29		16 46					17 16		17 29		17 46		
Gatwick Airport	d	16a12					16a42		16 45		17a15					17a45		17 45		18a15		
Brighton	a								17 21									18 21				

Please refer to Table T024 for the full service between Hertford North and Letchworth via Stevenage

Peterborough, Kings Lynn, Cambridge and Stevenage - London, Maidstone East, Gatwick Airport and Brighton

		TL	GN	TL	GN	TL	TL	TL		GR	GR	TL	GN	TL	GN	TL	TL	GN		TL	GR	GR	TL	GN	TL
		■		■		■	■	■		■ ■ ☕	■ ■ ☕	■		■		■	■			■	■ ■ ☕	■ ■ ☕	■		■
Peterborough ■	d			16 24				16 54		17 30				17 24						17 54	18 29				18 24
Huntingdon	d			16 41				17 11						17 41						18 11					18 41
St Neots	d			16 48				17 18						17 48						18 18					18 48
Sandy	d			16 56				17 26						17 56						18 26					18 56
Biggleswade	d			17 00				17 30						18 00						18 30					19 00
Arlesey	a			17 04				17 34						18 04						18 34					19 04
Kings Lynn	d		15 44										16 44					17 16						17 44	
Watlington	d		15 51										16 51											17 51	
Downham Market	d		15 58										16 58					17 29						17 58	
Littleport	d		16 08										17 08											18 08	
Ely	d		16 17										17 17					17 50						18 17	
Waterbeach	d		16 26										17 26					17 59						18 27	
Cambridge North	d		16 31				16 44						17 31				17 44							18 32	
Cambridge	a		16 37				16 50						17 37				17 50	18 07						18 36	
Cambridge	d	16 27	16 44			16 54	16 57					17 27	17 43			17 54	17 57	18 13					18 27	18 44	
Foxton	d	16 36					17 06					17 36					18 06						18 36		
Shepreth	d	16 38					17 08					17 38					18 08						18 38		
Meldreth	d	16 41					17 11					17 41					18 11						18 41		
Royston	d	16 48				17 09	17 18					17 48				18 09	18 16						18 48		
Ashwell & Morden	d	16 52					17 22					17 52					18 21						18 52		
Baldock	d	16 57				17 17	17 27					17 57				18 17	18 25						18 57		
Letchworth Garden City	a	17 00				17 20	17 30					18 00				18 20	18 28						19 00		
Hitchin ■	d	17 04		17 11		17 26	17 34	17 41				18 04		18 11		18 26	18 34			18 41			19 04		19 11
Stevenage ■	d	17 10		17 17	17 30	17 32	17 40	17 47		17 59	18 05	18 10		18 17	18 30	18 32	18 40			18 47	18 59	19 07	19 10		19 17
Knebworth	d	17 13					17 43					18 13					18 43						19 13		
Welwyn North	d	17 17					17 47					18 17					18 47						19 17		
Welwyn Garden City ■	d	17 22					17 52					18 22					18 52						19 22		
Hatfield	d	17 25					17 55					18 25					18 55						19 25		
Potters Bar	d	17 32					18 02					18 32					19 02						19 32		
Finsbury Park ⊖	a	17 44		17 37	18 19	17 51	18 14	18 07				18 44		18 36	19 22	18 51	19 14			19 07			19 44		19 37
London Kings Cross ■ ⊖	d	17a50	17a33				18a20			18a27	18a31	18a50	18a33				19a20	19a04			19a23	19a32	19a50	19a35	
St Pancras International	d			17 45		18 00		18 15						18 45		19 00				19 15					19 45
Farringdon	d			17 49		18 04		18 19						18 49		19 04				19 19					19 49
City Thameslink	d			17 51		18 06		18 21						18 51		19 06				19 21					19 51
London Blackfriars	d			17 54		18 09		18 24						18 54		19 09				19 24					19 54
London Bridge	a																								
Maidstone East	d																								
East Croydon	d			18 16		18 29		18 46						19 16		19 29				19 46					20 16
Gatwick Airport	d			18a45		18 45		19a15						19a45		19 45				20a14					20a42
Brighton	a					19 21										20 19									

		GN	GN	TL		TL	TL	GR	GR	TL	GN	TL	GN	GR		GN	GR	TL	TL	TL	GN	GR	TL	GN	
				■		■	■	■ ■ ☕	■ ■ ☕	■		■		■ ■ ☕			■ ■ ☕	■	■	■		■ ■ ☕	■		
Peterborough ■	d	18 32					18 52	19 30				19 24	19 42	19 51						19 54	20 19				
Huntingdon	d						19 10					19 41	19 56							20 11	20 33				
St Neots	d						19 17					19 48	20 04							20 18	20 41				
Sandy	d						19 25					19 56								20 26					
Biggleswade	d						19 29					20 00	20 15							20 30	20 51				
Arlesey	a						19 33					20 04								20 34					
Kings Lynn	d										18 44													19 44	
Watlington	d										18 51													19 51	
Downham Market	d										18 58													19 58	
Littleport	d										19 08													20 08	
Ely	d										19 17													20 18	
Waterbeach	d										19 26													20 28	
Cambridge North	d					18 50					19 31								19 48					20 33	
Cambridge	a					18 55					19 36								19 55					20 38	
Cambridge	d			18 53		18 57				19 27	19 44							19 54	19 57				20 27	20 44	
Foxton	d					19 06				19 36									20 06				20 36		
Shepreth	d					19 08				19 38									20 08				20 38		
Meldreth	d					19 11				19 41									20 11				20 41		
Royston	d			19 09		19 16				19 48								20 09	20 18				20 48		
Ashwell & Morden	d					19 21				19 52									20 22				20 52		
Baldock	d			19 17		19 25				19 57								20 17	20 27				20 57		
Letchworth Garden City	a			19 20		19 28				20 00								20 20	20 30				21 00		
Hitchin ■	d			19 26		19 33	19 39			20 04		20 11						20 26	20 34	20 41			21 04		
Stevenage ■	d	19 23	19 30	19 32		19 40	19 45	19 59	20 06	20 10		20 17		20 20		20 28	20 29	20 32	20 40	20 47		21 06	21 10		
Knebworth	d					19 43				20 13									20 43				21 13		
Welwyn North	d					19 47				20 17									20 47				21 17		
Welwyn Garden City ■	d					19 52				20 22									20 52				21 22		
Hatfield	d					19 55				20 25									20 55				21 25		
Potters Bar	d					20 02				20 32									21 02				21 32		
Finsbury Park ⊖	a		20 22	19 51		20 14	20 05			20 43		20 36				21 22		20 51	21 13	21 07			21 43		
London Kings Cross ■ ⊖	d	19a50				20a25		20a23	20a31	20a50	20a33		20a47	20a46			20a53		21a20		21a23	21a31	21a50	21a33	
St Pancras International	d			20 00			20 15					20 45						21 00		21 15					
Farringdon	d			20 04			20 19					20 49						21 04		21 19					
City Thameslink	d			20 06			20 21					20 51						21 06		21 21					
London Blackfriars	d			20 09			20 24					20 54						21 09		21 24					
London Bridge	a																								
Maidstone East	d																								
East Croydon	d			20 29			20 46					21 16						21 29		21 46					
Gatwick Airport	d			20 45			21a12					21a42						21 45		22a12					
Brighton	a			21 19														22 19							

Please refer to Table T024 for the full service between Hertford North and Letchworth via Stevenage

Table T025-R

Mondays to Fridays
21 May to 7 December

Peterborough, Kings Lynn, Cambridge and Stevenage - London, Maidstone East, Gatwick Airport and Brighton

		GR	TL	GN	TL	TL	GR	TL	TL	GN		TL	GN	GN	TL	TL	GR	TL	GR	TL		GN	TL	GN	TL
		■ ■ ☕	■		■	■	■ ■ ☕	■	■			■			■	■	■ ■ ☕	■	■ ■ ☕	■			■		■
Peterborough ■	d	20 46	20 24				21 16	20 54				21 24	21 41				22 16	21 54	22 39				22 24		
Huntingdon	d		20 41					21 11				21 41	21 55					22 11					22 41		
St Neots	d		20 48					21 18				21 48	22 04					22 18					22 48		
Sandy	d		20 56					21 26				21 56						22 26					22 56		
Biggleswade	d		21 00					21 30				22 00	22 13					22 30					23 00		
Arlesey	a		21 04					21 34				22 04						22 34					23 04		
Kings Lynn	d									20 44												21 44			
Watlington	d									20 51												21 51			
Downham Market	d									20 59												21 58			
Littleport	d									21 08												22 08			
Ely	d									21 17												22 17			
Waterbeach	d									21 26												22 26			
Cambridge North	d					20 44				21 31						21 44						22 31			
Cambridge	a					20 50				21 36						21 50						22 36			
Cambridge	d				20 54	20 57			21 27	21 44					21 54	21 57				22 27		22 44			22 54
Foxton	d					21 06			21 36							22 06				22 36					
Shepreth	d					21 08			21 38							22 08				22 38					
Meldreth	d					21 11			21 41							22 11				22 41					
Royston	d				21 08	21 18			21 48						22 09	22 18				22 48					23 09
Ashwell & Morden	d					21 22			21 52							22 22				22 52					
Baldock	d				21 16	21 27			21 57						22 17	22 27				22 57					23 17
Letchworth Garden City	a				21 19	21 30			22 00						22 20	22 30				23 00					23 20
Hitchin ■	d		21 11		21 24	21 34		21 41	22 04			22 11			22 26	22 34		22 41		23 04			23 11		23 26
Stevenage ■	d	21 15	21 17	21 28	21 29	21 40	21 45	21 47	22 10			22 17	22 24	22 28	22 32	22 40	22 45	22 47	23 08	23 10			23 17	23 28	23 32
Knebworth	d					21 43			22 13							22 43				23 14					
Welwyn North	d					21 47			22 17							22 47				23 18					
Welwyn Garden City ■	d					21 52			22 22							22 52				23 22					
Hatfield	d					21 55			22 25							22 55				23 26					
Potters Bar	d					22 02			22 32							23 02				23 32					
Finsbury Park ⊖	a		21 36	22 22	21 49	22 13		22 06	22 43			22 36		23 20	22 51	23 13		23 06		23 43			23 36	00 20	23 51
London Kings Cross ■ ⊖	d	21a39				22a20	22a08		22a50	22a32			22a46			23a20	23a09		23a30	23a50		23a34	23a43		23a58
St Pancras International	d		21 45		22 00			22 15				22 45			23 00			23 15							
Farringdon	d		21 49		22 04			22 19				22 49			23 04			23 19							
City Thameslink	d		21 51		22 06			22 21				22 51													
London Blackfriars	d		21 54		22 09			22 24				22 54			23 09			23 24							
London Bridge	a																								
Maidstone East	d																								
East Croydon	d		22 16		22 29			22 46				23 16			23 29			23 46							
Gatwick Airport	d		22a42		22 45			23a12				23a41			23 48			00a12							
Brighton	a				23 19										00 23										

		TL	TL	TL	TL	GN		TL
		■	■	■	■			■
Peterborough ■	d		22 54	23 20				
Huntingdon	d		23 11	23 35				
St Neots	d		23 18	23 42				
Sandy	d		23 26	23 50				
Biggleswade	d		23 30	23 53				
Arlesey	a		23 34	23 58				
Kings Lynn	d					22 44		
Watlington	d					22 51		
Downham Market	d					22 58		
Littleport	d					23 08		
Ely	d					23 17		
Waterbeach	d					23 26		
Cambridge North	d	22 44				23 31		
Cambridge	a	22 50				23 37		
Cambridge	d	22 57			23 35			23 54
Foxton	d	23 06			23 44			
Shepreth	d	23 08			23 46			
Meldreth	d	23 11			23 49			
Royston	d	23 17			23 54			00 09
Ashwell & Morden	d	23 22			23 58			
Baldock	d	23 26			00 03			00 17
Letchworth Garden City	a	23 29			00 06			00 20
Hitchin ■	d	23 34	23 44	00 06	00 10			00 28
Stevenage ■	d	23 40	23 50	00 12	00 16			00 34
Knebworth	d	23 43			00 19			
Welwyn North	d	23 47			00 23			
Welwyn Garden City ■	d	23 52			00 28			
Hatfield	d	23 55			00 31			
Potters Bar	d	00 02			00 38			
Finsbury Park ⊖	a	00 15	00 10	00 38	00 51			00 59
London Kings Cross ■ ⊖	d	00a21	00a18	00a45	00a57			01a06
St Pancras International	d							
Farringdon	d							
City Thameslink	d							
London Blackfriars	d							
London Bridge	a							
Maidstone East	d							
East Croydon	d							
Gatwick Airport	d							
Brighton	a							

Please refer to Table T024 for the full service between Hertford North and Letchworth via Stevenage

Table T025-R

Saturdays
26 May to 8 December

Peterborough, Kings Lynn, Cambridge and Stevenage - London, Maidstone East, Gatwick Airport and Brighton

	TL	TL	TL	TL	TL	GN	GN	TL	TL		TL	GN
Peterborough d					03 24				04 18			
Huntingdon d					03 39				04 33			
St Neots d					03 46				04 40			
Sandy d					03 54				04 48			
Biggleswade d					03 58				04 52			
Arlesey a					04 02				04 56			
Kings Lynn d												
Watlington d												
Downham Market d												
Littleport d												
Ely d												
Waterbeach d												
Cambridge North d												
Cambridge a												
Cambridge d											04 53	
Foxton d												
Shepreth d												
Meldreth d												
Royston d				00 09							05 09	
Ashwell & Morden d												
Baldock d			00 03	00 17							05 17	
Letchworth Garden City a			00 06	00 20							05 20	
Hitchin d		00 06	00 10	00 28	04 11			04 58	05 05		05 26	
Stevenage d		00 12	00 16	00 34	04 17	04 22	05 00	05 04	05 11		05 32	05 32
Knebworth d			00 19					05 07				
Welwyn North d			00 23					05 11				
Welwyn Garden City d			00 28					05 16	05 20			
Hatfield d			00 31					05 19				
Potters Bar d	00 02		00 38					05 26				
Finsbury Park a	00 15	00 38	00 51	00 59	04 45	05 04	05 52	05 39	05 34		05 51	06 25
London Kings Cross d	00a21	00a45	00a57	01a06	04a51	05a13		05a46				
St Pancras International d									05 45		06 00	
Farringdon d									05 49		06 04	
City Thameslink d												
London Blackfriars d									05 54		06 09	
London Bridge a												
Maidstone East d												
East Croydon d									06 16		06 29	
Gatwick Airport d									06a50		06 45	
Brighton a											07 22	

	TL	TL	GN	TL	TL	GN	TL		TL	TL	TL	GN
Peterborough d		04 54			05 24					05 54		
Huntingdon d		05 11			05 41					06 11		
St Neots d		05 18			05 48					06 18		
Sandy d		05 26			05 56					06 26		
Biggleswade d		05 30			06 00					06 30		
Arlesey a		05 34			06 04					06 34		
Kings Lynn d												05 44
Watlington d												05 51
Downham Market d												05 58
Littleport d												06 08
Ely d												06 17
Waterbeach d												06 27
Cambridge North d												06 32
Cambridge a												06 37
Cambridge d				05 27			05 54		05 59		06 29	06 44
Foxton d				05 36					06 08		06 38	
Shepreth d				05 38					06 10		06 40	
Meldreth d				05 41					06 13		06 43	
Royston d	05 18			05 48			06 09		06 18		06 48	
Ashwell & Morden d	05 22			05 52					06 22		06 52	
Baldock d	05 27			05 57			06 17		06 27		06 57	
Letchworth Garden City a	05 30			06 00			06 20		06 30		07 00	
Hitchin d	05 34	05 41		06 04	06 11		06 26		06 34	06 41	07 04	
Stevenage d	05 40	05 47	06 06	06 10	06 17	06 28	06 32		06 40	06 47	07 10	
Knebworth d	05 44			06 13					06 43		07 13	
Welwyn North d	05 47			06 17					06 47		07 17	
Welwyn Garden City d	05 52			06 22					06 52		07 22	
Hatfield d	05 56			06 25					06 55		07 25	
Potters Bar d	06 03			06 32					07 02		07 32	
Finsbury Park a	06 14	06 06	06 53	06 43	06 36	07 22	06 51		07 13	07 06	07 43	
London Kings Cross d	06a21			06a50					07a20		07a50	07a33
St Pancras International d		06 15			06 45		07 00			07 15		
Farringdon d		06 19			06 49		07 04			07 19		
City Thameslink d												
London Blackfriars d		06 24			06 54		07 09			07 24		
London Bridge a												
Maidstone East d												
East Croydon d		06 46			07 16		07 30			07 46		
Gatwick Airport d		07a12			07a42		07 45			08a12		
Brighton a							08 19					

	TL	GN	TL	TL	TL		TL	GN	TL	GN	TL	TL
Peterborough d	06 24				06 54				07 24			
Huntingdon d	06 41				07 11				07 41			
St Neots d	06 48				07 18				07 48			
Sandy d	06 56				07 26				07 56			
Biggleswade d	07 00				07 30				08 00			
Arlesey a	07 04				07 34				08 04			
Kings Lynn d								06 44				
Watlington d								06 51				
Downham Market d								06 58				
Littleport d								07 08				
Ely d								07 17				
Waterbeach d								07 27				
Cambridge North d				06 44				07 32				07 44
Cambridge a				06 50				07 36				07 50
Cambridge d			06 54	06 57			07 27	07 44			07 54	07 57
Foxton d				07 06			07 36					08 06
Shepreth d				07 08			07 38					08 08
Meldreth d				07 11			07 41					08 11
Royston d			07 09	07 18			07 48				08 09	08 18
Ashwell & Morden d				07 22			07 52					08 22
Baldock d			07 17	07 27			07 57				08 17	08 27
Letchworth Garden City a			07 20	07 30			08 00				08 20	08 30
Hitchin d	07 11		07 26	07 34	07 41		08 04		08 11		08 26	08 34
Stevenage d	07 17	07 28	07 32	07 40	07 47		08 10		08 17	08 28	08 32	08 40
Knebworth d				07 43			08 13					08 43
Welwyn North d				07 47			08 17					08 47
Welwyn Garden City d				07 52			08 22					08 52
Hatfield d				07 55			08 25					08 55
Potters Bar d				08 02			08 32					09 02
Finsbury Park a	07 36	08 22	07 51	08 13	08 07		08 43		08 37	09 22	08 51	09 13
London Kings Cross d				08a20			08a50	08a33				09a20
St Pancras International d	07 45		08 00		08 15				08 45		09 00	
Farringdon d	07 49		08 04		08 19				08 49		09 04	
City Thameslink d											09 06	
London Blackfriars d	07 54		08 09		08 24				08 54		09 09	
London Bridge a												
Maidstone East d												
East Croydon d	08 16		08 29		08 46				09 16		09 29	
Gatwick Airport d	08a42		08 45		09a12				09a42		09 45	
Brighton a			09 19								10 19	

	TL	GN	GR		GR	TL	GN	TL	GN	TL	TL	TL
Peterborough d	07 54	08 04	08 30					08 24				08 54
Huntingdon d	08 11	08 20						08 41				09 11
St Neots d	08 18	08 28						08 48				09 18
Sandy d	08 26							08 56				09 26
Biggleswade d	08 30	08 39						09 00				09 30
Arlesey a	08 34							09 04				09 34
Kings Lynn d							07 44					
Watlington d							07 51					
Downham Market d							07 58					
Littleport d							08 08					
Ely d							08 17					
Waterbeach d							08 27					
Cambridge North d							08 32				08 44	
Cambridge a							08 37				08 50	
Cambridge d						08 27	08 44			08 54	08 57	
Foxton d						08 36					09 06	
Shepreth d						08 38					09 08	
Meldreth d						08 41					09 11	
Royston d						08 48				09 09	09 18	
Ashwell & Morden d						08 52					09 22	
Baldock d						08 57				09 17	09 27	
Letchworth Garden City a						09 00				09 20	09 30	
Hitchin d	08 41					09 04		09 11		09 26	09 34	09 41
Stevenage d	08 47		08 59		09 04	09 10		09 17	09 28	09 32	09 40	09 47
Knebworth d						09 13					09 43	
Welwyn North d						09 17					09 47	
Welwyn Garden City d						09 22					09 52	
Hatfield d						09 25					09 55	
Potters Bar d						09 32					10 02	
Finsbury Park a	09 07					09 43		09 37	10 22	09 51	10 13	10 07
London Kings Cross d		09a16	09a21		09a29	09a50	09a33				10a20	
St Pancras International d	09 15							09 45		10 00		10 15
Farringdon d	09 19							09 49		10 04		10 19
City Thameslink d	09 21							09 51		10 06		10 21
London Blackfriars d	09 24							09 54		10 09		10 24
London Bridge a												
Maidstone East d												
East Croydon d	09 46							10 16		10 29		10 46
Gatwick Airport d	10a12							10a42		10 45		11a12
Brighton a										11 19		

Please refer to Table T024 for the full service between Hertford North and Letchworth via Stevenage

Table T025-R

Saturdays
26 May to 8 December

Peterborough, Kings Lynn, Cambridge and Stevenage - London, Maidstone East, Gatwick Airport and Brighton

	GN		GR	TL	GN	TL	GN	TL	TL	GN	TL	
Peterborough d	09 04					09 24					09 54	
Huntingdon d	09 20					09 41					10 11	
St Neots d	09 29					09 48					10 18	
Sandy d						09 56					10 26	
Biggleswade d	09 41					10 00					10 30	
Arlesey a						10 04					10 34	
Kings Lynn d					08 44					09 13		
Watlington d					08 51							
Downham Market d					08 58					09 25		
Littleport d					09 08							
Ely d					09 17					09 47		
Waterbeach d					09 27							
Cambridge North d					09 32				09 44	10 01		
Cambridge a					09 37				09 50	10 05		
Cambridge d				09 27	09 44			09 54	09 57	10 14		
Foxton d				09 36					10 06			
Shepreth d				09 38					10 08			
Meldreth d				09 41					10 11			
Royston d				09 48				10 09	10 18			
Ashwell & Morden d				09 52					10 22			
Baldock d				09 57				10 17	10 27			
Letchworth Garden City a				10 00				10 20	10 30			
Hitchin d				10 04		10 11		10 26	10 34		10 41	
Stevenage d			10 06	10 10		10 17	10 28	10 32	10 40		10 47	
Knebworth d				10 13					10 44			
Welwyn North d				10 17					10 47			
Welwyn Garden City d				10 22					10 52			
Hatfield d				10 25					10 56			
Potters Bar d				10 32					11 03			
Finsbury Park a				10 43		10 37	11 22	10 51	11 13		11 07	
London Kings Cross d	10a16		10a29	10a50	10a35				11a20	11a04		
St Pancras International d						10 45		11 00			11 15	
Farringdon d						10 49		11 04			11 19	
City Thameslink d						10 51		11 06			11 21	
London Blackfriars d						10 54		11 09			11 24	
London Bridge a												
Maidstone East d												
East Croydon d						11 16		11 29			11 46	
Gatwick Airport d						11a42		11 45			12a12	
Brighton a								12 19				

	GN	GR	TL	GN	TL	GN	TL	TL	GN		TL	GR
Peterborough d	10 04				10 24						10 53	11 36
Huntingdon d	10 20				10 41						11 11	
St Neots d	10 29				10 48						11 18	
Sandy d					10 56						11 26	
Biggleswade d	10 39				11 00						11 30	
Arlesey a					11 04						11 34	
Kings Lynn d				09 44					10 13			
Watlington d				09 51								
Downham Market d				09 58					10 25			
Littleport d				10 08								
Ely d				10 17					10 47			
Waterbeach d				10 27								
Cambridge North d				10 32				10 44	11 02			
Cambridge a				10 37				10 50	11 06			
Cambridge d			10 27	10 44			10 54	10 57	11 14			
Foxton d			10 36					11 06				
Shepreth d			10 38					11 08				
Meldreth d			10 41					11 11				
Royston d			10 48				11 09	11 18				
Ashwell & Morden d			10 52					11 22				
Baldock d			10 57				11 17	11 27				
Letchworth Garden City a			11 00				11 20	11 30				
Hitchin d			11 04		11 11		11 25	11 34			11 41	
Stevenage d		11 04	11 10		11 17	11 28	11 31	11 40			11 47	12 05
Knebworth d			11 13					11 43				
Welwyn North d			11 17					11 47				
Welwyn Garden City d			11 22					11 52				
Hatfield d			11 25					11 55				
Potters Bar d			11 32					12 02				
Finsbury Park a			11 43		11 37	12 22	11 50	12 13			12 07	
London Kings Cross d	11a13	11a29	11a50	11a33				12a20	12a05			12a28
St Pancras International d					11 45		12 00				12 15	
Farringdon d					11 49		12 04				12 19	
City Thameslink d					11 51		12 06				12 21	
London Blackfriars d					11 54		12 09				12 24	
London Bridge a												
Maidstone East d												
East Croydon d					12 16		12 29				12 46	
Gatwick Airport d					12a42		12 45				13a12	
Brighton a							13 19					

	GR	TL	GN	TL	GN	TL	TL		TL	GR	GR	TL
Peterborough d				11 24					11 54	12 30		
Huntingdon d				11 41					12 11			
St Neots d				11 48					12 18			
Sandy d				11 56					12 26			
Biggleswade d				12 00					12 30			
Arlesey a				12 04					12 34			
Kings Lynn d			10 44									
Watlington d			10 51									
Downham Market d			10 58									
Littleport d			11 08									
Ely d			11 17									
Waterbeach d			11 27									
Cambridge North d			11 32				11 44					
Cambridge a			11 37				11 50					
Cambridge d		11 27	11 44			11 54	11 57					12 27
Foxton d		11 36					12 06					12 36
Shepreth d		11 38					12 08					12 38
Meldreth d		11 41					12 11					12 41
Royston d		11 48				12 09	12 18					12 48
Ashwell & Morden d		11 52					12 22					12 52
Baldock d		11 57				12 17	12 27					12 57
Letchworth Garden City a		12 00				12 20	12 30					13 00
Hitchin d		12 04		12 11		12 26	12 34		12 41			13 04
Stevenage d	12 08	12 10		12 17	12 28	12 32	12 40		12 47	12 59	13 04	13 10
Knebworth d		12 13					12 43					13 14
Welwyn North d		12 18					12 47					13 17
Welwyn Garden City d		12 22					12 52					13 22
Hatfield d		12 26					12 55					13 26
Potters Bar d		12 32					13 02					13 33
Finsbury Park a		12 43		12 36	13 22	12 51	13 13		13 07			13 44
London Kings Cross d	12a31	12a50	12a34				13a20			13a21	13a29	13a51
St Pancras International d				12 45		13 00			13 15			
Farringdon d				12 49		13 04			13 19			
City Thameslink d				12 51		13 06			13 21			
London Blackfriars d				12 54		13 09			13 24			
London Bridge a												
Maidstone East d												
East Croydon d				13 16		13 29			13 46			
Gatwick Airport d				13a42		13 45			14a12			
Brighton a						14 19						

	GN	TL	GN	TL	TL		TL	GR	GR	TL	GN	TL
Peterborough d		12 24					12 54	13 30				13 24
Huntingdon d		12 41					13 11					13 41
St Neots d		12 48					13 18					13 48
Sandy d		12 56					13 26					13 56
Biggleswade d		13 00					13 30					14 00
Arlesey a		13 04					13 34					14 04
Kings Lynn d	11 44										12 44	
Watlington d	11 51										12 51	
Downham Market d	11 58										12 58	
Littleport d	12 08										13 08	
Ely d	12 17										13 17	
Waterbeach d	12 27										13 27	
Cambridge North d	12 32				12 44						13 32	
Cambridge a	12 37				12 50						13 37	
Cambridge d	12 44			12 54	12 57					13 27	13 44	
Foxton d					13 06					13 36		
Shepreth d					13 08					13 38		
Meldreth d					13 11					13 41		
Royston d				13 09	13 18					13 48		
Ashwell & Morden d					13 22					13 52		
Baldock d				13 17	13 27					13 57		
Letchworth Garden City a				13 20	13 30					14 00		
Hitchin d		13 11		13 26	13 34		13 41			14 04		14 11
Stevenage d		13 17	13 28	13 32	13 40		13 47	13 59	14 04	14 10		14 17
Knebworth d					13 43					14 13		
Welwyn North d					13 47					14 17		
Welwyn Garden City d					13 52					14 22		
Hatfield d					13 55					14 25		
Potters Bar d					14 02					14 32		
Finsbury Park a		13 37	14 22	13 51	14 13		14 06			14 43		14 37
London Kings Cross d	13a33				14a20			14a21	14a29	14a50	14a33	
St Pancras International d		13 45		14 00			14 15					14 45
Farringdon d		13 49		14 04			14 19					14 49
City Thameslink d		13 51		14 06			14 21					14 51
London Blackfriars d		13 54		14 09			14 24					14 54
London Bridge a												
Maidstone East d												
East Croydon d		14 16		14 29			14 46					15 16
Gatwick Airport d		14a42		14 45			15a12					15a42
Brighton a				15 19								

Please refer to Table T024 for the full service between Hertford North and Letchworth via Stevenage

Table T025-R

Saturdays

26 May to 8 December

Peterborough, Kings Lynn, Cambridge and Stevenage - London, Maidstone East, Gatwick Airport and Brighton

		GN	TL	TL	TL	GR	GR	TL	GN	TL	GN	TL	TL	TL	GR	GR	TL	GN	TL	GN	TL	TL
Peterborough	d				13 54	14 30				14 24				14 54		15 37			15 24			
Huntingdon	d				14 11					14 41				15 11					15 41			
St Neots	d				14 18					14 48				15 18					15 48			
Sandy	d				14 26					14 56				15 26					15 56			
Biggleswade	d				14 30					15 00				15 30					16 00			
Arlesey	a				14 34					15 04				15 34					16 04			
Kings Lynn	d								13 44									14 44				
Watlington	d								13 51									14 51				
Downham Market	d								13 58									14 58				
Littleport	d								14 08									15 08				
Ely	d								14 17									15 17				
Waterbeach	d								14 27									15 27				
Cambridge North	d			13 44					14 32				14 44					15 32				15 44
Cambridge	a			13 50					14 37				14 50					15 37				15 50
Cambridge	d		13 54	13 57				14 27	14 44			14 54	14 57				15 27	15 44			15 54	15 57
Foxton	d			14 06				14 36					15 06				15 36					16 06
Shepreth	d			14 08				14 38					15 08				15 38					16 08
Meldreth	d			14 11				14 41					15 11				15 41					16 11
Royston	d		14 09	14 18				14 48				15 09	15 18				15 48				16 09	16 18
Ashwell & Morden	d			14 22				14 52					15 22				15 52					16 22
Baldock	d		14 17	14 27				14 57				15 17	15 27				15 57				16 17	16 27
Letchworth Garden City	a		14 20	14 30				15 00				15 20	15 30				16 00				16 20	16 30
Hitchin	d		14 26	14 34	14 41			15 04		15 11		15 26	15 34	15 41			16 04		16 11		16 26	16 34
Stevenage	d	14 28	14 32	14 40	14 47	14 59	15 04	15 10		15 17	15 28	15 32	15 40	15 47	16 03	16 07	16 10		16 17	16 28	16 32	16 40
Knebworth	d			14 43				15 13					15 43				16 13					16 43
Welwyn North	d			14 47				15 17					15 47				16 17					16 48
Welwyn Garden City	d			14 52				15 22					15 52				16 22					16 53
Hatfield	d			14 55				15 25					15 55				16 26					16 56
Potters Bar	d			15 02				15 32					16 02				16 33					17 03
Finsbury Park ⊖	a	15 22	14 51	15 13	15 06			15 43		15 37	16 22	15 51	16 13	16 07			16 43		16 36	17 22	16 51	17 13
London Kings Cross ⊖	d			15a20		15a21	15a29	15a50	15a33				16a20		16a28	16a31	16a50	16a35				17a20
St Pancras International	d		15 00		15 15					15 45		16 00		16 15					16 45		17 00	
Farringdon	d		15 04		15 19					15 49		16 04		16 19					16 49		17 04	
City Thameslink	d		15 06		15 21					15 51		16 06		16 21					16 51		17 06	
London Blackfriars	d		15 09		15 24					15 54		16 09		16 24					16 54		17 09	
London Bridge	a																					
Maidstone East	d																					
East Croydon	d		15 29		15 46					16 16		16 29		16 46					17 16		17 29	
Gatwick Airport	d		15 45		16a12					16a42		16 45		17a12					17a42		17 45	
Brighton	a		16 19									17 19									18 19	

		TL	GR	GR	TL	GN	TL	GN	TL	TL	TL	GR	GR	TL	GN	TL	GN	TL	TL	TL	GR	GR	TL
Peterborough	d	15 54	16 30				16 24				16 54	17 34				17 24				17 56	18 30		
Huntingdon	d	16 11					16 41				17 11					17 41				18 12			
St Neots	d	16 18					16 48				17 18					17 48				18 19			
Sandy	d	16 26					16 56				17 26					17 56				18 27			
Biggleswade	d	16 30					17 00				17 30					18 00				18 31			
Arlesey	a	16 34					17 04				17 34					18 04				18 35			
Kings Lynn	d					15 44									16 44								
Watlington	d					15 51									16 51								
Downham Market	d					15 58									16 58								
Littleport	d					16 08									17 08								
Ely	d					16 17									17 17								
Waterbeach	d					16 27									17 27								
Cambridge North	d					16 32				16 44					17 32				17 44				
Cambridge	a					16 37				16 50					17 37				17 50				
Cambridge	d				16 27	16 44			16 54	16 57				17 27	17 44			17 54	17 57				18 27
Foxton	d				16 36					17 06				17 36					18 06				18 36
Shepreth	d				16 38					17 08				17 38					18 08				18 38
Meldreth	d				16 41					17 11				17 41					18 11				18 41
Royston	d				16 48				17 08	17 18				17 48				18 09	18 18				18 48
Ashwell & Morden	d				16 52					17 22				17 52					18 22				18 52
Baldock	d				16 57				17 16	17 27				17 57				18 17	18 27				18 57
Letchworth Garden City	a				17 00				17 19	17 30				18 00				18 20	18 30				19 00
Hitchin	d	16 41			17 04		17 11		17 25	17 34	17 41			18 04		18 11		18 26	18 34	18 41			19 04
Stevenage	d	16 47	16 59	17 04	17 10		17 17	17 28	17 32	17 40	17 47	18 03	18 08	18 10		18 17	18 28	18 32	18 40	18 47	18 59	19 09	19 10
Knebworth	d				17 13					17 43				18 13					18 43				19 13
Welwyn North	d				17 17					17 47				18 18					18 47				19 19
Welwyn Garden City	d				17 22					17 52				18 23					18 52				19 24
Hatfield	d				17 25					17 55				18 26					18 55				19 27
Potters Bar	d				17 32					18 02				18 32					19 02				19 34
Finsbury Park ⊖	a	17 06			17 43		17 37	18 22	17 51	18 13	18 07			18 43		18 36	19 22	18 51	19 13	19 07			19 44
London Kings Cross ⊖	d		17a21	17a29	17a50	17a33				18a20		18a27	18a30	18a50	18a34				19a20		19a21	19a31	19a51
St Pancras International	d	17 15					17 45		18 00		18 15					18 45		19 00		19 15			
Farringdon	d	17 19					17 49		18 04		18 19					18 49		19 04		19 19			
City Thameslink	d	17 21					17 51		18 06		18 21					18 51		19 06		19 21			
London Blackfriars	d	17 24					17 54		18 09		18 24					18 54		19 09		19 24			
London Bridge	a																						
Maidstone East	d																						
East Croydon	d	17 46					18 16		18 29		18 46					19 16		19 29		19 46			
Gatwick Airport	d	18a12					18a42		18 45		19a12					19a42		19 45		20a12			
Brighton	a								19 19									20 19					

Please refer to Table T024 for the full service between Hertford North and Letchworth via Stevenage

Table T025-R

Saturdays

26 May to 8 December

Peterborough, Kings Lynn, Cambridge and Stevenage - London, Maidstone East, Gatwick Airport and Brighton

		GN	TL	GN	TL	TL	TL	GR	GR	TL	GN	TL	GR	GN	GR	TL	TL	TL	GR	TL	GN	TL	GR
Peterborough	d		18 24				18 54	19 28				19 24	19 51					19 54				20 24	20 51
Huntingdon	d		18 41				19 11					19 41						20 11				20 41	
St Neots	d		18 48				19 18					19 48						20 18				20 48	
Sandy	d		18 56				19 26					19 56						20 26				20 56	
Biggleswade	d		19 00				19 30					20 00						20 30				21 00	
Arlesey	a		19 04				19 34					20 04						20 34				21 04	
Kings Lynn	d	17 44									18 44										19 44		
Watlington	d	17 51									18 51										19 51		
Downham Market	d	17 58									18 58										19 58		
Littleport	d	18 08									19 08										20 08		
Ely	d	18 17									19 17										20 17		
Waterbeach	d	18 27									19 27										20 27		
Cambridge North	d	18 32				18 44					19 32						19 44				20 32		
Cambridge	a	18 37				18 50					19 37						19 50				20 37		
Cambridge	d	18 44			18 54	18 57				19 27	19 44					19 54	19 57			20 27	20 44		
Foxton	d					19 06				19 36							20 06			20 36			
Shepreth	d					19 08				19 38							20 08			20 38			
Meldreth	d					19 11				19 41							20 11			20 41			
Royston	d				19 09	19 18				19 48						20 09	20 18			20 48			
Ashwell & Morden	d					19 22				19 52							20 22			20 52			
Baldock	d				19 17	19 27				19 57						20 17	20 27			20 57			
Letchworth Garden City	a				19 20	19 30				20 00						20 20	20 30			21 00			
Hitchin	d		19 11		19 26	19 34	19 41			20 04		20 11				20 26	20 34	20 41		21 04		21 11	
Stevenage	d		19 17	19 28	19 32	19 40	19 47	19 59	20 04	20 10		20 17	20 20	20 28	20 29	20 32	20 40	20 47	21 04	21 10		21 17	21 20
Knebworth	d					19 43				20 13							20 43			21 13			
Welwyn North	d					19 47				20 17							20 47			21 17			
Welwyn Garden City	d					19 52				20 22							20 52			21 22			
Hatfield	d					19 55				20 25							20 55			21 25			
Potters Bar	d					20 02				20 32							21 02			21 32			
Finsbury Park ⊖	a		19 36	20 22	19 51	20 13	20 06			20 43		20 36		21 22		20 51	21 13	21 07		21 43		21 36	
London Kings Cross ⊖	d	19a35				20a20		20a21	20a29	20a50	20a33		20a45		20a51		21a20		21a29	21a50	21a33		21a42
St Pancras International	d		19 45		20 00		20 15					20 45				21 00		21 15				21 45	
Farringdon	d		19 49		20 04		20 19					20 49				21 04		21 19				21 49	
City Thameslink	d		19 51		20 06		20 21					20 51											
London Blackfriars	d		19 54		20 09		20 24					20 54				21 09		21 24				21 54	
London Bridge	a																						
Maidstone East	d																						
East Croydon	d		20 16		20 29		20 46					21 16				21 29		21 46				22 16	
Gatwick Airport	d		20a42		20 45		21a12					21a42				21 45		22a12				22a42	
Brighton	a				21 19											22 19							

		GN	TL	TL	TL	GR	TL	TL	GN	TL	GN	TL	TL	TL	TL	GN	TL	GN	GN	TL	TL	TL
Peterborough	d				20 54	21 20				21 24				21 54			22 24				22 54	23 20
Huntingdon	d				21 11					21 41				22 11			22 41				23 09	23 35
St Neots	d				21 18					21 48				22 18			22 48				23 16	23 42
Sandy	d				21 26					21 56				22 26			22 56				23 24	23 50
Biggleswade	d				21 30					22 00				22 30			23 00				23 28	23 53
Arlesey	a				21 34					22 04				22 34			23 04				23 32	23 58
Kings Lynn	d								20 44							21 44						
Watlington	d								20 51							21 51						
Downham Market	d								20 58							21 58						
Littleport	d								21 08							22 08						
Ely	d								21 17							22 17						
Waterbeach	d								21 27							22 27						
Cambridge North	d			20 44					21 32				21 44			22 32				22 44		
Cambridge	a			20 50					21 37				21 50			22 37				22 50		
Cambridge	d		20 54	20 57			21 24	21 27	21 44			21 54	21 57		22 27	22 44			22 54	22 57		
Foxton	d			21 06				21 36					22 06		22 36					23 06		
Shepreth	d			21 08				21 38					22 08		22 38					23 08		
Meldreth	d			21 11				21 41					22 11		22 41					23 11		
Royston	d		21 09	21 18			21 39	21 48				22 09	22 18		22 48				23 09	23 18		
Ashwell & Morden	d			21 22				21 52					22 22		22 52					23 22		
Baldock	d		21 17	21 27			21 47	21 57				22 17	22 27		22 57				23 17	23 27		
Letchworth Garden City	a		21 20	21 30			21 50	22 00				22 20	22 30		23 00				23 20	23 30		
Hitchin	d		21 26	21 34	21 41		21 56	22 04		22 11		22 26	22 34	22 41	23 04		23 11		23 26	23 34	23 41	00 06
Stevenage	d	21 28	21 32	21 40	21 47	21 50	22 02	22 10		22 17	22 28	22 32	22 40	22 47	23 10		23 17	23 28	23 32	23 40	23 47	00 12
Knebworth	d			21 43				22 13					22 43		23 13					23 43		
Welwyn North	d			21 47				22 17					22 47		23 17					23 47		
Welwyn Garden City	d			21 52				22 22					22 52		23 22					23 52		
Hatfield	d			21 55				22 25					22 55		23 25					23 55		
Potters Bar	d			22 02				22 32					23 02		23 32					00 02		
Finsbury Park ⊖	a	22 22	21 51	22 13	22 06		22 21	22 43		22 36	23 20	22 51	23 13	23 06	23 43		23 36	00 20	23 51	00 15	00 11	00 38
London Kings Cross ⊖	d			22a20		22a12		22a50	22a33				23a20		23a50	23a33	23a43		23a58	00a24	00a21	00a45
St Pancras International	d		22 00		22 15		22 30			22 45		23 00		23 15								
Farringdon	d		22 04		22 19		22 34			22 49		23 04		23 19								
City Thameslink	d																					
London Blackfriars	d		22 09		22 24		22 39			22 54		23 09		23 24								
London Bridge	a																					
Maidstone East	d																					
East Croydon	d		22 29		22 46		22 59			23 16		23 29		23 46								
Gatwick Airport	d		22 45		23a12		23 15			23a41		23 48		00a12								
Brighton	a		23 19				23 49					00 23										

Please refer to Table T024 for the full service between Hertford North and Letchworth via Stevenage

Table T025-R

Peterborough, Kings Lynn, Cambridge and Stevenage - London, Maidstone East, Gatwick Airport and Brighton

Saturdays
26 May to 8 December

		TL	GN	TL
		■		■
Peterborough ■	d			
Huntingdon	d			
St Neots	d			
Sandy	d			
Biggleswade	d			
Arlesey	a			
Kings Lynn	d		22 57	
Watlington	d		23 04	
Downham Market	d		23 11	
Littleport	d		23 20	
Ely	d		23 29	
Waterbeach	d		23 38	
Cambridge North	d		23 43	
Cambridge	a		23 47	
Cambridge	d	23 35		23 54
Foxton	d	23 44		
Shepreth	d	23 46		
Meldreth	d	23 49		
Royston	d	23 54		00 09
Ashwell & Morden	d	23 58		
Baldock	d	00 03		00 17
Letchworth Garden City	a	00 06		00 20
Hitchin ■	d	00 10		00 26
Stevenage ■	d	00 16		00 32
Knebworth	d	00 19		
Welwyn North	d	00 23		
Welwyn Garden City ■	d	00 28		
Hatfield	d	00 31		
Potters Bar	d	00 38		
Finsbury Park ⊖	a	00 51		00 58
London Kings Cross ■ ⊖	d	00a58		01a05
St Pancras International	d			
Farringdon	d			
City Thameslink	d			
London Blackfriars	d			
London Bridge	a			
Maidstone East	d			
East Croydon	d			
Gatwick Airport	d			
Brighton	a			

Sundays
20 May to 2 December

		TL	TL	TL	TL	GN	GN	GN	GN	GN	GN	GN
		■	■	■	■	A (bus)	■ A	A (bus)	■ B	C	■	A (bus)
Peterborough ■	d					04 05		05 05	05 45			
Huntingdon	d					04 45		05 45	05 59			←
St Neots	d					05 15		06 15	06 07			06 15
Sandy	d					05 35		→	06 15			06 35
Biggleswade	d					05 45			06 19			06 45
Arlesey	a					06 05			06 24			07 05
Kings Lynn	d											
Watlington	d											
Downham Market	d											
Littleport	d											
Ely	d											
Waterbeach	d											
Cambridge North	d											
Cambridge	a											
Cambridge	d										06 41	
Foxton	d											
Shepreth	d											
Meldreth	d											
Royston	d				00 09						06 55	
Ashwell & Morden	d											
Baldock	d			00 03	00 17						07 03	
Letchworth Garden City	a			00 06	00 20						07 06	
Hitchin ■	d		00 06	00 10	00 26	06a23	06 33		06 33		07 11	07a23
Stevenage ■	d		00 12	00 16	00 32		06 39		06 39	06 59	07 17	
Knebworth	d			00 19			06 43		06 43			
Welwyn North	d			00 23			06 47		06 47			
Welwyn Garden City ■	d			00 28			06 52		06 53			
Hatfield	d			00 31			06 56		06 57			
Potters Bar	d	00 02		00 38			07 03		07 03			
Finsbury Park ⊖	a	00 15	00 38	00 51	00 58		07 13		07 13	07 53	07 41	
London Kings Cross ■ ⊖	d	00a24	00a45	00a58	01a05		07a23		07a23		07a51	
St Pancras International	d											
Farringdon	d											
City Thameslink	d											
London Blackfriars	d											
London Bridge	a											
Maidstone East	d											
East Croydon	d											
Gatwick Airport	d											
Brighton	a											

		GN	GN	GN	GN	GN	GN	GN	GN	GN	TL	GN
		C	■ A	B (bus)	■ B	■	C	■	A (bus)	C	■	■
Peterborough ■	d			06 05	06 42						07 45	
Huntingdon	d			06 45	06 57				←		08 00	
St Neots	d			07 15	07 04				07 15		08 07	
Sandy	d			→	07 12				07 35		08 15	
Biggleswade	d				07 16				07 45		08 19	
Arlesey	a				07 20				08 05		08 23	
Kings Lynn	d											
Watlington	d											
Downham Market	d											
Littleport	d											
Ely	d											
Waterbeach	d											
Cambridge North	d											
Cambridge	a											
Cambridge	d					06 54		07 28				07 54
Foxton	d					07 04						08 04
Shepreth	d					07 07						08 07
Meldreth	d					07 10						08 10
Royston	d					07 15		07 42				08 15
Ashwell & Morden	d					07 20						08 20
Baldock	d					07 25		07 50				08 25
Letchworth Garden City	a					07 28		07 53				08 28
Hitchin ■	d		07 30		07 30	07 34		07 58	08a23		08 30	08 34
Stevenage ■	d	07 29	07 36		07 36	07 40	07 59	08 04		08 29	08 36	08 40
Knebworth	d					07 44						08 44
Welwyn North	d					07 48						08 48
Welwyn Garden City ■	d					07 53						08 53
Hatfield	d					07 57						08 57
Potters Bar	d					08 04						09 04
Finsbury Park ⊖	a	08 23	07 59		07 59	08 14	08 50	08 24		09 20	08 55	09 14
London Kings Cross ■ ⊖	d		08a09		08a09	08a24		08a31			09a02	09a21
St Pancras International	d											
Farringdon	d											
City Thameslink	d											
London Blackfriars	d											
London Bridge	a											
Maidstone East	d											
East Croydon	d											
Gatwick Airport	d											
Brighton	a											

A from 16 September
B until 9 September
C until 21 October

Please refer to Table T024 for the full service between Hertford North and Letchworth via Stevenage

Table T025-R

Peterborough, Kings Lynn, Cambridge and Stevenage - London, Maidstone East, Gatwick Airport and Brighton

Sundays
20 May to 2 December

		GN	TL	GN	GN	TL	GR	GN	GN	GN	GN	TL
		A	■	■	A	■	■	■	■	■	A	■
Peterborough ■	d					08 45	09 11			09 15		
Huntingdon	d					09 00				09 29		
St Neots	d					09 07				09 37		
Sandy	d					09 15						
Biggleswade	d					09 19				09 46		
Arlesey	a					09 23						
Kings Lynn	d								08 26			
Watlington	d								08 33			
Downham Market	d								08 40			
Littleport	d								08 49			
Ely	d								08 57			
Waterbeach	d								09 07			
Cambridge North	d								09 12			
Cambridge	a								09 16			
Cambridge	d		08 28					08 54	09 22			09 28
Foxton	d							09 04				
Shepreth	d							09 07				
Meldreth	d							09 10				
Royston	d		08 42					09 15				09 42
Ashwell & Morden	d							09 20				
Baldock	d		08 50					09 25				09 50
Letchworth Garden City	a		08 53					09 28				09 53
Hitchin ■	d		08 58	09 05		09 30		09 34				09 58
Stevenage ■	d	08 59	09 04	09 11	09 29	09 36	09 40	09 40			09 59	10 04
Knebworth	d			09 15				09 44				
Welwyn North	d			09 19				09 47				
Welwyn Garden City ■	d			09 24				09 53				
Hatfield	d			09 28				09 57				
Potters Bar	d			09 34				10 04				
Finsbury Park ⊖	a	09 50	09 24	09 45	10 20	09 56		10 14			10 50	10 24
London Kings Cross ■ ⊖	d			09a52			10a04	10a21	10a10	10a17		
St Pancras International	d		09 35			10 05						10 35
Farringdon	d		09 39			10 09						10 39
City Thameslink	d											
London Blackfriars	d		09 44			10 14						10 44
London Bridge	a											
Maidstone East	d											
East Croydon	d		10 07			10 37						11 07
Gatwick Airport	d		10a27			11a02						11a27
Brighton	a											

		GN	GN	TL	GN	GN	GN	GN	TL	GR	GN	GN
		■	A	■	■	■	■	A	■	■	■	A
Peterborough ■	d			09 45			10 15			10 36		
Huntingdon	d			10 00			10 29					
St Neots	d			10 07			10 37					
Sandy	d			10 15								
Biggleswade	d			10 19			10 46					
Arlesey	a			10 23								
Kings Lynn	d					09 26						
Watlington	d					09 33						
Downham Market	d					09 40						
Littleport	d					09 49						
Ely	d					09 57						
Waterbeach	d					10 07						
Cambridge North	d					10 12						
Cambridge	a					10 16						
Cambridge	d				09 54	10 22			10 28			
Foxton	d				10 04							
Shepreth	d				10 07							
Meldreth	d				10 10							
Royston	d				10 15				10 42			
Ashwell & Morden	d				10 20							
Baldock	d				10 25				10 50			
Letchworth Garden City	a				10 28				10 53			
Hitchin ■	d	10 05		10 30	10 34				10 58		11 05	
Stevenage ■	d	10 11	10 29	10 36	10 40			10 59	11 04	11 05	11 11	11 29
Knebworth	d	10 15			10 44						11 15	
Welwyn North	d	10 19			10 48						11 19	
Welwyn Garden City ■	d	10 24			10 53						11 24	
Hatfield	d	10 28			10 57						11 28	
Potters Bar	d	10 34			11 04						11 34	
Finsbury Park ⊖	a	10 45	11 20	10 56	11 14			11 50	11 24		11 45	12 20
London Kings Cross ■ ⊖	d	10a52			11a21	11a10	11a17			11a31	11a52	
St Pancras International	d			11 05					11 35			
Farringdon	d			11 09					11 39			
City Thameslink	d											
London Blackfriars	d			11 14					11 44			
London Bridge	a											
Maidstone East	d											
East Croydon	d			11 37					12 07			
Gatwick Airport	d			12a02					12a27			
Brighton	a											

		TL	GN	GN	GN	GN	TL	GN	TL	GN	GN	GN
		■	■	■	■	A	■	A	■	■	■	A
Peterborough ■	d	10 45			11 15				11 45			
Huntingdon	d	11 00			11 29				12 00			
St Neots	d	11 07			11 37				12 07			
Sandy	d	11 15							12 15			
Biggleswade	d	11 19			11 46				12 19			
Arlesey	a	11 23							12 23			
Kings Lynn	d			10 26							11 26	
Watlington	d			10 33							11 33	
Downham Market	d			10 40							11 40	
Littleport	d			10 49							11 49	
Ely	d			10 57							11 57	
Waterbeach	d			11 07							12 07	
Cambridge North	d			11 12							12 12	
Cambridge	a			11 16							12 16	
Cambridge	d		10 54	11 22			11 28			11 54	12 22	
Foxton	d		11 04							12 04		
Shepreth	d		11 07							12 07		
Meldreth	d		11 10							12 10		
Royston	d		11 15				11 42			12 15		
Ashwell & Morden	d		11 20							12 20		
Baldock	d		11 25				11 50			12 25		
Letchworth Garden City	a		11 28				11 53			12 28		
Hitchin ■	d	11 30	11 34				11 58		12 30	12 34		
Stevenage ■	d	11 36	11 40			11 59	12 04	12 29	12 36	12 40		12 59
Knebworth	d		11 44							12 44		
Welwyn North	d		11 48							12 48		
Welwyn Garden City ■	d		11 53							12 53		
Hatfield	d		11 57							12 57		
Potters Bar	d		12 04							13 04		
Finsbury Park ⊖	a	11 56	12 14			12 50	12 24	13 20	12 56	13 14		13 50
London Kings Cross ■ ⊖	d		12a21	12a10	12a17					13a21	13a10	
St Pancras International	d	12 05					12 35		13 05			
Farringdon	d	12 09					12 39		13 09			
City Thameslink	d											
London Blackfriars	d	12 14					12 44		13 14			
London Bridge	a											
Maidstone East	d											
East Croydon	d	12 37					13 07		13 37			
Gatwick Airport	d	13a02					13a27		14a02			
Brighton	a											

		TL	GR	GN	TL	GN	GN	GN	TL	GN	TL
		■	■	A	■	■	■	A	■	A	■
Peterborough ■	d		12 39		12 45						13 45
Huntingdon	d				13 00						14 00
St Neots	d				13 07						14 07
Sandy	d				13 15						14 15
Biggleswade	d				13 19						14 19
Arlesey	a				13 23						14 23
Kings Lynn	d						12 26				
Watlington	d						12 33				
Downham Market	d						12 40				
Littleport	d						12 49				
Ely	d						12 57				
Waterbeach	d						13 07				
Cambridge North	d						13 12				
Cambridge	a						13 16				
Cambridge	d	12 28				12 54	13 22		13 28		
Foxton	d					13 04					
Shepreth	d					13 07					
Meldreth	d					13 10					
Royston	d	12 42				13 15			13 42		
Ashwell & Morden	d					13 20					
Baldock	d	12 50				13 25			13 50		
Letchworth Garden City	a	12 53				13 28			13 53		
Hitchin ■	d	12 58			13 30	13 34			13 58		14 30
Stevenage ■	d	13 04	13 08	13 29	13 36	13 40		13 59	14 04	14 29	14 36
Knebworth	d					13 44					
Welwyn North	d					13 48					
Welwyn Garden City ■	d					13 53					
Hatfield	d					13 57					
Potters Bar	d					14 04					
Finsbury Park ⊖	a	13 24		14 20	13 56	14 14		14 50	14 24	15 20	14 56
London Kings Cross ■ ⊖	d		13a31			14a21	14a10				
St Pancras International	d	13 35			14 05				14 35		15 05
Farringdon	d	13 39			14 09				14 39		15 09
City Thameslink	d										
London Blackfriars	d	13 44			14 14				14 44		15 14
London Bridge	a										
Maidstone East	d										
East Croydon	d	14 07			14 37				15 07		15 37
Gatwick Airport	d	14a27			15a02				15a27		16a02
Brighton	a										

A until 21 October

Please refer to Table T024 for the full service between Hertford North and Letchworth via Stevenage

Table T025-R

Sundays

20 May to 2 December

Peterborough, Kings Lynn, Cambridge and Stevenage - London, Maidstone East, Gatwick Airport and Brighton

		GN	GN	GN	GR	TL	GN	TL	GN	GN	GN	TL	GN	TL	GN	GN	GN	TL	GR	GN	TL	GN	GN
		■	■	A	■ ■	■	A	■	■	■	A	■	A	■	■	■	A	■	■ ■	A	■	■	■
Peterborough ■	d				14 34			14 45						15 45					16 36		16 45		
Huntingdon	d							15 00						16 00							17 00		
St Neots	d							15 07						16 07							17 07		
Sandy	d							15 15						16 15							17 15		
Biggleswade	d							15 19						16 19							17 19		
Arlesey	a							15 23						16 23							17 23		
Kings Lynn	d		13 26							14 26						15 26							16 26
Watlington	d		13 33							14 33						15 33							16 33
Downham Market	d		13 40							14 40						15 40							16 40
Littleport	d		13 49							14 49						15 49							16 49
Ely	d		13 57							14 57						15 57							16 57
Waterbeach	d		14 07							15 07						16 07							17 07
Cambridge North	d		14 12							15 12						16 12							17 12
Cambridge	a		14 16							15 16						16 16							17 16
Cambridge	d	13 54	14 22			14 28			14 54	15 22		15 28			15 54	16 22		16 28				16 54	17 22
Foxton	d	14 04							15 04						16 04							17 04	
Shepreth	d	14 07							15 07						16 07							17 07	
Meldreth	d	14 10							15 10						16 10							17 10	
Royston	d	14 15				14 42			15 15			15 42			16 15			16 42				17 15	
Ashwell & Morden	d	14 20							15 20						16 20							17 20	
Baldock	d	14 25				14 50			15 25			15 50			16 25			16 50				17 25	
Letchworth Garden City	a	14 28				14 53			15 28			15 53			16 28			16 53				17 28	
Hitchin ■	d	14 34				14 58		15 30	15 34			15 58		16 30	16 34			16 58			17 30	17 34	
Stevenage ■	d	14 40		14 59	15 03	15 06	15 29	15 36	15 40		15 59	16 04	16 29	16 36	16 41		16 59	17 04	17 06	17 29	17 36	17 40	
Knebworth	d	14 44							15 44						16 44							17 44	
Welwyn North	d	14 48							15 48						16 48							17 48	
Welwyn Garden City ■	d	14 53							15 53						16 53							17 53	
Hatfield	d	14 57							15 57						16 57							17 57	
Potters Bar	d	15 04							16 04						17 04							18 04	
Finsbury Park ⊖	a	15 14		15 50		15 25	16 20	15 56	16 14		16 50	16 24	17 20	16 56	17 14		17 50	17 24		18 20	17 56	18 14	
London Kings Cross ■ ⊖	d	15a21	15a10		15a25				16a21	16a10					17a21	17a11			17a30			18a21	18a10
St Pancras International	d					15 35		16 05				16 35		17 05				17 35			18 05		
Farringdon	d					15 39		16 09				16 39		17 09				17 39			18 09		
City Thameslink	d																						
London Blackfriars	d					15 44		16 14				16 44		17 14				17 44			18 14		
London Bridge	a																						
Maidstone East	d																						
East Croydon	d					16 07		16 37				17 07		17 37				18 07			18 37		
Gatwick Airport	d					16a27		17a02				17a27		18a02				18a27			19a02		
Brighton	a																						

		GN	TL	GR	GN	TL	GN	GN	GN	TL	GR	GN	GN	TL	GN	GN	GN	GR	TL	GN	TL	GN
		A	■	■ ■	A	■	■	■	A	■	■ ■	■	A	■	■	■	A	■ ■	■	A	■	■
Peterborough ■	d					17 45								18 45							19 45	
Huntingdon	d					18 00								19 00							20 00	
St Neots	d					18 07								19 07							20 07	
Sandy	d					18 15								19 15							20 15	
Biggleswade	d					18 19								19 19							20 19	
Arlesey	a					18 23								19 23							20 23	
Kings Lynn	d							17 26				17 54				18 26						
Watlington	d							17 33				18 01				18 33						
Downham Market	d							17 40				18 08				18 40						
Littleport	d							17 49				18 17				18 49						
Ely	d							17 57				18 26				18 57						
Waterbeach	d							18 07								19 07						
Cambridge North	d							18 12				18 38				19 12						
Cambridge	a							18 16				18 42				19 16						
Cambridge	d		17 28				17 54	18 22		18 28		18 43			18 54	19 22			19 28			19 54
Foxton	d						18 04								19 04							20 04
Shepreth	d						18 07								19 07							20 07
Meldreth	d						18 10								19 10							20 10
Royston	d		17 42				18 15			18 42					19 15				19 42			20 15
Ashwell & Morden	d						18 20								19 20							20 20
Baldock	d		17 50				18 25			18 50					19 25				19 50			20 25
Letchworth Garden City	a		17 53				18 28			18 53					19 28				19 53			20 28
Hitchin ■	d		17 58			18 30	18 34			18 58				19 30	19 34				19 58		20 30	20 34
Stevenage ■	d	17 59	18 04	18 04	18 29	18 36	18 40		18 59	19 04	19 09		19 29	19 36	19 40		19 59	20 03	20 04	20 29	20 36	20 40
Knebworth	d						18 44								19 44							20 44
Welwyn North	d						18 48								19 48							20 48
Welwyn Garden City ■	d						18 53								19 53							20 53
Hatfield	d						18 57								19 57							20 57
Potters Bar	d						19 04								20 04							21 04
Finsbury Park ⊖	a	18 50	18 26		19 20	18 56	19 14		19 50	19 24			20 20	19 55	20 14		20 50		20 25	21 20	20 56	21 14
London Kings Cross ■ ⊖	d			18a26			19a21	19a13			19a32	19a36			20a21	20a10		20a25				21a21
St Pancras International	d		18 35			19 05				19 35				20 05					20 35		21 05	
Farringdon	d		18 39			19 09				19 39				20 09					20 39		21 09	
City Thameslink	d																					
London Blackfriars	d		18 44			19 14				19 44				20 14					20 44		21 14	
London Bridge	a																					
Maidstone East	d																					
East Croydon	d		19 07			19 37				20 07				20 37					21 07		21 37	
Gatwick Airport	d		19a27			20a02				20a27				21a02					21a27		22a02	
Brighton	a																					

A until 21 October

Please refer to Table T024 for the full service between Hertford North and Letchworth via Stevenage

Table T025-R

Sundays

20 May to 2 December

Peterborough, Kings Lynn, Cambridge and Stevenage - London, Maidstone East, Gatwick Airport and Brighton

		GN	GN	TL	GR	GN	TL	GN	GN	GN	TL	GN	TL	GN	GR	GN	GR	GN	TL	GN	TL	GN
		■	A	■	■ ■	A	■	■	■	A	■	A	■	■	■ ■	■	■ ■	A	■	A	■	■
Peterborough ■	d						20 45						21 45		22 15		22 24				22 45	
Huntingdon	d						21 00						22 00								23 00	
St Neots	d						21 07						22 07								23 07	
Sandy	d						21 15						22 15								23 15	
Biggleswade	d						21 19						22 19								23 19	
Arlesey	a						21 23						22 23								23 23	
Kings Lynn	d	19 26							20 26							21 26						22 26
Watlington	d	19 33							20 33							21 33						22 33
Downham Market	d	19 40							20 40							21 40						22 40
Littleport	d	19 49							20 49							21 49						22 49
Ely	d	19 57							20 57							21 57						22 57
Waterbeach	d	20 07							21 07							22 07						23 07
Cambridge North	d	20 12							21 12							22 12						23 12
Cambridge	a	20 16							21 16							22 16						23 16
Cambridge	d	20 22		20 28				20 54	21 22		21 28			21 54		22 22			22 28			23 20
Foxton	d							21 04						22 04								23 30
Shepreth	d							21 07						22 07								23 33
Meldreth	d							21 10						22 10								23 36
Royston	d			20 42				21 15			21 42			22 15					22 42			23 41
Ashwell & Morden	d							21 20						22 20								23 46
Baldock	d			20 50				21 25			21 50			22 25					22 50			23 51
Letchworth Garden City	a			20 53				21 28			21 53			22 28					22 53			23 54
Hitchin ■	d			20 58			21 30	21 34			21 58		22 30	22 34					22 58		23 30	00 01
Stevenage ■	d		20 59	21 04	21 09	21 29	21 36	21 40		21 59	22 04	22 29	22 36	22 40	22 44		22 53	22 59	23 04	23 29	23 36	00 07
Knebworth	d							21 44						22 44								00 10
Welwyn North	d							21 47						22 48								00 14
Welwyn Garden City ■	d							21 53						22 53								00 19
Hatfield	d							21 57						22 57								00 23
Potters Bar	d							22 03						23 03								00 29
Finsbury Park ⊖	a		21 50	21 24		22 20	21 56	22 14		22 50	22 24	23 20	22 56	23 14				23 50	23 24	00 24	23 56	00 39
London Kings Cross ■ ⊖	d	21a10			21a31			22a21	22a10				23a03	23a21	23a09	23a13	23a15		23a31		00a03	00a49
St Pancras International	d			21 35			22 05				22 35											
Farringdon	d			21 39			22 09				22 39											
City Thameslink	d																					
London Blackfriars	d			21 44			22 14				22 44											
London Bridge	a																					
Maidstone East	d																					
East Croydon	d			22 07			22 37				23 08											
Gatwick Airport	d			22a26			23a02				23a35											
Brighton	a																					

A until 21 October

Please refer to Table T024 for the full service between Hertford North and Letchworth via Stevenage

Table T026-F

Mondays to Fridays
21 May to 7 December

London - Humberside, Yorkshire, North East England and Scotland

Miles	Miles	Miles			GR MO A	GR MO B	GR MX B	TP MO C	TP MX C	GR MO D	GR MO A	GR MX B	TP		XC	XC E	GR	XC F	TP G	GR	TP G	TP	TP C		XC H
0	—	—	**London Kings Cross** ⊖	d																					
27¼	—	—	**Stevenage**	d																					
76¼	—	—	**Peterborough**	a																					
—	—	—	Norwich	d																					
—	—	—	**Peterborough**	d																					
105¼	—	—	**Grantham**	a																					
—	—	—		d																					
120	—	—	**Newark North Gate**	a																					
—	—	—		d																					
—	—	—	**Lincoln**	a																					
138½	—	—	**Retford**	d																					
156	0	—	**Doncaster**	a																					
—	—	—	Selby	a																					
—	—	—	**Hull**	a																					
—	—	—	**Sheffield**	a																					
—	—	—	Pontefract Monkhill	a																					
—	—	—	Wakefield Kirkgate	a																					
—	19¾	—	**Wakefield Westgate**	d																					
—	29¾	—	**Leeds**	a																					
—	—	—	Mirfield	a																					
—	—	—	Brighouse	a																					
—	—	—	**Halifax**	a																					
—	—	—	Shipley	a																					
—	—	—	Bradford Forster Square	a																					
—	—	—	**Bradford Interchange**	a																					
—	—	—	Keighley	a																					
—	—	—	**Skipton**	a																					
—	—	—	**Doncaster**	d	00 04															06 15					07 03
188½	—	—	**York**	a	00 34															06 35					07 23
—	—	—	Scarborough	a																					
—	—	—	Harrogate	a																					
—	—	—	**Leeds**	d															06 00		06 17		06 52		
—	—	—	**York**	d						00 12	00 14	00 41	05 06					06 25	06 29	06 39	06 43	06 46	07 16		07 32
210¾	—	—	Thirsk	d									05 33									07 04	07 33		
218½	—	—	Northallerton	d						00s45	00s47	01s09	05 38						06 50		07 04	07 14	07 41		
232½	—	—	**Darlington**	a						00s59	01s01	01s23	05 53					06 51	07 01	07 06	07 15		07 53		07 58
—	—	—	Eaglescliffe	a																					
—	—	—	**Middlesbrough**	a									06 29									07 46			
—	—	—	**Darlington**	d				00 02	00 02									06 55	07 02	07 08	07 16		07 53		08 00
254½	—	—	**Durham**	d		00 07	00 14	00 18	00 25	01s17	01s19	01s42						07 13	07 18	07 26	07 33		08 10		08 18
260¼	—	—	Chester-le-Street	d				00 24	00 31										07 24		07 39		08 16		
268½	—	—	**Newcastle**	a		00 36	00 41	00 48	00 56	01 48	01 50	02 13						07 30	07 36	07 39	07 51		08 29		08 35
—	—	—	Hartlepool	a																					
—	—	—	**Sunderland**	a																					
—	—	—	**Newcastle**	d													06 22	07 35		07 43					
285	—	—	Morpeth	a													06 36	07 47							
303¼	—	—	Alnmouth for Alnwick	a													06 53			08 08					
335½	—	—	**Berwick-upon-Tweed**	a													07 17	08 20		08 30					
363¾	—	—	Dunbar 238	a													07 41			08 53					
393	—	0	**Edinburgh** 238	a													08 07	09 02		09 22					
—	—	—		d											06 24	07 27		09 12							
394¾	—	1¼	Haymarket 238	d												07 31		09 16							
437¾	—	—	Motherwell	a											07 04	08 14		09 54							
450¼	—	—	**Glasgow Central**	a											07 21	08 31		10 15							
—	—	—	**Stirling**	a																					
—	—	—	Perth	a																					
—	—	—	**Inverness**	a																					
—	—	—	Inverkeithing	a																					
—	—	26	Kirkcaldy	a																					
—	—	51	Leuchars	a																					
—	—	59¾	**Dundee**	a																					
—	—	76¼	Arbroath	a																					
—	—	90	Montrose	a																					
—	—	114¾	Stonehaven	a																					
—	—	130½	**Aberdeen**	a																					

A until 18 June. From London Kings Cross
B From London Kings Cross
C From Liverpool Lime Street
D from 25 June. From London Kings Cross
E From Dunbar
F ⊼ to Edinburgh
G From Manchester Airport
H from 23 July until 5 October. From Sheffield

Table T026-F

Mondays to Fridays
21 May to 7 December

London - Humberside, Yorkshire, North East England and Scotland

		XC A	GR	TP B	TP B	TP C	XC D	GR	GR		GR	EM E	TP B	XC F	GR	TP B	TP C	XC F	GR		GR	HT	GR	GR	EM E
London Kings Cross ⊖	d							05 55	06 12		06 33				07 00				07 03		07 06	07 26	07 30	07 33	
Stevenage	d							06 17	06 34		06 55										07 28			07 55	
Peterborough	a							06 46	07 03		07 24				07 46				07 49		07 57		08 16		
Norwich	d											05 50													06 51
Peterborough	d							06 47	07 05		07 25	07 29			07 48				07 53		08 00		08 18		08 25
Grantham	a							07 05	07 23		07 43	07 57									08 18	08 25		08 40	08 55
	d							07 06	07 24		07 44	07 58									08 19	08 27		08 41	08 56
Newark North Gate	a							07 18	07 36												08 31		08 45		
	d							07 19	07 37												08 32		08 46		
Lincoln	a																								
Retford	d							07 34	07 52												08 47	08 52			
Doncaster	a							07 48	08 06		08 16								08 42		09 01	09 05	09 10	09 13	
Selby	a																					09 26			
Hull	a																					10 06			
Sheffield	a											09 37													10 38
Pontefract Monkhill	a																								
Wakefield Kirkgate	a																								
Wakefield Westgate	d						07 48	08 07			08 36							08 48	09 02					09 32	
Leeds	a						08 01	08 22			08 51							09 02	09 17					09 45	
Mirfield	a																								
Brighouse	a																								
Halifax	a																								
Shipley	a																								
Bradford Forster Square	a																								
Bradford Interchange	a																								
Keighley	a																								
Skipton	a																								
Doncaster	d	07 04							08 12					08 19							09 02		09 11		
York	a	07 24							08 32					08 40	08 51						09 25		09 32		
Scarborough	a																								
Harrogate	a																								
Leeds	d		07 08	07 13	07 35	07 52	08 07						08 12			08 39	08 52	09 08							
York	d	07 32	07 36	07 38	08 04	08 18	08 30		08 35				08 38	08 50	08 55	09 03	09 18	09 31					09 35		
Thirsk	d			07 56									08 55												
Northallerton	d			08 04		08 39			08 54				09 02				09 39								
Darlington	a	07 58	08 04		08 34	08 50	08 57		09 07					09 16	09 22	09 33	09 51	09 58					10 03		
Eaglescliffe	a																								
Middlesbrough	a			08 36									09 38												
Darlington	d	08 00	08 06		08 35	08 51	08 58		09 08					09 17	09 24	09 34	09 51	10 00					10 05		
Durham	d	08 18	08 24		08 52	09 07	09 14		09 26					09 34		09 51	10 13	10 18					10 23		
Chester-le-Street	d					09 13																			
Newcastle	a	08 35	08 37		09 07	09 24	09 28		09 39					09 47	09 51	10 07	10 27	10 31					10 36		
Hartlepool	a																								
Sunderland	a																								
Newcastle	d		08 40				09 35		09 47						09 54			10 35					10 42		
Morpeth	a		08 53																						
Alnmouth for Alnwick	a						09 59																11 07		
Berwick-upon-Tweed	a		09 28				10 21								10 36										
Dunbar 238	a		09 53															11 38							
Edinburgh 238	a		10 20				11 06		11 12						11 20			12 03					12 08		
	d		10 28				11 11																		
Haymarket 238	d		10 33				11 16																		
Motherwell	a						11 54																		
Glasgow Central	a						12 12																		
Stirling	a																								
Perth	a																								
Inverness	a																								
Inverkeithing	a		10 47																						
Kirkcaldy	a		11 04																						
Leuchars	a		11 28																						
Dundee	a		11 43																						
Arbroath	a		12 00																						
Montrose	a		12 16																						
Stonehaven	a		12 39																						
Aberdeen	a		13 03																						

A until 20 July, from 8 October. From Derby
B From Manchester Airport
C From Liverpool Lime Street
D From Derby. ⊼ to Edinburgh
E To Liverpool Lime Street
F From Birmingham New Street

Please note, Network Rail have stated that further updates to this timetable are possible during the validity period.

Please note, Network Rail have stated that further updates to this timetable are possible during the validity period.

Table T026-F

Mondays to Fridays
21 May to 7 December

London - Humberside, Yorkshire, North East England and Scotland

Station		TP	XC	GR	TP	TP	XC	GR	GC	TP	XC	GR	GR	EM	EM	TP	XC	GR	TP	TP	XC	GR	GR
		A	B		A	C	D			E	F			G	H	A	I		A	E	J		
London Kings Cross ⊖	d			08 00				08 03	08 06			08 30	08 33					09 00				09 03	09 06
Stevenage	d												08 56										09 28
Peterborough	a							08 49				09 16						09 46				09 49	09 57
Norwich	d													07 57	07 57								
Peterborough	d							08 51				09 18		09 27	09 27			09 48				09 52	10 01
Grantham	a												09 40	09 55	09 55								10 20
	d												09 41	09 58	09 58								10 21
Newark North Gate	a											09 45											10 33
	d											09 46											10 34
Lincoln	a																						
Retford	d																						10 49
Doncaster	a							09 40				10 09	10 13									10 40	11 03
Selby	a																						
Hull	a																						
Sheffield	a													11 37	11 38								
Pontefract Monkhill	a																						
Wakefield Kirkgate	a																						
Wakefield Westgate	d						09 47	10 01					10 32								10 47	11 01	
Leeds	a						10 00	10 16					10 47								11 00	11 16	
Mirfield	a																						
Brighouse	a																						
Halifax	a																						
Shipley	a																						
Bradford Forster Square	a																						
Bradford Interchange	a																						
Keighley	a																						
Skipton	a																						
Doncaster	d		09 19									10 10					10 18						11 05
York	a		09 40	09 52					10 05			10 32					10 40	10 51					11 31
Scarborough	a																						
Harrogate	a										←												
Leeds	d	09 12			09 39	09 52	10 08			←	10 08					10 12			10 39	10 52	11 08		
York	d	09 39	09 46	09 54	10 02	10 18	→		10 07	10 18	10 31	10 35				10 39	10 46	10 54	11 02	11 18	11 31		
Thirsk	d	09 56				→			10 24							10 56							
Northallerton	d	10 07							10 32	10 40		10 55				11 07				11 40			
Darlington	a		10 12	10 22	10 33					10 52	10 58	11 07					11 13	11 22	11 33	11 51	11 58		
Eaglescliffe	a								10 50														
Middlesbrough	a	10 39														11 38							
Darlington	d		10 13	10 23	10 34					10 53	11 00	11 09					11 15	11 23	11 34	11 51	11 59		
Durham	d		10 30		10 50					11 09	11 17	11 26					11 33		11 50	12 07	12 16		
Chester-le-Street	d									11 15													
Newcastle	a		10 43	10 50	11 07					11 26	11 29	11 41					11 46	11 50	12 05	12 24	12 30		
Hartlepool	a								11 10														
Sunderland	a								11 40														
Newcastle	d			10 53							11 37							11 52			12 38		
Morpeth	a										11 49												
Alnmouth for Alnwick	a																						
Berwick-upon-Tweed	a			11 35							12 23							12 35					
Dunbar 238	a																				13 41		
Edinburgh 238	a			12 18							13 06							13 17			14 07		
	d										13 13												
Haymarket 238	d										13 17												
Motherwell	a										13 54												
Glasgow Central	a										14 12												
Stirling	a																						
Perth	a																						
Inverness	a																						
Inverkeithing	a																						
Kirkcaldy	a																						
Leuchars	a																						
Dundee	a																						
Arbroath	a																						
Montrose	a																						
Stonehaven	a																						
Aberdeen	a																						

A From Manchester Airport
B From Birmingham New Street
C From Liverpool Lime Street to Newcastle
D From Bath Spa to Glasgow Central
E From Liverpool Lime Street
F From Bath Spa
G from 23 July until 31 August. To Liverpool Lime Street
H until 20 July, from 3 September. To Liverpool Lime Street
I From Guildford
J From Plymouth

Table T026-F

Mondays to Fridays
21 May to 7 December

London - Humberside, Yorkshire, North East England and Scotland

Station		GR	GR	HT	EM	TP	XC	GR	TP	TP	XC	GR	GR	GR	GR	EM	GC	TP	XC	XC	GR	TP
					A	B	C		B	D	E					F		B	G	H		B
London Kings Cross ⊖	d	09 30	09 33	09 48				10 00				10 03	10 06	10 30	10 33		10 52				11 00	
Stevenage	d		09 56										10 28		10 56							
Peterborough	a	10 16										10 50	10 57	11 16								
Norwich	d				08 57											09 57						
Peterborough	d	10 18			10 28							10 51	11 01	11 18		11 28						
Grantham	a		10 40	10 49	10 58								11 20		11 40	12 01						
	d		10 41	10 50	11 00								11 21		11 41	12 02						
Newark North Gate	a	10 45											11 35	11 45								
	d	10 46												11 46								
Lincoln	a																					
Retford	d			11 11																		
Doncaster	a	11 09	11 13	11 25								11 40		12 09	12 13		12 27					
Selby	a			11 40																		
Hull	a			12 18																		
Sheffield	a				12 38											13 37						
Pontefract Monkhill	a																12 57					
Wakefield Kirkgate	a																13 14					
Wakefield Westgate	d		11 32								11 47	12 01			12 32							
Leeds	a		11 47								12 01	12 16			12 48							
Mirfield	a																13 27					
Brighouse	a																13 35					
Halifax	a																13 47					
Shipley	a																					
Bradford Forster Square	a																					
Bradford Interchange	a																14 03					
Keighley	a																					
Skipton	a																					
Doncaster	d	11 10					11 19							12 10					12 19	12 19		
York	a	11 32					11 40	11 51						12 32					12 40	12 40	12 51	
Scarborough	a																					
Harrogate	a																					
Leeds	d					11 12			11 39	11 52	12 08							12 12				12 39
York	d	11 35				11 38	11 46	11 54	12 02	12 18	12 31			12 35				12 38	12 46	12 46	12 54	13 02
Thirsk	d					11 56												12 56				
Northallerton	d					12 06				12 39				12 55				13 07				
Darlington	a	12 03					12 12	12 21		12 51	12 58			13 07					13 13	13 13	13 22	13 33
Eaglescliffe	a																					
Middlesbrough	a					12 38												13 39				
Darlington	d	12 05					12 13	12 23		12 52	13 00			13 09					13 14	13 14	13 23	13 34
Durham	d	12 22					12 30		12 47	13 08	13 17			13 26					13 32	13 32		13 51
Chester-le-Street	d									13 14												
Newcastle	a	12 38					12 42	12 50	13 04	13 26	13 29			13 39					13 45	13 45	13 50	14 07
Hartlepool	a																					
Sunderland	a																					
Newcastle	d	12 41						12 55			13 38			13 45							13 52	
Morpeth	a	12 55																				
Alnmouth for Alnwick	a	13 11									14 02											
Berwick-upon-Tweed	a							13 38			14 23										14 35	
Dunbar 238	a																					
Edinburgh 238	a	14 13						14 21			15 08			15 14							15 17	
	d							14 28			15 12											
Haymarket 238	d							14 33			15 17											
Motherwell	a										15 54											
Glasgow Central	a										16 12											
Stirling	a																					
Perth	a																					
Inverness	a																					
Inverkeithing	a							14 47														
Kirkcaldy	a							15 04														
Leuchars	a							15 29														
Dundee	a							15 46														
Arbroath	a							16 04														
Montrose	a							16 20														
Stonehaven	a							16 43														
Aberdeen	a							17 04														

A until 31 August, from 8 October. To Liverpool Lime Street
B From Manchester Airport
C From Plymouth
D From Liverpool Lime Street
E From Plymouth. ✠ to Edinburgh
F To Liverpool Lime Street
G from 23 July until 5 October. From Plymouth
H until 20 July, from 8 October. From Winchester

Table T026-F

Mondays to Fridays

21 May to 7 December

London - Humberside, Yorkshire, North East England and Scotland

		TP	XC	GR	GR	GC	XC	GR	GR	HT	EM	TP	XC	GR	TP	TP	XC	XC	GR	GR	GR	GR	EM
		A	B				C				D	E	C		E	A	F	G					D
London Kings Cross	d			11 03	11 06	11 27		11 30	11 33	11 48				12 00					12 03	12 06	12 30	12 33	
Stevenage	d				11 28				11 56											12 28		12 56	
Peterborough	a			11 50	11 57			12 16											12 50	12 57	13 16		
Norwich	d										10 57												11 57
Peterborough	d			11 53	11 59			12 18			12 26								12 52	13 01	13 18		13 26
Grantham	a				12 18				12 40	12 49	12 58									13 20		13 40	13 56
	d				12 19				12 41	12 50	12 59									13 21		13 41	13 58
Newark North Gate	a				12 31			12 45												13 34	13 45		
	d				12 32			12 46													13 46		
Lincoln	a																						
Retford	d				12 47					13 11													
Doncaster	a			12 40	13 03			13 09	13 13	13 25									13 40		14 09	14 13	
Selby	a									13 42													
Hull	a									14 17													
Sheffield	a										14 38												15 37
Pontefract Monkhill	a																						
Wakefield Kirkgate	a																						
Wakefield Westgate	d		12 47	13 01					13 32								13 47	13 47	14 01			14 32	
Leeds	a		13 00	13 16					13 48								14 00	14 00	14 16			14 48	
Mirfield	a																						
Brighouse	a																						
Halifax	a																						
Shipley	a																						
Bradford Forster Square	a																						
Bradford Interchange	a																						
Keighley	a																						
Skipton	a																						
Doncaster	d				13 05			13 10					13 19								14 11		
York	a				13 30	13 20		13 32					13 40	13 52							14 32		
Scarborough	a																						
Harrogate	a						←																
Leeds	d	12 52	13 08				13 08					13 12			13 39	13 52	14 08	14 08					
York	d	13 19	→			13 22	13 31	13 35				13 39	13 46	13 54	14 02	14 18	14 31	14 31			14 35		
Thirsk	d					13 38						13 56											
Northallerton	d	13 40				13 48						14 07				14 39					14 55		
Darlington	a	13 51					14 02	14 06					14 12	14 22	14 33	14 52	14 58	14 58			15 07		
Eaglescliffe	a					14 03																	
Middlesbrough	a											14 38											
Darlington	d	13 52					14 03	14 08					14 13	14 23	14 34	14 52	15 00	15 00			15 09		
Durham	d	14 12					14 19	14 25					14 31		14 50	15 11	15 17	15 17			15 26		
Chester-le-Street	d															15 17							
Newcastle	a	14 26					14 32	14 39					14 43	14 51	15 04	15 27	15 30	15 30			15 39		
Hartlepool	a					14 22																	
Sunderland	a					14 52																	
Newcastle	d						14 35	14 44						14 54			15 37	15 37					
Morpeth	a						14 47																
Alnmouth for Alnwick	a							15 09									16 01	16 01					
Berwick-upon-Tweed	a													15 37			16 23	16 23					
Dunbar 238	a						15 41																
Edinburgh 238	a						16 06	16 13						16 20			17 05	17 05					
	d													16 34			17 12	17 12					
Haymarket 238	d													16 39			17 16	17 16					
Motherwell	a																17 55	17 55					
Glasgow Central	a																18 11	18 11					
Stirling	a													17 19									
Perth	a													17 58									
Inverness	a													20 04									
Inverkeithing	a																						
Kirkcaldy	a																						
Leuchars	a																						
Dundee	a																						
Arbroath	a																						
Montrose	a																						
Stonehaven	a																						
Aberdeen	a																						

A From Liverpool Lime Street
B From Plymouth to Edinburgh
C From Plymouth
D To Liverpool Lime Street
E From Manchester Airport
F until 20 July, from 8 October. From Penzance
G from 23 July until 5 October. From Reading

Table T026-F

Mondays to Fridays

21 May to 7 December

London - Humberside, Yorkshire, North East England and Scotland

		TP	XC	GC	GR	TP	TP	XC	GR	GR	GR	GR	HT	EM	TP	XC	GR	TP	TP	XC	XC	GR
		A	B			A	C	D						E	A	F		A	C	G	H	
London Kings Cross	d			12 57	13 00				13 03	13 06	13 30	13 33	13 48				14 00					14 03
Stevenage	d									13 28		13 56										
Peterborough	a				13 46				13 49	13 58	14 17											14 50
Norwich	d													12 57								
Peterborough	d				13 48				13 52	14 00	14 18			14 26								14 51
Grantham	a									14 19		14 40	14 49	14 57								
	d									14 20		14 41	14 50	14 58								
Newark North Gate	a									14 32	14 45											
	d									14 33	14 46											
Lincoln	a																					
Retford	d									14 48			15 13									
Doncaster	a								14 39	15 02	15 09	15 13	15 26									15 40
Selby	a												15 43									
Hull	a												16 18									
Sheffield	a													16 37								
Pontefract Monkhill	a																					
Wakefield Kirkgate	a																					
Wakefield Westgate	d							14 47	15 01			15 32								15 47	15 47	16 00
Leeds	a							15 00	15 16			15 48								16 00	16 00	16 16
Mirfield	a																					
Brighouse	a																					
Halifax	a																					
Shipley	a																					
Bradford Forster Square	a																					
Bradford Interchange	a																					
Keighley	a																					
Skipton	a																					
Doncaster	d		14 19							15 04	15 11					15 19						
York	a		14 40	14 48	14 51					15 29	15 31					15 40	15 53					
Scarborough	a																					
Harrogate	a																					
Leeds	d	14 12				14 39	14 52	15 08							15 12			15 39	15 52	16 08	16 08	
York	d	14 38	14 46	14 51	14 54	15 02	15 18	15 31			15 35				15 38	15 46	15 55	16 02	16 18	16 31	16 31	
Thirsk	d	14 56		15 14											15 56							
Northallerton	d	15 07		15 27			15 39				15 55				16 07				16 39			
Darlington	a		15 13		15 21		15 50	15 58			16 07					16 13	16 23	16 33	16 52	16 58	16 58	
Eaglescliffe	a			15 43																		
Middlesbrough	a	15 38													16 38							
Darlington	d		15 15		15 23		15 51	16 00			16 09					16 15	16 24	16 34	16 52	17 00	17 00	
Durham	d		15 33			15 47	16 11	16 17			16 26					16 33		16 50	17 11	17 17	17 17	
Chester-le-Street	d																		17 17			
Newcastle	a		15 46		15 49	16 01	16 25	16 29			16 39					16 46	16 51	17 04	17 27	17 31	17 31	
Hartlepool	a			16 11																		
Sunderland	a			16 38																		
Newcastle	d				15 52			16 35			16 42						16 56			17 37	17 37	
Morpeth	a							16 47			16 55											
Alnmouth for Alnwick	a							17 02			17 10									18 01	18 01	
Berwick-upon-Tweed	a				16 34												17 39			18 23	18 23	
Dunbar 238	a							17 44														
Edinburgh 238	a				17 18			18 07			18 14						18 22			19 05	19 05	
	d							18 10									18 33			19 11	19 11	
Haymarket 238	d							18 15									18 38			19 16	19 16	
Motherwell	a																			19 54	19 54	
Glasgow Central	a																			20 15	20 15	
Stirling	a																					
Perth	a																					
Inverness	a																					
Inverkeithing	a							18 28									18 53					
Kirkcaldy	a							18 46									19 11					
Leuchars	a							19 22									19 39					
Dundee	a							19 35									19 53					
Arbroath	a							19 51									20 11					
Montrose	a							20 05									20 27					
Stonehaven	a							20 26									20 50					
Aberdeen	a							20 48									21 11					

A From Manchester Airport
B From Penzance
C From Liverpool Lime Street
D From Plymouth. ✕ to Edinburgh
E To Liverpool Lime Street
F From Plymouth
G until 20 July, from 8 October. From Penzance. ✕ to Edinburgh
H from 23 July until 5 October. From Reading

Please note, Network Rail have stated that further updates to this timetable are possible during the validity period.

Table T026-F

Mondays to Fridays

21 May to 7 December

London - Humberside, Yorkshire, North East England and Scotland

Station		GR	GR	GR	EM	GC	TP	XC	XC	GR	TP	TP	XC	GR	GR	GR	GR	HT	EM	TP	XC	GR	TP
					A		B	C	D		B	E	F						A	B	G		B
London Kings Cross ⊖	d	14 06	14 30	14 33		14 48				15 00				15 03	15 06	15 30	15 33	15 48				16 00	
Stevenage	d	14 28		14 56											15 28		15 56						
Peterborough	a	14 57	15 17											15 50	15 57	16 16							
Norwich	d				13 57														14 57				
Peterborough	d	15 01	15 19		15 28									15 51	16 00	16 18			16 27				
Grantham	a	15 19		15 41	15 59										16 19		16 40	16 48	16 57				
	d	15 20		15 42	16 01										16 20		16 41	16 49	16 58				
Newark North Gate	a	15 34	15 46												16 32	16 45							
	d		15 47												16 33	16 46							
Lincoln	a																						
Retford	d														16 48			17 11					
Doncaster	a		16 10	16 14		16 20								16 40	17 02	17 09	17 16	17 25					
Selby	a																	17 42					
Hull	a																	18 18					
Sheffield	a				17 37														18 38				
Pontefract Monkhill	a					16 52																	
Wakefield Kirkgate	a					17 10																	
Wakefield Westgate	d			16 33									16 47	17 01			17 35						
Leeds	a			16 48									17 00	17 16			17 49						
Mirfield	a					17 25																	
Brighouse	a					17 33																	
Halifax	a					17 48																	
Shipley	a																						
Bradford Forster Square	a																						
Bradford Interchange	a					18 04																	
Keighley	a																						
Skipton	a																						
Doncaster	d		16 11					16 19	16 19						17 04	17 10					17 19		
York	a		16 32					16 40	16 40	15 51					17 27	17 31					17 42	17 52	
Scarborough	a																						
Harrogate	a																						
Leeds	d						16 11				16 36	16 52	17 08							17 12			17 36
York	d		16 35				16 39	16 46	16 46	16 54	17 02	17 18	17 31			17 35				17 38	17 48	17 56	18 02
Thirsk	d						16 56													17 55			
Northallerton	d		16 55				17 07					17 39				17 55				18 07			
Darlington	a		17 07					17 13	17 13	17 22		17 51	17 58			18 08					18 14	18 23	18 33
Eaglescliffe	a																						
Middlesbrough	a						17 38													18 39			
Darlington	d		17 09					17 15	17 15	17 23		17 51	18 00			18 10					18 16	18 25	18 34
Durham	d		17 26					17 33	17 33		17 48	18 11	18 17			18 27					18 33		18 50
Chester-le-Street	d																						
Newcastle	a		17 39					17 46	17 46	17 50	18 02	18 27	18 33			18 40					18 47	18 51	19 04
Hartlepool	a																						
Sunderland	a																						
Newcastle	d									17 52			18 40			18 44						18 54	
Morpeth	a																						
Alnmouth for Alnwick	a															19 09							
Berwick-upon-Tweed	a									18 36			19 22									19 37	
Dunbar 238	a												19 45										
Edinburgh 238	a									19 16			20 08			20 13						20 20	
	d									19 25			20 14			20 17						20 32	
Haymarket 238	d									19 30			20 17			20 22						20 37	
Motherwell	a															21 03							
Glasgow Central	a															21 25							
Stirling	a									20 15													
Perth	a																						
Inverness	a																						
Inverkeithing	a												20 30									20 51	
Kirkcaldy	a																					21 09	
Leuchars	a												21 26									21 37	
Dundee	a												21 43									21 52	
Arbroath	a																					22 09	
Montrose	a																					22 25	
Stonehaven	a																					22 48	
Aberdeen	a																					23 10	

A To Liverpool Lime Street
B From Manchester Airport
C from 23 July until 5 October. From Penzance
D until 20 July, from 8 October. From Southampton Central
E From Liverpool Lime Street
F From Plymouth. ✠ to Edinburgh
G From Plymouth

Table T026-F

Mondays to Fridays

21 May to 7 December

London - Humberside, Yorkshire, North East England and Scotland

Station		TP	XC	XC	GR	GR	GC	GR	TP	XC	XC	GR	EM	GC	TP	GR	XC	XC	TP	TP	XC	GR	GR
		A	B	C					D	E	F		G		H		I	J	H	A	K		
London Kings Cross ⊖	d				16 03	16 06	16 27	16 30				16 33		16 48		17 00						17 03	17 18
Stevenage	d					16 28						16 55											
Peterborough	a				16 50	16 57		17 16														17 50	18 07
Norwich	d												15 48										
Peterborough	d				16 52	17 02		17 18					17 24									17 51	18 09
Grantham	a					17 21						17 40	17 57										18 28
	d					17 22						17 41	17 57										18 29
Newark North Gate	a					17 36		17 45															18 41
	d							17 46															18 42
Lincoln	a																						
Retford	d											18 04											
Doncaster	a				17 39		18 03	18 10				18 18										18 40	19 09
Selby	a																						19 26
Hull	a																						20 05
Sheffield	a												19 37										
Pontefract Monkhill	a																						
Wakefield Kirkgate	a						18 26																
Wakefield Westgate	d		17 47	17 47	18 01					18 17	18 17	18 36									18 50	19 01	
Leeds	a		18 00	18 01	18 15					18 34	18 34	18 52									19 03	19 17	
Mirfield	a						18 42																
Brighouse	a						18 50																
Halifax	a						19 03																
Shipley	a																						
Bradford Forster Square	a																						
Bradford Interchange	a						19 19																
Keighley	a																						
Skipton	a																						
Doncaster	d							18 16															
York	a							18 36						18 39		18 50							
Scarborough	a																						
Harrogate	a																←	←					
Leeds	d	17 52	18 07	18 07					18 11	18 38	18 38				←		18 38	18 38	18 39	18 52	19 08		
York	d	18 18	18 32	18 32				18 39	18 46	→	→			18 42	18 46	18 53	19 05	19 05	19 08	19 18	→		
Thirsk	d								→					18 59	19 03				19 26				
Northallerton	d	18 39						18 58						19 08	19 16					19 39			
Darlington	a	18 51	19 00	19 00				19 11								19 21	19 32	19 33	19 44	19 50			
Eaglescliffe	a													19 25									
Middlesbrough	a														19 51								
Darlington	d	18 52	19 02	19 02				19 12								19 22	19 33	19 34	19 45	19 51			
Durham	d	19 08	19 20	19 20				19 30									19 50	19 51	20 02	20 07			
Chester-le-Street	d	19 14																					
Newcastle	a	19 25	19 33	19 33				19 43								19 49	20 02	20 04	20 16	20 21			
Hartlepool	a													19 44									
Sunderland	a													20 22									
Newcastle	d		19 36	19 36				19 45								19 53	20 04	20 06					
Morpeth	a							19 59															
Alnmouth for Alnwick	a		20 01	20 01													20 28	20 31					
Berwick-upon-Tweed	a		20 25	20 25												20 36							
Dunbar 238	a																						
Edinburgh 238	a		21 08	21 08				21 12								21 21	21 29	21 35					
	d		21 14	21 14																			
Haymarket 238	d		21 19	21 19																			
Motherwell	a		22 04	22 04																			
Glasgow Central	a		22 21	22 21																			
Stirling	a																						
Perth	a																						
Inverness	a																						
Inverkeithing	a																						
Kirkcaldy	a																						
Leuchars	a																						
Dundee	a																						
Arbroath	a																						
Montrose	a																						
Stonehaven	a																						
Aberdeen	a																						

A From Liverpool Lime Street
B from 23 July until 5 October. From Reading. ✠ to Edinburgh
C until 20 July, from 8 October. From Plymouth. ✠ to Edinburgh
D From Manchester Airport to Middlesbrough
E from 23 July until 5 October. From Plymouth to Edinburgh
F until 20 July, from 8 October. From Southampton Central to Edinburgh
G To Liverpool Lime Street
H From Manchester Airport
I until 20 July, from 8 October. From Southampton Central. ✠ to Newcastle
J from 23 July until 5 October. From Plymouth. ✠ to Newcastle
K From Plymouth to Edinburgh

Table T026-F

Mondays to Fridays
21 May to 7 December

London - Humberside, Yorkshire, North East England and Scotland

Station		GR	XC A	GR	EM B	EM C	TP D	XC E	XC F	TP G	XC H	GR	GR	GR	GR	TP I	XC A	GR	GR	HT J	EM K	TP D
London Kings Cross	d	17 30		17 33								17 48	18 00	18 03	18 18			18 30	18 33	18 48		
Stevenage	d			17 55															18 55			
Peterborough	a	18 17										18 36		18 50	19 06			19 16				
Norwich	d				16 57	16 57															17 54	
Peterborough	d	18 19			18 26	18 26						18 38		18 53	19 08			19 18			19 26	
Grantham	a			18 41	18 52	18 54						19 05			19 26				19 40	19 53	19 58	
	d			18 42	18 55	18 57						19 06			19 27				19 41	19 53		
Newark North Gate	a	18 46												19 22				19 45				
	d	18 47												19 23				19 46				
Lincoln	a																					
Retford	d											19 29							20 04	20 15		
Doncaster	a			19 14								19 43		19 48				20 14	20 20	20 28		
Selby	a																			20 45		
Hull	a																			21 22		
Sheffield	a				20 28	20 28																
Pontefract Monkhill	a																					
Wakefield Kirkgate	a																					
Wakefield Westgate	d			19 33							19 47	20 02		20 07					20 40			
Leeds	a			19 47							20 02	20 17		20 21					20 54			
Mirfield	a																					
Brighouse	a																					
Halifax	a																					
Shipley	a																		21s18			
Bradford Forster Square	a																		21 29			
Bradford Interchange	a																					
Keighley	a													21s01								
Skipton	a													21 17								
Doncaster	d							19 19	19 19									20 16				
York	a	19 27						19 40	19 41				19 49		20 15			20 36				
Scarborough	a																					
Harrogate	a		←	20 23													←					
Leeds	d		19 08				19 12			19 52	20 08					←	20 08					20 12
York	d	19 30	19 33				19 36	19 43	19 43	20 22	→		19 52		20 18	20 22	20 32	20 39				20 40
Thirsk	d						19 55			→												21 02
Northallerton	d						20 06								20 37	20 43						21 12
Darlington	a	19 57	20 03					20 11	20 12				20 20		20 50	20 55	20 59	21 06				
Eaglescliffe	a																					
Middlesbrough	a						20 38															21 43
Darlington	d	19 59	20 05					20 12	20 12				20 22		20 51	20 56	21 01	21 08				
Durham	d	20 16	20 22					20 29	20 29						21 09	21 14	21 18	21 25				
Chester-le-Street	d															21 20						
Newcastle	a	20 29	20 35					20 42	20 44				20 48		21 22	21 30	21 33	21 38				
Hartlepool	a																					
Sunderland	a																					
Newcastle	d	20 33	20 38										20 51				21 35	21 41				
Morpeth	a		20 53															21 54				
Alnmouth for Alnwick	a	21 00															21 59	22 10				
Berwick-upon-Tweed	a		21 26										21 34									
Dunbar 238	a	21 42	21 50																			
Edinburgh 238	a	22 10	22 13										22 19				23 03	23 16				
	d																					
Haymarket 238	d																					
Motherwell	a																					
Glasgow Central	a																					
Stirling	a																					
Perth	a																					
Inverness	a																					
Inverkeithing	a																					
Kirkcaldy	a																					
Leuchars	a																					
Dundee	a																					
Arbroath	a																					
Montrose	a																					
Stonehaven	a																					
Aberdeen	a																					

A From Plymouth
B from 23 July until 5 October. To Manchester Piccadilly
C until 20 July, from 8 October. To Manchester Piccadilly
D From Manchester Airport
E until 20 July, from 8 October. From Reading
F from 23 July until 5 October. From Plymouth
G From Liverpool Lime Street to Newcastle
H From Plymouth to Edinburgh
I From Liverpool Lime Street
J To Beverley
K To Nottingham

Table T026-F

Mondays to Fridays
21 May to 7 December

London - Humberside, Yorkshire, North East England and Scotland

Station		XC A	GR	XC B	XC C	GR	GR	TP D	GC	GR FO	GR FX	GR	EM E	GC	TP F	XC G	XC H	GR	XC A	GR	HT	TP D	EM I
London Kings Cross	d		19 00			19 03	19 06		19 27	19 30	19 30	19 33		19 54				20 00		20 03	20 30		
Stevenage	d						19 28					19 55											
Peterborough	a					19 50	19 58			20 16	20 16									20 50			
Norwich	d												18 57										
Peterborough	d					19 52	20 00			20 18	20 18		20 27							20 52			
Grantham	a						20 19					20 40	20 58								21 29		
	d						20 20					20 41									21 30		
Newark North Gate	a						20 34			20 45	20 45									21 19			
	d						20 35			20 46	20 46									21 20			
Lincoln	a						21 01																
Retford	d																				21 52		
Doncaster	a					20 40				21 09	21 09	21 13		21 21						21 43	22 05		
Selby	a																				22 25		
Hull	a																				23 04		
Sheffield	a																						
Pontefract Monkhill	a																						
Wakefield Kirkgate	a													21 51									
Wakefield Westgate	d			20 48	20 48	21 01						21 31							21 47	22 06			22 16
Leeds	a			21 01	21 02	21 15						21 47							22 02	22 21			22 34
Mirfield	a													22 03									
Brighouse	a													22 11									
Halifax	a													22 25									
Shipley	a																						
Bradford Forster Square	a																						
Bradford Interchange	a													22 46									
Keighley	a																						
Skipton	a																						
Doncaster	d	20 20								21 10	21 10					21 19	21 19						
York	a	20 41	20 54						21 17	21 31	21 31					21 40	21 40	21 48					
Scarborough	a																						
Harrogate	a																						
Leeds	d							20 52							21 12							21 52	
York	d	20 48	20 57					21 18	21 22	21 33	21 33				21 40	21 46	21 46	21 53				22 18	
Thirsk	d								21 38						21 57								
Northallerton	d							21 39	21 47	21 53	21 53				22 07							22 39	
Darlington	a	21 14	21 24					21 50		22 05	22 05					22 12	22 12	22 21				22 50	
Eaglescliffe	a								22 02														
Middlesbrough	a														22 37								
Darlington	d	21 15	21 26					21 51		22 07	22 07					22 13	22 13	22 23				22 51	
Durham	d	21 32						22 07		22 24	22 24					22 30	22 30	22 41				23 07	
Chester-le-Street	d																					23 13	
Newcastle	a	21 45	21 52					22 22		22 37	22 37					22 48	22 48	22 54				23 24	
Hartlepool	a								22 22														
Sunderland	a								22 52									23 21					
Newcastle	d		21 55							22 40													
Morpeth	a									22 53													
Alnmouth for Alnwick	a									23 09													
Berwick-upon-Tweed	a		22 38							23 33													
Dunbar 238	a																						
Edinburgh 238	a		23 29							00 26													
	d																						
Haymarket 238	d																						
Motherwell	a																						
Glasgow Central	a																						
Stirling	a																						
Perth	a																						
Inverness	a																						
Inverkeithing	a																						
Kirkcaldy	a																						
Leuchars	a																						
Dundee	a																						
Arbroath	a																						
Montrose	a																						
Stonehaven	a																						
Aberdeen	a																						

A From Plymouth
B from 23 July until 5 October. From Southampton Central
C until 20 July, from 8 October. From Plymouth
D From Liverpool Lime Street
E To Nottingham
F From Manchester Airport
G from 23 July until 5 October. From Plymouth
H until 20 July, from 8 October. From Reading
I From St Pancras International

Table T026-F

Mondays to Fridays
21 May to 7 December

London - Humberside, Yorkshire, North East England and Scotland

		EM	GR		GR	EM	TP	XC	XC	GR	GR	GR	GR
		◇ A				◇ A	◇ B	◇ C	◇ D				
London Kings Cross ⊖	d		20 33		21 00					21 33	22 00	23 00	23 33
Stevenage	d		20 55		21 22					21 56			
Peterborough	a		21 24		21 51					22 25	22 47	23s44	00s16
Norwich	d												
Peterborough	d		21 25		21 53					22 23	22 49		
Grantham	a		21 43							22 47	23 08	00s13	00s45
	d		21 44							22 49	23 09		
Newark North Gate	a		21 56		22 20					23 01	23 21	00s25	00s57
	d		21 57		22 21					23 02	23 23		
Lincoln	a												
Retford	d									23 17			
Doncaster	a		22 22		22 44					23 36	23 51	00s58	01s24
Selby	a												
Hull	a												
Sheffield	a												
Pontefract Monkhill	a												
Wakefield Kirkgate	a												
Wakefield Westgate	d	22 34	22 41			22 49		22 54	23 13	23 55			
Leeds	a	22 49	22 57			23 06		23 07	23 26	00 08			02 34
Mirfield	a												
Brighouse	a												
Halifax	a												
Shipley	a												
Bradford Forster Square	a												
Bradford Interchange	a												
Keighley	a												
Skipton	a												
Doncaster	d				22 47						23 52		
York	a				23 08						00 38	01 32	
Scarborough	a												
Harrogate	a												
Leeds	d						22 52						
York	d				23 12		23 15				00 41		
Thirsk	d						23 39						
Northallerton	d				23 43		23 47				01s09		
Darlington	a				23 55		00 01				01s23		
Eaglescliffe	a												
Middlesbrough	a												
Darlington	d				23 57		00 02						
Durham	d				00 14		00 25				01s42		
Chester-le-Street	d						00 31						
Newcastle	a				00 41		00 56				02 13		
Hartlepool	a												
Sunderland	a												
Newcastle	d												
Morpeth	a												
Alnmouth for Alnwick	a												
Berwick-upon-Tweed	a												
Dunbar 238	a												
Edinburgh 238	a												
	d												
Haymarket 238	d												
Motherwell	a												
Glasgow Central	a												
Stirling	a												
Perth	a												
Inverness	a												
Inverkeithing	a												
Kirkcaldy	a												
Leuchars	a												
Dundee	a												
Arbroath	a												
Montrose	a												
Stonehaven	a												
Aberdeen	a												

A From St Pancras International
B From Liverpool Lime Street
C until 20 July, from 8 October. From Plymouth
D from 23 July until 5 October. From Plymouth

Table T026-F

Saturdays
26 May to 8 December

London - Humberside, Yorkshire, North East England and Scotland

		GR	TP	GR	TP	TP	XC	XC	GR	XC		GR	TP	TP	TP	GR	TP	XC	TP	TP		XC	XC	GR	GR
		A	◇ B	A	◇	◇ C	◇	◇		◇			◇ C	◇	◇ B		◇ C	◇ D	◇ C	◇ B		◇ E	◇ F		
London Kings Cross ⊖	d																							05 55	06 12
Stevenage	d																							06 17	06 34
Peterborough	a																							06 46	07 03
Norwich	d																								
Peterborough	d																							06 47	07 05
Grantham	a																							07 05	07 23
	d																							07 06	07 24
Newark North Gate	a																							07 18	07 36
	d																							07 19	07 37
Lincoln	a																								
Retford	d																							07 34	07 52
Doncaster	a																							07 48	08 06
Selby	a																								
Hull	a																								
Sheffield	a																								
Pontefract Monkhill	a																								
Wakefield Kirkgate	a																								
Wakefield Westgate	d																					07 46	07 46	08 07	
Leeds	a																					08 00	08 00	08 20	
Mirfield	a																								
Brighouse	a																								
Halifax	a																								
Shipley	a																								
Bradford Forster Square	a																								
Bradford Interchange	a																								
Keighley	a																								
Skipton	a																								
Doncaster	d											06 10						07 19							08 08
York	a											06 30						07 40							08 30
Scarborough	a																								
Harrogate	a																								
Leeds	d					06 00							06 15		06 52	07 08	07 13		07 35	07 52		08 06	08 07		
York	d			00 41	05 06	06 27						06 35	06 43	06 47	07 17	07 36	07 38	07 48	08 02	08 18		08 31	08 31		08 35
Thirsk	d				05 30									07 05	07 33		07 57								
Northallerton	d			01s09	05 38	06 48						06 55	07 04	07 14	07 41		08 05			08 39					08 54
Darlington	a			01s23	05 49	06 59						07 07	07 15		07 53	08 04		08 17	08 33	08 50		08 57	08 58		09 07
Eaglescliffe	a																								
Middlesbrough	a				06 29									07 47			08 36								
Darlington	d		00 02			07 00						07 09	07 16		07 55	08 06		08 18	08 34	08 51		08 58	08 59		09 08
Durham	d	00 14	00 25	01s42		07 17						07 26	07 33		08 10	08 24		08 35	08 50	09 07		09 15	09 15		09 26
Chester-le-Street	d		00 31			07 23							07 39		08 16					09 13					
Newcastle	a	00 41	00 56	02 13		07 35						07 39	07 51		08 29	08 37		08 48	09 04	09 24		09 28	09 28		09 39
Hartlepool	a																								
Sunderland	a																								
Newcastle	d								06 20	07 38		07 43				08 42						09 35	09 35		09 46
Morpeth	a								06 33	07 50						08 55									
Alnmouth for Alnwick	a								06 50			08 09										09 59	09 59		
Berwick-upon-Tweed	a								07 15	08 23		08 32				09 30						10 21	10 21		
Dunbar 238	a								07 39			08 55				09 54									
Edinburgh 238	a								08 03	09 05		09 18				10 24						11 03	11 03		11 07
	d						06 27	07 27		09 14						10 28						11 13	11 13		
Haymarket 238	d							07 31		09 18						10 33						11 17	11 17		
Motherwell	a						07 05	08 13		09 54												11 53	11 53		
Glasgow Central	a						07 22	08 30		10 14												12 12	12 12		
Stirling	a																								
Perth	a																								
Inverness	a																								
Inverkeithing	a															10 47									
Kirkcaldy	a															11 04									
Leuchars	a															11 28									
Dundee	a															11 43									
Arbroath	a															12 00									
Montrose	a															12 16									
Stonehaven	a															12 39									
Aberdeen	a															13 01									

A From London Kings Cross
B From Liverpool Lime Street
C From Manchester Airport
D From Derby
E from 8 September until 6 October. From Derby. to Edinburgh
F until 1 September, from 13 October. From Birmingham New Street. to Edinburgh

Please note, Network Rail have stated that further updates to this timetable are possible during the validity period.

Table T026-F

Saturdays
26 May to 8 December

London - Humberside, Yorkshire, North East England and Scotland

		GR	EM	TP	XC	XC	GR	TP	TP	XC	XC	GR	GR	HT	GR	GR	EM	TP	TP	XC	GR	TP	TP
		■ 1	◇	◇1	◇1	◇1	■ 1	◇1	◇1	◇1	◇1	■ 1	■ 1	◇1	■ 1	■ 1	◇	◇1	◇1	◇1	■ 1	◇1	◇1
			A	B	C	D		B	E	D	C						A	F	G	H		B	I
London Kings Cross 15 ⊖	d	06 30					07 00					07 03	07 06	07 26	07 30	07 35					08 00		
Stevenage 4	d	06 52											07 28			07 57							
Peterborough 8	a	07 21					07 46					07 51	07 57		08 16								
Norwich	d		05 50														06 53						
Peterborough 8	d	07 22	07 27				07 48					07 53	07 59		08 18		08 29						
Grantham 7	a	07 40	07 55										08 17	08 25		08 40	08 57						
	d	07 41	07 58										08 18	08 27		08 42	08 59						
Newark North Gate 7	a												08 30		08 45								
	d												08 31		08 46								
Lincoln	a																						
Retford 10	d												08 46	08 52									
Doncaster 7	a	08 13										08 39	09 00	09 05	09 09	09 13							
Selby	a													09 26									
Hull	a													10 07									
Sheffield 7 ⛴	a		09 37														10 37						
Pontefract Monkhill	a																						
Wakefield Kirkgate 4	a																						
Wakefield Westgate 7	d	08 37								08 47	08 47	09 01				09 32							
Leeds 10	a	08 50								09 01	09 01	09 15				09 45							
Mirfield	a																						
Brighouse	a																						
Halifax	a																						
Shipley	a																						
Bradford Forster Square	a																						
Bradford Interchange	a																						
Keighley	a																						
Skipton	a																						
Doncaster 7	d				08 19	08 19							09 02		09 11					09 19			
York 8	a				08 40	08 43	08 55						09 23		09 31					09 40	09 52		
Scarborough	a																						
Harrogate	a																						
Leeds 10	d			08 12				08 39	08 52	09 08	09 08							09 12	09 12			09 39	09 52
York 8	d			08 38	08 50	08 50	09 00	09 03	09 18	09 31	09 32				09 35			09 39	09 39	09 48	09 55	10 02	10 18
Thirsk	d			08 55														09 56	09 56				→
Northallerton	d			09 09					09 39									10 07	10 07				
Darlington 7	a				09 16	09 16	09 27	09 33	09 50	09 58	09 58				10 03					10 16	10 22	10 33	
Eaglescliffe	a																						
Middlesbrough	a			09 38														10 39	10 49				
Darlington 7	d				09 17	09 17	09 29	09 34	09 51	10 00	10 00				10 05					10 18	10 24	10 34	
Durham	d				09 34	09 34		09 51	10 07	10 17	10 17				10 22					10 35		10 50	
Chester-le-Street	d																						
Newcastle 8 ⛴	a				09 47	09 47	09 55	10 07	10 21	10 29	10 29				10 35					10 47	10 52	11 07	
Hartlepool	a																						
Sunderland ⛴	a																						
Newcastle 8 ⛴	d						09 58			10 35	10 35				10 40						10 55		
Morpeth	a																						
Alnmouth for Alnwick	a														11 05								
Berwick-upon-Tweed	a						10 40														11 37		
Dunbar 238	a									11 38	11 38												
Edinburgh 10 238 ⛴	a						11 25			12 05	12 05				12 08						12 24		
	d																						
Haymarket 238 ⛴	d																						
Motherwell	a																						
Glasgow Central 15	a																						
Stirling	a																						
Perth	a																						
Inverness	a																						
Inverkeithing	a																						
Kirkcaldy	a																						
Leuchars 3	a																						
Dundee	a																						
Arbroath	a																						
Montrose	a																						
Stonehaven	a																						
Aberdeen	a																						

A To Liverpool Lime Street
B From Manchester Airport
C until 6 October. From Birmingham New Street
D from 13 October. From Birmingham New Street
E From Liverpool Lime Street
F until 29 September. From Manchester Airport
G from 6 October. From Manchester Airport
H From Birmingham New Street
I From Liverpool Lime Street to Newcastle

Table T026-F

Saturdays
26 May to 8 December

London - Humberside, Yorkshire, North East England and Scotland

		XC	GR	GC	TP	XC	GR	GR	EM	TP	XC	XC	GR	TP	TP	XC	XC	GR	GR	GR	GR	HT
		◇1	■ 1	■ 1	◇1	◇1	■ 1	■ 1	◇	◇1	◇1	◇1	■ 1	◇1	◇1	◇1	◇1	■ 1	■ 1	■ 1	■ 1	◇1
		A			B	C			D	E	F	G		E	B	H	I					
London Kings Cross 15 ⊖	d		08 03	08 06			08 30	08 33					09 00					09 03	09 06	09 30	09 33	09 48
Stevenage 4	d							08 55											09 29		09 56	
Peterborough 8	a		08 49				09 16						09 46					09 50	09 58	10 16		
Norwich	d								07 57													
Peterborough 8	d		08 51				09 18		09 28				09 48					09 52	10 01	10 18		
Grantham 7	a							09 40	09 56										10 20		10 40	10 48
	d							09 41	09 56										10 21		10 41	10 49
Newark North Gate 7	a						09 45												10 33	10 45		
	d						09 46												10 34	10 46		
Lincoln	a																					
Retford 10	d																		10 49			11 11
Doncaster 7	a		09 42				10 09	10 13										10 38	11 04	11 09	11 13	11 24
Selby	a																					11 41
Hull	a																					12 18
Sheffield 7 ⛴	a								11 38													
Pontefract Monkhill	a																					
Wakefield Kirkgate 4	a																					
Wakefield Westgate 7	d	09 47	10 01					10 32								10 47	10 47	11 01			11 32	
Leeds 10	a	10 00	10 14					10 45								11 00	11 02	11 14			11 46	
Mirfield	a																					
Brighouse	a																					
Halifax	a																					
Shipley	a																					
Bradford Forster Square	a																					
Bradford Interchange	a																					
Keighley	a																					
Skipton	a																					
Doncaster 7	d						10 10				10 19	10 19							11 05	11 10		
York 8	a			10 05			10 31				10 40	10 40	10 51						11 26	11 31		
Scarborough	a																					
Harrogate	a					←																
Leeds 10	d	10 08			←	10 08				10 12				10 39	10 52	11 08	11 08					
York 8	d	→		10 14	10 18	10 32	10 36			10 39	10 48	10 48	10 54	11 02	11 18	11 32	11 32			11 35		
Thirsk	d			10 30						10 56												
Northallerton	d			10 45	10 40		10 55			11 07					11 39							
Darlington 7	a				10 53	10 59	11 08				11 14	11 14	11 22	11 33	11 50	11 58	11 58			12 04		
Eaglescliffe	a			11 04																		
Middlesbrough	a									11 38												
Darlington 7	d				10 53	11 00	11 09				11 16	11 16	11 23	11 34	11 51	11 59	11 59			12 06		
Durham	d				11 09	11 17	11 27				11 33	11 33		11 50	12 07	12 17	12 17			12 23		
Chester-le-Street	d				11 15																	
Newcastle 8 ⛴	a				11 26	11 29	11 40				11 45	11 45	11 50	12 08	12 24	12 31	12 31			12 36		
Hartlepool	a			11 23																		
Sunderland ⛴	a			11 50																		
Newcastle 8 ⛴	d					11 33	11 45						11 56			12 36	12 36			12 39		
Morpeth	a					11 45														12 52		
Alnmouth for Alnwick	a																			13 07		
Berwick-upon-Tweed	a					12 18							12 38									
Dunbar 238	a															13 39	13 39					
Edinburgh 10 238 ⛴	a					13 01	13 08						13 24			14 05	14 05			14 11		
	d					13 13																
Haymarket 238 ⛴	d					13 17																
Motherwell	a					13 54																
Glasgow Central 15	a					14 12																
Stirling	a																					
Perth	a																					
Inverness	a																					
Inverkeithing	a																					
Kirkcaldy	a																					
Leuchars 3	a																					
Dundee	a																					
Arbroath	a																					
Montrose	a																					
Stonehaven	a																					
Aberdeen	a																					

A From Bristol Temple Meads to Glasgow Central
B From Liverpool Lime Street
C From Bristol Temple Meads. ⚲ to Edinburgh
D To Liverpool Lime Street
E From Manchester Airport
F until 21 July, from 13 October. From Guildford
G from 28 July until 6 October. From Bristol Temple Meads
H until 1 September, from 13 October. From Plymouth
I from 8 September until 6 October. From Guildford

Table T026-F

Saturdays

26 May to 8 December

London - Humberside, Yorkshire, North East England and Scotland

Station		EM ◇ A	TP ◇1 B	XC ◇1 C	XC ◇1 D	GR 1	TP ◇1 B	TP ◇1 E	XC ◇1 F	XC ◇1 G	GR 1	GR 1	GR 1	GR 1	EM ◇ A	GC 1	TP ◇1 B	XC ◇1 C	XC ◇1 H	GR 1	TP ◇1 B	TP ◇1 E	XC ◇1 I
London Kings Cross 15 ⊖	d					10 00					10 03	10 06	10 30	10 35		10 48				11 00			
Stevenage 4	d											10 29		10 57									
Peterborough 8	a										10 50	10 58	11 16										
Norwich	d	08 57													09 57								
Peterborough 8	d	10 22									10 53	10 59	11 18		11 23								
Grantham 7	a	10 54										11 18		11 41	11 55								
	d	10 55										11 20		11 42	11 56								
Newark North Gate 7	a											11 32	11 45										
	d												11 46										
Lincoln	a																						
Retford 10	d																						
Doncaster 7	a										11 41		12 09	12 14		12 18							
Selby	a																						
Hull	a																						
Sheffield 7	a	12 38													13 37								
Pontefract Monkhill	a																						
Wakefield Kirkgate 4	a															12 49							
Wakefield Westgate 7	d								11 47	11 47	12 01			12 34									12 47
Leeds 10	a								12 00	12 00	12 14			12 47									13 00
Mirfield	a															13 01							
Brighouse	a															13 09							
Halifax	a															13 20							
Shipley	a																						
Bradford Forster Square	a																						
Bradford Interchange	a															13 37							
Keighley	a																						
Skipton	a																						
Doncaster 7	d			11 19	11 19								12 10					12 19	12 19				
York 8	a			11 40	11 40	11 51							12 31					12 40	12 40	12 50			
Scarborough	a																						
Harrogate	a																						
Leeds 10	d		11 12				11 39	11 52	12 08	12 08							12 12				12 39	12 52	13 08
York 8	d		11 38	11 49	11 49	11 54	12 02	12 18	12 32	12 32			12 34				12 38	12 48	12 48	12 54	13 02	13 18	→
Thirsk	d		11 56														12 56						
Northallerton	d		12 06					12 39					12 54				13 07					13 39	
Darlington 7	a			12 15	12 15	12 21	12 33	12 51	12 59	12 59			13 06					13 14	13 14	13 21	13 33	13 50	
Eaglescliffe	a																						
Middlesbrough	a		12 38														13 39						
Darlington 7	d			12 16	12 16	12 23	12 34	12 52	13 00	13 00			13 08					13 15	13 15	13 23	13 34	13 51	
Durham	d			12 33	12 33		12 50	13 08	13 17	13 17			13 25					13 32	13 32		13 50	14 07	
Chester-le-Street	d							13 14														14 13	
Newcastle 8	a			12 46	12 46	12 50	13 07	13 26	13 29	13 29			13 38					13 45	13 45	13 49	14 07	14 24	
Hartlepool	a																						
Sunderland	a																						
Newcastle 8	d					12 56			13 35	13 35			13 45							13 52			
Morpeth	a																						
Alnmouth for Alnwick	a								13 59	13 59													
Berwick-upon-Tweed	a					13 39			14 21	14 21										14 34			
Dunbar 238	a																						
Edinburgh 10 238	a					14 25			15 03	15 03			15 07							15 25			
	d					14 29			15 11	15 12													
Haymarket 238	d					14 34			15 16	15 16													
Motherwell	a								15 54	15 54													
Glasgow Central 15	a								16 12	16 12													
Stirling	a																						
Perth	a																						
Inverness	a																						
Inverkeithing	a					14 48																	
Kirkcaldy	a					15 05																	
Leuchars 3	a					15 30																	
Dundee	a					15 46																	
Arbroath	a					16 04																	
Montrose	a					16 20																	
Stonehaven	a					16 43																	
Aberdeen	a					17 04																	

A To Liverpool Lime Street
B From Manchester Airport
C from 28 July until 6 October. From Plymouth
D until 21 July, from 13 October. From Bournemouth
E From Liverpool Lime Street
F from 28 July until 6 October. From Bournemouth. ✠ to Edinburgh
G until 21 July, from 13 October. From Plymouth. ✠ to Edinburgh
H until 21 July, from 13 October. From Southampton Central
I From Plymouth to Edinburgh

Table T026-F

Saturdays

26 May to 8 December

London - Humberside, Yorkshire, North East England and Scotland

Station		GR 1	GR 1	GC 1	XC ◇1 A	GR 1	GR 1	HT ◇1	EM ◇ B	TP ◇1 C	XC ◇1 A	GR 1	TP ◇1 C	TP ◇1 D	XC ◇1 E	XC ◇1 F	GR 1	GR 1	GR 1	GR 1	EM ◇ B	TP ◇1 C
London Kings Cross 15 ⊖	d	11 03	11 06	11 27		11 30	11 35	11 46				12 00					12 03	12 06	12 30	12 35		
Stevenage 4	d		11 28				11 57											12 28		12 57		
Peterborough 8	a	11 50	11 57			12 16											12 50	12 57	13 16			
Norwich	d								10 57												11 57	
Peterborough 8	d	11 53	11 59			12 18			12 24								12 51	13 00	13 18		13 28	
Grantham 7	a		12 17				12 40	12 48	12 57									13 20		13 40	13 56	
	d		12 18				12 41	12 49	12 57									13 21		13 41	13 58	
Newark North Gate 7	a		12 30			12 45												13 34	13 45			
	d		12 31			12 46													13 46			
Lincoln	a																					
Retford 10	d		12 46					13 11														
Doncaster 7	a	12 40	13 03			13 09	13 15	13 24									13 41		14 09	14 13		
Selby	a							13 41														
Hull	a							14 16														
Sheffield 7	a								14 37												15 37	
Pontefract Monkhill	a																					
Wakefield Kirkgate 4	a																					
Wakefield Westgate 7	d	13 01					13 33								13 47	13 47	14 01			14 32		
Leeds 10	a	13 14					13 47								14 00	14 00	14 14			14 46		
Mirfield	a																					
Brighouse	a																					
Halifax	a																					
Shipley	a																					
Bradford Forster Square	a																					
Bradford Interchange	a																					
Keighley	a																					
Skipton	a																					
Doncaster 7	d		13 05			13 10					13 19								14 10			
York 8	a		13 28	13 19		13 31					13 40	13 51							14 31			
Scarborough	a																					
Harrogate	a				←																	
Leeds 10	d				13 08					13 12			13 39	13 52	14 08	14 08						14 12
York 8	d			13 21	13 32	13 35				13 38	13 46	13 54	14 02	14 18	14 32	14 32			14 35			14 38
Thirsk	d			13 37						13 56												14 56
Northallerton	d			13 47						14 07				14 39					14 55			15 07
Darlington 7	a				13 59	14 04					14 16	14 21	14 33	14 51	14 58	14 58			15 08			
Eaglescliffe	a			14 02																		
Middlesbrough	a									14 38												15 38
Darlington 7	d				14 00	14 06					14 17	14 23	14 34	14 52	15 00	15 00			15 09			
Durham	d				14 17	14 23					14 34		14 50	15 08	15 17	15 17			15 27			
Chester-le-Street	d													15 14								
Newcastle 8	a				14 29	14 37					14 46	14 50	15 04	15 27	15 29	15 29			15 40			
Hartlepool	a			14 21																		
Sunderland	a			14 51																		
Newcastle 8	d				14 33	14 40						14 56			15 35	15 35			15 45			
Morpeth	a				14 45																	
Alnmouth for Alnwick	a					15 05									15 59	15 59						
Berwick-upon-Tweed	a											15 39			16 21	16 21						
Dunbar 238	a				15 39																	
Edinburgh 10 238	a				16 02	16 07						16 24			17 05	17 05			17 08			
	d											16 34			17 13	17 13						
Haymarket 238	d											16 39			17 18	17 18						
Motherwell	a														17 54	17 54						
Glasgow Central 15	a														18 11	18 11						
Stirling	a											17 18										
Perth	a											17 58										
Inverness	a											20 03										
Inverkeithing	a																					
Kirkcaldy	a																					
Leuchars 3	a																					
Dundee	a																					
Arbroath	a																					
Montrose	a																					
Stonehaven	a																					
Aberdeen	a																					

A From Plymouth
B To Liverpool Lime Street
C From Manchester Airport
D From Liverpool Lime Street
E until 21 July, from 13 October. From Penzance. ✠ to Edinburgh
F from 28 July until 6 October. From Reading

Please note, Network Rail have stated that further updates to this timetable are possible during the validity period.

Table T026-F

Saturdays
26 May to 8 December

London - Humberside, Yorkshire, North East England and Scotland

		XC	GR	TP	TP	XC	XC	GR	GR	GC	TP	XC	XC	GR	GR	EM	TP	XC	GR	TP	TP	XC	XC
		◇■ A ⚲	■ ⊡	◇■ B ⚲	◇■ C ⚲	◇■ D ⚲	◇■ E ⚲	■ ⊡	■ ⊡	■ ⊡	◇■ F ⚲	◇■ G ⚲	◇■ H ⚲	■ ⊡	■ ⊡	◇ I	◇■ B ⚲	◇■ J ⚲	■ ⊡	◇■ B ⚲	◇■ F ⚲	◇■ K ⚲	◇■ L
London Kings Cross ⊖	d		13 00					13 03	13 06	13 18				13 30	13 35				14 00				
Stevenage	d														13 58								
Peterborough	a		13 46					13 49	13 53					14 16									
Norwich	d															12 57							
Peterborough	d		13 48					13 52	13 55					14 18		14 26							
Grantham	a								14 15						14 40	14 58							
	d								14 16						14 41	14 59							
Newark North Gate	a								14 28					14 45									
	d								14 33					14 46									
Lincoln	a																						
Retford	d								14 49														
Doncaster	a							14 40	15 03					15 09	15 13								
Selby	a																						
Hull	a																						
Sheffield	a															16 37							
Pontefract Monkhill	a																						
Wakefield Kirkgate	a																						
Wakefield Westgate	d					14 47	14 47	15 01							15 31							15 47	15 47
Leeds	a					15 00	15 00	15 14							15 45							16 00	16 00
Mirfield	a																						
Brighouse	a																						
Halifax	a																						
Shipley	a																						
Bradford Forster Square	a																						
Bradford Interchange	a																						
Keighley	a																						
Skipton	a																						
Doncaster	d	14 19							15 05					15 10				15 19					
York	a	14 40	14 51						15 26	15 12				15 31				15 40	15 50				
Scarborough	a																						
Harrogate	a											←	←										
Leeds	d			14 39	14 52	15 08	15 08				←	15 08	15 08				15 12			15 39	15 52	16 07	16 07
York	d	14 48	14 54	15 02	15 18	→	→			15 14	15 18	15 32	15 32	15 34			15 38	15 46	15 53	16 02	16 18	16 32	16 32
Thirsk	d				→					15 37							15 56						
Northallerton	d									15 46	15 39			15 54			16 07				16 39		
Darlington	a	15 14	15 21	15 33							15 50	15 59	15 59	16 06				16 15	16 21	16 33	16 51	16 58	16 58
Eaglescliffe	a									16 01													
Middlesbrough	a																16 38						
Darlington	d	15 15	15 23	15 34							15 51	16 00	16 00	16 08				16 16	16 23	16 34	16 52	17 00	17 00
Durham	d	15 32		15 50							16 07	16 17	16 17	16 25				16 33		16 50	17 08	17 17	17 17
Chester-le-Street	d																				17 14		
Newcastle	a	15 45	15 49	16 07							16 25	16 29	16 29	16 38				16 46	16 50	17 04	17 27	17 29	17 29
Hartlepool	a									16 22													
Sunderland	a									16 51													
Newcastle	d		15 59									16 32	16 32	16 41					16 57			17 35	17 35
Morpeth	a											16 44	16 44	16 54									
Alnmouth for Alnwick	a											16 59	16 59	17 09								18 00	18 00
Berwick-upon-Tweed	a		16 41																17 40			18 21	18 21
Dunbar 238	a											17 40	17 40										
Edinburgh 238	a		17 26									18 03	18 03	18 11					18 25			19 05	19 05
	d											18 11	18 11						18 33			19 12	19 12
Haymarket 238	d											18 15	18 15						18 38			19 17	19 17
Motherwell	a																					19 53	19 53
Glasgow Central	a																					20 15	20 15
Stirling	a																						
Perth	a																						
Inverness	a																						
Inverkeithing	a											18 28	18 28						18 53				
Kirkcaldy	a											18 43	18 43						19 11				
Leuchars	a											19 13	19 13						19 39				
Dundee	a											19 29	19 29						19 53				
Arbroath	a											19 45	19 45						20 11				
Montrose	a											20 01	20 03						20 27				
Stonehaven	a											20 22	20 24						20 50				
Aberdeen	a											20 42	20 44						21 11				

A From Penzance
B From Manchester Airport
C From Liverpool Lime Street to Newcastle
D until 21 July, from 13 October. From Plymouth to Aberdeen
E from 28 July until 6 October. From Southampton Central to Aberdeen
F From Liverpool Lime Street
G until 21 July, from 13 October. From Plymouth. ⚲ to Edinburgh
H from 28 July until 6 October. From Southampton Central. ⚲ to Edinburgh
I To Liverpool Lime Street
J From Plymouth
K until 21 July, from 13 October. From Penzance. ⚲ to Edinburgh
L from 28 July until 6 October. From Reading

Table T026-F

Saturdays
26 May to 8 December

London - Humberside, Yorkshire, North East England and Scotland

		GR	GR	GR	GR	HT	EM	TP	XC	GR	TP	TP	XC	XC	GR	GR	GR	GR	EM	GC	TP	XC	GR
		■ ⊡	■ ⊡	■ ⊡	■ ⊡	◇■ ⊠	◇ A	◇■ B ⚲	◇■ C ⚲	■ ⊡	◇■ B ⚲	◇■ D ⚲	◇■ E ⚲	◇■ F ⚲	■ ⊡	■ ⊡	■ ⊡	■ ⊡	◇ A	■ ⊡	◇■ B ⚲	◇■ G ⚲	■ ⊡
London Kings Cross ⊖	d	14 03	14 06	14 30	14 35	14 48				15 00					15 03	15 06	15 30	15 35		15 48			16 00
Stevenage	d		14 29		14 57											15 28		15 57					
Peterborough	a	14 50	14 58	15 16											15 50	15 57	16 16						
Norwich	d						13 57												14 57				
Peterborough	d	14 53	15 01	15 18			15 24								15 54	16 00	16 18		16 27				
Grantham	a		15 20		15 41	15 49	15 55									16 18		16 41	16 57				
	d		15 21		15 42	15 50	15 57									16 19		16 42	16 58				
Newark North Gate	a		15 34	15 45												16 31	16 45						
	d			15 46												16 32	16 46						
Lincoln	a																						
Retford	d					16 11										16 47							
Doncaster	a	15 40		16 09	16 14	16 25									16 42	17 01	17 09	17 14		17 18			
Selby	a					16 41																	
Hull	a					17 25																	
Sheffield	a						17 34												18 34				
Pontefract Monkhill	a																						
Wakefield Kirkgate	a																			17 44			
Wakefield Westgate	d	16 01			16 33								16 47	16 47	17 01			17 35					
Leeds	a	16 14			16 46								17 00	17 00	17 14			17 48					
Mirfield	a																			17 58			
Brighouse	a																			18 08			
Halifax	a																			18 20			
Shipley	a																						
Bradford Forster Square	a																						
Bradford Interchange	a																			18 38			
Keighley	a																						
Skipton	a																						
Doncaster	d			16 10					16 19							17 02	17 10					17 19	
York	a			16 32					16 40	16 51						17 23	17 31					17 40	17 50
Scarborough	a																						
Harrogate	a																						
Leeds	d							16 10			16 36	16 52	17 07	17 08							17 12		
York	d			16 35				16 39	16 48	16 54	17 02	17 18	17 30	17 30			17 34				17 38	17 45	17 54
Thirsk	d							16 56													17 55		
Northallerton	d			16 55				17 07				17 39					17 54				18 07		
Darlington	a			17 08					17 14	17 21	17 33	17 50	17 56	17 57			18 07					18 11	18 21
Eaglescliffe	a																						
Middlesbrough	a							17 38													18 39		
Darlington	d			17 09					17 15	17 23	17 34	17 51	17 57	17 58			18 08					18 12	18 23
Durham	d			17 27					17 32		17 50	18 07	18 14	18 14			18 25					18 29	
Chester-le-Street	d																						
Newcastle	a			17 40					17 45	17 49	18 04	18 21	18 29	18 29			18 38					18 41	18 49
Hartlepool	a																						
Sunderland	a																						
Newcastle	d			17 44						18 00			18 36	18 36			18 43						18 53
Morpeth	a																						
Alnmouth for Alnwick	a																19 08						
Berwick-upon-Tweed	a									18 43			19 18	19 18									19 35
Dunbar 238	a												19 41	19 41									
Edinburgh 238	a			19 08						19 26			20 04	20 04			20 10						20 19
	d												20 14	20 14									
Haymarket 238	d												20 18	20 18									
Motherwell	a																						
Glasgow Central	a																						
Stirling	a																						
Perth	a																						
Inverness	a																						
Inverkeithing	a												20 33	20 33									
Kirkcaldy	a												20 50	20 50									
Leuchars	a												21 26	21 26									
Dundee	a												21 43	21 43									
Arbroath	a																						
Montrose	a																						
Stonehaven	a																						
Aberdeen	a																						

A To Liverpool Lime Street
B From Manchester Airport
C From Penzance
D From Liverpool Lime Street
E from 28 July until 1 September. From Southampton Central. ⚲ to Edinburgh
F until 21 July, from 8 September. From Newquay. ⚲ to Edinburgh
G From Newquay

Please note, Network Rail have stated that further updates to this timetable are possible during the validity period.

Table T026-F

Saturdays

26 May to 8 December

London - Humberside, Yorkshire, North East England and Scotland

		TP	TP	XC	XC	GR	GR	GC	GR	TP	TP	XC	XC	XC	GR	EM	GC	TP	GR	XC	XC	XC
		◇ A	◇ B	◇ C	◇ D					◇ E	◇ F	◇ G	◇ H	◇ I		◇ J		◇ A		◇ G	◇ K	◇ L
London Kings Cross ⊖	d					16 03	16 06	16 27	16 30						16 33		16 48		17 00			
Stevenage	d						16 29								16 55							
Peterborough	a					16 54	17 00		17 17													
Norwich	d															15 52						
Peterborough	d					16 55	17 01		17 18							17 25						
Grantham	a						17 20								17 41	17 57						
	d						17 22								17 42	17 59						
Newark North Gate	a						17 34		17 45													
	d								17 47													
Lincoln	a																					
Retford	d														18 05							
Doncaster	a					17 42		18 03	18 10						18 19							
Selby	a																					
Hull	a																					
Sheffield	a															19 37						
Pontefract Monkhill	a																					
Wakefield Kirkgate	a							18 26														
Wakefield Westgate	d			17 48	17 48	18 01						18 17	18 17	18 17	18 38							
Leeds	a			18 01	18 01	18 14						18 33	18 33	18 33	18 51							
Mirfield	a							18 42														
Brighouse	a							18 50														
Halifax	a							19 03														
Shipley	a																					
Bradford Forster Square	a																					
Bradford Interchange	a							19 19														
Keighley	a																					
Skipton	a																					
Doncaster	d								18 12													
York	a								18 33								18 40		18 48			
Scarborough	a																					
Harrogate	a																			←	←	
Leeds	d	17 36	17 52	18 07	18 07					18 11	18 35	18 39	18 39	18 39				←		18 39	18 39	
York	d	18 02	18 18	18 32	18 32				18 35	18 46	19 14	→	→	→			18 43	18 46	18 55	19 07	19 08	
Thirsk	d									→	→						19 00	19 04				
Northallerton	d		18 39						18 58								19 10	19 16				←
Darlington	a	18 33	18 51	19 01	19 01				19 10										19 25	19 35	19 34	19 35
Eaglescliffe	a																19 26			→		
Middlesbrough	a																	19 51				
Darlington	d	18 34	18 52	19 02	19 02				19 12										19 26		19 35	19 35
Durham	d	18 50	19 08	19 19	19 19				19 29												19 52	19 52
Chester-le-Street	d		19 14																			
Newcastle	a	19 04	19 25	19 32	19 32				19 43										19 53		20 07	20 06
Hartlepool	a																19 47					
Sunderland	a																20 21					
Newcastle	d			19 35	19 35				19 45										19 55			20 10
Morpeth	a								19 59													
Alnmouth for Alnwick	a			20 00	20 00																	
Berwick-upon-Tweed	a			20 23	20 24														20 38			
Dunbar 238	a																					
Edinburgh 238	a			21 09	21 09				21 12										21 20			21 34
	d			21 14	21 14																	
Haymarket 238	d			21 19	21 19																	
Motherwell	a			21 56	21 56																	
Glasgow Central	a			22 19	22 19																	
Stirling	a																					
Perth	a																					
Inverness	a																					
Inverkeithing	a																					
Kirkcaldy	a																					
Leuchars	a																					
Dundee	a																					
Arbroath	a																					
Montrose	a																					
Stonehaven	a																					
Aberdeen	a																					

A From Manchester Airport
B From Liverpool Lime Street
C from 15 September until 6 October. From Reading. ⚲ to Edinburgh
D until 8 September, from 13 October. From Plymouth. ⚲ to Edinburgh
E From Manchester Airport to Middlesbrough
F From Manchester Airport to Newcastle
G from 28 July until 1 September. From Paignton to Edinburgh
H from 8 September until 6 October. From Plymouth to Edinburgh
I until 21 July, from 13 October. From Southampton Central to Newcastle
J To Liverpool Lime Street
K until 21 July, from 13 October. From Southampton Central
L from 28 July until 1 September. From Paignton

Table T026-F

Saturdays

26 May to 8 December

London - Humberside, Yorkshire, North East England and Scotland

		XC	TP	TP	XC	GR	GR	GR	XC	GR	HT	EM	TP	XC	XC	GR	TP	XC	GR	GR	GR	GR	EM
		◇ A	◇ B	◇ C	◇ D				◇ E		◇ F	◇ G	◇ B	◇ H	◇ I		◇ C	◇ J					◇ K
London Kings Cross ⊖	d					17 03	17 18	17 30		17 33	17 48					18 00			18 03	18 18	18 30	18 33	
Stevenage	d									17 55												18 55	
Peterborough	a					17 50	18 07	18 17											18 52	19 08	19 16		
Norwich	d											16 54											17 50
Peterborough	d					17 52	18 09	18 18				18 26							18 53	19 10	19 18		19 30
Grantham	a						18 28			18 41	18 48	18 55								19 28		19 41	19 57
	d						18 29			18 42	18 49	18 58								19 29		19 42	
Newark North Gate	a						18 41	18 46											19 20		19 47		
	d						18 42	18 47											19 22		19 48		
Lincoln	a																						
Retford	d										19 11									19 52		20 06	
Doncaster	a					18 40	19 04			19 14	19 24								19 47	20 06	20 12	20 21	
Selby	a						19 25				19 41												
Hull	a						20 03				20 18												
Sheffield	a											20 30											
Pontefract Monkhill	a																						
Wakefield Kirkgate	a																						
Wakefield Westgate	d				18 50	19 01				19 33								19 47	20 07	20 25		20 40	
Leeds	a				19 03	19 15				19 46								20 02	20 20	20 39		20 54	
Mirfield	a																						
Brighouse	a																						
Halifax	a																						
Shipley	a																						
Bradford Forster Square	a																						
Bradford Interchange	a																						
Keighley	a																		21s01				
Skipton	a																		21 17				
Doncaster	d													19 19	19 19						20 14		
York	a							19 28						19 40	19 42	19 51					20 34		
Scarborough	a																						
Harrogate	a	←							←													21 26	
Leeds	d	18 39	←	18 52	19 08				19 08				19 12				19 52	20 08					
York	d	19 08	19 14	19 18	→			19 30	19 36				19 40	19 45	19 45	19 53	20 18	20 32			20 37		
Thirsk	d			19 35									19 55										
Northallerton	d		19 35										20 06				20 39				20 56		
Darlington	a	19 36	19 47	19 52				19 58	20 04					20 13	20 15	20 21	20 50	20 58			21 09		
Eaglescliffe	a																						
Middlesbrough	a												20 38										
Darlington	d	19 36	19 48	19 53				19 59	20 05					20 14	20 15	20 22	20 51	20 59			21 10		
Durham	d	19 53	20 05	20 10				20 17	20 22					20 31	20 32		21 07	21 16			21 28		
Chester-le-Street	d																21 13						
Newcastle	a	20 07	20 18	20 24				20 30	20 35					20 44	20 47	20 49	21 24	21 28			21 41		
Hartlepool	a																						
Sunderland	a																						
Newcastle	d	20 10						20 33	20 37							20 51		21 32					
Morpeth	a								20 50							21 05							
Alnmouth for Alnwick	a															21 22		21 58					
Berwick-upon-Tweed	a								21 22							21 46							
Dunbar 238	a								21 46							22 10							
Edinburgh 238	a	21 34						21 56	22 09							22 36		22 59					
	d																						
Haymarket 238	d																						
Motherwell	a																						
Glasgow Central	a																						
Stirling	a																						
Perth	a																						
Inverness	a																						
Inverkeithing	a																						
Kirkcaldy	a																						
Leuchars	a																						
Dundee	a																						
Arbroath	a																						
Montrose	a																						
Stonehaven	a																						
Aberdeen	a																						

A from 8 September until 6 October. From Plymouth
B From Manchester Airport
C From Liverpool Lime Street
D From Plymouth to Edinburgh
E From Plymouth. ⚲ to Newcastle
F To Beverley
G To Manchester Piccadilly
H until 21 July, from 13 October. From Reading
I from 28 July until 6 October. From Plymouth
J From Plymouth. ⚲ to Leeds
K To Nottingham

Table T026-F

Saturdays

26 May to 8 December

London - Humberside, Yorkshire, North East England and Scotland

		TP	XC	GR	TP	TP	XC	XC	GR	GR	GC	GR	TP	GR	HT	EM	GC	XC	XC	GR	XC	XC
		◇1 A	◇1 B	1	◇1 C	◇1 D	◇1 E	◇1 F	1	1	1	1	◇1 A	1	◇1	◇ G	1	◇1 H	◇1 I	1	◇1 J	◇1 K
London Kings Cross 15 ⊖	d			19 00					19 03	19 06	19 27	19 30		19 33	19 48		19 57			20 00		
Stevenage 4	d									19 28				19 55								
Peterborough 8	a								19 49	19 57		20 16								20 46		
Norwich	d															18 57						
Peterborough 8	d								19 51	19 59		20 18				20 26				20 48		
Grantham 7	a									20 18				20 40	20 51	20 58						
	d									20 21				20 41	20 52							
Newark North Gate 7	a									20 34		20 45								21 15		
	d									20 36		20 46								21 16		
Lincoln	a									21 00												
Retford 10	d														21 14							
Doncaster 7	a								20 39			21 10		21 13	21 27		21 32			21 39		
Selby	a														21 44							
Hull	a														22 20							
Sheffield 7	a																					
Pontefract Monkhill	a																21 56					
Wakefield Kirkgate 4	a																22 20					
Wakefield Westgate 7	d						20 48	20 48	21 01					21 31							21 48	21 48
Leeds 10	a						21 01	21 02	21 14					21 45							22 02	22 03
Mirfield	a																22 31					
Brighouse	a																22 40					
Halifax	a																22 52					
Shipley	a													22s09								
Bradford Forster Square	a													22 18								
Bradford Interchange	a																23 08					
Keighley	a																					
Skipton	a																					
Doncaster 7	d		20 19									21 12						21 21	21 21	21 40		
York 8	a		20 40	20 48							21 20	21 33						21 42	21 42	22 02		
Scarborough	a																					
Harrogate	a																					
Leeds 10	d	20 12			20 52	21 12	21 19	21 19					←									
York 8	d	20 40	20 48	20 54	21 18	21 40	21a59	21a59			21 23	21 35	21 40					21 48	21 48	22 05		
Thirsk	d	21 02				→					21 39		21 57									
Northallerton	d	21 15			21 39						21 48	21 55	22 07									
Darlington 7	a		21 15	21 21	21 50							22 07						22 14	22 14	22 32		
Eaglescliffe	a										22 04											
Middlesbrough	a	21 43											22 37									
Darlington 7	d		21 16	21 23	21 51							22 09						22 15	22 15	22 34		
Durham	d		21 33		22 07							22 26						22 32	22 32	22 51		
Chester-le-Street	d																					
Newcastle 8	a		21 47	21 50	22 22							22 39						22 47	22 47	23 04		
Hartlepool	a										22 24											
Sunderland	a										22 49											
Newcastle 8	d																					
Morpeth	a																					
Alnmouth for Alnwick	a																					
Berwick-upon-Tweed	a																					
Dunbar 238	a																					
Edinburgh 10 238	a																					
	d																					
Haymarket 238	d																					
Motherwell	a																					
Glasgow Central 15	a																					
Stirling	a																					
Perth	a																					
Inverness	a																					
Inverkeithing	a																					
Kirkcaldy	a																					
Leuchars 3	a																					
Dundee	a																					
Arbroath	a																					
Montrose	a																					
Stonehaven	a																					
Aberdeen	a																					

A From Manchester Airport
B From Plymouth
C From Liverpool Lime Street
D From Manchester Airport to Middlesbrough
E from 28 July until 6 October. From Southampton Central. ⊼ to Leeds
F until 21 July, from 13 October. From Plymouth. ⊼ to Leeds
G To Nottingham
H from 28 July until 6 October. From Plymouth
I until 21 July, from 13 October. From Reading
J from 28 July until 6 October. From Reading
K until 21 July, from 13 October. From Plymouth

Table T026-F

Saturdays

26 May to 8 December

London - Humberside, Yorkshire, North East England and Scotland

		TP	EM	GR	GR	EM	GR	EM	XC	XC	GR
		◇1 A	◇1 B	1	1	C	1	◇1 B	◇1 D	◇1 E	1
London Kings Cross 15 ⊖	d			20 03	20 30		21 00				22 00
Stevenage 4	d										
Peterborough 8	a			20 50	21 17		21 47				22 46
Norwich	d										
Peterborough 8	d			20 52	21 18	21 27	21 48				22 48
Grantham 7	a			21 11	21 37	22 00					23 06
	d			21 12	21 38						23 07
Newark North Gate 7	a				21 50						23 19
	d				21 51						23 20
Lincoln	a										
Retford 10	d				22 07						23 34
Doncaster 7	a			21 44	22 21						23 48
Selby	a										
Hull	a										
Sheffield 7	a										
Pontefract Monkhill	a										
Wakefield Kirkgate 4	a										
Wakefield Westgate 7	d		21 58	22 06	22 41			22 49	23 13	23 23	00 07
Leeds 10	a		22 17	22 19	22 55			23 06	23 27	23 37	00 20
Mirfield	a										
Brighouse	a										
Halifax	a										
Shipley	a										
Bradford Forster Square	a										
Bradford Interchange	a										
Keighley	a										
Skipton	a										
Doncaster 7	d										
York 8	a						22 55				
Scarborough	a										
Harrogate	a										
Leeds 10	d	21 52									
York 8	d	22 21					22 57				
Thirsk	d										
Northallerton	d	22 42					23 18				
Darlington 7	a	22 54					23 31				
Eaglescliffe	a										
Middlesbrough	a										
Darlington 7	d	22 55					23 32				
Durham	d	23 11					23 50				
Chester-le-Street	d	23 17									
Newcastle 8	a	23 27					00 03				
Hartlepool	a										
Sunderland	a										
Newcastle 8	d										
Morpeth	a										
Alnmouth for Alnwick	a										
Berwick-upon-Tweed	a										
Dunbar 238	a										
Edinburgh 10 238	a										
	d										
Haymarket 238	d										
Motherwell	a										
Glasgow Central 15	a										
Stirling	a										
Perth	a										
Inverness	a										
Inverkeithing	a										
Kirkcaldy	a										
Leuchars 3	a										
Dundee	a										
Arbroath	a										
Montrose	a										
Stonehaven	a										
Aberdeen	a										

A From Liverpool Lime Street
B From St Pancras International
C From Spalding to Nottingham
D until 21 July, from 13 October. From Plymouth
E from 28 July until 6 October. From Plymouth

Table T026-F

Sundays
20 May to 2 December

London - Humberside, Yorkshire, North East England and Scotland

	GR	TP	TP	XC	TP	GR	TP	TP	XC	XC	GR	GR	XC	GR	TP	XC	XC	GR	TP	TP	TP	XC
	■ A	◇■ B	◇■ C	◇■	◇■	■	D	◇■ E	◇■ F	◇■ G	■	■	◇■	■	◇■ H	◇■ F	◇■ G	■	◇■ I	◇■ J	◇■ K	◇■ L
London Kings Cross ⊖ d																						
Stevenage d																						
Peterborough a																						
Norwich d																						
Peterborough d																						
Grantham a																						
Grantham d																						
Newark North Gate a																						
Newark North Gate d																						
Lincoln a																						
Retford d																						
Doncaster a																						
Selby a																						
Hull a																						
Sheffield a																						
Pontefract Monkhill a																						
Wakefield Kirkgate a																						
Wakefield Westgate d	00 07																					09 47
Leeds a	00 20																					10 02
Mirfield a																						
Brighouse a																						
Halifax a																						
Shipley a																						
Bradford Forster Square a																						
Bradford Interchange a																						
Keighley a																						
Skipton a																						
Doncaster d																		09 37				
York a																		09 57				
Scarborough a																						
Harrogate a																						
Leeds d		07 41												08 30	08 41	09 18	09 18		09 38	09 40	09 52	10 08
York d		08 14	08 14		08 38									09 00	09 04	09 44	09 44	10 00	10 04	10 04	10 18	10 32
Thirsk d					08 55														10 21	10 21		
Northallerton d					09 03									09 21					10 29	10 29	10 39	
Darlington a		08 45	08 45											09 33	09 44	10 10	10 10	10 27			10 51	10 58
Eaglescliffe a																						
Middlesbrough a					09 33														10 58	10 58		
Darlington d		08 46	08 46											09 36	09 45	10 11	10 11	10 29			10 52	10 59
Durham d		09 02	09 02											09 54	10 02	10 28	10 28	10 46			11 08	11 16
Chester-le-Street d															10 08						11 14	
Newcastle a		09 16	09 16											10 07	10 18	10 40	10 40	10 59			11 24	11 28
Hartlepool a																						
Sunderland a																						
Newcastle d											08 45	09 15	09 45	10 12		10 42	10 42	11 02				11 31
Morpeth a											08 58		09 57	10 25								11 43
Alnmouth for Alnwick a											09 14		10 12	10 42								
Berwick-upon-Tweed a											09 38	09 57		11 06		11 24	11 24	11 44				12 16
Dunbar 238 a											10 02			11 32								
Edinburgh 238 a											10 26	10 43	11 12	11 56		12 06	12 06	12 27				12 58
Edinburgh d				08 04		09 10	09 16	09 16	10 23	10 23						12 17	12 17					13 13
Haymarket 238 d				08 08		09 15	09a19	09a19								12 21	12 21					13 18
Motherwell a									11 03	11 03						12 59	12 59					13 54
Glasgow Central a										11 28							13 19					
Stirling a																						
Perth a																						
Inverness a																						
Inverkeithing a				08 24		09 31																
Kirkcaldy a				08 39		09 48																
Leuchars a				09 06		10 13																
Dundee a				09 19		10 27																
Arbroath a				09 35		10 45																
Montrose a				09 49		11 01																
Stonehaven a				10 10		11 24																
Aberdeen a				10 29		11 45																

A not 20 May. From London Kings Cross
B until 21 October. From Manchester Airport
C from 28 October
D from 24 June. To Manchester Airport
E until 17 June. To Manchester Airport
F until 9 September
G from 16 September
H From Manchester Airport
I until 9 September, from 28 October. From Manchester Airport
J from 16 September until 21 October. From Manchester Airport
K From Liverpool Lime Street
L until 9 September. From Sheffield. ⊼ to Edinburgh

Table T026-F

Sundays
20 May to 2 December

London - Humberside, Yorkshire, North East England and Scotland

	XC	GR	GR	TP	TP	XC	GR	GR	TP	GC	GR	TP	GR	TP	XC	XC	GR	EM	GR	HT	EM	TP
	◇■ A	■	■	◇■ B	◇■ C	◇■ D	■	■	◇■ E	■	■ F	◇■ B	■	◇■ C	◇■ G	◇■ H	■	◇ I	■	◇■ ☒	◇ J	◇■ K
London Kings Cross ⊖ d		08 48	09 00				09 03	09 30		09 52	10 00		10 03				10 07		10 30	10 48		
Stevenage d							09 25															
Peterborough a							09 54	10 16					10 50				10 54		11 16			
Norwich d																		09 47				
Peterborough d							09 55	10 18					10 51				10 58	11 14	11 18		←	
Grantham a							10 13										11 16	11 53		11 46	11 53	
Grantham d							10 14										11 17	11 56		11 47	11 56	
Newark North Gate a							10 26										11 29	→	11 45			
Newark North Gate d							10 27										11 30		11 46			
Lincoln a																						
Retford d								10 56												12 08		
Doncaster a							10 50	11 10					11 38				11 53		12 09	12 26		
Selby a																				12 44		
Hull a																				13 22		
Sheffield a																					13 33	
Pontefract Monkhill a																						
Wakefield Kirkgate a																						
Wakefield Westgate d	09 47					10 46	11 10								11 46	11 46	12 12					
Leeds a	10 02					10 59	11 24								11 59	11 59	12 26					
Mirfield a																						
Brighouse a																						
Halifax a																						
Shipley a																						
Bradford Forster Square a																						
Bradford Interchange a																						
Keighley a																						
Skipton a																						
Doncaster d								11 11					11 43						12 10			
York a		10 34	10 46					11 32		11 40	11 47		12 03						12 31			
Scarborough a																						
Harrogate a																						
Leeds d	10 08			10 39	10 52	11 07			11 12			11 36		11 51	12 08	12 08						12 11
York d	10 32	10 37	10 50	11 02	11 18	11 31		11 34	11 38	11 42	11 54	12 02	12 08	12 18	12 32	12 32			12 35			12 40
Thirsk d										11 59												12 56
Northallerton d					11 39				12 01	12 07				12 39					12 55			13 04
Darlington a	10 58	11 04	11 17	11 33	11 50	11 57		12 02			12 21		12 37	12 51	12 58	12 58			13 07			
Eaglescliffe a										12 23												
Middlesbrough a									12 30													13 34
Darlington d	10 59	11 06	11 19	11 34	11 51	11 58		12 03			12 23		12 39	12 52	12 59	12 59			13 09			
Durham d	11 16	11 24		11 50	12 07	12 15		12 21					12 56	13 08	13 16	13 16			13 26			
Chester-le-Street d														13 14								
Newcastle a	11 28	11 37	11 45	12 04	12 21	12 27		12 34			12 49	13 00	13 10	13 24	13 28	13 28			13 39			
Hartlepool a										12 45												
Sunderland a										13 10												
Newcastle d	11 31	11 40	11 51			12 30		12 38			12 52		13 15		13 31	13 31			13 42			
Morpeth a	11 43	11 53																				
Alnmouth for Alnwick a								13 03							13 55	13 55						
Berwick-upon-Tweed a	12 16		12 33								13 35				14 16	14 16						
Dunbar 238 a						13 34		13 46														
Edinburgh 238 a	12 58	13 06	13 16			14 01		14 16			14 19		14 36		14 58	14 58			15 06			
Edinburgh d	13 13										14 33				15 10	15 10						
Haymarket 238 d	13 18										14 39				15 14	15 14						
Motherwell a	13 54														15 55	15 55						
Glasgow Central a	14 14															16 12						
Stirling a																						
Perth a																						
Inverness a																						
Inverkeithing a											14 53											
Kirkcaldy a											15 10											
Leuchars a											15 34											
Dundee a											15 51											
Arbroath a											16 08											
Montrose a											16 24											
Stonehaven a											16 47											
Aberdeen a											17 06											

A from 16 September. From Sheffield. ⊼ to Edinburgh
B From Manchester Airport
C From Liverpool Lime Street
D From Birmingham New Street
E From Manchester Victoria
F The Northern Lights
G until 9 September. From Birmingham New Street. ⊼ to Edinburgh
H from 16 September. From Birmingham New Street. ⊼ to Edinburgh
I until 9 September. To Liverpool Lime Street
J until 9 September. From Norwich to Liverpool Lime Street
K From Manchester Oxford Road

Please note, Network Rail have stated that further updates to this timetable are possible during the validity period.

London - Humberside, Yorkshire, North East England and Scotland

		GR	TP	TP	XC	GR	GR	TP	XC	EM	GR	GC	TP	GR	TP	TP	XC	XC	XC	XC	GR	GR
		■1	◇1	◇1	◇1	■1	■1	◇1	◇1	◇	■1	■1	◇1	■1	◇1	◇1	◇1	◇1	◇1	◇1	■1	■1
			A	B	C			D	E	F			G	H	I	D	J	K	L	M		
London Kings Cross ⊖	d	11 00				11 03	11 22				11 30	11 50		12 00							12 03	12 22
Stevenage	d					11 25																
Peterborough	a					11 54					12 16										12 50	13 08
Norwich	d									10 47												
Peterborough	d					11 55				12 16	12 18										12 51	13 10
Grantham	a					12 13	12 22			12 46											13 09	
	d					12 14	12 24			12 52											13 10	
Newark North Gate	a					12 26															13 22	
	d					12 27															13 23	
Lincoln	a																					
Retford	d										12 56											
Doncaster	a					12 50					13 10	13 19									13 46	13 57
Selby	a																					
Hull	a																					
Sheffield	a									14 34												
Pontefract Monkhill	a																					
Wakefield Kirkgate	a											13 44										
Wakefield Westgate	d				12 46	13 10											13 32	13 32	13 46	13 46	14 05	
Leeds	a				13 00	13 24											13 46	13 46	14 00	14 00	14 18	
Mirfield	a											13 57										
Brighouse	a											14 05										
Halifax	a											14 17										
Shipley	a																					
Bradford Forster Square	a																					
Bradford Interchange	a											14 34										
Keighley	a																					
Skipton	a																					
Doncaster	d										13 11											13 59
York	a	12 46					13 12				13 32			13 47								14 19
Scarborough	a																					
Harrogate	a								←													
Leeds	d		12 39	12 52	13 05			←	13 05				13 12		13 39	13 52	14 05	14 05	14 05	14 05		
York	d	12 51	13 02	13 20	→		13 15	13 20	13 29		13 34		13 38	13 50	14 02	14 15	→	→	→	→		14 22
Thirsk	d			→									13 55									
Northallerton	d						13 34	13 41					14 03									
Darlington	a	13 18	13 33				13 47	13 52	13 56		14 02			14 18		14 45						14 49
Eaglescliffe	a																					
Middlesbrough	a												14 33									
Darlington	d	13 20	13 34				13 48	13 53	13 58		14 03			14 19		14 46						14 51
Durham	d		13 50				14 06	14 10	14 15		14 21				14 48	15 02						15 08
Chester-le-Street	d														14 54							
Newcastle	a	13 46	14 04				14 19	14 23	14 27		14 34			14 46	15 05	15 15						15 21
Hartlepool	a																					
Sunderland	a																					
Newcastle	d	13 49					14 25		14 31		14 40			14 50								
Morpeth	a						14 38		14 45													
Alnmouth for Alnwick	a										15 05											
Berwick-upon-Tweed	a	14 31												15 34								
Dunbar 238	a								15 39													
Edinburgh 238	a	15 14					15 56		16 03		16 07			16 18								
	d													16 32								
Haymarket 238	d													16 37								
Motherwell	a																					
Glasgow Central	a																					
Stirling	a													17 22								
Perth	a													17 59								
Inverness	a													20 09								
Inverkeithing	a																					
Kirkcaldy	a																					
Leuchars	a																					
Dundee	a																					
Arbroath	a																					
Montrose	a																					
Stonehaven	a																					
Aberdeen	a																					

A From Manchester Piccadilly
B From Liverpool Lime Street to Newcastle
C From Bristol Temple Meads to Edinburgh
D From Liverpool Lime Street
E From Bristol Temple Meads
F To Liverpool Lime Street
G From Manchester Oxford Road
H The Highland Chieftain
I From Manchester Airport
J from 22 July until 9 September. From Bristol Temple Meads to Motherwell
K from 16 September until 7 October. From Bristol Temple Meads to Glasgow Central
L until 15 July. From Bristol Temple Meads to Motherwell
M from 14 October. From Bristol Temple Meads to Glasgow Central

Table T026-F

Sundays

20 May to 2 December

London - Humberside, Yorkshire, North East England and Scotland

		XC	XC	XC	XC	GR	GR	HT	TP	XC	GR	TP	TP	XC	XC	GR	GR	TP	TP	TP	XC	XC	XC
		◇1	◇1	◇1	◇1	■1	■1	◇1	◇1	◇1	■1	◇1	◇1	◇1	◇1	■1	■1	◇1	◇1	◇1	◇1	◇1	◇1
		A	B	C	D				E	F		E	G	H	I			J	K	L	M	N	O
London Kings Cross ⊖	d					12 30	12 33	12 48			13 00					13 03	13 30						
Stevenage	d						12 56									13 25							
Peterborough	a					13 16										13 54	14 16						
Norwich	d																						
Peterborough	d					13 18										13 55	14 18						
Grantham	a						13 41	13 46								14 13							
	d						13 42	13 47								14 14							
Newark North Gate	a					13 45										14 26							
	d					13 46										14 27							
Lincoln	a																						
Retford	d							14 08									14 56						
Doncaster	a					14 09	14 18	14 23								14 50	15 10						
Selby	a							14 39															
Hull	a							15 18															
Sheffield	a																						
Pontefract Monkhill	a																						
Wakefield Kirkgate	a																						
Wakefield Westgate	d						14 38							14 45	14 47	15 11					15 36	15 36	15 47
Leeds	a						14 52							14 59	15 00	15 24					15 53	15 53	16 00
Mirfield	a																						
Brighouse	a																						
Halifax	a																						
Shipley	a																						
Bradford Forster Square	a																						
Bradford Interchange	a																						
Keighley	a																						
Skipton	a																						
Doncaster	d					14 10				14 19							15 11						
York	a					14 31				14 40	14 49						15 32						
Scarborough	a																						
Harrogate	a	←	←	←	←																		
Leeds	d	14 05	14 05	14 05	14 05				14 12			14 39	14 52	15 05	15 05			15 12	15 39	15 51	16 05	16 05	16 05
York	d	14 29	14 29	14 29	14 29	14 33			14 37	14 48	14 55	15 02	15 18	15 29	15 29		15 34	15 42	16 02	16 15	→	→	→
Thirsk	d								14 54									→	→	→			
Northallerton	d					14 53			15 02				15 39										
Darlington	a	14 55	14 55	14 55	14 55	15 05				15 16	15 23	15 33	15 50	15 55	15 55		16 02						
Eaglescliffe	a																						
Middlesbrough	a								15 31														
Darlington	d	14 57	14 57	14 57	14 57	15 07				15 17	15 24	15 34	15 51	15 56	15 56		16 03						
Durham	d	15 14	15 14	15 14	15 14	15 24				15 34		15 50	16 07	16 13	16 13		16 21						
Chester-le-Street	d																						
Newcastle	a	15 26	15 26	15 26	15 26	15 37				15 47	15 51	16 04	16 21	16 25	16 25		16 34						
Hartlepool	a																						
Sunderland	a																						
Newcastle	d	15 28	15 28	15 28	15 28	15 44					15 53			16 28	16 28		16 38						
Morpeth	a																						
Alnmouth for Alnwick	a	15 53	15 53	15 53	15 53									16 52	16 52		17 03						
Berwick-upon-Tweed	a	16 12	16 12	16 12	16 12						16 36												
Dunbar 238	a													17 35	17 35								
Edinburgh 238	a	16 55	16 55	16 55	16 55	17 06					17 18			17 58	17 58		18 06						
	d	17 11	17 11	17 11	17 11									18 13	18 13								
Haymarket 238	d	17 15	17 15	17 15	17 15									18 16	18 16								
Motherwell	a	17 51	17 51	17 52	17 52																		
Glasgow Central	a			18 13	18 13																		
Stirling	a																						
Perth	a																						
Inverness	a																						
Inverkeithing	a													18 28	18 28								
Kirkcaldy	a													18 44	18 44								
Leuchars	a													19 14	19 14								
Dundee	a													19 29	19 29								
Arbroath	a													19 46	19 46								
Montrose	a													20 00	20 00								
Stonehaven	a													20 22	20 22								
Aberdeen	a													20 42	20 42								

A from 22 July until 9 September. From Bristol Temple Meads
B until 15 July. From Bristol Temple Meads
C from 16 September until 7 October. From Bristol Temple Meads
D from 14 October. From Bristol Temple Meads
E From Manchester Airport
F until 15 July, from 14 October. From Birmingham New Street
G From Liverpool Lime Street
H from 22 July until 7 October. From Bristol Temple Meads. Trolley service to Edinburgh
I until 15 July, from 14 October. From Plymouth. Trolley service to Edinburgh
J From Manchester Airport to Middlesbrough
K From Manchester Airport to Newcastle
L From Liverpool Lime Street to Newcastle
M from 22 July until 9 September. From Plymouth to Motherwell
N from 16 September until 7 October. From Plymouth to Glasgow Central
O until 15 July. From Plymouth to Motherwell

Please note, Network Rail have stated that further updates to this timetable are possible during the validity period.

Sundays
20 May to 2 December

London - Humberside, Yorkshire, North East England and Scotland

Station		XC A	GR	GC	TP B	EM C	XC D	GR	TP B	TP E	XC F	XC G	XC H	XC I	GR	GR	HT	EM C	TP B	XC J	GR	TP B
London Kings Cross	d		13 33	13 48				14 00							14 03	14 30	14 48				15 00	
Stevenage	d		13 55																			
Peterborough	a		14 24												14 50	15 16						
Norwich	d																	13 47				
Peterborough	d		14 26			14 31									14 52	15 18		15 23				
Grantham	a		14 45			15 07									15 10		15 47	15 53				
	d		14 51			15 09									15 11		15 48	15 55				
Newark North Gate	a														15 23	15 45						
	d														15 24	15 46						
Lincoln	a																					
Retford	d		15 20														16 10					
Doncaster	a		15 34												15 47	16 09	16 27					
Selby	a																16 45					
Hull	a																17 22					
Sheffield	a					16 34												17 39				
Pontefract Monkhill	a																					
Wakefield Kirkgate	a																					
Wakefield Westgate	d	15 47	16 02												16 08							
Leeds	a	16 00	16 16												16 21							
Mirfield	a																					
Brighouse	a																					
Halifax	a																					
Shipley	a																					
Bradford Forster Square	a																					
Bradford Interchange	a																					
Keighley	a																					
Skipton	a																					
Doncaster	d						15 19									16 10				16 19		
York	a			15 37			15 40	15 47								16 31				16 40	16 47	
Scarborough	a																					
Harrogate	a										←	←	←	←								
Leeds	d	16 05			←				←	←	16 05	16 05	16 05	16 05					16 12			16 37
York	d	→		15 38	15 42		15 45	15 53	16 02	16 15	16 29	16 29	16 29	16 29		16 33			16 38	16 45	16 52	17 02
Thirsk	d			15 56	16 04														16 55			
Northallerton	d			16 06	16 14					16 36						16 53						
Darlington	a						16 11	16 20	16 33	16 48	16 55	16 55	16 55	16 55		17 05				17 11	17 19	17 33
Eaglescliffe	a			16 25																		
Middlesbrough	a				16 42														17 37			
Darlington	d						16 12	16 22	16 34	16 49	16 56	16 56	16 56	16 56		17 07				17 12	17 21	17 34
Durham	d						16 29		16 50	17 05	17 13	17 13	17 13	17 13		17 24				17 30		17 50
Chester-le-Street	d									17 11												
Newcastle	a						16 42	16 48	17 04	17 21	17 25	17 25	17 25	17 25		17 39				17 44	17 47	18 04
Hartlepool	a			16 45																		
Sunderland	a			17 11																		
Newcastle	d							16 52			17 28	17 28	17 28	17 28		17 43					17 50	
Morpeth	a										17 40	17 40	17 40	17 40								
Alnmouth for Alnwick	a										17 55	17 55	17 55	17 55								
Berwick-upon-Tweed	a							17 35			18 16	18 16	18 16	18 16							18 33	
Dunbar 238	a																					
Edinburgh 238	a							18 18			18 58	18 58	18 58	18 58		19 06					19 16	
	d							18 36			19 18	19 18	19 18	19 18								
Haymarket 238	d							18 41			19 23	19 23	19 23	19 23								
Motherwell	a										19 59	19 59	19 59	19 59								
Glasgow Central	a											20 19		20 19								
Stirling	a																					
Perth	a																					
Inverness	a																					
Inverkeithing	a							18 54														
Kirkcaldy	a							19 11														
Leuchars	a							19 36														
Dundee	a							19 50														
Arbroath	a							20 08														
Montrose	a							20 24														
Stonehaven	a							20 47														
Aberdeen	a							21 08														

A from 14 October. From Plymouth to Glasgow Central
B From Manchester Airport
C To Liverpool Lime Street
D until 15 July, from 14 October. From Birmingham New Street
E From Liverpool Lime Street
F from 22 July until 9 September. From Plymouth. ⚲ to Edinburgh
G from 16 September until 7 October. From Plymouth. ⚲ to Edinburgh
H until 15 July. From Plymouth. ⚲ to Edinburgh
I from 14 October. From Plymouth. ⚲ to Edinburgh
J until 15 July, from 14 October. From Guildford

Table T026-F

Sundays
20 May to 2 December

London - Humberside, Yorkshire, North East England and Scotland

Station		TP A	XC B	XC C	XC D	GR	GR	EM E	GC	TP F	XC G	GR	TP F	TP A	XC H	XC I	XC J	XC K	EM L	GR	GR M	GR N	TP O
London Kings Cross	d					15 03	15 30		15 50			16 00								16 05	16 30	16 30	
Stevenage	d					15 25																	
Peterborough	a					15 54	16 17													16 51	17 16	17 16	
Norwich	d							14 53															
Peterborough	d					15 55	16 18	16 24												16 53	17 18	17 18	
Grantham	a					16 13	16 37	16 54												17 11			
	d					16 14	16 38	16 56												17 12			
Newark North Gate	a					16 26														17 24	17 45	17 45	
	d					16 27														17 25	17 46	17 46	
Lincoln	a																						
Retford	d					16 42																	
Doncaster	a					16 56	17 10		17 17											17 48	18 09	18 09	
Selby	a																						
Hull	a																						
Sheffield	a							18 33															
Pontefract Monkhill	a																						
Wakefield Kirkgate	a								17 49														
Wakefield Westgate	d		16 46	16 46	16 46	17 15									17 36	17 36	17 45	17 45	18 01	18 10			
Leeds	a		16 59	16 59	17 00	17 28									17 54	17 54	18 00	18 00	18 15	18 24			
Mirfield	a								18 02														
Brighouse	a								18 10														
Halifax	a								18 24														
Shipley	a																						
Bradford Forster Square	a																						
Bradford Interchange	a								18 40														
Keighley	a																						
Skipton	a																						
Doncaster	d						17 12				17 19										18 10	18 10	
York	a						17 33				17 40	17 46									18 32	18 32	
Scarborough	a																						
Harrogate	a																						
Leeds	d	16 52	17 05	17 05	17 05					17 10			17 39	17 52	18 05	18 05	18 05	18 05					18 13
York	d	17 18	17 29	17 29	17 29		17 35			17 38	17 43	17 49	18 02	18 18	18 29	18 29	18 29	18 29			18 35	18 35	18 53
Thirsk	d									18 02													→
Northallerton	d	17 39								18 11				18 39							18 55	18 55	
Darlington	a	17 50	17 55	17 55	17 55		18 03				18 09	18 16	18 33	18 50	18 55	18 55	18 55	18 56			19 07	19 07	
Eaglescliffe	a																						
Middlesbrough	a									18 40													
Darlington	d	17 51	17 56	17 56	17 56		18 04				18 11	18 18	18 34	18 51	18 56	18 56	18 56	18 57			19 09	19 09	
Durham	d	18 07	18 13	18 13	18 13		18 22				18 28		18 50	19 07	19 13	19 13	19 13	19 15			19 26	19 26	
Chester-le-Street	d																						
Newcastle	a	18 21	18 25	18 25	18 25		18 35				18 41	18 45	19 04	19 21	19 25	19 25	19 25	19 27			19 39	19 39	
Hartlepool	a																						
Sunderland	a																						
Newcastle	d		18 28	18 32	18 32		18 38					18 50			19 32	19 32	19 32	19 32			19 42	19 42	
Morpeth	a																				19 55	19 55	
Alnmouth for Alnwick	a						19 04								19 56	19 56	19 56	19 56					
Berwick-upon-Tweed	a		19 10	19 14	19 14							19 32			20 18	20 18	20 18	20 19					
Dunbar 238	a		19 33	19 37	19 37																20 49	20 49	
Edinburgh 238	a		19 57	20 00	20 00		20 07					20 15			21 00	21 00	21 00	21 02			21 12	21 12	
	d														21 12	21 12	21 12	21 12				21 22	
Haymarket 238	d														21 17	21 17	21 17	21 17				21 26	
Motherwell	a														21 54	21 55	21 55	21 55				22 04	
Glasgow Central	a															22 12	22 12					22 24	
Stirling	a																						
Perth	a																						
Inverness	a																						
Inverkeithing	a																						
Kirkcaldy	a																						
Leuchars	a																						
Dundee	a																						
Arbroath	a																						
Montrose	a																						
Stonehaven	a																						
Aberdeen	a																						

A From Liverpool Lime Street
B until 15 July, from 14 October. From Penzance
C from 22 July until 2 September. From Plymouth
D from 9 September until 7 October. From Plymouth
E To Liverpool Lime Street
F From Manchester Airport
G until 15 July, from 14 October. From Reading
H from 22 July until 9 September. From Penzance. ⚲ to Edinburgh
I from 16 September until 7 October. From Penzance
J from 14 October. From Plymouth. ⚲ to Edinburgh
K until 15 July. From Plymouth. ⚲ to Edinburgh
L not 26 August. From St Pancras International
M until 9 September
N from 16 September
O From Manchester Airport to Middlesbrough

Table T026-F

Sundays

20 May to 2 December

London - Humberside, Yorkshire, North East England and Scotland

Station		TP	TP	XC	GR	EM	GC	GR	TP	TP	TP	XC	TP	XC	XC	XC	XC	XC	XC	GR	GR	GR	GR
		◇ A	◇ B	◇ C		◇ D			◇ E	◇ E	◇ B	◇ F	◇ G	◇ H	◇ I	◇ J	◇ K	◇ L	◇ M				
London Kings Cross	d				16 35		16 53	17 00												17 05	17 22	17 30	17 35
Stevenage	d				16 57																		17 57
Peterborough	a																			17 51		18 16	
Norwich	d					15 54																	
Peterborough	d					17 19														17 53		18 18	
Grantham	a				17 40	17 49															18 23	18 36	18 41
	d				17 41	17 55															18 25	18 37	18 43
Newark North Gate	a																			18 20	18 37		
	d																			18 21	18 38		
Lincoln	a																						
Retford	d				18 04																		
Doncaster	a				18 18															18 44	19 03	19 10	19 14
Selby	a																				19 22		
Hull	a																				20 00		
Sheffield	a					19 31																	
Pontefract Monkhill	a																						
Wakefield Kirkgate	a																						
Wakefield Westgate	d			18 33	18 39									18 45	18 45	18 47				19 04			19 34
Leeds	a			18 47	18 53									18 59	18 59	19 01				19 19			19 47
Mirfield	a																						
Brighouse	a																						
Halifax	a																						
Shipley	a																						
Bradford Forster Square	a																						
Bradford Interchange	a																						
Keighley	a																						
Skipton	a																						
Doncaster	d																					19 12	
York	a						18 41	18 47														19 32	
Scarborough	a																						
Harrogate	a											←											
Leeds	d	18 38	18 52	18 59					←	←	←	18 59		19 08	19 08	19 08							
York	d	19 02	19 18	→			18 43	18 50	18 53	19 02	19 18	19 23		19 32	19 32	19 32						19 37	
Thirsk	d	→	→				19 02		19 11				←										
Northallerton	d						19 13		19 19		19 44		19 44										
Darlington	a							19 17		19 35	→	19 49	19 55	19 59	19 59	19 59						20 04	
Eaglescliffe	a						19 31																
Middlesbrough	a								19 53								←	←					
Darlington	d							19 19		19 36		19 50	19 56	20 00	20 00	20 00	20 00	20 00				20 07	
Durham	d									19 53		20 07	20 12	→	→	20 17	20 19	20 19				20 25	
Chester-le-Street	d												20 18										
Newcastle	a							19 46		20 08		20 20	20 29			20 30	20 32	20 32				20 38	
Hartlepool	a						19 53																
Sunderland	a						20 21												←				
Newcastle	d							19 51								20 36	20 35	20 35	20 36			20 41	
Morpeth	a															→	20 47	20 47	20 49			20 54	
Alnmouth for Alnwick	a																					21 10	
Berwick-upon-Tweed	a							20 34									21 20	21 20	21 21				
Dunbar 238	a																21 43	21 45	21 44				
Edinburgh 238	a							21 17									22 06	22 07	22 07			22 13	
	d																						
Haymarket 238	d																						
Motherwell	a																						
Glasgow Central	a																						
Stirling	a																						
Perth	a																						
Inverness	a																						
Inverkeithing	a																						
Kirkcaldy	a																						
Leuchars	a																						
Dundee	a																						
Arbroath	a																						
Montrose	a																						
Stonehaven	a																						
Aberdeen	a																						

A From Manchester Airport to Newcastle
B From Liverpool Lime Street to Newcastle
C until 15 July, from 14 October. From Reading to Newcastle
D To Manchester Piccadilly
E From Manchester Airport
F until 15 July, from 14 October. From Reading
G From Liverpool Lime Street
H from 9 September until 7 October. From Plymouth to Edinburgh
I from 22 July until 2 September. From Plymouth to Edinburgh
J until 15 July, from 14 October. From Newquay to Edinburgh
K from 9 September until 7 October. From Plymouth
L from 22 July until 2 September. From Plymouth
M until 15 July, from 14 October. From Newquay

Table T026-F

Sundays

20 May to 2 December

London - Humberside, Yorkshire, North East England and Scotland

Station		HT	EM	TP	XC	GR	TP	TP	XC	XC	XC	GR	GC	GR	XC	XC	XC	GR	TP	XC	XC	GR
		◇ A	◇ B	◇ C	◇ D		◇ C	◇ E	◇ F	◇ G	◇ H				◇ I	◇ J	◇ K		◇ C	◇ L	◇ M	
London Kings Cross	d	17 47				18 00						18 03	18 22	18 27				18 30				18 35
Stevenage	d	18u09																				18 57
Peterborough	a					18 46						18 50										
Norwich	d		16 54																			
Peterborough	d		18 26			18 48						18 52										
Grantham	a	18 51	18 56																			19 39
	d	18 52	18 58																			19 41
Newark North Gate	a											19 19						19 45				
	d											19 21						19 46				
Lincoln	a																					
Retford	d	19 13																				20 04
Doncaster	a	19 27										19 48						20 09				20 18
Selby	a	19 45																				
Hull	a	20 20																				
Sheffield	a		20 31																			
Pontefract Monkhill	a																					
Wakefield Kirkgate	a																					
Wakefield Westgate	d								19 43	19 43	19 51	20 08									20 33	20 39
Leeds	a								19 57	19 57	20 04	20 21									20 47	20 52
Mirfield	a																					
Brighouse	a																					
Halifax	a																					
Shipley	a																					
Bradford Forster Square	a																					
Bradford Interchange	a																					
Keighley	a																					21s19
Skipton	a																					21 34
Doncaster	d				19 20													20 10		20 19		
York	a				19 46	19 54							20 12	20 18				20 32		20 40		
Scarborough	a																					
Harrogate	a											20 55			←	←	←					
Leeds	d			19 13			19 39	19 51	20 09	20 09	20 09				20 09	20 09	20 09		20 13			
York	d			19 40	19 54	19 59	20 02	20 14	→	→	→		20 18	20 27	20 32	20 32	20 32	20 36	20 37	20 48		
Thirsk	d			19 58									20 34						21 02			
Northallerton	d			20 06				20 35					20 42					20 56	21 18			
Darlington	a				20 20	20 26	20 34	20 48						20 54	21 00	21 00	21 00	21 08		21 14		
Eaglescliffe	a												21 02									
Middlesbrough	a			20 38															21 46			
Darlington	d				20 22	20 28	20 35	20 49						20 56	21 01	21 01	21 01	21 10		21 15		
Durham	d				20 38		20 51	21 06						21 13	21 18	21 18	21 18	21 27		21 33		
Chester-le-Street	d						20 57	21 12														
Newcastle	a				20 51	20 55	21 08	21 22						21 26	21 30	21 31	21 31	21 40		21 45		
Hartlepool	a												21 22									
Sunderland	a												21 53									
Newcastle	d				20 56	21 00									21 37	21 34	21 34	21 45				
Morpeth	a																					
Alnmouth for Alnwick	a														22 01	21 59	21 59					
Berwick-upon-Tweed	a					21 43												22 27				
Dunbar 238	a																					
Edinburgh 238	a				22 18	22 25									23 03	23 03	23 03	23 10				
	d																					
Haymarket 238	d																					
Motherwell	a																					
Glasgow Central	a																					
Stirling	a																					
Perth	a																					
Inverness	a																					
Inverkeithing	a																					
Kirkcaldy	a																					
Leuchars	a																					
Dundee	a																					
Arbroath	a																					
Montrose	a																					
Stonehaven	a																					
Aberdeen	a																					

A To Beverley
B To Manchester Piccadilly
C From Manchester Airport
D until 15 July, from 14 October. From Reading. 🛒 to Newcastle
E From Liverpool Lime Street
F from 22 July until 7 October, not 9 September.
G 9 September. From Newquay to Edinburgh
H until 15 July, from 14 October. From Plymouth to Edinburgh
I from 22 July until 7 October, not 9 September. From Newquay. 🛒 to Newcastle
J 9 September. From Newquay. 🛒 to Newcastle
K until 15 July, from 14 October. From Plymouth. 🛒 to Newcastle
L until 15 July, from 14 October. From Reading
M from 22 July until 7 October. From Plymouth

Please note, Network Rail have stated that further updates to this timetable are possible during the validity period.

Table T026-F

Sundays

20 May to 2 December

London - Humberside, Yorkshire, North East England and Scotland

		EM	GC	GR	TP	XC	GR	GR	GC	GR	XC	XC	TP	EM	GR	HT	EM	GR	XC	GR	TP	XC	GR
		◇ A			◇ B	◇ C					◇ D	◇ E	◇ B	◇ F		◇	◇ A		◇ G		◇ B	◇ D	
London Kings Cross ⊖	d		18 53	19 00			19 03	19 06	19 22	19 30					19 35	19 50		20 00		20 05			20 35
Stevenage	d							19 28							19 57								20 57
Peterborough	a						19 50	19 57		20 17					20 26			20 46		20 52			21 26
Norwich	d	17 54															18 56						
Peterborough	d	19 22					19 51	20 01		20 18					20 27		20 30	20 48		20 53			21 27
Grantham	a	19 52						20 20							20 45	20 50	21 00						21 45
	d							20 22							20 46	20 51							21 46
Newark North Gate	a						20 18	20 36		20 47													21 58
	d						20 19	20 37		20 48													21 59
Lincoln	a							21 01															
Retford	d															21 13				21 32			
Doncaster	a		20 24				20 42		20 58	21 12					21 18	21 27				21 47			22 22
Selby	a															21 43							
Hull	a															22 18							
Sheffield	a																						
Pontefract Monkhill	a																						
Wakefield Kirkgate	a		20 55						21 23														
Wakefield Westgate	d					20 48	21 03				21 08			21 33	21 39				21 49	22 06		22 10	22 41
Leeds	a					21 02	21 17				21 22			21 49	21 52				22 02	22 19		22 24	22 55
Mirfield	a		21 08						21 38														
Brighouse	a		21 16						21 45														
Halifax	a		21 29						21 57														
Shipley	a																						
Bradford Forster Square	a																						
Bradford Interchange	a		21 45						22 13														
Keighley	a																						
Skipton	a																						
Doncaster	d									21 16		21 23											
York	a			20 47						21 37		21 45						21 53					
Scarborough	a																						
Harrogate	a																						
Leeds	d				20 52	21 08							21 21								21 51		
York	d			20 52	21 18	21a31				21 39		21 46	21 49					21 56			22 18		
Thirsk	d												22 12										
Northallerton	d				21 39								22 21					22 30			22 39		
Darlington	a			21 20	21 50					22 19		22 25						22 42			22 50		
Eaglescliffe	a																						
Middlesbrough	a												22 52										
Darlington	d			21 22	21 51					22 20		22 26						22 43			22 51		
Durham	d				22 07					22 38		22 43						23 01			23 07		
Chester-le-Street	d																				23 13		
Newcastle	a			21 50	22 22					23 07		23 12						23 30			23 38		
Hartlepool	a																						
Sunderland	a																						
Newcastle	d			21 52																			
Morpeth	a			22 06																			
Alnmouth for Alnwick	a			22 23																			
Berwick-upon-Tweed	a			22 47																			
Dunbar 238	a			23 11																			
Edinburgh 238	a			23 36																			
	d																						
Haymarket 238	d																						
Motherwell	a																						
Glasgow Central	a																						
Stirling	a																						
Perth	a																						
Inverness	a																						
Inverkeithing	a																						
Kirkcaldy	a																						
Leuchars	a																						
Dundee	a																						
Arbroath	a																						
Montrose	a																						
Stonehaven	a																						
Aberdeen	a																						

A To Nottingham
B From Liverpool Lime Street
C until 15 July, from 14 October. From Plymouth. to Leeds
D from 22 July until 7 October. From Plymouth
E until 15 July, from 14 October. From Reading
F From St Pancras International
G until 15 July, from 14 October. From Plymouth

Table T026-F

Sundays

20 May to 2 December

London - Humberside, Yorkshire, North East England and Scotland

		GR	XC	TP	XC	GR	EM	EM	GR	GR	GR	GR	GR	GR
			◇ A	◇ B	◇ C		◇ D	◇ E		F	G	F	G	
London Kings Cross ⊖	d	21 00				21 05			21 35	22 00	22 00	22 05	22 05	22 35
Stevenage	d								21 57					
Peterborough	a	21 46				21 52			22 26	22 47	22 47	22 51	22 51	23s25
Norwich	d						20 52							
Peterborough	d	21 48				21 53	22 23		22 27	22 48	22 48	22 53	22 53	
Grantham	a						22 53		22 46			23 11	23 13	23s46
	d								22 48			23 12	23 14	
Newark North Gate	a					22 20			23 00			23 24	23 26	23s58
	d					22 21			23 01			23 25	23 28	
Lincoln	a													
Retford	d								23 17					
Doncaster	a					22 48			23 35	23 41	23 41	23 53	00 01	00s28
Selby	a													
Hull	a													
Sheffield	a													
Pontefract Monkhill	a													
Wakefield Kirkgate	a													
Wakefield Westgate	d		22 47		23 03	23 10		23 53	23 59					
Leeds	a		23 02		23 17	23 24		00 08	00 12					01 31
Mirfield	a													
Brighouse	a													
Halifax	a													
Shipley	a													
Bradford Forster Square	a													
Bradford Interchange	a													
Keighley	a													
Skipton	a													
Doncaster	d									23 43	23 43	23 54	00 04	
York	a	22 57								00 08	00 10	00 17	00 34	
Scarborough	a													
Harrogate	a													
Leeds	d			22 52										
York	d	23 02		23 17						00 12	00 14			
Thirsk	d			23 40										
Northallerton	d	23 37		23 48						00s45	00s47			
Darlington	a	23 48		00 01						00s59	01s01			
Eaglescliffe	a													
Middlesbrough	a													
Darlington	d	23 50		00 02										
Durham	d	00 07		00 18						01s17	01s19			
Chester-le-Street	d			00 24										
Newcastle	a	00 36		00 48						01 48	01 50			
Hartlepool	a													
Sunderland	a													
Newcastle	d													
Morpeth	a													
Alnmouth for Alnwick	a													
Berwick-upon-Tweed	a													
Dunbar 238	a													
Edinburgh 238	a													
	d													
Haymarket 238	d													
Motherwell	a													
Glasgow Central	a													
Stirling	a													
Perth	a													
Inverness	a													
Inverkeithing	a													
Kirkcaldy	a													
Leuchars	a													
Dundee	a													
Arbroath	a													
Montrose	a													
Stonehaven	a													
Aberdeen	a													

A until 15 July, from 14 October. From Penzance
B From Liverpool Lime Street
C from 22 July until 7 October. From Penzance
D To Nottingham
E From St Pancras International
F from 24 June
G until 17 June

Scotland, North East England, Yorkshire and Humberside - London

Miles	Miles	Miles	Station		XC MX	GR	EM	GR	EM	GR	GR	TP	GR	XC	GR	TP	GR	GR	GR	TP	TP	XC	XC
					◇ A		B		◇ C			◇ D		◇ E		◇ D		F		◇ D	◇ G	◇ H	I
—	—	0	Aberdeen	d																			
—	—	16¼	Stonehaven	d																			
—	—	40½	Montrose	d																			
—	—	54¼	Arbroath	d																			
—	—	71¼	Dundee	d																			
—	—	79½	Leuchars	d																			
—	—	104½	Kirkcaldy	d																			
—	—	—	Inverkeithing	a																			
—	—	—	Inverness	d																			
—	—	—	Perth	d																			
—	—	—	Stirling	a																			
0	—	—	Glasgow Central	d																			
12¾	—	—	Motherwell	a																			
56	—	129¾	Haymarket 238	d	00 03																		
57¼	—	130½	Edinburgh 238	a	00 08																		
—	—	—		d																			
86½	—	—	Dunbar 238	d																			
114¾	—	—	Berwick-upon-Tweed	d																			
147	—	—	Alnmouth for Alnwick	d																			
165¾	—	—	Morpeth	d																			
181¾	—	—	Newcastle	a																			
—	—	—	Sunderland	d															05 40				
—	—	—	Hartlepool	d																			
—	—	—	Newcastle	d							04 44	04 48			05 26				05 58	06 02		06 25	06 25
190	—	—	Chester-le-Street	d																06 11			
195¾	—	—	Durham	d							04 59	05 04			05 39				06 12	06 18		06 38	06 38
217¾	—	—	Darlington	a							05 15	05 22			05 56				06 30	06 36		06 54	06 54
—	—	—	Middlesbrough	d												05 43					06 22		
—	—	—	Eaglescliffe	a																			
—	—	—	Darlington	d							05 17	05 23			05 58				06 31	06 36		06 56	06 56
231¾	—	—	Northallerton	d							05 28	05 42			06 09	06 13					06 50		
239½	—	—	Thirsk	d								05 50				06 21					06 58		
—	—	—	York	a							05 57	06 07			06 29	06 39			06 58	07 07	07 16	07 24	07 24
—	—	—	Leeds	a								06 31				07 04				07 31	07 43		
—	—	—		d																			
—	—	—	Harrogate	d																			
—	—	—	Scarborough	a																			
—	—	—	York	d		04 40					05 59				06 31				07 01			07 26	07 26
294¼	—	—	Doncaster	a		05 05					06 21				06 53							07 51	07 51
—	—	—	Skipton	d																			
—	—	—	Keighley	d																			
—	—	—	Bradford Interchange	d																			
—	—	—	Bradford Forster Square	d														06 30					
—	—	—	Shipley	d														06u37					
—	—	—	Halifax	d																			
—	—	—	Brighouse	d																			
—	—	—	Mirfield	d																			
—	0	—	Leeds	d				05 05	05 19	05 30			06 05	06 16			06 40	07 00					
—	10	—	Wakefield Westgate	d				05 18	05 32	05 43			06 18	06 28			06 53	07 13					
—	—	—	Wakefield Kirkgate	d																			
—	—	—	Pontefract Monkhill	d																			
—	—	—	Sheffield	d																		08a14	08a15
—	—	—	Hull	d																			
—	—	—	Selby	a																			
—	29¾	—	Doncaster	d		05 07		05 37	05a55	06 02	06 22		06 37	06a45	06 54		07 14						
311¾	—	—	Retford	d				05 51					06 51										
—	—	—	Lincoln	d																			
330¼	—	—	Newark North Gate	a		05 34		06 05		06 24	06 45		07 05				07 36						
—	—	—		d		05 36		06 06		06 25	06 46		07 06				07 37						
344¾	—	—	Grantham	a		05 48		06 17		06 36	06 57		07 17		07 25								
—	—	—		d		05 49	05 51	06 18		06 38	06 58		07 18		07 26								
374	—	—	Peterborough	a		06 09	06 23	06 38		06 58	07 18		07 39		07 46				08 09				
—	—	—	Norwich	d																			
—	—	—	Peterborough	d		06 10		06 39		06 59	07 19		07 40		07 49				08 12				
422¾	—	—	Stevenage	d																			
450¼	—	—	London Kings Cross ⊖	a		07 00		07 28		07 49	08 10		08 31		08 40		08 51	08 59	09 07				

A From Aberdeen
B From Nottingham to Spalding
C To St Pancras International
D To Liverpool Lime Street
E To Southampton Central
F West Riding Limited
G To Manchester Airport
H from 23 July until 5 October. To Plymouth
I until 20 July, from 8 October. To Reading

Scotland, North East England, Yorkshire and Humberside - London

Station		HT	GR	GR	GR	EM	GR	GR	XC	TP	GR	GR	TP	GC	TP	GC	XC	EM	GR	GR	GR	XC	XC
		◇ A				◇ B	C		◇ D	◇ E		F	◇ G		◇ E		◇ D	◇ H				◇ I	◇ J
Aberdeen	d																						
Stonehaven	d																						
Montrose	d																						
Arbroath	d																						
Dundee	d																						
Leuchars	d																						
Kirkcaldy	d																						
Inverkeithing	a																						
Inverness	d																						
Perth	d																						
Stirling	a																						
Glasgow Central	d																						
Motherwell	a																						
Haymarket 238	d																						
Edinburgh 238	a																						
	d											05 40								05 48		06 06	06 06
Dunbar 238	d																			06 10			
Berwick-upon-Tweed	d										06 00									06 34		06 50	06 50
Alnmouth for Alnwick	d										06 21									06 55		07 11	07 11
Morpeth	d										06 38									07 11			
Newcastle	a										06 52	07 02								07 26		07 38	07 38
Sunderland	d															06 45							
Hartlepool	d															07 10							
Newcastle	d				06 30				06 45		06 55	07 05	07 08		07 14		07 25			07 29		07 40	07 40
Chester-le-Street	d																						
Durham	d				06 44				06 57		07 08				07 27		07 38			07 42		07 53	07 54
Darlington	a				07 01				07 14		07 26				07 45		07 54			08 00		08 10	08 10
Middlesbrough	d									06 50													
Eaglescliffe	a															07 28							
Darlington	d				07 03				07 15		07 32				07 45		07 56			08 01		08 11	08 12
Northallerton	d				07 15					07 19						07 51							
Thirsk	d									07 30						08 00							
York	a				07 34				07 41	07 50	07 59		08 06		08 16	08 19	08 23			08 28		08 42	08 42
Leeds	a								08 08	08 17			08 31		08 48							09 08	09 08
	d																						
Harrogate	d																		07 34				
Scarborough	a																						
York	d				07 37						08 02					08 21	08 27			08 31			
Doncaster	a																08 50			08 54			
Skipton	d							06 55															
Keighley	d							07u07															
Bradford Interchange	d													06 55									
Bradford Forster Square	d																						
Shipley	d							07u17															
Halifax	d													07 08									
Brighouse	d													07 19									
Mirfield	d													07 25									
Leeds	d			07 15				07 40	08 11										08 15		08 45	09 11	09 11
Wakefield Westgate	d			07 28				07 53	08 23										08 30		08 58	09 23	09 23
Wakefield Kirkgate	d													07 42									
Pontefract Monkhill	d													08 00									
Sheffield	d								08a54								09a19					09a53	09a53
Hull	d	06 26					07 00																
Selby	a	07 00					07 34																
Doncaster	d	07 17		07 47			07 58	08 14						08 31					08 49	08 56	09 19		
Retford	d	07 40									08 35												
Lincoln	d		07 30																				
Newark North Gate	a		07 55				08 22	08 38												09 19			
	d		07 57				08 24	08 39												09 20			
Grantham	a	08 00		08 17			08 35												09 19				
	d	08 01		08 18		08 27	08 36											09 10	09 21				
Peterborough	a		08 26		08 43	08 59		09 06										09 36		09 47	10 08		
Norwich	d					10a44												11a12					
Peterborough	d		08 29		08 44			09 08												09 50	10 10		
Stevenage	d		08 59	09 04															10 06				
London Kings Cross ⊖	a	09 15	09 24	09 31	09 37		09 53	09 58			10 01	09 40		10 09		10 14			10 31	10 40	11 01		

A From Beverley
B From Mansfield Woodhouse
C The Hull Executive
D To Southampton Central
E To Manchester Airport
F The Flying Scotsman
G To Liverpool Lime Street
H From Nottingham
I until 20 July, from 8 October. To Plymouth
J from 23 July until 5 October. To Reading

Table T026-R

Mondays to Fridays
21 May to 7 December

Scotland, North East England, Yorkshire and Humberside - London

		TP	GR	TP	TP	HT	GC	EM	GR	GR	XC	XC	GR	XC	XC	TP	GR	GR	TP	EM	GR	GC	TP
		A	B	C	A			D			E	F		G	H	A			C	D			A
Aberdeen	d																						
Stonehaven	d																						
Montrose	d																						
Arbroath	d																						
Dundee	d																						
Leuchars	d																						
Kirkcaldy	d																						
Inverkeithing	a																						
Inverness	d																						
Perth	d																						
Stirling	a																						
Glasgow Central	d													06 01	06 01								
Motherwell	a													06 16	06 16								
Haymarket 238	d		06 13											06 57	06 57								
Edinburgh 238	a		06 17											07 01	07 01								
	d		06 26							06 56	07 00	07 00		07 10	07 10		07 30						
Dunbar 238	d													07 32	07 32								
Berwick-upon-Tweed	d		07 10								07 43	07 43					08 12						
Alnmouth for Alnwick	d										08 03	08 04											
Morpeth	d										08 18	08 19											
Newcastle	a		07 53							08 22	08 32	08 34		08 36	08 39		08 55						
Sunderland	d																					08 42	
Hartlepool	d																					09 08	
Newcastle	d		07 57	08 01	08 15					08 25	08 35	08 36		08 43	08 43		08 58		09 02				09 18
Chester-le-Street	d				08 24																		
Durham	d			08 14	08 31					08 38	08 48	08 49		08 55	08 55				09 15				09 31
Darlington	a		08 25	08 32	08 48					08 55	09 03	09 05		09 11	09 11		09 26		09 32				09 49
Middlesbrough	d	07 57														08 57							
Eaglescliffe	a																					09 26	
Darlington	d		08 27	08 32	08 49					08 57	09 05	09 06		09 12	09 12		09 27		09 34				09 49
Northallerton	d	08 25		08 43						09 08						09 25			09 45			09 50	
Thirsk	d	08 33														09 33						09 59	
York	a	08 51	08 54	09 07	09 20					09 28	09 32	09 35		09 42	09 42	09 51	09 54		10 07			10 16	10 21
Leeds	a	09 15		09 31	09 46									10 07	10 07	10 15			10 31				10 46
	d																						
Harrogate	d																						
Scarborough	a																						
York	d		08 57							09 30	09 35	09 36					09 57	10 02				10 27	
Doncaster	a									09 52	09 58	09 58						10 23					
Skipton	d																						
Keighley	d																						
Bradford Interchange	d						07 56																
Bradford Forster Square	d																						
Shipley	d																						
Halifax	d						08 09																
Brighouse	d						08 24																
Mirfield	d						08 31																
Leeds	d								09 16				09 45	10 11	10 11						10 15		
Wakefield Westgate	d								09 29				09 58	10 23	10 23						10 28		
Wakefield Kirkgate	d						08 55																
Pontefract Monkhill	d																						
Sheffield	d							08 38			10a21	10a22		10a54	10a54					09 37			
Hull	d					08 23																	
Selby	a					08 57																	
Doncaster	d					09 25	09 30		09 48	09 53			10 18					10 26			10 47		
Retford	d					09 39												10 40					
Lincoln	d																						
Newark North Gate	a									10 16								10 54					
	d									10 17								10 55					
Grantham	a					10 00		10 06	10 18									11 06		11 07	11 17		
	d					10 01		10 11	10 19									11 07		11 10	11 18		
Peterborough	a							10 42		10 46			11 07					11 27		11 39			
Norwich	d							12a15												13a13			
Peterborough	d									10 49			11 10					11 28					
Stevenage	d								11 04									11 58			12 03		
London Kings Cross ⊖	a		10 48			11 09	11 15		11 31	11 39			12 01				11 49	12 22			12 30	12 32	

A To Manchester Airport
B From Stirling
C To Liverpool Lime Street
D From Liverpool Lime Street
E until 20 July, from 8 October. To Reading
F from 23 July until 5 October. To Plymouth
G until 20 July, from 8 October. To Plymouth. from Edinburgh
H from 23 July until 5 October. To Southampton Central

Table T026-R

Mondays to Fridays
21 May to 7 December

Scotland, North East England, Yorkshire and Humberside - London

		GR	TP	XC	XC	GR	XC	XC	XC	TP	GR	TP	TP	HT	GR	EM	EM	GR	GR	GC	XC	GR
			A	B	C		D	E	F	A		G	A			H	I				J	
Aberdeen	d																					
Stonehaven	d																					
Montrose	d																					
Arbroath	d																					
Dundee	d						06 32	06 32														
Leuchars	d						06 46	06 46														
Kirkcaldy	d						07 21	07 21														
Inverkeithing	a						07 38	07 38														
Inverness	d																					
Perth	d																					
Stirling	a																					
Glasgow Central	d	06 48	07 10																			
Motherwell	a	07 03	07 25																			
Haymarket 238	d	07 48					08 00	08 00														
Edinburgh 238	a	07 52					08 04	08 04														
	d	08 00					08 09	08 09			08 30								09 00			
Dunbar 238	d																					
Berwick-upon-Tweed	d						08 52	08 52			09 12											
Alnmouth for Alnwick	d	09 00																				
Morpeth	d						09 25	09 25														
Newcastle	a	09 27					09 39	09 40			09 55								10 24			
Sunderland	d																					
Hartlepool	d																					
Newcastle	d	09 29		09 35	09 35		09 42	09 42			09 58	10 02	10 15						10 26		10 35	
Chester-le-Street	d												10 24									
Durham	d	09 42		09 49	09 49		09 55	09 55				10 15	10 34						10 39		10 48	
Darlington	a	10 00		10 05	10 06		10 11	10 11			10 26	10 32							10 56		11 05	
Middlesbrough	d									09 57												
Eaglescliffe	a								←													
Darlington	d	10 01		10 06	10 07		10 13	10 12	10 13		10 28	10 33							10 57		11 06	
Northallerton	d						→			10 25		10 45							11 09			
Thirsk	d									10 33												
York	a	10 29		10 33	10 33			10 42	10 42	10 51	10 55	11 07	11 19						11 28		11 33	
Leeds	a							11 08	11 07	11 15		11 31	11 46									
	d																					
Harrogate	d																					
Scarborough	a																					
York	d	10 32		10 35	10 35						10 57								11 31		11 35	
Doncaster	a	10 54		10 58	10 58														11 53		11 57	
Skipton	d																					
Keighley	d																					
Bradford Interchange	d																			10 22		
Bradford Forster Square	d																					
Shipley	d																					
Halifax	d																			10 35		
Brighouse	d																			10 47		
Mirfield	d																			10 55		
Leeds	d					10 45		11 11	11 11									11 15				11 45
Wakefield Westgate	d					10 58		11 23	11 23									11 28				11 58
Wakefield Kirkgate	d																			11 14		
Pontefract Monkhill	d																			11 34		
Sheffield	d			11a21	11a21			11a53	11a53							10 37	10 38				12a21	
Hull	d													10 33								
Selby	a													11 07								
Doncaster	d	10 57				11 19								11 25				11 47	11 55	12 08		12 19
Retford	d													11 39								
Lincoln	d																					
Newark North Gate	a	11 20																	12 17			
	d	11 21													11 56				12 18			
Grantham	a													12 00	12 07	12 10	12 10	12 17				
	d													12 01	12 08	12 12	12 12	12 18				
Peterborough	a	11 48				12 07									12 28	12 40	12 40		12 46			13 07
Norwich	d															14a13	14a13					
Peterborough	d	11 50				12 10									12 30				12 47			13 10
Stevenage	d														12 59			13 04				
London Kings Cross ⊖	a	12 39				13 01					12 48			13 09	13 23			13 31	13 39	13 44		14 01

A To Manchester Airport
B from 23 July until 5 October. To Plymouth
C until 20 July, from 8 October. To Southampton Central
D from 23 July until 5 October. To Reading
E until 20 July, from 8 October. To Plymouth. from Edinburgh
F from 23 July until 5 October. From Dundee to Reading
G To Liverpool Lime Street
H until 31 August, from 8 October. From Liverpool Lime Street
I from 3 September until 5 October. From Liverpool Lime Street
J To Reading

Please note, Network Rail have stated that further updates to this timetable are possible during the validity period.

Table T026-R

Mondays to Fridays

21 May to 7 December

Scotland, North East England, Yorkshire and Humberside - London

		XC	XC	TP	GR	GR	TP	TP	EM	GR	GR	XC	GR	XC	XC	TP	TP	GR	TP	TP	HT	GR	EM
		◇ A	◇ B	◇ C			◇ D	◇ C	◇ E			◇ F		◇ G	◇ H	◇ C	◇ C		◇ D	◇ C	◇		◇ E
Aberdeen	d																	07 52					
Stonehaven	d																	08 10					
Montrose	d																	08 33					
Arbroath	d																	08 49					
Dundee	d																	09 07					
Leuchars	d																	09 21					
Kirkcaldy	d																	09 45					
Inverkeithing	a																	10 00					
Inverness	d																						
Perth	d																						
Stirling	a																						
Glasgow Central	d	07 48	07 48											09 00	09 00	09 06							
Motherwell	a	08 03	08 03											09 14	09 14	09 23							
Haymarket 238	d	08 51	08 51											09 54	09 54			10 20					
Edinburgh 238	a	08 56	08 56											09 58	09 58			10 25					
	d	09 08	09 08		09 30						10 00			10 10	10 10			10 30					
Dunbar 238	d	09 29	09 29																				
Berwick-upon-Tweed	d	09 53	09 53		10 12									10 51	10 51			11 13					
Alnmouth for Alnwick	d										11 00												
Morpeth	d													11 22	11 22								
Newcastle	a	10 37	10 37		10 55						11 27			11 36	11 38			11 56					
Sunderland	d																						
Hartlepool	d																						
Newcastle	d	10 42	10 42		10 58		11 02	11 18			11 29	11 35		11 42	11 42			11 59	12 03	12 18			
Chester-le-Street	d							11 27															
Durham	d	10 54	10 54				11 16	11 34			11 42	11 49		11 54	11 54				12 16	12 31			
Darlington	a	11 11	11 11		11 26		11 33				12 00	12 06		12 11	12 11			12 27	12 33	12 49			
Middlesbrough	d			10 55													11 55						
Eaglescliffe	a																						
Darlington	d	11 12	11 12		11 27		11 34				12 02	12 07		12 12	12 12			12 29	12 34	12 49			
Northallerton	d			11 25			11 45										12 25		12 45				
Thirsk	d			11 33													12 33						
York	a	11 42	11 42	11 51	11 54		12 07	12 19			12 29	12 33		12 41	12 41		12 51	12 56	13 07	13 21			
Leeds	a	12 07	12 07	12 15			12 31	12 46						13 08	13 08		13 15		13 31	13 46			
	d																						
Harrogate	d																						
Scarborough	a																						
York	d				11 58	12 02					12 32	12 35						12 58					
Doncaster	a					12 24					12 54	12 58											
Skipton	d																						
Keighley	d																						
Bradford Interchange	d																						
Bradford Forster Square	d																						
Shipley	d																						
Halifax	d																						
Brighouse	d																						
Mirfield	d																						
Leeds	d	12 11	12 11							12 15			12 45	13 11	13 11								
Wakefield Westgate	d	12 23	12 23							12 28			12 58	13 23	13 23								
Wakefield Kirkgate	d																						
Pontefract Monkhill	d																						
Sheffield	d	12a53	12a53						11 38			13a21		13a53	13a53								12 38
Hull	d																				12 33		
Selby	a																				13 07		
Doncaster	d					12 25				12 47	12 57		13 19								13 25		
Retford	d					12 40															13 39		
Lincoln	d																						
Newark North Gate	a					12 54					13 19												
	d					12 55					13 20											13 54	
Grantham	a					13 06			13 07	13 17											13 59	14 05	14 05
	d					13 07			13 09	13 18											14 00	14 06	14 11
Peterborough	a					13 27			13 39		13 48		14 08									14 27	14 39
Norwich	d								15a11														16a13
Peterborough	d					13 30					13 50		14 10									14 30	
Stevenage	d					13 59				14 04												14 59	
London Kings Cross ⊖	a				13 47	14 23				14 31	14 39		14 59					14 51			15 09	15 23	

- **A** from 23 July until 5 October. To Southampton Central
- **B** until 20 July, from 8 October. To Plymouth. from Edinburgh
- **C** To Manchester Airport
- **D** To Liverpool Lime Street
- **E** From Liverpool Lime Street
- **F** To Southampton Central
- **G** until 20 July, from 8 October. To Penzance. from Edinburgh
- **H** from 23 July until 5 October. To Reading

Table T026-R

Mondays to Fridays

21 May to 7 December

Scotland, North East England, Yorkshire and Humberside - London

		GR	GR	XC	GR	XC	XC	TP	GR	GC	GR	TP	TP	EM	GR	GR	XC	GR	XC	XC	TP	TP
				◇ A		◇ B	◇ C	◇ D	E			◇ F	◇ D	◇ G			◇ H		◇ I	◇ J	◇ D	◇ D
Aberdeen	d					08 20	08 20															
Stonehaven	d					08 38	08 38															
Montrose	d					08 59	08 59															
Arbroath	d					09 15	09 15															
Dundee	d					09 35	09 35															
Leuchars	d					09 48	09 48															
Kirkcaldy	d					10 18	10 18															
Inverkeithing	a					10 32	10 32															
Inverness	d								07 55													
Perth	d								09 57													
Stirling	a								10 29													
Glasgow Central	d																		11 00	11 00	11 09	
Motherwell	a																		11 14	11 14	11 23	
Haymarket 238	d					10 51	10 51		11 13										11 54	11 54		
Edinburgh 238	a					10 55	10 55		11 17										11 58	11 58		
	d					11 06	11 06		11 30							12 00			12 08	12 08		
Dunbar 238	d					11 28	11 28															
Berwick-upon-Tweed	d					11 51	11 51												12 50	12 50		
Alnmouth for Alnwick	d					12 12	12 12									13 00						
Morpeth	d																					
Newcastle	a					12 38	12 38		12 53							13 27			13 34	13 34		
Sunderland	d									12 28												
Hartlepool	d									12 53												
Newcastle	d		12 25	12 34		12 41	12 41		12 56			13 00	13 18			13 29	13 35		13 42	13 42		
Chester-le-Street	d											13 09										
Durham	d		12 38	12 47		12 54	12 54					13 16	13 31			13 42	13 49		13 54	13 54		
Darlington	a		12 55	13 03		13 10	13 10		13 24			13 33	13 49			14 00	14 06		14 11	14 11		
Middlesbrough	d							12 57														13 57
Eaglescliffe	a									13 11												
Darlington	d		12 57	13 05		13 12	13 12		13 25			13 34	13 49			14 01	14 07		14 12	14 12		
Northallerton	d		13 08					13 25		13 32		13 45										14 25
Thirsk	d							13 33		13 44												14 33
York	a		13 28	13 31		13 42	13 42	13 51	13 54	14 01		14 07	14 21			14 29	14 33		14 42	14 42		14 51
Leeds	a					14 07	14 07	14 15				14 32	14 46						15 07	15 07		15 15
	d																					
Harrogate	d																					
Scarborough	a																					
York	d		13 30	13 35					13 58	14 06	14 02					14 32	14 35					
Doncaster	a		13 52	13 57							14 23					14 54	14 58					
Skipton	d																					
Keighley	d																					
Bradford Interchange	d																					
Bradford Forster Square	d																					
Shipley	d																					
Halifax	d																					
Brighouse	d																					
Mirfield	d																					
Leeds	d	13 15			13 45	14 11	14 11								14 15			14 45	15 11	15 11		
Wakefield Westgate	d	13 28			13 58	14 23	14 23								14 28			14 58	15 23	15 23		
Wakefield Kirkgate	d																					
Pontefract Monkhill	d																					
Sheffield	d			14a21		14a54	14a54							13 37			15a21		15a54	15a54		
Hull	d																					
Selby	a																					
Doncaster	d	13 47	13 55		14 19						14 26				14 47	14 56		15 19				
Retford	d										14 41											
Lincoln	d																					
Newark North Gate	a		14 18								14 55					15 18						
	d		14 19								14 56					15 20						
Grantham	a	14 17									15 07			15 07	15 17							
	d	14 18									15 08			15 11	15 18							
Peterborough	a		14 46		15 08						15 28			15 38		15 48		16 08				
Norwich	d													17a13								
Peterborough	d		14 49		15 10						15 30					15 49		16 10				
Stevenage	d	15 04									15 59				16 04							
London Kings Cross ⊖	a	15 31	15 40		16 01				15 49	16 08	16 23				16 33	16 38		16 59				

- **A** To Reading
- **B** from 23 July until 5 October. To Guildford
- **C** until 20 July, from 8 October. To Penzance. from Edinburgh
- **D** To Manchester Airport
- **E** The Highland Chieftain
- **F** To Liverpool Lime Street
- **G** From Liverpool Lime Street
- **H** To Guildford
- **I** from 23 July until 5 October. To Reading
- **J** until 20 July, from 8 October. To Penzance. from Edinburgh

◇ from Edinburgh ■ to Edinburgh

Please note, Network Rail have stated that further updates to this timetable are possible during the validity period.

Table T026-R

Mondays to Fridays

21 May to 7 December

Scotland, North East England, Yorkshire and Humberside - London

		GR	TP	TP	GR	EM	GR	GR	XC	HT	GR	XC	TP	TP	GR	GC	GR	EM	GR	XC	TP	TP	GR
			A	B		C			D			E	B	A				C		D	F	B	
Aberdeen	d	09 52																					
Stonehaven	d	10 10																					
Montrose	d	10 33																					
Arbroath	d	10 49																					
Dundee	d	11 07																					
Leuchars	d	11 23																					
Kirkcaldy	d	11 47																					
Inverkeithing	a	12 02																					
Inverness	d																						
Perth	d																						
Stirling	a																						
Glasgow Central	d																						
Motherwell	a																						
Haymarket 238	d	12 22																					
Edinburgh 238	a	12 26																					
	d	12 30						13 00				13 07			13 30								14 00
Dunbar 238	d											13 32											
Berwick-upon-Tweed	d	13 13													14 12								
Alnmouth for Alnwick	d											14 13											15 00
Morpeth	d																						15 15
Newcastle	a	13 56						14 22				14 39			14 55								15 30
Sunderland	d																						
Hartlepool	d																						
Newcastle	d	13 59	14 03	14 15				14 25	14 36			14 42		14 52	14 59					15 03		15 15	15 33
Chester-le-Street	d			14 24																			
Durham	d		14 16	14 31				14 38	14 48			14 54		15 05						15 16		15 28	15 46
Darlington	a	14 27	14 33	14 49				14 55	15 05			15 11		15 22	15 26					15 32		15 46	16 04
Middlesbrough	d												14 55										
Eaglescliffe	a																				←		
Darlington	d	14 28	14 34	14 49				14 57	15 06			15 12		15 23	15 27					15 33	15 23	15 46	16 05
Northallerton	d		14 45					15 08					15 25	→								15 58	
Thirsk	d												15 33										
York	a	14 55	15 07	15 21				15 28	15 32			15 42	15 51		15 55					16 01	16 04	16 21	16 32
Leeds	a		15 31	15 46								16 07	16 15							16 30	16 32	16 46	
	d																						
Harrogate	d																						
Scarborough	a																						
York	d	14 58						15 31	15 35						15 59		16 03						16 35
Doncaster	a							15 53	15 58								16 25						16 56
Skipton	d																						
Keighley	d																						
Bradford Interchange	d															14 49							
Bradford Forster Square	d																						
Shipley	d																						
Halifax	d															15 04							
Brighouse	d															15 17							
Mirfield	d															15 24							
Leeds	d						15 15				15 45	16 11							16 15	16 40			
Wakefield Westgate	d						15 28				15 58	16 23							16 28	16 52			
Wakefield Kirkgate	d															15 39							
Pontefract Monkhill	d															15 55							
Sheffield	d					14 38			16a21			16a53						15 37		17a20			
Hull	d									15 12													
Selby	a									15 48													
Doncaster	d						15 47	15 56		16 05	16 19					16 22	16 26		16 47				16 58
Retford	d									16 19							16 41						
Lincoln	d																						
Newark North Gate	a							16 18									16 55						17 20
	d				15 56			16 20									16 56						17 21
Grantham	a				16 07	16 08	16 17			16 40							17 07	17 06	17 17				
	d				16 08	16 11	16 18			16 41							17 08	17 11	17 19				
Peterborough	a				16 28	16 39		16 48			17 08						17 28	17 42					17 49
Norwich	d					18a13												19a16					
Peterborough	d				16 29			16 49			17 10						17 30						17 50
Stevenage	d				16 59		17 04										17 59		18 05				
London Kings Cross	a	16 50			17 23		17 31	17 40		17 47	18 01				17 52	18 07	18 27		18 31				18 39

A To Liverpool Lime Street
B To Manchester Airport
C From Liverpool Lime Street
D To Reading
E until 11 October, FX from 15 October. To Reading
F From Newcastle to Liverpool Lime Street

Table T026-R

Mondays to Fridays

21 May to 7 December

Scotland, North East England, Yorkshire and Humberside - London

		GR	XC	XC	TP	TP	GR	GC	TP	TP	GR	EM	GR	GR	XC	HT	GR	XC	TP	GR	GR	TP	TP
			A	B	C	C			D	C		E			F			G	C			D	C
Aberdeen	d																						
Stonehaven	d																						
Montrose	d																						
Arbroath	d																						
Dundee	d																						
Leuchars	d																						
Kirkcaldy	d																						
Inverkeithing	a																						
Inverness	d																						
Perth	d																						
Stirling	a																						
Glasgow Central	d		13 00	13 00	13 09																		
Motherwell	a		13 15	13 15	13 23																		
Haymarket 238	d		13 55	13 55																			
Edinburgh 238	a		13 59	13 59																			
	d		14 09	14 09			14 30											15 08		15 30			
Dunbar 238	d																	15 29					
Berwick-upon-Tweed	d		14 50	14 50			15 12													16 12			
Alnmouth for Alnwick	d																						
Morpeth	d																						
Newcastle	a		15 37	15 37			15 55											16 33		16 55			
Sunderland	d							15 30															
Hartlepool	d							15 54															
Newcastle	d		15 41	15 41			15 59		16 03	16 15				16 25	16 35			16 41		16 59		17 03	17 17
Chester-le-Street	d									16 24													17 26
Durham	d		15 54	15 54					16 16	16 31				16 38	16 48			16 54				17 16	17 33
Darlington	a		16 10	16 10			16 26		16 32	16 48				16 55	17 04			17 10		17 26		17 32	17 50
Middlesbrough	d					15 57													16 57				
Eaglescliffe	a							16 13															
Darlington	d		16 12	16 12			16 28		16 33	16 49				16 57	17 06			17 12		17 27		17 33	17 51
Northallerton	d					16 25		16 33	16 44					17 09					17 25			17 44	
Thirsk	d					16 33		16 43											17 33				
York	a		16 42	16 42		16 51	16 56	17 00	17 07	17 20				17 28	17 32			17 41	17 51	17 54		18 07	18 22
Leeds	a		17 07	17 08		17 15			17 31	17 46								18 09	18 15			18 31	18 49
	d																						
Harrogate	d																						
Scarborough	a																						
York	d						16 58	17 06						17 31	17 35					17 58	18 02		
Doncaster	a													17 52	17 57						18 24		
Skipton	d																						
Keighley	d																						
Bradford Interchange	d																						
Bradford Forster Square	d																						
Shipley	d																						
Halifax	d																						
Brighouse	d																						
Mirfield	d																						
Leeds	d	16 45	17 10	17 10									17 14				17 45	18 11					
Wakefield Westgate	d	16 58	17 22	17 22									17 27				17 58	18 23					
Wakefield Kirkgate	d																						
Pontefract Monkhill	d																						
Sheffield	d		17a52	17a52								16 37			18a20			18a54					
Hull	d															17 09							
Selby	a															17 45							
Doncaster	d	17 18											17 46	17 56		18 03	18 18				18 25		
Retford	d												18 00			18 17					18 40		
Lincoln	d																						
Newark North Gate	a													18 18							18 54		
	d										17 54			18 19							18 55		
Grantham	a										18 05	18 09	18 22			18 37					19 06		
	d										18 06	18 11	18 23			18 38					19 07		
Peterborough	a	18 07									18 27	18 38		18 47			19 07				19 27		
Norwich	d											20a19											
Peterborough	d	18 09									18 29			18 49			19 10				19 30		
Stevenage	d										18 59		19 07								19 59		
London Kings Cross	a	19 01					18 49	19 08			19 23		19 32	19 41		19 47	20 01			19 55	20 23		

A until 20 July, from 8 October. To Plymouth. from Edinburgh
B from 23 July until 5 October. To Reading
C To Manchester Airport
D To Liverpool Lime Street
E From Liverpool Lime Street
F To Reading
G To Southampton Central

Table T026-R

Mondays to Fridays
21 May to 7 December

Scotland, North East England, Yorkshire and Humberside - London

Station		EM	GR	GR	XC	GR	XC	XC	TP	TP	GR	TP	GC	TP	GR	GR	HT	GR	EM	XC	XC	TP
		◇ A	■	■	◇■ B	■	◇■ C	◇■ D	◇■ E	◇■ E	■	◇■ F	■	◇■ E	■	■	◇■	■	◇ A	◇■ G	◇■ H	◇■ E
Aberdeen	d																					
Stonehaven	d																					
Montrose	d																					
Arbroath	d																					
Dundee	d																					
Leuchars 8	d																					
Kirkcaldy	d																					
Inverkeithing	a																					
Inverness	d																					
Perth	d																					
Stirling	a																					
Glasgow Central 15	d						15 00	15 00	15 09													
Motherwell	a						15 15	15 15	15 23													
Haymarket 238	d						15 56	15 56														
Edinburgh 15 238	a						16 01	16 01														
	d			16 00			16 06	16 06			16 30					17 00					17 07	
Dunbar 238	d																				17 29	
Berwick-upon-Tweed	d										17 12										17 52	
Alnmouth for Alnwick	d						17 05	17 05								18 00						
Morpeth	d						17 19	17 19													18 24	
Newcastle 8	a			17 22			17 33	17 33			17 55					18 27					18 38	
Sunderland	d												17 30									
Hartlepool	d												17 56									
Newcastle 8	d			17 26	17 32		17 41	17 41			17 59	18 03		18 15		18 29				18 35	18 43	
Chester-le-Street	d				17 41									18 24								
Durham	d			17 39	17 48		17 54	17 54				18 16		18 31		18 42				18 48	18 55	
Darlington 7	a			17 56	18 05		18 10	18 10			18 26	18 32		18 49		19 00				19 05	19 12	
Middlesbrough	d									17 57												18 57
Eaglescliffe	a												18 16									
Darlington 7	d			17 58	18 06		18 12	18 12			18 27	18 33		18 49		19 01				19 07	19 13	
Northallerton	d			18 09						18 25		18 44	18 41									19 25
Thirsk	d									18 33			18 51									19 33
York 8	a			18 29	18 33		18 38	18 40		18 51	18 54	19 07	19 09	19 21		19 28				19 33	19 39	19 52
Leeds	a						19 09	19 09		19 15		19 31		19 47							20 08	20 16
	d																					
Harrogate	d																					
Scarborough	a																					
York	d			18 31	18 36						18 58		19 12			19 31				19 36		
Doncaster 7	a			18 53	18 58											19 52				19 58		
Skipton	d																					
Keighley	d																					
Bradford Interchange	d																					
Bradford Forster Square	d																					
Shipley	d																					
Halifax	d																					
Brighouse	d																					
Mirfield	d																					
Leeds 10	d		18 15			18 45	19 11	19 11							19 16			19 45			20 11	
Wakefield Westgate 7	d		18 28			18 58	19 23	19 23							19 29			19 58			20 23	
Wakefield Kirkgate 4	d																					
Pontefract Monkhill	d																					
Sheffield 7	d	17 45			19a21		19a51	19a51											19 37	20a21	20a53	
Hull	d																19 12					
Selby	a																19 47					
Doncaster 7	d		18 47	18 55		19 19									19 48	19 54	20 04	20 17				
Retford 10	d																20 18					
Lincoln	d																					
Newark North Gate 7	a			19 17												20 16						
	d			19 19												20 17						
Grantham 7	a	19 07	19 17												20 18		20 39		21 07			
	d	19 10	19 18												20 19		20 40		21 10			
Peterborough 8	a	19 40		19 46		20 09										20 45		21 04	21 37			
Norwich	d	21a13																	23a18			
Peterborough 8	d			19 51		20 11										20 46		21 05				
Stevenage 4	d		20 06	20 20							20 29				21 06	21 15						
London Kings Cross 15 ⊖	a		20 31	20 46		20 59					20 53		21 08		21 31	21 39	21 48	21 56				

A From Liverpool Lime Street
B To Bristol Temple Meads
C until 31 August, from 8 October, not from 23 July until 27 July. To Birmingham New Street
D from 23 July until 27 July, from 3 September until 5 October. To Birmingham New Street
E To Manchester Airport
F To Liverpool Lime Street
G To Birmingham New Street
H To Birmingham New Street. to Leeds

Table T026-R

Mondays to Fridays
21 May to 7 December

Scotland, North East England, Yorkshire and Humberside - London

Station		TP	GR	XC	GR	XC	TP	TP	TP	GR	GR	TP	TP	GR	XC	TP FX	TP	TP	TP	GR	GR FO	XC	XC
		◇■ A	■	◇■ B	■	◇■ C	◇■ D	◇■	◇■ A	■	■	◇■ D	◇■ A	■	◇■	◇■ E	◇■	◇■ D	◇■	■	■	◇■	◇■
Aberdeen	d		14 52																	18 18			21 31
Stonehaven	d		15 10																	18 36			21 49
Montrose	d		15 33																	18 59			22 12
Arbroath	d		15 49																	19 15			22 28
Dundee	d		16 07																	19 33			22 48
Leuchars 8	d		16 22																	19 47			23 01
Kirkcaldy	d		16 46																	20 11			23 31
Inverkeithing	a		17 01																	20 26			23 45
Inverness	d																						
Perth	d																						
Stirling	a																						
Glasgow Central 15	d					17 00	17 10								19 00							21 05	
Motherwell	a					17 15	17 24								19 15							21 22	
Haymarket 238	d		17 21			17 55									19 55					20 46			00 03
Edinburgh 15 238	a		17 26			18 00									19 59					20 50		22 21	00 08
	d		17 31			18 08					18 30			19 36	20 03					21 00	22 00		
Dunbar 238	d		17 54			18 30					18 52				20 24					21 24	22 22		
Berwick-upon-Tweed	d		18 18			18 54					19 18			20 17	20 48					21 48	22 46		
Alnmouth for Alnwick	d					19 14					19 42			20 40	21 09					22 11	23 09		
Morpeth	d										20 00			20 57						22 28	23 26		
Newcastle 8	a		19 02			19 40					20 15			21 11	21 35					22 42	23 54		
Sunderland	d																						
Hartlepool	d																						
Newcastle 8	d	18 53	19 05	19 35		19 42			20 03		20 17		21 00	21 15	21 36			22 00		22 45			
Chester-le-Street	d												21 09										
Durham	d	19 06		19 50		19 55			20 16		20 30		21 16	21 29	21 50			22 14		22 59			
Darlington 7	a	19 22	19 33	20 06		20 11			20 32		20 48		21 32	21 46	22 08			22 30		23 19			
Middlesbrough	d							19 57				20 57				21 57	21 57		22 57				
Eaglescliffe	a																						
Darlington 7	d	19 23	19 34	20 07		20 13			20 33		20 49		21 33	21 48	22 09			22 31		23 20			
Northallerton	d	19 34						20 25	20 44			21 25	21 44	21 59		22 27	22 27	22 43	23 25	23s46			
Thirsk	d							20 33				21 33				22 35	22 35						
York 8	a	19 57	20 01	20 32		20 40		20 54	21 07		21 16	21 51	22 07	22 19	22 35	22 53	22 53	23 06	00 07	00 14			
Leeds	a	20 31				21 08			21 31			22 15	22 31			23 17	23 17	23 30		00 43			
	d															23 25							
Harrogate	d																						
Scarborough	a																						
York	d		20 04	20 36							21 19			22 21									
Doncaster 7	a		20 26	20 59							21 40			22 43									
Skipton	d																						
Keighley	d																						
Bradford Interchange	d																						
Bradford Forster Square	d																						
Shipley	d																						
Halifax	d																						
Brighouse	d																						
Mirfield	d															23a47							
Leeds 10	d				20 45	21 11																	
Wakefield Westgate 7	d				20 58	21 23																	
Wakefield Kirkgate 4	d																						
Pontefract Monkhill	d																						
Sheffield 7	d			21a24		21a53																	
Hull	d									20 28													
Selby	a									21 02													
Doncaster 7	d		20 27		21 17					21a22	21 42			22 44									
Retford 10	d				21 32																		
Lincoln	d																						
Newark North Gate 7	a										22 04			23 07									
	d										22 05			23 08									
Grantham 7	a				21 54						22 16			23 19									
	d				21 55						22 17			23 20									
Peterborough 8	a		21 15		22 15						22 37			23 46									
Norwich	d																						
Peterborough 8	d		21 16		22 16						22 39			23 47									
Stevenage 4	d		21 45		22 45						23 08			00s28									
London Kings Cross 15 ⊖	a		22 08		23 09						23 30			01 03									

A To Liverpool Lime Street
B To Birmingham New Street
C To Birmingham New Street. from Edinburgh to Leeds
D To Manchester Airport
E To Manchester Piccadilly

Please note, Network Rail have stated that further updates to this timetable are possible during the validity period.

Scotland, North East England, Yorkshire and Humberside - London

	XC	GR	EM	GR	GR	GR	TP	GR	XC	XC	GR	TP	HT	GR	GR	GR	TP	TP	XC	XC	GR	GR
	A		B				C		D	E		C	F		G		C	H	I	J		
Aberdeen d																						
Stonehaven d																						
Montrose d																						
Arbroath d																						
Dundee d																						
Leuchars d																						
Kirkcaldy d																						
Inverkeithing a																						
Inverness d																						
Perth d																						
Stirling a																						
Glasgow Central d																						
Motherwell a																						
Haymarket 238 d	00 03																					
Edinburgh 238 a	00 08																					
d																						
Dunbar 238 d																						
Berwick-upon-Tweed d																						
Alnmouth for Alnwick d																						
Morpeth d																						
Newcastle a																						
Sunderland d																						
Hartlepool d																						
Newcastle d						04 44	04 48				05 26					05 59	06 02		06 23	06 23		
Chester-le-Street d																	06 11					
Durham d						04 59	05 04				05 39					06 12	06 18		06 38	06 38		
Darlington a						05 15	05 22				05 56					06 30	06 36		06 54	06 54		
Middlesbrough d												05 43						06 22				
Eaglescliffe a																						
Darlington d						05 17	05 23				05 58					06 32	06 36		06 56	06 56		
Northallerton d						05 28	05 42				06 09	06 13						06 50				
Thirsk d							05 50					06 21						06 58				
York a						05 57	06 07				06 29	06 39				06 59	07 07	07 16	07 23	07 23		
Leeds a							06 31					07 04					07 31	07 43				
d																						
Harrogate d																						
Scarborough a																						
York d		04 40				05 59					06 31					07 01			07 25	07 25		
Doncaster a		05 04				06 21					06 53								07 49	07 49		
Skipton d																						
Keighley d																						
Bradford Interchange d																						
Bradford Forster Square d															06 30							
Shipley d															06u37							
Halifax d																						
Brighouse d																						
Mirfield d																						
Leeds d				05 05	05 30			06 05	06 17	06 17				06 40	07 00							07 15
Wakefield Westgate d				05 18	05 43			06 18	06 29	06 29				06 53	07 13							07 28
Wakefield Kirkgate d																						
Pontefract Monkhill d																						
Sheffield d																			08a15	08a15		
Hull d													06 17									
Selby a													06 51									
Doncaster d		05 07		05 37	06 03	06 22		06 37	06a45	06a45	06 54		07 10	07 14								07 47
Retford d				05 51				06 51														
Lincoln d																					07 30	
Newark North Gate a		05 34		06 05	06 26	06 45		07 05						07 36							07 56	
d		05 35		06 06	06 27	06 46		07 06						07 37							07 57	
Grantham a		05 46		06 17	06 39	06 57		07 17			07 25		07 40									08 17
d		05 47	05 51	06 18	06 40	06 58		07 18			07 26		07 41									08 18
Peterborough a		06 07	06 25	06 38	07 00	07 18		07 39			07 46					08 10					08 27	
Norwich d																						
Peterborough d		06 10		06 39	07 03	07 19		07 40			07 49					08 20					08 30	
Stevenage d																					08 59	09 04
London Kings Cross a		06 57		07 28	07 51	08 08		08 28			08 37		08 47	08 51	08 59	09 08					09 21	09 29

A From Aberdeen
B From Nottingham to Spalding
C To Liverpool Lime Street
D until 21 July, from 13 October. To Southampton Central
E from 28 July until 6 October. To Plymouth
F From Beverley
G West Riding Limited
H To Manchester Airport
I from 13 October. To Reading
J until 21 July. To Reading

Scotland, North East England, Yorkshire and Humberside - London

	GR	EM	GR	GR	EM	XC	XC	XC	XC	TP	GR	GC	TP	GC	TP	GR	GR	XC	XC	GR	XC	XC
		A	B		A	C	D	E	F	G			H		G			I	J		K	L
Aberdeen d																						
Stonehaven d																						
Montrose d																						
Arbroath d																						
Dundee d																						
Leuchars d																						
Kirkcaldy d																						
Inverkeithing a																						
Inverness d																						
Perth d																						
Stirling a																						
Glasgow Central d																						
Motherwell a																						
Haymarket 238 d																						
Edinburgh 238 a																						
d																	05 48				06 06	06 06
Dunbar 238 d																	06 10					
Berwick-upon-Tweed d																	06 34				06 49	06 49
Alnmouth for Alnwick d																	06 55				07 11	07 11
Morpeth d																	07 10					
Newcastle a																	07 25				07 37	07 37
Sunderland d														06 45								
Hartlepool d														07 09								
Newcastle d	06 30					06 43	06 45		06 45		06 55		06 59		07 18		07 27	07 35	07 35		07 41	07 41
Chester-le-Street d																						
Durham d	06 43					06 58	06 58		06 58		07 08		07 12		07 31		07 40	07 47	07 47		07 55	07 55
Darlington a	07 00					07 14	07 14		07 14		07 25		07 29		07 45		07 58	08 04	08 05		08 10	08 10
Middlesbrough d										06 50												
Eaglescliffe a								←						07 29								
Darlington d	07 02					07 16	07 15	07 16	07 16		07 27		07 30		07 45		07 59	08 05	08 05		08 13	08 13
Northallerton d	07 14					→				07 20			07 41	07 48							→	→
Thirsk d										07 30				07 57								
York a	07 33						07 41	07 43	07 43	07 48	07 54		08 03	08 14	08 20		08 26	08 31	08 33			
Leeds a							08 08	08 08	08 08	08 16			08 31		08 48							
d																						
Harrogate d																07 35						
Scarborough a																						
York d	07 39										07 57			08 19			08 30	08 35	08 35			
Doncaster a																	08 51	08 57	08 57			
Skipton d				06 55																		
Keighley d				07u09																		
Bradford Interchange d												06 55										
Bradford Forster Square d																						
Shipley d				07u19																		
Halifax d												07 09										
Brighouse d												07 20										
Mirfield d												07 28										
Leeds d				07 38			08 11	08 11	08 11							08 15				08 45		
Wakefield Westgate d							08 23	08 23	08 23							08 30				08 58		
Wakefield Kirkgate d												07 43										
Pontefract Monkhill d												08 00										
Sheffield d							08a52	08a52	08a52									09a23	09a20			
Hull d			07 00																			
Selby a			07 34																			
Doncaster d			07 58	08 10								08 32				08 49	08 53			09 19		
Retford d											08 29											
Lincoln d																						
Newark North Gate a			08 24	08 32													09 15					
d			08 25	08 33													09 18					
Grantham a			08 36													09 19						
d		08 29	08 38		09 10											09 21						
Peterborough a	08 45	08 59	08 58	09 01	09 36												09 45			10 08		
Norwich d		10a43			11a15																	
Peterborough d	08 50		09 00	09 03													09 50			10 09		
Stevenage d																10 06						
London Kings Cross a	09 37		09 47	09 54							09 59	10 05		10 18		10 29	10 37			10 59		

A From Nottingham
B The Hull Executive
C from 28 July until 8 September. To Southampton Central
D from 13 October. To Plymouth. (buffet) from Leeds
E from 28 July until 8 September. From Newcastle to Southampton Central
F from 15 September until 6 October. To Southampton Central
G To Manchester Airport
H To Liverpool Lime Street
I until 21 July, from 13 October. To Southampton Central
J from 28 July until 6 October. To Plymouth
K from 8 September until 6 October. To Reading
L from 28 July until 1 September. To Reading

Table T026-R

Saturdays
26 May to 8 December

Scotland, North East England, Yorkshire and Humberside - London

		XC	XC	XC	TP	GR	TP	TP	HT	EM	GR	GR	GR	EM	XC	XC	XC	XC	XC	XC	XC	TP
		◇ A	◇ B	◇ C	◇ D		◇ E	◇ D	◇	◇ F				◇ F	◇ G	◇ H	◇ I	◇ J	◇ K	◇ L	◇ M	◇ D
Aberdeen	d																					
Stonehaven	d																					
Montrose	d																					
Arbroath	d																					
Dundee	d																					
Leuchars	d																					
Kirkcaldy	d																					
Inverkeithing	a																					
Inverness	d																					
Perth	d																					
Stirling	a																					
Glasgow Central	d																	06 01	06 01	06 01	06 01	
Motherwell	a																	06 15	06 15	06 15	06 15	
Haymarket 238	d																	06 57	06 57	06 57	06 57	
Edinburgh 238	a																	07 01	07 01	07 01	07 01	
	d	06 06				06 26						06 54			07 00	07 00	07 00	07 07	07 07	07 07	07 07	
Dunbar 238	d																	07 29	07 29	07 29	07 29	
Berwick-upon-Tweed	d	06 49				07 09									07 43	07 43	07 43					
Alnmouth for Alnwick	d	07 11													08 03	08 03	08 03					
Morpeth	d														08 18	08 18	08 18					
Newcastle	a	07 38				07 52						08 22			08 32	08 34	08 34	08 37	08 38	08 38	08 38	
Sunderland	d																					
Hartlepool	d																					
Newcastle	d	07 41				07 56	08 01	08 15				08 25			08 35	08 35	08 35	08 41	08 41	08 41	08 41	
Chester-le-Street	d							08 24														
Durham	d	07 55					08 14	08 31				08 38			08 48	08 48	08 48	08 55	08 55	08 55	08 55	
Darlington	a	08 10				08 24	08 32	08 49				08 55			09 04	09 06	09 06	09 11	09 11	09 11	09 12	
Middlesbrough	d				07 57																	08 57
Eaglescliffe	a		←	←																		
Darlington	d	08 13	08 13	08 13		08 25	08 32	08 50				08 57			09 06	09 06	09 06	09 13	09 13	09 13	09 13	
Northallerton	d				08 25		08 43					09 08										09 25
Thirsk	d				08 33																	09 33
York	a	08 40	08 42	08 43	08 51	08 53	09 07	09 20				09 28			09 32	09 34	09 34	09 40	09 40	09 40	09 40	09 51
Leeds	a	09 08	09 08	09 08	09 15		09 31	09 46										10 09	10 09	10 09	10 09	10 15
	d																					
Harrogate	d																					
Scarborough	a																					
York	d					08 56						09 30			09 35	09 35	09 36					
Doncaster	a											09 52			09 57	09 58	09 58					
Skipton	d																					
Keighley	d																					
Bradford Interchange	d																					
Bradford Forster Square	d																					
Shipley	d																					
Halifax	d																					
Brighouse	d																					
Mirfield	d																					
Leeds	d	09 11	09 11	09 11							09 16		09 45					10 11	10 11	10 11	10 11	
Wakefield Westgate	d	09 23	09 23	09 23							09 29		09 58					10 23	10 23	10 23	10 23	
Wakefield Kirkgate	d																					
Pontefract Monkhill	d																					
Sheffield	d	09a51	09a51	09a51						08 37				09 37	10a20	10a21	10a21	10a51	10a51	10a52	10a51	
Hull	d								08 23													
Selby	a								08 57													
Doncaster	d								09 25		09 48	09 56	10 18									
Retford	d								09 39													
Lincoln	d																					
Newark North Gate	a											10 19										
	d											10 20										
Grantham	a								10 00	10 06	10 18			11 05								
	d								10 01	10 11	10 19			11 05								
Peterborough	a									10 38		10 47	11 07	11 36								
Norwich	d									12a13				13a13								
Peterborough	d											10 49	11 10									
Stevenage	d										11 04											
London Kings Cross ⊖	a					10 47			11 09		11 29	11 37	12 02									

A until 21 July, from 13 October. To Plymouth
B from 8 September until 6 October. From Edinburgh to Reading
C from 28 July until 1 September. From Edinburgh to Reading
D To Manchester Airport
E To Liverpool Lime Street
F From Liverpool Lime Street
G until 21 July, from 13 October. To Reading
H from 28 July until 8 September. To Paignton
I from 15 September until 6 October. To Plymouth
J until 21 July. To Paignton. ⚹ from Edinburgh
K from 8 September until 6 October. To Southampton Central
L from 13 October. To Plymouth. ⚹ from Edinburgh
M from 28 July until 1 September. To Southampton Central

Table T026-R

Saturdays
26 May to 8 December

Scotland, North East England, Yorkshire and Humberside - London

		GR	TP	GC	GC	GR	TP	GR	GR	TP	XC	XC	GR	XC	XC	TP	GR	TP	TP	HT	GR	EM	GR
			◇ A				◇ B			◇ B	◇ C	◇ D		◇ E	◇ F	◇ B		◇ A	◇ B	◇		◇ G	
Aberdeen	d																						
Stonehaven	d																						
Montrose	d																						
Arbroath	d																						
Dundee	d													06 32	06 32								
Leuchars	d													06 46	06 46								
Kirkcaldy	d													07 21	07 21								
Inverkeithing	a													07 36	07 36								
Inverness	d																						
Perth	d																						
Stirling	a																						
Glasgow Central	d								06 48	07 10													
Motherwell	a								07 03	07 25													
Haymarket 238	d								07 48					07 56	07 56								
Edinburgh 238	a								07 52					08 01	08 01								
	d	07 30							08 00					08 06	08 06		08 30						
Dunbar 238	d																						
Berwick-upon-Tweed	d	08 12												08 50	08 50		09 12						
Alnmouth for Alnwick	d								09 01					09 12	09 12								
Morpeth	d																						
Newcastle	a	08 55							09 27					09 39	09 39		09 55						
Sunderland	d				08 28																		
Hartlepool	d				08 53																		
Newcastle	d	08 58	09 02				09 18		09 30		09 35	09 35		09 42	09 42		09 59	10 02	10 17				
Chester-le-Street	d																		10 26				
Durham	d		09 15				09 31		09 43		09 49	09 50		09 56	09 56			10 15	10 33				
Darlington	a	09 26	09 32				09 49		10 00		10 05	10 06		10 12	10 12		10 27	10 33	10 50				
Middlesbrough	d															09 57							
Eaglescliffe	a				09 12																		
Darlington	d	09 27	09 34				09 49		10 02		10 07	10 08		10 14	10 14		10 29	10 33	10 51				
Northallerton	d		09 45		09 43											10 25		10 45					
Thirsk	d				09 54											10 33							
York	a	09 54	10 07		10 10		10 21		10 29		10 33	10 35		10 41	10 41	10 51	10 56	11 07	11 22				
Leeds	a		10 31				10 46							11 08	11 08	11 15		11 31	11 46				
	d																						
Harrogate	d																						
Scarborough	a																						
York	d	09 57			10 13	10 06			10 31		10 35	10 37					10 59						
Doncaster	a					10 28			10 53		10 58	11 00											
Skipton	d																						
Keighley	d																						
Bradford Interchange	d			08 51																			
Bradford Forster Square	d																						
Shipley	d																						
Halifax	d			09 05																			
Brighouse	d			09 16																			
Mirfield	d			09 24																			
Leeds	d							10 15					10 45	11 11	11 11								11 15
Wakefield Westgate	d							10 28					10 58	11 23	11 23								11 29
Wakefield Kirkgate	d			09 40																			
Pontefract Monkhill	d			09 57																			
Sheffield	d										11a21	11a23		11a51	11a51							10 36	
Hull	d																			10 33			
Selby	a																			11 07			
Doncaster	d			10 25		10 32		10 49	10 57				11 19							11 25			11 48
Retford	d					10 47														11 39			
Lincoln	d																						
Newark North Gate	a					11 01			11 20														
	d					11 02			11 21												11 54		
Grantham	a					11 13		11 19												11 59	12 05	12 05	12 18
	d					11 14		11 21												12 01	12 06	12 13	12 19
Peterborough	a					11 34			11 48				12 09								12 27	12 40	
Norwich	d																					14a12	
Peterborough	d					11 36			11 51				12 11								12 30		
Stevenage	d					12 05		12 08													12 59		13 04
London Kings Cross ⊖	a	11 46		11 58	12 10	12 28		12 31	12 44				12 58				12 50			13 09	13 21		13 29

A To Liverpool Lime Street
B To Manchester Airport
C until 8 September, from 13 October. To Southampton Central
D from 15 September until 6 October. To Plymouth
E from 28 July until 6 October. To Reading
F until 21 July, from 13 October. To Plymouth. ⚹ from Edinburgh
G From Liverpool Lime Street

Please note, Network Rail have stated that further updates to this timetable are possible during the validity period.

Table T026-R

Saturdays
26 May to 8 December

Scotland, North East England, Yorkshire and Humberside - London

	GR	GC	XC	GR	XC	XC	TP	GR	GR	TP	TP	EM	GR	GR	XC	XC	XC	GR	XC	XC	TP
			A		B	C	D			E	D	F			G	H	I		J	K	D
Aberdeen d																					
Stonehaven d																					
Montrose d																					
Arbroath d																					
Dundee d																					
Leuchars d																					
Kirkcaldy d																					
Inverkeithing a																					
Inverness d																					
Perth d																					
Stirling a																					
Glasgow Central d					07 48	07 48													09 00	09 00	09 07
Motherwell a					08 03	08 03													09 14	09 14	09 21
Haymarket 238 d					08 52	08 52													09 57	09 57	
Edinburgh 238 a					08 57	08 57													10 02	10 02	
d	09 00				09 08	09 08		09 30						10 00					10 05	10 05	
Dunbar 238 d					09 29	09 29															
Berwick-upon-Tweed d					09 53	09 53		10 12											10 47	10 47	
Alnmouth for Alnwick d														11 00							
Morpeth d																			11 21	11 21	
Newcastle a	10 23				10 37	10 37		10 56						11 27					11 35	11 35	
Sunderland d																					
Hartlepool d																					
Newcastle d	10 25		10 35		10 44	10 44		10 58		11 02	11 17			11 29	11 35	11 35	11 35		11 42	11 42	
Chester-le-Street d											11 26										
Durham d	10 38		10 48		10 56	10 56				11 16	11 33			11 42	11 49	11 49	11 49		11 55	11 55	
Darlington a	10 56		11 04		11 13	11 13		11 26		11 33	11 50			12 00	12 05	12 06	12 06		12 11	12 11	
Middlesbrough d							10 55														
Eaglescliffe a																					
Darlington d	10 57		11 06		11 14	11 14		11 28		11 34	11 51			12 01	12 06	12 06	12 07		12 12	12 12	
Northallerton d	11 09						11 25			11 45											
Thirsk d							11 33														
York a	11 28		11 31		11 40	11 40	11 51	11 55		12 07	12 22			12 28	12 32	12 34	12 34		12 38	12 39	
Leeds a					12 08	12 08	12 15			12 31	12 47								13 09	13 09	
d																					
Harrogate d																					
Scarborough a																					
York d	11 31		11 35					11 58	12 03					12 31	12 35	12 35	12 36				
Doncaster a	11 52		11 57						12 25					12 53	12 58	12 58	12 58				
Skipton d																					
Keighley d																					
Bradford Interchange d		10 21																			
Bradford Forster Square d																					
Shipley d																					
Halifax d		10 35																			
Brighouse d		10 48																			
Mirfield d		10 56																			
Leeds d				11 45	12 11	12 11							12 15					12 45	13 11	13 11	
Wakefield Westgate d				11 58	12 23	12 23							12 28					12 58	13 23	13 23	
Wakefield Kirkgate d		11 14																			
Pontefract Monkhill d		11 32																			
Sheffield d			12a20		12a53	12a53						11 37			13a21	13a21	13a21		13a52	13a51	
Hull d																					
Selby a																					
Doncaster d	11 54	12 06		12 18					12 26				12 47	12 55				13 18			
Retford d									12 41												
Lincoln d																					
Newark North Gate a	12 16								12 55					13 17							
d	12 17								12 56					13 19							
Grantham a									13 07			13 06	13 17								
d									13 08			13 11	13 18								
Peterborough a	12 45			13 07					13 28			13 38		13 46				14 07			
Norwich d												15a13									
Peterborough d	12 46			13 10					13 30					13 50				14 10			
Stevenage d									13 59				14 04								
London Kings Cross ⊖ a	13 37	13 44		13 59				13 47	14 21				14 29	14 37				14 59			

A To Reading
B from 28 July until 6 October. To Southampton Central
C until 21 July, from 13 October. To Plymouth. from Edinburgh
D To Manchester Airport
E To Liverpool Lime Street
F From Liverpool Lime Street
G until 21 July, from 13 October. To Southampton Central
H from 28 July until 1 September. To Penzance
I from 8 September until 6 October. To Penzance
J from 28 July until 6 October. To Reading
K until 21 July, from 13 October. To Penzance. from Edinburgh

Table T026-R

Saturdays
26 May to 8 December

Scotland, North East England, Yorkshire and Humberside - London

	TP	GR	TP	TP	GR	EM	GR	GR	XC	GR	XC	XC	GC	TP	GR	TP	TP	HT	GR	EM	GR	GR
	A		B	A		C			D		E	F		A	G	B	A		H	C		I
Aberdeen d		07 52									08 20	08 20										
Stonehaven d		08 10									08 38	08 38										
Montrose d		08 33									08 59	08 59										
Arbroath d		08 49									09 15	09 15										
Dundee d		09 07									09 35	09 35										
Leuchars d		09 21									09 48	09 48										
Kirkcaldy d		09 45									10 18	10 18										
Inverkeithing a		10 00									10 32	10 32										
Inverness d															07 55							
Perth d															09 57							
Stirling a															10 29							
Glasgow Central d																						
Motherwell a																						
Haymarket 238 d		10 21									10 50	10 50			11 13							
Edinburgh 238 a		10 25									10 55	10 55			11 17							
d		10 30						11 00			11 08	11 08			11 30							
Dunbar 238 d											11 29	11 29										
Berwick-upon-Tweed d		11 12									11 53	11 53										
Alnmouth for Alnwick d											12 13	12 13										
Morpeth d																						
Newcastle a		11 56						12 23			12 39	12 39			12 53							
Sunderland d													12 18									
Hartlepool d													12 43									
Newcastle d		11 58	12 03	12 18				12 25	12 35		12 44	12 44			12 56	13 00	13 18					
Chester-le-Street d																13 09						
Durham d			12 16	12 31				12 38	12 48		12 56	12 56				13 16	13 31					
Darlington a		12 26	12 33	12 49				12 56	13 04		13 13	13 13			13 24	13 33	13 49					
Middlesbrough d	11 55													12 57								
Eaglescliffe a													13 01									
Darlington d		12 28	12 34	12 49				12 57	13 06		13 14	13 14			13 25	13 34	13 49					
Northallerton d	12 25		12 45					13 09					13 21	13 25		13 45						
Thirsk d	12 33												13 31	13 33								
York a	12 51	12 55	13 07	13 21				13 28	13 31		13 41	13 41	13 48	13 51	13 55	14 07	14 21					
Leeds a	13 15		13 31	13 46							14 08	14 08		14 15		14 32	14 46					
d																						
Harrogate d																						
Scarborough a																						
York d		12 57						13 31	13 35				13 52		13 57				14 05			
Doncaster a								13 53	13 57										14 29			
Skipton d																						
Keighley d																						
Bradford Interchange d																						
Bradford Forster Square d																						
Shipley d																						
Halifax d																						
Brighouse d																						
Mirfield d																						
Leeds d							13 15			13 45	14 11	14 11									14 15	
Wakefield Westgate d							13 28			13 58	14 23	14 23									14 28	
Wakefield Kirkgate d																						
Pontefract Monkhill d																						
Sheffield d						12 37			14a21		14a51	14a51								13 37		
Hull d																		13 31				
Selby a																		14 05				
Doncaster d							13 47	13 54		14 18								14 25	14 30		14 47	
Retford d																		14 39	14 46			
Lincoln d																						
Newark North Gate a								14 17											15 00			
d					13 54			14 18											15 01			
Grantham a					14 05	14 05	14 17											15 00	15 12	15 07	15 17	
d					14 06	14 09	14 18											15 01	15 13	15 15	15 18	
Peterborough a					14 26	14 37		14 45		15 07									15 33	15 44		
Norwich d						16a12														17a12		←
Peterborough d					14 30			14 48		15 10									15 37			15 37
Stevenage d					14 59		15 04												→		16 03	16 07
London Kings Cross ⊖ a		14 49			15 21		15 29	15 37		15 59			15 44		15 48			16 09			16 28	16 31

A To Manchester Airport
B To Liverpool Lime Street
C From Liverpool Lime Street
D To Reading
E from 28 July until 6 October. To Guildford
F until 21 July, from 13 October. To Penzance. from Edinburgh
G The Highland Chieftain
H To London Kings Cross
I From York

Table T026-R

Saturdays

26 May to 8 December

Scotland, North East England, Yorkshire and Humberside - London

		GR	XC	GR	XC	XC	TP	TP	GR	TP	TP	GR	EM	GR	GR	XC	GR	XC	TP	TP	GR	HT	EM
			◇ A		◇ B	◇ C	◇ D	◇ D		◇ E	◇ D		◇ F			◇ G		◇ G	◇ D	◇ E		◇	◇ F
Aberdeen	d								09 52														
Stonehaven	d								10 10														
Montrose	d								10 33														
Arbroath	d								10 49														
Dundee	d								11 07														
Leuchars	d								11 23														
Kirkcaldy	d								11 47														
Inverkeithing	a								12 02														
Inverness	d																						
Perth	d																						
Stirling	a																						
Glasgow Central	d				11 00	11 00	11 09																
Motherwell	a				11 14	11 14	11 23																
Haymarket 238	d				11 54	11 54			12 22														
Edinburgh 238	a				11 58	11 58			12 26														
	d	12 00			12 05	12 05			12 30						13 00			13 09			13 30		
Dunbar 238	d																	13 30					
Berwick-upon-Tweed	d				12 47	12 47			13 12												14 11		
Alnmouth for Alnwick	d	13 00																14 12					
Morpeth	d				13 18	13 18																	
Newcastle	a	13 26			13 32	13 32			13 56						14 23			14 38			14 55		
Sunderland	d																						
Hartlepool	d																						
Newcastle	d	13 29	13 35		13 44	13 44			13 59	14 03	14 15				14 25	14 35		14 44		14 52	14 59		
Chester-le-Street	d										14 24												
Durham	d	13 42	13 48		13 56	13 56				14 16	14 31				14 38	14 48		14 56		15 05			
Darlington	a	13 59	14 04		14 13	14 13			14 27	14 33	14 49				14 56	15 04		15 13		15 22	15 26		
Middlesbrough	d							13 57											14 55				
Eaglescliffe	a																						
Darlington	d	14 01	14 06		14 14	14 14			14 28	14 34	14 49				14 57	15 06		15 14		15 23	15 27		
Northallerton	d							14 25		14 45					15 09				15 25	→			
Thirsk	d							14 33											15 33				
York	a	14 29	14 32		14 40	14 40		14 51	14 55	15 07	15 21				15 28	15 31		15 40	15 51		15 54		
Leeds	a				15 08	15 08		15 15		15 31	15 46							16 08	16 15				
	d																						
Harrogate	d																						
Scarborough	a																						
York	d	14 31	14 35						14 58						15 31	15 35					15 57		
Doncaster	a	14 53	14 57												15 52	15 57							
Skipton	d																						
Keighley	d																						
Bradford Interchange	d																						
Bradford Forster Square	d																						
Shipley	d																						
Halifax	d																						
Brighouse	d																						
Mirfield	d																						
Leeds	d			14 45	15 11	15 11								15 15			15 45	16 11					
Wakefield Westgate	d			14 58	15 23	15 23								15 28			15 58	16 23					
Wakefield Kirkgate	d																						
Pontefract Monkhill	d																						
Sheffield	d		15a21		15a51	15a51							14 37			16a20		16a51					15 37
Hull	d																					15 31	
Selby	a																					16 05	
Doncaster	d	14 54		15 19										15 47	15 54		16 19					16 24	
Retford	d																					16 38	
Lincoln	d																						
Newark North Gate	a	15 17													16 16								
	d	15 18										15 54			16 17								
Grantham	a											16 05	16 06	16 18								16 59	17 04
	d											16 06	16 08	16 19								17 00	17 06
Peterborough	a	15 45		16 10								16 26	16 39		16 45		17 08						17 36
Norwich	d												18a13										19a13
Peterborough	d	15 51		16 12								16 30			16 50		17 10						
Stevenage	d											16 59		17 04									
London Kings Cross ⊖	a	16 44		16 59					16 50			17 21		17 29	17 37		17 59				17 47	18 09	

A To Guildford
B from 28 July until 6 October. To Reading
C until 21 July, from 13 October. To Plymouth. from Edinburgh
D To Manchester Airport
E To Liverpool Lime Street
F From Liverpool Lime Street
G To Reading

Table T026-R

Saturdays

26 May to 8 December

Scotland, North East England, Yorkshire and Humberside - London

		GR	GR	XC	TP	TP	GR	GC	GR	XC	XC	TP	TP	GR	GC	TP	TP	GR	EM	GR	GR	XC
				◇ A	◇ B	◇ C				◇ D	◇ E	◇ C	◇ C			◇ F	◇ C		◇ G			◇ A
Aberdeen	d																					
Stonehaven	d																					
Montrose	d																					
Arbroath	d																					
Dundee	d																					
Leuchars	d																					
Kirkcaldy	d																					
Inverkeithing	a																					
Inverness	d																					
Perth	d																					
Stirling	a																					
Glasgow Central	d									13 00	13 00	13 09										
Motherwell	a									13 15	13 15	13 23										
Haymarket 238	d									13 55	13 55											
Edinburgh 238	a									13 59	13 59											
	d						14 00			14 05	14 05			14 30							15 00	
Dunbar 238	d																					
Berwick-upon-Tweed	d									14 47	14 47			15 11								
Alnmouth for Alnwick	d						15 00															
Morpeth	d						15 15			15 21	15 21											
Newcastle	a						15 30			15 35	15 35			15 55							16 23	
Sunderland	d														15 29							
Hartlepool	d														15 53							
Newcastle	d			15 05		15 15	15 32			15 44	15 44			15 57		16 03	16 15				16 25	16 35
Chester-le-Street	d																16 24					
Durham	d			15 18		15 28	15 45			15 56	15 56					16 16	16 31				16 38	16 48
Darlington	a			15 34		15 46	16 03			16 13	16 13			16 24		16 32	16 48				16 56	17 04
Middlesbrough	d												15 57									
Eaglescliffe	a				←										16 12							
Darlington	d			15 35	15 23	15 46	16 04			16 14	16 14			16 26		16 33	16 49				16 57	17 05
Northallerton	d					15 58							16 25		16 31	16 44					17 09	
Thirsk	d												16 33		16 43							
York	a			16 01	16 04	16 21	16 31			16 40	16 40		16 51	16 53	16 59	17 07	17 24				17 28	17 32
Leeds	a			16 30	16 32	16 46				17 08	17 08		17 15			17 31	17 46					
	d																					
Harrogate	d																					
Scarborough	a																					
York	d	16 02					16 34							16 57	17 06						17 31	17 35
Doncaster	a	16 27					16 55														17 53	17 57
Skipton	d																					
Keighley	d																					
Bradford Interchange	d							15 21														
Bradford Forster Square	d																					
Shipley	d																					
Halifax	d							15 35														
Brighouse	d							15 49														
Mirfield	d							15 56														
Leeds	d		16 15	16 40					16 45	17 10	17 10									17 14		
Wakefield Westgate	d		16 28	16 52					16 58	17 22	17 22									17 27		
Wakefield Kirkgate	d							16 14														
Pontefract Monkhill	d							16 35														
Sheffield	d			17a19						17a51	17a51								16 37			18a20
Hull	d																					
Selby	a																					
Doncaster	d	16 28	16 49				16 57	17 08	17 20											17 46	17 55	
Retford	d	16 43																		18 00		
Lincoln	d																					
Newark North Gate	a	16 57					17 19														18 19	
	d	16 58					17 20											17 54			18 20	
Grantham	a	17 09	17 19															18 05	18 09	18 22		
	d	17 10	17 21															18 06	18 11	18 23		
Peterborough	a	17 32					17 48		18 09									18 27	18 38		18 49	
Norwich	d																		20a16			
Peterborough	d	17 34					17 51		18 10									18 30			18 51	
Stevenage	d	18 03	18 08															18 59		19 09		
London Kings Cross ⊖	a	18 27	18 30				18 44	18 47	18 59					18 50	19 09			19 21		19 31	19 44	

A To Reading
B From Newcastle to Liverpool Lime Street
C To Manchester Airport
D from 28 July until 6 October. To Reading
E until 21 July, from 13 October. To Plymouth. from Edinburgh
F To Liverpool Lime Street
G From Liverpool Lime Street

Please note, Network Rail have stated that further updates to this timetable are possible during the validity period.

Table T026-R

Saturdays

26 May to 8 December

Scotland, North East England, Yorkshire and Humberside - London

Station		GR	XC	TP	GR	GR	TP	TP	EM	GR	GR	XC	GR	XC	XC	TP	TP	GR	GC	TP	TP	HT	GR
		■	◇	◇	■	■	◇	◇	◇	■	■	◇	■	◇	◇	◇	◇	■	■	◇	◇	◇	■
			A	B			C	B	D			E		F	G	B	B			C	B		
Aberdeen	d																						
Stonehaven	d																						
Montrose	d																						
Arbroath	d																						
Dundee	d																						
Leuchars	d																						
Kirkcaldy	d																						
Inverkeithing	a																						
Inverness	d																						
Perth	d																						
Stirling	a																						
Glasgow Central	d													15 00	15 00	15 09							
Motherwell	a													15 15	15 15	15 23							
Haymarket 238	d													15 56	15 56								
Edinburgh 238	a													16 00	16 00								
	d		15 08		15 30						16 00			16 05	16 05			16 30					
Dunbar 238	d		15 29																				
Berwick-upon-Tweed	d				16 12													17 12					
Alnmouth for Alnwick	d													17 05	17 05								
Morpeth	d													17 19	17 19								
Newcastle	a		16 33		16 55						17 23			17 33	17 33			17 55					
Sunderland	d																		17 29				
Hartlepool	d																		17 54				
Newcastle	d		16 44		16 59		17 03	17 17			17 25	17 32		17 44	17 44			17 58		18 03	18 15		
Chester-le-Street	d							17 26				17 41									18 24		
Durham	d		16 56				17 16	17 33			17 38	17 48		17 56	17 56					18 16	18 31		
Darlington	a		17 13		17 26		17 32	17 50			17 56	18 05		18 13	18 13			18 25		18 32	18 49		
Middlesbrough	d			16 57													17 57						
Eaglescliffe	a																		18 13				
Darlington	d		17 14		17 27		17 33	17 51			17 57	18 06		18 14	18 14			18 26		18 33	18 49		
Northallerton	d			17 25			17 44				18 09						18 25		18 32	18 44			
Thirsk	d			17 33													18 33		18 43				
York	a		17 40	17 51	17 54		18 07	18 22			18 28	18 31		18 40	18 40		18 51	18 53	18 59	19 07	19 21		
Leeds	a		18 08	18 15			18 31	18 49						19 09	19 09		19 15			19 31	19 47		
	d																						
Harrogate	d																						
Scarborough	a																						
York	d				17 58	18 02					18 31	18 35						18 56	19 02				
Doncaster	a					18 23					18 52	18 56											
Skipton	d																						
Keighley	d																						
Bradford Interchange	d																						
Bradford Forster Square	d																						
Shipley	d																						
Halifax	d																						
Brighouse	d																						
Mirfield	d																						
Leeds	d	17 45	18 11							18 15			18 45	19 11	19 11								19 16
Wakefield Westgate	d	17 58	18 23							18 28			18 58	19 23	19 23								19 29
Wakefield Kirkgate	d																						
Pontefract Monkhill	d																						
Sheffield	d		18a52						17 41			19a20		19a51	19a51								
Hull	d																					18 34	
Selby	a																					19 08	
Doncaster	d	18 19				18 25				18 47	18 56		19 23									19 27	19 48
Retford	d					18 39																19 41	
Lincoln	d																						
Newark North Gate	a					18 53					19 18												
	d					18 54					19 19												
Grantham	a					19 05			19 08	19 18												20 02	20 18
	d					19 06			19 09	19 19												20 04	20 19
Peterborough	a	19 08				19 26			19 39		19 47		20 12										
Norwich	d								21a13														
Peterborough	d	19 10				19 28					19 51		20 14										
Stevenage	d					19 59				20 04	20 20							20 29					21 04
London Kings Cross ⊖	a	19 59			19 47	20 21				20 29	20 45		21 07					20 51	20 59			21 14	21 29

A To Southampton Central
B To Manchester Airport
C To Liverpool Lime Street
D From Liverpool Lime Street
E To Bristol Temple Meads
F from 28 July until 6 October. To Birmingham New Street
G until 21 July, from 13 October. To Bristol Temple Meads. ✕ from Edinburgh

Table T026-R

Saturdays

26 May to 8 December

Scotland, North East England, Yorkshire and Humberside - London

Station		GR	GR	EM	XC	XC	XC	TP	TP	GR	XC	GR	XC	TP	GR	TP	TP	TP	GR	TP	XC	GR
		■	■	◇	◇	◇	◇	◇	◇	■	◇	■	◇	◇	■	◇	◇	◇	■	◇	◇	■
				A	B	C	D	E	F		B		G	E			F	E		F		
Aberdeen	d									14 52												
Stonehaven	d									15 10												
Montrose	d									15 33												
Arbroath	d									15 49												
Dundee	d									16 07												
Leuchars	d									16 22												
Kirkcaldy	d									16 46												
Inverkeithing	a									17 01												
Inverness	d																					
Perth	d																					
Stirling	a																					
Glasgow Central	d												17 00	17 09							19 00	
Motherwell	a												17 15	17 23							19 14	
Haymarket 238	d									17 21			17 55								19 53	
Edinburgh 238	a									17 26			18 00								20 00	
	d	17 00				17 08	17 08			17 31			18 08		18 30				19 00			20 00
Dunbar 238	d					17 31	17 31			17 54			18 30						19 21			20 22
Berwick-upon-Tweed	d					17 54	17 54			18 18			18 53		19 12				19 45			20 46
Alnmouth for Alnwick	d	18 00											19 14						20 08			21 09
Morpeth	d																		20 25			21 26
Newcastle	a	18 26				18 37	18 37			19 02			19 40		19 55				20 41			21 40
Sunderland	d																					
Hartlepool	d																					
Newcastle	d	18 29			18 36	18 44	18 44		18 53	19 04	19 35		19 45				20 00		20 43	21 00		
Chester-le-Street	d																20 09			21 09		
Durham	d	18 42			18 49	18 56	18 56		19 06		19 50		19 57				20 16		20 58	21 16		
Darlington	a	18 59			19 05	19 13	19 13		19 22	19 32	20 06		20 14				20 32		21 15	21 32		
Middlesbrough	d							18 57								20 03		20 52				
Eaglescliffe	a																					
Darlington	d	19 01			19 07	19 14	19 14		19 23	19 34	20 07		20 15				20 33		21 18	21 33		
Northallerton	d							19 25	19 34							20 32	20 44	21 20	21 31	21 44		
Thirsk	d							19 33								20 40		21 28				
York	a	19 28			19 33	19 40	19 40	19 51	19 57	20 01	20 33		20 41			21 04	21 07	21 50	21 51	22 07		
Leeds	a					20 08	20 08	20 16	20 31				21 08				21 31	22 15		22 31		
	d																					
Harrogate	d																					
Scarborough	a																					
York	d	19 31			19 36					20 03	20 35								21 55			
Doncaster	a	19 52			19 58					20 25	20 57								22 16			
Skipton	d																					
Keighley	d																					
Bradford Interchange	d																					
Bradford Forster Square	d																					
Shipley	d																					
Halifax	d																					
Brighouse	d																					
Mirfield	d																					
Leeds	d		19 45			20 11	20 11					20 15	21 11									
Wakefield Westgate	d		19 58			20 23	20 23					20 28	21 23									
Wakefield Kirkgate	d																					
Pontefract Monkhill	d																					
Sheffield	d			19 37	20a21	20a52	20a52				21a21		21a52									
Hull	d																					
Selby	a																					
Doncaster	d	19 54	20 17							20 27		20 48										
Retford	d											21 02										
Lincoln	d																					
Newark North Gate	a	20 16										21 16										
	d	20 17										21 17										
Grantham	a			21 06								21 28										
	d			21 07								21 29										
Peterborough	a	20 45	21 04	21 39						21 16		21 49										
Norwich	d			23a19																		
Peterborough	d	20 51	21 05							21 20		21 50										
Stevenage	d	21 20								21 50												
London Kings Cross ⊖	a	21 42	21 52							22 12		22 37										

A From Liverpool Lime Street
B To Birmingham New Street
C until 21 July, from 13 October. To Birmingham New Street. ✕ to Leeds
D from 28 July until 6 October. To Birmingham New Street
E To Manchester Airport
F To Liverpool Lime Street
G To Birmingham New Street. ✕ from Edinburgh to Leeds

Table T026-R

Scotland, North East England, Yorkshire and Humberside - London

Saturdays
26 May to 8 December

		XC	XC	TP	TP	TP	TP
		◇■	◇■	◇■	◇■ A	■	◇■
Aberdeen	d		21 31				
Stonehaven	d		21 49				
Montrose	d		22 12				
Arbroath	d		22 28				
Dundee	d		22 48				
Leuchars ■	d		23 02				
Kirkcaldy	d		23 32				
Inverkeithing	a		23 46				
Inverness	d						
Perth	d						
Stirling	a						
Glasgow Central ■	d	21 05					
Motherwell	a						
Haymarket 238	d	21 55	00 03				
Edinburgh ■ 238	a	22 00	00 08				
	d						
Dunbar 238	d						
Berwick-upon-Tweed	d						
Alnmouth for Alnwick	d						
Morpeth	d						
Newcastle ■	a						
Sunderland	d						
Hartlepool	d						
Newcastle ■	d				21 58	22 30	
Chester-le-Street	d				22 07	22 40	
Durham	d				22 14	22a46	
Darlington ■	a				22 30		
Middlesbrough	d			21 57			22 43
Eaglescliffe	a						
Darlington ■	d				22 31		
Northallerton	d			22 25	22 43		23 10
Thirsk	d			22 33			
York ■	a			22 51	23 06		23 32
Leeds	a			23 15	23 30		
	d						
Harrogate	d						
Scarborough	a						
York	d						
Doncaster ■	a						
Skipton	d						
Keighley	d						
Bradford Interchange	d						
Bradford Forster Square	d						
Shipley	d						
Halifax	d						
Brighouse	d						
Mirfield	d						
Leeds ■	d						
Wakefield Westgate ■	d						
Wakefield Kirkgate ■	d						
Pontefract Monkhill	d						
Sheffield ■	d						
Hull	d						
Selby	a						
Doncaster ■	d						
Retford ■	d						
Lincoln	d						
Newark North Gate ■	a						
	d						
Grantham ■	a						
	d						
Peterborough ■	a						
Norwich	d						
Peterborough ■	d						
Stevenage ■	d						
London Kings Cross ■ ⊖	a						

A To Manchester Piccadilly

Table T026-R

Scotland, North East England, Yorkshire and Humberside - London

Sundays
20 May to 2 December

		XC	GC	GR	GR	GC	GC	GR	TP	GR	TP	XC	GR	EM	HT	GR	TP	TP	GR	XC	GR	GR	XC
		◇■ A	B	■	■	■ C	■ B	■	◇■ D	■	◇■ E	◇■ F	■	◇ G	◇■	■	◇■ D	◇■ H	■	◇■ I	■	■	J
Aberdeen	d																						
Stonehaven	d																						
Montrose	d																						
Arbroath	d																						
Dundee	d																						
Leuchars ■	d																						
Kirkcaldy	d																						
Inverkeithing	a																						
Inverness	d																						
Perth	d																						
Stirling	a																						
Glasgow Central ■	d																						10 35
Motherwell	a																						11 05
Haymarket 238	d	00 03																					
Edinburgh ■ 238	a	00 08																					
	d																						
Dunbar 238	d																						
Berwick-upon-Tweed	d																						
Alnmouth for Alnwick	d																						
Morpeth	d																						
Newcastle ■	a																						
Sunderland	d																						
Hartlepool	d																						
Newcastle ■	d							07 54	08 00							08 55	09 03	09 17				09 25	
Chester-le-Street	d																	09 26					
Durham	d							08 08	08 13							09 08	09 16	09 33				09 38	
Darlington ■	a							08 26	08 30							09 25	09 33	09 50				09 55	
Middlesbrough	d										08 57												
Eaglescliffe	a																						
Darlington ■	d							08 27	08 31							09 28	09 34	09 51				09 57	
Northallerton	d								08 42		09 25						09 45					10 08	
Thirsk	d								08 50		09 33												
York ■	a							08 54	09 08		09 51					09 55	10 07	10 22				10 28	
Leeds	a								09 32		10 16						10 31	10 46					
	d																						
Harrogate	d																						
Scarborough	a																						
York	d			08 00				08 58								09 57				09 33		10 30	
Doncaster ■	a			08 21																		10 52	
Skipton	d																						
Keighley	d																						
Bradford Interchange	d					07 55	08 10																
Bradford Forster Square	d																						
Shipley	d																						
Halifax	d		07 37			08 10																	
Brighouse	d		07 57			08 21																	
Mirfield	d		08 12			08 28																	
Leeds ■	d				08 05					08 43		09 00	09 05						09 40	09 59	10 05		
Wakefield Westgate ■	d				08 18					08 56		09 11	09 18						09 53	10 12	10 18		
Wakefield Kirkgate ■	d		08a37			08 46	08 46																
Pontefract Monkhill	d																						
Sheffield ■	d																						
Hull	d														09 06								
Selby	a														09 39								
Doncaster ■	d			08 23	08 37	09 11	09 11			09 20		09a29	09 39		10 00					10a29	10 37	10 53	
Retford ■	d				08 51										10 14				10 22		10 52		
Lincoln	d																						
Newark North Gate ■	a				09 05								10 01						10 36		11 06	11 16	
	d				09 06								10 02						10 41		11 07	11 17	
Grantham ■	a				09 17								10 13		10 34						11 18		
	d				09 18								10 14	10 29	10 35						11 20		
Peterborough ■	a			09 10	09 38			10 03		10 07			10 34	11 06		11 05			11 09		11 40	11 44	
Norwich	d													12a52									
Peterborough ■	d			09 11	09 42			10 05		10 11			10 36			11 06			11 10		11 42	11 51	
Stevenage ■	d			09 40									11 05										
London Kings Cross ■ ⊖	a			10 04	10 31	10 40	10 40	10 52		11 06			11 31		11 41	11 53			11 58		12 31	12 38	

A not 20 May. From Aberdeen
B from 28 October
C until 21 October
D To Liverpool Lime Street
E To Manchester Oxford Road
F To Plymouth
G until 9 September. From Nottingham
H To Manchester Airport
I To Birmingham New Street
J until 9 September

Please note, Network Rail have stated that further updates to this timetable are possible during the validity period.

Table T026-R

Sundays

20 May to 2 December

Scotland, North East England, Yorkshire and Humberside - London

Station		GR	XC ◇A	TP ◇B	GC	GR	TP ◇C	TP ◇D	GR	GR	EM ◇E	HT ◇F	GR	XC ◇G	XC ◇H	TP ◇D	GR	TP ◇C	TP ◇D	EM ◇I	GR	GC	GR
Aberdeen	d																						
Stonehaven	d																						
Montrose	d																						
Arbroath	d																						
Dundee	d																						
Leuchars	d																						
Kirkcaldy	d																						
Inverkeithing	a																						
Inverness	d																						
Perth	d																						
Stirling	a																						
Glasgow Central	d																						
Motherwell	a																						
Haymarket 238	d																						
Edinburgh 238	a																						
	d									09 00				09 08	09 08		09 30				10 00		
Dunbar 238	d																						
Berwick-upon-Tweed	d													09 51	09 51		10 13						
Alnmouth for Alnwick	d																				11 00		
Morpeth	d																						
Newcastle	a									10 23				10 35	10 35		10 56				11 27		
Sunderland	d				09 20																		
Hartlepool	d				09 45																		
Newcastle	d		09 35			10 00	10 04	10 18		10 28				10 39	10 39		10 59	11 03	11 17		11 29		
Chester-le-Street	d							10 27											11 26				
Durham	d		09 47				10 17	10 34		10 41				10 53	10 53			11 16	11 33		11 42		
Darlington	a		10 04			10 27	10 34	10 50		10 58				11 08	11 08		11 27	11 33	11 50		12 00		
Middlesbrough	d			09 52												10 57							
Eaglescliffe	a				10 06																		
Darlington	d		10 05			10 28	10 35	10 51		11 00				11 10	11 10		11 28	11 34	11 51		12 01		
Northallerton	d			10 20	10 25		10 46			11 12						11 25		11 45					
Thirsk	d			10 28	10 34											11 33							
York	a		10 31	10 46	10 51	10 55	11 08	11 22		11 31				11 38	11 38	11 51	11 55	12 07	12 22		12 28		
Leeds	a		10 57	11 15			11 32	11 46						12 09	12 09	12 15		12 31	12 47				
	d																						
Harrogate	d																						
Scarborough	a																						
York	d				10 53	10 58				11 34							11 58				12 31		
Doncaster	a									11 55											12 52		
Skipton	d																						
Keighley	d																						
Bradford Interchange	d																					12 05	
Bradford Forster Square	d																						
Shipley	d																						
Halifax	d																					12 19	
Brighouse	d																					12 30	
Mirfield	d																					12 39	
Leeds	d	10 45	11 00						11 05				12 05	12 11	12 11								13 05
Wakefield Westgate	d	10 58	11 12						11 18				12 18	12 24	12 24								13 18
Wakefield Kirkgate	d																					12 56	
Pontefract Monkhill	d																						
Sheffield	d										1C 48			12a51									
Hull	d											11 13											
Selby	a											11 46											
Doncaster	d	11 17	11a28						11 39	11 57		12 04	12 37		12a41						12 54	13 21	13 37
Retford	d	11 34								12 11		12 18											
Lincoln	d																						
Newark North Gate	a								12 01				12 59								13 16		13 59
	d								12 03				13 00								13 17		14 00
Grantham	a								12 14		12 13	12 38	13 11										14 11
	d								12 15		12 23	12 39	13 12							13 15			14 12
Peterborough	a					12 02			12 36	12 50	12 54		13 32							13 41	13 45		14 32
Norwich	d										14a28									15a24			
Peterborough	d					12 04			12 39	12 51			13 34								13 51		14 34
Stevenage	d								13 08														15 03
London Kings Cross	a	12 57			12 42	12 51			13 31	13 38		13 43	14 21				13 47				14 38	14 54	15 25

A To Bristol Temple Meads
B To Manchester Oxford Road
C To Liverpool Lime Street
D To Manchester Airport
E until 9 September
F From Beverley
G until 15 July, from 14 October. To Plymouth
H from 22 July until 7 October. To Penzance
I From Nottingham

Table T026-R

Sundays

20 May to 2 December

Scotland, North East England, Yorkshire and Humberside - London

Station		XC ◇A	EM ◇	XC ◇B	TP ◇C	GR	TP ◇D	TP ◇C	GR	GR	XC ◇E	EM ◇F	XC ◇G	TP ◇C	GC	GR	GR	TP ◇D	TP ◇C	GR	GR	XC ◇H
Aberdeen	d																					
Stonehaven	d																					
Montrose	d																					
Arbroath	d																					
Dundee	d																					
Leuchars	d																					
Kirkcaldy	d																					
Inverkeithing	a																					
Inverness	d																					
Perth	d																					
Stirling	a																					
Glasgow Central	d																					
Motherwell	a																					
Haymarket 238	d																					
Edinburgh 238	a																					
	d	10 08		10 08		10 30			11 00		11 05		11 05			11 20	11 30				12 00	
Dunbar 238	d										11 26		11 26									
Berwick-upon-Tweed	d					11 12					11 50		11 50				12 12					
Alnmouth for Alnwick	d	11 07		11 07							12 10		12 10								13 00	
Morpeth	d	11 22		11 22												12 34						
Newcastle	a	11 36		11 36		11 55			12 23		12 36		12 36			12 48	12 56				13 27	
Sunderland	d														12 12							
Hartlepool	d														12 36							
Newcastle	d	11 40		11 40		11 58	12 03	12 17	12 25		12 40		12 40			12 51	13 01	13 05	13 10	13 15	13 29	13 35
Chester-le-Street	d							12 26														
Durham	d	11 52		11 52			12 16	12 33	12 38		12 53		12 53			13 05		13 18	13 23	13 28	13 42	13 47
Darlington	a	12 09		12 09		12 25	12 33	12 50	12 56		13 09		13 09			13 23	13 29	13 34	13 40	13 47	14 00	14 05
Middlesbrough	d				11 57									12 47								
Eaglescliffe	a														13 02							
Darlington	d	12 10		12 10		12 27	12 34	12 51	12 57		13 10		13 10			13 24	13 30	13 35	13 41	13 49	14 01	14 06
Northallerton	d				12 25		12 45		13 10					13 15	13 24			13 46	13 52	14 02		
Thirsk	d				12 33									13 24	13 33							
York	a	12 36		12 36	12 51	12 54	13 07	13 22	13 29		13 36		13 36	13 43	13 49	13 53	13 57	14 08	14 14	14 21	14 28	14 32
Leeds	a	13 08		13 08	13 15		13 31	13 46			14 08		14 08	14 16				14 32	14 46			
	d																					
Harrogate	d																					
Scarborough	a																					
York	d					12 56			13 32						13 52	13 56	14 00			14 24	14 31	14 35
Doncaster	a								13 53											14 45	14 52	14 56
Skipton	d																					
Keighley	d																					
Bradford Interchange	d																					
Bradford Forster Square	d																					
Shipley	d																					
Halifax	d																					
Brighouse	d																					
Mirfield	d																					
Leeds	d	13 11		13 11						14 05	14 11		14 11									
Wakefield Westgate	d	13 24		13 24						14 18	14 23		14 23									
Wakefield Kirkgate	d																					
Pontefract Monkhill	d																					
Sheffield	d		12 43	13a52								13 48	14a52									15a22
Hull	d																					
Selby	a																					
Doncaster	d	13a42							13 55	14 37	14a41									14 48	14 54	
Retford	d								14 09													
Lincoln	d																					
Newark North Gate	a									14 59											15 16	
	d									15 00											15 18	
Grantham	a		14 20							15 11		15 16										
	d		14 22							15 12		15 20										
Peterborough	a		14 51						14 48	15 32		15 51								15 36	15 46	
Norwich	d		16a35									17a26										
Peterborough	d								14 51	15 34										15 41	15 51	
Stevenage	d																					
London Kings Cross	a					14 43			15 38	16 21					15 42	15 45	15 49			16 30	16 38	

A from 22 July until 7 October. To Plymouth
B until 15 July, from 14 October. To Penzance
C To Manchester Airport
D To Liverpool Lime Street
E from 22 July until 7 October. To Penzance
F From Manchester Piccadilly
G until 15 July, from 14 October. To Plymouth
H until 15 July, from 14 October. To Reading

Table T026-R

Sundays

20 May to 2 December

Scotland, North East England, Yorkshire and Humberside - London

		EM	HT	GR	XC	XC	XC	XC	TP	TP	XC	GR	TP	GR	HT	GR	TP	TP	GR	GR	EM	XC	XC
		A	B	B	C	D	E	F	G	H	I		J	K		L	M	J			N	O	P
Aberdeen	d													09 47									
Stonehaven	d													10 05									
Montrose	d													10 28									
Arbroath	d													10 44									
Dundee	d													11 03									
Leuchars	d													11 17									
Kirkcaldy	d													11 41									
Inverkeithing	a													11 56									
Inverness	d																						
Perth	d																						
Stirling	a																						
Glasgow Central	d				10 55	10 55			11 01	11 08	11 40												
Motherwell	a				11 13	11 13			11 22	11 23	12 10												
Haymarket 238	d				11 53	11 53	11 53	11 53						12 18									12 56
Edinburgh 238	a				11 57	11 57	11 57	11 57						12 22									13 01
	d				12 08	12 08	12 08	12 08				12 20		12 30						13 00			13 08
Dunbar 238	d																						13 29
Berwick-upon-Tweed	d				12 49	12 49	12 49	12 49						13 13						13 43			
Alnmouth for Alnwick	d																						14 11
Morpeth	d											13 33											
Newcastle	a				13 34	13 34	13 34	13 34				13 47		13 56						14 26			14 37
Sunderland	d																						
Hartlepool	d																						
Newcastle	d				13 40	13 40	13 40	13 40				13 50		13 59			14 03	14 15	14 20	14 31		14 36	14 41
Chester-le-Street	d																						
Durham	d				13 53	13 53	13 53	13 53				14 04					14 16	14 28	14 33			14 48	14 53
Darlington	a				14 09	14 09	14 09	14 09						14 27			14 33	14 45	14 50	14 59		15 05	15 09
Middlesbrough	d												13 55										
Eaglescliffe	a																						
Darlington	d				14 10	14 10	14 10	14 10						14 30			14 34	14 46	14 52	15 00		15 06	15 10
Northallerton	d												14 23				14 45						
Thirsk	d												14 33										
York	a				14 36	14 36	14 36	14 36				14 46	14 50	14 57			15 07	15 17	15 20	15 27		15 32	15 37
Leeds	a				15 08	15 08	15 08	15 08					15 15				15 31	15 45					16 08
	d																						
Harrogate	d																						
Scarborough	a																						
York	d											14 49		14 59					15 23	15 30		15 35	
Doncaster	a																		15 44	15 52		15 57	
Skipton	d																						
Keighley	d																						
Bradford Interchange	d																						
Bradford Forster Square	d																						
Shipley	d																						
Halifax	d																						
Brighouse	d																						
Mirfield	d																						
Leeds	d	14 34		15 05	15 11	15 11	15 11	15 11								←							16 11
Wakefield Westgate	d	14a45		15 18	15 23	15 23	15 23	15 23								15 18							16 23
Wakefield Kirkgate	d			→																			
Pontefract Monkhill	d																						
Sheffield	d					15a51	15a51								←						14 41	16a20	16a52
Hull	d		14 36												14 36								
Selby	a		→												15 10								
Doncaster	d				15a42			15a42							15 28	15 37			15 46	15 53			
Retford	d														15 42					16 08			
Lincoln	d																						
Newark North Gate	a															15 59			16 08				
	d															16 00			16 09				
Grantham	a											15 39			16 05	16 11					16 20		
	d											15 40			16 06	16 12					16 22		
Peterborough	a															16 32			16 39	16 48	16 52		
Norwich	d																				18a30		
Peterborough	d															16 36			16 42	16 51			
Stevenage	d														16s51	17 06							
London Kings Cross ⊖	a											16 42		16 48	17 14	17 30			17 34	17 38			

A 5 August, 12 August, 26 August. To St Pancras International
B To London Kings Cross
C from 16 September until 7 October. To Plymouth
D from 14 October. To Penzance. 🍴 from Edinburgh
E until 15 July. From Motherwell to Penzance. 🍴 from Edinburgh
F from 22 July until 9 September. From Motherwell to Plymouth
G until 9 September. To Manchester Airport
H from 16 September. To Manchester Airport
I until 9 September
J To Manchester Airport
K The Northern Lights
L From Leeds
M To Liverpool Lime Street
N From Liverpool Lime Street
O until 15 July, from 14 October. To Reading
P until 15 July. From Motherwell to Plymouth

Table T026-R

Sundays

20 May to 2 December

Scotland, North East England, Yorkshire and Humberside - London

		XC	XC	XC	TP	TP	XC	TP	GC	GR	GR	TP	GC	TP	GR	EM	XC	GR	GC	GR	XC	XC
		A	B	C	D	E	F	G			H	I		G		J	K				L	M
Aberdeen	d																				11 10	11 10
Stonehaven	d																				11 27	11 27
Montrose	d																				11 48	11 48
Arbroath	d																				12 04	12 04
Dundee	d																				12 24	12 24
Leuchars	d																				12 37	12 37
Kirkcaldy	d																				13 07	13 07
Inverkeithing	a																				13 21	13 21
Inverness	d										09 40											
Perth	d										11 59											
Stirling	a										12 34											
Glasgow Central	d	12 02	12 02		13 08	13 14	13 25															
Motherwell	a	12 17	12 17		13 30	13 30	13 55															
Haymarket 238	d	12 56	12 56	12 56							13 17										13 38	13 38
Edinburgh 238	a	13 01	13 01	13 01							13 21										13 43	13 43
	d	13 08	13 08	13 08						13 19	13 30						13 55	14 00			14 08	14 08
Dunbar 238	d	13 29	13 29	13 29																		
Berwick-upon-Tweed	d										14 13						14 36				14 49	14 49
Alnmouth for Alnwick	d	14 11	14 11	14 11														15 00				
Morpeth	d																				15 20	15 20
Newcastle	a	14 37	14 37	14 37						14 42	14 56						15 19	15 28			15 35	15 35
Sunderland	d								14 12													
Hartlepool	d								14 38													
Newcastle	d	14 41	14 41	14 41						14 45	14 59	15 03		15 14			15 24	15 31			15 40	15 40
Chester-le-Street	d													15 23								
Durham	d	14 53	14 53	14 53						14 58		15 16		15 30			15 36	15 44			15 52	15 52
Darlington	a	15 09	15 09	15 09						15 15	15 27	15 33		15 47			15 53	16 01			16 09	16 09
Middlesbrough	d							14 48														
Eaglescliffe	a								15 04													
Darlington	d	15 10	15 10	15 10						15 18	15 28	15 34		15 48			15 54	16 03			16 10	16 10
Northallerton	d								15 24	15 32		15 45										
Thirsk	d							15 28	15 33													
York	a	15 40	15 40	15 40				15 46	15 49	15 54	15 58	16 07		16 19			16 22	16 30			16 37	16 37
Leeds	a	16 08	16 08	16 08				16 16				16 32		16 46							17 08	17 08
	d																					
Harrogate	d																					
Scarborough	a																					
York	d								15 52	15 57	16 01						16 25	16 32				
Doncaster	a																16 48	16 54				
Skipton	d																					
Keighley	d																					
Bradford Interchange	d												15 05						15 59			
Bradford Forster Square	d																					
Shipley	d																					
Halifax	d												15 20						16 13			
Brighouse	d												15 33						16 24			
Mirfield	d												15 40						16 31			
Leeds	d	16 11	16 11	16 11											16 16					16 45	17 11	17 11
Wakefield Westgate	d	16 23	16 23	16 23											16 29					16 58	17 23	17 23
Wakefield Kirkgate	d												16 02						16 45			
Pontefract Monkhill	d																					
Sheffield	d	16a52														15 39	17a19				17a51	
Hull	d																					
Selby	a																					
Doncaster	d		16a41	16a41									16 27		16 48			16 56	17 13	17 19		17a41
Retford	d																					
Lincoln	d																					
Newark North Gate	a																	17 19		17 43		
	d																	17 20		17 44		
Grantham	a														17 18	17 15						
	d														17 19	17 21						
Peterborough	a															17 50		17 47		18 12		
Norwich	d															19a28						
Peterborough	d																	17 51		18 14		
Stevenage	d														18 04							
London Kings Cross ⊖	a								17 44	17 46	17 51		17 56		18 26			18 38	18 45	19 03		

A from 14 October. To Plymouth
B from 16 September until 7 October. To Plymouth
C from 22 July until 9 September. From Motherwell to Plymouth
D until 9 September. To Manchester Airport
E from 16 September. To Manchester Airport
F until 9 September
G To Manchester Airport
H The Highland Chieftain
I To Liverpool Lime Street
J From Liverpool Lime Street
K until 15 July, from 14 October. To Reading
L until 15 July, from 14 October. To Plymouth. 🍴 from Edinburgh
M from 22 July until 7 October. To Plymouth. 🍴 from Edinburgh

Table T026-R

Sundays
20 May to 2 December

Scotland, North East England, Yorkshire and Humberside - London

		GR	TP	TP	HT	GR	TP	GR	EM	GR	GR	XC	GR	XC	XC	XC	XC	XC	TP	GR	TP	TP	GR
			A	B			A		C			D		E	F	G	H	I	A		B	A	
Aberdeen	d	11 47																					
Stonehaven	d	12 05																					
Montrose	d	12 28																					
Arbroath	d	12 44																					
Dundee	d	13 02																					
Leuchars	d	13 17																					
Kirkcaldy	d	13 42																					
Inverkeithing	a	14 00																					
Inverness	d																						
Perth	d																						
Stirling	a																						
Glasgow Central	d													13 48	13 48			14 35					
Motherwell	a													14 02	14 02			15 05					
Haymarket 238	d	14 21												14 42	14 42	14 42	14 42						
Edinburgh 238	a	14 26												14 47	14 47	14 47	14 47						
	d	14 30						14 50			15 00			15 08	15 08	15 08	15 08			15 30			
Dunbar 238	d													15 29	15 29	15 29	15 29						
Berwick-upon-Tweed	d							15 33												16 12			
Alnmouth for Alnwick	d																						
Morpeth	d													16 22	16 22	16 22	16 22						
Newcastle	a	15 53						16 16			16 23			16 36	16 36	16 36	16 36			16 55			
Sunderland	d																						
Hartlepool	d																						
Newcastle	d	15 56		16 00		16 04	16 12	16 20			16 27	16 35		16 40	16 40	16 40	16 40			17 01	17 05	17 13	
Chester-le-Street	d						16 21																
Durham	d			16 13		16 17	16 28	16 33			16 40	16 47		16 52	16 52	16 52	16 52				17 18	17 26	
Darlington	a			16 29		16 33	16 45	16 50			16 57	17 04		17 09	17 09	17 09	17 09			17 28	17 34	17 42	
Middlesbrough	d		15 54																16 57				
Eaglescliffe	a																						
Darlington	d			16 30		16 35	16 46	16 52			16 59	17 05		17 10	17 10	17 10	17 10			17 29	17 35	17 43	
Northallerton	d		16 23	16 41		16 47													17 25			17 55	
Thirsk	d		16 31																17 33				
York	a	16 47	16 52	17 03		17 08	17 17	17 19			17 27	17 31		17 40	17 40	17 40	17 40		17 51	17 56	18 07	18 17	
Leeds	a		17 16	17 31			17 44							18 09	18 09	18 09	18 09		18 15		18 32	18 46	
	d																						
Harrogate	d												17 07										
Scarborough	a																						
York	d	16 59				17 10		17 22			17 30	17 35								17 59			
Doncaster	a					17 34					17 52	17 57											
Skipton	d																						
Keighley	d																						
Bradford Interchange	d																						
Bradford Forster Square	d																						
Shipley	d																						
Halifax	d																						
Brighouse	d																						
Mirfield	d																						
Leeds	d									17 16			17 45	18 11	18 11	18 11	18 11						18 15
Wakefield Westgate	d									17 29			17 58	18 23	18 23	18 23	18 23						18 28
Wakefield Kirkgate	d																						
Pontefract Monkhill	d																						
Sheffield	d								16 43			18a20			18a52	18a52							
Hull	d				16 25																		
Selby	a				17 03																		
Doncaster	d				17 27	17 36				17 48	17 57		18 18	18a39			18a39						18 47
Retford	d				17 41					18 02													
Lincoln	d																						
Newark North Gate	a							18 02					18 43										
	d							18 03					18 44										
Grantham	a				18 01	18 07			18 16	18 24	18 29												19 17
	d				18 02	18 08			18 17	18 25	18 30												19 18
Peterborough	a							18 31	18 46		18 50		19 12										
Norwich	d								20a26														
Peterborough	d							18 33			18 52		19 14										
Stevenage	d				18s46					19 09													20 03
London Kings Cross ⊖	a	18 48			19 11	19 16		19 20		19 32	19 40		20 03							19 46			20 25

A To Manchester Airport
B To Liverpool Lime Street
C From Liverpool Lime Street
D until 15 July, from 14 October. To Reading
E from 16 September until 7 October. To Bristol Temple Meads. from Edinburgh
F from 14 October. To Plymouth. from Edinburgh
G until 15 July. From Motherwell to Plymouth. from Edinburgh
H from 22 July until 9 September. From Motherwell to Bristol Temple Meads. from Edinburgh
I until 9 September

Table T026-R

Sundays
20 May to 2 December

Scotland, North East England, Yorkshire and Humberside - London

		GR	EM	XC	GR	XC	XC	XC	XC	TP	TP	GR	XC	TP	GR	TP	TP	XC	HT	GR	GR	GR	XC
			A	B		C	D	E	F	G	H		I	J		K	J	L				M	N
Aberdeen	d														13 47								
Stonehaven	d														14 05								
Montrose	d														14 28								
Arbroath	d														14 44								
Dundee	d														15 02								
Leuchars	d														15 16								
Kirkcaldy	d														15 41								
Inverkeithing	a														15 56								
Inverness	d																						
Perth	d																						
Stirling	a																						
Glasgow Central	d					14 55	14 55			15 00	15 14		16 35										
Motherwell	a					15 12	15 12			15 21	15 30		17 05										
Haymarket 238	d					15 52	15 52	15 52	15 52						16 20								
Edinburgh 238	a					15 57	15 57	15 57	15 57						16 26								
	d	16 00				16 08	16 08	16 08	16 08			16 20			16 30						17 00		17 08
Dunbar 238	d																						17 29
Berwick-upon-Tweed	d														17 13								17 53
Alnmouth for Alnwick	d	17 00				17 08	17 08	17 08	17 08														
Morpeth	d					17 22	17 22	17 22	17 22			17 32											
Newcastle	a	17 27				17 36	17 36	17 36	17 36			17 46			17 56						18 23		18 36
Sunderland	d																						
Hartlepool	d																						
Newcastle	d	17 29		17 35		17 40	17 40	17 40	17 40			17 49			18 00	18 03	18 14	18 25			18 29		18 40
Chester-le-Street	d																18 23						
Durham	d	17 42		17 48		17 53	17 53	17 53	17 53							18 16	18 30	18 37			18 42		18 52
Darlington	a	18 00		18 05		18 10	18 10	18 10	18 10			18 16			18 28	18 33	18 47	18 54			19 00		19 08
Middlesbrough	d													17 56									
Eaglescliffe	a																						
Darlington	d	18 01		18 06		18 11	18 11	18 11	18 11			18 17			18 30	18 34	18 48	18 55			19 01		19 09
Northallerton	d											18 29		18 24		18 45					19 13		
Thirsk	d													18 32									
York	a	18 28		18 33		18 39	18 39	18 39	18 39			18 48		18 53	18 57	19 07	19 19	19 22			19 32		19 36
Leeds	a					19 08	19 08	19 08	19 08					19 17		19 31	19 46						20 08
	d																						
Harrogate	d																						
Scarborough	a																						
York	d	18 31		18 35								18 54			18 59			19 24			19 35		
Doncaster	a	18 52		18 57														19 50			19 56		
Skipton	d																						
Keighley	d																						
Bradford Interchange	d																						
Bradford Forster Square	d																						
Shipley	d																						
Halifax	d																						
Brighouse	d																						
Mirfield	d																						
Leeds	d				18 45	19 11	19 11	19 11	19 11											19 16		19 46	20 11
Wakefield Westgate	d				18 59	19 24	19 24	19 24	19 24											19 29		19 59	20 23
Wakefield Kirkgate	d																					→	
Pontefract Monkhill	d																						
Sheffield	d		17 40	19a20		19a52			19a52									20a16					20a51
Hull	d																		18 47				
Selby	a																		19 21				
Doncaster	d	18 55			19 20		19a40	19a40											19 40	19 48	19 58		
Retford	d																		19 54	20 02			
Lincoln	d																						
Newark North Gate	a	19 17			19 44																20 20		
	d	19 19			19 45																20 21		
Grantham	a		19 21									19 42							20 15	20 24			
	d		19 23									19 43							20 16	20 25			
Peterborough	a	19 46	19 55		20 13																20 49		
Norwich	d		21a35																				
Peterborough	d	19 51			20 14																20 51		
Stevenage	d																			21 09			
London Kings Cross ⊖	a	20 38			21 03							20 45			20 50				21 20	21 31	21 38		

A From Liverpool Lime Street
B until 15 July, from 14 October. To Guildford
C from 14 October. To Bristol Temple Meads. from Edinburgh
D from 16 September until 7 October. To Bristol Temple Meads
E from 22 July until 9 September. From Motherwell to Bristol Temple Meads
F until 15 July. From Motherwell to Bristol Temple Meads. from Edinburgh
G until 9 September. To Manchester Airport
H from 16 September. To Manchester Airport
I until 9 September
J To Manchester Airport
K To Liverpool Lime Street
L until 15 July, from 14 October. To Birmingham New Street
M To London Kings Cross
N from 22 July until 7 October. To Birmingham New Street

Please note, Network Rail have stated that further updates to this timetable are possible during the validity period.

Table T026-R

Sundays

20 May to 2 December

Scotland, North East England, Yorkshire and Humberside - London

		XC	GC	TP	GR	GR	TP	TP	EM	XC	GR	GR	XC	XC	TP	TP	GR	XC	TP	TP	GR	TP
		◇ A		◇ B		C	◇ D	◇	◇ E	◇ F			◇ G	◇ H	◇ I	◇ J		K	◇	◇ D		◇ D
Aberdeen	d																					
Stonehaven	d																					
Montrose	d																					
Arbroath	d																					
Dundee	d																					
Leuchars	d																					
Kirkcaldy	d																					
Inverkeithing	a																					
Inverness	d																					
Perth	d																					
Stirling	a																					
Glasgow Central	d												16 55		17 00	17 15		18 35				
Motherwell	a												17 12		17 21	17 29		19 05				
Haymarket 238	d												17 51	17 51								
Edinburgh 238	a												17 55	17 55								
	d	17 08			17 30						18 00		18 06	18 06			18 30				19 00	
Dunbar 238	d	17 29			17 52								18 28	18 28							19 22	
Berwick-upon-Tweed	d	17 53			18 16								18 52	18 52			19 13				19 46	
Alnmouth for Alnwick	d										19 01											
Morpeth	d												19 23	19 23								
Newcastle	a	18 36			18 59						19 28		19 38	19 38			19 56				20 29	
Sunderland	d		18 12																			
Hartlepool	d		18 40																			
Newcastle	d	18 40			19 02		19 06	19 20		19 26	19 30		19 41	19 41			20 00			20 04	20 33	21 00
Chester-le-Street	d																					21 09
Durham	d	18 52						19 33		19 39	19 44		19 53	19 53						20 17	20 46	21 16
Darlington	a	19 08			19 28		19 33	19 49		19 55	20 01		20 09	20 09			20 27			20 34	21 03	21 32
Middlesbrough	d			18 57															20 03			
Eaglescliffe	a		18 58																			
Darlington	d	19 09			19 29		19 34	19 50		19 56	20 03		20 10	20 10			20 29			20 35	21 05	21 33
Northallerton	d		19 21	19 26			19 45												20 32	20 46		21 44
Thirsk	d		19 30	19 35															20 40			
York	a	19 36	19 48	19 53	19 57		20 07	20 23		20 24	20 30		20 37	20 37			20 56		21 04	21 08	21 32	22 07
Leeds	a	20 08		20 17			20 33						21 08	21 08						21 32		22 32
	d																					
Harrogate	d																					
Scarborough	a																					
York	d		19 51		20 00					20 26	20 32						21 00				21 35	
Doncaster	a									20 48	20 54						21 21				21 56	
Skipton	d																					
Keighley	d																					
Bradford Interchange	d																					
Bradford Forster Square	d																					
Shipley	d																					
Halifax	d																					
Brighouse	d																					
Mirfield	d																					
Leeds	d	20 11				←						20 45	21 11	21 11								
Wakefield Westgate	d	20 23				19 59						20 58	21 23	21 23								
Wakefield Kirkgate	d																					
Pontefract Monkhill	d																					
Sheffield	d	20a51							19 40	21a17			21a51	21a51								
Hull	d																					
Selby	a																					
Doncaster	d					20 20					20 55	21 17					21 26				21 58	
Retford	d											21 31										
Lincoln	d																					
Newark North Gate	a					20 44					21 18						21 48				22 20	
	d					20 45					21 19						21 49				22 21	
Grantham	a				20 48				21 18			21 53					22 00				22 32	
	d				20 49				21 20			21 54					22 01				22 33	
Peterborough	a				21 09	21 13			21 52		21 46	22 14					22 21				22 53	
Norwich	d								23a25													
Peterborough	d				21 10	21 14					21 50	22 15					22 24				22 55	
Stevenage	d											22 44					22 53				23s33	
London Kings Cross ⊖	a		21 42		21 57	22 05					22 37	23 09					23 15				23 59	

A until 15 July, from 14 October. To Bristol Temple Meads. to Leeds
B To Manchester Airport
C From Leeds
D To Liverpool Lime Street
E From Liverpool Lime Street
F until 15 July, from 14 October. To Birmingham New Street
G from 16 September. To Birmingham New Street. from Edinburgh to Leeds
H until 9 September. From Motherwell to Birmingham New Street. from Edinburgh to Leeds
I until 9 September. To Manchester Airport
J from 16 September. To Manchester Airport
K until 9 September

Table T026-R

Sundays

20 May to 2 December

Scotland, North East England, Yorkshire and Humberside - London

		TP	GR	XC	XC	TP	TP	XC	GR	XC	XC	XC	TP	TP	TP
		◇ A		◇ B	◇ C	◇ D	◇ E	F		◇ B	◇ C	◇	◇	◇ G	◇
Aberdeen	d											21 29			
Stonehaven	d											21 46			
Montrose	d											22 07			
Arbroath	d											22 23			
Dundee	d											22 41			
Leuchars	d											22 54			
Kirkcaldy	d											23 24			
Inverkeithing	a											23 38			
Inverness	d														
Perth	d														
Stirling	a														
Glasgow Central	d			19 00		19 00	19 14	20 40		20 58					
Motherwell	a			19 14		19 23	19 29	21 10		21 17					
Haymarket 238	d			19 59	19 59					22 04	22 04	23 58			
Edinburgh 238	a			20 03	20 03					22 08	22 08	00 02			
	d		20 00	20 18	20 18				21 00						
Dunbar 238	d		20 23	20 40	20 40				21 23						
Berwick-upon-Tweed	d		20 47	21 04	21 04				21 47						
Alnmouth for Alnwick	d		21 10						22 09						
Morpeth	d		21 27												
Newcastle	a		21 41	21 48	21 48				22 36						
Sunderland	d														
Hartlepool	d														
Newcastle	d		21 44											22 00	
Chester-le-Street	d														
Durham	d		21 58											22 14	
Darlington	a		22 16											22 30	
Middlesbrough	d	21 21											22 07		23 00
Eaglescliffe	a														
Darlington	d		22 17											22 31	
Northallerton	d	21 49	22 31										22 36	22 43	23 28
Thirsk	d	21 57											22 44		
York	a	22 15	23 03										23 06	23 11	23 57
Leeds	a	22 39	23 33											23 39	
	d	22 40													
Harrogate	d														
Scarborough	a														
York	d														
Doncaster	a														
Skipton	d														
Keighley	d														
Bradford Interchange	d														
Bradford Forster Square	d														
Shipley	d														
Halifax	d														
Brighouse	d														
Mirfield	d	23a02													
Leeds	d														
Wakefield Westgate	d														
Wakefield Kirkgate	d														
Pontefract Monkhill	d														
Sheffield	d														
Hull	d														
Selby	a														
Doncaster	d														
Retford	d														
Lincoln	d														
Newark North Gate	a														
	d														
Grantham	a														
	d														
Peterborough	a														
Norwich	d														
Peterborough	d														
Stevenage	d														
London Kings Cross ⊖	a														

A To Manchester Piccadilly
B from 16 September
C until 9 September. From Motherwell
D until 9 September. To Manchester Airport
E from 16 September. To Manchester Airport
F until 9 September
G To Manchester Airport

Table T027-F

Mondays to Fridays

21 May to 21 September

Nottingham - Newark - Lincoln - Cleethorpes

Miles	Miles			EM	EM	EM	EM	EM	EM	EM	EM	EM	EM	EM	EM	EM	EM	EM	EM	EM	EM	EM	EM
						A				B	◇ C	◇ D	E	F			E	F	E	C	D		E
0	—	**Nottingham** 8	d		05 54	06 53		07 56		08 12	08 52	08 54	09 25	09 49			10 29	10 49	11 29	11 52	11 54		12 29
3	—	Carlton	d		06 01	06 59		08 02		08 19	08 58	09 00		09 55				10 55		11 58	12 00		
5	—	Burton Joyce	d		06 04	07 02		08 06						09 59						12 02	12 04		
9¼	—	Lowdham	d		06 09	07 07		08 10		08 27	09 05	09 07		10 04				11 02		12 07	12 09		
10	—	Thurgarton	d		06 13	07 11		08 14						10 08						12 11	12 13		
11	—	Bleasby	d		06 16	07 14		08 17						10 11						12 14	12 16		
12¾	—	Fiskerton	d		06 20	07 17		08 21			09 12	09 14		10 15				11 09		12 18	12 20		
13¾	—	Rolleston	d		06 22	07 19		08 23						10 17						12 20	12 22		
17¼	—	**Newark Castle**	d		06 30	07 27		08a30		08 40	09a20	09a22	09 52	10a25			10 51	11a18	11 53	12a29	12a31		12 53
—	0	**Newark North Gate** 7	a																				
—	—		d				07 42		08 31						09 57	10 50						12 06	
22¼	5	Collingham	d		06 39	07 35	07 51		08 40	08 49					10 05		11 04		12 01			12 15	13 02
25	—	Swinderby	d		06 43		07 56		08 45								11 09					12 19	
29¾	—	Hykeham	d		06 50	07 44	08 02		08 51	08 57					10 14		11 16		12 10			12 26	13 11
33¾	—	**Lincoln**	a		07 04	07 56	08 12		09 02	09 08			10 17		10 23	11 14	11 26		12 21			12 36	13 23
—	—		d	05 57			08 15								10 25							12 38	
48½	—	Market Rasen	d	06 13			08 32								10 42							12 54	
63½	—	Barnetby	a	06 30			08 49								10 58							13 10	
69½	—	Habrough	a	06 40			08 59								11 08							13 20	
77½	—	**Grimsby Town**	a	06 55			09 12								11 22							13 35	
80¾	—	**Cleethorpes**	a																				

		EM	EM	EM	EM	EM	EM	EM	EM	EM	EM	EM	EM	EM	EM	EM	EM	EM	EM	EM	EM	EM	EM
		F	A	E		F	E	C	D	◇ A	E	F		G	C	D		E		E	F		E
Nottingham 8	d	12 49		13 29		13 49	14 29	14 51	14 53		15 29	15 49		16 27	16 47	16 49		17 21	17 50	18 17	18 52		19 19
Carlton	d	12 55				13 55		14 59	15 01			15 55			16 53	16 55		17 27		18 23	18 59		19 25
Burton Joyce	d							15 02	15 04						16 57	16 59		17 31		18 27			19 29
Lowdham	d	13 02				14 02		15 08	15 10			16 02		16 38	17 02	17 04		17 36	18 01	18 31			19 33
Thurgarton	d							15 11	15 13						17 06	17 08				18 35			19 37
Bleasby	d							15 14	15 16						17 09	17 11				18 39			19 41
Fiskerton	d	13 09				14 09		15 18	15 20			16 09			17 13	17 15		17 43		18 42	19 11		19 44
Rolleston	d							15 20	15 22						17 15	17 17				18 45			19 47
Newark Castle	d	13a18		13 52		14a17	14 53	15a30	15a32		15 53	16a17		16 53	17a23	17a25		17 52	18 18	18 53	19a19		19 54
Newark North Gate 7	a																						
	d		13 02							15 28			16 46				17 28					19 35	
Collingham	d		13 11	14 00			15 04			15 37	16 02			17 02			17 36	18 01	18 27	19 03		19 44	20 03
Swinderby	d			14 04							16 07							18 06	18 32	19 06			
Hykeham	d			14 10			15 13			15 46	16 13		17 03				17 45	18 12	18 39	19 13			20 11
Lincoln	a		13 30	14 23			15 22			15 55	16 23		17 13	17 16			18 00	18 24	18 49	19 22		20 01	20 21
	d				14 37								17 22									20 02	
Market Rasen	d				14 54								17 39									20 19	
Barnetby	a				15 10								17 55									20 35	
Habrough	a				15 20								18 05									20 44	
Grimsby Town	a				15 34								18 18									20 56	
Cleethorpes	a																					21 04	

		EM	EM	GR	EM	EM
			◇1 H ⌶	8 1 I ⊏	E	
Nottingham 8	d		20 00		21 20	22 26
Carlton	d				21 28	22 32
Burton Joyce	d					22 35
Lowdham	d		20 11		21 34	22 40
Thurgarton	d					
Bleasby	d					22 45
Fiskerton	d				21 41	22 49
Rolleston	d					
Newark Castle	d		20 24		21 53	22 57
Newark North Gate 7	a					23 06
	d	20 04		20 35		23 10
Collingham	d	20 13	20 32		22 01	23 19
Swinderby	d					23 23
Hykeham	d				22 10	23 30
Lincoln	a	20 29	20 52	21 01	22 20	23 40
	d					
Market Rasen	d					
Barnetby	a					
Habrough	a					
Grimsby Town	a					
Cleethorpes	a					

A To Peterborough
B From Worksop
C from 3 September. From Derby
D until 31 August. From Matlock
E From Leicester
F From Matlock
G From Leicester to Sleaford
H From St Pancras International
I From London Kings Cross

For connections from London Kings Cross refer to Table T026

Table T027-F

Mondays to Fridays

24 September to 7 December

Nottingham - Newark - Lincoln - Cleethorpes

		EM	EM	EM	EM	EM	EM	EM	EM	EM	EM	EM	EM	EM	EM	EM	EM	EM	EM	EM	EM	EM	EM
				A				B	◇ C	D	C			D	C	D	C		D	C	A	D	
Nottingham 8	d		05 54	06 53		07 56		08 12	08 52	09 25	09 49			10 29	10 49	11 29	11 52		12 29	12 49		13 29	
Carlton	d		06 01	06 59		08 02		08 19	08 58		09 55				10 55		11 58			12 55			
Burton Joyce	d		06 04	07 02		08 06					09 59						12 02						
Lowdham	d		06 09	07 07		08 10		08 27	09 05		10 04				11 02		12 07			13 02			
Thurgarton	d		06 13	07 11		08 14					10 08						12 11						
Bleasby	d		06 16	07 14		08 17					10 11						12 14						
Fiskerton	d		06 20	07 17		08 21			09 12		10 15				11 09		12 18			13 09			
Rolleston	d		06 22	07 19		08 23					10 17						12 20						
Newark Castle	d		06 30	07 27		08a31		08 40	09a20	09 52	10a25			10 51	11a18	11 53	12a29		12 53	13a18		13 52	
Newark North Gate 7	a																						
	d				07 42		08 31					09 57	10 50					12 06			13 02		
Collingham	d		06 39	07 35	07 51		08 40	08 49				10 05		11 04		12 01		12 15	13 02		13 11	14 00	
Swinderby	d		06 43		07 56		08 45							11 09				12 19				14 04	
Hykeham	d		06 50	07 44	08 02		08 51	08 57				10 14		11 16		12 10		12 26	13 11			14 10	
Lincoln	a		07 04	07 56	08 12		09 02	09 08		10 19		10 23	11 14	11 30		12 23		12 36	13 25		13 30	14 25	
	d	05 57			08 15							10 25						12 38					14 37
Market Rasen	d	06 13			08 32							10 42						12 54					14 54
Barnetby	a	06 30			08 49							10 58						13 10					15 10
Habrough	a	06 40			08 59							11 08						13 20					15 20
Grimsby Town	a	06 55			09 12							11 22						13 35					15 34
Cleethorpes	a																						

		EM	EM	EM	EM	EM	EM	EM	EM	EM	EM	EM	EM	EM	EM	EM	EM	EM	EM	EM	EM	GR
		C	D	C	◇ A	D	C		E	F	G		D		D	C		H	I		◇1 J ⌶	8 1 K ⊏
Nottingham 8	d	13 49	14 29	14 51		15 29	15 49		16 27	16 47	16 49		17 21	17 50	18 17	18 52		19 19	19 20		20 00	
Carlton	d	13 55		14 59			15 55			16 53	16 55		17 27		18 23	18 59		19 25	19 26			
Burton Joyce	d			15 02						16 57	16 59		17 31		18 27			19 29	19 30			
Lowdham	d	14 02		15 08			16 02		16 38	17 02	17 04		17 36	18 01	18 31			19 33	19 34		20 11	
Thurgarton	d			15 11						17 06	17 08				18 35			19 37	19 38			
Bleasby	d			15 14						17 09	17 11				18 39			19 41	19 42			
Fiskerton	d	14 09		15 18			16 09			17 13	17 15		17 43		18 42	19 11		19 44	19 45			
Rolleston	d			15 20						17 15	17 17				18 45			19 47	19 48			
Newark Castle	d	14a17	14 53	15a30		15 53	16a17		16 53	17a23	17a25		17 52	18 18	18 53	19a19		19 54	19 55		20 24	
Newark North Gate 7	a																					
	d				15 28			16 46				17 28					19 35			20 04		20 35
Collingham	d		15 04		15 37	16 02			17 02			17 36	18 01	18 27	19 03		19 44	20 03	20 04	20 13	20 32	
Swinderby	d					16 07							18 06	18 32	19 06							
Hykeham	d		15 13		15 46	16 13		17 03				17 45	18 12	18 39	19 13			20 11	20 12			
Lincoln	a		15 24		15 55	16 25		17 13	17 18			18 00	18 26	18 51	19 24		20 01	20 23	20 24	20 29	20 52	21 01
	d							17 22									20 02					
Market Rasen	d							17 39									20 19					
Barnetby	a							17 55									20 35					
Habrough	a							18 05									20 44					
Grimsby Town	a							18 18									20 56					
Cleethorpes	a																21 04					

		EM	EM
		D	
Nottingham 8	d	21 20	22 26
Carlton	d	21 28	22 32
Burton Joyce	d		22 35
Lowdham	d	21 34	22 40
Thurgarton	d		
Bleasby	d		22 45
Fiskerton	d	21 41	22 49
Rolleston	d		
Newark Castle	d	21 53	22 57
Newark North Gate 7	a		23 06
	d		23 10
Collingham	d	22 01	23 19
Swinderby	d		23 23
Hykeham	d	22 10	23 30
Lincoln	a	22 22	23 40
	d		
Market Rasen	d		
Barnetby	a		
Habrough	a		
Grimsby Town	a		
Cleethorpes	a		

A To Peterborough
B From Worksop
C From Matlock
D From Leicester
E From Leicester to Sleaford
F until 5 October. From Derby
G from 8 October. From Matlock
H until 5 October. From Leicester
I from 8 October. From Leicester
J From St Pancras International
K From London Kings Cross

For connections from London Kings Cross refer to Table T026

Table T027-F

Saturdays 26 May to 22 September

Nottingham - Newark - Lincoln - Cleethorpes

		EM	EM	EM A	EM	EM	EM	EM	EM B	EM C	EM	EM D	EM B	EM C	EM	EM D	EM E	EM D	EM C	EM B	EM	EM D	EM E
Nottingham	d		05 55	06 53		07 58		08 11	08 52	08 54		09 22	09 49	09 51		10 29	10 52	11 29	11 53	11 55		12 29	12 49
Carlton	d		06 01	06 59		08 04			08 58	09 00		09 28	09 56	09 58			10 58		12 00	12 02			12 56
Burton Joyce	d		06 05	07 03		08 08							10 00	10 02					12 04	12 06			
Lowdham	d		06 10	07 07		08 12			09 05	09 07		09 34	10 04	10 06			11 06		12 08	12 10			13 02
Thurgarton	d		06 14	07 11		08 16							10 08	10 10					12 12	12 14			
Bleasby	d		06 17	07 14		08 19							10 12	10 14					12 16	12 18			
Fiskerton	d		06 20	07 18		08 22			09 12	09 14		09 42	10 15	10 17			11 13		12 19	12 21			13 09
Rolleston	d		06 22	07 20		08 24							10 18	10 20			11 15		12 22	12 24			
Newark Castle	d		06 30	07 26		08a32		08 42	09a20	09a22		09 51	10a26	10a28		10 51	11a23	11 55	12a31	12a33		12 53	13a19
Newark North Gate	a																						
	d						08 20				09 35				10 49						12 05		
Collingham	d		06 40	07 39			08 29	08 51			09 43	10 01				11 04		12 06			12 15	13 03	
Swinderby	d		06 44				08 34									11 08					12 19		
Hykeham	d		06 50	07 47			08 41	09 00				10 09				11 15		12 15			12 26	13 12	
Lincoln	a		07 03	07 58			08 55	09 09			09 59	10 19			11 17	11 25		12 26			12 36	13 22	
	d	05 38			08 08						10 06										12 36		
Market Rasen	d	05 54			08 25						10 23										12 54		
Barnetby	a	06 11			08 49						10 39										13 10		
Habrough	a	06 21			08 59						10 48										13 20		
Grimsby Town	a	06 36			09 12						11 02										13 34		
Cleethorpes	a																						

		EM A	EM D	EM	EM E	EM D	EM B	EM C	EM ◇ A	EM D	EM E	EM D	EM	EM E	EM D	EM E	EM	EM D	EM E	EM ◇ F	EM	GR G
Nottingham	d		13 29		13 49	14 19	14 50	14 52		15 28	15 49	16 21		16 49	17 29	17 48		18 17	18 57	19 29		
Carlton	d				13 55		14 56	14 58			15 55			16 55		17 54			19 04			
Burton Joyce	d						15 00	15 02						16 59		17 58						
Lowdham	d				14 03		15 05	15 07			16 03			17 04		18 03		18 30		19 40		
Thurgarton	d						15 09	15 11						17 08		18 07						
Bleasby	d						15 12	15 14						17 11		18 10						
Fiskerton	d				14 10		15 16	15 18			16 10			17 15		18 14			19 16			
Rolleston	d						15 18	15 20						17 17		18 16						
Newark Castle	d		13 51		14a18	14 42	15a26	15a28		15 54	16a18	16 43		17a25	17 50	18a24		18 43	19a25	19 53		
Newark North Gate	a																					
	d	13 02							15 29								18 07				20 30	20 36
Collingham	d	13 11	14 01			14 52			15 38	16 02		16 52			18 00		18 16	18 54		20 08	20 39	
Swinderby	d		14 05							16 07					18 04			19 01				
Hykeham	d		14 11			15 00				16 13					18 10			19 10				
Lincoln	a	13 30	14 24			15 11			15 56	16 25		17 08			18 23		18 34	19 23		20 26	20 54	21 00
	d			14 52									17 22				18 35				20 55	
Market Rasen	d			15 10									17 38				18 52				21a13	
Barnetby	a			15 26									17 54				19 08					
Habrough	a			15 36									18 02				19 18					
Grimsby Town	a			15 50									18 18				19 34					
Cleethorpes	a																					

		EM D	EM D
Nottingham	d	20 30	21 24
Carlton	d	20 36	21 30
Burton Joyce	d		21 34
Lowdham	d	20 41	21 38
Thurgarton	d		
Bleasby	d		21 43
Fiskerton	d	20 51	21 47
Rolleston	d		
Newark Castle	d	21 04	21 57
Newark North Gate	a		22 06
	d		22 09
Collingham	d	21 12	22 18
Swinderby	d		22 22
Hykeham	d	21 21	22 28
Lincoln	a	21 32	22 40
	d		
Market Rasen	d		
Barnetby	a		
Habrough	a		
Grimsby Town	a		
Cleethorpes	a		

A To Peterborough
B 8 September, 15 September, 22 September. From Derby
C until 1 September. From Matlock
D From Leicester
E From Matlock
F From St Pancras International
G From London Kings Cross

For connections from London Kings Cross refer to Table T026

Table T027-F

Saturdays 29 September to 8 December

Nottingham - Newark - Lincoln - Cleethorpes

		EM	EM	EM A	EM	EM	EM	EM	EM B	EM	EM C	EM B	EM	EM C	EM B	EM C	EM D	EM E	EM	EM C	EM B	EM A	EM C
Nottingham	d		05 55	06 53		07 58		08 11	08 52		09 22	09 49		10 29	10 52	11 29	11 53	11 55		12 29	12 49		13 29
Carlton	d		06 01	06 59		08 04			08 58		09 28	09 56			10 58		12 00	12 02			12 56		
Burton Joyce	d		06 05	07 03		08 08						10 00					12 04	12 06					
Lowdham	d		06 10	07 07		08 12			09 05		09 34	10 04			11 06		12 08	12 10			13 02		
Thurgarton	d		06 14	07 11		08 16						10 08					12 12	12 14					
Bleasby	d		06 17	07 14		08 19						10 12					12 16	12 18					
Fiskerton	d		06 20	07 18		08 22			09 12		09 42	10 15			11 13		12 19	12 21			13 09		
Rolleston	d		06 22	07 20		08 24						10 18			11 15		12 22	12 24					
Newark Castle	d		06 30	07 26		08a32		08 42	09a20		09 51	10a26		10 51	11a23	11 55	12a31	12a33		12 53	13a19		13 51
Newark North Gate	a																						
	d						08 20			09 35			10 49						12 05			13 02	
Collingham	d		06 40	07 39			08 29	08 51		09 43	10 01			11 04		12 06			12 15	13 03		13 11	14 01
Swinderby	d		06 44				08 34							11 08					12 19				14 05
Hykeham	d		06 50	07 47			08 41	09 00			10 09			11 15		12 15			12 26	13 12			14 11
Lincoln	a		07 03	07 58			08 55	09 09		09 59	10 19		11 17	11 27		12 28			12 36	13 24		13 30	14 26
	d	05 38			08 08					10 06									12 36				
Market Rasen	d	05 54			08 25					10 23									12 54				
Barnetby	a	06 11			08 49					10 39									13 10				
Habrough	a	06 21			08 59					10 48									13 20				
Grimsby Town	a	06 36			09 12					11 02									13 34				
Cleethorpes	a																						

		EM	EM B	EM C	EM B	EM ◇ A	EM C	EM B	EM C	EM	EM B	EM C	EM B	EM	EM C	EM B	EM ◇ F	EM	GR G	EM C	EM C
Nottingham	d		13 49	14 19	14 50		15 28	15 49	16 21		16 49	17 29	17 48		18 17	18 57	19 29			20 30	21 24
Carlton	d		13 55		14 56			15 55			16 55		17 54			19 04				20 36	21 30
Burton Joyce	d				15 00						16 59		17 58								21 34
Lowdham	d		14 03		15 05			16 03			17 04		18 03		18 30		19 40			20 41	21 38
Thurgarton	d				15 09						17 08		18 07								
Bleasby	d				15 12						17 11		18 10								21 43
Fiskerton	d		14 10		15 16			16 10			17 15		18 14			19 16				20 51	21 47
Rolleston	d				15 18						17 17		18 16								
Newark Castle	d		14a18	14 42	15a26		15 54	16a18	16 43		17a25	17 50	18a24		18 43	19a25	19 53			21 04	21 57
Newark North Gate	a																				22 06
	d					15 29								18 07				20 30	20 36		22 09
Collingham	d			14 52		15 38	16 02		16 52			18 00		18 16	18 54		20 08	20 39		21 12	22 18
Swinderby	d						16 07					18 04			19 01						22 22
Hykeham	d			15 00			16 13					18 10			19 10					21 21	22 28
Lincoln	a			15 11		15 56	16 27		17 10			18 25		18 34	19 25		20 26	20 54	21 00	21 33	22 40
	d	14 52								17 22				18 35				20 55			
Market Rasen	d	15 10								17 38				18 52				21a13			
Barnetby	a	15 26								17 54				19 08							
Habrough	a	15 36								18 02				19 18							
Grimsby Town	a	15 50								18 18				19 34							
Cleethorpes	a																				

Sundays 20 May to 9 September

		EM	EM	EM	EM	EM	EM	EM	EM	EM	EM	EM	EM	EM	EM	EM	EM	GR G	EM	EM	EM
Nottingham	d	09 30	10 30		11 30	12 30		13 30	14 35	15 29		16 33		17 27	18 36		19 35		20 39		22 28
Carlton	d	09 36			11 36				14 41					17 33							22 34
Burton Joyce	d	09 40			11 40				14 45					17 36							22 37
Lowdham	d	09 44	10 41		11 44	12 41		13 41	14 49	15 39		16 44		17 40	18 46		19 45		20 49		22 42
Thurgarton	d	09 48			11 48				14 53					17 44							22 46
Bleasby	d	09 51			11 51				14 57					17 47							22 49
Fiskerton	d	09 56			11 55				15 00					17 51							22 52
Rolleston	d	09 58			11 57				15 03					17 53							22 54
Newark Castle	d	10 06	10 55		12 06	12 54		13 54	15 13	15 59		16 59		18 01	19 02		19 58		21 03		23 03
Newark North Gate	a														19 12						23 13
	d			11 40			13 35				16 45		17 55		19 28	19 53		20 37		22 10	23 17
Collingham	d	10 17		11 48	12 17		13 43		15 26	16 08	16 53	17 08	18 04	18 10	19 37		20 07		21 12	22 19	23 25
Swinderby	d	10 22			12 22				15 31		16 58	17 12		18 15	19 42		20 12		21 17		23 30
Hykeham	d	10 28			12 28				15 37		17 04	17 18		18 21	19 48		20 18		21 23		23 36
Lincoln	a	10 40	11 22	12 07	12 41	13 25	14 02	14 23	15 50	16 26	17 16	17 31	18 20	18 33	19 57	20 19	20 30	21 01	21 35	22 37	23 48
	d			12 07						16 27			18 22								
Market Rasen	d			12 23						16 43			18 38								
Barnetby	a			12 38						16 58			18 53								
Habrough	a			12 51						17 06			19 01								
Grimsby Town	a			13 03						17 21			19 16								
Cleethorpes	a			13 15						17 31			19 25								

A To Peterborough
B From Matlock
C From Leicester
D not until 6 October. From Matlock
E 29 September, 6 October. From Derby
F From St Pancras International
G From London Kings Cross

For connections from London Kings Cross refer to Table T026

Table T027-F

Nottingham - Newark - Lincoln - Cleethorpes

Sundays

16 September to 2 December

		EM	EM	EM	EM	EM	EM	EM	EM	EM	EM	EM	EM	EM	EM	EM	EM	GR A	EM	EM	EM
Nottingham	d	09 30	10 30		11 30	12 30		13 30	14 35	15 30		16 33		17 27	18 36		19 35		20 39		22 28
Carlton	d	09 36			11 36				14 41					17 33							22 34
Burton Joyce	d	09 40			11 40				14 45					17 36							22 37
Lowdham	d	09 44	10 41		11 44	12 41		13 41	14 49	15 41		16 44		17 40	18 46		19 45		20 49		22 42
Thurgarton	d	09 48			11 48				14 53					17 44							22 46
Bleasby	d	09 51			11 51				14 57					17 47							22 49
Fiskerton	d	09 56			11 55				15 00					17 51							22 52
Rolleston	d	09 58			11 57				15 03					17 53							22 54
Newark Castle	d	10 06	10 55		12 06	12 54		13 54	15 13	15 56		16 59		18 01	19 02		19 58		21 03		23 03
Newark North Gate	a														19 12						23 13
	d			11 40			13 35				16 45		17 55		19 28	19 53		20 37		22 10	23 17
Collingham	d	10 17		11 48	12 17		13 43		15 26	16 08	16 53	17 08	18 04	18 10	19 37		20 07		21 12	22 19	23 25
Swinderby	d	10 22			12 22				15 31		16 58	17 12		18 15	19 42		20 12		21 17		23 30
Hykeham	d	10 28			12 28				15 37		17 04	17 18		18 21	19 48		20 18		21 23		23 36
Lincoln	a	10 40	11 22	12 07	12 41	13 25	14 02	14 23	15 50	16 26	17 16	17 31	18 20	18 33	19 57	20 19	20 30	21 01	21 35	22 37	23 48
	d																				
Market Rasen	d																				
Barnetby	a																				
Habrough	a																				
Grimsby Town	a																				
Cleethorpes	a																				

A From London Kings Cross

For connections from London Kings Cross refer to Table T026

Table T027-R

Cleethorpes - Lincoln - Newark - Nottingham

Mondays to Fridays

21 May to 21 September

Miles	Miles			EM	EM	EM	EM	EM ◇ A	EM	GR B	EM C	EM	EM	EM D	EM	EM	EM D	EM	EM ◇	EM D	EM	EM	EM D
0	—	**Cleethorpes**	d				05 49																
3¼	—	**Grimsby Town**	d				05 56					07 03							09 20				
11¼	—	Habrough	d				06 06					07 13							09 30				
17¾	—	Barnetby	d				06 16					07 22							09 39				
32¼	—	Market Rasen	d				06 32					07 39							09 55				
47	—	**Lincoln**	a				06 51					07 57							10 14				
—	—		d	05 26		06 46	06 54	07 05		07 30	07 36	07 59		08 36		09 07	09 37		10 16	10 36		11 35	11 40
51	—	Hykeham	d	05 34		06 54	07 01				07 44			08 44			09 45			10 44			
55¾	—	Swinderby	d	05 40			07 07				07 50			08 50			09 51			10 50			
58½	0	Collingham	d	05 45		07 04	07 12	07 20			07 55	08 15		08 55		09 22	09 56		10 31	10 55			
—	5	**Newark North Gate**	a	05 56			07 22			07 55		08 24				09 32			10 40			12 00	
—	—		d	05 59																			
63½	—	**Newark Castle**	d	06 09	06 42	07 14		07 30	07 39		08 06		08 41	09 08	09 39		10 07	10 47		11 07	11 39		12 07
67	—	Rolleston	d	06 15	06 48				07 46						09 46						11 46		
68	—	Fiskerton	d	06 18	06 51				07 48		08 13		08 48		09 48			10 54			11 48		
69¾	—	Bleasby	d	06 22	06 55				07 52						09 52						11 52		
70¾	—	Thurgarton	d	06 25	06 58				07 55						09 55						11 55		
71½	—	Lowdham	d	06 30	07 02			07 43	08 00		08 20		08 56		10 00			11 02			12 00		
75¾	—	Burton Joyce	d	06 34	07 06				08 04				09 00		10 04						12 04		
77¾	—	Carlton	d	06 38	07 11				08 08				09 05		10 08			11 08			12 08		
80¾	—	**Nottingham**	a	06 47	07 18	07 40		07 56	08 17		08 33		09 13	09 30	10 16		10 30	11 16		11 30	12 16		12 30

		EM	EM	EM D	EM	EM D	EM	EM D	EM	EM	EM D	EM	EM	EM D	EM	EM	EM D	EM	EM D	EM	EM	EM	EM
Cleethorpes	d																						
Grimsby Town	d		11 28							13 49						15 45				18 28			
Habrough	d		11 38							13 59						15 56				18 38			
Barnetby	d		11 47							14 09						16 05				18 48			
Market Rasen	d		12 03							14 25						16 22				19 04			
Lincoln	a		12 22							14 44						16 40				19 23			
	d		12 23	12 34		13 37		14 36		14 46	15 36		15 42	16 34		16 43	17 26	18 18	18 35	19 25		20 31	21 40
Hykeham	d			12 42		13 45		14 44			15 44			16 42			17 34	18 26	18 43	19 32		20 39	21 49
Swinderby	d			12 48				14 50			15 50			16 48			17 40			19 39			
Collingham	d		12 40	12 53		13 55		14 55		15 02	15 55			16 53		16 59	17 45	18 36	18 53	19 44		20 49	21 58
Newark North Gate	a		12 50							15 11			16 11			17 11		18 46		19 53			
	d																						
Newark Castle	d	12 47		13 05	13 47	14 07	14 39	15 06	15 47		16 08	16 39		17 05	17 39		17 56		19 03		19 47	20 58	22 07
Rolleston	d						14 46					16 46			17 46		18 02						
Fiskerton	d	12 54			13 54		14 48		15 54			16 48			17 48		18 04		19 10		19 54	21 05	22 17
Bleasby	d						14 52					16 52			17 52		18 08						
Thurgarton	d						14 55					16 55			17 55		18 11						
Lowdham	d	13 02			14 02		15 00		16 02			17 00		17 17	18 00		18 15		19 17		20 02	21 12	22 25
Burton Joyce	d						15 04					17 04			18 04		18 19						
Carlton	d	13 08			14 08		15 08		16 08			17 08		17 23	18 08		18 23		19 23		20 08	21 18	22 32
Nottingham	a	13 16		13 30	14 16	14 30	15 16	15 30	16 16		16 30	17 16		17 30	18 16		18 30		19 30		20 16	21 27	22 39

		EM	EM
Cleethorpes	d	21 17	
Grimsby Town	d	21 24	
Habrough	d	21 35	
Barnetby	d	21 44	
Market Rasen	d	22 00	
Lincoln	a	22 19	
	d		22 26
Hykeham	d		22 34
Swinderby	d		22 40
Collingham	d		22 45
Newark North Gate	a		
	d		
Newark Castle	d		22 55
Rolleston	d		
Fiskerton	d		23 02
Bleasby	d		23 05
Thurgarton	d		
Lowdham	d		23 11
Burton Joyce	d		23 15
Carlton	d		23 19
Nottingham	a		23 28

A To St Pancras International
B To London Kings Cross
C From Sleaford to Leicester
D To Leicester

For connections to London Kings Cross refer to Table T026

Table T027-R

Cleethorpes - Lincoln - Newark - Nottingham

Mondays to Fridays
24 September to 7 December

	EM	EM	EM	EM	EM	EM	GR	EM	EM	EM	EM	EM	EM	EM	EM	EM	EM	EM	EM	EM	EM	EM
		A			◇1 B	A	C	D		A	E	A		E	A	◇	E	A		E	A	
Cleethorpes d				05 49																		
Grimsby Town d				05 56					07 03							09 20						11 28
Habrough d				06 06					07 13							09 30						11 38
Barnetby d				06 16					07 22							09 39						11 47
Market Rasen d				06 32					07 39							09 55						12 03
Lincoln a				06 51					07 57							10 14						12 22
Lincoln d	05 26		06 46	06 54	07 05		07 30	07 36	07 59		08 36		09 07	09 37		10 16	10 36		11 35	11 40		12 23
Hykeham d	05 34		06 54	07 01				07 44			08 44			09 45			10 44					
Swinderby d	05 40			07 07				07 50			08 50			09 51			10 50					
Collingham d	05 45		07 04	07 12	07 20			07 55	08 15		08 55		09 22	09 56		10 31	10 55					12 40
Newark North Gate a	05 56			07 22			07 55		08 24				09 32			10 40			12 00			12 50
Newark North Gate d	05 59																					
Newark Castle d	06 09	06 42	07 14		07 30	07 39		08 06		08 41	09 08	09 39		10 07	10 47		11 07	11 39		12 07	12 47	
Rolleston d	06 15	06 48				07 46						09 46						11 46				
Fiskerton d	06 18	06 51				07 48		08 13		08 48		09 48			10 54			11 48			12 54	
Bleasby d	06 22	06 55				07 52						09 52						11 52				
Thurgarton d	06 25	06 58				07 55						09 55						11 55				
Lowdham d	06 30	07 02			07 43	08 00		08 20		08 56		10 00			11 02			12 00			13 02	
Burton Joyce d	06 34	07 06				08 04				09 00		10 04						12 04				
Carlton d	06 38	07 11				08 08				09 05		10 08			11 08			12 08			13 08	
Nottingham a	06 47	07 18	07 42		07 56	08 17		08 34		09 13	09 32	10 16		10 32	11 16		11 32	12 16		12 30	13 16	

	EM	EM	EM	EM	EM	EM	EM	EM	EM	EM	EM	EM	EM	EM	EM	EM	EM	EM	EM	EM	EM
	E	A	E	A	E	A		E	A		E	A		E		E		A	F	G	
Cleethorpes d																					
Grimsby Town d							13 49						15 45				18 28				
Habrough d							13 59						15 56				18 38				
Barnetby d							14 09						16 05				18 48				
Market Rasen d							14 25						16 22				19 04				
Lincoln a							14 44						16 40				19 23				
Lincoln d	12 34		13 37		14 36		14 46	15 36		15 42	16 34		16 43	17 26	18 18	18 35	19 25		20 31	20 31	21 40
Hykeham d	12 42		13 45		14 44			15 44			16 42			17 34	18 26	18 43	19 32		20 39	20 39	21 49
Swinderby d	12 48				14 50			15 50			16 48			17 40			19 39				
Collingham d	12 53		13 55		14 55		15 02	15 55			16 53		16 59	17 45	18 36	18 53	19 44		20 49	20 49	21 58
Newark North Gate a							15 11			16 11			17 11		18 46		19 53				
Newark North Gate d																					
Newark Castle d	13 05	13 47	14 07	14 39	15 06	15 47		16 08	16 39		17 05	17 39		17 56		19 03		19 47	20 58	20 58	22 07
Rolleston d				14 46					16 46			17 46		18 02							
Fiskerton d		13 54		14 48		15 54			16 48			17 48		18 04		19 10		19 54	21 05	21 05	22 17
Bleasby d				14 52					16 52			17 52		18 08							
Thurgarton d				14 55					16 55			17 55		18 11							
Lowdham d		14 02		15 00		16 02			17 00		17 17	18 00		18 15		19 17		20 02	21 12	21 12	22 25
Burton Joyce d				15 04					17 04			18 04		18 19							
Carlton d		14 08		15 08		16 08			17 08		17 23	18 08		18 23		19 23		20 08	21 18	21 18	22 32
Nottingham a	13 32	14 16	14 32	15 16	15 32	16 16		16 32	17 16		17 32	18 16		18 32		19 32		20 16	21 29	21 32	22 39

	EM	EM
Cleethorpes d	21 17	
Grimsby Town d	21 24	
Habrough d	21 35	
Barnetby d	21 44	
Market Rasen d	22 00	
Lincoln a	22 19	
Lincoln d		22 26
Hykeham d		22 34
Swinderby d		22 40
Collingham d		22 45
Newark North Gate a		
Newark North Gate d		
Newark Castle d		22 55
Rolleston d		
Fiskerton d		23 02
Bleasby d		23 05
Thurgarton d		
Lowdham d		23 11
Burton Joyce d		23 15
Carlton d		23 19
Nottingham a		23 30

A To Derby
B To St Pancras International
C To London Kings Cross
D From Sleaford to Leicester
E To Leicester
F until 5 October
G from 8 October

For connections to London Kings Cross refer to Table T026

Table T027-R

Cleethorpes - Lincoln - Newark - Nottingham

Saturdays
26 May to 22 September

	EM	EM	EM	GR	EM	EM	EM	EM	EM	EM	EM	EM	EM	EM	EM	EM	EM	EM	EM	EM	EM	EM
		◇1 A		B	C	D			E			E		◇	E			E			E	
Cleethorpes d																						
Grimsby Town d								06 50						09 20						11 28		
Habrough d								07 00						09 30						11 38		
Barnetby d								07 09						09 39						11 47		
Market Rasen d								07 26						09 55						12 03		
Lincoln a								07 44						10 14						12 22		
Lincoln d	05 26	07 04		07 30	07 36	07 36		07 46	08 35		09 01	09 36		10 15	10 36		11 35	11 40		12 23	12 36	
Hykeham d	05 34				07 44	07 44			08 43			09 44			10 44						12 44	
Swinderby d	05 40				07 50	07 50			08 49			09 50			10 50						12 50	
Collingham d	05 45	07 19			07 55	07 55		08 02	08 54		09 16	09 55		10 32	10 55					12 40	12 55	
Newark North Gate a	05 56			07 56				08 12			09 25			10 44			11 58			12 52		
Newark North Gate d	05 59																					
Newark Castle d	06 10	07 29	07 41		08 04	08 04	08 43		09 04	09 38		10 07	10 47		11 04	11 39		12 04	12 47		13 06	13 49
Rolleston d	06 16		07 47							09 45						11 46						
Fiskerton d	06 19		07 50				08 50			09 47			10 54		11 11	11 48			12 54			13 56
Bleasby d	06 22		07 54				08 55			09 51						11 52						
Thurgarton d	06 26		07 57							09 54						11 55						
Lowdham d	06 30	07 42	08 01				09 00			09 59			11 02		11 18	12 00			13 02			14 04
Burton Joyce d	06 34		08 06							10 03						12 04						
Carlton d	06 38		08 10				09 07			10 07			11 08		11 24	12 08			13 08			14 10
Nottingham a	06 47	07 57	08 17		08 28	08 29	09 17		09 31	10 15		10 30	11 16		11 31	12 16		12 27	13 16		13 29	14 18

	EM	EM	EM	EM	EM	EM	EM	EM	EM	EM	EM	EM	EM	EM	EM	EM	EM	EM
	E		E			E		E			E		E					
Cleethorpes d																		
Grimsby Town d					13 49					16 00					18 28		19 45	
Habrough d					13 59					16 10					18 38		19 55	
Barnetby d					14 09					16 19					18 47		20 04	
Market Rasen d					14 25					16 35					19 02		20 20	
Lincoln a					14 44					16 53					19 21		20 39	
Lincoln d	13 37		14 32		14 46	15 26		16 35		16 55	17 25		18 30		19 24	19 39		20 45
Hykeham d	13 45		14 40			15 33		16 43			17 33		18 38		19 32			
Swinderby d						15 39		16 50			17 39				19 38			
Collingham d	13 55		14 53		15 02	15 47		16 54		17 11	17 44		18 48		19 43			21 00
Newark North Gate a					15 11					17 22					19 53			
Newark North Gate d																		
Newark Castle d	14 05	14 39	15 04	15 47		15 59	16 38	17 05	17 39		17 55	18 47	18 59	19 47		20 04		21 10
Rolleston d		14 46					16 45		17 46		18 01							
Fiskerton d		14 48		15 54		16 06	16 47		17 48		18 03	18 54		19 54				
Bleasby d		14 52					16 51		17 52		18 06							
Thurgarton d		14 55					16 54		17 55		18 09							
Lowdham d		15 00		16 02		16 12	16 59	17 17	18 00		18 14	19 02		20 02		20 17		21 23
Burton Joyce d		15 04					17 03		18 04		18 18							
Carlton d		15 08		16 08		16 19	17 07		18 08		18 21	19 08		20 08				
Nottingham a	14 28	15 16	15 30	16 16		16 27	17 15	17 30	18 16		18 30	19 16	19 24	20 16		20 31		21 37

Saturdays
29 September to 8 December

	EM	EM	EM	GR	EM	EM	EM	EM	EM	EM	EM	EM	EM	EM	EM	EM	EM	EM	EM	EM	EM	EM
		◇1 A	F	B	G	F		E	F		E	F	◇	E	F		E	F		E	F	E
Cleethorpes d																						
Grimsby Town d							06 50						09 20						11 28			
Habrough d							07 00						09 30						11 38			
Barnetby d							07 09						09 39						11 47			
Market Rasen d							07 26						09 55						12 03			
Lincoln a							07 44						10 14						12 22			
Lincoln d	05 26	07 04		07 30	07 36		07 46	08 35		09 01	09 36		10 15	10 36		11 35	11 40		12 23	12 36		13 37
Hykeham d	05 34				07 44			08 43			09 44			10 44						12 44		13 45
Swinderby d	05 40				07 50			08 49			09 50			10 50						12 50		
Collingham d	05 45	07 19			07 55		08 02	08 54		09 16	09 55		10 32	10 55					12 40	12 55		13 55
Newark North Gate a	05 56			07 56			08 12			09 25			10 44			11 58			12 52			
Newark North Gate d	05 59																					
Newark Castle d	06 10	07 29	07 41		08 04	08 43		09 04	09 38		10 07	10 47		11 04	11 39		12 04	12 47		13 06	13 49	14 05
Rolleston d	06 16		07 47						09 45						11 46							
Fiskerton d	06 19		07 50			08 50			09 47			10 54		11 11	11 48			12 54			13 56	
Bleasby d	06 22		07 54			08 55			09 51						11 52							
Thurgarton d	06 26		07 57						09 54						11 55							
Lowdham d	06 30	07 42	08 01			09 00			09 59			11 02		11 18	12 00			13 02			14 04	
Burton Joyce d	06 34		08 06						10 03						12 04							
Carlton d	06 38		08 10			09 07			10 07			11 08		11 24	12 08			13 08			14 10	
Nottingham a	06 47	07 57	08 17		08 30	09 17		09 33	10 15		10 32	11 16		11 32	12 16		12 29	13 16		13 31	14 18	14 30

A To St Pancras International
B To London Kings Cross
C until 21 July, also 8 September, 15 September, 22 September. From Sleaford to Leicester
D from 28 July until 1 September. From Sleaford to Leicester
E To Leicester
F To Derby
G From Sleaford to Leicester

For connections to London Kings Cross refer to Table T026

Table T027-R

Saturdays

29 September to 8 December

Cleethorpes - Lincoln - Newark - Nottingham

		EM A	EM B	EM A	EM	EM B	EM A	EM B	EM A	EM	EM B	EM A	EM B	EM A	EM	EM	EM	EM
Cleethorpes	d																	
Grimsby Town	d				13 49					16 00					18 28		19 45	
Habrough	d				13 59					16 10					18 38		19 55	
Barnetby	d				14 09					16 19					18 47		20 04	
Market Rasen	d				14 25					16 35					19 02		20 20	
Lincoln	a				14 44					16 53					19 21		20 39	
	d		14 32		14 46	15 26		16 35		16 55	17 25		18 30		19 24	19 39		20 45
Hykeham	d		14 40			15 33		16 43			17 33		18 38		19 32			
Swinderby	d					15 39		16 50			17 39				19 38			
Collingham	d		14 53		15 02	15 47		16 54		17 11	17 44		18 48		19 43			21 00
Newark North Gate 7	a				15 11					17 22					19 53			
	d																	
Newark Castle	d	14 39	15 04	15 47		15 59	16 38	17 05	17 39		17 55	18 47	18 59	19 47		20 04		21 10
Rolleston	d	14 46					16 45		17 46		18 01							
Fiskerton	d	14 48		15 54		16 06	16 47		17 48		18 03	18 54		19 54				
Bleasby	d	14 52					16 51		17 52		18 06							
Thurgarton	d	14 55					16 54		17 55		18 09							
Lowdham	d	15 00		16 02		16 12	16 59	17 17	18 00		18 14	19 02		20 02		20 17		21 23
Burton Joyce	d	15 04					17 03		18 04		18 18							
Carlton	d	15 08		16 08		16 19	17 07		18 08		18 21	19 08		20 08				
Nottingham 8	a	15 16	15 32	16 16		16 29	17 15	17 32	18 16		18 32	19 16	19 26	20 16		20 33		21 37

Sundays

20 May to 9 September

		EM	EM	EM	EM	EM	EM	EM	EM	EM	EM	EM	EM	EM	EM	EM	EM	EM	EM	EM	EM
Cleethorpes	d									13 56							18 18			20 15	
Grimsby Town	d									14 03							18 25			20 22	
Habrough	d									14 13							18 35			20 33	
Barnetby	d									14 22							18 44			20 42	
Market Rasen	d									14 37							18 59			20 57	
Lincoln	a									14 56							19 18			21 15	
	d	08 47	09 59	11 05	11 10	11 56	12 45	13 00	14 17	15 08	15 44	16 15	16 56	17 09	18 05	19 03	19 22	20 05	21 00	21 23	22 10
Hykeham	d	08 55			11 18				14 25	15 16		16 23	17 04		18 13	19 11		20 13	21 08	21 31	22 18
Swinderby	d	09 01			11 24				14 31	15 22		16 29	17 10		18 19	19 17		20 19	21 14	21 37	22 24
Collingham	d	09 06		11 20	11 29		13 00		14 36	15 26	15 59	16 34	17 14	17 24	18 23	19 22		20 23	21 18	21 42	22 28
Newark North Gate 7	a	09 15		11 30			13 10			15 36	16 09			17 34			19 46		21 27	21 52	
	d	09 19								15 40									21 31		
Newark Castle	d	09 29	10 24		11 42	12 24		13 29	14 49	15 50		16 46	17 24		18 34	19 33		20 36	21 40		22 39
Rolleston	d	09 35			11 48				14 55			16 53			18 40						22 45
Fiskerton	d	09 38			11 51				14 57			16 55			18 42						22 47
Bleasby	d	09 41			11 54				15 01			16 59			18 46						22 50
Thurgarton	d	09 44			11 58				15 04			17 02			18 49						22 53
Lowdham	d	09 49	10 37		12 02	12 40		13 42	15 09	16 03		17 06	17 37		18 53	19 45		20 48	21 53		22 58
Burton Joyce	d	09 53			12 06				15 13			17 10			18 57						23 02
Carlton	d	09 57			12 10				15 17			17 14			19 01						23 05
Nottingham 8	a	10 08	10 53		12 21	12 57		13 57	15 29	16 20		17 26	17 54		19 11	20 05		21 03	22 09		23 16

Sundays

16 September to 2 December

		EM	EM	EM	EM	EM	EM	EM	EM	EM	EM	EM	EM	EM	EM	EM	EM	EM	EM	EM	EM
Cleethorpes	d																				
Grimsby Town	d																				
Habrough	d																				
Barnetby	d																				
Market Rasen	d																				
Lincoln	a																				
	d	08 47	09 59	11 05	11 10	11 56	12 45	13 00	14 17	15 08	15 44	16 15	16 56	17 09	18 05	19 03	19 22	20 05	21 00	21 26	22 10
Hykeham	d	08 55			11 18				14 25	15 16		16 23	17 04		18 13	19 11		20 13	21 08	21 34	22 18
Swinderby	d	09 01			11 24				14 31	15 22		16 29	17 10		18 19	19 17		20 19	21 14	21 40	22 24
Collingham	d	09 06		11 20	11 29		13 00		14 36	15 26	15 59	16 34	17 14	17 24	18 23	19 22		20 23	21 18	21 45	22 28
Newark North Gate 7	a	09 15		11 30			13 10			15 36	16 09			17 34			19 46		21 27	21 55	
	d	09 19								15 40									21 31		
Newark Castle	d	09 29	10 24		11 42	12 24		13 29	14 49	15 50		16 46	17 24		18 34	19 33		20 36	21 40		22 39
Rolleston	d	09 35			11 48				14 55			16 53			18 40						22 45
Fiskerton	d	09 38			11 51				14 57			16 55			18 42						22 47
Bleasby	d	09 41			11 54				15 01			16 59			18 46						22 50
Thurgarton	d	09 44			11 58				15 04			17 02			18 49						22 53
Lowdham	d	09 49	10 37		12 02	12 40		13 42	15 09	16 03		17 06	17 37		18 53	19 45		20 48	21 53		22 58
Burton Joyce	d	09 53			12 06				15 13			17 10			18 57						23 02
Carlton	d	09 57			12 10				15 17			17 14			19 01						23 05
Nottingham 8	a	10 08	10 53		12 21	12 57		13 57	15 29	16 20		17 26	17 54		19 11	20 05		21 03	22 09		23 16

A To Derby

B To Leicester

For connections to London Kings Cross refer to Table T026

Table T028-F

Mondays to Fridays

21 May to 7 December

Cleethorpes - Barton-on-Humber - Barnetby - Gainsborough Central

Miles	Miles			TP ◇1 A	EM B	NT	TP ◇1 A	EM B	NT	TP ◇1 A	TP ◇1 A	NT	EM ◇ B	TP ◇1 A	TP ◇1 A	NT	EM B	TP ◇1 A	TP ◇1 A	NT	TP ◇1 A	EM B	TP ◇1 A
0	0	**Cleethorpes**	d	05 07	05 49	05 59	06 26		07 00	07 26	08 26	08 55		09 26	10 26	10 55		11 26	12 26	12 55	13 26		14 26
1½	1½	New Clee	d			06x02			07x03			08x58				10x58				12x58			
2¼	2¼	Grimsby Docks	d			06 05			07 06			09 01				11 01				13 01			
3¼	3¼	**Grimsby Town**	a	05 14	05 55	06 07	06 33		07 08	07 33	08 33	09 03		09 33	10 33	11 03		11 33	12 33	13 03	13 33		14 33
—	—		d	05 15	05 56	06 08	06 34	07 03	07 09	07 34	08 34	09 04	09 20	09 34	10 34	11 04	11 28	11 34	12 34	13 04	13 34	13 49	14 34
5¼	5¼	Great Coates	d			06 12			07 13			09 08				11 08				13 08			
6½	6½	Healing	d			06 15			07 16			09 11				11 11				13 11			
7½	7½	Stallingborough	d			06 18			07 19			09 14				11 14				13 14			
11¼	11¼	Habrough	d		06 06	06 24	06 44	07 13	07 25	07 44	08 44	09 20	09 30		10 44	11 20	11 38		12 44	13 20		13 59	14 44
13	—	Ulceby	d			06 28			07 29			09 24				11 24				13 24			
15½	—	Thornton Abbey	d			06 33			07 34			09 29				11 29				13 29			
17¼	—	Goxhill	d			06 36			07 37			09 32				11 32				13 32			
19½	—	New Holland	d			06 41			07 42			09 37				11 37				13 37			
20¾	—	Barrow Haven	d			06 44			07 45			09 40				11 40				13 40			
22¾	—	**Barton-on-Humber**	a			06 50			07 51			09 46				11 46				13 46			
—	—	Barton-on-Humber	d																				
—	—	Hull Paragon Interchange	a																				
—	17¾	**Barnetby**	a	05 31	06 15		06 52	07 22		07 52	08 52		09 39	09 52	10 52		11 47	11 52	12 52		13 52	14 08	14 52
—	—		d																				
—	21½	Brigg	d																				
—	27¾	Kirton Lindsey	d																				
—	38	Gainsborough Central	a																				
—	—		d																				
—	48	Retford	a																				

		NT	TP ◇1 A	EM B	TP ◇1 A	NT	TP ◇1 A	EM B	TP ◇1 A	NT	TP ◇1 C	TP ◇1 A	NT	EM D
Cleethorpes	d	14 55	15 26		16 26	16 55	17 23		18 29	19 00	19 26	20 26	21 04	21 17
New Clee	d	14x58				16x58				19x03			21x07	
Grimsby Docks	d	15 01				17 01				19 06			21 10	
Grimsby Town	a	15 03	15 33		16 33	17 03	17 30		18 36	19 08	19 33	20 33	21 12	21 23
	d	15 04	15 34	15 45	16 34	17 04	17 31	18 28	18 37	19 09	19 34	20 34	21 13	21 24
Great Coates	d	15 08				17 08				19 13			21 17	
Healing	d	15 11				17 11				19 16			21 20	
Stallingborough	d	15 14				17 14				19 19			21 23	
Habrough	d	15 20		15 56	16 44	17 20	17 41	18 38		19 25	19 44		21 29	21 35
Ulceby	d	15 24				17 24				19 29			21 33	
Thornton Abbey	d	15 29				17 29				19 34			21 38	
Goxhill	d	15 32				17 32				19 37			21 41	
New Holland	d	15 37				17 37				19 42			21 46	
Barrow Haven	d	15 40				17 40				19 45			21 49	
Barton-on-Humber	a	15 46				17 46				19 51			21 55	
Barton-on-Humber	d													
Hull Paragon Interchange	a													
Barnetby	a		15 52	16 05	16 52		17 49	18 47	18 55		19 52	20 52		21 44
	d													
Brigg	d													
Kirton Lindsey	d													
Gainsborough Central	a													
	d													
Retford	a													

Saturdays

26 May to 8 December

		TP ◇1 A	NT	TP ◇1 A	EM B	NT	TP ◇1 A	TP ◇1 A	NT	EM ◇ B	TP ◇1 A	TP ◇1 A	NT	NT ◇ E	EM B	TP ◇1 A	TP ◇1 A	NT	TP ◇1 A	EM B	TP ◇1 A	NT	NT ◇ E
Cleethorpes	d	05 07	05 59	06 26		06 59	07 26	08 26	08 57		09 26	10 26	10 55	11 14		11 26	12 26	12 55	13 26		14 26	14 55	15 11
New Clee	d		06x02			07x02			09x00				10x58					12x58				14x58	
Grimsby Docks	d		06 05			07 05			09 03				11 01					13 01				15 01	
Grimsby Town	a	05 14	06 07	06 33		07 07	07 33	08 33	09 05		09 33	10 33	11 03	11 20		11 33	12 33	13 03	13 33		14 33	15 03	15 17
	d	05 15	06 08	06 34	06 50	07 08	07 34	08 34	09 06	09 20	09 34	10 34	11 04	11 21	11 28	11 34	12 34	13 04	13 34	13 49	14 34	15 04	15 18
Great Coates	d		06 12			07 12			09 10				11 08					13 08				15 08	
Healing	d		06 15			07 15			09 13				11 11					13 11				15 11	
Stallingborough	d		06 18			07 18			09 16				11 14					13 14				15 14	
Habrough	d		06 24	06 44	07 00	07 24	07 44	08 44	09 22	09 30		10 44	11 20	11 31	11 38		12 44	13 20		13 59	14 44	15 20	15 27
Ulceby	d		06 28			07 28			09 26				11 24					13 24				15 24	
Thornton Abbey	d		06 33			07 33			09 31				11 29					13 29				15 29	
Goxhill	d		06 36			07 36			09 34				11 32					13 32				15 32	
New Holland	d		06 41			07 41			09 39				11 37					13 37				15 37	
Barrow Haven	d		06 44			07 44			09 42				11 40					13 40				15 40	
Barton-on-Humber	a		06 50			07 50			09 48				11 46					13 46				15 46	
Barton-on-Humber	d																						
Hull Paragon Interchange	a																						
Barnetby	a	05 31		06 52	07 09		07 52	08 52		09 39	09 53	10 52		11 40	11 47	11 52	12 52		13 52	14 08	14 52		15 36
	d													11 42									15 38
Brigg	d													11 48									15 43
Kirton Lindsey	d													11 56									15 52
Gainsborough Central	a													12 09									16 10
	d																						
Retford	a																						

A To Manchester Airport

B To Newark North Gate

C To Manchester Piccadilly

D To Lincoln

E To Sheffield, via Retford

For Hull, Doncaster, Meadowhall, Sheffield, Manchester and Manchester Airport refer to Table T029

Table T028-F

Saturdays
26 May to 8 December

Cleethorpes - Barton-on-Humber - Barnetby - Gainsborough Central

		TP ◇1 A	EM B	TP ◇1 A	NT	TP ◇1 A	EM B	TP ◇1 A	NT	NT ◇ C	TP ◇1 D	EM E	TP ◇1 A	NT
Cleethorpes	d	15 26		16 26	16 55	17 26		18 29	18 56	19 17	19 26		20 26	21 04
New Clee	d				16x58				18x59					21x07
Grimsby Docks	d				17 01				19 02					21 10
Grimsby Town	a	15 33		16 33	17 03	17 33		18 36	19 04	19 23	19 33		20 33	21 12
	d	15 34	16 00	16 34	17 04	17 34	18 28	18 37	19 05	19 24	19 34	19 45	20 34	21 13
Great Coates	d				17 08				19 09					21 17
Healing	d				17 11				19 12					21 20
Stallingborough	d				17 14				19 15					21 23
Habrough	d		16 10	16 44	17 20	17 44	18 38		19 21	19 33	19 44	19 55		21 29
Ulceby	d				17 24				19 25					21 33
Thornton Abbey	d				17 29				19 30					21 38
Goxhill	d				17 32				19 33					21 41
New Holland	d				17 37				19 38					21 46
Barrow Haven	d				17 40				19 41					21 49
Barton-on-Humber	a				17 46				19 47					21 55
Barton-on-Humber	d													
Hull Paragon Interchange	a													
Barnetby	a	15 52	16 19	16 52		17 52	18 46	18 55		19 42	19 52	20 04	20 52	
	d									19 43				
Brigg	d									19 48				
Kirton Lindsey	d									19 57				
Gainsborough Central	a									20 15				
	d													
Retford	a													

Sundays
20 May to 2 December

		TP ◇1 A	NT	TP ◇1 A	TP ◇1 A	TP ◇1 A	NT	TP ◇1 A	EM F	TP ◇1 A	NT	TP ◇1 A	TP ◇1 A	TP ◇1 A	NT	EM G	TP ◇1 A	TP ◇1 A	EM G	TP ◇1 D
Cleethorpes	d	09 26	09 58	10 26	11 26	12 26	12 55	13 26	13 56	14 26	14 59	15 26	16 26	17 27	17 57	18 18	18 29	19 26	20 15	20 26
New Clee	d		10 02				12 59				15 03				18 01					
Grimsby Docks	d		10 04				13 01				15 05				18 03					
Grimsby Town	a	09 33	10 07	10 33	11 33	12 33	13 04	13 33	14 02	14 33	15 08	15 33	16 33	17 34	18 06	18 24	18 36	19 33	20 21	20 33
	d	09 34	10 07	10 34	11 34	12 34	13 04	13 34	14 03	14 34	15 08	15 34	16 34	17 35	18 06	18 25	18 37	19 34	20 22	20 34
Great Coates	d		10 11				13 08				15 12				18 10					
Healing	d		10 15				13 12				15 16				18 14					
Stallingborough	d		10 18				13 15				15 19				18 17					
Habrough	d		10 24	10 44		12 44	13 21		14 13	14 44	15 25		16 44	17 45	18 23	18 35			20 33	20 44
Ulceby	d		10 27				13 24				15 28				18 26					
Thornton Abbey	d		10 32				13 29				15 33				18 31					
Goxhill	d		10 36				13 33				15 37				18 35					
New Holland	d		10 41				13 38				15 42				18 40					
Barrow Haven	d		10 44				13 41				15 45				18 43					
Barton-on-Humber	a		10 50				13 46				15 50				18 48					
Barton-on-Humber	d																			
Hull Paragon Interchange	a																			
Barnetby	a	09 53		10 52	11 52	12 52		13 52	14 21	14 52		15 52	16 52	17 53		18 43	18 55	19 52	20 42	20 52
	d																			
Brigg	d																			
Kirton Lindsey	d																			
Gainsborough Central	a																			
	d																			
Retford	a																			

A To Manchester Airport
B To Newark North Gate
C To Sheffield. via Retford
D To Manchester Piccadilly
E To Lincoln
F until 9 September. To Nottingham
G until 9 September. To Newark North Gate

For Hull, Doncaster, Meadowhall, Sheffield, Manchester and Manchester Airport refer to Table T029

Table T028-R

Mondays to Fridays
21 May to 7 December

Gainsborough Central - Barnetby - Barton-on-Humber - Cleethorpes

Miles	Miles			EM A	NT	NT	TP ◇1 B	EM C	TP ◇1 B	NT	TP ◇1 B	EM C	TP ◇1 B	NT	TP ◇1 B	EM C	TP ◇1 B	NT	TP ◇1 B	EM A	TP ◇1 B	NT	TP ◇1 B
—	0	Retford	d																				
—	10	Gainsborough Central	a																				
—	—		d																				
—	20¼	Kirton Lindsey	d																				
—	26½	Brigg	d																				
—	30¼	**Barnetby**	d	06 31			08 16	08 50	09 20		10 19	10 59	11 17		12 17	13 11	13 17		14 17	15 11	15 17		16 17
—	—	Hull Paragon Interchange	d																				
—	—	Barton-on-Humber	a																				
0	—	**Barton-on-Humber**	d		06 58	07 56				09 50				11 50				13 50				15 50	
2	—	Barrow Haven	d		07 03	08 01				09 55				11 55				13 55				15 55	
3½	—	New Holland	d		07 07	08 05				09 59				11 59				13 59				15 59	
5½	—	Goxhill	d		07 12	08 10				10 04				12 04				14 04				16 04	
7¼	—	Thornton Abbey	d		07 16	08 14				10 08				12 08				14 08				16 08	
9¾	—	Ulceby	d		07 21	08 19				10 13				12 13				14 13				16 13	
11½	36¾	Habrough	d	06 40	07 25	08 23	08 28	08 59		10 17	10 28	11 08		12 17	12 26	13 20		14 17	14 26	15 20		16 17	16 26
15¼	—	Stallingborough	d		07 31	08 28				10 23				12 23				14 23				16 23	
16¼	—	Healing	d		07 34	08 31				10 26				12 26				14 26				16 26	
17½	—	Great Coates	d		07 37	08 34				10 29				12 29				14 29				16 29	
19½	44¾	**Grimsby Town**	a	06 55	07 42	08 39	08 44	09 12	09 39	10 34	10 41	11 22	11 37	12 34	12 39	13 35	13 37	14 34	14 39	15 34	15 37	16 34	16 39
—	—		d			08 39	08 45		09 40	10 34	10 42		11 38	12 34	12 40		13 38	14 34	14 40		15 38	16 34	16 40
20½	—	Grimsby Docks	d			08 42				10 37				12 37				14 37				16 37	
21¼	—	New Clee	d			08x44				10x39				12x39				14x39				16x39	
22¾	48	**Cleethorpes**	a			08 48	08 54		09 53	10 44	10 55		11 51	12 43	12 53		13 51	14 44	14 53		15 51	16 43	16 53

		TP ◇1 B	EM C	NT	TP ◇1 B	TP ◇1 B	TP ◇1 B	NT	EM C	TP ◇1 B	NT	TP ◇1 B	TP ◇1 B
Retford	d												
Gainsborough Central	a												
	d												
Kirton Lindsey	d												
Brigg	d												
Barnetby	d	17 17	17 56		18 21	19 18	20 17		20 35	21 17		22 27	23 25
Hull Paragon Interchange	d												
Barton-on-Humber	a												
Barton-on-Humber	d			17 55				20 03			22 02		
Barrow Haven	d			18 00				20 08			22 07		
New Holland	d			18 04				20 12			22 11		
Goxhill	d			18 09				20 17			22 17		
Thornton Abbey	d			18 13				20 21			22 20		
Ulceby	d			18 18				20 26			22 25		
Habrough	d		18 05	18 22	18 30			20 31	20 44	21 26	22 30	22 36	23 34
Stallingborough	d			18 28				20 37			22 36		
Healing	d			18 31				20 40			22 38		
Great Coates	d			18 34				20 43			22 41		
Grimsby Town	a	17 37	18 18	18 39	18 43	19 37	20 37	20 48	20 56	21 39	22 46	22 49	23 47
	d	17 38		18 39	18 44	19 38	20 38	20 48	20 57	21 40	22 47	22 50	23 48
Grimsby Docks	d			18 42				20 51			22 49		
New Clee	d			18x44				20x53			22x51		
Cleethorpes	a	17 51		18 48	18 55	19 51	20 51	20 57	21 04	21 53	22 55	23 03	00 01

Saturdays
26 May to 8 December

		EM A	NT	NT	TP ◇1 B	EM A	TP ◇1 B	NT ◇ D	NT	TP ◇1 B	EM C	TP ◇1 B	NT	TP ◇1 B	EM C	TP ◇1 B	NT ◇ D	NT	TP ◇1 B	TP ◇1 B	EM A	NT	TP ◇1 B
Retford	d																						
Gainsborough Central	a																						
	d							08 57									12 59						
Kirton Lindsey	d							09 10									13 12						
Brigg	d							09 23									13 21						
Barnetby	d	06 12			08 20	08 50	09 20	09 38		10 19	10 39	11 17		12 17	13 11	13 17	13 33		14 17	15 17	15 27		16 17
Hull Paragon Interchange	d																						
Barton-on-Humber	a																						
Barton-on-Humber	d		06 56	07 56					09 50				11 50					13 50				15 50	
Barrow Haven	d		07 01	08 01					09 55				11 55					13 55				15 55	
New Holland	d		07 05	08 05					09 59				11 59					13 59				15 59	
Goxhill	d		07 10	08 10					10 04				12 04					14 04				16 04	
Thornton Abbey	d		07 14	08 13					10 08				12 08					14 08				16 08	
Ulceby	d		07 19	08 18					10 13				12 13					14 13				16 13	
Habrough	d	06 21	07 23	08 22	08 29	08 59		09 47	10 17	10 28	10 48		12 17	12 26	13 20		13 41	14 17	14 26		15 37	16 17	16 26
Stallingborough	d		07 29	08 28					10 23				12 23					14 23				16 23	
Healing	d		07 32	08 30					10 26				12 26					14 26				16 26	
Great Coates	d		07 35	08 33					10 29				12 29					14 29				16 29	
Grimsby Town	a	06 36	07 40	08 38	08 43	09 12	09 39	09 59	10 34	10 41	11 02	11 37	12 34	12 39	13 34	13 37	13 54	14 34	14 39	15 37	15 50	16 34	16 39
	d		07 41	08 39	08 44		09 40	10 00	10 34	10 42		11 38	12 34	12 40		13 38	13 55	14 34	14 40	15 38		16 34	16 40
Grimsby Docks	d		07 44	08 41					10 37				12 37					14 37				16 37	
New Clee	d		07x46	08x43					10x39				12x39					14x39				16x39	
Cleethorpes	a		07 50	08 47	08 55		09 53	10 09	10 44	10 55		11 51	12 43	12 53		13 51	14 04	14 43	14 53	15 51		16 43	16 53

A From Lincoln
B From Manchester Airport
C From Newark North Gate
D From Sheffield. via Retford

For Hull, Doncaster, Meadowhall, Sheffield, Manchester and Manchester Airport refer to Table T029

Table T028-R

Gainsborough Central - Barnetby - Barton-on-Humber - Cleethorpes

Saturdays
26 May to 8 December

		TP ◇■ A	NT ◇ B	EM C	NT	TP ◇■ A	EM D	TP ◇■ A	TP ◇■ A	NT	TP ◇■ A	NT	TP ◇■ A	TP ◇■ A
Retford	d													
Gainsborough Central	a													
	d		16 57											
Kirton Lindsey	d		17 11											
Brigg	d		17 23											
Barnetby	d	17 17	17 34	17 54		18 21	19 09	19 18	20 17		21 17		22 30	23 25
Hull Paragon Interchange	d													
Barton-on-Humber	a													
Barton-on-Humber	d				17 55					20 03		22 02		
Barrow Haven	d				18 00					20 09		22 07		
New Holland	d				18 04					20 13		22 11		
Goxhill	d				18 09					20 18		22 16		
Thornton Abbey	d				18 13					20 22		22 20		
Ulceby	d				18 18					20 27		22 25		
Habrough	d		17 42	18 03	18 22	18 30	19 18			20 32	21 26	22 30	22 39	23 34
Stallingborough	d				18 28					20 38		22 35		
Healing	d				18 31					20 41		22 38		
Great Coates	d				18 34					20 44		22 41		
Grimsby Town	a	17 37	17 56	18 18	18 39	18 43	19 34	19 37	20 37	20 49	21 39	22 46	22 52	23 47
	d	17 38	17 57		18 39	18 44		19 39	20 38	20 49	21 40	22 47	22 53	23 48
Grimsby Docks	d				18 42					20 52		22 49		
New Clee	d				18x44					20x54		22x51		
Cleethorpes	a	17 51	18 07		18 48	18 55		19 51	20 51	20 58	21 53	22 55	23 06	00 01

Sundays
20 May to 2 December

		TP ◇■ A	TP ◇■ A	NT	TP ◇■ A	EM E	TP ◇■ A	NT	TP ◇■ A	TP ◇■ A	TP ◇■ A	NT	EM F	TP ◇■ A	TP ◇■ A	EM E	TP ◇■ A	NT	TP ◇■ A	TP ◇■ A	TP ◇■ A	TP ◇■ A
Retford	d																					
Gainsborough Central	a																					
	d																					
Kirton Lindsey	d																					
Brigg	d																					
Barnetby	d	10 18	11 20		12 19	12 43	13 17		14 17	15 17	16 18		16 58	17 17	18 17	18 53	19 17		20 17	21 17	22 17	23 19
Hull Paragon Interchange	d																					
Barton-on-Humber	a																					
Barton-on-Humber	d			11 05				13 49				16 15						19 11				
Barrow Haven	d			11 10				13 54				16 21						19 16				
New Holland	d			11 14				13 58				16 24						19 20				
Goxhill	d			11 19				14 03				16 29						19 25				
Thornton Abbey	d			11 23				14 07				16 33						19 29				
Ulceby	d			11 28				14 12				16 38						19 34				
Habrough	d	10 27		11 33	12 31	12 51		14 16	14 26		16 26	16 42	17 06		18 26	19 01		19 38		21 26	22 26	23 28
Stallingborough	d			11 38				14 22				16 48						19 44				
Healing	d			11 41				14 25				16 51						19 47				
Great Coates	d			11 44				14 28				16 54						19 50				
Grimsby Town	a	10 40	11 43	11 49	12 41	13 03	13 39	14 33	14 41	15 39	16 41	16 59	17 21	17 39	18 41	19 16	19 39	19 55	20 39	21 41	22 41	23 43
	d	10 41	11 44	11 50	12 42	13 05	13 40	14 33	14 42	15 40	16 42	16 59	17 22	17 40	18 42	19 16	19 40	19 55	20 40	21 42	22 42	23 44
Grimsby Docks	d			11 52				14 36				17 02						19 58				
New Clee	d			11 55				14 38				17 04						20 00				
Cleethorpes	a	10 53	11 56	12 00	12 56	13 15	13 51	14 43	14 53	15 51	16 53	17 09	17 31	17 51	18 53	19 25	19 51	20 04	20 51	21 53	22 53	23 53

A From Manchester Airport
B From Sheffield, via Retford
C From Lincoln
D From Newark North Gate
E until 9 September. From Newark North Gate
F until 9 September. From Nottingham

For Hull, Doncaster, Meadowhall, Sheffield, Manchester and Manchester Airport refer to Table T029

Table T029-F

Manchester Airport, Manchester, Sheffield and Meadowhall - Doncaster and Hull

Mondays to Fridays
21 May to 7 December

Miles	Miles	Miles	Miles			NT ◇ A	NT	NT ◇ A	NT	NT ■ ◇ B	NT ◇ A	NT	NT A	NT C	TP ◇■ D	NT ◇ A	NT E	XC ◇■ F	XC ◇■ G	NT H	NT I	TP ◇■	NT D	NT ◇ A
0	—	—	—	**Manchester Airport** 85	d																	05 48		
9¾	—	—	—	**Manchester Piccadilly** ■	d																	06 05		
15¾	—	—	—	Stockport 78	d																			
52½	—	—	—	**Sheffield** ■	a															←				
—	—	—	—		d	05 15	05 25			05 43		06 05	06 16				06 27	06 33	06 33					
56	—	—	—	**Meadowhall**	d	05 21	05 31			05 49		06 11	06 22				06 33			06 33				
58¾	—	—	—	Rotherham Central	d	05 28	05 37					06 17	06 28				→			06 40				
63¼	—	—	—	Swinton (S.Yorks)	d	05a38	05 46					06 26	06a38							06 48				
64½	—	—	—	Mexborough	d		05 49					06 29								06 51				
66¾	—	—	—	Conisbrough	d		05 53					06 33								06 55				
—	—	—	—	London Kings Cross	d																			
71½	—	—	—	**Doncaster** ■	a		06 02			06 12		06 42						06 59	07 00	07 04				
—	—	—	—	York ■ 26	a													07 23	07 24					
—	0	0	0	**Doncaster** 31	d			06 01	06 10	06 13	06 30	06 43		06 44		06 57				07 06	07 11			07 28
—	—	—	1¾	Bentley (S.Yorks) 31	a			06 04	06 14		06 33	06 47				07 00					07 14			07 31
—	—	—	4	Adwick 31	a			06 08	06 19		06 37	06 52				07 04					07 19			07 35
75½	—	4	—	Kirk Sandall	d					06 19				06 50						07 12				
78¼	—	6¾	—	Hatfield & Stainforth	d					06 24				06 55						07 17				
—	—	9¾	—	Thorne South	d									07 00										
—	—	15¾	—	Crowle	d									07 08										
—	—	19½	—	Althorpe	d									07 14										
—	23	23	—	**Scunthorpe**	a									07 22										
—	—	—	—		d																			
—	—	34	—	Barnetby 28	d																			
—	—	41	—	Habrough 28	d																			
—	—	49	—	**Grimsby Town** 28	a																			
—	—	—	—		d																			
—	52	52	—	**Cleethorpes** 28	a																			
81¼	—	—	—	Thorne North	d					06 30										07 23				
88¾	—	—	—	Goole	d					06 39										07 32				
92¼	—	—	—	Saltmarshe	d					06 43														
—	—	—	—	York ■ 33	d																		07 21	
—	18¼	—	—	**Selby**	a																	07 36	07 49	
—	—	—	—		d										06 45							07 41	07 50	
—	24½	—	—	Wressle	d																		07 57	
—	27	—	—	Howden	d																	07 50	08 02	
—	30	—	—	Eastrington	d																		08 07	
95½	32¼	—	—	Gilberdyke	d					06 51										07 42			08 13	
98	34¾	—	—	Broomfleet	d					06 55										07 47				
102	38¾	—	—	Brough	d					07 01					07 06					07 53		08 03	08 21	
105	41¾	—	—	Ferriby	d					07 06										07 57			08 25	
107¾	44½	—	—	Hessle	d					07 10										08 02			08 30	
112	49¼	—	—	**Hull**	a					07 21					07 23					08 13		08 20	08 39	

A To Leeds
B To Bridlington. ◇ to Thorne North ■ from Thorne North
C From Selby
D From Leeds
E To Beverley
F from 23 July until 5 October. To Newcastle
G until 20 July, from 8 October. From Derby to Newcastle
H From Sheffield to Beverley
I From Hull

For services between Barnetby, Habrough, Grimsby Town and Cleethorpes, refer to Table T028

Table T029-F

Mondays to Fridays
21 May to 7 December

Manchester Airport, Manchester, Sheffield and Meadowhall - Doncaster and Hull

	NT A	TP ◇■	NT		NT B	TP ◇■	NT C	XC ◇■ D 🛒	NT ◇ C	NT ◇ E	NT ■ F	NT	XC ◇■ G 🛒	NT	NT ◇ C	TP ◇■ H 🛒	NT	TP ◇■ 🛒	NT ◇ C		XC ◇■ I 🛒	NT ◇ J	NT	HT ◇■ ☒
Manchester Airport 85 ✈ d		05 54														06 53								
Manchester Piccadilly 10 d		06 17				06 44										07 18		07 47						
Stockport 78 d		06 24														07 28								
Sheffield 7 a		07 06														08 09								
d	07 01	07 08					07 14	07 21		07 24		07 31	07 52	08 06		08 10			08 15		08 22	08 25		
Meadowhall d	07 07	07 14			←		07 22			07 32		07 37		08 12		08 16			08 21			08 32		
Rotherham Central d	07 17				07 17		07 29					07 43		08 19					08 28					
Swinton (S.Yorks) d	↪				07 27		07a39					07 52		08 29					08a38					
Mexborough d					07 30							07 56		08 33										
Conisbrough d					07 34							08 00		08 37										
London Kings Cross d																								07 26
Doncaster 7 a		07 32			07 44					07 57		08 09	08 14	08 46		08 38						08 56		09 05
York 8 26 a								08 29					08 40								09 30			
Doncaster 31 d		07 33	07 42		07 53				07 59	08 01	08 10	08 10			08 26	08 40	08 44					08 58		09 07
Bentley (S.Yorks) 31 a					07 57				08 02			08 13			08 29									
Adwick 31 a					08 02				08 07			08 18			08 33									
Kirk Sandall d			07 48								08 16						08 50							
Hatfield & Stainforth d			07 53								08 21						08 55							
Thorne South d			07 58														09 00							
Crowle d			08 07														09 09							
Althorpe d			08 13														09 15							
Scunthorpe a		08 00	08 21													09 05	09 23							
d		08 00														09 06								
Barnetby 28 d		08 16														09 20								
Habrough 28 d		08 28																						
Grimsby Town 28 a		08 44														09 39								
d		08 45														09 40								
Cleethorpes 28 a		08 54														09 53								
Thorne North d										08 14	08 27													
Goole d										08 23	08 36											09 19		
Saltmarshe d										08 28	08 41													
York 8 33 d																							08 48	
Selby a						08 11												09 11					09 21	09 26
d						08 11												09 11					09 21	09 30
Wressle d																								
Howden d																							09 31	09 41
Eastrington d																								
Gilberdyke d										08 34	08 48												09 39	
Broomfleet d											08 53													
Brough d						08 30				08 41	08 59							09 30				09 37	09 47	09 53
Ferriby d										08 46	09 03											09 41		
Hessle d										08 50	09 08											09 46		
Hull a						08 45				09 00	09 19							09 45				09 58	10 04	10 06

A To Adwick
B From Sheffield
C To Leeds
D From Derby to Glasgow Central
E To Bridlington
F ■ from Thorne North
G From Birmingham New Street to Newcastle
H 🛒 to Sheffield
I From Birmingham New Street to Edinburgh
J To Scarborough

For services between Barnetby, Habrough, Grimsby Town and Cleethorpes, refer to Table T028

Table T029-F

Mondays to Fridays
21 May to 7 December

Manchester Airport, Manchester, Sheffield and Meadowhall - Doncaster and Hull

	NT	NT ◇ A	XC ◇■ B 🛒		NT ◇	NT C	TP ◇■ D 🛒	NT	NT E	TP ◇■ 🛒	NT A	XC ◇■ F 🛒	NT ◇ G	NT	NT	NT ◇ A	XC ◇■ H 🛒	NT C	TP ◇■ D 🛒		NT	NT E	TP ◇■ 🛒	NT ◇ A
Manchester Airport 85 ✈ d							07 53												08 53					
Manchester Piccadilly 10 d							08 19			08 47									09 19				09 47	
Stockport 78 d							08 28												09 28					
Sheffield 7 a							09 08												10 08					
d	08 30		08 51		08 54	09 06	09 10				09 15	09 21	09 24		09 30		09 52	10 05	10 10					10 15
Meadowhall d	08 36				09 01	09 12	09 16		←		09 21		09 32		09 36			10 11	10 16			←		10 21
Rotherham Central d	08 42				09 07	09 19			09 19		09 29				09 42			10 19				10 19		10 28
Swinton (S.Yorks) d	08 50				09 17	↪			09 28		09a38				09 50			↪				10 28		10a38
Mexborough d	08 54								09 31						09 54							10 31		
Conisbrough d	08 58								09 35						09 58							10 35		
London Kings Cross d																								
Doncaster 7 a	09 08		09 16				09 37		09 44				09 54		10 08		10 17		10 34			10 44		
York 8 26 a			09 40		10 14							10 30					10 40							
Doncaster 31 d	09 08	09 26					09 39	09 42	09 50				09 56		10 08	10 26			10 37		10 42	10 47		
Bentley (S.Yorks) 31 a		09 29							09 54							10 29						10 51		
Adwick 31 a		09 33							09 59							10 33						10 56		
Kirk Sandall d	09 15							09 48							10 15						10 48			
Hatfield & Stainforth d	09 20							09 53							10 20						10 53			
Thorne South d								09 58													10 58			
Crowle d								10 07													11 07			
Althorpe d								10 13													11 13			
Scunthorpe a							10 04	10 21											11 02		11 21			
d							10 05												11 03					
Barnetby 28 d							10 19												11 17					
Habrough 28 d							10 28																	
Grimsby Town 28 a							10 41												11 37					
d							10 42												11 38					
Cleethorpes 28 a							10 55												11 51					
Thorne North d	09 26														10 26									
Goole d	09 41												10 19		10 35									
Saltmarshe d																								
York 8 33 d														09 47										
Selby a										10 11				10 16									11 11	
d										10 11				10 17									11 11	
Wressle d																								
Howden d														10 27										
Eastrington d																								
Gilberdyke d	09 51													10 35	10 44									
Broomfleet d																								
Brough d	09 59									10 30			10 37	10 43	10 52								11 30	
Ferriby d	10 03														10 57									
Hessle d	10 08														11 02									
Hull a	10 18									10 45			10 51	11 00	11 14								11 45	

A To Leeds
B From Birmingham New Street to Newcastle
C To Adwick
D 🛒 to Sheffield
E From Sheffield
F From Bath Spa to Glasgow Central
G To Bridlington
H From Guildford to Newcastle

For services between Barnetby, Habrough, Grimsby Town and Cleethorpes, refer to Table T028

Table T029-F

Mondays to Fridays

21 May to 7 December

Manchester Airport, Manchester, Sheffield and Meadowhall - Doncaster and Hull

	XC ◇■ A	NT ◇ B	NT		NT	NT ◇ C	XC ◇■ D	HT ◇■ ⊠	NT E	TP ◇■ F	NT	NT G	TP ◇■	NT C	XC ◇■ H	NT ◇ B	NT	NT	NT ◇ C		XC ◇■ I	XC ◇■ J	NT ◇	NT E
Manchester Airport 85 d										09 53														
Manchester Piccadilly d										10 19			10 47											
Stockport 78 d										10 28														
Sheffield a										11 08														
d	10 21	10 24			10 30		10 54		11 05	11 10				11 15	11 21	11 24		11 30			11 52	11 52	11 59	12 05
Meadowhall d		10 32			10 36				11 11	11 16		←		11 21		11 32		11 36			⌇	⌇	12 05	12 11
Rotherham Central d					10 42				11 19			11 19		11 28				11 42			⌇	⌇	12 11	12 19
Swinton (S.Yorks) d					10 51				→			11 28		11a38				11 50			⌇	⌇	12 19	→
Mexborough d					10 55							11 31						11 54			⌇	⌇		
Conisbrough d					10 59							11 35						11 58			⌇	⌇		
London Kings Cross d								09 48													⌇	⌇		
Doncaster a		10 55			11 08		11 16	11 25		11 34		11 44				11 54		12 08			12 16	12 16		
York 26 a	11 30						11 40								12 30						12 40	12 40	13 12	
Doncaster 31 d		10 59			11 08	11 26		11 26		11 37	11 42	11 47				11 59		12 08	12 26					
Bentley (S.Yorks) 31 a						11 29						11 51							12 29					
Adwick 31 a						11 33						11 56							12 33					
Kirk Sandall d					11 15						11 48							12 15						
Hatfield & Stainforth d					11 20						11 53							12 20						
Thorne South d											11 58													
Crowle d											12 07													
Althorpe d											12 13													
Scunthorpe a										12 02	12 21													
d										12 03														
Barnetby 28 d										12 17														
Habrough 28 d										12 26														
Grimsby Town 28 a										12 39														
d										12 40														
Cleethorpes 28 a										12 53														
Thorne North d					11 26													12 26						
Goole d		11 19			11 35											12 19		12 35						
Saltmarshe d																								
York 33 d			10 50														11 47							
Selby a			11 16					11 40					12 11				12 16							
d			11 17					11 41					12 11				12 17							
Wressle d																								
Howden d			11 26					11 50									12 27							
Eastrington d																								
Gilberdyke d			11 35		11 44												12 35	12 45						
Broomfleet d																		12 49						
Brough d		11 37	11 43		11 52			12 02					12 30			12 37	12 43	12 55						
Ferriby d					11 57													13 00						
Hessle d					12 02													13 05						
Hull a		11 53	12 01		12 12			12 18					12 45			12 51	13 03	13 19						

A From Plymouth to Edinburgh
B To Bridlington
C To Leeds
D From Plymouth to Newcastle
E To Adwick
F ⚲ to Sheffield
G From Sheffield
H From Plymouth to Glasgow Central
I from 23 July until 5 October. From Plymouth to Newcastle
J until 20 July, from 8 October. From Winchester to Newcastle

For services between Barnetby, Habrough, Grimsby Town and Cleethorpes, refer to Table T028

Table T029-F

Mondays to Fridays

21 May to 7 December

Manchester Airport, Manchester, Sheffield and Meadowhall - Doncaster and Hull

	TP ◇■ A	NT	NT B		TP ◇■	NT ◇ C	XC ◇■ D	NT ◇ E	NT	NT	NT ◇ C	XC ◇■ F	HT ◇■ ⊠	NT G	TP ◇■ A	NT	NT B	TP ◇■	NT C		XC ◇■ H	XC ◇■ I	NT ◇ J	NT
Manchester Airport 85 d	10 53														11 53									
Manchester Piccadilly d	11 19				11 47										12 19			12 47						
Stockport 78 d	11 28														12 28									
Sheffield a	12 08														13 08									
d	12 10					12 15	12 21	12 24		12 30		12 52		13 05	13 10				13 15		13 21	13 21	13 24	
Meadowhall d	12 16		←			12 21		12 32		12 36				13 11	13 16		←		13 21		⌇	⌇	13 32	
Rotherham Central d			12 19			12 28				12 42				13 19			13 19		13 28		⌇	⌇		
Swinton (S.Yorks) d			12 28			12a38				12 50				→			13 28		13a38		⌇	⌇		
Mexborough d			12 31							12 54							13 31				⌇	⌇		
Conisbrough d			12 35							12 58							13 35				⌇	⌇		
London Kings Cross d													11 48								⌇	⌇		
Doncaster a	12 34		12 44					12 55		13 08		13 16	13 25		13 34		13 44				⌇	⌇	13 54	
York 26 a							13 30					13 40									14 30	14 30		
Doncaster 31 d	12 37	12 42	12 47					12 58		13 08	13 25		13 27		13 37	13 42	13 47						13 59	
Bentley (S.Yorks) 31 a			12 51								13 29						13 51							
Adwick 31 a			12 56								13 33						13 56							
Kirk Sandall d		12 48								13 15						13 48								
Hatfield & Stainforth d		12 53								13 20						13 53								
Thorne South d		12 58														13 58								
Crowle d		13 07														14 07								
Althorpe d		13 13														14 13								
Scunthorpe a	13 02	13 21													14 02	14 21								
d	13 03														14 03									
Barnetby 28 d	13 17														14 17									
Habrough 28 d															14 26									
Grimsby Town 28 a	13 37														14 39									
d	13 38														14 40									
Cleethorpes 28 a	13 51														14 53									
Thorne North d										13 26														
Goole d								13 19		13 36													14 19	
Saltmarshe d																								
York 33 d									12 50															13 47
Selby a					13 11				13 17				13 42					14 11						14 16
d					13 11				13 17				13 42					14 11						14 17
Wressle d																								
Howden d									13 27				13 52											14 27
Eastrington d																								
Gilberdyke d									13 35	13 44														14 35
Broomfleet d																								
Brough d					13 30			13 37	13 43	13 52			14 04					14 30					14 37	14 43
Ferriby d										13 57														
Hessle d										14 02														
Hull a					13 45			13 51	14 01	14 13			14 17					14 45					14 51	15 04

A ⚲ to Sheffield
B From Sheffield
C To Leeds
D From Plymouth to Edinburgh
E To Bridlington
F From Plymouth to Newcastle
G To Adwick
H until 20 July, from 8 October. From Penzance to Glasgow Central
I from 23 July until 5 October. From Reading to Glasgow Central
J To Scarborough

For services between Barnetby, Habrough, Grimsby Town and Cleethorpes, refer to Table T028

Table T029-F

Mondays to Fridays
21 May to 7 December

Manchester Airport, Manchester, Sheffield and Meadowhall - Doncaster and Hull

	NT	NT	XC	NT	TP	NT	NT	TP	NT	XC	NT	NT	NT	NT	XC	HT	NT	TP	NT	NT	TP	NT
		◇ A	◇1 B 🍴	C	◇1 D 🍴		E	◇1 🍴	◇ A	◇1 F 🍴	◇ G			◇ A	◇1 H 🍴	◇1 ☒	C	◇1 D 🍴		E	◇1 🍴	A
Manchester Airport 85 d					12 53													13 53				
Manchester Piccadilly 10 d					13 19			13 47										14 19			14 47	
Stockport 78 d					13 28													14 28				
Sheffield 7 a					14 08													15 08				
d	13 30		13 52	14 05	14 10				14 15	14 21	14 24		14 30		14 52		15 05	15 10				15 15
Meadowhall d	13 36			14 11	14 16		←		14 21		14 32		14 36				15 11	15 16		←		15 21
Rotherham Central d	13 42			14 19			14 19		14 28				14 42				15 19			15 19		15 28
Swinton (S.Yorks) d	13 50			→			14 28		14a38				14 50				→			15 28		15a38
Mexborough d	13 54						14 31						14 54							15 31		
Conisbrough d	13 58						14 35						14 58							15 35		
London Kings Cross d																13 48						
Doncaster 7 a	14 08		14 16		14 34		14 44				14 55		15 08		15 16	15 26		15 34		15 44		
York 8 26 a			14 40							15 30					15 40							
Doncaster 31 d	14 09	14 26			14 37	14 42	14 47				14 58		15 08	15 26		15 28		15 37	15 42	15 47		
Bentley (S.Yorks) 31 a		14 29					14 51							15 29						15 51		
Adwick 31 a		14 33					14 56							15 33						15 56		
Kirk Sandall d	14 15					14 48							15 15						15 48			
Hatfield & Stainforth d	14 20					14 53							15 20						15 53			
Thorne South d						14 58													15 58			
Crowle d						15 07													16 07			
Althorpe d						15 13													16 13			
Scunthorpe a					15 02	15 21												16 02	16 21			
d					15 03													16 03				
Barnetby 28 d					15 17													16 17				
Habrough 28 d																		16 26				
Grimsby Town 28 a					15 37													16 39				
d					15 38													16 40				
Cleethorpes 28 a					15 51													16 53				
Thorne North d	14 26												15 26									
Goole d	14 35										15 18		15 35									
Saltmarshe d	14 40																					
York 8 33 d												14 50										
Selby a								15 11				15 17				15 43					16 11	
d								15 11				15 17				15 43					16 11	
Wressle d																						
Howden d												15 27				15 53						
Eastrington d																						
Gilberdyke d	14 47											15 35	15 44									
Broomfleet d																						
Brough d	14 55							15 30			15 37	15 43	15 52			16 05					16 30	
Ferriby d	15 00												15 57									
Hessle d	15 05												16 02									
Hull a	15 17							15 45			15 51	16 00	16 14			16 18					16 45	

A To Leeds
B From Penzance to Newcastle
C To Adwick
D 🍴 to Sheffield
E From Sheffield
F From Plymouth to Aberdeen
G To Bridlington
H From Plymouth to Newcastle

For services between Barnetby, Habrough, Grimsby Town and Cleethorpes, refer to Table T028

Table T029-F

Mondays to Fridays
21 May to 7 December

Manchester Airport, Manchester, Sheffield and Meadowhall - Doncaster and Hull

	XC	XC	NT	NT	NT	NT	XC	XC	NT	TP	NT	NT	TP	NT	XC	NT	NT	NT	NT	XC	HT	NT
	◇1 A 🍴	1 B	◇ C			◇ D	◇1 E 🍴	1 F 🍴	G	◇1 H 🍴		I	◇1 🍴	◇ D	◇1 J 🍴	◇ K			◇ D	◇1 L 🍴	◇1 ☒	G
Manchester Airport 85 d										14 53												
Manchester Piccadilly 10 d										15 19			15 47									
Stockport 78 d										15 28												
Sheffield 7 a										16 08												
d	15 21	15 21	15 24		15 30		15 52	15 52	16 05	16 10				16 15	16 21	16 24		16 30		16 52		17 05
Meadowhall d			15 32		15 36				16 11	16 16		←		16 21		16 32		16 36				17 11
Rotherham Central d					15 42				16 19			16 19		16 28				16 42				17 19
Swinton (S.Yorks) d					15 50				→			16 28		16a38				16 50				→
Mexborough d					15 54							16 31						16 54				
Conisbrough d					15 58							16 35						16 58				
London Kings Cross d																					15 48	
Doncaster 7 a			15 57		16 08		16 17	16 17		16 34		16 45				16 54		17 08		17 13	17 25	
York 8 26 a	16 30	16 30					16 40	16 40							17 30					17 42		
Doncaster 31 d			15 59		16 08	16 26				16 37	16 42	16 47				16 59		17 08	17 26		17 27	
Bentley (S.Yorks) 31 a						16 29						16 51							17 29			
Adwick 31 a						16 33						16 56							17 33			
Kirk Sandall d					16 15						16 48							17 15				
Hatfield & Stainforth d					16 20						16 53							17 20				
Thorne South d											16 58											
Crowle d											17 07											
Althorpe d											17 13											
Scunthorpe a										17 02	17 21											
d										17 03												
Barnetby 28 d										17 17												
Habrough 28 d																						
Grimsby Town 28 a										17 37												
d										17 38												
Cleethorpes 28 a										17 51												
Thorne North d					16 26											17 10		17 26				
Goole d			16 19		16 35											17 21		17 35				
Saltmarshe d																		17 40				
York 8 33 d				15 47													16 48					
Selby a				16 16									17 11				17 17				17 42	
d				16 17									17 11				17 18				17 43	
Wressle d				16 25													17 25					
Howden d				16 30													17 30				17 52	
Eastrington d																						
Gilberdyke d				16 37	16 44												17 38	17 47				
Broomfleet d																						
Brough d			16 37	16 45	16 52								17 30			17 38	17 46	17 55			18 04	
Ferriby d					16 57													17 59				
Hessle d					17 02													18 04				
Hull a			16 51	17 02	17 13								17 45			17 52	18 03	18 14			18 18	

A until 20 July, from 8 October. From Penzance to Glasgow Central
B from 23 July until 5 October. From Reading to Glasgow Central
C To Bridlington
D To Leeds
E from 23 July until 5 October. From Penzance to Newcastle
F until 20 July, from 8 October. From Southampton Central to Newcastle
G To Adwick
H 🍴 to Sheffield
I From Sheffield
J From Plymouth to Dundee
K To Scarborough
L From Plymouth to Newcastle

For services between Barnetby, Habrough, Grimsby Town and Cleethorpes, refer to Table T028

Table T029-F

Mondays to Fridays
21 May to 7 December

Manchester Airport, Manchester, Sheffield and Meadowhall - Doncaster and Hull

	TP ◇■ A ⊼	NT	NT B	TP ◇■ ⊼	NT C	XC ◇■ D ⊼	NT ◇ E	NT	NT	NT ◇ C	XC ◇■ F ⊼	NT G	TP ◇■ A ⊼	NT	NT B	TP ◇■ ⊼	NT ◇ C	XC ◇■ F ⊼	NT ◇ H	NT	NT	NT ◇ C
Manchester Airport 85 d	15 53												16 53									
Manchester Piccadilly d	16 19			16 47									17 19			17 47						
Stockport 78 d	16 28												17 28									
Sheffield a	17 08												18 10									
d	17 10				17 15	17 21	17 24		17 30		17 50	18 05	18 11				18 15	18 21	18 24		18 30	
Meadowhall d	17 16		←		17 21		17 32		17 36			18 11	18 17		←		18 21		18 32		18 36	
Rotherham Central d			17 19		17 28				17 42			18 18			18 18		18 28				18 42	
Swinton (S.Yorks) d			17 28		17a38				17 50			→			18 27		18a38				18 50	
Mexborough d			17 31						17 54						18 31						18 54	
Conisbrough d			17 35						17 58						18 35						18 58	
London Kings Cross d																						
Doncaster a	17 34		17 44				17 57		13 09				18 35		18 45				18 56		19 08	
York 26 a						18 30					19 01							19 30				
Doncaster 31 d	17 38	17 42	17 48				18 02		18 09	18 28			18 37	18 42	18 48				18 58		19 09	19 28
Bentley (S.Yorks) 31 a			17 52							18 31					18 52							19 31
Adwick 31 a			17 57							18 35					18 57							19 35
Kirk Sandall d		17 48							18 16					18 48							19 15	
Hatfield & Stainforth d		17 53							18 21					18 53							19 20	
Thorne South d		17 58												18 58								
Crowle d		18 07												19 07								
Althorpe d		18 13												19 13								
Scunthorpe a	18 06	18 21											19 03	19 21								
d	18 07												19 03									
Barnetby 28 d	18 21												19 18									
Habrough 28 d	18 30																					
Grimsby Town 28 a	18 43												19 37									
d	18 44												19 38									
Cleethorpes 28 a	18 55												19 51									
Thorne North d							18 13		18 27												19 26	
Goole d							18 24		18 36										19 17		19 35	
Saltmarshe d																			19 22			
York 33 d								17 48												18 50		
Selby a				18 11				18 19								19 11				19 17		
d				18 12				18 20								19 11				19 18		
Wressle d																						
Howden d				18 21				18 31												19 27		
Eastrington d																						
Gilberdyke d							18 35	18 41	18 47										19 29	19 35	19 48	
Broomfleet d									18 51													
Brough d				18 34			18 42	18 49	18 57							19 30			19 36	19 43	19 56	
Ferriby d									19 01										19 41		20 00	
Hessle d									19 06										19 45		20 05	
Hull a				18 49			18 58	19 03	19 16							19 44			19 55	19 59	20 13	

A ⊼ to Sheffield
B From Sheffield
C To Leeds
D From Plymouth to Glasgow Central
E To Scarborough
F From Plymouth to Edinburgh
G To Adwick
H To Bridlington

For services between Barnetby, Habrough, Grimsby Town and Cleethorpes, refer to Table T028

Table T029-F

Mondays to Fridays
21 May to 7 December

Manchester Airport, Manchester, Sheffield and Meadowhall - Doncaster and Hull

	XC ◇■ A ⊼	XC ◇■ B ⊼	NT C	TP ◇■ D ⊼	NT	NT E	TP ◇■ ⊼	NT F	XC ◇■ G	NT ◇	NT	NT ◇ F	XC ◇■ H ⊼	HT ◇■ I ⊠	NT C	TP ◇■	NT	NT E	NT ◇ F	NT ◇ J	TP ◇■	NT
Manchester Airport 85 d				17 53												18 53						
Manchester Piccadilly d				18 19			18 47									19 19					19 47	
Stockport 78 d				18 28												19 28						
Sheffield a				19 09												20 09						
d	18 49	18 52	19 05	19 11				19 15	19 22	19 24	19 30		19 52		20 05	20 11			20 15	20 24		
Meadowhall d			19 11	19 17		←		19 21		19 32	19 36				20 11	20 17		←	20 21	20 32		
Rotherham Central d			19 19			19 19		19 28			19 42				20 19			20 19	20 28			
Swinton (S.Yorks) d			→			19 28		19a38			19 50				→			20 28	20a38			
Mexborough d						19 31					19 54							20 31				
Conisbrough d						19 35					19 58							20 35				
London Kings Cross d														18 48								
Doncaster a	19 17	19 17		19 37		19 44				19 54	20 08		20 13	20 28		20 35		20 44		20 54		
York 26 a	19 41	19 40							20 30				20 41									
Doncaster 31 d				19 37	19 42	19 54				19 59	20 08	20 28		20 30		20 36	20 42	20 48		20 58		
Bentley (S.Yorks) 31 a						19 58						20 31						20 52				
Adwick 31 a						20 03						20 35						20 57				
Kirk Sandall d					19 49						20 15						20 48					
Hatfield & Stainforth d					19 54						20 20						20 53					
Thorne South d					19 59												20 58					
Crowle d					20 08												21 07					
Althorpe d					20 14												21 13					
Scunthorpe a				20 03	20 22											21 02	21 21					
d				20 03												21 03						
Barnetby 28 d				20 17												21 17						
Habrough 28 d																21 26						
Grimsby Town 28 a				20 37												21 39						
d				20 38												21 40						
Cleethorpes 28 a				20 51												21 53						
Thorne North d											20 26											
Goole d										20 19	20 35									21 17		
Saltmarshe d																						
York 33 d																						20 45
Selby a							20 11							20 45							21 14	21 19
d							20 11							20 46							21 15	21 19
Wressle d																						21 26
Howden d														20 56							21 24	21 31
Eastrington d																						21 36
Gilberdyke d											20 44											
Broomfleet d																						
Brough d							20 30			20 37	20 52			21 08						21 33	21 39	21 46
Ferriby d											20 57											21 50
Hessle d											21 02											21 55
Hull a							20 48			20 52	21 14			21 22						21 49	21 52	22 05

A from 23 July until 5 October. From Plymouth to Newcastle
B until 20 July, from 8 October. From Reading to Newcastle
C To Adwick
D ⊼ to Sheffield
E From Sheffield
F To Leeds
G From Plymouth to Edinburgh
H From Plymouth to Newcastle
I To Beverley
J To Bridlington

For services between Barnetby, Habrough, Grimsby Town and Cleethorpes, refer to Table T028

Table T029-F

Mondays to Fridays

21 May to 7 December

Manchester Airport, Manchester, Sheffield and Meadowhall - Doncaster and Hull

	NT	NT	XC		XC	NT	TP	NT	TP	NT	NT	NT	HT	NT	XC	NT	TP	NT	TP		NT	NT	NT	NT
		◇	◇1		◇1		◇1		◇1			◇	◇1	◇	◇1		◇1		◇1		◇	◇		
		A	B		C	D		E		A		F		A	G	D		E			A		A	
Manchester Airport 85 d							19 53										20 53							
Manchester Piccadilly 10 d							20 19		20 47								21 19		21 47					
Stockport 78 d							20 28										21 28							
Sheffield 7 a							21 09										22 10							
d	20 30		20 52		20 52	21 05	21 11			21 15		21 28			21 52	22 07	22 11				22 15	22 28		
Meadowhall d	20 36					21 11	21 17	←		21 21		21 34				22 13	22 17	←			22 22	22 34		
Rotherham Central d	20 42					21 20		21 20		21 28						22 19		22 19			22 29			
Swinton (S.Yorks) d	20 50					→		21 35		21a38						→		22 29			22a41			
Mexborough d	20 54							21 39										22 33						
Conisbrough d	20 58							21 43										22 37						
London Kings Cross d													20 30											
Doncaster 7 a	21 08		21 19		21 19		21 45	21 52				21 57	22 05		22 25		22 36	22 46				22 55		
York 8 26 a			21 40		21 40										22 51									
Doncaster 31 d	21 08	21 28					21 47	21 54			21 54	21 59	22 07	22 32			22 37	22 47				22 57	23 24	
Bentley (S.Yorks) 31 a		21 31						21 58						22 35				22 50					23 27	
Adwick 31 a		21 35						22 03						22 39				22 55					23 31	
Kirk Sandall d	21 15										22 00						22 42							
Hatfield & Stainforth d	21 20										22 05						22 47							
Thorne South d											22 10						22 51							
Crowle d											22 19						23 00							
Althorpe d											22 25						23 05							
Scunthorpe a							22 12				22 33						23 10							
d							22 13										23 11							
Barnetby 28 d							22 27										23 25							
Habrough 28 d							22 36										23 34							
Grimsby Town 28 a							22 49										23 47							
d							22 50										23 48							
Cleethorpes 28 a							23 03										00 01							
Thorne North d	21 26																					23 08		
Goole d	21 36											22 20										23 17		
Saltmarshe d												22 24												
York 8 33 d																								22 46
Selby a									22 10				22 25						23 10					23 16
d									22 11				22 26						23 11					23 17
Wressle d																								
Howden d									22 20				22 35											23 26
Eastrington d																								
Gilberdyke d	21 46											22 31												23 35
Broomfleet d																								
Brough d	21 54								22 33			22 39	22 50						23 30			23 35		23 43
Ferriby d	21 59																							23 47
Hessle d	22 04																							23 52
Hull a	22 16								22 46			22 54	23 04						23 45			23 49		00 04

A To Leeds
B from 23 July until 5 October. From Plymouth to Newcastle
C until 20 July, from 8 October. From Reading to Newcastle
D To Adwick
E From Sheffield
F To Beverley
G From Plymouth

For services between Barnetby, Habrough, Grimsby Town and Cleethorpes, refer to Table T028

Table T029-F

Mondays to Fridays

21 May to 7 December

Manchester Airport, Manchester, Sheffield and Meadowhall - Doncaster and Hull

	NT	TP	NT	NT
		◇1		
			A	
Manchester Airport 85 d		21 53		
Manchester Piccadilly 10 d		22 19		
Stockport 78 d				
Sheffield 7 a		23 09		
d	23 05	23 10	23 15	23 27
Meadowhall d	23 11		23 21	23 33
Rotherham Central d	23 18		23 28	23 39
Swinton (S.Yorks) d	23 27		23a36	23 48
Mexborough d	23 30			23 51
Conisbrough d	23 34			23 55
London Kings Cross d				
Doncaster 7 a	23 43	23 52		00 04
York 8 26 a				
Doncaster 31 d				
Bentley (S.Yorks) 31 a				
Adwick 31 a				
Kirk Sandall d				
Hatfield & Stainforth d				
Thorne South d				
Crowle d				
Althorpe d				
Scunthorpe a				
d				
Barnetby 28 d				
Habrough 28 d				
Grimsby Town 28 a				
d				
Cleethorpes 28 a				
Thorne North d				
Goole d				
Saltmarshe d				
York 8 33 d				
Selby a				
d				
Wressle d				
Howden d				
Eastrington d				
Gilberdyke d				
Broomfleet d				
Brough d				
Ferriby d				
Hessle d				
Hull a				

A To Leeds

For services between Barnetby, Habrough, Grimsby Town and Cleethorpes, refer to Table T028

Table T029-F

Saturdays
26 May to 8 December

Manchester Airport, Manchester, Sheffield and Meadowhall - Doncaster and Hull

		NT	NT	NT	NT	NT	NT	TP	NT	NT	NT	NT	NT	NT	XC	XC	NT	NT	NT	TP	NT	NT	TP
						■																	
		◇		◇		◇	◇	◇■				◇			◇■	◇■		◇		◇■			◇■
		A		A		B	A			A	C	A	D	E	F	G	H	A	I			J	
Manchester Airport 85	d																			05 56			
Manchester Piccadilly	d							05 45												06 17			06 47
Stockport 78	d																			06 26			
Sheffield	a																			07 08			
	d	05 15	05 24			05 43			06 06	06 16			06 27		06 52	06 52			07 01	07 10			
Meadowhall	d	05 21	05 30			05 49			06 12	06 22			06 33						07 07	07 16		←	
Rotherham Central	d	05 28	05 36						06 18	06 28			06 40						07 17			07 17	
Swinton (S.Yorks)	d	05a38	05 45						06 26	06a38			06 48						→			07 27	
Mexborough	d		05 48						06 29				06 51									07 30	
Conisbrough	d		05 52						06 33				06 55									07 34	
London Kings Cross	d																						
Doncaster	a		06 01			06 12			06 41				07 04		07 13	07 13				07 35		07 44	
York 26	a														07 40	07 41							
Doncaster 31	d			06 01	06 11	06 13	06 30		06 42		06 44	06 57	07 06	07 11				07 28		07 37	07 42	07 53	
Bentley (S.Yorks) 31	a			06 04	06 15		06 33		06 45			07 00		07 14				07 31				07 57	
Adwick 31	a			06 08	06 19		06 37		06 50			07 04		07 19				07 35				08 02	
Kirk Sandall	d					06 19					06 50		07 12								07 48		
Hatfield & Stainforth	d					06 24					06 55		07 17								07 53		
Thorne South	d										07 00										07 58		
Crowle	d										07 08										08 07		
Althorpe	d										07 14										08 13		
Scunthorpe	a										07 22									08 03	08 21		
	d																			08 03			
Barnetby 28	d																			08 20			
Habrough 28	d																			08 29			
Grimsby Town 28	a																			08 43			
	d																			08 44			
Cleethorpes 28	a																			08 55			
Thorne North	d					06 30							07 23										
Goole	d					06 39							07 32										
Saltmarshe	d					06 43																	
York 33	d																07 21						
Selby	a							07 10									07 49						08 11
	d							07 11									07 50						08 11
Wressle	d																07 57						
Howden	d							07 20									08 02						
Eastrington	d																08 07						
Gilberdyke	d					06 51							07 42				08 13						
Broomfleet	d					06 55							07 47										
Brough	d					07 01		07 33					07 53				08 21						08 30
Ferriby	d					07 06							07 57				08 25						
Hessle	d					07 10							08 02				08 30						
Hull	a					07 22		07 46					08 13				08 39						08 45

A To Leeds
B To Bridlington. ◇ to Thorne North ■ from Thorne North
C From Selby
D To Beverley
E From Hull
F until 21 July, from 13 October. From Derby to Newcastle
G from 28 July until 6 October. To Newcastle
H From Leeds
I To Adwick
J From Sheffield

For services between Barnetby, Habrough, Grimsby Town and Cleethorpes, refer to Table T028

Table T029-F

Saturdays
26 May to 8 December

Manchester Airport, Manchester, Sheffield and Meadowhall - Doncaster and Hull

		NT	XC	XC	NT	NT	NT	NT	XC	XC	NT	NT	NT	TP	NT	TP	NT	XC	NT	NT	HT	NT	NT
							■																
			◇■	◇■	◇	◇			◇■	◇■	◇		◇	◇■		◇■	◇	◇■	◇		◇■		◇
		A	B	C	A	D	E		F	G	H		A	I			A	J	K				A
			🛒	🛒					🛒	🛒				🛒		🛒		🛒			☒		
Manchester Airport 85	d													06 53									
Manchester Piccadilly	d													07 19		07 47							
Stockport 78	d													07 28									
Sheffield	a													08 09									
	d	07 16	07 21	07 21		07 24		07 31	07 52	07 52	07 55	08 05		08 10			08 15	08 22	08 25			08 30	
Meadowhall	d	07 22				07 32		07 37				08 12		08 16			08 21		08 32			08 36	
Rotherham Central	d	07 34						07 43				08 19					08 28					08 42	
Swinton (S.Yorks)	d	07a44						07 52				08 29					08a38					08 50	
Mexborough	d							07 56				08 33										08 54	
Conisbrough	d							08 00				08 37										08 58	
London Kings Cross	d																				07 26		
Doncaster	a					07 57		08 09	08 13	08 13		08 46		08 38					08 56		09 05	09 12	
York 26	a		08 29	08 30					08 40	08 43								09 30					
Doncaster 31	d				07 59	08 01	08 10	08 10					08 26	08 40	08 44				08 58		09 07	09 13	09 26
Bentley (S.Yorks) 31	a				08 02			08 13					08 29										09 29
Adwick 31	a				08 07			08 18					08 33										09 33
Kirk Sandall	d						08 16								08 50							09 19	
Hatfield & Stainforth	d						08 21								08 55							09 24	
Thorne South	d														09 00								
Crowle	d														09 09								
Althorpe	d														09 15								
Scunthorpe	a													09 05	09 23								
	d													09 06									
Barnetby 28	d										09 38			09 20									
Habrough 28	d										09 47												
Grimsby Town 28	a										09 59			09 39									
	d										10 00			09 40									
Cleethorpes 28	a										10 09			09 53									
Thorne North	d					08 12	08 27															09 31	
Goole	d					08 21	08 36												09 19			09 40	
Saltmarshe	d					08 25	08 41																
York 33	d																			08 48			
Selby	a															09 11				09 20	09 26		
	d															09 11				09 20	09 30		
Wressle	d																						
Howden	d																			09 30	09 42		
Eastrington	d																						
Gilberdyke	d					08 32	08 48													09 38		09 53	
Broomfleet	d						08 53																
Brough	d					08 40	08 59									09 30			09 37	09 46	09 54	10 01	
Ferriby	d					08 44	09 03												09 41			10 06	
Hessle	d					08 49	09 08												09 46			10 11	
Hull	a					08 59	09 19									09 45			09 58	10 04	10 07	10 23	

A To Leeds
B from 8 September until 6 October. From Derby to Glasgow Central
C until 1 September, from 13 October. From Birmingham New Street to Glasgow Central
D To Bridlington
E ■ from Thorne North
F until 6 October. From Birmingham New Street to Newcastle
G from 13 October. From Birmingham New Street to Newcastle
H via Retford
I 🛒 to Sheffield
J From Birmingham New Street to Edinburgh
K To Scarborough

For services between Barnetby, Habrough, Grimsby Town and Cleethorpes, refer to Table T028

Table T029-F

Saturdays

26 May to 8 December

Manchester Airport, Manchester, Sheffield and Meadowhall - Doncaster and Hull

		XC	NT	NT	TP	NT	NT	TP		NT	XC	EM	NT	NT	NT	NT	XC	XC	NT	TP	NT	NT	TP	NT
		◇■	◇		◇■			◇■			◇■	◇■	◇			◇	◇■	◇■		◇■			◇■	◇
		A		B	C		D			E	F	G	H			E	I	J	B	C		D		E
		🛒			🛒			🛒			🛒	🛒					🛒			🛒			🛒	
Manchester Airport 85 ✈	d				07 53															08 53				
Manchester Piccadilly 10	d				08 19			08 47												09 19			09 47	
Stockport 78	d				08 28															09 28				
Sheffield 7	a				09 08															10 08				
	d	08 52	08 54	09 06	09 10					09 15	09 21	09 24	09 24		09 30		09 52	09 52	10 05	10 10				10 15
Meadowhall	d		09 01	09 12	09 16		←			09 21			09 32		09 36				10 11	10 16		←		10 21
Rotherham Central	d		09 07	09 19			09 19			09 29					09 42				10 19			10 19		10 28
Swinton (S.Yorks)	d		09 17	→			09 28			09a38					09 50				→			10 28		10a38
Mexborough	d						09 31								09 54							10 31		
Conisbrough	d						09 35								09 58							10 35		
London Kings Cross	d																							
Doncaster 7	a	09 15			09 37		09 44					09 53	09 54		10 08		10 15	10 15		10 34		10 44		
York 8 26	a	09 40	10 14								10 30	10 17					10 40	10 40						
Doncaster 31	d				09 39	09 42	09 50						09 56		10 08	10 26				10 37	10 42	10 47		
Bentley (S.Yorks) 31	a						09 54									10 29						10 51		
Adwick 31	a						09 59									10 33						10 56		
Kirk Sandall	d					09 48									10 15						10 48			
Hatfield & Stainforth	d					09 53									10 20						10 53			
Thorne South	d					09 58															10 58			
Crowle	d					10 07															11 07			
Althorpe	d					10 13															11 13			
Scunthorpe	a				10 04	10 21														11 02	11 21			
	d				10 05															11 03				
Barnetby 28	d				10 19															11 17				
Habrough 28	d				10 28																			
Grimsby Town 28	a				10 41															11 37				
	d				10 42															11 38				
Cleethorpes 28	a				10 55															11 51				
Thorne North	d														10 26									
Goole	d												10 19		10 35									
Saltmarshe	d																							
York 8 33	d													09 47										
Selby	a							10 11						10 16									11 11	
	d							10 11						10 17									11 11	
Wressle	d																							
Howden	d													10 27										
Eastrington	d																							
Gilberdyke	d													10 35	10 44									
Broomfleet	d																							
Brough	d							10 30					10 37	10 43	10 52								11 30	
Ferriby	d														10 57									
Hessle	d														11 02									
Hull	a							10 45					10 51	11 00	11 14								11 45	

A From Birmingham New Street to Newcastle
B To Adwick
C 🛒 to Sheffield
D From Sheffield
E To Leeds
F From Bristol Temple Meads to Glasgow Central
G From St Pancras International
H To Bridlington
I until 21 July, from 13 October. From Guildford to Newcastle
J from 28 July until 6 October. From Bristol Temple Meads to Newcastle

For services between Barnetby, Habrough, Grimsby Town and Cleethorpes, refer to Table T028

Table T029-F

Saturdays

26 May to 8 December

Manchester Airport, Manchester, Sheffield and Meadowhall - Doncaster and Hull

		XC	NT	NT	NT	NT	XC	XC		HT	NT	TP	NT	NT	TP	NT	XC	NT	NT	NT	NT	XC	XC	NT
		◇■	◇			◇	◇■	◇■		◇■		◇■			◇■		◇■	◇			◇	◇■	◇■	◇
		A	B			C	D	E			F	G		H		C	I	B			C	D	J	K
		🛒						🛒		☒		🛒			🛒		🛒						🛒	
Manchester Airport 85 ✈	d											09 53												
Manchester Piccadilly 10	d											10 19			10 47									
Stockport 78	d											10 28												
Sheffield 7	a											11 08												
	d	10 21	10 24		10 30		10 52	10 52			11 05	11 10				11 15	11 21	11 24		11 30		11 52	11 52	11 55
Meadowhall	d		10 32		10 36						11 11	11 16		←		11 21		11 32		11 36				
Rotherham Central	d				10 42						11 19			11 19		11 28				11 42				
Swinton (S.Yorks)	d				10 51						→			11 28		11a38				11 50				
Mexborough	d				10 55									11 31						11 54				
Conisbrough	d				10 59									11 35						11 58				
London Kings Cross	d									09 48														
Doncaster 7	a		10 55		11 08		11 15	11 15		11 24		11 34		11 44				11 54		12 08		12 13	12 13	
York 8 26	a	11 30					11 40	11 40									12 30					12 40	12 40	
Doncaster 31	d		10 59		11 08	11 26				11 26		11 37	11 42	11 47				11 59		12 08	12 26			
Bentley (S.Yorks) 31	a					11 29								11 51							12 29			
Adwick 31	a					11 33								11 56							12 33			
Kirk Sandall	d				11 15								11 48							12 15				
Hatfield & Stainforth	d				11 20								11 53							12 20				
Thorne South	d												11 58											
Crowle	d												12 07											
Althorpe	d												12 13											
Scunthorpe	a											12 02	12 21											
	d											12 03												
Barnetby 28	d											12 17												13 33
Habrough 28	d											12 26												13 41
Grimsby Town 28	a											12 39												13 54
	d											12 40												13 55
Cleethorpes 28	a											12 53												14 04
Thorne North	d				11 26															12 26				
Goole	d		11 19		11 35													12 19		12 35				
Saltmarshe	d																							
York 8 33	d			10 50															11 47					
Selby	a			11 16						11 41					12 11				12 16					
	d			11 17						11 41					12 11				12 17					
Wressle	d																							
Howden	d			11 26						11 51									12 27					
Eastrington	d																							
Gilberdyke	d			11 35	11 44														12 35	12 45				
Broomfleet	d																			12 49				
Brough	d		11 37	11 43	11 52					12 03					12 30			12 37	12 43	12 55				
Ferriby	d				11 57															13 00				
Hessle	d				12 02															13 05				
Hull	a		11 53	12 01	12 12					12 18					12 45			12 51	13 03	13 19				

A From Plymouth to Edinburgh
B To Bridlington
C To Leeds
D from 28 July until 6 October. From Plymouth to Newcastle
E until 21 July, from 13 October. From Bournemouth to Newcastle
F To Adwick
G 🛒 to Sheffield
H From Sheffield
I From Plymouth to Glasgow Central
J until 21 July, from 13 October. From Southampton Central to Newcastle
K via Retford

For services between Barnetby, Habrough, Grimsby Town and Cleethorpes, refer to Table T028

Table T029-F

Saturdays

26 May to 8 December

Manchester Airport, Manchester, Sheffield and Meadowhall - Doncaster and Hull

Station		NT ◇	NT A	TP ◇1 B ✠	NT	NT C	TP ◇1 ✠	NT ◇ D	XC ◇1 E ✠	NT ◇ F	NT	NT	NT ◇ D	XC ◇1 G ✠	HT ◇1 ⊠	NT A	TP ◇1 B ✠	NT	NT C	TP ◇1 ✠	NT D	XC ◇1 H ✠	XC ◇1 I
Manchester Airport 85	d			10 53													11 53						
Manchester Piccadilly 10	d			11 19			11 47										12 19			12 47			
Stockport 78	d			11 28													12 28						
Sheffield 7	a			12 08													13 08						
	d	11 59	12 05	12 10				12 15	12 21	12 24		12 30		12 52		13 05	13 10				13 15	13 21	13 21
Meadowhall	d	12 05	12 11	12 16		←		12 21		12 32		12 36				13 11	13 16		←		13 21		
Rotherham Central	d	12 11	12 19			12 19		12 28				12 42				13 19			13 19		13 28		
Swinton (S.Yorks)	d	12 19	→			12 28		12a38				12 50				→			13 28		13a38		
Mexborough	d					12 31						12 54							13 31				
Conisbrough	d					12 35						12 58							13 35				
London Kings Cross	d														11 46								
Doncaster 7	a			12 34		12 44				12 55		13 08		13 15	13 24		13 34		13 44				
York 8 26	a	13 12							13 30					13 40								14 30	14 30
Doncaster 31	d			12 37	12 42	12 47				12 58		13 08	13 25		13 26		13 37	13 42	13 47				
Bentley (S.Yorks) 31	a					12 51							13 29						13 51				
Adwick 31	a					12 56							13 33						13 56				
Kirk Sandall	d				12 48							13 15						13 48					
Hatfield & Stainforth	d				12 53							13 20						13 53					
Thorne South	d				12 58													13 58					
Crowle	d				13 07													14 07					
Althorpe	d				13 13													14 13					
Scunthorpe	a			13 02	13 21												14 02	14 21					
	d			13 03													14 03						
Barnetby 28	d			13 17													14 17						
Habrough 28	d																14 26						
Grimsby Town 28	a			13 37													14 39						
	d			13 38													14 40						
Cleethorpes 28	a			13 51													14 53						
Thorne North	d											13 26											
Goole	d									13 19		13 36											
Saltmarshe	d																						
York 8 33	d										12 50												
Selby	a						13 11				13 17				13 41					14 11			
	d						13 11				13 17				13 42					14 11			
Wressle	d																						
Howden	d										13 27				13 51								
Eastrington	d																						
Gilberdyke	d										13 35	13 44											
Broomfleet	d																						
Brough	d						13 30			13 37	13 43	13 52			14 03					14 30			
Ferriby	d											13 57											
Hessle	d											14 02											
Hull	a						13 45			13 51	14 01	14 13			14 16					14 45			

A To Adwick
B ✠ to Sheffield
C From Sheffield
D To Leeds
E From Plymouth to Edinburgh
F To Bridlington
G From Plymouth to Newcastle
H until 21 July, from 13 October. From Penzance to Glasgow Central
I from 28 July until 6 October. From Reading to Glasgow Central

For services between Barnetby, Habrough, Grimsby Town and Cleethorpes, refer to Table T028

Table T029-F

Saturdays

26 May to 8 December

Manchester Airport, Manchester, Sheffield and Meadowhall - Doncaster and Hull

Station		NT ◇ A	NT	NT	NT ◇ B	XC ◇1 C ✠	NT D	TP ◇1 E ✠	NT	NT F	TP ◇1 ✠	NT ◇ B	XC ◇1 G ✠	NT ◇ H	NT	NT	NT ◇ B	XC ◇1 I ✠	NT D	TP ◇1 E ✠	NT	NT F	TP ◇1 ✠
Manchester Airport 85	d							12 53												13 53			
Manchester Piccadilly 10	d							13 19			13 47									14 19			14 47
Stockport 78	d							13 28												14 28			
Sheffield 7	a							14 08												15 08			
	d	13 24		13 30		13 52	14 05	14 10				14 15	14 21	14 24		14 30		14 52	15 05	15 10			
Meadowhall	d	13 32		13 36			14 11	14 16		←		14 21		14 32		14 36			15 11	15 16		←	
Rotherham Central	d			13 42			14 19			14 19		14 28				14 42			15 19			15 19	
Swinton (S.Yorks)	d			13 50			→			14 28		14a38				14 50			→			15 28	
Mexborough	d			13 54						14 31						14 54						15 31	
Conisbrough	d			13 58						14 35						14 58						15 35	
London Kings Cross	d																						
Doncaster 7	a	13 54		14 08		14 15		14 34		14 44				14 55		15 08		15 15		15 34		15 44	
York 8 26	a					14 40							15 30					15 40					
Doncaster 31	d	13 59		14 09	14 26			14 37	14 42	14 47				14 58		15 08	15 26			15 37	15 42	15 47	
Bentley (S.Yorks) 31	a				14 29					14 51							15 29					15 51	
Adwick 31	a				14 33					14 56							15 33					15 56	
Kirk Sandall	d			14 15					14 48							15 15					15 48		
Hatfield & Stainforth	d			14 20					14 53							15 20					15 53		
Thorne South	d								14 58												15 58		
Crowle	d								15 07												16 07		
Althorpe	d								15 13												16 13		
Scunthorpe	a							15 02	15 21											16 02	16 21		
	d							15 03												16 03			
Barnetby 28	d							15 17												16 17			
Habrough 28	d																			16 26			
Grimsby Town 28	a							15 37												16 39			
	d							15 38												16 40			
Cleethorpes 28	a							15 51												16 53			
Thorne North	d			14 26												15 26							
Goole	d	14 19		14 35										15 18		15 35							
Saltmarshe	d			14 40																			
York 8 33	d		13 47												14 50								
Selby	a		14 16								15 11				15 17								16 11
	d		14 17								15 11				15 17								16 11
Wressle	d																						
Howden	d		14 27												15 27								
Eastrington	d																						
Gilberdyke	d		14 35	14 47											15 35	15 44							
Broomfleet	d																						
Brough	d	14 37	14 43	14 55							15 30			15 37	15 43	15 52							16 30
Ferriby	d			15 00												15 57							
Hessle	d			15 05												16 02							
Hull	a	14 51	15 04	15 17							15 45			15 51	16 00	16 14							16 45

A To Scarborough
B To Leeds
C From Penzance to Newcastle
D To Adwick
E ✠ to Sheffield
F From Sheffield
G From Plymouth to Aberdeen
H To Bridlington
I From Plymouth to Newcastle

For services between Barnetby, Habrough, Grimsby Town and Cleethorpes, refer to Table T028

Table T029-F

Saturdays
26 May to 8 December

Manchester Airport, Manchester, Sheffield and Meadowhall - Doncaster and Hull

	NT	XC	XC	NT	NT	NT	NT	XC	HT	NT	NT	TP	NT	NT	TP	NT	XC	XC	NT	NT	NT	NT
		◇■	◇■	◇			◇	◇■	◇■	◇		◇■			◇■	◇	◇■	◇■	◇			◇
	A	B 🛒	C	D			A	E 🛒	⊠	F	G	H 🛒		I	🛒	A	J 🛒	K 🛒	L			A
Manchester Airport 85 d												14 53										
Manchester Piccadilly d												15 19			15 47							
Stockport 78 d												15 28										
Sheffield a												16 08										
d	15 15	15 21	15 21	15 24		15 30		15 52		15 55	16 05	16 10				16 15	16 21	16 21	16 24		16 30	
Meadowhall d	15 21			15 32		15 36					16 11	16 16		←		16 21			16 32		16 36	
Rotherham Central d	15 28					15 42					16 19			16 19		16 28					16 42	
Swinton (S.Yorks) d	15a38					15 50					→			16 28		16a38					16 50	
Mexborough d						15 54								16 31							16 54	
Conisbrough d						15 58								16 35							16 58	
London Kings Cross d									14 48													
Doncaster a				15 57		16 08		16 16	16 25			16 34		16 45					16 54		17 08	
York 26 a		16 30	16 30					16 40									17 28	17 29				
Doncaster 31 d				15 59		16 08	16 26		16 26			16 37	16 42	16 47					16 59		17 08	17 26
Bentley (S.Yorks) 31 a							16 29							16 51								17 29
Adwick 31 a							16 33							16 56								17 33
Kirk Sandall d						16 15							16 48								17 15	
Hatfield & Stainforth d						16 20							16 53								17 20	
Thorne South d													16 58									
Crowle d													17 07									
Althorpe d													17 13									
Scunthorpe a												17 02	17 21									
d												17 03										
Barnetby 28 d										17 34		17 17										
Habrough 28 d										17 42												
Grimsby Town 28 a										17 56		17 37										
d										17 57		17 38										
Cleethorpes 28 a										18 07		17 51										
Thorne North d						16 26													17 10		17 26	
Goole d				16 19		16 35													17 21		17 35	
Saltmarshe d																					17 40	
York 33 d					15 47															16 48		
Selby a					16 16				16 41						17 11					17 17		
d					16 17				16 43						17 11					17 18		
Wressle d					16 25															17 25		
Howden d					16 30				16 53											17 30		
Eastrington d																						
Gilberdyke d					16 37	16 44														17 38	17 47	
Broomfleet d																						
Brough d				16 37	16 45	16 52			17 08						17 30				17 38	17 46	17 55	
Ferriby d						16 57															17 59	
Hessle d						17 02															18 04	
Hull a				16 51	17 02	17 13			17 25						17 45				17 52	18 03	18 14	

A To Leeds
B until 21 July, from 13 October. From Penzance to Glasgow Central
C from 28 July until 6 October. From Reading to Glasgow Central
D To Bridlington
E From Penzance to Newcastle
F via Retford
G To Adwick
H 🛒 to Sheffield
I From Sheffield
J from 28 July until 1 September. From Southampton Central to Dundee
K until 21 July, from 8 September. From Newquay to Dundee
L To Scarborough

For services between Barnetby, Habrough, Grimsby Town and Cleethorpes, refer to Table T028

Table T029-F

Saturdays
26 May to 8 December

Manchester Airport, Manchester, Sheffield and Meadowhall - Doncaster and Hull

	XC	NT	TP	NT	NT	TP	NT	XC	XC	NT	NT	NT	NT	XC	XC	NT	TP	NT	NT	TP	NT	XC
	◇■		◇■			◇■		◇■	◇■	◇			◇	◇■	◇■		◇■			◇■	◇	◇■
	A 🛒	B	C 🛒		D	🛒	E	F 🛒	G 🛒	H			E	I 🛒	J 🛒	B	C 🛒		D	🛒	E	K 🛒
Manchester Airport 85 d			15 53														16 53					
Manchester Piccadilly d			16 19			16 47											17 19			17 47		
Stockport 78 d			16 28														17 28					
Sheffield a			17 08														18 10					
d	16 52	17 05	17 10				17 15	17 21	17 21	17 24		17 30		17 48	17 50	18 05	18 11				18 15	18 21
Meadowhall d		17 11	17 16		←		17 21			17 32		17 36				18 11	18 17		←		18 21	
Rotherham Central d		17 19			17 19		17 28					17 42				18 18			18 18		18 28	
Swinton (S.Yorks) d		→			17 28		17a38					17 50				→			18 27		18a38	
Mexborough d					17 31							17 54							18 31			
Conisbrough d					17 35							17 58							18 35			
London Kings Cross d																						
Doncaster a	17 15		17 34		17 44					17 58		18 08					18 36		18 45			
York 26 a	17 40							18 29	18 30					19 05	19 05							19 30
Doncaster 31 d			17 38	17 42	17 48					18 00		18 08	18 28				18 37	18 42	18 48			
Bentley (S.Yorks) 31 a					17 52								18 31						18 52			
Adwick 31 a					17 57								18 35						18 57			
Kirk Sandall d				17 48								18 15						18 48				
Hatfield & Stainforth d				17 53								18 20						18 53				
Thorne South d				17 58														18 58				
Crowle d				18 07														19 07				
Althorpe d				18 13														19 13				
Scunthorpe a			18 06	18 21													19 03	19 21				
d			18 07														19 03					
Barnetby 28 d			18 21														19 18					
Habrough 28 d			18 30																			
Grimsby Town 28 a			18 43														19 37					
d			18 44														19 39					
Cleethorpes 28 a			18 55														19 51					
Thorne North d										18 11		18 26										
Goole d										18 22		18 35										
Saltmarshe d																						
York 33 d											17 48											
Selby a						18 11					18 19									19 11		
d						18 11					18 20									19 11		
Wressle d																						
Howden d						18 21					18 31											
Eastrington d																						
Gilberdyke d										18 35	18 41	18 47										
Broomfleet d												18 51										
Brough d						18 34				18 42	18 49	18 57								19 30		
Ferriby d												19 01										
Hessle d												19 06										
Hull a						18 49				18 58	19 03	19 16								19 44		

A From Newquay to Newcastle
B To Adwick
C 🛒 to Sheffield
D From Sheffield
E To Leeds
F from 28 July until 6 October. From Reading to Glasgow Central
G until 21 July, from 13 October. From Plymouth to Glasgow Central
H To Scarborough
I from 28 July until 6 October. From Plymouth to Edinburgh
J until 21 July, from 13 October. From Southampton Central to Newcastle
K From Plymouth to Edinburgh

For services between Barnetby, Habrough, Grimsby Town and Cleethorpes, refer to Table T028

Table T029-F

Saturdays

26 May to 8 December

Manchester Airport, Manchester, Sheffield and Meadowhall - Doncaster and Hull

	NT ◇ A	NT	NT	XC ◇■ B ⌶	XC ◇■ C ⌶	HT ◇■ D ☒	NT ◇ E		NT F	TP ◇■ G ⌶	NT	NT H	TP ◇■ ⌶	NT E	XC ◇■ I	NT ◇	NT	NT ◇ E	XC ◇■ J ⌶	NT F	TP ◇■	NT	NT H
Manchester Airport 85 ✈ d										17 53											18 53		
Manchester Piccadilly ■ d										18 19			18 47								19 19		
Stockport 78 d										18 28											19 28		
Sheffield ■ a										19 09											20 09		
d	18 24		18 30	18 52	18 52				19 05	19 11				19 15	19 21	19 24	19 30		19 52	20 05	20 11		
Meadowhall d	18 32		18 36						19 11	19 17		←		19 21		19 32	19 36			20 11	20 17		←
Rotherham Central d			18 42						19 19			19 19		19 28			19 42			20 19			20 19
Swinton (S.Yorks) d			18 50						→			19 28		19a38			19 50			→			20 28
Mexborough d			18 54									19 31					19 54						20 31
Conisbrough d			18 58									19 35					19 58						20 35
London Kings Cross d						17 48																	
Doncaster ■ a	18 56		19 08	19 13	19 13	19 24				19 37		19 44				19 54	20 08		20 13		20 35		20 46
York ■ 26 a				19 40	19 42										20 30				20 40				
Doncaster 31 d	19 00		19 09			19 26	19 28			19 37	19 42	19 54				19 59	20 09	20 28			20 36	20 42	20 48
Bentley (S.Yorks) 31 a							19 31					19 58						20 31					20 52
Adwick 31 a							19 35					20 03						20 35					20 57
Kirk Sandall d			19 15								19 49						20 16					20 48	
Hatfield & Stainforth d			19 20								19 54						20 21					20 53	
Thorne South d											19 59											20 58	
Crowle d											20 08											21 07	
Althorpe d											20 14											21 13	
Scunthorpe a										20 03	20 22										21 02	21 21	
d										20 03											21 03		
Barnetby 28 d										20 17											21 17		
Habrough 28 d																					21 26		
Grimsby Town 28 a										20 37											21 39		
d										20 38											21 40		
Cleethorpes 28 a										20 51											21 53		
Thorne North d			19 26														20 27						
Goole d	19 18		19 35													20 19	20 36						
Saltmarshe d	19 23																						
York ■ 33 d		18 50																					
Selby a		19 17				19 41							20 11										
d		19 18				19 43							20 11										
Wressle d																							
Howden d		19 27				19 53																	
Eastrington d																							
Gilberdyke d	19 29	19 35	19 48														20 45						
Broomfleet d																							
Brough d	19 36	19 43	19 56			20 05							20 30			20 37	20 53						
Ferriby d	19 41		20 00														20 58						
Hessle d	19 45		20 05														21 03						
Hull a	19 55	19 59	20 13			20 18							20 48			20 52	21 14						

A To Bridlington
B until 21 July, from 13 October. From Reading to Newcastle
C from 28 July until 6 October. From Plymouth to Newcastle
D To Beverley
E To Leeds
F To Adwick
G ⌶ to Sheffield
H From Sheffield
I From Plymouth to Edinburgh
J From Plymouth to Newcastle

For services between Barnetby, Habrough, Grimsby Town and Cleethorpes, refer to Table T028

Table T029-F

Saturdays

26 May to 8 December

Manchester Airport, Manchester, Sheffield and Meadowhall - Doncaster and Hull

	NT ◇ A	XC ◇■ B	NT ◇ C	TP ◇■	NT	NT	NT ◇ A		XC ◇■ D ⌶	XC ◇■ E	HT ◇■ ☒	NT F	TP ◇■	NT	NT G	TP ◇■	NT A	NT ◇ H	NT ◇ A	XC ◇■ I	XC ◇■ J	NT F	TP ◇■
Manchester Airport 85 ✈ d													19 56										20 53
Manchester Piccadilly ■ d				19 47									20 19			20 47							21 19
Stockport 78 d													20 28										21 28
Sheffield ■ a													21 09										22 10
d	20 15	20 21	20 24			20 30			20 52	20 52		21 05	21 11				21 15	21 28		22 03	22 03	22 07	22 11
Meadowhall d	20 21		20 32			20 36						21 11	21 17		←		21 21	21 34				22 13	22 17
Rotherham Central d	20 28					20 42						21 20			21 20		21 28					22 19	
Swinton (S.Yorks) d	20a38					20 50						→			21 28		21a38					→	
Mexborough d						20 54									21 39								
Conisbrough d						20 58									21 43								
London Kings Cross d											19 48												
Doncaster ■ a			20 54			21 08			21 21	21 21	21 27		21 48		21 53			21 57		22 24	22 24		22 36
York ■ 26 a		21 59							21 42	21 42										22 46	22 47		
Doncaster 31 d			20 58			21 08	21 28				21 29		21 50	21 54	21 55			21 59	22 32				22 37
Bentley (S.Yorks) 31 a							21 31								21 59				22 35				
Adwick 31 a							21 35								22 04				22 39				
Kirk Sandall d						21 15								22 00									22 42
Hatfield & Stainforth d						21 20								22 05									22 47
Thorne South d														22 10									22 51
Crowle d														22 19									23 00
Althorpe d														22 25									23 05
Scunthorpe a													22 15	22 33									23 10
d													22 16										23 11
Barnetby 28 d													22 30										23 25
Habrough 28 d													22 39										23 34
Grimsby Town 28 a													22 52										23 47
d													22 53										23 48
Cleethorpes 28 a													23 06										00 01
Thorne North d						21 26																	
Goole d			21 17			21 36												22 20					
Saltmarshe d																		22 24					
York ■ 33 d					20 45																		
Selby a				21 14	21 19						21 44					22 10							
d				21 15	21 19						21 44					22 11							
Wressle d					21 26																		
Howden d				21 24	21 31						21 54					22 20							
Eastrington d					21 36																		
Gilberdyke d						21 47												22 31					
Broomfleet d																							
Brough d			21 33	21 39	21 46	21 55					22 06					22 33		22 39					
Ferriby d					21 50	21 59																	
Hessle d					21 55	22 04																	
Hull a			21 49	21 52	22 05	22 14					22 20					22 46		22 54					

A To Leeds
B From Plymouth
C To Bridlington
D from 28 July until 6 October. From Plymouth to Newcastle
E until 21 July, from 13 October. From Reading to Newcastle
F To Adwick
G From Sheffield
H To Beverley
I until 21 July, from 13 October. From Southampton Central
J from 28 July until 6 October. From Plymouth

For services between Barnetby, Habrough, Grimsby Town and Cleethorpes, refer to Table T028

Table T029-F

Saturdays

26 May to 8 December

Manchester Airport, Manchester, Sheffield and Meadowhall - Doncaster and Hull

		NT	TP	NT		XC	XC	NT	NT	XC	NT	NT	TP	NT
			◇■	◇		◇■	◇■	◇		◇■			◇■	
		A		B		C	D		B	E				
Manchester Airport 85 ✈	d												21 53	
Manchester Piccadilly ■	d		21 47										22 19	
Stockport 78	d													
Sheffield ■	a												23 10	
	d			22 15		22 24	22 24	22 28		22 42		23 05	23 10	23 27
Meadowhall	d	←		22 21				22 34				23 11		23 33
Rotherham Central	d	22 19		22 28								23 18		23 39
Swinton (S.Yorks)	d	22 29		22a41								23 27		23 48
Mexborough	d	22 33										23 30		23 51
Conisbrough	d	22 37										23 34		23 55
London Kings Cross	d													
Doncaster ■	a	22 46				22 48	22 50	22 55		23 03		23 43	23 52	00 04
York ■ 26	a													
Doncaster 31	d	22 47						22 57	23 24					
Bentley (S.Yorks) 31	a	22 50							23 27					
Adwick 31	a	22 55							23 31					
Kirk Sandall	d													
Hatfield & Stainforth	d													
Thorne South	d													
Crowle	d													
Althorpe	d													
Scunthorpe	a													
	d													
Barnetby 28	d													
Habrough 28	d													
Grimsby Town 28	a													
	d													
Cleethorpes 28	a													
Thorne North	d							23 08						
Goole	d							23 17						
Saltmarshe	d													
York ■ 33	d										22 46			
Selby	a		23 10								23 16			
	d		23 11								23 17			
Wressle	d													
Howden	d										23 26			
Eastrington	d													
Gilberdyke	d										23 35			
Broomfleet	d													
Brough	d		23 30					23 35			23 43			
Ferriby	d										23 47			
Hessle	d										23 52			
Hull	a		23 45					23 49			00 04			

A From Sheffield
B To Leeds
C until 21 July. From Bournemouth to Leeds
D from 13 October. From Plymouth to Leeds
E from 28 July until 6 October. From Plymouth to Leeds

For services between Barnetby, Habrough, Grimsby Town and Cleethorpes, refer to Table T028

Table T029-F

Sundays

20 May to 2 December

Manchester Airport, Manchester, Sheffield and Meadowhall - Doncaster and Hull

		TP	NT	NT	NT	NT	NT	TP		TP	TP	XC	NT	TP	TP	NT	NT	NT	NT	NT	TP	TP	TP	TP
		◇■		◇	◇			◇■		◇■	◇■	◇■	◇	◇■	◇■						◇■	◇■	◇■	◇■
		A	B		C			D		E	F	G	H	I	J	C		K			L	E	M	N
		🛒						🛒		🛒	🛒	🛒		🛒	🛒						🛒	🛒	🛒	🛒
Manchester Airport 85 ✈	d							07 49			07 49										08 46			
Manchester Piccadilly ■	d							08 12		08 12	08 13			08 47							09 10	09 10	09 47	
Stockport 78	d							08 22		08 22	08 23										09 18	09 18		
Sheffield ■	a							09 08		09 08	09 08										10 08	10 08		
	d		08 06	08 36			09 06	09 10		09 10	09 10	09 21	09 25			09 35		10 02	10 06		10 10	10 10		
Meadowhall	d		08 12	08 43			09 12	09 16		09 16	09 16		09 31			09 41		10a07	10 12		10 16	10 16		
Rotherham Central	d		08 18				09 18									09 47			10 18					
Swinton (S.Yorks)	d		08 26				09 28									09a55			10 27					
Mexborough	d		08 29				09 31												10 31					
Conisbrough	d		08 33				09 35												10 35					
London Kings Cross	d																							
Doncaster ■	a			09 03			09 45	09 36		09 36	09 36		09 50						10 44		10 36	10 36		
York ■ 26	a											10 30												
Doncaster 31	d			09 05	09 25			09 38		09 38	09 38		09 52							10 16	10 38	10 38		
Bentley (S.Yorks) 31	a				09 28																			
Adwick 31	a				09 32																			
Kirk Sandall	d		08 52																	10 22				
Hatfield & Stainforth	d		08 57																	10 27				
Thorne South	d																							
Crowle	d																							
Althorpe	d																							
Scunthorpe	a							10 03		10 03	10 03										11 03	11 03		
	d							10 04		10 04	10 04										11 04	11 04		
Barnetby 28	d							10 18		10 18	10 18										11 20	11 20		
Habrough 28	d							10 27		10 27	10 27													
Grimsby Town 28	a							10 40		10 40	10 40										11 43	11 43		
	d							10 41		10 41	10 41										11 44	11 44		
Cleethorpes 28	a							10 53		10 53	10 53										11 56	11 56		
Thorne North	d		09 03																	10 32				
Goole	d		09 12	09 24									10 11							10 41				
Saltmarshe	d																							
York ■ 33	d					08 51											10 01							
Selby	a					09 21								10 07			10 19						11 07	
	d	09 06				09 21								10 08	10 08		10 20						11 09	11 09
Wressle	d																							
Howden	d					09 31											10 28							
Eastrington	d																							
Gilberdyke	d		09 21																	10 50				
Broomfleet	d																							
Brough	d	09 24	09 29	09 38		09 44							10 26	10 33	10 33		10 41			10 58			11 28	11 28
Ferriby	d																			11 03				
Hessle	d																			11 07				
Hull	a	09 38	09 43	09 53		09 59							10 40	10 48	10 48		10 55			11 19			11 42	11 42

A From Leeds
B To Scarborough
C To Leeds
D from 16 September until 21 October. 🛒 to Sheffield
E from 28 October. 🛒 to Sheffield
F until 9 September. 🛒 to Sheffield
G To Motherwell
H To Bridlington
I from 16 September
J until 9 September. From Manchester Victoria
K From Retford
L until 21 October. 🛒 to Sheffield
M until 9 September
N from 16 September. From Manchester Victoria

For services between Barnetby, Habrough, Grimsby Town and Cleethorpes, refer to Table T028

Table T029-F

Sundays

20 May to 2 December

Manchester Airport, Manchester, Sheffield and Meadowhall - Doncaster and Hull

	XC	NT	NT	NT	NT	TP	TP	XC	NT	EM	NT	NT	NT	HT	NT	TP	TP	TP	XC	NT	NT	XC
	◇1 A 🛒	◇ B			◇ C	◇1 D 🛒	◇1 🛒	◇1 E 🛒	C	◇1 F ☕		◇		◇1 ☒		◇1 D 🛒	◇1 G 🛒	◇1 H 🛒	◇1 I 🛒	◇ B		◇1 J 🛒
Manchester Airport 85 ✈ d						09 56										10 55						
Manchester Piccadilly 10 d						10 14	10 47									11 19	11 47	11 48				
Stockport 78 d						10 23										11 29						
Sheffield 7 a						11 05										12 09						
d	10 21	10 25		11 06		11 10		11 21	11 24	11 31		11 34			12 06	12 10			12 21	12 25		12 51
Meadowhall d		10 31		11 12		11 16			11 30			11 40			12 12	12 16				12 31		
Rotherham Central d				11 18					11 40						12 18							
Swinton (S.Yorks) d				11 27					11a51						12 28							
Mexborough d				11 31											12 31							
Conisbrough d				11 35											12 35							
London Kings Cross d														10 48								
Doncaster 7 a		10 50		11 44		11 36				11 52		11 58		12 26	12 45	12 34				12 50		13 13
York 8 26 a	11 29							12 30		12 15									13 27			14 27
Doncaster 31 d		10 54	11 15		11 25	11 39						12 03	12 15	12 30		12 37				12 55	13 15	
Bentley (S.Yorks) 31 a					11 28																	
Adwick 31 a					11 32																	
Kirk Sandall d			11 21										12 21								13 21	
Hatfield & Stainforth d			11 26										12 26								13 26	
Thorne South d																						
Crowle d																						
Althorpe d																						
Scunthorpe a						12 04										13 02						
d						12 05										13 03						
Barnetby 28 d						12 19										13 17						
Habrough 28 d						12 31																
Grimsby Town 28 a						12 41										13 39						
d						12 42										13 40						
Cleethorpes 28 a						12 56										13 51						
Thorne North d			11 31										12 31								13 31	
Goole d		11 17	11 40									12 26	12 40							13 19	13 40	
Saltmarshe d																						
York 8 33 d											11 51											
Selby a							12 07				12 13			12 44			13 09	13 09				
d							12 08				12 16			12 45			13 10	13 10				
Wressle d																						
Howden d											12 24			12 55								
Eastrington d																						
Gilberdyke d			11 49										12 49								13 49	
Broomfleet d																						
Brough d		11 33	11 57				12 27				12 38	12 44	12 57	13 08			13 29	13 29		13 34	13 57	
Ferriby d																						
Hessle d																						
Hull a		11 47	12 14				12 41				12 52	12 58	13 14	13 22			13 43	13 43		13 49	14 14	

A From Birmingham New Street to Edinburgh
B To Scarborough
C To Leeds
D 🛒 to Sheffield
E From Birmingham New Street to Motherwell
F From Leicester
G from 16 September
H until 9 September
I From Bristol Temple Meads to Edinburgh
J from 22 July until 7 October. From Bristol Temple Meads to Motherwell

For services between Barnetby, Habrough, Grimsby Town and Cleethorpes, refer to Table T028

Table T029-F

Sundays

20 May to 2 December

Manchester Airport, Manchester, Sheffield and Meadowhall - Doncaster and Hull

	NT	NT	TP	TP	XC	NT	NT	NT	XC	XC	NT	HT	NT	TP	TP	XC	NT	NT	NT	XC	XC	XC
		◇ A	◇1 B 🛒	◇1 🛒	◇1 C 🛒	◇ D	A		◇1 E 🛒	◇1 F 🛒		◇1 ☒		◇1 B 🛒	◇1 🛒	◇1 G 🛒	◇ H		◇ A	◇1 E 🛒	◇1 I 🛒	◇1 E 🛒
Manchester Airport 85 ✈ d			11 56											12 56								
Manchester Piccadilly 10 d			12 19	12 47										13 19	13 47							
Stockport 78 d			12 28											13 28								
Sheffield 7 a			13 08											14 08								
d	13 06		13 10		13 21	13 25	13 31		13 52	13 52			14 06	14 10		14 21	14 25			14 52	14 54	
Meadowhall d	13 12		13 16			13 31	13 37						14 12	14 16			14 31					
Rotherham Central d	13 18						13 43						14 18									
Swinton (S.Yorks) d	13 27						13a51						14 27									
Mexborough d	13 31												14 31									
Conisbrough d	13 35												14 35									
London Kings Cross d												12 48										←
Doncaster 7 a	13 44		13 34			13 51			14 14	14 14		14 23	14 44	14 34			14 57			15 18	15 16	15 18
York 8 26 a					14 27				14 40	15 27						15 27				→	16 27	15 40
Doncaster 31 d		13 25	13 37			13 53					14 15	14 25		14 37			15 02	15 15	15 25			
Bentley (S.Yorks) 31 a		13 28																	15 28			
Adwick 31 a		13 32																	15 32			
Kirk Sandall d											14 21							15 21				
Hatfield & Stainforth d											14 26							15 26				
Thorne South d																						
Crowle d																						
Althorpe d																						
Scunthorpe a			14 02											15 02								
d			14 03											15 03								
Barnetby 28 d			14 17											15 17								
Habrough 28 d			14 26																			
Grimsby Town 28 a			14 41											15 39								
d			14 42											15 40								
Cleethorpes 28 a			14 53											15 51								
Thorne North d											14 31							15 31				
Goole d						14 12					14 40						15 21	15 40				
Saltmarshe d																						
York 8 33 d								13 51														
Selby a				14 07				14 18				14 39			15 07							
d				14 08				14 18				14 39			15 08							
Wressle d																						
Howden d								14 27				14 49										
Eastrington d																						
Gilberdyke d											14 49							15 49				
Broomfleet d																						
Brough d				14 27		14 31		14 40			14 57	15 03			15 27		15 36	15 57				
Ferriby d																						
Hessle d																						
Hull a				14 41		14 46		14 56			15 14	15 18			15 41		15 50	16 14				

A To Leeds
B 🛒 to Sheffield
C until 15 July, from 14 October. From Bristol Temple Meads to Motherwell
D To Bridlington
E until 15 July, from 14 October. From Birmingham New Street to Newcastle
F from 22 July until 7 October. From Bristol Temple Meads to Aberdeen
G until 15 July, from 14 October. From Plymouth to Aberdeen
H To Scarborough
I from 22 July until 7 October. From Plymouth to Motherwell

For services between Barnetby, Habrough, Grimsby Town and Cleethorpes, refer to Table T028

Table T029-F

Sundays
20 May to 2 December

Manchester Airport, Manchester, Sheffield and Meadowhall - Doncaster and Hull

		NT	TP	TP	XC	NT	NT	NT	XC	XC	NT	HT	NT	TP	TP	NT	XC	NT	NT	XC	XC	XC	NT
			◇■ A	◇■	◇■ B	◇ C	D		◇■ E	◇■ F		◇■		◇■ A	◇■	◇ G	◇■ H	◇ I		◇■ J	◇■ K	◇■ L	
Manchester Airport 85	d		13 56											14 56									
Manchester Piccadilly	d		14 19	14 47										15 19	15 47								
Stockport 78	d		14 28											15 28									
Sheffield	a		15 08											16 08									
	d	15 06	15 10		15 21	15 25	15 31		15 52	15 52			16 06	16 10		16 13	16 21	16 25		16 52	16 52	16 52	17 06
Meadowhall	d	15 12	15 16			15 31	15 37						16 12	16 16		16 20		16 32					17 12
Rotherham Central	d	15 18					15 43						16 18			16 28							17 18
Swinton (S.Yorks)	d	15 27					15a51						16 27			16 38							17 27
Mexborough	d	15 31											16 30										17 31
Conisbrough	d	15 35											16 34										17 35
London Kings Cross	d											14 48											
Doncaster	a	15 44	15 35			15 49			16 11	16 14		16 27	16 44	16 34				16 54		17 12	17 12	17 15	17 44
York 26	a				16 27				17 27	16 40						17 36	17 27			18 27	18 27	17 40	
Doncaster 31	d		15 37			15 51					16 15	16 31		16 37				16 55	17 15				
Bentley (S.Yorks) 31	a																						
Adwick 31	a																						
Kirk Sandall	d										16 21								17 21				
Hatfield & Stainforth	d										16 26								17 26				
Thorne South	d																						
Crowle	d																						
Althorpe	d																						
Scunthorpe	a		16 03											17 02									
	d		16 03											17 03									
Barnetby 28	d		16 18											17 17									
Habrough 28	d		16 26																				
Grimsby Town 28	a		16 41											17 39									
	d		16 42											17 40									
Cleethorpes 28	a		16 53											17 51									
Thorne North	d										16 31								17 31				
Goole	d					16 11					16 40							17 15	17 40				
Saltmarshe	d																						
York 33	d							15 51															
Selby	a			16 07				16 19				16 45			17 07								
	d			16 08				16 19				16 45			17 08								
Wressle	d																						
Howden	d							16 28				16 55											
Eastrington	d																						
Gilberdyke	d										16 49								17 49				
Broomfleet	d																						
Brough	d			16 27		16 31		16 40			16 57	17 08			17 27			17 29	17 57				
Ferriby	d																						
Hessle	d																						
Hull	a			16 41		16 46		16 58			17 14	17 22			17 41			17 45	18 14				

A to Sheffield
B until 15 July, from 14 October. From Plymouth to Motherwell
C To Bridlington
D To Leeds
E from 22 July until 7 October. From Plymouth to Edinburgh
F until 15 July, from 14 October. From Guildford to Newcastle
G via Pontefract Baghill
H until 15 July, from 14 October. From Penzance to Edinburgh
I To Scarborough
J from 22 July until 9 September. From Penzance to Motherwell
K from 16 September until 7 October. From Penzance to Glasgow Central
L until 15 July, from 14 October. From Reading to Newcastle

For services between Barnetby, Habrough, Grimsby Town and Cleethorpes, refer to Table T028

Table T029-F

Sundays
20 May to 2 December

Manchester Airport, Manchester, Sheffield and Meadowhall - Doncaster and Hull

		NT	TP	TP	XC	NT	NT	NT	NT	XC	XC	NT	TP	TP	XC	NT	GR	NT	XC	XC	NT	NT	HT
		◇ A	◇■ B	◇■	◇■ C		◇ D		A	◇■ E	◇■ F		◇■ B	◇■	◇■ G	◇ D	■		◇■ H	◇■ I	◇ J	◇ A	◇■ K
Manchester Airport 85	d		15 56										16 56										
Manchester Piccadilly	d		16 19	16 47									17 19	17 47									
Stockport 78	d		16 28										17 28										
Sheffield	a		17 08										18 09										
	d		17 10		17 21		17 25		17 31	17 52	17 52	18 06	18 11		18 21	18 25			18 52	18 52	18 58		
Meadowhall	d		17 16				17 31		17 37			18 12	18 17			18 31					19 04		
Rotherham Central	d								17 43			18 18									19 12		
Swinton (S.Yorks)	d								17a52			18 27									19 20		
Mexborough	d											18 31											
Conisbrough	d											18 35											
London Kings Cross	d																17 22						17 47
Doncaster	a		17 34				17 50			18 11	18 14	18 45	18 35			18 50	19 03		19 17	19 17			19 27
York 26	a				18 27					19 30	19 21				19 30				19 46	20 30	20 16		
Doncaster 31	d	17 26	17 37				18 02	18 15					18 37			18 52	19 05	19 15				19 29	19 30
Bentley (S.Yorks) 31	a	17 29																				19 32	
Adwick 31	a	17 33																				19 36	
Kirk Sandall	d							18 21										19 21					
Hatfield & Stainforth	d							18 26										19 26					
Thorne South	d																						
Crowle	d																						
Althorpe	d																						
Scunthorpe	a		18 02										19 02										
	d		18 03										19 03										
Barnetby 28	d		18 17										19 17										
Habrough 28	d		18 26																				
Grimsby Town 28	a		18 41										19 39										
	d		18 42										19 40										
Cleethorpes 28	a		18 53										19 51										
Thorne North	d							18 31										19 31					
Goole	d						18 21	18 40								19 11		19 40					
Saltmarshe	d																						
York 33	d					17 51																	
Selby	a			18 05		18 10								19 07			19 22						19 45
	d			18 06		18 11								19 08			19 24						19 46
Wressle	d																						
Howden	d					18 19																	19 55
Eastrington	d																						
Gilberdyke	d							18 49										19 49					
Broomfleet	d																						
Brough	d			18 26		18 31	18 36	18 57						19 27		19 31	19 47	19 57					20 07
Ferriby	d																						
Hessle	d																						
Hull	a			18 40		18 45	18 51	19 14						19 41		19 46	20 00	20 14					20 20

A To Leeds
B to Sheffield
C until 15 July, from 14 October. From Plymouth to Motherwell
D To Bridlington
E from 22 July until 7 October. From Plymouth to Edinburgh
F until 15 July, from 14 October. From Reading to Newcastle
G until 15 July, from 14 October. From Newquay to Edinburgh
H until 15 July, from 14 October. From Reading to Edinburgh
I from 22 July until 7 October. From Newquay to Edinburgh
J via Pontefract Baghill
K To Beverley

For services between Barnetby, Habrough, Grimsby Town and Cleethorpes, refer to Table T028

Table T029-F

Sundays

20 May to 2 December

Manchester Airport, Manchester, Sheffield and Meadowhall - Doncaster and Hull

	NT	TP	TP	XC	NT	NT	XC		XC	NT	NT	NT	TP	TP	XC	NT	NT	XC	HT	NT	TP	TP	NT
		◇■ A 🍴	◇■ 🍴	◇■ B 🍴	◇ C	D	◇■ E		◇■ F 🍴				◇■	◇■	◇■ G	◇		◇■ E	◇■ ☒		◇■	◇■	◇
Manchester Airport 85 d		17 56											18 56								19 56		
Manchester Piccadilly d		18 19	18 47										19 19	19 47							20 18	20 47	
Stockport 78 d		18 28											19 28								20 28		
Sheffield a		19 09											20 09								21 09		
d	19 06	19 11		19 20	19 27	19 31	19 52		19 53		20 06		20 11		20 22	20 25		20 54		21 06	21 11		21 25
Meadowhall d	19 12	19 17			19 33	19 37					20 12		20 17			20 31				21 12	21 17		21 31
Rotherham Central d	19 18					19 43					20 20									21 18			
Swinton (S.Yorks) d	19 28					19a51					20 29									21 28			
Mexborough d	19 32										20 32									21 32			
Conisbrough d	19 36										20 36									21 36			
London Kings Cross d																			19 50				
Doncaster a	19 45	19 35			19 54		20 14		20 13		20 46		20 35			20 50		21 20	21 27	21 45	21 35		21 50
York 26 a				20 30			20 40								21 31			21 45					
Doncaster 31 d		19 37			19 56							20 15	20 37			20 52	21 15		21 28		21 37		21 52
Bentley (S.Yorks) 31 a																							
Adwick 31 a																							
Kirk Sandall d												20 21					21 21						
Hatfield & Stainforth d												20 26					21 26						
Thorne South d																							
Crowle d																							
Althorpe d																							
Scunthorpe a		20 02											21 02								22 02		
d		20 03											21 03								22 03		
Barnetby 28 d		20 17											21 17								22 17		
Habrough 28 d													21 26								22 26		
Grimsby Town 28 a		20 39											21 41								22 41		
d		20 40											21 42								22 42		
Cleethorpes 28 a		20 51											21 53								22 53		
Thorne North d												20 31					21 31						
Goole d					20 15							20 40				21 15	21 40						22 16
Saltmarshe d																							
York 33 d										20 05													
Selby a			20 07							20 23				21 06					21 43			22 07	
d			20 08							20 24				21 06					21 44			22 08	
Wressle d																							
Howden d										20 32									21 53				
Eastrington d																							
Gilberdyke d												20 49					21 49						
Broomfleet d																							
Brough d			20 27		20 31					20 45		20 57		21 24		21 29	21 57		22 05			22 27	22 31
Ferriby d																							
Hessle d																							
Hull a			20 41		20 46					21 01		21 14		21 38		21 44	22 14		22 18			22 41	22 46

A 🍴 to Sheffield
B until 15 July, from 14 October. From Plymouth to Edinburgh
C To Beverley
D To Leeds
E until 15 July, from 14 October. From Reading to Newcastle
F from 22 July until 7 October. From Plymouth to Leeds
G until 15 July, from 14 October. From Plymouth

For services between Barnetby, Habrough, Grimsby Town and Cleethorpes, refer to Table T028

Table T029-F

Sundays

20 May to 2 December

Manchester Airport, Manchester, Sheffield and Meadowhall - Doncaster and Hull

	NT	NT	NT	NT	NT		TP	TP	NT	TP	NT
		◇ A			A		◇■	◇■	◇	◇■	
Manchester Airport 85 d							20 55			21 56	
Manchester Piccadilly d							21 19	21 47		22 19	
Stockport 78 d							21 28			22 27	
Sheffield a							22 11			23 09	
d		21 31	22 08				22 12		22 25	23 11	23 30
Meadowhall d		21 37	22 14				22 18		22 31		23 36
Rotherham Central d		21 49	22 20								23 42
Swinton (S.Yorks) d		21a57	22 30								23 51
Mexborough d			22 33								23 54
Conisbrough d			22 37								23 58
London Kings Cross d											
Doncaster a			22 47				22 36		22 50	23 40	00 06
York 26 a											
Doncaster 31 d	22 15				22 29		22 39		22 52		
Bentley (S.Yorks) 31 a					22 32						
Adwick 31 a					22 36						
Kirk Sandall d	22 21										
Hatfield & Stainforth d	22 26										
Thorne South d											
Crowle d											
Althorpe d											
Scunthorpe a							23 04				
d							23 05				
Barnetby 28 d							23 19				
Habrough 28 d							23 28				
Grimsby Town 28 a							23 43				
d							23 44				
Cleethorpes 28 a							23 53				
Thorne North d	22 31										
Goole d	22 40								23 15		
Saltmarshe d											
York 33 d				22 19							
Selby a				22 37				23 07			
d				22 38				23 08			
Wressle d											
Howden d				22 46							
Eastrington d											
Gilberdyke d	22 49			22 53					23 24		
Broomfleet d											
Brough d	22 57			23 02				23 27	23 32		
Ferriby d				23 06					23 36		
Hessle d				23 11					23 41		
Hull a	23 14			23 23				23 41	23 52		

A To Leeds

For services between Barnetby, Habrough, Grimsby Town and Cleethorpes, refer to Table T028

Table T029-R

Mondays to Fridays

21 May to 7 December

Hull - Doncaster - Meadowhall, Sheffield, Manchester and Manchester Airport

Miles	Miles	Miles	Miles			NT	NT	NT	TP	EM	NT	NT	NT	TP	NT	TP		NT	XC	NT	NT	NT	HT	NT	TP
						MX	MX	MX																	
							◇		◇1	◇1			◇	◇1		◇1			◇1				◇1	◇	◇1
						A	B	C		D	E		C	F				G	H		I		J		
										⊠				🍴					🍴				⊠		🍴
0	0	—	—	**Hull**	d										05 24	05 35					05 58	06 19	06 26	06 30	06 40
4¾	4¾	—	—	Hessle	d										05 31						06 05				
7½	7½	—	—	Ferriby	d										05 36						06 10				
10½	10½	—	—	Brough	d										05 41	05 47					06 15	06 30	06 38	06 43	06 52
14½	14½	—	—	Broomfleet	d																				
17	17	—	—	Gilberdyke	d										05 49	05 54					06 23	06 38			
—	19¼	—	—	Eastrington	d																				
—	22¼	—	—	Howden	d											06 01						06 45	06 51		
—	25	—	—	Wressle	d																				
—	31	—	—	**Selby**	a											06 11						06 55	07 00		07 11
—	—	—	—		d											06 11		06 18				06 56	07 01		07 12
—	—	—	—	York 8	33 a																	07 28			
20¾	—	—	—	Saltmarshe	d										05 54						06 28				
23¾	—	—	—	Goole	d										05 59						06 33			06 58	
31	—	—	—	Thorne North	d										06 10										
—	—	0	—	**Cleethorpes**	28 d									05 07											
—	—	3	—	**Grimsby Town**	28 d									05 15											
—	—	11	—	Habrough	28 d																				
—	—	18	—	Barnetby	28 d									05 32											
—	—	29	—	**Scunthorpe**	a									05 47											
—	—	—	—		d									05 47											
—	—	32½	—	Althorpe	d									05 52											
—	—	36¼	—	Crowle	d									05 58											
—	—	42¼	—	Thorne South	d									06 06											
34¾	—	45¾	—	Hatfield & Stainforth	d									06 12	06 16						06 45				
37	—	48	—	Kirk Sandall	d										06 20						06 50				
—	—	—	0	Adwick	31 d															06 47					
—	—	—	2¼	Bentley (S.Yorks)	31 d															06 51					
41	49¼	52	4	**Doncaster 7**	31 a									06 23	06 30			06 41		06 56	07 00		07 15	07 19	
—	—	—	—	London Kings Cross 15 ⊖	26 a																		09 15		
—	—	—	—	York 8	26 d																				
—	—	—	—	**Doncaster 7**	d				05 38	05 57	06 03	06 06		06 23	06 37				06 46	06 58				07 19	
45¾	—	—	—	Conisbrough	d							06 13			06 44					07 06					
48	—	—	—	Mexborough	d							06 18			06 49					07 10					
49¾	—	—	—	Swinton (S.Yorks)	d			00 03				06 21	06 31		06 52					07 13					
53¾	—	—	—	Rotherham Central	d			00 11				06 29	06 41	06 46	06 59					07 22					
56½	—	—	—	**Meadowhall** 🚊	d	00 04	00 09	00 17	06 00			06 35	06 50	06 54	07 10					07 30				07 38	
60	—	—	—	**Sheffield 7** 🚊	a	00 13	00 17	00 26	06 08	06 23	06 36	06 45	06 59	07 07	07 18				07 12	07 38				07 47	
—	—	—	—		d				06 09					07 08											
96¾	—	—	—	Stockport	78 a				06 53					07 53											
102¾	—	—	—	**Manchester Piccadilly 10** 🚊	a				07 02					08 03		07 37									08 40
112½	—	—	—	**Manchester Airport** 85 ✈🚊	a				07 26					08 26											

A From Doncaster
B From Hull
C From Leeds
D From Leeds to St Pancras International
E To Lincoln
F 🍴 from Sheffield
G To Scunthorpe
H From Leeds to Southampton Central
I To Adwick
J From Beverley

For services between Barnetby, Habrough, Grimsby Town and Cleethorpes, refer to Table T028

Table T029-R

Mondays to Fridays

21 May to 7 December

Hull - Doncaster - Meadowhall, Sheffield, Manchester and Manchester Airport

		XC	XC	NT	NT	NT	TP	NT	GR	NT	XC	XC	NT	NT	TP	XC		NT	NT	NT	TP	NT	NT	XC	NT
		▣							▣			▣										▣			
		1	◇1				◇1		1		◇1	1		◇	◇1	◇1					◇1			◇1	
		A	B	C			D		E		F	G		H		I			C		D	J		I	
		🍴					🍴		🍽		🍴	🍴			🍴	🍴					🍴			🍴	
Hull	d							06 48	07 00	07 06				07 25	07 38							07 53	08 08		
Hessle	d							06 55		07 13												08 00			
Ferriby	d							07 00		07 18												08 05			
Brough	d							07 05	07 14	07 23				07 37	07 50							08 10	08 20		
Broomfleet	d									07 28												08 15			
Gilberdyke	d							07 12		07 33												08 20	08 27		
Eastrington	d									07 37															
Howden	d									07 42					08 02								08 34		
Wressle	d									07 46															
Selby	a								07 34	07 55					08 12								08 46		
	d								07 38	07 55					08 12								08 47		
York 8	33 a									08 31													09 19		
Saltmarshe	d																								
Goole	d							07 22						07 52								08 30			
Thorne North	d							07 31						08 00								08 38			
Cleethorpes	28 d						06 26														07 26				
Grimsby Town	28 d						06 34														07 34				
Habrough	28 d						06 44														07 44				
Barnetby	28 d						06 53														07 53				
Scunthorpe	a						07 08														08 08				
	d					06 48	07 08											07 48			08 08				
Althorpe	d					06 53												07 53							
Crowle	d					07 00												08 00							
Thorne South	d					07 08												08 08							
Hatfield & Stainforth	d					07 14		07 37										08 14				08 44			
Kirk Sandall	d					07 18		07 41										08 18				08 49			
Adwick	31 d				07 16								07 49							08 21					08 52
Bentley (S.Yorks)	31 d				07 20								07 53							08 25					08 56
Doncaster 7	31 a				07 25	07 28	07 38	07 51	07 54				07 58	08 19				08 28		08 30	08 39	08 58			09 02
London Kings Cross 15 ⊖	26 a								09 53																
York 8	26 d	06 45	06 45								07 26	07 26				07 43								08 27	
Doncaster 7	d				07 26		07 42				07 53	07 53	08 00	08 22						08 32	08 42			08 53	09 04
Conisbrough	d				07 34								08 11							08 39					09 12
Mexborough	d				07 38								08 15							08 44					09 17
Swinton (S.Yorks)	d			07 34	07 41								08 20						08 36	08 47					09 20
Rotherham Central	d			07 44	07 56								08 28						08 44	08 57					09 29
Meadowhall 🚊	d			07 50	08 03		07 59						08 34	08 40					08 51	09 05	09 01				09 35
Sheffield 7 🚊	a	07 51	07 51	07 57	08 11		08 06				08 14	08 15	08 44	08 49		08 54			09 00	09 14	09 08			09 19	09 44
	d						08 08														09 11				
Stockport	78 a						08 53														09 52				
Manchester Piccadilly 10 🚊	a						09 02								09 40						10 02				
Manchester Airport 85 ✈🚊	a						09 26														10 26				

A from 23 July until 5 October. To Reading
B until 20 July, from 8 October. To Plymouth
C From Leeds
D 🍴 from Sheffield
E The Hull Executive
F from 23 July until 5 October. From Newcastle to Plymouth
G until 20 July, from 8 October. From Newcastle to Reading
H From Bridlington
I From Newcastle to Southampton Central
J ▣ from Thorne North

For services between Barnetby, Habrough, Grimsby Town and Cleethorpes, refer to Table T028

Table T029-R

Mondays to Fridays

21 May to 7 December

Hull - Doncaster - Meadowhall, Sheffield, Manchester and Manchester Airport

	HT ◇1 A ⊠	NT ◇ B	HT ◇1 C ⊠	TP ◇1 🛒	XC ◇1 D 🛒	NT	NT ◇ E	NT	TP ◇1 F 🛒	XC ◇1 G 🛒	XC ◇1 H 🛒	NT I	NT	NT ◇ J	TP ◇1 🛒		XC ◇1 K 🛒	NT	NT E	NT	TP ◇1 F 🛒	XC ◇1 L 🛒	NT ◇	NT
Hull d	08 23	08 27		08 40								08 53	09 10	09 27	09 40									09 51
Hessle d												09 00												10 00
Ferriby d												09 05												10 05
Brough d	08 35	08 40		08 52								09 10	09 22	09 39	09 52									10 10
Broomfleet d																								
Gilberdyke d												09 18	09 29											10 17
Eastrington d																								
Howden d	08 46												09 36											
Wressle d																								
Selby a	08 57			09 11									09 47		10 11									
d	09 01			09 11									09 47		10 12									
York 8 33 a													10 22											
Saltmarshe d												09 23												
Goole d		08 55										09 28		09 54										10 28
Thorne North d												09 37												10 37
Cleethorpes 28 d									08 26												09 26			
Grimsby Town 28 d									08 34												09 34			
Habrough 28 d									08 44															
Barnetby 28 d									08 53												09 53			
Scunthorpe a									09 08												10 08			
d						08 52			09 08									09 48			10 08			
Althorpe d						08 57												09 53						
Crowle d						09 04												10 00						
Thorne South d						09 12												10 08						
Hatfield & Stainforth d						09 18						09 43						10 14						10 43
Kirk Sandall d						09 22						09 47						10 18						10 47
Adwick 31 d								09 25												10 24				
Bentley (S.Yorks) 31 d			←					09 29												10 28				
Doncaster 7 31 a	09 24	09 19	09 24			09 32		09 34	09 38			10 00		10 19				10 28		10 33	10 39			10 59
London Kings Cross 15 ⊖26 a	→		11 09																					
York 8 26 d					08 44					09 35	09 36						09 44					10 35	10 15	
Doncaster 7 d		09 20						09 35	09 42	09 59	10 00	10 04		10 20						10 35	10 42	10 59		11 04
Conisbrough d								09 42				10 11								10 42				11 12
Mexborough d								09 47				10 16								10 47				11 17
Swinton (S.Yorks) d							09 36	09 50				10 19							10 36	10 50			11 10	11 20
Rotherham Central d							09 44	09 58				10 28							10 44	10 58			11 18	11 28
Meadowhall 🚊 d		09 38					09 50	10 06	10 01			10 34		10 38					10 50	11 06	11 02		11 24	11 34
Sheffield 7 🚊 a		09 48			09 53		09 58	10 14	10 08	10 21	10 22	10 44		10 48			10 54		10 58	11 14	11 08	11 21	11 31	11 44
d									10 10												11 11			
Stockport 78 a									10 52												11 52			
Manchester Piccadilly 10 🚊 a				10 40					11 02						11 40						12 02			
Manchester Airport 85 ✈🚊 a									11 26												12 26			

A To London Kings Cross
B From Scarborough
C From Hull
D From Edinburgh to Reading
E From Leeds
F 🛒 from Sheffield
G until 20 July, from 8 October. From Edinburgh to Reading
H from 23 July until 5 October. From Edinburgh to Plymouth
I From Beverley
J From Bridlington
K From Glasgow Central to Southampton Central
L From Newcastle to Southampton Central

For services between Barnetby, Habrough, Grimsby Town and Cleethorpes, refer to Table T028

Table T029-R

Mondays to Fridays

21 May to 7 December

Hull - Doncaster - Meadowhall, Sheffield, Manchester and Manchester Airport

	NT	NT ◇ A	HT ◇1 ⊠	TP ◇1	XC ◇1 B 🛒	NT	NT ◇ C	NT	TP ◇1 D 🛒	XC ◇1 E 🛒	NT	NT	NT ◇ F	TP ◇1 🛒	XC ◇1 G 🛒		NT	NT C	NT	TP ◇1 D 🛒	XC ◇1 H 🛒	NT	NT	NT ◇ A
Hull d	10 10	10 27	10 33	10 40							10 53	11 10	11 27	11 40								11 51	12 10	12 27
Hessle d											11 00											11 58		
Ferriby d											11 05											12 03		
Brough d	10 22	10 39	10 45	10 52							11 10	11 22	11 39	11 52								12 08	12 22	12 39
Broomfleet d																						12 13		
Gilberdyke d	10 29										11 17	11 28										12 18	12 29	
Eastrington d																								
Howden d	10 36		10 56									11 35											12 36	
Wressle d																								
Selby a	10 47		11 07	11 11								11 47		12 11									12 47	
d	10 47		11 08	11 12								11 47		12 12									12 47	
York 8 33 a	11 12											12 22											13 19	
Saltmarshe d											11 23													
Goole d		10 54									11 28		11 54									12 28		12 54
Thorne North d											11 37											12 37		
Cleethorpes 28 d									10 26											11 26				
Grimsby Town 28 d									10 34											11 34				
Habrough 28 d									10 44															
Barnetby 28 d									10 53											11 53				
Scunthorpe a									11 08											12 08				
d						10 48			11 08								11 48			12 08				
Althorpe d						10 53											11 53							
Crowle d						11 00											12 00							
Thorne South d						11 08											12 08							
Hatfield & Stainforth d						11 14					11 43						12 14					12 43		
Kirk Sandall d						11 18					11 47						12 18					12 47		
Adwick 31 d								11 24											12 24					
Bentley (S.Yorks) 31 d								11 28											12 28					
Doncaster 7 31 a		11 19	11 23			11 28		11 33	11 38		11 58		12 19				12 28		12 33	12 40		12 58		13 19
London Kings Cross 15 ⊖26 a			13 09																					
York 8 26 d					10 44					11 35					11 44						12 35			
Doncaster 7 d		11 19						11 35	11 42	11 59	12 03		12 20						12 35	12 42	12 59	13 04		13 20
Conisbrough d								11 42			12 10								12 42			13 12		
Mexborough d								11 47			12 15								12 47			13 16		
Swinton (S.Yorks) d							11 36	11 50			12 18							12 36	12 50			13 19		
Rotherham Central d							11 44	11 58			12 28							12 44	12 58			13 28		
Meadowhall 🚊 d		11 38					11 50	12 06	12 02		12 34		12 39					12 50	13 06	13 02		13 34		13 38
Sheffield 7 🚊 a		11 48			11 53		11 58	12 14	12 08	12 21	12 44		12 48		12 53			12 58	13 14	13 08	13 21	13 44		13 48
d									12 11											13 11				
Stockport 78 a									12 52											13 52				
Manchester Piccadilly 10 🚊 a				12 40					13 02					13 40						14 02				
Manchester Airport 85 ✈🚊 a									13 26											14 26				

A From Bridlington
B From Dundee to Reading
C From Leeds
D 🛒 from Sheffield
E From Newcastle to Reading
F From Scarborough
G From Glasgow Central to Southampton Central
H From Newcastle to Southampton Central

For services between Barnetby, Habrough, Grimsby Town and Cleethorpes, refer to Table T028

Table T029-R

Mondays to Fridays
21 May to 7 December

Hull - Doncaster - Meadowhall, Sheffield, Manchester and Manchester Airport

			HT ◇1 ⊠	TP ◇1	XC ◇1 A	NT	NT ◇ B	NT	TP ◇1 C	XC ◇1 D	NT ◇	NT	NT	NT ◇ E	TP ◇1	XC ◇1 F	NT		NT B	NT	TP ◇1 C	XC ◇1 G	NT	NT	NT ◇ E	TP ◇1
Hull		d	12 33	12 40								12 53	13 10	13 24	13 40								13 53	14 09	14 27	14 40
Hessle		d										13 00											14 00			
Ferriby		d										13 05											14 05			
Brough		d	12 45	12 52								13 10	13 23	13 36	13 52								14 10	14 22	14 39	14 52
Broomfleet		d																					14 15			
Gilberdyke		d										13 18	13 31										14 20	14 29		
Eastrington		d											13 35													
Howden		d	12 56										13 40											14 36		
Wressle		d											13 45													
Selby		a	13 07	13 11									13 55		14 11									14 47		15 11
		d	13 07	13 12									13 56		14 12									14 47		15 12
York 8	33	a											14 20											15 11		
Saltmarshe		d										13 23														
Goole		d										13 28		13 54									14 28		14 54	
Thorne North		d										13 37											14 37			
Cleethorpes	28	d							12 26												13 26					
Grimsby Town	28	d							12 34												13 34					
Habrough	28	d							12 44																	
Barnetby	28	d							12 53												13 53					
Scunthorpe		a							13 08												14 08					
		d				12 48			13 08								13 48				14 08					
Althorpe		d				12 53											13 53									
Crowle		d				13 00											14 00									
Thorne South		d				13 08											14 08									
Hatfield & Stainforth		d				13 14						13 43					14 14						14 43			
Kirk Sandall		d				13 18						13 47					14 18						14 47			
Adwick	31	d						13 24												14 24						
Bentley (S.Yorks)	31	d						13 28												14 28						
Doncaster 7	31	a	13 23			13 28		13 33	13 38			13 58		14 19			14 28			14 33	14 38		14 58		15 19	
London Kings Cross 15	⊖26	a	15 09																							
York 8	26	d			12 44					13 35	13 13					13 44						14 35				
Doncaster 7		d						13 35	13 42	13 59		14 05		14 20						14 35	14 42	14 59	15 04		15 20	
Conisbrough		d						13 42				14 12								14 42			15 12			
Mexborough		d						13 47				14 17								14 47			15 16			
Swinton (S.Yorks)		d					13 36	13 50			14 10	14 20							14 36	14 50			15 19			
Rotherham Central		d					13 44	13 58			14 18	14 28							14 44	14 58			15 28			
Meadowhall		d					13 50	14 06	14 02		14 24	14 34		14 38					14 50	15 06	15 02		15 34		15 38	
Sheffield 7		a			13 53		13 58	14 14	14 08	14 21	14 31	14 44		14 48		14 54			14 58	15 14	15 08	15 21	15 44		15 48	
		d							14 11												15 11					
Stockport	78	a							14 52												15 52					
Manchester Piccadilly 10		a		14 40					15 02						15 40						16 02					16 40
Manchester Airport	85 ✈	a							15 26												16 26					

A From Glasgow Central to Reading
B From Leeds
C trolley from Sheffield
D From Newcastle to Reading
E From Bridlington
F From Aberdeen to Guildford
G From Newcastle to Guildford

For services between Barnetby, Habrough, Grimsby Town and Cleethorpes, refer to Table T028

Table T029-R

Mondays to Fridays
21 May to 7 December

Hull - Doncaster - Meadowhall, Sheffield, Manchester and Manchester Airport

			XC ◇1 A	NT	NT ◇ B	NT	TP ◇1 C	XC ◇1 D	NT	HT ◇1 ⊠	NT	NT ◇ E	TP ◇1	XC ◇1 F	NT	NT B	NT		TP ◇1 C	XC ◇1 D	NT	NT	NT ◇ G	TP ◇1	XC ◇1 A	NT
Hull		d							14 53	15 12	15 18	15 25	15 40								15 53	16 10	16 27	16 40		
Hessle		d							15 00												16 01					
Ferriby		d							15 05												16 05					
Brough		d							15 10	15 24	15 30	15 37	15 52								16 10	16 22	16 39	16 52		
Broomfleet		d																			16 16					
Gilberdyke		d							15 18		15 39										16 20	16 29				
Eastrington		d																								
Howden		d								15 38	15 46											16 36				
Wressle		d																								
Selby		a								15 48	15 56		16 11									16 46		17 11		
		d								15 48	15 57		16 12									16 47		17 12		
York 8	33	a									16 29											17 23				
Saltmarshe		d							15 23																	
Goole		d							15 28			15 54									16 29		16 54			
Thorne North		d							15 37												16 37					
Cleethorpes	28	d					14 26												15 26							
Grimsby Town	28	d					14 34												15 34							
Habrough	28	d					14 44																			
Barnetby	28	d					14 53												15 53							
Scunthorpe		a					15 08												16 08							
		d		14 48			15 08								15 48				16 08							16 48
Althorpe		d		14 53											15 53											16 53
Crowle		d		15 00											16 00											17 00
Thorne South		d		15 08											16 08											17 08
Hatfield & Stainforth		d		15 14					15 43						16 14						16 43					17 14
Kirk Sandall		d		15 18					15 47						16 18						16 48					17 18
Adwick	31	d				15 24											16 24									
Bentley (S.Yorks)	31	d				15 28											16 28									
Doncaster 7	31	a		15 28		15 33	15 38		15 58	16 04		16 20			16 28		16 33		16 38		17 01		17 19			17 28
London Kings Cross 15	⊖26	a								17 47																
York 8	26	d	14 44					15 35						15 44						16 05					16 44	
Doncaster 7		d				15 35	15 42	15 59	16 04			16 21					16 35		16 42		17 04		17 20			
Conisbrough		d				15 42			16 12								16 42				17 12					
Mexborough		d				15 47			16 16								16 47				17 16					
Swinton (S.Yorks)		d			15 36	15 50			16 19							16 36	16 50				17 19					
Rotherham Central		d			15 44	15 58			16 28							16 44	16 58				17 28					
Meadowhall		d			15 50	16 06	16 02		16 34			16 38				16 50	17 06		17 02		17 34		17 38			
Sheffield 7		a	15 54		15 58	16 14	16 08	16 21	16 44			16 48		16 53		16 58	17 14		17 08	17 20	17 44		17 48		17 52	
		d					16 11												17 11							
Stockport	78	a					16 52												17 52							
Manchester Piccadilly 10		a					17 02						17 40						18 02					18 40		
Manchester Airport	85 ✈	a					17 26												18 26							

A From Glasgow Central to Reading
B From Leeds
C trolley from Sheffield
D From Newcastle to Reading
E From Bridlington
F until 11 October, FX from 15 October. From Edinburgh to Reading
G From Scarborough

For services between Barnetby, Habrough, Grimsby Town and Cleethorpes, refer to Table T028

Hull - Doncaster - Meadowhall, Sheffield, Manchester and Manchester Airport

		NT	NT	TP	XC	NT	HT	NT	NT	TP	XC	XC	NT	NT	NT	TP	XC	NT	NT	NT	TP	XC	NT	NT
		A		◇1 B 🍴	◇1 C 🍴		◇1 ⊠		◇ D	◇1 🍴	◇1 E 🍴	◇1 F 🍴		A		◇1	◇1 G 🍴			◇ D	◇1	◇1 H 🍴		◇ A
Hull	d					16 53	17 09	17 15	17 27	17 40								17 52	18 10	18 27	18 38			
Hessle	d					17 00		17 22										17 59						
Ferriby	d					17 05		17 27										18 04						
Brough	d					17 10	17 21	17 32	17 39	17 52								18 09	18 22	18 39	18 52			
Broomfleet	d					17 15												18 14						
Gilberdyke	d					17 20		17 39										18 19	18 29					
Eastrington	d							17 44																
Howden	d						17 35	17 48											18 36					
Wressle	d							17 53																
Selby	a						17 45	18 03		18 11									18 47		19 11			
	d						17 46	18 03		18 12									18 47		19 12			
York 8 33	a							18 34											19 20					
Saltmarshe	d																	18 24						
Goole	d					17 28			17 54									18 29		18 54				
Thorne North	d					17 37												18 38						
Cleethorpes 28	d			16 26												17 23								
Grimsby Town 28	d			16 34												17 31								
Habrough 28	d			16 44												17 41								
Barnetby 28	d			16 53												17 50								
Scunthorpe	a			17 08												18 08								
	d			17 08									17 48			18 08							18 48	
Althorpe	d												17 53										18 53	
Crowle	d												18 00										19 00	
Thorne South	d												18 08										19 08	
Hatfield & Stainforth	d					17 43							18 14					18 44					19 14	
Kirk Sandall	d					17 47							18 18					18 48					19 18	
Adwick 31	d		17 24												18 24									
Bentley (S.Yorks) 31	d		17 28												18 28									
Doncaster 7 31	a		17 33	17 38		17 58	18 01		18 19				18 28		18 33	18 38		18 59		19 20			19 28	
London Kings Cross 15 ⊖26	a						19 47																	
York 8 26	d				17 35						17 45	17 45					18 36					18 45		
Doncaster 7	d		17 35	17 42	17 58	18 04			18 22						18 35	18 42	18 59	19 04		19 20				
Conisbrough	d		17 42			18 12									18 42			19 12						
Mexborough	d		17 47			18 16									18 47			19 16						
Swinton (S.Yorks)	d	17 35	17 50			18 19								18 36	18 50			19 19						19 36
Rotherham Central	d	17 45	17 58			18 28								18 44	18 58			19 28						19 44
Meadowhall ⇌	d	17 50	18 06	18 02		18 34			18 40					18 50	19 06	19 02		19 34		19 38				19 50
Sheffield 7 ⇌	a	17 58	18 14	18 08	18 20	18 44			18 49		18 51	18 54		18 58	19 14	19 08	19 21	19 44		19 48		19 51		19 58
	d			18 11												19 11								
Stockport 78	a			18 52												19 52								
Manchester Piccadilly 10 ⇌	a			19 02						19 40						20 02					20 40			
Manchester Airport 85 ✈⇌	a			19 26												20 26								

A From Leeds
B 🍴 from Sheffield
C From Newcastle to Reading
D From Bridlington
E until 20 July, from 3 September. From Edinburgh to Southampton Central
F from 23 July until 31 August. From Edinburgh to Southampton Central
G From Newcastle to Bristol Temple Meads
H From Glasgow Central to Birmingham New Street

For services between Barnetby, Habrough, Grimsby Town and Cleethorpes, refer to Table T028

Hull - Doncaster - Meadowhall, Sheffield, Manchester and Manchester Airport

		NT	TP	XC	NT	HT	NT	NT	NT	TP	XC	XC	NT	NT	NT	TP	XC	NT	GR	TP	XC	NT	NT	NT
			◇1	◇1 A 🍴	B	◇1 ⊠	C		◇ D	◇1	◇1 E	◇1 F		G		◇1	◇1 A 🍴	■ H	■ 1 ☕	◇1	◇1 I		◇ G	
Hull	d				18 53	19 12		19 16	19 27	19 40								19 55	20 28	20 40				
Hessle	d				19 00													20 02						
Ferriby	d				19 05													20 07						
Brough	d				19 10	19 24		19 31	19 39	19 52								20 12	20 42	20 52				
Broomfleet	d																							
Gilberdyke	d				19 18			19 38										20 19						
Eastrington	d																							
Howden	d					19 37		19 45																
Wressle	d																							
Selby	a					19 47		19 56		20 11									21 02	21 11				
	d					19 47		19 56		20 12									21 04	21 12				
York 8 33	a							20 27																
Saltmarshe	d				19 23																			
Goole	d				19 28				19 54									20 29						
Thorne North	d				19 37													20 38						
Cleethorpes 28	d		18 29													19 26								
Grimsby Town 28	d		18 37													19 34								
Habrough 28	d															19 44								
Barnetby 28	d		18 56													19 53								
Scunthorpe	a		19 08													20 08								
	d		19 08										19 48			20 08						20 48		
Althorpe	d												19 53									20 53		
Crowle	d												20 00									21 00		
Thorne South	d												20 08									21 08		
Hatfield & Stainforth	d				19 43								20 14					20 44				21 14		
Kirk Sandall	d				19 47								20 18					20 48				21 18		
Adwick 31	d	19 24													20 24									21 24
Bentley (S.Yorks) 31	d	19 28					←								20 28									21 28
Doncaster 7 31	a	19 33	19 41		20 05	20 03	20 05		20 19				20 28		20 33	20 38		21 02	21 22			21 28		21 33
London Kings Cross 15 ⊖26	a				→	21 48																		
York 8 26	d			19 36							19 45	19 45					20 36				20 45			
Doncaster 7	d	19 35	19 42	19 59			20 06		20 21						20 35	20 42	21 01	21 04						21 35
Conisbrough	d	19 43					20 14								20 42			21 11						21 42
Mexborough	d	19 47					20 18								20 47			21 16						21 47
Swinton (S.Yorks)	d	19 50					20 21							20 36	20 50			21 19					21 36	21 50
Rotherham Central	d	19 58					20 30							20 44	21 00			21 29					21 44	21 58
Meadowhall ⇌	d	20 06	20 02				20 36		20 39					20 50	21 08	21 04		21 35					21 50	22 06
Sheffield 7 ⇌	a	20 14	20 08	20 21			20 45		20 48		20 52	20 53		20 58	21 18	21 09	21 24	21 43			21 53		21 59	22 16
	d		20 11													21 11								
Stockport 78	a		20 52													21 52								
Manchester Piccadilly 10 ⇌	a		21 01							21 40						22 09				22 38				
Manchester Airport 85 ✈⇌	a		21 26																	23 00				

A From Newcastle to Birmingham New Street
B To Sheffield
C From Hull
D From Scarborough
E until 20 July, from 8 October. From Edinburgh to Bristol Temple Meads
F from 23 July until 5 October. From Edinburgh to Birmingham New Street
G From Leeds
H ■ from Thorne North
I From Glasgow Central to Birmingham New Street

For services between Barnetby, Habrough, Grimsby Town and Cleethorpes, refer to Table T028

Table T029-R

Mondays to Fridays
21 May to 7 December

Hull - Doncaster - Meadowhall, Sheffield, Manchester and Manchester Airport

		TP	NT	TP	NT	TP	TP	NT	NT		NT	NT	NT	NT	NT	NT
						FO	FX									
		◇1	◇	◇1		◇1	◇1						◇			◇
			A					B	C				C	C		D
Hull	d		21 23	21 40		22 24	22 24	22 30								22 48
Hessle	d															22 55
Ferriby	d															22 59
Brough	d		21 38	21 52		22 36	22 36	22 42								23 04
Broomfleet	d															
Gilberdyke	d															23 11
Eastrington	d															
Howden	d							22 54								
Wressle	d															
Selby	a			22 11		22 55	22 55	23 04								
	d			22 12		22 56	22 56									
York 8 33	a															
Saltmarshe	d															
Goole	d		21 53													23 19
Thorne North	d		22 01													23 29
Cleethorpes 28	d	20 26														
Grimsby Town 28	d	20 34														
Habrough 28	d															
Barnetby 28	d	20 53														
Scunthorpe	a	21 08														
	d	21 08			21 48							22 48				
Althorpe	d				21 53							22 53				
Crowle	d				22 00							23 00				
Thorne South	d				22 08							23 08				
Hatfield & Stainforth	d		22 07		22 14							23 14				23 34
Kirk Sandall	d		22 11		22 18							23 18				23 39
Adwick 31	d										22 23					
Bentley (S.Yorks) 31	d										22 27					
Doncaster 7 31	a	21 38	22 25		22 29						22 31	23 28				23 47
London Kings Cross 15 ⊖26	a															
York 8 26	d															
Doncaster 7	d	21 42	22 26								22 37				23 35	23 51
Conisbrough	d										22 44				23 42	
Mexborough	d										22 49				23 47	
Swinton (S.Yorks)	d								22 41		22 52		23 18	23 31	23 50	
Rotherham Central	d								22 50		22 59		23 28	23 40	23 57	
Meadowhall ⇌	d	22 02	22 44						22 56		23 06		23 34	23 47	00 04	00 09
Sheffield 7 ⇌	a	22 08	22 53						23 04		23 15		23 42	23 55	00 13	00 17
	d	22 11														
Stockport 78	a	22 52														
Manchester Piccadilly 10 ⇌	a	23 01		23 53		00 42	01 02									
Manchester Airport 85 ✈⇌	a	23 26														

A From Bridlington
B To Leeds
C From Leeds
D ◇ from Thorne North

For services between Barnetby, Habrough, Grimsby Town and Cleethorpes, refer to Table T028

Table T029-R

Saturdays
26 May to 8 December

Hull - Doncaster - Meadowhall, Sheffield, Manchester and Manchester Airport

		NT	NT	NT	TP	NT	NT	NT		TP	NT	TP	NT	XC	XC	NT	NT	HT	NT	NT	XC	XC	TP	XC
			◇		◇1					◇1		◇1		◇1	◇1			◇1		◇	◇1	◇1	◇1	◇1
		A	B	C		D		C		E			F	G	H		I	J			K	L		M
										⚒				⚒				☒			⚒		⚒	⚒
Hull	d										05 24	05 35					05 58	06 17	06 22	06 30			06 40	
Hessle	d										05 31						06 05							
Ferriby	d										05 36						06 10							
Brough	d										05 41	05 47					06 15	06 29	06 33	06 43			06 52	
Broomfleet	d																							
Gilberdyke	d										05 49	05 54					06 23		06 41					
Eastrington	d																							
Howden	d											06 00						06 40	06 48					
Wressle	d																							
Selby	a											06 10						06 51	06 58				07 11	
	d											06 11	06 18					06 51	06 59				07 12	
York 8 33	a																		07 31					
Saltmarshe	d										05 54						06 28							
Goole	d										05 59						06 33			06 58				
Thorne North	d										06 10													
Cleethorpes 28	d									05 07														
Grimsby Town 28	d									05 15														
Habrough 28	d																							
Barnetby 28	d									05 32														
Scunthorpe	a									05 47														
	d									05 47														
Althorpe	d									05 52														
Crowle	d									05 58														
Thorne South	d									06 06														
Hatfield & Stainforth	d									06 12	06 16						06 45							
Kirk Sandall	d										06 20						06 50							
Adwick 31	d															06 48								
Bentley (S.Yorks) 31	d															06 52								
Doncaster 7 31	a									06 23	06 30		06 41			06 57	07 00	07 09		07 19				
London Kings Cross 15 ⊖26	a																	08 47						
York 8 26	d																				06 20	06 20		06 45
Doncaster 7	d				05 38	06 02	06 06			06 23	06 32			06 51	06 51	06 58				07 19				
Conisbrough	d						06 13				06 39					07 06								
Mexborough	d						06 18				06 44					07 10								
Swinton (S.Yorks)	d			00 03			06 21	06 31			06 47					07 13								
Rotherham Central	d			00 11			06 29	06 41		06 47	06 55					07 22								
Meadowhall ⇌	d	00 04	00 09	00 17	06 00		06 35	06 50		06 51	07 03					07 30				07 38				
Sheffield 7 ⇌	a	00 13	00 17	00 26	06 08	06 26	06 45	06 59		07 07	07 11			07 17	07 17	07 38				07 47	07 51	07 51		07 51
	d				06 09					07 08														
Stockport 78	a				06 52					07 52														
Manchester Piccadilly 10 ⇌	a				07 02					08 02		07 37											08 40	
Manchester Airport 85 ✈⇌	a				07 26					08 26														

A From Doncaster
B From Hull
C From Leeds
D To Lincoln
E ⚒ from Sheffield
F To Scunthorpe
G until 21 July, from 13 October. From Leeds to Southampton Central
H from 28 July until 6 October. From Leeds to Plymouth
I To Adwick
J From Beverley
K from 15 September until 6 October. To Reading
L from 13 October. To Plymouth
M from 28 July until 8 September. To Reading

For services between Barnetby, Habrough, Grimsby Town and Cleethorpes, refer to Table T028

Hull - Doncaster - Meadowhall, Sheffield, Manchester and Manchester Airport

		XC	NT	NT	NT	TP	NT	GR	NT	XC	XC	XC	XC	NT	NT	TP	XC	XC	XC	NT	NT	NT	TP
		◇■ A	B			◇■ C		■ ■ D		◇■ E	F	◇■ G	◇■ H		◇ I	◇■	◇■ J	◇■ K	◇■ L		B		◇■ C
Hull	d						06 48	07 00	07 06						07 25	07 38							
Hessle	d						06 55		07 13														
Ferriby	d						07 00		07 18														
Brough	d						07 05	07 14	07 23						07 37	07 50							
Broomfleet	d								07 28														
Gilberdyke	d						07 12		07 33														
Eastrington	d								07 37														
Howden	d								07 42							08 02							
Wressle	d								07 46														
Selby	a							07 34	07 55							08 13							
	d							07 37	07 55							08 13							
York ■ 33	a								08 31														
Saltmarshe	d																						
Goole	d						07 22								07 52								
Thorne North	d						07 31								08 00								
Cleethorpes 28	d					06 26																	07 26
Grimsby Town 28	d					06 34																	07 34
Habrough 28	d					06 44																	07 44
Barnetby 28	d					06 53																	07 53
Scunthorpe	a					07 08																	08 08
	d				06 48	07 08														07 48			08 08
Althorpe	d				06 53															07 53			
Crowle	d				07 00															08 00			
Thorne South	d				07 08															08 08			
Hatfield & Stainforth	d				07 14		07 37													08 14			
Kirk Sandall	d				07 18		07 41													08 18			
Adwick 31	d			07 16										07 49								08 21	
Bentley (S.Yorks) 31	d			07 20										07 53								08 25	
Doncaster ■ 31	a			07 25	07 28	07 38	07 51	07 53						08 00	08 19					08 28		08 30	08 38
London Kings Cross ■ ⊖26	a							09 47															
York ■ 26	d	06 45								07 25	07 25	07 25	07 35				07 45	07 44	07 45				
Doncaster ■	d			07 26		07 42				07 51	07 51	07 51	07 58	08 02	08 22							08 32	08 42
Conisbrough	d			07 34										08 11								08 39	
Mexborough	d			07 38										08 15								08 44	
Swinton (S.Yorks)	d		07 36	07 41										08 20							08 36	08 47	
Rotherham Central	d		07 44	07 49										08 28							08 44	08 57	
Meadowhall	d		07 50	07 56		07 59								08 34	08 40						08 51	09 05	09 01
Sheffield ■	a	07 51	07 58	08 04		08 06				08 15	08 15	08 15	08 20	08 44	08 49		08 51	08 52	08 52		09 00	09 15	09 08
	d					08 08																	09 11
Stockport 78	a					08 53																	09 52
Manchester Piccadilly ■	a					09 02										09 48							10 02
Manchester Airport 85	a					09 26																	10 26

A until 21 July. To Plymouth
B From Leeds
C ⌶ from Sheffield
D The Hull Executive
E until 21 July. From Newcastle to Reading
F from 13 October. From Newcastle to Reading
G from 15 September until 6 October. To Plymouth
H from 28 July until 8 September. To Penzance
I From Bridlington
J until 21 July. To Penzance
K from 28 July until 6 October. From Newcastle to Southampton Central
L from 13 October. From Newcastle to Plymouth

For services between Barnetby, Habrough, Grimsby Town and Cleethorpes, refer to Table T028

Hull - Doncaster - Meadowhall, Sheffield, Manchester and Manchester Airport

		NT	NT	XC	XC	NT	HT	NT	HT	TP	XC	NT	NT	NT	TP	XC	XC	XC	NT	NT	NT	TP	XC
		■ A		◇■ B ⌶	◇■ C ⌶		◇■ D ⊠	◇ E	◇■ F ⊠	◇■ ⌶	◇■ G ⌶		◇ H		◇■ I ⌶	◇■ J ⌶	◇■ K	◇■ L	M		◇ N	◇■ ⌶	◇■ O ⌶
Hull	d	07 53	08 08				08 23	08 27		08 40									08 53	09 10	09 27	09 40	
Hessle	d	08 00																	09 00				
Ferriby	d	08 05																	09 05				
Brough	d	08 10	08 20				08 35	08 40		08 52									09 10	09 22	09 39	09 52	
Broomfleet	d	08 15																					
Gilberdyke	d	08 20	08 27																09 18	09 29			
Eastrington	d																						
Howden	d		08 34				08 46													09 36			
Wressle	d																						
Selby	a		08 46				08 57			09 11										09 47		10 11	
	d		08 47				09 03			09 11										09 47		10 12	
York ■ 33	a		09 19																	10 22			
Saltmarshe	d																		09 23				
Goole	d	08 30						08 55											09 28		09 54		
Thorne North	d	08 38																	09 37				
Cleethorpes 28	d														08 26								
Grimsby Town 28	d														08 34								
Habrough 28	d														08 44								
Barnetby 28	d														08 53								
Scunthorpe	a														09 08								
	d											08 52			09 08								
Althorpe	d											08 57											
Crowle	d											09 04											
Thorne South	d											09 12											
Hatfield & Stainforth	d	08 44										09 18							09 43				
Kirk Sandall	d	08 49										09 22							09 47				
Adwick 31	d					08 52								09 25									
Bentley (S.Yorks) 31	d					08 56			←					09 29									
Doncaster ■ 31	a	08 58				09 02	09 24	09 19	09 24			09 32		09 34	09 38				10 00		10 19		
London Kings Cross ■ ⊖26	a						→		11 09														
York ■ 26	d			08 35	08 35						08 45					09 35	09 35	09 36					09 45
Doncaster ■	d			08 58	09 01	09 04		09 20						09 35	09 42	09 58	09 58	09 59	10 04		10 20		
Conisbrough	d					09 12								09 42					10 11				
Mexborough	d					09 17								09 47					10 16				
Swinton (S.Yorks)	d					09 20							09 36	09 50					10 19				
Rotherham Central	d					09 29							09 44	09 58					10 28				
Meadowhall	d					09 35		09 38					09 50	10 06	10 01				10 34		10 38		
Sheffield ■	a			09 20	09 23	09 44		09 48			09 51		09 58	10 14	10 08	10 20	10 21	10 21	10 44		10 48		10 51
	d														10 10								
Stockport 78	a														10 52								
Manchester Piccadilly ■	a									10 40					11 02							11 40	
Manchester Airport 85	a														11 26								

A ■ from Thorne North
B from 28 July until 6 October. From Newcastle to Plymouth
C until 21 July, from 13 October. From Newcastle to Southampton Central
D To London Kings Cross
E From Scarborough
F From Hull
G From Edinburgh to Reading
H From Leeds
I ⌶ from Sheffield
J until 21 July, from 13 October. From Edinburgh to Reading
K from 28 July until 8 September. From Edinburgh to Paignton
L from 15 September until 6 October. From Edinburgh to Plymouth
M From Beverley
N From Bridlington
O until 6 October. From Glasgow Central to Southampton Central

For services between Barnetby, Habrough, Grimsby Town and Cleethorpes, refer to Table T028

Table T029-R

Saturdays
26 May to 8 December

Hull - Doncaster - Meadowhall, Sheffield, Manchester and Manchester Airport

	XC ◇■ A ✠	NT	NT B	NT	TP ◇■ C ✠	XC ◇■ D ✠	XC ◇■ E ✠	NT ◇	NT	NT	NT ◇ F	HT ◇■ ⊠	TP ◇■ ✠	XC ◇■ G ✠	XC ◇■ H ✠	NT	NT ◇ B	NT	TP ◇■ C ✠	XC ◇■ I ✠	NT	NT
Hull d									09 51	10 10	10 27	10 33	10 40								10 53	11 10
Hessle d									10 00												11 00	
Ferriby d									10 05												11 05	
Brough d									10 10	10 22	10 39	10 45	10 52								11 10	11 22
Broomfleet d																						
Gilberdyke d									10 17	10 29											11 17	11 28
Eastrington d																						
Howden d										10 36		10 56										11 35
Wressle d																						
Selby a										10 47		11 07	11 11									11 47
d										10 47		11 08	11 12									11 47
York ■ 33 a										11 12												12 22
Saltmarshe d																					11 23	
Goole d									10 28		10 54										11 28	
Thorne North d									10 37												11 37	
Cleethorpes 28 d					09 26														10 26			
Grimsby Town 28 d					09 34														10 34			
Habrough 28 d																			10 44			
Barnetby 28 d					09 53														10 53			
Scunthorpe a					10 08														11 08			
d		09 48			10 08											10 48			11 08			
Althorpe d		09 53														10 53						
Crowle d		10 00														11 00						
Thorne South d		10 08														11 08						
Hatfield & Stainforth d		10 14							10 43							11 14					11 43	
Kirk Sandall d		10 18							10 47							11 18					11 47	
Adwick 31 d				10 24														11 24				
Bentley (S.Yorks) 31 d				10 28														11 28				
Doncaster ■ 31 a		10 28		10 33	10 39				10 59		11 19	11 23				11 28		11 33	11 38		11 58	
London Kings Cross ■ ⊖26 a												13 09										
York ■ 26 d	09 45					10 35	10 37	10 15						10 45	10 45					11 35		
Doncaster ■ d	⌇			10 35	10 42	10 59	11 01		11 04		11 20			⌇	⌇			11 35	11 42	11 58	12 03	
Conisbrough d	⌇			10 42		⌇	⌇		11 12					⌇	⌇			11 42			12 10	
Mexborough d	⌇			10 47		⌇	⌇		11 17					⌇	⌇			11 47			12 15	
Swinton (S.Yorks) d	⌇		10 36	10 50		⌇	⌇	11 10	11 20					⌇	⌇		11 36	11 50			12 18	
Rotherham Central d	⌇		10 44	10 58		⌇	⌇	11 18	11 28					⌇	⌇		11 44	11 58			12 28	
Meadowhall ⇌ d	⌇		10 50	11 06	11 02	⌇	⌇	11 24	11 34		11 38			⌇	⌇		11 50	12 06	12 02		12 34	
Sheffield ■ ⇌ a	10 52		10 58	11 14	11 09	11 21	11 23	11 31	11 44		11 48			11 51	11 53		11 58	12 14	12 08	12 20	12 44	
d					11 11														12 11			
Stockport 78 a					11 52														12 52			
Manchester Piccadilly ■ ⇌ a					12 02								12 40						13 02			
Manchester Airport 85 ✈⇌ a					12 26														13 26			

A from 13 October. From Glasgow Central to Plymouth
B From Leeds
C ✠ from Sheffield
D until 8 September, from 13 October. From Newcastle to Southampton Central
E from 15 September until 6 October. From Newcastle to Plymouth
F From Bridlington
G from 28 July. From Dundee to Reading
H until 21 July. From Dundee to Newquay
I From Newcastle to Reading

For services between Barnetby, Habrough, Grimsby Town and Cleethorpes, refer to Table T028

Table T029-R

Saturdays
26 May to 8 December

Hull - Doncaster - Meadowhall, Sheffield, Manchester and Manchester Airport

	NT ◇ A	TP ◇■ ✠	XC ◇■ B ✠	NT	NT C	NT	TP ◇■ D ✠	XC ◇■ E ✠	XC ◇■ F ✠	NT	NT	NT ◇ G	TP ◇■ ✠	XC ◇■ H ✠	XC ◇■ I ✠	NT	NT ◇ C	NT	TP ◇■ D ✠	XC ◇■ J ✠	NT ◇	NT
Hull d	11 27	11 40								11 51	12 10	12 27	12 40									12 53
Hessle d										11 58												13 00
Ferriby d										12 03												13 05
Brough d	11 39	11 52								12 08	12 22	12 39	12 52									13 10
Broomfleet d										12 13												
Gilberdyke d										12 18	12 29											13 18
Eastrington d																						
Howden d											12 36											
Wressle d																						
Selby a		12 11									12 47		13 11									
d		12 12									12 47		13 12									
York ■ 33 a											13 19											
Saltmarshe d																						13 23
Goole d	11 54									12 28		12 54										13 28
Thorne North d										12 37												13 37
Cleethorpes 28 d							11 26												12 26			
Grimsby Town 28 d							11 34												12 34			
Habrough 28 d																			12 44			
Barnetby 28 d							11 53												12 53			
Scunthorpe a							12 08												13 08			
d				11 48			12 08									12 48			13 08			
Althorpe d				11 53												12 53						
Crowle d				12 00												13 00						
Thorne South d				12 08												13 08						
Hatfield & Stainforth d				12 14						12 43						13 14						13 43
Kirk Sandall d				12 18						12 47						13 18						13 47
Adwick 31 d						12 24												13 24				
Bentley (S.Yorks) 31 d						12 28												13 28				
Doncaster ■ 31 a	12 19			12 28		12 33	12 40			12 58		13 19				13 28		13 33	13 38			13 58
London Kings Cross ■ ⊖26 a																						
York ■ 26 d			11 45					12 35	12 36					12 45	12 45					13 35	13 13	
Doncaster ■ d	12 20					12 35	12 42	12 59	12 59	13 04		13 20		⌇	⌇			13 35	13 42	13 58		14 05
Conisbrough d						12 42		⌇	⌇	13 12				⌇	⌇			13 42				14 12
Mexborough d						12 47		⌇	⌇	13 16				⌇	⌇			13 47				14 17
Swinton (S.Yorks) d					12 36	12 50		⌇	⌇	13 19				⌇	⌇		13 36	13 50			14 10	14 20
Rotherham Central d					12 44	12 58		⌇	⌇	13 28				⌇	⌇		13 44	13 58			14 18	14 28
Meadowhall ⇌ d	12 39				12 50	13 06	13 02	⌇	⌇	13 34		13 38		⌇	⌇		13 50	14 06	14 02		14 24	14 34
Sheffield ■ ⇌ a	12 48		12 53		12 58	13 14	13 08	13 21	13 21	13 44		13 48		13 51	13 52		13 58	14 14	14 08	14 21	14 31	14 44
d							13 11												14 11			
Stockport 78 a							13 52												14 52			
Manchester Piccadilly ■ ⇌ a		13 40					14 02						14 40						15 03			
Manchester Airport 85 ✈⇌ a							14 26												15 26			

A From Scarborough
B From Glasgow Central to Southampton Central
C From Leeds
D ✠ from Sheffield
E until 1 September, from 13 October. From Newcastle to Southampton Central
F from 8 September until 6 October. From Newcastle to Penzance
G From Bridlington
H until 21 July, from 13 October. From Glasgow Central to Penzance
I from 28 July until 6 October. From Glasgow Central to Reading
J From Newcastle to Reading

For services between Barnetby, Habrough, Grimsby Town and Cleethorpes, refer to Table T028

Table T029-R

Saturdays
26 May to 8 December

Hull - Doncaster - Meadowhall, Sheffield, Manchester and Manchester Airport

		NT	NT ◇ A	HT ◇1 ⊠	TP ◇1 🍴	XC ◇1 B 🍴	NT	NT C		NT	TP ◇1 D 🍴	XC ◇1 E 🍴	NT	NT	NT ◇ A	TP ◇1 🍴	XC ◇1 F 🍴	NT	NT ◇ C	NT	TP ◇1 D 🍴	XC ◇1 G 🍴	NT	NT
Hull	d	13 10	13 24	13 31	13 40								13 53	14 09	14 27	14 40							14 53	15 18
Hessle	d												14 00										15 00	
Ferriby	d												14 05										15 05	
Brough	d	13 23	13 36	13 43	13 52								14 10	14 22	14 39	14 52							15 10	15 30
Broomfleet	d												14 15											
Gilberdyke	d	13 31											14 20	14 29									15 18	15 39
Eastrington	d	13 35																						
Howden	d	13 40		13 55										14 36										15 46
Wressle	d	13 45																						
Selby	a	13 55		14 05	14 11									14 47		15 11								15 56
	d	13 56		14 06	14 12									14 47		15 12								15 57
York 8 33	a	14 20												15 11										16 29
Saltmarshe	d																						15 23	
Goole	d		13 54										14 28		14 54								15 28	
Thorne North	d												14 37										15 37	
Cleethorpes 28	d										13 26										14 26			
Grimsby Town 28	d										13 34										14 34			
Habrough 28	d																				14 44			
Barnetby 28	d										13 53										14 53			
Scunthorpe	a										14 08										15 08			
	d						13 48				14 08							14 48			15 08			
Althorpe	d						13 53											14 53						
Crowle	d						14 00											15 00						
Thorne South	d						14 08											15 08						
Hatfield & Stainforth	d						14 14						14 43					15 14					15 43	
Kirk Sandall	d						14 18						14 47					15 18					15 47	
Adwick 31	d									14 24										15 24				
Bentley (S.Yorks) 31	d									14 28										15 28				
Doncaster 7 31	a		14 19	14 24			14 28			14 33	14 38		14 58		15 19			15 28		15 33	15 38		15 58	
London Kings Cross 15 ⊖26	a			16 09																				
York 8 26	d					13 45						14 35					14 45					15 35		
Doncaster 7	d		14 20							14 35	14 42	14 59	15 04		15 20					15 35	15 42	15 58	16 04	
Conisbrough	d									14 42			15 12							15 42			16 12	
Mexborough	d									14 47			15 16							15 47			16 16	
Swinton (S.Yorks)	d							14 36		14 50			15 19						15 36	15 50			16 19	
Rotherham Central	d							14 44		14 58			15 28						15 44	15 58			16 28	
Meadowhall 🚌	d		14 38					14 50		15 06	15 02		15 34		15 38				15 50	16 06	16 02		16 34	
Sheffield 7 🚌	a		14 48			14 51		14 58		15 14	15 08	15 21	15 44		15 48		15 51		15 58	16 14	16 08	16 20	16 44	
	d										15 11										16 11			
Stockport 78	a										15 52										16 52			
Manchester Piccadilly 10 🚌	a				15 40						16 02					16 40					17 02			
Manchester Airport 85 ✈🚌	a										16 26										17 26			

A From Bridlington
B From Aberdeen to Guildford
C From Leeds
D 🍴 from Sheffield
E From Newcastle to Guildford
F From Glasgow Central to Reading
G From Newcastle to Reading

For services between Barnetby, Habrough, Grimsby Town and Cleethorpes, refer to Table T028

Table T029-R

Saturdays
26 May to 8 December

Hull - Doncaster - Meadowhall, Sheffield, Manchester and Manchester Airport

		NT ◇ A	HT ◇1 ⊠	TP ◇1 🍴	XC ◇1 B 🍴	NT	NT C	NT		TP ◇1 D 🍴	XC ◇1 E 🍴	NT	NT	NT ◇ F	TP ◇1 🍴	XC ◇1 G 🍴	NT	NT C	NT	TP ◇1 D 🍴	XC ◇1 E 🍴	NT	NT	EM ◇1 H 🍴
Hull	d	15 25	15 31	15 40								15 53	16 10	16 27	16 40							16 53	17 15	
Hessle	d											16 01										17 00	17 22	
Ferriby	d											16 05										17 05	17 27	
Brough	d	15 37	15 43	15 52								16 10	16 22	16 39	16 52							17 10	17 32	
Broomfleet	d											16 16										17 15		
Gilberdyke	d											16 20	16 29									17 20	17 39	
Eastrington	d																						17 44	
Howden	d		15 55										16 36										17 48	
Wressle	d																						17 53	
Selby	a		16 05	16 11									16 46		17 11								18 03	
	d		16 06	16 12									16 47		17 12								18 03	
York 8 33	a												17 23										18 37	
Saltmarshe	d																							
Goole	d	15 54										16 29		16 54								17 28		
Thorne North	d											16 37										17 37		
Cleethorpes 28	d									15 26										16 26				
Grimsby Town 28	d									15 34										16 34				
Habrough 28	d																			16 44				
Barnetby 28	d									15 53										16 53				
Scunthorpe	a									16 08										17 08				
	d					15 48				16 08							16 48			17 08				
Althorpe	d					15 53											16 53							
Crowle	d					16 00											17 00							
Thorne South	d					16 08											17 08							
Hatfield & Stainforth	d					16 14						16 43					17 14					17 43		
Kirk Sandall	d					16 18						16 48					17 18					17 47		
Adwick 31	d							16 24											17 24					
Bentley (S.Yorks) 31	d							16 28											17 28					
Doncaster 7 31	a	16 19	16 23			16 28		16 33		16 38		17 01		17 19			17 28		17 33	17 38		17 58		
London Kings Cross 15 ⊖26	a		18 09																					
York 8 26	d				15 45						16 04					16 45					17 35			17 50
Doncaster 7	d	16 20						16 35		16 42		17 04		17 20					17 35	17 42	17 58	18 04		18 19
Conisbrough	d							16 42				17 12							17 42			18 12		
Mexborough	d							16 47				17 16							17 47			18 16		
Swinton (S.Yorks)	d						16 36	16 50				17 19						17 35	17 50			18 19		
Rotherham Central	d						16 44	16 58				17 28						17 45	17 58			18 28		
Meadowhall 🚌	d	16 38					16 50	17 06		17 02		17 34		17 38				17 50	18 06	18 02		18 34		
Sheffield 7 🚌	a	16 48			16 51		16 58	17 14		17 08	17 19	17 44		17 48		17 51		17 58	18 14	18 08	18 20	18 44		18 43
	d									17 11										18 11				
Stockport 78	a									17 52										18 52				
Manchester Piccadilly 10 🚌	a			17 40						18 02					18 40					19 02				
Manchester Airport 85 ✈🚌	a									18 26										19 26				

A From Bridlington
B From Edinburgh to Reading
C From Leeds
D 🍴 from Sheffield
E From Newcastle to Reading
F From Scarborough
G From Glasgow Central to Reading
H From Scarborough to St Pancras International

For services between Barnetby, Habrough, Grimsby Town and Cleethorpes, refer to Table T028

Table T029-R

Saturdays
26 May to 8 December

Hull - Doncaster - Meadowhall, Sheffield, Manchester and Manchester Airport

	NT	TP	XC	XC	NT	NT	NT	TP	XC	NT	NT	NT	HT	TP	XC	NT	NT	NT	TP	XC	NT	NT
	◇	◇[1]	◇[1]	◇[1]				◇[1]	◇[1]			◇	◇[1]	◇[1]	◇[1]		◇		◇[1]	◇[1]		
	A		B	C		D			E			A			F		D			G		
		🍴	🍴	🍴					🍴				☒		🍴					🍴		
Hull d	17 27	17 40								17 52	18 10	18 27	18 34	18 40							18 53	19 16
Hessle d										17 59											19 00	
Ferriby d										18 04											19 05	
Brough d	17 39	17 52								18 09	18 22	18 39	18 46	18 52							19 10	19 31
Broomfleet d										18 14												
Gilberdyke d										18 19	18 29										19 18	19 38
Eastrington d																						
Howden d											18 36		18 57									19 45
Wressle d																						
Selby a		18 11									18 47		19 08	19 13								19 56
d		18 12									18 47		19 09	19 14								19 56
York [8] 33 a											19 20											20 27
Saltmarshe d										18 24											19 23	
Goole d	17 54									18 29		18 54									19 28	
Thorne North d										18 38											19 37	
Cleethorpes 28 d								17 26											18 29			
Grimsby Town 28 d								17 34											18 37			
Habrough 28 d								17 44														
Barnetby 28 d								17 53											18 56			
Scunthorpe a								18 08											19 08			
d					17 48			18 08								18 48			19 08			
Althorpe d					17 53											18 53						
Crowle d					18 00											19 00						
Thorne South d					18 08											19 08						
Hatfield & Stainforth d					18 14					18 44						19 14					19 43	
Kirk Sandall d					18 18					18 48						19 18					19 47	
Adwick 31 d							18 24											19 24				
Bentley (S.Yorks) 31 d							18 28											19 28				
Doncaster [7] 31 a	18 19				18 28		18 33	18 38		18 59		19 19	19 26			19 28		19 33	19 41		19 58	
London Kings Cross [15] ⊖26 a													21 14									
York [8] 26 d			17 45	17 45					18 35						18 45					19 36		
Doncaster [7] d	18 22						18 35	18 42	18 58	19 04		19 20						19 35	19 42	19 59	20 03	
Conisbrough d							18 42			19 12								19 43			20 12	
Mexborough d							18 47			19 16								19 47			20 16	
Swinton (S.Yorks) d						18 36	18 50			19 19							19 36	19 50			20 19	
Rotherham Central d						18 44	18 58			19 28							19 44	19 58			20 28	
Meadowhall d	18 40					18 50	19 06	19 02		19 34		19 38					19 50	20 06	20 02		20 34	
Sheffield [7] a	18 49		18 52	18 53		18 58	19 14	19 08	19 20	19 44		19 48			19 51		19 58	20 14	20 08	20 21	20 44	
d								19 11											20 11			
Stockport 78 a								19 52											20 52			
Manchester Piccadilly [10] a		19 40						20 03						20 40					21 04			
Manchester Airport 85 a								20 26											21 26			

A From Bridlington
B from 28 July until 6 October. From Edinburgh to Southampton Central
C until 21 July, from 13 October. From Edinburgh to Plymouth
D From Leeds
E From Newcastle to Bristol Temple Meads
F From Glasgow Central to Birmingham New Street
G From Newcastle to Birmingham New Street

For services between Barnetby, Habrough, Grimsby Town and Cleethorpes, refer to Table T028

Table T029-R

Saturdays
26 May to 8 December

Hull - Doncaster - Meadowhall, Sheffield, Manchester and Manchester Airport

	NT	TP	XC	XC	NT	NT	NT	TP	XC	NT	TP	XC	NT	NT	NT	TP	NT	TP	NT	TP	TP	NT
										■												
	◇	◇[1]	◇[1]	◇[1]				◇[1]	◇[1]		◇[1]	◇[1]		◇		◇[1]	◇	◇[1]		◇[1]	◇[1]	
	A		B	C		D			E	F		G		D			H			I	J	K
Hull d	19 27	19 40								19 55	20 40						21 23	21 40		22 24	22 24	22 30
Hessle d										20 02												
Ferriby d										20 07												
Brough d	19 39	19 52								20 12	20 52						21 38	21 52		22 36	22 36	22 42
Broomfleet d																						
Gilberdyke d										20 19												
Eastrington d																						
Howden d																						22 54
Wressle d																						
Selby a		20 11									21 11							22 11		22 55	22 55	23 04
d		20 12									21 12							22 12		22 56	22 56	
York [8] 33 a																						
Saltmarshe d																						
Goole d	19 54									20 29							21 53					
Thorne North d										20 38							22 01					
Cleethorpes 28 d								19 26								20 26						
Grimsby Town 28 d								19 34								20 34						
Habrough 28 d								19 44														
Barnetby 28 d								19 53								20 53						
Scunthorpe a								20 08								21 08						
d					19 48			20 08					20 48			21 08			21 48			
Althorpe d					19 53								20 53						21 53			
Crowle d					20 00								21 00						22 00			
Thorne South d					20 08								21 08						22 08			
Hatfield & Stainforth d					20 14					20 44			21 14				22 07		22 14			
Kirk Sandall d					20 18					20 48			21 18				22 11		22 18			
Adwick 31 d							20 24								21 24							
Bentley (S.Yorks) 31 d							20 28								21 28							
Doncaster [7] 31 a	20 19				20 28		20 33	20 38		20 58			21 28		21 33	21 38	22 25		22 29			
London Kings Cross [15] ⊖26 a																						
York [8] 26 d			19 45	19 45					20 35			20 45										
Doncaster [7] d	20 21						20 35	20 42	20 59	21 04					21 35	21 42	22 26					
Conisbrough d							20 42			21 11					21 42							
Mexborough d							20 47			21 16					21 47							
Swinton (S.Yorks) d						20 36	20 50			21 19				21 36	21 50							
Rotherham Central d						20 44	21 00			21 29				21 44	21 58							
Meadowhall d	20 39					20 50	21 08	21 04		21 35				21 50	22 06	22 02	22 44					
Sheffield [7] a	20 48		20 52	20 52		20 58	21 18	21 09	21 21	21 43		21 52		21 59	22 16	22 08	22 53					
d								21 11								22 11						
Stockport 78 a								21 52								22 54						
Manchester Piccadilly [10] a		21 40						22 04			22 38					23 03		23 53		00 37	00 42	
Manchester Airport 85 a											23 00					23 26						

A From Scarborough
B until 21 July, from 13 October. From Edinburgh to Birmingham New Street
C from 28 July until 6 October. From Edinburgh to Birmingham New Street
D From Leeds
E From Newcastle to Birmingham New Street
F ■ from Thorne North
G From Glasgow Central to Birmingham New Street
H From Bridlington
I from 27 October
J until 20 October
K To Leeds

For services between Barnetby, Habrough, Grimsby Town and Cleethorpes, refer to Table T028

Saturdays

26 May to 8 December

Hull - Doncaster - Meadowhall, Sheffield, Manchester and Manchester Airport

			NT	NT	NT	NT	NT	NT	NT
						◇			◇
			A			A	A		B
Hull		d							22 48
Hessle		d							22 55
Ferriby		d							22 59
Brough		d							23 04
Broomfleet		d							
Gilberdyke		d							23 11
Eastrington		d							
Howden		d							
Wressle		d							
Selby		a							
		d							
York 8	33	a							
Saltmarshe		d							
Goole		d							23 19
Thorne North		d							23 29
Cleethorpes	28	d							
Grimsby Town	28	d							
Habrough	28	d							
Barnetby	28	d							
Scunthorpe		a							
		d			22 48				
Althorpe		d			22 53				
Crowle		d			23 00				
Thorne South		d			23 08				
Hatfield & Stainforth		d			23 14				23 34
Kirk Sandall		d			23 18				23 39
Adwick	31	d		22 23					
Bentley (S.Yorks)	31	d		22 27					
Doncaster 7	31	a		22 31	23 28				23 47
London Kings Cross 15	⊖26	a							
York 8	26	d							
Doncaster 7		d		22 37				23 35	23 49
Conisbrough		d		22 44				23 42	
Mexborough		d		22 49				23 47	
Swinton (S.Yorks)		d	22 41	22 52		22 59	23 31	23 50	
Rotherham Central		d	22 50	22 59		23 08	23 40	23 57	
Meadowhall		d	22 56	23 06		23 13	23 47	00 04	00 08
Sheffield 7		a	23 04	23 15		23 23	23 55	00 13	00 17
		d							
Stockport	78	a							
Manchester Piccadilly 10		a							
Manchester Airport	85	a							

A From Leeds

B ◇ from Thorne North

For services between Barnetby, Habrough, Grimsby Town and Cleethorpes, refer to Table T028

Table T029-R

Sundays

20 May to 2 December

Hull - Doncaster - Meadowhall, Sheffield, Manchester and Manchester Airport

			NT	NT	NT	NT	TP	NT	NT		XC	XC	NT	NT	HT	TP	NT	NT	XC	NT	TP	TP	NT	NT	XC
				◇			◇1		◇		◇1	◇1			◇1	◇1		◇	◇1		◇1	◇1		◇	◇1
			A	B					C		D	E				F	C		G			F			H
							🍴				🍴	🍴			☒	🍴			🍴		🍴	🍴			🍴
Hull		d				08 31	08 41							08 45	09 06			09 27			09 43		09 59	10 29	
Hessle		d												08 52											
Ferriby		d												08 57											
Brough		d				08 43	08 54							09 02	09 18			09 39			09 55		10 11	10 41	
Broomfleet		d																							
Gilberdyke		d				08 50								09 10									10 19		
Eastrington		d																							
Howden		d				08 57									09 30										
Wressle		d																							
Selby		a				09 07	09 14								09 39						10 14				
		d				09 07	09 15								09 40						10 15				
York 8	33	a				09 42																			
Saltmarshe		d																							
Goole		d											09 00	09 18				09 54					10 28	10 56	
Thorne North		d											09 09	09 27				10 03					10 36		
Cleethorpes	28	d																				09 26			
Grimsby Town	28	d																				09 34			
Habrough	28	d																							
Barnetby	28	d																				09 53			
Scunthorpe		a																				10 08			
		d																				10 09			
Althorpe		d																							
Crowle		d																							
Thorne South		d																							
Hatfield & Stainforth		d											09 14										10 42		
Kirk Sandall		d											09 19										10 47		
Adwick	31	d																							
Bentley (S.Yorks)	31	d																							
Doncaster 7	31	a											09 29	09 43	09 58			10 19				10 39	10 57	11 19	
London Kings Cross 15	⊖26	a													11 41										
York 8	26	d																	09 33						10 33
Doncaster 7		d			08 07			09 03			09 31	09 31		09 37		09 45		10 21	10 30	10 35		10 43		11 22	11 30
Conisbrough		d			08 14			09 10						09 45						10 42					
Mexborough		d			08 19			09 15						09 50						10 47					
Swinton (S.Yorks)		d			08 22			09 18	09 31					09 53			10 13			10 50					
Rotherham Central		d			08 31			09 26	09 39					10 01			10 24			10 59					
Meadowhall		d	00 04	00 08	08 37			09 33	09 45					10 09		10 05	10 29	10 39		11 07		11 02		11 40	
Sheffield 7		a	00 13	00 17	08 45			09 41	09 53		09 55	09 56		10 17		10 12	10 38	10 49	10 52	11 15		11 10		11 49	11 53
		d														10 14						11 11			
Stockport	78	a																				11 56			
Manchester Piccadilly 10		a					10 40									11 03					11 39	12 10			
Manchester Airport	85	a														11 26						12 27			

A not 20 May. From Doncaster

B not 20 May. From Hull

C From Leeds

D from 22 July until 2 September. From Leeds to Plymouth

E until 15 July, from 9 September. From Leeds to Plymouth

F 🍴 from Sheffield

G To Birmingham New Street

H From Newcastle to Bristol Temple Meads

For services between Barnetby, Habrough, Grimsby Town and Cleethorpes, refer to Table T028

Table T029-R

Sundays

20 May to 2 December

Hull - Doncaster - Meadowhall, Sheffield, Manchester and Manchester Airport

		NT	TP ◇1 A	TP ◇1 B	NT ◇ C	NT	TP ◇1 D	TP ◇1 E		NT	HT ◇1 F ⊠	NT ◇ G	XC ◇1 H	TP ◇1	NT C	NT	TP ◇1 I	XC ◇1 J	NT	NT ◇ K	NT	TP ◇1	XC ◇1 L	NT
Hull	d	10 33	10 43	10 43						10 59	11 13	11 29		11 43					11 59	12 29	12 33	12 44		
Hessle	d																							
Ferriby	d																							
Brough	d	10 46	10 55	10 55						11 11	11 25	11 41		11 55					12 11	12 41	12 47	12 56		
Broomfleet	d																							
Gilberdyke	d									11 19									12 19					
Eastrington	d																							
Howden	d	10 58									11 36										12 59			
Wressle	d																							
Selby	a	11 08	11 14	11 14							11 46			12 14							13 08	13 15		
	d	11 09	11 15	11 15							11 47			12 15							13 09	13 16		
York 8 33	a	11 39																			13 43			
Saltmarshe	d																							
Goole	d									11 28		11 56							12 28	12 56				
Thorne North	d									11 36									12 36					
Cleethorpes 28	d						10 26	10 26									11 26							
Grimsby Town 28	d						10 34	10 34									11 34							
Habrough 28	d						10 44	10 44																
Barnetby 28	d						10 53	10 53									11 53							
Scunthorpe	a						11 08	11 08									12 08							
	d						11 08	11 08									12 08							
Althorpe	d																							
Crowle	d																							
Thorne South	d																							
Hatfield & Stainforth	d									11 42									12 42					
Kirk Sandall	d									11 47									12 47					
Adwick 31	d																							
Bentley (S.Yorks) 31	d																							
Doncaster 7 31	a						11 38	11 38		11 57	12 02	12 19					12 38		12 57	13 21				
London Kings Cross 15 ⊖26	a										13 43													
York 8 26	d												11 41					11 41					12 45	
Doncaster 7	d					11 34	11 43	11 43				12 21				12 33	12 43	12 54		13 23				13 33
Conisbrough	d					11 41										12 40								13 40
Mexborough	d					11 46										12 45								13 45
Swinton (S.Yorks)	d				11 35	11 49									12 34	12 48								13 48
Rotherham Central	d				11 43	11 59									12 45	12 58								13 59
Meadowhall	d				11 50	12 06	12 02	12 02				12 39			12 51	13 05	13 01			13 41				14 06
Sheffield 7	a				11 57	12 13	12 08	12 08				12 48	12 51		12 58	13 12	13 07	13 17		13 50			13 52	14 13
	d						12 11	12 11									13 11							
Stockport 78	a						12 52	12 52									13 52							
Manchester Piccadilly 10	a		12 39	12 41			13 02	13 04						13 39			14 02					14 39		
Manchester Airport 85	a						13 26	13 26									14 26							

A until 9 September
B from 16 September
C From Leeds
D until 9 September. ⚒ from Sheffield
E from 16 September. ⚒ from Sheffield
F From Beverley
G From Scarborough
H until 15 July, from 14 October. From Edinburgh to Plymouth
I ⚒ from Sheffield
J from 22 July until 7 October. From Edinburgh to Penzance
K From Bridlington
L until 15 July, from 14 October. From Edinburgh to Penzance

For services between Barnetby, Habrough, Grimsby Town and Cleethorpes, refer to Table T028

Table T029-R

Sundays

20 May to 2 December

Hull - Doncaster - Meadowhall, Sheffield, Manchester and Manchester Airport

		TP ◇1 A	XC ◇1 B	NT	NT ◇ C	XC ◇1 D	TP ◇1	XC ◇1 E		NT F	NT	TP ◇1 A	XC ◇1 G	NT	NT	EM ◇1 H	XC ◇1 I	NT ◇ J	HT ◇1 ⊠	TP ◇1	XC ◇1 K	NT	TP ◇1 A	XC ◇1 L
Hull	d			12 59	13 29		13 43							13 59	14 24			14 29	14 36	14 43				
Hessle	d																							
Ferriby	d																							
Brough	d			13 11	13 41		13 55							14 11	14 36			14 41	14 48	14 55				
Broomfleet	d																							
Gilberdyke	d			13 19										14 19										
Eastrington	d																							
Howden	d														14 48				14 59					
Wressle	d																							
Selby	a						14 14								14 57				15 10	15 14				
	d						14 15								14 59				15 10	15 15				
York 8 33	a														15 25									
Saltmarshe	d																							
Goole	d			13 28	13 56									14 28				14 56						
Thorne North	d			13 36										14 36										
Cleethorpes 28	d	12 26										13 26											14 26	
Grimsby Town 28	d	12 34										13 34											14 34	
Habrough 28	d	12 44																					14 44	
Barnetby 28	d	12 53										13 53											14 53	
Scunthorpe	a	13 08										14 08											15 08	
	d	13 08										14 08											15 08	
Althorpe	d																							
Crowle	d																							
Thorne South	d																							
Hatfield & Stainforth	d			13 42										14 42										
Kirk Sandall	d			13 47										14 47										
Adwick 31	d																							
Bentley (S.Yorks) 31	d																							
Doncaster 7 31	a	13 38		13 57	14 19							14 38		14 57				15 19	15 27				15 38	
London Kings Cross 15 ⊖26	a																		17 14					
York 8 26	d		12 42			13 43		13 45					13 45				14 35				14 44			14 44
Doncaster 7	d	13 44	13 54		14 21						14 33	14 44	14 54				15 00	15 21				15 33	15 43	15 54
Conisbrough	d										14 40											15 40		
Mexborough	d										14 45											15 45		
Swinton (S.Yorks)	d									14 34	14 48					15 05						15 48		
Rotherham Central	d									14 44	14 59											15 59		
Meadowhall	d	14 02			14 39					14 49	15 06	15 02						15 39				16 06	16 02	
Sheffield 7	a	14 08	14 17		14 48	14 52		14 52		14 57	15 13	15 08	15 16			15 19	15 22	15 48			15 51	16 13	16 08	16 16
	d	14 11										15 11											16 11	
Stockport 78	a	14 53										15 53											16 53	
Manchester Piccadilly 10	a	15 03					15 39					16 02								16 39			17 02	
Manchester Airport 85	a	15 26										16 26											17 26	

A ⚒ from Sheffield
B from 22 July until 7 October. From Edinburgh to Plymouth
C From Scarborough
D until 15 July. From Edinburgh to Plymouth
E from 14 October. From Edinburgh to Plymouth
F From Leeds
G from 22 July until 7 October. From Edinburgh to Penzance
H not 5 August, 12 August, 26 August. From Leeds to St Pancras International
I until 15 July, from 14 October. From Newcastle to Reading
J From Bridlington
K until 15 July, from 14 October. From Glasgow Central to Penzance
L from 22 July until 7 October. From Glasgow Central to Plymouth

For services between Barnetby, Habrough, Grimsby Town and Cleethorpes, refer to Table T028

Table T029-R

Sundays 20 May to 2 December

Hull - Doncaster - Meadowhall, Sheffield, Manchester and Manchester Airport

		NT	XC	NT	XC	TP	NT	NT	TP	XC	NT	XC	HT	NT	HT	NT	XC	TP	NT	TP	XC	NT	XC
Notes			◇1 A 🛒	◇ B	◇1 C 🛒	◇1 🛒	D		◇1 E 🛒	◇1 F		◇1 G 🛒	◇1 H ⊠	◇ I	◇1 J ⊠		◇1 K 🛒	◇1 🛒		◇1 E 🛒	◇1 L 🛒		◇1 A 🛒
Hull	d	14 59		15 29		15 43					15 54		16 25	16 29		16 35		16 43				16 59	
Hessle	d										16 01												
Ferriby	d										16 06												
Brough	d	15 11		15 41		15 55					16 11		16 37	16 41		16 47		16 55				17 11	
Broomfleet	d																						
Gilberdyke	d	15 19									16 19											17 19	
Eastrington	d																						
Howden	d												16 49			16 59							
Wressle	d																						
Selby	a					16 14							17 03			17 08		17 14					
	d					16 15							17 04			17 09		17 15					
York 8 33	a															17 41							
Saltmarshe	d																						
Goole	d	15 28		15 56							16 27			16 56								17 28	
Thorne North	d	15 36									16 36											17 36	
Cleethorpes 28	d								15 26											16 26			
Grimsby Town 28	d								15 34											16 34			
Habrough 28	d																			16 44			
Barnetby 28	d								15 53											16 53			
Scunthorpe	a								16 08											17 08			
	d								16 08											17 08			
Althorpe	d																						
Crowle	d																						
Thorne South	d																						
Hatfield & Stainforth	d	15 42									16 42											17 42	
Kirk Sandall	d	15 47									16 47											17 47	
Adwick 31	d																						
Bentley (S.Yorks) 31	d														←								
Doncaster 7 31	a	15 57		16 19					16 38		16 57		17 25	17 19	17 25					17 38		17 57	
London Kings Cross 15 ⊖26	a												→		19 11								
York 8 26	d		15 35		15 42					15 42		16 25					16 41				16 41		17 35
Doncaster 7	d		15 58	16 22				16 35	16 42	16 46		16 51		17 21					17 33	17 43	17 46		17 58
Conisbrough	d							16 42											17 40				
Mexborough	d							16 47											17 45				
Swinton (S.Yorks)	d						16 34	16 50											17 48				
Rotherham Central	d						16 43	16 59											17 57				
Meadowhall	d			16 40			16 49	17 06	17 02					17 39					18 03	18 02			
Sheffield 7	a		16 20	16 49	16 52		16 56	17 14	17 09	17 17		17 19		17 48			17 51		18 10	18 08	18 15		18 20
	d								17 11											18 11			
Stockport 78	a								17 53											18 53			
Manchester Piccadilly 10	a					17 39			18 03									18 39		19 03			
Manchester Airport 85	a								18 26											19 26			

A until 5 July, from 14 October. From Newcastle to Reading
B From Scarborough
C until 15 July, from 14 October. From Glasgow Central to Plymouth
D From Leeds
E 🛒 from Sheffield
F from 22 July until 7 October. From Glasgow Central to Plymouth
G until 15 July, from 14 October. From Edinburgh to Reading
H To London Kings Cross
I From Bridlington
J From Hull
K until 15 July, from 14 October. From Aberdeen to Plymouth
L from 22 July until 7 October. From Aberdeen to Plymouth

For services between Barnetby, Habrough, Grimsby Town and Cleethorpes, refer to Table T028

Table T029-R

Sundays 20 May to 2 December

Hull - Doncaster - Meadowhall, Sheffield, Manchester and Manchester Airport

		EM	NT	TP	XC	NT	NT	TP	NT	NT	XC	XC	NT	NT	TP	XC	HT	NT	TP	XC	XC	NT	XC
Notes		◇1 A	◇ B	◇1 🛒	◇1 C 🛒	D		◇1		◇	◇1 E 🛒	◇1 F 🛒	◇ G		◇1	◇1 H 🛒	◇1 ⊠		◇1	◇1 I 🛒	◇1 J 🛒		◇1 K 🛒
Hull	d		17 29	17 43					17 59				18 29	18 35	18 43		18 47					18 59	
Hessle	d																						
Ferriby	d																						
Brough	d		17 41	17 55					18 11				18 41	18 47	18 55		18 59					19 11	
Broomfleet	d																						
Gilberdyke	d								18 19													19 19	
Eastrington	d																						
Howden	d													18 59			19 10						
Wressle	d																						
Selby	a			18 14										19 08	19 14		19 21						
	d			18 15										19 09	19 15		19 22						
York 8 33	a													19 41									
Saltmarshe	d																						
Goole	d		17 56						18 28				18 56									19 28	
Thorne North	d								18 36													19 36	
Cleethorpes 28	d							17 27											18 29				
Grimsby Town 28	d							17 35											18 37				
Habrough 28	d							17 45															
Barnetby 28	d							17 54											18 56				
Scunthorpe	a							18 09											19 08				
	d							18 09											19 08				
Althorpe	d																						
Crowle	d																						
Thorne South	d																						
Hatfield & Stainforth	d								18 42													19 42	
Kirk Sandall	d								18 47													19 47	
Adwick 31	d																						
Bentley (S.Yorks) 31	d																						
Doncaster 7 31	a		18 19					18 39	18 57				19 19				19 38		19 41			19 57	
London Kings Cross 15 ⊖26	a																21 20						
York 8 26	d	17 48			17 44					18 01	17 44	18 35				18 45				18 45	18 45		19 24
Doncaster 7	d	18 13	18 22				18 29	18 44			18 58	18 58	19 21					19 33	19 42	19 47	19 54		19 54
Conisbrough	d						18 36											19 40					
Mexborough	d						18 41											19 45					
Swinton (S.Yorks)	d					18 35	18 44			18 54								19 48					
Rotherham Central	d					18 44	18 53			19 03								19 57					
Meadowhall	d		18 40			18 50	18 59	19 02		19 08			19 39					20 03	20 02				
Sheffield 7	a	18 39	18 49		18 52	18 57	19 06	19 08		19 19	19 20	19 20	19 48			19 52		20 10	20 08	20 13	20 16		20 16
	d							19 11											20 11				
Stockport 78	a							19 53											20 53				
Manchester Piccadilly 10	a			19 39				20 04							20 39				21 04				
Manchester Airport 85	a							20 26											21 26				

A not 5 August, 12 August, 26 August. To St Pancras International
B From Scarborough
C until 15 July, from 14 October. From Glasgow Central to Plymouth
D From Leeds
E from 22 July until 7 October. From Glasgow Central to Bristol Temple Meads
F until 15 July, from 14 October. From Newcastle to Guildford
G From Bridlington
H until 15 July, from 14 October. From Glasgow Central to Bristol Temple Meads
I from 22 July until 2 September. From Motherwell to Bristol Temple Meads
J from 9 September until 7 October. From Glasgow Central to Bristol Temple Meads
K until 15 July, from 14 October. From Newcastle to Birmingham New Street

For services between Barnetby, Habrough, Grimsby Town and Cleethorpes, refer to Table T028

Table T029-R

Sundays
20 May to 2 December

Hull - Doncaster - Meadowhall, Sheffield, Manchester and Manchester Airport

	NT ◇ A	NT	TP ◇■	XC ◇■ B	XC ◇■ C	NT D	NT	TP ◇■	NT	XC ◇■ E	NT ◇ F	XC ◇■ G	NT ◇ H	TP ◇■	NT	TP ◇■	NT ◇ A	NT	NT	TP ◇■ I	NT ◇ D	NT
Hull d	19 29	19 35	19 43						19 54		20 29			20 53			21 29	21 35	21 59	22 30		
Hessle d									20 01													
Ferriby d									20 06													
Brough d	19 41	19 47	19 55						20 11		20 41			21 05			21 41	21 47	22 11	22 42		
Broomfleet d																						
Gilberdyke d									20 19										22 19			
Eastrington d																						
Howden d		19 59																21 59				
Wressle d																						
Selby a		20 08	20 14											21 24				22 08		23 01		
d		20 09	20 15											21 25				22 09				
York ■ 33 a		20 41																22 41				
Saltmarshe d																						
Goole d	19 56								20 27		20 56						21 56		22 28			
Thorne North d									20 36										22 36			
Cleethorpes 28 d								19 26								20 26						
Grimsby Town 28 d								19 34								20 34						
Habrough 28 d																20 44						
Barnetby 28 d								19 53								20 53						
Scunthorpe a								20 08								21 08						
d								20 08								21 08						
Althorpe d																						
Crowle d																						
Thorne South d																						
Hatfield & Stainforth d									20 42										22 42			
Kirk Sandall d									20 47										22 47			
Adwick 31 d																						
Bentley (S.Yorks) 31 d																						
Doncaster ■ 31 a	20 19							20 38	20 57		21 19					21 38	22 19		22 57			
London Kings Cross ■ ⊖26 a																						
York ■ 26 d				19 45	19 45					20 26		20 45	20 48									
Doncaster ■ d	20 21						20 28	20 42		20 51	21 21				21 33	21 44	22 21					22 40
Conisbrough d							20 35								21 40							22 47
Mexborough d							20 40								21 45							22 52
Swinton (S.Yorks) d						20 34	20 43						21 45		21 49						22 34	22 55
Rotherham Central d						20 43	20 52								22 00						22 43	23 04
Meadowhall d	20 39					20 49	20 58	21 02			21 39		21 55		22 06	22 02	22 42				22 49	23 11
Sheffield ■ a	20 48			20 51	20 51	20 56	21 05	21 08		21 17	21 48	21 51	22 03		22 13	22 10	22 51				22 56	23 20
d								21 11								22 13						
Stockport 78 a								21 56								23 03						
Manchester Piccadilly ■ a			21 39					22 05						23 08		23 16						
Manchester Airport 85 a								22 26														

	NT
Hull d	22 54
Hessle d	23 01
Ferriby d	23 06
Brough d	23 11
Broomfleet d	
Gilberdyke d	23 19
Eastrington d	
Howden d	
Wressle d	
Selby a	
d	
York ■ 33 a	
Saltmarshe d	
Goole d	23 27
Thorne North d	23 36
Cleethorpes 28 d	
Grimsby Town 28 d	
Habrough 28 d	
Barnetby 28 d	
Scunthorpe a	
d	
Althorpe d	
Crowle d	
Thorne South d	
Hatfield & Stainforth d	23 42
Kirk Sandall d	23 47
Adwick 31 d	
Bentley (S.Yorks) 31 d	
Doncaster ■ 31 a	23 57
London Kings Cross ■ ⊖26 a	
York ■ 26 d	
Doncaster ■ d	
Conisbrough d	
Mexborough d	
Swinton (S.Yorks) d	
Rotherham Central d	
Meadowhall d	
Sheffield ■ a	
d	
Stockport 78 a	
Manchester Piccadilly ■ a	
Manchester Airport 85 a	

A From Scarborough
B from 22 July until 7 October. From Edinburgh to Birmingham New Street
C until 15 July, from 14 October. From Edinburgh to Bristol Temple Meads
D From Leeds
E until 15 July, from 14 October. From Newcastle to Birmingham New Street
F From Bridlington
G From Glasgow Central to Birmingham New Street
H via Pontefract Baghill
I To Huddersfield

For services between Barnetby, Habrough, Grimsby Town and Cleethorpes, refer to Table T028

Table T030-F

Mondays to Fridays
21 May to 7 December

Lincoln - Retford - Sheffield

Miles		NT	NT ◇ A	NT	NT ◇ A	NT ◇ A	NT ◇ A	NT ◇ A	NT ◇ A	NT ◇ A	NT ◇ A	NT ◇ A	NT ◇ A	NT ◇ A	NT ◇ A	NT ◇ A	NT	NT ◇ A	NT ◇	NT ◇	NT	NT
0	**Lincoln** 18 d			07 02	07 22	08 22	09 19	10 20	11 20	12 20	13 20	14 20	15 20	16 20	17 22	18 22		19 23	20 19	21 29		
6	Saxilby 18 d			07 10	07 31	08 32	09 29	10 29	11 29	12 30	13 30	14 29	15 30	16 29	17 31	18 31		19 32	20 28	21 37		
15½	Gainsborough Lea Road 18 d			07 23	07 44	08 44	09 41	10 42	11 42	12 42	13 42	14 41	15 42	16 42	17 44	18 44		19 45	20 40	21 50		
25	**Retford** ■ a			07 35	07 56	08 57	09 56	10 56	11 56	12 57	13 57	14 56	15 57	16 56	17 56	18 56		19 57	20 53	22 02		
—	d	06 14	06 56	07 36	07 57	08 57	09 56	10 57	11 57	12 57	13 57	14 56	15 57	16 57	17 57	18 57	19 29	19 58	20 53	22 04	22 51	
32¾	Worksop d	06 26	07 09	07 48	08 08	09 08	10 08	11 08	12 08	13 09	14 09	15 08	16 09	17 08	18 08	19 08	19 39	20 09	21 05	22 16	23 03	23 22
34¾	Shireoaks d	06 31	07 13	07 52	08 12	09 13	10 12	11 13	12 13	13 13	14 13	15 12	16 13	17 13	18 12	19 12	19 43	20 13	21 10	22 20	23 08	23 26
37¾	Kiveton Park d	06 36	07 18	07 57	08 18	09 18	10 18	11 18	12 18	13 19	14 19	15 18	16 19	17 18	18 18	19 18	19 49	20 19	21 15	22 26	23 13	23 31
39	Kiveton Bridge d	06 39	07 21	08 01	08 21	09 21	10 21	11 21	12 21	13 22	14 22	15 21	16 22	17 21	18 21	19 21	19 52	20 22	21 18	22 29	23 17	23 35
43¼	Woodhouse d	06 45	07 28	08 07	08 27	09 28	10 27	11 28	12 28	13 28	14 28	15 27	16 28	17 28	18 27	19 27	19 59	20 28	21 24	22 35	23 23	23 41
46¼	Darnall d	06 50	07 33	08 12	08 32	09 33	10 32	11 33	12 33	13 33	14 33	15 32	16 33	17 33	18 32	19 32	20 04	20 33	21 29	22 40	23 28	23 48
48½	**Sheffield** ■ a	06 56	07 41	08 20	08 41	09 42	10 38	11 42	12 42	13 42	14 42	15 42	16 42	17 42	18 41	19 41	20 11	20 41	21 38	22 48	23 36	23 58
—	Meadowhall 34 a		07 53		08 51	09 53	10 54	11 50	12 51	13 51	14 51	15 50	16 51	17 51	18 50	19 50		20 50				

	NT
Lincoln 18 d	22 42
Saxilby 18 d	22 50
Gainsborough Lea Road 18 d	23 05
Retford ■ a	23 17
d	23 18
Worksop d	23 30
Shireoaks d	23 34
Kiveton Park d	23 39
Kiveton Bridge d	23 43
Woodhouse d	23 50
Darnall d	23 55
Sheffield ■ a	00 03
Meadowhall 34 a	

Saturdays
26 May to 8 December

	NT	NT ◇ A	NT	NT ◇ A	NT ◇ A	NT ◇ A	NT ◇ A	NT ◇ A	NT ◇ B	NT ◇ A	NT ◇ A	NT ◇ A	NT ◇ A	NT ◇ B	NT ◇ A	NT ◇ A	NT ◇ A	NT	NT ◇ A	NT ◇ B	NT ◇	NT ◇
Lincoln 18 d			06 42	07 22	08 22	09 19	10 20	11 20		12 20	13 20	14 20	15 20		16 20	17 22	18 22		19 23		20 19	21 29
Saxilby 18 d			06 50	07 31	08 32	09 29	10 29	11 29		12 30	13 30	14 29	15 30		16 29	17 31	18 31		19 32		20 28	21 37
Gainsborough Lea Road 18 d			07 03	07 44	08 44	09 41	10 42	11 42		12 42	13 42	14 41	15 42		16 42	17 44	18 44		19 45		20 40	21 50
Retford ■ a			07 15	07 56	08 57	09 56	10 56	11 56		12 57	13 57	14 56	15 57		16 56	17 56	18 56		19 57		20 53	22 02
d	06 14	06 56	07 16	07 57	08 57	09 56	10 57	11 57		12 57	13 57	14 56	15 57		16 57	17 57	18 57	19 29	19 58	20 32	20 53	22 04
Worksop d	06 26	07 09	07 28	08 08	09 08	10 08	11 08	12 08	12 42	13 09	14 09	15 08	16 09	16 42	17 08	18 08	19 08	19 39	20 09	20 43	21 05	22 16
Shireoaks d	06 31	07 13	07 32	08 12	09 13	10 12	11 13	12 13	12 46	13 13	14 13	15 12	16 13	16 47	17 13	18 12	19 12	19 43	20 13	20 47	21 10	22 20
Kiveton Park d	06 36	07 18	07 37	08 18	09 18	10 18	11 18	12 18	12 52	13 19	14 19	15 18	16 19	16 53	17 18	18 18	19 18	19 49	20 19	20 53	21 15	22 26
Kiveton Bridge d	06 39	07 21	07 41	08 21	09 21	10 21	11 21	12 21	12 55	13 22	14 22	15 21	16 22	16 56	17 21	18 21	19 21	19 52	20 22	20 56	21 18	22 29
Woodhouse d	06 45	07 28	07 47	08 27	09 28	10 27	11 28	12 28	13 02	13 28	14 28	15 27	16 28	17 03	17 28	18 27	19 27	19 59	20 28	21 02	21 24	22 35
Darnall d	06 50	07 33	07 52	08 32	09 33	10 32	11 33	12 33	13 08	13 33	14 33	15 32	16 33	17 08	17 33	18 32	19 32	20 04	20 33	21 07	21 29	22 40
Sheffield ■ a	06 56	07 41	08 00	08 41	09 42	10 38	11 42	12 42	13 17	13 42	14 42	15 42	16 42	17 17	17 42	18 41	19 41	20 11	20 41	21 15	21 38	22 48
Meadowhall 34 a		07 53		08 50	09 53	10 54	11 50	12 51		13 51	14 51	15 50	16 51		17 51	18 50	19 50		20 50			

	NT	NT	NT
Lincoln 18 d			22 44
Saxilby 18 d			22 52
Gainsborough Lea Road 18 d			23 05
Retford ■ a			23 17
d	22 51		23 18
Worksop d	23 03	23 22	23 30
Shireoaks d	23 08	23 26	23 34
Kiveton Park d	23 13	23 31	23 39
Kiveton Bridge d	23 17	23 35	23 43
Woodhouse d	23 23	23 41	23 50
Darnall d	23 28	23 48	23 55
Sheffield ■ a	23 36	23 58	00 03
Meadowhall 34 a			

Sundays
20 May to 2 December

	NT	NT ◇ C	NT ◇ C	NT ◇ C	NT ◇ C	NT	NT ◇ C	NT	NT ◇	NT	NT ◇	NT	NT ◇	NT ◇	NT
Lincoln 18 d		10 14	11 14	12 14	13 14		14 14	15 12	16 09	17 14	18 21	19 20	20 17	21 20	21 51
Saxilby 18 d		10 23	11 23	12 23	13 23		14 23	15 21	16 19	17 23	18 30	19 29	20 26	21 29	22 00
Gainsborough Lea Road 18 d		10 35	11 35	12 35	13 35		14 35	15 33	16 32	17 35	18 42	19 41	20 39	21 41	22 12
Retford ■ a		10 50	11 50	12 50	13 50		14 50	15 48	16 46	17 50	18 57	19 56	20 53	21 56	22 27
d	09 12	10 50	11 50	12 50	13 50	14 14	14 50	15 48	16 47	17 50	18 57	19 56	20 54	21 56	22 27
Worksop d	09 26	11 02	12 02	13 02	14 02	14 28	15 02	16 00	16 59	18 02	19 09	20 08	21 06	22 08	22 39
Shireoaks d	09 30	11 07	12 07	13 07	14 07	14 33	15 07	16 05	17 03	18 07		20 13		22 12	22 43
Kiveton Park d	09 36	11 12	12 12	13 12	14 12	14 38	15 12	16 11	17 09	18 12	19 18	20 18	21 14	22 18	22 49
Kiveton Bridge d	09 39	11 15	12 15	13 15	14 15	14 41	15 15	16 14	17 12	18 15	19 21	20 21	21 17	22 21	22 52
Woodhouse d	09 45	11 22	12 22	13 22	14 22	14 48	15 22	16 20	17 18	18 22		20 28		22 28	22 59
Darnall d	09 50				14 27		15 27		17 23	18 27		20 33		22 33	23 04
Sheffield ■ a	09 59	11 34	12 34	13 34	14 36	15 01	15 36	16 33	17 32	18 36	19 37	20 41	21 34	22 42	23 12
Meadowhall 34 a	10 07	11 45	12 45	13 44	14 44		15 44								

A To Leeds
B From Cleethorpes. via Retford
C To Huddersfield

For connections from London Kings Cross refer to Table T026

Table T030-R

Mondays to Fridays

21 May to 7 December

Sheffield - Retford - Lincoln

Miles		NT	NT	EM	NT	NT	NT	NT	NT	NT	NT	NT	NT	NT	NT	NT	NT	NT	NT	NT	NT	NT
							◇	◇	◇	◇	◇	◇	◇	◇	◇	◇	◇		◇	◇	◇	
					A	B	C	C	C	C	C	C	C	C	C	C	C		C			
—	Meadowhall 34 d					06 40	07 27	08 28	09 28	10 28	11 27	12 28	13 27	14 28	15 28	16 28	17 27		18 28			
0	**Sheffield** ■ d	05 45	06 10		06 38	06 58	07 39	08 38	09 38	10 39	11 37	12 38	13 37	14 38	15 38	16 38	17 37	17 54	18 42	19 48	20 59	21 42
2¼	Darnall d	05 50			06 45	07 04	07 45	08 43	09 46	10 44	11 43	12 43	13 43	14 43	15 43	16 43	17 43	18 00	18 48	19 56	21 05	21 47
5¼	Woodhouse d	05 55			06 50	07 09	07 50	08 48	09 51	10 49	11 48	12 48	13 48	14 48	15 48	16 48	17 48	18 05	18 53	20 02	21 10	21 53
9½	Kiveton Bridge d	06 01			06 57	07 16	07 56	08 55	09 57	10 56	11 54	12 55	13 54	14 55	15 55	16 55	17 54	18 12	18 59	20 09	21 16	21 59
10¾	Kiveton Park d	06 04	06 26		07 00	07 19	07 59	08 58	10 00	10 59	11 57	12 58	13 57	14 58	15 58	16 58	17 57	18 15	19 02	20 12	21 19	22 03
13¾	Shireoaks d	06 08			07 05	07 24	08 04	09 02	10 05	11 03	12 02	13 02	14 02	15 02	16 02	17 02	18 02	18 21	19 08	20 17	21 24	22 08
15¾	Worksop d	06 13	06 34	06 52	07 10	07 29	08 08	09 07	10 09	11 08	12 06	13 07	14 06	15 07	16 07	17 07	18 07	18 27	19 13	20 22	21 29	22 14
23½	**Retford** ■ a	06 23	06 49		07 20	07 40	08 18	09 16	10 19	11 18	12 16	13 16	14 16	15 16	16 16	17 16	18 16	18 39	19 22	20 31	21 39	22 28
—	d	06 24			07 20		08 18	09 17	10 19	11 19	12 16	13 17	14 16	15 17	16 17	17 17	18 17		19 24	20 32	21 39	
33	Gainsborough Lea Road 18 a	06 39			07 35		08 33	09 32	10 34	11 34	12 31	13 34	14 31	15 36	16 35	17 32	18 38		19 41	20 47	21 54	
42½	Saxilby 18 a	06 51			07 50		08 45	09 44	10 46	11 46	12 42	13 49	14 43	15 48	16 47	17 44	18 52		19 55	20 58	22 06	
48½	**Lincoln** 18 a	07 07		09 08	08 05		08 56	09 56	10 59	11 58	12 55	14 01	14 55	16 00	16 59	17 56	19 05		20 07	21 10	22 17	

Saturdays

26 May to 8 December

	NT	NT	NT	NT	NT	NT	NT	NT	NT	NT	NT	NT	NT	NT	NT	NT	NT	NT	NT	NT
					◇	◇	◇	◇	◇	◇	◇	◇	◇	◇	◇		◇	◇	◇	
			A	B	C	C	C	C	C	C	C	C	C	C	C		C			
Meadowhall 34 d				06 40	07 27	08 28	09 28	10 28	11 27	12 28	13 27	14 28	15 28	16 28	17 27		18 28			
Sheffield ■ d	05 45	06 13	06 38	06 58	07 39	08 38	09 38	10 39	11 37	12 38	13 37	14 38	15 38	16 38	17 37	17 54	18 42	19 48	20 59	21 42
Darnall d	05 50		06 45	07 04	07 45	08 43	09 46	10 44	11 43	12 43	13 43	14 43	15 43	16 43	17 43	18 00	18 48	19 56	21 05	21 47
Woodhouse d	05 55		06 50	07 09	07 50	08 48	09 51	10 49	11 48	12 48	13 48	14 48	15 48	16 48	17 48	18 05	18 53	20 02	21 10	21 53
Kiveton Bridge d	06 01		06 57	07 16	07 56	08 55	09 57	10 56	11 54	12 55	13 54	14 55	15 55	16 55	17 54	18 12	18 59	20 09	21 16	21 59
Kiveton Park d	06 04	06 28	07 00	07 19	07 59	08 58	10 00	10 59	11 57	12 58	13 57	14 58	15 58	16 58	17 57	18 15	19 02	20 12	21 19	22 03
Shireoaks d	06 08		07 05	07 24	08 04	09 02	10 05	11 03	12 02	13 02	14 02	15 02	16 02	17 02	18 02	18 21	19 08	20 17	21 24	22 08
Worksop d	06 13	06 36	07 10	07 29	08 08	09 07	10 09	11 08	12 06	13 07	14 06	15 07	16 07	17 07	18 07	18 27	19 13	20 22	21 29	22 14
Retford ■ a	06 23	06 52	07 20	07 40	08 18	09 16	10 19	11 18	12 16	13 16	14 16	15 16	16 16	17 16	18 16	18 39	19 22	20 31	21 39	22 28
d	06 24		07 20		08 18	09 17	10 19	11 19	12 16	13 17	14 16	15 17	16 17	17 17	18 17		19 24	20 32	21 39	
Gainsborough Lea Road 18 a	06 39		07 35		08 33	09 32	10 34	11 34	12 31	13 34	14 31	15 36	16 35	17 32	18 38		19 41	20 47	21 54	
Saxilby 18 a	06 51		07 47		08 45	09 44	10 46	11 46	12 42	13 49	14 43	15 48	16 47	17 44	18 52		19 55	20 58	22 06	
Lincoln 18 a	07 07		08 02		08 56	09 56	10 59	11 58	12 55	14 01	14 55	16 00	16 59	17 56	19 05		20 07	21 10	22 17	

Sundays

20 May to 2 December

	NT	NT	NT	NT	NT	NT	NT	NT	NT	NT	NT	NT	NT	NT	NT
	◇		◇		◇		◇	◇	◇	◇	◇		◇		◇
					D		D	D	D	D	D				
Meadowhall 34 d					12 27		13 17	14 25	15 16	16 21	17 17				
Sheffield ■ d	08 45	09 41	10 41	11 41	12 44	13 14	13 36	14 41	15 41	16 37	17 35	18 43	19 24	20 24	21 24
Darnall d		09 46		11 46		13 19				16 43		18 48		20 29	21 29
Woodhouse d		09 52		11 51		13 25				16 47		18 53		20 34	21 34
Kiveton Bridge d		09 58	10 55	11 58	12 58	13 31	13 52	14 55	15 55	16 55	17 50	19 00	19 38	20 41	21 41
Kiveton Park d		10 02	10 58	12 01	13 01	13 35	13 57	14 58	15 58	16 58	17 53	19 04	19 41	20 45	21 45
Shireoaks d		10 07		12 06		13 40				17 03		19 09		20 50	21 50
Worksop d	09 08	10 12	11 07	12 11	13 10	13 45	14 06	15 07	16 07	17 08	18 02	19 14	19 50	20 55	21 55
Retford ■ a	09 18	10 21	11 16	12 21	13 19	14 00	14 15	15 17	16 16	17 18	18 12	19 24	19 59	21 05	22 04
d	09 18	10 22	11 17	12 21	13 20		14 16	15 17	16 17	17 18	18 12	19 24	20 00	21 05	22 05
Gainsborough Lea Road 18 a	09 33	10 36	11 31	12 36	13 34		14 30	15 32	16 31	17 33	18 27	19 39	20 14	21 19	22 19
Saxilby 18 a	09 45	10 48	11 44	12 48	13 47		14 43	15 44	16 44	17 46	18 40	19 51	20 27	21 31	22 32
Lincoln 18 a	09 57	11 00	11 56	13 00	13 58		14 55	15 57	16 57	17 58	18 52	20 07	20 39	21 44	22 45

A From Doncaster
B From Barnsley
C From Leeds
D From Huddersfield

For connections to London Kings Cross refer to Table T026

Table T031-F

Mondays to Fridays

21 May to 7 December

Sheffield, Doncaster and Wakefield - Leeds

Miles	Miles		NT MX	NT MX	NT	NT MX	NT MO	NT	NT	NT	NT	NT	NT	NT	NT	NT	NT	NT	NT	NT	NT	NT	XC
					◇			◇		◇				◇	◇	◇		◇				◇	◇■ ⊤
—	0	**Sheffield** ■ 29 d			05 15	05 30	05 30				06 02	06 05	06 16	06 19		06 45			07 01	07 04	07 14	07 18	07 21
—	3½	Meadowhall 29 d			05 21	05 36	05 36				06 08	06 11	06 22	06 25		06 51			07 07	07 10	07 22	07 25	
—	6¼	Rotherham Central 29 d			05 28							06 17	06 28						07 17		07 29		
—	10¾	Swinton (S.Yorks) 29 d			05 38							06 26	06 38						07 27		07 39		
—	13	Bolton-upon-Dearne d			05 43								06 43								07 43		
—	14¼	Goldthorpe d			05 46								06 46								07 46		
—	15	Thurnscoe d			05 49								06 49								07 49		
—	18½	Moorthorpe d			05 55								06 55								08 01		
0	—	**Doncaster** ■ d						06 01	06 10	06 30		06 43			06 57		07 11	07 28	07 53				
1¾	—	Bentley (S.Yorks) d						06 05	06 14	06 33		06 47			07 00		07 14	07 31	07 57				
4	—	Adwick a						06 08	06 19	06 37		06 52			07 04		07 19	07 35	08 02				
—	—	d						06 09		06 37					07 04			07 35					
8¾	—	South Elmsall d						06 15		06 42					07 09			07 40					
13¾	22¼	Fitzwilliam d			06 01			06 20		06 48			07 01		07 15			07 45			08 07		
18	27	Sandal & Agbrigg d			06 08			06 26		06 54			07 08		07 21			07 51			08 14		
19¾	28¾	**Wakefield Westgate** ■ 32,39 a			06 12			06 30		06 58			07 12		07 25			07 55			08 18		07 47
—	—	d	00 01	00 12	06 13			06 31		06 59			07 13		07 26			07 56			08 19		07 48
—	—	Pontefract Monkhill 32 d																→			→		
—	—	Wakefield Kirkgate ■ 32,34,39 a				06 14	06 16				06 48			06 54		07 22				07 49		07 57	
—	—	d				06 16	06 17				06 49			06 55		07 23				07 50		07 57	
22½	31¼	Outwood d	00 04	00 17	06 18			06 35		07 03			07 18		07 30								
29¾	38¾	**Leeds** ■ 32,34 a	00 17	00 29	06 30	06 43	06 45	06 47		07 14	07 25		07 30	07 16	07 42	07 43				08 25		08 17	08 01

	NT	GR	NT	NT	NT	NT	GR	NT	NT	NT	XC	NT	GR	NT	GR	NT	NT	NT	NT	NT	NT	XC	NT
	◇	■ ■ ⊡		◇		◇	■ ■ ⊡		◇	◇	◇■ ⊤	◇	■ ■ ⊡	◇	■ ■ ⊡	◇		◇			◇	◇■ ⊤	◇
Sheffield ■ 29 d					07 31	07 47		08 03	08 15	08 18	08 22					08 46	09 03		09 06	09 15	09 18	09 21	
Meadowhall 29 d					07 37	07 54		08 09	08 21	08 25						08 53	09 09		09 12	09 21	09 24		
Rotherham Central 29 d					07 43				08 28										09 19	09 29			
Swinton (S.Yorks) 29 d					07 52				08 38										09 28	09 38			
Bolton-upon-Dearne d									08 43											09 43			
Goldthorpe d									08 46											09 46			
Thurnscoe d									08 49											09 49			
Moorthorpe d									08 55											09 55			
Doncaster ■ d		07 50		07 59	08 10		08 18					08 26	08 43		09 15			09 26	09 50				
Bentley (S.Yorks) d				08 03	08 13							08 29						09 29	09 54				
Adwick a				08 07	08 18							08 33						09 33	09 59				
d				08 07								08 33						09 33					
South Elmsall d				08 12								08 40						09 39					
Fitzwilliam d				08 17					09 01			08 46						09 45		10 01			
Sandal & Agbrigg d	←		←	08 23					09 08			08 51		←				09 50		10 08			←
Wakefield Westgate ■ 32,39 a	07 55	08 06	08 18	08 27			08 34		09 12		08 47	08 55	09 00	09 12	09 31			09 54		10 12		09 46	09 54
d	07 56	08 07	08 19	08 28			08 36		09 13		08 48	08 56	09 02	09 13	09 32			09 55		10 13		09 47	09 55
Pontefract Monkhill 32 d									→									→		→			
Wakefield Kirkgate ■ 32,34,39 a						08 25		08 48		08 57						09 26	09 48				09 56		
d						08 25		08 49		08 58						09 26	09 49				09 56		
Outwood d	08 00		08 24	08 32								09 00		09 18									09 59
Leeds ■ 32,34 a	08 12	08 22	08 36	08 44		08 46	08 51	09 24		09 17	09 02	09 12	09 17	09 30	09 45	09 46	10 24				10 16	10 00	10 11

	GR	NT	NT	GR	NT	NT	NT	NT	NT	XC	NT	GR	NT	NT	GR	NT	NT	NT	NT	NT	XC	NT
	■ ■ ⊡		◇	■ ■ ⊡		◇		◇	◇	◇■ ⊤	◇	■ ■ ⊡	◇	◇	■ ■ ⊡		◇			◇	◇■ ⊤	◇
Sheffield ■ 29 d			09 48		10 02		10 05	10 15	10 18	10 21				10 49		11 02		11 05	11 15	11 18	11 21	
Meadowhall 29 d			09 54		10 08		10 11	10 21	10 24					10 57		11 08		11 11	11 21	11 24		
Rotherham Central 29 d							10 19	10 28										11 19	11 28			
Swinton (S.Yorks) 29 d							10 28	10 38										11 28	11 38			
Bolton-upon-Dearne d								10 43											11 43			
Goldthorpe d								10 46											11 46			
Thurnscoe d								10 49											11 49			
Moorthorpe d								10 55											11 55			
Doncaster ■ d	09 44			10 15		10 26	10 47					10 43			11 15		11 26	11 47				
Bentley (S.Yorks) d						10 29	10 51										11 29	11 51				
Adwick a						10 33	10 56										11 33	11 56				
d						10 33											11 33					
South Elmsall d						10 39											11 39					
Fitzwilliam d						10 45		11 01									11 45		12 01			
Sandal & Agbrigg d		←				10 50		11 08			←		←				11 50		12 08			←
Wakefield Westgate ■ 32,39 a	10 00	10 12		10 31		10 54		11 12		10 46	10 54	11 00	11 12		11 31		11 54		12 12		11 46	11 54
d	10 01	10 13		10 32		10 55		11 13		10 47	10 55	11 01	11 13		11 32		11 55		12 13		11 47	11 55
Pontefract Monkhill 32 d						→		→									→		→			
Wakefield Kirkgate ■ 32,34,39 a			10 26		10 48				10 55					11 27		11 48				11 55		
d			10 26		10 49				10 55					11 27		11 49				11 55		
Outwood d		10 18									10 59		11 18									11 59
Leeds ■ 32,34 a	10 16	10 30	10 46	10 47	11 24				11 15	11 00	11 11	11 16	11 30	11 47	11 47	12 24				12 15	12 01	12 11

Table T031-F

Mondays to Fridays

21 May to 7 December

Sheffield, Doncaster and Wakefield - Leeds

	GR		NT	NT	GR	NT	NT	GC	NT	NT	NT	XC	NT	GR	NT	NT	GR		NT	NT	NT	NT	NT	XC
				◇			◇			◇	◇	◇	◇		◇	◇				◇			◇	◇ A
Sheffield 29 d				11 45		12 02			12 05	12 15	12 18	12 21				12 45			13 02		13 05	13 15	13 18	13 21
Meadowhall 29 d				11 51		12 08			12 11	12 21	12 24					12 51			13 08		13 11	13 21	13 24	
Rotherham Central 29 d									12 19	12 28											13 19	13 28		
Swinton (S.Yorks) 29 d									12 28	12 38											13 28	13 38		
Bolton-upon-Dearne d										12 43												13 43		
Goldthorpe d										12 46												13 46		
Thurnscoe d										12 49												13 49		
Moorthorpe d										12 55												13 55		
Doncaster d	11 43				12 15		12 26	12 35	12 47					12 43			13 15			13 25	13 47			
Bentley (S.Yorks) d							12 29		12 51											13 29	13 51			
Adwick a							12 33		12 56											13 33	13 56			
d							12 33													13 33				
South Elmsall d							12 39													13 39				
Fitzwilliam d							12 45			13 01										13 45		14 01		
Sandal & Agbrigg d			←				12 50			13 08			←		←					13 50		14 08		
Wakefield Westgate 32,39 a	11 59		12 12		12 31		12 54			13 12		12 46	12 54	13 00	13 12		13 31			13 54		14 12		13 46
d	12 01		12 13		12 32		12 55			13 13		12 47	12 55	13 01	13 13		13 32			13 55		14 13		13 47
Pontefract Monkhill 32 d							→	12 58		→										→		→		
Wakefield Kirkgate 32,34,39 a				12 26		12 48		13 14			12 55					13 26			13 48				13 55	
d				12 26		12 49					12 55					13 27			13 49				13 55	
Outwood d			12 18										12 59		13 18									
Leeds 32,34 a	12 16		12 30	12 46	12 48	13 24					13 15	13 00	13 11	13 16	13 30	13 46	13 48		14 24				14 15	14 00

	XC	NT	GR	NT	NT	GR	NT	NT	NT		NT	NT	XC	NT	GR	NT	NT	GR	NT	NT	NT	NT	NT	XC
	◇ B	◇			◇			◇			◇	◇	◇	◇		◇	◇			◇			◇	◇ A
Sheffield 29 d	13 21				13 45		14 02		14 05		14 15	14 18	14 21				14 45		15 02		15 05	15 15	15 18	15 21
Meadowhall 29 d					13 51		14 08		14 11		14 21	14 24					14 51		15 08		15 11	15 21	15 24	
Rotherham Central 29 d									14 19		14 28										15 19	15 28		
Swinton (S.Yorks) 29 d									14 28		14 38										15 28	15 38		
Bolton-upon-Dearne d											14 43											15 43		
Goldthorpe d											14 46											15 46		
Thurnscoe d											14 49											15 49		
Moorthorpe d											14 55											15 55		
Doncaster d			13 43			14 15		14 26	14 47						14 43			15 15		15 26	15 47			
Bentley (S.Yorks) d								14 29	14 51											15 29	15 51			
Adwick a								14 33	14 56											15 33	15 56			
d								14 33												15 33				
South Elmsall d								14 39												15 39				
Fitzwilliam d								14 45			15 01									15 45		16 01		
Sandal & Agbrigg d		←		←				14 50			15 08			←		←				15 50		16 08		
Wakefield Westgate 32,39 a	13 46	13 54	13 59	14 12		14 31		14 54			15 12		14 46	14 54	14 59	15 12		15 31		15 54		16 12		15 46
d	13 47	13 55	14 01	14 13		14 32		14 55			15 13		14 47	14 55	15 01	15 13		15 32		15 55		16 13		15 47
Pontefract Monkhill 32 d								→			→									→		→		
Wakefield Kirkgate 32,34,39 a					14 26		14 48					14 55					15 26		15 48				15 55	
d					14 27		14 49					14 55					15 27		15 49				15 55	
Outwood d		13 59		14 18										14 59		15 18								
Leeds 32,34 a	14 00	14 11	14 16	14 30	14 46	14 48	15 24					15 15	15 00	15 11	15 16	15 30	15 46	15 48	16 24				16 15	16 00

	XC		NT	GR	NT	NT	GR	NT	GC	NT	NT	NT	NT	XC	NT	GR	NT		NT	GR	NT	NT	NT	NT
	B		◇			◇				◇		◇	◇	◇	◇		◇		◇			◇		
Sheffield 29 d	15 21					15 45		16 02			16 05	16 15	16 18	16 21					16 45		17 02		17 05	17 15
Meadowhall 29 d						15 51		16 08			16 11	16 21	16 24						16 51		17 08		17 11	17 21
Rotherham Central 29 d											16 19	16 28											17 19	17 28
Swinton (S.Yorks) 29 d											16 28	16 38											17 28	17 38
Bolton-upon-Dearne d												16 43												17 43
Goldthorpe d												16 46												17 46
Thurnscoe d												16 49												17 49
Moorthorpe d												16 55												17 55
Doncaster d				15 43			16 15		16 23	16 26	16 47					16 43				17 17		17 26	17 48	
Bentley (S.Yorks) d										16 29	16 51											17 29	17 52	
Adwick a										16 33	16 56											17 33	17 57	
d										16 33												17 33		
South Elmsall d										16 39												17 39		
Fitzwilliam d										16 45		17 01										17 45		18 01
Sandal & Agbrigg d			←		←					16 50		17 08			←		←					17 50		18 08
Wakefield Westgate 32,39 a	15 46		15 54	15 59	16 12		16 31			16 54		17 14		16 46	16 54	16 59	17 14			17 33		17 54		18 12
d	15 47		15 55	16 00	16 13		16 33			16 55		17 15		16 47	16 55	17 01	17 15			17 35		17 55		18 12
Pontefract Monkhill 32 d									16 54	→		→										→		→
Wakefield Kirkgate 32,34,39 a						16 26		16 48	17 10				16 55						17 26		17 48			
d						16 26		16 49					16 55						17 27		17 49			
Outwood d			15 59		16 18										16 59		17 20							
Leeds 32,34 a	16 00		16 11	16 16	16 30	16 46	16 48	17 24					17 15	17 00	17 12	17 16	17 32		17 46	17 49	18 24			

A until 20 July, from 8 October

B from 23 July until 5 October

Table T031-F

Mondays to Fridays

21 May to 7 December

Sheffield, Doncaster and Wakefield - Leeds

	NT		XC	XC	NT	GR	NT	GC	NT	XC	GR	NT	NT	NT	NT	NT	XC		NT	GR	NT	NT	GR	NT
	◇		◇ A	◇ B	◇				◇	◇			◇		◇	◇	◇		◇		◇	◇		
Sheffield 29 d	17 18		17 21	17 21					17 45	17 50		18 02		18 05	18 15	18 18	18 21					18 45		19 02
Meadowhall 29 d	17 24								17 51			18 08		18 11	18 21	18 24						18 51		19 08
Rotherham Central 29 d														18 18	18 28									
Swinton (S.Yorks) 29 d														18 27	18 38									
Bolton-upon-Dearne d															18 43									
Goldthorpe d															18 46									
Thurnscoe d															18 49									
Moorthorpe d															18 55									
Doncaster d						17 41		18 04			18 19		18 28	18 48						18 43			19 16	
Bentley (S.Yorks) d													18 31	18 52										
Adwick a													18 35	18 57										
d													18 35											
South Elmsall d													18 40											
Fitzwilliam d													18 46		19 01									
Sandal & Agbrigg d					←		←						18 51		19 08				←		←			
Wakefield Westgate 32,39 a			17 45	17 46	17 54	17 59	18 12			18 16	18 35		18 55		19 13		18 48		18 55	19 00	19 13		19 32	
d			17 47	17 47	17 55	18 01	18 12			18 17	18 36		18 56		19 13		18 50		18 56	19 01	19 13		19 33	
Pontefract Monkhill 32 d													→		→									
Wakefield Kirkgate 32,34,39 a	17 55							18 26	18 27			18 48				18 55						19 26		19 48
d	17 55								18 27			18 49				18 55						19 26		19 49
Outwood d					17 59		18 17												19 00		19 18			
Leeds 32,34 a	18 15		18 00	18 01	18 12	18 15	18 30		18 47	18 34	18 52	19 24				19 15	19 03		19 14	19 17	19 30	19 46	19 47	20 24

	NT	NT	NT	NT	XC	NT	GR	GR	NT		NT	GR	NT	NT	NT	NT	NT	XC	XC	NT	GR	NT	NT	GR
	◇			◇	◇	◇					◇			◇		◇	◇	◇ A	◇ B	◇		◇	◇	
Sheffield 29 d		19 05	19 15	19 18	19 22						19 45		20 02		20 05	20 15	20 18	20 21	20 21				20 45	
Meadowhall 29 d		19 11	19 21	19 24							19 51		20 08		20 11	20 21	20 24						20 51	
Rotherham Central 29 d		19 19	19 28												20 19	20 28								
Swinton (S.Yorks) 29 d		19 28	19 38												20 28	20 38								
Bolton-upon-Dearne d			19 43													20 43								
Goldthorpe d			19 46													20 46								
Thurnscoe d			19 49													20 49								
Moorthorpe d			19 55													20 55								
Doncaster d	19 28	19 54					19 45	19 50				20 22		20 28	20 48						20 42			21 14
Bentley (S.Yorks) d	19 31	19 58												20 31	20 52									
Adwick a	19 35	20 03												20 35	20 57									
d	19 35													20 35										
South Elmsall d	19 40													20 40										
Fitzwilliam d	19 45		20 07											20 45		21 01								
Sandal & Agbrigg d	19 51		20 14			←			←					20 51		21 08				←		←		
Wakefield Westgate 32,39 a	19 55		20 18		19 46	19 55	20 01	20 06	20 18			20 38		20 55		21 13		20 46	20 47	20 55	20 59	21 13		21 30
d	19 55		20 19		19 47	19 55	20 02	20 07	20 19			20 40		20 55		21 14		20 48	20 48	20 55	21 01	21 14		21 31
Pontefract Monkhill 32 d	→		→											→		→								
Wakefield Kirkgate 32,34,39 a				19 55							20 26		20 48				20 55						21 26	
d				19 55							20 26		20 49				20 55						21 26	
Outwood d						20 00			20 24											21 00		21 19		
Leeds 32,34 a				20 15	20 02	20 13	20 17	20 21	20 36		20 46	20 54	21 24				21 15	21 01	21 02	21 13	21 15	21 30	21 46	21 47

	NT		GC	NT	NT	NT	NT	XC	NT	GR	NT	EM	EM	GR	NT	NT	NT		NT	NT	EM	XC	NT	NT
				◇			◇	◇	◇			◇	◇		◇		◇ A		◇ B	◇	◇	◇ B	◇	
Sheffield 29 d	21 02				21 05	21 15	21 18	21 21				21 32	22 04			22 07	22 15		22 15	22 18	22 21	22 24		22 31
Meadowhall 29 d	21 08				21 11	21 21	21 24									22 13	22 22		22 22	22 24				22 37
Rotherham Central 29 d					21 20	21 28										22 19	22 29		22 29					
Swinton (S.Yorks) 29 d					21 35	21 38										22 29	22 38		22 41					
Bolton-upon-Dearne d						21 43											22 42		22 45					
Goldthorpe d						21 46											22 45		22 48					
Thurnscoe d						21 49											22 48		22 51					
Moorthorpe d						21 55											22 54		22 57					
Doncaster d			21 24	21 28	21 54					21 45				22 23	22 32	22 47								
Bentley (S.Yorks) d				21 31	21 58										22 35	22 50								
Adwick a				21 35	22 03										22 39	22 55								
d				21 35											22 39									
South Elmsall d				21 40											22 45									
Fitzwilliam d				21 45		22 01									22 51		23 10		23 03					
Sandal & Agbrigg d				21 51		22 08			←		←				22 56		23 17		23 09				←	
Wakefield Westgate 32,39 a				21 55		22 12		21 46	21 55	22 05	22 12	22 15	22 33	22 39	23 00		23 21		23 13		22 48	22 53	23 00	
d				21 55		22 12		21 47	21 55	22 06	22 12	22 16	22 34	22 41	23 01		23 21		23 14		22 49	22 54	23 01	
Pontefract Monkhill 32 d				→		→									→		→		→					
Wakefield Kirkgate 32,34,39 a	21 48		21 51				21 55													22 55				23 16
d	21 49						21 55													22 55				23 17
Outwood d									22 00		22 18												23 05	
Leeds 32,34 a	22 24						22 15	22 02	22 12	22 21	22 30	22 34	22 49	22 57						23 14	23 06	23 07	23 18	23 53

A from 23 July until 5 October

B until 20 July, from 8 October

Sheffield, Doncaster and Wakefield - Leeds

Mondays to Fridays
21 May to 7 December

	XC	NT	NT	GR	NT	NT FO	NT FX	NT
	◇1 A	◇ B	◇ A	1 ☕				
Sheffield 29 d	22 46					23 15	23 15	23 18
Meadowhall 29 d						23 21	23 21	23 24
Rotherham Central 29 d						23 28	23 28	
Swinton (S.Yorks) 29 d						23 36	23 36	
Bolton-upon-Dearne d						23 40	23 40	
Goldthorpe d						23 44	23 44	
Thurnscoe d						23 47	23 47	
Moorthorpe d						23 53	23 53	
Doncaster d				23 37	23 24			
Bentley (S.Yorks) d					23 27			
Adwick a					23 31			
d					23 31			
South Elmsall d					23 36			
Fitzwilliam d					23 50	23 59	23 59	
Sandal & Agbrigg d		←	←		23 56			
Wakefield Westgate 32,39 a	23 12	23 13	23 21	23 54	23 59		00 11	
d	23 13	23 14	23 21	23 55	00 01		00 12	
Pontefract Monkhill 32 d								
Wakefield Kirkgate 32,34,39 a								00 03
d								
Outwood d		23 19	23 26		00 04		00 17	
Leeds 32,34 a	23 26	23 31	23 39	00 08	00 17	00 28	00 29	

Saturdays
26 May to 8 December

	NT	NT	NT	NT	NT	NT	NT	NT	NT	NT	NT	NT	NT	NT	NT	NT	NT	NT	XC	NT	GR	NT	NT
		◇		◇		◇				◇	◇	◇		◇				◇	◇1 🚲	◇	1 ☕		◇
Sheffield 29 d		05 15	05 30				06 03	06 06	06 16	06 19		06 45			07 01	07 04	07 16	07 18	07 21				
Meadowhall 29 d		05 21	05 36				06 09	06 12	06 22	06 25		06 51			07 07	07 10	07 22	07 25					
Rotherham Central 29 d		05 28						06 18	06 28						07 17		07 34						
Swinton (S.Yorks) 29 d		05 38						06 26	06 38						07 27		07 44						
Bolton-upon-Dearne d		05 43							06 43								07 49						
Goldthorpe d		05 46							06 46								07 52						
Thurnscoe d		05 49							06 49								07 55						
Moorthorpe d		05 55							06 55								08 01						
Doncaster d				06 01	06 11	06 30		06 42			06 57		07 11	07 28	07 53						07 50		07 59
Bentley (S.Yorks) d				06 05	06 15	06 33		06 45			07 00		07 14	07 31	07 57								08 03
Adwick a				06 08	06 19	06 37		06 50			07 04		07 19	07 35	08 02								08 07
d				06 09		06 37					07 04			07 35									08 07
South Elmsall d				06 15		06 42					07 09			07 40									08 12
Fitzwilliam d		06 01		06 20		06 48			07 01		07 15			07 45			08 07						08 17
Sandal & Agbrigg d		06 08		06 26		06 54			07 08		07 21			07 51			08 14			←		←	08 23
Wakefield Westgate 32,39 a		06 12		06 30		06 58			07 12		07 25			07 55			08 18		07 45	07 55	08 06	08 18	08 27
d	00 01	06 13		06 31		06 59			07 13		07 26			07 56			08 19		07 46	07 56	08 07	08 19	08 28
Pontefract Monkhill 32 d														→			→						
Wakefield Kirkgate 32,34,39 a			06 14				06 49			06 54		07 22				07 50		07 57					
d			06 16				06 50			06 55		07 23				07 51		07 57					
Outwood d	00 04	06 18		06 35		07 03			07 18		07 30									08 00		08 24	08 32
Leeds 32,34 a	00 17	06 30	06 43	06 47		07 14	07 25		07 30	07 16	07 42	07 43				08 26		08 17	08 00	08 12	08 20	08 36	08 44

	NT	NT	GR	NT	NT	NT	XC	NT	GR	NT	GR	NT	NT	NT	NT	NT	NT	XC	NT	GR	NT	GR
		◇	1 ☕		◇	◇	◇1 🚲	◇	1 ☕	◇	1 ☕	◇		◇			◇	◇1 🚲	◇	1 ☕		1 ☕
Sheffield 29 d	07 31	07 45		08 02	08 15	08 18	08 22					08 45	09 03		09 06	09 15	09 18	09 21				
Meadowhall 29 d	07 37	07 54		08 09	08 21	08 25						08 51	09 09		09 12	09 21	09 24					
Rotherham Central 29 d	07 43				08 28										09 19	09 29						
Swinton (S.Yorks) 29 d	07 52				08 38										09 28	09 38						
Bolton-upon-Dearne d					08 43											09 43						
Goldthorpe d					08 46											09 46						
Thurnscoe d					08 49											09 49						
Moorthorpe d					08 55											09 55						
Doncaster d	08 10		08 17					08 26	08 43		09 15			09 26	09 50					09 44		10 15
Bentley (S.Yorks) d	08 13							08 29						09 29	09 54							
Adwick a	08 18							08 33						09 33	09 59							
d								08 33						09 33								
South Elmsall d								08 40						09 39								
Fitzwilliam d					09 01			08 46						09 45		10 01						
Sandal & Agbrigg d					09 08			08 51		←				09 50		10 08			←		←	
Wakefield Westgate 32,39 a			08 35		09 12		08 46	08 55	08 59	09 12	09 31			09 54		10 12		09 46	09 54	10 00	10 12	10 31
d			08 37		09 13		08 47	08 56	09 01	09 13	09 32			09 55		10 13		09 47	09 55	10 01	10 13	10 32
Pontefract Monkhill 32 d					→									→		→						
Wakefield Kirkgate 32,34,39 a		08 25		08 48		08 57						09 26	09 48				09 56					
d		08 25		08 49		08 58						09 26	09 49				09 56					
Outwood d								09 00		09 18									09 59		10 18	
Leeds 32,34 a		08 46	08 50	09 24		09 17	09 01	09 12	09 15	09 30	09 45	09 46	10 24				10 16	10 00	10 11	10 14	10 30	10 45

A from 23 July until 5 October
B until 20 July, from 8 October

Sheffield, Doncaster and Wakefield - Leeds

Saturdays
26 May to 8 December

	NT	NT	NT	NT	NT	NT	XC	XC	NT	GR	NT	GR	NT	NT	NT	NT	NT	NT	XC	NT	GR	NT
	◇		◇		◇	◇	◇1 A 🚲	◇1 B 🚲	◇	1 ☕	◇	1 ☕	◇		◇			◇	◇1 🚲	◇	1 ☕	
Sheffield 29 d	09 48	10 02		10 05	10 15	10 18	10 21	10 21					10 49	11 02		11 05	11 15	11 18	11 21			
Meadowhall 29 d	09 54	10 08		10 11	10 21	10 24							10 57	11 08		11 11	11 21	11 24				
Rotherham Central 29 d				10 19	10 28											11 19	11 28					
Swinton (S.Yorks) 29 d				10 28	10 38											11 28	11 38					
Bolton-upon-Dearne d					10 43												11 43					
Goldthorpe d					10 46												11 46					
Thurnscoe d					10 49												11 49					
Moorthorpe d					10 55												11 55					
Doncaster d			10 26	10 47						10 42		11 15			11 26	11 47					11 43	
Bentley (S.Yorks) d			10 29	10 51											11 29	11 51						
Adwick a			10 33	10 56											11 33	11 56						
d			10 33												11 33							
South Elmsall d			10 39												11 39							
Fitzwilliam d			10 45		11 01										11 45		12 01					
Sandal & Agbrigg d			10 50		11 08				←		←				11 50		12 08			←		←
Wakefield Westgate 32,39 a			10 54		11 12		10 46	10 46	10 54	11 00	11 12	11 31			11 54		12 12		11 46	11 54	12 00	12 12
d			10 55		11 13		10 47	10 47	10 55	11 01	11 13	11 32			11 55		12 13		11 47	11 55	12 01	12 13
Pontefract Monkhill 32 d			→		→										→		→					
Wakefield Kirkgate 32,34,39 a	10 26	10 48				10 55							11 27	11 48				11 55				
d	10 26	10 49				10 55							11 27	11 49				11 55				
Outwood d									10 59		11 18									11 59		12 18
Leeds 32,34 a	10 46	11 24				11 15	11 00	11 02	11 11	11 14	11 30	11 46	11 47	12 24				12 15	12 00	12 11	12 14	12 30

	NT	GR	NT	GC	NT	NT	NT	NT	XC	NT	GR	NT	NT	GR	NT	NT	NT	NT	NT	XC	XC	NT	GR
	◇	1 ☕		1 ☕	◇		◇	◇	◇1 🚲	◇	1 ☕	◇	◇	1 ☕		◇			◇	◇1 C 🚲	◇1 D	◇	1 ☕
Sheffield 29 d	11 45		12 02			12 05	12 15	12 18	12 21				12 45		13 02		13 05	13 15	13 18	13 21	13 21		
Meadowhall 29 d	11 51		12 08			12 11	12 21	12 24					12 51		13 08		13 11	13 21	13 24				
Rotherham Central 29 d						12 19	12 28										13 19	13 28					
Swinton (S.Yorks) 29 d						12 28	12 38										13 28	13 38					
Bolton-upon-Dearne d							12 43											13 43					
Goldthorpe d							12 46											13 46					
Thurnscoe d							12 49											13 49					
Moorthorpe d							12 55											13 55					
Doncaster d		12 16		12 22	12 26	12 47					12 43			13 16		13 25	13 47						13 43
Bentley (S.Yorks) d					12 29	12 51										13 29	13 51						
Adwick a					12 33	12 56										13 33	13 56						
d					12 33											13 33							
South Elmsall d					12 39											13 39							
Fitzwilliam d					12 45		13 01									13 45		14 01					
Sandal & Agbrigg d					12 50		13 08			←		←				13 50		14 08				←	
Wakefield Westgate 32,39 a		12 32			12 54		13 12		12 46	12 54	13 00	13 12		13 32		13 54		14 12		13 46	13 46	13 54	13 59
d		12 34			12 55		13 13		12 47	12 55	13 01	13 13		13 33		13 55		14 13		13 47	13 47	13 55	14 01
Pontefract Monkhill 32 d					→		→									→		→					
Wakefield Kirkgate 32,34,39 a	12 26		12 48	12 49				12 55					13 26		13 48				13 55				
d	12 26		12 49					12 55					13 27		13 49				13 55				
Outwood d										12 59		13 18										13 59	
Leeds 32,34 a	12 46	12 47	13 24					13 15	13 00	13 11	13 14	13 30	13 46	13 47	14 24				14 15	14 00	14 00	14 11	14 14

	NT	NT	GR	NT	NT	NT	NT	NT	XC	NT	GR	NT	GR	NT	NT	NT	NT	NT	NT	XC	XC	NT
		◇	1 ☕		◇		◇	◇	◇1 🚲	◇	1 ☕	◇	1 ☕	◇		◇			◇	◇1 C 🚲	◇1 D	◇
Sheffield 29 d		13 45		14 02		14 05	14 15	14 18	14 21					14 45	15 02		15 05	15 15	15 18	15 21	15 21	
Meadowhall 29 d		13 51		14 08		14 11	14 21	14 24						14 51	15 08		15 11	15 21	15 24			
Rotherham Central 29 d						14 19	14 28										15 19	15 28				
Swinton (S.Yorks) 29 d						14 28	14 38										15 28	15 38				
Bolton-upon-Dearne d							14 43											15 43				
Goldthorpe d							14 46											15 46				
Thurnscoe d							14 49											15 49				
Moorthorpe d							14 55											15 55				
Doncaster d			14 15		14 26	14 47					14 43		15 14			15 26	15 47					
Bentley (S.Yorks) d					14 29	14 51										15 29	15 51					
Adwick a					14 33	14 56										15 33	15 56					
d					14 33											15 33						
South Elmsall d					14 39											15 39						
Fitzwilliam d					14 45		15 01									15 45		16 01				
Sandal & Agbrigg d	←				14 50		15 08			←		←				15 50		16 08				←
Wakefield Westgate 32,39 a	14 12		14 31		14 54		15 12		14 46	14 54	14 59	15 12	15 30			15 54		16 12		15 46	15 46	15 54
d	14 13		14 32		14 55		15 13		14 47	14 55	15 01	15 13	15 31			15 55		16 13		15 47	15 47	15 55
Pontefract Monkhill 32 d					→		→									→		→				
Wakefield Kirkgate 32,34,39 a		14 26		14 48				14 55						15 26	15 48				15 55			
d		14 27		14 49				14 55						15 27	15 49				15 55			
Outwood d	14 18									14 59		15 18										15 59
Leeds 32,34 a	14 30	14 46	14 46	15 24				15 15	15 00	15 11	15 14	15 30	15 45	15 46	16 24				16 15	16 00	16 00	16 11

A until 1 September, from 13 October
B from 8 September until 6 October
C until 21 July, from 13 October
D from 28 July until 6 October

Sheffield, Doncaster and Wakefield - Leeds

Saturdays
26 May to 8 December

Station			GR	NT	NT	GR	NT	NT	NT	NT	NT	XC	NT	GR	NT	NT	GR	GC	NT	NT	NT	NT	NT	XC
			■ ☕		◇	■ ☕		◇		◇	◇	◇■ 🍴	◇	■ ☕	◇	◇	■ ☕	■ ☕		◇			◇	◇■ A 🍴
Sheffield	29	d			15 45		16 02		16 05	16 15	16 18	16 21				16 45			17 02		17 05	17 15	17 18	17 21
Meadowhall	29	d			15 51		16 08		16 11	16 21	16 24					16 51			17 08		17 11	17 21	17 24	
Rotherham Central	29	d							16 19	16 28											17 19	17 28		
Swinton (S.Yorks)	29	d							16 28	16 38											17 28	17 38		
Bolton-upon-Dearne		d								16 43												17 43		
Goldthorpe		d								16 46												17 46		
Thurnscoe		d								16 49												17 49		
Moorthorpe		d								16 55												17 55		
Doncaster		d	15 43			16 15		16 26	16 47					16 44			17 16	17 22		17 26	17 48			
Bentley (S.Yorks)		d						16 29	16 51											17 29	17 52			
Adwick		a						16 33	16 56											17 33	17 57			
		d						16 33												17 33				
South Elmsall		d						16 39												17 39				
Fitzwilliam		d						16 45		17 01										17 45		18 01		
Sandal & Agbrigg		d		←				16 50		17 08			←		←					17 50		18 08		
Wakefield Westgate	32,39	a	15 59	16 12		16 32		16 54		17 14		16 46	16 54	17 00	17 14		17 34			17 54		18 12		17 45
		d	16 01	16 13		16 33		16 55		17 15		16 47	16 55	17 01	17 15		17 35			17 55		18 12		17 48
Pontefract Monkhill	32	d						→		→										→		→		
Wakefield Kirkgate	32,34,39	a			16 26		16 48				16 55					17 26		17 44	17 48				17 55	
		d			16 26		16 49				16 55					17 27			17 49				17 55	
Outwood		d		16 18									16 59		17 20									
Leeds	32,34	a	16 14	16 30	16 46	16 46	17 24				17 15	17 00	17 12	17 14	17 32	17 46	17 48		18 24				18 15	18 01

Station			XC	NT	GR	NT	GC	NT	XC	XC	GR	NT	NT	NT	NT	NT	XC	NT	GR	NT	NT	GR	NT	NT	NT
			◇■ B 🍴	◇	■ ☕		■ ☕	◇	◇■ A 🍴	◇■ B 🍴	■ ☕		◇		◇	◇	◇■ 🍴	◇	■ ☕	◇	◇	■ ☕		◇	
Sheffield	29	d	17 21					17 45	17 48	17 50		18 02		18 05	18 15	18 18	18 21				18 45		19 02		19 05
Meadowhall	29	d						17 51				18 08		18 11	18 21	18 24					18 51		19 08		19 11
Rotherham Central	29	d												18 18	18 28										19 19
Swinton (S.Yorks)	29	d												18 27	18 38										19 28
Bolton-upon-Dearne		d													18 43										
Goldthorpe		d													18 46										
Thurnscoe		d													18 49										
Moorthorpe		d													18 55										
Doncaster		d			17 43		18 05				18 20		18 28	18 48					18 43			19 16		19 28	19 54
Bentley (S.Yorks)		d											18 31	18 52										19 31	19 58
Adwick		a											18 35	18 57										19 35	20 03
		d											18 35											19 35	
South Elmsall		d											18 40											19 40	
Fitzwilliam		d											18 46		19 01									19 45	
Sandal & Agbrigg		d		←		←							18 51		19 08			←		←				19 51	
Wakefield Westgate	32,39	a	17 47	17 54	17 59	18 12			18 16	18 16	18 36		18 55		19 13		18 49	18 55	19 00	19 13		19 32		19 55	
		d	17 48	17 55	18 01	18 12			18 17	18 17	18 38		18 56		19 13		18 50	18 56	19 01	19 13		19 33		19 55	
Pontefract Monkhill	32	d											→		→									→	
Wakefield Kirkgate	32,34,39	a					18 26	18 27				18 48				18 55					19 26		19 48		
		d						18 27				18 49				18 55					19 26		19 49		
Outwood		d		17 59		18 17												19 00		19 18					
Leeds	32,34	a	18 01	18 12	18 14	18 30		18 47	18 33	18 33	18 51	19 24				19 15	19 03	19 14	19 15	19 30	19 46	19 46	20 24		

Station			NT	NT	XC	NT	GR	NT	GR	NT	GR	NT	NT	NT	NT	NT	XC	XC	NT	GR	NT	GR	NT	NT
				◇	◇■ 🍴	◇	■ ☕		■ ☕	◇	■ ☕		◇		◇	◇	◇■ A 🍴	◇■ B 🍴	◇	■ ☕	◇	■ ☕	◇	
Sheffield	29	d	19 15	19 18	19 21					19 45		20 02		20 05	20 15	20 18	20 21	20 21					20 45	21 02
Meadowhall	29	d	19 21	19 24						19 51		20 08		20 11	20 21	20 24							20 51	21 08
Rotherham Central	29	d	19 28											20 19	20 28									
Swinton (S.Yorks)	29	d	19 38											20 28	20 38									
Bolton-upon-Dearne		d	19 43												20 43									
Goldthorpe		d	19 46												20 46									
Thurnscoe		d	19 49												20 49									
Moorthorpe		d	19 55												20 55									
Doncaster		d					19 50		20 07		20 22		20 28	20 48						20 42		21 14		
Bentley (S.Yorks)		d											20 31	20 52										
Adwick		a											20 35	20 57										
		d											20 35											
South Elmsall		d											20 40											
Fitzwilliam		d	20 07										20 45		21 01									
Sandal & Agbrigg		d	20 14			←		←					20 51		21 08				←		←			
Wakefield Westgate	32,39	a	20 18		19 46	19 55	20 06	20 18	20 23		20 39		20 55		21 13		20 46	20 47	20 55	20 59	21 13	21 30		
		d	20 19		19 47	19 55	20 07	20 19	20 25		20 40		20 55		21 14		20 48	20 48	20 55	21 01	21 14	21 31		
Pontefract Monkhill	32	d	→										→		→									
Wakefield Kirkgate	32,34,39	a		19 55						20 26		20 48				20 55							21 26	21 48
		d		19 55						20 26		20 49				20 55							21 26	21 49
Outwood		d				20 00		20 24											21 00		21 19			
Leeds	32,34	a		20 15	20 02	20 13	20 20	20 36	20 39	20 46	20 54	21 24				21 15	21 01	21 02	21 13	21 14	21 30	21 45	21 46	22 24

A from 28 July until 6 October
B until 21 July, from 13 October

Table T031-F

Sheffield, Doncaster and Wakefield - Leeds

Saturdays
26 May to 8 December

Station			NT	GC	NT	NT	NT	XC	XC	NT	EM	GR	NT	GR	NT	NT	NT	NT	EM	NT	NT	XC	NT	XC
			◇	■ ☕			◇	◇■ A	◇■ B	◇	◇■ 🍴	■ ☕		■ ☕	◇		◇	◇	◇■ 🍴	◇	◇	◇■ B		◇■ A
Sheffield	29	d			21 05	21 15	21 18	21 21	21 21		21 24					22 07	22 15	22 18	22 21			22 24	22 31	22 42
Meadowhall	29	d			21 11	21 21	21 24									22 13	22 21	22 24					22 37	
Rotherham Central	29	d			21 20	21 28										22 19	22 28							
Swinton (S.Yorks)	29	d			21 28	21 38										22 29	22 41							
Bolton-upon-Dearne		d				21 43											22 45							
Goldthorpe		d				21 46											22 48							
Thurnscoe		d				21 49											22 51							
Moorthorpe		d				21 55											22 57							
Doncaster		d	21 28	21 34	21 55							21 45		22 23	22 32	22 47						22 56		23 04
Bentley (S.Yorks)		d	21 31		21 59										22 35	22 50								
Adwick		a	21 35		22 04										22 39	22 55								
		d	21 35												22 39									
South Elmsall		d	21 40												22 45									
Fitzwilliam		d	21 45			22 01									22 51									
Sandal & Agbrigg		d	21 51			22 08				←			←		22 56					←	←			
Wakefield Westgate	32,39	a	21 55			22 12		21 46	21 47	21 55	21 57	22 05	22 12	22 40	23 00		23 09		22 48	23 00	23 09	23 12		23 22
		d	21 55			22 12		21 48	21 48	21 55	21 58	22 06	22 12	22 41	23 01		23 09		22 49	23 01	23 09	23 13		23 23
Pontefract Monkhill	32	d	→	22 03		→									→		→							
Wakefield Kirkgate	32,34,39	a		22 20			21 55											22 55					23 16	
		d					21 55											22 55					23 17	
Outwood		d								22 00			22 18							23 05				
Leeds	32,34	a					22 15	22 02	22 03	22 12	22 17	22 19	22 30	22 55				23 14	23 06	23 18	23 25	23 27	23 53	23 37

Station			NT	GR
				■ ☕
Sheffield	29	d		
Meadowhall	29	d		
Rotherham Central	29	d		
Swinton (S.Yorks)	29	d		
Bolton-upon-Dearne		d		
Goldthorpe		d		
Thurnscoe		d		
Moorthorpe		d		
Doncaster		d	23 24	23 50
Bentley (S.Yorks)		d	23 27	
Adwick		a	23 31	
		d	23 31	
South Elmsall		d	23 36	
Fitzwilliam		d	23 41	
Sandal & Agbrigg		d	23 47	
Wakefield Westgate	32,39	a	23 51	00 06
		d	23 51	00 07
Pontefract Monkhill	32	d		
Wakefield Kirkgate	32,34,39	a		
		d		
Outwood		d	23 57	
Leeds	32,34	a	00 09	00 20

Sundays
20 May to 2 December

Station			GR	NT	NT	XC	NT	NT	NT	XC	GR	NT	NT	XC	NT	GR	NT	NT	XC	GR	NT	XC	GC	NT	XC
			■ C ☕		◇	◇■ 🍴	◇		◇	◇■ 🍴	■ ☕		◇	◇■ 🍴	◇	■ ☕		◇	◇■ 🍴	■ ☕		◇■ D 🍴	■ ☕	◇	◇■ E 🍴
Sheffield	29	d		08 39	09 17	09 21		09 35	10 17	10 21		10 51	11 16	11 21			11 24	12 16	12 21		12 44	12 51		13 17	13 21
Meadowhall	29	d		08 45	09 23			09 41	10 23			10 57	11 22				11 30	12 23			12 50			13 23	
Rotherham Central	29	d						09 47									11 40								
Swinton (S.Yorks)	29	d						09 55									11 51								
Bolton-upon-Dearne		d						10 00									11 56								
Goldthorpe		d						10 02									11 58								
Thurnscoe		d						10 05									12 01								
Moorthorpe		d						10 10									12 06								
Doncaster		d					09 25				10 52				11 25	11 55				12 52		13 14	13 21		
Bentley (S.Yorks)		d					09 28								11 28										
Adwick		a					09 32								11 32										
		d					09 32								11 32										
South Elmsall		d					09 38								11 38										
Fitzwilliam		d					09 45	10 17							11 44		12 13								
Sandal & Agbrigg		d					09 51	10 23							11 50		12 19								
Wakefield Westgate	32,39	a				09 45	09 55	10 27		10 45	11 08			11 45	11 54	12 11	12 23		12 45	13 08		13 30			13 44
		d	00 07			09 47	09 55	10 27		10 46	11 10			11 46	11 55	12 12	12 23		12 46	13 10		13 32			13 46
Pontefract Monkhill	32	d																							
Wakefield Kirkgate	32,34,39	a		09 22	09 57				10 52			11 31	11 51					12 58			13 28		13 44	13 52	
		d		09 23	09 59				10 53			11 32	11 52					12 58			13 29			13 53	
Outwood		d					10 00	10 32							12 00		12 28								
Leeds	32,34	a	00 20	09 56	10 24	10 02	10 13	10 47	11 12	10 59	11 24	12 08	12 11	11 59	12 13	12 26	12 41	13 22	13 00	13 24	14 04	13 46		14 18	14 00

A from 28 July until 6 October
B until 21 July, from 13 October
C not 20 May
D from 22 July until 7 October
E until 15 July, from 14 October

20 May to 2 December

Sheffield, Doncaster and Wakefield - Leeds

		NT	GR	NT	GR	XC	NT	XC	GR	NT	XC	NT	XC	NT	GR	GR	NT	XC	XC	NT	XC	GR	NT	XC
		◇				◇ A	◇	◇ B			◇ A	◇	◇ B	◇				◇ C	◇ D	◇	◇ B			◇ E
Sheffield 29	d			13 31		13 52	14 17	14 21		14 44	14 54	15 17	15 21				15 31	15 52	15 52	16 17	16 21		16 44	16 52
Meadowhall 29	d			13 37			14 23			14 50		15 23					15 37			16 23			16 50	
Rotherham Central 29	d			13 43													15 43							
Swinton (S.Yorks) 29	d			13 51													15 51							
Bolton-upon-Dearne	d			13 56													15 56							
Goldthorpe	d			13 58													15 58							
Thurnscoe	d			14 01													16 01							
Moorthorpe	d			14 06													16 09							
Doncaster	d	13 25	13 48		14 20	14 25			14 54		15 19			15 25	15 36	15 50		16 21	16 21			16 58		17 18
Bentley (S.Yorks)	d	13 28												15 28										
Adwick	a	13 32												15 32										
	d	13 32												15 32										
South Elmsall	d	13 38												15 38										
Fitzwilliam	d	13 44		14 13										15 45			16 15							
Sandal & Agbrigg	d	13 50		14 19										15 51			16 21							
Wakefield Westgate 32,39	a	13 54	14 04	14 23	14 36	14 44		14 45	15 10		15 35		15 45	15 55	16 00	16 06	16 25	16 40	16 40		16 45	17 14		17 33
	d	13 55	14 05	14 23	14 38	14 45		14 47	15 11		15 36		15 47	15 56	16 02	16 08	16 26	16 46	16 46		16 46	17 15		17 36
Pontefract Monkhill 32	d																							
Wakefield Kirkgate 32,34,39	a						14 52			15 28		15 52								16 53			17 28	
	d						14 53			15 29		15 55								16 54			17 29	
Outwood	d	14 00		14 28										16 01			16 31							
Leeds 32,34	a	14 14	14 18	14 43	14 52	14 59	15 17	15 00	15 24	16 04	15 53	16 15	16 00	16 14	16 16	16 21	16 44	16 59	17 00	17 17	16 59	17 28	18 04	17 54

		XC	GC	NT	XC	NT	NT	EM	GR	NT	XC	GR	XC	NT	XC	GR	GR	NT	XC	NT	XC	NT	GR
		◇ F		◇	◇ B	◇		◇ G			◇ B		◇ A	◇	◇ B				◇ A	◇	◇ B	◇	
Sheffield 29	d	16 52		17 18	17 21		17 31	17 34			17 52		17 52	18 17	18 21			18 45	18 52	19 17	19 20		
Meadowhall 29	d			17 23			17 37							18 23				18 51		19 23			
Rotherham Central 29	d						17 43																
Swinton (S.Yorks) 29	d						17 52																
Bolton-upon-Dearne	d						17 57																
Goldthorpe	d						18 00																
Thurnscoe	d						18 03																
Moorthorpe	d						18 08																
Doncaster	d	17 18	17 22			17 26			17 52		18 17	18 21	18 25			18 45	19 16		19 21			19 29	19 50
Bentley (S.Yorks)	d					17 29																19 32	
Adwick	a					17 33																19 36	
	d					17 33																19 36	
South Elmsall	d					17 39																19 42	
Fitzwilliam	d					17 45	18 14															19 47	
Sandal & Agbrigg	d					17 51	18 20			←												19 53	
Wakefield Westgate 32,39	a	17 33			17 44	17 55	18 24	18 00	18 08	18 24	18 32	18 37	18 43		18 45	19 03	19 32		19 38		19 49	19 57	20 06
	d	17 36			17 45	17 56	18 25	18 01	18 10	18 25	18 33	18 39	18 45		18 47	19 04	19 34		19 43		19 51	19 57	20 08
Pontefract Monkhill 32	d						→																
Wakefield Kirkgate 32,34,39	a		17 49	17 52										18 52				19 28		19 52			
	d			17 53										18 53				19 29		19 53			
Outwood	d					18 01				18 30												20 02	
Leeds 32,34	a	17 54		18 17	18 00	18 14		18 15	18 24	18 44	18 47	18 53	18 59	19 15	19 01	19 19	19 47	20 04	19 57	20 15	20 04	20 15	20 21

		NT	XC	GR	NT	XC	GC	GR	XC	GC	EM	GR	NT	XC	GR	NT	XC	NT	GR	XC	NT	XC	GR	NT
			◇ A		◇	◇ B			◇ A		◇		◇	◇ B		◇	◇ A	◇		◇ B		◇ A		◇
Sheffield 29	d	19 31	19 53		20 17	20 22			20 40		21 03		21 17	21 21		21 31	21 41			22 21		22 39		22 44
Meadowhall 29	d	19 37			20 23								21 23			21 37								22 50
Rotherham Central 29	d	19 43														21 49								
Swinton (S.Yorks) 29	d	19 51														21 57								
Bolton-upon-Dearne	d	19 56														22 01								
Goldthorpe	d	19 58														22 04								
Thurnscoe	d	20 01														22 07								
Moorthorpe	d	20 06														22 12								
Doncaster	d		20 15	20 20			20 26	20 44		21 00		21 21			21 48				22 24		22 29		22 50	
Bentley (S.Yorks)	d																				22 32			
Adwick	a																				22 36			
	d																				22 36			
South Elmsall	d																				22 42			
Fitzwilliam	d	20 13														22 18					22 47			
Sandal & Agbrigg	d	20 19														22 24		←			22 53			
Wakefield Westgate 32,39	a	20 23	20 32	20 38		20 45		21 02	21 07		21 32	21 37		21 48	22 05	22 28	22 09	22 28	22 40	22 47	22 57	23 02	23 08	
	d	20 25	20 33	20 39		20 48		21 03	21 08		21 33	21 39		21 49	22 06	22 29	22 10	22 29	22 41	22 47	22 57	23 03	23 10	
Pontefract Monkhill 32	d															→								
Wakefield Kirkgate 32,34,39	a				20 52		20 55			21 23			21 52											23 31
	d				20 53								21 53											23 32
Outwood	d	20 30																22 34			23 02			
Leeds 32,34	a	20 44	20 47	20 52	21 14	21 02		21 17	21 22		21 49	21 52	22 14	22 02	22 19		22 24	22 47	22 55	23 02	23 15	23 17	23 24	00 07

A from 22 July until 7 October
B until 15 July, from 14 October
C from 22 July until 2 September
D from 9 September until 7 October
E from 22 July until 9 September
F from 16 September until 7 October
G not 26 August

20 May to 2 December

Sheffield, Doncaster and Wakefield - Leeds

		EM	GR
		◇	
Sheffield 29	d	23 26	
Meadowhall 29	d		
Rotherham Central 29	d		
Swinton (S.Yorks) 29	d		
Bolton-upon-Dearne	d		
Goldthorpe	d		
Thurnscoe	d		
Moorthorpe	d		
Doncaster	d		23 37
Bentley (S.Yorks)	d		
Adwick	a		
	d		
South Elmsall	d		
Fitzwilliam	d		
Sandal & Agbrigg	d		
Wakefield Westgate 32,39	a	23 52	23 57
	d	23 53	23 59
Pontefract Monkhill 32	d		
Wakefield Kirkgate 32,34,39	a		
	d		
Outwood	d		
Leeds 32,34	a	00 08	00 12

Table T031-R

Mondays to Fridays

21 May to 7 December

Leeds - Wakefield, Doncaster and Sheffield

Miles	Miles	Station		NT MX	GR	EM	GR	NT	XC	NT	GR	XC	XC	XC	NT	NT	NT	EM	EM	NT	NT	GR	NT	GR
									A			B	A	B				C	D					E
0	0	Leeds 32,34	d		05 05	05 19	05 30	05 34	05 48	05 55	06 05	06 11	06 16	06 16		06 25	06 30	06 33	06 33	06 39		06 40	06 47	07 00
7½	7½	Outwood	d					05 45								06 34					←		06 58	
—	—	Wakefield Kirkgate 32,34,39	a							06 28							07 01			06 55	07 01			
—	—		d							06 28							07 01			06 56	07 01			
—	—	Pontefract Monkhill	d														→							
10	10	Wakefield Westgate 32,39	a		05 17	05 31	05 42	05 49	06 00		06 17	06 22	06 27	06 27		06 38		06 44	06 45			06 52	07 02	07 12
—	—		d		05 18	05 32	05 43	05 50	06 01		06 18	06 23	06 28	06 28		06 38		06 47	06 47			06 53	07 02	
11¾	11¾	Sandal & Agbrigg	d					05 53								06 41							07 06	
16½	16½	Fitzwilliam	d					06 01								06 48							07 13	
21	—	South Elmsall	d													06 53								
25¾	—	Adwick	a													06 58								
—	—		d	00 05											06 47	06 59								
28	—	Bentley (S.Yorks)	d	00 09											06 51	07 03								
29¾	—	Doncaster	a	00 16	05 35	05 55	06 00				06 35		06 44	06 45	06 56	07 10						07 12		
—	20¾	Moorthorpe	d					06 15															07 19	
—	23¾	Thurnscoe	d					06 21															07 25	
—	24½	Goldthorpe	d					06 23															07 27	
—	25¾	Bolton-upon-Dearne	d					06 26															07 30	
—	28	Swinton (S.Yorks) 29	a					06 31							07 13								07 34	
—	32½	Rotherham Central 29	a					06 40							07 21								07 43	
—	35¼	Meadowhall 29	a					06 50		07 07					07 27					07 27	07 42		07 49	
—	38¾	Sheffield 29	a			06 23		06 59	06 29	07 16		06 51	07 12	07 12	07 38			07 21	07 22	07 35	07 54		07 57	

Station		NT	XC	XC	NT	GR	NT	NT	GC	NT	NT	NT	NT	GR	NT	NT	XC	NT	GR	NT	NT	GC	NT
			A	B																			
Leeds 32,34	d	07 03	07 10	07 10		07 15		07 22		07 30	07 38			07 40	07 48	08 04	08 11		08 15		08 22		08 30
Outwood	d							07 31					←		07 59						08 31		
Wakefield Kirkgate 32,34,39	a	07 21								08 01	07 54		08 01			08 21							09 01
	d	07 22							07 42	08 01	07 55		08 01			08 22						08 55	09 01
Pontefract Monkhill	d								08 00	→													→
Wakefield Westgate 32,39	a		07 21	07 22		07 27		07 35						07 52	08 03		08 22		08 28		08 35		
	d		07 23	07 23		07 28		07 35						07 53	08 03		08 23		08 30		08 35		
Sandal & Agbrigg	d							07 38							08 07						08 38		
Fitzwilliam	d							07 45							08 14						08 46		
South Elmsall	d							07 50													08 51		
Adwick	a							07 55													08 56		
	d				07 16		07 49	07 56										08 21		08 52	08 57		
Bentley (S.Yorks)	d				07 20		07 53	08 00										08 25		08 56	09 01		
Doncaster	a				07 25	07 45	07 58	08 07	08 28					08 11				08 30	08 47	09 02	09 07	09 24	
Moorthorpe	d														08 20								
Thurnscoe	d														08 26								
Goldthorpe	d														08 29								
Bolton-upon-Dearne	d														08 32								
Swinton (S.Yorks) 29	a				07 41		08 20								08 36			08 47		09 20			
Rotherham Central 29	a				07 48		08 28					←			08 44			08 55		09 28			
Meadowhall 29	a	07 52			08 02		08 34				08 27	08 34	08 42		08 50	08 52		09 05		09 34			
Sheffield 29	a	08 00	07 51	07 51	08 11		→				08 35	08 44	08 57		09 00	09 03	08 54	09 14		→			

Station		NT	NT	NT	GR	NT	NT	XC	NT	GR	NT	NT	NT	NT	GR	NT	NT	XC	NT	GR	NT	NT	NT	NT
Leeds 32,34	d	08 38			08 45	08 48	09 04	09 11		09 16	09 22	09 29	09 38		09 45	09 48	10 04	10 11		10 15	10 21		10 30	10 38
Outwood	d			←		08 59					09 31			←		09 59					10 30			
Wakefield Kirkgate 32,34,39	a	08 54		09 01			09 21					10 00	09 54	10 00			10 21						11 01	10 54
	d	08 55		09 01			09 22					10 00	09 55	10 00			10 22						11 01	10 55
Pontefract Monkhill	d											→											→	
Wakefield Westgate 32,39	a				08 57	09 03		09 22		09 28	09 35				09 57	10 03		10 22		10 27	10 34			
	d				08 58	09 03		09 23		09 29	09 35				09 58	10 03		10 23		10 28	10 34			
Sandal & Agbrigg	d					09 07					09 38					10 07					10 37			
Fitzwilliam	d					09 14					09 45					10 14					10 44			
South Elmsall	d										09 50										10 50			
Adwick	a										09 56										10 55			
	d								09 25		09 56								10 24		10 56			
Bentley (S.Yorks)	d								09 29		10 00								10 28		11 00			
Doncaster	a				09 16				09 34	09 46	10 06				10 16				10 33	10 45	11 06			
Moorthorpe	d					09 20										10 20						11 01		
Thurnscoe	d					09 26										10 26								
Goldthorpe	d					09 29										10 29								
Bolton-upon-Dearne	d					09 32										10 32								
Swinton (S.Yorks) 29	a					09 36			09 50							10 36			10 50			11 10		
Rotherham Central 29	a		←			09 44			09 57							10 44			10 57			11 18		
Meadowhall 29	a	09 27	09 34	09 41		09 50	09 52		10 05				10 28	10 42		10 50	10 52		11 05			11 24		11 26
Sheffield 29	a	09 35	09 44	09 50		09 58	10 02	09 53	10 14				10 35	10 52		10 58	11 02	10 54	11 14			11 31		11 34

A from 23 July until 5 October
B until 20 July, from 8 October
C until 27 July, from 8 October
D from 30 July until 5 October
E West Riding Limited

Table T031-R

Mondays to Fridays

21 May to 7 December

Leeds - Wakefield, Doncaster and Sheffield

Station		NT	GR	NT	GC	NT	XC	NT	GR	NT	NT	NT	NT	GR	NT	NT	XC	NT	GR	NT	NT	NT	NT	GR
Leeds 32,34	d		10 45	10 48		11 04	11 11		11 15	11 21	11 30	11 38		11 45	11 48	12 04	12 11		12 15	12 21	12 30	12 38		12 45
Outwood	d	←		10 59						11 30			←		11 59					12 30			←	
Wakefield Kirkgate 32,34,39	a	11 01				11 21					12 01	11 54	12 01			12 21					13 01	12 54	13 01	
	d	11 01			11 14	11 22					12 01	11 55	12 01			12 22					13 01	12 55	13 01	
Pontefract Monkhill	d				11 34						→										→			
Wakefield Westgate 32,39	a		10 57	11 03			11 22		11 27	11 34				11 57	12 03		12 22		12 27	12 34				12 57
	d		10 58	11 03			11 23		11 28	11 34				11 58	12 03		12 23		12 28	12 34				12 58
Sandal & Agbrigg	d			11 07						11 37					12 07					12 37				
Fitzwilliam	d			11 14						11 44					12 14					12 44				
South Elmsall	d									11 50										12 50				
Adwick	a									11 55										12 55				
	d							11 24		11 56								12 24		12 56				
Bentley (S.Yorks)	d							11 28		12 00								12 28		13 00				
Doncaster	a		11 15		12 04			11 33	11 45	12 06				12 15				12 33	12 45	13 06				13 16
Moorthorpe	d			11 20											12 20									
Thurnscoe	d			11 26											12 26									
Goldthorpe	d			11 29											12 29									
Bolton-upon-Dearne	d			11 32											12 32									
Swinton (S.Yorks) 29	a			11 36				11 50							12 36			12 50						
Rotherham Central 29	a			11 44				11 57							12 44			12 57						
Meadowhall 29	a	11 41		11 50		11 52		12 05				12 27	12 41		12 50	12 52		13 05				13 26	13 41	
Sheffield 29	a	11 50		11 58		12 02	11 53	12 14				12 35	12 50		12 58	13 02	12 53	13 14				13 34	13 50	

Station		NT	NT	XC	NT	GR	NT	NT	NT	NT	NT	GR	NT	NT	XC	NT	GR	NT	NT	NT	NT	GR	NT
Leeds 32,34	d	12 48	13 04	13 11		13 15	13 21		13 30	13 38		13 45	13 48	14 04	14 11		14 15	14 21	14 30	14 38		14 45	14 48
Outwood	d	12 59					13 30				←		13 59					14 30			←		14 59
Wakefield Kirkgate 32,34,39	a		13 23						14 01	13 54	14 01			14 21					15 01	14 54	15 01		
	d		13 23						14 01	13 55	14 01			14 22					15 01	14 55	15 01		
Pontefract Monkhill	d								→										→				
Wakefield Westgate 32,39	a	13 03		13 22		13 27	13 34					13 57	14 03		14 22		14 27	14 34				14 57	15 03
	d	13 03		13 23		13 28	13 34					13 58	14 03		14 23		14 28	14 35				14 58	15 03
Sandal & Agbrigg	d	13 07					13 37						14 07					14 38					15 07
Fitzwilliam	d	13 14					13 44						14 14					14 45					15 14
South Elmsall	d						13 50											14 50					
Adwick	a						13 55											14 55					
	d				13 24		13 56									14 24		14 56					
Bentley (S.Yorks)	d				13 28		14 00									14 28		15 00					
Doncaster	a				13 33	13 45	14 06					14 15				14 33	14 45	15 06				15 15	
Moorthorpe	d	13 20						13 59					14 20										15 20
Thurnscoe	d	13 26											14 26										15 26
Goldthorpe	d	13 29											14 29										15 29
Bolton-upon-Dearne	d	13 32											14 32										15 32
Swinton (S.Yorks) 29	a	13 36			13 50			14 10					14 36			14 50							15 36
Rotherham Central 29	a	13 44			13 57			14 18					14 44			14 57							15 44
Meadowhall 29	a	13 50	13 53		14 05			14 24		14 27	14 41		14 50	14 52		15 05				15 27	15 41		15 50
Sheffield 29	a	13 58	14 02	13 53	14 14			14 31		14 35	14 50		14 58	15 02	14 54	15 14				15 35	15 50		15 58

Station		NT	XC	NT	GR	NT	GC	NT	NT	NT	GR	NT	NT	XC	NT	GR	NT	NT	NT	XC	NT	GR	NT	NT
														A										
Leeds 32,34	d	15 04	15 11		15 15	15 21		15 30	15 38		15 45	15 48	16 04	16 11		16 15	16 21	16 29	16 38	16 40		16 45	16 48	17 03
Outwood	d					15 30				←		15 59					16 30				←		17 00	
Wakefield Kirkgate 32,34,39	a	15 21						16 01	15 54	16 01			16 21					17 01	16 54		17 01			17 22
	d	15 22					15 39	16 01	15 55	16 01			16 22					17 01	16 55		17 01			17 22
Pontefract Monkhill	d						15 55	→										→						
Wakefield Westgate 32,39	a		15 22		15 27	15 34					15 57	16 03		16 22		16 27	16 34			16 51		16 57	17 04	
	d		15 23		15 28	15 35					15 58	16 03		16 23		16 28	16 34			16 52		16 58	17 04	
Sandal & Agbrigg	d					15 38						16 07					16 37						17 08	
Fitzwilliam	d					15 45						16 14					16 44						17 14	
South Elmsall	d					15 50											16 49							
Adwick	a					15 55											16 54							
	d			15 24		15 56									16 24		16 55							
Bentley (S.Yorks)	d			15 28		16 00									16 28		16 59							
Doncaster	a			15 33	15 45	16 06	16 17				16 15				16 33	16 45	17 06					17 16		
Moorthorpe	d											16 20											17 20	
Thurnscoe	d											16 26											17 26	
Goldthorpe	d											16 29											17 28	
Bolton-upon-Dearne	d											16 32											17 31	
Swinton (S.Yorks) 29	a			15 50								16 36			16 50								17 35	
Rotherham Central 29	a			15 57								16 44			16 57								17 44	
Meadowhall 29	a	15 52		16 05					16 27	16 41		16 50	16 52		17 05				17 26		17 41		17 50	17 53
Sheffield 29	a	16 02	15 54	16 14					16 35	16 50		16 58	17 02	16 53	17 14				17 34	17 20	17 50		17 58	18 02

A until 11 October, FX from 15 October

Table T031-R

Mondays to Fridays
21 May to 7 December

Leeds - Wakefield, Doncaster and Sheffield

	XC	NT	GR	NT	NT	NT	NT	GR	NT	NT	NT		NT	XC	XC	NT	GR	NT	NT	NT	NT	NT	GR	NT
	◇■		■	◇		◇		■			◇		◇	◇■ A	◇■ B		■	◇ C	◇ D		◇		■	◇
Leeds 32,34 d	17 10		17 14	17 22	17 30	17 38		17 45	17 48		17 57		18 03	18 11	18 11		18 15	18 23	18 23	18 30	18 38		18 45	18 48
Outwood d				17 31			←		17 59		18 06							18 32	18 32			←		18 59
Wakefield Kirkgate 32,34,39 a					18 01	17 54	18 01						18 20							19 01	18 55	19 01		
d					18 01	17 55	18 01						18 21							19 01	18 56	19 01		
Pontefract Monkhill d					→															→				
Wakefield Westgate 32,39 a	17 21		17 26	17 35				17 57	18 03		18 10			18 22	18 22		18 27	18 36	18 36				18 57	19 03
d	17 22		17 27	17 35				17 58	18 03		18 10			18 23	18 23		18 28	18 36	18 36				18 58	19 03
Sandal & Agbrigg d				17 38					18 07		18 13							18 39	18 39					19 07
Fitzwilliam d				17 45					18 14		18 20							18 46	18 47					19 14
South Elmsall d				17 50							18 25							18 51	18 53					
Adwick a				17 55							18 30							18 56	18 58					
d		17 24		17 56						18 24	18 31							18 57	18 59					
Bentley (S.Yorks) d		17 28		18 00						18 28	18 35							19 01	19 03					
Doncaster a		17 33	17 44	18 09				18 15		18 33	18 42						18 45	19 08	19 10				19 17	
Moorthorpe d									18 20															19 20
Thurnscoe d									18 26															19 26
Goldthorpe d									18 29															19 29
Bolton-upon-Dearne d									18 32															19 32
Swinton (S.Yorks) 29 a		17 50							18 36	18 50														19 36
Rotherham Central 29 a		17 57							18 44	18 57						←								19 44
Meadowhall 29 a		18 05				18 27	18 41		18 50	19 05			18 51			19 05					19 26	19 41		19 50
Sheffield 29 a	17 52	18 14				18 35	18 50		18 58	→			19 00	18 51	18 54	19 14					19 35	19 50		19 58

	NT	XC	NT		GR	NT	NT	GR	NT	NT	XC	XC	NT	NT	NT	GR	NT	NT	XC		NT	NT	NT	NT
	◇	◇■			■	◇		■		◇	◇■ E	◇■ F		◇		■	◇	◇	◇■			◇		
Leeds 32,34 d	19 03	19 11			19 16	19 22	19 30	19 45	19 48	20 03	20 11	20 11		20 23	20 30	20 45	20 48	21 03	21 11			21 22	21 30	21 48
Outwood d						19 31			19 59					20 32			20 59					21 31		21 59
Wakefield Kirkgate 32,34,39 a	19 20						20 01			20 20					21 01			21 20					22 01	
d	19 21						20 01			20 21					21 01			21 21					22 01	
Pontefract Monkhill d																								
Wakefield Westgate 32,39 a		19 22			19 28	19 35		19 57	20 03		20 22	20 22		20 36		20 57	21 03		21 22			21 35		22 03
d		19 23			19 29	19 35		19 58	20 03		20 23	20 23		20 36		20 58	21 03		21 23			21 35		22 03
Sandal & Agbrigg d						19 38			20 07					20 39			21 07					21 38		22 07
Fitzwilliam d						19 45			20 14					20 46			21 14					21 45		22 14
South Elmsall d						19 50								20 51								21 50		
Adwick a						19 55								20 56								21 55		
d			19 24			19 56							20 24	20 57							21 24	21 56		
Bentley (S.Yorks) d			19 28			20 00							20 28	21 01							21 28	22 00		
Doncaster a			19 33		19 46	20 07		20 15					20 33	21 08		21 15					21 33	22 07		
Moorthorpe d									20 20								21 20							22 26
Thurnscoe d									20 26								21 26							22 32
Goldthorpe d									20 29								21 29							22 34
Bolton-upon-Dearne d									20 32								21 32							22 37
Swinton (S.Yorks) 29 a			19 50						20 36				20 50				21 36				21 50			22 41
Rotherham Central 29 a			19 57						20 44				20 57				21 44				21 57			22 49
Meadowhall 29 a	19 51		20 05				20 41		20 50	20 51			21 07		21 41		21 50	21 51			22 05		22 44	22 55
Sheffield 29 a	20 00	19 51	20 14				20 50		20 58	21 00	20 52	20 53	21 18		21 50		21 59	22 02	21 53		22 16		22 58	23 04

	NT	NT	NT	NT	NT	NT	NT	NT
		◇	◇					
Leeds 32,34 d		22 22	22 30	22 32	22 44	23 00	23 10	23 31
Outwood d		22 31	22 41		22 55		23 21	23 40
Wakefield Kirkgate 32,34,39 a				23 03		23 32		
d				23 04		23 32		
Pontefract Monkhill d								
Wakefield Westgate 32,39 a		22 35	22 45		22 59		23 25	23 44
d		22 35	22 45		22 59		23 26	23 44
Sandal & Agbrigg d		22 38	22 49		23 03		23 29	23 47
Fitzwilliam d		22 45	22 56		23 09		23 37	23 54
South Elmsall d		22 50						23 59
Adwick a		22 55						00 04
d	22 23	22 56						00 05
Bentley (S.Yorks) d	22 27	23 00						00 09
Doncaster a	22 31	23 07						00 16
Moorthorpe d			23 02		23 16		23 45	
Thurnscoe d			23 08		23 22		23 51	
Goldthorpe d			23 11		23 24		23 53	
Bolton-upon-Dearne d			23 14		23 27		23 56	
Swinton (S.Yorks) 29 a	22 52		23 18		23 31		00 01	
Rotherham Central 29 a	22 59		23 28		23 39		00 11	
Meadowhall 29 a	23 06		23 34	23 43	23 45	00 12	00 17	
Sheffield 29 a	23 15		23 42	23 52	23 55	00 21	00 26	

A until 20 July, from 3 September
B from 23 July until 31 August
C until 31 August, from 8 October
D from 3 September until 5 October
E until 20 July, from 8 October
F from 23 July until 5 October

Table T031-R

Saturdays
26 May to 8 December

Leeds - Wakefield, Doncaster and Sheffield

	NT	GR	GR	NT	XC	NT	GR		XC	XC	XC	NT	NT	NT	EM	NT	NT	GR	NT	GR	NT	XC	NT	
		■	■		◇■ A		■		◇■ B	◇■ B	◇■ A		◇		◇■	◇		■		■ C	◇	◇■		
Leeds 32,34 d		05 05	05 30	05 34	05 49	05 55	06 05		06 11	06 17	06 17		06 25	06 30	06 34	06 39		06 40	06 48	07 00	07 03	07 11		
Outwood d				05 45									06 34				←		06 59					
Wakefield Kirkgate 32,34,39 a						06 28								07 01		06 55	07 01				07 21			
d						06 28								07 01		06 56	07 01				07 22			
Pontefract Monkhill d														→										
Wakefield Westgate 32,39 a		05 17	05 42	05 49	06 00		06 17		06 22	06 28	06 28		06 38		06 45			06 52	07 03	07 12		07 22		
d		05 18	05 43	05 50	06 01		06 18		06 23	06 29	06 29		06 38		06 46			06 53	07 03			07 23		
Sandal & Agbrigg d				05 53									06 41						07 07					
Fitzwilliam d				06 01									06 48						07 14					
South Elmsall d													06 53											
Adwick a													06 58											
d	00 05											06 48	06 59										07 16	
Bentley (S.Yorks) d	00 09											06 52	07 03										07 20	
Doncaster a	00 16	05 35	06 00				06 35			06 45	06 45	06 57	07 10					07 12					07 25	
Moorthorpe d				06 15															07 20					
Thurnscoe d				06 21															07 26					
Goldthorpe d				06 23															07 29					
Bolton-upon-Dearne d				06 26															07 32					
Swinton (S.Yorks) 29 a				06 31								07 13							07 36				07 41	
Rotherham Central 29 a				06 40								07 21							07 44				07 48	
Meadowhall 29 a				06 50		07 07						07 27				07 27	07 42		07 50		07 52		07 55	
Sheffield 29 a				06 59	06 29	07 16			06 51	07 17	07 17	07 38			07 22	07 35	07 55		07 58		08 00	07 51	08 04	

	GR	NT	NT	GC	NT	NT	EM	NT	NT	NT	NT	XC	XC	NT	GR		NT	NT	NT	NT	NT	NT	GR	NT
	■		◇	■		◇	◇■				◇	◇■ D	◇■ E		■			◇		◇			■	◇
Leeds 32,34 d	07 15		07 22		07 30	07 38	07 40			07 48	08 04	08 11	08 11		08 15			08 22	08 30	08 38			08 45	08 48
Outwood d			07 31						←	07 59								08 31				←		08 59
Wakefield Kirkgate 32,34,39 a					08 01	07 54			08 01		08 21								09 01	08 54		09 01		
d				07 43	08 01	07 55			08 01		08 22								09 01	08 55		09 01		
Pontefract Monkhill d				08 00	→														→					
Wakefield Westgate 32,39 a	07 27		07 35				07 51			08 03		08 22	08 22		08 28			08 35					08 57	09 03
d	07 28		07 35				07 53			08 03		08 23	08 23		08 30			08 35					08 58	09 03
Sandal & Agbrigg d			07 38							08 07								08 38						09 07
Fitzwilliam d			07 45							08 14								08 46						09 14
South Elmsall d			07 50															08 51						
Adwick a			07 55															08 56						
d		07 49	07 56											08 21			08 52	08 57						
Bentley (S.Yorks) d		07 53	08 00											08 25			08 56	09 01						
Doncaster a	07 45	08 00	08 07	08 29										08 30	08 47		09 02	09 07					09 15	
Moorthorpe d										08 20														09 20
Thurnscoe d										08 26														09 26
Goldthorpe d										08 29														09 29
Bolton-upon-Dearne d										08 32														09 32
Swinton (S.Yorks) 29 a		08 20								08 36				08 47			09 20							09 36
Rotherham Central 29 a		08 28						←		08 44				08 55			09 28				←			09 44
Meadowhall 29 a		08 34				08 27		08 34	08 42	08 50	08 52			09 05			09 34			09 27	09 34	09 41		09 50
Sheffield 29 a		→				08 35	08 24	08 44	08 58	09 00	09 03	08 51	08 52	09 15			→			09 35	09 44	09 50		09 58

	NT	XC	NT	GR	NT	GC	NT		NT	NT	GR	NT	NT	XC	XC	NT	GR	NT	NT	NT	NT	NT	GR	
	◇	◇■		■	◇	■			◇		■		◇	◇■ F	◇■ G		■	◇	◇		◇		■	
Leeds 32,34 d	09 04	09 11		09 16	09 22		09 29		09 38		09 45	09 48	10 04	10 11	10 11		10 15	10 21		10 30	10 38		10 45	
Outwood d					09 31					←		09 59						10 30				←		
Wakefield Kirkgate 32,34,39 a	09 21						10 00		09 54	10 00			10 21							11 01	10 54	11 01		
d	09 22					09 40	10 00		09 55	10 00			10 22							11 01	10 55	11 01		
Pontefract Monkhill d						09 57	→													→				
Wakefield Westgate 32,39 a		09 22		09 28	09 35						09 57	10 03		10 21	10 21		10 27	10 34					10 57	
d		09 23		09 29	09 35						09 58	10 03		10 23	10 23		10 28	10 34					10 58	
Sandal & Agbrigg d					09 38							10 07						10 37						
Fitzwilliam d					09 45							10 14						10 44						
South Elmsall d					09 50													10 50						
Adwick a					09 56													10 55						
d			09 25		09 56											10 24		10 56						
Bentley (S.Yorks) d			09 29		10 00											10 28		11 00						
Doncaster a			09 34	09 46	10 06	10 23					10 15					10 33	10 45	11 06					11 16	
Moorthorpe d												10 20							11 01					
Thurnscoe d												10 26												
Goldthorpe d												10 29												
Bolton-upon-Dearne d												10 32												
Swinton (S.Yorks) 29 a			09 50									10 36				10 50			11 10					
Rotherham Central 29 a			09 57									10 44				10 57			11 18					
Meadowhall 29 a	09 52		10 05						10 28	10 42		10 50	10 52			11 05			11 24		11 26	11 41		
Sheffield 29 a	10 02	09 51	10 14						10 35	10 52		10 58	11 02	10 51	10 52	11 14			11 31		11 34	11 50		

A from 28 July until 6 October
B until 21 July, from 13 October
C West Riding Limited
D until 21 July
E from 28 July
F until 6 October
G from 13 October

Leeds - Wakefield, Doncaster and Sheffield

		NT	GC	NT	XC	XC	NT	GR	NT	NT	NT	NT	GR	NT	NT	XC	NT	GR	NT	NT	NT	NT	GR
		◇	1	◇	◇1 A	◇1 B		1	◇		◇		1		◇	◇1		1	◇		◇		1
Leeds 10 32,34	d	10 48		11 04	11 11	11 11		11 15	11 21	11 30	11 38		11 45	11 48	12 04	12 11		12 15	12 21	12 30	12 38		12 45
Outwood	d	10 59							11 30			←		11 59					12 30			←	
Wakefield Kirkgate 4 32,34,39	a			11 21						12 01	11 54	12 01			12 21					13 01	12 54	13 01	
	d		11 14	11 22						12 01	11 55	12 01			12 22					13 01	12 55	13 01	
Pontefract Monkhill	d		11 32							→										→			
Wakefield Westgate 7 32,39	a	11 03			11 22	11 22		11 28	11 34				11 57	12 03		12 22		12 27	12 34				12 57
	d	11 03			11 23	11 23		11 29	11 34				11 58	12 03		12 23		12 28	12 34				12 58
Sandal & Agbrigg	d	11 07							11 37					12 07					12 37				
Fitzwilliam	d	11 14							11 44					12 14					12 44				
South Elmsall	d								11 50										12 50				
Adwick	a								11 55										12 55				
	d						11 24		11 56								12 24		12 56				
Bentley (S.Yorks)	d						11 28		12 00								12 28		13 00				
Doncaster 7	a		12 03				11 33	11 46	12 06				12 15				12 33	12 45	13 06				13 16
Moorthorpe	d	11 20												12 20									
Thurnscoe	d	11 26												12 26									
Goldthorpe	d	11 29												12 29									
Bolton-upon-Dearne	d	11 32												12 32									
Swinton (S.Yorks) 29	a	11 36					11 50							12 36			12 50						
Rotherham Central 29	a	11 44					11 57							12 44			12 57						
Meadowhall 29	a	11 50		11 52			12 05				12 27	12 41		12 50	12 52		13 05				13 26	13 41	
Sheffield 7 29	a	11 58		12 02	11 51	11 53	12 14				12 35	12 50		12 58	13 02	12 53	13 14				13 34	13 50	

		NT	NT	XC	XC	NT	GR	NT	NT	NT	NT	NT	GR	NT	NT	XC	NT	GR	NT	NT	NT	NT	GR	NT
		◇	◇	◇1 C	◇1 D		1	◇	◇		◇		1		◇	◇1		1	◇		◇		1	◇
Leeds 10 32,34	d	12 48	13 04	13 11	13 11		13 15	13 21		13 30	13 38		13 45	13 48	14 04	14 11		14 15	14 21	14 30	14 38		14 45	14 48
Outwood	d	12 59						13 30				←		13 59					14 30			←		14 59
Wakefield Kirkgate 4 32,34,39	a		13 23							14 01	13 54	14 01			14 21					15 01	14 54	15 01		
	d		13 23							14 01	13 55	14 01			14 22					15 01	14 55	15 01		
Pontefract Monkhill	d									→										→				
Wakefield Westgate 7 32,39	a	13 03		13 22	13 22		13 27	13 34					13 57	14 03		14 22		14 27	14 34				14 57	15 03
	d	13 03		13 23	13 23		13 28	13 34					13 58	14 03		14 23		14 28	14 35				14 58	15 03
Sandal & Agbrigg	d	13 07						13 37						14 07					14 38					15 07
Fitzwilliam	d	13 14						13 44						14 14					14 45					15 14
South Elmsall	d							13 50											14 50					
Adwick	a							13 55											14 55					
	d					13 24		13 56									14 24		14 56					
Bentley (S.Yorks)	d					13 28		14 00									14 28		15 00					
Doncaster 7	a					13 33	13 45	14 06					14 15				14 33	14 45	15 06				15 15	
Moorthorpe	d	13 20							13 59					14 20										15 20
Thurnscoe	d	13 26												14 26										15 26
Goldthorpe	d	13 29												14 29										15 29
Bolton-upon-Dearne	d	13 32												14 32										15 32
Swinton (S.Yorks) 29	a	13 36				13 50			14 10					14 36			14 50							15 36
Rotherham Central 29	a	13 44				13 57			14 18					14 44			14 57							15 44
Meadowhall 29	a	13 50	13 53			14 05			14 24		14 27	14 41		14 50	14 52		15 05				15 27	15 41		15 50
Sheffield 7 29	a	13 58	14 02	13 51	13 52	14 14			14 31		14 35	14 50		14 58	15 02	14 51	15 14				15 35	15 50		15 58

		NT	XC	NT	GR	NT	NT	NT	NT	GR	NT	GC	NT	XC	NT	GR	NT	NT	NT	XC	NT	GR	NT
		◇	◇1		1	◇		◇		1		1	◇	◇1		1	◇		◇	◇1		1	
Leeds 10 32,34	d	15 04	15 11		15 15	15 21	15 30	15 38		15 45	15 48		16 04	16 11		16 15	16 21	16 29	16 38	16 40		16 45	16 48
Outwood	d					15 30			←		15 59						16 30				←		17 00
Wakefield Kirkgate 4 32,34,39	a	15 21					16 01	15 54	16 01				16 21					17 01	16 54		17 01		
	d	15 22					16 01	15 55	16 01			16 14	16 22					17 01	16 55		17 01		
Pontefract Monkhill	d						→					16 35						→					
Wakefield Westgate 7 32,39	a		15 22		15 27	15 34				15 57	16 03			16 22		16 27	16 34			16 51		16 57	17 04
	d		15 23		15 28	15 35				15 58	16 03			16 23		16 28	16 34			16 52		16 58	17 04
Sandal & Agbrigg	d					15 38					16 07						16 37						17 08
Fitzwilliam	d					15 45					16 14						16 44						17 14
South Elmsall	d					15 50											16 49						
Adwick	a					15 55											16 54						
	d			15 24		15 56									16 24		16 55						
Bentley (S.Yorks)	d			15 28		16 00									16 28		16 59						
Doncaster 7	a			15 33	15 45	16 06				16 16		17 06			16 33	16 45	17 06					17 16	
Moorthorpe	d										16 20												17 20
Thurnscoe	d										16 26												17 26
Goldthorpe	d										16 29												17 28
Bolton-upon-Dearne	d										16 32												17 31
Swinton (S.Yorks) 29	a			15 50							16 36				16 50								17 35
Rotherham Central 29	a			15 57							16 44				16 57								17 44
Meadowhall 29	a	15 52		16 05				16 27	16 41		16 50		16 52		17 05				17 26		17 41		17 50
Sheffield 7 29	a	16 02	15 51	16 14				16 35	16 50		16 58		17 02	16 51	17 14				17 34	17 19	17 50		17 58

A from 28 July
B until 21 July
C until 21 July, from 13 October
D from 28 July until 6 October

Table T031-R

Saturdays
26 May to 8 December

Leeds - Wakefield, Doncaster and Sheffield

		NT	XC	NT	GR	NT	NT	NT	NT	GR	NT	NT	NT	NT	XC	XC	NT	GR	NT	NT	NT	NT	GR
		◇	◇1		1	◇		◇		1			◇	◇	◇1 A	◇1 B		1	◇		◇		1
Leeds 10 32,34	d	17 03	17 10		17 14	17 22	17 30	17 38		17 45	17 48		17 57	18 03	18 11	18 11		18 15	18 23	18 30	18 38		18 45
Outwood	d					17 31			←		17 59		18 06						18 32			←	
Wakefield Kirkgate 4 32,34,39	a	17 22					18 01	17 54	18 01					18 20						19 01	18 55	19 01	
	d	17 22					18 01	17 55	18 01					18 21						19 01	18 56	19 01	
Pontefract Monkhill	d						→													→			
Wakefield Westgate 7 32,39	a		17 21		17 26	17 35				17 57	18 03		18 10		18 22	18 22		18 27	18 36				18 57
	d		17 22		17 27	17 35				17 58	18 03		18 10		18 23	18 23		18 28	18 36				18 58
Sandal & Agbrigg	d					17 38					18 07		18 13						18 39				
Fitzwilliam	d					17 45					18 14		18 20						18 46				
South Elmsall	d					17 50							18 25						18 51				
Adwick	a					17 55							18 30						18 56				
	d			17 24		17 56						18 24	18 31						18 57				
Bentley (S.Yorks)	d			17 28		18 00						18 28	18 35						19 01				
Doncaster 7	a			17 33	17 44	18 06				18 16		18 33	18 42					18 46	19 08				19 15
Moorthorpe	d										18 20												
Thurnscoe	d										18 26												
Goldthorpe	d										18 29												
Bolton-upon-Dearne	d										18 32												
Swinton (S.Yorks) 29	a			17 50							18 36	18 50											
Rotherham Central 29	a			17 57							18 44	18 57					←						
Meadowhall 29	a	17 53		18 05				18 27	18 41		18 50	19 05		18 51			19 05				19 26	19 41	
Sheffield 7 29	a	18 02	17 51	18 14				18 35	18 50		18 58	→		19 00	18 52	18 53	19 14				19 35	19 50	

		NT	NT	XC	NT	GR	NT	NT	GR	NT	NT	XC	NT	GR	NT	NT	NT	NT	XC	NT	NT	NT	NT	NT
		◇	◇	◇1		1	◇		1		◇	◇1		1	◇		◇	◇	◇1		◇			
Leeds 10 32,34	d	18 48	19 03	19 11		19 16	19 22	19 30	19 45	19 48	20 03	20 11		20 15	20 23	20 30	20 48	21 03	21 11		21 22	21 30	21 48	
Outwood	d	18 59					19 31			19 59					20 32		20 59				21 31		21 59	
Wakefield Kirkgate 4 32,34,39	a		19 20					20 01			20 20					21 01		21 20				22 01		
	d		19 21					20 01			20 21					21 01		21 21				22 01		
Pontefract Monkhill	d																							
Wakefield Westgate 7 32,39	a	19 03		19 22		19 28	19 35		19 57	20 03		20 22		20 27	20 36		21 03		21 22		21 35		22 03	
	d	19 03		19 23		19 29	19 35		19 58	20 03		20 23		20 28	20 36		21 03		21 23		21 35		22 03	
Sandal & Agbrigg	d	19 07					19 38			20 07					20 39		21 07				21 38		22 07	
Fitzwilliam	d	19 14					19 45			20 14					20 46		21 14				21 45		22 14	
South Elmsall	d						19 50								20 51						21 50			
Adwick	a						19 55								20 56						21 55			
	d				19 24		19 56						20 24		20 57					21 24	21 56			22 23
Bentley (S.Yorks)	d				19 28		20 00						20 28		21 01					21 28	22 00			22 27
Doncaster 7	a				19 33	19 46	20 07		20 15				20 33	20 46	21 08					21 33	22 07			22 31
Moorthorpe	d	19 20								20 20							21 20						22 26	
Thurnscoe	d	19 26								20 26							21 26						22 32	
Goldthorpe	d	19 29								20 29							21 29						22 34	
Bolton-upon-Dearne	d	19 32								20 32							21 32						22 37	
Swinton (S.Yorks) 29	a	19 36			19 50					20 36			20 50				21 36			21 50			22 41	22 52
Rotherham Central 29	a	19 44			19 57					20 44			20 57				21 44			21 57			22 49	22 59
Meadowhall 29	a	19 50	19 51		20 05			20 41		20 50	20 51		21 07			21 41	21 50	21 51		22 05		22 44	22 55	23 06
Sheffield 7 29	a	19 58	20 00	19 51	20 14			20 50		20 58	21 00	20 52	21 18			21 50	21 59	22 02	21 52	22 16		22 58	23 04	23 15

		NT	NT	NT	NT
		◇	◇		
Leeds 10 32,34	d	22 13	22 22	22 32	22 44
Outwood	d	22 24	22 31		22 55
Wakefield Kirkgate 4 32,34,39	a			23 03	
	d			23 04	
Pontefract Monkhill	d				
Wakefield Westgate 7 32,39	a	22 28	22 35		22 59
	d	22 28	22 35		22 59
Sandal & Agbrigg	d	22 32	22 38		23 03
Fitzwilliam	d	22 38	22 45		23 09
South Elmsall	d		22 50		
Adwick	a		22 55		
	d		22 56		
Bentley (S.Yorks)	d		23 00		
Doncaster 7	a		23 07		
Moorthorpe	d	22 44			23 16
Thurnscoe	d	22 50			23 22
Goldthorpe	d	22 52			23 24
Bolton-upon-Dearne	d	22 55			23 27
Swinton (S.Yorks) 29	a	22 59			23 31
Rotherham Central 29	a	23 07			23 39
Meadowhall 29	a	23 13		23 43	23 45
Sheffield 7 29	a	23 23		23 52	23 55

A from 28 July until 6 October
B until 21 July, from 13 October

Table T031-R

Sundays

20 May to 2 December

Leeds - Wakefield, Doncaster and Sheffield

	GR	XC	NT	GC	NT	GR	NT		XC	XC	GR	NT	NT	GR	EM	XC	GR	NT	NT	NT	NT	GR	EM
		◇	◇				◇		◇ A	◇ B		◇			◇	◇		◇		◇	◇		◇
Leeds 32,34 d	08 05	08 10	08 21		08 33	08 43	08 45		09 00	09 00	09 05	09 08	09 29	09 40	09 50	09 59	10 05	10 08	10 18	10 21	10 31	10 45	10 50
Outwood d			08 30				08 56													10 30	10 42		
Wakefield Kirkgate 32,34,39 a					09 02							09 24						10 24	10 47				
d				08 46	09 02							09 24						10 24	10 47				
Pontefract Monkhill d																							
Wakefield Westgate 32,39 a	08 17	08 22	08 34			08 55	09 00		09 11	09 11	09 17		09 42	09 52	10 01	10 10	10 17			10 34	10 46	10 57	11 01
d	08 18	08 23	08 34			08 56	09 00		09 11	09 11	09 18		09 42		10 02	10 12	10 18			10 34	10 47	10 58	11 03
Sandal & Agbrigg d			08 37				09 04													10 37	10 51		
Fitzwilliam d			08 44				09 10						09 50							10 44	10 57		
South Elmsall d			08 49																	10 49			
Adwick a			08 54																	10 54			
d			08 55																	10 55			
Bentley (S.Yorks) d			08 59																	10 59			
Doncaster a	08 35		09 07	09 09		09 14			09 29	09 29	09 37					10 29	10 35			11 06		11 16	
Moorthorpe d							09 16						09 57								11 17		
Thurnscoe d							09 22						10 03								11 23		
Goldthorpe d							09 24						10 05								11 26		
Bolton-upon-Dearne d							09 27						10 08								11 29		
Swinton (S.Yorks) 29 a							09 31						10 12								11 33		
Rotherham Central 29 a							09 38						10 21								11 43		
Meadowhall 29 a					09 40		09 45					09 56	10 29					10 55	11 29		11 49		
Sheffield 29 a		08 52			09 49		09 53		09 55	09 56		10 03	10 38		10 30	10 52		11 03	11 38		11 57		11 30

	XC	GR	NT	NT	GR	NT	XC	XC	NT	NT	GC	GR	NT	XC	XC		NT	GR	NT	XC	XC	NT	NT	EM
	◇		◇			◇	◇ C	◇ D		◇			◇	◇ C	◇ D				◇	◇ C	◇ D		◇	◇ E
Leeds 32,34 d	11 00	11 05	11 08	11 48	12 05	12 08	12 11	12 11	12 16	12 22		13 05	13 08	13 11	13 11		13 48	14 05	14 08	14 11	14 11	14 17	14 21	14 34
Outwood d				11 59						12 31							13 59						14 30	
Wakefield Kirkgate 32,34,39 a			11 24			12 24			12 46				13 24						14 24			14 46		
d			11 24			12 24			12 46		12 56		13 24						14 24			14 46		
Pontefract Monkhill d																								
Wakefield Westgate 32,39 a	11 11	11 17		12 03	12 17		12 22	12 22		12 35		13 17		13 22	13 22		14 03	14 17		14 22	14 22		14 34	14 45
d	11 12	11 18		12 03	12 18		12 24	12 24		12 35		13 18		13 24	13 24		14 03	14 18		14 23	14 23		14 34	14 47
Sandal & Agbrigg d				12 07						12 38							14 07						14 37	
Fitzwilliam d				12 13						12 45							14 13						14 44	
South Elmsall d										12 50													14 49	
Adwick a										12 55													14 54	
d										12 56													14 55	
Bentley (S.Yorks) d										13 00													14 59	
Doncaster a	11 28	11 35			12 35			12 41		13 07	13 19	13 35			13 42			14 35			14 41		15 06	
Moorthorpe d				12 19													14 19							
Thurnscoe d				12 25													14 25							
Goldthorpe d				12 27													14 27							
Bolton-upon-Dearne d				12 30													14 30							
Swinton (S.Yorks) 29 a				12 34													14 34							15 03
Rotherham Central 29 a				12 42													14 43							
Meadowhall 29 a			11 56	12 50		12 56			13 28				13 56				14 49		14 56			15 28		
Sheffield 29 a	11 53		12 03	12 58		13 03	12 51	13 17	13 38				14 03	13 52	14 17		14 57		15 03	14 52	15 16	15 38		

	EM	GR	NT	XC	XC	NT	GC		NT	XC	XC	GR	GC	NT	NT	GR	NT	XC	XC	GR	GR	NT	NT
	◇ F		◇	◇ C	◇ D				◇	◇ C	◇ D				◇		◇	◇ C	◇ D				◇
Leeds 32,34 d	14 34	15 05	15 08	15 11	15 11	15 42			16 08	16 11	16 11	16 16		16 17	16 23	16 45	17 08	17 11	17 11	17 16	17 45	17 47	18 08
Outwood d						15 53									16 32							18 00	
Wakefield Kirkgate 32,34,39 a			15 24						16 24					16 48			17 24						18 24
d			15 24				16 02		16 24				16 45	16 48			17 24						18 25
Pontefract Monkhill d																							
Wakefield Westgate 32,39 a	14 45	15 17		15 22	15 22	15 57				16 22	16 22	16 28			16 36	16 57		17 22	17 22	17 28	17 57	18 04	
d	14 47	15 18		15 23	15 23	15 57				16 23	16 23	16 29			16 36	16 58		17 23	17 23	17 29	17 58	18 04	
Sandal & Agbrigg d						16 01									16 39							18 08	
Fitzwilliam d						16 07									16 46							18 14	
South Elmsall d															16 51								
Adwick a															16 56								
d															16 57								
Bentley (S.Yorks) d															17 01								
Doncaster a		15 35			15 42		16 25				16 41	16 46	17 11		17 08	17 16			17 41	17 46	18 15		
Moorthorpe d						16 13																18 20	
Thurnscoe d						16 19																18 26	
Goldthorpe d						16 21																18 28	
Bolton-upon-Dearne d						16 24																18 31	
Swinton (S.Yorks) 29 a	15 03					16 28																18 35	
Rotherham Central 29 a						16 42																18 44	
Meadowhall 29 a			15 56			16 48			16 56					17 28			17 56					18 49	18 55
Sheffield 29 a	15 19		16 03	15 51	16 16	16 56			17 05	16 52	17 17			17 38			18 03	17 51	18 15			18 57	19 03

A from 22 July until 2 September
B until 15 July, from 9 September
C until 15 July, from 14 October
D from 22 July until 7 October
E 5 August, 12 August, 26 August
F not 5 August, 12 August, 26 August

Table T031-R

Sundays

20 May to 2 December

Leeds - Wakefield, Doncaster and Sheffield

	XC	NT	XC	NT	GR	NT	GR		NT	XC	XC	XC	GR	GR	NT	NT	XC	NT	NT	GR	NT	NT	XC
	◇ A	◇	◇ B			◇			◇	◇ A	◇ C	◇ D				◇	◇		◇		◇ E	◇	◇
Leeds 32,34 d	18 11		18 11	18 13	18 15	18 21	18 45		19 08	19 11	19 11	19 11	19 16	19 46	19 48	20 08	20 11	20 17	20 22	20 45		21 08	21 11
Outwood d						18 30									19 59				20 31				
Wakefield Kirkgate 32,34,39 a				18 52					19 24							20 24		20 46				21 28	
d				18 52					19 24							20 24		20 46				21 29	
Pontefract Monkhill d																							
Wakefield Westgate 32,39 a	18 22		18 22		18 27	18 34	18 57			19 22	19 22	19 22	19 28	19 58	20 03		20 22		20 35	20 57			21 22
d	18 23		18 23		18 28	18 34	18 59			19 24	19 24	19 24	19 29	19 59	20 03		20 23		20 35	20 58			21 23
Sandal & Agbrigg d						18 37									20 07				20 38				
Fitzwilliam d						18 44									20 13				20 45				
South Elmsall d						18 49													20 50				
Adwick a						18 54													20 55				
d						18 55													20 56				
Bentley (S.Yorks) d						18 59													21 00				
Doncaster a			18 39		18 45	19 06	19 17				19 40	19 40	19 46	20 17					21 07	21 15			
Moorthorpe d		18 44													20 19						21 36		
Thurnscoe d															20 25								
Goldthorpe d															20 27								
Bolton-upon-Dearne d															20 30								
Swinton (S.Yorks) 29 a		18 53													20 34						21 45		
Rotherham Central 29 a		19 02													20 43								
Meadowhall 29 a		19 08		19 33					19 56						20 48	20 54		21 27			21 55	21 59	
Sheffield 29 a	18 52	19 19	19 20	19 43					20 03	19 52	20 13	20 16			20 56	21 02	20 51	21 37			22 03	22 07	21 51

	NT	NT	NT	NT
	◇	◇	◇	
Leeds 32,34 d	21 21	21 48	22 08	22 18
Outwood d	21 30	21 59		
Wakefield Kirkgate 32,34,39 a			22 24	22 47
d			22 24	22 47
Pontefract Monkhill d				
Wakefield Westgate 32,39 a	21 34	22 03		
d	21 34	22 03		
Sandal & Agbrigg d	21 37	22 07		
Fitzwilliam d	21 44	22 13		
South Elmsall d	21 49			
Adwick a	21 54			
d	21 55			
Bentley (S.Yorks) d	21 59			
Doncaster a	22 06			
Moorthorpe d		22 19		
Thurnscoe d		22 25		
Goldthorpe d		22 27		
Bolton-upon-Dearne d		22 30		
Swinton (S.Yorks) 29 a		22 34		
Rotherham Central 29 a		22 43		
Meadowhall 29 a		22 48	22 55	23 26
Sheffield 29 a		22 56	23 03	23 35

A until 15 July, from 14 October
B from 22 July until 7 October
C from 22 July until 2 September
D from 9 September until 7 October
E via Pontefract Baghill

Table T032-F

Mondays to Fridays

21 May to 7 December

Bradford, Leeds and Wakefield - Pontefract, Knottingley and Goole

Miles	Miles			NT	NT	NT	NT	NT	NT	GC	NT	NT	NT	NT	NT	NT	NT	NT	NT	NT	NT	NT	GC
						A		A				A			A			A			A		
—	—	Bradford Interchange 41	d							06 55													10 22
—	—	Halifax 41	d							07 08													10 35
—	—	Brighouse 41	d							07 19													10 47
—	—	Mirfield	d							07 25													10 55
0	—	**Leeds** 31	d	05 24	05 47	05 55	06 18	06 30	06 58		07 28	07 30	07 58	08 28	08 30	08 58	09 28	09 29	09 58	10 28	10 30	10 58	
6	—	Woodlesford	d		05 57	06 04		06 39	07 07			07 39	08 07		08 39	09 07		09 38	10 07		10 39	11 07	
10¾	—	Castleford	a		06 05	06 14		06 48	07 17			07 48	08 16		08 47	09 16		09 47	10 16		10 48	11 16	
—	—		d		06 08	06 17		06 50	07 19			07 50	08 18		08 50	09 18		09 49	10 18		10 50	11 18	
12¼	—	Glasshoughton	d		06 13				07 24				08 23			09 23			10 23			11 23	
—	0	**Wakefield Westgate** 31,39	d	05 38			06 34				07 42			08 42			09 42			10 42			
—	1	Wakefield Kirkgate 31,34,39	a	05 41		06 28	06 37	07 01		07 41	07 47	08 01		08 45	09 01		09 45	10 00		10 45	11 01		11 13
—	—		d	05 42			06 37			07 42	07 49			08 45			09 45			10 45			11 14
—	5¼	Streethouse	d	05 51			06 46				07 57			08 54			09 54			10 54			
—	7	Featherstone	d	05 55			06 50				08 01			08 58			09 58			10 58			
—	9	Pontefract Tanshelf	d	05 59			06 54				08 05			09 02			10 02			11 02			
14	9¾	Pontefract Monkhill	a	06 01	06 17		06 56		07 29	07 59	08 08		08 28	09 05		09 28	10 04		10 28	11 04		11 28	11 32
—	—		d	06 02	06 18		06 57		07 29	08 00	08 08		08 28	09 05		09 28	10 05		10 28	11 05		11 28	11 34
—	—	London Kings Cross ⊖26	a							10 09													13 44
16	—	**Knottingley**	a	06 08	06 24		07 03		07 35		08 14		08 34	09 11		09 34	10 11		10 34	11 11		11 34	
—	—		d																				
20¾	—	Whitley Bridge	d																				
22	—	Hensall	d																				
25¾	—	Snaith	d																				
28½	—	Rawcliffe	d																				
32½	—	**Goole**	a																				

		NT	NT	NT		NT	NT	NT	GC	NT	NT	NT	NT	NT	NT	NT	NT	NT	NT	NT	NT	NT
			A		and at the same minutes past each hour until		A				A			A			A	◇		A		
Bradford Interchange 41	d								14 49													
Halifax 41	d								15 04													
Brighouse 41	d								15 17													
Mirfield	d								15 24													
Leeds 31	d	11 28	11 30	11 58		14 28	14 30	14 58		15 28	15 30	15 58	16 28	16 29	16 58	17 29	17 30	17 58	18 28	18 30	18 58	19 28
Woodlesford	d		11 39	12 07			14 39	15 07			15 39	16 07		16 38	17 07		17 39	18 07		18 39	19 07	
Castleford	a		11 48	12 16			14 48	15 16			15 48	16 16		16 47	17 16		17 48	18 16		18 48	19 16	
	d		11 50	12 18			14 50	15 18			15 50	16 18		16 49	17 18		17 50	18 18		18 50	19 18	
Glasshoughton	d			12 23				15 23				16 23			17 23			18 23			19 23	
Wakefield Westgate 31,39	d	11 42				14 42				15 42			16 42			17 43			18 42			19 42
Wakefield Kirkgate 31,34,39	a	11 45	12 01			14 45	15 01		15 38	15 45	16 01		16 45	17 01		17 46	18 01		18 45	19 01		19 46
	d	11 45				14 45			15 39	15 45			16 45			17 46			18 45			19 47
Streethouse	d	11 54				14 54				15 55			16 54			17 55			18 54			19 57
Featherstone	d	11 58				14 58				15 59			16 58			17 59			18 58			20 01
Pontefract Tanshelf	d	12 02				15 02				16 02			17 02			18 03			19 02			20 05
Pontefract Monkhill	a	12 04		12 28		15 04		15 28	15 54	16 05		16 29	17 04		17 28	18 05		18 28	19 04		19 28	20 07
	d	12 05		12 28		15 05		15 28	15 55	16 05		16 29	17 05		17 28	18 06		18 28	19 05		19 28	20 08
London Kings Cross ⊖26	a								18 07													
Knottingley	a	12 11		12 34		15 11		15 34		16 11		16 35	17 11		17 34	18 12		18 35	19 11		19 34	20 14
	d																	18 36				
Whitley Bridge	d																	18 42				
Hensall	d																	18 46				
Snaith	d																	18 53				
Rawcliffe	d																	18 58				
Goole	a																	19 07				

		NT	NT	NT	NT	NT	NT	NT	NT	NT	NT	NT	NT
		A			A			A		A		A	
Bradford Interchange 41	d												
Halifax 41	d												
Brighouse 41	d												
Mirfield	d												
Leeds 31	d	19 30	19 58	20 28	20 30	20 58	21 28	21 30	22 03	22 32	22 50	23 00	23 16
Woodlesford	d	19 39	20 07		20 39	21 07		21 39	22 12	22 41		23 09	23 27
Castleford	a	19 48	20 16		20 48	21 16		21 48	22 21	22 50		23 18	23 36
	d	19 50	20 18		20 50	21 18		21 50	22 23	22 53		23 20	23 38
Glasshoughton	d		20 23			21 23			22 28				23 43
Wakefield Westgate 31,39	d			20 42			21 42				23 04		
Wakefield Kirkgate 31,34,39	a	20 01		20 45	21 01		21 45	22 01		23 03	23 07	23 32	
	d			20 45			21 45				23 08		
Streethouse	d			20 54			21 54				23 16		
Featherstone	d			20 58			21 58				23 20		
Pontefract Tanshelf	d			21 02			22 02				23 24		
Pontefract Monkhill	a		20 28	21 04		21 30	22 04		22 33		23 27		23 47
	d		20 28	21 05		21 30	22 05		22 33		23 27		23 47
London Kings Cross ⊖26	a												
Knottingley	a		20 34	21 11		21 37	22 11		22 39		23 33		23 53
	d												
Whitley Bridge	d												
Hensall	d												
Snaith	d												
Rawcliffe	d												
Goole	a												

A To Sheffield

Table T032-F

Saturdays

26 May to 8 December

Bradford, Leeds and Wakefield - Pontefract, Knottingley and Goole

		NT	NT	NT	NT	NT	NT	GC	NT	NT	NT	NT	NT	NT	GC	NT	NT	NT	NT	NT	NT	GC
				A		A				A			A				A			A		
Bradford Interchange 41	d							06 55							08 51							10 21
Halifax 41	d							07 09							09 05							10 35
Brighouse 41	d							07 20							09 16							10 48
Mirfield	d							07 28							09 24							10 56
Leeds 31	d	05 24	05 47	05 55	06 18	06 30	06 58		07 28	07 30	07 58	08 28	08 30	08 58		09 28	09 29	09 58	10 28	10 30	10 58	
Woodlesford	d		05 57	06 04		06 39	07 07			07 39	08 07		08 39	09 07			09 38	10 07		10 39	11 07	
Castleford	a		06 05	06 14		06 48	07 17			07 48	08 16		08 47	09 16			09 47	10 16		10 48	11 16	
	d		06 08	06 17		06 50	07 19			07 50	08 18		08 50	09 18			09 49	10 18		10 50	11 18	
Glasshoughton	d		06 13				07 24				08 23			09 23				10 23			11 23	
Wakefield Westgate 31,39	d	05 38			06 34				07 42			08 42				09 42			10 42			
Wakefield Kirkgate 31,34,39	a	05 41		06 28	06 37	07 01		07 42	07 47	08 01		08 45	09 01		09 39	09 45	10 00		10 45	11 01		11 11
	d	05 42			06 37			07 43	07 49			08 45			09 40	09 45			10 45			11 14
Streethouse	d	05 51			06 46				07 57			08 54				09 54			10 54			
Featherstone	d	05 55			06 50				08 01			08 58				09 58			10 58			
Pontefract Tanshelf	d	05 59			06 54				08 05			09 02				10 02			11 02			
Pontefract Monkhill	a	06 01	06 17		06 56		07 29	07 59	08 08		08 28	09 05		09 28	09 55	10 04		10 28	11 04		11 28	11 30
	d	06 02	06 18		06 57		07 29	08 00	08 08		08 28	09 05		09 28	09 57	10 05		10 28	11 05		11 28	11 32
London Kings Cross ⊖26	a							10 05							11 58							13 44
Knottingley	a	06 08	06 24		07 03		07 35		08 14		08 34	09 11		09 34		10 11		10 34	11 11		11 34	
	d																					
Whitley Bridge	d																					
Hensall	d																					
Snaith	d																					
Rawcliffe	d																					
Goole	a																					

		NT	NT	NT		NT	NT	NT	NT	NT	NT	GC	NT	NT	NT	NT	NT	NT	NT	NT	NT	NT
			A		and at the same minutes past each hour until		A			A				A			A	◇		A		
Bradford Interchange 41	d											15 21										
Halifax 41	d											15 35										
Brighouse 41	d											15 49										
Mirfield	d											15 56										
Leeds 31	d	11 28	11 30	11 58		14 28	14 30	14 58	15 28	15 30	15 58		16 28	16 29	16 58	17 29	17 30	17 58	18 28	18 30	18 58	19 28
Woodlesford	d		11 39	12 07			14 39	15 07		15 39	16 07			16 38	17 07		17 39	18 07		18 39	19 07	
Castleford	a		11 48	12 16			14 48	15 16		15 48	16 16			16 47	17 16		17 48	18 16		18 48	19 16	
	d		11 50	12 18			14 50	15 18		15 50	16 18			16 49	17 18		17 50	18 18		18 50	19 18	
Glasshoughton	d			12 23				15 23			16 23				17 23			18 23			19 23	
Wakefield Westgate 31,39	d	11 42				14 42			15 42				16 42			17 43			18 42			19 42
Wakefield Kirkgate 31,34,39	a	11 45	12 01			14 45	15 01		15 45	16 01		16 11	16 45	17 01		17 46	18 01		18 45	19 01		19 46
	d	11 45				14 45			15 45			16 14	16 45			17 46			18 45			19 47
Streethouse	d	11 54				14 54			15 55				16 54			17 55			18 54			19 57
Featherstone	d	11 58				14 58			15 59				16 58			17 59			18 58			20 01
Pontefract Tanshelf	d	12 02				15 02			16 02				17 02			18 03			19 02			20 05
Pontefract Monkhill	a	12 04		12 28		15 04		15 28	16 05		16 29	16 33	17 04		17 28	18 05		18 28	19 04		19 28	20 07
	d	12 05		12 28		15 05		15 28	16 05		16 29	16 35	17 05		17 28	18 06		18 28	19 05		19 28	20 08
London Kings Cross ⊖26	a											18 47										
Knottingley	a	12 11		12 34		15 11		15 34	16 11		16 35		17 11		17 34	18 12		18 35	19 11		19 34	20 14
	d																	18 36				
Whitley Bridge	d																	18 42				
Hensall	d																	18 46				
Snaith	d																	18 53				
Rawcliffe	d																	18 58				
Goole	a																	19 07				

		NT	NT	NT	NT	NT	NT	NT	NT	NT	NT	NT
		A			A			A		A		
Bradford Interchange 41	d											
Halifax 41	d											
Brighouse 41	d											
Mirfield	d											
Leeds 31	d	19 30	19 58	20 28	20 30	20 58	21 28	21 30	22 03	22 32	22 50	23 00
Woodlesford	d	19 39	20 07		20 39	21 07		21 39	22 12	22 41		23 09
Castleford	a	19 48	20 16		20 48	21 16		21 48	22 21	22 50		23 18
	d	19 50	20 18		20 50	21 18		21 50	22 23	22 53		
Glasshoughton	d		20 23			21 23			22 28			
Wakefield Westgate 31,39	d			20 42			21 42				23 04	
Wakefield Kirkgate 31,34,39	a	20 01		20 45	21 01		21 45	22 01		23 03	23 07	
	d			20 45			21 45				23 08	
Streethouse	d			20 54			21 54				23 16	
Featherstone	d			20 58			21 58				23 20	
Pontefract Tanshelf	d			21 02			22 02				23 24	
Pontefract Monkhill	a		20 28	21 04		21 30	22 04		22 33		23 27	
	d		20 28	21 05		21 30	22 05		22 33		23 27	
London Kings Cross ⊖26	a											
Knottingley	a		20 34	21 11		21 37	22 11		22 39		23 33	
	d											
Whitley Bridge	d											
Hensall	d											
Snaith	d											
Rawcliffe	d											
Goole	a											

A To Sheffield

Table T032-F

Sundays

20 May to 2 December

Bradford, Leeds and Wakefield - Pontefract, Knottingley and Goole

Station		NT A	NT	NT	NT A	NT	NT	NT A	NT	NT	NT A	NT
Bradford Interchange 41	d											
Halifax 41	d											
Brighouse 41	d											
Mirfield	d											
Leeds ■10 31	d	08 33	08 52	09 14	10 18	10 25	11 16	12 16	12 26	13 16	14 17	14 25
Woodlesford	d	08 41		09 24	10 26		11 25	12 25		13 25	14 25	
Castleford	a	08 49		09 32	10 34		11 33	12 33		13 33	14 33	
	d	08 52		09 35	10 37		11 36	12 36		13 36	14 36	
Glasshoughton	d			09 40			11 41			13 41		
Wakefield Westgate ■7 31,39	d		09 06			10 39			12 40			14 39
Wakefield Kirkgate ■4 31,34,39	a	09 02	09 09		10 47	10 42		12 46	12 43		14 46	14 42
	d		09 12			10 42			12 43			14 42
Streethouse	d		09 20			10 49			12 50			14 49
Featherstone	d		09 24			10 53			12 54			14 53
Pontefract Tanshelf	d		09 28			10 57			12 58			14 57
Pontefract Monkhill	a		09 31	09 44		10 59	11 45		13 00	13 45		14 59
	d		09 31	09 44		11 00	11 45		13 01	13 45		15 00
London Kings Cross ■15 ⊖26	a											
Knottingley	a		09 36	09 50		11 05	11 51		13 06	13 51		15 05
	d											
Whitley Bridge	d											
Hensall	d											
Snaith	d											
Rawcliffe	d											
Goole	a											

Station		NT	NT A	NT	NT	NT A	NT	NT	NT A	NT	NT	NT A
Bradford Interchange 41	d											
Halifax 41	d											
Brighouse 41	d											
Mirfield	d											
Leeds ■10 31	d	15 16	16 17	16 28	17 16	18 13	18 25	19 17	20 17	20 25	21 17	22 18
Woodlesford	d	15 25	16 25		17 25	18 21		19 25	20 25		21 25	22 26
Castleford	a	15 33	16 33		17 33	18 31		19 33	20 33		21 33	22 34
	d	15 36	16 37		17 36	18 42		19 36	20 36		21 36	22 37
Glasshoughton	d	15 41			17 41			19 41			21 41	
Wakefield Westgate ■7 31,39	d			16 49			18 39			20 39		
Wakefield Kirkgate ■4 31,34,39	a		16 48	16 52		18 52	18 42		20 46	20 42		22 47
	d			16 53			18 42			20 43		
Streethouse	d			17 00			18 49			20 50		
Featherstone	d			17 04			18 53			20 54		
Pontefract Tanshelf	d			17 07			18 57			20 57		
Pontefract Monkhill	a	15 45		17 10	17 45		18 59	19 45		21 00	21 45	
	d	15 45		17 10	17 45		19 00	19 45		21 00	21 45	
London Kings Cross ■15 ⊖26	a											
Knottingley	a	15 51		17 16	17 51		19 05	19 51		21 05	21 51	
	d											
Whitley Bridge	d											
Hensall	d											
Snaith	d											
Rawcliffe	d											
Goole	a											

Station		NT
Bradford Interchange 41	d	
Halifax 41	d	
Brighouse 41	d	
Mirfield	d	
Leeds ■10 31	d	22 25
Woodlesford	d	
Castleford	a	
	d	
Glasshoughton	d	
Wakefield Westgate ■7 31,39	d	22 39
Wakefield Kirkgate ■4 31,34,39	a	22 42
	d	22 42
Streethouse	d	22 49
Featherstone	d	22 53
Pontefract Tanshelf	d	22 57
Pontefract Monkhill	a	22 59
	d	23 00
London Kings Cross ■15 ⊖26	a	
Knottingley	a	23 05
	d	
Whitley Bridge	d	
Hensall	d	
Snaith	d	
Rawcliffe	d	
Goole	a	

A To Sheffield

Table T032-R

Mondays to Fridays

21 May to 7 December

Goole, Knottingley and Pontefract - Wakefield and Leeds, Bradford

Miles	Miles	Station		NT	NT A	NT	NT	NT	NT A	NT	NT	NT ◇	NT A
0	—	**Goole**	d									07 42	
4	—	Rawcliffe	d									07 50	
6¾	—	Snaith	d									07 55	
10½	—	Hensall	d									08 02	
12¼	—	Whitley Bridge	d									08 05	
16½	—	**Knottingley**	a									08 12	
—	—		d	06 12		06 39		07 15		07 30	07 48	08 13	
—	—	London Kings Cross ■15 ⊖26	d										
18½	0	Pontefract Monkhill	a	06 16		06 43		07 19		07 34	07 52	08 17	
—	—		d	06 16		06 44		07 19		07 35	07 53	08 17	
—	0¾	Pontefract Tanshelf	d			06 46				07 37			
—	2¾	Featherstone	d			06 51				07 42			
—	4½	Streethouse	d			06 54				07 45			
—	8¾	Wakefield Kirkgate ■4 31,34,39	a			07 04				07 57			
—	—		d		06 49	07 05			07 50	07 58			08 49
—	9¾	**Wakefield Westgate** ■7 31,39	a			07 08				08 01			
20	—	Glasshoughton	d	06 24				07 24			08 03	08 22	
21½	—	Castleford	a	06 29	06 59			07 29	08 00		08 08	08 27	08 59
—	—		d	06 32	07 02		07 13	07 32	08 03		08 11	08 30	09 02
26½	—	Woodlesford	d	06 41	07 11		07 22	07 41	08 12		08 23	08 39	09 11
32½	—	**Leeds** ■10 31	a	06 52	07 25	07 24	07 38	07 52	08 25	08 16	08 34	08 50	09 24
—	—	Mirfield	a										
—	—	Brighouse 41	a										
—	—	Halifax 41	a										
—	—	Bradford Interchange 41	a										

Miles	Miles	Station		NT	NT	NT A	NT	NT	NT A	NT	NT	NT A	NT
0	—	**Goole**	d										
4	—	Rawcliffe	d										
6¾	—	Snaith	d										
10½	—	Hensall	d										
12¼	—	Whitley Bridge	d										
16½	—	**Knottingley**	a										
—	—		d	08 39	09 15		09 39	10 15		10 39	11 15		11 39
—	—	London Kings Cross ■15 ⊖26	d										
18½	0	Pontefract Monkhill	a	08 43	09 19		09 43	10 19		10 43	11 19		11 43
—	—		d	08 44	09 19		09 44	10 19		10 44	11 19		11 44
—	0¾	Pontefract Tanshelf	d	08 46			09 46			10 46			11 46
—	2¾	Featherstone	d	08 51			09 51			10 51			11 51
—	4½	Streethouse	d	08 54			09 54			10 54			11 54
—	8¾	Wakefield Kirkgate ■4 31,34,39	a	09 04			10 04			11 04			12 04
—	—		d	09 04		09 49	10 04		10 49	11 04		11 49	12 04
—	9¾	**Wakefield Westgate** ■7 31,39	a	09 08			10 08			11 08			12 08
20	—	Glasshoughton	d		09 24			10 24			11 24		
21½	—	Castleford	a		09 29	09 59		10 29	10 59		11 29	11 59	
—	—		d		09 32	10 02		10 32	11 02		11 32	12 02	
26½	—	Woodlesford	d		09 41	10 11		10 41	11 11		11 41	12 11	
32½	—	**Leeds** ■10 31	a	09 24	09 51	10 24	10 24	10 52	11 24	11 24	11 52	12 24	12 24
—	—	Mirfield	a										
—	—	Brighouse 41	a										
—	—	Halifax 41	a										
—	—	Bradford Interchange 41	a										

Station		NT	NT A	NT	GC ■ 1 ⊡	NT	NT A	NT	NT	NT A	NT	NT
Goole	d											
Rawcliffe	d											
Snaith	d											
Hensall	d											
Whitley Bridge	d											
Knottingley	a											
	d	12 15		12 39		13 15		13 39	14 15		14 39	15 15
London Kings Cross ■15 ⊖26	d				10 52							
Pontefract Monkhill	a	12 19		12 43	12 57	13 19		13 43	14 19		14 43	15 19
	d	12 19		12 44	12 58	13 19		13 44	14 19		14 44	15 19
Pontefract Tanshelf	d			12 46				13 46			14 46	
Featherstone	d			12 51				13 51			14 51	
Streethouse	d			12 54				13 54			14 54	
Wakefield Kirkgate ■4 31,34,39	a			13 04	13 14			14 04			15 04	
	d		12 49	13 04	13 15		13 49	14 04		14 49	15 04	
Wakefield Westgate ■7 31,39	a			13 08				14 08			15 08	
Glasshoughton	d	12 24				13 24			14 24			15 24
Castleford	a	12 29	12 59			13 29	13 59		14 29	14 59		15 29
	d	12 32	13 02			13 32	14 02		14 32	15 02		15 32
Woodlesford	d	12 41	13 11			13 41	14 11		14 41	15 11		15 41
Leeds ■10 31	a	12 52	13 24	13 24		13 52	14 24	14 24	14 52	15 24	15 24	15 52
Mirfield	a				13 27							
Brighouse 41	a				13 35							
Halifax 41	a				13 47							
Bradford Interchange 41	a				14 03							

Station		NT A	NT	NT	NT A	NT	GC ■ 1 ⊡	NT	NT A	NT	NT	NT A
Goole	d											
Rawcliffe	d											
Snaith	d											
Hensall	d											
Whitley Bridge	d											
Knottingley	a											
	d		15 39	16 14		16 41		17 15		17 39	18 16	
London Kings Cross ■15 ⊖26	d						14 48					
Pontefract Monkhill	a		15 43	16 18		16 45	16 52	17 19		17 43	18 20	
	d		15 44	16 18		16 46	16 54	17 19		17 44	18 20	
Pontefract Tanshelf	d		15 46			16 48				17 46		
Featherstone	d		15 51			16 53				17 51		
Streethouse	d		15 54			16 56				17 54		
Wakefield Kirkgate ■4 31,34,39	a		16 04			17 06	17 10			18 04		
	d	15 49	16 04		16 49	17 06	17 11		17 49	18 04		18 49
Wakefield Westgate ■7 31,39	a		16 08			17 10				18 08		
Glasshoughton	d			16 23				17 24			18 25	
Castleford	a	15 59		16 28	16 59			17 29	17 59		18 30	18 59
	d	16 02		16 31	17 02			17 32	18 02		18 33	19 02
Woodlesford	d	16 11		16 40	17 11			17 41	18 11		18 42	19 11
Leeds ■10 31	a	16 24	16 24	16 51	17 24	17 25		17 52	18 24	18 23	18 53	19 24
Mirfield	a						17 25					
Brighouse 41	a						17 33					
Halifax 41	a						17 48					
Bradford Interchange 41	a						18 04					

Station		NT	NT	NT A	NT	NT ◇	NT A	NT	NT	NT A	NT	NT	NT	NT	NT A
Goole	d					19 44									
Rawcliffe	d					19 52									
Snaith	d					19 57									
Hensall	d					20 04									
Whitley Bridge	d					20 07									
Knottingley	a					20 14									
	d	18 39	19 15		19 39	20 15		20 40	21 15		21 45	22 15	22 47	23 09	
London Kings Cross ■15 ⊖26	d														
Pontefract Monkhill	a	18 43	19 19		19 43	20 19		20 44	21 19		21 49	22 19	22 51	23 13	
	d	18 44	19 19		19 44	20 19		20 45	21 19		21 50	22 19	22 52	23 14	
Pontefract Tanshelf	d	18 46			19 46			20 47			21 52		22 54		
Featherstone	d	18 51			19 51			20 52			21 57		22 59		
Streethouse	d	18 54			19 54			20 55			22 00		23 02		
Wakefield Kirkgate ■4 31,34,39	a	19 04			20 04			21 05			22 12		23 12		
	d	19 04		19 49	20 06		20 49	21 05		21 49	22 13		23 13		23 17
Wakefield Westgate ■7 31,39	a	19 08			20 11			21 09			22 16		23 16		
Glasshoughton	d		19 24			20 24			21 24			22 24		23 19	
Castleford	a		19 29	19 59		20 29	20 59		21 29	21 59		22 29		23 24	23 30
	d		19 32	20 02		20 32	21 02		21 32	22 02		22 32		23 26	23 32
Woodlesford	d		19 41	20 11		20 41	21 11		21 41	22 11		22 41		23 36	23 41
Leeds ■10 31	a	19 24	19 52	20 24	20 26	20 52	21 24	21 26	21 55	22 24		22 52		23 47	23 53
Mirfield	a														
Brighouse 41	a														
Halifax 41	a														
Bradford Interchange 41	a														

A From Sheffield

Table T032-R

Saturdays
26 May to 8 December

Goole, Knottingley and Pontefract - Wakefield and Leeds, Bradford

		NT	NT	NT	NT	NT	NT	NT	NT	NT		NT	NT	NT	NT	NT	NT		NT	NT	NT		NT	NT
			A				A			◇		A			A				A				A	
Goole	d									07 42														
Rawcliffe	d									07 50														
Snaith	d									07 55														
Hensall	d									08 02														
Whitley Bridge	d									08 05														
Knottingley	a									08 12														
	d	06 12		06 39		07 15		07 30	07 48	08 13			08 39	09 15		09 39	10 15			14 39	15 15			15 39
London Kings Cross ⊖26	d																	and at						
Pontefract Monkhill	a	06 16		06 43		07 19		07 34	07 52	08 17			08 43	09 19		09 43	10 19	the same		14 43	15 19			15 43
	d	06 16		06 44		07 19		07 35	07 53	08 17			08 44	09 19		09 44	10 19	minutes		14 44	15 19			15 44
Pontefract Tanshelf	d			06 46				07 37					08 46			09 46		past		14 46				15 46
Featherstone	d			06 51				07 42					08 51			09 51		each		14 51				15 51
Streethouse	d			06 54				07 45					08 54			09 54		hour until		14 54				15 54
Wakefield Kirkgate 31,34,39	a			07 04				07 57					09 04			10 04				15 04				16 04
	d		06 50	07 05			07 51	07 58				08 49	09 04		09 49	10 04			14 49	15 04			15 49	16 04
Wakefield Westgate 31,39	a			07 08				08 01					09 08			10 08				15 08				16 08
Glasshoughton	d	06 24				07 24			08 03	08 22				09 24			10 24				15 24			
Castleford	a	06 29	07 00			07 29	08 01		08 08	08 27		08 59		09 29	09 59		10 29		14 59		15 29		15 59	
	d	06 32	07 03		07 13	07 32	08 04		08 11	08 30		09 02		09 32	10 02		10 32		15 02		15 32		16 02	
Woodlesford	d	06 41	07 12		07 22	07 41	08 13		08 23	08 39		09 11		09 41	10 11		10 41		15 11		15 41		16 11	
Leeds	31 a	06 52	07 25	07 24	07 38	07 52	08 26	08 16	08 34	08 50		09 24	09 24	09 51	10 24	10 24	10 52		15 24	15 24	15 52		16 24	16 24
Mirfield	a																							
Brighouse	41 a																							
Halifax	41 a																							
Bradford Interchange	41 a																							

		NT	NT	NT	NT	NT	NT	NT		NT	NT	NT	NT	NT	NT	NT	NT	NT		NT	NT	GC	NT	NT	NT
			A			A				A			A		◇	A				A					
Goole	d														19 44										
Rawcliffe	d														19 52										
Snaith	d														19 57										
Hensall	d														20 04										
Whitley Bridge	d														20 07										
Knottingley	a														20 14										
	d	16 14		16 41	17 15		17 39	18 16			18 39	19 15		19 39	20 15		20 40	21 15			21 45		22 15	22 47	23 09
London Kings Cross ⊖26	d																					19 57			
Pontefract Monkhill	a	16 18		16 45	17 19		17 43	18 20			18 43	19 19		19 43	20 19		20 44	21 19			21 49	21 56	22 19	22 51	23 13
	d	16 18		16 46	17 19		17 44	18 20			18 44	19 19		19 44	20 19		20 45	21 19			21 50	22 03	22 19	22 52	23 14
Pontefract Tanshelf	d			16 48			17 46				18 46			19 46			20 47				21 52			22 54	
Featherstone	d			16 53			17 51				18 51			19 51			20 52				21 57			22 59	
Streethouse	d			16 56			17 54				18 54			19 54			20 55				22 00			23 02	
Wakefield Kirkgate 31,34,39	a			17 06			18 04				19 04			20 04			21 05				22 12	22 20		23 12	
	d		16 49	17 06		17 49	18 04			18 49	19 04		19 49	20 06		20 49	21 05			21 49	22 13	22 21		23 13	
Wakefield Westgate 31,39	a			17 10			18 08				19 08			20 11			21 09				22 16			23 16	
Glasshoughton	d	16 23			17 24			18 25				19 24			20 24			21 24					22 24		23 19
Castleford	a	16 28	16 59		17 29	17 59		18 30		18 59		19 29	19 59		20 29	20 59		21 29		21 59			22 29		23 24
	d	16 31	17 02		17 32	18 02		18 33		19 02		19 32	20 02		20 32	21 02		21 32		22 02			22 32		23 26
Woodlesford	d	16 40	17 11		17 41	18 11		18 42		19 11		19 41	20 11		20 41	21 11		21 41		22 11			22 41		23 36
Leeds	31 a	16 51	17 24	17 25	17 52	18 24	18 23	18 53		19 24	19 24	19 52	20 24	20 26	20 52	21 24	21 26	21 55		22 24			22 52		23 47
Mirfield	a																					22 31			
Brighouse	41 a																					22 40			
Halifax	41 a																					22 52			
Bradford Interchange	41 a																					23 08			

		NT
		A
Goole	d	
Rawcliffe	d	
Snaith	d	
Hensall	d	
Whitley Bridge	d	
Knottingley	a	
	d	
London Kings Cross ⊖26	d	
Pontefract Monkhill	a	
	d	
Pontefract Tanshelf	d	
Featherstone	d	
Streethouse	d	
Wakefield Kirkgate 31,34,39	a	
	d	23 17
Wakefield Westgate 31,39	a	
Glasshoughton	d	
Castleford	a	23 30
	d	23 32
Woodlesford	d	23 41
Leeds	31 a	23 53
Mirfield	a	
Brighouse	41 a	
Halifax	41 a	
Bradford Interchange	41 a	

A From Sheffield

Table T032-R

Sundays
20 May to 2 December

Goole, Knottingley and Pontefract - Wakefield and Leeds, Bradford

		NT	NT	NT	NT	NT	NT	NT	NT	NT		NT	NT	NT	NT	NT	NT	NT	NT	NT		NT	NT	NT	NT
		A				A			A				A			A			A					A	
Goole	d																								
Rawcliffe	d																								
Snaith	d																								
Hensall	d																								
Whitley Bridge	d																								
Knottingley	a																								
	d		09 22	09 42	10 28		11 12	12 28		13 10		14 28		15 12	16 28		17 20	18 28		19 12		20 28	21 12		22 28
London Kings Cross ⊖26	d																								
Pontefract Monkhill	a		09 26	09 46	10 32		11 16	12 32		13 14		14 32		15 16	16 32		17 24	18 32		19 16		20 32	21 16		22 32
	d		09 26	09 46	10 32		11 16	12 32		13 14		14 32		15 16	16 32		17 24	18 32		19 16		20 32	21 16		22 32
Pontefract Tanshelf	d			09 49			11 19			13 17				15 19			17 27			19 19			21 19		
Featherstone	d			09 53			11 22			13 20				15 22			17 30			19 22			21 22		
Streethouse	d			09 56			11 26			13 24				15 26			17 34			19 26			21 26		
Wakefield Kirkgate 31,34,39	a			10 05			11 35			13 33				15 35			17 43			19 35			21 35		
	d	09 23		10 07		11 32	11 36		13 29	13 35			15 29	15 36		17 29	17 44		19 29	19 36			21 36		
Wakefield Westgate 31,39	a			10 11			11 39			13 39				15 39			17 47			19 39			21 40		
Glasshoughton	d		09 33		10 37			12 37				14 37			16 37			18 37				20 37			22 37
Castleford	a	09 33	09 38		10 41	11 42		12 41	13 39			14 41	15 39		16 41	17 40		18 41	19 39			20 41			22 41
	d	09 36	09 41		10 44	11 44		12 44	13 42			14 44	15 41		16 44	17 42		18 44	19 42			20 44		21 44	22 44
Woodlesford	d	09 45	09 50		10 53	11 54		12 53	13 51			14 53	15 51		16 53	17 51		18 53	19 51			20 53		21 54	22 53
Leeds	31 a	09 56	10 00	10 27	11 03	12 08	11 56	13 03	14 04	13 54		15 03	16 04	15 56	17 03	18 04	18 04	19 03	20 04	19 54		21 03	21 56	22 11	23 03
Mirfield	a																								
Brighouse	41 a																								
Halifax	41 a																								
Bradford Interchange	41 a																								

A From Sheffield

Table T033-F

Mondays to Fridays
21 May to 7 December

Sheffield and Selby - York

Local services only

Miles	Miles		NT	NT	NT	NT	NT	NT	NT	NT	NT	NT	NT	NT	NT	NT	NT	NT	NT	NT	NT	NT
					◇		◇		◇	◇		◇		◇		◇	◇		◇		◇	
			A		B		B		B			B		B		B			B		B	
0	—	Sheffield 7 29,31 d								08 54							11 59					
3½	—	Meadowhall 29,31 d								09 01							12 05					
6¾	—	Rotherham Central 29,31 d								09 07							12 11					
10¾	—	Swinton (S.Yorks) 29,31 d								09 17							12 19					
18½	—	Moorthorpe 31 d								09 26							12 29					
25½	—	Pontefract Baghill d								09 35							12 37					
—	—	Hull 29 d		06 19		07 06		08 08			09 10		10 10		11 10			12 10		13 10		14 09
—	0	Selby d		06 56		07 55		08 47			09 47		10 47		11 47			12 47		13 56		14 47
33¾	8¼	Sherburn-in-Elmet d		07 09		08 09		09 01		09 49	10 01				12 01		12 52	13 01				
36	10½	Church Fenton d	06 56	07 14	07 48	08 14	08 48	09 05	09 48	09 54	10 05	10 48		11 48	12 05	12 48	12 56	13 05	13 48		14 48	
38	12½	Ulleskelf d		07 18	07 53	08 18				09 58							13 00					
46¾	21	York 8 29 a	07 11	07 28	08 06	08 31	09 02	09 19	10 01	10 14	10 22	11 01	11 12	12 00	12 22	13 01	13 12	13 19	14 01	14 20	15 00	15 11

	NT	NT	NT	NT	NT	NT	NT	NT	NT	NT	NT	NT	NT	NT	NT	NT
	◇		◇				◇		◇		◇		◇	◇	◇	
	B		B		A		B		B		B		B	B	B	
Sheffield 7 29,31 d																
Meadowhall 29,31 d																
Rotherham Central 29,31 d																
Swinton (S.Yorks) 29,31 d																
Moorthorpe 31 d																
Pontefract Baghill d																
Hull 29 d		15 18		16 10		17 15		18 10		19 16						
Selby d		15 57		16 47		18 03		18 47		19 56		20 46				23 44
Sherburn-in-Elmet d		16 12		17 01		18 18		19 01		20 11		21 01				
Church Fenton d	15 48	16 17	16 48	17 05	18 04	18 22	18 48	19 05	19 48	20 15	20 48	21 09	21 47	22 47	23 50	
Ulleskelf d																
York 8 29 a	16 02	16 29	17 00	17 23	18 17	18 34	19 01	19 20	20 00	20 27	20 59	21 26	22 00	23 01	00 03	00 08

Saturdays
26 May to 8 December

	NT	NT	NT	NT	NT	NT	NT	NT	NT	NT	NT	NT	NT	NT	NT	NT	NT	NT	NT	NT	NT	NT
		◇		◇		◇	◇		◇		◇		◇	◇		◇		◇		◇		◇
		B		B		B			B		B		B			B		B		B		B
Sheffield 7 29,31 d							08 54							11 59								
Meadowhall 29,31 d							09 01							12 05								
Rotherham Central 29,31 d							09 07							12 11								
Swinton (S.Yorks) 29,31 d							09 17							12 19								
Moorthorpe 31 d							09 26							12 29								
Pontefract Baghill d							09 35							12 37								
Hull 29 d	06 22		07 06		08 08			09 10		10 10		11 10			12 10		13 10		14 09		15 18	
Selby d	06 59		07 55		08 47			09 47		10 47		11 47			12 47		13 56		14 47		15 57	
Sherburn-in-Elmet d	07 12		08 09		09 01		09 49	10 01				12 01		12 52	13 01						16 12	
Church Fenton d	07 17	07 48	08 14	08 48	09 05	09 48	09 54	10 05	10 48		11 48	12 05	12 48	12 56	13 05	13 48		14 48		15 48	16 17	16 48
Ulleskelf d	07 21	07 53	08 18				09 58							13 00								
York 8 29 a	07 31	08 06	08 31	09 02	09 19	10 01	10 14	10 22	11 01	11 12	12 00	12 22	13 01	13 12	13 19	14 02	14 20	15 00	15 11	16 00	16 29	17 00

	NT	NT	NT	NT	NT	NT	NT	NT	NT	NT	NT	NT	NT
		◇			◇		◇		◇		◇	◇	◇
		B	A		B		B		B		B	B	B
Sheffield 7 29,31 d													
Meadowhall 29,31 d													
Rotherham Central 29,31 d													
Swinton (S.Yorks) 29,31 d													
Moorthorpe 31 d													
Pontefract Baghill d													
Hull 29 d	16 10			17 15		18 10		19 16					
Selby d	16 47			18 03		18 47		19 56		20 46			
Sherburn-in-Elmet d	17 01			18 18		19 01		20 11		21 01			
Church Fenton d	17 05	17 48	18 04	18 23	18 48	19 05	19 48	20 15	20 48	21 09	21 47	22 48	23 50
Ulleskelf d													
York 8 29 a	17 23	18 00	18 17	18 37	19 00	19 20	20 00	20 27	20 59	21 26	22 00	23 01	00 03

Sundays
20 May to 2 December

	NT	NT	NT	NT	NT	NT	NT	NT	NT	NT	NT	NT	NT	NT	NT	NT	NT	NT	NT	NT	NT	NT
			◇	◇		◇	◇		◇	◇		◇	◇	◇		◇	◇		◇	◇		◇
	A		C	D		E	E		E	E		E	E	F		E	E		E	F		E
Sheffield 7 29,31 d														16 13						18 58		
Meadowhall 29,31 d														16 20						19 04		
Rotherham Central 29,31 d														16 28						19 12		
Swinton (S.Yorks) 29,31 d														16 38						19 20		
Moorthorpe 31 d														16 53						19 29		
Pontefract Baghill d														17 01						19 37		
Hull 29 d		08 31			10 33			12 33			14 24				16 35			18 35			19 35	
Selby d		09 07			11 09			13 09			14 59				17 09			19 09			20 09	
Sherburn-in-Elmet d		09 25			11 22			13 26						17 15				19 24		19 52		
Church Fenton d	08 34		09 48	10 46	11 26	11 47	12 48		13 48	14 48		15 48	16 46	17 20	17 26	17 48	18 48		19 46	19 56	20 26	20 48
Ulleskelf d		09 31						13 32						17 24				19 30		20 00		
York 8 29 a	08 47	09 42	10 05	10 59	11 39	12 00	13 01	13 43	14 01	15 01	15 25	16 01	17 00	17 36	17 41	18 01	19 01	19 41	19 59	20 16	20 41	21 01

A From Leeds
B From Manchester Victoria
C From Halifax
D From Blackburn
E From Blackpool North
F via Pontefract Baghill

Table T033-F

Sundays
20 May to 2 December

Sheffield and Selby - York

Local services only

	NT	NT	NT
	◇		
	A		B
Sheffield 7 29,31 d			
Meadowhall 29,31 d			
Rotherham Central 29,31 d			
Swinton (S.Yorks) 29,31 d			
Moorthorpe 31 d			
Pontefract Baghill d			
Hull 29 d		21 35	
Selby d		22 09	
Sherburn-in-Elmet d		22 23	
Church Fenton d	21 46	22 27	22 48
Ulleskelf d			
York 8 29 a	22 03	22 41	23 04

A From Blackpool North
B From Leeds

Table T033-R

Mondays to Fridays
21 May to 7 December

York - Selby and Sheffield

Local services only

Miles	Miles			NT	NT	NT	NT	NT	NT	NT	NT	NT	NT	NT	NT	NT	NT	NT	NT	NT	NT	NT	NT
														◇						◇			
				A		A	A	B	A		A		A			A		A			A		A
0	0	York	29 d	05 18	05 40	06 24	07 13	07 21	08 16	08 48	09 15	09 47	10 15	10 15	10 50	11 15	11 47	12 15	12 50	13 13	13 15	13 47	14 15
8¾	8¾	Ulleskelf	d				07 22			08 58				10 25						13 23			
10¾	10¾	Church Fenton	a	05 29		06 35	07 26	07 32	08 28	09 02	09 27	09 58	10 28	10 29		11 27	11 58	12 27		13 27	13 27	13 58	14 27
—	—		d					07 33		09 02		09 59		10 29			11 59			13 27		13 59	
12¾	12¾	Sherburn-in-Elmet	d					07 37		09 06		10 03		10 33			12 03			13 31		14 03	
—	21	**Selby**	a		06 06			07 49		09 21		10 16			11 16		12 16		13 17			14 16	
—	—	Hull	29 a					08 39		10 04		11 00			12 01		13 03		14 01			15 04	
21¼	—	Pontefract Baghill	d											10 49						13 47			
28¼	—	Moorthorpe	31 a											11 00						13 58			
36	—	Swinton (S.Yorks)	29,31 a											11 10						14 10			
40½	—	Rotherham Central	29,31 a											11 18						14 18			
43¼	—	Meadowhall	29,31 ⇌ a											11 24						14 24			
46¾	—	**Sheffield**	29,31 ⇌ a											11 31						14 31			

		NT	NT	NT	NT	NT	NT	NT	NT	NT	NT	NT	NT	NT	NT	NT	NT	NT
			A		A		A			A		A		A	A		C	
York	29 d	14 50	15 15	15 47	16 15	16 48	17 15	17 48	18 50	19 15	19 50	20 20	20 45	21 15	22 17	22 46	23 15	23 19
Ulleskelf	d							17 58								22 55		
Church Fenton	a		15 27	15 58	16 27	16 59	17 27	18 02		19 27	20 01	20 32	20 56	21 30	22 29	22 59	23 29	
	d			15 59		17 00		18 03			20 02		20 57			22 59		
Sherburn-in-Elmet	d			16 03		17 04		18 07			20 08		21 01			23 03		
Selby	a	15 17		16 16		17 17		18 19	19 17		20 20		21 19			23 16		23 40
Hull	29 a	16 00		17 02		18 03		19 03	19 59				22 05			00 04		
Pontefract Baghill	d																	
Moorthorpe	31 a																	
Swinton (S.Yorks)	29,31 a																	
Rotherham Central	29,31 a																	
Meadowhall	29,31 ⇌ a																	
Sheffield	29,31 ⇌ a																	

Saturdays
26 May to 8 December

		NT	NT	NT	NT	NT	NT	NT	NT	NT	NT	NT	NT	NT	NT	NT	NT	NT	NT	NT	NT	NT	NT	NT	NT
											◇							◇					
		A		A	A	B	A		A			A		A		A			A		A		A
York	29 d	05 18	05 40	06 24	07 13	07 21	08 16	08 48	09 19	09 47	10 15	10 17	10 50	11 17	11 47	12 17	12 50	13 13	13 17	13 47	14 17	14 50	15 17
Ulleskelf	d				07 22			08 58			10 25							13 23					
Church Fenton	a	05 29		06 35	07 26	07 32	08 28	09 02	09 30	09 58	10 29	10 29		11 29	11 58	12 29		13 27	13 29	13 58	14 29		15 29
	d					07 33		09 02		09 59	10 29				11 59			13 27		13 59			
Sherburn-in-Elmet	d					07 37		09 06		10 03	10 33				12 03			13 31		14 03			
Selby	a		06 06			07 49		09 20		10 16			11 16		12 16		13 17			14 16		15 17	
Hull	29 a					08 39		10 04		11 00			12 01		13 03		14 01			15 04		16 00	
Pontefract Baghill	d										10 49							13 47					
Moorthorpe	31 a										11 00							13 58					
Swinton (S.Yorks)	29,31 a										11 10							14 10					
Rotherham Central	29,31 a										11 18							14 18					
Meadowhall	29,31 ⇌ a										11 24							14 24					
Sheffield	29,31 ⇌ a										11 31							14 31					

		NT	NT	NT	NT	NT	NT	NT	NT	NT	NT	NT	NT	NT	NT	NT	NT	NT
			A		A		A		A		A		A	A		C	
York	29 d	15 47	16 17	16 48	17 19	17 48	18 21	18 50	19 17	19 50	20 20	20 45	21 19	22 17	22 46	23 15	23 19
Ulleskelf	d					17 58									22 55		
Church Fenton	a	15 58	16 29	16 59	17 31	18 02	18 32		19 29	20 01	20 32	20 56	21 31	22 29	22 59	23 29	
	d	15 59		17 00		18 03				20 02		20 57			22 59		
Sherburn-in-Elmet	d	16 03		17 04		18 07				20 08		21 01			23 03		
Selby	a	16 16		17 17		18 19		19 17		20 20		21 19			23 16		23 40
Hull	29 a	17 02		18 03		19 03		19 59				22 05			00 04		
Pontefract Baghill	d																
Moorthorpe	31 a																
Swinton (S.Yorks)	29,31 a																
Rotherham Central	29,31 a																
Meadowhall	29,31 ⇌ a																
Sheffield	29,31 ⇌ a																

Sundays
20 May to 2 December

		NT	NT	NT	NT	NT	NT	NT	NT	NT	NT	NT	NT	NT	NT	NT	NT	NT	NT	NT	NT	NT	NT
		◇		◇		◇	◇		◇	◇		◇	◇		◇	◇		◇	◇	◇		◇	◇
		D		D		D	D		D	D		D	D		D	D			D	D		D	E
York	29 d	08 15	08 51	09 14	10 01	10 17	11 17	11 51	12 17	13 17	13 51	14 17	15 14	15 51	16 17	17 22	17 51	18 01	18 22	19 14	20 05	20 22	20 48
Ulleskelf	d		09 01											16 00				18 11					20 58
Church Fenton	a	08 26	09 04	09 25		10 28	11 28		12 29	13 29	14 02	14 28	15 25	16 03	16 28	17 33		18 15	18 34	19 25		20 33	21 02
	d		09 05								14 02			16 03				18 19					21 02
Sherburn-in-Elmet	d		09 09								14 06			16 07				18 22					21 06
Selby	a		09 21		10 19			12 13			14 18			16 19			18 10				20 23		
Hull	29 a		09 59		10 55			12 52			14 56			16 58			18 45				21 01		
Pontefract Baghill	d																	18 34					21 24
Moorthorpe	31 a																	18 44					21 36
Swinton (S.Yorks)	29,31 a																	18 53					21 45
Rotherham Central	29,31 a																	19 02					
Meadowhall	29,31 ⇌ a																	19 08					21 55
Sheffield	29,31 ⇌ a																	19 19					22 03

A To Huddersfield
B From Leeds
C To Leeds
D To Blackpool North
E via Pontefract Baghill

Table T033-R

Sundays
20 May to 2 December

York - Selby and Sheffield

Local services only

		NT	NT	NT
				◇
		A		A
York	29 d	21 17	22 19	22 21
Ulleskelf	d			
Church Fenton	a	21 28		22 32
	d			
Sherburn-in-Elmet	d			
Selby	a		22 37	
Hull	29 a		23 23	
Pontefract Baghill	d			
Moorthorpe	31 a			
Swinton (S.Yorks)	29,31 a			
Rotherham Central	29,31 a			
Meadowhall	29,31 ⇌ a			
Sheffield	29,31 ⇌ a			

A To Leeds

21 May to 20 July

Nottingham and Sheffield - Barnsley - Huddersfield and Leeds

Miles	Miles	Station			NT MX ◇ A	NT ◇	NT	NT B	NT MX	NT MO	NT	NT ◇ C	NT		NT	NT D	NT	NT ◇	NT E	NT	NT ◇	NT D	NT		TP ◇1 F	NT
0	—	**Nottingham** [8]		d																						
—	—	Ilkeston		d																						
12	—	Langley Mill		d																						
18¼	—	Alfreton		d																						
28¼	—	Chesterfield		d																		06 25				
33½	—	Dronfield		d	00 02																	06 32				
40½	0	**Sheffield** [7]	29,31	a	00 16																	06 42				
—	—			d		05 15	05 18	05 25	05 30	05 30	05 37	05 43	05 51		06 02	06 05	06 16	06 19	06 27	06 30	06 45	07 01	07 04		07 08	07 14
44	3½	**Meadowhall** [4]	29,31	a		05 20	05 23	05 30	05 35	05 35	05 43	05 48	05 56		06 07	06 10	06 21	06 24	06 32	06 35	06 50	07 06	07 09		07 13	07 19
—	—			d		05 21	05 24		05 36	05 36	05 44		05 57		06 08		06 22	06 25		06 36	06 51		07 10			07 22
47¾	7¼	Chapeltown		d			05 30		05 42	05 42	05 50				06 14					06 42			07 16			
51	10½	Elsecar		d			05 35		05 48	05 48	05 56				06 20					06 48			07 22			
52½	12	Wombwell		d			05 39		05 51	05 51	05 59				06 23					06 51			07 25			
56½	16	**Barnsley**		a			05 45		05 57	05 57	06 05		06 12		06 29			06 39		06 57	07 06		07 31			
—	—			d					05 58	06 00	06 06				06 30			06 39		07 00	07 06		07 32			
—	19	Dodworth		d							06 12									07 06						
—	20¼	Silkstone Common		d							06 15									07 09						
—	23½	Penistone		d							06 21									07 16						
—	27½	Denby Dale		d							06 28									07 23						
—	29¾	Shepley		d							06 33									07 28						
—	30¾	Stocksmoor		d							06 36									07 31						
—	32¾	Brockholes		d							06 40									07 35						
—	33¾	Honley		d							06 42									07 37						
—	34¾	Berry Brow		d							06 45									07 40						
—	35¾	Lockwood		d							06 48									07 43						
—	37	**Huddersfield**		a							06 52									07 47						
60	—	Darton		d					06 03	06 05					06 35								07 37			
67½	—	**Wakefield Kirkgate** [4]	31	a					06 14	06 16					06 48			06 54			07 22		07 49			
—	—			d					06 16	06 17					06 49			06 55			07 23		07 50			
70½	—	Normanton		d					06 21	06 22					06 54			06 59			07 27		07 55			
74	—	Castleford	32	a											06 59								08 00			
78¾	—	Woodlesford	32	a					06 29	06 30					07 11								08 12			
84¾	—	**Leeds** [10]	31,32	a		06 30			06 43	06 45					07 25		07 30	07 16			07 43		08 25			08 36

Station			NT ◇	NT ◇ C	EM ◇ G	NT D	NT	NT ◇ H	EM ◇1 I		NT	NT B	TP ◇1 F	NT ◇	NT ◇	NT ◇ J	NT K	NT	EM ◇ G		NT ◇ L	NT ◇ M	NT	NT D	TP ◇1 F	NT
Nottingham [8]		d	06 17		06 39										07 18				07 46							
Ilkeston		d	06 29												07 30				07 59							
Langley Mill		d	06 36												07 37											
Alfreton		d	06 44		07 00										07 45				08 10							
Chesterfield		d	06 54		07 10				07 43						07 57				08 20							
Dronfield		d	07 01		07 18				07 49						08 04				08 27							
Sheffield [7]	29,31	a	07 11		07 28				08 00						08 15				08 38							
		d	07 18	07 24		07 31	07 35	07 47			08 03	08 06	08 10	08 15	08 18	08 25	08 30	08 35			08 46	08 54	09 03	09 06	09 10	09 15
Meadowhall [4]	29,31	a	07 23	07 31		07 36	07 40	07 53			08 08	08 11	08 16	08 21	08 24	08 31	08 35	08 40			08 51	09 00	09 08	09 11	09 15	09 20
		d	07 25				07 41	07 54			08 09			08 21	08 25			08 41			08 53		09 09			09 21
Chapeltown		d					07 47				08 15							08 47					09 15			
Elsecar		d					07 53				08 21							08 53					09 21			
Wombwell		d					07 56				08 24							08 56					09 24			
Barnsley		a	07 41				08 02	08 10			08 30				08 40			09 02			09 10		09 30			
		d	07 42				08 03	08 11			08 31				08 41			09 03			09 11		09 31			
Dodworth		d					08 09											09 09								
Silkstone Common		d					08 12											09 12								
Penistone		d					08 19											09 19								
Denby Dale		d					08 26											09 26								
Shepley		d					08 31											09 31								
Stocksmoor		d					08 34											09 34								
Brockholes		d					08 38											09 38								
Honley		d					08 40											09 40								
Berry Brow		d					08 43											09 43								
Lockwood		d					08 46											09 46								
Huddersfield		a					08 50											09 50								
Darton		d									08 36												09 36			
Wakefield Kirkgate [4]	31	a	07 57					08 25			08 48					08 57					09 26		09 48			
		d	07 57					08 25			08 49					08 58					09 26		09 49			
Normanton		d						08 30			08 54												09 54			
Castleford	32	a									08 59												09 59			
Woodlesford	32	a									09 11												10 11			
Leeds [10]	31,32	a	08 17					08 46			09 24			09 30	09 17						09 46		10 24			10 30

A From Nottingham
B To Doncaster
C To Bridlington
D To Adwick
E To Beverley
F From Manchester Airport to Cleethorpes
G To Liverpool Lime Street
H From Retford
I From Derby
J To Scarborough
K To Hull
L From Lincoln
M To York

21 May to 20 July

Nottingham and Sheffield - Barnsley - Huddersfield and Leeds

Station			NT ◇	NT ◇ A	NT B		NT	EM ◇ C	NT ◇ D	NT	NT E	TP ◇1 F	NT ◇	NT ◇	NT ◇ A		NT B	NT	EM ◇ C	NT ◇ D	NT	NT E	TP ◇1 F	NT	NT ◇
Nottingham [8]		d	08 17					08 47						09 17					09 47						10 17
Ilkeston		d	08 29											09 29											10 29
Langley Mill		d	08 36											09 36											10 36
Alfreton		d	08 44					09 08						09 44					10 08						10 44
Chesterfield		d	08 55					09 20						09 55					10 20						10 55
Dronfield		d	09 02											10 02											11 02
Sheffield [7]	29,31	a	09 13					09 37						10 13					10 38						11 13
		d	09 18	09 24	09 30		09 35		09 48	10 02	10 05	10 10	10 15	10 18	10 24		10 30	10 35		10 49	11 02	11 05	11 10	11 15	11 18
Meadowhall [4]	29,31	a	09 23	09 31	09 35		09 40		09 53	10 07	10 10	10 16	10 20	10 23	10 31		10 35	10 40		10 54	11 07	11 10	11 16	11 20	11 23
		d	09 24				09 41		09 54	10 08			10 21	10 24				10 41		10 57	11 08			11 21	11 24
Chapeltown		d					09 47			10 14								10 47			11 14				
Elsecar		d					09 53			10 20								10 53			11 20				
Wombwell		d					09 56			10 23								10 56			11 23				
Barnsley		a	09 40				10 02		10 10	10 29				10 39				11 02		11 11	11 29				11 39
		d	09 41				10 03		10 11	10 30				10 40				11 03		11 12	11 30				11 40
Dodworth		d					10 09											11 09							
Silkstone Common		d					10 12											11 12							
Penistone		d					10 19											11 19							
Denby Dale		d					10 26											11 26							
Shepley		d					10 31											11 31							
Stocksmoor		d					10 34											11 34							
Brockholes		d					10 38											11 38							
Honley		d					10 40											11 40							
Berry Brow		d					10 43											11 43							
Lockwood		d					10 46											11 46							
Huddersfield		a					10 50											11 50							
Darton		d								10 35											11 35				
Wakefield Kirkgate [4]	31	a	09 56						10 26	10 48				10 55						11 27	11 48				11 55
		d	09 56						10 26	10 49				10 55						11 27	11 49				11 55
Normanton		d								10 54											11 54				
Castleford	32	a								10 59											11 59				
Woodlesford	32	a								11 11											12 11				
Leeds [10]	31,32	a	10 16						10 46	11 24			11 30	11 15						11 47	12 24			12 30	12 15

Station			NT ◇ A	NT B	NT	EM ◇ C	NT ◇ D	NT ◇ G	NT	NT E	TP ◇1 F		NT ◇	NT ◇	NT ◇ A	NT B	NT	EM ◇ C	NT ◇ D	NT	NT E		TP ◇1 F	NT	NT ◇	NT ◇ H
Nottingham [8]		d				10 51								11 17				11 47							12 17	
Ilkeston		d												11 29											12 29	
Langley Mill		d												11 36											12 36	
Alfreton		d				11 12								11 44				12 08							12 44	
Chesterfield		d				11 22								11 55				12 20							12 55	
Dronfield		d												12 02											13 02	
Sheffield [7]	29,31	a				11 38								12 13				12 38							13 13	
		d	11 24	11 30	11 35		11 45	11 59	12 02	12 05	12 10		12 15	12 18	12 24	12 30	12 35		12 45	13 02	13 05		13 10	13 15	13 18	13 24
Meadowhall [4]	29,31	a	11 31	11 35	11 40		11 50	12 04	12 07	12 10	12 16		12 20	12 23	12 31	12 35	12 40		12 51	13 07	13 10		13 16	13 20	13 23	13 31
		d			11 41		11 51		12 08				12 21	12 24			12 41		12 51	13 08				13 21	13 24	
Chapeltown		d			11 47				12 14								12 47			13 14						
Elsecar		d			11 53				12 20								12 53			13 20						
Wombwell		d			11 56				12 23								12 56			13 23						
Barnsley		a			12 02		12 10		12 29					12 39			13 02		13 11	13 29					13 39	
		d			12 03		12 11		12 30					12 40			13 03		13 11	13 30					13 40	
Dodworth		d			12 09												13 09									
Silkstone Common		d			12 12												13 12									
Penistone		d			12 19												13 19									
Denby Dale		d			12 26												13 26									
Shepley		d			12 31												13 31									
Stocksmoor		d			12 34												13 34									
Brockholes		d			12 38												13 38									
Honley		d			12 40												13 40									
Berry Brow		d			12 43												13 43									
Lockwood		d			12 46												13 46									
Huddersfield		a			12 50												13 50									
Darton		d							12 35											13 35						
Wakefield Kirkgate [4]	31	a					12 26		12 48					12 55					13 26	13 48					13 55	
		d					12 26		12 49					12 55					13 27	13 49					13 55	
Normanton		d							12 54											13 54						
Castleford	32	a							12 59											13 59						
Woodlesford	32	a							13 11											14 11						
Leeds [10]	31,32	a					12 46		13 24				13 30	13 15					13 46	14 24				14 30	14 15	

A To Bridlington
B To Hull
C From Norwich to Liverpool Lime Street
D From Lincoln
E To Adwick
F From Manchester Airport to Cleethorpes
G To York
H To Scarborough

Table T034-F

Mondays to Fridays
21 May to 20 July

Nottingham and Sheffield - Barnsley - Huddersfield and Leeds

		NT	NT	EM	NT	NT	NT	TP	NT	NT	NT	NT	NT	EM	NT	NT	NT	TP	NT	NT	NT	NT	NT
				◇	◇			◇1	◇	◇	◇			◇	◇			◇1		◇	◇		
		A		B	C		D	E			F	A		B	C		D	E			F	A	
Nottingham	d			12 47						13 17				13 47						14 17			
Ilkeston	d			13 00						13 29										14 29			
Langley Mill	d									13 36										14 36			
Alfreton	d			13 10						13 44				14 08						14 44			
Chesterfield	d			13 21						13 55				14 20						14 55			
Dronfield	d									14 02										15 02			
Sheffield 29,31	a			13 37						14 13				14 38						15 13			
	d	13 30	13 35		13 45	14 02	14 05	14 10	14 15	14 18	14 24	14 30	14 35		14 45	15 02	15 05	15 10	15 15	15 18	15 24	15 30	15 35
Meadowhall 29,31	a	13 35	13 40		13 51	14 07	14 10	14 16	14 20	14 23	14 31	14 35	14 40		14 51	15 07	15 10	15 16	15 20	15 23	15 31	15 35	15 40
	d		13 41		13 51	14 08			14 21	14 24			14 41		14 51	15 08			15 21	15 24			15 41
Chapeltown	d		13 47			14 14							14 47			15 14							15 47
Elsecar	d		13 53			14 20							14 53			15 20							15 53
Wombwell	d		13 56			14 23							14 56			15 23							15 56
Barnsley	a		14 02		14 11	14 29				14 39			15 02		15 11	15 29				15 39			16 02
	d		14 03		14 11	14 30				14 40			15 03		15 11	15 30				15 40			16 03
Dodworth	d		14 09										15 09										16 09
Silkstone Common	d		14 12										15 12										16 12
Penistone	d		14 19										15 19										16 19
Denby Dale	d		14 26										15 26										16 26
Shepley	d		14 31										15 31										16 31
Stocksmoor	d		14 34										15 34										16 34
Brockholes	d		14 38										15 38										16 38
Honley	d		14 40										15 40										16 40
Berry Brow	d		14 43										15 43										16 43
Lockwood	d		14 46										15 46										16 46
Huddersfield	a		14 50										15 50										16 50
Darton	d					14 35										15 35							
Wakefield Kirkgate 31	a				14 26	14 48				14 55					15 26	15 48				15 55			
	d				14 27	14 49				14 55					15 27	15 49				15 55			
Normanton	d					14 54										15 54							
Castleford 32	a					14 59										15 59							
Woodlesford 32	a					15 11										16 11							
Leeds 31,32	a				14 46	15 24			15 30	15 15					15 46	16 24			16 30	16 15			

		EM	NT	NT	NT	TP	NT	NT	NT	NT	NT	EM	NT	NT	NT	TP	NT	NT	NT	NT	EM	NT
		◇	◇			◇1	◇	◇	◇			◇	◇			◇1		◇			◇	◇
		B	C		D	E			G	A		B	C		D	E		G	A		B	C
Nottingham	d	14 47						15 17				15 47									16 47	
Ilkeston	d							15 29				16 00										
Langley Mill	d							15 36														
Alfreton	d	15 08						15 44				16 10									17 08	
Chesterfield	d	15 20						15 55				16 20									17 20	
Dronfield	d							16 02														
Sheffield 29,31	a	15 37						16 13				16 37									17 37	
	d		15 45	16 02	16 05	16 10	16 15	16 18	16 24	16 30	16 35		16 45	17 02	17 05	17 10	17 15	17 24	17 30	17 35		17 45
Meadowhall 29,31	a		15 50	16 07	16 10	16 16	16 20	16 23	16 31	16 35	16 40		16 51	17 07	17 10	17 16	17 20	17 31	17 35	17 40		17 51
	d		15 51	16 08			16 21	16 24			16 41		16 51	17 08			17 21			17 41		17 51
Chapeltown	d			16 14							16 47			17 14						17 47		
Elsecar	d			16 20							16 53			17 20						17 53		
Wombwell	d			16 23							16 56			17 23						17 56		
Barnsley	a		16 10	16 29				16 39			17 02		17 11	17 29						18 02		18 10
	d		16 11	16 30				16 40			17 03		17 11	17 30						18 03		18 11
Dodworth	d										17 09									18 09		
Silkstone Common	d										17 12									18 13		
Penistone	d										17 19									18 23		
Denby Dale	d										17 26									18 29		
Shepley	d										17 31									18 34		
Stocksmoor	d										17 33									18 37		
Brockholes	d										17 37									18 41		
Honley	d										17 40									18 43		
Berry Brow	d										17 43									18 46		
Lockwood	d										17 45									18 49		
Huddersfield	a										17 50									18 54		
Darton	d			16 35										17 35								
Wakefield Kirkgate 31	a		16 26	16 48				16 55					17 26	17 48								18 27
	d		16 26	16 49				16 55					17 27	17 49								18 27
Normanton	d			16 54										17 54								
Castleford 32	a			16 59										17 59								
Woodlesford 32	a			17 11										18 11								
Leeds 31,32	a		16 46	17 24			17 32	17 15					17 46	18 24			18 30					18 47

A To Hull
B From Norwich to Liverpool Lime Street
C From Lincoln
D To Adwick
E From Manchester Airport to Cleethorpes
F To Bridlington
G To Scarborough

Table T034-F

Mondays to Fridays
21 May to 20 July

Nottingham and Sheffield - Barnsley - Huddersfield and Leeds

		NT	NT	TP	NT	NT	NT	NT	NT	EM	NT	NT	NT	TP	NT	NT	NT	NT	NT	EM	NT	NT	NT
				◇1	◇	◇	◇			◇	◇			◇1		◇	◇			◇	◇		
			A	B			C	D		E	F		A	B			D	D		E	F		A
Nottingham	d					17 17				17 47						18 17				18 47			
Ilkeston	d					17 29										18 29							
Langley Mill	d					17 36				18 03						18 36							
Alfreton	d					17 44				18 11						18 44				19 08			
Chesterfield	d					17 55				18 20						18 55				19 20			
Dronfield	d					18 02										19 02							
Sheffield 29,31	a					18 13				18 38						19 13				19 37			
	d	18 02	18 05	18 11	18 15	18 18	18 24	18 30	18 35		18 45	19 02	19 05	19 11	19 15	19 18	19 24	19 30	19 35		19 45	20 02	20 05
Meadowhall 29,31	a	18 07	18 10	18 17	18 20	18 23	18 31	18 35	18 40		18 50	19 07	19 10	19 16	19 20	19 23	19 31	19 35	19 40		19 50	20 07	20 10
	d	18 08			18 21	18 24			18 41		18 51	19 08			19 21	19 24			19 41		19 51	20 08	
Chapeltown	d	18 14							18 47			19 14							19 47			20 14	
Elsecar	d	18 20							18 53			19 20							19 53			20 20	
Wombwell	d	18 23							18 56			19 23							19 56			20 23	
Barnsley	a	18 29				18 39			19 02		19 10	19 29				19 39			20 02		20 10	20 29	
	d	18 30				18 40			19 03		19 11	19 30				19 40			20 03		20 11	20 30	
Dodworth	d								19 09										20 09				
Silkstone Common	d								19 12										20 12				
Penistone	d								19 19										20 19				
Denby Dale	d								19 26										20 26				
Shepley	d								19 31										20 31				
Stocksmoor	d								19 34										20 34				
Brockholes	d								19 38										20 38				
Honley	d								19 40										20 40				
Berry Brow	d								19 43										20 43				
Lockwood	d								19 46										20 46				
Huddersfield	a								19 50										20 50				
Darton	d	18 35										19 35										20 35	
Wakefield Kirkgate 31	a	18 48				18 55					19 26	19 48				19 55					20 26	20 48	
	d	18 49				18 55					19 26	19 49				19 55					20 26	20 49	
Normanton	d	18 54										19 54										20 54	
Castleford 32	a	18 59										19 59										20 59	
Woodlesford 32	a	19 11										20 11										21 11	
Leeds 31,32	a	19 24			19 30	19 15					19 46	20 24			20 36	20 15					20 46	21 24	

		TP	NT	NT	NT	EM	NT	NT	NT	NT	NT	TP	NT	NT	NT	EM	NT	EM	NT	TP	NT	NT
		◇1	◇	◇	◇	◇			◇			◇1		◇	◇	◇1		◇1		◇1	◇	◇
		B			C	G	D		F		A	B			H	I		I	A	B		
Nottingham	d			19 17		19 41								20 17		20 33		21 08				21 12
Ilkeston	d			19 29										20 29								21 29
Langley Mill	d			19 36										20 36		20 52		21 25				21 36
Alfreton	d			19 44		20 02								20 44		21 00		21 33				21 44
Chesterfield	d			19 55		20 12								20 55		21 11		21 44				21 55
Dronfield	d			20 02										21 02								22 02
Sheffield 29,31	a			20 13		20 28								21 13		21 27		21 58				22 13
	d	20 11	20 15	20 18	20 24		20 30	20 35	20 45	21 02	21 05	21 11	21 15	21 18	21 28	21 32	21 35	22 04	22 07	22 11	22 15	22 18
Meadowhall 29,31	a	20 16	20 20	20 23	20 31		20 35	20 40	20 50	21 07	21 10	21 16	21 20	21 23	21 33		21 40		22 12	22 16	22 21	22 23
	d		20 21	20 24				20 41	20 51	21 08			21 21	21 24			21 41				22 22	22 24
Chapeltown	d							20 47		21 14							21 47					
Elsecar	d							20 53		21 20							21 53					
Wombwell	d							20 56		21 23							21 56					
Barnsley	a			20 39				21 02	21 10	21 29				21 39			22 02					22 39
	d			20 40				21 03	21 11	21 30				21 40			22 03					22 40
Dodworth	d							21 09									22 09					
Silkstone Common	d							21 12									22 12					
Penistone	d							21 19									22 19					
Denby Dale	d							21 26									22 26					
Shepley	d							21 31									22 31					
Stocksmoor	d							21 34									22 34					
Brockholes	d							21 38									22 38					
Honley	d							21 40									22 40					
Berry Brow	d							21 43									22 43					
Lockwood	d							21 46									22 46					
Huddersfield	a							21 50									22 50					
Darton	d									21 35												
Wakefield Kirkgate 31	a			20 55					21 26	21 48				21 55								22 55
	d			20 55					21 26	21 49				21 55								22 55
Normanton	d									21 54												
Castleford 32	a									21 59												
Woodlesford 32	a									22 11												
Leeds 31,32	a		21 30	21 15					21 46	22 24			22 30	22 15		22 34		22 49			23 31	23 14

A To Adwick
B From Manchester Airport to Cleethorpes
C To Bridlington
D To Hull
E From Norwich to Liverpool Lime Street
F From Lincoln
G From Norwich to Manchester Piccadilly
H To Beverley
I From St Pancras International

Table T034-F

Mondays to Fridays

21 May to 20 July

Nottingham and Sheffield - Barnsley - Huddersfield and Leeds

	NT ◇ A	NT	NT	NT B	NT FO	NT FX	NT	NT B	NT ◇
Nottingham d									23 18
Ilkeston d									23 30
Langley Mill d									23 36
Alfreton d									23 44
Chesterfield d									23 54
Dronfield d									00 02
Sheffield 29,31 a									00 16
Sheffield d	22 28	22 31	22 38	23 05	23 15	23 15	23 18	23 27	
Meadowhall 29,31 a	22 33	22 36	22 43	23 10	23 20	23 20	23 23	23 32	
Meadowhall d		22 37	22 44		23 21	23 21	23 24		
Chapeltown d		22 43	22 51				23 30		
Elsecar d		22 48	22 57				23 35		
Wombwell d		22 52	23 01				23 39		
Barnsley a		22 59	23 07				23 46		
Barnsley d		22 59	23 07				23 46		
Dodworth d			23 13						
Silkstone Common d			23 17						
Penistone d			23 26						
Denby Dale d			23 33						
Shepley d			23 38						
Stocksmoor d			23 40						
Brockholes d			23 44						
Honley d			23 47						
Berry Brow d			23 50						
Lockwood d			23 52						
Huddersfield a			23 57						
Darton d		23 04					23 51		
Wakefield Kirkgate 31 a		23 16					00 03		
Wakefield Kirkgate d		23 17							
Normanton d		23 21							
Castleford 32 a		23 30							
Woodlesford 32 a		23 41							
Leeds 31,32 a		23 53			00 28	00 29			

Mondays to Fridays

23 July to 31 August

	NT MX ◇ C	NT ◇	NT	NT B	NT MX	NT MO	NT	NT ◇ D	NT	NT	NT E	NT	NT ◇	NT F	NT	NT ◇	NT E	NT	TP ◇■ G	NT	NT ◇	NT ◇ D
Nottingham d																					06 17	
Ilkeston d																					06 29	
Langley Mill d																					06 36	
Alfreton d																					06 44	
Chesterfield d																06 25					06 54	
Dronfield d	00 02															06 32					07 01	
Sheffield 29,31 a	00 16															06 42					07 11	
Sheffield d		05 15	05 18	05 25	05 30	05 30	05 37	05 43	05 51	06 02	06 05	06 16	06 19	06 27	06 30	06 45	07 01	07 04	07 08	07 14	07 18	07 24
Meadowhall 29,31 a		05 20	05 23	05 30	05 35	05 35	05 43	05 48	05 56	06 07	06 10	06 21	06 24	06 32	06 35	06 50	07 06	07 09	07 13	07 19	07 23	07 31
Meadowhall d		05 21	05 24		05 36	05 36	05 44		05 57	06 08		06 22	06 25		06 36	06 51		07 10		07 22	07 25	
Chapeltown d			05 30		05 42	05 42	05 50			06 14					06 42			07 16				
Elsecar d			05 35		05 48	05 48	05 56			06 20					06 48			07 22				
Wombwell d			05 39		05 51	05 51	05 59			06 23					06 51			07 25				
Barnsley a			05 45		05 57	05 57	06 05		06 12	06 29			06 39		06 57	07 06		07 31			07 41	
Barnsley d					05 58	06 00	06 06			06 30			06 39		07 00	07 06		07 32			07 42	
Dodworth d							06 12								07 06							
Silkstone Common d							06 15								07 09							
Penistone d							06 21								07 16							
Denby Dale d							06 28								07 23							
Shepley d							06 33								07 28							
Stocksmoor d							06 36								07 31							
Brockholes d							06 40								07 35							
Honley d							06 42								07 37							
Berry Brow d							06 45								07 40							
Lockwood d							06 48								07 43							
Huddersfield a							06 52								07 47							
Darton d					06 03	06 05				06 35								07 37				
Wakefield Kirkgate 31 a					06 14	06 16				06 48			06 54			07 22		07 49			07 57	
Wakefield Kirkgate d					06 16	06 17				06 49			06 55			07 23		07 50			07 57	
Normanton d					06 21	06 22				06 54			06 59			07 27		07 55				
Castleford 32 a										06 59								08 00				
Woodlesford 32 a					06 29	06 30				07 11								08 12				
Leeds 31,32 a		06 30			06 43	06 45				07 25		07 30	07 16			07 43		08 25		08 36	08 17	

A To Hull
B To Doncaster
C From Nottingham
D To Bridlington
E To Adwick
F To Beverley
G From Manchester Airport to Cleethorpes

Table T034-F

Mondays to Fridays

23 July to 31 August

Nottingham and Sheffield - Barnsley - Huddersfield and Leeds

	EM ◇ A	NT B	NT	NT ◇ C	EM ◇■ D	NT	NT E	TP ◇■ F	NT ◇	NT ◇	NT ◇ G	NT H	NT	EM ◇ A	NT ◇ I	NT ◇ J	NT	NT B	TP ◇■ F	NT	NT ◇	NT ◇ K
Nottingham d	06 39									07 18				07 46							08 17	
Ilkeston d										07 30				07 59							08 29	
Langley Mill d										07 37											08 36	
Alfreton d	07 00									07 45				08 10							08 44	
Chesterfield d	07 10				07 43					07 57				08 20							08 55	
Dronfield d	07 18				07 49					08 04				08 27							09 02	
Sheffield 29,31 a	07 28				08 00					08 15				08 38							09 13	
Sheffield d		07 31	07 35	07 47		08 03	08 06	08 10	08 15	08 18	08 25	08 30	08 35		08 46	08 54	09 03	09 06	09 10	09 15	09 18	09 24
Meadowhall 29,31 a		07 36	07 40	07 53		08 08	08 11	08 16	08 21	08 24	08 31	08 35	08 40		08 51	09 00	09 08	09 11	09 15	09 20	09 23	09 31
Meadowhall d			07 41	07 54		08 09			08 21	08 25			08 41		08 53		09 09			09 21	09 24	
Chapeltown d			07 47			08 15							08 47				09 15					
Elsecar d			07 53			08 21							08 53				09 21					
Wombwell d			07 56			08 24							08 56				09 24					
Barnsley a			08 02	08 10		08 30				08 40			09 02		09 10		09 30				09 40	
Barnsley d			08 03	08 11		08 31				08 41			09 03		09 11		09 31				09 41	
Dodworth d			08 09										09 09									
Silkstone Common d			08 12										09 12									
Penistone d			08 19										09 19									
Denby Dale d			08 26										09 26									
Shepley d			08 31										09 31									
Stocksmoor d			08 34										09 34									
Brockholes d			08 38										09 38									
Honley d			08 40										09 40									
Berry Brow d			08 43										09 43									
Lockwood d			08 46										09 46									
Huddersfield a			08 50										09 50									
Darton d						08 36											09 36					
Wakefield Kirkgate 31 a				08 25		08 48				08 57					09 26		09 48				09 56	
Wakefield Kirkgate d				08 25		08 49				08 58					09 26		09 49				09 56	
Normanton d				08 30		08 54											09 54					
Castleford 32 a						08 59											09 59					
Woodlesford 32 a						09 11											10 11					
Leeds 31,32 a				08 46		09 24			09 30	09 17					09 46		10 24			10 30	10 16	

	NT H	NT	EM ◇ L	NT ◇ I	NT	NT B	TP ◇■ F	NT ◇	NT ◇	NT ◇ K	NT H	NT	EM ◇ L	NT ◇ I	NT	NT B	TP ◇■ F	NT	NT ◇	NT ◇ K	NT H
Nottingham d			08 47						09 19				09 47						10 17		
Ilkeston d									09 31										10 29		
Langley Mill d									09 38										10 36		
Alfreton d			09 08						09 46				10 08						10 44		
Chesterfield d			09 20						09 56				10 20						10 55		
Dronfield d									10 03										11 02		
Sheffield 29,31 a			09 37						10 13				10 38						11 13		
Sheffield d	09 30	09 35		09 48	10 02	10 05	10 10	10 15	10 18	10 24	10 30	10 35		10 49	11 02	11 05	11 10	11 15	11 18	11 24	11 30
Meadowhall 29,31 a	09 35	09 40		09 53	10 07	10 10	10 16	10 20	10 23	10 31	10 35	10 40		10 54	11 07	11 10	11 16	11 20	11 23	11 31	11 35
Meadowhall d		09 41		09 54	10 08			10 21	10 24			10 41		10 57	11 08			11 21	11 24		
Chapeltown d		09 47			10 14							10 47			11 14						
Elsecar d		09 53			10 20							10 53			11 20						
Wombwell d		09 56			10 23							10 56			11 23						
Barnsley a		10 02		10 10	10 29				10 39			11 02		11 11	11 29				11 39		
Barnsley d		10 03		10 11	10 30				10 40			11 03		11 12	11 30				11 40		
Dodworth d		10 09										11 09									
Silkstone Common d		10 12										11 12									
Penistone d		10 19										11 19									
Denby Dale d		10 26										11 26									
Shepley d		10 31										11 31									
Stocksmoor d		10 34										11 34									
Brockholes d		10 38										11 38									
Honley d		10 40										11 40									
Berry Brow d		10 43										11 43									
Lockwood d		10 46										11 46									
Huddersfield a		10 50										11 50									
Darton d					10 35										11 35						
Wakefield Kirkgate 31 a				10 26	10 48				10 55					11 27	11 48				11 55		
Wakefield Kirkgate d				10 26	10 49				10 55					11 27	11 49				11 55		
Normanton d					10 54										11 54						
Castleford 32 a					10 59										11 59						
Woodlesford 32 a					11 11										12 11						
Leeds 31,32 a				10 46	11 24			11 30	11 15					11 47	12 24			12 30	12 15		

A To Liverpool Lime Street
B To Adwick
C From Retford
D until 27 July. From Derby
E To Doncaster
F From Manchester Airport to Cleethorpes
G To Scarborough
H To Hull
I From Lincoln
J To York
K To Bridlington
L From Norwich to Liverpool Lime Street

Table T034-F

Mondays to Fridays

23 July to 31 August

Nottingham and Sheffield - Barnsley - Huddersfield and Leeds

		NT	EM ◇ A	NT ◇ B	NT ◇ C	NT	NT D	TP ◇1 E	NT ◇	NT ◇	NT ◇ F	NT G	NT	EM ◇ A	NT ◇ B	NT	NT D	TP ◇1 E	NT	NT ◇	NT ◇ H	NT G	NT
Nottingham 8	d		10 47							11 17				11 47						12 17			
Ilkeston	d									11 29										12 29			
Langley Mill	d									11 36										12 36			
Alfreton	d		11 09							11 44				12 08						12 44			
Chesterfield	d		11 21							11 55				12 20						12 55			
Dronfield	d									12 02										13 02			
Sheffield 7 29,31	a		11 37							12 13				12 38						13 13			
	d	11 35		11 45	11 59	12 02	12 05	12 10	12 15	12 18	12 24	12 30	12 35		12 45	13 02	13 05	13 10	13 15	13 18	13 24	13 30	13 35
Meadowhall 4 29,31	a	11 40		11 50	12 04	12 07	12 10	12 16	12 20	12 23	12 31	12 35	12 40		12 51	13 07	13 10	13 16	13 20	13 23	13 31	13 35	13 40
	d	11 41		11 51		12 08			12 21	12 24			12 41		12 51	13 08			13 21	13 24			13 41
Chapeltown	d	11 47				12 14							12 47			13 14							13 47
Elsecar	d	11 53				12 20							12 53			13 20							13 53
Wombwell	d	11 56				12 23							12 56			13 23							13 56
Barnsley	a	12 02		12 10		12 29				12 39			13 02		13 11	13 29				13 39			14 02
	d	12 03		12 11		12 30				12 40			13 03		13 11	13 30				13 40			14 03
Dodworth	d	12 09											13 09										14 09
Silkstone Common	d	12 12											13 12										14 12
Penistone	d	12 19											13 19										14 19
Denby Dale	d	12 26											13 26										14 26
Shepley	d	12 31											13 31										14 31
Stocksmoor	d	12 34											13 34										14 34
Brockholes	d	12 38											13 38										14 38
Honley	d	12 40											13 40										14 40
Berry Brow	d	12 43											13 43										14 43
Lockwood	d	12 46											13 46										14 46
Huddersfield	a	12 50											13 50										14 50
Darton	d					12 35										13 35							
Wakefield Kirkgate 4 31	a			12 26		12 48				12 55					13 26	13 48				13 55			
	d			12 26		12 49				12 55					13 27	13 49				13 55			
Normanton	d					12 54										13 54							
Castleford 32	a					12 59										13 59							
Woodlesford 32	a					13 11										14 11							
Leeds 10 31,32	a			12 46		13 24			13 30	13 15					13 46	14 24			14 30	14 15			

		EM ◇ A	NT ◇ B	NT	NT D	TP ◇1 E	NT ◇	NT ◇	NT ◇ F	NT G	NT	EM ◇ A	NT ◇ B	NT	NT D	TP ◇1 E	NT	NT ◇	NT ◇ F	NT G	NT	EM ◇ A
Nottingham 8	d	12 47						13 17				13 47						14 17				14 47
Ilkeston	d	13 00						13 29										14 29				
Langley Mill	d							13 36										14 36				
Alfreton	d	13 10						13 44				14 08						14 44				15 08
Chesterfield	d	13 21						13 55				14 20						14 55				15 20
Dronfield	d							14 02										15 02				
Sheffield 7 29,31	a	13 37						14 13				14 38						15 13				15 37
	d		13 45	14 02	14 05	14 10	14 15	14 18	14 24	14 30	14 35		14 45	15 02	15 05	15 10	15 15	15 18	15 24	15 30	15 35	
Meadowhall 4 29,31	a		13 51	14 07	14 10	14 16	14 20	14 23	14 31	14 35	14 40		14 51	15 07	15 10	15 16	15 20	15 23	15 31	15 35	15 40	
	d		13 51	14 08			14 21	14 24			14 41		14 51	15 08			15 21	15 24			15 41	
Chapeltown	d			14 14							14 47			15 14							15 47	
Elsecar	d			14 20							14 53			15 20							15 53	
Wombwell	d			14 23							14 56			15 23							15 56	
Barnsley	a		14 11	14 29				14 39			15 02		15 11	15 29				15 39			16 02	
	d		14 11	14 30				14 40			15 03		15 11	15 30				15 40			16 03	
Dodworth	d										15 09										16 09	
Silkstone Common	d										15 12										16 12	
Penistone	d										15 19										16 19	
Denby Dale	d										15 26										16 26	
Shepley	d										15 31										16 31	
Stocksmoor	d										15 34										16 34	
Brockholes	d										15 38										16 38	
Honley	d										15 40										16 40	
Berry Brow	d										15 43										16 43	
Lockwood	d										15 46										16 46	
Huddersfield	a										15 50										16 50	
Darton	d			14 35										15 35								
Wakefield Kirkgate 4 31	a		14 26	14 48				14 55					15 26	15 48				15 55				
	d		14 27	14 49				14 55					15 27	15 49				15 55				
Normanton	d			14 54										15 54								
Castleford 32	a			14 59										15 59								
Woodlesford 32	a			15 11										16 11								
Leeds 10 31,32	a		14 46	15 24			15 30	15 15					15 46	16 24			16 30	16 15				

A From Norwich to Liverpool Lime Street
B From Lincoln
C To York
D To Adwick
E From Manchester Airport to Cleethorpes
F To Bridlington
G To Hull
H To Scarborough

Table T034-F

Mondays to Fridays

23 July to 31 August

Nottingham and Sheffield - Barnsley - Huddersfield and Leeds

		NT ◇ A	NT	NT B	TP ◇1 C	NT ◇	NT ◇	NT ◇ D	NT E	NT	EM ◇ F	NT ◇ A	NT	NT B	TP ◇1 C	NT	NT ◇ G	NT ◇ D	NT E	NT	EM ◇ F	NT ◇ A	NT
Nottingham 8	d						15 17				15 47						16 17				16 47		
Ilkeston	d						15 29				16 00						16 29						
Langley Mill	d						15 36										16 36						
Alfreton	d						15 44				16 10						16 44				17 08		
Chesterfield	d						15 55				16 20						16 55				17 20		
Dronfield	d						16 02										17 02						
Sheffield 7 29,31	a						16 13				16 37						17 13				17 37		
	d	15 45	16 02	16 05	16 10	16 15	16 18	16 24	16 30	16 35		16 45	17 02	17 05	17 10	17 15	17 18	17 24	17 30	17 35		17 45	18 02
Meadowhall 4 29,31	a	15 50	16 07	16 10	16 16	16 20	16 23	16 31	16 35	16 40		16 51	17 07	17 10	17 16	17 20	17 23	17 31	17 35	17 40		17 51	18 07
	d	15 51	16 08			16 21	16 24			16 41		16 51	17 08			17 21	17 24			17 41		17 51	18 08
Chapeltown	d		16 14							16 47			17 14							17 47			18 14
Elsecar	d		16 20							16 53			17 20							17 53			18 20
Wombwell	d		16 23							16 56			17 23							17 56			18 23
Barnsley	a	16 10	16 29				16 39			17 02		17 11	17 29				17 39			18 02		18 10	18 29
	d	16 11	16 30				16 40			17 03		17 11	17 30				17 40			18 03		18 11	18 30
Dodworth	d									17 09										18 09			
Silkstone Common	d									17 12										18 13			
Penistone	d									17 19										18 23			
Denby Dale	d									17 26										18 29			
Shepley	d									17 31										18 34			
Stocksmoor	d									17 33										18 37			
Brockholes	d									17 37										18 41			
Honley	d									17 40										18 43			
Berry Brow	d									17 43										18 46			
Lockwood	d									17 45										18 49			
Huddersfield	a									17 50										18 54			
Darton	d		16 35										17 35										18 35
Wakefield Kirkgate 4 31	a	16 26	16 48				16 55					17 26	17 48				17 55					18 27	18 48
	d	16 26	16 49				16 55					17 27	17 49				17 55					18 27	18 49
Normanton	d		16 54										17 54										18 54
Castleford 32	a		16 59										17 59										18 59
Woodlesford 32	a		17 11										18 11										19 11
Leeds 10 31,32	a	16 46	17 24			17 32	17 15					17 46	18 24			18 30	18 15					18 47	19 24

		NT B	TP ◇1 C	NT ◇	NT ◇	NT ◇ H	NT E	NT	EM ◇ F	NT ◇ A	NT	NT B	TP ◇1 C	NT	NT ◇	NT ◇ E	NT E	NT	EM ◇ F	NT ◇ A	NT	NT B	TP ◇1 C
Nottingham 8	d				17 17				17 47						18 17				18 47				
Ilkeston	d				17 29										18 29								
Langley Mill	d				17 36				18 03						18 36								
Alfreton	d				17 44				18 11						18 44				19 08				
Chesterfield	d				17 55				18 20						18 55				19 20				
Dronfield	d				18 02										19 02								
Sheffield 7 29,31	a				18 13				18 38						19 13				19 37				
	d	18 05	18 11	18 15	18 18	18 24	18 30	18 35		18 45	19 02	19 05	19 11	19 15	19 18	19 24	19 30	19 35		19 45	20 02	20 05	20 11
Meadowhall 4 29,31	a	18 10	18 17	18 20	18 23	18 31	18 35	18 40		18 50	19 07	19 10	19 16	19 20	19 23	19 31	19 35	19 40		19 50	20 07	20 10	20 16
	d			18 21	18 24			18 41		18 51	19 08			19 21	19 24			19 41		19 51	20 08		
Chapeltown	d							18 47			19 14							19 47			20 14		
Elsecar	d							18 53			19 20							19 53			20 20		
Wombwell	d							18 56			19 23							19 56			20 23		
Barnsley	a				18 39			19 02		19 10	19 29				19 39			20 02		20 10	20 29		
	d				18 40			19 03		19 11	19 30				19 40			20 03		20 11	20 30		
Dodworth	d							19 09										20 09					
Silkstone Common	d							19 12										20 12					
Penistone	d							19 19										20 19					
Denby Dale	d							19 26										20 26					
Shepley	d							19 31										20 31					
Stocksmoor	d							19 34										20 34					
Brockholes	d							19 38										20 38					
Honley	d							19 40										20 40					
Berry Brow	d							19 43										20 43					
Lockwood	d							19 46										20 46					
Huddersfield	a							19 50										20 50					
Darton	d										19 35										20 35		
Wakefield Kirkgate 4 31	a				18 55					19 26	19 48				19 55					20 26	20 48		
	d				18 55					19 26	19 49				19 55					20 26	20 49		
Normanton	d										19 54										20 54		
Castleford 32	a										19 59										20 59		
Woodlesford 32	a										20 11										21 11		
Leeds 10 31,32	a			19 30	19 15					19 46	20 24			20 36	20 15					20 46	21 24		

A From Lincoln
B To Adwick
C From Manchester Airport to Cleethorpes
D To Scarborough
E To Hull
F From Norwich to Liverpool Lime Street
G from 30 July
H To Bridlington

Table T034-F

Mondays to Fridays

23 July to 31 August

Nottingham and Sheffield - Barnsley - Huddersfield and Leeds

		NT ◇	NT ◇	NT ◇ A	EM ◇ B	NT C	NT	NT ◇ D	NT	NT E	TP ◇1 F	NT	NT ◇	NT ◇ G	NT	EM ◇1 H	NT E	TP ◇1 F	NT ◇	NT ◇	NT ◇ C	NT
Nottingham 8	d		19 17		19 41								20 17			21 08				21 12		
Ilkeston	d		19 29										20 29							21 29		
Langley Mill	d		19 36										20 36			21 25				21 36		
Alfreton	d		19 44		20 02								20 44			21 33				21 44		
Chesterfield	d		19 55		20 12								20 55			21 44				21 55		
Dronfield	d		20 02										21 02							22 02		
Sheffield 7 29,31	a		20 13		20 28								21 13			21 58				22 13		
	d	20 15	20 18	20 24		20 30	20 35	20 45	21 02	21 05	21 11	21 15	21 18	21 28	21 35	22 04	22 07	22 11	22 15	22 18	22 28	22 31
Meadowhall 4 29,31	a	20 20	20 23	20 31		20 35	20 40	20 50	21 07	21 10	21 16	21 20	21 23	21 33	21 40		22 12	22 16	22 21	22 23	22 33	22 36
	d	20 21	20 24				20 41	20 51	21 08			21 21	21 24		21 41				22 22	22 24		22 37
Chapeltown	d						20 47		21 14						21 47							22 43
Elsecar	d						20 53		21 20						21 53							22 48
Wombwell	d						20 56		21 23						21 56							22 52
Barnsley	a		20 39				21 02	21 10	21 29				21 39		22 02					22 39		22 59
	d		20 40				21 03	21 11	21 30				21 40		22 03					22 40		22 59
Dodworth	d						21 09								22 09							
Silkstone Common	d						21 12								22 12							
Penistone	d						21 19								22 19							
Denby Dale	d						21 26								22 26							
Shepley	d						21 31								22 31							
Stocksmoor	d						21 34								22 34							
Brockholes	d						21 38								22 38							
Honley	d						21 40								22 40							
Berry Brow	d						21 43								22 43							
Lockwood	d						21 46								22 46							
Huddersfield	a						21 50								22 50							
Darton	d								21 35													23 04
Wakefield Kirkgate 4 31	a		20 55					21 26	21 48				21 55							22 55		23 16
	d		20 55					21 26	21 49				21 55							22 55		23 17
Normanton	d								21 54													23 21
Castleford 32	a								21 59													23 30
Woodlesford 32	a								22 11													23 41
Leeds 10 31,32	a	21 30	21 15					21 46	22 24			22 30	22 15			22 49			23 39	23 14		23 53

		NT	NT I	NT FO	NT FX	NT	NT I	NT ◇
Nottingham 8	d							23 18
Ilkeston	d							23 30
Langley Mill	d							23 36
Alfreton	d							23 44
Chesterfield	d							23 54
Dronfield	d							00 02
Sheffield 7 29,31	a							00 16
	d	22 38	23 05	23 15	23 15	23 18	23 27	
Meadowhall 4 29,31	a	22 43	23 10	23 20	23 20	23 23	23 32	
	d	22 44		23 21	23 21	23 24		
Chapeltown	d	22 51				23 30		
Elsecar	d	22 57				23 35		
Wombwell	d	23 01				23 39		
Barnsley	a	23 07				23 46		
	d	23 07				23 46		
Dodworth	d	23 13						
Silkstone Common	d	23 17						
Penistone	d	23 26						
Denby Dale	d	23 33						
Shepley	d	23 38						
Stocksmoor	d	23 40						
Brockholes	d	23 44						
Honley	d	23 47						
Berry Brow	d	23 50						
Lockwood	d	23 52						
Huddersfield	a	23 57						
Darton	d					23 51		
Wakefield Kirkgate 4 31	a					00 03		
	d							
Normanton	d							
Castleford 32	a							
Woodlesford 32	a							
Leeds 10 31,32	a			00 28	00 29			

A To Bridlington
B From Norwich to Manchester Piccadilly
C To Hull
D From Lincoln
E To Adwick
F From Manchester Airport to Cleethorpes
G To Beverley
H From St Pancras International
I To Doncaster

Table T034-F

Mondays to Fridays

3 September to 5 October

Nottingham and Sheffield - Barnsley - Huddersfield and Leeds

		NT MX ◇ A	NT ◇	NT	NT B	NT MX	NT MO	NT	NT ◇ C	NT	NT	NT D	NT	NT ◇	NT E	NT	NT ◇	NT D	NT	TP ◇1 F	NT	NT ◇	NT ◇ C
Nottingham 8	d																					06 17	
Ilkeston	d																					06 29	
Langley Mill	d																					06 36	
Alfreton	d																					06 44	
Chesterfield	d																06 25					06 54	
Dronfield	d	00 02															06 32					07 01	
Sheffield 7 29,31	a	00 16															06 42					07 11	
	d		05 15	05 18	05 25	05 30	05 30	05 37	05 43	05 51	06 02	06 05	06 16	06 19	06 27	06 30	06 45	07 01	07 04	07 08	07 14	07 18	07 24
Meadowhall 4 29,31	a		05 20	05 23	05 30	05 35	05 35	05 43	05 48	05 56	06 07	06 10	06 21	06 24	06 32	06 35	06 50	07 06	07 09	07 13	07 19	07 23	07 31
	d		05 21	05 24		05 36	05 36	05 44		05 57	06 08		06 22	06 25		06 36	06 51		07 10		07 22	07 25	
Chapeltown	d			05 30		05 42	05 42	05 50			06 14					06 42			07 16				
Elsecar	d			05 35		05 48	05 48	05 56			06 20					06 48			07 22				
Wombwell	d			05 39		05 51	05 51	05 59			06 23					06 51			07 25				
Barnsley	a			05 45		05 57	05 57	06 05		06 12	06 29			06 39		06 57	07 06		07 31			07 41	
	d					05 58	06 00	06 06			06 30			06 39		07 00	07 06		07 32			07 42	
Dodworth	d							06 12								07 06							
Silkstone Common	d							06 15								07 09							
Penistone	d							06 21								07 16							
Denby Dale	d							06 28								07 23							
Shepley	d							06 33								07 28							
Stocksmoor	d							06 36								07 31							
Brockholes	d							06 40								07 35							
Honley	d							06 42								07 37							
Berry Brow	d							06 45								07 40							
Lockwood	d							06 48								07 43							
Huddersfield	a							06 52								07 47							
Darton	d					06 03	06 05				06 35								07 37				
Wakefield Kirkgate 4 31	a					06 14	06 16				06 48			06 54			07 22		07 49			07 57	
	d					06 16	06 17				06 49			06 55			07 23		07 50			07 57	
Normanton	d					06 21	06 22				06 54			06 59			07 27		07 55				
Castleford 32	a										06 59								08 00				
Woodlesford 32	a					06 29	06 30				07 11								08 12				
Leeds 10 31,32	a		06 30			06 43	06 45				07 25		07 30	07 16			07 43		08 25		08 36	08 17	

		EM ◇ G	NT D	NT	NT ◇ H	NT	NT B	TP ◇1 F	NT ◇	NT ◇	NT ◇ I	NT J	NT	EM ◇ G	NT ◇ K	NT ◇ L	NT	NT D	TP ◇1 F	NT	NT ◇	NT ◇ C	NT J
Nottingham 8	d	06 39								07 18				07 46							08 17		
Ilkeston	d									07 30				07 59							08 29		
Langley Mill	d									07 37											08 36		
Alfreton	d	07 00								07 45				08 10							08 44		
Chesterfield	d	07 10								07 57				08 20							08 55		
Dronfield	d	07 18								08 04				08 27							09 02		
Sheffield 7 29,31	a	07 28								08 15				08 38							09 13		
	d		07 31	07 35	07 47	08 03	08 06	08 10	08 15	08 18	08 25	08 30	08 35		08 46	08 54	09 03	09 06	09 10	09 15	09 18	09 24	09 30
Meadowhall 4 29,31	a		07 36	07 40	07 53	08 08	08 11	08 16	08 21	08 24	08 31	08 35	08 40		08 51	09 00	09 08	09 11	09 15	09 20	09 23	09 31	09 35
	d			07 41	07 54	08 09			08 21	08 25			08 41		08 53		09 09			09 21	09 24		
Chapeltown	d			07 47		08 15							08 47				09 15						
Elsecar	d			07 53		08 21							08 53				09 21						
Wombwell	d			07 56		08 24							08 56				09 24						
Barnsley	a			08 02	08 10	08 30				08 40			09 02		09 10		09 30				09 40		
	d			08 03	08 11	08 31				08 41			09 03		09 11		09 31				09 41		
Dodworth	d			08 09									09 09										
Silkstone Common	d			08 12									09 12										
Penistone	d			08 19									09 19										
Denby Dale	d			08 26									09 26										
Shepley	d			08 31									09 31										
Stocksmoor	d			08 34									09 34										
Brockholes	d			08 38									09 38										
Honley	d			08 40									09 40										
Berry Brow	d			08 43									09 43										
Lockwood	d			08 46									09 46										
Huddersfield	a			08 50									09 50										
Darton	d					08 36											09 36						
Wakefield Kirkgate 4 31	a				08 25	08 48				08 57					09 26		09 48				09 56		
	d				08 25	08 49				08 58					09 26		09 49				09 56		
Normanton	d				08 30	08 54											09 54						
Castleford 32	a					08 59											09 59						
Woodlesford 32	a					09 11											10 11						
Leeds 10 31,32	a				08 46	09 24			09 30	09 17					09 46		10 24			10 30	10 16		

A From Nottingham
B To Doncaster
C To Bridlington
D To Adwick
E To Beverley
F From Manchester Airport to Cleethorpes
G To Liverpool Lime Street
H From Retford
I To Scarborough
J To Hull
K From Lincoln
L To York

Table T034-F

Mondays to Fridays

3 September to 5 October

Nottingham and Sheffield - Barnsley - Huddersfield and Leeds

		NT		EM	NT	NT	NT	TP	NT	NT	NT	NT		NT	EM	NT	NT	NT	TP	NT	NT	NT		NT	NT
				◇	◇			◇1	◇	◇	◇				◇	◇			◇1		◇	◇			
				A	B		C	D			E	F			A	B		C	D			E		F	
Nottingham 8	d			08 47						09 19					09 47						10 17				
Ilkeston	d									09 31											10 31				
Langley Mill	d									09 38											10 38				
Alfreton	d			09 09						09 46					10 08						10 46				
Chesterfield	d			09 20						09 56					10 20						10 56				
Dronfield	d									10 03											11 03				
Sheffield 7 29,31	a			09 37						10 13					10 38						11 13				
	d	09 35			09 48	10 02	10 05	10 10	10 15	10 18	10 24	10 30		10 35		10 49	11 02	11 05	11 10	11 15	11 18	11 24		11 30	11 35
Meadowhall 4 29,31	a	09 40			09 53	10 07	10 10	10 16	10 20	10 23	10 31	10 35		10 40		10 54	11 07	11 10	11 16	11 20	11 23	11 31		11 35	11 40
	d	09 41			09 54	10 08			10 21	10 24				10 41		10 57	11 08			11 21	11 24				11 41
Chapeltown	d	09 47				10 14								10 47			11 14								11 47
Elsecar	d	09 53				10 20								10 53			11 20								11 53
Wombwell	d	09 56				10 23								10 56			11 23								11 56
Barnsley	a	10 02			10 10	10 29				10 39				11 02		11 11	11 29				11 39				12 02
	d	10 03			10 11	10 30				10 40				11 03		11 12	11 30				11 40				12 03
Dodworth	d	10 09												11 09											12 09
Silkstone Common	d	10 12												11 12											12 12
Penistone	d	10 19												11 19											12 19
Denby Dale	d	10 26												11 26											12 26
Shepley	d	10 31												11 31											12 31
Stocksmoor	d	10 34												11 34											12 34
Brockholes	d	10 38												11 38											12 38
Honley	d	10 40												11 40											12 40
Berry Brow	d	10 43												11 43											12 43
Lockwood	d	10 46												11 46											12 46
Huddersfield	a	10 50												11 50											12 50
Darton	d					10 35											11 35								
Wakefield Kirkgate 4 31	a				10 26	10 48				10 55						11 27	11 48				11 55				
	d				10 26	10 49				10 55						11 27	11 49				11 55				
Normanton	d					10 54											11 54								
Castleford 32	a					10 59											11 59								
Woodlesford 32	a					11 11											12 11								
Leeds 10 31,32	a				10 46	11 24			11 30	11 15						11 47	12 24			12 30	12 15				

		EM	NT	NT	NT	NT	TP	NT		NT	NT	NT	NT	NT	NT	NT	TP	NT		NT	NT	NT	NT	EM	NT
		◇	◇	◇			◇1	◇		◇	◇			◇			◇1			◇	◇			◇	◇
		A	B	G		C	D				E	F		B		C	D				H	F		A	B
Nottingham 8	d	10 51								11 17										12 17				12 47	
Ilkeston	d									11 31										12 32				13 00	
Langley Mill	d									11 37										12 38					
Alfreton	d	11 12								11 45										12 46				13 10	
Chesterfield	d	11 22								11 56										12 56				13 21	
Dronfield	d									12 02										13 03					
Sheffield 7 29,31	a	11 38								12 13										13 13				13 37	
	d		11 45	11 59	12 02	12 05	12 10	12 15		12 18	12 24	12 30	12 35	12 45	13 02	13 05	13 10	13 15		13 18	13 24	13 30	13 35		13 45
Meadowhall 4 29,31	a		11 50	12 04	12 07	12 10	12 16	12 20		12 23	12 31	12 35	12 40	12 51	13 07	13 10	13 16	13 20		13 23	13 31	13 35	13 40		13 51
	d		11 51		12 08			12 21		12 24			12 41	12 51	13 08			13 21		13 24			13 41		13 51
Chapeltown	d				12 14								12 47		13 14								13 47		
Elsecar	d				12 20								12 53		13 20								13 53		
Wombwell	d				12 23								12 56		13 23								13 56		
Barnsley	a		12 10		12 29					12 39			13 02	13 11	13 29					13 39			14 02		14 11
	d		12 11		12 30					12 40			13 03	13 11	13 30					13 40			14 03		14 11
Dodworth	d												13 09										14 09		
Silkstone Common	d												13 12										14 12		
Penistone	d												13 19										14 19		
Denby Dale	d												13 26										14 26		
Shepley	d												13 31										14 31		
Stocksmoor	d												13 34										14 34		
Brockholes	d												13 38										14 38		
Honley	d												13 40										14 40		
Berry Brow	d												13 43										14 43		
Lockwood	d												13 46										14 46		
Huddersfield	a												13 50										14 50		
Darton	d				12 35										13 35										
Wakefield Kirkgate 4 31	a		12 26		12 48					12 55				13 26	13 48					13 55					14 26
	d		12 26		12 49					12 55				13 27	13 49					13 55					14 27
Normanton	d				12 54										13 54										
Castleford 32	a				12 59										13 59										
Woodlesford 32	a				13 11										14 11										
Leeds 10 31,32	a		12 46		13 24			13 30		13 15				13 46	14 24			14 30		14 15					14 46

A From Norwich to Liverpool Lime Street
B From Lincoln
C To Adwick
D From Manchester Airport to Cleethorpes
E To Bridlington
F To Hull
G To York
H To Scarborough

Table T034-F

Mondays to Fridays

3 September to 5 October

Nottingham and Sheffield - Barnsley - Huddersfield and Leeds

		NT	NT	TP		NT	NT	NT	NT	NT	EM	NT	NT	NT		TP	NT	NT	NT	NT	NT	EM	NT	NT	
				◇1		◇	◇	◇			◇	◇				◇1		◇	◇			◇	◇		
			A	B				C	D		E	F		A		B			C	D		E	F		
Nottingham 8	d						13 17				13 47							14 17				14 47			
Ilkeston	d						13 31											14 32							
Langley Mill	d						13 38											14 38							
Alfreton	d						13 46				14 10							14 46				15 08			
Chesterfield	d						13 56				14 20							14 56				15 20			
Dronfield	d						14 03											15 03							
Sheffield 7 29,31	a						14 13				14 38							15 13				15 37			
	d	14 02	14 05	14 10		14 15	14 18	14 24	14 30	14 35		14 45	15 02	15 05		15 10	15 15	15 18	15 24	15 30	15 35		15 45	16 02	
Meadowhall 4 29,31	a	14 07	14 10	14 16		14 20	14 23	14 31	14 35	14 40		14 51	15 07	15 10		15 16	15 20	15 23	15 31	15 35	15 40		15 50	16 07	
	d	14 08				14 21	14 24			14 41		14 51	15 08				15 21	15 24			15 41		15 51	16 08	
Chapeltown	d	14 14								14 47			15 14								15 47			16 14	
Elsecar	d	14 20								14 53			15 20								15 53			16 20	
Wombwell	d	14 23								14 56			15 23								15 56			16 23	
Barnsley	a	14 29					14 39			15 02		15 11	15 29					15 39			16 02		16 10	16 29	
	d	14 30					14 40			15 03		15 11	15 30					15 40			16 03		16 11	16 30	
Dodworth	d									15 09											16 09				
Silkstone Common	d									15 12											16 12				
Penistone	d									15 19											16 19				
Denby Dale	d									15 26											16 26				
Shepley	d									15 31											16 31				
Stocksmoor	d									15 34											16 34				
Brockholes	d									15 38											16 38				
Honley	d									15 40											16 40				
Berry Brow	d									15 43											16 43				
Lockwood	d									15 46											16 46				
Huddersfield	a									15 50											16 50				
Darton	d	14 35											15 35											16 35	
Wakefield Kirkgate 4 31	a	14 48					14 55					15 26	15 48					15 55					16 26	16 48	
	d	14 49					14 55					15 27	15 49					15 55					16 26	16 49	
Normanton	d	14 54											15 54											16 54	
Castleford 32	a	14 59											15 59											16 59	
Woodlesford 32	a	15 11											16 11											17 11	
Leeds 10 31,32	a	15 24				15 30	15 15					15 46	16 24				16 30	16 15					16 46	17 24	

		NT	TP	NT	NT	NT	NT	NT	EM	NT		NT	NT	TP	NT	NT	NT	NT	NT	EM		NT	NT	NT	TP
			◇1	◇	◇	◇			◇	◇				◇1		◇	◇			◇		◇			◇1
		A	B			G	D		E	F			A	B			G	D		E		F		A	B
Nottingham 8	d				15 17				15 47							16 17				16 47					
Ilkeston	d				15 31				16 00							16 31									
Langley Mill	d				15 38											16 38									
Alfreton	d				15 46				16 10							16 46				17 08					
Chesterfield	d				15 56				16 20							16 56				17 20					
Dronfield	d				16 03											17 03									
Sheffield 7 29,31	a				16 13				16 37							17 13				17 37					
	d	16 05	16 10	16 15	16 18	16 24	16 30	16 35		16 45		17 02	17 05	17 10	17 15	17 18	17 24	17 30	17 35			17 45	18 02	18 05	18 11
Meadowhall 4 29,31	a	16 10	16 16	16 20	16 23	16 31	16 35	16 40		16 51		17 07	17 10	17 16	17 20	17 23	17 31	17 35	17 40			17 51	18 07	18 10	18 17
	d			16 21	16 24			16 41		16 51		17 08			17 21	17 24			17 41			17 51	18 08		
Chapeltown	d							16 47				17 14							17 47				18 14		
Elsecar	d							16 53				17 20							17 53				18 20		
Wombwell	d							16 56				17 23							17 56				18 23		
Barnsley	a				16 39			17 02		17 11		17 29				17 39			18 02			18 10	18 29		
	d				16 40			17 03		17 11		17 30				17 40			18 03			18 11	18 30		
Dodworth	d							17 09											18 09						
Silkstone Common	d							17 12											18 13						
Penistone	d							17 19											18 23						
Denby Dale	d							17 26											18 29						
Shepley	d							17 31											18 34						
Stocksmoor	d							17 33											18 37						
Brockholes	d							17 37											18 41						
Honley	d							17 40											18 43						
Berry Brow	d							17 43											18 46						
Lockwood	d							17 45											18 49						
Huddersfield	a							17 50											18 54						
Darton	d											17 35											18 35		
Wakefield Kirkgate 4 31	a				16 55					17 26		17 48				17 55						18 27	18 48		
	d				16 55					17 27		17 49				17 55						18 27	18 49		
Normanton	d											17 54											18 54		
Castleford 32	a											17 59											18 59		
Woodlesford 32	a											18 11											19 11		
Leeds 10 31,32	a			17 32	17 15					17 46		18 24			18 30	18 15						18 47	19 24		

A To Adwick
B From Manchester Airport to Cleethorpes
C To Bridlington
D To Hull
E From Norwich to Liverpool Lime Street
F From Lincoln
G To Scarborough

Table T034-F

Mondays to Fridays
3 September to 5 October

Nottingham and Sheffield - Barnsley - Huddersfield and Leeds

Station		NT ◇	NT ◇	NT ◇ A	NT B	NT	EM ◇ C	NT ◇ D	NT	NT E	TP ◇[1] F	NT	NT ◇	NT ◇ B	NT B	NT	EM ◇ C	NT ◇ D	NT	NT E	TP ◇[1] F	NT ◇	NT ◇
Nottingham [8] ⇌	d		17 17				17 47						18 17				18 47						19 17
Ilkeston	d		17 31										18 32										19 30
Langley Mill	d		17 38				18 04						18 38										19 37
Alfreton	d		17 46				18 12						18 46				19 08						19 45
Chesterfield	d		17 56				18 22						18 56				19 20						19 55
Dronfield	d		18 03										19 03										20 02
Sheffield [7] 29,31 ⇌	a		18 13				18 38						19 13				19 37						20 13
	d	18 15	18 18	18 24	18 30	18 35		18 45	19 02	19 05	19 11	19 15	19 18	19 24	19 30	19 35		19 45	20 02	20 05	20 11	20 15	20 18
Meadowhall [4] 29,31 ⇌	a	18 20	18 23	18 31	18 35	18 40		18 50	19 07	19 10	19 16	19 20	19 23	19 31	19 35	19 40		19 50	20 07	20 10	20 16	20 20	20 23
	d	18 21	18 24			18 41		18 51	19 08			19 21	19 24			19 41		19 51	20 08			20 21	20 24
Chapeltown	d					18 47			19 14							19 47			20 14				
Elsecar	d					18 53			19 20							19 53			20 20				
Wombwell	d					18 56			19 23							19 56			20 23				
Barnsley	a		18 39			19 02		19 10	19 29				19 39			20 02		20 10	20 29				20 39
	d		18 40			19 03		19 11	19 30				19 40			20 03		20 11	20 30				20 40
Dodworth	d					19 09										20 09							
Silkstone Common	d					19 12										20 12							
Penistone	d					19 19										20 19							
Denby Dale	d					19 26										20 26							
Shepley	d					19 31										20 31							
Stocksmoor	d					19 34										20 34							
Brockholes	d					19 38										20 38							
Honley	d					19 40										20 40							
Berry Brow	d					19 43										20 43							
Lockwood	d					19 46										20 46							
Huddersfield	a					19 50										20 50							
Darton	d								19 35										20 35				
Wakefield Kirkgate [4] 31	a		18 55					19 26	19 48				19 55					20 26	20 48				20 55
	d		18 55					19 26	19 49				19 55					20 26	20 49				20 55
Normanton	d								19 54										20 54				
Castleford 32	a								19 59										20 59				
Woodlesford 32	a								20 11										21 11				
Leeds [10] 31,32	a	19 30	19 15					19 46	20 24			20 36	20 15					20 46	21 24			21 30	21 15

Station		NT ◇ A	EM ◇ G	NT B	NT	NT ◇ D	NT	NT E	TP ◇[1] F	NT	NT ◇	NT ◇ H	NT	EM ◇[1] I	NT E	TP ◇[1] F	NT ◇	NT ◇	NT ◇ B	NT	NT	NT J
Nottingham [8] ⇌	d		19 40								20 17			21 08				21 12				
Ilkeston	d										20 29							21 29				
Langley Mill	d										20 36			21 25				21 36				
Alfreton	d		20 02								20 44			21 33				21 44				
Chesterfield	d		20 12								20 54			21 44				21 55				
Dronfield	d										21 02							22 02				
Sheffield [7] 29,31 ⇌	a		20 28								21 13			21 58				22 13				
	d	20 24		20 30	20 35	20 45	21 02	21 05	21 11	21 15	21 18	21 28	21 35	22 04	22 07	22 11	22 15	22 18	22 28	22 31	22 38	23 05
Meadowhall [4] 29,31 ⇌	a	20 31		20 35	20 40	20 50	21 07	21 10	21 16	21 20	21 23	21 33	21 40		22 12	22 16	22 21	22 23	22 33	22 36	22 43	23 10
	d				20 41	20 51	21 08			21 21	21 24		21 41				22 22	22 24		22 37	22 44	
Chapeltown	d				20 47		21 14						21 47							22 43	22 51	
Elsecar	d				20 53		21 20						21 53							22 48	22 57	
Wombwell	d				20 56		21 23						21 56							22 52	23 01	
Barnsley	a				21 02	21 10	21 29				21 39		22 02					22 39		22 59	23 07	
	d				21 03	21 11	21 30				21 40		22 03					22 40		22 59	23 07	
Dodworth	d				21 09								22 09								23 13	
Silkstone Common	d				21 12								22 12								23 17	
Penistone	d				21 19								22 19								23 26	
Denby Dale	d				21 26								22 26								23 33	
Shepley	d				21 31								22 31								23 38	
Stocksmoor	d				21 34								22 34								23 40	
Brockholes	d				21 38								22 38								23 44	
Honley	d				21 40								22 40								23 47	
Berry Brow	d				21 43								22 43								23 50	
Lockwood	d				21 46								22 46								23 52	
Huddersfield	a				21 50								22 50								23 57	
Darton	d						21 35													23 04		
Wakefield Kirkgate [4] 31	a					21 26	21 48				21 55							22 55		23 16		
	d					21 26	21 49				21 55							22 55		23 17		
Normanton	d						21 54													23 21		
Castleford 32	a						21 59													23 30		
Woodlesford 32	a						22 11													23 41		
Leeds [10] 31,32	a					21 46	22 24			22 30	22 15			22 49			23 39	23 14		23 53		

A To Bridlington
B To Hull
C From Norwich to Liverpool Lime Street
D From Lincoln
E To Adwick
F From Manchester Airport to Cleethorpes
G From Norwich to Manchester Piccadilly
H To Beverley
I From St Pancras International
J To Doncaster

Table T034-F

Mondays to Fridays
3 September to 5 October

Nottingham and Sheffield - Barnsley - Huddersfield and Leeds

Station		NT FO	NT FX	NT	NT A	NT ◇
Nottingham [8] ⇌	d					23 18
Ilkeston	d					23 30
Langley Mill	d					23 36
Alfreton	d					23 44
Chesterfield	d					23 54
Dronfield	d					00 02
Sheffield [7] 29,31 ⇌	a					00 16
	d	23 15	23 15	23 18	23 27	
Meadowhall [4] 29,31 ⇌	a	23 20	23 20	23 23	23 32	
	d	23 21	23 21	23 24		
Chapeltown	d			23 30		
Elsecar	d			23 35		
Wombwell	d			23 39		
Barnsley	a			23 46		
	d			23 46		
Dodworth	d					
Silkstone Common	d					
Penistone	d					
Denby Dale	d					
Shepley	d					
Stocksmoor	d					
Brockholes	d					
Honley	d					
Berry Brow	d					
Lockwood	d					
Huddersfield	a					
Darton	d			23 51		
Wakefield Kirkgate [4] 31	a			00 03		
	d					
Normanton	d					
Castleford 32	a					
Woodlesford 32	a					
Leeds [10] 31,32	a	00 28	00 29			

Mondays to Fridays
8 October to 7 December

Station		NT MX ◇ B	NT ◇	NT	NT A	NT MX	NT MO	NT	NT ◇ C	NT	NT	NT D	NT	NT ◇	NT E	NT	NT ◇	NT D	NT	TP ◇[1] F	NT	NT ◇	NT ◇ C
Nottingham [8] ⇌	d																					06 17	
Ilkeston	d																					06 29	
Langley Mill	d																					06 36	
Alfreton	d																					06 44	
Chesterfield	d																06 25					06 54	
Dronfield	d	00 02															06 32					07 01	
Sheffield [7] 29,31 ⇌	a	00 16															06 42					07 11	
	d		05 15	05 18	05 25	05 30	05 30	05 37	05 43	05 51	06 02	06 05	06 16	06 19	06 27	06 30	06 45	07 01	07 04	07 08	07 14	07 18	07 24
Meadowhall [4] 29,31 ⇌	a		05 20	05 23	05 30	05 35	05 35	05 43	05 48	05 56	06 07	06 10	06 21	06 24	06 32	06 35	06 50	07 06	07 09	07 13	07 19	07 23	07 31
	d		05 21	05 24		05 36	05 36	05 44		05 57	06 08		06 22	06 25		06 36	06 51		07 10		07 22	07 25	
Chapeltown	d			05 30		05 42	05 42	05 50			06 14					06 42			07 16				
Elsecar	d			05 35		05 48	05 48	05 56			06 20					06 48			07 22				
Wombwell	d			05 39		05 51	05 51	05 59			06 23					06 51			07 25				
Barnsley	a			05 45		05 57	05 57	06 05		06 12	06 29			06 39		06 57	07 06		07 31			07 41	
	d					05 58	06 00	06 06			06 30			06 39		07 00	07 06		07 32			07 42	
Dodworth	d							06 12								07 06							
Silkstone Common	d							06 15								07 09							
Penistone	d							06 21								07 16							
Denby Dale	d							06 28								07 23							
Shepley	d							06 33								07 28							
Stocksmoor	d							06 36								07 31							
Brockholes	d							06 40								07 35							
Honley	d							06 42								07 37							
Berry Brow	d							06 45								07 40							
Lockwood	d							06 48								07 43							
Huddersfield	a							06 52								07 47							
Darton	d					06 03	06 05				06 35								07 37				
Wakefield Kirkgate [4] 31	a					06 14	06 16				06 48			06 54			07 22		07 49			07 57	
	d					06 16	06 17				06 49			06 55			07 23		07 50			07 57	
Normanton	d					06 21	06 22				06 54			06 59			07 27		07 55				
Castleford 32	a										06 59								08 00				
Woodlesford 32	a					06 29	06 30				07 11								08 12				
Leeds [10] 31,32	a		06 30			06 43	06 45				07 25		07 30	07 16			07 43		08 25		08 36	08 17	

A To Doncaster
B From Nottingham
C To Bridlington
D To Adwick
E To Beverley
F From Manchester Airport to Cleethorpes

Nottingham and Sheffield - Barnsley - Huddersfield and Leeds

Station		EM ◇ A	NT B	NT	NT ◇ C	EM ◇1 D	NT	NT E	TP ◇1 F	NT ◇	NT ◇	NT ◇ G	NT H	NT	EM ◇ A	NT ◇ I	NT ◇ J	NT	NT B	TP ◇1 F	NT	NT ◇	NT ◇ K
Nottingham	d	06 39									07 18				07 46							08 17	
Ilkeston	d										07 30				07 59							08 29	
Langley Mill	d										07 37											08 36	
Alfreton	d	07 00									07 45				08 10							08 44	
Chesterfield	d	07 10				07 42					07 57				08 20							08 55	
Dronfield	d	07 18				07 49					08 04				08 27							09 02	
Sheffield 29,31	a	07 28				08 00					08 15				08 38							09 13	
	d		07 31	07 35	07 47		08 03	08 06	08 10	08 15	08 18	08 25	08 30	08 35		08 46	08 54	09 03	09 06	09 10	09 15	09 18	09 24
Meadowhall 29,31	a		07 36	07 40	07 53		08 08	08 11	08 16	08 21	08 24	08 31	08 35	08 40		08 51	09 00	09 08	09 11	09 15	09 20	09 23	09 31
	d			07 41	07 54		08 09			08 21	08 25			08 41		08 53		09 09			09 21	09 24	
Chapeltown	d			07 47			08 15							08 47				09 15					
Elsecar	d			07 53			08 21							08 53				09 21					
Wombwell	d			07 56			08 24							08 56				09 24					
Barnsley	a			08 02	08 10		08 30				08 40			09 02		09 10		09 30				09 40	
	d			08 03	08 11		08 31				08 41			09 03		09 11		09 31				09 41	
Dodworth	d			08 09										09 09									
Silkstone Common	d			08 12										09 12									
Penistone	d			08 19										09 19									
Denby Dale	d			08 26										09 26									
Shepley	d			08 31										09 31									
Stocksmoor	d			08 34										09 34									
Brockholes	d			08 38										09 38									
Honley	d			08 40										09 40									
Berry Brow	d			08 43										09 43									
Lockwood	d			08 46										09 46									
Huddersfield	a			08 50										09 50									
Darton	d						08 36											09 36					
Wakefield Kirkgate 31	a				08 25		08 48				08 57					09 26		09 48				09 56	
	d				08 25		08 49				08 58					09 26		09 49				09 56	
Normanton	d				08 30		08 54											09 54					
Castleford 32	a						08 59											09 59					
Woodlesford 32	a						09 11											10 11					
Leeds 31,32	a				08 46		09 24			09 30	09 17					09 46		10 24			10 30	10 16	

Station		NT H	NT	EM ◇ L	NT ◇ I	NT	NT B	TP ◇1 F	NT ◇	NT ◇	NT ◇ K	NT H	NT	EM ◇ L	NT ◇ I	NT	NT B	TP ◇1 F	NT	NT ◇	NT ◇ K	NT H
Nottingham	d			08 47						09 17				09 47						10 17		
Ilkeston	d									09 29										10 29		
Langley Mill	d									09 36										10 36		
Alfreton	d			09 08						09 44				10 08						10 44		
Chesterfield	d			09 20						09 55				10 20						10 55		
Dronfield	d									10 02										11 02		
Sheffield 29,31	a			09 37						10 13				10 38						11 13		
	d	09 30	09 35		09 48	10 02	10 05	10 10	10 15	10 18	10 24	10 30	10 35		10 49	11 02	11 05	11 10	11 15	11 18	11 24	11 30
Meadowhall 29,31	a	09 35	09 40		09 53	10 07	10 10	10 16	10 20	10 23	10 31	10 35	10 40		10 54	11 07	11 10	11 16	11 20	11 23	11 31	11 35
	d		09 41		09 54	10 08			10 21	10 24			10 41		10 57	11 08			11 21	11 24		
Chapeltown	d		09 47			10 14							10 47			11 14						
Elsecar	d		09 53			10 20							10 53			11 20						
Wombwell	d		09 56			10 23							10 56			11 23						
Barnsley	a		10 02		10 10	10 29				10 39			11 02		11 11	11 29				11 39		
	d		10 03		10 11	10 30				10 40			11 03		11 12	11 30				11 40		
Dodworth	d		10 09										11 09									
Silkstone Common	d		10 12										11 12									
Penistone	d		10 19										11 19									
Denby Dale	d		10 26										11 26									
Shepley	d		10 31										11 31									
Stocksmoor	d		10 34										11 34									
Brockholes	d		10 38										11 38									
Honley	d		10 40										11 40									
Berry Brow	d		10 43										11 43									
Lockwood	d		10 46										11 46									
Huddersfield	a		10 50										11 50									
Darton	d					10 35										11 35						
Wakefield Kirkgate 31	a				10 26	10 48				10 55					11 27	11 48				11 55		
	d				10 26	10 49				10 55					11 27	11 49				11 55		
Normanton	d					10 54										11 54						
Castleford 32	a					10 59										11 59						
Woodlesford 32	a					11 11										12 11						
Leeds 31,32	a				10 46	11 24			11 30	11 15					11 47	12 24			12 30	12 15		

A To Liverpool Lime Street
B To Adwick
C From Retford
D From Derby
E To Doncaster
F From Manchester Airport to Cleethorpes
G To Scarborough
H To Hull
I From Lincoln
J To York
K To Bridlington
L From Norwich to Liverpool Lime Street

Nottingham and Sheffield - Barnsley - Huddersfield and Leeds

Station		NT	EM ◇ A	NT ◇ B	NT ◇ C	NT	NT D	TP ◇1 E	NT ◇	NT ◇	NT ◇ F	NT G	NT	EM ◇ A	NT ◇ B	NT	NT D	TP ◇1 E	NT	NT ◇	NT ◇ H	NT G	NT
Nottingham	d		10 51							11 17				11 47						12 17			
Ilkeston	d									11 29										12 29			
Langley Mill	d									11 36										12 36			
Alfreton	d		11 12							11 44				12 08						12 44			
Chesterfield	d		11 22							11 55				12 20						12 55			
Dronfield	d									12 02										13 02			
Sheffield 29,31	a		11 38							12 13				12 38						13 13			
	d	11 35		11 45	11 59	12 02	12 05	12 10	12 15	12 18	12 24	12 30	12 35		12 45	13 02	13 05	13 10	13 15	13 18	13 24	13 30	13 35
Meadowhall 29,31	a	11 40		11 50	12 04	12 07	12 10	12 16	12 20	12 23	12 31	12 35	12 40		12 51	13 07	13 10	13 16	13 20	13 23	13 31	13 35	13 40
	d	11 41		11 51		12 08			12 21	12 24			12 41		12 51	13 08			13 21	13 24			13 41
Chapeltown	d	11 47				12 14							12 47			13 14							13 47
Elsecar	d	11 53				12 20							12 53			13 20							13 53
Wombwell	d	11 56				12 23							12 56			13 23							13 56
Barnsley	a	12 02		12 10		12 29				12 39			13 02		13 11	13 29				13 39			14 02
	d	12 03		12 11		12 30				12 40			13 03		13 11	13 30				13 40			14 03
Dodworth	d	12 09											13 09										14 09
Silkstone Common	d	12 12											13 12										14 12
Penistone	d	12 19											13 19										14 19
Denby Dale	d	12 26											13 26										14 26
Shepley	d	12 31											13 31										14 31
Stocksmoor	d	12 34											13 34										14 34
Brockholes	d	12 38											13 38										14 38
Honley	d	12 40											13 40										14 40
Berry Brow	d	12 43											13 43										14 43
Lockwood	d	12 46											13 46										14 46
Huddersfield	a	12 50											13 50										14 50
Darton	d					12 35										13 35							
Wakefield Kirkgate 31	a			12 26		12 48				12 55					13 26	13 48				13 55			
	d			12 26		12 49				12 55					13 27	13 49				13 55			
Normanton	d					12 54										13 54							
Castleford 32	a					12 59										13 59							
Woodlesford 32	a					13 11										14 11							
Leeds 31,32	a			12 46		13 24			13 30	13 15					13 46	14 24			14 30	14 15			

Station		EM ◇ A	NT ◇ B	NT	NT D	TP ◇1 E	NT ◇	NT ◇	NT ◇ F	NT G	NT	EM ◇ A	NT ◇ B	NT	NT D	TP ◇1 E	NT	NT ◇	NT ◇ F	NT G	NT	EM ◇ A
Nottingham	d	12 47						13 17				13 47						14 17				14 47
Ilkeston	d	13 00						13 29										14 29				
Langley Mill	d							13 36										14 36				
Alfreton	d	13 10						13 44				14 10						14 44				15 08
Chesterfield	d	13 21						13 55				14 20						14 55				15 20
Dronfield	d							14 02										15 02				
Sheffield 29,31	a	13 37						14 13				14 38						15 13				15 37
	d		13 45	14 02	14 05	14 10	14 15	14 18	14 24	14 30	14 35		14 45	15 02	15 05	15 10	15 15	15 18	15 24	15 30	15 35	
Meadowhall 29,31	a		13 51	14 07	14 10	14 16	14 20	14 23	14 31	14 35	14 40		14 51	15 07	15 10	15 16	15 20	15 23	15 31	15 35	15 40	
	d		13 51	14 08			14 21	14 24			14 41		14 51	15 08			15 21	15 24			15 41	
Chapeltown	d			14 14							14 47			15 14							15 47	
Elsecar	d			14 20							14 53			15 20							15 53	
Wombwell	d			14 23							14 56			15 23							15 56	
Barnsley	a		14 11	14 29				14 39			15 02		15 11	15 29				15 39			16 02	
	d		14 11	14 30				14 40			15 03		15 11	15 30				15 40			16 03	
Dodworth	d										15 09										16 09	
Silkstone Common	d										15 12										16 12	
Penistone	d										15 19										16 19	
Denby Dale	d										15 26										16 26	
Shepley	d										15 31										16 31	
Stocksmoor	d										15 34										16 34	
Brockholes	d										15 38										16 38	
Honley	d										15 40										16 40	
Berry Brow	d										15 43										16 43	
Lockwood	d										15 46										16 46	
Huddersfield	a										15 50										16 50	
Darton	d			14 35										15 35								
Wakefield Kirkgate 31	a		14 26	14 48				14 55					15 26	15 48				15 55				
	d		14 27	14 49				14 55					15 27	15 49				15 55				
Normanton	d			14 54										15 54								
Castleford 32	a			14 59										15 59								
Woodlesford 32	a			15 11										16 11								
Leeds 31,32	a		14 46	15 24			15 30	15 15					15 46	16 24			16 30	16 15				

A From Norwich to Liverpool Lime Street
B From Lincoln
C To York
D To Adwick
E From Manchester Airport to Cleethorpes
F To Bridlington
G To Hull
H To Scarborough

Nottingham and Sheffield - Barnsley - Huddersfield and Leeds

		NT	NT	NT	TP	NT	NT	NT	NT	NT	EM	NT	NT	NT	TP	NT	NT	NT	NT	NT	EM	NT	NT
		◇			◇■	◇	◇	◇			◇	◇			◇■		◇	◇			◇	◇	
		A		B	C			D	E		F	A		B	C			D	E		F	A	
Nottingham 8	d						15 17				15 47						16 17				16 47		
Ilkeston	d						15 29				16 00						16 29						
Langley Mill	d						15 36										16 36						
Alfreton	d						15 44				16 10						16 44				17 08		
Chesterfield	d						15 55				16 20						16 55				17 20		
Dronfield	d						16 02										17 02						
Sheffield 7 29,31	a						16 13				16 37						17 13				17 37		
	d	15 45	16 02	16 05	16 10	16 15	16 18	16 24	16 30	16 35		16 45	17 02	17 05	17 10	17 15	17 18	17 24	17 30	17 35		17 45	18 02
Meadowhall 4 29,31	a	15 50	16 07	16 10	16 16	16 20	16 23	16 31	16 35	16 40		16 51	17 07	17 10	17 16	17 20	17 23	17 31	17 35	17 40		17 51	18 07
	d	15 51	16 08			16 21	16 24			16 41		16 51	17 08			17 21	17 24			17 41		17 51	18 08
Chapeltown	d		16 14							16 47			17 14							17 47			18 14
Elsecar	d		16 20							16 53			17 20							17 53			18 20
Wombwell	d		16 23							16 56			17 23							17 56			18 23
Barnsley	a	16 10	16 29				16 39			17 02		17 11	17 29				17 39			18 02		18 10	18 29
	d	16 11	16 30				16 40			17 03		17 11	17 30				17 40			18 03		18 11	18 30
Dodworth	d									17 09										18 09			
Silkstone Common	d									17 12										18 13			
Penistone	d									17 19										18 23			
Denby Dale	d									17 26										18 29			
Shepley	d									17 31										18 34			
Stocksmoor	d									17 33										18 37			
Brockholes	d									17 37										18 41			
Honley	d									17 40										18 43			
Berry Brow	d									17 43										18 46			
Lockwood	d									17 45										18 49			
Huddersfield	a									17 50										18 54			
Darton	d		16 35										17 35										18 35
Wakefield Kirkgate 4 31	a	16 26	16 48				16 55					17 26	17 48				17 55					18 27	18 48
	d	16 26	16 49				16 55					17 27	17 49				17 55					18 27	18 49
Normanton	d		16 54										17 54										18 54
Castleford 32	a		16 59										17 59										18 59
Woodlesford 32	a		17 11										18 11										19 11
Leeds 10 31,32	a	16 46	17 24			17 32	17 15					17 46	18 24			18 30	18 15					18 47	19 24

		NT	TP	NT	NT	NT	NT	NT	EM	NT	NT	NT	TP	NT	NT	NT	NT	NT	EM	NT	NT	NT	TP
			◇■	◇	◇	◇			◇	◇			◇■		◇	◇			◇	◇			◇■
		B	C			G	E		F	A		B	C			E	E		F	A		B	C
Nottingham 8	d				17 17				17 47						18 17				18 47				
Ilkeston	d				17 29										18 29								
Langley Mill	d				17 36				18 03						18 36								
Alfreton	d				17 44				18 11						18 44				19 08				
Chesterfield	d				17 55				18 20						18 55				19 20				
Dronfield	d				18 02										19 02								
Sheffield 7 29,31	a				18 13				18 38						19 13				19 37				
	d	18 05	18 11	18 15	18 18	18 24	18 30	18 35		18 45	19 02	19 05	19 11	19 15	19 18	19 24	19 30	19 35		19 45	20 02	20 05	20 11
Meadowhall 4 29,31	a	18 10	18 17	18 20	18 23	18 31	18 35	18 40		18 50	19 07	19 10	19 16	19 20	19 23	19 31	19 35	19 40		19 50	20 07	20 10	20 16
	d			18 21	18 24			18 41		18 51	19 08			19 21	19 24			19 41		19 51	20 08		
Chapeltown	d							18 47			19 14							19 47			20 14		
Elsecar	d							18 53			19 20							19 53			20 20		
Wombwell	d							18 56			19 23							19 56			20 23		
Barnsley	a				18 39			19 02		19 10	19 29				19 39			20 02		20 10	20 29		
	d				18 40			19 03		19 11	19 30				19 40			20 03		20 11	20 30		
Dodworth	d							19 09										20 09					
Silkstone Common	d							19 12										20 12					
Penistone	d							19 19										20 19					
Denby Dale	d							19 26										20 26					
Shepley	d							19 31										20 31					
Stocksmoor	d							19 34										20 34					
Brockholes	d							19 38										20 38					
Honley	d							19 40										20 40					
Berry Brow	d							19 43										20 43					
Lockwood	d							19 46										20 46					
Huddersfield	a							19 50										20 50					
Darton	d										19 35										20 35		
Wakefield Kirkgate 4 31	a				18 55					19 26	19 48				19 55					20 26	20 48		
	d				18 55					19 26	19 49				19 55					20 26	20 49		
Normanton	d										19 54										20 54		
Castleford 32	a										19 59										20 59		
Woodlesford 32	a										20 11										21 11		
Leeds 10 31,32	a			19 30	19 15					19 46	20 24			20 36	20 15					20 46	21 24		

A From Lincoln
B To Adwick
C From Manchester Airport to Cleethorpes
D To Scarborough
E To Hull
F From Norwich to Liverpool Lime Street
G To Bridlington

Table T034-F

Mondays to Fridays

8 October to 7 December

Nottingham and Sheffield - Barnsley - Huddersfield and Leeds

		NT	NT	NT	EM	NT	NT	NT	NT	NT	TP	NT	NT	NT	EM	NT	EM	NT	TP	NT	NT	NT
		◇	◇	◇	◇			◇			◇■		◇	◇	◇■		◇■		◇■	◇	◇	◇
				A	B	C		D		E	F			G	H		H	E	F			C
Nottingham 8	d		19 17		19 39								20 17		20 33		21 08				21 12	
Ilkeston	d		19 29										20 29								21 29	
Langley Mill	d		19 36										20 36		20 52		21 25				21 36	
Alfreton	d		19 44		20 01								20 44		21 00		21 33				21 44	
Chesterfield	d		19 55		20 11								20 54		21 11		21 44				21 55	
Dronfield	d		20 02										21 02								22 02	
Sheffield 7 29,31	a		20 13		20 28								21 13		21 27		21 58				22 13	
	d	20 15	20 18	20 24		20 30	20 35	20 45	21 02	21 05	21 11	21 15	21 18	21 28	21 32	21 35	22 04	22 07	22 11	22 15	22 18	22 28
Meadowhall 4 29,31	a	20 20	20 23	20 31		20 35	20 40	20 50	21 07	21 10	21 16	21 20	21 23	21 33		21 40		22 12	22 16	22 21	22 23	22 33
	d	20 21	20 24				20 41	20 51	21 08			21 21	21 24			21 41				22 22	22 24	
Chapeltown	d						20 47		21 14							21 47						
Elsecar	d						20 53		21 20							21 53						
Wombwell	d						20 56		21 23							21 56						
Barnsley	a		20 39				21 02	21 10	21 29				21 39			22 02					22 39	
	d		20 40				21 03	21 11	21 30				21 40			22 03					22 40	
Dodworth	d						21 09									22 09						
Silkstone Common	d						21 12									22 12						
Penistone	d						21 19									22 19						
Denby Dale	d						21 26									22 26						
Shepley	d						21 31									22 31						
Stocksmoor	d						21 34									22 34						
Brockholes	d						21 38									22 38						
Honley	d						21 40									22 40						
Berry Brow	d						21 43									22 43						
Lockwood	d						21 46									22 46						
Huddersfield	a						21 50									22 50						
Darton	d								21 35													
Wakefield Kirkgate 4 31	a		20 55					21 26	21 48				21 55								22 55	
	d		20 55					21 26	21 49				21 55								22 55	
Normanton	d								21 54													
Castleford 32	a								21 59													
Woodlesford 32	a								22 11													
Leeds 10 31,32	a	21 30	21 15					21 46	22 24			22 30	22 15		22 34		22 49			23 31	23 14	

		NT	NT	NT	NT	NT	NT	NT	NT
					FO	FX			
									◇
				I				I	
Nottingham 8	d								23 18
Ilkeston	d								23 30
Langley Mill	d								23 36
Alfreton	d								23 44
Chesterfield	d								23 54
Dronfield	d								00 02
Sheffield 7 29,31	a								00 16
	d	22 31	22 38	23 05	23 15	23 15	23 18	23 27	
Meadowhall 4 29,31	a	22 36	22 43	23 10	23 20	23 20	23 23	23 32	
	d	22 37	22 44		23 21	23 21	23 24		
Chapeltown	d	22 43	22 51				23 30		
Elsecar	d	22 48	22 57				23 35		
Wombwell	d	22 52	23 01				23 39		
Barnsley	a	22 59	23 07				23 46		
	d	22 59	23 07				23 46		
Dodworth	d		23 13						
Silkstone Common	d		23 17						
Penistone	d		23 26						
Denby Dale	d		23 33						
Shepley	d		23 38						
Stocksmoor	d		23 40						
Brockholes	d		23 44						
Honley	d		23 47						
Berry Brow	d		23 50						
Lockwood	d		23 52						
Huddersfield	a		23 57						
Darton	d	23 04					23 51		
Wakefield Kirkgate 4 31	a	23 16					00 03		
	d	23 17							
Normanton	d	23 21							
Castleford 32	a	23 30							
Woodlesford 32	a	23 41							
Leeds 10 31,32	a	23 53			00 28	00 29			

A To Bridlington
B From Norwich to Manchester Piccadilly
C To Hull
D From Lincoln
E To Adwick
F From Manchester Airport to Cleethorpes
G To Beverley
H From St Pancras International
I To Doncaster

Table T034-F

Saturdays
26 May to 16 June

Nottingham and Sheffield - Barnsley - Huddersfield and Leeds

		NT	NT	NT	NT	NT	NT	NT	NT	NT	NT	NT	NT	NT	NT	NT	NT	NT	TP	NT	NT	NT	EM
		◇	◇					◇					◇			◇			◇1		◇	◇	◇
		A			B			C			D			E			D		F			C	G
Nottingham 8	d																				06 17		06 40
Ilkeston	d																				06 29		
Langley Mill	d																				06 36		
Alfreton	d																				06 44		07 01
Chesterfield	d															06 25					06 54		07 11
Dronfield	d	00 02														06 32					07 01		07 19
Sheffield 7 29,31	a	00 16														06 42					07 11		07 29
	d		05 15	05 18	05 24	05 30	05 37	05 43	05 51	06 03	06 06	06 16	06 19	06 27	06 30	06 45	07 01	07 04	07 10	07 16	07 18	07 24	
Meadowhall 4 29,31	a		05 20	05 23	05 29	05 35	05 43	05 48	05 56	06 08	06 11	06 21	06 24	06 32	06 35	06 50	07 06	07 09	07 15	07 21	07 23	07 31	
	d		05 21	05 24		05 36	05 44		05 57	06 09		06 22	06 25		06 36	06 51		07 10		07 22	07 25		
Chapeltown	d			05 30		05 42	05 50			06 16					06 42			07 17					
Elsecar	d			05 35		05 48	05 56			06 22					06 48			07 23					
Wombwell	d			05 39		05 51	05 59			06 25					06 51			07 26					
Barnsley	a			05 45		05 57	06 05		06 12	06 31			06 39		06 57	07 06		07 32			07 41		
	d					05 58	06 06			06 32			06 39		07 00	07 06		07 33			07 42		
Dodworth	d						06 12								07 06								
Silkstone Common	d						06 15								07 09								
Penistone	d						06 21								07 16								
Denby Dale	d						06 28								07 23								
Shepley	d						06 33								07 28								
Stocksmoor	d						06 36								07 31								
Brockholes	d						06 40								07 35								
Honley	d						06 42								07 37								
Berry Brow	d						06 45								07 40								
Lockwood	d						06 48								07 43								
Huddersfield	a						06 52								07 47								
Darton	d					06 03				06 37								07 38					
Wakefield Kirkgate 4 31	a					06 14				06 49			06 54			07 22		07 50			07 57		
	d					06 16				06 50			06 55			07 23		07 51			07 57		
Normanton	d					06 21				06 55			06 59			07 27		07 56					
Castleford 32	a									07 00								08 01					
Woodlesford 32	a					06 29				07 12								08 13					
Leeds 10 31,32	a		06 30			06 43				07 25		07 30	07 16			07 43		08 26		08 36	08 17		

		NT	NT	NT	EM	NT	NT	TP	NT	NT	NT	NT	NT	EM	NT	NT	NT	NT	TP	NT	NT	NT	NT
				◇	◇1			◇1	◇	◇	◇			◇	◇	◇			◇1		◇	◇	
		D		H	I		B	F			J	K		G	L	M		D	F			C	K
Nottingham 8	d									07 18				07 46							08 17		
Ilkeston	d									07 30				07 59							08 29		
Langley Mill	d									07 37											08 36		
Alfreton	d									07 45				08 09							08 44		
Chesterfield	d				07 43					07 57				08 20							08 55		
Dronfield	d				07 49					08 04				08 26							09 02		
Sheffield 7 29,31	a				07 59					08 15				08 37							09 13		
	d	07 31	07 35	07 45		08 02	08 05	08 10	08 15	08 18	08 25	08 30	08 35		08 45	08 54	09 03	09 06	09 10	09 15	09 18	09 24	09 30
Meadowhall 4 29,31	a	07 36	07 40	07 53		08 08	08 11	08 15	08 20	08 24	08 31	08 35	08 40		08 50	09 00	09 08	09 11	09 16	09 20	09 23	09 31	09 35
	d		07 41	07 54		08 09			08 21	08 25			08 41		08 51		09 09			09 21	09 24		
Chapeltown	d		07 47			08 15							08 47				09 15						
Elsecar	d		07 53			08 21							08 53				09 21						
Wombwell	d		07 56			08 24							08 56				09 24						
Barnsley	a		08 02	08 10		08 30				08 40			09 02		09 10		09 30				09 40		
	d		08 03	08 11		08 31				08 41			09 03		09 11		09 31				09 41		
Dodworth	d		08 09										09 09										
Silkstone Common	d		08 12										09 12										
Penistone	d		08 19										09 19										
Denby Dale	d		08 26										09 26										
Shepley	d		08 31										09 31										
Stocksmoor	d		08 34										09 34										
Brockholes	d		08 38										09 38										
Honley	d		08 40										09 40										
Berry Brow	d		08 43										09 43										
Lockwood	d		08 46										09 46										
Huddersfield	a		08 50										09 50										
Darton	d					08 36											09 36						
Wakefield Kirkgate 4 31	a			08 25		08 48				08 57					09 26		09 48				09 56		
	d			08 25		08 49				08 58					09 26		09 49				09 56		
Normanton	d			08 30		08 54											09 54						
Castleford 32	a					08 59											09 59						
Woodlesford 32	a					09 11											10 11						
Leeds 10 31,32	a			08 46		09 24			09 30	09 17					09 46		10 24			10 30	10 16		

A From Nottingham
B To Doncaster
C To Bridlington
D To Adwick
E To Beverley
F From Manchester Airport to Cleethorpes
G To Liverpool Lime Street
H From Retford
I From Derby
J To Scarborough
K To Hull
L From Lincoln
M To York

Table T034-F

Saturdays
26 May to 16 June

Nottingham and Sheffield - Barnsley - Huddersfield and Leeds

		NT	EM	NT	NT	NT	TP	NT	NT	NT	NT	NT	EM	NT	NT	NT	TP	NT	NT	NT	NT	NT
			◇	◇			◇1	◇	◇	◇			◇	◇			◇1		◇	◇		
			A	B		C	D			E	F		A	B		C	D			E	F	
Nottingham 8	d		08 47						09 17				09 47						10 17			
Ilkeston	d								09 29										10 29			
Langley Mill	d								09 36										10 36			
Alfreton	d		09 08						09 44				10 08						10 44			
Chesterfield	d		09 20						09 55				10 20						10 55			
Dronfield	d								10 02										11 02			
Sheffield 7 29,31	a		09 37						10 13				10 37						11 13			
	d	09 35		09 48	10 02	10 05	10 10	10 15	10 18	10 24	10 30	10 35		10 49	11 02	11 05	11 10	11 15	11 18	11 24	11 30	11 35
Meadowhall 4 29,31	a	09 40		09 53	10 07	10 10	10 16	10 20	10 23	10 31	10 35	10 40		10 54	11 07	11 10	11 16	11 20	11 23	11 31	11 35	11 40
	d	09 41		09 54	10 08			10 21	10 24			10 41		10 57	11 08			11 21	11 24			11 41
Chapeltown	d	09 47			10 14							10 47			11 14							11 47
Elsecar	d	09 53			10 20							10 53			11 20							11 53
Wombwell	d	09 56			10 23							10 56			11 23							11 56
Barnsley	a	10 02		10 10	10 29				10 39			11 02		11 11	11 29				11 39			12 02
	d	10 03		10 11	10 30				10 40			11 03		11 12	11 30				11 40			12 03
Dodworth	d	10 09										11 09										12 09
Silkstone Common	d	10 12										11 12										12 12
Penistone	d	10 19										11 19										12 19
Denby Dale	d	10 26										11 26										12 26
Shepley	d	10 31										11 31										12 31
Stocksmoor	d	10 34										11 34										12 34
Brockholes	d	10 38										11 38										12 38
Honley	d	10 40										11 40										12 40
Berry Brow	d	10 43										11 43										12 43
Lockwood	d	10 46										11 46										12 46
Huddersfield	a	10 50										11 50										12 50
Darton	d				10 35										11 35							
Wakefield Kirkgate 4 31	a			10 26	10 48				10 55					11 27	11 48				11 55			
	d			10 26	10 49				10 55					11 27	11 49				11 55			
Normanton	d				10 54										11 54							
Castleford 32	a				10 59										11 59							
Woodlesford 32	a				11 11										12 11							
Leeds 10 31,32	a			10 46	11 24			11 30	11 15					11 47	12 24			12 30	12 15			

		EM	NT	NT	NT	NT	TP	NT	NT	NT	NT	NT	EM	NT	NT	NT	TP	NT	NT	NT	NT	NT	EM
		◇	◇	◇			◇1	◇	◇	◇			◇	◇			◇1		◇	◇			◇
		A	B	G		C	D			E	F		A	B		C	D			H	F		A
Nottingham 8	d	10 46							11 17				11 47						12 17				12 47
Ilkeston	d								11 29										12 29				13 00
Langley Mill	d								11 36										12 36				
Alfreton	d	11 08							11 44				12 08						12 44				13 10
Chesterfield	d	11 20							11 55				12 20						12 55				13 21
Dronfield	d								12 02										13 02				
Sheffield 7 29,31	a	11 38							12 13				12 38						13 13				13 37
	d		11 45	11 59	12 02	12 05	12 10	12 15	12 18	12 24	12 30	12 35		12 45	13 02	13 05	13 10	13 15	13 18	13 24	13 30	13 35	
Meadowhall 4 29,31	a		11 50	12 04	12 07	12 10	12 16	12 20	12 23	12 31	12 35	12 40		12 51	13 07	13 10	13 16	13 20	13 23	13 31	13 35	13 40	
	d		11 51		12 08			12 21	12 24			12 41		12 51	13 08			13 21	13 24			13 41	
Chapeltown	d				12 14							12 47			13 14							13 47	
Elsecar	d				12 20							12 53			13 20							13 53	
Wombwell	d				12 23							12 56			13 23							13 56	
Barnsley	a		12 10		12 29				12 39			13 02		13 11	13 29				13 39			14 02	
	d		12 11		12 30				12 40			13 03		13 11	13 30				13 40			14 03	
Dodworth	d											13 09										14 09	
Silkstone Common	d											13 12										14 12	
Penistone	d											13 19										14 19	
Denby Dale	d											13 26										14 26	
Shepley	d											13 31										14 31	
Stocksmoor	d											13 34										14 34	
Brockholes	d											13 38										14 38	
Honley	d											13 40										14 40	
Berry Brow	d											13 43										14 43	
Lockwood	d											13 46										14 46	
Huddersfield	a											13 50										14 50	
Darton	d				12 35										13 35								
Wakefield Kirkgate 4 31	a		12 26		12 48				12 55					13 26	13 48				13 55				
	d		12 26		12 49				12 55					13 27	13 49				13 55				
Normanton	d				12 54										13 54								
Castleford 32	a				12 59										13 59								
Woodlesford 32	a				13 11										14 11								
Leeds 10 31,32	a		12 46		13 24			13 30	13 15					13 46	14 24			14 30	14 15				

A From Norwich to Liverpool Lime Street
B From Lincoln
C To Adwick
D From Manchester Airport to Cleethorpes
E To Bridlington
F To Hull
G To York
H To Scarborough

Table T034-F

Saturdays
26 May to 16 June

Nottingham and Sheffield - Barnsley - Huddersfield and Leeds

		NT	NT	NT		TP	NT	NT	NT	NT	NT	EM	NT	NT		NT	TP	NT	NT	NT	NT	NT	EM	NT	
		◇				◇1	◇	◇	◇			◇	◇				◇1		◇	◇			◇	◇	
		A		B		C			D	E		F	A			B	C			D	E		F	A	
Nottingham ⇌	d							13 17				13 47							14 17				14 47		
Ilkeston	d							13 29											14 29						
Langley Mill	d							13 36											14 36						
Alfreton	d							13 44				14 08							14 44				15 08		
Chesterfield	d							13 55				14 20							14 55				15 20		
Dronfield	d							14 02											15 02						
Sheffield 29,31 ⇌	a							14 13				14 37							15 13				15 37		
	d	13 45	14 02	14 05		14 10	14 15	14 18	14 24	14 30	14 35		14 45	15 02		15 05	15 10	15 15	15 18	15 24	15 30	15 35		15 45	
Meadowhall 29,31 ⇌	a	13 51	14 07	14 10		14 16	14 20	14 23	14 31	14 35	14 40		14 51	15 07		15 10	15 16	15 20	15 23	15 31	15 35	15 40		15 50	
	d	13 51	14 08				14 21	14 24			14 41		14 51	15 08				15 21	15 24			15 41		15 51	
Chapeltown	d		14 14								14 47			15 14								15 47			
Elsecar	d		14 20								14 53			15 20								15 53			
Wombwell	d		14 23								14 56			15 23								15 56			
Barnsley	a	14 11	14 29					14 39			15 02		15 11	15 29					15 39			16 02		16 10	
	d	14 11	14 30					14 40			15 03		15 11	15 30					15 40			16 03		16 11	
Dodworth	d										15 09											16 09			
Silkstone Common	d										15 12											16 12			
Penistone	d										15 19											16 19			
Denby Dale	d										15 26											16 26			
Shepley	d										15 31											16 31			
Stocksmoor	d										15 34											16 34			
Brockholes	d										15 38											16 38			
Honley	d										15 40											16 40			
Berry Brow	d										15 43											16 43			
Lockwood	d										15 46											16 46			
Huddersfield	a										15 50											16 50			
Darton	d		14 35											15 35											
Wakefield Kirkgate 31	a	14 26	14 48					14 55					15 26	15 48					15 55					16 26	
	d	14 27	14 49					14 55					15 27	15 49					15 55					16 26	
Normanton	d		14 54											15 54											
Castleford 32	a		14 59											15 59											
Woodlesford 32	a		15 11											16 11											
Leeds 31,32	a	14 46	15 24				15 30	15 15					15 46	16 24				16 30	16 15					16 46	

		NT	NT	TP	NT	NT	NT	NT	NT	EM		NT	NT	NT	TP	NT	NT	NT	NT	EM		NT	NT	NT	NT
				◇1	◇	◇	◇			◇		◇			◇1		◇	◇		◇			◇		
			B	C			G	E		F		A		B	C			G	E	F			A		B
Nottingham ⇌	d					15 17				15 47							16 17			16 44					
Ilkeston	d					15 29				16 00							16 29								
Langley Mill	d					15 36											16 36								
Alfreton	d					15 44				16 10							16 44			17 05					
Chesterfield	d					15 55				16 21							16 55			17 15					
Dronfield	d					16 02											17 02								
Sheffield 29,31 ⇌	a					16 13				16 37							17 13			17 34					
	d	16 02	16 05	16 10	16 15	16 18	16 24	16 30	16 35			16 45	17 02	17 05	17 10	17 15	17 18	17 24	17 30			17 35	17 45	18 02	18 05
Meadowhall 29,31 ⇌	a	16 07	16 10	16 16	16 20	16 23	16 31	16 35	16 40			16 51	17 07	17 10	17 16	17 20	17 23	17 31	17 35			17 40	17 51	18 07	18 10
	d	16 08			16 21	16 24			16 41			16 51	17 08			17 21	17 24					17 41	17 51	18 08	
Chapeltown	d	16 14							16 47				17 14									17 47		18 14	
Elsecar	d	16 20							16 53				17 20									17 53		18 20	
Wombwell	d	16 23							16 56				17 23									17 56		18 23	
Barnsley	a	16 29				16 39			17 02			17 11	17 29				17 39					18 02	18 10	18 29	
	d	16 30				16 40			17 03			17 11	17 30				17 40					18 03	18 11	18 30	
Dodworth	d								17 09													18 09			
Silkstone Common	d								17 12													18 13			
Penistone	d								17 19													18 23			
Denby Dale	d								17 26													18 29			
Shepley	d								17 31													18 34			
Stocksmoor	d								17 33													18 37			
Brockholes	d								17 37													18 41			
Honley	d								17 40													18 43			
Berry Brow	d								17 43													18 46			
Lockwood	d								17 45													18 49			
Huddersfield	a								17 50													18 54			
Darton	d	16 35											17 35											18 35	
Wakefield Kirkgate 31	a	16 48				16 55						17 26	17 48				17 55						18 27	18 48	
	d	16 49				16 55						17 27	17 49				17 55						18 27	18 49	
Normanton	d	16 54											17 54											18 54	
Castleford 32	a	16 59											17 59											18 59	
Woodlesford 32	a	17 11											18 11											19 11	
Leeds 31,32	a	17 24			17 32	17 15						17 46	18 24			18 30	18 15						18 47	19 24	

A From Lincoln
B To Adwick
C From Manchester Airport to Cleethorpes
D To Bridlington
E To Hull
F From Norwich to Liverpool Lime Street
G To Scarborough

Table T034-F

Saturdays
26 May to 16 June

Nottingham and Sheffield - Barnsley - Huddersfield and Leeds

		TP	NT	NT	NT	NT		EM	NT	NT	NT	NT	TP	NT	NT	NT		NT	NT	EM	NT	NT	NT	TP	NT
		◇1	◇	◇	◇			◇		◇			◇1		◇	◇				◇	◇			◇1	◇
		A			B	C		D		E		F	A			C		C		D	E		F	A	
Nottingham ⇌	d			17 17				17 44							18 17					18 47					
Ilkeston	d			17 29											18 29										
Langley Mill	d			17 36				18 00							18 36										
Alfreton	d			17 44				18 08							18 44					19 08					
Chesterfield	d			17 55				18 18							18 55					19 20					
Dronfield	d			18 02											19 02										
Sheffield 29,31 ⇌	a			18 13				18 34							19 13					19 37					
	d	18 11	18 15	18 18	18 24	18 30			18 35	18 45	19 02	19 05	19 11	19 15	19 18	19 24		19 30	19 35		19 45	20 02	20 05	20 11	20 15
Meadowhall 29,31 ⇌	a	18 17	18 20	18 23	18 31	18 35			18 40	18 50	19 07	19 10	19 16	19 20	19 23	19 31		19 35	19 40		19 50	20 07	20 10	20 16	20 20
	d		18 21	18 24					18 41	18 51	19 08			19 21	19 24				19 41		19 51	20 08			20 21
Chapeltown	d								18 47		19 14								19 47			20 14			
Elsecar	d								18 53		19 20								19 53			20 20			
Wombwell	d								18 56		19 23								19 56			20 23			
Barnsley	a			18 39					19 02	19 10	19 29				19 39				20 02		20 10	20 29			
	d			18 40					19 03	19 11	19 30				19 40				20 03		20 11	20 30			
Dodworth	d								19 09										20 09						
Silkstone Common	d								19 12										20 12						
Penistone	d								19 19										20 19						
Denby Dale	d								19 26										20 26						
Shepley	d								19 31										20 31						
Stocksmoor	d								19 34										20 34						
Brockholes	d								19 38										20 38						
Honley	d								19 40										20 40						
Berry Brow	d								19 43										20 43						
Lockwood	d								19 46										20 46						
Huddersfield	a								19 50										20 50						
Darton	d										19 35											20 35			
Wakefield Kirkgate 31	a			18 55						19 26	19 48				19 55						20 26	20 48			
	d			18 55						19 26	19 49				19 55						20 26	20 49			
Normanton	d										19 54											20 54			
Castleford 32	a										19 59											20 59			
Woodlesford 32	a										20 11											21 11			
Leeds 31,32	a		19 30	19 15						19 46	20 24			20 36	20 15						20 46	21 24			21 30

		NT		NT	EM	NT	NT	NT	NT	NT	TP	NT		NT	EM	NT	NT	NT	TP	NT	NT	NT		NT	NT
		◇		◇	◇			◇			◇1			◇	◇1	◇			◇1	◇	◇	◇			
				B	G	C		E		F	A				H 🚲	I		F	A			C			
Nottingham ⇌	d	19 17			19 36									20 17	20 25						21 12				
Ilkeston	d	19 29												20 29							21 29				
Langley Mill	d	19 36												20 36	20 49						21 36				
Alfreton	d	19 44			20 01									20 44	20 57						21 44				
Chesterfield	d	19 55			20 11									20 55	21 07						21 55				
Dronfield	d	20 02												21 02							22 02				
Sheffield 29,31 ⇌	a	20 13			20 30									21 13	21 23						22 13				
	d	20 18		20 24		20 30	20 35	20 45	21 02	21 05	21 11	21 15		21 18	21 24	21 28	21 35	22 07	22 11	22 15	22 18	22 28		22 31	22 38
Meadowhall 29,31 ⇌	a	20 23		20 31		20 35	20 40	20 50	21 07	21 10	21 16	21 20		21 23		21 33	21 40	22 12	22 16	22 20	22 23	22 33		22 36	22 43
	d	20 24					20 41	20 51	21 08			21 21		21 24			21 41			22 21	22 24			22 37	22 44
Chapeltown	d						20 47		21 14								21 47							22 43	22 51
Elsecar	d						20 53		21 20								21 53							22 48	22 57
Wombwell	d						20 56		21 23								21 56							22 52	23 01
Barnsley	a	20 39					21 02	21 10	21 29					21 39			22 02				22 39			22 59	23 07
	d	20 40					21 03	21 11	21 30					21 40			22 03				22 40			22 59	23 07
Dodworth	d						21 09										22 09								23 13
Silkstone Common	d						21 12										22 12								23 17
Penistone	d						21 19										22 19								23 26
Denby Dale	d						21 26										22 26								23 33
Shepley	d						21 31										22 31								23 38
Stocksmoor	d						21 34										22 34								23 40
Brockholes	d						21 38										22 38								23 44
Honley	d						21 40										22 40								23 47
Berry Brow	d						21 43										22 43								23 50
Lockwood	d						21 46										22 46								23 52
Huddersfield	a						21 50										22 50								23 57
Darton	d								21 35															23 04	
Wakefield Kirkgate 31	a	20 55						21 26	21 48					21 55							22 55			23 16	
	d	20 55						21 26	21 49					21 55							22 55			23 17	
Normanton	d								21 54															23 21	
Castleford 32	a								21 59															23 30	
Woodlesford 32	a								22 11															23 41	
Leeds 31,32	a	21 15						21 46	22 24			22 30		22 15	22 17					23 25	23 14			23 53	

A From Manchester Airport to Cleethorpes
B To Bridlington
C To Hull
D From Norwich to Liverpool Lime Street
E From Lincoln
F To Adwick
G From Norwich to Manchester Piccadilly
H From St Pancras International
I To Beverley

Table T034-F

Saturdays
26 May to 16 June

Nottingham and Sheffield - Barnsley - Huddersfield and Leeds

Station		NT	NT	NT
		A	A	◇
Nottingham 8	d			23 18
Ilkeston	d			23 30
Langley Mill	d			23 36
Alfreton	d			23 44
Chesterfield	d			23 54
Dronfield	d			00 02
Sheffield 7 29,31	a			00 16
	d	23 05	23 27	
Meadowhall 4 29,31	a	23 10	23 32	
	d			
Chapeltown	d			
Elsecar	d			
Wombwell	d			
Barnsley	a			
	d			
Dodworth	d			
Silkstone Common	d			
Penistone	d			
Denby Dale	d			
Shepley	d			
Stocksmoor	d			
Brockholes	d			
Honley	d			
Berry Brow	d			
Lockwood	d			
Huddersfield	a			
Darton	d			
Wakefield Kirkgate 4 31	a			
	d			
Normanton	d			
Castleford 32	a			
Woodlesford 32	a			
Leeds 10 31,32	a			

Saturdays
23 June to 21 July

Station		NT	NT	NT	NT	NT	NT	NT	NT	NT	NT	NT	NT	NT	NT	NT	NT	NT	TP	NT	NT	NT	EM
		◇ B	◇		A			◇ C			D		◇	E		◇	D		◇1 F		◇	◇ C	◇ G
Nottingham 8	d																				06 17		06 40
Ilkeston	d																				06 29		
Langley Mill	d																				06 36		
Alfreton	d																				06 44		07 01
Chesterfield	d															06 25					06 54		07 11
Dronfield	d	00 02														06 32					07 01		07 18
Sheffield 7 29,31	a	00 16														06 42					07 11		07 28
	d		05 15	05 18	05 24	05 30	05 37	05 43	05 51	06 03	06 06	06 16	06 19	06 27	06 30	06 45	07 01	07 04	07 10	07 16	07 18	07 24	
Meadowhall 4 29,31	a		05 20	05 23	05 29	05 35	05 43	05 48	05 56	06 08	06 11	06 21	06 24	06 32	06 35	06 50	07 06	07 09	07 15	07 21	07 23	07 31	
	d		05 21	05 24		05 36	05 44		05 57	06 09		06 22	06 25		06 36	06 51		07 10		07 22	07 25		
Chapeltown	d			05 30		05 42	05 50			06 16					06 42			07 17					
Elsecar	d			05 35		05 48	05 56			06 22					06 48			07 23					
Wombwell	d			05 39		05 51	05 59			06 25					06 51			07 26					
Barnsley	a			05 45		05 57	06 05		06 12	06 31			06 39		06 57	07 06		07 32			07 41		
	d					05 58	06 06			06 32			06 39		07 00	07 06		07 33			07 42		
Dodworth	d						06 12								07 06								
Silkstone Common	d						06 15								07 09								
Penistone	d						06 21								07 16								
Denby Dale	d						06 28								07 23								
Shepley	d						06 33								07 28								
Stocksmoor	d						06 36								07 31								
Brockholes	d						06 40								07 35								
Honley	d						06 42								07 37								
Berry Brow	d						06 45								07 40								
Lockwood	d						06 48								07 43								
Huddersfield	a						06 52								07 47								
Darton	d					06 03				06 37								07 38					
Wakefield Kirkgate 4 31	a					06 14				06 49			06 54			07 22		07 50			07 57		
	d					06 16				06 50			06 55			07 23		07 51			07 57		
Normanton	d					06 21				06 55			06 59			07 27		07 56					
Castleford 32	a									07 00								08 01					
Woodlesford 32	a					06 29				07 12								08 13					
Leeds 10 31,32	a		06 30			06 43				07 25		07 30	07 16			07 43		08 26		08 36	08 17		

A To Doncaster
B From Nottingham
C To Bridlington
D To Adwick
E To Beverley
F From Manchester Airport to Cleethorpes
G To Liverpool Lime Street

Table T034-F

Saturdays
23 June to 21 July

Nottingham and Sheffield - Barnsley - Huddersfield and Leeds

Station		NT	NT	NT	EM	NT	NT	TP	NT	NT	NT	NT	NT	EM	NT	NT	NT	NT	TP	NT	NT	NT	NT
		A		◇ B	◇1 C ⚭		D	◇1 E	◇	◇	◇ F	G		◇ H	◇ I	◇ J		A	◇1 E		◇	◇ K	G
Nottingham 8	d									07 18				07 46							08 17		
Ilkeston	d									07 30				07 59							08 29		
Langley Mill	d									07 37											08 36		
Alfreton	d									07 45				08 09							08 44		
Chesterfield	d				07 43					07 57				08 20							08 55		
Dronfield	d				07 49					08 04				08 26							09 02		
Sheffield 7 29,31	a				07 59					08 15				08 37							09 13		
	d	07 31	07 35	07 45		08 02	08 05	08 10	08 15	08 18	08 25	08 30	08 35		08 45	08 54	09 03	09 06	09 10	09 15	09 18	09 24	09 30
Meadowhall 4 29,31	a	07 36	07 40	07 53		08 08	08 11	08 15	08 20	08 24	08 31	08 35	08 40		08 50	09 00	09 08	09 11	09 16	09 20	09 23	09 31	09 35
	d		07 41	07 54		08 09			08 21	08 25			08 41		08 51		09 09			09 21	09 24		
Chapeltown	d		07 47			08 15							08 47				09 15						
Elsecar	d		07 53			08 21							08 53				09 21						
Wombwell	d		07 56			08 24							08 56				09 24						
Barnsley	a		08 02	08 10		08 30				08 40			09 02		09 10		09 30				09 40		
	d		08 03	08 11		08 31				08 41			09 03		09 11		09 31				09 41		
Dodworth	d		08 09										09 09										
Silkstone Common	d		08 12										09 12										
Penistone	d		08 19										09 19										
Denby Dale	d		08 26										09 26										
Shepley	d		08 31										09 31										
Stocksmoor	d		08 34										09 34										
Brockholes	d		08 38										09 38										
Honley	d		08 40										09 40										
Berry Brow	d		08 43										09 43										
Lockwood	d		08 46										09 46										
Huddersfield	a		08 50										09 50										
Darton	d					08 36											09 36						
Wakefield Kirkgate 4 31	a			08 25		08 48				08 57					09 26		09 48				09 56		
	d			08 25		08 49				08 58					09 26		09 49				09 56		
Normanton	d			08 30		08 54											09 54						
Castleford 32	a					08 59											09 59						
Woodlesford 32	a					09 11											10 11						
Leeds 10 31,32	a			08 46		09 24			09 30	09 17					09 46		10 24			10 30	10 16		

Station		NT	EM	NT	NT	NT	TP	NT	NT	NT	NT	NT	EM	NT	NT	NT	TP	NT	NT	NT	NT	NT
			◇ L	◇ I		A	◇1 E	◇	◇	◇ K	G		◇ L	◇ I		A	◇1 E		◇	◇ K	G	
Nottingham 8	d		08 47						09 17				09 47						10 17			
Ilkeston	d								09 29										10 29			
Langley Mill	d								09 36										10 36			
Alfreton	d		09 08						09 44				10 08						10 44			
Chesterfield	d		09 20						09 55				10 20						10 55			
Dronfield	d								10 02										11 02			
Sheffield 7 29,31	a		09 37						10 13				10 37						11 13			
	d	09 35		09 48	10 02	10 05	10 10	10 15	10 18	10 24	10 30	10 35		10 49	11 02	11 05	11 10	11 15	11 18	11 24	11 30	11 35
Meadowhall 4 29,31	a	09 40		09 53	10 07	10 10	10 16	10 20	10 23	10 31	10 35	10 40		10 54	11 07	11 10	11 16	11 20	11 23	11 31	11 35	11 40
	d	09 41		09 54	10 08			10 21	10 24			10 41		10 57	11 08			11 21	11 24			11 41
Chapeltown	d	09 47			10 14							10 47			11 14							11 47
Elsecar	d	09 53			10 20							10 53			11 20							11 53
Wombwell	d	09 56			10 23							10 56			11 23							11 56
Barnsley	a	10 02		10 10	10 29				10 39			11 02		11 11	11 29				11 39			12 02
	d	10 03		10 11	10 30				10 40			11 03		11 12	11 30				11 40			12 03
Dodworth	d	10 09										11 09										12 09
Silkstone Common	d	10 12										11 12										12 12
Penistone	d	10 19										11 19										12 19
Denby Dale	d	10 26										11 26										12 26
Shepley	d	10 31										11 31										12 31
Stocksmoor	d	10 34										11 34										12 34
Brockholes	d	10 38										11 38										12 38
Honley	d	10 40										11 40										12 40
Berry Brow	d	10 43										11 43										12 43
Lockwood	d	10 46										11 46										12 46
Huddersfield	a	10 50										11 50										12 50
Darton	d				10 35										11 35							
Wakefield Kirkgate 4 31	a			10 26	10 48				10 55					11 27	11 48				11 55			
	d			10 26	10 49				10 55					11 27	11 49				11 55			
Normanton	d				10 54										11 54							
Castleford 32	a				10 59										11 59							
Woodlesford 32	a				11 11										12 11							
Leeds 10 31,32	a			10 46	11 24			11 30	11 15					11 47	12 24			12 30	12 15			

A To Adwick
B From Retford
C From Derby
D To Doncaster
E From Manchester Airport to Cleethorpes
F To Scarborough
G To Hull
H To Liverpool Lime Street
I From Lincoln
J To York
K To Bridlington
L From Norwich to Liverpool Lime Street

Table T034-F

Saturdays
23 June to 21 July

Nottingham and Sheffield - Barnsley - Huddersfield and Leeds

Station		EM ◇ A	NT ◇ B	NT ◇ C	NT	NT D	TP ◇■ E	NT ◇		NT ◇	NT ◇ F	NT G	NT	EM ◇ A	NT ◇ B	NT	NT D	TP ◇■ E		NT	NT ◇	NT ◇ H	NT G	NT	EM ◇ A
Nottingham 8 ⇌	d	10 46								11 17				11 47							12 17				12 47
Ilkeston	d									11 29											12 29				13 00
Langley Mill	d									11 36											12 36				
Alfreton	d	11 08								11 44				12 08							12 44				13 10
Chesterfield	d	11 20								11 55				12 20							12 55				13 21
Dronfield	d									12 02											13 02				
Sheffield 7 29,31 ⇌	a	11 38								12 13				12 38							13 13				13 37
	d		11 45	11 59	12 02	12 05	12 10	12 15		12 18	12 24	12 30	12 35		12 45	13 02	13 05	13 10		13 15	13 18	13 24	13 30	13 35	
Meadowhall 4 29,31 ⇌	a		11 50	12 04	12 07	12 10	12 16	12 20		12 23	12 31	12 35	12 40		12 51	13 07	13 10	13 16		13 20	13 23	13 31	13 35	13 40	
	d		11 51		12 08			12 21		12 24			12 41		12 51	13 08				13 21	13 24			13 41	
Chapeltown	d				12 14								12 47			13 14								13 47	
Elsecar	d				12 20								12 53			13 20								13 53	
Wombwell	d				12 23								12 56			13 23								13 56	
Barnsley	a		12 10		12 29					12 39			13 02		13 11	13 29					13 39			14 02	
	d		12 11		12 30					12 40			13 03		13 11	13 30					13 40			14 03	
Dodworth	d												13 09											14 09	
Silkstone Common	d												13 12											14 12	
Penistone	d												13 19											14 19	
Denby Dale	d												13 26											14 26	
Shepley	d												13 31											14 31	
Stocksmoor	d												13 34											14 34	
Brockholes	d												13 38											14 38	
Honley	d												13 40											14 40	
Berry Brow	d												13 43											14 43	
Lockwood	d												13 46											14 46	
Huddersfield	a												13 50											14 50	
Darton	d				12 35											13 35									
Wakefield Kirkgate 4 31	a		12 26		12 48					12 55					13 26	13 48					13 55				
	d		12 26		12 49					12 55					13 27	13 49					13 55				
Normanton	d				12 54											13 54									
Castleford 32	a				12 59											13 59									
Woodlesford 32	a				13 11											14 11									
Leeds 10 31,32	a		12 46		13 24			13 30		13 15					13 46	14 24				14 30	14 15				

Station		NT ◇ B	NT	NT D		TP ◇■ E	NT ◇	NT ◇	NT ◇ F	NT G	NT	EM ◇ A	NT ◇ B	NT		NT D	TP ◇■ E	NT	NT ◇	NT ◇ F	NT G	NT	EM ◇ A	NT ◇ B	
Nottingham 8 ⇌	d							13 17				13 47							14 17				14 47		
Ilkeston	d							13 29											14 29						
Langley Mill	d							13 36											14 36						
Alfreton	d							13 44				14 08							14 44				15 08		
Chesterfield	d							13 55				14 20							14 55				15 20		
Dronfield	d							14 02											15 02						
Sheffield 7 29,31 ⇌	a							14 13				14 37							15 13				15 37		
	d	13 45	14 02	14 05		14 10	14 15	14 18	14 24	14 30	14 35		14 45	15 02		15 05	15 10	15 15	15 18	15 24	15 30	15 35		15 45	
Meadowhall 4 29,31 ⇌	a	13 51	14 07	14 10		14 16	14 20	14 23	14 31	14 35	14 40		14 51	15 07		15 10	15 16	15 20	15 23	15 31	15 35	15 40		15 50	
	d	13 51	14 08				14 21	14 24			14 41		14 51	15 08				15 21	15 24			15 41		15 51	
Chapeltown	d		14 14								14 47			15 14								15 47			
Elsecar	d		14 20								14 53			15 20								15 53			
Wombwell	d		14 23								14 56			15 23								15 56			
Barnsley	a	14 11	14 29					14 39			15 02		15 11	15 29					15 39			16 02		16 10	
	d	14 11	14 30					14 40			15 03		15 11	15 30					15 40			16 03		16 11	
Dodworth	d										15 09											16 09			
Silkstone Common	d										15 12											16 12			
Penistone	d										15 19											16 19			
Denby Dale	d										15 26											16 26			
Shepley	d										15 31											16 31			
Stocksmoor	d										15 34											16 34			
Brockholes	d										15 38											16 38			
Honley	d										15 40											16 40			
Berry Brow	d										15 43											16 43			
Lockwood	d										15 46											16 46			
Huddersfield	a										15 50											16 50			
Darton	d		14 35											15 35											
Wakefield Kirkgate 4 31	a	14 26	14 48					14 55					15 26	15 48					15 55					16 26	
	d	14 27	14 49					14 55					15 27	15 49					15 55					16 26	
Normanton	d		14 54											15 54											
Castleford 32	a		14 59											15 59											
Woodlesford 32	a		15 11											16 11											
Leeds 10 31,32	a	14 46	15 24				15 30	15 15					15 46	16 24				16 30	16 15					16 46	

A From Norwich to Liverpool Lime Street
B From Lincoln
C To York
D To Adwick
E From Manchester Airport to Cleethorpes
F To Bridlington
G To Hull
H To Scarborough

Table T034-F

Saturdays
23 June to 21 July

Nottingham and Sheffield - Barnsley - Huddersfield and Leeds

Station		NT	NT A	TP ◇■ B	NT ◇	NT ◇	NT ◇ C	NT D	NT	EM ◇ E		NT ◇ F	NT	NT A	TP ◇■ B	NT	NT ◇	NT ◇ C	NT D	EM ◇ E		NT	NT ◇ F	NT	NT A
Nottingham 8 ⇌	d					15 17				15 47							16 17			16 44					
Ilkeston	d					15 29				16 00							16 29								
Langley Mill	d					15 36											16 36								
Alfreton	d					15 44				16 10							16 44			17 05					
Chesterfield	d					15 55				16 21							16 55			17 15					
Dronfield	d					16 02											17 02								
Sheffield 7 29,31 ⇌	a					16 13				16 37							17 13			17 34					
	d	16 02	16 05	16 10	16 15	16 18	16 24	16 30	16 35			16 45	17 02	17 05	17 10	17 15	17 18	17 24	17 30			17 35	17 45	18 02	18 05
Meadowhall 4 29,31 ⇌	a	16 07	16 10	16 16	16 20	16 23	16 31	16 35	16 40			16 51	17 07	17 10	17 16	17 20	17 23	17 31	17 35			17 40	17 51	18 07	18 10
	d	16 08			16 21	16 24			16 41			16 51	17 08			17 21	17 24					17 41	17 51	18 08	
Chapeltown	d	16 14							16 47				17 14									17 47		18 14	
Elsecar	d	16 20							16 53				17 20									17 53		18 20	
Wombwell	d	16 23							16 56				17 23									17 56		18 23	
Barnsley	a	16 29				16 39			17 02			17 11	17 29				17 39					18 02	18 10	18 29	
	d	16 30				16 40			17 03			17 11	17 30				17 40					18 03	18 11	18 30	
Dodworth	d								17 09													18 09			
Silkstone Common	d								17 12													18 13			
Penistone	d								17 19													18 23			
Denby Dale	d								17 26													18 29			
Shepley	d								17 31													18 34			
Stocksmoor	d								17 33													18 37			
Brockholes	d								17 37													18 41			
Honley	d								17 40													18 43			
Berry Brow	d								17 43													18 46			
Lockwood	d								17 45													18 49			
Huddersfield	a								17 50													18 54			
Darton	d	16 35											17 35											18 35	
Wakefield Kirkgate 4 31	a	16 48				16 55						17 26	17 48				17 55						18 27	18 48	
	d	16 49				16 55						17 27	17 49				17 55						18 27	18 49	
Normanton	d	16 54											17 54											18 54	
Castleford 32	a	16 59											17 59											18 59	
Woodlesford 32	a	17 11											18 11											19 11	
Leeds 10 31,32	a	17 24			17 32	17 15						17 46	18 24			18 30	18 15						18 47	19 24	

Station		TP ◇■ B	NT ◇	NT ◇	NT ◇ G	NT D		EM ◇ E	NT	NT ◇ F	NT	NT A	TP ◇■ B	NT	NT ◇	NT ◇ D		NT D	NT	EM ◇ E	NT ◇ F	NT	NT A	TP ◇■ B	NT ◇
Nottingham 8 ⇌	d			17 17				17 44							18 17					18 47					
Ilkeston	d			17 29											18 29										
Langley Mill	d			17 36				18 00							18 36										
Alfreton	d			17 44				18 08							18 44					19 08					
Chesterfield	d			17 55				18 18							18 55					19 20					
Dronfield	d			18 02											19 02										
Sheffield 7 29,31 ⇌	a			18 13				18 34							19 13					19 37					
	d	18 11	18 15	18 18	18 24	18 30			18 35	18 45	19 02	19 05	19 11	19 15	19 18	19 24		19 30	19 35		19 45	20 02	20 05	20 11	20 15
Meadowhall 4 29,31 ⇌	a	18 17	18 20	18 23	18 31	18 35			18 40	18 50	19 07	19 10	19 16	19 20	19 23	19 31		19 35	19 40		19 50	20 07	20 10	20 16	20 20
	d		18 21	18 24					18 41	18 51	19 08			19 21	19 24				19 41		19 51	20 08			20 21
Chapeltown	d								18 47		19 14								19 47			20 14			
Elsecar	d								18 53		19 20								19 53			20 20			
Wombwell	d								18 56		19 23								19 56			20 23			
Barnsley	a			18 39					19 02	19 10	19 29				19 39				20 02		20 10	20 29			
	d			18 40					19 03	19 11	19 30				19 40				20 03		20 11	20 30			
Dodworth	d								19 09										20 09						
Silkstone Common	d								19 12										20 12						
Penistone	d								19 19										20 19						
Denby Dale	d								19 26										20 26						
Shepley	d								19 31										20 31						
Stocksmoor	d								19 34										20 34						
Brockholes	d								19 38										20 38						
Honley	d								19 40										20 40						
Berry Brow	d								19 43										20 43						
Lockwood	d								19 46										20 46						
Huddersfield	a								19 50										20 50						
Darton	d										19 35											20 35			
Wakefield Kirkgate 4 31	a			18 55						19 26	19 48				19 55						20 26	20 48			
	d			18 55						19 26	19 49				19 55						20 26	20 49			
Normanton	d										19 54											20 54			
Castleford 32	a										19 59											20 59			
Woodlesford 32	a										20 11											21 11			
Leeds 10 31,32	a		19 30	19 15						19 46	20 24			20 36	20 15						20 46	21 24			21 30

A To Adwick
B From Manchester Airport to Cleethorpes
C To Scarborough
D To Hull
E From Norwich to Liverpool Lime Street
F From Lincoln
G To Bridlington

Table T034-F

Saturdays
23 June to 21 July

Nottingham and Sheffield - Barnsley - Huddersfield and Leeds

	NT	NT	EM	NT	NT	NT	NT	NT	TP	NT	NT	EM	NT	NT	NT	TP	NT	NT	NT	NT	NT
	◇	◇ A	◇ B	C		◇ D		E	◇1 F		◇	◇1 G	◇ H		E	◇1 F	◇	◇	◇ C		
Nottingham d	19 17		19 36								20 17	20 25						21 12			
Ilkeston d	19 29										20 29							21 29			
Langley Mill d	19 36										20 36	20 49						21 36			
Alfreton d	19 44		20 01								20 44	20 57						21 44			
Chesterfield d	19 55		20 11								20 55	21 07						21 55			
Dronfield d	20 02										21 02							22 02			
Sheffield 29,31 a	20 13		20 30								21 13	21 23						22 13			
d	20 18	20 24		20 30	20 35	20 45	21 02	21 05	21 11	21 15	21 18	21 24	21 28	21 35	22 07	22 11	22 15	22 18	22 28	22 31	22 38
Meadowhall 29,31 a	20 23	20 31		20 35	20 40	20 50	21 07	21 10	21 16	21 20	21 23		21 33	21 40	22 12	22 16	22 20	22 23	22 33	22 36	22 43
d	20 24				20 41	20 51	21 08			21 21	21 24			21 41			22 21	22 24		22 37	22 44
Chapeltown d					20 47		21 14							21 47						22 43	22 51
Elsecar d					20 53		21 20							21 53						22 48	22 57
Wombwell d					20 56		21 23							21 56						22 52	23 01
Barnsley a	20 39				21 02	21 10	21 29				21 39			22 02				22 39		22 59	23 07
d	20 40				21 03	21 11	21 30				21 40			22 03				22 40		22 59	23 07
Dodworth d					21 09									22 09							23 13
Silkstone Common d					21 12									22 12							23 17
Penistone d					21 19									22 19							23 26
Denby Dale d					21 26									22 26							23 33
Shepley d					21 31									22 31							23 38
Stocksmoor d					21 34									22 34							23 40
Brockholes d					21 38									22 38							23 44
Honley d					21 40									22 40							23 47
Berry Brow d					21 43									22 43							23 50
Lockwood d					21 46									22 46							23 52
Huddersfield a					21 50									22 50							23 57
Darton d							21 35													23 04	
Wakefield Kirkgate 31 a	20 55					21 26	21 48				21 55							22 55		23 16	
d	20 55					21 26	21 49				21 55							22 55		23 17	
Normanton d							21 54													23 21	
Castleford 32 a							21 59													23 30	
Woodlesford 32 a							22 11													23 41	
Leeds 31,32 a	21 15					21 46	22 24			22 30	22 15	22 17					23 25	23 14		23 53	

	NT	NT	NT
	I	I	◇
Nottingham d			23 18
Ilkeston d			23 30
Langley Mill d			23 36
Alfreton d			23 44
Chesterfield d			23 54
Dronfield d			00 02
Sheffield 29,31 a			00 16
d	23 05	23 27	
Meadowhall 29,31 a	23 10	23 32	
d			
Chapeltown d			
Elsecar d			
Wombwell d			
Barnsley a			
d			
Dodworth d			
Silkstone Common d			
Penistone d			
Denby Dale d			
Shepley d			
Stocksmoor d			
Brockholes d			
Honley d			
Berry Brow d			
Lockwood d			
Huddersfield a			
Darton d			
Wakefield Kirkgate 31 a			
d			
Normanton d			
Castleford 32 a			
Woodlesford 32 a			
Leeds 31,32 a			

A To Bridlington
B From Norwich to Manchester Piccadilly
C To Hull
D From Lincoln
E To Adwick
F From Manchester Airport to Cleethorpes
G From St Pancras International
H To Beverley
I To Doncaster

Table T034-F

Saturdays
28 July to 1 September

Nottingham and Sheffield - Barnsley - Huddersfield and Leeds

	NT	NT	NT	NT	NT	NT	NT	NT	NT	NT	NT	NT	NT	NT	NT	NT	NT	TP	NT	NT	NT	EM
	◇ A	◇		B			◇ C			D		◇	E		◇	D		◇1 F		◇	◇ C	◇ G
Nottingham d																				06 17		06 40
Ilkeston d																				06 29		
Langley Mill d																				06 36		
Alfreton d																				06 44		07 01
Chesterfield d															06 25					06 54		07 11
Dronfield d	00 02														06 32					07 01		07 18
Sheffield 29,31 a	00 16														06 42					07 11		07 28
d		05 15	05 18	05 24	05 30	05 37	05 43	05 51	06 03	06 06	06 16	06 19	06 27	06 30	06 45	07 01	07 04	07 10	07 16	07 18	07 24	
Meadowhall 29,31 a		05 20	05 23	05 29	05 35	05 43	05 48	05 56	06 08	06 11	06 21	06 24	06 32	06 35	06 50	07 06	07 09	07 15	07 21	07 23	07 31	
d		05 21	05 24		05 36	05 44		05 57	06 09		06 22	06 25		06 36	06 51		07 10		07 22	07 25		
Chapeltown d			05 30		05 42	05 50			06 16					06 42			07 17					
Elsecar d			05 35		05 48	05 56			06 22					06 48			07 23					
Wombwell d			05 39		05 51	05 59			06 25					06 51			07 26					
Barnsley a			05 45		05 57	06 05		06 12	06 31			06 39		06 57	07 06		07 32			07 41		
d					05 58	06 06			06 32			06 39		07 00	07 06		07 33			07 42		
Dodworth d						06 12								07 06								
Silkstone Common d						06 15								07 09								
Penistone d						06 21								07 16								
Denby Dale d						06 28								07 23								
Shepley d						06 33								07 28								
Stocksmoor d						06 36								07 31								
Brockholes d						06 40								07 35								
Honley d						06 42								07 37								
Berry Brow d						06 45								07 40								
Lockwood d						06 48								07 43								
Huddersfield a						06 52								07 47								
Darton d					06 03				06 37								07 38					
Wakefield Kirkgate 31 a					06 14				06 49			06 54			07 22		07 50			07 57		
d					06 16				06 50			06 55			07 23		07 51			07 57		
Normanton d					06 21				06 55			06 59			07 27		07 56					
Castleford 32 a									07 00								08 01					
Woodlesford 32 a					06 29				07 12								08 13					
Leeds 31,32 a		06 30			06 43				07 25		07 30	07 16			07 43		08 26		08 36	08 17		

	NT	NT	NT	EM	NT	NT	TP	NT	NT	NT	NT	NT	EM	NT	NT	NT	NT	TP	NT	NT	NT	NT
	D		◇ H	◇1 I		B	◇1 F	◇	◇	◇ J	K		◇ G	◇ L	◇ M		D	◇1 F		◇	◇ C	K
Nottingham d									07 18				07 46							08 17		
Ilkeston d									07 30				07 59							08 29		
Langley Mill d									07 37											08 36		
Alfreton d									07 45				08 09							08 44		
Chesterfield d				07 43					07 57				08 20							08 55		
Dronfield d				07 49					08 04				08 26							09 02		
Sheffield 29,31 a				07 59					08 15				08 37							09 13		
d	07 31	07 35	07 45		08 02	08 05	08 10	08 15	08 18	08 25	08 30	08 35		08 45	08 54	09 03	09 06	09 10	09 15	09 18	09 24	09 30
Meadowhall 29,31 a	07 36	07 40	07 53		08 08	08 11	08 15	08 20	08 24	08 31	08 35	08 40		08 50	09 00	09 08	09 11	09 16	09 20	09 23	09 31	09 35
d		07 41	07 54		08 09			08 21	08 25			08 41		08 51		09 09			09 21	09 24		
Chapeltown d		07 47			08 15							08 47				09 15						
Elsecar d		07 53			08 21							08 53				09 21						
Wombwell d		07 56			08 24							08 56				09 24						
Barnsley a		08 02	08 10		08 30				08 40			09 02		09 10		09 30				09 40		
d		08 03	08 11		08 31				08 41			09 03		09 11		09 31				09 41		
Dodworth d		08 09										09 09										
Silkstone Common d		08 12										09 12										
Penistone d		08 19										09 19										
Denby Dale d		08 26										09 26										
Shepley d		08 31										09 31										
Stocksmoor d		08 34										09 34										
Brockholes d		08 38										09 38										
Honley d		08 40										09 40										
Berry Brow d		08 43										09 43										
Lockwood d		08 46										09 46										
Huddersfield a		08 50										09 50										
Darton d					08 36											09 36						
Wakefield Kirkgate 31 a			08 25		08 48				08 57					09 26		09 48				09 56		
d			08 25		08 49				08 58					09 26		09 49				09 56		
Normanton d			08 30		08 54											09 54						
Castleford 32 a					08 59											09 59						
Woodlesford 32 a					09 11											10 11						
Leeds 31,32 a			08 46		09 24			09 30	09 17					09 46		10 24			10 30	10 16		

A From Nottingham
B To Doncaster
C To Bridlington
D To Adwick
E To Beverley
F From Manchester Airport to Cleethorpes
G To Liverpool Lime Street
H From Retford
I From Derby
J To Scarborough
K To Hull
L From Lincoln
M To York

Table T034-F

Saturdays

28 July to 1 September

Nottingham and Sheffield - Barnsley - Huddersfield and Leeds

	NT	EM ◇ A	NT ◇ B	NT	NT C	TP ◇■ D	NT ◇	NT ◇	NT ◇ E	NT F	NT	EM ◇ A	NT ◇ B	NT	NT C	TP ◇■ D	NT	NT ◇	NT ◇ E	NT F	NT
Nottingham ■ d		08 47						09 16				09 47						10 17			
Ilkeston d								09 32										10 31			
Langley Mill d								09 37										10 38			
Alfreton d		09 08						09 45				10 08						10 46			
Chesterfield d		09 20						09 56				10 20						10 56			
Dronfield d								10 02										11 03			
Sheffield ■ 29,31 a		09 37						10 13				10 37						11 13			
d	09 35		09 48	10 02	10 05	10 10	10 15	10 18	10 24	10 30	10 35		10 49	11 02	11 05	11 10	11 15	11 18	11 24	11 30	11 35
Meadowhall ■ 29,31 a	09 40		09 53	10 07	10 10	10 16	10 20	10 23	10 31	10 35	10 40		10 54	11 07	11 10	11 16	11 20	11 23	11 31	11 35	11 40
d	09 41		09 54	10 08			10 21	10 24			10 41		10 57	11 08			11 21	11 24			11 41
Chapeltown d	09 47			10 14							10 47			11 14							11 47
Elsecar d	09 53			10 20							10 53			11 20							11 53
Wombwell d	09 56			10 23							10 56			11 23							11 56
Barnsley a	10 02		10 10	10 29				10 39			11 02		11 11	11 29				11 39			12 02
d	10 03		10 11	10 30				10 40			11 03		11 12	11 30				11 40			12 03
Dodworth d	10 09										11 09										12 09
Silkstone Common d	10 12										11 12										12 12
Penistone d	10 19										11 19										12 19
Denby Dale d	10 26										11 26										12 26
Shepley d	10 31										11 31										12 31
Stocksmoor d	10 34										11 34										12 34
Brockholes d	10 38										11 38										12 38
Honley d	10 40										11 40										12 40
Berry Brow d	10 43										11 43										12 43
Lockwood d	10 46										11 46										12 46
Huddersfield a	10 50										11 50										12 50
Darton d				10 35										11 35							
Wakefield Kirkgate ■ 31 a			10 26	10 48				10 55					11 27	11 48				11 55			
d			10 26	10 49				10 55					11 27	11 49				11 55			
Normanton d				10 54										11 54							
Castleford 32 a				10 59										11 59							
Woodlesford 32 a				11 11										12 11							
Leeds ■ 31,32 a			10 46	11 24			11 30	11 15					11 47	12 24			12 30	12 15			

	EM ◇ A	NT ◇ B	NT ◇ G	NT	NT C	TP ◇■ D	NT ◇	NT ◇	NT ◇ E	NT F	NT	EM ◇ A	NT ◇ B	NT	NT C	TP ◇■ D	NT	NT ◇	NT ◇ H	NT F	NT	EM ◇ A
Nottingham ■ d	10 46							11 17				11 47						12 17				12 47
Ilkeston d								11 32										12 31				13 00
Langley Mill d								11 38										12 38				
Alfreton d	11 08							11 46				12 08						12 46				13 10
Chesterfield d	11 20							11 56				12 20						12 56				13 21
Dronfield d								12 03										13 03				
Sheffield ■ 29,31 a	11 38							12 13				12 38						13 14				13 37
d		11 45	11 59	12 02	12 05	12 10	12 15	12 18	12 24	12 30	12 35		12 45	13 02	13 05	13 10	13 15	13 18	13 24	13 30	13 35	
Meadowhall ■ 29,31 a		11 50	12 04	12 07	12 10	12 16	12 20	12 23	12 31	12 35	12 40		12 51	13 07	13 10	13 16	13 20	13 23	13 31	13 35	13 40	
d		11 51		12 08			12 21	12 24			12 41		12 51	13 08			13 21	13 24			13 41	
Chapeltown d				12 14							12 47			13 14							13 47	
Elsecar d				12 20							12 53			13 20							13 53	
Wombwell d				12 23							12 56			13 23							13 56	
Barnsley a		12 10		12 29				12 39			13 02		13 11	13 29				13 39			14 02	
d		12 11		12 30				12 40			13 03		13 11	13 30				13 40			14 03	
Dodworth d											13 09										14 09	
Silkstone Common d											13 12										14 12	
Penistone d											13 19										14 19	
Denby Dale d											13 26										14 26	
Shepley d											13 31										14 31	
Stocksmoor d											13 34										14 34	
Brockholes d											13 38										14 38	
Honley d											13 40										14 40	
Berry Brow d											13 43										14 43	
Lockwood d											13 46										14 46	
Huddersfield a											13 50										14 50	
Darton d				12 35										13 35								
Wakefield Kirkgate ■ 31 a		12 26		12 48				12 55					13 26	13 48				13 55				
d		12 26		12 49				12 55					13 27	13 49				13 55				
Normanton d				12 54										13 54								
Castleford 32 a				12 59										13 59								
Woodlesford 32 a				13 11										14 11								
Leeds ■ 31,32 a		12 46		13 24			13 30	13 15					13 46	14 24			14 30	14 15				

A From Norwich to Liverpool Lime Street
B From Lincoln
C To Adwick
D From Manchester Airport to Cleethorpes
E To Bridlington
F To Hull
G To York
H To Scarborough

Table T034-F

Saturdays

28 July to 1 September

Nottingham and Sheffield - Barnsley - Huddersfield and Leeds

	NT ◇ A	NT	NT B	TP ◇■ C	NT ◇	NT ◇	NT ◇ D	NT E	NT	EM ◇ F	NT ◇ A	NT	NT B	TP ◇■ C	NT	NT ◇	NT ◇ D	NT E	NT	EM ◇ F	NT ◇ A
Nottingham ■ d						13 17				13 47						14 17				14 47	
Ilkeston d						13 32										14 31					
Langley Mill d						13 38										14 38					
Alfreton d						13 46				14 08						14 46				15 08	
Chesterfield d						13 56				14 20						14 56				15 20	
Dronfield d						14 03										15 03					
Sheffield ■ 29,31 a						14 13				14 37						15 13				15 37	
d	13 45	14 02	14 05	14 10	14 15	14 18	14 24	14 30	14 35		14 45	15 02	15 05	15 10	15 15	15 18	15 24	15 30	15 35		15 45
Meadowhall ■ 29,31 a	13 51	14 07	14 10	14 16	14 20	14 23	14 31	14 35	14 40		14 51	15 07	15 10	15 16	15 20	15 23	15 31	15 35	15 40		15 50
d	13 51	14 08			14 21	14 24			14 41		14 51	15 08			15 21	15 24			15 41		15 51
Chapeltown d		14 14							14 47			15 14							15 47		
Elsecar d		14 20							14 53			15 20							15 53		
Wombwell d		14 23							14 56			15 23							15 56		
Barnsley a	14 11	14 29				14 39			15 02		15 11	15 29				15 39			16 02		16 10
d	14 11	14 30				14 40			15 03		15 11	15 30				15 40			16 03		16 11
Dodworth d									15 09										16 09		
Silkstone Common d									15 12										16 12		
Penistone d									15 19										16 19		
Denby Dale d									15 26										16 26		
Shepley d									15 31										16 31		
Stocksmoor d									15 34										16 34		
Brockholes d									15 38										16 38		
Honley d									15 40										16 40		
Berry Brow d									15 43										16 43		
Lockwood d									15 46										16 46		
Huddersfield a									15 50										16 50		
Darton d		14 35										15 35									
Wakefield Kirkgate ■ 31 a	14 26	14 48				14 55					15 26	15 48				15 55					16 26
d	14 27	14 49				14 55					15 27	15 49				15 55					16 26
Normanton d		14 54										15 54									
Castleford 32 a		14 59										15 59									
Woodlesford 32 a		15 11										16 11									
Leeds ■ 31,32 a	14 46	15 24			15 30	15 15					15 46	16 24			16 30	16 15					16 46

	NT	NT B	TP ◇■ C	NT ◇	NT ◇	NT ◇ G	NT E	NT	EM ◇ F	NT ◇ A	NT	NT B	TP ◇■ C	NT	NT ◇	NT ◇ G	NT E	EM ◇ F	NT	NT ◇ A	NT	NT B
Nottingham ■ d					15 17				15 47						16 17			16 44				
Ilkeston d					15 31				16 00						16 31							
Langley Mill d					15 38										16 38							
Alfreton d					15 46				16 10						16 46			17 05				
Chesterfield d					15 56				16 21						16 56			17 15				
Dronfield d					16 03										17 03							
Sheffield ■ 29,31 a					16 13				16 37						17 13			17 34				
d	16 02	16 05	16 10	16 15	16 18	16 24	16 30	16 35		16 45	17 02	17 05	17 10	17 15	17 18	17 24	17 30		17 35	17 45	18 02	18 05
Meadowhall ■ 29,31 a	16 07	16 10	16 16	16 20	16 23	16 31	16 35	16 40		16 51	17 07	17 10	17 16	17 20	17 23	17 31	17 35		17 40	17 51	18 07	18 10
d	16 08			16 21	16 24			16 41		16 51	17 08			17 21	17 24				17 41	17 51	18 08	
Chapeltown d	16 14							16 47			17 14								17 47		18 14	
Elsecar d	16 20							16 53			17 20								17 53		18 20	
Wombwell d	16 23							16 56			17 23								17 56		18 23	
Barnsley a	16 29				16 39			17 02		17 11	17 29				17 39				18 02	18 10	18 29	
d	16 30				16 40			17 03		17 11	17 30				17 40				18 03	18 11	18 30	
Dodworth d								17 09											18 09			
Silkstone Common d								17 12											18 13			
Penistone d								17 19											18 23			
Denby Dale d								17 26											18 29			
Shepley d								17 31											18 34			
Stocksmoor d								17 33											18 37			
Brockholes d								17 37											18 41			
Honley d								17 40											18 43			
Berry Brow d								17 43											18 46			
Lockwood d								17 45											18 49			
Huddersfield a								17 50											18 54			
Darton d	16 35										17 35										18 35	
Wakefield Kirkgate ■ 31 a	16 48				16 55					17 26	17 48				17 55					18 27	18 48	
d	16 49				16 55					17 27	17 49				17 55					18 27	18 49	
Normanton d	16 54										17 54										18 54	
Castleford 32 a	16 59										17 59										18 59	
Woodlesford 32 a	17 11										18 11										19 11	
Leeds ■ 31,32 a	17 24			17 32	17 15					17 46	18 24			18 30	18 15					18 47	19 24	

A From Lincoln
B To Adwick
C From Manchester Airport to Cleethorpes
D To Bridlington
E To Hull
F From Norwich to Liverpool Lime Street
G To Scarborough

Table T034-F

Nottingham and Sheffield - Barnsley - Huddersfield and Leeds

Saturdays
28 July to 1 September

	TP	NT	NT	NT	NT	EM	NT	NT	NT	NT	TP	NT	NT	NT	NT	NT	EM	NT	NT	NT	TP	NT
	◇1	◇	◇	◇		◇		◇			◇1		◇	◇			◇	◇			◇1	◇
	A			B	C	D		E		F	A			C	C		D	E		F	A	
Nottingham d			17 17			17 44							18 17				18 47					
Ilkeston d			17 31										18 31									
Langley Mill d			17 38			18 00							18 38									
Alfreton d			17 46			18 08							18 46				19 08					
Chesterfield d			17 56			18 18							18 56				19 20					
Dronfield d			18 03										19 03									
Sheffield 29,31 a			18 14			18 34							19 13				19 37					
d	18 11	18 15	18 18	18 24	18 30		18 35	18 45	19 02	19 05	19 11	19 15	19 18	19 24	19 30	19 35		19 45	20 02	20 05	20 11	20 15
Meadowhall 29,31 a	18 17	18 20	18 23	18 31	18 35		18 40	18 50	19 07	19 10	19 16	19 20	19 23	19 31	19 35	19 40		19 50	20 07	20 10	20 16	20 20
d		18 21	18 24				18 41	18 51	19 08			19 21	19 24			19 41		19 51	20 08			20 21
Chapeltown d							18 47		19 14							19 47			20 14			
Elsecar d							18 53		19 20							19 53			20 20			
Wombwell d							18 56		19 23							19 56			20 23			
Barnsley a			18 39				19 02	19 10	19 29				19 39			20 02		20 10	20 29			
d			18 40				19 03	19 11	19 30				19 40			20 03		20 11	20 30			
Dodworth d							19 09									20 09						
Silkstone Common d							19 12									20 12						
Penistone d							19 19									20 19						
Denby Dale d							19 26									20 26						
Shepley d							19 31									20 31						
Stocksmoor d							19 34									20 34						
Brockholes d							19 38									20 38						
Honley d							19 40									20 40						
Berry Brow d							19 43									20 43						
Lockwood d							19 46									20 46						
Huddersfield a							19 50									20 50						
Darton d									19 35										20 35			
Wakefield Kirkgate 31 a			18 55					19 26	19 48				19 55					20 26	20 48			
d			18 55					19 26	19 49				19 55					20 26	20 49			
Normanton d									19 54										20 54			
Castleford 32 a									19 59										20 59			
Woodlesford 32 a									20 11										21 11			
Leeds 31,32 a		19 30	19 15					19 46	20 24			20 36	20 15					20 46	21 24			21 30

	NT	NT	EM	NT	NT	NT	NT	NT	TP	NT	NT	EM	NT	NT	NT	TP	NT	NT	NT	NT	NT
	◇	◇	◇			◇			◇1		◇	◇1	◇			◇1	◇	◇	◇		
		B	G	C		E		F	A			H	I		F	A			C		
Nottingham d	19 17		19 36								20 17	20 25						21 12			
Ilkeston d	19 31										20 29							21 29			
Langley Mill d	19 38										20 36	20 49						21 36			
Alfreton d	19 46		20 01								20 44	20 57						21 44			
Chesterfield d	19 56		20 11								20 54	21 07						21 55			
Dronfield d	20 03										21 02							22 02			
Sheffield 29,31 a	20 13		20 30								21 13	21 23						22 13			
d	20 18	20 24		20 30	20 35	20 45	21 02	21 05	21 11	21 15	21 18	21 24	21 28	21 35	22 07	22 11	22 15	22 18	22 28	22 31	22 38
Meadowhall 29,31 a	20 23	20 31		20 35	20 40	20 50	21 07	21 10	21 16	21 20	21 23		21 33	21 40	22 12	22 16	22 20	22 23	22 33	22 36	22 43
d	20 24				20 41	20 51	21 08			21 21	21 24			21 41			22 21	22 24		22 37	22 44
Chapeltown d					20 47		21 14							21 47						22 43	22 51
Elsecar d					20 53		21 20							21 53						22 48	22 57
Wombwell d					20 56		21 23							21 56						22 52	23 01
Barnsley a	20 39				21 02	21 10	21 29				21 39			22 02				22 39		22 59	23 07
d	20 40				21 03	21 11	21 30				21 40			22 03				22 40		22 59	23 07
Dodworth d					21 09									22 09							23 13
Silkstone Common d					21 12									22 12							23 17
Penistone d					21 19									22 19							23 26
Denby Dale d					21 26									22 26							23 33
Shepley d					21 31									22 31							23 38
Stocksmoor d					21 34									22 34							23 40
Brockholes d					21 38									22 38							23 44
Honley d					21 40									22 40							23 47
Berry Brow d					21 43									22 43							23 50
Lockwood d					21 46									22 46							23 52
Huddersfield a					21 50									22 50							23 57
Darton d							21 35													23 04	
Wakefield Kirkgate 31 a	20 55					21 26	21 48				21 55							22 55		23 16	
d	20 55					21 26	21 49				21 55							22 55		23 17	
Normanton d							21 54													23 21	
Castleford 32 a							21 59													23 30	
Woodlesford 32 a							22 11													23 41	
Leeds 31,32 a	21 15					21 46	22 24			22 30	22 15	22 17					23 25	23 14		23 53	

A From Manchester Airport to Cleethorpes
B To Bridlington
C To Hull
D From Norwich to Liverpool Lime Street
E From Lincoln
F To Adwick
G From Norwich to Manchester Piccadilly
H From St Pancras International
I To Beverley

Table T034-F

Nottingham and Sheffield - Barnsley - Huddersfield and Leeds

Saturdays
28 July to 1 September

	NT	NT	NT
			◇
	A	A	
Nottingham d			23 18
Ilkeston d			23 30
Langley Mill d			23 36
Alfreton d			23 44
Chesterfield d			23 54
Dronfield d			00 02
Sheffield 29,31 a			00 16
d	23 05	23 27	
Meadowhall 29,31 a	23 10	23 32	
d			
Chapeltown d			
Elsecar d			
Wombwell d			
Barnsley a			
d			
Dodworth d			
Silkstone Common d			
Penistone d			
Denby Dale d			
Shepley d			
Stocksmoor d			
Brockholes d			
Honley d			
Berry Brow d			
Lockwood d			
Huddersfield a			
Darton d			
Wakefield Kirkgate 31 a			
d			
Normanton d			
Castleford 32 a			
Woodlesford 32 a			
Leeds 31,32 a			

Saturdays
8 September to 8 December

	NT	NT	NT	NT	NT	NT	NT	NT	NT	NT	NT	NT	NT	NT	NT	NT	NT	TP	NT	NT	NT	EM
	◇	◇					◇					◇			◇			◇1		◇	◇	◇
	B			A			C			D			E			D		F			C	G
Nottingham d																				06 17		06 40
Ilkeston d																				06 29		
Langley Mill d																				06 36		
Alfreton d																				06 44		07 01
Chesterfield d															06 25					06 54		07 11
Dronfield d	00 02														06 32					07 01		07 18
Sheffield 29,31 a	00 16														06 42					07 11		07 28
d		05 15	05 18	05 24	05 30	05 37	05 43	05 51	06 03	06 06	06 16	06 19	06 27	06 30	06 45	07 01	07 04	07 10	07 16	07 18	07 24	
Meadowhall 29,31 a		05 20	05 23	05 29	05 35	05 43	05 48	05 56	06 08	06 11	06 21	06 24	06 32	06 35	06 50	07 06	07 09	07 15	07 21	07 23	07 31	
d		05 21	05 24		05 36	05 44		05 57	06 09		06 22	06 25		06 36	06 51		07 10		07 22	07 25		
Chapeltown d			05 30		05 42	05 50			06 16					06 42			07 17					
Elsecar d			05 35		05 48	05 56			06 22					06 48			07 23					
Wombwell d			05 39		05 51	05 59			06 25					06 51			07 26					
Barnsley a			05 45		05 57	06 05		06 12	06 31			06 39		06 57	07 06		07 32			07 41		
d					05 58	06 06			06 32			06 39		07 00	07 06		07 33			07 42		
Dodworth d						06 12								07 06								
Silkstone Common d						06 15								07 09								
Penistone d						06 21								07 16								
Denby Dale d						06 28								07 23								
Shepley d						06 33								07 28								
Stocksmoor d						06 36								07 31								
Brockholes d						06 40								07 35								
Honley d						06 42								07 37								
Berry Brow d						06 45								07 40								
Lockwood d						06 48								07 43								
Huddersfield a						06 52								07 47								
Darton d					06 03				06 37								07 38					
Wakefield Kirkgate 31 a					06 14				06 49			06 54			07 22		07 50			07 57		
d					06 16				06 50			06 55			07 23		07 51			07 57		
Normanton d					06 21				06 55			06 59			07 27		07 56					
Castleford 32 a									07 00								08 01					
Woodlesford 32 a					06 29				07 12								08 13					
Leeds 31,32 a		06 30			06 43				07 25		07 30	07 16			07 43		08 26		08 36	08 17		

A To Doncaster
B From Nottingham
C To Bridlington
D To Adwick
E To Beverley
F From Manchester Airport to Cleethorpes
G To Liverpool Lime Street

Table T034-F

Saturdays

8 September to 8 December

Nottingham and Sheffield - Barnsley - Huddersfield and Leeds

	NT A	NT	NT ◇ B	EM ◇■ C	NT	NT D	TP ◇■ E	NT ◇	NT ◇	NT ◇ F	NT G	NT	EM ◇ H	NT ◇ I	NT ◇ J	NT	NT A	TP ◇■ E	NT	NT ◇	NT ◇ K	NT G
Nottingham 8 d									07 18				07 46							08 17		
Ilkeston d									07 30				07 59							08 29		
Langley Mill d									07 37											08 36		
Alfreton d									07 45				08 09							08 44		
Chesterfield d				07 43					07 57				08 20							08 55		
Dronfield d				07 49					08 04				08 26							09 02		
Sheffield 7 29,31 a				07 59					08 15				08 37							09 13		
d	07 31	07 35	07 45		08 02	08 05	08 10	08 15	08 18	08 25	08 30	08 35		08 45	08 54	09 03	09 06	09 10	09 15	09 18	09 24	09 30
Meadowhall 4 29,31 a	07 36	07 40	07 53		08 08	08 11	08 15	08 20	08 24	08 31	08 35	08 40		08 50	09 00	09 08	09 11	09 16	09 20	09 23	09 31	09 35
d		07 41	07 54		08 09			08 21	08 25			08 41		08 51		09 09			09 21	09 24		
Chapeltown d		07 47			08 15							08 47				09 15						
Elsecar d		07 53			08 21							08 53				09 21						
Wombwell d		07 56			08 24							08 56				09 24						
Barnsley a		08 02	08 10		08 30				08 40			09 02		09 10		09 30				09 40		
d		08 03	08 11		08 31				08 41			09 03		09 11		09 31				09 41		
Dodworth d		08 09										09 09										
Silkstone Common d		08 12										09 12										
Penistone d		08 19										09 19										
Denby Dale d		08 26										09 26										
Shepley d		08 31										09 31										
Stocksmoor d		08 34										09 34										
Brockholes d		08 38										09 38										
Honley d		08 40										09 40										
Berry Brow d		08 43										09 43										
Lockwood d		08 46										09 46										
Huddersfield a		08 50										09 50										
Darton d					08 36											09 36						
Wakefield Kirkgate 4 31 a			08 25		08 48				08 57					09 26		09 48				09 56		
d			08 25		08 49				08 58					09 26		09 49				09 56		
Normanton d			08 30		08 54											09 54						
Castleford 32 a					08 59											09 59						
Woodlesford 32 a					09 11											10 11						
Leeds 10 31,32 a			08 46		09 24			09 30	09 17					09 46		10 24			10 30	10 16		

	NT	EM ◇ L	NT ◇ I	NT	NT A	TP ◇■ E	NT ◇	NT ◇	NT ◇ K	NT G	NT	EM ◇ L	NT ◇ I	NT	NT A	TP ◇■ E	NT	NT ◇	NT ◇ K	NT G	NT
Nottingham 8 d		08 47						09 19				09 47						10 17			
Ilkeston d								09 31										10 29			
Langley Mill d								09 38										10 36			
Alfreton d		09 08						09 46				10 08						10 44			
Chesterfield d		09 20						09 57				10 20						10 55			
Dronfield d								10 04										11 02			
Sheffield 7 29,31 a		09 37						10 14				10 37						11 13			
d	09 35		09 48	10 02	10 05	10 10	10 15	10 18	10 24	10 30	10 35		10 49	11 02	11 05	11 10	11 15	11 18	11 24	11 30	11 35
Meadowhall 4 29,31 a	09 40		09 53	10 07	10 10	10 16	10 20	10 23	10 31	10 35	10 40		10 54	11 07	11 10	11 16	11 20	11 23	11 31	11 35	11 40
d	09 41		09 54	10 08			10 21	10 24			10 41		10 57	11 08			11 21	11 24			11 41
Chapeltown d	09 47			10 14							10 47			11 14							11 47
Elsecar d	09 53			10 20							10 53			11 20							11 53
Wombwell d	09 56			10 23							10 56			11 23							11 56
Barnsley a	10 02		10 10	10 29				10 39			11 02		11 11	11 29				11 39			12 02
d	10 03		10 11	10 30				10 40			11 03		11 12	11 30				11 40			12 03
Dodworth d	10 09										11 09										12 09
Silkstone Common d	10 12										11 12										12 12
Penistone d	10 19										11 19										12 19
Denby Dale d	10 26										11 26										12 26
Shepley d	10 31										11 31										12 31
Stocksmoor d	10 34										11 34										12 34
Brockholes d	10 38										11 38										12 38
Honley d	10 40										11 40										12 40
Berry Brow d	10 43										11 43										12 43
Lockwood d	10 46										11 46										12 46
Huddersfield a	10 50										11 50										12 50
Darton d				10 35										11 35							
Wakefield Kirkgate 4 31 a			10 26	10 48				10 55					11 27	11 48				11 55			
d			10 26	10 49				10 55					11 27	11 49				11 55			
Normanton d				10 54										11 54							
Castleford 32 a				10 59										11 59							
Woodlesford 32 a				11 11										12 11							
Leeds 10 31,32 a			10 46	11 24			11 30	11 15					11 47	12 24			12 30	12 15			

A To Adwick
B From Retford
C From Derby
D To Doncaster
E From Manchester Airport to Cleethorpes
F To Scarborough
G To Hull
H To Liverpool Lime Street
I From Lincoln
J To York
K To Bridlington
L From Norwich to Liverpool Lime Street

Table T034-F

Saturdays

8 September to 8 December

Nottingham and Sheffield - Barnsley - Huddersfield and Leeds

	EM ◇ A	NT ◇ B	NT ◇ C	NT	NT D	TP ◇■ E	NT ◇	NT ◇	NT ◇ F	NT G	NT	EM ◇ A	NT ◇ B	NT	NT D	TP ◇■ E	NT	NT ◇	NT ◇ H	NT G	NT	EM ◇ A
Nottingham 8 d	10 46							11 17				11 47						12 17				12 47
Ilkeston d								11 29										12 29				13 00
Langley Mill d								11 36										12 36				
Alfreton d	11 08							11 44				12 08						12 44				13 10
Chesterfield d	11 20							11 55				12 20						12 55				13 21
Dronfield d								12 02										13 02				
Sheffield 7 29,31 a	11 38							12 13				12 38						13 13				13 37
d		11 45	11 59	12 02	12 05	12 10	12 15	12 18	12 24	12 30	12 35		12 45	13 02	13 05	13 10	13 15	13 18	13 24	13 30	13 35	
Meadowhall 4 29,31 a		11 50	12 04	12 07	12 10	12 16	12 20	12 23	12 31	12 35	12 40		12 51	13 07	13 10	13 16	13 20	13 23	13 31	13 35	13 40	
d		11 51		12 08			12 21	12 24			12 41		12 51	13 08			13 21	13 24			13 41	
Chapeltown d				12 14							12 47			13 14							13 47	
Elsecar d				12 20							12 53			13 20							13 53	
Wombwell d				12 23							12 56			13 23							13 56	
Barnsley a		12 10		12 29				12 39			13 02		13 11	13 29				13 39			14 02	
d		12 11		12 30				12 40			13 03		13 11	13 30				13 40			14 03	
Dodworth d											13 09										14 09	
Silkstone Common d											13 12										14 12	
Penistone d											13 19										14 19	
Denby Dale d											13 26										14 26	
Shepley d											13 31										14 31	
Stocksmoor d											13 34										14 34	
Brockholes d											13 38										14 38	
Honley d											13 40										14 40	
Berry Brow d											13 43										14 43	
Lockwood d											13 46										14 46	
Huddersfield a											13 50										14 50	
Darton d				12 35										13 35								
Wakefield Kirkgate 4 31 a		12 26		12 48				12 55					13 26	13 48				13 55				
d		12 26		12 49				12 55					13 27	13 49				13 55				
Normanton d				12 54										13 54								
Castleford 32 a				12 59										13 59								
Woodlesford 32 a				13 11										14 11								
Leeds 10 31,32 a		12 46		13 24			13 30	13 15					13 46	14 24			14 30	14 15				

	NT ◇ B	NT	NT D	TP ◇■ E	NT ◇	NT ◇	NT ◇ F	NT G	NT	EM ◇ A	NT ◇ B	NT	NT D	TP ◇■ E	NT	NT ◇	NT ◇ F	NT G	NT	EM ◇ A	NT ◇ B
Nottingham 8 d						13 17				13 47						14 17				14 47	
Ilkeston d						13 29										14 29					
Langley Mill d						13 36										14 36					
Alfreton d						13 44				14 08						14 44				15 08	
Chesterfield d						13 55				14 20						14 55				15 20	
Dronfield d						14 02										15 02					
Sheffield 7 29,31 a						14 13				14 37						15 13				15 37	
d	13 45	14 02	14 05	14 10	14 15	14 18	14 24	14 30	14 35		14 45	15 02	15 05	15 10	15 15	15 18	15 24	15 30	15 35		15 45
Meadowhall 4 29,31 a	13 51	14 07	14 10	14 16	14 20	14 23	14 31	14 35	14 40		14 51	15 07	15 10	15 16	15 20	15 23	15 31	15 35	15 40		15 50
d	13 51	14 08			14 21	14 24			14 41		14 51	15 08			15 21	15 24			15 41		15 51
Chapeltown d		14 14							14 47			15 14							15 47		
Elsecar d		14 20							14 53			15 20							15 53		
Wombwell d		14 23							14 56			15 23							15 56		
Barnsley a	14 11	14 29				14 39			15 02		15 11	15 29				15 39			16 02		16 10
d	14 11	14 30				14 40			15 03		15 11	15 30				15 40			16 03		16 11
Dodworth d									15 09										16 09		
Silkstone Common d									15 12										16 12		
Penistone d									15 19										16 19		
Denby Dale d									15 26										16 26		
Shepley d									15 31										16 31		
Stocksmoor d									15 34										16 34		
Brockholes d									15 38										16 38		
Honley d									15 40										16 40		
Berry Brow d									15 43										16 43		
Lockwood d									15 46										16 46		
Huddersfield a									15 50										16 50		
Darton d		14 35										15 35									
Wakefield Kirkgate 4 31 a	14 26	14 48				14 55					15 26	15 48				15 55					16 26
d	14 27	14 49				14 55					15 27	15 49				15 55					16 26
Normanton d		14 54										15 54									
Castleford 32 a		14 59										15 59									
Woodlesford 32 a		15 11										16 11									
Leeds 10 31,32 a	14 46	15 24			15 30	15 15					15 46	16 24			16 30	16 15					16 46

A From Norwich to Liverpool Lime Street
B From Lincoln
C To York
D To Adwick
E From Manchester Airport to Cleethorpes
F To Bridlington
G To Hull
H To Scarborough

Table T034-F

Saturdays

8 September to 8 December

Nottingham and Sheffield - Barnsley - Huddersfield and Leeds

		NT	NT	TP	NT	NT	NT	NT	NT	EM	NT	NT	NT	TP	NT	NT	NT	NT	EM	NT	NT	NT	NT
				◇[1]	◇	◇	◇			◇	◇			◇[1]		◇	◇		◇		◇		
			A	B			C	D		E	F		A	B			C	D	E		F		A
Nottingham [8]	d					15 17				15 47						16 17			16 44				
Ilkeston	d					15 29				16 00						16 29							
Langley Mill	d					15 36										16 36							
Alfreton	d					15 44				16 10						16 44			17 05				
Chesterfield	d					15 55				16 21						16 55			17 15				
Dronfield	d					16 02										17 02							
Sheffield [7] 29,31	a					16 13				16 37						17 13			17 34				
	d	16 02	16 05	16 10	16 15	16 18	16 24	16 30	16 35		16 45	17 02	17 05	17 10	17 15	17 18	17 24	17 30		17 35	17 45	18 02	18 05
Meadowhall [4] 29,31	a	16 07	16 10	16 16	16 20	16 23	16 31	16 35	16 40		16 51	17 07	17 10	17 16	17 20	17 23	17 31	17 35		17 40	17 51	18 07	18 10
	d	16 08			16 21	16 24			16 41		16 51	17 08			17 21	17 24				17 41	17 51	18 08	
Chapeltown	d	16 14							16 47			17 14								17 47		18 14	
Elsecar	d	16 20							16 53			17 20								17 53		18 20	
Wombwell	d	16 23							16 56			17 23								17 56		18 23	
Barnsley	a	16 29				16 39			17 02		17 11	17 29				17 39				18 02	18 10	18 29	
	d	16 30				16 40			17 03		17 11	17 30				17 40				18 03	18 11	18 30	
Dodworth	d								17 09											18 09			
Silkstone Common	d								17 12											18 13			
Penistone	d								17 19											18 23			
Denby Dale	d								17 26											18 29			
Shepley	d								17 31											18 34			
Stocksmoor	d								17 33											18 37			
Brockholes	d								17 37											18 41			
Honley	d								17 40											18 43			
Berry Brow	d								17 43											18 46			
Lockwood	d								17 45											18 49			
Huddersfield	a								17 50											18 54			
Darton	d	16 35										17 35										18 35	
Wakefield Kirkgate [4] 31	a	16 48				16 55					17 26	17 48				17 55					18 27	18 48	
	d	16 49				16 55					17 27	17 49				17 55					18 27	18 49	
Normanton	d	16 54										17 54										18 54	
Castleford 32	a	16 59										17 59										18 59	
Woodlesford 32	a	17 11										18 11										19 11	
Leeds [10] 31,32	a	17 24			17 32	17 15					17 46	18 24			18 30	18 15					18 47	19 24	

		TP	NT	NT	NT	NT	EM	NT	NT	NT	NT	TP	NT	NT	NT	NT	NT	EM	NT	NT	NT	TP	NT
		◇[1]	◇	◇	◇		◇		◇			◇[1]		◇	◇			◇	◇			◇[1]	◇
		B			G	D	E		F		A	B			D	D		E	F		A	B	
Nottingham [8]	d			17 17			17 44							18 17				18 47					
Ilkeston	d			17 29										18 29									
Langley Mill	d			17 36			18 00							18 36									
Alfreton	d			17 44			18 08							18 44				19 08					
Chesterfield	d			17 55			18 18							18 55				19 20					
Dronfield	d			18 02										19 02									
Sheffield [7] 29,31	a			18 13			18 34							19 13				19 37					
	d	18 11	18 15	18 18	18 24	18 30		18 35	18 45	19 02	19 05	19 11	19 15	19 18	19 24	19 30	19 35		19 45	20 02	20 05	20 11	20 15
Meadowhall [4] 29,31	a	18 17	18 20	18 23	18 31	18 35		18 40	18 50	19 07	19 10	19 16	19 20	19 23	19 31	19 35	19 40		19 50	20 07	20 10	20 16	20 20
	d		18 21	18 24				18 41	18 51	19 08			19 21	19 24			19 41		19 51	20 08			20 21
Chapeltown	d							18 47		19 14							19 47			20 14			
Elsecar	d							18 53		19 20							19 53			20 20			
Wombwell	d							18 56		19 23							19 56			20 23			
Barnsley	a			18 39				19 02	19 10	19 29				19 39			20 02		20 10	20 29			
	d			18 40				19 03	19 11	19 30				19 40			20 03		20 11	20 30			
Dodworth	d							19 09									20 09						
Silkstone Common	d							19 12									20 12						
Penistone	d							19 19									20 19						
Denby Dale	d							19 26									20 26						
Shepley	d							19 31									20 31						
Stocksmoor	d							19 34									20 34						
Brockholes	d							19 38									20 38						
Honley	d							19 40									20 40						
Berry Brow	d							19 43									20 43						
Lockwood	d							19 46									20 46						
Huddersfield	a							19 50									20 50						
Darton	d									19 35										20 35			
Wakefield Kirkgate [4] 31	a			18 55					19 26	19 48				19 55					20 26	20 48			
	d			18 55					19 26	19 49				19 55					20 26	20 49			
Normanton	d									19 54										20 54			
Castleford 32	a									19 59										20 59			
Woodlesford 32	a									20 11										21 11			
Leeds [10] 31,32	a		19 30	19 15					19 46	20 24			20 36	20 15					20 46	21 24			21 30

A To Adwick
B From Manchester Airport to Cleethorpes
C To Scarborough
D To Hull
E From Norwich to Liverpool Lime Street
F From Lincoln
G To Bridlington

Table T034-F

Saturdays

8 September to 8 December

Nottingham and Sheffield - Barnsley - Huddersfield and Leeds

		NT	NT	EM	NT	NT	NT	NT	NT	TP	NT	NT	EM	EM	NT	NT	NT	TP	NT	NT	NT	NT
		◇	◇	◇			◇			◇[1]		◇	◇[1]	◇[1]	◇			◇[1]	◇	◇	◇	
			A	B	C		D		E	F			G	H	I		E	F			C	
Nottingham [8]	d	19 17		19 36								20 17	20 25	20 25						21 12		
Ilkeston	d	19 29										20 29								21 29		
Langley Mill	d	19 36										20 36	20 49	20 43						21 36		
Alfreton	d	19 44		20 01								20 44	20 57	20 51						21 44		
Chesterfield	d	19 55		20 11								20 55	21 07	21 09						21 55		
Dronfield	d	20 02										21 02								22 02		
Sheffield [7] 29,31	a	20 13		20 30								21 13	21 23	21 23						22 13		
	d	20 18	20 24		20 30	20 35	20 45	21 02	21 05	21 11	21 15	21 18	21 24	21 24	21 28	21 35	22 07	22 11	22 15	22 18	22 28	22 31
Meadowhall [4] 29,31	a	20 23	20 31		20 35	20 40	20 50	21 07	21 10	21 16	21 20	21 23			21 33	21 40	22 12	22 16	22 20	22 23	22 33	22 36
	d	20 24				20 41	20 51	21 08			21 21	21 24				21 41			22 21	22 24		22 37
Chapeltown	d					20 47		21 14								21 47						22 43
Elsecar	d					20 53		21 20								21 53						22 48
Wombwell	d					20 56		21 23								21 56						22 52
Barnsley	a	20 39				21 02	21 10	21 29				21 39				22 02				22 39		22 59
	d	20 40				21 03	21 11	21 30				21 40				22 03				22 40		22 59
Dodworth	d					21 09										22 09						
Silkstone Common	d					21 12										22 12						
Penistone	d					21 19										22 19						
Denby Dale	d					21 26										22 26						
Shepley	d					21 31										22 31						
Stocksmoor	d					21 34										22 34						
Brockholes	d					21 38										22 38						
Honley	d					21 40										22 40						
Berry Brow	d					21 43										22 43						
Lockwood	d					21 46										22 46						
Huddersfield	a					21 50										22 50						
Darton	d							21 35														23 04
Wakefield Kirkgate [4] 31	a	20 55					21 26	21 48				21 55								22 55		23 16
	d	20 55					21 26	21 49				21 55								22 55		23 17
Normanton	d							21 54														23 21
Castleford 32	a							21 59														23 30
Woodlesford 32	a							22 11														23 41
Leeds [10] 31,32	a	21 15					21 46	22 24			22 30	22 15	22 17	22 17					23 25	23 14		23 53

		NT	NT	NT	NT
					◇
			J	J	
Nottingham [8]	d				23 18
Ilkeston	d				23 30
Langley Mill	d				23 36
Alfreton	d				23 44
Chesterfield	d				23 54
Dronfield	d				00 02
Sheffield [7] 29,31	a				00 16
	d	22 38	23 05	23 27	
Meadowhall [4] 29,31	a	22 43	23 10	23 32	
	d	22 44			
Chapeltown	d	22 51			
Elsecar	d	22 57			
Wombwell	d	23 01			
Barnsley	a	23 07			
	d	23 07			
Dodworth	d	23 13			
Silkstone Common	d	23 17			
Penistone	d	23 26			
Denby Dale	d	23 33			
Shepley	d	23 38			
Stocksmoor	d	23 40			
Brockholes	d	23 44			
Honley	d	23 47			
Berry Brow	d	23 50			
Lockwood	d	23 52			
Huddersfield	a	23 57			
Darton	d				
Wakefield Kirkgate [4] 31	a				
	d				
Normanton	d				
Castleford 32	a				
Woodlesford 32	a				
Leeds [10] 31,32	a				

A To Bridlington
B From Norwich to Manchester Piccadilly
C To Hull
D From Lincoln
E To Adwick
F From Manchester Airport to Cleethorpes
G until 6 October. From St Pancras International
H from 13 October. From St Pancras International
I To Beverley
J To Doncaster

Table T034-F

Sundays
20 May to 2 December

Nottingham and Sheffield - Barnsley - Huddersfield and Leeds

		NT ◇ A	NT B	NT ◇ C	NT	NT D	TP ◇■ E	NT ◇	NT ◇ F	NT	NT	NT G	NT D	TP ◇■ E	NT ◇ H	NT ◇ B	EM ◇ I	NT	NT	NT D	TP ◇■ E	NT ◇	NT
Nottingham ■	d														09 19		09 47					10 13	
Ilkeston	d														09 32							10 26	
Langley Mill	d														09 37							10 31	
Alfreton	d														09 45		10 05					10 39	
Chesterfield	d														09 55		10 18					10 50	
Dronfield	d	00 02													10 02		10 25					10 57	
Sheffield ■ 29,31	a	00 16													10 15		10 37					11 10	
	d		08 06	08 36	08 39	09 06	09 10	09 17	09 25	09 35	09 38	10 02	10 06	10 10	10 17	10 25		10 38	10 51	11 06	11 10	11 16	11 24
Meadowhall ■ 29,31	a		08 11	08 41	08 44	09 11	09 15	09 22	09 30	09 40	09 44	10 07	10 11	10 15	10 22	10 30		10 43	10 56	11 11	11 15	11 21	11 29
	d				08 45			09 23		09 41	09 45				10 23			10 45	10 57			11 22	11 30
Chapeltown	d				08 51						09 51							10 51					
Elsecar	d				08 57						09 57							10 56					
Wombwell	d				09 00						10 00							11 00					
Barnsley	a				09 06			09 37			10 06				10 37			11 05	11 11			11 36	
	d				09 06			09 38			10 06				10 37			11 06	11 12			11 36	
Dodworth	d										10 12							11 12					
Silkstone Common	d										10 16							11 16					
Penistone	d										10 23							11 23					
Denby Dale	d										10 30							11 29					
Shepley	d										10 35							11 34					
Stocksmoor	d										10 37							11 37					
Brockholes	d										10 41							11 41					
Honley	d										10 44							11 43					
Berry Brow	d										10 47							11 46					
Lockwood	d										10 49							11 49					
Huddersfield	a										10 54							11 54					
Darton	d				09 11			09 43											11 17				
Wakefield Kirkgate ■ 31	a				09 22			09 57							10 52				11 31			11 51	
	d				09 23			09 59							10 53				11 32			11 52	
Normanton	d				09 28			10 04											11 37				
Castleford 32	a				09 33														11 42				
Woodlesford 32	a				09 45														11 54				
Leeds ■ 31,32	a				09 56			10 24		10 47					11 12				12 08			12 11	12 41

		NT ◇ C	EM ◇ I	NT ◇ J	NT D	TP ◇■ E	NT ◇	NT ◇ B	EM ◇ I	NT ◇ J	NT	NT D	TP ◇■ E	NT ◇	NT ◇ F	NT	EM ◇ K	NT ◇ J	NT D	TP ◇■ E	NT ◇	NT ◇ B	EM ◇ K
Nottingham ■	d		10 48				11 16		11 44					12 19			12 40				13 19		13 42
Ilkeston	d						11 31		11 56					12 32							13 32		
Langley Mill	d						11 36							12 37			12 56				13 37		13 58
Alfreton	d		11 09				11 44		12 08					12 45			13 04				13 45		14 06
Chesterfield	d		11 19				11 55		12 18					12 56			13 17				13 56		14 16
Dronfield	d						12 02							13 03							14 03		
Sheffield ■ 29,31	a		11 35				12 14		12 35					13 15			13 33				14 15		14 34
	d	11 34		11 39	12 06	12 10	12 16	12 25		12 39	12 44	13 06	13 10	13 17	13 25	13 31		13 39	14 06	14 10	14 17	14 25	
Meadowhall ■ 29,31	a	11 39		11 45	12 11	12 16	12 22	12 30		12 45	12 49	13 11	13 15	13 22	13 30	13 36		13 44	14 11	14 15	14 22	14 30	
	d			11 45			12 23			12 45	12 50			13 23		13 37		13 45			14 23		
Chapeltown	d			11 51						12 51	12 56							13 51					
Elsecar	d			11 57						12 57	13 02							13 56					
Wombwell	d			12 00						13 00	13 06							14 00					
Barnsley	a			12 06			12 37			13 06	13 11			13 37				14 05			14 37		
	d			12 06			12 37			13 06	13 12			13 37				14 06			14 37		
Dodworth	d			12 12						13 12								14 12					
Silkstone Common	d			12 16						13 16								14 16					
Penistone	d			12 23						13 23								14 23					
Denby Dale	d			12 30						13 30								14 29					
Shepley	d			12 35						13 35								14 34					
Stocksmoor	d			12 37						13 37								14 37					
Brockholes	d			12 41						13 41								14 41					
Honley	d			12 44						13 44								14 43					
Berry Brow	d			12 47						13 47								14 46					
Lockwood	d			12 49						13 49								14 49					
Huddersfield	a			12 55						13 55								14 54					
Darton	d										13 17												
Wakefield Kirkgate ■ 31	a						12 58				13 28			13 52							14 52		
	d						12 58				13 29			13 53							14 53		
Normanton	d										13 34												
Castleford 32	a										13 39												
Woodlesford 32	a										13 51												
Leeds ■ 31,32	a						13 22				14 04			14 18		14 43					15 17		

A not 20 May. From Nottingham
B To Scarborough
C To Hull
D To Doncaster
E From Manchester Airport to Cleethorpes
F To Bridlington
G From Retford
H To Carlisle
I To Liverpool Lime Street
J From Lincoln
K From Norwich to Liverpool Lime Street

Table T034-F

Sundays
20 May to 2 December

Nottingham and Sheffield - Barnsley - Huddersfield and Leeds

		NT ◇ A	NT	NT B	TP ◇■ C	NT ◇	NT ◇ D	NT	NT ◇ A	EM ◇ E	NT B	TP ◇■ C	NT ◇ F	NT ◇	NT ◇ G	EM ◇ H	NT	NT	NT B	TP ◇■ C	NT ◇	NT ◇ D
Nottingham ■	d					14 19				14 47				15 19		15 47					16 19	
Ilkeston	d					14 32								15 32							16 32	
Langley Mill	d					14 37				15 03				15 37							16 37	
Alfreton	d					14 45				15 11				15 45		16 08					16 45	
Chesterfield	d					14 56				15 21				15 56		16 18					16 56	
Dronfield	d					15 03								16 03							17 03	
Sheffield ■ 29,31	a					15 15				15 39				16 15		16 34					17 15	
	d	14 39	14 44	15 06	15 10	15 17	15 25	15 31	15 38		16 06	16 10	16 13	16 17	16 25		16 39	16 44	17 06	17 10	17 18	17 25
Meadowhall ■ 29,31	a	14 44	14 49	15 11	15 15	15 22	15 30	15 36	15 44		16 11	16 16	16 20	16 22	16 30		16 44	16 49	17 11	17 15	17 22	17 30
	d	14 45	14 50			15 23		15 37	15 44					16 23			16 45	16 50			17 23	
Chapeltown	d		14 56						15 50									16 56				
Elsecar	d		15 02						15 56									17 02				
Wombwell	d		15 06						15 59									17 06				
Barnsley	a	14 59	15 11			15 37			16 05					16 37			16 59	17 11			17 37	
	d	15 00	15 12			15 37			16 05					16 37			17 00	17 12			17 37	
Dodworth	d	15 06							16 11								17 06					
Silkstone Common	d	15 10							16 15								17 10					
Penistone	d	15 17							16 21								17 17					
Denby Dale	d	15 23							16 28								17 23					
Shepley	d	15 28							16 33								17 28					
Stocksmoor	d	15 31							16 35								17 31					
Brockholes	d	15 35							16 39								17 35					
Honley	d	15 37							16 42								17 38					
Berry Brow	d	15 40							16 45								17 40					
Lockwood	d	15 43							16 47								17 43					
Huddersfield	a	15 48							16 53								17 49					
Darton	d		15 17															17 17				
Wakefield Kirkgate ■ 31	a		15 28			15 52								16 53				17 28			17 52	
	d		15 29			15 55								16 54				17 29			17 53	
Normanton	d		15 34															17 34				
Castleford 32	a		15 39															17 40				
Woodlesford 32	a		15 51															17 51				
Leeds ■ 31,32	a		16 04			16 15		16 44						17 17				18 04			18 17	

		NT	EM ◇ I	NT	NT B	TP ◇■ C	NT ◇	NT ◇ D	EM ◇ I	NT	NT	NT ◇ F	NT B	TP ◇■ C	NT ◇	NT ◇ J	EM ◇ K	NT	NT	NT B	TP ◇■ C	NT ◇	NT ◇ L
Nottingham ■	d		16 42				17 19		17 39						18 19		18 40					19 19	
Ilkeston	d		16 57				17 32								18 32							19 32	
Langley Mill	d		17 03				17 37		17 57						18 37		18 56					19 37	
Alfreton	d		17 11				17 45		18 05						18 45		19 04					19 45	
Chesterfield	d		17 22				17 56		18 16						18 56		19 15					19 56	
Dronfield	d						18 03								19 03							20 03	
Sheffield ■ 29,31	a		17 39				18 15		18 33						19 14		19 31					20 15	
	d	17 31		17 42	18 06	18 11	18 17	18 25		18 39	18 45	18 58	19 06	19 11	19 17	19 27		19 31	19 39	20 06	20 11	20 17	20 25
Meadowhall ■ 29,31	a	17 36		17 47	18 11	18 16	18 22	18 30		18 44	18 50	19 03	19 11	19 16	19 22	19 32		19 36	19 44	20 11	20 16	20 22	20 30
	d	17 37		17 48			18 23			18 45	18 51				19 23			19 37	19 45			20 23	
Chapeltown	d			17 54							18 57								19 51				
Elsecar	d			17 59							19 02								19 56				
Wombwell	d			18 03							19 06								20 00				
Barnsley	a			18 08			18 37			18 59	19 11				19 37				20 05			20 37	
	d			18 09			18 37			19 00	19 12				19 37				20 06			20 37	
Dodworth	d			18 15						19 06									20 12				
Silkstone Common	d			18 19						19 10									20 16				
Penistone	d			18 25						19 17									20 23				
Denby Dale	d			18 31						19 23									20 29				
Shepley	d			18 36						19 28									20 34				
Stocksmoor	d			18 39						19 31									20 37				
Brockholes	d			18 43						19 35									20 41				
Honley	d			18 45						19 37									20 43				
Berry Brow	d			18 48						19 40									20 46				
Lockwood	d			18 51						19 43									20 49				
Huddersfield	a			18 56						19 47									20 53				
Darton	d										19 17												
Wakefield Kirkgate ■ 31	a						18 52				19 28				19 52							20 52	
	d						18 53				19 29				19 53							20 53	
Normanton	d										19 34												
Castleford 32	a										19 39												
Woodlesford 32	a										19 51												
Leeds ■ 31,32	a	18 44					19 15				20 04				20 15			20 44				21 14	

A From Lincoln
B To Doncaster
C From Manchester Airport to Cleethorpes
D To Bridlington
E To Liverpool Lime Street
F To York, via Pontefract Baghill
G To Scarborough
H From Peterborough to Liverpool Lime Street
I From Norwich to Liverpool Lime Street
J To Beverley
K From Norwich to Manchester Piccadilly
L To Hull

Table T034-F

Sundays
20 May to 2 December

Nottingham and Sheffield - Barnsley - Huddersfield and Leeds

		EM ◇ A	NT	NT B	TP ◇■ C	NT ◇	NT ◇ D	NT ◇	NT	NT B	TP ◇■ C	NT ◇ D	NT ◇	NT B	NT ◇
Nottingham ■	d	19 43				20 19							21 33		22 33
Ilkeston	d					20 32							21 52		22 52
Langley Mill	d					20 37							21 57		22 57
Alfreton	d	20 04				20 45							22 05		23 05
Chesterfield	d	20 14				20 56							22 16		23 16
Dronfield	d					21 03							22 23		23 23
Sheffield ■ 29,31	a	20 31				21 15							22 34		23 35
	d		20 48	21 06	21 11	21 17	21 25	21 31	21 44	22 08	22 12	22 25	22 44	23 30	
Meadowhall ■ 29,31	a		20 53	21 11	21 16	21 22	21 30	21 36	21 50	22 13	22 18	22 30	22 49	23 35	
	d		20 54			21 23		21 37	21 50				22 50		
Chapeltown	d		21 00						21 56				22 56		
Elsecar	d		21 05						22 02				23 01		
Wombwell	d		21 09						22 05				23 05		
Barnsley	a		21 14			21 37			22 11				23 11		
	d		21 15			21 37							23 12		
Dodworth	d														
Silkstone Common	d														
Penistone	d														
Denby Dale	d														
Shepley	d														
Stocksmoor	d														
Brockholes	d														
Honley	d														
Berry Brow	d														
Lockwood	d														
Huddersfield	a														
Darton	d		21 20										23 17		
Wakefield Kirkgate ■ 31	a					21 52							23 31		
	d					21 53							23 32		
Normanton	d		21 37										23 37		
Castleford 32	a		21 42										23 42		
Woodlesford 32	a		21 54										23 54		
Leeds ■ 31,32	a		22 11			22 14		22 47					00 07		

A From Norwich to Manchester Piccadilly
B To Doncaster
C From Manchester Airport to Cleethorpes
D To Hull

Table T034-R

Mondays to Fridays
21 May to 20 July

Leeds and Huddersfield - Barnsley - Sheffield and Nottingham

Miles	Miles			NT MX A	EM MO ◇ B	EM MX ◇ B	NT MX C	NT MX ◇ D	NT MX E	NT MX E	NT ◇	NT	NT ◇	TP ◇■ F	NT	NT C	NT G	NT ◇	NT ◇	TP ◇■ H	NT	NT D	NT I
0	—	**Leeds** ■ 31,32	d															05 34			05 55		06 30
6	—	Woodlesford 32	d																		06 04		06 39
10¼	—	Castleford 32	d																		06 17		06 50
14¼	—	Normanton	d																		06 23		06 56
17¼	—	Wakefield Kirkgate ■ 31	a																		06 28		07 01
—	—		d																		06 28		07 01
24¼	—	Darton	d																		06 39		→
—	0	**Huddersfield**	d																				
—	1¼	Lockwood	d																				
—	2¼	Berry Brow	d																				
—	3¼	Honley	d																				
—	4¼	Brockholes	d																				
—	6¼	Stocksmoor	d																				
—	7¼	Shepley	d																				
—	9½	Denby Dale	d																				
—	13½	Penistone	d																				
—	16¼	Silkstone Common	d																				
—	18	Dodworth	d																				
28¼	21	**Barnsley**	a																		06 46		
—	—		d									05 23			05 52		06 20				06 46		
32¼	25	Wombwell	d									05 28			05 57		06 25				06 52		
33¾	26½	Elsecar	d						00 01			05 32			06 01		06 29				06 56		
37	29¾	Chapeltown	d						00 06			05 37			06 06		06 34				07 01		
40¼	33½	**Meadowhall** 29,31	a						00 12			05 43			06 11		06 39	06 50			07 07		
—	—		d	00 01			00 04	00 09	00 12	00 17		05 43		06 00	06 12	06 35	06 40	06 50		06 54	07 07	07 10	
44¼	37	**Sheffield** ■ 29,31	a	00 08			00 13	00 17	00 21	00 26		05 53		06 08	06 20	06 45	06 48	06 59		07 07	07 16	07 18	
—	—		d								05 15		06 03						07 02				
51¼	—	Dronfield	d								05 24		06 13						07 11				
56½	—	Chesterfield	d			00 02					05 30		06 19						07 17				
66½	—	Alfreton	d								05 45		06 29						07 28				
72¼	—	Langley Mill	d		00 02						05 53		06 36						07 35				
—	—	Ilkeston	d								05 58		06 41						07 40				
84¼	—	**Nottingham**	a		00 23	00 45					06 11		07 00						07 53				

		EM ◇■ J	NT	NT ◇ K	NT L	NT ◇ D	NT E	NT	NT ◇	TP ◇■ H	NT L	NT	NT I	NT ◇ K	EM ◇ M	NT L	NT ◇ N	NT E	NT	NT ◇	TP ◇■ H	NT L	NT
Leeds ■ 31,32	d	06 33		06 39				06 47	07 03				07 30	07 38					07 48	08 04			
Woodlesford 32	d												07 39										
Castleford 32	d												07 50										
Normanton	d						←						07 56					←					
Wakefield Kirkgate ■ 31	a			06 55			07 01		07 21				08 01	07 54				08 01		08 21			
	d			06 56			07 01		07 22				08 01	07 55				08 01		08 22			
Darton	d						07 14						→					08 14					
Huddersfield	d		06 12									07 12											08 12
Lockwood	d		06 15									07 15											08 15
Berry Brow	d		06 18									07 18											08 18
Honley	d		06 21									07 21											08 21
Brockholes	d		06 24									07 24											08 24
Stocksmoor	d		06 28									07 28											08 28
Shepley	d		06 30									07 30											08 30
Denby Dale	d		06 35									07 35											08 35
Penistone	d		06 43									07 43											08 43
Silkstone Common	d		06 48									07 48											08 48
Dodworth	d		06 52									07 52											08 52
Barnsley	a		06 59	07 11			07 21		07 37			07 59		08 10				08 21		08 38			08 59
	d		07 01	07 12			07 22		07 38			08 00		08 11				08 21		08 38			09 00
Wombwell	d		07 06				07 27					08 05						08 27					09 05
Elsecar	d		07 10				07 31					08 09						08 31					09 09
Chapeltown	d		07 16				07 37					08 15						08 36					09 15
Meadowhall 29,31	a		07 21	07 27			07 42	07 49	07 52			08 20		08 27				08 42	08 50	08 52			09 20
	d		07 22	07 27	07 30	07 38	07 47	07 50	07 53	07 59	08 03	08 21		08 28		08 34	08 40	08 48	08 51	08 55	09 01	09 05	09 21
Sheffield ■ 29,31	a	07 21	07 29	07 35	07 38	07 47	07 54	07 57	08 00	08 06	08 11	08 29		08 35		08 44	08 49	08 57	09 00	09 03	09 08	09 14	09 28
	d	07 24							08 03						08 38					09 06			
Dronfield	d								08 13											09 16			
Chesterfield	d	07 37							08 19						08 54					09 22			
Alfreton	d	07 48							08 33						09 05					09 33			
Langley Mill	d	07 57							08 41											09 40			
Ilkeston	d								08 46											09 45			
Nottingham	a	08 24							08 59						09 27					09 59			

A From Huddersfield
B From Liverpool Lime Street
C From Doncaster
D From Hull
E From Leeds
F From Doncaster to Manchester Airport
G To Retford Low Level
H From Cleethorpes to Manchester Airport
I To Sheffield
J To St Pancras International
K To Lincoln
L From Adwick
M From Liverpool Lime Street to Norwich
N From Bridlington

Leeds and Huddersfield - Barnsley - Sheffield and Nottingham

		NT		NT	EM	NT	NT	NT	NT	NT	TP	NT		NT	NT	NT	EM	NT	NT	NT	NT	NT		TP	NT
				◇	◇		◇		◇	◇	◇1					◇	◇		◇			◇		◇1	
		A		B	C	D	E	F			G	D			A	B	C	H	I	F				G	D
Leeds 10	31,32 d	08 30		08 38					08 48	09 04					09 29	09 38					09 48	10 04			
Woodlesford	32 d	08 39													09 38										
Castleford	32 d	08 50													09 49										
Normanton	d	08 56						←							09 55					←					
Wakefield Kirkgate 4	31 a	09 01		08 54				09 01		09 21					10 00	09 54				10 00		10 21			
	d	09 01		08 55				09 01		09 22					10 00	09 55				10 00		10 22			
Darton	d	→						09 13							→					10 16					
Huddersfield	d													09 12											
Lockwood	d													09 15											
Berry Brow	d													09 18											
Honley	d													09 21											
Brockholes	d													09 24											
Stocksmoor	d													09 28											
Shepley	d													09 30											
Denby Dale	d													09 35											
Penistone	d													09 43											
Silkstone Common	d													09 48											
Dodworth	d													09 52											
Barnsley	a			09 10				09 20		09 37				09 59		10 11				10 22		10 37			
	d			09 11				09 20		09 38				10 00		10 12				10 23		10 38			
Wombwell	d							09 26						10 05						10 28					
Elsecar	d							09 30						10 09						10 32					
Chapeltown	d							09 35						10 15						10 37					
Meadowhall	29,31 ⇌ a			09 27				09 41	09 50	09 52				10 20		10 28				10 42	10 50	10 52			
	d			09 28		09 35	09 38	09 41	09 50	09 53	10 01	10 06		10 21		10 28		10 34	10 38	10 43	10 50	10 53		11 02	11 06
Sheffield 7	29,31 ⇌ a			09 35		09 44	09 48	09 50	09 58	10 02	10 08	10 14		10 28		10 35		10 44	10 48	10 52	10 58	11 02		11 08	11 14
	d				09 37					10 05							10 37					11 05			
Dronfield	d									10 15												11 15			
Chesterfield	d				09 51					10 22							10 54					11 22			
Alfreton	d				10 01					10 32							11 05					11 32			
Langley Mill	d									10 40												11 40			
Ilkeston	d				10 11					10 45												11 45			
Nottingham	a				10 26					10 58							11 26					11 58			

		NT	NT	NT	NT	EM	NT	NT		NT	NT	NT	TP	NT	NT	NT	NT	EM		NT	NT	NT	NT	NT	TP
			◇		◇	◇		◇			◇	◇	◇1				◇	◇			◇			◇	◇1
			J	A	B	C	K	I		F			G	D		A	B	C		K	E	F			G
Leeds 10	31,32 d			10 30	10 38						10 48	11 04				11 30	11 38						11 48	12 04	
Woodlesford	32 d			10 39												11 39									
Castleford	32 d			10 50												11 50									
Normanton	d			10 56						←						11 56						←			
Wakefield Kirkgate 4	31 a			11 01	10 54					11 01		11 21				12 01	11 54					12 01		12 21	
	d			11 01	10 55					11 01		11 22				12 01	11 55					12 01		12 22	
Darton	d			→						11 13						→						12 13			
Huddersfield	d	10 12													11 12										
Lockwood	d	10 15													11 15										
Berry Brow	d	10 18													11 18										
Honley	d	10 21													11 21										
Brockholes	d	10 24													11 24										
Stocksmoor	d	10 28													11 28										
Shepley	d	10 30													11 30										
Denby Dale	d	10 35													11 35										
Penistone	d	10 43													11 43										
Silkstone Common	d	10 48													11 48										
Dodworth	d	10 52													11 52										
Barnsley	a	10 59			11 09					11 20		11 37			11 59		12 10					12 20		12 37	
	d	11 00			11 11					11 20		11 38			12 00		12 11					12 20		12 38	
Wombwell	d	11 05								11 26					12 05							12 26			
Elsecar	d	11 09								11 30					12 09							12 30			
Chapeltown	d	11 15								11 35					12 15							12 35			
Meadowhall	29,31 ⇌ a	11 20			11 26					11 41	11 50	11 52			12 20		12 26					12 41	12 50	12 52	
	d	11 21	11 24		11 27		11 34	11 38		11 41	11 50	11 53	12 02	12 06	12 21		12 27			12 34	12 39	12 42	12 50	12 53	13 02
Sheffield 7	29,31 ⇌ a	11 28	11 31		11 34		11 44	11 48		11 50	11 58	12 02	12 08	12 14	12 28		12 34			12 44	12 48	12 50	12 58	13 02	13 08
	d					11 38						12 05						12 38						13 05	
Dronfield	d											12 15												13 15	
Chesterfield	d					11 54						12 22						12 52						13 22	
Alfreton	d					12 05						12 32						13 03						13 32	
Langley Mill	d											12 40												13 40	
Ilkeston	d											12 45												13 45	
Nottingham	a					12 29						12 58						13 27						13 58	

A To Sheffield
B To Lincoln
C From Liverpool Lime Street to Norwich
D From Adwick
E From Scarborough
F From Leeds
G From Cleethorpes to Manchester Airport
H From Beverley
I From Bridlington
J From York
K From Hull

Leeds and Huddersfield - Barnsley - Sheffield and Nottingham

		NT	NT	NT		NT	EM	NT	NT	NT	NT	NT	TP	NT		NT	NT	NT	NT	EM	NT	NT	NT	NT
						◇	◇		◇		◇	◇	◇1				◇		◇	◇		◇		
		A		B		C	D	E	F	G			H	A			I	B	C	D	E	F	G	
Leeds 10	31,32 d			12 30		12 38					12 48	13 04						13 30	13 38					13 48
Woodlesford	32 d			12 39														13 39						
Castleford	32 d			12 50														13 50						
Normanton	d			12 56						←								13 56					←	
Wakefield Kirkgate 4	31 a			13 01		12 54				13 01		13 23						14 01	13 54				14 01	
	d			13 01		12 55				13 01		13 23						14 01	13 55				14 01	
Darton	d			→						13 13								→					14 13	
Huddersfield	d		12 12													13 12								
Lockwood	d		12 15													13 15								
Berry Brow	d		12 18													13 18								
Honley	d		12 21													13 21								
Brockholes	d		12 24													13 24								
Stocksmoor	d		12 28													13 28								
Shepley	d		12 30													13 30								
Denby Dale	d		12 35													13 35								
Penistone	d		12 43													13 43								
Silkstone Common	d		12 48													13 48								
Dodworth	d		12 52													13 52								
Barnsley	a		12 59			13 10				13 20		13 39				13 59			14 10				14 20	
	d		13 00			13 11				13 20		13 39				14 00			14 11				14 20	
Wombwell	d		13 05							13 26						14 05							14 26	
Elsecar	d		13 09							13 30						14 09							14 30	
Chapeltown	d		13 15							13 35						14 15							14 35	
Meadowhall	29,31 ⇌ a		13 20			13 26				13 41	13 50	13 53				14 20			14 26				14 41	14 50
	d	13 06	13 21			13 27		13 34	13 38	13 41	13 50	13 54	14 02	14 06		14 21	14 24		14 27		14 34	14 38	14 41	14 50
Sheffield 7	29,31 ⇌ a	13 14	13 28			13 34		13 44	13 48	13 50	13 58	14 02	14 08	14 14		14 28	14 31		14 34		14 44	14 48	14 50	14 58
	d						13 37					14 05								14 38				
Dronfield	d											14 15												
Chesterfield	d						13 52					14 22								14 52				
Alfreton	d						14 03					14 32								15 03				
Langley Mill	d											14 40												
Ilkeston	d											14 45								15 13				
Nottingham	a						14 27					14 58								15 28				

		NT	TP	NT	NT	NT	NT	EM	NT	NT		NT	NT	NT	TP	NT	NT	NT	NT	EM		NT	NT	NT	NT
		◇	◇1				◇	◇		◇			◇	◇	◇1				◇	◇			◇		
			H	A		B	C	D	E	F		G			H	A		B	C	D		E	F	G	
Leeds 10	31,32 d	14 04				14 30	14 38						14 48	15 04				15 30	15 38						15 48
Woodlesford	32 d					14 39												15 39							
Castleford	32 d					14 50												15 50							
Normanton	d					14 56						←						15 56						←	
Wakefield Kirkgate 4	31 a	14 21				15 01	14 54					15 01		15 21				16 01	15 54					16 01	
	d	14 22				15 01	14 55					15 01		15 22				16 01	15 55					16 01	
Darton	d					→						15 13						→						16 13	
Huddersfield	d				14 12												15 12								
Lockwood	d				14 15												15 15								
Berry Brow	d				14 18												15 18								
Honley	d				14 21												15 21								
Brockholes	d				14 24												15 24								
Stocksmoor	d				14 28												15 28								
Shepley	d				14 30												15 30								
Denby Dale	d				14 35												15 35								
Penistone	d				14 43												15 43								
Silkstone Common	d				14 48												15 48								
Dodworth	d				14 52												15 52								
Barnsley	a	14 37			14 59		15 10					15 20		15 37			15 59		16 10					16 20	
	d	14 38			15 00		15 11					15 20		15 38			16 00		16 11					16 20	
Wombwell	d				15 05							15 26					16 05							16 26	
Elsecar	d				15 09							15 30					16 09							16 30	
Chapeltown	d				15 15							15 35					16 15							16 35	
Meadowhall	29,31 ⇌ a	14 52			15 20		15 26					15 41	15 50	15 52			16 20		16 27					16 41	16 50
	d	14 53	15 02	15 06	15 21		15 27		15 34	15 38		15 41	15 50	15 53	16 02	16 06	16 21		16 28			16 34	16 38	16 41	16 50
Sheffield 7	29,31 ⇌ a	15 02	15 08	15 14	15 28		15 34		15 44	15 48		15 50	15 58	16 02	16 08	16 14	16 28		16 35			16 44	16 48	16 50	16 58
	d	15 05						15 37						16 05						16 37					
Dronfield	d	15 15												16 15						16 48					
Chesterfield	d	15 22						15 53						16 22						16 53					
Alfreton	d	15 32						16 05						16 32						17 04					
Langley Mill	d	15 40												16 40											
Ilkeston	d	15 45												16 45											
Nottingham	a	15 58						16 27						16 58						17 27					

A From Adwick
B To Sheffield
C To Lincoln
D From Liverpool Lime Street to Norwich
E From Hull
F From Bridlington
G From Leeds
H From Cleethorpes to Manchester Airport
I From York

Table T034-R

Mondays to Fridays
21 May to 20 July

Leeds and Huddersfield - Barnsley - Sheffield and Nottingham

			NT	TP	NT	NT	NT	NT	NT	EM	NT	NT	NT	NT	TP	NT	NT	NT	NT	NT	NT	NT	EM	NT
			◇	◇1				◇		◇	◇			◇	◇1				◇		◇		◇	
				A	B		C	D	E	F	G	H			A	B		C	D	E	I	H	J	
Leeds 10	31,32	d	16 04				16 29	16 38					16 48	17 03				17 30	17 38					17 48
Woodlesford	32	d					16 38											17 39						
Castleford	32	d					16 49											17 50						
Normanton		d					16 56					←		17 17				17 56				←		
Wakefield Kirkgate 4	31	a	16 21				17 01	16 54				17 01		17 22				18 01	17 54			18 01		
		d	16 22				17 01	16 55				17 01		17 22				18 01	17 55			18 01		
Darton		d					→					17 13						→				18 13		
Huddersfield		d				16 12											17 12							
Lockwood		d				16 15											17 15							
Berry Brow		d				16 18											17 18							
Honley		d				16 21											17 21							
Brockholes		d				16 24											17 24							
Stocksmoor		d				16 28											17 28							
Shepley		d				16 30											17 30							
Denby Dale		d				16 35											17 35							
Penistone		d				16 43											17 43							
Silkstone Common		d				16 48											17 48							
Dodworth		d				16 52											17 52							
Barnsley		a	16 37			16 59		17 09				17 20		17 37			17 59		18 10			18 20		
		d	16 38			17 00		17 11				17 20		17 38			18 00		18 11			18 20		
Wombwell		d				17 05						17 26					18 05					18 26		
Elsecar		d				17 09						17 30					18 09					18 30		
Chapeltown		d				17 15						17 35					18 15					18 35		
Meadowhall	29,31 ⇌	a	16 52			17 20		17 26				17 41	17 50	17 53			18 20		18 27			18 41		18 50
		d	16 53	17 02	17 06	17 21		17 27	17 34		17 38	17 41	17 50	17 54	18 02	18 06	18 21		18 28	18 34	18 40	18 41		18 50
Sheffield 7	29,31 ⇌	a	17 02	17 08	17 14	17 28		17 34	17 44		17 48	17 50	17 58	18 02	18 08	18 14	18 28		18 35	18 44	18 49	18 50		18 58
		d	17 05							17 45				18 03									18 53	
Dronfield		d	17 15							17 55				18 13										
Chesterfield		d	17 22							18 01				18 19									19 08	
Alfreton		d	17 32							18 11				18 30									19 19	
Langley Mill		d	17 40											18 37										
Ilkeston		d	17 45											18 42										
Nottingham		a	17 58							18 31				18 55									19 39	

			NT	TP	NT	NT	NT	NT	NT	EM	NT	NT	NT	NT	NT	TP	NT	NT	EM	NT	NT	NT	NT
			◇	◇1					◇	◇		◇		◇	◇	◇1			◇		◇		
				A	B			C		F	E	I	H			A	B		J	E	G		
Leeds 10	31,32	d	18 03					18 30	18 38					18 48	19 03							19 30	19 48
Woodlesford	32	d						18 39														19 39	
Castleford	32	d						18 50														19 50	
Normanton		d						18 56	18 51				←									19 56	
Wakefield Kirkgate 4	31	a	18 20					19 01	18 55				19 01		19 20							20 01	
		d	18 21					19 01	18 56				19 01		19 21							20 01	
Darton		d						→					19 13									20 13	
Huddersfield		d				17 50	18 15											19 12					
Lockwood		d				17 53	18 18											19 15					
Berry Brow		d				17 56	18 21											19 18					
Honley		d				17 59	18 24											19 21					
Brockholes		d				18 02	18 27											19 24					
Stocksmoor		d				18 06	18 31											19 28					
Shepley		d				18 08	18 34											19 30					
Denby Dale		d				18 13	18 39											19 35					
Penistone		d				18 27	18 46											19 43					
Silkstone Common		d				18 32	18 52											19 48					
Dodworth		d				18 36	18 55											19 52					
Barnsley		a	18 36			18 44	19 02		19 12				19 20		19 36			19 59				20 20	
		d	18 37			18 45	19 02		19 13				19 20		19 37			20 00				20 20	
Wombwell		d				18 50	19 08						19 26					20 05				20 26	
Elsecar		d				18 54	19 12						19 30					20 09				20 30	
Chapeltown		d				18 59	19 17						19 35					20 15				20 35	
Meadowhall	29,31 ⇌	a	18 51			19 06	19 23		19 26				19 41	19 50	19 51			20 20				20 41	20 50
		d	18 53	19 02	19 06	19 09	19 23		19 27		19 34	19 38	19 41	19 50	19 53	20 02	20 06	20 21		20 36	20 39	20 41	20 50
Sheffield 7	29,31 ⇌	a	19 00	19 08	19 14	19 17	19 31		19 35		19 44	19 48	19 50	19 58	20 00	20 08	20 14	20 28		20 45	20 48	20 50	20 58
		d	19 05							19 37					20 02				20 41				
Dronfield		d	19 15												20 12								
Chesterfield		d	19 21							19 52					20 18				20 56				
Alfreton		d	19 31							20 03					20 28				21 08				
Langley Mill		d	19 39												20 36								
Ilkeston		d	19 44												20 41								
Nottingham		a	19 57							20 27					20 55				21 33				

A From Cleethorpes to Manchester Airport
B From Adwick
C To Sheffield
D To Lincoln
E From Hull
F From Liverpool Lime Street to Norwich
G From Scarborough
H From Leeds
I From Bridlington
J From Liverpool Lime Street

Table T034-R

Mondays to Fridays
21 May to 20 July

Leeds and Huddersfield - Barnsley - Sheffield and Nottingham

			NT	TP	NT	NT	EM	NT	NT	NT	NT	TP	NT	NT	NT	NT	NT	NT	EM	NT	NT	NT	NT	NT
			◇	◇1			◇	■		◇	◇	◇1			◇				◇	◇				
				A	B		C	D				E	B		F			B	C					
Leeds 10	31,32	d	20 03						20 30	20 48	21 03					21 30	21 48			22 30	22 32	22 44		23 00
Woodlesford	32	d							20 39							21 39					22 41			23 09
Castleford	32	d							20 50							21 50					22 53			23 20
Normanton		d							20 56							21 56					22 58			23 27
Wakefield Kirkgate 4	31	a	20 20						21 01		21 20					22 01					23 03			23 32
		d	20 21						21 01		21 21					22 01					23 04			23 32
Darton		d							21 13							22 13					23 15			23 43
Huddersfield		d				20 12								21 12									22 51	
Lockwood		d				20 15								21 15									22 54	
Berry Brow		d				20 18								21 18									22 57	
Honley		d				20 21								21 21									23 00	
Brockholes		d				20 24								21 24									23 03	
Stocksmoor		d				20 28								21 28									23 07	
Shepley		d				20 30								21 30									23 09	
Denby Dale		d				20 35								21 35									23 14	
Penistone		d				20 43								21 43									23 24	
Silkstone Common		d				20 48								21 48									23 29	
Dodworth		d				20 52								21 52									23 33	
Barnsley		a	20 36			20 59			21 20		21 36			21 59		22 20					23 22		23 39	23 50
		d	20 37			21 00			21 20		21 37			22 00		22 20					23 22		23 40	23 50
Wombwell		d				21 05			21 26					22 05		22 26					23 28		23 45	23 56
Elsecar		d				21 09			21 30					22 09		22 30					23 32		23 49	00 01
Chapeltown		d				21 15			21 35					22 15		22 35					23 37		23 54	00 06
Meadowhall	29,31 ⇌	a	20 51			21 20			21 41	21 50	21 51			22 20		22 44	22 55			23 34	23 43	23 45	23 59	00 12
		d	20 53	21 04	21 08	21 21		21 35	21 41	21 50	21 54	22 02	22 06	22 21	22 44	22 48	22 56	23 06		23 34	23 43	23 47	00 01	00 12
Sheffield 7	29,31 ⇌	a	21 00	21 09	21 18	21 28		21 43	21 50	21 59	22 02	22 08	22 16	22 28	22 53	22 58	23 04	23 15		23 42	23 52	23 55	00 08	00 21
		d	21 02				21 37				22 03								23 37					
Dronfield		d	21 12				21 49				22 13													
Chesterfield		d	21 18				21 55				22 20								00 02					
Alfreton		d					22 05				22 31													
Langley Mill		d					22 13				22 38													
Ilkeston		d					22 18				22 43													
Nottingham		a	22 06				22 31				22 57								00 45					

			NT
Leeds 10	31,32	d	23 10
Woodlesford	32	d	
Castleford	32	d	
Normanton		d	
Wakefield Kirkgate 4	31	a	
		d	
Darton		d	
Huddersfield		d	
Lockwood		d	
Berry Brow		d	
Honley		d	
Brockholes		d	
Stocksmoor		d	
Shepley		d	
Denby Dale		d	
Penistone		d	
Silkstone Common		d	
Dodworth		d	
Barnsley		a	
		d	
Wombwell		d	
Elsecar		d	
Chapeltown		d	
Meadowhall	29,31 ⇌	a	00 17
		d	00 17
Sheffield 7	29,31 ⇌	a	00 26
		d	
Dronfield		d	
Chesterfield		d	
Alfreton		d	
Langley Mill		d	
Ilkeston		d	
Nottingham		a	

A From Cleethorpes to Manchester Piccadilly
B From Adwick
C From Liverpool Lime Street
D From Hull
E From Cleethorpes to Manchester Airport
F From Bridlington

Table T034-R

Mondays to Fridays
23 July to 31 August

Leeds and Huddersfield - Barnsley - Sheffield and Nottingham

		NT MX A	EM MO ◇ B	EM MX ◇ B	NT MX C	NT MX ◇ D	NT MX E	NT MX E	NT ◇	NT	NT ◇	TP ◇1 F	NT	NT C	NT G	NT ◇	NT ◇	TP ◇1 H	NT	NT D	NT I	EM ◇1 J	EM ◇1 K
Leeds 31,32	d															05 34			05 55		06 30	06 33	06 33
Woodlesford 32	d																		06 04		06 39		
Castleford 32	d																		06 17		06 50		
Normanton	d																		06 23		06 56		
Wakefield Kirkgate 31	a																		06 28		07 01		
	d																		06 28		07 01		
Darton	d																		06 39		→		
Huddersfield	d																						
Lockwood	d																						
Berry Brow	d																						
Honley	d																						
Brockholes	d																						
Stocksmoor	d																						
Shepley	d																						
Denby Dale	d																						
Penistone	d																						
Silkstone Common	d																						
Dodworth	d																						
Barnsley	a																		06 46				
	d									05 23			05 52		06 20				06 46				
Wombwell	d									05 28			05 57		06 25				06 52				
Elsecar	d						00 01			05 32			06 01		06 29				06 56				
Chapeltown	d						00 06			05 37			06 06		06 34				07 01				
Meadowhall 29,31	a						00 12			05 43			06 11		06 39	06 50			07 07				
	d	00 01			00 04	00 09	00 12	00 17		05 43		06 00	06 12	06 35	06 40	06 50		06 54	07 07	07 10			
Sheffield 29,31	a	00 08			00 13	00 17	00 21	00 26		05 53		06 08	06 20	06 45	06 48	06 59		07 07	07 16	07 18		07 21	07 22
	d								05 15		06 03						07 02					07 24	07 32
Dronfield	d								05 24		06 13						07 11						
Chesterfield	d			00 02					05 30		06 19						07 17					07 37	07 46
Alfreton	d								05 45		06 29						07 28					07 48	07 57
Langley Mill	d		00 02						05 53		06 36						07 35					07 57	08 05
Ilkeston	d								05 58		06 41						07 40						
Nottingham	a		00 23	00 45					06 11		07 00						07 53					08 24	08 24

		NT	NT ◇ L	NT M	NT ◇ D	NT E	NT	NT ◇	TP ◇1 H	NT M	NT	NT I	NT ◇ L	EM ◇ N	NT M	NT ◇ O	NT E	NT	NT ◇	TP ◇1 H	NT M	NT	NT I
Leeds 31,32	d		06 39				06 47	07 03				07 30	07 38					07 48	08 04				08 30
Woodlesford 32	d											07 39											08 39
Castleford 32	d											07 50											08 50
Normanton	d					←						07 56					←						08 56
Wakefield Kirkgate 31	a		06 55			07 01		07 21				08 01	07 54				08 01		08 21				09 01
	d		06 56			07 01		07 22				08 01	07 55				08 01		08 22				09 01
Darton	d					07 14						→					08 14						→
Huddersfield	d	06 12									07 12											08 12	
Lockwood	d	06 15									07 15											08 15	
Berry Brow	d	06 18									07 18											08 18	
Honley	d	06 21									07 21											08 21	
Brockholes	d	06 24									07 24											08 24	
Stocksmoor	d	06 28									07 28											08 28	
Shepley	d	06 30									07 30											08 30	
Denby Dale	d	06 35									07 35											08 35	
Penistone	d	06 43									07 43											08 43	
Silkstone Common	d	06 48									07 48											08 48	
Dodworth	d	06 52									07 52											08 52	
Barnsley	a	06 59	07 11			07 21		07 37			07 59		08 10				08 21		08 38			08 59	
	d	07 01	07 12			07 22		07 38			08 00		08 11				08 21		08 38			09 00	
Wombwell	d	07 06				07 27					08 05						08 27					09 05	
Elsecar	d	07 10				07 31					08 09						08 31					09 09	
Chapeltown	d	07 16				07 37					08 15						08 36					09 15	
Meadowhall 29,31	a	07 21	07 27			07 42	07 49	07 52			08 20		08 27				08 42	08 50	08 52			09 20	
	d	07 22	07 27	07 30	07 38	07 47	07 50	07 53	07 59	08 03	08 21		08 28		08 34	08 40	08 48	08 51	08 55	09 01	09 05	09 21	
Sheffield 29,31	a	07 29	07 35	07 38	07 47	07 54	07 57	08 00	08 06	08 11	08 29		08 35		08 44	08 49	08 57	09 00	09 03	09 08	09 14	09 28	
	d							08 03						08 38					09 06				
Dronfield	d							08 13											09 16				
Chesterfield	d							08 19						08 54					09 22				
Alfreton	d							08 33						09 05					09 33				
Langley Mill	d							08 41											09 40				
Ilkeston	d							08 46											09 45				
Nottingham	a							08 59						09 27					09 59				

- **A** From Huddersfield
- **B** From Liverpool Lime Street
- **C** From Doncaster
- **D** From Hull
- **E** From Leeds
- **F** From Doncaster to Manchester Airport
- **G** To Retford Low Level
- **H** From Cleethorpes to Manchester Airport
- **I** To Sheffield
- **J** until 27 July. To St Pancras International
- **K** from 30 July. To St Pancras International
- **L** To Lincoln
- **M** From Adwick
- **N** From Liverpool Lime Street to Norwich
- **O** From Bridlington

Table T034-R

Mondays to Fridays
23 July to 31 August

Leeds and Huddersfield - Barnsley - Sheffield and Nottingham

		NT ◇ A	EM ◇ B	NT C	NT ◇ D	NT E	NT ◇	NT ◇	TP ◇1 F	NT C	NT	NT G	NT ◇ A	EM ◇ B	NT H	NT ◇ I	NT E	NT	NT ◇	TP ◇1 F	NT C	NT
Leeds 31,32	d	08 38					08 48	09 04				09 29	09 38					09 48	10 04			
Woodlesford 32	d											09 38										
Castleford 32	d											09 49										
Normanton	d					←						09 55					←					
Wakefield Kirkgate 31	a	08 54				09 01		09 21				10 00	09 54				10 00		10 21			
	d	08 55				09 01		09 22				10 00	09 55				10 00		10 22			
Darton	d					09 13						→					10 16					
Huddersfield	d										09 12											10 12
Lockwood	d										09 15											10 15
Berry Brow	d										09 18											10 18
Honley	d										09 21											10 21
Brockholes	d										09 24											10 24
Stocksmoor	d										09 28											10 28
Shepley	d										09 30											10 30
Denby Dale	d										09 35											10 35
Penistone	d										09 43											10 43
Silkstone Common	d										09 48											10 48
Dodworth	d										09 52											10 52
Barnsley	a	09 10				09 20		09 37			09 59		10 11				10 22		10 37			10 59
	d	09 11				09 20		09 38			10 00		10 12				10 23		10 38			11 00
Wombwell	d					09 26					10 05						10 28					11 05
Elsecar	d					09 30					10 09						10 32					11 09
Chapeltown	d					09 35					10 15						10 37					11 15
Meadowhall 29,31	a	09 27				09 41	09 50	09 52			10 20		10 28				10 42	10 50	10 52			11 20
	d	09 28		09 35	09 38	09 41	09 50	09 53	10 01	10 06	10 21		10 28		10 34	10 38	10 43	10 50	10 53	11 02	11 06	11 21
Sheffield 29,31	a	09 35		09 44	09 48	09 50	09 58	10 02	10 08	10 14	10 28		10 35		10 44	10 48	10 52	10 58	11 02	11 08	11 14	11 28
	d		09 37					10 05						10 37					11 05			
Dronfield	d							10 15											11 15			
Chesterfield	d		09 51					10 22						10 54					11 22			
Alfreton	d		10 01					10 32						11 05					11 32			
Langley Mill	d							10 40											11 40			
Ilkeston	d		10 11					10 45											11 45			
Nottingham	a		10 26					10 58						11 26					11 58			

		NT ◇ J	NT G	NT ◇ A	EM ◇ B	NT K	NT ◇ I	NT E	NT ◇	NT ◇	TP ◇1 F	NT C	NT	NT G	NT ◇ A	EM ◇ B	NT K	NT ◇ D	NT E	NT	NT ◇	TP ◇1 F	NT C
Leeds 31,32	d		10 30	10 38					10 48	11 04				11 30	11 38					11 48	12 04		
Woodlesford 32	d		10 39											11 39									
Castleford 32	d		10 50											11 50									
Normanton	d		10 56					←						11 56					←				
Wakefield Kirkgate 31	a		11 01	10 54				11 01		11 21				12 01	11 54				12 01		12 21		
	d		11 01	10 55				11 01		11 22				12 01	11 55				12 01		12 22		
Darton	d		→					11 13						→					12 13				
Huddersfield	d												11 12										
Lockwood	d												11 15										
Berry Brow	d												11 18										
Honley	d												11 21										
Brockholes	d												11 24										
Stocksmoor	d												11 28										
Shepley	d												11 30										
Denby Dale	d												11 35										
Penistone	d												11 43										
Silkstone Common	d												11 48										
Dodworth	d												11 52										
Barnsley	a			11 09				11 20		11 37			11 59		12 10				12 20		12 37		
	d			11 11				11 20		11 38			12 00		12 11				12 20		12 38		
Wombwell	d							11 26					12 05						12 26				
Elsecar	d							11 30					12 09						12 30				
Chapeltown	d							11 35					12 15						12 35				
Meadowhall 29,31	a			11 26				11 41	11 50	11 52			12 20		12 26				12 41	12 50	12 52		
	d	11 24		11 27		11 34	11 38	11 41	11 50	11 53	12 02	12 06	12 21		12 27		12 34	12 39	12 42	12 50	12 53	13 02	13 06
Sheffield 29,31	a	11 31		11 34		11 44	11 48	11 50	11 58	12 02	12 08	12 14	12 28		12 34		12 44	12 48	12 50	12 58	13 02	13 08	13 14
	d				11 38					12 05						12 38					13 05		
Dronfield	d									12 15											13 15		
Chesterfield	d				11 54					12 22						12 52					13 22		
Alfreton	d				12 05					12 32						13 03					13 32		
Langley Mill	d									12 40											13 40		
Ilkeston	d									12 45											13 45		
Nottingham	a				12 29					12 58						13 27					13 58		

- **A** To Lincoln
- **B** From Liverpool Lime Street to Norwich
- **C** From Adwick
- **D** From Scarborough
- **E** From Leeds
- **F** From Cleethorpes to Manchester Airport
- **G** To Sheffield
- **H** From Beverley
- **I** From Bridlington
- **J** From York
- **K** From Hull

Leeds and Huddersfield - Barnsley - Sheffield and Nottingham

	NT	NT A	NT ◇ B	EM ◇ C	NT D	NT ◇ E	NT F	NT ◇	NT ◇	TP ◇1 G	NT H	NT	NT ◇ I	NT A	NT ◇ B	EM ◇ C	NT D	NT ◇ E	NT F	NT	NT ◇
Leeds 10 31,32 d		12 30	12 38					12 48	13 04					13 30	13 38					13 48	14 04
Woodlesford 32 d		12 39												13 39							
Castleford 32 d		12 50												13 50							
Normanton d		12 56					←							13 56					←		
Wakefield Kirkgate 4 31 a		13 01	12 54				13 01		13 23					14 01	13 54				14 01		14 21
d		13 01	12 55				13 01		13 23					14 01	13 55				14 01		14 22
Darton d		→					13 13							→					14 13		
Huddersfield d	12 12											13 12									
Lockwood d	12 15											13 15									
Berry Brow d	12 18											13 18									
Honley d	12 21											13 21									
Brockholes d	12 24											13 24									
Stocksmoor d	12 28											13 28									
Shepley d	12 30											13 30									
Denby Dale d	12 35											13 35									
Penistone d	12 43											13 43									
Silkstone Common d	12 48											13 48									
Dodworth d	12 52											13 52									
Barnsley a	12 59		13 10				13 20		13 39			13 59			14 10				14 20		14 37
d	13 00		13 11				13 20		13 39			14 00			14 11				14 20		14 38
Wombwell d	13 05						13 26					14 05							14 26		
Elsecar d	13 09						13 30					14 09							14 30		
Chapeltown d	13 15						13 35					14 15							14 35		
Meadowhall 29,31 ⇌ a	13 20		13 26				13 41	13 50	13 53			14 20			14 26				14 41	14 50	14 52
d	13 21		13 27		13 34	13 38	13 41	13 50	13 54	14 02	14 06	14 21	14 24		14 27		14 34	14 38	14 41	14 50	14 53
Sheffield 7 29,31 ⇌ a	13 28		13 34		13 44	13 48	13 50	13 58	14 02	14 08	14 14	14 28	14 31		14 34		14 44	14 48	14 50	14 58	15 02
d				13 37					14 05							14 38					15 05
Dronfield d									14 15												15 15
Chesterfield d				13 52					14 22							14 52					15 22
Alfreton d				14 03					14 32							15 03					15 32
Langley Mill d									14 40												15 40
Ilkeston d									14 45							15 13					15 45
Nottingham a				14 27					14 58							15 28					15 58

	TP ◇1 G	NT H	NT	NT A	NT ◇ B	EM ◇ C	NT D	NT ◇ E	NT F	NT ◇	NT ◇	TP ◇1 G	NT H	NT	NT A	NT ◇ B	EM ◇ C	NT D	NT ◇ E	NT F	NT	NT ◇
Leeds 10 31,32 d				14 30	14 38					14 48	15 04				15 30	15 38					15 48	16 04
Woodlesford 32 d				14 39											15 39							
Castleford 32 d				14 50											15 50							
Normanton d				14 56					←						15 56					←		
Wakefield Kirkgate 4 31 a				15 01	14 54				15 01		15 21				16 01	15 54				16 01		16 21
d				15 01	14 55				15 01		15 22				16 01	15 55				16 01		16 22
Darton d				→					15 13						→					16 13		
Huddersfield d			14 12											15 12								
Lockwood d			14 15											15 15								
Berry Brow d			14 18											15 18								
Honley d			14 21											15 21								
Brockholes d			14 24											15 24								
Stocksmoor d			14 28											15 28								
Shepley d			14 30											15 30								
Denby Dale d			14 35											15 35								
Penistone d			14 43											15 43								
Silkstone Common d			14 48											15 48								
Dodworth d			14 52											15 52								
Barnsley a			14 59		15 10				15 20		15 37			15 59		16 10				16 20		16 37
d			15 00		15 11				15 20		15 38			16 00		16 11				16 20		16 38
Wombwell d			15 05						15 26					16 05						16 26		
Elsecar d			15 09						15 30					16 09						16 30		
Chapeltown d			15 15						15 35					16 15						16 35		
Meadowhall 29,31 ⇌ a			15 20		15 26				15 41	15 50	15 52			16 20		16 27				16 41	16 50	16 52
d	15 02	15 06	15 21		15 27		15 34	15 38	15 41	15 50	15 53	16 02	16 06	16 21		16 28		16 34	16 38	16 41	16 50	16 53
Sheffield 7 29,31 ⇌ a	15 08	15 14	15 28		15 34		15 44	15 48	15 50	15 58	16 02	16 08	16 14	16 28		16 35		16 44	16 48	16 50	16 58	17 02
d						15 37					16 05						16 37					17 05
Dronfield d											16 15						16 48					17 15
Chesterfield d						15 53					16 22						16 53					17 22
Alfreton d						16 05					16 32						17 04					17 32
Langley Mill d											16 40											17 40
Ilkeston d											16 45											17 45
Nottingham a						16 27					16 58						17 27					17 58

A To Sheffield
B To Lincoln
C From Liverpool Lime Street to Norwich
D From Hull
E From Bridlington
F From Leeds
G From Cleethorpes to Manchester Airport
H From Adwick
I From York

Table T034-R

Mondays to Fridays
23 July to 31 August

Leeds and Huddersfield - Barnsley - Sheffield and Nottingham

	TP ◇1 A	NT B	NT	NT C	NT ◇ D	NT E	EM ◇ F	NT ◇ G	NT H	NT	NT ◇	TP ◇1 A	NT B	NT	NT C	NT ◇ D	NT E	NT ◇ I	NT H	EM ◇ J	NT	NT ◇
Leeds 10 31,32 d				16 29	16 38					16 48	17 03				17 30	17 38					17 48	18 03
Woodlesford 32 d				16 38											17 39							
Castleford 32 d				16 49											17 50							
Normanton d				16 56					←		17 17				17 56				←			
Wakefield Kirkgate 4 31 a				17 01	16 54				17 01		17 22				18 01	17 54			18 01			18 20
d				17 01	16 55				17 01		17 22				18 01	17 55			18 01			18 21
Darton d				→					17 13						→				18 13			
Huddersfield d			16 12											17 12								
Lockwood d			16 15											17 15								
Berry Brow d			16 18											17 18								
Honley d			16 21											17 21								
Brockholes d			16 24											17 24								
Stocksmoor d			16 28											17 28								
Shepley d			16 30											17 30								
Denby Dale d			16 35											17 35								
Penistone d			16 43											17 43								
Silkstone Common d			16 48											17 48								
Dodworth d			16 52											17 52								
Barnsley a			16 59		17 09				17 20		17 37			17 59		18 10			18 20			18 36
d			17 00		17 11				17 20		17 38			18 00		18 11			18 20			18 37
Wombwell d			17 05						17 26					18 05					18 26			
Elsecar d			17 09						17 30					18 09					18 30			
Chapeltown d			17 15						17 35					18 15					18 35			
Meadowhall 29,31 ⇌ a			17 20		17 26				17 41	17 50	17 53			18 20		18 27			18 41		18 50	18 51
d	17 02	17 06	17 21		17 27	17 34		17 38	17 41	17 50	17 54	18 02	18 06	18 21		18 28	18 34	18 40	18 41		18 50	18 53
Sheffield 7 29,31 ⇌ a	17 08	17 14	17 28		17 34	17 44		17 48	17 50	17 58	18 02	18 08	18 14	18 28		18 35	18 44	18 49	18 50		18 58	19 00
d							17 45				18 03									18 53		19 05
Dronfield d							17 55				18 13											19 15
Chesterfield d							18 01				18 19									19 08		19 21
Alfreton d							18 11				18 30									19 19		19 31
Langley Mill d											18 37											19 39
Ilkeston d											18 42											19 44
Nottingham a							18 31				18 55									19 39		19 57

	TP ◇1 A	NT B	NT	NT	NT C	NT ◇	EM ◇ F	NT E	NT ◇ I	NT H	NT ◇	NT ◇	TP ◇1 A	NT B	NT	EM ◇ J	NT E	NT ◇ G	NT	NT	NT ◇
Leeds 10 31,32 d					18 30	18 38					18 48	19 03							19 30	19 48	20 03
Woodlesford 32 d					18 39														19 39		
Castleford 32 d					18 50														19 50		
Normanton d					18 56	18 51				←									19 56		
Wakefield Kirkgate 4 31 a					19 01	18 55				19 01		19 20							20 01		20 20
d					19 01	18 56				19 01		19 21							20 01		20 21
Darton d					→					19 13									20 13		
Huddersfield d			17 50	18 15											19 12						
Lockwood d			17 53	18 18											19 15						
Berry Brow d			17 56	18 21											19 18						
Honley d			17 59	18 24											19 21						
Brockholes d			18 02	18 27											19 24						
Stocksmoor d			18 06	18 31											19 28						
Shepley d			18 08	18 34											19 30						
Denby Dale d			18 13	18 39											19 35						
Penistone d			18 27	18 46											19 43						
Silkstone Common d			18 32	18 52											19 48						
Dodworth d			18 36	18 55											19 52						
Barnsley a			18 44	19 02		19 12				19 20		19 36			19 59				20 20		20 36
d			18 45	19 02		19 13				19 20		19 37			20 00				20 20		20 37
Wombwell d			18 50	19 08						19 26					20 05				20 26		
Elsecar d			18 54	19 12						19 30					20 09				20 30		
Chapeltown d			18 59	19 17						19 35					20 15				20 35		
Meadowhall 29,31 ⇌ a			19 06	19 23		19 26				19 41	19 50	19 51			20 20				20 41	20 50	20 51
d	19 02	19 06	19 09	19 23		19 27		19 34	19 38	19 41	19 50	19 53	20 02	20 06	20 21		20 36	20 39	20 41	20 50	20 53
Sheffield 7 29,31 ⇌ a	19 08	19 14	19 17	19 31		19 35		19 44	19 48	19 50	19 58	20 00	20 08	20 14	20 28		20 45	20 48	20 50	20 58	21 00
d							19 37					20 02				20 41					21 02
Dronfield d												20 12									21 12
Chesterfield d							19 52					20 21				20 56					21 18
Alfreton d							20 03					20 32				21 08					
Langley Mill d												20 40									
Ilkeston d												20 45									
Nottingham a							20 27					20 59				21 33					22 06

A From Cleethorpes to Manchester Airport
B From Adwick
C To Sheffield
D To Lincoln
E From Hull
F From Liverpool Lime Street to Norwich
G From Scarborough
H From Leeds
I From Bridlington
J From Liverpool Lime Street

23 July to 31 August

Leeds and Huddersfield - Barnsley - Sheffield and Nottingham

	TP ◇1 A	NT B	NT	EM ◇ C	NT D	NT	NT ◇	NT ◇	TP ◇1 E	NT B	NT	NT ◇ F	NT	NT	NT B	EM ◇ C	NT ◇	NT	NT	NT	NT	NT
Leeds 10 31,32 d						20 30	20 48	21 03					21 30	21 48			22 30	22 32	22 44		23 00	23 10
Woodlesford 32 d						20 39							21 39					22 41			23 09	
Castleford 32 d						20 50							21 50					22 53			23 20	
Normanton d						20 56							21 56					22 58			23 27	
Wakefield Kirkgate 4 31 a						21 01		21 20					22 01					23 03			23 32	
d						21 01		21 21					22 01					23 04			23 32	
Darton d						21 13							22 13					23 15			23 43	
Huddersfield d			20 12								21 12									22 51		
Lockwood d			20 15								21 15									22 54		
Berry Brow d			20 18								21 18									22 57		
Honley d			20 21								21 21									23 00		
Brockholes d			20 24								21 24									23 03		
Stocksmoor d			20 28								21 28									23 07		
Shepley d			20 30								21 30									23 09		
Denby Dale d			20 35								21 35									23 14		
Penistone d			20 43								21 43									23 24		
Silkstone Common d			20 48								21 48									23 29		
Dodworth d			20 52								21 52									23 33		
Barnsley a			20 59			21 20		21 36			21 59		22 20					23 22		23 39	23 50	
d			21 00			21 20		21 37			22 00		22 20					23 22		23 40	23 50	
Wombwell d			21 05			21 26					22 05		22 26					23 28		23 45	23 56	
Elsecar d			21 09			21 30					22 09		22 30					23 32		23 49	00 01	
Chapeltown d			21 15			21 35					22 15		22 35					23 37		23 54	00 06	
Meadowhall 29,31 a			21 20			21 41	21 50	21 51			22 20		22 44	22 55			23 34	23 43	23 45	23 59	00 12	00 17
d	21 04	21 08	21 21		21 35	21 41	21 50	21 54	22 02	22 06	22 21	22 44	22 48	22 56	23 06		23 34	23 43	23 47	00 01	00 12	00 17
Sheffield 7 29,31 a	21 09	21 18	21 28		21 43	21 50	21 59	22 02	22 08	22 16	22 28	22 53	22 58	23 04	23 15		23 42	23 52	23 55	00 08	00 21	00 26
d				21 37				22 03								23 37						
Dronfield d				21 49				22 13														
Chesterfield d				21 55				22 20								00 02						
Alfreton d				22 05				22 31														
Langley Mill d				22 13				22 38														
Ilkeston d				22 18				22 43														
Nottingham a				22 31				22 57								00 45						

Mondays to Fridays

3 September to 5 October

	NT MX G	EM MO ◇ C	EM MX ◇ C	NT MX H	NT MX ◇ D	NT MX I	NT MX I	NT ◇	NT	NT ◇	TP ◇1 J	NT	NT H	NT K	NT ◇	NT ◇	TP ◇1 E	NT	NT D	NT L	EM ◇1 M	NT
Leeds 10 31,32 d															05 34			05 55		06 30	06 33	
Woodlesford 32 d																		06 04		06 39		
Castleford 32 d																		06 17		06 50		
Normanton d																		06 23		06 56		
Wakefield Kirkgate 4 31 a																		06 28		07 01		
d																		06 28		07 01		
Darton d																		06 39		→		
Huddersfield d																						06 12
Lockwood d																						06 15
Berry Brow d																						06 18
Honley d																						06 21
Brockholes d																						06 24
Stocksmoor d																						06 28
Shepley d																						06 30
Denby Dale d																						06 35
Penistone d																						06 43
Silkstone Common d																						06 48
Dodworth d																						06 52
Barnsley a																		06 46				06 59
d									05 23			05 52		06 20				06 46				07 01
Wombwell d									05 28			05 57		06 25				06 52				07 06
Elsecar d						00 01			05 32			06 01		06 29				06 56				07 10
Chapeltown d						00 06			05 37			06 06		06 34				07 01				07 16
Meadowhall 29,31 a						00 12			05 43			06 11		06 39	06 50			07 07				07 21
d	00 01			00 04	00 09	00 12	00 17		05 43		06 00	06 12	06 35	06 40	06 50		06 54	07 07	07 10			07 22
Sheffield 7 29,31 a	00 08			00 13	00 17	00 21	00 26		05 53		06 08	06 20	06 45	06 48	06 59		07 07	07 16	07 18		07 22	07 29
d								05 15		06 03						07 02					07 30	
Dronfield d								05 24		06 13						07 11						
Chesterfield d			00 02					05 30		06 19						07 17					07 46	
Alfreton d								05 45		06 29						07 28					07 57	
Langley Mill d		00 02						05 53		06 36						07 35					08 05	
Ilkeston d								05 58		06 41						07 40						
Nottingham a		00 23	00 45					06 11		07 00						07 53					08 24	

A From Cleethorpes to Manchester Piccadilly
B From Adwick
C From Liverpool Lime Street
D From Hull
E From Cleethorpes to Manchester Airport
F From Bridlington
G From Huddersfield
H From Doncaster
I From Leeds
J From Doncaster to Manchester Airport
K To Retford Low Level
L To Sheffield
M To St Pancras International

3 September to 5 October

Leeds and Huddersfield - Barnsley - Sheffield and Nottingham

	NT ◇ A	NT B	NT ◇ C	NT D	NT	NT ◇	TP ◇1 E	NT B	NT	NT F	NT ◇ A	EM ◇ G	NT B	NT ◇ H	NT D	NT	NT ◇	TP ◇1 E	NT B	NT	NT F	NT ◇ A
Leeds 10 31,32 d	06 39				06 47	07 03				07 30	07 38					07 48	08 04				08 30	08 38
Woodlesford 32 d										07 39											08 39	
Castleford 32 d										07 50											08 50	
Normanton d				←						07 56					←						08 56	
Wakefield Kirkgate 4 31 a	06 55			07 01		07 21				08 01	07 54				08 01		08 21				09 01	08 54
d	06 56			07 01		07 22				08 01	07 55				08 01		08 22				09 01	08 55
Darton d				07 14						→					08 14						→	
Huddersfield d									07 12											08 12		
Lockwood d									07 15											08 15		
Berry Brow d									07 18											08 18		
Honley d									07 21											08 21		
Brockholes d									07 24											08 24		
Stocksmoor d									07 28											08 28		
Shepley d									07 30											08 30		
Denby Dale d									07 35											08 35		
Penistone d									07 43											08 43		
Silkstone Common d									07 48											08 48		
Dodworth d									07 52											08 52		
Barnsley a	07 11			07 21		07 37			07 59		08 10				08 21		08 38			08 59		09 10
d	07 12			07 22		07 38			08 00		08 11				08 21		08 38			09 00		09 11
Wombwell d				07 27					08 05						08 27					09 05		
Elsecar d				07 31					08 09						08 31					09 09		
Chapeltown d				07 37					08 15						08 36					09 15		
Meadowhall 29,31 a	07 27			07 42	07 49	07 52			08 20		08 27				08 42	08 50	08 52			09 20		09 27
d	07 27	07 30	07 38	07 47	07 50	07 53	07 59	08 03	08 21		08 28		08 34	08 40	08 48	08 51	08 55	09 01	09 05	09 21		09 28
Sheffield 7 29,31 a	07 35	07 38	07 47	07 54	07 57	08 00	08 06	08 11	08 29		08 35		08 44	08 49	08 57	09 00	09 03	09 08	09 14	09 28		09 35
d						08 03						08 38					09 06					
Dronfield d						08 13											09 16					
Chesterfield d						08 21						08 54					09 22					
Alfreton d						08 33						09 05					09 33					
Langley Mill d						08 41											09 40					
Ilkeston d						08 46											09 45					
Nottingham a						08 59						09 27					09 59					

	EM ◇ G	NT B	NT ◇ I	NT D	NT ◇	NT ◇	TP ◇1 E	NT B	NT	NT F	NT ◇ A	EM ◇ G	NT J	NT ◇ H	NT D	NT	NT ◇	TP ◇1 E	NT B	NT	NT ◇ K
Leeds 10 31,32 d					08 48	09 04				09 29	09 38					09 48	10 04				
Woodlesford 32 d										09 38											
Castleford 32 d										09 49											
Normanton d				←						09 55					←						
Wakefield Kirkgate 4 31 a				09 01		09 21				10 00	09 54				10 00		10 21				
d				09 01		09 22				10 00	09 55				10 00		10 22				
Darton d				09 13						→					10 16						
Huddersfield d									09 12											10 12	
Lockwood d									09 15											10 15	
Berry Brow d									09 18											10 18	
Honley d									09 21											10 21	
Brockholes d									09 24											10 24	
Stocksmoor d									09 28											10 28	
Shepley d									09 30											10 30	
Denby Dale d									09 35											10 35	
Penistone d									09 43											10 43	
Silkstone Common d									09 48											10 48	
Dodworth d									09 52											10 52	
Barnsley a				09 20		09 37			09 59		10 11				10 22		10 37			10 59	
d				09 20		09 38			10 00		10 12				10 23		10 38			11 00	
Wombwell d				09 26					10 05						10 28					11 05	
Elsecar d				09 30					10 09						10 32					11 09	
Chapeltown d				09 35					10 15						10 37					11 15	
Meadowhall 29,31 a				09 41	09 50	09 52			10 20		10 28				10 42	10 50	10 52			11 20	
d		09 35	09 38	09 41	09 50	09 53	10 01	10 06	10 21		10 28		10 34	10 38	10 43	10 50	10 53	11 02	11 06	11 21	11 24
Sheffield 7 29,31 a		09 44	09 48	09 50	09 58	10 02	10 08	10 14	10 28		10 35		10 44	10 48	10 52	10 58	11 02	11 08	11 14	11 28	11 31
d	09 37					10 05						10 38					11 05				
Dronfield d						10 15											11 15				
Chesterfield d	09 51					10 22						10 54					11 22				
Alfreton d	10 02					10 32						11 05					11 33				
Langley Mill d						10 40											11 42				
Ilkeston d	10 12					10 45											11 47				
Nottingham a	10 28					10 58						11 27					12 00				

A To Lincoln
B From Adwick
C From Hull
D From Leeds
E From Cleethorpes to Manchester Airport
F To Sheffield
G From Liverpool Lime Street to Norwich
H From Bridlington
I From Scarborough
J From Beverley
K From York

Table T034-R

Mondays to Fridays

3 September to 5 October

Leeds and Huddersfield - Barnsley - Sheffield and Nottingham

	NT	NT	EM	NT	NT	NT	NT	NT	TP	NT	NT	NT
	A	◇ B	◇ C	D	◇ E	F	◇	◇	◇1 G	H		A
Leeds 10 31,32 d	10 30	10 38					10 48	11 04				11 30
Woodlesford 32 d	10 39											11 39
Castleford 32 d	10 50											11 50
Normanton d	10 56					←						11 56
Wakefield Kirkgate 4 31 a	11 01	10 54				11 01		11 21				12 01
d	11 01	10 55				11 01		11 22				12 01
Darton d	→					11 13						→
Huddersfield d											11 12	
Lockwood d											11 15	
Berry Brow d											11 18	
Honley d											11 21	
Brockholes d											11 24	
Stocksmoor d											11 28	
Shepley d											11 30	
Denby Dale d											11 35	
Penistone d											11 43	
Silkstone Common d											11 48	
Dodworth d											11 52	
Barnsley a		11 09				11 20		11 37			11 59	
d		11 11				11 20		11 38			12 00	
Wombwell d						11 26					12 05	
Elsecar d						11 30					12 09	
Chapeltown d						11 35					12 15	
Meadowhall 29,31 ⇌ a		11 26				11 41	11 50	11 52			12 20	
d		11 27		11 34	11 38	11 41	11 50	11 53	12 02	12 06	12 21	
Sheffield 7 29,31 ⇌ a		11 34		11 44	11 48	11 50	11 58	12 02	12 08	12 14	12 28	
d			11 38					12 05				
Dronfield d								12 15				
Chesterfield d			11 54					12 22				
Alfreton d			12 05					12 32				
Langley Mill d								12 40				
Ilkeston d								12 45				
Nottingham a			12 29					13 00				

	NT	EM	NT	NT	NT	NT	NT	TP	NT	NT
	◇ B	◇ C	D	◇ I	F		◇	◇1 G	H	
Leeds 10 31,32 d	11 38					11 48	12 04			
Woodlesford 32 d										
Castleford 32 d										
Normanton d					←					
Wakefield Kirkgate 4 31 a	11 54				12 01		12 21			
d	11 55				12 01		12 22			
Darton d					12 13					
Huddersfield d										12 12
Lockwood d										12 15
Berry Brow d										12 18
Honley d										12 21
Brockholes d										12 24
Stocksmoor d										12 28
Shepley d										12 30
Denby Dale d										12 35
Penistone d										12 43
Silkstone Common d										12 48
Dodworth d										12 52
Barnsley a	12 10				12 20		12 37			12 59
d	12 11				12 20		12 38			13 00
Wombwell d					12 26					13 05
Elsecar d					12 30					13 09
Chapeltown d					12 35					13 15
Meadowhall 29,31 ⇌ a	12 26				12 41	12 50	12 52			13 20
d	12 27		12 34	12 39	12 42	12 50	12 53	13 02	13 06	13 21
Sheffield 7 29,31 ⇌ a	12 34		12 44	12 48	12 50	12 58	13 02	13 08	13 14	13 28
d		12 38					13 05			
Dronfield d							13 15			
Chesterfield d		12 52					13 22			
Alfreton d		13 03					13 32			
Langley Mill d							13 40			
Ilkeston d							13 45			
Nottingham a		13 27					13 58			

	NT	NT	EM	NT	NT	NT	NT	NT	TP	NT	NT
	A	◇ B	◇ C	D	◇ E	F	◇	◇	◇1 G	H	
Leeds 10 31,32 d	12 30	12 38					12 48	13 04			
Woodlesford 32 d	12 39										
Castleford 32 d	12 50										
Normanton d	12 56					←					
Wakefield Kirkgate 4 31 a	13 01	12 54				13 01		13 23			
d	13 01	12 55				13 01		13 23			
Darton d	→					13 13					
Huddersfield d											13 12
Lockwood d											13 15
Berry Brow d											13 18
Honley d											13 21
Brockholes d											13 24
Stocksmoor d											13 28
Shepley d											13 30
Denby Dale d											13 35
Penistone d											13 43
Silkstone Common d											13 48
Dodworth d											13 52
Barnsley a		13 10				13 20		13 39			13 59
d		13 11				13 20		13 39			14 00
Wombwell d						13 26					14 05
Elsecar d						13 30					14 09
Chapeltown d						13 35					14 15
Meadowhall 29,31 ⇌ a		13 26				13 41	13 50	13 53			14 20
d		13 27		13 34	13 38	13 41	13 50	13 54	14 02	14 06	14 21
Sheffield 7 29,31 ⇌ a		13 34		13 44	13 48	13 50	13 58	14 02	14 08	14 14	14 28
d			13 37					14 05			
Dronfield d								14 15			
Chesterfield d			13 52					14 22			
Alfreton d			14 03					14 32			
Langley Mill d								14 40			
Ilkeston d								14 45			
Nottingham a			14 27					14 58			

	NT	NT	NT	EM	NT	NT	NT	NT	NT	TP
	◇ J	A	◇ B	◇ C	D	◇ E	F		◇	◇1 G
Leeds 10 31,32 d		13 30	13 38					13 48	14 04	
Woodlesford 32 d		13 39								
Castleford 32 d		13 50								
Normanton d		13 56					←			
Wakefield Kirkgate 4 31 a		14 01	13 54				14 01		14 21	
d		14 01	13 55				14 01		14 22	
Darton d		→					14 13			
Huddersfield d										
Lockwood d										
Berry Brow d										
Honley d										
Brockholes d										
Stocksmoor d										
Shepley d										
Denby Dale d										
Penistone d										
Silkstone Common d										
Dodworth d										
Barnsley a			14 10				14 20		14 37	
d			14 11				14 20		14 38	
Wombwell d							14 26			
Elsecar d							14 30			
Chapeltown d							14 35			
Meadowhall 29,31 ⇌ a			14 26				14 41	14 50	14 52	
d	14 24		14 27		14 34	14 38	14 41	14 50	14 53	15 02
Sheffield 7 29,31 ⇌ a	14 31		14 34		14 44	14 48	14 50	14 58	15 02	15 08
d				14 38					15 05	
Dronfield d									15 15	
Chesterfield d				14 52					15 22	
Alfreton d				15 03					15 32	
Langley Mill d									15 40	
Ilkeston d				15 13					15 45	
Nottingham a				15 28					15 58	

A To Sheffield
B To Lincoln
C From Liverpool Lime Street to Norwich
D From Hull
E From Bridlington
F From Leeds
G From Cleethorpes to Manchester Airport
H From Adwick
I From Scarborough
J From York

Table T034-R

Mondays to Fridays

3 September to 5 October

Leeds and Huddersfield - Barnsley - Sheffield and Nottingham

	NT	NT	NT	NT	EM	NT	NT	NT	NT	NT	TP
	A		B	◇ C	◇ D	E	◇ F	G	◇	◇	◇1 H
Leeds 10 31,32 d			14 30	14 38					14 48	15 04	
Woodlesford 32 d			14 39								
Castleford 32 d			14 50								
Normanton d			14 56					←			
Wakefield Kirkgate 4 31 a			15 01	14 54				15 01		15 21	
d			15 01	14 55				15 01		15 22	
Darton d			→					15 13			
Huddersfield d		14 12									
Lockwood d		14 15									
Berry Brow d		14 18									
Honley d		14 21									
Brockholes d		14 24									
Stocksmoor d		14 28									
Shepley d		14 30									
Denby Dale d		14 35									
Penistone d		14 43									
Silkstone Common d		14 48									
Dodworth d		14 52									
Barnsley a		14 59		15 10				15 20		15 37	
d		15 00		15 11				15 20		15 38	
Wombwell d		15 05						15 26			
Elsecar d		15 09						15 30			
Chapeltown d		15 15						15 35			
Meadowhall 29,31 ⇌ a		15 20		15 26				15 41	15 50	15 52	
d	15 06	15 21		15 27		15 34	15 38	15 41	15 50	15 53	16 02
Sheffield 7 29,31 ⇌ a	15 14	15 28		15 34		15 44	15 48	15 50	15 58	16 02	16 08
d					15 37					16 05	
Dronfield d										16 15	
Chesterfield d					15 53					16 22	
Alfreton d					16 05					16 32	
Langley Mill d										16 40	
Ilkeston d										16 45	
Nottingham a					16 29					16 58	

	NT	NT	NT	NT	EM	NT	NT	NT	NT	NT	TP
	A		B	◇ C	◇ D	E	◇ F	G		◇	◇1 H
Leeds 10 31,32 d			15 30	15 38					15 48	16 04	
Woodlesford 32 d			15 39								
Castleford 32 d			15 50								
Normanton d			15 56					←			
Wakefield Kirkgate 4 31 a			16 01	15 54				16 01		16 21	
d			16 01	15 55				16 01		16 22	
Darton d			→					16 13			
Huddersfield d		15 12									
Lockwood d		15 15									
Berry Brow d		15 18									
Honley d		15 21									
Brockholes d		15 24									
Stocksmoor d		15 28									
Shepley d		15 30									
Denby Dale d		15 35									
Penistone d		15 43									
Silkstone Common d		15 48									
Dodworth d		15 52									
Barnsley a		15 59		16 10				16 20		16 37	
d		16 00		16 11				16 20		16 38	
Wombwell d		16 05						16 26			
Elsecar d		16 09						16 30			
Chapeltown d		16 15						16 35			
Meadowhall 29,31 ⇌ a		16 20		16 27				16 41	16 50	16 52	
d	16 06	16 21		16 28		16 34	16 38	16 41	16 50	16 53	17 02
Sheffield 7 29,31 ⇌ a	16 14	16 28		16 35		16 44	16 48	16 50	16 58	17 02	17 08
d					16 37					17 05	
Dronfield d					16 48					17 15	
Chesterfield d					16 53					17 22	
Alfreton d					17 04					17 32	
Langley Mill d										17 40	
Ilkeston d										17 45	
Nottingham a					17 27					18 00	

	NT	NT	NT	NT	NT	EM	NT	NT	NT	NT	TP
	A		B	◇ C	E	◇ D	◇ I	G		◇	◇1 H
Leeds 10 31,32 d			16 29	16 38					16 48	17 03	
Woodlesford 32 d			16 38								
Castleford 32 d			16 49								
Normanton d			16 56					←		17 17	
Wakefield Kirkgate 4 31 a			17 01	16 54				17 01		17 22	
d			17 01	16 55				17 01		17 22	
Darton d			→					17 13			
Huddersfield d		16 12									
Lockwood d		16 15									
Berry Brow d		16 18									
Honley d		16 21									
Brockholes d		16 24									
Stocksmoor d		16 28									
Shepley d		16 30									
Denby Dale d		16 35									
Penistone d		16 43									
Silkstone Common d		16 48									
Dodworth d		16 52									
Barnsley a		16 59		17 09				17 20		17 37	
d		17 00		17 11				17 20		17 38	
Wombwell d		17 05						17 26			
Elsecar d		17 09						17 30			
Chapeltown d		17 15						17 35			
Meadowhall 29,31 ⇌ a		17 20		17 26				17 41	17 50	17 53	
d	17 06	17 21		17 27	17 34		17 38	17 41	17 50	17 54	18 02
Sheffield 7 29,31 ⇌ a	17 14	17 28		17 34	17 44		17 48	17 50	17 58	18 02	18 08
d						17 45				18 03	
Dronfield d						17 55				18 13	
Chesterfield d						18 01				18 19	
Alfreton d						18 11				18 30	
Langley Mill d										18 37	
Ilkeston d										18 42	
Nottingham a						18 33				18 55	

	NT	NT	NT	NT	NT	NT	NT	EM	NT	NT	TP
	A		B	◇ C	E	◇ F	G	◇ J		◇	◇1 H
Leeds 10 31,32 d			17 30	17 38					17 48	18 03	
Woodlesford 32 d			17 39								
Castleford 32 d			17 50								
Normanton d			17 56				←				
Wakefield Kirkgate 4 31 a			18 01	17 54			18 01			18 20	
d			18 01	17 55			18 01			18 21	
Darton d			→				18 13				
Huddersfield d		17 12									
Lockwood d		17 15									
Berry Brow d		17 18									
Honley d		17 21									
Brockholes d		17 24									
Stocksmoor d		17 28									
Shepley d		17 30									
Denby Dale d		17 35									
Penistone d		17 43									
Silkstone Common d		17 48									
Dodworth d		17 52									
Barnsley a		17 59		18 10			18 20			18 36	
d		18 00		18 11			18 20			18 37	
Wombwell d		18 05					18 26				
Elsecar d		18 09					18 30				
Chapeltown d		18 15					18 35				
Meadowhall 29,31 ⇌ a		18 20		18 27			18 41		18 50	18 51	
d	18 06	18 21		18 28	18 34	18 40	18 41		18 50	18 53	19 02
Sheffield 7 29,31 ⇌ a	18 14	18 28		18 35	18 44	18 49	18 50		18 58	19 00	19 08
d								18 53		19 05	
Dronfield d										19 15	
Chesterfield d								19 15		19 21	
Alfreton d								19 27		19 31	
Langley Mill d										19 39	
Ilkeston d										19 44	
Nottingham a								19 50		19 57	

A From Adwick
B To Sheffield
C To Lincoln
D From Liverpool Lime Street to Norwich
E From Hull
F From Bridlington
G From Leeds
H From Cleethorpes to Manchester Airport
I From Scarborough
J From Liverpool Lime Street

3 September to 5 October

Leeds and Huddersfield - Barnsley - Sheffield and Nottingham

	NT		NT	NT	NT	NT	EM	NT	NT	NT	NT		NT	TP	NT	NT	EM	NT	NT	NT	NT		NT	TP
						◇	◇		◇		◇		◇	◇■			◇		◇				◇	◇■
	A				B		C	D	E	F				G	A		H	D	I					J
Leeds ■ 31,32 d					18 30	18 38					18 48		19 03							19 30	19 48		20 03	
Woodlesford 32 d					18 39															19 39				
Castleford 32 d					18 50															19 50				
Normanton d					18 56	18 51				←										19 56				
Wakefield Kirkgate ■ 31 a					19 01	18 55				19 01			19 20							20 01			20 20	
d					19 01	18 56				19 01			19 21							20 01			20 21	
Darton d					→					19 13										20 13				
Huddersfield d			17 50	18 15												19 12								
Lockwood d			17 53	18 18												19 15								
Berry Brow d			17 56	18 21												19 18								
Honley d			17 59	18 24												19 21								
Brockholes d			18 02	18 27												19 24								
Stocksmoor d			18 06	18 31												19 28								
Shepley d			18 08	18 34												19 30								
Denby Dale d			18 13	18 39												19 35								
Penistone d			18 27	18 46												19 43								
Silkstone Common d			18 32	18 52												19 48								
Dodworth d			18 36	18 55												19 52								
Barnsley a			18 44	19 02		19 12				19 20			19 36			19 59				20 20			20 36	
d			18 45	19 02		19 13				19 20			19 37			20 00				20 20			20 37	
Wombwell d			18 50	19 08						19 26						20 05				20 26				
Elsecar d			18 54	19 12						19 30						20 09				20 30				
Chapeltown d			18 59	19 17						19 35						20 15				20 35				
Meadowhall 29,31 ⇌ a			19 06	19 23		19 26				19 41	19 50		19 51			20 20				20 41	20 50		20 51	
d	19 06		19 09	19 23		19 27		19 34	19 38	19 41	19 50		19 53	20 02	20 06	20 21		20 36	20 39	20 41	20 50		20 53	21 04
Sheffield ■ 29,31 ⇌ a	19 14		19 17	19 31		19 35		19 44	19 48	19 50	19 58		20 00	20 08	20 14	20 28		20 45	20 48	20 50	20 58		21 00	21 09
d							19 37						20 02				20 41						21 02	
Dronfield d													20 12										21 12	
Chesterfield d							19 52						20 18				20 56						21 18	
Alfreton d							20 03						20 28				21 08							
Langley Mill d													20 36											
Ilkeston d													20 41											
Nottingham a							20 27						20 55				21 33						21 59	

	NT	NT	EM	NT	NT	NT	NT		TP	NT	NT	NT	NT	NT	NT	EM	NT		NT	NT	NT	NT	NT	
				■																				
			◇			◇	◇		◇■			◇				◇	◇							
	A		H	D					G	A		E			A	H								
Leeds ■ 31,32 d					20 30	20 48	21 03						21 30	21 48			22 30		22 32	22 44		23 00	23 10	
Woodlesford 32 d					20 39								21 39						22 41			23 09		
Castleford 32 d					20 50								21 50						22 53			23 20		
Normanton d					20 56								21 56						22 58			23 27		
Wakefield Kirkgate ■ 31 a					21 01		21 20						22 01						23 03			23 32		
d					21 01		21 21						22 01						23 04			23 32		
Darton d					21 13								22 13						23 15			23 43		
Huddersfield d		20 12									21 12										22 51			
Lockwood d		20 15									21 15										22 54			
Berry Brow d		20 18									21 18										22 57			
Honley d		20 21									21 21										23 00			
Brockholes d		20 24									21 24										23 03			
Stocksmoor d		20 28									21 28										23 07			
Shepley d		20 30									21 30										23 09			
Denby Dale d		20 35									21 35										23 14			
Penistone d		20 43									21 43										23 24			
Silkstone Common d		20 48									21 48										23 29			
Dodworth d		20 52									21 52										23 33			
Barnsley a		20 59			21 20		21 36				21 59		22 20						23 22		23 39	23 50		
d		21 00			21 20		21 37				22 00		22 20						23 22		23 40	23 50		
Wombwell d		21 05			21 26						22 05		22 26						23 28		23 45	23 56		
Elsecar d		21 09			21 30						22 09		22 30						23 32		23 49	00 01		
Chapeltown d		21 15			21 35						22 15		22 35						23 37		23 54	00 06		
Meadowhall 29,31 ⇌ a		21 20			21 41	21 50	21 51				22 20		22 44	22 55			23 34		23 43	23 45	23 59	00 12	00 17	
d	21 08	21 21		21 35	21 41	21 50	21 54		22 02	22 06	22 21	22 44	22 48	22 56	23 06		23 34		23 43	23 47	00 01	00 12	00 17	
Sheffield ■ 29,31 ⇌ a	21 18	21 28		21 43	21 50	21 59	22 02		22 08	22 16	22 28	22 53	22 58	23 04	23 15		23 42		23 52	23 55	00 08	00 21	00 26	
d			21 37				22 03									23 37								
Dronfield d			21 49				22 13																	
Chesterfield d			21 55				22 20									00 02								
Alfreton d			22 05				22 30																	
Langley Mill d			22 13				22 38																	
Ilkeston d			22 18				22 43																	
Nottingham a			22 31				22 57									00 45								

A From Adwick
B To Sheffield
C From Liverpool Lime Street to Norwich
D From Hull
E From Bridlington
F From Leeds
G From Cleethorpes to Manchester Airport
H From Liverpool Lime Street
I From Scarborough
J From Cleethorpes to Manchester Piccadilly

8 October to 7 December

Leeds and Huddersfield - Barnsley - Sheffield and Nottingham

	NT MX	EM MO	EM MX	NT MX	NT MX	NT MX	NT MX	NT	NT		NT	TP	NT	NT	NT	NT	NT	TP	NT		NT	NT	EM	NT
		◇	◇		◇			◇			◇	◇■				◇	◇	◇■					◇■	
	A	B	B	C	D	E	E					F		C	G			H			D	I	J ⚲	
Leeds ■ 31,32 d																05 34			05 55			06 30	06 33	
Woodlesford 32 d																			06 04			06 39		
Castleford 32 d																			06 17			06 50		
Normanton d																			06 23			06 56		
Wakefield Kirkgate ■ 31 a																			06 28			07 01		
d																			06 28			07 01		
Darton d																			06 39			→		
Huddersfield d																								06 12
Lockwood d																								06 15
Berry Brow d																								06 18
Honley d																								06 21
Brockholes d																								06 24
Stocksmoor d																								06 28
Shepley d																								06 30
Denby Dale d																								06 35
Penistone d																								06 43
Silkstone Common d																								06 48
Dodworth d																								06 52
Barnsley a																			06 46					06 59
d									05 23				05 52		06 20				06 46					07 01
Wombwell d									05 28				05 57		06 25				06 52					07 06
Elsecar d						00 01			05 32				06 01		06 29				06 56					07 10
Chapeltown d						00 06			05 37				06 06		06 34				07 01					07 16
Meadowhall 29,31 ⇌ a						00 12			05 43				06 11		06 39	06 50			07 07					07 21
d	00 01			00 04	00 09	00 12	00 17		05 43			06 00	06 12	06 35	06 40	06 50		06 54	07 07		07 10			07 22
Sheffield ■ 29,31 ⇌ a	00 08			00 13	00 17	00 21	00 26		05 53			06 08	06 20	06 45	06 48	06 59		07 07	07 16		07 18		07 21	07 29
d								05 15			06 03						07 02						07 24	
Dronfield d								05 24			06 13						07 11							
Chesterfield d			00 02					05 30			06 19						07 17						07 37	
Alfreton d								05 45			06 29						07 28						07 48	
Langley Mill d		00 02						05 53			06 36						07 35						07 57	
Ilkeston d								05 58			06 41						07 40							
Nottingham a		00 23	00 45					06 11			07 00						07 53						08 24	

	NT	NT	NT	NT	NT		NT	TP	NT	NT	NT	NT	EM	NT	NT		NT	NT	NT	TP	NT	NT	NT	NT
	◇		◇				◇	◇■				◇	◇		◇				◇	◇■				◇
	K	L	D	E				H	L		I	K	M	L	N		E			H	L		I	K
Leeds ■ 31,32 d	06 39				06 47		07 03				07 30	07 38						07 48	08 04				08 30	08 38
Woodlesford 32 d											07 39												08 39	
Castleford 32 d											07 50												08 50	
Normanton d				←							07 56						←						08 56	
Wakefield Kirkgate ■ 31 a	06 55			07 01			07 21				08 01	07 54					08 01		08 21				09 01	08 54
d	06 56			07 01			07 22				08 01	07 55					08 01		08 22				09 01	08 55
Darton d				07 14							→						08 14						→	
Huddersfield d										07 12												08 12		
Lockwood d										07 15												08 15		
Berry Brow d										07 18												08 18		
Honley d										07 21												08 21		
Brockholes d										07 24												08 24		
Stocksmoor d										07 28												08 28		
Shepley d										07 30												08 30		
Denby Dale d										07 35												08 35		
Penistone d										07 43												08 43		
Silkstone Common d										07 48												08 48		
Dodworth d										07 52												08 52		
Barnsley a	07 11			07 21			07 37			07 59		08 10					08 21		08 38			08 59		09 10
d	07 12			07 22			07 38			08 00		08 11					08 21		08 38			09 00		09 11
Wombwell d				07 27						08 05							08 27					09 05		
Elsecar d				07 31						08 09							08 31					09 09		
Chapeltown d				07 37						08 15							08 36					09 15		
Meadowhall 29,31 ⇌ a	07 27			07 42	07 49		07 52			08 20		08 27					08 42	08 50	08 52			09 20		09 27
d	07 27	07 30	07 38	07 47	07 50		07 53	07 59	08 03	08 21		08 28		08 34	08 40		08 48	08 51	08 55	09 01	09 05	09 21		09 28
Sheffield ■ 29,31 ⇌ a	07 35	07 38	07 47	07 54	07 57		08 00	08 06	08 11	08 29		08 35		08 44	08 49		08 57	09 00	09 03	09 08	09 14	09 28		09 35
d							08 03						08 38						09 06					
Dronfield d							08 13												09 16					
Chesterfield d							08 21						08 54						09 22					
Alfreton d							08 33						09 05						09 33					
Langley Mill d							08 41												09 40					
Ilkeston d							08 46												09 45					
Nottingham a							08 59						09 28						09 59					

A From Huddersfield
B From Liverpool Lime Street
C From Doncaster
D From Hull
E From Leeds
F From Doncaster to Manchester Airport
G To Retford Low Level
H From Cleethorpes to Manchester Airport
I To Sheffield
J To St Pancras International
K To Lincoln
L From Adwick
M From Liverpool Lime Street to Norwich
N From Bridlington

Table T034-R

Mondays to Fridays

8 October to 7 December

Leeds and Huddersfield - Barnsley - Sheffield and Nottingham

		EM	NT	NT	NT	NT	NT	TP	NT	NT	NT	NT	EM	NT	NT	NT	NT	NT	TP	NT	NT	NT
		◇		◇		◇	◇	◇1				◇	◇		◇			◇	◇1			◇
		A	B	C	D			E	B		F	G	A	H	I	D			E	B		J
Leeds 10	31,32 d					08 48	09 04				09 29	09 38					09 48	10 04				
Woodlesford	32 d										09 38											
Castleford	32 d										09 49											
Normanton	d				←						09 55					←						
Wakefield Kirkgate 4	31 a				09 01		09 21				10 00	09 54				10 00		10 21				
	d				09 01		09 22				10 00	09 55				10 00		10 22				
Darton	d				09 13						→					10 16						
Huddersfield	d									09 12											10 12	
Lockwood	d									09 15											10 15	
Berry Brow	d									09 18											10 18	
Honley	d									09 21											10 21	
Brockholes	d									09 24											10 24	
Stocksmoor	d									09 28											10 28	
Shepley	d									09 30											10 30	
Denby Dale	d									09 35											10 35	
Penistone	d									09 43											10 43	
Silkstone Common	d									09 48											10 48	
Dodworth	d									09 52											10 52	
Barnsley	a				09 20		09 37			09 59		10 11				10 22		10 37			10 59	
	d				09 20		09 38			10 00		10 12				10 23		10 38			11 00	
Wombwell	d				09 26					10 05						10 28					11 05	
Elsecar	d				09 30					10 09						10 32					11 09	
Chapeltown	d				09 35					10 15						10 37					11 15	
Meadowhall	29,31 a				09 41	09 50	09 52			10 20		10 28				10 42	10 50	10 52			11 20	
	d		09 35	09 38	09 41	09 50	09 53	10 01	10 06	10 21		10 28		10 34	10 38	10 43	10 50	10 53	11 02	11 06	11 21	11 24
Sheffield 7	29,31 a		09 44	09 48	09 50	09 58	10 02	10 08	10 14	10 28		10 35		10 44	10 48	10 52	10 58	11 02	11 08	11 14	11 28	11 31
	d	09 37					10 05						10 37					11 05				
Dronfield	d						10 15											11 15				
Chesterfield	d	09 51					10 22						10 54					11 22				
Alfreton	d	10 01					10 32						11 05					11 32				
Langley Mill	d						10 40											11 40				
Ilkeston	d	10 11					10 45											11 45				
Nottingham	a	10 26					10 58						11 26					11 58				

		NT	NT	EM	NT	NT	NT	NT	NT	TP	NT	NT	NT	NT	EM	NT	NT	NT	NT	NT	TP	NT	NT
			◇	◇		◇		◇	◇	◇1				◇	◇		◇			◇	◇1		
		F	G	A	K	I	D			E	B		F	G	A	K	C	D			E	B	
Leeds 10	31,32 d	10 30	10 38					10 48	11 04				11 30	11 38					11 48	12 04			
Woodlesford	32 d	10 39											11 39										
Castleford	32 d	10 50											11 50										
Normanton	d	10 56					←						11 56					←					
Wakefield Kirkgate 4	31 a	11 01	10 54				11 01		11 21				12 01	11 54				12 01		12 21			
	d	11 01	10 55				11 01		11 22				12 01	11 55				12 01		12 22			
Darton	d	→					11 13						→					12 13					
Huddersfield	d											11 12											12 12
Lockwood	d											11 15											12 15
Berry Brow	d											11 18											12 18
Honley	d											11 21											12 21
Brockholes	d											11 24											12 24
Stocksmoor	d											11 28											12 28
Shepley	d											11 30											12 30
Denby Dale	d											11 35											12 35
Penistone	d											11 43											12 43
Silkstone Common	d											11 48											12 48
Dodworth	d											11 52											12 52
Barnsley	a		11 09				11 20		11 37			11 59		12 10				12 20		12 37			12 59
	d		11 11				11 20		11 38			12 00		12 11				12 20		12 38			13 00
Wombwell	d						11 26					12 05						12 26					13 05
Elsecar	d						11 30					12 09						12 30					13 09
Chapeltown	d						11 35					12 15						12 35					13 15
Meadowhall	29,31 a		11 26				11 41	11 50	11 52			12 20		12 26				12 41	12 50	12 52			13 20
	d		11 27		11 34	11 38	11 41	11 50	11 53	12 02	12 06	12 21		12 27		12 34	12 39	12 42	12 50	12 53	13 02	13 06	13 21
Sheffield 7	29,31 a		11 34		11 44	11 48	11 50	11 58	12 02	12 08	12 14	12 28		12 34		12 44	12 48	12 50	12 58	13 02	13 08	13 14	13 28
	d			11 38					12 05						12 38					13 05			
Dronfield	d								12 15											13 15			
Chesterfield	d			11 54					12 22						12 52					13 22			
Alfreton	d			12 05					12 32						13 03					13 32			
Langley Mill	d								12 40											13 40			
Ilkeston	d								12 45											13 45			
Nottingham	a			12 29					12 58						13 27					13 58			

A From Liverpool Lime Street to Norwich
B From Adwick
C From Scarborough
D From Leeds
E From Cleethorpes to Manchester Airport
F To Sheffield
G To Lincoln
H From Beverley
I From Bridlington
J From York
K From Hull

Table T034-R

Mondays to Fridays

8 October to 7 December

Leeds and Huddersfield - Barnsley - Sheffield and Nottingham

		NT	NT	EM	NT	NT	NT	NT	NT	TP	NT	NT	NT	NT	NT	EM	NT	NT	NT	NT	NT	TP
			◇	◇		◇		◇	◇	◇1			◇		◇	◇		◇			◇	◇1
		A	B	C	D	E	F			G	H		I	A	B	C	D	E	F			G
Leeds 10	31,32 d	12 30	12 38					12 48	13 04					13 30	13 38					13 48	14 04	
Woodlesford	32 d	12 39												13 39								
Castleford	32 d	12 50												13 50								
Normanton	d	12 56					←							13 56					←			
Wakefield Kirkgate 4	31 a	13 01	12 54				13 01		13 23					14 01	13 54				14 01		14 21	
	d	13 01	12 55				13 01		13 23					14 01	13 55				14 01		14 22	
Darton	d	→					13 13							→					14 13			
Huddersfield	d											13 12										
Lockwood	d											13 15										
Berry Brow	d											13 18										
Honley	d											13 21										
Brockholes	d											13 24										
Stocksmoor	d											13 28										
Shepley	d											13 30										
Denby Dale	d											13 35										
Penistone	d											13 43										
Silkstone Common	d											13 48										
Dodworth	d											13 52										
Barnsley	a		13 10				13 20		13 39			13 59			14 10				14 20		14 37	
	d		13 11				13 20		13 39			14 00			14 11				14 20		14 38	
Wombwell	d						13 26					14 05							14 26			
Elsecar	d						13 30					14 09							14 30			
Chapeltown	d						13 35					14 15							14 35			
Meadowhall	29,31 a		13 26				13 41	13 50	13 53			14 20			14 26				14 41	14 50	14 52	
	d		13 27		13 34	13 38	13 41	13 50	13 54	14 02	14 06	14 21	14 24		14 27		14 34	14 38	14 41	14 50	14 53	15 02
Sheffield 7	29,31 a		13 34		13 44	13 48	13 50	13 58	14 02	14 08	14 14	14 28	14 31		14 34		14 44	14 48	14 50	14 58	15 02	15 08
	d			13 37					14 05							14 38					15 05	
Dronfield	d								14 15												15 15	
Chesterfield	d			13 52					14 22							14 52					15 22	
Alfreton	d			14 03					14 32							15 03					15 32	
Langley Mill	d								14 40												15 40	
Ilkeston	d								14 45							15 13					15 45	
Nottingham	a			14 27					14 58							15 28					15 58	

		NT	NT	NT	NT	EM	NT	NT	NT	NT	NT	TP	NT	NT	NT	NT	EM	NT	NT	NT	NT	NT	TP
					◇	◇		◇		◇	◇	◇1				◇	◇		◇			◇	◇1
		H		A	B	C	D	E	F			G	H		A	B	C	D	E	F			G
Leeds 10	31,32 d			14 30	14 38					14 48	15 04				15 30	15 38					15 48	16 04	
Woodlesford	32 d			14 39											15 39								
Castleford	32 d			14 50											15 50								
Normanton	d			14 56					←						15 56					←			
Wakefield Kirkgate 4	31 a			15 01	14 54				15 01		15 21				16 01	15 54				16 01		16 21	
	d			15 01	14 55				15 01		15 22				16 01	15 55				16 01		16 22	
Darton	d			→					15 13						→					16 13			
Huddersfield	d		14 12											15 12									
Lockwood	d		14 15											15 15									
Berry Brow	d		14 18											15 18									
Honley	d		14 21											15 21									
Brockholes	d		14 24											15 24									
Stocksmoor	d		14 28											15 28									
Shepley	d		14 30											15 30									
Denby Dale	d		14 35											15 35									
Penistone	d		14 43											15 43									
Silkstone Common	d		14 48											15 48									
Dodworth	d		14 52											15 52									
Barnsley	a		14 59		15 10				15 20		15 37			15 59		16 10				16 20		16 37	
	d		15 00		15 11				15 20		15 38			16 00		16 11				16 20		16 38	
Wombwell	d		15 05						15 26					16 05						16 26			
Elsecar	d		15 09						15 30					16 09						16 30			
Chapeltown	d		15 15						15 35					16 15						16 35			
Meadowhall	29,31 a		15 20		15 26				15 41	15 50	15 52			16 20		16 27				16 41	16 50	16 52	
	d	15 06	15 21		15 27		15 34	15 38	15 41	15 50	15 53	16 02	16 06	16 21		16 28		16 34	16 38	16 41	16 50	16 53	17 02
Sheffield 7	29,31 a	15 14	15 28		15 34		15 44	15 48	15 50	15 58	16 02	16 08	16 14	16 28		16 35		16 44	16 48	16 50	16 58	17 02	17 08
	d					15 37					16 05						16 37					17 05	
Dronfield	d										16 15						16 48					17 15	
Chesterfield	d					15 53					16 22						16 53					17 22	
Alfreton	d					16 05					16 32						17 04					17 32	
Langley Mill	d										16 40											17 40	
Ilkeston	d										16 45											17 45	
Nottingham	a					16 27					16 58						17 27					18 00	

A To Sheffield
B To Lincoln
C From Liverpool Lime Street to Norwich
D From Hull
E From Bridlington
F From Leeds
G From Cleethorpes to Manchester Airport
H From Adwick
I From York

Table T034-R

Mondays to Fridays

8 October to 7 December

Leeds and Huddersfield - Barnsley - Sheffield and Nottingham

	NT A	NT	NT B	NT ◇ C	NT D	EM ◇ E	NT ◇ F	NT G	NT	NT ◇	TP ◇1 H	NT A	NT	NT B	NT ◇ C	NT D	NT ◇ I	NT G	EM ◇ J	NT	NT ◇	TP ◇1 H
Leeds 10 31,32 d			16 29	16 38					16 48	17 03				17 30	17 38					17 48	18 03	
Woodlesford 32 d			16 38											17 39								
Castleford 32 d			16 49											17 50								
Normanton d			16 56					←		17 17				17 56				←				
Wakefield Kirkgate 4 31 a			17 01	16 54				17 01		17 22				18 01	17 54			18 01			18 20	
d			17 01	16 55				17 01		17 22				18 01	17 55			18 01			18 21	
Darton d			↦					17 13						↦				18 13				
Huddersfield d		16 12											17 12									
Lockwood d		16 15											17 15									
Berry Brow d		16 18											17 18									
Honley d		16 21											17 21									
Brockholes d		16 24											17 24									
Stocksmoor d		16 28											17 28									
Shepley d		16 30											17 30									
Denby Dale d		16 35											17 35									
Penistone d		16 43											17 43									
Silkstone Common d		16 48											17 48									
Dodworth d		16 52											17 52									
Barnsley a		16 59		17 09				17 20		17 37			17 59		18 10			18 20			18 36	
d		17 00		17 11				17 20		17 38			18 00		18 11			18 20			18 37	
Wombwell d		17 05						17 26					18 05					18 26				
Elsecar d		17 09						17 30					18 09					18 30				
Chapeltown d		17 15						17 35					18 15					18 35				
Meadowhall 29,31 ⇌ a		17 20		17 26				17 41	17 50	17 53			18 20		18 27			18 41		18 50	18 51	
d	17 06	17 21		17 27	17 34		17 38	17 41	17 50	17 54	18 02	18 06	18 21		18 28	18 34	18 40	18 41		18 50	18 53	19 02
Sheffield 7 29,31 ⇌ a	17 14	17 28		17 34	17 44		17 48	17 50	17 58	18 02	18 08	18 14	18 28		18 35	18 44	18 49	18 50		18 58	19 00	19 08
d						17 45				18 03									18 52		19 05	
Dronfield d						17 55				18 13											19 15	
Chesterfield d						18 01				18 19									19 07		19 21	
Alfreton d						18 11				18 30									19 19		19 31	
Langley Mill d										18 37											19 39	
Ilkeston d										18 42											19 44	
Nottingham a						18 31				18 55									19 40		19 57	

	NT A	NT	NT	NT B	NT ◇	EM ◇ E	NT D	NT ◇ I	NT G	NT ◇	NT ◇	TP ◇1 H	NT A	NT	EM ◇ J	NT D	NT ◇ F	NT	NT	NT ◇	TP ◇1 K
Leeds 10 31,32 d				18 30	18 38					18 48	19 03							19 30	19 48	20 03	
Woodlesford 32 d				18 39														19 39			
Castleford 32 d				18 50														19 50			
Normanton d				18 56	18 51				←									19 56			
Wakefield Kirkgate 4 31 a				19 01	18 55				19 01		19 20							20 01		20 20	
d				19 01	18 56				19 01		19 21							20 01		20 21	
Darton d				↦					19 13									20 13			
Huddersfield d		17 50	18 15											19 12							
Lockwood d		17 53	18 18											19 15							
Berry Brow d		17 56	18 21											19 18							
Honley d		17 59	18 24											19 21							
Brockholes d		18 02	18 27											19 24							
Stocksmoor d		18 06	18 31											19 28							
Shepley d		18 08	18 34											19 30							
Denby Dale d		18 13	18 39											19 35							
Penistone d		18 27	18 46											19 43							
Silkstone Common d		18 32	18 52											19 48							
Dodworth d		18 36	18 55											19 52							
Barnsley a		18 44	19 02		19 12				19 20		19 36			19 59				20 20		20 36	
d		18 45	19 02		19 13				19 20		19 37			20 00				20 20		20 37	
Wombwell d		18 50	19 08						19 26					20 05				20 26			
Elsecar d		18 54	19 12						19 30					20 09				20 30			
Chapeltown d		18 59	19 17						19 35					20 15				20 35			
Meadowhall 29,31 ⇌ a		19 06	19 23		19 26				19 41	19 50	19 51			20 20				20 41	20 50	20 51	
d	19 06	19 09	19 23		19 27		19 34	19 38	19 41	19 50	19 53	20 02	20 06	20 21		20 36	20 39	20 41	20 50	20 53	21 04
Sheffield 7 29,31 ⇌ a	19 14	19 17	19 31		19 35		19 44	19 48	19 50	19 58	20 00	20 08	20 14	20 28		20 45	20 48	20 50	20 58	21 00	21 09
d						19 37					20 02				20 41					21 02	
Dronfield d											20 12									21 12	
Chesterfield d						19 52					20 18				20 56					21 18	
Alfreton d						20 03					20 28				21 08						
Langley Mill d											20 36										
Ilkeston d											20 41										
Nottingham a						20 27					20 55				21 34					22 01	

A From Adwick
B To Sheffield
C To Lincoln
D From Hull
E From Liverpool Lime Street to Norwich
F From Scarborough
G From Leeds
H From Cleethorpes to Manchester Airport
I From Bridlington
J From Liverpool Lime Street
K From Cleethorpes to Manchester Piccadilly

Table T034-R

Mondays to Fridays

8 October to 7 December

Leeds and Huddersfield - Barnsley - Sheffield and Nottingham

	NT A	NT	EM ◇ B	NT ■ C	NT	NT ◇	NT ◇	TP ◇1 D	NT A	NT	NT ◇ E	NT	NT	NT A	EM ◇ B	NT ◇	NT	NT	NT	NT	NT
Leeds 10 31,32 d					20 30	20 48	21 03					21 30	21 48			22 30	22 32	22 44		23 00	23 10
Woodlesford 32 d					20 39							21 39					22 41			23 09	
Castleford 32 d					20 50							21 50					22 53			23 20	
Normanton d					20 56							21 56					22 58			23 27	
Wakefield Kirkgate 4 31 a					21 01		21 20					22 01					23 03			23 32	
d					21 01		21 21					22 01					23 04			23 32	
Darton d					21 13							22 13					23 15			23 43	
Huddersfield d		20 12								21 12									22 51		
Lockwood d		20 15								21 15									22 54		
Berry Brow d		20 18								21 18									22 57		
Honley d		20 21								21 21									23 00		
Brockholes d		20 24								21 24									23 03		
Stocksmoor d		20 28								21 28									23 07		
Shepley d		20 30								21 30									23 09		
Denby Dale d		20 35								21 35									23 14		
Penistone d		20 43								21 43									23 24		
Silkstone Common d		20 48								21 48									23 29		
Dodworth d		20 52								21 52									23 33		
Barnsley a		20 59			21 20		21 36			21 59		22 20					23 22		23 39	23 50	
d		21 00			21 20		21 37			22 00		22 20					23 22		23 40	23 50	
Wombwell d		21 05			21 26					22 05		22 26					23 28		23 45	23 56	
Elsecar d		21 09			21 30					22 09		22 30					23 32		23 49	00 01	
Chapeltown d		21 15			21 35					22 15		22 35					23 37		23 54	00 06	
Meadowhall 29,31 ⇌ a		21 20			21 41	21 50	21 51			22 20		22 44	22 55			23 34	23 43	23 45	23 59	00 12	00 17
d	21 08	21 21		21 35	21 41	21 50	21 54	22 02	22 06	22 21	22 44	22 48	22 56	23 06		23 34	23 43	23 47	00 01	00 12	00 17
Sheffield 7 29,31 ⇌ a	21 18	21 28		21 43	21 50	21 59	22 02	22 08	22 16	22 28	22 53	22 58	23 04	23 15		23 42	23 52	23 55	00 08	00 21	00 26
d			21 37				22 03								23 37						
Dronfield d			21 49				22 13														
Chesterfield d			21 55				22 20								00 02						
Alfreton d			22 05				22 31														
Langley Mill d			22 13				22 38														
Ilkeston d			22 18				22 43														
Nottingham a			22 31				22 57								00 45						

Saturdays

26 May to 8 December

	NT F	EM ◇ B	NT G	NT ◇ C	NT H	NT H	NT ◇	NT	NT ◇	TP ◇1 I	NT	NT G	NT J	NT	NT ◇	TP ◇1 D	NT C	NT	NT K	EM ◇1 L ⊠	NT	NT ◇ M
Leeds 10 31,32 d														05 34				05 55	06 30	06 34		06 39
Woodlesford 32 d																		06 04	06 39			
Castleford 32 d																		06 17	06 50			
Normanton d																		06 23	06 56			
Wakefield Kirkgate 4 31 a																		06 28	07 01			06 55
d																		06 28	07 01			06 56
Darton d																		06 39	↦			
Huddersfield d																					06 12	
Lockwood d																					06 15	
Berry Brow d																					06 18	
Honley d																					06 21	
Brockholes d																					06 24	
Stocksmoor d																					06 28	
Shepley d																					06 30	
Denby Dale d																					06 35	
Penistone d																					06 43	
Silkstone Common d																					06 48	
Dodworth d																					06 52	
Barnsley a																		06 46			06 59	07 11
d								05 23			05 52		06 20					06 46			07 01	07 12
Wombwell d								05 28			05 57		06 25					06 52			07 06	
Elsecar d					00 01			05 32			06 01		06 29					06 56			07 10	
Chapeltown d					00 06			05 37			06 06		06 34					07 01			07 16	
Meadowhall 29,31 ⇌ a					00 12			05 43			06 11		06 39	06 50				07 07			07 21	07 27
d	00 01		00 04	00 09	00 12	00 17		05 43		06 00	06 12	06 35	06 40	06 50		06 51	07 03	07 07			07 22	07 27
Sheffield 7 29,31 ⇌ a	00 08		00 13	00 17	00 21	00 26		05 53		06 08	06 20	06 45	06 48	06 59		07 07	07 11	07 16		07 22	07 29	07 35
d							05 15		06 01						07 02					07 37		
Dronfield d							05 24		06 13						07 11							
Chesterfield d		00 02					05 30		06 19						07 17					07 50		
Alfreton d							05 45		06 29						07 28					08 01		
Langley Mill d							05 53		06 36						07 35					08 09		
Ilkeston d							05 58		06 41						07 40							
Nottingham a		00 45					06 11		07 00						07 53					08 25		

A From Adwick
B From Liverpool Lime Street
C From Hull
D From Cleethorpes to Manchester Airport
E From Bridlington
F From Huddersfield
G From Doncaster
H From Leeds
I From Doncaster to Manchester Airport
J To Retford Low Level
K To Sheffield
L To St Pancras International
M To Lincoln

Leeds and Huddersfield - Barnsley - Sheffield and Nottingham

	NT A	NT ◇ B	NT C	NT	NT ◇	NT A	TP ◇1 D	NT	NT E	NT ◇ F	EM ◇1 G	EM ◇ H	EM ◇ I	NT A	NT ◇ J	NT C	NT	NT ◇	TP ◇1 D	NT A	NT	NT E
Leeds 10 31,32 d				06 48	07 03				07 30	07 38	07 40						07 48	08 04				08 30
Woodlesford 32 d									07 39													08 39
Castleford 32 d									07 50													08 50
Normanton d			←						07 56							←						08 56
Wakefield Kirkgate 4 31 a			07 01		07 21				08 01	07 54						08 01		08 21				09 01
d			07 01		07 22				08 01	07 55						08 01		08 22				09 01
Darton d			07 14						→							08 14						→
Huddersfield d								07 12													08 12	
Lockwood d								07 15													08 15	
Berry Brow d								07 18													08 18	
Honley d								07 21													08 21	
Brockholes d								07 24													08 24	
Stocksmoor d								07 28													08 28	
Shepley d								07 30													08 30	
Denby Dale d								07 35													08 35	
Penistone d								07 43													08 43	
Silkstone Common d								07 48													08 48	
Dodworth d								07 52													08 52	
Barnsley a			07 21		07 37			07 59		08 10						08 21		08 38			08 59	
d			07 22		07 38			08 00		08 11						08 21		08 38			09 00	
Wombwell d			07 27					08 05								08 27					09 05	
Elsecar d			07 31					08 09								08 31					09 09	
Chapeltown d			07 37					08 15								08 36					09 15	
Meadowhall 29,31 ⇌ a			07 42	07 50	07 52			08 20		08 27						08 42	08 50	08 52			09 20	
d	07 30	07 38	07 47	07 50	07 53	07 56	07 59	08 21		08 28				08 34	08 40	08 49	08 51	08 55	09 01	09 05	09 21	
Sheffield 7 29,31 ⇌ a	07 38	07 47	07 55	07 58	08 00	08 04	08 06	08 29		08 35	08 24			08 44	08 49	08 58	09 00	09 03	09 08	09 15	09 28	
d					08 03						08 34	08 37	08 37					09 06				
Dronfield d					08 13													09 16				
Chesterfield d					08 19						08 47	08 52	08 54					09 22				
Alfreton d					08 29						08 57	09 03	09 05					09 33				
Langley Mill d					08 37													09 40				
Ilkeston d					08 42													09 45				
Nottingham a					08 55						09 22	09 27	09 27					09 59				

	NT ◇ F	EM ◇ K	NT A	NT ◇ L	NT C	NT ◇	NT ◇	TP ◇1 D	NT A	NT	NT E	NT ◇ F	EM ◇ K	NT M	NT ◇ J	NT C	NT	NT ◇	TP ◇1 D	NT A	NT
Leeds 10 31,32 d	08 38					08 48	09 04				09 29	09 38					09 48	10 04			
Woodlesford 32 d											09 38										
Castleford 32 d											09 49										
Normanton d					←						09 55					←					
Wakefield Kirkgate 4 31 a	08 54				09 01		09 21				10 00	09 54				10 00		10 21			
d	08 55				09 01		09 22				10 00	09 55				10 00		10 22			
Darton d					09 13						→					10 16					
Huddersfield d										09 12											10 12
Lockwood d										09 15											10 15
Berry Brow d										09 18											10 18
Honley d										09 21											10 21
Brockholes d										09 24											10 24
Stocksmoor d										09 28											10 28
Shepley d										09 30											10 30
Denby Dale d										09 35											10 35
Penistone d										09 43											10 43
Silkstone Common d										09 48											10 48
Dodworth d										09 52											10 52
Barnsley a	09 10				09 20		09 37			09 59		10 11				10 22		10 37			10 59
d	09 11				09 20		09 38			10 00		10 12				10 23		10 38			11 00
Wombwell d					09 26					10 05						10 28					11 05
Elsecar d					09 30					10 09						10 32					11 09
Chapeltown d					09 35					10 15						10 37					11 15
Meadowhall 29,31 ⇌ a	09 27				09 41	09 50	09 52			10 20		10 28				10 42	10 50	10 52			11 20
d	09 28		09 35	09 38	09 41	09 50	09 53	10 01	10 06	10 21		10 28		10 34	10 38	10 43	10 50	10 53	11 02	11 06	11 21
Sheffield 7 29,31 ⇌ a	09 35		09 44	09 48	09 50	09 58	10 02	10 08	10 14	10 28		10 35		10 44	10 48	10 52	10 58	11 02	11 09	11 14	11 28
d		09 37					10 05						10 36					11 05			
Dronfield d							10 15											11 15			
Chesterfield d		09 52					10 22						10 52					11 22			
Alfreton d		10 03					10 32						11 02					11 32			
Langley Mill d							10 40											11 40			
Ilkeston d							10 45											11 45			
Nottingham a		10 27					10 58						11 27					11 58			

A From Adwick
B From Hull
C From Leeds
D From Cleethorpes to Manchester Airport
E To Sheffield
F To Lincoln
G To St Pancras International
H from 23 June. From Liverpool Lime Street to Norwich
I until 16 June. From Liverpool Lime Street to Norwich
J From Bridlington
K From Liverpool Lime Street to Norwich
L From Scarborough
M From Beverley

Table T034-R

Saturdays
26 May to 8 December

Leeds and Huddersfield - Barnsley - Sheffield and Nottingham

	NT ◇ A	NT B	NT ◇ C	EM ◇ D	NT E	NT ◇ F	NT G	NT ◇	NT ◇	TP ◇1 H	NT I	NT	NT B	NT ◇ C	EM ◇ D	NT E	NT ◇ J	NT G	NT	NT ◇	TP ◇1 H	NT I
Leeds 10 31,32 d		10 30	10 38					10 48	11 04				11 30	11 38					11 48	12 04		
Woodlesford 32 d		10 39											11 39									
Castleford 32 d		10 50											11 50									
Normanton d		10 56					←						11 56					←				
Wakefield Kirkgate 4 31 a		11 01	10 54				11 01		11 21				12 01	11 54				12 01		12 21		
d		11 01	10 55				11 01		11 22				12 01	11 55				12 01		12 22		
Darton d		→					11 13						→					12 13				
Huddersfield d												11 12										
Lockwood d												11 15										
Berry Brow d												11 18										
Honley d												11 21										
Brockholes d												11 24										
Stocksmoor d												11 28										
Shepley d												11 30										
Denby Dale d												11 35										
Penistone d												11 43										
Silkstone Common d												11 48										
Dodworth d												11 52										
Barnsley a			11 09				11 20		11 37			11 59		12 10				12 20		12 37		
d			11 11				11 20		11 38			12 00		12 11				12 20		12 38		
Wombwell d							11 26					12 05						12 26				
Elsecar d							11 30					12 09						12 30				
Chapeltown d							11 35					12 15						12 35				
Meadowhall 29,31 ⇌ a			11 26				11 41	11 50	11 52			12 20		12 26				12 41	12 50	12 52		
d	11 24		11 27		11 34	11 38	11 41	11 50	11 53	12 02	12 06	12 21		12 27		12 34	12 39	12 42	12 50	12 53	13 02	13 06
Sheffield 7 29,31 ⇌ a	11 31		11 34		11 44	11 48	11 50	11 58	12 02	12 08	12 14	12 28		12 34		12 44	12 48	12 50	12 58	13 02	13 08	13 14
d				11 37					12 05						12 37					13 05		
Dronfield d									12 15											13 15		
Chesterfield d				11 52					12 22						12 52					13 22		
Alfreton d				12 02					12 32						13 02					13 32		
Langley Mill d									12 40											13 40		
Ilkeston d				12 12					12 45						13 12					13 45		
Nottingham a				12 27					12 58						13 27					13 58		

	NT	NT B	NT ◇ C	EM ◇ D	NT E	NT ◇ F	NT G	NT ◇	NT ◇	TP ◇1 H	NT I	NT	NT ◇ A	NT B	NT ◇ C	EM ◇ D	NT E	NT ◇ F	NT G	NT	NT ◇
Leeds 10 31,32 d		12 30	12 38					12 48	13 04					13 30	13 38					13 48	14 04
Woodlesford 32 d		12 39												13 39							
Castleford 32 d		12 50												13 50							
Normanton d		12 56					←							13 56					←		
Wakefield Kirkgate 4 31 a		13 01	12 54				13 01		13 23					14 01	13 54				14 01		14 21
d		13 01	12 55				13 01		13 23					14 01	13 55				14 01		14 22
Darton d		→					13 13							→					14 13		
Huddersfield d	12 12											13 12									
Lockwood d	12 15											13 15									
Berry Brow d	12 18											13 18									
Honley d	12 21											13 21									
Brockholes d	12 24											13 24									
Stocksmoor d	12 28											13 28									
Shepley d	12 30											13 30									
Denby Dale d	12 35											13 35									
Penistone d	12 43											13 43									
Silkstone Common d	12 48											13 48									
Dodworth d	12 52											13 52									
Barnsley a	12 59		13 10				13 20		13 39			13 59			14 10				14 20		14 37
d	13 00		13 11				13 20		13 39			14 00			14 11				14 20		14 38
Wombwell d	13 05						13 26					14 05							14 26		
Elsecar d	13 09						13 30					14 09							14 30		
Chapeltown d	13 15						13 35					14 15							14 35		
Meadowhall 29,31 ⇌ a	13 20		13 26				13 41	13 50	13 53			14 20			14 26				14 41	14 50	14 52
d	13 21		13 27		13 34	13 38	13 41	13 50	13 54	14 02	14 06	14 21	14 24		14 27		14 34	14 38	14 41	14 50	14 53
Sheffield 7 29,31 ⇌ a	13 28		13 34		13 44	13 48	13 50	13 58	14 02	14 08	14 14	14 28	14 31		14 34		14 44	14 48	14 50	14 58	15 02
d				13 37					14 05							14 37					15 05
Dronfield d									14 15												15 15
Chesterfield d				13 52					14 22							14 54					15 22
Alfreton d				14 03					14 32							15 04					15 32
Langley Mill d									14 40												15 40
Ilkeston d									14 45												15 45
Nottingham a				14 27					14 58							15 28					15 58

A From York
B To Sheffield
C To Lincoln
D From Liverpool Lime Street to Norwich
E From Hull
F From Bridlington
G From Leeds
H From Cleethorpes to Manchester Airport
I From Adwick
J From Scarborough

Leeds and Huddersfield - Barnsley - Sheffield and Nottingham

		TP ◇■ A	NT B	NT	NT C	NT ◇ D	EM ◇ E	NT F	NT ◇ G	NT H	NT ◇	NT ◇	TP ◇■ A	NT B	NT	NT C	NT ◇ D	EM ◇ E	NT F	NT ◇ G	NT H	NT	NT ◇
Leeds ■	31,32 d				14 30	14 38					14 48	15 04				15 30	15 38					15 48	16 04
Woodlesford	32 d				14 39											15 39							
Castleford	32 d				14 50											15 50							
Normanton	d				14 56					←						15 56					←		
Wakefield Kirkgate ■	31 a				15 01	14 54				15 01		15 21				16 01	15 54				16 01		16 21
	d				15 01	14 55				15 01		15 22				16 01	15 55				16 01		16 22
Darton	d				→					15 13						→					16 13		
Huddersfield	d			14 12											15 12								
Lockwood	d			14 15											15 15								
Berry Brow	d			14 18											15 18								
Honley	d			14 21											15 21								
Brockholes	d			14 24											15 24								
Stocksmoor	d			14 28											15 28								
Shepley	d			14 30											15 30								
Denby Dale	d			14 35											15 35								
Penistone	d			14 43											15 43								
Silkstone Common	d			14 48											15 48								
Dodworth	d			14 52											15 52								
Barnsley	a			14 59		15 10				15 20		15 37			15 59		16 10				16 20		16 37
	d			15 00		15 11				15 20		15 38			16 00		16 11				16 20		16 38
Wombwell	d			15 05						15 26					16 05						16 26		
Elsecar	d			15 09						15 30					16 09						16 30		
Chapeltown	d			15 15						15 35					16 15						16 35		
Meadowhall	29,31 ⇌ a			15 20		15 26				15 41	15 50	15 52			16 20		16 27				16 41	16 50	16 52
	d	15 02	15 06	15 21		15 27		15 34	15 38	15 41	15 50	15 53	16 02	16 06	16 21		16 28		16 34	16 38	16 41	16 50	16 53
Sheffield ■	29,31 ⇌ a	15 08	15 14	15 28		15 34		15 44	15 48	15 50	15 58	16 02	16 08	16 14	16 28		16 35		16 44	16 48	16 50	16 58	17 02
	d						15 37					16 05						16 37					17 05
Dronfield	d											16 15						16 48					17 15
Chesterfield	d						15 52					16 22						16 53					17 22
Alfreton	d						16 03					16 32						17 04					17 32
Langley Mill	d											16 40											17 40
Ilkeston	d											16 45											17 45
Nottingham	a						16 27					16 58						17 27					17 58

		TP ◇■ A	NT B	NT	NT C	NT ◇ D	EM ◇ E	NT F	NT ◇ I	NT H	NT	NT ◇	TP ◇■ A	NT B	NT	NT C	NT ◇ D	EM ◇ J	NT F	NT ◇ G	NT H	NT	NT ◇
Leeds ■	31,32 d				16 29	16 38					16 48	17 03				17 30	17 38					17 48	18 03
Woodlesford	32 d				16 38											17 39							
Castleford	32 d				16 49											17 50							
Normanton	d				16 56					←		17 17				17 56					←		
Wakefield Kirkgate ■	31 a				17 01	16 54				17 01		17 22				18 01	17 54				18 01		18 20
	d				17 01	16 55				17 01		17 22				18 01	17 55				18 01		18 21
Darton	d				→					17 13						→					18 13		
Huddersfield	d			16 12											17 12								
Lockwood	d			16 15											17 15								
Berry Brow	d			16 18											17 18								
Honley	d			16 21											17 21								
Brockholes	d			16 24											17 24								
Stocksmoor	d			16 28											17 28								
Shepley	d			16 30											17 30								
Denby Dale	d			16 35											17 35								
Penistone	d			16 43											17 43								
Silkstone Common	d			16 48											17 48								
Dodworth	d			16 52											17 52								
Barnsley	a			16 59		17 09				17 20		17 37			17 59		18 10				18 20		18 36
	d			17 00		17 11				17 20		17 38			18 00		18 11				18 20		18 37
Wombwell	d			17 05						17 26					18 05						18 26		
Elsecar	d			17 09						17 30					18 09						18 30		
Chapeltown	d			17 15						17 35					18 15						18 35		
Meadowhall	29,31 ⇌ a			17 20		17 26				17 41	17 50	17 53			18 20		18 27				18 41	18 50	18 51
	d	17 02	17 06	17 21		17 27		17 34	17 38	17 41	17 50	17 54	18 02	18 06	18 21		18 28		18 34	18 40	18 41	18 50	18 53
Sheffield ■	29,31 ⇌ a	17 08	17 14	17 28		17 34		17 44	17 48	17 50	17 58	18 02	18 08	18 14	18 28		18 35		18 44	18 49	18 50	18 58	19 00
	d						17 41					18 03						18 40					19 05
Dronfield	d						17 51					18 13											19 15
Chesterfield	d						17 57					18 19						18 57					19 21
Alfreton	d						18 08					18 30						19 08					19 31
Langley Mill	d											18 37											19 39
Ilkeston	d											18 42											19 44
Nottingham	a						18 29					18 55						19 29					19 57

A From Cleethorpes to Manchester Airport
B From Adwick
C To Sheffield
D To Lincoln
E From Liverpool Lime Street to Norwich
F From Hull
G From Bridlington
H From Leeds
I From Scarborough
J From Liverpool Lime Street

Leeds and Huddersfield - Barnsley - Sheffield and Nottingham

		TP ◇■ A	NT B	NT	NT	NT C	NT ◇	EM ◇ D	NT E	NT ◇ F	NT G	NT ◇	NT ◇	TP ◇■ A	NT B	NT	EM ◇ H	NT E	NT ◇ I	NT	NT	NT ◇ J
Leeds ■	31,32 d					18 30	18 38					18 48	19 03							19 30	19 48	20 03
Woodlesford	32 d					18 39														19 39		
Castleford	32 d					18 50														19 50		
Normanton	d					18 56	18 51				←									19 56		
Wakefield Kirkgate ■	31 a					19 01	18 55				19 01		19 20							20 01		20 20
	d					19 01	18 56				19 01		19 21							20 01		20 21
Darton	d					→					19 13									20 13		
Huddersfield	d			17 50	18 15											19 12						
Lockwood	d			17 53	18 18											19 15						
Berry Brow	d			17 56	18 21											19 18						
Honley	d			17 59	18 24											19 21						
Brockholes	d			18 02	18 27											19 24						
Stocksmoor	d			18 06	18 31											19 28						
Shepley	d			18 08	18 34											19 30						
Denby Dale	d			18 13	18 39											19 35						
Penistone	d			18 27	18 46											19 43						
Silkstone Common	d			18 32	18 52											19 48						
Dodworth	d			18 36	18 55											19 52						
Barnsley	a			18 44	19 02		19 12				19 20		19 36			19 59				20 20		20 36
	d			18 45	19 02		19 13				19 20		19 37			20 00				20 20		20 37
Wombwell	d			18 50	19 08						19 26					20 05				20 26		
Elsecar	d			18 54	19 12						19 30					20 09				20 30		
Chapeltown	d			18 59	19 17						19 35					20 15				20 35		
Meadowhall	29,31 ⇌ a			19 06	19 23		19 26				19 41	19 50	19 51			20 20				20 41	20 50	20 51
	d	19 02	19 06	19 09	19 23		19 27		19 34	19 38	19 41	19 50	19 53	20 02	20 06	20 21		20 34	20 39	20 41	20 50	20 53
Sheffield ■	29,31 ⇌ a	19 08	19 14	19 17	19 31		19 35		19 44	19 48	19 50	19 58	20 00	20 08	20 14	20 28		20 44	20 48	20 50	20 58	21 00
	d							19 37					20 02				20 39					21 02
Dronfield	d												20 12									21 12
Chesterfield	d							19 52					20 18				20 54					21 18
Alfreton	d							20 03					20 28				21 05					
Langley Mill	d												20 36									
Ilkeston	d												20 41									
Nottingham	a							20 27					20 55				21 33					21 47

		NT ◇ K	TP ◇■ L	NT B	NT	EM ◇ H	NT ■ E	NT	NT ◇	NT ◇	TP ◇■ A	NT B	NT	EM ◇ H	NT ◇ F	NT	NT	NT B	NT ◇	EM ◇ H	NT	NT	NT
Leeds ■	31,32 d	20 03						20 30	20 48	21 03						21 30	21 48		22 13		22 32	22 44	
Woodlesford	32 d							20 39								21 39					22 41		
Castleford	32 d							20 50								21 50					22 53		
Normanton	d							20 56								21 56					22 58		
Wakefield Kirkgate ■	31 a	20 20						21 01		21 20						22 01					23 03		
	d	20 21						21 01		21 21						22 01					23 04		
Darton	d							21 13								22 13					23 15		
Huddersfield	d				20 12								21 12										22 51
Lockwood	d				20 15								21 15										22 54
Berry Brow	d				20 18								21 18										22 57
Honley	d				20 21								21 21										23 00
Brockholes	d				20 24								21 24										23 03
Stocksmoor	d				20 28								21 28										23 07
Shepley	d				20 30								21 30										23 09
Denby Dale	d				20 35								21 35										23 14
Penistone	d				20 43								21 43										23 24
Silkstone Common	d				20 48								21 48										23 29
Dodworth	d				20 52								21 52										23 33
Barnsley	a	20 36			20 59			21 20		21 36			21 59			22 20					23 22		23 39
	d	20 37			21 00			21 20		21 37			22 00			22 20					23 22		23 40
Wombwell	d				21 05			21 26					22 05			22 26					23 28		23 45
Elsecar	d				21 09			21 30					22 09			22 30					23 32		23 49
Chapeltown	d				21 15			21 35					22 15			22 35					23 37		23 54
Meadowhall	29,31 ⇌ a	20 51			21 20			21 41	21 50	21 51			22 20			22 44	22 55		23 13		23 43	23 45	23 59
	d	20 53	21 04	21 08	21 21		21 35	21 41	21 50	21 54	22 02	22 06	22 21		22 44	22 48	22 56	23 06	23 13		23 43	23 47	00 01
Sheffield ■	29,31 ⇌ a	21 00	21 09	21 18	21 28		21 43	21 50	21 59	22 02	22 08	22 16	22 28		22 53	22 58	23 04	23 15	23 23		23 52	23 55	00 08
	d	21 02				21 38				22 03				22 42						23 38			
Dronfield	d	21 12				21 49				22 13													
Chesterfield	d	21 18				21 54				22 20				22 56						23 53			
Alfreton	d					22 05				22 31				23 07									
Langley Mill	d					22 13				22 38													
Ilkeston	d					22 18				22 43													
Nottingham	a	22 08				22 34				22 57				23 28						00 30			

A From Cleethorpes to Manchester Airport
B From Adwick
C To Sheffield
D From Liverpool Lime Street to Norwich
E From Hull
F From Bridlington
G From Leeds
H From Liverpool Lime Street
I From Scarborough
J from 8 September until 6 October
K until 1 September, from 13 October
L From Cleethorpes to Manchester Piccadilly

Sundays
20 May to 2 December

Leeds and Huddersfield - Barnsley - Sheffield and Nottingham

	NT	NT	NT	NT	NT	NT	NT	NT	NT		TP	NT	NT	NT	EM	EM	NT	NT	TP		NT	NT	NT	NT
	A	B	◇ C	D	◇	D		◇	◇		◇1 E	F			◇1 G	◇ H	◇ I	◇	◇1 J		D			◇ I
Leeds 10 31,32 d							08 33	08 45	09 08					09 29	09 50			10 08					10 18	
Woodlesford 32 d							08 41																10 26	
Castleford 32 d							08 52																10 37	
Normanton d							08 57																10 42	
Wakefield Kirkgate 4 31 a							09 02		09 24									10 24					10 47	
d							09 02		09 24									10 24					10 47	
Darton d							09 13																11 01	
Huddersfield d													09 10									10 15		
Lockwood d													09 13									10 18		
Berry Brow d													09 16									10 21		
Honley d													09 19									10 24		
Brockholes d													09 22									10 27		
Stocksmoor d													09 26									10 31		
Shepley d													09 28									10 34		
Denby Dale d													09 33									10 39		
Penistone d													09 41									10 46		
Silkstone Common d													09 46									10 52		
Dodworth d													09 50									10 55		
Barnsley a							09 19		09 40				09 57					10 40				11 02	11 09	
d							09 20		09 41				09 58					10 41				11 02	11 09	
Wombwell d							09 25						10 03										11 14	
Elsecar d							09 29						10 07										11 18	
Chapeltown d							09 34						10 12										11 23	
Meadowhall 29,31 a							09 40	09 45	09 56				10 17	10 29				10 55				11 18	11 29	
d	00 01	00 04	00 08	08 37		09 33	09 41	09 45	09 56		10 05	10 09	10 18	10 29			10 39	10 55	11 02		11 07	11 19	11 29	11 40
Sheffield 7 29,31 a	00 06	00 13	00 17	08 45		09 41	09 49	09 53	10 03		10 12	10 17	10 27	10 38	10 30		10 49	11 03	11 10		11 15	11 26	11 38	11 49
d					09 05				10 06						10 35	10 48		11 06						
Dronfield d					09 15				10 16									11 16						
Chesterfield d					09 21				10 22						10 48	11 04		11 22						
Alfreton d					09 32				10 32							11 14		11 32						
Langley Mill d					09 39				10 40									11 40						
Ilkeston d					09 44				10 45									11 45						
Nottingham a					10 00				11 00						11 21	11 39		12 00						

	NT	NT	TP	NT	NT		EM	NT	NT	NT	TP	NT	NT	NT	EM		NT	NT	TP	NT	NT	EM	NT	NT
	◇	◇	◇1 J	D	◇ K		◇ L	◇ M		◇	◇1 J	D	◇ K		◇ N		◇ O	◇	◇1 J	D	◇ K	◇ P	◇ M	
Leeds 10 31,32 d	10 31	11 08							11 48	12 08				12 16				13 08						13 48
Woodlesford 32 d														12 25										
Castleford 32 d														12 36										
Normanton d														12 41										
Wakefield Kirkgate 4 31 a		11 24								12 24				12 46				13 24						
d		11 24								12 24				12 46				13 24						
Darton d														13 00										
Huddersfield d					11 19								12 12								13 19			
Lockwood d					11 22								12 15								13 22			
Berry Brow d					11 25								12 18								13 25			
Honley d					11 28								12 21								13 28			
Brockholes d					11 31								12 24								13 31			
Stocksmoor d					11 35								12 28								13 35			
Shepley d					11 37								12 30								13 37			
Denby Dale d					11 42								12 35								13 42			
Penistone d					11 50								12 43								13 50			
Silkstone Common d					11 55								12 48								13 55			
Dodworth d					11 59								12 52								13 59			
Barnsley a		11 40			12 06					12 40			12 59	13 08				13 40			14 06			
d		11 41			12 07					12 41			13 00	13 08				13 41			14 07			
Wombwell d					12 12									13 13							14 12			
Elsecar d					12 16									13 18							14 16			
Chapeltown d					12 21									13 23							14 21			
Meadowhall 29,31 a	11 49	11 56			12 26				12 50	12 56			13 12	13 28				13 56			14 24			14 49
d	11 50	11 56	12 02	12 06	12 27			12 39	12 51	12 56	13 01	13 05	13 17	13 28			13 41	13 56	14 02	14 06	14 25		14 39	14 49
Sheffield 7 29,31 a	11 57	12 03	12 08	12 13	12 37			12 48	12 58	13 03	13 07	13 12	13 30	13 38			13 50	14 03	14 08	14 13	14 38		14 48	14 57
d		12 06					12 43			13 06					13 48			14 06				14 41		
Dronfield d		12 16								13 16								14 16						
Chesterfield d		12 22					12 57			13 22					14 02			14 22				14 55		
Alfreton d		12 32					13 08			13 32					14 12			14 32				15 08		
Langley Mill d		12 40								13 40								14 40				15 15		
Ilkeston d		12 45								13 45					14 22			14 45						
Nottingham a		13 00					13 34			14 00					14 35			15 00				15 32		

A not 20 May. From Huddersfield
B not 20 May. From Doncaster
C not 20 May. From Hull
D From Doncaster
E From Doncaster to Manchester Airport
F From Goole
G To St Pancras International
H until 9 September. To Norwich
I From Hull
J From Cleethorpes to Manchester Airport
K To Lincoln
L To Norwich
M From Scarborough
N From Manchester Piccadilly to Norwich
O From Bridlington
P From Liverpool Lime Street to Norwich

Sundays
20 May to 2 December

Leeds and Huddersfield - Barnsley - Sheffield and Nottingham

	NT		TP	NT	NT	NT	EM	NT	NT	TP	NT		NT	EM	NT	NT	NT	TP	NT	NT	NT		EM	NT
	◇		◇1 A	B	◇ C		◇ D	◇ E	◇	◇1 A	B		◇ C	◇ D	◇ F		◇	◇1 A	B	◇ C			◇ D	◇ E
Leeds 10 31,32 d	14 08					14 17			15 08							15 42	16 08				16 17			
Woodlesford 32 d						14 25															16 25			
Castleford 32 d						14 36															16 37			
Normanton d						14 41															16 42			
Wakefield Kirkgate 4 31 a	14 24					14 46			15 24								16 24				16 48			
d	14 24					14 46			15 24								16 24				16 48			
Darton d						15 00															17 02			
Huddersfield d					14 15								15 15							16 15				
Lockwood d					14 18								15 18							16 18				
Berry Brow d					14 21								15 21							16 21				
Honley d					14 24								15 24							16 24				
Brockholes d					14 27								15 27							16 27				
Stocksmoor d					14 31								15 31							16 31				
Shepley d					14 33								15 33							16 33				
Denby Dale d					14 38								15 38							16 38				
Penistone d					14 46								15 46							16 46				
Silkstone Common d					14 51								15 51							16 51				
Dodworth d					14 55								15 55							16 55				
Barnsley a	14 40				15 02	15 07			15 40				16 02				16 40			17 02	17 09			
d	14 41				15 03	15 10			15 41				16 03				16 41			17 03	17 09			
Wombwell d						15 15							16 08								17 14			
Elsecar d						15 19							16 12								17 18			
Chapeltown d						15 24							16 17								17 23			
Meadowhall 29,31 a	14 56				15 15	15 28			15 56				16 20			16 48	16 56			17 17	17 28			
d	14 56		15 02	15 06	15 16	15 29		15 39	15 56	16 02	16 06		16 21		16 40	16 49	16 56	17 02	17 06	17 17	17 29			17 39
Sheffield 7 29,31 a	15 03		15 08	15 13	15 26	15 38		15 48	16 03	16 08	16 13		16 33		16 49	16 56	17 05	17 09	17 14	17 26	17 38			17 48
d	15 06						15 39		16 06					16 43			17 06						17 40	
Dronfield d	15 16								16 16								17 16							
Chesterfield d	15 22						15 53		16 22					16 57			17 22						17 54	
Alfreton d	15 32						16 03		16 32					17 07			17 32						18 05	
Langley Mill d	15 40						16 11		16 40					17 15			17 40						18 12	
Ilkeston d	15 45								16 45								17 45						18 17	
Nottingham a	16 00						16 28		17 00					17 30			18 00						18 34	

	NT	TP	NT	NT	EM	EM	NT		NT	NT	NT	TP	NT	NT	EM	NT	NT		NT	TP	NT	NT	EM	NT
	◇	◇1 A	B		◇ G	◇ H	◇ F			◇ I	B	◇1 A	◇ J		◇ D		◇ E		◇	◇1 A	B		◇ K	◇ F
Leeds 10 31,32 d	17 08								17 47	18 08						18 13			19 08					
Woodlesford 32 d																18 21								
Castleford 32 d																18 42								
Normanton d																18 47								
Wakefield Kirkgate 4 31 a	17 24									18 24						18 52			19 24					
d	17 24									18 25						18 52			19 24					
Darton d																19 06								
Huddersfield d				17 15										18 15								19 15		
Lockwood d				17 18										18 18								19 18		
Berry Brow d				17 21										18 21								19 21		
Honley d				17 24										18 24								19 24		
Brockholes d				17 27										18 27								19 27		
Stocksmoor d				17 31										18 32								19 31		
Shepley d				17 33										18 34								19 33		
Denby Dale d				17 39										18 39								19 38		
Penistone d				17 47										18 47								19 46		
Silkstone Common d				17 52										18 52								19 51		
Dodworth d				17 56										18 56								19 55		
Barnsley a	17 40			18 02						18 41				19 03		19 14			19 40			20 02		
d	17 41			18 03						18 41				19 04		19 14			19 41			20 03		
Wombwell d				18 08												19 19						20 08		
Elsecar d				18 12												19 23						20 12		
Chapeltown d				18 17												19 28						20 17		
Meadowhall 29,31 a	17 56			18 22					18 49	18 55				19 18		19 33			19 56			20 22		
d	17 56	18 02	18 03	18 23			18 40		18 50	18 57	18 59	19 02	19 08	19 20		19 34	19 39		19 56	20 02	20 03	20 23		20 39
Sheffield 7 29,31 a	18 03	18 08	18 10	18 33			18 49		18 57	19 03	19 06	19 08	19 19	19 29		19 43	19 48		20 03	20 08	20 10	20 33		20 48
d	18 06				18 40	18 45				19 06					19 40				20 06				20 40	
Dronfield d	18 16									19 16									20 16					
Chesterfield d	18 22				18 54	18 59				19 22					19 54				20 22				20 54	
Alfreton d	18 32				19 05	19 10				19 32					20 05				20 32				21 05	
Langley Mill d	18 40				19 12	19 17				19 40					20 12				20 40				21 12	
Ilkeston d	18 45									19 45									20 45					
Nottingham a	19 00				19 33	19 38				20 00					20 30				21 00				21 33	

A From Cleethorpes to Manchester Airport
B From Doncaster
C To Lincoln
D From Liverpool Lime Street to Norwich
E From Bridlington
F From Scarborough
G not 5 August, 12 August, 26 August. From Liverpool Lime Street
H 5 August, 12 August, 26 August. From Liverpool Lime Street
I From Carlisle
J From York
K From Liverpool Lime Street

Table T034-R

Leeds and Huddersfield - Barnsley - Sheffield and Nottingham

Sundays
20 May to 2 December

Station			NT	NT ◇	NT A		TP ◇■ B	NT	EM ◇ C	NT ◇ D	NT ◇ E	NT ◇	TP ◇■ F	NT A	NT		NT ◇ G	NT ◇	NT ◇	NT A	EM ◇ C	NT
Leeds 10	31,32	d	19 48	20 08				20 17				21 08						21 48	22 08			22 18
Woodlesford	32	d						20 25														22 26
Castleford	32	d						20 36														22 37
Normanton		d						20 41														22 42
Wakefield Kirkgate 4	31	a		20 24				20 46				21 28							22 24			22 47
		d		20 24				20 46				21 29							22 24			22 47
Darton		d						21 00														22 58
Huddersfield		d																				
Lockwood		d																				
Berry Brow		d																				
Honley		d																				
Brockholes		d																				
Stocksmoor		d																				
Shepley		d																				
Denby Dale		d																				
Penistone		d																				
Silkstone Common		d																				
Dodworth		d																				
Barnsley		a		20 40				21 08				21 45							22 40			23 05
		d		20 41				21 08				21 45			22 19				22 41			23 05
Wombwell		d						21 13							22 24							23 10
Elsecar		d						21 17							22 28							23 14
Chapeltown		d						21 22							22 33							23 19
Meadowhall	29,31 ⇌	a	20 48	20 54				21 27				21 59			22 38			22 48	22 55			23 26
		d	20 49	20 54	20 58		21 02	21 28		21 39	21 55	22 00	22 02	22 06	22 39		22 42	22 49	22 55	23 11		23 26
Sheffield 7	29,31 ⇌	a	20 56	21 02	21 05		21 08	21 37		21 48	22 03	22 07	22 10	22 13	22 49		22 51	22 56	23 03	23 20		23 35
		d		21 06					21 40			22 09									23 30	
Dronfield		d		21 16					21 50			22 19										
Chesterfield		d		21 22					21 56			22 25									23 44	
Alfreton		d		21 32					22 06			22 36									23 55	
Langley Mill		d		21 40					22 14			22 43									00 02	
Ilkeston		d		21 45								22 48										
Nottingham		a		22 00					22 36			23 07									00 23	

A From Doncaster
B From Cleethorpes to Manchester Airport
C From Liverpool Lime Street
D From Bridlington
E From York, via Pontefract Baghill
F From Cleethorpes to Manchester Piccadilly
G From Scarborough

Table T035-F

York - Harrogate - Leeds

Mondays to Fridays
21 May to 7 December

Miles	Station			NT	NT	NT	NT	NT	GR ■ A	NT	NT	NT		NT	NT	NT	NT	NT	NT	NT	NT	NT		NT	NT
0	**York 8**	40	d					06 49						07 56			08 46	09 11		10 11		11 11	and at the same minutes past each hour until		14 11
3	Poppleton		d					06 54						08 01			08 53	09 16		10 16		11 16			14 16
8¾	Hammerton		d					07 02						08 09			09 01	09 24		10 24		11 24			14 24
10¼	Cattal		d					07 05						08 12			09 05	09 27		10 27		11 27			14 27
16¾	**Knaresborough**		a					07 13						08 20			09 13	09 35		10 35		11 35			14 35
—			d				06 55	07 14		07 40		08 09		08 21		08 59	09 13	09 36	10 06	10 36	11 06	11 36		14 06	14 36
18¼	Starbeck		d				06 58	07 17		07 43		08 12		08 25		09 02	09 17	09 39	10 09	10 39	11 09	11 39		14 09	14 39
20½	**Harrogate**		a				07 03	07 22		07 48		08 17		08 29		09 07	09 21	09 44	10 14	10 44	11 14	11 44		14 14	14 44
—			d	06 03	06 32	06 55	07 04	07 23	07 34	07 49	08 04	08 18		08 31		09 08	09 23	09 45	10 15	10 45	11 15	11 45		14 15	14 45
21½	Hornbeam Park		d	06 05	06 34	06 57	07 07	07 26		07 52	08 06	08 21		08 33		09 11	09 25	09 48	10 18	10 48	11 18	11 48		14 18	14 48
23¾	Pannal		d	06 10	06 40	07 02	07 12	07 31		07 57	08 11					09 16	09 31	09 53	10 23	10 53	11 23	11 53		14 23	14 53
27	Weeton		d	06 15	06 45	07 07	07 17	07 36		08 02	08 16					09 21	09 36	09 58	10 28	10 58	11 28	11 58		14 28	14 58
33	Horsforth		d	06 24	06 53	07 16	07 26	07 45	07u52	08 11	08 25	08 36		08 48	09 05	09 30	09 44	10 07	10 37	11 07	11 37	12 07		14 37	15 07
35¾	Headingley		d	06 28	06 58		07 30	07 49			08 29	08 40		08 53	09 09	09 34	09 49	10 11	10 41	11 11	11 41	12 11		14 41	15 11
36½	Burley Park		d	06 31	07 00		07 33	07 52			08 32	08 43		08 55	09 11	09 37	09 51	10 14	10 44	11 14	11 44	12 14		14 44	15 14
38¾	**Leeds 10**	40	a	06 40	07 10	07 28	07 42	08 01	08 03	08 24	08 41	08 52		09 05	09 18	09 46	10 01	10 23	10 53	11 23	11 53	12 24		14 53	15 24

Station			NT	NT	NT	NT	NT	NT	NT	NT	NT		NT	NT	NT	NT	NT	NT	NT	NT
York 8	40	d		15 11		16 11		17 11			17 42		18 11		19 11		20 11	21 11	22 11	22 44
Poppleton		d		15 16		16 16		17 16			17 49		18 16		19 16		20 16	21 16	22 16	22 49
Hammerton		d		15 24		16 24		17 24			17 57		18 24		19 24		20 24	21 24	22 24	22 57
Cattal		d		15 27		16 27		17 27			18 00		18 28		19 27		20 27	21 27	22 27	23 00
Knaresborough		a		15 35		16 35		17 35			18 08		18 36		19 35		20 35	21 35	22 35	23 08
		d	15 06	15 36	16 06	16 36	17 06	17 36			18 09		18 37	19 06	19 36	20 06	20 36	21 36	22 36	23 09
Starbeck		d	15 09	15 39	16 09	16 39	17 09	17 39			18 12		18 40	19 09	19 39	20 09	20 39	21 39	22 39	23 13
Harrogate		a	15 14	15 44	16 14	16 44	17 14	17 44			18 17		18 45	19 14	19 44	20 14	20 44	21 44	22 44	23 17
		d	15 15	15 45	16 15	16 45	17 15	17 45		18 10	18 18		18 46	19 15	19 45	20 15	20 45	21 45	22 45	23 19
Hornbeam Park		d	15 18	15 48	16 18	16 48	17 18	17 48		18 12	18 21		18 49	19 18	19 48	20 18	20 48	21 48	22 48	23 21
Pannal		d	15 23	15 53	16 23	16 53	17 23	17 53		18 17	18 26		18 54	19 23	19 53	20 23	20 53	21 53	22 53	23 27
Weeton		d	15 28	15 58	16 28	16 58	17 28	17 58		18 22	18 31		18 59	19 28	19 58	20 28	20 58	21 58	22 58	23 32
Horsforth		d	15 37	16 07	16 37	17 07	17 37	18 07	18 22	18 30	18 40		19 08	19 37	20 07	20 37	21 07	22 07	23 07	23 40
Headingley		d	15 41	16 11	16 41	17 11		18 11	18 26	18 34			19 12	19 41	20 11	20 41	21 11	22 11	23 11	23 45
Burley Park		d	15 44	16 14	16 44	17 14		18 14	18 29	18 37			19 15	19 44	20 14	20 44	21 14	22 14	23 14	23 47
Leeds 10	40	a	15 53	16 23	16 53	17 23	17 50	18 23	18 35	18 44	18 53		19 24	19 53	20 24	20 54	21 24	22 24	23 23	23 56

Saturdays
26 May to 8 December

Station			NT	NT	NT	NT	NT	GR ■ A	NT	NT	NT		NT	NT	NT	NT	NT	NT	NT	NT	NT		NT	NT
York 8	40	d					06 49						07 56			08 46	09 11		10 11		11 11	and at the same minutes past each hour until		14 11
Poppleton		d					06 54						08 01			08 53	09 16		10 16		11 16			14 16
Hammerton		d					07 02						08 09			09 01	09 24		10 24		11 24			14 24
Cattal		d					07 05						08 12			09 05	09 27		10 27		11 27			14 27
Knaresborough		a					07 13						08 20			09 13	09 35		10 35		11 35			14 35
		d				06 55	07 14		07 40		08 09		08 21		08 59	09 13	09 36	10 06	10 36	11 06	11 36		14 06	14 36
Starbeck		d				06 58	07 17		07 43		08 12		08 25		09 02	09 17	09 39	10 09	10 39	11 09	11 39		14 09	14 39
Harrogate		a				07 03	07 22		07 48		08 17		08 29		09 07	09 21	09 44	10 14	10 44	11 14	11 44		14 14	14 44
		d	06 03	06 32	06 55	07 04	07 23	07 35	07 49	08 04	08 18		08 31		09 08	09 23	09 45	10 15	10 45	11 15	11 45		14 15	14 45
Hornbeam Park		d	06 05	06 34	06 57	07 07	07 26		07 52	08 06	08 21		08 33		09 11	09 25	09 48	10 18	10 48	11 18	11 48		14 18	14 48
Pannal		d	06 10	06 40	07 02	07 12	07 31		07 57	08 11					09 16	09 31	09 53	10 23	10 53	11 23	11 53		14 23	14 53
Weeton		d	06 15	06 45	07 07	07 17	07 36		08 02	08 16					09 21	09 36	09 58	10 28	10 58	11 28	11 58		14 28	14 58
Horsforth		d	06 24	06 53	07 16	07 26	07 45	07u54	08 11	08 25	08 36		08 48	09 05	09 30	09 44	10 07	10 37	11 07	11 37	12 07		14 37	15 07
Headingley		d	06 28	06 58		07 30	07 49			08 29	08 40		08 53	09 09	09 34	09 49	10 11	10 41	11 11	11 41	12 11		14 41	15 11
Burley Park		d	06 31	07 00		07 33	07 52			08 32	08 43		08 55	09 11	09 37	09 51	10 14	10 44	11 14	11 44	12 14		14 44	15 14
Leeds 10	40	a	06 40	07 10	07 28	07 42	08 01	08 07	08 24	08 41	08 52		09 05	09 18	09 46	10 01	10 23	10 53	11 23	11 53	12 24		14 53	15 24

Station			NT	NT	NT	NT	NT	NT	NT	NT	NT		NT	NT	NT	NT	NT	NT	NT	NT
York 8	40	d		15 11		16 11		17 11			17 42		18 11		19 11		20 11	21 11	22 11	22 44
Poppleton		d		15 16		16 16		17 16			17 49		18 16		19 16		20 16	21 16	22 16	22 49
Hammerton		d		15 24		16 24		17 24			17 57		18 24		19 24		20 24	21 24	22 24	22 57
Cattal		d		15 27		16 27		17 27			18 00		18 28		19 27		20 27	21 27	22 27	23 00
Knaresborough		a		15 35		16 35		17 35			18 08		18 36		19 35		20 35	21 35	22 35	23 08
		d	15 06	15 36	16 06	16 36	17 06	17 36			18 09		18 37	19 06	19 36	20 06	20 36	21 36	22 36	23 09
Starbeck		d	15 09	15 39	16 09	16 39	17 09	17 39			18 12		18 40	19 09	19 39	20 09	20 39	21 39	22 39	23 13
Harrogate		a	15 14	15 44	16 14	16 44	17 14	17 44			18 17		18 45	19 14	19 44	20 14	20 44	21 44	22 44	23 17
		d	15 15	15 45	16 15	16 45	17 15	17 45		18 10	18 18		18 46	19 15	19 45	20 15	20 45	21 45	22 45	23 19
Hornbeam Park		d	15 18	15 48	16 18	16 48	17 18	17 48		18 12	18 21		18 49	19 18	19 48	20 18	20 48	21 48	22 48	23 21
Pannal		d	15 23	15 53	16 23	16 53	17 23	17 53		18 17	18 26		18 54	19 23	19 53	20 23	20 53	21 53	22 53	23 27
Weeton		d	15 28	15 58	16 28	16 58	17 28	17 58		18 22	18 31		18 59	19 28	19 58	20 28	20 58	21 58	22 58	23 32
Horsforth		d	15 37	16 07	16 37	17 07	17 37	18 07	18 22	18 30	18 40		19 08	19 37	20 07	20 37	21 07	22 07	23 07	23 40
Headingley		d	15 41	16 11	16 41	17 11		18 11	18 26	18 34			19 12	19 41	20 11	20 41	21 11	22 11	23 11	23 45
Burley Park		d	15 44	16 14	16 44	17 14		18 14	18 29	18 37			19 15	19 44	20 14	20 44	21 14	22 14	23 14	23 47
Leeds 10	40	a	15 53	16 23	16 53	17 23	17 50	18 23	18 35	18 44	18 53		19 24	19 53	20 24	20 54	21 24	22 24	23 23	23 56

A To London Kings Cross

Table T035-F

Sundays

20 May to 2 December

York - Harrogate - Leeds

		NT	NT	NT	NT	NT		NT	NT	NT	NT	NT	NT
York 8	40 d					10 47			11 47		12 47		13 47
Poppleton	d					10 52			11 52		12 52		13 52
Hammerton	d					11 00			12 00		13 00		14 00
Cattal	d					11 03			12 03		13 03		14 03
Knaresborough	a					11 11			12 11		13 11		14 11
	d				10 42	11 12		11 42	12 12	12 42	13 12	13 42	14 12
Starbeck	d				10 45	11 15		11 45	12 15	12 45	13 16	13 45	14 15
Harrogate	a				10 50	11 20		11 50	12 20	12 50	13 20	13 50	14 20
	d	09 22	09 52	10 22	10 51	11 21		11 51	12 21	12 51	13 22	13 51	14 21
Hornbeam Park	d	09 24	09 54	10 24	10 54	11 24		11 54	12 24	12 54	13 24	13 54	14 24
Pannal	d	09 30	10 00	10 30	10 59	11 29		11 59	12 29	12 59	13 30	13 59	14 29
Weeton	d	09 35	10 05	10 35	11 04	11 34		12 04	12 34	13 04	13 35	14 04	14 34
Horsforth	d	09 43	10 13	10 43	11 13	11 43		12 13	12 43	13 13	13 43	14 13	14 43
Headingley	d	09 48	10 18	10 48	11 17	11 47		12 17	12 47	13 17	13 48	14 17	14 47
Burley Park	d	09 50	10 20	10 50	11 21	11 50		12 20	12 50	13 20	13 50	14 20	14 50
Leeds 10	40 a	10 00	10 30	11 00	11 30	12 00		12 29	13 00	13 29	14 00	14 29	15 00

		NT	NT	NT		NT	NT	GR ■ 1 A ☕	NT	NT	NT	NT	NT
York 8	40 d		14 47			15 47			16 47		17 47		18 47
Poppleton	d		14 52			15 52			16 52		17 52		18 52
Hammerton	d		15 00			16 00			17 00		18 00		19 00
Cattal	d		15 03			16 03			17 03		18 03		19 03
Knaresborough	a		15 11			16 12			17 11		18 11		19 12
	d	14 42	15 12	15 42		16 12	16 42		17 12	17 42	18 12	18 42	19 12
Starbeck	d	14 45	15 15	15 45		16 16	16 45		17 15	17 45	18 15	18 45	19 15
Harrogate	a	14 50	15 20	15 50		16 20	16 50		17 20	17 50	18 20	18 50	19 20
	d	14 51	15 21	15 51		16 22	16 51	17 07	17 21	17 51	18 21	18 51	19 21
Hornbeam Park	d	14 54	15 24	15 54		16 24	16 54		17 24	17 54	18 24	18 54	19 24
Pannal	d	14 59	15 29	15 59		16 30	16 59		17 29	17 59	18 29	18 59	19 29
Weeton	d	15 04	15 34	16 04		16 35	17 04		17 34	18 04	18 34	19 04	19 34
Horsforth	d	15 13	15 43	16 13		16 43	17 13		17 43	18 13	18 43	19 13	19 43
Headingley	d	15 17	15 47	16 17		16 48	17 17		17 47	18 17	18 47	19 17	19 47
Burley Park	d	15 20	15 50	16 20		16 50	17 20		17 50	18 20	18 50	19 20	19 50
Leeds 10	40 a	15 29	16 00	16 29		17 00	17 29	17 33	18 00	18 29	19 00	19 29	20 00

		NT		NT	NT	NT	NT	NT
York 8	40 d			19 46		20 47	21 42	
Poppleton	d			19 52		20 52	21 47	
Hammerton	d			20 00		21 00	21 55	
Cattal	d			20 03		21 03	22 02	
Knaresborough	a			20 11		21 11	22 10	
	d	19 42		20 12	20 42	21 12	22 11	
Starbeck	d	19 45		20 15	20 45	21 15	22 14	
Harrogate	a	19 50		20 20	20 50	21 20	22 19	
	d	19 51		20 21	20 51	21 21	22 20	23 12
Hornbeam Park	d	19 54		20 24	20 54	21 24	22 23	23 15
Pannal	d	19 59		20 29	20 59	21 29	22 28	23 20
Weeton	d	20 04		20 34	21 04	21 34	22 33	23 25
Horsforth	d	20 13		20 43	21 13	21 43	22 42	23 34
Headingley	d	20 17		20 47	21 17	21 47	22 46	23 38
Burley Park	d	20 20		20 50	21 20	21 50	22 49	23 42
Leeds 10	40 a	20 29		21 00	21 29	21 59	22 59	23 51

A To London Kings Cross

Table T035-R

Mondays to Fridays

21 May to 7 December

Leeds - Harrogate - York

Miles			NT MX A	NT B	NT	NT	NT	NT	NT		NT	NT	NT
0	**Leeds** 10	40 d		06 02	06 23	06 33	07 00	07 15	07 45		08 09	08 29	08 45
2¼	Burley Park	d		06 07		06 38	07 05	07 20	07 50		08 14	08 34	08 49
3	Headingley	d		06 10		06 41	07 08	07 23	07 53		08 17	08 37	08 52
5¾	Horsforth	d		06 15	06 33	06 47	07 13	07 28	07 58		08 22	08 42	08a58
11¾	Weeton	d		06 23		06 55	07 21	07 36	08 06			08 50	
15	Pannal	d	00 05	06 29		07 01	07 27	07 42	08 12			08 56	
17¼	Hornbeam Park	d	00 10	06 35		07 06	07 32	07 47	08 17		08 37	09 01	
18¼	**Harrogate**	a	00 16	06 38	06 51	07 09	07 38	07 50	08 20		08 40	09 04	
—		d		06 39		07 10	07 40	07 52	08 22		08 41	09 07	
20½	Starbeck	d		06 44		07 15	07 44	07 56	08 26		08 46	09 11	
22	**Knaresborough**	a		06 48		07 19	07 51	08 01	08 31		08 53	09 16	
—		d		06 49		07 20		08 01	08 31			09 16	
28½	Cattal	d		07 00		07 28		08 09	08 39			09 24	
30	Hammerton	d		07 05		07 32		08 13	08 43			09 28	
35¾	Poppleton	d		07 12		07 39		08 21	08 51			09 36	
38¾	**York** 8	40 a		07 19		07 48		08 30	09 01			09 46	

Miles			NT	NT		NT	NT	NT		NT	NT	NT	NT
0	**Leeds** 10	40 d	08 59	09 29	and at the same minutes past each hour until	14 59	15 29	15 59		16 29	16 45	16 59	17 09
2¼	Burley Park	d	09 04	09 34		15 04	15 34	16 04		16 34	16 50	17 04	17 14
3	Headingley	d	09 07	09 37		15 07	15 37	16 07		16 37	16 53	17 07	17 17
5¾	Horsforth	d	09 12	09 42		15 12	15 42	16 12		16 42	16a59	17 12	17 22
11¾	Weeton	d	09 20	09 50		15 20	15 50	16 20		16 50		17 20	17 30
15	Pannal	d	09 26	09 56		15 26	15 56	16 26		16 56		17 26	17 36
17¼	Hornbeam Park	d	09 31	10 01		15 31	16 01	16 31		17 01		17 31	17 41
18¼	**Harrogate**	a	09 34	10 04		15 34	16 04	16 34		17 04		17 34	17 46
—		d	09 36	10 06		15 36	16 06	16 36		17 06		17 36	17 48
20½	Starbeck	d	09 40	10 10		15 40	16 10	16 40		17 10		17 40	17 52
22	**Knaresborough**	a	09 47	10 15		15 47	16 15	16 47		17 15		17 47	17 56
—		d		10 15			16 15			17 15			
28½	Cattal	d		10 23			16 23			17 23			
30	Hammerton	d		10 27			16 27			17 27			
35¾	Poppleton	d		10 35			16 35			17 35			
38¾	**York** 8	40 a		10 46			16 46			17 47			

		NT	NT	NT	NT	NT		NT	NT	NT	GR ■ 1 C ☕	NT	NT	NT	NT
Leeds 10	40 d	17 29	17 39	17 53	17 59	18 09		18 29	18 59	19 29	19 59	20 30	21 29	22 39	23 39
Burley Park	d	17 34	17 44	17 58	18 03	18 14		18 34	19 04	19 34		20 35	21 34	22 44	23 44
Headingley	d	17 37	17 47	18 01	18 07	18 17		18 37	19 07	19 37		20 38	21 37	22 47	23 46
Horsforth	d	17 42	17 52	18 06	18a13	18 22		18 42	19 12	19 42		20 43	21 42	22 52	23 52
Weeton	d	17 50	18 00	18 14		18 30		18 50	19 20	19 50		20 51	21 50	23 00	23 59
Pannal	d	17 56	18 06	18 20		18 36		18 56	19 26	19 56		20 57	21 56	23 06	00 05
Hornbeam Park	d	18 01	18 11	18 25		18 41		19 01	19 31	20 01		21 02	22 01	23 11	00 10
Harrogate	a	18 04	18 14	18 28		18 44		19 04	19 34	20 04	20 23	21 05	22 04	23 17	00 16
	d	18 06	18 16	18 30		18 46		19 06	19 36	20 06		21 07	22 06		
Starbeck	d	18 10	18 20	18 34		18 50		19 10	19 40	20 10		21 11	22 10		
Knaresborough	a	18 15	18 27	18 39		18 57		19 15	19 47	20 15		21 16	22 15		
	d	18 15		18 39				19 15		20 15		21 16	22 15		
Cattal	d	18 23		18 47				19 23		20 23		21 24	22 23		
Hammerton	d	18 27		18 51				19 27		20 27		21 28	22 27		
Poppleton	d	18 35		18 58				19 35		20 35		21 36	22 35		
York 8	40 a	18 46		19 06				19 46		20 47		21 46	22 47		

Saturdays

26 May to 8 December

		NT A	NT B	NT	NT	NT	NT	NT	NT	NT		NT
Leeds 10	40 d		06 02	06 23	06 33	07 00	07 15	07 45	08 09	08 29		08 45
Burley Park	d		06 07		06 38	07 05	07 20	07 50	08 14	08 34		08 49
Headingley	d		06 10		06 41	07 08	07 23	07 53	08 17	08 37		08 52
Horsforth	d		06 15	06 33	06 47	07 13	07 28	07 58	08 22	08 42		08a58
Weeton	d		06 23		06 55	07 21	07 36	08 06		08 50		
Pannal	d	00 05	06 29		07 01	07 27	07 42	08 12		08 56		
Hornbeam Park	d	00 10	06 35		07 06	07 32	07 47	08 17	08 37	09 01		
Harrogate	a	00 16	06 38	06 51	07 09	07 38	07 50	08 20	08 40	09 04		
	d		06 39		07 10	07 40	07 52	08 22	08 41	09 07		
Starbeck	d		06 44		07 15	07 44	07 56	08 26	08 46	09 11		
Knaresborough	a		06 48		07 19	07 51	08 01	08 31	08 53	09 16		
	d		06 49		07 20		08 01	08 31		09 16		
Cattal	d		07 00		07 28		08 09	08 39		09 24		
Hammerton	d		07 05		07 32		08 13	08 43		09 28		
Poppleton	d		07 12		07 39		08 21	08 51		09 36		
York 8	40 a		07 19		07 48		08 30	09 01		09 46		

		NT	NT		NT	NT	NT	NT	NT		NT	NT	NT
Leeds 10	40 d	08 59	09 29	and at the same minutes past each hour until	14 59	15 29	15 59	16 29	16 45		16 59	17 09	17 29
Burley Park	d	09 04	09 34		15 04	15 34	16 04	16 34	16 50		17 04	17 14	17 34
Headingley	d	09 07	09 37		15 07	15 37	16 07	16 37	16 53		17 07	17 17	17 37
Horsforth	d	09 12	09 42		15 12	15 42	16 12	16 42	16a59		17 12	17 22	17 42
Weeton	d	09 20	09 50		15 20	15 50	16 20	16 50			17 20	17 30	17 50
Pannal	d	09 26	09 56		15 26	15 56	16 26	16 56			17 26	17 36	17 56
Hornbeam Park	d	09 31	10 01		15 31	16 01	16 31	17 01			17 31	17 41	18 01
Harrogate	a	09 34	10 04		15 34	16 04	16 34	17 04			17 34	17 46	18 04
	d	09 36	10 06		15 36	16 06	16 36	17 06			17 36	17 48	18 06
Starbeck	d	09 40	10 10		15 40	16 10	16 40	17 10			17 40	17 52	18 10
Knaresborough	a	09 47	10 15		15 47	16 15	16 47	17 15			17 47	17 56	18 15
	d		10 15			16 15		17 15					18 15
Cattal	d		10 23			16 23		17 23					18 23
Hammerton	d		10 27			16 27		17 27					18 27
Poppleton	d		10 35			16 35		17 35					18 35
York 8	40 a		10 46			16 46		17 47					18 46

		NT	NT	NT	NT	NT	NT		NT	NT	GR ■ 1 C ☕	NT	NT	NT
Leeds 10	40 d	17 39	17 53	17 59	18 09	18 29	18 59		19 29	20 30	21 01	21 29	22 39	23 39
Burley Park	d	17 44	17 58	18 03	18 14	18 34	19 04		19 34	20 35		21 34	22 44	23 44
Headingley	d	17 47	18 01	18 07	18 17	18 37	19 07		19 37	20 38		21 37	22 47	23 46
Horsforth	d	17 52	18 06	18a13	18 22	18 42	19 12		19 42	20 43		21 42	22 52	23 52
Weeton	d	18 00	18 14		18 30	18 50	19 20		19 50	20 51		21 50	23 00	23 59
Pannal	d	18 06	18 20		18 36	18 56	19 26		19 56	20 57		21 56	23 06	00 05
Hornbeam Park	d	18 11	18 25		18 41	19 01	19 31		20 01	21 02		22 01	23 11	00 10
Harrogate	a	18 14	18 28		18 44	19 04	19 34		20 04	21 05	21 26	22 04	23 17	00 16
	d	18 16	18 30		18 46	19 06	19 36		20 06	21 07		22 06		
Starbeck	d	18 20	18 34		18 50	19 10	19 40		20 10	21 11		22 10		
Knaresborough	a	18 27	18 39		18 57	19 15	19 47		20 15	21 16		22 15		
	d		18 39			19 15			20 15	21 16		22 15		
Cattal	d		18 47			19 23			20 23	21 24		22 23		
Hammerton	d		18 51			19 27			20 27	21 28		22 27		
Poppleton	d		18 58			19 35			20 35	21 36		22 35		
York 8	40 a		19 06			19 46			20 47	21 46		22 47		

A From Leeds B To Hull C From London Kings Cross

Table T035-R

Sundays

20 May to 2 December

Leeds - Harrogate - York

	NT	NT	NT	NT	NT		NT	NT		NT	NT	NT	NT	NT	NT	NT	NT	GR		NT	NT	NT
	A																	■ 1 B ⚿				
Leeds 10 40 d		09 02	10 05	10 36	11 05	and at the same minutes past each hour until	15 36	16 05		16 36	17 05	17 36	18 05	18 36	19 05	19 35	20 05	20 31		21 31	22 26	23 15
Burley Park d		09 07	10 10	10 41	11 10		15 41	16 10		16 41	17 10	17 41	18 10	18 41	19 10	19 41	20 10			21 36	22 31	23 20
Headingley d		09 10	10 13	10 44	11 13		15 44	16 13		16 44	17 13	17 44	18 13	18 44	19 13	19 44	20 13			21 39	22 34	23 23
Horsforth d		09 15	10 18	10 49	11 18		15 49	16 18		16 50	17 18	17 49	18 18	18 49	19 18	19 49	20 18			21 44	22 39	23 28
Weeton d		09 23	10 26	10 57	11 26		15 57	16 26		16 58	17 26	17 57	18 26	18 57	19 26	19 57	20 26			21 52	22 47	23 36
Pannal d	00 05	09 29	10 32	11 03	11 32		16 03	16 32		17 04	17 32	18 03	18 32	19 03	19 32	20 03	20 32			21 58	22 53	23 42
Hornbeam Park d	00 10	09 35	10 38	11 09	11 38		16 09	16 38		17 09	17 38	18 09	18 38	19 09	19 38	20 09	20 38			22 04	22 59	23 48
Harrogate a	00 16	09 38	10 41	11 12	11 41		16 12	16 41		17 12	17 41	18 12	18 41	19 12	19 41	20 12	20 41	20 55		22 07	23 05	23 54
d		09 42	10 42	11 13	11 42		16 13	16 42		17 14	17 42	18 13	18 42	19 13	19 42	20 13	20 42			22 08		
Starbeck d		09 47	10 47	11 18	11 47		16 18	16 47		17 18	17 47	18 18	18 47	19 18	19 47	20 18	20 47			22 13		
Knaresborough a		09 51	10 51	11 24	11 51		16 24	16 51		17 25	17 51	18 24	18 51	19 24	19 51	20 24	20 51			22 19		
d		09 52	10 52		11 52			16 52			17 52		18 52		19 52		20 52					
Cattal d		10 00	11 00		12 00			17 00			18 00		19 00		20 00		21 00					
Hammerton d		10 04	11 04		12 04			17 04			18 04		19 04		20 04		21 04					
Poppleton d		10 11	11 12		12 11			17 11			18 11		19 15		20 11		21 11					
York 8 40 a		10 20	11 20		12 20			17 20			18 20		19 25		20 20		21 20					

A From Leeds

B From London Kings Cross

Table T036-F

Mondays to Fridays

21 May to 7 December

Leeds and Bradford - Skipton

Miles	Miles		NT	NT	NT	NT	NT	NT	NT	NT	NT		NT	NT	NT	NT	NT	NT	NT	NT	NT		NT	NT
			◇ A ⚲								◇ A ⚲				◇ B					◇ A ⚲				
0	—	**Leeds** 10 37 d	05 17		06 26		06 56		07 23		07 48		07 52		08 19	08 26		08 56		09 19	09 26			09 54
4¼	—	Kirkstall Forge d																						
7¾	—	Apperley Bridge d																						
—	0	**Bradford Forster Square** 37 d		06 03		06 41		07 11		07 41				08 11			08 41		09 11				09 41	
—	1¾	Frizinghall 37 d		06 06		06 44		07 14		07 44				08 14			08 44		09 14				09 44	
10¾	2¾	Shipley 37 a	05 29	06 10	06 42	06 48	07 09	07 18	07 36	07 48	08 01		08 07	08 18	08 31	08 37	08 49	09 07	09 18	09 31	09 37		09 48	10 07
—	—	d	05 30	06 11	06 42	06 49	07 10	07 19	07 37	07 49	08 02		08 08	08 19	08 32	08 38	08 49	09 08	09 19	09 32	09 38		09 49	10 08
11½	—	Saltaire d	05 32	06 13	06 45	06 52	07 12	07 22	07 39	07 52			08 10	08 22		08 40	08 52	09 10	09 22		09 40		09 52	10 10
13¾	—	Bingley d	05 37	06 17	06 49	06 56	07 15	07 26	07 43	07 56	08 06		08 14	08 26	08 37	08 44	08 56	09 14	09 26	09 37	09 44		09 56	10 14
14½	—	Crossflatts d	05 39	06 19	06 51	06 58	07 17	07 28	07 46	07 58			08 17	08 28		08 47	08 59	09 17	09 28		09 47		09 58	10 17
17	—	Keighley d	05 44	06 24	06 56	07 03	07 22	07 33	07 50	08 03	08 12		08 21	08 33	08 42	08 51	09 03	09 21	09 33	09 42	09 51		10 03	10 21
20	—	Steeton & Silsden d	05 48	06 28	07 00	07 07	07 26	07 37	07 55	08 07			08 26	08 37		08 56	09 08	09 26	09 37		09 56		10 07	10 26
23¼	—	Cononley d	05 53	06 32	07 05	07 12	07 30	07 42	07 59	08 12			08 30	08 42		09 00	09 12	09 30	09 42		10 00		10 12	10 30
26¼	—	**Skipton** a	06 00	06 41	07 12	07 20	07 39	07 50	08 08	08 20	08 24		08 39	08 50	08 55	09 09	09 21	09 39	09 51	09 57	10 09		10 20	10 39

	NT	NT	NT	NT	NT	NT	NT		NT	NT	NT	NT	NT	NT	NT	NT	NT		NT	NT	NT	NT	NT	NT
		◇ C			◇ A ⚲								◇ B						◇ A ⚲					◇ C
Leeds 10 37 d		10 18	10 26		10 49	10 54			11 26		11 56		12 20	12 26		12 56			13 18	13 26		13 56		14 18
Kirkstall Forge d																								
Apperley Bridge d																								
Bradford Forster Square 37 d	10 11			10 41			11 11			11 41		12 11			12 41		13 11				13 41		14 11	
Frizinghall 37 d	10 14			10 44			11 14			11 44		12 14			12 44		13 14				13 44		14 14	
Shipley 37 a	10 18	10 32	10 37	10 48	11 01	11 07	11 18		11 37	11 48	12 08	12 18	12 32	12 37	12 48	13 07	13 18		13 32	13 37	13 48	14 08	14 18	14 32
d	10 19	10 33	10 38	10 49	11 03	11 08	11 19		11 38	11 49	12 08	12 19	12 33	12 38	12 49	13 08	13 19		13 33	13 38	13 49	14 08	14 19	14 33
Saltaire d	10 22		10 40	10 52		11 10	11 22		11 40	11 52	12 11	12 22		12 40	12 52	13 10	13 22			13 40	13 52	14 11	14 22	
Bingley d	10 26	10 37	10 44	10 56	11 07	11 14	11 26		11 44	11 56	12 15	12 26	12 37	12 44	12 56	13 14	13 26		13 37	13 44	13 56	14 15	14 26	14 38
Crossflatts d	10 28		10 47	10 58		11 17	11 28		11 47	11 58	12 17	12 28		12 47	12 58	13 17	13 28			13 47	13 58	14 17	14 28	
Keighley d	10 33	10 43	10 51	11 03	11 13	11 21	11 33		11 51	12 03	12 22	12 33	12 43	12 51	13 03	13 21	13 33		13 43	13 51	14 03	14 22	14 33	14 43
Steeton & Silsden d	10 37		10 56	11 07		11 26	11 37		11 56	12 07	12 26	12 37		12 56	13 07	13 26	13 37			13 56	14 07	14 26	14 37	
Cononley d	10 42		11 00	11 12		11 30	11 42		12 00	12 12	12 31	12 42		13 00	13 12	13 30	13 42			14 00	14 12	14 31	14 42	
Skipton a	10 50	10 55	11 09	11 20	11 25	11 39	11 50		12 09	12 21	12 39	12 51	12 56	13 09	13 20	13 39	13 50		13 55	14 09	14 21	14 39	14 51	14 57

	NT	NT	NT		NT	NT	NT	NT	NT	NT	NT	NT	NT		NT	NT	NT	NT	NT	NT	NT	NT	NT	
						◇ A ⚲							◇ A ⚲					◇ C					◇ A ⚲	
Leeds 10 37 d	14 26		14 56			15 18	15 26		15 56		16 26		16 49		16 56		17 18	17 25		17 41	17 56		18 19	
Kirkstall Forge d																	17 25			17 48				
Apperley Bridge d																								
Bradford Forster Square 37 d		14 41			15 11			15 41		16 11		16 41				17 11			17 41			18 11		
Frizinghall 37 d		14 44			15 14			15 44		16 14		16 44				17 14			17 44			18 14		
Shipley 37 a	14 37	14 48	15 08		15 18	15 32	15 37	15 48	16 08	16 18	16 37	16 48	17 01		17 07	17 18	17 32	17 37	17 48	17 55	18 07	18 18	18 31	
d	14 38	14 49	15 08		15 19	15 33	15 38	15 49	16 08	16 19	16 38	16 49	17 02		17 08	17 19	17 33	17 39	17 49	17 56	18 08	18 19	18 32	
Saltaire d	14 40	14 52	15 11		15 22		15 40	15 52	16 11	16 22	16 40	16 52			17 10	17 22	17 35		17 52	17 58	18 10	18 22		
Bingley d	14 44	14 56	15 15		15 26	15 37	15 44	15 56	16 15	16 26	16 44	16 56	17 07		17 14	17 26	17 39	17 45	17 56	18 02	18 14	18 26	18 36	
Crossflatts d	14 47	14 58	15 17		15 28		15 47	15 58	16 17	16 28	16 47	16 58			17 17	17 28	17 42		17 58	18 05	18 17	18 28		
Keighley d	14 51	15 03	15 22		15 33	15 43	15 51	16 03	16 22	16 33	16 51	17 03	17 13		17 21	17 33	17 46	17 52	18 03	18 09	18 21	18 33	18 42	
Steeton & Silsden d	14 56	15 07	15 26		15 37	15 47	15 56	16 07	16 26	16 37	16 56	17 07			17 26	17 37	17 51	17 56	18 07	18 14	18 26	18 37		
Cononley d	15 00	15 12	15 31		15 42	15 52	16 00	16 12	16 31	16 42	17 00	17 12			17 30	17 42	17 55		18 12	18 18	18 30	18 42		
Skipton a	15 09	15 20	15 39		15 50	15 59	16 09	16 20	16 39	16 50	17 09	17 20	17 25		17 39	17 50	18 04	18 07	18 20	18 27	18 39	18 50	18 54	

	NT	NT	NT	NT	NT	NT	NT	NT	NT		NT	NT	GR	NT	NT	NT	NT	NT	NT		NT	NT	NT	NT
					◇ B			◇ D ⚲					■ 1 E ⚿											
Leeds 10 37 d	18 26		18 56		19 18	19 26		19 49	19 56			20 26	20 39		20 56		21 26	21 56			22 26	22 56		23 20
Kirkstall Forge d						19 33			20 03			20 33					21 33				22 33			23 27
Apperley Bridge d						19 37			20 07			20 37			21 04		21 37				22 37			23 31
Bradford Forster Square 37 d		18 41		19 11			19 41				20 11			20 48		21 11			22 11				23 11	
Frizinghall 37 d		18 44		19 14			19 44				20 14			20 51		21 14			22 14				23 14	
Shipley 37 a	18 37	18 48	19 07	19 18	19 31	19 42	19 48	20 01	20 12		20 18	20 42		20 55	21 09	21 18	21 42	22 07	22 18		22 42	23 07	23 18	23 36
d	18 38	18 49	19 09	19 19	19 32	19 42	19 49	20 02	20 12		20 19	20 42		20 56	21 09	21 19	21 42	22 08	22 19		22 42	23 08	23 19	23 36
Saltaire d	18 40	18 52	19 12	19 22		19 45	19 52		20 15		20 22	20 45		20 59	21 12	21 22	21 45	22 10	22 22		22 45	23 10	23 22	23 38
Bingley d	18 44	18 56	19 16	19 26	19 37	19 49	19 56	20 07	20 19		20 26	20 49		21 03	21 16	21 26	21 49	22 14	22 26		22 49	23 14	23 26	23 42
Crossflatts d	18 47	18 58	19 18	19 28		19 51	19 58		20 21		20 28	20 51		21 05	21 18	21 28	21 51	22 17	22 28		22 51	23 17	23 28	23 44
Keighley d	18 51	19 03	19 23	19 33	19 43	19 56	20 03	20 12	20 26		20 33	20 56	21s01	21 10	21 23	21 33	21 56	22 21	22 33		22 56	23 21	23 33	23 49
Steeton & Silsden d	18 56	19 07	19 27	19 37		20 00	20 07		20 30		20 37	21 00		21 14	21 27	21 37	22 00	22 26	22 37		23 00	23 26	23 37	23 53
Cononley d	19 00	19 12	19 32	19 42		20 05	20 12		20 35		20 42	21 05		21 19	21 32	21 42	22 05	22 30	22 42		23 05	23 30	23 42	23 57
Skipton a	19 09	19 20	19 40	19 50	19 57	20 13	20 20	20 26	20 43		20 50	21 13	21 17	21 27	21 40	21 50	22 13	22 39	22 50		23 13	23 39	23 50	00 05

A To Carlisle

B To Lancaster

C To Morecambe

D To Ribblehead

E From London Kings Cross

Table T036-F

Leeds and Bradford - Skipton

Saturdays
26 May to 8 December

			NT	NT	NT	NT	NT	NT	NT	NT	NT	NT	NT	NT	NT	NT	NT	NT	NT	NT	NT	NT	NT	NT
				◇ A							◇ A			◇ B					◇ A					◇ C
Leeds	37	d		06 20	06 26		06 56		07 23		07 48	07 52		08 19	08 26		08 56		09 19	09 26		09 54		10 18
Kirkstall Forge		d																						
Apperley Bridge		d																						
Bradford Forster Square	37	d	06 03			06 41		07 11		07 41			08 11			08 41		09 11			09 41		10 11	
Frizinghall	37	d	06 06			06 44		07 14		07 44			08 14			08 44		09 14			09 44		10 14	
Shipley	37	a	06 10	06 32	06 42	06 48	07 09	07 18	07 36	07 48	08 01	08 07	08 18	08 31	08 37	08 49	09 07	09 18	09 31	09 37	09 48	10 07	10 18	10 32
		d	06 11	06 33	06 42	06 49	07 10	07 19	07 37	07 49	08 02	08 08	08 19	08 32	08 38	08 49	09 08	09 19	09 32	09 38	09 49	10 08	10 19	10 33
Saltaire		d	06 13	06 35	06 45	06 52	07 12	07 22	07 39	07 52		08 10	08 22		08 40	08 52	09 10	09 22		09 40	09 52	10 10	10 22	
Bingley		d	06 17	06 40	06 49	06 56	07 15	07 26	07 43	07 56	08 06	08 14	08 26	08 37	08 44	08 56	09 14	09 26	09 37	09 44	09 56	10 14	10 26	10 37
Crossflatts		d	06 19	06 42	06 51	06 58	07 17	07 28	07 46	07 58		08 17	08 28		08 47	08 59	09 17	09 28		09 47	09 58	10 17	10 28	
Keighley		d	06 24	06 47	06 56	07 03	07 22	07 33	07 50	08 03	08 12	08 21	08 33	08 42	08 51	09 03	09 21	09 33	09 42	09 51	10 03	10 21	10 33	10 43
Steeton & Silsden		d	06 28	06 51	07 00	07 07	07 26	07 37	07 55	08 07		08 26	08 37		08 56	09 08	09 26	09 37		09 56	10 07	10 26	10 37	
Cononley		d	06 32	06 56	07 05	07 12	07 30	07 42	07 59	08 12		08 30	08 42		09 00	09 12	09 30	09 42		10 00	10 12	10 30	10 42	
Skipton		a	06 41	07 03	07 12	07 20	07 39	07 50	08 08	08 20	08 24	08 39	08 50	08 55	09 09	09 21	09 39	09 51	09 57	10 09	10 20	10 39	10 50	10 55

			NT	NT	NT	NT	NT	NT	NT	NT	NT	NT	NT	NT	NT	NT	NT	NT	NT	NT	NT	NT	NT
					◇ A							◇ B					◇ A					◇ C	
Leeds	37	d	10 26		10 49	10 54		11 26		11 56		12 20	12 26		12 56		13 18	13 26		13 56		14 18	14 26
Kirkstall Forge		d																					
Apperley Bridge		d																					
Bradford Forster Square	37	d		10 41			11 11		11 41		12 11			12 41		13 11			13 41		14 11		
Frizinghall	37	d		10 44			11 14		11 44		12 14			12 44		13 14			13 44		14 14		
Shipley	37	a	10 37	10 48	11 01	11 07	11 18	11 37	11 48	12 08	12 18	12 32	12 37	12 48	13 07	13 18	13 32	13 37	13 48	14 08	14 18	14 32	14 37
		d	10 38	10 49	11 03	11 08	11 19	11 38	11 49	12 08	12 19	12 33	12 38	12 49	13 08	13 19	13 33	13 38	13 49	14 08	14 19	14 33	14 38
Saltaire		d	10 40	10 52		11 10	11 22	11 40	11 52	12 11	12 22		12 40	12 52	13 10	13 22		13 40	13 52	14 11	14 22		14 40
Bingley		d	10 44	10 56	11 07	11 14	11 26	11 44	11 56	12 15	12 26	12 37	12 44	12 56	13 14	13 26	13 37	13 44	13 56	14 15	14 26	14 38	14 44
Crossflatts		d	10 47	10 58		11 17	11 28	11 47	11 58	12 17	12 28		12 47	12 58	13 17	13 28		13 47	13 58	14 17	14 28		14 47
Keighley		d	10 51	11 03	11 13	11 21	11 33	11 51	12 03	12 22	12 33	12 43	12 51	13 03	13 21	13 33	13 43	13 51	14 03	14 22	14 33	14 43	14 51
Steeton & Silsden		d	10 56	11 07		11 26	11 37	11 56	12 07	12 26	12 37		12 56	13 07	13 26	13 37		13 56	14 07	14 26	14 37		14 56
Cononley		d	11 00	11 12		11 30	11 42	12 00	12 12	12 31	12 42		13 00	13 12	13 30	13 42		14 00	14 12	14 31	14 42		15 00
Skipton		a	11 09	11 20	11 25	11 39	11 50	12 09	12 21	12 39	12 51	12 56	13 09	13 20	13 39	13 50	13 55	14 09	14 21	14 39	14 51	14 57	15 09

			NT	NT	NT	NT	NT	NT	NT	NT	NT	NT	NT	NT	NT	NT	NT	NT	NT	NT	NT	NT	NT	NT
						◇ A							◇ A				◇ C					◇ A		
Leeds	37	d		14 56		15 18	15 26		15 56		16 26		16 49	16 56		17 18	17 25		17 41	17 56		18 19	18 26	
Kirkstall Forge		d														17 25			17 48					
Apperley Bridge		d																						
Bradford Forster Square	37	d	14 41		15 11			15 41		16 11		16 41			17 11			17 41			18 11			18 41
Frizinghall	37	d	14 44		15 14			15 44		16 14		16 44			17 14			17 44			18 14			18 44
Shipley	37	a	14 48	15 08	15 18	15 32	15 37	15 48	16 08	16 18	16 37	16 48	17 01	17 07	17 18	17 32	17 37	17 48	17 55	18 07	18 18	18 31	18 37	18 46
		d	14 49	15 08	15 19	15 33	15 38	15 49	16 08	16 19	16 38	16 49	17 02	17 08	17 19	17 33	17 39	17 49	17 56	18 08	18 19	18 32	18 38	18 49
Saltaire		d	14 52	15 11	15 22		15 40	15 52	16 11	16 22	16 40	16 52		17 10	17 22	17 35		17 52	17 58	18 10	18 22		18 40	18 52
Bingley		d	14 56	15 15	15 26	15 37	15 44	15 56	16 15	16 26	16 44	16 56	17 07	17 14	17 26	17 39	17 45	17 56	18 02	18 14	18 26	18 36	18 44	18 56
Crossflatts		d	14 58	15 17	15 28		15 47	15 58	16 17	16 28	16 47	16 58		17 17	17 28	17 42		17 58	18 05	18 17	18 28		18 47	18 58
Keighley		d	15 03	15 22	15 33	15 43	15 51	16 03	16 22	16 33	16 51	17 03	17 13	17 21	17 33	17 46	17 52	18 03	18 09	18 21	18 33	18 42	18 51	19 03
Steeton & Silsden		d	15 07	15 26	15 37	15 47	15 56	16 07	16 26	16 37	16 56	17 07		17 26	17 37	17 51	17 56	18 07	18 14	18 26	18 37		18 56	19 07
Cononley		d	15 12	15 31	15 42	15 52	16 00	16 12	16 31	16 42	17 00	17 12		17 30	17 42	17 55		18 12	18 18	18 30	18 42		19 00	19 12
Skipton		a	15 20	15 39	15 50	15 59	16 09	16 20	16 39	16 50	17 09	17 20	17 25	17 39	17 50	18 04	18 07	18 20	18 27	18 39	18 50	18 54	19 09	19 20

			NT	NT	NT	NT	NT	NT	NT	NT	NT	GR	NT	NT	NT	NT	NT	NT	NT	NT	NT	NT
					◇ B			◇ D				E										
Leeds	37	d	18 56		19 18	19 26		19 49	19 56		20 26	20 39		20 56		21 26	21 54		22 26	22 56		23 20
Kirkstall Forge		d				19 33			20 03		20 33					21 33			22 33			23 27
Apperley Bridge		d				19 37			20 07		20 37			21 04		21 37			22 37			23 31
Bradford Forster Square	37	d		19 11			19 41			20 11			20 48		21 11			22 11			23 11	
Frizinghall	37	d		19 14			19 44			20 14			20 51		21 14			22 14			23 14	
Shipley	37	a	19 07	19 18	19 31	19 42	19 48	20 01	20 12	20 18	20 42		20 55	21 09	21 18	21 42	22 05	22 18	22 42	23 07	23 18	23 36
		d	19 09	19 19	19 32	19 42	19 49	20 02	20 12	20 19	20 42		20 56	21 09	21 19	21 42	22 08	22 19	22 42	23 08	23 19	23 36
Saltaire		d	19 12	19 22		19 45	19 52		20 15	20 22	20 45		20 59	21 12	21 22	21 45	22 10	22 22	22 45	23 10	23 22	23 38
Bingley		d	19 16	19 26	19 37	19 49	19 56	20 07	20 19	20 26	20 49		21 03	21 16	21 26	21 49	22 14	22 26	22 49	23 14	23 26	23 42
Crossflatts		d	19 18	19 28		19 51	19 58		20 21	20 28	20 51		21 05	21 18	21 28	21 51	22 17	22 28	22 51	23 17	23 28	23 44
Keighley		d	19 23	19 33	19 43	19 56	20 03	20 12	20 26	20 33	20 56	21s01	21 10	21 23	21 33	21 56	22 21	22 33	22 56	23 21	23 33	23 49
Steeton & Silsden		d	19 27	19 37		20 00	20 07		20 30	20 37	21 00		21 14	21 27	21 37	22 00	22 26	22 37	23 00	23 26	23 37	23 53
Cononley		d	19 32	19 42		20 05	20 12		20 35	20 42	21 05		21 19	21 32	21 42	22 05	22 30	22 42	23 05	23 30	23 42	23 57
Skipton		a	19 40	19 50	19 57	20 13	20 20	20 26	20 43	20 50	21 13	21 17	21 27	21 40	21 50	22 13	22 39	22 50	23 13	23 39	23 50	00 05

A To Carlisle
B To Lancaster
C To Morecambe
D To Ribblehead
E From London Kings Cross

Table T036-F

Leeds and Bradford - Skipton

Sundays
20 May to 2 December

			NT	NT	NT	NT	NT	NT	NT	NT	NT	NT	NT	NT	NT	NT	NT	NT	NT	NT	NT	NT	NT	NT
			◇ A	◇ B			◇ A		◇ C					◇ B			◇ A			◇ B			◇ A	
Leeds	37	d	08 30	08 59		10 16	10 24		11 15	11 26		11 57	12 16	12 28		13 16	13 24		14 16	14 24		15 16	15 24	
Kirkstall Forge		d																						
Apperley Bridge		d																						
Bradford Forster Square	37	d			09 48			10 48			11 48				12 48			13 48			14 48			15 48
Frizinghall	37	d			09 51			10 51			11 51				12 51			13 51			14 51			15 51
Shipley	37	a	08 42	09 12	09 55	10 27	10 36	10 55	11 27	11 37	11 55	12 08	12 27	12 40	12 55	13 27	13 36	13 55	14 27	14 36	14 55	15 27	15 36	15 55
		d	08 43	09 13	09 56	10 28	10 37	10 56	11 32	11 38	11 56	12 10	12 28	12 41	12 56	13 28	13 37	13 56	14 28	14 37	14 56	15 28	15 37	15 56
Saltaire		d	08 45	09 15	09 59	10 30		10 59		11 40	11 59		12 30		12 59	13 30		13 59	14 30		14 59	15 30		15 59
Bingley		d	08 50	09 20	10 03	10 34	10 41	11 03	11 37	11 44	12 03	12 14	12 34	12 45	13 03	13 34	13 41	14 03	14 34	14 41	15 03	15 34	15 41	16 03
Crossflatts		d	08 52	09 22	10 05	10 36		11 05		11 46	12 05		12 36		13 05	13 36		14 05	14 36		15 05	15 36		16 05
Keighley		d	08 57	09 27	10 09	10 41	10 47	11 09	11 42	11 51	12 09	12 19	12 41	12 51	13 09	13 41	13 47	14 09	14 41	14 47	15 09	15 41	15 47	16 09
Steeton & Silsden		d	09 01	09 31	10 13	10 45		11 13		11 55	12 13		12 45		13 13	13 45		14 13	14 45		15 13	15 45		16 13
Cononley		d	09 06	09 36	10 18	10 49		11 18		11 59	12 18		12 49		13 18	13 49		14 18	14 49		15 18	15 49		16 18
Skipton		a	09 14	09 43	10 26	10 58	11 00	11 26	11 55	12 08	12 26	12 33	12 58	13 03	13 26	13 58	14 00	14 26	14 58	14 59	15 26	15 58	16 00	16 26

			NT	NT	NT	NT	NT	NT	NT	NT	NT	NT	NT	NT	NT	GR	NT	NT	NT	NT	NT
				◇ B			◇ A				◇ B					D					
Leeds	37	d	16 12	16 22		17 16	17 24		18 16		18 52	19 16		20 16		21 00	21 16		22 20		23 22
Kirkstall Forge		d																			
Apperley Bridge		d																			
Bradford Forster Square	37	d			16 48			17 48		18 48			19 48		20 48			21 48		22 48	
Frizinghall	37	d			16 51			17 51		18 51			19 51		20 51			21 51		22 51	
Shipley	37	a	16 23	16 34	16 55	17 27	17 36	17 55	18 28	18 55	19 04	19 27	19 55	20 27	20 55		21 27	21 55	22 31	22 55	23 33
		d	16 24	16 37	16 56	17 28	17 37	17 56	18 28	18 56	19 05	19 28	19 56	20 28	20 56		21 28	21 56	22 32	22 56	23 34
Saltaire		d	16 26		16 59	17 30		17 59	18 31	18 59		19 30	19 59	20 30	20 59		21 30	21 59	22 34	22 59	23 36
Bingley		d	16 30	16 41	17 03	17 34	17 41	18 03	18 35	19 03	19 09	19 34	20 03	20 34	21 03		21 34	22 03	22 38	23 03	23 40
Crossflatts		d	16 32		17 05	17 36		18 05	18 37	19 05		19 36	20 05	20 36	21 05		21 36	22 05	22 40	23 05	23 42
Keighley		d	16 37	16 47	17 09	17 40	17 47	18 09	18 41	19 09	19 16	19 41	20 09	20 41	21 09	21s19	21 41	22 09	22 45	23 09	23 47
Steeton & Silsden		d	16 41		17 13	17 44		18 13	18 45	19 13		19 45	20 13	20 45	21 13		21 45	22 13	22 49	23 13	23 51
Cononley		d	16 45		17 18	17 49		18 18	18 50	19 18		19 49	20 18	20 49	21 18		21 49	22 18	22 53	23 18	23 55
Skipton		a	16 54	17 01	17 26	17 58	18 00	18 26	18 58	19 26	19 33	19 58	20 26	20 58	21 26	21 34	21 58	22 26	23 02	23 26	00 04

A To Lancaster
B To Carlisle
C From Nottingham to Carlisle
D From London Kings Cross

Table T036-R

Skipton - Bradford and Leeds

Mondays to Fridays

21 May to 7 December

Miles	Miles	Station		NT	NT	NT	NT	NT	GR ■ A	NT	NT	NT	NT	NT	NT	NT ◇ B	NT ◇ C	NT	NT	NT	NT	NT	NT
0	—	**Skipton**	d	05 45	06 04	06 18	06 34	06 40	06 55	07 01	07 09	07 16	07 30	07 36	07 44	07 55	08 05	08 09	08 15	08 34	08 47	09 04	09 17
3	—	Cononley	d	05 50	06 09	06 23	06 39	06 45		07 06	07 14	07 21	07 35	07 41	07 49			08 14	08 20	08 39	08 52	09 09	09 22
6¼	—	Steeton & Silsden	d	05 55	06 14	06 28	06 44	06 50		07 11	07 19	07 26	07 40	07 46	07 54		08 12	08 19	08 25	08 44	08 57	09 14	09 27
9¼	—	Keighley	d	05 59	06 18	06 32	06 48	06 54	07u07	07 15	07 23	07 30	07 44	07 50	07 58	08 05	08 17	08 24	08 30	08 48	09 01	09 18	09 31
11¾	—	Crossflatts	d	06 03	06 22	06 36	06 52	06 58		07 19	07 27	07 34	07 48	07 54	08 02			08 28	08 34	08 52	09 05	09 22	09 35
12½	—	Bingley	d	06 05	06 24	06 38	06 54	07 00		07 21	07 29	07 36	07 50	07 56	08 04	08 10	08 22	08 30	08 36	08 54	09 07	09 24	09 37
14¾	—	Saltaire	d	06 10	06 29	06 43	06 59	07 05		07 26	07 34	07 40	07 54	08 01	08 09			08 35	08 41	08 59	09 12	09 29	09 42
15½	0	Shipley	a	06 12	06 31	06 46	07 02	07 07		07 28	07 37	07 43	07 57	08 04	08 11	08 15	08 27	08 37	08 44	09 01	09 14	09 31	09 44
—	—		d	06 13	06 32	06 46	07 03	07 08	07u17	07 29	07 37	07 44	07 58	08 04	08 12	08 15	08 28	08 38	08 44	09 02	09 15	09 32	09 45
—	1	Frizinghall 37	d		06 35		07 08				07 41			08 08					08 48	09 05		09 35	
—	2¾	**Bradford Forster Square** 37	a		06 41		07 14				07 47			08 14					08 54	09 11		09 40	
18½	—	Apperley Bridge	d									07 48											
22	—	Kirkstall Forge	d																				
26½	—	**Leeds** 10 37	a	06 27		07 02		07 23	07 31	07 44		07 59	08 13		08 28	08 33	08 43	08 53			09 29		10 01

Station		NT	NT	NT	NT	NT ◇ B	NT	NT	NT	NT	NT	NT	NT ◇ C	NT	NT	NT	NT	NT ◇ B	NT	NT	NT	NT	NT D
Skipton	d	09 34	09 47	10 04	10 17	10 25	10 34	10 47	11 04	11 17	11 34	11 47	11 59	12 04	12 17	12 34	12 47	12 55	13 04	13 17	13 34	13 47	13 59
Cononley	d	09 39	09 52	10 09	10 22		10 39	10 52	11 09	11 22	11 39	11 52		12 09	12 22	12 39	12 52		13 09	13 22	13 39	13 52	
Steeton & Silsden	d	09 44	09 57	10 14	10 27		10 44	10 57	11 14	11 27	11 44	11 57		12 14	12 27	12 44	12 57		13 14	13 27	13 44	13 57	
Keighley	d	09 48	10 01	10 18	10 31	10 38	10 48	11 01	11 18	11 31	11 48	12 01	12 09	12 18	12 31	12 48	13 01	13 08	13 18	13 31	13 48	14 01	14 09
Crossflatts	d	09 52	10 05	10 22	10 35		10 52	11 05	11 22	11 35	11 52	12 05		12 22	12 35	12 52	13 05		13 22	13 35	13 52	14 05	
Bingley	d	09 54	10 07	10 24	10 37	10 45	10 54	11 07	11 24	11 37	11 54	12 07	12 16	12 24	12 37	12 54	13 07	13 13	13 24	13 37	13 54	14 07	14 14
Saltaire	d	09 59	10 12	10 29	10 42		10 59	11 12	11 29	11 42	11 59	12 12		12 29	12 42	12 59	13 12		13 29	13 42	13 59	14 12	
Shipley	a	10 01	10 14	10 32	10 44	10 49	11 01	11 14	11 32	11 44	12 01	12 14	12 20	12 32	12 44	13 01	13 14	13 19	13 32	13 44	14 01	14 14	14 19
	d	10 02	10 15	10 32	10 45	10 50	11 02	11 15	11 32	11 45	12 02	12 15	12 21	12 32	12 45	13 02	13 15	13 20	13 32	13 45	14 02	14 15	14 20
Frizinghall 37	d	10 05		10 36			11 05		11 36		12 05			12 36		13 05			13 36		14 05		
Bradford Forster Square 37	a	10 11		10 42			11 11		11 41		12 11			12 42		13 11			13 42		14 11		
Apperley Bridge	d																						
Kirkstall Forge	d																						
Leeds 10 37	a		10 29		10 59	11 08		11 31		12 01		12 30	12 37		12 59		13 30	13 38		14 00		14 30	14 38

Station		NT	NT	NT	NT	NT	NT	NT	NT	NT ◇ B	NT	NT	NT ◇ C	NT	NT	NT ◇ B	NT	NT	NT	NT	NT	NT
Skipton	d	14 04	14 17	14 34	14 47	15 04	15 17	15 34	15 47	16 00	16 04	16 17	16 28	16 34	16 47	16 59	17 04	17 17	17 34	17 47	18 03	18 17
Cononley	d	14 09	14 22	14 39	14 52	15 09	15 22	15 39	15 52		16 09	16 22		16 39	16 52		17 09	17 22	17 39	17 52	18 08	18 22
Steeton & Silsden	d	14 14	14 27	14 44	14 57	15 14	15 27	15 44	15 57		16 14	16 27		16 44	16 57		17 14	17 27	17 44	17 57	18 13	18 27
Keighley	d	14 18	14 31	14 48	15 01	15 18	15 31	15 48	16 01	16 10	16 18	16 31	16 38	16 48	17 01	17 09	17 18	17 31	17 48	18 01	18 17	18 31
Crossflatts	d	14 22	14 35	14 52	15 05	15 22	15 35	15 52	16 05		16 22	16 35		16 52	17 05		17 22	17 35	17 52	18 05	18 21	18 35
Bingley	d	14 24	14 37	14 54	15 07	15 24	15 37	15 54	16 07	16 15	16 24	16 37	16 44	16 54	17 07	17 14	17 24	17 37	17 54	18 07	18 23	18 37
Saltaire	d	14 29	14 42	14 59	15 12	15 29	15 42	15 59	16 12		16 29	16 42		16 59	17 12		17 29	17 42	17 59	18 12	18 28	18 42
Shipley	a	14 32	14 44	15 01	15 14	15 32	15 44	16 01	16 14	16 19	16 32	16 44	16 48	17 01	17 14	17 19	17 32	17 44	18 01	18 14	18 31	18 44
	d	14 32	14 45	15 02	15 15	15 32	15 45	16 02	16 15	16 20	16 32	16 45	16 49	17 02	17 15	17 20	17 32	17 45	18 02	18 15	18 31	18 45
Frizinghall 37	d	14 36		15 05		15 36		16 05			16 36			17 05			17 36		18 05		18 35	
Bradford Forster Square 37	a	14 42		15 11		15 42		16 11			16 42			17 11			17 42		18 11		18 42	
Apperley Bridge	d																					
Kirkstall Forge	d																					
Leeds 10 37	a		14 59		15 30		15 59		16 30	16 38		16 59	17 03		17 29	17 38		18 00		18 29		18 59

Station		NT ◇ B	NT	NT	NT ◇ D	NT	NT	NT	NT	NT	NT	NT ◇ B	NT	NT	NT	NT	NT ◇ D	NT	NT ◇ B	NT ◇ E	NT	NT
Skipton	d	18 29	18 41	18 47	18 59	19 04	19 17	19 34	19 47	20 04	20 17	20 29	20 34	20 47	21 17	21 34	21 43	21 48	22 10	22 26	22 34	22 47
Cononley	d		18 46	18 52		19 09	19 22	19 39	19 52	20 09	20 22		20 39	20 52	21 22	21 39		21 53		22 31	22 39	22 52
Steeton & Silsden	d		18 51	18 57		19 14	19 27	19 44	19 57	20 14	20 27		20 44	20 57	21 27	21 44		21 58		22 36	22 44	22 57
Keighley	d	18 39	18 55	19 01	19 09	19 18	19 31	19 48	20 01	20 18	20 31	20 39	20 48	21 01	21 31	21 48	21 55	22 02	22 20	22 41	22 48	23 01
Crossflatts	d		18 59	19 05		19 22	19 35	19 52	20 05	20 22	20 35		20 52	21 05	21 35	21 52		22 06		22 45	22 52	23 05
Bingley	d	18 44	19 01	19 07	19 14	19 24	19 37	19 54	20 07	20 24	20 37	20 44	20 54	21 07	21 37	21 54	22 00	22 08	22 25	22 47	22 54	23 07
Saltaire	d		19 06	19 12		19 29	19 42	19 59	20 12	20 29	20 42		20 59	21 12	21 42	21 59		22 13		22 51	22 59	23 12
Shipley	a	18 50	19 09	19 14	19 19	19 32	19 44	20 01	20 14	20 32	20 44	20 50	21 02	21 14	21 44	22 01	22 05	22 15	22 32	22 54	23 02	23 14
	d	18 50	19 09	19 15	19 20	19 32	19 46	20 02	20 16	20 32	20 45	20 51	21 02	21 15	21 45	22 02	22 06	22 16	22 32	22 55	23 02	23 15
Frizinghall 37	d		19 13			19 36		20 05		20 36			21 06			22 05					23 06	
Bradford Forster Square 37	a		19 19			19 42		20 11		20 42			21 12			22 11					23 12	
Apperley Bridge	d								20 21		20 49			21 19	21 49			22 20				23 19
Kirkstall Forge	d										20 54			21 24	21 54			22 25				23 24
Leeds 10 37	a	19 06		19 29	19 36		20 00		20 32		21 02	21 06		21 32	22 02		22 22	22 34	22 49	23 12		23 32

A To London Kings Cross
B From Carlisle
C From Lancaster
D From Morecambe
E From Ribblehead

Table T036-R

Skipton - Bradford and Leeds

Saturdays

26 May to 8 December

Station		NT	NT	NT	NT	NT	GR ■ A	NT	NT	NT	NT	NT	NT	NT ◇ B	NT ◇ C	NT	NT	NT	NT	NT	NT	NT	NT
Skipton	d	05 45	06 04	06 18	06 34	06 40	06 55	07 01	07 09	07 16	07 30	07 36	07 44	07 55	08 05	08 09	08 15	08 34	08 47	09 04	09 17	09 34	09 47
Cononley	d	05 50	06 09	06 23	06 39	06 45		07 06	07 14	07 21	07 35	07 41	07 49			08 14	08 20	08 39	08 52	09 09	09 22	09 39	09 52
Steeton & Silsden	d	05 55	06 14	06 28	06 44	06 50		07 11	07 19	07 26	07 40	07 46	07 54	08 03	08 12	08 19	08 25	08 44	08 57	09 14	09 27	09 44	09 57
Keighley	d	05 59	06 18	06 32	06 48	06 54	07u09	07 15	07 23	07 30	07 44	07 50	07 58	08 08	08 17	08 24	08 30	08 48	09 01	09 18	09 31	09 48	10 01
Crossflatts	d	06 03	06 22	06 36	06 52	06 58		07 19	07 27	07 34	07 48	07 54	08 02			08 28	08 34	08 52	09 05	09 22	09 35	09 52	10 05
Bingley	d	06 05	06 24	06 38	06 54	07 00		07 21	07 29	07 36	07 50	07 56	08 04	08 13	08 22	08 30	08 36	08 54	09 07	09 24	09 37	09 54	10 07
Saltaire	d	06 10	06 29	06 43	06 59	07 05		07 26	07 34	07 40	07 54	08 01	08 09			08 35	08 41	08 59	09 12	09 29	09 42	09 59	10 12
Shipley	a	06 12	06 31	06 46	07 02	07 07		07 28	07 37	07 43	07 57	08 04	08 11	08 18	08 27	08 37	08 44	09 01	09 14	09 31	09 44	10 01	10 14
	d	06 13	06 32	06 46	07 03	07 08	07u19	07 29	07 37	07 44	07 58	08 04	08 12	08 19	08 28	08 38	08 44	09 02	09 15	09 32	09 45	10 02	10 15
Frizinghall 37	d		06 35		07 08				07 41			08 08					08 48	09 05		09 35		10 05	
Bradford Forster Square 37	a		06 41		07 14				07 47			08 14					08 54	09 11		09 40		10 11	
Apperley Bridge	d									07 48													
Kirkstall Forge	d																						
Leeds 10 37	a	06 27		07 02		07 23	07 33	07 44		07 59	08 13		08 28	08 35	08 43	08 53			09 29		10 01		10 29

Station		NT ◇ D	NT	NT	NT	NT	NT	NT	NT ◇ D	NT	NT	NT ◇ C	NT	NT	NT	NT	NT ◇ D	NT	NT	NT	NT	NT E
Skipton	d	09 56	10 04	10 17	10 34	10 47	11 04	11 17	11 28	11 34	11 47	11 59	12 04	12 17	12 34	12 47	12 55	13 04	13 17	13 34	13 47	13 59
Cononley	d		10 09	10 22	10 39	10 52	11 09	11 22		11 39	11 52		12 09	12 22	12 39	12 52		13 09	13 22	13 39	13 52	
Steeton & Silsden	d		10 14	10 27	10 44	10 57	11 14	11 27		11 44	11 57		12 14	12 27	12 44	12 57		13 14	13 27	13 44	13 57	
Keighley	d	10 09	10 18	10 31	10 48	11 01	11 18	11 31	11 38	11 48	12 01	12 09	12 18	12 31	12 48	13 01	13 08	13 18	13 31	13 48	14 01	14 09
Crossflatts	d		10 22	10 35	10 52	11 05	11 22	11 35		11 52	12 05		12 22	12 35	12 52	13 05		13 22	13 35	13 52	14 05	
Bingley	d	10 13	10 24	10 37	10 54	11 07	11 24	11 37	11 45	11 54	12 07	12 16	12 24	12 37	12 54	13 07	13 13	13 24	13 37	13 54	14 07	14 14
Saltaire	d		10 29	10 42	10 59	11 12	11 29	11 42		11 59	12 12		12 29	12 42	12 59	13 12		13 29	13 42	13 59	14 12	
Shipley	a	10 20	10 32	10 44	11 01	11 14	11 32	11 44	11 49	12 01	12 14	12 20	12 32	12 44	13 01	13 14	13 19	13 32	13 44	14 01	14 14	14 19
	d	10 20	10 32	10 45	11 02	11 15	11 32	11 45	11 50	12 02	12 15	12 21	12 32	12 45	13 02	13 15	13 20	13 32	13 45	14 02	14 15	14 20
Frizinghall 37	d		10 36		11 05		11 36			12 05			12 36		13 05			13 36		14 05		
Bradford Forster Square 37	a		10 42		11 11		11 41			12 11			12 42		13 11			13 42		14 11		
Apperley Bridge	d																					
Kirkstall Forge	d																					
Leeds 10 37	a	10 37		10 59		11 31		12 01	12 05		12 30	12 37		12 59		13 30	13 38		14 00		14 30	14 38

Station		NT	NT	NT	NT	NT	NT	NT	NT	NT ◇ D	NT	NT	NT ◇ C	NT	NT	NT ◇ D	NT	NT	NT	NT	NT	NT	NT ◇ D
Skipton	d	14 04	14 17	14 34	14 47	15 04	15 17	15 34	15 47	16 00	16 04	16 17	16 28	16 34	16 47	16 59	17 04	17 17	17 34	17 47	18 03	18 17	18 29
Cononley	d	14 09	14 22	14 39	14 52	15 09	15 22	15 39	15 52		16 09	16 22		16 39	16 52		17 09	17 22	17 39	17 52	18 08	18 22	
Steeton & Silsden	d	14 14	14 27	14 44	14 57	15 14	15 27	15 44	15 57		16 14	16 27		16 44	16 57		17 14	17 27	17 44	17 57	18 13	18 27	
Keighley	d	14 18	14 31	14 48	15 01	15 18	15 31	15 48	16 01	16 10	16 18	16 31	16 38	16 48	17 01	17 09	17 18	17 31	17 48	18 01	18 17	18 31	18 39
Crossflatts	d	14 22	14 35	14 52	15 05	15 22	15 35	15 52	16 05		16 22	16 35		16 52	17 05		17 22	17 35	17 52	18 05	18 21	18 35	
Bingley	d	14 24	14 37	14 54	15 07	15 24	15 37	15 54	16 07	16 15	16 24	16 37	16 44	16 54	17 07	17 14	17 24	17 37	17 54	18 07	18 23	18 37	18 44
Saltaire	d	14 29	14 42	14 59	15 12	15 29	15 42	15 59	16 12		16 29	16 42		16 59	17 12		17 29	17 42	17 59	18 12	18 28	18 42	
Shipley	a	14 32	14 44	15 01	15 14	15 32	15 44	16 01	16 14	16 19	16 32	16 44	16 48	17 01	17 14	17 19	17 32	17 44	18 01	18 14	18 31	18 44	18 50
	d	14 32	14 45	15 02	15 15	15 32	15 45	16 02	16 15	16 20	16 32	16 45	16 49	17 02	17 15	17 20	17 32	17 45	18 02	18 15	18 31	18 45	18 50
Frizinghall 37	d	14 36		15 05		15 36		16 05			16 36			17 05			17 36		18 05		18 35		
Bradford Forster Square 37	a	14 42		15 11		15 42		16 11			16 42			17 11			17 42		18 11		18 42		
Apperley Bridge	d																						
Kirkstall Forge	d																						
Leeds 10 37	a		14 59		15 30		15 59		16 30	16 38		16 59	17 03		17 29	17 38		18 00		18 29		18 59	19 06

Station		NT	NT	NT ◇ E	NT	NT	NT	NT	NT	NT	NT ◇ D	NT	NT	NT	NT	NT ◇ E	NT	NT ◇ D	NT ◇ B	NT	NT
Skipton	d	18 41	18 47	18 59	19 04	19 17	19 34	19 47	20 04	20 17	20 29	20 34	20 47	21 17	21 34	21 43	21 48	22 10	22 26	22 34	22 47
Cononley	d	18 46	18 52		19 09	19 22	19 39	19 52	20 09	20 22		20 39	20 52	21 22	21 39		21 53		22 31	22 39	22 52
Steeton & Silsden	d	18 51	18 57		19 14	19 27	19 44	19 57	20 14	20 27		20 44	20 57	21 27	21 44		21 58		22 36	22 44	22 57
Keighley	d	18 55	19 01	19 09	19 18	19 31	19 48	20 01	20 18	20 31	20 39	20 48	21 01	21 31	21 48	21 55	22 02	22 20	22 41	22 48	23 01
Crossflatts	d	18 59	19 05		19 22	19 35	19 52	20 05	20 22	20 35		20 52	21 05	21 35	21 52		22 06		22 45	22 52	23 05
Bingley	d	19 01	19 07	19 14	19 24	19 37	19 54	20 07	20 24	20 37	20 44	20 54	21 07	21 37	21 54	22 00	22 08	22 25	22 47	22 54	23 07
Saltaire	d	19 06	19 12		19 29	19 42	19 59	20 12	20 29	20 42		20 59	21 12	21 42	21 59		22 13		22 51	22 59	23 12
Shipley	a	19 09	19 14	19 19	19 32	19 44	20 01	20 14	20 32	20 44	20 50	21 02	21 14	21 44	22 01	22 05	22 15	22 30	22 54	23 02	23 14
	d	19 09	19 15	19 20	19 32	19 46	20 02	20 16	20 32	20 45	20 51	21 02	21 15	21 45	22 02	22 06	22 16	22 30	22 54	23 02	23 15
Frizinghall 37	d	19 13			19 36		20 05		20 36			21 06			22 05					23 06	
Bradford Forster Square 37	a	19 19			19 42		20 11		20 42			21 12			22 11					23 12	
Apperley Bridge	d							20 21		20 49			21 19	21 49			22 20				23 19
Kirkstall Forge	d									20 54			21 24	21 54			22 25				23 24
Leeds 10 37	a		19 29	19 36		20 00		20 32		21 02	21 06		21 32	22 02		22 22	22 34	22 48	23 11		23 32

A To London Kings Cross
B From Ribblehead
C From Lancaster
D From Carlisle
E From Morecambe

Table T036-R

Sundays

20 May to 2 December

Skipton - Bradford and Leeds

			NT	NT	NT	NT	NT		NT	NT	NT	NT ◇ A	NT	NT ◇ B	NT	NT	NT		NT	NT ◇ B	NT	NT	NT ◇ A	NT	NT	NT
Skipton		d	08 32	08 42	09 12	09 42	10 12		10 30	10 42	11 12	11 30	11 42	11 56	12 12	12 42	13 12		13 42	13 56	14 12	14 42	14 58	15 12	15 42	16 07
Cononley		d	08 37	08 47	09 17	09 47	10 17			10 47	11 17		11 47		12 17	12 47	13 17		13 47		14 17	14 47		15 17	15 47	
Steeton & Silsden		d	08 42	08 52	09 22	09 52	10 22			10 52	11 22		11 52		12 22	12 52	13 22		13 52		14 22	14 52		15 22	15 52	
Keighley		d	08 46	08 56	09 26	09 56	10 26		10 40	10 56	11 26	11 40	11 56	12 06	12 26	12 56	13 26		13 56	14 06	14 26	14 56	15 08	15 26	15 56	16 17
Crossflatts		d	08 50	09 00	09 30	10 00	10 30			11 00	11 30		12 00		12 30	13 00	13 30		14 00		14 30	15 00		15 30	16 00	
Bingley		d	08 52	09 02	09 32	10 02	10 32		10 44	11 02	11 32	11 44	12 02	12 11	12 32	13 02	13 32		14 02	14 11	14 32	15 02	15 13	15 32	16 02	16 21
Saltaire		d	08 57	09 07	09 37	10 07	10 37			11 07	11 37		12 07		12 37	13 07	13 37		14 07		14 37	15 07		15 37	16 07	
Shipley		a	08 59	09 10	09 39	10 10	10 39		10 49	11 10	11 39	11 49	12 10	12 15	12 39	13 10	13 39		14 10	14 15	14 39	15 10	15 17	15 39	16 10	16 26
		d	09 00	09 10	09 40	10 10	10 40		10 49	11 10	11 40	11 49	12 10	12 16	12 40	13 10	13 40		14 10	14 16	14 40	15 10	15 18	15 40	16 10	16 26
Frizinghall	37	d		09 14		10 14				11 14			12 14			13 14			14 14			15 14			16 14	
Bradford Forster Square	37	a		09 20		10 20				11 20			12 20			13 20			14 20			15 20			16 20	
Apperley Bridge		d																								
Kirkstall Forge		d																								
Leeds 10	37	a	09 14		09 54		10 54		11 06		11 54	12 06		12 36	12 54		13 54			14 36	14 54		15 36	15 54		16 45

			NT		NT	NT ◇ B	NT ◇ C	NT	NT	NT ◇ A	NT	NT	NT ◇ B		NT	NT ◇ A	NT	NT	NT	NT ◇ B	NT	NT	NT		NT	
Skipton		d	16 12		16 42	16 55	17 09	17 14	17 42	17 58	18 12	18 42	18 56		19 12	19 30	19 42	20 12	20 42	21 07	21 22	21 42	22 12		23 12	
Cononley		d	16 17		16 47			17 19	17 47		18 17	18 47			19 17		19 47	20 17	20 47		21 27	21 47	22 17		23 18	
Steeton & Silsden		d	16 22		16 52			17 24	17 52		18 22	18 52			19 22		19 52	20 22	20 52		21 32	21 52	22 22		23 22	
Keighley		d	16 26		16 56	17 05	17 19	17 28	17 56	18 08	18 26	18 56	19 06		19 26	19 40	19 56	20 26	20 56	21 17	21 36	21 56	22 26		23 27	
Crossflatts		d	16 30		17 00			17 32	18 00		18 30	19 00			19 30		20 00	20 30	21 00		21 40	22 00	22 30		23 31	
Bingley		d	16 32		17 02	17 10	17 23	17 34	18 02	18 13	18 32	19 02	19 11		19 32	19 45	20 02	20 32	21 02	21 22	21 42	22 02	22 32		23 34	
Saltaire		d	16 37		17 07			17 39	18 07		18 37	19 07			19 37		20 07	20 37	21 07		21 47	22 07	22 37		23 39	
Shipley		a	16 39		17 10	17 15	17 28	17 41	18 10	18 17	18 39	19 10	19 16		19 39	19 49	20 10	20 39	21 10	21 27	21 49	22 10	22 39		23 42	
		d	16 40		17 10	17 16	17 28	17 42	18 10	18 18	18 40	19 10	19 17		19 40	19 50	20 10	20 40	21 10	21 28	21 50	22 10	22 39		23 42	
Frizinghall	37	d			17 14				18 14			19 14					20 14		21 14			22 14				
Bradford Forster Square	37	a			17 20				18 20			19 20					20 20		21 20			22 20				
Apperley Bridge		d																								
Kirkstall Forge		d																								
Leeds 10	37	a	16 54			17 39	17 50	17 56		18 32	18 54		19 37		19 54	20 07		20 54		21 47	22 04		22 54		23 57	

A From Carlisle
B From Lancaster
C From Carlisle to Nottingham

Table T037-F

Mondays to Fridays

21 May to 7 December

Leeds - Shipley and Bradford

Miles	Miles			NT	NT ◇	NT ◇ 🛒	NT	NT ◇	NT ◇	NT	NT ◇	NT		NT	NT	NT ◇	NT ◇	NT	NT	NT	NT	NT		NT ◇	NT
0	0	**Leeds** 10	d	05 01	05 12	05 17		05 36	05 55	06 02	06 18			06 26	06 30	06 37	06 52		06 56		07 06	07 12		07 13	07 23
4¼	—	Kirkstall Forge	d												06 37							07 18			
7¼	—	Apperley Bridge	d												06 41							07 23			
10¾	—	**Shipley**	a			05 29								06 42	06 45				07 09			07 27			07 36
—	—		d				06 13					06 32			06 46			07 03		07 14		07 27			
11¾	—	Frizinghall	d				06 16					06 35			06 48			07 08		07 17		07 30			
—	4	Bramley	d	05 09	05 21			05 45		06 10	06 26					06 46					07 14			07 21	
—	5¾	New Pudsey	d	05 14	05 25			05 49	06 04	06 15	06 30					06 50	07 01				07 19			07 29	
—	9½	**Bradford Interchange**	a	05 22	05 35			06 00	06 13	06 27	06 39					07 01	07 11				07 28			07 38	
13¾	—	**Bradford Forster Square**	a				06 22					06 41			06 55			07 14		07 23		07 37			

		NT	NT ◇	NT	NT	NT ◇ 🛒	NT	NT		NT	NT ◇	NT	NT	NT ◇	NT ◇	NT	NT	NT ◇		NT	NT	NT ◇	NT	NT	NT
Leeds 10	d		07 36		07 42	07 48		07 52			07 52	08 07	08 12	08 18	08 19	08 26		08 36			08 42	08 51		08 56	
Kirkstall Forge	d				07 49								08 18								08 49				
Apperley Bridge	d				07 53								08 23								08 53				
Shipley	a				07 57	08 01		08 07					08 27		08 31	08 37					08 57			09 07	
	d	07 37		07 44	07 58		08 04			08 11			08 27				08 44			08 49	08 58		09 02		09 14
Frizinghall	d	07 41		07 47	08 00		08 08			08 14			08 30				08 48			08 52	09 00		09 05		09 17
Bramley	d		07 45									08 15		08 26				08 45							
New Pudsey	d		07 49								08 01	08 20		08 30				08 49				09 00			
Bradford Interchange	a		07 59								08 10	08 31		08 39				08 59				09 09			
Bradford Forster Square	a	07 47		07 53	08 07		08 14			08 20			08 37				08 54			08 57	09 07		09 11		09 23

		NT	NT	NT ◇		NT ◇ 🛒	NT	NT	NT	NT ◇	NT	NT ◇	NT	NT		NT	NT	NT	NT ◇	NT ◇	NT	NT	NT	NT ◇	
Leeds 10	d	09 07	09 12	09 19		09 19		09 26		09 36	09 42	09 51		09 54			10 07	10 12	10 18	10 18		10 26		10 36	
Kirkstall Forge	d		09 18								09 49							10 19							
Apperley Bridge	d		09 23								09 53							10 23							
Shipley	a		09 27			09 31		09 37			09 57			10 07				10 27		10 32		10 37			
	d		09 28				09 32		09 44		09 58		10 02			10 14		10 28			10 32		10 44		
Frizinghall	d		09 30				09 35		09 47		10 00		10 05			10 17		10 30			10 36		10 47		
Bramley	d	09 15		09 27						09 45							10 15		10 26					10 45	
New Pudsey	d	09 20		09 31						09 49		10 00					10 20		10 30					10 49	
Bradford Interchange	a	09 30		09 42						09 59		10 09					10 30		10 39					10 59	
Bradford Forster Square	a		09 37				09 40		09 53		10 07		10 11			10 23		10 37			10 42		10 53		

		NT	NT ◇ 🛒	NT	NT ◇	NT	NT	NT	NT	NT ◇		NT	NT	NT	NT ◇	NT	NT ◇	NT	NT	NT		NT	NT	NT ◇	NT ◇
Leeds 10	d	10 42	10 49		10 51	10 54		11 07	11 12	11 18			11 26		11 36	11 42	11 51		11 56			12 07	12 12	12 18	12 20
Kirkstall Forge	d	10 49							11 19							11 49							12 19		
Apperley Bridge	d	10 53							11 23							11 53							12 23		
Shipley	a	10 57	11 01			11 07			11 27				11 37			11 57			12 08				12 27		12 32
	d	10 58		11 02			11 14		11 28			11 32		11 44		11 58		12 02		12 14			12 28		
Frizinghall	d	11 00		11 05			11 17		11 30			11 36		11 47		12 00		12 05		12 17			12 30		
Bramley	d							11 15		11 26					11 45							12 15		12 26	
New Pudsey	d				11 00			11 20		11 30					11 49		12 00					12 20		12 30	
Bradford Interchange	a				11 09			11 30		11 39					11 59		12 09					12 30		12 39	
Bradford Forster Square	a	11 07		11 11			11 23		11 37			11 41		11 53		12 07		12 11		12 23			12 37		

		NT	NT	NT	NT ◇	NT		NT ◇	NT	NT	NT	NT	NT	NT ◇	NT ◇ 🛒	NT		NT	NT	NT ◇	NT	NT ◇	NT	NT	NT
Leeds 10	d		12 26		12 36	12 42		12 51		12 56		13 07	13 12	13 18	13 18			13 26		13 36	13 42	13 51		13 56	
Kirkstall Forge	d					12 49							13 19								13 49				
Apperley Bridge	d					12 53							13 23								13 53				
Shipley	a		12 37			12 57				13 07			13 27		13 32			13 37			13 57			14 08	
	d	12 32		12 44		12 58			13 02		13 14		13 28			13 32			13 44		13 58		14 02		14 14
Frizinghall	d	12 36		12 47		13 00			13 05		13 17		13 30			13 36			13 47		14 00		14 05		14 17
Bramley	d				12 45							13 15		13 26						13 45					
New Pudsey	d				12 49			13 00				13 20		13 30						13 49		14 00			
Bradford Interchange	a				12 59			13 09				13 30		13 39						13 59		14 09			
Bradford Forster Square	a	12 42		12 53		13 07			13 11		13 23		13 37			13 42			13 53		14 07		14 11		14 23

		NT		NT	NT ◇	NT ◇	NT	NT	NT	NT ◇	NT	NT ◇		NT	NT	NT	NT	NT	NT ◇	NT ◇ 🛒	NT	NT		NT	NT ◇
Leeds 10	d	14 07		14 12	14 18	14 18		14 26		14 36	14 42	14 51			14 56		15 07	15 12	15 18	15 18		15 26			15 36
Kirkstall Forge	d			14 19							14 49							15 19							
Apperley Bridge	d			14 23							14 53							15 23							
Shipley	a			14 27		14 32		14 37			14 57				15 08			15 27		15 32		15 37			
	d			14 28			14 32		14 44		14 58			15 02		15 14		15 28			15 32			15 44	
Frizinghall	d			14 30			14 36		14 47		15 00			15 05		15 17		15 30			15 36			15 47	
Bramley	d	14 15			14 26					14 45							15 15		15 26						15 45
New Pudsey	d	14 20			14 30					14 49		15 00					15 20		15 30						15 49
Bradford Interchange	a	14 30			14 39					14 59		15 09					15 30		15 39						15 59
Bradford Forster Square	a			14 37			14 42		14 53		15 07			15 11		15 23		15 37			15 42			15 53	

Table T037-F

Mondays to Fridays

21 May to 7 December

Leeds - Shipley and Bradford

		NT	NT ◇	NT	NT	NT	NT	NT	NT ◇	NT	NT	NT	NT ◇	NT	NT ◇ 🛒	NT	NT ◇	NT	NT	NT	NT	NT
Leeds [10]	d	15 42	15 51		15 56		16 07	16 12	16 18		16 26		16 36	16 42	16 49		16 51	16 56		17 07	17 12	17 18
Kirkstall Forge	d	15 49						16 19						16 49								17 25
Apperley Bridge	d	15 53						16 23						16 53							17 21	
Shipley	a	15 57			16 08			16 27			16 37			16 57	17 01			17 07			17 25	17 32
	d	15 58		16 02		16 14		16 28		16 32		16 44		16 58		17 02			17 14		17 26	
Frizinghall	d	16 00		16 05		16 17		16 30		16 36		16 47		17 00		17 05			17 17		17 29	
Bramley	d						16 15		16 26				16 45							17 15		
New Pudsey	d		16 00				16 20		16 30				16 49				17 00			17 20		
Bradford Interchange	a		16 09				16 30		16 39				16 59				17 09			17 30		
Bradford Forster Square	a	16 07		16 11		16 23		16 37		16 42		16 53		17 07		17 11			17 23		17 36	

		NT	NT ◇	NT	NT ◇	NT	NT ◇	NT	NT	NT	NT ◇	NT	NT	NT	NT	NT ◇ 🛒	NT	NT ◇	NT	NT	NT ◇	NT	NT ◇
Leeds [10]	d		17 18	17 25	17 25		17 36	17 36	17 41		17 51	17 56		18 09	18 12	18 19		18 20	18 26		18 36	18 42	18 51
Kirkstall Forge	d							17 43	17 48						18 19							18 49	
Apperley Bridge	d							17 47							18 23							18 53	
Shipley	a				17 37			17 51	17 55			18 07			18 27	18 31			18 37			18 57	
	d	17 32				17 44		17 52		18 02			18 15		18 28		18 31			18 44		18 58	
Frizinghall	d	17 36				17 47		17 54		18 05			18 17		18 31		18 35			18 47		19 00	
Bramley	d		17 26	17 32			17 45							18 17				18 28			18 45		
New Pudsey	d		17 30	17 38			17 49				18 00			18 22				18 32			18 49		19 00
Bradford Interchange	a		17 39	17 47			17 59				18 11			18 32				18 41			19 00		19 09
Bradford Forster Square	a	17 42				17 53		18 01		18 11			18 23		18 38		18 42			18 53		19 07	

		NT	NT	NT	NT	NT	NT ◇	NT	NT	NT	NT ◇	NT ◇ 🛒	NT	NT ◇	NT	NT	NT	NT ◇	NT	NT	NT	NT ◇	NT ◇
Leeds [10]	d	18 56		19 07		19 12	19 18		19 26		19 36	19 49		19 51	19 56		20 07	20 19		20 26		20 39	20 49
Kirkstall Forge	d					19 18			19 33						20 03					20 33			
Apperley Bridge	d					19 23			19 37						20 07					20 37			
Shipley	a	19 07				19 27	19 31		19 42			20 01			20 12					20 42			
	d		19 09		19 14	19 28		19 32		19 46			20 02			20 16			20 32		20 48		
Frizinghall	d		19 13		19 17	19 30		19 36		19 49			20 05			20 19			20 36		20 51		
Bramley	d			19 15							19 45						20 15	20 27				20 47	
New Pudsey	d			19 20							19 49			20 00			20 20	20 31				20 51	20 58
Bradford Interchange	a			19 32							19 59			20 09			20 31	20 40				21 00	21 08
Bradford Forster Square	a		19 19		19 23	19 37		19 42		19 55			20 11			20 25			20 42		20 57		

		NT	NT	NT	GR ■ [1] ⊐	NT	NT ◇	NT	NT	NT ◇	NT	NT	NT	NT ◇	NT	NT ◇	NT	NT	NT ◇	NT	NT	NT
Leeds [10]	d		20 56		21 06	21 07	21 18	21 26		21 39		21 56		22 00	22 07	22 18	22 26		22 38		22 56	
Kirkstall Forge	d							21 33									22 33					
Apperley Bridge	d		21 04					21 37									22 37					
Shipley	a		21 09		21s18			21 42				22 07					22 42				23 07	
	d	21 02		21 14					21 48		22 02		22 15					22 46		23 02		23 14
Frizinghall	d	21 06		21 17					21 51		22 05		22 17					22 49		23 06		23 17
Bramley	d					21 15	21 26			21 48					22 15	22 26			22 46			
New Pudsey	d					21 20	21 30			21 52				22 09	22 20	22 30			22 51			
Bradford Interchange	a					21 30	21 39			22 02				22 18	22 30	22 41			23 00			
Bradford Forster Square	a	21 12		21 23	21 29				21 57		22 11		22 23					22 55		23 12		23 23

		NT	NT	NT
Leeds [10]	d	23 07	23 20	23 38
Kirkstall Forge	d		23 27	
Apperley Bridge	d		23 31	
Shipley	a		23 36	
	d			
Frizinghall	d			
Bramley	d	23 15		23 45
New Pudsey	d	23 20		23 50
Bradford Interchange	a	23 30		23 58
Bradford Forster Square	a			

Saturdays

26 May to 8 December

		NT ◇	NT	NT ◇	NT ◇	NT	NT	NT ◇	NT ◇ 🛒	NT	NT	NT	NT ◇	NT ◇	NT	NT	NT	NT	NT	NT ◇	NT	NT	NT ◇
Leeds [10]	d	05 02	05 08	05 36	05 55	06 02		06 18	06 20		06 26	06 30	06 38	06 52		06 56		07 06	07 12	07 13	07 23		07 36
Kirkstall Forge	d											06 37							07 18				
Apperley Bridge	d											06 41							07 23				
Shipley	a								06 32		06 42	06 45				07 09			07 27		07 36		
	d						06 13			06 32		06 46			07 03		07 14		07 27			07 37	
Frizinghall	d						06 16			06 35		06 48			07 08		07 17		07 30			07 41	
Bramley	d	05 11	05 16	05 45		06 10		06 26					06 47					07 14		07 21			07 45
New Pudsey	d	05 15	05 21	05 49	06 04	06 15		06 30					06 51	07 01				07 19		07 29			07 49
Bradford Interchange	a	05 24	05 32	06 00	06 13	06 27		06 39					07 01	07 11				07 28		07 38			07 59
Bradford Forster Square	a						06 22			06 41		06 55			07 14		07 23		07 37			07 47	

Table T037-F

Saturdays

26 May to 8 December

Leeds - Shipley and Bradford

		NT	NT	NT ◇ 🛒	NT	NT	NT	NT ◇	NT	NT	NT ◇	NT ◇	NT	NT	NT ◇	NT	NT	NT ◇	NT	NT	NT	NT
Leeds [10]	d		07 42	07 48		07 52		07 52	08 07	08 12	08 18	08 19	08 26		08 36		08 42	08 51		08 56		09 07
Kirkstall Forge	d		07 49							08 18							08 49					
Apperley Bridge	d		07 53							08 23							08 53					
Shipley	a		07 57	08 01		08 07				08 27		08 31	08 37				08 57			09 07		
	d	07 44	07 58		08 04		08 11			08 27				08 44		08 49	08 58		09 02		09 14	
Frizinghall	d	07 47	08 00		08 08		08 14			08 30				08 48		08 52	09 00		09 05		09 17	
Bramley	d								08 15		08 26				08 45							09 15
New Pudsey	d							08 01	08 20		08 30				08 49			09 00				09 20
Bradford Interchange	a							08 10	08 30		08 39				08 59			09 09				09 30
Bradford Forster Square	a	07 53	08 07		08 14		08 20			08 37				08 54		08 57	09 07		09 11		09 23	

		NT	NT ◇	NT ◇ 🛒	NT	NT	NT	NT ◇	NT	NT ◇	NT	NT	NT	NT	NT	NT ◇	NT ◇	NT	NT	NT	NT ◇	NT	NT ◇ 🛒
Leeds [10]	d	09 12	09 19	09 19		09 26		09 36	09 42	09 51		09 54		10 07	10 12	10 18	10 18		10 26		10 36	10 42	10 49
Kirkstall Forge	d	09 18							09 49						10 19							10 49	
Apperley Bridge	d	09 23							09 53						10 23							10 53	
Shipley	a	09 27		09 31		09 37			09 57			10 07			10 27		10 32		10 37			10 57	11 01
	d	09 28			09 32		09 44		09 58		10 02		10 14		10 28			10 32		10 44		10 58	
Frizinghall	d	09 30			09 35		09 47		10 00		10 05		10 17		10 30			10 36		10 47		11 00	
Bramley	d		09 27					09 45						10 15		10 26					10 45		
New Pudsey	d		09 31					09 49		10 00				10 20		10 30					10 49		
Bradford Interchange	a		09 40					09 59		10 09				10 30		10 39					10 59		
Bradford Forster Square	a	09 37			09 40		09 53		10 07		10 11		10 23		10 37			10 42		10 53		11 07	

		NT	NT ◇	NT	NT	NT	NT	NT ◇	NT	NT	NT	NT ◇	NT	NT ◇	NT	NT	NT	NT	NT	NT ◇	NT ◇	NT
Leeds [10]	d		10 51	10 54		11 07	11 12	11 18		11 26		11 36	11 42	11 51		11 56		12 07	12 12	12 18	12 20	
Kirkstall Forge	d						11 19						11 49						12 19			
Apperley Bridge	d						11 23						11 53						12 23			
Shipley	a			11 07			11 27			11 37			11 57			12 08			12 27		12 32	
	d	11 02			11 14		11 28		11 32		11 44		11 58		12 02		12 14		12 28			12 32
Frizinghall	d	11 05			11 17		11 30		11 36		11 47		12 00		12 05		12 17		12 30			12 36
Bramley	d					11 15		11 26				11 45						12 15		12 26		
New Pudsey	d		11 00			11 20		11 30				11 49		12 00				12 20		12 30		
Bradford Interchange	a		11 09			11 30		11 39				11 59		12 09				12 30		12 39		
Bradford Forster Square	a	11 11			11 23		11 37		11 41		11 53		12 07		12 11		12 23		12 37			12 42

		NT	NT	NT ◇	NT	NT ◇	NT	NT	NT	NT	NT	NT ◇	NT ◇ 🛒	NT	NT	NT	NT ◇	NT	NT ◇	NT	NT	NT	NT
Leeds [10]	d	12 26		12 36	12 42	12 51		12 56		13 07	13 12	13 18	13 18		13 26		13 36	13 42	13 51		13 56		14 07
Kirkstall Forge	d				12 49						13 19							13 49					
Apperley Bridge	d				12 53						13 23							13 53					
Shipley	a	12 37			12 57			13 07			13 27		13 32		13 37			13 57			14 08		
	d		12 44		12 58		13 02		13 14		13 28			13 32		13 44		13 58		14 02		14 14	
Frizinghall	d		12 47		13 00		13 05		13 17		13 30			13 36		13 47		14 00		14 05		14 17	
Bramley	d			12 45						13 15		13 26					13 45						14 15
New Pudsey	d			12 49		13 00				13 20		13 30					13 49		14 00				14 20
Bradford Interchange	a			12 59		13 09				13 30		13 40					13 59		14 09				14 30
Bradford Forster Square	a		12 53		13 07		13 11		13 23		13 37			13 42		13 53		14 07		14 11		14 23	

		NT	NT ◇	NT ◇	NT	NT	NT	NT ◇	NT	NT ◇	NT	NT	NT	NT	NT	NT ◇	NT ◇ 🛒	NT	NT	NT	NT ◇	NT	NT ◇
Leeds [10]	d	14 12	14 18	14 18		14 26		14 36	14 42	14 51		14 56		15 07	15 12	15 18	15 18		15 26		15 36	15 42	15 51
Kirkstall Forge	d	14 19							14 49						15 19							15 49	
Apperley Bridge	d	14 23							14 53						15 23							15 53	
Shipley	a	14 27		14 32		14 37			14 57			15 08			15 27		15 32		15 37			15 57	
	d	14 28			14 32		14 44		14 58		15 02		15 14		15 28			15 32		15 44		15 58	
Frizinghall	d	14 30			14 36		14 47		15 00		15 05		15 17		15 30			15 36		15 47		16 00	
Bramley	d		14 26					14 45						15 15		15 26					15 45		
New Pudsey	d		14 30					14 49		15 00				15 20		15 30					15 49		16 00
Bradford Interchange	a		14 39					14 59		15 09				15 30		15 39					15 59		16 09
Bradford Forster Square	a	14 37			14 42		14 53		15 07		15 11		15 23		15 37			15 42		15 53		16 07	

		NT	NT	NT	NT	NT	NT ◇	NT	NT	NT	NT ◇	NT	NT ◇ 🛒	NT	NT ◇	NT	NT	NT	NT	NT	NT	NT ◇
Leeds [10]	d		15 56		16 07	16 12	16 18		16 26		16 36	16 42	16 49		16 51	16 56		17 07	17 12	17 18		17 18
Kirkstall Forge	d					16 19						16 49								17 25		
Apperley Bridge	d					16 23						16 53							17 21			
Shipley	a		16 08			16 27			16 37			16 57	17 01			17 07			17 25	17 32		
	d	16 02		16 14		16 28		16 32		16 44		16 58		17 02			17 14		17 26		17 32	
Frizinghall	d	16 05		16 17		16 30		16 36		16 47		17 00		17 05			17 17		17 29		17 36	
Bramley	d				16 15		16 26				16 45							17 15				17 26
New Pudsey	d				16 20		16 30				16 49				17 00			17 20				17 30
Bradford Interchange	a				16 30		16 39				16 59				17 09			17 30				17 39
Bradford Forster Square	a	16 11		16 23		16 37		16 42		16 53		17 07		17 11			17 23		17 36		17 42	

Table T037-F

Leeds - Shipley and Bradford

Saturdays

26 May to 8 December

		NT	NT	NT		NT	NT	NT	NT	NT	NT	NT	NT	NT		NT	NT	NT	NT	NT	NT	NT	NT	NT	
		◇		◇					◇					◇		◇ 🚲				◇		◇			
Leeds 10	d	17 25		17 36		17 36	17 41		17 51	17 56		18 09	18 12	18 18		18 19		18 26		18 36	18 42	18 51	18 56		
Kirkstall Forge	d					17 43	17 48						18 19								18 49				
Apperley Bridge	d					17 47							18 23								18 53				
Shipley	a	17 37				17 51	17 55			18 07			18 27			18 31		18 37			18 57		19 07		
	d		17 44			17 52		18 02			18 15		18 28				18 31		18 44		18 58			19 09	
Frizinghall	d		17 47			17 54		18 05			18 17		18 31				18 35		18 47		19 00			19 13	
Bramley	d			17 45								18 17		18 27						18 45					
New Pudsey	d			17 49					18 00			18 22		18 31						18 49		19 00			
Bradford Interchange	a			17 59					18 11			18 32		18 42						19 00		19 09			
Bradford Forster Square	a		17 53			18 01		18 11			18 23		18 38				18 42		18 53		19 07			19 19	

		NT	NT	NT	NT	NT	NT	NT	NT	NT		NT	NT	NT	NT	NT	NT	NT	NT	NT		NT	NT	NT	NT
					◇				◇	◇ 🚲			◇				◇					◇	◇		
Leeds 10	d	19 09		19 12	19 18		19 26		19 36	19 49			19 51	19 56		20 07	20 19		20 26			20 39	20 49		20 56
Kirkstall Forge	d			19 18			19 33							20 03					20 33						
Apperley Bridge	d			19 23			19 37							20 07					20 37						21 04
Shipley	a			19 27	19 31		19 42			20 01				20 12					20 42						21 09
	d		19 14	19 28		19 32		19 46				20 02			20 16			20 32		20 48				21 02	
Frizinghall	d		19 17	19 30		19 36		19 49				20 05			20 19			20 36		20 51				21 06	
Bramley	d	19 17							19 45							20 15	20 27					20 47			
New Pudsey	d	19 22							19 49				20 00			20 20	20 31					20 51	20 58		
Bradford Interchange	a	19 32							19 59				20 09			20 31	20 40					21 00	21 08		
Bradford Forster Square	a		19 23	19 37		19 42		19 55				20 11			20 25			20 42		20 57				21 12	

		NT	NT	NT	NT	NT		NT	NT	NT	GR	NT	NT	NT	NT	NT		NT	NT	NT	NT	NT	NT	NT	
				◇				◇			■ 1 ⊡		◇		◇				◇						
Leeds 10	d		21 07	21 18	21 26			21 39		21 54	21 58		22 00	22 07	22 18	22 26			22 38		22 56		23 03	23 20	
Kirkstall Forge	d				21 33											22 33								23 27	
Apperley Bridge	d				21 37											22 37								23 31	
Shipley	a				21 42					22 05	22s09					22 42					23 07			23 36	
	d	21 14				21 48			22 02			22 15						22 46		23 02		23 14			
Frizinghall	d	21 17				21 51			22 05			22 17						22 49		23 06		23 17			
Bramley	d		21 15	21 26				21 48						22 15	22 26				22 46				23 13		
New Pudsey	d		21 20	21 30				21 52					22 09	22 20	22 30				22 51				23 18		
Bradford Interchange	a		21 30	21 39				22 02					22 18	22 30	22 41				23 00				23 27		
Bradford Forster Square	a	21 23				21 57			22 11		22 18	22 23						22 55		23 12		23 23			

Sundays

20 May to 2 December

		NT	NT	NT	NT	NT	NT	NT	NT	NT		NT	NT	NT	NT	NT	NT	NT	NT	NT		NT	NT	NT	NT
		■	◇	◇				◇		◇		◇			◇				◇	◇				◇	
Leeds 10	d	07 57	08 18	08 30	08 36	08 57		08 59		09 02		09 18	09 41	09 53	10 02			10 16	10 16	10 24		10 41	10 48	11 02	
Kirkstall Forge	d				08 43								09 48									10 48			
Apperley Bridge	d				08 47								09 52									10 52			
Shipley	a			08 42	08 51			09 12					09 57					10 27		10 36		10 56			
	d				08 52		09 10		09 17				09 57			10 10	10 16					10 57			11 10
Frizinghall	d				08 54		09 14		09 19				10 00			10 14	10 19					10 59			11 14
Bramley	d	08 05	08 26							09 10		09 26			10 10				10 24					11 09	
New Pudsey	d	08 09	08 31			09 07				09 14		09 31		10 03	10 14				10 29				10 58	11 14	
Bradford Interchange	a	08 18	08 39			09 16				09 25		09 39		10 12	10 24				10 37				11 07	11 25	
Bradford Forster Square	a				09 01		09 20		09 25				10 07			10 20	10 25					11 06			11 20

		NT	NT	NT	NT	NT		NT	NT	NT	NT	NT	NT	NT	NT	NT		NT	NT	NT	NT	NT	NT	NT	NT
			◇	◇							◇			◇	◇				◇				◇	◇	
Leeds 10	d		11 15	11 18	11 26	11 41		11 51	11 57		12 02		12 16	12 18	12 28	12 41		12 51	13 08			13 16	13 21	13 24	13 41
Kirkstall Forge	d					11 48										12 48									13 48
Apperley Bridge	d					11 52										12 52									13 52
Shipley	a		11 27		11 37	11 56			12 08				12 27		12 40	12 56						13 27		13 36	13 56
	d	11 16				11 57				12 10		12 16				12 57				13 10	13 16				13 57
Frizinghall	d	11 19				11 59				12 14		12 19				12 59				13 14	13 19				13 59
Bramley	d			11 26							12 10			12 26					13 16				13 29		
New Pudsey	d			11 31				12 01			12 14			12 31				13 01	13 20				13 34		
Bradford Interchange	a			11 39				12 10			12 25			12 39				13 10	13 29				13 42		
Bradford Forster Square	a	11 25				12 06				12 20		12 25				13 06				13 20	13 25				14 06

		NT		NT	NT	NT	NT	NT	NT	NT	NT	NT		NT	NT	NT	NT	NT	NT	NT	NT	NT		NT	NT
				◇				◇	◇	◇				◇				◇	◇			◇			
Leeds 10	d	13 51		14 08			14 16	14 18	14 24	14 37	14 41	14 51		15 03			15 16	15 17	15 24	15 41	15 51	16 03			
Kirkstall Forge	d										14 48									15 48					
Apperley Bridge	d										14 52									15 52					
Shipley	a						14 27		14 36		14 56						15 27		15 36	15 56					
	d				14 10	14 16					14 57				15 10	15 16				15 57				16 10	16 16
Frizinghall	d				14 14	14 19					14 59				15 14	15 19				15 59				16 14	16 19
Bramley	d			14 16				14 26						15 11				15 25				16 11			
New Pudsey	d	14 01		14 20				14 31		14 46		15 01		15 16				15 30			16 01	16 16			
Bradford Interchange	a	14 10		14 29				14 42		14 54		15 10		15 25				15 42			16 10	16 25			
Bradford Forster Square	a				14 20	14 25					15 06				15 20	15 25				16 06				16 20	16 25

Table T037-F

Leeds - Shipley and Bradford

Sundays

20 May to 2 December

		NT	NT	NT		NT	NT	NT	NT	NT	NT	NT	NT	NT		NT	NT	NT	NT	NT	NT	NT	NT	NT	
			◇	◇				◇				◇	◇				◇				◇			◇	
Leeds 10	d	16 12	16 19	16 22		16 41	16 51	17 03			17 16	17 19	17 24	17 45		17 51	18 03			18 16	18 28	18 41	18 51	18 52	
Kirkstall Forge	d					16 48								17 52								18 48			
Apperley Bridge	d					16 52								17 56								18 52			
Shipley	a	16 23		16 34		16 56					17 27		17 36	18 00						18 28		18 56		19 04	
	d					16 57			17 10	17 17				18 01				18 10	18 16			18 57			
Frizinghall	d					16 59			17 14	17 20				18 03				18 14	18 19			18 59			
Bramley	d		16 27					17 11				17 27					18 11				18 36				
New Pudsey	d		16 32				17 01	17 16				17 31				18 01	18 16				18 41		19 01		
Bradford Interchange	a		16 40				17 10	17 25				17 40				18 10	18 25				18 49		19 10		
Bradford Forster Square	a					17 06			17 20	17 26				18 10				18 20	18 25			19 06			

		NT	NT	NT	NT	NT	NT	NT	NT	NT		NT	NT	NT	NT	NT	NT	NT	NT	NT		NT	NT	NT	NT
			◇			◇			◇					◇			◇					◇			
Leeds 10	d		19 04		19 16	19 19	19 42	19 51	20 03				20 16	20 27	20 41	21 01	21 08			21 16		21 27	21 42	22 01	
Kirkstall Forge	d						19 49								20 48								21 49		
Apperley Bridge	d						19 53								20 52								21 53		
Shipley	a				19 27		19 57						20 27		20 56					21 27			21 59		
	d	19 10		19 16			19 58			20 10		20 18			20 57			21 10	21 17				21 59		22 10
Frizinghall	d	19 14		19 19			20 00			20 14		20 20			20 59			21 14	21 19				22 02		22 14
Bramley	d		19 12			19 27			20 11					20 35			21 16					21 35			
New Pudsey	d		19 16			19 32		20 01	20 16					20 40		21 11	21 20					21 40		22 11	
Bradford Interchange	a		19 25			19 41		20 10	20 25					20 48		21 22	21 29					21 49		22 22	
Bradford Forster Square	a	19 20		19 25			20 07			20 20		20 26			21 06			21 20	21 25				22 08		22 20

		NT	NT	NT	NT	NT		NT
			◇					
Leeds 10	d		22 17	22 20	22 41	22 50		23 22
Kirkstall Forge	d				22 48			
Apperley Bridge	d				22 52			
Shipley	a			22 31	22 56			23 33
	d	22 16			22 57			
Frizinghall	d	22 19			22 59			
Bramley	d		22 25					
New Pudsey	d		22 30			23 00		
Bradford Interchange	a		22 38			23 09		
Bradford Forster Square	a	22 25			23 07			

Table T037-R

Mondays to Fridays
21 May to 7 December

Bradford and Shipley - Leeds

Miles	Miles			NT MX ◇	NT MX ◇	NT	NT	NT	NT	NT		GR ■ A ☕	NT	NT	NT	NT	NT	NT ◇	NT	GR ■ ☕		NT	NT	NT ◇	NT
0	—	**Bradford Forster Square**	d			05 46	05 58	06 03				06 30		06 41	06 46		06 56					07 11	07 16		
—	0	**Bradford Interchange**	d		00 31					06 22						06 50		07 02						07 17	
—	3½	New Pudsey	d	00 09						06 30						06 59		07 11						07 25	
—	5½	Bramley	d	00 12						06 34								07 14						07 29	
1¾	—	Frizinghall	d			05 49	06 01	06 06						06 44	06 49		06 59					07 14	07 19		
2¾	—	**Shipley**	a			05 53	06 05	06 10						06 48	06 53		07 03					07 18	07 23		
—	—		d				06 06		06 13			06u37	06 46				07 03		07 08	07u17					07 29
5¾	—	Apperley Bridge	d				06 10										07 08								
9¼	—	Kirkstall Forge	d				06 15										07 12								
13½	9½	**Leeds** 🔟	a	00 21	00 50		06 24		06 27	06 43		06 52	07 02			07 12	07 21	07 23	07 23	07 31				07 40	07 44

		NT	NT ◇	NT	NT	NT		NT	NT	NT	NT	NT ◇	NT	NT ◇ 🚲	NT	NT		NT ◇	NT ◇	NT	NT ◇	NT	NT	NT	NT
Bradford Forster Square	d	07 28			07 41			07 47			07 54				08 11	08 16						08 34	08 41	08 46	
Bradford Interchange	d		07 29			07 45				07 52		08 00						08 17			08 29				08 51
New Pudsey	d		07 38			07 54				08 01		08 09						08 27			08 38				09 00
Bramley	d		07 42			07 57				08 04		08 12						08 30			08 42				
Frizinghall	d	07 31			07 44			07 50			07 57				08 14	08 19						08 37	08 44	08 49	
Shipley	a	07 35			07 48			07 54			08 01				08 18	08 23						08 41	08 49	08 53	
	d	07 35		07 44					07 58		08 02		08 12	08 15					08 28	08 38		08 42			
Apperley Bridge	d	07 40		07 48							08 06											08 46			
Kirkstall Forge	d	07 45									08 11											08 51			
Leeds 🔟	a	07 53	07 56	07 59		08 08			08 13	08 15	08 19	08 21	08 28	08 33				08 38	08 43	08 53	08 54	08 59			09 08

		NT ◇		NT	NT	NT	NT	NT ◇	NT ◇	NT	NT	NT		NT	NT	NT ◇	NT	NT	NT	NT	NT ◇	NT ◇		NT	NT
Bradford Forster Square	d			09 00		09 11	09 16			09 30		09 41		09 46			10 00		10 11	10 16				10 30	
Bradford Interchange	d	09 00						09 18	09 29						09 51	10 00					10 18	10 30			
New Pudsey	d	09 09						09 26	09 38						10 00	10 09					10 26	10 39			
Bramley	d	09 12						09 30	09 42							10 12					10 32	10 43			
Frizinghall	d			09 03		09 14	09 19			09 33		09 44		09 49			10 03		10 14	10 19				10 33	
Shipley	a			09 07		09 18	09 23			09 37		09 48		09 53			10 07		10 18	10 23				10 37	
	d			09 08	09 15					09 38	09 45						10 08	10 15						10 38	10 45
Apperley Bridge	d			09 12						09 42							10 12							10 42	
Kirkstall Forge	d			09 17						09 47							10 17							10 47	
Leeds 🔟	a	09 21		09 26	09 29			09 42	09 51	09 56	10 01				10 10	10 21	10 27	10 29			10 43	10 54		10 56	10 59

		NT	NT ◇ 🚲	NT	NT	NT ◇	NT	NT		NT	NT	NT ◇	NT ◇	NT	NT	NT	NT	NT		NT ◇	NT	NT	NT	NT ◇	NT ◇
Bradford Forster Square	d	10 41		10 46			11 00			11 11	11 16			11 30		11 41	11 46				12 00		12 11		
Bradford Interchange	d				10 51	11 00						11 18	11 28					11 51		12 00					12 15
New Pudsey	d				11 00	11 09						11 26	11 38					11 59		12 09					12 24
Bramley	d					11 12						11 30	11 42							12 12					12 28
Frizinghall	d	10 44		10 49			11 03			11 14	11 19			11 33		11 44	11 49				12 03		12 14		
Shipley	a	10 48		10 53			11 07			11 18	11 23			11 37		11 48	11 53				12 07		12 18		
	d		10 50				11 08	11 15						11 38	11 45						12 08	12 15		12 21	
Apperley Bridge	d						11 13							11 42							12 13				
Kirkstall Forge	d						11 18							11 47							12 18				
Leeds 🔟	a		11 08		11 09	11 21	11 27	11 31				11 39	11 51	11 56	12 01			12 09		12 21	12 27	12 30		12 37	12 38

		NT	NT ◇	NT		NT	NT	NT	NT	NT ◇	NT	NT	NT	NT ◇ 🚲		NT ◇	NT	NT ◇	NT	NT	NT	NT	NT	NT ◇	
Bradford Forster Square	d	12 16		12 30			12 41	12 46			13 00		13 11				13 16		13 30		13 41	13 46			
Bradford Interchange	d		12 29						12 50	13 00						13 15		13 29					13 51	14 00	
New Pudsey	d		12 38						12 59	13 09						13 24		13 38					14 00	14 09	
Bramley	d		12 42							13 12						13 28		13 42						14 12	
Frizinghall	d	12 19		12 33			12 44	12 49			13 03		13 14				13 19		13 33		13 44	13 49			
Shipley	a	12 23		12 37			12 48	12 53			13 07		13 18				13 23		13 37		13 48	13 53			
	d			12 38		12 45					13 08	13 15		13 20					13 38	13 45					
Apperley Bridge	d			12 42							13 13								13 42						
Kirkstall Forge	d			12 47							13 18								13 47						
Leeds 🔟	a		12 53	12 56		12 59			13 08	13 21	13 27	13 30		13 38		13 38		13 51	13 56	14 00			14 10	14 21	

		NT	NT	NT	NT	NT ◇	NT	NT ◇	NT	NT		NT	NT	NT	NT ◇	NT	NT	NT	NT ◇	NT		NT ◇	NT	NT	NT
Bradford Forster Square	d	14 00		14 11			14 16		14 30			14 41	14 46			15 00		15 11		15 16			15 30		15 41
Bradford Interchange	d					14 15		14 29						14 51	15 00				15 15			15 29			
New Pudsey	d					14 24		14 38						15 00	15 09				15 24			15 38			
Bramley	d					14 28		14 42							15 12				15 28			15 42			
Frizinghall	d	14 03		14 14			14 19		14 33			14 44	14 49			15 03		15 14		15 19			15 33		15 44
Shipley	a	14 07		14 18			14 23		14 37			14 48	14 53			15 07		15 18		15 23			15 37		15 48
	d	14 08	14 15		14 20				14 38	14 45						15 08	15 15						15 38	15 45	
Apperley Bridge	d	14 13							14 42							15 13							15 42		
Kirkstall Forge	d	14 18							14 47							15 18							15 47		
Leeds 🔟	a	14 27	14 30		14 38	14 38		14 53	14 56	14 59				15 10	15 21	15 27	15 30		15 37			15 51	15 56	15 59	

A West Riding Limited

Table T037-R

Mondays to Fridays
21 May to 7 December

Bradford and Shipley - Leeds

		NT		NT	NT ◇	NT	NT	NT	NT ◇ 🚲	NT ◇	NT	NT ◇		NT	NT	NT	NT ◇	NT	NT	NT ◇	NT	NT		NT	NT ◇ 🚲
Bradford Forster Square	d	15 46				16 00		16 11			16 16			16 30		16 41		16 46			17 00			17 11	
Bradford Interchange	d			15 50	16 00					16 16		16 29							16 52	17 00					
New Pudsey	d			15 59	16 09					16 25		16 38							17 01	17 09					
Bramley	d				16 12					16 29		16 42								17 12					
Frizinghall	d	15 49				16 03		16 14			16 19			16 33		16 44		16 49			17 03			17 14	
Shipley	a	15 53				16 07		16 18			16 23			16 37		16 48		16 53			17 07			17 18	
	d					16 08	16 15		16 20					16 38	16 45		16 49				17 08	17 15			17 20
Apperley Bridge	d					16 13								16 42							17 12				
Kirkstall Forge	d					16 18								16 47							17 17				
Leeds 🔟	a			16 09	16 21	16 27	16 30		16 38	16 39		16 53		16 56	16 59		17 03		17 10	17 21	17 27	17 29			17 38

		NT	NT ◇	NT ◇	NT	NT	NT	NT		NT	NT ◇	NT	NT	NT	NT	NT ◇	NT ◇	NT		NT	NT	NT ◇ 🚲	NT	NT	NT ◇
Bradford Forster Square	d	17 16			17 30		17 41	17 49				18 00		18 11	18 16			18 30			18 41			18 46	
Bradford Interchange	d		17 17	17 29						17 52	18 00					18 19	18 31						18 46		19 00
New Pudsey	d		17 26	17 38						18 01	18 08					18 28	18 40						18 55		19 09
Bramley	d		17 30	17 42							18 12					18 32	18 44								19 12
Frizinghall	d	17 19			17 33		17 44	17 52				18 03		18 14	18 19			18 33			18 44			18 49	
Shipley	a	17 23			17 37		17 48	17 56				18 07		18 18	18 23			18 37			18 48			18 53	
	d				17 38	17 45						18 08	18 15					18 38		18 45		18 50			
Apperley Bridge	d				17 42							18 12						18 42							
Kirkstall Forge	d				17 47							18 17						18 47							
Leeds 🔟	a		17 39	17 53	17 57	18 00				18 10	18 21	18 26	18 29			18 41	18 55	18 56		18 59		19 06	19 07		19 21

		NT	NT	NT		NT ◇	NT ◇	NT	NT ◇	NT	NT	NT	NT	NT		NT ◇	NT	NT	NT	NT ◇	NT ◇	NT	NT	NT ◇ 🚲	
Bradford Forster Square	d	19 00		19 11				19 16		19 30		19 41		19 46				20 11	20 16			20 30			
Bradford Interchange	d						19 15		19 31				19 46			20 00				20 17	20 30				
New Pudsey	d						19 24		19 40				19 55			20 09				20 26	20 39				
Bramley	d						19 28		19 44							20 12				20 30	20 43				
Frizinghall	d	19 03		19 14				19 19		19 33		19 44		19 49				20 14	20 19			20 33			
Shipley	a	19 07		19 18				19 23		19 37		19 48		19 53				20 18	20 23			20 37			
	d	19 08	19 15			19 20				19 38	19 46						20 16						20 45	20 51	
Apperley Bridge	d	19 12								19 42							20 21						20 49		
Kirkstall Forge	d	19 17								19 47													20 54		
Leeds 🔟	a	19 27	19 29			19 36	19 37		19 53	19 56	20 00		20 06			20 21	20 32			20 39	20 53		21 02	21 06	

		NT	NT	NT ◇	NT	NT	NT ◇	NT	NT	NT ◇		NT	NT	NT ◇	NT ◇	NT	NT	NT ◇	NT	NT ◇ 🚲		NT	NT ◇	NT ◇ 🚲	NT ◇
Bradford Forster Square	d	20 48				21 11		21 16	21 28								22 11		22 16			22 25			
Bradford Interchange	d		20 52	20 59			21 15			21 29			21 50	21 56				22 15					22 29		23 01
New Pudsey	d		21 01	21 08			21 24			21 38			21 59	22 05				22 24					22 38		23 10
Bramley	d			21 12			21 28			21 42				22 09				22 28					22 42		23 13
Frizinghall	d	20 51				21 14		21 19	21 31								22 14		22 19			22 28			
Shipley	a	20 55				21 18		21 24	21 35								22 18		22 23			22 32			
	d				21 15							21 45			22 06	22 16				22 32				22 55	
Apperley Bridge	d				21 19							21 49				22 20									
Kirkstall Forge	d				21 24							21 54				22 25									
Leeds 🔟	a		21 10	21 21	21 32		21 37			21 52		22 02	22 09	22 18	22 22	22 34		22 38		22 49			22 53	23 12	23 22

		NT	NT	NT	NT ◇	NT		NT ◇
Bradford Forster Square	d			23 11		23 16		
Bradford Interchange	d	23 08			23 16			23 59
New Pudsey	d	23 17			23 24			00 09
Bramley	d	23 21			23 28			00 12
Frizinghall	d			23 14		23 19		
Shipley	a			23 18		23 23		
	d		23 15					
Apperley Bridge	d		23 19					
Kirkstall Forge	d		23 24					
Leeds 🔟	a	23 30	23 32		23 37			00 21

Saturdays
26 May to 8 December

		NT ◇	NT ◇	NT	NT	NT	NT	NT	GR ■ A ☕	NT		NT	NT	NT	NT	NT ◇	NT	NT	GR ■ ☕	NT		NT ◇	NT	NT	NT ◇
Bradford Forster Square	d			05 46	05 58	06 03			06 30			06 41	06 46		06 56			07 11		07 16				07 28	
Bradford Interchange	d		00 31					06 22						06 50		07 02						07 17			07 29
New Pudsey	d	00 09						06 30						06 59		07 11						07 25			07 38
Bramley	d	00 12						06 34								07 14						07 29			07 42
Frizinghall	d			05 49	06 01	06 06						06 44	06 49		06 59			07 14		07 19				07 31	
Shipley	a			05 53	06 05	06 10						06 48	06 53		07 03			07 18		07 23				07 35	
	d				06 06		06 13		06u37	06 46					07 03		07 08		07u19				07 29	07 35	
Apperley Bridge	d				06 10										07 08									07 40	
Kirkstall Forge	d				06 15										07 12									07 45	
Leeds 🔟	a	00 21	00 50		06 24		06 27	06 43	06 52	07 02				07 12	07 21	07 23	07 23		07 33			07 40	07 44	07 53	07 56

A West Riding Limited

Table T037-R

Saturdays

26 May to 8 December

Bradford and Shipley - Leeds

		NT		NT	NT	NT	NT	NT	NT	NT	NT	NT		NT	NT	NT	NT	NT	NT	NT	NT	NT		NT	NT
									◇			◇			◇	◇		◇						◇	
Bradford Forster Square	d			07 41	07 47			07 54			08 11			08 16					08 34	08 41	08 46				09 00
Bradford Interchange	d						07 52		08 00						08 17			08 29				08 48		09 00	
New Pudsey	d						08 01		08 09						08 27			08 38				08 57		09 09	
Bramley	d						08 04		08 12						08 30			08 42				09 01		09 12	
Frizinghall	d			07 44	07 50			07 57			08 14			08 19					08 37	08 44	08 49				09 03
Shipley	a			07 48	07 54			08 01			08 18			08 23					08 41	08 49	08 53				09 07
	d	07 44				07 58		08 02		08 12		08 19				08 28	08 38		08 42						09 08
Apperley Bridge	d	07 48						08 06											08 46						09 12
Kirkstall Forge	d							08 11											08 51						09 17
Leeds 10	a	07 59				08 13	08 15	08 19	08 21	08 28		08 35			08 38	08 43	08 53	08 54	08 59			09 09		09 21	09 26

		NT	NT	NT	NT	NT	NT	NT		NT	NT	NT	NT	NT	NT	NT	NT	NT		NT	NT	NT	NT	NT	NT
					◇	◇							◇				◇ trolley			◇	◇				
Bradford Forster Square	d		09 11	09 16			09 30			09 41	09 46			10 00		10 11		10 16				10 30		10 41	10 46
Bradford Interchange	d				09 18	09 29						09 49	10 00							10 18	10 30				
New Pudsey	d				09 26	09 38						09 58	10 09							10 26	10 39				
Bramley	d				09 30	09 42						10 02	10 12							10 32	10 43				
Frizinghall	d		09 14	09 19			09 33			09 44	09 49			10 03		10 14		10 19				10 33		10 44	10 49
Shipley	a		09 18	09 23			09 37			09 48	09 53			10 07		10 18		10 23				10 37		10 48	10 53
	d	09 15					09 38	09 45						10 08	10 15		10 20					10 38	10 45		
Apperley Bridge	d						09 42							10 12								10 42			
Kirkstall Forge	d						09 47							10 17								10 47			
Leeds 10	a	09 29			09 42	09 52	09 56	10 01				10 10	10 21	10 27	10 29		10 37			10 43	10 54	10 56	10 59		

		NT	NT	NT		NT	NT	NT	NT	NT	NT	NT	NT	NT		NT	NT	NT	NT	NT	NT	NT	NT	NT	
			◇						◇	◇				◇ trolley				◇				◇	◇		
Bradford Forster Square	d			11 00			11 11	11 16			11 30		11 41			11 46			12 00		12 11			12 16	
Bradford Interchange	d	10 51	11 00						11 18	11 28							11 51	12 00					12 15		
New Pudsey	d	11 00	11 09						11 26	11 38							11 59	12 09					12 24		
Bramley	d		11 12						11 30	11 42								12 12					12 28		
Frizinghall	d			11 03			11 14	11 19			11 33		11 44			11 49			12 03		12 14			12 19	
Shipley	a			11 07			11 18	11 23			11 37		11 48			11 53			12 07		12 18			12 23	
	d			11 08		11 15					11 38	11 45		11 50					12 08	12 15		12 21			
Apperley Bridge	d			11 13							11 42								12 13						
Kirkstall Forge	d			11 18							11 47								12 18						
Leeds 10	a	11 09	11 21	11 27		11 31			11 39	11 51	11 56	12 01		12 05			12 09	12 21	12 27	12 30		12 37	12 38		

		NT	NT	NT	NT	NT	NT	NT	NT	NT		NT	NT	NT	NT	NT	NT	NT	NT	NT		NT	NT	NT	NT
		◇						◇					◇ trolley	◇		◇							◇		
Bradford Forster Square	d		12 30		12 41	12 46			13 00			13 11			13 16		13 30		13 41	13 46				14 00	
Bradford Interchange	d	12 29					12 50	13 00						13 15		13 29						13 50	14 00		
New Pudsey	d	12 38					12 59	13 09						13 24		13 38						13 59	14 09		
Bramley	d	12 42						13 12						13 28		13 42							14 12		
Frizinghall	d		12 33		12 44	12 49			13 03			13 14			13 19		13 33		13 44	13 49				14 03	
Shipley	a		12 37		12 48	12 53			13 07			13 18			13 23		13 37		13 48	13 53				14 07	
	d		12 38	12 45					13 08	13 15			13 20				13 38	13 45						14 08	14 15
Apperley Bridge	d		12 42						13 13								13 42							14 13	
Kirkstall Forge	d		12 47						13 18								13 47							14 18	
Leeds 10	a	12 53	12 56	12 59			13 08	13 21	13 27	13 30			13 38	13 38		13 51	13 56	14 00				14 09	14 21	14 27	14 30

		NT	NT	NT	NT	NT		NT	NT	NT	NT	NT	NT	NT	NT	NT		NT	NT	NT	NT	NT	NT	NT	NT
				◇		◇							◇					◇		◇					
Bradford Forster Square	d	14 11			14 16			14 30		14 41	14 46			15 00		15 11			15 16		15 30		15 41	15 46	
Bradford Interchange	d			14 15		14 29						14 51	15 00					15 15		15 29					15 50
New Pudsey	d			14 24		14 38						15 00	15 09					15 24		15 38					15 59
Bramley	d			14 28		14 42							15 12					15 28		15 42					
Frizinghall	d	14 14			14 19			14 33		14 44	14 49			15 03		15 14			15 19		15 33		15 44	15 49	
Shipley	a	14 18			14 23			14 37		14 48	14 53			15 07		15 18			15 23		15 37		15 48	15 53	
	d		14 20					14 38	14 45					15 08	15 15						15 38	15 45			
Apperley Bridge	d							14 42						15 13							15 42				
Kirkstall Forge	d							14 47						15 18							15 47				
Leeds 10	a		14 38	14 38		14 53		14 56	14 59			15 09	15 22	15 27	15 30			15 37		15 51	15 56	15 59			16 09

		NT		NT	NT	NT	NT	NT	NT	NT	NT	NT		NT	NT	NT	NT	NT	NT	NT	NT	NT		NT	NT
		◇					◇ trolley	◇		◇					◇			◇				◇ trolley			◇
Bradford Forster Square	d			16 00		16 11			16 16		16 30			16 41		16 46			17 00		17 11			17 16	
Bradford Interchange	d	16 00						16 16		16 29							16 52	17 00							17 17
New Pudsey	d	16 09						16 25		16 38							17 01	17 09							17 26
Bramley	d	16 12						16 29		16 42								17 12							17 30
Frizinghall	d			16 03		16 14			16 19		16 33			16 44		16 49			17 03		17 14			17 19	
Shipley	a			16 07		16 18			16 23		16 37			16 48		16 53			17 07		17 18			17 23	
	d			16 08	16 15		16 20				16 38	16 45			16 49				17 08	17 15		17 20			
Apperley Bridge	d			16 13							16 42								17 12						
Kirkstall Forge	d			16 18							16 47								17 17						
Leeds 10	a	16 21		16 27	16 30		16 38	16 39		16 53	16 56	16 59			17 03		17 10	17 21	17 27	17 29		17 38			17 39

Table T037-R

Saturdays

26 May to 8 December

Bradford and Shipley - Leeds

		NT	NT	NT		NT	NT	NT	NT	NT	NT	NT	NT	NT		NT	NT	NT	NT	NT	NT	NT	NT	NT	
		◇							◇					◇		◇				◇ trolley			◇		
Bradford Forster Square	d		17 30			17 41	17 49			18 00		18 11	18 16				18 30		18 41			18 46		19 00	
Bradford Interchange	d	17 29						17 52	18 00					18 19		18 31					18 46		19 00		
New Pudsey	d	17 38						18 01	18 08					18 28		18 40					18 55		19 09		
Bramley	d	17 42							18 12					18 32		18 44							19 12		
Frizinghall	d		17 33			17 44	17 52			18 03		18 14	18 19				18 33		18 44			18 49		19 03	
Shipley	a		17 37			17 48	17 56			18 07		18 18	18 23				18 37		18 48			18 53		19 07	
	d		17 38	17 45						18 08	18 15						18 38	18 45		18 50				19 08	
Apperley Bridge	d		17 42							18 12							18 42							19 12	
Kirkstall Forge	d		17 47							18 17							18 47							19 17	
Leeds 10	a	17 53	17 57	18 00				18 10	18 21	18 26	18 29			18 41		18 55	18 56	18 59		19 06	19 07		19 21	19 27	

		NT	NT	NT	NT	NT	NT	NT	NT	NT		NT	NT	NT	NT	NT	NT	NT	NT	NT		NT	NT	NT	NT
				◇	◇		◇							◇				◇	◇				◇ trolley		
Bradford Forster Square	d		19 11			19 16		19 30		19 41			19 46			20 11	20 16			20 30				20 48	
Bradford Interchange	d				19 15		19 31					19 46		20 00				20 17	20 30						20 50
New Pudsey	d				19 24		19 40					19 55		20 09				20 26	20 39						20 59
Bramley	d				19 28		19 44							20 12				20 30	20 43						
Frizinghall	d		19 14			19 19		19 33		19 44			19 49			20 14	20 19			20 33				20 51	
Shipley	a		19 18			19 23		19 37		19 48			19 53			20 18	20 23			20 37				20 55	
	d	19 15		19 20				19 38	19 46						20 16							20 45	20 51		
Apperley Bridge	d							19 42							20 21							20 49			
Kirkstall Forge	d							19 47														20 54			
Leeds 10	a	19 29		19 36	19 37		19 53	19 56	20 00			20 06		20 21	20 32			20 39	20 52			21 02	21 06		21 08

		NT	NT	NT	NT	NT		NT	NT	NT	NT	NT	NT	NT	NT	NT		NT	NT	NT	NT	NT	NT	NT	NT
		◇			◇				◇			◇	◇			◇			◇ trolley		◇		◇ trolley	◇	
Bradford Forster Square	d			21 11		21 16		21 28							22 11			22 16		22 25					
Bradford Interchange	d	20 59			21 15				21 29		21 50	22 00				22 15					22 29	22 50		23 01	
New Pudsey	d	21 08			21 24				21 38		21 59	22 09				22 24					22 38	22 59		23 10	
Bramley	d	21 12			21 28				21 42			22 12				22 28					22 42			23 13	
Frizinghall	d			21 14		21 19		21 31							22 14			22 19		22 28					
Shipley	a			21 18		21 24		21 35							22 18			22 23		22 32					
	d		21 15							21 45			22 06	22 16					22 30				22 54		23 15
Apperley Bridge	d		21 19							21 49				22 20											23 19
Kirkstall Forge	d		21 24							21 54				22 25											23 24
Leeds 10	a	21 21	21 32		21 37				21 52	22 02	22 09	22 21	22 22	22 34		22 38			22 48		22 53	23 11	23 11	23 22	23 32

		NT		NT	NT
				◇	
Bradford Forster Square	d	23 11			23 16
Bradford Interchange	d			23 16	
New Pudsey	d			23 24	
Bramley	d			23 28	
Frizinghall	d	23 14			23 19
Shipley	a	23 18			23 23
	d				
Apperley Bridge	d				
Kirkstall Forge	d				
Leeds 10	a			23 37	

Sundays

20 May to 2 December

		NT	NT	NT	NT	NT	NT	NT	NT	NT		NT	NT	NT	NT	NT	NT	NT	NT	NT		NT	NT	NT	NT
		◇		◇						◇					◇				◇						◇
Bradford Forster Square	d				09 13			09 38	09 48				10 13			10 38		10 48				11 13		11 38	
Bradford Interchange	d	00 06		09 00		09 30				10 00		10 18			10 38				10 59	11 07					11 39
New Pudsey	d	00 15		09 09		09 39				10 09		10 27			10 47				11 08	11 16					11 50
Bramley	d	00 18				09 43						10 31			10 50					11 20					11 53
Frizinghall	d				09 16			09 41	09 51				10 16			10 41		10 51				11 16		11 41	
Shipley	a				09 20			09 45	09 55				10 20			10 45		10 55				11 20		11 45	
	d		09 00		09 21		09 40						10 21	10 40			10 49					11 21	11 40		
Apperley Bridge	d				09 26								10 26									11 26			
Kirkstall Forge	d				09 31								10 31									11 32			
Leeds 10	a	00 28	09 14	09 18	09 39	09 52	09 54			10 19		10 38	10 40	10 54	10 59		11 06		11 19	11 28		11 40	11 54		12 02

		NT	NT	NT	NT	NT		NT	NT	NT	NT	NT	NT	NT	NT	NT		NT	NT	NT	NT	NT	NT	NT	NT
		◇		◇	◇						◇		◇						◇		◇		◇		
Bradford Forster Square	d		11 48					12 13		12 38		12 48			13 13			13 38		13 48				14 13	
Bradford Interchange	d			12 00		12 16					12 39		13 00	13 17					13 47		14 00	14 10			
New Pudsey	d			12 09		12 25					12 50		13 09	13 26					13 56		14 09	14 19			
Bramley	d					12 29					12 54			13 30					14 00			14 23			
Frizinghall	d		11 51					12 16		12 41		12 51			13 16			13 41		13 51				14 16	
Shipley	a		11 55					12 20		12 45		12 55			13 20			13 45		13 55				14 20	
	d	11 49			12 16			12 21	12 40						13 20	13 40							14 16	14 21	14 40
Apperley Bridge	d							12 26							13 25									14 26	
Kirkstall Forge	d							12 31							13 30									14 31	
Leeds 10	a	12 06		12 19	12 36	12 37		12 40	12 54		13 05		13 19	13 38	13 39	13 54			14 11		14 23	14 31	14 36	14 40	14 54

Table T037-R

Sundays

20 May to 2 December

Bradford and Shipley - Leeds

		NT	NT ◇	NT	NT ◇	NT ◇	NT	NT	NT	NT ◇	NT	NT	NT ◇	NT	NT	NT	NT	NT ◇	NT	NT	NT ◇	NT	NT ◇
Bradford Forster Square	d	14 38		14 48				15 13			15 38	15 48			16 13				16 38	16 48			
Bradford Interchange	d		14 42		15 00		15 17			15 38			15 56	16 14				16 38			17 00	17 17	
New Pudsey	d		14 51		15 09		15 26			15 50			16 04	16 23				16 50			17 09	17 26	
Bramley	d		14 54				15 30			15 54				16 27				16 53				17 30	
Frizinghall	d	14 41		14 51				15 16			15 41	15 51			16 16				16 41	16 51			
Shipley	a	14 45		14 55				15 20			15 45	15 55			16 20				16 45	16 55			
	d					15 18		15 22	15 40						16 21	16 26	16 40						17 16
Apperley Bridge	d							15 27							16 26								
Kirkstall Forge	d							15 32							16 31								
Leeds	a		15 05		15 19	15 36	15 38	15 41	15 54	16 03			16 15	16 35	16 40	16 45	16 54	17 03			17 19	17 38	17 39

		NT	NT ◇	NT	NT	NT ◇	NT	NT ◇	NT ◇	NT	NT	NT	NT	NT ◇	NT	NT ◇	NT ◇	NT	NT	NT	NT	NT ◇
Bradford Forster Square	d	17 13			17 38		17 48				18 14		18 38		18 48				19 13		19 38	
Bradford Interchange	d					17 39		18 00		18 17				18 48		18 59		19 17				
New Pudsey	d					17 53		18 09		18 26				18 57		19 08		19 26				
Bramley	d					17 57				18 30				19 00				19 30				
Frizinghall	d	17 16			17 41		17 51				18 17		18 41		18 51				19 16		19 41	
Shipley	a	17 20			17 45		17 55				18 21		18 45		18 55				19 20		19 45	
	d	17 21	17 28	17 42					18 18		18 22	18 40					19 17		19 21	19 40		19 50
Apperley Bridge	d	17 26									18 27								19 26			
Kirkstall Forge	d	17 31									18 32								19 31			
Leeds	a	17 40	17 50	17 56		18 07		18 20	18 32	18 38	18 41	18 54		19 09		19 18	19 37	19 38	19 40	19 54		20 07

		NT ◇	NT	NT ◇	NT	NT	NT	NT ◇	NT	NT	NT ◇	NT	NT	NT ◇	NT	NT	NT ◇	NT	NT ◇	NT	NT	NT ◇	NT
Bradford Forster Square	d		19 48			20 13			20 38	20 48			21 13		21 38			21 48		22 13			
Bradford Interchange	d	19 42		19 57	20 17			20 37			21 00	21 15					21 40		21 59		22 22	22 29	
New Pudsey	d	19 55		20 05	20 26			20 46			21 09	21 24					21 52		22 08		22 31	22 38	
Bramley	d	19 58			20 30			20 50				21 28					21 55				22 35	22 41	
Frizinghall	d		19 51			20 16			20 41	20 51			21 16		21 41			21 51		22 16			
Shipley	a		19 55			20 20			20 45	20 55			21 20		21 45			21 55		22 20			
	d					20 21	20 40						21 21	21 28		21 50				22 21			22 39
Apperley Bridge	d					20 26							21 26							22 26			
Kirkstall Forge	d					20 31							21 31							22 31			
Leeds	a	20 07		20 17	20 38	20 40	20 54	20 59			21 19	21 36	21 40	21 47		22 04	22 04		22 18	22 40	22 43	22 50	22 54

		NT	NT	NT ◇	NT	NT	NT	NT ◇
Bradford Forster Square	d	22 38	22 48			23 15		
Bradford Interchange	d			23 00	23 17			23 38
New Pudsey	d			23 09	23 26			23 47
Bramley	d				23 30			23 50
Frizinghall	d	22 41	22 51			23 18		
Shipley	a	22 45	22 55			23 22		
	d					23 23	23 42	
Apperley Bridge	d					23 29		
Kirkstall Forge	d					23 35		
Leeds	a			23 22	23 38	23 48	23 57	23 59

Table T038-F

Mondays to Fridays

21 May to 7 December

Leeds and Bradford - Ilkley

Miles	Miles			NT	NT	NT	NT	NT	NT	NT	NT	NT	NT	NT	NT	NT	NT	NT	NT	NT	NT	NT	NT
0	—	**Leeds**	37 d		05 59	06 38		07 03		07 29	07 34		07 58		08 32		09 03		09 33		10 03		10 33
4¼	—	Kirkstall Forge	37 d																				
—	0	**Bradford Forster Square**	37 d	05 46			06 46		07 16			07 47		08 16		08 46		09 16		09 46		10 16	
—	1¾	Frizinghall	37 d	05 49			06 49		07 19			07 50		08 19		08 49		09 19		09 49		10 19	
—	2¾	Shipley	37 d	05 53			06 53		07 23			07 54		08 23		08 53		09 23		09 53		10 23	
—	4¼	Baildon	d	05 56			06 56		07 26			07 57		08 26		08 56		09 26		09 56		10 26	
10¼	7½	Guiseley	d	06 02	06 11	06 50	07 02	07 15	07 32	07 41	07 48	08 03	08 10	08 32	08 45	09 02	09 15	09 32	09 45	10 02	10 15	10 32	10 45
11½	8¾	Menston	d	06 05	06 14	06 53	07 05	07 18	07 35	07 44	07 52	08 06	08 13	08 35	08 48	09 05	09 18	09 35	09 48	10 05	10 18	10 35	10 48
13	10¼	Burley-in-Wharfedale	d	06 08	06 17	06 56	07 08	07 21	07 38	07 47	07 56	08 09	08 18	08 38	08 51	09 08	09 21	09 38	09 51	10 08	10 21	10 38	10 51
15¼	12½	Ben Rhydding	d	06 11	06 20	06 59	07 11	07 24	07 41	07 50	07 59	08 13	08 21	08 41	08 55	09 11	09 24	09 41	09 54	10 11	10 24	10 41	10 54
16¼	13½	**Ilkley**	a	06 17	06 27	07 06	07 17	07 31	07 47	07 57	08 05	08 18	08 27	08 47	09 02	09 17	09 31	09 47	10 01	10 17	10 31	10 47	11 01

		NT	NT	NT	NT	NT	NT	NT	NT	NT	NT	NT	NT	NT		NT	NT	NT	NT	NT	NT	NT	NT
Leeds	37 d		11 03		11 33		12 03		12 33		13 03		13 33	and at the same minutes past each hour until		16 03		16 33		17 03	17 15	
Kirkstall Forge	37 d																					
Bradford Forster Square	37 d	10 46		11 16		11 46		12 16		12 46		13 16			15 46		16 16		16 46			17 16
Frizinghall	37 d	10 49		11 19		11 49		12 19		12 49		13 19			15 49		16 19		16 49			17 19
Shipley	37 d	10 53		11 23		11 53		12 23		12 53		13 23			15 53		16 23		16 53			17 24
Baildon	d	10 56		11 26		11 56		12 26		12 56		13 26			15 56		16 26		16 56			17 27
Guiseley	d	11 02	11 15	11 32	11 45	12 02	12 15	12 32	12 45	13 02	13 15	13 32	13 45		16 02	16 15	16 32	16 45	17 02	17 15	17 28	17 35
Menston	d	11 05	11 18	11 35	11 48	12 05	12 18	12 35	12 48	13 05	13 18	13 35	13 48		16 05	16 18	16 35	16 48	17 05	17 18	17 31	17 38
Burley-in-Wharfedale	d	11 08	11 21	11 38	11 51	12 08	12 21	12 38	12 51	13 08	13 21	13 38	13 51		16 08	16 21	16 38	16 51	17 08	17 21	17 34	17 44
Ben Rhydding	d	11 11	11 24	11 41	11 54	12 11	12 24	12 41	12 54	13 11	13 24	13 41	13 54		16 11	16 24	16 41	16 54	17 11	17 24	17 37	17 47
Ilkley	a	11 17	11 31	11 47	12 00	12 17	12 31	12 47	13 00	13 17	13 31	13 47	14 01		16 17	16 31	16 47	17 01	17 17	17 31	17 44	17 53

		NT	NT	NT	NT	NT	NT	NT	NT	NT	NT	NT	NT	NT	NT	NT	NT	NT	NT	NT	NT	NT
Leeds	37 d	17 33	17 47		18 03		18 33		19 03		19 33		20 03		20 33	21 03		21 33		22 33		23 33
Kirkstall Forge	37 d																					
Bradford Forster Square	37 d			17 49		18 16		18 46		19 16		19 46		20 16			21 16		22 16		23 16	
Frizinghall	37 d			17 52		18 19		18 49		19 19		19 49		20 19			21 19		22 19		23 19	
Shipley	37 d			17 56		18 23		18 54		19 24		19 53		20 23			21 24		22 23		23 23	
Baildon	d			17 59		18 26		18 57		19 27		19 56		20 26			21 27		22 26		23 26	
Guiseley	d	17 47	17 59	18 06	18 15	18 32	18 45	19 03	19 15	19 33	19 45	20 02	20 15	20 32	20 45	21 15	21 33	21 45	22 32	22 45	23 32	23 45
Menston	d	17 50	18 02	18 09	18 18	18 35	18 48	19 06	19 18	19 36	19 48	20 05	20 18	20 35	20 48	21 18	21 36	21 48	22 35	22 48	23 35	23 48
Burley-in-Wharfedale	d	17 53	18 05	18 15	18 23	18 38	18 51	19 09	19 21	19 39	19 51	20 08	20 21	20 38	20 51	21 21	21 38	21 51	22 38	22 51	23 38	23 51
Ben Rhydding	d	17 57	18 09	18 18	18 27	18 41	18 54	19 12	19 24	19 42	19 54	20 11	20 24	20 41	20 54	21 24	21 42	21 54	22 41	22 54	23 41	23 54
Ilkley	a	18 04	18 16	18 24	18 34	18 47	19 01	19 18	19 31	19 48	20 01	20 17	20 31	20 47	21 01	21 31	21 47	22 01	22 47	23 01	23 47	00 01

Saturdays

26 May to 8 December

		NT	NT	NT	NT	NT	NT	NT	NT	NT	NT	NT	NT	NT	NT	NT	NT	NT	NT	NT	NT	NT	NT
Leeds	37 d		05 59	06 38		07 03		07 29	07 34		07 58		08 32		09 03		09 33		10 03		10 33		11 03
Kirkstall Forge	37 d																						
Bradford Forster Square	37 d	05 46			06 46		07 16			07 47		08 16		08 46		09 16		09 46		10 16		10 46	
Frizinghall	37 d	05 49			06 49		07 19			07 50		08 19		08 49		09 19		09 49		10 19		10 49	
Shipley	37 d	05 53			06 53		07 23			07 54		08 23		08 53		09 23		09 53		10 23		10 53	
Baildon	d	05 56			06 56		07 26			07 57		08 26		08 56		09 26		09 56		10 26		10 56	
Guiseley	d	06 02	06 11	06 50	07 02	07 15	07 32	07 41	07 48	08 03	08 10	08 32	08 45	09 02	09 15	09 32	09 45	10 02	10 15	10 32	10 45	11 02	11 15
Menston	d	06 05	06 14	06 53	07 05	07 18	07 35	07 44	07 52	08 06	08 13	08 35	08 48	09 05	09 18	09 35	09 48	10 05	10 18	10 35	10 48	11 05	11 18
Burley-in-Wharfedale	d	06 08	06 17	06 56	07 08	07 21	07 38	07 47	07 56	08 09	08 18	08 38	08 51	09 08	09 21	09 38	09 51	10 08	10 21	10 38	10 51	11 08	11 21
Ben Rhydding	d	06 11	06 20	06 59	07 11	07 24	07 41	07 50	07 59	08 13	08 21	08 41	08 55	09 11	09 24	09 41	09 54	10 11	10 24	10 41	10 54	11 11	11 24
Ilkley	a	06 17	06 27	07 06	07 17	07 31	07 47	07 57	08 05	08 18	08 27	08 47	09 02	09 17	09 31	09 47	10 01	10 17	10 31	10 47	11 01	11 17	11 31

		NT	NT	NT	NT	NT	NT	NT	NT	NT	NT		NT	NT	NT	NT	NT	NT	NT	NT	NT	NT
Leeds	37 d		11 33		12 03		12 33		13 03		13 33	and at the same minutes past each hour until		16 03		16 33		17 03	17 15		17 33	17 47
Kirkstall Forge	37 d																					
Bradford Forster Square	37 d	11 16		11 46		12 16		12 46		13 16			15 46		16 16		16 46			17 16		
Frizinghall	37 d	11 19		11 49		12 19		12 49		13 19			15 49		16 19		16 49			17 19		
Shipley	37 d	11 23		11 53		12 23		12 53		13 23			15 53		16 23		16 53			17 24		
Baildon	d	11 26		11 56		12 26		12 56		13 26			15 56		16 26		16 56			17 27		
Guiseley	d	11 32	11 45	12 02	12 15	12 32	12 45	13 02	13 15	13 32	13 45		16 02	16 15	16 32	16 45	17 02	17 15	17 28	17 35	17 47	17 59
Menston	d	11 35	11 48	12 05	12 18	12 35	12 48	13 05	13 18	13 35	13 48		16 05	16 18	16 35	16 48	17 05	17 18	17 31	17 38	17 50	18 02
Burley-in-Wharfedale	d	11 38	11 51	12 08	12 21	12 38	12 51	13 08	13 21	13 38	13 51		16 08	16 21	16 38	16 51	17 08	17 21	17 34	17 44	17 53	18 05
Ben Rhydding	d	11 41	11 54	12 11	12 24	12 41	12 54	13 11	13 24	13 41	13 54		16 11	16 24	16 41	16 54	17 11	17 24	17 37	17 47	17 57	18 09
Ilkley	a	11 47	12 00	12 17	12 31	12 47	13 00	13 17	13 31	13 47	14 01		16 17	16 31	16 47	17 01	17 17	17 31	17 44	17 53	18 04	18 16

		NT	NT	NT	NT	NT	NT	NT	NT	NT	NT	NT	NT	NT	NT	NT	NT	NT	NT	NT
Leeds	37 d		18 03		18 33		19 03		19 33		20 03		20 33	21 03		21 33		22 33		23 33
Kirkstall Forge	37 d																			
Bradford Forster Square	37 d	17 49		18 16		18 46		19 16		19 46		20 16			21 16		22 16		23 16	
Frizinghall	37 d	17 52		18 19		18 49		19 19		19 49		20 19			21 19		22 19		23 19	
Shipley	37 d	17 56		18 23		18 54		19 24		19 53		20 23			21 24		22 23		23 23	
Baildon	d	17 59		18 26		18 57		19 27		19 56		20 26			21 27		22 26		23 26	
Guiseley	d	18 06	18 15	18 32	18 45	19 03	19 15	19 33	19 45	20 02	20 15	20 32	20 45	21 15	21 33	21 45	22 32	22 45	23 32	23 45
Menston	d	18 09	18 18	18 35	18 48	19 06	19 18	19 36	19 48	20 05	20 18	20 35	20 48	21 18	21 36	21 48	22 35	22 48	23 35	23 48
Burley-in-Wharfedale	d	18 15	18 23	18 38	18 51	19 09	19 21	19 39	19 51	20 08	20 21	20 38	20 51	21 21	21 38	21 51	22 38	22 51	23 38	23 51
Ben Rhydding	d	18 18	18 27	18 41	18 54	19 12	19 24	19 42	19 54	20 11	20 24	20 41	20 54	21 24	21 42	21 54	22 41	22 54	23 41	23 54
Ilkley	a	18 24	18 34	18 47	19 01	19 18	19 31	19 48	20 01	20 17	20 31	20 47	21 01	21 31	21 47	22 01	22 47	23 01	23 47	00 01

Table T038-F

Sundays

20 May to 2 December

Leeds and Bradford - Ilkley

		NT	NT	NT		NT	NT	NT	NT	NT	NT		NT	NT	NT	NT
Leeds 10	37 d	09 15		10 12	and at the same minutes past each hour until		15 12		16 16		17 12	and at the same minutes past each hour until		22 12		23 18
Kirkstall Forge	37 d															
Bradford Forster Square	37 d		09 38			14 38		15 38		16 38			21 38		22 38	
Frizinghall	37 d		09 41			14 41		15 41		16 41			21 41		22 41	
Shipley	37 d		09 45			14 45		15 45		16 45			21 45		22 45	
Baildon	d		09 48			14 48		15 48		16 48			21 48		22 48	
Guiseley	d	09 26	09 54	10 24		14 54	15 24	15 54	16 28	16 54	17 24		21 54	22 24	22 54	23 30
Menston	d	09 29	09 57	10 27		14 57	15 27	15 57	16 31	16 57	17 27		21 57	22 27	22 57	23 33
Burley-in-Wharfedale	d	09 32	10 00	10 30		15 00	15 30	16 00	16 34	17 00	17 30		22 00	22 30	23 00	23 36
Ben Rhydding	d	09 36	10 03	10 33		15 03	15 33	16 03	16 37	17 03	17 33		22 03	22 33	23 03	23 39
Ilkley	a	09 41	10 09	10 40		15 09	15 40	16 09	16 44	17 09	17 40		22 09	22 40	23 09	23 46

Table T038-R

Sundays

20 May to 2 December

Ilkley - Bradford and Leeds

		NT	NT	NT		NT	NT	NT	NT	NT	NT	NT	NT	NT	NT	NT	NT	NT	NT	NT
Ilkley	d	08 30	08 53	09 21	and at the same minutes past each hour until	15 53	16 21	16 53	17 21	17 53	18 21	18 53	19 21	19 53	20 21	20 53	21 21	21 53	22 21	23 21
Ben Rhydding	d	08 32	08 55	09 23		15 55	16 23	16 55	17 23	17 55	18 23	18 55	19 23	19 55	20 23	20 55	21 23	21 55	22 23	23 23
Burley-in-Wharfedale	d	08 37	09 00	09 28		16 00	16 28	17 00	17 29	18 00	18 28	19 00	19 28	20 00	20 28	21 00	21 28	22 00	22 28	23 28
Menston	d	08 41	09 04	09 32		16 04	16 32	17 04	17 33	18 04	18 32	19 04	19 32	20 04	20 32	21 04	21 32	22 04	22 32	23 32
Guiseley	d	08 44	09 07	09 35		16 07	16 35	17 07	17 36	18 07	18 35	19 07	19 35	20 07	20 35	21 07	21 35	22 07	22 35	23 35
Baildon	d		09 13			16 13		17 14		18 13		19 13		20 14		21 13		22 13		
Shipley	37 a		09 16			16 16		17 17		18 16		19 16		20 17		21 16		22 16		
Frizinghall	37 a		09 19			16 19		17 20		18 19		19 19		20 20		21 19		22 19		
Bradford Forster Square	37 a		09 25			16 25		17 26		18 25		19 25		20 26		21 25		22 25		
Kirkstall Forge	37 d																			
Leeds 10	37 a	08 59		09 50			16 50		17 51		18 50		19 49		20 50		21 52		22 50	23 52

Table T038-R

Mondays to Fridays

21 May to 7 December

Ilkley - Bradford and Leeds

Miles	Miles			NT	NT	NT	NT	NT	NT	NT	NT	NT	NT	NT	NT	NT	NT	NT	NT	NT	NT	NT	NT
0	0	**Ilkley**	d	05 50	06 02	06 40	06 51	07 09	07 21	07 37	07 48	07 55	08 08	08 17	08 25	08 40	08 51	09 10	09 21	09 40	09 51	10 10	10 21
1	1	Ben Rhydding	d	05 52	06 04	06 42	06 53	07 11	07 23	07 39	07 50	07 57	08 10	08 19	08 27	08 42	08 53	09 12	09 23	09 42	09 53	10 12	10 23
3¼	3¼	Burley-in-Wharfedale	d	05 57	06 09	06 47	06 58	07 16	07 28	07 44	07 55	08 02	08 15	08 24	08 32	08 47	08 58	09 17	09 28	09 47	09 58	10 17	10 28
4¾	4¾	Menston	d	06 01	06 13	06 51	07 02	07 20	07 31	07 48	07 59	08 06	08 19	08 28	08 36	08 51	09 02	09 21	09 32	09 51	10 02	10 21	10 32
6	6	Guiseley	d	06 04	06 16	06 54	07 05	07 23	07 35	07 52	08 02	08 09	08 22	08 31	08 39	08 54	09 05	09 24	09 35	09 54	10 05	10 24	10 35
—	9¼	Baildon	d	06 10			07 11		07 41		08 08				08 45		09 11		09 41		10 11		10 41
—	10¼	Shipley	37 a	06 13			07 14		07 44		08 11				08 48		09 14		09 44		10 14		10 44
—	11¼	Frizinghall	37 a	06 16			07 17		07 47		08 14				08 52		09 17		09 47		10 17		10 47
—	13½	**Bradford Forster Square**	37 a	06 22			07 23		07 53		08 20				08 57		09 23		09 53		10 23		10 53
12	—	Kirkstall Forge	37 d																				
16¼	—	**Leeds** 10	37 a		06 31	07 10		07 37		08 05		08 24	08 37	08 48		09 08		09 38		10 08		10 38	

		NT	NT	NT	NT	NT		NT	NT	NT	NT	NT	NT	NT	NT	NT	NT	NT	NT	NT	NT	NT
Ilkley	d	10 40	10 51	11 10	11 21	11 40	and at the same minutes past each hour until	13 51	14 10	14 21	14 40	14 51	15 10	15 21	15 40	15 51	16 10	16 21	16 40	16 51	17 12	17 21
Ben Rhydding	d	10 42	10 53	11 12	11 23	11 42		13 53	14 12	14 23	14 42	14 53	15 12	15 23	15 42	15 53	16 12	16 23	16 42	16 53	17 14	17 23
Burley-in-Wharfedale	d	10 47	10 58	11 17	11 28	11 47		13 58	14 17	14 28	14 47	14 58	15 17	15 28	15 47	15 58	16 17	16 28	16 47	16 58	17 19	17 28
Menston	d	10 51	11 02	11 21	11 32	11 51		14 02	14 21	14 32	14 51	15 02	15 21	15 32	15 51	16 02	16 21	16 32	16 51	17 02	17 23	17 32
Guiseley	d	10 54	11 05	11 24	11 35	11 54		14 05	14 24	14 35	14 54	15 05	15 24	15 35	15 54	16 05	16 24	16 35	16 54	17 05	17 27	17 35
Baildon	d		11 11		11 41			14 11		14 41		15 11		15 41		16 11		16 41		17 11		17 41
Shipley	37 a		11 14		11 44			14 14		14 44		15 14		15 44		16 14		16 44		17 14		17 44
Frizinghall	37 a		11 17		11 47			14 17		14 47		15 17		15 47		16 17		16 47		17 17		17 47
Bradford Forster Square	37 a		11 23		11 53			14 23		14 53		15 23		15 53		16 23		16 53		17 23		17 53
Kirkstall Forge	37 d																					
Leeds 10	37 a	11 11		11 41		12 08			14 41		15 08		15 38		16 11		16 40		17 08		17 41	

		NT	NT	NT	NT	NT	NT	NT	NT	NT	NT	NT	NT	NT	NT	NT	NT	NT	NT	NT	NT
Ilkley	d	17 43	17 51	18 04	18 11	18 21	18 40	18 51	19 11	19 23	19 40	19 53	20 10	20 40	20 51	21 10	21 37	21 51	22 10	22 51	23 18
Ben Rhydding	d	17 45	17 53	18 06	18 13	18 23	18 42	18 53	19 13	19 25	19 42	19 55	20 12	20 42	20 53	21 12	21 39	21 53	22 12	22 53	23 20
Burley-in-Wharfedale	d	17 50	17 58	18 11	18 18	18 28	18 47	18 58	19 18	19 30	19 47	20 00	20 17	20 47	20 58	21 17	21 44	21 58	22 17	22 58	23 25
Menston	d	17 54	18 02	18 15	18 22	18 32	18 51	19 02	19 22	19 34	19 51	20 04	20 21	20 51	21 02	21 21	21 48	22 02	22 21	23 02	23 29
Guiseley	d	17 58	18 06	18 18	18 25	18 35	18 54	19 05	19 25	19 37	19 54	20 07	20 24	20 54	21 05	21 24	21 51	22 05	22 24	23 05	23 32
Baildon	d		18 11			18 41		19 11		19 43		20 13			21 11			22 11		23 11	
Shipley	37 a		18 14			18 44		19 14		19 46		20 16			21 14			22 14		23 14	
Frizinghall	37 a		18 17			18 47		19 17		19 49		20 19			21 17			22 17		23 17	
Bradford Forster Square	37 a		18 23			18 53		19 23		19 55		20 25			21 23			22 23		23 23	
Kirkstall Forge	37 d																				
Leeds 10	37 a	18 12		18 33	18 39		19 11		19 40		20 08		20 38	21 09		21 38	22 07		22 38		23 46

Saturdays

26 May to 8 December

		NT	NT	NT	NT	NT	NT	NT	NT	NT	NT	NT	NT	NT	NT	NT	NT	NT	NT	NT	NT	NT
Ilkley	d	05 50	06 02	06 40	06 51	07 09	07 21	07 37	07 48	07 55	08 08	08 17	08 25	08 40	08 51	09 10	09 21	09 40	09 51	10 10	10 21	10 40
Ben Rhydding	d	05 52	06 04	06 42	06 53	07 11	07 23	07 39	07 50	07 57	08 10	08 19	08 27	08 42	08 53	09 12	09 23	09 42	09 53	10 12	10 23	10 42
Burley-in-Wharfedale	d	05 57	06 09	06 47	06 58	07 16	07 28	07 44	07 55	08 02	08 15	08 24	08 32	08 47	08 58	09 17	09 28	09 47	09 58	10 17	10 28	10 47
Menston	d	06 01	06 13	06 51	07 02	07 20	07 31	07 48	07 59	08 06	08 19	08 28	08 36	08 51	09 02	09 21	09 32	09 51	10 02	10 21	10 32	10 51
Guiseley	d	06 04	06 16	06 54	07 05	07 23	07 35	07 52	08 02	08 09	08 22	08 31	08 39	08 54	09 05	09 24	09 35	09 54	10 05	10 24	10 35	10 54
Baildon	d	06 10			07 11		07 41		08 08				08 45		09 11		09 41		10 11		10 41	
Shipley	37 a	06 13			07 14		07 44		08 11				08 48		09 14		09 44		10 14		10 44	
Frizinghall	37 a	06 16			07 17		07 47		08 14				08 52		09 17		09 47		10 17		10 47	
Bradford Forster Square	37 a	06 22			07 23		07 53		08 20				08 57		09 23		09 53		10 23		10 53	
Kirkstall Forge	37 d																					
Leeds 10	37 a		06 31	07 10		07 37		08 05		08 24	08 37	08 48		09 08		09 38		10 08		10 38		11 11

		NT	NT	NT	NT		NT	NT	NT	NT	NT	NT	NT	NT	NT	NT	NT	NT	NT	NT	NT	NT
Ilkley	d	10 51	11 10	11 21	11 40	and at the same minutes past each hour until	13 51	14 10	14 21	14 40	14 51	15 10	15 21	15 40	15 51	16 10	16 21	16 40	16 51	17 12	17 21	17 43
Ben Rhydding	d	10 53	11 12	11 23	11 42		13 53	14 12	14 23	14 42	14 53	15 12	15 23	15 42	15 53	16 12	16 23	16 42	16 53	17 14	17 23	17 45
Burley-in-Wharfedale	d	10 58	11 17	11 28	11 47		13 58	14 17	14 28	14 47	14 58	15 17	15 28	15 47	15 58	16 17	16 28	16 47	16 58	17 19	17 28	17 50
Menston	d	11 02	11 21	11 32	11 51		14 02	14 21	14 32	14 51	15 02	15 21	15 32	15 51	16 02	16 21	16 32	16 51	17 02	17 23	17 32	17 54
Guiseley	d	11 05	11 24	11 35	11 54		14 05	14 24	14 35	14 54	15 05	15 24	15 35	15 54	16 05	16 24	16 35	16 54	17 05	17 27	17 35	17 58
Baildon	d	11 11		11 41			14 11		14 41		15 11		15 41		16 11		16 41		17 11		17 41	
Shipley	37 a	11 14		11 44			14 14		14 44		15 14		15 44		16 14		16 44		17 14		17 44	
Frizinghall	37 a	11 17		11 47			14 17		14 47		15 17		15 47		16 17		16 47		17 17		17 47	
Bradford Forster Square	37 a	11 23		11 53			14 23		14 53		15 23		15 53		16 23		16 53		17 23		17 53	
Kirkstall Forge	37 d																					
Leeds 10	37 a		11 41		12 08			14 41		15 08		15 38		16 11		16 40		17 08		17 41		18 12

		NT	NT	NT	NT	NT	NT	NT	NT	NT	NT	NT	NT	NT	NT	NT	NT	NT	NT	NT
Ilkley	d	17 51	18 04	18 11	18 21	18 40	18 51	19 11	19 23	19 40	19 53	20 10	20 40	20 51	21 10	21 37	21 51	22 10	22 51	23 18
Ben Rhydding	d	17 53	18 06	18 13	18 23	18 42	18 53	19 13	19 25	19 42	19 55	20 12	20 42	20 53	21 12	21 39	21 53	22 12	22 53	23 20
Burley-in-Wharfedale	d	17 58	18 11	18 18	18 28	18 47	18 58	19 18	19 30	19 47	20 00	20 17	20 47	20 58	21 17	21 44	21 58	22 17	22 58	23 25
Menston	d	18 02	18 15	18 22	18 32	18 51	19 02	19 22	19 34	19 51	20 04	20 21	20 51	21 02	21 21	21 48	22 02	22 21	23 02	23 29
Guiseley	d	18 06	18 18	18 25	18 35	18 54	19 05	19 25	19 37	19 54	20 07	20 24	20 54	21 05	21 24	21 51	22 05	22 24	23 05	23 32
Baildon	d	18 11			18 41		19 11		19 43		20 13			21 11			22 11		23 11	
Shipley	37 a	18 14			18 44		19 14		19 46		20 16			21 14			22 14		23 14	
Frizinghall	37 a	18 17			18 47		19 17		19 49		20 19			21 17			22 17		23 17	
Bradford Forster Square	37 a	18 23			18 53		19 23		19 55		20 25			21 23			22 23		23 23	
Kirkstall Forge	37 d																			
Leeds 10	37 a		18 33	18 39		19 11		19 40		20 08		20 38	21 09		21 38	22 07		22 38		23 46

Table T039-F

Mondays to Fridays
21 May to 7 December

Liverpool, Manchester Airport and Manchester - Huddersfield - Wakefield, Leeds, Hull, York, Scarborough, Middlesbrough and Newcastle

Miles	Miles	Miles	Miles	Miles			TP MX ◇■	TP MO ◇■	TP MX ◇■	TP MO ◇■	TP MX ◇■	TP MX ◇■	TP MO ◇■	TP ◇■	TP ◇■	TP ◇■	TP ◇■	TP ◇■	NT ◇	TP ◇■	NT			TP ◇■	
0	—	—	—	—	**Liverpool Lime Street** 10 90	d														05 20					
10¾	—	—	—	—	Lea Green 90	d														05 32					
15¾	—	—	—	—	Newton-le-Willows 90	d														05 38					
—	—	—	—	—	**Manchester Airport**	d						00 38	00 45		04 22	05 03								05 48	
34¾	—	—	—	—	**Manchester Piccadilly** 10	d						00 53	01 00		04 36	05 17		05 45						06 05	
—	—	—	—	—	Manchester Oxford Road	d										05 20								06 09	
—	—	—	—	0	**Manchester Victoria**	a										05 26				05 57				06 14	
—	—	—	—	—		d										05 27			05 45	05 59				06 17	
—	—	—	—	6½	Ashton-under-Lyne	d																			
42¾	—	—	—	7¾	**Stalybridge**	a												05 57							
—	—	—	—	—		d												05 57							
45	—	—	—	10½	Mossley (Grtr Manchester)	d																			
47½	—	—	—	12¾	Greenfield	d																			
53¾	—	—	—	18¾	Marsden	d												06 10							
55¾	—	—	—	21¼	Slaithwaite	d												06 13							
60¼	—	—	—	25¾	**Huddersfield**	a									05 36	05 54		06 18		06 26				06 44	
—	—	—	—	—		d				00 18	00 43				05 40	05 56		06 20		06 27	06 38			06 45	
62¼	—	—	—	27¾	Deighton	d												06 23			06 42				
65¾	—	—	—	30¾	Mirfield	d															06 46				
—	—	—	—	—	Wakefield Kirkgate	a															07 04				
66¾	—	—	—	—	Ravensthorpe	d																			
68¼	—	—	—	—	**Dewsbury**	a					00s51							06 30		06 35				06 53	
—	—	—	—	—		d			00 07									06 31		06 36				06 54	
69¾	—	—	—	—	Batley	d												06 34							
73	—	—	—	—	Morley	d																			
74½	—	—	—	—	Cottingley	d																			
77½	0	—	0	—	**Leeds** 10	a			00 22	00 35	01 05	01 59	02 06		05 59	06 15		06 45	07 23	06 49				07 07	
—	—	—	—	—		d	00 11	00 14	00 24	00 39	01 14	02 05	02 11		06 00	06 17			07 24	06 52				07 13	07 17
84¾	7¼	—	7¼	—	Garforth 40	d													→						
—	20¾	—	—	—	Selby 29,40	a																			07 36
—	29½	—	—	—	Howden 29	a																			07 50
—	41¼	—	—	—	Brough 29	a																			08 03
—	51¾	—	—	—	**Hull** 29	a																			08 20
103	—	0	25½	—	**York** 8 26	a	00 51	00 45	01 05	01 03	01 55	02 46	02 38		06 23	06 39				07 16				07 35	
—	—	—	—	—		d								05 06	06 29	06 43	06 46			07 16				07 38	
—	—	—	46½	—	Malton	d																			
—	—	—	64¾	—	Seamer 43	d																			
—	—	—	67½	—	**Scarborough** 43	a																			
125½	—	22¼	—	—	Thirsk	a								05 33			07 03			07 33				07 56	
133	—	30½	—	—	Northallerton 26	a								05 38	06 49	07 04	07 13			07 41				08 03	
147	—	—	—	—	**Darlington** 8 26	a								05 53	07 01	07 15				07 53					
—	—	42¼	—	—	Yarm	d											07 27							08 17	
—	—	47½	—	—	Thornaby 44	a								06 20			07 37							08 28	
—	—	50¾	—	—	**Middlesbrough** 44	a								06 29			07 46							08 36	
169	—	—	—	—	Durham 26	a									07 18	07 32				08 10					
174¾	—	—	—	—	Chester-le-Street 26	a									07 24	07 38				08 16					
183	—	—	—	—	**Newcastle** 8 26	a									07 36	07 51				08 29					

Table T039-F

Mondays to Fridays
21 May to 7 December

Liverpool, Manchester Airport and Manchester - Huddersfield - Wakefield, Leeds, Hull, York, Scarborough, Middlesbrough and Newcastle

		TP ◇■		NT	TP ◇■			TP ◇■	TP ◇■	NT		TP ◇■ ⫟			NT		TP ◇■ ⫟	TP ◇■		NT	TP ◇■ ⫟			TP ◇■ ⫟	TP ◇■ ⫟
Liverpool Lime Street 10 90	d				05 56							06 25									06 56				
Lea Green 90	d																				07 08				
Newton-le-Willows 90	d											06 43													
Manchester Airport	d							06 19									06 47							07 19	
Manchester Piccadilly 10	d	06 17						06 34	06 44								07 05	07 17						07 35	07 47
Manchester Oxford Road	d							06 38									07 08							07 38	
Manchester Victoria	a				06 30			06 45				07 00					07 14				07 31			07 45	
	d			06 26	06 32			06 47		06 53		07 02					07 17			07 23	07 32			07 47	
Ashton-under-Lyne	d			06 35						07 03										07 33					
Stalybridge	a	06 29		06 40					06 58	07 07								07 30		07 37					07 59
	d	06 30							06 59									07 30							08 00
Mossley (Grtr Manchester)	d								07 04																08 04
Greenfield	d	06 36																07 36							
Marsden	d	06 44																07 44							
Slaithwaite	d								07 15																08 15
Huddersfield	a	06 51			06 59			07 14	07 21			07 29					07 44	07 51			07 59			08 14	08 21
	d	06 52			07 00			07 15	07 22			07 30			07 38		07 45	07 52			08 00			08 15	08 22
Deighton	d	06 55													07 42			07 55							
Mirfield	d	07 00													07 46			08 00							
Wakefield Kirkgate	a														08 01										
Ravensthorpe	d	07 03																08 03							
Dewsbury	a	07 06							07 31								07 53	08 06						08 23	08 30
	d	07 10							07 32								07 54	08 10						08 24	08 31
Batley	d	07 12							07 35									08 13							08 34
Morley	d	07 17																08 18							
Cottingley	d	07 21																08 21							
Leeds 10	a	07 28			07 19			07 34	07 46			07 49					08 07	08 30			08 19			08 37	08 45
	d				07 21			07 35	07 48			07 52					08 12				08 21			08 39	08 48
Garforth 40	d							07 43	07 56																08 56
Selby 29,40	a								08 11																09 11
Howden 29	a																								
Brough 29	a								08 30																09 30
Hull 29	a								08 45																09 45
York 8 26	a				07 43			08 02				08 16					08 35				08 43			09 01	
	d				07 45			08 04				08 18					08 38				08 45			09 03	
Malton	d				08 08																09 08				
Seamer 43	d				08 25																09 25				
Scarborough 43	a				08 35																09 35				
Thirsk	a																08 54								
Northallerton 26	a											08 38					09 02								
Darlington 8 26	a							08 34				08 50												09 33	
Yarm	d																09 21								
Thornaby 44	a																09 30								
Middlesbrough 44	a																09 38								
Durham 26	a							08 52				09 07												09 51	
Chester-le-Street 26	a											09 13													
Newcastle 8 26	a							09 07				09 24												10 07	

Table T039-F

Mondays to Fridays
21 May to 7 December

Liverpool, Manchester Airport and Manchester - Huddersfield - Wakefield, Leeds, Hull, York, Scarborough, Middlesbrough and Newcastle

Station	Table		NT	TP ◇1 ✠	NT ◇	NT	TP ◇1 ✠	TP ◇1	NT	TP ◇1 ✠	NT ◇	TP ◇1 ✠	TP ◇1 ✠	NT	TP ◇1 ✠	NT ◇
Liverpool Lime Street 10	90	d		07 25						07 54					08 25	
Lea Green	90	d								08 07						
Newton-le-Willows	90	d		07 42											08 42	
Manchester Airport		d					07 47					08 17				
Manchester Piccadilly 10		d					08 05	08 17				08 35	08 47			
Manchester Oxford Road		d					08 08					08 38				
Manchester Victoria		a		08 01			08 14			08 31		08 45			09 01	
		d	07 52	08 03			08 17		08 20	08 32	08 38	08 46		08 52	09 02	
Ashton-under-Lyne		d	08 03						08 33					09 02		
Stalybridge		a	08 07					08 29	08 37				08 59	09 07		
		d						08 30					09 00			
Mossley (Grtr Manchester)		d											09 04			
Greenfield		d						08 36								
Marsden		d						08 44								
Slaithwaite		d											09 15			
Huddersfield		a		08 29			08 46	08 51		08 59		09 14	09 21		09 29	
		d		08 30		08 38	08 46	08 52		09 00		09 15	09 22		09 30	
Deighton		d				08 42		08 55								
Mirfield		d			08 38	08 47		09 00			09 40					09 40
Wakefield Kirkgate		a				09 01					→					
Ravensthorpe		d			08 41			09 03								
Dewsbury		a			08 44		08 55	09 06					09 30			09 45
		d			08 45		08 55	09 11					09 31			09 45
Batley		d						09 13					09 34			
Morley		d			08 52			09 18								09 52
Cottingley		d			08 55											09 56
Leeds 10		a		08 49	09 03		09 08	09 30		09 19		09 34	09 45		09 49	10 04
		d		08 52			09 12			09 21		09 39	09 48		09 52	
Garforth	40	d											09 56			
Selby	29,40	a											10 11			
Howden	29	a														
Brough	29	a											10 30			
Hull	29	a											10 45			
York 8	26	a		09 17			09 34			09 43		10 01			10 17	
		d		09 18			09 39			09 45		10 02			10 18	
Malton		d								10 08						
Seamer	43	d								10 25						
Scarborough	43	a								10 35						
Thirsk		a					09 55									
Northallerton	26	a		09 39			10 06								10 39	
Darlington 5	26	a		09 51								10 33			10 52	
Yarm		d					10 20									
Thornaby	44	a					10 31									
Middlesbrough	44	a					10 39									
Durham	26	a		10 13								10 50			11 09	
Chester-le-Street	26	a													11 15	
Newcastle 8	26	a		10 27								11 07			11 26	

Table T039-F

Mondays to Fridays
21 May to 7 December

Liverpool, Manchester Airport and Manchester - Huddersfield - Wakefield, Leeds, Hull, York, Scarborough, Middlesbrough and Newcastle

Station	Table		TP ◇1 ✠	TP ◇1	NT	TP ◇1 ✠	NT ◇	TP ◇1 ✠	TP ◇1 ✠	NT	TP ◇1 ✠	NT ◇	NT	TP ◇1 ✠	TP ◇1	NT	TP ◇1 ✠	NT ◇	TP ◇1 ✠
Liverpool Lime Street 10	90	d				08 56					09 25						09 56		
Lea Green	90	d				09 08											10 08		
Newton-le-Willows	90	d									09 43								
Manchester Airport		d	08 47					09 19						09 47					10 19
Manchester Piccadilly 10		d	09 05	09 17				09 35	09 47					10 05	10 17				10 35
Manchester Oxford Road		d	09 08					09 38						10 08					10 38
Manchester Victoria		a	09 14			09 31		09 45			10 01			10 14			10 30		10 45
		d	09 17		09 24	09 32	09 37	09 47		09 53	10 02			10 17		10 23	10 32	10 37	10 47
Ashton-under-Lyne		d			09 34					10 03						10 33			
Stalybridge		a		09 30	09 38				09 59	10 07					10 29	10 37			
		d		09 30					10 00						10 30				
Mossley (Grtr Manchester)		d							10 04										
Greenfield		d		09 36											10 36				
Marsden		d		09 44											10 44				
Slaithwaite		d							10 15										
Huddersfield		a	09 46	09 51		09 59		10 14	10 21		10 29			10 45	10 51		10 59		11 14
		d	09 46	09 52		10 00		10 15	10 22		10 30		10 38	10 46	10 52		11 00		11 15
Deighton		d		09 55								←	10 42		10 55				
Mirfield		d		10 00			10 39					10 39	10 46		11 00			11 39	
Wakefield Kirkgate		a					→						11 01					→	
Ravensthorpe		d		10 03											11 03				
Dewsbury		a	09 55	10 06					10 30			10 44		10 55	11 06				
		d	09 55	10 11					10 31			10 44		10 55	11 11				
Batley		d		10 13					10 34						11 13				
Morley		d		10 18								10 51			11 18				
Cottingley		d										10 55							
Leeds 10		a	10 08	10 30		10 19		10 34	10 45		10 49	11 03		11 08	11 30		11 19		11 35
		d	10 12			10 21		10 39	10 48		10 52			11 12			11 21		11 39
Garforth	40	d							10 56										
Selby	29,40	a							11 11										
Howden	29	a																	
Brough	29	a							11 30										
Hull	29	a							11 45										
York 8	26	a	10 35			10 43		11 01			11 17			11 35			11 43		12 01
		d	10 39			10 45		11 02			11 18			11 38			11 45		12 02
Malton		d				11 08											12 08		
Seamer	43	d				11 25											12 25		
Scarborough	43	a				11 35											12 35		
Thirsk		a	10 55											11 55					
Northallerton	26	a	11 06								11 39			12 06					
Darlington 5	26	a						11 33			11 51								
Yarm		d	11 21											12 19					
Thornaby	44	a	11 30											12 30					
Middlesbrough	44	a	11 38											12 38					
Durham	26	a						11 50			12 07								12 47
Chester-le-Street	26	a																	
Newcastle 8	26	a						12 05			12 24								13 04

Table T039-F

Mondays to Fridays
21 May to 7 December

Liverpool, Manchester Airport and Manchester - Huddersfield - Wakefield, Leeds, Hull, York, Scarborough, Middlesbrough and Newcastle

			TP ◇1	NT		TP ◇1			NT ◇	NT		TP ◇1	TP ◇1	NT	TP ◇1		NT ◇	TP ◇1	TP ◇1	NT	TP ◇1		NT ◇	NT
Liverpool Lime Street 10	90	d				10 25									10 56						11 25			
Lea Green	90	d													11 08									
Newton-le-Willows	90	d				10 43															11 42			
Manchester Airport		d										10 47						11 19						
Manchester Piccadilly 10		d	10 47									11 05	11 17					11 35	11 47					
Manchester Oxford Road		d										11 08						11 38						
Manchester Victoria		a				11 01						11 14			11 31			11 45			12 01			
		d		10 53		11 02						11 17		11 23	11 32		11 37	11 47		11 53	12 02			
Ashton-under-Lyne		d		11 03										11 33						12 03				
Stalybridge		a	10 59	11 07									11 29	11 37					11 59	12 07				
		d	11 00										11 30						12 00					
Mossley (Grtr Manchester)		d	11 04																12 04					
Greenfield		d											11 36											
Marsden		d											11 44											
Slaithwaite		d	11 15																12 15					
Huddersfield		a	11 21			11 29						11 46	11 51		11 59			12 15	12 22		12 29			
		d	11 22			11 30				11 38		11 46	11 52		12 00			12 15	12 22		12 30			12 38
Deighton		d							←	11 42			11 55										←	12 42
Mirfield		d							11 39	11 46			12 00				12 39						12 39	12 46
Wakefield Kirkgate		a								12 01							→							13 01
Ravensthorpe		d											12 03											
Dewsbury		a	11 30						11 44			11 55	12 06						12 31				12 44	
		d	11 31						11 44			11 55	12 11						12 31				12 44	
Batley		d	11 34										12 13						12 34					
Morley		d							11 51				12 18										12 51	
Cottingley		d							11 55														12 55	
Leeds 10		a	11 45			11 49			12 03			12 08	12 30		12 19			12 35	12 46		12 49		13 03	
		d	11 48			11 52						12 12			12 21			12 39	12 48		12 52			
Garforth	40	d	11 56																12 56					
Selby	29,40	a	12 11																13 11					
Howden	29	a																						
Brough	29	a	12 30																13 30					
Hull	29	a	12 45																13 45					
York 8	26	a				12 17						12 35			12 43			13 01			13 17			
		d				12 18						12 38			12 45			13 02			13 19			
Malton		d													13 08									
Seamer	43	d													13 25									
Scarborough	43	a													13 35									
Thirsk		a										12 55												
Northallerton	26	a				12 39						13 06									13 39			
Darlington 8	26	a				12 51												13 33			13 51			
Yarm		d										13 21												
Thornaby	44	a										13 31												
Middlesbrough	44	a										13 39												
Durham	26	a				13 08												13 51			14 11			
Chester-le-Street	26	a				13 14																		
Newcastle 8	26	a				13 26												14 07			14 26			

Table T039-F

Mondays to Fridays
21 May to 7 December

Liverpool, Manchester Airport and Manchester - Huddersfield - Wakefield, Leeds, Hull, York, Scarborough, Middlesbrough and Newcastle

			TP ◇1	TP ◇1		NT	TP ◇1		NT ◇	TP ◇1	TP ◇1	NT		TP ◇1			NT ◇	NT	TP ◇1	TP ◇1		NT	TP ◇1		NT ◇	TP ◇1
Liverpool Lime Street 10	90	d					11 56							12 25									12 56			
Lea Green	90	d					12 08																13 08			
Newton-le-Willows	90	d												12 43												
Manchester Airport		d	11 47							12 19									12 47							13 19
Manchester Piccadilly 10		d	12 05	12 17						12 35	12 47								13 05	13 17						13 35
Manchester Oxford Road		d	12 08							12 38									13 08							13 38
Manchester Victoria		a	12 14				12 31			12 45				13 01					13 14				13 31			13 45
		d	12 17			12 23	12 32		12 37	12 47		12 53		13 02					13 17			13 23	13 32		13 37	13 47
Ashton-under-Lyne		d				12 33						13 03										13 33				
Stalybridge		a		12 29		12 37					12 59	13 07								13 29		13 37				
		d		12 30							13 00									13 30						
Mossley (Grtr Manchester)		d									13 04															
Greenfield		d		12 36																13 36						
Marsden		d		12 44																13 44						
Slaithwaite		d									13 15															
Huddersfield		a	12 46	12 51			12 59			13 14	13 21			13 29					13 46	13 51			13 59			14 14
		d	12 46	12 52			13 00			13 15	13 22			13 30				13 38	13 46	13 52			14 00			14 15
Deighton		d		12 55													←	13 42		13 55						
Mirfield		d		13 00					13 39								13 39	13 46		14 00					14 39	
Wakefield Kirkgate		a							→									14 01							→	
Ravensthorpe		d		13 03																14 03						
Dewsbury		a	12 55	13 06							13 30						13 44		13 54	14 06						
		d	12 55	13 11							13 31						13 44		13 55	14 11						
Batley		d		13 13							13 34									14 13						
Morley		d		13 18													13 51			14 18						
Cottingley		d															13 55									
Leeds 10		a	13 08	13 30			13 19			13 34	13 45			13 49			14 03		14 07	14 30			14 19			14 37
		d	13 12				13 21			13 39	13 48			13 52					14 12				14 21			14 39
Garforth	40	d									13 56															
Selby	29,40	a									14 11															
Howden	29	a																								
Brough	29	a									14 30															
Hull	29	a									14 45															
York 8	26	a	13 35				13 43			14 01				14 17					14 34				14 43			15 01
		d	13 39				13 45			14 02				14 18					14 38				14 45			15 02
Malton		d					14 08																15 08			
Seamer	43	d					14 25																15 25			
Scarborough	43	a					14 35																15 35			
Thirsk		a	13 55																14 55							
Northallerton	26	a	14 06											14 39					15 06							
Darlington 8	26	a								14 33				14 52												
Yarm		d	14 20																15 21							
Thornaby	44	a	14 30																15 30							
Middlesbrough	44	a	14 38																15 38							
Durham	26	a								14 50				15 10												15 47
Chester-le-Street	26	a												15 16												
Newcastle 8	26	a								15 04				15 27												16 01

Table T039-F

Mondays to Fridays
21 May to 7 December

Liverpool, Manchester Airport and Manchester - Huddersfield - Wakefield, Leeds, Hull, York, Scarborough, Middlesbrough and Newcastle

		TP	NT		TP			NT	NT	TP	TP		NT	TP		NT	TP	TP	NT		TP			NT	NT
		◇1			◇1			◇		◇1	◇1			◇1		◇	◇1	◇1			◇1			◇	
Liverpool Lime Street 10	90 d				13 25									13 56							14 25				
Lea Green	90 d													14 08											
Newton-le-Willows	90 d				13 43																14 43				
Manchester Airport	d									13 47							14 19								
Manchester Piccadilly 10	d	13 47								14 05	14 17						14 35	14 47							
Manchester Oxford Road	d									14 08							14 38								
Manchester Victoria	a				14 01					14 14				14 31			14 45				15 01				
	d		13 53		14 02					14 17			14 23	14 33		14 36	14 47		14 53		15 02				
Ashton-under-Lyne	d		14 03										14 33						15 03						
Stalybridge	a	13 59	14 07								14 29		14 37					14 59	15 07						
	d	14 00									14 30							15 00							
Mossley (Grtr Manchester)	d	14 04																15 04							
Greenfield	d										14 36														
Marsden	d										14 44														
Slaithwaite	d	14 15																15 15							
Huddersfield	a	14 21			14 29					14 46	14 51			14 59			15 14	15 21			15 29				
	d	14 22			14 30				14 38	14 46	14 52			15 00			15 15	15 22			15 30				15 38
Deighton	d							←	14 42		14 55													←	15 42
Mirfield	d							14 39	14 46		15 00					15 38								15 38	15 46
Wakefield Kirkgate	a								15 01							→									16 01
Ravensthorpe	d										15 03														
Dewsbury	a	14 30						14 44		14 55	15 06							15 31						15 43	
	d	14 31						14 44		14 55	15 11							15 31						15 43	
Batley	d	14 34									15 13							15 34							
Morley	d							14 51			15 18													15 50	
Cottingley	d							14 55																15 54	
Leeds 10	a	14 45			14 49			15 03		15 08	15 30			15 19			15 35	15 45			15 49			16 02	
	d	14 48			14 52					15 12				15 21			15 39	15 48			15 52				
Garforth	40 d	14 56																15 56							
Selby	29,40 a	15 11																16 11							
Howden	29 a																								
Brough	29 a	15 30																16 30							
Hull	29 a	15 45																16 45							
York 8	26 a				15 17					15 34				15 43			16 01				16 17				
	d				15 18					15 38				15 45			16 02				16 18				
Malton	d													16 08											
Seamer	43 d													16 25											
Scarborough	43 a													16 35											
Thirsk	a									15 55															
Northallerton	26 a				15 39					16 06											16 39				
Darlington 6	26 a				15 50												16 33				16 52				
Yarm	d									16 20															
Thornaby	44 a									16 30															
Middlesbrough	44 a									16 38															
Durham	26 a				16 10												16 50				17 11				
Chester-le-Street	26 a																				17 17				
Newcastle 8	26 a				16 25												17 04				17 27				

Table T039-F

Mondays to Fridays
21 May to 7 December

Liverpool, Manchester Airport and Manchester - Huddersfield - Wakefield, Leeds, Hull, York, Scarborough, Middlesbrough and Newcastle

		TP	TP		NT	TP		NT	TP	TP	NT		TP			NT	NT		TP	TP		NT	TP		NT
		◇1	◇1			◇1		◇	◇1	◇1			◇1			◇			◇1	◇1			◇1		◇
Liverpool Lime Street 10	90 d					14 56							15 25										15 56		
Lea Green	90 d					15 08																	16 08		
Newton-le-Willows	90 d												15 43												
Manchester Airport	d	14 47							15 19										15 47						
Manchester Piccadilly 10	d	15 05	15 17						15 35	15 47									16 05	16 17					
Manchester Oxford Road	d	15 08							15 38										16 08						
Manchester Victoria	a	15 14				15 31			15 45				16 01						16 15				16 30		
	d	15 17			15 23	15 32		15 36	15 47		15 53		16 02						16 17			16 23	16 32		16 37
Ashton-under-Lyne	d				15 33						16 03											16 33			
Stalybridge	a		15 29		15 37					15 59	16 07									16 29		16 37			
	d		15 30							16 00										16 30					
Mossley (Grtr Manchester)	d									16 04															
Greenfield	d		15 36																	16 36					
Marsden	d		15 44																	16 44					
Slaithwaite	d									16 15															
Huddersfield	a	15 46	15 51			15 59			16 14	16 21			16 29						16 44	16 51			16 59		
	d	15 46	15 52			16 00			16 15	16 22			16 30				16 38		16 45	16 52			17 00		
Deighton	d		15 55													←	16 42			16 55					
Mirfield	d		16 00					16 39								16 39	16 46			17 00					17 39
Wakefield Kirkgate	a							→									17 01								→
Ravensthorpe	d		16 03																	17 03					
Dewsbury	a	15 55	16 06							16 30						16 44			16 53	17 06					
	d	15 55	16 11							16 31						16 44			16 54	17 11					
Batley	d		16 13							16 34										17 13					
Morley	d		16 18													16 51				17 18					
Cottingley	d															16 55									
Leeds 10	a	16 08	16 30			16 17			16 34	16 45			16 49			17 03			17 07	17 28			17 19		
	d	16 11				16 21			16 36	16 48			16 52						17 12				17 21		
Garforth	40 d								16 45	16 56															
Selby	29,40 a									17 11															
Howden	29 a																								
Brough	29 a									17 30															
Hull	29 a									17 45															
York 8	26 a	16 35				16 43			17 01				17 17						17 36				17 43		
	d	16 39				16 45			17 02				17 18						17 38				17 44		
Malton	d					17 08																	18 08		
Seamer	43 d					17 25																	18 25		
Scarborough	43 a					17 35																	18 35		
Thirsk	a	16 55																	17 55						
Northallerton	26 a	17 06											17 39						18 07						
Darlington 6	26 a												17 51												
Yarm	d	17 21																	18 21						
Thornaby	44 a	17 30																	18 31						
Middlesbrough	44 a	17 38																	18 39						
Durham	26 a								17 48				18 11												
Chester-le-Street	26 a																								
Newcastle 8	26 a								18 02				18 27												

Table T039-F

Mondays to Fridays

21 May to 7 December

Liverpool, Manchester Airport and Manchester - Huddersfield - Wakefield, Leeds, Hull, York, Scarborough, Middlesbrough and Newcastle

Station			TP ◇1 ✠	TP ◇1 ✠	NT	TP ◇1 ✠	NT ◇	NT	TP ◇1 ✠	TP ◇1	NT	TP ◇1 ✠	TP ◇1 ✠	NT ◇	TP ◇1 ✠	TP ◇1 ✠	NT
Liverpool Lime Street 10	90	d				16 25						16 56					
Lea Green	90	d										17 08					
Newton-le-Willows	90	d				16 43											
Manchester Airport		d	16 19						16 47						17 19		
Manchester Piccadilly 10		d	16 35	16 47					17 05	17 17					17 35	17 47	
Manchester Oxford Road		d	16 38						17 08						17 38		
Manchester Victoria		a	16 45			17 01			17 14			17 30			17 45		
		d	16 47		16 53	17 02			17 17		17 23	17 31		17 37	17 47		17 53
Ashton-under-Lyne		d			17 03						17 33						18 03
Stalybridge		a		16 59	17 07					17 29	17 37	17 42				17 59	18 07
		d		17 00						17 30		17 42				18 00	
Mossley (Grtr Manchester)		d		17 04						17 34						18 04	
Greenfield		d								17 38							
Marsden		d								17 45							
Slaithwaite		d		17 15												18 15	
Huddersfield		a	17 14	17 21		17 29			17 44	17 53		18 00			18 14	18 21	
		d	17 15	17 22		17 30		17 38	17 45	17 53		18 01			18 15	18 22	
Deighton		d					←	17 42		17 57							
Mirfield		d					17 39	17 46		18 01				18 39			
Wakefield Kirkgate		a						18 01						→			
Ravensthorpe		d								18 04							
Dewsbury		a		17 30			17 44		17 53	18 07						18 30	
		d		17 31			17 44		17 54	18 11						18 31	
Batley		d		17 34						18 14						18 34	
Morley		d					17 51			18 19							
Cottingley		d					17 55										
Leeds 10		a	17 34	17 45		17 49	18 03		18 07	18 28		18 20			18 34	18 45	
		d	17 36	17 48		17 52			18 11			18 21			18 39	18 48	
Garforth	40	d	17 45	17 56												18 56	
Selby	29,40	a		18 11												19 11	
Howden	29	a		18 21													
Brough	29	a		18 34												19 30	
Hull	29	a		18 49									←			19 44	
York 8	26	a	18 01			18 16			18 37			18 43	18 37		19 05		
		d	18 02			18 18			18 46			18 45	18 46		19 08		
Malton		d							→			19 08					
Seamer	43	d										19 25					
Scarborough	43	a										19 35					
Thirsk		a											19 03		19 25		
Northallerton	26	a				18 38							19 13				
Darlington 8	26	a	18 33			18 51									19 44		
Yarm		d											19 30				
Thornaby	44	a											19 42				
Middlesbrough	44	a											19 51				
Durham	26	a	18 50			19 08									20 01		
Chester-le-Street	26	a				19 14											
Newcastle 8	26	a	19 04			19 25									20 16		

Table T039-F

Mondays to Fridays

21 May to 7 December

Liverpool, Manchester Airport and Manchester - Huddersfield - Wakefield, Leeds, Hull, York, Scarborough, Middlesbrough and Newcastle

Station			TP ◇1 ✠	NT ◇	NT	TP ◇1 ✠	TP ◇1	NT	TP ◇1 ✠	NT ◇	TP ◇1 ✠	TP ◇1 ✠	NT	TP ◇1	NT ◇	NT	TP ◇1	TP ◇1
Liverpool Lime Street 10	90	d	17 26						17 56					18 26				
Lea Green	90	d							18 08									
Newton-le-Willows	90	d	17 42											18 44				
Manchester Airport		d				17 47					18 19						18 47	
Manchester Piccadilly 10		d				18 05	18 17				18 35	18 47					19 05	19 17
Manchester Oxford Road		d				18 08					18 38						19 08	
Manchester Victoria		a	18 00			18 15			18 31		18 45			19 01			19 14	
		d	18 02			18 17		18 22	18 32	18 37	18 47		18 53	19 02			19 16	
Ashton-under-Lyne		d						18 32					19 03					
Stalybridge		a					18 29	18 36				18 59	19 07					19 29
		d					18 30					19 00						19 30
Mossley (Grtr Manchester)		d										19 04						
Greenfield		d					18 36											19 36
Marsden		d					18 44											19 44
Slaithwaite		d										19 15						
Huddersfield		a	18 29			18 44	18 51		18 59		19 14	19 21		19 29			19 46	19 51
		d	18 30		18 38	18 45	18 52		19 00		19 15	19 22		19 30		19 38	19 46	19 52
Deighton		d		←	18 42		18 55								←	19 42		19 55
Mirfield		d		18 39	18 46		19 00			19 39					19 39	19 46		20 00
Wakefield Kirkgate		a			19 01					→						20 01		
Ravensthorpe		d					19 03											20 03
Dewsbury		a		18 44		18 53	19 06					19 31			19 44		19 55	20 06
		d		18 44		18 54	19 10					19 31			19 44		19 55	20 10
Batley		d					19 12					19 34						20 12
Morley		d		18 51			19 17								19 51			20 17
Cottingley		d		18 55											19 55			
Leeds 10		a	18 49	19 03		19 08	19 27		19 19		19 36	19 45		19 49	20 03		20 08	20 26
		d	18 52			19 12			19 21		19 38	19 48		19 52			20 12	
Garforth	40	d										19 56						
Selby	29,40	a										20 11						
Howden	29	a																
Brough	29	a										20 30						
Hull	29	a										20 48						
York 8	26	a	19 16			19 34			19 43		20 05			20 16			20 34	
		d	19 18			19 36			19 44					20 22			20 40	
Malton		d							20 08									
Seamer	43	d							20 25									
Scarborough	43	a							20 35									
Thirsk		a				19 54											21 02	
Northallerton	26	a	19 38			20 05								20 43			21 12	
Darlington 8	26	a	19 50											20 55				
Yarm		d				20 20											21 25	
Thornaby	44	a				20 30											21 34	
Middlesbrough	44	a				20 38											21 43	
Durham	26	a	20 07											21 13				
Chester-le-Street	26	a												21 19				
Newcastle 8	26	a	20 21											21 30				

Table T039-F

Liverpool, Manchester Airport and Manchester - Huddersfield - Wakefield, Leeds, Hull, York, Scarborough, Middlesbrough and Newcastle

Station	Table		NT	TP ◇1	NT ◇	TP ◇1	TP ◇1	NT	TP ◇1	NT ◇	NT	TP ◇1	TP ◇1	NT	TP ◇1	NT ◇	TP ◇1	TP ◇1
Liverpool Lime Street 10	90	d		18 56					19 25						19 56			
Lea Green	90	d		19 08											20 08			
Newton-le-Willows	90	d							19 43									
Manchester Airport		d				19 19						19 47					20 19	
Manchester Piccadilly 10		d				19 35	19 47					20 05	20 17				20 35	20 47
Manchester Oxford Road		d				19 38						20 08					20 38	
Manchester Victoria		a		19 31		19 45			20 01			20 14			20 31		20 45	
		d	19 24	19 32	19 37	19 47		19 53	20 02			20 17		20 19	20 32	20 37	20 47	
Ashton-under-Lyne		d	19 35					20 03						20 30				
Stalybridge		a	19 39				19 59	20 07					20 30	20 35				21 00
		d					20 00						20 30					21 00
Mossley (Grtr Manchester)		d					20 04											21 04
Greenfield		d											20 36					
Marsden		d											20 44					
Slaithwaite		d					20 15											21 15
Huddersfield		a		19 59		20 14	20 21		20 29			20 46	20 51		20 59		21 15	21 21
		d		20 00		20 15	20 22		20 30		20 38	20 46	20 52		21 00		21 16	21 22
Deighton		d								←	20 42		20 55					
Mirfield		d			20 39					20 39	20 46		21 00			21 39		
Wakefield Kirkgate		a			→						21 01					→		
Ravensthorpe		d											21 03					
Dewsbury		a					20 30			20 44		20 55	21 06					21 30
		d					20 31			20 44		20 55	21 10					21 31
Batley		d					20 34						21 12					21 34
Morley		d								20 51			21 17					
Cottingley		d								20 55								
Leeds 10		a		20 19		20 34	20 45		20 49	21 03		21 08	21 27		21 19		21 35	21 46
		d		20 21		20 39	20 48		20 52			21 12			21 21		21 37	21 48
Garforth	40	d					20 56											
Selby	29,40	a					21 14											22 10
Howden	29	a					21 24											22 20
Brough	29	a					21 38											22 33
Hull	29	a					21 52											22 46
York 8	26	a		20 43		21 05			21 16			21 34			21 43		22 04	
		d		20 44					21 18			21 40			21 45			
Malton		d		21 08											22 08			
Seamer	43	d		21 25											22 25			
Scarborough	43	a		21 35											22 35			
Thirsk		a										21 56						
Northallerton	26	a							21 38			22 06						
Darlington 8	26	a							21 50									
Yarm		d										22 20						
Thornaby	44	a										22 29						
Middlesbrough	44	a										22 37						
Durham	26	a							22 07									
Chester-le-Street	26	a																
Newcastle 8	26	a							22 22									

Table T039-F

Liverpool, Manchester Airport and Manchester - Huddersfield - Wakefield, Leeds, Hull, York, Scarborough, Middlesbrough and Newcastle

Station	Table		NT	TP ◇1	NT ◇	NT	TP ◇1	TP ◇1	NT ◇	NT	TP ◇1	TP ◇1	NT	NT	NT	TP ◇1	TP ◇1	TP ◇1	TP ◇1
Liverpool Lime Street 10	90	d		20 24								21 24						22 24	
Lea Green	90	d		20 36								21 36						22 36	
Newton-le-Willows	90	d		20 43								21 44						22 42	
Manchester Airport		d					20 45									22 07			22 47
Manchester Piccadilly 10		d					21 05	21 17			21 47					22 22	22 35		23 05
Manchester Oxford Road		d					21 08									22 25	22 38		23 08
Manchester Victoria		a		21 01			21 14					22 01				22 31	22 43	23 00	23 14
		d	20 53	21 02			21 17		21 20	21 23		22 02		22 07	22 14	22 32	22 45	23 02	23 17
Ashton-under-Lyne		d	21 03							21 33				22 17	22 30				
Stalybridge		a	21 07					21 31		21 37	21 59			22 21	22 35		22 56		23 30
		d						21 32			22 00						22 56		23 31
Mossley (Grtr Manchester)		d									22 04						23 00		23 36
Greenfield		d						21 38			22 08						23 04		23 40
Marsden		d						21 45									23 12		23 48
Slaithwaite		d									22 17						23 15		23 51
Huddersfield		a		21 29			21 45	21 53			22 22	22 29				22 59	23 21	23 29	23 57
		d		21 30		21 38	21 46	21 53			22 23	22 30	22 38			23 00	23 21	23 30	23 58
Deighton		d			←	21 42		21 57					22 42				23 25		
Mirfield		d			21 39	21 46		22 01					22 46				23 29		
Wakefield Kirkgate		a				22 01							23 06						
Ravensthorpe		d						22 04									23 32		
Dewsbury		a			21 44			22 07			22 31					23 08	23 35		00 06
		d			21 44			22 10			22 32					23 09	23 36		00 07
Batley		d						22 13			22 34						23 39		
Morley		d			21 51			22 18									23 44		
Cottingley		d			21 55												23 47		
Leeds 10		a		21 49	22 03		22 06	22 27	22 53		22 46	22 49				23 22	23 56	00 07	00 22
		d		21 52			22 07				22 48	22 52				23 23		00 11	00 24
Garforth	40	d																	
Selby	29,40	a									23 10								
Howden	29	a																	
Brough	29	a									23 29								
Hull	29	a									23 45								
York 8	26	a		22 16			22 31					23 14				23 50		00 51	01 05
		d		22 18			22 45					23 15							
Malton		d					23 08												
Seamer	43	d					23 25												
Scarborough	43	a					23 35												
Thirsk		a										23 39							
Northallerton	26	a		22 38								23 47							
Darlington 8	26	a		22 50								00 01							
Yarm		d																	
Thornaby	44	a																	
Middlesbrough	44	a																	
Durham	26	a		23 07								00 18							
Chester-le-Street	26	a		23 13								00 30							
Newcastle 8	26	a		23 24								00 56							

Table T039-F

Mondays to Fridays

21 May to 7 December

Liverpool, Manchester Airport and Manchester - Huddersfield - Wakefield, Leeds, Hull, York, Scarborough, Middlesbrough and Newcastle

Station	Table		NT	TP FO ◇1	TP FX ◇1
Liverpool Lime Street 10	90	d			
Lea Green	90	d			
Newton-le-Willows	90	d			
Manchester Airport		d		23 19	23 19
Manchester Piccadilly 10		d		23 35	23 35
Manchester Oxford Road		d		23 38	23 38
Manchester Victoria		a		23 45	23 45
		d	23 29	23 47	23 47
Ashton-under-Lyne		d	23 39		
Stalybridge		a	23 43		
		d			
Mossley (Grtr Manchester)		d			
Greenfield		d			
Marsden		d			
Slaithwaite		d			
Huddersfield		a		00 14	00 34
		d		00 15	00 43
Deighton		d			
Mirfield		d			
Wakefield Kirkgate		a			
Ravensthorpe		d			
Dewsbury		a		00s23	00s51
		d			
Batley		d			
Morley		d			
Cottingley		d			
Leeds 10		a		00 37	01 05
		d		00 45	01 14
Garforth	40	d			
Selby	29,40	a			
Howden	29	a			
Brough	29	a			
Hull	29	a			
York 8	26	a		01 26	01 55
		d			
Malton		d			
Seamer	43	d			
Scarborough	43	a			
Thirsk		a			
Northallerton	26	a			
Darlington 8	26	a			
Yarm		d			
Thornaby	44	a			
Middlesbrough	44	a			
Durham	26	a			
Chester-le-Street	26	a			
Newcastle 8	26	a			

Table T039-F

Saturdays

26 May to 8 December

Liverpool, Manchester Airport and Manchester - Huddersfield - Wakefield, Leeds, Hull, York, Scarborough, Middlesbrough and Newcastle

Station	Table		TP ◇1	TP ◇1	TP ◇1	TP ◇1	TP ◇1	TP ◇1	TP ◇1	TP ◇1	TP ◇1	TP ◇1	NT	TP ◇1	TP ◇1	NT	TP ◇1	NT ◇	TP ◇1	TP ◇1	NT
Liverpool Lime Street 10	90	d										05 20					05 56				
Lea Green	90	d										05 32					06 08				
Newton-le-Willows	90	d										05 38									
Manchester Airport		d				00 38		04 12	04 54					05 48					06 19		
Manchester Piccadilly 10		d				00 55		04 26	05 10		05 45			06 05	06 17				06 35	06 47	
Manchester Oxford Road		d							05 13					06 09					06 38		
Manchester Victoria		a							05 19			05 57		06 16			06 31		06 45		
		d							05 20			05 59		06 17		06 26	06 32	06 37	06 47		06 53
Ashton-under-Lyne		d														06 35					07 03
Stalybridge		a									05 57				06 29	06 40				06 59	07 07
		d									05 57				06 30					07 00	
Mossley (Grtr Manchester)		d																		07 04	
Greenfield		d													06 36						
Marsden		d									06 10				06 44						
Slaithwaite		d									06 13									07 15	
Huddersfield		a				01 24		05 32	05 47		06 18	06 26		06 44	06 51		06 59		07 14	07 21	
		d			00 15	01 25		05 40	05 54		06 20	06 27	06 38	06 45	06 52		07 00		07 15	07 22	
Deighton		d									06 23		06 42		06 55						
Mirfield		d											06 46		07 00			07 40			
Wakefield Kirkgate		a											07 04								
Ravensthorpe		d													07 03						
Dewsbury		a			00s23						06 30	06 35		06 53	07 06			07 45			
		d		00 07							06 31	06 36		06 54	07 10			07 45			
Batley		d									06 34				07 12						
Morley		d													07 17			07 52			
Cottingley		d													07 21			07 56			
Leeds 10		a		00 22	00 37	02 02		05 59	06 14		06 45	06 49		07 07	07 28		07 19	08 04	07 34	07 45	
		d	00 11	00 24	00 45	02 05		06 00	06 15		06 48	06 52		07 13			07 21		07 35	07 48	
Garforth	40	d									06 57									07 56	
Selby	29,40	a									07 10									08 11	
Howden	29	a									07 20										
Brough	29	a									07 33									08 30	
Hull	29	a									07 46									08 45	
York 8	26	a	00 51	01 05	01 26	02 43		06 23	06 39			07 16		07 35			07 43		08 00		
		d					05 06	06 27	06 43	06 47		07 17		07 38			07 45		08 02		
Malton		d															08 08				
Seamer	43	d															08 25				
Scarborough	43	a															08 35				
Thirsk		a					05 30			07 04		07 33		07 56							
Northallerton	26	a					05 38	06 48	07 04	07 13		07 41		08 04							
Darlington 8	26	a					05 49	06 59	07 15			07 53							08 33		
Yarm		d								07 27				08 18							
Thornaby	44	a					06 20			07 38				08 28							
Middlesbrough	44	a					06 29			07 47				08 36							
Durham	26	a						07 16	07 32			08 10							08 50		
Chester-le-Street	26	a						07 22	07 38			08 16									
Newcastle 8	26	a						07 35	07 51			08 29							09 04		

Table T039-F

Saturdays
26 May to 8 December

Liverpool, Manchester Airport and Manchester - Huddersfield - Wakefield, Leeds, Hull, York, Scarborough, Middlesbrough and Newcastle

		TP	NT	TP	TP	NT	TP	NT	TP	TP	NT	TP	NT	NT	TP	TP	TP	NT	NT
		◇■ ✠		◇■ ✠	◇■		◇■ ✠	◇	◇■ ✠	◇■ ✠		◇■ ✠	◇		◇■ A ✠	◇■ B ✠	◇■		◇
Liverpool Lime Street ■ 90	d	06 25					06 56					07 25							
Lea Green 90	d						07 08												
Newton-le-Willows 90	d	06 43										07 42							
Manchester Airport	d			06 47					07 19						07 47	07 47			
Manchester Piccadilly ■	d			07 05	07 17				07 35	07 47					08 05	08 05	08 17		
Manchester Oxford Road	d			07 08					07 38						08 08	08 08			
Manchester Victoria	a	07 00		07 14			07 31		07 44			08 01			08 15	08 15			
	d	07 02		07 17		07 23	07 32	07 36	07 46		07 52	08 03			08 17	08 17		08 20	08 21
Ashton-under-Lyne	d					07 33					08 03							08 33	
Stalybridge	a				07 29	07 37				07 59	08 07						08 29	08 37	
	d				07 30					08 00							08 30		
Mossley (Grtr Manchester)	d									08 04									
Greenfield	d				07 36												08 36		
Marsden	d				07 44												08 44		
Slaithwaite	d									08 15									
Huddersfield	a	07 29		07 44	07 51		07 59		08 14	08 21		08 29			08 46	08 46	08 51		
	d	07 30	07 38	07 45	07 52		08 00		08 15	08 22		08 30		08 38	08 46	08 46	08 52		
Deighton	d		07 42		07 55								←	08 42			08 55		
Mirfield	d		07 46		08 00			08 38					08 38	08 47			09 00		
Wakefield Kirkgate	a		08 01					→						09 01					
Ravensthorpe	d				08 03								08 41				09 03		
Dewsbury	a			07 53	08 06				08 23	08 30			08 44		08 55	08 55	09 06		
	d			07 54	08 10				08 24	08 31			08 45		08 55	08 55	09 11		
Batley	d				08 13					08 34							09 13		
Morley	d				08 18								08 52				09 18		
Cottingley	d				08 21								08 55						
Leeds ■	a	07 49		08 07	08 30		08 19		08 37	08 45		08 49	09 03		09 08	09 08	09 30		09 52
	d	07 52		08 12			08 21		08 39	08 48		08 52			09 12	09 12			09 55
Garforth 40	d									08 56									→
Selby 29,40	a									09 11									
Howden 29	a																		
Brough 29	a									09 30									
Hull 29	a									09 45									
York ■ 26	a	08 16		08 35			08 43		09 01			09 16			09 34	09 34			
	d	08 18		08 38			08 45		09 03			09 18			09 39	09 39			
Malton	d						09 08												
Seamer 43	d						09 25												
Scarborough 43	a						09 35												
Thirsk	a			08 55											09 55	09 55			
Northallerton 26	a	08 38		09 09								09 38			10 06	10 06			
Darlington ■ 26	a	08 50							09 33			09 50							
Yarm	d			09 21											10 20	10 32			
Thornaby 44	a			09 30											10 31	10 42			
Middlesbrough 44	a			09 38											10 39	10 49			
Durham 26	a	09 07							09 50			10 07							
Chester-le-Street 26	a	09 13																	
Newcastle ■ 26	a	09 24							10 07			10 21							

A until 29 September
B from 6 October

Table T039-F

Saturdays
26 May to 8 December

Liverpool, Manchester Airport and Manchester - Huddersfield - Wakefield, Leeds, Hull, York, Scarborough, Middlesbrough and Newcastle

		TP	NT	TP	TP	NT	TP	NT	NT	TP	TP	NT	TP	NT	TP	TP	NT	TP
		◇■ ✠	◇	◇■ ✠	◇■ ✠		◇■ ✠	◇		◇■ ✠	◇■		◇■ ✠	◇	◇■ ✠	◇■ ✠		◇■ ✠
Liverpool Lime Street ■ 90	d	07 54					08 25						08 56					09 25
Lea Green 90	d	08 07											09 08					
Newton-le-Willows 90	d						08 42											09 43
Manchester Airport	d			08 17						08 47					09 19			
Manchester Piccadilly ■	d			08 35	08 47					09 05	09 17				09 35	09 47		
Manchester Oxford Road	d			08 38						09 08					09 38			
Manchester Victoria	a	08 31		08 45			09 01			09 15			09 31		09 45			10 01
	d	08 33	08 38	08 46		08 52	09 02			09 17		09 24	09 32	09 37	09 47		09 53	10 02
Ashton-under-Lyne	d					09 02						09 34					10 03	
Stalybridge	a				08 59	09 07					09 29	09 38				09 59	10 07	
	d				09 00						09 30					10 00		
Mossley (Grtr Manchester)	d				09 04											10 04		
Greenfield	d										09 36							
Marsden	d										09 44							
Slaithwaite	d				09 15											10 15		
Huddersfield	a	08 59		09 14	09 21		09 29			09 46	09 51		09 59		10 14	10 21		10 29
	d	09 00		09 15	09 22		09 30		09 38	09 46	09 52		10 00		10 15	10 22		10 30
Deighton	d							←	09 42		09 55							
Mirfield	d		09 40					09 40	09 46		10 00			10 39				
Wakefield Kirkgate	a		→						10 01					→				
Ravensthorpe	d										10 03							
Dewsbury	a				09 30			09 45		09 55	10 06					10 30		
	d				09 31			09 45		09 55	10 11					10 31		
Batley	d				09 34						10 13					10 34		
Morley	d							09 52			10 18							
Cottingley	d							09 56										
Leeds ■	a	09 19		09 34	09 45		09 49	10 04		10 08	10 30		10 19		10 34	10 45		10 49
	d	09 21		09 39	09 48		09 52			10 12			10 21		10 39	10 48		10 52
Garforth 40	d				09 56											10 56		
Selby 29,40	a				10 11											11 11		
Howden 29	a																	
Brough 29	a				10 30											11 30		
Hull 29	a				10 45											11 45		
York ■ 26	a	09 43		10 01			10 17			10 35			10 43		11 01			11 17
	d	09 45		10 02			10 18			10 39			10 45		11 02			11 18
Malton	d	10 08											11 08					
Seamer 43	d	10 25											11 25					
Scarborough 43	a	10 35											11 35					
Thirsk	a									10 56								
Northallerton 26	a						10 40			11 07								11 38
Darlington ■ 26	a			10 33			10 53								11 33			11 50
Yarm	d									11 21								
Thornaby 44	a									11 30								
Middlesbrough 44	a									11 38								
Durham 26	a			10 50			11 09								11 50			12 07
Chester-le-Street 26	a						11 15											
Newcastle ■ 26	a			11 07			11 26								12 08			12 24

Table T039-F

Saturdays
26 May to 8 December

Liverpool, Manchester Airport and Manchester - Huddersfield - Wakefield, Leeds, Hull, York, Scarborough, Middlesbrough and Newcastle

Station			NT ◇	NT	TP ◇1	TP ◇1	NT	TP ◇1	NT ◇	TP ◇1	TP ◇1	NT	TP ◇1	NT ◇	NT	TP ◇1	TP ◇1	NT
Liverpool Lime Street 10	90	d						09 56					10 25					
Lea Green	90	d						10 08										
Newton-le-Willows	90	d											10 43					
Manchester Airport		d			09 47					10 19						10 47		
Manchester Piccadilly 10		d			10 05	10 17				10 35	10 47					11 05	11 17	
Manchester Oxford Road		d			10 08					10 38						11 08		
Manchester Victoria		a			10 14			10 30		10 45			11 01			11 14		
		d			10 17		10 23	10 32	10 37	10 47		10 53	11 02			11 17		11 23
Ashton-under-Lyne		d					10 33					11 03						11 33
Stalybridge		a				10 29	10 37				10 59	11 07					11 29	11 37
		d				10 30					11 00						11 30	
Mossley (Grtr Manchester)		d									11 04							
Greenfield		d				10 36											11 36	
Marsden		d				10 44											11 44	
Slaithwaite		d									11 15							
Huddersfield		a			10 45	10 51		10 59		11 14	11 21		11 29			11 46	11 51	
		d		10 38	10 46	10 52		11 00		11 15	11 22		11 30		11 38	11 46	11 52	
Deighton		d	←	10 42		10 55								←	11 42		11 55	
Mirfield		d	10 39	10 46		11 00			11 39					11 39	11 46		12 00	
Wakefield Kirkgate		a		11 01					→						12 01			
Ravensthorpe		d				11 03											12 03	
Dewsbury		a	10 44		10 55	11 06					11 30			11 44		11 55	12 06	
		d	10 44		10 55	11 11					11 31			11 44		11 55	12 11	
Batley		d				11 13					11 34						12 13	
Morley		d	10 51			11 18								11 51			12 18	
Cottingley		d	10 55											11 55				
Leeds 10		a	11 03		11 08	11 30		11 19		11 34	11 45		11 49	12 03		12 08	12 30	
		d			11 12			11 21		11 39	11 48		11 52			12 12		
Garforth	40	d									11 56							
Selby	29,40	a									12 11							
Howden	29	a																
Brough	29	a									12 30							
Hull	29	a									12 45							
York 8	26	a			11 35			11 43		12 01			12 17			12 35		
		d			11 38			11 45		12 02			12 18			12 38		
Malton		d						12 08										
Seamer	43	d						12 25										
Scarborough	43	a						12 35										
Thirsk		a			11 55											12 55		
Northallerton	26	a			12 05								12 39			13 06		
Darlington 5	26	a								12 33			12 51					
Yarm		d			12 19											13 21		
Thornaby	44	a			12 30											13 31		
Middlesbrough	44	a			12 38											13 39		
Durham	26	a								12 50			13 08					
Chester-le-Street	26	a											13 14					
Newcastle 8	26	a								13 07			13 26					

Table T039-F

Saturdays
26 May to 8 December

Liverpool, Manchester Airport and Manchester - Huddersfield - Wakefield, Leeds, Hull, York, Scarborough, Middlesbrough and Newcastle

Station			TP ◇1	NT ◇	TP ◇1	TP ◇1	NT	TP ◇1	NT ◇	NT	TP ◇1	TP ◇1	NT	TP ◇1	NT ◇	TP ◇1	TP ◇1	NT	TP ◇1
Liverpool Lime Street 10	90	d	10 56					11 25						11 56					12 25
Lea Green	90	d	11 08											12 08					
Newton-le-Willows	90	d						11 42											12 43
Manchester Airport		d			11 19						11 47					12 19			
Manchester Piccadilly 10		d			11 35	11 47					12 05	12 17				12 35	12 47		
Manchester Oxford Road		d			11 38						12 08					12 38			
Manchester Victoria		a	11 30		11 45			12 00			12 14			12 31		12 45			13 01
		d	11 32	11 37	11 47		11 53	12 02			12 17		12 23	12 32	12 37	12 47		12 53	13 02
Ashton-under-Lyne		d					12 03						12 33					13 03	
Stalybridge		a				11 59	12 07					12 29	12 37				12 59	13 07	
		d				12 00						12 30					13 00		
Mossley (Grtr Manchester)		d				12 04											13 04		
Greenfield		d										12 36							
Marsden		d										12 44							
Slaithwaite		d				12 15											13 15		
Huddersfield		a	11 59		12 15	12 22		12 29			12 46	12 51		12 59		13 14	13 21		13 29
		d	12 00		12 15	12 22		12 30		12 38	12 46	12 52		13 00		13 15	13 22		13 30
Deighton		d							←	12 42		12 55							
Mirfield		d		12 39					12 39	12 46		13 00			13 39				
Wakefield Kirkgate		a		→						13 01					→				
Ravensthorpe		d										13 03							
Dewsbury		a				12 31			12 44		12 55	13 06					13 30		
		d				12 31			12 44		12 55	13 11					13 31		
Batley		d				12 34						13 13					13 34		
Morley		d							12 51			13 18							
Cottingley		d							12 55										
Leeds 10		a	12 19		12 35	12 46		12 50	13 03		13 08	13 30		13 19		13 34	13 45		13 49
		d	12 21		12 39	12 48		12 52			13 12			13 21		13 39	13 48		13 52
Garforth	40	d				12 56											13 56		
Selby	29,40	a				13 11											14 11		
Howden	29	a																	
Brough	29	a				13 30											14 30		
Hull	29	a				13 45											14 45		
York 8	26	a	12 43		13 01			13 16			13 34			13 43		14 01			14 17
		d	12 45		13 02			13 18			13 38			13 44		14 02			14 18
Malton		d	13 08											14 08					
Seamer	43	d	13 25											14 25					
Scarborough	43	a	13 35											14 35					
Thirsk		a									13 55								
Northallerton	26	a						13 38			14 06								14 38
Darlington 5	26	a			13 33			13 50								14 33			14 51
Yarm		d									14 20								
Thornaby	44	a									14 30								
Middlesbrough	44	a									14 38								
Durham	26	a			13 50			14 07								14 50			15 08
Chester-le-Street	26	a						14 13											15 14
Newcastle 8	26	a			14 07			14 24								15 04			15 27

Table T039-F

Saturdays
26 May to 8 December

Liverpool, Manchester Airport and Manchester - Huddersfield - Wakefield, Leeds, Hull, York, Scarborough, Middlesbrough and Newcastle

			NT ◇	NT	TP ◇1 🍴	TP ◇1	NT	TP ◇1 🍴	NT ◇	TP ◇1 🍴	TP ◇1 🍴	NT	TP ◇1 🍴	NT ◇	NT	TP ◇1 🍴	TP ◇1	NT
Liverpool Lime Street 10	90	d						12 56					13 25					
Lea Green	90	d						13 08										
Newton-le-Willows	90	d											13 43					
Manchester Airport		d			12 47					13 19						13 47		
Manchester Piccadilly 10		d			13 05	13 17				13 35	13 47					14 05	14 17	
Manchester Oxford Road		d			13 08					13 38						14 08		
Manchester Victoria		a			13 14			13 31		13 45			14 01			14 14		
		d			13 17		13 23	13 32	13 37	13 47		13 53	14 02			14 17		14 23
Ashton-under-Lyne		d					13 33					14 03						14 33
Stalybridge		a				13 29	13 37				13 59	14 07					14 29	14 37
		d				13 30					14 00						14 30	
Mossley (Grtr Manchester)		d									14 04							
Greenfield		d				13 36											14 36	
Marsden		d				13 44											14 44	
Slaithwaite		d									14 15							
Huddersfield		a			13 46	13 51		13 59		14 14	14 21		14 29			14 46	14 51	
		d		13 38	13 46	13 52		14 00		14 15	14 22		14 30		14 38	14 46	14 52	
Deighton		d	←	13 42		13 55								←	14 42		14 55	
Mirfield		d	13 39	13 46		14 00			14 39					14 39	14 46		15 00	
Wakefield Kirkgate		a		14 01					→						15 01			
Ravensthorpe		d				14 03											15 03	
Dewsbury		a	13 44		13 55	14 06					14 30			14 44		14 55	15 06	
		d	13 44		13 55	14 11					14 31			14 44		14 55	15 11	
Batley		d				14 13					14 34						15 13	
Morley		d	13 51			14 18								14 51			15 18	
Cottingley		d	13 55											14 55				
Leeds 10		a	14 03		14 08	14 30		14 19		14 34	14 45		14 49	15 03		15 08	15 30	
		d			14 12			14 21		14 39	14 48		14 52			15 12		
Garforth	40	d									14 56							
Selby	29,40	a									15 11							
Howden	29	a																
Brough	29	a									15 30							
Hull	29	a									15 45							
York 8	26	a			14 34			14 43		15 01			15 17			15 34		
		d			14 38			14 44		15 02			15 18			15 38		
Malton		d						15 08										
Seamer	43	d						15 25										
Scarborough	43	a						15 35										
Thirsk		a			14 55											15 55		
Northallerton	26	a			15 06								15 39			16 06		
Darlington 5	26	a								15 33			15 50					
Yarm		d			15 21											16 20		
Thornaby	44	a			15 30											16 30		
Middlesbrough	44	a			15 38											16 38		
Durham	26	a								15 50			16 07					
Chester-le-Street	26	a																
Newcastle 8	26	a								16 07			16 25					

Table T039-F

Saturdays
26 May to 8 December

Liverpool, Manchester Airport and Manchester - Huddersfield - Wakefield, Leeds, Hull, York, Scarborough, Middlesbrough and Newcastle

			TP ◇1 🍴	NT ◇	TP ◇1 🍴	TP ◇1 🍴	NT	TP ◇1 🍴	NT ◇	NT	TP ◇1 🍴	TP ◇1	NT	TP ◇1 🍴	NT ◇	TP ◇1 🍴	TP ◇1 🍴	NT	TP ◇1 🍴
Liverpool Lime Street 10	90	d	13 56					14 25						14 56					15 25
Lea Green	90	d	14 08											15 08					
Newton-le-Willows	90	d						14 43											15 44
Manchester Airport		d			14 19						14 47					15 19			
Manchester Piccadilly 10		d			14 35	14 47					15 05	15 17				15 35	15 47		
Manchester Oxford Road		d			14 38						15 08					15 38			
Manchester Victoria		a	14 31		14 45			15 01			15 14			15 31		15 45			16 01
		d	14 32	14 36	14 47		14 53	15 02			15 17		15 23	15 32	15 36	15 47		15 53	16 02
Ashton-under-Lyne		d					15 03						15 33					16 03	
Stalybridge		a				14 59	15 07					15 29	15 37				15 59	16 07	
		d				15 00						15 30					16 00		
Mossley (Grtr Manchester)		d				15 04											16 04		
Greenfield		d										15 36							
Marsden		d										15 44							
Slaithwaite		d				15 15											16 15		
Huddersfield		a	14 59		15 14	15 21		15 29			15 46	15 51		15 59		16 14	16 21		16 29
		d	15 00		15 15	15 22		15 30		15 38	15 46	15 52		16 00		16 15	16 22		16 30
Deighton		d							←	15 42		15 55							
Mirfield		d		15 38					15 38	15 46		16 00			16 39				
Wakefield Kirkgate		a		→						16 01					→				
Ravensthorpe		d										16 03							
Dewsbury		a				15 31			15 43		15 55	16 06					16 30		
		d				15 31			15 43		15 55	16 11					16 31		
Batley		d				15 34						16 13					16 34		
Morley		d							15 50			16 18							
Cottingley		d							15 54										
Leeds 10		a	15 19		15 35	15 45		15 49	16 02		16 08	16 28		16 19		16 34	16 45		16 49
		d	15 21		15 39	15 48		15 52			16 10			16 21		16 36	16 48		16 52
Garforth	40	d				15 56										16 44	16 56		
Selby	29,40	a				16 11											17 11		
Howden	29	a																	
Brough	29	a				16 30											17 30		
Hull	29	a				16 45											17 45		
York 8	26	a	15 43		16 01			16 17			16 35			16 43		17 01			17 17
		d	15 44		16 02			16 18			16 39			16 45		17 02			17 18
Malton		d	16 08											17 08					
Seamer	43	d	16 25											17 25					
Scarborough	43	a	16 35											17 35					
Thirsk		a									16 55								
Northallerton	26	a						16 39			17 06								17 39
Darlington 5	26	a			16 33			16 51								17 33			17 50
Yarm		d									17 21								
Thornaby	44	a									17 30								
Middlesbrough	44	a									17 38								
Durham	26	a			16 50			17 08								17 50			18 07
Chester-le-Street	26	a						17 14											
Newcastle 8	26	a			17 04			17 27								18 04			18 21

Table T039-F

Saturdays
26 May to 8 December

Liverpool, Manchester Airport and Manchester - Huddersfield - Wakefield, Leeds, Hull, York, Scarborough, Middlesbrough and Newcastle

Station		NT ◇	NT	TP ◇1 ⚲	NT	TP ◇1 ⚲	NT ◇	TP ◇1 ⚲	TP ◇1 ⚲	NT	TP ◇1 ⚲	NT ◇	NT	TP ◇1 ⚲	TP ◇1	NT
Liverpool Lime Street 10	90 d					15 56					16 25					
Lea Green	90 d					16 08										
Newton-le-Willows	90 d										16 43					
Manchester Airport	d			15 47				16 19						16 47		
Manchester Piccadilly 10	d			16 05				16 35	16 47					17 05	17 17	
Manchester Oxford Road	d			16 08				16 38						17 08		
Manchester Victoria	a			16 14		16 31		16 45			17 01			17 14		
	d			16 17	16 23	16 32	16 37	16 47		16 53	17 02			17 17		17 23
Ashton-under-Lyne	d				16 33					17 03						17 33
Stalybridge	a				16 37				16 59	17 07					17 29	17 37
	d								17 00						17 30	
Mossley (Grtr Manchester)	d								17 04						17 34	
Greenfield	d														17 38	
Marsden	d														17 45	
Slaithwaite	d								17 15							
Huddersfield	a			16 44		16 59		17 14	17 21		17 29			17 44	17 53	
	d		16 38	16 45		17 00		17 15	17 22		17 30		17 38	17 45	17 53	
Deighton	d	←	16 42									←	17 42		17 57	
Mirfield	d	16 39	16 46				17 39					17 39	17 46		18 01	
Wakefield Kirkgate	a		17 01				→						18 01			
Ravensthorpe	d														18 04	
Dewsbury	a	16 44		16 53					17 30			17 44		17 53	18 07	
	d	16 44		16 54					17 31			17 44		17 54	18 11	
Batley	d								17 34						18 14	
Morley	d	16 51										17 51			18 19	
Cottingley	d	16 55										17 55				
Leeds 10	a	17 03		17 07		17 19		17 34	17 45		17 49	18 03		18 07	18 28	
	d			17 12		17 21		17 36	17 48		17 52			18 11		
Garforth	40 d							17 45	17 56							
Selby	29,40 a								18 11							
Howden	29 a								18 20							
Brough	29 a								18 33							
Hull	29 a								18 49							
York 8	26 a			17 36		17 43		18 01			18 16			18 37		
	d			17 38		17 44		18 02			18 18			18 46		
Malton	d					18 08								→		
Seamer	43 d					18 25										
Scarborough	43 a					18 35										
Thirsk	a			17 55												
Northallerton	26 a			18 06							18 38					
Darlington 8	26 a							18 33			18 51					
Yarm	d			18 21												
Thornaby	44 a			18 31												
Middlesbrough	44 a			18 39												
Durham	26 a							18 50			19 08					
Chester-le-Street	26 a										19 14					
Newcastle 8	26 a							19 04			19 25					

Table T039-F

Saturdays
26 May to 8 December

Liverpool, Manchester Airport and Manchester - Huddersfield - Wakefield, Leeds, Hull, York, Scarborough, Middlesbrough and Newcastle

Station		TP ◇1 ⚲	TP ◇1 ⚲	NT ◇	TP ◇1 ⚲	TP ◇1 ⚲	NT	TP ◇1 ⚲	NT ◇	NT	TP ◇1 ⚲	TP ◇1	NT	TP ◇1 ⚲	NT ◇	TP ◇1 ⚲	TP ◇1 ⚲	NT
Liverpool Lime Street 10	90 d	16 56						17 26						17 56				
Lea Green	90 d	17 08												18 08				
Newton-le-Willows	90 d							17 42										
Manchester Airport	d				17 19						17 47					18 19		
Manchester Piccadilly 10	d				17 35	17 47					18 05	18 17				18 35	18 47	
Manchester Oxford Road	d				17 38						18 08					18 38		
Manchester Victoria	a	17 30			17 45			18 00			18 15			18 31		18 45		
	d	17 31		17 37	17 47		17 53	18 02			18 17		18 22	18 32	18 37	18 47		18 53
Ashton-under-Lyne	d						18 03						18 32					19 03
Stalybridge	a	17 42				17 59	18 07					18 29	18 36				18 59	19 07
	d	17 42				18 00						18 30					19 00	
Mossley (Grtr Manchester)	d					18 04											19 04	
Greenfield	d											18 36						
Marsden	d											18 44						
Slaithwaite	d					18 15											19 15	
Huddersfield	a	18 00			18 14	18 21		18 29			18 45	18 51		18 59		19 14	19 21	
	d	18 01			18 15	18 22		18 30		18 38	18 45	18 52		19 00		19 15	19 22	
Deighton	d								←	18 42		18 55						
Mirfield	d			18 39					18 39	18 46		19 00			19 39			
Wakefield Kirkgate	a			→						19 01					→			
Ravensthorpe	d											19 03						
Dewsbury	a					18 30			18 44		18 54	19 06					19 30	
	d					18 31			18 44		18 54	19 10					19 31	
Batley	d					18 34						19 12					19 34	
Morley	d								18 51			19 17						
Cottingley	d								18 55									
Leeds 10	a	18 20			18 34	18 45		18 49	19 03		19 08	19 27		19 19		19 34	19 45	
	d	18 21			18 35	18 48		18 52			19 12			19 21		19 39	19 48	
Garforth	40 d					18 56											19 56	
Selby	29,40 a					19 11											20 11	
Howden	29 a																	
Brough	29 a					19 30											20 30	
Hull	29 a		←			19 44											20 48	
York 8	26 a	18 43	18 37		19 01			19 16			19 34			19 43		20 05		
	d	18 45	18 46		19 14			19 18			19 40			19 44				
Malton	d	19 08												20 08				
Seamer	43 d	19 25												20 25				
Scarborough	43 a	19 35												20 35				
Thirsk	a		19 03					19 34			19 54							
Northallerton	26 a		19 16		19 35						20 06							
Darlington 8	26 a				19 47			19 52										
Yarm	d		19 30								20 20							
Thornaby	44 a		19 43								20 30							
Middlesbrough	44 a		19 51								20 38							
Durham	26 a				20 04			20 09										
Chester-le-Street	26 a																	
Newcastle 8	26 a				20 18			20 24										

Table T039-F

Saturdays

26 May to 8 December

Liverpool, Manchester Airport and Manchester - Huddersfield - Wakefield, Leeds, Hull, York, Scarborough, Middlesbrough and Newcastle

Station			TP ◇1	NT ◇	NT	TP ◇1	TP ◇1	NT	TP ◇1	NT ◇	TP ◇1	TP ◇1	NT	TP ◇1	NT ◇	NT	TP ◇1
Liverpool Lime Street 10	90	d	18 26						18 56					19 25			
Lea Green	90	d							19 08								
Newton-le-Willows	90	d	18 43											19 43			
Manchester Airport		d				18 47					19 19						19 47
Manchester Piccadilly 10		d				19 05	19 17				19 35	19 47					20 07
Manchester Oxford Road		d				19 08					19 38						20 10
Manchester Victoria		a	19 02			19 14			19 31		19 45			20 01			20 16
		d	19 03			19 17		19 24	19 32	19 37	19 47		19 53	20 02			20 17
Ashton-under-Lyne		d						19 35					20 03				
Stalybridge		a					19 29	19 39				19 59	20 07				
		d					19 30					20 00					
Mossley (Grtr Manchester)		d										20 04					
Greenfield		d					19 36										
Marsden		d					19 44										
Slaithwaite		d										20 15					
Huddersfield		a	19 30			19 46	19 51		19 59		20 14	20 21		20 29			20 46
		d	19 31		19 38	19 46	19 52		20 00		20 15	20 22		20 30		20 38	20 46
Deighton		d		←	19 42		19 55								←	20 42	
Mirfield		d		19 39	19 46		20 00			20 39					20 39	20 46	
Wakefield Kirkgate		a			20 01					→						21 01	
Ravensthorpe		d					20 03										
Dewsbury		a		19 44		19 55	20 06					20 30			20 44		20 55
		d		19 44		19 55	20 10					20 31			20 44		20 55
Batley		d					20 12					20 34					
Morley		d		19 51			20 17								20 51		
Cottingley		d		19 55											20 55		
Leeds 10		a	19 50	20 03		20 08	20 26		20 19		20 34	20 45		20 49	21 03		21 08
		d	19 52			20 12			20 21		20 39	20 48		20 52			21 12
Garforth	40	d										20 56					
Selby	29,40	a										21 14					
Howden	29	a										21 24					
Brough	29	a										21 38					
Hull	29	a										21 52					
York 8	26	a	20 16			20 34			20 43		21 05			21 16			21 34
		d	20 18			20 40			20 44					21 18			21 40
Malton		d							21 08								
Seamer	43	d							21 25								
Scarborough	43	a							21 35								
Thirsk		a				21 02											21 56
Northallerton	26	a	20 38			21 12								21 38			22 06
Darlington 5	26	a	20 50											21 50			
Yarm		d				21 28											22 20
Thornaby	44	a				21 34											22 28
Middlesbrough	44	a				21 43											22 37
Durham	26	a	21 07											22 07			
Chester-le-Street	26	a	21 13														
Newcastle 8	26	a	21 24											22 22			

Table T039-F

Saturdays

26 May to 8 December

Liverpool, Manchester Airport and Manchester - Huddersfield - Wakefield, Leeds, Hull, York, Scarborough, Middlesbrough and Newcastle

Station			TP ◇1	NT	TP ◇1	NT ◇	TP ◇1	TP ◇1	NT	TP ◇1	NT ◇	NT	TP ◇1	NT	TP ◇1	TP ◇1	TP ◇1	NT
Liverpool Lime Street 10	90	d			19 56					20 24							21 24	
Lea Green	90	d			20 08					20 36							21 36	
Newton-le-Willows	90	d								20 43							21 42	
Manchester Airport		d					20 19								21 06			
Manchester Piccadilly 10		d	20 17				20 35	20 47					21 17		21 22	21 47		
Manchester Oxford Road		d					20 38								21 25			
Manchester Victoria		a			20 31		20 45			21 01					21 30		22 00	
		d		20 19	20 32	20 37	20 47		20 53	21 02				21 23	21 32		22 02	
Ashton-under-Lyne		d		20 30					21 03					21 33				
Stalybridge		a	20 30	20 35				20 59	21 07				21 29	21 37		21 59		
		d	20 30					21 00					21 30			22 00		
Mossley (Grtr Manchester)		d						21 04								22 04		
Greenfield		d	20 36										21 36			22 08		
Marsden		d	20 44										21 44					
Slaithwaite		d						21 15								22 17		
Huddersfield		a	20 51		20 59		21 14	21 21		21 29			21 51		21 59	22 22	22 29	
		d	20 52		21 00		21 15	21 22		21 30		21 38	21 52		22 00	22 23	22 30	22 38
Deighton		d	20 55								←	21 42	21 55					22 42
Mirfield		d	21 00			21 39					21 39	21 46	22 00					22 46
Wakefield Kirkgate		a				→						22 01						23 01
Ravensthorpe		d	21 03										22 03					
Dewsbury		a	21 06					21 30			21 44		22 06			22 31		
		d	21 10					21 31			21 44		22 10			22 32		
Batley		d	21 12					21 34					22 13			22 34		
Morley		d	21 17								21 51		22 18					
Cottingley		d									21 55							
Leeds 10		a	21 27		21 19		21 34	21 45		21 49	22 03		22 27		22 19	22 46	22 49	
		d			21 21		21 39	21 48		21 52					22 21	22 48	22 52	
Garforth	40	d																
Selby	29,40	a						22 10								23 10		
Howden	29	a						22 20										
Brough	29	a						22 33								23 29		
Hull	29	a						22 46								23 45		
York 8	26	a			21 45		22 03			22 16					22 43		23 17	
		d			21 47					22 21					22 45			
Malton		d			22 12										23 08			
Seamer	43	d			22 29										23 25			
Scarborough	43	a			22 37										23 35			
Thirsk		a																
Northallerton	26	a								22 41								
Darlington 5	26	a								22 54								
Yarm		d																
Thornaby	44	a																
Middlesbrough	44	a																
Durham	26	a								23 11								
Chester-le-Street	26	a								23 17								
Newcastle 8	26	a								23 27								

Table T039-F

Saturdays
26 May to 8 December

Liverpool, Manchester Airport and Manchester - Huddersfield - Wakefield, Leeds, Hull, York, Scarborough, Middlesbrough and Newcastle

		NT	TP	NT	TP	TP	NT	TP	TP	TP	TP	TP	NT
			◇1		◇1	◇1		◇1	◇1	◇1	◇1		
								A	B	B	B	A 🚌	
Liverpool Lime Street	90 d					22 24							23 21
Lea Green	90 d					22 36							23 46
Newton-le-Willows	90 d					22 42							23 56
Manchester Airport	d		22 07					23 07	23 07	23 19		23 20	
Manchester Piccadilly	d		22 22		22 44			23 26	23 26	23 35		23 45	
Manchester Oxford Road	d		22 25					23 29	23 29	23 38			
Manchester Victoria	a		22 31			23 00		23 35	23 35	23 45			00 17
	d	22 06	22 32	22 34		23 02	23 29	23 37	23 37	23 47			
Ashton-under-Lyne	d	22 16		22 44			23 39						
Stalybridge	a	22 20		22 49	22 56		23 43	23 48	23 48				
	d				22 56			23 48	23 48				
Mossley (Grtr Manchester)	d				23 00			23 52	23 52				
Greenfield	d				23 04			23a56	23 56				
Marsden	d				23 12				00 04				
Slaithwaite	d				23 15				00 07		←		
Huddersfield	a		22 59		23 21	23 29			00 13	00 17	00 13	00 45	
	d		23 00		23 21	23 30			00 20	00 17	00 20	00 45	
Deighton	d				23 25				→				
Mirfield	d				23 29								
Wakefield Kirkgate	a												
Ravensthorpe	d				23 32								
Dewsbury	a		23 08		23 35						00 29	01 10	
	d		23 09		23 40						00 29	01 10	
Batley	d				23 43								
Morley	d				23 48								
Cottingley	d				23 51								
Leeds	a		23 22		23 59	23 49				00 36	00 42	01 35	
	d		23 23			23 53				00 39	00 44	01 35	
Garforth	40 d												
Selby	29,40 a												
Howden	29 a												
Brough	29 a												
Hull	29 a												
York	26 a		23 50			00 24				01 05	01 10	02 25	
	d												
Malton	d												
Seamer	43 d												
Scarborough	43 a												
Thirsk	a												
Northallerton	26 a												
Darlington	26 a												
Yarm	d												
Thornaby	44 a												
Middlesbrough	44 a												
Durham	26 a												
Chester-le-Street	26 a												
Newcastle	26 a												

A from 27 October
B until 20 October

Table T039-F

Sundays
20 May to 2 December

Liverpool, Manchester Airport and Manchester - Huddersfield - Wakefield, Leeds, Hull, York, Scarborough, Middlesbrough and Newcastle

		TP	TP	TP	TP	TP	TP	TP	TP	TP	TP	TP	TP	TP	TP	TP	TP	TP	TP	TP	TP	TP	TP	TP
			◇1	◇1			◇1			◇1		◇1		◇1		◇1		◇1		◇1	◇1		◇1	
		A 🚌	B	B	A 🚌	A 🚌	C	A 🚌	A 🚌	C	A 🚌	C	A 🚌	A	A 🚌	C	A 🚌	C	A 🚌		A 🛒	A 🚌	C 🛒	A 🚌
Liverpool Lime Street	90 d																							
Lea Green	90 d																							
Newton-le-Willows	90 d																							
Manchester Airport	d						01 00	01 00	03 30	04 22			04 55		06 05	06 27						07 00	07 27	
Manchester Piccadilly	d						01 23	01 25	03 55	04 40			05 20		06 30	06 44		07 14				07 25	07 44	
Manchester Oxford Road	d																							
Manchester Victoria	a																							
	d																							
Ashton-under-Lyne	d																							
Stalybridge	a														06 55	06 57		07 26				07 50	07 57	
	d														06 55	06 57		07 26				07 50	07 57	
Mossley (Grtr Manchester)	d																							
Greenfield	d																							
Marsden	d			00 04																				
Slaithwaite	d			00 07													←							←
Huddersfield	a			00 13			01 52	02 25	04 55	05 09			06 20		07 40	07 15	07 40	07 44				08 35	08 15	08 35
	d	00 15	00 17	00 20		00 45	01 53	02 25	04 55	05 10			06 20		07 40	07 16	07 40	07 45				08 35	08 16	08 35
Deighton	d														→			07 48				→		
Mirfield	d																	07 53						
Wakefield Kirkgate	a																							
Ravensthorpe	d				←													07 56	←					
Dewsbury	a	00 40		00 29	00 40	01 10							06 45			07 25	08 05	07 59	08 05				08 25	
	d	00 40		00 29	00 40	01 10							06 45			07 25	08 05	07 59	08 05				08 25	
Batley	d	→															→	08 02						
Morley	d																	08 07						
Cottingley	d										←	←						08 10						
Leeds	a		00 36	00 42	01 05	01 35	02 12	03 00	05 30	05 29	05 30	05 29	07 10			07 38		08 18	08 30				08 38	09 10
	d		00 39	00 44	01 05	01 35	02 13	03 00	05 30	05 31	05 30	05 31	07 10			07 41					08 41		08 41	
Garforth	40 d								→	→														
Selby	29,40 a																							
Howden	29 a																							
Brough	29 a																							
Hull	29 a																							
York	26 a		01 05	01 10	01 55	02 25	02 40	03 50			06 20	05 55	08 00			08 06					09 03		09 03	
	d													08 14		08 14				08 38	09 04		09 04	
Malton	d																							
Seamer	43 d																							
Scarborough	43 a																							
Thirsk	a																			08 54				
Northallerton	26 a																			09 03				
Darlington	26 a													08 45		08 45					09 44		09 44	
Yarm	d																			09 16				
Thornaby	44 a																			09 25				
Middlesbrough	44 a																			09 33				
Durham	26 a													09 02		09 02					10 01		10 01	
Chester-le-Street	26 a																				10 07		10 07	
Newcastle	26 a													09 16		09 16					10 18		10 18	

A from 28 October
B from 27 May until 21 October
C until 21 October

Table T039-F

Sundays
20 May to 2 December

Liverpool, Manchester Airport and Manchester - Huddersfield - Wakefield, Leeds, Hull, York, Scarborough, Middlesbrough and Newcastle

Station			TP ◇1 A	TP A (bus)	NT	TP ◇1 B	TP ◇1 C	TP ◇1 D	TP ◇1 B	TP ◇1 C	TP ◇1 E	TP ◇1 B	TP ◇1 F	TP ◇1 C	TP ◇1	TP ◇1	TP ◇1	TP ◇1	TP ◇1 C	TP ◇1 F	TP ◇1	NT
Liverpool Lime Street 10	90	d													08 12		08 56				09 23	
Lea Green	90	d													08 28		09 09					
Newton-le-Willows	90	d													08 34						09 39	
Manchester Airport		d				07 46	07 46				08 22	08 25						09 19				
Manchester Piccadilly 10		d		08 00		08 04	08 06	08 13		←	08 36	08 38	08 47			09 13		09 33	09 47			
Manchester Oxford Road		d				08 07	08 09		←	08 09	08 39	08 41						09 37				
Manchester Victoria		a				08 13	→		08 13	08 15	08 47	08 50			08 55		09 30	09 43			09 57	
		d			08 17	08 25			08 25	08 25	08 48	08 50		08 52	08 57		09 32	09 46		09 50	10 02	10 07
Ashton-under-Lyne		d			08 27	→																10 16
Stalybridge		a		08 25	08 33			08 25					09 01	09 03		09 25			09 59	10 02		10 23
		d		08 25				08 25					09 01	09 04		09 26			10 00	10 02		
Mossley (Grtr Manchester)		d		08 32				08 29					09 06			09 30			10 04	10 07		
Greenfield		d		08 48				08 33								09 34						
Marsden		d		09 15				08 42								09 42						
Slaithwaite		d		09 25				08 46					09 17			09 46			10 15	10 19		
Huddersfield		a		09 45				08 51	08 59	08 59	09 14	09 18	09 22	09 22	09 29	09 52	09 59	10 14	10 24	10 24	10 29	
		d						08 52	09 00	09 00	09 15	09 19	09 23	09 23	09 30	09 52	10 00	10 15	10 25	10 25	10 30	
Deighton		d						08 55								09 56						
Mirfield		d						09 00								10 00						
Wakefield Kirkgate		a																				
Ravensthorpe		d						09 03								10 03						
Dewsbury		a						09 06					09 32	09 32		10 06			10 33	10 33		
		d						09 10					09 32	09 32		10 12			10 34	10 34		
Batley		d						09 13								10 14						
Morley		d						09 18								10 19						
Cottingley		d						09 21								10 22						
Leeds 10		a						09 28	09 19	09 19	09 35	09 37	09 43	09 43	09 47	10 28	10 19	10 34	10 45	10 45	10 49	
		d	09 21						09 21	09 21	09 38	09 40	09 47	09 47	09 52		10 21	10 39	10 48	10 48	10 52	
Garforth	40	d																				
Selby	29,40	a											10 07	10 07					11 07	11 07		
Howden	29	a																				
Brough	29	a											10 32	10 32					11 27	11 27		
Hull	29	a											10 48	10 48					11 42	11 42		
York 8	26	a	09 44						09 44	09 44	10 03	10 03			10 16		10 43	11 01			11 16	
		d	09 46						09 46	09 46	10 04	10 04			10 18		10 45	11 02			11 18	
Malton		d	10 09						10 09	10 09							11 08					
Seamer	43	d	10 26						10 26	10 26							11 25					
Scarborough	43	a	10 36						10 36	10 36							11 35					
Thirsk		a									10 20	10 20										
Northallerton	26	a									10 28	10 28			10 38						11 38	
Darlington 8	26	a													10 51			11 33			11 50	
Yarm		d																				
Thornaby	44	a									10 49	10 49										
Middlesbrough	44	a									10 58	10 58										
Durham	26	a													11 08			11 50			12 07	
Chester-le-Street	26	a													11 14							
Newcastle 8	26	a													11 24			12 04			12 21	

A from 28 October
B from 16 September until 21 October
C until 9 September
D until 21 October
E until 9 September, from 28 October
F from 16 September

Table T039-F

Sundays
20 May to 2 December

Liverpool, Manchester Airport and Manchester - Huddersfield - Wakefield, Leeds, Hull, York, Scarborough, Middlesbrough and Newcastle

Station			TP ◇1	TP ◇1	TP ◇1	TP ◇1 A	TP ◇1 B	TP ◇1	TP ◇1	NT	TP ◇1	TP ◇1	TP ◇1	TP ◇1	TP ◇1 A	TP ◇1 B	TP ◇1	NT	TP ◇1	TP ◇1 A	TP ◇1 B	TP ◇1
Liverpool Lime Street 10	90	d			09 55				10 24				10 52				11 25					11 52
Lea Green	90	d			10 08								11 05									12 04
Newton-le-Willows	90	d							10 43								11 43					
Manchester Airport		d				10 19	10 20															
Manchester Piccadilly 10		d		10 17		10 36	10 37	10 47				11 17		11 40	11 47	11 48				12 13	12 17	
Manchester Oxford Road		d				10 39	10 40				11 10								12 09			
Manchester Victoria		a			10 31	10 45	10 46		11 00		11 16		11 28				12 00		12 15			12 28
		d	10 16		10 32	10 47	10 47		11 02	11 07	11 17		11 32				12 02	12 07	12 17			12 30
Ashton-under-Lyne		d								11 16								12 16				
Stalybridge		a		10 29				10 59		11 23		11 29			12 00	12 00		12 23		12 29	12 29	
		d		10 30				11 00				11 30			12 00	12 00				12 30	12 30	
Mossley (Grtr Manchester)		d						11 04							12 04	12 04						
Greenfield		d		10 36								11 36								12 36	12 36	
Marsden		d		10 44								11 44								12 44	12 44	
Slaithwaite		d						11 15							12 15	12 15						
Huddersfield		a	10 44	10 52	10 59	11 14	11 14	11 21	11 29		11 47	11 52	11 59	12 14	12 21	12 21	12 29		12 44	12 52	12 52	12 59
		d	10 45	10 52	11 00	11 15	11 15	11 22	11 30		11 47	11 52	12 00	12 15	12 22	12 22	12 30		12 45	12 52	12 52	13 00
Deighton		d		10 56								11 56								12 56	12 56	
Mirfield		d		11 00								12 00								13 00	13 00	
Wakefield Kirkgate		a																				
Ravensthorpe		d		11 03								12 03								13 03	13 03	
Dewsbury		a	10 53	11 06				11 30			11 56	12 06			12 30	12 30			12 53	13 06	13 06	
		d	10 54	11 12				11 31			11 56	12 12			12 31	12 31			12 54	13 12	13 12	
Batley		d		11 14								12 14								13 14	13 14	
Morley		d		11 19								12 19								13 19	13 19	
Cottingley		d		11 22								12 22								13 22	13 22	
Leeds 10		a	11 07	11 28	11 19	11 34	11 34	11 43	11 49		12 07	12 28	12 19	12 34	12 44	12 44	12 50		13 07	13 28	13 28	13 19
		d	11 12		11 21	11 36	11 36	11 47	11 51		12 11		12 21	12 39	12 48	12 48	12 52		13 12			13 21
Garforth	40	d																				
Selby	29,40	a						12 07							13 09	13 09						
Howden	29	a																				
Brough	29	a						12 26							13 28	13 28						
Hull	29	a						12 41							13 43	13 43						
York 8	26	a	11 34		11 43	12 01	12 01		12 14		12 35		12 43	13 01			13 15		13 35			13 43
		d	11 38		11 44	12 02	12 02		12 18		12 40		12 45	13 02			13 20		13 38			13 45
Malton		d			12 08								13 08									14 08
Seamer	43	d			12 25								13 25									14 25
Scarborough	43	a			12 35								13 35									14 35
Thirsk		a									12 56								13 55			
Northallerton	26	a	12 00						12 38		13 04						13 40		14 03			
Darlington 8	26	a							12 51					13 33			13 52					
Yarm		d	12 14																14 16			
Thornaby	44	a	12 22								13 24								14 25			
Middlesbrough	44	a	12 30								13 34								14 33			
Durham	26	a							13 08					13 50			14 09					
Chester-le-Street	26	a							13 14													
Newcastle 8	26	a				13 00	13 00		13 24					14 04			14 23					

A from 16 September
B until 9 September

Table T039-F

Sundays

20 May to 2 December

Liverpool, Manchester Airport and Manchester - Huddersfield - Wakefield, Leeds, Hull, York, Scarborough, Middlesbrough and Newcastle

		TP	TP	TP	NT	TP	TP	TP	TP	TP	TP	TP	NT	TP	TP	TP	TP	TP	TP	NT	TP
		◇1	◇1	◇1		◇1	◇1	◇1	◇1	◇1	◇1	◇1		◇1	◇1	◇1	◇1	◇1	◇1		◇1
						A	B														
		✠	✠	✠		✠	✠		✠	✠	✠	✠		✠		✠	✠	✠	✠		✠
Liverpool Lime Street 10	90 d			12 24					12 52			13 25				13 52			14 25		
Lea Green	90 d								13 04							14 04					
Newton-le-Willows	90 d			12 43								13 43							14 43		
Manchester Airport ✈	d	12 19				12 47				13 19				13 47			14 19				14 47
Manchester Piccadilly 10	d	12 35	12 47			13 05		13 17		13 35	13 47			14 05	14 17		14 35	14 47			15 05
Manchester Oxford Road	d	12 38				13 09	13 09			13 38				14 09			14 38				15 09
Manchester Victoria	a	12 45		13 00		13 15	13 15		13 30	13 45		14 00		14 15		14 30	14 45		15 01		15 14
	d	12 47		13 02	13 06	13 17	13 17		13 32	13 47		14 02	14 06	14 17		14 32	14 47		15 02	15 06	15 17
Ashton-under-Lyne	d				13 15								14 16							15 16	
Stalybridge	a		13 00		13 22			13 29			14 00		14 23		14 29			14 59		15 22	
	d		13 00					13 30			14 00				14 30			15 00			
Mossley (Grtr Manchester)	d		13 04								14 04							15 04			
Greenfield	d							13 36							14 36						
Marsden	d							13 44							14 44						
Slaithwaite	d		13 15								14 15							15 15			
Huddersfield	a	13 14	13 21	13 29		13 47	13 47	13 52	13 59	14 14	14 21	14 29		14 47	14 52	14 59	15 14	15 21	15 29		15 47
	d	13 15	13 22	13 30		13 47	13 47	13 52	14 00	14 15	14 22	14 30		14 47	14 52	15 00	15 15	15 22	15 30		15 47
Deighton	d							13 56							14 56						
Mirfield	d							14 00							15 00						
Wakefield Kirkgate	a																				
Ravensthorpe	d							14 03							15 03						
Dewsbury	a		13 30			13 56	13 56	14 06			14 30			14 56	15 06			15 30			15 56
	d		13 31			13 56	13 56	14 12			14 31			14 56	15 12			15 31			15 56
Batley	d							14 14							15 14						
Morley	d							14 19							15 19						
Cottingley	d							14 22							15 22						
Leeds 10	a	13 34	13 44	13 49		14 07	14 07	14 28	14 19	14 34	14 44	14 49		15 07	15 28	15 19	15 34	15 44	15 49		16 07
	d	13 39	13 48	13 52		14 12	14 12		14 21	14 39	14 48	14 52		15 12		15 21	15 39	15 48	15 51		16 12
Garforth	40 d																				
Selby	29,40 a		14 07								15 07							16 07			
Howden	29 a																				
Brough	29 a		14 26								15 26							16 26			
Hull	29 a		14 41								15 41							16 41			
York 8	26 a	14 01		14 14		14 34	14 34		14 43	15 01		15 15		15 35		15 44	16 01		16 13		16 34
	d	14 02		14 15		14 37	14 37		14 45	15 02		15 18		15 42		15 46	16 02		16 15		16 38
Malton	d								15 08							16 09					
Seamer	43 d								15 25							16 26					
Scarborough	43 a								15 35							16 36					
Thirsk	a					14 54	14 54							16 04							16 54
Northallerton	26 a					15 02	15 02					15 38		16 14					16 35		
Darlington 5	26 a			14 45						15 33		15 50					16 33		16 48		
Yarm	d					15 15	15 15														17 18
Thornaby	44 a					15 23	15 23							16 36							17 30
Middlesbrough	44 a					15 31	15 31							16 42							17 37
Durham	26 a	14 47		15 02						15 50		16 07					16 50		17 05		
Chester-le-Street	26 a	14 53																	17 11		
Newcastle 8	26 a	15 05		15 15						16 04		16 21					17 04		17 21		

A until 9 September

B from 16 September

Table T039-F

Sundays

20 May to 2 December

Liverpool, Manchester Airport and Manchester - Huddersfield - Wakefield, Leeds, Hull, York, Scarborough, Middlesbrough and Newcastle

		TP	TP	TP	TP	TP	NT	TP	TP	TP	TP	TP	TP	NT	TP	TP	TP	TP	TP	TP	TP
		◇1	◇1	◇1	◇1	◇1		◇1	◇1	◇1	◇1	◇1	◇1		◇1	◇1	◇1	◇1	◇1	◇1	◇1
			✠	✠	✠	✠		✠		✠	✠	✠	✠		✠		✠	✠	✠	✠	✠
Liverpool Lime Street 10	90 d		14 52			15 25				15 52			16 25				16 52				17 25
Lea Green	90 d		15 04							16 04							17 04				
Newton-le-Willows	90 d					15 43							16 43								17 43
Manchester Airport ✈	d			15 19				15 47			16 19				16 47				17 19		
Manchester Piccadilly 10	d	15 17		15 35	15 47			16 05	16 17		16 35	16 47			17 05	17 17			17 35	17 47	
Manchester Oxford Road	d			15 38				16 09			16 38				17 09				17 38		
Manchester Victoria	a		15 30	15 45		16 00		16 14		16 30	16 45		17 00		17 14		17 30		17 45		18 00
	d		15 32	15 47		16 02	16 06	16 17		16 32	16 47		17 02	17 06	17 17		17 32		17 47		18 02
Ashton-under-Lyne	d						16 16							17 16							
Stalybridge	a	15 29			16 00		16 22		16 29			16 59		17 22		17 29				18 00	
	d	15 30			16 00				16 30			17 00				17 30				18 00	
Mossley (Grtr Manchester)	d				16 04							17 04								18 04	
Greenfield	d	15 36							16 36							17 36					
Marsden	d	15 44							16 44							17 44					
Slaithwaite	d				16 15							17 15								18 15	
Huddersfield	a	15 52	15 59	16 14	16 21	16 29		16 47	16 52	16 59	17 14	17 21	17 29		17 47	17 52	17 59		18 14	18 21	18 29
	d	15 52	16 00	16 15	16 22	16 30		16 47	16 52	17 00	17 15	17 22	17 29		17 47	17 52	18 00		18 15	18 22	18 30
Deighton	d	15 56							16 56							17 56					
Mirfield	d	16 00							17 00							18 00					
Wakefield Kirkgate	a																				
Ravensthorpe	d	16 03							17 03							18 03					
Dewsbury	a	16 06			16 30			16 56	17 06			17 30			17 56	18 06				18 30	
	d	16 12			16 31			16 56	17 12			17 31			17 56	18 12				18 31	
Batley	d	16 14							17 14							18 14					
Morley	d	16 19							17 19							18 19					
Cottingley	d	16 22							17 22							18 22					
Leeds 10	a	16 28	16 19	16 34	16 44	16 49		17 07	17 28	17 19	17 34	17 44	17 46		18 07	18 28	18 19		18 34	18 44	18 49
	d		16 21	16 37	16 48	16 52		17 10		17 21	17 39	17 47	17 52		18 13		18 21		18 38	18 48	18 52
Garforth	40 d																				
Selby	29,40 a				17 07							18 05								19 07	
Howden	29 a																				
Brough	29 a				17 26							18 25								19 26	
Hull	29 a				17 41							18 40						←		19 41	
York 8	26 a		16 43	16 59		17 16		17 32		17 43	18 01		18 16		18 35		18 43	18 35	19 01		19 16
	d		16 45	17 02		17 18		17 38		17 45	18 02		18 18		18 53		18 45	18 53	19 02		19 18
Malton	d		17 08							18 08					→		19 08				
Seamer	43 d		17 25							18 25							19 25				
Scarborough	43 a		17 35							18 35							19 35				
Thirsk	a							18 01										19 10			
Northallerton	26 a					17 38		18 11					18 38					19 17			19 43
Darlington 5	26 a			17 33		17 50					18 33		18 50						19 35		19 55
Yarm	d							18 25										19 34			
Thornaby	44 a							18 33										19 46			
Middlesbrough	44 a							18 40										19 53			
Durham	26 a			17 50		18 07					18 50		19 07						19 52		20 12
Chester-le-Street	26 a																				20 18
Newcastle 8	26 a			18 04		18 21					19 04		19 21						20 08		20 29

Table T039-F

Sundays
20 May to 2 December

Liverpool, Manchester Airport and Manchester - Huddersfield - Wakefield, Leeds, Hull, York, Scarborough, Middlesbrough and Newcastle

Station	Table	a/d	NT	TP	TP	TP	TP	TP	TP	NT	TP	TP	TP	TP	TP	TP	NT	TP	TP	TP	TP
				◇1	◇1	◇1	◇1	◇1	◇1		◇1	◇1	◇1	◇1	◇1	◇1		◇1	◇1	◇1	◇1
Liverpool Lime Street 10	90	d				17 52			18 25				18 52			19 25			19 52		
Lea Green	90	d				18 04							19 04						20 04		
Newton-le-Willows	90	d							18 43							19 43					
Manchester Airport		d		17 47			18 19				18 47			19 19						20 19	
Manchester Piccadilly 10		d		18 07	18 17		18 35	18 47			19 05	19 17		19 35	19 47			20 17		20 35	20 47
Manchester Oxford Road		d		18 10			18 38				19 09			19 38						20 38	
Manchester Victoria		a		18 16		18 30	18 45		19 00		19 14		19 30	19 45		20 00			20 30	20 45	
		d	18 06	18 17		18 32	18 47		19 02	19 06	19 17		19 32	19 47		20 02	20 06		20 32	20 47	
Ashton-under-Lyne		d	18 16							19 15							20 16				
Stalybridge		a	18 22		18 29			19 00		19 22		19 29			20 00		20 22	20 29			21 00
		d			18 30			19 00				19 30			20 00			20 30			21 00
Mossley (Grtr Manchester)		d						19 04							20 04						21 04
Greenfield		d			18 36							19 36						20 36			
Marsden		d			18 44							19 44						20 44			
Slaithwaite		d						19 15							20 15						21 15
Huddersfield		a		18 47	18 52	18 59	19 14	19 21	19 29		19 47	19 52	19 59	20 14	20 21	20 29		20 52	20 59	21 14	21 21
		d		18 47	18 52	19 00	19 15	19 22	19 30		19 47	19 52	20 00	20 15	20 22	20 30		20 52	21 00	21 15	21 22
Deighton		d			18 56							19 56						20 56			
Mirfield		d			19 00							20 00						21 00			
Wakefield Kirkgate		a																			
Ravensthorpe		d			19 03							20 03						21 03			
Dewsbury		a		18 56	19 06			19 30			19 56	20 06			20 30			21 06			21 30
		d		18 56	19 12			19 31			19 56	20 12			20 31			21 12			21 31
Batley		d			19 14							20 14						21 14			
Morley		d			19 19							20 19						21 19			
Cottingley		d			19 22							20 22						21 22			
Leeds 10		a		19 08	19 28	19 19	19 34	19 44	19 49		20 07	20 28	20 19	20 34	20 44	20 49		21 28	21 19	21 34	21 42
		d		19 13		19 21	19 39	19 48	19 51		20 13		20 21	20 39	20 46	20 52			21 21	21 39	21 47
Garforth	40	d																			
Selby	29,40	a						20 07							21 06						22 07
Howden	29	a																			
Brough	29	a						20 26							21 24						22 26
Hull	29	a						20 41							21 38						22 41
York 8	26	a		19 35		19 43	20 01		20 13		20 35		20 43	21 03		21 16			21 46	22 01	
		d		19 40		19 45	20 02		20 14		20 37		20 45			21 18			21 49	22 04	
Malton		d				20 08							21 08							22 27	
Seamer	43	d				20 25							21 25							22 46	
Scarborough	43	a				20 35							21 35							22 54	
Thirsk		a		19 57							21 02								22 12		
Northallerton	26	a		20 05					20 35		21 17					21 38			22 21		
Darlington 5	26	a					20 34		20 48							21 50					
Yarm		d		20 19							21 31								22 34		
Thornaby	44	a		20 30							21 39								22 43		
Middlesbrough	44	a		20 38							21 46								22 52		
Durham	26	a					20 51		21 05							22 07					
Chester-le-Street	26	a					20 57		21 11												
Newcastle 8	26	a					21 08		21 22							22 22					

Table T039-F

Sundays
20 May to 2 December

Liverpool, Manchester Airport and Manchester - Huddersfield - Wakefield, Leeds, Hull, York, Scarborough, Middlesbrough and Newcastle

Station	Table	a/d	TP	NT	TP	TP	TP	TP	TP	NT	TP	TP	TP	NT	TP
			◇1		◇1	◇1	◇1	◇1	◇1		◇1	◇1	◇1		◇1
Liverpool Lime Street 10	90	d	20 24			20 52			21 24				22 20		
Lea Green	90	d	20 36						21 36				22 34		
Newton-le-Willows	90	d	20 43						21 42				22 40		
Manchester Airport		d					21 04				22 06	22 19			23 27
Manchester Piccadilly 10		d			21 17		21 22	21 47			22 23	22 35			23 41
Manchester Oxford Road		d					21 25				22 26	22 38			23 44
Manchester Victoria		a	21 00			21 27	21 31		22 00		22 32	22 44	22 58		23 49
		d	21 02	21 07			21 32		22 02	22 07	22 33	22 45	23 02	23 06	23 51
Ashton-under-Lyne		d		21 16						22 16				23 15	
Stalybridge		a		21 23	21 29			21 59		22 23		22 56		23 22	
		d			21 30			22 00				22 56			
Mossley (Grtr Manchester)		d						22 04				23 00			
Greenfield		d			21 36			22 08				23 04			
Marsden		d			21 44							23 12			
Slaithwaite		d						22 17				23 15			
Huddersfield		a	21 29		21 52		21 59	22 22	22 29		23 00	23 21	23 29		00 17
		d	21 30		21 52		22 00	22 23	22 30		23 00	23 21	23 30		00 18
Deighton		d			21 56							23 25			
Mirfield		d			22 00							23 29			
Wakefield Kirkgate		a													
Ravensthorpe		d			22 03							23 32			
Dewsbury		a			22 06			22 31			23 09	23 35			
		d			22 12			22 32			23 09	23 36			
Batley		d			22 14							23 39			
Morley		d			22 19							23 44			
Cottingley		d			22 22							23 47			
Leeds 10		a	21 47		22 28		22 19	22 45	22 49		23 22	23 54	00 13		00 35
		d	21 51				22 21	22 47	22 52		23 24	23 56	00 14		00 39
Garforth	40	d													
Selby	29,40	a						23 07							
Howden	29	a													
Brough	29	a						23 26							
Hull	29	a						23 41							
York 8	26	a	22 13				22 43		23 14		23 51	00 23	00 45		01 03
		d	22 18				22 45		23 17						
Malton		d					23 08								
Seamer	43	d					23 25								
Scarborough	43	a					23 35								
Thirsk		a							23 40						
Northallerton	26	a	22 38						23 48						
Darlington 5	26	a	22 50						00 01						
Yarm		d													
Thornaby	44	a													
Middlesbrough	44	a													
Durham	26	a	23 07						00 18						
Chester-le-Street	26	a	23 13						00 24						
Newcastle 8	26	a	23 38						00 48						

Table T039-R

Mondays to Fridays

21 May to 7 December

Newcastle, Middlesborough, Scarborough, York, Hull, Leeds and Wakefield - Huddersfield - Manchester, Manchester Airport and Liverpool

			TP	TP	TP	TP	TP	TP	NT	TP	TP	TP	TP	TP	TP	TP	NT	TP	TP	TP	TP	TP	TP	NT	TP	TP
			MO	MX	MO	MX	MX	MO																		
			◇1	◇1	◇1	◇1	◇1	◇1		◇1	◇1	◇1	◇1	◇1	◇1	◇1		◇1 🚲	◇1	◇1 🚲	◇1 🚲	◇1 🚲	◇1 🚲		◇1	◇1 🚲
Newcastle 8	26	d											04 48								06 02					
Chester-le-Street	26	a																			06 11					
Durham	26	a											05 03								06 18					
Middlesbrough	44	d																05 43					06 22			
Thornaby	44	a																05 48					06 27			
Yarm		a																05 56					06 35			
Darlington 5	26	a											05 22								06 36					
Northallerton	26	a											05 42					06 13					06 50			
Thirsk		a											05 50					06 21					06 58			
Scarborough	43	d																		06 00						06 42
Seamer	43	d																		06 05						06 47
Malton		d																		06 24						07 06
York 8	26	a											06 07					06 39		06 49	07 07		07 16			07 31
		d	01 38	01 38	02 52	02 52	03 50	03 50		05 05	05 38	05 47	06 09		06 22			06 41		06 51	07 09		07 18			07 38
Hull	29	a																								
Brough	29	a																								
Howden	29	a																								
Selby	29,40	a																								
Garforth	40	d												06 27								07 28				07 54
Leeds 10		a	02 05	02 18	03 19	03 32	04 15	04 15		05 43	06 03	06 12	06 31	06 37	06 47			07 04		07 16	07 31	07 37	07 43			08 03
		d	02 05	02 20	03 20	03 35	04 16	04 17		05 46	06 06	06 14	06 33	06 39	06 50	06 53		07 06		07 18	07 34	07 40	07 48		07 53	08 06
Cottingley		d																	←							
Morley		d														07 00			07 00						08 00	
Batley		d										06 24				→			07 04			07 49			→	
Dewsbury		a								05 57		06 26		06 49					07 07	07 28		07 52	07 58			
		d								05 57		06 27		06 50					07 07	07 29		07 52	07 59			
Ravensthorpe		a																	07 10							
Wakefield Kirkgate		d																								
Mirfield		d																	07 14							
Deighton		d																	07 23							
Huddersfield		a	02 40	02 40	03 55	03 56	04 50	04 50		06 06	06 23	06 36	06 51	06 58	07 07			07 23	07 27	07 37	07 51	08 01	08 07			08 23
		d	02 41	02 41	03 58	03 58	04 53	04 53	06 00	06 07	06 24	06 36	06 52	06 59	07 08		07 12	07 24	07 28	07 38	07 52	08 01	08 08	08 11		08 24
Slaithwaite		d							06 06					07 05								08 07				
Marsden		d							06 11								07 22		07 36					08 21		
Greenfield		d							06 27								07 30		07 44					08 29		
Mossley (Grtr Manchester)		d												07 17			07 35		07 48			08 19		08 33		
Stalybridge		a							06 36	06 25				07 21			07 39		07 52			08 23		08 38		
		d								06 25				07 21					07 52			08 23				
Ashton-under-Lyne		d																								
Manchester Victoria		a					05 38	05 38		06 38	06 54	07 09	07 23		07 38			07 54		08 08	08 22		08 38			08 53
		d					05 39	05 39		06 40	06 56	07 10	07 24		07 39			07 55		08 10	08 24		08 39			08 54
Manchester Oxford Road		d					05 46	05 46		06 49		07 16			07 47					08 16			08 47			
Manchester Piccadilly		d	03 43	03 43	04 59	04 59	05 50	05 50	06 56	06 55		07 20		07a37	07 51		07 55		08a07	08 20		08a40	08 51	08 55		
Manchester Airport		a	04 00	04 00	05 15	05 15	06 09	06 10		07 08		07 38			08 07					08 36			09 09			
Newton-le-Willows	90	d											07 41								08 41					
Lea Green	90	d									07 19							08 16								09 16
Liverpool Lime Street 10	90	a									07 35		08 02					08 32			09 02					09 32

Table T039-R

Mondays to Fridays

21 May to 7 December

Newcastle, Middlesborough, Scarborough, York, Hull, Leeds and Wakefield - Huddersfield - Manchester, Manchester Airport and Liverpool

			TP	TP	TP	TP	TP	TP	TP	TP	TP	TP	TP	TP	TP	TP	TP	TP	TP	TP	TP	TP	TP	TP	TP	TP
			◇1	◇1 🚲	◇1 🚲	◇1 🚲	◇1 🚲	◇1	◇1 🚲	◇1	◇1 🚲	◇1 🚲	◇1 🚲	◇1 🚲	◇1	◇1 🚲	◇1	◇1 🚲	◇1 🚲	◇1 🚲	◇1 🚲	◇1	◇1 🚲	◇1	◇1 🚲	◇1 🚲
Newcastle 8	26	d			07 08		07 14					08 01		08 15					09 02		09 18					10 02
Chester-le-Street	26	a												08 24												
Durham	26	a					07 26					08 14		08 30					09 15		09 30					10 14
Middlesbrough	44	d		06 50							07 57							08 57							09 57	
Thornaby	44	a		06 55							08 02							09 02							10 02	
Yarm		a		07 03							08 10							09 10							10 10	
Darlington 5	26	a					07 45					08 32		08 48					09 32		09 49					10 32
Northallerton	26	a		07 19							08 24	08 43						09 24	09 45						10 24	10 44
Thirsk		a		07 29							08 33							09 33							10 33	
Scarborough	43	d							07 38							08 46							09 46			
Seamer	43	d							07 43							08 52							09 52			
Malton		d							08 02							09 11							10 11			
York 8	26	a		07 50	08 06		08 16		08 27		08 51	09 07		09 20		09 36		09 51	10 07		10 21		10 36		10 51	11 07
		d		07 52	08 09		08 22		08 37		08 52	09 09		09 22		09 39		09 52	10 09		10 22		10 38		10 52	11 09
Hull	29	a																								
Brough	29	a																								
Howden	29	a																								
Selby	29,40	a																								
Garforth	40	d				08 28	08 39						09 28							10 28						
Leeds 10		a		08 17	08 31	08 38	08 48		09 03		09 15	09 31	09 38	09 46		10 03		10 15	10 31	10 38	10 46		11 03		11 15	11 31
		d		08 19	08 34	08 40	08 50	08 53	09 06		09 18	09 34	09 40	09 50	09 53	10 06		10 18	10 34	10 40	10 50	10 53	11 06		11 18	11 34
Cottingley		d	←							←							←							←		
Morley		d	08 00					09 00		09 00					10 00		10 00					11 00		11 00		
Batley		d	08 04			08 49		→		09 04			09 49		→		10 04			10 49		→		11 04		
Dewsbury		a	08 07	08 30		08 52				09 07	09 28		09 52				10 07	10 28		10 52				11 07	11 28	
		d	08 07	08 30		08 52				09 07	09 29		09 52				10 07	10 29		10 52				11 07	11 29	
Ravensthorpe		a	08 10							09 10							10 10							11 10		
Wakefield Kirkgate		d																								
Mirfield		d	08 14							09 14							10 13							11 14		
Deighton		d	08 23							09 24							10 24							11 24		
Huddersfield		a	08 27	08 38	08 51	09 01	09 07		09 23	09 27	09 37	09 51	10 01	10 07		10 23	10 28	10 37	10 51	11 01	11 07		11 23	11 27	11 37	11 51
		d	08 28	08 39	08 52	09 01	09 08		09 24	09 28	09 38	09 52	10 01	10 08		10 24	10 29	10 38	10 52	11 01	11 08		11 24	11 29	11 38	11 52
Slaithwaite		d				09 07							10 07							11 07						
Marsden		d	08 36							09 36							10 37							11 37		
Greenfield		d	08 44							09 44							10 45							11 45		
Mossley (Grtr Manchester)		d	08 48			09 19				09 48			10 19							11 19						
Stalybridge		a	08 52			09 23				09 52			10 23				10 51			11 23				11 51		
		d	08 52			09 23				09 52			10 23				10 52			11 23				11 52		
Ashton-under-Lyne		d																								
Manchester Victoria		a		09 08	09 21		09 38		09 53		10 08	10 22		10 38		10 54		11 08	11 22		11 39		11 54		12 08	12 22
		d		09 10	09 23		09 39		09 55		10 09	10 24		10 39		10 56		11 09	11 24		11 39		11 56		12 09	12 24
Manchester Oxford Road		d		09 16			09 46				10 15			10 46				11 15			11 47				12 15	
Manchester Piccadilly		d	09a09	09 20		09a40	09 51			10a08	10 20		10a40	10 50			11a07	11 20		11a40	11 51			12a10	12 20	
Manchester Airport		a		09 36			10 08				10 36			11 09				11 36			12 09				12 39	
Newton-le-Willows	90	d			09 41							10 42							11 43							12 42
Lea Green	90	d							10 16							11 16							12 16			
Liverpool Lime Street 10	90	a			10 02				10 33			11 02				11 32			12 02				12 35			13 02

Table T039-R

Mondays to Fridays
21 May to 7 December

Newcastle, Middlesborough, Scarborough, York, Hull, Leeds and Wakefield - Huddersfield - Manchester, Manchester Airport and Liverpool

	TP	TP	TP	TP	TP	TP	TP	TP	TP	TP	TP	TP	TP	TP	TP		TP	TP	TP	TP	TP	TP	TP	TP
	◇■	◇■	◇■	◇■	◇■	◇■	◇■	◇■	◇■	◇■	◇■	◇■	◇■	◇■	◇■		◇■	◇■	◇■	◇■	◇■	◇■	◇■	◇■
	A																							
	✠	✠		✠		✠	✠	✠	✠		✠		✠	✠	✠		✠		✠		✠	✠	✠	✠
Newcastle ■ 26 ⛴ d		10 15					11 02		11 18					12 03			12 18					13 00		13 18
Chester-le-Street 26 a		10 24							11 27													13 09		
Durham 26 a		10 33					11 15		11 33					12 15			12 31					13 15		13 31
Middlesbrough 44 d						10 55							11 55								12 57			
Thornaby 44 a						11 00							12 00								13 02			
Yarm a						11 10							12 10								13 10			
Darlington ■ 26 a							11 33							12 33			12 49					13 33		13 49
Northallerton 26 a						11 24	11 45						12 24	12 45							13 24	13 45		
Thirsk a						11 33							12 33								13 33			
Scarborough 43 d				10 46							11 46								12 46					
Seamer 43 d				10 52							11 52								12 52					
Malton d				11 11							12 11								13 11					
York ■ 26 a		11 19		11 36		11 51	12 07		12 19		12 36		12 51	13 07			13 21		13 36		13 51	14 07		14 21
d		11 22		11 38		11 52	12 09		12 22		12 38		12 52	13 09			13 22		13 38		13 52	14 09		14 22
Hull 29 a																								
Brough 29 a																								
Howden 29 a																								
Selby 29,40 a																								
Garforth 40 d	11 28							12 28							13 28								14 28	
Leeds ■ a	11 38	11 46		12 03		12 15	12 31	12 38	12 46		13 04		13 15	13 31	13 38		13 46		14 03		14 15	14 32	14 38	14 46
d	11 40	11 50	11 53	12 06		12 18	12 34	12 40	12 50	12 53	13 06		13 18	13 34	13 40		13 50	13 53	14 06		14 18	14 34	14 40	14 50
Cottingley d					←							←								←				
Morley d			12 00		12 00					13 00		13 00						14 00		14 00				
Batley d	11 49		→		12 04			12 49		→		13 04			13 49			→		14 04			14 49	
Dewsbury a	11 52				12 07	12 28		12 52				13 07	13 28		13 52					14 07	14 28		14 52	
d	11 52				12 07	12 29		12 52				13 07	13 29		13 52					14 07	14 29		14 52	
Ravensthorpe a					12 10							13 10								14 10				
Wakefield Kirkgate d																								
Mirfield d					12 14							13 14								14 14				
Deighton d					12 24							13 24								14 24				
Huddersfield a	12 01	12 07		12 23	12 27	12 37	12 51	13 01	13 07		13 23	13 27	13 37	13 51	14 01		14 07		14 23	14 27	14 37	14 51	15 01	15 07
d	12 01	12 08		12 24	12 29	12 38	12 52	13 01	13 08		13 24	13 29	13 38	13 52	14 01		14 08		14 24	14 29	14 38	14 52	15 01	15 08
Slaithwaite d	12 07							13 07							14 07								15 07	
Marsden d					12 37							13 37								14 37				
Greenfield d					12 45							13 45								14 45				
Mossley (Grtr Manchester) d	12 19							13 19							14 19								15 19	
Stalybridge a	12 23				12 51			13 23				13 51			14 23					14 51			15 23	
d	12 23				12 52			13 23				13 52			14 23					14 52			15 23	
Ashton-under-Lyne ⛴ d																								
Manchester Victoria ⛴ a		12 38		12 54		13 08	13 22		13 38		13 54		14 08	14 22			14 38		14 54		15 08	15 22		15 39
d		12 39		12 56		13 09	13 24		13 39		13 56		14 09	14 24			14 39		14 56		15 09	15 24		15 40
Manchester Oxford Road d		12 46				13 15			13 46				14 15				14 46				15 15			15 46
Manchester Piccadilly d	12a40	12 50			13a08	13 20		13a40	13 50			14a08	14 20		14a40		14 50			15a08	15 20		15a40	15 50
Manchester Airport ⛴✈ a		13 09				13 36			14 08				14 36				15 08				15 36			16 09
Newton-le-Willows 90 d							13 42							14 42								15 42		
Lea Green 90 d				13 16							14 16								15 17					
Liverpool Lime Street ■ 90 a				13 35			14 02				14 32			15 02					15 33			16 02		

A ✠ from Leeds

Table T039-R

Mondays to Fridays
21 May to 7 December

Newcastle, Middlesborough, Scarborough, York, Hull, Leeds and Wakefield - Huddersfield - Manchester, Manchester Airport and Liverpool

	TP	TP	TP	TP	TP	TP	TP		TP	TP	TP	TP	TP	TP	TP	NT	TP	TP	TP	TP	TP	TP	TP	TP
	◇■	◇■	◇■	◇■	◇■	◇■	◇■		◇■	◇■	◇■	◇■	◇■	◇■	◇■		◇■	◇■	◇■	◇■	◇■	◇■	◇■	◇■
		✠		✠	✠	✠	✠			✠		✠	✠	✠	✠			✠		✠	✠	✠	✠	
Newcastle ■ 26 ⛴ d					14 03		14 15						14 52		15 15						16 03		16 15	
Chester-le-Street 26 a							14 24																16 24	
Durham 26 a					14 15		14 30						15 04		15 28						16 15		16 31	
Middlesbrough 44 d				13 57								14 55								15 57				
Thornaby 44 a				14 02								15 00								16 02				
Yarm a				14 10								15 10								16 10				
Darlington ■ 26 a					14 33		14 49						15 22		15 46						16 32		16 48	
Northallerton 26 a				14 24	14 45							15 24			15 58					16 24	16 44			
Thirsk a				14 33								15 33								16 33				
Scarborough 43 d		13 46								14 46								15 46						
Seamer 43 d		13 52								14 52								15 52						
Malton d		14 11								15 11								16 11						
York ■ 26 a		14 36		14 51	15 07		15 21			15 36		15 51	16 04		16 21			16 36		16 51	17 07		17 20	
d		14 38		14 52	15 09		15 22			15 38		15 52	16 09		16 22			16 38		16 52	17 09		17 22	
Hull 29 a																								
Brough 29 a																								
Howden 29 a																								
Selby 29,40 a																								
Garforth 40 d						15 28								16 28								17 28		
Leeds ■ a		15 03		15 15	15 31	15 38	15 46			16 03		16 15	16 32	16 37	16 46			17 03	←	17 15	17 31	17 37	17 46	
d	14 53	15 06		15 18	15 34	15 40	15 50		15 53	16 06		16 18	16 34	16 40	16 50		16 52	17 06		17 18	17 34	17 40	17 49	17 52
Cottingley d			←								←						16 58		16 58					17 57
Morley d	15 00		15 00						16 00		16 00						→		17 01					→
Batley d	→		15 04			15 49			→		16 04			16 49					17 06			17 49		
Dewsbury a			15 07	15 28		15 52					16 07	16 28		16 52					17 08	17 28		17 52		
d			15 07	15 29		15 52					16 07	16 29		16 52					17 09	17 29		17 52		
Ravensthorpe a			15 10								16 10								17 11					
Wakefield Kirkgate d																								
Mirfield d			15 14								16 14								17 15					
Deighton d			15 24								16 24								17 24					
Huddersfield a		15 23	15 27	15 37	15 51	16 01	16 07			16 23	16 27	16 37	16 52	17 01	17 07			17 23	17 28	17 37	17 52	18 01	18 07	
d		15 24	15 29	15 38	15 52	16 01	16 08			16 24	16 29	16 38	16 52	17 01	17 08	17 13		17 24	17 29	17 38	17 52	18 01	18 08	
Slaithwaite d						16 07								17 07		17 19						18 07		
Marsden d			15 37								16 37					17 24			17 37					
Greenfield d			15 45								16 45					17 32			17 45					
Mossley (Grtr Manchester) d						16 19								17 19								18 19		
Stalybridge a			15 51			16 23					16 51			17 23		17 37			17 51			18 23		
d			15 52			16 23					16 52			17 23					17 52			18 23		
Ashton-under-Lyne ⛴ d																								
Manchester Victoria ⛴ a		15 53		16 08	16 22		16 38			16 54		17 08	17 22		17 38			17 54		18 08	18 22		18 38	
d		15 55		16 09	16 24		16 39			16 56		17 09	17 24		17 39			17 56		18 10	18 23		18 39	
Manchester Oxford Road d				16 15			16 46					17 15			17 46					18 16			18 46	
Manchester Piccadilly d			16a07	16 20		16a40	16 50				17a07	17 20		17a40	17 50	17 54			18a07	18 20		18a40	18 51	
Manchester Airport ⛴✈ a				16 36			17 09					17 36			18 08					18 36			19 09	
Newton-le-Willows 90 d					16 42								17 40								18 41			
Lea Green 90 d		16 16								17 23								18 16						
Liverpool Lime Street ■ 90 a		16 32			17 02					17 39			18 05					18 32			19 02			

Table T039-R

Newcastle, Middlesborough, Scarborough, York, Hull, Leeds and Wakefield - Huddersfield - Manchester, Manchester Airport and Liverpool

			NT	TP	TP	TP	TP	TP	TP	TP	TP	TP	TP	TP	TP	TP	TP	TP	TP	TP	TP	TP	TP	TP	TP	TP
				◇■	◇■	◇■	◇■	◇■	◇■	◇■	◇■	◇■	◇■	◇■	◇■	◇■	◇■	◇■	◇■	◇■	◇■	◇■	◇■	◇■	◇■	◇■
				⚲		⚲	⚲	⚲	⚲																	
Newcastle ■	26 ⇌	d					17 03		17 17					18 03		18 15					18 53					
Chester-le-Street	26	a							17 26							18 24										
Durham	26	a					17 15		17 32					18 15		18 31					19 05					
Middlesbrough	44	d				16 57							17 57							18 57						19 57
Thornaby	44	a				17 02							18 02							19 02						20 02
Yarm		a				17 10							18 10							19 10						20 10
Darlington ■	26	a					17 32		17 50					18 32		18 49					19 22					
Northallerton	26	a				17 24	17 44						18 24	18 44						19 25	19 34					20 24
Thirsk		a				17 33							18 33							19 33						20 33
Scarborough	43	d		16 46							17 50							18 50						19 46		
Seamer	43	d		16 52							17 55							18 55						19 52		
Malton		d		17 11							18 14							19 13						20 11		
York ■	26	a		17 36		17 51	18 07		18 22		18 39		18 51	19 07		19 21		19 39		19 52	19 57			20 36		20 54
		d		17 38		17 52	18 09		18 24		18 41		18 52	19 09		19 22		19 40		19 52	20 09			20 38		
Hull	29	a																								
Brough	29	a																								
Howden	29	a																								
Selby	29,40	a																								
Garforth	40	d						18 28							19 28							20 28				
Leeds ■		a		18 04	←	18 15	18 31	18 38	18 49		19 05		19 15	19 31	19 38	19 47		20 03		20 16	20 31	20 38		21 03		
		d		18 06		18 18	18 34	18 40	18 50	18 53	19 06		19 18	19 34	19 40	19 51	19 53	20 06		20 18	20 34	20 40	20 53	21 06		
Cottingley		d			17 57							←							←						←	
Morley		d			18 00					19 00		19 00					20 00		20 00				21 00		21 00	
Batley		d			18 05			18 49		→		19 04			19 49		→		20 04			20 49	→		21 04	
Dewsbury		a			18 07	18 28		18 52				19 07	19 28		19 52				20 07	20 28		20 52			21 07	
		d			18 08	18 29		18 52				19 07	19 29		19 52				20 07	20 29		20 52			21 07	
Ravensthorpe		a			18 10							19 10							20 10						21 10	
Wakefield Kirkgate		d																								
Mirfield		d			18 14							19 14							20 14						21 14	
Deighton		d			18 23							19 24							20 23						21 23	
Huddersfield		a		18 23	18 27	18 37	18 53	19 01	19 07		19 24	19 27	19 37	19 51	20 01	20 08		20 23	20 27	20 37	20 51	21 01		21 23	21 27	
		d	18 13	18 24	18 29	18 38	18 53	19 01	19 08		19 24	19 29	19 38	19 52	20 01	20 09		20 24	20 29	20 38	20 52	21 01		21 24	21 29	
Slaithwaite		d	18 19					19 07							20 07							21 07				
Marsden		d	18 24		18 37							19 37							20 40						21 37	
Greenfield		d	18 32		18 45							19 45							20 47						21 45	
Mossley (Grtr Manchester)		d						19 19							20 19							21 19				
Stalybridge		a	18 37		18 51			19 23				19 51			20 23				20 53			21 23			21 51	
		d			18 52			19 23				19 52			20 23				20 54			21 23			21 52	
Ashton-under-Lyne	⇌	d																								
Manchester Victoria	⇌	a		18 54		19 08	19 23		19 38		19 54		20 08	20 22		20 39		21 00		21 09	21 22			21 55		
		d		18 56		19 10	19 25		19 39		19 56		20 10	20 24		20 40				21 10	21 24			21 55		
Manchester Oxford Road		d				19 15			19 46				20 16			20 47				21 16				22 01		
Manchester Piccadilly		d	18 54		19a08	19 21		19a40	19 50			20a08	20 20		20a40	20 51			21a09	21 20		21a40		22 05	22a07	
Manchester Airport	⇌✈	a				19 36			20 08				20 36			21 13				21 36				22 22		
Newton-le-Willows	90	d					19 43							20 40							21 40					
Lea Green	90	d		19 16							20 16			20 46							21 46					
Liverpool Lime Street ■	90	a		19 34			20 03				20 32			21 03							22 03					

Table T039-R

Mondays to Fridays
21 May to 7 December

Newcastle, Middlesborough, Scarborough, York, Hull, Leeds and Wakefield - Huddersfield - Manchester, Manchester Airport and Liverpool

			TP	TP	TP	TP	TP	TP	TP		TP	TP	TP	TP	TP	TP	TP	TP	TP	TP	TP
														FO	FX		FO	FX	FX		
			◇■	◇■	◇■	◇■	◇■	◇■	◇■		◇■	◇■	◇■	◇■	◇■	◇■	◇■	◇■	◇■	◇■	◇■
Newcastle ■	26 ⇌	d	20 03						21 00							22 00					
Chester-le-Street	26	a							21 09												
Durham	26	a	20 15						21 15							22 14					
Middlesbrough	44	d						20 57					21 57		21 57						22 57
Thornaby	44	a						21 02					22 02		22 02						23 02
Yarm		a						21 10					22 10		22 10						23 10
Darlington ■	26	a	20 32						21 32							22 30					
Northallerton	26	a	20 44					21 24	21 44				22 26		22 26	22 42					23 24
Thirsk		a						21 33					22 34		22 34						
Scarborough	43	d				20 50						21 46								22 46	
Seamer	43	d				20 55						21 51								22 52	
Malton		d				21 14						22 12								23 12	
York ■	26	a	21 07			21 40		21 51	22 07			22 36	22 53		22 53	23 06				23 35	00 07
		d	21 09			21 40		21 52	22 09			22 38	22 54		22 54	23 07					
Hull	29	a																			
Brough	29	a																			
Howden	29	a																			
Selby	29,40	a																			
Garforth	40	d																			
Leeds ■		a	21 31			22 03		22 15	22 31			23 02	23 17		23 17	23 30					
		d	21 34	21 38	21 53	22 06		22 17	22 34		22 40	23 04		23 25	23 25	23 35					
Cottingley		d					←				22 45			23 30	23 30						
Morley		d			22 00		22 00				22 48			23 34	23 34						
Batley		d		21 49	→		22 04				22 53			23 38	23 38						
Dewsbury		a		21 52			22 07	22 27			22 55	23 14		23 41	23 41	23 45	←	←	←		
		d		21 52			22 07	22 28			22 56	23 15		23 41	23 41	23 46					
Ravensthorpe		a					22 10				22 58			23 44	23 44		23 44	23 44	23 44		
Wakefield Kirkgate		d												→	→						
Mirfield		d					22 14				23 02						23 48	23 48	23 48		
Deighton		d					22 23				23 07						23 55	23 55	23 55		
Huddersfield		a	21 51	22 01		22 23	22 27	22 37	22 51		23 10	23 23				23 54	23 58	23 59	23 59		
		d	21 52	22 01		22 24	22 28	22 38	22 52		23 11	23 24				23 55	23 59	00 03	00 03		
Slaithwaite		d		22 07			22 33				23 16						00 05				
Marsden		d					22 37				23 20						00 09				
Greenfield		d					22 44				23 27						00 16				
Mossley (Grtr Manchester)		d		22 19			22 48				23 31						00 20				
Stalybridge		a		22 23			22 52				23 35						00 24				
		d		22 23			22 53				23 36						00 24				
Ashton-under-Lyne	⇌	d																			
Manchester Victoria	⇌	a	22 22			22 54		23 07	23 21			23 54				00 25					
		d	22 24			22 55		23 09	23 23							00 27					
Manchester Oxford Road		d						23 24													
Manchester Piccadilly		d		22 43			23a08	23 28			23a53					00 37	00a42	01a02	01a02		
Manchester Airport	⇌✈	a		23 00				23 44								00 52					
Newton-le-Willows	90	d	22 41			23 12			23 40												
Lea Green	90	d	22 47			23 18			23 46												
Liverpool Lime Street ■	90	a	23 04			23 36			00 03												

Table T039-R

Saturdays

26 May to 8 December

Newcastle, Middlesborough, Scarborough, York, Hull, Leeds and Wakefield - Huddersfield - Manchester, Manchester Airport and Liverpool

		TP	TP	TP	TP	TP	TP	TP	TP	TP	TP	TP	TP	TP	TP	TP	TP	TP	TP	TP	TP	TP	TP	TP
		◇1	◇1	◇1	◇1	◇1	◇1	◇1	◇1	◇1	◇1	◇1	◇1	◇1	◇1	◇1	◇1	◇1	◇1	◇1	◇1	◇1	◇1	◇1
													🚲		🚲	🚲	🚲	🚲		🚲		🚲	🚲	🚲
Newcastle 8	26 ⇌ d								04 48							06 02							06 59	
Chester-le-Street	26 a															06 11								
Durham	26 a								05 03							06 18							07 11	
Middlesbrough	44 d												05 43					06 22				06 50		
Thornaby	44 a												05 48					06 27				06 55		
Yarm	a												05 56					06 35				07 03		
Darlington 8	26 a								05 22							06 36							07 29	
Northallerton	26 a								05 42				06 12					06 49				07 19	07 41	
Thirsk	a								05 50				06 20					06 58				07 28		
Scarborough	43 d														06 00					06 47				
Seamer	43 d														06 05					06 52				
Malton	d														06 24					07 11				
York 8	26 a								06 07				06 39		06 49	07 07		07 16		07 36		07 48	08 03	
	d		01 38	02 52	03 53	05 05	05 38	05 47	06 09		06 22		06 41		06 51	07 09		07 18		07 38		07 50	08 09	
Hull	29 a																							
Brough	29 a																							
Howden	29 a																							
Selby	29,40 a																							
Garforth	40 d									06 27							07 28			07 54				08 30
Leeds 10	a		02 18	03 18	04 36	05 43	06 03	06 12	06 31	06 37	06 47		07 04		07 16	07 31	07 37	07 43		08 03		08 16	08 31	08 40
	d		02 18	03 19	04 39	05 46	06 06	06 14	06 33	06 39	06 50	06 53	07 06		07 18	07 34	07 40	07 48	07 53	08 06		08 19	08 34	08 43
Cottingley	d													←							←			
Morley	d											07 00		07 00					08 00		08 00			
Batley	d							06 24				→		07 04			07 49		→		08 04			08 52
Dewsbury	a					05 57		06 26		06 50				07 07	07 28		07 52	07 59			08 07	08 29		08 55
	d					05 57		06 27		06 50				07 07	07 29		07 52	07 59			08 07	08 30		08 56
Ravensthorpe	a													07 10							08 10			
Wakefield Kirkgate	d																							
Mirfield	d													07 14							08 14			
Deighton	d													07 23							08 23			
Huddersfield	a		02 56	03 55	05 11	06 06	06 23	06 36	06 52	06 59	07 07		07 23	07 27	07 37	07 51	08 01	08 08		08 23	08 27	08 38	08 51	09 05
	d		02 56	03 55	05 12	06 07	06 24	06 36	06 52	06 59	07 08		07 24	07 28	07 38	07 52	08 01	08 08		08 24	08 28	08 39	08 52	09 05
Slaithwaite	d	00 05								07 05							08 07							09 12
Marsden	d	00 09												07 36							08 36			
Greenfield	d	00 16												07 44							08 44			
Mossley (Grtr Manchester)	d	00 20								07 17				07 48			08 19				08 48			09 25
Stalybridge	a	00 24				06 25				07 21				07 52			08 23				08 52			09 30
	d	00 24				06 25				07 21				07 52			08 23				08 52			09 30
Ashton-under-Lyne	⇌ d																							
Manchester Victoria	⇌ a				05 42	06 38	06 54	07 09	07 23		07 38		07 54		08 08	08 22		08 38		08 54		09 08	09 21	
	d				05 44	06 40	06 56	07 10	07 23		07 39		07 55		08 10	08 24		08 39		08 56		09 10	09 23	
Manchester Oxford Road	d				05 51	06 49		07 16			07 47				08 16			08 46				09 16		
Manchester Piccadilly	d	00a42	03 34	04 34	05 55	06 55		07 20		07a37	07 51			08a07	08 20		08a40	08 50			09a09	09 20		09a48
Manchester Airport	⇌✈ a		03 52	04 50	06 11	07 08		07 38			08 09				08 36			09 09				09 36		
Newton-le-Willows	90 d								07 41							08 41							09 41	
Lea Green	90 d						07 19						08 16							09 16				
Liverpool Lime Street 10	90 a						07 35		08 02				08 32			09 02				09 32			10 09	

Table T039-R

Saturdays

26 May to 8 December

Newcastle, Middlesborough, Scarborough, York, Hull, Leeds and Wakefield - Huddersfield - Manchester, Manchester Airport and Liverpool

		TP	TP	TP	TP	TP	TP	TP	TP	TP	TP	TP	TP	TP	TP	TP	TP	TP	TP	TP	TP	TP	TP
		◇1	◇1	◇1	◇1	◇1	◇1	◇1	◇1	◇1	◇1	◇1	◇1	◇1	◇1	◇1	◇1	◇1	◇1	◇1	◇1	◇1	◇1
																						A	
		🚲		🚲		🚲	🚲	🚲	🚲		🚲		🚲	🚲	🚲	🚲		🚲		🚲	🚲		🚲
Newcastle 8	26 ⇌ d	07 18					08 01		08 15					09 02		09 18					10 02		
Chester-le-Street	26 a								08 24														
Durham	26 a	07 30					08 14		08 31					09 15		09 30					10 15		
Middlesbrough	44 d					07 57							08 57							09 57			
Thornaby	44 a					08 02							09 02							10 02			
Yarm	a					08 10							09 10							10 10			
Darlington 8	26 a	07 45					08 32		08 49					09 32		09 49					10 33		
Northallerton	26 a					08 24	08 43						09 24	09 45						10 25	10 45		
Thirsk	a					08 33							09 33							10 33			
Scarborough	43 d			07 46							08 50							09 46				10 27	
Seamer	43 d			07 52							08 55							09 52					
Malton	d			08 11							09 13							10 11					
York 8	26 a	08 20		08 36		08 51	09 07		09 20		09 39		09 51	10 07		10 21		10 36		10 51	11 07	11 13	
	d	08 22		08 38		08 52	09 09		09 22		09 41		09 52	10 09		10 22		10 38		10 52	11 09		
Hull	29 a																						
Brough	29 a																						
Howden	29 a																						
Selby	29,40 a																						
Garforth	40 d	08 39						09 28							10 28								11 28
Leeds 10	a	08 48		09 03		09 15	09 31	09 38	09 46		10 04		10 15	10 31	10 38	10 46		11 04		11 15	11 31		11 38
	d	08 50	08 53	09 06		09 18	09 34	09 40	09 50	09 53	10 06		10 18	10 34	10 40	10 50	10 53	11 06		11 18	11 34		11 40
Cottingley	d				←							←							←				
Morley	d		09 00		09 00					10 00		10 00					11 00		11 00				
Batley	d		→		09 04			09 49		→		10 04			10 49		→		11 04				11 49
Dewsbury	a				09 07	09 28		09 52				10 07	10 28		10 52				11 07	11 28			11 52
	d				09 07	09 29		09 52				10 07	10 29		10 52				11 07	11 29			11 52
Ravensthorpe	a				09 10							10 10							11 10				
Wakefield Kirkgate	d																						
Mirfield	d				09 14							10 14							11 14				
Deighton	d				09 24							10 24							11 24				
Huddersfield	a	09 07		09 23	09 27	09 37	09 51	10 01	10 07		10 23	10 28	10 37	10 51	11 01	11 07		11 23	11 27	11 37	11 51		12 01
	d	09 08		09 24	09 28	09 38	09 52	10 01	10 08		10 24	10 29	10 38	10 52	11 01	11 08		11 24	11 29	11 38	11 52		12 01
Slaithwaite	d							10 07							11 07								12 07
Marsden	d				09 36							10 37							11 37				
Greenfield	d				09 44							10 45							11 45				
Mossley (Grtr Manchester)	d				09 48			10 19							11 19								12 19
Stalybridge	a				09 52			10 23				10 51			11 23				11 51				12 23
	d				09 52			10 23				10 52			11 23				11 52				12 23
Ashton-under-Lyne	⇌ d																						
Manchester Victoria	⇌ a	09 38		09 53		10 09	10 22		10 38		10 54		11 08	11 22		11 39		11 54		12 08	12 22		
	d	09 39		09 56		10 09	10 24		10 39		10 56		11 09	11 24		11 39		11 56		12 09	12 24		
Manchester Oxford Road	d	09 46				10 15			10 46				11 15			11 47				12 15			
Manchester Piccadilly	d	09 50			10a08	10 20		10a40	10 50			11a07	11 20		11a40	11 51			12a10	12 20			12a40
Manchester Airport	⇌✈ a	10 08				10 36			11 09				11 36			12 09				12 39			
Newton-le-Willows	90 d						10 42							11 42							12 42		
Lea Green	90 d			10 16							11 16							12 16					
Liverpool Lime Street 10	90 a			10 32			11 02				11 32			12 02				12 35			13 02		

A from 23 June until 8 September

Table T039-R

Saturdays
26 May to 8 December

Newcastle, Middlesborough, Scarborough, York, Hull, Leeds and Wakefield - Huddersfield - Manchester, Manchester Airport and Liverpool

Station			TP ◇1 🛒	TP ◇1	TP ◇1 🛒	TP ◇1	TP ◇1 🛒	TP ◇1 🛒	TP ◇1 🛒	TP ◇1 🛒	TP ◇1	TP ◇1 🛒	TP ◇1	TP ◇1 🛒	TP ◇1 🛒	TP ◇1 A	TP ◇1 🛒	TP ◇1 🛒	TP ◇1	TP ◇1 🛒	TP ◇1	TP ◇1 🛒	TP ◇1 🛒	TP ◇1 🛒	TP ◇1 🛒
Newcastle 8	26 ⛴	d	10 17					11 02		11 17					12 03			12 18					13 00		13 18
Chester-le-Street	26	a	10 26							11 26													13 09		
Durham	26	a	10 32					11 15		11 32					12 15			12 31					13 15		13 31
Middlesbrough	44	d					10 55							11 55								12 57			
Thornaby	44	a					11 02							12 02								13 02			
Yarm		a					11 10							12 10								13 10			
Darlington 8	26	a	10 50					11 33		11 50					12 33			12 49					13 33		13 49
Northallerton	26	a					11 24	11 45						12 24	12 45							13 24	13 45		
Thirsk		a					11 33							12 33								13 33			
Scarborough	43	d			10 46							11 46				12 25				12 46					
Seamer	43	d			10 52							11 52								12 52					
Malton		d			11 11							12 11				12 47				13 11					
York 8	26	a	11 22		11 36		11 51	12 07		12 22		12 36		12 51	13 07	13 14		13 21		13 36		13 51	14 07		14 21
		d	11 24		11 38		11 52	12 09		12 24		12 38		12 52	13 09			13 22		13 38		13 52	14 09		14 22
Hull	29	a																							
Brough	29	a																							
Howden	29	a																							
Selby	29,40	a																							
Garforth	40	d							12 28								13 28							14 28	
Leeds 10		a	11 46		12 04		12 15	12 31	12 38	12 47		13 04		13 15	13 31		13 38	13 46		14 04		14 15	14 32	14 38	14 46
		d	11 50	11 53	12 06		12 18	12 34	12 40	12 50	12 53	13 06		13 18	13 34		13 40	13 50	13 53	14 06		14 18	14 34	14 40	14 50
Cottingley		d				←							←								←				
Morley		d		12 00		12 00					13 00		13 00						14 00		14 00				
Batley		d		→		12 04			12 49		→		13 04				13 49		→		14 04			14 49	
Dewsbury		a				12 07	12 28		12 52				13 07	13 28			13 52				14 07	14 28		14 52	
		d				12 07	12 29		12 52				13 07	13 29			13 52				14 07	14 29		14 52	
Ravensthorpe		a				12 10							13 10								14 10				
Wakefield Kirkgate		d																							
Mirfield		d				12 14							13 14								14 14				
Deighton		d				12 24							13 24								14 24				
Huddersfield		a	12 07		12 23	12 27	12 37	12 51	13 01	13 07		13 23	13 27	13 37	13 51		14 01	14 07		14 23	14 27	14 37	14 51	15 01	15 07
		d	12 08		12 24	12 29	12 38	12 52	13 01	13 08		13 24	13 29	13 38	13 52		14 01	14 08		14 24	14 29	14 38	14 52	15 01	15 08
Slaithwaite		d							13 07								14 07							15 07	
Marsden		d				12 37							13 37								14 37				
Greenfield		d				12 45							13 45								14 45				
Mossley (Grtr Manchester)		d							13 19								14 19							15 19	
Stalybridge		a				12 51			13 23				13 51				14 23				14 51			15 23	
		d				12 52			13 23				13 52				14 23				14 52			15 23	
Ashton-under-Lyne	⛴	d																							
Manchester Victoria	⛴	a	12 39		12 54		13 08	13 22		13 38		13 54		14 08	14 22			14 38		14 54		15 08	15 22		15 38
		d	12 40		12 56		13 09	13 24		13 40		13 56		14 09	14 24			14 39		14 56		15 09	15 24		15 40
Manchester Oxford Road		d	12 47				13 15			13 47				14 15				14 46				15 15			15 46
Manchester Piccadilly		d	12 51			13a08	13 20		13a40	13 51			14a08	14 20			14a40	14 50			15a08	15 20		15a40	15 50
Manchester Airport	⛴✈	a	13 09				13 36			14 08				14 36				15 08				15 36			16 09
Newton-le-Willows	90	d						13 42							14 42								15 42		
Lea Green	90	d			13 16							14 16								15 16					
Liverpool Lime Street 10	90	a			13 35			14 02				14 36			15 02					15 32			16 02		

A from 23 June until 8 September

Table T039-R

Saturdays
26 May to 8 December

Newcastle, Middlesborough, Scarborough, York, Hull, Leeds and Wakefield - Huddersfield - Manchester, Manchester Airport and Liverpool

Station			TP ◇1	TP ◇1 🛒	TP ◇1	TP ◇1 🛒	TP ◇1 🛒	TP ◇1 🛒	TP ◇1 🛒	TP ◇1	TP ◇1 🛒	TP ◇1	TP ◇1 🛒	TP ◇1 🛒	TP ◇1 🛒	TP ◇1 🛒	TP ◇1	TP ◇1 🛒	TP ◇1	TP ◇1 🛒	TP ◇1 🛒	TP ◇1 🛒	TP ◇1 🛒	TP ◇1
Newcastle 8	26 ⛴	d					14 03		14 15					14 52		15 15					16 03		16 15	
Chester-le-Street	26	a							14 24														16 24	
Durham	26	a					14 15		14 30					15 04		15 28					16 15		16 31	
Middlesbrough	44	d				13 57							14 55							15 57				
Thornaby	44	a				14 02							15 02							16 02				
Yarm		a				14 10							15 10							16 10				
Darlington 8	26	a					14 33		14 49					15 22		15 46					16 32		16 48	
Northallerton	26	a				14 24	14 45						15 24			15 58				16 24	16 44			
Thirsk		a				14 33							15 33							16 33				
Scarborough	43	d		13 46							14 46							15 46						
Seamer	43	d		13 52							14 52							15 52						
Malton		d		14 11							15 11							16 11						
York 8	26	a		14 36		14 51	15 07		15 21		15 36		15 51	16 04		16 21		16 36		16 51	17 07		17 24	
		d		14 38		14 52	15 09		15 22		15 38		15 52	16 09		16 22		16 38		16 52	17 09		17 25	
Hull	29	a																						
Brough	29	a																						
Howden	29	a																						
Selby	29,40	a																						
Garforth	40	d						15 28							16 28							17 28		
Leeds 10		a		15 04		15 15	15 31	15 38	15 46		16 04		16 15	16 32	16 37	16 46		17 04	←	17 15	17 31	17 37	17 46	
		d	14 53	15 06		15 18	15 34	15 40	15 50	15 53	16 06		16 18	16 34	16 40	16 50	16 52	17 06		17 18	17 34	17 40	17 49	17 52
Cottingley		d			←							←					16 58		16 58					17 57
Morley		d	15 00		15 00					16 00		16 00					→		17 01					→
Batley		d	→		15 04			15 49		→		16 04			16 49				17 06			17 49		
Dewsbury		a			15 07	15 28		15 52				16 07	16 28		16 52				17 08	17 28		17 52		
		d			15 07	15 29		15 52				16 07	16 29		16 52				17 09	17 29		17 52		
Ravensthorpe		a			15 10							16 10							17 11					
Wakefield Kirkgate		d																						
Mirfield		d			15 14							16 14							17 15					
Deighton		d			15 24							16 24							17 24					
Huddersfield		a		15 23	15 27	15 37	15 51	16 01	16 07		16 23	16 27	16 37	16 52	17 01	17 07		17 23	17 28	17 37	17 52	18 01	18 07	
		d		15 24	15 29	15 38	15 52	16 01	16 08		16 24	16 29	16 38	16 52	17 01	17 08		17 24	17 29	17 38	17 52	18 01	18 08	
Slaithwaite		d						16 07							17 07							18 07		
Marsden		d			15 37							16 37							17 37					
Greenfield		d			15 45							16 45							17 45					
Mossley (Grtr Manchester)		d						16 19							17 19							18 19		
Stalybridge		a			15 51			16 23				16 51			17 23				17 51			18 23		
		d			15 52			16 23				16 52			17 23				17 52			18 23		
Ashton-under-Lyne	⛴	d																						
Manchester Victoria	⛴	a		15 54		16 09	16 22		16 39		16 54		17 08	17 22		17 38		17 54		18 08	18 22		18 38	
		d		15 55		16 09	16 23		16 40		16 56		17 09	17 24		17 39		17 56		18 10	18 23		18 39	
Manchester Oxford Road		d				16 15			16 46				17 15			17 46				18 16			18 46	
Manchester Piccadilly		d			16a07	16 20		16a40	16 51			17a07	17 20		17a40	17 50			18a07	18 20		18a40	18 50	
Manchester Airport	⛴✈	a				16 36			17 09				17 36			18 08				18 36			19 09	
Newton-le-Willows	90	d					16 42							17 40							18 41			
Lea Green	90	d		16 16							17 16							18 16						
Liverpool Lime Street 10	90	a		16 32			17 02				17 32			18 05				18 32			19 02			

Table T039-R

Saturdays
26 May to 8 December

Newcastle, Middlesborough, Scarborough, York, Hull, Leeds and Wakefield - Huddersfield - Manchester, Manchester Airport and Liverpool

			TP	TP	TP	TP	TP	TP	TP	TP	TP	TP	TP	TP	TP	TP	TP
			◇1	◇1	◇1	◇1	◇1	◇1	◇1	◇1	◇1	◇1	◇1	◇1	◇1	◇1	◇1
			🍴		🍴	🍴	🍴	🍴									
Newcastle 8	26	d				17 03		17 17					18 03		18 15		
Chester-le-Street	26	a						17 26							18 24		
Durham	26	a				17 15		17 32					18 15		18 31		
Middlesbrough	44	d			16 57							17 57					
Thornaby	44	a			17 02							18 02					
Yarm		a			17 10							18 10					
Darlington 5	26	a				17 32		17 50					18 32		18 49		
Northallerton	26	a			17 24	17 44						18 24	18 44				
Thirsk		a			17 33							18 33					
Scarborough	43	d	16 46							17 50							18 50
Seamer	43	d	16 52							17 55							18 55
Malton		d	17 11							18 14							19 13
York 8	26	a	17 36		17 51	18 07		18 22		18 39		18 51	19 07		19 21		19 39
		d	17 38		17 52	18 09		18 24		18 41		18 52	19 09		19 22		19 40
Hull	29	a															
Brough	29	a															
Howden	29	a															
Selby	29,40	a															
Garforth	40	d					18 28							19 29			
Leeds 10		a	18 03	←	18 15	18 31	18 38	18 49		19 05		19 15	19 31	19 38	19 47		20 03
		d	18 06		18 18	18 34	18 40	18 50	18 53	19 06		19 18	19 34	19 40	19 50	19 53	20 06
Cottingley		d		17 57							←						
Morley		d		18 00					19 00		19 00					20 00	
Batley		d		18 05			18 49		→		19 04			19 49		→	
Dewsbury		a		18 07	18 28		18 52				19 07	19 28		19 52			
		d		18 08	18 29		18 52				19 07	19 29		19 52			
Ravensthorpe		a		18 10							19 10						
Wakefield Kirkgate		d															
Mirfield		d		18 14							19 14						
Deighton		d		18 23							19 24						
Huddersfield		a	18 23	18 27	18 37	18 53	19 01	19 07		19 24	19 27	19 37	19 51	20 01	20 07		20 23
		d	18 24	18 29	18 38	18 53	19 01	19 08		19 24	19 29	19 38	19 52	20 01	20 08		20 24
Slaithwaite		d					19 07							20 07			
Marsden		d		18 37							19 37						
Greenfield		d		18 45							19 45						
Mossley (Grtr Manchester)		d					19 19							20 19			
Stalybridge		a		18 51			19 23				19 51			20 23			
		d		18 52			19 23				19 52			20 23			
Ashton-under-Lyne		d															
Manchester Victoria		a	18 54		19 08	19 23		19 38		19 54		20 09	20 22		20 38		21 01
		d	18 56		19 10	19 25		19 39		19 56		20 10	20 24		20 39		
Manchester Oxford Road		d			19 16			19 46				20 16			20 46		
Manchester Piccadilly		d		19a08	19 22		19a40	19 50			20a08	20 20		20a40	20 50		
Manchester Airport		a			19 36			20 07				20 36			21 12		
Newton-le-Willows	90	d				19 43							20 40				
Lea Green	90	d	19 16							20 16			20 46				
Liverpool Lime Street 10	90	a	19 34			20 03				20 32			21 03				

			TP	TP	TP	TP	TP	TP	TP	TP
			◇1	◇1	◇1	◇1	◇1	◇1	◇1	◇1
Newcastle 8	26	d			18 53					
Chester-le-Street	26	a								
Durham	26	a			19 05					
Middlesbrough	44	d		18 57						20 03
Thornaby	44	a		19 02						20 08
Yarm		a		19 10						20 16
Darlington 5	26	a			19 22					
Northallerton	26	a		19 24	19 34					20 31
Thirsk		a		19 33						20 40
Scarborough	43	d						19 46		
Seamer	43	d						19 52		
Malton		d						20 11		
York 8	26	a		19 51	19 57			20 36		21 04
		d		19 52	20 09			20 38		
Hull	29	a								
Brough	29	a								
Howden	29	a								
Selby	29,40	a								
Garforth	40	d				20 28				
Leeds 10		a		20 16	20 31	20 38		21 03		
		d		20 18	20 34	20 40	20 53	21 06		
Cottingley		d	←						←	
Morley		d	20 00				21 00		21 00	
Batley		d	20 04			20 49	→		21 04	
Dewsbury		a	20 07	20 28		20 52			21 07	
		d	20 07	20 29		20 52			21 07	
Ravensthorpe		a	20 10						21 10	
Wakefield Kirkgate		d								
Mirfield		d	20 14						21 14	
Deighton		d	20 23						21 23	
Huddersfield		a	20 27	20 37	20 51	21 01		21 23	21 27	
		d	20 29	20 38	20 52	21 01		21 24	21 29	
Slaithwaite		d				21 07				
Marsden		d	20 40						21 37	
Greenfield		d	20 47						21 45	
Mossley (Grtr Manchester)		d				21 19				
Stalybridge		a	20 53			21 23			21 51	
		d	20 54			21 23			21 52	
Ashton-under-Lyne		d								
Manchester Victoria		a		21 09	21 22			21 54		
		d		21 11	21 24			21 55		
Manchester Oxford Road		d		21 16				22 01		
Manchester Piccadilly		d	21a09	21 20		21a40		22 05	22a07	
Manchester Airport		a		21 36				22 22		
Newton-le-Willows	90	d			21 40					
Lea Green	90	d			21 46					
Liverpool Lime Street 10	90	a			22 03					

Table T039-R

Saturdays
26 May to 8 December

Newcastle, Middlesborough, Scarborough, York, Hull, Leeds and Wakefield - Huddersfield - Manchester, Manchester Airport and Liverpool

			TP	TP	TP	TP	TP	TP	TP	TP	TP	TP	TP	TP	TP	TP	TP	TP	TP	TP	TP
			◇1	◇1	◇1	◇1	◇1	◇1	◇1	◇1	◇1	◇1	◇1	◇1	◇1	◇1	◇1	◇1	1	◇1	◇1
													A	B	A	B	A	B			
Newcastle 8	26	d	20 00						21 00						21 58	21 58			22 30		
Chester-le-Street	26	a	20 09						21 09						22 07	22 07			22 39		
Durham	26	a	20 15						21 15						22 14	22 14			22 46		
Middlesbrough	44	d						20 52				21 57								22 43	
Thornaby	44	a						20 57				22 02								22 48	
Yarm		a						21 05				22 10								22 55	
Darlington 5	26	a	20 32						21 32						22 30	22 30					
Northallerton	26	a	20 44					21 19	21 44			22 24			22 42	22 42				23 10	
Thirsk		a						21 28				22 32									
Scarborough	43	d				20 50					21 46										22 46
Seamer	43	d				20 55					21 51										22 52
Malton		d				21 14					22 08										23 12
York 8	26	a	21 07			21 39		21 50	22 07		22 36	22 51			23 06	23 06				23 32	23 35
		d	21 09			21 40		21 52	22 09		22 38	22 52			23 07	23 07					
Hull	29	a																			
Brough	29	a																			
Howden	29	a																			
Selby	29,40	a																			
Garforth	40	d																			
Leeds 10		a	21 31			22 03		22 15	22 31		23 00	23 15			23 30	23 30					
		d	21 34	21 38	21 53	22 06		22 17	22 34	22 40	23 02		23 25	23 25	23 35	23 35					
Cottingley		d					←			22 45			23 30	23 30							
Morley		d			22 00		22 00			22 48			23 34	23 34							
Batley		d		21 49	→		22 04			22 53			23 38	23 38							
Dewsbury		a		21 52			22 07	22 27		22 56	23 12		23 41	23 41	23 45	23 45	←	←			
		d		21 52			22 07	22 28		22 56	23 13		23 41	23 41	23 46	23 46					
Ravensthorpe		a					22 10			22 58			23 44	23 44			23 44	23 44			
Wakefield Kirkgate		d											→	→							
Mirfield		d					22 14			23 02							23 47	23 47			
Deighton		d					22 23			23 07							23 55	23 55			
Huddersfield		a	21 51	22 01		22 23	22 27	22 37	22 51	23 11	23 21				23 54	23 54	23 58	23 58			
		d	21 52	22 01		22 24	22 28	22 38	22 52	23 11	23 22				23 55	23 55	23 59	23 59			
Slaithwaite		d		22 07			22 33			23 16							00 04	00 05			
Marsden		d					22 37			23 20							00 08	00 09			
Greenfield		d					22 44			23 27								00 16			
Mossley (Grtr Manchester)		d		22 19			22 48			23 31								00 20			
Stalybridge		a		22 23			22 52			23 36							00 20	00 24			
		d		22 23			22 53			23 36							00 20	00 25			
Ashton-under-Lyne		d																			
Manchester Victoria		a	22 22			22 54		23 07	23 21												
		d	22 23			22 55		23 10	23 23												
Manchester Oxford Road		d						23 24													
Manchester Piccadilly		d		22 42			23a08	23 27		23a53	23a54				00a27	00 35	00a37	00a42			
Manchester Airport		a		23 00				23 44								00 52					
Newton-le-Willows	90	d	22 40			23 12			23 40												
Lea Green	90	d	22 46			23 18			23 46												
Liverpool Lime Street 10	90	a	23 03			23 34			00 03												

A from 27 October
B until 20 October

Table T039-R

Sundays
20 May to 2 December

Newcastle, Middlesborough, Scarborough, York, Hull, Leeds and Wakefield - Huddersfield - Manchester, Manchester Airport and Liverpool

			TP	TP	TP	TP	TP	TP	TP	TP	TP	TP	TP	TP	TP	TP	TP	TP	TP	TP	TP	TP	TP	TP	TP
			◇1	◇1		◇1		◇1			◇1			◇1		◇1			◇1			◇1	◇1	◇1	
			A	B	A	C	A	C	A	A	C	A	A	C	A	C	A	A	C	A	A	C	D	E	A
					🚌		🚌		🚌	🚌		🚌	🚌		🚌		🚌	🚌	🛒	🚌	🚌	🛒			🚌
Newcastle 8	26 ⛴	d																							
Chester-le-Street	26	a																							
Durham	26	a																							
Middlesbrough	44	d																							
Thornaby	44	a																							
Yarm		a																							
Darlington 5	26	a																							
Northallerton	26	a																							
Thirsk		a																							
Scarborough	43	d																							
Seamer	43	d																							
Malton		d																							
York 8	26	a																							
		d			01 30	02 25	03 30	04 00		04 55	05 15		05 55	06 19				06 55	07 17			07 53			
Hull	29	a																							
Brough	29	a																							
Howden	29	a																							
Selby	29,40	a																							
Garforth	40	d										←			←	←					←				
Leeds 10		a			02 20	02 50	04 20	04 25		05 45	05 40	05 45	06 45	06 44	06 45	06 44		07 45	07 43		07 45	08 18			
		d			02 20	02 53	04 20	04 28		05 45	05 43	05 45	06 45	06 46	06 45	06 46		07 45	07 45		07 45	08 21	08 25	08 25	08 25
Cottingley		d								→			→	→				→					08 30	08 30	08 40
Morley		d																					08 33	08 33	→
Batley		d															←						08 38	08 38	
Dewsbury		a									05 53	06 10			07 10	06 57	07 10		07 55		08 10		08 40	08 40	
		d									05 54	06 10			07 10	06 57	07 10		07 56		08 10		08 41	08 41	
Ravensthorpe		a													→								08 43	08 43	
Wakefield Kirkgate		d																							
Mirfield		d																					08 47	08 47	
Deighton		d							←														08 52	08 52	
Huddersfield		a			02 55	03 10	04 55	04 45	04 55		06 02	06 35				07 06	07 35		08 04		08 35	08 39	08 55	08 55	
		d			02 55	03 11	04 55	04 46	04 55		06 03	06 35				07 07	07 35		08 05		08 35	08 39	08 56	08 56	
Slaithwaite		d	00 04	00 05			→																09 02	09 02	
Marsden		d	00 08	00 09																			09 06	09 06	
Greenfield		d		00 16																			09 13	09 13	
Mossley (Grtr Manchester)		d		00 20																←			09 17	09 17	
Stalybridge		a	00 20	00 24								07 25				07 25	08 25		08 23	08 25	09s20		09 21	09 21	
		d	00 20	00 25								07 25				07 25	08 25		08 24	08 25			09 22	09 22	
Ashton-under-Lyne	⛴	d															→								
Manchester Victoria	⛴	a																	08 37			09 09	09 35		
		d																	08 38			09 10			
Manchester Oxford Road		d																	08 46						
Manchester Piccadilly		d	00a37	00a42	03 55	03 47		05 21	05 55		06 36	07 45				07 50			08 56	08s45	09a45			09a39	
Manchester Airport	⛴✈	a			04 20	04 02		05 36	06 20		06 52	08 10				08 04			09 10	09 10					
Newton-le-Willows	90	d																				09 27			
Lea Green	90	d																							
Liverpool Lime Street 10	90	a																				09 48			

A from 28 October
B from 27 May until 21 October
C until 21 October
D from 16 September until 21 October
E until 9 September

Table T039-R

Sundays
20 May to 2 December

Newcastle, Middlesborough, Scarborough, York, Hull, Leeds and Wakefield - Huddersfield - Manchester, Manchester Airport and Liverpool

			TP	TP	TP	TP	TP	TP	TP	TP	TP	TP	TP	TP	TP	TP	TP	TP	TP	TP	TP	TP	TP	TP
			◇1	◇1	◇1	◇1		◇1	◇1	◇1	◇1	◇1	◇1	◇1	◇1	◇1	◇1	◇1	◇1	◇1	◇1	◇1	◇1	◇1
			A	B	C		A	A															C	D
			🛒	🛒	🛒	🛒	🚌	🛒	🛒	🛒	🛒	🛒		🛒		🛒	🛒	🛒	🛒		🛒		🛒	🛒
Newcastle 8	26 ⛴	d								08 00							09 03		09 17					
Chester-le-Street	26	a																	09 26					
Durham	26	a								08 12							09 15		09 32					
Middlesbrough	44	d														08 57							09 52	09 52
Thornaby	44	a														09 02							09 57	09 57
Yarm		a														09 10							10 05	10 05
Darlington 5	26	a								08 30							09 33		09 50					
Northallerton	26	a								08 42						09 24	09 45						10 19	10 19
Thirsk		a								08 50						09 33							10 28	10 28
Scarborough	43	d												08 50							09 44			
Seamer	43	d												08 55							09 50			
Malton		d												09 13							10 10			
York 8	26	a								09 08				09 39		09 51	10 07		10 22		10 35		10 46	10 46
		d	08 10	08 22	08 22	08 39			08 52	09 09		09 20		09 41		09 53	10 09		10 24		10 36		10 52	10 52
Hull	29	a																						
Brough	29	a																						
Howden	29	a																						
Selby	29,40	a																						
Garforth	40	d																						
Leeds 10		a	08 32	08 45	08 45	09 02	←		09 14	09 32		09 45		10 04	←	10 16	10 31		10 46		11 00	←	11 15	11 15
		d		08 47	08 47	09 04			09 16	09 34	09 40	09 48	09 53	10 06		10 18	10 34	10 40	10 50	10 53	11 06		11 18	11 18
Cottingley		d					08 40						09 58		09 58					10 58		10 58		
Morley		d					08 50						→		10 01					→		11 01		
Batley		d					09 00								10 06							11 06		
Dewsbury		a		08 58	08 58		09 08		09 27		09 50				10 08	10 28		10 50				11 08	11 28	11 28
		d		08 58	08 58		09 08		09 27		09 51				10 09	10 29		10 51				11 09	11 29	11 29
Ravensthorpe		a					09 15								10 11							11 11		
Wakefield Kirkgate		d																						
Mirfield		d					09 20								10 15							11 15		
Deighton		d					09 30								10 23							11 24		
Huddersfield		a		09 07	09 07	09 21	09 39		09 36	09 51	09 59	10 05		10 23	10 27	10 37	10 51	10 59	11 07		11 23	11 27	11 38	11 38
		d		09 07	09 08	09 22			09 37	09 52	10 00	10 08		10 24	10 29	10 38	10 52	11 00	11 08		11 24	11 29	11 38	11 38
Slaithwaite		d									10 05							11 06						
Marsden		d													10 37							11 37		
Greenfield		d						09 15			10 15				10 45							11 45		
Mossley (Grtr Manchester)		d						09 19			10 19							11 18						
Stalybridge		a						09 23	09 55		10 23				10 51			11 22				11 51		
		d						09 24	09 55		10 23				10 52			11 22				11 52		
Ashton-under-Lyne	⛴	d																						
Manchester Victoria	⛴	a			09 39	09 54			10 09	10 22				10 54		11 09	11 22		11 38		11 54		12 09	12 09
		d			09 40	09 56			10 10	10 24				10 56		11 10	11 24		11 39		11 56		12 10	12 10
Manchester Oxford Road		d			09 47				10a16							11a17			11 47				12 16	12a17
Manchester Piccadilly		d		09 52	09 52			09 52			10a40	10a42			11a07			11a39	11 52			12a07	12 20	
Manchester Airport	⛴✈	a		10 07	10 05			10 07											12 08				12 37	
Newton-le-Willows	90	d								10 42							11 40							
Lea Green	90	d				10 16								11 22							12 17			
Liverpool Lime Street 10	90	a				10 32				11 02				11 42			12 01				12 33			

A from 28 October
B from 16 September until 21 October
C until 9 September
D from 16 September

Table T039-R

Sundays
20 May to 2 December

Newcastle, Middlesborough, Scarborough, York, Hull, Leeds and Wakefield - Huddersfield - Manchester, Manchester Airport and Liverpool

		TP	TP	TP	TP	TP	TP	TP	TP	TP	TP	TP	TP	TP	TP	TP	TP	TP	TP	TP	TP	TP	TP	TP
		◇1	◇1	◇1	◇1	◇1	◇1	◇1	◇1	◇1	◇1	◇1	◇1	◇1	◇1	◇1	◇1	◇1	◇1	◇1	◇1	◇1	◇1	◇1
		🛒	🛒	🛒		🛒		🛒	🛒	🛒	🛒		🛒		🛒	🛒	🛒	🛒		🛒		🛒	🛒	🛒
Newcastle ■	26 ⇌ d	10 04		10 18					11 03		11 17					12 03		12 17					13 05	
Chester-le-Street	26 a			10 27							11 26							12 26						
Durham	26 a	10 16		10 33					11 16		11 32					12 15		12 32					13 17	
Middlesbrough	44 d							10 57							11 57							12 47		
Thornaby	44 a							11 02							12 02							12 52		
Yarm	a							11 10							12 10							13 00		
Darlington ■	26 a	10 34		10 50					11 33		11 50					12 33		12 50					13 34	
Northallerton	26 a	10 46						11 24	11 45						12 24	12 45						13 14	13 46	
Thirsk	a							11 33							12 33							13 23		
Scarborough	43 d					10 46							11 46							12 46				
Seamer	43 d					10 52							11 52							12 52				
Malton	d					11 11							12 11							13 11				
York ■	26 a	11 08		11 22		11 36		11 51	12 07		12 22		12 36		12 51	13 07		13 22		13 36		13 43	14 08	
	d	11 10		11 24		11 38		11 52	12 09		12 24		12 38		12 52	13 09		13 24		13 38		13 53	14 10	
Hull	29 a																							
Brough	29 a																							
Howden	29 a																							
Selby	29,40 a																							
Garforth	40 d																							
Leeds ■	a	11 32		11 46		12 04	←	12 15	12 31		12 47		13 04	←	13 15	13 31		13 46		14 04	←	14 16	14 32	
	d	11 34	11 40	11 50	11 53	12 06		12 18	12 34	12 40	12 50	12 53	13 06		13 18	13 34	13 40	13 50	13 53	14 06		14 19	14 34	14 40
Cottingley	d				11 58		11 58					12 58		12 58					13 58		13 58			
Morley	d				→		12 01					→		13 01					→		14 01			
Batley	d						12 06							13 06							14 06			
Dewsbury	a		11 50				12 08	12 28		12 50				13 08	13 28		13 50				14 08	14 29		14 50
	d		11 51				12 09	12 29		12 51				13 09	13 29		13 51				14 09	14 30		14 51
Ravensthorpe	a						12 11							13 11							14 11			
Wakefield Kirkgate	d																							
Mirfield	d						12 15							13 15							14 15			
Deighton	d						12 24							13 24							14 24			
Huddersfield	a	11 51	11 59	12 07		12 23	12 27	12 38	12 51	12 59	13 07		13 23	13 27	13 38	13 51	13 59	14 07		14 23	14 27	14 38	14 51	14 59
	d	11 52	12 00	12 08		12 24	12 29	12 38	12 52	13 00	13 08		13 24	13 29	13 38	13 52	14 00	14 08		14 24	14 29	14 39	14 52	15 00
Slaithwaite	d		12 06							13 06							14 06							15 06
Marsden	d						12 37							13 37							14 37			
Greenfield	d						12 45							13 45							14 45			
Mossley (Grtr Manchester)	d		12 18							13 18							14 18							15 18
Stalybridge	a		12 22				12 51			13 22				13 51			14 22				14 51			15 22
	d		12 22				12 52			13 22				13 52			14 22				14 52			15 22
Ashton-under-Lyne	⇌ d																							
Manchester Victoria	⇌ a	12 22		12 38		12 54		13 09	13 22		13 38		13 54		14 09	14 22		14 38		14 54		15 09	15 22	
	d	12 27		12 40		12 56		13 10	13 24		13 40		13 56		14 10	14 24		14 40		14 56		15 10	15 24	
Manchester Oxford Road	d			12 49				13 16			13 47				14 16			14 47				15 16		
Manchester Piccadilly	d		12a39	12 53			13a07	13 20		13a39	13 51			14a07	14 20		14a39	14 51			15a07	15 20		15a39
Manchester Airport	⇌✈ a			13 06				13 38			14 06				14 38			15 05				15 38		
Newton-le-Willows	90 d	12 43							13 40							14 42							15 40	
Lea Green	90 d					13 17							14 17							15 17				
Liverpool Lime Street ■	90 a	13 04				13 33			14 01				14 33			15 02				15 33			16 02	

Table T039-R

Sundays
20 May to 2 December

Newcastle, Middlesborough, Scarborough, York, Hull, Leeds and Wakefield - Huddersfield - Manchester, Manchester Airport and Liverpool

		TP	TP	TP	TP	TP	TP	TP	TP	TP	TP	TP	TP	TP	TP	TP	TP	TP	TP	TP	TP	TP	TP
		◇1	◇1	◇1	◇1	◇1	◇1	◇1	◇1	◇1	◇1	◇1	◇1	◇1	◇1	◇1	◇1	◇1	◇1	◇1	◇1	◇1	◇1
		🛒		🛒		🛒	🛒	🛒	🛒		🛒		🛒	🛒	🛒	🛒		🛒		🛒	🛒	🛒	🛒
Newcastle ■	26 ⇌ d	13 10					14 03		14 15					15 03		15 14					16 00		16 12
Chester-le-Street	26 a															15 23							16 21
Durham	26 a	13 22					14 15		14 27					15 15		15 29					16 12		16 27
Middlesbrough	44 d					13 55							14 48							15 54			
Thornaby	44 a					14 00							14 53							15 59			
Yarm	a					14 08							15 01							16 07			
Darlington ■	26 a	13 40					14 33		14 45					15 33		15 47					16 29		16 45
Northallerton	26 a	13 52				14 23	14 45							15 45						16 22	16 41		
Thirsk	a					14 31							15 28							16 31			
Scarborough	43 d			13 46							14 46							15 46					
Seamer	43 d			13 52							14 52							15 52					
Malton	d			14 11							15 11							16 11					
York ■	26 a	14 14		14 36		14 50	15 07		15 17		15 36		15 46	16 07		16 19		16 36		16 52	17 03		17 17
	d	14 24		14 38		14 52	15 09		15 21		15 38		15 54	16 09		16 24		16 38		16 54	17 09		17 18
Hull	29 a																						
Brough	29 a																						
Howden	29 a																						
Selby	29,40 a																						
Garforth	40 d																						
Leeds ■	a	14 46		15 04	←	15 15	15 31		15 45		16 04	←	16 16	16 32		16 46		17 04	←	17 16	17 31		17 44
	d	14 50	14 53	15 06		15 18	15 34	15 40	15 50	15 53	16 06		16 19	16 34	16 40	16 50	16 53	17 06		17 18	17 34	17 40	17 49
Cottingley	d		14 58		14 58					15 58		15 58					16 58		16 58				
Morley	d		→		15 01					→		16 01					→		17 01				
Batley	d				15 06							16 06							17 06				
Dewsbury	a				15 08	15 28		15 50				16 08	16 30		16 50				17 08	17 28		17 50	
	d				15 09	15 29		15 51				16 09	16 30		16 51				17 09	17 29		17 51	
Ravensthorpe	a				15 11							16 11							17 11				
Wakefield Kirkgate	d																						
Mirfield	d				15 15							16 15							17 15				
Deighton	d				15 24							16 24							17 24				
Huddersfield	a	15 07		15 23	15 27	15 38	15 51	15 59	16 07		16 23	16 27	16 39	16 51	16 59	17 07		17 23	17 27	17 38	17 51	17 59	18 07
	d	15 08		15 24	15 29	15 38	15 52	16 00	16 08		16 24	16 29	16 39	16 52	17 00	17 08		17 24	17 29	17 38	17 52	18 00	18 08
Slaithwaite	d							16 06							17 06							18 06	
Marsden	d				15 37							16 37							17 37				
Greenfield	d				15 45							16 45							17 45				
Mossley (Grtr Manchester)	d							16 18							17 18							18 18	
Stalybridge	a				15 51			16 22				16 51			17 22				17 51			18 22	
	d				15 52			16 22				16 52			17 22				17 52			18 22	
Ashton-under-Lyne	⇌ d																						
Manchester Victoria	⇌ a	15 38		15 54		16 09	16 22		16 38		16 54		17 09	17 22		17 38		17 54		18 09	18 22		18 38
	d	15 40		15 56		16 10	16 24		16 40		16 56		17 10	17 24		17 40		17 56		18 10	18 24		18 40
Manchester Oxford Road	d	15 47				16 16			16 47				17 16			17 47				18 16			18 47
Manchester Piccadilly	d	15 51			16a07	16 20		16a39	16 51			17a07	17 20		17a39	17 51			18a07	18 20		18a39	18 51
Manchester Airport	⇌✈ a	16 05				16 38			17 06				17 38			18 05				18 38			19 06
Newton-le-Willows	90 d						16 42							17 41							18 41		
Lea Green	90 d			16 17							17 17							18 17					
Liverpool Lime Street ■	90 a			16 33			17 02				17 33			18 02				18 33			19 02		

Table T039-R

Sundays
20 May to 2 December

Newcastle, Middlesborough, Scarborough, York, Hull, Leeds and Wakefield - Huddersfield - Manchester, Manchester Airport and Liverpool

	TP ◇■	TP ◇■ 🛒	TP ◇■	TP ◇■ 🛒	TP ◇■ 🛒	TP ◇■ 🛒	TP ◇■ 🛒	TP ◇■	TP ◇■	TP ◇■	TP ◇■	TP ◇■	TP ◇■	TP ◇■	TP ◇■
Newcastle ■ 26 d					17 05		17 13					18 03		18 14	
Chester-le-Street 26 a														18 23	
Durham 26 a					17 17		17 25					18 15		18 29	
Middlesbrough 44 d				16 57							17 56				
Thornaby 44 a				17 02							18 01				
Yarm a				17 10							18 09				
Darlington ■ 26 a					17 34		17 42					18 33		18 47	
Northallerton 26 a				17 24			17 54				18 23	18 45			
Thirsk a				17 33							18 32				
Scarborough 43 d		16 46							17 50						
Seamer 43 d		16 52							17 55						
Malton d		17 11							18 14						
York ■ 26 a		17 36		17 51	18 07		18 17		18 39		18 53	19 07		19 19	
d		17 38		17 52	18 09		18 19		18 40		18 55	19 09		19 20	
Hull 29 a															
Brough 29 a															
Howden 29 a															
Selby 29,40 a															
Garforth 40 d															
Leeds 10 a		18 04	←	18 15	18 32		18 46		19 04	←	19 17	19 31		19 46	
d	17 53	18 06		18 16	18 34	18 40	18 50	18 53	19 05		19 19	19 34	19 40	19 50	19 53
Cottingley d	17 58		17 58					18 58		18 58					19 58
Morley d	→		18 01					→		19 01					→
Batley d			18 06							19 06					
Dewsbury a			18 08	18 28		18 50				19 08	19 29		19 50		
d			18 09	18 29		18 51				19 09	19 30		19 51		
Ravensthorpe a			18 11							19 11					
Wakefield Kirkgate d															
Mirfield d			18 15							19 15					
Deighton d			18 24							19 24					
Huddersfield a		18 23	18 27	18 38	18 51	18 59	19 07		19 24	19 27	19 38	19 51	19 59	20 07	
d		18 24	18 29	18 38	18 52	19 00	19 08		19 24	19 29	19 39	19 52	20 00	20 08	
Slaithwaite d						19 06							20 06		
Marsden d			18 37							19 38					
Greenfield d			18 45							19 45					
Mossley (Grtr Manchester) d						19 18							20 18		
Stalybridge a			18 51			19 22				19 51			20 22		
d			18 52			19 22				19 52			20 22		
Ashton-under-Lyne d															
Manchester Victoria a		18 54		19 09	19 22		19 38		19 54		20 09	20 22		20 38	
d		18 56		19 10	19 24		19 40		19 56		20 10	20 24		20 40	
Manchester Oxford Road d				19 16			19 47				20 16			20 47	
Manchester Piccadilly d			19a07	19 20		19a39	19 51			20a07	20 20		20a39	20 51	
Manchester Airport a				19 38			20 05				20 39			21 11	
Newton-le-Willows 90 d					19 41							20 40			
Lea Green 90 d		19 17							20 17			20 46			
Liverpool Lime Street 10 90 a		19 33			20 02				20 33			21 03			

	TP ◇■	TP ◇■	TP ◇■	TP ◇■	TP ◇■	TP ◇■	TP ◇■	TP ◇■
Newcastle ■ 26 d				19 06		19 20		
Chester-le-Street 26 a								
Durham 26 a						19 32		
Middlesbrough 44 d			18 57					
Thornaby 44 a			19 02					
Yarm a			19 10					
Darlington ■ 26 a				19 33		19 49		
Northallerton 26 a			19 26	19 45				
Thirsk a			19 35					
Scarborough 43 d	18 50							19 46
Seamer 43 d	18 55							19 52
Malton d	19 14							20 11
York ■ 26 a	19 39		19 53	20 07		20 23		20 36
d	19 41		19 54	20 09				20 38
Hull 29 a								
Brough 29 a								
Howden 29 a								
Selby 29,40 a								
Garforth 40 d								
Leeds 10 a	20 04	←	20 17	20 33				21 04
d	20 05		20 18	20 34	20 40		20 53	21 06
Cottingley d		19 58					20 58	
Morley d		20 01					→	
Batley d		20 06						
Dewsbury a		20 08	20 29		20 50			
d		20 09	20 29		20 51			
Ravensthorpe a		20 11						
Wakefield Kirkgate d								
Mirfield d		20 16						
Deighton d		20 23						
Huddersfield a	20 23	20 28	20 38	20 51	20 59			21 23
d	20 24	20 29	20 38	20 52	21 00			21 24
Slaithwaite d					21 06			
Marsden d		20 37						
Greenfield d		20 45						
Mossley (Grtr Manchester) d					21 18			
Stalybridge a		20 51			21 22			
d		20 52			21 22			
Ashton-under-Lyne d								
Manchester Victoria a	20 54		21 09	21 22				21 54
d	20 56		21 10	21 23				21 56
Manchester Oxford Road d			21 16					
Manchester Piccadilly d		21a07	21 21		21a39			
Manchester Airport a			21 37					
Newton-le-Willows 90 d				21 40				
Lea Green 90 d	21 17			21 46				22 17
Liverpool Lime Street 10 90 a	21 33			22 03				22 33

Table T039-R

Sundays
20 May to 2 December

Newcastle, Middlesborough, Scarborough, York, Hull, Leeds and Wakefield - Huddersfield - Manchester, Manchester Airport and Liverpool

	TP ◇■	TP ◇■	TP ◇■	TP ◇■	TP ◇■	TP ◇■	TP ◇■	TP ◇■	TP ◇■	TP ◇■	TP ◇■	TP ◇■	TP ◇■
Newcastle ■ 26 d			20 04				21 00					22 00	
Chester-le-Street 26 a							21 09						
Durham 26 a			20 16				21 15					22 14	
Middlesbrough 44 d		20 03						21 21			22 07		23 00
Thornaby 44 a		20 08						21 26			22 12		23 05
Yarm a		20 16						21 34			22 20		23 13
Darlington ■ 26 a			20 34				21 32					22 30	
Northallerton 26 a		20 31	20 46				21 44	21 48			22 35	22 42	23 27
Thirsk a		20 39						21 57			22 44		
Scarborough 43 d					20 50				21 48				
Seamer 43 d					20 56				21 53				
Malton d					21 14				22 12				
York ■ 26 a		21 04	21 08		21 39		22 07	22 15	22 38		23 06	23 11	23 57
d			21 10		21 41		22 09	22 16	22 39			23 13	
Hull 29 a													
Brough 29 a													
Howden 29 a													
Selby 29,40 a													
Garforth 40 d													
Leeds 10 a	←		21 32		22 04	←	22 32	22 39	23 02			23 39	
d			21 34	21 53	22 06		22 34	22 40	23 04	23 25		23 40	
Cottingley d	20 58			21 58		21 58		22 45		23 30			
Morley d	21 01			→		22 01		22 48		23 34			
Batley d	21 06					22 06		22 53		23 38			
Dewsbury a	21 08					22 08		22 56	23 14	23 41		23 51	
d	21 09					22 09		22 56	23 15	23 41		23 51	
Ravensthorpe a	21 11					22 11		22 59		23 44			
Wakefield Kirkgate d													
Mirfield d	21 15					22 15		23 03		23 48			
Deighton d	21 24					22 24		23 07		23 52			
Huddersfield a	21 27		21 51		22 23	22 27	22 51	23 11	23 23	23 57		23 59	
d	21 28		21 52		22 24	22 28	22 52	23 11	23 24			00 01	
Slaithwaite d	21 33					22 33		23 17					
Marsden d	21 37					22 37		23 21					
Greenfield d	21 45					22 44		23 28					
Mossley (Grtr Manchester) d	21 48					22 48		23 32					
Stalybridge a	21 52					22 52		23 36					
d	21 53					22 53		23 36					
Ashton-under-Lyne d													
Manchester Victoria a			22 22		22 54		23 22		23 54			00 31	
d			22 24		22 55		23 24		23 56			00 32	
Manchester Oxford Road d					23 04								
Manchester Piccadilly d	22a08				23 10	23a08		23a51	00 06			00 44	
Manchester Airport a					23 25				00 23			00 59	
Newton-le-Willows 90 d			22 40				23 40						
Lea Green 90 d			22 46				23 46						
Liverpool Lime Street 10 90 a			23 04				00 03						

York and Selby - Leeds

Mondays to Fridays
21 May to 7 December

Miles	Miles		GR MX	TP MO	TP MX	TP MO	TP MX	TP	TP	NT	TP	TP	NT	TP	TP	TP	NT	TP	XC	XC	TP	NT	TP
			1 ⊡	◇1	◇1	◇1	◇1	◇1	◇1		◇1	◇1	◇	◇1	◇1	◇1		◇1 ⊼	1 A ⊼	◇1 B	◇1 ⊼	◇	◇1 ⊼
0	—	York 33 d	00 16	01 38	01 38	02 52	02 52	03 50	05 05	05 18	05 38	05 47		06 09		06 22	06 24	06 41	06 45	06 45	06 51		07 09
8¾	—	Ulleskelf 33 d																					
10¾	—	Church Fenton 33 d								05 32							06 35						
—	0	Selby d											05 50		06 11							06 50	
—	7¾	South Milford d											06 01									07 03	
15¾	11	Micklefield d								05 39			06 07				06 43					07 08	
17¼	12¾	East Garforth d								05 44			06 11				06 47					07 12	
18	13¾	Garforth d								05 46			06 13		06 27		06 49					07 15	
21	16¾	Cross Gates d								05 51			06 18				06 54					07 19	
25½	20¾	Leeds a	00 43	02 05	02 18	03 19	03 32	04 15	05 43	05 59	06 03	06 12	06 26	06 31	06 37	06 47	07 02	07 04	07 07	07 07	07 16	07 27	07 31
—	—	Bradford Interchange 37 a								06 27			07 01				07 28					07 59	

	TP	NT	NT	TP	TP	XC	TP	NT	TP	TP	NT	TP	NT	NT	TP	XC	TP	NT	TP	TP	NT	TP
	◇1 ⊼			◇1 ⊼	◇1 ⊼	◇1 ⊼	◇1 ⊼	◇	◇1 ⊼	◇1 ⊼		◇1 ⊼			◇1 ⊼	◇1 ⊼	◇1 ⊼	◇	◇1 ⊼	◇1 ⊼		◇1 ⊼
York 33 d			07 13	07 18	07 38	07 43	07 52		08 09		08 16	08 22			08 37	08 44	08 52		09 09		09 15	09 22
Ulleskelf 33 d			07 22																			
Church Fenton 33 d			07 32								08 34										09 33	
Selby d	07 12	07 19						07 51		08 12			08 23					08 52		09 11		
South Milford d		07 30						08 02					08 34					09 03				
Micklefield d		07 36	07 40					08 08										09 09			09 40	
East Garforth d		07 40	07 45					08 12						←				09 13			09 45	
Garforth d	07 28	07 42	07 47		07 54			08 14		08 28	08 48	08 39	08 43	08 48				09 15		09 28	09 47	
Cross Gates d		07 47	07 52	07 35			08 09	08 19			→		08 47	08 52	08 57			09 20			09 52	
Leeds a	07 37	07 55	08 00	07 43	08 03	08 08	08 17	08 28	08 31	08 38		08 48	08 55	09 00	09 03	09 08	09 15	09 28	09 31	09 38	10 00	09 46
Bradford Interchange 37 a			08 31					08 59						09 30				09 59			10 30	

	TP	XC	TP	NT	TP	TP	NT	TP	TP	XC	XC	TP	NT	TP	TP	NT	TP	TP	XC	TP	NT	TP
	◇1 ⊼	◇1 ⊼	◇1 ⊼	◇	◇1 ⊼	◇1 ⊼		◇1 ⊼	◇1 ⊼	◇1 A ⊼	◇1 B ⊼	◇1 ⊼	◇	◇1 ⊼	◇1		◇1 ⊼	◇1 ⊼	◇1 ⊼	◇1 ⊼	◇	◇1 ⊼
York 33 d	09 39	09 44	09 52		10 09		10 15	10 22	10 38	10 44	10 44	10 52		11 09		11 15	11 22	11 38	11 44	11 52		12 09
Ulleskelf 33 d																						
Church Fenton 33 d							10 33									11 33						
Selby d				09 52		10 12							10 52		11 12						11 52	
South Milford d				10 03									11 03								12 03	
Micklefield d				10 09			10 40						11 09			11 40					12 09	
East Garforth d				10 13			10 45						11 13			11 45					12 13	
Garforth d				10 15		10 28	10 47						11 15		11 28	11 47					12 15	
Cross Gates d				10 20			10 52						11 20			11 52					12 20	
Leeds a	10 03	10 07	10 15	10 28	10 31	10 38	11 00	10 46	11 03	11 07	11 08	11 15	11 28	11 31	11 38	12 00	11 46	12 03	12 07	12 15	12 28	12 31
Bradford Interchange 37 a				10 59			11 30						11 59			12 30					12 59	

	TP	NT	TP	TP	XC	TP	NT	TP	TP	NT	TP	TP	XC	TP	NT	TP	TP	NT	TP	TP	XC	TP
	◇1 ⊼		◇1 ⊼	◇1 ⊼	◇1 ⊼	◇1 ⊼	◇	◇1 ⊼	◇1 ⊼		◇1 ⊼	◇1 ⊼	◇1 ⊼	◇1 ⊼	◇	◇1 ⊼	◇1 ⊼		◇1 ⊼	◇1 ⊼	◇1 ⊼	◇1 ⊼
York 33 d		12 15	12 22	12 38	12 44	12 52		13 09		13 15	13 22	13 38	13 44	13 52		14 09		14 15	14 22	14 38	14 44	14 52
Ulleskelf 33 d																						
Church Fenton 33 d		12 35								13 33								14 33				
Selby d	12 12						12 52		13 12						13 52		14 12					
South Milford d							13 03								14 03							
Micklefield d		12 42					13 09			13 40					14 09			14 40				
East Garforth d		12 46					13 13			13 45					14 13			14 45				
Garforth d	12 28	12 48					13 15		13 28	13 47					14 15		14 28	14 47				
Cross Gates d		12 53					13 20			13 52					14 20			14 52				
Leeds a	12 38	13 01	12 46	13 04	13 08	13 15	13 28	13 31	13 38	14 00	13 46	14 03	14 07	14 15	14 28	14 32	14 38	15 00	14 46	15 03	15 07	15 15
Bradford Interchange 37 a		13 30					13 59			14 30					14 59			15 30				

	NT	TP	TP	NT	TP	TP	XC	TP	NT	XC	TP	TP	NT	TP	TP	XC	XC	TP	NT	TP	TP	NT
	◇	◇1 ⊼	◇1 ⊼		◇1 ⊼	◇1 ⊼	◇1 C ⊼	◇1 ⊼	◇	◇1 ⊼	◇1 ⊼	◇1 ⊼		◇1 ⊼	◇1 ⊼	◇1 B ⊼	◇1 A ⊼	◇1 ⊼	◇	◇1 ⊼	◇1 ⊼	
York 33 d		15 09		15 15	15 22	15 38	15 44	15 52		16 05	16 09		16 15	16 22	16 38	16 44	16 44	16 52		17 09		17 15
Ulleskelf 33 d																						
Church Fenton 33 d				15 33									16 33									17 33
Selby d	14 52		15 12						15 52			16 12							16 52		17 12	
South Milford d	15 03								16 03										17 03			
Micklefield d	15 09			15 40					16 09				16 40						17 09			17 40
East Garforth d	15 13			15 45					16 13				16 45						17 13			17 45
Garforth d	15 15		15 28	15 47					16 15			16 28	16 47						17 15		17 28	17 47
Cross Gates d	15 20			15 52					16 20				16 52						17 20			17 52
Leeds a	15 28	15 31	15 38	16 00	15 46	16 03	16 07	16 15	16 28	16 30	16 32	16 37	17 00	16 46	17 03	17 07	17 08	17 15	17 28	17 31	17 37	18 02
Bradford Interchange 37 a	15 59			16 30					16 59				17 30						17 59			18 32

A from 23 July until 5 October
B until 20 July, from 8 October
C until 11 October, FX from 15 October

Table T040-F

York and Selby - Leeds

Mondays to Fridays
21 May to 7 December

	TP	TP	XC	TP	NT	TP	TP	TP	NT	TP	XC	TP	NT	TP	TP	NT	TP	TP	XC	TP	NT	TP
	◇1 ⊼	◇1 ⊼	◇1 ⊼	◇1 ⊼	◇	◇1 ⊼	◇1 ⊼	◇1 ⊼		◇1	◇1 ⊼	◇1	◇	◇1	◇1		◇1	◇1	◇1 ⊼	◇1	◇	◇1
York 33 d	17 22	17 38	17 45	17 52		18 09		18 24		18 41	18 45	18 52		19 09		19 15	19 22	19 40	19 45	19 52		20 09
Ulleskelf 33 d																						
Church Fenton 33 d																19 33						
Selby d					17 52		18 12		18 23				18 52		19 12						19 51	
South Milford d					18 03				18 35				19 03								20 04	
Micklefield d					18 09				18 41				19 09			19 40					20 09	
East Garforth d					18 13				18 45				19 13			19 45					20 13	
Garforth d					18 15		18 28		18 48				19 15		19 28	19 47					20 16	
Cross Gates d					18 20				18 52				19 20			19 52					20 20	
Leeds a	17 46	18 04	18 09	18 15	18 28	18 31	18 38	18 49	18 59	19 05	19 09	19 15	19 28	19 31	19 38	20 00	19 47	20 03	20 08	20 16	20 28	20 31
Bradford Interchange 37 a					19 00				19 32				19 59			20 31					21 00	

	TP	NT	TP	XC	NT	TP	TP	NT	TP	TP	NT	TP	TP	NT	TP	TP	TP	TP	NT	NT
	◇1		◇1	◇1 ⊼	◇	◇1	◇1		◇1	◇1	◇	◇1	◇1		◇1	◇1	◇1	◇1	■	
York 33 d		20 20	20 38	20 45		21 09		21 15	21 40	21 52		22 09		22 17	22 38	22 54		23 07		23 15
Ulleskelf 33 d																				
Church Fenton 33 d		20 33						21 33						22 30						23 29
Selby d	20 12				20 52		21 12				21 52		22 12				22 56		23 05	
South Milford d					21 03						22 03								23 15	
Micklefield d		20 40			21 09			21 40			22 09			22 37					23 23	23 37
East Garforth d		20 45			21 13			21 45			22 13			22 42					23 27	23 41
Garforth d	20 28	20 47			21 15			21 47			22 15			22 44					23 30	23 43
Cross Gates d		20 52			21 20			21 52			22 20			22 49					23 34	23 48
Leeds a	20 38	21 00	21 03	21 08	21 28	21 31	21 37	22 00	22 03	22 15	22 28	22 31	22 37	22 57	23 02	23 17	23 21	23 30	23 42	23 57
Bradford Interchange 37 a		21 30			22 02			22 30			23 00			23 30						

Saturdays
26 May to 8 December

	GR	TP	TP	TP	TP	NT	TP	TP	NT	TP	TP	XC	XC	TP	NT	TP	XC	XC	TP	NT	TP	TP	NT
	1 ⊡	◇1	◇1	◇1	◇1		◇1	◇1	◇	◇1	◇1	◇1 A ⊼	◇1 B	◇1		◇1 ⊼	◇1 C ⊼	◇1 D	◇1 ⊼	◇	◇1 ⊼	◇1 ⊼	
York 33 d	00 16	01 38	02 52	03 53	05 05	05 18	05 38	05 47		06 09		06 20	06 20	06 22	06 24	06 41	06 45	06 45	06 51		07 09		
Ulleskelf 33 d																							
Church Fenton 33 d						05 32									06 35								
Selby d									05 50		06 11									06 50		07 12	07 19
South Milford d									06 01											07 03			07 30
Micklefield d						05 39			06 07						06 43					07 08			07 36
East Garforth d						05 44			06 11						06 47					07 12			07 40
Garforth d						05 46			06 13		06 27				06 49					07 15		07 28	07 42
Cross Gates d						05 51			06 18						06 54					07 19			07 47
Leeds a	00 43	02 18	03 18	04 36	05 43	05 59	06 03	06 12	06 26	06 31	06 37	06 59	06 59	06 47	07 02	07 04	07 09	07 09	07 16	07 27	07 31	07 37	07 55
Bradford Interchange 37 a						06 27			07 01						07 28					07 59			

	NT	TP	TP	XC	XC	TP	NT	TP	TP	NT	TP	NT	NT	TP	XC	TP	NT	TP	TP	NT	TP	TP
		◇1 ⊼	◇1 ⊼	◇1 E ⊼	◇1 F	◇1 ⊼	◇	◇1 ⊼	◇1 ⊼		◇1 ⊼			◇1 ⊼	◇1 ⊼	◇1 ⊼	◇	◇1 ⊼	◇1 ⊼		◇1 ⊼	◇1 ⊼
York 33 d	07 13	07 18	07 38	07 44	07 45	07 51		08 09		08 16	08 22			08 38	08 45	08 52		09 09		09 19	09 22	09 41
Ulleskelf 33 d	07 22																					
Church Fenton 33 d	07 32									08 34										09 35		
Selby d							07 51		08 13			08 23					08 52		09 11			
South Milford d							08 02					08 34					09 03					
Micklefield d	07 40						08 08										09 09			09 42		
East Garforth d	07 45						08 12						←				09 13			09 47		
Garforth d	07 47		07 54				08 14		08 30	08 48	08 39	08 43	08 48				09 15		09 28	09 49		
Cross Gates d	07 52	07 35				08 09	08 19			→		08 47	08 52	08 57			09 20			09 54		
Leeds a	08 00	07 43	08 03	08 08	08 08	08 16	08 28	08 31	08 40		08 48	08 55	08 59	09 03	09 08	09 15	09 28	09 31	09 38	10 02	09 46	10 04
Bradford Interchange 37 a	08 30						08 59						09 30				09 59			10 30		

	XC	TP	NT	TP	TP	NT	TP	TP	XC	TP	NT	TP	TP	NT	TP	TP	XC	TP	NT	TP	TP	NT
	◇1 ⊼	◇1 ⊼	◇	◇1 ⊼	◇1 ⊼		◇1 ⊼	◇1 ⊼	◇1 ⊼	◇1 ⊼	◇	◇1 ⊼	◇1 ⊼		◇1 ⊼	◇1 ⊼	◇1 ⊼	◇1 ⊼	◇	◇1 ⊼	◇1 ⊼	
York 33 d	09 45	09 52		10 09		10 17	10 22	10 38	10 45	10 52		11 09		11 17	11 24	11 38	11 45	11 52		12 09		12 17
Ulleskelf 33 d																						
Church Fenton 33 d						10 35								11 35								12 35
Selby d			09 52		10 12						10 52		11 12						11 52		12 12	
South Milford d			10 03								11 03								12 03			
Micklefield d			10 09			10 42					11 09			11 42					12 09			12 42
East Garforth d			10 13			10 47					11 13			11 47					12 13			12 47
Garforth d			10 15		10 28	10 49					11 15		11 28	11 49					12 15		12 28	12 49
Cross Gates d			10 20			10 54					11 20			11 54					12 20			12 54
Leeds a	10 09	10 15	10 28	10 31	10 38	11 02	10 46	11 04	11 08	11 15	11 28	11 31	11 38	12 01	11 46	12 04	12 08	12 15	12 28	12 31	12 38	13 02
Bradford Interchange 37 a			10 59			11 30					11 59			12 30					12 59			13 30

A from 15 September until 6 October
B from 13 October
C from 28 July until 8 September
D until 21 July
E from 28 July until 6 October
F until 21 July, from 13 October

Table T040-F

York and Selby - Leeds

Saturdays
26 May to 8 December

			TP	TP	XC	TP	NT	TP	TP	NT	TP	TP	XC	TP	NT	TP	TP	NT	TP	TP	XC	TP	NT	TP
			◇■ 🛒	◇■ 🛒	◇■ 🛒	◇■ 🛒	◇	◇■ 🛒	◇■ 🛒		◇■ 🛒	◇■ 🛒	◇■ 🛒	◇■ 🛒	◇	◇■ 🛒	◇■ 🛒		◇■ 🛒	◇■ 🛒	◇■ 🛒	◇■ 🛒	◇	◇■ 🛒
York 8	33	d	12 24	12 38	12 45	12 52		13 09		13 17	13 22	13 38	13 45	13 52		14 09		14 17	14 22	14 38	14 45	14 52		15 09
Ulleskelf	33	d																						
Church Fenton	33	d								13 35								14 35						
Selby		d					12 52		13 12						13 52		14 12						14 52	
South Milford		d					13 03								14 03								15 03	
Micklefield		d					13 09			13 42					14 09			14 42					15 09	
East Garforth		d					13 13			13 47					14 13			14 47					15 13	
Garforth		d					13 15		13 28	13 49					14 15		14 28	14 49					15 15	
Cross Gates		d					13 20			13 54					14 20			14 54					15 20	
Leeds 10		a	12 47	13 04	13 09	13 15	13 28	13 31	13 38	14 02	13 46	14 04	14 08	14 15	14 28	14 32	14 38	15 02	14 46	15 04	15 08	15 15	15 28	15 31
Bradford Interchange	37	a					13 59			14 30					14 59			15 30					15 59	

			TP	NT	TP	TP	XC	TP	NT	XC	TP	TP	NT	TP	TP	XC	TP	NT	TP	TP	NT	TP	TP	XC
			◇■ 🛒		◇■ 🛒	◇■ 🛒	◇■ 🛒	◇■ 🛒	◇	◇■ 🛒	◇■ 🛒	◇■ 🛒		◇■ 🛒	◇■ 🛒	◇■ 🛒	◇■ 🛒	◇	◇■ 🛒	◇■ 🛒		◇■ 🛒	◇■ 🛒	◇■ 🛒
York 8	33	d		15 17	15 22	15 38	15 45	15 52		16 04	16 09		16 17	16 22	16 38	16 45	16 52		17 09		17 19	17 25	17 38	17 45
Ulleskelf	33	d																						
Church Fenton	33	d		15 35									16 35								17 32			
Selby		d	15 12						15 52			16 12						16 52		17 12				
South Milford		d							16 03									17 03						
Micklefield		d		15 42					16 08				16 42					17 09			17 39			
East Garforth		d		15 47					16 12				16 47					17 13			17 44			
Garforth		d	15 28	15 49					16 15			16 28	16 49					17 15		17 28	17 46			
Cross Gates		d		15 54					16 19				16 54					17 20			17 51			
Leeds 10		a	15 38	16 02	15 46	16 04	16 08	16 15	16 27	16 30	16 32	16 37	17 02	16 46	17 04	17 08	17 15	17 28	17 31	17 37	18 01	17 46	18 03	18 08
Bradford Interchange	37	a		16 30					16 59				17 30					17 59			18 32			

			TP	NT	TP	TP	NT	TP	TP	XC	TP	NT	TP	TP	NT	TP	TP	XC	XC	TP	NT	TP	TP	NT	TP
			◇■ 🛒	◇	◇■ 🛒	◇■ 🛒		◇■ 🛒	◇■	◇■ 🛒	◇■	◇	◇■	◇■		◇■	◇■	◇■ A 🛒	◇■ B	◇■	◇	◇■	◇■		◇■
York 8	33	d	17 52		18 09		18 21	18 24	18 41	18 45	18 52		19 09		19 17	19 22	19 40	19 45	19 45	19 52		20 09		20 20	20 38
Ulleskelf	33	d																							
Church Fenton	33	d					18 37								19 35									20 33	
Selby		d		17 52		18 12						18 52		19 14							19 51		20 12		
South Milford		d		18 03								19 03									20 04				
Micklefield		d		18 09			18 45					19 09			19 42						20 09			20 40	
East Garforth		d		18 13			18 49					19 13			19 47						20 13			20 45	
Garforth		d		18 15		18 28	18 51					19 15		19 29	19 49						20 16		20 28	20 47	
Cross Gates		d		18 20			18 56					19 20			19 54						20 20			20 52	
Leeds 10		a	18 15	18 28	18 31	18 38	19 04	18 49	19 05	19 09	19 15	19 28	19 31	19 38	20 02	19 47	20 03	20 08	20 08	20 16	20 28	20 31	20 38	21 00	21 03
Bradford Interchange	37	a		19 00			19 32					19 59			20 31						21 00			21 30	

			XC	NT	TP	TP	NT	TP	TP	NT	TP	TP	NT	NT	TP	TP	TP	TP	NT	NT
			◇■ 🛒	◇	◇■	◇■		◇■	◇■	◇	◇■	◇■			◇■	◇■	◇■	◇■	■	
York 8	33	d	20 45		21 09		21 19	21 40	21 52		22 09		22 17	22 17	22 38	22 52		23 07		23 15
Ulleskelf	33	d																		
Church Fenton	33	d					21 32						22 30	22 30						23 29
Selby		d		20 52		21 12				21 52		22 12					22 56		23 05	
South Milford		d		21 03						22 03									23 15	
Micklefield		d		21 09			21 39			22 09			22 37	22 37					23 23	23 37
East Garforth		d		21 13			21 44			22 13			22 42	22 42					23 27	23 41
Garforth		d		21 15			21 46			22 15			22 44	22 44					23 30	23 43
Cross Gates		d		21 20			21 51			22 20			22 49	22 49					23 34	23 48
Leeds 10		a	21 08	21 28	21 31	21 37	22 00	22 03	22 15	22 28	22 31	22 37	22 57	22 57	23 00	23 15	23 21	23 30	23 42	23 57
Bradford Interchange	37	a		22 02			22 30			23 00			23 27							

Sundays
20 May to 2 December

			TP	TP	TP	TP	TP	TP	TP	TP	TP	TP	TP	TP	NT	TP	TP	TP	TP	TP	NT	TP	XC	TP	TP
			C 🚌	◇■ D	C 🚌	◇■ D	C 🚌	◇■ D	C 🚌	◇■ D	C 🚌	◇■ D 🛒	◇■ D 🛒	◇■ C 🛒	◇	◇■ D 🛒	◇■ 🛒	◇■ 🛒	◇■ 🛒	◇■ 🛒	◇	◇■ 🛒	◇■ 🛒	◇■ 🛒	◇■ 🛒
York 8	33	d	01 30	02 25	03 30	04 00	04 55	05 15	05 55	06 19	06 55	07 17	07 53	08 10	08 15	08 22	08 39	08 52	09 09		09 14	09 20	09 33	09 41	09 53
Ulleskelf	33	d																							
Church Fenton	33	d													08 32						09 31				
Selby		d																		09 15					
South Milford		d																							
Micklefield		d													08 40										
East Garforth		d													08 44										
Garforth		d													08 46						09 41				
Cross Gates		d													08 51										
Leeds 10		a	02 20	02 50	04 20	04 25	05 45	05 40	06 45	06 44	07 45	07 43	08 18	08 32	09 00	08 45	09 02	09 14	09 32	09 37	09 53	09 45	09 57	10 04	10 16
Bradford Interchange	37	a													09 25						10 24				

A until 21 July, from 13 October
B from 23 July until 6 October
C from 28 October
D until 21 October

Table T040-F

York and Selby - Leeds

Sundays
20 May to 2 December

			NT	TP	TP	NT	TP	XC	TP	TP	NT	TP	TP	NT	TP	TP	XC	TP	TP	TP	NT	TP	TP	XC
				◇■ 🛒	◇■ 🛒	◇	◇■ 🛒	◇■ 🛒	◇■ 🛒	◇■ 🛒		◇■ 🛒	◇■ 🛒	◇	◇■ 🛒	◇■ 🛒	◇■ 🛒	◇■ 🛒	◇■ 🛒	◇■ 🛒	◇	◇■ 🛒	◇■ 🛒	◇■ A 🛒
York 8	33	d		10 09		10 17	10 24	10 33	10 36	10 52		11 10		11 17	11 24	11 38	11 41	11 52	12 09		12 17	12 24	12 38	12 42
Ulleskelf	33	d																						
Church Fenton	33	d				10 34								11 34							12 35			
Selby		d	09 52		10 15						10 52		11 15							12 15				
South Milford		d	10 03								11 04													
Micklefield		d	10 08								11 09			11 42							12 42			
East Garforth		d	10 13								11 13			11 45							12 46			
Garforth		d	10 15								11 15			11 48							12 48			
Cross Gates		d	10 20								11 20			11 52							12 53			
Leeds 10		a	10 28	10 31	10 37	10 55	10 46	10 57	11 00	11 15	11 28	11 32	11 37	12 00	11 46	12 04	12 09	12 15	12 31	12 37	13 01	12 47	13 04	13 08
Bradford Interchange	37	a				11 25								12 25							13 29			

			XC	TP	TP	TP	NT	TP	TP	XC	XC	TP	NT	TP	TP	NT	TP	TP	XC	TP	TP	TP	NT	TP
			◇■ B 🛒	◇■ 🛒	◇■ 🛒	◇■ 🛒	◇	◇■ 🛒	◇■ 🛒	◇■ C 🛒	◇■ D 🛒	◇■ 🛒		◇■ 🛒	◇■ 🛒	◇	◇■ 🛒	◇■ 🛒	◇■ 🛒	◇■ 🛒	◇■ 🛒	◇■ 🛒	◇	◇■ 🛒
York 8	33	d	12 45	12 52	13 09		13 17	13 24	13 38	13 43	13 45	13 53		14 10		14 17	14 24	14 38	14 44	14 52	15 09		15 14	15 21
Ulleskelf	33	d																						
Church Fenton	33	d					13 35									14 34							15 32	
Selby		d				13 16							13 52		14 15							15 15		
South Milford		d											14 03											
Micklefield		d					13 42									14 41							15 39	
East Garforth		d					13 46									14 45							15 43	
Garforth		d					13 48									14 48							15 46	
Cross Gates		d					13 53									14 53							15 51	
Leeds 10		a	13 08	13 15	13 31	13 38	14 01	13 46	14 04	14 08	14 08	14 16	14 25	14 32	14 37	15 01	14 46	15 04	15 08	15 15	15 31	15 37	15 59	15 45
Bradford Interchange	37	a					14 29									15 25							16 25	

			TP	XC	XC	TP	NT	TP	TP	NT	TP	TP	XC	TP	TP	TP	TP	NT	TP	XC	TP	NT	TP	TP
			◇■ 🛒	◇■ B 🛒	◇■ A	◇■ 🛒		◇■ 🛒	◇■ 🛒	◇	◇■ 🛒	◇■ 🛒	◇■ 🛒	◇■ 🛒	◇■ 🛒	◇■ 🛒	◇■ 🛒	◇	◇■ 🛒	◇■ 🛒	◇■ 🛒		◇■ 🛒	◇■ 🛒
York 8	33	d	15 38	15 42	15 42	15 54		16 09		16 17	16 24	16 38	16 41	16 54	17 09		17 18	17 22	17 38	17 44	17 52		18 09	
Ulleskelf	33	d																						
Church Fenton	33	d								16 35								17 34						
Selby		d					15 56		16 15							17 15						18 00		18 15
South Milford		d					16 07															18 11		
Micklefield		d								16 42								17 41						
East Garforth		d								16 46								17 45						
Garforth		d								16 48								17 48						
Cross Gates		d								16 53								17 53						
Leeds 10		a	16 04	16 08	16 08	16 16	16 24	16 32	16 37	17 01	16 46	17 04	17 08	17 16	17 31	17 37	17 44	18 01	18 04	18 09	18 15	18 27	18 32	18 37
Bradford Interchange	37	a								17 25								18 25						

			TP	NT	TP	XC	TP	TP	TP	NT	TP	TP	XC	XC	TP	NT	TP	TP	NT	TP	XC	TP	TP	NT
			◇■ 🛒	◇	◇■	◇■ 🛒	◇■	◇■	◇■	◇	◇■	◇■	◇■ A	◇■ B 🛒	◇■		◇■	◇■	◇	◇■	◇■ 🛒	◇■	◇■	
York 8	33	d	18 19	18 22	18 40	18 45	18 55	19 09		19 14	19 20	19 41	19 45	19 45	19 54		20 09		20 22	20 38	20 45	21 10		21 17
Ulleskelf	33	d																						
Church Fenton	33	d		18 34						19 31									20 34					21 33
Selby		d							19 15							19 53		20 15					21 25	
South Milford		d														20 04								
Micklefield		d		18 42						19 39									20 41					21 41
East Garforth		d		18 46						19 43									20 45					21 46
Garforth		d		18 48						19 45									20 48					21 48
Cross Gates		d		18 53						19 50									20 53					21 53
Leeds 10		a	18 46	19 01	19 04	19 08	19 17	19 31	19 37	20 00	19 46	20 04	20 08	20 08	20 17	20 21	20 33	20 37	21 00	21 04	21 08	21 32	21 47	22 01
Bradford Interchange	37	a		19 25						20 25									21 29					

			TP	NT	TP	TP	NT	TP	NT	TP	GR	TP
			◇■		◇■	◇■	◇	◇■		◇■	■ ■ 🍴	◇■
York 8	33	d	21 41		22 09	22 16	22 21	22 39			23 07	23 13
Ulleskelf	33	d										
Church Fenton	33	d					22 33					
Selby		d		21 53					22 49	23 02		
South Milford		d		22 04					23 00			
Micklefield		d					22 40					
East Garforth		d					22 44					
Garforth		d					22 47					
Cross Gates		d					22 52					
Leeds 10		a	22 04	22 20	22 32	22 39	23 00	23 02	23 16	23 24	23 33	23 39
Bradford Interchange	37	a										

A from 22 July until 7 October
B until 15 July, from 14 October
C until 15 July
D from 22 July

Table T040-R

Leeds - Selby and York

Mondays to Fridays
21 May to 7 December

Miles	Miles		TP	TP	TP	TP	TP	TP	TP	TP	NT	TP	TP	TP	NT	TP	NT	GR	TP	TP	TP	NT
			MX	MO	MX	MO	MX	MO A	MX	MO												
—	—	Bradford Interchange 37 d																				07 02
0	0	**Leeds** d	00 11	00 14	00 24	00 39	01 14	01 35	02 05	02 11	05 40	06 00	06 17	06 24	06 32	06 52	07 01	07 08	07 13	07 17	07 21	07 24
4¼	4¼	Cross Gates d									05 47				06 38							07 30
7¼	7¼	Garforth d									05 52				06 44		07 11					07 36
8	8	East Garforth d									05 54				06 46							07 38
9	9	Micklefield d									05 58				06 50							07 42
—	12¾	South Milford d									06 03						07 18					
—	20¾	**Selby** a									06 15			06 45			07 31			07 36		
14¾	—	Church Fenton 33 a													06 56							07 48
16½	—	Ulleskelf 33 a																				07 53
25½	—	**York** 33 a	00 51	00 45	01 05	01 03	01 55	02 25	02 46	02 38		06 23	06 39		07 11	07 16		07 31	07 35		07 43	08 06

	TP	TP	TP	NT	XC	TP	TP	NT	TP	TP	TP	NT	XC	TP	TP	NT	TP	TP	TP	NT	XC	TP
Bradford Interchange 37 d								08 00				08 29				09 00				09 29		
Leeds d	07 35	07 48	07 52	07 55	08 07	08 12	08 21	08 24	08 39	08 48	08 52	08 55	09 08	09 12	09 21	09 24	09 39	09 48	09 52	09 55	10 08	10 12
Cross Gates d				08 02				08 31				09 01				09 30				10 01		
Garforth d	07 43	07 56		08 07				08 36		08 56		09 07				09 36		09 56		10 07		
East Garforth d				08 09				08 38				09 09				09 38				10 09		
Micklefield d				08 13				08 42				09 13				09 42				10 13		
South Milford d				08 18								09 18								10 18		
Selby a		08 11		08 31						09 11		09 30						10 11		10 30		
Church Fenton 33 a								08 48								09 48						
Ulleskelf 33 a																						
York 33 a	08 02		08 16		08 29	08 35	08 43	09 02	09 01		09 17		09 30	09 34	09 43	10 01	10 01		10 17		10 30	10 35

	TP	NT	TP	TP	TP	NT	XC	TP	TP	NT	TP	TP	TP	NT	XC	TP	TP	NT	TP	TP	TP	NT
Bradford Interchange 37 d		10 00				10 30				11 00				11 28				12 00				12 29
Leeds d	10 21	10 24	10 39	10 48	10 52	10 55	11 08	11 12	11 21	11 24	11 39	11 48	11 52	11 55	12 08	12 12	12 21	12 24	12 39	12 48	12 52	12 55
Cross Gates d		10 30				11 02				11 30				12 01				12 30				13 01
Garforth d		10 36		10 56		11 07				11 36		11 56		12 07				12 36		12 56		13 07
East Garforth d		10 38				11 09				11 38				12 09				12 38				13 09
Micklefield d		10 42				11 13				11 42				12 13				12 42				13 13
South Milford d						11 18								12 18								13 18
Selby a				11 11		11 31						12 11		12 30						13 11		13 32
Church Fenton 33 a		10 48								11 48								12 48				
Ulleskelf 33 a																						
York 33 a	10 43	11 01	11 01		11 17		11 30	11 35	11 43	12 00	12 01		12 17		12 30	12 35	12 43	13 01	13 01		13 17	

	XC	TP	TP	NT	TP	TP	TP	NT	XC	XC	TP	TP	NT	TP	TP	TP	NT	XC	TP	TP	NT	TP	TP
									B	C													
Bradford Interchange 37 d				13 00				13 29					14 00				14 29				15 00		
Leeds d	13 08	13 12	13 21	13 24	13 39	13 48	13 52	13 55	14 08	14 08	14 12	14 21	14 24	14 39	14 48	14 52	14 55	15 08	15 12	15 21	15 24	15 39	15 48
Cross Gates d				13 30				14 01					14 30				15 01				15 30		
Garforth d				13 36		13 56		14 07					14 36		14 56		15 07				15 36		15 56
East Garforth d				13 38				14 09					14 38				15 09				15 38		
Micklefield d				13 42				14 13					14 42				15 13				15 42		
South Milford d								14 18									15 18						
Selby a						14 11		14 30							15 11		15 30						16 11
Church Fenton 33 a				13 48									14 48								15 48		
Ulleskelf 33 a																							
York 33 a	13 30	13 35	13 43	14 01	14 01		14 17		14 30	14 30	14 34	14 43	15 00	15 01		15 17		15 30	15 34	15 43	16 02	16 01	

	TP	NT	XC	XC	TP	TP	NT	TP	TP	TP	NT	XC	TP	TP	NT	TP	NT	TP	TP	NT	XC	TP
			B	C																		
Bradford Interchange 37 d		15 29					16 00				16 29				17 00					17 29		
Leeds d	15 52	15 55	16 08	16 08	16 11	16 21	16 24	16 36	16 48	16 52	16 55	17 08	17 12	17 21	17 25	17 36	17 40	17 48	17 52	17 55	18 07	18 11
Cross Gates d		16 01			16 17		16 30				17 01		17 18		17 31		17 46			18 01		18 17
Garforth d		16 07					16 36	16 45	16 56		17 07				17 37	17 45	17 52	17 56		18 07		
East Garforth d		16 09					16 38				17 09				17 39		17 54			18 09		
Micklefield d		16 13					16 42				17 13				17 44		17 58			18 13		
South Milford d		16 18									17 18				17 51					18 18		
Selby a		16 30							17 11		17 30				18 08			18 11		18 30		
Church Fenton 33 a							16 48										18 04					
Ulleskelf 33 a																						
York 33 a	16 17		16 30	16 30	16 35	16 43	17 00	17 01		17 17		17 30	17 36	17 43		18 01	18 17		18 16		18 30	18 37

A from 29 October
B until 20 July, from 8 October
C from 23 July until 5 October

Table T040-R

Leeds - Selby and York

Mondays to Fridays
21 May to 7 December

	TP	NT	XC	TP	TP	TP	NT	XC	TP	TP	NT	TP	TP	TP	NT	XC	TP	TP	NT	TP	TP	TP
Bradford Interchange 37 d		18 00					18 31				19 00				19 31				20 00			
Leeds d	18 21	18 24	18 38	18 39	18 48	18 52	18 55	19 08	19 12	19 21	19 24	19 38	19 48	19 52	19 55	20 08	20 12	20 21	20 24	20 39	20 48	20 52
Cross Gates d		18 31					19 01				19 30				20 01				20 30			
Garforth d		18 36			18 56		19 07				19 36		19 56		20 07				20 36		20 56	
East Garforth d		18 38					19 09				19 38				20 09				20 38			
Micklefield d		18 42					19 13				19 42				20 13				20 41			
South Milford d							19 18								20 18							
Selby a					19 11		19 30						20 11		20 30						21 14	
Church Fenton 33 a		18 48									19 48								20 47			
Ulleskelf 33 a																						
York 33 a	18 43	19 01	19 01	19 05		19 16		19 30	19 34	19 43	20 00	20 05		20 16		20 30	20 34	20 43	20 59	21 05		21 16

	NT	TP	TP	NT	TP	TP	TP	NT	TP	NT	TP	TP	TP	NT
Bradford Interchange 37 d	20 30			20 59				21 29		21 56				23 01
Leeds d	20 55	21 12	21 21	21 23	21 37	21 48	21 52	21 55	22 07	22 21	22 48	22 52	23 23	23 26
Cross Gates d	21 01			21 30				22 01		22 27				23 33
Garforth d	21 07			21 35				22 07		22 33				23 38
East Garforth d	21 09			21 37				22 09		22 35				23 40
Micklefield d	21 13			21 41				22 13		22 41				23 44
South Milford d	21 18					22 01		22 18			23 01			
Selby a	21 30					22 10		22 30			23 10			
Church Fenton 33 a				21 47						22 47				23 50
Ulleskelf 33 a														
York 33 a		21 34	21 43	22 00	22 04		22 16		22 31	23 01		23 14	23 50	00 03

Saturdays
26 May to 8 December

	TP	TP	TP	TP	NT	TP	TP	TP	TP	NT	GR	TP	TP	NT	TP	TP	TP	NT	XC	XC	TP	TP	NT
																			A	B			
Bradford Interchange 37 d														07 02									08 00
Leeds d	00 11	00 24	00 45	02 05	05 40	06 00	06 15	06 48	06 52	07 01	07 08	07 13	07 21	07 24	07 35	07 48	07 52	07 55	08 06	08 07	08 12	08 21	08 24
Cross Gates d					05 47									07 30				08 02					08 31
Garforth d					05 52			06 57		07 11				07 36		07 56		08 07					08 36
East Garforth d					05 54									07 38				08 09					08 38
Micklefield d					05 58									07 42				08 13					08 42
South Milford d					06 03					07 18								08 18					
Selby a					06 15			07 10		07 31						08 11		08 31					
Church Fenton 33 a														07 48									08 48
Ulleskelf 33 a														07 53									
York 33 a	00 51	01 05	01 26	02 43		06 23	06 39		07 16		07 31	07 35	07 43	08 06	08 00		08 16		08 29	08 30	08 35	08 43	09 02

	TP	TP	TP	NT	XC	TP	TP	NT	TP	TP	TP	NT	XC	TP	TP	NT	TP	TP	TP	NT	XC	TP
Bradford Interchange 37 d				08 29				09 00				09 29				10 00				10 30		
Leeds d	08 39	08 48	08 52	08 55	09 08	09 12	09 21	09 24	09 39	09 48	09 52	09 55	10 08	10 12	10 21	10 24	10 39	10 48	10 52	10 55	11 08	11 12
Cross Gates d				09 01				09 30				10 01				10 30				11 02		
Garforth d		08 56		09 07				09 36		09 56		10 07				10 36		10 56		11 07		
East Garforth d				09 09				09 38				10 09				10 38				11 09		
Micklefield d				09 13				09 42				10 13				10 42				11 13		
South Milford d				09 18								10 18								11 18		
Selby a		09 11		09 30						10 11		10 30						11 11		11 31		
Church Fenton 33 a								09 48								10 48						
Ulleskelf 33 a																						
York 33 a	09 01		09 16		09 30	09 34	09 43	10 01	10 01		10 17		10 30	10 35	10 43	11 01	11 01		11 17		11 30	11 35

	TP	NT	TP	TP	TP	NT	XC	TP	TP	NT	TP	TP	TP	NT	XC	TP	TP	NT	TP	TP	TP	NT
Bradford Interchange 37 d		11 00				11 28				12 00				12 29				13 00				13 29
Leeds d	11 21	11 24	11 39	11 48	11 52	11 55	12 08	12 12	12 21	12 24	12 39	12 48	12 52	12 55	13 08	13 12	13 21	13 24	13 39	13 48	13 52	13 55
Cross Gates d		11 30				12 01				12 30				13 01				13 30				14 01
Garforth d		11 36		11 56		12 07				12 36		12 56		13 07				13 36		13 56		14 07
East Garforth d		11 38				12 09				12 38				13 09				13 38				14 09
Micklefield d		11 42				12 13				12 42				13 13				13 42				14 13
South Milford d						12 18								13 18								14 18
Selby a				12 11		12 30						13 11		13 30						14 11		14 30
Church Fenton 33 a		11 48								12 48								13 48				
Ulleskelf 33 a																						
York 33 a	11 43	12 00	12 01		12 17		12 30	12 35	12 43	13 01	13 01		13 16		13 30	13 34	13 43	14 02	14 01		14 17	

A from 8 September until 6 October
B until 1 September, from 13 October

Leeds - Selby and York

Saturdays
26 May to 8 December

	XC	XC	TP	TP	NT	TP	TP	TP	NT	XC	TP	TP	NT	TP	TP	TP	NT	XC	XC	TP	TP	NT
	◇■	◇■	◇■	◇■	◇	◇■	◇■	◇■	◇	◇■	◇■	◇■	◇	◇■	◇■	◇■	◇	◇■	◇■	◇■	◇■	◇
	A	B																A	B			
	🍴		🍴	🍴		🍴	🍴	🍴		🍴	🍴	🍴		🍴	🍴	🍴		🍴		🍴	🍴	
Bradford Interchange 37 d					14 00				14 29				15 00				15 29					16 00
Leeds ■ d	14 08	14 08	14 12	14 21	14 24	14 39	14 48	14 52	14 55	15 08	15 12	15 21	15 24	15 39	15 48	15 52	15 55	16 07	16 07	16 10	16 21	16 24
Cross Gates d					14 30				15 01				15 30				16 01			16 17		16 30
Garforth d					14 36		14 56		15 07				15 36		15 56		16 07					16 36
East Garforth d					14 38				15 09				15 38				16 09					16 38
Micklefield d					14 42				15 13				15 42				16 13					16 42
South Milford d									15 18								16 18					
Selby a							15 11		15 30						16 11		16 30					
Church Fenton 33 a					14 48								15 48									16 48
Ulleskelf 33 a																						
York ■ 33 a	14 30	14 30	14 34	14 43	15 00	15 01		15 17		15 30	15 34	15 43	16 00	16 01		16 17		16 30	16 30	16 35	16 43	17 00

	TP	TP	TP	NT	XC	XC	TP	TP	NT	TP	NT	TP	TP	NT	XC	XC	TP	TP	NT	TP	XC	TP
	◇■	◇■	◇■	◇	◇■	◇■	◇■	◇■	◇	◇■		◇■	◇■	◇	◇■	◇■	◇■	◇■	◇	◇■	◇■	◇■
					C	D									B	A						
	🍴	🍴	🍴		🍴	🍴	🍴	🍴		🍴		🍴	🍴		🍴	🍴	🍴	🍴		🍴	🍴	🍴
Bradford Interchange 37 d				16 29					17 00					17 29					18 00			
Leeds ■ d	16 36	16 48	16 52	16 55	17 07	17 08	17 12	17 21	17 24	17 36	17 40	17 48	17 52	17 55	18 07	18 07	18 11	18 21	18 24	18 35	18 39	18 48
Cross Gates d				17 01			17 18		17 30		17 46			18 01			18 17		18 31			
Garforth d	16 44	16 56		17 07					17 36	17 45	17 52	17 56		18 07					18 36			18 56
East Garforth d				17 09					17 38		17 54			18 09					18 38			
Micklefield d				17 13					17 42		17 58			18 13					18 42			
South Milford d				17 18										18 18								
Selby a		17 11		17 30								18 11		18 30								19 11
Church Fenton 33 a									17 48		18 04								18 48			
Ulleskelf 33 a																						
York ■ 33 a	17 01		17 17		17 28	17 29	17 36	17 43	18 00	18 01	18 17		18 16		18 29	18 30	18 37	18 43	19 00	19 01	19 05	

	TP	NT	XC	TP	TP	NT	TP	TP	TP	NT	XC	TP	TP	NT	TP	TP	TP	NT	TP	XC	TP	NT	TP
	◇■	◇	◇■	◇■	◇■	◇	◇■	◇■	◇■	◇	◇■	◇■	◇■	◇	◇■	◇■	◇■	◇	◇■	◇■	◇■	◇	◇■
	🍴		🍴	🍴	🍴		🍴	🍴															
Bradford Interchange 37 d		18 31				19 00				19 31				20 00				20 30				20 59	
Leeds ■ d	18 52	18 55	19 08	19 12	19 21	19 24	19 39	19 48	19 52	19 55	20 08	20 12	20 21	20 24	20 39	20 48	20 52	20 55	21 12	21 19	21 21	21 23	21 39
Cross Gates d		19 01				19 30				20 01				20 30				21 01				21 30	
Garforth d		19 07				19 36		19 56		20 07				20 36		20 56		21 07				21 35	
East Garforth d		19 09				19 38				20 09				20 38				21 09				21 37	
Micklefield d		19 13				19 42				20 13				20 41				21 13				21 41	
South Milford d		19 18								20 18								21 18					
Selby a		19 30						20 11		20 30						21 14		21 30					
Church Fenton 33 a						19 48								20 47								21 47	
Ulleskelf 33 a																							
York ■ 33 a	19 16		19 30	19 34	19 43	20 00	20 05		20 16		20 30	20 34	20 43	20 59	21 05		21 16		21 34	21 59	21 45	22 00	22 03

	TP	TP	NT	TP	NT	TP	TP	TP	NT	TP
	◇■	◇■	◇	◇■	◇	◇■	◇■	◇■	◇	◇■
Bradford Interchange 37 d			21 29		22 00				23 01	
Leeds ■ d	21 48	21 52	21 55	22 21	22 24	22 48	22 52	23 23	23 26	23 53
Cross Gates d			22 01		22 30				23 33	
Garforth d			22 07		22 36				23 38	
East Garforth d			22 09		22 38				23 40	
Micklefield d			22 13		22 42				23 44	
South Milford d	22 01		22 18			23 01				
Selby a	22 10		22 30			23 10				
Church Fenton 33 a					22 48				23 50	
Ulleskelf 33 a										
York ■ 33 a		22 16		22 43	23 01		23 17	23 50	00 03	00 24

Sundays
20 May to 2 December

	TP	TP	TP	TP	TP	TP	TP	TP	TP	NT	GR	TP	TP	NT	XC	TP	NT	TP	TP	TP	TP	NT	XC
	◇■	◇■		◇■			◇■		◇■		■	◇■	◇■		◇■	◇■	◇	◇■	◇■	◇■	◇■		◇■
	E	E	F	G	F	F	G	F	G									H	I				
			🚌		🚌	🚌		🚌			🍴	🍴	🍴		🍴	🍴		🍴	🍴	🍴	🍴		🍴
Bradford Interchange 37 d																	09 00						
Leeds ■ d	00 39	00 44	01 05	02 13	03 00	05 30	05 31	07 10	07 41	08 10	08 30	08 41	08 46	08 52	09 18	09 21	09 24	09 38	09 40	09 47	09 52	10 01	10 08
Cross Gates d										08 17				08 58			09 31						
Garforth d										08 22				09 04			09 36						
East Garforth d										08 24				09 06			09 38						
Micklefield d										08 28				09 10			09 42					10 12	
South Milford d														09 14								10 18	
Selby a													09 05	09 27						10 07		10 30	
Church Fenton 33 a										08 33							09 47						
Ulleskelf 33 a																							
York ■ 33 a	01 05	01 10	01 55	02 40	03 50	06 20	05 55	08 00	08 06	08 47	08 55	09 03			09 40	09 44	10 05	10 03	10 03		10 16		10 30

A until 21 July, from 13 October
B from 28 July until 6 October
C from 28 July until 1 September
D until 21 July, from 8 September
E from 27 May until 21 October
F from 28 October
G until 21 October
H until 9 September, from 28 October
I from 16 September until 21 October

Table T040-R

Leeds - Selby and York

Sundays
20 May to 2 December

	TP	NT	TP	TP	TP	XC	TP	TP	NT	TP	TP	TP	XC	TP	TP	NT	TP	TP	TP	NT	XC	TP
	◇■	◇	◇■	◇■	◇■	◇■	◇■	◇■	◇	◇■	◇■	◇■	◇■	◇■	◇■	◇	◇■	◇■	◇■		◇■	◇■
	🍴		🍴	🍴	🍴	🍴	🍴	🍴		🍴	🍴	🍴	🍴	🍴	🍴		🍴	🍴	🍴		🍴	🍴
Bradford Interchange 37 d		10 00							10 59							12 00						
Leeds ■ d	10 21	10 24	10 39	10 48	10 52	11 07	11 12	11 21	11 24	11 36	11 47	11 51	12 08	12 11	12 21	12 24	12 39	12 48	12 52	13 00	13 05	13 12
Cross Gates d		10 31							11 30							12 31						
Garforth d		10 36							11 35							12 36						
East Garforth d									11 37							12 38						
Micklefield d		10 40							11 41							12 42						
South Milford d																				13 14		
Selby a				11 07							12 07							13 09		13 27		
Church Fenton 33 a		10 46							11 46							12 47						
Ulleskelf 33 a																						
York ■ 33 a	10 43	10 59	11 01		11 16	11 29	11 34	11 43	12 00	12 01		12 14	12 30	12 35	12 43	13 01	13 01		13 15		13 27	13 35

	TP	NT	TP	TP	TP	XC	TP	TP	NT	TP	TP	TP	NT	XC	TP	TP	NT	TP	TP	TP	XC	TP
	◇■	◇	◇■	◇■	◇■	◇■	◇■	◇■	◇	◇■	◇■	◇■		◇■	◇■	◇■	◇	◇■	◇■	◇■	◇■	◇■
	🍴		🍴	🍴	🍴	🍴	🍴	🍴		🍴	🍴	🍴		🍴	🍴	🍴		🍴	🍴	🍴	🍴	🍴
Bradford Interchange 37 d		13 00							14 00								15 00					
Leeds ■ d	13 21	13 24	13 39	13 48	13 52	14 05	14 12	14 21	14 24	14 39	14 48	14 52	15 00	15 05	15 12	15 21	15 24	15 39	15 48	15 51	16 05	16 12
Cross Gates d		13 31							14 31								15 31					
Garforth d		13 36							14 36								15 36					
East Garforth d		13 38							14 38								15 38					
Micklefield d		13 42							14 42								15 42					
South Milford d													15 14									
Selby a				14 07							15 07		15 27						16 07			
Church Fenton 33 a		13 47							14 47								15 47					
Ulleskelf 33 a																						
York ■ 33 a	13 43	14 01	14 01		14 14	14 27	14 34	14 43	15 01	15 01		15 15		15 27	15 35	15 44	16 01	16 01		16 13	16 27	16 34

	TP	NT	TP	TP	TP	NT	XC	TP	TP	NT	TP	TP	TP	XC	XC	TP	TP	NT	TP	TP	TP	XC
	◇■	◇	◇■	◇■	◇■		◇■	◇■	◇■	◇	◇■	◇■	◇■	◇■	◇■	◇■	◇■	◇	◇■	◇■	◇■	◇■
														A	B							C
	🍴		🍴	🍴	🍴		🍴	🍴	🍴		🍴	🍴	🍴	🍴		🍴	🍴		🍴	🍴	🍴	🍴
Bradford Interchange 37 d		15 56								17 00								18 00				
Leeds ■ d	16 21	16 24	16 37	16 48	16 52	16 58	17 05	17 10	17 21	17 24	17 39	17 47	17 52	18 05	18 05	18 13	18 21	18 24	18 38	18 48	18 52	18 59
Cross Gates d		16 30								17 31								18 31				
Garforth d		16 35								17 36								18 36				
East Garforth d		16 37								17 38								18 38				
Micklefield d		16 41								17 42								18 42				
South Milford d						17 12																
Selby a				17 07		17 25						18 05								19 07		
Church Fenton 33 a		16 46								17 47								18 47				
Ulleskelf 33 a																						
York ■ 33 a	16 43	17 00	16 59		17 16		17 27	17 32	17 43	18 01	18 01		18 16	18 27	18 27	18 35	18 43	19 01	19 01		19 16	19 21

	NT	XC	TP	TP	NT	TP	TP	TP	XC	TP	TP	NT	TP	TP	TP	NT	XC	TP	NT	TP	TP	TP
		◇■	◇■	◇■	◇	◇■	◇■	◇■	◇■	◇■	◇■	◇	◇■	◇■	◇■		◇■	◇■	◇	◇■	◇■	◇■
																	C					
		🍴	🍴	🍴		🍴	🍴		🍴													
Bradford Interchange 37 d					18 59							19 57							21 00			
Leeds ■ d	19 03	19 08	19 13	19 21	19 24	19 39	19 48	19 51	20 09	20 13	20 21	20 24	20 39	20 46	20 52	20 56	21 08	21 21	21 24	21 39	21 47	21 51
Cross Gates d					19 30							20 31							21 30			
Garforth d					19 35							20 36							21 35			
East Garforth d					19 37							20 38							21 37			
Micklefield d					19 41							20 42							21 41			
South Milford d	19 17															21 18						
Selby a	19 31						20 07							21 06		21 32					22 07	
Church Fenton 33 a					19 46							20 47							21 46			
Ulleskelf 33 a																						
York ■ 33 a		19 30	19 35	19 43	19 59	20 01		20 13	20 30	20 35	20 43	21 01	21 03		21 16		21 31	21 46	22 03	22 01		22 13

	NT	TP	NT	TP	TP	TP	TP
		◇■		◇■	◇■	◇■	◇■
Bradford Interchange 37 d							
Leeds ■ d	21 55	22 21	22 24	22 47	22 52	23 24	23 56
Cross Gates d			22 30				
Garforth d			22 36				
East Garforth d			22 38				
Micklefield d			22 42				
South Milford d	22 10						
Selby a	22 24			23 07			
Church Fenton 33 a			22 48				
Ulleskelf 33 a							
York ■ 33 a		22 43	23 04		23 14	23 51	00 23

A until 9 September, from 14 October
B from 16 September until 7 October
C until 15 July, from 14 October

Manchester Victoria, Rochdale, Blackpool North and Huddersfield - Bradford and Leeds via Brighouse and Halifax

Miles	Miles	Miles	Miles		NT MX ◇ A	NT	NT	NT ◇	NT ◇	NT B	NT	NT ◇	NT	NT ◇	NT	NT	NT ◇	NT ◇	NT B	NT C	NT ◇	NT ◇ D
0	—	—	—	**Manchester Victoria** d				05 45		06 00	06 09	06 23		06 37	06 42		06 55		07 04	07 09	07 21	07 36
4	—	—	—	Moston d				05 52			06 16				06 50					07 16		
6	—	—	—	Mills Hill d				05 57			06 20				06 54					07 20		
8¾	—	—	—	Castleton d				06 02			06 26				07 00					07 25		
10½	—	—	—	**Rochdale** a				06 06		06 13	06 31	06 36		06 50	07 05		07 08		07 17	07 31	07 34	07 49
—	—	—	—	d				06 06		06 14		06 36		06 51			07 09		07 18		07 34	07 50
12¾	—	—	—	Smithy Bridge d				06 10		06 18				06 55			07 13		07 22			07 54
13¾	—	—	—	Littleborough d				06 14		06 21				06 58			07 16		07 25			07 57
17¼	—	—	—	Walsden d				06 20						07 04					07 31			08 03
19¼	—	—	—	Todmorden d				06 23		06 29		06 47		07 08			07 23		07 35		07 45	08 06
—	0	—	—	**Blackpool North** 97 d					05 19													
—	3	—	—	Poulton-le-Fylde 97 d					05 25													
—	17½	—	—	**Preston** 8 97 d					05 44									06 48				
—	29½	—	—	Blackburn 97 d					06 03									07 04				
—	35¾	—	—	Accrington 97 d					06 11									07 12				
—	42	—	—	Burnley Manchester Road 97 a					06 20	06 45								07 21	07 51			
—	—	—	—	d					06 20									07 21				
23½	54½	—	0	**Hebden Bridge** a				06 30	06 42			06 54		07 14			07 30	07 43			07 54	08 13
—	—	—	—	d		05 47		06 30	06 42			06 54	07 02	07 15			07 30	07 43			07 55	08 13
24¾	56	—	1¼	Mytholmroyd d	00 01	05 50			06 46			06 57	07 09	07 18				07 47			07 58	08 16
28¾	60	—	5¼	Sowerby Bridge d	00 07	05 56			06 52			07 03	07 17	07 24				07 53			08 04	08 22
—	—	0	—	**Huddersfield** 39 d			06 07									07 10						
—	—	—	—	London Kings Cross 15 ⊖26 d																		
—	—	5¼	11	Brighouse d			06 22							07 33		07 18						08 31
—	—	—	15	Mirfield 39 a										07 40								08 38
—	—	—	—	d										07 40								08 38
—	—	—	18	Dewsbury 39 a										07 45								08 44
32¼	63½	10½	—	**Halifax** a	00 14	06 03	06 32	06 42	06 58			07 10	07 25			07 34	07 42	07 59			08 11	
—	—	—	—	d	00 15	06 03	06 33	06 43	06 59			07 11	07 26			07 34	07 43	08 00			08 12	
—	—	—	—	Low Moor d		06 11	06 40						07 33			07 42						
40¼	71½	—	—	**Bradford Interchange** a	00 29	06 19	06 48	06 57	07 13			07 26	07 41			07 49	07 57	08 15			08 27	
—	—	—	—	d	00 31	06 22	06 50	07 02	07 17			07 29	07 45			07 52	08 00	08 17			08 29	
43¾	75	—	—	New Pudsey 37 a		06 30	06 59	07 10	07 25			07 38	07 53			08 00	08 08	08 25			08 38	
45¾	77	—	—	Bramley 37 a		06 34		07 14	07 29			07 42	07 57			08 04	08 12	08 30			08 42	
49¾	81	—	27½	**Leeds** 10 37,39 a	00 50	06 43	07 12	07 23	07 40			07 56	08 08	08 04		08 15	08 21	08 38			08 54	09 03
—	—	—	—	Selby 40 a																	09 30	
—	—	—	—	York 8 40 a				08 06									09 02					

	NT E	NT	NT ◇	NT ◇	NT F	NT E	NT ◇	NT ◇ D	NT E	NT	NT ◇	NT ◇	NT F	NT C	NT ◇	NT ◇ G	NT E	NT	NT ◇	NT ◇	NT F	NT C
Manchester Victoria d	07 42		07 55		08 04	08 10	08 21	08 38	08 42		08 58		09 04	09 09	09 20	09 37	09 42		09 58		10 04	10 09
Moston d	07 50					08 17			08 50					09 16			09 50					10 16
Mills Hill d	07 54					08 21			08 54					09 20			09 54					10 20
Castleton d	08 00					08 26			09 00					09 25			10 00					10 25
Rochdale a	08 06		08 08		08 17	08 31	08 34	08 51	09 06		09 12		09 17	09 31	09 33	09 50	10 06		10 12		10 17	10 31
d			08 09		08 18		08 34	08 52			09 12		09 18		09 34	09 51			10 12		10 18	
Smithy Bridge d			08 13		08 22			08 56					09 22			09 55					10 22	
Littleborough d			08 16		08 25			08 59					09 25			09 58					10 25	
Walsden d					08 31			09 05					09 31			10 04						
Todmorden d			08 23		08 35		08 45	09 08			09 23		09 35		09 44	10 07			10 23		10 33	
Blackpool North 97 d																						
Poulton-le-Fylde 97 d																						
Preston 8 97 d				07 50								08 50								09 48		
Blackburn 97 d				08 06								09 06								10 05		
Accrington 97 d				08 14								09 14								10 13		
Burnley Manchester Road 97 a				08 22	08 51							09 22	09 50							10 21	10 48	
d				08 23								09 23								10 22		
Hebden Bridge a			08 30	08 44			08 54	09 15			09 30	09 44			09 54	10 14			10 30	10 44		
d			08 30	08 45			08 55	09 15			09 30	09 45			09 54	10 14			10 30	10 45		
Mytholmroyd d				08 48			08 58	09 18				09 48			09 58	10 17				10 48		
Sowerby Bridge d				08 54			09 04	09 24				09 54			10 04	10 23				10 54		
Huddersfield 39 d		08 08								09 08								10 08				
London Kings Cross 15 ⊖26 d																						
Brighouse d		08 17						09 33		09 18						10 32		10 17				
Mirfield 39 a								09 40								10 39						
d								09 40								10 39						
Dewsbury 39 a								09 45								10 44						
Halifax a		08 30	08 42	09 01			09 11			09 33	09 42	10 01			10 11			10 33	10 42	11 01		
d		08 30	08 43	09 01			09 12			09 34	09 43	10 01			10 12			10 34	10 43	11 01		
Low Moor d		08 38								09 41								10 41				
Bradford Interchange a		08 49	08 57	09 15			09 27			09 49	09 57	10 15			10 27			10 49	10 57	11 15		
d		08 51	09 00	09 18			09 29			09 51	10 00	10 18			10 30			10 51	11 00	11 18		
New Pudsey 37 a		09 00	09 08	09 26			09 38			10 00	10 08	10 26			10 38			11 00	11 08	11 26		
Bramley 37 a			09 12	09 30			09 42				10 12	10 32			10 42				11 12	11 30		
Leeds 10 37,39 a		09 08	09 21	09 42			09 51	10 04		10 10	10 21	10 43			10 54	11 03		11 09	11 21	11 39		
Selby 40 a							10 30								11 31							
York 8 40 a			10 01								11 01								12 00			

A From Manchester Victoria
B To Blackburn
C From Blackburn
D From Wigan North Western
E From Clitheroe
F From Southport to Blackburn
G From Southport

For connections from Liverpool Lime Street refer to Table T090

Manchester Victoria, Rochdale, Blackpool North and Huddersfield - Bradford and Leeds via Brighouse and Halifax

	NT ◇	NT ◇ A	NT B	NT	NT ◇	NT ◇	NT C	NT D	NT ◇	NT ◇ A	NT B	NT	NT ◇	NT ◇	NT C	NT D	NT ◇	NT ◇ A	NT B	NT	NT ◇	GC 1st class
Manchester Victoria d	10 20	10 37	10 42		10 58		11 04	11 09	11 15	11 37	11 42		11 58		12 04	12 09	12 20	12 37	12 42		12 57	
Moston d			10 50					11 16			11 49					12 16			12 50			
Mills Hill d			10 54					11 20			11 53					12 20			12 54			
Castleton d			11 00					11 25			11 59					12 26			13 00			
Rochdale a	10 33	10 50	11 06		11 12		11 17	11 31	11 33	11 50	12 03		12 12		12 17	12 32	12 34	12 50	13 06		13 10	
d	10 33	10 51			11 12		11 18		11 36	11 51			12 12		12 18		12 35	12 51			13 10	
Smithy Bridge d		10 55					11 22			11 55					12 22			12 55				
Littleborough d		10 58					11 25			11 58					12 25			12 58				
Walsden d		11 04								12 04								13 04				
Todmorden d	10 44	11 07			11 23		11 33		11 46	12 07			12 23		12 33		12 45	13 07			13 21	
Blackpool North 97 d																						
Poulton-le-Fylde 97 d																						
Preston 8 97 d						10 47								11 47								
Blackburn 97 d						11 03								12 03								
Accrington 97 d						11 11								12 11								
Burnley Manchester Road 97 a						11 20	11 49							12 20	12 49							
d						11 20								12 20								
Hebden Bridge a	10 53	11 14			11 30	11 42			11 55	12 14			12 30	12 42			12 53	13 14			13 28	
d	10 54	11 14			11 30	11 42			11 55	12 14			12 30	12 42			12 54	13 14			13 28	
Mytholmroyd d	10 57	11 17				11 46			11 59	12 17				12 46			12 57	13 17				
Sowerby Bridge d	11 03	11 23				11 52			12 05	12 23				12 52			13 03	13 23				
Huddersfield 39 d				11 08								12 08								13 08		
London Kings Cross 15 ⊖26 d																						10 52
Brighouse d		11 32		11 17						12 32		12 17						13 32		13 18		13 36
Mirfield 39 a		11 39								12 39								13 39				
d		11 39								12 39								13 39				
Dewsbury 39 a		11 44								12 44								13 44				
Halifax a	11 10			11 33	11 42	11 58			12 12			12 32	12 42	12 58			13 10			13 33	13 40	13 47
d	11 11			11 33	11 43	11 59			12 13			12 33	12 43	12 59			13 11			13 34	13 41	13 48
Low Moor d				11 41								12 40								13 41		13 55
Bradford Interchange a	11 25			11 48	11 57	12 13			12 27			12 48	12 57	13 13			13 27			13 49	13 57	14 03
d	11 28			11 51	12 00	12 15			12 29			12 50	13 00	13 15			13 29			13 51	14 00	
New Pudsey 37 a	11 38			11 59	12 08	12 23			12 38			12 59	13 08	13 23			13 38			14 00	14 08	
Bramley 37 a	11 42				12 12	12 27			12 42				13 12	13 27			13 42				14 12	
Leeds 10 37,39 a	11 51	12 03		12 09	12 21	12 38			12 53	13 03		13 08	13 21	13 38			13 51	14 03		14 10	14 21	
Selby 40 a	12 30								13 32								14 30					
York 8 40 a					13 01								14 01								15 00	

	NT ◇	NT C	NT D	NT ◇	NT ◇ A	NT B	NT	NT ◇	NT ◇	NT C	NT D	NT ◇	NT ◇ A	NT B	NT	NT ◇	NT ◇	NT C	NT D	NT ◇	NT ◇ A
Manchester Victoria d		13 04	13 09	13 20	13 37	13 42		13 58		14 04	14 09	14 20	14 36	14 43		14 58		15 04	15 09	15 20	15 36
Moston d			13 16			13 50					14 16			14 53					15 16		
Mills Hill d			13 20			13 54					14 20			14 57					15 20		
Castleton d			13 25			14 00					14 25			15 03					15 25		
Rochdale a		13 17	13 31	13 33	13 50	14 06		14 12		14 17	14 31	14 33	14 49	15 08		15 12		15 17	15 31	15 33	15 49
d		13 18		13 34	13 51			14 12		14 18		14 34	14 50			15 12		15 18		15 34	15 49
Smithy Bridge d		13 22			13 55					14 22			14 54					15 22			15 53
Littleborough d		13 25			13 58					14 25			14 57					15 25			15 56
Walsden d					14 04								15 03								16 02
Todmorden d		13 33		13 44	14 07			14 23		14 33		14 44	15 06			15 23		15 33		15 44	16 06
Blackpool North 97 d																					
Poulton-le-Fylde 97 d																					
Preston 8 97 d	12 47								13 47								14 47				
Blackburn 97 d	13 03								14 03								15 04				
Accrington 97 d	13 11								14 11								15 12				
Burnley Manchester Road 97 a	13 20	13 49							14 20	14 49							15 21	15 48			
d	13 20								14 20								15 21				
Hebden Bridge a	13 42			13 53	14 14			14 30	14 42			14 53	15 13			15 30	15 43			15 53	16 14
d	13 42			13 54	14 14			14 30	14 42			14 54	15 13			15 30	15 43			15 54	16 14
Mytholmroyd d	13 46			13 57	14 17				14 46			14 57	15 16				15 47			15 57	16 17
Sowerby Bridge d	13 52			14 03	14 23				14 52			15 03	15 22				15 53			16 03	16 23
Huddersfield 39 d							14 08								15 08						
London Kings Cross 15 ⊖26 d																					
Brighouse d					14 32		14 18						15 31		15 17						16 32
Mirfield 39 a					14 39								15 38								16 39
d					14 39								15 38								16 39
Dewsbury 39 a					14 44								15 43								16 44
Halifax a	13 58			14 10			14 32	14 42	14 58			15 10			15 32	15 42	15 59			16 10	
d	13 59			14 11			14 33	14 43	14 59			15 11			15 33	15 43	16 00			16 11	
Low Moor d							14 40								15 40						
Bradford Interchange a	14 13			14 27			14 48	14 57	15 13			15 27			15 48	15 57	16 14			16 27	
d	14 15			14 29			14 51	15 00	15 15			15 29			15 50	16 00	16 16			16 29	
New Pudsey 37 a	14 23			14 38			15 00	15 08	15 23			15 38			15 59	16 08	16 24			16 38	
Bramley 37 a	14 27			14 42				15 12	15 27			15 42				16 12	16 28			16 42	
Leeds 10 37,39 a	14 38			14 53	15 03		15 10	15 21	15 37			15 51	16 02		16 09	16 21	16 39			16 53	17 03
Selby 40 a				15 30								16 30								17 30	
York 8 40 a								16 02								17 00					

A From Southport
B From Clitheroe
C From Southport to Blackburn
D From Blackburn

For connections from Liverpool Lime Street refer to Table T090

Manchester Victoria, Rochdale, Blackpool North and Huddersfield - Bradford and Leeds via Brighouse and Halifax

		NT A	NT	NT ◇	NT ◇	NT B	NT C	NT ◇	NT ◇ D	NT A	NT	NT ◇	GC	NT ◇	NT B	NT C	NT ◇	NT ◇ D	NT A	NT	NT ◇	NT ◇	GC
Manchester Victoria	d	15 42		15 58		16 04	16 09	16 20	16 37	16 42		16 55			17 04	17 09	17 22	17 37	17 42		17 55		
Moston	d	15 49					16 16			16 54						17 16			17 50				
Mills Hill	d	15 53					16 20	16 29		16 59						17 20	17 31		17 54				
Castleton	d	15 58					16 25			17 05						17 25	17 37		18 00				
Rochdale	a	16 03		16 12		16 17	16 31	16 36	16 50	17 10		17 08			17 17	17 31	17 40	17 50	18 06		18 08		
	d			16 12		16 18		16 36	16 51			17 08			17 18		17 41	17 51			18 08		
Smithy Bridge	d					16 22			16 55			17 12			17 22			17 55			18 12		
Littleborough	d					16 25			16 58			17 16			17 25			17 58			18 16		
Walsden	d					16 31			17 04						17 31			18 04					
Todmorden	d			16 23		16 35		16 47	17 07			17 23			17 35		17 51	18 07			18 23		
Blackpool North	97 d																						
Poulton-le-Fylde	97 d																						
Preston	97 d				15 47									16 47								17 35	
Blackburn	97 d				16 04									17 04								18 03	
Accrington	97 d				16 12									17 12								18 11	
Burnley Manchester Road	97 a				16 21	16 50								17 21	17 51							18 20	
	d				16 21									17 21								18 20	
Hebden Bridge	a			16 30	16 44			16 55	17 14			17 30		17 46			17 58	18 14			18 30	18 42	
	d			16 30	16 44			16 55	17 14			17 30		17 46			17 58	18 14			18 30	18 42	
Mytholmroyd	d				16 48			16 59	17 17					17 50			18 01	18 17				18 46	
Sowerby Bridge	d				16 54			17 05	17 23					17 56			18 07	18 23				18 52	
Huddersfield	39 d		16 08								17 08									18 08			
London Kings Cross 15 ⊖	26 d												14 48										16 27
Brighouse	d		16 17						17 32		17 17		17 35					18 32		18 17			18 51
Mirfield	39 a								17 39									18 39					
	d								17 39									18 39					
Dewsbury	39 a								17 44									18 44					
Halifax	a		16 34	16 42	17 00			17 12			17 34	17 42	17 48	18 02			18 14			18 28	18 42	18 58	19 03
	d		16 35	16 43	17 01			17 13			17 35	17 43	17 50	18 03			18 15			18 28	18 43	18 59	19 04
Low Moor	d		16 42								17 42		17 57							18 36			19 12
Bradford Interchange	a		16 50	16 57	17 15			17 27			17 50	17 57	18 04	18 17			18 29			18 43	18 57	19 13	19 19
	d		16 52	17 00	17 17			17 29			17 52	18 00		18 19			18 31			18 46	19 00	19 15	
New Pudsey	37 a		17 01	17 08	17 25			17 38			18 01	18 08		18 27			18 40			18 54	19 08	19 23	
Bramley	37 a			17 12	17 29			17 42				18 12		18 31			18 44				19 12	19 27	
Leeds 10	37,39 a		17 10	17 21	17 39			17 53	18 03		18 10	18 21		18 41			18 55	19 03		19 07	19 21	19 37	
Selby	40 a			18 08				18 30									19 30						
York 8	40 a											19 01									20 00		

		NT B	NT ◇	NT ◇ D	NT A	NT	NT ◇	NT ◇	NT B	NT A	NT ◇	NT ◇ D	NT A	NT	NT ◇	NT ◇	NT B	NT C	NT ◇	NT ◇ D	NT A	NT
Manchester Victoria	d	18 04	18 22	18 37	18 42		18 55		19 04	19 08	19 26	19 37	19 41		19 58		20 04	20 09	20 25	20 37	20 42	
Moston	d				18 50					19 16			19 49					20 16			20 50	
Mills Hill	d		18 31		18 54					19 20			19 53					20 20			20 54	
Castleton	d		18 37		19 00					19 26			19 59					20 25			21 00	
Rochdale	a	18 17	18 40	18 50	19 06		19 08		19 17	19 32	19 39	19 50	20 05		20 12		20 17	20 31	20 38	20 50	21 05	
	d	18 18	18 41	18 51			19 08		19 18		19 39	19 51			20 12		20 18		20 38	20 51		
Smithy Bridge	d	18 22		18 55			19 12		19 22			19 55					20 22			20 55		
Littleborough	d	18 25		18 58			19 16		19 25			19 58					20 25			20 58		
Walsden	d	18 31		19 04								20 04								21 04		
Todmorden	d	18 35	18 51	19 07			19 23		19 33		19 50	20 07			20 23		20 33		20 49	21 07		
Blackpool North	97 d																					
Poulton-le-Fylde	97 d																					
Preston 8	97 d							18 47								19 47						
Blackburn	97 d							19 03								20 03						
Accrington	97 d							19 11								20 10						
Burnley Manchester Road	97 a	18 51						19 20	19 48							20 19	20 48					
	d							19 20								20 19						
Hebden Bridge	a		18 58	19 14			19 30	19 42			19 56	20 14			20 30	20 41			20 55	21 14		
	d		18 58	19 14			19 30	19 42			19 57	20 14			20 30	20 41			20 56	21 14		
Mytholmroyd	d		19 01	19 17				19 46			20 00	20 17				20 44			20 59	21 17		
Sowerby Bridge	d		19 07	19 23				19 52			20 06	20 23				20 50			21 05	21 23		
Huddersfield	39 d					18 56								20 08								21 08
London Kings Cross 15 ⊖	26 d																					
Brighouse	d			19 32		19 09						20 32		20 18						21 32		21 17
Mirfield	39 a			19 39								20 39								21 39		
	d			19 39								20 39								21 39		
Dewsbury	39 a			19 44								20 44								21 44		
Halifax	a		19 14			19 24	19 42	19 58			20 13			20 33	20 42	20 56			21 12			21 32
	d		19 15			19 26	19 43	19 59			20 14			20 33	20 43	20 57			21 13			21 33
Low Moor	d					19 34								20 41								21 40
Bradford Interchange	a		19 29			19 43	19 57	20 13			20 28			20 48	20 57	21 11			21 27			21 48
	d		19 31			19 46	20 00	20 17			20 30			20 52	20 59	21 15			21 29			21 50
New Pudsey	37 a		19 40			19 54	20 08	20 25			20 39			21 01	21 08	21 23			21 38			21 59
Bramley	37 a		19 44				20 12	20 29			20 43				21 12	21 27			21 42			
Leeds 10	37,39 a		19 53	20 03		20 06	20 21	20 39			20 53	21 03		21 10	21 21	21 37			21 52	22 03		22 09
Selby	40 a		20 30								21 30								22 30			
York 8	40 a						20 59								22 00							

A From Clitheroe
B From Southport to Blackburn
C From Blackburn
D From Southport

For connections from Liverpool Lime Street refer to Table T090

Manchester Victoria, Rochdale, Blackpool North and Huddersfield - Bradford and Leeds via Brighouse and Halifax

		NT ◇	NT ◇	NT A	NT ◇	GC	NT B	NT ◇	NT	NT ◇	NT C	NT	NT ◇	NT C	NT ◇	NT
Manchester Victoria	d	20 55		21 04	21 20		21 38	21 58			22 04	22 42	22 58	23 04	23 20	23 32
Moston	d						21 46					22 50				23 40
Mills Hill	d						21 50					22 54				23 44
Castleton	d						21 56					23 00				23 50
Rochdale	a	21 09		21 17	21 33		22 01	22 12			22 17	23 05	23 12	23 17	23 33	23 55
	d	21 09		21 18	21 33			22 12			22 18		23 12	23 18	23 34	
Smithy Bridge	d			21 22							22 22			23 22	23 38	
Littleborough	d			21 25							22 25			23 25	23 41	
Walsden	d			21 31							22 31				23 47	
Todmorden	d	21 20		21 35	21 44			22 23			22 35		23 23	23 33	23 51	
Blackpool North	97 d															
Poulton-le-Fylde	97 d															
Preston 8	97 d		20 47							21 47						
Blackburn	97 d		21 03							22 03						
Accrington	97 d		21 11							22 11						
Burnley Manchester Road	97 a		21 20	21 51						22 20	22 51			23 49		
	d		21 20							22 20						
Hebden Bridge	a	21 27	21 42		21 53			22 30		22 42			23 30		23 57	
	d	21 27	21 42		21 54			22 30		22 42			23 30		23 58	
Mytholmroyd	d		21 46		21 57					22 46					00 01	
Sowerby Bridge	d		21 52		22 03					22 52					00 07	
Huddersfield	39 d								22 27							
London Kings Cross 15 ⊖	26 d					19 54										
Brighouse	d					22 12			22 35							
Mirfield	39 a															
	d															
Dewsbury	39 a															
Halifax	a	21 39	21 58		22 10	22 25		22 42	22 49	22 58			23 42		00 14	
	d	21 40	21 59		22 11	22 26		22 43	22 51	22 59			23 43		00 15	
Low Moor	d					22 36			22 58							
Bradford Interchange	a	21 54	22 13		22 27	22 46		22 58	23 06	23 13			23 57		00 29	
	d	21 56	22 15		22 29			23 01	23 08	23 16			23 59		00 31	
New Pudsey	37 a	22 05	22 23		22 38			23 09	23 17	23 24			00 08			
Bramley	37 a	22 09	22 27		22 42			23 13	23 21	23 28			00 12			
Leeds 10	37,39 a	22 18	22 38		22 53			23 22	23 30	23 37			00 21		00 50	
Selby	40 a															
York 8	40 a	23 01						00 03								

Saturdays
26 May to 8 December

		NT ◇ D	NT	NT	NT ◇	NT ◇	NT C	NT	NT ◇	NT ◇	NT	NT	NT ◇	NT ◇	NT C	NT E	NT ◇	NT ◇ F	NT B	NT	NT ◇	NT ◇	NT G
Manchester Victoria	d				05 45		06 00	06 09	06 23	06 37	06 42		06 55		07 04	07 09	07 21	07 36	07 42		07 55		08 04
Moston	d				05 52			06 16			06 50					07 16			07 50				
Mills Hill	d				05 57			06 20			06 54					07 20			07 54				
Castleton	d				06 02			06 26			07 00					07 25			08 00				
Rochdale	a				06 06		06 13	06 31	06 36	06 50	07 05		07 08		07 17	07 31	07 34	07 49	08 06		08 08		08 17
	d				06 06		06 14		06 36	06 51			07 09		07 18		07 34	07 50			08 09		08 18
Smithy Bridge	d				06 10		06 18			06 55			07 13		07 22			07 54			08 13		08 22
Littleborough	d				06 14		06 21			06 58			07 16		07 25			07 57			08 16		08 25
Walsden	d				06 20					07 04					07 31			08 03					08 31
Todmorden	d				06 23		06 29		06 47	07 08			07 23		07 35		07 45	08 06			08 23		08 35
Blackpool North	97 d					05 19																	
Poulton-le-Fylde	97 d					05 25																	
Preston 8	97 d					05 44								06 48								07 50	
Blackburn	97 d					06 03								07 04								08 06	
Accrington	97 d					06 11								07 12								08 14	
Burnley Manchester Road	97 a					06 20	06 45							07 21	07 51							08 22	08 51
	d					06 20								07 21								08 23	
Hebden Bridge	a				06 30	06 42			06 54	07 14			07 30	07 43			07 54	08 13			08 30	08 44	
	d		05 47		06 30	06 42			06 54	07 15			07 30	07 43			07 55	08 13			08 30	08 45	
Mytholmroyd	d	00 01	05 50			06 46			06 57	07 18				07 47			07 58	08 16				08 48	
Sowerby Bridge	d	00 07	05 56			06 52			07 03	07 24				07 53			08 04	08 22				08 54	
Huddersfield	39 d			06 07								07 10								08 09			
London Kings Cross 15 ⊖	26 d																						
Brighouse	d			06 22						07 33		07 19						08 31		08 17			
Mirfield	39 a									07 40								08 38					
	d									07 40								08 38					
Dewsbury	39 a									07 45								08 44					
Halifax	a	00 14	06 03	06 32	06 42	06 58			07 10			07 34	07 42	07 59			08 11			08 28	08 42	09 01	
	d	00 15	06 03	06 33	06 43	06 59			07 11			07 34	07 43	08 00			08 12			08 28	08 43	09 01	
Low Moor	d		06 11	06 40								07 42								08 36			
Bradford Interchange	a	00 29	06 19	06 48	06 57	07 13			07 26			07 49	07 57	08 15			08 27			08 46	08 57	09 15	
	d	00 31	06 22	06 50	07 02	07 17			07 29			07 52	08 00	08 17			08 29			08 48	09 00	09 18	
New Pudsey	37 a		06 30	06 59	07 10	07 25			07 38			08 00	08 08	08 25			08 38			08 57	09 08	09 26	
Bramley	37 a		06 34		07 14	07 29			07 42			08 04	08 12	08 30			08 42			09 01	09 12	09 30	
Leeds 10	37,39 a	00 50	06 43	07 12	07 23	07 40			07 56	08 04		08 15	08 21	08 38			08 54	09 03		09 09	09 21	09 42	
Selby	40 a																09 30						
York 8	40 a				08 06								09 02								10 01		

A From Kirkby to Blackburn
B From Clitheroe
C To Blackburn
D From Manchester Victoria
E From Blackburn
F From Wigan North Western
G From Southport to Blackburn

For connections from Liverpool Lime Street refer to Table T090

Table T041-F

Saturdays
26 May to 8 December

Manchester Victoria, Rochdale, Blackpool North and Huddersfield - Bradford and Leeds via Brighouse and Halifax

Station		NT	NT	NT	NT	NT	NT	NT	NT	NT	NT	NT	NT	NT	NT	NT	NT	NT	NT	NT	NT	NT	NT
		A	◇	◇ B	A		◇	◇	C	D	◇	◇ E	A		◇	◇	C	D	◇	◇ E	A		◇
Manchester Victoria	d	08 10	08 21	08 38	08 42		08 58		09 04	09 09	09 20	09 37	09 42		09 58		10 04	10 09	10 20	10 37	10 42		10 58
Moston	d	08 17			08 50					09 16			09 50					10 16			10 50		
Mills Hill	d	08 21			08 54					09 20			09 54					10 20			10 54		
Castleton	d	08 26			09 00					09 25			10 00					10 25			11 00		
Rochdale	a	08 31	08 34	08 51	09 06		09 12		09 17	09 31	09 33	09 50	10 06		10 12		10 17	10 31	10 33	10 50	11 06		11 12
	d		08 34	08 52			09 12		09 18		09 34	09 51			10 12		10 18		10 33	10 51			11 12
Smithy Bridge	d			08 56					09 22			09 55					10 22			10 55			
Littleborough	d			08 59					09 25			09 58					10 25			10 58			
Walsden	d			09 05					09 31			10 04								11 04			
Todmorden	d		08 45	09 08			09 23		09 35		09 44	10 07			10 23		10 33		10 44	11 07			11 23
Blackpool North	97 d																						
Poulton-le-Fylde	97 d																						
Preston 8	97 d							08 50								09 48							
Blackburn	97 d							09 06								10 05							
Accrington	97 d							09 14								10 13							
Burnley Manchester Road	97 a							09 22	09 50							10 21	10 48						
	d							09 23								10 22							
Hebden Bridge	a		08 54	09 15			09 30	09 44			09 54	10 14			10 30	10 44			10 53	11 14			11 30
	d		08 55	09 15			09 30	09 45			09 54	10 14			10 30	10 45			10 54	11 14			11 30
Mytholmroyd	d		08 58	09 18				09 48			09 58	10 17				10 48			10 57	11 17			
Sowerby Bridge	d		09 04	09 24				09 54			10 04	10 23				10 54			11 03	11 23			
Huddersfield	39 d					09 10								10 08								11 08	
London Kings Cross 15 ⊖	26 d																						
Brighouse	d			09 33		09 18						10 32		10 17						11 32		11 17	
Mirfield	39 a			09 40								10 39								11 39			
	d			09 40								10 39								11 39			
Dewsbury	39 a			09 45								10 44								11 44			
Halifax	a		09 11			09 31	09 42	10 01			10 11			10 33	10 42	11 01			11 10			11 33	11 42
	d		09 12			09 32	09 43	10 01			10 12			10 34	10 43	11 01			11 11			11 33	11 43
Low Moor	d					09 39								10 41								11 41	
Bradford Interchange	a		09 27			09 47	09 57	10 15			10 27			10 49	10 57	11 15			11 25			11 48	11 57
	d		09 29			09 49	10 00	10 18			10 30			10 51	11 00	11 18			11 28			11 51	12 00
New Pudsey	37 a		09 38			09 58	10 08	10 26			10 38			11 00	11 08	11 26			11 38			11 59	12 08
Bramley	37 a		09 42			10 02	10 12	10 32			10 42				11 12	11 30			11 42				12 12
Leeds 10	37,39 a		09 52	10 04		10 10	10 21	10 43			10 54	11 03		11 09	11 21	11 39			11 51	12 03		12 09	12 21
Selby	40 a		10 30								11 31								12 30				
York 8	40 a						11 01								12 00								13 01

Station		NT	NT	NT	NT	NT	NT	NT	NT	NT	NT	NT	NT	GC	NT	NT	NT	NT	NT	NT	NT	NT
		◇	C	D	◇	◇ E	A		◇	◇	C	D	◇	■ 1 ⊐	◇ E	A		◇	◇	C	D	◇
Manchester Victoria	d		11 04	11 09	11 20	11 37	11 42		11 58		12 04	12 09	12 20		12 37	12 42		12 58		13 04	13 09	13 20
Moston	d			11 16			11 49					12 16				12 50					13 16	
Mills Hill	d			11 20			11 53					12 20				12 54					13 20	
Castleton	d			11 25			11 59					12 26				13 00					13 25	
Rochdale	a		11 17	11 31	11 36	11 50	12 03		12 12		12 17	12 32	12 34		12 50	13 06		13 12		13 17	13 31	13 33
	d		11 18		11 36	11 51			12 12		12 18		12 35		12 51			13 12		13 18		13 34
Smithy Bridge	d		11 22			11 55					12 22				12 55					13 22		
Littleborough	d		11 25			11 58					12 25				12 58					13 25		
Walsden	d					12 04									13 04							
Todmorden	d		11 33		11 47	12 07			12 23		12 33		12 45		13 07			13 23		13 33		13 44
Blackpool North	97 d																					
Poulton-le-Fylde	97 d																					
Preston 8	97 d	10 47								11 47									12 47			
Blackburn	97 d	11 03								12 03									13 03			
Accrington	97 d	11 11								12 11									13 11			
Burnley Manchester Road	97 a	11 20	11 49							12 20	12 49								13 20	13 49		
	d	11 20								12 20									13 20			
Hebden Bridge	a	11 42			11 55	12 14			12 30	12 42			12 53		13 14			13 30	13 42			13 53
	d	11 42			11 55	12 14			12 30	12 42			12 54		13 14			13 30	13 42			13 54
Mytholmroyd	d	11 46			11 59	12 17				12 46			12 57		13 17				13 46			13 57
Sowerby Bridge	d	11 52			12 05	12 23				12 52			13 03		13 23				13 52			14 03
Huddersfield	39 d							12 08									13 08					
London Kings Cross 15 ⊖	26 d													10 48								
Brighouse	d					12 32		12 17						13 10	13 32		13 18					
Mirfield	39 a					12 39									13 39							
	d					12 39									13 39							
Dewsbury	39 a					12 44									13 44							
Halifax	a	11 58			12 12			12 32	12 42	12 58			13 10	13 20			13 33	13 42	13 58			14 10
	d	11 59			12 13			12 33	12 43	12 59			13 11	13 22			13 33	13 43	13 59			14 11
Low Moor	d							12 40						13 29			13 40					
Bradford Interchange	a	12 13			12 27			12 48	12 57	13 13			13 27	13 37			13 48	13 57	14 13			14 27
	d	12 15			12 29			12 50	13 00	13 15			13 29				13 50	14 00	14 15			14 29
New Pudsey	37 a	12 23			12 38			12 59	13 08	13 23			13 38				13 59	14 08	14 23			14 38
Bramley	37 a	12 27			12 42				13 12	13 27			13 42					14 12	14 27			14 42
Leeds 10	37,39 a	12 38			12 53	13 03		13 08	13 21	13 38			13 51		14 03		14 09	14 21	14 38			14 53
Selby	40 a				13 30								14 30									15 30
York 8	40 a								14 02									15 00				

A From Clitheroe
B From Wigan North Western
C From Southport to Blackburn
D From Blackburn
E From Southport

For connections from Liverpool Lime Street refer to Table T090

Table T041-F

Saturdays
26 May to 8 December

Manchester Victoria, Rochdale, Blackpool North and Huddersfield - Bradford and Leeds via Brighouse and Halifax

Station		NT	NT	NT	NT	NT	NT	NT	NT	NT	NT	NT	NT	NT	NT	NT	NT	NT	NT	NT	NT	NT	NT
		◇ A	B		◇	◇	C	D	◇	◇ A	B		◇	◇	C	D	◇	◇ A	B		◇	◇	C
Manchester Victoria	d	13 37	13 42		13 58		14 04	14 09	14 20	14 36	14 43		14 58		15 04	15 09	15 20	15 36	15 42		15 58		16 04
Moston	d		13 50					14 16			14 53					15 16			15 49				
Mills Hill	d		13 54					14 20			14 57					15 20			15 53				
Castleton	d		14 00					14 25			15 03					15 25			15 58				
Rochdale	a	13 50	14 06		14 12		14 17	14 31	14 33	14 49	15 08		15 12		15 17	15 31	15 33	15 49	16 03		16 12		16 17
	d	13 51			14 12		14 18		14 34	14 50			15 12		15 18		15 34	15 49			16 12		16 18
Smithy Bridge	d	13 55					14 22			14 54					15 22			15 53					16 22
Littleborough	d	13 58					14 25			14 57					15 25			15 56					16 25
Walsden	d	14 04								15 03								16 02					16 31
Todmorden	d	14 07			14 23		14 33		14 44	15 06			15 23		15 33		15 44	16 06			16 23		16 35
Blackpool North	97 d																						
Poulton-le-Fylde	97 d																						
Preston 8	97 d					13 47								14 47								15 47	
Blackburn	97 d					14 03								15 04								16 04	
Accrington	97 d					14 11								15 12								16 12	
Burnley Manchester Road	97 a					14 20	14 49							15 21	15 48							16 21	16 50
	d					14 20								15 21								16 21	
Hebden Bridge	a	14 14			14 30	14 42			14 53	15 13			15 30	15 43			15 53	16 14			16 30	16 44	
	d	14 14			14 30	14 42			14 54	15 13			15 30	15 43			15 54	16 14			16 30	16 44	
Mytholmroyd	d	14 17				14 46			14 57	15 16				15 47			15 57	16 17				16 48	
Sowerby Bridge	d	14 23				14 52			15 03	15 22				15 53			16 03	16 23				16 54	
Huddersfield	39 d			14 10								15 08								16 08			
London Kings Cross 15 ⊖	26 d																						
Brighouse	d	14 32		14 18						15 31		15 17						16 32		16 17			
Mirfield	39 a	14 39								15 38								16 39					
	d	14 39								15 38								16 39					
Dewsbury	39 a	14 44								15 43								16 44					
Halifax	a			14 32	14 42	14 58			15 10			15 32	15 42	15 59			16 10			16 34	16 42	17 00	
	d			14 33	14 43	14 59			15 11			15 33	15 43	16 00			16 11			16 35	16 43	17 01	
Low Moor	d			14 40								15 40								16 42			
Bradford Interchange	a			14 48	14 57	15 13			15 27			15 48	15 57	16 14			16 27			16 50	16 57	17 15	
	d			14 51	15 00	15 15			15 29			15 50	16 00	16 16			16 29			16 52	17 00	17 17	
New Pudsey	37 a			15 00	15 08	15 23			15 38			15 59	16 08	16 24			16 38			17 01	17 08	17 25	
Bramley	37 a				15 12	15 27			15 42				16 12	16 28			16 42				17 12	17 29	
Leeds 10	37,39 a	15 03		15 09	15 22	15 37			15 51	16 02		16 09	16 21	16 39			16 53	17 03		17 10	17 21	17 39	
Selby	40 a								16 30								17 30						
York 8	40 a				16 00								17 00								18 00		

Station		NT	NT	NT	NT	NT	NT	NT	NT	NT	NT	GC	NT	NT	NT	NT	NT	GC	NT	NT	NT	NT
		D	◇	◇ A	B		◇	◇	C	D	◇	■ 1 ⊐	◇ A	B		◇	◇	■ 1 ⊐	C	◇	◇ A	B
Manchester Victoria	d	16 09	16 20	16 37	16 42		16 55		17 04	17 09	17 22		17 37	17 42		17 55			18 04	18 22	18 37	18 42
Moston	d	16 16			16 54					17 16				17 50								18 50
Mills Hill	d	16 20	16 29		16 59					17 20	17 31			17 54						18 31		18 54
Castleton	d	16 25			17 05					17 25	17 37			18 00						18 37		19 00
Rochdale	a	16 31	16 36	16 50	17 10		17 08		17 17	17 31	17 40		17 50	18 06		18 08			18 17	18 40	18 50	19 06
	d		16 36	16 51			17 08		17 18		17 41		17 51			18 08			18 18	18 41	18 51	
Smithy Bridge	d			16 55			17 12		17 22				17 55			18 12			18 22		18 55	
Littleborough	d			16 58			17 16		17 25				17 58			18 16			18 25		18 58	
Walsden	d			17 04					17 31				18 04						18 31		19 04	
Todmorden	d		16 47	17 07			17 23		17 35		17 51		18 07			18 23			18 35	18 51	19 07	
Blackpool North	97 d																					
Poulton-le-Fylde	97 d																					
Preston 8	97 d							16 47									17 35					
Blackburn	97 d							17 04									18 03					
Accrington	97 d							17 12									18 11					
Burnley Manchester Road	97 a							17 21	17 51								18 20		18 51			
	d							17 21									18 20					
Hebden Bridge	a		16 55	17 14			17 30	17 46			17 58		18 14			18 30	18 42			18 58	19 14	
	d		16 55	17 14			17 30	17 46			17 58		18 14			18 30	18 42			18 58	19 14	
Mytholmroyd	d		16 59	17 17				17 50			18 01		18 17				18 46			19 01	19 17	
Sowerby Bridge	d		17 05	17 23				17 56			18 07		18 23				18 52			19 07	19 23	
Huddersfield	39 d					17 08									18 08							
London Kings Cross 15 ⊖	26 d											15 48						16 27				
Brighouse	d			17 32		17 17						18 09	18 32		18 17			18 51			19 32	
Mirfield	39 a			17 39									18 39								19 39	
	d			17 39									18 39								19 39	
Dewsbury	39 a			17 44									18 44								19 44	
Halifax	a		17 12			17 34	17 42	18 02			18 14	18 20			18 28	18 42	18 58	19 03		19 14		
	d		17 13			17 35	17 43	18 03			18 15	18 22			18 28	18 43	18 59	19 04		19 15		
Low Moor	d					17 42						18 30			18 36			19 12				
Bradford Interchange	a		17 27			17 50	17 57	18 17			18 29	18 38			18 43	18 57	19 13	19 19		19 29		
	d		17 29			17 52	18 00	18 19			18 31				18 46	19 00	19 15			19 31		
New Pudsey	37 a		17 38			18 01	18 08	18 27			18 40				18 54	19 08	19 23			19 40		
Bramley	37 a		17 42				18 12	18 31			18 44					19 12	19 27			19 44		
Leeds 10	37,39 a		17 53	18 03		18 10	18 21	18 41			18 55		19 03		19 07	19 21	19 37			19 53	20 03	
Selby	40 a		18 30								19 30									20 30		
York 8	40 a						19 00									20 00						

A From Southport
B From Clitheroe
C From Southport to Blackburn
D From Blackburn

For connections from Liverpool Lime Street refer to Table T090

Table T041-F

Saturdays
26 May to 8 December

Manchester Victoria, Rochdale, Blackpool North and Huddersfield - Bradford and Leeds via Brighouse and Halifax

		NT	NT	NT	NT	NT	NT	NT	NT	NT	NT	NT	NT	NT	NT	NT	NT	NT	NT	NT	NT	NT	NT
			◇	◇	A	B	◇	◇ C	B		◇	◇	A	D	◇	◇ C	B		◇	◇	E	◇	B
Manchester Victoria	d		18 55		19 04	19 08	19 24	19 37	19 41		19 58		20 04	20 09	20 25	20 37	20 42		20 58		21 04	21 20	21 38
Moston	d					19 16			19 49					20 16			20 50						21 46
Mills Hill	d					19 20			19 53					20 20			20 54						21 50
Castleton	d					19 26			19 59					20 25			21 00						21 56
Rochdale	a		19 08		19 17	19 32	19 37	19 50	20 05		20 12		20 17	20 31	20 38	20 50	21 05		21 12		21 17	21 33	22 01
	d		19 08		19 18		19 37	19 51			20 12		20 18		20 38	20 51			21 12		21 18	21 33	
Smithy Bridge	d		19 12		19 22			19 55					20 22			20 55					21 22		
Littleborough	d		19 16		19 25			19 58					20 25			20 58					21 25		
Walsden	d							20 04								21 04					21 31		
Todmorden	d		19 23		19 33		19 49	20 07			20 23		20 33		20 49	21 07			21 23		21 35	21 44	
Blackpool North 97	d																						
Poulton-le-Fylde 97	d																						
Preston 8 97	d			18 47								19 47								20 47			
Blackburn 97	d			19 03								20 03								21 03			
Accrington 97	d			19 11								20 10								21 11			
Burnley Manchester Road 97	a			19 20	19 48							20 19	20 48							21 20	21 51		
	d			19 20								20 19								21 20			
Hebden Bridge	a		19 30	19 42			19 56	20 14			20 30	20 41			20 55	21 14			21 30	21 42		21 53	
	d		19 30	19 42			19 57	20 14			20 30	20 41			20 56	21 14			21 30	21 42		21 54	
Mytholmroyd	d			19 46			20 00	20 17				20 44			20 59	21 17				21 46		21 57	
Sowerby Bridge	d			19 52			20 06	20 23				20 50			21 05	21 23				21 52		22 03	
Huddersfield 39	d	18 56								20 08								21 08					
London Kings Cross 15 ⊖26	d																						
Brighouse	d	19 09						20 32		20 18						21 32		21 17					
Mirfield 39	a							20 39								21 39							
	d							20 39								21 39							
Dewsbury 39	a							20 44								21 44							
Halifax	a	19 24	19 42	19 58			20 13			20 32	20 42	20 56			21 12			21 32	21 42	21 58		22 10	
	d	19 26	19 43	19 59			20 14			20 33	20 43	20 57			21 13			21 33	21 43	21 59		22 11	
Low Moor	d	19 34								20 40								21 40					
Bradford Interchange	a	19 43	19 57	20 13			20 28			20 48	20 57	21 11			21 27			21 48	21 57	22 13		22 27	
	d	19 46	20 00	20 17			20 30			20 50	20 59	21 15			21 29			21 50	22 00	22 15		22 29	
New Pudsey 37	a	19 54	20 08	20 25			20 39			20 59	21 08	21 23			21 38			21 59	22 08	22 23		22 38	
Bramley 37	a		20 12	20 29			20 43				21 12	21 27			21 42				22 12	22 27		22 42	
Leeds 10 37,39	a	20 06	20 21	20 39			20 52	21 03		21 08	21 21	21 37			21 52	22 03		22 09	22 21	22 38		22 53	
Selby 40	a						21 30								22 30								
York 8 40	a		20 59								22 00								23 01				

		NT	NT	GC	NT	NT	NT	NT	NT	NT
			◇		◇	F	F	◇	F	
Manchester Victoria	d		21 58			22 04	22 42	22 58	23 04	23 32
Moston	d						22 49			23 40
Mills Hill	d						22 53			23 44
Castleton	d						22 59			23 50
Rochdale	a		22 12			22 17	23 02	23 11	23 17	23 55
	d		22 12			22 18	23 03	23 12	23 18	
Smithy Bridge	d					22 22			23 22	
Littleborough	d					22 25			23 25	
Walsden	d					22 31		23 21		
Todmorden	d		22 23			22 35	23 15	23 25	23 33	
Blackpool North 97	d									
Poulton-le-Fylde 97	d									
Preston 8 97	d				21 47					
Blackburn 97	d				22 03					
Accrington 97	d				22 11					
Burnley Manchester Road 97	a				22 20	22 51	23 30		23 49	
	d				22 20					
Hebden Bridge	a		22 30		22 42			23 31		
	d		22 30		22 42			23 32		
Mytholmroyd	d				22 46			23 35		
Sowerby Bridge	d				22 52			23 41		
Huddersfield 39	d	22 08								
London Kings Cross 15 ⊖26	d			19 57						
Brighouse	d	22 17		22 41						
Mirfield 39	a									
	d									
Dewsbury 39	a									
Halifax	a	22 32	22 42	22 52	22 58			23 48		
	d	22 32	22 43	22 53	22 59			23 48		
Low Moor	d	22 40		23 01						
Bradford Interchange	a	22 47	22 58	23 08	23 13			00 03		
	d	22 50	23 01		23 16			00 06		
New Pudsey 37	a	22 58	23 09		23 24			00 14		
Bramley 37	a		23 13		23 28			00 18		
Leeds 10 37,39	a	23 11	23 22		23 37			00 28		
Selby 40	a									
York 8 40	a		00 03							

A From Southport to Blackburn
B From Clitheroe
C From Southport
D From Blackburn
E From Kirkby to Blackburn
F To Blackburn

For connections from Liverpool Lime Street refer to Table T090

Table T041-F

Sundays
20 May to 2 December

Manchester Victoria, Rochdale, Blackpool North and Huddersfield - Bradford and Leeds via Brighouse and Halifax

		NT	GC	NT	NT	NT	NT	NT	NT	NT	NT	NT	NT	NT	NT	NT	NT	NT	NT	NT	NT	NT	NT
		◇ A	B	◇		◇	C	D		◇	◇	E		◇	◇	E		◇	◇	E		◇	◇
Manchester Victoria	d						08 33	08 59		09 30		10 00		10 30		11 01		11 30		12 01		12 38	
Moston	d						08 40	09 06				10 07				11 08				12 08			
Mills Hill	d						08 44	09 10				10 11				11 12				12 12			
Castleton	d						08 50	09 16				10 17				11 17				12 18			
Rochdale	a						08 53	09 19		09 43		10 20		10 44		11 21		11 43		12 21		12 51	
	d						08 54	09 20		09 43		10 21		10 44		11 21		11 43		12 21		12 51	
Smithy Bridge	d						08 58	09 24				10 25				11 25				12 25			
Littleborough	d						09 01	09 27		09 49		10 28		10 50		11 28		11 49		12 28		12 57	
Walsden	d									09 55				10 56				11 55				13 03	
Todmorden	d						09 09	09 35		09 58		10 36		10 59		11 36		11 58		12 36		13 06	
Blackpool North 97	d										09 05				10 05				11 05				12 05
Poulton-le-Fylde 97	d										09 11				10 11				11 11				12 11
Preston 8 97	d										09 30				10 30				11 30				12 30
Blackburn 97	d					08 48					09 47				10 47				11 47				12 47
Accrington 97	d					08 56					09 55				10 55				11 55				12 55
Burnley Manchester Road 97	a					09 04	09 25	09 51			10 04	10 52			11 04	11 52			12 04	12 52			13 04
	d					09 05					10 04				11 04				12 04				13 04
Hebden Bridge	a					09 27				10 05	10 27			11 06	11 27			12 05	12 27			13 13	13 27
	d					09 27				10 05	10 27			11 06	11 27			12 05	12 27			13 13	13 27
Mytholmroyd	d					09 31				10 08	10 31			11 09	11 31			12 08	12 31			13 16	13 31
Sowerby Bridge	d					09 37				10 14	10 37			11 15	11 37			12 14	12 37			13 22	13 37
Huddersfield 39	d				08 46				09 34				10 21				11 34				12 34		
London Kings Cross 15 ⊖26	d																						
Brighouse	d				08 54				09 44				10 31				11 44				12 44		
Mirfield 39	a																						
	d																						
Dewsbury 39	a																						
Halifax	a				09 07	09 43			09 57	10 21	10 43		10 47	11 22	11 43		11 56	12 21	12 43		12 57	13 29	13 43
	d			08 44	09 08	09 44			09 58	10 22	10 44		10 50	11 23	11 44		11 57	12 22	12 44		12 58	13 30	13 44
Low Moor	d		07 45		09 16				10 05				10 57				12 04				13 05		
Bradford Interchange	a		08 03	08 57	09 26	09 57			10 13	10 35	10 57		11 05	11 36	11 57		12 12	12 36	12 57		13 13	13 45	13 57
	d	00 06		09 00	09 30	10 00			10 18	10 38	10 59		11 07	11 39	12 00		12 16	12 39	13 00		13 17	13 47	14 00
New Pudsey 37	a	00 14		09 08	09 38	10 08			10 26	10 46	11 07		11 16	11 49	12 08		12 24	12 50	13 08		13 25	13 56	14 08
Bramley 37	a	00 18			09 43				10 31	10 50			11 20	11 53			12 29	12 54			13 30	14 00	
Leeds 10 37,39	a	00 28		09 18	09 52	10 19			10 38	10 59	11 19		11 28	12 02	12 19		12 37	13 05	13 19		13 38	14 11	14 23
Selby 40	a																						
York 8 40	a			10 05		10 59					12 00				13 01				14 01				15 01

		NT	NT	GC	NT	NT	NT	NT	NT	NT	NT	NT	NT	NT	NT	NT	NT	NT	NT	NT	GC	NT	NT
		E			◇	◇	E		◇	◇	E		◇	◇	E		◇	◇	E			◇	◇
Manchester Victoria	d	13 02			13 32		14 02		14 30		15 02		15 27		16 02		16 30		17 02			17 30	
Moston	d	13 09					14 09				15 09				16 09				17 09				
Mills Hill	d	13 13					14 13				15 13				16 13				17 13				
Castleton	d	13 18					14 18				15 18				16 18				17 18				
Rochdale	a	13 22			13 45		14 22		14 43		15 22		15 40		16 22		16 43		17 22			17 43	
	d	13 22			13 45		14 22		14 43		15 22		15 40		16 22		16 43		17 22			17 43	
Smithy Bridge	d	13 26					14 26				15 26				16 26				17 26				
Littleborough	d	13 29			13 51		14 29		14 49		15 29		15 46		16 29		16 49		17 29			17 49	
Walsden	d				13 57				14 55				15 52				16 55					17 55	
Todmorden	d	13 37			14 00		14 37		14 58		15 37		15 55		16 37		16 58		17 37			17 58	
Blackpool North 97	d					13 05				13 52				15 05				16 05					17 05
Poulton-le-Fylde 97	d					13 11				13 58				15 11				16 11					17 11
Preston 8 97	d					13 30				14 18				15 30				16 30					17 30
Blackburn 97	d					13 47				14 39				15 47				16 47					17 47
Accrington 97	d					13 55				14 47				15 55				16 55					17 55
Burnley Manchester Road 97	a	13 52				14 04	14 52			14 55	15 52			16 04	16 52			17 04	17 52				18 04
	d					14 04				14 56				16 04				17 04					18 04
Hebden Bridge	a				14 07	14 27			15 05	15 21			16 02	16 27			17 05	17 27				18 08	18 27
	d				14 07	14 27			15 05	15 23			16 02	16 27			17 05	17 27				18 08	18 27
Mytholmroyd	d				14 10	14 31			15 08	15 26			16 05	16 31			17 08	17 31				18 12	18 31
Sowerby Bridge	d				14 16	14 37			15 14	15 32			16 11	16 37			17 14	17 37				18 22	18 37
Huddersfield 39	d		13 34					14 34				15 34				16 34				17 34			
London Kings Cross 15 ⊖26	d			11 50																	15 50		
Brighouse	d		13 42	14 06				14 44				15 43				16 44				17 44	18 11		
Mirfield 39	a																						
	d																						
Dewsbury 39	a																						
Halifax	a		13 52	14 17	14 23	14 43		14 57	15 21	15 39		15 55	16 18	16 43		16 57	17 21	17 43		17 57	18 24	18 30	18 43
	d		13 53	14 18	14 24	14 44		14 58	15 22	15 39		15 56	16 19	16 44		16 58	17 22	17 44		17 58	18 25	18 31	18 44
Low Moor	d		14 00	14 26				15 05				16 03				17 05				18 05	18 33		
Bradford Interchange	a		14 08	14 34	14 39	14 57		15 13	15 35	15 53		16 12	16 35	16 57		17 13	17 36	17 57		18 13	18 40	18 45	18 57
	d		14 10		14 42	15 00		15 17	15 38	15 56		16 14	16 38	17 00		17 17	17 39	18 00		18 17		18 48	18 59
New Pudsey 37	a		14 19		14 50	15 08		15 25	15 49	16 04		16 23	16 49	17 08		17 25	17 52	18 08		18 25		18 56	19 07
Bramley 37	a		14 23		14 54			15 30	15 54			16 27	16 53			17 30	17 57			18 30		19 00	
Leeds 10 37,39	a		14 31		15 05	15 19		15 38	16 03	16 15		16 35	17 03	17 19		17 38	18 07	18 20		18 38		19 09	19 18
Selby 40	a																						
York 8 40	a					16 01				17 00				18 01				19 01					19 59

A From Manchester Victoria
B from 28 October
C To Blackburn
D From Wigan Wallgate to Blackburn
E From Southport to Blackburn

For connections from Liverpool Lime Street refer to Table T090

Table T041-F

Sundays
20 May to 2 December

Manchester Victoria, Rochdale, Blackpool North and Huddersfield - Bradford and Leeds via Brighouse and Halifax

Station		NT	NT	NT	NT	NT	NT	NT	NT	NT	NT	NT	GC	NT	GC	NT	NT	NT	NT	NT	NT	NT
				◇	◇			◇	◇			◇		◇				◇	◇			◇
		A				A				A						A				A		
Manchester Victoria	d	18 02		18 30		19 02		19 30		20 02		20 30				21 02		21 18		22 02		22 30
Moston	d	18 09				19 09				20 09						21 09				22 09		
Mills Hill	d	18 13				19 13				20 13						21 13				22 13		
Castleton	d	18 18				19 18				20 18						21 18				22 18		
Rochdale	a	18 22		18 43		19 22		19 43		20 22		20 43				21 22		21 31		22 22		22 43
	d	18 22		18 43		19 22		19 43		20 22		20 43				21 22		21 31		22 22		22 43
Smithy Bridge	d	18 26				19 26				20 26						21 26				22 26		
Littleborough	d	18 29		18 49		19 29		19 49		20 29		20 49				21 29		21 37		22 29		22 49
Walsden	d			18 55				19 55				20 55						21 43				22 55
Todmorden	d	18 37		18 58		19 37		19 58		20 37		20 58				21 37		21 46		22 37		22 58
Blackpool North	97 d				17 52				19 05					20 00					21 05			
Poulton-le-Fylde	97 d				17 58				19 11					20 06					21 11			
Preston	97 d				18 19				19 30					20 29					21 30			
Blackburn	97 d				18 36				19 47					20 46					21 47			
Accrington	97 d				18 45				19 55					20 54					21 55			
Burnley Manchester Road	97 a	18 52			18 58	19 52			20 04	20 52				21 03		21 52			22 04	22 52		
	d				18 58				20 04					21 03					22 04			
Hebden Bridge	a			19 05	19 23			20 05	20 27			21 05		21 26				21 54	22 27			23 05
	d			19 05	19 24			20 05	20 27			21 05		21 26				21 54	22 27			23 05
Mytholmroyd	d			19 08	19 27			20 08	20 31			21 08		21 30				21 57	22 31			23 08
Sowerby Bridge	d			19 14	19 33			20 14	20 37			21 14		21 36				22 03	22 37			23 14
Huddersfield	39 d		18 34				19 34				20 34						21 43				22 34	
London Kings Cross ⊖26	d												18 53		19 22							
Brighouse	d		18 44				19 44				20 44		21 18		21 46		21 51				22 44	
Mirfield	39 a																					
	d																					
Dewsbury	39 a																					
Halifax	a		18 57	19 21	19 40		19 57	20 21	20 43		20 55	21 21	21 29	21 42	21 57		22 04	22 10	22 43		22 57	23 21
	d		18 58	19 22	19 40		19 58	20 22	20 44		20 56	21 22	21 30	21 43	21 58		22 05	22 11	22 44		22 58	23 22
Low Moor	d		19 05				20 05				21 03		21 38		22 06		22 12				23 05	
Bradford Interchange	a		19 13	19 39	19 54		20 13	20 35	20 57		21 12	21 37	21 45	21 57	22 13		22 20	22 25	22 57		23 13	23 35
	d		19 17	19 42	19 57		20 17	20 37	21 00		21 15	21 40		21 59			22 22	22 29	23 00		23 17	23 38
New Pudsey	37 a		19 25	19 54	20 05		20 25	20 46	21 08		21 23	21 51		22 07			22 31	22 37	23 08		23 25	23 46
Bramley	37 a		19 30	19 58			20 30	20 50			21 28	21 55					22 35	22 41			23 30	23 50
Leeds	37,39 a		19 38	20 07	20 17		20 38	20 59	21 19		21 36	22 04		22 18			22 43	22 50	23 22		23 38	23 59
Selby	40 a																					
York	40 a				21 01				22 03													

Station		NT
		B
Manchester Victoria	d	23 02
Moston	d	23 09
Mills Hill	d	23 13
Castleton	d	23 19
Rochdale	a	23 23
	d	
Smithy Bridge	d	
Littleborough	d	
Walsden	d	
Todmorden	d	
Blackpool North	97 d	
Poulton-le-Fylde	97 d	
Preston	97 d	
Blackburn	97 d	
Accrington	97 d	
Burnley Manchester Road	97 a	
	d	
Hebden Bridge	a	
	d	
Mytholmroyd	d	
Sowerby Bridge	d	
Huddersfield	39 d	
London Kings Cross ⊖26	d	
Brighouse	d	
Mirfield	39 a	
	d	
Dewsbury	39 a	
Halifax	a	
	d	
Low Moor	d	
Bradford Interchange	a	
	d	
New Pudsey	37 a	
Bramley	37 a	
Leeds	37,39 a	
Selby	40 a	
York	40 a	

A From Southport to Blackburn
B From Southport

For connections from Liverpool Lime Street refer to Table T090

Table T041-R

Mondays to Fridays
21 May to 7 December

Leeds and Bradford - Huddersfield, Blackpool North, Rochdale and Manchester Victoria via Halifax and Brighouse

Miles	Miles	Miles	Miles	Station		NT MO	NT MX	NT MX	NT	NT	NT	NT	NT	NT	NT	NT	NT	NT	NT	NT	NT	GC	NT
											◇	◇		◇			◇		◇	◇			◇
						A	B	A	C			D	E		F	G				H	E		
—	—	—	—	York	40 d													05 18					
—	—	—	—	Selby	40 d																		05 50
0	0	—	0	Leeds	37,39 d					05 01	05 12	05 19		05 36			05 55	06 02	06 18	06 21			06 37
4	4	—	—	Bramley	37 d					05 09	05 21			05 45				06 10	06 26				06 46
5¾	5¾	—	—	New Pudsey	37 d					05 14	05 25			05 49			06 04	06 15	06 30				06 50
9½	9½	—	—	Bradford Interchange	37 a					05 22	05 35			06 00			06 13	06 27	06 39				07 01
—	—	—	—		d		00 01			05 25	05 37			06 03			06 16	06 29	06 41			06 55	07 05
—	—	—	—	Low Moor	d					05 31								06 36				07 01	
17½	17½	0	—	Halifax	a		00 14			05 38	05 49			06 15			06 27	06 43	06 53			07 08	07 17
—	—	—	—		d		00 14			05 39	05 50			06 15			06 28	06 43	06 54			07 08	07 17
—	—	—	9¼	Dewsbury	39 d							05 38								06 38			
—	—	—	12¼	Mirfield	39 a							05 44								06 44			
—	—	—	—		d							05 45								06 47			
—	—	5¼	16¼	Brighouse	d					05 53		05 55						06 57		06 59		07 19	
—	—	—	—	London Kings Cross ⊖26	a																	10 09	
—	—	10½	—	Huddersfield	39 a					06 12								07 15					
21	21	—	22	Sowerby Bridge	d						05 57	06 06		06 23			06 35			07 11			07 24
25	25	—	26	Mytholmroyd	d						06 03	06 12		06 28			06 41			07 16			07 30
26¼	26¼	—	27¼	Hebden Bridge	a		00 26				06 06	06 15		06 31			06 44		07 06	07 20			07 33
—	—	—	—		d						06 07	06 15		06 32			06 45		07 06	07 20			07 34
—	39	—	—	Burnley Manchester Road	97 a												07 04						
—	—	—	—		d										06 38		07 04						
—	45¼	—	—	Accrington	97 a												07 13						
—	51½	—	—	Blackburn	97 a												07 21						
—	63½	—	—	Preston	97 a												07 44						
—	78	—	—	Poulton-le-Fylde	97 a																		
—	81	—	—	Blackpool North	97 a																		
30½	—	—	—	Todmorden	d			00 04			06 14	06 23		06 39	06 55				07 15				07 41
32	—	—	—	Walsden	d							06 26											
36	—	—	—	Littleborough	d			00 11			06 22	06 32			07 02				07 22	07 31			
37	—	—	—	Smithy Bridge	d			00 14				06 35			07 04					07 34			
39¼	—	—	—	Rochdale	a			00 18			06 27	06 39		06 49	07 08				07 27	07 38			07 51
—	—	—	—		d			00 18	05 53		06 27	06 39	06 42	06 50	07 09	07 14			07 28	07 38	07 42		07 51
41	—	—	—	Castleton	d				05 56				06 45			07 17					07 45		
43¾	—	—	—	Mills Hill	d				06 01				06 50			07 22					07 50		
45¾	—	—	—	Moston	d	00 01			06 05				06 54			07 26					07 54		
49¾	—	—	—	Manchester Victoria	a	00 11		00 33	06 13		06 43	06 54	07 03	07 06	07 23	07 35			07 43	07 53	08 03		08 07

Station		NT	NT	NT	NT	NT	NT	NT	GC	NT	NT	NT	NT	NT	NT	NT	NT	NT	NT	NT	NT	NT	NT
				◇		◇	◇			◇			◇		◇	◇		◇			◇		◇
		F	G				H	E			F	G				H	E		F	G			
York	40 d				06 24									07 13								08 16	
Selby	40 d									06 50								07 51					
Leeds	37,39 d			06 52	07 06	07 13	07 21			07 36			07 52	08 07	08 18	08 21		08 36			08 51	09 07	09 19
Bramley	37 d				07 14	07 21				07 45				08 15	08 26			08 45				09 15	09 27
New Pudsey	37 d			07 01	07 19	07 29				07 49			08 01	08 20	08 30			08 49			09 00	09 20	09 31
Bradford Interchange	37 a			07 11	07 28	07 38				07 59			08 10	08 31	08 39			08 59			09 09	09 30	09 42
	d			07 14	07 33	07 41			07 56	08 03			08 13	08 33	08 41			09 03			09 11	09 33	09 45
Low Moor	d				07 39				08 02					08 40								09 39	
Halifax	a			07 26	07 46	07 53			08 09	08 15			08 24	08 47	08 53			09 15			09 23	09 46	09 57
	d			07 26	07 47	07 54			08 09	08 15			08 25	08 47	08 54			09 15			09 23	09 47	09 57
Dewsbury	39 d						07 38									08 38							
Mirfield	39 a						07 43									08 44							
	d						07 43									08 44							
Brighouse	d				08 01		07 55		08 24					09 01		08 56						10 01	
London Kings Cross ⊖26	a								11 15														
Huddersfield	39 a				08 16									09 17								10 16	
Sowerby Bridge	d			07 34			08 06			08 22			08 32			09 06		09 22			09 31		
Mytholmroyd	d			07 40			08 12			08 28			08 38			09 12		09 28			09 37		
Hebden Bridge	a			07 43		08 06	08 15			08 31			08 41		09 06	09 15		09 31			09 40		10 09
	d			07 43		08 06	08 15			08 32			08 42		09 06	09 15		09 32			09 40		10 10
Burnley Manchester Road	97 a			08 04									09 03								10 02		
	d	07 32		08 04							08 38		09 03						09 38		10 03		
Accrington	97 a			08 13									09 12								10 11		
Blackburn	97 a			08 22									09 21								10 20		
Preston	97 a			08 46									09 43								10 38		
Poulton-le-Fylde	97 a																						
Blackpool North	97 a																						
Todmorden	d	07 49				08 15	08 23			08 39	08 55				09 15	09 23		09 39	09 55				10 18
Walsden	d	07 52					08 26									09 26							10 21
Littleborough	d	07 59				08 23	08 32				09 02					09 32			10 02				10 27
Smithy Bridge	d	08 02					08 34				09 05					09 34			10 05				
Rochdale	a	08 06				08 28	08 38			08 49	09 09				09 25	09 38		09 49	10 09				10 32
	d	08 06	08 14			08 28	08 39	08 42		08 49	09 09	09 14			09 26	09 39	09 42	09 49	10 09	10 14			10 33
Castleton	d		08 17					08 45				09 17					09 45			10 17			
Mills Hill	d		08 22			08 35		08 50				09 22					09 50			10 22			
Moston	d		08 26					08 53				09 26					09 54			10 26			
Manchester Victoria	a	08 24	08 35			08 47	08 54	09 03		09 04	09 24	09 35			09 43	09 54	10 03	10 06	10 24	10 35			10 50

A From Blackburn
B From Leeds
C To Kirkby
D To Wigan Wallgate
E To Blackburn
F From Blackburn to Southport
G To Clitheroe
H To Southport

For connections to Liverpool Lime Street refer to Table T090

Leeds and Bradford - Huddersfield, Blackpool North, Rochdale and Manchester Victoria via Halifax and Brighouse

Station	NT	NT	NT	NT	NT	NT	GC	NT	NT	NT	NT	NT	NT	NT	NT	NT	NT	NT	NT	NT ThX	NT ThO	NT
	◇ A	B	◇	C	D	◇			◇	◇ A	B	◇	C	D	◇		◇	◇ A	B	◇	◇	C
York 40 d								09 15								10 15						
Selby 40 d			08 52									09 52								10 52	10 52	
Leeds 37,39 d	09 20		09 36			09 51		10 07	10 18	10 20		10 36			10 51	11 07	11 18	11 20		11 36	11 36	
Bramley 37 d			09 45					10 15	10 26			10 45				11 15	11 26			11 45	11 45	
New Pudsey 37 d			09 49			10 00		10 20	10 30			10 49			11 00	11 20	11 30			11 49	11 49	
Bradford Interchange 37 a			09 59			10 09		10 30	10 39			10 59			11 09	11 30	11 39			11 59	11 59	
d			10 03			10 12	10 22	10 33	10 41			11 03			11 12	11 33	11 41			12 03	12 03	
Low Moor d							10 28	10 39								11 39						
Halifax a			10 15			10 24	10 35	10 46	10 53			11 15			11 23	11 46	11 53			12 15	12 15	
d			10 15			10 24	10 35	10 47	10 54			11 15			11 24	11 47	11 54			12 15	12 15	
Dewsbury 39 d	09 38									10 38								11 38				
Mirfield 39 a	09 44									10 44								11 44				
d	09 44									10 44								11 44				
Brighouse d	09 55						10 47	11 01		10 55						12 01		11 55				
London Kings Cross ⊖26 a							13 44															
Huddersfield 39 a								11 16								12 16						
Sowerby Bridge d	10 09		10 22			10 32				11 06		11 22			11 31			12 06		12 22	12 22	
Mytholmroyd d	10 15		10 28			10 38				11 12		11 28			11 37			12 12		12 28	12 28	
Hebden Bridge a	10 18		10 31			10 41			11 06	11 15		11 31			11 40		12 06	12 15		12 31	12 31	
d	10 18		10 32			10 41			11 06	11 15		11 32			11 41		12 06	12 15		12 32	12 32	
Burnley Manchester Road 97 a						11 02									12 02							
d				10 38		11 03							11 38		12 03							12 38
Accrington 97 a						11 11									12 11							
Blackburn 97 a						11 20									12 20							
Preston 97 a						11 39									12 39							
Poulton-le-Fylde 97 a																						
Blackpool North 97 a																						
Todmorden d	10 26		10 39	10 55					11 14	11 23		11 39	11 55				12 15	12 23		12 39	12 39	12 55
Walsden d										11 26								12 26				
Littleborough d				11 02						11 32			12 02					12 32				13 02
Smithy Bridge d	10 34			11 05						11 35			12 05					12 35				13 05
Rochdale a	10 38		10 49	11 09					11 24	11 39		11 49	12 09				12 25	12 39		12 49	12 51	13 09
d	10 38	10 42	10 49	11 09	11 16				11 24	11 39	11 42	11 49	12 09	12 17			12 26	12 39	12 42	12 49	12 52	13 09
Castleton d		10 45			11 19						11 45			12 20					12 45			
Mills Hill d		10 50			11 24				11 31		11 50			12 25					12 50			
Moston d		10 54			11 27						11 54			12 29					12 54			
Manchester Victoria a	10 53	11 03	11 05	11 24	11 39				11 43	11 54	12 03	12 04	12 24	12 39			12 45	12 54	13 03	13 05	13 15	13 24

Station	NT	NT	NT	NT	NT	NT	NT	NT	NT	NT	NT	NT	NT	NT	NT	NT	NT	NT	NT	NT	NT
	D	◇		◇	◇ A	B	◇	C	D	◇		◇	◇ A	B	◇	C	D	◇		◇	◇ A
York 40 d			11 15								12 15								13 15		
Selby 40 d							11 52								12 52						
Leeds 37,39 d		11 51	12 07	12 18	12 20		12 36			12 51	13 07	13 18	13 20		13 36			13 51	14 07	14 18	14 20
Bramley 37 d			12 15	12 26			12 45				13 15	13 26			13 45				14 15	14 26	
New Pudsey 37 d		12 00	12 20	12 30			12 49			13 00	13 20	13 30			13 49			14 00	14 20	14 30	
Bradford Interchange 37 a		12 09	12 30	12 39			12 59			13 09	13 30	13 39			13 59			14 09	14 30	14 39	
d		12 12	12 33	12 41			13 03			13 12	13 33	13 41			14 04			14 12	14 33	14 41	
Low Moor d			12 39								13 39								14 39		
Halifax a		12 23	12 46	12 53			13 15			13 23	13 46	13 53			14 16			14 23	14 46	14 53	
d		12 24	12 47	12 54			13 15			13 24	13 47	13 54			14 16			14 24	14 47	14 54	
Dewsbury 39 d					12 38								13 38								14 38
Mirfield 39 a					12 44								13 44								14 44
d					12 44								13 44								14 44
Brighouse d			13 01		12 55						14 01		13 55						15 01		14 55
London Kings Cross ⊖26 a																					
Huddersfield 39 a			13 16								14 16								15 16		
Sowerby Bridge d		12 31			13 06		13 22			13 31			14 06		14 23			14 31			15 06
Mytholmroyd d		12 37			13 12		13 28			13 37			14 12		14 29			14 37			15 12
Hebden Bridge a		12 40		13 06	13 15		13 31			13 40		14 06	14 15		14 32			14 40		15 06	15 15
d		12 41		13 06	13 15		13 32			13 41		14 06	14 15		14 33			14 41		15 06	15 15
Burnley Manchester Road 97 a		13 02								14 02								15 02			
d		13 03						13 38		14 03						14 38		15 03			
Accrington 97 a		13 11								14 11								15 11			
Blackburn 97 a		13 20								14 20								15 20			
Preston 97 a		13 38								14 38								15 38			
Poulton-le-Fylde 97 a																					
Blackpool North 97 a																					
Todmorden d				13 15	13 23		13 39	13 55				14 14	14 23		14 40	14 55				15 15	15 23
Walsden d					13 26								14 26								15 26
Littleborough d					13 32			14 02					14 32			15 02					15 32
Smithy Bridge d					13 35			14 05					14 35			15 05					15 35
Rochdale a				13 25	13 39		13 49	14 09				14 24	14 39		14 50	15 09				15 25	15 39
d	13 16			13 26	13 39	13 42	13 49	14 09	14 13			14 25	14 39	14 42	14 50	15 09	15 16			15 26	15 39
Castleton d	13 19					13 45			14 16					14 45			15 19				
Mills Hill d	13 24					13 50			14 21					14 50			15 24				
Moston d	13 28					13 54			14 25					14 54			15 28				
Manchester Victoria a	13 39			13 43	13 54	14 03	14 10	14 24	14 35			14 43	14 54	15 03	15 05	15 24	15 39			15 43	15 54

A To Southport
B To Blackburn
C From Blackburn to Southport
D To Clitheroe

For connections to Liverpool Lime Street refer to Table T090

Table T041-R

Mondays to Fridays

21 May to 7 December

Leeds and Bradford - Huddersfield, Blackpool North, Rochdale and Manchester Victoria via Halifax and Brighouse

Station	NT	GC	NT	NT	NT	NT	NT	NT	NT	NT	NT	NT	NT	NT	NT	NT	NT	NT	NT	NT	NT	NT
	A		◇	B	A	◇		◇	C	◇ D	◇	E	A	◇ F		◇	◇ D	◇	C	G	A	◇
York 40 d							14 15								15 15							
Selby 40 d			13 52								14 52							15 52				
Leeds 37,39 d			14 36			14 51	15 07	15 18		15 20	15 36			15 51	16 07	16 18	16 20	16 36				16 51
Bramley 37 d			14 45				15 15	15 26			15 45				16 15	16 26		16 45				
New Pudsey 37 d			14 49			15 00	15 20	15 30			15 49			16 00	16 20	16 30		16 49				17 00
Bradford Interchange 37 a			14 59			15 09	15 30	15 39			15 59			16 09	16 30	16 39		16 59				17 09
d		14 49	15 03			15 12	15 33	15 41			16 03			16 13	16 33	16 41		17 03				17 13
Low Moor d		14 55					15 39								16 39							
Halifax a		15 02	15 15			15 23	15 46	15 53			16 15			16 25	16 46	16 53		17 15				17 25
d		15 04	15 15			15 24	15 47	15 54			16 15			16 25	16 47	16 54		17 15				17 25
Dewsbury 39 d										15 38							16 38					
Mirfield 39 a										15 44							16 45					
d										15 44							16 46					
Brighouse d		15 17					16 01			15 55					17 01		16 55					
London Kings Cross ⊖26 a		18 07																				
Huddersfield 39 a							16 16								17 16							
Sowerby Bridge d			15 22			15 31				16 06	16 22			16 33			17 07	17 22				17 33
Mytholmroyd d			15 28			15 37				16 12	16 28			16 39			17 12	17 28				17 39
Hebden Bridge a			15 31			15 40		16 06		16 15	16 31			16 42		17 06	17 15	17 31				17 42
d			15 32			15 41		16 06		16 15	16 32			16 42		17 06	17 16	17 32				17 42
Burnley Manchester Road 97 a						16 02								17 02								18 02
d				15 38		16 03						16 36		17 03						17 38		18 03
Accrington 97 a						16 11								17 11								18 11
Blackburn 97 a						16 20								17 20								18 20
Preston 97 a						16 38								17 41								18 38
Poulton-le-Fylde 97 a																						
Blackpool North 97 a																						
Todmorden d			15 39	15 55				16 15		16 23	16 39	16 53				17 14	17 23	17 39		17 55		
Walsden d										16 26		16 56					17 26					
Littleborough d				16 02						16 32		17 02				17 22	17 33			18 02		
Smithy Bridge d				16 05						16 35		17 05				17 24	17 35			18 05		
Rochdale a			15 49	16 09				16 25		16 39	16 49	17 09				17 28	17 39	17 49		18 09		
d	15 42		15 49	16 09	16 14			16 26	16 34	16 39	16 49	17 09	17 14			17 29	17 40	17 49	17 53	18 09	18 18	
Castleton d	15 45				16 17								17 17						17 56		18 21	
Mills Hill d	15 50				16 22				16 40				17 22						18 01			
Moston d	15 54				16 26								17 26						18 05			
Manchester Victoria a	16 03		16 05	16 24	16 35			16 41	17 02	16 54	17 04	17 24	17 35			17 44	17 54	18 04	18 14	18 24	18 34	

Station	NT	NT	NT	NT	NT	NT	NT	NT	NT	NT	NT	NT	NT	NT	NT	NT	NT	NT	NT	NT	NT
		◇	◇ D		◇	B	A	◇		◇	◇ H	C	◇	B	A	◇		◇ I	C	◇	J
York 40 d	16 15								17 15												
Selby 40 d					16 52								17 52				18 23			18 52	
Leeds 37,39 d	17 07	17 18	17 21	17 25	17 36			17 51	18 09	18 20	18 23		18 36			18 51	19 07	19 21		19 36	
Bramley 37 d	17 15	17 26		17 32	17 45				18 17	18 28			18 45				19 15			19 45	
New Pudsey 37 d	17 20	17 30		17 38	17 49			18 00	18 22	18 32			18 49			19 00	19 20			19 49	
Bradford Interchange 37 a	17 30	17 39		17 47	17 59			18 11	18 32	18 41			19 00			19 09	19 32			19 59	
d	17 33	17 41		17 54	18 03			18 14	18 35	18 43			19 03			19 12	19 35			20 03	
Low Moor d	17 39								18 41								19 41				
Halifax a	17 46	17 53		18 06	18 15			18 25	18 48	18 55			19 15			19 24	19 48			20 15	
d	17 47	17 54		18 06	18 15			18 26	18 49	18 56			19 15			19 24	19 49			20 15	
Dewsbury 39 d			17 38								18 40							19 38			
Mirfield 39 a			17 45								18 46							19 44			
d			17 45								18 46							19 44			
Brighouse d	18 01		17 56						19 02		18 57						20 02	19 56			
London Kings Cross ⊖26 a																					
Huddersfield 39 a	18 16								19 18								20 18				
Sowerby Bridge d			18 06	18 14	18 22			18 33			19 09		19 22			19 32		20 08		20 22	
Mytholmroyd d			18 12	18 20	18 28			18 39			19 14		19 28			19 38		20 14		20 28	
Hebden Bridge a		18 06	18 15	18 23	18 31			18 42		19 08	19 17		19 31			19 41		20 17		20 31	
d		18 06	18 15		18 32			18 43		19 08	19 18		19 32			19 41		20 17		20 32	
Burnley Manchester Road 97 a								19 03								20 02					
d						18 38		19 04						19 38		20 03					20 36
Accrington 97 a								19 12								20 11					
Blackburn 97 a								19 21								20 20					
Preston 97 a								19 40								20 38					
Poulton-le-Fylde 97 a																					
Blackpool North 97 a																					
Todmorden d		18 14	18 23		18 39	18 55				19 15	19 25		19 39	19 55				20 25		20 39	20 53
Walsden d			18 26								19 28							20 28			20 56
Littleborough d			18 32			19 02				19 23				20 02							21 02
Smithy Bridge d			18 35			19 05					19 35			20 05				20 35			21 05
Rochdale a		18 24	18 39		18 49	19 09				19 28	19 39		19 49	20 09				20 39		20 49	21 09
d		18 24	18 39		18 49	19 09	19 14			19 28	19 40	19 42	19 49	20 09	20 14			20 39	20 42	20 49	21 09
Castleton d							19 17					19 45			20 17				20 45		
Mills Hill d		18 31					19 22					19 50			20 22				20 50		
Moston d		18 34					19 26					19 54			20 26				20 53		
Manchester Victoria a		18 45	18 54		19 04	19 24	19 35			19 44	19 54	20 03	20 05	20 24	20 35			20 54	21 02	21 04	21 24

A To Clitheroe
B From Blackburn to Southport
C To Blackburn
D To Southport
E From Blackburn to Wigan North Western
F To Barrow-in-Furness
G From Blackburn to Kirkby
H To Wigan North Western
I To Wigan Wallgate
J From Blackburn to Wigan Wallgate

For connections to Liverpool Lime Street refer to Table T090

Table T041-R

Mondays to Fridays
21 May to 7 December

Leeds and Bradford - Huddersfield, Blackpool North, Rochdale and Manchester Victoria via Halifax and Brighouse

		NT	NT	NT	NT	NT	NT	NT	NT	NT	NT	NT	NT	NT FO	NT FX	NT	NT	NT	NT	NT	NT	NT	NT
		A	◇		◇	◇ B		◇	C	◇		◇	◇	D	E	◇	F	◇		◇		◇	
York 🅱	40 d			19 15							20 20								21 15				22 17
Selby	40 d							19 51								20 52						21 52	
Leeds	37,39 d		19 51	20 07	20 19	20 21		20 39		20 49	21 07	21 18	21 21			21 39		22 00	22 07	22 18	22 21	22 38	23 07
Bramley	37 d			20 15	20 27			20 47			21 15	21 26				21 48			22 15	22 26		22 46	23 15
New Pudsey	37 d		20 00	20 20	20 31			20 51		20 58	21 20	21 30				21 52		22 09	22 20	22 30		22 51	23 20
Bradford Interchange	37 a		20 09	20 31	20 40			21 00		21 08	21 30	21 39				22 02		22 18	22 30	22 41		23 00	23 30
	d		20 11	20 34	20 42			21 02		21 11	21 33	21 41				22 04		22 20	22 33	22 45		23 03	23 33
Low Moor	d			20 40							21 39								22 39				23 39
Halifax	a		20 23	20 47	20 54			21 16		21 23	21 46	21 53				22 16		22 32	22 46	22 57		23 15	23 46
	d		20 23	20 48	20 55			21 16		21 23	21 47	21 54				22 17		22 32	22 47	22 58		23 15	23 47
Dewsbury	39 d					20 38							21 38								22 38		
Mirfield	39 a					20 44							21 44								22 44		
	d					20 44							21 44								22 44		
Brighouse	d			21 01		20 56					22 01		21 56						23 01		22 56		23 57
London Kings Cross 🅱 ⊖26	a																						
Huddersfield	39 a			21 16							22 16								23 16				00 09
Sowerby Bridge	d		20 31			21 07		21 24		21 32			22 06			22 24		22 40			23 11		
Mytholmroyd	d		20 37			21 13		21 30		21 38			22 12			22 30		22 46			23 16		
Hebden Bridge	a		20 40		21 07	21 16		21 33		21 41		22 06	22 15			22 33		22 49		23 10	23 19	23 27	
	d		20 40		21 07	21 16		21 33		21 41		22 06	22 15			22 33		22 49		23 10		23 28	
Burnley Manchester Road	97 a		21 02							22 02								23 10					
	d		21 03						21 41	22 03							22 38	23 11					
Accrington	97 a		21 11							22 11								23 19					
Blackburn	97 a		21 20							22 20								23 28					
Preston 🅱	97 a		21 39							22 42								23 46					
Poulton-le-Fylde	97 a																	00 03					
Blackpool North	97 a																	00 11					
Todmorden	d				21 16	21 24		21 41	21 58			22 15	22 23			22 41	22 55			23 19		23 35	
Walsden	d					21 27			22 01				22 26				22 58					23 38	
Littleborough	d				21 23				22 07				22 32				23 04					23 44	
Smithy Bridge	d					21 34			22 10				22 35				23 07					23 47	
Rochdale	a				21 28	21 38		21 51	22 14			22 25	22 39			22 51	23 11			23 29		23 51	
	d	21 15			21 28	21 39	21 42	21 52	22 14			22 26	22 39	22 43	22 43	22 52	23 11			23 30		23 51	
Castleton	d	21 18					21 45							22 46	22 46		23 14						
Mills Hill	d	21 23					21 50							22 51	22 51		23 20						
Moston	d				21 37		21 54							22 55	22a55		23 24						
Manchester Victoria	a	21 33			21 47	21 53	22 03	22 08	22 29			22 43	22 54	23 06		23 11	23 33			23 48		00 07	

		NT	NT
			G
York 🅱	40 d		
Selby	40 d		
Leeds	37,39 d	23 38	
Bramley	37 d	23 45	
New Pudsey	37 d	23 50	
Bradford Interchange	37 a	23 58	
	d	00 01	
Low Moor	d		
Halifax	a	00 14	
	d	00 14	
Dewsbury	39 d		
Mirfield	39 a		
	d		
Brighouse	d		
London Kings Cross 🅱 ⊖26	a		
Huddersfield	39 a		
Sowerby Bridge	d		
Mytholmroyd	d		
Hebden Bridge	a	00 26	
Burnley Manchester Road	97 a		
	d		23 45
Accrington	97 a		
Blackburn	97 a		
Preston 🅱	97 a		
Poulton-le-Fylde	97 a		
Blackpool North	97 a		
Todmorden	d		00 04
Walsden	d		
Littleborough	d		00 11
Smithy Bridge	d		00 14
Rochdale	a		00 18
	d		00 18
Castleton	d		
Mills Hill	d		
Moston	d		
Manchester Victoria	a		00 33

A To Clitheroe
B To Southport
C From Blackburn to Southport
D To Blackburn
E To Newton Heath T.M.D.
F From Blackburn to Wigan Wallgate
G From Blackburn

For connections to Liverpool Lime Street refer to Table T090

Table T041-R

Saturdays
26 May to 8 December

Leeds and Bradford - Huddersfield, Blackpool North, Rochdale and Manchester Victoria via Halifax and Brighouse

		NT	NT	NT	NT	NT	NT	NT	NT	NT	NT	NT	NT	NT	NT	NT	GC	NT	NT	NT	NT	NT	NT
		A	B	C	◇		◇ D	E	◇	F	G	◇		◇	◇ H	E	■ ■	◇	F	G	◇		◇
York 🅱	40 d												05 18									06 24	
Selby	40 d																	05 50					
Leeds	37,39 d				05 02	05 08	05 19		05 36			05 55	06 02	06 18	06 21			06 38			06 52	07 06	07 13
Bramley	37 d				05 11	05 16			05 45				06 10	06 26				06 47				07 14	07 21
New Pudsey	37 d				05 15	05 21			05 49			06 04	06 15	06 30				06 51			07 01	07 19	07 29
Bradford Interchange	37 a				05 24	05 32			06 00			06 13	06 27	06 39				07 01			07 11	07 28	07 38
	d	00 01			05 26	05 34			06 03			06 16	06 29	06 41			06 55	07 05			07 14	07 33	07 41
Low Moor	d					05 41							06 36				07 01					07 39	
Halifax	a	00 14			05 38	05 48			06 15			06 27	06 43	06 53			07 08	07 17			07 26	07 46	07 53
	d	00 14			05 39	05 48			06 15			06 28	06 43	06 54			07 09	07 17			07 26	07 47	07 54
Dewsbury	39 d						05 38								06 38								
Mirfield	39 a						05 44								06 44								
	d						05 45								06 47								
Brighouse	d					05 59	05 55						06 57		06 59		07 20					08 01	
London Kings Cross 🅱 ⊖26	a																10 05						
Huddersfield	39 a					06 20							07 15									08 16	
Sowerby Bridge	d				05 46		06 06		06 23			06 35			07 11			07 24			07 34		
Mytholmroyd	d				05 52		06 12		06 28			06 41			07 16			07 30			07 40		
Hebden Bridge	a	00 26			05 55		06 15		06 31			06 44		07 06	07 20			07 33			07 43		08 06
	d				05 56		06 15		06 32			06 45		07 06	07 20			07 34			07 43		08 06
Burnley Manchester Road	97 a											07 04									08 04		
	d									06 38		07 04							07 32		08 04		
Accrington	97 a											07 13									08 13		
Blackburn	97 a											07 21									08 22		
Preston 🅱	97 a											07 44									08 46		
Poulton-le-Fylde	97 a																						
Blackpool North	97 a																						
Todmorden	d		00 04		06 04		06 23		06 39	06 55				07 15				07 41	07 49				08 15
Walsden	d						06 26												07 52				
Littleborough	d		00 11		06 11		06 32			07 02				07 22	07 31				07 59				08 23
Smithy Bridge	d		00 14				06 35			07 04					07 34				08 02				
Rochdale	a		00 18		06 16		06 39		06 49	07 08				07 27	07 38			07 51	08 06				08 28
	d		00 18	05 53	06 17		06 39	06 42	06 50	07 09	07 14			07 28	07 38	07 42		07 51	08 06	08 14			08 28
Castleton	d			05 56				06 45			07 17					07 45				08 17			
Mills Hill	d			06 01				06 50			07 22					07 50				08 22			08 35
Moston	d			06 05				06 54			07 26					07 54				08 26			
Manchester Victoria	a		00 33	06 13	06 35		06 54	07 03	07 06	07 23	07 35			07 43	07 53	08 03		08 07	08 24	08 35			08 47

		NT	NT	NT	NT	NT	NT	NT	NT	NT	NT	GC	NT	NT	NT	NT	NT	NT	NT	NT	NT	NT	NT
		◇ H	E	◇	F	G	◇		◇	◇ H	E	■ ■	◇	F	G	◇		◇	◇ H	E	◇	F	G
York 🅱	40 d							07 13									08 16						
Selby	40 d			06 50									07 51								08 52		
Leeds	37,39 d	07 21		07 36			07 52	08 07	08 18	08 21			08 36			08 51	09 07	09 19	09 20		09 36		
Bramley	37 d			07 45				08 15	08 26				08 45				09 15	09 27			09 45		
New Pudsey	37 d			07 49			08 01	08 20	08 30				08 49			09 00	09 20	09 31			09 49		
Bradford Interchange	37 a			07 59			08 10	08 30	08 39				08 59			09 09	09 30	09 40			09 59		
	d			08 03			08 13	08 33	08 41			08 51	09 03			09 11	09 33	09 42			10 03		
Low Moor	d							08 39				08 57					09 39						
Halifax	a			08 15			08 24	08 46	08 53			09 04	09 15			09 23	09 46	09 54			10 15		
	d			08 15			08 25	08 47	08 54			09 05	09 15			09 23	09 47	09 55			10 15		
Dewsbury	39 d	07 38								08 38									09 38				
Mirfield	39 a	07 43								08 44									09 44				
	d	07 43								08 44									09 44				
Brighouse	d	07 55						09 01		08 56		09 16					10 01		09 55				
London Kings Cross 🅱 ⊖26	a											11 58											
Huddersfield	39 a							09 17									10 16						
Sowerby Bridge	d	08 06		08 22			08 32			09 06			09 22			09 31			10 09		10 22		
Mytholmroyd	d	08 12		08 28			08 38			09 12			09 28			09 37			10 15		10 28		
Hebden Bridge	a	08 15		08 31			08 41		09 06	09 15			09 31			09 40		10 07	10 18		10 31		
	d	08 15		08 32			08 42		09 06	09 15			09 32			09 40		10 07	10 18		10 32		
Burnley Manchester Road	97 a						09 03									10 02							
	d				08 38		09 03							09 38		10 03						10 38	
Accrington	97 a						09 12									10 11							
Blackburn	97 a						09 21									10 20							
Preston 🅱	97 a						09 43									10 38							
Poulton-le-Fylde	97 a																						
Blackpool North	97 a																						
Todmorden	d	08 23		08 39	08 55				09 15	09 23			09 39	09 55				10 16	10 26		10 39	10 55	
Walsden	d	08 26								09 26													
Littleborough	d	08 32			09 02					09 32				10 02								11 02	
Smithy Bridge	d	08 34			09 05					09 34				10 05					10 34			11 05	
Rochdale	a	08 38		08 49	09 09				09 25	09 38			09 49	10 09				10 26	10 38		10 49	11 09	
	d	08 39	08 42	08 49	09 09	09 14			09 26	09 39	09 42		09 49	10 09	10 14			10 27	10 38	10 42	10 49	11 09	11 13
Castleton	d		08 45			09 17					09 45				10 17					10 45			11 16
Mills Hill	d		08 50			09 22					09 50				10 22					10 50			
Moston	d		08 53			09 26					09 54				10 26					10 54			11 23
Manchester Victoria	a	08 54	09 03	09 04	09 24	09 35			09 43	09 54	10 03		10 05	10 24	10 35			10 44	10 53	11 03	11 05	11 24	11 32

A From Leeds
B From Blackburn
C To Kirkby
D To Wigan Wallgate
E To Blackburn
F From Blackburn to Southport
G To Clitheroe
H To Southport

For connections to Liverpool Lime Street refer to Table T090

Leeds and Bradford - Huddersfield, Blackpool North, Rochdale and Manchester Victoria via Halifax and Brighouse

	NT	GC	NT	NT	NT	NT	NT	NT	NT	NT	NT	NT	NT	NT	NT	NT	NT	NT	NT	NT	NT
	◇	1		◇	◇		◇			◇		◇	◇		◇			◇		◇	◇
					A	B		C	D				A	B		C	D				A
York 40 d			09 19								10 17								11 17		
Selby 40 d							09 52								10 52						
Leeds 37,39 d	09 51		10 07	10 18	10 20		10 36			10 51	11 07	11 18	11 20		11 36			11 51	12 07	12 18	12 20
Bramley 37 d			10 15	10 26			10 45				11 15	11 26			11 45				12 15	12 26	
New Pudsey 37 d	10 00		10 20	10 30			10 49			11 00	11 20	11 30			11 49			12 00	12 20	12 30	
Bradford Interchange 37 a	10 09		10 30	10 39			10 59			11 09	11 30	11 39			11 59			12 09	12 30	12 39	
d	10 12	10 21	10 33	10 41			11 03			11 12	11 33	11 41			12 03			12 12	12 33	12 41	
Low Moor d		10 27	10 39								11 39								12 39		
Halifax a	10 24	10 34	10 46	10 53			11 15			11 23	11 46	11 53			12 15			12 23	12 46	12 53	
d	10 24	10 35	10 47	10 54			11 15			11 24	11 47	11 54			12 15			12 24	12 47	12 54	
Dewsbury 39 d					10 38								11 38								12 38
Mirfield 39 a					10 44								11 44								12 44
d					10 44								11 44								12 44
Brighouse d		10 48	11 01		10 55						12 01		11 55						13 01		12 55
London Kings Cross ⊖26 a		13 44																			
Huddersfield 39 a			11 16								12 16								13 16		
Sowerby Bridge d	10 32				11 06		11 22			11 31			12 06		12 22			12 31			13 06
Mytholmroyd d	10 38				11 12		11 28			11 37			12 12		12 28			12 37			13 12
Hebden Bridge a	10 41			11 06	11 15		11 31			11 40		12 06	12 15		12 31			12 40		13 06	13 15
d	10 41			11 06	11 15		11 32			11 41		12 06	12 15		12 32			12 41		13 06	13 15
Burnley Manchester Road 97 a	11 02									12 02								13 02			
d	11 03							11 38		12 03						12 38		13 03			
Accrington 97 a	11 11									12 11								13 11			
Blackburn 97 a	11 20									12 20								13 20			
Preston 97 a	11 39									12 39								13 38			
Poulton-le-Fylde 97 a																					
Blackpool North 97 a																					
Todmorden d				11 14	11 23		11 39	11 55				12 15	12 23		12 39	12 55				13 15	13 23
Walsden d					11 26								12 26								13 26
Littleborough d					11 32			12 02					12 32			13 02					13 32
Smithy Bridge d					11 35			12 05					12 35			13 05					13 35
Rochdale a				11 24	11 39		11 49	12 09				12 25	12 39		12 49	13 09				13 25	13 39
d				11 24	11 39	11 42	11 49	12 09	12 17			12 26	12 39	12 42	12 49	13 09	13 16			13 26	13 39
Castleton d						11 45			12 20					12 45			13 19				
Mills Hill d				11 31		11 50			12 25					12 50			13 24				
Moston d						11 54			12 29					12 54			13 28				
Manchester Victoria a				11 43	11 54	12 03	12 04	12 24	12 39			12 45	12 54	13 03	13 05	13 24	13 39			13 43	13 54

	NT	NT	NT	NT	NT	NT	NT	NT	NT	NT	NT	NT	NT	NT	NT	NT	NT	NT	NT	NT	NT	GC
		◇			◇		◇	◇		◇			◇		◇	◇		◇			◇	1
	B		C	D				A	B		C	D				A	D		C	D		
York 40 d						12 17								13 17								
Selby 40 d		11 52								12 52								13 52				
Leeds 37,39 d		12 36			12 51	13 07	13 18	13 20		13 36			13 51	14 07	14 18	14 20		14 36			14 51	
Bramley 37 d		12 45				13 15	13 26			13 45				14 15	14 26			14 45				
New Pudsey 37 d		12 49			13 00	13 20	13 30			13 49			14 00	14 20	14 30			14 49			15 00	
Bradford Interchange 37 a		12 59			13 09	13 30	13 40			13 59			14 09	14 30	14 39			14 59			15 09	
d		13 03			13 12	13 33	13 42			14 04			14 12	14 33	14 41			15 03			15 12	15 21
Low Moor d						13 39								14 39								15 27
Halifax a		13 15			13 23	13 46	13 54			14 16			14 23	14 46	14 53			15 15			15 23	15 34
d		13 15			13 24	13 47	13 55			14 16			14 24	14 47	14 54			15 15			15 24	15 35
Dewsbury 39 d								13 38								14 38						
Mirfield 39 a								13 44								14 44						
d								13 44								14 44						
Brighouse d						14 01		13 55						15 01		14 55						15 49
London Kings Cross ⊖26 a																						18 47
Huddersfield 39 a						14 16								15 16								
Sowerby Bridge d		13 22			13 31			14 06		14 23			14 31			15 06		15 22			15 31	
Mytholmroyd d		13 28			13 37			14 12		14 29			14 37			15 12		15 28			15 37	
Hebden Bridge a		13 31			13 40		14 07	14 15		14 32			14 40		15 06	15 15		15 31			15 40	
d		13 32			13 41		14 07	14 15		14 33			14 41		15 06	15 15		15 32			15 41	
Burnley Manchester Road 97 a					14 02								15 02								16 02	
d			13 38		14 03						14 38		15 03						15 38		16 03	
Accrington 97 a					14 11								15 11								16 11	
Blackburn 97 a					14 20								15 20								16 20	
Preston 97 a					14 38								15 38								16 38	
Poulton-le-Fylde 97 a																						
Blackpool North 97 a																						
Todmorden d		13 39	13 55				14 15	14 23		14 40	14 55				15 15	15 23		15 39	15 55			
Walsden d								14 26								15 26						
Littleborough d			14 02					14 32			15 02					15 32			16 02			
Smithy Bridge d			14 05					14 35			15 05					15 35			16 05			
Rochdale a		13 49	14 09				14 25	14 39		14 50	15 09				15 25	15 39		15 49	16 09			
d	13 42	13 49	14 09	14 13			14 25	14 39	14 42	14 50	15 09	15 14			15 26	15 39	15 42	15 49	16 09	16 14		
Castleton d	13 45			14 16					14 45			15 17					15 45			16 17		
Mills Hill d	13 50			14 21					14 50			15 22					15 50			16 22		
Moston d	13 54			14 25					14 54			15 26					15 54			16 26		
Manchester Victoria a	14 03	14 10	14 24	14 35			14 43	14 54	15 03	15 05	15 24	15 35			15 43	15 54	16 03	16 05	16 24	16 35		

A To Southport
B To Blackburn
C From Blackburn to Southport
D To Clitheroe

For connections to Liverpool Lime Street refer to Table T090

Leeds and Bradford - Huddersfield, Blackpool North, Rochdale and Manchester Victoria via Halifax and Brighouse

	NT	NT	NT	NT	NT	NT	NT	NT	NT	NT	NT	NT	NT	NT	NT	NT	NT	NT	NT	NT	NT
		◇	◇		◇			◇		◇	◇	◇				◇		◇	◇	◇	
			A	B		C	D	E			A		B	F	D				A		G
York 40 d	14 17								15 17								16 17				
Selby 40 d					14 52							15 52								16 52	
Leeds 37,39 d	15 07	15 18	15 20		15 36			15 51	16 07	16 18	16 20	16 36				16 51	17 07	17 18	17 21	17 36	
Bramley 37 d	15 15	15 26			15 45				16 15	16 26		16 45					17 15	17 26		17 45	
New Pudsey 37 d	15 20	15 30			15 49			16 00	16 20	16 30		16 49				17 00	17 20	17 30		17 49	
Bradford Interchange 37 a	15 30	15 39			15 59			16 09	16 30	16 39		16 59				17 09	17 30	17 39		17 59	
d	15 33	15 41			16 03			16 13	16 33	16 41		17 03				17 13	17 33	17 41		18 03	
Low Moor d	15 39								16 39								17 39				
Halifax a	15 46	15 53			16 15			16 25	16 46	16 53		17 15				17 25	17 46	17 53		18 15	
d	15 47	15 54			16 15			16 25	16 47	16 54		17 15				17 25	17 47	17 54		18 15	
Dewsbury 39 d			15 38								16 38								17 38		
Mirfield 39 a			15 44								16 45								17 45		
d			15 44								16 46								17 45		
Brighouse d	16 01		15 55						17 01		16 55						18 01		17 56		
London Kings Cross ⊖26 a																					
Huddersfield 39 a	16 16								17 16								18 16				
Sowerby Bridge d			16 06		16 22			16 33			17 07	17 22				17 33			18 06	18 22	
Mytholmroyd d			16 12		16 28			16 39			17 12	17 28				17 39			18 12	18 28	
Hebden Bridge a		16 06	16 15		16 31			16 42		17 06	17 15	17 31				17 42		18 06	18 15	18 31	
d		16 06	16 15		16 32			16 42		17 06	17 16	17 32				17 42		18 06	18 15	18 32	
Burnley Manchester Road 97 a								17 02								18 02					
d						16 36		17 03						17 38		18 03					18 38
Accrington 97 a								17 11								18 11					
Blackburn 97 a								17 20								18 20					
Preston 97 a								17 41								18 38					
Poulton-le-Fylde 97 a																					
Blackpool North 97 a																					
Todmorden d		16 15	16 23		16 39	16 53				17 14	17 23	17 39		17 55				18 14	18 23	18 39	18 55
Walsden d			16 26			16 56					17 26								18 26		
Littleborough d			16 32			17 02				17 22	17 33			18 02					18 32		19 02
Smithy Bridge d			16 35			17 05				17 24	17 35			18 05					18 35		19 05
Rochdale a		16 25	16 39		16 49	17 09				17 28	17 39	17 49		18 09				18 24	18 39	18 49	19 09
d		16 26	16 39	16 42	16 49	17 09	17 14			17 29	17 40	17 49	17 53	18 09	18 18			18 24	18 39	18 49	19 09
Castleton d				16 45			17 17						17 56		18 21						
Mills Hill d				16 50			17 22						18 01					18 31			
Moston d				16 54			17 26						18 05					18 34			
Manchester Victoria a		16 41	16 54	17 03	17 05	17 24	17 35			17 44	17 54	18 04	18 14	18 24	18 34			18 45	18 54	19 04	19 24

	NT	NT	NT	NT	NT	NT	NT	NT	NT	NT	NT	NT	NT	NT	NT	NT	NT	NT	NT	NT	NT	NT
		◇		◇	◇		◇			◇		◇		◇			◇		◇	◇		◇
	D				H	B		G	D			I	B		J	D				A	D	
York 40 d			17 19								18 21							19 17				
Selby 40 d							17 52							18 52								19 51
Leeds 37,39 d		17 51	18 09	18 18	18 23		18 36			18 51	19 09	19 21		19 36			19 51	20 07	20 19	20 21		20 39
Bramley 37 d			18 17	18 27			18 45				19 17			19 45				20 15	20 27			20 47
New Pudsey 37 d		18 00	18 22	18 31			18 49			19 00	19 22			19 49			20 00	20 20	20 31			20 51
Bradford Interchange 37 a		18 11	18 32	18 42			19 00			19 09	19 32			19 59			20 09	20 31	20 40			21 00
d		18 14	18 35	18 44			19 03			19 12	19 35			20 03			20 11	20 34	20 42			21 02
Low Moor d			18 41								19 41							20 40				
Halifax a		18 25	18 48	18 56			19 15			19 24	19 48			20 15			20 23	20 47	20 54			21 16
d		18 26	18 49	18 57			19 15			19 24	19 49			20 15			20 23	20 48	20 55			21 16
Dewsbury 39 d					18 40							19 38								20 38		
Mirfield 39 a					18 46							19 44								20 44		
d					18 46							19 44								20 44		
Brighouse d			19 02		18 57						20 02	19 56						21 01		20 56		
London Kings Cross ⊖26 a																						
Huddersfield 39 a			19 18								20 18							21 16				
Sowerby Bridge d		18 33			19 09		19 22			19 32		20 08		20 22			20 31			21 07		21 24
Mytholmroyd d		18 39			19 14		19 28			19 38		20 14		20 28			20 37			21 13		21 30
Hebden Bridge a		18 42		19 09	19 17		19 31			19 41		20 17		20 31			20 40		21 07	21 16		21 33
d		18 43		19 09	19 18		19 32			19 41		20 17		20 32			20 40		21 07	21 16		21 33
Burnley Manchester Road 97 a		19 03								20 02							21 02					
d		19 04						19 38		20 03					20 36		21 03					
Accrington 97 a		19 12								20 11							21 11					
Blackburn 97 a		19 21								20 20							21 20					
Preston 97 a		19 40								20 38							21 39					
Poulton-le-Fylde 97 a																						
Blackpool North 97 a																						
Todmorden d				19 16	19 25		19 39	19 55				20 25		20 39	20 53				21 16	21 24		21 41
Walsden d					19 28							20 28			20 56					21 27		
Littleborough d				19 24				20 02							21 02				21 23			
Smithy Bridge d					19 35			20 05				20 35			21 05					21 34		
Rochdale a				19 29	19 39		19 49	20 09				20 39		20 49	21 09				21 28	21 38		21 51
d	19 14			19 29	19 40	19 42	19 49	20 09	20 14			20 39	20 42	20 49	21 09	21 19			21 28	21 39	21 42	21 52
Castleton d	19 17					19 45			20 17				20 45			21 22					21 45	
Mills Hill d	19 22					19 50			20 22				20 50			21 27					21 50	
Moston d	19 26					19 54			20 26				20 53						21 37		21 54	
Manchester Victoria a	19 35			19 45	19 54	20 03	20 05	20 24	20 35			20 54	21 02	21 04	21 24	21 37			21 47	21 53	22 03	22 08

A To Southport
B To Blackburn
C From Blackburn to Wigan North Western
D To Clitheroe
E To Barrow-in-Furness
F From Blackburn to Kirkby
G From Blackburn to Southport
H To Wigan North Western
I To Wigan Wallgate
J From Blackburn to Wigan Wallgate

For connections to Liverpool Lime Street refer to Table T090

Table T041-R

Leeds and Bradford - Huddersfield, Blackpool North, Rochdale and Manchester Victoria via Halifax and Brighouse

Saturdays
26 May to 8 December

		NT A	NT ◇	NT	NT ◇	NT ◇	NT B	NT ◇	NT C	NT ◇	NT	NT ◇	NT	NT ◇	NT	NT C
York	40 d			20 20							21 19				22 17	
Selby	40 d							20 52						21 52		
Leeds	37,39 d		20 49	21 07	21 18	21 21		21 39		22 00	22 07	22 18	22 21	22 38	23 03	
Bramley	37 d			21 15	21 26			21 48			22 15	22 26		22 46	23 13	
New Pudsey	37 d		20 58	21 20	21 30			21 52		22 09	22 20	22 30		22 51	23 18	
Bradford Interchange	37 a		21 08	21 30	21 39			22 02		22 18	22 30	22 41		23 00	23 27	
	d		21 11	21 33	21 41			22 04		22 20	22 33	22 45		23 03	23 29	
Low Moor	d			21 39							22 39				23 36	
Halifax	a		21 23	21 46	21 53			22 16		22 32	22 46	22 57		23 15	23 43	
	d		21 23	21 47	21 54			22 17		22 32	22 47	22 58		23 15	23 43	
Dewsbury	39 d					21 38							22 38			
Mirfield	39 a					21 44							22 44			
	d					21 44							22 44			
Brighouse	d			22 01		21 56					23 01		22 56		23 54	
London Kings Cross ⊖26	a															
Huddersfield	39 a			22 16							23 16				00 05	
Sowerby Bridge	d		21 32			22 06		22 24		22 40			23 11			
Mytholmroyd	d		21 38			22 12		22 30		22 46			23 16			
Hebden Bridge	a		21 41		22 06	22 15		22 33		22 49		23 10	23 19	23 27		
	d		21 41		22 06	22 15		22 33		22 49		23 10		23 28		
Burnley Manchester Road	97 a		22 02							23 10						
	d	21 41	22 03						22 38	23 11						23 38
Accrington	97 a		22 11							23 19						
Blackburn	97 a		22 20							23 28						
Preston	97 a		22 42							23 46						
Poulton-le-Fylde	97 a									00 03						
Blackpool North	97 a									00 11						
Todmorden	d	21 58			22 15	22 23		22 41	22 55			23 19		23 35		23 55
Walsden	d	22 01				22 26			22 58					23 38		
Littleborough	d	22 07				22 32			23 04					23 44		00 02
Smithy Bridge	d	22 10				22 35			23 07					23 47		00 05
Rochdale	a	22 14			22 25	22 39		22 51	23 11			23 29		23 51		00 09
	d	22 14			22 26	22 39	22 43	22 52	23 11			23 30		23 51		00 09
Castleton	d						22 46		23 14							
Mills Hill	d						22 51		23 20							
Moston	d						22 55		23 24							
Manchester Victoria	a	22 29			22 43	22 54	23 06	23 11	23 33			23 48		00 07		00 24

Sundays
20 May to 2 December

		NT D	GC E	GC F	NT	NT C	NT A	NT ◇	NT	NT A	NT ◇	NT ◇	NT	NT A	NT ◇	NT ◇	NT	NT A	NT ◇	NT ◇	GC	NT	NT A
York	40 d										08 15				09 14				10 17				
Selby	40 d																						
Leeds	37,39 d				07 57			08 18	08 57		09 02	09 18	09 53		10 02	10 16	10 48		11 02	11 18		11 51	
Bramley	37 d				08 05			08 26			09 10	09 26			10 10	10 24			11 09	11 26			
New Pudsey	37 d				08 09			08 31	09 07		09 14	09 31	10 03		10 14	10 29	10 58		11 14	11 31		12 01	
Bradford Interchange	37 a				08 18			08 39	09 16		09 25	09 39	10 12		10 24	10 37	11 07		11 25	11 39		12 10	
	d			07 55	08 20			08 42	09 19		09 27	09 42	10 14		10 27	10 40	11 10		11 27	11 42	12 05	12 13	
Low Moor	d			08 02	08 27				09 25				10 21				11 16				12 11	12 19	
Halifax	a			08 09	08 35			08 54	09 32		09 40	09 54	10 28		10 38	10 52	11 23		11 39	11 54	12 18	12 26	
	d		07 37	08 10				08 54	09 33		09 40	09 54	10 28		10 39	10 53	11 24		11 39	11 54	12 19	12 27	
Dewsbury	39 d																						
Mirfield	39 a																						
	d																						
Brighouse	d		07a57	08 21					09 44				10 42				11 34				12 30	12 37	
London Kings Cross ⊖26	a			10 40																	14 54		
Huddersfield	39 a								09 55				10 56				11 45					12 48	
Sowerby Bridge	d							09 01			09 48	10 01			10 47	11 00			11 47	12 01			
Mytholmroyd	d							09 07			09 54	10 07			10 53	11 06			11 53	12 07			
Hebden Bridge	a							09 10			09 57	10 10			10 56	11 09			11 56	12 10			
	d							09 11			09 57	10 11			10 56	11 09			11 56	12 11			
Burnley Manchester Road	97 a										10 20				11 20				12 20				
	d					08 07	08 32			09 32	10 20			10 32	11 20			11 32	12 20				12 32
Accrington	97 a										10 29				11 29				12 29				
Blackburn	97 a										10 38				11 38				12 38				
Preston	97 a										10 57				11 57				12 57				
Poulton-le-Fylde	97 a										11 15				12 15				13 15				
Blackpool North	97 a										11 22				12 22				13 22				
Todmorden	d					08 24	08 49	09 19		09 49		10 19		10 49		11 18		11 49		12 19			12 49
Walsden	d							09 22				10 22				11 21				12 22			
Littleborough	d	00 02				08 31	08 56	09 28		09 56		10 28		10 56		11 28		11 56		12 28			12 56
Smithy Bridge	d	00 05				08 34	08 58			09 58				10 58				11 58					12 58
Rochdale	a	00 09				08 38	09 02	09 33		10 02		10 33		11 02		11 33		12 02		12 33			13 02
	d	00 09				08 38	09 03	09 34		10 03		10 34		11 03		11 34		12 03		12 34			13 03
Castleton	d					08 41	09 06			10 06				11 06				12 06					13 06
Mills Hill	d					08 47	09 11			10 11				11 11				12 11					13 11
Moston	d					08 50	09 15			10 15				11 15				12 15					13 15
Manchester Victoria	a	00 24				08 59	09 24	09 49		10 24		10 49		11 24		11 49		12 24		12 49			13 24

A From Blackburn to Southport
B To Blackburn
C From Blackburn
D From Blackburn
E from 28 October. To Wakefield Kirkgate
F until 21 October

For connections to Liverpool Lime Street refer to Table T090

Table T041-R

Leeds and Bradford - Huddersfield, Blackpool North, Rochdale and Manchester Victoria via Halifax and Brighouse

Sundays
20 May to 2 December

		NT ◇	NT ◇	NT	NT A	NT ◇	NT ◇	NT	NT A	NT ◇	NT ◇	NT ◇	GC	NT	NT A	NT ◇	NT ◇	GC	NT	NT A	NT ◇	NT ◇	NT
York	40 d	11 17				12 17				13 17						14 17					15 14		
Selby	40 d																						
Leeds	37,39 d	12 02	12 18	12 51		13 08	13 21	13 51		14 08	14 18	14 37		14 51		15 03	15 17		15 51		16 03	16 19	16 51
Bramley	37 d	12 10	12 26			13 16	13 29			14 16	14 26					15 11	15 25				16 11	16 27	
New Pudsey	37 d	12 14	12 31	13 01		13 20	13 34	14 01		14 20	14 31	14 46		15 01		15 16	15 30		16 01		16 16	16 32	17 01
Bradford Interchange	37 a	12 25	12 39	13 10		13 29	13 42	14 10		14 29	14 42	14 54		15 10		15 25	15 42		16 10		16 25	16 40	17 10
	d	12 27	12 42	13 13		13 31	13 45	14 13		14 31	14 45	14 58	15 05	15 13		15 27	15 45	15 59	16 13		16 27	16 43	17 13
Low Moor	d			13 19				14 19					15 11	15 19				16 05	16 19				17 19
Halifax	a	12 39	12 54	13 26		13 43	13 57	14 26		14 43	14 57	15 09	15 18	15 26		15 39	15 57	16 12	16 26		16 39	16 55	17 26
	d	12 39	12 54	13 27		13 43	13 57	14 27		14 43	14 57	15 13	15 20	15 27		15 39	15 57	16 13	16 27		16 39	16 55	17 27
Dewsbury	39 d																						
Mirfield	39 a																						
	d																						
Brighouse	d			13 37				14 37					15 33	15 37				16 24	16 37				17 37
London Kings Cross ⊖26	a												17 56					18 45					
Huddersfield	39 a			13 48				14 48						15 48					16 48				17 46
Sowerby Bridge	d	12 47	13 01			13 51	14 04			14 51	15 04					15 47	16 04				16 47	17 02	
Mytholmroyd	d	12 53	13 07			13 57	14 10			14 57	15 10					15 53	16 10				16 53	17 08	
Hebden Bridge	a	12 56	13 10			14 00	14 13			15 00	15 13	15 25				15 56	16 13				16 56	17 13	
	d	12 56	13 11			14 00	14 14			15 00	15 14	15 28				15 56	16 14				16 56	17 14	
Burnley Manchester Road	97 a	13 20				14 21				15 21						16 20					17 20		
	d	13 20			13 32	14 21			14 32	15 21					15 32	16 20				16 32	17 20		
Accrington	97 a	13 29				14 30				15 30						16 29					17 29		
Blackburn	97 a	13 38				14 39				15 39						16 38					17 38		
Preston	97 a	13 57				14 57				15 57						16 57					17 57		
Poulton-le-Fylde	97 a	14 15				15 15				16 15						17 15					18 15		
Blackpool North	97 a	14 22				15 22				16 22						17 22					18 22		
Todmorden	d		13 19		13 49		14 22		14 49		15 22	15 35			15 49		16 22			16 49		17 22	
Walsden	d		13 22				14 25				15 25						16 25					17 25	
Littleborough	d		13 28		13 56		14 31		14 56		15 31				15 56		16 31			16 56		17 31	
Smithy Bridge	d				13 58				14 58						15 58					16 58			
Rochdale	a		13 33		14 02		14 36		15 02		15 36	15 46			16 02		16 36			17 02		17 36	
	d		13 34		14 03		14 37		15 03		15 37	15 46			16 03		16 37			17 03		17 37	
Castleton	d				14 06				15 06						16 06					17 06			
Mills Hill	d				14 11				15 11						16 11					17 11			
Moston	d				14 15				15 15						16 15					17 15			
Manchester Victoria	a		13 49		14 24		14 52		15 24		15 52	16 06			16 24		16 52			17 24		17 52	

		NT A	NT ◇	NT ◇	NT	NT A	NT ◇	NT ◇	NT	NT A	NT ◇	NT ◇	NT	NT A	NT ◇	NT ◇	NT	NT B	NT ◇	NT ◇	NT	NT B
York	40 d		16 17				17 22				18 22				19 14				20 22			
Selby	40 d																					
Leeds	37,39 d		17 03	17 19	17 51		18 03	18 28	18 51		19 04	19 19	19 51		20 03	20 27	21 01		21 08	21 27	22 01	
Bramley	37 d		17 11	17 27			18 11	18 36			19 12	19 27			20 11	20 35			21 16	21 35		
New Pudsey	37 d		17 16	17 31	18 01		18 16	18 41	19 01		19 16	19 32	20 01		20 16	20 40	21 11		21 20	21 40	22 11	
Bradford Interchange	37 a		17 25	17 40	18 10		18 25	18 49	19 10		19 25	19 41	20 10		20 25	20 48	21 22		21 29	21 49	22 22	
	d		17 27	17 42	18 13		18 27	18 52	19 13		19 27	19 44	20 13		20 27	20 51	21 25		21 32	21 53	22 24	
Low Moor	d				18 19				19 19				20 19				21 31				22 31	
Halifax	a		17 39	17 54	18 26		18 39	19 04	19 26		19 39	19 56	20 26		20 39	21 08	21 38		21 44	22 05	22 38	
	d		17 39	17 55	18 27		18 39	19 04	19 27		19 39	19 56	20 27		20 39	21 08	21 39		21 45	22 06	22 38	
Dewsbury	39 d																					
Mirfield	39 a																					
	d																					
Brighouse	d				18 37				19 37				20 37				21 49				22 49	
London Kings Cross ⊖26	a																					
Huddersfield	39 a				18 48				19 48				20 48				22 07				23 00	
Sowerby Bridge	d		17 47	18 02			18 47	19 11			19 47	20 03			20 47	21 16			21 52	22 13		
Mytholmroyd	d		17 53	18 08			18 53	19 17			19 53	20 09			20 53	21 22			21 58	22 19		
Hebden Bridge	a		17 56	18 13			18 56	19 20			19 56	20 12			20 56	21 25			22 01	22 22		
	d		17 56	18 13			18 56	19 21			19 56	20 13			20 56	21 26			22 02	22 22		
Burnley Manchester Road	97 a		18 20				19 20				20 20				21 20				22 24			
	d	17 32	18 20			18 32	19 20			19 32	20 20			20 36	21 20			21 33	22 25			22 33
Accrington	97 a		18 29				19 29				20 29				21 29				22 33			
Blackburn	97 a		18 38				19 38				20 38				21 38				22 42			
Preston	97 a		18 57				19 57				20 57				21 59				23 01			
Poulton-le-Fylde	97 a		19 15				20 15				21 15				22 17				23 19			
Blackpool North	97 a		19 22				20 22				21 22				22 24				23 26			
Todmorden	d	17 49		18 21		18 49		19 28		19 49		20 21		20 55		21 34		21 50		22 30		22 50
Walsden	d			18 24				19 31				20 24				21 37				22 33		
Littleborough	d	17 56		18 30		18 56		19 38		19 56		20 30		21 02		21 43		21 57		22 39		22 57
Smithy Bridge	d	17 58				18 58				19 58				21 05				21 59				22 59
Rochdale	a	18 02		18 35		19 02		19 43		20 02		20 35		21 09		21 48		22 03		22 44		23 03
	d	18 03		18 36		19 03		19 43		20 03		20 36		21 09		21 49		22 04		22 45		23 04
Castleton	d	18 06				19 06				20 06				21 12				22 07				23 07
Mills Hill	d	18 11				19 11				20 11				21 18				22 12				23 12
Moston	d	18 15				19 15				20 15				21 21				22 16				23 16
Manchester Victoria	a	18 24		18 51		19 24		19 59		20 24		20 51		21 30		22 04		22 25		23 00		23 25

A From Blackburn to Southport
B From Blackburn

For connections to Liverpool Lime Street refer to Table T090

Table T041-R

Sundays
20 May to 2 December

Leeds and Bradford - Huddersfield, Blackpool North, Rochdale and Manchester Victoria via Halifax and Brighouse

			NT	NT	NT
			◇		A
York	40	d			
Selby	40	d			
Leeds	37,39	d	22 17	22 50	
Bramley	37	d	22 25		
New Pudsey	37	d	22 30	23 00	
Bradford Interchange	37	a	22 38	23 09	
		d	22 41	23 11	
Low Moor		d		23 18	
Halifax		a	22 53	23 25	
		d	22 53	23 25	
Dewsbury	39	d			
Mirfield	39	a			
		d			
Brighouse		d		23 36	
London Kings Cross	⊖26	a			
Huddersfield	39	a		23 47	
Sowerby Bridge		d	23 00		
Mytholmroyd		d	23 06		
Hebden Bridge		a	23 09		
		d	23 10		
Burnley Manchester Road	97	a			
		d			23 19
Accrington	97	a			
Blackburn	97	a			
Preston	97	a			
Poulton-le-Fylde	97	a			
Blackpool North	97	a			
Todmorden		d	23 18		23 35
Walsden		d	23 21		
Littleborough		d	23 27		23 42
Smithy Bridge		d			23 45
Rochdale		a	23 32		23 49
		d	23 33		23 49
Castleton		d			23 52
Mills Hill		d			23 57
Moston		d			00 01
Manchester Victoria		a	23 48		00 11

A From Blackburn

For connections to Liverpool Lime Street refer to Table T090

Table T042-F

Mondays to Fridays
21 May to 7 December

Leeds - Morecambe and Carlisle

Miles	Miles	Miles				NT	NT	NT	NT	NT	NT	NT	NT	NT	NT	NT	NT	NT	NT	NT	NT	NT
							◇	◇	◇	◇	◇	◇	◇	◇	◇	◇	◇ A	◇	◇	◇	◇	◇
							🍴	🍴		🍴		🍴		🍴		🍴		🍴		🍴		🍴
0	0	—	**Leeds**	36,37	d		05 17	07 48	08 19	09 19	10 18	10 49	12 20	13 18	14 18	15 18	15 51	16 49	17 25	18 19	19 18	19 49
10¾	10¾	—	Shipley	36,37	d		05 30	08 02	08 32	09 32	10 33	11 03	12 33	13 33	14 33	15 33		17 02	17 39	18 32	19 32	20 02
13¾	13¾	—	Bingley	36	d		05 37	08 06	08 37	09 37	10 37	11 07	12 37	13 37	14 38	15 37		17 07	17 45	18 36	19 37	20 07
17	17	—	Keighley	36	d		05 44	08 12	08 42	09 42	10 43	11 13	12 43	13 43	14 43	15 43		17 13	17 52	18 42	19 43	20 12
26¼	26¼	—	**Skipton**	36	a		06 00	08 24	08 55	09 57	10 55	11 25	12 56	13 55	14 57	15 59		17 25	18 07	18 54	19 57	20 26
—	—	—	Skipton		d	05 22	06 02	08 26	08 56	09 59	10 57	11 27	12 58	13 57	14 58	16 00		17 27	18 08	18 56	20 00	20 27
30	30	—	Gargrave		a	05 27			09 02	10 04	11 02	11 32	13 03		15 04			17 32	18 14	19 01	20 05	20 33
—	—	0	Blackpool North	97	d																	
—	—	17½	Preston	97	d												17 45					
—	—	29¾	Blackburn	94,97	d																	
—	—	39½	Clitheroe	94	d																	
36	36	53	Hellifield		d	05 37	06 13		09 10	10 13	11 11	11 41	13 12	14 08	15 13	16 12		17 41	18 22	19 10	20 14	20 42
37¼	37¼	—	Long Preston		d	05 40			09 13	10 15	11 14	11 44	13 15		15 15			17 43	18 25	19 12	20 17	20 44
—	41	—	Giggleswick		d	05 48			09 21		11 22		13 23		15 23				18 33		20 25	
—	47¾	—	Clapham (Nth Yorkshire)		d	05 56			09 29		11 30		13 31		15 31				18 41		20 34	
—	51	—	Bentham		d	06 03			09 35		11 36		13 37		15 38				18 48		20 40	
—	54¼	—	Wennington		d	06 08			09 40		11 42		13 43		15 43				18 53		20 46	
—	64	—	Carnforth	82	d	06 24			09 57		12 01		14 01		15 59				19 14		21 05	
—	70	—	**Lancaster**	65,82,98	a	06 32			10 05		12 10		14 13		16 08		18 02		19 23		21 13	
—	72½	—	Bare Lane	98	d						12 20				16 28				19 46			
—	74	—	**Morecambe**	98	a						12 24				16 32				19 50			
—	78¼	—	Heysham Port	⛴	a																	
41	—	—	Settle		d		06 21	08 49		10 22		11 51		14 17		16 19		17 49		19 18		20 50
47¼	—	—	Horton-in-Ribblesdale		d		06 29	08 58		10 31		11 59		14 26		16 28		17 58		19 27		20 59
52	—	—	Ribblehead		d		06 37	09 06		10 39		12 07		14 34		16 36		18 06		19 35		21a09
58	—	—	Dent		d		06 47	09 15		10 48		12 17		14 43		16 45		18 15		19 44		
61½	—	—	Garsdale		d		06 52	09 21		10 54		12 22		14 49		16 51		18 21		19 50		
71¼	—	—	Kirkby Stephen		d		07 05	09 34		11 06		12 35		15 01		17 03		18 33		20 02		
82	—	—	Appleby		d		07 17	09 47		11 19		12 48		15 14		17 16		18 46		20 15		
93	—	—	Langwathby		d		07 31	10 01				13 02		15 28		17 30		19 00		20 28		
97¼	—	—	Lazonby & Kirkoswald		d		07 37	10 07				13 08		15 34		17 35		19 05		20 34		
102¾	—	—	Armathwaite		d		07 45	10 14				13 16		15 42		17 43		19 13		20 41		
112¾	—	—	**Carlisle**	65	a		08 04	10 30		12 01		13 33		16 01		17 58		19 28		20 58		

Saturdays
26 May to 8 December

			NT	NT	NT	NT	NT	NT	NT	NT	NT	NT	NT	NT	NT	NT	NT	NT	NT
				◇	◇	◇	◇	◇	◇	◇	◇	◇	◇	◇ A	◇	◇	◇	◇	◇
				🍴	🍴		🍴		🍴		🍴		🍴		🍴		🍴		🍴
Leeds	36,37	d		06 20	07 48	08 19	09 19	10 18	10 49	12 20	13 18	14 18	15 18	15 51	16 49	17 25	18 19	19 18	19 49
Shipley	36,37	d		06 33	08 02	08 32	09 32	10 33	11 03	12 33	13 33	14 33	15 33		17 02	17 39	18 32	19 32	20 02
Bingley	36	d		06 40	08 06	08 37	09 37	10 37	11 07	12 37	13 37	14 38	15 37		17 07	17 45	18 36	19 37	20 07
Keighley	36	d		06 47	08 12	08 42	09 42	10 43	11 13	12 43	13 43	14 43	15 43		17 13	17 52	18 42	19 43	20 12
Skipton	36	a		07 03	08 24	08 55	09 57	10 55	11 25	12 56	13 55	14 57	15 59		17 25	18 07	18 54	19 57	20 26
Skipton		d	05 19	07 05	08 26	08 56	09 59	10 57	11 27	12 58	13 57	14 58	16 00		17 27	18 08	18 56	20 00	20 27
Gargrave		a	05 24			09 02	10 04	11 02	11 32	13 03		15 04			17 32	18 14	19 01	20 05	20 33
Blackpool North	97	d																	
Preston	97	d												17 45					
Blackburn	94,97	d																	
Clitheroe	94	d																	
Hellifield		d	05 34	07 16		09 10	10 13	11 11	11 41	13 12	14 08	15 13	16 12		17 41	18 22	19 10	20 14	20 42
Long Preston		d	05 37			09 13	10 15	11 14	11 44	13 15		15 15			17 43	18 25	19 12	20 17	20 44
Giggleswick		d	05 45			09 21		11 22		13 23		15 23				18 33		20 25	
Clapham (Nth Yorkshire)		d	05 54			09 29		11 30		13 31		15 31				18 41		20 34	
Bentham		d	06 01			09 35		11 36		13 37		15 38				18 48		20 40	
Wennington		d	06 06			09 40		11 42		13 43		15 43				18 53		20 46	
Carnforth	82	d	06 22			09 57		12 01		14 02		15 59				19 10		21 05	
Lancaster	65,82,98	a	06 32			10 05		12 10		14 13		16 08		18 02		19 19		21 13	
Bare Lane	98	d						12 20				16 28				19 41			
Morecambe	98	a						12 24				16 32				19 45			
Heysham Port	⛴	a																	
Settle		d		07 25	08 49		10 22		11 51		14 17		16 19		17 49		19 18		20 50
Horton-in-Ribblesdale		d		07 33	08 58		10 31		11 59		14 26		16 28		17 58		19 27		20 59
Ribblehead		d		07 41	09 06		10 39		12 07		14 34		16 36		18 06		19 35		21a09
Dent		d		07 51	09 15		10 48		12 17		14 43		16 45		18 15		19 44		
Garsdale		d		07 56	09 21		10 54		12 22		14 49		16 51		18 21		19 50		
Kirkby Stephen		d		08 09	09 34		11 06		12 35		15 01		17 03		18 33		20 02		
Appleby		d		08 21	09 47		11 19		12 48		15 14		17 16		18 46		20 15		
Langwathby		d		08 35	10 01				13 02		15 28		17 30		19 00		20 28		
Lazonby & Kirkoswald		d		08 41	10 07				13 08		15 34		17 35		19 05		20 34		
Armathwaite		d		08 49	10 14				13 16		15 42		17 43		19 13		20 41		
Carlisle	65	a		09 04	10 30		12 01		13 33		16 01		17 58		19 28		20 58		

A To Barrow-in-Furness

Table T042-F

Sundays
20 May to 2 December

Leeds - Morecambe and Carlisle

		NT	NT	NT	NT	NT	NT	NT	NT	NT	NT	NT	NT
		◇	◇	◇	◇	◇	◇	◇	◇	◇	◇	◇	◇
				🛒		A							
Leeds [10]	36,37 d	08 30	08 59		10 24	11 15	12 28	13 24	14 24	15 24	16 22	17 24	18 52
Shipley	36,37 d	08 43	09 13		10 37	11 32	12 41	13 37	14 37	15 37	16 37	17 37	19 05
Bingley	36 d	08 50	09 20		10 41	11 37	12 45	13 41	14 41	15 41	16 41	17 41	19 09
Keighley	36 d	08 57	09 27		10 47	11 42	12 51	13 47	14 47	15 47	16 47	17 47	19 16
Skipton	36 a	09 14	09 43		11 00	11 55	13 03	14 00	14 59	16 00	17 01	18 00	19 33
Skipton	d	09 15	09 45		11 02	11 55	13 05	14 02	15 02	16 02	17 01	18 02	19 33
Gargrave	a	09 21	09 50		11 07		13 11	14 07	15 07	16 07		18 07	
Blackpool North	97 d			08 40									
Preston [8]	97 d			09 07									
Blackburn	94,97 d			09 28									
Clitheroe	94 d			09 52									
Hellifield	d	09 29	09 59	10 16	11 16	12 07	13 19	14 16	15 16	16 16	17 12	18 16	19 44
Long Preston	d	09 32			11 18		13 22	14 18	15 19	16 18		18 18	
Giggleswick	d	09 39			11 26			14 26		16 26		18 26	
Clapham (Nth Yorkshire)	d	09 47			11 34			14 34		16 34		18 34	
Bentham	d	09 54			11 40			14 40		16 40		18 40	
Wennington	d	09 59			11 45			14 45		16 45		18 45	
Carnforth	82 d	10 15			12 02			15 02		17 02		19 02	
Lancaster [8]	65,82,98 a	10 25			12 13			15 13		17 13		19 13	
Bare Lane	98 d												
Morecambe	98 a												
Heysham Port	⛴ a												
Settle	d		10 07	10 34		12 16	13 28		15 25		17 20		19 52
Horton-in-Ribblesdale	d		10 16	10 43			13 37		15 34		17 29		20 01
Ribblehead	d		10 24	10 51			13 45		15 42		17 37		20 09
Dent	d		10 34	11 01			13 55		15 52		17 47		20 19
Garsdale	d		10 40	11 07			14 01		15 57		17 52		20 24
Kirkby Stephen	d		10 53	11 20		12 54	14 14		16 10		18 05		20 37
Appleby	d		11 06	11 33		13 08	14 26		16 23		18 18		20 50
Langwathby	d		11 20	11 47			14 40		16 37		18 32		21 04
Lazonby & Kirkoswald	d		11 26	11 53			14 46		16 43		18 38		21 10
Armathwaite	d		11 34	12 01			14 54		16 51		18 46		21 18
Carlisle [8]	65 a		11 52	12 16		13 47	15 11		17 08		19 02		21 38

A From Nottingham

Table T042-R

Sundays
20 May to 2 December

Carlisle and Morecambe - Leeds

		NT	NT	NT	NT	NT	NT	NT	NT	NT	NT	NT	NT
		◇	◇	◇	◇		◇	◇	◇	◇	◇	◇	◇
				A			A	B		A		🛒	
Carlisle [8]	65 d	09 25			12 50			15 02	16 07		17 25	17 48	
Armathwaite	d	09 39			13 04			15 16			17 39	18 02	
Lazonby & Kirkoswald	d	09 46			13 11			15 23			17 46	18 09	
Langwathby	d	09 53			13 18			15 30			17 53	18 15	
Appleby	d	10 07			13 32			15 44	16 44		18 08	18 31	
Kirkby Stephen	d	10 21			13 46			15 57	16 57		18 22	18 44	
Garsdale	d	10 34			13 59			16 12			18 35	18 57	
Dent	d	10 40			14 05			16 18			18 41	19 03	
Ribblehead	d	10 49			14 14			16 27			18 50	19 12	
Horton-in-Ribblesdale	d	10 56			14 21			16 34			18 57	19 19	
Settle	d	11 04			14 29			16 44	17 34		19 06	19 27	
Heysham Port	⛴ d					13 05							
Morecambe	98 d			12 36		13 25	15 36			17 36			
Bare Lane	98 d			12 40		13 29	15 40			17 40			
Lancaster [8]	65,82,98 d		10 41			13a35							19 51
Carnforth	82 d		10 51	12 51			15 51			17 51			20 01
Wennington	d		11 05	13 05			16 05			18 05			20 15
Bentham	d		11 11	13 11			16 10			18 11			20 21
Clapham (Nth Yorkshire)	d		11 17	13 17			16 17			18 17			20 27
Giggleswick	d		11 26	13 26			16 25			18 26			20 36
Long Preston	d	11 10	11 34	13 34	14 35		16 34	16 50		18 34			20 44
Hellifield	d	11 13	11 37	13 37	14 38		16 37	16 53	17 42	18 37	19 13	19 37	20 47
Clitheroe	94 a											19 59	
Blackburn	94,97 a											20 25	
Preston [8]	97 a											20 46	
Blackpool North	97 a											21 14	
Gargrave	d	11 21	11 46	13 46	14 46		16 45	17 01		18 46			20 56
Skipton	a	11 30	11 54	13 54	14 55		16 54	17 09	17 57	18 54	19 28		21 04
Skipton	36 d	11 30	11 56	13 56	14 58		16 55	17 09	17 58	18 56	19 30		21 07
Keighley	36 d	11 40	12 06	14 06	15 08		17 05	17 19	18 08	19 06	19 40		21 17
Bingley	36 d	11 44	12 11	14 11	15 13		17 10	17 23	18 13	19 11	19 45		21 22
Shipley	36,37 d	11 49	12 16	14 16	15 18		17 16	17 28	18 18	19 17	19 50		21 28
Leeds [10]	36,37 a	12 06	12 36	14 36	15 36		17 39	17 50	18 32	19 37	20 07		21 47

A From Lancaster
B To Nottingham

Table T042-R

Mondays to Fridays
21 May to 7 December

Carlisle and Morecambe - Leeds

Miles	Miles	Miles																					
					NT	NT	NT	NT	NT	NT	NT	NT	NT	NT	NT	NT	NT	NT	NT	NT	NT	NT
					◇	◇	◇	◇	◇			◇	◇	◇	◇	◇	◇	◇	◇	◇		
													A									
					🛒		🛒		🛒			🛒		🛒	🛒		🛒		🛒	🛒		
0	—	—	**Carlisle [8]**	65 d	05 51		08 24		10 49			14 04		14 50	16 19		18 24		20 18			
10	—	—	Armathwaite	d	06 05		08 38		11 04					15 04	16 35		18 38					
15½	—	—	Lazonby & Kirkoswald	d	06 12		08 45		11 12					15 11	16 42		18 45					
19¾	—	—	Langwathby	d	06 19		08 52		11 18					15 18	16 49		18 52		20 43			
30¾	—	—	Appleby	d	06 33		09 06		11 33			14 41		15 32	17 03		19 06		20 57			
41½	—	—	Kirkby Stephen	d	06 46		09 20		11 46			14 55		15 46	17 17		19 20		21 11			
51¼	—	—	Garsdale	d	07 00		09 33		12 05					15 59	17 30		19 33		21 24			
54¾	—	—	Dent	d	07 05		09 38		12 10					16 04	17 35		19 38					
60¾	—	—	Ribblehead	d	07 14		09 48		12 19					16 14	17 45		19 48			21 45		
65½	—	—	Horton-in-Ribblesdale	d	07 21		09 54		12 26					16 20	17 51		19 54			21 51		
71¾	—	—	Settle	d	07 29		10 02		12 34			15 32		16 28	17 59		20 02		21 48	21 59		
—	0	—	Heysham Port	⛴ d							13 20											
—	4¼	—	**Morecambe**	98 d						12 32	13 38		15 04			17 31		20 10				22 52
—	5¾	—	Bare Lane	98 d						12 36	13 42		15 08			17 35		20 14				22 56
—	8¼	—	**Lancaster [8]**	65,82,98 d		06 48		10 45		12 45	13a48					17 45		20 30			21 34	23 03
—	14¼	—	Carnforth	82 d		06 59		10 55		12 55			15 23			17 55		20 40			21 44	
—	24	—	Wennington	d		07 12		11 09		13 08			15 37			18 09		20 54			21 58	
—	27¼	—	Bentham	d		07 18		11 15		13 14			15 43			18 15		21 00			22 03	
—	30½	—	Clapham (Nth Yorkshire)	d		07 25		11 21		13 20			15 49			18 21		21 06			22 10	
—	37¼	—	Giggleswick	d		07 34		11 32		13 31			16 00			18 32		21 17			22 20	
75½	41	—	Long Preston	d	07 34	07 43		11 38		13 37		15 40	16 10	16 34		18 38	20 08	21 23		22 05	22 27	
76¾	42¼	0	Hellifield	d	07 37	07 46	10 10	11 41		13 40		15 43	16 13	16 37	18 07	18 41	20 11	21 26		22 08	22 29	
—	—	13½	Clitheroe	94 a																		
—	—	23¼	Blackburn	94,97 a																		
—	—	35½	Preston [8]	97 a																		23 24
—	—	53	Blackpool North	97 a																		
82¾	48¼	—	Gargrave	d	07 45	07 55		11 50		13 49		15 51	16 21	16 45		18 50	20 19	21 34		22 16	22 38	
86½	52	—	Skipton	a	07 53	08 03	10 24	11 57	12 53	13 56		15 58	16 27	16 54	18 23	18 57	20 27	21 41	22 09	22 25	22 45	
—	—	—	**Skipton**	36 d	07 55	08 05	10 25	11 59	12 55	13 59		16 00	16 28	16 59	18 29	18 59	20 29	21 43	22 10	22 26		
95¾	61¼	—	Keighley	36 d	08 05	08 17	10 38	12 09	13 08	14 09		16 10	16 38	17 09	18 39	19 09	20 39	21 55	22 20	22 41		
99	67½	—	Bingley	36 d	08 10	08 22	10 45	12 16	13 13	14 14		16 15	16 44	17 14	18 44	19 14	20 44	22 00	22 25	22 47		
102	67½	—	Shipley	36,37 d	08 15	08 28	10 50	12 21	13 20	14 20		16 20	16 49	17 20	18 50	19 20	20 51	22 06	22 32	22 55		
112¾	78¼	—	**Leeds [10]**	36,37 a	08 33	08 43	11 08	12 37	13 38	14 38		16 38	17 03	17 38	19 06	19 36	21 06	22 22	22 49	23 12		

Saturdays
26 May to 8 December

		NT	NT	NT	NT	NT	NT	NT	NT	NT	NT	NT	NT	NT	NT	NT	NT	NT	NT
		◇	◇	◇	◇	◇	◇			◇	◇	◇	◇	◇	◇	◇	◇	◇	
											A								
				🛒	🛒		🛒			🛒		🛒	🛒		🛒		🛒	🛒	
Carlisle [8]	65 d			07 49	09 27		10 49			14 04		14 50	16 19		18 24		20 19		
Armathwaite	d			08 06	09 41		11 04					15 04	16 35		18 38				
Lazonby & Kirkoswald	d			08 13	09 48		11 12					15 11	16 42		18 45				
Langwathby	d			08 19	09 55		11 18					15 18	16 49		18 52		20 43		
Appleby	d			08 34	10 09		11 33			14 41		15 32	17 03		19 06		20 57		
Kirkby Stephen	d			08 47	10 23		11 46			14 55		15 46	17 17		19 20		21 11		
Garsdale	d			09 01	10 36		12 05					15 59	17 30		19 33		21 24		
Dent	d			09 06	10 41		12 10					16 04	17 35		19 38				
Ribblehead	d	07 14		09 15	10 51		12 19					16 14	17 45		19 48			21 45	
Horton-in-Ribblesdale	d	07 20		09 22	10 57		12 26					16 20	17 51		19 54			21 53	
Settle	d	07 28		09 30	11 05		12 34			15 32		16 28	17 59		20 02		21 48	22 01	
Heysham Port	⛴ d								13 20										
Morecambe	98 d							12 32	13 38		15 04			17 31		20 10			
Bare Lane	98 d							12 36	13 42		15 08			17 35		20 14			
Lancaster [8]	65,82,98 d		06 48			10 45		12 45	13a48					17 45		20 30			21 34
Carnforth	82 d		06 59			10 55		12 55			15 23			17 55		20 40			21 44
Wennington	d		07 12			11 09		13 08			15 37			18 09		20 54			21 58
Bentham	d		07 18			11 15		13 14			15 43			18 15		21 00			22 03
Clapham (Nth Yorkshire)	d		07 25			11 21		13 20			15 49			18 21		21 06			22 10
Giggleswick	d		07 34			11 32		13 31			16 00			18 32		21 17			22 20
Long Preston	d	07 34	07 43			11 38		13 37		15 40	16 10	16 34		18 38	20 08	21 23		22 07	22 27
Hellifield	d	07 37	07 46	09 37	11 13	11 41		13 40		15 43	16 13	16 37	18 07	18 41	20 11	21 26		22 10	22 29
Clitheroe	94 a																		
Blackburn	94,97 a																		
Preston [8]	97 a																		
Blackpool North	97 a																		
Gargrave	d	07 45	07 55			11 50		13 49		15 51	16 21	16 45		18 50	20 19	21 34		22 18	22 38
Skipton	a	07 53	08 03	09 52	11 27	11 57	12 53	13 56		15 58	16 27	16 54	18 23	18 57	20 27	21 41	22 09	22 26	22 45
Skipton	36 d	07 55	08 05	09 56	11 28	11 59	12 55	13 59		16 00	16 28	16 59	18 29	18 59	20 29	21 43	22 10	22 26	
Keighley	36 d	08 08	08 17	10 09	11 38	12 09	13 08	14 09		16 10	16 38	17 09	18 39	19 09	20 39	21 55	22 20	22 41	
Bingley	36 d	08 13	08 22	10 13	11 45	12 16	13 13	14 14		16 15	16 44	17 14	18 44	19 14	20 44	22 00	22 25	22 47	
Shipley	36,37 d	08 19	08 28	10 20	11 50	12 21	13 20	14 20		16 20	16 49	17 20	18 50	19 20	20 51	22 06	22 30	22 54	
Leeds [10]	36,37 a	08 35	08 43	10 37	12 05	12 37	13 38	14 38		16 38	17 03	17 38	19 06	19 36	21 06	22 22	22 48	23 11	

A From Lancaster

Table T043-F

Hull - Beverley, Bridlington and Scarborough

Mondays to Fridays

21 May to 7 December

Miles			NT	NT	NT	NT	NT ■ A	NT	NT A	NT	NT ◇ A	NT	NT ◇ A
0	**Hull**	d	05 58	06 16	06 43	06 54	07 25	07 57	08 15	08 27	09 01	09 30	10 01
4	Cottingham	d	06 05	06 23	06 50	07 01	07 33	08 05	08 21	08 34	09 08	09 37	10 08
8¼	**Beverley**	d	06 12	06 30	06 57	07a07	07 39	08 11	08a27	08 41	09 14	09 44	10 14
11¼	Arram	d		06 35				08 16					
16¼	Hutton Cranswick	d	06 21	06 41	07 06		07 48	08 23		08 50	09 24	09 53	10 23
19½	Driffield	d	06 26	06 47	07 11		07 53	08 29		08 55	09 29	09 58	10 28
21½	Nafferton	d	06 30		07 15		07 58	08 33		08 59	09 33	10 02	10 32
31	**Bridlington**	a	06 44	07 01	07 27		08 10	08 47		09 11	09 46	10 14	10 43
—		d			07 33					09 14			10 43
34½	Bempton	d			07 39					09 20			10 50
41¾	Hunmanby	d			07 50					09 31			10 59
44½	Filey	d			07 55					09 36			11 04
51	Seamer	39 d			08 04					09 47			11 14
53¾	**Scarborough**	39 a			08 12					09 54			11 21

		NT	NT ◇ A	NT	NT ◇ A	NT	NT ◇ A	NT	NT ◇ A	NT	NT ◇ A
Hull	d	10 30	10 56	11 30	11 56	12 30	12 56	13 30	13 56	14 30	14 56
Cottingham	d	10 37	11 03	11 37	12 03	12 37	13 03	13 37	14 03	14 37	15 03
Beverley	d	10 44	11 09	11 44	12 09	12 44	13 09	13 44	14 09	14 44	15 09
Arram	d	10 48	11 14						14 14		
Hutton Cranswick	d	10 55	11 20		12 18		13 18		14 20	14 53	15 18
Driffield	d	11 01	11 26	11 56	12 24	12 56	13 24	13 56	14 26	14 58	15 23
Nafferton	d		11 30		12 28		13 28		14 30	15 02	15 27
Bridlington	a	11 15	11 43	12 10	12 41	13 10	13 41	14 10	14 43	15 14	15 38
	d			12 13				14 13			15 39
Bempton	d			12 20				14 20			15 45
Hunmanby	d										15 55
Filey	d			12 36				14 36			16 00
Seamer	39 d			12 47				14 47			16 10
Scarborough	39 a			12 54				14 54			16 17

		NT	NT ◇ A	NT	NT ◇ A	NT	NT	NT ◇ A	NT	NT ◇ A	NT	NT ◇ A	HT ◇■ B ⊠	NT ◇ A	NT ◇ A	NT
Hull	d	15 30	15 56	16 30	16 56	17 18	17 36	17 57	18 16	19 04	19 30	19 59	21 31	21 57	22 56	23 15
Cottingham	d	15 37	16 03	16 37	17 03	17 25	17 43	18 04	18 23	19 11	19 37	20 06	21 38	22 04	23 03	23 22
Beverley	d	15 44	16 09	16 44	17 09	17 32	17 50	18 10	18 30	19 17	19 44	20 17	21a44	22 10	23a08	23a28
Arram	d							18 15				20 22				
Hutton Cranswick	d		16 18		17 18	17 41		18 21		19 26		20 28		22 19		
Driffield	d	15 56	16 24	16 56	17 24	17 46	18 06	18 28	18 44	19 32	19 56	20 34		22 25		
Nafferton	d		16 28		17 28	17 50		18 32		19 36		20 38		22 29		
Bridlington	a	16 10	16 41	17 10	17 41	18 04	18 20	18 43	18 59	19 47	20 10	20 51		22 42		
	d			17 13				18 43		19 47						
Bempton	d			17 20				18 50		19 54						
Hunmanby	d			17 30				19 00		20 04						
Filey	d			17 36				19 05		20 09						
Seamer	39 d			17 47				19 14		20 19						
Scarborough	39 a			17 54				19 22		20 26						

Saturdays

26 May to 8 December

		NT	NT	NT	NT	NT ■ A	NT	NT A	NT	NT ◇ A	NT	NT ◇ A
Hull	d	05 58	06 16	06 43	06 54	07 25	07 57	08 15	08 27	09 01	09 30	10 01
Cottingham	d	06 05	06 23	06 50	07 01	07 33	08 05	08 21	08 34	09 08	09 37	10 08
Beverley	d	06 12	06 30	06 57	07a07	07 39	08 11	08a27	08 41	09 14	09 44	10 14
Arram	d		06 35				08 16					
Hutton Cranswick	d	06 21	06 41	07 06		07 48	08 23		08 50	09 23	09 53	10 23
Driffield	d	06 26	06 47	07 11		07 53	08 29		08 55	09 29	09 58	10 28
Nafferton	d	06 30		07 15		07 58	08 33		08 59	09 33	10 02	10 32
Bridlington	a	06 44	07 01	07 27		08 10	08 47		09 11	09 46	10 14	10 43
	d			07 33					09 14			10 43
Bempton	d			07 39					09 20			10 50
Hunmanby	d			07 50					09 31			10 59
Filey	d			07 55					09 36			11 04
Seamer	39 d			08 04					09 47			11 14
Scarborough	39 a			08 12					09 54			11 21

		NT	NT ◇ A	NT	NT ◇ A	NT	NT ◇ A	NT	NT ◇ A	NT	NT ◇ A	NT
Hull	d	10 30	10 56	11 30	11 56	12 30	12 56	13 30	13 56	14 30	14 56	15 30
Cottingham	d	10 37	11 03	11 37	12 03	12 37	13 03	13 37	14 03	14 37	15 03	15 37
Beverley	d	10 44	11 09	11 44	12 09	12 44	13 09	13 44	14 09	14 44	15 09	15 44
Arram	d	10 48	11 14						14 14			
Hutton Cranswick	d	10 55	11 20		12 18		13 18		14 20	14 53	15 18	
Driffield	d	11 01	11 26	11 56	12 24	12 56	13 24	13 56	14 26	14 58	15 23	15 56
Nafferton	d		11 30		12 28		13 28		14 30	15 02	15 27	
Bridlington	a	11 15	11 43	12 10	12 41	13 10	13 41	14 10	14 43	15 14	15 38	16 10
	d			12 13				14 13			15 39	
Bempton	d			12 20				14 20			15 45	
Hunmanby	d										15 55	
Filey	d			12 36				14 36			16 00	
Seamer	39 d			12 47				14 47			16 10	
Scarborough	39 a			12 54				14 54			16 17	

		NT ◇ A	NT	NT ◇ A	NT	NT	NT ◇ A	NT	NT ◇ A	NT	NT ◇ A	HT ◇■ B ⊠	NT ◇ A	NT ◇ A	NT
Hull	d	15 56	16 30	16 56	17 18	17 36	17 57	18 16	19 04	19 30	19 59	20 28	21 57	22 56	23 15
Cottingham	d	16 03	16 37	17 03	17 25	17 43	18 04	18 23	19 11	19 37	20 06	20 35	22 04	23 03	23 22
Beverley	d	16 09	16 44	17 09	17 32	17 50	18 10	18 30	19 17	19 44	20 17	20a41	22 10	23a08	23a28
Arram	d						18 15				20 22				
Hutton Cranswick	d	16 18		17 18	17 41		18 21		19 26		20 28		22 19		
Driffield	d	16 24	16 56	17 24	17 46	18 06	18 28	18 44	19 32	19 56	20 34		22 25		
Nafferton	d	16 28		17 28	17 50		18 32		19 36		20 38		22 29		
Bridlington	a	16 41	17 10	17 41	18 04	18 20	18 43	18 59	19 47	20 10	20 51		22 42		
	d		17 13				18 43		19 47						
Bempton	d		17 20				18 50		19 54						
Hunmanby	d		17 30				19 00		20 04						
Filey	d		17 36				19 05		20 09						
Seamer	39 d		17 47				19 14		20 19						
Scarborough	39 a		17 54				19 22		20 26						

A From Sheffield

B From London Kings Cross

Table T043-F

Hull - Beverley, Bridlington and Scarborough

Sundays

20 May to 2 December

		NT	NT A	NT ◇ A	NT ◇ A	NT	NT ◇ A	NT ◇ A	NT ◇ A	NT ◇ A	NT	NT ◇ A	NT ◇ A	NT ◇ A	HT ◇■ B ⊠	NT ◇ A
Hull	d	08 36	09 48	10 52	11 52	12 52	13 52	14 52	15 52	16 52	17 25	17 52	18 52	19 52	20 28	20 52
Cottingham	d	08 43	09 56	11 00	12 00	12 59	14 00	15 00	16 00	17 00	17 33	18 00	19 01	20 00	20 35	21 00
Beverley	d	08 49	10 04	11 06	12 06	13 05	14 06	15 06	16 06	17 06	17 39	18 06	19 07	20 06	20a41	21a06
Arram	d	08 53														
Hutton Cranswick	d	08 59	10 15		12 15		14 15		16 15		17 48	18 15		20 15		
Driffield	d	09 05	10 21	11 18	12 21	13 17	14 21	15 18	16 21	17 18	17 54	18 21	19 19	20 21		
Nafferton	d	09 09	10 25		12 25		14 25		16 25		17 58	18 25		20 25		
Bridlington	a	09 22	10 37	11 33	12 37	13 30	14 37	15 33	16 37	17 33	18 14	18 37	19 34	20 37		
	d	09 23	10 46		12 45		14 45		16 45			18 45				
Bempton	d	09 29	10 53		12 52		14 52		16 52			18 52				
Hunmanby	d	09 39	11 03		13 02		15 02		17 02			19 02				
Filey	d	09 44	11 08		13 07		15 07		17 07			19 07				
Seamer	39 d	09 58	11 20		13 19		15 19		17 19			19 19				
Scarborough	39 a	10 04	11 26		13 25		15 25		17 25			19 25				

A From Sheffield

B From London Kings Cross

Table T043-R

Mondays to Fridays

21 May to 7 December

Scarborough, Bridlington and Beverley - Hull

Miles			HT ◇1 A ☒	NT	NT ◇ B	NT	NT	NT ◇ B	NT	NT B	NT ◇ B	NT	NT ◇ B	NT	NT ◇ B	NT	NT ◇ B	NT	NT ◇ B	NT	NT ◇ B	NT	NT ◇ B
0	**Scarborough**	39 d						06 55				08 26			10 00			11 26				13 25	
2¾	Seamer	39 d						07 00				08 31			10 05			11 31				13 31	
9¼	Filey	d						07 10				08 41			10 15			11 41				13 41	
12	Hunmanby	d						07 15				08 46			10 20			11 46				13 46	
19¾	Bempton	d						07 25				08 56			10 30			11 56				13 55	
22¾	**Bridlington**	a						07 32				09 03			10 37			12 04				14 03	
—		d			06 31		07 03	07 33	07 49		08 35	09 04	09 35	10 00	10 38	11 04	11 35	12 04	12 32	13 04	13 35	14 04	14 35
32¾	Nafferton	d			06 41		07 14	07 44	08 00		08 45		09 45	10 11	10 48		11 45		12 42		13 45		14 45
24¾	Driffield	d			06 45		07 18	07 48	08 04		08 49	09 18	09 49	10 16	10 52	11 18	11 49	12 18	12 46	13 18	13 49	14 18	14 49
37½	Hutton Cranswick	d			06 50		07 23	07 53	08 09		08 54		09 54	10 21	10 57		11 54		12 51		13 54		14 54
42½	Arram	d					07 30		08 16		09 01						12 01						
45½	**Beverley**	d	06 00	06 23	07 00	07 22	07 35	08 02	08 21	08 36	09 06	09 30	10 04	10 30	11 07	11 30	12 06	12 30	13 01	13 30	14 04	14 30	15 04
49¾	Cottingham	d	06 06	06 29	07 06	07 28	07 42	08 09	08 27	08 42	09 12	09 36	10 10	10 36	11 13	11 37	12 12	12 36	13 07	13 36	14 10	14 36	15 10
53¾	**Hull**	a	06 15	06 38	07 16	07 38	07 53	08 22	08 36	08 50	09 22	09 47	10 21	10 47	11 23	11 47	12 22	12 47	13 17	13 47	14 20	14 47	15 22

		NT	NT ◇ B	NT	NT ◇ B	NT	NT ◇ B	NT	NT	NT ◇ B	NT	NT	NT ◇ B	NT	NT	NT	NT
Scarborough	39 d		14 58			16 25				17 58				20 24		21 11	
Seamer	39 d		15 03			16 30				18 03				20 30		21 17	
Filey	d		15 13			16 40				18 13				20 40		21 28	
Hunmanby	d		15 18			16 45				18 18				20 44		21 33	
Bempton	d		15 28			16 54				18 28				20 54		21 43	
Bridlington	a		15 35			17 02				18 34				21 01		21 50	
	d	15 00	15 36	16 04	16 33	17 02	17 35	18 04	18 22	18 35	19 04	19 33	20 35	21 02	21 36	21 55	23 02
Nafferton	d	15 11	15 46		16 43		17 45	18 15		18 45		19 44	20 45		21 47		23 13
Driffield	d	15 16	15 50	16 18	16 47	17 16	17 49	18 19	18 35	18 49	19 18	19 49	20 49	21 15	21 52	22 09	23 18
Hutton Cranswick	d	15 21	15 55		16 52	17 21	17 54	18 24		18 54		19 54	20 54		21 57		23 23
Arram	d				16 59	17 27											
Beverley	d	15 30	16 05	16 30	17 04	17 32	18 04	18 34	18 47	19 04	19 30	20 04	21 04	21 28	22 07	22 21	23 33
Cottingham	d	15 36	16 11	16 36	17 10	17 38	18 10	18 40	18 53	19 10	19 36	20 10	21 10	21 34	22 13	22 27	23 39
Hull	a	15 47	16 23	16 47	17 22	17 48	18 21	18 50	19 03	19 20	19 49	20 21	21 20	21 44	22 23	22 37	23 49

Saturdays

26 May to 8 December

		HT ◇1 A ☒	NT	NT ◇ B	NT	NT	NT ◇ B	NT	NT B	NT ◇ B	NT	NT ◇ B	NT	NT ◇ B	NT	NT ◇ B	NT	NT ◇ B	NT	NT ◇ B	NT	NT ◇ B	NT
Scarborough	39 d						06 55				08 26			10 00			11 26				13 25		
Seamer	39 d						07 00				08 31			10 05			11 31				13 31		
Filey	d						07 10				08 41			10 15			11 41				13 41		
Hunmanby	d						07 15				08 46			10 20			11 46				13 46		
Bempton	d						07 25				08 56			10 30			11 56				13 55		
Bridlington	a						07 32				09 03			10 37			12 04				14 03		
	d			06 31		07 03	07 33	07 49		08 35	09 04	09 35	10 00	10 38	11 04	11 35	12 04	12 32	13 04	13 35	14 04	14 35	15 00
Nafferton	d			06 41		07 14	07 44	08 00		08 45		09 45	10 11	10 48		11 45		12 42		13 45		14 45	15 11
Driffield	d			06 45		07 18	07 48	08 04		08 49	09 18	09 49	10 16	10 52	11 18	11 49	12 18	12 46	13 18	13 49	14 18	14 49	15 16
Hutton Cranswick	d			06 50		07 23	07 53	08 09		08 54		09 54	10 21	10 57		11 54		12 51		13 54		14 54	15 21
Arram	d					07 30		08 16		09 01						12 01							
Beverley	d	05 57	06 23	07 00	07 22	07 35	08 02	08 21	08 36	09 06	09 30	10 04	10 30	11 07	11 30	12 06	12 30	13 01	13 30	14 04	14 30	15 04	15 30
Cottingham	d	06 03	06 29	07 06	07 28	07 42	08 09	08 27	08 42	09 12	09 36	10 10	10 36	11 13	11 37	12 12	12 36	13 07	13 36	14 10	14 36	15 10	15 36
Hull	a	06 12	06 38	07 16	07 38	07 53	08 22	08 36	08 50	09 22	09 47	10 21	10 47	11 23	11 47	12 22	12 47	13 17	13 47	14 20	14 47	15 22	15 47

		NT ◇ B	NT	NT ◇ B	NT	NT ◇ B	NT	NT	NT ◇ B	NT	NT	NT ◇ B	NT	NT	NT	NT
Scarborough	39 d	14 58			16 25				17 58				20 24		21 11	
Seamer	39 d	15 03			16 30				18 03				20 30		21 17	
Filey	d	15 13			16 40				18 13				20 40		21 28	
Hunmanby	d	15 18			16 45				18 18				20 44		21 33	
Bempton	d	15 28			16 54				18 28				20 54		21 43	
Bridlington	a	15 35			17 02				18 34				21 01		21 50	
	d	15 36	16 04	16 33	17 02	17 35	18 04	18 22	18 35	19 04	19 33	20 35	21 02	21 36	21 55	23 02
Nafferton	d	15 46		16 43		17 45	18 15		18 45		19 44	20 45		21 47		23 13
Driffield	d	15 50	16 18	16 47	17 16	17 49	18 19	18 35	18 49	19 18	19 49	20 49	21 15	21 52	22 09	23 18
Hutton Cranswick	d	15 55		16 52	17 21	17 54	18 24		18 54		19 54	20 54		21 57		23 23
Arram	d			16 59	17 27											
Beverley	d	16 05	16 30	17 04	17 32	18 04	18 34	18 47	19 04	19 30	20 04	21 04	21 28	22 07	22 21	23 33
Cottingham	d	16 11	16 36	17 10	17 38	18 10	18 40	18 53	19 10	19 36	20 10	21 10	21 34	22 13	22 27	23 39
Hull	a	16 23	16 47	17 22	17 48	18 21	18 50	19 03	19 20	19 49	20 21	21 20	21 44	22 23	22 37	23 49

A To London Kings Cross

B To Sheffield

Table T043-R

Sundays

20 May to 2 December

Scarborough, Bridlington and Beverley - Hull

		NT	HT ◇1 A ☒	NT ◇ B	NT ◇ B	NT ◇ B	NT ◇ B	NT ◇ B	NT ◇ B	NT ◇ B	NT ◇ B	NT	NT ◇ B	NT ◇ B	NT ◇ B	NT	NT
Scarborough	39 d			10 09		12 08		14 08		16 08			18 08		20 08		
Seamer	39 d			10 14		12 13		14 13		16 13			18 13		20 13		
Filey	d			10 24		12 23		14 23		16 23			18 23		20 23		
Hunmanby	d			10 29		12 28		14 28		16 28			18 28		20 28		
Bempton	d			10 38		12 37		14 37		16 37			18 37		20 37		
Bridlington	a			10 46		12 45		14 45		16 45			18 45		20 45		
	d	09 57		10 47	11 42	12 46	13 42	14 46	15 42	16 46	17 42	18 27	18 46	19 42	20 46		21 15
Nafferton	d	10 07			11 53		13 53		15 53		17 53	18 38		19 53			21 25
Driffield	d	10 11		11 00	11 57	12 59	13 57	14 59	15 57	16 59	17 57	18 42	18 59	19 57	20 59		21 29
Hutton Cranswick	d	10 16			12 02		14 02		16 02		18 02	18 47		20 02			21 34
Arram	d																
Beverley	d	10 26	10 52	11 13	12 12	13 12	14 12	15 12	16 12	17 12	18 12	18 57	19 12	20 12	21 12	21 30	21 44
Cottingham	d	10 32	10 58	11 19	12 18	13 18	14 18	15 18	16 18	17 18	18 18	19 03	19 18	20 18	21 18	21 36	21 50
Hull	a	10 43	11 05	11 26	12 26	13 26	14 26	15 26	16 26	17 26	18 26	19 14	19 26	20 26	21 26	21 47	22 01

A To London Kings Cross

B To Sheffield

Saltburn and Middlesbrough - Darlington, Bishop Auckland, Sunderland and Newcastle

Miles	Miles		GR ■ A	TP ◇■ B	NT ◇ C	TP ◇■ D	NT	NT	NT ◇ C	TP ◇■ D	NT	NT	NT	NT E	NT ◇ C	TP ◇■ D	NT	NT E	NT	TP ◇■ D	NT	NT F
0	—	**Saltburn** d							06 18				06 58		07 18		07 41		08 17		08 44	09 00
2	—	Marske d							06 22				07 02		07 22		07 45		08 21		08 48	09 04
2½	—	Longbeck d							06 25				07 05		07 25		07 48		08 24		08 51	09 07
4	—	Redcar East d							06 28				07 08		07 28		07 51		08 27		08 54	09 10
5	—	**Redcar Central** d							06 31				07 11		07 31		07 54		08 30		08 57	09 13
6¾	—	British Steel Redcar § d															07 57					
10	—	South Bank d							06 38				07 18		07 38		08 03				09 04	
12½	0	**Middlesbrough** a							06 44				07 25		07 44		08 09		08 42		09 10	09 25
—	—	d		05 43	05 47	06 22			06 45	06 50	06 59		07 25	07 34	07 45	07 57	08 10	08 21	08 43	08 57	09 10	
15¾	3¼	Thornaby d		05a48	05 52	06a27			06 50	06a55	07 04		07 30	07 39	07 50	08a02	08 15	08 26	08 48	09a02	09 15	
—	—	London Kings Cross ⊖26 d																				
18¾	—	Eaglescliffe a			05 57				06 55				07 35		07 56		08 20		08 53		09 20	
—	—	d			05 58				06 55				07 37		07 57		08 20		08 53		09 21	
19½	—	Allens West d			06 01				06 58				07 39		08 00		08 23		08 56		09 23	
22	—	Tees-side Airport d																				
23¾	—	Dinsdale d			06 07				07 04				07 47		08 06		08 29		09 02		09 30	
27½	—	**Darlington** 26 a			06 19				07 19				07 55		08 17		08 38		09 11		09 38	
—	—	d			06 20		06 24		07 21			07 40			08 19		08 40				09 40	
—	—	Durham d			06 41				07 42						08 40							
—	—	Chester-le-Street d			06 48				07 49						08 48							
28¾	—	North Road d					06 27					07 43					08 43				09 43	
33¼	—	Heighington d					06 35					07 51					08 51				09 51	
34½	—	Newton Aycliffe d					06 38					07 54					08 54				09 54	
36¾	—	Shildon d					06 43					07 59					08 59				09 59	
39½	—	**Bishop Auckland** a					06 50					08 06					09 06				10 06	
—	5½	Stockton d									07 10			07 45				08 32				
—	10	Billingham d									07 18			07 53				08 41				
—	15	Seaton Carew d									07 24			07 59				08 47				
—	17¼	**Hartlepool** d						06 53			07 30			08 04				08 54				
—	30	Seaham d						07 09			07 46			08 20				09 10				
—	35¼	**Sunderland** a						07 18			07 55			08 29				09 19				
—	—	d	05 40					07 19			07 56			08 30				09 20				
—	44½	Heworth d						07 33			08 10			08 45				09 34				
—	47¼	**Newcastle** 26,45 a	05 56		06 59			07 40	07 59		08 19			08 54	09 00			09 41				
—	—	Metrocentre 48 a			07 09			07 49	08 14					09 04	09 20			09 54				
—	—	Hexham 48 a			07 42			08 16	08 39					09 38	09 47			10 28				

	NT E	NT	TP ◇■ D	NT	NT	GC ■	NT	TP ◇■ D	NT	NT E	NT	TP ◇■ D	NT	NT E	NT	TP ◇■ D	NT	NT	NT	GC ■	TP ◇■ D	NT
Saltburn d		09 17		09 44			10 17		10 44		11 17		11 44		12 17		12 44		13 17			13 44
Marske d		09 21		09 48			10 21		10 48		11 21		11 48		12 21		12 48		13 21			13 48
Longbeck d		09 24		09 51			10 24		10 51		11 24		11 51		12 24		12 51		13 24			13 51
Redcar East d		09 27		09 54			10 27		10 54		11 27		11 54		12 27		12 54		13 27			13 54
Redcar Central d		09 30		09 57			10 30		10 57		11 30		11 57		12 30		12 57		13 30			13 57
British Steel Redcar § d																						
South Bank d				10 04					11 04				12 04				13 04					14 04
Middlesbrough a		09 42		10 10			10 42		11 10		11 42		12 10		12 42		13 10		13 42			14 10
d	09 35	09 43	09 57	10 10	10 33		10 43	10 55	11 10	11 35	11 43	11 55	12 10	12 35	12 43	12 57	13 10	13 33	13 43		13 57	14 10
Thornaby d	09 41	09 48	10a02	10 15	10 38		10 48	11a00	11 15	11 40	11 48	12a00	12 15	12 40	12 48	13a02	13 15	13 38	13 48		14a02	14 15
London Kings Cross ⊖26 d						08 06														11 27		
Eaglescliffe a		09 53		10 20		10 50	10 53		11 20		11 53		12 20		12 53		13 22		13 53	14 03		14 20
d		09 53		10 21		10 51	10 53		11 21		11 53		12 21		12 53		13 22		13 53	14 04		14 21
Allens West d		09 56		10 23			10 56		11 23		11 56		12 23		12 56		13 25		13 56			14 23
Tees-side Airport d																						
Dinsdale d		10 02		10 30			11 02		11 30		12 02		12 30		13 02		13 31		14 02			14 30
Darlington 26 a		10 11		10 38			11 11		11 38		12 11		12 38		13 11		13 39		14 11			14 38
d				10 40					11 40				12 40				13 41					14 40
Durham d																						
Chester-le-Street d																						
North Road d				10 43					11 43				12 43				13 44					14 43
Heighington d				10 51					11 51				12 51				13 52					14 51
Newton Aycliffe d				10 54					11 54				12 54				13 55					14 54
Shildon d				10 59					11 59				12 59				14 00					14 59
Bishop Auckland a				11 06					12 06				13 06				14 07					15 06
Stockton d	09 47				10 45					11 46				12 46				13 44				
Billingham d	09 54				10 52					11 53				12 54				13 52				
Seaton Carew d	10 00				10 58					11 59				13 00				13 58				
Hartlepool d	10 05				11 04	11 15				12 05				13 05				14 03		14 23		
Seaham d	10 21				11 19					12 20				13 21				14 19				
Sunderland a	10 30				11 29	11 40				12 29				13 30				14 28		14 52		
d	10 30				11 30					12 30				13 30				14 30				
Heworth d	10 45				11 45					12 45				13 45				14 45				
Newcastle 26,45 a	10 52				11 52					12 52				13 52				14 52				
Metrocentre 48 a	11 03				12 03					13 03				14 03				15 05				
Hexham 48 a	11 37				12 37					13 37				14 37				15 40				

§ For authorised access only to BSC Redcar
A To London Kings Cross
B To Liverpool Lime Street
C To Carlisle
D To Manchester Airport
E From Nunthorpe
F To Nunthorpe

For services between Middlesbrough and Nunthorpe, refer to Table T045

Table T044-F

Mondays to Fridays

21 May to 7 December

Saltburn and Middlesbrough - Darlington, Bishop Auckland, Sunderland and Newcastle

	NT A	NT	TP ◇■ B	NT	NT ◇ C	GC ■	NT	TP ◇■ B	NT	NT D	NT	TP ◇■ B	NT	NT ◇ E	NT	TP ◇■ B	NT	NT F	NT	TP ◇■ B	NT
Saltburn d		14 17		14 44			15 17		15 44		16 17		16 42		17 17		17 44		18 17		18 44
Marske d		14 21		14 48			15 21		15 48		16 21		16 46		17 21		17 48		18 21		18 48
Longbeck d		14 24		14 51			15 24		15 51		16 24		16 49		17 24		17 51		18 24		18 51
Redcar East d		14 27		14 54			15 27		15 54		16 27		16 52		17 27		17 54		18 27		18 54
Redcar Central d		14 30		14 57			15 30		15 57		16 30		16 55		17 30		17 57		18 30		18 57
British Steel Redcar § d													16 58								
South Bank d				15 04					16 04				17 04				18 04				19 04
Middlesbrough a		14 42		15 10			15 42		16 10		16 42		17 10		17 42		18 10		18 42		19 10
d	14 36	14 43	14 55	15 10	15 32		15 43	15 57	16 10	16 35	16 43	16 57	17 10	17 34	17 43	17 57	18 10	18 33	18 43	18 57	19 10
Thornaby d	14 42	14 48	15a00	15 15	15 38		15 48	16a02	16 15	16 40	16 48	17a02	17 15	17 39	17 48	18a02	18 16	18 39	18 48	19a02	19 15
London Kings Cross ⊖26 d						12 57															
Eaglescliffe a		14 53		15 20		15 43	15 53		16 20		16 53		17 20		17 53		18 21		18 53		19 20
d		14 53		15 21		15 46	15 53		16 21		16 53		17 21		17 53		18 22		18 53		19 21
Allens West d		14 56		15 23			15 56		16 23		16 56		17 23		17 56		18 24		18 56		19 23
Tees-side Airport d																					
Dinsdale d		15 02		15 30			16 02		16 30		17 02		17 30		18 02		18 31		19 02		19 30
Darlington 26 a		15 11		15 38			16 11		16 38		17 11		17 38		18 11		18 39		19 12		19 39
d				15 40					16 40				17 40				18 41				19 41
Durham d																					
Chester-le-Street d																					
North Road d				15 43					16 43				17 43				18 44				19 44
Heighington d				15 51					16 51				17 51				18 52				19 52
Newton Aycliffe d				15 54					16 54				17 54				18 55				19 55
Shildon d				15 59					16 59				17 59				19 00				20 00
Bishop Auckland a				16 06					17 06				18 06				19 07				20 07
Stockton d	14 48				15 44					16 46				17 45				18 44			
Billingham d	14 55				15 51					16 54				17 52				18 52			
Seaton Carew d	15 01				15 57					17 00				17 58				18 58			
Hartlepool d	15 07				16 03	16 13				17 05				18 04				19 03			
Seaham d	15 22				16 18					17 21				18 19				19 19			
Sunderland a	15 31				16 29	16 38				17 30				18 29				19 28			
d	15 32				16 30					17 30				18 29				19 28			
Heworth d	15 45				16 45					17 45				18 42				19 40			
Newcastle 26,45 a	15 52				16 52					17 52				18 49				19 47			
Metrocentre 48 a	16 03				17 03					18 04				19 01				19 57			
Hexham 48 a	16 37				17 36					18 38				19 35							

	GC ■	NT D	NT	TP ◇■ G	NT	NT D	NT	TP ◇■ B	NT	NT	NT	GC ■	GR ■	TP ◇■ H	NT	NT	TP ◇■ G	NT
Saltburn d			19 17		19 44		20 17		20 47		21 18				21 44			22 44
Marske d			19 21		19 48		20 21		20 51		21 22				21 48			22 48
Longbeck d			19 24		19 51		20 24		20 54		21 25				21 51			22 51
Redcar East d			19 27		19 54		20 27		20 57		21 28				21 54			22 54
Redcar Central d			19 30		19 57		20 30		21 00		21 31				21 57			22 57
British Steel Redcar § d																		
South Bank d					20 04				21 07						22 04			23 04
Middlesbrough a			19 42		20 10		20 45		21 13		21 42				22 11			23 10
d		19 34	19 43	19 57	20 10	20 35	20 45	20 57	21 15	21 35	21 46			21 57		22 16	22 57	23 10
Thornaby d		19 40	19 48	20a02	20 15	20 40	20 50	21a02	21 20	21 40	21 51			22a02		22 22	23a02	23 15
London Kings Cross ⊖26 d	16 48											19 27	20 00					
Eaglescliffe a	19 25		19 53		20 20		20 56		21 25		21 56	22 02				22 27		23 20
d	19 26		19 53		20 21		20 56		21 25		21 57	22 03				22 27		23 21
Allens West d			19 56		20 23		20 59		21 28		22 00					22 30		23 23
Tees-side Airport d																		
Dinsdale d			20 02		20 30		21 05		21 34		22 06					22 36		23 30
Darlington 26 a			20 11		20 38		21 14		21 44		22 18		22 21			22 44		23 38
d					20 40								22 23					
Durham d													22 41					
Chester-le-Street d																		
North Road d					20 43													
Heighington d					20 51													
Newton Aycliffe d					20 54													
Shildon d					20 59													
Bishop Auckland a					21 06													
Stockton d		19 46				20 45				21 46								
Billingham d		19 54				20 53				21 53								
Seaton Carew d		20 00				20 59				21 59								
Hartlepool d	19 51	20 05				21 04				22 05		22 26						
Seaham d		20 21				21 20				22 20								
Sunderland a	20 22	20 30				21 29				22 30		22 52	23 21					
d		20 30				21 29				22 30								
Heworth d		20 44				21 45				22 44								
Newcastle 26,45 a		20 51				21 52				22 51								
Metrocentre 48 a		21 01				22 02				23 01								
Hexham 48 a										23 36								

§ For authorised access only to BSC Redcar
A From Danby
B To Manchester Airport
C From Nunthorpe to Carlisle
D From Nunthorpe
E From Whitby
F From Battersby
G To York
H To Manchester Piccadilly

For services between Middlesbrough and Nunthorpe, refer to Table T045

Table T044-F

Saturdays

26 May to 8 December

Saltburn and Middlesbrough - Darlington, Bishop Auckland, Sunderland and Newcastle

		TP	NT	TP	NT	NT	TP	NT	NT	NT	NT	NT	TP	NT	NT	NT	TP	NT	NT	NT	NT	TP	NT
		◇1 A 🛒		◇1 B 🛒		◇ C	◇1 B 🛒				D	◇ C	◇1 B 🛒		D		◇1 B 🛒		E	D		◇1 B 🛒	
Saltburn	d					06 18				06 58		07 18		07 41		08 17		08 44	09 00		09 17		09 44
Marske	d					06 22				07 02		07 22		07 45		08 21		08 48	09 04		09 21		09 48
Longbeck	d					06 25				07 05		07 25		07 48		08 24		08 51	09 07		09 24		09 51
Redcar East	d					06 28				07 08		07 28		07 51		08 27		08 54	09 10		09 27		09 54
Redcar Central	d					06 31				07 11		07 31		07 54		08 30		08 57	09 13		09 30		09 57
British Steel Redcar §	d													07 57									
South Bank	d					06 38				07 18		07 38		08 03				09 04					10 04
Middlesbrough	a					06 44				07 25		07 44		08 09		08 42		09 10	09 25		09 42		10 10
	d	05 43	05 47	06 22		06 45	06 50	06 59		07 25	07 34	07 45	07 57	08 10	08 25	08 43	08 57	09 10		09 35	09 43	09 57	10 10
Thornaby	d	05a48	05 52	06a27		06 50	06a55	07 04		07 30	07 39	07 50	08a02	08 15	08 31	08 48	09a02	09 15		09 41	09 48	10a02	10 15
London Kings Cross 15 ⊖26	d																						
Eaglescliffe	a		05 57			06 55				07 35		07 56		08 20		08 53		09 20			09 53		10 20
	d		05 58			06 55				07 37		07 57		08 20		08 53		09 21			09 53		10 21
Allens West	d		06 01			06 58				07 39		08 00		08 23		08 56		09 23			09 56		10 23
Tees-side Airport	d																						
Dinsdale	d		06 07			07 04				07 47		08 06		08 29		09 02		09 30			10 02		10 30
Darlington 7 26	a		06 16			07 19				07 55		08 19		08 38		09 11		09 38			10 11		10 38
	d		06 24			07 21			07 40			08 20		08 40				09 40					10 40
Durham	d					07 42						08 42											
Chester-le-Street	d					07 49						08 49											
North Road	d		06 27						07 43					08 43				09 43					10 43
Heighington	d		06 35						07 51					08 51				09 51					10 51
Newton Aycliffe	d		06 38						07 54					08 54				09 54					10 54
Shildon	d		06 43						07 59					08 59				09 59					10 59
Bishop Auckland	a		06 50						08 06					09 06				10 06					11 06
Stockton	d							07 10			07 45				08 37					09 47			
Billingham	d							07 18			07 53				08 45					09 54			
Seaton Carew	d							07 24			07 59				08 51					10 00			
Hartlepool	d				06 50			07 30			08 04				08 59					10 05			
Seaham	d				07 06			07 46			08 20				09 15					10 21			
Sunderland ⇌	a				07 15			07 55			08 29				09 24					10 30			
	d				07 16			07 56			08 30				09 28					10 30			
Heworth ⇌	d				07 26			08 10			08 45				09 43					10 45			
Newcastle 8 26,45 ⇌	a				07 35	07 59		08 19			08 54	09 01			09 53					10 52			
Metrocentre 48	a				07 48	08 14					09 04	09 22			10 03					11 03			
Hexham 48	a				08 16	08 39					09 38	09 47			10 37					11 37			

		NT	NT	GC	TP	NT	NT	NT	TP	NT	NT	NT	TP	NT	NT	NT	GC	TP	NT	NT	NT	TP
				■ 1 🍴	◇1 B 🛒		D		◇1 B 🛒		D		◇1 B 🛒				■ 1 🍴	◇1 B 🛒		F		◇1 B 🛒
Saltburn	d		10 17			10 44		11 17		11 44		12 17		12 44		13 17			13 44		14 17	
Marske	d		10 21			10 48		11 21		11 48		12 21		12 48		13 21			13 48		14 21	
Longbeck	d		10 24			10 51		11 24		11 51		12 24		12 51		13 24			13 51		14 24	
Redcar East	d		10 27			10 54		11 27		11 54		12 27		12 54		13 27			13 54		14 27	
Redcar Central	d		10 30			10 57		11 30		11 57		12 30		12 57		13 30			13 57		14 30	
British Steel Redcar §	d																					
South Bank	d					11 04				12 04				13 04					14 04			
Middlesbrough	a		10 42			11 10		11 42		12 10		12 42		13 10		13 42			14 10		14 42	
	d	10 33	10 43		10 55	11 10	11 35	11 43	11 55	12 10	12 35	12 43	12 57	13 10	13 33	13 43		13 57	14 10	14 36	14 43	14 55
Thornaby	d	10 38	10 48		11a02	11 15	11 40	11 48	12a02	12 15	12 40	12 48	13a02	13 15	13 38	13 48		14a02	14 15	14 42	14 48	15a02
London Kings Cross 15 ⊖26	d			08 06													11 27					
Eaglescliffe	a		10 53	11 04		11 20		11 53		12 20		12 53		13 22		13 54	14 02		14 20		14 53	
	d		10 53	11 05		11 21		11 53		12 21		12 53		13 22		13 54	14 03		14 21		14 53	
Allens West	d		10 56			11 23		11 56		12 23		12 56		13 25		13 56			14 23		14 56	
Tees-side Airport	d																					
Dinsdale	d		11 02			11 30		12 02		12 30		13 02		13 31		14 02			14 30		15 02	
Darlington 7 26	a		11 11			11 38		12 11		12 38		13 11		13 39		14 11			14 38		15 11	
	d					11 40				12 40				13 41					14 40			
Durham	d																					
Chester-le-Street	d																					
North Road	d					11 43				12 43				13 44					14 43			
Heighington	d					11 51				12 51				13 52					14 51			
Newton Aycliffe	d					11 54				12 54				13 55					14 54			
Shildon	d					11 59				12 59				14 00					14 59			
Bishop Auckland	a					12 06				13 06				14 07					15 06			
Stockton	d	10 45					11 46				12 46				13 44					14 48		
Billingham	d	10 52					11 53				12 54				13 52					14 55		
Seaton Carew	d	10 58					11 59				13 00				13 58					15 01		
Hartlepool	d	11 04		11 24			12 05				13 05				14 03		14 23			15 07		
Seaham	d	11 19					12 20				13 21				14 19					15 22		
Sunderland ⇌	a	11 29		11 50			12 29				13 30				14 28		14 51			15 31		
	d	11 30					12 30				13 30				14 30					15 32		
Heworth ⇌	d	11 45					12 45				13 45				14 45					15 45		
Newcastle 8 26,45 ⇌	a	11 52					12 52				13 52				14 52					15 52		
Metrocentre 48	a	12 03					13 03				14 03				15 03					16 03		
Hexham 48	a	12 37					13 37				14 37				15 37					16 37		

§ For authorised access only to BSC Redcar
A To Liverpool Lime Street
B To Manchester Airport
C To Carlisle
D From Nunthorpe
E To Nunthorpe
F From Danby

For services between Middlesbrough and Nunthorpe, refer to Table T045

Table T044-F

Saturdays

26 May to 8 December

Saltburn and Middlesbrough - Darlington, Bishop Auckland, Sunderland and Newcastle

		NT	NT	NT	GC	TP	NT	NT	NT	TP	NT	NT	NT	TP	NT	NT	NT	TP	NT	GC	NT	NT
			◇ A		■ 1 🍴	◇1 B 🛒		C		◇1 B 🛒		◇ D		◇1 B		E		◇1 B		■ 1 🍴	C	
Saltburn	d	14 44		15 17			15 44		16 17		16 42		17 17		17 44		18 17		18 44			19 17
Marske	d	14 48		15 21			15 48		16 21		16 46		17 21		17 48		18 21		18 48			19 21
Longbeck	d	14 51		15 24			15 51		16 24		16 49		17 24		17 51		18 24		18 51			19 24
Redcar East	d	14 54		15 27			15 54		16 27		16 52		17 27		17 54		18 27		18 54			19 27
Redcar Central	d	14 57		15 30			15 57		16 30		16 55		17 30		17 57		18 30		18 57			19 30
British Steel Redcar §	d										16 58											
South Bank	d	15 04					16 04				17 04				18 04				19 04			
Middlesbrough	a	15 10		15 42			16 10		16 42		17 10		17 42		18 10		18 42		19 10			19 42
	d	15 10	15 32	15 43		15 57	16 10	16 35	16 43	16 57	17 10	17 34	17 43	17 57	18 10	18 33	18 43	18 57	19 10		19 31	19 43
Thornaby	d	15 15	15 38	15 48		16a02	16 15	16 40	16 48	17a02	17 15	17 39	17 48	18a02	18 16	18 39	18 48	19a02	19 15		19 36	19 48
London Kings Cross 15 ⊖26	d				13 18															16 48		
Eaglescliffe	a	15 20		15 53	16 01		16 20		16 53		17 20		17 53		18 21		18 53		19 20	19 26		19 53
	d	15 21		15 53	16 02		16 21		16 53		17 21		17 53		18 22		18 53		19 21	19 27		19 53
Allens West	d	15 23		15 56			16 23		16 56		17 23		17 56		18 24		18 56		19 23			19 56
Tees-side Airport	d																					
Dinsdale	d	15 30		16 02			16 30		17 02		17 30		18 02		18 31		19 02		19 30			20 02
Darlington 7 26	a	15 38		16 11			16 38		17 11		17 38		18 11		18 39		19 12		19 39			20 11
	d	15 40					16 40				17 40				18 41				19 41			
Durham	d																					
Chester-le-Street	d																					
North Road	d	15 43					16 43				17 43				18 44				19 44			
Heighington	d	15 51					16 51				17 51				18 52				19 52			
Newton Aycliffe	d	15 54					16 54				17 54				18 55				19 55			
Shildon	d	15 59					16 59				17 59				19 00				20 00			
Bishop Auckland	a	16 06					17 06				18 06				19 07				20 07			
Stockton	d		15 44					16 46				17 45				18 44					19 46	
Billingham	d		15 51					16 54				17 52				18 52					19 54	
Seaton Carew	d		15 57					17 00				17 58				18 58					20 00	
Hartlepool	d		16 03		16 23			17 05				18 04				19 03				19 57	20 05	
Seaham	d		16 18					17 21				18 19				19 19					20 21	
Sunderland ⇌	a		16 29		16 51			17 30				18 29				19 28				20 21	20 30	
	d		16 30					17 30				18 29				19 28					20 30	
Heworth ⇌	d		16 45					17 45				18 42				19 40					20 44	
Newcastle 8 26,45 ⇌	a		16 52					17 52				18 49				19 47					20 51	
Metrocentre 48	a		17 03					18 04				19 01				19 57					21 01	
Hexham 48	a		17 36					18 38				19 35										

		TP	NT	NT	NT	TP	NT	NT	GC	NT	TP	NT	TP	NT
		◇1 F		C		◇1 B			■ 1 🍴		◇1 G		◇1 F	
Saltburn	d		19 44		20 17		20 47			21 18		21 44		22 44
Marske	d		19 48		20 21		20 51			21 22		21 48		22 48
Longbeck	d		19 51		20 24		20 54			21 25		21 51		22 51
Redcar East	d		19 54		20 27		20 57			21 28		21 54		22 54
Redcar Central	d		19 57		20 30		21 00			21 31		21 57		22 57
British Steel Redcar §	d													
South Bank	d		20 04				21 07					22 04		23 04
Middlesbrough	a		20 10		20 45		21 13			21 42				23 10
	d	20 03	20 10	20 35	20 45	20 52	21 15	21 35			21 57		22 43	23 10
Thornaby	d	20a08	20 15	20 40	20 50	20a57	21 20	21 40			22a02	22 22	22a48	23 15
London Kings Cross 15 ⊖26	d								19 27					
Eaglescliffe	a		20 20		20 55		21 25		22 04			22 27		23 20
	d		20 21		20 55		21 25		22 05			22 27		23 21
Allens West	d		20 23		20 58		21 28					22 30		23 23
Tees-side Airport	d													
Dinsdale	d		20 30		21 04		21 34					22 36		23 30
Darlington 7 26	a		20 38		21 13		21 44					22 45		23 38
	d		20 40											
Durham	d													
Chester-le-Street	d													
North Road	d		20 43											
Heighington	d		20 51											
Newton Aycliffe	d		20 54											
Shildon	d		20 59											
Bishop Auckland	a		21 06											
Stockton	d			20 45				21 45						
Billingham	d			20 53				21 53						
Seaton Carew	d			20 59				21 59						
Hartlepool	d			21 04				22 04	22 25					
Seaham	d			21 20				22 20						
Sunderland ⇌	a			21 29				22 28	22 49					
	d			21 29				22 29						
Heworth ⇌	d			21 42				22 42						
Newcastle 8 26,45 ⇌	a			21 51				22 49						
Metrocentre 48	a			22 01										
Hexham 48	a													

§ For authorised access only to BSC Redcar
A From Nunthorpe to Carlisle
B To Manchester Airport
C From Nunthorpe
D From Whitby
E From Battersby
F To York
G To Leeds

For services between Middlesbrough and Nunthorpe, refer to Table T045

Table T044-F

Sundays
20 May to 2 December

Saltburn and Middlesbrough - Darlington, Bishop Auckland, Sunderland and Newcastle

		NT	NT	NT	NT	TP	NT	NT	NT	TP	NT	NT	TP	NT	NT	NT	GC	TP	NT	NT	TP	NT	NT
					◇ A	◇■ B		◇ A		◇■ B		◇ C	◇■ D		◇ A	E	■ ■	◇■ D		◇ C	◇■ D		F
Saltburn	d								09 16		09 44			10 44					11 49			12 44	
Marske	d								09 20		09 48			10 48					11 53			12 48	
Longbeck	d								09 23		09 51			10 51					11 56			12 51	
Redcar East	d								09 26		09 54			10 54					11 59			12 54	
Redcar Central	d								09 29		09 57			10 57					12 02			12 57	
British Steel Redcar §	d																						
South Bank	d								09 36		10 04			11 04					12 09			13 04	
Middlesbrough	a								09 43		10 10			11 10					12 15			13 10	
	d			08 25	08 32	08 57	09 11	09 35		09 52	10 10	10 33	10 57	11 10	11 33	11 52		11 57	12 15	12 33	12 47	13 10	
Thornaby	d			08 30	08 38	09a02	09 16	09 40		09a57	10 15	10 39	11a02	11 15	11 38	11 57		12a02	12 20	12 38	12a52	13 15	
London Kings Cross ⊖26	d																09 52						
Eaglescliffe	a			08 35			09 21				10 20			11 20		12 02	12 23		12 25			13 20	
	d			08 35			09 22				10 21			11 21		12 02	12 24		12 26			13 21	13 29
Allens West	d			08 38			09 24				10 23			11 23		12 05			12 28			13 23	
Tees-side Airport	d																						
Dinsdale	d			08 44			09 31				10 30			11 30		12 11			12 35			13 30	
Darlington ■ 26	a			08 53			09 39				10 38			11 38		12 20			12 42			13 38	
	d	07 35	08 40				09 41				10 40			11 40								13 40	
Durham	d																						
Chester-le-Street	d																						
North Road	d	07 38	08 43				09 44				10 43			11 43								13 43	
Heighington	d	07 46	08 51				09 52				10 51			11 51								13 51	
Newton Aycliffe	d	07 49	08 54				09 55				10 54			11 54								13 54	
Shildon	d	07 54	08 59				10 00				10 59			11 59								13 59	
Bishop Auckland	a	08 01	09 06				10 07				11 06			12 06								14 06	
Stockton	d				08 44			09 46				10 44			11 44					12 44			13 34
Billingham	d				08 53			09 54				10 52			11 53					12 53			13 41
Seaton Carew	d				08 59			10 00				10 58			11 59					12 59			13 47
Hartlepool	d				09 04			10 05				11 03			12 04		12 46			13 04			13a54
Seaham	d				09 20			10 21				11 19			12 20					13 20			
Sunderland	a				09 29			10 29				11 27			12 28		13 10			13 28			
	d				09 30			10 30				11 28			12 29					13 29			
Heworth	d				09 42			10 42				11 41			12 41					13 41			
Newcastle ■ 26,45	a				09 50			10 50				11 49			12 50					13 50			
Metrocentre 48	a				10 02			11 02				12 03			13 02					14 02			
Hexham 48	a				10 35			11 33				12 36			13 33					14 35			

		NT	TP	NT	NT	NT	TP	NT	NT	TP	NT	GC	NT	TP	NT	NT	NT	TP	NT	NT	NT	TP	NT
		◇ C	◇■ D		◇ G	H	◇■ D		◇ C	◇■ D		■ ■	◇ C	◇■ D		F	◇ G	◇■ D		◇ C	H	◇■ D	
Saltburn	d			13 44				14 44			15 44				16 44				17 44				18 44
Marske	d			13 48				14 48			15 48				16 48				17 48				18 48
Longbeck	d			13 51				14 51			15 51				16 51				17 51				18 51
Redcar East	d			13 54				14 54			15 54				16 54				17 54				18 54
Redcar Central	d			13 57				14 57			15 57				16 57				17 57				18 57
British Steel Redcar §	d																						
South Bank	d			14 04				15 04			16 04				17 04				18 04				19 04
Middlesbrough	a			14 10				15 10			16 10				17 10				18 10				19 10
	d	13 32	13 55	14 10	14 33		14 48	15 10	15 33	15 54	16 10		16 33	16 57	17 10		17 33	17 56	18 10	18 33		18 57	19 10
Thornaby	d	13 38	14a00	14 15	14 38		14a53	15 15	15 38	15a59	16 15		16 38	17a02	17 15		17 38	18a01	18 15	18 38		19a02	19 15
London Kings Cross ⊖26	d											13 48											
Eaglescliffe	a			14 20				15 20			16 20	16 25			17 20				18 20				19 20
	d			14 21		14 48		15 21			16 21	16 26			17 21	17 31			18 21		18 43		19 21
Allens West	d			14 23		14 50		15 23			16 23				17 23				18 23		18 46		19 23
Tees-side Airport	d					14 55																	
Dinsdale	d			14 30		14 59		15 30			16 30				17 30				18 30		18 52		19 30
Darlington ■ 26	a			14 38		15 08		15 37			16 38				17 38				18 38		18 59		19 37
	d			14 40				15 39			16 40				17 40				18 40				19 40
Durham	d																						
Chester-le-Street	d																						
North Road	d			14 43				15 42			16 43				17 43				18 43				19 43
Heighington	d			14 51				15 50			16 51				17 51				18 51				19 51
Newton Aycliffe	d			14 54				15 53			16 54				17 54				18 54				19 54
Shildon	d			14 59				15 58			16 59				17 59				18 59				19 58
Bishop Auckland	a			15 06				16 05			17 06				18 06				19 06				20 04
Stockton	d	13 44			14 44				15 44				16 44			17 37	17 44			18 44			
Billingham	d	13 52			14 53				15 53				16 53			17 44	17 53			18 53			
Seaton Carew	d	13 58			14 59				15 59				16 59			17 50	17 59			18 59			
Hartlepool	d	14 04			15 04				16 04			16 46	17 04			17a56	18 04			19 04			
Seaham	d	14 19			15 20				16 20				17 20				18 20			19 20			
Sunderland	a	14 27			15 28				16 28			17 11	17 29				18 28			19 28			
	d	14 28			15 29				16 29				17 30				18 29			19 29			
Heworth	d	14 40			15 41				16 41				17 42				18 41			19 41			
Newcastle ■ 26,45	a	14 49			15 49				16 49				17 50				18 49			19 50			
Metrocentre 48	a	15 02			16 02				17 02				18 02				19 02			20 02			
Hexham 48	a	15 33			16 35				17 33				18 35				19 33			20 35			

§ For authorised access only to BSC Redcar
A To Carlisle
B To Manchester Oxford Road
C From Nunthorpe to Carlisle
D To Manchester Airport
E From Whitby
F From Darlington
G From Whitby to Carlisle
H From Hartlepool

For services between Middlesbrough and Nunthorpe, refer to Table T045

Table T044-F

Sundays
20 May to 2 December

Saltburn and Middlesbrough - Darlington, Bishop Auckland, Sunderland and Newcastle

		GC	NT	TP	NT	NT	GC	NT	TP	NT	TP	NT	TP	NT
		■ ■	◇ A	◇■ B			■ ■		◇■ C		◇■ B		◇■ B	
Saltburn	d				19 44			20 44				21 44		22 56
Marske	d				19 48			20 48				21 48		23 00
Longbeck	d				19 51			20 51				21 51		23 03
Redcar East	d				19 54			20 54				21 54		23 06
Redcar Central	d				19 57			20 57				21 57		23 09
British Steel Redcar §	d													
South Bank	d				20 04			21 04				22 04		23 16
Middlesbrough	a				20 10			21 10				22 10		23 22
	d		19 33	20 03	20 10	20 33		21 10	21 21	21 33	22 07	22 11	23 00	23 22
Thornaby	d		19 38	20a08	20 15	20 38		21 15	21a26	21 39	22a12	22 16	23a05	23 27
London Kings Cross ⊖26	d	16 53					18 22							
Eaglescliffe	a	19 31			20 20		21 02	21 20				22 21		23 32
	d	19 33			20 21		21 03	21 21				22 21		23 33
Allens West	d				20 23			21 23				22 24		23 35
Tees-side Airport	d													
Dinsdale	d				20 30			21 30				22 30		23 42
Darlington ■ 26	a				20 38			21 39				22 40		23 51
	d													
Durham	d													
Chester-le-Street	d													
North Road	d													
Heighington	d													
Newton Aycliffe	d													
Shildon	d													
Bishop Auckland	a													
Stockton	d		19 44			20 44				21 44				
Billingham	d		19 53			20 53				21 53				
Seaton Carew	d		19 59			20 59				21 59				
Hartlepool	d	19 55	20 04			21 04	21 28			22 04				
Seaham	d		20 20			21 20				22 20				
Sunderland	a	20 21	20 29			21 28	21 53			22 28				
	d		20 30			21 29				22 29				
Heworth	d		20 42			21 41				22 42				
Newcastle ■ 26,45	a		20 50			21 49				22 50				
Metrocentre 48	a		21 08											
Hexham 48	a		21 41											

§ For authorised access only to BSC Redcar
A To Carlisle
B To York
C To Manchester Piccadilly

For services between Middlesbrough and Nunthorpe, refer to Table T045

Newcastle, Sunderland, Bishop Auckland and Darlington - Middlesbrough and Saltburn

Miles	Miles		NT	NT	TP	NT	GR	NT	NT	NT	NT	GC	TP	NT	NT	TP	NT	NT	NT	GC	TP	NT
			MX A		◇■ B		■ ■ ☕	C		D		■ ■ ☕	◇■ B			◇■ E		D		■ ■ ☕	◇■ E 🛒	
—	—	Hexham 48 d													06 09			06 48				
—	—	Metrocentre 48 d	00 13												06 42			07 21				
—	0	**Newcastle ■** 26,45 ⛴ d	00a23							06 05					06 54			07 41				
—	2¾	Heworth ⛴ d								06 12					07 01			07 48				
—	12	**Sunderland** ⛴ a								06 25					07 13			08 01				
—	—	d					05 40			06 25		06 45			07 14			08 01		08 42		
—	17¾	Seaham d								06 33					07 21			08 09				
—	30	**Hartlepool** d										07 10			07 37			08 25		09 08		
—	32¼	Seaton Carew d								07 01					07 42			08 29				
—	37¼	Billingham d								07 08					07 49			08 36				
—	41¾	Stockton d								07 16					07 56			08 43				
0	—	**Bishop Auckland** d												07 09					08 11			
2¾	—	Shildon d												07 14					08 16			
5	—	Newton Aycliffe d												07 19					08 21			
6¼	—	Heighington d												07 23					08 25			
10½	—	North Road d												07 31					08 33			
—	—	Chester-le-Street 26 d																				
—	—	Durham 26 d					06 12															
12	—	**Darlington ■** 26 a					06 30							07 37					08 38			
—	—	d			06 02	06 14	06 31	06 34			07 12			07 38			08 18		08 40			09 18
15¾	—	Dinsdale d				06 20		06 40			07 18			07 44			08 24		08 46			09 24
20	—	Allens West d				06 27		06 47			07 25			07 51			08 33		08 53			09 31
20¾	—	Eaglescliffe a				06 29		06 49			07 27	07 28		07 54			08 35		08 55	09 26		09 33
—	—	d				06 29		06 49			07 27	07 32		07 54			08 35		08 55	09 28		09 33
—	—	London Kings Cross ■ ⊖26 a					09 07					10 14								12 32		
23¾	44	Thornaby d			06 20	06 35		06 54		07 25	07 33		07 37	07 59	08 03	08 28	08 41	08 48	09 01		09 31	09 39
27	47¾	**Middlesbrough** a			06 29	06 41		07 00		07 33	07 39		07 46	08 05	08 10	08 36	08 47	08 54	09 07		09 38	09 45
—	—	d		06 22		06 46			07 09		07 40			08 06	08 14		08 48		09 07			09 46
29½	—	South Bank d		06 26					07 13		07 44			08 10	08 19				09 12			
32¾	—	British Steel Redcar § d													08 24							
34½	—	**Redcar Central** d		06 34		06 56			07 21		07 52			08 18	08 28		08 58		09 19			09 56
35½	—	Redcar East d		06 36		06 59			07 23		07 54			08 20	08 31		09 01		09 22			09 59
37	—	Longbeck d		06 40		07 03			07 27		07 58			08 24	08 35		09 05		09 26			10 03
37½	—	Marske d		06 42		07 04			07 29		08 00			08 26	08 36		09 06		09 27			10 04
39½	—	**Saltburn** a		06 49		07 11			07 36		08 08			08 33	08 43		09 12		09 34			10 11

	NT	NT	TP	NT	NT	NT	TP	NT	NT	NT	TP	NT	NT	NT	GC	TP	NT	NT	NT	TP	NT	NT
			◇■ E 🛒		F		◇■ E 🛒		D		◇■ E 🛒		G		■ ■ ☕	◇■ E 🛒				◇■ E 🛒		D
Hexham 48 d					08 57				09 57				10 57					11 57				12 57
Metrocentre 48 d					09 29				10 30				11 30					12 30				13 30
Newcastle ■ 26,45 ⛴ d	08 29				09 41				10 41				11 41					12 41				13 41
Heworth ⛴ d	08 36				09 48				10 48				11 48					12 48				13 48
Sunderland ⛴ a	08 51				10 01				11 01				12 01					13 01				14 01
d	08 53				10 01				11 01				12 01		12 28			13 01				14 03
Seaham d	09 01				10 08				11 09				12 09					13 09				14 10
Hartlepool d	09 20				10 25				11 25				12 25		12 53			13 25				14 28
Seaton Carew d	09 25				10 29				11 29				12 29					13 29				14 33
Billingham d	09 32				10 36				11 36				12 36					13 36				14 40
Stockton d	09 39				10 43				11 43				12 43					13 43				14 47
Bishop Auckland d		09 11				10 11				11 11				12 11					13 11			
Shildon d		09 16				10 16				11 16				12 16					13 16			
Newton Aycliffe d		09 21				10 21				11 21				12 21					13 21			
Heighington d		09 25				10 25				11 25				12 25					13 25			
North Road d		09 33				10 33				11 33				12 33					13 33			
Chester-le-Street 26 d																						
Durham 26 d																						
Darlington ■ 26 a		09 38				10 38				11 38				12 38					13 38			
d		09 40		10 17		10 40		11 18		11 40		12 18		12 40			13 18		13 40		14 18	
Dinsdale d		09 46		10 23		10 46		11 24		11 46		12 24		12 46			13 24		13 46		14 24	
Allens West d		09 53		10 30		10 53		11 31		11 53		12 31		12 53			13 31		13 53		14 31	
Eaglescliffe a		09 55		10 32		10 55		11 33		11 55		12 33		12 55	13 11		13 33		13 55		14 33	
d		09 55		10 32		10 55		11 33		11 55		12 33		12 55	13 13		13 33		13 55		14 33	
London Kings Cross ■ ⊖26 a															16 08							
Thornaby d	09 45	10 01	10 31	10 38	10 48	11 01	11 31	11 39	11 48	12 01	12 30	12 39	12 48	13 01		13 32	13 39	13 48	14 01	14 30	14 39	14 52
Middlesbrough a	09 53	10 07	10 39	10 45	10 54	11 07	11 38	11 45	11 54	12 07	12 38	12 45	12 54	13 07		13 39	13 45	13 55	14 07	14 38	14 45	14 58
d		10 08		10 46		11 07		11 46		12 07		12 46		13 07			13 46		14 07		14 46	
South Bank d		10 12				11 12				12 12				13 12					14 12			
British Steel Redcar § d																						
Redcar Central d		10 20		10 56		11 19		11 56		12 19		12 56		13 19			13 56		14 19		14 56	
Redcar East d		10 22		10 59		11 22		11 59		12 22		12 59		13 22			13 59		14 22		14 59	
Longbeck d		10 26		11 03		11 26		12 03		12 26		13 03		13 26			14 03		14 26		15 03	
Marske d		10 28		11 04		11 27		12 04		12 27		13 04		13 27			14 04		14 27		15 04	
Saltburn a		10 35		11 11		11 34		12 11		12 34		13 11		13 34			14 11		14 34		15 11	

§ For authorised access only to BSC Redcar
A From Hexham
B From York
C To Whitby
D To Nunthorpe
E From Manchester Airport
F From Carlisle to Nunthorpe
G To Danby

For services between Nunthorpe and Middlesbrough, refer to Table T045

Newcastle, Sunderland, Bishop Auckland and Darlington - Middlesbrough and Saltburn

	NT	TP	NT	NT	NT	GC	TP	NT	NT	NT	TP	NT	NT	NT	GC	NT	TP	NT	NT	NT	NT
		◇■ A 🛒		B		■ ■ ☕	◇■ A 🛒		C		◇■ A 🛒		D		■ ■ ☕		◇■ A 🛒		B		
Hexham 48 d									14 57				16 00						16 57		
Metrocentre 48 d									15 30				16 32						17 30		
Newcastle ■ 26,45 ⛴ d				14 41					15 41				16 43			17 23			17 41		
Heworth ⛴ d				14 48					15 48				16 50			17 30			17 48		
Sunderland ⛴ a				15 01					16 01				17 02			17 50			18 01		
d				15 01		15 30			16 01				17 03		17 30	17 50			18 01		
Seaham d				15 09					16 09				17 10			17 58			18 09		
Hartlepool d				15 25		15 54			16 25				17 26		17 56	18 14			18 25		
Seaton Carew d				15 29					16 29				17 31			18 18			18 29		
Billingham d				15 36					16 36				17 38			18 25			18 36		
Stockton d				15 43					16 43				17 45			18a34			18 43		
Bishop Auckland d	14 11				15 11					16 11				17 11						18 11	
Shildon d	14 16				15 16					16 16				17 16						18 16	
Newton Aycliffe d	14 21				15 21					16 21				17 21						18 21	
Heighington d	14 25				15 25					16 25				17 25						18 25	
North Road d	14 33				15 33					16 33				17 33						18 33	
Chester-le-Street 26 d																					
Durham 26 d																					
Darlington ■ 26 a	14 38				15 38					16 38				17 38						18 38	
d	14 40		15 18		15 40			16 18		16 40		17 18		17 40				18 18		18 40	19 18
Dinsdale d	14 46		15 24		15 46			16 24		16 46		17 24		17 46				18 24		18 46	19 23
Allens West d	14 53		15 31		15 53			16 31		16 53		17 31		17 53				18 31		18 53	19 30
Eaglescliffe a	14 56		15 33		15 55	16 13		16 33		16 55		17 33		17 55	18 16			18 33		18 55	19 32
d	14 56		15 33		15 55	16 15		16 33		16 55		17 33		17 55	18 17			18 33		18 55	19 32
London Kings Cross ■ ⊖26 a						19 08									21 08						
Thornaby d	15 01	15 30	15 39	15 48	16 01		16 30	16 39	16 48	17 01	17 30	17 39	17 50	18 01			18 31	18 39	18 48	19 01	19 39
Middlesbrough a	15 07	15 38	15 45	15 54	16 07		16 38	16 45	16 54	17 07	17 38	17 45	17 56	18 07			18 39	18 45	18 54	19 07	19 45
d	15 08		15 46		16 07			16 46		17 07		17 46		18 07				18 46		19 07	19 46
South Bank d	15 12				16 12					17 12				18 12						19 12	
British Steel Redcar § d														18 17							
Redcar Central d	15 20		15 56		16 19			16 56		17 19		17 56		18 21				18 56		19 19	19 56
Redcar East d	15 22		15 59		16 22			16 59		17 22		17 59		18 24				18 59		19 22	19 59
Longbeck d	15 26		16 03		16 26			17 03		17 26		18 03		18 28				19 03		19 26	20 03
Marske d	15 28		16 04		16 27			17 04		17 27		18 04		18 29				19 04		19 27	20 04
Saltburn a	15 35		16 11		16 34			17 11		17 34		18 11		18 36				19 11		19 34	20 11

	TP	NT	NT	TP	NT	NT	NT	TP	NT	NT	TP	NT	NT	NT	GR
	◇■ A 🛒	B		◇■ A 🛒				◇■ A			◇■ A	◇ E	◇ E		■ ■ F ☕
Hexham 48 d		17 59				19 00			19 59			21 00	21 59		
Metrocentre 48 d		18 33				19 32			20 32			21 33	22 32		
Newcastle ■ 26,45 ⛴ d		18 48				19 48			20 48			21 48	22 45		23 00
Heworth ⛴ d		18 55				19 55			20 55			21 55	22 52		
Sunderland ⛴ a		19 08				20 08			21 07			22 07	23 05		23 21
d		19 08				20 08			21 08			22 08			
Seaham d		19 16				20 16			21 16			22 16			
Hartlepool d		19 32				20 32			21 32			22 32			
Seaton Carew d		19 36				20 36			21 36			22 36			
Billingham d		19 43				20 43			21 43			22 43			
Stockton d		19 50				20 50			21 50			22 50			
Bishop Auckland d			19 11				20 11			21 11					
Shildon d			19 16				20 16			21 16					
Newton Aycliffe d			19 21				20 21			21 21					
Heighington d			19 25				20 25			21 25					
North Road d			19 33				20 33			21 33					
Chester-le-Street 26 d															
Durham 26 d															
Darlington ■ 26 a			19 38				20 38			21 38					
d			19 40		20 18		20 40			21 40				22 40	
Dinsdale d			19 46		20 24		20 46			21 46				22 46	
Allens West d			19 53		20 31		20 53			21 53				22 53	
Eaglescliffe a			19 55		20 33		20 55			21 55				22 55	
d			19 55		20 33		20 55			21 55				22 55	
London Kings Cross ■ ⊖26 a															
Thornaby d	19 43	19 55	20 01	20 30	20 39	20 55	21 01	21 34	21 55	22 01	22 30	22 56		23 01	
Middlesbrough a	19 51	20 01	20 07	20 38	20 45	21 02	21 09	21 43	22 01	22 07	22 37	23 01		23 07	
d			20 07		20 46		21 09			22 07					
South Bank d			20 12				21 14			22 12					
British Steel Redcar § d															
Redcar Central d			20 19		20 56		21 21			22 19					
Redcar East d			20 22		20 59		21 24			22 22					
Longbeck d			20 26		21 03		21 28			22 26					
Marske d			20 27		21 04		21 29			22 27					
Saltburn a			20 34		21 11		21 36			22 34					

§ For authorised access only to BSC Redcar
A From Manchester Airport
B To Nunthorpe
C To Battersby
D To Whitby
E From Carlisle
F From London Kings Cross

For services between Nunthorpe and Middlesbrough, refer to Table T045

Newcastle, Sunderland, Bishop Auckland and Darlington - Middlesbrough and Saltburn

	NT A	NT	TP ◇■ B	NT	NT C	NT	NT D	NT	GC ■		TP ◇■ B	NT	NT	TP ◇■ E	NT	NT D	NT	GC ■	TP ◇■ E		NT	NT	NT	TP ◇■ F
Hexham 48 d													06 09			06 48								
Metrocentre 48 d	00 13												06 42			07 21								
Newcastle 26,45 d	00a23						06 00						06 54			07 36						08 33		
Heworth d							06 06						07 02			07 42						08 40		
Sunderland a							06 20						07 20			07 55						08 52		
d							06 22		06 45				07 20			08 01		08 28				08 54		
Seaham d							06 29						07 28			08 09						09 02		
Hartlepool d									07 09				07 44			08 25		08 53				09 18		
Seaton Carew d							07 05						07 48			08 29						09 23		
Billingham d							07 12						07 55			08 36						09 30		
Stockton d							07 20						08 02			08 43						09 37		
Bishop Auckland d												07 07					08 11						09 11	
Shildon d												07 12					08 16						09 16	
Newton Aycliffe d												07 17					08 21						09 21	
Heighington d												07 21					08 25						09 25	
North Road d												07 29					08 33						09 33	
Chester-le-Street 26 d																								
Durham 26 d																								
Darlington 26 a												07 34					08 38						09 38	
d			06 02	06 14	06 34			07 12				07 36			08 18		08 40				09 18		09 40	
Dinsdale d				06 20	06 40			07 18				07 42			08 24		08 46				09 24		09 46	
Allens West d				06 27	06 47			07 25				07 49			08 33		08 53				09 31		09 53	
Eaglescliffe a				06 29	06 49			07 27	07 29			07 51			08 35		08 55	09 12			09 33		09 55	
d				06 29	06 49			07 27	07 30			07 51			08 35		08 55	09 16			09 33		09 55	
London Kings Cross ⊖26 a									10 18									12 10						
Thornaby d			06 20	06 35	06 54		07 25	07 33			07 39	07 57	08 08	08 28	08 41	08 48	09 01		09 31		09 39	09 43	10 01	10 31
Middlesbrough a			06 29	06 41	07 00		07 33	07 39			07 47	08 03	08 14	08 36	08 47	08 54	09 07		09 38		09 45	09 50	10 07	10 39
d		06 22		06 46		07 09		07 40				08 06	08 14		08 48		09 07				09 46		10 08	
South Bank d		06 26				07 13		07 44				08 10	08 19				09 12						10 12	
British Steel Redcar § d													08 24											
Redcar Central d		06 34		06 56		07 21		07 52				08 18	08 28		08 58		09 19				09 56		10 20	
Redcar East d		06 36		06 59		07 23		07 54				08 20	08 31		09 01		09 22				09 59		10 22	
Longbeck d		06 40		07 03		07 27		07 58				08 24	08 35		09 05		09 26				10 03		10 26	
Marske d		06 42		07 04		07 29		08 00				08 26	08 36		09 06		09 27				10 04		10 28	
Saltburn a		06 49		07 11		07 36		08 08				08 33	08 43		09 12		09 34				10 11		10 35	

	NT	TP ◇■ G	NT H	NT	TP ◇■ E		NT	NT D	NT	TP ◇■ E	NT	NT I	NT	GC ■	TP ◇■ E		NT	NT	NT	TP ◇■ E	NT	NT D	NT	TP ◇■ E
Hexham 48 d			08 57					09 57				10 57						11 57				12 57		
Metrocentre 48 d			09 29					10 30				11 30						12 30				13 30		
Newcastle 26,45 d			09 41					10 41				11 41						12 41				13 41		
Heworth d			09 48					10 48				11 48						12 48				13 48		
Sunderland a			10 01					11 01				12 01						13 01				14 01		
d			10 01					11 03				12 01		12 18				13 01				14 03		
Seaham d			10 08					11 10				12 09						13 09				14 10		
Hartlepool d			10 25					11 29				12 25		12 43				13 25				14 28		
Seaton Carew d			10 29					11 34				12 29						13 29				14 33		
Billingham d			10 36					11 41				12 36						13 36				14 40		
Stockton d			10 43					11 48				12 43						13 43				14 47		
Bishop Auckland d				10 11					11 11				12 11						13 11				14 11	
Shildon d				10 16					11 16				12 16						13 16				14 16	
Newton Aycliffe d				10 21					11 21				12 21						13 21				14 21	
Heighington d				10 25					11 25				12 25						13 25				14 25	
North Road d				10 33					11 33				12 33						13 33				14 33	
Chester-le-Street 26 d																								
Durham 26 d																								
Darlington 26 a				10 38					11 38				12 38						13 38				14 38	
d	10 17			10 40			11 18		11 40		12 18		12 40				13 18		13 40		14 18		14 40	
Dinsdale d	10 23			10 46			11 24		11 46		12 24		12 46				13 24		13 46		14 24		14 46	
Allens West d	10 30			10 53			11 31		11 53		12 31		12 53				13 31		13 53		14 31		14 53	
Eaglescliffe a	10 32			10 55			11 33		11 55		12 33		12 55	13 01			13 33		13 55		14 33		14 56	
d	10 32			10 55			11 33		11 55		12 33		12 55	13 02			13 33		13 55		14 33		14 56	
London Kings Cross ⊖26 a														15 44										
Thornaby d	10 38	10 42	10 48	11 01	11 30		11 39	11 53	12 01	12 30	12 39	12 48	13 01		13 32		13 39	13 48	14 01	14 30	14 39	14 52	15 01	15 30
Middlesbrough a	10 45	10 49	10 54	11 07	11 38		11 45	11 59	12 07	12 38	12 45	12 54	13 07		13 39		13 45	13 55	14 07	14 38	14 45	14 58	15 07	15 38
d	10 46			11 07			11 46		12 07		12 46		13 07				13 46		14 07		14 46		15 08	
South Bank d				11 12					12 12				13 12						14 12				15 12	
British Steel Redcar § d																								
Redcar Central d	10 56			11 19			11 56		12 19		12 56		13 19				13 56		14 19		14 56		15 20	
Redcar East d	10 59			11 22			11 59		12 22		12 59		13 22				13 59		14 22		14 59		15 22	
Longbeck d	11 03			11 26			12 03		12 26		13 03		13 26				14 03		14 26		15 03		15 26	
Marske d	11 04			11 27			12 04		12 27		13 04		13 27				14 04		14 27		15 04		15 28	
Saltburn a	11 11			11 34			12 11		12 34		13 11		13 34				14 11		14 34		15 11		15 35	

§ For authorised access only to BSC Redcar
A From Hexham
B From York
C To Whitby
D To Nunthorpe
E From Manchester Airport
F until 29 September. From Manchester Airport
G from 6 October. From Manchester Airport
H From Carlisle to Nunthorpe
I To Danby

For services between Nunthorpe and Middlesbrough, refer to Table T045

Table T044-R

Saturdays
26 May to 8 December

Newcastle, Sunderland, Bishop Auckland and Darlington - Middlesbrough and Saltburn

	NT		NT A	NT	GC ■	TP ◇■ B	NT	NT C	NT	TP ◇■ B	NT		NT D	NT	GC ■	NT	TP ◇■ B	NT	NT A	NT	NT		TP ◇■ B	NT A
Hexham 48 d			13 57					14 57					16 00						16 57					17 59
Metrocentre 48 d			14 30					15 30					16 32						17 30					18 33
Newcastle 26,45 d			14 41					15 41					16 43			17 23			17 41					18 48
Heworth d			14 48					15 48					16 50			17 30			17 48					18 55
Sunderland a			15 01					16 01					17 02			17 50			18 01					19 08
d			15 01		15 29			16 03					17 03		17 29	17 50			18 01					19 08
Seaham d			15 09					16 10					17 10			17 58			18 09					19 16
Hartlepool d			15 25		15 53			16 28					17 26		17 54	18 14			18 25					19 32
Seaton Carew d			15 29					16 32					17 31			18 18			18 29					19 36
Billingham d			15 36					16 39					17 38			18 25			18 36					19 43
Stockton d			15 43					16 46					17 45			18a34			18 43					19 50
Bishop Auckland d				15 11					16 11					17 11						18 11				
Shildon d				15 16					16 16					17 16						18 16				
Newton Aycliffe d				15 21					16 21					17 21						18 21				
Heighington d				15 25					16 25					17 25						18 25				
North Road d				15 33					16 33					17 33						18 33				
Chester-le-Street 26 d																								
Durham 26 d																								
Darlington 26 a				15 38					16 38					17 38						18 38				
d	15 18			15 40			16 18		16 40		17 18			17 40				18 18		18 40	19 18			
Dinsdale d	15 24			15 46			16 24		16 46		17 24			17 46				18 24		18 46	19 23			
Allens West d	15 31			15 53			16 31		16 53		17 31			17 53				18 31		18 53	19 30			
Eaglescliffe a	15 33			15 55	16 12		16 33		16 55		17 33			17 55	18 13			18 33		18 55	19 32			
d	15 33			15 55	16 13		16 33		16 55		17 33			17 55	18 14			18 33		18 55	19 32			
London Kings Cross ⊖26 a					19 09										20 59									
Thornaby d	15 39		15 48	16 01		16 30	16 39	16 51	17 01	17 30	17 39		17 50	18 01			18 31	18 39	18 48	19 01	19 39		19 43	19 55
Middlesbrough a	15 45		15 54	16 07		16 38	16 45	16 57	17 07	17 38	17 45		17 56	18 07			18 39	18 45	18 54	19 07	19 45		19 51	20 01
d	15 46			16 07			16 46		17 07		17 46			18 07				18 46		19 07	19 46			
South Bank d				16 12					17 12					18 12						19 12				
British Steel Redcar § d														18 17										
Redcar Central d	15 56			16 19			16 56		17 19		17 56			18 21				18 56		19 19	19 56			
Redcar East d	15 59			16 22			16 59		17 22		17 59			18 24				18 59		19 22	19 59			
Longbeck d	16 03			16 26			17 03		17 26		18 03			18 28				19 03		19 26	20 03			
Marske d	16 04			16 27			17 04		17 27		18 04			18 29				19 04		19 27	20 04			
Saltburn a	16 11			16 34			17 11		17 34		18 11			18 36				19 11		19 34	20 11			

	NT	TP ◇■ B	NT	NT	NT	TP ◇■ B	NT		NT	TP ◇■ B	NT ◇ E	NT	NT
Hexham 48 d				19 00			19 59				21 00		
Metrocentre 48 d				19 32			20 32				21 33		
Newcastle 26,45 d				19 48			20 48				21 48	22 32	
Heworth d				19 55			20 55				21 55	22 39	
Sunderland a				20 08			21 07				22 07	22 51	
d				20 08			21 08				22 08	22 53	
Seaham d				20 16			21 16				22 16	23 00	
Hartlepool d				20 32			21 32				22 32	23a17	
Seaton Carew d				20 36			21 36				22 36		
Billingham d				20 43			21 43				22 43		
Stockton d				20 50			21 50				22 50		
Bishop Auckland d	19 11				20 11				21 11				
Shildon d	19 16				20 16				21 16				
Newton Aycliffe d	19 21				20 21				21 21				
Heighington d	19 25				20 25				21 25				
North Road d	19 33				20 33				21 33				
Chester-le-Street 26 d													
Durham 26 d													
Darlington 26 a	19 38				20 38				21 38				
d	19 40		20 18		20 40				21 40				22 40
Dinsdale d	19 46		20 24		20 46				21 46				22 46
Allens West d	19 53		20 31		20 53				21 53				22 53
Eaglescliffe a	19 55		20 33		20 55				21 55				22 55
d	19 55		20 33		20 55				21 55				22 55
London Kings Cross ⊖26 a													
Thornaby d	20 01	20 30	20 39	20 55	21 01	21 34	21 55		22 01	22 29	22 55		23 01
Middlesbrough a	20 07	20 38	20 45	21 02	21 09	21 43	22 01		22 07	22 37	23 01		23 09
d	20 07		20 46		21 09				22 07				
South Bank d	20 12				21 14				22 12				
British Steel Redcar § d													
Redcar Central d	20 19		20 56		21 21				22 19				
Redcar East d	20 22		20 59		21 24				22 22				
Longbeck d	20 26		21 03		21 28				22 26				
Marske d	20 27		21 04		21 29				22 27				
Saltburn a	20 34		21 11		21 36				22 34				

§ For authorised access only to BSC Redcar
A To Nunthorpe
B From Manchester Airport
C To Battersby
D To Whitby
E From Carlisle

For services between Nunthorpe and Middlesbrough, refer to Table T045

Table T044-R

Sundays

20 May to 2 December

Newcastle, Sunderland, Bishop Auckland and Darlington - Middlesbrough and Saltburn

	NT A	NT	NT	TP ◇ B	NT C	NT	GC	NT A	TP ◇ D	NT	NT ◇ E	NT	TP ◇ F	NT ◇ E	NT	GC	NT G	TP ◇ H	NT ◇ I	NT	TP ◇ H	NT ◇ J
Hexham 48 d											09 44			10 46					11 44			
Metrocentre 48 d											10 18			11 18					12 18			
Newcastle 26,45 d					08 30			09 32			10 30			11 30					12 30			13 30
Heworth d					08 37			09 39			10 37			11 37					12 37			13 37
Sunderland a					08 49			09 53			10 50			11 49					12 51			13 51
d					08 50		09 20	09 53			10 50			11 50		12 12			12 51			13 52
Seaham d					08 57			10 01			10 58			11 57					12 59			13 59
Hartlepool d					09 13		09 45	10 17			11 14			12 13		12 36			13 15			14 15
Seaton Carew d					09 18			10 21			11 18			12 18					13 19			14 20
Billingham d					09 25			10 28			11 25			12 25					13 26			14 27
Stockton d					09 32			10 35			11 32			12 32					13 33			14 34
Bishop Auckland d			08 11			09 11				10 11		11 11			12 11							
Shildon d			08 16			09 16				10 16		11 16			12 16							
Newton Aycliffe d			08 21			09 21				10 21		11 21			12 21							
Heighington d			08 25			09 25				10 25		11 25			12 25							
North Road d			08 33			09 33				10 33		11 33			12 33							
Chester-le-Street 26 d																						
Durham 26 d																						
Darlington 26 a			08 38			09 38				10 38		11 38			12 38							
d	08 10		08 40			09 40				10 40		11 40			12 40		13 13			13 34		
Dinsdale d	08 16		08 46			09 46				10 46		11 46			12 46		13 19			13 39		
Allens West d	08 23		08 53			09 53				10 53		11 53			12 53		13 26			13 46		
Eaglescliffe a	08 25		08 55			09 55	10 06			10 55		11 55			12 55	13 02	13 28			13 48		
d	08 25		08 55			09 55	10 07			10 55		11 55			12 55	13 04				13 48		
London Kings Cross ⊖26 a							12 42									15 42						
Thornaby d	08a30		09 01	09 26	09 37	10 01		10 41	10 49	11 01	11 38	12 01	12 23	12 37	13 01			13 27	13 39	13 54	14 25	14 39
Middlesbrough a			09 07	09 33	09 43	10 07		10 47	10 58	11 07	11 44	12 07	12 30	12 43	13 07			13 34	13 45	14 00	14 33	14 45
d		08 45	09 07			10 07				11 07		12 07			13 07					14 00		
South Bank d		08 49	09 12			10 12				11 12		12 12			13 12					14 05		
British Steel Redcar § d																						
Redcar Central d		08 57	09 19			10 19				11 19		12 19			13 19					14 12		
Redcar East d		08 59	09 22			10 22				11 22		12 22			13 22					14 15		
Longbeck d		09 03	09 26			10 26				11 26		12 26			13 26					14 19		
Marske d		09 05	09 27			10 27				11 27		12 27			13 27					14 20		
Saltburn a		09 12	09 34			10 34				11 34		12 34			13 34					14 27		

	NT K	NT	GC	TP ◇ D	NT ◇ E	NT	TP ◇ D	NT ◇ I	NT	NT G	TP ◇ D	NT ◇ E	NT	TP ◇ D	NT ◇ L	NT K	NT	GC	NT ◇ L	TP ◇ D	NT	TP ◇ D
Hexham 48 d					13 44			14 46				15 44			16 46				17 44			
Metrocentre 48 d					14 18			15 18				16 18			17 17				18 18			
Newcastle 26,45 d					14 30			15 30				16 30			17 27				18 30			
Heworth d					14 37			15 37				16 37			17 34				18 37			
Sunderland a					14 51			15 51				16 51			17 49				18 51			
d			14 12		14 51			15 52				16 51			17 50			18 12	18 51			
Seaham d					14 59			15 59				16 59			17 57				18 59			
Hartlepool d	14 24		14 38		15 15			16 15				17 15			18 13	18 19		18 40	19 15			
Seaton Carew d	14 28				15 19			16 20				17 19			18 18	18 23			19 19			
Billingham d	14 35				15 26			16 27				17 26			18 25	18 30			19 26			
Stockton d	14 42				15 33			16 34				17 33			18 32	18 37			19 33			
Bishop Auckland d		14 11				15 11			16 11				17 11				18 11				19 11	
Shildon d		14 16				15 16			16 16				17 16				18 16				19 16	
Newton Aycliffe d		14 21				15 21			16 21				17 21				18 21				19 21	
Heighington d		14 25				15 25			16 25				17 25				18 25				19 25	
North Road d		14 33				15 33			16 33				17 33				18 33				19 33	
Chester-le-Street 26 d																						
Durham 26 d																						
Darlington 26 a		14 38				15 38			16 38				17 38				18 38				19 38	
d		14 40				15 40			16 40	17 16			17 40				18 40				19 40	
Dinsdale d		14 46				15 46			16 46	17 22			17 46				18 46				19 46	
Allens West d		14 53				15 53			16 53	17 29			17 53				18 53				19 53	
Eaglescliffe a	14 47	14 55	15 04			15 55			16 55	17 31			17 55			18 43	18 55	18 58			19 55	
d		14 55	15 05			15 55			16 55				17 55				18 55	19 02			19 55	
London Kings Cross ⊖26 a			17 44															21 42				
Thornaby d		15 01		15 24	15 39	16 01	16 36	16 39	17 01		17 30	17 39	18 01	18 33	18 38		19 02		19 39	19 47	20 01	20 30
Middlesbrough a		15 07		15 31	15 45	16 07	16 42	16 47	17 07		17 37	17 45	18 07	18 40	18 46		19 08		19 46	19 53	20 07	20 38
d		15 07				16 07			17 07				18 07				19 08				20 07	
South Bank d		15 12				16 12			17 12				18 12				19 13				20 12	
British Steel Redcar § d																						
Redcar Central d		15 19				16 19			17 19				18 19				19 20				20 19	
Redcar East d		15 22				16 22			17 22				18 22				19 23				20 22	
Longbeck d		15 26				16 26			17 26				18 26				19 27				20 26	
Marske d		15 27				16 27			17 27				18 27				19 28				20 27	
Saltburn a		15 34				16 34			17 34				18 34				19 35				20 34	

§ For authorised access only to BSC Redcar
A To Whitby
B From York
C To Nunthorpe
D From Manchester Airport
E From Carlisle to Nunthorpe
F From Manchester Victoria
G To Hartlepool
H From Manchester Oxford Road
I From Carlisle to Whitby
J not from 27 May until 3 June. To Nunthorpe
K To Darlington
L From Carlisle

For services between Nunthorpe and Middlesbrough, refer to Table T045

Table T044-R

Sundays

20 May to 2 December

Newcastle, Sunderland, Bishop Auckland and Darlington - Middlesbrough and Saltburn

	NT ◇ A	NT	TP ◇ B	NT ◇ A	NT	NT	NT ◇ A	TP ◇ C	NT
Hexham 48 d	18 47			19 45			20 45		
Metrocentre 48 d	19 18			20 18		20 58	21 18		
Newcastle 26,45 d	19 30			20 30		21 15	21 30		
Heworth d	19 37			20 37			21 37		
Sunderland a	19 51			20 51			21 51		
d	19 51			20 51			21 51		
Seaham d	19 59			20 59			21 59		
Hartlepool d	20 15			21 15			22 15		
Seaton Carew d	20 19			21 19			22 19		
Billingham d	20 26			21 26			22 26		
Stockton d	20 33			21 33			22 33		
Bishop Auckland d		20 11							
Shildon d		20 16							
Newton Aycliffe d		20 21							
Heighington d		20 25							
North Road d		20 33							
Chester-le-Street 26 d						21 25			
Durham 26 d						21 33			
Darlington 26 a		20 38				21 54			
d		20 40			21 27	21 57			22 52
Dinsdale d		20 46			21 33	22 03			22 58
Allens West d		20 53			21 40	22 10			23 05
Eaglescliffe a		20 55			21 42	22 12			23 07
d		20 55			21 42	22 12			23 07
London Kings Cross ⊖26 a									
Thornaby d	20 39	21 01	21 40	21 41	21 49	22 18	22 38	22 44	23 13
Middlesbrough a	20 45	21 07	21 46	21 49	21 58	22 24	22 44	22 52	23 20
d		21 07				22 24			
South Bank d		21 12				22 29			
British Steel Redcar § d									
Redcar Central d		21 19				22 36			
Redcar East d		21 22				22 39			
Longbeck d		21 26				22 43			
Marske d		21 27				22 44			
Saltburn a		21 34				22 51			

§ For authorised access only to BSC Redcar
A From Carlisle
B From Manchester Airport
C From Liverpool Lime Street

For services between Nunthorpe and Middlesbrough, refer to Table T045

Table T045-F

Middlesbrough and Pickering - Whitby

Mondays to Fridays
21 May to 7 December

Miles	Miles			NT	NT	NT	NT	NT	NY [1] A	NY [1] A	NT	NT	NT	NT	NY [1] A	NY [1] B	NT	NT	NT	NY [1] C	NT	NY [1] B	NT
—	—	Newcastle [8] 44	d			06 05	07 41					09 41	10 41	11 41				13 41	14 41		15 41		16 43
0	—	**Middlesbrough**	d	06 53	07 05	07 34	08 55	09 34			10 20	10 55	11 55	12 55			14 02	14 58	15 55		17 00		17 56
2½	—	James Cook	d	06 57	07 09	07 38	08 59	09 38			10 24	10 59	11 59	12 59			14 06	15 03	15 59		17 04		18 01
3	—	Marton	d		07 12	07 41	09 02	09 41			10 27	11 02	12 02	13 02			14 09	15 06	16 02		17 07		18 04
4	—	Gypsy Lane	d			07 44	09 05				10 30	11 05	12 05				14 12	15 09	16 05		17 10		18 07
4½	—	Nunthorpe	d	07a05	07 19	07a47	09a09	09a48			10 34	11a09	12a09	13 13			14 19	15a12	16a09		17 17		18 10
8½	—	Great Ayton	d		07 26						10 41						14 26				17 24		18 17
11	—	Battersby	a		07 32						10 47			13 24			14 32				17 30		18 23
—	—		d		07 35						10 50			13 27			14 35						18 26
12¾	—	Kildale	d		07 40						10 55						14 40						18 31
16½	—	Commondale	d		07 47						11 03						14 47						18 38
18½	—	Castleton Moor	d		07 51						11 06						14 51						18 42
20	—	Danby	d		07 55						11 10			13a43			14 55						18 45
23½	—	Lealholm	d		08 01						11 16						15 01						18 52
25½	—	Glaisdale	a		08 06						11 21						15 06						18 57
—	—		d		08 09						11 24						15 09						18 59
27¼	—	Egton	d		08 13						11 28						15 13						19 03
—	0	**Pickering** §	d							09 25					12 00	13 00				15 00		16 00	
—	6	Levisham §	d							09 44					12 20	13 20				15 20		16 20	
—	14½	Goathland §	d							10 10					12 50	14 00				16 00		16 50	
28¾	18	Grosmont	d		08 17				09 19	10 40	11 32				13 15	14 31	15 17			16 30		17 15	19 07
32	21¼	Sleights	d		08 26						11 40						15 25						19 16
33½	22¾	Ruswarp	d		08 31						11 45						15 30						19 20
35	24¼	**Whitby**	a		08 37				09 45	11 10	11 51				13 45	14 56	15 36			16 55		17 45	19 27

		NT	NT ◇ D	NT FX
Newcastle [8] 44	d	17 41	18 48	
Middlesbrough	d	18 55	20 01	21 20
James Cook	d	18 59	20 06	21 24
Marton	d	19 02	20 09	21 27
Gypsy Lane	d	19 05	20 12	21 30
Nunthorpe	d	19a09	20a15	21a33
Great Ayton	d			
Battersby	a			
	d			
Kildale	d			
Commondale	d			
Castleton Moor	d			
Danby	d			
Lealholm	d			
Glaisdale	a			
	d			
Egton	d			
Pickering §	d			
Levisham §	d			
Goathland §	d			
Grosmont	d			
Sleights	d			
Ruswarp	d			
Whitby	a			

Saturdays
26 May to 8 December

		NT	NT	NT	NT	NT	NY [1]	NY [1]	NT	NT	NT	NT	NY [1]	NY [1] E	NT	NT	NT	NY [1] F	NT	NY [1] E	NT	NT	NT ◇ D
Newcastle [8] 44	d			06 00	07 36					09 41	10 41	11 41				13 41	14 41		15 41		16 43	17 41	18 48
Middlesbrough	d	06 53	07 05	07 34	08 55	09 34			10 20	10 55	11 59	12 55			14 02	14 58	15 55		17 00		17 56	18 55	20 01
James Cook	d	06 57	07 09	07 38	08 59	09 38			10 24	10 59	12 04	12 59			14 06	15 03	15 59		17 04		18 01	18 59	20 06
Marton	d		07 12	07 41	09 02	09 41			10 27	11 02	12 07	13 02			14 09	15 06	16 02		17 07		18 04	19 02	20 09
Gypsy Lane	d			07 44	09 05				10 30	11 05	12 10				14 12	15 09	16 05		17 10		18 07	19 05	20 12
Nunthorpe	d	07a05	07 19	07a47	09a09	09a48			10 34	11a09	12a13	13 13			14 19	15a12	16a09		17 17		18 10	19a09	20a15
Great Ayton	d		07 26						10 41						14 26				17 24		18 17		
Battersby	a		07 32						10 47			13 24			14 32				17 30		18 23		
	d		07 35						10 50			13 27			14 35						18 26		
Kildale	d		07 40						10 55						14 40						18 31		
Commondale	d		07 47						11 03						14 47						18 38		
Castleton Moor	d		07 51						11 06						14 51						18 42		
Danby	d		07 55						11 10			13a43			14 55						18 45		
Lealholm	d		08 01						11 16						15 01						18 52		
Glaisdale	a		08 06						11 21						15 06						18 57		
	d		08 09						11 24						15 09						18 59		
Egton	d		08 13						11 28						15 13						19 03		
Pickering §	d							09 25					12 00	13 00				15 00		16 00			
Levisham §	d							09 44					12 20	13 20				15 20		16 20			
Goathland §	d							10 10					12 50	14 00				16 00		16 50			
Grosmont	d		08 17				09 19	10 40	11 32				13 15	14 31	15 17			16 30		17 15	19 07		
Sleights	d		08 26						11 40						15 25						19 16		
Ruswarp	d		08 31						11 45						15 30						19 20		
Whitby	a		08 37				09 45	11 10	11 51				13 45	14 53	15 36			16 52		17 45	19 26		

§ North Yorkshire Moors Railway. For full service between Grosmont and Pickering please see separate publicity

A until 3 December

B from 28 May until 1 June, from 23 July until 31 August

C until 20 July, from 3 September until 3 December, not from 28 May until 1 June

D ◇ from Middlesbrough

E from 28 July until 1 September

F until 21 July, from 8 September, not 2 June

For connections to Darlington refer to Table T044

Table T045-F

Middlesbrough and Pickering - Whitby

Saturdays
26 May to 8 December

		NT
Newcastle [8] 44	d	
Middlesbrough	d	21 20
James Cook	d	21 24
Marton	d	21 27
Gypsy Lane	d	21 30
Nunthorpe	d	21a33
Great Ayton	d	
Battersby	a	
	d	
Kildale	d	
Commondale	d	
Castleton Moor	d	
Danby	d	
Lealholm	d	
Glaisdale	a	
	d	
Egton	d	
Pickering §	d	
Levisham §	d	
Goathland §	d	
Grosmont	d	
Sleights	d	
Ruswarp	d	
Whitby	a	

Sundays
20 May to 2 December

		NY [1]	NT	NT	NY [1]	NT	NT ◇	NT ◇	NY [1]	NT ◇	NT ◇ A	NT ◇	NY [1]	NT ◇	NT ◇
Newcastle [8] 44	d			08 30		09 32	10 30	11 30		12 30	13 30	14 30		15 30	16 30
Middlesbrough	d			09 51		10 48	11 50	12 50		13 46	14 52	15 46		16 48	17 51
James Cook	d		08 45	09 55		10 53	11 54	12 54		13 51	14 56	15 51		16 52	17 55
Marton	d		08 48	09 58		10 56	11 57	12 57		13 54	14 59	15 54		16 55	17 58
Gypsy Lane	d		08 51	10 01		10 59	12 00	13 00		13 57	15 02	15 57		16 58	18 01
Nunthorpe	d		08 54	10a05		11 02	12a04	13a04		14 03	15a06	16a00		17 05	18a05
Great Ayton	d		09 01			11 09				14 10				17 12	
Battersby	a		09 07			11 15				14 16				17 18	
	d		09 10			11 28				14 19				17 21	
Kildale	d		09 15			11 33				14 24				17 26	
Commondale	d		09 23			11 41				14 31				17 34	
Castleton Moor	d		09 26			11 44				14 35				17 37	
Danby	d		09 30			11 48				14 38				17 41	
Lealholm	d		09 36			11 54				14 45				17 47	
Glaisdale	a		09 41			11 59				14 50				17 52	
	d		09 44			12 02				14 52				17 55	
Egton	d		09 48			12 06				14 56				17 59	
Pickering §	d				09 45				12 00				15 00		
Levisham §	d				10 05				12 20				15 26		
Goathland §	d				10 35				12 50				15 53		
Grosmont	d	08 34	09 52		10 50	12 10			13 19	15 00			16 18	18 03	
Sleights	d		10 00			12 18				15 09				18 11	
Ruswarp	d		10 05			12 23				15 13				18 16	
Whitby	a	08 59	10 11		11 17	12 29			13 44	15 20			16 43	18 22	

§ North Yorkshire Moors Railway. For full service between Grosmont and Pickering please see separate publicity

A not from 27 May until 3 June

For connections to Darlington refer to Table T044

Table T045-R

Whitby - Pickering and Middlesbrough

Mondays to Fridays

21 May to 7 December

Miles	Miles	Station		NT	NT	NT	NT	NY ■ A 🛒	NT	NT	NT	NY ■ A 🛒	NT
0	0	**Whitby**	d				08 45	10 00			11 58	12 45	
1½	1½	Ruswarp	d				08 49				12 02		
3	3	Sleights	d				08 54				12 07		
6¼	6¼	Grosmont	d				09 02	10 30			12 15	13 30	
—	9¾	Goathland §	a					10 50				13 45	
—	18¾	Levisham §	a					11 16				14 16	
—	24¼	**Pickering** §	a					11 40				14 40	
7¾	—	Egton	d				09 06				12 19		
9½	—	Glaisdale	a				09 10				12 23		
—	—		d				09 13				12 26		
11½	—	Lealholm	d				09 18				12 31		
15	—	Danby	d				09 25				12 38		13 50
16½	—	Castleton Moor	d				09 28				12 41		
18¾	—	Commondale	d				09 32				12 45		
22¼	—	Kildale	d				09 39				12 52		
24	—	Battersby	a				09 44				12 57		14 05
—	—		d				09 47				13 00		14 08
26½	—	Great Ayton	d				09 53				13 06		
30½	—	Nunthorpe	d	07 20	08 05	09 20	10 00		11 18	12 19	13 15		14 20
31	—	Gypsy Lane	d	07 22	08 07	09 22	10 02		11 21	12 21	13 17		14 22
32	—	Marton	d	07 25	08 10	09 25	10 05		11 24	12 24	13 21		14 25
32½	—	James Cook	d	07 28	08 13	09 28	10 08		11 26	12 27	13 24		14 28
35	—	**Middlesbrough**	a	07 33	08 19	09 34	10 15		11 33	12 33	13 29		14 35
—	—	Newcastle ■ 44	a	08 54	09 41	10 52			12 52	13 52			15 52

Station		NY ■ A 🛒	NT ◇	NT	NT ◇	NY ■ B 🛒	NY ■ C 🛒	NT	NY ■ B 🛒	NT	NT
Whitby	d	14 00			15 59	16 40	17 10		18 00		
Ruswarp	d				16 03						
Sleights	d				16 08						
Grosmont	d	14 30			16 17	17 09	17 39		18 35		
Goathland §	a	14 45				17 24	17 54		18 50		
Levisham §	a	15 16				17 50	18 20		19 15		
Pickering §	a	15 40				18 10	18 40		19 35		
Egton	d				16 21						
Glaisdale	a				16 25						
	d				16 28						
Lealholm	d				16 33						
Danby	d				16 40						
Castleton Moor	d				16 44						
Commondale	d				16 47						
Kildale	d				16 55						
Battersby	a				17 01						
	d				17 04			17 45			
Great Ayton	d				17 09			17 50			
Nunthorpe	d		15 16	16 18	17 17			18 15		19 18	20 20
Gypsy Lane	d		15 18	16 20	17 19			18 17		19 20	20 22
Marton	d		15 21	16 23	17 22			18 20		19 23	20 25
James Cook	d		15 24	16 26	17 25			18 23		19 26	20 28
Middlesbrough	a		15 30	16 32	17 31			18 30		19 32	20 34
Newcastle ■ 44	a		16 52	17 52	18 49			19 47		20 51	21 52

Station		NT	NT FX
Whitby	d	19 34	
Ruswarp	d	19 38	
Sleights	d	19 43	
Grosmont	d	19 51	
Goathland §	a		
Levisham §	a		
Pickering §	a		
Egton	d	19 55	
Glaisdale	a	19 59	
	d	20 02	
Lealholm	d	20 07	
Danby	d	20 14	
Castleton Moor	d	20 17	
Commondale	d	20 21	
Kildale	d	20 28	
Battersby	a	20 33	
	d	20 36	
Great Ayton	d	20 42	
Nunthorpe	d	20 51	21 38
Gypsy Lane	d	20 53	21 40
Marton	d	20 56	21 43
James Cook	d	20 59	21 46
Middlesbrough	a	21 06	21 52
Newcastle ■ 44	a		

Saturdays

26 May to 8 December

Station		NT	NT	NT	NT	NY ■ 🛒	NT	NT	NT	NY ■ 🛒	NT	NY ■ 🛒
Whitby	d				08 45	10 00			11 58	12 45		14 00
Ruswarp	d				08 49				12 02			
Sleights	d				08 54				12 07			
Grosmont	d				09 02	10 30			12 15	13 30		14 30
Goathland §	a					10 48				13 45		14 45
Levisham §	a					11 16				14 16		15 16
Pickering §	a					11 40				14 40		15 40
Egton	d				09 06				12 19			
Glaisdale	a				09 10				12 23			
	d				09 13				12 26			
Lealholm	d				09 18				12 31			
Danby	d				09 25				12 38		13 50	
Castleton Moor	d				09 28				12 41			
Commondale	d				09 32				12 45			
Kildale	d				09 39				12 52			
Battersby	a				09 44				12 57		14 05	
	d				09 47				13 00		14 08	
Great Ayton	d				09 53				13 06			
Nunthorpe	d	07 20	08 05	09 20	10 00		11 18	12 19	13 15		14 20	
Gypsy Lane	d	07 22	08 07	09 22	10 02		11 21	12 21	13 17		14 22	
Marton	d	07 25	08 10	09 25	10 05		11 24	12 24	13 21		14 25	
James Cook	d	07 28	08 13	09 28	10 08		11 26	12 27	13 24		14 28	
Middlesbrough	a	07 33	08 19	09 34	10 15		11 33	12 33	13 29		14 35	
Newcastle ■ 44	a	08 54	09 53	10 52			12 52	13 52			15 52	

Station		NT ◇	NT	NT ◇	NY ■ D 🛒	NY ■ E 🛒	NT	NY ■ D 🛒	NT	NT	NT	NT
Whitby	d			15 59	16 40	17 10		18 00			19 34	
Ruswarp	d			16 03							19 38	
Sleights	d			16 08							19 43	
Grosmont	d			16 17	17 09	17 39		18 35			19 51	
Goathland §	a				17 24	17 54		18 50				
Levisham §	a				17 50	18 20		19 15				
Pickering §	a				18 10	18 40		19 35				
Egton	d			16 21							19 55	
Glaisdale	a			16 25							19 59	
	d			16 28							20 02	
Lealholm	d			16 33							20 07	
Danby	d			16 40							20 14	
Castleton Moor	d			16 44							20 17	
Commondale	d			16 47							20 21	
Kildale	d			16 55							20 28	
Battersby	a			17 01							20 33	
	d			17 04			17 45				20 36	
Great Ayton	d			17 09			17 50				20 42	
Nunthorpe	d	15 16	16 18	17 17			18 15		19 17	20 20	20 51	21 40
Gypsy Lane	d	15 18	16 20	17 19			18 17		19 19	20 22	20 53	21 42
Marton	d	15 21	16 23	17 22			18 20		19 22	20 25	20 56	21 45
James Cook	d	15 24	16 26	17 25			18 23		19 25	20 28	20 59	21 48
Middlesbrough	a	15 30	16 32	17 31			18 30		19 29	20 34	21 05	21 53
Newcastle ■ 44	a	16 52	17 52	18 49			19 47		20 51	21 51		

§ North Yorkshire Moors Railway. For full service between Grosmont and Pickering please see separate publicity

A until 3 December

B from 28 May until 1 June, from 23 July until 31 August

C until 20 July, from 3 September until 3 December, not from 28 May until 1 June

D from 28 July until 1 September

E until 21 July, from 8 September, not 2 June

For connections to Darlington refer to Table T044

Table T045-R

Whitby - Pickering and Middlesbrough

Sundays

20 May to 2 December

Station		NY ■ 🛒	NT ◇	NT	NY ■ 🛒	NT ◇	NT ◇	NT ◇	NY ■ 🛒	NT ◇	NT ◇	NT ◇	NY ■ 🛒	NT ◇	NT
Whitby	d	09 14		10 18	11 32			12 46	13 57			15 50	16 58		18 28
Ruswarp	d			10 22				12 50				15 54	17 12		18 32
Sleights	d			10 27				12 55				15 59			18 37
Grosmont	d	10 07		10 35	12 30			13 03	14 40			16 07	17 30		18 45
Goathland §	a	10 22			12 45				14 55				17 45		
Levisham §	a	10 58			13 16				15 23				18 09		
Pickering §	a	11 22			13 40				15 45				18 30		
Egton	d			10 39				13 07				16 11			18 49
Glaisdale	a			10 43				13 11				16 15			18 53
	d			10 46				13 14				16 18			18 56
Lealholm	d			10 51				13 19				16 23			19 01
Danby	d			10 58				13 26				16 30			19 08
Castleton Moor	d			11 01				13 30				16 34			19 11
Commondale	d			11 05				13 33				16 37			19 15
Kildale	d			11 12				13 41				16 45			19 22
Battersby	a			11 20				13 46				16 50			19 27
	d			11 23				13 49				16 53			19 30
Great Ayton	d			11 29				13 55				16 58			19 36
Nunthorpe	d		10 18	11 36		12 17	13 17	14 05		15 19	16 19	17 08		18 17	19 43
Gypsy Lane	d		10 20	11 38		12 19	13 19	14 07		15 21	16 21	17 10		18 19	19 45
Marton	d		10 23	11 41		12 22	13 22	14 10		15 24	16 24	17 13		18 22	19 48
James Cook	d		10 26	11 44		12 25	13 25	14 13		15 27	16 27	17 16		18 25	19 51
Middlesbrough	a		10 32	11 50		12 31	13 31	14 19		15 32	16 32	17 23		18 32	19 58
Newcastle ■ 44	a		11 49			13 50	14 49	15 49		16 49	17 50	18 49		19 50	

§ North Yorkshire Moors Railway. For full service between Grosmont and Pickering please see separate publicity

For connections to Darlington refer to Table T044

Table T047-F

Mondays to Fridays

21 May to 7 December

Stansted Airport - Leicester - Birmingham New Street

Miles	Miles			XC ■	XC ■	XC ◇■	XC ■	XC ◇■	XC ■ A	XC ■	XC ◇■	XC ■	XC ◇■ B	XC ■	EM ◇ C	XC ◇■ B	XC ■	XC ◇■ B	XC ■	XC ◇■ B	XC ■	XC ◇■ B	XC ■
0	—	**Stansted Airport** ✈	d					05 16			06 12		07 21			08 21		09 21		10 27		11 27	
10½	—	Audley End	d					05 37			06 24		07 37			08 38		09 39		10 40		11 40	
24½	—	Cambridge	d			05 15		05 55			06 56		08 01			09 01		10 00		11 01		12 01	
39¼	—	Ely ■	d			05 30		06 10			07 12		08 16			09 15		10 15		11 15		12 15	
54¾	—	March	d			05 46		06 28			07 29		08 33			09 33		10 32		11 32		12 32	
69¾	—	Peterborough ■	d			06 10		06 52			07 52		08 52			09 52		10 52		11 52		12 52	
81¾	—	Stamford	d			06 23		07 05			08 05		09 05			10 05		11 05		12 05		13 05	
95½	—	Oakham	d			06 37		07 19			08 19		09 19		09 48	10 19		11 19		12 19		13 19	
106¾	—	Melton Mowbray	d			06 48		07 30			08 30		09 30		10a02	10 30		11 30		12 30		13 30	
121½	0	**Leicester**	a			07 08		07 46			08 46		09 46			10 46		11 46		12 46		13 46	
—	—		d	06 18	06 43	07 10	07 22	07 50		08 18	08 48	09 13	09 48	10 18		10 48	11 18	11 48	12 18	12 48	13 18	13 48	14 18
—	4	South Wigston	d	06 24	06 49		07 28	07 56						10 24					12 24				14 24
—	7	Narborough	d	06 29	06 54		07 33	08 01		08 27		09 23		10 29			11 27		12 29		13 27		14 29
—	15	Hinckley	d	06 38	07 03		07 42	08 10		08 36		09 31		10 38			11 36		12 38		13 36		14 38
140	18½	Nuneaton	d	06 45	07 10	07 30	07 49	08 17		08 43	09 10	09 43	10 10	10 45		11 10	11 43	12 10	12 45	13 10	13 43	14 10	14 45
151½	30	Coleshill Parkway	d	06 59	07 24	07 44	08 03	08 31		08 57	09 24	09 57	10 24	10 59		11 24	11 57	12 24	12 59	13 24	13 57	14 24	14 59
—	32¼	Water Orton	d		07 29		08 08		08 42			10 02					12 02				14 02		
161¼	39¾	**Birmingham New Street** ■	a	07 14	07 44	07 58	08 18	08 45	08 55	09 14	09 38	10 14	10 38	11 14		11 38	12 14	12 38	13 14	13 38	14 14	14 38	15 14

		XC ◇■ B	XC ■	XC ◇■ B	XC ■	XC ◇■ B	XC ■	LE ■	XC ◇■ B	XC ■	XC ◇■ B	XC ■	XC ◇■ B	XC ■	EM ◇■ D	XC ◇■	XC ■	XC ◇■	XC ■	EM E	XC ◇■
Stansted Airport ✈	d	12 27		13 27		14 27		15 10	15 27		16 27		17 27			18 21		19 21			20 21
Audley End	d	12 40		13 40		14 40		15 24	15 40		16 40		17 40			18 38		19 38			20 39
Cambridge	d	13 01		14 01		15 01		15 44	16 01		17 01		18 01			19 00		20 01			21 01
Ely ■	d	13 15		14 15		15 15		16a03	16 15		17 15		18 15			19 15		20 15			21 16
March	d	13 32		14 32		15 32			16 32		17 32		18 34			19 33		20 32			21 34
Peterborough ■	d	13 52		14 52		15 52			16 52		17 52		18 52			19 52		20 52		21 31	21 59
Stamford	d	14 05		15 05		16 05			17 05		18 05		19 05			20 05		21 05		21 45	22 12
Oakham	d	14 19		15 19		16 19			17 19		18 19		19 19		19 26	20 19		21 19		22 01	22 26
Melton Mowbray	d	14 30		15 30		16 30			17 30		18 30		19 30		19a36	20 30		21 30		22a12	22 37
Leicester	a	14 46		15 46		16 46			17 46		18 46		19 46			20 46		21 45			22 53
	d	14 48	15 18	15 48	16 18	16 48	17 18		17 48	18 18	18 48	19 18	19 48	20 18		20 48	21 16	21 47	22 27		22 55
South Wigston	d				16 24		17 24		17 56	18 24		19 24		20 24			21 22		22 33		
Narborough	d		15 27		16 29		17 29		18 01	18 29		19 29		20 29			21 27		22 38		
Hinckley	d		15 36		16 38		17 38		18 09	18 38		19 38		20 38			21 36		22 47		
Nuneaton	d	15 10	15 43	16 10	16 45	17 10	17 45		18 17	18 45	19 10	19 45	20 10	20 44		21 10	21 43	22 10	22 54		23 14
Coleshill Parkway	d	15 24	15 57	16 24	16 59	17 24	17 59		18 31	18 59	19 24	19 59	20 24	21 00		21 24	21 58	22 24	23 08		23 29
Water Orton	d		16 02																		
Birmingham New Street ■	a	15 38	16 14	16 38	17 14	17 38	18 14		18 44	19 14	19 38	20 14	20 38	21 14		21 38	22 14	22 38	23 22		23 42

Saturdays

26 May to 8 December

		XC ■	XC ■	XC ◇■	XC ◇■	XC ■ A	XC ■	XC ◇■	XC ■	XC ◇■ B	XC ■	XC ◇■ B	XC ■	XC ◇■ B	XC ■	XC ◇■ B	XC ■	XC ◇■ B	XC ■	XC ◇■ B	XC ■	XC ◇■ B	XC ■
Stansted Airport ✈	d				05 25			06 27		07 27		08 27		09 27		10 27		11 27		12 27		13 27	
Audley End	d				05 37			06 40		07 40		08 40		09 40		10 40		11 40		12 40		13 40	
Cambridge	d			05 15	05 55			06 57		08 01		09 01		10 01		11 01		12 01		13 01		14 01	
Ely ■	d			05 30	06 10			07 12		08 15		09 15		10 15		11 15		12 15		13 15		14 15	
March	d			05 46	06 28			07 29		08 32		09 32		10 32		11 32		12 32		13 32		14 32	
Peterborough ■	d			06 10	06 52			07 52		08 52		09 52		10 52		11 52		12 52		13 52		14 52	
Stamford	d			06 23	07 05			08 05		09 05		10 05		11 05		12 05		13 05		14 05		15 05	
Oakham	d			06 35	07 19			08 19		09 19		10 19		11 19		12 19		13 19		14 19		15 19	
Melton Mowbray	d			06 46	07 30			08 30		09 30		10 30		11 30		12 30		13 30		14 30		15 30	
Leicester	a			07 05	07 46			08 46		09 46		10 46		11 46		12 46		13 46		14 46		15 46	
	d	05 49	06 49	07 09	07 48		08 18	08 48	09 18	09 48	10 18	10 48	11 18	11 48	12 18	12 48	13 18	13 48	14 18	14 48	15 18	15 48	16 18
South Wigston	d	05 54	06 55				08 25				10 24				12 24				14 24				16 24
Narborough	d	05 59	07 00				08 30		09 27		10 29		11 27		12 29		13 27		14 29		15 27		16 29
Hinckley	d	06 08	07 08				08 38		09 36		10 37		11 36		12 37		13 36		14 37		15 36		16 37
Nuneaton	d	06 14	07 14	07 29	08 10		08 46	09 10	09 43	10 10	10 44	11 10	11 43	12 10	12 44	13 10	13 43	14 10	14 44	15 10	15 43	16 10	16 44
Coleshill Parkway	d	06 30	07 30	07 47	08 25		09 01	09 25	09 58	10 25	11 00	11 25	11 58	12 25	13 00	13 25	13 58	14 25	15 00	15 25	15 58	16 25	17 00
Water Orton	d		07 35			08 42			10 02				12 02				14 02				16 02		
Birmingham New Street ■	a	06 43	07 47	08 03	08 38	08 55	09 14	09 38	10 14	10 38	11 14	11 38	12 14	12 38	13 14	13 38	14 14	14 38	15 14	15 38	16 14	16 38	17 14

		XC ◇■ B	XC ■	XC ◇■ B	XC ■	XC ◇■ B	XC ■	XC ◇■ B	XC ■	XC ◇■	XC ■	XC ◇■	XC ■
Stansted Airport ✈	d	14 27		15 27		16 27		17 27		18 27		19 27	
Audley End	d	14 40		15 40		16 40		17 40		18 40		19 40	
Cambridge	d	15 01		16 01		17 01		18 01		19 01		20 01	
Ely ■	d	15 15		16 15		17 15		18 15		19 15		20 16	
March	d	15 32		16 32		17 32		18 34		19 32		20 32	
Peterborough ■	d	15 52		16 52		17 52		18 52		19 52		20 52	
Stamford	d	16 05		17 05		18 05		19 05		20 05		21 05	
Oakham	d	16 19		17 19		18 19		19 19		20 19		21 19	
Melton Mowbray	d	16 30		17 30		18 30		19 30		20 30		21 30	
Leicester	a	16 46		17 46		18 46		19 46		20 46		21 46	
	d	16 48	17 18	17 51	18 18	18 48	19 18	19 48	20 18	20 48	21 18	21 48	22 20
South Wigston	d		17 24		18 24		19 24		20 24		21 24		22 26
Narborough	d		17 29		18 29		19 29		20 29		21 29		22 31
Hinckley	d		17 37		18 37		19 37		20 37		21 37		22 39
Nuneaton	d	17 10	17 44	18 10	18 44	19 10	19 44	20 10	20 44	21 10	21 44	22 10	22 46
Coleshill Parkway	d	17 25	18 00	18 25	19 00	19 25	20 00	20 25	21 00	21 25	22 00	22 25	23 01
Water Orton	d												
Birmingham New Street ■	a	17 38	18 14	18 38	19 14	19 38	20 13	20 38	21 13	21 38	22 14	22 38	23 14

A From Nottingham
B 🍴 from Peterborough
C From Corby
D From St Pancras International
E From Spalding to Nottingham

Table T047-F

Sundays

20 May to 2 December

Stansted Airport - Leicester - Birmingham New Street

		XC ■	XC ■	XC ■	XC ◇■	XC ■	XC ◇■	XC ■	XC ◇■ A	XC ■	XC ◇■ A	XC ■	XC ◇■ A	XC ■	XC ◇■ A	XC ■	XC ◇■ A	XC ■	XC ◇■	XC ■	XC ◇■	XC ◇■	XC ■
Stansted Airport ✈	d				10 25		11 25		12 25		13 25		14 25		15 25		16 25		17 25		18 25	19 25	
Audley End	d				10 39		11 39		12 39		13 39		14 39		15 39		16 39		17 39		18 39	19 39	
Cambridge	d				11 00		12 00		13 00		14 00		15 00		16 00		17 00		18 00		19 00	20 00	
Ely ■	d				11 15		12 15		13 15		14 15		15 15		16 15		17 15		18 15		19 15	20 15	
March	d				11 32		12 32		13 32		14 32		15 32		16 32		17 32		18 32		19 32	20 32	
Peterborough ■	d				11 53		12 53		13 53		14 53		15 53		16 53		17 53		18 53		19 53	20 53	
Stamford	d				12 06		13 06		14 06		15 06		16 06		17 06		18 06		19 06		20 06	21 06	
Oakham	d				12 20		13 20		14 20		15 20		16 20		17 20		18 20		19 20		20 20	21 20	
Melton Mowbray	d				12 31		13 31		14 31		15 31		16 31		17 31		18 31		19 31		20 31	21 31	
Leicester	a				12 48		13 48		14 48		15 48		16 48		17 49		18 48		19 48		20 48	21 48	
	d	10 22	11 19	12 19	12 50	13 19	13 49	14 19	14 50	15 19	15 50	16 19	16 50	17 19	17 50	18 19	18 50	19 19	19 50	20 19	20 50	21 50	22 19
South Wigston	d			12 24				14 24				16 24		17 25				19 24		20 24			22 24
Narborough	d	10 31	11 28	12 29		13 28		14 29		15 28		16 29		17 30		18 28		19 29		20 29			22 29
Hinckley	d	10 39	11 36	12 38		13 36		14 38		15 36		16 38		17 38		18 36		19 37		20 38			22 38
Nuneaton	d	10 46	11 44	12 45	13 10	13 43	14 09	14 45	15 09	15 43	16 09	16 45	17 09	17 45	18 09	18 43	19 09	19 43	20 10	20 44	21 10	22 10	22 45
Coleshill Parkway	d	11 02	11 59	13 00	13 25	13 59	14 25	15 00	15 25	15 59	16 25	17 00	17 25	18 00	18 25	18 59	19 25	19 59	20 25	21 00	21 25	22 25	23 00
Water Orton	d																						
Birmingham New Street ■	a	11 15	12 15	13 15	13 38	14 15	14 38	15 15	15 38	16 15	16 38	17 15	17 38	18 15	18 38	19 15	19 38	20 15	20 38	21 15	21 38	22 38	23 15

A 🍴 from Peterborough

Table T047-R

Birmingham New Street - Leicester - Stansted Airport

Mondays to Fridays
21 May to 7 December

Miles	Miles			EM	EM	XC	XC	EM	XC	XC	XC	XC	XC	XC	XC	XC	XC	XC	XC	XC	XC	XC
				◇	◇■	◇■	■	◇	◇■	■	◇■	■	◇■	■	◇■	■	◇■	■	◇■	■	◇■	■
				A	B			A	C		C				C		C		C		C	
					🛒				🛒		🛒		🛒		🛒		🛒		🛒		🛒	
0	0	**Birmingham New Street** ■	d			05 19	05 50		06 22	06 52	07 22	07 52	08 22	08 52	09 22	09 52	10 22	10 52	11 22	11 52	12 22	12 52
—	7½	Water Orton	d											09 03				11 03				13 04
9¾	9¾	Coleshill Parkway	d			05 34	06 03		06 36	07 06	07 35	08 06	08 36	09 07	09 36	10 08	10 36	11 07	11 36	12 08	12 36	13 08
21¼	21¼	Nuneaton	d			05 49	06 18		06 53	07 23	07 50	08 25	08 52	09 23	09 52	10 23	10 52	11 23	11 52	12 23	12 52	13 23
—	24¾	Hinckley	d			05 55	06 25			07 30	07 57	08 31		09 30		10 30		11 30		12 30		13 29
—	32¾	Narborough	d			06 04	06 33			07 38	08 05	08 39		09 38		10 38		11 38		12 38		13 38
—	35¾	South Wigston	d				06 38			07 43	08 10	08 44				10 43				12 43		
39¾	39¾	**Leicester**	a			06 14	06 45		07 15	07 50	08 16	08 50	09 12	09 50	10 16	10 50	11 14	11 50	12 14	12 51	13 14	13 51
—	—		d			06 15			07 18		08 18		09 18		10 18		11 18		12 18		13 18	
54½	—	Melton Mowbray	d	05 36	06 03	06 32		06 53	07 35		08 35		09 35		10 35		11 35		12 35		13 35	
65¾	—	Oakham	d	05 49	06a14	06 43		07 05	07 46		08 46		09 46		10 46		11 46		12 46		13 46	
79½	—	Stamford	d	06 05		06 57		07 19	08 00		09 00		10 00		11 00		12 00		13 00		14 00	
91¼	—	Peterborough ■	d	06 27		07 12		07 38	08 18		09 18		10 19		11 18		12 19		13 19		14 19	
106½	—	March	d	06 43		07 31		07 54	08 34		09 34		10 35		11 34		12 35		13 35		14 35	
122	—	Ely ■	d	07a02		07 52		08a12	08 54		09 52		10 53		11 53		12 53		13 53		14 53	
136¾	—	Cambridge	d			08 13			09 15		10 10		11 11		12 11		13 11		14 11		15 11	
150¾	—	Audley End	d			08 27			09 29		10 25		11 25		12 25		13 25		14 25		15 25	
161¼	—	**Stansted Airport** ✈	a			08 39			09 43		10 40		11 40		12 40		13 40		14 40		15 40	

		XC	XC	XC	XC	XC	XC	XC	EM	XC	XC	XC	XC	XC	XC	XC	XC	XC	XC	XC	XC	XC	XC
		◇■	■	◇■	■	◇■	■	■	◇■	◇■	◇■	■	◇■	■	◇■	■	◇■	■	◇■	■	◇■	■	■
		C		C		C			D	C				E	F								
		🛒		🛒		🛒			🛒	🛒					🛒								
Birmingham New Street ■	d	13 22	13 52	14 22	14 52	15 22	15 52	16 09		16 22	16 52	17 09	17 22	17 39	17 49	17 52	18 22	18 52	19 22	19 52	20 25	20 52	22 22
Water Orton	d				15 03			16 20				17 23		17a50	17a59	18 05				20 05			
Coleshill Parkway	d	13 36	14 08	14 36	15 07	15 36	16 08	16 24		16 36	17 06	17 26	17 36			18 08	18 36	19 07	19 36	20 08	20 38	21 06	22 36
Nuneaton	d	13 52	14 23	14 52	15 23	15 52	16 23	16 40		16 52	17 23	17 41	17 51			18 23	18 52	19 23	19 52	20 23	20 53	21 23	22 53
Hinckley	d		14 30		15 30		16 30	16 46			17 30	17 48	17 57			18 30		19 30		20 30		21 30	23 00
Narborough	d		14 38		15 38		16 38	16 55			17 38		18 06			18 38		19 38		20 38		21 38	23 08
South Wigston	d		14 43				16 43					17 59				18 43		19 43		20 43		21 43	23 13
Leicester	a	14 14	14 50	15 16	15 50	16 14	16 50	17 08		17 16	17 51	18 05	18 16			18 50	19 13	19 55	20 17	20 49	21 15	21 50	23 20
	d	14 18		15 18		16 18				17 18	17 53		18 17				19 18		20 18		21 18		
Melton Mowbray	d	14 35		15 35		16 35			17 09	17 35	18 16		18 35				19 35		20 35		21 35		
Oakham	d	14 46		15 46		16 46			17a21	17 46	18 29		18 46				19 46		20 46		21 46		
Stamford	d	15 00		16 00		17 00				18 00	18 43		19 00				20 00		21 00		22 00		
Peterborough ■	d	15 19		16 19		17 18				18 18	18 59		19 19				20 19		21 16		22 18		
March	d	15 35		16 35		17 37				18 34	19 15		19 35				20 35		21 32		22 36		
Ely ■	d	15 53		16 53		17 59				18 52	19 34		19 53				20 53		21 52		22 54		
Cambridge	d	16 11		17 11		18 18				19 10	19a50		20 11				21 11		22 10		23a10		
Audley End	d	16 25		17 25		18 32				19 25			20 25				21 25		22 25				
Stansted Airport ✈	a	16 40		17 40		18 54				19 40			20 39				21 40		22 52				

Saturdays
26 May to 8 December

		EM	XC	XC	EM	XC	XC	XC	XC	XC	XC	XC	XC	XC	XC	XC	XC	XC	XC	XC	XC	XC	XC
		◇	◇■	■	◇	◇■	■	◇■	■	◇■	■	◇■	■	◇■	■	◇■	■	◇■	■	◇■	■	◇■	■
		A			A	C		C		G		C		C		C		C		C		C	
						🛒		🛒		🛒		🛒		🛒		🛒		🛒		🛒		🛒	
Birmingham New Street ■	d		05 22	05 52		06 22	06 52	07 22	07 52	08 22	08 52	09 22	09 52	10 22	10 52	11 22	11 52	12 22	12 52	13 22	13 52	14 22	14 52
Water Orton	d						07 02				09 02				11 02				13 02				15 02
Coleshill Parkway	d		05 36	06 06		06 36	07 06	07 36	08 06	08 36	09 07	09 36	10 07	10 36	11 07	11 36	12 07	12 36	13 07	13 36	14 07	14 36	15 07
Nuneaton	d		05 52	06 21		06 52	07 22	07 52	08 23	08 52	09 23	09 52	10 23	10 52	11 23	11 52	12 23	12 52	13 23	13 52	14 23	14 52	15 23
Hinckley	d			06 28			07 29		08 29		09 29		10 29		11 29		12 29		13 29		14 29		15 29
Narborough	d			06 36			07 37		08 38		09 38		10 38		11 38		12 38		13 38		14 38		15 38
South Wigston	d			06 41			07 42		08 43				10 43				12 43				14 43		
Leicester	a		06 12	06 47		07 15	07 49	08 13	08 49	09 13	09 50	10 13	10 52	11 13	11 48	12 12	12 50	13 14	13 50	14 14	14 50	15 13	15 48
	d		06 15			07 18		08 19		09 18		10 18		11 18		12 18		13 18		14 18		15 18	
Melton Mowbray	d	05 40	06 32		06 53	07 35		08 36		09 35		10 35		11 35		12 35		13 35		14 35		15 35	
Oakham	d	05 52	06 43		07 05	07 46		08 47		09 46		10 46		11 46		12 46		13 46		14 46		15 46	
Stamford	d	06 08	06 57		07 19	08 00		09 01		10 00		11 00		12 00		13 00		14 00		15 00		16 00	
Peterborough ■	d	06 27	07 13		07 35	08 19		09 18		10 18		11 19		12 19		13 19		14 19		15 19		16 19	
March	d	06 43	07 32		07 53	08 35		09 34		10 34		11 35		12 35		13 35		14 35		15 35		16 35	
Ely ■	d	07a03	07 53		08a13	08 53		09 55		10 52		11 53		12 53		13 53		14 53		15 53		16 53	
Cambridge	d		08 10			09 11		10 11		11 11		12 11		13 11		14 11		15 11		16 11		17 11	
Audley End	d		08 25			09 25		10 26		11 26		12 25		13 25		14 25		15 25		16 25		17 25	
Stansted Airport ✈	a		08 39			09 40		10 40		11 40		12 40		13 40		14 40		15 40		16 40		17 40	

A From Nottingham to Norwich
B To St Pancras International
C 🛒 to Peterborough
D From Derby to Kettering
E until 20 July, from 3 September. To Derby
F from 23 July until 31 August. From Cardiff Central to Nottingham
G From Gloucester. 🛒 to Peterborough

Table T047-R

Birmingham New Street - Leicester - Stansted Airport

Saturdays
26 May to 8 December

		XC	XC	XC	XC	XC	XC	XC	XC	XC	XC	XC	XC	XC
		◇■	■	◇■	■	◇■	■	◇■	■	◇■	■	◇■	■	■
				A										
		🛒		🛒										
Birmingham New Street ■	d	15 22	15 52	16 22	16 52	17 22	17 52	18 22	18 52	19 22	19 52	20 22	20 52	22 22
Water Orton	d				17 02						20 02			
Coleshill Parkway	d	15 36	16 07	16 36	17 07	17 36	18 05	18 36	19 05	19 36	20 07	20 36	21 05	22 36
Nuneaton	d	15 52	16 23	16 52	17 23	17 52	18 22	18 52	19 22	19 52	20 23	20 52	21 22	22 52
Hinckley	d		16 29		17 29		18 29		19 29		20 29		21 29	22 59
Narborough	d		16 38		17 38		18 38		19 38		20 38		21 38	23 08
South Wigston	d		16 43				18 43		19 43		20 43		21 43	23 12
Leicester	a	16 14	16 50	17 13	17 50	18 12	18 50	19 13	19 50	20 13	20 50	21 12	21 51	23 18
	d	16 18		17 18		18 18		19 18		20 18		21 16		
Melton Mowbray	d	16 35		17 35		18 35		19 35		20 35		21 33		
Oakham	d	16 46		17 46		18 46		19 46		20 46		21 44		
Stamford	d	17 00		18 00		19 00		20 00		21 00		21 58		
Peterborough ■	d	17 18		18 19		19 19		20 19		21 19		22 14		
March	d	17 37		18 35		19 35		20 35		21 35		22 29		
Ely ■	d	18 00		18 53		19 54		20 53		21 53		22 48		
Cambridge	d	18 17		19 11		20 11		21 11		22 11		23a03		
Audley End	d	18 33		19 25		20 25		21 25		22 25				
Stansted Airport ✈	a	18 53		19 40		20 40		21 40		22 40				

Sundays
20 May to 2 December

		XC	XC	XC	XC	XC	XC	XC	XC	XC	XC	XC	XC	XC	XC	XC	XC	XC	XC	XC	XC	XC	XC
		■	■	◇■	■	◇■	■	◇■	■	◇■	■	◇■	■	◇■	■	◇■	■	◇■	■	◇■	■	◇■	■
				A		A		A		A		A											
				🛒		🛒		🛒		🛒		🛒											
Birmingham New Street ■	d	09 52	10 52	11 22	11 52	12 22	12 52	13 22	13 52	14 22	14 52	15 22	15 52	16 22	16 52	17 22	17 52	18 22	18 52	19 22	19 52	20 22	20 52
Water Orton	d																						
Coleshill Parkway	d	10 05	11 05	11 36	12 05	12 36	13 05	13 36	14 05	14 36	15 05	15 36	16 05	16 36	17 05	17 36	18 05	18 36	19 05	19 36	20 05	20 36	21 05
Nuneaton	d	10 22	11 22	11 52	12 22	12 52	13 22	13 52	14 22	14 52	15 22	15 52	16 22	16 52	17 22	17 52	18 22	18 52	19 22	19 52	20 22	20 52	21 22
Hinckley	d	10 29	11 29		12 29		13 29		14 29		15 29		16 29		17 29		18 29		19 29		20 29		21 29
Narborough	d	10 37	11 37		12 37		13 37		14 37		15 37		16 37		17 37		18 37		19 37		20 37		21 37
South Wigston	d	10 42			12 42				14 42				16 42		17 42		18 42		19 42		20 42		21 42
Leicester	a	10 48	11 48	12 16	12 48	13 12	13 48	14 13	14 48	15 15	15 48	16 12	16 48	17 13	17 48	18 15	18 48	19 14	19 48	20 13	20 48	21 13	21 48
	d			12 19		13 19		14 19		15 19		16 19		17 16		18 19		19 19		20 19		21 16	
Melton Mowbray	d			12 36		13 36		14 36		15 36		16 36		17 36		18 36		19 36		20 36		21 36	
Oakham	d			12 47		13 47		14 47		15 47		16 47		17 48		18 48		19 48		20 48		21 47	
Stamford	d			13 01		14 01		15 01		16 01		17 01		18 01		19 02		20 01		21 01		22 01	
Peterborough ■	d			13 18		14 18		15 18		16 18		17 18		18 18		19 18		20 18		21 18		22 16	
March	d			13 34		14 34		15 34		16 34		17 34		18 34		19 34		20 34		21 34		22 32	
Ely ■	d			13 52		14 52		15 52		16 52		17 52		18 52		19 52		20 52		21 52		22 51	
Cambridge	d			14 10		15 10		16 10		17 10		18 10		19 10		20 10		21 10		22 10		23a06	
Audley End	d			14 25		15 25		16 25		17 25		18 25		19 25		20 25		21 25		22 25			
Stansted Airport ✈	a			14 45		15 45		16 45		17 45		18 45		19 45		20 45		21 45		22 45			

		XC
		◇■
		B
Birmingham New Street ■	d	21 52
Water Orton	d	
Coleshill Parkway	d	22 05
Nuneaton	d	22 22
Hinckley	d	22 29
Narborough	d	22 37
South Wigston	d	22 42
Leicester	a	22 48
	d	
Melton Mowbray	d	
Oakham	d	
Stamford	d	
Peterborough ■	d	
March	d	
Ely ■	d	
Cambridge	d	
Audley End	d	
Stansted Airport ✈	a	

A 🛒 to Peterborough
B From Cardiff Central

Table T048-F

21 May to 7 December

Chathill and Morpeth - Newcastle - Metrocentre, Hexham and Carlisle

Miles	Miles			NT	GR	NT	GR	NT	XC	NT	NT	NT	XC	NT	NT	GR	NT	XC	NT	NT	NT
					■ 1		■ 1	◇	◇1		◇	◇	◇1			■ 1	◇	◇1			
0	—	**Chathill**	d									07 10									
11¼	—	Alnmouth for Alnwick 26	d		06 21		06 55		07 11			07 22	08 03			09 00					
17½	—	Acklington	d									07 39									
22¾	—	Widdrington	d									07 46									
27½	—	Pegswood	d									07 52									
39½	—	**Morpeth** 26	d		06 38		07 11					07 56	08 18	08 52				09 25			09 52
36¼	—	Cramlington	d									08 05		09 00							10 00
45½	—	Manors	d									08 16		09 11							10 11
46	—	**Newcastle** 8 26	a		06 52		07 26		07 38			08 21	08 32	09 17		09 27		09 40			10 17
—	—	Sunderland 26,44	d							07 19					08 30					09 20	
—	0	**Newcastle** 8	d	06 00		06 30		07 01		07 41	08 05	08 23			08 56		09 13		09 28	09 45	
48¼	2¼	Dunston	d	06 05											09 01					09 51	
49½	3½	**Metrocentre**	a	06 08		06 37		07 09		07 49	08 14	08 30			09 04		09 20		09 36	09 54	
—	—		d	06 09		06 38		07 09		07 49	08 14	08 31			09 05		09 21			09 54	
—	5½	Blaydon	d	06 13				07 13				08 35			09 09					09 58	
—	9¾	Wylam	d	06 19				07 20				08 41			09 15					10 04	
—	12	Prudhoe	d	06 23		06 49		07 24		07 59	08 25	08a46			09 19		09 33			10 09	
—	14½	Stocksfield	d	06 28				07 29		08 04					09 24					10 13	
—	16¾	Riding Mill	d	06 32				07 33		08 08					09 28					10 18	
—	19¼	Corbridge	d	06 36				07 37			08 34				09 32					10 22	
—	22¼	**Hexham**	a	06 42		07 00		07 42		08 16	08 39				09 38		09 47			10 28	
—	—		d			07 01		07 43			08 40						09 47				
—	30	Haydon Bridge	d			07 10		07 52			08 49						09 56				
—	33¾	Bardon Mill	d			07 16					08 55										
—	38½	Haltwhistle	d			07 24		08 03			09 02						10 08				
—	50¾	Brampton (Cumbria)	d			07 39		08 18									10 23				
—	57½	Wetheral	d			07 48		08 27									10 32				
—	61¾	**Carlisle** 8	a			07 57		08 37			09 33						10 40				

		NT	NT	NT	NT	GR	NT	XC	NT	NT	NT	XC	NT	NT	NT	NT	GR	NT	NT	NT	NT	XC
		◇				■ 1	◇	◇1				◇1	◇				■ 1	◇				◇1
Chathill	d																					
Alnmouth for Alnwick 26	d					11 00						12 12					13 00					14 13
Acklington	d																					
Widdrington	d																					
Pegswood	d																					
Morpeth 26	d				10 51			11 22			11 52					12 52					13 52	
Cramlington	d				11 00						12 00					13 00					14 00	
Manors	d				11 11						12 11					13 12					14 12	
Newcastle 8 26	a				11 15	11 27		11 38			12 14	12 38				13 19	13 27				14 19	14 39
Sunderland 26,44	d			10 30						11 30					12 30					13 30		
Newcastle 8	d	10 13	10 28	10 55			11 15		11 28	11 55			12 16	12 28	12 55			13 15	13 28	13 55		
Dunston	d			11 00						12 00					13 00					14 00		
Metrocentre	a	10 22	10 36	11 03			11 24		11 36	12 03			12 23	12 36	13 03			13 24	13 36	14 03		
	d	10 22		11 04			11 24			12 04			12 24		13 04			13 24		14 04		
Blaydon	d			11 08						12 08					13 08					14 08		
Wylam	d			11 14						12 14					13 14					14 14		
Prudhoe	d	10 33		11 18			11 35			12 18			12 35		13 18			13 35		14 18		
Stocksfield	d			11 23						12 23					13 23					14 23		
Riding Mill	d			11 27						12 27					13 27					14 27		
Corbridge	d			11 31						12 31					13 31					14 31		
Hexham	a	10 46		11 37			11 47			12 37			12 47		13 37			13 47		14 37		
	d	10 46					11 47						12 47					13 47				
Haydon Bridge	d	10 55					11 57						12 56					13 57				
Bardon Mill	d						12 03											14 03				
Haltwhistle	d	11 07					12 10						13 08					14 10				
Brampton (Cumbria)	d	11 22											13 23									
Wetheral	d	11 31											13 32									
Carlisle 8	a	11 39					12 43						13 41					14 40				

For connections to and from London Kings Cross refer to Table T026

Table T048-F

21 May to 7 December

Chathill and Morpeth - Newcastle - Metrocentre, Hexham and Carlisle

		NT	NT	NT	NT	GR	NT	NT	NT	NT	NT	NT	NT	NT	NT	NT	XC	NT	NT	NT	GR	XC	NT
		◇				■ 1		◇			◇		◇				◇1		◇	◇	■ 1	◇1	◇
Chathill	d																						
Alnmouth for Alnwick 26	d					15 00											17 05				18 00		
Acklington	d																						
Widdrington	d																						
Pegswood	d																						
Morpeth 26	d				14 51	15 15	15 52								16 52		17 19			17 51		18 24	
Cramlington	d				15 00		16 00								17 00					18 00			
Manors	d				15 14		16 12								17 11					18 11			
Newcastle 8 26	a				15 19	15 30	16 19								17 16		17 33			18 16	18 27	18 38	
Sunderland 26,44	d			14 30						15 32			16 30					17 30					18 29
Newcastle 8	d	14 15	14 28	14 55				15 15	15 28	15 55	16 15	16 28	16 55	17 10	17 23	17 28		17 54	18 10	18 23			18 52
Dunston	d			15 02						16 00		16 33	17 00			17 33		18 01					18 58
Metrocentre	a	14 24	14 36	15 05				15 24	15 36	16 03	16 24	16 37	17 03	17 19	17 30	17 37		18 04	18 19	18 30			19 01
	d	14 24		15 06				15 24		16 04	16 24		17 04	17 19	17 31			18 04	18 19	18 31			19 01
Blaydon	d			15 10						16 08			17 08		17 35			18 08		18 35			19 05
Wylam	d			15 16						16 14			17 14	17 27	17 41			18 15	18 27	18 41			19 11
Prudhoe	d	14 35		15 21				15 35		16 18	16 35		17 18	17 32	17 46			18 19	18 32	18 46			19 16
Stocksfield	d			15 25						16 23			17 23	17 36	17 50			18 24	18 36	18 50			19 20
Riding Mill	d			15 30						16 27			17 27	17 41	17 55			18 28	18 41	18 55			19 25
Corbridge	d			15 34						16 31			17 31	17 45	17 59			18 32	18 45	18 59			19 29
Hexham	a	14 47		15 40				15 47		16 37	16 47		17 36	17 52	18 04			18 38	18 50	19 04			19 35
	d	14 47						15 47			16 47		17 37		18 04				18 50	19 04			
Haydon Bridge	d	14 56						15 57			16 56		17 46		18 13					19 13			
Bardon Mill	d							16 03					17 52		18 20					19 20			
Haltwhistle	d	15 08						16 10			17 08		17 59		18 27				19 09	19 27			
Brampton (Cumbria)	d	15 23									17 23		18 15		18 42					19 43			
Wetheral	d	15 32									17 32		18 24		18 51					19 51			
Carlisle 8	a	15 41						16 40			17 41		18 33		19 00				19 39	20 00			

		NT	XC	NT	GR	NT	NT	GR	NT	XC	NT	NT	GR	NT	NT	GR FO
		◇	◇1		■ 1	◇		■ 1	◇	◇1			■ 1			■ 1
Chathill	d					19 15										
Alnmouth for Alnwick 26	d		19 14		19 42	19 27		20 40		21 09			22 11			23 09
Acklington	d					19 35										
Widdrington	d					19 42										
Pegswood	d					19 48										
Morpeth 26	d	18 54			20 00	19 52		20 57	21 00			21 57	22 28	22 55		23 26
Cramlington	d	19 03				20 00			21 08			22 06		23 04		
Manors	d	19 14				20 11			21 19			22 17		23 15		
Newcastle 8 26	a	19 19	19 40		20 15	20 16		21 11	21 21	21 35		22 21	22 42	23 19		23 54
Sunderland 26,44	d			19 28			20 30				21 29				22 30	
Newcastle 8	d	19 23		19 49		20 25	20 53		21 23		21 54	22 23			22 53	
Dunston	d			19 54			20 58				21 59	22 28			22 58	
Metrocentre	a	19 30		19 57		20 32	21 01		21 30		22 02	22 32			23 01	
	d	19 31				20 33			21 31						23 02	
Blaydon	d	19 35				20 37			21 35						23 06	
Wylam	d	19 41				20 43			21 41						23 12	
Prudhoe	d	19 46				20 48			21 46						23 17	
Stocksfield	d	19 50				20 52			21 50						23 21	
Riding Mill	d	19 55				20 57			21 55						23 26	
Corbridge	d	19 59				21 01			21 59						23 30	
Hexham	a	20 04				21 06			22 04						23 36	
	d	20 04				21 06			22 04							
Haydon Bridge	d	20 13				21 15			22 13							
Bardon Mill	d	20 20							22 20							
Haltwhistle	d	20 27				21 27			22 27							
Brampton (Cumbria)	d	20 43							22 42							
Wetheral	d	20 51							22 51							
Carlisle 8	a	21 01				21 57			23 00							

For connections to and from London Kings Cross refer to Table T026

Table T048-F

Saturdays

26 May to 8 December

Chathill and Morpeth - Newcastle - Metrocentre, Hexham and Carlisle

Station			NT	NT	GR	NT			XC	NT	NT	NT		XC	NT	NT	GR		XC	NT	NT	NT	NT	NT	NT	NT
					1 ⊏				◇1 ⊼		◇	◇		◇1			1 ⊏		◇1 ⊼	◇				◇		
Chathill		d										07 10														
Alnmouth for Alnwick	26	d			06 55				07 11			07 22		08 03			09 01		09 12							
Acklington		d										07 39														
Widdrington		d										07 46														
Pegswood		d										07 52														
Morpeth	26	d			07 10							07 56		08 18	08 52								09 52			
Cramlington		d										08 05			09 00								10 00			
Manors		d										08 16			09 11								10 11			
Newcastle ■	26 ⇌	a			07 25				07 38			08 21		08 34	09 17		09 27		09 39				10 17			
Sunderland	26,44 ⇌	d								07 16						08 30						09 28				10 30
Newcastle ■	⇌	d	05 58	06 30		07 02				07 41	08 05	08 23				08 56				09 13	09 28	09 55		10 13	10 28	10 55
Dunston		d	06 05													09 01						10 00				11 00
Metrocentre		a	06 08	06 37		07 09				07 48	08 14	08 30				09 04				09 22	09 36	10 03		10 22	10 36	11 03
		d	06 09	06 38		07 10				07 49	08 14	08 31				09 05				09 22		10 04		10 22		11 04
Blaydon		d	06 13			07 14						08 35				09 09						10 08				11 08
Wylam		d	06 19			07 21						08 41				09 15						10 14				11 14
Prudhoe		d	06 23	06 49		07 25				07 59	08 25	08a46				09 19				09 33		10 18		10 33		11 18
Stocksfield		d	06 28			07 30				08 04						09 24						10 23				11 23
Riding Mill		d	06 32			07 34				08 08						09 28						10 27				11 27
Corbridge		d	06 36			07 38					08 34					09 32						10 31				11 31
Hexham		a	06 42	07 00		07 43				08 16	08 39					09 38				09 47		10 37		10 46		11 37
		d		07 01		07 44					08 40									09 47				10 46		
Haydon Bridge		d		07 10		07 53					08 49									09 56				10 55		
Bardon Mill		d		07 16							08 55															
Haltwhistle		d		07 24		08 04					09 02									10 08				11 07		
Brampton (Cumbria)		d		07 39		08 19														10 23				11 22		
Wetheral		d		07 48		08 28														10 32				11 31		
Carlisle ■		a		07 57		08 38					09 33									10 40				11 39		

Station			NT		GR	NT	XC	NT	NT	NT	XC	NT	NT		NT	NT	GR	NT	XC	NT	NT	NT	XC		NT	NT
					1 ⊏	◇	◇1 ⊼				◇1 ⊼	◇					1 ⊏	◇	◇1 ⊼				◇1 ⊼		◇	
Chathill		d																								
Alnmouth for Alnwick	26	d			11 00						12 13						13 00						14 12			
Acklington		d																								
Widdrington		d																								
Pegswood		d																								
Morpeth	26	d	10 51				11 21			11 52						12 52			13 18			13 52				
Cramlington		d	11 00							12 00						13 00						14 00				
Manors		d	11 11							12 11						13 12						14 12				
Newcastle ■	26 ⇌	a	11 15		11 27		11 35			12 14	12 39					13 19	13 26		13 32			14 19	14 38			
Sunderland	26,44 ⇌	d							11 30						12 30						13 30					
Newcastle ■	⇌	d				11 15		11 28	11 55			12 16	12 28		12 55			13 15		13 28	13 55				14 15	14 28
Dunston		d							12 00						13 00						14 00					
Metrocentre		a				11 24		11 36	12 03			12 23	12 36		13 03			13 24		13 36	14 03				14 24	14 36
		d				11 24			12 04			12 24			13 04			13 24			14 04				14 24	
Blaydon		d							12 08						13 08						14 08					
Wylam		d							12 14						13 14						14 14					
Prudhoe		d				11 35			12 18			12 35			13 18			13 35			14 18				14 35	
Stocksfield		d							12 23						13 23						14 23					
Riding Mill		d							12 27						13 27						14 27					
Corbridge		d							12 31						13 31						14 31					
Hexham		a				11 47			12 37			12 47			13 37			13 47			14 37				14 47	
		d				11 47						12 47						13 47							14 47	
Haydon Bridge		d				11 57						12 56						13 57							14 56	
Bardon Mill		d				12 03												14 03								
Haltwhistle		d				12 10						13 08						14 10							15 08	
Brampton (Cumbria)		d										13 23													15 23	
Wetheral		d										13 32													15 32	
Carlisle ■		a				12 43						13 41						14 40							15 41	

For connections to and from London Kings Cross refer to Table T026

Table T048-F

Saturdays

26 May to 8 December

Chathill and Morpeth - Newcastle - Metrocentre, Hexham and Carlisle

Station			NT	NT	GR		NT	XC	NT	NT	NT	NT	NT	NT	NT		NT	NT	XC	NT	NT	NT	GR	NT	NT
					1 ⊏		◇	◇1 ⊼				◇		◇					◇1 ⊼		◇	◇	1 ⊏	◇	◇
Chathill		d																							
Alnmouth for Alnwick	26	d			15 00														17 05				18 00		
Acklington		d																							
Widdrington		d																							
Pegswood		d																							
Morpeth	26	d		14 51	15 15			15 21			15 52						16 52		17 19			17 51			18 54
Cramlington		d		15 00							16 00						17 00					18 00			19 03
Manors		d		15 14							16 12						17 11					18 11			19 14
Newcastle ■	26 ⇌	a		15 19	15 30			15 35			16 19						17 16		17 33			18 16	18 26		19 19
Sunderland	26,44 ⇌	d	14 30							15 32				16 30						17 30				18 29	
Newcastle ■	⇌	d	14 55				15 15		15 28	15 55		16 15	16 26	16 55	17 10		17 23	17 28		17 54	18 10	18 23		18 52	19 23
Dunston		d	15 00							16 00			16 31	17 00				17 33		18 01				18 58	
Metrocentre		a	15 03				15 24		15 36	16 03		16 24	16 35	17 03	17 19		17 30	17 37		18 04	18 19	18 30		19 01	19 30
		d	15 04				15 24			16 04		16 24		17 04	17 19		17 31			18 04	18 19	18 31		19 01	19 31
Blaydon		d	15 08							16 08				17 08			17 35			18 08		18 35		19 05	19 35
Wylam		d	15 14							16 14				17 14	17 27		17 41			18 15	18 27	18 41		19 11	19 41
Prudhoe		d	15 18				15 35			16 18		16 35		17 18	17 32		17 46			18 19	18 32	18 46		19 16	19 46
Stocksfield		d	15 23							16 23				17 23	17 36		17 50			18 24	18 36	18 50		19 20	19 50
Riding Mill		d	15 27							16 27				17 27	17 41		17 55			18 28	18 41	18 55		19 25	19 55
Corbridge		d	15 31							16 31				17 31	17 45		17 59			18 32	18 45	18 59		19 29	19 59
Hexham		a	15 37				15 47			16 37		16 47		17 36	17 52		18 04			18 38	18 50	19 04		19 35	20 04
		d					15 47					16 47		17 37			18 04				18 50	19 04			20 04
Haydon Bridge		d					15 57					16 56		17 46			18 13					19 13			20 13
Bardon Mill		d					16 03							17 52			18 20					19 20			20 20
Haltwhistle		d					16 10					17 08		17 59			18 27				19 09	19 27			20 27
Brampton (Cumbria)		d										17 23		18 15			18 42					19 43			20 43
Wetheral		d										17 32		18 24			18 51					19 51			20 51
Carlisle ■		a					16 40					17 41		18 33			19 00				19 39	20 00			21 01

Station			XC	NT	NT	GR	NT	NT	NT	GR	NT		NT	NT
			◇1 ⊼		◇	1 ⊏		◇	◇	1 ⊏				
Chathill		d			19 30									
Alnmouth for Alnwick	26	d	19 14		19 42	20 08				21 09				
Acklington		d			19 50									
Widdrington		d			19 57									
Pegswood		d			20 03									
Morpeth	26	d			20 07	20 25		20 51	20 51	21 26			21 57	22 55
Cramlington		d			20 15			20 59	21 00				22 06	23 04
Manors		d			20 26			21 10	21 11				22 17	23 15
Newcastle ■	26 ⇌	a	19 40		20 31	20 41		21 15	21 16	21 40			22 21	23 19
Sunderland	26,44 ⇌	d		19 28			20 30				21 29			
Newcastle ■	⇌	d		19 49	20 33		20 53	21 23			21 53		22 33	
Dunston		d		19 54			20 58				21 58		22 38	
Metrocentre		a		19 57	20 40		21 01	21 30			22 01		22 41	
		d			20 41			21 31					22 42	
Blaydon		d			20 45			21 35					22 46	
Wylam		d			20 51			21 41					22 52	
Prudhoe		d			20 56			21 46					22 57	
Stocksfield		d			21 00			21 50					23 01	
Riding Mill		d			21 05			21 55					23 06	
Corbridge		d			21 09			21 59					23 10	
Hexham		a			21 14			22 04					23 17	
		d			21 14			22 04						
Haydon Bridge		d			21 23			22 13						
Bardon Mill		d						22 20						
Haltwhistle		d			21 35			22 27						
Brampton (Cumbria)		d						22 42						
Wetheral		d						22 51						
Carlisle ■		a			22 05			23 00						

For connections to and from London Kings Cross refer to Table T026

Chathill and Morpeth - Newcastle - Metrocentre, Hexham and Carlisle

		NT	NT	NT	NT	NT	NT	NT	GR	XC	NT	NT	NT	XC	GR	NT	NT	NT	GR	GR	NT	NT	NT
		◇		◇			◇		■	◇■		◇		◇■	■		◇		■	■		◇	
Chathill	d																						
Alnmouth for Alnwick 26	d								11 00	11 07				12 10					13 00				
Acklington	d																						
Widdrington	d																						
Pegswood	d																						
Morpeth 26	d		09 05		09 50					11 22			11 50		12 34					13 33			13 50
Cramlington	d		09 14		09 59								11 59										13 59
Manors	d		09 25		10 10								12 10										14 10
Newcastle ■ 26	a		09 28		10 13				11 27	11 36			12 13	12 36	12 48				13 27	13 47			14 13
Sunderland 26,44	d			09 30			10 30					11 28					12 29					13 29	
Newcastle ■	d	08 45	09 30	09 55	10 15	10 35	10 55	11 15			11 35	11 55	12 15			12 35	12 55	13 15			13 35	13 55	14 15
Dunston	d		09 35		10 21			11 21					12 21					13 21					14 21
Metrocentre	a	08 52	09 39	10 02	10 24	10 43	11 02	11 24			11 43	12 03	12 24			12 43	13 02	13 24			13 43	14 02	14 24
	d	08 53		10 03			11 03					12 03					13 03					14 03	
Blaydon	d	08 57		10 07								12 07										14 07	
Wylam	d	09 03		10 13			11 11					12 13					13 11					14 13	
Prudhoe	d	09 07		10 17			11 15					12 18					13 15					14 17	
Stocksfield	d	09 12		10 22			11 20					12 22					13 20					14 22	
Riding Mill	d	09 16		10 26			11 24					12 27					13 24					14 26	
Corbridge	d	09 20		10 30			11 28					12 31					13 28					14 30	
Hexham	a	09 25		10 35			11 33					12 36					13 33					14 35	
	d	09 26		10 36			11 34					12 36					13 34					14 36	
Haydon Bridge	d	09 35		10 45			11 43										13 43						
Bardon Mill	d	09 41		10 51			11 49										13 49						
Haltwhistle	d	09 48		10 58			11 56					12 55					13 56					14 54	
Brampton (Cumbria)	d	10 04		11 14								13 11										15 10	
Wetheral	d	10 13		11 23								13 19										15 19	
Carlisle ■	a	10 22		11 32			12 29					13 28					14 29					15 28	

		XC	NT	NT	NT	GR	XC	NT	NT	NT	XC	NT	NT	NT	GR	XC	GR	NT	NT	NT	NT
		◇■		◇		■	◇■		◇		◇■		◇		■	◇■	■		◇		
Chathill	d																				
Alnmouth for Alnwick 26	d	14 11				15 00									17 00	17 08					
Acklington	d																				
Widdrington	d																				
Pegswood	d																				
Morpeth 26	d						15 20			15 50	16 22					17 22	17 32			17 50	
Cramlington	d									15 59										17 59	
Manors	d									16 10										18 10	
Newcastle ■ 26	a	14 37				15 28	15 35			16 13	16 36				17 27	17 36	17 46			18 13	
Sunderland 26,44	d			14 28					15 29				16 29						17 30		
Newcastle ■	d		14 35	14 55	15 15			15 35	15 55	16 15		16 35	16 55	17 15				17 32	17 55	18 15	18 35
Dunston	d				15 21					16 21				17 21						18 21	
Metrocentre	a		14 43	15 02	15 24			15 43	16 02	16 24		16 43	17 02	17 24				17 40	18 02	18 24	18 43
	d			15 03					16 03				17 03						18 03		
Blaydon	d								16 07										18 07		
Wylam	d			15 11					16 13				17 11						18 13		
Prudhoe	d			15 15					16 17				17 15						18 17		
Stocksfield	d			15 20					16 22				17 20						18 22		
Riding Mill	d			15 24					16 26				17 24						18 26		
Corbridge	d			15 28					16 30				17 28						18 30		
Hexham	a			15 33					16 35				17 33						18 35		
	d			15 34					16 36				17 34						18 36		
Haydon Bridge	d			15 43									17 43								
Bardon Mill	d			15 49									17 49								
Haltwhistle	d			15 56					16 54				17 56						18 54		
Brampton (Cumbria)	d								17 10										19 10		
Wetheral	d								17 19										19 19		
Carlisle ■	a			16 27					17 30				18 27						19 28		

For connections to and from London Kings Cross refer to Table T026

Chathill and Morpeth - Newcastle - Metrocentre, Hexham and Carlisle

		NT	NT	GR	XC	NT	NT	NT	NT	GR	NT	GR
		◇		■	◇■	◇			◇	■		■
Chathill	d											
Alnmouth for Alnwick 26	d			19 01						21 10		22 09
Acklington	d											
Widdrington	d											
Pegswood	d											
Morpeth 26	d				19 23		19 50			21 27	21 40	
Cramlington	d						19 59				21 49	
Manors	d						20 10				22 00	
Newcastle ■ 26	a			19 28	19 38		20 13			21 41	22 03	22 36
Sunderland 26,44	d	18 29				19 29			20 30			
Newcastle ■	d	18 55	19 15			19 55	20 15	20 35	21 00			
Dunston	d		19 20				20 21		21 05			
Metrocentre	a	19 02	19 24			20 02	20 24	20 43	21 08			
	d	19 03				20 03			21 09			
Blaydon	d					20 07			21 13			
Wylam	d	19 11				20 13			21 19			
Prudhoe	d	19 15				20 17			21 23			
Stocksfield	d	19 20				20 22			21 28			
Riding Mill	d	19 24				20 26			21 32			
Corbridge	d	19 28				20 30			21 36			
Hexham	a	19 33				20 35			21 41			
	d	19 34				20 36			21 42			
Haydon Bridge	d	19 43				20 45			21 51			
Bardon Mill	d	19 49				20 51			21 57			
Haltwhistle	d	19 56				20 58			22 04			
Brampton (Cumbria)	d					21 14			22 20			
Wetheral	d					21 23			22 29			
Carlisle ■	a	20 27				21 32			22 38			

For connections to and from London Kings Cross refer to Table T026

Table T048-R

Mondays to Fridays
21 May to 7 December

Carlisle, Hexham and Metrocentre - Newcastle - Morpeth and Chathill

Miles	Miles	Station		NT MX	NT	NT	GR	NT	XC ◇	GR	NT ◇	SR	NT	GR	NT	NT	SR	NT	NT ◇	NT	NT	XC ◇	NT ◇
0	—	**Carlisle**	d								06 30	06 57				08 03	08 26		08 46				09 46
4¼	—	Wetheral	d								06 37	07 04				08 10			08 53				09 53
11	—	Brampton (Cumbria)	d								06 47	07 14				08 20			09 03				10 03
23¼	—	Haltwhistle	d								07 02	07 29				08 35	08 55		09 18				10 18
28	—	Bardon Mill	d								07 09	07 36				08 42							
31½	—	Haydon Bridge	d								07 15	07 41				08 47			09 29				10 28
39½	—	**Hexham**	a								07 24	07 50				08 56	09 13		09 38				10 38
—	—		d			06 09		06 48			07 25	07 51	08 25			08 57	09 14		09 39	09 57			10 38
42½	—	Corbridge	d			06 14		06 53			07 29	07 55	08 30			09 01				10 02			
45	—	Riding Mill	d			06 18		06 57			07 34	08 00	08 34			09 06				10 06			
47¼	—	Stocksfield	d			06 22		07 01			07 38	08 04	08 38			09 10				10 10			
49¾	—	Prudhoe	d			06 27		07 06			07 42	08 08	08 43		08 52	09 14	09 25		09 51	10 15			10 50
52	—	Wylam	d	00 04		06 31		07 10			07 47	08 13			08 57	09 19				10 19			
56¼	—	Blaydon	d			06 37		07 16			07 53	08 19			09 03	09 25				10 25			
58¼	—	**Metrocentre**	a	00 13		06 42		07 21			07 57	08 24	08 54		09 07	09 29	09 37		10 02	10 30			11 02
—	—		d	00 13		06 42		07 21			07 58	08 25	08 55		09 08	09 29	09 37	09 45	10 03	10 30	10 45		11 02
59½	1¼	Dunston	d			06 45		07 24			08 01	08 28			09 11			09 48			10 48		
61¼	3½	**Newcastle**	a	00 23		06 52		07 32			08 09	08 38	09 04		09 17	09 39	09 48	09 54	10 12	10 39	10 54		11 12
—	—	Sunderland 26,44	a			07 13		08 01								10 01				11 01			
—	—	**Newcastle** 26	d		05 55		06 22		07 35	07 43	08 20			08 40	09 20							09 35	
—	4	Manors	d		05 57						08 22				09 22								
—	13¼	Cramlington	d		06 08						08 33				09 33								
—	20	**Morpeth** 26	d		06 16		06 38		07a47		08a42			08a53	09a41								
—	22	Pegswood	d																				
—	26¾	Widdrington	d																				
—	32	Acklington	d																				
—	38¼	Alnmouth for Alnwick 26	d		06 34		06a53			08a08												09a59	
—	49½	**Chathill**	a		06 47																		

Station		NT	NT	NT	GR	NT ◇	NT	NT	NT	XC ◇	NT ◇	NT	NT	NT	GR	NT ◇	NT	NT	NT	XC ◇	NT ◇	NT	NT
Carlisle	d					10 46					11 46					12 47					13 46		
Wetheral	d										11 53										13 53		
Brampton (Cumbria)	d										12 03										14 03		
Haltwhistle	d					11 14					12 18					13 15					14 18		
Bardon Mill	d					11 21										13 22							
Haydon Bridge	d					11 27					12 28					13 28					14 28		
Hexham	a					11 37					12 38					13 38					14 38		
	d	10 57				11 38	11 57				12 38	12 57				13 38	13 57				14 38	14 57	
Corbridge	d	11 02					12 02					13 02					14 02					15 02	
Riding Mill	d	11 06					12 06					13 06					14 06					15 06	
Stocksfield	d	11 10					12 10					13 10					14 10					15 10	
Prudhoe	d	11 15				11 50	12 15				12 50	13 15				13 50	14 15				14 50	15 15	
Wylam	d	11 19					12 19					13 19					14 19					15 19	
Blaydon	d	11 25					12 25					13 25					14 25					15 25	
Metrocentre	a	11 30				12 02	12 30				13 02	13 30				14 02	14 30				15 02	15 29	
	d	11 30	11 45			12 02	12 30	12 45			13 02	13 30	13 45			14 02	14 30	14 45			15 02	15 30	15 45
Dunston	d		11 48					12 48					13 48					14 48					15 48
Newcastle	a	11 39	12 00			12 11	12 39	12 54			13 12	13 39	13 54			14 11	14 47	14 54			15 12	15 39	15 54
Sunderland 26,44	a	12 01					13 01					14 01										16 01	
Newcastle 26	d			10 20	10 42				11 19	11 37				12 20	12 41				13 16	13 38			
Manors	d			10 22					11 21					12 22					13 18				
Cramlington	d			10 33					11 32					12 33					13 29				
Morpeth 26	d			10a41					11a41	11a49				12a42	12 57				13a38				
Pegswood	d																						
Widdrington	d																						
Acklington	d																						
Alnmouth for Alnwick 26	d				11a07										13a11					14a02			
Chathill	a																						

For connections to and from London Kings Cross refer to Table T026

Table T048-R

Mondays to Fridays
21 May to 7 December

Carlisle, Hexham and Metrocentre - Newcastle - Morpeth and Chathill

Station		NT	XC ◇	GR	NT ◇	NT	NT	NT	XC ◇	NT ◇	NT	NT	XC ◇	GR	NT	XC ◇	NT	NT ◇	NT	NT	GR
Carlisle	d				14 46					15 46								16 47			
Wetheral	d									15 53											
Brampton (Cumbria)	d									16 03											
Haltwhistle	d				15 14					16 18								17 15			
Bardon Mill	d				15 21													17 22			
Haydon Bridge	d				15 27					16 28								17 28			
Hexham	a				15 37					16 38								17 38			
	d				15 38	16 00				16 38	16 57							17 38	17 59		
Corbridge	d					16 04					17 02								18 03		
Riding Mill	d					16 09					17 06								18 08		
Stocksfield	d					16 13					17 10								18 12		
Prudhoe	d				15 50	16 17				16 50	17 15							17 50	18 16		
Wylam	d					16 22					17 19								18 21		
Blaydon	d					16 27					17 25								18 26		
Metrocentre	a				16 02	16 32				17 02	17 30							18 02	18 31		
	d				16 02	16 32	16 45			17 02	17 30						17 45	18 02	18 33		
Dunston	d						16 48										17 48				
Newcastle	a				16 11	16 41	16 54			17 11	17 39						17 54	18 11	18 42		
Sunderland 26,44	a					17 02					18 01								19 08		
Newcastle 26	d	14 20	14 35	14 44				15 20	15 37			16 19	16 35	16 42	17 20	17 37	17 56			18 20	18 44
Manors	d	14 22						15 22				16 21			17 22		17 58			18 22	
Cramlington	d	14 33						15 33				16 32			17 33		18 09			18 33	
Morpeth 26	d	14a42	14a47					15a42				16a41	16 48	16 57	17a42		18 17			18a41	
Pegswood	d																18 21				
Widdrington	d																18 27				
Acklington	d																18 33				
Alnmouth for Alnwick 26	d			15a09					16a01				17a02	17a10		18a01	18 41				19a09
Chathill	a																18 54				

Station		NT ◇	NT	SR	XC ◇	GR	XC ◇	NT	NT	GR	XC ◇	NT	NT ◇	XC ◇	GR	NT	NT ◇	NT	NT ◇	GR FO	NT
Carlisle	d	17 45		18 41									20 09				21 05		22 04		
Wetheral	d	17 52		18 48													21 14		22 11		
Brampton (Cumbria)	d	18 02		18 58													21 24		22 21		
Haltwhistle	d	18 17		19 13									20 37				21 39		22 35		
Bardon Mill	d	18 25		19 20									20 44						22 43		
Haydon Bridge	d	18 30		19 26									20 50				21 50		22 48		
Hexham	a	18 39		19 36									21 00				21 59		22 57		
	d	18 39	19 00	19 36					19 59				21 00				21 59		22 57		23 42
Corbridge	d		19 04						20 03				21 05				22 04		23 02		23 47
Riding Mill	d		19 09						20 08				21 09				22 08		23 06		23 51
Stocksfield	d		19 13						20 12				21 13				22 12		23 10		23 55
Prudhoe	d	18 51	19 17	19 48					20 16				21 18				22 17		23 15		23 59
Wylam	d		19 22						20 21				21 22				22 21		23 19		00 04
Blaydon	d		19 27						20 26				21 28				22 27		23 25		
Metrocentre	a	19 02	19 32	20 01					20 31				21 33				22 32		23 30		00 13
	d	19 03	19 32	20 01				20 05	20 32			21 09	21 33			22 10	22 32	23 00	23 30		00 13
Dunston	d	19 06						20 08				21 12				22 13		23 03			
Newcastle	a	19 14	19 41	20 13				20 13	20 41			21 18	21 43			22 19	22 42	23 09	23 40		00 23
Sunderland 26,44	a		20 08						21 07				22 07				23 05				
Newcastle 26	d	19 20			19 36	19 45	20 06	20 20		20 33	20 38	21 20		21 35	21 41	22 21				22 40	
Manors	d	19 22						20 22				21 22				22 23					
Cramlington	d	19 32						20 33				21 33				22 34					
Morpeth 26	d	19a40				19a59		20a41			20a53	21a41			21 57	22a43				22 56	
Pegswood	d																				
Widdrington	d																				
Acklington	d																				
Alnmouth for Alnwick 26	d				20a01		20a31			21a00				21a59	22a10					23a09	
Chathill	a																				

For connections to and from London Kings Cross refer to Table T026

Table T048-R

Saturdays

26 May to 8 December

Carlisle, Hexham and Metrocentre - Newcastle - Morpeth and Chathill

	NT	NT	NT	GR	NT		XC	GR	NT	SR	NT	GR
				1			◇1	1	◇			1
Carlisle d									06 30	06 57		
Wetheral d									06 37	07 04		
Brampton (Cumbria) d									06 47	07 14		
Haltwhistle d									07 02	07 29		
Bardon Mill d									07 09	07 36		
Haydon Bridge d									07 15	07 41		
Hexham a									07 24	07 50		
d			06 09		06 48				07 25	07 52	08 25	
Corbridge d			06 14		06 53				07 29	07 56	08 30	
Riding Mill d			06 18		06 57				07 34	08 01	08 34	
Stocksfield d			06 22		07 01				07 38	08 05	08 38	
Prudhoe d			06 27		07 06				07 42	08 09	08 43	
Wylam d	00 04		06 31		07 10				07 47	08 14		
Blaydon d			06 37		07 16				07 53	08 20		
Metrocentre a	00 13		06 42		07 21				07 57	08 24	08 54	
d	00 13		06 42		07 21				07 58	08 25	08 55	
Dunston d			06 45		07 24				08 01	08 28		
Newcastle a	00 23		06 52		07 32				08 09	08 42	09 04	
Sunderland 26,44 a			07 20		07 55							
Newcastle 26 d		05 55		06 20			07 38	07 43	08 20			08 42
Manors d		05 57							08 22			
Cramlington d		06 08							08 33			
Morpeth 26 d		06 16		06 36			07a50		08a42			08a55
Pegswood d												
Widdrington d												
Acklington d												
Alnmouth for Alnwick 26 d		06 34		06a50				08a09				
Chathill a		06 47										

	NT	NT	NT		NT	NT	NT	NT	XC	NT	NT	NT
			◇			◇			◇1	◇		
Carlisle d		08 03	08 27			08 46				09 46		
Wetheral d		08 10				08 53				09 53		
Brampton (Cumbria) d		08 20				09 03				10 03		
Haltwhistle d		08 35	08 55			09 18				10 18		
Bardon Mill d		08 42										
Haydon Bridge d		08 47				09 29				10 28		
Hexham a		08 56	09 14			09 38				10 38		
d		08 57	09 14			09 39	09 57			10 38	10 57	
Corbridge d		09 01					10 02				11 02	
Riding Mill d		09 06					10 06				11 06	
Stocksfield d		09 10					10 10				11 10	
Prudhoe d	08 52	09 14	09 26			09 51	10 15			10 50	11 15	
Wylam d	08 57	09 19					10 19				11 19	
Blaydon d	09 03	09 25					10 25				11 25	
Metrocentre a	09 07	09 29	09 38			10 02	10 30			11 02	11 30	
d	09 08	09 29	09 38		09 45	10 03	10 30	10 45		11 02	11 30	11 45
Dunston d	09 11				09 48			10 48				11 48
Newcastle a	09 17	09 39	09 50		09 54	10 12	10 39	10 54		11 12	11 39	12 00
Sunderland 26,44 a		10 01					11 01				12 01	
Newcastle 26 d	09 20								09 35			
Manors d	09 22											
Cramlington d	09 33											
Morpeth 26 d	09a41											
Pegswood d												
Widdrington d												
Acklington d												
Alnmouth for Alnwick 26 d									09a59			
Chathill a												

	NT		GR	NT	NT	NT	NT	XC	NT	NT	NT	
			1	◇				◇1	◇			
Carlisle d				10 46					11 46			
Wetheral d									11 53			
Brampton (Cumbria) d									12 03			
Haltwhistle d				11 14					12 18			
Bardon Mill d				11 21								
Haydon Bridge d				11 27					12 28			
Hexham a				11 37					12 38			
d				11 38	11 57				12 38	12 57		
Corbridge d					12 02					13 02		
Riding Mill d					12 06					13 06		
Stocksfield d					12 10					13 10		
Prudhoe d				11 50	12 15				12 50	13 15		
Wylam d					12 19					13 19		
Blaydon d					12 25					13 25		
Metrocentre a				12 02	12 30				13 02	13 30		
d				12 02	12 30	12 45			13 02	13 30	13 45	
Dunston d						12 48					13 48	
Newcastle a				12 11	12 39	12 54			13 12	13 39	13 54	
Sunderland 26,44 a					13 01					14 01		
Newcastle 26 d	10 18		10 40				11 19	11 33				
Manors d	10 21						11 21					
Cramlington d	10 31						11 32					
Morpeth 26 d	10a40						11a41	11a45				
Pegswood d												
Widdrington d												
Acklington d												
Alnmouth for Alnwick 26 d			11a05									
Chathill a												

	NT	GR	NT	NT	NT	NT	XC	NT	NT		NT	NT
		1	◇				◇1	◇				
Carlisle d			12 47					13 46				
Wetheral d								13 53				
Brampton (Cumbria) d								14 03				
Haltwhistle d			13 15					14 18				
Bardon Mill d			13 22									
Haydon Bridge d			13 28					14 28				
Hexham a			13 38					14 38				
d			13 38	13 57				14 38	14 57			
Corbridge d				14 02					15 02			
Riding Mill d				14 06					15 06			
Stocksfield d				14 10					15 10			
Prudhoe d			13 50	14 15				14 50	15 15			
Wylam d				14 19					15 19			
Blaydon d				14 25					15 25			
Metrocentre a			14 02	14 30				15 02	15 29			
d			14 02	14 30	14 45			15 02	15 30		15 45	
Dunston d					14 48						15 48	
Newcastle a			14 11	14 39	14 54			15 12	15 39		15 54	
Sunderland 26,44 a				15 01					16 01			
Newcastle 26 d	12 20	12 39				13 16	13 35					14 20
Manors d	12 22					13 18						14 22
Cramlington d	12 33					13 29						14 33
Morpeth 26 d	12a42	12 53				13a38						14a42
Pegswood d												
Widdrington d												
Acklington d												
Alnmouth for Alnwick 26 d		13a07					13a59					
Chathill a												

For connections to and from London Kings Cross refer to Table T026

Table T048-R

Saturdays

26 May to 8 December

Carlisle, Hexham and Metrocentre - Newcastle - Morpeth and Chathill

	XC	GR	NT			XC	NT	NT	NT	NT	NT	XC
	◇1	1				◇1			◇			◇1
Carlisle d									15 46			
Wetheral d									15 53			
Brampton (Cumbria) d									16 03			
Haltwhistle d									16 18			
Bardon Mill d												
Haydon Bridge d									16 28			
Hexham a									16 38			
d							16 00		16 38	16 57		
Corbridge d							16 04			17 02		
Riding Mill d							16 09			17 06		
Stocksfield d							16 13			17 10		
Prudhoe d							16 17		16 50	17 15		
Wylam d							16 22			17 19		
Blaydon d							16 27			17 25		
Metrocentre a							16 32		17 02	17 30		
d							16 32	16 45	17 02	17 30		
Dunston d								16 48				
Newcastle a							16 41	16 54	17 11	17 39		
Sunderland 26,44 a							17 02			18 01		
Newcastle 26 d	14 33	14 40	15 20			15 35					16 19	16 32
Manors d			15 22								16 21	
Cramlington d			15 33								16 32	
Morpeth 26 d	14a45		15a42								16a41	16 45
Pegswood d												
Widdrington d												
Acklington d												
Alnmouth for Alnwick 26 d		15a05				15a59						16a59
Chathill a												

	GR		NT		XC	NT	NT	NT	NT	GR	NT	
	1				◇1		◇			1	◇	
Carlisle d							16 47				17 45	
Wetheral d											17 52	
Brampton (Cumbria) d											18 02	
Haltwhistle d							17 15				18 17	
Bardon Mill d							17 22				18 25	
Haydon Bridge d							17 28				18 30	
Hexham a							17 38				18 39	
d							17 38	17 59			18 39	
Corbridge d								18 03				
Riding Mill d								18 08				
Stocksfield d								18 12				
Prudhoe d							17 50	18 16			18 51	
Wylam d								18 21				
Blaydon d								18 26				
Metrocentre a							18 02	18 31			19 02	
d						17 45	18 02	18 33			19 03	
Dunston d						17 48					19 06	
Newcastle a						17 54	18 11	18 42			19 14	
Sunderland 26,44 a								19 08				
Newcastle 26 d	16 41		17 20		17 35	18 03			18 20	18 43	19 20	
Manors d			17 22			18 05			18 22		19 22	
Cramlington d			17 33			18 16			18 33		19 32	
Morpeth 26 d	16 55		17a42			18 24			18a41		19a40	
Pegswood d						18 28						
Widdrington d						18 34						
Acklington d						18 40						
Alnmouth for Alnwick 26 d	17a09				18a00	18 48				19a08		
Chathill a						19 01						

	NT	XC	GR	NT	SR	NT	XC	GR	NT		NT	XC	NT	NT	NT	NT
		◇1	1				◇1	1			◇	◇1		◇	◇	
Carlisle d					18 49						20 09			21 05	22 04	
Wetheral d					18 59									21 14	22 11	
Brampton (Cumbria) d					19 09									21 24	22 21	
Haltwhistle d					19 24						20 37			21 39	22 35	
Bardon Mill d					19 31						20 44				22 43	
Haydon Bridge d					19 36						20 50			21 50	22 48	
Hexham a					19 45						21 00			21 59	22 57	
d	19 00				19 46	19 59					21 00			21 59	22 57	23 25
Corbridge d	19 04					20 03					21 05			22 04	23 02	23 30
Riding Mill d	19 09					20 08					21 09			22 08	23 06	23 34
Stocksfield d	19 13					20 12					21 13			22 12	23 10	23 38
Prudhoe d	19 17				19 58	20 16					21 18			22 17	23 15	23 43
Wylam d	19 22					20 21					21 22			22 21	23 19	
Blaydon d	19 27					20 26					21 28			22 27	23 25	
Metrocentre a	19 32				20 10	20 31					21 33			22 32	23 30	23 55
d	19 32			20 05	20 10	20 32			21 09		21 33		22 09	22 32	23 30	23 55
Dunston d				20 08	20 13				21 12				22 12	22 35		
Newcastle a	19 41			20 13	20 19	20 41			21 18		21 43		22 19	22 46	23 40	00 05
Sunderland 26,44 a	20 08					21 07					22 07					
Newcastle 26 d		19 35	19 45	20 19			20 37	20 51	21 19			21 32	22 20			
Manors d				20 21					21 21				22 22			
Cramlington d				20 32					21 32				22 33			
Morpeth 26 d			19a59	20a40			20a50	21 07	21a41				22a41			
Pegswood d																
Widdrington d																
Acklington d																
Alnmouth for Alnwick 26 d		20a00						21a22				21a58				
Chathill a																

For connections to and from London Kings Cross refer to Table T026

Table T048-R

Sundays

20 May to 2 December

Carlisle, Hexham and Metrocentre - Newcastle - Morpeth and Chathill

		NT	GR	NT	XC	NT		NT	GR	NT	NT	NT	NT	XC	GR	NT		NT	GR	NT	NT	NT	NT	XC	NT
			1		◇1			◇	1			◇		◇1	1			◇	1			◇		◇1	
Carlisle 8	d							08 50				09 55						10 54				11 55			
Wetheral	d							08 57										11 01							
Brampton (Cumbria)	d							09 07										11 11							
Haltwhistle	d							09 22				10 24						11 26				12 24			
Bardon Mill	d							09 29				10 30										12 30			
Haydon Bridge	d							09 35				10 36										12 36			
Hexham	a							09 44				10 45						11 44				12 45			
	d							09 44				10 46						11 44				12 46			
Corbridge	d							09 49				10 50						11 49				12 50			
Riding Mill	d							09 53				10 55						11 53				12 55			
Stocksfield	d							09 57				10 59						11 57				12 59			
Prudhoe	d							10 02				11 03						12 02				13 03			
Wylam	d							10 06				11 08						12 06				13 08			
Blaydon	d							10 12										12 12							
Metrocentre	a							10 17				11 17						12 17				13 17			
	d					09 50		10 18		10 38	10 58	11 18	11 38			11 58		12 18		12 38	12 58	13 18	13 38		13 58
Dunston	d					09 53				10 41			11 41							12 41			13 41		
Newcastle 8	a					09 59		10 28		10 48	11 06	11 28	11 48			12 07		12 28		12 48	13 06	13 28	13 49		14 06
Sunderland 26,44	a							10 50				11 49						12 51							
Newcastle 8 26	d	08 30	08 45	09 19	09 45				10 12	11 05				11 31	11 40				12 38	12 56				13 31	
Manors	d	08 32		09 21						11 07										12 58					
Cramlington	d	08 43		09 32						11 18										13 09					
Morpeth 26	d	08a51	09 01	09a40	09 58				10 28	11a26				11a43	11a53					13a17					
Pegswood	d																								
Widdrington	d																								
Acklington	d																								
Alnmouth for Alnwick 26	d		09a14		10a12				10a42										13a03					13a55	
Chathill	a																								

		NT		GR	XC	GR	NT	NT	NT	NT	XC	NT		NT	XC	GR	NT	NT	NT	NT	XC	NT		NT	GR
		◇		1	◇1	1			◇		◇1			◇	◇1	1			◇		◇1			◇	1
Carlisle 8	d	12 54							13 55					14 54					15 55					16 54	
Wetheral	d	13 01												15 01										17 01	
Brampton (Cumbria)	d	13 11												15 11										17 11	
Haltwhistle	d	13 26							14 24					15 26					16 24					17 26	
Bardon Mill	d								14 30										16 30						
Haydon Bridge	d								14 36										16 36						
Hexham	a	13 44							14 45					15 44					16 45					17 44	
	d	13 44							14 46					15 44					16 46					17 44	
Corbridge	d	13 49							14 50					15 49					16 50					17 49	
Riding Mill	d	13 53							14 55					15 53					16 55					17 53	
Stocksfield	d	13 57							14 59					15 57					16 59					17 57	
Prudhoe	d	14 02							15 03					16 02					17 03					18 02	
Wylam	d	14 06							15 08					16 06					17 08					18 06	
Blaydon	d	14 12												16 12										18 12	
Metrocentre	a	14 17							15 17					16 17					17 16					18 17	
	d	14 18					14 38	14 58	15 18	15 38		15 58		16 18			16 38	16 58	17 17	17 38		17 58		18 18	
Dunston	d						14 41			15 41							16 41			17 41					
Newcastle 8	a	14 28					14 48	15 06	15 28	15 47		16 08		16 28			16 48	17 06	17 25	17 47		18 07		18 28	
Sunderland 26,44	a	14 51							15 51					16 51					17 49					18 51	
Newcastle 8 26	d			14 25	14 31	14 40	14 56				15 28				16 28	16 38	16 56				17 28				18 38
Manors	d						14 58										16 58								
Cramlington	d						15 09										17 09								
Morpeth 26	d			14a38	14a45		15a17										17a17				17 41				
Pegswood	d																								
Widdrington	d																								
Acklington	d																								
Alnmouth for Alnwick 26	d					15a05					15a53				16a52	17a03					17a55				19a04
Chathill	a																								

For connections to and from London Kings Cross refer to Table T026

Table T048-R

Sundays

20 May to 2 December

Carlisle, Hexham and Metrocentre - Newcastle - Morpeth and Chathill

		NT	NT	NT	NT	NT		XC		GR		XC	GR	NT	NT	NT	NT			XC	GR
				◇		◇		◇1		1		◇1	1			◇	◇			◇1	1
Carlisle 8	d			17 56		18 55										19 51	20 38				
Wetheral	d					19 02										19 58	20 45				
Brampton (Cumbria)	d					19 12										20 08	20 55				
Haltwhistle	d			18 25		19 27										20 23	21 10				
Bardon Mill	d			18 31												20 30	21 17				
Haydon Bridge	d			18 37												20 36	21 22				
Hexham	a			18 46		19 45										20 45	21 31				
	d			18 47		19 45										20 45	21 32				
Corbridge	d			18 51		19 50										20 50	21 36				
Riding Mill	d			18 56		19 54										20 54	21 41				
Stocksfield	d			19 00		19 58										20 58	21 45				
Prudhoe	d			19 04		20 03										21 03	21 49				
Wylam	d			19 09		20 07										21 07	21 54				
Blaydon	d					20 13										21 13	21 59				
Metrocentre	a			19 17		20 17										21 17	22 04				
	d	18 38	18 58	19 18	19 48	20 18								20 38	20 58	21 18	22 04				
Dunston	d	18 41			19 51									20 41			22 07				
Newcastle 8	a	18 48	19 06	19 28	19 57	20 28								20 48	21 06	21 28	22 15				
Sunderland 26,44	a			19 51		20 51										21 51					
Newcastle 8 26	d	19 00						19 32		19 42		20 36	20 41	21 04						21 37	21 52
Manors	d	19 02												21 07							
Cramlington	d	19 13												21 18							
Morpeth 26	d	19a21								19a55		20a49	20 57	21a27							22 08
Pegswood	d																				
Widdrington	d																				
Acklington	d																				
Alnmouth for Alnwick 26	d							19a56					21a10							22a01	22a23
Chathill	a																				

For connections to and from London Kings Cross refer to Table T026

Table T049-F

Mondays to Fridays

21 May to 7 December

East Anglia - East Midlands - North West England

Miles			EM ◇	EM ◇ A	EM ◇ B	EM ◇	EM ◇ C	EM ◇ D	EM ◇ C	EM ◇ D	EM ◇ E	EM ◇ F	EM ◇ C
0	**Norwich**	d					05 50	05 50	06 51	06 51	07 57	07 57	08 57
30½	Thetford	d					06 24	06 24	07 19	07 19	08 24	08 24	09 24
53¾	Ely 6	d					06 51	06 51	07 44	07 44	08 51	08 51	09 50
69	March	d					07 07	07 07	08 00	08 00	09 07	09 07	
83¾	**Peterborough 8**	a					07 25	07 25	08 22	08 22	09 25	09 25	10 26
—		d					07 29	07 29	08 25	08 25	09 27	09 27	10 28
113	Grantham 7	a					07 57	07 57	08 55	08 55	09 55	09 55	10 58
—	East Midlands Parkway	a											
134¾	**Nottingham 8**	a					08 40	08 40	09 27	09 27	10 35	10 35	11 34
—		d	05 23	06 39	06 39	07 46	08 47	08 47	09 47	09 47	10 47	10 51	11 47
141	Ilkeston	d				07 59							
146¾	Langley Mill	a											
154	Alfreton	a		06 59	06 59	08 10	09 08	09 09	10 08	10 08	11 09	11 11	12 08
163¾	Chesterfield	a	05 51	07 10	07 10	08 20	09 20	09 20	10 20	10 20	11 21	11 22	12 20
176¾	**Sheffield 7**	a	06 15	07 28	07 28	08 38	09 37	09 37	10 38	10 38	11 37	11 38	12 38
—		d	06 18	07 32	07 33	08 41	09 40	09 40	10 40	10 41	11 41	11 41	12 41
212	Stockport	a	07 24	08 25	08 25	09 25	10 25	10 25	11 25	11 25	12 25	12 25	13 25
218	**Manchester Piccadilly 10**	a	07 38	08 37	08 37	09 37	10 37	10 37	11 37	11 37	12 37	12 37	13 37
219	Manchester Oxford Road	a	07 42	08 41	08 41	09 41	10 41	10 41	11 41	11 41	12 41	12 41	13 41
235	Warrington Central	a	07 58	08 58	08 58	09 58	10 58	10 58	11 58	11 58	12 58	12 58	13 58
241	Widnes	a	08 06	09 06	09 06	10 06	11 06	11 06	12 06	12 06	13 06	13 06	14 06
248	Liverpool South Parkway 7	a	08 20	09 15	09 15	10 15	11 15	11 15	12 15	12 15	13 15	13 15	14 15
254	**Liverpool Lime Street 10**	a	08 34	09 28	09 28	10 31	11 32	11 32	12 32	12 32	13 32	13 32	14 32

Miles			EM ◇	EM ◇ G	EM ◇ H	EM ◇	EM ◇	EM ◇	EM ◇ C	EM ◇ D	EM ◇	EM ◇ I
0	**Norwich**	d	09 57	10 57	10 57	11 57	12 57	13 57	14 57	14 57	15 48	16 57
30½	Thetford	d	10 24	11 24	11 24	12 24	13 24	14 24	15 24	15 24	16 23	17 27
53¾	Ely 6	d	10 51	11 51	11 51	12 50	13 50	14 48	15 50	15 50	16 49	17 52
69	March	d		12 08	12 08							
83¾	**Peterborough 8**	a	11 27	12 24	12 24	13 23	14 25	15 27	16 25	16 25	17 22	18 25
—		d	11 28	12 26	12 26	13 26	14 26	15 28	16 27	16 27	17 24	18 26
113	Grantham 7	a	12 01	12 58	12 58	13 56	14 57	15 59	16 57	16 57	17 57	18 52
—	East Midlands Parkway	a										
134¾	**Nottingham 8**	a	12 35	13 36	13 36	14 35	15 34	16 35	17 35	17 35	18 35	19 28
—		d	12 47	13 47	13 47	14 47	15 47	16 47	17 47	17 47	18 47	19 40
141	Ilkeston	d	13 00				16 00					→
146¾	Langley Mill	a							18 02	18 04		
154	Alfreton	a	13 10	14 08	14 09	15 08	16 10	17 08	18 10	18 12	19 08	
163¾	Chesterfield	a	13 20	14 20	14 20	15 20	16 20	17 20	18 20	18 21	19 20	
176¾	**Sheffield 7**	a	13 37	14 38	14 38	15 37	16 37	17 37	18 38	18 38	19 37	
—		d	13 40	14 41	14 41	15 40	16 40	17 40	18 40	18 40	19 40	
212	Stockport	a	14 25	15 25	15 25	16 25	17 25	18 25	19 25	19 25	20 25	
218	**Manchester Piccadilly 10**	a	14 37	15 37	15 37	16 37	17 37	18 37	19 37	19 37	20 37	
219	Manchester Oxford Road	a	14 41	15 41	15 41	16 41	17 41	18 41	19 41	19 41	20 41	
235	Warrington Central	a	14 58	15 58	15 58	16 58	18 03	18 58	19 58	19 58	20 58	
241	Widnes	a	15 06	16 06	16 06	17 06	18 11	19 06	20 06	20 06	21 06	
248	Liverpool South Parkway 7	a	15 15	16 15	16 15	17 15	18 22	19 20	20 16	20 16	21 19	
254	**Liverpool Lime Street 10**	a	15 32	16 32	16 32	17 32	18 36	19 35	20 34	20 34	21 36	

		EM ◇ J	EM ◇ K	EM ◇ L	EM ◇ M	EM ◇ N	EM ◇	EM ◇	EM O
Norwich	d	16 57	16 57			16 57	17 54	18 57	
Thetford	d	17 27	17 27			17 27	18 27	19 24	
Ely 6	d	17 52	17 52			17 52	18 52	19 52	
March	d						19 08		
Peterborough 8	a	18 25	18 25			18 25	19 26	20 25	
	d	18 26	18 26			18 26	19 26	20 27	21 31
Grantham 7	a	18 52	18 54			18 54	19 58	20 58	
East Midlands Parkway	a			←	←				
Nottingham 8	a	19 28	19 35	19 28	19 28	19 35	20 31	21 36	23 00
	d	19 41	19 39	19 40	19 41	19 41			
Ilkeston	d	→							
Langley Mill	a								
Alfreton	a		20 00	20 01	20 01	20 01			
Chesterfield	a		20 11	20 12	20 12	20 12			
Sheffield 7	a		20 28	20 28	20 28	20 28			
	d		20 31	20 31	20 31	20 31			
Stockport	a		21 25	21 25	21 25	21 25			
Manchester Piccadilly 10	a		21 36	21 36	21 36	21 36			
Manchester Oxford Road	a								
Warrington Central	a								
Widnes	a								
Liverpool South Parkway 7	a								
Liverpool Lime Street 10	a								

Saturdays

26 May to 8 December

		EM ◇	EM ◇ P	EM ◇ Q	EM ◇	EM ◇	EM ◇	EM ◇	EM ◇	EM ◇
Norwich	d					05 50	06 53	07 57	08 57	09 57
Thetford	d					06 23	07 22	08 24	09 24	10 24
Ely 6	d					06 51	07 48	08 48	09 46	10 48
March	d					07 07	08 04	09 05		
Peterborough 8	a					07 25	08 27	09 22	10 21	11 19
	d					07 27	08 29	09 28	10 22	11 23
Grantham 7	a					07 55	08 57	09 56	10 54	11 55
East Midlands Parkway	a									
Nottingham 8	a					08 39	09 35	10 35	11 36	12 35
	d	05 20	06 40	06 40	07 46	08 47	09 47	10 46	11 47	12 47
Ilkeston	d				07 59					13 00
Langley Mill	a									
Alfreton	a		07 00	07 00	08 09	09 08	10 08	11 08	12 08	13 10
Chesterfield	a	05 49	07 11	07 11	08 19	09 20	10 20	11 20	12 20	13 20
Sheffield 7	a	06 15	07 28	07 29	08 37	09 37	10 37	11 38	12 38	13 37
	d	06 20	07 32	07 33	08 40	09 40	10 40	11 40	12 40	13 40
Stockport	a	07 26	08 25	08 25	09 25	10 26	11 25	12 25	13 25	14 25
Manchester Piccadilly 10	a	07 39	08 37	08 37	09 37	10 37	11 37	12 37	13 37	14 37
Manchester Oxford Road	a	07 42	08 41	08 41	09 41	10 41	11 41	12 41	13 41	14 41
Warrington Central	a	07 58	08 58	08 58	09 58	10 58	11 58	12 58	13 58	14 58
Widnes	a	08 06	09 06	09 06	10 06	11 06	12 06	13 06	14 06	15 06
Liverpool South Parkway 7	a	08 20	09 15	09 15	10 15	11 15	12 15	13 15	14 15	15 15
Liverpool Lime Street 10	a	08 33	09 31	09 31	10 31	11 32	12 32	13 32	14 32	15 31

		EM ◇	EM ◇	EM ◇	EM ◇	EM ◇	EM ◇	EM ◇	EM ◇	EM ◇	EM O
Norwich	d	10 57	11 57	12 57	13 57	14 57	15 52	16 54	17 50	18 57	
Thetford	d	11 24	12 24	13 24	14 24	15 24	16 23	17 24	18 23	19 24	
Ely 6	d	11 48	12 51	13 48	14 48	15 47	16 47	17 47	18 48	19 48	
March	d	12 05							19 05		
Peterborough 8	a	12 21	13 26	14 25	15 23	16 25	17 23	18 23	19 24	20 23	
	d	12 24	13 28	14 26	15 24	16 27	17 25	18 26	19 30	20 26	21 27
Grantham 7	a	12 57	13 56	14 58	15 55	16 57	17 57	18 55	19 57	20 58	22 00
East Midlands Parkway	a										
Nottingham 8	a	13 35	14 33	15 35	16 35	17 35	18 34	19 31	20 36	21 32	22 32
	d	13 47	14 47	15 47	16 44	17 44	18 47	19 36			
Ilkeston	d			16 00							
Langley Mill	a					17 59					
Alfreton	a	14 08	15 08	16 10	17 05	18 08	19 08	20 01			
Chesterfield	a	14 20	15 20	16 20	17 15	18 18	19 20	20 11			
Sheffield 7	a	14 37	15 37	16 37	17 34	18 34	19 37	20 30			
	d	14 40	15 40	16 40	17 38	18 37	19 40	20 34			
Stockport	a	15 25	16 25	17 25	18 25	19 25	20 25	21 19			
Manchester Piccadilly 10	a	15 37	16 37	17 37	18 37	19 37	20 37	21 29			
Manchester Oxford Road	a	15 41	16 41	17 41	18 41	19 41	20 41				
Warrington Central	a	15 58	16 58	18 03	18 58	19 58	20 58				
Widnes	a	16 06	17 06	18 11	19 06	20 06	21 06				
Liverpool South Parkway 7	a	16 15	17 15	18 22	19 20	20 18	21 19				
Liverpool Lime Street 10	a	16 32	17 32	18 36	19 36	20 33	21 32				

A until 27 July, from 8 October
B from 30 July until 5 October
C until 31 August, from 8 October
D from 3 September until 5 October
E from 23 July until 31 August
F until 20 July, from 3 September
G until 31 August
H from 3 September
I from 3 September until 5 October. To Manchester Piccadilly
J from 23 July until 31 August. To Manchester Piccadilly
K from 8 October
L from 3 September until 5 October. From Norwich
M from 23 July until 31 August. From Norwich
N until 20 July
O From Spalding
P from 23 June
Q until 16 June

Table T049-F

Sundays

20 May to 2 December

East Anglia - East Midlands - North West England

		EM ◇	EM ◇	EM ◇	EM ◇ A	EM ◇ B	EM ◇	EM ◇	EM ◇
Norwich	d				09 47		10 47		
Thetford	d				10 15		11 14		
Ely 6	d				10 41		11 39		
March	d								
Peterborough 8	a				11 13		12 11		
	d				11 14		12 16		14 31
Grantham 7	a				11 53		12 46		15 07
East Midlands Parkway	a								
Nottingham 8	a				12 30		13 30		15 39
	d	09 47	10 48	11 44	12 40	12 40	13 42	14 47	15 47
Ilkeston	d			11 56					
Langley Mill	a				12 56	12 56	13 57	15 02	
Alfreton	a	10 04	11 08	12 07	13 04	13 04	14 05	15 10	16 07
Chesterfield	a	10 18	11 19	12 18	13 17	13 17	14 16	15 21	16 18
Sheffield 7	a	10 37	11 35	12 35	13 33	13 33	14 34	15 39	16 34
	d	10 41	11 39	12 39	13 38	13 38	14 37	15 43	16 39
Stockport	a	11 26	12 25	13 25	14 26	14 26	15 25	16 25	17 28
Manchester Piccadilly 10	a	11 37	12 37	13 37	14 37	14 37	15 37	16 37	17 38
Manchester Oxford Road	a	11 41	12 41	13 41	14 41	14 41	15 41	16 41	17 41
Warrington Central	a	11 58	12 58	13 58	14 58	14 58	15 58	16 58	17 58
Widnes	a	12 06	13 06	14 06	15 06	15 06	16 06	17 06	18 06
Liverpool South Parkway 7	a	12 16	13 16	14 16	15 16	15 16	16 16	17 16	18 16
Liverpool Lime Street 10	a	12 30	13 30	14 32	15 30	15 30	16 30	17 30	18 30

		EM ◇	EM ◇	EM ◇	EM ◇	EM ◇	EM ◇	EM ◇
Norwich	d	13 47	14 53	15 54	16 54	17 54	18 56	20 52
Thetford	d	14 14	15 20	16 21	17 21	18 21	19 23	21 19
Ely 6	d	14 40	15 46		17 49	18 47	19 49	21 44
March	d		16 03					
Peterborough 8	a	15 13	16 20	17 12	18 20	19 20	20 23	22 16
	d	15 23	16 24	17 19	18 26	19 22	20 30	22 23
Grantham 7	a	15 53	16 54	17 49	18 56	19 52	21 00	22 53
East Midlands Parkway	a							
Nottingham 8	a	16 24	17 31	18 27	19 33	20 31	21 34	23 28
	d	16 42	17 39	18 40	19 43			
Ilkeston	d	16 57						
Langley Mill	a	17 03	17 56	18 55				
Alfreton	a	17 11	18 04	19 03	20 03			
Chesterfield	a	17 21	18 15	19 14	20 13			
Sheffield 7	a	17 39	18 33	19 31	20 31			
	d	17 44	18 37	19 35	20 35			
Stockport	a	18 25	19 25	20 26	21 25			
Manchester Piccadilly 10	a	18 37	19 37	20 38	21 37			
Manchester Oxford Road	a	18 41	19 42					
Warrington Central	a	18 58	19 59					
Widnes	a	19 06	20 07					
Liverpool South Parkway 7	a	19 16	20 17					
Liverpool Lime Street 10	a	19 30	20 31					

A until 9 September

B from 16 September

North West England - East Midlands - East Anglia

Mondays to Fridays
21 May to 7 December

Miles			EM MO	EM MX	EM	EM	EM	EM	EM	EM	EM	EM	EM	EM	EM	EM	EM	EM	EM	EM	EM	EM	EM
			◇ A	◇ A	◇	B	◇		◇ C	◇	◇ D	◇ E	◇ F	◇ G	◇ H	◇ F	◇ I	◇	◇	◇	◇	◇ F	◇ G
0	**Liverpool Lime Street**	d									06 47	06 47	07 42	07 42	08 52	08 52		09 52	10 52	11 52	12 52	13 52	13 52
6	Liverpool South Parkway	d									06 58	06 58	07 53	07 53	09 03	09 03		10 03	11 03	12 03	13 03	14 03	14 03
12	Widnes	d									07 07	07 07	08 05	08 05	09 11	09 11		10 11	11 11	12 11	13 11	14 11	14 11
18	Warrington Central	d									07 15	07 15	08 13	08 13	09 19	09 19		10 19	11 19	12 19	13 19	14 19	14 19
34	Manchester Oxford Road	d									07 38	07 38	08 38	08 38	09 38	09 38		10 38	11 38	12 38	13 38	14 38	14 38
35	**Manchester Piccadilly**	d									07 42	07 42	08 43	08 43	09 42	09 42		10 42	11 42	12 42	13 42	14 42	14 42
41	Stockport	d									07 54	07 54	08 54	08 54	09 54	09 54	←	10 54	11 54	12 54	13 54	14 54	14 54
77	**Sheffield**	a									08 34	08 34	09 35	09 35	10 32	10 34	10 32	11 35	12 35	13 34	14 35	15 34	15 34
—		d									08 38	08 38	09 37	09 37	10 38	10 37	10 38	11 38	12 38	13 37	14 38	15 37	15 37
89	Chesterfield	d		00 02							08 54	08 54	09 51	09 51	→	10 54	10 54	11 54	12 52	13 52	14 52	15 53	15 53
100	Alfreton	d									09 05	09 05	10 01	10 02		11 05	11 05	12 05	13 03	14 03	15 03	16 05	16 05
—	Langley Mill	d	00 02																				
113	Ilkeston	d											10 11	10 12							15 13		
118	**Nottingham**	a	00 23	00 45							09 27	09 28	10 26	10 28		11 26	11 27	12 29	13 27	14 27	15 28	16 27	16 29
—		d			04 56	05 07	06 10	06 53	07 52	08 35	09 34	09 34	10 34	10 34		11 34	11 34	12 34	13 34	14 34	15 34	16 35	16 35
—	East Midlands Parkway	d					06 21																
141	Grantham	d				05 51			08 27	09 10	10 11	10 11	11 10	11 10		12 12	12 12	13 09	14 11	15 11	16 11	17 11	17 11
170	**Peterborough**	a			06 21	06 23	07 33	09 23	08 59	09 36	10 42	10 42	11 39	11 39		12 40	12 40	13 39	14 39	15 38	16 39	17 42	17 42
—		d			06 27		07 38		09 03	09 40	10 45	10 45	11 41	11 41		12 42	12 42	13 41	14 41	15 40	16 41	17 44	17 44
—	March	a			06 42		07 53																
200	Ely	a			07 02		08 12		09 42	10 13	11 19	11 19	12 13	12 13		13 14	13 14	14 13	15 14	16 13	17 13	18 19	18 19
—	Ipswich	d																					
223	Thetford	a			07 33		08 38		10 09	10 39	11 43	11 43	12 38	12 38		13 40	13 40	14 38	15 39	16 39	17 40	18 43	18 43
254	**Norwich**	a			08 13		09 15		10 44	11 12	12 15	12 15	13 13	13 13		14 13	14 13	15 11	16 13	17 13	18 13	19 16	19 16

		EM	EM	EM	EM	EM	EM	EM	EM	EM	EM	EM
		◇	◇ F	◇ G	◇ E	◇ J	◇ G	◇	◇ D	◇ E	◇	◇
Liverpool Lime Street	d	14 52	15 52	15 52	16 52	16 52	16 52	17 52	18 52	18 52	19 52	21 37
Liverpool South Parkway	d	15 03	16 03	16 03	17 03	17 03	17 03	18 03	19 03	19 03	20 03	21 48
Widnes	d	15 11	16 11	16 11	17 11	17 11	17 11	18 11	19 11	19 11	20 11	21 56
Warrington Central	d	15 19	16 19	16 19	17 19	17 19	17 19	18 19	19 19	19 19	20 19	22 04
Manchester Oxford Road	d	15 38	16 38	16 38	17 38	17 38	17 38	18 38	19 38	19 38	20 38	22 24
Manchester Piccadilly	d	15 42	16 42	16 42	17 42	17 42	17 42	18 42	19 42	19 42	20 42	22 28
Stockport	d	15 54	16 54	16 54	17 54	17 54	17 54	18 54	19 54	19 54	20 54	22 38
Sheffield	a	16 34	17 39	17 39	18 48	18 49	18 49	19 35	20 35	20 35	21 35	23 35
	d	16 37	17 45	17 45	18 52	18 53	18 53	19 37	20 41	20 41	21 37	23 37
Chesterfield	d	16 53	18 01	18 01	19 07	19 08	19 15	19 52	20 56	20 56	21 55	00 02
Alfreton	d	17 04	18 11	18 11	19 19	19 19	19 27	20 03	21 08	21 08	22 05	
Langley Mill	d										22 13	
Ilkeston	d										22 18	
Nottingham	a	17 27	18 31	18 33	19 40	19 39	19 50	20 27	21 33	21 34	22 31	00 45
	d	17 34	18 37	18 37				20 34				
East Midlands Parkway	d											
Grantham	d	18 11	19 10	19 10				21 10				
Peterborough	a	18 38	19 40	19 40				21 37				
	d	18 45	19 42	19 42				21 39				
March	a	18 59										
Ely	a	19 19	20 15	20 15				22 13				
Ipswich	d											
Thetford	a	19 44	20 38	20 38				22 38				
Norwich	a	20 19	21 13	21 13				23 18				

Saturdays
26 May to 8 December

		EM	EM	EM	EM	EM	EM	EM	EM	EM	EM	EM	EM	EM	EM	EM	EM	EM	EM	EM	EM	EM	EM
		◇ A	◇	B	◇		◇	◇	◇ K	◇ L	◇	◇	◇	◇	◇	◇	◇	◇	◇	◇	◇	◇	◇
Liverpool Lime Street	d								06 47	06 47	07 42	08 52	09 52	10 52	11 52	12 52	13 52	14 52	15 52	16 52	17 52	18 52	19 52
Liverpool South Parkway	d								06 58	06 58	07 52	09 03	10 03	11 03	12 03	13 03	14 03	15 03	16 03	17 03	18 03	19 03	20 03
Widnes	d								07 07	07 07	08 05	09 11	10 11	11 11	12 11	13 11	14 11	15 11	16 11	17 11	18 11	19 11	20 11
Warrington Central	d								07 15	07 15	08 13	09 19	10 19	11 19	12 19	13 19	14 19	15 19	16 19	17 19	18 19	19 19	20 19
Manchester Oxford Road	d								07 38	07 38	08 39	09 38	10 39	11 38	12 38	13 38	14 38	15 38	16 38	17 38	18 38	19 38	20 39
Manchester Piccadilly	d								07 42	07 42	08 43	09 42	10 43	11 42	12 42	13 42	14 42	15 42	16 42	17 42	18 42	19 42	20 43
Stockport	d								07 55	07 55	08 54	09 54	10 54	11 54	12 54	13 54	14 54	15 54	16 54	17 54	18 54	19 55	20 55
Sheffield	a								08 35	08 35	09 34	10 34	11 35	12 35	13 34	14 33	15 34	16 34	17 37	18 37	19 34	20 34	21 35
	d								08 37	08 37	09 37	10 36	11 37	12 37	13 37	14 37	15 37	16 37	17 41	18 40	19 37	20 39	21 38
Chesterfield	d	00 02							08 52	08 54	09 52	10 52	11 52	12 52	13 52	14 54	15 52	16 53	17 57	18 57	19 52	20 54	21 54
Alfreton	d								09 03	09 05	10 03	11 02	12 02	13 02	14 03	15 04	16 03	17 04	18 08	19 08	20 03	21 05	22 05
Langley Mill	d																						22 13
Ilkeston	d												12 12	13 12									22 18
Nottingham	a	00 45							09 27	09 27	10 27	11 27	12 27	13 27	14 27	15 28	16 27	17 27	18 29	19 29	20 27	21 33	22 34
	d		05 05	05 07	06 07	06 53	07 45	08 35	09 34	09 34	10 34	11 34	12 34	13 34	14 34	15 34	16 34	17 34	18 37		20 34		
East Midlands Parkway	d				06 20																		
Grantham	d			05 51			08 29	09 10	10 11	10 11	11 05	12 13	13 11	14 09	15 15	16 08	17 06	18 11	19 09		21 07		
Peterborough	a		06 24	06 25	07 33	09 24	08 59	09 36	10 38	10 38	11 36	12 40	13 38	14 37	15 44	16 39	17 36	18 38	19 39		21 39		
	d		06 27		07 35		09 00	09 45	10 40	10 40	11 41	12 44	13 40	14 41	15 45	16 39	17 40	18 44	19 41		21 40		
March	a		06 42		07 52													19 00					
Ely	a		07 03		08 13		09 34	10 19	11 13	11 13	12 13	13 19	14 13	15 14	16 19	17 13	18 13	19 19	20 14		22 13		
Ipswich	d																						
Thetford	a		07 30		08 37		10 06	10 43	11 37	11 37	12 38	13 43	14 37	15 40	16 43	17 37	18 37	19 43	20 38		22 37		
Norwich	a		08 13		09 15		10 43	11 15	12 13	12 13	13 13	14 12	15 13	16 12	17 12	18 13	19 13	20 16	21 13		23 19		

A From Liverpool Lime Street
B To Spalding
C From Mansfield Woodhouse
D until 5 October
E from 8 October
F until 31 August, from 8 October
G from 3 September until 5 October
H from 3 September until 5 October. To Norwich
I from 3 September until 5 October. From Liverpool Lime Street
J until 31 August
K from 23 June
L until 16 June

Table T049-R

North West England - East Midlands - East Anglia

Saturdays
26 May to 8 December

		EM	EM
		◇	◇
Liverpool Lime Street	d	20 49	21 37
Liverpool South Parkway	d	21 00	21 48
Widnes	d	21 08	21 56
Warrington Central	d	21 16	22 04
Manchester Oxford Road	d	21 37	22 24
Manchester Piccadilly	d	21 41	22 28
Stockport	d	21 52	22 38
Sheffield	a	22 31	23 35
	d	22 42	23 38
Chesterfield	d	22 56	23 53
Alfreton	d	23 07	
Langley Mill	d		
Ilkeston	d		
Nottingham	a	23 28	00 30
	d		
East Midlands Parkway	d		
Grantham	d		
Peterborough	a		
	d		
March	a		
Ely	a		
Ipswich	d		
Thetford	a		
Norwich	a		

Sundays
20 May to 2 December

		EM	EM	EM	EM	EM	EM	EM	EM	EM	EM	EM	EM	EM	EM	EM
		◇ A	◇ A	◇	◇	◇	◇	◇	◇	◇	◇ B	◇ C	◇	◇	◇	◇
Liverpool Lime Street	d						12 52	13 52	14 52	15 52	16 52	16 52	17 52	18 52	19 52	21 16
Liverpool South Parkway	d						13 03	14 03	15 03	16 03	17 03	17 03	18 03	19 03	20 03	21 26
Widnes	d						13 11	14 11	15 11	16 11	17 11	17 11	18 11	19 11	20 11	21 34
Warrington Central	d						13 19	14 19	15 19	16 19	17 19	17 19	18 19	19 19	20 19	21 42
Manchester Oxford Road	d						13 39	14 39	15 38	16 38	17 38	17 38	18 38	19 38	20 38	22 07
Manchester Piccadilly	d					12 43	13 43	14 43	15 42	16 42	17 42	17 42	18 42	19 42	20 43	22 11
Stockport	d					12 55	13 51	14 54	15 53	16 54	17 54	17 54	18 53	19 54	20 53	22 30
Sheffield	a					13 37	14 37	15 35	16 37	17 35	18 36	18 36	19 35	20 35	21 34	23 26
	d		10 48		12 43	13 48	14 41	15 39	16 43	17 40	18 40	18 45	19 40	20 40	21 40	23 30
Chesterfield	d		11 04		12 57	14 02	14 55	15 53	16 57	17 54	18 54	18 59	19 54	20 54	21 56	23 44
Alfreton	d		11 14		13 08	14 12	15 08	16 03	17 07	18 05	19 05	19 10	20 05	21 05	22 06	23 55
Langley Mill	d						15 15	16 11	17 15	18 12	19 12	19 17	20 12	21 12	22 14	00 02
Ilkeston	d					14 22				18 17						
Nottingham	a		11 39		13 34	14 35	15 32	16 28	17 30	18 34	19 33	19 38	20 30	21 33	22 36	00 23
	d	09 52	11 39	12 40	13 47	14 45	15 50	16 45	17 36	18 46			20 45			
East Midlands Parkway	d															
Grantham	d	10 29	12 23	13 15	14 22	15 20	16 22	17 21	18 17	19 23			21 20			
Peterborough	a	11 06	12 54	13 41	14 51	15 51	16 52	17 50	18 46	19 55			21 52			
	d	11 09	12 56	13 43	14 58	15 58	16 59	17 57	18 49	19 57			21 54			
March	a	11 25						18 12								
Ely	a	11 43	13 31	14 16	15 31	16 31	17 32	18 31	19 22	20 32			22 27			
Ipswich	d															
Thetford	a	12 12	13 55	14 43	16 01	16 55	17 56	18 55	19 51	20 56			22 51			
Norwich	a	12 52	14 28	15 24	16 35	17 26	18 30	19 28	20 26	21 35			23 25			

A until 9 September
B not 5 August, 12 August, 26 August
C 5 August, 12 August, 26 August

Table T050-F

Mondays to Fridays

21 May to 7 December

Derby - Stoke-on-Trent and Crewe

Miles			NT ◇ A	NT ◇ A	LM ■ B	EM C	EM D	EM E	NT ◇ A	LM ■ B	EM F	EM D	EM G	EM H	EM I	NT A	LM ■ J	EM F	EM D	EM E	EM H	NT A	LM ■ J
0	**Derby 6**	d				06 40		06 40			07 39		07 39	07 40	07 41			08 42		08 42	08 42		
1¼	Peartree	d									07 43		07 43	07 43	07 44								
11¼	Tutbury & Hatton	d				06 54	06 54	06 54			07 56	07 56	07 56	07 56	07 56			08 56	08 56	08 56	08 57		
19	Uttoxeter	d				07 05	07 05	07 05			08 07	08 07	08 07	08 07	08 07			09 07	09 07	09 07	09 08		
30	Blythe Bridge	d				07 19	07 19	07 19			08 21	08 21	08 21	08 21	08 21			09 21	09 21	09 21	09 22		
33½	Longton	d				07 25	07 25	07 25			08 27	08 27	08 27	08 27	08 27			09 27	09 27	09 27	09 28		
36	**Stoke-on-Trent**	a				07 32	07 32	07 32			08 32	08 32	08 32	08 32	08 32			09 33	09 33	09 33	09 34		
—		d	06 29	06 58	07 16	07 33	07 33	07 33	07 56	08 12	08 34	08 34	08 34	08 34	08 34	08 56	09 12	09 34	09 34	09 34	09 35	09 56	10 02
38¾	Longport	d	06 33			07 38	07 38	07 38	08 00		08 39	08 39	08 39	08 39	08 39			09 39	09 39	09 39	09 40		
42¼	Kidsgrove	d	06a37	07a05	07 24	07 44	07 44	07 44	08a04	08 21	08 45	08 45	08 45	08 45	08 45	09a03	09 21	09 45	09 45	09 45	09 46	10a03	10 11
44½	Alsager	d			07 28	07 48	07 48	07 48		08 25	08 49	08 49	08 49	08 49	08 49		09 25	09 49	09 49	09 49	09 50		10 15
51	**Crewe 10**	a			07 38	07 59	07 59	08 00		08 34	08 59	08 59	09 02	08 59	09 02		09 34	10 00	10 01	10 04	10 01		10 24

		EM F	EM D	EM G	EM I	EM H	NT A	LM ■ J	EM C	EM D	EM G	EM I	NT A	LM ■ J	EM C	EM D	EM G	EM I	NT A	LM ■ J	EM F	EM D	EM E
Derby 6	d	09 42		09 42	09 43	09 42			10 42		10 42	10 43			11 42		11 42	11 43			12 42		12 42
Peartree	d																						
Tutbury & Hatton	d	09 56	09 56	09 56	09 56	09 57			10 56	10 56	10 56	10 56			11 56	11 56	11 56	11 56			12 56	12 56	12 56
Uttoxeter	d	10 07	10 07	10 07	10 07	10 08			11 07	11 07	11 07	11 07			12 07	12 07	12 07	12 07			13 07	13 07	13 07
Blythe Bridge	d	10 21	10 21	10 21	10 21	10 22			11 21	11 21	11 21	11 21			12 21	12 21	12 21	12 21			13 21	13 21	13 21
Longton	d	10 27	10 27	10 27	10 27	10 28			11 27	11 27	11 27	11 27			12 27	12 27	12 27	12 27			13 27	13 27	13 27
Stoke-on-Trent	a	10 33	10 33	10 33	10 33	10 34			11 33	11 33	11 33	11 33			12 33	12 33	12 33	12 33			13 33	13 33	13 33
	d	10 34	10 34	10 34	10 34	10 35	10 56	11 02	11 34	11 34	11 34	11 34	11 56	12 02	12 34	12 34	12 34	12 34	12 58	13 02	13 34	13 34	13 34
Longport	d	10 39	10 39	10 39	10 39	10 40			11 39	11 39	11 39	11 39			12 39	12 39	12 39	12 39			13 39	13 39	13 39
Kidsgrove	d	10 45	10 45	10 45	10 45	10 46	11a03	11 11	11 45	11 45	11 45	11 45	12a03	12 11	12 45	12 45	12 45	12 45	13a05	13 11	13 45	13 45	13 45
Alsager	d	10 49	10 49	10 49	10 49	10 50		11 15	11 49	11 49	11 49	11 49		12 15	12 49	12 49	12 49	12 49		13 15	13 49	13 49	13 49
Crewe 10	a	11 01	11 01	11 04	11 04	11 01		11 24	12 01	12 01	12 04	12 04		12 24	13 01	13 01	13 04	13 04		13 24	14 01	14 01	14 04

		EM H	NT A	LM ■ J	EM C	EM D	EM E	NT A	LM ■ J	EM C	EM D	EM E	NT A	LM ■ J	EM C	EM D	EM E	NT A	LM ■ J	EM H	EM D	EM F
Derby 6	d	12 43			13 42		13 42			14 42		14 42			15 42		15 42			16 42		16 42
Peartree	d																			16 44		16 44
Tutbury & Hatton	d	12 57			13 56	13 56	13 56			14 56	14 56	14 56			15 56	15 56	15 56			16 55	16 55	16 56
Uttoxeter	d	13 08			14 07	14 07	14 07			15 07	15 07	15 07			16 07	16 07	16 07			17 06	17 06	17 07
Blythe Bridge	d	13 22			14 21	14 21	14 21			15 21	15 21	15 21			16 21	16 21	16 21			17 21	17 21	17 21
Longton	d	13 28			14 27	14 27	14 27			15 27	15 27	15 27			16 27	16 27	16 27			17 27	17 27	17 28
Stoke-on-Trent	a	13 34			14 33	14 33	14 33			15 33	15 33	15 33			16 33	16 33	16 33			17 33	17 33	17 33
	d	13 35	13 56	14 02	14 34	14 34	14 34	14 56	15 02	15 34	15 34	15 34	15 56	16 02	16 34	16 34	16 34	16 56	17 02	17 34	17 34	17 35
Longport	d	13 40			14 39	14 39	14 39			15 39	15 39	15 39			16 39	16 39	16 39			17 39	17 39	17 40
Kidsgrove	d	13 46	14a03	14 11	14 45	14 45	14 45	15a03	15 11	15 45	15 45	15 45	16a03	16 11	16 45	16 45	16 45	17a03	17 11	17 46	17 46	17 46
Alsager	d	13 50		14 15	14 49	14 49	14 49		15 15	15 49	15 49	15 49		16 15	16 49	16 49	16 49		17 15	17 50	17 50	17 50
Crewe 10	a	14 02		14 24	15 01	15 01	15 04		15 24	16 01	16 01	16 04		16 24	17 01	17 01	17 04		17 24	18 01	18 01	18 03

		EM E	NT A	LM ■ J	EM H	EM D	EM F	EM E	NT ◇ A	LM ■ J	EM C	EM D	EM E	NT ◇ A	LM ■ J	LM ■ K	EM F	EM D	EM E	EM H	NT ◇ A	LM ■ J	EM C
Derby 6	d	16 42			17 42		17 42	17 42			18 42		18 42				19 42		19 42	19 43			20 42
Peartree	d	16 44			17 44		17 44	17 44															
Tutbury & Hatton	d	16 56			17 56	17 56	17 56	17 56			18 56	18 56	18 56				19 56	19 56	19 56	19 56			20 56
Uttoxeter	d	17 07			18 07	18 07	18 07	18 07			19 07	19 07	19 07				20 07	20 07	20 07	20 07			21 07
Blythe Bridge	d	17 21			18 20	18 21	18 22	18 22			19 21	19 21	19 21				20 21	20 21	20 21	20 22			21 21
Longton	d	17 28			18 27	18 27	18 27	18 27			19 27	19 27	19 27				20 27	20 27	20 27	20 27			21 27
Stoke-on-Trent	a	17 33			18 32	18 32	18 33	18 33			19 33	19 33	19 33				20 33	20 33	20 33	20 34			21 33
	d	17 35	17 56	18 02	18 34	18 34	18 34	18 34	18 58	19 07	19 34	19 34	19 34	19 58	20 02	20 07	20 34	20 34	20 34	20 34	20 58	21 12	21 34
Longport	d	17 40			18 39	18 39	18 39	18 39			19 39	19 39	19 39				20 39	20 39	20 39	20 39			21 39
Kidsgrove	d	17 46	18a03	18 11	18 45	18 45	18 46	18 46	19a05		19 45	19 45	19 45	20a05		20 15	20 45	20 45	20 45	20 46	21a05	21 21	21 45
Alsager	d	17 50		18 15	18 49	18 49	18 50	18 50			19 49	19 49	19 49			20 20	20 49	20 49	20 49	20 50		21 25	21 49
Crewe 10	a	18 05		18 24	19 01	19 01	19 02	19 05		19 26	20 01	20 01	20 04		20 25	20 32	21 01	21 01	21 04	21 01		21 34	21 59

		EM D	EM E	LM ■ J	VT ◇■ J	NT ◇ A	LM ■ J
Derby 6	d		20 42				
Peartree	d						
Tutbury & Hatton	d	20 56	20 56				
Uttoxeter	d	21 07	21 07				
Blythe Bridge	d	21 21	21 21				
Longton	d	21 27	21 27				
Stoke-on-Trent	a	21 33	21 33				
	d	21 34	21 34	22 02	22 11	22 20	22 51
Longport	d	21 39	21 39				
Kidsgrove	d	21 45	21 45	22 11		22a27	
Alsager	d	21 49	21 49	22 15			
Crewe 10	a	21 59	22 04	22 24	22 30		23 10

A To Manchester Piccadilly
B From Northampton
C until 20 July, from 3 September until 21 September
D from 23 July until 31 August
E from 24 September
F from 3 September until 21 September
G from 24 September until 5 October
H until 20 July
I from 8 October
J From London Euston
K From Birmingham New Street

Table T050-F

Saturdays

26 May to 8 December

Derby - Stoke-on-Trent and Crewe

		NT ◇ A	LM ■ B	EM C	EM D	EM E	NT ◇ A	LM ■ B	EM F	EM G	EM H	EM I	NT A	LM ■ J	EM C	EM I	NT A	LM ■ J	
Derby 6	d			06 40	06 40	06 40			07 38	07 40	07 40	07 40			08 42	08 42			and at the same minutes past each hour until
Peartree	d								07 44	07 44	07 44	07 44							
Tutbury & Hatton	d			06 56	06 56	06 58			07 55	07 55	07 56	07 56			08 56	08 56			
Uttoxeter	d			07 07	07 07	07 09			08 07	08 07	08 07	08 07			09 07	09 07			
Blythe Bridge	d			07 21	07 21	07 23			08 21	08 21	08 22	08 22			09 21	09 21			
Longton	d			07 28	07 28	07 30			08 27	08 27	08 27	08 27			09 27	09 27			
Stoke-on-Trent	a			07 34	07 34	07 36			08 32	08 32	08 33	08 33			09 33	09 33			
	d	06 58	07 15	07 34	07 34	07 36	07 56	08 15	08 34	08 34	08 34	08 34	08 56	09 15	09 34	09 34	09 56	10 02	
Longport	d			07 39	07 39	07 41	08 00		08 39	08 39	08 39	08 39			09 39	09 39			
Kidsgrove	d	07a05	07 23	07 45	07 45	07 47	08a04	08 23	08 45	08 45	08 46	08 46	09a03	09 23	09 45	09 45	10a03	10 11	
Alsager	d		07 27	07 49	07 49	07 51		08 27	08 49	08 49	08 50	08 50		09 28	09 49	09 49		10 15	
Crewe 10	a		07 37	07 59	08 00	08 02		08 37	08 59	08 59	09 00	09 03		09 37	10 01	10 04		10 24	

		EM C	EM I	NT ◇ A	LM ■ J	EM C	EM K	EM I	NT ◇ A	LM ■ J	EM C	EM I	NT A	LM ■ J	EM C	EM I	NT ◇ A	LM ■ J	EM C	EM I	NT A	LM ■ J	EM C
Derby 6	d	11 42	11 42			12 42		12 42			13 42	13 42			14 42	14 42			15 42	15 42			16 42
Peartree	d																						
Tutbury & Hatton	d	11 56	11 56			12 56	12 56	12 56			13 56	13 56			14 56	14 56			15 56	15 56			16 55
Uttoxeter	d	12 07	12 07			13 07	13 07	13 07			14 07	14 07			15 07	15 07			16 07	16 07			17 07
Blythe Bridge	d	12 21	12 21			13 21	13 21	13 21			14 21	14 21			15 21	15 21			16 21	16 21			17 21
Longton	d	12 27	12 27			13 27	13 27	13 27			14 27	14 27			15 27	15 27			16 27	16 27			17 27
Stoke-on-Trent	a	12 33	12 33			13 33	13 33	13 33			14 33	14 33			15 33	15 33			16 33	16 33			17 32
	d	12 34	12 34	12 56	13 02	13 34	13 34	13 34	13 58	14 02	14 34	14 34	14 56	15 02	15 34	15 34	15 58	16 02	16 34	16 34	16 56	17 02	17 34
Longport	d	12 39	12 39			13 39	13 39	13 39			14 39	14 39			15 39	15 39			16 39	16 39			17 39
Kidsgrove	d	12 45	12 45	13a03	13 11	13 45	13 45	13 45	14a05	14 11	14 45	14 45	15a03	15 11	15 45	15 45	16a05	16 11	16 45	16 45	17a03	17 11	17 45
Alsager	d	12 49	12 49		13 15	13 49	13 49	13 49		14 15	14 49	14 49		15 15	15 49	15 49		16 15	16 49	16 49		17 15	17 49
Crewe 10	a	13 01	13 04		13 24	14 01	14 01	14 04		14 24	15 01	15 04		15 24	16 01	16 04		16 24	17 01	17 03		17 24	18 01

		EM I	NT A	LM ■ J	EM L	EM H	EM I	NT ◇ A	LM ■ J	EM C	EM I	NT ◇ A	LM ■ J	EM C	EM D	EM E	NT ◇ A	LM ■ J	LM ■ M	EM C	EM I	NT ◇ A
Derby 6	d	16 42			17 42	17 42	17 42			18 42	18 42			19 42	19 42	19 43				20 42	20 42	
Peartree	d				17 45	17 45	17 45															
Tutbury & Hatton	d	16 55			17 57	17 58	17 58			18 56	18 56			19 56	19 56	19 56				20 56	20 56	
Uttoxeter	d	17 07			18 06	18 07	18 07			19 07	19 07			20 07	20 07	20 07				21 07	21 07	
Blythe Bridge	d	17 21			18 21	18 21	18 21			19 21	19 21			20 21	20 21	20 21				21 21	21 21	
Longton	d	17 27			18 27	18 28	18 28			19 27	19 27			20 27	20 27	20 27				21 27	21 27	
Stoke-on-Trent	a	17 32			18 32	18 33	18 33			19 33	19 33			20 33	20 33	20 33				21 33	21 33	
	d	17 34	17 56	18 02	18 34	18 34	18 34	18 58	19 02	19 34	19 34	19 58	20 02	20 34	20 34	20 34	20 58	21 02	21 27	21 34	21 34	22 55
Longport	d	17 39			18 39	18 39	18 39			19 39	19 39			20 39	20 39	20 39				21 39	21 39	
Kidsgrove	d	17 45	18a03	18 11	18 45	18 46	18 46	19a05	19 11	19 45	19 45	20a05	20 11	20 45	20 45	20 45	21a05		21 35	21 45	21 45	23a02
Alsager	d	17 49		18 15	18 49	18 50	18 50		19 15	19 49	19 49		20 15	20 49	20 49	20 49			21 40	21 49	21 49	
Crewe 10	a	18 04		18 24	19 01	19 02	19 05		19 27	20 01	20 04		20 24	21 01	21 04	21 04		21 22	21 49	22 01	22 04	

Sundays

20 May to 2 December

		NT ◇ A	LM ■ B	LM ■ J	LM ■ J	NT ◇ A	LM ■ B	EM N	EM O	EM P	LM ■ J	NT ◇ A	EM N	EM O	EM P	LM ■ J	EM N	EM O	EM P	LM ■ J	EM Q	EM O	LM ■ J
Derby 6	d							14 38		14 40			15 38		15 40		16 38		16 41		17 41		
Peartree	d																						
Tutbury & Hatton	d							14 52	14 52	14 54			15 52	15 52	15 54		16 52	16 52	16 55		17 55	17 55	
Uttoxeter	d							15 03	15 03	15 05			16 03	16 03	16 05		17 03	17 03	17 06		18 06	18 06	
Blythe Bridge	d							15 17	15 17	15 19			16 17	16 17	16 19		17 17	17 17	17 20		18 20	18 20	
Longton	d							15 23	15 23	15 25			16 23	16 23	16 25		17 23	17 23	17 26		18 26	18 26	
Stoke-on-Trent	a							15 30	15 30	15 32			16 31	16 31	16 33		17 30	17 30	17 33		18 33	18 33	
	d	10 30	11 17	12 41	13 17	13 25	14 41	15 32	15 32	15 32	15 41	16 30	16 33	16 33	16 33	16 41	17 32	17 32	17 33	17 41	18 34	18 34	18 41
Longport	d							15 37	15 37	15 37			16 38	16 38	16 38		17 37	17 37	17 38		18 39	18 39	
Kidsgrove	d	10a37	11 25	12 49	13 25	13a32	14 49	15 44	15 44	15 44	15 51	16a37	16 45	16 45	16 45	16 51	17 44	17 44	17 45	17 51	18 45	18 45	18 52
Alsager	d		11 30	12 53	13 30		14 54	15 48	15 48	15 48	15 55		16 49	16 49	16 49	16 55	17 48	17 48	17 49	17 55	18 49	18 49	18 56
Crewe 10	a		11 41	13 03	13 41		15 03	16 02	16 02	16 02	16 05		17 02	17 02	17 02	17 05	18 04	18 04	18 05	18 05	19 01	19 01	19 06

		EM Q	EM O	LM ■ J	NT ◇ A	EM Q	EM O	LM ■ J	EM Q	EM O	LM ■ J	LM ■ J	NT ◇ A
Derby 6	d	18 41				19 41			20 40				
Peartree	d												
Tutbury & Hatton	d	18 55	18 55			19 55	19 55		20 54	20 54			
Uttoxeter	d	19 05	19 05			20 06	20 06		21 05	21 05			
Blythe Bridge	d	19 19	19 19			20 20	20 20		21 19	21 19			
Longton	d	19 26	19 26			20 26	20 26		21 25	21 25			
Stoke-on-Trent	a	19 33	19 33			20 34	20 34		21 33	21 33			
	d	19 33	19 33	19 41	20 30	20 34	20 34	20 41	21 33	21 33	21 41	22 41	23 00
Longport	d	19 38	19 38			20 39	20 39		21 38	21 38			
Kidsgrove	d	19 45	19 45	19 52	20a37	20 46	20 46	20 52	21 44	21 44	21 52	22 49	23a07
Alsager	d	19 49	19 49	19 56		20 50	20 50	20 56	21 49	21 49	21 56	22 53	
Crewe 10	a	20 02	20 02	20 06		21 00	21 00	21 06	22 00	22 00	22 06	23 03	

A To Manchester Piccadilly
B From Northampton
C until 21 July, also 8 September, 15 September, 22 September
D 29 September, 6 October
E from 13 October
F until 16 June
G from 23 June until 21 July
H 8 September, 15 September, 22 September
I from 29 September
J From London Euston
K from 28 July until 1 September
L until 21 July
M From Birmingham New Street
N from 9 September
O from 22 July until 2 September
P until 15 July
Q until 15 July, from 9 September

Table T050-R

Crewe and Stoke-on-Trent - Derby

Mondays to Fridays

21 May to 7 December

Miles	Station		NT A	EM B	EM C	EM D	NT ◇ E	LM 1 F	LM 1 G	EM B	EM H	EM I	EM D	NT ◇ E	LM 1 G	EM B	EM H	EM J	EM I	EM K	NT ◇ E	LM 1 G	EM B
0	**Crewe**	d		06 07	06 07	06 07		06 35	06 52	06 58	06 58	06 58	06 58		07 55	08 07	08 07	08 07	08 07	08 07		09 02	09 07
6¼	Alsager	d		06 16	06 16	06 16		06 44		07 07	07 07	07 07	07 07		08 04	08 16	08 16	08 16	08 16	08 16		09 11	09 16
8½	Kidsgrove	d	06 13	06 21	06 21	06 21	06 26	06 48		07 12	07 12	07 12	07 12	07 21	08 08	08 21	08 21	08 21	08 21	08 21	08 29	09 15	09 21
12	Longport	d		06 27	06 27	06 27				07 18	07 18	07 18	07 18			08 27	08 27	08 27	08 27	08 27			09 27
15	**Stoke-on-Trent**	a	06 23	06 31	06 31	06 31	06 37	06 56	07 16	07 23	07 23	07 23	07 23	07 31	08 17	08 31	08 31	08 31	08 31	08 31	08 40	09 23	09 31
—		d		06 33	06 33	06 33				07 24	07 24	07 24	07 24			08 33	08 33	08 33	08 33	08 33			09 33
17½	Longton	d		06 40	06 40	06 40				07 30	07 30	07 30	07 30			08 39	08 39	08 39	08 39	08 39			09 39
20¾	Blythe Bridge	d		06 46	06 46	06 46				07 36	07 36	07 36	07 36			08 45	08 45	08 45	08 45	08 45			09 45
31¾	Uttoxeter	d		06 58	06 58	06 58				07 49	07 49	07 49	07 49			08 58	08 58	08 58	08 58	08 58			09 58
39½	Tutbury & Hatton	d		07a07	07 07	07 07				07a58	07 58	07 58	07 58			09a07	09 07	09 07	09 07	09 07			10a07
49½	Peartree	d			07 20	07 20																	
51	**Derby**	a			07 25	07 26					08 16	08 17	08 18				09 21	09 23	09 25	09 27			

Station		EM H	EM D	EM I	NT ◇ E	LM 1 G	EM B	EM H	EM L	NT ◇ E	LM 1 G	EM B	EM H	EM L	NT ◇ E	LM 1 G	EM B	EM C	EM J	EM K	NT ◇ E	LM 1 G
Crewe	d	09 07	09 07	09 07		10 02	10 07	10 07	10 07		11 02	11 07	11 07	11 07		12 02	12 07	12 07	12 07	12 07		13 02
Alsager	d	09 16	09 16	09 16		10 11	10 16	10 16	10 16		11 11	11 16	11 16	11 16		12 11	12 16	12 16	12 16	12 16		13 11
Kidsgrove	d	09 21	09 21	09 21	09 31	10 15	10 21	10 21	10 21	10 31	11 15	11 21	11 21	11 21	11 31	12 15	12 21	12 21	12 21	12 21	12 31	13 15
Longport	d	09 27	09 27	09 27			10 27	10 27	10 27			11 27	11 27	11 27			12 27	12 27	12 27	12 27		
Stoke-on-Trent	a	09 31	09 31	09 31	09 41	10 23	10 31	10 31	10 31	10 41	11 23	11 31	11 31	11 31	11 41	12 23	12 31	12 31	12 31	12 31	12 41	13 23
	d	09 33	09 33	09 33			10 33	10 33	10 33			11 33	11 33	11 33			12 33	12 33	12 33	12 33		
Longton	d	09 39	09 39	09 39			10 39	10 39	10 39			11 39	11 39	11 39			12 39	12 39	12 39	12 39		
Blythe Bridge	d	09 45	09 45	09 45			10 45	10 45	10 45			11 45	11 45	11 45			12 45	12 45	12 45	12 45		
Uttoxeter	d	09 58	09 58	09 58			10 58	10 58	10 58			11 58	11 58	11 58			12 58	12 58	12 58	12 58		
Tutbury & Hatton	d	10 07	10 07	10 07			11a07	11 07	11 07			12a07	12 07	12 07			13a07	13 07	13 07	13 07		
Peartree	d																					
Derby	a	10 21	10 23	10 24				11 21	11 23				12 21	12 23				13 23	13 25	13 28		

Station		EM B	EM H	EM L	NT ◇ E	LM 1 G	EM B	EM I	EM H	EM D	NT ◇ E	LM 1 G	EM B	EM I	EM K	EM H	EM J	NT ◇ E	LM 1 G	EM B	EM H	EM I	EM D
Crewe	d	13 07	13 07	13 07		14 02	14 07	14 07	14 07	14 07		15 02	15 07	15 07	15 07	15 07	15 07		16 02	16 07	16 07	16 07	16 07
Alsager	d	13 16	13 16	13 16		14 11	14 16	14 16	14 16	14 16		15 11	15 16	15 16	15 16	15 16	15 16		16 11	16 16	16 16	16 16	16 16
Kidsgrove	d	13 21	13 21	13 21	13 31	14 15	14 21	14 21	14 21	14 21	14 31	15 15	15 21	15 21	15 21	15 21	15 21	15 31	16 15	16 21	16 21	16 21	16 21
Longport	d	13 27	13 27	13 27			14 27	14 27	14 27	14 27			15 27	15 27	15 27	15 27	15 27			16 27	16 27	16 27	16 27
Stoke-on-Trent	a	13 31	13 31	13 31	13 41	14 23	14 31	14 31	14 31	14 31	14 41	15 23	15 31	15 31	15 31	15 31	15 31	15 41	16 23	16 31	16 31	16 31	16 31
	d	13 33	13 33	13 33			14 33	14 33	14 33	14 33			15 33	15 33	15 33	15 33	15 33			16 33	16 33	16 33	16 33
Longton	d	13 39	13 39	13 39			14 39	14 39	14 39	14 39			15 39	15 39	15 39	15 39	15 39			16 39	16 39	16 39	16 39
Blythe Bridge	d	13 45	13 45	13 45			14 45	14 45	14 45	14 45			15 45	15 45	15 45	15 45	15 45			16 45	16 45	16 45	16 45
Uttoxeter	d	13 58	13 58	13 58			14 58	14 58	14 58	14 58			15 58	15 58	15 58	15 58	15 58			16 58	16 58	16 58	16 58
Tutbury & Hatton	d	14a07	14 07	14 07			15a07	15 07	15 07	15 07			16a07	16 07	16 07	16 07	16 07			17a07	17 07	17 07	17 07
Peartree	d													16 19	16 19	16 19	16 19						
Derby	a		14 21	14 23				15 23	15 26	15 28				16 24	16 25	16 26	16 28				17 22	17 23	17 24

Station		NT ◇ E	LM 1 G	EM B	EM H	EM D	EM I	NT ◇ E	LM 1 G	EM B	EM H	EM J	EM I	EM K	NT ◇ E	LM 1 M	EM B	EM C	EM D	NT ◇ E	LM 1 M	NT ◇ E	EM B
Crewe	d		17 02	17 07	17 07	17 07	17 07		18 02	18 07	18 07	18 07	18 07	18 07		19 02	19 07	19 07	19 07		20 10		20 45
Alsager	d		17 11	17 16	17 16	17 16	17 16		18 11	18 16	18 16	18 16	18 16	18 16		19 11	19 16	19 16	19 16		20 19		20 58
Kidsgrove	d	16 31	17 15	17 21	17 21	17 21	17 21	17 31	18 15	18 21	18 21	18 21	18 21	18 21	18 31	19 15	19 21	19 21	19 21	19 31	20 23	20 31	21 07
Longport	d			17 27	17 27	17 27	17 27			18 27	18 27	18 27	18 27	18 27			19 27	19 27	19 27				21 12
Stoke-on-Trent	a	16 41	17 23	17 31	17 31	17 31	17 31	17 41	18 25	18 31	18 31	18 31	18 31	18 31	18 41	19 23	19 31	19 31	19 31	19 41	20 31	20 41	21 16
	d			17 33	17 33	17 33	17 33			18 33	18 33	18 33	18 33	18 33			19 33	19 33	19 33				21 18
Longton	d			17 39	17 39	17 39	17 39			18 39	18 39	18 39	18 39	18 39			19 39	19 39	19 39				21 24
Blythe Bridge	d			17 45	17 45	17 45	17 45			18 45	18 45	18 45	18 45	18 45			19 45	19 45	19 45				21 30
Uttoxeter	d			17 58	17 58	17 58	17 58			18 58	18 58	18 58	18 58	18 58			19 58	19 58	19 58				21 42
Tutbury & Hatton	d			18a07	18 07	18 07	18 07			19a07	19 07	19 07	19 07	19 07			20a07	20 07	20 07				21a51
Peartree	d																						
Derby	a				18 21	18 23	18 26				19 21	19 23	19 25	19 26				20 25	20 27				

Station		EM N	EM J	NT ◇ E	NT ◇ E
Crewe	d	20 45	20 45		
Alsager	d	20 58	20 58		
Kidsgrove	d	21 07	21 07	21 31	22 31
Longport	d	21 12	21 12		
Stoke-on-Trent	a	21 16	21 16	21 41	22 41
	d	21 18	21 18		
Longton	d	21 24	21 24		
Blythe Bridge	d	21 30	21 30		
Uttoxeter	d	21 42	21 42		
Tutbury & Hatton	d	21 51	21 51		
Peartree	d				
Derby	a	22 08	22 09		

A From Macclesfield
B from 23 July until 31 August
C until 20 July, from 3 September until 21 September
D from 24 September
E From Manchester Piccadilly
F To Birmingham New Street
G To London Euston
H from 3 September until 21 September
I until 20 July
J from 24 September until 5 October
K from 8 October
L until 20 July, from 24 September
M To Northampton
N until 20 July, from 3 September, not from 24 September until 5 October

Table T050-R

Crewe and Stoke-on-Trent - Derby

Saturdays

26 May to 8 December

Station		NT A	LM 1 B	EM C	EM D	EM E	EM F	NT ◇ G	LM 1 B	EM H	EM I	EM J	EM K	EM F	LM 1 B	NT ◇ G	LM 1 B	EM H	EM J	EM E	EM F	NT ◇ G	LM 1 B
Crewe	d		06 01	06 07	06 07	06 07	06 07		07 00	07 07	07 07	07 07	07 07	07 07	07 18		08 02	08 07	08 07	08 07	08 07		09 02
Alsager	d			06 16	06 16	06 16	06 16		07 08	07 16	07 16	07 16	07 16	07 16			08 11	08 16	08 16	08 16	08 16		09 11
Kidsgrove	d	06 08		06 21	06 21	06 21	06 21	06 26	07 14	07 21	07 21	07 21	07 21	07 21		07 32	08 15	08 21	08 21	08 21	08 21	08 29	09 15
Longport	d			06 27	06 27	06 27	06 27			07 27	07 27	07 27	07 27	07 27				08 27	08 27	08 27	08 27		
Stoke-on-Trent	a	06 18	06 23	06 31	06 31	06 31	06 31	06 37	07 22	07 31	07 31	07 31	07 31	07 31	07 37	07 42	08 23	08 31	08 31	08 31	08 31	08 40	09 23
	d			06 33	06 33	06 33	06 33			07 33	07 33	07 33	07 33	07 33				08 33	08 33	08 33	08 33		
Longton	d			06 39	06 39	06 39	06 39			07 39	07 39	07 39	07 39	07 39				08 39	08 39	08 39	08 39		
Blythe Bridge	d			06 45	06 45	06 45	06 45			07 45	07 45	07 45	07 45	07 45				08 45	08 45	08 45	08 45		
Uttoxeter	d			06 58	06 58	06 58	06 58			07 58	07 58	07 58	07 58	07 58				08 58	08 58	08 58	08 58		
Tutbury & Hatton	d			07 07	07 07	07 07	07a08			08 07	08 07	08 07	08 07	08a11				09 07	09 07	09 07	09a08		
Peartree	d			07 20	07 20	07 20																	
Derby	a			07 23	07 24	07 28				08 21	08 24	08 26	08 28					09 21	09 23	09 27			

Station		EM L	EM F	NT ◇ G	LM 1 B	EM H	EM J	EM K	EM I	EM F	NT ◇ G	LM 1 B	EM J	EM H	EM I	EM K	EM F	NT ◇ G	LM 1 B	EM J	EM H	EM I
Crewe	d	09 07	09 07		10 02	10 07	10 07	10 07	10 07	10 07		11 02	11 07	11 07	11 07	11 07	11 07		12 02	12 07	12 07	12 07
Alsager	d	09 16	09 16		10 11	10 16	10 16	10 16	10 16	10 16		11 11	11 16	11 16	11 16	11 16	11 16		12 11	12 16	12 16	12 16
Kidsgrove	d	09 21	09 21	09 31	10 15	10 21	10 21	10 21	10 21	10 21	10 31	11 15	11 21	11 21	11 21	11 21	11 21	11 31	12 15	12 21	12 21	12 21
Longport	d	09 27	09 27			10 27	10 27	10 27	10 27	10 27			11 27	11 27	11 27	11 27	11 27			12 27	12 27	12 27
Stoke-on-Trent	a	09 31	09 31	09 41	10 23	10 31	10 31	10 31	10 31	10 31	10 41	11 23	11 31	11 31	11 31	11 31	11 31	11 41	12 23	12 31	12 31	12 31
	d	09 33	09 33			10 33	10 33	10 33	10 33	10 33			11 33	11 33	11 33	11 33	11 33			12 33	12 33	12 33
Longton	d	09 39	09 39			10 39	10 39	10 39	10 39	10 39			11 39	11 39	11 39	11 39	11 39			12 39	12 39	12 39
Blythe Bridge	d	09 45	09 45			10 45	10 45	10 45	10 45	10 45			11 45	11 45	11 45	11 45	11 45			12 45	12 45	12 45
Uttoxeter	d	09 58	09 58			10 58	10 58	10 58	10 58	10 58			11 58	11 58	11 58	11 58	11 58			12 58	12 58	12 58
Tutbury & Hatton	d	10 07	10a08			11 07	11 07	11 07	11 07	11a09			12 07	12 07	12 07	12 07	12a08			13 07	13 07	13 07
Peartree	d																					
Derby	a	10 23				11 21	11 24	11 27	11 28				12 23	12 24	12 26	12 27				13 23	13 24	13 26

Station		EM K	EM F	NT ◇ G	LM 1 B	EM H	EM J	EM E	EM F	NT ◇ G	LM 1 B	EM F	EM H	EM J	EM E	NT ◇ G	LM 1 B	EM F	EM J	EM H	EM E	NT ◇ G	LM 1 B
Crewe	d	12 07	12 07		13 02	13 07	13 07	13 07	13 07		14 02	14 07	14 07	14 07	14 07		15 02	15 07	15 07	15 07	15 07		16 02
Alsager	d	12 16	12 16		13 11	13 16	13 16	13 16	13 16		14 11	14 16	14 16	14 16	14 16		15 11	15 16	15 16	15 16	15 16		16 11
Kidsgrove	d	12 21	12 21	12 31	13 15	13 21	13 21	13 21	13 21	13 31	14 15	14 21	14 21	14 21	14 21	14 31	15 15	15 21	15 21	15 21	15 21	15 31	16 15
Longport	d	12 27	12 27			13 27	13 27	13 27	13 27			14 27	14 27	14 27	14 27			15 27	15 27	15 27	15 27		
Stoke-on-Trent	a	12 31	12 31	12 41	13 23	13 31	13 31	13 31	13 31	13 41	14 23	14 32	14 32	14 32	14 32	14 41	15 23	15 31	15 31	15 31	15 31	15 41	16 23
	d	12 33	12 33			13 33	13 33	13 33	13 33			14 33	14 33	14 33	14 33			15 33	15 33	15 33	15 33		
Longton	d	12 39	12 39			13 39	13 39	13 39	13 39			14 39	14 39	14 39	14 39			15 39	15 39	15 39	15 39		
Blythe Bridge	d	12 45	12 45			13 45	13 45	13 45	13 45			14 45	14 45	14 45	14 45			15 45	15 45	15 45	15 45		
Uttoxeter	d	12 58	12 58			13 58	13 58	13 58	13 58			14 58	14 58	14 58	14 58			15 58	15 58	15 58	15 58		
Tutbury & Hatton	d	13 07	13a08			14 07	14 07	14 07	14a08			15a07	15 07	15 07	15 07			16a07	16 07	16 07	16 07		
Peartree	d																		16 20	16 20	16 20		
Derby	a	13 27				14 21	14 23	14 27					15 22	15 23	15 27				16 23	16 25	16 27		

Station		EM H	EM J	EM E	EM F	NT ◇ G	LM 1 B	EM H	EM J	EM I	EM K	EM F	NT ◇ G	LM 1 M	EM H	EM J	EM E	EM F	NT ◇ G	LM 1 B	EM F	EM H
Crewe	d	16 07	16 07	16 07	16 07		17 02	17 07	17 07	17 07	17 07	17 07		18 02	18 07	18 07	18 07	18 07		19 02	19 07	19 07
Alsager	d	16 16	16 16	16 16	16 16		17 11	17 16	17 16	17 16	17 16	17 16		18 11	18 16	18 16	18 16	18 16		19 11	19 16	19 16
Kidsgrove	d	16 21	16 21	16 21	16 21	16 31	17 15	17 21	17 21	17 21	17 21	17 21	17 31	18 15	18 21	18 21	18 21	18 21	18 31	19 15	19 21	19 21
Longport	d	16 27	16 27	16 27	16 27			17 27	17 27	17 27	17 27	17 27			18 27	18 27	18 27	18 27			19 27	19 27
Stoke-on-Trent	a	16 31	16 31	16 31	16 31	16 41	17 23	17 31	17 31	17 31	17 31	17 31	17 41	18 23	18 31	18 31	18 31	18 31	18 41	19 23	19 31	19 31
	d	16 33	16 33	16 33	16 33			17 33	17 33	17 33	17 33	17 33			18 33	18 33	18 33	18 33			19 33	19 33
Longton	d	16 39	16 39	16 39	16 39			17 39	17 39	17 39	17 39	17 39			18 39	18 39	18 39	18 39			19 39	19 39
Blythe Bridge	d	16 45	16 45	16 45	16 45			17 45	17 45	17 45	17 45	17 45			18 45	18 45	18 45	18 45			19 45	19 45
Uttoxeter	d	16 58	16 58	16 58	16 58			17 58	17 58	17 58	17 58	17 58			18 58	18 58	18 58	18 58			19 58	19 58
Tutbury & Hatton	d	17 07	17 07	17 07	17a08			18 07	18 07	18 07	18 07	18a08			19 07	19 07	19 07	19a08			20a07	20 07
Peartree	d																					
Derby	a	17 21	17 23	17 27				18 21	18 23	18 27	18 28				19 21	19 23	19 27					20 21

Station		EM J	EM K	EM I	NT ◇ G	NT ◇ G	EM F	EM N	EM K	EM I	NT G	NT ◇ G
Crewe	d	19 07	19 07	19 07			20 45	20 45	20 45	20 45		
Alsager	d	19 16	19 16	19 16			20 54	20 54	20 54	20 54		
Kidsgrove	d	19 21	19 21	19 21	19 31	20 31	21 08	21 08	21 08	21 08	21 31	22 31
Longport	d	19 27	19 27	19 27			21 14	21 14	21 14	21 14		
Stoke-on-Trent	a	19 31	19 31	19 31	19 41	20 41	21 18	21 18	21 18	21 18	21 41	22 41
	d	19 33	19 33	19 33			21 19	21 19	21 19	21 19		
Longton	d	19 39	19 39	19 39			21 25	21 25	21 25	21 25		
Blythe Bridge	d	19 45	19 45	19 45			21 31	21 31	21 31	21 31		
Uttoxeter	d	19 58	19 58	19 58			21 44	21 44	21 44	21 44		
Tutbury & Hatton	d	20 07	20 07	20 07			21a53	21 53	21 53	21 53		
Peartree	d											
Derby	a	20 22	20 23	20 24				22 10	22 12	22 13		

A From Macclesfield
B To London Euston
C until 16 June
D from 23 June until 21 July, also 8 September, 15 September, 22 September
E from 29 September
F from 28 July until 1 September
G From Manchester Piccadilly
H 8 September, 15 September, 22 September
I 29 September, 6 October
J until 21 July
K from 13 October
L until 21 July, from 8 September
M To Northampton
N until 21 July, also 8 September, 15 September, 22 September

Table T050-R

Sundays
20 May to 2 December

Crewe and Stoke-on-Trent - Derby

		NT	NT	LM	LM	LM	NT	LM	LM	EM	EM	LM	EM	EM	EM	NT	LM	EM	EM	LM	EM	EM	LM
		◇		■	■	■	◇	■	■			■				◇	■			■			■
		A	A	B	B	B	A	B	B	C	D	B	E	F	D	A	B	C	D	B	C	D	B
Crewe ■	d			09 32	10 37	11 37		12 37	13 37	14 04	14 04	14 32	15 05	15 05	15 05		15 37	16 08	16 08	16 37	17 08	17 08	17 37
Alsager	d			09 41	10 46	11 46		12 46	13 46	14 13	14 13	14 41	15 14	15 14	15 14		15 46	16 17	16 17	16 46	17 17	17 17	17 46
Kidsgrove	d	09 36	09 36	09 45	10 50	11 50	12 26	12 50	13 50	14 18	14 18	14 45	15 21	15 21	15 21	15 30	15 50	16 22	16 22	16 50	17 22	17 22	17 50
Longport	d									14 24	14 24		15 26	15 26	15 26			16 29	16 29		17 29	17 29	
Stoke-on-Trent	a	09 44	09 44	09 53	10 58	11 58	12 37	12 58	13 58	14 29	14 29	14 53	15 30	15 30	15 30	15 40	15 58	16 35	16 35	16 58	17 33	17 33	17 58
	d									14 29	14 29		15 32	15 32	15 32			16 35	16 35		17 35	17 35	
Longton	d									14 35	14 35		15 38	15 38	15 38			16 41	16 41		17 41	17 41	
Blythe Bridge	d									14 41	14 41		15 44	15 44	15 44			16 47	16 47		17 47	17 47	
Uttoxeter	d									14 54	14 54		15 57	15 57	15 57			16 59	16 59		17 59	17 59	
Tutbury & Hatton	d									15 03	15a04		16 06	16 06	16a07			17 08	17a09		18 08	18a09	
Peartree	d																						
Derby ■	a									15 19			16 23	16 24				17 27			18 28		

		EM	EM	LM	EM	EM	EM	NT	LM	EM	EM	LM	EM	EM	EM	NT
				■				◇	■			■				◇
		C	D	B	E	F	D	A	B	C	D	G	E	F	D	A
Crewe ■	d	18 08	18 08	18 37	19 08	19 08	19 08		19 37	20 15	20 15	20 42	21 16	21 16	21 16	
Alsager	d	18 17	18 17	18 46	19 17	19 17	19 17		19 46	20 24	20 24	20 51	21 25	21 25	21 25	
Kidsgrove	d	18 22	18 22	18 50	19 22	19 22	19 22	19 30	19 50	20 30	20 30	20 55	21 31	21 31	21 31	22 42
Longport	d	18 29	18 29		19 29	19 29	19 29			20 35	20 35		21 36	21 36	21 36	
Stoke-on-Trent	a	18 34	18 34	18 58	19 33	19 33	19 33	19 42	19 58	20 40	20 40	21 03	21 40	21 40	21 40	22 53
	d	18 35	18 35		19 35	19 35	19 35			20 40	20 40		21 42	21 42	21 42	
Longton	d	18 41	18 41		19 41	19 41	19 41			20 46	20 46		21 48	21 48	21 48	
Blythe Bridge	d	18 47	18 47		19 47	19 47	19 47			20 52	20 52		21 54	21 54	21 54	
Uttoxeter	d	18 59	18 59		19 59	19 59	19 59			21 05	21 05		22 06	22 06	22 06	
Tutbury & Hatton	d	19 08	19a09		20 08	20 08	20a09			21 14	21a15		22 15	22 15	22a16	
Peartree	d															
Derby ■	a	19 28			20 27	20 28				21 34			22 32	22 36		

A From Manchester Piccadilly
B To London Euston
C until 15 July, from 9 September
D from 22 July until 2 September
E from 14 October
F until 15 July, from 9 September until 7 October
G To Northampton

Table T051-F

Mondays to Fridays
21 May to 20 July

Scotland, The North East, North West England - The South West and South Coast

		XC	XC	XC	XC	XC	XC	XC	XC	XC	XC	XC	XC	VT	VT	XC	XC	XC	XC	XC	XC	VT	XC
		◇■	◇■	◇■	◇■	◇■	◇■	◇■	◇■	◇■	◇■	◇■	◇■	◇■	◇■	◇■	◇■	◇■	◇■	■	■ ■	◇■	◇■
					A						B		B										C
				⊤	⊤	⊤		⊤	⊤	⊤	⊤	⊤	⊤	⊠	⊠	⊤		⊤	⊤		⊤	⊠	⊤
Aberdeen	d																						
Stonehaven	d																						
Montrose	d																						
Arbroath	d																						
Dundee	d																						
Leuchars ■	d																						
Cupar	d																						
Ladybank	d																						
Markinch	d																						
Kirkcaldy	d																						
Inverkeithing	d																						
Glasgow Central ■	d																						
Motherwell	d																						
Haymarket	d																						
Edinburgh ■	d																						
Haymarket	d																						
Lockerbie	d																						
Carlisle ■	d																						
Penrith North Lakes	d																						
Oxenholme Lake District	d																						
Lancaster ■	d																					06 58	
Preston ■	d													06 17								07 17	
Wigan North Western	d													06 28								07 28	
Warrington Bank Quay	d													06 39								07 39	
M'chester Piccadilly ■	d							05 11				06 00			06 27				07 05		07 27		
Stockport	d											06 08			06 35				07 13		07 36		
Wilmslow	d											06 16											
Crewe ■	d							05 47				06 39		07 01								08 01	
Macclesfield	d														06 48				07 26		07 49		
Congleton	d																						
Stoke-on-Trent	d							06 07							07 06				07 44		08 07		
Stafford	d							06 25				07 01			07 24				08 01		08 25		
Wolverhampton ■	d							06 41				07 16		07 37	07 45				08 17		08 41	08 45	
Dunbar	d																						
Berwick-upon-Tweed	d																						
Alnmouth for Alnwick	d																						
Morpeth	d																						
Newcastle ■	d																						
Chester-le-Street	d																						
Durham	d																						
Darlington ■	d																						
York ■	d																						06 45
Leeds ■	d															06 11		06 16					07 10
Wakefield Westgate ■	d															06 23		06 28					07 23
Doncaster ■	d																	06 46					
Sheffield ■	d										05 59					06 53		07 18					07 53
Chesterfield	d										06 26					07 06		07 30					08 06
Nottingham ■	d									06 00			06 37				07 04			07 37			
Derby ■	d						06 10			06 36	06 48		07 06			07 27	07 36	07 50		08 06			08 28
Burton-on-Trent	d						06 20			06 48	06 58		07 17			07 38	07 50	08 00		08 18			08 38
Tamworth	d						06 31		←	07 01	07 09		07 30			07 50	08 03	08 11		08 30			08 50
Birmingham New Street ■	a						06 52	06 57	06 52	07 25	07 27	07 33	07 53	07 56	08 07	08 08	08 25	08 27	08 33	08 55	08 58	09 05	09 10
Birmingham New Street ■	d	05 00	05 37	06 04	06 33	06 42	07 12	07 04	07 12	07 30	07 33	07 42	08 04		08 10	08 12	08 30	08 33	08 42		09 04	09 10	09 17
Cheltenham Spa ■	a	06 01	06 36			07 21	→		07 51	08 10		08 24				08 50	09 10		09 24				09 58
Gloucester ■	a	06 12	06 53							08 20							09 20						
Bristol Parkway ■	a					07 54			08 26			08 54				09 25			09 55				10 30
Bristol Temple Meads ■	a					08 06			08 40			09 11				09 39			10 08				10 43
Newport (South Wales)	a	07 06	07 52							09 13							10 11						
Cardiff Central ■	a	07 22	08 08							09 29							10 27						
Weston-super-Mare	a																						
Taunton	a					08 42			09 14							10 15							11 16
Tiverton Parkway	a					08 54			09 26							10 28							11 29
Exeter St Davids ■	a					09 07			09 40							10 42							11 43
Dawlish	a																						
Teignmouth	a																						
Newton Abbot	a					09 27			09 59							11 04							12 04
Torquay	a					09 39																	
Paignton	a					09 47																	
Totnes	a								10 14							11 17							12 18
Plymouth	a								10 42							11 44							12 47
Liskeard ■	a																						
Bodmin Parkway	a																						
Lostwithiel	a																						
Par	a																						
St Austell	a																						
Truro	a																						
Redruth	a																						
Camborne	a																						
Hayle	a																						
St Erth	a																						
Penzance	a																						
Birmingham International	d			06 14				07 14					08 14		08 21						09 14	09 20	
Coventry	d			06 25				07 25					08 25		08a31						09 25	09a30	
Leamington Spa ■	d			06 37	07 00			07 38			08 00		08 38					09 00			09 39		
Banbury	a			06 53	07 18			07 54			08 16		08 55					09 18			09 55		
Oxford	a			07 14	07 41			08 14			08 39		09 15					09 41			10 14		
Reading ■	a			07 40	08 09			08 40			09 08		09 42					10 10			10 42		
Guildford	a																						
Basingstoke	a			08 08	08 41			09 10					10 09					10 39			11 09		
Winchester	a			08 24	08 56			09 25					10 24					10 54			11 24		
Southampton Airport Pkway	a			08 33	09 08			09 34					10 33					11 07			11 33		
Southampton Central	a			08 44	09 18			09 43					10 43					11 17			11 43		
Brockenhurst ■	a			08 59				09 58					10 58								11 58		
Bournemouth	a			09 15				10 13					11 13								12 13		

A ⊤ from Reading
B ⊤ from Birmingham New Street
C ⊤ from Leeds

Table T051-F

Mondays to Fridays
21 May to 20 July

Scotland, The North East, North West England - The South West and South Coast

Station		XC	XC	XC	XC	XC	VT	XC	XC	XC	XC	XC	XC	VT	XC	XC	XC	XC	XC	XC	VT	XC	XC
		◇1 A 🍴	◇1 B 🍴	◇1 🍴	1	◇1 🍴	◇1 ⊠	◇1 🍴	◇1 🍴	◇1 🍴	◇1 🍴	1	◇1 🍴	◇1 ⊠	◇1 🍴	◇1 🍴	◇1 🍴	◇1 🍴	1	◇1 🍴	◇1 ⊠	◇1 C 🍴	◇1 🍴
Aberdeen	d																						
Stonehaven	d																						
Montrose	d																						
Arbroath	d																						
Dundee	d																						
Leuchars	d																						
Cupar	d																						
Ladybank	d																						
Markinch	d																						
Kirkcaldy	d																						
Inverkeithing	d																						
Glasgow Central	d						05 49														08 00	06 01	
Motherwell	d						06 04															06 17	
Haymarket	d																					06 57	
Edinburgh	d													06 52	06 06		07 00					07 10	
Haymarket	d													06 57									
Lockerbie	d																						
Carlisle	d						07 03							08 08							09 11		
Penrith North Lakes	d						07 18							08 22									
Oxenholme Lake District	d						07 42																
Lancaster	d						07 57							08 57							09 56		
Preston	d						08 17							09 17							10 17		
Wigan North Western	d						08 28							09 28							10 28		
Warrington Bank Quay	d						08 39							09 39							10 39		
M'chester Piccadilly	d			08 05		08 27					09 05		09 27					10 05		10 27			
Stockport	d			08 13		08 36					09 13		09 36					10 13		10 36			
Wilmslow	d																						
Crewe	d						09 01							10 01							11 01		
Macclesfield	d			08 26		08 49					09 26		09 49					10 26		10 49			
Congleton	d																						
Stoke-on-Trent	d			08 44		09 07					09 44		10 07					10 44		11 07			
Stafford	d			09 01		09 25					10 01		10 25					11 01		11 25			
Wolverhampton	d			09 17		09 42	09 45				10 17		10 41	10 45				11 17		11 41	11 45		
Dunbar	d																					07 32	
Berwick-upon-Tweed	d														06 50		07 43						
Alnmouth for Alnwick	d														07 11		08 03						
Morpeth	d																08 18						
Newcastle	d		06 25					06 45		07 25					07 40		08 35					08 43	
Chester-le-Street	d																						
Durham	d		06 38					06 57		07 38					07 53		08 48					08 55	
Darlington	d		06 56					07 15		07 56					08 11		09 05					09 12	
York	d		07 26					07 43		08 27					08 44		09 35					09 44	
Leeds	d							08 11							09 11							10 11	
Wakefield Westgate	d							08 23							09 23							10 23	
Doncaster	d		07 53							08 53							09 59						
Sheffield	d		08 18					08 54		09 24					09 55		10 24					10 55	
Chesterfield	d		08 30					09 07							10 08							11 07	
Nottingham	d	08 09			08 39				09 07			09 41				10 07			10 41				11 07
Derby	d	08 38	08 53		09 10			09 26	09 39	09 53		10 10			10 30	10 38	10 53		11 10			11 28	11 37
Burton-on-Trent	d	08 50			09 22			09 38	09 52			10 21				10 49			11 21				11 49
Tamworth	d	09 03			09 34				10 04			10 33			10 50	11 02			11 33				12 02
Birmingham New Street	a	09 24	09 27	09 33	09 55	09 58	10 05	10 08	10 24	10 27	10 33	10 55	10 58	11 05	11 09	11 24	11 27	11 33	11 55	11 58	12 05	12 07	12 24
Birmingham New Street	d	09 30	09 33	09 42		10 04	10 10	10 17	10 30	10 33	10 42		11 04	11 10	11 17	11 30	11 33	11 42		12 04	12 10	12 17	12 30
Cheltenham Spa	a	10 10		10 24				10 59	11 10		11 24				11 56	12 10		12 24				13 01	13 10
Gloucester	a	10 20							11 20							12 20							13 20
Bristol Parkway	a			10 56				11 31			11 55				12 28			12 56				13 30	
Bristol Temple Meads	a			11 10				11 42			12 05				12 42			13 10				13 41	
Newport (South Wales)	a	11 11							12 10							13 09							14 11
Cardiff Central	a	11 29							12 26							13 26							14 26
Weston-super-Mare	a			11 32																			
Taunton	a			11 58				12 14							13 16							14 15	
Tiverton Parkway	a			12 10				12 26							13 28							14 27	
Exeter St Davids	a			12 24				12 40							13 43							14 40	
Dawlish	a			12 36																			
Teignmouth	a			12 41																			
Newton Abbot	a			12 48				12 59							14 03							15 00	
Torquay	a			13 00																			
Paignton	a			13 08																			
Totnes	a							13 11							14 16							15 12	
Plymouth	a							13 38							14 43							15 40	
Liskeard	a																						
Bodmin Parkway	a																						
Lostwithiel	a																						
Par	a																						
St Austell	a																						
Truro	a																						
Redruth	a																						
Camborne	a																						
Hayle	a																						
St Erth	a																						
Penzance	a																						
Birmingham International	d					10 14	10 20						11 14	11 20						12 14	12 20		
Coventry	d					10 25	10a30						11 25	11a30						12 25	12a30		
Leamington Spa	d		10 00			10 38				11 00			11 38				12 01			12 38			
Banbury	a		10 17			10 54				11 17			11 54				12 18			12 54			
Oxford	a		10 40			11 13				11 41			12 14				12 40			13 14			
Reading	a		11 09			11 40				12 08			12 42				13 08			13 40			
Guildford	a																						
Basingstoke	a					12 09				12 39			13 09							14 09			
Winchester	a					12 24				12 54			13 24							14 25			
Southampton Airport Pkwy	a					12 33				13 08			13 33							14 34			
Southampton Central	a					12 41				13 17			13 41							14 41			
Brockenhurst	a					12 57							13 56							14 56			
Bournemouth	a					13 12							14 11							15 11			

A 🍴 from Birmingham New Street
B ◇ from Birmingham New Street 1 to Birmingham New Street
C 🍴 from Edinburgh

Please check the 'Additional Notes to Individual Tables' …

Table T051-F

Mondays to Fridays
21 May to 20 July

Scotland, The North East, North West England - The South West and South Coast

Station		XC	XC	XC	XC	VT	XC	XC	XC	XC	XC	XC	VT	XC	XC	XC	XC	XC	XC	VT	XC	XC
		◇1 🍴	◇1 🍴	1	◇1 🍴	◇1 ⊠	◇1 A 🍴	◇1 🍴	◇1 🍴	◇1 🍴	1	◇1 🍴	◇1 ⊠	◇1 A 🍴	◇1 🍴	◇1 🍴	◇1 🍴	1 🍴	◇1 🍴	◇1 ☕	◇1 B 🍴	◇1 🍴
Aberdeen	d																					
Stonehaven	d																					
Montrose	d																					
Arbroath	d																					
Dundee	d						06 32															
Leuchars	d						06 46															
Cupar	d						06 54															
Ladybank	d						07 03															
Markinch	d						07 11															
Kirkcaldy	d						07 21															
Inverkeithing	d						07 40															
Glasgow Central	d												10 00	07 48							09 00	
Motherwell	d													08 08							09 15	
Haymarket	d						08 00							08 51							09 54	
Edinburgh	d					08 51	08 09							09 08						10 52	10 10	
Haymarket	d					08 57														10 57		
Lockerbie	d																					
Carlisle	d					10 08							11 12							12 08		
Penrith North Lakes	d												11 27									
Oxenholme Lake District	d					10 42														12 43		
Lancaster	d					10 57														12 57		
Preston	d					11 17							12 18							13 17		
Wigan North Western	d					11 28							12 29							13 28		
Warrington Bank Quay	d					11 39							12 40							13 39		
M'chester Piccadilly	d		11 05		11 27					12 05		12 27					13 05		13 27			
Stockport	d		11 13		11 36					12 13		12 36					13 13		13 36			
Wilmslow	d																					
Crewe	d					12 01							13 01							14 01		
Macclesfield	d		11 26		11 49					12 26		12 49					13 26		13 49			
Congleton	d																					
Stoke-on-Trent	d		11 44		12 07					12 44		13 07					13 44		14 07			
Stafford	d		12 01		12 25					13 01		13 26					14 01		14 25			
Wolverhampton	d		12 17		12 41	12 45				13 17		13 41	13 45				14 17		14 41	14 45		
Dunbar	d													09 29								
Berwick-upon-Tweed	d						08 52							09 53							10 51	
Alnmouth for Alnwick	d																					
Morpeth	d						09 25														11 22	
Newcastle	d	09 35					09 42		10 35					10 42		11 35					11 42	
Chester-le-Street	d																					
Durham	d	09 49					09 55		10 48					10 54		11 49					11 54	
Darlington	d	10 07					10 12		11 06					11 12		12 07					12 12	
York	d	10 35					10 44		11 35					11 44		12 35					12 44	
Leeds	d						11 11							12 11							13 11	
Wakefield Westgate	d						11 23							12 23							13 23	
Doncaster	d	10 59							11 59							12 59						
Sheffield	d	11 24					11 55		12 24					12 55		13 24					13 55	
Chesterfield	d						12 08							13 07							14 07	
Nottingham	d			11 41				12 07			12 41				13 07			13 41				14 07
Derby	d	11 53		12 10			12 29	12 37	12 53		13 10			13 28	13 37	13 53		14 10			14 28	14 37
Burton-on-Trent	d			12 21				12 49			13 24			13 38	13 49			14 21				14 50
Tamworth	d			12 33			12 49	13 02			13 35				14 02			14 33			14 47	15 02
Birmingham New Street	a	12 27	12 33	12 55	12 58	13 05	13 08	13 24	13 27	13 33	13 55	13 58	14 05	14 08	14 24	14 27	14 34	14 55	14 58	15 05	15 08	15 25
Birmingham New Street	d	12 33	12 42		13 04	13 10	13 17	13 30	13 33	13 42		14 04	14 10	14 17	14 30	14 33	14 42		15 04	15 10	15 17	15 30
Cheltenham Spa	a		13 24				14 00	14 10		14 24				14 58	15 10		15 24				15 58	16 10
Gloucester	a							14 22							15 20							16 22
Bristol Parkway	a		13 56				14 28			14 56				15 29			15 56				16 30	
Bristol Temple Meads	a		14 08				14 43			15 10				15 41			16 11				16 43	
Newport (South Wales)	a							15 12							16 12							17 11
Cardiff Central	a							15 30							16 30							17 30
Weston-super-Mare	a																					
Taunton	a						15 16			15 44				16 14							17 16	
Tiverton Parkway	a						15 29			15 56				16 26							17 28	
Exeter St Davids	a						15 43			16 12				16 40							17 42	
Dawlish	a																					
Teignmouth	a																					
Newton Abbot	a						16 03							17 04							18 11	
Torquay	a																					
Paignton	a																					
Totnes	a						16 17							17 16							18 23	
Plymouth	a						16 45							17 42							18 49	
Liskeard	a																				19 23	
Bodmin Parkway	a																				19 35	
Lostwithiel	a																					
Par	a																				19 45	
St Austell	a																				19 51	
Truro	a																				20 07	
Redruth	a																				20 28	
Camborne	a																				20 34	
Hayle	a																					
St Erth	a																				20 44	
Penzance	a																				20 54	
Birmingham International	d				13 14	13 20						14 14	14 20						15 14	15 20		
Coventry	d				13 25	13a30						14 25	14a29						15 25	15a30		
Leamington Spa	d	13 00			13 38				14 00			14 38				15 00			15 38			
Banbury	a	13 18			13 54				14 17			14 54				15 17			15 54			
Oxford	a	13 41			14 13				14 40			15 14				15 40			16 14			
Reading	a	14 09			14 40				15 08			15 41				16 11			16 40			
Guildford	a																					
Basingstoke	a	14 40			15 09							16 09				16 40			17 09			
Winchester	a	14 56			15 24							16 24				16 57			17 24			
Southampton Airport Pkwy	a	15 09			15 33							16 33				17 08			17 33			
Southampton Central	a	15 17			15 41							16 41				17 17			17 41			
Brockenhurst	a				15 57							16 57							17 57			
Bournemouth	a				16 12							17 12							18 15			

A 🍴 from Edinburgh
B 🍴 from Edinburgh to Plymouth

Table T051-F

Mondays to Fridays

21 May to 20 July

Scotland, The North East, North West England - The South West and South Coast

		XC	XC	XC	XC	XC	VT	XC	XC	XC	XC	XC	XC	VT	XC	XC	XC	XC	XC	XC	XC	VT	XC
		◇1 ☕	◇1 A ☕	1	◇1 ☕	◇1 B ☕	◇1 🍽	◇1 C ☕	◇1 ☕	◇1 D ☕	◇1 ☕	1 ☕	◇1 ☕	◇1 🍽	◇1 E ☕	◇1	◇1 ☕	◇1 ☕	1 ☕	◇1 ☕	◇1 ☕	◇1 🍽	◇1 ☕
Aberdeen	d					08 20																	
Stonehaven	d					08 38																	
Montrose	d					08 59																	
Arbroath	d					09 15																	
Dundee	d					09 35																	
Leuchars	d					09 48																	
Cupar	d					09 55																	
Ladybank	d					10 02																	
Markinch	d					10 09																	
Kirkcaldy	d					10 18																	
Inverkeithing	d					10 33																	
Glasgow Central	d						12 00								11 00							14 00	
Motherwell	d														11 15								
Haymarket	d					10 51									11 54								
Edinburgh	d					11 06								12 52	12 08						13 07		
Haymarket	d													12 57									
Lockerbie	d																						
Carlisle	d						13 11							14 08								15 11	
Penrith North Lakes	d													14 22									
Oxenholme Lake District	d																					15 45	
Lancaster	d						13 57							14 57								16 17	
Preston	d						14 17							15 17								16 28	
Wigan North Western	d						14 29							15 28								16 39	
Warrington Bank Quay	d						14 40							15 39									
M'chester Piccadilly	d		14 05		14 27						15 05		15 27					16 05		16 27			
Stockport	d		14 13		14 36						15 13		15 36					16 13		16 36			
Wilmslow	d																						
Crewe	d						15 01							16 01								17 01	
Macclesfield	d		14 26		14 49						15 26		15 49					16 26		16 49			
Congleton	d																						
Stoke-on-Trent	d		14 44		15 07						15 44		16 07					16 44		17 07			
Stafford	d		15 01		15 25						16 01		16 25					17 01		17 25			
Wolverhampton	d		15 17		15 41		15 45				16 17		16 41	16 45				17 17		17 41		17 45	
Dunbar	d					11 28															13 32		
Berwick-upon-Tweed	d					11 51									12 50								
Alnmouth for Alnwick	d					12 12															14 13		
Morpeth	d																						
Newcastle	d	12 34				12 41				13 35					13 42		14 36				14 42		
Chester-le-Street	d																						
Durham	d	12 47				12 54				13 49					13 54		14 48				14 54		
Darlington	d	13 05				13 12				14 07					14 12		15 06				15 12		
York	d	13 35				13 44				14 35					14 44		15 35				15 44		
Leeds	d					14 11									15 11						16 11		
Wakefield Westgate	d					14 23									15 23						16 23		
Doncaster	d	13 59								14 59							15 59						
Sheffield	d	14 24				14 55				15 24					15 55		16 24				16 55		
Chesterfield	d					15 07									16 07						17 07		
Nottingham	d			14 41					15 07			15 41				16 07			16 41				
Derby	d	14 53		15 10		15 28			15 37	15 53		16 10			16 28	16 37	16 53		17 10		17 29		
Burton-on-Trent	d			15 24		15 38			15 49			16 21				16 49			17 24		17 39		
Tamworth	d			15 35				←	16 02			16 33			16 47	17 02			17 35				←
Birmingham New Street	a	15 27	15 33	15 55	15 58	16 03	16 05	16 03	16 25	16 28	16 33	16 55	16 58	17 05	17 08	17 25	17 28	17 33	17 55	17 58	18 04	18 05	18 04
Birmingham New Street	d	15 33	15 42		16 04	16 12	16 10	16 12	16 30	16 33	16 42		17 04	17 10	17 12	17 30	17 33	17 42		18 04	18 12	18 10	18 12
Cheltenham Spa	a		16 24			→		16 49	17 14		17 24				17 51	18 16		18 24			→		18 51
Gloucester	a								17 24							18 28							19 01
Bristol Parkway	a		16 56					17 25			17 56				18 28			18 54					19 31
Bristol Temple Meads	a		17 10					17 40			18 07				18 42			19 06					19 43
Newport (South Wales)	a								18 10							19 14							
Cardiff Central	a								18 27							19 33							
Weston-super-Mare	a																						
Taunton	a		17 44					18 15							19 15								20 16
Tiverton Parkway	a		17 56					18 27							19 27								20 28
Exeter St Davids	a		18 11					18 41							19 42								20 41
Dawlish	a		18 23																				
Teignmouth	a		18 28																				
Newton Abbot	a		18 35					19 05							20 02								21 01
Torquay	a		18 47																				
Paignton	a		18 55																				
Totnes	a							19 17							20 14								21 13
Plymouth	a							19 43							20 40								21 39
Liskeard	a							20 11							21 12								
Bodmin Parkway	a							20 23							21 24								
Lostwithiel	a														21 30								
Par	a							20 33							21 36								
St Austell	a							20 40							21 43								
Truro	a							21 00							22 01								
Redruth	a							21 17							22 13								
Camborne	a							21 24							22 19								
Hayle	a														22 27								
St Erth	a							21 34							22 31								
Penzance	a							21 43							22 41								
Birmingham International	d				16 14		16 20						17 14	17 20						18 14		18 20	
Coventry	d				16 25		16a30						17 25	17a30						18 25		18a30	
Leamington Spa	d	16 01			16 38					17 00			17 38				18 01			18 38			
Banbury	a	16 17			16 54					17 17			17 54				18 18			18 55			
Oxford	a	16 40			17 13					17 40			18 14				18 40			19 13			
Reading	a	17 08			17 40					18 09			18 44				19 10			19 41			
Guildford	a									18 59													
Basingstoke	a				18 09								19 09							20 09			
Winchester	a				18 25								19 24							20 25			
Southampton Airport Pkway	a				18 33								19 33							20 34			
Southampton Central	a				18 43								19 42							20 42			
Brockenhurst	a				18 58								19 56							20 58			
Bournemouth	a				19 12								20 11							21 15			

A ☕ to Bristol Temple Meads
B ☕ ◇ from Edinburgh 1 to Edinburgh
C ☕ to Plymouth
D ☕ to Reading
E ☕ from Edinburgh to Plymouth

Table T051-F

Mondays to Fridays

21 May to 20 July

Scotland, The North East, North West England - The South West and South Coast

		XC	XC	XC	XC	XC	VT	XC	XC	XC	XC	XC	XC	VT	XC	XC FX	XC FO	XC	XC	XC	XC	VT
		◇1	◇1 ☕	◇1 A ☕	1 ☕	◇1 B ☕	1 🍽	◇1 C ☕	◇1	◇1 ☕	◇1 A ☕	1 ☕	◇1 D ☕	◇1 ⊠	◇1 D ☕	◇1	◇1	◇1 D ☕	◇1 D ☕	1 ☕	◇1 D ☕	1 ⊠
Aberdeen	d																					
Stonehaven	d																					
Montrose	d																					
Arbroath	d																					
Dundee	d																					
Leuchars	d																					
Cupar	d																					
Ladybank	d																					
Markinch	d																					
Kirkcaldy	d																					
Inverkeithing	d																					
Glasgow Central	d							13 00						16 00								
Motherwell	d							13 16														
Haymarket	d							13 55														
Edinburgh	d						14 52	14 09							15 08							16 52
Haymarket	d						14 58															16 57
Lockerbie	d																					
Carlisle	d						16 08							17 11								18 08
Penrith North Lakes	d						16 21															
Oxenholme Lake District	d													17 45								18 42
Lancaster	d						16 57															18 59
Preston	d						17 17							18 17								19 17
Wigan North Western	d						17 28							18 28								19 31
Warrington Bank Quay	d						17 39							18 39								19 41
M'chester Piccadilly	d			17 05		17 27					18 05		18 27						19 05		19 27	
Stockport	d			17 13		17 35					18 13		18 36						19 13		19 36	
Wilmslow	d					17 45																
Crewe	d					18 07	18 01							19 01								20 03
Macclesfield	d			17 26							18 26								19 26		19 49	
Congleton	d												18 55									
Stoke-on-Trent	d			17 44							18 44		19 07						19 44		20 07	
Stafford	d			18 01		18 25					19 01		19 25						20 01		20 25	
Wolverhampton	d			18 17		18 41	18 45				19 17		19 41	19 45					20 17		20 44	20 47
Dunbar	d														15 29							
Berwick-upon-Tweed	d							14 50														
Alnmouth for Alnwick	d																					
Morpeth	d																					
Newcastle	d		15 03					15 41		16 35					16 41			17 32				
Chester-le-Street	d																	17 41				
Durham	d		15 16					15 54		16 48					16 54			17 48				
Darlington	d		15 33					16 12		17 06					17 12			18 06				
York	d		16 05					16 44		17 35					17 45			18 36				
Leeds	d		16 40					17 10							18 11							
Wakefield Westgate	d		16 52					17 22							18 23							
Doncaster	d									17 58								18 59				
Sheffield	d		17 24					17 55		18 24					18 58			19 24				
Chesterfield	d							18 07							19 11							
Nottingham	d	17 07			17 41				18 07			18 41				19 07	19 07			19 36		
Derby	d	17 37	17 53		18 13			18 29	18 37	18 53		19 08			19 30	19 37	19 37	19 54		20 10		
Burton-on-Trent	d	17 49			18 27				18 49			19 21			19 41	19 49	19 49			20 21		
Tamworth	d	18 02			18 38			18 49	19 02			19 33				20 03	20 03			20 33		
Birmingham New Street	a	18 23	18 28	18 33	18 57	18 58	19 05	19 08	19 24	19 27	19 33	19 55	19 58	20 05	20 07	20 25	20 25	20 28	20 33	20 55	21 00	21 05
Birmingham New Street	d	18 30	18 33	18 42		19 04	19 10	19 12	19 30	19 33	19 42		20 04	20 10	20 12	20 30	20 30	20 34	20 42		21 04	21 10
Cheltenham Spa	a	19 13		19 24				19 50	20 11		20 24				20 52	21 10	21 10		21 25			
Gloucester	a	19 23							20 20							21 19	21 19					
Bristol Parkway	a			19 56				20 30			20 55				21 25				22 01			
Bristol Temple Meads	a			20 09				20 42			21 05				21 36				22 14			
Newport (South Wales)	a	20 11		20 47					21 11							22 12	22 13					
Cardiff Central	a	20 28		21 03					21 28							22 35	22 30					
Weston-super-Mare	a																					
Taunton	a							21 19			21 43				22 15							
Tiverton Parkway	a							21 31			21 55				22 27							
Exeter St Davids	a							21 45			22 09				22 41							
Dawlish	a																					
Teignmouth	a																					
Newton Abbot	a							22 05			22 28				23 01							
Torquay	a																					
Paignton	a																					
Totnes	a							22 17			22 40				23 18							
Plymouth	a							22 45			23 07				23 44							
Liskeard	a																					
Bodmin Parkway	a																					
Lostwithiel	a																					
Par	a																					
St Austell	a																					
Truro	a																					
Redruth	a																					
Camborne	a																					
Hayle	a																					
St Erth	a																					
Penzance	a																					
Birmingham International	d					19 14	19 20						20 14	20 20							21 14	21 20
Coventry	d					19 25	19a30						20 25	20a30							21 25	21a30
Leamington Spa	d		19 01			19 38				20 02			20 38					21 00			21 38	
Banbury	a		19 17			19 54				20 19			20 55					21 17			21 54	
Oxford	a		19 41			20 13				20 40			21 14					21 40			22 14	
Reading	a		20 09			20 41				21 07			21 42					22 16			22 42	
Guildford	a																					
Basingstoke	a					21 09							22 09					22 39			23 06	
Winchester	a					21 24							22 24					22 56			23 24	
Southampton Airport Pkway	a					21 33							22 33					23 12			23 36	
Southampton Central	a					21 40							22 42					23 20			23 43	
Brockenhurst	a					21 56							22 56									
Bournemouth	a					22 15							23 19									

A ☕ to Bristol Temple Meads
B ☕ to Reading
C ☕ from Edinburgh to Bristol Temple Meads
D ☕ to Birmingham New Street

Table T051-F

Mondays to Fridays

21 May to 20 July

Scotland, The North East, North West England - The South West and South Coast

		XC	XC	XC	VT	XC	XC	XC	XC	XC	VT	XC	XC	XC	XC
		◇1	◇1	◇1	◇1	1	◇1	◇1	◇1	◇1	◇1	◇1	1	◇1	◇1
		A							B					C	
		✠	✠		⊠				✠	✠	⊠			✠	
Aberdeen	d														
Stonehaven	d														
Montrose	d														
Arbroath	d														
Dundee	d														
Leuchars	d														
Cupar	d														
Ladybank	d														
Markinch	d														
Kirkcaldy	d														
Inverkeithing	d														
Glasgow Central	d	15 00			17 40									17 00	
Motherwell	d	15 16												17 16	
Haymarket	d	15 56												17 55	
Edinburgh	d	16 06							17 07		18 52			18 08	
Haymarket	d										18 56				
Lockerbie	d				18 33										
Carlisle	d				18 57						20 07				
Penrith North Lakes	d														
Oxenholme Lake District	d				19 33						20 42				
Lancaster	d				19 47						20 56				
Preston	d				20 08						21 17				
Wigan North Western	d				20 19						21 28				
Warrington Bank Quay	d				20 32						21 39				
M'chester Piccadilly	d			20 05			20 27					21 27			22 07
Stockport	d			20 13			20 36					21 36			22 16
Wilmslow	d														
Crewe	d				20 53						22 01				
Macclesfield	d			20 26			20 49					21 49			22 29
Congleton	d														
Stoke-on-Trent	d			20 44			21 07					22 08			22 47
Stafford	d			21 01	21 14		21 25					22 26			23 04
Wolverhampton	d			21 17	21 32		21 41				22 33	22 42			23 18
Dunbar	d								17 29					18 30	
Berwick-upon-Tweed	d								17 52					18 54	
Alnmouth for Alnwick	d	17 05												19 14	
Morpeth	d	17 19							18 24						
Newcastle	d	17 41	18 35						18 43	19 35				19 42	
Chester-le-Street	d														
Durham	d	17 54	18 48						18 55	19 50				19 55	
Darlington	d	18 12	19 07						19 13	20 07				20 13	
York	d	18 45	19 36						19 45	20 36				20 45	
Leeds	d	19 11							20 11					21 11	
Wakefield Westgate	d	19 23							20 23					21 23	
Doncaster	d		19 59							21 01					
Sheffield	d	19 58	20 24						20 56	21 29				22 01	
Chesterfield	d	20 10							21 08	21 41				22 25	
Nottingham	d					20 40							21 39		
Derby	d	20 29	20 54			21 10			21 28	22 02			22 12	22 45	
Burton-on-Trent	d					21 24			21 40				22 23	22 56	
Tamworth	d	20 47				21 34			21 50				22 35	23 07	
Birmingham New Street	a	21 07	21 29	21 33	21 54	21 57	22 00		22 09	22 51	22 52	22 59	23 01	23 26	23 35
Birmingham New Street	d	21 12						22 04	22 12						
Cheltenham Spa	a	21 51							22 51						
Gloucester	a	22 02													
Bristol Parkway	a	22 33							23 21						
Bristol Temple Meads	a	22 43							23 41						
Newport (South Wales)	a														
Cardiff Central	a														
Weston-super-Mare	a														
Taunton	a														
Tiverton Parkway	a														
Exeter St Davids	a														
Dawlish	a														
Teignmouth	a														
Newton Abbot	a														
Torquay	a														
Paignton	a														
Totnes	a														
Plymouth	a														
Liskeard	a														
Bodmin Parkway	a														
Lostwithiel	a														
Par	a														
St Austell	a														
Truro	a														
Redruth	a														
Camborne	a														
Hayle	a														
St Erth	a														
Penzance	a														
Birmingham International	d							22 14							
Coventry	d							22 25							
Leamington Spa	d							22 38							
Banbury	a							22 54							
Oxford	a							23 14							
Reading	a							23 49							
Guildford	a														
Basingstoke	a														
Winchester	a														
Southampton Airport Pkway	a														
Southampton Central	a														
Brockenhurst	a														
Bournemouth	a														

A ✠ to Birmingham New Street B ✠ to Leeds C ✠ from Edinburgh to Leeds

Table T051-F

Mondays to Fridays

23 July to 31 August

Scotland, The North East, North West England - The South West and South Coast

		XC	XC	XC	XC	XC	XC	XC	XC	XC	XC	XC	XC	VT	VT	XC	XC	XC	XC	XC	XC	VT	XC
		◇1	◇1	◇1	◇1	◇1	◇1	◇1	◇1	◇1	◇1	◇1	◇1	◇1	◇1	◇1	◇1	◇1	◇1	1	■ 1	◇1	◇1
					A						B		B										
				✠	✠	✠		✠	✠	✠	✠	✠	✠	⊠	⊠	✠		✠	✠		✠	⊠	✠
Aberdeen	d																						
Stonehaven	d																						
Montrose	d																						
Arbroath	d																						
Dundee	d																						
Leuchars	d																						
Cupar	d																						
Ladybank	d																						
Markinch	d																						
Kirkcaldy	d																						
Inverkeithing	d																						
Glasgow Central	d																						
Motherwell	d																						
Haymarket	d																						
Edinburgh	d																						
Haymarket	d																						
Lockerbie	d																						
Carlisle	d																						
Penrith North Lakes	d																						
Oxenholme Lake District	d																						
Lancaster	d																					06 58	
Preston	d													06 17								07 17	
Wigan North Western	d													06 28								07 28	
Warrington Bank Quay	d													06 39								07 39	
M'chester Piccadilly	d							05 11				06 00			06 27				07 05		07 27		
Stockport	d											06 08			06 35				07 13		07 36		
Wilmslow	d											06 16											
Crewe	d							05 47				06 39		07 01								08 01	
Macclesfield	d														06 48				07 26		07 49		
Congleton	d																						
Stoke-on-Trent	d							06 07							07 06				07 44		08 07		
Stafford	d							06 25				07 01			07 24				08 01		08 25		
Wolverhampton	d							06 41				07 16		07 37	07 45				08 17		08 41	08 45	
Dunbar	d																						
Berwick-upon-Tweed	d																						
Alnmouth for Alnwick	d																						
Morpeth	d																						
Newcastle	d																						
Chester-le-Street	d																						
Durham	d																						
Darlington	d																						
York	d																						
Leeds	d															05 48							06 16
Wakefield Westgate	d															06 01							06 28
Doncaster	d																						06 46
Sheffield	d										05 40					06 30							07 18
Chesterfield	d										06 05					06 44							07 32
Nottingham	d									06 00			06 37				07 04			07 37			
Derby	d																						
Burton-on-Trent	d						06 20			06 48	06 58		07 19			07 38	07 50	08 00		08 18			08 38
Tamworth	d						06 31		←	07 01	07 09		07 30			07 50	08 03	08 11		08 30			08 50
Birmingham New Street	a						06 52	06 57	06 52	07 25	07 27	07 33	07 53	07 56	08 07	08 08	08 25	08 27	08 33	08 55	08 58	09 05	09 10
Birmingham New Street	d	05 00	05 37	06 04	06 33	06 42	07 12	07 04	07 12	07 30	07 33	07 42	08 04		08 10	08 12	08 30	08 33	08 42		09 04	09 10	09 17
Cheltenham Spa	a	06 01	06 36			07 21	↪		07 51	08 10		08 24				08 50	09 10		09 24				09 58
Gloucester	a	06 12	06 53							08 20							09 20						
Bristol Parkway	a					07 54			08 26			08 54				09 25			09 55				10 30
Bristol Temple Meads	a					08 06			08 40			09 11				09 39			10 08				10 43
Newport (South Wales)	a	07 06	07 52							09 13							10 11						
Cardiff Central	a	07 22	08 08							09 29							10 27						
Weston-super-Mare	a																						
Taunton	a					08 42			09 14							10 15							11 16
Tiverton Parkway	a					08 54			09 26							10 28							11 29
Exeter St Davids	a					09 07			09 40							10 42							11 43
Dawlish	a																						
Teignmouth	a																						
Newton Abbot	a					09 27			09 59							11 04							12 04
Torquay	a					09 39																	
Paignton	a					09 47																	
Totnes	a								10 14							11 17							12 18
Plymouth	a								10 42							11 44							12 47
Liskeard	a																						
Bodmin Parkway	a																						
Lostwithiel	a																						
Par	a																						
St Austell	a																						
Truro	a																						
Redruth	a																						
Camborne	a																						
Hayle	a																						
St Erth	a																						
Penzance	a																						
Birmingham International	d			06 14				07 14					08 14		08 21						09 14	09 20	
Coventry	d			06 25				07 25					08 25		08a31						09 25	09a30	
Leamington Spa	d			06 37	07 00			07 38			08 00		08 38					09 00			09 39		
Banbury	a			06 53	07 18			07 54			08 16		08 55					09 18			09 55		
Oxford	a			07 14	07 41			08 14			08 39		09 15					09 41			10 14		
Reading	a			07 40	08 09			08 40			09 08		09 42					10 10			10 42		
Guildford	a																						
Basingstoke	a			08 08	08 41			09 10					10 09					10 39			11 09		
Winchester	a			08 24	08 56			09 25					10 24					10 54			11 24		
Southampton Airport Pkway	a			08 33	09 08			09 34					10 33					11 07			11 33		
Southampton Central	a			08 44	09 18			09 43					10 43					11 17			11 43		
Brockenhurst	a			08 59				09 58					10 58								11 58		
Bournemouth	a			09 15				10 13					11 13								12 13		

A ✠ from Reading B ✠ from Birmingham New Street

Scotland, The North East, North West England - The South West and South Coast

		XC	XC	XC	XC	XC	VT	XC	XC	XC	XC	XC	XC	VT	XC	XC	XC	XC	XC	XC	VT	XC	XC
		◇■	■ ◇■	◇■	■	◇■	◇■	◇■	◇■	◇■	◇■	■	◇■	◇■	◇■	◇■	◇■	◇■	■	◇■	◇■	◇■	◇■
		A	B																				
		⊼	⊼	⊼		⊼	⊠	⊼	⊼	⊼	⊼		⊼	⊠	⊼	⊼	⊼	⊼		⊼	⊠	⊼	⊼
Aberdeen	d																						
Stonehaven	d																						
Montrose	d																						
Arbroath	d																						
Dundee	d																						
Leuchars ■	d																						
Cupar	d																						
Ladybank	d																						
Markinch	d																						
Kirkcaldy	d																						
Inverkeithing	d																						
Glasgow Central ■	d						05 49														08 00		
Motherwell	d						06 04																
Haymarket	d																						
Edinburgh ■	d													06 52			06 06					07 00	
Haymarket	d													06 57									
Lockerbie	d																						
Carlisle ■	d						07 03							08 08							09 11		
Penrith North Lakes	d						07 18							08 22									
Oxenholme Lake District	d						07 42																
Lancaster ■	d						07 57							08 57							09 56		
Preston ■	d						08 17							09 17							10 17		
Wigan North Western	d						08 28							09 28							10 28		
Warrington Bank Quay	d						08 39							09 39							10 39		
M'chester Piccadilly ■	d			08 05		08 27					09 05		09 27					10 05		10 27			
Stockport	d			08 13		08 36					09 13		09 36					10 13		10 36			
Wilmslow	d																						
Crewe ■	d						09 01							10 01							11 01		
Macclesfield	d			08 26		08 49					09 26		09 49					10 26		10 49			
Congleton	d																						
Stoke-on-Trent	d			08 44		09 07					09 44		10 07					10 44		11 07			
Stafford	d			09 01		09 25					10 01		10 25					11 01		11 25			
Wolverhampton ■	d			09 17		09 42	09 45				10 17		10 41	10 45				11 17		11 41	11 45		
Dunbar	d																						
Berwick-upon-Tweed	d																06 50					07 43	
Alnmouth for Alnwick	d																07 11					08 04	
Morpeth	d																					08 19	
Newcastle ■	d							06 25		06 45					07 25		07 40					08 36	
Chester-le-Street	d																						
Durham	d							06 38		06 57					07 38		07 54					08 49	
Darlington ■	d							06 56		07 15					07 56		08 12					09 06	
York ■	d		06 45					07 26		07 43					08 27		08 44					09 36	
Leeds ■	d		07 10							08 11							09 11						
Wakefield Westgate ■	d		07 23							08 23							09 23						
Doncaster ■	d							07 53							08 53							10 00	
Sheffield ■	d		07 53					08 18		08 54					09 24		09 55					10 24	
Chesterfield	d		08 06					08 33		09 07					09 36		10 07					10 38	
Nottingham ■	d	08 12			08 41				09 07			09 41				10 07			10 41				11 07
Derby ■	d																						
Burton-on-Trent	d	08 49	09 01		09 22			09 38	09 50	10 01		10 21			10 39	10 49	11 00		11 21			11 36	11 49
Tamworth	d	09 02			09 34				10 02			10 33			10 50	11 02			11 33				12 02
Birmingham New Street ■	a	09 24	09 27	09 33	09 55	09 58	10 05	10 08	10 24	10 27	10 33	10 55	10 58	11 05	11 08	11 24	11 27	11 33	11 55	11 58	12 05	12 09	12 24
Birmingham New Street ■	d	09 30	09 33	09 42		10 04	10 10	10 17	10 30	10 33	10 42		11 04	11 10	11 17	11 30	11 33	11 42		12 04	12 10	12 17	12 30
Cheltenham Spa ■	a	10 10		10 24				10 59	11 10		11 24				11 57	12 10		12 24				13 00	13 10
Gloucester ■	a	10 20							11 20							12 20							13 20
Bristol Parkway ■	a			10 56				11 31			11 55				12 28			12 56				13 30	
Bristol Temple Meads ■	a			11 10				11 42			12 05				12 42			13 10				13 42	
Newport (South Wales)	a	11 11							12 10							13 09							14 11
Cardiff Central ■	a	11 28							12 26							13 26							14 26
Weston-super-Mare	a			11 32																			
Taunton	a			11 58				12 14							13 16							14 16	
Tiverton Parkway	a			12 10				12 26							13 28							14 28	
Exeter St Davids ■	a			12 24				12 40							13 43							14 43	
Dawlish	a			12 36																			
Teignmouth	a			12 41																			
Newton Abbot	a			12 48				12 59							14 03							15 03	
Torquay	a			13 00																			
Paignton	a			13 08																			
Totnes	a							13 11							14 16							15 16	
Plymouth	a							13 38							14 43							15 43	
Liskeard ■	a																						
Bodmin Parkway	a																						
Lostwithiel	a																						
Par	a																						
St Austell	a																						
Truro	a																						
Redruth	a																						
Camborne	a																						
Hayle	a																						
St Erth	a																						
Penzance	a																						
Birmingham International	d					10 14	10 20						11 14	11 20						12 14	12 20		
Coventry	d					10 25	10a30						11 25	11a30						12 25	12a30		
Leamington Spa ■	d		10 00			10 38				11 00			11 38				12 01			12 38			
Banbury	a		10 17			10 54				11 17			11 54				12 18			12 54			
Oxford	a		10 40			11 13				11 41			12 14				12 40			13 14			
Reading ■	a		11 09			11 40				12 08			12 42				13 08			13 40			
Guildford	a																						
Basingstoke	a					12 09				12 39			13 09							14 09			
Winchester	a					12 24				12 54			13 24							14 25			
Southampton Airport Pkway	a					12 33				13 08			13 33							14 34			
Southampton Central	a					12 41				13 17			13 41							14 41			
Brockenhurst ■	a					12 57							13 56							14 56			
Bournemouth	a					13 12							14 11							15 11			

A ⊼ from Birmingham New Street

B ◇ from Birmingham New Street ■ to Birmingham New Street

Scotland, The North East, North West England - The South West and South Coast

		XC	XC	XC	XC	VT	XC	XC	XC	XC	XC	XC	VT	XC	XC	XC	XC	XC	XC	VT	XC	XC
		◇■	◇■	■	◇■	◇■	◇■	◇■	◇■	◇■	■	◇■	◇■	◇■	◇■	◇■	◇■	■	◇■	◇■	◇■	◇■
																					A	
		⊼	⊼		⊼	⊠	⊼	⊼	⊼	⊼		⊼	⊠	⊼	⊼	⊼	⊼	⊼	⊼	☐	⊼	⊼
Aberdeen	d																					
Stonehaven	d																					
Montrose	d																					
Arbroath	d																					
Dundee	d								06 32													
Leuchars ■	d								06 46													
Cupar	d								06 54													
Ladybank	d								07 03													
Markinch	d								07 11													
Kirkcaldy	d								07 21													
Inverkeithing	d								07 40													
Glasgow Central ■	d	06 01											10 00			07 48						
Motherwell	d	06 17														08 08						
Haymarket	d	06 57							08 00							08 51						
Edinburgh ■	d	07 10				08 51			08 09							09 08				10 52		
Haymarket	d					08 57														10 57		
Lockerbie	d																					
Carlisle ■	d					10 08							11 12							12 08		
Penrith North Lakes	d												11 27									
Oxenholme Lake District	d					10 42														12 43		
Lancaster ■	d					10 57														12 57		
Preston ■	d					11 17							12 18							13 17		
Wigan North Western	d					11 28							12 29							13 28		
Warrington Bank Quay	d					11 39							12 40							13 39		
M'chester Piccadilly ■	d		11 05		11 27					12 05		12 27					13 05		13 27			
Stockport	d		11 13		11 36					12 13		12 36					13 13		13 36			
Wilmslow	d																					
Crewe ■	d					12 01							13 01							14 01		
Macclesfield	d		11 26		11 49					12 26		12 49					13 26		13 49			
Congleton	d																					
Stoke-on-Trent	d		11 44		12 07					12 44		13 07					13 44		14 07			
Stafford	d		12 01		12 25					13 01		13 26					14 01		14 25			
Wolverhampton ■	d		12 17		12 41	12 45				13 17		13 41	13 45				14 17		14 41	14 45		
Dunbar	d	07 32														09 29						
Berwick-upon-Tweed	d								08 52							09 53						
Alnmouth for Alnwick	d																					
Morpeth	d								09 25													
Newcastle ■	d	08 43					09 35		09 42					10 35		10 42					11 35	
Chester-le-Street	d																					
Durham	d	08 55					09 49		09 55					10 48		10 54					11 49	
Darlington ■	d	09 12					10 06		10 13					11 06		11 12					12 07	
York ■	d	09 44					10 35		10 44					11 35		11 44					12 35	
Leeds ■	d	10 11							11 11							12 11						
Wakefield Westgate ■	d	10 23							11 23							12 23						
Doncaster ■	d						10 59							11 59							12 59	
Sheffield ■	d	10 55					11 24		11 55					12 24		12 55					13 24	
Chesterfield	d	11 07					11 38		12 07					12 36		13 07					13 36	
Nottingham ■	d			11 41				12 07			12 41				13 07			13 41				14 07
Derby ■	d																					
Burton-on-Trent	d	12 02		12 21			12 38	12 49	13 01		13 24			13 38	13 49	14 02		14 21			14 36	14 50
Tamworth	d			12 33			12 49	13 02			13 35				14 02			14 33			14 47	15 02
Birmingham New Street ■	a	12 27	12 33	12 55	12 58	13 05	13 08	13 24	13 27	13 33	13 55	13 58	14 05	14 08	14 24	14 27	14 34	14 55	14 58	15 05	15 08	15 25
Birmingham New Street ■	d	12 33	12 42		13 04	13 10	13 17	13 30	13 33	13 42		14 04	14 10	14 17	14 30	14 33	14 42		15 04	15 10	15 17	15 30
Cheltenham Spa ■	a		13 24				14 00	14 10		14 24				14 58	15 10		15 24				15 58	16 10
Gloucester ■	a							14 22							15 20							16 22
Bristol Parkway ■	a		13 56				14 28			14 56				15 29			15 56				16 30	
Bristol Temple Meads ■	a		14 08				14 42			15 10				15 41			16 11				16 43	
Newport (South Wales)	a							15 12							16 12							17 11
Cardiff Central ■	a							15 30							16 30							17 30
Weston-super-Mare	a																					
Taunton	a						15 16			15 44				16 14							17 16	
Tiverton Parkway	a						15 28			15 56				16 26							17 28	
Exeter St Davids ■	a						15 43			16 12				16 40							17 42	
Dawlish	a																					
Teignmouth	a																					
Newton Abbot	a						16 03							17 04							18 11	
Torquay	a																					
Paignton	a																					
Totnes	a						16 16							17 16							18 23	
Plymouth	a						16 45							17 42							18 49	
Liskeard ■	a																				19 23	
Bodmin Parkway	a																				19 35	
Lostwithiel	a																					
Par	a																				19 45	
St Austell	a																				19 51	
Truro	a																				20 07	
Redruth	a																				20 28	
Camborne	a																				20 34	
Hayle	a																					
St Erth	a																				20 44	
Penzance	a																				20 54	
Birmingham International	d				13 14	13 20						14 14	14 20						15 14	15 20		
Coventry	d				13 25	13a30						14 25	14a29						15 25	15a30		
Leamington Spa ■	d	13 00			13 38				14 00			14 38				15 00			15 38			
Banbury	a	13 18			13 54				14 17			14 54				15 17			15 54			
Oxford	a	13 41			14 13				14 40			15 14				15 40			16 14			
Reading ■	a	14 09			14 40				15 08			15 41				16 11			16 40			
Guildford	a																					
Basingstoke	a	14 40			15 09							16 09				16 40			17 09			
Winchester	a	14 56			15 24							16 24				16 57			17 24			
Southampton Airport Pkway	a	15 09			15 33							16 33				17 08			17 33			
Southampton Central	a	15 17			15 41							16 41				17 17			17 41			
Brockenhurst ■	a				15 57							16 57							17 57			
Bournemouth	a				16 12							17 12							18 15			

A ⊼ to Plymouth

Table T051-F

Mondays to Fridays
23 July to 31 August

Scotland, The North East, North West England - The South West and South Coast

		XC	XC	XC	XC	XC	VT	XC	XC	XC	XC	XC	XC	VT	XC	XC	XC	XC	XC	XC	VT	XC	XC
		◇■ 🛒	◇■ A 🛒	■	◇■ 🛒	◇■ 🛒	◇■ 🍴	◇■ B 🛒	◇■ 🛒	◇■ C 🛒	◇■ 🛒	■ 🛒	◇■ 🛒	◇■ 🍴	◇■ B 🛒	◇■	◇■ 🛒	◇■ 🛒	■ 🛒	◇■ 🛒	◇■ 🍴	◇■ 🛒	◇■
Aberdeen	d									08 20													
Stonehaven	d									08 38													
Montrose	d									08 59													
Arbroath	d									09 15													
Dundee	d									09 35													
Leuchars ■	d									09 48													
Cupar	d									09 55													
Ladybank	d									10 02													
Markinch	d									10 09													
Kirkcaldy	d									10 18													
Inverkeithing	d									10 33													
Glasgow Central ■	d	09 00					12 00										11 00				14 00		
Motherwell	d	09 15															11 15						
Haymarket	d	09 54								10 51							11 54						
Edinburgh ■	d	10 10								11 06				12 52			12 08						
Haymarket	d													12 57									
Lockerbie	d																						
Carlisle ■	d						13 11							14 08							15 11		
Penrith North Lakes	d													14 22									
Oxenholme Lake District	d																				15 45		
Lancaster ■	d						13 57							14 57									
Preston ■	d						14 17							15 17							16 17		
Wigan North Western	d						14 29							15 28							16 28		
Warrington Bank Quay	d						14 40							15 39							16 39		
M'chester Piccadilly ■	d		14 05		14 27						15 05		15 27					16 05		16 27			
Stockport	d		14 13		14 36						15 13		15 36					16 13		16 36			
Wilmslow	d																						
Crewe ■	d						15 01							16 01							17 01		
Macclesfield	d		14 26		14 49						15 26		15 49					16 26		16 49			
Congleton	d																						
Stoke-on-Trent	d		14 44		15 07						15 44		16 07					16 44		17 07			
Stafford	d		15 01		15 25						16 01		16 25					17 01		17 25			
Wolverhampton ■	d		15 17		15 41		15 45				16 17		16 41	16 45				17 17		17 41	17 45		
Dunbar	d									11 28													
Berwick-upon-Tweed	d	10 51								11 51							12 50						
Alnmouth for Alnwick	d									12 12													
Morpeth	d	11 22																					
Newcastle ■	d	11 42				12 34				12 41					13 35		13 42					14 36	
Chester-le-Street	d																						
Durham	d	11 54				12 47				12 54					13 49		13 54					14 48	
Darlington ■	d	12 12				13 05				13 12					14 07		14 12					15 06	
York ■	d	12 44				13 35				13 44					14 35		14 44					15 35	
Leeds ■	d	13 11								14 11							15 11						
Wakefield Westgate ■	d	13 23								14 23							15 23						
Doncaster ■	d					13 59									14 59							15 59	
Sheffield ■	d	13 55				14 24				14 55					15 24		15 55					16 24	
Chesterfield	d	14 07				14 36				15 07					15 36		16 07					16 36	
Nottingham ■	d			14 41					15 07			15 41				16 07			16 41				17 07
Derby ■	d																						
Burton-on-Trent	d	15 01		15 24		15 38			15 49	16 01		16 21			16 36	16 49	17 01		17 24			17 39	17 49
Tamworth	d			15 35				←	16 02			16 33			16 47	17 02			17 35				18 02
Birmingham New Street ■	a	15 27	15 33	15 54	15 58	16 03	16 05	16 03	16 25	16 28	16 33	16 55	16 58	17 05	17 08	17 25	17 28	17 33	17 55	17 58	18 05	18 05	18 23
Birmingham New Street ■	d	15 33	15 42		16 04	16 12	16 10	16 12	16 30	16 33	16 42		17 04	17 10	17 12	17 30	17 33	17 42		18 04	18 10	18 12	18 30
Cheltenham Spa ■	a		16 24			→		16 49	17 13		17 24				17 51	18 16		18 24				18 51	19 13
Gloucester ■	a								17 23							18 28						19 01	19 23
Bristol Parkway ■	a		16 56					17 25			17 56				18 28			18 54				19 31	
Bristol Temple Meads ■	a		17 10					17 40			18 07				18 42			19 06				19 43	
Newport (South Wales)	a								18 10							19 14							20 11
Cardiff Central ■	a								18 27							19 33							20 28
Weston-super-Mare	a																						
Taunton	a		17 44					18 15							19 15							20 16	
Tiverton Parkway	a		17 56					18 27							19 27							20 28	
Exeter St Davids ■	a		18 11					18 41							19 42							20 41	
Dawlish	a		18 23																				
Teignmouth	a		18 28																				
Newton Abbot	a		18 35					19 05							20 02							21 01	
Torquay	a		18 47																				
Paignton	a		18 55																				
Totnes	a							19 17							20 14							21 13	
Plymouth	a							19 43							20 40							21 39	
Liskeard ■	a							20 11							21 12								
Bodmin Parkway	a							20 23							21 24								
Lostwithiel	a														21 30								
Par	a							20 33							21 36								
St Austell	a							20 40							21 43								
Truro	a							21 00							22 01								
Redruth	a							21 17							22 13								
Camborne	a							21 24							22 19								
Hayle	a														22 27								
St Erth	a							21 34							22 31								
Penzance	a							21 43							22 41								
Birmingham International ✈	d				16 14		16 20						17 14	17 20						18 14	18 20		
Coventry	d				16 25		16a30						17 25	17a30						18 25	18a30		
Leamington Spa ■	d	16 01			16 38					17 00			17 38				18 01			18 38			
Banbury	a	16 17			16 54					17 17			17 54				18 18			18 55			
Oxford	a	16 40			17 13					17 40			18 14				18 40			19 13			
Reading ■	a	17 08			17 40					18 09			18 44				19 10			19 41			
Guildford	a									18 59													
Basingstoke	a				18 09								19 09							20 09			
Winchester	a				18 25								19 24							20 25			
Southampton Airport Pkway ✈	a				18 33								19 33							20 34			
Southampton Central	a				18 43								19 42							20 42			
Brockenhurst ■	a				18 58								19 56							20 58			
Bournemouth	a				19 12								20 11							21 15			

A 🛒 to Bristol Temple Meads B 🛒 to Plymouth C 🛒 to Reading

Table T051-F

Mondays to Fridays
23 July to 31 August

Scotland, The North East, North West England - The South West and South Coast

		XC	XC	XC	XC	VT	XC	XC	XC	XC	XC	XC	VT	XC	XC FX	XC FO	XC	XC	XC	XC	VT	XC
		◇■ 🛒	◇■ A 🛒	■ 🛒	◇■ B 🛒	■ ■ 🍴	◇■ A 🛒	◇■	◇■ 🛒	◇■ A 🛒	■ 🛒	◇■ C 🛒	◇■ ☒	◇■ C 🛒	◇■	◇■	◇■ C 🛒	◇■ C 🛒	■ 🛒	◇■ C 🛒	■ ■ ☒	◇■ C 🛒
Aberdeen	d																					
Stonehaven	d																					
Montrose	d																					
Arbroath	d																					
Dundee	d																					
Leuchars ■	d																					
Cupar	d																					
Ladybank	d																					
Markinch	d																					
Kirkcaldy	d																					
Inverkeithing	d																					
Glasgow Central ■	d								13 00				16 00									
Motherwell	d								13 16													
Haymarket	d								13 55													
Edinburgh ■	d	13 07				14 52			14 09								15 08				16 52	
Haymarket	d					14 58															16 57	
Lockerbie	d																					
Carlisle ■	d					16 08							17 11								18 08	
Penrith North Lakes	d					16 21																
Oxenholme Lake District	d												17 45								18 42	
Lancaster ■	d					16 57															18 59	
Preston ■	d					17 17							18 17								19 17	
Wigan North Western	d					17 28							18 28								19 31	
Warrington Bank Quay	d					17 39							18 39								19 41	
M'chester Piccadilly ■	d		17 05		17 27					18 05		18 27						19 05		19 27		
Stockport	d		17 13		17 35					18 13		18 36						19 13		19 36		
Wilmslow	d				17 45																	
Crewe ■	d				18 07	18 01							19 01								20 03	
Macclesfield	d		17 26							18 26								19 26		19 49		
Congleton	d											18 55										
Stoke-on-Trent	d		17 44							18 44		19 07						19 44		20 07		
Stafford	d		18 01		18 25					19 01		19 25						20 01		20 25		
Wolverhampton ■	d		18 17		18 41	18 45				19 17		19 41	19 45					20 17		20 44	20 47	
Dunbar	d	13 32															15 29					
Berwick-upon-Tweed	d								14 50													
Alnmouth for Alnwick	d	14 13																					
Morpeth	d																					
Newcastle ■	d	14 42					15 03		15 41					16 35			16 41					17 32
Chester-le-Street	d																					17 41
Durham	d	14 54					15 16		15 54					16 48			16 54					17 48
Darlington ■	d	15 12					15 33		16 12					17 06			17 12					18 06
York ■	d	15 44					16 05		16 44					17 35			17 45					18 36
Leeds ■	d	16 11					16 40		17 10								18 11					
Wakefield Westgate ■	d	16 23					16 52		17 22								18 23					
Doncaster ■	d													17 58								18 59
Sheffield ■	d	16 55					17 24		17 55					18 24			18 58					19 24
Chesterfield	d	17 07					17 36		18 07					18 36			19 12					19 36
Nottingham ■	d			17 41				18 07			18 41				19 07	19 07			19 36			
Derby ■	d																					
Burton-on-Trent	d	18 01		18 27			18 37	18 49	19 01		19 21			19 41	19 49	19 49	20 06		20 21			20 37
Tamworth	d			18 38			18 49	19 02			19 33				20 03	20 03			20 33			20 47
Birmingham New Street ■	a	18 27	18 33	18 57	18 58	19 05	19 08	19 24	19 27	19 33	19 55	19 58	20 05	20 07	20 25	20 25	20 28	20 33	20 55	21 00	21 05	21 07
Birmingham New Street ■	d	18 33	18 42		19 04	19 10	19 12	19 30	19 33	19 42		20 04	20 10	20 12	20 30	20 30	20 34	20 42		21 04	21 10	21 12
Cheltenham Spa ■	a		19 24				19 50	20 11		20 24				20 52	21 10	21 10		21 25				21 51
Gloucester ■	a							20 20							21 19	21 19						22 02
Bristol Parkway ■	a		19 56				20 30			20 55				21 25				22 01				22 33
Bristol Temple Meads ■	a		20 09				20 42			21 05				21 36				22 14				22 43
Newport (South Wales)	a		20 47					21 11							22 12	22 13						
Cardiff Central ■	a		21 03					21 28							22 35	22 30						
Weston-super-Mare	a																					
Taunton	a						21 19			21 43				22 15								
Tiverton Parkway	a						21 31			21 55				22 27								
Exeter St Davids ■	a						21 45			22 09				22 41								
Dawlish	a																					
Teignmouth	a																					
Newton Abbot	a						22 05			22 28				23 01								
Torquay	a																					
Paignton	a																					
Totnes	a						22 17			22 40				23 18								
Plymouth	a						22 45			23 07				23 44								
Liskeard ■	a																					
Bodmin Parkway	a																					
Lostwithiel	a																					
Par	a																					
St Austell	a																					
Truro	a																					
Redruth	a																					
Camborne	a																					
Hayle	a																					
St Erth	a																					
Penzance	a																					
Birmingham International ✈	d				19 14	19 20						20 14	20 20							21 14	21 20	
Coventry	d				19 25	19a30						20 25	20a30							21 25	21a30	
Leamington Spa ■	d	19 01			19 38				20 02			20 38					21 00			21 38		
Banbury	a	19 17			19 54				20 19			20 55					21 17			21 54		
Oxford	a	19 41			20 13				20 40			21 14					21 40			22 14		
Reading ■	a	20 09			20 41				21 07			21 42					22 16			22 42		
Guildford	a																					
Basingstoke	a				21 09							22 09					22 39			23 06		
Winchester	a				21 24							22 24					22 56			23 24		
Southampton Airport Pkway ✈	a				21 33							22 33					23 12			23 36		
Southampton Central	a				21 40							22 42					23 20			23 43		
Brockenhurst ■	a				21 56							22 56										
Bournemouth	a				22 15							23 19										

A 🛒 to Bristol Temple Meads B 🛒 to Reading C 🛒 to Birmingham New Street

Table T051-F

Mondays to Fridays
23 July to 31 August

Scotland, The North East, North West England - The South West and South Coast

		XC	XC	VT	XC	XC	XC	XC	XC FO	XC FX	VT	XC	XC	XC	XC	XC
		◇1	◇1	◇1	1	◇1	◇1	◇1	◇1 A	◇1 A	◇1	◇1	◇1	1	◇1	◇1 B
		⊼		⊠				⊼	⊼	⊼	⊠	⊼				⊼
Aberdeen	d															
Stonehaven	d															
Montrose	d															
Arbroath	d															
Dundee	d															
Leuchars	d															
Cupar	d															
Lacybank	d															
Markinch	d															
Kirkcaldy	d															
Inverkeithing	d															
Glasgow Central	d	15 00		17 40												17 00
Motherwell	d	15 16														17 16
Haymarket	d	15 56														17 55
Edinburgh	d	16 06							17 07	17 07	18 52					18 08
Haymarket	d										18 56					
Lockerbie	d			18 33												
Carlisle	d			18 57							20 07					
Penrith North Lakes	d															
Oxenholme Lake District	d			19 33							20 42					
Lancaster	d			19 47							20 56					
Preston	d			20 08							21 17					
Wigan North Western	d			20 19							21 28					
Warrington Bank Quay	d			20 32							21 39					
M'chester Piccadilly	d		20 05			20 27							21 27		22 07	
Stockport	d		20 13			20 36							21 36		22 16	
Wilmslow	d															
Crewe	d			20 53							22 01					
Macclesfield	d		20 26			20 49							21 49		22 29	
Congleton	d															
Stoke-on-Trent	d		20 44			21 07							22 08		22 47	
Stafford	d		21 01	21 14		21 25							22 26		23 04	
Wolverhampton	d		21 17	21 32		21 41					22 33		22 42		23 18	
Dunbar	d								17 29	17 29						18 30
Berwick-upon-Tweed	d								17 52	17 52						18 54
Alnmouth for Alnwick	d	17 05														19 14
Morpeth	d	17 19							18 24	18 24						
Newcastle	d	17 41						18 35	18 43	18 43		19 35				19 42
Chester-le-Street	d															
Durham	d	17 54						18 48	18 55	18 55		19 50				19 55
Darlington	d	18 12						19 07	19 13	19 13		20 07				20 13
York	d	18 45						19 36	19 45	19 45		20 36				20 45
Leeds	d	19 11							20 11	20 11						21 11
Wakefield Westgate	d	19 23							20 23	20 23						21 23
Doncaster	d							19 59				21 01				
Sheffield	d	19 58						20 24	20 58	20 58		21 27				22 01
Chesterfield	d	20 10						20 36	21 10	21 10		21 39				22 25
Nottingham	d				20 40									21 39		
Derby	d															
Burton-on-Trent	d	21 05			21 24			21 40	22 09	22 10		22 31		22 23		23 24
Tamworth	d				21 34			21 50						22 35		23 35
Birmingham New Street	a	21 29	21 33	21 54	21 57	22 00		22 09	22 36	22 48	22 52	22 55	22 59	23 01	23 35	23 50
Birmingham New Street	d						22 04	22 12								
Cheltenham Spa	a							22 51								
Gloucester	a															
Bristol Parkway	a							23 21								
Bristol Temple Meads	a							23 41								
Newport (South Wales)	a															
Cardiff Central	a															
Weston-super-Mare	a															
Taunton	a															
Tiverton Parkway	a															
Exeter St Davids	a															
Dawlish	a															
Teignmouth	a															
Newton Abbot	a															
Torquay	a															
Paignton	a															
Totnes	a															
Plymouth	a															
Liskeard	a															
Bodmin Parkway	a															
Lostwithiel	a															
Par	a															
St Austell	a															
Truro	a															
Redruth	a															
Camborne	a															
Hayle	a															
St Erth	a															
Penzance	a															
Birmingham International	d						22 14									
Coventry	d						22 25									
Leamington Spa	d						22 38									
Banbury	a						22 54									
Oxford	a						23 14									
Reading	a						23 49									
Guildford	a															
Basingstoke	a															
Winchester	a															
Southampton Airport Pkway	a															
Southampton Central	a															
Brockenhurst	a															
Bournemouth	a															

A ⊼ to Leeds
B ⊼ from Edinburgh to Leeds

Table T051-F

Mondays to Fridays
3 September to 5 October

Scotland, The North East, North West England - The South West and South Coast

		XC	XC	XC	XC	XC	XC	XC	XC	XC	XC	XC	XC	VT	VT	XC	XC	XC	XC	XC	XC	VT	XC
		◇1	◇1	◇1	◇1 A	◇1	◇1	◇1	◇1	◇1	◇1 B	◇1	◇1 B	◇1	◇1	◇1	◇1	◇1	◇1	1	■ 1	◇1	◇1
				⊼	⊼	⊼		⊼	⊼	⊼	⊼	⊼	⊼	⊠	⊠	⊼		⊼	⊼		⊼	⊠	⊼
Aberdeen	d																						
Stonehaven	d																						
Montrose	d																						
Arbroath	d																						
Dundee	d																						
Leuchars	d																						
Cupar	d																						
Ladybank	d																						
Markinch	d																						
Kirkcaldy	d																						
Inverkeithing	d																						
Glasgow Central	d																						
Motherwell	d																						
Haymarket	d																						
Edinburgh	d																						
Haymarket	d																						
Lockerbie	d																						
Carlisle	d																						
Penrith North Lakes	d																						
Oxenholme Lake District	d																						
Lancaster	d																					06 58	
Preston	d													06 17								07 17	
Wigan North Western	d													06 28								07 28	
Warrington Bank Quay	d													06 39								07 39	
M'chester Piccadilly	d							05 11				06 00			06 27				07 05		07 27		
Stockport	d											06 08			06 35				07 13		07 36		
Wilmslow	d											06 16											
Crewe	d							05 47				06 39		07 01								08 01	
Macclesfield	d														06 48				07 26		07 49		
Congleton	d																						
Stoke-on-Trent	d							06 07							07 06				07 44		08 07		
Stafford	d							06 25				07 01			07 24				08 01		08 25		
Wolverhampton	d							06 41				07 16		07 37	07 45				08 17		08 41	08 45	
Dunbar	d																						
Berwick-upon-Tweed	d																						
Alnmouth for Alnwick	d																						
Morpeth	d																						
Newcastle	d																						
Chester-le-Street	d																						
Durham	d																						
Darlington	d																						
York	d																						
Leeds	d															05 48							06 16
Wakefield Westgate	d															06 01							06 28
Doncaster	d																						06 46
Sheffield	d										05 40					06 30							07 18
Chesterfield	d										05 52					06 44							07 32
Nottingham	d									05 57			06 37				07 04			07 37			
Derby	d						06 10			06 36	06 44		07 07			07 27	07 36	07 50		08 06			08 28
Burton-on-Trent	d						06 20			06 48	06 58		07 17			07 38	07 50	08 00		08 18			08 38
Tamworth	d						06 31		←	07 01	07 09		07 30			07 50	08 03	08 11		08 30			08 50
Birmingham New Street	a						06 52	06 57	06 52	07 25	07 27	07 33	07 53	07 56	08 07	08 08	08 25	08 27	08 33	08 55	08 58	09 05	09 10
Birmingham New Street	d	05 00	05 37	06 04	06 33	06 42	07 12	07 04	07 12	07 30	07 33	07 42	08 04		08 10	08 12	08 30	08 33	08 42		09 04	09 10	09 17
Cheltenham Spa	a	06 01	06 36			07 21	→		07 51	08 10		08 24				08 50	09 10		09 24				09 58
Gloucester	a	06 12	06 53							08 20							09 20						
Bristol Parkway	a					07 54			08 26			08 54				09 25			09 55				10 30
Bristol Temple Meads	a					08 06			08 40			09 11				09 39			10 08				10 43
Newport (South Wales)	a	07 06	07 52							09 13							10 11						
Cardiff Central	a	07 22	08 08							09 29							10 27						
Weston-super-Mare	a																						
Taunton	a					08 42			09 14							10 15							11 16
Tiverton Parkway	a					08 54			09 26							10 28							11 29
Exeter St Davids	a					09 07			09 40							10 42							11 43
Dawlish	a																						
Teignmouth	a																						
Newton Abbot	a					09 27			09 59							11 04							12 04
Torquay	a					09 39																	
Paignton	a					09 47																	
Totnes	a								10 14							11 17							12 18
Plymouth	a								10 42							11 44							12 47
Liskeard	a																						
Bodmin Parkway	a																						
Lostwithiel	a																						
Par	a																						
St Austell	a																						
Truro	a																						
Redruth	a																						
Camborne	a																						
Hayle	a																						
St Erth	a																						
Penzance	a																						
Birmingham International	d			06 14				07 14					08 14		08 21						09 14	09 20	
Coventry	d			06 25				07 25					08 25		08a31						09 25	09a30	
Leamington Spa	d			06 37	07 00			07 38			08 00		08 38					09 00			09 39		
Banbury	a			06 53	07 18			07 54			08 16		08 55					09 18			09 55		
Oxford	a			07 14	07 41			08 14			08 39		09 15					09 41			10 14		
Reading	a			07 40	08 09			08 40			09 08		09 42					10 10			10 42		
Guildford	a																						
Basingstoke	a			08 08	08 41			09 10					10 09					10 39			11 09		
Winchester	a			08 24	08 56			09 25					10 24					10 54			11 24		
Southampton Airport Pkway	a			08 33	09 08			09 34					10 33					11 07			11 33		
Southampton Central	a			08 44	09 18			09 43					10 43					11 17			11 43		
Brockenhurst	a			08 59				09 58					10 58								11 58		
Bournemouth	a			09 15				10 13					11 13								12 13		

A ⊼ from Reading
B ⊼ from Birmingham New Street

Table T051-F

Mondays to Fridays
3 September to 5 October

Scotland, The North East, North West England - The South West and South Coast

		XC	XC	XC	XC	XC	VT	XC	XC	XC	XC	XC	XC	VT	XC	XC	XC	XC	XC	XC	VT	XC	XC
		◇■ A ⊼	■ ◇■ B ⊼	◇■ ⊼	■	◇■ ⊼	◇■ ⊠	◇■ ⊼	◇■ ⊼	◇■ ⊼	◇■ ⊼	■	◇■ ⊼	◇■ ⊠	◇■ ⊼	◇■ ⊼	◇■ ⊼	◇■ ⊼	■	◇■ ⊼	◇■ ⊠	◇■ ⊼	◇■ ⊼
Aberdeen	d																						
Stonehaven	d																						
Montrose	d																						
Arbroath	d																						
Dundee	d																						
Leuchars ■	d																						
Cupar	d																						
Ladybank	d																						
Markinch	d																						
Kirkcaldy	d																						
Inverkeithing	d																						
Glasgow Central ■	d						05 49														08 00		
Motherwell	d						06 04																
Haymarket	d																						
Edinburgh ■	d													06 52			06 06					07 00	
Haymarket	d													06 57									
Lockerbie	d																						
Carlisle ■	d						07 03							08 08							09 11		
Penrith North Lakes	d						07 18							08 22									
Oxenholme Lake District	d						07 42																
Lancaster ■	d						07 57							08 57							09 56		
Preston ■	d						08 17							09 17							10 17		
Wigan North Western	d						08 28							09 28							10 28		
Warrington Bank Quay	d						08 39							09 39							10 39		
M'chester Piccadilly ■	d			08 05		08 27					09 05		09 27					10 05		10 27			
Stockport	d			08 13		08 36					09 13		09 36					10 13		10 36			
Wilmslow	d																						
Crewe ■	d						09 01							10 01							11 01		
Macclesfield	d			08 26		08 49					09 26		09 49					10 26		10 49			
Congleton	d																						
Stoke-on-Trent	d			08 44		09 07					09 44		10 07					10 44		11 07			
Stafford	d			09 01		09 25					10 01		10 25					11 01		11 25			
Wolverhampton ■	d			09 17		09 42	09 45				10 17		10 41	10 45				11 17		11 41	11 45		
Dunbar	d																						
Berwick-upon-Tweed	d																06 50					07 43	
Alnmouth for Alnwick	d																07 11					08 04	
Morpeth	d																					08 19	
Newcastle ■	d							06 25		06 45					07 25		07 40					08 36	
Chester-le-Street	d																						
Durham	d							06 38		06 57					07 38		07 54					08 49	
Darlington ■	d							06 56		07 15					07 56		08 12					09 06	
York ■	d		06 45					07 26		07 43					08 27		08 44					09 36	
Leeds ■	d		07 10							08 11							09 11						
Wakefield Westgate ■	d		07 23							08 23							09 23						
Doncaster ■	d							07 53							08 53							10 00	
Sheffield ■	d		07 53					08 18		08 54					09 24		09 55					10 24	
Chesterfield	d		08 06					08 33		09 08					09 36		10 07					10 40	
Nottingham ■	d	08 09			08 41				09 07			09 41				10 04			10 41				11 04
Derby ■	d	08 37	08 53		09 11			09 27	09 39	09 51		10 10			10 28	10 37	10 53		11 10			11 29	11 37
Burton-on-Trent	d	08 49			09 22			09 38	09 52			10 21				10 49			11 21				11 49
Tamworth	d	09 02			09 34				10 03			10 33			10 50	11 02			11 33				12 02
Birmingham New Street ■	a	09 24	09 27	09 33	09 55	09 58	10 05	10 08	10 24	10 27	10 33	10 55	10 58	11 05	11 08	11 24	11 27	11 33	11 55	11 58	12 05	12 07	12 24
Birmingham New Street ■	d	09 30	09 33	09 42		10 04	10 10	10 17	10 30	10 33	10 42		11 04	11 10	11 17	11 30	11 33	11 42		12 04	12 10	12 17	12 30
Cheltenham Spa ■	a	10 10		10 24				10 59	11 10		11 24				11 57	12 10		12 24				13 00	13 10
Gloucester ■	a	10 20							11 20							12 20							13 20
Bristol Parkway ■	a			10 56				11 31			11 55				12 28			12 56				13 30	
Bristol Temple Meads ■	a			11 10				11 42			12 05				12 42			13 10				13 42	
Newport (South Wales)	a	11 11							12 10							13 09							14 11
Cardiff Central ■	a	11 28							12 26							13 26							14 26
Weston-super-Mare	a			11 32																			
Taunton	a			11 58				12 14							13 16							14 16	
Tiverton Parkway	a			12 10				12 26							13 28							14 28	
Exeter St Davids ■	a			12 24				12 40							13 43							14 43	
Dawlish	a			12 36																			
Teignmouth	a			12 41																			
Newton Abbot	a			12 48				12 59							14 03							15 03	
Torquay	a			13 00																			
Paignton	a			13 08																			
Totnes	a							13 11							14 16							15 16	
Plymouth	a							13 38							14 43							15 43	
Liskeard ■	a																						
Bodmin Parkway	a																						
Lostwithiel	a																						
Par	a																						
St Austell	a																						
Truro	a																						
Redruth	a																						
Camborne	a																						
Hayle	a																						
St Erth	a																						
Penzance	a																						
Birmingham International ✈	d					10 14	10 20						11 14	11 20						12 14	12 20		
Coventry	d					10 25	10a30						11 25	11a30						12 25	12a30		
Leamington Spa ■	d		10 00			10 38				11 00			11 38				12 01			12 38			
Banbury	a		10 17			10 54				11 17			11 54				12 18			12 54			
Oxford	a		10 40			11 13				11 41			12 14				12 40			13 14			
Reading ■	a		11 09			11 40				12 08			12 42				13 08			13 40			
Guildford	a																						
Basingstoke	a					12 09				12 39			13 09							14 09			
Winchester	a					12 24				12 54			13 24							14 25			
Southampton Airport Pkway ✈	a					12 33				13 08			13 33							14 34			
Southampton Central	a					12 41				13 17			13 41							14 41			
Brockenhurst ■	a					12 57							13 56							14 56			
Bournemouth	a					13 12							14 11							15 11			

A ⊼ from Birmingham New Street

B ◇ from Birmingham New Street ■ to Birmingham New Street

Table T051-F

Mondays to Fridays
3 September to 5 October

Scotland, The North East, North West England - The South West and South Coast

		XC	XC	XC	XC	VT	XC	XC	XC	XC	XC	XC	VT	XC	XC	XC	XC	XC	XC	VT	XC	XC
		◇■ ⊼	◇■ ⊼	■	◇■ ⊼	◇■ ⊠	◇■ ⊼	◇■ ⊼	◇■ ⊼	◇■ ⊼	■	◇■ ⊼	◇■ ⊠	◇■ ⊼	◇■ ⊼	◇■ ⊼	◇■ ⊼	■ ⊼	◇■ ⊼	◇■ ⊡	◇■ A ⊼	◇■ ⊼
Aberdeen	d																					
Stonehaven	d																					
Montrose	d																					
Arbroath	d																					
Dundee	d								06 32													
Leuchars ■	d								06 46													
Cupar	d								06 54													
Ladybank	d								07 03													
Markinch	d								07 11													
Kirkcaldy	d								07 21													
Inverkeithing	d								07 40													
Glasgow Central ■	d	06 01											10 00			07 48						
Motherwell	d	06 17														08 08						
Haymarket	d	06 57							08 00							08 51						
Edinburgh ■	d	07 10				08 51			08 09							09 08				10 52		
Haymarket	d					08 57														10 57		
Lockerbie	d																					
Carlisle ■	d					10 08							11 12							12 08		
Penrith North Lakes	d												11 27									
Oxenholme Lake District	d					10 42														12 43		
Lancaster ■	d					10 57														12 57		
Preston ■	d					11 17							12 18							13 17		
Wigan North Western	d					11 28							12 29							13 28		
Warrington Bank Quay	d					11 39							12 40							13 39		
M'chester Piccadilly ■	d		11 05		11 27					12 05		12 27					13 05		13 27			
Stockport	d		11 13		11 36					12 13		12 36					13 13		13 36			
Wilmslow	d																					
Crewe ■	d					12 01							13 01							14 01		
Macclesfield	d		11 26		11 49					12 26		12 49					13 26		13 49			
Congleton	d																					
Stoke-on-Trent	d		11 44		12 07					12 44		13 07					13 44		14 07			
Stafford	d		12 01		12 25					13 01		13 26					14 01		14 25			
Wolverhampton ■	d		12 17		12 41	12 45				13 17		13 41	13 45				14 17		14 41	14 45		
Dunbar	d	07 32														09 29						
Berwick-upon-Tweed	d								08 52							09 53						
Alnmouth for Alnwick	d																					
Morpeth	d								09 25													
Newcastle ■	d	08 43					09 35		09 42					10 35		10 42					11 35	
Chester-le-Street	d																					
Durham	d	08 55					09 49		09 55					10 48		10 54					11 49	
Darlington ■	d	09 12					10 06		10 13					11 06		11 12					12 07	
York ■	d	09 44					10 35		10 44					11 35		11 44					12 35	
Leeds ■	d	10 11							11 11							12 11						
Wakefield Westgate ■	d	10 23							11 23							12 23						
Doncaster ■	d						10 59							11 59							12 59	
Sheffield ■	d	10 55					11 24		11 55					12 24		12 55					13 24	
Chesterfield	d	11 07					11 38		12 07					12 36		13 07					13 36	
Nottingham ■	d			11 41				12 04			12 41				13 04			13 41				14 04
Derby ■	d	11 53		12 10			12 29	12 37	12 53		13 10			13 28	13 36	13 52		14 10			14 28	14 37
Burton-on-Trent	d			12 21				12 49			13 24			13 38	13 49			14 21				14 50
Tamworth	d			12 33			12 49	13 02			13 35				14 02			14 33			14 47	15 02
Birmingham New Street ■	a	12 27	12 33	12 55	12 58	13 05	13 08	13 24	13 27	13 33	13 55	13 58	14 05	14 08	14 24	14 27	14 34	14 55	14 58	15 05	15 08	15 25
Birmingham New Street ■	d	12 33	12 42		13 04	13 10	13 17	13 30	13 33	13 42		14 04	14 10	14 17	14 30	14 33	14 42		15 04	15 10	15 17	15 30
Cheltenham Spa ■	a		13 24				14 00	14 10		14 24				14 58	15 10		15 24				15 58	16 10
Gloucester ■	a							14 22							15 20							16 22
Bristol Parkway ■	a		13 56				14 28			14 56				15 29			15 56				16 30	
Bristol Temple Meads ■	a		14 08				14 42			15 10				15 41			16 11				16 43	
Newport (South Wales)	a							15 12							16 12							17 11
Cardiff Central ■	a							15 30							16 30							17 30
Weston-super-Mare	a																					
Taunton	a						15 16			15 44				16 14							17 16	
Tiverton Parkway	a						15 28			15 56				16 26							17 28	
Exeter St Davids ■	a						15 43			16 12				16 40							17 42	
Dawlish	a																					
Teignmouth	a																					
Newton Abbot	a						16 03							17 04							18 11	
Torquay	a																					
Paignton	a																					
Totnes	a						16 16							17 16							18 23	
Plymouth	a						16 45							17 42							18 49	
Liskeard ■	a																				19 23	
Bodmin Parkway	a																				19 35	
Lostwithiel	a																					
Par	a																				19 45	
St Austell	a																				19 51	
Truro	a																				20 07	
Redruth	a																				20 28	
Camborne	a																				20 34	
Hayle	a																					
St Erth	a																				20 44	
Penzance	a																				20 54	
Birmingham International ✈	d				13 14	13 20						14 14	14 20						15 14	15 20		
Coventry	d				13 25	13a30						14 25	14a29						15 25	15a30		
Leamington Spa ■	d	13 00			13 38				14 00			14 38				15 00			15 38			
Banbury	a	13 18			13 54				14 17			14 54				15 17			15 54			
Oxford	a	13 41			14 13				14 40			15 14				15 40			16 14			
Reading ■	a	14 09			14 40				15 08			15 41				16 11			16 40			
Guildford	a																					
Basingstoke	a	14 40			15 09							16 09				16 40			17 09			
Winchester	a	14 56			15 24							16 24				16 57			17 24			
Southampton Airport Pkway ✈	a	15 09			15 33							16 33				17 08			17 33			
Southampton Central	a	15 17			15 41							16 41				17 17			17 41			
Brockenhurst ■	a				15 57							16 57							17 57			
Bournemouth	a				16 12							17 12							18 15			

A ⊼ to Plymouth

Table T051-F

Mondays to Fridays
3 September to 5 October

Scotland, The North East, North West England - The South West and South Coast

		XC	XC	XC	XC	XC	VT	XC	XC	XC	XC	XC	XC	VT	XC	XC	XC	XC	XC	XC	VT	XC	XC
		◇1	◇1	1	◇1	◇1	◇1	◇1	◇1	◇1	◇1	1	◇1	◇1	◇1	◇1	◇1	◇1	1	◇1	◇1	◇1	◇1
			A					B		C					B								
		🛒	🛒		🛒	🛒	⊡	🛒	🛒	🛒	🛒	🛒	🛒	⊡	🛒		🛒	🛒	🛒	🛒	⊡	🛒	
Aberdeen	d									08 20													
Stonehaven	d									08 38													
Montrose	d									08 59													
Arbroath	d									09 15													
Dundee	d									09 35													
Leuchars	d									09 48													
Cupar	d									09 55													
Ladybank	d									10 02													
Markinch	d									10 09													
Kirkcaldy	d									10 18													
Inverkeithing	d									10 33													
Glasgow Central	d	09 00					12 00										11 00				14 00		
Motherwell	d	09 15															11 15						
Haymarket	d	09 54								10 51							11 54						
Edinburgh	d	10 10								11 06				12 52			12 08						
Haymarket	d													12 57									
Lockerbie	d																						
Carlisle	d						13 11							14 08							15 11		
Penrith North Lakes	d													14 22									
Oxenholme Lake District	d																				15 45		
Lancaster	d						13 57							14 57									
Preston	d						14 17							15 17							16 17		
Wigan North Western	d						14 29							15 28							16 28		
Warrington Bank Quay	d						14 40							15 39							16 39		
M'chester Piccadilly	d		14 05		14 27						15 05		15 27					16 05		16 27			
Stockport	d		14 13		14 36						15 13		15 36					16 13		16 36			
Wilmslow	d																						
Crewe	d						15 01							16 01							17 01		
Macclesfield	d		14 26		14 49						15 26		15 49					16 26		16 49			
Congleton	d																						
Stoke-on-Trent	d		14 44		15 07						15 44		16 07					16 44		17 07			
Stafford	d		15 01		15 25						16 01		16 25					17 01		17 25			
Wolverhampton	d		15 17		15 41		15 45				16 17		16 41	16 45				17 17		17 41	17 45		
Dunbar	d									11 28													
Berwick-upon-Tweed	d	10 51								11 51							12 50						
Alnmouth for Alnwick	d									12 12													
Morpeth	d	11 22																					
Newcastle	d	11 42				12 34				12 41					13 35		13 42					14 36	
Chester-le-Street	d																						
Durham	d	11 54				12 47				12 54					13 49		13 54					14 48	
Darlington	d	12 12				13 05				13 12					14 07		14 12					15 06	
York	d	12 44				13 35				13 44					14 35		14 44					15 35	
Leeds	d	13 11								14 11							15 11						
Wakefield Westgate	d	13 23								14 23							15 23						
Doncaster	d					13 59									14 59							15 59	
Sheffield	d	13 55				14 24				14 55					15 24		15 55					16 24	
Chesterfield	d	14 07				14 36				15 07					15 36		16 07					16 36	
Nottingham	d			14 41					15 04			15 41				16 04			16 41				17 04
Derby	d	14 53		15 10		15 27			15 37	15 53		16 10			16 28	16 37	16 53		17 10			17 29	17 37
Burton-on-Trent	d			15 24		15 38			15 49			16 21				16 49			17 24			17 39	17 49
Tamworth	d			15 35				←	16 02			16 33			16 47	17 02			17 35				18 02
Birmingham New Street	a	15 27	15 33	15 54	15 58	16 03	16 05	16 03	16 25	16 28	16 33	16 55	16 58	17 05	17 08	17 25	17 28	17 33	17 55	17 58	18 05	18 05	18 23
Birmingham New Street	d	15 33	15 42		16 04	16 12	16 10	16 12	16 30	16 33	16 42		17 04	17 10	17 12	17 30	17 33	17 42		18 04	18 10	18 12	18 30
Cheltenham Spa	a		16 24			→		16 49	17 14		17 24				17 51	18 16		18 24				18 51	19 13
Gloucester	a								17 24							18 28						19 01	19 23
Bristol Parkway	a		16 56					17 25			17 56				18 28			18 54				19 31	
Bristol Temple Meads	a		17 10					17 40			18 07				18 42			19 06				19 43	
Newport (South Wales)	a								18 10							19 14							20 11
Cardiff Central	a								18 27							19 33							20 28
Weston-super-Mare	a																						
Taunton	a		17 44					18 15							19 15							20 16	
Tiverton Parkway	a		17 56					18 27							19 27							20 28	
Exeter St Davids	a		18 11					18 41							19 42							20 41	
Dawlish	a		18 23																				
Teignmouth	a		18 28																				
Newton Abbot	a		18 35					19 05							20 02							21 01	
Torquay	a		18 47																				
Paignton	a		18 55																				
Totnes	a							19 17							20 14							21 13	
Plymouth	a							19 43							20 40							21 39	
Liskeard	a							20 11							21 12								
Bodmin Parkway	a							20 23							21 24								
Lostwithiel	a														21 30								
Par	a							20 33							21 36								
St Austell	a							20 40							21 43								
Truro	a							21 00							22 01								
Redruth	a							21 17							22 13								
Camborne	a							21 24							22 19								
Hayle	a														22 27								
St Erth	a							21 34							22 31								
Penzance	a							21 43							22 41								
Birmingham International	d				16 14		16 20						17 14	17 20						18 14	18 20		
Coventry	d				16 25		16a30						17 25	17a30						18 25	18a30		
Leamington Spa	d	16 01			16 38					17 00			17 38				18 01			18 38			
Banbury	a	16 17			16 54					17 17			17 54				18 18			18 55			
Oxford	a	16 40			17 13					17 40			18 14				18 40			19 13			
Reading	a	17 08			17 40					18 09			18 44				19 10			19 41			
Guildford	a									18 59													
Basingstoke	a				18 09								19 09							20 09			
Winchester	a				18 25								19 24							20 25			
Southampton Airport Pkway	a				18 33								19 33							20 34			
Southampton Central	a				18 43								19 42							20 42			
Brockenhurst	a				18 58								19 56							20 58			
Bournemouth	a				19 12								20 11							21 15			

A 🛒 to Bristol Temple Meads B 🛒 to Plymouth C 🛒 to Reading

Table T051-F

Mondays to Fridays
3 September to 5 October

Scotland, The North East, North West England - The South West and South Coast

		XC	XC	XC	XC	VT	XC	XC	XC	XC	XC	XC	VT	XC	XC FX	XC FO	XC	XC	XC	XC	VT	XC
		◇1	◇1	1	◇1	1	◇1	◇1	◇1	◇1	1	◇1	◇1	◇1	◇1	◇1	◇1	◇1	1	◇1	1	◇1
			A		B		A			A		C		C			C	C		C		C
		🛒	🛒	🛒	🛒	⊡	🛒		🛒	🛒	🛒	🛒	⊠	🛒			🛒	🛒	🛒	🛒	⊠	🛒
Aberdeen	d																					
Stonehaven	d																					
Montrose	d																					
Arbroath	d																					
Dundee	d																					
Leuchars	d																					
Cupar	d																					
Ladybank	d																					
Markinch	d																					
Kirkcaldy	d																					
Inverkeithing	d																					
Glasgow Central	d								13 00				16 00									
Motherwell	d								13 16													
Haymarket	d								13 55													
Edinburgh	d	13 07				14 52			14 09								15 08				16 52	
Haymarket	d					14 58															16 57	
Lockerbie	d																					
Carlisle	d					16 08							17 11								18 08	
Penrith North Lakes	d					16 21																
Oxenholme Lake District	d												17 45								18 42	
Lancaster	d					16 57															18 59	
Preston	d					17 17							18 17								19 17	
Wigan North Western	d					17 28							18 28								19 31	
Warrington Bank Quay	d					17 39							18 39								19 41	
M'chester Piccadilly	d		17 05		17 27					18 05		18 27						19 05		19 27		
Stockport	d		17 13		17 35					18 13		18 36						19 13		19 36		
Wilmslow	d				17 45																	
Crewe	d				18 07	18 01							19 01								20 03	
Macclesfield	d		17 26							18 26								19 26		19 49		
Congleton	d											18 55										
Stoke-on-Trent	d		17 44							18 44		19 07						19 44		20 07		
Stafford	d		18 01		18 25					19 01		19 25						20 01		20 25		
Wolverhampton	d		18 17		18 41	18 45				19 17		19 41	19 45					20 17		20 44	20 47	
Dunbar	d	13 32															15 29					
Berwick-upon-Tweed	d								14 50													
Alnmouth for Alnwick	d	14 13																				
Morpeth	d																					
Newcastle	d	14 42					15 03		15 41					16 35			16 41					17 32
Chester-le-Street	d																					17 41
Durham	d	14 54					15 16		15 54					16 48			16 54					17 48
Darlington	d	15 12					15 33		16 12					17 06			17 12					18 06
York	d	15 44					16 05		16 44					17 35			17 45					18 36
Leeds	d	16 11					16 40		17 10								18 11					
Wakefield Westgate	d	16 23					16 52		17 22								18 23					
Doncaster	d													17 58								18 59
Sheffield	d	16 55					17 24		17 55					18 24			18 58					19 24
Chesterfield	d	17 07					17 36		18 07					18 36			19 12					19 36
Nottingham	d			17 41				18 04			18 41				19 04	19 04			19 36			
Derby	d	17 52		18 13			18 29	18 37	18 53		19 10			19 29	19 37	19 37	19 54		20 10			20 29
Burton-on-Trent	d			18 27				18 49			19 21			19 41	19 49	19 49			20 21			
Tamworth	d			18 38			18 49	19 02			19 33				20 03	20 03			20 33			20 47
Birmingham New Street	a	18 27	18 33	18 57	18 58	19 05	19 08	19 24	19 27	19 33	19 55	19 58	20 05	20 07	20 25	20 25	20 28	20 33	20 55	21 00	21 05	21 07
Birmingham New Street	d	18 33	18 42		19 04	19 10	19 12	19 30	19 33	19 42		20 04	20 10	20 12	20 30	20 30	20 34	20 42		21 04	21 10	21 12
Cheltenham Spa	a		19 24				19 50	20 11		20 24				20 52	21 10	21 10		21 25				21 51
Gloucester	a							20 20							21 19	21 19						22 02
Bristol Parkway	a		19 56				20 30			20 55				21 25				22 01				22 33
Bristol Temple Meads	a		20 09				20 42			21 05				21 36				22 14				22 43
Newport (South Wales)	a		20 47					21 11							22 12	22 13						
Cardiff Central	a		21 03					21 28							22 35	22 30						
Weston-super-Mare	a																					
Taunton	a						21 19			21 43				22 15								
Tiverton Parkway	a						21 31			21 55				22 27								
Exeter St Davids	a						21 45			22 09				22 41								
Dawlish	a																					
Teignmouth	a																					
Newton Abbot	a						22 05			22 28				23 01								
Torquay	a																					
Paignton	a																					
Totnes	a						22 17			22 40				23 18								
Plymouth	a						22 45			23 07				23 44								
Liskeard	a																					
Bodmin Parkway	a																					
Lostwithiel	a																					
Par	a																					
St Austell	a																					
Truro	a																					
Redruth	a																					
Camborne	a																					
Hayle	a																					
St Erth	a																					
Penzance	a																					
Birmingham International	d				19 14	19 20						20 14	20 20							21 14	21 20	
Coventry	d				19 25	19a30						20 25	20a30							21 25	21a30	
Leamington Spa	d	19 01			19 38				20 02			20 38					21 00			21 38		
Banbury	a	19 17			19 54				20 19			20 55					21 17			21 54		
Oxford	a	19 41			20 13				20 40			21 14					21 40			22 14		
Reading	a	20 09			20 41				21 07			21 42					22 16			22 42		
Guildford	a																					
Basingstoke	a				21 09							22 09					22 39			23 06		
Winchester	a				21 24							22 24					22 56			23 24		
Southampton Airport Pkway	a				21 33							22 33					23 12			23 36		
Southampton Central	a				21 40							22 42					23 20			23 43		
Brockenhurst	a				21 56							22 56										
Bournemouth	a				22 15							23 19										

A 🛒 to Bristol Temple Meads B 🛒 to Reading C 🛒 to Birmingham New Street

Scotland, The North East, North West England - The South West and South Coast

		XC	XC	VT	XC	XC	XC	XC	XC	XC	VT	XC	XC	XC	XC	XC
									FO	FX						
		◇■	◇■	◇■	■	◇■	◇■	◇■	◇■	◇■	◇■	◇■	◇■	■	◇■	◇■
									A	A						B
		⊼		⊠				⊼	⊼	⊼	⊠	⊼				⊼
Aberdeen	d															
Stonehaven	d															
Montrose	d															
Arbroath	d															
Dundee	d															
Leuchars ■	d															
Cupar	d															
Ladybank	d															
Markinch	d															
Kirkcaldy	d															
Inverkeithing	d															
Glasgow Central ■	d	15 00		17 40												17 00
Motherwell	d	15 16														17 16
Haymarket	d	15 56														17 55
Edinburgh ■	d	16 06							17 07	17 07	18 52					18 08
Haymarket	d										18 56					
Lockerbie	d			18 33												
Carlisle ■	d			18 57							20 07					
Penrith North Lakes	d															
Oxenholme Lake District	d			19 33							20 42					
Lancaster ■	d			19 47							20 56					
Preston ■	d			20 08							21 17					
Wigan North Western	d			20 19							21 28					
Warrington Bank Quay	d			20 32							21 39					
M'chester Piccadilly ■	d		20 05			20 27							21 27		22 07	
Stockport	d		20 13			20 36							21 36		22 16	
Wilmslow	d															
Crewe ■	d			20 53							22 01					
Macclesfield	d		20 26			20 49							21 49		22 29	
Congleton	d															
Stoke-on-Trent	d		20 44			21 07							22 08		22 47	
Stafford	d		21 01	21 14		21 25							22 26		23 04	
Wolverhampton ■	d		21 17	21 32		21 41					22 33		22 42		23 18	
Dunbar	d								17 29	17 29						18 30
Berwick-upon-Tweed	d								17 52	17 52						18 54
Alnmouth for Alnwick	d	17 05														19 14
Morpeth	d	17 19							18 24	18 24						
Newcastle ■	d	17 41						18 35	18 43	18 43		19 35				19 42
Chester-le-Street	d															
Durham	d	17 54						18 48	18 55	18 55		19 50				19 55
Darlington ■	d	18 12						19 07	19 13	19 13		20 07				20 13
York ■	d	18 45						19 36	19 45	19 45		20 36				20 45
Leeds ■	d	19 11							20 11	20 11						21 11
Wakefield Westgate ■	d	19 23							20 23	20 23						21 23
Doncaster ■	d							19 59				21 01				
Sheffield ■	d	19 58						20 24	20 58	20 58		21 29				22 01
Chesterfield	d	20 10						20 36	21 10	21 10		21 41				22 25
Nottingham ■	d				20 40									21 39		
Derby ■	d	20 55			21 10			21 29	22 02	22 02		22 23		22 12		23 14
Burton-on-Trent	d				21 24			21 40						22 23		23 24
Tamworth	d				21 34			21 50						22 35		23 35
Birmingham New Street ■	a	21 29	21 33	21 54	21 57	22 00		22 09	22 36	22 48	22 52	22 55	22 59	23 01	23 35	23 50
Birmingham New Street ■	d						22 04	22 12								
Cheltenham Spa ■	a							22 51								
Gloucester ■	a															
Bristol Parkway ■	a							23 21								
Bristol Temple Meads ■	a							23 41								
Newport (South Wales)	a															
Cardiff Central ■	a															
Weston-super-Mare	a															
Taunton	a															
Tiverton Parkway	a															
Exeter St Davids ■	a															
Dawlish	a															
Teignmouth	a															
Newton Abbot	a															
Torquay	a															
Paignton	a															
Totnes	a															
Plymouth	a															
Liskeard ■	a															
Bodmin Parkway	a															
Lostwithiel	a															
Par	a															
St Austell	a															
Truro	a															
Redruth	a															
Camborne	a															
Hayle	a															
St Erth	a															
Penzance	a															
Birmingham International ✈	d						22 14									
Coventry	d						22 25									
Leamington Spa ■	d						22 38									
Banbury	a						22 54									
Oxford	a						23 14									
Reading ■	a						23 49									
Guildford	a															
Basingstoke	a															
Winchester	a															
Southampton Airport Pkway ✈	a															
Southampton Central	a															
Brockenhurst ■	a															
Bournemouth	a															

A ⊼ to Leeds
B ⊼ from Edinburgh to Leeds

Scotland, The North East, North West England - The South West and South Coast

		XC	XC	XC	XC	XC	XC	XC	XC	XC	XC	XC	XC	VT	VT	XC	XC	XC	XC	XC	XC	VT	XC
		◇■	◇■	◇■	◇■	◇■	◇■	◇■	◇■	◇■	◇■	◇■	◇■	◇■	◇■	◇■	◇■	◇■	◇■	■	■ ■	◇■	◇■
					A						B		B										C
				⊼	⊼	⊼		⊼	⊼	⊼	⊼	⊼	⊼	⊠	⊠	⊼		⊼	⊼		⊼	⊠	⊼
Aberdeen	d																						
Stonehaven	d																						
Montrose	d																						
Arbroath	d																						
Dundee	d																						
Leuchars ■	d																						
Cupar	d																						
Ladybank	d																						
Markinch	d																						
Kirkcaldy	d																						
Inverkeithing	d																						
Glasgow Central ■	d																						
Motherwell	d																						
Haymarket	d																						
Edinburgh ■	d																						
Haymarket	d																						
Lockerbie	d																						
Carlisle ■	d																						
Penrith North Lakes	d																						
Oxenholme Lake District	d																						
Lancaster ■	d																					06 58	
Preston ■	d													06 17								07 17	
Wigan North Western	d													06 28								07 28	
Warrington Bank Quay	d													06 39								07 39	
M'chester Piccadilly ■	d							05 11				06 00			06 27				07 05		07 27		
Stockport	d											06 08			06 35				07 13		07 36		
Wilmslow	d											06 16											
Crewe ■	d							05 47				06 39		07 01								08 01	
Macclesfield	d														06 48				07 26		07 49		
Congleton	d																						
Stoke-on-Trent	d							06 07							07 06				07 44		08 07		
Stafford	d							06 25				07 01			07 24				08 01		08 25		
Wolverhampton ■	d							06 41				07 16		07 37	07 45				08 17		08 41	08 45	
Dunbar	d																						
Berwick-upon-Tweed	d																						
Alnmouth for Alnwick	d																						
Morpeth	d																						
Newcastle ■	d																						
Chester-le-Street	d																						
Durham	d																						
Darlington ■	d																						
York ■	d																						06 45
Leeds ■	d															06 11		06 16					07 10
Wakefield Westgate ■	d															06 23		06 28					07 23
Doncaster ■	d																	06 46					
Sheffield ■	d										05 59					06 53		07 18					07 53
Chesterfield	d										06 26					07 06		07 30					08 06
Nottingham ■	d									06 00			06 37				07 04			07 37			
Derby ■	d						06 10			06 36	06 48		07 06			07 27	07 36	07 50		08 06			08 28
Burton-on-Trent	d						06 20			06 48	06 58		07 17			07 38	07 50	08 00		08 18			08 38
Tamworth	d						06 31		←	07 01	07 09		07 30			07 50	08 03	08 11		08 30			08 50
Birmingham New Street ■	a						06 52	06 57	06 52	07 25	07 27	07 33	07 53	07 56	08 07	08 08	08 25	08 27	08 33	08 55	08 58	09 05	09 10
Birmingham New Street ■	d	05 00	05 37	06 04	06 33	06 42	07 12	07 04	07 12	07 30	07 33	07 42	08 04		08 10	08 12	08 30	08 33	08 42		09 04	09 10	09 17
Cheltenham Spa ■	a	06 01	06 36			07 21	→		07 51	08 10		08 24				08 50	09 10		09 24				09 58
Gloucester ■	a	06 12	06 53							08 20							09 20						
Bristol Parkway ■	a					07 54			08 26			08 54				09 25			09 55				10 30
Bristol Temple Meads ■	a					08 06			08 40			09 11				09 39			10 08				10 43
Newport (South Wales)	a	07 06	07 52							09 13							10 11						
Cardiff Central ■	a	07 22	08 08							09 29							10 27						
Weston-super-Mare	a																						
Taunton	a					08 42			09 14							10 15							11 16
Tiverton Parkway	a					08 54			09 26							10 28							11 29
Exeter St Davids ■	a					09 07			09 40							10 42							11 43
Dawlish	a																						
Teignmouth	a																						
Newton Abbot	a					09 27			09 59							11 04							12 04
Torquay	a					09 39																	
Paignton	a					09 47																	
Totnes	a								10 14							11 17							12 18
Plymouth	a								10 42							11 44							12 47
Liskeard ■	a																						
Bodmin Parkway	a																						
Lostwithiel	a																						
Par	a																						
St Austell	a																						
Truro	a																						
Redruth	a																						
Camborne	a																						
Hayle	a																						
St Erth	a																						
Penzance	a																						
Birmingham International ✈	d			06 14				07 14					08 14		08 21						09 14	09 20	
Coventry	d			06 25				07 25					08 25		08a31						09 25	09a30	
Leamington Spa ■	d			06 37	07 00			07 38			08 00		08 38					09 00			09 39		
Banbury	a			06 53	07 18			07 54			08 16		08 55					09 18			09 55		
Oxford	a			07 14	07 41			08 14			08 39		09 15					09 41			10 14		
Reading ■	a			07 40	08 09			08 40			09 08		09 42					10 10			10 42		
Guildford	a																						
Basingstoke	a			08 08	08 41			09 10					10 09					10 39			11 09		
Winchester	a			08 24	08 56			09 25					10 24					10 54			11 24		
Southampton Airport Pkway ✈	a			08 33	09 08			09 34					10 33					11 07			11 33		
Southampton Central	a			08 44	09 18			09 43					10 43					11 17			11 43		
Brockenhurst ■	a			08 59				09 58					10 58								11 58		
Bournemouth	a			09 15				10 13					11 13								12 13		

A ⊼ from Reading
B ⊼ from Birmingham New Street
C ⊼ from Leeds

Scotland, The North East, North West England - The South West and South Coast

		XC	XC	XC	XC	XC	VT	XC	XC	XC	XC	XC	XC	VT	XC	XC	XC	XC	XC	XC	VT	XC	XC
		◇1 A ✠	■ ◇1 B ✠	◇1 ✠	1	◇1 ✠	◇1 ⊠	◇1 ✠	◇1 ✠	◇1 ✠	◇1 ✠	1	◇1 ✠	◇1 ⊠	◇1 ✠	◇1 ✠	◇1 ✠	◇1 ✠	1	◇1 ✠	◇1 ⊠	◇1 C ✠	◇1 ✠
Aberdeen	d																						
Stonehaven	d																						
Montrose	d																						
Arbroath	d																						
Dundee	d																						
Leuchars	d																						
Cupar	d																						
Ladybank	d																						
Markinch	d																						
Kirkcaldy	d																						
Inverkeithing	d																						
Glasgow Central	d						05 49														08 00	06 01	
Motherwell	d						06 04															06 17	
Haymarket	d																					06 57	
Edinburgh	d													06 52	06 06		07 00					07 10	
Haymarket	d													06 57									
Lockerbie	d																						
Carlisle	d						07 03							08 08							09 11		
Penrith North Lakes	d						07 18							08 22									
Oxenholme Lake District	d						07 42																
Lancaster	d						07 57							08 57							09 56		
Preston	d						08 17							09 17							10 17		
Wigan North Western	d						08 28							09 28							10 28		
Warrington Bank Quay	d						08 39							09 39							10 39		
M'chester Piccadilly	d			08 05		08 27					09 05		09 27					10 05		10 27			
Stockport	d			08 13		08 36					09 13		09 36					10 13		10 36			
Wilmslow	d																						
Crewe	d						09 01							10 01							11 01		
Macclesfield	d			08 26		08 49					09 26		09 49					10 26		10 49			
Congleton	d																						
Stoke-on-Trent	d			08 44		09 07					09 44		10 07					10 44		11 07			
Stafford	d			09 01		09 25					10 01		10 25					11 01		11 25			
Wolverhampton	d			09 17		09 42	09 45				10 17		10 41	10 45				11 17		11 41	11 45		
Dunbar	d																					07 32	
Berwick-upon-Tweed	d														06 50		07 43						
Alnmouth for Alnwick	d														07 11		08 03						
Morpeth	d																08 18						
Newcastle	d		06 25					06 45		07 25					07 40		08 35					08 43	
Chester-le-Street	d																						
Durham	d		06 38					06 57		07 38					07 53		08 48					08 55	
Darlington	d		06 56					07 15		07 56					08 11		09 05					09 12	
York	d		07 26					07 43		08 27					08 44		09 35					09 44	
Leeds	d							08 11							09 11							10 11	
Wakefield Westgate	d							08 23							09 23							10 23	
Doncaster	d		07 53							08 53							09 59						
Sheffield	d		08 18					08 54		09 24					09 55		10 24					10 55	
Chesterfield	d		08 30					09 07							10 08							11 07	
Nottingham	d	08 09			08 40				09 07			09 41				10 07			10 41				11 07
Derby	d	08 38	08 53		09 11			09 26	09 39	09 53		10 10			10 29	10 38	10 53		11 10			11 28	11 37
Burton-on-Trent	d	08 50			09 22			09 38	09 52			10 21				10 49			11 21				11 49
Tamworth	d	09 03			09 34				10 03			10 33			10 50	11 02			11 33				12 02
Birmingham New Street	a	09 24	09 27	09 33	09 55	09 58	10 05	10 08	10 24	10 27	10 33	10 55	10 58	11 05	11 09	11 24	11 27	11 33	11 55	11 58	12 05	12 07	12 24
Birmingham New Street	d	09 30	09 33	09 42		10 04	10 10	10 17	10 30	10 33	10 42		11 04	11 10	11 17	11 30	11 33	11 42		12 04	12 10	12 17	12 30
Cheltenham Spa	a	10 10		10 24				10 59	11 10		11 24				11 56	12 10		12 24				13 01	13 10
Gloucester	a	10 20							11 20							12 20							13 20
Bristol Parkway	a			10 56				11 31			11 55				12 28			12 56				13 30	
Bristol Temple Meads	a			11 10				11 42			12 05				12 42			13 10				13 41	
Newport (South Wales)	a	11 11							12 10							13 09							14 11
Cardiff Central	a	11 28							12 26							13 26							14 26
Weston-super-Mare	a			11 32																			
Taunton	a			11 58				12 14							13 16							14 15	
Tiverton Parkway	a			12 10				12 26							13 28							14 27	
Exeter St Davids	a			12 24				12 40							13 43							14 40	
Dawlish	a			12 36																			
Teignmouth	a			12 41																			
Newton Abbot	a			12 48				12 59							14 03							15 00	
Torquay	a			13 00																			
Paignton	a			13 08																			
Totnes	a							13 11							14 16							15 12	
Plymouth	a							13 38							14 43							15 40	
Liskeard	a																						
Bodmin Parkway	a																						
Lostwithiel	a																						
Par	a																						
St Austell	a																						
Truro	a																						
Redruth	a																						
Camborne	a																						
Hayle	a																						
St Erth	a																						
Penzance	a																						
Birmingham International	d					10 14	10 20						11 14	11 20						12 14	12 20		
Coventry	d					10 25	10a30						11 25	11a30						12 25	12a30		
Leamington Spa	d		10 00			10 38				11 00			11 38				12 01			12 38			
Banbury	a		10 17			10 54				11 17			11 54				12 18			12 54			
Oxford	a		10 40			11 13				11 41			12 14				12 40			13 14			
Reading	a		11 09			11 40				12 08			12 42				13 08			13 40			
Guildford	a																						
Basingstoke	a					12 09				12 39			13 09							14 09			
Winchester	a					12 24				12 54			13 24							14 25			
Southampton Airport Pkway	a					12 33				13 08			13 33							14 34			
Southampton Central	a					12 41				13 17			13 41							14 41			
Brockenhurst	a					12 57							13 56							14 56			
Bournemouth	a					13 12							14 11							15 11			

A ✠ from Birmingham New Street

B ◇ from Birmingham New Street ■ to Birmingham New Street

C ✠ from Edinburgh

Table T051-F

Mondays to Fridays

8 October to 7 December

Scotland, The North East, North West England - The South West and South Coast

		XC	XC	XC	XC	VT	XC	XC	XC	XC	XC	XC	VT	XC	XC	XC	XC	XC	XC	VT	XC	XC
		◇1 ✠	◇1 ✠	1	◇1 ✠	◇1 ⊠	◇1 A ✠	◇1 ✠	◇1 ✠	◇1 ✠	1	◇1 ✠	◇1 ⊠	◇1 A ✠	◇1 ✠	◇1 ✠	◇1 ✠	1 ✠	◇1 ✠	◇1 ⊡	◇1 B ✠	◇1 ✠
Aberdeen	d																					
Stonehaven	d																					
Montrose	d																					
Arbroath	d																					
Dundee	d						06 32															
Leuchars	d						06 46															
Cupar	d						06 54															
Ladybank	d						07 03															
Markinch	d						07 11															
Kirkcaldy	d						07 21															
Inverkeithing	d						07 40															
Glasgow Central	d												10 00	07 48							09 00	
Motherwell	d													08 08							09 15	
Haymarket	d						08 00							08 51							09 54	
Edinburgh	d					08 51	08 09							09 08						10 52	10 10	
Haymarket	d					08 57														10 57		
Lockerbie	d																					
Carlisle	d					10 08							11 12							12 08		
Penrith North Lakes	d												11 27									
Oxenholme Lake District	d					10 42														12 43		
Lancaster	d					10 57														12 57		
Preston	d					11 17							12 18							13 17		
Wigan North Western	d					11 28							12 29							13 28		
Warrington Bank Quay	d					11 39							12 40							13 39		
M'chester Piccadilly	d		11 05		11 27					12 05		12 27					13 05		13 27			
Stockport	d		11 13		11 36					12 13		12 36					13 13		13 36			
Wilmslow	d																					
Crewe	d					12 01							13 01							14 01		
Macclesfield	d		11 26		11 49					12 26		12 49					13 26		13 49			
Congleton	d																					
Stoke-on-Trent	d		11 44		12 07					12 44		13 07					13 44		14 07			
Stafford	d		12 01		12 25					13 01		13 26					14 01		14 25			
Wolverhampton	d		12 17		12 41	12 45				13 17		13 41	13 45				14 17		14 41	14 45		
Dunbar	d													09 29								
Berwick-upon-Tweed	d						08 52							09 53							10 51	
Alnmouth for Alnwick	d																					
Morpeth	d						09 25														11 22	
Newcastle	d	09 35					09 42		10 35					10 42		11 35					11 42	
Chester-le-Street	d																					
Durham	d	09 49					09 55		10 48					10 54		11 49					11 54	
Darlington	d	10 07					10 12		11 06					11 12		12 07					12 12	
York	d	10 35					10 44		11 35					11 44		12 35					12 44	
Leeds	d						11 11							12 11							13 11	
Wakefield Westgate	d						11 23							12 23							13 23	
Doncaster	d	10 59							11 59							12 59						
Sheffield	d	11 24					11 55		12 24					12 55		13 24					13 55	
Chesterfield	d						12 08							13 07							14 07	
Nottingham	d			11 41				12 07			12 41				13 07			13 41				14 07
Derby	d	11 53		12 10			12 29	12 37	12 53		13 10			13 28	13 37	13 53		14 10			14 28	14 37
Burton-on-Trent	d			12 21				12 49			13 24			13 38	13 49			14 21				14 50
Tamworth	d			12 33			12 49	13 02			13 35				14 02			14 33			14 47	15 02
Birmingham New Street	a	12 27	12 33	12 55	12 58	13 05	13 08	13 24	13 27	13 33	13 55	13 58	14 05	14 08	14 24	14 27	14 34	14 55	14 58	15 05	15 08	15 25
Birmingham New Street	d	12 33	12 42		13 04	13 10	13 17	13 30	13 33	13 42		14 04	14 10	14 17	14 30	14 33	14 42		15 04	15 10	15 17	15 30
Cheltenham Spa	a		13 24				14 00	14 10		14 24				14 58	15 10		15 24				15 58	16 10
Gloucester	a							14 22							15 20							16 22
Bristol Parkway	a		13 56				14 28			14 56				15 29			15 56				16 30	
Bristol Temple Meads	a		14 08				14 42			15 10				15 41			16 11				16 43	
Newport (South Wales)	a							15 12							16 12							17 11
Cardiff Central	a							15 30							16 30							17 30
Weston-super-Mare	a																					
Taunton	a						15 16			15 44				16 14							17 16	
Tiverton Parkway	a						15 28			15 56				16 26							17 28	
Exeter St Davids	a						15 43			16 12				16 40							17 42	
Dawlish	a																					
Teignmouth	a																					
Newton Abbot	a						16 03							17 04							18 11	
Torquay	a																					
Paignton	a																					
Totnes	a						16 16							17 16							18 23	
Plymouth	a						16 45							17 42							18 49	
Liskeard	a																				19 23	
Bodmin Parkway	a																				19 35	
Lostwithiel	a																					
Par	a																				19 45	
St Austell	a																				19 51	
Truro	a																				20 07	
Redruth	a																				20 28	
Camborne	a																				20 34	
Hayle	a																					
St Erth	a																				20 44	
Penzance	a																				20 54	
Birmingham International	d				13 14	13 20						14 14	14 20						15 14	15 20		
Coventry	d				13 25	13a30						14 25	14a29						15 25	15a30		
Leamington Spa	d	13 00			13 38				14 00			14 38				15 00			15 38			
Banbury	a	13 18			13 54				14 17			14 54				15 17			15 54			
Oxford	a	13 41			14 13				14 40			15 14				15 40			16 14			
Reading	a	14 09			14 40				15 08			15 41				16 11			16 40			
Guildford	a																					
Basingstoke	a	14 40			15 09							16 09				16 40			17 09			
Winchester	a	14 56			15 24							16 24				16 57			17 24			
Southampton Airport Pkway	a	15 09			15 33							16 33				17 08			17 33			
Southampton Central	a	15 17			15 41							16 41				17 17			17 41			
Brockenhurst	a				15 57							16 57							17 57			
Bournemouth	a				16 12							17 12							18 15			

A ✠ from Edinburgh

B ✠ from Edinburgh to Plymouth

Table T051-F

Mondays to Fridays

8 October to 7 December

Scotland, The North East, North West England - The South West and South Coast

		XC	XC	XC	XC	XC	VT	XC	XC	XC	XC	XC	XC	VT	XC	XC	XC	XC	XC	XC	XC FX	VT	XC FX
		◇■ ⚒	◇■ A ⚒	■	◇■ ⚒	■ ◇■ B ⚒	◇■ ⊡	◇■ C ⚒	◇■ ⚒	◇■ D ⚒	◇■ ⚒	■ ⚒	◇■ ⚒	◇■ ⊡	◇■ E ⚒	◇■	◇■ ⚒	◇■ ⚒	■ ⚒	◇■ ⚒	◇■ ⚒	◇■ ⊡	◇■ ⚒
Aberdeen	d					08 20																	
Stonehaven	d					08 38																	
Montrose	d					08 59																	
Arbroath	d					09 15																	
Dundee	d					09 35																	
Leuchars ■	d					09 48																	
Cupar	d					09 55																	
Ladybank	d					10 02																	
Markinch	d					10 09																	
Kirkcaldy	d					10 18																	
Inverkeithing	d					10 33																	
Glasgow Central ■	d						12 00								11 00							14 00	
Motherwell	d														11 15								
Haymarket	d					10 51									11 54								
Edinburgh ■	d					11 06								12 52	12 08						13 07		
Haymarket	d													12 57									
Lockerbie	d																						
Carlisle ■	d						13 11							14 08								15 11	
Penrith North Lakes	d													14 22									
Oxenholme Lake District	d																					15 45	
Lancaster ■	d						13 57							14 57									
Preston ■	d						14 17							15 17								16 17	
Wigan North Western	d						14 29							15 28								16 28	
Warrington Bank Quay	d						14 40							15 39								16 39	
M'chester Piccadilly ■	d		14 05		14 27						15 05		15 27					16 05		16 27			
Stockport	d		14 13		14 36						15 13		15 36					16 13		16 36			
Wilmslow	d																						
Crewe ■	d						15 01							16 01								17 01	
Macclesfield	d		14 26		14 49						15 26		15 49					16 26		16 49			
Congleton	d																						
Stoke-on-Trent	d		14 44		15 07						15 44		16 07					16 44		17 07			
Stafford	d		15 01		15 25						16 01		16 25					17 01		17 25			
Wolverhampton ■	d		15 17		15 41		15 45				16 17		16 41	16 45				17 17		17 41		17 45	
Dunbar	d					11 28															13 32		
Berwick-upon-Tweed	d					11 51									12 50								
Alnmouth for Alnwick	d					12 12															14 13		
Morpeth	d																						
Newcastle ■	d	12 34				12 41				13 35					13 42		14 36				14 42		
Chester-le-Street	d																						
Durham	d	12 47				12 54				13 49					13 54		14 48				14 54		
Darlington ■	d	13 05				13 12				14 07					14 12		15 06				15 12		
York ■	d	13 35				13 44				14 35					14 44		15 35				15 44		
Leeds ■	d					14 11									15 11						16 11		
Wakefield Westgate ■	d					14 23									15 23						16 23		
Doncaster ■	d	13 59								14 59							15 59						
Sheffield ■	d	14 24				14 55				15 24					15 55		16 24				16 55		
Chesterfield	d					15 07									16 07						17 07		
Nottingham ■	d			14 41					15 07			15 41				16 07			16 41				
Derby ■	d	14 53		15 10		15 28			15 37	15 53		16 10			16 28	16 37	16 53		17 10		17 27		
Burton-on-Trent	d			15 24		15 38			15 49			16 21				16 49			17 24		17 39		
Tamworth	d			15 35				←	16 02			16 33			16 47	17 02			17 35				←
Birmingham New Street ■	a	15 27	15 33	15 54	15 58	16 03	16 05	16 03	16 25	16 28	16 33	16 55	16 58	17 05	17 08	17 25	17 28	17 33	17 55	17 58	18 04	18 05	18 04
Birmingham New Street ■	d	15 33	15 42		16 04	16 12	16 10	16 12	16 30	16 33	16 42		17 04	17 10	17 12	17 30	17 33	17 42		18 04	18 12	18 10	18 12
Cheltenham Spa ■	a		16 24			→		16 49	17 14		17 24				17 51	18 16		18 24			→		18 51
Gloucester ■	a								17 24							18 28							19 01
Bristol Parkway ■	a		16 56					17 25			17 56				18 28			18 54					19 31
Bristol Temple Meads ■	a		17 10					17 40			18 07				18 42			19 06					19 43
Newport (South Wales)	a								18 10							19 14							
Cardiff Central ■	a								18 27							19 33							
Weston-super-Mare	a																						
Taunton	a		17 44					18 15							19 15								20 16
Tiverton Parkway	a		17 56					18 27							19 27								20 28
Exeter St Davids ■	a		18 11					18 41							19 42								20 41
Dawlish	a		18 23																				
Teignmouth	a		18 28																				
Newton Abbot	a		18 35					19 05							20 02								21 01
Torquay	a		18 47																				
Paignton	a		18 55																				
Totnes	a							19 17							20 14								21 13
Plymouth	a							19 43							20 40								21 39
Liskeard ■	a							20 11							21 12								
Bodmin Parkway	a							20 23							21 24								
Lostwithiel	a														21 30								
Par	a							20 33							21 36								
St Austell	a							20 40							21 43								
Truro	a							21 00							22 01								
Redruth	a							21 17							22 13								
Camborne	a							21 24							22 19								
Hayle	a														22 27								
St Erth	a							21 34							22 31								
Penzance	a							21 43							22 41								
Birmingham International	d				16 14		16 20						17 14	17 20						18 14		18 20	
Coventry	d				16 25		16a30						17 25	17a30						18 25		18a30	
Leamington Spa ■	d	16 01			16 38					17 00			17 38				18 01			18 38			
Banbury	a	16 17			16 54					17 17			17 54				18 18			18 55			
Oxford	a	16 40			17 13					17 40			18 14				18 40			19 13			
Reading ■	a	17 08			17 40					18 09			18 44				19 10			19 41			
Guildford	a									18 59													
Basingstoke	a				18 09								19 09							20 09			
Winchester	a				18 25								19 24							20 25			
Southampton Airport Pkway	a				18 33								19 33							20 34			
Southampton Central	a				18 43								19 42							20 42			
Brockenhurst ■	a				18 58								19 56							20 58			
Bournemouth	a				19 12								20 11							21 15			

A ⚒ to Bristol Temple Meads
B ⚒ ◇ from Edinburgh ■ to Edinburgh
C ⚒ to Plymouth
D ⚒ to Reading
E ⚒ from Edinburgh to Plymouth

Table T051-F

Mondays to Fridays

8 October to 7 December

Scotland, The North East, North West England - The South West and South Coast

		XC	XC	XC	XC	XC	VT	XC	XC	XC	XC	XC	XC	VT	XC	XC FX	XC FO	XC	XC	XC	XC	VT
		◇■	◇■ ⚒	◇■ A ⚒	■ ⚒	◇■ B ⚒	■ ■ ⊡	◇■ C ⚒	◇■	◇■ ⚒	◇■ A ⚒	■ ⚒	◇■ D ⚒	◇■ ⊠	◇■ D ⚒	◇■	◇■	◇■ D ⚒	◇■ D ⚒	■ ⚒	◇■ D ⚒	■ ■ ⊠
Aberdeen	d																					
Stonehaven	d																					
Montrose	d																					
Arbroath	d																					
Dundee	d																					
Leuchars ■	d																					
Cupar	d																					
Ladybank	d																					
Markinch	d																					
Kirkcaldy	d																					
Inverkeithing	d																					
Glasgow Central ■	d							13 00						16 00								
Motherwell	d							13 16														
Haymarket	d							13 55														
Edinburgh ■	d						14 52	14 09							15 08							16 52
Haymarket	d						14 58															16 57
Lockerbie	d																					
Carlisle ■	d						16 08							17 11								18 08
Penrith North Lakes	d						16 21															
Oxenholme Lake District	d													17 45								18 42
Lancaster ■	d						16 57															18 59
Preston ■	d						17 17							18 17								19 17
Wigan North Western	d						17 28							18 28								19 31
Warrington Bank Quay	d						17 39							18 39								19 41
M'chester Piccadilly ■	d			17 05		17 27					18 05		18 27						19 05		19 27	
Stockport	d			17 13		17 35					18 13		18 36						19 13		19 36	
Wilmslow	d					17 45																
Crewe ■	d					18 07	18 01							19 01								20 03
Macclesfield	d			17 26							18 26								19 26		19 49	
Congleton	d												18 55									
Stoke-on-Trent	d			17 44							18 44		19 07						19 44		20 07	
Stafford	d			18 01		18 25					19 01		19 25						20 01		20 25	
Wolverhampton ■	d			18 17		18 41	18 45				19 17		19 41	19 45					20 17		20 44	20 47
Dunbar	d														15 29							
Berwick-upon-Tweed	d							14 50														
Alnmouth for Alnwick	d																					
Morpeth	d																					
Newcastle ■	d		15 03					15 41		16 35					16 41			17 32				
Chester-le-Street	d																	17 41				
Durham	d		15 16					15 54		16 48					16 54			17 48				
Darlington ■	d		15 33					16 12		17 06					17 12			18 06				
York ■	d		16 05					16 44		17 35					17 45			18 36				
Leeds ■	d		16 40					17 10							18 11							
Wakefield Westgate ■	d		16 52					17 22							18 23							
Doncaster ■	d									17 58								18 59				
Sheffield ■	d		17 24					17 55		18 24					18 56			19 24				
Chesterfield	d							18 07							19 11							
Nottingham ■	d	17 07			17 41				18 07			18 41				19 07	19 07			19 36		
Derby ■	d	17 37	17 53		18 13			18 29	18 37	18 53		19 10			19 30	19 37	19 37	19 54		20 10		
Burton-on-Trent	d	17 49			18 27				18 49			19 21			19 41	19 49	19 49			20 21		
Tamworth	d	18 02			18 38			18 49	19 02			19 33				20 03	20 03			20 33		
Birmingham New Street ■	a	18 23	18 27	18 33	18 57	18 58	19 05	19 08	19 24	19 27	19 33	19 55	19 58	20 05	20 07	20 25	20 25	20 28	20 33	20 55	21 00	21 05
Birmingham New Street ■	d	18 30	18 33	18 42		19 04	19 10	19 12	19 30	19 33	19 42		20 04	20 10	20 12	20 30	20 30	20 34	20 42		21 04	21 10
Cheltenham Spa ■	a	19 13		19 24				19 50	20 11		20 24				20 52	21 10	21 10		21 25			
Gloucester ■	a	19 23							20 20							21 19	21 19					
Bristol Parkway ■	a			19 56				20 30			20 55				21 25				22 01			
Bristol Temple Meads ■	a			20 09				20 42			21 05				21 36				22 14			
Newport (South Wales)	a	20 11		20 47					21 11							22 12	22 13					
Cardiff Central ■	a	20 28		21 03					21 28							22 35	22 30					
Weston-super-Mare	a																					
Taunton	a							21 19			21 43				22 15							
Tiverton Parkway	a							21 31			21 55				22 27							
Exeter St Davids ■	a							21 45			22 09				22 41							
Dawlish	a																					
Teignmouth	a																					
Newton Abbot	a							22 05			22 28				23 01							
Torquay	a																					
Paignton	a																					
Totnes	a							22 17			22 40				23 18							
Plymouth	a							22 45			23 07				23 44							
Liskeard ■	a																					
Bodmin Parkway	a																					
Lostwithiel	a																					
Par	a																					
St Austell	a																					
Truro	a																					
Redruth	a																					
Camborne	a																					
Hayle	a																					
St Erth	a																					
Penzance	a																					
Birmingham International	d					19 14	19 20						20 14	20 20							21 14	21 20
Coventry	d					19 25	19a30						20 25	20a30							21 25	21a30
Leamington Spa ■	d		19 01			19 38				20 02			20 38					21 00			21 38	
Banbury	a		19 17			19 54				20 19			20 55					21 17			21 54	
Oxford	a		19 41			20 13				20 40			21 14					21 40			22 14	
Reading ■	a		20 09			20 41				21 07			21 42					22 16			22 42	
Guildford	a																					
Basingstoke	a					21 09							22 09					22 39			23 06	
Winchester	a					21 24							22 24					22 56			23 24	
Southampton Airport Pkway	a					21 33							22 33					23 12			23 36	
Southampton Central	a					21 40							22 42					23 20			23 43	
Brockenhurst ■	a					21 56							22 56									
Bournemouth	a					22 15							23 19									

A ⚒ to Bristol Temple Meads
B ⚒ to Reading
C ⚒ from Edinburgh to Bristol Temple Meads
D ⚒ to Birmingham New Street

Table T051-F

Mondays to Fridays
8 October to 7 December

Scotland, The North East, North West England - The South West and South Coast

		XC ◇■ A ✠	XC ◇■ ✠	XC ◇■	VT ◇■ ⊠	XC ■	XC ◇■	XC ◇■	XC ◇■ B ✠	XC ◇■ ✠	VT ◇■ ⊠	XC ◇■	XC ■	XC ◇■ C ✠	XC ◇■
Aberdeen	d														
Stonehaven	d														
Montrose	d														
Arbroath	d														
Dundee	d														
Leuchars	d														
Cupar	d														
Ladybank	d														
Markinch	d														
Kirkcaldy	d														
Inverkeithing	d														
Glasgow Central	d	15 00			17 40									17 00	
Motherwell	d	15 16												17 16	
Haymarket	d	15 56												17 55	
Edinburgh	d	16 06							17 07		18 52			18 08	
Haymarket	d										18 56				
Lockerbie	d				18 33										
Carlisle	d				18 57						20 07				
Penrith North Lakes	d														
Oxenholme Lake District	d				19 33						20 42				
Lancaster	d				19 47						20 56				
Preston	d				20 08						21 17				
Wigan North Western	d				20 19						21 28				
Warrington Bank Quay	d				20 32						21 39				
M'chester Piccadilly	d			20 05			20 27					21 27			22 07
Stockport	d			20 13			20 36					21 36			22 16
Wilmslow	d														
Crewe	d				20 53						22 01				
Macclesfield	d			20 26			20 49					21 49			22 29
Congleton	d														
Stoke-on-Trent	d			20 44			21 07					22 08			22 47
Stafford	d			21 01	21 14		21 25					22 26			23 04
Wolverhampton	d			21 17	21 32		21 41				22 33	22 42			23 18
Dunbar	d								17 29					18 30	
Berwick-upon-Tweed	d								17 52					18 54	
Alnmouth for Alnwick	d	17 05												19 14	
Morpeth	d	17 19							18 24						
Newcastle	d	17 41	18 35						18 43	19 35				19 42	
Chester-le-Street	d														
Durham	d	17 54	18 48						18 55	19 50				19 55	
Darlington	d	18 12	19 07						19 13	20 07				20 13	
York	d	18 45	19 36						19 45	20 36				20 45	
Leeds	d	19 11							20 11					21 11	
Wakefield Westgate	d	19 23							20 23					21 23	
Doncaster	d		19 59							21 01					
Sheffield	d	19 58	20 24						20 58	21 29				22 01	
Chesterfield	d	20 10							21 10	21 41				22 25	
Nottingham	d					20 40							21 39		
Derby	d	20 29	20 54			21 10			21 30	22 02			22 12	22 45	
Burton-on-Trent	d					21 24			21 40				22 23	22 56	
Tamworth	d	20 47				21 34			21 50				22 35	23 07	
Birmingham New Street	a	21 07	21 29	21 33	21 54	21 57	22 00		22 09	22 51	22 52	22 59	23 01	23 26	23 35
Birmingham New Street	d	21 12						22 04	22 12						
Cheltenham Spa	a	21 51							22 51						
Gloucester	a	22 02													
Bristol Parkway	a	22 33							23 21						
Bristol Temple Meads	a	22 43							23 41						
Newport (South Wales)	a														
Cardiff Central	a														
Weston-super-Mare	a														
Taunton	a														
Tiverton Parkway	a														
Exeter St Davids	a														
Dawlish	a														
Teignmouth	a														
Newton Abbot	a														
Torquay	a														
Paignton	a														
Totnes	a														
Plymouth	a														
Liskeard	a														
Bodmin Parkway	a														
Lostwithiel	a														
Par	a														
St Austell	a														
Truro	a														
Redruth	a														
Camborne	a														
Hayle	a														
St Erth	a														
Penzance	a														
Birmingham International ✈	d							22 14							
Coventry	d							22 25							
Leamington Spa	d							22 38							
Banbury	a							22 54							
Oxford	a							23 14							
Reading	a							23 49							
Guildford	a														
Basingstoke	a														
Winchester	a														
Southampton Airport Pkway ✈	a														
Southampton Central ⛴	a														
Brockenhurst	a														
Bournemouth	a														

A ✠ to Birmingham New Street
B ✠ to Leeds
C ✠ from Edinburgh to Leeds

Table T051-F

Saturdays
26 May to 21 July

Scotland, The North East, North West England - The South West and South Coast

		XC ◇■	XC ◇■	XC ◇■ ✠	XC ◇■ A ✠	XC ◇■ ✠	XC ◇■	XC ◇■ ✠	XC ◇■ ✠	XC ◇■ B ✠	XC ◇■ B ✠	XC ◇■ ✠	XC ◇■ C ✠	VT ◇■ ⊐	XC ◇■ ✠	XC ◇■	XC ◇■ ✠	XC ◇■ D ✠	XC ■	XC ◇■ ✠	VT ◇■ ⊐	XC ◇■ E ✠	XC ◇■ B ✠
Aberdeen	d																						
Stonehaven	d																						
Montrose	d																						
Arbroath	d																						
Dundee	d																						
Leuchars	d																						
Cupar	d																						
Ladybank	d																						
Markinch	d																						
Kirkcaldy	d																						
Inverkeithing	d																						
Glasgow Central	d																						
Motherwell	d																						
Haymarket	d																						
Edinburgh	d																						
Haymarket	d																						
Lockerbie	d																						
Carlisle	d																						
Penrith North Lakes	d																						
Oxenholme Lake District	d																						
Lancaster	d																				06 58		
Preston	d													06 17							07 17		
Wigan North Western	d													06 28							07 28		
Warrington Bank Quay	d													06 39							07 39		
M'chester Piccadilly	d							05 11				06 00						07 05		07 27			
Stockport	d											06 08						07 13		07 36			
Wilmslow	d																						
Crewe	d							05 47						07 01							08 01		
Macclesfield	d											06 21						07 26		07 49			
Congleton	d																						
Stoke-on-Trent	d							06 08				06 39						07 44		08 07			
Stafford	d							06 26				07 01						08 01		08 25			
Wolverhampton	d							06 41				07 17		07 45				08 17		08 41	08 45		
Dunbar	d																						
Berwick-upon-Tweed	d																						
Alnmouth for Alnwick	d																						
Morpeth	d																						
Newcastle	d																						
Chester-le-Street	d																						
Durham	d																						
Darlington	d																						
York	d																					06 45	
Leeds	d														06 11		06 17					07 11	
Wakefield Westgate	d														06 23		06 29					07 23	
Doncaster	d																06 51						
Sheffield	d										05 45				06 53		07 18					07 56	
Chesterfield	d										05 57				07 06		07 30					08 08	
Nottingham	d									05 58			06 37			06 58			07 37				08 07
Derby	d						06 10			06 36	06 47		07 06		07 27	07 36	07 51		08 06			08 28	08 37
Burton-on-Trent	d						06 20			06 48	06 58		07 17		07 38	07 50	08 00		08 18			08 38	08 49
Tamworth	d						06 31		←	07 01	07 09		07 30		07 49	08 02	08 12		08 30			08 49	09 02
Birmingham New Street	a						06 50	06 57	06 50	07 24	07 28	07 33	07 52	08 05	08 08	08 24	08 27	08 33	08 55	08 58	09 05	09 08	09 24
Birmingham New Street	d	05 00	05 42	06 04	06 33	06 42	07 12	07 04	07 12	07 30	07 33	07 42	08 04	08 10	08 12	08 30	08 33	08 42		09 04		09 12	09 30
Cheltenham Spa	a	06 02	06 42			07 24	→		07 51	08 10		08 24			08 51	09 10		09 24				09 51	10 10
Gloucester	a	06 12	06 52							08 20						09 20							10 20
Bristol Parkway	a					07 53			08 24			08 54			09 24			09 53				10 29	
Bristol Temple Meads	a					08 05			08 38			09 07			09 39			10 04				10 42	
Newport (South Wales)	a	07 05	07 48							09 06						10 05							11 06
Cardiff Central	a	07 21	08 04							09 23						10 21							11 24
Weston-super-Mare	a																						
Taunton	a					08 42			09 15						10 16			11 00				11 15	
Tiverton Parkway	a					08 54			09 27						10 29			11 12				11 27	
Exeter St Davids	a					09 07			09 40						10 43			11 26				11 41	
Dawlish	a														11 01								
Teignmouth	a														11 07								
Newton Abbot	a					09 28			10 00						11 15			11 52				12 01	
Torquay	a					09 39									11 27								
Paignton	a					09 47									11 37								
Totnes	a								10 12									12 04				12 14	
Plymouth	a								10 39									12 33				12 41	
Liskeard	a																	13 04					
Bodmin Parkway	a																	13 20					
Lostwithiel	a																						
Par	a																	13 32					
St Austell	a																						
Truro	a																						
Redruth	a																						
Camborne	a																						
Hayle	a																						
St Erth	a																						
Penzance	a																						
Birmingham International ✈	d			06 14				07 14					08 14	08 20						09 14			
Coventry	d			06 25				07 25					08 25	08a30						09 25			
Leamington Spa	d			06 38	07 00			07 38			08 01		08 38				09 00			09 38			
Banbury	a			06 54	07 17			07 54			08 17		08 54				09 17			09 55			
Oxford	a			07 14	07 40			08 14			08 39		09 14				09 41			10 15			
Reading	a			07 41	08 09			08 41			09 09		09 40				10 08			10 41			
Guildford	a																						
Basingstoke	a			08 08	08 39			09 09					10 09				10 40			11 09			
Winchester	a			08 24	08 58			09 25					10 24				10 56			11 25			
Southampton Airport Pkway ✈	a			08 32	09 08			09 33					10 33				11 08			11 33			
Southampton Central ⛴	a			08 41	09 17			09 41					10 41				11 17			11 41			
Brockenhurst	a			08 56				09 57					10 57							11 57			
Bournemouth	a			09 14				10 11					11 13							12 12			

A ✠ from Reading
B ✠ from Birmingham New Street
C ✠ from Derby
D ✠ to Plymouth
E ✠ from Leeds

Table T051-F

Saturdays
26 May to 21 July

Scotland, The North East, North West England - The South West and South Coast

		XC ◇1	XC ◇1	XC 1	XC ◇1	VT ◇1	XC ◇1 A	XC ◇1	XC ◇1	XC ◇1	XC 1	XC ◇1	VT ◇1	XC ◇1	XC ◇1	XC ◇1	XC ◇1	XC 1	XC ◇1	VT ◇1	XC ◇1 B	XC ◇1	XC ◇1
Aberdeen	d																						
Stonehaven	d																						
Montrose	d																						
Arbroath	d																						
Dundee	d																						
Leuchars	d																						
Cupar	d																						
Ladybank	d																						
Markinch	d																						
Kirkcaldy	d																						
Inverkeithing	d																						
Glasgow Central	d					05 50														08 00	06 01		
Motherwell	d					06 05															06 16		
Haymarket	d																				06 57		
Edinburgh	d												06 52	06 06		07 00					07 07		
Haymarket	d												06 56										
Lockerbie	d																						
Carlisle	d					07 02							08 07							09 11			
Penrith North Lakes	d					07 17							08 22										
Oxenholme Lake District	d					07 41																	
Lancaster	d					07 56							08 57							09 58			
Preston	d					08 17							09 17							10 17			
Wigan North Western	d					08 28							09 28							10 29			
Warrington Bank Quay	d					08 39							09 39							10 41			
M'chester Piccadilly	d		08 05		08 27					09 05		09 27					10 05		10 27				
Stockport	d		08 13		08 36					09 13		09 37					10 13		10 36				
Wilmslow	d																						
Crewe	d					09 01							10 01							11 02			
Macclesfield	d		08 26		08 49					09 26		09 50					10 26		10 49				
Congleton	d																						
Stoke-on-Trent	d		08 44		09 07					09 44		10 08					10 44		11 07				
Stafford	d		09 01		09 25					10 01		10 25					11 01		11 25				
Wolverhampton	d		09 17		09 41	09 45				10 17		10 41	10 45				11 17		11 41	11 45			
Dunbar	d																				07 29		
Berwick-upon-Tweed	d													06 49		07 43							
Alnmouth for Alnwick	d													07 11		08 03							
Morpeth	d															08 18							
Newcastle	d	06 23							07 35					07 41		08 35					08 41		09 35
Chester-le-Street	d																						
Durham	d	06 38							07 47					07 55		08 48					08 55		09 49
Darlington	d	06 56							08 05					08 13		09 06					09 13		10 07
York	d	07 25					07 45		08 35					08 45		09 35					09 45		10 35
Leeds	d						08 11							09 11							10 11		
Wakefield Westgate	d						08 23							09 23							10 23		
Doncaster	d	07 51							09 01							09 58							10 59
Sheffield	d	08 22					08 53		09 24					09 53		10 24					10 53		11 24
Chesterfield	d	08 34					09 05							10 06							11 05		
Nottingham	d			08 41				09 07			09 41				10 06			10 41				11 06	
Derby	d	08 53		09 10			09 29	09 36	09 53		10 10			10 28	10 37	10 53		11 10			11 28	11 37	11 53
Burton-on-Trent	d			09 22			09 41	09 49			10 21				10 49			11 21			11 41	11 49	
Tamworth	d			09 34				10 02			10 33			10 49	11 02			11 33				12 02	
Birmingham New Street	a	09 27	09 33	09 56	09 58	10 05	10 06	10 24	10 27	10 33	10 55	10 58	11 05	11 08	11 24	11 27	11 33	11 55	11 59	12 05	12 08	12 24	12 27
Birmingham New Street	d	09 33	09 42		10 04	10 10	10 12	10 30	10 33	10 42		11 04	11 10	11 12	11 30	11 33	11 42		12 04	12 10	12 12	12 30	12 33
Cheltenham Spa	a		10 24				10 51	11 10		11 24				11 53	12 10		12 24				12 51	13 10	
Gloucester	a							11 20							12 20							13 20	
Bristol Parkway	a		10 54				11 25			11 53				12 29			12 53				13 24		
Bristol Temple Meads	a		11 09				11 39			12 04				12 42			13 09				13 39		
Newport (South Wales)	a							12 05							13 05							14 06	
Cardiff Central	a							12 23							13 21							14 22	
Weston-super-Mare	a		11 29																				
Taunton	a		11 59				12 16							13 16							14 16		
Tiverton Parkway	a		12 11				12 29							13 29							14 29		
Exeter St Davids	a		12 25				12 43							13 43							14 43		
Dawlish	a		12 38																		14 57		
Teignmouth	a		12 43																		15 03		
Newton Abbot	a		12 50				13 04							14 03							15 11		
Torquay	a		13 02																		15 23		
Paignton	a		13 10																		15 33		
Totnes	a						13 17							14 17									
Plymouth	a						13 45							14 45									
Liskeard	a						14 10																
Bodmin Parkway	a						14 22																
Lostwithiel	a																						
Par	a						14 33																
St Austell	a						14 41																
Truro	a						14 58																
Redruth	a						15 11																
Camborne	a						15 18																
Hayle	a																						
St Erth	a						15 28																
Penzance	a						15 38																
Birmingham International	d				10 14	10 20						11 14	11 20						12 14	12 20			
Coventry	d				10 25	10a30						11 25	11a30						12 25	12a30			
Leamington Spa	d	10 00			10 38				11 00			11 38				12 00			12 38				13 00
Banbury	a	10 17			10 54				11 17			11 54				12 17			12 54				13 17
Oxford	a	10 41			11 14				11 41			12 15				12 41			13 14				13 41
Reading	a	11 10			11 38				12 06			12 42				13 09			13 40				14 08
Guildford	a																						
Basingstoke	a				12 09				12 40			13 09							14 09				14 40
Winchester	a				12 24				12 55			13 24							14 24				14 56
Southampton Airport Pkway	a				12 33				13 08			13 33							14 32				15 07
Southampton Central	a				12 41				13 17			13 41							14 41				15 17
Brockenhurst	a				12 57							13 57							14 57				
Bournemouth	a				13 12							14 12							15 12				

A from Leeds to Plymouth
B from Edinburgh

Table T051-F

Saturdays
26 May to 21 July

Scotland, The North East, North West England - The South West and South Coast

		XC ◇1	XC 1	XC ◇1	VT ◇1	XC ◇1 A	XC ◇1	XC ◇1	XC ◇1	XC 1	XC ◇1	XC ◇1 A	VT ◇1	XC ◇1 B	XC ◇1	XC ◇1	XC ◇1	XC 1	XC ◇1	VT ◇1	XC ◇1 C	XC ◇1
Aberdeen	d																					
Stonehaven	d																					
Montrose	d																					
Arbroath	d																					
Dundee	d					06 32																
Leuchars	d					06 46																
Cupar	d					06 54																
Ladybank	d					07 03																
Markinch	d					07 11																
Kirkcaldy	d					07 21																
Inverkeithing	d					07 38																
Glasgow Central	d											07 48	10 00								09 00	
Motherwell	d											08 08									09 15	
Haymarket	d					07 56						08 52									09 57	
Edinburgh	d				08 53	08 06						09 08								10 52	10 05	
Haymarket	d				08 58															10 57		
Lockerbie	d																					
Carlisle	d				10 08								11 11							12 08		
Penrith North Lakes	d												11 25									
Oxenholme Lake District	d				10 42															12 43		
Lancaster	d				10 57															12 57		
Preston	d				11 16								12 17							13 17		
Wigan North Western	d				11 29								12 28							13 28		
Warrington Bank Quay	d				11 40								12 39							13 39		
M'chester Piccadilly	d	11 05		11 27					12 05		12 27						13 05		13 27			
Stockport	d	11 13		11 36					12 13		12 36						13 13		13 36			
Wilmslow	d																					
Crewe	d				12 00								13 01							14 01		
Macclesfield	d	11 26		11 49					12 26		12 49						13 26		13 49			
Congleton	d																					
Stoke-on-Trent	d	11 44		12 07					12 44		13 07						13 44		14 07			
Stafford	d	12 01		12 25					13 01		13 25						14 01		14 25			
Wolverhampton	d	12 17		12 41	12 45				13 17		13 41		13 45				14 17		14 41	14 45		
Dunbar	d											09 29										
Berwick-upon-Tweed	d					08 50						09 53									10 47	
Alnmouth for Alnwick	d					09 12																
Morpeth	d																				11 21	
Newcastle	d					09 42		10 35				10 44				11 35					11 42	
Chester-le-Street	d																					
Durham	d					09 56		10 48				10 56				11 49					11 55	
Darlington	d					10 14		11 06				11 14				12 06					12 12	
York	d					10 45		11 35				11 45				12 35					12 45	
Leeds	d					11 11						12 11									13 11	
Wakefield Westgate	d					11 23						12 23									13 23	
Doncaster	d							11 58								12 59						
Sheffield	d					11 55		12 24				12 55				13 24					13 53	
Chesterfield	d					12 07						13 07									14 06	
Nottingham	d		11 41				12 06			12 41					13 06			13 41				14 06
Derby	d		12 10			12 28	12 37	12 53		13 10		13 28			13 37	13 53		14 10			14 28	14 37
Burton-on-Trent	d		12 21				12 49			13 24		13 38			13 49			14 21				14 49
Tamworth	d		12 33			12 49	13 02			13 35				←	14 02			14 33			14 49	15 02
Birmingham New Street	a	12 34	12 55	12 58	13 05	13 08	13 24	13 27	13 34	13 55	13 58	14 03	14 05	14 03	14 24	14 27	14 35	14 55	14 58	15 05	15 08	15 24
Birmingham New Street	d	12 42		13 04	13 10	13 12	13 30	13 33	13 42		14 04	14 12	14 10	14 12	14 30	14 33	14 42		15 04	15 10	15 12	15 30
Cheltenham Spa	a	13 25				13 51	14 10		14 24			→		14 51	15 10		15 24				15 50	16 10
Gloucester	a						14 20								15 20							16 20
Bristol Parkway	a	13 54				14 26			14 54								15 54				16 29	
Bristol Temple Meads	a	14 05				14 40			15 09					16 31			16 07				16 43	
Newport (South Wales)	a						15 09								16 06							17 08
Cardiff Central	a						15 26								16 25							17 24
Weston-super-Mare	a																					
Taunton	a					15 15			15 42					17 17							17 17	
Tiverton Parkway	a					15 27			15 54					17 30							17 30	
Exeter St Davids	a					15 40			16 07					17 44							17 44	
Dawlish	a								16 34													
Teignmouth	a								16 40													
Newton Abbot	a					16 04			16 47					18 10							18 10	
Torquay	a								16 59													
Paignton	a								17 10													
Totnes	a					16 16								18 23							18 23	
Plymouth	a					16 43								18 51							18 51	
Liskeard	a					17 12								19 19							19 19	
Bodmin Parkway	a					17 27								19 32							19 32	
Lostwithiel	a																					
Par	a					17 39								19 43							19 43	
St Austell	a													19 50							19 50	
Truro	a													20 09							20 09	
Redruth	a													20 22							20 22	
Camborne	a													20 30							20 30	
Hayle	a																					
St Erth	a													20 40							20 40	
Penzance	a													20 53							20 52	
Birmingham International	d			13 14	13 20						14 14		14 20						15 14	15 20		
Coventry	d			13 25	13a30						14 25		14a29						15 25	15a30		
Leamington Spa	d			13 38				14 00			14 38					15 00			15 38			
Banbury	a			13 54				14 18			14 55					15 21			15 54			
Oxford	a			14 14				14 40			15 15					15 41			16 14			
Reading	a			14 41				15 08			15 40					16 09			16 42			
Guildford	a																					
Basingstoke	a			15 09							16 09					16 40			17 09			
Winchester	a			15 24							16 24					16 55			17 24			
Southampton Airport Pkway	a			15 33							16 33					17 08			17 33			
Southampton Central	a			15 41							16 41					17 17			17 41			
Brockenhurst	a			15 57							16 57								17 57			
Bournemouth	a			16 12							17 12								18 12			

A from Edinburgh
B to Plymouth
C [illegible]

Table T051-F

Saturdays
26 May to 21 July

Scotland, The North East, North West England - The South West and South Coast

Station		XC ◇1 ✠	XC ◇1 ✠	XC 1	XC ◇1 ✠	XC ◇1 A ✠	VT ◇1 ⊡	XC ◇1 B ✠	XC ◇1 ✠	XC ◇1 C ✠	XC ◇1 ✠	XC 1 ✠	XC ◇1 ✠	VT ◇1 ⊡	XC ◇1 A ✠	XC ◇1	XC ◇1 ✠	XC ◇1 ✠	XC 1 ✠	XC ◇1 ✠	VT ◇1 ⊡	XC ◇1 ✠	XC ◇1
Aberdeen	d					08 20																	
Stonehaven	d					08 38																	
Montrose	d					08 59																	
Arbroath	d					09 15																	
Dundee	d					09 35																	
Leuchars	d					09 48																	
Cupar	d					09 55																	
Ladybank	d					10 02																	
Markinch	d					10 09																	
Kirkcaldy	d					10 18																	
Inverkeithing	d					10 33																	
Glasgow Central	d						12 00								11 00						14 00		
Motherwell	d														11 15								
Haymarket	d					10 50									11 54								
Edinburgh	d					11 08								12 52	12 05							13 09	
Haymarket	d													12 58									
Lockerbie	d																						
Carlisle	d						13 13							14 08							15 11		
Penrith North Lakes	d													14 22									
Oxenholme Lake District	d																				15 45		
Lancaster	d						14 00							14 56									
Preston	d						14 20							15 17							16 17		
Wigan North Western	d						14 32							15 28							16 28		
Warrington Bank Quay	d						14 43							15 39							16 39		
M'chester Piccadilly	d		14 05		14 27						15 05		15 27					16 05		16 27			
Stockport	d		14 13		14 36						15 13		15 36					16 13		16 36			
Wilmslow	d																						
Crewe	d						15 03							16 01							17 01		
Macclesfield	d		14 26		14 49						15 26		15 49					16 26		16 49			
Congleton	d																						
Stoke-on-Trent	d		14 44		15 07						15 44		16 07					16 44		17 07			
Stafford	d		15 01		15 26						16 01		16 25					17 01		17 25			
Wolverhampton	d		15 17		15 41		15 45				16 17		16 41	16 45				17 17		17 41	17 45		
Dunbar	d					11 29																13 30	
Berwick-upon-Tweed	d					11 53									12 47								
Alnmouth for Alnwick	d					12 13																14 12	
Morpeth	d														13 18								
Newcastle	d	12 35				12 44				13 35					13 44		14 35					14 44	
Chester-le-Street	d																						
Durham	d	12 48				12 56				13 48					13 56		14 48					14 56	
Darlington	d	13 06				13 14				14 06					14 14		15 06					15 14	
York	d	13 35				13 45				14 35					14 45		15 35					15 45	
Leeds	d					14 11									15 11							16 11	
Wakefield Westgate	d					14 23									15 23							16 23	
Doncaster	d	13 58								14 59							15 58						
Sheffield	d	14 25				14 55				15 24					15 55		16 24					16 55	
Chesterfield	d					15 07									16 07							17 07	
Nottingham	d			14 41					15 06			15 41				16 06			16 41				17 06
Derby	d	14 54		15 10		15 28			15 37	15 53		16 10			16 28	16 37	16 53		17 10			17 28	17 37
Burton-on-Trent	d			15 24		15 38			15 49			16 21				16 49			17 24			17 38	17 49
Tamworth	d			15 35				←	16 02			16 33			16 48	17 02			17 35				18 02
Birmingham New Street	a	15 27	15 33	15 55	15 58	16 03	16 05	16 03	16 24	16 27	16 33	16 55	16 58	17 05	17 07	17 24	17 27	17 33	17 55	17 58	18 05	18 07	18 24
Birmingham New Street	d	15 33	15 42		16 04	16 12	16 10	16 12	16 30	16 33	16 42		17 04	17 10	17 12	17 30	17 33	17 42		18 04	18 10	18 12	18 30
Cheltenham Spa	a		16 24			→		16 50	17 09		17 24				17 51	18 16		18 24				18 51	19 10
Gloucester	a								17 20							18 25							19 20
Bristol Parkway	a		16 53					17 25			17 53				18 29			18 53				19 24	
Bristol Temple Meads	a		17 08					17 39			18 04				18 43			19 08				19 39	
Newport (South Wales)	a								18 06							19 10							20 03
Cardiff Central	a								18 24							19 30							20 20
Weston-super-Mare	a																						
Taunton	a							18 15							19 15							20 15	
Tiverton Parkway	a							18 27							19 27							20 27	
Exeter St Davids	a							18 41							19 44							20 40	
Dawlish	a																						
Teignmouth	a																						
Newton Abbot	a							19 04							20 05							21 00	
Torquay	a																						
Paignton	a																						
Totnes	a							19 16							20 17							21 12	
Plymouth	a							19 42							20 43							21 38	
Liskeard	a							20 10															
Bodmin Parkway	a							20 22															
Lostwithiel	a							20 27															
Par	a							20 34															
St Austell	a							20 40															
Truro	a							21 00															
Redruth	a							21 12															
Camborne	a							21 18															
Hayle	a							21 26															
St Erth	a							21 30															
Penzance	a							21 40															
Birmingham International	d				16 14		16 20						17 14	17 20						18 14	18 20		
Coventry	d				16 25		16a30						17 25	17a30						18 25	18a30		
Leamington Spa	d	16 02			16 38					17 00			17 38				18 02			18 38			
Banbury	a	16 18			16 54					17 17			17 54				18 18			18 54			
Oxford	a	16 40			17 14					17 40			18 14				18 41			19 14			
Reading	a	17 10			17 39					18 10			18 43				19 10			19 41			
Guildford	a									19 01													
Basingstoke	a				18 09								19 09							20 09			
Winchester	a				18 24								19 24							20 25			
Southampton Airport Pkway	a				18 33								19 33							20 33			
Southampton Central	a				18 41								19 41							20 41			
Brockenhurst	a				18 57								19 57							20 57			
Bournemouth	a				19 12								20 12							21 12			

A ✠ from Edinburgh
B ✠ to Plymouth
C ✠ to Reading

Table T051-F

Saturdays
26 May to 21 July

Scotland, The North East, North West England - The South West and South Coast

Station		XC ◇1 ✠	XC ◇1 A ✠	XC 1 ✠	XC ◇1 B ✠	XC ◇1 C ✠	XC ◇1	XC ◇1 ✠	XC ◇1 D ✠	XC 1 ✠	XC ◇1 D ✠	XC ◇1 D ✠	XC ◇1	XC ◇1 D ✠	XC ◇1 D ✠	XC 1 ✠	XC ◇1 D ✠	XC ◇1 C ✠	XC ◇1 ✠	XC ◇1	VT ◇1 ⊡	XC 1
Aberdeen	d																					
Stonehaven	d																					
Montrose	d																					
Arbroath	d																					
Dundee	d																					
Leuchars	d																					
Cupar	d																					
Ladybank	d																					
Markinch	d																					
Kirkcaldy	d																					
Inverkeithing	d																					
Glasgow Central	d					13 00												15 00			18 00	
Motherwell	d					13 16												15 16				
Haymarket	d					13 55												15 56				
Edinburgh	d					14 05						15 08						16 05				
Haymarket	d																					
Lockerbie	d																					
Carlisle	d																				19 11	
Penrith North Lakes	d																					
Oxenholme Lake District	d																					
Lancaster	d																				19 58	
Preston	d																				20 17	
Wigan North Western	d																				20 28	
Warrington Bank Quay	d																				20 39	
M'chester Piccadilly	d		17 05		17 27				18 05		18 27				19 05		19 27			20 05		
Stockport	d		17 13		17 36				18 13		18 36				19 13		19 36			20 13		
Wilmslow	d																					
Crewe	d																				21 01	
Macclesfield	d		17 26						18 26						19 26		19 49			20 26		
Congleton	d				17 55						18 55											
Stoke-on-Trent	d		17 44		18 07				18 44		19 07				19 44		20 07			20 44		
Stafford	d		18 01		18 25				19 01		19 25				20 01		20 25			21 01		
Wolverhampton	d		18 17		18 41				19 17		19 41				20 17		20 41			21 17	21 34	
Dunbar	d											15 29										
Berwick-upon-Tweed	d					14 47																
Alnmouth for Alnwick	d																	17 05				
Morpeth	d					15 21												17 19				
Newcastle	d	15 05				15 44		16 35				16 44		17 32				17 44	18 36			
Chester-le-Street	d													17 41								
Durham	d	15 18				15 56		16 48				16 56		17 48				17 56	18 49			
Darlington	d	15 35				16 14		17 05				17 14		18 06				18 14	19 07			
York	d	16 04				16 45		17 35				17 45		18 35				18 45	19 36			
Leeds	d	16 40				17 10						18 11						19 11				
Wakefield Westgate	d	16 52				17 22						18 23						19 23				
Doncaster	d							17 58						18 58					19 59			
Sheffield	d	17 24				17 55		18 23				18 55		19 24				19 55	20 24			
Chesterfield	d					18 07						19 07						20 07				
Nottingham	d			17 41			18 06			18 41			19 06			19 34						20 38
Derby	d	17 53		18 10		18 29	18 37	18 53		19 10		19 29	19 39	19 54		20 10		20 28	20 53			21 06
Burton-on-Trent	d			18 24			18 49			19 21		19 39	19 50			20 22						21 24
Tamworth	d			18 35		18 47	19 02			19 33			20 02			20 34		20 46				21 35
Birmingham New Street	a	18 27	18 33	18 55	18 58	19 07	19 24	19 27	19 33	19 55	19 59	20 06	20 24	20 27	20 33	20 55	20 58	21 04	21 25	21 33	21 51	21 56
Birmingham New Street	d	18 33	18 42		19 04	19 12	19 30	19 33	19 42		20 04	20 12	20 30	20 33	20 42		21 04	21 12				
Cheltenham Spa	a		19 24			19 51	20 10		20 24			20 51	21 10		21 24			21 51				
Gloucester	a						20 20						21 20					22 01				
Bristol Parkway	a		19 54			20 29			20 53			21 22			21 58			22 32				
Bristol Temple Meads	a		20 05			20 42			21 04			21 34			22 12			22 42				
Newport (South Wales)	a		20 44				21 09						22 18									
Cardiff Central	a		21 00				21 26						22 42									
Weston-super-Mare	a																					
Taunton	a					21 15						22 15										
Tiverton Parkway	a					21 27						22 29										
Exeter St Davids	a					21 43						22 44										
Dawlish	a																					
Teignmouth	a																					
Newton Abbot	a					22 04						23 11										
Torquay	a																					
Paignton	a																					
Totnes	a					22 20						23 27										
Plymouth	a					22 50						23 56										
Liskeard	a																					
Bodmin Parkway	a																					
Lostwithiel	a																					
Par	a																					
St Austell	a																					
Truro	a																					
Redruth	a																					
Camborne	a																					
Hayle	a																					
St Erth	a																					
Penzance	a																					
Birmingham International	d				19 14						20 14						21 14					
Coventry	d				19 25						20 25						21 25					
Leamington Spa	d	19 00			19 38			20 03			20 38			21 00			21 38					
Banbury	a	19 17			19 54			20 19			20 54			21 19			21 54					
Oxford	a	19 41			20 14			20 40			21 14			21 41			22 14					
Reading	a	20 08			20 41			21 08			21 42			22 14			22 45					
Guildford	a																					
Basingstoke	a				21 09						22 08			22 39			23 07					
Winchester	a				21 24						22 26			22 56			23 24					
Southampton Airport Pkway	a				21 32						22 34			23 12			23 32					
Southampton Central	a				21 40						22 42			23 20			23 41					
Brockenhurst	a				21 56						22 59											
Bournemouth	a				22 15						23 19											

A ✠ to Bristol Temple Meads
B ✠ to Reading
C ✠ from Edinburgh
D ✠ to Birmingham New Street

Table T051-F

Saturdays

26 May to 21 July

Scotland, The North East, North West England - The South West and South Coast

		XC	XC	XC	XC	VT	VT	XC	XC	XC
		◇1	◇1	◇1	◇1	◇1	◇1	◇1	1	◇1
			A							B
			🍴			🍽	🍽			🍴
Aberdeen	d									
Stonehaven	d									
Montrose	d									
Arbroath	d									
Dundee	d									
Leuchars	d									
Cupar	d									
Ladybank	d									
Markinch	d									
Kirkcaldy	d									
Inverkeithing	d									
Glasgow Central	d					18 40				17 00
Motherwell	d									17 16
Haymarket	d									17 55
Edinburgh	d		17 08				18 52			18 08
Haymarket	d						18 56			
Lockerbie	d									
Carlisle	d					19 49	20 09			
Penrith North Lakes	d					20 03	20 23			
Oxenholme Lake District	d					20 26	20 47			
Lancaster	d					20 41	21 02			
Preston	d					21 01	21 22			
Wigan North Western	d					21 12	21 33			
Warrington Bank Quay	d					21 23	21 44			
M'chester Piccadilly	d	20 27		21 05				21 27		
Stockport	d	20 36		21 13				21 35		
Wilmslow	d									
Crewe	d					21 44	22 06			
Macclesfield	d	20 49		21 26				21 49		
Congleton	d									
Stoke-on-Trent	d	21 08		21 44				22 07		
Stafford	d	21 25		22 01		22 08	22 25	22 30		
Wolverhampton	d	21 42		22 17		22 23	22 40	22 45		
Dunbar	d		17 31							18 30
Berwick-upon-Tweed	d		17 54							18 53
Alnmouth for Alnwick	d									19 14
Morpeth	d									
Newcastle	d		18 44		19 35					19 45
Chester-le-Street	d									
Durham	d		18 56		19 50					19 57
Darlington	d		19 14		20 07					20 15
York	d		19 45		20 35					20 45
Leeds	d		20 11							21 11
Wakefield Westgate	d		20 23							21 23
Doncaster	d				20 59					
Sheffield	d		20 55		21 25					21 55
Chesterfield	d		21 07		21 37					22 07
Nottingham	d								21 39	
Derby	d		21 28		21 56				22 12	22 26
Burton-on-Trent	d		21 38						22 22	22 37
Tamworth	d		21 49						22 35	22 47
Birmingham New Street	a	21 59	22 06	22 33	22 44	22 48	22 58	23 01	23 02	23 06
Birmingham New Street	d									
Cheltenham Spa	a									
Gloucester	a									
Bristol Parkway	a									
Bristol Temple Meads	a									
Newport (South Wales)	a									
Cardiff Central	a									
Weston-super-Mare	a									
Taunton	a									
Tiverton Parkway	a									
Exeter St Davids	a									
Dawlish	a									
Teignmouth	a									
Newton Abbot	a									
Torquay	a									
Paignton	a									
Totnes	a									
Plymouth	a									
Liskeard	a									
Bodmin Parkway	a									
Lostwithiel	a									
Par	a									
St Austell	a									
Truro	a									
Redruth	a									
Camborne	a									
Hayle	a									
St Erth	a									
Penzance	a									
Birmingham International	d									
Coventry	d									
Leamington Spa	d									
Banbury	a									
Oxford	a									
Reading	a									
Guildford	a									
Basingstoke	a									
Winchester	a									
Southampton Airport Pkwy	a									
Southampton Central	a									
Brockenhurst	a									
Bournemouth	a									

A 🍴 to Leeds

B 🍴 from Edinburgh to Leeds

Table T051-F

Saturdays

28 July to 1 September

Scotland, The North East, North West England - The South West and South Coast

		XC	XC	XC	XC	XC	XC	XC	XC	XC	XC	XC	XC	VT	XC	XC	XC	XC	XC	XC	VT	XC	XC
		◇1	◇1	◇1	◇1	◇1	◇1	◇1	◇1	◇1	◇1	◇1	◇1	◇1	◇1	◇1	◇1	◇1	1	◇1	◇1	◇1	◇1
					A					B	B							C					B
				🍴	🍴	🍴		🍴	🍴	🍴	🍴	🍴		🍽	🍴		🍴	🍴		🍴	🍽		🍴
Aberdeen	d																						
Stonehaven	d																						
Montrose	d																						
Arbroath	d																						
Dundee	d																						
Leuchars	d																						
Cupar	d																						
Ladybank	d																						
Markinch	d																						
Kirkcaldy	d																						
Inverkeithing	d																						
Glasgow Central	d																						
Motherwell	d																						
Haymarket	d																						
Edinburgh	d																						
Haymarket	d																						
Lockerbie	d																						
Carlisle	d																						
Penrith North Lakes	d																						
Oxenholme Lake District	d																						
Lancaster	d																				06 58		
Preston	d													06 17							07 17		
Wigan North Western	d													06 28							07 28		
Warrington Bank Quay	d													06 39							07 39		
M'chester Piccadilly	d							05 11				06 00						07 05		07 27			
Stockport	d											06 08						07 13		07 36			
Wilmslow	d																						
Crewe	d							05 47						07 01							08 01		
Macclesfield	d											06 21						07 26		07 49			
Congleton	d																						
Stoke-on-Trent	d							06 08				06 39						07 44		08 07			
Stafford	d							06 26				07 01						08 01		08 25			
Wolverhampton	d							06 41				07 17		07 45				08 17		08 41	08 45		
Dunbar	d																						
Berwick-upon-Tweed	d																						
Alnmouth for Alnwick	d																						
Morpeth	d																						
Newcastle	d																						
Chester-le-Street	d																						
Durham	d																						
Darlington	d																						
York	d																						
Leeds	d														05 49							06 17	
Wakefield Westgate	d														06 01							06 29	
Doncaster	d																					06 51	
Sheffield	d														06 30							07 18	
Chesterfield	d														06 44							07 32	
Nottingham	d									05 58			06 37			06 58			07 37				08 07
Derby	d																						
Burton-on-Trent	d						06 20			06 48	06 58		07 17		07 38	07 50	08 00		08 18			08 38	08 49
Tamworth	d						06 31		←	07 01	07 09		07 30		07 49	08 02	08 12		08 30			08 49	09 02
Birmingham New Street	a						06 50	06 57	06 50	07 24	07 28	07 33	07 52	08 05	08 08	08 24	08 27	08 33	08 55	08 58	09 05	09 08	09 24
Birmingham New Street	d	05 00	05 42	06 04	06 33	06 42	07 12	07 04	07 12	07 30	07 33	07 42	08 04	08 10	08 12	08 30	08 33	08 42		09 04		09 12	09 30
Cheltenham Spa	a	06 02	06 42			07 24	→		07 51	08 10		08 24			08 51	09 10		09 24				09 51	10 10
Gloucester	a	06 12	06 52							08 20						09 20							10 20
Bristol Parkway	a					07 53			08 24			08 54			09 24			09 53				10 29	
Bristol Temple Meads	a					08 05			08 38			09 07			09 39			10 04				10 43	
Newport (South Wales)	a	07 05	07 48							09 06						10 05							11 06
Cardiff Central	a	07 21	08 04							09 23						10 21							11 24
Weston-super-Mare	a																						
Taunton	a					08 42			09 15						10 16			11 00				11 16	
Tiverton Parkway	a					08 54			09 27						10 29			11 12				11 29	
Exeter St Davids	a					09 07			09 40						10 43			11 26				11 43	
Dawlish	a														11 01								
Teignmouth	a														11 07								
Newton Abbot	a					09 28			10 00						11 15			11 52				12 03	
Torquay	a					09 39									11 27								
Paignton	a					09 47									11 37								
Totnes	a								10 12									12 04				12 16	
Plymouth	a								10 39									12 33				12 44	
Liskeard	a																	13 04					
Bodmin Parkway	a																	13 20					
Lostwithiel	a																						
Par	a																	13 32					
St Austell	a																						
Truro	a																						
Redruth	a																						
Camborne	a																						
Hayle	a																						
St Erth	a																						
Penzance	a																						
Birmingham International	d			06 14				07 14					08 14	08 20						09 14			
Coventry	d			06 25				07 25					08 25	08a30						09 25			
Leamington Spa	d			06 38	07 00			07 38			08 01		08 38				09 00			09 38			
Banbury	a			06 54	07 17			07 54			08 17		08 54				09 17			09 55			
Oxford	a			07 14	07 40			08 14			08 39		09 14				09 40			10 15			
Reading	a			07 41	08 09			08 41			09 09		09 40				10 08			10 41			
Guildford	a																						
Basingstoke	a			08 08	08 39			09 09					10 09				10 40			11 09			
Winchester	a			08 24	08 58			09 25					10 24				10 56			11 25			
Southampton Airport Pkwy	a			08 32	09 08			09 33					10 33				11 08			11 33			
Southampton Central	a			08 41	09 17			09 41					10 41				11 17			11 41			
Brockenhurst	a			08 56				09 57					10 57							11 57			
Bournemouth	a			09 14				10 11					11 13							12 12			

A 🍴 from Reading

B 🍴 from Birmingham New Street

C 🍴 to Plymouth

Table T051-F

Saturdays
28 July to 1 September

Scotland, The North East, North West England - The South West and South Coast

		XC ◇1 ⊼	XC ◇1 ⊼	XC 1	XC ◇1 ⊼	VT ◇1 ⊡	XC ◇1	XC ◇1 ⊼	XC ◇1 ⊼	XC ◇1 ⊼	XC 1	XC ◇1 ⊼	VT ◇1 ⊡	XC ◇1 ⊼	XC ◇1 ⊼	XC ◇1 ⊼	XC ◇1 ⊼	XC 1	XC ◇1 ⊼	VT ◇1 ⊡	XC ◇1	XC ◇1 ⊼	XC ◇1 ⊼
Aberdeen	d																						
Stonehaven	d																						
Montrose	d																						
Arbroath	d																						
Dundee	d																						
Leuchars 8	d																						
Cupar	d																						
Ladybank	d																						
Markinch	d																						
Kirkcaldy	d																						
Inverkeithing	d																						
Glasgow Central 15	d					05 50														08 00			06 01
Motherwell	d					06 05																	06 16
Haymarket	d																						06 57
Edinburgh 10	d												06 52			06 06					07 00		07 07
Haymarket	d												06 56										
Lockerbie	d																						
Carlisle 8	d					07 02							08 07							09 11			
Penrith North Lakes	d					07 17							08 22										
Oxenholme Lake District	d					07 41																	
Lancaster 6	d					07 56							08 57							09 58			
Preston 8	d					08 17							09 17							10 17			
Wigan North Western	d					08 28							09 28							10 29			
Warrington Bank Quay	d					08 39							09 39							10 41			
M'chester Piccadilly 10	d		08 05		08 27					09 05		09 27					10 05		10 27				
Stockport	d		08 13		08 36					09 13		09 37					10 13		10 36				
Wilmslow	d																						
Crewe 10	d					09 01							10 01							11 02			
Macclesfield	d		08 26		08 49					09 26		09 50					10 26		10 49				
Congleton	d																						
Stoke-on-Trent	d		08 44		09 07					09 44		10 08					10 44		11 07				
Stafford	d		09 01		09 25					10 01		10 25					11 01		11 25				
Wolverhampton 7	d		09 17		09 41	09 45				10 17		10 41	10 45				11 17		11 41	11 45			
Dunbar	d																						07 29
Berwick-upon-Tweed	d															06 49					07 43		
Alnmouth for Alnwick	d															07 11					08 03		
Morpeth	d																				08 18		
Newcastle 8	d								06 43					07 35		07 41					08 35		08 41
Chester-le-Street	d																						
Durham	d								06 58					07 47		07 55					08 48		08 55
Darlington 7	d								07 16					08 05		08 13					09 06		09 13
York 8	d	06 45					07 35		07 44					08 35		08 45					09 35		09 45
Leeds 10	d	07 11							08 11							09 11							10 11
Wakefield Westgate 7	d	07 23							08 23							09 23							10 23
Doncaster 7	d						07 58							08 58							09 58		
Sheffield 7	d	07 56					08 22		08 53					09 24		09 53					10 24		10 55
Chesterfield	d	08 08					08 35		09 05					09 38		10 05					10 37		11 07
Nottingham 8	d			08 41				09 04			09 41				10 04			10 41				11 04	
Derby 6	d																						
Burton-on-Trent	d	09 02		09 22			09 41	09 49	10 01		10 21			10 37	10 49	11 01		11 21			11 41	11 49	12 03
Tamworth	d			09 34				10 02			10 33			10 49	11 02			11 33				12 02	
Birmingham New Street 12	a	09 27	09 33	09 56	09 58	10 05	10 06	10 24	10 27	10 33	10 55	10 58	11 05	11 08	11 24	11 27	11 33	11 55	11 59	12 05	12 08	12 24	12 27
Birmingham New Street 12	d	09 33	09 42		10 04	10 10	10 12	10 30	10 33	10 42		11 04	11 10	11 12	11 30	11 33	11 42		12 04	12 10	12 12	12 30	12 33
Cheltenham Spa 4	a		10 24				10 51	11 10		11 24				11 53	12 10		12 24				12 51	13 10	
Gloucester 7	a							11 20							12 20							13 20	
Bristol Parkway 7	a		10 54				11 25			11 53				12 29			12 53				13 24		
Bristol Temple Meads 10	a		11 09				11 39			12 04				12 42			13 09				13 39		
Newport (South Wales)	a							12 05							13 05							14 06	
Cardiff Central 7	a							12 23							13 21							14 22	
Weston-super-Mare	a		11 29																				
Taunton	a		11 59				12 16							13 16							14 16		
Tiverton Parkway	a		12 11				12 29							13 29							14 29		
Exeter St Davids 6	a		12 25				12 43							13 43							14 43		
Dawlish	a		12 38																		14 57		
Teignmouth	a		12 43																		15 03		
Newton Abbot	a		12 50				13 04							14 03							15 11		
Torquay	a		13 02																		15 23		
Paignton	a		13 10																		15 33		
Totnes	a						13 17							14 17									
Plymouth	a						13 45							14 45									
Liskeard 6	a						14 10																
Bodmin Parkway	a						14 22																
Lostwithiel	a																						
Par	a						14 33																
St Austell	a						14 41																
Truro	a						14 58																
Redruth	a						15 11																
Camborne	a						15 18																
Hayle	a																						
St Erth	a						15 28																
Penzance	a						15 38																
Birmingham International ✈	d				10 14	10 20						11 14	11 20						12 14	12 20			
Coventry	d				10 25	10a30						11 25	11a30						12 25	12a30			
Leamington Spa 8	d	10 00			10 38				11 00			11 38				12 00			12 38				13 00
Banbury	a	10 17			10 54				11 17			11 54				12 17			12 54				13 17
Oxford	a	10 41			11 14				11 41			12 15				12 41			13 14				13 41
Reading 7	a	11 10			11 38				12 06			12 42				13 09			13 40				14 08
Guildford	a																						
Basingstoke	a				12 09				12 40			13 09							14 09				14 40
Winchester	a				12 24				12 55			13 24							14 24				14 56
Southampton Airport Pkwy ✈	a				12 33				13 08			13 33							14 32				15 07
Southampton Central ⛴	a				12 41				13 17			13 41							14 41				15 17
Brockenhurst 3	a				12 57							13 57							14 57				
Bournemouth	a				13 12							14 12							15 12				

Table T051-F

Saturdays
28 July to 1 September

Scotland, The North East, North West England - The South West and South Coast

		XC ◇1 ⊼	XC 1	XC ◇1 ⊼	VT ◇1 ⊡	XC ◇1 ⊼	XC ◇1 ⊼	XC ◇1 ⊼	XC ◇1 ⊼	XC 1	XC ◇1 ⊼	XC ◇1 ⊼	VT ◇1 ⊡	XC ◇1 A ⊼	XC ◇1 ⊼	XC ◇1 ⊼	XC ◇1 ⊼	XC 1 ⊼	XC ◇1 ⊼	VT ◇1 ⊡	XC ◇1 A ⊼	XC ◇1 ⊼
Aberdeen	d																					
Stonehaven	d																					
Montrose	d																					
Arbroath	d																					
Dundee	d							06 32														
Leuchars 8	d							06 46														
Cupar	d							06 54														
Ladybank	d							07 03														
Markinch	d							07 11														
Kirkcaldy	d							07 21														
Inverkeithing	d							07 38														
Glasgow Central 15	d												10 00			07 48						
Motherwell	d															08 08						
Haymarket	d							07 56								08 52						
Edinburgh 10	d				08 53			08 06								09 08				10 52		
Haymarket	d				08 58															10 57		
Lockerbie	d																					
Carlisle 8	d				10 08								11 11							12 08		
Penrith North Lakes	d												11 25									
Oxenholme Lake District	d				10 42															12 43		
Lancaster 6	d				10 57															12 57		
Preston 8	d				11 16								12 17							13 17		
Wigan North Western	d				11 29								12 28							13 28		
Warrington Bank Quay	d				11 40								12 39							13 39		
M'chester Piccadilly 10	d	11 05		11 27					12 05		12 27						13 05		13 27			
Stockport	d	11 13		11 36					12 13		12 36						13 13		13 36			
Wilmslow	d																					
Crewe 10	d				12 00								13 01							14 01		
Macclesfield	d	11 26		11 49					12 26		12 49						13 26		13 49			
Congleton	d																					
Stoke-on-Trent	d	11 44		12 07					12 44		13 07						13 44		14 07			
Stafford	d	12 01		12 25					13 01		13 25						14 01		14 25			
Wolverhampton 7	d	12 17		12 41	12 45				13 17		13 41		13 45				14 17		14 41	14 45		
Dunbar	d															09 29						
Berwick-upon-Tweed	d							08 50								09 53						
Alnmouth for Alnwick	d							09 12														
Morpeth	d																					
Newcastle 8	d					09 35		09 42				10 35				10 44					11 35	
Chester-le-Street	d																					
Durham	d					09 49		09 56				10 48				10 56					11 49	
Darlington 7	d					10 07		10 14				11 06				11 14					12 06	
York 8	d					10 35		10 45				11 35				11 45					12 35	
Leeds 10	d							11 11								12 11						
Wakefield Westgate 7	d							11 23								12 23						
Doncaster 7	d					10 59						11 58									12 59	
Sheffield 7	d					11 24		11 55				12 24				12 55					13 23	
Chesterfield	d					11 36		12 07				12 36				13 07					13 37	
Nottingham 8	d		11 41				12 04			12 41					13 04			13 41				14 04
Derby 6	d																					
Burton-on-Trent	d		12 21			12 37	12 49	13 01		13 24		13 38			13 49	14 01		14 21			14 37	14 49
Tamworth	d		12 33			12 49	13 02			13 35				←	14 02			14 33			14 49	15 02
Birmingham New Street 12	a	12 34	12 55	12 58	13 05	13 08	13 24	13 27	13 34	13 55	13 58	14 03	14 05	14 03	14 24	14 27	14 35	14 55	14 58	15 05	15 08	15 24
Birmingham New Street 12	d	12 42		13 04	13 10	13 12	13 30	13 33	13 42		14 04	14 12	14 10	14 12	14 30	14 33	14 42		15 04	15 10	15 12	15 30
Cheltenham Spa 4	a	13 25				13 51	14 10		14 24			→		14 51	15 10		15 24				15 50	16 10
Gloucester 7	a						14 20								15 20							16 20
Bristol Parkway 7	a	13 54				14 26			14 54					15 24			15 54				16 29	
Bristol Temple Meads 10	a	14 05				14 40			15 09					15 38			16 07				16 43	
Newport (South Wales)	a						15 09								16 06							17 08
Cardiff Central 7	a						15 26								16 25							17 24
Weston-super-Mare	a																					
Taunton	a					15 15			15 42					16 14							17 17	
Tiverton Parkway	a					15 27			15 54					16 26							17 30	
Exeter St Davids 6	a					15 40			16 07					16 40							17 44	
Dawlish	a								16 34													
Teignmouth	a								16 40													
Newton Abbot	a					16 04			16 47					17 00							18 10	
Torquay	a								16 59													
Paignton	a								17 10													
Totnes	a					16 16								17 12							18 23	
Plymouth	a					16 43								17 39							18 51	
Liskeard 6	a					17 12								18 04							19 19	
Bodmin Parkway	a					17 27								18 16							19 32	
Lostwithiel	a																					
Par	a					17 39								18 27							19 43	
St Austell	a													18 33							19 50	
Truro	a													18 50							20 09	
Redruth	a													19 07							20 22	
Camborne	a													19 14							20 30	
Hayle	a													19 22								
St Erth	a													19 26							20 40	
Penzance	a													19 36							20 52	
Birmingham International ✈	d			13 14	13 20						14 14		14 20						15 14	15 20		
Coventry	d			13 25	13a30						14 25		14a29						15 25	15a30		
Leamington Spa 8	d			13 38				14 00			14 38					15 00			15 38			
Banbury	a			13 54				14 18			14 55					15 21			15 54			
Oxford	a			14 14				14 40			15 15					15 41			16 14			
Reading 7	a			14 41				15 08			15 40					16 09			16 42			
Guildford	a																					
Basingstoke	a			15 09							16 09					16 40			17 09			
Winchester	a			15 24							16 24					16 55			17 24			
Southampton Airport Pkwy ✈	a			15 33							16 33					17 08			17 33			
Southampton Central ⛴	a			15 41							16 41					17 17			17 41			
Brockenhurst 3	a			15 57							16 57								17 57			
Bournemouth	a			16 12							17 12								18 12			

A ⊼ to Plymouth

Table T051-F

Saturdays

28 July to 1 September

Scotland, The North East, North West England - The South West and South Coast

		XC	XC	XC	XC	XC	VT	XC	XC	XC	XC	XC	XC	VT	XC	XC	XC	XC	XC	XC	VT	XC	XC
		◇1	◇1	1	◇1	◇1	◇1	◇1	◇1	◇1	◇1	1	◇1	◇1	◇1	◇1	◇1	◇1	1	◇1	◇1	◇1	◇1
								A		B													
Aberdeen	d									08 20													
Stonehaven	d									08 38													
Montrose	d									08 59													
Arbroath	d									09 15													
Dundee	d									09 35													
Leuchars	d									09 48													
Cupar	d									09 55													
Ladybank	d									10 02													
Markinch	d									10 09													
Kirkcaldy	d									10 18													
Inverkeithing	d									10 33													
Glasgow Central	d	09 00					12 00										11 00				14 00		
Motherwell	d	09 15															11 15						
Haymarket	d	09 57								10 50							11 54						
Edinburgh	d	10 05								11 08				12 52			12 05						
Haymarket	d													12 58									
Lockerbie	d																						
Carlisle	d						13 13							14 08							15 11		
Penrith North Lakes	d													14 22									
Oxenholme Lake District	d																				15 45		
Lancaster	d						14 00							14 56									
Preston	d						14 20							15 17							16 17		
Wigan North Western	d						14 32							15 28							16 28		
Warrington Bank Quay	d						14 43							15 39							16 39		
M'chester Piccadilly	d		14 05		14 27						15 05		15 27					16 05		16 27			
Stockport	d		14 13		14 36						15 13		15 36					16 13		16 36			
Wilmslow	d																						
Crewe	d						15 03							16 01							17 01		
Macclesfield	d		14 26		14 49						15 26		15 49					16 26		16 49			
Congleton	d																						
Stoke-on-Trent	d		14 44		15 07						15 44		16 07					16 44		17 07			
Stafford	d		15 01		15 26						16 01		16 25					17 01		17 25			
Wolverhampton	d		15 17		15 41		15 45				16 17		16 41	16 45				17 17		17 41	17 45		
Dunbar	d									11 29													
Berwick-upon-Tweed	d	10 47								11 53							12 47						
Alnmouth for Alnwick	d									12 13													
Morpeth	d	11 21															13 18						
Newcastle	d	11 42				12 35				12 44					13 35		13 44					14 35	
Chester-le-Street	d																						
Durham	d	11 55				12 48				12 56					13 48		13 56					14 48	
Darlington	d	12 12				13 06				13 14					14 06		14 14					15 06	
York	d	12 45				13 35				13 45					14 35		14 45					15 35	
Leeds	d	13 11								14 11							15 11						
Wakefield Westgate	d	13 23								14 23							15 23						
Doncaster	d					13 58									14 59							15 58	
Sheffield	d	13 54				14 25				14 55					15 24		15 55					16 24	
Chesterfield	d	14 06				14 37				15 07					15 36		16 07					16 36	
Nottingham	d			14 41					15 04			15 41				16 04			16 41				17 04
Derby	d																						
Burton-on-Trent	d	15 01		15 24		15 38			15 49	16 01		16 21			16 37	16 49	17 01		17 24			17 38	17 49
Tamworth	d			15 35				←	16 02			16 33			16 48	17 02			17 35				18 02
Birmingham New Street	a	15 27	15 33	15 55	15 58	16 03	16 05	16 03	16 24	16 27	16 33	16 55	16 58	17 05	17 07	17 24	17 27	17 33	17 55	17 58	18 05	18 07	18 24
Birmingham New Street	d	15 33	15 42		16 04	16 12	16 10	16 12	16 30	16 33	16 42		17 04	17 10	17 12	17 30	17 33	17 42		18 04	18 10	18 12	18 30
Cheltenham Spa	a		16 24			→		16 50	17 09		17 24				17 51	18 16		18 24				18 51	19 10
Gloucester	a								17 20							18 25							19 20
Bristol Parkway	a		16 53					17 25			17 53				18 29			18 53				19 24	
Bristol Temple Meads	a		17 08					17 39			18 04				18 43			19 08				19 39	
Newport (South Wales)	a								18 06							19 10							20 03
Cardiff Central	a								18 24							19 30							20 20
Weston-super-Mare	a																						
Taunton	a							18 15							19 15							20 15	
Tiverton Parkway	a							18 27							19 27							20 27	
Exeter St Davids	a							18 41							19 44							20 40	
Dawlish	a																						
Teignmouth	a																						
Newton Abbot	a							19 04							20 05							21 00	
Torquay	a																						
Paignton	a																						
Totnes	a							19 16							20 17							21 12	
Plymouth	a							19 42							20 43							21 38	
Liskeard	a							20 10															
Bodmin Parkway	a							20 22															
Lostwithiel	a							20 27															
Par	a							20 34															
St Austell	a							20 40															
Truro	a							21 00															
Redruth	a							21 12															
Camborne	a							21 18															
Hayle	a							21 26															
St Erth	a							21 30															
Penzance	a							21 40															
Birmingham International	d				16 14		16 20						17 14	17 20						18 14	18 20		
Coventry	d				16 25		16a30						17 25	17a30						18 25	18a30		
Leamington Spa	d	16 02			16 38					17 00			17 38				18 02			18 38			
Banbury	a	16 18			16 54					17 17			17 54				18 18			18 54			
Oxford	a	16 40			17 14					17 40			18 14				18 41			19 14			
Reading	a	17 10			17 39					18 10			18 43				19 10			19 41			
Guildford	a									19 01													
Basingstoke	a				18 09								19 09							20 09			
Winchester	a				18 24								19 24							20 25			
Southampton Airport Pkway	a				18 33								19 33							20 33			
Southampton Central	a				18 41								19 41							20 41			
Brockenhurst	a				18 57								19 57							20 57			
Bournemouth	a				19 12								20 12							21 12			

A to Plymouth B to Reading

Table T051-F

Saturdays

28 July to 1 September

Scotland, The North East, North West England - The South West and South Coast

		XC	XC	XC	XC	XC	XC	XC	XC	XC	XC	XC	XC	XC	XC	XC	XC	XC	XC	XC	VT	XC
		◇1	◇1	1	◇1	◇1	◇1	◇1	◇1	1	◇1	◇1	◇1	◇1	◇1	1	◇1	◇1	◇1	◇1	◇1	1
			A		B				C		C	C		C	C		C					
Aberdeen	d																					
Stonehaven	d																					
Montrose	d																					
Arbroath	d																					
Dundee	d																					
Leuchars	d																					
Cupar	d																					
Ladybank	d																					
Markinch	d																					
Kirkcaldy	d																					
Inverkeithing	d																					
Glasgow Central	d							13 00											15 00		18 00	
Motherwell	d							13 16											15 16			
Haymarket	d							13 55											15 56			
Edinburgh	d	13 09						14 05						15 08					16 05			
Haymarket	d																					
Lockerbie	d																					
Carlisle	d																				19 11	
Penrith North Lakes	d																					
Oxenholme Lake District	d																					
Lancaster	d																				19 58	
Preston	d																				20 17	
Wigan North Western	d																				20 28	
Warrington Bank Quay	d																				20 39	
M'chester Piccadilly	d		17 05		17 27				18 05		18 27				19 05		19 27			20 05		
Stockport	d		17 13		17 36				18 13		18 36				19 13		19 36			20 13		
Wilmslow	d																					
Crewe	d																				21 01	
Macclesfield	d		17 26						18 26						19 26		19 49			20 26		
Congleton	d				17 55						18 55											
Stoke-on-Trent	d		17 44		18 07				18 44		19 07				19 44		20 07			20 44		
Stafford	d		18 01		18 25				19 01		19 25				20 01		20 25			21 01		
Wolverhampton	d		18 17		18 41				19 17		19 41				20 17		20 41			21 17	21 34	
Dunbar	d	13 30												15 29								
Berwick-upon-Tweed	d							14 47														
Alnmouth for Alnwick	d	14 12																	17 05			
Morpeth	d							15 21											17 19			
Newcastle	d	14 44				15 05		15 44				16 35		16 44				17 32	17 44			
Chester-le-Street	d																	17 41				
Durham	d	14 56				15 18		15 56				16 48		16 56				17 48	17 56			
Darlington	d	15 14				15 35		16 14				17 05		17 14				18 06	18 14			
York	d	15 45				16 04		16 45				17 35		17 45				18 35	18 45			
Leeds	d	16 11				16 40		17 10						18 11					19 11			
Wakefield Westgate	d	16 23				16 52		17 22						18 23					19 23			
Doncaster	d											17 58						18 58				
Sheffield	d	16 55				17 24		17 55				18 24		18 55				19 24	19 55			
Chesterfield	d	17 07				17 36		18 07				18 36		19 07				19 36	20 07			
Nottingham	d			17 41			18 04			18 41			19 04			19 34						20 37
Derby	d																					
Burton-on-Trent	d	18 01		18 24		18 37	18 49	19 01		19 21		19 39	19 50	20 02		20 22		20 36	21 01			21 24
Tamworth	d			18 35		18 47	19 02			19 33			20 02			20 34		20 46				21 35
Birmingham New Street	a	18 27	18 33	18 55	18 58	19 07	19 24	19 27	19 33	19 55	19 59	20 06	20 24	20 27	20 33	20 55	20 58	21 04	21 25	21 33	21 51	21 56
Birmingham New Street	d	18 33	18 42		19 04	19 12	19 30	19 33	19 42		20 04	20 12	20 30	20 33	20 42		21 04	21 12				
Cheltenham Spa	a		19 24			19 51	20 10		20 24			20 51	21 10		21 24			21 51				
Gloucester	a						20 20						21 20					22 01				
Bristol Parkway	a		19 54			20 29			20 53			21 22			21 58			22 32				
Bristol Temple Meads	a		20 05			20 42			21 04			21 34			22 12			22 42				
Newport (South Wales)	a		20 44				21 09						22 18									
Cardiff Central	a		21 00				21 26						22 42									
Weston-super-Mare	a																					
Taunton	a					21 15						22 15										
Tiverton Parkway	a					21 27						22 29										
Exeter St Davids	a					21 43						22 44										
Dawlish	a																					
Teignmouth	a																					
Newton Abbot	a					22 04						23 11										
Torquay	a																					
Paignton	a																					
Totnes	a					22 20						23 27										
Plymouth	a					22 50						23 56										
Liskeard	a																					
Bodmin Parkway	a																					
Lostwithiel	a																					
Par	a																					
St Austell	a																					
Truro	a																					
Redruth	a																					
Camborne	a																					
Hayle	a																					
St Erth	a																					
Penzance	a																					
Birmingham International	d				19 14						20 14						21 14					
Coventry	d				19 25						20 25						21 25					
Leamington Spa	d	19 00			19 38			20 03			20 38			21 00			21 38					
Banbury	a	19 17			19 54			20 19			20 54			21 19			21 54					
Oxford	a	19 41			20 14			20 40			21 14			21 41			22 14					
Reading	a	20 08			20 41			21 08			21 42			22 14			22 45					
Guildford	a																					
Basingstoke	a				21 09						22 08			22 39			23 07					
Winchester	a				21 24						22 26			22 56			23 24					
Southampton Airport Pkway	a				21 32						22 34			23 12			23 32					
Southampton Central	a				21 40						22 42			23 20			23 41					
Brockenhurst	a				21 56						22 59											
Bournemouth	a				22 15						23 19											

A to Bristol Temple Meads B to Reading C to Birmingham New Street

Table T051-F

Saturdays
28 July to 1 September

Scotland, The North East, North West England - The South West and South Coast

		XC	XC	XC	XC	VT	VT	XC	XC	XC	XC
		◇■	◇■	◇■	◇■	◇■	◇■	◇■	■	◇■	◇■
											A
			🍴			🛒	🛒				🍴
Aberdeen	d										
Stonehaven	d										
Montrose	d										
Arbroath	d										
Dundee	d										
Leuchars	d										
Cupar	d										
Ladybank	d										
Markinch	d										
Kirkcaldy	d										
Inverkeithing	d										
Glasgow Central	d					18 40					17 00
Motherwell	d										17 16
Haymarket	d										17 55
Edinburgh	d			17 08			18 52				18 08
Haymarket	d						18 56				
Lockerbie	d										
Carlisle	d					19 49	20 09				
Penrith North Lakes	d					20 03	20 23				
Oxenholme Lake District	d					20 26	20 47				
Lancaster	d					20 41	21 02				
Preston	d					21 01	21 22				
Wigan North Western	d					21 12	21 33				
Warrington Bank Quay	d					21 23	21 44				
M'chester Piccadilly	d	20 27			21 05			21 27			
Stockport	d	20 36			21 13			21 35			
Wilmslow	d										
Crewe	d					21 44	22 06				
Macclesfield	d	20 49			21 26			21 49			
Congleton	d										
Stoke-on-Trent	d	21 08			21 44			22 07			
Stafford	d	21 25			22 01	22 08	22 25	22 30			
Wolverhampton	d	21 42			22 17	22 23	22 40	22 45			
Dunbar	d			17 31							18 30
Berwick-upon-Tweed	d			17 54							18 53
Alnmouth for Alnwick	d										19 14
Morpeth	d										
Newcastle	d		18 36	18 44						19 35	19 45
Chester-le-Street	d										
Durham	d		18 49	18 56						19 50	19 57
Darlington	d		19 07	19 14						20 07	20 15
York	d		19 36	19 45						20 35	20 45
Leeds	d			20 11							21 11
Wakefield Westgate	d			20 23							21 23
Doncaster	d		19 59							20 59	
Sheffield	d		20 24	20 55						21 25	21 55
Chesterfield	d		20 36	21 07						21 37	22 07
Nottingham	d								21 39		
Derby	d										
Burton-on-Trent	d		21 38	21 57					22 22	22 29	23 00
Tamworth	d		21 49						22 35		23 10
Birmingham New Street	a	21 59	22 06	22 21	22 33	22 48	22 58	23 01	23 02	23 05	23 32
Birmingham New Street	d										
Cheltenham Spa	a										
Gloucester	a										
Bristol Parkway	a										
Bristol Temple Meads	a										
Newport (South Wales)	a										
Cardiff Central	a										
Weston-super-Mare	a										
Taunton	a										
Tiverton Parkway	a										
Exeter St Davids	a										
Dawlish	a										
Teignmouth	a										
Newton Abbot	a										
Torquay	a										
Paignton	a										
Totnes	a										
Plymouth	a										
Liskeard	a										
Bodmin Parkway	a										
Lostwithiel	a										
Par	a										
St Austell	a										
Truro	a										
Redruth	a										
Camborne	a										
Hayle	a										
St Erth	a										
Penzance	a										
Birmingham International	d										
Coventry	d										
Leamington Spa	d										
Banbury	a										
Oxford	a										
Reading	a										
Guildford	a										
Basingstoke	a										
Winchester	a										
Southampton Airport Pkway	a										
Southampton Central	a										
Brockenhurst	a										
Bournemouth	a										

A 🍴 from Edinburgh to Leeds

Table T051-F

Saturdays
8 September to 6 October

Scotland, The North East, North West England - The South West and South Coast

		XC	XC	XC	XC	XC	XC	XC	XC	XC	XC	XC	XC	VT	XC	XC	XC	XC	XC	XC	XC	XC	VT
		◇■	◇■	◇■	◇■	◇■	◇■	◇■	◇■	◇■	◇■	◇■	◇■	◇■	◇■	◇■	◇■	◇■	◇■	◇■	■	◇■	◇■
					A					B	B		C		D	E			D	F			
				🍴	🍴	🍴		🍴	🍴	🍴	🍴	🍴	🍴	🛒	🍴	🍴		🍴	🍴	🍴		🍴	🛒
Aberdeen	d																						
Stonehaven	d																						
Montrose	d																						
Arbroath	d																						
Dundee	d																						
Leuchars	d																						
Cupar	d																						
Ladybank	d																						
Markinch	d																						
Kirkcaldy	d																						
Inverkeithing	d																						
Glasgow Central	d																						
Motherwell	d																						
Haymarket	d																						
Edinburgh	d																						
Haymarket	d																						
Lockerbie	d																						
Carlisle	d																						
Penrith North Lakes	d																						
Oxenholme Lake District	d																						
Lancaster	d																						06 58
Preston	d													06 17									07 17
Wigan North Western	d													06 28									07 28
Warrington Bank Quay	d													06 39									07 39
M'chester Piccadilly	d							05 11				06 00							07 05	07 05		07 27	
Stockport	d											06 08							07 13	07 13		07 36	
Wilmslow	d																						
Crewe	d							05 47						07 01									08 01
Macclesfield	d											06 21							07 26	07 26		07 49	
Congleton	d																						
Stoke-on-Trent	d							06 08				06 39							07 44	07 44		08 07	
Stafford	d							06 26				07 01							08 01	08 01		08 25	
Wolverhampton	d							06 41				07 17		07 45					08 17	08 17		08 41	08 45
Dunbar	d																						
Berwick-upon-Tweed	d																						
Alnmouth for Alnwick	d																						
Morpeth	d																						
Newcastle	d																						
Chester-le-Street	d																						
Durham	d																						
Darlington	d																						
York	d																						
Leeds	d														05 49	05 49							
Wakefield Westgate	d														06 01	06 01							
Doncaster	d																						
Sheffield	d														06 30	06 30							
Chesterfield	d														06 44	06 44							
Nottingham	d									05 58			06 37				07 02				07 37		
Derby	d						06 10			06 36	06 48		07 06		07 27	07 27	07 36	07 50			08 06		
Burton-on-Trent	d						06 20			06 48	06 58		07 17		07 38	07 38	07 50	08 00			08 18		
Tamworth	d						06 31		←	07 01	07 09		07 30		07 49	07 49	08 02	08 12			08 30		
Birmingham New Street	a						06 50	06 57	06 50	07 24	07 28	07 33	07 52	08 05	08 08	08 08	08 24	08 27	08 33	08 33	08 55	08 58	09 05
Birmingham New Street	d	05 00	05 42	06 04	06 33	06 42	07 12	07 04	07 12	07 30	07 33	07 42	08 04	08 10	08 12	08 12	08 30	08 33	08 42	08 42		09 04	
Cheltenham Spa	a	06 02	06 42			07 24	→		07 51	08 10		08 24			08 51	08 51	09 10		09 24	09 24			
Gloucester	a	06 12	06 52							08 20							09 20						
Bristol Parkway	a					07 53			08 24			08 54			09 24	09 24			09 53	09 53			
Bristol Temple Meads	a					08 05			08 38			09 07			09 39	09 39			10 04	10 04			
Newport (South Wales)	a	07 05	07 48							09 06							10 05						
Cardiff Central	a	07 21	08 04							09 23							10 21						
Weston-super-Mare	a																						
Taunton	a					08 42			09 15						10 16	10 16				11 00			
Tiverton Parkway	a					08 54			09 27						10 29	10 29				11 12			
Exeter St Davids	a					09 07			09 40						10 43	10 43				11 26			
Dawlish	a															11 01							
Teignmouth	a															11 07							
Newton Abbot	a					09 28			10 00						11 09	11 15				11 52			
Torquay	a					09 39										11 27							
Paignton	a					09 47										11 37							
Totnes	a								10 12						11 22					12 04			
Plymouth	a								10 39						11 51					12 33			
Liskeard	a																			13 04			
Bodmin Parkway	a																			13 20			
Lostwithiel	a																						
Par	a																			13 32			
St Austell	a																						
Truro	a																						
Redruth	a																						
Camborne	a																						
Hayle	a																						
St Erth	a																						
Penzance	a																						
Birmingham International	d			06 14				07 14					08 14	08 20								09 14	
Coventry	d			06 25				07 25					08 25	08a30								09 25	
Leamington Spa	d			06 38	07 00			07 38			08 01		08 38					09 00				09 38	
Banbury	a			06 54	07 17			07 54			08 17		08 54					09 17				09 55	
Oxford	a			07 14	07 40			08 14			08 39		09 14					09 40				10 15	
Reading	a			07 41	08 09			08 41			09 09		09 40					10 08				10 41	
Guildford	a																						
Basingstoke	a			08 08	08 39			09 09					10 09					10 40				11 09	
Winchester	a			08 24	08 58			09 25					10 24					10 56				11 25	
Southampton Airport Pkway	a			08 32	09 08			09 33					10 33					11 08				11 33	
Southampton Central	a			08 41	09 17			09 41					10 41					11 17				11 41	
Brockenhurst	a			08 56				09 57					10 57									11 57	
Bournemouth	a			09 14				10 11					11 13									12 12	

A 🍴 from Reading
B 🍴 from Birmingham New Street
C 🍴 from Derby
D not 8 September
E 8 September
F 8 September. 🍴 to Plymouth

Table T051-F

Saturdays
8 September to 6 October

Scotland, The North East, North West England - The South West and South Coast

Station		XC ◇1 ✠	XC ◇1 A ✠	XC ◇1 B ✠	XC ◇1 C ✠	XC ◇1 ✠	XC 1	XC ◇1 ✠	XC ◇1 B	VT ◇1 ⊡	XC ◇1 C	XC ◇1 ✠	XC ◇1 C ✠	XC ◇1 B ✠	XC ◇1 ✠	XC 1	XC ◇1 ✠	VT ◇1 ⊡	XC ◇1 ✠	XC ◇1 ✠	XC ◇1 ✠	XC ◇1 ✠	XC 1
Aberdeen	d																						
Stonehaven	d																						
Montrose	d																						
Arbroath	d																						
Dundee	d																						
Leuchars	d																						
Cupar	d																						
Ladybank	d																						
Markinch	d																						
Kirkcaldy	d																						
Inverkeithing	d																						
Glasgow Central	d									05 50													
Motherwell	d									06 05													
Haymarket	d																						
Edinburgh	d																	06 52			06 06		
Haymarket	d																	06 56					
Lockerbie	d																						
Carlisle	d									07 02								08 07					
Penrith North Lakes	d									07 17								08 22					
Oxenholme Lake District	d									07 41													
Lancaster	d									07 56								08 57					
Preston	d									08 17								09 17					
Wigan North Western	d									08 28								09 28					
Warrington Bank Quay	d									08 39								09 39					
M'chester Piccadilly	d					08 05		08 27							09 05		09 27					10 05	
Stockport	d					08 13		08 36							09 13		09 37					10 13	
Wilmslow	d																						
Crewe	d									09 01								10 01					
Macclesfield	d					08 26		08 49							09 26		09 50					10 26	
Congleton	d																						
Stoke-on-Trent	d					08 44		09 07							09 44		10 08					10 44	
Stafford	d					09 01		09 25							10 01		10 25					11 01	
Wolverhampton	d					09 17		09 41		09 45					10 17		10 41	10 45				11 17	
Dunbar	d																						
Berwick-upon-Tweed	d																				06 49		
Alnmouth for Alnwick	d																				07 11		
Morpeth	d																						
Newcastle	d												06 43	06 45					07 35		07 41		
Chester-le-Street	d																						
Durham	d												06 58	06 58					07 47		07 55		
Darlington	d												07 16	07 16					08 05		08 13		
York	d			06 20	06 45				07 25		07 35		07 44	07 44					08 35		08 45		
Leeds	d	06 17		07 11	07 11								08 11	08 11							09 11		
Wakefield Westgate	d	06 29		07 23	07 23								08 23	08 23							09 23		
Doncaster	d	06 51							07 51		07 58								08 58				
Sheffield	d	07 18		07 56	07 56				08 22		08 22		08 54	08 53					09 24		09 53		
Chesterfield	d	07 32		08 08	08 08				08 35		08 35		09 06	09 06					09 37		10 05		
Nottingham	d		08 07				08 41					09 04				09 41				10 04			10 41
Derby	d	08 28	08 37	08 53	08 53		09 10		09 24		09 30	09 37	09 51	09 51		10 10			10 28	10 37	10 53		11 10
Burton-on-Trent	d	08 38	08 49				09 22		09 34		09 41	09 49				10 21				10 49			11 21
Tamworth	d	08 49	09 02				09 34					10 02				10 33			10 49	11 02			11 33
Birmingham New Street	a	09 08	09 24	09 27	09 27	09 33	09 56	09 58	10 00	10 05	10 06	10 24	10 27	10 27	10 33	10 55	10 58	11 05	11 08	11 24	11 27	11 33	11 55
Birmingham New Street	d	09 12	09 30	09 33	09 33	09 42		10 04	10 05	10 10	10 12	10 30	10 33	10 33	10 42		11 04	11 10	11 12	11 30	11 33	11 42	
Cheltenham Spa	a	09 51	10 10			10 24			10 44		10 51	11 10			11 24				11 53	12 10		12 24	
Gloucester	a		10 20									11 20								12 20			
Bristol Parkway	a	10 29				10 54			11 19		11 25				11 53				12 29			12 53	
Bristol Temple Meads	a	10 43				11 09			11 33		11 39				12 04				12 42			13 09	
Newport (South Wales)	a		11 06									12 05								13 05			
Cardiff Central	a		11 24									12 23								13 21			
Weston-super-Mare	a					11 29																	
Taunton	a	11 16				11 59			12 09		12 16								13 16				
Tiverton Parkway	a	11 29				12 11			12 21		12 29								13 29				
Exeter St Davids	a	11 43				12 25			12 34		12 43								13 43				
Dawlish	a					12 38																	
Teignmouth	a					12 43																	
Newton Abbot	a	12 03				12 50			12 54		13 04								14 03				
Torquay	a					13 02																	
Paignton	a					13 10																	
Totnes	a	12 16							13 06		13 17								14 17				
Plymouth	a	12 44							13 33		13 45								14 45				
Liskeard	a										14 10												
Bodmin Parkway	a										14 22												
Lostwithiel	a																						
Par	a										14 33												
St Austell	a										14 41												
Truro	a										14 58												
Redruth	a										15 11												
Camborne	a										15 18												
Hayle	a																						
St Erth	a										15 28												
Penzance	a										15 38												
Birmingham International	d							10 14		10 20							11 14	11 20					
Coventry	d							10 25		10a30							11 25	11a30					
Leamington Spa	d			10 00	10 00			10 38					11 00	11 00			11 38				12 00		
Banbury	a			10 17	10 17			10 54					11 17	11 17			11 54				12 17		
Oxford	a			10 41	10 41			11 14					11 41	11 41			12 15				12 41		
Reading	a			11 10	11 10			11 38					12 06	12 06			12 42				13 09		
Guildford	a																						
Basingstoke	a							12 09					12 40	12 40			13 09						
Winchester	a							12 24					12 55	12 55			13 24						
Southampton Airport Pkway	a							12 33					13 08	13 08			13 33						
Southampton Central	a							12 41					13 17	13 17			13 41						
Brockenhurst	a							12 57									13 57						
Bournemouth	a							13 12									14 12						

A ✠ from Birmingham New Street
B not 8 September
C 8 September

NRT MAY 2018 EDITION

Table T051-F

Saturdays
8 September to 6 October

Scotland, The North East, North West England - The South West and South Coast

Station		XC ◇1 ✠	VT ◇1 ⊡	XC ◇1 A	XC ◇1 B	XC ◇1 ✠	XC ◇1 ✠	XC ◇1 ✠	XC 1	XC ◇1 ✠	VT ◇1 ⊡	XC ◇1 A ✠	XC ◇1 B ✠	XC ◇1 ✠	XC ◇1 ✠	XC ◇1 A ✠	XC ◇1 B ✠	XC 1	XC ◇1 ✠	XC ◇1 B ✠	XC ◇1 A ✠	VT ◇1 ⊡
Aberdeen	d																					
Stonehaven	d																					
Montrose	d																					
Arbroath	d																					
Dundee	d														06 32							
Leuchars	d														06 46							
Cupar	d														06 54							
Ladybank	d														07 03							
Markinch	d														07 11							
Kirkcaldy	d														07 21							
Inverkeithing	d														07 38							
Glasgow Central	d		08 00				06 01															10 00
Motherwell	d						06 16															
Haymarket	d						06 57								07 56							
Edinburgh	d			07 00	07 00		07 07				08 53				08 06							
Haymarket	d										08 58											
Lockerbie	d																					
Carlisle	d		09 11								10 08											11 11
Penrith North Lakes	d																					11 25
Oxenholme Lake District	d										10 42											
Lancaster	d		09 58								10 57											
Preston	d		10 17								11 16											12 17
Wigan North Western	d		10 29								11 29											12 28
Warrington Bank Quay	d		10 41								11 40											12 39
M'chester Piccadilly	d	10 27						11 05		11 27						12 05	12 05		12 27			
Stockport	d	10 36						11 13		11 36						12 13	12 13		12 36			
Wilmslow	d																					
Crewe	d		11 02								12 00											13 01
Macclesfield	d	10 49						11 26		11 49						12 26	12 26		12 49			
Congleton	d																					
Stoke-on-Trent	d	11 07						11 44		12 07						12 44	12 44		13 07			
Stafford	d	11 25						12 01		12 25						13 01	13 01		13 25			
Wolverhampton	d	11 41	11 45					12 17		12 41	12 45					13 17	13 17		13 41			13 45
Dunbar	d						07 29															
Berwick-upon-Tweed	d			07 43	07 43										08 50							
Alnmouth for Alnwick	d			08 03	08 03										09 12							
Morpeth	d			08 18	08 18																	
Newcastle	d			08 35	08 35		08 41					09 35	09 35		09 42					10 35	10 35	
Chester-le-Street	d																					
Durham	d			08 48	08 48		08 55					09 49	09 50		09 56					10 48	10 48	
Darlington	d			09 06	09 06		09 13					10 07	10 08		10 14					11 06	11 06	
York	d			09 35	09 36		09 45					10 35	10 37		10 45					11 35	11 35	
Leeds	d						10 11								11 11							
Wakefield Westgate	d						10 23								11 23							
Doncaster	d			09 58	09 59							10 59	11 01							11 58	11 58	
Sheffield	d			10 24	10 24		10 55					11 24	11 24		11 55					12 24	12 24	
Chesterfield	d			10 37	10 37		11 07					11 38	11 38		12 07					12 36	12 36	
Nottingham	d					11 04			11 41					12 04				12 41				
Derby	d			11 29	11 29	11 37	11 53		12 10			12 29	12 29	12 37	12 53			13 10		13 28	13 28	
Burton-on-Trent	d			11 41	11 41	11 49			12 21					12 49				13 24		13 38	13 38	
Tamworth	d					12 02			12 33			12 49	12 49	13 02				13 35				
Birmingham New Street	a	11 59	12 05	12 08	12 08	12 24	12 27	12 34	12 55	12 58	13 05	13 08	13 08	13 24	13 27	13 34	13 34	13 55	13 58	14 04	14 04	14 05
Birmingham New Street	d	12 04	12 10	12 12	12 12	12 30	12 33	12 42		13 04	13 10	13 12	13 12	13 30	13 33	13 42	13 42		14 04	14 12	14 12	14 10
Cheltenham Spa	a			12 51	12 51	13 10		13 25				13 51	13 50	14 10		14 24	14 24			↦	↦	
Gloucester	a					13 20								14 20								
Bristol Parkway	a			13 24	13 24			13 54				14 26	14 26			14 54	14 54					
Bristol Temple Meads	a			13 39	13 39			14 05				14 40	14 41			15 09	15 09					
Newport (South Wales)	a					14 06								15 09								
Cardiff Central	a					14 22								15 26								
Weston-super-Mare	a																					
Taunton	a			14 16	14 16							15 15	15 16			15 42	15 42					
Tiverton Parkway	a			14 29	14 29							15 27	15 28			15 54	15 54					
Exeter St Davids	a			14 43	14 43							15 40	15 43			16 07	16 09					
Dawlish	a			14 57												16 34						
Teignmouth	a			15 03												16 40						
Newton Abbot	a			15 11	15 04							16 04	16 03			16 47						
Torquay	a			15 23												16 59						
Paignton	a			15 33												17 10						
Totnes	a				15 17							16 16	16 16									
Plymouth	a				15 45							16 43	16 43									
Liskeard	a											17 12										
Bodmin Parkway	a											17 27										
Lostwithiel	a																					
Par	a											17 39										
St Austell	a																					
Truro	a																					
Redruth	a																					
Camborne	a																					
Hayle	a																					
St Erth	a																					
Penzance	a																					
Birmingham International	d	12 14	12 20							13 14	13 20								14 14			14 20
Coventry	d	12 25	12a30							13 25	13a30								14 25			14a29
Leamington Spa	d	12 38					13 00			13 38					14 00				14 38			
Banbury	a	12 54					13 17			13 54					14 18				14 55			
Oxford	a	13 14					13 41			14 14					14 40				15 15			
Reading	a	13 40					14 08			14 41					15 08				15 40			
Guildford	a																					
Basingstoke	a	14 09					14 40			15 09									16 09			
Winchester	a	14 24					14 56			15 24									16 24			
Southampton Airport Pkway	a	14 32					15 07			15 33									16 33			
Southampton Central	a	14 41					15 17			15 41									16 41			
Brockenhurst	a	14 57								15 57									16 57			
Bournemouth	a	15 12								16 12									17 12			

A 8 September
B not 8 September

Scotland, The North East, North West England - The South West and South Coast

		XC ◇■ A 🛒	XC ◇■ B 🛒	XC ◇■ 🛒	XC ◇■ 🛒	XC ◇■ 🛒	XC ■ 🛒	XC ◇■ 🛒	VT ◇■ 🍽	XC ◇■ C 🛒	XC ◇■ 🛒	XC ◇■ 🛒	XC ◇■ A 🛒	XC ◇■ D 🛒	XC ■	XC ◇■ 🛒	XC ◇■ 🛒	VT ◇■ 🍽	XC ◇■ C 🛒	XC ◇■ 🛒	XC ◇■ E 🛒	XC ◇■ 🛒	XC ■ 🛒
Aberdeen	d																				08 20		
Stonehaven	d																				08 38		
Montrose	d																				08 59		
Arbroath	d																				09 15		
Dundee	d																				09 35		
Leuchars	d																				09 48		
Cupar	d																				09 55		
Ladybank	d																				10 02		
Markinch	d																				10 09		
Kirkcaldy	d																				10 18		
Inverkeithing	d																				10 33		
Glasgow Central	d				07 48							09 00						12 00					
Motherwell	d				08 08							09 15											
Haymarket	d				08 52							09 57									10 50		
Edinburgh	d				09 08				10 52			10 05									11 08		
Haymarket	d								10 57														
Lockerbie	d																						
Carlisle	d								12 08									13 13					
Penrith North Lakes	d																						
Oxenholme Lake District	d								12 43														
Lancaster	d								12 57									14 00					
Preston	d								13 17									14 20					
Wigan North Western	d								13 28									14 32					
Warrington Bank Quay	d								13 39									14 43					
M'chester Piccadilly	d					13 05		13 27					14 05	14 05		14 27						15 05	
Stockport	d					13 13		13 36					14 13	14 13		14 36						15 13	
Wilmslow	d																						
Crewe	d								14 01									15 03					
Macclesfield	d					13 26		13 49					14 26	14 26		14 49						15 26	
Congleton	d																						
Stoke-on-Trent	d					13 44		14 07					14 44	14 44		15 07						15 44	
Stafford	d					14 01		14 25					15 01	15 01		15 26						16 01	
Wolverhampton	d					14 17		14 41	14 45				15 17	15 17		15 41		15 45				16 17	
Dunbar	d				09 29																11 29		
Berwick-upon-Tweed	d				09 53							10 47									11 53		
Alnmouth for Alnwick	d																				12 13		
Morpeth	d											11 21											
Newcastle	d				10 44					11 35		11 42					12 35				12 44		
Chester-le-Street	d																						
Durham	d				10 56					11 49		11 55					12 48				12 56		
Darlington	d				11 14					12 07		12 12					13 06				13 14		
York	d				11 45					12 36		12 45					13 35				13 45		
Leeds	d				12 11							13 11									14 11		
Wakefield Westgate	d				12 23							13 23									14 23		
Doncaster	d									12 59							13 58						
Sheffield	d				12 55					13 23		13 54					14 25				14 55		
Chesterfield	d				13 07					13 37		14 06					14 37				15 07		
Nottingham	d			13 04			13 41				14 04				14 41					15 04			15 41
Derby	d			13 37	13 53		14 10			14 26	14 37	14 53			15 10		15 27			15 37	15 53		16 10
Burton-on-Trent	d			13 49			14 21				14 49				15 24		15 38			15 49			16 21
Tamworth	d	←	←	14 02			14 33			14 49	15 02				15 35				←	16 02			16 33
Birmingham New Street	a	14 04	14 04	14 24	14 27	14 35	14 55	14 58	15 05	15 08	15 24	15 27	15 33	15 33	15 55	15 58	16 03	16 05	16 03	16 24	16 27	16 33	16 55
Birmingham New Street	d	14 12	14 12	14 30	14 33	14 42		15 04	15 10	15 12	15 30	15 33	15 42	15 42		16 04	16 12	16 10	16 12	16 30	16 33	16 42	
Cheltenham Spa	a	14 51	14 51	15 10		15 24				15 50	16 10		16 24	16 24			→		16 50	17 09		17 24	
Gloucester	a			15 20							16 20									17 20			
Bristol Parkway	a	15 24	15 24			15 54				16 29			16 53	16 53					17 25			17 53	
Bristol Temple Meads	a	15 38	15 38			16 07				16 43			17 07	17 08					17 39			18 04	
Newport (South Wales)	a			16 06							17 08									18 06			
Cardiff Central	a			16 25							17 24									18 24			
Weston-super-Mare	a																						
Taunton	a	16 14	16 14							17 17			17 40						18 15				
Tiverton Parkway	a	16 26	16 26							17 30			17 52						18 27				
Exeter St Davids	a	16 40	16 40							17 44			18 05						18 41				
Dawlish	a												18 18										
Teignmouth	a												18 23										
Newton Abbot	a	17 00	17 00							18 10			18 30						19 04				
Torquay	a												18 41										
Paignton	a												18 49										
Totnes	a	17 12	17 12							18 23									19 16				
Plymouth	a	17 39	17 39							18 51									19 42				
Liskeard	a		18 04							19 19									20 10				
Bodmin Parkway	a		18 16							19 32									20 22				
Lostwithiel	a																		20 27				
Par	a		18 27							19 43									20 34				
St Austell	a		18 33							19 50									20 40				
Truro	a		18 50							20 09									21 00				
Redruth	a		19 07							20 22									21 12				
Camborne	a		19 14							20 30									21 18				
Hayle	a		19 22																21 26				
St Erth	a		19 26							20 40									21 30				
Penzance	a		19 36							20 52									21 40				
Birmingham International	d							15 14	15 20							16 14		16 20					
Coventry	d							15 25	15a30							16 25		16a30					
Leamington Spa	d				15 00			15 38				16 02				16 38					17 00		
Banbury	a				15 21			15 54				16 18				16 54					17 17		
Oxford	a				15 41			16 14				16 40				17 14					17 40		
Reading	a				16 09			16 42				17 10				17 39					18 10		
Guildford	a																				19 01		
Basingstoke	a				16 40			17 09								18 09							
Winchester	a				16 55			17 24								18 24							
Southampton Airport Pkway	a				17 08			17 33								18 33							
Southampton Central	a				17 17			17 41								18 41							
Brockenhurst	a							17 57								18 57							
Bournemouth	a							18 12								19 12							

A not 8 September
B 8 September. 🛒 to Plymouth
C 🛒 to Plymouth
D 8 September
E 🛒 to Reading

Table T051-F

Saturdays
8 September to 6 October

Scotland, The North East, North West England - The South West and South Coast

		XC ◇■ 🛒	VT ◇■ 🍽	XC ◇■ A 🛒	XC ◇■ B 🛒	XC ◇■	XC ◇■ 🛒	XC ◇■ C 🛒	XC ◇■ A 🛒	XC ■ 🛒	XC ◇■ 🛒	VT ◇■ 🍽	XC ◇■ 🛒	XC ◇■	XC ◇■ 🛒	XC ◇■ D 🛒	XC ■ 🛒	XC ◇■ E 🛒	XC ◇■ 🛒	XC ◇■	XC ◇■ 🛒	XC ◇■ F 🛒
Aberdeen	d																					
Stonehaven	d																					
Montrose	d																					
Arbroath	d																					
Dundee	d																					
Leuchars	d																					
Cupar	d																					
Ladybank	d																					
Markinch	d																					
Kirkcaldy	d																					
Inverkeithing	d																					
Glasgow Central	d						11 00					14 00									13 00	
Motherwell	d						11 15														13 16	
Haymarket	d						11 54														13 55	
Edinburgh	d		12 52				12 05								13 09						14 05	
Haymarket	d		12 58																			
Lockerbie	d																					
Carlisle	d		14 08									15 11										
Penrith North Lakes	d		14 22																			
Oxenholme Lake District	d											15 45										
Lancaster	d		14 56																			
Preston	d		15 17									16 17										
Wigan North Western	d		15 28									16 28										
Warrington Bank Quay	d		15 39									16 39										
M'chester Piccadilly	d	15 27						16 05	16 05		16 27					17 05		17 27				18 05
Stockport	d	15 36						16 13	16 13		16 36					17 13		17 36				18 13
Wilmslow	d																					
Crewe	d		16 01									17 01										
Macclesfield	d	15 49						16 26	16 26		16 49					17 26						18 26
Congleton	d																	17 55				
Stoke-on-Trent	d	16 07						16 44	16 44		17 07					17 44		18 07				18 44
Stafford	d	16 25						17 01	17 01		17 25					18 01		18 25				19 01
Wolverhampton	d	16 41	16 45					17 17	17 17		17 41	17 45				18 17		18 41				19 17
Dunbar	d														13 30							
Berwick-upon-Tweed	d						12 47														14 47	
Alnmouth for Alnwick	d														14 12							
Morpeth	d						13 18														15 21	
Newcastle	d			13 35	13 35		13 44						14 35		14 44				15 05		15 44	
Chester-le-Street	d																					
Durham	d			13 48	13 48		13 56						14 48		14 56				15 18		15 56	
Darlington	d			14 06	14 06		14 14						15 06		15 14				15 35		16 14	
York	d			14 35	14 35		14 45						15 35		15 45				16 04		16 45	
Leeds	d						15 11								16 11				16 40		17 10	
Wakefield Westgate	d						15 23								16 23				16 52		17 22	
Doncaster	d			14 59	14 59								15 58									
Sheffield	d			15 24	15 24		15 55						16 24		16 55				17 24		17 55	
Chesterfield	d			15 36	15 36		16 07						16 36		17 07				17 36		18 07	
Nottingham	d					16 04				16 41				17 04			17 41			18 04		
Derby	d			16 28	16 28	16 37	16 53			17 10			17 29	17 37	17 53		18 10		18 29	18 37	18 53	
Burton-on-Trent	d					16 49				17 24			17 38	17 49			18 24			18 49		
Tamworth	d			16 48	16 48	17 02				17 35				18 02			18 35		18 47	19 02		
Birmingham New Street	a	16 58	17 05	17 07	17 07	17 24	17 27	17 33	17 33	17 55	17 58	18 05	18 07	18 24	18 27	18 33	18 55	18 58	19 07	19 24	19 27	19 33
Birmingham New Street	d	17 04	17 10	17 12	17 12	17 30	17 33	17 42	17 42		18 04	18 10	18 12	18 30	18 33	18 42		19 04	19 12	19 30	19 33	19 42
Cheltenham Spa	a			17 51	17 51	18 16		18 24	18 24				18 51	19 10		19 24			19 51	20 10		20 24
Gloucester	a					18 25								19 20						20 20		
Bristol Parkway	a			18 29	18 29			18 53	18 53				19 24			19 54			20 29			20 53
Bristol Temple Meads	a			18 43	18 43			19 05	19 08				19 39			20 05			20 42			21 04
Newport (South Wales)	a					19 10								20 03		20 44				21 09		
Cardiff Central	a					19 30								20 20		21 00				21 26		
Weston-super-Mare	a																					
Taunton	a			19 15	19 15								20 15						21 15			
Tiverton Parkway	a			19 27	19 27								20 27						21 27			
Exeter St Davids	a			19 44	19 44								20 40						21 43			
Dawlish	a																					
Teignmouth	a																					
Newton Abbot	a			20 05	20 05								21 00						22 04			
Torquay	a																					
Paignton	a																					
Totnes	a			20 17	20 17								21 12						22 20			
Plymouth	a			20 43	20 43								21 38						22 50			
Liskeard	a				21 23																	
Bodmin Parkway	a				21 36																	
Lostwithiel	a																					
Par	a				21 46																	
St Austell	a				21 52																	
Truro	a				22 16																	
Redruth	a				22 28																	
Camborne	a				22 34																	
Hayle	a																					
St Erth	a				22 44																	
Penzance	a				22 54																	
Birmingham International	d	17 14	17 20								18 14	18 20						19 14				
Coventry	d	17 25	17a30								18 25	18a30						19 25				
Leamington Spa	d	17 38					18 02				18 38				19 00			19 38			20 03	
Banbury	a	17 54					18 18				18 54				19 17			19 54			20 19	
Oxford	a	18 14					18 41				19 14				19 41			20 14			20 40	
Reading	a	18 43					19 10				19 41				20 08			20 41			21 08	
Guildford	a																					
Basingstoke	a	19 09									20 09							21 09				
Winchester	a	19 24									20 25							21 24				
Southampton Airport Pkway	a	19 33									20 33							21 32				
Southampton Central	a	19 41									20 41							21 40				
Brockenhurst	a	19 57									20 57							21 56				
Bournemouth	a	20 12									21 12							22 15				

A 8 September
B not 8 September. 🛒 to Plymouth
C not 8 September
D 🛒 to Bristol Temple Meads
E 🛒 to Reading
F 8 September. 🛒 to Birmingham New Street

Scotland, The North East, North West England - The South West and South Coast

Station		XC	XC	XC	XC	XC	XC	XC	XC	XC	XC	XC	XC	VT	XC	XC	XC	XC	XC	VT	VT	XC	XC
		◇1	1	◇1	◇1	◇1	◇1	◇1	1	◇1	◇1	◇1	◇1	◇1	1	◇1	◇1	◇1	◇1	◇1	◇1	◇1	1
		A		B	B		B	B		B													
		✠	✠	✠	✠		✠	✠	✠	✠	✠	✠		⊡			✠			⊡	⊡		
Aberdeen	d																						
Stonehaven	d																						
Montrose	d																						
Arbroath	d																						
Dundee	d																						
Leuchars	d																						
Cupar	d																						
Ladybank	d																						
Markinch	d																						
Kirkcaldy	d																						
Inverkeithing	d																						
Glasgow Central	d											15 00		18 00						18 40			
Motherwell	d											15 16											
Haymarket	d											15 56											
Edinburgh	d						15 08					16 05						17 08			18 52		
Haymarket	d																				18 56		
Lockerbie	d																						
Carlisle	d													19 11						19 49	20 09		
Penrith North Lakes	d																			20 03	20 23		
Oxenholme Lake District	d																			20 26	20 47		
Lancaster	d													19 58						20 41	21 02		
Preston	d													20 17						21 01	21 22		
Wigan North Western	d													20 28						21 12	21 33		
Warrington Bank Quay	d													20 39						21 23	21 44		
M'chester Piccadilly	d	18 05		18 27				19 05		19 27			20 05			20 27			21 05			21 27	
Stockport	d	18 13		18 36				19 13		19 36			20 13			20 36			21 13			21 35	
Wilmslow	d																						
Crewe	d													21 01						21 44	22 06		
Macclesfield	d	18 26						19 26		19 49			20 26			20 49			21 26			21 49	
Congleton	d			18 55																			
Stoke-on-Trent	d	18 44		19 07				19 44		20 07			20 44			21 08			21 44			22 07	
Stafford	d	19 01		19 25				20 01		20 25			21 01			21 25			22 01	22 08	22 25	22 30	
Wolverhampton	d	19 17		19 41				20 17		20 41			21 17	21 34		21 42			22 17	22 23	22 40	22 45	
Dunbar	d						15 29											17 31					
Berwick-upon-Tweed	d																	17 54					
Alnmouth for Alnwick	d											17 05											
Morpeth	d											17 19											
Newcastle	d				16 35		16 44				17 32	17 44					18 36	18 44					
Chester-le-Street	d										17 41												
Durham	d				16 48		16 56				17 48	17 56					18 49	18 56					
Darlington	d				17 05		17 14				18 06	18 14					19 07	19 14					
York	d				17 35		17 45				18 35	18 45					19 36	19 45					
Leeds	d						18 11					19 11						20 11					
Wakefield Westgate	d						18 23					19 23						20 23					
Doncaster	d				17 58						18 58						19 59						
Sheffield	d				18 24		18 55				19 24	19 55					20 24	20 55					
Chesterfield	d				18 36		19 07				19 36	20 07					20 36	21 07					
Nottingham	d		18 41			19 04			19 34						20 40								21 39
Derby	d		19 10		19 29	19 37	19 54		20 11		20 28	20 53			21 10		21 28	21 50					22 12
Burton-on-Trent	d		19 21		19 39	19 49			20 22						21 24		21 38						22 22
Tamworth	d		19 33			20 02			20 34		20 46				21 35		21 49						22 35
Birmingham New Street	a	19 33	19 55	19 59	20 06	20 24	20 27	20 33	20 55	20 58	21 04	21 25	21 33	21 51	21 56	21 59	22 06	22 21	22 33	22 48	22 58	23 01	23 02
Birmingham New Street	d	19 42		20 04	20 12	20 30	20 33	20 42		21 04	21 12												
Cheltenham Spa	a	20 24			20 51	21 10		21 24			21 51												
Gloucester	a					21 20					22 01												
Bristol Parkway	a	20 53			21 22			21 58			22 32												
Bristol Temple Meads	a	21 04			21 34			22 12			22 42												
Newport (South Wales)	a					22 18																	
Cardiff Central	a					22 42																	
Weston-super-Mare	a																						
Taunton	a	21 41			22 15																		
Tiverton Parkway	a	21 53			22 29																		
Exeter St Davids	a	22 07			22 44																		
Dawlish	a																						
Teignmouth	a																						
Newton Abbot	a	22 26			23 11																		
Torquay	a																						
Paignton	a																						
Totnes	a	22 38			23 27																		
Plymouth	a	23 05			23 56																		
Liskeard	a																						
Bodmin Parkway	a																						
Lostwithiel	a																						
Par	a																						
St Austell	a																						
Truro	a																						
Redruth	a																						
Camborne	a																						
Hayle	a																						
St Erth	a																						
Penzance	a																						
Birmingham International	d			20 14						21 14													
Coventry	d			20 25						21 25													
Leamington Spa	d			20 38			21 00			21 38													
Banbury	a			20 54			21 19			21 54													
Oxford	a			21 14			21 41			22 14													
Reading	a			21 42			22 14			22 45													
Guildford	a																						
Basingstoke	a			22 08			22 39			23 07													
Winchester	a			22 26			22 56			23 24													
Southampton Airport Pkway	a			22 34			23 12			23 32													
Southampton Central	a			22 42			23 20			23 41													
Brockenhurst	a			22 59																			
Bournemouth	a			23 19																			

A not 8 September. ✠ to Birmingham New Street   B ✠ to Birmingham New Street

Please check the 'Additional Notes to Individual Tables' section for any other general notes that apply to this Table

Scotland, The North East, North West England - The South West and South Coast

Station		XC	XC
		◇1	◇1
			A
			✠
Aberdeen	d		
Stonehaven	d		
Montrose	d		
Arbroath	d		
Dundee	d		
Leuchars	d		
Cupar	d		
Ladybank	d		
Markinch	d		
Kirkcaldy	d		
Inverkeithing	d		
Glasgow Central	d		17 00
Motherwell	d		17 16
Haymarket	d		17 55
Edinburgh	d		18 08
Haymarket	d		
Lockerbie	d		
Carlisle	d		
Penrith North Lakes	d		
Oxenholme Lake District	d		
Lancaster	d		
Preston	d		
Wigan North Western	d		
Warrington Bank Quay	d		
M'chester Piccadilly	d		
Stockport	d		
Wilmslow	d		
Crewe	d		
Macclesfield	d		
Congleton	d		
Stoke-on-Trent	d		
Stafford	d		
Wolverhampton	d		
Dunbar	d		18 30
Berwick-upon-Tweed	d		18 53
Alnmouth for Alnwick	d		19 14
Morpeth	d		
Newcastle	d	19 35	19 45
Chester-le-Street	d		
Durham	d	19 50	19 57
Darlington	d	20 07	20 15
York	d	20 35	20 45
Leeds	d		21 11
Wakefield Westgate	d		21 23
Doncaster	d	20 59	
Sheffield	d	21 25	21 55
Chesterfield	d	21 37	22 07
Nottingham	d		
Derby	d	22 23	22 50
Burton-on-Trent	d		23 00
Tamworth	d		23 10
Birmingham New Street	a	23 05	23 32
Birmingham New Street	d		
Cheltenham Spa	a		
Gloucester	a		
Bristol Parkway	a		
Bristol Temple Meads	a		
Newport (South Wales)	a		
Cardiff Central	a		
Weston-super-Mare	a		
Taunton	a		
Tiverton Parkway	a		
Exeter St Davids	a		
Dawlish	a		
Teignmouth	a		
Newton Abbot	a		
Torquay	a		
Paignton	a		
Totnes	a		
Plymouth	a		
Liskeard	a		
Bodmin Parkway	a		
Lostwithiel	a		
Par	a		
St Austell	a		
Truro	a		
Redruth	a		
Camborne	a		
Hayle	a		
St Erth	a		
Penzance	a		
Birmingham International	d		
Coventry	d		
Leamington Spa	d		
Banbury	a		
Oxford	a		
Reading	a		
Guildford	a		
Basingstoke	a		
Winchester	a		
Southampton Airport Pkway	a		
Southampton Central	a		
Brockenhurst	a		
Bournemouth	a		

A ✠ from Edinburgh to Leeds

Table T051-F

Scotland, The North East, North West England - The South West and South Coast

Saturdays
13 October to 8 December

		XC	XC	XC	XC	XC	XC	XC	XC	XC	XC	XC	XC	VT	XC	XC	XC	XC	XC	XC	VT	XC	XC
		◇■	◇■	◇■	◇■	◇■	◇■	◇■	◇■	◇■	◇■	◇■	◇■	◇■	◇■	◇■	◇■	◇■	■	◇■	◇■	◇■	◇■
					A					B	B		C									D	B
				✠	✠	✠		✠	✠	✠	✠	✠	✠	⊡	✠		✠	✠		✠	⊡	✠	✠
Aberdeen	d																						
Stonehaven	d																						
Montrose	d																						
Arbroath	d																						
Dundee	d																						
Leuchars ■	d																						
Cupar	d																						
Ladybank	d																						
Markinch	d																						
Kirkcaldy	d																						
Inverkeithing	d																						
Glasgow Central ■	d																						
Motherwell	d																						
Haymarket	d																						
Edinburgh ■	d																						
Haymarket	d																						
Lockerbie	d																						
Carlisle ■	d																						
Penrith North Lakes	d																						
Oxenholme Lake District	d																						
Lancaster ■	d																				06 58		
Preston ■	d													06 17							07 17		
Wigan North Western	d													06 28							07 28		
Warrington Bank Quay	d													06 39							07 39		
M'chester Piccadilly ■	d							05 11				06 00						07 05		07 27			
Stockport	d											06 08						07 13		07 36			
Wilmslow	d																						
Crewe ■	d							05 47						07 01							08 01		
Macclesfield	d											06 21						07 26		07 49			
Congleton	d																						
Stoke-on-Trent	d							06 08				06 39						07 44		08 07			
Stafford	d							06 26				07 01						08 01		08 25			
Wolverhampton ■	d							06 41				07 17		07 45				08 17		08 41	08 45		
Dunbar	d																						
Berwick-upon-Tweed	d																						
Alnmouth for Alnwick	d																						
Morpeth	d																						
Newcastle ■	d																						
Chester-le-Street	d																						
Durham	d																						
Darlington ■	d																						
York ■	d																					06 20	
Leeds ■	d														06 11		06 17					07 11	
Wakefield Westgate ■	d														06 23		06 29					07 23	
Doncaster ■	d																06 51						
Sheffield ■	d														06 53		07 18					07 56	
Chesterfield	d														07 06		07 30					08 08	
Nottingham ■	d									05 58			06 37			06 58			07 37				08 09
Derby ■	d						06 10			06 36	06 48		07 06		07 27	07 36	07 51		08 06			08 28	08 37
Burton-on-Trent	d						06 20			06 48	06 58		07 17		07 38	07 50	08 00		08 18			08 38	08 49
Tamworth	d						06 31		←	07 01	07 09		07 30		07 49	08 02	08 12		08 30			08 49	09 02
Birmingham New Street ■	a						06 50	06 57	06 50	07 24	07 28	07 33	07 52	08 05	08 08	08 24	08 27	08 33	08 55	08 58	09 05	09 08	09 24
Birmingham New Street ■	d	05 00	05 42	06 04	06 33	06 42	07 12	07 04	07 12	07 30	07 33	07 42	08 04	08 10	08 12	08 30	08 33	08 42		09 04		09 12	09 30
Cheltenham Spa ■	a	06 02	06 42			07 24	→		07 51	08 10		08 24			08 51	09 10		09 24				09 51	10 10
Gloucester ■	a	06 12	06 52							08 20						09 20							10 20
Bristol Parkway ■	a					07 53			08 24			08 54			09 24			09 53				10 29	
Bristol Temple Meads ■	a					08 05			08 38			09 07			09 39			10 04				10 42	
Newport (South Wales)	a	07 05	07 48							09 06						10 05							11 06
Cardiff Central ■	a	07 21	08 04							09 23						10 21							11 24
Weston-super-Mare	a																						
Taunton	a					08 42			09 15						10 16							11 15	
Tiverton Parkway	a					08 54			09 27						10 29							11 27	
Exeter St Davids ■	a					09 07			09 40						10 43							11 41	
Dawlish	a																						
Teignmouth	a																						
Newton Abbot	a					09 28			10 00						11 09							12 01	
Torquay	a					09 39																	
Paignton	a					09 47																	
Totnes	a								10 12						11 22							12 14	
Plymouth	a								10 39						11 51							12 41	
Liskeard ■	a																						
Bodmin Parkway	a																						
Lostwithiel	a																						
Par	a																						
St Austell	a																						
Truro	a																						
Redruth	a																						
Camborne	a																						
Hayle	a																						
St Erth	a																						
Penzance	a																						
Birmingham International ✈	d			06 14				07 14					08 14	08 20						09 14			
Coventry	d			06 25				07 25					08 25	08a30						09 25			
Leamington Spa ■	d			06 38	07 00			07 38			08 01		08 38				09 00			09 38			
Banbury	a			06 54	07 17			07 54			08 17		08 54				09 17			09 55			
Oxford	a			07 14	07 40			08 14			08 39		09 14				09 41			10 15			
Reading ■	a			07 41	08 09			08 41			09 09		09 40				10 08			10 41			
Guildford	a																						
Basingstoke	a			08 08	08 39			09 09					10 09				10 40			11 09			
Winchester	a			08 24	08 58			09 25					10 24				10 56			11 25			
Southampton Airport Pkway ✈	a			08 32	09 08			09 33					10 33				11 08			11 33			
Southampton Central	a			08 41	09 17			09 41					10 41				11 17			11 41			
Brockenhurst ■	a			08 56				09 57					10 57							11 57			
Bournemouth	a			09 14				10 11					11 13							12 12			

A ✠ from Reading
B ✠ from Birmingham New Street
C ✠ from Derby
D ✠ from Leeds

Table T051-F

Scotland, The North East, North West England - The South West and South Coast

Saturdays
13 October to 8 December

		XC	XC	XC	XC	VT	XC	XC	XC	XC	XC	XC	VT	XC	XC	XC	XC	XC	XC	VT	XC	XC	XC
		◇■	◇■	■	◇■	◇■	◇■	◇■	◇■	◇■	■	◇■	◇■	◇■	◇■	◇■	◇■	■	◇■	◇■	◇■	◇■	◇■
		A					B														C		
		✠	✠		✠	⊡	✠	✠	✠	✠		✠	⊡	✠	✠	✠	✠		✠	⊡	✠	✠	✠
Aberdeen	d																						
Stonehaven	d																						
Montrose	d																						
Arbroath	d																						
Dundee	d																						
Leuchars ■	d																						
Cupar	d																						
Ladybank	d																						
Markinch	d																						
Kirkcaldy	d																						
Inverkeithing	d																						
Glasgow Central ■	d					05 50														08 00	06 01		
Motherwell	d					06 05															06 16		
Haymarket	d																				06 57		
Edinburgh ■	d												06 52	06 06		07 00					07 07		
Haymarket	d												06 56										
Lockerbie	d																						
Carlisle ■	d					07 02							08 07							09 11			
Penrith North Lakes	d					07 17							08 22										
Oxenholme Lake District	d					07 41																	
Lancaster ■	d					07 56							08 57							09 58			
Preston ■	d					08 17							09 17							10 17			
Wigan North Western	d					08 28							09 28							10 29			
Warrington Bank Quay	d					08 39							09 39							10 41			
M'chester Piccadilly ■	d		08 05		08 27					09 05		09 27					10 05		10 27				
Stockport	d		08 13		08 36					09 13		09 37					10 13		10 36				
Wilmslow	d																						
Crewe ■	d					09 01							10 01							11 02			
Macclesfield	d		08 26		08 49					09 26		09 50					10 26		10 49				
Congleton	d																						
Stoke-on-Trent	d		08 44		09 07					09 44		10 08					10 44		11 07				
Stafford	d		09 01		09 25					10 01		10 25					11 01		11 25				
Wolverhampton ■	d		09 17		09 41	09 45				10 17		10 41	10 45				11 17		11 41	11 45			
Dunbar	d																				07 29		
Berwick-upon-Tweed	d													06 49		07 43							
Alnmouth for Alnwick	d													07 11		08 03							
Morpeth	d															08 18							
Newcastle ■	d	06 23					06 45		07 35					07 41		08 35					08 41		09 35
Chester-le-Street	d																						
Durham	d	06 38					06 58		07 47					07 55		08 48					08 55		09 49
Darlington ■	d	06 56					07 15		08 05					08 13		09 06					09 13		10 07
York ■	d	07 25					07 45		08 35					08 45		09 35					09 45		10 35
Leeds ■	d						08 11							09 11							10 11		
Wakefield Westgate ■	d						08 23							09 23							10 23		
Doncaster ■	d	07 51							09 01							09 58							10 59
Sheffield ■	d	08 22					08 54		09 24					09 53		10 24					10 54		11 24
Chesterfield	d	08 34					09 07							10 06							11 07		
Nottingham ■	d			08 41				09 07			09 41				10 06			10 41				11 06	
Derby ■	d	08 53		09 10			09 31	09 36	09 53		10 10			10 29	10 37	10 53		11 09			11 30	11 37	11 53
Burton-on-Trent	d			09 22			09 41	09 49			10 21				10 49			11 21			11 41	11 49	
Tamworth	d			09 34				10 02			10 33			10 49	11 02			11 33				12 02	
Birmingham New Street ■	a	09 27	09 33	09 56	09 58	10 05	10 06	10 24	10 27	10 33	10 55	10 58	11 05	11 08	11 24	11 27	11 33	11 55	11 59	12 05	12 08	12 24	12 27
Birmingham New Street ■	d	09 33	09 42		10 04	10 10	10 12	10 30	10 33	10 42		11 04	11 10	11 12	11 30	11 33	11 42		12 04	12 10	12 12	12 30	12 33
Cheltenham Spa ■	a		10 24				10 51	11 10		11 24				11 53	12 10		12 24				12 51	13 10	
Gloucester ■	a							11 20							12 20							13 20	
Bristol Parkway ■	a		10 54				11 25			11 53				12 29			12 53				13 24		
Bristol Temple Meads ■	a		11 09				11 39			12 04				12 42			13 09				13 39		
Newport (South Wales)	a							12 05							13 05							14 06	
Cardiff Central ■	a							12 23							13 21							14 22	
Weston-super-Mare	a		11 29																				
Taunton	a		11 59				12 15							13 16							14 16		
Tiverton Parkway	a		12 11				12 27							13 29							14 29		
Exeter St Davids ■	a		12 25				12 41							13 43							14 43		
Dawlish	a		12 38																				
Teignmouth	a		12 43																				
Newton Abbot	a		12 50				13 00							14 03							15 04		
Torquay	a		13 02																				
Paignton	a		13 10																				
Totnes	a						13 12							14 17							15 17		
Plymouth	a						13 39							14 45							15 45		
Liskeard ■	a																						
Bodmin Parkway	a																						
Lostwithiel	a																						
Par	a																						
St Austell	a																						
Truro	a																						
Redruth	a																						
Camborne	a																						
Hayle	a																						
St Erth	a																						
Penzance	a																						
Birmingham International ✈	d				10 14	10 20						11 14	11 20						12 14	12 20			
Coventry	d				10 25	10a30						11 25	11a30						12 25	12a30			
Leamington Spa ■	d	10 00			10 38				11 00			11 38				12 00			12 38				13 00
Banbury	a	10 17			10 54				11 17			11 54				12 17			12 54				13 17
Oxford	a	10 41			11 14				11 41			12 15				12 41			13 14				13 41
Reading ■	a	11 10			11 38				12 06			12 42				13 09			13 40				14 08
Guildford	a																						
Basingstoke	a				12 09				12 40			13 09							14 09				14 40
Winchester	a				12 24				12 55			13 24							14 24				14 56
Southampton Airport Pkway ✈	a				12 33				13 08			13 33							14 32				15 07
Southampton Central	a				12 41				13 17			13 41							14 41				15 17
Brockenhurst ■	a				12 57							13 57							14 57				
Bournemouth	a				13 12							14 12							15 12				

A ■ ✠ ◇ from Birmingham New Street
B ✠ from Leeds
C ✠ from Edinburgh

Table T051-F

Saturdays

13 October to 8 December

Scotland, The North East, North West England - The South West and South Coast

		XC ◇1 🛒	XC 1	XC ◇1 🛒	VT ◇1 🍽	XC ◇1 A 🛒	XC ◇1 🛒	XC ◇1 🛒	XC ◇1 🛒	XC 1	XC ◇1 🛒	XC ◇1 A 🛒	VT ◇1 🍽	XC ◇1 🛒	XC ◇1 🛒	XC ◇1 🛒	XC ◇1 🛒	XC 1 🛒	XC ◇1 🛒	VT ◇1 🍽	XC ◇1 B 🛒	XC ◇1 🛒
Aberdeen	d																					
Stonehaven	d																					
Montrose	d																					
Arbroath	d																					
Dundee	d					06 32																
Leuchars	d					06 46																
Cupar	d					06 54																
Ladybank	d					07 03																
Markinch	d					07 11																
Kirkcaldy	d					07 21																
Inverkeithing	d					07 38																
Glasgow Central	d											07 48	10 00								09 00	
Motherwell	d											08 08									09 15	
Haymarket	d					07 56						08 52									09 57	
Edinburgh	d				08 53	08 06						09 08								10 52	10 05	
Haymarket	d				08 58															10 57		
Lockerbie	d																					
Carlisle	d				10 08								11 11							12 08		
Penrith North Lakes	d												11 25									
Oxenholme Lake District	d				10 42															12 43		
Lancaster	d				10 57															12 57		
Preston	d				11 16								12 17							13 17		
Wigan North Western	d				11 29								12 28							13 28		
Warrington Bank Quay	d				11 40								12 39							13 39		
M'chester Piccadilly	d	11 05		11 27					12 05		12 27						13 05		13 27			
Stockport	d	11 13		11 36					12 13		12 36						13 13		13 36			
Wilmslow	d																					
Crewe	d				12 00								13 01							14 01		
Macclesfield	d	11 26		11 49					12 26		12 49						13 26		13 49			
Congleton	d																					
Stoke-on-Trent	d	11 44		12 07					12 44		13 07						13 44		14 07			
Stafford	d	12 01		12 25					13 01		13 25						14 01		14 25			
Wolverhampton	d	12 17		12 41	12 45				13 17		13 41		13 45				14 17		14 41	14 45		
Dunbar	d											09 29										
Berwick-upon-Tweed	d					08 50						09 53									10 47	
Alnmouth for Alnwick	d					09 12																
Morpeth	d																				11 21	
Newcastle	d					09 42		10 35				10 44				11 35					11 42	
Chester-le-Street	d																					
Durham	d					09 56		10 48				10 56				11 49					11 55	
Darlington	d					10 14		11 06				11 14				12 06					12 12	
York	d					10 45		11 35				11 45				12 35					12 45	
Leeds	d					11 11						12 11									13 11	
Wakefield Westgate	d					11 23						12 23									13 23	
Doncaster	d							11 58								12 59						
Sheffield	d					11 55		12 24				12 55				13 24					13 53	
Chesterfield	d					12 09						13 07									14 06	
Nottingham	d		11 41				12 06			12 41					13 06			13 41				14 06
Derby	d		12 10			12 30	12 37	12 53		13 10		13 28			13 37	13 53		14 10			14 30	14 37
Burton-on-Trent	d		12 21				12 49			13 24		13 38			13 49			14 21				14 49
Tamworth	d		12 33			12 49	13 02			13 35				←	14 02			14 33			14 49	15 02
Birmingham New Street	a	12 34	12 55	12 58	13 05	13 08	13 24	13 27	13 34	13 55	13 58	14 03	14 05	14 03	14 24	14 27	14 35	14 55	14 58	15 05	15 08	15 24
Birmingham New Street	d	12 42		13 04	13 10	13 12	13 30	13 33	13 42		14 04	14 12	14 10	14 12	14 30	14 33	14 42		15 04	15 10	15 12	15 30
Cheltenham Spa	a	13 25				13 50	14 10		14 24			→		14 51	15 10		15 24				15 50	16 10
Gloucester	a						14 20								15 20							16 20
Bristol Parkway	a	13 54				14 26			14 54					15 24			15 54				16 29	
Bristol Temple Meads	a	14 05				14 41			15 09					15 38			16 07				16 43	
Newport (South Wales)	a						15 09								16 06							17 08
Cardiff Central	a						15 26								16 25							17 24
Weston-super-Mare	a																					
Taunton	a					15 16			15 42					16 14							17 17	
Tiverton Parkway	a					15 28			15 54					16 26							17 30	
Exeter St Davids	a					15 43			16 09					16 40							17 44	
Dawlish	a																					
Teignmouth	a																					
Newton Abbot	a					16 03								17 00							18 10	
Torquay	a																					
Paignton	a																					
Totnes	a					16 16								17 12							18 23	
Plymouth	a					16 43								17 39							18 51	
Liskeard	a																				19 19	
Bodmin Parkway	a																				19 32	
Lostwithiel	a																					
Par	a																				19 43	
St Austell	a																				19 50	
Truro	a																				20 09	
Redruth	a																				20 22	
Camborne	a																				20 30	
Hayle	a																					
St Erth	a																				20 40	
Penzance	a																				20 52	
Birmingham International	d			13 14	13 20						14 14		14 20						15 14	15 20		
Coventry	d			13 25	13a30						14 25		14a29						15 25	15a30		
Leamington Spa	d			13 38				14 00			14 38					15 00			15 38			
Banbury	a			13 54				14 18			14 55					15 21			15 54			
Oxford	a			14 14				14 40			15 15					15 41			16 14			
Reading	a			14 41				15 08			15 40					16 09			16 42			
Guildford	a																					
Basingstoke	a			15 09							16 09					16 40			17 09			
Winchester	a			15 24							16 24					16 55			17 24			
Southampton Airport Pkway	a			15 33							16 33					17 08			17 33			
Southampton Central	a			15 41							16 41					17 17			17 41			
Brockenhurst	a			15 57							16 57								17 57			
Bournemouth	a			16 12							17 12								18 12			

A 🛒 from Edinburgh
B 🛒 from Edinburgh to Plymouth

Table T051-F

Saturdays

13 October to 8 December

Scotland, The North East, North West England - The South West and South Coast

		XC ◇1 🛒	XC ◇1 🛒	XC 1	XC ◇1 🛒	XC ◇1 A 🛒	VT ◇1 🍽	XC ◇1 B 🛒	XC ◇1 🛒	XC ◇1 C 🛒	XC ◇1 🛒	XC 1 🛒	XC ◇1 🛒	VT ◇1 🍽	XC ◇1 D 🛒	XC ◇1	XC ◇1 🛒	XC ◇1 🛒	XC 1 🛒	XC ◇1 🛒	VT ◇1 🍽	XC ◇1 🛒	XC ◇1
Aberdeen	d					08 20																	
Stonehaven	d					08 38																	
Montrose	d					08 59																	
Arbroath	d					09 15																	
Dundee	d					09 35																	
Leuchars	d					09 48																	
Cupar	d					09 55																	
Ladybank	d					10 02																	
Markinch	d					10 09																	
Kirkcaldy	d					10 18																	
Inverkeithing	d					10 33																	
Glasgow Central	d						12 00								11 00						14 00		
Motherwell	d														11 15								
Haymarket	d					10 50									11 54								
Edinburgh	d					11 08								12 52	12 05							13 09	
Haymarket	d													12 58									
Lockerbie	d																						
Carlisle	d						13 13							14 08							15 11		
Penrith North Lakes	d													14 22									
Oxenholme Lake District	d																				15 45		
Lancaster	d						14 00							14 56									
Preston	d						14 20							15 17							16 17		
Wigan North Western	d						14 32							15 28							16 28		
Warrington Bank Quay	d						14 43							15 39							16 39		
M'chester Piccadilly	d		14 05		14 27						15 05		15 27					16 05		16 27			
Stockport	d		14 13		14 36						15 13		15 36					16 13		16 36			
Wilmslow	d																						
Crewe	d						15 03							16 01							17 01		
Macclesfield	d		14 26		14 49						15 26		15 49					16 26		16 49			
Congleton	d																						
Stoke-on-Trent	d		14 44		15 07						15 44		16 07					16 44		17 07			
Stafford	d		15 01		15 26						16 01		16 25					17 01		17 25			
Wolverhampton	d		15 17		15 41		15 45				16 17		16 41	16 45				17 17		17 41	17 45		
Dunbar	d					11 29																13 30	
Berwick-upon-Tweed	d					11 53									12 47								
Alnmouth for Alnwick	d					12 13																14 12	
Morpeth	d														13 18								
Newcastle	d	12 35				12 44				13 35					13 44		14 35					14 44	
Chester-le-Street	d																						
Durham	d	12 48				12 56				13 48					13 56		14 48					14 56	
Darlington	d	13 06				13 14				14 06					14 14		15 06					15 14	
York	d	13 35				13 45				14 35					14 45		15 35					15 45	
Leeds	d					14 11									15 11							16 11	
Wakefield Westgate	d					14 23									15 23							16 23	
Doncaster	d	13 58								14 59							15 58						
Sheffield	d	14 25				14 55				15 24					15 55		16 24					16 55	
Chesterfield	d					15 07									16 07							17 07	
Nottingham	d			14 41					15 06			15 41				16 06			16 41				17 06
Derby	d	14 54		15 10		15 28			15 37	15 53		16 10			16 28	16 37	16 53		17 10			17 28	17 37
Burton-on-Trent	d			15 24		15 38			15 49			16 21				16 49			17 24			17 38	17 49
Tamworth	d			15 35				←	16 02			16 33			16 48	17 02			17 35				18 02
Birmingham New Street	a	15 27	15 33	15 55	15 58	16 03	16 05	16 03	16 24	16 27	16 33	16 55	16 58	17 05	17 07	17 24	17 27	17 33	17 55	17 58	18 05	18 07	18 24
Birmingham New Street	d	15 33	15 42		16 04	16 12	16 10	16 12	16 30	16 33	16 42		17 04	17 10	17 12	17 30	17 33	17 42		18 04	18 10	18 12	18 30
Cheltenham Spa	a		16 24			→		16 50	17 09		17 24				17 51	18 16		18 24				18 51	19 10
Gloucester	a								17 20							18 25							19 20
Bristol Parkway	a		16 53					17 25			17 53				18 29			18 53				19 24	
Bristol Temple Meads	a		17 07					17 39			18 04				18 43			19 05				19 39	
Newport (South Wales)	a								18 06							19 10							20 03
Cardiff Central	a								18 24							19 30							20 20
Weston-super-Mare	a																						
Taunton	a		17 40					18 15							19 15							20 15	
Tiverton Parkway	a		17 52					18 27							19 27							20 27	
Exeter St Davids	a		18 05					18 41							19 44							20 40	
Dawlish	a		18 18																				
Teignmouth	a		18 23																				
Newton Abbot	a		18 30					19 04							20 05							21 00	
Torquay	a		18 41																				
Paignton	a		18 49																				
Totnes	a							19 16							20 17							21 12	
Plymouth	a							19 42							20 43							21 38	
Liskeard	a							20 10							21 23								
Bodmin Parkway	a							20 22							21 36								
Lostwithiel	a							20 27															
Par	a							20 34							21 46								
St Austell	a							20 40							21 52								
Truro	a							21 00							22 16								
Redruth	a							21 12							22 28								
Camborne	a							21 18							22 34								
Hayle	a							21 26															
St Erth	a							21 30							22 44								
Penzance	a							21 40							22 54								
Birmingham International	d				16 14		16 20						17 14	17 20						18 14	18 20		
Coventry	d				16 25		16a30						17 25	17a30						18 25	18a30		
Leamington Spa	d	16 02			16 38					17 00			17 38				18 02			18 38			
Banbury	a	16 18			16 54					17 17			17 54				18 18			18 54			
Oxford	a	16 40			17 14					17 40			18 14				18 41			19 14			
Reading	a	17 10			17 39					18 10			18 43				19 10			19 41			
Guildford	a									19 01													
Basingstoke	a				18 09								19 09							20 09			
Winchester	a				18 24								19 24							20 25			
Southampton Airport Pkway	a				18 33								19 33							20 33			
Southampton Central	a				18 41								19 41							20 41			
Brockenhurst	a				18 57								19 57							20 57			
Bournemouth	a				19 12								20 12							21 12			

A 🛒 from Edinburgh
B 🛒 to Plymouth
C 🛒 to Reading
D 🛒 from Edinburgh to Plymouth

Table T051-F

Saturdays
13 October to 8 December

Scotland, The North East, North West England - The South West and South Coast

		XC ◇1 ✠	XC ◇1 A ✠	XC 1 ✠	XC ◇1 B ✠	XC ◇1 C ✠	XC ◇1	XC ◇1 ✠	XC ◇1 D ✠	XC 1 ✠	XC ◇1 D ✠	XC ◇1 D ✠	XC ◇1	XC ◇1 D ✠	XC ◇1 D ✠	XC 1 ✠	XC ◇1 D ✠	XC ◇1 C ✠	XC ◇1 ✠	XC ◇1	VT ◇1 🍴	XC 1
Aberdeen	d																					
Stonehaven	d																					
Montrose	d																					
Arbroath	d																					
Dundee	d																					
Leuchars 8	d																					
Cupar	d																					
Ladybank	d																					
Markinch	d																					
Kirkcaldy	d																					
Inverkeithing	d																					
Glasgow Central 15	d					13 00												15 00			18 00	
Motherwell	d					13 16												15 16				
Haymarket	d					13 55												15 56				
Edinburgh 10	d					14 05						15 08						16 05				
Haymarket	d																					
Lockerbie	d																					
Carlisle 8	d																				19 11	
Penrith North Lakes	d																					
Oxenholme Lake District	d																					
Lancaster 8	d																				19 58	
Preston 8	d																				20 17	
Wigan North Western	d																				20 28	
Warrington Bank Quay	d																				20 39	
M'chester Piccadilly 10	d		17 05		17 27				18 05		18 27				19 05		19 27			20 05		
Stockport	d		17 13		17 36				18 13		18 36				19 13		19 36			20 13		
Wilmslow	d																					
Crewe 10	d																				21 01	
Macclesfield	d		17 26						18 26						19 26		19 49			20 26		
Congleton	d				17 55						18 55											
Stoke-on-Trent	d		17 44		18 07				18 44		19 07				19 44		20 07			20 44		
Stafford	d		18 01		18 25				19 01		19 25				20 01		20 25			21 01		
Wolverhampton 7	d		18 17		18 41				19 17		19 41				20 17		20 41			21 17	21 34	
Dunbar	d											15 29										
Berwick-upon-Tweed	d					14 47																
Alnmouth for Alnwick	d																	17 05				
Morpeth	d					15 21												17 19				
Newcastle 8	d	15 05				15 44		16 35				16 44		17 32				17 44	18 36			
Chester-le-Street	d													17 41								
Durham	d	15 18				15 56		16 48				16 56		17 48				17 56	18 49			
Darlington 7	d	15 35				16 14		17 05				17 14		18 06				18 14	19 07			
York 8	d	16 04				16 45		17 35				17 45		18 35				18 45	19 36			
Leeds 10	d	16 40				17 10						18 11						19 11				
Wakefield Westgate 7	d	16 52				17 22						18 23						19 23				
Doncaster 7	d							17 58						18 58					19 59			
Sheffield 7	d	17 24				17 55		18 23				18 55		19 24				19 55	20 24			
Chesterfield	d					18 07						19 07						20 07				
Nottingham 8	d			17 41			18 06			18 41			19 06			19 29						20 40
Derby 8	d	17 53		18 10		18 29	18 37	18 53		19 10		19 29	19 39	19 54		20 10		20 28	20 53			21 09
Burton-on-Trent	d			18 24			18 49			19 21		19 39	19 50			20 22						21 24
Tamworth	d			18 35		18 47	19 02			19 33			20 02			20 34		20 46				21 35
Birmingham New Street 12	a	18 27	18 33	18 55	18 58	19 07	19 24	19 27	19 33	19 55	19 59	20 06	20 24	20 27	20 33	20 55	20 58	21 04	21 25	21 33	21 51	21 56
Birmingham New Street 12	d	18 33	18 42		19 04	19 12	19 30	19 33	19 42		20 04	20 12	20 30	20 33	20 42		21 04	21 12				
Cheltenham Spa 4	a		19 24			19 51	20 10		20 24			20 51	21 10		21 24			21 51				
Gloucester 7	a						20 20						21 20					22 01				
Bristol Parkway 7	a		19 54			20 29			20 53			21 22			21 58			22 32				
Bristol Temple Meads 10	a		20 05			20 42			21 04			21 34			22 12			22 42				
Newport (South Wales)	a		20 44				21 09						22 18									
Cardiff Central 7	a		21 00				21 26						22 42									
Weston-super-Mare	a																					
Taunton	a					21 15			21 41			22 15										
Tiverton Parkway	a					21 27			21 53			22 29										
Exeter St Davids 6	a					21 43			22 07			22 44										
Dawlish	a																					
Teignmouth	a																					
Newton Abbot	a					22 04			22 26			23 11										
Torquay	a																					
Paignton	a																					
Totnes	a					22 20			22 38			23 27										
Plymouth	a					22 50			23 05			23 56										
Liskeard 6	a																					
Bodmin Parkway	a																					
Lostwithiel	a																					
Par	a																					
St Austell	a																					
Truro	a																					
Redruth	a																					
Camborne	a																					
Hayle	a																					
St Erth	a																					
Penzance	a																					
Birmingham International	d				19 14						20 14						21 14					
Coventry	d				19 25						20 25						21 25					
Leamington Spa 8	d	19 00			19 38			20 03			20 38			21 00			21 38					
Banbury	a	19 17			19 54			20 19			20 54			21 19			21 54					
Oxford	a	19 41			20 14			20 40			21 14			21 41			22 14					
Reading 7	a	20 08			20 41			21 08			21 42			22 14			22 45					
Guildford	a																					
Basingstoke	a				21 09						22 08			22 39			23 07					
Winchester	a				21 24						22 26			22 56			23 24					
Southampton Airport Pkway	a				21 32						22 34			23 12			23 32					
Southampton Central	a				21 40						22 42			23 20			23 41					
Brockenhurst 3	a				21 56						22 59											
Bournemouth	a				22 15						23 19											

A ✠ to Bristol Temple Meads
B ✠ to Reading
C ✠ from Edinburgh
D ✠ to Birmingham New Street

Table T051-F

Saturdays
13 October to 8 December

Scotland, The North East, North West England - The South West and South Coast

		XC ◇1	XC ◇1 A ✠	XC ◇1	XC ◇1	VT ◇1 🍴	VT ◇1 🍴	XC ◇1	XC 1	XC ◇1 B ✠
Aberdeen	d									
Stonehaven	d									
Montrose	d									
Arbroath	d									
Dundee	d									
Leuchars 8	d									
Cupar	d									
Ladybank	d									
Markinch	d									
Kirkcaldy	d									
Inverkeithing	d									
Glasgow Central 15	d					18 40				17 00
Motherwell	d									17 16
Haymarket	d									17 55
Edinburgh 10	d		17 08				18 52			18 08
Haymarket	d						18 56			
Lockerbie	d									
Carlisle 8	d					19 49	20 09			
Penrith North Lakes	d					20 03	20 23			
Oxenholme Lake District	d					20 26	20 47			
Lancaster 8	d					20 41	21 02			
Preston 8	d					21 01	21 22			
Wigan North Western	d					21 12	21 33			
Warrington Bank Quay	d					21 23	21 44			
M'chester Piccadilly 10	d	20 27		21 05				21 27		
Stockport	d	20 36		21 13				21 35		
Wilmslow	d									
Crewe 10	d					21 44	22 06			
Macclesfield	d	20 49		21 26				21 49		
Congleton	d									
Stoke-on-Trent	d	21 08		21 44				22 07		
Stafford	d	21 25		22 01		22 08	22 25	22 30		
Wolverhampton 7	d	21 42		22 17		22 23	22 40	22 45		
Dunbar	d		17 31							18 30
Berwick-upon-Tweed	d		17 54							18 53
Alnmouth for Alnwick	d									19 14
Morpeth	d									
Newcastle 8	d		18 44		19 35					19 45
Chester-le-Street	d									
Durham	d		18 56		19 50					19 57
Darlington 7	d		19 14		20 07					20 15
York 8	d		19 45		20 35					20 45
Leeds 10	d		20 11							21 11
Wakefield Westgate 7	d		20 23							21 23
Doncaster 7	d				20 59					
Sheffield 7	d		20 55		21 25					21 55
Chesterfield	d		21 07		21 37					22 07
Nottingham 8	d								21 39	
Derby 8	d		21 28		21 56				22 12	22 26
Burton-on-Trent	d		21 38						22 22	22 37
Tamworth	d		21 49						22 35	22 47
Birmingham New Street 12	a	21 59	22 06	22 33	22 44	22 48	22 58	23 01	23 02	23 06
Birmingham New Street 12	d									
Cheltenham Spa 4	a									
Gloucester 7	a									
Bristol Parkway 7	a									
Bristol Temple Meads 10	a									
Newport (South Wales)	a									
Cardiff Central 7	a									
Weston-super-Mare	a									
Taunton	a									
Tiverton Parkway	a									
Exeter St Davids 6	a									
Dawlish	a									
Teignmouth	a									
Newton Abbot	a									
Torquay	a									
Paignton	a									
Totnes	a									
Plymouth	a									
Liskeard 6	a									
Bodmin Parkway	a									
Lostwithiel	a									
Par	a									
St Austell	a									
Truro	a									
Redruth	a									
Camborne	a									
Hayle	a									
St Erth	a									
Penzance	a									
Birmingham International	d									
Coventry	d									
Leamington Spa 8	d									
Banbury	a									
Oxford	a									
Reading 7	a									
Guildford	a									
Basingstoke	a									
Winchester	a									
Southampton Airport Pkway	a									
Southampton Central	a									
Brockenhurst 3	a									
Bournemouth	a									

A ✠ to Leeds
B ✠ from Edinburgh to Leeds

Table T051-F

Sundays 20 May to 15 July

Scotland, The North East, North West England - The South West and South Coast

		XC	XC	XC	XC	XC	XC	XC	XC	VT	XC	XC	XC	XC	VT	XC	XC	XC	XC	XC	XC	VT	XC
		◇1	◇1	◇1	◇1	◇1	◇1	◇1	◇1	◇1	◇1	◇1	◇1	◇1	◇1	◇1	◇1	◇1	◇1	◇1	◇1	◇1	◇1
			A										B					B					
		🛒	🛒	🛒	🛒	🛒	🛒	🛒	🛒	⊡	🛒	🛒	🛒	🛒	⊡	🛒	🛒	🛒	🛒	🛒	🛒	⊡	🛒
Aberdeen	d																						
Stonehaven	d																						
Montrose	d																						
Arbroath	d																						
Dundee	d																						
Leuchars	d																						
Cupar	d																						
Ladybank	d																						
Markinch	d																						
Kirkcaldy	d																						
Inverkeithing	d																						
Glasgow Central	d																						
Motherwell	d																						
Haymarket	d																						
Edinburgh	d																						09 08
Haymarket	d																						
Lockerbie	d																						
Carlisle	d																						
Penrith North Lakes	d																						
Oxenholme Lake District	d																						
Lancaster	d																					11 58	
Preston	d									10 17					11 17							12 17	
Wigan North Western	d									10 28					11 28							12 28	
Warrington Bank Quay	d									10 39					11 40							12 39	
M'chester Piccadilly	d			08 27			09 27				10 26					11 27					12 26		
Stockport	d			08 36			09 36				10 36					11 36					12 35		
Wilmslow	d			08 43																			
Crewe	d			09 05						11 02					12 02							13 01	
Macclesfield	d						09 49				10 49					11 49					12 49		
Congleton	d																						
Stoke-on-Trent	d						10 07				11 07					12 07					13 07		
Stafford	d			09 26			10 25				11 27					12 25					13 25		
Wolverhampton	d			09 41			10 41			11 32	11 42				12 32	12 41					13 41	13 45	
Dunbar	d																						
Berwick-upon-Tweed	d																						09 51
Alnmouth for Alnwick	d																						
Morpeth	d																						
Newcastle	d																09 35						10 39
Chester-le-Street	d																						
Durham	d																09 47						10 53
Darlington	d																10 05						11 10
York	d											09 33					10 33						11 41
Leeds	d					08 10			09 00			09 59					11 00						12 11
Wakefield Westgate	d					08 23			09 11			10 12					11 12						12 24
Doncaster	d								09 31			10 30					11 30						
Sheffield	d					08 54			09 57			10 55					11 57						12 57
Chesterfield	d					09 07			10 09			11 08					12 09						13 09
Nottingham	d							09 54					11 11					12 10					
Derby	d					09 28		10 18	10 33			11 29	11 36				12 29	12 36					13 32
Burton-on-Trent	d							10 30				11 40	11 47					12 47					13 43
Tamworth	d							10 42	10 53				12 00				12 48	13 00					
Birmingham New Street	a			09 57		10 18	10 57	11 03	11 21	11 50	11 58	12 06	12 21		12 50	12 57	13 06	13 21			13 57	14 06	14 09
Birmingham New Street	d	09 04	09 30	10 04	10 12	10 30	11 04	11 12	11 30		12 04	12 12	12 30	12 33		13 04	13 12	13 30	13 33	13 42	14 04	14 10	14 12
Cheltenham Spa	a		10 08		10 52	11 09		11 52	12 09			12 50	13 10				13 51	14 10		14 23			14 50
Gloucester	a				11 02			12 02					13 20					14 20					
Bristol Parkway	a		10 37			11 39			12 39			13 21					14 20			14 53			15 23
Bristol Temple Meads	a		10 48			11 51			12 50			13 32					14 31			15 08			15 34
Newport (South Wales)	a				11 47			12 44					14 06					15 01					
Cardiff Central	a				12 09			13 07					14 27					15 27					
Weston-super-Mare	a																						
Taunton	a		11 29			12 25			13 25			14 15					15 14						16 14
Tiverton Parkway	a		11 41			12 35			13 36			14 27					15 26						16 26
Exeter St Davids	a		11 54			12 52			13 52			14 42					15 39						16 40
Dawlish	a																						
Teignmouth	a																						
Newton Abbot	a		12 14			13 12			14 12			15 02					16 00						17 01
Torquay	a																						
Paignton	a																						
Totnes	a		12 26			13 25			14 25			15 15					16 12						17 14
Plymouth	a		12 52			13 52			14 52			15 42					16 38						17 42
Liskeard	a		13 17																				
Bodmin Parkway	a		13 29																				
Lostwithiel	a																						
Par	a		13 39																				
St Austell	a		13 45																				
Truro	a		14 06																				
Redruth	a		14 19																				
Camborne	a		14 25																				
Hayle	a																						
St Erth	a		14 36																				
Penzance	a		14 47																				
Birmingham International	d	09 14		10 14			11 14				12 14			12 44		13 14					14 14	14 20	
Coventry	d	09 25		10 25			11 25				12 25			12 55		13 25					14 25	14a30	
Leamington Spa	d	09 38		10 38			11 38				12 38			13 08		13 38			13 59		14 38		
Banbury	a	09 54		10 54			11 54				12 54			13 24		13 54			14 15		14 54		
Oxford	a	10 14		11 14			12 14				13 14			13 43		14 14			14 35		15 14		
Reading	a	10 42		11 40			12 41				13 42			14 11		14 41			15 02		15 40		
Guildford	a																						
Basingstoke	a	11 09		12 09			13 09				14 09					15 09					16 09		
Winchester	a	11 24		12 25			13 24				14 24					15 24					16 24		
Southampton Airport Pkwy	a	11 33		12 34			13 33				14 33					15 33					16 33		
Southampton Central	a	11 42		12 43			13 42				14 42					15 43					16 42		
Brockenhurst	a	12 06		13 07			14 06				15 06					16 03					17 06		
Bournemouth	a	12 26		13 26			14 26				15 26					16 26					17 26		

A 🛒 to Plymouth
B 🛒 from Birmingham New Street

Table T051-F

Sundays 20 May to 15 July

Scotland, The North East, North West England - The South West and South Coast

		XC	XC	XC	XC	XC	VT	XC	XC	XC	XC	XC	XC	VT	XC	XC	XC	XC	XC	XC	VT	XC	XC
		◇1	◇1	◇1	◇1	◇1	◇1	◇1	◇1	◇1	◇1	◇1	◇1	◇1	◇1	◇1	◇1	◇1	◇1	◇1	◇1	◇1	◇1
		A						B												C		B	D
		🛒	🛒	🛒	🛒	🛒	⊡	🛒	🛒	🛒	🛒	🛒	🛒	⊡	🛒		🛒	🛒	🛒	🛒	⊡	🛒	🛒
Aberdeen	d																						
Stonehaven	d																						
Montrose	d																						
Arbroath	d																						
Dundee	d																						
Leuchars	d																						
Cupar	d																						
Ladybank	d																						
Markinch	d																						
Kirkcaldy	d																						
Inverkeithing	d																						
Glasgow Central	d																						
Motherwell	d																			11 14			
Haymarket	d																			11 53			
Edinburgh	d					10 08	10 51						11 05							12 08	12 51		
Haymarket	d						10 55														12 55		
Lockerbie	d																						
Carlisle	d						12 07							13 07							14 07		
Penrith North Lakes	d																				14 22		
Oxenholme Lake District	d						12 43																
Lancaster	d						12 57							13 56							14 57		
Preston	d						13 17							14 17							15 17		
Wigan North Western	d						13 28							14 28							15 28		
Warrington Bank Quay	d						13 39							14 39							15 39		
M'chester Piccadilly	d			13 05	13 27						14 05	14 27						15 05	15 27				
Stockport	d			13 13	13 36						14 13	14 36						15 13	15 36				
Wilmslow	d																						
Crewe	d						14 01							15 01							16 01		
Macclesfield	d			13 26	13 49						14 26	14 49						15 26	15 49				
Congleton	d																						
Stoke-on-Trent	d			13 45	14 07						14 44	15 07						15 44	16 07				
Stafford	d			14 02	14 25						15 01	15 25						16 01	16 25				
Wolverhampton	d			14 17	14 41		14 45				15 17	15 41		15 45				16 17	16 41		16 45		
Dunbar	d												11 26										
Berwick-upon-Tweed	d												11 50							12 49			
Alnmouth for Alnwick	d					11 07							12 10										
Morpeth	d					11 22																	
Newcastle	d					11 40							12 40				13 35			13 40			
Chester-le-Street	d																						
Durham	d					11 52							12 53				13 47			13 53			
Darlington	d					12 10							13 10				14 06			14 10			
York	d					12 45							13 43				14 35			14 44			
Leeds	d					13 11							14 11							15 11			
Wakefield Westgate	d					13 24							14 23							15 23			
Doncaster	d																15 00						
Sheffield	d					13 57				14 22			14 55				15 24			15 55			
Chesterfield	d					14 09				14 32			15 07							16 07			
Nottingham	d	13 10							14 10							15 10							16 10
Derby	d	13 38	13 55			14 29			14 34	14 53			15 26			15 34	15 53			16 27			16 34
Burton-on-Trent	d	13 49							14 47				15 37			15 47							16 47
Tamworth	d	14 00				14 48		←	15 00						←	16 00				16 46		←	17 00
Birmingham New Street	a	14 22	14 27	14 33	14 57	15 05	15 06	15 05	15 20	15 26	15 33	15 57	16 01	16 06	16 01	16 21	16 26	16 33	16 57	17 03	17 06	17 03	17 19
Birmingham New Street	d	14 30	14 33	14 42	15 04	15 12	15 10	15 12	15 30	15 33	15 42	16 04	16 12	16 10	16 12	16 30	16 33	16 42	17 04	17 12	17 10	17 12	17 30
Cheltenham Spa	a	15 10		15 24		→		15 51	16 10		16 24		→		16 51	17 10		17 24		→		17 51	18 10
Gloucester	a	15 22							16 20							17 20							18 20
Bristol Parkway	a			15 55				16 20			16 54				17 20			18 03				18 20	
Bristol Temple Meads	a			16 09				16 32			17 08				17 31			18 14				18 35	
Newport (South Wales)	a	16 06							17 04							18 06							19 05
Cardiff Central	a	16 29							17 26							18 29							19 27
Weston-super-Mare	a																						
Taunton	a			16 44				17 14							18 17							19 17	
Tiverton Parkway	a			16 56				17 26							18 29							19 29	
Exeter St Davids	a			17 09				17 40							18 45							19 45	
Dawlish	a			17 24																			
Teignmouth	a			17 29																			
Newton Abbot	a			17 36				18 00							19 05							20 07	
Torquay	a			17 48																			
Paignton	a			17 56																			
Totnes	a							18 12							19 17							20 19	
Plymouth	a							18 38							19 43							20 45	
Liskeard	a							19 15														21 12	
Bodmin Parkway	a							19 27														21 24	
Lostwithiel	a																						
Par	a							19 37														21 34	
St Austell	a							19 43														21 40	
Truro	a							20 00														21 58	
Redruth	a							20 11														22 10	
Camborne	a							20 18														22 16	
Hayle	a																						
St Erth	a							20 30														22 29	
Penzance	a							20 39														22 42	
Birmingham International	d		14 44		15 14		15 20					16 14		16 19			16 44		17 14		17 20		
Coventry	d		14 55		15 25		15a30					16 25		16a30			16 55		17 25		17a29		
Leamington Spa	d		15 09		15 38					15 59		16 38					17 09		17 38				
Banbury	a		15 26		15 54					16 15		16 54					17 25		17 54				
Oxford	a		15 45		16 14					16 35		17 14					17 44		18 14				
Reading	a		16 11		16 41					17 01		17 41					18 10		18 41				
Guildford	a																						
Basingstoke	a				17 09							18 09							19 09				
Winchester	a				17 24							18 24							19 24				
Southampton Airport Pkwy	a				17 33							18 33							19 33				
Southampton Central	a				17 42							18 44							19 42				
Brockenhurst	a				18 06							19 03							20 06				
Bournemouth	a				18 26							19 26							20 26				

A 🛒 from Birmingham New Street
B 🛒 to Plymouth
C 🛒 from Edinburgh
D 🛒 to Birmingham New Street

Scotland, The North East, North West England - The South West and South Coast

		XC	XC	XC	XC	VT	XC	XC	XC	XC	XC	XC	VT	XC	XC	XC	XC	XC	XC	VT	XC	XC
		◇1	◇1	◇1	◇1	◇1	◇1	◇1	◇1	◇1	◇1	◇1	◇1	◇1	◇1	◇1	◇1	◇1	◇1	◇1	◇1	◇1
								A		B	C	D		B	A		A	C	D		B	
		⊼	⊼	⊼	⊼	🍴	⊼	⊼	⊼	⊼	⊼	⊼	🍴	⊼	⊼	⊼	⊼	⊼	⊼	🍴	⊼	⊼
Aberdeen	d											11 10										
Stonehaven	d											11 27										
Montrose	d											11 48										
Arbroath	d											12 04										
Dundee	d											12 24										
Leuchars	d											12 37										
Cupar	d											12 44										
Ladybank	d											12 51										
Markinch	d											12 58										
Kirkcaldy	d											13 07										
Inverkeithing	d											13 22										
Glasgow Central	d																					
Motherwell	d				12 18														14 03			
Haymarket	d				12 56							13 38							14 42			
Edinburgh	d				13 08				13 55			14 08	14 51						15 08			
Haymarket	d												14 56									
Lockerbie	d																					
Carlisle	d					15 05							16 07							17 05		
Penrith North Lakes	d												16 22									
Oxenholme Lake District	d					15 45														17 44		
Lancaster	d												16 57									
Preston	d					16 17							17 17							18 17		
Wigan North Western	d					16 29							17 29							18 28		
Warrington Bank Quay	d					16 40							17 40							18 39		
M'chester Piccadilly	d		16 05	16 27						17 05	17 27						18 05	18 27				
Stockport	d		16 13	16 36						17 13	17 36						18 13	18 36				
Wilmslow	d																					
Crewe	d					17 01							18 01							19 01		
Macclesfield	d		16 26	16 49						17 26	17 49						18 26	18 49				
Congleton	d																					
Stoke-on-Trent	d		16 44	17 07						17 45	18 07						18 45	19 07				
Stafford	d		17 01	17 25						18 02	18 25						19 02	19 25				
Wolverhampton	d		17 15	17 41		17 45				18 17	18 41		18 45				19 17	19 41		19 45		
Dunbar	d				13 29														15 29			
Berwick-upon-Tweed	d								14 36			14 49										
Alnmouth for Alnwick	d				14 11																	
Morpeth	d											15 20							16 22			
Newcastle	d	14 36			14 41				15 24			15 40				16 35			16 40			
Chester-le-Street	d																					
Durham	d	14 48			14 53				15 36			15 52				16 47			16 52			
Darlington	d	15 06			15 10				15 54			16 10				17 05			17 10			
York	d	15 35			15 42				16 25			16 41				17 35			17 44			
Leeds	d				16 11							17 11							18 11			
Wakefield Westgate	d				16 23							17 23							18 23			
Doncaster	d	15 58							16 51							17 58						
Sheffield	d	16 24			16 55				17 24			17 55				18 24			18 55			
Chesterfield	d				17 07							18 07							19 07			
Nottingham	d							17 10							18 10							19 10
Derby	d	16 54			17 27			17 35	17 54			18 26			18 35	18 54			19 27			19 35
Burton-on-Trent	d				17 37			17 47							18 47				19 38			19 47
Tamworth	d						←	18 00				18 45		←	19 00						←	19 59
Birmingham New Street	a	17 26	17 32	17 57	18 01	18 05	18 01	18 19	18 26	18 33	18 57	19 03	19 06	19 03	19 21	19 28	19 33	19 57	20 02	20 06	20 02	20 21
Birmingham New Street	d	17 33	17 42	18 04	18 12	18 10	18 12	18 30	18 33	18 42	19 04	19 12	19 10	19 12	19 30	19 33	19 42	20 04	20 12	20 10	20 12	
Cheltenham Spa	a		18 24		→		18 51	19 11		19 24		→		19 51	20 10		20 24		→		20 51	
Gloucester	a							19 26							20 19							
Bristol Parkway	a		18 54				19 21			20 03				20 20			20 56				21 20	
Bristol Temple Meads	a		19 08				19 32			20 14				20 31			21 06				21 30	
Newport (South Wales)	a							20 06							21 06							
Cardiff Central	a							20 30							21 27							
Weston-super-Mare	a									20 37												
Taunton	a						20 17			20 58				21 14							22 14	
Tiverton Parkway	a						20 29			21 13				21 26							22 27	
Exeter St Davids	a						20 43			21 29				21 40							22 46	
Dawlish	a									21 41												
Teignmouth	a									21 47												
Newton Abbot	a						21 01			21 54				21 59							23 06	
Torquay	a									22 05												
Paignton	a									22 14												
Totnes	a						21 13							22 11							23 18	
Plymouth	a						21 41							22 38							23 46	
Liskeard	a																					
Bodmin Parkway	a																					
Lostwithiel	a																					
Par	a																					
St Austell	a																					
Truro	a																					
Redruth	a																					
Camborne	a																					
Hayle	a																					
St Erth	a																					
Penzance	a																					
Birmingham International	d			18 14		18 20			18 44		19 14		19 20			19 44		20 14		20 20		
Coventry	d			18 25		18a30			18 55		19 25		19a30			19 55		20 25		20a30		
Leamington Spa	d	17 59		18 38					19 09		19 38					20 09		20 38				
Banbury	a	18 16		18 54					19 25		19 54					20 25		20 54				
Oxford	a	18 35		19 14					19 44		20 14					20 44		21 14				
Reading	a	19 05		19 40					20 08		20 41					21 12		21 38				
Guildford	a																					
Basingstoke	a			20 09							21 08							22 09				
Winchester	a			20 24							21 24							22 23				
Southampton Airport Pkway	a			20 33							21 33							22 33				
Southampton Central	a			20 43							21 42							22 42				
Brockenhurst	a			21 06							22 06											
Bournemouth	a			21 26							22 26											

A ⊼ to Birmingham New Street
B ⊼ to Bristol Temple Meads
C ⊼ to Reading
D ⊼ from Edinburgh

Scotland, The North East, North West England - The South West and South Coast

		XC	XC	VT	XC	XC	XC	XC	XC	XC	XC	XC	VT	XC	VT	XC	XC
		◇1	◇1	◇1	◇1	◇1	◇1	◇1	◇1	◇1	◇1	◇1	◇1	◇1	◇1	◇1	◇1
		A	A		A	B				C						D	
		⊼	⊼	🍴	⊼	⊼		⊼		⊼			🍴		🍴	⊼	
Aberdeen	d																
Stonehaven	d																
Montrose	d																
Arbroath	d																
Dundee	d																
Leuchars	d																
Cupar	d																
Ladybank	d																
Markinch	d																
Kirkcaldy	d																
Inverkeithing	d																
Glasgow Central	d												18 31				
Motherwell	d					15 13										17 13	
Haymarket	d					15 52										17 51	
Edinburgh	d			16 51		16 08				17 08					18 51	18 06	
Haymarket	d			16 55											18 56		
Lockerbie	d																
Carlisle	d			18 07									19 48		20 07		
Penrith North Lakes	d														20 22		
Oxenholme Lake District	d			18 42									20 23				
Lancaster	d			18 57									20 37		20 57		
Preston	d			19 17									20 57		21 17		
Wigan North Western	d			19 28									21 08		21 29		
Warrington Bank Quay	d			19 39									21 19		21 39		
M'chester Piccadilly	d		19 05		19 27				20 05					21 05			22 05
Stockport	d		19 13		19 36				20 14					21 13			22 13
Wilmslow	d																
Crewe	d			20 01									21 41		22 01		
Macclesfield	d		19 26		19 49				20 27					21 26			22 26
Congleton	d																
Stoke-on-Trent	d		19 45		20 06				20 45					21 45			22 45
Stafford	d		20 02		20 26				21 02				22 01	22 05			23 02
Wolverhampton	d		20 17	20 33	20 41				21 17				22 16	22 19	22 32		23 17
Dunbar	d									17 29						18 28	
Berwick-upon-Tweed	d									17 53						18 52	
Alnmouth for Alnwick	d					17 08											
Morpeth	d					17 22										19 23	
Newcastle	d	17 35				17 40		18 25		18 40		19 26				19 41	
Chester-le-Street	d																
Durham	d	17 48				17 53		18 37		18 52		19 39				19 53	
Darlington	d	18 06				18 11		18 55		19 09		19 56				20 10	
York	d	18 35				18 45		19 24		19 45		20 26				20 45	
Leeds	d					19 11				20 11						21 11	
Wakefield Westgate	d					19 24				20 23						21 23	
Doncaster	d	18 58						19 54				20 51					
Sheffield	d	19 24				19 55		20 21		20 54		21 20				21 54	
Chesterfield	d					20 07				21 06		21 32				22 06	
Nottingham	d						20 10				21 10						
Derby	d	19 56				20 27	20 35	20 54		21 26	21 37	21 53				22 26	
Burton-on-Trent	d						20 47			21 37	21 48	22 03				22 37	
Tamworth	d					20 46	20 59			21 47	22 00	22 14				22 47	
Birmingham New Street	a	20 27	20 33	20 51	20 57	21 03	21 18	21 26	21 33	22 05	22 23	22 31	22 33	22 36	22 53	23 05	23 33
Birmingham New Street	d	20 33	20 42		21 04	21 12			21 42	22 11							
Cheltenham Spa	a		21 24			21 51			22 23	22 52							
Gloucester	a					22 04											
Bristol Parkway	a		21 59			22 35			22 52	23 22							
Bristol Temple Meads	a		22 10			22 46			23 02	23 33							
Newport (South Wales)	a																
Cardiff Central	a																
Weston-super-Mare	a																
Taunton	a																
Tiverton Parkway	a																
Exeter St Davids	a																
Dawlish	a																
Teignmouth	a																
Newton Abbot	a																
Torquay	a																
Paignton	a																
Totnes	a																
Plymouth	a																
Liskeard	a																
Bodmin Parkway	a																
Lostwithiel	a																
Par	a																
St Austell	a																
Truro	a																
Redruth	a																
Camborne	a																
Hayle	a																
St Erth	a																
Penzance	a																
Birmingham International	d				21 14												
Coventry	d				21 24												
Leamington Spa	d	21 00			21 36												
Banbury	a	21 17			21 52												
Oxford	a	21 38			22 11												
Reading	a	22 06			22 38												
Guildford	a	22 42															
Basingstoke	a																
Winchester	a																
Southampton Airport Pkway	a																
Southampton Central	a																
Brockenhurst	a																
Bournemouth	a																

A ⊼ to Birmingham New Street
B ⊼ from Edinburgh to Birmingham New Street
C ⊼ to Leeds
D ⊼ from Edinburgh to Leeds

Table T051-F

Sundays

22 July to 2 September

Scotland, The North East, North West England - The South West and South Coast

		XC	XC	XC	XC	XC	XC	XC	XC	VT	XC	XC	XC	XC	XC	VT	XC	XC	XC	XC	XC	XC	VT
			A										B						B				
Aberdeen	d																						
Stonehaven	d																						
Montrose	d																						
Arbroath	d																						
Dundee	d																						
Leuchars	d																						
Cupar	d																						
Ladybank	d																						
Markinch	d																						
Kirkcaldy	d																						
Inverkeithing	d																						
Glasgow Central	d																						
Motherwell	d																						
Haymarket	d																						
Edinburgh	d																						
Haymarket	d																						
Lockerbie	d																						
Carlisle	d																						
Penrith North Lakes	d																						
Oxenholme Lake District	d																						
Lancaster	d																						11 58
Preston	d									10 17						11 17							12 17
Wigan North Western	d									10 28						11 28							12 28
Warrington Bank Quay	d									10 39						11 40							12 39
M'chester Piccadilly	d			08 27			09 27				10 26						11 27					12 26	
Stockport	d			08 36			09 36				10 36						11 36					12 35	
Wilmslow	d			08 43																			
Crewe	d			09 05						11 02						12 02							13 01
Macclesfield	d						09 49				10 49						11 49					12 49	
Congleton	d																						
Stoke-on-Trent	d						10 07				11 07						12 07					13 07	
Stafford	d			09 26			10 25				11 27						12 25					13 25	
Wolverhampton	d			09 41			10 41			11 32	11 42					12 32	12 41					13 41	13 45
Dunbar	d																						
Berwick-upon-Tweed	d																						
Alnmouth for Alnwick	d																						
Morpeth	d																						
Newcastle	d																				09 35		
Chester-le-Street	d																						
Durham	d																				09 47		
Darlington	d																				10 05		
York	d													09 33							10 33		
Leeds	d					08 10			09 00					09 59							11 00		
Wakefield Westgate	d					08 23			09 11					10 12							11 12		
Doncaster	d								09 31					10 30							11 30		
Sheffield	d					08 55			09 57					10 55							11 57		
Chesterfield	d					09 08			10 10					11 08							12 09		
Nottingham	d							09 54					11 11						12 10				
Derby	d																						
Burton-on-Trent	d					10 00		10 29	11 00				11 47	12 02					12 47		13 03		
Tamworth	d							10 42	11 12				12 00	12 13					13 00		13 13		
Birmingham New Street	a			09 57		10 26	10 57	11 02	11 30	11 50	11 58		12 21	12 32		12 50	12 57		13 21		13 31	13 57	14 06
Birmingham New Street	d	09 04	09 30	10 04	10 12	10 30	11 04	11 12	11 30		12 04	12 12	12 30		12 33		13 04	13 12	13 30	13 33	13 42	14 04	14 10
Cheltenham Spa	a		10 08		10 52	11 09		11 52	12 09			12 50	13 10					13 51	14 10		14 23		
Gloucester	a				11 02			12 02					13 20						14 20				
Bristol Parkway	a		10 37			11 39			12 39			13 21						14 20			14 53		
Bristol Temple Meads	a		10 48			11 51			12 51			13 32						14 31			15 08		
Newport (South Wales)	a				11 47			12 44					14 06						15 01				
Cardiff Central	a				12 09			13 07					14 27						15 28				
Weston-super-Mare	a																						
Taunton	a		11 29			12 25			13 25			14 15						15 14					
Tiverton Parkway	a		11 41			12 35			13 36			14 27						15 26					
Exeter St Davids	a		11 54			12 52			13 52			14 42						15 39					
Dawlish	a																						
Teignmouth	a																						
Newton Abbot	a		12 14			13 12			14 12			15 02						16 00					
Torquay	a																						
Paignton	a																						
Totnes	a		12 26			13 25			14 25			15 15						16 12					
Plymouth	a		12 52			13 52			14 52			15 42						16 38					
Liskeard	a		13 17																				
Bodmin Parkway	a		13 29																				
Lostwithiel	a																						
Par	a		13 39																				
St Austell	a		13 45																				
Truro	a		14 06																				
Redruth	a		14 19																				
Camborne	a		14 25																				
Hayle	a																						
St Erth	a		14 36																				
Penzance	a		14 47																				
Birmingham International	d	09 14		10 14			11 14				12 14				12 44		13 14					14 14	14 20
Coventry	d	09 25		10 25			11 25				12 25				12 55		13 25					14 25	14a30
Leamington Spa	d	09 38		10 38			11 38				12 38				13 08		13 38			13 59		14 38	
Banbury	a	09 54		10 54			11 54				12 54				13 24		13 54			14 15		14 54	
Oxford	a	10 14		11 14			12 14				13 14				13 43		14 14			14 35		15 14	
Reading	a	10 42		11 40			12 41				13 42				14 11		14 41			15 02		15 40	
Guildford	a																						
Basingstoke	a	11 09		12 09			13 09				14 09						15 09					16 09	
Winchester	a	11 24		12 25			13 24				14 24						15 24					16 24	
Southampton Airport Pkway	a	11 33		12 34			13 33				14 33						15 33					16 33	
Southampton Central	a	11 42		12 43			13 42				14 42						15 43					16 42	
Brockenhurst	a	12 06		13 07			14 06				15 06						16 03					17 06	
Bournemouth	a	12 26		13 26			14 26				15 26						16 26					17 26	

A to Plymouth B from Birmingham New Street

Table T051-F

Sundays

22 July to 2 September

Scotland, The North East, North West England - The South West and South Coast

		XC	XC	XC	XC	XC	XC	VT	XC	XC	XC	XC	XC	XC	VT	XC	XC	XC	XC	XC	XC	VT	XC
			A						B														B
Aberdeen	d																						
Stonehaven	d																						
Montrose	d																						
Arbroath	d																						
Dundee	d																						
Leuchars	d																						
Cupar	d																						
Ladybank	d																						
Markinch	d																						
Kirkcaldy	d																						
Inverkeithing	d																						
Glasgow Central	d																						
Motherwell	d																						
Haymarket	d																						
Edinburgh	d						09 08	10 51						10 08							11 05	12 51	
Haymarket	d							10 55														12 55	
Lockerbie	d																						
Carlisle	d							12 07							13 07							14 07	
Penrith North Lakes	d																					14 22	
Oxenholme Lake District	d							12 43															
Lancaster	d							12 57							13 56							14 57	
Preston	d							13 17							14 17							15 17	
Wigan North Western	d							13 28							14 28							15 28	
Warrington Bank Quay	d							13 39							14 39							15 39	
M'chester Piccadilly	d				13 05	13 27						14 05	14 27						15 05	15 27			
Stockport	d				13 13	13 36						14 13	14 36						15 13	15 36			
Wilmslow	d																						
Crewe	d							14 01							15 01							16 01	
Macclesfield	d				13 26	13 49						14 26	14 49						15 26	15 49			
Congleton	d																						
Stoke-on-Trent	d				13 45	14 07						14 44	15 07						15 44	16 07			
Stafford	d				14 02	14 25						15 01	15 25						16 01	16 25			
Wolverhampton	d				14 17	14 41		14 45				15 17	15 41		15 45				16 17	16 41		16 45	
Dunbar	d																				11 26		
Berwick-upon-Tweed	d						09 51														11 50		
Alnmouth for Alnwick	d													11 07							12 10		
Morpeth	d													11 22									
Newcastle	d						10 39							11 40							12 40		
Chester-le-Street	d																						
Durham	d						10 53							11 52							12 53		
Darlington	d						11 10							12 10							13 10		
York	d						11 41							12 42							13 45		
Leeds	d						12 11							13 11							14 11		
Wakefield Westgate	d						12 24							13 24							14 23		
Doncaster	d						12 54							13 54							14 54		
Sheffield	d						13 24							14 22							15 24		
Chesterfield	d						13 36							14 34							15 36		
Nottingham	d		13 10							14 10							15 10						
Derby	d																						
Burton-on-Trent	d		13 49				14 37			14 47				15 37			15 47				16 35		
Tamworth	d		14 00				14 48		←	15 00						←	16 00				16 46		←
Birmingham New Street	a		14 22		14 33	14 57	15 05	15 06	15 05	15 20		15 33	15 57	16 01	16 06	16 01	16 21		16 33	16 57	17 03	17 06	17 03
Birmingham New Street	d	14 12	14 30	14 33	14 42	15 04	15 12	15 10	15 12	15 30	15 33	15 42	16 04	16 12	16 10	16 12	16 30	16 33	16 42	17 04	17 12	17 10	17 12
Cheltenham Spa	a	14 50	15 10		15 24		→		15 51	16 10		16 24		→		16 51	17 10		17 24		→		17 51
Gloucester	a		15 22							16 20							17 20						
Bristol Parkway	a	15 23			15 55				16 20			16 54				17 20			18 03				18 20
Bristol Temple Meads	a	15 34			16 09				16 32			17 08				17 31			18 14				18 35
Newport (South Wales)	a		16 06							17 04							18 06						
Cardiff Central	a		16 29							17 26							18 29						
Weston-super-Mare	a																						
Taunton	a	16 14			16 44				17 14							18 17							19 17
Tiverton Parkway	a	16 26			16 56				17 26							18 29							19 29
Exeter St Davids	a	16 40			17 09				17 40							18 45							19 45
Dawlish	a				17 24																		
Teignmouth	a				17 29																		
Newton Abbot	a	17 01			17 36				18 00							19 05							20 07
Torquay	a				17 48																		
Paignton	a				17 56																		
Totnes	a	17 14							18 12							19 17							20 19
Plymouth	a	17 42							18 38							19 43							20 45
Liskeard	a								19 15														21 12
Bodmin Parkway	a								19 27														21 24
Lostwithiel	a																						
Par	a								19 37														21 34
St Austell	a								19 43														21 40
Truro	a								20 00														21 58
Redruth	a								20 11														22 10
Camborne	a								20 18														22 16
Hayle	a																						
St Erth	a								20 30														22 29
Penzance	a								20 39														22 42
Birmingham International	d			14 44		15 14		15 20					16 14		16 19			16 44		17 14		17 20	
Coventry	d			14 55		15 25		15a30					16 25		16a30			16 55		17 25		17a29	
Leamington Spa	d			15 09		15 38					15 59		16 38					17 09		17 38			
Banbury	a			15 26		15 54					16 15		16 54					17 25		17 54			
Oxford	a			15 45		16 14					16 35		17 14					17 44		18 14			
Reading	a			16 11		16 41					17 01		17 41					18 10		18 41			
Guildford	a																						
Basingstoke	a					17 09							18 09							19 09			
Winchester	a					17 24							18 24							19 24			
Southampton Airport Pkway	a					17 33							18 33							19 33			
Southampton Central	a					17 42							18 44							19 42			
Brockenhurst	a					18 06							19 03							20 06			
Bournemouth	a					18 26							19 26							20 26			

A from Birmingham New Street B to Plymouth

Scotland, The North East, North West England - The South West and South Coast

	XC ◇1 A ⚒	XC ◇1 ⚒	XC ◇1 ⚒	XC ◇1 ⚒	XC ◇1 ⚒	VT ◇1 ⊡	XC ◇1 ⚒	XC ◇1 A ⚒	XC ◇1 ⚒	XC ◇1 B ⚒	XC ◇1 C ⚒	XC ◇1	VT ◇1 ⊡	XC ◇1	XC ◇1 A ⚒	XC ◇1 ⚒	XC ◇1 A ⚒	XC ◇1 C ⚒	XC ◇1 D ⚒	VT ◇1 ⊡	XC ◇1 B ⚒
Aberdeen d																			11 10		
Stonehaven d																			11 27		
Montrose d																			11 48		
Arbroath d																			12 04		
Dundee d																			12 24		
Leuchars d																			12 37		
Cupar d																			12 44		
Ladybank d																			12 51		
Markinch d																			12 58		
Kirkcaldy d																			13 07		
Inverkeithing d																			13 22		
Glasgow Central d																					
Motherwell d					11 14							12 18									
Haymarket d					11 53							12 56							13 38		
Edinburgh d					12 08							13 08	14 51						14 08		
Haymarket d													14 56								
Lockerbie d																					
Carlisle d						15 05							16 07							17 05	
Penrith North Lakes d													16 22								
Oxenholme Lake District d						15 45														17 44	
Lancaster d													16 57								
Preston d						16 17							17 17							18 17	
Wigan North Western d						16 29							17 29							18 28	
Warrington Bank Quay d						16 40							17 40							18 39	
M'chester Piccadilly d			16 05	16 27						17 05	17 27						18 05	18 27			
Stockport d			16 13	16 36						17 13	17 36						18 13	18 36			
Wilmslow d																					
Crewe d						17 01							18 01							19 01	
Macclesfield d			16 26	16 49						17 26	17 49						18 26	18 49			
Congleton d																					
Stoke-on-Trent d			16 44	17 07						17 45	18 07						18 45	19 07			
Stafford d			17 01	17 25						18 02	18 25						19 02	19 25			
Wolverhampton d			17 15	17 41		17 45				18 17	18 41		18 45				19 17	19 41		19 45	
Dunbar d												13 29									
Berwick-upon-Tweed d					12 49														14 49		
Alnmouth for Alnwick d												14 11									
Morpeth d																			15 20		
Newcastle d					13 40							14 41							15 40		
Chester-le-Street d																					
Durham d					13 53							14 53							15 52		
Darlington d					14 10							15 10							16 10		
York d					14 44							15 42							16 41		
Leeds d					15 11							16 11							17 11		
Wakefield Westgate d					15 23							16 23							17 23		
Doncaster d					15 54							16 46							17 46		
Sheffield d					16 24							17 19							18 24		
Chesterfield d					16 36							17 31							18 36		
Nottingham d	16 10							17 10							18 10						
Derby d																					
Burton-on-Trent d	16 47				17 37			17 47				18 35			18 47				19 38		
Tamworth d	17 00						←	18 00				18 45		←	19 00						←
Birmingham New Street a	17 19		17 32	17 57	18 01	18 05	18 01	18 19		18 33	18 57	19 03	19 06	19 03	19 21		19 33	19 57	20 02	20 06	20 02
Birmingham New Street d	17 30	17 33	17 42	18 04	18 12	18 10	18 12	18 30	18 33	18 42	19 04	19 12	19 10	19 12	19 30	19 33	19 42	20 04	20 12	20 10	20 12
Cheltenham Spa a	18 10		18 24		→		18 51	19 11		19 24		→		19 51	20 10		20 24		→		20 51
Gloucester a	18 20							19 26							20 19						
Bristol Parkway a			18 54				19 21			20 03				20 20			20 56				21 20
Bristol Temple Meads a			19 08				19 32			20 14				20 31			21 06				21 30
Newport (South Wales) a	19 05							20 06							21 06						
Cardiff Central a	19 27							20 30							21 27						
Weston-super-Mare a										20 37											
Taunton a							20 17			20 58				21 14							22 14
Tiverton Parkway a							20 29			21 13				21 26							22 27
Exeter St Davids a							20 43			21 29				21 39							22 46
Dawlish a										21 41											
Teignmouth a										21 47											
Newton Abbot a							21 01			21 54				21 59							23 06
Torquay a										22 05											
Paignton a										22 14											
Totnes a							21 13							22 11							23 18
Plymouth a							21 41							22 38							23 46
Liskeard a																					
Bodmin Parkway a																					
Lostwithiel a																					
Par a																					
St Austell a																					
Truro a																					
Redruth a																					
Camborne a																					
Hayle a																					
St Erth a																					
Penzance a																					
Birmingham International d				18 14		18 20			18 44		19 14		19 20			19 44		20 14		20 20	
Coventry d				18 25		18a30			18 55		19 25		19a30			19 55		20 25		20a30	
Leamington Spa d		17 59		18 38					19 09		19 38					20 09		20 38			
Banbury a		18 16		18 54					19 25		19 54					20 25		20 54			
Oxford a		18 35		19 14					19 44		20 14					20 44		21 14			
Reading a		19 05		19 40					20 08		20 41					21 12		21 38			
Guildford a																					
Basingstoke a				20 09							21 08							22 09			
Winchester a				20 24							21 24							22 23			
Southampton Airport Pkway a				20 33							21 33							22 33			
Southampton Central a				20 43							21 42							22 42			
Brockenhurst a				21 06							22 06										
Bournemouth a				21 26							22 26										

A ⚒ to Birmingham New Street
B ⚒ to Bristol Temple Meads
C ⚒ to Reading
D ⚒ from Edinburgh

Table T051-F

Sundays

22 July to 2 September

Scotland, The North East, North West England - The South West and South Coast

	XC ◇1 ⚒	XC	XC ◇1 A ⚒	VT ◇1 ⊡	XC ◇1 A ⚒	XC ◇1 B ⚒	XC ◇1	XC ◇1	XC ◇1 ⚒	XC ◇1	XC ◇1	VT ◇1 ⊡	XC ◇1	VT ◇1 ⊡	XC ◇1 C ⚒	XC ◇1
Aberdeen d																
Stonehaven d																
Montrose d																
Arbroath d																
Dundee d																
Leuchars d																
Cupar d																
Ladybank d																
Markinch d																
Kirkcaldy d																
Inverkeithing d																
Glasgow Central d												18 31				
Motherwell d						14 03			15 13						17 13	
Haymarket d						14 42			15 52						17 51	
Edinburgh d				16 51		15 08			16 08		17 08			18 51	18 06	
Haymarket d				16 55										18 56		
Lockerbie d																
Carlisle d				18 07								19 48		20 07		
Penrith North Lakes d														20 22		
Oxenholme Lake District d				18 42								20 23				
Lancaster d				18 57								20 37		20 57		
Preston d				19 17								20 57		21 17		
Wigan North Western d				19 28								21 08		21 29		
Warrington Bank Quay d				19 39								21 19		21 39		
M'chester Piccadilly d			19 05		19 27			20 05					21 05			22 05
Stockport d			19 13		19 36			20 14					21 13			22 13
Wilmslow d																
Crewe d				20 01								21 41		22 01		
Macclesfield d			19 26		19 49			20 27					21 26			22 26
Congleton d																
Stoke-on-Trent d			19 45		20 06			20 45					21 45			22 45
Stafford d			20 02		20 26			21 02				22 01	22 05			23 02
Wolverhampton d			20 17	20 33	20 41			21 17				22 16	22 19	22 32		23 17
Dunbar d						15 29					17 29				18 28	
Berwick-upon-Tweed d											17 53				18 52	
Alnmouth for Alnwick d									17 08							
Morpeth d						16 22			17 22						19 23	
Newcastle d						16 40			17 40		18 40				19 41	
Chester-le-Street d																
Durham d						16 52			17 53		18 52				19 53	
Darlington d						17 10			18 11		19 09				20 10	
York d						17 44			18 45		19 45				20 45	
Leeds d						18 11			19 11		20 11				21 11	
Wakefield Westgate d						18 23			19 24		20 23				21 23	
Doncaster d						18 58			19 47							
Sheffield d						19 24			20 21		20 54				21 54	
Chesterfield d						19 36			20 33		21 06				22 06	
Nottingham d	19 10						20 10			21 10						
Derby d																
Burton-on-Trent d	19 47					20 35	20 47		21 37	21 48	22 03				22 59	
Tamworth d	19 59					20 46	20 59		21 47	22 00	22 14				23 10	
Birmingham New Street a	20 21		20 33	20 51	20 57	21 03	21 18	21 33	22 05	22 23	22 31	22 33	22 36	22 53	23 27	23 33
Birmingham New Street d		20 33	20 42		21 04	21 12		21 42	22 12							
Cheltenham Spa a			21 24			21 51		22 23	22 52							
Gloucester a						22 04										
Bristol Parkway a			21 59			22 35		22 52	23 22							
Bristol Temple Meads a			22 10			22 46		23 02	23 33							
Newport (South Wales) a																
Cardiff Central a																
Weston-super-Mare a																
Taunton a																
Tiverton Parkway a																
Exeter St Davids a																
Dawlish a																
Teignmouth a																
Newton Abbot a																
Torquay a																
Paignton a																
Totnes a																
Plymouth a																
Liskeard a																
Bodmin Parkway a																
Lostwithiel a																
Par a																
St Austell a																
Truro a																
Redruth a																
Camborne a																
Hayle a																
St Erth a																
Penzance a																
Birmingham International d					21 14											
Coventry d					21 24											
Leamington Spa d		21 00			21 36											
Banbury a		21 17			21 52											
Oxford a		21 38			22 11											
Reading a		22 06			22 38											
Guildford a		22 42														
Basingstoke a																
Winchester a																
Southampton Airport Pkway a																
Southampton Central a																
Brockenhurst a																
Bournemouth a																

A ⚒ to Birmingham New Street
B ⚒ from Edinburgh to Birmingham New Street
C ⚒ from Edinburgh to Leeds

Table T051-F

Sundays
9 September to 7 October

Scotland, The North East, North West England - The South West and South Coast

		XC	XC A	XC	XC	XC	XC	XC	XC	VT	XC	XC	XC B	XC	XC	VT	XC	XC	XC B	XC	XC	XC	VT
Aberdeen	d																						
Stonehaven	d																						
Montrose	d																						
Arbroath	d																						
Dundee	d																						
Leuchars	d																						
Cupar	d																						
Ladybank	d																						
Markinch	d																						
Kirkcaldy	d																						
Inverkeithing	d																						
Glasgow Central	d																						
Motherwell	d																						
Haymarket	d																						
Edinburgh	d																						
Haymarket	d																						
Lockerbie	d																						
Carlisle	d																						
Penrith North Lakes	d																						
Oxenholme Lake District	d																						
Lancaster	d																						11 58
Preston	d									10 17						11 17							12 17
Wigan North Western	d									10 28						11 28							12 28
Warrington Bank Quay	d									10 39						11 40							12 39
M'chester Piccadilly	d			08 27			09 27				10 26						11 27					12 26	
Stockport	d			08 36			09 36				10 36						11 36					12 35	
Wilmslow	d			08 43																			
Crewe	d			09 05						11 02						12 02							13 01
Macclesfield	d						09 49				10 49						11 49					12 49	
Congleton	d																						
Stoke-on-Trent	d						10 07				11 07						12 07					13 07	
Stafford	d			09 26			10 25				11 27						12 25					13 25	
Wolverhampton	d			09 41			10 41			11 32	11 42					12 32	12 41					13 41	13 45
Dunbar	d																						
Berwick-upon-Tweed	d																						
Alnmouth for Alnwick	d																						
Morpeth	d																						
Newcastle	d																				09 35		
Chester-le-Street	d																						
Durham	d																				09 47		
Darlington	d																				10 05		
York	d													09 33							10 33		
Leeds	d					08 10			09 00					09 59							11 00		
Wakefield Westgate	d					08 23			09 11					10 12							11 12		
Doncaster	d								09 31					10 30							11 30		
Sheffield	d					08 55			09 58					10 55							11 57		
Chesterfield	d					09 08			10 11					11 08							12 09		
Nottingham	d							09 54					11 11						12 10				
Derby	d					09 52		10 18	10 52				11 36	11 50					12 35		12 54		
Burton-on-Trent	d							10 29					11 47	12 02					12 47				
Tamworth	d							10 42	11 12				12 00	12 13					13 00		13 13		
Birmingham New Street	a			09 57		10 26	10 57	11 02	11 30	11 50	11 58		12 21	12 32		12 50	12 57		13 21		13 31	13 57	14 06
Birmingham New Street	d	09 04	09 30	10 04	10 12	10 30	11 04	11 12	11 30		12 04	12 12	12 30		12 33		13 04	13 12	13 30	13 33	13 42	14 04	14 10
Cheltenham Spa	a		10 08		10 52	11 09		11 52	12 09			12 50	13 10					13 51	14 10		14 23		
Gloucester	a				11 02			12 02					13 20						14 20				
Bristol Parkway	a		10 37			11 39			12 39			13 21						14 20			14 53		
Bristol Temple Meads	a		10 48			11 51			12 51			13 32						14 31			15 08		
Newport (South Wales)	a				11 47			12 44					14 06						15 01				
Cardiff Central	a				12 09			13 07					14 27						15 28				
Weston-super-Mare	a																						
Taunton	a		11 29			12 25			13 25			14 15						15 14					
Tiverton Parkway	a		11 41			12 35			13 36			14 27						15 26					
Exeter St Davids	a		11 54			12 52			13 52			14 42						15 39					
Dawlish	a																						
Teignmouth	a																						
Newton Abbot	a		12 14			13 12			14 12			15 02						16 00					
Torquay	a																						
Paignton	a																						
Totnes	a		12 26			13 25			14 25			15 15						16 12					
Plymouth	a		12 52			13 52			14 52			15 42						16 38					
Liskeard	a		13 17																				
Bodmin Parkway	a		13 29																				
Lostwithiel	a																						
Par	a		13 39																				
St Austell	a		13 45																				
Truro	a		14 06																				
Redruth	a		14 19																				
Camborne	a		14 25																				
Hayle	a																						
St Erth	a		14 36																				
Penzance	a		14 47																				
Birmingham International	d	09 14		10 14			11 14				12 14				12 44		13 14					14 14	14 20
Coventry	d	09 25		10 25			11 25				12 25				12 55		13 25					14 25	14a30
Leamington Spa	d	09 38		10 38			11 38				12 38				13 08		13 38			13 59		14 38	
Banbury	a	09 54		10 54			11 54				12 54				13 24		13 54			14 15		14 54	
Oxford	a	10 14		11 14			12 14				13 14				13 43		14 14			14 35		15 14	
Reading	a	10 42		11 40			12 41				13 42				14 11		14 41			15 02		15 40	
Guildford	a																						
Basingstoke	a	11 09		12 09			13 09				14 09						15 09					16 09	
Winchester	a	11 24		12 25			13 24				14 24						15 24					16 24	
Southampton Airport Pkway	a	11 33		12 34			13 33				14 33						15 33					16 33	
Southampton Central	a	11 42		12 43			13 42				14 42						15 43					16 42	
Brockenhurst	a	12 06		13 07			14 06				15 06						16 03					17 06	
Bournemouth	a	12 26		13 26			14 26				15 26						16 26					17 26	

A ✠ to Plymouth
B ✠ from Birmingham New Street

Table T051-F

Sundays
9 September to 7 October

Scotland, The North East, North West England - The South West and South Coast

		XC	XC A	XC B	XC C	XC	XC	XC	VT	XC D	XC	XC	XC	XC	XC	VT C	VT B	XC	XC	XC B	XC C	XC	XC
Aberdeen	d																						
Stonehaven	d																						
Montrose	d																						
Arbroath	d																						
Dundee	d																						
Leuchars	d																						
Cupar	d																						
Ladybank	d																						
Markinch	d																						
Kirkcaldy	d																						
Inverkeithing	d																						
Glasgow Central	d															11 55							
Motherwell	d																						
Haymarket	d																						
Edinburgh	d							09 08	10 51						10 08								
Haymarket	d								10 55														
Lockerbie	d																						
Carlisle	d								12 07							13 07	13 07						
Penrith North Lakes	d																						
Oxenholme Lake District	d								12 43														
Lancaster	d								12 57							13 56	13 56						
Preston	d								13 17							14 17	14 17						
Wigan North Western	d								13 28							14 28	14 28						
Warrington Bank Quay	d								13 39							14 39	14 39						
M'chester Piccadilly	d					13 05	13 27						14 05	14 27								15 05	15 27
Stockport	d					13 13	13 36						14 13	14 36								15 13	15 36
Wilmslow	d																						
Crewe	d								14 01							15 01	15 01						
Macclesfield	d					13 26	13 49						14 26	14 49								15 26	15 49
Congleton	d																						
Stoke-on-Trent	d					13 45	14 07						14 44	15 07								15 44	16 07
Stafford	d					14 02	14 25						15 01	15 25								16 01	16 25
Wolverhampton	d					14 17	14 41		14 45				15 17	15 41		15 45	15 45					16 17	16 41
Dunbar	d																						
Berwick-upon-Tweed	d							09 51															
Alnmouth for Alnwick	d														11 07								
Morpeth	d														11 22								
Newcastle	d							10 39							11 40								
Chester-le-Street	d																						
Durham	d							10 53							11 52								
Darlington	d							11 10							12 10								
York	d							11 41							12 42								
Leeds	d							12 11							13 11								
Wakefield Westgate	d							12 24							13 24								
Doncaster	d							12 54							13 54								
Sheffield	d							13 24							14 22								
Chesterfield	d							13 36							14 34								
Nottingham	d		13 10								14 10								15 10				
Derby	d	13 32	13 38	13 55	13 55			14 29			14 34	14 53			15 26				15 34	15 54	15 54		
Burton-on-Trent	d	13 43	13 49								14 47				15 37				15 47				
Tamworth	d		14 00					14 48		←	15 00							←	16 00				
Birmingham New Street	a	14 09	14 22	14 27	14 27	14 33	14 57	15 05	15 06	15 05	15 20	15 26	15 33	15 57	16 01	16 06	16 06	16 01	16 21	16 26	16 26	16 33	16 57
Birmingham New Street	d	14 12	14 30	14 33	14 33	14 42	15 04	15 12	15 10	15 12	15 30	15 33	15 42	16 04	16 12	16 10	16 10	16 12	16 30	16 33	16 33	16 42	17 04
Cheltenham Spa	a	14 50	15 10			15 24		→		15 51	16 10		16 24		→			16 51	17 10			17 24	
Gloucester	a		15 22								16 20								17 20				
Bristol Parkway	a	15 23				15 55				16 20			16 54					17 20				18 03	
Bristol Temple Meads	a	15 34				16 09				16 32			17 08					17 31				18 14	
Newport (South Wales)	a		16 06								17 04								18 06				
Cardiff Central	a		16 29								17 26								18 29				
Weston-super-Mare	a																						
Taunton	a	16 14				16 44				17 14								18 17					
Tiverton Parkway	a	16 26				16 56				17 26								18 29					
Exeter St Davids	a	16 40				17 09				17 40								18 45					
Dawlish	a					17 24																	
Teignmouth	a					17 29																	
Newton Abbot	a	17 01				17 36				18 00								19 05					
Torquay	a					17 48																	
Paignton	a					17 56																	
Totnes	a	17 14								18 12								19 17					
Plymouth	a	17 42								18 38								19 43					
Liskeard	a									19 15													
Bodmin Parkway	a									19 27													
Lostwithiel	a																						
Par	a									19 37													
St Austell	a									19 43													
Truro	a									20 00													
Redruth	a									20 11													
Camborne	a									20 18													
Hayle	a																						
St Erth	a									20 30													
Penzance	a									20 39													
Birmingham International	d			14 44	14 44		15 14		15 20					16 14		16 19	16 19			16 44	16 44		17 14
Coventry	d			14 55	14 55		15 25		15a30					16 25		16a30	16a30			16 55	16 55		17 25
Leamington Spa	d			15 09	15 09		15 38					15 59		16 38						17 09	17 09		17 38
Banbury	a			15 26	15 26		15 54					16 15		16 54						17 25	17 25		17 54
Oxford	a			15 45	15 45		16 14					16 35		17 14						17 44	17 44		18 14
Reading	a			16 11	16 12		16 41					17 01		17 41						18 10	18 12		18 41
Guildford	a																						
Basingstoke	a						17 09							18 09									19 09
Winchester	a						17 24							18 24									19 24
Southampton Airport Pkway	a						17 33							18 33									19 33
Southampton Central	a						17 42							18 44									19 42
Brockenhurst	a						18 06							19 03									20 06
Bournemouth	a						18 26							19 26									20 26

A ✠ from Birmingham New Street
B 9 September
C not 9 September
D ✠ to Plymouth

Table T051-F

Sundays

9 September to 7 October

Scotland, The North East, North West England - The South West and South Coast

		XC	VT	XC	XC	XC	XC	XC	XC	XC	VT	VT	XC	XC	XC	XC	XC	XC	XC	XC	XC	VT
		◇1	◇1	◇1	◇1	◇1	◇1	◇1	◇1	◇1	◇1	◇1	◇1	◇1	◇1	◇1	◇1	◇1	◇1	◇1	◇1	◇1
				A	B				C	D	D	C	C	D	B		E	F	G	C	D	
		🍴	☕	🍴	🍴	🍴	🍴	🍴	🍴	🍴	☕	☕	🍴	🍴	🍴	🍴	🍴	🍴	🍴			☕
Aberdeen	d																					
Stonehaven	d																					
Montrose	d																					
Arbroath	d																					
Dundee	d																					
Leuchars	d																					
Cupar	d																					
Ladybank	d																					
Markinch	d																					
Kirkcaldy	d																					
Inverkeithing	d																					
Glasgow Central	d								10 55			13 55								12 02		
Motherwell	d								11 14	11 14										12 18	12 18	
Haymarket	d								11 53	11 53										12 56	12 56	
Edinburgh	d	11 05	12 51						12 08	12 08										13 08	13 08	14 51
Haymarket	d		12 55																			14 56
Lockerbie	d																					
Carlisle	d		14 07								15 05	15 11										16 07
Penrith North Lakes	d		14 22																			16 22
Oxenholme Lake District	d										15 45	15 45										
Lancaster	d		14 57																			16 57
Preston	d		15 17								16 17	16 17										17 17
Wigan North Western	d		15 28								16 29	16 29										17 29
Warrington Bank Quay	d		15 39								16 40	16 40										17 40
M'chester Piccadilly	d						16 05	16 27									17 05	17 05	17 27			
Stockport	d						16 13	16 36									17 13	17 13	17 36			
Wilmslow	d																					
Crewe	d		16 01								17 01	17 01										18 01
Macclesfield	d						16 26	16 49									17 26	17 26	17 49			
Congleton	d																					
Stoke-on-Trent	d						16 44	17 07									17 45	17 45	18 07			
Stafford	d						17 01	17 25									18 02	18 02	18 25			
Wolverhampton	d		16 45				17 15	17 41			17 45	17 45					18 17	18 17	18 41			18 45
Dunbar	d	11 26																		13 29	13 29	
Berwick-upon-Tweed	d	11 50							12 49	12 49												
Alnmouth for Alnwick	d	12 10																		14 11	14 11	
Morpeth	d																					
Newcastle	d	12 40							13 40	13 40										14 41	14 41	
Chester-le-Street	d																					
Durham	d	12 53							13 53	13 53										14 53	14 53	
Darlington	d	13 10							14 10	14 10										15 10	15 10	
York	d	13 45							14 44	14 44										15 42	15 42	
Leeds	d	14 11							15 11	15 11										16 11	16 11	
Wakefield Westgate	d	14 23							15 23	15 23										16 23	16 23	
Doncaster	d	14 54							15 54	15 54										16 46	16 46	
Sheffield	d	15 24							16 24	16 24										17 19	17 19	
Chesterfield	d	15 36							16 36	16 36										17 31	17 31	
Nottingham	d				16 10										17 10							
Derby	d	16 27			16 34	16 55			17 26	17 26					17 35	17 55				18 26	18 26	
Burton-on-Trent	d				16 47				17 37	17 37					17 47							
Tamworth	d	16 46		←	17 00								←	←	18 00					18 45	18 45	
Birmingham New Street	a	17 03	17 06	17 03	17 19	17 26	17 32	17 57	18 01	18 01	18 05	18 05	18 01	18 01	18 19	18 26	18 33	18 33	18 57	19 03	19 03	19 06
Birmingham New Street	d	17 12	17 10	17 12	17 30	17 33	17 42	18 04	18 12	18 12	18 10	18 10	18 12	18 12	18 30	18 33	18 42	18 42	19 04	19 12	19 12	19 10
Cheltenham Spa	a	→		17 51	18 10		18 24		→	→			18 51	18 51	19 11		19 24	19 24		→	→	
Gloucester	a				18 20										19 26							
Bristol Parkway	a			18 20			18 54						19 21	19 21			20 03	20 03				
Bristol Temple Meads	a			18 35			19 08						19 32	19 32			20 14	20 14				
Newport (South Wales)	a				19 05										20 06							
Cardiff Central	a				19 27										20 30							
Weston-super-Mare	a																20 37	20 37				
Taunton	a			19 17									20 17	20 17			20 58	20 58				
Tiverton Parkway	a			19 29									20 29	20 29			21 11	21 13				
Exeter St Davids	a			19 45									20 43	20 43			21 27	21 29				
Dawlish	a																21 41	21 41				
Teignmouth	a																21 46	21 47				
Newton Abbot	a			20 07									21 01	21 01			21 53	21 54				
Torquay	a																	22 05				
Paignton	a																	22 14				
Totnes	a			20 19									21 13	21 13								
Plymouth	a			20 45									21 41	21 41			22 37					
Liskeard	a			21 12																		
Bodmin Parkway	a			21 24																		
Lostwithiel	a																					
Par	a			21 34																		
St Austell	a			21 40																		
Truro	a			21 58																		
Redruth	a			22 10																		
Camborne	a			22 16																		
Hayle	a																					
St Erth	a			22 29																		
Penzance	a			22 42																		
Birmingham International	d		17 20					18 14			18 20	18 20				18 44			19 14			19 20
Coventry	d		17a29					18 25			18a30	18a30				18 55			19 25			19a30
Leamington Spa	d					17 59		18 38								19 09			19 38			
Banbury	a					18 16		18 54								19 25			19 54			
Oxford	a					18 35		19 14								19 44			20 14			
Reading	a					19 05		19 40								20 08			20 41			
Guildford	a																					
Basingstoke	a							20 09											21 08			
Winchester	a							20 24											21 24			
Southampton Airport Pkway	a							20 33											21 33			
Southampton Central	a							20 43											21 42			
Brockenhurst	a							21 06											22 06			
Bournemouth	a							21 26											22 26			

A 🍴 to Plymouth
B 🍴 to Birmingham New Street
C not 9 September
D 9 September
E not 9 September. 🍴 to Bristol Temple Meads
F 9 September. 🍴 to Bristol Temple Meads
G 🍴 to Reading

Table T051-F

Sundays

9 September to 7 October

Scotland, The North East, North West England - The South West and South Coast

		XC	XC	XC	XC	XC	XC	XC	XC	VT	VT	XC	XC	XC	XC	VT	XC	XC	XC	XC	XC	XC	XC
		◇1	◇1	◇1	◇1	◇1	◇1	◇1	◇1	◇1	◇1	◇1	◇1	◇1	◇1	◇1	◇1	◇1	◇1	◇1	◇1	◇1	◇1
		A	B	C	A	B	C	D	E	A	B	F		C	C		C	G	H				B
				🍴	🍴	🍴	🍴	🍴	🍴	☕	☕	🍴	🍴	🍴	🍴	☕	🍴	🍴	🍴		🍴		🍴
Aberdeen	d								11 10														
Stonehaven	d								11 27														
Montrose	d								11 48														
Arbroath	d								12 04														
Dundee	d								12 24														
Leuchars	d								12 37														
Cupar	d								12 44														
Ladybank	d								12 51														
Markinch	d								12 58														
Kirkcaldy	d								13 07														
Inverkeithing	d								13 22														
Glasgow Central	d										15 57							13 48					14 55
Motherwell	d																	14 03	14 03				15 13
Haymarket	d								13 38									14 42	14 42				15 52
Edinburgh	d								14 08							16 51		15 08	15 08				16 08
Haymarket	d															16 55							
Lockerbie	d																						
Carlisle	d									17 05	17 10					18 07							
Penrith North Lakes	d																						
Oxenholme Lake District	d									17 44	17 44					18 42							
Lancaster	d															18 57							
Preston	d									18 17	18 17					19 17							
Wigan North Western	d									18 28	18 28					19 28							
Warrington Bank Quay	d									18 39	18 39					19 39							
M'chester Piccadilly	d						18 05	18 27							19 05		19 27					20 05	
Stockport	d						18 13	18 36							19 13		19 36					20 14	
Wilmslow	d																						
Crewe	d									19 01	19 01					20 01							
Macclesfield	d						18 26	18 49							19 26		19 49					20 27	
Congleton	d																						
Stoke-on-Trent	d						18 45	19 07							19 45		20 06					20 45	
Stafford	d						19 02	19 25							20 02		20 26					21 02	
Wolverhampton	d						19 17	19 41		19 45	19 45				20 17	20 33	20 41					21 17	
Dunbar	d																	15 29	15 29				
Berwick-upon-Tweed	d								14 49														
Alnmouth for Alnwick	d																						17 08
Morpeth	d								15 20									16 22	16 22				17 22
Newcastle	d								15 40									16 40	16 40				17 40
Chester-le-Street	d																						
Durham	d								15 52									16 52	16 52				17 53
Darlington	d								16 10									17 10	17 10				18 11
York	d								16 41									17 44	17 44				18 45
Leeds	d								17 11									18 11	18 11				19 11
Wakefield Westgate	d								17 23									18 23	18 23				19 24
Doncaster	d								17 46									18 58	18 58				19 54
Sheffield	d								18 24									19 24	19 24				20 21
Chesterfield	d								18 36									19 36	19 36				20 33
Nottingham	d			18 10									19 10							20 10			
Derby	d			18 35	18 55	18 55			19 27				19 35	19 55				20 27	20 27	20 35	20 54		21 26
Burton-on-Trent	d			18 46					19 38				19 46							20 46			21 37
Tamworth	d	←	←	19 00								←	19 58					20 46	20 46	20 59			21 47
Birmingham New Street	a	19 03	19 03	19 21	19 28	19 28	19 33	19 57	20 02	20 06	20 06	20 02	20 21	20 27	20 33	20 51	20 57	21 03	21 03	21 18	21 26	21 33	22 05
Birmingham New Street	d	19 12	19 12	19 30	19 33	19 33	19 42	20 04	20 12	20 10	20 10	20 12		20 33	20 42		21 04	21 12	21 12			21 42	22 12
Cheltenham Spa	a	19 51	19 51	20 10			20 24		→			20 51			21 24			21 51	21 51			22 23	22 52
Gloucester	a			20 19														22 04	22 04				
Bristol Parkway	a	20 20	20 20				20 56					21 20			21 59			22 35	22 35			22 52	23 22
Bristol Temple Meads	a	20 31	20 31				21 06					21 30			22 10			22 46	22 46			23 02	23 33
Newport (South Wales)	a			21 06																			
Cardiff Central	a			21 27																			
Weston-super-Mare	a																						
Taunton	a	21 14	21 14									22 14											
Tiverton Parkway	a	21 26	21 26									22 27											
Exeter St Davids	a	21 39	21 39									22 46											
Dawlish	a																						
Teignmouth	a																						
Newton Abbot	a	21 59	21 59									23 06											
Torquay	a																						
Paignton	a																						
Totnes	a	22 11	22 17									23 18											
Plymouth	a	22 38	22 45									23 46											
Liskeard	a																						
Bodmin Parkway	a																						
Lostwithiel	a																						
Par	a																						
St Austell	a																						
Truro	a																						
Redruth	a																						
Camborne	a																						
Hayle	a																						
St Erth	a																						
Penzance	a																						
Birmingham International	d				19 44	19 44		20 14		20 20	20 20						21 14						
Coventry	d				19 55	19 55		20 25		20a30	20a30						21 24						
Leamington Spa	d				20 09	20 09		20 38						21 00			21 36						
Banbury	a				20 25	20 25		20 54						21 17			21 52						
Oxford	a				20 44	20 44		21 14						21 38			22 11						
Reading	a				21 12	21 13		21 38						22 06			22 38						
Guildford	a													22 42									
Basingstoke	a							22 09															
Winchester	a							22 23															
Southampton Airport Pkway	a							22 33															
Southampton Central	a							22 42															
Brockenhurst	a																						
Bournemouth	a																						

A 9 September
B not 9 September
C 🍴 to Birmingham New Street
D 🍴 to Reading
E 🍴 from Edinburgh
F 🍴 to Bristol Temple Meads
G not 9 September. 🍴 from Edinburgh to Birmingham New Street
H 9 September. 🍴 from Edinburgh to Birmingham New Street

Table T051-F

Sundays

9 September to 7 October

Scotland, The North East, North West England - The South West and South Coast

		XC	XC	XC	VT	VT	XC	VT	XC	XC	XC
		◇■	◇■	◇■	◇■	◇■	◇■	◇■	◇■	◇■	◇■
		A			A	B			C	D	
Aberdeen	d										
Stonehaven	d										
Montrose	d										
Arbroath	d										
Dundee	d										
Leuchars	d										
Cupar	d										
Ladybank	d										
Markinch	d										
Kirkcaldy	d										
Inverkeithing	d										
Glasgow Central	d				18 31	18 37			16 55		
Motherwell	d	15 13							17 13	17 13	
Haymarket	d	15 52							17 51	17 51	
Edinburgh	d	16 08		17 08				18 51	18 06	18 06	
Haymarket	d							18 56			
Lockerbie	d										
Carlisle	d				19 48	19 48		20 07			
Penrith North Lakes	d							20 22			
Oxenholme Lake District	d				20 23	20 23					
Lancaster	d				20 37	20 37		20 57			
Preston	d				20 57	20 57		21 17			
Wigan North Western	d				21 08	21 08		21 29			
Warrington Bank Quay	d				21 19	21 19		21 39			
M'chester Piccadilly	d						21 05				22 05
Stockport	d						21 13				22 13
Wilmslow	d										
Crewe	d				21 41	21 41		22 01			
Macclesfield	d						21 26				22 26
Congleton	d										
Stoke-on-Trent	d						21 45				22 45
Stafford	d				22 01	22 01	22 05				23 02
Wolverhampton	d				22 16	22 16	22 19	22 32			23 17
Dunbar	d			17 29					18 28	18 28	
Berwick-upon-Tweed	d			17 53					18 52	18 52	
Alnmouth for Alnwick	d	17 08									
Morpeth	d	17 22							19 23	19 23	
Newcastle	d	17 40		18 40					19 41	19 41	
Chester-le-Street	d										
Durham	d	17 53		18 52					19 53	19 53	
Darlington	d	18 11		19 09					20 10	20 10	
York	d	18 45		19 45					20 45	20 45	
Leeds	d	19 11		20 11					21 11	21 11	
Wakefield Westgate	d	19 24		20 23					21 23	21 23	
Doncaster	d	19 54									
Sheffield	d	20 21		20 54					21 54	21 54	
Chesterfield	d	20 33		21 06					22 06	22 06	
Nottingham	d		21 10								
Derby	d	21 26	21 37	21 53					22 48	22 48	
Burton-on-Trent	d	21 37	21 48	22 03					22 59	22 59	
Tamworth	d	21 47	22 00	22 14					23 10	23 10	
Birmingham New Street	a	22 05	22 23	22 31	22 33	22 33	22 36	22 53	23 27	23 27	23 33
Birmingham New Street	d	22 12									
Cheltenham Spa	a	22 52									
Gloucester	a										
Bristol Parkway	a	23 22									
Bristol Temple Meads	a	23 33									
Newport (South Wales)	a										
Cardiff Central	a										
Weston-super-Mare	a										
Taunton	a										
Tiverton Parkway	a										
Exeter St Davids	a										
Dawlish	a										
Teignmouth	a										
Newton Abbot	a										
Torquay	a										
Paignton	a										
Totnes	a										
Plymouth	a										
Liskeard	a										
Bodmin Parkway	a										
Lostwithiel	a										
Par	a										
St Austell	a										
Truro	a										
Redruth	a										
Camborne	a										
Hayle	a										
St Erth	a										
Penzance	a										
Birmingham International	d										
Coventry	d										
Leamington Spa	d										
Banbury	a										
Oxford	a										
Reading	a										
Guildford	a										
Basingstoke	a										
Winchester	a										
Southampton Airport Pkwy	a										
Southampton Central	a										
Brockenhurst	a										
Bournemouth	a										

A 9 September
B not 9 September
C not 9 September. ⊼ from Edinburgh to Leeds
D 9 September. ⊼ from Edinburgh to Leeds

Table T051-F

Sundays

14 October to 2 December

Scotland, The North East, North West England - The South West and South Coast

		XC	XC	XC	XC	XC	XC	XC	XC	VT	XC	XC	XC	XC	VT	XC	XC	XC	XC	XC	XC	VT	XC
		◇■	◇■	◇■	◇■	◇■	◇■	◇■	◇■	◇■	◇■	◇■	◇■	◇■	◇■	◇■	◇■	◇■	◇■	◇■	◇■	◇■	◇■
			A										B					B					
Aberdeen	d																						
Stonehaven	d																						
Montrose	d																						
Arbroath	d																						
Dundee	d																						
Leuchars	d																						
Cupar	d																						
Ladybank	d																						
Markinch	d																						
Kirkcaldy	d																						
Inverkeithing	d																						
Glasgow Central	d																						
Motherwell	d																						
Haymarket	d																						
Edinburgh	d																						09 08
Haymarket	d																						
Lockerbie	d																						
Carlisle	d																						
Penrith North Lakes	d																						
Oxenholme Lake District	d																						
Lancaster	d																					11 58	
Preston	d									10 17					11 17							12 17	
Wigan North Western	d									10 28					11 28							12 28	
Warrington Bank Quay	d									10 39					11 40							12 39	
M'chester Piccadilly	d			08 27			09 27				10 26					11 27					12 26		
Stockport	d			08 36			09 36				10 36					11 36					12 35		
Wilmslow	d			08 43																			
Crewe	d			09 05						11 02					12 02							13 01	
Macclesfield	d						09 49				10 49					11 49					12 49		
Congleton	d																						
Stoke-on-Trent	d						10 07				11 07					12 07					13 07		
Stafford	d			09 26			10 25				11 27					12 25					13 25		
Wolverhampton	d			09 41			10 41			11 32	11 42				12 32	12 41					13 41	13 45	
Dunbar	d																						
Berwick-upon-Tweed	d																						
Alnmouth for Alnwick	d																						09 51
Morpeth	d																						
Newcastle	d																09 35						10 39
Chester-le-Street	d																						
Durham	d																09 47						10 53
Darlington	d																10 05						11 10
York	d											09 33					10 33						11 41
Leeds	d					08 10			09 00			09 59					11 00						12 11
Wakefield Westgate	d					08 23			09 11			10 12					11 12						12 24
Doncaster	d								09 31			10 30					11 30						
Sheffield	d					08 54			09 57			10 55					11 57						12 57
Chesterfield	d					09 07			10 09			11 08					12 09						13 09
Nottingham	d							09 54					11 11					12 10					
Derby	d					09 28		10 18	10 33			11 29	11 36				12 29	12 36					13 32
Burton-on-Trent	d							10 29				11 40	11 47					12 47					13 43
Tamworth	d							10 42	10 53				12 00				12 48	13 00					
Birmingham New Street	a			09 57		10 18	10 57	11 02	11 21	11 50	11 58	12 06	12 21		12 50	12 57	13 06	13 21			13 57	14 06	14 09
Birmingham New Street	d	09 04	09 30	10 04	10 12	10 30	11 04	11 12	11 30		12 04	12 12	12 30	12 33		13 04	13 12	13 30	13 33	13 42	14 04	14 10	14 12
Cheltenham Spa	a		10 08		10 52	11 09		11 52	12 09			12 50	13 10				13 51	14 10		14 23			14 50
Gloucester	a				11 02			12 02					13 20					14 20					
Bristol Parkway	a		10 37			11 39			12 39			13 21					14 20			14 53			15 23
Bristol Temple Meads	a		10 48			11 51			12 50			13 32					14 31			15 08			15 34
Newport (South Wales)	a				11 47			12 44					14 06					15 01					
Cardiff Central	a				12 09			13 07					14 27					15 28					
Weston-super-Mare	a																						
Taunton	a		11 29			12 25			13 25			14 15					15 14						16 14
Tiverton Parkway	a		11 41			12 35			13 36			14 27					15 26						16 26
Exeter St Davids	a		11 54			12 52			13 52			14 42					15 39						16 40
Dawlish	a																						
Teignmouth	a																						
Newton Abbot	a		12 14			13 12			14 12			15 02					16 00						17 01
Torquay	a																						
Paignton	a																						
Totnes	a		12 26			13 25			14 25			15 15					16 12						17 14
Plymouth	a		12 52			13 52			14 52			15 42					16 38						17 42
Liskeard	a		13 17																				
Bodmin Parkway	a		13 29																				
Lostwithiel	a																						
Par	a		13 39																				
St Austell	a		13 45																				
Truro	a		14 06																				
Redruth	a		14 19																				
Camborne	a		14 25																				
Hayle	a																						
St Erth	a		14 36																				
Penzance	a		14 47																				
Birmingham International	d	09 14		10 14			11 14				12 14			12 44		13 14					14 14	14 20	
Coventry	d	09 25		10 25			11 25				12 25			12 55		13 25					14 25	14a30	
Leamington Spa	d	09 38		10 38			11 38				12 38			13 08		13 38			13 59		14 38		
Banbury	a	09 54		10 54			11 54				12 54			13 24		13 54			14 15		14 54		
Oxford	a	10 14		11 14			12 14				13 14			13 43		14 14			14 35		15 14		
Reading	a	10 42		11 40			12 41				13 42			14 11		14 41			15 02		15 40		
Guildford	a																						
Basingstoke	a	11 09		12 09			13 09				14 09					15 09					16 09		
Winchester	a	11 24		12 25			13 24				14 24					15 24					16 24		
Southampton Airport Pkwy	a	11 33		12 34			13 33				14 33					15 33					16 33		
Southampton Central	a	11 42		12 43			13 42				14 42					15 43					16 42		
Brockenhurst	a	12 06		13 07			14 06				15 06					16 03					17 06		
Bournemouth	a	12 26		13 26			14 26				15 26					16 26					17 26		

A ⊼ to Plymouth
B ⊼ from Birmingham New Street

Table T051-F

Sundays

14 October to 2 December

Scotland, The North East, North West England - The South West and South Coast

		XC ◇1 A	XC ◇1	XC ◇1	XC ◇1	XC ◇1	VT ◇1	XC ◇1 B	XC ◇1	XC ◇1	XC ◇1	XC ◇1	XC ◇1	VT ◇1	XC ◇1	XC ◇1	XC ◇1	XC ◇1	XC ◇1	XC ◇1 C	VT ◇1	XC ◇1 B	XC ◇1 D
Aberdeen	d																						
Stonehaven	d																						
Montrose	d																						
Arbroath	d																						
Dundee	d																						
Leuchars	d																						
Cupar	d																						
Ladybank	d																						
Markinch	d																						
Kirkcaldy	d																						
Inverkeithing	d																						
Glasgow Central	d													11 55						10 55			
Motherwell	d																			11 14			
Haymarket	d																			11 53			
Edinburgh	d					10 08	10 51						11 05							12 08	12 51		
Haymarket	d						10 55														12 55		
Lockerbie	d																						
Carlisle	d						12 07							13 07							14 07		
Penrith North Lakes	d																				14 22		
Oxenholme Lake District	d						12 43																
Lancaster	d						12 57							13 56							14 57		
Preston	d						13 17							14 17							15 17		
Wigan North Western	d						13 28							14 28							15 28		
Warrington Bank Quay	d						13 39							14 39							15 39		
M'chester Piccadilly	d			13 05	13 27						14 05	14 27						15 05	15 27				
Stockport	d			13 13	13 36						14 13	14 36						15 13	15 36				
Wilmslow	d																						
Crewe	d						14 01							15 01							16 01		
Macclesfield	d			13 26	13 49						14 26	14 49						15 26	15 49				
Congleton	d																						
Stoke-on-Trent	d			13 45	14 07						14 44	15 07						15 44	16 07				
Stafford	d			14 02	14 25						15 01	15 25						16 01	16 25				
Wolverhampton	d			14 17	14 41		14 45				15 17	15 41		15 45				16 17	16 41		16 45		
Dunbar	d												11 26										
Berwick-upon-Tweed	d												11 50							12 49			
Alnmouth for Alnwick	d					11 07							12 10										
Morpeth	d					11 22																	
Newcastle	d					11 40							12 40				13 35			13 40			
Chester-le-Street	d																						
Durham	d					11 52							12 53				13 47			13 53			
Darlington	d					12 10							13 10				14 06			14 10			
York	d					12 45							13 45				14 35			14 44			
Leeds	d					13 11							14 11							15 11			
Wakefield Westgate	d					13 24							14 23							15 23			
Doncaster	d																15 00						
Sheffield	d					13 57				14 22			14 55				15 24			15 55			
Chesterfield	d					14 09				14 32			15 07							16 07			
Nottingham	d	13 10							14 10							15 10							16 10
Derby	d	13 38	13 55			14 29			14 34	14 53			15 26			15 34	15 53			16 27			16 34
Burton-on-Trent	d	13 49							14 47				15 37			15 47							16 47
Tamworth	d	14 00				14 48		←	15 00						←	16 00				16 46		←	17 00
Birmingham New Street	a	14 22	14 27	14 33	14 57	15 05	15 06	15 05	15 20	15 26	15 33	15 57	16 01	16 06	16 01	16 21	16 26	16 33	16 57	17 03	17 06	17 03	17 19
Birmingham New Street	d	14 30	14 33	14 42	15 04	15 12	15 10	15 12	15 30	15 33	15 42	16 04	16 12	16 10	16 12	16 30	16 33	16 42	17 04	17 12	17 10	17 12	17 30
Cheltenham Spa	a	15 10		15 24		→		15 51	16 10		16 24		→		16 51	17 10		17 24		→		17 51	18 10
Gloucester	a	15 22							16 20							17 20							18 20
Bristol Parkway	a			15 55				16 20			16 54				17 20			18 03				18 20	
Bristol Temple Meads	a			16 09				16 32			17 08				17 31			18 14				18 35	
Newport (South Wales)	a	16 06							17 04							18 06							19 05
Cardiff Central	a	16 29							17 26							18 29							19 27
Weston-super-Mare	a																						
Taunton	a			16 44				17 14							18 17							19 17	
Tiverton Parkway	a			16 56				17 26							18 29							19 29	
Exeter St Davids	a			17 09				17 40							18 45							19 45	
Dawlish	a			17 24																			
Teignmouth	a			17 29																			
Newton Abbot	a			17 36				18 00							19 05							20 07	
Torquay	a			17 48																			
Paignton	a			17 56																			
Totnes	a							18 12							19 17							20 19	
Plymouth	a							18 38							19 43							20 45	
Liskeard	a							19 15														21 12	
Bodmin Parkway	a							19 27														21 24	
Lostwithiel	a																						
Par	a							19 37														21 34	
St Austell	a							19 43														21 40	
Truro	a							20 00														21 58	
Redruth	a							20 11														22 10	
Camborne	a							20 18														22 16	
Hayle	a																						
St Erth	a							20 30														22 29	
Penzance	a							20 39														22 42	
Birmingham International	d		14 44		15 14		15 20					16 14		16 19			16 44		17 14		17 20		
Coventry	d		14 55		15 25		15a30					16 25		16a30			16 55		17 25		17a29		
Leamington Spa	d		15 09		15 38					15 59		16 38					17 09		17 38				
Banbury	a		15 26		15 54					16 15		16 54					17 25		17 54				
Oxford	a		15 45		16 14					16 35		17 14					17 44		18 14				
Reading	a		16 12		16 41					17 01		17 41					18 12		18 41				
Guildford	a																						
Basingstoke	a				17 09							18 09							19 09				
Winchester	a				17 24							18 24							19 24				
Southampton Airport Pkway	a				17 33							18 33							19 33				
Southampton Central	a				17 42							18 44							19 42				
Brockenhurst	a				18 06							19 03							20 06				
Bournemouth	a				18 26							19 26							20 26				

A from Birmingham New Street
B to Plymouth
C from Edinburgh
D to Birmingham New Street

Table T051-F

Sundays

14 October to 2 December

Scotland, The North East, North West England - The South West and South Coast

		XC ◇1	XC ◇1	XC ◇1	XC ◇1	VT ◇1	XC ◇1	XC ◇1 A	XC ◇1	XC ◇1 B	XC ◇1 C	XC ◇1 D	VT ◇1	XC ◇1 B	XC ◇1 A	XC ◇1	XC ◇1 A	XC ◇1 C	XC ◇1 D	VT ◇1	XC ◇1 B	XC ◇1
Aberdeen	d											11 10										
Stonehaven	d											11 27										
Montrose	d											11 48										
Arbroath	d											12 04										
Dundee	d											12 24										
Leuchars	d											12 37										
Cupar	d											12 44										
Ladybank	d											12 51										
Markinch	d											12 58										
Kirkcaldy	d											13 07										
Inverkeithing	d											13 22										
Glasgow Central	d				12 02	13 55													13 48	15 57		
Motherwell	d				12 18														14 03			
Haymarket	d				12 56							13 38							14 42			
Edinburgh	d				13 08				13 55			14 08	14 51						15 08			
Haymarket	d												14 56									
Lockerbie	d																					
Carlisle	d					15 11							16 07							17 10		
Penrith North Lakes	d												16 22									
Oxenholme Lake District	d					15 45														17 44		
Lancaster	d												16 57									
Preston	d					16 17							17 17							18 17		
Wigan North Western	d					16 29							17 29							18 28		
Warrington Bank Quay	d					16 40							17 40							18 39		
M'chester Piccadilly	d		16 05	16 27						17 05	17 27						18 05	18 27				
Stockport	d		16 13	16 36						17 13	17 36						18 13	18 36				
Wilmslow	d																					
Crewe	d					17 01							18 01							19 01		
Macclesfield	d		16 26	16 49						17 26	17 49						18 26	18 49				
Congleton	d																					
Stoke-on-Trent	d		16 44	17 07						17 45	18 07						18 45	19 07				
Stafford	d		17 01	17 25						18 02	18 25						19 02	19 25				
Wolverhampton	d		17 15	17 41		17 45				18 17	18 41		18 45				19 17	19 41		19 45		
Dunbar	d				13 29														15 29			
Berwick-upon-Tweed	d								14 36			14 49										
Alnmouth for Alnwick	d				14 11																	
Morpeth	d											15 20							16 22			
Newcastle	d	14 36			14 41				15 24			15 40				16 35			16 40			
Chester-le-Street	d																					
Durham	d	14 48			14 53				15 36			15 52				16 47			16 52			
Darlington	d	15 06			15 10				15 54			16 10				17 05			17 10			
York	d	15 35			15 42				16 25			16 41				17 35			17 44			
Leeds	d				16 11							17 11							18 11			
Wakefield Westgate	d				16 23							17 23							18 23			
Doncaster	d	15 58							16 51							17 58						
Sheffield	d	16 24			16 55				17 24			17 55				18 24			18 55			
Chesterfield	d				17 07							18 07							19 07			
Nottingham	d							17 10							18 10							19 10
Derby	d	16 54			17 27			17 35	17 54			18 26			18 35	18 54			19 27			19 35
Burton-on-Trent	d				17 37			17 47							18 47				19 38			19 46
Tamworth	d						←	18 00				18 45		←	19 00						←	19 58
Birmingham New Street	a	17 26	17 32	17 57	18 01	18 05	18 01	18 19	18 26	18 33	18 57	19 03	19 06	19 03	19 21	19 28	19 33	19 57	20 02	20 06	20 02	20 21
Birmingham New Street	d	17 33	17 42	18 04	18 12	18 10	18 12	18 30	18 33	18 42	19 04	19 12	19 10	19 12	19 30	19 33	19 42	20 04	20 12	20 10	20 12	
Cheltenham Spa	a		18 24		→		18 51	19 11		19 24		→		19 51	20 10		20 24		→		20 51	
Gloucester	a							19 26							20 19							
Bristol Parkway	a		18 54				19 21			20 03				20 20			20 56				21 20	
Bristol Temple Meads	a		19 08				19 32			20 14				20 31			21 06				21 30	
Newport (South Wales)	a							20 06							21 06							
Cardiff Central	a							20 30							21 27							
Weston-super-Mare	a									20 37												
Taunton	a						20 17			20 58				21 14							22 14	
Tiverton Parkway	a						20 29			21 11				21 26							22 27	
Exeter St Davids	a						20 43			21 27				21 39							22 46	
Dawlish	a									21 41												
Teignmouth	a									21 46												
Newton Abbot	a						21 01			21 53				21 59							23 06	
Torquay	a																					
Paignton	a																					
Totnes	a						21 13							22 17							23 18	
Plymouth	a						21 41			22 37				22 45							23 46	
Liskeard	a																					
Bodmin Parkway	a																					
Lostwithiel	a																					
Par	a																					
St Austell	a																					
Truro	a																					
Redruth	a																					
Camborne	a																					
Hayle	a																					
St Erth	a																					
Penzance	a																					
Birmingham International	d			18 14		18 20			18 44		19 14		19 20			19 44		20 14		20 20		
Coventry	d			18 25		18a30			18 55		19 25		19a30			19 55		20 25		20a30		
Leamington Spa	d	17 59		18 38					19 09		19 38					20 09		20 38				
Banbury	a	18 16		18 54					19 25		19 54					20 25		20 54				
Oxford	a	18 35		19 14					19 44		20 14					20 44		21 14				
Reading	a	19 05		19 40					20 08		20 41					21 13		21 38				
Guildford	a																					
Basingstoke	a			20 09							21 08							22 09				
Winchester	a			20 24							21 24							22 23				
Southampton Airport Pkway	a			20 33							21 33							22 33				
Southampton Central	a			20 43							21 42							22 42				
Brockenhurst	a			21 06							22 06											
Bournemouth	a			21 26							22 26											

A to Birmingham New Street
B to Bristol Temple Meads
C to Reading
D from Edinburgh

Table T051-F

Sundays

14 October to 2 December

Scotland, The North East, North West England - The South West and South Coast

		XC	XC	VT	XC	XC	XC	XC	XC	XC	XC	XC	VT	XC	VT	XC	XC
		◇1	◇1	◇1	◇1	◇1	◇1	◇1	◇1	◇1	◇1	◇1	◇1	◇1	◇1	◇1	◇1
		A ✠	A ✠	⊡	A ✠	B ✠		✠		C ✠			⊡		⊡	D ✠	
Aberdeen	d																
Stonehaven	d																
Montrose	d																
Arbroath	d																
Dundee	d																
Leuchars	d																
Cupar	d																
Ladybank	d																
Markinch	d																
Kirkcaldy	d																
Inverkeithing	d																
Glasgow Central	d					14 55							18 37			16 55	
Motherwell	d					15 13										17 13	
Haymarket	d					15 52										17 51	
Edinburgh	d			16 51		16 08				17 08					18 51	18 06	
Haymarket	d			16 55											18 56		
Lockerbie	d																
Carlisle	d			18 07									19 48		20 07		
Penrith North Lakes	d														20 22		
Oxenholme Lake District	d			18 42									20 23				
Lancaster	d			18 57									20 37		20 57		
Preston	d			19 17									20 57		21 17		
Wigan North Western	d			19 28									21 08		21 29		
Warrington Bank Quay	d			19 39									21 19		21 39		
M'chester Piccadilly	d		19 05		19 27				20 05					21 05			22 05
Stockport	d		19 13		19 36				20 14					21 13			22 13
Wilmslow	d																
Crewe	d			20 01									21 41		22 01		
Macclesfield	d		19 26		19 49				20 27					21 26			22 26
Congleton	d																
Stoke-on-Trent	d		19 45		20 06				20 45					21 45			22 45
Stafford	d		20 02		20 26				21 02				22 01	22 05			23 02
Wolverhampton	d		20 17	20 33	20 41				21 17				22 16	22 19	22 32		23 17
Dunbar	d									17 29						18 28	
Berwick-upon-Tweed	d									17 53						18 52	
Alnmouth for Alnwick	d					17 08											
Morpeth	d					17 22										19 23	
Newcastle	d	17 35				17 40		18 25		18 40		19 26				19 41	
Chester-le-Street	d																
Durham	d	17 48				17 53		18 37		18 52		19 39				19 53	
Darlington	d	18 06				18 11		18 55		19 09		19 56				20 10	
York	d	18 35				18 45		19 24		19 45		20 26				20 45	
Leeds	d					19 11				20 11						21 11	
Wakefield Westgate	d					19 24				20 23						21 23	
Doncaster	d	18 58						19 54				20 51					
Sheffield	d	19 24				19 55		20 21		20 54		21 20				21 54	
Chesterfield	d					20 07				21 06		21 32				22 06	
Nottingham	d						20 10				21 10						
Derby	d	19 56				20 27	20 35	20 54		21 26	21 37	21 53				22 26	
Burton-on-Trent	d						20 46			21 37	21 48	22 03				22 37	
Tamworth	d					20 46	20 59			21 47	22 00	22 14				22 47	
Birmingham New Street	a	20 27	20 33	20 51	20 57	21 03	21 18	21 26	21 33	22 05	22 23	22 31	22 33	22 36	22 53	23 05	23 33
Birmingham New Street	d	20 33	20 42		21 04	21 12			21 42	22 11							
Cheltenham Spa	a		21 24			21 51			22 23	22 52							
Gloucester	a					22 04											
Bristol Parkway	a		21 59			22 35			22 52	23 22							
Bristol Temple Meads	a		22 10			22 46			23 02	23 33							
Newport (South Wales)	a																
Cardiff Central	a																
Weston-super-Mare	a																
Taunton	a																
Tiverton Parkway	a																
Exeter St Davids	a																
Dawlish	a																
Teignmouth	a																
Newton Abbot	a																
Torquay	a																
Paignton	a																
Totnes	a																
Plymouth	a																
Liskeard	a																
Bodmin Parkway	a																
Lostwithiel	a																
Par	a																
St Austell	a																
Truro	a																
Redruth	a																
Camborne	a																
Hayle	a																
St Erth	a																
Penzance	a																
Birmingham International	d				21 14												
Coventry	d				21 24												
Leamington Spa	d	21 00			21 36												
Banbury	a	21 17			21 52												
Oxford	a	21 38			22 11												
Reading	a	22 06			22 38												
Guildford	a	22 42															
Basingstoke	a																
Winchester	a																
Southampton Airport Pkway	a																
Southampton Central	a																
Brockenhurst	a																
Bournemouth	a																

A ✠ to Birmingham New Street
B ✠ from Edinburgh to Birmingham New Street
C ✠ to Leeds
D ✠ from Edinburgh to Leeds

Table T051-R

Mondays to Fridays

21 May to 20 July

South Coast and the South West - North West England, The North East and Scotland

		XC	XC	VT	XC	XC	XC	XC	XC	XC	VT	XC	XC	XC	XC	XC	XC	VT	XC	XC	XC	XC	XC
		◇1	◇1	◇1	1	◇1	◇1	1	◇1	◇1	◇1	1	◇1	◇1	1	◇1	◇1	◇1	1	◇1	◇1	◇1	◇1
			A ✠	⊠		✠	✠		✠	✠	⊠	✠	✠	✠		B ✠	✠	⊠	✠	B ✠		✠	
Bournemouth	d																						
Brockenhurst	d																						
Southampton Central	d															05 15							
Southampton Airport Pkway	d															05 22							
Winchester	d															05 31							
Basingstoke	d															05 47							
Guildford	d																			06 01			
Reading	d															06 15				06 45			
Oxford	d															06 38				07 08			
Banbury	d															06 57				07 26			
Leamington Spa	d															07 14				07 43			
Coventry	d															07 27		07 42					
Birmingham International	d															07 38		07 53					
Penzance	d																						
St Erth	d																						
Hayle	d																						
Camborne	d																						
Redruth	d																						
Truro	d																						
St Austell	d																						
Par	d																						
Lostwithiel	d																						
Bodmin Parkway	d																						
Liskeard	d																						
Plymouth	d																						
Totnes	d																						
Paignton	d																						
Torquay	d																						
Newton Abbot	d																						
Teignmouth	d																						
Dawlish	d																						
Exeter St Davids	d																						
Tiverton Parkway	d																						
Taunton	d																						
Weston-super-Mare	d																						
Cardiff Central	d																						06 40
Newport (South Wales)	d																						06 55
Bristol Temple Meads	d																06 27					07 00	
Bristol Parkway	d																06 39					07 10	
Gloucester	d																				07 10		07 46
Cheltenham Spa	d																07 10				07 21	07 41	07 57
Birmingham New Street	a															07 48	07 56	08 09		08 12	08 17	08 26	08 45
Birmingham New Street	d	05 57	06 00	06 15	06 19	06 30	06 30	06 49	06 51	07 03	07 15	07 19	07 30	07 31	07 49	07 57	08 03	08 15	08 19	08 30		08 31	08 49
Tamworth	d				06 39			07 07		07 19		07 39			08 07		08 19		08 36				09 09
Burton-on-Trent	d				06 51			07 20		07 31		07 50			08 19		08 29		08 48				09 20
Derby	a		06 33		07 04		07 11	07 35		07 42		08 05	08 09		08 37		08 41		09 02	09 07			09 32
Nottingham	a				07 38			08 09				08 34			09 08				09 28				10 05
Chesterfield	a		06 53				07 31			08 02			08 31				09 02						
Sheffield	a		07 15				07 45			08 19			08 48				09 17			09 50			
Doncaster	a						08 14						09 16							10 17			
Wakefield Westgate	a		07 47							08 47							09 46						
Leeds	a		08 01							09 02							10 00						
York	a		08 29				08 40			09 30			09 40				10 30			10 40			
Darlington	a		08 57				09 16			09 58			10 12				10 58			11 13			
Durham	a		09 13				09 33			10 17			10 29				11 15			11 31			
Chester-le-Street	a																						
Newcastle	a		09 28				09 47			10 31			10 43				11 29			11 46			
Morpeth	a																11 49						
Alnmouth for Alnwick	a		09 59																				
Berwick-upon-Tweed	a		10 21														12 23						
Dunbar	a									11 38													
Wolverhampton	d	06 15		06 37		06 48			07 10		07 37			07 49		08 15		08 37				08 49	
Stafford	a	06 27				06 59			07 21					08 02		08 27						09 02	
Stoke-on-Trent	a	06 44				07 19								08 18		08 43						09 18	
Congleton	a	06 56																					
Macclesfield	a	07 05				07 37								08 36		09 01						09 36	
Crewe	a			07 08					07 42		08 08							09 07					
Wilmslow	a								08 00														
Stockport	a	07 19				07 49			08 13					08 49		09 13						09 49	
M'chester Piccadilly	a	07 28				07 59			08 24					08 59		09 25						09 59	
Warrington Bank Quay	a			07 26							08 26							09 26					
Wigan North Western	a			07 37							08 37							09 37					
Preston	a			07 51							08 51							09 51					
Lancaster	a			08 07							09 07							10 07					
Oxenholme Lake District	a			08 21														10 21					
Penrith North Lakes	a										09 43												
Carlisle	a			09 00							09 59							10 59					
Lockerbie	a																						
Haymarket	a			10 12														12 16					
Edinburgh	a		11 06	10 18						12 03							13 06	12 22					
Haymarket	a		11 15														13 16						
Motherwell	a		11 54														13 54						
Glasgow Central	a		12 12								11 15						14 12						
Inverkeithing	a																						
Kirkcaldy	a																						
Markinch	a																						
Ladybank	a																						
Cupar	a																						
Leuchars	a																						
Dundee	a																						
Arbroath	a																						
Montrose	a																						
Stonehaven	a																						
Aberdeen	a																						

A ✠ to Edinburgh
B ✠ from Reading

South Coast and the South West - North West England, The North East and Scotland

		XC	XC	VT	XC	XC	XC	XC	XC	XC	VT	XC	XC	XC	XC	XC	XC	VT	XC	XC	XC	XC	XC
		◇1	◇1	◇1	1	◇1	◇1	◇1	◇1	◇1	◇1	1	◇1	◇1	◇1	◇1	◇1	◇1	1	◇1	◇1	◇1	■ 1
		A					B			C			A	D									
		T	T	⊠	T	T	T		T	T	⊠	T	T	T		T	T	⊠	T	T	T	T	T
Bournemouth	d								06 30							07 30							08 45
Brockenhurst	d								06 45							07 50							09 00
Southampton Central	d	06 15							07 15							08 15							09 16
Southampton Airport Pkway	d	06 22							07 22							08 22							09 23
Winchester	d	06 31							07 31				08 12			08 31							09 32
Basingstoke	d	06 47							07 47				08 28			08 47							09 49
Guildford	d																						
Reading	d	07 15				07 46			08 15				08 50			09 15				09 45			10 15
Oxford	d	07 39				08 12			08 39				09 15			09 39				10 15			10 39
Banbury	d	07 57				08 30			08 57				09 34			09 57				10 32			10 57
Leamington Spa	d	08 14				08 47			09 14				09 51			10 14				10 50			11 14
Coventry	d	08 27		08 42					09 27		09 42					10 27		10 42					11 27
Birmingham International	d	08 38		08 53					09 38		09 53					10 38		10 53					11 38
Penzance	d																						
St Erth	d																						
Hayle	d																						
Camborne	d																						
Redruth	d																						
Truro	d																						
St Austell	d																						
Par	d																						
Lostwithiel	d																						
Bodmin Parkway	d																						
Liskeard	d																						
Plymouth	d		05 20							06 25							07 25						
Totnes	d		05 45							06 50							07 50						
Paignton	d													07 01									
Torquay	d													07 07									
Newton Abbot	d		06 02							07 03				07 18			08 03						
Teignmouth	d													07 25									
Dawlish	d													07 30									
Exeter St Davids	d		06 24							07 24				07 44			08 24						
Tiverton Parkway	d		06 37							07 37				07 57			08 37						
Taunton	d		06 51							07 51				08 12			08 51						
Weston-super-Mare	d													08 35									
Cardiff Central	d						07 00	07 45							08 45							09 45	
Newport (South Wales)	d						07 14	08 02							09 00							10 00	
Bristol Temple Meads	d		07 30				08 00			08 30				09 00			09 30				10 00		
Bristol Parkway	d		07 40				08 10			08 40				09 10			09 40				10 10		
Gloucester	d							08 49							09 50							10 50	
Cheltenham Spa	d		08 11				08 41	09 00		09 12				09 42	10 01		10 11				10 41	11 01	
Birmingham New Street	a	08 48	08 56	09 05		09 18	09 26	09 45	09 49	09 58	10 04		10 18	10 23	10 45	10 48	10 56	11 04		11 18	11 26	11 45	11 48
Birmingham New Street	d	08 57	09 03	09 15	09 19	09 30	09 31	09 49	09 57	10 03	10 15	10 19	10 30	10 31	10 49	10 57	11 03	11 15	11 19	11 30	11 31	11 49	11 57
Tamworth	d				09 36			10 07		10 19		10 36			11 09				11 36			12 07	
Burton-on-Trent	d		09 27		09 48			10 19				10 48			11 21		11 26		11 48			12 19	
Derby	a		09 38		10 01	10 04		10 37		10 41		11 00	11 05		11 34		11 38		12 00	12 05		12 37	
Nottingham	a				10 28			11 04				11 28			12 06				12 28			13 05	
Chesterfield	a		10 02							11 02							12 02						
Sheffield	a		10 18			10 50				11 17			11 46				12 17			12 46			
Doncaster	a					11 16							12 16							13 16			
Wakefield Westgate	a		10 46							11 46							12 46						
Leeds	a		11 00							12 01							13 00						
York	a		11 30			11 40				12 30			12 40				13 30			13 40			
Darlington	a		11 58			12 12				12 58			13 13				14 02			14 12			
Durham	a		12 15			12 29				13 15			13 31				14 18			14 30			
Chester-le-Street	a																						
Newcastle	a		12 30			12 42				13 29			13 45				14 32			14 43			
Morpeth	a																14 47						
Alnmouth for Alnwick	a									14 02													
Berwick-upon-Tweed	a									14 23													
Dunbar	a		13 41														15 41						
Wolverhampton	d	09 15		09 37			09 49		10 15		10 37			10 49		11 15		11 37			11 49		12 15
Stafford	a	09 27					10 01		10 27					11 02		11 27					12 02		12 27
Stoke-on-Trent	a	09 43					10 17		10 43					11 18		11 43					12 18		12 43
Congleton	a																						
Macclesfield	a	10 01					10 36		11 01					11 36		12 01					12 36		13 01
Crewe	a			10 08							11 08							12 07					
Wilmslow	a																						
Stockport	a	10 13					10 49		11 13					11 49		12 13					12 49		13 12
M'chester Piccadilly	a	10 25					11 00		11 24					11 59		12 25					12 59		13 25
Warrington Bank Quay	a			10 26							11 26							12 26					
Wigan North Western	a			10 37							11 37							12 37					
Preston	a			10 51							11 51							12 51					
Lancaster	a			11 07							12 07							13 07					
Oxenholme Lake District	a										12 20							13 21					
Penrith North Lakes	a			11 44																			
Carlisle	a			12 00							12 59							13 59					
Lockerbie	a																						
Haymarket	a										14 12												
Edinburgh	a		14 07							15 08	14 19						16 06						
Haymarket	a									15 16													
Motherwell	a									15 54								14 58					
Glasgow Central	a			13 15						16 12								15 15					
Inverkeithing	a																						
Kirkcaldy	a																						
Markinch	a																						
Ladybank	a																						
Cupar	a																						
Leuchars	a																						
Dundee	a																						
Arbroath	a																						
Montrose	a																						
Stonehaven	a																						
Aberdeen	a																						

A T from Reading
B T from Bristol Temple Meads
C T to Edinburgh
D T from Newton Abbot

South Coast and the South West - North West England, The North East and Scotland

		XC	VT	XC	XC	XC	XC	XC	XC	VT	XC	XC	XC	XC	XC	XC	VT	XC	XC	XC	XC	XC
		◇1	◇1	1	◇1	◇1	◇1	◇1	◇1	◇1	1	◇1	◇1	◇1	◇1	■ ◇1	◇1	1	■ 1	◇1	◇1	◇1
		A							B							C						
		T	☕	T	T	T		T	T	⊠	T	T	T	T	T	T	⊠		T	T	T	T
Bournemouth	d							09 45							10 45							11 45
Brockenhurst	d							10 00							11 00							12 00
Southampton Central	d				09 46			10 17							11 17				11 46			12 17
Southampton Airport Pkway	d				09 55			10 24							11 24				11 53			12 24
Winchester	d				10 03			10 33							11 33				12 02			12 33
Basingstoke	d				10 19			10 49							11 49				12 18			12 49
Guildford	d																					
Reading	d				10 45			11 15				11 45			12 15				12 45			13 15
Oxford	d				11 13			11 39				12 13			12 39				13 13			13 39
Banbury	d				11 30			11 57				12 32			12 57				13 31			13 57
Leamington Spa	d				11 48			12 14				12 50			13 14				13 48			14 14
Coventry	d		11 42					12 27		12 42					13 27		13 42					14 27
Birmingham International	d		11 53					12 38		12 53					13 38		13 53					14 38
Penzance	d	06 28														08 28						
St Erth	d	06 36														08 36						
Hayle	d																					
Camborne	d	06 46														08 46						
Redruth	d	06 52														08 52						
Truro	d	07 04														09 04						
St Austell	d	07 20														09 20						
Par	d	07 27														09 27						
Lostwithiel	d																					
Bodmin Parkway	d	07 37														09 37						
Liskeard	d	07 53														09 50						
Plymouth	d	08 25							09 25							10 25						
Totnes	d	08 50							09 50							10 50						
Paignton	d												10 07									
Torquay	d												10 13									
Newton Abbot	d	09 03							10 03				10 24			11 03						
Teignmouth	d												10 31									
Dawlish	d												10 36									
Exeter St Davids	d	09 24							10 23				10 50			11 24						
Tiverton Parkway	d	09 38							10 37				11 03			11 37						
Taunton	d	09 51							10 51				11 17			11 51						
Weston-super-Mare	d																					
Cardiff Central	d						10 45							11 45							12 45	
Newport (South Wales)	d						11 00							12 00							13 01	
Bristol Temple Meads	d	10 30				11 00			11 30				12 00			12 30				13 00		
Bristol Parkway	d	10 40				11 10			11 40				12 10			12 40				13 10		
Gloucester	d						11 50							12 48							13 50	
Cheltenham Spa	d	11 11				11 42	12 01		12 11				12 41	12 58		13 11				13 41	14 01	
Birmingham New Street	a	11 58	12 05		12 18	12 26	12 45	12 48	12 56	13 05		13 18	13 26	13 45	13 48	13 56	14 05		14 18	14 23	14 45	14 48
Birmingham New Street	d	12 03	12 15	12 19	12 30	12 31	12 49	12 57	13 03	13 15	13 19	13 30	13 31	13 49	13 57	14 03	14 15	14 19	14 30	14 31	14 49	14 57
Tamworth	d	12 19		12 36			13 09				13 36			14 09		14 19		14 36			15 09	
Burton-on-Trent	d			12 48			13 19		13 28		13 48			14 21				14 48			15 21	
Derby	a	12 42		13 00	13 05		13 36		13 39		14 00	14 05		14 36		14 41		15 00	15 05		15 35	
Nottingham	a			13 28			14 03				14 28			15 03				15 28			16 03	
Chesterfield	a	13 02							14 02							15 02						
Sheffield	a	13 17			13 46				14 17			14 46				15 17			15 46			
Doncaster	a				14 16							15 16							16 17			
Wakefield Westgate	a	13 46							14 46							15 46						
Leeds	a	14 00							15 00							16 00						
York	a	14 30			14 40				15 30			15 40				16 30			16 40			
Darlington	a	14 58			15 13				15 58			16 13				16 58			17 13			
Durham	a	15 15			15 31				16 15			16 31				17 15			17 31			
Chester-le-Street	a																					
Newcastle	a	15 30			15 46				16 29			16 46				17 31			17 46			
Morpeth	a								16 47													
Alnmouth for Alnwick	a	16 01							17 02							18 01						
Berwick-upon-Tweed	a	16 23														18 23						
Dunbar	a								17 44													
Wolverhampton	d		12 37			12 49		13 15		13 37			13 49		14 15		14 37			14 49		15 15
Stafford	a					13 02		13 27					14 02		14 27					15 02		15 27
Stoke-on-Trent	a					13 18		13 43					14 18		14 43					15 18		15 43
Congleton	a																					
Macclesfield	a					13 36		14 01					14 36		15 01					15 36		16 01
Crewe	a		13 08							14 07							15 07					
Wilmslow	a																					
Stockport	a					13 49		14 13					14 49		15 13					15 49		16 13
M'chester Piccadilly	a					13 59		14 25					14 59		15 25					15 59		16 25
Warrington Bank Quay	a		13 26							14 26							15 26					
Wigan North Western	a		13 37							14 37							15 37					
Preston	a		13 51							14 51							15 51					
Lancaster	a		14 07							15 07							16 07					
Oxenholme Lake District	a									15 21												
Penrith North Lakes	a		14 42														16 44					
Carlisle	a		14 59							16 00							17 00					
Lockerbie	a																					
Haymarket	a		16 13														18 14					
Edinburgh	a	17 05	16 20						18 07							19 05	18 22					
Haymarket	a	17 15							18 13							19 15						
Motherwell	a	17 55														19 54						
Glasgow Central	a	18 11								17 15						20 15						
Inverkeithing	a								18 28													
Kirkcaldy	a								18 46													
Markinch	a								18 56													
Ladybank	a								19 04													
Cupar	a								19 15													
Leuchars	a								19 22													
Dundee	a								19 35													
Arbroath	a								19 51													
Montrose	a								20 05													
Stonehaven	a								20 26													
Aberdeen	a								20 48													

A T from Plymouth
B T to Edinburgh
C T from Plymouth to Edinburgh ◇ from Plymouth ■ to Plymouth

South Coast and the South West - North West England, The North East and Scotland

Station		XC ◇1 A ✕	VT ◇1 ☕	XC 1	XC ◇1 ✕	XC ■ ◇1 B ✕	XC ◇1 ✕	XC ◇1 ✕	XC ◇1 A ✕	VT ■ 1 ☕	XC 1	XC ◇1 C ✕	XC ◇1 ✕	XC ◇1 ✕	XC ◇1 ✕	XC ◇1 ✕	VT ■ 1 ☕	XC 1	XC ◇1 ✕	XC ◇1 ✕	XC 1	XC ◇1 ✕	XC ◇1 ✕
Bournemouth	d							12 45							13 45								14 45
Brockenhurst	d							13 00							14 00								15 00
Southampton Central	d							13 16				13 46			14 17								15 16
Southampton Airport Pkway	d							13 23				13 54			14 24								15 23
Winchester	d							13 32				14 03			14 33								15 32
Basingstoke	d							13 49				14 19			14 49								15 48
Guildford	d																						
Reading	d				13 45			14 15				14 45			15 15				15 45				16 15
Oxford	d				14 13			14 39				15 13			15 39				16 13				16 39
Banbury	d				14 31			14 57				15 32			15 57				16 31				16 57
Leamington Spa	d				14 50			15 14				15 50			16 14				16 48				17 14
Coventry	d		14 42					15 27		15 42					16 27		16 42						17 27
Birmingham International	d		14 53					15 38		15 53					16 38		16 53						17 38
Penzance	d					09 35																	
St Erth	d					09 43																	
Hayle	d					09 47																	
Camborne	d					09 56																	
Redruth	d					10 03																	
Truro	d					10 15																	
St Austell	d					10 31																	
Par	d					10 38																	
Lostwithiel	d					10 45																	
Bodmin Parkway	d					10 51																	
Liskeard	d					11 04																	
Plymouth	d	11 25				11 50			12 25							13 25							
Totnes	d	11 50				12 15			12 51							13 51							
Paignton	d																			14 04			
Torquay	d																			14 10			
Newton Abbot	d	12 03				12 28			13 04							14 04				14 21			
Teignmouth	d																			14 28			
Dawlish	d																			14 33			
Exeter St Davids	d	12 24				12 50			13 24							14 24				14 48			
Tiverton Parkway	d	12 38				13 06			13 38							14 38				15 02			
Taunton	d	12 51				13 22			13 51							14 51				15 15			
Weston-super-Mare	d																			15 39			
Cardiff Central	d						13 45							14 45								15 45	
Newport (South Wales)	d						14 00							15 00								16 00	
Bristol Temple Meads	d	13 30				14 00			14 30				15 00			15 30				16 00			
Bristol Parkway	d	13 40				14 10			14 40				15 10			15 40				16 10			
Gloucester	d						14 50							15 50								16 50	
Cheltenham Spa	d	14 11				14 41	15 01		15 11				15 42	16 01		16 11				16 41		17 01	
Birmingham New Street	a	14 56	15 05		15 18	15 23	15 45	15 48	15 56	16 05		16 18	16 23	16 45	16 48	16 56	17 05		17 18	17 23		17 45	17 48
Birmingham New Street	d	15 03	15 15	15 19	15 30	15 31	15 49	15 57	16 03	16 15	16 19	16 30	16 31	16 49	16 57	17 03	17 15	17 19	17 30	17 31	17 39	17 49	17 57
Tamworth	d			15 36			16 09		16 20		16 36			17 09				17 36			18 03	18 09	
Burton-on-Trent	d	15 26		15 48			16 21				16 48			17 21		17 26		17 48			18 14	18 21	
Derby	a	15 41		16 00	16 05		16 36		16 41		17 00	17 05		17 36		17 40		18 00	18 05		18 30	18 35	
Nottingham	a			16 28			17 03				17 31			18 04				18 32				19 03	
Chesterfield	a	16 02							17 03							18 02							
Sheffield	a	16 18			16 44				17 18			17 46				18 18			18 44				
Doncaster	a				17 13														19 17				
Wakefield Westgate	a	16 46							17 46			18 16				18 48							
Leeds	a	17 00							18 01			18 34				19 03							
York	a	17 30			17 42				18 30			19 01				19 30			19 40				
Darlington	a	17 58			18 14				19 00			19 32				20 03			20 11				
Durham	a	18 15			18 31				19 19			19 49				20 21			20 28				
Chester-le-Street	a																						
Newcastle	a	18 33			18 47				19 33			20 02				20 35			20 42				
Morpeth	a															20 53							
Alnmouth for Alnwick	a								20 01			20 28											
Berwick-upon-Tweed	a	19 22							20 25							21 26							
Dunbar	a	19 45														21 50							
Wolverhampton	d		15 37			15 49		16 15		16 37			16 49		17 15		17 37			17 49			18 15
Stafford	a					16 02		16 27					17 02		17 27					18 02			18 27
Stoke-on-Trent	a					16 18		16 43					17 18		17 43					18 18			18 43
Congleton	a																						
Macclesfield	a					16 36		17 01					17 36		18 01					18 36			19 01
Crewe	a		16 07							17 08							18 08						
Wilmslow	a																						
Stockport	a					16 49		17 13					17 49		18 13					18 49			19 13
M'chester Piccadilly	a					16 59		17 25					17 59		18 25					18 59			19 24
Warrington Bank Quay	a		16 26							17 26							18 26						
Wigan North Western	a		16 37							17 37							18 37						
Preston	a		16 51							17 52							18 51						
Lancaster	a		17 07							18 08							19 07						
Oxenholme Lake District	a		17 21							18 23							19 21						
Penrith North Lakes	a		17 46							18 47													
Carlisle	a		18 03							19 04							20 00						
Lockerbie	a																						
Haymarket	a									20 14													
Edinburgh	a	20 08							21 08	20 23		21 29				22 13							
Haymarket	a	20 16							21 17														
Motherwell	a								22 04														
Glasgow Central	a		19 23						22 21								21 15						
Inverkeithing	a	20 30																					
Kirkcaldy	a																						
Markinch	a	21 00																					
Ladybank	a	21 08																					
Cupar	a	21 19																					
Leuchars	a	21 26																					
Dundee	a	21 43																					
Arbroath	a																						
Montrose	a																						
Stonehaven	a																						
Aberdeen	a																						

A ✕ to Edinburgh

B ✕ ◇ from Plymouth ■ to Plymouth

C ✕ to Newcastle

South Coast and the South West - North West England, The North East and Scotland

Station		XC ◇1 A ✕	VT ◇1 ☕	XC 1	XC ◇1 ✕	XC ◇1 ✕	XC ◇1 B ✕	XC ◇1 ✕	XC ◇1 ✕	VT ◇1 ☕	XC 1	XC ◇1 B ✕	XC ◇1 ✕	XC ◇1 B ✕	XC ◇1 ✕	XC ◇1 B ✕	VT ◇1 ⊠	XC ◇1 B ✕	XC ◇1 ✕	XC ◇1 B ✕	XC ◇1 B ✕	XC ◇1 B ✕
Bournemouth	d							15 45							16 45						17 45	
Brockenhurst	d							16 00							17 00						18 00	
Southampton Central	d				15 46			16 17							17 17			17 46			18 15	
Southampton Airport Pkway	d				15 53			16 24							17 24			17 53			18 22	
Winchester	d				16 02			16 33							17 33			18 02			18 31	
Basingstoke	d				16 18			16 49							17 49			18 18			18 47	
Guildford	d																					
Reading	d				16 45			17 15				17 45			18 15			18 45			19 15	
Oxford	d				17 13			17 39				18 10			18 39			19 13			19 39	
Banbury	d				17 33			17 57				18 27			18 57			19 30			19 57	
Leamington Spa	d				17 51			18 14				18 45			19 14			19 48			20 14	
Coventry	d		17 42					18 27		18 42					19 27		19 42				20 27	
Birmingham International	d		17 53					18 38		18 53					19 38		19 53				20 38	
Penzance	d																					
St Erth	d																					
Hayle	d																					
Camborne	d																					
Redruth	d																					
Truro	d																					
St Austell	d																					
Par	d																					
Lostwithiel	d																					
Bodmin Parkway	d																					
Liskeard	d																					
Plymouth	d	14 25							15 25							16 25						17 25
Totnes	d	14 50							15 51							16 50						17 51
Paignton	d																					
Torquay	d																					
Newton Abbot	d	15 03							16 04							17 03						18 04
Teignmouth	d																					
Dawlish	d																					
Exeter St Davids	d	15 24							16 24				16 54			17 24						18 25
Tiverton Parkway	d	15 37							16 38				17 08			17 37						18 39
Taunton	d	15 51							16 51				17 22			17 50						18 52
Weston-super-Mare	d																					
Cardiff Central	d						16 45							17 45						18 45		
Newport (South Wales)	d						17 00							18 00						19 00		
Bristol Temple Meads	d	16 30				17 00			17 30				18 00			18 30			19 00			19 30
Bristol Parkway	d	16 40				17 10			17 40				18 10			18 40			19 10			19 40
Gloucester	d						17 50							18 46						19 45		
Cheltenham Spa	d	17 11				17 42	18 01		18 11				18 41	18 57		19 11			19 41	19 58		20 11
Birmingham New Street	a	17 56	18 05		18 18	18 23	18 45	18 48	18 56	19 05		19 18	19 23	19 45	19 48	19 56	20 06	20 18	20 23	20 40	20 48	20 51
Birmingham New Street	d	18 03	18 15	18 19	18 30	18 31	18 49	18 57	19 03	19 15	19 19	19 30	19 31	19 49	19 57	20 03	20 15	20 30	20 31	20 49	20 57	21 03
Tamworth	d	18 19		18 36			19 09				19 36			20 09		20 19				21 09		21 19
Burton-on-Trent	d			18 48			19 21		19 29		19 48			20 21						21 21		21 30
Derby	a	18 39		19 04	19 07		19 34		19 38		20 03	20 08		20 36		20 39		21 09		21 31		21 43
Nottingham	a			19 31			20 04				20 28			21 03						22 04		
Chesterfield	a	19 02			19 27				20 03							21 06		21 37				22 06
Sheffield	a	19 18			19 40				20 18			20 37				21 19		21 50				22 22
Doncaster	a				20 13							21 19						22 25				
Wakefield Westgate	a	19 46							20 47							21 46						22 53
Leeds	a	20 02							21 02							22 02						23 07
York	a	20 30			20 41							21 40						22 51				
Darlington	a	20 59			21 14							22 12										
Durham	a	21 17			21 31							22 29										
Chester-le-Street	a																					
Newcastle	a	21 33			21 45							22 48										
Morpeth	a																					
Alnmouth for Alnwick	a	21 59																				
Berwick-upon-Tweed	a																					
Dunbar	a																					
Wolverhampton	d		18 37			18 49		19 15		19 37			19 49		20 15		20 37		20 49		21 15	
Stafford	a					19 02		19 27					20 02		20 27		20 50		21 02		21 28	
Stoke-on-Trent	a					19 18		19 43					20 19		20 43				21 18		21 45	
Congleton	a																					
Macclesfield	a					19 36		20 01					20 36		21 01				21 36		22 02	
Crewe	a		19 07							20 07							21 15					
Wilmslow	a																					
Stockport	a					19 49		20 13					20 48		21 13				21 49		22 15	
M'chester Piccadilly	a					19 59		20 25					20 59		21 25				21 59		22 25	
Warrington Bank Quay	a		19 26							20 26												
Wigan North Western	a		19 37							20 37												
Preston	a		19 51							20 51												
Lancaster	a		20 07							21 07												
Oxenholme Lake District	a									21 22												
Penrith North Lakes	a		20 44																			
Carlisle	a		21 00							22 00												
Lockerbie	a																					
Haymarket	a		22 13																			
Edinburgh	a	23 03	22 19																			
Haymarket	a																					
Motherwell	a																					
Glasgow Central	a									23 17												
Inverkeithing	a																					
Kirkcaldy	a																					
Markinch	a																					
Ladybank	a																					
Cupar	a																					
Leuchars	a																					
Dundee	a																					
Arbroath	a																					
Montrose	a																					
Stonehaven	a																					
Aberdeen	a																					

A ✕ to Leeds

B ✕ to Birmingham New Street

Table T051-R

Mondays to Fridays
21 May to 20 July

South Coast and the South West - North West England, The North East and Scotland

		VT	XC	XC	XC	XC	XC	XC	XC	XC	XC	XC	XC	XC	XC	XC
		◇1	◇1	◇1	◇1	◇1	◇1	1	◇1	◇1	◇1	◇1	1	◇1	◇1	◇1
					A		B									
		⊡			🛒		🛒									
Bournemouth	d				18 45						19 45					
Brockenhurst	d				19 00						20 00					
Southampton Central	d				19 16						20 17					
Southampton Airport Pkway	d				19 23						20 24					
Winchester	d				19 32						20 33					
Basingstoke	d				19 49						20 49					
Guildford	d															
Reading	d		19 45		20 12				20 45		21 11				21 45	
Oxford	d		20 13		20 39				21 14		21 36				22 30	
Banbury	d		20 32		20 57				21 33		21 54				22 48	
Leamington Spa	d		20 50		21 14				21 53		22 12				23 05	
Coventry	d	20 42			21 27						22 25				23 17	
Birmingham International	d	20 53			21 38						22 35				23 27	
Penzance	d															
St Erth	d															
Hayle	d															
Camborne	d															
Redruth	d															
Truro	d															
St Austell	d															
Par	d															
Lostwithiel	d															
Bodmin Parkway	d															
Liskeard	d															
Plymouth	d						18 25									
Totnes	d						18 50									
Paignton	d													20 14		
Torquay	d													20 20		
Newton Abbot	d						19 03							20 31		
Teignmouth	d															
Dawlish	d															
Exeter St Davids	d						19 24							20 52		
Tiverton Parkway	d						19 37							21 05		
Taunton	d						19 51							21 19		
Weston-super-Mare	d															
Cardiff Central	d					19 50						21 05				21 50
Newport (South Wales)	d					20 05						21 21				22 05
Bristol Temple Meads	d			20 00			20 30							22 00		
Bristol Parkway	d			20 10			20 40							22 10		
Gloucester	d			20 46		20 59						22 04				22 47
Cheltenham Spa	d			20 56		21 11	21 17					22 15		22 42		22 58
Birmingham New Street	a	21 04	21 23	21 37	21 48	21 51	22 02		22 18		22 45	23 05		23 43	23 56	23 59
Birmingham New Street	d	21 15			21 57			22 03		22 30			23 09			
Tamworth	d							22 27					23 28			
Burton-on-Trent	d							22 39					23 40			
Derby	a							22 51					23 53			
Nottingham	a							23 27					00 16			
Chesterfield	a															
Sheffield	a															
Doncaster	a															
Wakefield Westgate	a															
Leeds	a															
York	a															
Darlington	a															
Durham	a															
Chester-le-Street	a															
Newcastle	a															
Morpeth	a															
Alnmouth for Alnwick	a															
Berwick-upon-Tweed	a															
Dunbar	a															
Wolverhampton	d	21 37			22 15					22 48						
Stafford	a	21 52			22 27					23 00						
Stoke-on-Trent	a	22 10			22 43					23 17						
Congleton	a															
Macclesfield	a				23 01											
Crewe	a	22 30														
Wilmslow	a															
Stockport	a				23 13											
M'chester Piccadilly	a				23 25					00 11						
Warrington Bank Quay	a															
Wigan North Western	a															
Preston	a															
Lancaster	a															
Oxenholme Lake District	a															
Penrith North Lakes	a															
Carlisle	a															
Lockerbie	a															
Haymarket	a															
Edinburgh	a															
Haymarket	a															
Motherwell	a															
Glasgow Central	a															
Inverkeithing	a															
Kirkcaldy	a															
Markinch	a															
Ladybank	a															
Cupar	a															
Leuchars	a															
Dundee	a															
Arbroath	a															
Montrose	a															
Stonehaven	a															
Aberdeen	a															

A 🛒 to Reading
B 🛒 to Bristol Temple Meads

Table T051-R

Mondays to Fridays
23 July to 31 August

South Coast and the South West - North West England, The North East and Scotland

		XC	XC	VT	XC	XC	XC	XC	XC	XC	VT	XC	XC	XC	XC	XC	XC	VT	XC	XC	XC	XC	XC
		◇1	◇1	◇1	1	◇1	◇1	1	◇1	◇1	◇1	1	◇1	◇1	1	◇1	◇1	◇1	1	◇1	◇1	◇1	◇1
																A							
			🛒	⊠		🛒	🛒		🛒	🛒	⊠	🛒	🛒	🛒		🛒	🛒	⊠	🛒	🛒		🛒	
Bournemouth	d																						
Brockenhurst	d																						
Southampton Central	d															05 15							
Southampton Airport Pkway	d															05 22							
Winchester	d															05 31							
Basingstoke	d															05 47							
Guildford	d																			06 01			
Reading	d															06 15				06 45			
Oxford	d															06 38				07 08			
Banbury	d															06 57				07 26			
Leamington Spa	d															07 14				07 43			
Coventry	d															07 27		07 42					
Birmingham International	d															07 38		07 53					
Penzance	d																						
St Erth	d																						
Hayle	d																						
Camborne	d																						
Redruth	d																						
Truro	d																						
St Austell	d																						
Par	d																						
Lostwithiel	d																						
Bodmin Parkway	d																						
Liskeard	d																						
Plymouth	d																						
Totnes	d																						
Paignton	d																						
Torquay	d																						
Newton Abbot	d																						
Teignmouth	d																						
Dawlish	d																						
Exeter St Davids	d																						
Tiverton Parkway	d																						
Taunton	d																						
Weston-super-Mare	d																						
Cardiff Central	d																						06 40
Newport (South Wales)	d																						06 55
Bristol Temple Meads	d																06 27					07 00	
Bristol Parkway	d																06 39					07 10	
Gloucester	d																				07 10		07 46
Cheltenham Spa	d																07 10				07 21	07 41	07 57
Birmingham New Street	a															07 48	07 56	08 09		08 12	08 17	08 26	08 45
Birmingham New Street	d	05 57	06 00	06 15	06 19	06 30	06 30	06 49	06 51	07 03	07 15	07 19	07 30	07 31	07 49	07 57	08 03	08 15	08 19	08 30		08 31	08 49
Tamworth	d				06 39		06 46	07 07		07 19		07 39			08 07		08 20		08 36				09 09
Burton-on-Trent	d		06 28		06 51		06 57	07 20		07 31		07 50	07 55		08 19		08 31		08 48	08 54			09 21
Derby	a																						
Nottingham	a				07 38			08 09				08 34			09 07				09 25				10 03
Chesterfield	a		07 21				08 00			08 25			08 59				09 24			10 00			
Sheffield	a		07 45				08 19			08 48			09 17				09 50			10 18			
Doncaster	a		08 14							09 16							10 17						
Wakefield Westgate	a						08 47						09 46							10 46			
Leeds	a						09 02						10 00							11 00			
York	a		08 40				09 30			09 40			10 30				10 40			11 30			
Darlington	a		09 16				09 58			10 12			10 58				11 13			11 58			
Durham	a		09 33				10 17			10 29			11 15				11 31			12 15			
Chester-le-Street	a																						
Newcastle	a		09 47				10 31			10 43			11 29				11 46			12 30			
Morpeth	a												11 49										
Alnmouth for Alnwick	a																						
Berwick-upon-Tweed	a												12 23										
Dunbar	a						11 38													13 41			
Wolverhampton	d	06 15		06 37		06 48			07 10		07 37			07 49		08 15		08 37				08 49	
Stafford	a	06 27				06 59			07 21					08 02		08 27						09 02	
Stoke-on-Trent	a	06 44				07 19								08 18		08 43						09 18	
Congleton	a	06 56																					
Macclesfield	a	07 05				07 37								08 36		09 01						09 36	
Crewe	a			07 08					07 42		08 08							09 07					
Wilmslow	a								08 00														
Stockport	a	07 19				07 49			08 13					08 49		09 13						09 49	
M'chester Piccadilly	a	07 28				07 59			08 24					08 59		09 25						09 59	
Warrington Bank Quay	a			07 26							08 26							09 26					
Wigan North Western	a			07 37							08 37							09 37					
Preston	a			07 51							08 51							09 51					
Lancaster	a			08 07							09 07							10 07					
Oxenholme Lake District	a			08 21														10 21					
Penrith North Lakes	a										09 43												
Carlisle	a			09 00							09 59							10 59					
Lockerbie	a																						
Haymarket	a			10 12														12 16					
Edinburgh	a			10 18			12 03						13 06					12 22		14 07			
Haymarket	a												13 16										
Motherwell	a												13 54										
Glasgow Central	a										11 15		14 12										
Inverkeithing	a																						
Kirkcaldy	a																						
Markinch	a																						
Ladybank	a																						
Cupar	a																						
Leuchars	a																						
Dundee	a																						
Arbroath	a																						
Montrose	a																						
Stonehaven	a																						
Aberdeen	a																						

A 🛒 from Reading

Table T051-R

South Coast and the South West - North West England, The North East and Scotland

Mondays to Fridays
23 July to 31 August

		XC	XC	VT	XC	XC	XC	XC	XC	XC	VT	XC	XC	XC	XC	XC	XC	VT	XC	XC	XC	XC	XC
		◇1	◇1	◇1	1	◇1	◇1	◇1	◇1	◇1	◇1	1	◇1	◇1	◇1	◇1	◇1	◇1	1	◇1	◇1	◇1	■ 1
		A				B	C							D									
		⊼	⊼	⊠	⊼	⊼	⊼		⊼		⊠	⊼	⊼	⊼		⊼	⊼	⊠	⊼		⊼	⊼	⊼
Bournemouth	d								06 30							07 30							08 45
Brockenhurst 3	d								06 45							07 50							09 00
Southampton Central	d	06 15							07 15							08 15							09 16
Southampton Airport Pkway	d	06 22							07 22							08 22							09 23
Winchester	d	06 31							07 31				08 12			08 31							09 32
Basingstoke	d	06 47							07 47				08 28			08 47							09 49
Guildford	d																						
Reading 7	d	07 15				07 46			08 15				08 50			09 15				09 45			10 15
Oxford	d	07 39				08 12			08 39				09 15			09 39				10 15			10 39
Banbury	d	07 57				08 30			08 57				09 34			09 57				10 32			10 57
Leamington Spa 3	d	08 14				08 47			09 14				09 51			10 14				10 50			11 14
Coventry	d	08 27		08 42					09 27		09 42					10 27		10 42					11 27
Birmingham International	d	08 38		08 53					09 38		09 53					10 38		10 53					11 38
Penzance	d																						
St Erth	d																						
Hayle	d																						
Camborne	d																						
Redruth	d																						
Truro	d																						
St Austell	d																						
Par	d																						
Lostwithiel	d																						
Bodmin Parkway	d																						
Liskeard 3	d																						
Plymouth	d		05 20							06 25							07 25						
Totnes	d		05 45							06 50							07 50						
Paignton	d													07 01									
Torquay	d													07 07									
Newton Abbot	d		06 02							07 03				07 18			08 03						
Teignmouth	d													07 25									
Dawlish	d													07 30									
Exeter St Davids 6	d		06 24							07 24				07 44			08 24						
Tiverton Parkway	d		06 37							07 37				07 57			08 37						
Taunton	d		06 51							07 51				08 12			08 51						
Weston-super-Mare	d													08 35									
Cardiff Central 7	d						07 00	07 45							08 45							09 45	
Newport (South Wales)	d						07 14	08 02							09 00							10 00	
Bristol Temple Meads 10	d		07 30				08 00			08 30				09 00			09 30				10 00		
Bristol Parkway 7	d		07 40				08 10			08 40				09 10			09 40				10 10		
Gloucester 7	d							08 49							09 50							10 50	
Cheltenham Spa	d		08 11				08 41	09 00		09 12				09 42	10 01		10 11				10 41	11 01	
Birmingham New Street 12	a	08 48	08 56	09 05		09 18	09 26	09 45	09 49	09 58	10 04		10 18	10 23	10 45	10 48	10 56	11 04		11 18	11 26	11 45	11 48
Birmingham New Street 12	d	08 57	09 03	09 15	09 19	09 30	09 31	09 49	09 57	10 03	10 15	10 19	10 30	10 31	10 49	10 57	11 03	11 15	11 19	11 30	11 31	11 49	11 57
Tamworth	d				09 36			10 07		10 19		10 36			11 09				11 36			12 07	
Burton-on-Trent	d		09 27		09 48	09 52		10 19		10 29		10 48	10 55		11 21		11 26		11 48	11 52		12 19	
Derby 6	a																						
Nottingham 6	a				10 25			11 03				11 25			12 07				12 25			13 03	
Chesterfield	a		10 22			10 59				11 25			11 59				12 24			12 59			
Sheffield 7	a		10 50			11 17				11 46			12 17				12 46			13 17			
Doncaster 7	a		11 16							12 16							13 16						
Wakefield Westgate 7	a					11 46							12 46							13 46			
Leeds 10	a					12 01							13 00							14 00			
York 8	a		11 40			12 30				12 40			13 30				13 40			14 30			
Darlington 7	a		12 12			12 58				13 13			14 02				14 12			14 58			
Durham	a		12 29			13 15				13 31			14 18				14 30			15 15			
Chester-le-Street	a																						
Newcastle 8	a		12 42			13 29				13 45			14 32				14 43			15 30			
Morpeth	a												14 47										
Alnmouth for Alnwick	a					14 02														16 01			
Berwick-upon-Tweed	a					14 23														16 23			
Dunbar	a												15 41										
Wolverhampton 7	d	09 15		09 37			09 49		10 15		10 37			10 49		11 15		11 37			11 49		12 15
Stafford	a	09 27					10 01		10 27					11 02		11 27					12 02		12 27
Stoke-on-Trent	a	09 43					10 17		10 43					11 18		11 43					12 18		12 43
Congleton	a																						
Macclesfield	a	10 01					10 36		11 01					11 36		12 01					12 36		13 01
Crewe 10	a			10 08							11 08							12 07					
Wilmslow	a																						
Stockport	a	10 13					10 49		11 13					11 49		12 13					12 49		13 12
M'chester Piccadilly 10	a	10 25					11 00		11 24					11 59		12 25					12 59		13 25
Warrington Bank Quay	a			10 26							11 26							12 26					
Wigan North Western	a			10 37							11 37							12 37					
Preston 8	a			10 51							11 51							12 51					
Lancaster 6	a			11 07							12 07							13 07					
Oxenholme Lake District	a										12 20							13 21					
Penrith North Lakes	a			11 44																			
Carlisle 8	a			12 00							12 59							13 59					
Lockerbie	a																						
Haymarket	a										14 12												
Edinburgh 10	a					15 08					14 19		16 06							17 05			
Haymarket	a					15 16														17 15			
Motherwell	a					15 54												14 58		17 55			
Glasgow Central 15	a			13 15		16 12												15 15		18 11			
Inverkeithing	a																						
Kirkcaldy	a																						
Markinch	a																						
Ladybank	a																						
Cupar	a																						
Leuchars 3	a																						
Dundee	a																						
Arbroath	a																						
Montrose	a																						
Stonehaven	a																						
Aberdeen	a																						

A ⊼ from Reading
B ⊼ to Edinburgh
C ⊼ from Bristol Temple Meads
D ⊼ from Newton Abbot

Table T051-R

South Coast and the South West - North West England, The North East and Scotland

Mondays to Fridays
23 July to 31 August

		XC	VT	XC	XC	XC	XC	XC	XC	VT	XC	XC	XC	XC	XC	XC	VT	XC	XC	XC	XC	XC
		◇1	◇1	1	◇1	◇1	◇1	◇1	◇1	◇1	1	■ 1	◇1	◇1	◇1	■ ◇1	◇1	1	◇1	◇1	◇1	◇1
					A											B			A			
		⊼	⊡	⊼	⊼	⊼		⊼	⊼	⊠	⊼		⊼	⊼	⊼	⊼	⊠		⊼	⊼	⊼	⊼
Bournemouth	d							09 45							10 45							11 45
Brockenhurst 3	d							10 00							11 00							12 00
Southampton Central	d				09 46			10 17							11 17				11 46			12 17
Southampton Airport Pkway	d				09 55			10 24							11 24				11 53			12 24
Winchester	d				10 03			10 33							11 33				12 02			12 33
Basingstoke	d				10 19			10 49							11 49				12 18			12 49
Guildford	d																					
Reading 7	d				10 45			11 15				11 45			12 15				12 45			13 15
Oxford	d				11 13			11 39				12 13			12 39				13 13			13 39
Banbury	d				11 30			11 57				12 32			12 57				13 31			13 57
Leamington Spa 3	d				11 48			12 14				12 50			13 14				13 48			14 14
Coventry	d		11 42					12 27		12 42					13 27		13 42					14 27
Birmingham International	d		11 53					12 38		12 53					13 38		13 53					14 38
Penzance	d	06 28														08 28						
St Erth	d	06 36														08 36						
Hayle	d																					
Camborne	d	06 46														08 46						
Redruth	d	06 52														08 52						
Truro	d	07 04														09 04						
St Austell	d	07 20														09 20						
Par	d	07 27														09 27						
Lostwithiel	d																					
Bodmin Parkway	d	07 37														09 37						
Liskeard 3	d	07 53														09 50						
Plymouth	d	08 25							09 25							10 25						
Totnes	d	08 50							09 50							10 50						
Paignton	d												10 07									
Torquay	d												10 13									
Newton Abbot	d	09 03							10 03				10 24			11 03						
Teignmouth	d												10 31									
Dawlish	d												10 36									
Exeter St Davids 6	d	09 24							10 23				10 50			11 24						
Tiverton Parkway	d	09 38							10 37				11 03			11 37						
Taunton	d	09 51							10 51				11 17			11 51						
Weston-super-Mare	d																					
Cardiff Central 7	d						10 45							11 45							12 45	
Newport (South Wales)	d						11 00							12 00							13 01	
Bristol Temple Meads 10	d	10 30				11 00			11 30				12 00			12 30				13 00		
Bristol Parkway 7	d	10 40				11 10			11 40				12 10			12 40				13 10		
Gloucester 7	d						11 50							12 48							13 50	
Cheltenham Spa	d	11 11				11 42	12 01		12 11				12 41	12 58		13 11				13 41	14 01	
Birmingham New Street 12	a	11 58	12 05		12 18	12 26	12 45	12 48	12 56	13 05		13 18	13 26	13 45	13 48	13 56	14 05		14 18	14 23	14 45	14 48
Birmingham New Street 12	d	12 03	12 15	12 19	12 30	12 31	12 49	12 57	13 03	13 15	13 19	13 30	13 31	13 49	13 57	14 03	14 15	14 19	14 30	14 31	14 49	14 57
Tamworth	d	12 19		12 36			13 09				13 36			14 09		14 19		14 36			15 09	
Burton-on-Trent	d	12 31		12 48	12 54		13 19		13 28		13 48	13 53		14 21		14 30		14 48	14 53		15 21	
Derby 6	a																					
Nottingham 6	a			13 25			14 03				14 25			15 03				15 25			16 03	
Chesterfield	a	13 32			13 59				14 24			15 00				15 31			16 01			
Sheffield 7	a	13 46			14 17				14 46			15 17				15 46			16 18			
Doncaster 7	a	14 16							15 16							16 17						
Wakefield Westgate 7	a				14 46							15 46							16 46			
Leeds 10	a				15 00							16 00							17 00			
York 8	a	14 40			15 30				15 40			16 30				16 40			17 30			
Darlington 7	a	15 13			15 58				16 13			16 58				17 13			17 58			
Durham	a	15 31			16 15				16 31			17 15				17 31			18 15			
Chester-le-Street	a																					
Newcastle 8	a	15 46			16 29				16 46			17 31				17 46			18 33			
Morpeth	a				16 47																	
Alnmouth for Alnwick	a				17 02							18 01										
Berwick-upon-Tweed	a											18 23							19 22			
Dunbar	a				17 44														19 45			
Wolverhampton 7	d		12 37			12 49		13 15		13 37			13 49		14 15		14 37			14 49		15 15
Stafford	a					13 02		13 27					14 02		14 27					15 02		15 27
Stoke-on-Trent	a					13 18		13 43					14 18		14 43					15 18		15 43
Congleton	a																					
Macclesfield	a					13 36		14 01					14 36		15 01					15 36		16 01
Crewe 10	a		13 08							14 07							15 07					
Wilmslow	a																					
Stockport	a					13 49		14 13					14 49		15 13					15 49		16 13
M'chester Piccadilly 10	a					13 59		14 25					14 59		15 25					15 59		16 25
Warrington Bank Quay	a		13 26							14 26							15 26					
Wigan North Western	a		13 37							14 37							15 37					
Preston 8	a		13 51							14 51							15 51					
Lancaster 6	a		14 07							15 07							16 07					
Oxenholme Lake District	a									15 21												
Penrith North Lakes	a		14 42														16 44					
Carlisle 8	a		14 59							16 00							17 00					
Lockerbie	a																					
Haymarket	a		16 13														18 14					
Edinburgh 10	a		16 20		18 07							19 05					18 22		20 08			
Haymarket	a				18 13							19 15							20 16			
Motherwell	a											19 54										
Glasgow Central 15	a									17 15		20 15										
Inverkeithing	a				18 28														20 30			
Kirkcaldy	a				18 46																	
Markinch	a				18 56														21 00			
Ladybank	a				19 04														21 08			
Cupar	a				19 15														21 19			
Leuchars 3	a				19 22														21 26			
Dundee	a				19 35														21 43			
Arbroath	a				19 51																	
Montrose	a				20 05																	
Stonehaven	a				20 26																	
Aberdeen	a				20 48																	

A ⊼ to Edinburgh
B ◇ from Plymouth ■ to Plymouth

Table T051-R

Mondays to Fridays

23 July to 31 August

South Coast and the South West - North West England, The North East and Scotland

		XC ◇■ ⚒	VT ◇■ 🍴	XC ■	XC ◇■ A ⚒	XC ■ ◇■ B ⚒	XC ◇■ ⚒	XC ◇■ ⚒	XC ◇■ C ⚒	VT ■ ■ 🍴	XC ■	XC ◇■ ⚒	XC ◇■ ⚒	XC ◇■ ⚒	XC ◇■ ⚒	XC ◇■ ⚒	VT ■ ■ 🍴	XC ■	XC ◇■ D ⚒	XC ◇■ ⚒	XC ◇■ ⚒	XC ◇■ ⚒	XC ◇■ ⚒
Bournemouth	d							12 45							13 45							14 45	
Brockenhurst ■	d							13 00							14 00							15 00	
Southampton Central ⛴	d							13 16				13 46			14 17							15 16	
Southampton Airport Pkway ✈	d							13 23				13 54			14 24							15 23	
Winchester	d							13 32				14 03			14 33							15 32	
Basingstoke	d							13 49				14 19			14 49							15 48	
Guildford	d																						
Reading ■	d				13 45			14 15				14 45			15 15				15 45			16 15	
Oxford	d				14 13			14 39				15 13			15 39				16 13			16 39	
Banbury	d				14 31			14 57				15 32			15 57				16 31			16 57	
Leamington Spa ■	d				14 50			15 14				15 50			16 14				16 48			17 14	
Coventry	d		14 42					15 27		15 42					16 27		16 42					17 27	
Birmingham International ✈	d		14 53					15 38		15 53					16 38		16 53					17 38	
Penzance	d					09 35																	
St Erth	d					09 43																	
Hayle	d					09 47																	
Camborne	d					09 56																	
Redruth	d					10 03																	
Truro	d					10 15																	
St Austell	d					10 31																	
Par	d					10 38																	
Lostwithiel	d					10 45																	
Bodmin Parkway	d					10 51																	
Liskeard ■	d					11 04																	
Plymouth	d	11 25				11 50			12 25							13 25							14 25
Totnes	d	11 50				12 15			12 51							13 51							14 50
Paignton	d																			14 04			
Torquay	d																			14 10			
Newton Abbot	d	12 03				12 28			13 04							14 04				14 21			15 03
Teignmouth	d																			14 28			
Dawlish	d																			14 33			
Exeter St Davids ■	d	12 24				12 50			13 24							14 24				14 48			15 24
Tiverton Parkway	d	12 38				13 06			13 38							14 38				15 02			15 37
Taunton	d	12 51				13 22			13 51							14 51				15 15			15 51
Weston-super-Mare	d																			15 39			
Cardiff Central ■	d						13 45							14 45							15 45		
Newport (South Wales)	d						14 00							15 00							16 00		
Bristol Temple Meads ■	d	13 30				14 00			14 30				15 00			15 30				16 00			16 30
Bristol Parkway ■	d	13 40				14 10			14 40				15 10			15 40				16 10			16 40
Gloucester ■	d						14 50							15 50							16 50		
Cheltenham Spa	d	14 11				14 41	15 01		15 11				15 42	16 01		16 11				16 41	17 01		17 11
Birmingham New Street ■	a	14 56	15 05		15 18	15 23	15 45	15 48	15 56	16 05		16 18	16 23	16 45	16 48	16 56	17 05		17 18	17 23	17 45	17 48	17 56
Birmingham New Street ■	d	15 03	15 15	15 19	15 30	15 31	15 49	15 57	16 03	16 15	16 19	16 30	16 31	16 49	16 57	17 03	17 15	17 19	17 30	17 31	17 49	17 57	18 03
Tamworth	d			15 36			16 09		16 20		16 36			17 09				17 36			18 10		18 19
Burton-on-Trent	d	15 27		15 48	16 05		16 21		16 32		16 48	16 53		17 21		17 26		17 48	17 52		18 21		18 29
Derby ■	a																						
Nottingham ■ 🚊	a			16 25			17 03				17 31			18 03				18 31			19 04		
Chesterfield	a	16 35			16 59				17 33			17 58				18 26			18 59				19 21
Sheffield ■ 🚊	a	16 48			17 18				17 48			18 18				18 44			19 18				19 40
Doncaster ■	a	17 13														19 17							20 13
Wakefield Westgate ■	a				17 45				18 16			18 48							19 46				
Leeds ■	a				18 00				18 34			19 03							20 02				
York ■	a	17 42			18 30				19 01			19 30				19 41			20 30				20 41
Darlington ■	a	18 14			19 00				19 33			20 03				20 12			20 59				21 14
Durham	a	18 31			19 19				19 50			20 21				20 29			21 17				21 31
Chester-le-Street	a																						
Newcastle ■	a	18 47			19 33				20 04			20 35				20 44			21 33				21 45
Morpeth	a											20 53											
Alnmouth for Alnwick	a				20 01				20 31										21 59				
Berwick-upon-Tweed	a				20 25							21 26											
Dunbar	a											21 50											
Wolverhampton ■ 🚊	d		15 37			15 49		16 15		16 37			16 49		17 15		17 37			17 49		18 15	
Stafford	a					16 02		16 27					17 02		17 27					18 02		18 27	
Stoke-on-Trent	a					16 18		16 43					17 18		17 43					18 18		18 43	
Congleton	a																						
Macclesfield	a					16 36		17 01					17 36		18 01					18 36		19 01	
Crewe ■	a		16 07							17 08							18 08						
Wilmslow	a																						
Stockport	a					16 49		17 13					17 49		18 13					18 49		19 13	
M'chester Piccadilly ■ 🚊	a					16 59		17 25					17 59		18 25					18 59		19 24	
Warrington Bank Quay	a		16 26							17 26							18 26						
Wigan North Western	a		16 37							17 37							18 37						
Preston ■	a		16 51							17 52							18 51						
Lancaster ■	a		17 07							18 08							19 07						
Oxenholme Lake District	a		17 21							18 23							19 21						
Penrith North Lakes	a		17 46							18 47													
Carlisle ■	a		18 03							19 04							20 00						
Lockerbie	a																						
Haymarket 🚊	a									20 14													
Edinburgh ■	a				21 08				21 35	20 23		22 13							23 03				
Haymarket 🚊	a				21 17																		
Motherwell	a				22 04																		
Glasgow Central ■	a		19 23		22 21												21 15						
Inverkeithing	a																						
Kirkcaldy	a																						
Markinch	a																						
Ladybank	a																						
Cupar	a																						
Leuchars ■	a																						
Dundee	a																						
Arbroath	a																						
Montrose	a																						
Stonehaven	a																						
Aberdeen	a																						

A ⚒ to Edinburgh

B ⚒ ◇ from Plymouth ■ to Plymouth

C ⚒ to Newcastle

D ⚒ to Leeds

Table T051-R

Mondays to Fridays

23 July to 31 August

South Coast and the South West - North West England, The North East and Scotland

		VT ◇■ 🍴	XC ■	XC ◇■ ⚒	XC ◇■ ⚒	XC ◇■ A ⚒	XC ◇■ ⚒	XC ◇■ ⚒	VT ◇■ 🍴	XC ■	XC ◇■ A ⚒	XC ◇■ ⚒	XC ◇■ A ⚒	XC ◇■ ⚒	XC ◇■ A ⚒	VT ◇■ ⊠	XC ◇■ ⚒	XC ◇■ ⚒	XC ◇■ A ⚒	XC ◇■ A ⚒	XC ◇■ A ⚒	VT ◇■ 🍴
Bournemouth	d						15 45							16 45						17 45		
Brockenhurst ■	d						16 00							17 00						18 00		
Southampton Central ⛴	d			15 46			16 17							17 17			17 46			18 15		
Southampton Airport Pkway ✈	d			15 53			16 24							17 24			17 53			18 22		
Winchester	d			16 02			16 33							17 33			18 02			18 31		
Basingstoke	d			16 18			16 49							17 49			18 18			18 47		
Guildford	d																					
Reading ■	d			16 45			17 15				17 45			18 15			18 45			19 15		
Oxford	d			17 13			17 39				18 10			18 39			19 13			19 39		
Banbury	d			17 33			17 57				18 27			18 57			19 30			19 57		
Leamington Spa ■	d			17 51			18 14				18 45			19 14			19 48			20 14		
Coventry	d	17 42					18 27		18 42					19 27		19 42				20 27		20 42
Birmingham International ✈	d	17 53					18 38		18 53					19 38		19 53				20 38		20 53
Penzance	d																					
St Erth	d																					
Hayle	d																					
Camborne	d																					
Redruth	d																					
Truro	d																					
St Austell	d																					
Par	d																					
Lostwithiel	d																					
Bodmin Parkway	d																					
Liskeard ■	d																					
Plymouth	d							15 25							16 25						17 25	
Totnes	d							15 51							16 50						17 51	
Paignton	d																					
Torquay	d																					
Newton Abbot	d							16 04							17 03						18 04	
Teignmouth	d																					
Dawlish	d																					
Exeter St Davids ■	d							16 24				16 54			17 24						18 25	
Tiverton Parkway	d							16 38				17 08			17 37						18 39	
Taunton	d							16 51				17 22			17 50						18 52	
Weston-super-Mare	d																					
Cardiff Central ■	d					16 45							17 45						18 45			
Newport (South Wales)	d					17 00							18 00						19 00			
Bristol Temple Meads ■	d				17 00			17 30				18 00			18 30			19 00			19 30	
Bristol Parkway ■	d				17 10			17 40				18 10			18 40			19 10			19 40	
Gloucester ■	d					17 50							18 46						19 45			
Cheltenham Spa	d				17 42	18 01		18 11				18 41	18 57		19 11			19 41	19 58		20 11	
Birmingham New Street ■	a	18 05		18 18	18 23	18 45	18 48	18 56	19 05		19 18	19 23	19 45	19 48	19 56	20 06	20 18	20 23	20 40	20 48	20 51	21 04
Birmingham New Street ■	d	18 15	18 19	18 30	18 31	18 49	18 57	19 03	19 15	19 19	19 30	19 31	19 49	19 57	20 03	20 15		20 31	20 49	20 57	21 03	21 15
Tamworth	d		18 36			19 09				19 36			20 09		20 19				21 09		21 19	
Burton-on-Trent	d		18 48	18 52		19 21		19 30		19 48	19 52		20 21		20 30				21 21		21 30	
Derby ■	a																					
Nottingham ■ 🚊	a		19 31			20 04				20 25			21 03						22 02			
Chesterfield	a			19 59				20 22			20 58				21 25						22 25	
Sheffield ■ 🚊	a			20 18				20 38			21 16				21 50						22 44	
Doncaster ■	a							21 19							22 25							
Wakefield Westgate ■	a			20 46							21 46										23 12	
Leeds ■	a			21 01							22 02										23 26	
York ■	a							21 40							22 51							
Darlington ■	a							22 12														
Durham	a							22 29														
Chester-le-Street	a																					
Newcastle ■	a							22 48														
Morpeth	a																					
Alnmouth for Alnwick	a																					
Berwick-upon-Tweed	a																					
Dunbar	a																					
Wolverhampton ■ 🚊	d	18 37			18 49		19 15		19 37			19 49		20 15		20 37		20 49		21 15		21 37
Stafford	a				19 02		19 27					20 02		20 27		20 50		21 02		21 28		21 52
Stoke-on-Trent	a				19 18		19 43					20 19		20 43				21 18		21 45		22 10
Congleton	a																					
Macclesfield	a				19 36		20 01					20 36		21 01				21 36		22 02		
Crewe ■	a	19 07							20 07							21 15						22 30
Wilmslow	a																					
Stockport	a				19 49		20 13					20 48		21 13				21 49		22 15		
M'chester Piccadilly ■ 🚊	a				19 59		20 25					20 59		21 25				21 59		22 25		
Warrington Bank Quay	a	19 26							20 26													
Wigan North Western	a	19 37							20 37													
Preston ■	a	19 51							20 51													
Lancaster ■	a	20 07							21 07													
Oxenholme Lake District	a								21 22													
Penrith North Lakes	a	20 44																				
Carlisle ■	a	21 00							22 00													
Lockerbie	a																					
Haymarket 🚊	a	22 13																				
Edinburgh ■	a	22 19																				
Haymarket 🚊	a																					
Motherwell	a																					
Glasgow Central ■	a								23 17													
Inverkeithing	a																					
Kirkcaldy	a																					
Markinch	a																					
Ladybank	a																					
Cupar	a																					
Leuchars ■	a																					
Dundee	a																					
Arbroath	a																					
Montrose	a																					
Stonehaven	a																					
Aberdeen	a																					

A ⚒ to Birmingham New Street

Table T051-R

South Coast and the South West - North West England, The North East and Scotland

Mondays to Fridays
23 July to 31 August

		XC	XC	XC	XC	XC	XC	XC	XC	XC	XC	XC	XC	XC	XC
		◇1	◇1	◇1	◇1	◇1	1	◇1	◇1	◇1	◇1	1	◇1	◇1	◇1
				A		B									
				🍴		🍴									
Bournemouth	d			18 45						19 45					
Brockenhurst	d			19 00						20 00					
Southampton Central	d			19 16						20 17					
Southampton Airport Pkway	d			19 23						20 24					
Winchester	d			19 32						20 33					
Basingstoke	d			19 49						20 49					
Guildford	d														
Reading	d	19 45		20 12				20 45		21 11				21 45	
Oxford	d	20 13		20 39				21 14		21 36				22 30	
Banbury	d	20 32		20 57				21 33		21 54				22 48	
Leamington Spa	d	20 50		21 14				21 53		22 12				23 05	
Coventry	d			21 27						22 25				23 17	
Birmingham International	d			21 38						22 35				23 27	
Penzance	d														
St Erth	d														
Hayle	d														
Camborne	d														
Redruth	d														
Truro	d														
St Austell	d														
Par	d														
Lostwithiel	d														
Bodmin Parkway	d														
Liskeard	d														
Plymouth	d					18 25									
Totnes	d					18 50									
Paignton	d												20 14		
Torquay	d												20 20		
Newton Abbot	d					19 03							20 31		
Teignmouth	d														
Dawlish	d														
Exeter St Davids	d					19 24							20 52		
Tiverton Parkway	d					19 37							21 05		
Taunton	d					19 51							21 19		
Weston-super-Mare	d														
Cardiff Central	d				19 50						21 05				21 50
Newport (South Wales)	d				20 05						21 21				22 05
Bristol Temple Meads	d		20 00			20 30							22 00		
Bristol Parkway	d		20 10			20 40							22 10		
Gloucester	d		20 46		20 59						22 04				22 47
Cheltenham Spa	d		20 56		21 11	21 17					22 15		22 42		22 58
Birmingham New Street	a	21 23	21 37	21 48	21 51	22 02		22 18		22 45	23 05		23 43	23 56	23 59
Birmingham New Street	d			21 57			22 03		22 30			23 09			
Tamworth	d						22 27					23 28			
Burton-on-Trent	d						22 39					23 40			
Derby	a														
Nottingham	a						23 27					00 19			
Chesterfield	a														
Sheffield	a														
Doncaster	a														
Wakefield Westgate	a														
Leeds	a														
York	a														
Darlington	a														
Durham	a														
Chester-le-Street	a														
Newcastle	a														
Morpeth	a														
Alnmouth for Alnwick	a														
Berwick-upon-Tweed	a														
Dunbar	a														
Wolverhampton	d			22 15					22 48						
Stafford	a			22 27					23 00						
Stoke-on-Trent	a			22 43					23 17						
Congleton	a														
Macclesfield	a			23 01											
Crewe	a														
Wilmslow	a														
Stockport	a			23 13											
M'chester Piccadilly	a			23 25					00 11						
Warrington Bank Quay	a														
Wigan North Western	a														
Preston	a														
Lancaster	a														
Oxenholme Lake District	a														
Penrith North Lakes	a														
Carlisle	a														
Lockerbie	a														
Haymarket	a														
Edinburgh	a														
Haymarket	a														
Motherwell	a														
Glasgow Central	a														
Inverkeithing	a														
Kirkcaldy	a														
Markinch	a														
Ladybank	a														
Cupar	a														
Leuchars	a														
Dundee	a														
Arbroath	a														
Montrose	a														
Stonehaven	a														
Aberdeen	a														

A 🍴 to Reading
B 🍴 to Bristol Temple Meads

Table T051-R

South Coast and the South West - North West England, The North East and Scotland

Mondays to Fridays
3 September to 5 October

		XC	XC	VT	XC	XC	XC	XC	XC	XC	VT	XC	XC	XC	XC	XC	XC	VT	XC	XC	XC	XC	XC
		◇1	◇1	◇1	1	◇1	◇1	1	◇1	◇1	◇1	1	◇1	◇1	1	◇1	◇1	◇1	1	◇1	◇1	◇1	◇1
																A							
			🍴	⊠		🍴	🍴		🍴	🍴	⊠	🍴	🍴	🍴		🍴	🍴	⊠	🍴	🍴		🍴	
Bournemouth	d																						
Brockenhurst	d																						
Southampton Central	d															05 15							
Southampton Airport Pkway	d															05 22							
Winchester	d															05 31							
Basingstoke	d															05 47							
Guildford	d																			06 01			
Reading	d															06 15				06 45			
Oxford	d															06 38				07 08			
Banbury	d															06 57				07 26			
Leamington Spa	d															07 14				07 43			
Coventry	d															07 27		07 42					
Birmingham International	d															07 38		07 53					
Penzance	d																						
St Erth	d																						
Hayle	d																						
Camborne	d																						
Redruth	d																						
Truro	d																						
St Austell	d																						
Par	d																						
Lostwithiel	d																						
Bodmin Parkway	d																						
Liskeard	d																						
Plymouth	d																						
Totnes	d																						
Paignton	d																						
Torquay	d																						
Newton Abbot	d																						
Teignmouth	d																						
Dawlish	d																						
Exeter St Davids	d																						
Tiverton Parkway	d																						
Taunton	d																						
Weston-super-Mare	d																						
Cardiff Central	d																						06 40
Newport (South Wales)	d																						06 55
Bristol Temple Meads	d																06 27					07 00	
Bristol Parkway	d																06 39					07 10	
Gloucester	d																				07 10		07 46
Cheltenham Spa	d																07 10				07 21	07 41	07 57
Birmingham New Street	a															07 48	07 56	08 09		08 12	08 17	08 26	08 45
Birmingham New Street	d	05 57	06 00	06 15	06 19	06 30	06 30	06 49	06 51	07 03	07 15	07 19	07 30	07 31	07 49	07 57	08 03	08 15	08 19	08 30		08 31	08 49
Tamworth	d				06 39			07 07		07 19		07 39			08 07		08 19		08 36				09 09
Burton-on-Trent	d				06 51			07 20		07 31		07 50			08 19		08 29		08 48				09 21
Derby	a		06 49		07 03		07 11	07 35		07 42		08 05	08 10		08 36		08 42		09 00	09 12			09 34
Nottingham	a				07 38			08 12				08 35			09 07				09 28				10 03
Chesterfield	a		07 28				08 01			08 31			08 59				09 27			10 01			
Sheffield	a		07 46				08 19			08 48			09 17				09 50			10 18			
Doncaster	a		08 14							09 16							10 17						
Wakefield Westgate	a						08 47						09 46							10 46			
Leeds	a						09 02						10 00							11 00			
York	a		08 40				09 30			09 40			10 30				10 40			11 30			
Darlington	a		09 16				09 58			10 12			10 58				11 13			11 58			
Durham	a		09 33				10 17			10 29			11 15				11 31			12 15			
Chester-le-Street	a																						
Newcastle	a		09 47				10 31			10 43			11 29				11 46			12 30			
Morpeth	a												11 49										
Alnmouth for Alnwick	a																						
Berwick-upon-Tweed	a												12 23										
Dunbar	a						11 38													13 41			
Wolverhampton	d	06 15		06 37		06 48			07 10		07 37			07 49		08 15		08 37				08 49	
Stafford	a	06 27				06 59			07 21					08 02		08 27						09 02	
Stoke-on-Trent	a	06 44				07 19								08 18		08 43						09 18	
Congleton	a	06 56																					
Macclesfield	a	07 05				07 37								08 36		09 01						09 36	
Crewe	a			07 08					07 42		08 08							09 07					
Wilmslow	a								08 00														
Stockport	a	07 19				07 49			08 13					08 49		09 13						09 49	
M'chester Piccadilly	a	07 28				07 59			08 24					08 59		09 25						09 59	
Warrington Bank Quay	a			07 26							08 26							09 26					
Wigan North Western	a			07 37							08 37							09 37					
Preston	a			07 51							08 51							09 51					
Lancaster	a			08 07							09 07							10 07					
Oxenholme Lake District	a			08 21														10 21					
Penrith North Lakes	a										09 43												
Carlisle	a			09 00							09 59							10 59					
Lockerbie	a																						
Haymarket	a			10 12														12 16					
Edinburgh	a			10 18			12 03						13 06					12 22		14 07			
Haymarket	a												13 16										
Motherwell	a												13 54										
Glasgow Central	a										11 15		14 12										
Inverkeithing	a																						
Kirkcaldy	a																						
Markinch	a																						
Ladybank	a																						
Cupar	a																						
Leuchars	a																						
Dundee	a																						
Arbroath	a																						
Montrose	a																						
Stonehaven	a																						
Aberdeen	a																						

A 🍴 from Reading

Table T051-R

Mondays to Fridays
3 September to 5 October

South Coast and the South West - North West England, The North East and Scotland

		XC	XC	VT	XC	XC	XC	XC	XC	XC	VT	XC	XC	XC	XC	XC	XC	VT	XC	XC	XC	XC	XC
		A				B	C							D									
Bournemouth	d								06 30							07 30							08 45
Brockenhurst	d								06 45							07 50							09 00
Southampton Central	d	06 15							07 15							08 15							09 16
Southampton Airport Pkway	d	06 22							07 22							08 22							09 23
Winchester	d	06 31							07 31				08 12			08 31							09 32
Basingstoke	d	06 47							07 47				08 28			08 47							09 49
Guildford	d																						
Reading	d	07 15				07 46			08 15				08 50			09 15				09 45			10 15
Oxford	d	07 39				08 12			08 39				09 15			09 39				10 15			10 39
Banbury	d	07 57				08 30			08 57				09 34			09 57				10 32			10 57
Leamington Spa	d	08 14				08 47			09 14				09 51			10 14				10 50			11 14
Coventry	d	08 27		08 42					09 27		09 42					10 27		10 42					11 27
Birmingham International	d	08 38		08 53					09 38		09 53					10 38		10 53					11 38
Penzance	d																						
St Erth	d																						
Hayle	d																						
Camborne	d																						
Redruth	d																						
Truro	d																						
St Austell	d																						
Par	d																						
Lostwithiel	d																						
Bodmin Parkway	d																						
Liskeard	d																						
Plymouth	d		05 20							06 25							07 25						
Totnes	d		05 45							06 50							07 50						
Paignton	d													07 01									
Torquay	d													07 07									
Newton Abbot	d		06 02							07 03				07 18			08 03						
Teignmouth	d													07 25									
Dawlish	d													07 30									
Exeter St Davids	d		06 24							07 24				07 44			08 24						
Tiverton Parkway	d		06 37							07 37				07 57			08 37						
Taunton	d		06 51							07 51				08 12			08 51						
Weston-super-Mare	d													08 35									
Cardiff Central	d						07 00	07 45							08 45							09 45	
Newport (South Wales)	d						07 14	08 02							09 00							10 00	
Bristol Temple Meads	d		07 30				08 00			08 30				09 00			09 30				10 00		
Bristol Parkway	d		07 40				08 10			08 40				09 10			09 40				10 10		
Gloucester	d							08 49							09 50							10 50	
Cheltenham Spa	d		08 11				08 41	09 00		09 12				09 42	10 01		10 11				10 41	11 01	
Birmingham New Street	a	08 48	08 56	09 05		09 18	09 26	09 45	09 49	09 58	10 04		10 18	10 23	10 45	10 48	10 56	11 04		11 18	11 26	11 45	11 48
Birmingham New Street	d	08 57	09 03	09 15	09 19	09 30	09 31	09 49	09 57	10 03	10 15	10 19	10 30	10 31	10 49	10 57	11 03	11 15	11 19	11 30	11 31	11 49	11 57
Tamworth	d				09 36			10 07		10 19		10 36			11 09				11 36			12 07	
Burton-on-Trent	d		09 27		09 48			10 19				10 48			11 21		11 26		11 48			12 19	
Derby	a		09 46		10 00	10 12		10 37		10 45		11 00	11 12		11 35		11 47		12 00	12 12		12 36	
Nottingham	a				10 31			11 03				11 29			12 07				12 30			13 03	
Chesterfield	a		10 33			11 01				11 27			12 00				12 30			13 01			
Sheffield	a		10 48			11 17				11 46			12 17				12 46			13 17			
Doncaster	a		11 16							12 16							13 16						
Wakefield Westgate	a					11 46							12 46							13 46			
Leeds	a					12 01							13 00							14 00			
York	a		11 40			12 30				12 40			13 30				13 40			14 30			
Darlington	a		12 12			12 58				13 13			14 02				14 12			14 58			
Durham	a		12 29			13 15				13 31			14 18				14 30			15 15			
Chester-le-Street	a																						
Newcastle	a		12 42			13 29				13 45			14 32				14 43			15 30			
Morpeth	a												14 47										
Alnmouth for Alnwick	a					14 02														16 01			
Berwick-upon-Tweed	a					14 23														16 23			
Dunbar	a												15 41										
Wolverhampton	d	09 15		09 37			09 49		10 15		10 37			10 49		11 15		11 37			11 49		12 15
Stafford	a	09 27					10 01		10 27					11 02		11 27					12 02		12 27
Stoke-on-Trent	a	09 43					10 17		10 43					11 18		11 43					12 18		12 43
Congleton	a																						
Macclesfield	a	10 01					10 36		11 01					11 36		12 01					12 36		13 01
Crewe	a			10 08							11 08							12 07					
Wilmslow	a																						
Stockport	a	10 13					10 49		11 13					11 49		12 13					12 49		13 12
M'chester Piccadilly	a	10 25					11 00		11 24					11 59		12 25					12 59		13 25
Warrington Bank Quay	a			10 26							11 26							12 26					
Wigan North Western	a			10 37							11 37							12 37					
Preston	a			10 51							11 51							12 51					
Lancaster	a			11 07							12 07							13 07					
Oxenholme Lake District	a										12 20							13 21					
Penrith North Lakes	a			11 44																			
Carlisle	a			12 00							12 59							13 59					
Lockerbie	a																						
Haymarket	a										14 12												
Edinburgh	a					15 08					14 19		16 06							17 05			
Haymarket	a					15 16														17 15			
Motherwell	a					15 54												14 58		17 55			
Glasgow Central	a			13 15		16 12												15 15		18 11			
Inverkeithing	a																						
Kirkcaldy	a																						
Markinch	a																						
Ladybank	a																						
Cupar	a																						
Leuchars	a																						
Dundee	a																						
Arbroath	a																						
Montrose	a																						
Stonehaven	a																						
Aberdeen	a																						

A from Reading
B to Edinburgh
C from Bristol Temple Meads
D from Newton Abbot

Table T051-R

Mondays to Fridays
3 September to 5 October

South Coast and the South West - North West England, The North East and Scotland

		XC	VT	XC	XC	XC	XC	XC	XC	VT	XC	XC	XC	XC	XC	XC	VT	XC	XC	XC	XC	XC
					A											B			A			
Bournemouth	d							09 45							10 45							11 45
Brockenhurst	d							10 00							11 00							12 00
Southampton Central	d				09 46			10 17							11 17				11 46			12 17
Southampton Airport Pkway	d				09 55			10 24							11 24				11 53			12 24
Winchester	d				10 03			10 33							11 33				12 02			12 33
Basingstoke	d				10 19			10 49							11 49				12 18			12 49
Guildford	d																					
Reading	d				10 45			11 15				11 45			12 15				12 45			13 15
Oxford	d				11 13			11 39				12 13			12 39				13 13			13 39
Banbury	d				11 30			11 57				12 32			12 57				13 31			13 57
Leamington Spa	d				11 48			12 14				12 50			13 14				13 48			14 14
Coventry	d		11 42					12 27		12 42					13 27		13 42					14 27
Birmingham International	d		11 53					12 38		12 53					13 38		13 53					14 38
Penzance	d	06 28														08 28						
St Erth	d	06 36														08 36						
Hayle	d																					
Camborne	d	06 46														08 46						
Redruth	d	06 52														08 52						
Truro	d	07 04														09 04						
St Austell	d	07 20														09 20						
Par	d	07 27														09 27						
Lostwithiel	d																					
Bodmin Parkway	d	07 37														09 37						
Liskeard	d	07 53														09 50						
Plymouth	d	08 25							09 25							10 25						
Totnes	d	08 50							09 50							10 50						
Paignton	d												10 07									
Torquay	d												10 13									
Newton Abbot	d	09 03							10 03				10 24			11 03						
Teignmouth	d												10 31									
Dawlish	d												10 36									
Exeter St Davids	d	09 24							10 23				10 50			11 24						
Tiverton Parkway	d	09 38							10 37				11 03			11 37						
Taunton	d	09 51							10 51				11 17			11 51						
Weston-super-Mare	d																					
Cardiff Central	d						10 45							11 45							12 45	
Newport (South Wales)	d						11 00							12 00							13 01	
Bristol Temple Meads	d	10 30				11 00			11 30				12 00			12 30				13 00		
Bristol Parkway	d	10 40				11 10			11 40				12 10			12 40				13 10		
Gloucester	d						11 50							12 48							13 50	
Cheltenham Spa	d	11 11				11 42	12 01		12 11				12 41	12 58		13 11				13 41	14 01	
Birmingham New Street	a	11 58	12 05		12 18	12 26	12 45	12 48	12 56	13 05		13 18	13 26	13 45	13 48	13 56	14 05		14 18	14 23	14 45	14 48
Birmingham New Street	d	12 03	12 15	12 19	12 30	12 31	12 49	12 57	13 03	13 15	13 19	13 30	13 31	13 49	13 57	14 03	14 15	14 19	14 30	14 31	14 49	14 57
Tamworth	d	12 19		12 36			13 09				13 36			14 09		14 19		14 36			15 09	
Burton-on-Trent	d			12 48			13 19		13 28		13 48			14 21				14 48			15 21	
Derby	a	12 46		13 00	13 13		13 35		13 39		14 00	14 12		14 35		14 43		15 00	15 12		15 34	
Nottingham	a			13 31			14 03				14 32			15 03				15 29			16 03	
Chesterfield	a	13 32			14 01				14 25			15 01				15 26			16 01			
Sheffield	a	13 46			14 17				14 46			15 17				15 46			16 18			
Doncaster	a	14 16							15 16							16 17						
Wakefield Westgate	a				14 46							15 46							16 46			
Leeds	a				15 00							16 00							17 00			
York	a	14 40			15 30				15 40			16 30				16 40			17 30			
Darlington	a	15 13			15 58				16 13			16 58				17 13			17 58			
Durham	a	15 31			16 15				16 31			17 15				17 31			18 15			
Chester-le-Street	a																					
Newcastle	a	15 46			16 29				16 46			17 31				17 46			18 33			
Morpeth	a				16 47																	
Alnmouth for Alnwick	a				17 02							18 01										
Berwick-upon-Tweed	a											18 23							19 22			
Dunbar	a				17 44														19 45			
Wolverhampton	d		12 37			12 49		13 15		13 37			13 49		14 15		14 37			14 49		15 15
Stafford	a					13 02		13 27					14 02		14 27					15 02		15 27
Stoke-on-Trent	a					13 18		13 43					14 18		14 43					15 18		15 43
Congleton	a																					
Macclesfield	a					13 36		14 01					14 36		15 01					15 36		16 01
Crewe	a		13 08							14 07							15 07					
Wilmslow	a																					
Stockport	a					13 49		14 13					14 49		15 13					15 49		16 13
M'chester Piccadilly	a					13 59		14 25					14 59		15 25					15 59		16 25
Warrington Bank Quay	a		13 26							14 26							15 26					
Wigan North Western	a		13 37							14 37							15 37					
Preston	a		13 51							14 51							15 51					
Lancaster	a		14 07							15 07							16 07					
Oxenholme Lake District	a									15 21												
Penrith North Lakes	a		14 42														16 44					
Carlisle	a		14 59							16 00							17 00					
Lockerbie	a																					
Haymarket	a		16 13														18 14					
Edinburgh	a		16 20		18 07							19 05					18 22		20 08			
Haymarket	a				18 13							19 15							20 16			
Motherwell	a											19 54										
Glasgow Central	a									17 15		20 15										
Inverkeithing	a				18 28														20 30			
Kirkcaldy	a				18 46																	
Markinch	a				18 56														21 00			
Ladybank	a				19 04														21 08			
Cupar	a				19 15														21 19			
Leuchars	a				19 22														21 26			
Dundee	a				19 35														21 43			
Arbroath	a				19 51																	
Montrose	a				20 05																	
Stonehaven	a				20 26																	
Aberdeen	a				20 48																	

A to Edinburgh
B ◇ from Plymouth ■ to Plymouth

South Coast and the South West - North West England, The North East and Scotland

Station		XC	VT	XC	XC	XC	XC	XC	XC	VT	XC	XC	XC	XC	XC	XC	VT	XC	XC	XC	XC	XC	XC
					A	B			C										D				
Bournemouth	d							12 45							13 45								14 45
Brockenhurst	d							13 00							14 00								15 00
Southampton Central	d							13 16				13 46			14 17								15 16
Southampton Airport Pkway	d							13 23				13 54			14 24								15 23
Winchester	d							13 32				14 03			14 33								15 32
Basingstoke	d							13 49				14 19			14 49								15 48
Guildford	d																						
Reading	d				13 45			14 15				14 45			15 15				15 45				16 15
Oxford	d				14 13			14 39				15 13			15 39				16 13				16 39
Banbury	d				14 31			14 57				15 32			15 57				16 31				16 57
Leamington Spa	d				14 50			15 14				15 50			16 14				16 48				17 14
Coventry	d		14 42					15 27		15 42					16 27		16 42						17 27
Birmingham International	d		14 53					15 38		15 53					16 38		16 53						17 38
Penzance	d					09 35																	
St Erth	d					09 43																	
Hayle	d					09 47																	
Camborne	d					09 56																	
Redruth	d					10 03																	
Truro	d					10 15																	
St Austell	d					10 31																	
Par	d					10 38																	
Lostwithiel	d					10 45																	
Bodmin Parkway	d					10 51																	
Liskeard	d					11 04																	
Plymouth	d	11 25				11 50			12 25							13 25							
Totnes	d	11 50				12 15			12 51							13 51							
Paignton	d																			14 04			
Torquay	d																			14 10			
Newton Abbot	d	12 03				12 28			13 04							14 04				14 21			
Teignmouth	d																			14 28			
Dawlish	d																			14 33			
Exeter St Davids	d	12 24				12 50			13 24							14 24				14 48			
Tiverton Parkway	d	12 38				13 06			13 38							14 38				15 02			
Taunton	d	12 51				13 22			13 51							14 51				15 15			
Weston-super-Mare	d																			15 39			
Cardiff Central	d						13 45							14 45								15 45	
Newport (South Wales)	d						14 00							15 00								16 00	
Bristol Temple Meads	d	13 30				14 00			14 30				15 00			15 30				16 00			
Bristol Parkway	d	13 40				14 10			14 40				15 10			15 40				16 10			
Gloucester	d						14 50							15 50								16 50	
Cheltenham Spa	d	14 11				14 41	15 01		15 11				15 42	16 01		16 11				16 41		17 01	
Birmingham New Street	a	14 56	15 05		15 18	15 23	15 45	15 48	15 56	16 05		16 18	16 23	16 45	16 48	16 56	17 05		17 18	17 23		17 45	17 48
Birmingham New Street	d	15 03	15 15	15 19	15 30	15 31	15 49	15 57	16 03	16 15	16 19	16 30	16 31	16 49	16 57	17 03	17 15	17 19	17 30	17 31	17 39	17 49	17 57
Tamworth	d			15 36			16 09		16 20		16 36			17 09				17 36			18 03	18 09	
Burton-on-Trent	d	15 26		15 48			16 21				16 48			17 21		17 26		17 48			18 14	18 21	
Derby	a	15 44		16 02	16 14		16 35		16 42		17 00	17 12		17 35		17 44		18 01	18 12		18 29	18 34	
Nottingham	a			16 29			17 03				17 32			18 04				18 35				19 03	
Chesterfield	a	16 25			17 02				17 33			18 01				18 29			19 01				
Sheffield	a	16 48			17 18				17 48			18 18				18 44			19 18				
Doncaster	a	17 13														19 17							
Wakefield Westgate	a				17 45				18 16			18 48							19 46				
Leeds	a				18 00				18 34			19 03							20 02				
York	a	17 42			18 30				19 01			19 30				19 41			20 30				
Darlington	a	18 14			19 00				19 33			20 03				20 12			20 59				
Durham	a	18 31			19 19				19 50			20 21				20 29			21 17				
Chester-le-Street	a																						
Newcastle	a	18 47			19 33				20 04			20 35				20 44			21 33				
Morpeth	a											20 53											
Alnmouth for Alnwick	a				20 01				20 31										21 59				
Berwick-upon-Tweed	a				20 25							21 26											
Dunbar	a											21 50											
Wolverhampton	d		15 37			15 49		16 15		16 37			16 49		17 15		17 37			17 49			18 15
Stafford	a					16 02		16 27					17 02		17 27					18 02			18 27
Stoke-on-Trent	a					16 18		16 43					17 18		17 43					18 18			18 43
Congleton	a																						
Macclesfield	a					16 36		17 01					17 36		18 01					18 36			19 01
Crewe	a		16 07							17 08							18 08						
Wilmslow	a																						
Stockport	a					16 49		17 13					17 49		18 13					18 49			19 13
M'chester Piccadilly	a					16 59		17 25					17 59		18 25					18 59			19 24
Warrington Bank Quay	a		16 26							17 26							18 26						
Wigan North Western	a		16 37							17 37							18 37						
Preston	a		16 51							17 52							18 51						
Lancaster	a		17 07							18 08							19 07						
Oxenholme Lake District	a		17 21							18 23							19 21						
Penrith North Lakes	a		17 46							18 47													
Carlisle	a		18 03							19 04							20 00						
Lockerbie	a																						
Haymarket	a									20 14													
Edinburgh	a				21 08				21 35	20 23		22 13							23 03				
Haymarket	a				21 17																		
Motherwell	a				22 04																		
Glasgow Central	a		19 23		22 21												21 15						
Inverkeithing	a																						
Kirkcaldy	a																						
Markinch	a																						
Ladybank	a																						
Cupar	a																						
Leuchars	a																						
Dundee	a																						
Arbroath	a																						
Montrose	a																						
Stonehaven	a																						
Aberdeen	a																						

A to Edinburgh
B ◇ from Plymouth ■ to Plymouth
C to Newcastle
D to Leeds

South Coast and the South West - North West England, The North East and Scotland

Station		XC	VT	XC	XC	XC	XC	XC	XC	VT	XC	XC	XC	XC	XC	XC	VT	XC	XC	XC	XC	XC
							A					A		A		A				A	A	A
Bournemouth	d							15 45							16 45						17 45	
Brockenhurst	d							16 00							17 00						18 00	
Southampton Central	d				15 46			16 17							17 17			17 46			18 15	
Southampton Airport Pkway	d				15 53			16 24							17 24			17 53			18 22	
Winchester	d				16 02			16 33							17 33			18 02			18 31	
Basingstoke	d				16 18			16 49							17 49			18 18			18 47	
Guildford	d																					
Reading	d				16 45			17 15				17 45			18 15			18 45			19 15	
Oxford	d				17 13			17 39				18 10			18 39			19 13			19 39	
Banbury	d				17 33			17 57				18 27			18 57			19 30			19 57	
Leamington Spa	d				17 51			18 14				18 45			19 14			19 48			20 14	
Coventry	d		17 42					18 27		18 42					19 27		19 42				20 27	
Birmingham International	d		17 53					18 38		18 53					19 38		19 53				20 38	
Penzance	d																					
St Erth	d																					
Hayle	d																					
Camborne	d																					
Redruth	d																					
Truro	d																					
St Austell	d																					
Par	d																					
Lostwithiel	d																					
Bodmin Parkway	d																					
Liskeard	d																					
Plymouth	d	14 25							15 25							16 25						17 25
Totnes	d	14 50							15 51							16 50						17 51
Paignton	d																					
Torquay	d																					
Newton Abbot	d	15 03							16 04							17 03						18 04
Teignmouth	d																					
Dawlish	d																					
Exeter St Davids	d	15 24							16 24				16 54			17 24						18 25
Tiverton Parkway	d	15 37							16 38				17 08			17 37						18 39
Taunton	d	15 51							16 51				17 22			17 50						18 52
Weston-super-Mare	d																					
Cardiff Central	d						16 45							17 45						18 45		
Newport (South Wales)	d						17 00							18 00						19 00		
Bristol Temple Meads	d	16 30				17 00			17 30				18 00			18 30			19 00			19 30
Bristol Parkway	d	16 40				17 10			17 40				18 10			18 40			19 10			19 40
Gloucester	d						17 50							18 46						19 45		
Cheltenham Spa	d	17 11				17 42	18 01		18 11				18 41	18 57		19 11			19 41	19 58		20 11
Birmingham New Street	a	17 56	18 05		18 18	18 23	18 45	18 48	18 56	19 05		19 18	19 23	19 45	19 48	19 56	20 06	20 18	20 23	20 40	20 48	20 51
Birmingham New Street	d	18 03	18 15	18 19	18 30	18 31	18 49	18 57	19 03	19 15	19 19	19 30	19 31	19 49	19 57	20 03	20 15		20 31	20 49	20 57	21 03
Tamworth	d	18 19		18 36			19 09				19 36			20 09		20 19				21 09		21 19
Burton-on-Trent	d			18 48			19 21		19 29		19 48			20 21		20 30				21 21		21 30
Derby	a	18 41		19 00	19 12		19 35		19 43		20 02	20 13		20 34		20 42				21 33		21 42
Nottingham	a			19 31			20 04				20 30			21 04						22 10		
Chesterfield	a	19 24			20 00				20 29			21 03				21 30						22 25
Sheffield	a	19 40			20 18				20 49			21 18				21 50						22 44
Doncaster	a	20 13							21 19							22 25						
Wakefield Westgate	a				20 46							21 46										23 12
Leeds	a				21 01							22 02										23 26
York	a	20 41							21 40							22 51						
Darlington	a	21 14							22 12													
Durham	a	21 31							22 29													
Chester-le-Street	a																					
Newcastle	a	21 45							22 48													
Morpeth	a																					
Alnmouth for Alnwick	a																					
Berwick-upon-Tweed	a																					
Dunbar	a																					
Wolverhampton	d		18 37			18 49		19 15		19 37			19 49		20 15		20 37		20 49		21 15	
Stafford	a					19 02		19 27					20 02		20 27		20 50		21 02		21 28	
Stoke-on-Trent	a					19 18		19 43					20 19		20 43				21 18		21 45	
Congleton	a																					
Macclesfield	a					19 36		20 01					20 36		21 01				21 36		22 02	
Crewe	a		19 07							20 07							21 15					
Wilmslow	a																					
Stockport	a					19 49		20 13					20 48		21 13				21 49		22 15	
M'chester Piccadilly	a					19 59		20 25					20 59		21 25				21 59		22 25	
Warrington Bank Quay	a		19 26							20 26												
Wigan North Western	a		19 37							20 37												
Preston	a		19 51							20 51												
Lancaster	a		20 07							21 07												
Oxenholme Lake District	a									21 22												
Penrith North Lakes	a		20 44																			
Carlisle	a		21 00							22 00												
Lockerbie	a																					
Haymarket	a		22 13																			
Edinburgh	a		22 19																			
Haymarket	a																					
Motherwell	a																					
Glasgow Central	a									23 17												
Inverkeithing	a																					
Kirkcaldy	a																					
Markinch	a																					
Ladybank	a																					
Cupar	a																					
Leuchars	a																					
Dundee	a																					
Arbroath	a																					
Montrose	a																					
Stonehaven	a																					
Aberdeen	a																					

A to Birmingham New Street

Table T051-R

Mondays to Fridays
3 September to 5 October

South Coast and the South West - North West England, The North East and Scotland

		VT	XC	XC	XC	XC	XC	XC	XC	XC	XC	XC	XC	XC	XC	XC
		◇1	◇1	◇1	◇1	◇1	◇1	1	◇1	◇1	◇1	◇1	1	◇1	◇1	◇1
					A ✠		B ✠									
Bournemouth	d				18 45						19 45					
Brockenhurst	d				19 00						20 00					
Southampton Central	d				19 16						20 17					
Southampton Airport Pkway	d				19 23						20 24					
Winchester	d				19 32						20 33					
Basingstoke	d				19 49						20 49					
Guildford	d															
Reading	d		19 45		20 12				20 45		21 11				21 45	
Oxford	d		20 13		20 39				21 14		21 36				22 30	
Banbury	d		20 32		20 57				21 33		21 54				22 48	
Leamington Spa	d		20 50		21 14				21 53		22 12				23 05	
Coventry	d	20 42			21 27						22 25				23 17	
Birmingham International	d	20 53			21 38						22 35				23 27	
Penzance	d															
St Erth	d															
Hayle	d															
Camborne	d															
Redruth	d															
Truro	d															
St Austell	d															
Par	d															
Lostwithiel	d															
Bodmin Parkway	d															
Liskeard	d															
Plymouth	d						18 25									
Totnes	d						18 50									
Paignton	d													20 14		
Torquay	d													20 20		
Newton Abbot	d						19 03							20 31		
Teignmouth	d															
Dawlish	d															
Exeter St Davids	d						19 24							20 52		
Tiverton Parkway	d						19 37							21 05		
Taunton	d						19 51							21 19		
Weston-super-Mare	d															
Cardiff Central	d					19 50						21 05				21 50
Newport (South Wales)	d					20 05						21 21				22 05
Bristol Temple Meads	d			20 00			20 30							22 00		
Bristol Parkway	d			20 10			20 40							22 10		
Gloucester	d			20 46		20 59						22 04				22 47
Cheltenham Spa	d			20 56		21 11	21 17					22 15		22 42		22 58
Birmingham New Street	a	21 04	21 23	21 37	21 48	21 51	22 02		22 18		22 45	23 05		23 43	23 56	23 59
Birmingham New Street	d	21 15			21 57			22 03		22 30			23 09			
Tamworth	d							22 27					23 28			
Burton-on-Trent	d							22 39					23 40			
Derby	a							22 51					23 53			
Nottingham	a							23 27					00 16			
Chesterfield	a															
Sheffield	a															
Doncaster	a															
Wakefield Westgate	a															
Leeds	a															
York	a															
Darlington	a															
Durham	a															
Chester-le-Street	a															
Newcastle	a															
Morpeth	a															
Alnmouth for Alnwick	a															
Berwick-upon-Tweed	a															
Dunbar	a															
Wolverhampton	d	21 37			22 15					22 48						
Stafford	a	21 52			22 27					23 00						
Stoke-on-Trent	a	22 10			22 43					23 17						
Congleton	a															
Macclesfield	a				23 01											
Crewe	a	22 30														
Wilmslow	a															
Stockport	a				23 13											
M'chester Piccadilly	a				23 25					00 11						
Warrington Bank Quay	a															
Wigan North Western	a															
Preston	a															
Lancaster	a															
Oxenholme Lake District	a															
Penrith North Lakes	a															
Carlisle	a															
Lockerbie	a															
Haymarket	a															
Edinburgh	a															
Haymarket	a															
Motherwell	a															
Glasgow Central	a															
Inverkeithing	a															
Kirkcaldy	a															
Markinch	a															
Ladybank	a															
Cupar	a															
Leuchars	a															
Dundee	a															
Arbroath	a															
Montrose	a															
Stonehaven	a															
Aberdeen	a															

A ✠ to Reading
B ✠ to Bristol Temple Meads

Table T051-R

Mondays to Fridays
8 October to 7 December

South Coast and the South West - North West England, The North East and Scotland

		XC	XC	VT	XC	XC	XC	XC	XC	XC	VT	XC	XC	XC	XC	XC	XC	VT	XC	XC	XC	XC	XC
		◇1	◇1	◇1	1	◇1	◇1	1	◇1	◇1	◇1	1	◇1	◇1	1	◇1	◇1	◇1	1	◇1	◇1	◇1	◇1
			A ✠	⊠		✠	✠		✠	✠	⊠	✠	✠	✠		B ✠	✠	⊠	✠	B ✠		✠	
Bournemouth	d																						
Brockenhurst	d																						
Southampton Central	d															05 15							
Southampton Airport Pkway	d															05 22							
Winchester	d															05 31							
Basingstoke	d															05 47							
Guildford	d																			06 01			
Reading	d															06 15				06 45			
Oxford	d															06 38				07 08			
Banbury	d															06 57				07 26			
Leamington Spa	d															07 14				07 43			
Coventry	d															07 27		07 42					
Birmingham International	d															07 38		07 53					
Penzance	d																						
St Erth	d																						
Hayle	d																						
Camborne	d																						
Redruth	d																						
Truro	d																						
St Austell	d																						
Par	d																						
Lostwithiel	d																						
Bodmin Parkway	d																						
Liskeard	d																						
Plymouth	d																						
Totnes	d																						
Paignton	d																						
Torquay	d																						
Newton Abbot	d																						
Teignmouth	d																						
Dawlish	d																						
Exeter St Davids	d																						
Tiverton Parkway	d																						
Taunton	d																						
Weston-super-Mare	d																						
Cardiff Central	d																						06 40
Newport (South Wales)	d																						06 55
Bristol Temple Meads	d																06 27					07 00	
Bristol Parkway	d																06 39					07 10	
Gloucester	d																				07 10		07 46
Cheltenham Spa	d																07 10				07 21	07 41	07 57
Birmingham New Street	a															07 48	07 56	08 09		08 12	08 17	08 26	08 45
Birmingham New Street	d	05 57	06 00	06 15	06 19	06 30	06 30	06 49	06 51	07 03	07 15	07 19	07 30	07 31	07 49	07 57	08 03	08 15	08 19	08 30		08 31	08 49
Tamworth	d				06 39			07 07		07 19		07 39			08 07		08 19		08 36				09 09
Burton-on-Trent	d				06 51			07 20		07 31		07 50			08 19		08 29		08 48				09 20
Derby	a		06 33		07 04		07 11	07 35		07 42		08 04	08 09		08 36		08 41		09 01	09 05			09 33
Nottingham	a				07 38			08 12				08 34			09 07				09 28				10 05
Chesterfield	a		06 58				07 31			08 02			08 31				09 02						
Sheffield	a		07 15				07 45			08 19			08 48				09 17			09 50			
Doncaster	a						08 14						09 16							10 17			
Wakefield Westgate	a		07 47							08 47							09 46						
Leeds	a		08 01							09 02							10 00						
York	a		08 29				08 40			09 30			09 40				10 30			10 40			
Darlington	a		08 57				09 16			09 58			10 12				10 58			11 13			
Durham	a		09 13				09 33			10 17			10 29				11 15			11 31			
Chester-le-Street	a																						
Newcastle	a		09 28				09 47			10 31			10 43				11 29			11 46			
Morpeth	a																11 49						
Alnmouth for Alnwick	a		09 59																				
Berwick-upon-Tweed	a		10 21														12 23						
Dunbar	a									11 38													
Wolverhampton	d	06 15		06 37		06 48			07 10		07 37			07 49		08 15		08 37				08 49	
Stafford	a	06 27				06 59			07 21					08 02		08 27						09 02	
Stoke-on-Trent	a	06 44				07 19								08 18		08 43						09 18	
Congleton	a	06 56																					
Macclesfield	a	07 05				07 37								08 36		09 01						09 36	
Crewe	a			07 08					07 42		08 08							09 07					
Wilmslow	a								08 00														
Stockport	a	07 19				07 49			08 13					08 49		09 13						09 49	
M'chester Piccadilly	a	07 28				07 59			08 24					08 59		09 25						09 59	
Warrington Bank Quay	a			07 26							08 26							09 26					
Wigan North Western	a			07 37							08 37							09 37					
Preston	a			07 51							08 51							09 51					
Lancaster	a			08 07							09 07							10 07					
Oxenholme Lake District	a			08 21														10 21					
Penrith North Lakes	a										09 43												
Carlisle	a			09 00							09 59							10 59					
Lockerbie	a																						
Haymarket	a			10 12														12 16					
Edinburgh	a		11 06	10 18						12 03							13 06	12 22					
Haymarket	a		11 15														13 16						
Motherwell	a		11 54														13 54						
Glasgow Central	a		12 12								11 15						14 12						
Inverkeithing	a																						
Kirkcaldy	a																						
Markinch	a																						
Ladybank	a																						
Cupar	a																						
Leuchars	a																						
Dundee	a																						
Arbroath	a																						
Montrose	a																						
Stonehaven	a																						
Aberdeen	a																						

A ✠ to Edinburgh
B ✠ from Reading

South Coast and the South West - North West England, The North East and Scotland

		XC	XC	VT	XC	XC	XC	XC	XC	XC	VT	XC	XC	XC	XC	XC	XC	VT	XC	XC	XC	XC	XC
		◇■ A ⊼	◇■ ⊼	◇■ ⊠	■ ⊼	◇■ ⊼	◇■ B ⊼	◇■	◇■ ⊼	◇■ C ⊼	◇■ ⊠	■ ⊼	◇■ A ⊼	◇■ D ⊼	◇■	◇■ ⊼	◇■ ⊼	◇■ ⊠	■ ⊼	◇■ ⊼	◇■ ⊼	◇■ ⊼	■ ■ ⊼
Bournemouth	d								06 30							07 30							08 45
Brockenhurst	d								06 45							07 50							09 00
Southampton Central	d	06 15							07 15							08 15							09 16
Southampton Airport Pkway	d	06 22							07 22							08 22							09 23
Winchester	d	06 31							07 31				08 12			08 31							09 32
Basingstoke	d	06 47							07 47				08 28			08 47							09 49
Guildford	d																						
Reading	d	07 15				07 46			08 15				08 50			09 15				09 45			10 15
Oxford	d	07 39				08 12			08 39				09 15			09 39				10 15			10 39
Banbury	d	07 57				08 30			08 57				09 34			09 57				10 32			10 57
Leamington Spa	d	08 14				08 47			09 14				09 51			10 14				10 50			11 14
Coventry	d	08 27		08 42					09 27		09 42					10 27		10 42					11 27
Birmingham International	d	08 38		08 53					09 38		09 53					10 38		10 53					11 38
Penzance	d																						
St Erth	d																						
Hayle	d																						
Camborne	d																						
Redruth	d																						
Truro	d																						
St Austell	d																						
Par	d																						
Lostwithiel	d																						
Bodmin Parkway	d																						
Liskeard	d																						
Plymouth	d		05 20							06 25							07 25						
Totnes	d		05 45							06 50							07 50						
Paignton	d													07 01									
Torquay	d													07 07									
Newton Abbot	d		06 02							07 03				07 18			08 03						
Teignmouth	d													07 25									
Dawlish	d													07 30									
Exeter St Davids	d		06 24							07 24				07 44			08 24						
Tiverton Parkway	d		06 37							07 37				07 57			08 37						
Taunton	d		06 51							07 51				08 12			08 51						
Weston-super-Mare	d													08 35									
Cardiff Central	d						07 00	07 45							08 45							09 45	
Newport (South Wales)	d						07 14	08 02							09 00							10 00	
Bristol Temple Meads	d		07 30				08 00			08 30				09 00			09 30				10 00		
Bristol Parkway	d		07 40				08 10			08 40				09 10			09 40				10 10		
Gloucester	d							08 49							09 50							10 50	
Cheltenham Spa	d		08 11				08 41	09 00		09 12				09 42	10 01		10 11				10 41	11 01	
Birmingham New Street	a	08 48	08 56	09 05		09 18	09 26	09 45	09 49	09 58	10 04		10 18	10 23	10 45	10 48	10 56	11 04		11 18	11 26	11 45	11 48
Birmingham New Street	d	08 57	09 03	09 15	09 19	09 30	09 31	09 49	09 57	10 03	10 15	10 19	10 30	10 31	10 49	10 57	11 03	11 15	11 19	11 30	11 31	11 49	11 57
Tamworth	d				09 36			10 07		10 19		10 36			11 09				11 36			12 07	
Burton-on-Trent	d		09 27		09 48			10 19				10 48			11 21		11 26		11 48			12 19	
Derby	a		09 41		10 01	10 05		10 37		10 41		11 01	11 05		11 35		11 40		12 01	12 05		12 36	
Nottingham	a				10 28			11 04				11 28			12 07				12 28			13 03	
Chesterfield	a		10 02							11 01							12 02						
Sheffield	a		10 18			10 48				11 17			11 46				12 17			12 46			
Doncaster	a					11 16							12 16							13 16			
Wakefield Westgate	a		10 46							11 46							12 46						
Leeds	a		11 00							12 01							13 00						
York	a		11 30			11 40				12 30			12 40				13 30			13 40			
Darlington	a		11 58			12 12				12 58			13 13				14 02			14 12			
Durham	a		12 15			12 29				13 15			13 31				14 18			14 30			
Chester-le-Street	a																						
Newcastle	a		12 30			12 42				13 29			13 45				14 32			14 43			
Morpeth	a																14 47						
Alnmouth for Alnwick	a									14 02													
Berwick-upon-Tweed	a									14 23													
Dunbar	a		13 41														15 41						
Wolverhampton	d	09 15		09 37			09 49		10 15		10 37			10 49		11 15		11 37			11 49		12 15
Stafford	a	09 27					10 01		10 27					11 02		11 27					12 02		12 27
Stoke-on-Trent	a	09 43					10 17		10 43					11 18		11 43					12 18		12 43
Congleton	a																						
Macclesfield	a	10 01					10 36		11 01					11 36		12 01					12 36		13 01
Crewe	a			10 08							11 08							12 07					
Wilmslow	a																						
Stockport	a	10 13					10 49		11 13					11 49		12 13					12 49		13 12
M'chester Piccadilly	a	10 25					11 00		11 24					11 59		12 25					12 59		13 25
Warrington Bank Quay	a			10 26							11 26							12 26					
Wigan North Western	a			10 37							11 37							12 37					
Preston	a			10 51							11 51							12 51					
Lancaster	a			11 07							12 07							13 07					
Oxenholme Lake District	a										12 20							13 21					
Penrith North Lakes	a			11 44																			
Carlisle	a			12 00							12 59							13 59					
Lockerbie	a																						
Haymarket	a										14 12												
Edinburgh	a		14 07							15 08	14 19						16 06						
Haymarket	a									15 16													
Motherwell	a									15 54								14 58					
Glasgow Central	a			13 15						16 12								15 15					
Inverkeithing	a																						
Kirkcaldy	a																						
Markinch	a																						
Ladybank	a																						
Cupar	a																						
Leuchars	a																						
Dundee	a																						
Arbroath	a																						
Montrose	a																						
Stonehaven	a																						
Aberdeen	a																						

A ⊼ from Reading
B ⊼ from Bristol Temple Meads
C ⊼ to Edinburgh
D ⊼ from Newton Abbot

South Coast and the South West - North West England, The North East and Scotland

		XC	VT	XC	XC	XC	XC	XC	XC	VT	XC	XC	XC	XC	XC	XC	VT	XC	XC	XC	XC	XC
		◇■ A ⊼	◇■ ℝ	■ ⊼	◇■ ⊼	◇■ ⊼	◇■	◇■ ⊼	◇■ B ⊼	◇■ ⊠	■ ⊼	◇■ ⊼	◇■ ⊼	◇■ ⊼	◇■ ⊼	■ ◇■ C ⊼	◇■ ⊠	■	■ ■ ⊼	◇■ ⊼	◇■ ⊼	◇■ ⊼
Bournemouth	d							09 45							10 45							11 45
Brockenhurst	d							10 00							11 00							12 00
Southampton Central	d				09 46			10 17							11 17				11 46			12 17
Southampton Airport Pkway	d				09 55			10 24							11 24				11 53			12 24
Winchester	d				10 03			10 33							11 33				12 02			12 33
Basingstoke	d				10 19			10 49							11 49				12 18			12 49
Guildford	d																					
Reading	d				10 45			11 15				11 45			12 15				12 45			13 15
Oxford	d				11 13			11 39				12 13			12 39				13 13			13 39
Banbury	d				11 30			11 57				12 32			12 57				13 31			13 57
Leamington Spa	d				11 48			12 14				12 50			13 14				13 48			14 14
Coventry	d		11 42					12 27		12 42					13 27		13 42					14 27
Birmingham International	d		11 53					12 38		12 53					13 38		13 53					14 38
Penzance	d	06 28														08 28						
St Erth	d	06 36														08 36						
Hayle	d																					
Camborne	d	06 46														08 46						
Redruth	d	06 52														08 52						
Truro	d	07 04														09 04						
St Austell	d	07 20														09 20						
Par	d	07 27														09 27						
Lostwithiel	d																					
Bodmin Parkway	d	07 37														09 37						
Liskeard	d	07 53														09 50						
Plymouth	d	08 25							09 25							10 25						
Totnes	d	08 50							09 50							10 50						
Paignton	d												10 07									
Torquay	d												10 13									
Newton Abbot	d	09 03							10 03				10 24			11 03						
Teignmouth	d												10 31									
Dawlish	d												10 36									
Exeter St Davids	d	09 24							10 23				10 50			11 24						
Tiverton Parkway	d	09 38							10 37				11 03			11 37						
Taunton	d	09 51							10 51				11 17			11 51						
Weston-super-Mare	d																					
Cardiff Central	d						10 45							11 45							12 45	
Newport (South Wales)	d						11 00							12 00							13 01	
Bristol Temple Meads	d	10 30				11 00			11 30				12 00			12 30				13 00		
Bristol Parkway	d	10 40				11 10			11 40				12 10			12 40				13 10		
Gloucester	d						11 50							12 48							13 50	
Cheltenham Spa	d	11 11				11 42	12 01		12 11				12 41	12 58		13 11				13 41	14 01	
Birmingham New Street	a	11 58	12 05		12 18	12 26	12 45	12 48	12 56	13 05		13 18	13 26	13 45	13 48	13 56	14 05		14 18	14 23	14 45	14 48
Birmingham New Street	d	12 03	12 15	12 19	12 30	12 31	12 49	12 57	13 03	13 15	13 19	13 30	13 31	13 49	13 57	14 03	14 15	14 19	14 30	14 31	14 49	14 57
Tamworth	d	12 19		12 36			13 09				13 36			14 09		14 19		14 36			15 09	
Burton-on-Trent	d			12 48			13 19		13 28		13 48			14 21				14 48			15 21	
Derby	a	12 41		13 01	13 05		13 36		13 39		14 01	14 05		14 35		14 41		15 01	15 05		15 34	
Nottingham	a			13 28			14 03				14 28			15 03				15 28			16 03	
Chesterfield	a	13 02							14 02							15 02						
Sheffield	a	13 17			13 46				14 17			14 46				15 17			15 46			
Doncaster	a				14 16							15 16							16 17			
Wakefield Westgate	a	13 46							14 46							15 46						
Leeds	a	14 00							15 00							16 00						
York	a	14 30			14 40				15 30			15 40				16 30			16 40			
Darlington	a	14 58			15 13				15 58			16 13				16 58			17 13			
Durham	a	15 15			15 31				16 15			16 31				17 15			17 31			
Chester-le-Street	a																					
Newcastle	a	15 30			15 46				16 29			16 46				17 31			17 46			
Morpeth	a								16 47													
Alnmouth for Alnwick	a	16 01							17 02							18 01						
Berwick-upon-Tweed	a	16 23														18 23						
Dunbar	a								17 44													
Wolverhampton	d		12 37			12 49		13 15		13 37			13 49		14 15		14 37			14 49		15 15
Stafford	a					13 02		13 27					14 02		14 27					15 02		15 27
Stoke-on-Trent	a					13 18		13 43					14 18		14 43					15 18		15 43
Congleton	a																					
Macclesfield	a					13 36		14 01					14 36		15 01					15 36		16 01
Crewe	a		13 08							14 07							15 07					
Wilmslow	a																					
Stockport	a					13 49		14 13					14 49		15 13					15 49		16 13
M'chester Piccadilly	a					13 59		14 25					14 59		15 25					15 59		16 25
Warrington Bank Quay	a		13 26							14 26							15 26					
Wigan North Western	a		13 37							14 37							15 37					
Preston	a		13 51							14 51							15 51					
Lancaster	a		14 07							15 07							16 07					
Oxenholme Lake District	a									15 21												
Penrith North Lakes	a		14 42														16 44					
Carlisle	a		14 59							16 00							17 00					
Lockerbie	a																					
Haymarket	a		16 13														18 14					
Edinburgh	a	17 05	16 20						18 07							19 05	18 22					
Haymarket	a	17 15							18 13							19 15						
Motherwell	a	17 55														19 54						
Glasgow Central	a	18 11								17 15						20 15						
Inverkeithing	a								18 28													
Kirkcaldy	a								18 46													
Markinch	a								18 56													
Ladybank	a								19 04													
Cupar	a								19 15													
Leuchars	a								19 22													
Dundee	a								19 35													
Arbroath	a								19 51													
Montrose	a								20 05													
Stonehaven	a								20 26													
Aberdeen	a								20 48													

A ⊼ from Plymouth
B ⊼ to Edinburgh
C ⊼ from Plymouth to Edinburgh ◇ from Plymouth ■ to Plymouth

Table T051-R

Mondays to Fridays
8 October to 7 December

South Coast and the South West - North West England, The North East and Scotland

		XC	VT	XC	XC	XC	XC	XC	XC	VT	XC	XC	XC	XC	XC	XC	VT	XC	XC	XC	XC	XC	XC
		◇■	◇■	■	◇■	■ ◇■	◇■	◇■	◇■	■ ■	■	◇■	◇■	◇■	◇■	◇■	■ ■	■	◇■	◇■	■	◇■	◇■
		A				B			A			C											
		✠	☐		✠	✠	✠	✠	✠	☐		✠	✠	✠	✠	✠	☐		✠	✠		✠	✠
Bournemouth	d							12 45							13 45								14 45
Brockenhurst	d							13 00							14 00								15 00
Southampton Central	d							13 16				13 46			14 17								15 16
Southampton Airport Pkway	d							13 23				13 54			14 24								15 23
Winchester	d							13 32				14 03			14 33								15 32
Basingstoke	d							13 49				14 19			14 49								15 48
Guildford	d																						
Reading	d				13 45			14 15				14 45			15 15				15 45				16 15
Oxford	d				14 13			14 39				15 13			15 39				16 13				16 39
Banbury	d				14 31			14 57				15 32			15 57				16 31				16 57
Leamington Spa	d				14 50			15 14				15 50			16 14				16 48				17 14
Coventry	d		14 42					15 27		15 42					16 27		16 42						17 27
Birmingham International	d		14 53					15 38		15 53					16 38		16 53						17 38
Penzance	d					09 35																	
St Erth	d					09 43																	
Hayle	d					09 47																	
Camborne	d					09 56																	
Redruth	d					10 03																	
Truro	d					10 15																	
St Austell	d					10 31																	
Par	d					10 38																	
Lostwithiel	d					10 45																	
Bodmin Parkway	d					10 51																	
Liskeard	d					11 04																	
Plymouth	d	11 25				11 50			12 25							13 25							
Totnes	d	11 50				12 15			12 51							13 51							
Paignton	d																			14 04			
Torquay	d																			14 10			
Newton Abbot	d	12 03				12 28			13 04							14 04				14 21			
Teignmouth	d																			14 28			
Dawlish	d																			14 33			
Exeter St Davids	d	12 24				12 50			13 24							14 24				14 48			
Tiverton Parkway	d	12 38				13 06			13 38							14 38				15 02			
Taunton	d	12 51				13 22			13 51							14 51				15 15			
Weston-super-Mare	d																			15 39			
Cardiff Central	d						13 45							14 45								15 45	
Newport (South Wales)	d						14 00							15 00								16 00	
Bristol Temple Meads	d	13 30				14 00			14 30				15 00			15 30				16 00			
Bristol Parkway	d	13 40				14 10			14 40				15 10			15 40				16 10			
Gloucester	d						14 50							15 50								16 50	
Cheltenham Spa	d	14 11				14 41	15 01		15 11				15 42	16 01		16 11				16 41		17 01	
Birmingham New Street	a	14 56	15 05		15 18	15 23	15 45	15 48	15 56	16 05		16 18	16 23	16 45	16 48	16 56	17 05		17 18	17 23		17 45	17 48
Birmingham New Street	d	15 03	15 15	15 19	15 30	15 31	15 49	15 57	16 03	16 15	16 19	16 30	16 31	16 49	16 57	17 03	17 15	17 19	17 30	17 31	17 39	17 49	17 57
Tamworth	d			15 36			16 09		16 20		16 36			17 09				17 36			18 03	18 09	
Burton-on-Trent	d	15 26		15 48			16 21				16 48			17 21		17 26		17 48			18 14	18 21	
Derby	a	15 40		16 02	16 06		16 35		16 41		17 00	17 05		17 35		17 40		18 01	18 05		18 29	18 34	
Nottingham	a			16 28			17 03				17 31			18 04				18 31				19 05	
Chesterfield	a	16 02							17 03							18 02							
Sheffield	a	16 18			16 44				17 18			17 46				18 18			18 44				
Doncaster	a				17 13														19 17				
Wakefield Westgate	a	16 46							17 46			18 16				18 48							
Leeds	a	17 00							18 01			18 34				19 03							
York	a	17 30			17 42				18 30			19 01				19 30			19 40				
Darlington	a	17 58			18 14				19 00			19 32				20 03			20 11				
Durham	a	18 15			18 31				19 19			19 49				20 21			20 28				
Chester-le-Street	a																						
Newcastle	a	18 33			18 47				19 33			20 02				20 35			20 42				
Morpeth	a															20 53							
Alnmouth for Alnwick	a								20 01			20 28											
Berwick-upon-Tweed	a	19 22							20 25							21 26							
Dunbar	a	19 45														21 50							
Wolverhampton	d		15 37			15 49		16 15		16 37			16 49		17 15		17 37			17 49			18 15
Stafford	a					16 02		16 27					17 02		17 27					18 02			18 27
Stoke-on-Trent	a					16 18		16 43					17 18		17 43					18 18			18 43
Congleton	a																						
Macclesfield	a					16 36		17 01					17 36		18 01					18 36			19 01
Crewe	a		16 07							17 08							18 08						
Wilmslow	a																						
Stockport	a					16 49		17 13					17 49		18 13					18 49			19 13
M'chester Piccadilly	a					16 59		17 25					17 59		18 25					18 59			19 24
Warrington Bank Quay	a		16 26							17 26							18 26						
Wigan North Western	a		16 37							17 37							18 37						
Preston	a		16 51							17 52							18 51						
Lancaster	a		17 07							18 08							19 07						
Oxenholme Lake District	a		17 21							18 23							19 21						
Penrith North Lakes	a		17 46							18 47													
Carlisle	a		18 03							19 04							20 00						
Lockerbie	a																						
Haymarket	a									20 14													
Edinburgh	a	20 08							21 08	20 23		21 29				22 13							
Haymarket	a	20 16							21 17														
Motherwell	a								22 04														
Glasgow Central	a		19 23						22 21								21 15						
Inverkeithing	a	20 30																					
Kirkcaldy	a																						
Markinch	a	21 00																					
Ladybank	a	21 08																					
Cupar	a	21 19																					
Leuchars	a	21 26																					
Dundee	a	21 43																					
Arbroath	a																						
Montrose	a																						
Stonehaven	a																						
Aberdeen	a																						

A ✠ to Edinburgh
B ✠ ◇ from Plymouth ■ to Plymouth
C ✠ to Newcastle

Table T051-R

Mondays to Fridays
8 October to 7 December

South Coast and the South West - North West England, The North East and Scotland

		XC	VT	XC	XC	XC	XC	XC	XC	VT	XC	XC	XC	XC	XC	XC	VT	XC	XC	XC	XC	XC
		◇■	◇■	■	◇■	◇■	◇■	◇■	◇■	◇■	■	◇■	◇■	◇■	◇■	◇■	◇■	◇■	◇■	◇■	◇■	◇■
		A					B					B		B		B		B		B	B	B
		✠	☐		✠	✠	✠	✠	✠	☐		✠	✠	✠	✠	✠	⊠	✠	✠	✠	✠	✠
Bournemouth	d							15 45							16 45						17 45	
Brockenhurst	d							16 00							17 00						18 00	
Southampton Central	d				15 46			16 17							17 17			17 46			18 15	
Southampton Airport Pkway	d				15 53			16 24							17 24			17 53			18 22	
Winchester	d				16 02			16 33							17 33			18 02			18 31	
Basingstoke	d				16 18			16 49							17 49			18 18			18 47	
Guildford	d																					
Reading	d				16 45			17 15				17 45			18 15			18 45			19 15	
Oxford	d				17 13			17 39				18 10			18 39			19 13			19 39	
Banbury	d				17 33			17 57				18 27			18 57			19 30			19 57	
Leamington Spa	d				17 51			18 14				18 45			19 14			19 48			20 14	
Coventry	d		17 42					18 27		18 42					19 27		19 42				20 27	
Birmingham International	d		17 53					18 38		18 53					19 38		19 53				20 38	
Penzance	d																					
St Erth	d																					
Hayle	d																					
Camborne	d																					
Redruth	d																					
Truro	d																					
St Austell	d																					
Par	d																					
Lostwithiel	d																					
Bodmin Parkway	d																					
Liskeard	d																					
Plymouth	d	14 25							15 25							16 25						17 25
Totnes	d	14 50							15 51							16 50						17 51
Paignton	d																					
Torquay	d																					
Newton Abbot	d	15 03							16 04							17 03						18 04
Teignmouth	d																					
Dawlish	d																					
Exeter St Davids	d	15 24							16 24				16 54			17 24						18 25
Tiverton Parkway	d	15 37							16 38				17 08			17 37						18 39
Taunton	d	15 51							16 51				17 22			17 50						18 52
Weston-super-Mare	d																					
Cardiff Central	d						16 45							17 45						18 45		
Newport (South Wales)	d						17 00							18 00						19 00		
Bristol Temple Meads	d	16 30				17 00			17 30				18 00			18 30			19 00			19 30
Bristol Parkway	d	16 40				17 10			17 40				18 10			18 40			19 10			19 40
Gloucester	d						17 50							18 46						19 45		
Cheltenham Spa	d	17 11				17 42	18 01		18 11				18 41	18 57		19 11			19 41	19 58		20 11
Birmingham New Street	a	17 56	18 05		18 18	18 23	18 45	18 48	18 56	19 05		19 18	19 23	19 45	19 48	19 56	20 06	20 18	20 23	20 40	20 48	20 51
Birmingham New Street	d	18 03	18 15	18 19	18 30	18 31	18 49	18 57	19 03	19 15	19 19	19 30	19 31	19 49	19 57	20 03	20 15	20 30	20 31	20 49	20 57	21 03
Tamworth	d	18 19		18 36			19 09				19 36			20 09		20 19				21 09		21 19
Burton-on-Trent	d			18 48			19 21		19 29		19 48			20 21						21 21		21 30
Derby	a	18 40		19 00	19 05		19 38		19 42		20 02	20 06		20 34		20 38		21 09		21 36		21 43
Nottingham	a			19 34			20 08				20 28			21 04						22 12		
Chesterfield	a	19 02			19 27				20 03							21 02		21 37				22 06
Sheffield	a	19 18			19 40				20 18			20 44				21 17		21 50				22 22
Doncaster	a				20 13							21 19						22 25				
Wakefield Westgate	a	19 46							20 47							21 46						22 53
Leeds	a	20 02							21 02							22 02						23 07
York	a	20 30			20 41							21 40						22 51				
Darlington	a	20 59			21 14							22 12										
Durham	a	21 17			21 31							22 29										
Chester-le-Street	a																					
Newcastle	a	21 33			21 45							22 48										
Morpeth	a																					
Alnmouth for Alnwick	a	21 59																				
Berwick-upon-Tweed	a																					
Dunbar	a																					
Wolverhampton	d		18 37			18 49		19 15		19 37			19 49		20 15		20 37		20 49		21 15	
Stafford	a					19 02		19 27					20 02		20 27		20 50		21 02		21 28	
Stoke-on-Trent	a					19 18		19 43					20 19		20 43				21 18		21 45	
Congleton	a																					
Macclesfield	a					19 36		20 01					20 36		21 01				21 36		22 02	
Crewe	a		19 07							20 07							21 15					
Wilmslow	a																					
Stockport	a					19 49		20 13					20 48		21 13				21 49		22 15	
M'chester Piccadilly	a					19 59		20 25					20 59		21 25				21 59		22 25	
Warrington Bank Quay	a		19 26							20 26												
Wigan North Western	a		19 37							20 37												
Preston	a		19 51							20 51												
Lancaster	a		20 07							21 07												
Oxenholme Lake District	a									21 22												
Penrith North Lakes	a		20 44																			
Carlisle	a		21 00							22 00												
Lockerbie	a																					
Haymarket	a		22 13																			
Edinburgh	a	23 03	22 19																			
Haymarket	a																					
Motherwell	a																					
Glasgow Central	a									23 17												
Inverkeithing	a																					
Kirkcaldy	a																					
Markinch	a																					
Ladybank	a																					
Cupar	a																					
Leuchars	a																					
Dundee	a																					
Arbroath	a																					
Montrose	a																					
Stonehaven	a																					
Aberdeen	a																					

A ✠ to Leeds
B ✠ to Birmingham New Street

Table T051-R

Mondays to Fridays

8 October to 7 December

South Coast and the South West - North West England, The North East and Scotland

		VT	XC	XC	XC	XC	XC	XC	XC	XC	XC	XC	XC	XC	XC	XC
		◇1	◇1	◇1	◇1	◇1	◇1	1	◇1	◇1	◇1	◇1	1	◇1	◇1	◇1
					A		B									
Bournemouth	d				18 45						19 45					
Brockenhurst	d				19 00						20 00					
Southampton Central	d				19 16						20 17					
Southampton Airport Pkway	d				19 23						20 24					
Winchester	d				19 32						20 33					
Basingstoke	d				19 49						20 49					
Guildford	d															
Reading	d		19 45		20 12				20 45		21 11				21 45	
Oxford	d		20 13		20 39				21 14		21 36				22 30	
Banbury	d		20 32		20 57				21 33		21 54				22 48	
Leamington Spa	d		20 50		21 14				21 53		22 12				23 05	
Coventry	d	20 42			21 27						22 25				23 17	
Birmingham International	d	20 53			21 38						22 35				23 27	
Penzance	d															
St Erth	d															
Hayle	d															
Camborne	d															
Redruth	d															
Truro	d															
St Austell	d															
Par	d															
Lostwithiel	d															
Bodmin Parkway	d															
Liskeard	d															
Plymouth	d						18 25									
Totnes	d						18 50									
Paignton	d													20 14		
Torquay	d													20 20		
Newton Abbot	d						19 03							20 31		
Teignmouth	d															
Dawlish	d															
Exeter St Davids	d						19 24							20 52		
Tiverton Parkway	d						19 37							21 05		
Taunton	d						19 51							21 19		
Weston-super-Mare	d															
Cardiff Central	d					19 50						21 05				21 50
Newport (South Wales)	d					20 05						21 21				22 05
Bristol Temple Meads	d			20 00			20 30							22 00		
Bristol Parkway	d			20 10			20 40							22 10		
Gloucester	d			20 46		20 59						22 04				22 47
Cheltenham Spa	d			20 56		21 11	21 17					22 15		22 42		22 58
Birmingham New Street	a	21 04	21 23	21 37	21 48	21 51	22 02		22 18		22 45	23 05		23 43	23 56	23 59
Birmingham New Street	d	21 15			21 57			22 03		22 30			23 09			
Tamworth	d							22 27					23 28			
Burton-on-Trent	d							22 39					23 40			
Derby	a							22 52					23 53			
Nottingham	a							23 27					00 16			
Chesterfield	a															
Sheffield	a															
Doncaster	a															
Wakefield Westgate	a															
Leeds	a															
York	a															
Darlington	a															
Durham	a															
Chester-le-Street	a															
Newcastle	a															
Morpeth	a															
Alnmouth for Alnwick	a															
Berwick-upon-Tweed	a															
Dunbar	a															
Wolverhampton	d	21 37			22 15					22 48						
Stafford	a	21 52			22 27					23 00						
Stoke-on-Trent	a	22 10			22 43					23 17						
Congleton	a															
Macclesfield	a				23 01											
Crewe	a	22 30														
Wilmslow	a															
Stockport	a				23 13											
M'chester Piccadilly	a				23 25					00 11						
Warrington Bank Quay	a															
Wigan North Western	a															
Preston	a															
Lancaster	a															
Oxenholme Lake District	a															
Penrith North Lakes	a															
Carlisle	a															
Lockerbie	a															
Haymarket	a															
Edinburgh	a															
Haymarket	a															
Motherwell	a															
Glasgow Central	a															
Inverkeithing	a															
Kirkcaldy	a															
Markinch	a															
Ladybank	a															
Cupar	a															
Leuchars	a															
Dundee	a															
Arbroath	a															
Montrose	a															
Stonehaven	a															
Aberdeen	a															

A 🛒 to Reading

B 🛒 to Bristol Temple Meads

Table T051-R

Saturdays

26 May to 21 July

South Coast and the South West - North West England, The North East and Scotland

		XC	XC	VT	XC	XC	XC	XC	XC	XC	VT	XC	VT	XC	XC	XC	XC	XC	XC	VT	XC	XC	XC
		◇1	◇1	◇1	1	◇1	◇1	1	◇1	◇1	◇1	1	◇1	◇1	◇1	1	◇1	◇1	◇1	◇1	1	◇1	◇1
			A														B	A				B	
Bournemouth	d																						
Brockenhurst	d																						
Southampton Central	d																05 09						
Southampton Airport Pkway	d																05 16						
Winchester	d																05 25						
Basingstoke	d																05 41						
Guildford	d																					06 09	
Reading	d																06 15					06 47	
Oxford	d																06 39					07 12	
Banbury	d																06 57					07 29	
Leamington Spa	d																07 14					07 47	
Coventry	d																07 27						
Birmingham International	d																07 38						
Penzance	d																						
St Erth	d																						
Hayle	d																						
Camborne	d																						
Redruth	d																						
Truro	d																						
St Austell	d																						
Par	d																						
Lostwithiel	d																						
Bodmin Parkway	d																						
Liskeard	d																						
Plymouth	d																						
Totnes	d																						
Paignton	d																						
Torquay	d																						
Newton Abbot	d																						
Teignmouth	d																						
Dawlish	d																						
Exeter St Davids	d																						
Tiverton Parkway	d																						
Taunton	d																						
Weston-super-Mare	d																						
Cardiff Central	d																						
Newport (South Wales)	d																						
Bristol Temple Meads	d																	06 15					07 00
Bristol Parkway	d																	06 25					07 10
Gloucester	d																	07 00	07 06				
Cheltenham Spa	d																	07 11	07 17				07 41
Birmingham New Street	a																07 48	07 56	08 07			08 18	08 25
Birmingham New Street	d	05 57	05 58	06 15	06 19	06 30	06 31	06 49	06 57	07 03	07 15	07 19	07 21	07 30	07 31	07 49	07 57	08 03		08 15	08 19	08 30	08 31
Tamworth	d		06 14		06 39	06 46		07 07		07 19		07 39		07 46		08 07		08 19			08 36		
Burton-on-Trent	d		06 25		06 51	06 56		07 19		07 31		07 50		07 56		08 19		08 29			08 48		
Derby	a		06 35		07 03	07 09		07 35		07 41		08 05		08 08		08 35		08 41			09 00	09 05	
Nottingham	a				07 38			08 06				08 34				09 07					09 28		
Chesterfield	a		06 58			07 31				08 02				08 31				09 02					
Sheffield	a		07 15			07 46				08 19				08 44				09 17				09 44	
Doncaster	a					08 13								09 15								10 15	
Wakefield Westgate	a		07 45							08 46								09 46					
Leeds	a		08 00							09 01								10 00					
York	a		08 30			08 40				09 30				09 40				10 30				10 40	
Darlington	a		08 58			09 16				09 58				10 16				10 59				11 14	
Durham	a		09 14			09 33				10 15				10 33				11 15				11 31	
Chester-le-Street	a																						
Newcastle	a		09 28			09 47				10 29				10 47				11 29				11 45	
Morpeth	a																	11 45					
Alnmouth for Alnwick	a		09 59																				
Berwick-upon-Tweed	a		10 21															12 18					
Dunbar	a									11 38													
Wolverhampton	d	06 15		06 37			06 49		07 15		07 37		07 41		07 49		08 15			08 37			08 49
Stafford	a	06 27					07 02		07 29				07 58		08 02		08 27						09 02
Stoke-on-Trent	a	06 44					07 18								08 18		08 43						09 18
Congleton	a	06 57																					
Macclesfield	a	07 05					07 36								08 36		09 01						09 36
Crewe	a			07 08					07 50		08 06		08 18							09 08			
Wilmslow	a								08 07														
Stockport	a	07 18					07 49		08 16						08 50		09 13						09 49
M'chester Piccadilly	a	07 28					07 59		08 29						08 59		09 25						09 59
Warrington Bank Quay	a			07 26							08 26		08 40							09 26			
Wigan North Western	a			07 37							08 37		08 51							09 38			
Preston	a			07 51							08 51		09 09							09 51			
Lancaster	a			08 07							09 09									10 07			
Oxenholme Lake District	a			08 21																10 21			
Penrith North Lakes	a										09 46												
Carlisle	a			09 00							10 01									10 59			
Lockerbie	a																						
Haymarket	a			10 13																12 17			
Edinburgh	a		11 03	10 18						12 05								13 01		12 22			
Haymarket	a		11 16															13 16					
Motherwell	a		11 53															13 54					
Glasgow Central	a		12 12								11 15							14 12					
Inverkeithing	a																						
Kirkcaldy	a																						
Markinch	a																						
Ladybank	a																						
Cupar	a																						
Leuchars	a																						
Dundee	a																						
Arbroath	a																						
Montrose	a																						
Stonehaven	a																						
Aberdeen	a																						

A 🛒 to Edinburgh

B 🛒 from Reading

Table T051-R

South Coast and the South West - North West England, The North East and Scotland

		XC	XC	XC	VT	XC	XC	XC	XC	XC	XC	VT	XC	XC	XC	XC	XC	XC	VT	XC	XC	XC	XC
		◇1	◇1	◇1	◇1	1	◇1	◇1	◇1	◇1	◇1	◇1	1	◇1	◇1	◇1	◇1	◇1	◇1	1	◇1	◇1	◇1
							A	B			C			A	D								
			⚲	⚲	⊡	⚲	⚲	⚲		⚲	⚲	⊡	⚲	⚲	⚲		⚲	⚲	⊡	⚲	⚲	⚲	⚲
Bournemouth	d						06 25			06 37							07 47						
Brockenhurst 3	d						06 39			06 55							08 02						
Southampton Central	d		06 20				06 53			07 20				07 47			08 20						
Southampton Airport Pkway	d		06 27				07 01			07 27				07 54			08 27						
Winchester	d		06 36				07 09			07 36				08 03			08 36						
Basingstoke	d		06 52				07 25			07 52				08 19			08 52						
Guildford	d																						
Reading 7	d		07 15				07 47			08 15				08 45			09 15				09 45		
Oxford	d		07 40				08 12			08 40				09 12			09 40				10 12		
Banbury	d		07 57				08 29			08 57				09 29			09 57				10 29		
Leamington Spa 3	d		08 14				08 47			09 14				09 47			10 14				10 47		
Coventry	d		08 27		08 42					09 27		09 42					10 27		10 42				
Birmingham International	d		08 38		08 53					09 38		09 53					10 38		10 53				
Penzance	d																						
St Erth	d																						
Hayle	d																						
Camborne	d																						
Redruth	d																						
Truro	d																						
St Austell	d																						
Par	d																						
Lostwithiel	d																						
Bodmin Parkway	d																						
Liskeard 3	d																						
Plymouth	d			05 25							06 25							07 25					
Totnes	d			05 50							06 50							07 50					
Paignton	d														07 02								
Torquay	d														07 08								
Newton Abbot	d			06 03							07 03				07 19			08 03					
Teignmouth	d														07 26								
Dawlish	d														07 31								
Exeter St Davids 6	d			06 23							07 23				07 45			08 23					
Tiverton Parkway	d			06 37							07 37				07 58			08 37					
Taunton	d			06 50							07 50				08 11			08 50					
Weston-super-Mare	d																						
Cardiff Central 7	d	06 40						07 00	07 45							08 45							09 45
Newport (South Wales)	d	06 55						07 15	08 00							09 00							09 59
Bristol Temple Meads 10	d			07 30				08 00			08 30				09 00			09 30				10 00	
Bristol Parkway 7	d			07 40				08 10			08 40				09 10			09 40				10 10	
Gloucester 7	d	07 46							08 50							09 50							10 50
Cheltenham Spa	d	07 57		08 11				08 41	09 01		09 11				09 41	10 01		10 11				10 41	11 01
Birmingham New Street 12	a	08 45	08 48	08 56	09 05		09 18	09 26	09 45	09 48	09 56	10 04		10 18	10 25	10 45	10 48	10 56	11 04		11 18	11 26	11 45
Birmingham New Street 12	d	08 49	08 57	09 03	09 15	09 19	09 30	09 31	09 49	09 57	10 03	10 15	10 19	10 30	10 31	10 49	10 57	11 03	11 15	11 19	11 30	11 31	11 49
Tamworth	d	09 09				09 36			10 07		10 19		10 36			11 09				11 36			12 07
Burton-on-Trent	d	09 21		09 28		09 48			10 19				10 48			11 21		11 28		11 48			12 19
Derby 6	a	09 35		09 39		10 00	10 05		10 36		10 39		11 00	11 05		11 37		11 39		12 00	12 05		12 36
Nottingham 8	a	10 03				10 28			11 03				11 28			12 03				12 28			13 03
Chesterfield	a			10 02							11 02							12 02					
Sheffield 7	a			10 17			10 46				11 17			11 44				12 17			12 44		
Doncaster 7	a						11 15							12 13							13 15		
Wakefield Westgate 7	a			10 46							11 46							12 46					
Leeds 10	a			11 00							12 00							13 00					
York 8	a			11 30			11 40				12 30			12 40				13 30			13 40		
Darlington 7	a			11 58			12 15				12 59			13 14				13 59			14 16		
Durham	a			12 15			12 32				13 16			13 31				14 16			14 33		
Chester-le-Street	a																						
Newcastle 8	a			12 31			12 46				13 29			13 45				14 29			14 46		
Morpeth	a																	14 45					
Alnmouth for Alnwick	a										13 59												
Berwick-upon-Tweed	a										14 21												
Dunbar	a			13 39														15 39					
Wolverhampton 7	d		09 15		09 37			09 49		10 15		10 37			10 49		11 15		11 37			11 49	
Stafford	a		09 27					10 02		10 27					11 02		11 27					12 02	
Stoke-on-Trent	a		09 43					10 18		10 43					11 18		11 43					12 18	
Congleton	a																						
Macclesfield	a		10 01					10 36		11 01					11 36		12 01					12 36	
Crewe 10	a				10 08							11 08							12 07				
Wilmslow	a																						
Stockport	a		10 13					10 49		11 13					11 49		12 13					12 49	
M'chester Piccadilly 10	a		10 24					11 00		11 25					11 59		12 25					12 59	
Warrington Bank Quay	a				10 26							11 26							12 26				
Wigan North Western	a				10 37							11 37							12 37				
Preston 8	a				10 51							11 51							12 52				
Lancaster 8	a				11 07							12 07							13 08				
Oxenholme Lake District	a											12 20							13 21				
Penrith North Lakes	a				11 44																		
Carlisle 8	a				12 00							12 59							14 00				
Lockerbie	a																						
Haymarket	a											14 11											
Edinburgh 10	a			14 05							15 03	14 17						16 02					
Haymarket	a										15 15												
Motherwell	a										15 54								14 58				
Glasgow Central 15	a				13 15						16 12								15 15				
Inverkeithing	a																						
Kirkcaldy	a																						
Markinch	a																						
Ladybank	a																						
Cupar	a																						
Leuchars 3	a																						
Dundee	a																						
Arbroath	a																						
Montrose	a																						
Stonehaven	a																						
Aberdeen	a																						

A ⚲ from Reading
B ⚲ from Bristol Temple Meads
C ⚲ to Edinburgh
D ⚲ from Newton Abbot

Table T051-R

South Coast and the South West - North West England, The North East and Scotland

		XC	XC	VT	XC	XC	XC	XC	XC	XC	VT	XC	XC	XC	XC	XC	XC	VT	XC	XC	XC	XC
		◇1	◇1	◇1	1	◇1	◇1	◇1	◇1	◇1	◇1	1	◇1	◇1	◇1	◇1	◇1	◇1	1	◇1	◇1	◇1
			A							B							A					
		⚲	⚲	⊡	⚲	⚲	⚲		⚲	⚲	⊡	⚲	⚲	⚲	⚲	⚲	⚲	⊡		⚲	⚲	⚲
Bournemouth	d	08 47							09 47							10 47						
Brockenhurst 3	d	09 02							10 02							11 02						
Southampton Central	d	09 18				09 47			10 17							11 20				11 47		
Southampton Airport Pkway	d	09 25				09 54			10 24							11 27				11 54		
Winchester	d	09 34				10 03			10 33							11 36				12 03		
Basingstoke	d	09 52				10 19			10 52							11 52				12 19		
Guildford	d																					
Reading 7	d	10 15				10 45			11 15				11 45			12 15				12 45		
Oxford	d	10 40				11 12			11 40				12 12			12 40				13 12		
Banbury	d	10 57				11 29			11 57				12 29			12 57				13 29		
Leamington Spa 3	d	11 14				11 47			12 14				12 47			13 14				13 47		
Coventry	d	11 27		11 42					12 27		12 42					13 27		13 42				
Birmingham International	d	11 38		11 53					12 38		12 53					13 38		13 53				
Penzance	d		06 30														08 28					
St Erth	d		06 38														08 36					
Hayle	d		06 41																			
Camborne	d		06 51														08 46					
Redruth	d		06 57														08 52					
Truro	d		07 09														09 04					
St Austell	d		07 25														09 20					
Par	d		07 32														09 27					
Lostwithiel	d		07 39																			
Bodmin Parkway	d		07 46														09 37					
Liskeard 3	d		07 58														09 50					
Plymouth	d		08 25				08 39			09 18							10 25					
Totnes	d		08 50				09 04			09 43							10 50					
Paignton	d													10 06								
Torquay	d													10 12								
Newton Abbot	d		09 03				09 17			09 56				10 23			11 03					
Teignmouth	d									10 03				10 30								
Dawlish	d									10 09				10 35								
Exeter St Davids 6	d		09 23				09 45			10 25				10 49			11 23					
Tiverton Parkway	d		09 37				09 58			10 38				11 02			11 36					
Taunton	d		09 50				10 11			10 51				11 17			11 50					
Weston-super-Mare	d						10 33															
Cardiff Central 7	d							10 45							11 45							12 45
Newport (South Wales)	d							11 00							12 00							13 00
Bristol Temple Meads 10	d		10 30				11 00			11 30				12 00			12 30				13 00	
Bristol Parkway 7	d		10 40				11 10			11 40				12 10			12 40				13 10	
Gloucester 7	d							11 50							12 48							13 50
Cheltenham Spa	d		11 11				11 41	12 01		12 11				12 41	12 59		13 11				13 41	14 01
Birmingham New Street 12	a	11 48	11 56	12 05		12 18	12 26	12 45	12 48	12 56	13 05		13 18	13 26	13 45	13 48	13 56	14 05		14 18	14 26	14 45
Birmingham New Street 12	d	11 57	12 03	12 15	12 19	12 30	12 31	12 49	12 57	13 03	13 15	13 19	13 30	13 31	13 49	13 57	14 03	14 15	14 19	14 30	14 31	14 49
Tamworth	d		12 19		12 36			13 09				13 36			14 09		14 19		14 36			15 09
Burton-on-Trent	d				12 48			13 21		13 27		13 48			14 21				14 48			15 21
Derby 6	a		12 39		13 00	13 05		13 36		13 39		14 00	14 05		14 36		14 39		15 00	15 05		15 36
Nottingham 8	a				13 28			14 03				14 28			15 03				15 28			16 03
Chesterfield	a		13 02							14 02							15 02					
Sheffield 7	a		13 17			13 48				14 18			14 44				15 17			15 44		
Doncaster 7	a					14 15							15 15							16 16		
Wakefield Westgate 7	a		13 46							14 46							15 46					
Leeds 10	a		14 00							15 00							16 00					
York 8	a		14 30			14 40				15 30			15 40				16 30			16 40		
Darlington 7	a		14 58			15 14				15 59			16 15				16 58			17 14		
Durham	a		15 15			15 31				16 16			16 32				17 15			17 31		
Chester-le-Street	a																					
Newcastle 8	a		15 29			15 45				16 29			16 46				17 29			17 45		
Morpeth	a									16 44												
Alnmouth for Alnwick	a		15 59							16 59							18 00					
Berwick-upon-Tweed	a		16 21														18 21					
Dunbar	a									17 40												
Wolverhampton 7	d	12 15		12 37			12 49		13 15		13 37			13 49		14 15		14 37			14 49	
Stafford	a	12 27					13 02		13 27					14 02		14 27					15 02	
Stoke-on-Trent	a	12 43					13 18		13 43					14 18		14 43					15 18	
Congleton	a																					
Macclesfield	a	13 01					13 36		14 01					14 36		15 01					15 36	
Crewe 10	a			13 08							14 08							15 07				
Wilmslow	a																					
Stockport	a	13 13					13 49		14 13					14 49		15 13					15 49	
M'chester Piccadilly 10	a	13 25					13 59		14 25					14 59		15 25					15 59	
Warrington Bank Quay	a			13 26							14 26							15 26				
Wigan North Western	a			13 37							14 37							15 37				
Preston 8	a			13 51							14 51							15 51				
Lancaster 8	a			14 07							15 07							16 07				
Oxenholme Lake District	a										15 21											
Penrith North Lakes	a			14 42														16 43				
Carlisle 8	a			14 59							16 00							17 00				
Lockerbie	a																					
Haymarket	a			16 16														18 14				
Edinburgh 10	a		17 05	16 23						18 03							19 05	18 22				
Haymarket	a		17 17							18 14							19 16					
Motherwell	a		17 54														19 53					
Glasgow Central 15	a		18 11								17 15						20 15					
Inverkeithing	a									18 28												
Kirkcaldy	a									18 43												
Markinch	a									18 52												
Ladybank	a									18 59												
Cupar	a									19 06												
Leuchars 3	a									19 13												
Dundee	a									19 29												
Arbroath	a									19 45												
Montrose	a									20 01												
Stonehaven	a									20 22												
Aberdeen	a									20 42												

A ⚲ from Plymouth to Edinburgh
B ⚲ to Edinburgh

Table T051-R

Saturdays
26 May to 21 July

South Coast and the South West - North West England, The North East and Scotland

	XC	XC	VT	XC	XC	XC	XC	XC	XC	VT	XC	XC	XC	XC	XC	XC	VT	XC	XC	XC	XC	XC
	◇1	◇1	◇1	1	◇1	◇1	◇1	◇1	◇1	■ 1	1	◇1	◇1	◇1	◇1	◇1	■ 1	1	◇1	◇1	◇1	◇1
		A							A							B						
	⊼	⊼	⊡		⊼	⊼	⊼	⊼	⊼	⊡		⊼	⊼	⊼	⊼	⊼	⊡		⊼	⊼	⊼	⊼
Bournemouth d	11 47							12 47							13 47							14 47
Brockenhurst d	12 02							13 02							14 02							15 02
Southampton Central d	12 20							13 18				13 47			14 20							15 18
Southampton Airport Pkway d	12 27							13 25				13 54			14 27							15 25
Winchester d	12 36							13 34				14 03			14 36							15 34
Basingstoke d	12 52							13 52				14 19			14 52							15 52
Guildford d																						
Reading d	13 15				13 45			14 15				14 45			15 15				15 45			16 15
Oxford d	13 40				14 11			14 40				15 12			15 40				16 11			16 40
Banbury d	13 57				14 29			14 57				15 29			15 57				16 29			16 57
Leamington Spa d	14 14				14 47			15 14				15 47			16 14				16 47			17 14
Coventry d	14 27		14 42					15 27		15 42					16 27		16 42					17 27
Birmingham International d	14 38		14 53					15 38		15 53					16 38		16 53					17 38
Penzance d																						
St Erth d																						
Hayle d																						
Camborne d																						
Redruth d																						
Truro d																						
St Austell d																						
Par d		10 31																				
Lostwithiel d																						
Bodmin Parkway d		10 43																				
Liskeard d		10 55																				
Plymouth d		11 25														13 25						
Totnes d		11 50														13 51						
Paignton d									12 35											13 55		
Torquay d									12 42											14 01		
Newton Abbot d		12 03							12 54							14 03				14 12		
Teignmouth d									13 02											14 19		
Dawlish d									13 09											14 24		
Exeter St Davids d		12 23							13 23							14 25				14 37		
Tiverton Parkway d		12 36							13 37							14 38				14 50		
Taunton d		12 50							13 50							14 52				15 03		
Weston-super-Mare d																				15 29		
Cardiff Central d							13 45							14 45							15 45	
Newport (South Wales) d							14 00							15 00							16 00	
Bristol Temple Meads d		13 30				14 00			14 30				15 00			15 30				16 00		
Bristol Parkway d		13 40				14 10			14 40				15 10			15 40				16 10		
Gloucester d							14 50							15 50							16 50	
Cheltenham Spa d		14 11				14 41	15 01		15 11				15 41	16 01		16 11				16 41	17 01	
Birmingham New Street a	14 48	14 56	15 05		15 18	15 26	15 45	15 48	15 56	16 05		16 18	16 26	16 45	16 48	16 56	17 05		17 18	17 26	17 45	17 48
Birmingham New Street d	14 57	15 03	15 15	15 19	15 30	15 31	15 49	15 57	16 03	16 15	16 19	16 30	16 31	16 49	16 57	17 03	17 15	17 19	17 30	17 31	17 49	17 57
Tamworth d				15 36			16 09		16 19		16 36			17 09				17 36			18 09	
Burton-on-Trent d		15 27		15 48			16 21				16 48	16 54		17 21		17 26		17 48			18 21	
Derby a		15 40		16 00	16 05		16 36		16 40		17 00	17 05		17 36		17 39		18 00	18 05		18 36	
Nottingham a				16 28			17 03				17 31			18 04				18 31			19 03	
Chesterfield a		16 02							17 03							18 02						
Sheffield a		16 18			16 44				17 17			17 45				18 17			18 44			
Doncaster a					17 15														19 13			
Wakefield Westgate a		16 46							17 47			18 16				18 49						
Leeds a		17 00							18 01			18 33				19 03						
York a		17 29			17 40				18 30			19 05				19 30			19 40			
Darlington a		17 57			18 11				19 01			19 34				20 04			20 13			
Durham a		18 13			18 28				19 18			19 51				20 21			20 30			
Chester-le-Street a																						
Newcastle a		18 29			18 41				19 32			20 07				20 35			20 44			
Morpeth a																20 50						
Alnmouth for Alnwick a									20 00													
Berwick-upon-Tweed a		19 18							20 24							21 22						
Dunbar a		19 41														21 46						
Wolverhampton d	15 15		15 37			15 49		16 15		16 37			16 49		17 15		17 37			17 49		18 15
Stafford a	15 27					16 02		16 27					17 02		17 27					18 02		18 27
Stoke-on-Trent a	15 43					16 18		16 43					17 18		17 43					18 18		18 43
Congleton a																						
Macclesfield a	16 01					16 36		17 01					17 36		18 01					18 36		19 01
Crewe a			16 08							17 08							18 07					
Wilmslow a																						
Stockport a	16 13					16 49		17 13					17 49		18 13					18 49		19 13
M'chester Piccadilly a	16 25					16 59		17 25					17 59		18 25					18 59		19 24
Warrington Bank Quay a			16 26							17 26							18 26					
Wigan North Western a			16 37							17 37							18 37					
Preston a			16 51							17 51							18 51					
Lancaster a			17 07							18 07							19 08					
Oxenholme Lake District a			17 21							18 21							19 22					
Penrith North Lakes a										18 47												
Carlisle a			18 00							19 04							20 01					
Lockerbie a																						
Haymarket a										20 14												
Edinburgh a		20 04							21 09	20 21						22 09						
Haymarket a		20 17							21 17													
Motherwell a									21 56													
Glasgow Central a			19 15						22 19								21 15					
Inverkeithing a		20 33																				
Kirkcaldy a		20 50																				
Markinch a		21 00																				
Ladybank a		21 08																				
Cupar a		21 19																				
Leuchars a		21 26																				
Dundee a		21 43																				
Arbroath a																						
Montrose a																						
Stonehaven a																						
Aberdeen a																						

A ⊼ to Edinburgh
B ⊼ to Newcastle

Table T051-R

Saturdays
26 May to 21 July

South Coast and the South West - North West England, The North East and Scotland

	XC	VT	XC	XC	XC	XC	XC	XC	VT	XC	XC	XC	XC	XC	XC	VT	XC	XC	XC	XC	XC
	◇1	◇1	1	◇1	◇1	◇1	◇1	◇1	◇1	1	◇1	◇1	◇1	◇1	◇1	◇1	◇1	◇1	◇1	◇1	◇1
	A					B		A			B		B	B	B		B	B	B	B	B
	⊼	⊡		⊼	⊼	⊼	⊼	⊼	⊡		⊼	⊼	⊼	⊼	⊼	⊡	⊼	⊼	⊼	⊼	⊼
Bournemouth d							15 47							16 47							17 47
Brockenhurst d							16 02							17 02							18 02
Southampton Central d				15 47			16 20							17 20			17 47				18 20
Southampton Airport Pkway d				15 54			16 27							17 27			17 54				18 27
Winchester d				16 03			16 36							17 36			18 03				18 36
Basingstoke d				16 18			16 52							17 52			18 18				18 52
Guildford d																					
Reading d				16 45			17 15				17 45			18 15			18 45				19 15
Oxford d				17 12			17 40				18 12			18 40			19 12				19 40
Banbury d				17 29			17 57				18 29			18 57			19 29				19 57
Leamington Spa d				17 47			18 14				18 47			19 14			19 47				20 14
Coventry d		17 42					18 27		18 42					19 27		19 42					20 27
Birmingham International d		17 53					18 38		18 53					19 38		19 53					20 38
Penzance d																					
St Erth d																					
Hayle d																					
Camborne d																					
Redruth d																					
Truro d																					
St Austell d																					
Par d																				16 27	
Lostwithiel d																					
Bodmin Parkway d																				16 38	
Liskeard d																				16 51	
Plymouth d	14 25							15 25												17 25	
Totnes d	14 50							15 51												17 50	
Paignton d															16 37						
Torquay d															16 44						
Newton Abbot d	15 03							16 04							16 56					18 03	
Teignmouth d															17 04						
Dawlish d															17 10						
Exeter St Davids d	15 23							16 24							17 24					18 23	
Tiverton Parkway d	15 37							16 38							17 38					18 37	
Taunton d	15 50							16 51							17 51					18 50	
Weston-super-Mare d																					
Cardiff Central d						16 45							17 45						18 45		
Newport (South Wales) d						17 00							18 00						19 00		
Bristol Temple Meads d	16 30				17 00			17 30				18 00			18 30			19 00		19 30	
Bristol Parkway d	16 40				17 10			17 40				18 10			18 39			19 10		19 40	
Gloucester d						17 50							18 46						19 46		
Cheltenham Spa d	17 12				17 41	18 01		18 13				18 41	18 57		19 11			19 41	19 57	20 12	
Birmingham New Street a	17 56	18 05		18 18	18 26	18 45	18 48	18 56	19 05		19 18	19 26	19 45	19 48	19 58	20 06	20 18	20 26	20 42	20 49	20 48
Birmingham New Street d	18 03	18 15	18 19	18 30	18 31	18 49	18 57	19 03	19 15	19 19	19 30	19 31	19 49	19 57	20 03	20 15	20 30	20 31	20 49	20 57	21 03
Tamworth d	18 19		18 36			19 09				19 36			20 09		20 19				21 09		21 19
Burton-on-Trent d			18 48			19 21		19 27		19 48			20 21						21 21		21 30
Derby a	18 40		19 00	19 05		19 35		19 41		20 00	20 05		20 33		20 40		21 24		21 32		21 42
Nottingham a			19 31			20 04				20 28			21 03						22 04		
Chesterfield a	19 02			19 34				20 03			20 34				21 02		21 46				22 07
Sheffield a	19 17			19 47				20 18			20 47				21 17		21 59				22 21
Doncaster a				20 13							21 21						22 24				22 48
Wakefield Westgate a	19 46							20 47							21 47						23 12
Leeds a	20 02							21 02							22 03						23 27
York a	20 30			20 40				21 59			21 42						22 46				
Darlington a	20 58			21 15							22 14										
Durham a	21 15			21 32							22 31										
Chester-le-Street a																					
Newcastle a	21 28			21 47							22 47										
Morpeth a																					
Alnmouth for Alnwick a	21 58																				
Berwick-upon-Tweed a																					
Dunbar a																					
Wolverhampton d		18 37			18 49		19 15		19 37			19 49		20 15		20 37		20 49		21 17	
Stafford a					19 02		19 27					20 02		20 27		20 50		21 02		21 29	
Stoke-on-Trent a					19 18		19 43					20 18		20 43				21 18		21 46	
Congleton a																					
Macclesfield a					19 36		20 01					20 36		21 01				21 36		22 04	
Crewe a		19 08							20 09							21 10					
Wilmslow a																					
Stockport a					19 49		20 13					20 49		21 13				21 49		22 16	
M'chester Piccadilly a					19 59		20 25					20 59		21 24				21 59		22 33	
Warrington Bank Quay a		19 26							20 26												
Wigan North Western a		19 37							20 37												
Preston a		19 54							20 52												
Lancaster a																					
Oxenholme Lake District a																					
Penrith North Lakes a																					
Carlisle a																					
Lockerbie a																					
Haymarket a																					
Edinburgh a	22 59																				
Haymarket a																					
Motherwell a																					
Glasgow Central a																					
Inverkeithing a																					
Kirkcaldy a																					
Markinch a																					
Ladybank a																					
Cupar a																					
Leuchars a																					
Dundee a																					
Arbroath a																					
Montrose a																					
Stonehaven a																					
Aberdeen a																					

A ⊼ to Leeds
B ⊼ to Birmingham New Street

Table T051-R

Saturdays
26 May to 21 July

South Coast and the South West - North West England, The North East and Scotland

		XC ◇■	XC ◇■	XC ◇■ A ✠	XC ◇■ B ✠	XC ◇■	XC ◇■	XC ◇■	XC ◇■	XC ◇■		XC ■	XC ◇■
Bournemouth	d				18 47					19 47			
Brockenhurst ■	d				19 02					20 02			
Southampton Central	d				19 20					20 19			
Southampton Airport Pkway ✈	d				19 27					20 26			
Winchester	d				19 36					20 36			
Basingstoke	d				19 52					20 52			
Guildford	d												
Reading ■	d	19 45			20 15		20 45			21 15			21 45
Oxford	d	20 12			20 40		21 12			21 39			22 12
Banbury	d	20 30			20 57		21 29			21 57			22 29
Leamington Spa ■	d	20 48			21 14		21 49			22 14			22 47
Coventry	d				21 27		22 01			22 26			
Birmingham International ✈	d				21 38		22 11			22 37			
Penzance	d			16 25									
St Erth	d			16 34									
Hayle	d												
Camborne	d			16 45									
Redruth	d			16 52									
Truro	d			17 05									
St Austell	d			17 22									
Par	d			17 29									
Lostwithiel	d												
Bodmin Parkway	d			17 41									
Liskeard ■	d			17 54									
Plymouth	d			18 25									
Totnes	d			18 51									
Paignton	d		18 08										
Torquay	d		18 15										
Newton Abbot	d		18 27	19 04									
Teignmouth	d												
Dawlish	d												
Exeter St Davids ■	d		18 49	19 24									
Tiverton Parkway	d		19 05	19 38									
Taunton	d		19 18	19 51									
Weston-super-Mare	d												
Cardiff Central ■	d					20 00			20 50				
Newport (South Wales)	d					20 15			21 05				
Bristol Temple Meads ■	d		20 00	20 30									
Bristol Parkway ■	d		20 10	20 40									
Gloucester ■	d					21 07			21 49				
Cheltenham Spa	d		20 41	21 11		21 18			21 59				
Birmingham New Street ■	a	21 16	21 38	21 51	21 48	22 07	22 21		22 42	22 47			23 17
Birmingham New Street ■	d			21 56	21 57	22 10		22 31				22 49	
Tamworth	d					22 27						23 08	
Burton-on-Trent	d					22 39						23 20	
Derby ■	a			22 29		22 53						23 33	
Nottingham ■	a					23 27							
Chesterfield	a			22 54									
Sheffield ■	a			23 11									
Doncaster ■	a												
Wakefield Westgate ■	a												
Leeds ■	a			23 55									
York ■	a												
Darlington ■	a												
Durham	a												
Chester-le-Street	a												
Newcastle ■	a												
Morpeth	a												
Alnmouth for Alnwick	a												
Berwick-upon-Tweed	a												
Dunbar	a												
Wolverhampton ■	d				22 15			22 49					
Stafford	a				22 27			23 01					
Stoke-on-Trent	a				22 43			23 19					
Congleton	a												
Macclesfield	a				23 01			23 38					
Crewe ■	a												
Wilmslow	a												
Stockport	a				23 13			23 53					
M'chester Piccadilly ■	a				23 29			00 10					
Warrington Bank Quay	a												
Wigan North Western	a												
Preston ■	a												
Lancaster ■	a												
Oxenholme Lake District	a												
Penrith North Lakes	a												
Carlisle ■	a												
Lockerbie	a												
Haymarket	a												
Edinburgh ■	a												
Haymarket	a												
Motherwell	a												
Glasgow Central ■	a												
Inverkeithing	a												
Kirkcaldy	a												
Markinch	a												
Ladybank	a												
Cupar	a												
Leuchars ■	a												
Dundee	a												
Arbroath	a												
Montrose	a												
Stonehaven	a												
Aberdeen	a												

A ✠ to Bristol Temple Meads
B ✠ to Reading

Table T051-R

Saturdays
28 July to 1 September

South Coast and the South West - North West England, The North East and Scotland

		XC ◇■	XC ◇■ ✠	VT ◇■ 🍴	XC ■	XC ◇■ ✠	XC ◇■ ✠	XC ■	XC ◇■ ✠	XC ◇■ ✠		VT ◇■ 🍴	XC ■ ✠	VT ◇■ 🍴	XC ◇■ A ✠	XC ◇■ ✠	XC ■	XC ◇■ B ✠	XC ◇■	XC ◇■		VT ◇■ 🍴	XC ■ ✠	XC ◇■ ✠	XC ◇■ ✠
Bournemouth	d																								
Brockenhurst ■	d																								
Southampton Central	d																	05 09							
Southampton Airport Pkway ✈	d																	05 16							
Winchester	d																	05 25							
Basingstoke	d																	05 41							
Guildford	d																							06 09	
Reading ■	d																	06 15						06 47	
Oxford	d																	06 39						07 12	
Banbury	d																	06 57						07 29	
Leamington Spa ■	d																	07 14						07 47	
Coventry	d																	07 27							
Birmingham International ✈	d																	07 38							
Penzance	d																								
St Erth	d																								
Hayle	d																								
Camborne	d																								
Redruth	d																								
Truro	d																								
St Austell	d																								
Par	d																								
Lostwithiel	d																								
Bodmin Parkway	d																								
Liskeard ■	d																								
Plymouth	d																								
Totnes	d																								
Paignton	d																								
Torquay	d																								
Newton Abbot	d																								
Teignmouth	d																								
Dawlish	d																								
Exeter St Davids ■	d																								
Tiverton Parkway	d																								
Taunton	d																								
Weston-super-Mare	d																								
Cardiff Central ■	d																								
Newport (South Wales)	d																								
Bristol Temple Meads ■	d																		06 15						07 00
Bristol Parkway ■	d																		06 25						07 10
Gloucester ■	d																		07 00	07 06					
Cheltenham Spa	d																		07 11	07 17					07 41
Birmingham New Street ■	a																	07 48	07 56	08 07				08 18	08 25
Birmingham New Street ■	d	05 57	05 58	06 15	06 19	06 30	06 31	06 49	06 57	07 03		07 15	07 19	07 21	07 30	07 31	07 49	07 57	08 03			08 15	08 19	08 30	08 31
Tamworth	d		06 14		06 39	06 46		07 07		07 19			07 39		07 46		08 07		08 19				08 36		
Burton-on-Trent	d		06 25		06 51	06 56		07 19		07 31			07 50		07 56		08 19		08 29				08 48	08 53	
Derby ■	a																								
Nottingham ■	a				07 38			08 06					08 34				09 06						09 30		
Chesterfield	a		07 20			08 02				08 25					09 00				09 33					10 03	
Sheffield ■	a		07 44			08 19				08 44					09 17				09 46					10 17	
Doncaster ■	a		08 13							09 15									10 15						
Wakefield Westgate ■	a					08 46									09 46									10 46	
Leeds ■	a					09 01									10 00									11 00	
York ■	a		08 40			09 30				09 40					10 30				10 40					11 30	
Darlington ■	a		09 16			09 58				10 16					10 59				11 14					11 58	
Durham	a		09 33			10 15				10 33					11 15				11 31					12 15	
Chester-le-Street	a																								
Newcastle ■	a		09 47			10 29				10 47					11 29				11 45					12 31	
Morpeth	a														11 45										
Alnmouth for Alnwick	a																								
Berwick-upon-Tweed	a														12 18										
Dunbar	a					11 38																		13 39	
Wolverhampton ■	d	06 15		06 37			06 49		07 15			07 37		07 41		07 49		08 15				08 37			08 49
Stafford	a	06 27					07 02		07 29					07 58		08 02		08 27							09 02
Stoke-on-Trent	a	06 44					07 18									08 18		08 43							09 18
Congleton	a	06 57																							
Macclesfield	a	07 05					07 36									08 36		09 01							09 36
Crewe ■	a			07 08					07 50			08 06		08 18								09 08			
Wilmslow	a								08 07																
Stockport	a	07 18					07 49		08 16							08 50		09 13							09 49
M'chester Piccadilly ■	a	07 28					07 59		08 29							08 59		09 25							09 59
Warrington Bank Quay	a			07 26								08 26		08 40								09 26			
Wigan North Western	a			07 37								08 37		08 51								09 38			
Preston ■	a			07 51								08 51		09 09								09 51			
Lancaster ■	a			08 07								09 09										10 07			
Oxenholme Lake District	a			08 21																		10 21			
Penrith North Lakes	a											09 46													
Carlisle ■	a			09 00								10 01										10 59			
Lockerbie	a																								
Haymarket	a			10 13																		12 17			
Edinburgh ■	a			10 18		12 05									13 01							12 22		14 05	
Haymarket	a														13 16										
Motherwell	a														13 54										
Glasgow Central ■	a											11 15			14 12										
Inverkeithing	a																								
Kirkcaldy	a																								
Markinch	a																								
Ladybank	a																								
Cupar	a																								
Leuchars ■	a																								
Dundee	a																								
Arbroath	a																								
Montrose	a																								
Stonehaven	a																								
Aberdeen	a																								

A ✠ to Edinburgh
B ✠ from Reading

Table T051-R

Saturdays

28 July to 1 September

South Coast and the South West - North West England, The North East and Scotland

		XC	XC	XC	VT	XC	XC	XC	XC	XC	XC	VT	XC	XC	XC	XC	XC	XC	VT	XC	XC	XC	XC
		◇1	◇1	◇1	◇1	1	◇1	◇1	◇1	◇1	◇1	◇1	1	◇1	◇1	◇1	◇1	◇1	◇1	1	◇1	◇1	◇1
							A	B							C								
			🛒		☕	🛒	🛒	🛒		🛒		☕	🛒	🛒	🛒		🛒	🛒	☕	🛒		🛒	🛒
Bournemouth	d						06 25			06 37							07 47						
Brockenhurst	d						06 39			06 55							08 02						
Southampton Central	d		06 20				06 53			07 20				07 47			08 20						
Southampton Airport Pkway	d		06 27				07 01			07 27				07 54			08 27						
Winchester	d		06 36				07 09			07 36				08 03			08 36						
Basingstoke	d		06 52				07 25			07 52				08 19			08 52						
Guildford	d																						
Reading	d		07 15				07 47			08 15				08 45			09 15				09 45		
Oxford	d		07 40				08 12			08 40				09 12			09 40				10 12		
Banbury	d		07 57				08 29			08 57				09 29			09 57				10 29		
Leamington Spa	d		08 14				08 47			09 14				09 47			10 14				10 47		
Coventry	d		08 27		08 42					09 27		09 42					10 27		10 42				
Birmingham International	d		08 38		08 53					09 38		09 53					10 38		10 53				
Penzance	d																						
St Erth	d																						
Hayle	d																						
Camborne	d																						
Redruth	d																						
Truro	d																						
St Austell	d																						
Par	d																						
Lostwithiel	d																						
Bodmin Parkway	d																						
Liskeard	d																						
Plymouth	d			05 25							06 25							07 25					
Totnes	d			05 50							06 50							07 50					
Paignton	d														07 02								
Torquay	d														07 08								
Newton Abbot	d			06 03							07 03				07 19			08 03					
Teignmouth	d														07 26								
Dawlish	d														07 31								
Exeter St Davids	d			06 23							07 23				07 45			08 23					
Tiverton Parkway	d			06 37							07 37				07 58			08 37					
Taunton	d			06 50							07 50				08 11			08 50					
Weston-super-Mare	d																						
Cardiff Central	d	06 40						07 00	07 45							08 45							09 45
Newport (South Wales)	d	06 55						07 15	08 00							09 00							09 59
Bristol Temple Meads	d			07 30				08 00			08 30				09 00			09 30				10 00	
Bristol Parkway	d			07 40				08 10			08 40				09 10			09 40				10 10	
Gloucester	d	07 46							08 50							09 50							10 50
Cheltenham Spa	d	07 57		08 11				08 41	09 01		09 11				09 41	10 01		10 11				10 41	11 01
Birmingham New Street	a	08 45	08 48	08 56	09 05		09 18	09 26	09 45	09 48	09 56	10 04		10 18	10 25	10 45	10 48	10 56	11 04		11 18	11 26	11 45
Birmingham New Street	d	08 49	08 57	09 03	09 15	09 19	09 30	09 31	09 49	09 57	10 03	10 15	10 19	10 30	10 31	10 49	10 57	11 03	11 15	11 19	11 30	11 31	11 49
Tamworth	d	09 09				09 36			10 07		10 19		10 36			11 09				11 36			12 07
Burton-on-Trent	d	09 21		09 28		09 48	09 55		10 19		10 29		10 48	10 53		11 21		11 28		11 48	11 56		12 19
Derby	a																						
Nottingham	a	10 03				10 31			11 03				11 30			12 03				12 30			13 03
Chesterfield	a			10 32			11 01				11 32			12 01				12 32			13 01		
Sheffield	a			10 47			11 17				11 45			12 17				12 45			13 18		
Doncaster	a			11 15							12 13							13 15					
Wakefield Westgate	a						11 46							12 46							13 46		
Leeds	a						12 00							13 00							14 00		
York	a			11 40			12 30				12 40			13 30				13 40			14 30		
Darlington	a			12 15			12 59				13 14			13 59				14 16			14 58		
Durham	a			12 32			13 16				13 31			14 16				14 33			15 15		
Chester-le-Street	a																						
Newcastle	a			12 46			13 29				13 45			14 29				14 46			15 29		
Morpeth	a													14 45									
Alnmouth for Alnwick	a						13 59														15 59		
Berwick-upon-Tweed	a						14 21														16 21		
Dunbar	a													15 39									
Wolverhampton	d		09 15		09 37			09 49		10 15		10 37			10 49		11 15		11 37			11 49	
Stafford	a		09 27					10 02		10 27					11 02		11 27					12 02	
Stoke-on-Trent	a		09 43					10 18		10 43					11 18		11 43					12 18	
Congleton	a																						
Macclesfield	a		10 01					10 36		11 01					11 36		12 01					12 36	
Crewe	a				10 08							11 08							12 07				
Wilmslow	a																						
Stockport	a		10 13					10 49		11 13					11 49		12 13					12 49	
M'chester Piccadilly	a		10 24					11 00		11 25					11 59		12 25					12 59	
Warrington Bank Quay	a				10 26							11 26							12 26				
Wigan North Western	a				10 37							11 37							12 37				
Preston	a				10 51							11 51							12 52				
Lancaster	a				11 07							12 07							13 08				
Oxenholme Lake District	a											12 20							13 21				
Penrith North Lakes	a				11 44																		
Carlisle	a				12 00							12 59							14 00				
Lockerbie	a																						
Haymarket	a											14 11											
Edinburgh	a						15 03					14 17		16 02							17 05		
Haymarket	a						15 15														17 17		
Motherwell	a						15 54												14 58		17 54		
Glasgow Central	a				13 15		16 12												15 15		18 11		
Inverkeithing	a																						
Kirkcaldy	a																						
Markinch	a																						
Ladybank	a																						
Cupar	a																						
Leuchars	a																						
Dundee	a																						
Arbroath	a																						
Montrose	a																						
Stonehaven	a																						
Aberdeen	a																						

A 🛒 to Edinburgh
B 🛒 from Bristol Temple Meads
C 🛒 from Newton Abbot

Table T051-R

Saturdays

28 July to 1 September

South Coast and the South West - North West England, The North East and Scotland

		XC	XC	VT	XC	XC	XC	XC	XC	XC	VT	XC	XC	XC	XC	XC	XC	VT	XC	XC	XC	XC
		◇1	◇1	◇1	1	◇1	◇1	◇1	◇1	◇1	◇1	1	◇1	◇1	◇1	◇1	◇1	◇1	1	◇1	◇1	◇1
						A														A		
		🛒	🛒	☕	🛒	🛒	🛒		🛒	🛒	☕	🛒		🛒	🛒	🛒	🛒	☕		🛒	🛒	🛒
Bournemouth	d	08 47							09 47							10 47						
Brockenhurst	d	09 02							10 02							11 02						
Southampton Central	d	09 18				09 47			10 17							11 20				11 47		
Southampton Airport Pkway	d	09 25				09 54			10 24							11 27				11 54		
Winchester	d	09 34				10 03			10 33							11 36				12 03		
Basingstoke	d	09 52				10 19			10 52							11 52				12 19		
Guildford	d																					
Reading	d	10 15				10 45			11 15				11 45			12 15				12 45		
Oxford	d	10 40				11 12			11 40				12 12			12 40				13 12		
Banbury	d	10 57				11 29			11 57				12 29			12 57				13 29		
Leamington Spa	d	11 14				11 47			12 14				12 47			13 14				13 47		
Coventry	d	11 27		11 42					12 27		12 42					13 27		13 42				
Birmingham International	d	11 38		11 53					12 38		12 53					13 38		13 53				
Penzance	d		06 30														08 28					
St Erth	d		06 38														08 36					
Hayle	d		06 41																			
Camborne	d		06 51														08 46					
Redruth	d		06 57														08 52					
Truro	d		07 09														09 04					
St Austell	d		07 25														09 20					
Par	d		07 32														09 27					
Lostwithiel	d		07 39																			
Bodmin Parkway	d		07 46														09 37					
Liskeard	d		07 58														09 50					
Plymouth	d		08 25				08 39			09 18							10 25					
Totnes	d		08 50				09 04			09 43							10 50					
Paignton	d													10 06								
Torquay	d													10 12								
Newton Abbot	d		09 03				09 17			09 56				10 23			11 03					
Teignmouth	d									10 03				10 30								
Dawlish	d									10 09				10 35								
Exeter St Davids	d		09 23				09 45			10 25				10 49			11 23					
Tiverton Parkway	d		09 37				09 58			10 38				11 02			11 36					
Taunton	d		09 50				10 11			10 51				11 17			11 50					
Weston-super-Mare	d						10 33															
Cardiff Central	d							10 45							11 45							12 45
Newport (South Wales)	d							11 00							12 00							13 00
Bristol Temple Meads	d		10 30				11 00			11 30				12 00			12 30				13 00	
Bristol Parkway	d		10 40				11 10			11 40				12 10			12 40				13 10	
Gloucester	d							11 50							12 48							13 50
Cheltenham Spa	d		11 11				11 41	12 01		12 11				12 41	12 59		13 11				13 41	14 01
Birmingham New Street	a	11 48	11 56	12 05		12 18	12 26	12 45	12 48	12 56	13 05		13 18	13 26	13 45	13 48	13 56	14 05		14 18	14 26	14 45
Birmingham New Street	d	11 57	12 03	12 15	12 19	12 30	12 31	12 49	12 57	13 03	13 15	13 19	13 30	13 31	13 49	13 57	14 03	14 15	14 19	14 30	14 31	14 49
Tamworth	d		12 19		12 36			13 09				13 36			14 09		14 19		14 36			15 09
Burton-on-Trent	d		12 29		12 48	12 57		13 21		13 27		13 48	13 55		14 21		14 29		14 48	14 55		15 21
Derby	a																					
Nottingham	a				13 30			14 03				14 30			15 03				15 30			16 03
Chesterfield	a		13 32			14 01				14 32			15 02				15 32			16 01		
Sheffield	a		13 45			14 17				14 45			15 17				15 45			16 17		
Doncaster	a		14 15							15 15							16 16					
Wakefield Westgate	a					14 46							15 46							16 46		
Leeds	a					15 00							16 00							17 00		
York	a		14 40			15 30				15 40			16 30				16 40			17 28		
Darlington	a		15 14			15 59				16 15			16 58				17 14			17 56		
Durham	a		15 31			16 16				16 32			17 15				17 31			18 13		
Chester-le-Street	a																					
Newcastle	a		15 45			16 29				16 46			17 29				17 45			18 29		
Morpeth	a					16 44																
Alnmouth for Alnwick	a					16 59							18 00									
Berwick-upon-Tweed	a												18 21							19 18		
Dunbar	a					17 40														19 41		
Wolverhampton	d	12 15		12 37			12 49		13 15		13 37			13 49		14 15		14 37			14 49	
Stafford	a	12 27					13 02		13 27					14 02		14 27					15 02	
Stoke-on-Trent	a	12 43					13 18		13 43					14 18		14 43					15 18	
Congleton	a																					
Macclesfield	a	13 01					13 36		14 01					14 36		15 01					15 36	
Crewe	a			13 08							14 08							15 07				
Wilmslow	a																					
Stockport	a	13 13					13 49		14 13					14 49		15 13					15 49	
M'chester Piccadilly	a	13 25					13 59		14 25					14 59		15 25					15 59	
Warrington Bank Quay	a			13 26							14 26							15 26				
Wigan North Western	a			13 37							14 37							15 37				
Preston	a			13 51							14 51							15 51				
Lancaster	a			14 07							15 07							16 07				
Oxenholme Lake District	a										15 21											
Penrith North Lakes	a			14 42														16 43				
Carlisle	a			14 59							16 00							17 00				
Lockerbie	a																					
Haymarket	a			16 16														18 14				
Edinburgh	a			16 23		18 03							19 05					18 22		20 04		
Haymarket	a					18 14							19 16							20 17		
Motherwell	a												19 53									
Glasgow Central	a										17 15		20 15									
Inverkeithing	a					18 28														20 33		
Kirkcaldy	a					18 43														20 50		
Markinch	a					18 52														21 00		
Ladybank	a					18 59														21 08		
Cupar	a					19 06														21 19		
Leuchars	a					19 13														21 26		
Dundee	a					19 29														21 43		
Arbroath	a					19 45																
Montrose	a					20 03																
Stonehaven	a					20 24																
Aberdeen	a					20 44																

A 🛒 to Edinburgh

Table T051-R

Saturdays
28 July to 1 September

South Coast and the South West - North West England, The North East and Scotland

		XC	XC	VT	XC	XC	XC	XC	XC	XC	VT	XC	XC	XC	XC	XC	XC	VT	XC	XC	XC	XC	XC
		◇1	◇1	◇1	1	◇1	◇1	◇1	◇1	◇1	1	1	◇1	◇1	◇1	◇1	◇1	1	1	◇1	◇1	◇1	◇1
						A							B							C			
		✠	✠	⊡		✠	✠	✠	✠	✠	⊡		✠	✠	✠	✠	✠	⊡		✠	✠	✠	✠
Bournemouth	d	11 47							12 47							13 47							14 47
Brockenhurst	d	12 02							13 02							14 02							15 02
Southampton Central	d	12 20							13 18				13 47			14 20							15 18
Southampton Airport Pkway	d	12 27							13 25				13 54			14 27							15 25
Winchester	d	12 36							13 34				14 03			14 36							15 34
Basingstoke	d	12 52							13 52				14 19			14 52							15 52
Guildford	d																						
Reading	d	13 15				13 45			14 15				14 45			15 15				15 45			16 15
Oxford	d	13 40				14 11			14 40				15 12			15 40				16 11			16 40
Banbury	d	13 57				14 29			14 57				15 29			15 57				16 29			16 57
Leamington Spa	d	14 14				14 47			15 14				15 47			16 14				16 47			17 14
Coventry	d	14 27		14 42					15 27		15 42					16 27		16 42					17 27
Birmingham International	d	14 38		14 53					15 38		15 53					16 38		16 53					17 38
Penzance	d																						
St Erth	d																						
Hayle	d																						
Camborne	d																						
Redruth	d																						
Truro	d																						
St Austell	d																						
Par	d		10 31																				
Lostwithiel	d																						
Bodmin Parkway	d		10 43																				
Liskeard	d		10 55																				
Plymouth	d		11 25														13 25						
Totnes	d		11 50														13 51						
Paignton	d									12 35											13 55		
Torquay	d									12 42											14 01		
Newton Abbot	d		12 03							12 54							14 03				14 12		
Teignmouth	d									13 02											14 19		
Dawlish	d									13 09											14 24		
Exeter St Davids	d		12 23							13 23							14 25				14 37		
Tiverton Parkway	d		12 36							13 37							14 38				14 50		
Taunton	d		12 50							13 50							14 52				15 03		
Weston-super-Mare	d																				15 29		
Cardiff Central	d							13 45							14 45							15 45	
Newport (South Wales)	d							14 00							15 00							16 00	
Bristol Temple Meads	d		13 30				14 00			14 30				15 00			15 30				16 00		
Bristol Parkway	d		13 40				14 10			14 40				15 10			15 40				16 10		
Gloucester	d							14 50							15 50							16 50	
Cheltenham Spa	d		14 11				14 41	15 01		15 11				15 41	16 01		16 11				16 41	17 01	
Birmingham New Street	a	14 48	14 56	15 05		15 18	15 26	15 45	15 48	15 56	16 05		16 18	16 26	16 45	16 48	16 56	17 05		17 18	17 26	17 45	17 48
Birmingham New Street	d	14 57	15 03	15 15	15 19	15 30	15 31	15 49	15 57	16 03	16 15	16 19	16 30	16 31	16 49	16 57	17 03	17 15	17 19	17 30	17 31	17 49	17 57
Tamworth	d				15 36			16 09		16 19		16 36			17 09				17 36			18 09	
Burton-on-Trent	d		15 27		15 48	15 55		16 21		16 31		16 48	16 54		17 21		17 26		17 48	17 56		18 21	
Derby	a																						
Nottingham	a				16 30			17 03				17 32			18 03				18 32			19 03	
Chesterfield	a		16 32			17 01				17 25			18 01				18 22			19 01			
Sheffield	a		16 45			17 17				17 40			18 17				18 47			19 17			
Doncaster	a		17 15														19 13						
Wakefield Westgate	a					17 45				18 16			18 49							19 46			
Leeds	a					18 01				18 33			19 03							20 02			
York	a		17 40			18 29				19 05			19 30				19 42			20 30			
Darlington	a		18 11			19 01				19 35			20 04				20 15			20 58			
Durham	a		18 28			19 18				19 52			20 21				20 32			21 15			
Chester-le-Street	a																						
Newcastle	a		18 41			19 32				20 06			20 35				20 47			21 28			
Morpeth	a												20 50										
Alnmouth for Alnwick	a					20 00														21 58			
Berwick-upon-Tweed	a					20 24							21 22										
Dunbar	a												21 46										
Wolverhampton	d	15 15		15 37			15 49		16 15		16 37			16 49		17 15		17 37			17 49		18 15
Stafford	a	15 27					16 02		16 27					17 02		17 27					18 02		18 27
Stoke-on-Trent	a	15 43					16 18		16 43					17 18		17 43					18 18		18 43
Congleton	a																						
Macclesfield	a	16 01					16 36		17 01					17 36		18 01					18 36		19 01
Crewe	a			16 08							17 08							18 07					
Wilmslow	a																						
Stockport	a	16 13					16 49		17 13					17 49		18 13					18 49		19 13
M'chester Piccadilly	a	16 25					16 59		17 25					17 59		18 25					18 59		19 24
Warrington Bank Quay	a			16 26							17 26							18 26					
Wigan North Western	a			16 37							17 37							18 37					
Preston	a			16 51							17 51							18 51					
Lancaster	a			17 07							18 07							19 08					
Oxenholme Lake District	a			17 21							18 21							19 22					
Penrith North Lakes	a										18 47												
Carlisle	a			18 00							19 04							20 01					
Lockerbie	a																						
Haymarket	a										20 14												
Edinburgh	a					21 09				21 34	20 21		22 09							22 59			
Haymarket	a					21 17																	
Motherwell	a					21 56																	
Glasgow Central	a			19 15		22 19												21 15					
Inverkeithing	a																						
Kirkcaldy	a																						
Markinch	a																						
Ladybank	a																						
Cupar	a																						
Leuchars	a																						
Dundee	a																						
Arbroath	a																						
Montrose	a																						
Stonehaven	a																						
Aberdeen	a																						

A ✠ to Edinburgh B ✠ to Newcastle C ✠ to Leeds

Table T051-R

Saturdays
28 July to 1 September

South Coast and the South West - North West England, The North East and Scotland

		XC	VT	XC	XC	XC	XC	XC	XC	VT	XC	XC	XC	XC	XC	XC	VT	XC	XC	XC	XC	XC
		◇1	◇1	1	◇1	◇1	◇1	◇1	◇1	◇1	1	◇1	◇1	◇1	◇1	◇1	◇1	◇1	◇1	◇1	◇1	◇1
					A		B					B		B	B	B			B	B	B	B
		✠	⊡		✠	✠	✠	✠	✠	⊡		✠	✠	✠	✠	✠	⊡	✠	✠	✠	✠	✠
Bournemouth	d							15 47							16 47							17 47
Brockenhurst	d							16 02							17 02							18 02
Southampton Central	d				15 47			16 20							17 20			17 47				18 20
Southampton Airport Pkway	d				15 54			16 27							17 27			17 54				18 27
Winchester	d				16 03			16 36							17 36			18 03				18 36
Basingstoke	d				16 18			16 52							17 52			18 18				18 52
Guildford	d																					
Reading	d				16 45			17 15				17 45			18 15			18 45				19 15
Oxford	d				17 12			17 40				18 12			18 40			19 12				19 40
Banbury	d				17 29			17 57				18 29			18 57			19 29				19 57
Leamington Spa	d				17 47			18 14				18 47			19 14			19 47				20 14
Coventry	d		17 42					18 27		18 42					19 27		19 42					20 27
Birmingham International	d		17 53					18 38		18 53					19 38		19 53					20 38
Penzance	d																					
St Erth	d																					
Hayle	d																					
Camborne	d																					
Redruth	d																					
Truro	d																					
St Austell	d																					
Par	d																				16 27	
Lostwithiel	d																					
Bodmin Parkway	d																				16 38	
Liskeard	d																				16 51	
Plymouth	d	14 25							15 25												17 25	
Totnes	d	14 50							15 51												17 50	
Paignton	d															16 37						
Torquay	d															16 44						
Newton Abbot	d	15 03							16 04							16 56					18 03	
Teignmouth	d															17 04						
Dawlish	d															17 10						
Exeter St Davids	d	15 23							16 24							17 24					18 23	
Tiverton Parkway	d	15 37							16 38							17 38					18 37	
Taunton	d	15 50							16 51							17 51					18 50	
Weston-super-Mare	d																					
Cardiff Central	d						16 45							17 45						18 45		
Newport (South Wales)	d						17 00							18 00						19 00		
Bristol Temple Meads	d	16 30				17 00			17 30				18 00			18 30			19 00		19 30	
Bristol Parkway	d	16 40				17 10			17 40				18 10			18 39			19 10		19 40	
Gloucester	d						17 50							18 46						19 46		
Cheltenham Spa	d	17 12				17 41	18 01		18 13				18 41	18 57		19 11			19 41	19 57	20 12	
Birmingham New Street	a	17 56	18 05		18 18	18 26	18 45	18 48	18 55	19 05		19 18	19 26	19 45	19 48	19 58	20 06	20 18	20 26	20 42	20 49	20 48
Birmingham New Street	d	18 03	18 15	18 19	18 30	18 31	18 49	18 57	19 03	19 15	19 19	19 30	19 31	19 49	19 57	20 03	20 15		20 31	20 49	20 57	21 03
Tamworth	d	18 19		18 36			19 09				19 36			20 09		20 19				21 09		21 19
Burton-on-Trent	d	18 29		18 48	18 56		19 21		19 26		19 48	19 54		20 21		20 30				21 21		21 30
Derby	a																					
Nottingham	a			19 32			20 04				20 30			21 03						22 04		
Chesterfield	a	19 32			20 05				20 24			21 01				21 26						22 22
Sheffield	a	19 47			20 18				20 49			21 17				22 01						22 36
Doncaster	a	20 13							21 21							22 24						23 03
Wakefield Westgate	a				20 46							21 46										23 22
Leeds	a				21 01							22 02										23 37
York	a	20 40			21 59				21 42							22 47						
Darlington	a	21 15							22 14													
Durham	a	21 32							22 31													
Chester-le-Street	a																					
Newcastle	a	21 47							22 47													
Morpeth	a																					
Alnmouth for Alnwick	a																					
Berwick-upon-Tweed	a																					
Dunbar	a																					
Wolverhampton	d		18 37			18 49		19 15		19 37			19 49		20 15		20 37		20 49		21 17	
Stafford	a					19 02		19 27					20 02		20 27		20 50		21 02		21 29	
Stoke-on-Trent	a					19 18		19 43					20 18		20 43				21 18		21 46	
Congleton	a																					
Macclesfield	a					19 36		20 01					20 36		21 01				21 36		22 04	
Crewe	a		19 08							20 09							21 10					
Wilmslow	a																					
Stockport	a					19 49		20 13					20 49		21 13				21 49		22 16	
M'chester Piccadilly	a					19 59		20 25					20 59		21 24				21 59		22 33	
Warrington Bank Quay	a		19 26							20 26												
Wigan North Western	a		19 37							20 37												
Preston	a		19 54							20 52												
Lancaster	a																					
Oxenholme Lake District	a																					
Penrith North Lakes	a																					
Carlisle	a																					
Lockerbie	a																					
Haymarket	a																					
Edinburgh	a																					
Haymarket	a																					
Motherwell	a																					
Glasgow Central	a																					
Inverkeithing	a																					
Kirkcaldy	a																					
Markinch	a																					
Ladybank	a																					
Cupar	a																					
Leuchars	a																					
Dundee	a																					
Arbroath	a																					
Montrose	a																					
Stonehaven	a																					
Aberdeen	a																					

A ✠ to Leeds B ✠ to Birmingham New Street

Saturdays

28 July to 1 September

South Coast and the South West - North West England, The North East and Scotland

		XC ◇1	XC ◇1	XC ◇1 A 🍴	XC ◇1 B 🍴	XC ◇1	XC ◇1	XC ◇1	XC ◇1	XC ◇1	XC 1	XC ◇1
Bournemouth	d				18 47					19 47		
Brockenhurst	d				19 02					20 02		
Southampton Central	d				19 20					20 19		
Southampton Airport Pkway	d				19 27					20 26		
Winchester	d				19 36					20 36		
Basingstoke	d				19 52					20 52		
Guildford	d											
Reading	d	19 45			20 15		20 45			21 15		21 45
Oxford	d	20 12			20 40		21 12			21 39		22 12
Banbury	d	20 30			20 57		21 29			21 57		22 29
Leamington Spa	d	20 48			21 14		21 49			22 14		22 47
Coventry	d				21 27		22 01			22 26		
Birmingham International	d				21 38		22 11			22 37		
Penzance	d			16 25								
St Erth	d			16 34								
Hayle	d											
Camborne	d			16 45								
Redruth	d			16 52								
Truro	d			17 05								
St Austell	d			17 22								
Par	d			17 29								
Lostwithiel	d											
Bodmin Parkway	d			17 41								
Liskeard	d			17 54								
Plymouth	d			18 25								
Totnes	d			18 51								
Paignton	d		18 08									
Torquay	d		18 15									
Newton Abbot	d		18 27	19 04								
Teignmouth	d											
Dawlish	d											
Exeter St Davids	d		18 49	19 24								
Tiverton Parkway	d		19 05	19 38								
Taunton	d		19 18	19 51								
Weston-super-Mare	d											
Cardiff Central	d					20 00			20 50			
Newport (South Wales)	d					20 15			21 05			
Bristol Temple Meads	d		20 00	20 30								
Bristol Parkway	d		20 10	20 40								
Gloucester	d					21 07			21 49			
Cheltenham Spa	d		20 41	21 11		21 18			21 59			
Birmingham New Street	a	21 16	21 38	21 51	21 48	22 07	22 21		22 42	22 47		23 17
Birmingham New Street	d			21 56	21 57	22 10		22 31			22 49	
Tamworth	d					22 27					23 08	
Burton-on-Trent	d			22 20		22 39					23a19	
Derby	a											
Nottingham	a					23 27						
Chesterfield	a			23 15								
Sheffield	a			23 30								
Doncaster	a											
Wakefield Westgate	a											
Leeds	a			00 10								
York	a											
Darlington	a											
Durham	a											
Chester-le-Street	a											
Newcastle	a											
Morpeth	a											
Alnmouth for Alnwick	a											
Berwick-upon-Tweed	a											
Dunbar	a											
Wolverhampton	d				22 15			22 49				
Stafford	a				22 27			23 01				
Stoke-on-Trent	a				22 43			23 19				
Congleton	a											
Macclesfield	a				23 01			23 38				
Crewe	a											
Wilmslow	a											
Stockport	a				23 13			23 53				
M'chester Piccadilly	a				23 29			00 10				
Warrington Bank Quay	a											
Wigan North Western	a											
Preston	a											
Lancaster	a											
Oxenholme Lake District	a											
Penrith North Lakes	a											
Carlisle	a											
Lockerbie	a											
Haymarket	a											
Edinburgh	a											
Haymarket	a											
Motherwell	a											
Glasgow Central	a											
Inverkeithing	a											
Kirkcaldy	a											
Markinch	a											
Ladybank	a											
Cupar	a											
Leuchars	a											
Dundee	a											
Arbroath	a											
Montrose	a											
Stonehaven	a											
Aberdeen	a											

A 🍴 to Bristol Temple Meads
B 🍴 to Reading

Table T051-R

Saturdays

8 September to 6 October

South Coast and the South West - North West England, The North East and Scotland

		XC ◇1	XC ◇1 🍴	VT ◇1 ☕	XC 1	XC ◇1 🍴	XC ◇1 🍴	XC 1	XC ◇1 🍴	XC ◇1 🍴	VT ◇1 ☕	XC 1 🍴	VT ◇1 ☕	XC ◇1 A 🍴	XC ◇1 🍴	XC 1	XC ◇1 B 🍴	XC ◇1	XC ◇1	VT ◇1 ☕	XC 1 🍴	XC ◇1 🍴	XC ◇1 🍴
Bournemouth	d																						
Brockenhurst	d																						
Southampton Central	d																05 09						
Southampton Airport Pkway	d																05 16						
Winchester	d																05 25						
Basingstoke	d																05 41						
Guildford	d																					06 09	
Reading	d																06 15					06 47	
Oxford	d																06 39					07 12	
Banbury	d																06 57					07 29	
Leamington Spa	d																07 14					07 47	
Coventry	d																07 27						
Birmingham International	d																07 38						
Penzance	d																						
St Erth	d																						
Hayle	d																						
Camborne	d																						
Redruth	d																						
Truro	d																						
St Austell	d																						
Par	d																						
Lostwithiel	d																						
Bodmin Parkway	d																						
Liskeard	d																						
Plymouth	d																						
Totnes	d																						
Paignton	d																						
Torquay	d																						
Newton Abbot	d																						
Teignmouth	d																						
Dawlish	d																						
Exeter St Davids	d																						
Tiverton Parkway	d																						
Taunton	d																						
Weston-super-Mare	d																						
Cardiff Central	d																						
Newport (South Wales)	d																						
Bristol Temple Meads	d																	06 15					07 00
Bristol Parkway	d																	06 25					07 10
Gloucester	d																	07 00	07 06				
Cheltenham Spa	d																	07 11	07 17				07 41
Birmingham New Street	a																07 48	07 56	08 07			08 18	08 25
Birmingham New Street	d	05 57	05 58	06 15	06 19	06 30	06 31	06 49	06 57	07 03	07 15	07 19	07 21	07 30	07 31	07 49	07 57	08 03		08 15	08 19	08 30	08 31
Tamworth	d		06 14		06 39	06 46		07 07		07 19		07 39		07 46		08 07		08 19			08 36		
Burton-on-Trent	d		06 26		06 51	06 56		07 19		07 31		07 50		07 56		08 19		08 29			08 48		
Derby	a		06 49		07 03	07 13		07 35		07 45		08 05		08 11		08 36		08 42			09 00	09 13	
Nottingham	a				07 38			08 06				08 34				09 07					09 30		
Chesterfield	a		07 28			08 02				08 31				09 03				09 32				09 58	
Sheffield	a		07 44			08 19				08 44				09 17				09 49				10 17	
Doncaster	a		08 13							09 15								10 15					
Wakefield Westgate	a					08 46								09 46								10 46	
Leeds	a					09 01								10 00								11 02	
York	a		08 40			09 30				09 40				10 30				10 40				11 30	
Darlington	a		09 16			09 58				10 16				10 59				11 14				11 58	
Durham	a		09 33			10 15				10 33				11 15				11 31				12 15	
Chester-le-Street	a																						
Newcastle	a		09 47			10 29				10 47				11 29				11 45				12 31	
Morpeth	a													11 45									
Alnmouth for Alnwick	a																						
Berwick-upon-Tweed	a													12 18									
Dunbar	a					11 38																13 39	
Wolverhampton	d	06 15		06 37			06 49		07 15		07 37		07 41		07 49		08 15			08 37			08 49
Stafford	a	06 27					07 02		07 29				07 58		08 02		08 27						09 02
Stoke-on-Trent	a	06 44					07 18								08 18		08 43						09 18
Congleton	a	06 57																					
Macclesfield	a	07 05					07 36								08 36		09 01						09 36
Crewe	a			07 08					07 50		08 06		08 18							09 08			
Wilmslow	a								08 07														
Stockport	a	07 18					07 49		08 16						08 50		09 13						09 49
M'chester Piccadilly	a	07 28					07 59		08 29						08 59		09 25						09 59
Warrington Bank Quay	a			07 26							08 26		08 40							09 26			
Wigan North Western	a			07 37							08 37		08 51							09 38			
Preston	a			07 51							08 51		09 09							09 51			
Lancaster	a			08 07							09 09									10 07			
Oxenholme Lake District	a			08 21																10 21			
Penrith North Lakes	a										09 46												
Carlisle	a			09 00							10 01									10 59			
Lockerbie	a																						
Haymarket	a			10 13																12 17			
Edinburgh	a			10 18		12 05								13 01						12 22		14 05	
Haymarket	a													13 16									
Motherwell	a													13 54									
Glasgow Central	a										11 15			14 12									
Inverkeithing	a																						
Kirkcaldy	a																						
Markinch	a																						
Ladybank	a																						
Cupar	a																						
Leuchars	a																						
Dundee	a																						
Arbroath	a																						
Montrose	a																						
Stonehaven	a																						
Aberdeen	a																						

A 🍴 to Edinburgh
B 🍴 from Reading

Table T051-R

Saturdays

8 September to 6 October

South Coast and the South West - North West England, The North East and Scotland

		XC	XC	XC	VT	XC	XC	XC	XC	XC	XC	VT	XC	XC	XC	XC	XC	XC	VT	XC	XC	XC	XC
		◇■	◇■	◇■	◇■	■	◇■	◇■	◇■	◇■	◇■	◇■	■	◇■	◇■	◇■	◇■	◇■	◇■	■	◇■	◇■	◇■
							A	B							C								
			🍴		☕	🍴	🍴	🍴		🍴		☕	🍴	🍴	🍴		🍴	🍴	☕	🍴		🍴	🍴
Bournemouth	d						06 25			06 37							07 47						
Brockenhurst	d						06 39			06 55							08 02						
Southampton Central	d		06 20				06 53			07 20				07 47			08 20						
Southampton Airport Pkway	d		06 27				07 01			07 27				07 54			08 27						
Winchester	d		06 36				07 09			07 36				08 03			08 36						
Basingstoke	d		06 52				07 25			07 52				08 19			08 52						
Guildford	d																						
Reading	d		07 15				07 47			08 15				08 45			09 15				09 45		
Oxford	d		07 40				08 12			08 40				09 12			09 40				10 12		
Banbury	d		07 57				08 29			08 57				09 29			09 57				10 29		
Leamington Spa	d		08 14				08 47			09 14				09 47			10 14				10 47		
Coventry	d		08 27		08 42					09 27		09 42					10 27		10 42				
Birmingham International	d		08 38		08 53					09 38		09 53					10 38		10 53				
Penzance	d																						
St Erth	d																						
Hayle	d																						
Camborne	d																						
Redruth	d																						
Truro	d																						
St Austell	d																						
Par	d																						
Lostwithiel	d																						
Bodmin Parkway	d																						
Liskeard	d																						
Plymouth	d			05 25							06 25							07 25					
Totnes	d			05 50							06 50							07 50					
Paignton	d														07 02								
Torquay	d														07 08								
Newton Abbot	d			06 03							07 03				07 19			08 03					
Teignmouth	d														07 26								
Dawlish	d														07 31								
Exeter St Davids	d			06 23							07 23				07 45			08 23					
Tiverton Parkway	d			06 37							07 37				07 58			08 37					
Taunton	d			06 50							07 50				08 11			08 50					
Weston-super-Mare	d																						
Cardiff Central	d	06 40						07 00	07 45							08 45							09 45
Newport (South Wales)	d	06 55						07 15	08 00							09 00							09 59
Bristol Temple Meads	d			07 30				08 00			08 30				09 00			09 30				10 00	
Bristol Parkway	d			07 40				08 10			08 40				09 10			09 40				10 10	
Gloucester	d	07 46							08 50							09 50							10 50
Cheltenham Spa	d	07 57		08 11				08 41	09 01		09 11				09 41	10 01		10 11				10 41	11 01
Birmingham New Street	a	08 45	08 48	08 56	09 05		09 18	09 26	09 45	09 48	09 56	10 04		10 18	10 25	10 45	10 48	10 56	11 04		11 18	11 26	11 45
Birmingham New Street	d	08 49	08 57	09 03	09 15	09 19	09 30	09 31	09 49	09 57	10 03	10 15	10 19	10 30	10 31	10 49	10 57	11 03	11 15	11 19	11 30	11 31	11 49
Tamworth	d	09 09				09 36			10 07		10 19		10 36			11 09				11 36			12 07
Burton-on-Trent	d	09 21		09 28		09 48			10 19				10 48			11 21		11 26		11 48			12 19
Derby	a	09 36		09 45		10 01	10 13		10 36		10 45		11 00	11 13		11 36		11 42		12 01	12 13		12 36
Nottingham	a	10 03				10 30			11 03				11 30			12 03				12 28			13 03
Chesterfield	a			10 32			10 59				11 32			11 59				12 37			12 59		
Sheffield	a			10 47			11 17				11 45			12 17				12 50			13 17		
Doncaster	a			11 15							12 13							13 15					
Wakefield Westgate	a						11 46							12 46							13 46		
Leeds	a						12 00							13 00							14 00		
York	a			11 40			12 30				12 40			13 30				13 40			14 30		
Darlington	a			12 15			12 59				13 14			13 59				14 16			14 58		
Durham	a			12 32			13 16				13 31			14 16				14 33			15 15		
Chester-le-Street	a																						
Newcastle	a			12 46			13 29				13 45			14 29				14 46			15 29		
Morpeth	a													14 45									
Alnmouth for Alnwick	a						13 59														15 59		
Berwick-upon-Tweed	a						14 21														16 21		
Dunbar	a													15 39									
Wolverhampton	d		09 15		09 37			09 49		10 15		10 37			10 49		11 15		11 37			11 49	
Stafford	a		09 27					10 02		10 27					11 02		11 27					12 02	
Stoke-on-Trent	a		09 43					10 18		10 43					11 18		11 43					12 18	
Congleton	a																						
Macclesfield	a		10 01					10 36		11 01					11 36		12 01					12 36	
Crewe	a				10 08							11 08							12 07				
Wilmslow	a																						
Stockport	a		10 13					10 49		11 13					11 49		12 13					12 49	
M'chester Piccadilly	a		10 24					11 00		11 25					11 59		12 25					12 59	
Warrington Bank Quay	a				10 26							11 26							12 26				
Wigan North Western	a				10 37							11 37							12 37				
Preston	a				10 51							11 51							12 52				
Lancaster	a				11 07							12 07							13 08				
Oxenholme Lake District	a											12 20							13 21				
Penrith North Lakes	a				11 44																		
Carlisle	a				12 00							12 59							14 00				
Lockerbie	a																						
Haymarket	a											14 11											
Edinburgh	a						15 03					14 17		16 02							17 05		
Haymarket	a						15 15														17 17		
Motherwell	a						15 54												14 58		17 54		
Glasgow Central	a				13 15		16 12												15 15		18 11		
Inverkeithing	a																						
Kirkcaldy	a																						
Markinch	a																						
Ladybank	a																						
Cupar	a																						
Leuchars	a																						
Dundee	a																						
Arbroath	a																						
Montrose	a																						
Stonehaven	a																						
Aberdeen	a																						

A 🍴 to Edinburgh   B 🍴 from Bristol Temple Meads   C 🍴 from Newton Abbot

Table T051-R

Saturdays

8 September to 6 October

South Coast and the South West - North West England, The North East and Scotland

		XC	XC	VT	XC	XC	XC	XC	XC	XC	VT	XC	XC	XC	XC	XC	XC	VT	XC
		◇■	◇■	◇■	■	◇■	◇■	◇■	◇■	◇■	◇■	■	◇■	◇■	◇■	◇■	◇■	◇■	■
		🍴	🍴	☕	🍴	🍴	🍴		🍴	🍴	☕	🍴		🍴	🍴	🍴	🍴	☕	
Bournemouth	d	08 47							09 47							10 47			
Brockenhurst	d	09 02							10 02							11 02			
Southampton Central	d	09 18				09 47			10 17							11 20			
Southampton Airport Pkway	d	09 25				09 54			10 24							11 27			
Winchester	d	09 34				10 03			10 33							11 36			
Basingstoke	d	09 52				10 19			10 52							11 52			
Guildford	d																		
Reading	d	10 15				10 45			11 15				11 45			12 15			
Oxford	d	10 40				11 12			11 40				12 12			12 40			
Banbury	d	10 57				11 29			11 57				12 29			12 57			
Leamington Spa	d	11 14				11 47			12 14				12 47			13 14			
Coventry	d	11 27		11 42					12 27		12 42					13 27		13 42	
Birmingham International	d	11 38		11 53					12 38		12 53					13 38		13 53	
Penzance	d		06 30														08 28		
St Erth	d		06 38														08 36		
Hayle	d		06 41																
Camborne	d		06 51														08 46		
Redruth	d		06 57														08 52		
Truro	d		07 09														09 04		
St Austell	d		07 25														09 20		
Par	d		07 32														09 27		
Lostwithiel	d		07 39																
Bodmin Parkway	d		07 46														09 37		
Liskeard	d		07 58														09 50		
Plymouth	d		08 25				08 39			09 25							10 25		
Totnes	d		08 50				09 04			09 50							10 50		
Paignton	d													10 06					
Torquay	d													10 12					
Newton Abbot	d		09 03				09 17			10 03				10 23			11 03		
Teignmouth	d													10 30					
Dawlish	d													10 35					
Exeter St Davids	d		09 23				09 45			10 24				10 49			11 23		
Tiverton Parkway	d		09 37				09 58			10 37				11 02			11 36		
Taunton	d		09 50				10 11			10 50				11 17			11 50		
Weston-super-Mare	d						10 33												
Cardiff Central	d							10 45							11 45				
Newport (South Wales)	d							11 00							12 00				
Bristol Temple Meads	d		10 30				11 00			11 30				12 00			12 30		
Bristol Parkway	d		10 40				11 10			11 40				12 10			12 40		
Gloucester	d							11 50							12 48				
Cheltenham Spa	d		11 11				11 41	12 01		12 11				12 41	12 59		13 11		
Birmingham New Street	a	11 48	11 56	12 05		12 18	12 26	12 45	12 48	12 56	13 05		13 18	13 26	13 45	13 48	13 56	14 05	
Birmingham New Street	d	11 57	12 03	12 15	12 19	12 30	12 31	12 49	12 57	13 03	13 15	13 19	13 30	13 31	13 49	13 57	14 03	14 15	14 19
Tamworth	d		12 19		12 36			13 09				13 36			14 09		14 19		14 36
Burton-on-Trent	d				12 48			13 21		13 27		13 48			14 21				14 48
Derby	a		12 42		13 01	13 05		13 35		13 38		14 02	14 13		14 35		14 42		15 00
Nottingham	a				13 28			14 03				14 28			15 03				15 28
Chesterfield	a		13 30			13 46				14 19			14 59				15 25		
Sheffield	a		13 45			14 17				14 45			15 17				15 45		
Doncaster	a		14 15							15 15							16 16		
Wakefield Westgate	a					14 46							15 46						
Leeds	a					15 00							16 00						
York	a		14 40			15 30				15 40			16 30				16 40		
Darlington	a		15 14			15 59				16 15			16 58				17 14		
Durham	a		15 31			16 16				16 32			17 15				17 31		
Chester-le-Street	a																		
Newcastle	a		15 45			16 29				16 46			17 29				17 45		
Morpeth	a					16 44													
Alnmouth for Alnwick	a					16 59							18 00						
Berwick-upon-Tweed	a												18 21						
Dunbar	a					17 40													
Wolverhampton	d	12 15		12 37			12 49		13 15		13 37			13 49		14 15		14 37	
Stafford	a	12 27					13 02		13 27					14 02		14 27			
Stoke-on-Trent	a	12 43					13 18		13 43					14 18		14 43			
Congleton	a																		
Macclesfield	a	13 01					13 36		14 01					14 36		15 01			
Crewe	a			13 08							14 08							15 07	
Wilmslow	a																		
Stockport	a	13 13					13 49		14 13					14 49		15 13			
M'chester Piccadilly	a	13 25					13 59		14 25					14 59		15 25			
Warrington Bank Quay	a			13 26							14 26							15 26	
Wigan North Western	a			13 37							14 37							15 37	
Preston	a			13 51							14 51							15 51	
Lancaster	a			14 07							15 07							16 07	
Oxenholme Lake District	a										15 21								
Penrith North Lakes	a			14 42														16 43	
Carlisle	a			14 59							16 00							17 00	
Lockerbie	a																		
Haymarket	a			16 16														18 14	
Edinburgh	a			16 23		18 03							19 05					18 22	
Haymarket	a					18 14							19 16						
Motherwell	a												19 53						
Glasgow Central	a										17 15		20 15						
Inverkeithing	a					18 28													
Kirkcaldy	a					18 43													
Markinch	a					18 52													
Ladybank	a					18 59													
Cupar	a					19 06													
Leuchars	a					19 13													
Dundee	a					19 29													
Arbroath	a					19 45													
Montrose	a					20 03													
Stonehaven	a					20 24													
Aberdeen	a					20 44													

Saturdays
8 September to 6 October

South Coast and the South West - North West England, The North East and Scotland

		XC	XC	XC	XC	XC	VT	XC	XC	XC	XC	XC	XC	VT	XC	XC	XC	XC
		◇■	◇■	◇■	◇■	◇■	◇■	■	◇■	◇■	◇■	◇■	◇■	■	■	◇■	◇■	◇■
		⊼	⊼	⊼	⊼	⊼	⊡		⊼	⊼	⊼	⊼	⊼	⊡		⊼	⊼	⊼
Bournemouth	d				11 47							12 47						
Brockenhurst ■	d				12 02							13 02						
Southampton Central	d	11 47			12 20							13 18				13 47		
Southampton Airport Pkway	d	11 54			12 27							13 25				13 54		
Winchester	d	12 03			12 36							13 34				14 03		
Basingstoke	d	12 19			12 52							13 52				14 19		
Guildford	d																	
Reading ■	d	12 45			13 15				13 45			14 15				14 45		
Oxford	d	13 12			13 40				14 11			14 40				15 12		
Banbury	d	13 29			13 57				14 29			14 57				15 29		
Leamington Spa ■	d	13 47			14 14				14 47			15 14				15 47		
Coventry	d				14 27		14 42					15 27		15 42				
Birmingham International	d				14 38		14 53					15 38		15 53				
Penzance	d									09 43								
St Erth	d									09 51								
Hayle	d																	
Camborne	d									10 01								
Redruth	d									10 07								
Truro	d									10 19								
St Austell	d									10 35								
Par	d					10 31				10 41								
Lostwithiel	d									10 48								
Bodmin Parkway	d					10 43				10 55								
Liskeard ■	d					10 55				11 15								
Plymouth	d					11 25				11 48			12 25					
Totnes	d					11 50				12 13			12 51					
Paignton	d																	
Torquay	d																	
Newton Abbot	d					12 03				12 25			13 03					
Teignmouth	d																	
Dawlish	d																	
Exeter St Davids ■	d					12 23				12 48			13 23					
Tiverton Parkway	d					12 36				13 02			13 37					
Taunton	d					12 50				13 15			13 50					
Weston-super-Mare	d																	
Cardiff Central ■	d			12 45							13 45							14 45
Newport (South Wales)	d			13 00							14 00							15 00
Bristol Temple Meads ■	d		13 00			13 30				14 00			14 30				15 00	
Bristol Parkway ■	d		13 10			13 40				14 10			14 40				15 10	
Gloucester ■	d			13 50							14 50							15 50
Cheltenham Spa	d		13 41	14 01		14 11				14 41	15 01		15 11				15 41	16 01
Birmingham New Street ■	a	14 18	14 26	14 45	14 48	14 56	15 05		15 18	15 26	15 45	15 48	15 56	16 05		16 18	16 26	16 45
Birmingham New Street ■	d	14 30	14 31	14 49	14 57	15 03	15 15		15 30	15 31	15 49	15 57	16 03	16 15	16 19	16 30	16 31	16 49
Tamworth	d			15 09							16 09		16 19		16 36			17 09
Burton-on-Trent	d			15 21		15 27					16 21				16 48	16 58		17 21
Derby ■	a	15 05		15 35		15 45			16 13		16 36		16 45		17 02	17 13		17 36
Nottingham ■	a			16 03							17 03				17 31			18 03
Chesterfield	a	15 46				16 24			16 59				17 30			17 59		
Sheffield ■	a	16 17				16 45			17 17				17 46			18 16		
Doncaster ■	a					17 15												
Wakefield Westgate ■	a	16 46							17 45				18 16			18 49		
Leeds ■	a	17 00							18 01				18 33			19 03		
York ■	a	17 29				17 40			18 29				19 05			19 30		
Darlington ■	a	17 57				18 11			19 01				19 36			20 04		
Durham	a	18 13				18 28			19 18				19 53			20 21		
Chester-le-Street	a																	
Newcastle ■	a	18 29				18 41			19 32				20 07			20 35		
Morpeth	a															20 50		
Alnmouth for Alnwick	a								20 00									
Berwick-upon-Tweed	a	19 18							20 24							21 22		
Dunbar	a	19 41														21 46		
Wolverhampton ■	d		14 49		15 15		15 37			15 49		16 15		16 37			16 49	
Stafford	a		15 02		15 27					16 02		16 27					17 02	
Stoke-on-Trent	a		15 18		15 43					16 18		16 43					17 18	
Congleton	a																	
Macclesfield	a		15 36		16 01					16 36		17 01					17 36	
Crewe ■	a						16 08							17 08				
Wilmslow	a																	
Stockport	a		15 49		16 13					16 49		17 13					17 49	
M'chester Piccadilly ■	a		15 59		16 25					16 59		17 25					17 59	
Warrington Bank Quay	a						16 26							17 26				
Wigan North Western	a						16 37							17 37				
Preston ■	a						16 51							17 51				
Lancaster ■	a						17 07							18 07				
Oxenholme Lake District	a						17 21							18 21				
Penrith North Lakes	a													18 47				
Carlisle ■	a						18 00							19 04				
Lockerbie	a																	
Haymarket	a													20 14				
Edinburgh ■	a	20 04							21 09				21 34	20 21		22 09		
Haymarket	a	20 17							21 17									
Motherwell	a								21 56									
Glasgow Central ■	a						19 15		22 19									
Inverkeithing	a	20 33																
Kirkcaldy	a	20 50																
Markinch	a	21 00																
Ladybank	a	21 08																
Cupar	a	21 19																
Leuchars ■	a	21 26																
Dundee	a	21 43																
Arbroath	a																	
Montrose	a																	
Stonehaven	a																	
Aberdeen	a																	

Saturdays
8 September to 6 October

South Coast and the South West - North West England, The North East and Scotland

		XC	XC	VT	XC	XC	XC	XC	XC	XC	VT	XC	XC	XC	XC	XC	XC	VT	XC	XC	XC
		◇■	◇■	■ ■	■	◇■	◇■	◇■	◇■	◇■	◇■	■	◇■	◇■	◇■	◇■	◇■	◇■	■	◇■	◇■
		⊼	⊼	⊡		⊼	⊼	⊼	⊼	⊼	⊡		⊼	⊼	⊼	⊼	⊼	⊡		⊼	⊼
Bournemouth	d	13 47							14 47							15 47					
Brockenhurst ■	d	14 02							15 02							16 02					
Southampton Central	d	14 20							15 18				15 47			16 20					
Southampton Airport Pkway	d	14 27							15 25				15 54			16 27					
Winchester	d	14 36							15 34				16 03			16 36					
Basingstoke	d	14 52							15 52				16 18			16 52					
Guildford	d																				
Reading ■	d	15 15				15 45			16 15				16 45			17 15				17 45	
Oxford	d	15 40				16 11			16 40				17 12			17 40				18 12	
Banbury	d	15 57				16 29			16 57				17 29			17 57				18 29	
Leamington Spa ■	d	16 14				16 47			17 14				17 47			18 14				18 47	
Coventry	d	16 27		16 42					17 27		17 42					18 27		18 42			
Birmingham International	d	16 38		16 53					17 38		17 53					18 38		18 53			
Penzance	d																				
St Erth	d																				
Hayle	d																				
Camborne	d																				
Redruth	d																				
Truro	d																				
St Austell	d																				
Par	d																				
Lostwithiel	d																				
Bodmin Parkway	d																				
Liskeard ■	d																				
Plymouth	d		13 25							14 25							15 25				
Totnes	d		13 51							14 50							15 51				
Paignton	d						13 55														
Torquay	d						14 01														
Newton Abbot	d		14 03				14 12			15 03							16 04				
Teignmouth	d						14 19														
Dawlish	d						14 24														
Exeter St Davids ■	d		14 25				14 37			15 23							16 24				16 53
Tiverton Parkway	d		14 38				14 50			15 37							16 38				17 07
Taunton	d		14 52				15 03			15 50							16 51				17 21
Weston-super-Mare	d						15 29														
Cardiff Central ■	d							15 45							16 45						
Newport (South Wales)	d							16 00							17 00						
Bristol Temple Meads ■	d		15 30				16 00			16 30				17 00			17 30				18 00
Bristol Parkway ■	d		15 40				16 10			16 40				17 10			17 40				18 10
Gloucester ■	d							16 50							17 50						
Cheltenham Spa	d		16 11				16 41	17 01		17 12				17 41	18 01		18 13				18 41
Birmingham New Street ■	a	16 48	16 56	17 05		17 18	17 26	17 45	17 48	17 56	18 05		18 18	18 26	18 45	18 48	18 55	19 05		19 18	19 26
Birmingham New Street ■	d	16 57	17 03	17 15	17 19	17 30	17 31	17 49	17 57	18 03	18 15	18 19	18 30	18 31	18 49	18 57	19 03	19 15	19 19	19 30	19 31
Tamworth	d				17 36			18 09		18 19		18 36			19 09				19 36		
Burton-on-Trent	d		17 27		17 48			18 21				18 48			19 21		19 29		19 48		
Derby ■	a		17 42		18 01	18 13		18 36		18 42		19 00	19 13		19 35		19 42		20 00	20 13	
Nottingham ■	a				18 31			19 03				19 31			20 04				20 28		
Chesterfield	a		18 25			18 59				19 25			20 04				20 27			20 59	
Sheffield ■	a		18 47			19 17				19 47			20 18				20 49			21 16	
Doncaster ■	a		19 13							20 13							21 21				
Wakefield Westgate ■	a					19 46							20 46							21 46	
Leeds ■	a					20 02							21 01							22 02	
York ■	a		19 42			20 30				20 40			21 59				21 42				
Darlington ■	a		20 15			20 58				21 15							22 14				
Durham	a		20 32			21 15				21 32							22 31				
Chester-le-Street	a																				
Newcastle ■	a		20 47			21 28				21 47							22 47				
Morpeth	a																				
Alnmouth for Alnwick	a					21 58															
Berwick-upon-Tweed	a																				
Dunbar	a																				
Wolverhampton ■	d	17 15		17 37			17 49		18 15		18 37			18 49		19 15		19 37			19 49
Stafford	a	17 27					18 02		18 27					19 02		19 27					20 02
Stoke-on-Trent	a	17 43					18 18		18 43					19 18		19 43					20 18
Congleton	a																				
Macclesfield	a	18 01					18 36		19 01					19 36		20 01					20 36
Crewe ■	a			18 07							19 08							20 09			
Wilmslow	a																				
Stockport	a	18 13					18 49		19 13					19 49		20 13					20 49
M'chester Piccadilly ■	a	18 25					18 59		19 24					19 59		20 25					20 59
Warrington Bank Quay	a			18 26							19 26							20 26			
Wigan North Western	a			18 37							19 37							20 37			
Preston ■	a			18 51							19 54							20 52			
Lancaster ■	a			19 08																	
Oxenholme Lake District	a			19 22																	
Penrith North Lakes	a																				
Carlisle ■	a			20 01																	
Lockerbie	a																				
Haymarket	a																				
Edinburgh ■	a					22 59															
Haymarket	a																				
Motherwell	a																				
Glasgow Central ■	a			21 15																	
Inverkeithing	a																				
Kirkcaldy	a																				
Markinch	a																				
Ladybank	a																				
Cupar	a																				
Leuchars ■	a																				
Dundee	a																				
Arbroath	a																				
Montrose	a																				
Stonehaven	a																				
Aberdeen	a																				

Table T051-R

Saturdays

8 September to 6 October

South Coast and the South West - North West England, The North East and Scotland

		XC ◇1	XC ◇1	XC ◇1	VT ◇1	XC ◇1	XC ◇1	XC ◇1	XC ◇1	XC ◇1	XC ◇1	XC ◇1	XC ◇1	XC ◇1	XC ◇1	XC ◇1	XC ◇1	XC ◇1
Bournemouth	d		16 47						17 47	17 47				18 47				
Brockenhurst 3	d		17 02						18 02	18 02				19 02				
Southampton Central	d		17 20			17 47			18 20	18 20				19 20				
Southampton Airport Pkway	d		17 27			17 54			18 27	18 27				19 27				
Winchester	d		17 36			18 03			18 36	18 36				19 36				
Basingstoke	d		17 52			18 18			18 52	18 52				19 52				
Guildford	d																	
Reading 7	d		18 15			18 45			19 15	19 15	19 45			20 15		20 45		
Oxford	d		18 40			19 12			19 40	19 40	20 12			20 40		21 12		
Banbury	d		18 57			19 29			19 57	19 57	20 30			20 57		21 29		
Leamington Spa 3	d		19 14			19 47			20 14	20 14	20 48			21 14		21 49		
Coventry	d		19 27		19 42				20 27	20 27				21 27		22 01		
Birmingham International	d		19 38		19 53				20 38	20 38				21 38		22 11		
Penzance	d												16 25					
St Erth	d												16 34					
Hayle	d																	
Camborne	d												16 45					
Redruth	d												16 52					
Truro	d												17 05					
St Austell	d												17 22					
Par	d												17 29					
Lostwithiel	d																	
Bodmin Parkway	d												17 41					
Liskeard 3	d												17 54					
Plymouth	d			16 25									18 25					
Totnes	d			16 51									18 51					
Paignton	d											18 08						
Torquay	d											18 15						
Newton Abbot	d			17 04								18 27	19 04					
Teignmouth	d																	
Dawlish	d																	
Exeter St Davids 6	d			17 24								18 49	19 24					
Tiverton Parkway	d			17 38								19 05	19 38					
Taunton	d			17 51								19 18	19 51					
Weston-super-Mare	d																	
Cardiff Central 7	d	17 45						18 45							20 00			20 50
Newport (South Wales)	d	18 00						19 00							20 15			21 05
Bristol Temple Meads 10	d			18 30			19 00					20 00	20 30					
Bristol Parkway 7	d			18 39			19 10					20 10	20 40					
Gloucester 7	d	18 46						19 46							21 07			21 49
Cheltenham Spa	d	18 57		19 11			19 41	19 57				20 41	21 11		21 18			21 59
Birmingham New Street 12	a	19 45	19 48	19 58	20 06	20 18	20 26	20 42	20 48	20 48	21 16	21 38	21 51	21 48	22 07	22 21		22 42
Birmingham New Street 12	d	19 49	19 57	20 03	20 15		20 31	20 49	20 57	21 03			21 56	21 57	22 10		22 31	
Tamworth	d	20 09		20 19				21 09		21 19					22 27			
Burton-on-Trent	d	20 21						21 21		21 30					22 39			
Derby 6	a	20 33		20 40				21 33		21 42			22 28		22 53			
Nottingham 6	a	21 03						22 04							23 27			
Chesterfield	a			21 23						22 24			23 11					
Sheffield 7	a			22 01						22 39			23 30					
Doncaster 7	a			22 24						23 03								
Wakefield Westgate 7	a									23 22								
Leeds 10	a									23 37			00 10					
York 8	a			22 47														
Darlington 7	a																	
Durham	a																	
Chester-le-Street	a																	
Newcastle 8	a																	
Morpeth	a																	
Alnmouth for Alnwick	a																	
Berwick-upon-Tweed	a																	
Dunbar	a																	
Wolverhampton 7	d		20 15		20 37		20 49		21 17					22 15			22 49	
Stafford	a		20 27		20 50		21 02		21 29					22 27			23 01	
Stoke-on-Trent	a		20 43				21 18		21 46					22 43			23 19	
Congleton	a																	
Macclesfield	a		21 01				21 36		22 04					23 01			23 38	
Crewe 10	a				21 10													
Wilmslow	a																	
Stockport	a		21 13				21 49		22 16					23 13			23 53	
M'chester Piccadilly 10	a		21 24				21 59		22 33					23 29			00 10	
Warrington Bank Quay	a																	
Wigan North Western	a																	
Preston 8	a																	
Lancaster 6	a																	
Oxenholme Lake District	a																	
Penrith North Lakes	a																	
Carlisle 8	a																	
Lockerbie	a																	
Haymarket	a																	
Edinburgh 10	a																	
Haymarket	a																	
Motherwell	a																	
Glasgow Central 15	a																	
Inverkeithing	a																	
Kirkcaldy	a																	
Markinch	a																	
Ladybank	a																	
Cupar	a																	
Leuchars 3	a																	
Dundee	a																	
Arbroath	a																	
Montrose	a																	
Stonehaven	a																	
Aberdeen	a																	

Table T051-R

Saturdays

8 September to 6 October

South Coast and the South West - North West England, The North East and Scotland

		XC ◇1	XC 1	XC ◇1
Bournemouth	d	19 47		
Brockenhurst 3	d	20 02		
Southampton Central	d	20 19		
Southampton Airport Pkway	d	20 26		
Winchester	d	20 36		
Basingstoke	d	20 52		
Guildford	d			
Reading 7	d	21 15		21 45
Oxford	d	21 39		22 12
Banbury	d	21 57		22 29
Leamington Spa 3	d	22 14		22 47
Coventry	d	22 26		
Birmingham International	d	22 37		
Penzance	d			
St Erth	d			
Hayle	d			
Camborne	d			
Redruth	d			
Truro	d			
St Austell	d			
Par	d			
Lostwithiel	d			
Bodmin Parkway	d			
Liskeard 3	d			
Plymouth	d			
Totnes	d			
Paignton	d			
Torquay	d			
Newton Abbot	d			
Teignmouth	d			
Dawlish	d			
Exeter St Davids 6	d			
Tiverton Parkway	d			
Taunton	d			
Weston-super-Mare	d			
Cardiff Central 7	d			
Newport (South Wales)	d			
Bristol Temple Meads 10	d			
Bristol Parkway 7	d			
Gloucester 7	d			
Cheltenham Spa	d			
Birmingham New Street 12	a	22 47		23 17
Birmingham New Street 12	d		22 49	
Tamworth	d		23 08	
Burton-on-Trent	d		23 20	
Derby 6	a		23 33	
Nottingham 6	a			
Chesterfield	a			
Sheffield 7	a			
Doncaster 7	a			
Wakefield Westgate 7	a			
Leeds 10	a			
York 8	a			
Darlington 7	a			
Durham	a			
Chester-le-Street	a			
Newcastle 8	a			
Morpeth	a			
Alnmouth for Alnwick	a			
Berwick-upon-Tweed	a			
Dunbar	a			
Wolverhampton 7	d			
Stafford	a			
Stoke-on-Trent	a			
Congleton	a			
Macclesfield	a			
Crewe 10	a			
Wilmslow	a			
Stockport	a			
M'chester Piccadilly 10	a			
Warrington Bank Quay	a			
Wigan North Western	a			
Preston 8	a			
Lancaster 6	a			
Oxenholme Lake District	a			
Penrith North Lakes	a			
Carlisle 8	a			
Lockerbie	a			
Haymarket	a			
Edinburgh 10	a			
Haymarket	a			
Motherwell	a			
Glasgow Central 15	a			
Inverkeithing	a			
Kirkcaldy	a			
Markinch	a			
Ladybank	a			
Cupar	a			
Leuchars 3	a			
Dundee	a			
Arbroath	a			
Montrose	a			
Stonehaven	a			
Aberdeen	a			

South Coast and the South West - North West England, The North East and Scotland

Station		XC	XC	VT	XC	XC	XC	XC	XC	XC	VT	XC	VT	XC	XC	XC	XC	XC	XC	VT	XC	XC	XC
		◇1	◇1	◇1	1	◇1	◇1	1	◇1	◇1	◇1	1	◇1	◇1	◇1	1	◇1	◇1	◇1	◇1	1	◇1	◇1
			A														B	A				B	
			🛒	🍽		🛒	🛒		🛒	🛒	🍽	🛒	🍽	🛒	🛒		🛒	🛒		🍽	🛒	🛒	🛒
Bournemouth	d																						
Brockenhurst	d																						
Southampton Central	d																05 09						
Southampton Airport Pkway	d																05 16						
Winchester	d																05 25						
Basingstoke	d																05 41						
Guildford	d																					06 09	
Reading	d																06 15					06 47	
Oxford	d																06 39					07 12	
Banbury	d																06 57					07 29	
Leamington Spa	d																07 14					07 47	
Coventry	d																07 27						
Birmingham International	d																07 38						
Penzance	d																						
St Erth	d																						
Hayle	d																						
Camborne	d																						
Redruth	d																						
Truro	d																						
St Austell	d																						
Par	d																						
Lostwithiel	d																						
Bodmin Parkway	d																						
Liskeard	d																						
Plymouth	d																						
Totnes	d																						
Paignton	d																						
Torquay	d																						
Newton Abbot	d																						
Teignmouth	d																						
Dawlish	d																						
Exeter St Davids	d																						
Tiverton Parkway	d																						
Taunton	d																						
Weston-super-Mare	d																						
Cardiff Central	d																						
Newport (South Wales)	d																						
Bristol Temple Meads	d																	06 15					07 00
Bristol Parkway	d																	06 25					07 10
Gloucester	d																	07 00	07 06				
Cheltenham Spa	d																	07 11	07 17				07 41
Birmingham New Street	a																07 48	07 56	08 07			08 18	08 25
Birmingham New Street	d	05 57	05 58	06 15	06 19	06 30	06 31	06 49	06 57	07 03	07 15	07 19	07 21	07 30	07 31	07 49	07 57	08 03		08 15	08 19	08 30	08 31
Tamworth	d		06 14		06 39	06 46		07 07		07 19		07 39		07 46		08 07		08 19			08 36		
Burton-on-Trent	d		06 25		06 51	06 56		07 19		07 31		07 50		07 56		08 19		08 29			08 48		
Derby	a		06 35		07 03	07 09		07 35		07 41		08 05		08 08		08 35		08 41			09 00	09 05	
Nottingham	a				07 38			08 06				08 34				09 07					09 28		
Chesterfield	a		06 58			07 31				08 02				08 31				09 02					
Sheffield	a		07 15			07 46				08 19				08 44				09 17				09 44	
Doncaster	a					08 13								09 15								10 15	
Wakefield Westgate	a		07 45							08 46								09 46					
Leeds	a		08 00							09 01								10 00					
York	a		08 30			08 43				09 30				09 40				10 30				10 40	
Darlington	a		08 58			09 16				09 58				10 16				10 59				11 14	
Durham	a		09 14			09 33				10 15				10 33				11 15				11 31	
Chester-le-Street	a																						
Newcastle	a		09 28			09 47				10 29				10 47				11 29				11 45	
Morpeth	a																	11 45					
Alnmouth for Alnwick	a		09 59																				
Berwick-upon-Tweed	a		10 21															12 18					
Dunbar	a									11 38													
Wolverhampton	d	06 15		06 37			06 49		07 15		07 37		07 41		07 49		08 15			08 37			08 49
Stafford	a	06 27					07 02		07 29				07 58		08 02		08 27						09 02
Stoke-on-Trent	a	06 44					07 18								08 18		08 43						09 18
Congleton	a	06 57																					
Macclesfield	a	07 05					07 36								08 36		09 01						09 36
Crewe	a			07 08					07 50		08 06		08 18							09 08			
Wilmslow	a								08 07														
Stockport	a	07 18					07 49		08 16						08 50		09 13						09 49
M'chester Piccadilly	a	07 28					07 59		08 29						08 59		09 25						09 59
Warrington Bank Quay	a			07 26							08 26		08 40							09 26			
Wigan North Western	a			07 37							08 37		08 51							09 38			
Preston	a			07 51							08 51		09 09							09 51			
Lancaster	a			08 07							09 09									10 07			
Oxenholme Lake District	a			08 21																10 21			
Penrith North Lakes	a										09 46												
Carlisle	a			09 00							10 01									10 59			
Lockerbie	a																						
Haymarket	a			10 13																12 17			
Edinburgh	a		11 03	10 18						12 05								13 01		12 22			
Haymarket	a		11 16															13 16					
Motherwell	a		11 53															13 54					
Glasgow Central	a		12 12								11 15							14 12					
Inverkeithing	a																						
Kirkcaldy	a																						
Markinch	a																						
Ladybank	a																						
Cupar	a																						
Leuchars	a																						
Dundee	a																						
Arbroath	a																						
Montrose	a																						
Stonehaven	a																						
Aberdeen	a																						

A 🛒 to Edinburgh
B 🛒 from Reading

South Coast and the South West - North West England, The North East and Scotland

Station		XC	XC	XC	VT	XC	XC	XC	XC	XC	XC	VT	XC	XC	XC	XC	XC	XC	VT	XC	XC	XC	XC
		◇1	◇1	◇1	◇1	1	◇1	◇1	◇1	◇1	◇1	◇1	1	◇1	◇1	◇1	◇1	◇1	◇1	1	◇1	◇1	◇1
							A	B			C			A	D								
			🛒	🛒	🍽	🛒	🛒	🛒		🛒	🛒	🍽	🛒	🛒	🛒		🛒	🛒	🍽	🛒	🛒	🛒	🛒
Bournemouth	d						06 25			06 37							07 47						
Brockenhurst	d						06 39			06 55							08 02						
Southampton Central	d		06 20				06 53			07 20				07 47			08 20						
Southampton Airport Pkway	d		06 27				07 01			07 27				07 54			08 27						
Winchester	d		06 36				07 09			07 36				08 03			08 36						
Basingstoke	d		06 52				07 25			07 52				08 19			08 52						
Guildford	d																						
Reading	d		07 15				07 47			08 15				08 45			09 15				09 45		
Oxford	d		07 40				08 12			08 40				09 12			09 40				10 12		
Banbury	d		07 57				08 29			08 57				09 29			09 57				10 29		
Leamington Spa	d		08 14				08 47			09 14				09 47			10 14				10 47		
Coventry	d		08 27		08 42					09 27		09 42					10 27		10 42				
Birmingham International	d		08 38		08 53					09 38		09 53					10 38		10 53				
Penzance	d																						
St Erth	d																						
Hayle	d																						
Camborne	d																						
Redruth	d																						
Truro	d																						
St Austell	d																						
Par	d																						
Lostwithiel	d																						
Bodmin Parkway	d																						
Liskeard	d																						
Plymouth	d			05 25							06 25							07 25					
Totnes	d			05 50							06 50							07 50					
Paignton	d														07 02								
Torquay	d														07 08								
Newton Abbot	d			06 03							07 03				07 19			08 03					
Teignmouth	d														07 26								
Dawlish	d														07 31								
Exeter St Davids	d			06 23							07 23				07 45			08 23					
Tiverton Parkway	d			06 37							07 37				07 58			08 37					
Taunton	d			06 50							07 50				08 11			08 50					
Weston-super-Mare	d																						
Cardiff Central	d	06 40						07 00	07 45							08 45							09 45
Newport (South Wales)	d	06 55						07 15	08 00							09 00							09 59
Bristol Temple Meads	d			07 30				08 00			08 30				09 00			09 30				10 00	
Bristol Parkway	d			07 40				08 10			08 40				09 10			09 40				10 10	
Gloucester	d	07 46							08 50							09 50							10 50
Cheltenham Spa	d	07 57		08 11				08 41	09 01		09 11				09 41	10 01		10 11				10 41	11 01
Birmingham New Street	a	08 45	08 48	08 56	09 05		09 18	09 26	09 45	09 48	09 56	10 04		10 18	10 25	10 45	10 48	10 56	11 04		11 18	11 26	11 45
Birmingham New Street	d	08 49	08 57	09 03	09 15	09 19	09 30	09 31	09 49	09 57	10 03	10 15	10 19	10 30	10 31	10 49	10 57	11 03	11 15	11 19	11 30	11 31	11 49
Tamworth	d	09 09				09 36			10 07		10 19		10 36			11 09				11 36			12 07
Burton-on-Trent	d	09 21		09 28		09 48			10 19				10 48			11 21		11 28		11 48			12 19
Derby	a	09 34		09 39		10 00	10 06		10 34		10 38		11 00	11 05		11 34		11 38		12 01	12 05		12 35
Nottingham	a	10 03				10 28			11 03				11 28			12 03				12 28			13 02
Chesterfield	a			10 02							11 02							12 02					
Sheffield	a			10 17			10 46				11 17			11 44				12 17			12 44		
Doncaster	a						11 15							12 13							13 15		
Wakefield Westgate	a			10 46							11 46							12 46					
Leeds	a			11 00							12 00							13 00					
York	a			11 30			11 40				12 30			12 40				13 30			13 40		
Darlington	a			11 58			12 15				12 59			13 14				13 59			14 16		
Durham	a			12 15			12 32				13 16			13 31				14 16			14 33		
Chester-le-Street	a																						
Newcastle	a			12 31			12 46				13 29			13 45				14 29			14 46		
Morpeth	a																	14 45					
Alnmouth for Alnwick	a										13 59												
Berwick-upon-Tweed	a										14 21												
Dunbar	a			13 39														15 39					
Wolverhampton	d		09 15		09 37			09 49		10 15		10 37			10 49		11 15		11 37			11 49	
Stafford	a		09 27					10 02		10 27					11 02		11 27					12 02	
Stoke-on-Trent	a		09 43					10 18		10 43					11 18		11 43					12 18	
Congleton	a																						
Macclesfield	a		10 01					10 36		11 01					11 36		12 01					12 36	
Crewe	a				10 08							11 08							12 07				
Wilmslow	a																						
Stockport	a		10 13					10 49		11 13					11 49		12 13					12 49	
M'chester Piccadilly	a		10 24					11 00		11 25					11 59		12 25					12 59	
Warrington Bank Quay	a				10 26							11 26							12 26				
Wigan North Western	a				10 37							11 37							12 37				
Preston	a				10 51							11 51							12 52				
Lancaster	a				11 07							12 07							13 08				
Oxenholme Lake District	a											12 20							13 21				
Penrith North Lakes	a				11 44																		
Carlisle	a				12 00							12 59							14 00				
Lockerbie	a																						
Haymarket	a											14 11											
Edinburgh	a			14 05							15 03	14 17						16 02					
Haymarket	a										15 15												
Motherwell	a										15 54								14 58				
Glasgow Central	a				13 15						16 12								15 15				
Inverkeithing	a																						
Kirkcaldy	a																						
Markinch	a																						
Ladybank	a																						
Cupar	a																						
Leuchars	a																						
Dundee	a																						
Arbroath	a																						
Montrose	a																						
Stonehaven	a																						
Aberdeen	a																						

A 🛒 from Reading
B 🛒 from Bristol Temple Meads
C 🛒 to Edinburgh
D 🛒 from Newton Abbot

Table T051-R

Saturdays

13 October to 8 December

South Coast and the South West - North West England, The North East and Scotland

		XC		XC	VT	XC	XC	XC	XC	XC	XC	VT		XC	XC	XC	XC	XC	XC	VT	XC	XC		XC	XC
		◇1		◇1	◇1	1	◇1	◇1	◇1	◇1	◇1	◇1		1	◇1	◇1	◇1	◇1	◇1	◇1	1	◇1		◇1	◇1
				A							B								A						
		✠		✠	☕	✠	✠	✠		✠	✠	☕		✠	✠	✠	✠	✠	✠	☕		✠		✠	✠
Bournemouth	d	08 47								09 47								10 47							
Brockenhurst	d	09 02								10 02								11 02							
Southampton Central	d	09 18					09 47			10 17								11 20				11 47			
Southampton Airport Pkway	d	09 25					09 54			10 24								11 27				11 54			
Winchester	d	09 34					10 03			10 33								11 36				12 03			
Basingstoke	d	09 52					10 19			10 52								11 52				12 19			
Guildford	d																								
Reading	d	10 15					10 45			11 15					11 45			12 15				12 45			
Oxford	d	10 40					11 12			11 40					12 12			12 40				13 12			
Banbury	d	10 57					11 29			11 57					12 29			12 57				13 29			
Leamington Spa	d	11 14					11 47			12 14					12 47			13 14				13 47			
Coventry	d	11 27			11 42					12 27		12 42						13 27		13 42					
Birmingham International	d	11 38			11 53					12 38		12 53						13 38		13 53					
Penzance	d			06 30															08 28						
St Erth	d			06 38															08 36						
Hayle	d			06 41																					
Camborne	d			06 51															08 46						
Redruth	d			06 57															08 52						
Truro	d			07 09															09 04						
St Austell	d			07 25															09 20						
Par	d			07 32															09 27						
Lostwithiel	d			07 39																					
Bodmin Parkway	d			07 46															09 37						
Liskeard	d			07 58															09 50						
Plymouth	d			08 25							09 25								10 25						
Totnes	d			08 50							09 50								10 50						
Paignton	d															10 06									
Torquay	d															10 12									
Newton Abbot	d			09 03							10 03					10 23			11 03						
Teignmouth	d															10 30									
Dawlish	d															10 35									
Exeter St Davids	d			09 23							10 24					10 49			11 23						
Tiverton Parkway	d			09 37							10 37					11 02			11 36						
Taunton	d			09 50							10 50					11 17			11 50						
Weston-super-Mare	d																								
Cardiff Central	d								10 45								11 45								12 45
Newport (South Wales)	d								11 00								12 00								13 00
Bristol Temple Meads	d			10 30				11 00			11 30					12 00			12 30					13 00	
Bristol Parkway	d			10 40				11 10			11 40					12 10			12 40					13 10	
Gloucester	d								11 50								12 48								13 50
Cheltenham Spa	d			11 11				11 41	12 01		12 11					12 41	12 59		13 11					13 41	14 01
Birmingham New Street	a	11 48		11 56	12 05		12 18	12 26	12 45	12 48	12 56	13 05			13 18	13 26	13 45	13 48	13 56	14 05		14 18		14 26	14 45
Birmingham New Street	d	11 57		12 03	12 15	12 19	12 30	12 31	12 49	12 57	13 03	13 15		13 19	13 30	13 31	13 49	13 57	14 03	14 15	14 19	14 30		14 31	14 49
Tamworth	d			12 19		12 36			13 09					13 36			14 09		14 19		14 36				15 09
Burton-on-Trent	d					12 48			13 21		13 27			13 48			14 21				14 48				15 21
Derby	a			12 38		13 01	13 05		13 34		13 38			14 00	14 05		14 34		14 38		15 00	15 05			15 35
Nottingham	a					13 28			14 03					14 28			15 03				15 28				16 03
Chesterfield	a			13 02							14 02								15 02						
Sheffield	a			13 17			13 48				14 18				14 44				15 17			15 44			
Doncaster	a						14 15								15 15							16 16			
Wakefield Westgate	a			13 46							14 46								15 46						
Leeds	a			14 00							15 00								16 00						
York	a			14 30			14 40				15 30				15 40				16 30			16 40			
Darlington	a			14 58			15 14				15 59				16 15				16 58			17 14			
Durham	a			15 15			15 31				16 16				16 32				17 15			17 31			
Chester-le-Street	a																								
Newcastle	a			15 29			15 45				16 29				16 46				17 29			17 45			
Morpeth	a										16 44														
Alnmouth for Alnwick	a			15 59							16 59								18 00						
Berwick-upon-Tweed	a			16 21															18 21						
Dunbar	a										17 40														
Wolverhampton	d	12 15			12 37			12 49		13 15		13 37				13 49		14 15		14 37				14 49	
Stafford	a	12 27						13 02		13 27						14 02		14 27						15 02	
Stoke-on-Trent	a	12 43						13 18		13 43						14 18		14 43						15 18	
Congleton	a																								
Macclesfield	a	13 01						13 36		14 01						14 36		15 01						15 36	
Crewe	a				13 08							14 08								15 07					
Wilmslow	a																								
Stockport	a	13 13						13 49		14 13						14 49		15 13						15 49	
M'chester Piccadilly	a	13 25						13 59		14 25						14 59		15 25						15 59	
Warrington Bank Quay	a				13 26							14 26								15 26					
Wigan North Western	a				13 37							14 37								15 37					
Preston	a				13 51							14 51								15 51					
Lancaster	a				14 07							15 07								16 07					
Oxenholme Lake District	a											15 21													
Penrith North Lakes	a				14 42															16 43					
Carlisle	a				14 59							16 00								17 00					
Lockerbie	a																								
Haymarket	a				16 16															18 14					
Edinburgh	a			17 05	16 23						18 03								19 05	18 22					
Haymarket	a			17 17							18 14								19 16						
Motherwell	a			17 54															19 53						
Glasgow Central	a			18 11								17 15							20 15						
Inverkeithing	a										18 28														
Kirkcaldy	a										18 43														
Markinch	a										18 52														
Ladybank	a										18 59														
Cupar	a										19 06														
Leuchars	a										19 13														
Dundee	a										19 29														
Arbroath	a										19 45														
Montrose	a										20 01														
Stonehaven	a										20 22														
Aberdeen	a										20 42														

A ✠ from Plymouth to Edinburgh
B ✠ to Edinburgh

Table T051-R

Saturdays

13 October to 8 December

South Coast and the South West - North West England, The North East and Scotland

		XC	XC	VT	XC	XC	XC	XC		XC	XC	VT	XC	XC	XC	XC	XC	XC		VT	XC	XC	XC	XC	XC
		◇1	◇1	◇1	1	◇1	◇1	◇1		◇1	◇1	■ 1	1	◇1	◇1	◇1	◇1	◇1		■ 1	1	◇1	◇1	◇1	◇1
			A				B				A							C							
		✠	✠	☕		✠	✠	✠		✠	✠	☕		✠	✠	✠	✠	✠		☕		✠	✠	✠	✠
Bournemouth	d	11 47								12 47							13 47								14 47
Brockenhurst	d	12 02								13 02							14 02								15 02
Southampton Central	d	12 20								13 18				13 47			14 20								15 18
Southampton Airport Pkway	d	12 27								13 25				13 54			14 27								15 25
Winchester	d	12 36								13 34				14 03			14 36								15 34
Basingstoke	d	12 52								13 52				14 19			14 52								15 52
Guildford	d																								
Reading	d	13 15				13 45				14 15				14 45			15 15					15 45			16 15
Oxford	d	13 40				14 11				14 40				15 12			15 40					16 11			16 40
Banbury	d	13 57				14 29				14 57				15 29			15 57					16 29			16 57
Leamington Spa	d	14 14				14 47				15 14				15 47			16 14					16 47			17 14
Coventry	d	14 27		14 42						15 27		15 42					16 27			16 42					17 27
Birmingham International	d	14 38		14 53						15 38		15 53					16 38			16 53					17 38
Penzance	d						09 43																		
St Erth	d						09 51																		
Hayle	d																								
Camborne	d						10 01																		
Redruth	d						10 07																		
Truro	d						10 19																		
St Austell	d						10 35																		
Par	d						10 41																		
Lostwithiel	d						10 48																		
Bodmin Parkway	d						10 55																		
Liskeard	d						11 15																		
Plymouth	d		11 25				11 48				12 25							13 25							
Totnes	d		11 50				12 13				12 51							13 51							
Paignton	d																						13 55		
Torquay	d																						14 01		
Newton Abbot	d		12 03				12 25				13 03							14 03					14 12		
Teignmouth	d																						14 19		
Dawlish	d																						14 24		
Exeter St Davids	d		12 23				12 48				13 23							14 25					14 37		
Tiverton Parkway	d		12 36				13 02				13 37							14 38					14 50		
Taunton	d		12 50				13 15				13 50							14 52					15 03		
Weston-super-Mare	d																						15 29		
Cardiff Central	d							13 45								14 45								15 45	
Newport (South Wales)	d							14 00								15 00								16 00	
Bristol Temple Meads	d		13 30				14 00				14 30				15 00			15 30					16 00		
Bristol Parkway	d		13 40				14 10				14 40				15 10			15 40					16 10		
Gloucester	d							14 50								15 50								16 50	
Cheltenham Spa	d		14 11				14 41	15 01			15 11				15 41	16 01		16 11					16 41	17 01	
Birmingham New Street	a	14 48	14 56	15 05		15 18	15 26	15 45		15 48	15 56	16 05		16 18	16 26	16 45	16 48	16 56		17 05		17 18	17 26	17 45	17 48
Birmingham New Street	d	14 57	15 03	15 15	15 19	15 30	15 31	15 49		15 57	16 03	16 15	16 19	16 30	16 31	16 49	16 57	17 03		17 15	17 19	17 30	17 31	17 49	17 57
Tamworth	d				15 36			16 09			16 19		16 36			17 09					17 36			18 09	
Burton-on-Trent	d		15 27		15 48			16 21					16 48	16 54		17 21		17 26			17 48			18 21	
Derby	a		15 40		16 00	16 06		16 34			16 40		17 00	17 05		17 36		17 40			18 00	18 05		18 36	
Nottingham	a				16 28			17 03					17 31			18 04					18 31			19 03	
Chesterfield	a		16 02								17 03							18 02							
Sheffield	a		16 18			16 44					17 17			17 45				18 17				18 44			
Doncaster	a					17 15																19 13			
Wakefield Westgate	a		16 46								17 47			18 16				18 49							
Leeds	a		17 00								18 01			18 33				19 03							
York	a		17 29			17 40					18 30			19 05				19 30				19 40			
Darlington	a		17 57			18 11					19 01			19 34				20 04				20 13			
Durham	a		18 13			18 28					19 18			19 51				20 21				20 30			
Chester-le-Street	a																								
Newcastle	a		18 29			18 41					19 32			20 07				20 35				20 44			
Morpeth	a																	20 50							
Alnmouth for Alnwick	a										20 00														
Berwick-upon-Tweed	a		19 18								20 24							21 22							
Dunbar	a		19 41															21 46							
Wolverhampton	d	15 15		15 37			15 49			16 15		16 37			16 49		17 15			17 37			17 49		18 15
Stafford	a	15 27					16 02			16 27					17 02		17 27						18 02		18 27
Stoke-on-Trent	a	15 43					16 18			16 43					17 18		17 43						18 18		18 43
Congleton	a																								
Macclesfield	a	16 01					16 36			17 01					17 36		18 01						18 36		19 01
Crewe	a			16 08								17 08								18 07					
Wilmslow	a																								
Stockport	a	16 13					16 49			17 13					17 49		18 13						18 49		19 13
M'chester Piccadilly	a	16 25					16 59			17 25					17 59		18 25						18 59		19 24
Warrington Bank Quay	a			16 26								17 26								18 26					
Wigan North Western	a			16 37								17 37								18 37					
Preston	a			16 51								17 51								18 51					
Lancaster	a			17 07								18 07								19 08					
Oxenholme Lake District	a			17 21								18 21								19 22					
Penrith North Lakes	a											18 47													
Carlisle	a			18 00								19 04								20 01					
Lockerbie	a																								
Haymarket	a											20 14													
Edinburgh	a		20 04								21 09	20 21						22 09							
Haymarket	a		20 17								21 17														
Motherwell	a										21 56														
Glasgow Central	a			19 15							22 19									21 15					
Inverkeithing	a		20 33																						
Kirkcaldy	a		20 50																						
Markinch	a		21 00																						
Ladybank	a		21 08																						
Cupar	a		21 19																						
Leuchars	a		21 26																						
Dundee	a		21 43																						
Arbroath	a																								
Montrose	a																								
Stonehaven	a																								
Aberdeen	a																								

A ✠ to Edinburgh
B ✠ from Plymouth
C ✠ to Newcastle

Table T051-R

Saturdays
13 October to 8 December

South Coast and the South West - North West England, The North East and Scotland

		XC ◇1 A 🛒	VT ◇1 🍴	XC 1	XC ◇1 🛒	XC ◇1 🛒	XC ◇1 B 🛒	XC ◇1 🛒	XC ◇1 A 🛒	VT ◇1 🍴	XC 1	XC ◇1 B 🛒	XC ◇1 🛒	XC ◇1 B 🛒	XC ◇1 B 🛒	XC ◇1 B 🛒	VT ◇1 🍴	XC ◇1 B 🛒	XC ◇1 B 🛒	XC ◇1 B 🛒	XC ◇1 B 🛒	XC ◇1 B 🛒
Bournemouth	d							15 47							16 47						17 47	
Brockenhurst	d							16 02							17 02						18 02	
Southampton Central	d				15 47			16 20							17 20			17 47			18 20	
Southampton Airport Pkway	d				15 54			16 27							17 27			17 54			18 27	
Winchester	d				16 03			16 36							17 36			18 03			18 36	
Basingstoke	d				16 18			16 52							17 52			18 18			18 52	
Guildford	d																					
Reading	d				16 45			17 15				17 45			18 15			18 45			19 15	
Oxford	d				17 12			17 40				18 12			18 40			19 12			19 40	
Banbury	d				17 29			17 57				18 29			18 57			19 29			19 57	
Leamington Spa	d				17 47			18 14				18 47			19 14			19 47			20 14	
Coventry	d		17 42					18 27		18 42					19 27		19 42				20 27	
Birmingham International	d		17 53					18 38		18 53					19 38		19 53				20 38	
Penzance	d																					
St Erth	d																					
Hayle	d																					
Camborne	d																					
Redruth	d																					
Truro	d																					
St Austell	d																					
Par	d																					
Lostwithiel	d																					
Bodmin Parkway	d																					
Liskeard	d																					
Plymouth	d	14 25							15 25							16 25						17 25
Totnes	d	14 50							15 51							16 51						17 51
Paignton	d																					
Torquay	d																					
Newton Abbot	d	15 03							16 04							17 04						18 04
Teignmouth	d																					
Dawlish	d																					
Exeter St Davids	d	15 23							16 24				16 53			17 24						18 24
Tiverton Parkway	d	15 37							16 38				17 07			17 38						18 38
Taunton	d	15 50							16 51				17 21			17 51						18 51
Weston-super-Mare	d																					
Cardiff Central	d						16 45							17 45						18 45		
Newport (South Wales)	d						17 00							18 00						19 00		
Bristol Temple Meads	d	16 30				17 00			17 30				18 00			18 30			19 00			19 30
Bristol Parkway	d	16 40				17 10			17 40				18 10			18 39			19 10			19 40
Gloucester	d						17 50							18 46						19 46		
Cheltenham Spa	d	17 12				17 41	18 01		18 13				18 41	18 57		19 11			19 41	19 57		20 12
Birmingham New Street	a	17 56	18 05		18 18	18 26	18 45	18 48	18 56	19 05		19 18	19 26	19 45	19 48	19 58	20 06	20 18	20 26	20 42	20 48	20 51
Birmingham New Street	d	18 03	18 15	18 19	18 30	18 31	18 49	18 57	19 03	19 15	19 19	19 30	19 31	19 49	19 57	20 03	20 15	20 30	20 31	20 49	20 57	21 03
Tamworth	d	18 19		18 36			19 09				19 36			20 09		20 19				21 09		21 19
Burton-on-Trent	d			18 48			19 21		19 27		19 48			20 21						21 21		21 30
Derby	a	18 40		19 00	19 05		19 32		19 39		20 00	20 05		20 33		20 40		21 24		21 32		21 43
Nottingham	a			19 31			20 04				20 28			21 03						22 04		
Chesterfield	a	19 02			19 34				20 03			20 34				21 04		21 46				22 07
Sheffield	a	19 17			19 47				20 18			20 47				21 19		21 59				22 22
Doncaster	a				20 13							21 21						22 24				22 50
Wakefield Westgate	a	19 46							20 47							21 47						23 12
Leeds	a	20 02							21 02							22 03						23 27
York	a	20 30			20 40				21 59			21 42						22 46				
Darlington	a	20 58			21 15							22 14										
Durham	a	21 15			21 32							22 31										
Chester-le-Street	a																					
Newcastle	a	21 28			21 47							22 47										
Morpeth	a																					
Alnmouth for Alnwick	a	21 58																				
Berwick-upon-Tweed	a																					
Dunbar	a																					
Wolverhampton	d		18 37			18 49		19 15		19 37			19 49		20 15		20 37		20 49		21 17	
Stafford	a					19 02		19 27					20 02		20 27		20 50		21 02		21 29	
Stoke-on-Trent	a					19 18		19 43					20 18		20 43				21 18		21 46	
Congleton	a																					
Macclesfield	a					19 36		20 01					20 36		21 01				21 36		22 04	
Crewe	a		19 08							20 09							21 10					
Wilmslow	a																					
Stockport	a					19 49		20 13					20 49		21 13				21 49		22 16	
M'chester Piccadilly	a					19 59		20 25					20 59		21 24				21 59		22 33	
Warrington Bank Quay	a		19 26							20 26												
Wigan North Western	a		19 37							20 37												
Preston	a		19 54							20 52												
Lancaster	a																					
Oxenholme Lake District	a																					
Penrith North Lakes	a																					
Carlisle	a																					
Lockerbie	a																					
Haymarket	a																					
Edinburgh	a	22 59																				
Haymarket	a																					
Motherwell	a																					
Glasgow Central	a																					
Inverkeithing	a																					
Kirkcaldy	a																					
Markinch	a																					
Ladybank	a																					
Cupar	a																					
Leuchars	a																					
Dundee	a																					
Arbroath	a																					
Montrose	a																					
Stonehaven	a																					
Aberdeen	a																					

A 🛒 to Leeds
B 🛒 to Birmingham New Street

Table T051-R

Saturdays
13 October to 8 December

South Coast and the South West - North West England, The North East and Scotland

		XC ◇1	XC ◇1	XC ◇1 A 🛒	XC ◇1 B 🛒	XC ◇1	XC ◇1	XC ◇1	XC ◇1	XC ◇1	XC 1	XC ◇1
Bournemouth	d			18 47						19 47		
Brockenhurst	d			19 02						20 02		
Southampton Central	d			19 20						20 19		
Southampton Airport Pkway	d			19 27						20 26		
Winchester	d			19 36						20 36		
Basingstoke	d			19 52						20 52		
Guildford	d											
Reading	d	19 45		20 15			20 45			21 15		21 45
Oxford	d	20 12		20 40			21 12			21 39		22 12
Banbury	d	20 30		20 57			21 29			21 57		22 29
Leamington Spa	d	20 48		21 14			21 49			22 14		22 47
Coventry	d			21 27			22 01			22 26		
Birmingham International	d			21 38			22 11			22 37		
Penzance	d											
St Erth	d											
Hayle	d											
Camborne	d											
Redruth	d											
Truro	d											
St Austell	d											
Par	d											
Lostwithiel	d											
Bodmin Parkway	d											
Liskeard	d											
Plymouth	d				18 25							
Totnes	d				18 50							
Paignton	d											
Torquay	d											
Newton Abbot	d				19 03							
Teignmouth	d											
Dawlish	d											
Exeter St Davids	d				19 23							
Tiverton Parkway	d				19 37							
Taunton	d				19 50							
Weston-super-Mare	d											
Cardiff Central	d					20 00			20 50			
Newport (South Wales)	d					20 15			21 05			
Bristol Temple Meads	d		20 00		20 30							
Bristol Parkway	d		20 10		20 40							
Gloucester	d					21 07			21 49			
Cheltenham Spa	d		20 41		21 11	21 18			21 59			
Birmingham New Street	a	21 16	21 38	21 48	21 52	22 07	22 21		22 42	22 47		23 17
Birmingham New Street	d			21 57		22 10		22 31			22 49	
Tamworth	d					22 27					23 08	
Burton-on-Trent	d					22 39					23 20	
Derby	a					22 53					23 33	
Nottingham	a					23 27						
Chesterfield	a											
Sheffield	a											
Doncaster	a											
Wakefield Westgate	a											
Leeds	a											
York	a											
Darlington	a											
Durham	a											
Chester-le-Street	a											
Newcastle	a											
Morpeth	a											
Alnmouth for Alnwick	a											
Berwick-upon-Tweed	a											
Dunbar	a											
Wolverhampton	d			22 15				22 49				
Stafford	a			22 27				23 01				
Stoke-on-Trent	a			22 43				23 19				
Congleton	a											
Macclesfield	a			23 01				23 38				
Crewe	a											
Wilmslow	a											
Stockport	a			23 13				23 53				
M'chester Piccadilly	a			23 29				00 10				
Warrington Bank Quay	a											
Wigan North Western	a											
Preston	a											
Lancaster	a											
Oxenholme Lake District	a											
Penrith North Lakes	a											
Carlisle	a											
Lockerbie	a											
Haymarket	a											
Edinburgh	a											
Haymarket	a											
Motherwell	a											
Glasgow Central	a											
Inverkeithing	a											
Kirkcaldy	a											
Markinch	a											
Ladybank	a											
Cupar	a											
Leuchars	a											
Dundee	a											
Arbroath	a											
Montrose	a											
Stonehaven	a											
Aberdeen	a											

A 🛒 to Reading
B 🛒 to Bristol Temple Meads

Table T051-R

Sundays 20 May to 15 July

South Coast and the South West - North West England, The North East and Scotland

		VT	XC	XC	VT	XC	XC	VT	XC	XC	VT	XC	XC	XC	VT	XC	XC	XC	XC	VT	XC	XC	XC
		◇■	◇■	◇■	◇■	◇■	◇■	◇■	◇■	◇■	◇■	◇■	◇■	◇■	◇■	◇■	◇■	◇■	◇■	◇■	◇■	◇■	◇■
							A										B		A				B
Bournemouth	d																	09 40					
Brockenhurst	d																	09 57					
Southampton Central	d												09 15					10 15					
Southampton Airport Pkwy	d												09 22					10 22					
Winchester	d												09 31					10 31					
Basingstoke	d												09 47					10 47					
Guildford	d																						
Reading	d								09 12				10 11					11 11					
Oxford	d								09 37				10 37					11 37					
Banbury	d								09 55				10 55					11 55					
Leamington Spa	d								10 12				11 12					12 12					
Coventry	d								10 29				11 29					12 28					
Birmingham International	d								10 40				11 41					12 40					
Penzance	d																						
St Erth	d																						
Hayle	d																						
Camborne	d																						
Redruth	d																						
Truro	d																						
St Austell	d																						
Par	d																						
Lostwithiel	d																						
Bodmin Parkway	d																						
Liskeard	d																						
Plymouth	d																		09 25				
Totnes	d																		09 50				
Paignton	d																						
Torquay	d																						
Newton Abbot	d																		10 03				
Teignmouth	d																						
Dawlish	d																						
Exeter St Davids	d																		10 23				
Tiverton Parkway	d																		10 37				
Taunton	d																		10 50				
Weston-super-Mare	d																						
Cardiff Central	d																10 45						11 45
Newport (South Wales)	d																11 06						12 05
Bristol Temple Meads	d									09 15				10 30					11 30				
Bristol Parkway	d									09 25				10 40					11 40				
Gloucester	d									10 00							11 50						12 50
Cheltenham Spa	d									10 12				11 11			12 01		12 11				13 01
Birmingham New Street	a								10 50	10 49			11 51	11 48			12 45	12 50	12 49				13 45
Birmingham New Street	d	08 45	09 01	09 03	09 20	10 01	10 03	10 20	11 01	11 03	11 20	11 49	11 57	12 03	12 20	12 30	12 49	12 57	13 03	13 20	13 30	13 30	13 49
Tamworth	d			09 19			10 18					12 07		12 19			13 07						14 07
Burton-on-Trent	d			09 28			10 29			11 25		12 19					13 19		13 26				14 19
Derby	a			09 41			10 40			11 37		12 34		12 38		13 01	13 33		13 37			14 01	14 34
Nottingham	a											13 00					14 00						15 00
Chesterfield	a			10 02			11 02			12 02				13 02		13 29			14 02			14 29	
Sheffield	a			10 18			11 17			12 18				13 18		13 43			14 17			14 45	
Doncaster	a															14 14						15 18	
Wakefield Westgate	a			10 45			11 45			12 45				13 44					14 45				
Leeds	a			10 59			11 59			13 00				14 00					15 00				
York	a			11 29			12 30			13 27				14 27		14 40			15 27			15 40	
Darlington	a			11 57			12 58			13 56				14 55		15 16			15 55			16 11	
Durham	a			12 14			13 15			14 13				15 13		15 33			16 12			16 28	
Chester-le-Street	a																						
Newcastle	a			12 27			13 28			14 27				15 26		15 47			16 25			16 42	
Morpeth	a									14 45													
Alnmouth for Alnwick	a						13 55							15 53					16 52				
Berwick-upon-Tweed	a						14 16							16 12									
Dunbar	a			13 34						15 39									17 35				
Wolverhampton	d	09 04	09 19		09 37	10 19		10 37	11 19		11 37		12 16		12 37			13 16		13 37	13 49		
Stafford	a	09 17	09 32			10 32			11 31				12 28					13 28			14 02		
Stoke-on-Trent	a		09 51			10 48			11 48				12 45					13 44			14 18		
Congleton	a																						
Macclesfield	a		10 09			11 08			12 09				13 04					14 04			14 36		
Crewe	a	09 35			10 07			11 10			12 07				13 07					14 07			
Wilmslow	a																						
Stockport	a		10 22			11 22			12 24				13 16					14 16			14 50		
M'chester Piccadilly	a		10 38			11 33			12 41				13 29					14 29			14 59		
Warrington Bank Quay	a	09 54			10 26			11 28			12 26				13 26					14 26			
Wigan North Western	a	10 05			10 37			11 39			12 37				13 37					14 37			
Preston	a	10 20			10 51			11 53			12 51				13 51					14 50			
Lancaster	a				11 16			12 09			13 07				14 08					15 08			
Oxenholme Lake District	a				11 32			12 22			13 21									15 22			
Penrith North Lakes	a														14 44								
Carlisle	a				12 11			13 01			14 00				15 00					16 01			
Lockerbie	a																						
Haymarket	a							14 16							16 14								
Edinburgh	a			14 01			14 58	14 21		16 03				16 55	16 20				17 58				
Haymarket	a						15 13							17 14					18 16				
Motherwell	a						15 55							17 51									
Glasgow Central	a										15 19									17 19			
Inverkeithing	a																		18 28				
Kirkcaldy	a																		18 44				
Markinch	a																		18 53				
Ladybank	a																		19 01				
Cupar	a																		19 07				
Leuchars	a																		19 14				
Dundee	a																		19 29				
Arbroath	a																		19 46				
Montrose	a																		20 00				
Stonehaven	a																		20 22				
Aberdeen	a																		20 42				

A to Edinburgh
B from Birmingham New Street

Table T051-R

Sundays 20 May to 15 July

South Coast and the South West - North West England, The North East and Scotland

		XC	XC	VT	XC	XC	XC	XC	XC	VT	XC	XC	XC	XC	XC	VT	XC	XC	XC	XC	XC	VT	XC
		◇■	◇■	◇■	◇■	◇■	◇■	◇■	◇■	◇■	◇■	◇■	◇■	◇■	◇■	◇■	◇■	◇■	◇■	◇■	◇■	◇■	◇■
			A		B		C		D				C		A								E
Bournemouth	d	10 40						11 40						12 40						13 40			
Brockenhurst	d	10 57						11 57						12 57						13 57			
Southampton Central	d	11 15						12 15						13 15						14 15			
Southampton Airport Pkwy	d	11 22						12 22						13 22						14 22			
Winchester	d	11 31						12 31						13 31						14 31			
Basingstoke	d	11 47						12 47						13 47						14 47			
Guildford	d				12 14																		
Reading	d	12 11			12 54			13 11			13 41			14 10			14 41			15 11			15 41
Oxford	d	12 37			13 17			13 37			14 06			14 37			15 06			15 37			16 06
Banbury	d	12 55			13 35			13 55			14 24			14 55			15 24			15 55			16 24
Leamington Spa	d	13 12			13 52			14 12			14 41			15 12			15 41			16 12			16 41
Coventry	d	13 27		13 42				14 27		14 42	14 54			15 27		15 42	15 54			16 27		16 42	16 54
Birmingham International	d	13 38		13 53				14 38		14 53	15 04			15 38		15 53	16 04			16 38		16 53	17 04
Penzance	d								09 30														
St Erth	d								09 38														
Hayle	d																						
Camborne	d								09 48														
Redruth	d								09 54														
Truro	d								10 08														
St Austell	d								10 24														
Par	d								10 31												12 23		
Lostwithiel	d																						
Bodmin Parkway	d								10 41												12 35		
Liskeard	d								10 54												12 48		
Plymouth	d		10 25						11 25			12 00			12 24			12 52			13 25		
Totnes	d		10 50						11 50						12 50						13 50		
Paignton	d					10 50																	
Torquay	d					10 56																	
Newton Abbot	d		11 03			11 08			12 03			12 36			13 03			13 27			14 03		
Teignmouth	d					11 15																	
Dawlish	d					11 20																	
Exeter St Davids	d		11 23			11 33			12 23			12 56			13 23			13 47			14 23		
Tiverton Parkway	d		11 37			11 47			12 37			13 10			13 37						14 36		
Taunton	d		11 52			12 00			12 50			13 23			13 50						14 49		
Weston-super-Mare	d					12 21																	
Cardiff Central	d						12 45						13 45						14 45				
Newport (South Wales)	d						13 05						14 05						15 05				
Bristol Temple Meads	d		12 30			13 00			13 30			14 00			14 30			15 00			15 30		
Bristol Parkway	d		12 40			13 10			13 40			14 10			14 40			15 10			15 40		
Gloucester	d						13 50						14 50						15 50				
Cheltenham Spa	d		13 11			13 41	14 01		14 11			14 41	15 01		15 11			15 40	16 01		16 11		
Birmingham New Street	a	13 48	13 48	14 04	14 19	14 27	14 45	14 48	14 48	15 04	15 14	15 27	15 45	15 48	15 49	16 05	16 14	16 27	16 45	16 48	16 49	17 04	17 14
Birmingham New Street	d	13 57	14 03	14 15	14 30	14 31	14 49	14 57	15 03	15 15	15 30	15 31	15 49	15 57	16 03	16 15	16 30	16 31	16 49	16 57	17 03	17 15	17 30
Tamworth	d		14 19				15 09						16 07		16 19				17 07				
Burton-on-Trent	d						15 21		15 25				16 19						17 19		17 25		
Derby	a		14 39		15 01		15 33		15 37		16 01		16 34		16 40		17 02		17 33		17 36		18 02
Nottingham	a						16 00						17 00						18 00				
Chesterfield	a		15 02						16 02						17 03						18 01		
Sheffield	a		15 17		15 45				16 18		16 42				17 19		17 41				18 19		18 42
Doncaster	a				16 14						17 15						18 14						19 17
Wakefield Westgate	a		15 45						16 45						17 44		18 32				18 45		
Leeds	a		16 00						16 59						18 00		18 47				19 01		
York	a		16 27		16 40				17 27		17 40				18 27		19 21				19 30		19 46
Darlington	a		16 55		17 11				17 55		18 09				18 56		19 49				19 59		20 20
Durham	a		17 12		17 29				18 12		18 26				19 14		20 06				20 16		20 37
Chester-le-Street	a																						
Newcastle	a		17 25		17 44				18 25		18 41				19 27		20 20				20 30		20 51
Morpeth	a		17 40																		20 49		
Alnmouth for Alnwick	a		17 55												19 56								
Berwick-upon-Tweed	a		18 16						19 10						20 19						21 21		
Dunbar	a								19 33												21 44		
Wolverhampton	d	14 15		14 37		14 49		15 15		15 37		15 49		16 15		16 37		16 49		17 15		17 37	
Stafford	a	14 27				15 02		15 27				16 02		16 27				17 02		17 28			
Stoke-on-Trent	a	14 44				15 18		15 44				16 18		16 44				17 18		17 45			
Congleton	a																						
Macclesfield	a	15 01				15 36		16 04				16 36		17 04				17 36		18 04			
Crewe	a			15 07						16 08						17 07						18 07	
Wilmslow	a																						
Stockport	a	15 14				15 50		16 16				16 50		17 16				17 50		18 16			
M'chester Piccadilly	a	15 24				15 59		16 29				16 59		17 29				17 59		18 29			
Warrington Bank Quay	a			15 26						16 26						17 26						18 26	
Wigan North Western	a			15 37						16 37						17 37						18 37	
Preston	a			15 51						16 51						17 51						18 51	
Lancaster	a			16 08						17 07						18 07						19 07	
Oxenholme Lake District	a									17 21						18 22						19 21	
Penrith North Lakes	a			16 44												18 47							
Carlisle	a			17 00						18 01						19 03						20 00	
Lockerbie	a																						
Haymarket	a			18 11												20 16							
Edinburgh	a		18 58	18 20					19 57						21 02	20 22					22 07		22 18
Haymarket	a		19 22												21 16								
Motherwell	a		19 59												21 55								
Glasgow Central	a									19 20												21 22	
Inverkeithing	a																						
Kirkcaldy	a																						
Markinch	a																						
Ladybank	a																						
Cupar	a																						
Leuchars	a																						
Dundee	a																						
Arbroath	a																						
Montrose	a																						
Stonehaven	a																						
Aberdeen	a																						

A to Edinburgh
B from Reading
C from Birmingham New Street
D from Plymouth
E to Newcastle

Table T051-R

Sundays
20 May to 15 July

South Coast and the South West - North West England, The North East and Scotland

		XC	XC	XC	XC	VT	XC	XC	XC	XC	XC	VT	XC	XC	XC	XC	XC	VT	XC	XC	XC	XC
		◇1	◇1	◇1	◇1	◇1	◇1	◇1	◇1	◇1	◇1	1	◇1	◇1	◇1	◇1	◇1	◇1	◇1	◇1	◇1	◇1
			A		B		C	D	A		E		A		A	A	A				A	A
		✠	✠	✠	✠	🛒	✠	✠	✠	✠	✠	🛒	✠	✠	✠	✠	✠	🛒	✠	✠	✠	✠
Bournemouth	d			14 40						15 40						16 40						17 40
Brockenhurst	d			14 57						15 57						16 57						17 57
Southampton Central	d			15 15						16 15						17 15						18 15
Southampton Airport Pkway	d			15 22						16 22						17 22						18 22
Winchester	d			15 31						16 31						17 31						18 31
Basingstoke	d			15 47						16 47						17 47						18 47
Guildford	d																					
Reading	d			16 11			16 41			17 11			17 41			18 11			18 41			19 11
Oxford	d			16 37			17 06			17 37			18 06			18 37			19 06			19 37
Banbury	d			16 55			17 24			17 55			18 24			18 55			19 24			19 55
Leamington Spa	d			17 12			17 41			18 12			18 41			19 12			19 41			20 12
Coventry	d			17 27		17 45	17 54			18 27		18 45	18 54			19 27		19 42	19 54			20 27
Birmingham International	d			17 38		17 55	18 04			18 38		18 55	19 04			19 38		19 53	20 04			20 38
Penzance	d							12 30														
St Erth	d							12 38														
Hayle	d							12 42														
Camborne	d							12 51														
Redruth	d							12 58														
Truro	d							13 09														
St Austell	d							13 26														
Par	d							13 32														
Lostwithiel	d							13 39														
Bodmin Parkway	d							13 46														
Liskeard	d							13 58														
Plymouth	d				14 25			14 35			15 24						16 25					
Totnes	d				14 51			15 01			15 50						16 51					
Paignton	d																					
Torquay	d																					
Newton Abbot	d				15 04			15 13			16 03						17 04					
Teignmouth	d																					
Dawlish	d																					
Exeter St Davids	d				15 24			15 32			16 25						17 25					
Tiverton Parkway	d				15 37			15 46			16 39						17 39					
Taunton	d				15 51			15 59			16 52						17 51					
Weston-super-Mare	d							16 29														
Cardiff Central	d		15 45						16 45						17 45						18 45	
Newport (South Wales)	d		16 05						17 03						18 04						19 03	
Bristol Temple Meads	d	16 00			16 30			17 00			17 30			18 00			18 30			19 00		
Bristol Parkway	d	16 10			16 40			17 10			17 40			18 10			18 40			19 10		
Gloucester	d		16 50						17 50						18 50						19 50	
Cheltenham Spa	d	16 41	17 01		17 12			17 41	18 01		18 11			18 41	19 01		19 11			19 41	20 01	
Birmingham New Street	a	17 26	17 45	17 48	17 49	18 05	18 14	18 27	18 45	18 48	18 50	19 05	19 14	19 26	19 45	19 48	19 50	20 04	20 14	20 27	20 45	20 48
Birmingham New Street	d	17 31	17 49	17 57	18 03	18 15	18 30	18 31	18 49	18 57	19 03	19 15	19 30	19 31	19 49	19 57	20 03	20 15		20 31	20 49	20 57
Tamworth	d		18 07		18 19				19 09						20 07		20 19				21 06	
Burton-on-Trent	d		18 19						19 21		19 26				20 19						21 19	
Derby	a		18 33		18 39		19 03		19 33		19 40		20 01		20 33		20 40				21 33	
Nottingham	a		18 58						20 00						20 56						22 00	
Chesterfield	a				19 04						20 02						21 03					
Sheffield	a				19 20		19 38				20 18		20 38				21 18					
Doncaster	a						20 14						21 20									
Wakefield Westgate	a				19 49						20 45						21 48					
Leeds	a				20 04						21 02						22 02					
York	a				20 30		20 40				21 31		21 45									
Darlington	a				21 00		21 14						22 25									
Durham	a				21 17		21 32						22 42									
Chester-le-Street	a																					
Newcastle	a				21 31		21 45						23 12									
Morpeth	a																					
Alnmouth for Alnwick	a				21 59																	
Berwick-upon-Tweed	a																					
Dunbar	a																					
Wolverhampton	d	17 49		18 15		18 37		18 49		19 15		19 37		19 49		20 15		20 37		20 52		21 17
Stafford	a	18 02		18 27				19 02		19 27				20 02		20 27		20 51		21 05		21 29
Stoke-on-Trent	a	18 18		18 44				19 18		19 44				20 18		20 44				21 21		21 45
Congleton	a																					
Macclesfield	a	18 36		19 04				19 36		20 04				20 36		21 02				21 39		22 03
Crewe	a					19 07						20 07						21 10				
Wilmslow	a																					
Stockport	a	18 50		19 17				19 50		20 16				20 50		21 15				21 52		22 15
M'chester Piccadilly	a	18 59		19 28				19 59		20 28				20 59		21 29				22 02		22 26
Warrington Bank Quay	a					19 26						20 26										
Wigan North Western	a					19 37						20 37										
Preston	a					19 51						20 51										
Lancaster	a					20 07						21 08										
Oxenholme Lake District	a											21 22										
Penrith North Lakes	a					20 44																
Carlisle	a					20 59						22 01										
Lockerbie	a											22 20										
Haymarket	a					22 14																
Edinburgh	a				23 03	22 19																
Haymarket	a																					
Motherwell	a											23 04										
Glasgow Central	a											23 24										
Inverkeithing	a																					
Kirkcaldy	a																					
Markinch	a																					
Ladybank	a																					
Cupar	a																					
Leuchars	a																					
Dundee	a																					
Arbroath	a																					
Montrose	a																					
Stonehaven	a																					
Aberdeen	a																					

A ✠ to Birmingham New Street
B ✠ to Newcastle
C ✠ to Sheffield
D ✠ from Plymouth
E ✠ to Leeds

Table T051-R

Sundays
20 May to 15 July

South Coast and the South West - North West England, The North East and Scotland

		XC	VT	XC	XC	XC	XC	XC	XC	XC	XC	XC	XC
		◇1	◇1	◇1	◇1	◇1	◇1	◇1	◇1	◇1	◇1	◇1	◇1
		A			B		C	B					
		✠	🛒		✠		✠	✠					
Bournemouth	d						18 40			19 40			
Brockenhurst	d						18 57			19 57			
Southampton Central	d						19 15			20 15			
Southampton Airport Pkway	d						19 22			20 22			
Winchester	d						19 31			20 31			
Basingstoke	d						19 47			20 47			
Guildford	d												
Reading	d			19 41			20 11		20 41	21 11		21 41	
Oxford	d			20 06			20 37		21 06	21 37		22 06	
Banbury	d			20 24			20 55		21 24	21 55		22 24	
Leamington Spa	d			20 41			21 12		21 41	22 12		22 41	
Coventry	d		20 42	20 54			21 27		21 53	22 24		22 54	
Birmingham International	d		20 53	21 04			21 38		22 03	22 34		23 04	
Penzance	d	15 30											
St Erth	d	15 38											
Hayle	d												
Camborne	d	15 49											
Redruth	d	15 55											
Truro	d	16 07											
St Austell	d	16 23											
Par	d	16 30											
Lostwithiel	d												
Bodmin Parkway	d	16 40											
Liskeard	d	16 52											
Plymouth	d	17 25						18 25					
Totnes	d	17 50						18 52					
Paignton	d				18 20								
Torquay	d				18 26								
Newton Abbot	d	18 03			18 37			19 05					
Teignmouth	d												
Dawlish	d												
Exeter St Davids	d	18 23			18 58			19 25					
Tiverton Parkway	d	18 37			19 11			19 38					
Taunton	d	18 50			19 24			19 52					
Weston-super-Mare	d												
Cardiff Central	d					19 45					20 45		
Newport (South Wales)	d					20 03					21 05		
Bristol Temple Meads	d	19 30			20 00			20 30					22 10
Bristol Parkway	d	19 40			20 09			20 40					22 20
Gloucester	d					20 50					21 50		
Cheltenham Spa	d	20 11			20 40	21 01		21 11			22 01		22 49
Birmingham New Street	a	20 52	21 05	21 15	21 18	21 45	21 48	21 48	22 14	22 43	22 45	23 14	23 40
Birmingham New Street	d	21 03	21 15				21 57	22 03					
Tamworth	d	21 19						22 19					
Burton-on-Trent	d	21 29											
Derby	a	21 41						22 40					
Nottingham	a												
Chesterfield	a	22 02						23 02					
Sheffield	a	22 18						23 18					
Doncaster	a												
Wakefield Westgate	a	22 47											
Leeds	a	23 02						00 09					
York	a												
Darlington	a												
Durham	a												
Chester-le-Street	a												
Newcastle	a												
Morpeth	a												
Alnmouth for Alnwick	a												
Berwick-upon-Tweed	a												
Dunbar	a												
Wolverhampton	d		21 37				22 15						
Stafford	a		21 55				22 27						
Stoke-on-Trent	a						22 44						
Congleton	a												
Macclesfield	a						23 01						
Crewe	a		22 16										
Wilmslow	a												
Stockport	a						23 14						
M'chester Piccadilly	a						23 24						
Warrington Bank Quay	a		22 36										
Wigan North Western	a		22 47										
Preston	a		23 01										
Lancaster	a												
Oxenholme Lake District	a												
Penrith North Lakes	a												
Carlisle	a												
Lockerbie	a												
Haymarket	a												
Edinburgh	a												
Haymarket	a												
Motherwell	a												
Glasgow Central	a												
Inverkeithing	a												
Kirkcaldy	a												
Markinch	a												
Ladybank	a												
Cupar	a												
Leuchars	a												
Dundee	a												
Arbroath	a												
Montrose	a												
Stonehaven	a												
Aberdeen	a												

A ✠ from Plymouth to Birmingham New Street
B ✠ to Bristol Temple Meads
C ✠ to Reading

Table T051-R

Sundays
22 July to 2 September

South Coast and the South West - North West England, The North East and Scotland

		XC	VT	XC	VT	XC	XC	VT	XC	XC	XC	VT	XC	XC	XC	VT	XC	XC	XC	VT	XC	XC	XC
		◇■	◇■	◇■	◇■	◇■	◇■	◇■	◇■	◇■	◇■	◇■	◇■	◇■	◇■	◇■	◇■	◇■	◇■	◇■	◇■	◇■	◇■
						A									A		B		A			B	
		🛒	🍽	🛒	🍽	🛒	🛒	🍽	🛒	🛒	🛒	🍽	🛒	🛒	🛒	🍽	🛒	🛒	🛒	🍽	🛒	🛒	🛒
Bournemouth	d																	09 40					10 40
Brockenhurst	d																	09 57					10 57
Southampton Central	d													09 15				10 15					11 15
Southampton Airport Pkway	d													09 22				10 22					11 22
Winchester	d													09 31				10 31					11 31
Basingstoke	d													09 47				10 47					11 47
Guildford	d																						
Reading	d									09 12				10 11				11 11					12 11
Oxford	d									09 37				10 37				11 37					12 37
Banbury	d									09 55				10 55				11 55					12 55
Leamington Spa	d									10 12				11 12				12 12					13 12
Coventry	d									10 29				11 29				12 28					13 27
Birmingham International	d									10 40				11 41				12 40					13 38
Penzance	d																						
St Erth	d																						
Hayle	d																						
Camborne	d																						
Redruth	d																						
Truro	d																						
St Austell	d																						
Par	d																						
Lostwithiel	d																						
Bodmin Parkway	d																						
Liskeard	d																						
Plymouth	d																		09 25				
Totnes	d																		09 50				
Paignton	d																						
Torquay	d																						
Newton Abbot	d																		10 03				
Teignmouth	d																						
Dawlish	d																						
Exeter St Davids	d																		10 23				
Tiverton Parkway	d																		10 37				
Taunton	d																		10 50				
Weston-super-Mare	d																						
Cardiff Central	d																10 45					11 45	
Newport (South Wales)	d																11 06					12 05	
Bristol Temple Meads	d										09 15				10 30				11 30				
Bristol Parkway	d										09 25				10 40				11 40				
Gloucester	d										10 00						11 50					12 50	
Cheltenham Spa	d										10 12				11 11		12 01		12 11			13 01	
Birmingham New Street	a									10 50	10 49			11 51	11 48		12 45	12 50	12 49			13 45	13 48
Birmingham New Street	d	08 44	08 45	09 01	09 20	09 44	10 01	10 20	10 49	11 01	11 10	11 20	11 49	11 57	12 03	12 20	12 49	12 57	13 03	13 20	13 30	13 49	13 57
Tamworth	d	09 01				10 00							12 07		12 19		13 07					14 07	
Burton-on-Trent	d	09 11				10 10			11 11		11 32		12 19		12 29		13 19		13 26			14 19	
Derby	a																						
Nottingham	a												12 56				13 56					14 58	
Chesterfield	a	10 02				11 02			12 03		12 23				13 21				14 21				
Sheffield	a	10 18				11 17			12 18		12 42				13 43				14 45				
Doncaster	a										13 13				14 14				15 16				
Wakefield Westgate	a	10 45				11 45			12 45		13 30				14 44				15 35				
Leeds	a	10 59				11 59			13 00		13 46				14 59				15 53				
York	a	11 29				12 30			13 27		14 27				15 27				16 27				
Darlington	a	11 57				12 58			13 56		14 55				15 55				16 55				
Durham	a	12 14				13 15			14 13		15 13				16 12				17 12				
Chester-le-Street	a																						
Newcastle	a	12 27				13 28			14 27		15 26				16 25				17 25				
Morpeth	a								14 45										17 40				
Alnmouth for Alnwick	a					13 55					15 53				16 52				17 55				
Berwick-upon-Tweed	a					14 16					16 12								18 16				
Dunbar	a	13 34							15 39						17 35								
Wolverhampton	d		09 04	09 19	09 37		10 19	10 37		11 19		11 37		12 16		12 37		13 16		13 37	13 49		14 15
Stafford	a		09 17	09 32			10 32			11 31				12 28				13 28			14 02		14 27
Stoke-on-Trent	a			09 51			10 48			11 48				12 45				13 44			14 18		14 44
Congleton	a																						
Macclesfield	a			10 09			11 08			12 09				13 04				14 04			14 36		15 01
Crewe	a		09 35		10 07			11 10				12 07				13 07				14 07			
Wilmslow	a																						
Stockport	a			10 22			11 22			12 24				13 16				14 16			14 50		15 14
M'chester Piccadilly	a			10 38			11 33			12 41				13 29				14 29			14 59		15 24
Warrington Bank Quay	a		09 54		10 26			11 28				12 26				13 26				14 26			
Wigan North Western	a		10 05		10 37			11 39				12 37				13 37				14 37			
Preston	a		10 20		10 51			11 53				12 51				13 51				14 50			
Lancaster	a				11 16			12 09				13 07				14 08				15 08			
Oxenholme Lake District	a				11 32			12 22				13 21								15 22			
Penrith North Lakes	a															14 44							
Carlisle	a				12 11			13 01				14 00				15 00				16 01			
Lockerbie	a																						
Haymarket	a							14 16								16 14							
Edinburgh	a	14 01				14 58		14 21	16 03		16 55				17 58	16 20			18 58				
Haymarket	a					15 13					17 14				18 16				19 22				
Motherwell	a					15 55					17 51								19 59				
Glasgow Central	a											15 19								17 19			
Inverkeithing	a														18 28								
Kirkcaldy	a														18 44								
Markinch	a														18 53								
Ladybank	a														19 01								
Cupar	a														19 07								
Leuchars	a														19 14								
Dundee	a														19 29								
Arbroath	a														19 46								
Montrose	a														20 00								
Stonehaven	a														20 22								
Aberdeen	a														20 42								

A 🛒 to Edinburgh
B 🛒 from Birmingham New Street

Table T051-R

Sundays
22 July to 2 September

South Coast and the South West - North West England, The North East and Scotland

		XC	VT	XC	XC	XC	XC	XC	VT	XC	XC	XC	XC	XC	VT	XC	XC	XC	XC	XC	VT	XC	XC
		◇■	◇■	◇■	◇■	◇■	◇■	◇■	◇■	◇■	◇■	◇■	◇■	◇■	◇■	◇■	◇■	◇■	◇■	◇■	◇■	◇■	◇■
				A		B		C				B								D			
		🛒	🍽	🛒	🛒	🛒	🛒	🛒	🍽	🛒	🛒	🛒	🛒	🛒	🍽	🛒	🛒	🛒	🛒	🛒	🍽	🛒	🛒
Bournemouth	d						11 40						12 40						13 40				
Brockenhurst	d						11 57						12 57						13 57				
Southampton Central	d						12 15						13 15						14 15				
Southampton Airport Pkway	d						12 22						13 22						14 22				
Winchester	d						12 31						13 31						14 31				
Basingstoke	d						12 47						13 47						14 47				
Guildford	d			12 14																			
Reading	d			12 54			13 11			13 41			14 10			14 41			15 11			15 41	
Oxford	d			13 17			13 37			14 06			14 37			15 06			15 37			16 06	
Banbury	d			13 35			13 55			14 24			14 55			15 24			15 55			16 24	
Leamington Spa	d			13 52			14 12			14 41			15 12			15 41			16 12			16 41	
Coventry	d		13 42				14 27		14 42	14 54			15 27		15 42	15 54			16 27		16 42	16 54	
Birmingham International	d		13 53				14 38		14 53	15 04			15 38		15 53	16 04			16 38		16 53	17 04	
Penzance	d							09 30															
St Erth	d							09 38															
Hayle	d																						
Camborne	d							09 48															
Redruth	d							09 54															
Truro	d							10 08															
St Austell	d							10 24															
Par	d							10 31												12 23			
Lostwithiel	d																						
Bodmin Parkway	d							10 41												12 35			
Liskeard	d							10 54												12 48			
Plymouth	d	10 25						11 25			12 00			12 25			12 52			13 25			
Totnes	d	10 50						11 50						12 50						13 50			
Paignton	d				10 50																		
Torquay	d				10 56																		
Newton Abbot	d	11 03			11 08			12 03			12 36			13 03			13 27			14 03			
Teignmouth	d				11 15																		
Dawlish	d				11 20																		
Exeter St Davids	d	11 23			11 33			12 23			12 56			13 23			13 47			14 23			
Tiverton Parkway	d	11 37			11 47			12 37			13 10			13 37						14 36			
Taunton	d	11 52			12 00			12 50			13 23			13 50						14 49			
Weston-super-Mare	d				12 21																		
Cardiff Central	d					12 45						13 45						14 45					
Newport (South Wales)	d					13 05						14 05						15 05					
Bristol Temple Meads	d	12 30			13 00			13 30			14 00			14 30			15 00			15 30			16 00
Bristol Parkway	d	12 40			13 10			13 40			14 10			14 40			15 10			15 40			16 10
Gloucester	d					13 50						14 50						15 50					
Cheltenham Spa	d	13 11			13 41	14 01		14 11			14 41	15 01		15 11			15 40	16 01		16 11			16 41
Birmingham New Street	a	13 48	14 04	14 18	14 27	14 45	14 48	14 48	15 04	15 14	15 27	15 45	15 48	15 48	16 05	16 14	16 27	16 45	16 48	16 49	17 04	17 14	17 26
Birmingham New Street	d	14 03	14 15		14 31	14 49	14 57	15 03	15 15		15 31	15 49	15 57	16 03	16 15		16 31	16 49	16 57	17 03	17 15		17 31
Tamworth	d	14 19				15 09						16 07		16 19				17 07					
Burton-on-Trent	d	14 30				15 21		15 25				16 19		16 29				17 19		17 25			
Derby	a																						
Nottingham	a					16 00						16 56						17 56					
Chesterfield	a	15 25						16 23						17 26						18 27			
Sheffield	a	15 45						16 41						17 43						18 42			
Doncaster	a	16 11						17 12						18 11						19 17			
Wakefield Westgate	a	16 40						17 33						18 43						19 38			
Leeds	a	16 59						17 54						18 59						19 57			
York	a	17 27						18 27						19 30						20 30			
Darlington	a	17 55						18 55						19 59						21 00			
Durham	a	18 12						19 12						20 18						21 17			
Chester-le-Street	a																						
Newcastle	a	18 25						19 25						20 32						21 30			
Morpeth	a													20 47									
Alnmouth for Alnwick	a							19 56												22 01			
Berwick-upon-Tweed	a	19 14						20 18						21 20									
Dunbar	a	19 37												21 45									
Wolverhampton	d		14 37		14 49		15 15		15 37		15 49		16 15		16 37		16 49		17 15		17 37		17 49
Stafford	a				15 02		15 27				16 02		16 27				17 02		17 28				18 02
Stoke-on-Trent	a				15 18		15 44				16 18		16 44				17 18		17 45				18 18
Congleton	a																						
Macclesfield	a				15 36		16 04				16 36		17 04				17 36		18 04				18 36
Crewe	a		15 07						16 08						17 07						18 07		
Wilmslow	a																						
Stockport	a				15 50		16 16				16 50		17 16				17 50		18 16				18 50
M'chester Piccadilly	a				15 59		16 29				16 59		17 29				17 59		18 29				18 59
Warrington Bank Quay	a		15 26						16 26						17 26						18 26		
Wigan North Western	a		15 37						16 37						17 37						18 37		
Preston	a		15 51						16 51						17 51						18 51		
Lancaster	a		16 08						17 07						18 07						19 07		
Oxenholme Lake District	a								17 21						18 22						19 21		
Penrith North Lakes	a		16 44												18 47								
Carlisle	a		17 00						18 01						19 03						20 00		
Lockerbie	a																						
Haymarket	a		18 11												20 16								
Edinburgh	a	20 00	18 20					21 00						22 07	20 22					23 03			
Haymarket	a							21 16															
Motherwell	a							21 54															
Glasgow Central	a								19 20												21 22		
Inverkeithing	a																						
Kirkcaldy	a																						
Markinch	a																						
Ladybank	a																						
Cupar	a																						
Leuchars	a																						
Dundee	a																						
Arbroath	a																						
Montrose	a																						
Stonehaven	a																						
Aberdeen	a																						

A 🛒 from Reading
B 🛒 from Birmingham New Street
C 🛒 from Plymouth to Edinburgh
D 🛒 to Newcastle

Sundays

22 July to 2 September

South Coast and the South West - North West England, The North East and Scotland

	XC	XC	XC	VT	XC	XC	XC	XC	XC	VT	XC	XC	XC	XC	XC	VT	XC	XC	XC	XC	XC
	◇1	◇1	◇1	◇1	◇1	◇1	◇1	◇1	◇1	■ 1	◇1	◇1	◇1	◇1	◇1	◇1	◇1	◇1	◇1	◇1	◇1
	A					B	A						A	A	A				A	A	C
	✠	✠	✠	🍽	✠	✠	✠	✠	✠	🍽	✠	✠	✠	✠	✠	🍽	✠	✠	✠	✠	✠
Bournemouth d		14 40						15 40						16 40						17 40	
Brockenhurst d		14 57						15 57						16 57						17 57	
Southampton Central d		15 15						16 15						17 15						18 15	
Southampton Airport Pkway d		15 22						16 22						17 22						18 22	
Winchester d		15 31						16 31						17 31						18 31	
Basingstoke d		15 47						16 47						17 47						18 47	
Guildford d																					
Reading d		16 11			16 41			17 11			17 41			18 11			18 41			19 11	
Oxford d		16 37			17 06			17 37			18 06			18 37			19 06			19 37	
Banbury d		16 55			17 24			17 55			18 24			18 55			19 24			19 55	
Leamington Spa d		17 12			17 41			18 12			18 41			19 12			19 41			20 12	
Coventry d		17 27		17 45	17 54			18 27		18 45	18 54			19 27		19 42	19 54			20 27	
Birmingham International d		17 38		17 55	18 04			18 38		18 55	19 04			19 38		19 53	20 04			20 38	
Penzance d						12 30															15 30
St Erth d						12 38															15 38
Hayle d						12 42															
Camborne d						12 51															15 49
Redruth d						12 58															15 55
Truro d						13 09															16 07
St Austell d						13 26															16 23
Par d						13 32															16 30
Lostwithiel d						13 39															
Bodmin Parkway d						13 46															16 40
Liskeard d						13 58															16 52
Plymouth d			14 25			14 35			15 24						16 25						17 25
Totnes d			14 51			15 01			15 50						16 51						17 50
Paignton d																					
Torquay d																					
Newton Abbot d			15 04			15 13			16 03						17 04						18 03
Teignmouth d																					
Dawlish d																					
Exeter St Davids d			15 24			15 32			16 25						17 25						18 23
Tiverton Parkway d			15 37			15 46			16 39						17 39						18 37
Taunton d			15 51			15 59			16 52						17 52						18 50
Weston-super-Mare d						16 29															
Cardiff Central d	15 45						16 45						17 45						18 45		
Newport (South Wales) d	16 05						17 03						18 04						19 03		
Bristol Temple Meads d			16 30			17 00			17 30			18 00			18 30			19 00			19 30
Bristol Parkway d			16 40			17 10			17 40			18 10			18 40			19 10			19 40
Gloucester d	16 50						17 50						18 50						19 50		
Cheltenham Spa d	17 01		17 12			17 41	18 01		18 11			18 41	19 01		19 11			19 41	20 01		20 11
Birmingham New Street a	17 45	17 48	17 49	18 05	18 14	18 27	18 45	18 48	18 50	19 05	19 14	19 26	19 45	19 48	19 50	20 04	20 14	20 27	20 45	20 48	20 52
Birmingham New Street d	17 49	17 57	18 03	18 15		18 31	18 49	18 57	19 03	19 15		19 31	19 49	19 57	20 03	20 15		20 31	20 49	20 57	21 03
Tamworth d	18 07		18 19				19 09						20 07		20 19				21 06		21 19
Burton-on-Trent d	18 19		18 30				19 21		19 26				20 19		20 30				21 19		21 29
Derby a																					
Nottingham a	18 56						19 58						20 56						21 56		
Chesterfield a			19 25						20 21						21 26						22 21
Sheffield a			19 43						20 38						21 39						22 37
Doncaster a			20 13																		
Wakefield Westgate a			20 32						21 07						22 09						23 02
Leeds a			20 47						21 22						22 24						23 17
York a																					
Darlington a																					
Durham a																					
Chester-le-Street a																					
Newcastle a																					
Morpeth a																					
Alnmouth for Alnwick a																					
Berwick-upon-Tweed a																					
Dunbar a																					
Wolverhampton d		18 15		18 37		18 49		19 15		19 37		19 49		20 15		20 37		20 52		21 17	
Stafford a		18 27				19 02		19 27				20 02		20 27		20 51		21 05		21 29	
Stoke-on-Trent a		18 44				19 18		19 44				20 18		20 44				21 21		21 45	
Congleton a																					
Macclesfield a		19 04				19 36		20 04				20 36		21 02				21 39		22 03	
Crewe a				19 07						20 07						21 10					
Wilmslow a																					
Stockport a		19 17				19 50		20 16				20 50		21 15				21 52		22 15	
M'chester Piccadilly a		19 28				19 59		20 28				20 59		21 29				22 02		22 26	
Warrington Bank Quay a				19 26						20 26											
Wigan North Western a				19 37						20 37											
Preston a				19 51						20 51											
Lancaster a				20 07						21 08											
Oxenholme Lake District a										21 22											
Penrith North Lakes a				20 44																	
Carlisle a				20 59						22 01											
Lockerbie a										22 20											
Haymarket a				22 14																	
Edinburgh a				22 19																	
Haymarket a																					
Motherwell a										23 04											
Glasgow Central a										23 24											
Inverkeithing a																					
Kirkcaldy a																					
Markinch a																					
Ladybank a																					
Cupar a																					
Leuchars a																					
Dundee a																					
Arbroath a																					
Montrose a																					
Stonehaven a																					
Aberdeen a																					

A ✠ to Birmingham New Street
B ✠ from Plymouth
C ✠ from Plymouth to Birmingham New Street

Sundays

22 July to 2 September

South Coast and the South West - North West England, The North East and Scotland

	VT	XC	XC	XC	XC	XC	XC	XC	XC	XC	XC
	◇1	◇1	◇1	◇1	◇1	◇1	◇1	◇1	◇1	◇1	◇1
			A		B	A					
	🍽		✠		✠	✠					
Bournemouth d					18 40			19 40			
Brockenhurst d					18 57			19 57			
Southampton Central d					19 15			20 15			
Southampton Airport Pkway d					19 22			20 22			
Winchester d					19 31			20 31			
Basingstoke d					19 47			20 47			
Guildford d											
Reading d		19 41			20 11		20 41	21 11		21 41	
Oxford d		20 06			20 37		21 06	21 37		22 06	
Banbury d		20 24			20 55		21 24	21 55		22 24	
Leamington Spa d		20 41			21 12		21 41	22 12		22 41	
Coventry d	20 42	20 54			21 27		21 53	22 24		22 54	
Birmingham International d	20 53	21 04			21 38		22 03	22 34		23 04	
Penzance d											
St Erth d											
Hayle d											
Camborne d											
Redruth d											
Truro d											
St Austell d											
Par d											
Lostwithiel d											
Bodmin Parkway d											
Liskeard d											
Plymouth d						18 25					
Totnes d						18 52					
Paignton d			18 20								
Torquay d			18 26								
Newton Abbot d			18 37			19 05					
Teignmouth d											
Dawlish d											
Exeter St Davids d			18 58			19 25					
Tiverton Parkway d			19 11			19 38					
Taunton d			19 24			19 52					
Weston-super-Mare d											
Cardiff Central d				19 45					20 45		
Newport (South Wales) d				20 03					21 05		
Bristol Temple Meads d			20 00			20 30					22 10
Bristol Parkway d			20 09			20 40					22 20
Gloucester d				20 50					21 50		
Cheltenham Spa d			20 40	21 01		21 11			22 01		22 49
Birmingham New Street a	21 05	21 15	21 18	21 45	21 48	21 48	22 14	22 43	22 45	23 14	23 40
Birmingham New Street d	21 15				21 57	22 03					
Tamworth d						22 19					
Burton-on-Trent d						22a30					
Derby a											
Nottingham a											
Chesterfield a											
Sheffield a											
Doncaster a											
Wakefield Westgate a											
Leeds a											
York a											
Darlington a											
Durham a											
Chester-le-Street a											
Newcastle a											
Morpeth a											
Alnmouth for Alnwick a											
Berwick-upon-Tweed a											
Dunbar a											
Wolverhampton d	21 37				22 15						
Stafford a	21 55				22 27						
Stoke-on-Trent a					22 44						
Congleton a											
Macclesfield a					23 01						
Crewe a	22 16										
Wilmslow a											
Stockport a					23 14						
M'chester Piccadilly a					23 24						
Warrington Bank Quay a	22 36										
Wigan North Western a	22 47										
Preston a	23 01										
Lancaster a											
Oxenholme Lake District a											
Penrith North Lakes a											
Carlisle a											
Lockerbie a											
Haymarket a											
Edinburgh a											
Haymarket a											
Motherwell a											
Glasgow Central a											
Inverkeithing a											
Kirkcaldy a											
Markinch a											
Ladybank a											
Cupar a											
Leuchars a											
Dundee a											
Arbroath a											
Montrose a											
Stonehaven a											
Aberdeen a											

A ✠ to Bristol Temple Meads
B ✠ to Reading

Sundays

9 September to 7 October

South Coast and the South West - North West England, The North East and Scotland

Station		XC	VT	XC	VT	VT	XC	XC	XC	VT	XC	XC	XC	XC	VT	VT	XC	XC	XC	VT	XC	XC	XC
		◇1	◇1	◇1	◇1	◇1	◇1	◇1	◇1	◇1	◇1	◇1	◇1	◇1	◇1	◇1	◇1	◇1	◇1	◇1	◇1	◇1	◇1
					A	B	C	D					B	A	A	B			E			F	
Bournemouth	d																						09 40
Brockenhurst	d																						09 57
Southampton Central	d																	09 15					10 15
Southampton Airport Pkway	d																	09 22					10 22
Winchester	d																	09 31					10 31
Basingstoke	d																	09 47					10 47
Guildford	d																						
Reading	d											09 12						10 11					11 11
Oxford	d											09 37						10 37					11 37
Banbury	d											09 55						10 55					11 55
Leamington Spa	d											10 12						11 12					12 12
Coventry	d											10 29						11 29					12 28
Birmingham International	d											10 40						11 41					12 40
Penzance	d																						
St Erth	d																						
Hayle	d																						
Camborne	d																						
Redruth	d																						
Truro	d																						
St Austell	d																						
Par	d																						
Lostwithiel	d																						
Bodmin Parkway	d																						
Liskeard	d																						
Plymouth	d																						
Totnes	d																						
Paignton	d																						
Torquay	d																						
Newton Abbot	d																						
Teignmouth	d																						
Dawlish	d																						
Exeter St Davids	d																						
Tiverton Parkway	d																						
Taunton	d																						
Weston-super-Mare	d																						
Cardiff Central	d																					10 45	
Newport (South Wales)	d																					11 06	
Bristol Temple Meads	d												09 15	09 15					10 30				
Bristol Parkway	d												09 25	09 25					10 40				
Gloucester	d												10 00	10 00								11 50	
Cheltenham Spa	d												10 12	10 12					11 11			12 01	
Birmingham New Street	a											10 50	10 49	10 49				11 51	11 48			12 45	12 50
Birmingham New Street	d	08 44	08 45	09 01	09 20	09 20	09 44	09 44	10 01	10 20	10 49	11 01	11 10	11 10	11 20	11 20	11 49	11 57	12 03	12 20	12 30	12 49	12 57
Tamworth	d	09 01					10 00	10 00									12 07		12 19			13 07	
Burton-on-Trent	d	09 11					10 10	10 10			11 11		11 32	11 32			12 19					13 19	
Derby	a	09 23					10 23	10 23			11 23		11 44	11 44			12 34		12 39		13 01	13 33	
Nottingham	a																13 00					14 00	
Chesterfield	a	10 02					11 02	11 02			12 03		12 24	12 24					13 20				
Sheffield	a	10 18					11 17	11 17			12 18		12 42	12 42					13 43				
Doncaster	a												13 13	13 13					14 14				
Wakefield Westgate	a	10 45					11 45	11 45			12 45		13 30	13 30					14 44				
Leeds	a	10 59					11 59	11 59			13 00		13 46	13 46					14 59				
York	a	11 29					12 30	12 30			13 27		14 27	14 27					15 27				
Darlington	a	11 57					12 58	12 58			13 56		14 55	14 55					15 55				
Durham	a	12 14					13 15	13 15			14 13		15 13	15 13					16 12				
Chester-le-Street	a																						
Newcastle	a	12 27					13 28	13 28			14 27		15 26	15 26					16 25				
Morpeth	a										14 45												
Alnmouth for Alnwick	a						13 55	13 55					15 53	15 53					16 52				
Berwick-upon-Tweed	a						14 16	14 16					16 12	16 12									
Dunbar	a	13 34									15 39								17 35				
Wolverhampton	d		09 04	09 19	09 37	09 37			10 19	10 37		11 19			11 37	11 37		12 16		12 37			13 16
Stafford	a		09 17	09 32					10 32			11 31						12 28					13 28
Stoke-on-Trent	a			09 51					10 48			11 48						12 45					13 44
Congleton	a																						
Macclesfield	a			10 09					11 08			12 09						13 04					14 04
Crewe	a		09 35		10 07	10 07				11 10					12 07	12 07				13 07			
Wilmslow	a																						
Stockport	a			10 22					11 22			12 24						13 16					14 16
M'chester Piccadilly	a			10 38					11 33			12 41						13 29					14 29
Warrington Bank Quay	a		09 54		10 26	10 26				11 28					12 26	12 26				13 26			
Wigan North Western	a		10 05		10 37	10 37				11 39					12 37	12 37				13 37			
Preston	a		10 20		10 51	10 51				11 53					12 51	12 51				13 51			
Lancaster	a				11 16	11 16				12 09					13 07	13 07				14 08			
Oxenholme Lake District	a				11 32	11 32				12 22					13 21	13 21							
Penrith North Lakes	a																			14 44			
Carlisle	a				12 10	12 11				13 01					14 00	14 00				15 00			
Lockerbie	a																						
Haymarket	a									14 16										16 14			
Edinburgh	a	14 01					14 58	14 58		14 21	16 03		16 55	16 55					17 58	16 20			
Haymarket	a						15 13	15 13					17 14	17 14					18 16				
Motherwell	a						15 55	15 55					17 51	17 52									
Glasgow Central	a				13 27			16 12						18 13	15 16	15 19							
Inverkeithing	a																		18 28				
Kirkcaldy	a																		18 44				
Markinch	a																		18 53				
Ladybank	a																		19 01				
Cupar	a																		19 07				
Leuchars	a																		19 14				
Dundee	a																		19 29				
Arbroath	a																		19 46				
Montrose	a																		20 00				
Stonehaven	a																		20 22				
Aberdeen	a																		20 42				

A not 9 September
B 9 September
C 9 September. 🛒 to Edinburgh
D not 9 September. 🛒 to Edinburgh
E 🛒 to Edinburgh
F 🛒 from Birmingham New Street

Table T051-R

Sundays

9 September to 7 October

South Coast and the South West - North West England, The North East and Scotland

Station		XC	XC	VT	VT	XC	XC	XC	XC	XC	VT	XC	XC	XC	XC	XC	XC	VT	VT	XC	XC	XC	XC
		◇1	◇1	◇1	◇1	◇1	◇1	◇1	◇1	◇1	◇1	◇1	◇1	◇1	◇1	◇1	◇1	◇1	◇1	◇1	◇1	◇1	◇1
		A	B	C	D			E				F		E		G	H	C	D			E	
Bournemouth	d								10 40						11 40								12 40
Brockenhurst	d								10 57						11 57								12 57
Southampton Central	d								11 15						12 15								13 15
Southampton Airport Pkway	d								11 22						12 22								13 22
Winchester	d								11 31						12 31								13 31
Basingstoke	d								11 47						12 47								13 47
Guildford	d											12 14											
Reading	d								12 11			12 54			13 11					13 41			14 10
Oxford	d								12 37			13 17			13 37					14 06			14 37
Banbury	d								12 55			13 35			13 55					14 24			14 55
Leamington Spa	d								13 12			13 52			14 12					14 41			15 12
Coventry	d								13 27		13 42				14 27			14 42	14 42	14 54			15 27
Birmingham International	d								13 38		13 53				14 38			14 53	14 53	15 04			15 38
Penzance	d															09 30	09 30						
St Erth	d															09 38	09 38						
Hayle	d																						
Camborne	d															09 48	09 48						
Redruth	d															09 54	09 54						
Truro	d															10 08	10 08						
St Austell	d															10 24	10 24						
Par	d															10 31	10 31						
Lostwithiel	d																						
Bodmin Parkway	d															10 41	10 41						
Liskeard	d															10 54	10 54						
Plymouth	d	09 25	09 25							10 25						11 25	11 25				12 00		
Totnes	d	09 50	09 50							10 50						11 50	11 50						
Paignton	d												10 50										
Torquay	d												10 56										
Newton Abbot	d	10 03	10 03							11 03			11 08			12 03	12 03				12 36		
Teignmouth	d												11 15										
Dawlish	d												11 20										
Exeter St Davids	d	10 23	10 23							11 23			11 33			12 23	12 23				12 56		
Tiverton Parkway	d	10 37	10 37							11 37			11 47			12 37	12 37				13 10		
Taunton	d	10 50	10 50							11 52			12 00			12 50	12 50				13 23		
Weston-super-Mare	d												12 21										
Cardiff Central	d							11 45						12 45								13 45	
Newport (South Wales)	d							12 05						13 05								14 05	
Bristol Temple Meads	d	11 30	11 30							12 30			13 00			13 30	13 30				14 00		
Bristol Parkway	d	11 40	11 40							12 40			13 10			13 40	13 40				14 10		
Gloucester	d							12 50						13 50								14 50	
Cheltenham Spa	d	12 11	12 11					13 01		13 11			13 41	14 01		14 11	14 11				14 41	15 01	
Birmingham New Street	a	12 49	12 49					13 45	13 48	13 48	14 04	14 18	14 27	14 45	14 48	14 48	14 48	15 04	15 04	15 14	15 27	15 45	15 48
Birmingham New Street	d	13 03	13 03	13 20	13 20	13 30	13 30	13 49	13 57	14 03	14 15	14 30	14 31	14 49	14 57	15 03	15 03	15 15	15 15	15 30	15 31	15 49	15 57
Tamworth	d							14 07		14 19				15 09								16 07	
Burton-on-Trent	d	13 26	13 26					14 19						15 21		15 25	15 25					16 19	
Derby	a	13 42	13 42			14 01		14 34		14 43		15 02		15 33		15 42	15 42			16 02		16 34	
Nottingham	a							15 00						16 00								17 00	
Chesterfield	a	14 22	14 22							15 26						16 22	16 22						
Sheffield	a	14 45	14 45							15 45						16 41	16 41						
Doncaster	a	15 16	15 16							16 11						17 12	17 12						
Wakefield Westgate	a	15 35	15 35							16 40						17 33	17 33						
Leeds	a	15 53	15 53							17 00						17 54	17 54						
York	a	16 27	16 27							17 27						18 27	18 27						
Darlington	a	16 55	16 55							17 55						18 55	18 55						
Durham	a	17 12	17 12							18 12						19 12	19 12						
Chester-le-Street	a																						
Newcastle	a	17 25	17 25							18 25						19 25	19 25						
Morpeth	a	17 40	17 40																				
Alnmouth for Alnwick	a	17 55	17 55													19 56	19 56						
Berwick-upon-Tweed	a	18 16	18 16							19 14						20 18	20 18						
Dunbar	a									19 37													
Wolverhampton	d			13 37	13 37		13 49		14 15		14 37		14 49		15 15			15 37	15 37		15 49		16 15
Stafford	a						14 02		14 27				15 02		15 27						16 02		16 27
Stoke-on-Trent	a						14 18		14 44				15 18		15 44						16 18		16 44
Congleton	a																						
Macclesfield	a						14 36		15 01				15 36		16 04						16 36		17 04
Crewe	a			14 07	14 07						15 07							16 08	16 08				
Wilmslow	a																						
Stockport	a						14 50		15 14				15 50		16 16						16 50		17 16
M'chester Piccadilly	a						14 59		15 24				15 59		16 29						16 59		17 29
Warrington Bank Quay	a			14 26	14 26						15 26							16 26	16 26				
Wigan North Western	a			14 37	14 37						15 37							16 37	16 37				
Preston	a			14 50	14 50						15 51							16 51	16 51				
Lancaster	a			15 08	15 08						16 08							17 07	17 07				
Oxenholme Lake District	a			15 22	15 22													17 21	17 21				
Penrith North Lakes	a										16 44												
Carlisle	a			16 01	16 01						17 00							18 01	18 01				
Lockerbie	a																						
Haymarket	a										18 11												
Edinburgh	a	18 58	18 58							20 00	18 20					21 00	21 00						
Haymarket	a	19 22	19 22													21 16	21 16						
Motherwell	a	19 59	19 59													21 54	21 55						
Glasgow Central	a		20 19	17 15	17 19												22 12	19 13	19 20				
Inverkeithing	a																						
Kirkcaldy	a																						
Markinch	a																						
Ladybank	a																						
Cupar	a																						
Leuchars	a																						
Dundee	a																						
Arbroath	a																						
Montrose	a																						
Stonehaven	a																						
Aberdeen	a																						

A 9 September. 🛒 to Edinburgh
B not 9 September. 🛒 to Edinburgh
C not 9 September
D 9 September
E 🛒 from Birmingham New Street
F 🛒 from Reading
G 9 September. 🛒 from Plymouth to Edinburgh
H not 9 September. 🛒 from Plymouth to Birmingham New Street

Sundays

9 September to 7 October

South Coast and the South West - North West England, The North East and Scotland

		XC	VT	XC	XC	XC	XC	XC	XC	VT	VT	XC	XC	XC	XC	XC	VT	XC	XC	XC	XC	XC
								A	B	C	D			E					F	E		
Bournemouth	d						13 40								14 40						15 40	
Brockenhurst	d						13 57								14 57						15 57	
Southampton Central	d						14 15								15 15						16 15	
Southampton Airport Pkway	d						14 22								15 22						16 22	
Winchester	d						14 31								15 31						16 31	
Basingstoke	d						14 47								15 47						16 47	
Guildford	d																					
Reading	d			14 41			15 11					15 41			16 11			16 41			17 11	
Oxford	d			15 06			15 37					16 06			16 37			17 06			17 37	
Banbury	d			15 24			15 55					16 24			16 55			17 24			17 55	
Leamington Spa	d			15 41			16 12					16 41			17 12			17 41			18 12	
Coventry	d		15 42	15 54			16 27			16 42	16 42	16 54			17 27		17 45	17 54			18 27	
Birmingham International	d		15 53	16 04			16 38			16 53	16 53	17 04			17 38		17 55	18 04			18 38	
Penzance	d																		12 30			
St Erth	d																		12 38			
Hayle	d																		12 42			
Camborne	d																		12 51			
Redruth	d																		12 58			
Truro	d																		13 09			
St Austell	d																		13 26			
Par	d								12 23										13 32			
Lostwithiel	d																		13 39			
Bodmin Parkway	d								12 35										13 46			
Liskeard	d								12 48										13 58			
Plymouth	d	12 25			12 52			13 25	13 25							14 25			14 35			15 24
Totnes	d	12 50						13 50	13 50							14 51			15 01			15 50
Paignton	d																					
Torquay	d																					
Newton Abbot	d	13 03			13 27			14 03	14 03							15 04			15 13			16 03
Teignmouth	d																					
Dawlish	d																					
Exeter St Davids	d	13 23			13 47			14 23	14 23							15 24			15 32			16 25
Tiverton Parkway	d	13 37						14 36	14 36							15 37			15 46			16 39
Taunton	d	13 50						14 49	14 49							15 51			15 59			16 52
Weston-super-Mare	d																		16 29			
Cardiff Central	d					14 45								15 45						16 45		
Newport (South Wales)	d					15 05								16 05						17 03		
Bristol Temple Meads	d	14 30			15 00			15 30	15 30				16 00			16 30			17 00			17 30
Bristol Parkway	d	14 40			15 10			15 40	15 40				16 10			16 40			17 10			17 40
Gloucester	d					15 50								16 50						17 50		
Cheltenham Spa	d	15 11			15 40	16 01		16 11	16 11				16 41	17 01		17 12			17 41	18 01		18 11
Birmingham New Street	a	15 48	16 05	16 14	16 27	16 45	16 48	16 49	16 49	17 04	17 04	17 14	17 26	17 45	17 48	17 49	18 05	18 14	18 27	18 45	18 48	18 50
Birmingham New Street	d	16 03	16 15	16 30	16 31	16 49	16 57	17 03	17 03	17 15	17 15	17 30	17 31	17 49	17 57	18 03	18 15	18 30	18 31	18 49	18 57	19 03
Tamworth	d	16 19				17 07								18 07		18 19				19 09		
Burton-on-Trent	d					17 19		17 34	17 34					18 19						19 21		19 26
Derby	a	16 44		17 03		17 33		17 44	17 44			18 03		18 33		18 39		19 04		19 33		19 39
Nottingham	a					18 00								18 58						20 00		
Chesterfield	a	17 26						18 26	18 26							19 26						20 21
Sheffield	a	17 43						18 42	18 42							19 43						20 38
Doncaster	a	18 11						19 17	19 17							20 13						
Wakefield Westgate	a	18 43						19 38	19 38							20 32						21 07
Leeds	a	18 59						19 57	19 57							20 47						21 22
York	a	19 30						20 30	20 30													
Darlington	a	19 59						21 00	21 00													
Durham	a	20 18						21 17	21 17													
Chester-le-Street	a																					
Newcastle	a	20 32						21 30	21 31													
Morpeth	a	20 47																				
Alnmouth for Alnwick	a							22 01	21 59													
Berwick-upon-Tweed	a	21 20																				
Dunbar	a	21 43																				
Wolverhampton	d		16 37		16 49		17 15			17 37	17 37		17 49		18 15		18 37		18 49		19 15	
Stafford	a				17 02		17 28						18 02		18 27				19 02		19 27	
Stoke-on-Trent	a				17 18		17 45						18 18		18 44				19 18		19 44	
Congleton	a																					
Macclesfield	a				17 36		18 04						18 36		19 04				19 36		20 04	
Crewe	a		17 07							18 07	18 07						19 07					
Wilmslow	a																					
Stockport	a				17 50		18 16						18 50		19 17				19 50		20 16	
M'chester Piccadilly	a				17 59		18 29						18 59		19 28				19 59		20 28	
Warrington Bank Quay	a		17 26							18 26	18 26						19 26					
Wigan North Western	a		17 37							18 37	18 37						19 37					
Preston	a		17 51							18 51	18 51						19 51					
Lancaster	a		18 07							19 07	19 07						20 07					
Oxenholme Lake District	a		18 22							19 21	19 21											
Penrith North Lakes	a		18 47														20 44					
Carlisle	a		19 03							20 00	20 00						20 59					
Lockerbie	a																					
Haymarket	a		20 16														22 14					
Edinburgh	a	22 06	20 22					23 03	23 03								22 19					
Haymarket	a																					
Motherwell	a																					
Glasgow Central	a									21 12	21 22											
Inverkeithing	a																					
Kirkcaldy	a																					
Markinch	a																					
Ladybank	a																					
Cupar	a																					
Leuchars	a																					
Dundee	a																					
Arbroath	a																					
Montrose	a																					
Stonehaven	a																					
Aberdeen	a																					

A not 9 September. ⊼ to Newcastle
B 9 September. ⊼ to Newcastle
C not 9 September
D 9 September
E ⊼ to Birmingham New Street
F ⊼ from Plymouth

Sundays

9 September to 7 October

South Coast and the South West - North West England, The North East and Scotland

		VT	VT	XC	XC	XC	XC	XC	VT	XC	XC	XC	XC	XC	VT	XC	XC	XC	XC	XC	XC	XC	XC
		A	B	C		C	C	C				C	C	D			E		F	E			
Bournemouth	d						16 40						17 40						18 40			19 40	
Brockenhurst	d						16 57						17 57						18 57			19 57	
Southampton Central	d						17 15						18 15						19 15			20 15	
Southampton Airport Pkway	d						17 22						18 22						19 22			20 22	
Winchester	d						17 31						18 31						19 31			20 31	
Basingstoke	d						17 47						18 47						19 47			20 47	
Guildford	d																						
Reading	d			17 41			18 11			18 41			19 11			19 41			20 11		20 41	21 11	
Oxford	d			18 06			18 37			19 06			19 37			20 06			20 37		21 06	21 37	
Banbury	d			18 24			18 55			19 24			19 55			20 24			20 55		21 24	21 55	
Leamington Spa	d			18 41			19 12			19 41			20 12			20 41			21 12		21 41	22 12	
Coventry	d	18 45	18 45	18 54			19 27		19 42	19 54			20 27		20 42	20 54			21 27		21 53	22 24	
Birmingham International	d	18 55	18 55	19 04			19 38		19 53	20 04			20 38		20 53	21 04			21 38		22 03	22 34	
Penzance	d													15 30									
St Erth	d													15 38									
Hayle	d																						
Camborne	d													15 49									
Redruth	d													15 55									
Truro	d													16 07									
St Austell	d													16 23									
Par	d													16 30									
Lostwithiel	d																						
Bodmin Parkway	d													16 40									
Liskeard	d													16 52									
Plymouth	d							16 25						17 25						18 25			
Totnes	d							16 51						17 50						18 52			
Paignton	d																18 20						
Torquay	d																18 26						
Newton Abbot	d							17 04						18 03			18 37			19 05			
Teignmouth	d																						
Dawlish	d																						
Exeter St Davids	d							17 25						18 23			18 58			19 25			
Tiverton Parkway	d							17 39						18 37			19 11			19 38			
Taunton	d							17 51						18 50			19 24			19 52			
Weston-super-Mare	d																						
Cardiff Central	d					17 45						18 45						19 45					20 45
Newport (South Wales)	d					18 04						19 03						20 03					21 05
Bristol Temple Meads	d				18 00			18 30			19 00			19 30			20 00			20 30			
Bristol Parkway	d				18 10			18 40			19 10			19 40			20 09			20 40			
Gloucester	d					18 50						19 50						20 50					21 50
Cheltenham Spa	d				18 41	19 01		19 11			19 41	20 01		20 11			20 40	21 01		21 11			22 01
Birmingham New Street	a	19 05	19 05	19 14	19 26	19 45	19 48	19 50	20 04	20 14	20 27	20 45	20 48	20 52	21 05	21 15	21 18	21 45	21 48	21 48	22 14	22 43	22 45
Birmingham New Street	d	19 15	19 15	19 30	19 31	19 49	19 57	20 03	20 15		20 31	20 49	20 57	21 03	21 15				21 57	22 03			
Tamworth	d					20 07		20 19				21 06		21 19						22 19			
Burton-on-Trent	d					20 19						21 19		21 29									
Derby	a			20 03		20 34		20 40				21 33		21 41						22 40			
Nottingham	a					21 00						22 00											
Chesterfield	a							21 21						22 22									
Sheffield	a							21 38						22 37									
Doncaster	a																						
Wakefield Westgate	a							22 09						23 02									
Leeds	a							22 24						23 17									
York	a																						
Darlington	a																						
Durham	a																						
Chester-le-Street	a																						
Newcastle	a																						
Morpeth	a																						
Alnmouth for Alnwick	a																						
Berwick-upon-Tweed	a																						
Dunbar	a																						
Wolverhampton	d	19 37	19 37		19 49		20 15		20 37		20 52		21 17		21 37				22 15				
Stafford	a				20 02		20 27		20 51		21 05		21 29		21 55				22 27				
Stoke-on-Trent	a				20 18		20 44				21 21		21 45						22 44				
Congleton	a																						
Macclesfield	a				20 36		21 02				21 39		22 03						23 01				
Crewe	a	20 07	20 07						21 10						22 16								
Wilmslow	a																						
Stockport	a				20 50		21 15				21 52		22 15						23 14				
M'chester Piccadilly	a				20 59		21 29				22 02		22 26						23 24				
Warrington Bank Quay	a	20 26	20 26												22 36								
Wigan North Western	a	20 37	20 37												22 47								
Preston	a	20 51	20 51												23 01								
Lancaster	a	21 08	21 08																				
Oxenholme Lake District	a	21 22	21 22																				
Penrith North Lakes	a																						
Carlisle	a	22 01	22 01																				
Lockerbie	a	22 20	22 20																				
Haymarket	a																						
Edinburgh	a																						
Haymarket	a																						
Motherwell	a	23 04	23 04																				
Glasgow Central	a	23 21	23 24																				
Inverkeithing	a																						
Kirkcaldy	a																						
Markinch	a																						
Ladybank	a																						
Cupar	a																						
Leuchars	a																						
Dundee	a																						
Arbroath	a																						
Montrose	a																						
Stonehaven	a																						
Aberdeen	a																						

A not 9 September
B 9 September
C ⊼ to Birmingham New Street
D ⊼ from Plymouth to Birmingham New Street
E ⊼ to Bristol Temple Meads
F ⊼ to Reading

Table T051-R

Sundays

9 September to 7 October

South Coast and the South West - North West England, The North East and Scotland

Station		XC	XC
Bournemouth	d		
Brockenhurst	d		
Southampton Central	d		
Southampton Airport Pkway	d		
Winchester	d		
Basingstoke	d		
Guildford	d		
Reading	d	21 41	
Oxford	d	22 06	
Banbury	d	22 24	
Leamington Spa	d	22 41	
Coventry	d	22 54	
Birmingham International	d	23 04	
Penzance	d		
St Erth	d		
Hayle	d		
Camborne	d		
Redruth	d		
Truro	d		
St Austell	d		
Par	d		
Lostwithiel	d		
Bodmin Parkway	d		
Liskeard	d		
Plymouth	d		
Totnes	d		
Paignton	d		
Torquay	d		
Newton Abbot	d		
Teignmouth	d		
Dawlish	d		
Exeter St Davids	d		
Tiverton Parkway	d		
Taunton	d		
Weston-super-Mare	d		
Cardiff Central	d		
Newport (South Wales)	d		
Bristol Temple Meads	d		22 10
Bristol Parkway	d		22 20
Gloucester	d		
Cheltenham Spa	d		22 49
Birmingham New Street	a	23 14	23 40
Birmingham New Street	d		
Tamworth	d		
Burton-on-Trent	d		
Derby	a		
Nottingham	a		
Chesterfield	a		
Sheffield	a		
Doncaster	a		
Wakefield Westgate	a		
Leeds	a		
York	a		
Darlington	a		
Durham	a		
Chester-le-Street	a		
Newcastle	a		
Morpeth	a		
Alnmouth for Alnwick	a		
Berwick-upon-Tweed	a		
Dunbar	a		
Wolverhampton	d		
Stafford	a		
Stoke-on-Trent	a		
Congleton	a		
Macclesfield	a		
Crewe	a		
Wilmslow	a		
Stockport	a		
M'chester Piccadilly	a		
Warrington Bank Quay	a		
Wigan North Western	a		
Preston	a		
Lancaster	a		
Oxenholme Lake District	a		
Penrith North Lakes	a		
Carlisle	a		
Lockerbie	a		
Haymarket	a		
Edinburgh	a		
Haymarket	a		
Motherwell	a		
Glasgow Central	a		
Inverkeithing	a		
Kirkcaldy	a		
Markinch	a		
Ladybank	a		
Cupar	a		
Leuchars	a		
Dundee	a		
Arbroath	a		
Montrose	a		
Stonehaven	a		
Aberdeen	a		

Table T051-R

Sundays

14 October to 2 December

South Coast and the South West - North West England, The North East and Scotland

Station		VT	XC	XC	VT	XC	XC	VT	XC	XC	VT	XC	XC	XC	VT	XC	XC	XC	XC	VT	XC	XC	XC
							A										B		A				B
Bournemouth	d																	09 40					
Brockenhurst	d																	09 57					
Southampton Central	d												09 15					10 15					
Southampton Airport Pkway	d												09 22					10 22					
Winchester	d												09 31					10 31					
Basingstoke	d												09 47					10 47					
Guildford	d																						
Reading	d								09 12				10 11					11 11					
Oxford	d								09 37				10 37					11 37					
Banbury	d								09 55				10 55					11 55					
Leamington Spa	d								10 12				11 12					12 12					
Coventry	d								10 29				11 29					12 28					
Birmingham International	d								10 40				11 41					12 40					
Penzance	d																						
St Erth	d																						
Hayle	d																						
Camborne	d																						
Redruth	d																						
Truro	d																						
St Austell	d																						
Par	d																						
Lostwithiel	d																						
Bodmin Parkway	d																						
Liskeard	d																						
Plymouth	d																		09 25				
Totnes	d																		09 50				
Paignton	d																						
Torquay	d																						
Newton Abbot	d																		10 03				
Teignmouth	d																						
Dawlish	d																						
Exeter St Davids	d																		10 23				
Tiverton Parkway	d																		10 37				
Taunton	d																		10 50				
Weston-super-Mare	d																						
Cardiff Central	d																10 45						11 45
Newport (South Wales)	d																11 06						12 05
Bristol Temple Meads	d									09 15				10 30					11 30				
Bristol Parkway	d									09 25				10 40					11 40				
Gloucester	d									10 00							11 50						12 50
Cheltenham Spa	d									10 12				11 11			12 01		12 11				13 01
Birmingham New Street	a								10 50	10 49			11 51	11 48			12 45	12 50	12 49				13 45
Birmingham New Street	d	08 45	09 01	09 03	09 20	10 01	10 03	10 20	11 01	11 03	11 20	11 49	11 57	12 03	12 20	12 30	12 49	12 57	13 03	13 20	13 30	13 30	13 49
Tamworth	d			09 19			10 18					12 07		12 19			13 07						14 07
Burton-on-Trent	d			09 28			10 29			11 25		12 19					13 19		13 26				14 19
Derby	a			09 41			10 40			11 37		12 34		12 38		13 01	13 33		13 37			14 01	14 34
Nottingham	a											13 00					14 00						14 59
Chesterfield	a			10 02			11 02			12 02				13 02		13 29			14 02			14 29	
Sheffield	a			10 18			11 17			12 18				13 18		13 43			14 17			14 45	
Doncaster	a															14 14						15 18	
Wakefield Westgate	a			10 45			11 45			12 45				13 44					14 45				
Leeds	a			10 59			11 59			13 00				14 00					15 00				
York	a			11 29			12 30			13 27				14 27		14 40			15 27			15 40	
Darlington	a			11 57			12 58			13 56				14 55		15 16			15 55			16 11	
Durham	a			12 14			13 15			14 13				15 13		15 33			16 12			16 28	
Chester-le-Street	a																						
Newcastle	a			12 27			13 28			14 27				15 26		15 47			16 25			16 42	
Morpeth	a									14 45													
Alnmouth for Alnwick	a						13 55							15 53					16 52				
Berwick-upon-Tweed	a						14 16							16 12									
Dunbar	a			13 34						15 39									17 35				
Wolverhampton	d	09 04	09 19		09 37	10 19		10 37	11 19		11 37		12 16		12 37			13 16		13 37	13 49		
Stafford	a	09 17	09 32			10 32			11 31				12 28					13 28			14 02		
Stoke-on-Trent	a		09 51			10 48			11 48				12 45					13 44			14 18		
Congleton	a																						
Macclesfield	a		10 09			11 08			12 09				13 04					14 04			14 36		
Crewe	a	09 35			10 07			11 10			12 07				13 07					14 07			
Wilmslow	a																						
Stockport	a		10 22			11 22			12 24				13 16					14 16			14 50		
M'chester Piccadilly	a		10 38			11 33			12 41				13 29					14 29			14 59		
Warrington Bank Quay	a	09 54			10 26			11 28			12 26				13 26					14 26			
Wigan North Western	a	10 05			10 37			11 39			12 37				13 37					14 37			
Preston	a	10 20			10 51			11 53			12 51				13 51					14 50			
Lancaster	a				11 16			12 09			13 07				14 08					15 08			
Oxenholme Lake District	a				11 32			12 22			13 21									15 22			
Penrith North Lakes	a														14 44								
Carlisle	a				12 10			13 01			14 00				15 00					16 01			
Lockerbie	a																						
Haymarket	a							14 16							16 14								
Edinburgh	a			14 01			14 58	14 21		16 03				16 55	16 20				17 58				
Haymarket	a						15 13							17 14					18 16				
Motherwell	a						15 55							17 52									
Glasgow Central	a				13 27		16 12				15 16			18 13						17 15			
Inverkeithing	a																		18 28				
Kirkcaldy	a																		18 44				
Markinch	a																		18 53				
Ladybank	a																		19 01				
Cupar	a																		19 07				
Leuchars	a																		19 14				
Dundee	a																		19 29				
Arbroath	a																		19 46				
Montrose	a																		20 00				
Stonehaven	a																		20 22				
Aberdeen	a																		20 42				

A to Edinburgh

B from Birmingham New Street

South Coast and the South West - North West England, The North East and Scotland

		XC	XC	VT	XC	XC	XC	XC	XC	VT	XC	XC	XC	XC	XC	VT	XC	XC	XC	XC	XC	VT	XC
		◇1	◇1	◇1	◇1	◇1	◇1	◇1	◇1	◇1	◇1	◇1	◇1	◇1	◇1	◇1	◇1	◇1	◇1	◇1	◇1	◇1	◇1
			A		B		C		D				C		A								E
		✕	✕	⊡	✕	✕	✕	✕	✕	⊡	✕	✕	✕	✕	✕	⊡	✕	✕	✕	✕	✕	⊡	✕
Bournemouth	d	10 40						11 40						12 40						13 40			
Brockenhurst 3	d	10 57						11 57						12 57						13 57			
Southampton Central	d	11 15						12 15						13 15						14 15			
Southampton Airport Pkwy	d	11 22						12 22						13 22						14 22			
Winchester	d	11 31						12 31						13 31						14 31			
Basingstoke	d	11 47						12 47						13 47						14 47			
Guildford	d				12 14																		
Reading 7	d	12 11			12 54			13 11			13 41			14 10			14 41			15 11			15 41
Oxford	d	12 37			13 17			13 37			14 06			14 37			15 06			15 37			16 06
Banbury	d	12 55			13 35			13 55			14 24			14 55			15 24			15 55			16 24
Leamington Spa 8	d	13 12			13 52			14 12			14 41			15 12			15 41			16 12			16 41
Coventry	d	13 27		13 42				14 27		14 42	14 54			15 27		15 42	15 54			16 27		16 42	16 54
Birmingham International	d	13 38		13 53				14 38		14 53	15 04			15 38		15 53	16 04			16 38		16 53	17 04
Penzance	d								09 30														
St Erth	d								09 38														
Hayle	d																						
Camborne	d								09 48														
Redruth	d								09 54														
Truro	d								10 06														
St Austell	d								10 22														
Par	d								10 29														
Lostwithiel	d																						
Bodmin Parkway	d								10 39														
Liskeard 6	d								10 52														
Plymouth	d		10 25						11 25			12 00			12 25			12 52			13 25		
Totnes	d		10 50						11 50						12 50						13 50		
Paignton	d					10 50																	
Torquay	d					10 56																	
Newton Abbot	d		11 03			11 08			12 03			12 36			13 03			13 27			14 03		
Teignmouth	d					11 15																	
Dawlish	d					11 20																	
Exeter St Davids 6	d		11 23			11 33			12 23			12 56			13 23			13 47			14 23		
Tiverton Parkway	d		11 37			11 47			12 37			13 10			13 37						14 36		
Taunton	d		11 52			12 00			12 50			13 23			13 50						14 49		
Weston-super-Mare	d					12 21																	
Cardiff Central 7	d						12 45						13 45						14 45				
Newport (South Wales)	d						13 05						14 05						15 05				
Bristol Temple Meads 10	d		12 30			13 00			13 30			14 00			14 30			15 00			15 30		
Bristol Parkway 7	d		12 40			13 10			13 40			14 10			14 40			15 10			15 40		
Gloucester 7	d						13 50						14 50						15 50				
Cheltenham Spa	d		13 11			13 41	14 01		14 11			14 41	15 01		15 11			15 40	16 01		16 11		
Birmingham New Street 12	a	13 48	13 48	14 04	14 19	14 27	14 45	14 48	14 48	15 04	15 14	15 27	15 45	15 48	15 48	16 05	16 14	16 27	16 45	16 48	16 49	17 04	17 14
Birmingham New Street 12	d	13 57	14 03	14 15	14 30	14 31	14 49	14 57	15 03	15 15	15 30	15 31	15 49	15 57	16 03	16 15	16 30	16 31	16 49	16 57	17 03	17 15	17 30
Tamworth	d		14 19				15 09						16 07		16 19				17 07				
Burton-on-Trent	d						15 21		15 25				16 19						17 19		17 25		
Derby 6	a		14 39		15 01		15 33		15 37		16 01		16 34		16 38		17 02		17 33		17 36		18 02
Nottingham 8	a						16 00						17 00						18 00				
Chesterfield	a		15 02						16 02						17 02						18 01		
Sheffield 7	a		15 17		15 45				16 18		16 42				17 18		17 41				18 19		18 42
Doncaster 7	a				16 14						17 15						18 14						19 17
Wakefield Westgate 7	a		15 45						16 45						17 44		18 32				18 45		
Leeds 10	a		16 00						16 59						18 00		18 47				19 01		
York 8	a		16 27		16 40				17 27		17 40				18 27		19 21				19 30		19 46
Darlington 7	a		16 55		17 11				17 55		18 09				18 55		19 49				19 59		20 20
Durham	a		17 12		17 29				18 12		18 26				19 12		20 06				20 16		20 37
Chester-le-Street	a																						
Newcastle 8	a		17 25		17 44				18 25		18 41				19 25		20 20				20 32		20 51
Morpeth	a		17 40																		20 48		
Alnmouth for Alnwick	a		17 55												19 56								
Berwick-upon-Tweed	a		18 16						19 10						20 18						21 21		
Dunbar	a								19 33												21 44		
Wolverhampton 7	d	14 15		14 37		14 49		15 15		15 37		15 49		16 15		16 37		16 49		17 15		17 37	
Stafford	a	14 27				15 02		15 27				16 02		16 27				17 02		17 28			
Stoke-on-Trent	a	14 44				15 18		15 44				16 18		16 44				17 18		17 45			
Congleton	a																						
Macclesfield	a	15 01				15 36		16 04				16 36		17 04				17 36		18 04			
Crewe 10	a			15 07						16 08						17 07						18 07	
Wilmslow	a																						
Stockport	a	15 14				15 50		16 16				16 50		17 16				17 50		18 16			
M'chester Piccadilly 10	a	15 24				15 59		16 29				16 59		17 29				17 59		18 29			
Warrington Bank Quay	a			15 26						16 26						17 26						18 26	
Wigan North Western	a			15 37						16 37						17 37						18 37	
Preston 8	a			15 51						16 51						17 51						18 51	
Lancaster 6	a			16 08						17 07						18 07						19 07	
Oxenholme Lake District	a									17 21						18 22						19 21	
Penrith North Lakes	a			16 44												18 47							
Carlisle 8	a			17 00						18 01						19 03						20 00	
Lockerbie	a																						
Haymarket	a			18 11												20 16							
Edinburgh 10	a		18 58	18 20					19 57						21 00	20 22					22 07		22 18
Haymarket	a		19 22												21 16								
Motherwell	a		19 59												21 55								
Glasgow Central 15	a		20 19							19 13					22 12							21 12	
Inverkeithing	a																						
Kirkcaldy	a																						
Markinch	a																						
Ladybank	a																						
Cupar	a																						
Leuchars 8	a																						
Dundee	a																						
Arbroath	a																						
Montrose	a																						
Stonehaven	a																						
Aberdeen	a																						

A ✕ to Edinburgh
B ✕ from Reading
C ✕ from Birmingham New Street
D ✕ from Plymouth
E ✕ to Newcastle

South Coast and the South West - North West England, The North East and Scotland

		XC	XC	XC	XC	VT	XC	XC	XC	XC	XC	VT	XC	XC	XC	XC	XC	VT	XC	XC	XC	XC
		◇1	◇1	◇1	◇1	◇1	◇1	◇1	◇1	◇1	◇1	■ 1	◇1	◇1	◇1	◇1	◇1	◇1	◇1	◇1	◇1	◇1
			A		B		C	D	A		E		A		A	A	A				A	A
		✕	✕	✕	✕	⊡	✕	✕	✕	✕	✕	⊡	✕	✕	✕	✕	✕	⊡	✕	✕	✕	✕
Bournemouth	d			14 40						15 40						16 40						17 40
Brockenhurst 3	d			14 57						15 57						16 57						17 57
Southampton Central	d			15 15						16 15						17 15						18 15
Southampton Airport Pkwy	d			15 22						16 22						17 22						18 22
Winchester	d			15 31						16 31						17 31						18 31
Basingstoke	d			15 47						16 47						17 47						18 47
Guildford	d																					
Reading 7	d			16 11			16 41			17 11			17 41			18 11			18 41			19 11
Oxford	d			16 37			17 06			17 37			18 06			18 37			19 06			19 37
Banbury	d			16 55			17 24			17 55			18 24			18 55			19 24			19 55
Leamington Spa 8	d			17 12			17 41			18 12			18 41			19 12			19 41			20 12
Coventry	d			17 27		17 45	17 54			18 27		18 45	18 54			19 27		19 42	19 54			20 27
Birmingham International	d			17 38		17 55	18 04			18 38		18 55	19 04			19 38		19 53	20 04			20 38
Penzance	d							12 30														
St Erth	d							12 38														
Hayle	d							12 42														
Camborne	d							12 51														
Redruth	d							12 58														
Truro	d							13 09														
St Austell	d							13 26														
Par	d							13 32														
Lostwithiel	d							13 39														
Bodmin Parkway	d							13 46														
Liskeard 6	d							13 58														
Plymouth	d				14 25			14 35			15 24						16 25					
Totnes	d				14 51			15 01			15 50						16 51					
Paignton	d																					
Torquay	d																					
Newton Abbot	d				15 04			15 13			16 03						17 04					
Teignmouth	d																					
Dawlish	d																					
Exeter St Davids 6	d				15 24			15 32			16 25						17 25					
Tiverton Parkway	d				15 37			15 46			16 39						17 39					
Taunton	d				15 51			15 59			16 52						17 51					
Weston-super-Mare	d							16 29														
Cardiff Central 7	d		15 45						16 45						17 45						18 45	
Newport (South Wales)	d		16 05						17 03						18 04						19 03	
Bristol Temple Meads 10	d	16 00			16 30			17 00			17 30			18 00			18 30			19 00		
Bristol Parkway 7	d	16 10			16 40			17 10			17 40			18 10			18 40			19 10		
Gloucester 7	d		16 50						17 50						18 50						19 50	
Cheltenham Spa	d	16 41	17 01		17 12			17 41	18 01		18 11			18 41	19 01		19 11			19 41	20 01	
Birmingham New Street 12	a	17 26	17 45	17 48	17 49	18 05	18 14	18 27	18 45	18 48	18 50	19 05	19 14	19 26	19 45	19 48	19 50	20 04	20 14	20 27	20 45	20 48
Birmingham New Street 12	d	17 31	17 49	17 57	18 03	18 15	18 30	18 31	18 49	18 57	19 03	19 15	19 30	19 31	19 49	19 57	20 03	20 15		20 31	20 49	20 57
Tamworth	d		18 07		18 19				19 09						20 07		20 19				21 06	
Burton-on-Trent	d		18 19						19 21		19 26				20 19						21 19	
Derby 6	a		18 33		18 39		19 03		19 33		19 40		20 01		20 34		20 40				21 33	
Nottingham 8	a		18 58						20 00						21 00						22 00	
Chesterfield	a				19 04						20 02						21 03					
Sheffield 7	a				19 20		19 38				20 18		20 38				21 18					
Doncaster 7	a						20 14						21 20									
Wakefield Westgate 7	a				19 49						20 45						21 48					
Leeds 10	a				20 04						21 02						22 02					
York 8	a				20 30		20 40				21 31		21 45									
Darlington 7	a				21 00		21 14						22 25									
Durham	a				21 17		21 32						22 42									
Chester-le-Street	a																					
Newcastle 8	a				21 31		21 45						23 12									
Morpeth	a																					
Alnmouth for Alnwick	a				21 59																	
Berwick-upon-Tweed	a																					
Dunbar	a																					
Wolverhampton 7	d	17 49		18 15		18 37		18 49		19 15		19 37		19 49		20 15		20 37		20 52		21 17
Stafford	a	18 02		18 27				19 02		19 27				20 02		20 27		20 51		21 05		21 29
Stoke-on-Trent	a	18 18		18 44				19 18		19 44				20 18		20 44				21 21		21 45
Congleton	a																					
Macclesfield	a	18 36		19 04				19 36		20 04				20 36		21 02				21 39		22 03
Crewe 10	a					19 07						20 07						21 10				
Wilmslow	a																					
Stockport	a	18 50		19 17				19 50		20 16				20 50		21 15				21 52		22 15
M'chester Piccadilly 10	a	18 59		19 28				19 59		20 28				20 59		21 29				22 02		22 26
Warrington Bank Quay	a					19 26						20 26										
Wigan North Western	a					19 37						20 37										
Preston 8	a					19 51						20 51										
Lancaster 6	a					20 07						21 08										
Oxenholme Lake District	a											21 22										
Penrith North Lakes	a					20 44																
Carlisle 8	a					20 59						22 01										
Lockerbie	a											22 20										
Haymarket	a					22 14																
Edinburgh 10	a				23 03	22 19																
Haymarket	a																					
Motherwell	a											23 04										
Glasgow Central 15	a											23 21										
Inverkeithing	a																					
Kirkcaldy	a																					
Markinch	a																					
Ladybank	a																					
Cupar	a																					
Leuchars 8	a																					
Dundee	a																					
Arbroath	a																					
Montrose	a																					
Stonehaven	a																					
Aberdeen	a																					

A ✕ to Birmingham New Street
B ✕ to Newcastle
C ✕ to Sheffield
D ✕ from Plymouth
E ✕ to Leeds

Table T051-R

Sundays

14 October to 2 December

South Coast and the South West - North West England, The North East and Scotland

		XC	VT	XC	XC	XC	XC	XC		XC	XC	XC	XC	XC
		◇■	◇■	◇■	◇■	◇■	◇■	◇■		◇■	◇■	◇■	◇■	◇■
		A			B		C	B						
		✠	⊞		✠		✠	✠						
Bournemouth	d						18 40				19 40			
Brockenhurst ■	d						18 57				19 57			
Southampton Central	d						19 15				20 15			
Southampton Airport Pkway ✈	d						19 22				20 22			
Winchester	d						19 31				20 31			
Basingstoke	d						19 47				20 47			
Guildford	d													
Reading ■	d			19 41			20 11			20 41	21 11		21 41	
Oxford	d			20 06			20 37			21 06	21 37		22 06	
Banbury	d			20 24			20 55			21 24	21 55		22 24	
Leamington Spa ■	d			20 41			21 12			21 41	22 12		22 41	
Coventry	d		20 42	20 54			21 27			21 53	22 24		22 54	
Birmingham International ✈	d		20 53	21 04			21 38			22 03	22 34		23 04	
Penzance	d	15 30												
St Erth	d	15 38												
Hayle	d													
Camborne	d	15 49												
Redruth	d	15 55												
Truro	d	16 07												
St Austell	d	16 23												
Par	d	16 30												
Lostwithiel	d													
Bodmin Parkway	d	16 40												
Liskeard ■	d	16 52												
Plymouth	d	17 25						18 25						
Totnes	d	17 50						18 52						
Paignton	d				18 20									
Torquay	d				18 26									
Newton Abbot	d	18 03			18 37			19 05						
Teignmouth	d													
Dawlish	d													
Exeter St Davids ■	d	18 23			18 58			19 25						
Tiverton Parkway	d	18 37			19 11			19 38						
Taunton	d	18 50			19 24			19 52						
Weston-super-Mare	d													
Cardiff Central ■	d					19 45						20 45		
Newport (South Wales)	d					20 03						21 05		
Bristol Temple Meads ■	d	19 30			20 00			20 30						22 10
Bristol Parkway ■	d	19 40			20 09			20 40						22 20
Gloucester ■	d					20 50						21 50		
Cheltenham Spa	d	20 11			20 40	21 01		21 11				22 01		22 49
Birmingham New Street ■	a	20 52	21 05	21 15	21 18	21 45	21 48	21 48		22 14	22 43	22 45	23 14	23 40
Birmingham New Street ■	d	21 03	21 15				21 57	22 03						
Tamworth	d	21 19						22 19						
Burton-on-Trent	d	21 29												
Derby ■	a	21 41						22 40						
Nottingham ■	a													
Chesterfield	a	22 02						23 02						
Sheffield ■	a	22 18						23 18						
Doncaster ■	a													
Wakefield Westgate ■	a	22 47												
Leeds ■	a	23 02						00 09						
York ■	a													
Darlington ■	a													
Durham	a													
Chester-le-Street	a													
Newcastle ■	a													
Morpeth	a													
Alnmouth for Alnwick	a													
Berwick-upon-Tweed	a													
Dunbar	a													
Wolverhampton ■	d		21 37				22 15							
Stafford	a		21 55				22 27							
Stoke-on-Trent	a						22 44							
Congleton	a													
Macclesfield	a						23 01							
Crewe ■	a		22 16											
Wilmslow	a													
Stockport	a						23 14							
M'chester Piccadilly ■	a						23 24							
Warrington Bank Quay	a		22 36											
Wigan North Western	a		22 47											
Preston ■	a		23 01											
Lancaster ■	a													
Oxenholme Lake District	a													
Penrith North Lakes	a													
Carlisle ■	a													
Lockerbie	a													
Haymarket	a													
Edinburgh ■	a													
Haymarket	a													
Motherwell	a													
Glasgow Central ■	a													
Inverkeithing	a													
Kirkcaldy	a													
Markinch	a													
Ladybank	a													
Cupar	a													
Leuchars ■	a													
Dundee	a													
Arbroath	a													
Montrose	a													
Stonehaven	a													
Aberdeen	a													

A ✠ from Plymouth to Birmingham New Street
B ✠ to Bristol Temple Meads
C ✠ to Reading

Table T052-F

Mondays to Fridays

21 May to 7 December

Brighton and Gatwick Airport - London, Stevenage, Cambridge, Luton and Bedford

Miles	Miles	Miles	Miles	Miles			TL	TL	TL	TL	TL	TL	TL	TL	TL	TL		TL	TL	TL	TL	TL	TL	TL	TL
							MX	MO	MX	MX	MX	MX	MO	MX	MX	MO		MX							
								■		■			■	■	■	■		■	■	■	■	■	■	■	■
							A	B	A	B	C	C	B	D	B	B		B		E	E	E	E	E	E
0	—	—	—	—	Brighton ■	d													00 04						
—	—	—	—	—	Horsham	d																			
24¼	—	—	—	—	Gatwick Airport ■ ✈	d									00 04	00 21		00 21	00 42	01 46	02 21	02 46	03 21	03 46	04 21
40½	—	—	—	—	East Croydon	d							00 10	00 10	00 23	00 40		00 40	01 10	02 10	02 40	03 10	03 40	04 10	04 40
—	—	—	—	—	Rainham Kt	d																			
—	—	—	—	—	Dartford	d																			
—	—	—	—	—	Abbey Wood	d																			
—	—	—	—	—	Woolwich Arsenal	d																			
—	—	—	—	—	Greenwich	d																			
—	—	—	—	—	Maidstone East	d																			
—	—	—	—	—	Sevenoaks	d																			
—	—	—	—	—	Swanley	d																			
—	—	—	—	—	St Mary Cray	d																			
—	—	—	—	—	Orpington	d																			
—	—	—	—	—	Bromley South	d																			
—	—	—	—	—	Catford	d					00 06	00 06													
—	—	—	22¾	—	Peckham Rye ■ 195	d					00 14	00 14													
—	—	—	23¾	—	Denmark Hill ■ 195	d					00 17	00 17													
—	0	0	—	—	Sutton ■ 179	d																			
—	—	—	—	—	Wimbledon	d																			
—	9½	6	—	—	Streatham ■	d																			
—	11	7½	—	—	Tulse Hill ■	d																			
—	12	8½	—	—	Herne Hill ■ 173,179	d																			
—	13	9½	—	—	Loughborough Jn 173,179	d																			
50½	15	11¼	26¼	—	Elephant & Castle ⊖173,179	d			00 04		00 24	00 24													
—	—	—	—	—	London Bridge	d																			
51½	16	12½	27¼	—	**London Blackfriars**	a			00 08		00 29	00 33	00 36	00 36	00 49	01 06		01 07	01 36	02 36	03 06	03 36	04 06	04 36	05 06
—	—	—	—	—	**London Blackfriars** ■ ⊖	d	00 02	00 06	00 09	00 22	00 29		00 36	00 37	00 50	01 06		01 08	01 36	02 36	03 06	03 36	04 06	04 36	05 06
52	—	—	—	—	**City Thameslink** ■	d					00 31														05 08
—	—	—	—	—	**Farringdon** ■ ⊖	d	00 06	00 11	00 13	00 25	00 34			00 41											05 11
—	—	—	—	—	St Pancras International	d	00 11	00 16	00 18	00 30	00 38		00 46	00 46	01 01	01 16		01 16	01 44	02 44	03 14	03 44	04 14	04 44	05 16
—	—	—	—	—	Finsbury Park	a					00 44			00 52											
—	—	—	—	—	Welwyn Garden City	a								01 12											
—	—	—	—	—	Stevenage	a								01 21											
—	—	—	—	—	Hitchin	a								01 30											
—	—	—	—	—	Letchworth Garden City	a																			
—	—	—	—	—	Royston	a																			
—	—	—	—	—	Cambridge	a																			
—	—	—	—	—	Huntingdon	a								01 59											
—	—	—	—	—	Peterborough	a								02 17											
—	—	—	—	—	Kentish Town	a		00 20	00 22				00 50		01 05				01 48	02 48		03 48		04 48	
—	—	—	—	—	West Hampstead Thameslink	a	00 19	00 24	00 26	00 39			00 54		01 09	01 24		01 24	01 52	02 52	03 22	03 52	04 22	04 52	05 24
—	—	—	—	—	Elstree & Borehamwood	a		00 39	00 41				01 09		01 24				02 07	03 07		04 07		05 07	
—	—	—	—	—	St Albans City	a	00 35	00 49	00 51	00 56			01 19		01 34	01 40		01 40	02 17	03 17	03 40	04 17	04 40	05 17	05 40
—	—	—	—	—	Harpenden	a	00 42	00 57	00 58	01 02			01 27		01 40	01 47		01 47	02 25	03 25	03 47	04 25	04 47	05 25	05 47
83¼	—	—	—	29¼	Luton Airport Parkway ■ ✈	a	00 47	01 02	01 03	01 07			01 32		01 45	01 52		01 52	02 30	03 30	03 52	04 30	04 52	05 30	05 52
84¼	30¼	—	—	30¼	Luton ■	a	00 51	01 06	01 07	01 11			01 36		01 49	01 56		01 56	02 34	03 34	03 56	04 34	04 56	05 34	05 56
—	—	—	—	—	Bedford	a	01 18	01 31	01 32	01 36			02 01		02 14	02 21		02 21	02 59	03 59	04 21	05 01	05 21	05 59	06 21

A From Sutton (Surrey)
B From Brighton
C From Sevenoaks
D From Horsham
E From Three Bridges

Table T052-F

Mondays to Fridays

21 May to 7 December

Brighton and Gatwick Airport - London, Stevenage, Cambridge, Luton and Bedford

Station		TL	TL ■	TL	TL ■ A	TL B	TL	TL ■	TL	TL ■ A	TL	TL B	TL ■	TL	TL ■	TL ■ C	TL	TL	TL ■ A	TL	TL ■	TL	TL ■ A
Brighton ■	d		04 12					05 06							05 26						05 52		
Horsham	d												05 25										
Gatwick Airport ■	d		04 41		05 19			05 46		05 33			05 49		06 06				05 56		06 25		06 13
East Croydon	d		05 10		05 40			06 01		06 03			06 16		06 21	06 25			06 31		06 40		06 46
Rainham Kt	d																					05 30	
Dartford	d					05 15						05 45										06 15	
Abbey Wood	d					05 28						05 58										06 28	
Woolwich Arsenal	d					05 34						06 04										06 34	
Greenwich	d					05 47						06 17										06 47	
Maidstone East	d																						
Sevenoaks	d										05 22									05 52			
Swanley	d										05 41									06 11			
St Mary Cray	d										05 45									06 15			
Orpington	d	04 33		05 03			05 33										06 03						
Bromley South	d	04 43		05 13			05 43				05 53						06 13			06 23			
Catford	d	04 55		05 25			05 55				06 05						06 25			06 35			
Peckham Rye ■ 195	d	05 04		05 34			06 04				06 14						06 34			06 44			
Denmark Hill ■ 195	d	05 07		05 37			06 07				06 17						06 37			06 47			
Sutton ■ 179	d								05 46					05 49				06 16					
Wimbledon	d													06 07									
Streatham ■	d								06 03					06 18				06 33					
Tulse Hill ■	d								06 08					06 23				06 38					
Herne Hill ■ 173,179	d								06 12					06 27				06 42					
Loughborough Jn 173,179	d								06 15					06 30				06 45					
Elephant & Castle ⊖173,179	d	05 14		05 44			06 14		06 19		06 24			06 34			06 44	06 49		06 54			
London Bridge	d		05 25		05 55	05 58		06 16		06 21		06 28	06 31		06 35	06 41			06 51		06 54	06 58	07 01
London Blackfriars	a	05 19	05 31	05 49	06 01	06 04	06 19	06 21	06 24	06 26	06 29	06 34	06 36	06 39	06 41	06 46	06 49	06 54	06 56	06 59	07 01	07 04	07 06
London Blackfriars ■ ⊖	d	05 19	05 31	05 49	06 01	06 04	06 19	06 22	06 24	06 27		06 34	06 37	06 39	06 42	06 47	06 49	06 54	06 57		07 02	07 04	07 07
City Thameslink ■	d	05 21	05 33	05 51	06 03	06 06	06 21	06 24	06 26	06 29		06 36	06 39	06 41	06 44	06 49	06 51	06 56	06 59		07 04	07 06	07 09
Farringdon ■ ⊖	d	05 24	05 36	05 54	06 06	06 09	06 24	06 26	06 29	06 31		06 39	06 41	06 44	06 46	06 51	06 54	06 59	07 01		07 06	07 09	07 11
St Pancras International	d	05 28	05 40	05 58	06 10	06 13	06 28	06 31	06 33	06 36		06 43	06 46	06 48	06 51	06 56	06 58	07 03	07 06		07 11	07 13	07 16
Finsbury Park	a							06 40					06 52										07 22
Welwyn Garden City	a																						
Stevenage	a							07 01					07 13										07 43
Hitchin	a							07 08					07 19										07 49
Letchworth Garden City	a							07 13															
Royston	a							07 24															
Cambridge	a							07 39															
Huntingdon	a												07 48										08 18
Peterborough	a												08 06										08 40
Kentish Town	a	05 33		06 03		06 18			06 38					06 53				07 08					
West Hampstead Thameslink	a	05 37	05 48	06 07	06 18	06 22	06 36		06 43	06 44		06 51		06 57			07 06	07 13				07 21	
Elstree & Borehamwood	a	05 51		06 21		06 36	06 50		06 58			07 05		07 12			07 20	07 28				07 36	
St Albans City	a	06 01	06 00	06 31	06 30	06 46	07 00		07 08	06 56		07 15		07 22	07 09	07 14	07 30	07 38	07 24		07 28	07 46	
Harpenden	a	06 11	06 07	06 41	06 36		07 09			07 03		07 26				07 20	07 39				07 34	07 56	
Luton Airport Parkway ■	a	06 16	06 12	06 46	06 42		07 14			07 08		07 31			07 18	07 26	07 44		07 33		07 39	08 01	
Luton ■	a	06 20	06 16	06 51	06 46		07 20			07 12		07 36			07 22	07 30	07 50		07 37		07 43	08 06	
Bedford	a		06 42		07 12					07 38					07 42	07 54			07 58		08 11		

A From Three Bridges
B From Gillingham (Kent)
C From East Grinstead

Table T052-F

Mondays to Fridays

21 May to 7 December

Brighton and Gatwick Airport - London, Stevenage, Cambridge, Luton and Bedford

Station		TL	TL ■ A	TL	TL ■	TL	TL ■	TL	TL ■	TL	TL ■	TL	TL ■ A	TL	TL	TL ■	TL	TL ■	TL	TL ■	TL	TL ■ A
Brighton ■	d				06 05				06 22									06 48				
Horsham	d						06 04									06 34						
Gatwick Airport ■	d				06 46		06 29		06 55		06 43					06 59		07 25		07 13		
East Croydon	d		06 51		07 01		07 01		07 10		07 16		07 25			07 31		07 40		07 46		07 55
Rainham Kt	d									06 00									06 30			
Dartford	d									06 46									07 15			
Abbey Wood	d									06 58									07 28			
Woolwich Arsenal	d									07 04									07 34			
Greenwich	d									07 17									07 47			
Maidstone East	d																					
Sevenoaks	d							06 22									06 52					
Swanley	d							06 41									07 11					
St Mary Cray	d							06 45									07 15					
Orpington	d			06 29										06 59								
Bromley South	d			06 43				06 53						07 13			07 23					
Catford	d			06 55				07 05						07 25			07 35					
Peckham Rye ■ 195	d			07 04				07 14						07 34			07 44					
Denmark Hill ■ 195	d			07 07				07 17						07 37			07 47					
Sutton ■ 179	d	06 19				06 46						06 49			07 16						07 19	
Wimbledon	d	06 37										07 07									07 37	
Streatham ■	d	06 48				07 03						07 18			07 33						07 48	
Tulse Hill ■	d	06 53				07 08						07 23			07 38						07 53	
Herne Hill ■ 173,179	d	06 57				07 12						07 27			07 42						07 57	
Loughborough Jn 173,179	d	07 00				07 15						07 30			07 45						08 00	
Elephant & Castle ⊖173,179	d	07 04		07 14		07 19		07 24				07 34		07 44	07 49		07 54				08 04	
London Bridge	d		07 06		07 16		07 21		07 24	07 28	07 31		07 41			07 51		07 54	07 58	08 01		08 11
London Blackfriars	a	07 09	07 11	07 19	07 21	07 24	07 26	07 29	07 31	07 34	07 36	07 39	07 46	07 49	07 54	07 56	07 59	08 01	08 04	08 06	08 09	08 16
London Blackfriars ■ ⊖	d	07 09	07 12	07 19	07 22	07 24	07 27		07 32	07 34	07 37	07 39	07 47	07 49	07 54	07 57		08 02	08 04	08 07	08 09	08 17
City Thameslink ■	d	07 11	07 14	07 21	07 24	07 26	07 29		07 34	07 36	07 39	07 41	07 49	07 51	07 56	07 59		08 04	08 06	08 09	08 11	08 19
Farringdon ■ ⊖	d	07 14	07 16	07 24	07 26	07 29	07 31		07 36	07 39	07 41	07 44	07 51	07 54	07 59	08 01		08 06	08 09	08 11	08 14	08 21
St Pancras International	d	07 18	07 21	07 28	07 31	07 33	07 36		07 41	07 43	07 46	07 48	07 56	07 58	08 03	08 06		08 11	08 13	08 16	08 18	08 26
Finsbury Park	a				07 37						07 52									08 22		
Welwyn Garden City	a																					
Stevenage	a				08 01						08 13									08 43		
Hitchin	a				08 08						08 19									08 49		
Letchworth Garden City	a				08 13																	
Royston	a				08 24																	
Cambridge	a				08 39																	
Huntingdon	a										08 48									09 18		
Peterborough	a										09 05									09 35		
Kentish Town	a	07 23		07 33						07 48				08 03					08 18			
West Hampstead Thameslink	a	07 27	07 29	07 37		07 43				07 52		07 58		08 07	08 13				08 22		08 29	
Elstree & Borehamwood	a	07 40		07 51		07 56				08 06		08 11		08 21	08 26				08 36		08 41	
St Albans City	a	07 51	07 41	08 01		08 06	07 54		07 58	08 16		08 21	08 13	08 31	08 36	08 25		08 29	08 46		08 51	08 43
Harpenden	a		07 47	08 11					08 06	08 24			08 20	08 39				08 35	08 55			08 51
Luton Airport Parkway ■	a		07 53	08 17			08 01		08 12	08 29			08 25	08 44		08 33		08 40	09 01			08 56
Luton ■	a		07 57	08 20			08 05		08 15	08 34			08 29	08 50		08 37		08 44	09 04			09 00
Bedford	a		08 21				08 30		08 39				08 54			09 00		09 09				09 24

A From East Grinstead

Table T052-F

Mondays to Fridays

21 May to 7 December

Brighton and Gatwick Airport - London, Stevenage, Cambridge, Luton and Bedford

		TL	TL ■	TL	TL ■	TL	TL ■	TL	TL ■	TL		TL ■ A	TL	TL	TL ■	TL	TL	TL ■	TL	TL ■	TL ■ A		TL	TL ■	TL
Brighton ■	d		07 07				07 18													07 59				08 07	
Horsham	d				07 04										07 34										
Gatwick Airport ■ ✈	d		07 46		07 29		07 55		07 43						07 59			08 13		08 36				08 46	
East Croydon	d		08 01		08 01		08 10		08 16			08 25			08 31			08 46		08 51	08 55			09 01	
Rainham Kt	d							06 56									07 30								
Dartford	d							07 45									08 15								
Abbey Wood	d							07 57									08 28								
Woolwich Arsenal	d							08 04									08 34								
Greenwich	d							08 17									08 47								
Maidstone East	d																								
Sevenoaks	d					07 18										07 52									
Swanley	d					07 37										08 11									
St Mary Cray	d					07 41										08 15									
Orpington	d	07 30											08 03										08 29		
Bromley South	d	07 43				07 53							08 13			08 23							08 43		
Catford	d	07 55				08 05							08 25			08 35							08 55		
Peckham Rye ■ 195	d	08 04				08 14							08 34			08 44							09 04		
Denmark Hill ■ 195	d	08 07				08 17							08 37			08 47							09 07		
Sutton ■ 179	d			07 46						07 49				08 16					08 19						08 46
Wimbledon	d									08 07									08 37						
Streatham ■	d			08 03						08 18				08 33					08 48						09 03
Tulse Hill ■	d			08 08						08 23				08 38					08 53						09 08
Herne Hill ■ 173,179	d			08 12						08 27				08 42					08 57						09 12
Loughborough Jn 173,179	d			08 15						08 30				08 45					09 00						09 15
Elephant & Castle ⊖ 173,179	d	08 14		08 19		08 24				08 34			08 44	08 49		08 54			09 04				09 14		09 19
London Bridge	d		08 16		08 21		08 24	08 28	08 31			08 41			08 51		08 58	09 01		09 05	09 11			09 16	
London Blackfriars	a	08 19	08 21	08 24	08 26	08 29	08 31	08 34	08 36	08 39		08 46	08 49	08 54	08 56	08 59	09 04	09 06	09 09	09 11	09 16		09 19	09 21	09 24
London Blackfriars ■ ⊖	d	08 19	08 22	08 24	08 27		08 32	08 34	08 37	08 39		08 47	08 49	08 54	08 57		09 04	09 07	09 09	09 12	09 17		09 19	09 22	09 24
City Thameslink ■	d	08 21	08 24	08 26	08 29		08 34	08 36	08 39	08 41		08 49	08 51	08 56	08 59		09 06	09 09	09 11	09 14	09 19		09 21	09 24	09 26
Farringdon ■ ⊖	d	08 24	08 26	08 29	08 31		08 36	08 39	08 41	08 44		08 51	08 54	08 59	09 01		09 09	09 11	09 14	09 16	09 21		09 24	09 26	09 29
St Pancras International	d	08 28	08 31	08 33	08 36		08 41	08 43	08 46	08 48		08 56	08 58	09 03	09 06		09 13	09 16	09 18	09 21	09 26		09 28	09 31	09 33
Finsbury Park	a		08 37						08 52									09 22						09 41	
Welwyn Garden City	a																								
Stevenage	a		09 01						09 13									09 43						10 01	
Hitchin	a		09 08						09 19									09 49						10 08	
Letchworth Garden City	a		09 14																					10 14	
Royston	a		09 24																					10 24	
Cambridge	a		09 42																					10 40	
Huntingdon	a								09 48									10 18							
Peterborough	a								10 05									10 40							
Kentish Town	a	08 33						08 48					09 03				09 18						09 33		
West Hampstead Thameslink	a	08 37		08 43				08 52		08 58			09 07	09 14			09 22		09 28				09 37		09 44
Elstree & Borehamwood	a	08 51		08 56						09 11			09 21	09 26					09 41				09 51		09 55
St Albans City	a	09 01		09 06	08 54		08 59			09 21		09 15	09 31	09 36	09 24				09 51		09 45		10 01		10 06
Harpenden	a	09 10					09 05					09 21	09 37		09 31					09 43	09 51		10 07		
Luton Airport Parkway ■ ✈	a	09 15			09 02		09 11					09 26	09 42		09 36					09 48	09 56		10 12		
Luton ■	a	09 20			09 06		09 15					09 30	09 49		09 40					09 52	10 00		10 19		
Bedford	a				09 28		09 38					09 54			10 05					10 16	10 26				

A From East Grinstead

Table T052-F

Mondays to Fridays

21 May to 7 December

Brighton and Gatwick Airport - London, Stevenage, Cambridge, Luton and Bedford

		TL ■	TL	TL	TL ■	TL	TL ■	TL ■ A		TL	TL	TL ■	TL	TL	TL ■	TL	TL ■	TL	TL ■		TL	TL ■	TL	TL	TL ■
Brighton ■	d						08 28										09 02		09 08						
Horsham	d	08 04										08 34			08 55										09 25
Gatwick Airport ■ ✈	d	08 29			08 43		09 06					08 59			09 19		09 36		09 46			09 33			09 49
East Croydon	d	09 01			09 16		09 21	09 25				09 31			09 45		09 51		10 01			10 03			10 15
Rainham Kt	d			08 01										08 30										09 00	
Dartford	d			08 46										09 15										09 45	
Abbey Wood	d			08 58										09 28										09 58	
Woolwich Arsenal	d			09 04										09 34										10 04	
Greenwich	d			09 17										09 47										10 17	
Maidstone East	d																								
Sevenoaks	d		08 22										08 52										09 22		
Swanley	d		08 41										09 11										09 41		
St Mary Cray	d		08 45										09 15										09 45		
Orpington	d									09 03								09 33							
Bromley South	d		08 53							09 13			09 23					09 43					09 53		
Catford	d		09 05							09 25			09 35					09 55					10 05		
Peckham Rye ■ 195	d		09 14							09 34			09 44					10 04					10 14		
Denmark Hill ■ 195	d		09 17							09 37			09 47					10 07					10 17		
Sutton ■ 179	d					08 49					09 16					09 19					09 46				
Wimbledon	d					09 07										09 37									
Streatham ■	d					09 18					09 33					09 48					10 03				
Tulse Hill ■	d					09 23					09 38					09 53					10 08				
Herne Hill ■ 173,179	d					09 27					09 42					09 57					10 12				
Loughborough Jn 173,179	d					09 30					09 45					10 00					10 15				
Elephant & Castle ⊖ 173,179	d		09 24			09 34				09 44	09 49		09 54			10 04		10 14			10 19		10 24		
London Bridge	d	09 21		09 28	09 31		09 35	09 41				09 51		09 58	10 01		10 05		10 16			10 21		10 28	10 31
London Blackfriars	a	09 26	09 29	09 34	09 36	09 39	09 41	09 46		09 49	09 54	09 56	09 59	10 04	10 06	10 09	10 11	10 19	10 21		10 24	10 26	10 29	10 34	10 36
London Blackfriars ■ ⊖	d	09 27		09 34	09 37	09 39	09 42	09 47		09 49	09 54	09 57		10 04	10 07	10 09	10 12	10 19	10 22		10 24	10 27		10 34	10 37
City Thameslink ■	d	09 29		09 36	09 39	09 41	09 44	09 49		09 51	09 56	09 59		10 06	10 09	10 11	10 14	10 21	10 24		10 26	10 29		10 36	10 39
Farringdon ■ ⊖	d	09 31		09 39	09 41	09 44	09 46	09 51		09 54	09 59	10 01		10 09	10 11	10 14	10 16	10 24	10 26		10 29	10 31		10 39	10 41
St Pancras International	d	09 36		09 43	09 46	09 48	09 51	09 56		09 58	10 03	10 06		10 13	10 16	10 18	10 21	10 28	10 31		10 33	10 36		10 43	10 46
Finsbury Park	a				09 52										10 22				10 37						10 52
Welwyn Garden City	a																								
Stevenage	a				10 13										10 43				11 01						11 13
Hitchin	a				10 18										10 49				11 08						11 20
Letchworth Garden City	a																		11 14						
Royston	a																		11 24						
Cambridge	a																		11 40						
Huntingdon	a				10 48										11 18										11 48
Peterborough	a				11 05										11 39										12 05
Kentish Town	a			09 48		09 53				10 03	10 08					10 23		10 33			10 38				
West Hampstead Thameslink	a	09 44		09 52		09 58					10 14			10 21		10 29	10 29				10 44			10 51	
Elstree & Borehamwood	a			10 06		10 13					10 28			10 35		10 43					10 58			11 05	
St Albans City	a	09 56		10 19		10 23		10 15			10 38	10 25		10 45		10 53	10 41				11 08	10 54		11 15	
Harpenden	a	10 02		10 27			10 13	10 21				10 31		10 51			10 47					11 02		11 21	
Luton Airport Parkway ■ ✈	a	10 07		10 32			10 18	10 26				10 37		10 56			10 52					11 07		11 26	
Luton ■	a	10 11		10 36			10 22	10 30				10 40		11 01			10 56					11 11		11 31	
Bedford	a	10 36					10 44	10 55				11 05					11 21					11 36			

A From East Grinstead

Table T052-F

Mondays to Fridays

21 May to 7 December

Brighton and Gatwick Airport - London, Stevenage, Cambridge, Luton and Bedford

		TL	TL ■	TL	TL A	TL B	TL ■	TL	TL	TL ■	TL	TL ■	TL	TL ■	TL A	TL B	TL ■	TL	TL	TL ■	TL	TL ■	TL
Brighton	d		09 25									09 58		10 08								10 26	
Horsham	d									09 55										10 25			
Gatwick Airport ✈	d		10 06				10 03			10 19		10 36		10 46			10 33			10 49		11 06	
East Croydon	d		10 21				10 33			10 45		10 51		11 01			11 03			11 15		11 21	
Rainham Kt	d								09 28										09 58				
Dartford	d								10 15										10 45				
Abbey Wood	d								10 28										10 58				
Woolwich Arsenal	d								10 34										11 04				
Greenwich	d								10 47										11 17				
Maidstone East	d																						
Sevenoaks	d							09 52										10 22					
Swanley	d							10 11										10 41					
St Mary Cray	d							10 15										10 45					
Orpington	d			10 03									10 33										11 03
Bromley South	d			10 13				10 23					10 43					10 53					11 13
Catford	d			10 25				10 35					10 55					11 05					11 25
Peckham Rye 195	d			10 34				10 44					11 04					11 14					11 34
Denmark Hill 195	d			10 37				10 47					11 07					11 17					11 37
Sutton 179	d	09 49			10 16	10 16					10 19				10 46	10 46					10 49		
Wimbledon	d	10 07									10 37										11 07		
Streatham	d	10 18			10 33	10 33					10 48				11 03	11 03					11 18		
Tulse Hill	d	10 23			10 38	10 38					10 53				11 08	11 08					11 23		
Herne Hill 173,179	d	10 27			10 42	10 42					10 57				11 12	11 12					11 27		
Loughborough Jn 173,179	d	10 30			10 45	10 45					11 00				11 15	11 15					11 30		
Elephant & Castle ⊖ 173,179	d	10 34		10 44	10 49	10 49		10 54			11 04		11 14		11 19	11 19		11 24			11 34		11 44
London Bridge	d		10 35				10 51		10 58	11 01		11 05		11 16			11 21		11 28	11 31		11 35	
London Blackfriars	a	10 39	10 41	10 49	10 54	10 54	10 56	10 59	11 04	11 06	11 09	11 11	11 19	11 21	11 24	11 24	11 26	11 29	11 34	11 36	11 39	11 41	11 49
London Blackfriars ⊖	d	10 39	10 42	10 49	10 54	10 54	10 57		11 04	11 07	11 09	11 12	11 19	11 22	11 24	11 24	11 27		11 34	11 37	11 39	11 42	11 49
City Thameslink	d	10 41	10 44	10 51	10 56	10 56	10 59		11 06	11 09	11 11	11 14	11 21	11 24	11 26	11 26	11 29		11 36	11 39	11 41	11 44	11 51
Farringdon ⊖	d	10 44	10 46	10 54	10 59	10 59	11 01		11 09	11 11	11 14	11 16	11 24	11 26	11 29	11 29	11 31		11 39	11 41	11 44	11 46	11 54
St Pancras International	d	10 48	10 51	10 58	11 03	11 03	11 06		11 13	11 16	11 18	11 21	11 28	11 31	11 33	11 33	11 36		11 43	11 46	11 48	11 51	11 58
Finsbury Park	a									11 22				11 37						11 52			
Welwyn Garden City	a																						
Stevenage	a									11 43				12 01						12 13			
Hitchin	a									11 49				12 08						12 19			
Letchworth Garden City	a													12 14									
Royston	a													12 24									
Cambridge	a													12 40									
Huntingdon	a									12 18										12 48			
Peterborough	a									12 39										13 05			
Kentish Town	a	10 53		11 03	11 08	11 08					11 23		11 33		11 38	11 38					11 53		12 03
West Hampstead Thameslink	a	10 59	10 59		11 14	11 14			11 21		11 29	11 29			11 42	11 44			11 51		11 59	11 59	
Elstree & Borehamwood	a	11 13			11 27	11 28			11 35		11 43				11 55	11 58			12 05		12 13		
St Albans City	a	11 23	11 11		11 37	11 38	11 24		11 45		11 53	11 41			12 05	12 08	11 54		12 15		12 23	12 11	
Harpenden	a		11 17				11 31		11 51			11 47					12 01		12 21			12 17	
Luton Airport Parkway ✈	a		11 22				11 36		11 56			11 52					12 06		12 26			12 22	
Luton	a		11 26				11 40		12 01			11 56					12 10		12 31			12 26	
Bedford	a		11 51				12 05					12 21					12 35					12 51	

A until 20 July, from 8 October

B from 23 July until 5 October

Table T052-F

Mondays to Fridays

21 May to 7 December

Brighton and Gatwick Airport - London, Stevenage, Cambridge, Luton and Bedford

		TL	TL ■	TL	TL	TL ■	TL	TL ■	TL	TL ■	TL	TL ■	TL	TL	TL ■	TL	TL ■	TL	TL A	TL B	TL ■	TL	TL
Brighton	d							10 58		11 08							11 26						
Horsham	d					10 55									11 25								
Gatwick Airport ✈	d		11 03			11 19		11 36		11 46		11 33			11 49		12 06				12 03		
East Croydon	d		11 33			11 45		11 51		12 01		12 03			12 15		12 21				12 33		
Rainham Kt	d				10 28									10 58									11 28
Dartford	d				11 15									11 45									12 15
Abbey Wood	d				11 28									11 58									12 28
Woolwich Arsenal	d				11 34									12 04									12 34
Greenwich	d				11 47									12 17									12 47
Maidstone East	d																						
Sevenoaks	d			10 52									11 22									11 52	
Swanley	d			11 11									11 41									12 11	
St Mary Cray	d			11 15									11 45									12 15	
Orpington	d								11 33									12 03					
Bromley South	d			11 23					11 43				11 53					12 13				12 23	
Catford	d			11 35					11 55				12 05					12 25				12 35	
Peckham Rye 195	d			11 44					12 04				12 14					12 34				12 44	
Denmark Hill 195	d			11 47					12 07				12 17					12 37				12 47	
Sutton 179	d	11 16					11 19				11 46					11 49			12 16	12 16			
Wimbledon	d						11 37									12 07							
Streatham	d	11 33					11 48				12 03					12 18			12 33	12 33			
Tulse Hill	d	11 38					11 53				12 08					12 23			12 38	12 38			
Herne Hill 173,179	d	11 42					11 57				12 12					12 27			12 42	12 42			
Loughborough Jn 173,179	d	11 45					12 00				12 15					12 30			12 45	12 45			
Elephant & Castle ⊖ 173,179	d	11 49		11 54			12 04		12 14		12 19		12 24			12 34		12 44	12 49	12 49		12 54	
London Bridge	d		11 51		11 58	12 01		12 05		12 16		12 21		12 28	12 31		12 35				12 51		12 58
London Blackfriars	a	11 54	11 56	11 59	12 04	12 06	12 09	12 11	12 19	12 21	12 24	12 26	12 29	12 34	12 36	12 39	12 41	12 49	12 54	12 54	12 56	12 59	13 04
London Blackfriars ⊖	d	11 54	11 57		12 04	12 07	12 09	12 12	12 19	12 22	12 24	12 27		12 34	12 37	12 39	12 42	12 49	12 54	12 54	12 57		13 04
City Thameslink	d	11 56	11 59		12 06	12 09	12 11	12 14	12 21	12 24	12 26	12 29		12 36	12 39	12 41	12 44	12 51	12 56	12 56	12 59		13 06
Farringdon ⊖	d	11 59	12 01		12 09	12 11	12 14	12 16	12 24	12 26	12 29	12 31		12 39	12 41	12 44	12 46	12 54	12 59	12 59	13 01		13 09
St Pancras International	d	12 03	12 06		12 13	12 16	12 18	12 21	12 28	12 31	12 33	12 36		12 43	12 46	12 48	12 51	12 58	13 03	13 03	13 06		13 13
Finsbury Park	a					12 22				12 37					12 52								
Welwyn Garden City	a																						
Stevenage	a					12 43				13 01					13 13								
Hitchin	a					12 49				13 08					13 19								
Letchworth Garden City	a									13 14													
Royston	a									13 24													
Cambridge	a									13 40													
Huntingdon	a					13 18									13 48								
Peterborough	a					13 39									14 05								
Kentish Town	a	12 08					12 23		12 33		12 38					12 53		13 03	13 08	13 08			
West Hampstead Thameslink	a	12 14			12 21		12 29	12 29			12 44			12 51		12 59	12 59		13 14	13 14			13 21
Elstree & Borehamwood	a	12 28			12 35		12 43				12 58			13 05		13 13			13 27	13 28			13 35
St Albans City	a	12 38	12 24		12 45		12 53	12 41			13 08	12 54		13 15		13 23	13 11		13 37	13 38	13 24		13 45
Harpenden	a		12 31		12 51			12 47				13 01		13 21			13 17				13 31		13 51
Luton Airport Parkway ✈	a		12 36		12 56			12 52				13 06		13 26			13 22				13 36		13 56
Luton	a		12 40		13 01			12 56				13 10		13 31			13 26				13 40		14 01
Bedford	a		13 05					13 21				13 35					13 51				14 05		

A until 20 July, from 8 October

B from 23 July until 5 October

Table T052-F

Mondays to Fridays

21 May to 7 December

Brighton and Gatwick Airport - London, Stevenage, Cambridge, Luton and Bedford

		TL ■	TL	TL ■	TL	TL ■	TL A	TL B	TL ■	TL	TL	TL ■	TL	TL ■	TL	TL C	TL D	TL ■	TL	TL	TL ■	TL
Brighton ■	d			11 58		12 08								12 26								
Horsham	d	11 55										12 23									12 55	
Gatwick Airport ■ ✈	d	12 19		12 36		12 46			12 33			12 49		13 06				13 03			13 19	
East Croydon	d	12 45		12 51		13 01			13 03			13 15		13 21				13 33			13 45	
Rainham Kt	d										11 58									12 28		
Dartford	d										12 45									13 15		
Abbey Wood	d										12 58									13 28		
Woolwich Arsenal	d										13 04									13 34		
Greenwich	d										13 17									13 47		
Maidstone East	d																					
Sevenoaks	d									12 22									12 52			
Swanley	d									12 41									13 11			
St Mary Cray	d									12 45									13 15			
Orpington	d				12 33										13 03							
Bromley South	d				12 43					12 53					13 13				13 23			
Catford	d				12 55					13 05					13 25				13 35			
Peckham Rye ■ 195	d				13 04					13 14					13 34				13 44			
Denmark Hill ■ 195	d				13 07					13 17					13 37				13 47			
Sutton ■ 179	d		12 19				12 46	12 46					12 49			13 16	13 16					13 19
Wimbledon	d		12 37										13 07									13 37
Streatham ■	d		12 48				13 03	13 03					13 18			13 33	13 33					13 48
Tulse Hill ■	d		12 53				13 08	13 08					13 23			13 38	13 38					13 53
Herne Hill ■ 173,179	d		12 57				13 12	13 12					13 27			13 42	13 42					13 57
Loughborough Jn 173,179	d		13 00				13 15	13 15					13 30			13 45	13 45					14 00
Elephant & Castle ⊖173,179	d		13 04		13 14		13 19	13 19		13 24			13 34		13 44	13 49	13 49		13 54			14 04
London Bridge	d	13 01		13 05		13 16			13 21		13 28	13 31		13 35				13 51		13 58	14 01	
London Blackfriars	a	13 06	13 09	13 11	13 19	13 21	13 24	13 24	13 26	13 29	13 34	13 36	13 39	13 41	13 49	13 54	13 54	13 56	13 59	14 04	14 06	14 09
London Blackfriars ■ ⊖	d	13 07	13 09	13 12	13 19	13 22	13 24	13 24	13 27		13 34	13 37	13 39	13 42	13 49	13 54	13 54	13 57		14 04	14 07	14 09
City Thameslink ■	d	13 09	13 11	13 14	13 21	13 24	13 26	13 26	13 29		13 36	13 39	13 41	13 44	13 51	13 56	13 56	13 59		14 06	14 09	14 11
Farringdon ■ ⊖	d	13 11	13 14	13 16	13 24	13 26	13 29	13 29	13 31		13 39	13 41	13 44	13 46	13 54	13 59	13 59	14 01		14 09	14 11	14 14
St Pancras International	d	13 16	13 18	13 21	13 28	13 31	13 33	13 33	13 36		13 43	13 46	13 48	13 51	13 58	14 03	14 03	14 06		14 13	14 16	14 18
Finsbury Park	a	13 22				13 37						13 52									14 22	
Welwyn Garden City	a																					
Stevenage	a	13 43				14 01						14 13									14 43	
Hitchin	a	13 49				14 08						14 18									14 49	
Letchworth Garden City	a					14 14																
Royston	a					14 24																
Cambridge	a					14 40																
Huntingdon	a	14 18										14 48									15 18	
Peterborough	a	14 39										15 05									15 39	
Kentish Town	a		13 23		13 33		13 38	13 38					13 53		14 03	14 08	14 08					14 23
West Hampstead Thameslink	a		13 29	13 29			13 42	13 44			13 51		13 59	13 59		14 14	14 14			14 21		14 29
Elstree & Borehamwood	a		13 43				13 55	13 58			14 05		14 13			14 27	14 28			14 35		14 43
St Albans City	a		13 53	13 41			14 05	14 08	13 54		14 15		14 23	14 11		14 37	14 38	14 24		14 45		14 53
Harpenden	a			13 47					14 01		14 21			14 17				14 31		14 51		
Luton Airport Parkway ■ ✈	a			13 52					14 06		14 26			14 22				14 36		14 56		
Luton ■	a			13 56					14 10		14 31			14 26				14 40		15 01		
Bedford	a			14 21					14 35					14 51				15 05				

A until 20 July, from 8 October
B from 23 July until 5 October
C until 27 July
D from 30 July

Table T052-F

Mondays to Fridays

21 May to 7 December

Brighton and Gatwick Airport - London, Stevenage, Cambridge, Luton and Bedford

		TL ■	TL	TL ■	TL A	TL B	TL ■	TL	TL	TL ■	TL	TL ■	TL	TL	TL ■	TL	TL	TL ■	TL	TL ■	TL	TL ■	TL
Brighton ■	d	12 58		13 08								13 26								13 58		14 08	
Horsham	d									13 25								13 55					
Gatwick Airport ■ ✈	d	13 36		13 46			13 33			13 49		14 06			14 03			14 19		14 36		14 46	
East Croydon	d	13 51		14 01			14 03			14 15		14 21			14 33			14 45		14 52		15 01	
Rainham Kt	d								12 58								13 28						
Dartford	d								13 45								14 15						
Abbey Wood	d								13 58								14 28						
Woolwich Arsenal	d								14 04								14 34						
Greenwich	d								14 17								14 47						
Maidstone East	d																						
Sevenoaks	d							13 22								13 52							
Swanley	d							13 41								14 11							
St Mary Cray	d							13 45								14 15							
Orpington	d		13 33										14 03								14 33		
Bromley South	d		13 43					13 53					14 13			14 23					14 43		
Catford	d		13 55					14 05					14 25			14 35					14 55		
Peckham Rye ■ 195	d		14 04					14 14					14 34			14 44					15 04		
Denmark Hill ■ 195	d		14 07					14 17					14 37			14 47					15 07		
Sutton ■ 179	d				13 46	13 46					13 49			14 16					14 18				14 46
Wimbledon	d										14 07								14 36				
Streatham ■	d				14 03	14 03					14 18			14 33					14 46				15 03
Tulse Hill ■	d				14 08	14 08					14 23			14 38					14 53				15 08
Herne Hill ■ 173,179	d				14 12	14 12					14 27			14 42					14 57				15 12
Loughborough Jn 173,179	d				14 15	14 15					14 30			14 45					15 00				15 15
Elephant & Castle ⊖173,179	d		14 14		14 19	14 19		14 24			14 34		14 44	14 49		14 54			15 04		15 14		15 19
London Bridge	d	14 05		14 16			14 21		14 28	14 31		14 35			14 51		14 58	15 01		15 05		15 16	
London Blackfriars	a	14 11	14 19	14 21	14 24	14 24	14 26	14 29	14 34	14 36	14 39	14 41	14 49	14 54	14 56	14 59	15 04	15 06	15 09	15 11	15 19	15 21	15 24
London Blackfriars ■ ⊖	d	14 12	14 19	14 22	14 24	14 24	14 27		14 34	14 37	14 39	14 42	14 49	14 54	14 57		15 04	15 07	15 09	15 12	15 19	15 22	15 24
City Thameslink ■	d	14 14	14 21	14 24	14 26	14 26	14 29		14 36	14 39	14 41	14 44	14 51	14 56	14 59		15 06	15 09	15 11	15 14	15 21	15 24	15 26
Farringdon ■ ⊖	d	14 16	14 24	14 26	14 29	14 29	14 31		14 39	14 41	14 44	14 46	14 54	14 59	15 01		15 09	15 11	15 14	15 16	15 24	15 26	15 29
St Pancras International	d	14 21	14 28	14 31	14 33	14 33	14 36		14 43	14 46	14 48	14 51	14 58	15 03	15 06		15 13	15 16	15 18	15 21	15 28	15 31	15 33
Finsbury Park	a			14 37						14 52								15 22				15 37	
Welwyn Garden City	a																						
Stevenage	a			15 01						15 13								15 43				16 01	
Hitchin	a			15 08						15 19								15 49				16 08	
Letchworth Garden City	a			15 14																		16 14	
Royston	a			15 24																		16 24	
Cambridge	a			15 40																		16 40	
Huntingdon	a									15 48								16 18					
Peterborough	a									16 05								16 39					
Kentish Town	a		14 33		14 38	14 38					14 53		15 03	15 08					15 23		15 33		15 38
West Hampstead Thameslink	a	14 29			14 42	14 44			14 51		14 59	14 59		15 14			15 21		15 29	15 29			15 44
Elstree & Borehamwood	a				14 55	14 58			15 05		15 13			15 28			15 35		15 43				15 58
St Albans City	a	14 41			15 05	15 08	14 54		15 15		15 23	15 11		15 38	15 24		15 45		15 53	15 41			16 08
Harpenden	a	14 47					15 01		15 21			15 17			15 31		15 51			15 47			
Luton Airport Parkway ■ ✈	a	14 52					15 06		15 26			15 22			15 36		15 56			15 52			
Luton ■	a	14 56					15 10		15 31			15 26			15 40		16 01			15 56			
Bedford	a	15 21					15 35					15 52			16 05					16 21			

A until 27 July
B from 30 July

Table T052-F

Mondays to Fridays

21 May to 7 December

Brighton and Gatwick Airport - London, Stevenage, Cambridge, Luton and Bedford

		TL ■	TL	TL	TL ■	TL	TL ■	TL	TL		TL ■	TL	TL	TL ■	TL	TL ■	TL ■	TL	TL ■	TL		TL ■	TL	TL	TL ■
Brighton ■	d						14 26									14 56			15 08						
Horsham	d				14 25									14 55											15 25
Gatwick Airport ■ ✈	d	14 33			14 49		15 06				15 03			15 19		15 36	15 27		15 46			15 33			15 49
East Croydon (tram)	d	15 03			15 15		15 21				15 33			15 45		15 51	15 54		16 01			16 03			16 15
Rainham Kt	d			13 58									14 28											14 58	
Dartford	d			14 45									15 15											15 45	
Abbey Wood	d			14 58									15 28											15 58	
Woolwich Arsenal	d			15 04									15 34											16 04	
Greenwich	d			15 17									15 47											16 17	
Maidstone East	d																								
Sevenoaks	d		14 22									14 52											15 22		
Swanley	d		14 41									15 11											15 41		
St Mary Cray	d		14 45									15 15											15 45		
Orpington	d							15 03										15 33							
Bromley South	d		14 53					15 13				15 23						15 43					15 53		
Catford	d		15 05					15 25				15 35						15 55					16 05		
Peckham Rye ■ 195	d		15 14					15 34				15 44						16 04					16 14		
Denmark Hill ■ 195	d		15 17					15 37				15 47						16 07					16 17		
Sutton ■ 179	d					14 49			15 16						15 19					15 46					
Wimbledon	d					15 07									15 37										
Streatham ■	d					15 18			15 33						15 48					16 03					
Tulse Hill ■	d					15 23			15 38						15 53					16 08					
Herne Hill ■ 173,179	d					15 27			15 42						15 57					16 12					
Loughborough Jn 173,179	d					15 30			15 45						16 00					16 15					
Elephant & Castle ⊖173,179	d		15 24			15 34		15 44	15 49			15 54			16 04			16 14		16 19			16 24		
London Bridge	d	15 21		15 28	15 31		15 35				15 51		15 58	16 01		16 05	16 11		16 16			16 21		16 28	16 31
London Blackfriars	a	15 26	15 29	15 34	15 36	15 39	15 41	15 49	15 54		15 56	15 59	16 04	16 06	16 09	16 11	16 16	16 19	16 21	16 24		16 26	16 29	16 34	16 36
London Blackfriars ■ ⊖	d	15 27		15 34	15 37	15 39	15 42	15 49	15 54		15 57		16 04	16 07	16 09	16 12	16 17	16 19	16 22	16 24		16 27		16 34	16 37
City Thameslink ■	d	15 29		15 36	15 39	15 41	15 44	15 51	15 56		15 59		16 06	16 09	16 11	16 14	16 19	16 21	16 24	16 26		16 29		16 36	16 39
Farringdon ■ ⊖	d	15 31		15 39	15 41	15 44	15 46	15 54	15 59		16 01		16 09	16 11	16 14	16 16	16 21	16 24	16 26	16 29		16 31		16 39	16 41
St Pancras International	d	15 36		15 43	15 46	15 48	15 51	15 58	16 03		16 06		16 13	16 16	16 18	16 21	16 26	16 28	16 31	16 33		16 36		16 43	16 46
Finsbury Park	a				15 52									16 22					16 37						16 52
Welwyn Garden City	a																								
Stevenage	a				16 13									16 43					17 01						17 13
Hitchin	a				16 19									16 49					17 08						17 19
Letchworth Garden City	a																		17 14						
Royston	a																		17 24						
Cambridge	a																		17 40						
Huntingdon	a				16 48									17 18											17 48
Peterborough	a				17 05									17 35											18 05
Kentish Town	a					15 53		16 03	16 08				16 18					16 33						16 48	
West Hampstead Thameslink	a			15 51		15 59	15 59		16 14				16 22		16 29			16 37		16 44		16 44		16 52	
Elstree & Borehamwood	a			16 05		16 13			16 28				16 37		16 41			16 52		16 56				17 07	
St Albans City	a	15 54		16 19		16 23	16 14		16 38		16 24		16 46		16 52	16 39	16 44	17 01		17 07		16 56		17 16	
Harpenden	a	16 01		16 27			16 20				16 30		16 54				16 50	17 07				17 02		17 26	
Luton Airport Parkway ■ ✈	a	16 06		16 32			16 25				16 36		17 00				16 56	17 13				17 07		17 31	
Luton ■	a	16 10		16 36			16 29				16 40		17 05			16 49	17 00	17 19				17 11		17 36	
Bedford	a	16 35					16 53				17 06					17 06	17 26					17 35			

Table T052-F

Mondays to Fridays

21 May to 7 December

Brighton and Gatwick Airport - London, Stevenage, Cambridge, Luton and Bedford

		TL	TL ■	TL ■	TL	TL	TL ■		TL	TL	TL ■	TL	TL ■	TL ■	TL	TL ■	TL	TL ■		TL	TL ■ A	TL	TL ■	TL	TL ■
Brighton ■	d		15 26										15 58			16 08									16 26
Horsham	d										15 55												16 25		
Gatwick Airport ■ ✈	d		16 06	15 57			16 03				16 19		16 36	16 27		16 46		16 33			16 54		16 49		17 06
East Croydon (tram)	d		16 21	16 24			16 33				16 45		16 51	16 54		17 01		17 03			17 10		17 15		17 21
Rainham Kt	d									15 28												16 00			
Dartford	d									16 15												16 45			
Abbey Wood	d									16 28												16 58			
Woolwich Arsenal	d									16 34												17 04			
Greenwich	d									16 47												17 17			
Maidstone East	d																								
Sevenoaks	d								15 52											16 22					
Swanley	d								16 11											16 41					
St Mary Cray	d								16 15											16 45					
Orpington	d				16 03										16 33										
Bromley South	d				16 13				16 23						16 43					16 53					
Catford	d				16 25				16 35						16 55					17 05					
Peckham Rye ■ 195	d				16 34				16 44						17 04					17 14					
Denmark Hill ■ 195	d				16 37				16 47						17 07					17 17					
Sutton ■ 179	d	15 49				16 16						16 19					16 46							16 49	
Wimbledon	d	16 07										16 37												17 07	
Streatham ■	d	16 18				16 33						16 48					17 03							17 18	
Tulse Hill ■	d	16 23				16 38						16 53					17 08							17 23	
Herne Hill ■ 173,179	d	16 27				16 42						16 57					17 12							17 27	
Loughborough Jn 173,179	d	16 30				16 45						17 00					17 15							17 30	
Elephant & Castle ⊖173,179	d	16 34			16 44	16 49			16 54			17 04			17 14		17 19			17 24				17 34	
London Bridge	d		16 35	16 41			16 51			16 57	17 01		17 05	17 11		17 16		17 21			17 24	17 28	17 31		17 35
London Blackfriars	a	16 39	16 41	16 46	16 49	16 54	16 56		16 59	17 02	17 06	17 09	17 11	17 16	17 19	17 21	17 24	17 26		17 29	17 31	17 34	17 36	17 39	17 41
London Blackfriars ■ ⊖	d	16 39	16 42	16 47	16 49	16 54	16 57			17 03	17 07	17 09	17 12	17 17	17 19	17 22	17 24	17 27			17 32	17 34	17 37	17 39	17 42
City Thameslink ■	d	16 41	16 44	16 49	16 51	16 56	16 59			17 05	17 09	17 11	17 14	17 19	17 21	17 24	17 26	17 29			17 34	17 36	17 39	17 41	17 44
Farringdon ■ ⊖	d	16 44	16 46	16 51	16 54	16 59	17 01			17 07	17 11	17 14	17 16	17 21	17 24	17 26	17 29	17 31			17 36	17 39	17 41	17 44	17 46
St Pancras International	d	16 48	16 51	16 56	16 58	17 03	17 06			17 12	17 16	17 18	17 21	17 26	17 28	17 31	17 33	17 36			17 41	17 43	17 46	17 48	17 51
Finsbury Park	a										17 22					17 37							17 52		
Welwyn Garden City	a																								
Stevenage	a										17 43					18 01							18 13		
Hitchin	a										17 49					18 08							18 19		
Letchworth Garden City	a															18 14									
Royston	a															18 25									
Cambridge	a															18 43									
Huntingdon	a										18 18												18 48		
Peterborough	a										18 34												19 05		
Kentish Town	a				17 03										17 33							17 48			
West Hampstead Thameslink	a	16 58			17 07	17 14						17 29			17 37		17 43					17 52		17 58	
Elstree & Borehamwood	a	17 11			17 22	17 26						17 41			17 52		17 56					18 07		18 11	
St Albans City	a	17 22	17 10	17 14	17 31	17 37	17 24			17 29		17 52	17 39	17 44	18 01		18 07	17 54			17 58	18 19		18 23	18 09
Harpenden	a			17 20	17 41		17 30			17 35			17 45	17 50	18 09			18 00			18 05	18 25			
Luton Airport Parkway ■ ✈	a			17 26	17 46					17 41				17 56	18 15						18 10	18 31			
Luton ■	a		17 20	17 30	17 50		17 36			17 45			17 52	18 00	18 21			18 06			18 14	18 35			18 18
Bedford	a		17 38	17 55			17 58			18 09			18 15	18 25				18 28			18 41				18 36

A From Three Bridges

Table T052-F

Mondays to Fridays

21 May to 7 December

Brighton and Gatwick Airport - London, Stevenage, Cambridge, Luton and Bedford

		TL ■	TL	TL	TL ■	TL	TL ■ A	TL	TL ■	TL	TL ■	TL ■	TL	TL ■	TL	TL ■ B	TL ■ C	TL	TL	TL ■	TL	TL ■	TL ■ D
Brighton ■	d										16 58			17 08								17 26	
Horsham	d								16 55											17 25			
Gatwick Airport ■ ✈	d	16 57			17 03		17 24		17 19		17 36	17 27		17 46		17 33	17 33			17 49		18 06	
East Croydon	d	17 25			17 33		17 40		17 45		17 51	17 54		18 01		18 03	18 03			18 15		18 21	18 25
Rainham Kt	d							16 30											17 00				
Dartford	d							17 15											17 45				
Abbey Wood	d							17 28											17 58				
Woolwich Arsenal	d							17 34											18 04				
Greenwich	d							17 47											18 17				
Maidstone East	d																						
Sevenoaks	d					16 52												17 22					
Swanley	d					17 11												17 41					
St Mary Cray	d					17 15												17 45					
Orpington	d		17 03										17 33										
Bromley South	d		17 13			17 23							17 43					17 53					
Catford	d		17 25			17 35							17 55					18 05					
Peckham Rye ■	195 d		17 34			17 44							18 04					18 14					
Denmark Hill ■	195 d		17 37			17 47							18 07					18 17					
Sutton ■	179 d			17 16						17 19					17 46						17 49		
Wimbledon	d									17 37											18 07		
Streatham ■	d			17 33						17 48					18 03						18 18		
Tulse Hill ■	d			17 38						17 53					18 08						18 23		
Herne Hill ■	173,179 d			17 42						17 57					18 12						18 27		
Loughborough Jn	173,179 d			17 45						18 00					18 15						18 30		
Elephant & Castle ⊖	173,179 d		17 44	17 49		17 54				18 04			18 14		18 19			18 24			18 34		
London Bridge	d	17 41			17 51		17 54	17 58	18 01		18 05	18 11		18 16		18 21	18 21		18 28	18 31		18 35	18 41
London Blackfriars	a	17 46	17 49	17 54	17 56	17 59	18 01	18 04	18 06	18 09	18 11	18 16	18 19	18 21	18 24	18 26	18 26	18 29	18 34	18 36	18 39	18 41	18 46
London Blackfriars ■ ⊖	d	17 47	17 49	17 54	17 57		18 02	18 04	18 07	18 09	18 12	18 17	18 19	18 22	18 24	18 27	18 27		18 34	18 37	18 39	18 42	18 47
City Thameslink ■	d	17 49	17 51	17 56	17 59		18 04	18 06	18 09	18 11	18 14	18 19	18 21	18 24	18 26	18 29	18 29		18 36	18 39	18 41	18 44	18 49
Farringdon ■ ⊖	d	17 51	17 54	17 59	18 01		18 06	18 09	18 11	18 14	18 16	18 21	18 24	18 26	18 29	18 31	18 31		18 39	18 41	18 44	18 46	18 51
St Pancras International	d	17 56	17 58	18 03	18 06		18 11	18 13	18 16	18 18	18 21	18 26	18 28	18 31	18 33	18 36	18 36		18 43	18 46	18 48	18 51	18 56
Finsbury Park	a								18 22					18 37						18 52			
Welwyn Garden City	a																						
Stevenage	a								18 43					19 01						19 13			
Hitchin	a								18 49					19 08						19 19			
Letchworth Garden City	a													19 14									
Royston	a													19 25									
Cambridge	a													19 42									
Huntingdon	a								19 18											19 48			
Peterborough	a								19 41											20 05			
Kentish Town	a		18 03					18 18					18 33						18 48				
West Hampstead Thameslink	a		18 07	18 14				18 22		18 28			18 37		18 44				18 52		18 58		
Elstree & Borehamwood	a		18 22	18 26				18 37		18 41			18 52		18 56				19 07		19 11		
St Albans City	a	18 15	18 31	18 37	18 24		18 28	18 46		18 52	18 39	18 44	19 01		19 07	18 54	18 54		19 16		19 22	19 09	19 14
Harpenden	a	18 22	18 41		18 30		18 36	18 54				18 50	19 09			19 01	19 01		19 26				19 20
Luton Airport Parkway ■ ✈	a	18 27	18 46				18 41	19 00				18 56	19 15			19 07	19 07		19 31				19 26
Luton ■	a	18 31	18 51		18 36		18 45	19 05			18 49	19 00	19 21			19 11	19 11		19 36			19 19	19 30
Bedford	a	18 56			18 58		19 15				19 06	19 25				19 39	19 42					19 36	19 55

A From Three Bridges
B from 18 June
C until 15 June
D From East Grinstead

Table T052-F

Mondays to Fridays

21 May to 7 December

Brighton and Gatwick Airport - London, Stevenage, Cambridge, Luton and Bedford

		TL	TL A	TL B	TL ■	TL	TL	TL ■	TL	TL ■	TL ■ C	TL	TL ■	TL A	TL B	TL ■	TL	TL	TL ■	TL	TL ■	TL ■ C	TL
Brighton ■	d									17 58			18 08								18 26		
Horsham	d							17 55											18 25				
Gatwick Airport ■ ✈	d				18 03			18 19		18 36			18 46			18 33			18 49		19 06		
East Croydon	d				18 33			18 45		18 51	18 55		19 01			19 03			19 15		19 21	19 24	
Rainham Kt	d						17 28											18 00					
Dartford	d						18 15											18 46					
Abbey Wood	d						18 28											18 59					
Woolwich Arsenal	d						18 34											19 05					
Greenwich	d						18 47											19 18					
Maidstone East	d																						
Sevenoaks	d					17 52											18 22						
Swanley	d					18 11											18 41						
St Mary Cray	d					18 15											18 45						
Orpington	d	18 02										18 33											19 03
Bromley South	d	18 13				18 23						18 43					18 53						19 13
Catford	d	18 25				18 35						18 55					19 05						19 25
Peckham Rye ■	195 d	18 34				18 44						19 04					19 14						19 34
Denmark Hill ■	195 d	18 37				18 47						19 07					19 17						19 37
Sutton ■	179 d		18 16	18 16					18 19					18 46	18 46					18 49			
Wimbledon	d								18 37											19 07			
Streatham ■	d		18 33	18 33					18 48					19 03	19 03					19 18			
Tulse Hill ■	d		18 38	18 38					18 53					19 08	19 08					19 23			
Herne Hill ■	173,179 d		18 42	18 42					18 57					19 12	19 12					19 27			
Loughborough Jn	173,179 d		18 45	18 45					19 00					19 15	19 15					19 30			
Elephant & Castle ⊖	173,179 d	18 44	18 49	18 49		18 54			19 04			19 14		19 19	19 19		19 24			19 34			19 44
London Bridge	d				18 51		18 58	19 01		19 05	19 11		19 16			19 21		19 28	19 31		19 35	19 41	
London Blackfriars	a	18 49	18 54	18 54	18 56	18 59	19 04	19 06	19 09	19 11	19 16	19 19	19 21	19 24	19 24	19 26	19 29	19 34	19 36	19 39	19 41	19 46	19 49
London Blackfriars ■ ⊖	d	18 49	18 54	18 54	18 57		19 04	19 07	19 09	19 12	19 17	19 19	19 22	19 24	19 24	19 27		19 34	19 37	19 39	19 42	19 47	19 49
City Thameslink ■	d	18 51	18 56	18 56	18 59		19 06	19 09	19 11	19 14	19 19	19 21	19 24	19 26	19 26	19 29		19 36	19 39	19 41	19 44	19 49	19 51
Farringdon ■ ⊖	d	18 54	18 59	18 59	19 01		19 09	19 11	19 14	19 16	19 21	19 24	19 26	19 29	19 29	19 31		19 39	19 41	19 44	19 46	19 51	19 54
St Pancras International	d	18 58	19 03	19 03	19 06		19 13	19 16	19 18	19 21	19 26	19 28	19 31	19 33	19 33	19 36		19 43	19 46	19 48	19 51	19 56	19 58
Finsbury Park	a							19 22					19 37						19 52				
Welwyn Garden City	a																						
Stevenage	a							19 43					20 01						20 12				
Hitchin	a							19 49					20 08						20 19				
Letchworth Garden City	a												20 14										
Royston	a												20 25										
Cambridge	a												20 43										
Huntingdon	a							20 18											20 48				
Peterborough	a							20 35											21 05				
Kentish Town	a	19 03					19 18							19 38	19 38					19 53			
West Hampstead Thameslink	a	19 07	19 14	19 14			19 22		19 29			19 36		19 42	19 44	19 44		19 51		19 59			20 06
Elstree & Borehamwood	a	19 22	19 25	19 26			19 37		19 42					19 55	19 58			20 05		20 13			
St Albans City	a	19 31	19 36	19 37	19 24		19 49		19 53	19 39	19 45			20 05	20 08	19 56		20 15		20 23	20 09	20 14	
Harpenden	a	19 41			19 31		19 57			19 45	19 51					20 02		20 27			20 15	20 20	
Luton Airport Parkway ■ ✈	a	19 46			19 36		20 02				19 57					20 07		20 32				20 26	
Luton ■	a	19 51			19 40		20 06			19 52	20 01					20 11		20 36			20 22	20 30	
Bedford	a				20 05					20 14	20 26					20 36					20 44	20 57	

A until 27 July
B from 30 July
C From East Grinstead

Table T052-F

Mondays to Fridays

21 May to 7 December

Brighton and Gatwick Airport - London, Stevenage, Cambridge, Luton and Bedford

Station		TL	TL 1	TL	TL	TL 1	TL	TL 1	TL	TL 1	TL	TL 1	TL	TL	TL 1	TL	TL 1	TL	TL	TL 1	TL	TL
Brighton 10	d							18 58		19 08							19 26					
Horsham	d					18 55									19 25							
Gatwick Airport 10 ✈	d		19 03			19 19		19 36		19 46		19 33			19 49		20 06			20 03		
East Croydon	d		19 33			19 45		19 51		20 01		20 03			20 15		20 21			20 33		
Rainham Kt	d				18 30									18 58								19 28
Dartford	d				19 15									19 45								20 15
Abbey Wood	d				19 28									19 58								20 28
Woolwich Arsenal	d				19 34									20 04								20 34
Greenwich	d				19 47									20 17								20 47
Maidstone East	d																					
Sevenoaks	d			18 52									19 22								19 52	
Swanley	d			19 11									19 41								20 11	
St Mary Cray	d			19 15									19 45								20 15	
Orpington	d								19 33									20 03				
Bromley South	d			19 23					19 43				19 53					20 13			20 23	
Catford	d			19 35					19 55				20 05					20 25			20 35	
Peckham Rye 4 195	d			19 44					20 04				20 14					20 34			20 44	
Denmark Hill 4 195	d			19 47					20 07				20 17					20 37			20 47	
Sutton 4 179	d	19 16					19 19				19 46					19 49			20 16			
Wimbledon	d						19 37									20 07						
Streatham 4	d	19 33					19 48				20 03					20 18			20 33			
Tulse Hill 3	d	19 38					19 53				20 08					20 23			20 38			
Herne Hill 4 173,179	d	19 42					19 57				20 12					20 27			20 42			
Loughborough Jn 173,179	d	19 45					20 00				20 15					20 30			20 45			
Elephant & Castle ⊖173,179	d	19 49		19 54			20 04		20 14		20 19		20 24			20 34		20 44	20 49		20 54	
London Bridge	d		19 51		19 58	20 01		20 05		20 16		20 21		20 28	20 31		20 35			20 51		20 58
London Blackfriars	a	19 54	19 56	19 59	20 04	20 06	20 09	20 11	20 19	20 21	20 24	20 26	20 29	20 34	20 36	20 39	20 41	20 49	20 54	20 56	20 59	21 04
London Blackfriars 3 ⊖	d	19 54	19 57		20 04	20 07	20 09	20 12	20 19	20 22	20 24	20 27		20 34	20 37	20 39	20 42	20 49	20 54	20 57		21 04
City Thameslink 3	d	19 56	19 59		20 06	20 09	20 11	20 14	20 21	20 24	20 26	20 29		20 36	20 39	20 41	20 44	20 51	20 56	20 59		21 06
Farringdon 3 ⊖	d	19 59	20 01		20 09	20 11	20 14	20 16	20 24	20 26	20 29	20 31		20 39	20 41	20 44	20 46	20 54	20 59	21 01		21 09
St Pancras International	d	20 03	20 06		20 13	20 16	20 18	20 21	20 28	20 31	20 33	20 36		20 43	20 46	20 48	20 51	20 58	21 03	21 06		21 13
Finsbury Park	a					20 22				20 37					20 52							
Welwyn Garden City	a																					
Stevenage	a					20 43				21 01					21 13							
Hitchin	a					20 49				21 08					21 19							
Letchworth Garden City	a									21 14												
Royston	a									21 24												
Cambridge	a									21 40												
Huntingdon	a					21 18									21 48							
Peterborough	a					21 35									22 05							
Kentish Town	a	20 08					20 23		20 33		20 38					20 53		21 03	21 08			21 18
West Hampstead Thameslink	a	20 14			20 21		20 29	20 29			20 44			20 51		20 59	20 59		21 14			21 22
Elstree & Borehamwood	a	20 28			20 35		20 43				20 58			21 05		21 13			21 28			21 38
St Albans City	a	20 38	20 24		20 45		20 53	20 41			21 08	20 54		21 15		21 23	21 11		21 38	21 24		21 48
Harpenden	a		20 31		20 51			20 47				21 01		21 21			21 17			21 31		21 57
Luton Airport Parkway 7 ✈	a		20 36		20 56			20 52				21 06		21 26			21 22			21 36		22 02
Luton 10	a		20 40		21 01			20 56				21 10		21 31			21 26			21 40		22 06
Bedford	a		21 05					21 21				21 35					21 51			22 05		

Table T052-F

Mondays to Fridays

21 May to 7 December

Brighton and Gatwick Airport - London, Stevenage, Cambridge, Luton and Bedford

Station		TL 1	TL 1	TL	TL	TL 1	TL	TL 1	TL	TL	TL 1	TL	TL 1	TL	TL	TL 1	TL	TL	TL 1	TL	TL 1	TL	TL 1
Brighton 10	d		19 58			20 08							20 26								20 58		21 08
Horsham	d	19 55									20 25								20 55				
Gatwick Airport 10 ✈	d	20 19	20 36			20 46		20 33			20 49		21 06			21 03			21 19		21 36		21 46
East Croydon	d	20 46	20 51			21 01		21 03			21 15		21 21			21 33			21 45		21 51		22 01
Rainham Kt	d									19 58								20 28					
Dartford	d									20 45								21 15					
Abbey Wood	d									20 58								21 28					
Woolwich Arsenal	d									21 04								21 34					
Greenwich	d									21 17								21 47					
Maidstone East	d																						
Sevenoaks	d								20 22								20 52						
Swanley	d								20 41								21 11						
St Mary Cray	d								20 45								21 15						
Orpington	d				20 33									21 03								21 33	
Bromley South	d				20 43				20 53					21 13			21 23					21 43	
Catford	d				20 55				21 05					21 25			21 35					21 55	
Peckham Rye 4 195	d				21 04				21 14					21 34			21 44					22 04	
Denmark Hill 4 195	d				21 07				21 17					21 37			21 47					22 07	
Sutton 4 179	d			20 21			20 46					20 49			21 16					21 19			
Wimbledon	d			20 43								21 07								21 37			
Streatham 4	d			20 54			21 03					21 18			21 33					21 48			
Tulse Hill 3	d			20 59			21 08					21 23			21 38					21 53			
Herne Hill 4 173,179	d			21 04			21 12					21 27			21 42					21 57			
Loughborough Jn 173,179	d			21 07			21 15					21 30			21 45					22 00			
Elephant & Castle ⊖173,179	d			21 11	21 14		21 19		21 24			21 34		21 44	21 49		21 54			22 04		22 14	
London Bridge	d	21 01	21 05			21 16		21 21		21 28	21 31		21 35			21 51		21 58	22 01		22 05		22 16
London Blackfriars	a	21 06	21 11	21 16	21 19	21 21	21 24	21 26	21 29	21 34	21 36	21 39	21 41	21 49	21 54	21 56	21 59	22 04	22 06	22 09	22 11	22 19	22 21
London Blackfriars 3 ⊖	d	21 07	21 12	21 17	21 19	21 22	21 24	21 27		21 34	21 37	21 39	21 42	21 49	21 54	21 57		22 04	22 07	22 09	22 12	22 19	22 22
City Thameslink 3	d	21 09	21 14	21 19	21 21	21 24	21 26	21 29		21 36	21 39	21 41	21 44	21 51	21 56	21 59		22 06	22 09	22 11	22 14	22 21	22 24
Farringdon 3 ⊖	d	21 11	21 16	21 21	21 24	21 26	21 29	21 31		21 39	21 41	21 44	21 46	21 54	21 59	22 01		22 09	22 11	22 14	22 16	22 24	22 26
St Pancras International	d	21 16	21 21	21 26	21 28	21 31	21 33	21 36		21 43	21 46	21 48	21 51	21 58	22 03	22 06		22 13	22 16	22 18	22 21	22 28	22 31
Finsbury Park	a	21 22				21 37					21 52								22 22				22 37
Welwyn Garden City	a																						
Stevenage	a	21 43				22 01					22 13								22 43				23 02
Hitchin	a	21 49				22 08					22 19								22 49				23 09
Letchworth Garden City	a					22 14																	23 14
Royston	a					22 24																	23 25
Cambridge	a					22 40																	23 41
Huntingdon	a	22 18									22 48								23 18				
Peterborough	a	22 35									23 05								23 37				
Kentish Town	a				21 33		21 38					21 53		22 03	22 08					22 23		22 33	
West Hampstead Thameslink	a		21 29	21 34			21 44			21 51		21 59	21 59		22 14			22 21		22 29	22 29		
Elstree & Borehamwood	a			21 44			21 58			22 05		22 13			22 28			22 35		22 43			
St Albans City	a		21 41	21 54			22 08	21 54		22 15		22 23	22 11		22 38	22 24		22 45		22 53	22 41		
Harpenden	a		21 47					22 01		22 21			22 17			22 31		22 51			22 47		
Luton Airport Parkway 7 ✈	a		21 52					22 06		22 26			22 22			22 36		22 56			22 52		
Luton 10	a		21 56					22 10		22 30			22 26			22 40		23 01			22 56		
Bedford	a		22 21					22 35		22 55			22 51			23 05					23 21		

Table T052-F

Mondays to Fridays

21 May to 7 December

Brighton and Gatwick Airport - London, Stevenage, Cambridge, Luton and Bedford

		TL	TL ■	TL	TL	TL ■	TL	TL ■	TL	TL	TL	TL	TL ■	TL ■	TL	TL	TL ■	TL	TL	TL	TL ■	TL ■	TL
Brighton 10	d							21 26						21 58			22 08					22 26	
Horsham	d					21 25							21 55								22 25		
Gatwick Airport 10 ✈	d		21 33			21 49		22 06					22 19	22 36			22 46				22 49	23 06	
East Croydon	d		22 03			22 15		22 21					22 45	22 51			23 01				23 15	23 21	
Rainham Kt	d				20 58							21 28								22 00			
Dartford	d				21 45							22 15								22 45			
Abbey Wood	d				21 58							22 28								22 58			
Woolwich Arsenal	d				22 04							22 34								23 04			
Greenwich	d				22 17							22 47								23 17			
Maidstone East	d																						
Sevenoaks	d			21 22							21 52								22 22				
Swanley	d			21 41							22 11								22 41				
St Mary Cray	d			21 45							22 15								22 45				
Orpington	d								22 03							22 33							
Bromley South	d			21 53					22 13		22 23					22 43			22 53				
Catford	d			22 05					22 25		22 35					22 55			23 05				
Peckham Rye 4	195 d			22 14					22 34		22 44					23 04			23 14				
Denmark Hill 4	195 d			22 17					22 37		22 47					23 07			23 17				
Sutton 4	179 d	21 46					21 49			22 18					22 19			22 48					22 49
Wimbledon	d						22 07								22 41								23 11
Streatham 4	d	22 03					22 18			22 35					22 52			23 05					23 22
Tulse Hill 3	d	22 08					22 23			22 40					22 57			23 10					23 27
Herne Hill 4	173,179 d	22 12					22 27			22 44					23 04			23 14					23 34
Loughborough Jn	173,179 d	22 15					22 30			22 47					23 07			23 17					23 37
Elephant & Castle ⊖	173,179 d	22 19		22 24			22 34		22 44	22 51	22 54				23 11	23 14		23 21	23 24				23 41
London Bridge	d		22 21		22 28	22 31		22 35				22 58	23 01	23 05			23 16			23 28	23 31	23 35	
London Blackfriars	a	22 24	22 26	22 29	22 34	22 36	22 39	22 41	22 49	22 56	22 59	23 04	23 06	23 11	23 16	23 19	23 21	23 26	23 29	23 34	23 36	23 41	23 46
London Blackfriars 3 ⊖	d	22 24	22 27		22 34	22 37	22 39	22 42	22 49	22 59		23 04	23 07	23 12	23 17		23 22	23 27		23 34	23 37	23 42	23 49
City Thameslink 3	d	22 26	22 29		22 36	22 39	22 41	22 44	22 51														
Farringdon 3 ⊖	d	22 29	22 31		22 39	22 41	22 44	22 46	22 54	23 04		23 09	23 11	23 16	23 21		23 26	23 31		23 39	23 41	23 46	23 53
St Pancras International	d	22 33	22 36		22 43	22 46	22 48	22 51	22 58	23 08		23 13	23 16	23 21	23 26		23 31	23 36		23 43	23 46	23 51	23 58
Finsbury Park	a					22 52							23 22				23 37				23 52		
Welwyn Garden City	a																						
Stevenage	a					23 14							23 43				00 01				00 13		
Hitchin	a					23 20							23 49				00 08				00 22		
Letchworth Garden City	a																00 14						
Royston	a																00 24						
Cambridge	a																00 40						
Huntingdon	a					23 48							00 18								00 50		
Peterborough	a					00 07							00 37								01 09		
Kentish Town	a	22 38					22 53			23 13					23 30			23 40					00 01
West Hampstead Thameslink	a	22 44			22 51		23 02	22 59	23 06	23 17		23 21		23 29	23 34			23 44		23 51		23 59	00 06
Elstree & Borehamwood	a	22 58					23 16			23 31					23 49			23 59					00 21
St Albans City	a	23 08	22 54				23 26	23 15		23 41				23 46	23 58			00 09				00 16	00 31
Harpenden	a	23 15	23 01				23 33	23 22		23 48				23 52	00 06			00 16				00 22	00 38
Luton Airport Parkway 7 ✈	a	23 20	23 06				23 38	23 27		23 53				23 57	00 11			00 21				00 27	00 43
Luton 10	a	23 24	23 10				23 42	23 31		23 57				00 01	00 15			00 25				00 31	00 47
Bedford	a	23 48	23 35				00 03	23 55		00 18				00 26	00 40			00 46				00 56	01 10

Table T052-F

Mondays to Fridays

21 May to 7 December

Brighton and Gatwick Airport - London, Stevenage, Cambridge, Luton and Bedford

		TL	TL	TL	TL	TL ■	TL	TL	TL ■	TL ■	TL ■
Brighton 10	d					22 56				23 24	23 42
Horsham	d								23 11		
Gatwick Airport 10 ✈	d					23 34			23 35	00 04	00 21
East Croydon	d					23 53			00 10	00 23	00 40
Rainham Kt	d										
Dartford	d										
Abbey Wood	d										
Woolwich Arsenal	d										
Greenwich	d										
Maidstone East	d										
Sevenoaks	d		22 52				23 22	23 22			
Swanley	d		23 11				23 41	23 41			
St Mary Cray	d		23 15				23 45	23 45			
Orpington	d	23 03									
Bromley South	d	23 13	23 23				23 53	23 53			
Catford	d	23 25	23 35				00 06	00 06			
Peckham Rye 4	195 d	23 34	23 44				00 14	00 14			
Denmark Hill 4	195 d	23 37	23 47				00 17	00 17			
Sutton 4	179 d			23 18	23 19						
Wimbledon	d				23 37						
Streatham 4	d			23 35	23 48						
Tulse Hill 3	d			23 40	23 53						
Herne Hill 4	173,179 d			23 44	23 57						
Loughborough Jn	173,179 d			23 47							
Elephant & Castle ⊖	173,179 d	23 44	23 54	23 54	00 04		00 24	00 24			
London Bridge	d										
London Blackfriars	a	23 49	23 59	00 01	00 08	00 18	00 29	00 33	00 36	00 49	01 07
London Blackfriars 3 ⊖	d			00 02	00 09	00 22	00 29		00 37	00 50	01 08
City Thameslink 3	d						00 31				
Farringdon 3 ⊖	d			00 06	00 13	00 25	00 34		00 41		
St Pancras International	d			00 11	00 18	00 30	00 38		00 46	01 01	01 16
Finsbury Park	a						00 44		00 52		
Welwyn Garden City	a								01 12		
Stevenage	a								01 21		
Hitchin	a								01 30		
Letchworth Garden City	a										
Royston	a										
Cambridge	a										
Huntingdon	a								01 59		
Peterborough	a								02 17		
Kentish Town	a				00 22					01 05	
West Hampstead Thameslink	a			00 19	00 26	00 39				01 09	01 24
Elstree & Borehamwood	a				00 41					01 24	
St Albans City	a			00 35	00 51	00 56				01 34	01 40
Harpenden	a			00 42	00 58	01 02				01 40	01 47
Luton Airport Parkway 7 ✈	a			00 47	01 03	01 07				01 45	01 52
Luton 10	a			00 51	01 07	01 11				01 49	01 56
Bedford	a			01 18	01 32	01 36				02 14	02 21

Brighton and Gatwick Airport - London, Stevenage, Cambridge, Luton and Bedford

		TL	TL	TL	TL	TL	TL	TL	TL	TL	TL	TL	TL	TL	TL	TL	TL	TL	TL	TL	TL	TL	TL
				■			■	■	■	■	■	■	■	■	■	■		■	■		■		■
		A	A	B	C	C	D	B	B		E	E	E	E	E	E			E	F			E
Brighton 10	d									00 04								04 12			05 06		
Horsham	d																						
Gatwick Airport 10 ✈	d							00 04	00 21	00 42	01 46	02 21	02 46	03 21	03 46	04 21		04 41	05 20		05 46		05 33
East Croydon	d						00 10	00 23	00 40	01 10	02 10	02 40	03 10	03 40	04 10	04 40		05 10	05 39		06 01		06 03
Rainham Kt	d																						
Dartford	d																			05 15			
Abbey Wood	d																			05 28			
Woolwich Arsenal	d																			05 34			
Greenwich	d																			05 47			
Maidstone East	d																						
Sevenoaks	d																						
Swanley	d																						
St Mary Cray	d																						
Orpington	d																						
Bromley South	d																						
Catford	d				00 06	00 06																	
Peckham Rye 4 195	d				00 14	00 14																	
Denmark Hill 4 195	d				00 17	00 17																	
Sutton 4 179	d																					05 46	
Wimbledon	d																						
Streatham 4	d																					06 03	
Tulse Hill 5	d																					06 08	
Herne Hill 4 173,179	d																					06 12	
Loughborough Jn 173,179	d																					06 15	
Elephant & Castle ⊖ 173,179	d		00 04		00 24	00 24																06 19	
London Bridge	d																	05 26	05 55	05 58	06 16		06 21
London Blackfriars	a		00 08		00 29	00 33	00 36	00 49	01 07	01 36	02 36	03 06	03 36	04 06	04 36	05 06		05 31	06 01	06 04	06 21	06 24	06 26
London Blackfriars 3 ⊖	d	00 02	00 09	00 22	00 29		00 37	00 50	01 08	01 36	02 36	03 06	03 36	04 06	04 36	05 06	05 27	05 32	06 02	06 04	06 22	06 24	06 27
City Thameslink 3	d				00 31																		
Farringdon 3 ⊖	d	00 06	00 13	00 25	00 34		00 41									05 11	05 31	05 36	06 06	06 09	06 26	06 29	06 31
St Pancras International	d	00 11	00 18	00 30	00 38		00 46	01 01	01 16	01 44	02 44	03 14	03 44	04 14	04 44	05 16	05 36	05 41	06 11	06 13	06 31	06 33	06 36
Finsbury Park	a				00 44		00 52														06 37		
Welwyn Garden City	a						01 12																
Stevenage	a						01 21														07 01		
Hitchin	a						01 30														07 08		
Letchworth Garden City	a																				07 13		
Royston	a																				07 24		
Cambridge	a																				07 39		
Huntingdon	a						01 59																
Peterborough	a						02 17																
Kentish Town	a		00 22					01 05		01 48	02 48		03 48	04 18	04 48		05 40			06 18		06 38	
West Hampstead Thameslink	a	00 19	00 26	00 39				01 09	01 24	01 52	02 52	03 22	03 52	04 22	04 52	05 24	05 44	05 48	06 19	06 22		06 44	06 44
Elstree & Borehamwood	a		00 41					01 24		02 07	03 07		04 07	04 37	05 07		05 58			06 36		06 58	
St Albans City	a	00 35	00 51	00 56				01 34	01 40	02 17	03 17	03 40	04 17	04 47	05 17	05 40	06 08	06 00	06 31	06 45		07 08	06 56
Harpenden	a	00 42	00 58	01 02				01 40	01 47	02 25	03 25	03 47	04 25	04 55	05 25	05 47		06 06	06 37	06 51			07 03
Luton Airport Parkway 7 ✈	a	00 47	01 03	01 07				01 45	01 52	02 30	03 30	03 52	04 30	05 00	05 30	05 52		06 11	06 42	06 56			07 08
Luton 10	a	00 51	01 07	01 11				01 49	01 56	02 34	03 34	03 56	04 34	05 04	05 34	05 56		06 15	06 46	07 01			07 12
Bedford	a	01 18	01 32	01 36				02 14	02 21	02 59	03 59	04 21	05 01	05 33	05 59	06 21		06 41	07 11				07 37

A From Sutton (Surrey)
B From Brighton
C From Sevenoaks
D From Horsham
E From Three Bridges
F From Gillingham (Kent)

Brighton and Gatwick Airport - London, Stevenage, Cambridge, Luton and Bedford

		TL	TL	TL	TL	TL	TL	TL	TL	TL	TL	TL	TL	TL	TL	TL	TL	TL	TL	TL	TL	TL	TL
				■		■		■			■		■		■		■			■		■	
			A																				
Brighton 10	d					05 26							05 58		06 08							06 26	
Horsham	d			05 25							05 55									06 25			
Gatwick Airport 10 ✈	d			05 49		06 06		06 03			06 19		06 36		06 46		06 33			06 49		07 06	
East Croydon	d			06 15		06 21		06 33			06 45		06 51		07 01		07 03			07 15		07 21	
Rainham Kt	d									05 28									05 58				
Dartford	d		05 45							06 15									06 45				
Abbey Wood	d		05 58							06 28									06 58				
Woolwich Arsenal	d		06 04							06 34									07 04				
Greenwich	d		06 17							06 47									07 17				
Maidstone East	d																						
Sevenoaks	d	05 22							05 52									06 22					
Swanley	d	05 41							06 11									06 41					
St Mary Cray	d	05 45							06 15									06 45					
Orpington	d													06 33									07 03
Bromley South	d	05 53							06 23					06 43				06 53					07 13
Catford	d	06 05							06 35					06 55				07 05					07 25
Peckham Rye 4 195	d	06 14							06 44					07 04				07 14					07 34
Denmark Hill 4 195	d	06 17							06 47					07 07				07 17					07 37
Sutton 4 179	d				05 49		06 16					06 19				06 46					06 49		
Wimbledon	d				06 07							06 37									07 07		
Streatham 4	d				06 18		06 33					06 48				07 03					07 18		
Tulse Hill 5	d				06 23		06 38					06 53				07 08					07 23		
Herne Hill 4 173,179	d				06 27		06 42					06 57				07 12					07 27		
Loughborough Jn 173,179	d				06 30		06 45					07 00				07 15					07 30		
Elephant & Castle ⊖ 173,179	d	06 24			06 34		06 49		06 54			07 04		07 14		07 19		07 24			07 34		07 44
London Bridge	d		06 28	06 31		06 35		06 51		06 58	07 01		07 05		07 16		07 21		07 28	07 31		07 35	
London Blackfriars	a	06 29	06 34	06 36	06 39	06 41	06 54	06 56	06 59	07 04	07 06	07 09	07 11	07 19	07 21	07 24	07 26	07 29	07 34	07 36	07 39	07 41	07 49
London Blackfriars 3 ⊖	d		06 34	06 37	06 39	06 42	06 54	06 57		07 04	07 07	07 09	07 12	07 19	07 22	07 24	07 27		07 34	07 37	07 39	07 42	07 49
City Thameslink 3	d																						
Farringdon 3 ⊖	d		06 39	06 41	06 44	06 46	06 59	07 01		07 09	07 11	07 14	07 16	07 24	07 26	07 29	07 31		07 39	07 41	07 44	07 46	07 54
St Pancras International	d		06 43	06 46	06 48	06 51	07 03	07 06		07 13	07 16	07 18	07 21	07 28	07 31	07 33	07 36		07 43	07 46	07 48	07 51	07 58
Finsbury Park	a			06 52							07 22				07 37					07 52			
Welwyn Garden City	a																						
Stevenage	a			07 13							07 43				08 01					08 13			
Hitchin	a			07 19							07 49				08 08					08 19			
Letchworth Garden City	a														08 14								
Royston	a														08 24								
Cambridge	a														08 40								
Huntingdon	a			07 48							08 18									08 48			
Peterborough	a			08 05							08 39									09 05			
Kentish Town	a				06 53		07 08					07 23		07 33		07 38					07 53		08 03
West Hampstead Thameslink	a		06 51		06 59	06 59	07 14			07 21		07 29	07 29			07 44			07 51		07 59	07 59	
Elstree & Borehamwood	a		07 05		07 13		07 28			07 35		07 43				07 58			08 05		08 13		
St Albans City	a		07 15		07 23	07 11	07 38	07 24		07 45		07 53	07 41			08 08	07 54		08 15		08 23	08 11	
Harpenden	a		07 21			07 17		07 31		07 51			07 47				08 01		08 21			08 17	
Luton Airport Parkway 7 ✈	a		07 26			07 22		07 36		07 56			07 52				08 06		08 26			08 22	
Luton 10	a		07 31			07 26		07 40		08 01			07 56				08 10		08 31			08 26	
Bedford	a					07 51		08 05					08 21				08 35					08 51	

A From Gillingham (Kent)

Table T052-F

Saturdays

26 May to 8 December

Brighton and Gatwick Airport - London, Stevenage, Cambridge, Luton and Bedford

		TL	TL ■	TL	TL	TL ■	TL	TL ■	TL	TL ■	TL	TL ■	TL	TL	TL ■	TL	TL ■	TL	TL	TL ■	TL	TL	TL ■
Brighton	d							06 58		07 08							07 26						
Horsham	d					06 55									07 25								07 55
Gatwick Airport ✈	d		07 03			07 19		07 36		07 46		07 33			07 49		08 06			08 03			08 19
East Croydon	d		07 33			07 45		07 51		08 01		08 03			08 15		08 21			08 33			08 45
Rainham Kt	d				06 28									06 58								07 28	
Dartford	d				07 15									07 45								08 15	
Abbey Wood	d				07 28									07 58								08 28	
Woolwich Arsenal	d				07 34									08 04								08 34	
Greenwich	d				07 47									08 17								08 47	
Maidstone East	d																						
Sevenoaks	d			06 52									07 22								07 52		
Swanley	d			07 11									07 41								08 11		
St Mary Cray	d			07 15									07 45								08 15		
Orpington	d								07 33									08 03					
Bromley South	d			07 23					07 43				07 53					08 13			08 23		
Catford	d			07 35					07 55				08 05					08 25			08 35		
Peckham Rye (195)	d			07 44					08 04				08 14					08 34			08 44		
Denmark Hill (195)	d			07 47					08 07				08 17					08 37			08 47		
Sutton (179)	d	07 16					07 19				07 46					07 49			08 16				
Wimbledon	d						07 37									08 07							
Streatham	d	07 33					07 48				08 03					08 18			08 33				
Tulse Hill	d	07 38					07 53				08 08					08 23			08 38				
Herne Hill (173,179)	d	07 42					07 57				08 12					08 27			08 42				
Loughborough Jn (173,179)	d	07 45					08 00				08 15					08 30			08 45				
Elephant & Castle ⊖ (173,179)	d	07 49		07 54			08 04		08 14		08 19		08 24			08 34		08 44	08 49		08 54		
London Bridge	d		07 51		07 58	08 01		08 05		08 16		08 21		08 28	08 31		08 35			08 51		08 58	09 01
London Blackfriars	a	07 54	07 56	07 59	08 04	08 06	08 09	08 11	08 19	08 21	08 24	08 26	08 29	08 34	08 36	08 39	08 41	08 49	08 54	08 56	08 59	09 04	09 06
London Blackfriars ⊖	d	07 54	07 57		08 04	08 07	08 09	08 12	08 19	08 22	08 24	08 27		08 34	08 37	08 39	08 42	08 49	08 54	08 57		09 04	09 07
City Thameslink	d																					09 06	09 09
Farringdon ⊖	d	07 59	08 01		08 09	08 11	08 14	08 16	08 24	08 26	08 29	08 31		08 39	08 41	08 44	08 46	08 54	08 59	09 01		09 09	09 11
St Pancras International	d	08 03	08 06		08 13	08 16	08 18	08 21	08 28	08 31	08 33	08 36		08 43	08 46	08 48	08 51	08 58	09 03	09 06		09 13	09 16
Finsbury Park	a					08 22				08 37					08 52								09 22
Welwyn Garden City	a																						
Stevenage	a					08 43				09 01					09 13								09 43
Hitchin	a					08 49				09 08					09 19								09 49
Letchworth Garden City	a									09 14													
Royston	a									09 24													
Cambridge	a									09 40													
Huntingdon	a					09 18									09 48								10 18
Peterborough	a					09 36									10 05								10 40
Kentish Town	a	08 08					08 23		08 33		08 38					08 53		09 03	09 08				
West Hampstead Thameslink	a	08 14			08 21		08 29	08 29			08 44			08 51		08 59	08 59		09 14			09 21	
Elstree & Borehamwood	a	08 28			08 35		08 43				08 58			09 05		09 13			09 28			09 35	
St Albans City	a	08 38	08 24		08 45		08 53	08 41			09 08	08 54		09 15		09 23	09 11		09 38	09 24		09 45	
Harpenden	a		08 31		08 51			08 47				09 01		09 21			09 17			09 31		09 51	
Luton Airport Parkway ✈	a		08 36		08 56			08 52				09 06		09 26			09 22			09 36		09 56	
Luton	a		08 40		09 01			08 56				09 10		09 31			09 26			09 40		10 01	
Bedford	a		09 05					09 21				09 35					09 51			10 05			

Table T052-F

Saturdays

26 May to 8 December

Brighton and Gatwick Airport - London, Stevenage, Cambridge, Luton and Bedford

		TL	TL ■	TL	TL ■	TL	TL ■	TL	TL	TL ■	TL	TL ■	TL	TL	TL ■	TL	TL	TL ■	TL	TL ■	TL	TL ■	TL
Brighton	d		07 58		08 08							08 26								08 58		09 08	
Horsham	d									08 25								08 55					
Gatwick Airport ✈	d		08 36		08 46		08 33			08 49		09 06			09 03			09 19		09 36		09 46	
East Croydon	d		08 51		09 01		09 03			09 15		09 21			09 33			09 45		09 51		10 01	
Rainham Kt	d								07 58								08 28						
Dartford	d								08 45								09 15						
Abbey Wood	d								08 58								09 28						
Woolwich Arsenal	d								09 04								09 34						
Greenwich	d								09 17								09 47						
Maidstone East	d																						
Sevenoaks	d							08 22								08 52							
Swanley	d							08 41								09 11							
St Mary Cray	d							08 45								09 15							
Orpington	d			08 33									09 03								09 33		
Bromley South	d			08 43				08 53					09 13			09 23					09 43		
Catford	d			08 55				09 05					09 25			09 35					09 55		
Peckham Rye (195)	d			09 04				09 14					09 34			09 44					10 04		
Denmark Hill (195)	d			09 07				09 17					09 37			09 47					10 07		
Sutton (179)	d	08 19				08 46					08 49			09 16					09 19				09 46
Wimbledon	d	08 37									09 07								09 37				
Streatham	d	08 48				09 03					09 18			09 33					09 48				10 03
Tulse Hill	d	08 53				09 08					09 23			09 38					09 53				10 08
Herne Hill (173,179)	d	08 57				09 12					09 27			09 42					09 57				10 12
Loughborough Jn (173,179)	d	09 00				09 15					09 30			09 45					10 00				10 15
Elephant & Castle ⊖ (173,179)	d	09 04		09 14		09 19		09 24			09 34		09 44	09 49		09 54			10 04		10 14		10 19
London Bridge	d		09 05		09 16		09 21		09 28	09 31		09 35			09 51		09 58	10 01		10 05		10 16	
London Blackfriars	a	09 09	09 11	09 19	09 21	09 24	09 26	09 29	09 34	09 36	09 39	09 41	09 49	09 54	09 56	09 59	10 04	10 06	10 09	10 11	10 19	10 21	10 24
London Blackfriars ⊖	d	09 09	09 12	09 19	09 22	09 24	09 27		09 34	09 37	09 39	09 42	09 49	09 54	09 57		10 04	10 07	10 09	10 12	10 19	10 22	10 24
City Thameslink	d	09 11	09 14	09 21	09 24	09 26	09 29		09 36	09 39	09 41	09 44	09 51	09 56	09 59		10 06	10 09	10 11	10 14	10 21	10 24	10 26
Farringdon ⊖	d	09 14	09 16	09 24	09 26	09 29	09 31		09 39	09 41	09 44	09 46	09 54	09 59	10 01		10 09	10 11	10 14	10 16	10 24	10 26	10 29
St Pancras International	d	09 18	09 21	09 28	09 31	09 33	09 36		09 43	09 46	09 48	09 51	09 58	10 03	10 06		10 13	10 16	10 18	10 21	10 28	10 31	10 33
Finsbury Park	a				09 37					09 52								10 22				10 37	
Welwyn Garden City	a																						
Stevenage	a				10 01					10 13								10 43				11 01	
Hitchin	a				10 08					10 19								10 49				11 08	
Letchworth Garden City	a				10 14																	11 14	
Royston	a				10 24																	11 24	
Cambridge	a				10 40																	11 40	
Huntingdon	a									10 48								11 18					
Peterborough	a									11 05								11 39					
Kentish Town	a	09 23		09 33		09 38					09 53		10 03	10 08					10 23		10 33		10 38
West Hampstead Thameslink	a	09 29	09 29			09 44			09 51		09 59	09 59		10 14			10 21		10 29	10 29			10 44
Elstree & Borehamwood	a	09 43				09 58			10 05		10 13			10 28			10 35		10 43				10 58
St Albans City	a	09 53	09 41			10 08	09 54		10 15		10 23	10 11		10 38	10 24		10 45		10 53	10 41			11 08
Harpenden	a		09 47				10 01		10 21			10 17			10 31		10 51			10 47			
Luton Airport Parkway ✈	a		09 52				10 06		10 26			10 22			10 36		10 56			10 52			
Luton	a		09 56				10 10		10 31			10 26			10 40		11 01			10 56			
Bedford	a		10 21				10 35					10 51			11 05					11 21			

Table T052-F

Saturdays

26 May to 8 December

Brighton and Gatwick Airport - London, Stevenage, Cambridge, Luton and Bedford

		TL ■	TL		TL	TL ■	TL	TL ■	TL	TL	TL ■	TL	TL	TL ■		TL	TL ■	TL	TL ■	TL	TL ■	TL	TL	TL ■	TL
Brighton ■	d							09 26									09 58		10 08						
Horsham	d					09 25								09 55										10 25	
Gatwick Airport ■ ✈	d	09 33				09 49		10 06			10 03			10 19			10 36		10 46		10 33			10 49	
East Croydon	d	10 03				10 15		10 21			10 33			10 45			10 51		11 01		11 03			11 15	
Rainham Kt	d				08 58								09 28										09 58		
Dartford	d				09 45								10 15										10 45		
Abbey Wood	d				09 58								10 28										10 58		
Woolwich Arsenal	d				10 04								10 34										11 04		
Greenwich	d				10 17								10 47										11 17		
Maidstone East	d																								
Sevenoaks	d		09 22									09 52										10 22			
Swanley	d		09 41									10 11										10 41			
St Mary Cray	d		09 45									10 15										10 45			
Orpington	d								10 03									10 33							
Bromley South	d		09 53						10 13			10 23						10 43				10 53			
Catford	d		10 05						10 25			10 35						10 55				11 05			
Peckham Rye ■ 195	d		10 14						10 34			10 44						11 04				11 14			
Denmark Hill ■ 195	d		10 17						10 37			10 47						11 07				11 17			
Sutton ■ 179	d						09 49			10 16						10 19				10 46					10 49
Wimbledon	d						10 07									10 37									11 07
Streatham ■	d						10 18			10 33						10 48				11 03					11 18
Tulse Hill ■	d						10 23			10 38						10 53				11 08					11 23
Herne Hill ■ 173,179	d						10 27			10 42						10 57				11 12					11 27
Loughborough Jn 173,179	d						10 30			10 45						11 00				11 15					11 30
Elephant & Castle ⊖ 173,179	d		10 24				10 34		10 44	10 49		10 54				11 04		11 14		11 19		11 24			11 34
London Bridge	d	10 21			10 28	10 31		10 35			10 51		10 58	11 01			11 05		11 16		11 21		11 28	11 31	
London Blackfriars	a	10 26	10 29		10 34	10 36	10 39	10 41	10 49	10 54	10 56	10 59	11 04	11 06		11 09	11 11	11 19	11 21	11 24	11 26	11 29	11 34	11 36	11 39
London Blackfriars ■ ⊖	d	10 27			10 34	10 37	10 39	10 42	10 49	10 54	10 57		11 04	11 07		11 09	11 12	11 19	11 22	11 24	11 27		11 34	11 37	11 39
City Thameslink ■	d	10 29			10 36	10 39	10 41	10 44	10 51	10 56	10 59		11 06	11 09		11 11	11 14	11 21	11 24	11 26	11 29		11 36	11 39	11 41
Farringdon ■ ⊖	d	10 31			10 39	10 41	10 44	10 46	10 54	10 59	11 01		11 09	11 11		11 14	11 16	11 24	11 26	11 29	11 31		11 39	11 41	11 44
St Pancras International	d	10 36			10 43	10 46	10 48	10 51	10 58	11 03	11 06		11 13	11 16		11 18	11 21	11 28	11 31	11 33	11 36		11 43	11 46	11 48
Finsbury Park	a					10 52								11 22					11 37					11 53	
Welwyn Garden City	a																								
Stevenage	a					11 13								11 43					12 01					12 13	
Hitchin	a					11 18								11 49					12 08					12 19	
Letchworth Garden City	a																		12 14						
Royston	a																		12 24						
Cambridge	a																		12 40						
Huntingdon	a					11 48								12 18										12 48	
Peterborough	a					12 05								12 39										13 05	
Kentish Town	a						10 53		11 03	11 08						11 23		11 33		11 38					11 53
West Hampstead Thameslink	a				10 51		10 59	10 59		11 14			11 21			11 29	11 29			11 44			11 51		11 59
Elstree & Borehamwood	a				11 05		11 13			11 28			11 35			11 43				11 58			12 05		12 13
St Albans City	a	10 54			11 15		11 23	11 11		11 38	11 24		11 45			11 53	11 41			12 08	11 54		12 15		12 23
Harpenden	a	11 01			11 21			11 17			11 31		11 51				11 47				12 01		12 21		
Luton Airport Parkway ■ ✈	a	11 06			11 26			11 22			11 36		11 56				11 52				12 06		12 26		
Luton ■	a	11 10			11 31			11 26			11 40		12 01				11 56				12 10		12 31		
Bedford	a	11 35						11 51			12 05						12 21				12 35				

Table T052-F

Saturdays

26 May to 8 December

Brighton and Gatwick Airport - London, Stevenage, Cambridge, Luton and Bedford

			TL ■	TL	TL	TL ■	TL	TL	TL ■	TL	TL ■	TL		TL ■	TL	TL ■	TL	TL	TL ■	TL	TL ■	TL	TL		TL ■
Brighton ■	d		10 26								10 58			11 08							11 26				
Horsham	d								10 55										11 25						
Gatwick Airport ■ ✈	d		11 06			11 03			11 19		11 36			11 46		11 33			11 49		12 06				12 03
East Croydon	d		11 21			11 33			11 45		11 51			12 01		12 03			12 15		12 21				12 33
Rainham Kt	d							10 28										10 58							
Dartford	d							11 15										11 45							
Abbey Wood	d							11 28										11 58							
Woolwich Arsenal	d							11 34										12 04							
Greenwich	d							11 47										12 17							
Maidstone East	d																								
Sevenoaks	d						10 52										11 22								
Swanley	d						11 11										11 41								
St Mary Cray	d						11 15										11 45								
Orpington	d			11 03								11 33										12 03			
Bromley South	d			11 13			11 23					11 43					11 53					12 13			
Catford	d			11 25			11 35					11 55					12 05					12 25			
Peckham Rye ■ 195	d			11 34			11 44					12 04					12 14					12 34			
Denmark Hill ■ 195	d			11 37			11 47					12 07					12 17					12 37			
Sutton ■ 179	d				11 16					11 19					11 46					11 49			12 16		
Wimbledon	d									11 37										12 07					
Streatham ■	d				11 33					11 48					12 03					12 18			12 33		
Tulse Hill ■	d				11 38					11 53					12 08					12 23			12 38		
Herne Hill ■ 173,179	d				11 42					11 57					12 12					12 27			12 42		
Loughborough Jn 173,179	d				11 45					12 00					12 15					12 30			12 45		
Elephant & Castle ⊖ 173,179	d			11 44	11 49		11 54			12 04		12 14			12 19		12 24			12 34		12 44	12 49		
London Bridge	d		11 35			11 51		11 58	12 01		12 05			12 16		12 21		12 28	12 31		12 35				12 51
London Blackfriars	a		11 41	11 49	11 54	11 56	11 59	12 04	12 06	12 09	12 11	12 19		12 21	12 24	12 26	12 29	12 34	12 36	12 39	12 41	12 49	12 54		12 56
London Blackfriars ■ ⊖	d		11 42	11 49	11 54	11 57		12 04	12 07	12 09	12 12	12 19		12 22	12 24	12 27		12 34	12 37	12 39	12 42	12 49	12 54		12 57
City Thameslink ■	d		11 44	11 51	11 56	11 59		12 06	12 09	12 11	12 14	12 21		12 24	12 26	12 29		12 36	12 39	12 41	12 44	12 51	12 56		12 59
Farringdon ■ ⊖	d		11 46	11 54	11 59	12 01		12 09	12 11	12 14	12 16	12 24		12 26	12 29	12 31		12 39	12 41	12 44	12 46	12 54	12 59		13 01
St Pancras International	d		11 51	11 58	12 03	12 06		12 13	12 16	12 18	12 21	12 28		12 31	12 33	12 36		12 43	12 46	12 48	12 51	12 58	13 03		13 06
Finsbury Park	a								12 22					12 37					12 52						
Welwyn Garden City	a																								
Stevenage	a								12 43					13 01					13 14						
Hitchin	a								12 49					13 08					13 20						
Letchworth Garden City	a													13 14											
Royston	a													13 24											
Cambridge	a													13 40											
Huntingdon	a								13 18										13 49						
Peterborough	a								13 39										14 05						
Kentish Town	a			12 03	12 08					12 23		12 33			12 38					12 53		13 03	13 08		
West Hampstead Thameslink	a		11 59		12 14			12 21		12 29	12 29				12 44			12 51		12 59	12 59		13 14		
Elstree & Borehamwood	a				12 28			12 35		12 43					12 58			13 05		13 13			13 28		
St Albans City	a		12 11		12 38	12 24		12 45		12 53	12 41				13 08	12 54		13 15		13 23	13 11		13 38		13 23
Harpenden	a		12 17			12 31		12 51			12 47					13 01		13 21			13 17				13 30
Luton Airport Parkway ■ ✈	a		12 22			12 36		12 56			12 52					13 06		13 26			13 22				13 35
Luton ■	a		12 26			12 40		13 01			12 56					13 10		13 31			13 26				13 39
Bedford	a		12 51			13 05					13 21					13 36					13 51				14 05

Table T052-F

Saturdays

26 May to 8 December

Brighton and Gatwick Airport - London, Stevenage, Cambridge, Luton and Bedford

			TL	TL	TL ■	TL	TL ■	TL	TL ■	TL	TL ■	TL	TL	TL ■	TL	TL ■	TL	TL	TL ■	TL	TL	TL ■	TL	TL ■
Brighton ■		d					11 58		12 08							12 26								12 58
Horsham		d			11 55									12 25								12 55		
Gatwick Airport ■ ✈		d			12 19		12 36		12 46		12 33			12 49		13 06			13 03			13 19		13 36
East Croydon		d			12 45		12 51		13 01		13 03			13 15		13 21			13 33			13 45		13 51
Rainham Kt		d		11 28									11 58								12 28			
Dartford		d		12 15									12 45								13 15			
Abbey Wood		d		12 28									12 58								13 28			
Woolwich Arsenal		d		12 34									13 04								13 34			
Greenwich		d		12 47									13 17								13 47			
Maidstone East		d																						
Sevenoaks		d	11 52									12 22								12 52				
Swanley		d	12 11									12 41								13 11				
St Mary Cray		d	12 15									12 45								13 15				
Orpington		d						12 33									13 03							
Bromley South		d	12 23					12 43				12 53					13 13			13 23				
Catford		d	12 35					12 55				13 05					13 25			13 35				
Peckham Rye ■	195	d	12 44					13 04				13 14					13 34			13 44				
Denmark Hill ■	195	d	12 47					13 07				13 17					13 37			13 47				
Sutton ■	179	d				12 19				12 46					12 49			13 16					13 19	
Wimbledon		d				12 37									13 07								13 37	
Streatham ■		d				12 48				13 03					13 18			13 33					13 48	
Tulse Hill ■		d				12 53				13 08					13 23			13 38					13 53	
Herne Hill ■	173,179	d				12 57				13 12					13 27			13 42					13 57	
Loughborough Jn	173,179	d				13 00				13 15					13 30			13 45					14 00	
Elephant & Castle ⊖	173,179	d	12 54			13 04		13 14		13 19		13 24			13 34		13 44	13 49		13 54			14 04	
London Bridge		d		12 58	13 01		13 05		13 16		13 21		13 28	13 31		13 35			13 51		13 58	14 01		14 05
London Blackfriars		a	12 59	13 04	13 06	13 09	13 11	13 19	13 21	13 24	13 26	13 29	13 34	13 36	13 39	13 41	13 49	13 54	13 56	13 59	14 04	14 06	14 09	14 11
London Blackfriars ■ ⊖		d		13 04	13 07	13 09	13 12	13 19	13 22	13 24	13 27		13 34	13 37	13 39	13 42	13 49	13 54	13 57		14 04	14 07	14 09	14 12
City Thameslink ■		d		13 06	13 09	13 11	13 14	13 21	13 24	13 26	13 29		13 36	13 39	13 41	13 44	13 51	13 56	13 59		14 06	14 09	14 11	14 14
Farringdon ■ ⊖		d		13 09	13 11	13 14	13 16	13 24	13 26	13 29	13 31		13 39	13 41	13 44	13 46	13 54	13 59	14 01		14 09	14 11	14 14	14 16
St Pancras International		d		13 13	13 16	13 18	13 21	13 28	13 31	13 33	13 36		13 43	13 46	13 48	13 51	13 58	14 03	14 06		14 13	14 16	14 18	14 21
Finsbury Park		a			13 22				13 37					13 52								14 22		
Welwyn Garden City		a																						
Stevenage		a			13 43				14 01					14 13								14 43		
Hitchin		a			13 49				14 08					14 19								14 49		
Letchworth Garden City		a							14 14															
Royston		a							14 24															
Cambridge		a							14 40															
Huntingdon		a			14 18									14 48								15 18		
Peterborough		a			14 40									15 05								15 39		
Kentish Town		a				13 23		13 33		13 38					13 53		14 03	14 08					14 23	
West Hampstead Thameslink		a		13 21		13 29	13 29			13 44			13 51		13 59	13 59		14 14			14 21		14 29	14 29
Elstree & Borehamwood		a		13 35		13 43				13 58			14 05		14 13			14 28			14 35		14 43	
St Albans City		a		13 45		13 53	13 41			14 08	13 54		14 15		14 23	14 11		14 38	14 24		14 45		14 53	14 41
Harpenden		a		13 51			13 47				14 01		14 21			14 17			14 31		14 51			14 47
Luton Airport Parkway ■ ✈		a		13 56			13 52				14 06		14 26			14 22			14 36		14 56			14 52
Luton ■		a		14 01			13 56				14 10		14 31			14 26			14 40		15 01			14 56
Bedford		a					14 21				14 36					14 51			15 06					15 21

Table T052-F

Saturdays

26 May to 8 December

Brighton and Gatwick Airport - London, Stevenage, Cambridge, Luton and Bedford

			TL	TL ■	TL	TL ■	TL	TL	TL ■	TL	TL ■	TL	TL	TL ■	TL	TL	TL ■	TL	TL ■	TL	TL ■	TL	TL ■	TL
Brighton ■		d		13 08							13 26								13 58		14 08			
Horsham		d							13 25								13 55							
Gatwick Airport ■ ✈		d		13 46		13 33			13 49		14 06			14 03			14 19		14 36		14 46		14 33	
East Croydon		d		14 01		14 03			14 15		14 21			14 33			14 45		14 51		15 01		15 03	
Rainham Kt		d						12 58								13 28								
Dartford		d						13 45								14 15								
Abbey Wood		d						13 58								14 28								
Woolwich Arsenal		d						14 04								14 34								
Greenwich		d						14 17								14 47								
Maidstone East		d																						
Sevenoaks		d					13 22								13 52									14 22
Swanley		d					13 41								14 11									14 41
St Mary Cray		d					13 45								14 15									14 45
Orpington		d	13 33									14 03								14 33				
Bromley South		d	13 43				13 53					14 13			14 23					14 43				14 53
Catford		d	13 55				14 05					14 25			14 35					14 55				15 05
Peckham Rye ■	195	d	14 04				14 14					14 34			14 44					15 04				15 14
Denmark Hill ■	195	d	14 07				14 17					14 37			14 47					15 07				15 17
Sutton ■	179	d			13 46					13 49			14 16					14 19				14 46		
Wimbledon		d								14 07								14 37						
Streatham ■		d			14 03					14 18			14 33					14 48				15 03		
Tulse Hill ■		d			14 08					14 23			14 38					14 53				15 08		
Herne Hill ■	173,179	d			14 12					14 27			14 42					14 57				15 12		
Loughborough Jn	173,179	d			14 15					14 30			14 45					15 00				15 15		
Elephant & Castle ⊖	173,179	d	14 14		14 19		14 24			14 34		14 44	14 49		14 54			15 04		15 14		15 19		15 24
London Bridge		d		14 16		14 21		14 28	14 31		14 35			14 51		14 58	15 01		15 05		15 16		15 21	
London Blackfriars		a	14 19	14 21	14 24	14 26	14 29	14 34	14 36	14 39	14 41	14 49	14 54	14 56	14 59	15 04	15 06	15 09	15 11	15 19	15 21	15 24	15 26	15 29
London Blackfriars ■ ⊖		d	14 19	14 22	14 24	14 27		14 34	14 37	14 39	14 42	14 49	14 54	14 57		15 04	15 07	15 09	15 12	15 19	15 22	15 24	15 27	
City Thameslink ■		d	14 21	14 24	14 26	14 29		14 36	14 39	14 41	14 44	14 51	14 56	14 59		15 06	15 09	15 11	15 14	15 21	15 24	15 26	15 29	
Farringdon ■ ⊖		d	14 24	14 26	14 29	14 31		14 39	14 41	14 44	14 46	14 54	14 59	15 01		15 09	15 11	15 14	15 16	15 24	15 26	15 29	15 31	
St Pancras International		d	14 28	14 31	14 33	14 36		14 43	14 46	14 48	14 51	14 58	15 03	15 06		15 13	15 16	15 18	15 21	15 28	15 31	15 33	15 36	
Finsbury Park		a		14 37					14 52								15 22				15 37			
Welwyn Garden City		a																						
Stevenage		a		15 01					15 13								15 43				16 01			
Hitchin		a		15 08					15 19								15 49				16 08			
Letchworth Garden City		a		15 14																	16 14			
Royston		a		15 24																	16 24			
Cambridge		a		15 40																	16 40			
Huntingdon		a							15 48								16 18							
Peterborough		a							16 07								16 40							
Kentish Town		a	14 33		14 38					14 53		15 03	15 08					15 23		15 33		15 38		
West Hampstead Thameslink		a			14 44			14 51		14 59	14 59		15 14			15 21		15 29	15 29			15 44		
Elstree & Borehamwood		a			14 58			15 05		15 13			15 28			15 35		15 43				15 58		
St Albans City		a			15 08	14 54		15 15		15 23	15 11		15 38	15 24		15 45		15 53	15 41			16 08	15 54	
Harpenden		a				15 01		15 21			15 17			15 31		15 51			15 47				16 01	
Luton Airport Parkway ■ ✈		a				15 06		15 26			15 22			15 36		15 56			15 52				16 06	
Luton ■		a				15 10		15 31			15 26			15 40		16 01			15 56				16 10	
Bedford		a				15 36					15 51			16 06					16 21				16 36	

Table T052-F

Saturdays

26 May to 8 December

Brighton and Gatwick Airport - London, Stevenage, Cambridge, Luton and Bedford

		TL	TL ■	TL	TL ■	TL		TL	TL ■	TL	TL	TL ■	TL	TL ■	TL	TL ■	TL		TL ■	TL	TL	TL ■	TL	TL ■	TL
Brighton ■	d				14 26									14 58		15 08								15 26	
Horsham	d		14 25									14 55										15 25			
Gatwick Airport ■ ✈	d		14 49		15 06				15 03			15 19		15 36		15 46			15 33			15 49		16 06	
East Croydon	d		15 15		15 21				15 33			15 45		15 51		16 01			16 03			16 15		16 21	
Rainham Kt	d	13 58									14 28										14 58				
Dartford	d	14 45									15 15										15 45				
Abbey Wood	d	14 58									15 28										15 58				
Woolwich Arsenal	d	15 04									15 34										16 04				
Greenwich	d	15 17									15 47										16 17				
Maidstone East	d																								
Sevenoaks	d									14 52										15 22					
Swanley	d									15 11										15 41					
St Mary Cray	d									15 15										15 45					
Orpington	d					15 03									15 33										16 03
Bromley South	d					15 13				15 23					15 43					15 53					16 13
Catford	d					15 25				15 35					15 55					16 05					16 25
Peckham Rye ■ 195	d					15 34				15 44					16 04					16 14					16 34
Denmark Hill ■ 195	d					15 37				15 47					16 07					16 17					16 37
Sutton ■ 179	d			14 49				15 16					15 19				15 46						15 49		
Wimbledon	d			15 07									15 37										16 07		
Streatham ■	d			15 18				15 33					15 48				16 03						16 18		
Tulse Hill ■	d			15 23				15 38					15 53				16 08						16 23		
Herne Hill ■ 173,179	d			15 27				15 42					15 57				16 12						16 27		
Loughborough Jn 173,179	d			15 30				15 45					16 00				16 15						16 30		
Elephant & Castle ⊖173,179	d			15 34		15 44		15 49		15 54			16 04		16 14		16 19			16 24			16 34		16 44
London Bridge	d	15 28	15 31		15 35				15 51		15 58	16 01		16 05		16 16			16 21		16 28	16 31		16 35	
London Blackfriars	a	15 34	15 36	15 39	15 41	15 49		15 54	15 56	15 59	16 04	16 06	16 09	16 11	16 19	16 21	16 24		16 26	16 29	16 34	16 36	16 39	16 41	16 49
London Blackfriars ■ ⊖	d	15 34	15 37	15 39	15 42	15 49		15 54	15 57		16 04	16 07	16 09	16 12	16 19	16 22	16 24		16 27		16 34	16 37	16 39	16 42	16 49
City Thameslink ■	d	15 36	15 39	15 41	15 44	15 51		15 56	15 59		16 06	16 09	16 11	16 14	16 21	16 24	16 26		16 29		16 36	16 39	16 41	16 44	16 51
Farringdon ■ ⊖	d	15 39	15 41	15 44	15 46	15 54		15 59	16 01		16 09	16 11	16 14	16 16	16 24	16 26	16 29		16 31		16 39	16 41	16 44	16 46	16 54
St Pancras International	d	15 43	15 46	15 48	15 51	15 58		16 03	16 06		16 13	16 16	16 18	16 21	16 28	16 31	16 33		16 36		16 43	16 46	16 48	16 51	16 58
Finsbury Park	a		15 52									16 22				16 37						16 52			
Welwyn Garden City	a																								
Stevenage	a		16 13									16 42				17 01						17 13			
Hitchin	a		16 19									16 48				17 08						17 19			
Letchworth Garden City	a															17 14									
Royston	a															17 24									
Cambridge	a															17 40									
Huntingdon	a		16 48									17 17										17 48			
Peterborough	a		17 05									17 33										18 04			
Kentish Town	a			15 53		16 03		16 08					16 23		16 33		16 38						16 53		17 03
West Hampstead Thameslink	a	15 51		15 59	15 59			16 14			16 21		16 29	16 29			16 44				16 51		16 59	16 59	
Elstree & Borehamwood	a	16 05		16 13				16 28			16 35		16 43				16 58				17 05		17 13		
St Albans City	a	16 15		16 23	16 11			16 38	16 24		16 45		16 53	16 41			17 08		16 54		17 15		17 23	17 11	
Harpenden	a	16 21			16 17				16 31		16 51			16 47					17 01		17 21			17 17	
Luton Airport Parkway ■ ✈	a	16 26			16 22				16 36		16 56			16 52					17 06		17 26			17 22	
Luton ■	a	16 31			16 26				16 40		17 01			16 56					17 10		17 31			17 26	
Bedford	a				16 51				17 06					17 21					17 35					17 51	

Table T052-F

Saturdays

26 May to 8 December

Brighton and Gatwick Airport - London, Stevenage, Cambridge, Luton and Bedford

		TL	TL ■	TL		TL	TL ■	TL	TL ■	TL	TL ■	TL	TL ■	TL	TL		TL ■	TL	TL ■	TL	TL	TL ■	TL	TL	TL ■
Brighton ■	d								15 58		16 08								16 26						
Horsham	d						15 55										16 25								16 55
Gatwick Airport ■ ✈	d		16 03				16 19		16 36		16 46		16 33				16 49		17 06			17 03			17 19
East Croydon	d		16 33				16 45		16 51		17 01		17 03				17 15		17 21			17 33			17 45
Rainham Kt	d					15 28									15 58									16 28	
Dartford	d					16 15									16 45									17 15	
Abbey Wood	d					16 28									16 58									17 28	
Woolwich Arsenal	d					16 34									17 04									17 34	
Greenwich	d					16 47									17 17									17 47	
Maidstone East	d																								
Sevenoaks	d			15 52										16 22									16 52		
Swanley	d			16 11										16 41									17 11		
St Mary Cray	d			16 15										16 45									17 15		
Orpington	d									16 33										17 03					
Bromley South	d			16 23						16 43				16 53						17 13			17 23		
Catford	d			16 35						16 55				17 05						17 25			17 35		
Peckham Rye ■ 195	d			16 44						17 04				17 14						17 34			17 44		
Denmark Hill ■ 195	d			16 47						17 07				17 17						17 37			17 47		
Sutton ■ 179	d	16 16						16 19				16 46						16 49			17 16				
Wimbledon	d							16 37										17 07							
Streatham ■	d	16 33						16 48				17 03						17 18			17 33				
Tulse Hill ■	d	16 38						16 53				17 08						17 23			17 38				
Herne Hill ■ 173,179	d	16 42						16 57				17 12						17 27			17 42				
Loughborough Jn 173,179	d	16 45						17 00				17 15						17 30			17 45				
Elephant & Castle ⊖173,179	d	16 49		16 54				17 04		17 14		17 19		17 24				17 34		17 44	17 49		17 54		
London Bridge	d		16 51			16 58	17 01		17 05		17 16		17 21		17 28		17 31		17 35			17 51		17 58	18 01
London Blackfriars	a	16 54	16 56	16 59		17 04	17 06	17 09	17 11	17 19	17 21	17 24	17 26	17 29	17 34		17 36	17 39	17 41	17 49	17 54	17 56	17 59	18 04	18 06
London Blackfriars ■ ⊖	d	16 54	16 57			17 04	17 07	17 09	17 12	17 19	17 22	17 24	17 27		17 34		17 37	17 39	17 42	17 49	17 54	17 57		18 04	18 07
City Thameslink ■	d	16 56	16 59			17 06	17 09	17 11	17 14	17 21	17 24	17 26	17 29		17 36		17 39	17 41	17 44	17 51	17 56	17 59		18 06	18 09
Farringdon ■ ⊖	d	16 59	17 01			17 09	17 11	17 14	17 16	17 24	17 26	17 29	17 31		17 39		17 41	17 44	17 46	17 54	17 59	18 01		18 09	18 11
St Pancras International	d	17 03	17 06			17 13	17 16	17 18	17 21	17 28	17 31	17 33	17 36		17 43		17 46	17 48	17 51	17 58	18 03	18 06		18 13	18 16
Finsbury Park	a						17 22				17 37						17 52								18 22
Welwyn Garden City	a																								
Stevenage	a						17 43				18 02						18 13								18 43
Hitchin	a						17 49				18 08						18 19								18 49
Letchworth Garden City	a										18 14														
Royston	a										18 24														
Cambridge	a										18 40														
Huntingdon	a						18 18										18 48								19 18
Peterborough	a						18 37										19 05								19 34
Kentish Town	a	17 08						17 23		17 33		17 38						17 53		18 03	18 08				
West Hampstead Thameslink	a	17 14				17 21		17 29	17 29			17 44			17 51			17 59	17 59		18 14			18 21	
Elstree & Borehamwood	a	17 28				17 35		17 43				17 58			18 05			18 13			18 28			18 35	
St Albans City	a	17 38	17 24			17 45		17 53	17 41			18 08	17 54		18 15			18 23	18 11		18 38	18 24		18 45	
Harpenden	a		17 31			17 51			17 47				18 01		18 21				18 17			18 31		18 51	
Luton Airport Parkway ■ ✈	a		17 36			17 56			17 52				18 06		18 26				18 22			18 36		18 56	
Luton ■	a		17 40			18 01			17 56				18 10		18 31				18 26			18 40		19 01	
Bedford	a		18 06						18 21				18 35						18 51			19 05			

Table T052-F

Saturdays

26 May to 8 December

Brighton and Gatwick Airport - London, Stevenage, Cambridge, Luton and Bedford

	TL		TL 1	TL	TL 1	TL	TL 1	TL	TL	TL 1	TL	TL 1		TL	TL	TL 1	TL	TL	TL 1	TL	TL 1	TL	TL 1	
Brighton 10 d			16 58		17 08							17 26									17 58		18 08	
Horsham d										17 25									17 55					
Gatwick Airport 10 ✈ d			17 36		17 46		17 33			17 49		18 06				18 03			18 19		18 36		18 46	
East Croydon d			17 51		18 01		18 03			18 15		18 21				18 33			18 45		18 51		19 01	
Rainham Kt d									16 58									17 28						
Dartford d									17 45									18 15						
Abbey Wood d									17 58									18 28						
Woolwich Arsenal d									18 04									18 34						
Greenwich d									18 17									18 47						
Maidstone East d																								
Sevenoaks d								17 22									17 52							
Swanley d								17 41									18 11							
St Mary Cray d								17 45									18 15							
Orpington d				17 33										18 03								18 33		
Bromley South d				17 43				17 53						18 13			18 23					18 43		
Catford d				17 55				18 05						18 25			18 35					18 55		
Peckham Rye 4 195 d				18 04				18 14						18 34			18 44					19 04		
Denmark Hill 4 195 d				18 07				18 17						18 37			18 47					19 07		
Sutton 4 179 d	17 19					17 46					17 49				18 16					18 19				
Wimbledon d	17 37										18 07									18 37				
Streatham 4 d	17 48					18 03					18 18				18 33					18 48				
Tulse Hill 3 d	17 53					18 08					18 23				18 38					18 53				
Herne Hill 4 173,179 d	17 57					18 12					18 27				18 42					18 57				
Loughborough Jn 173,179 d	18 00					18 15					18 30				18 45					19 00				
Elephant & Castle ⊖173,179 d	18 04			18 14		18 19		18 24			18 34			18 44	18 49		18 54			19 04		19 14		
London Bridge d			18 05		18 16		18 21		18 28	18 31		18 35				18 51		18 58	19 01		19 05		19 16	
London Blackfriars a	18 09		18 11	18 19	18 21	18 24	18 26	18 29	18 34	18 36	18 39	18 41		18 49	18 54	18 56	18 59	19 04	19 06	19 09	19 11	19 19	19 21	
London Blackfriars 3 ⊖ d	18 09		18 12	18 19	18 22	18 24	18 27		18 34	18 37	18 39	18 42		18 49	18 54	18 57		19 04	19 07	19 09	19 12	19 19	19 22	
City Thameslink 3 d	18 11		18 14	18 21	18 24	18 26	18 29		18 36	18 39	18 41	18 44		18 51	18 56	18 59		19 06	19 09	19 11	19 14	19 21	19 24	
Farringdon 3 ⊖ d	18 14		18 16	18 24	18 26	18 29	18 31		18 39	18 41	18 44	18 46		18 54	18 59	19 01		19 09	19 11	19 14	19 16	19 24	19 26	
St Pancras International d	18 18		18 21	18 28	18 31	18 33	18 36		18 43	18 46	18 48	18 51		18 58	19 03	19 06		19 13	19 16	19 18	19 21	19 28	19 31	
Finsbury Park a					18 38					18 52									19 22				19 37	
Welwyn Garden City a																								
Stevenage a					19 01					19 13									19 42				20 01	
Hitchin a					19 08					19 19									19 48				20 08	
Letchworth Garden City a					19 14																		20 14	
Royston a					19 24																		20 24	
Cambridge a					19 40																		20 40	
Huntingdon a										19 48									20 17					
Peterborough a										20 04									20 33					
Kentish Town a	18 23			18 33		18 38					18 53			19 03	19 08					19 23		19 33		
West Hampstead Thameslink a	18 29		18 29			18 44			18 51		18 59	18 59			19 14			19 21		19 29	19 29			
Elstree & Borehamwood a	18 43					18 58			19 05		19 13				19 28			19 35		19 43				
St Albans City a	18 53		18 41			19 08	18 54		19 15		19 23	19 11			19 38	19 24		19 45		19 53	19 41			
Harpenden a			18 47				19 01		19 21			19 17				19 31		19 51			19 47			
Luton Airport Parkway 7 ✈ a			18 52				19 06		19 26			19 22				19 36		19 56			19 52			
Luton 10 a			18 56				19 10		19 31			19 26				19 40		20 01			19 56			
Bedford a			19 21				19 35					19 51				20 05					20 21			

Table T052-F

Saturdays

26 May to 8 December

Brighton and Gatwick Airport - London, Stevenage, Cambridge, Luton and Bedford

	TL	TL 1	TL	TL	TL 1	TL	TL 1	TL	TL	TL 1		TL	TL	TL 1	TL	TL 1	TL	TL 1	TL	TL 1	TL		TL	TL 1
Brighton 10 d							18 26									18 58		19 08						
Horsham d					18 25									18 55										19 25
Gatwick Airport 10 ✈ d		18 33			18 49		19 06			19 03				19 19		19 36		19 46		19 33				19 49
East Croydon d		19 03			19 15		19 21			19 33				19 45		19 51		20 01		20 03				20 15
Rainham Kt d				17 58									18 28										18 58	
Dartford d				18 45									19 15										19 45	
Abbey Wood d				18 58									19 28										19 58	
Woolwich Arsenal d				19 04									19 34										20 04	
Greenwich d				19 17									19 47										20 17	
Maidstone East d																								
Sevenoaks d			18 22									18 52									19 22			
Swanley d			18 41									19 11									19 41			
St Mary Cray d			18 45									19 15									19 45			
Orpington d								19 03									19 33							
Bromley South d			18 53					19 13				19 23					19 43				19 53			
Catford d			19 05					19 25				19 35					19 55				20 05			
Peckham Rye 4 195 d			19 14					19 34				19 44					20 04				20 14			
Denmark Hill 4 195 d			19 17					19 37				19 47					20 07				20 17			
Sutton 4 179 d	18 46					18 49			19 16						19 19				19 46					
Wimbledon d						19 07									19 37									
Streatham 4 d	19 03					19 18			19 33						19 48				20 03					
Tulse Hill 3 d	19 08					19 23			19 38						19 53				20 08					
Herne Hill 4 173,179 d	19 12					19 27			19 42						19 57				20 12					
Loughborough Jn 173,179 d	19 15					19 30			19 45						20 00				20 15					
Elephant & Castle ⊖173,179 d	19 19		19 24			19 34		19 44	19 49			19 54			20 04		20 14		20 19		20 24			
London Bridge d		19 21		19 28	19 31		19 35			19 51			19 58	20 01		20 05		20 16		20 21			20 28	20 31
London Blackfriars a	19 24	19 26	19 29	19 34	19 36	19 39	19 41	19 49	19 54	19 56		19 59	20 04	20 06	20 09	20 11	20 19	20 21	20 24	20 26	20 29		20 34	20 36
London Blackfriars 3 ⊖ d	19 24	19 27		19 34	19 37	19 39	19 42	19 49	19 54	19 57			20 04	20 07	20 09	20 12	20 19	20 22	20 24	20 27			20 34	20 37
City Thameslink 3 d	19 26	19 29		19 36	19 39	19 41	19 44	19 51	19 56	19 59			20 06	20 09	20 11	20 14	20 21	20 24	20 26	20 29			20 36	20 39
Farringdon 3 ⊖ d	19 29	19 31		19 39	19 41	19 44	19 46	19 54	19 59	20 01			20 09	20 11	20 14	20 16	20 24	20 26	20 29	20 31			20 39	20 41
St Pancras International d	19 33	19 36		19 43	19 46	19 48	19 51	19 58	20 03	20 06			20 13	20 16	20 18	20 21	20 28	20 31	20 33	20 36			20 43	20 46
Finsbury Park a					19 52									20 22				20 37						20 52
Welwyn Garden City a																								
Stevenage a					20 13									20 43				21 01						21 13
Hitchin a					20 19									20 49				21 08						21 19
Letchworth Garden City a																		21 14						
Royston a																		21 24						
Cambridge a																		21 40						
Huntingdon a					20 48									21 18										21 48
Peterborough a					21 04									21 34										22 05
Kentish Town a	19 38					19 53		20 03	20 08						20 23		20 33		20 38					
West Hampstead Thameslink a	19 44			19 51		19 59	19 59		20 14				20 21		20 29	20 29			20 44				20 51	
Elstree & Borehamwood a	19 58			20 05		20 13			20 28				20 35		20 43				20 58				21 05	
St Albans City a	20 08	19 54		20 15		20 23	20 11		20 38	20 24			20 45		20 53	20 41			21 08	20 54			21 15	
Harpenden a		20 01		20 21			20 17			20 31			20 51			20 47				21 01			21 21	
Luton Airport Parkway 7 ✈ a		20 06		20 26			20 22			20 36			20 56			20 52				21 06			21 26	
Luton 10 a		20 10		20 31			20 26			20 40			21 01			20 56				21 10			21 31	
Bedford a		20 35					20 51			21 05						21 21				21 35				

Saturdays

26 May to 8 December

Brighton and Gatwick Airport - London, Stevenage, Cambridge, Luton and Bedford

	TL	TL ■	TL	TL	TL ■	TL	TL	TL ■		TL	TL ■	TL	TL ■	TL	TL ■	TL	TL	TL ■	TL		TL ■	TL	TL	TL ■
Brighton ■ d		19 26									19 58		20 08								20 26			
Horsham d								19 55										20 25						
Gatwick Airport ■ ✈ d		20 06			20 03			20 19			20 36		20 46		20 33			20 49			21 06			21 03
East Croydon d		20 21			20 33			20 45			20 51		21 01		21 03			21 15			21 21			21 33
Rainham Kt d							19 28										19 58							
Dartford d							20 15										20 45							
Abbey Wood d							20 28										20 58							
Woolwich Arsenal d							20 34										21 04							
Greenwich d							20 47										21 17							
Maidstone East d																								
Sevenoaks d						19 52										20 22								
Swanley d						20 11										20 41								
St Mary Cray d						20 15										20 45								
Orpington d			20 03									20 33										21 03		
Bromley South d			20 13			20 23						20 43				20 53						21 13		
Catford d			20 25			20 35						20 55				21 05						21 25		
Peckham Rye ■ 195 d			20 34			20 44						21 04				21 14						21 34		
Denmark Hill ■ 195 d			20 37			20 47						21 07				21 17						21 37		
Sutton ■ 179 d	19 49			20 16						20 19				20 46					20 49				21 16	
Wimbledon d	20 07									20 37									21 07					
Streatham ■ d	20 18			20 33						20 48				21 03					21 18				21 33	
Tulse Hill ■ d	20 23			20 38						20 53				21 08					21 23				21 38	
Herne Hill ■ 173,179 d	20 27			20 42						20 57				21 12					21 27				21 42	
Loughborough Jn 173,179 d	20 30			20 45						21 00				21 15					21 30				21 45	
Elephant & Castle ⊖173,179 d	20 34		20 44	20 49		20 54				21 04		21 14		21 19		21 24			21 34			21 44	21 49	
London Bridge d		20 35			20 51		20 58	21 01			21 05		21 16		21 21		21 28	21 31			21 35			21 51
London Blackfriars a	20 39	20 41	20 49	20 54	20 56	20 59	21 04	21 06		21 09	21 11	21 19	21 21	21 24	21 26	21 29	21 34	21 36	21 39		21 41	21 49	21 54	21 56
London Blackfriars ■ ⊖ d	20 39	20 42	20 49	20 54	20 57		21 04	21 07		21 09	21 12	21 19	21 22	21 24	21 27		21 34	21 37	21 39		21 42	21 49	21 54	21 57
City Thameslink ■ d	20 41	20 44	20 51	20 56	20 59																			
Farringdon ■ ⊖ d	20 44	20 46	20 54	20 59	21 01		21 09	21 11		21 14	21 16	21 24	21 26	21 29	21 31		21 39	21 41	21 44		21 46	21 54	21 59	22 01
St Pancras International d	20 48	20 51	20 58	21 03	21 06		21 13	21 16		21 18	21 21	21 28	21 31	21 33	21 36		21 43	21 46	21 48		21 51	21 58	22 03	22 06
Finsbury Park a								21 22					21 37					21 52						
Welwyn Garden City a																								
Stevenage a								21 43					22 01					22 13						
Hitchin a								21 49					22 08					22 19						
Letchworth Garden City a													22 14											
Royston a													22 24											
Cambridge a													22 40											
Huntingdon a								22 18										22 48						
Peterborough a								22 39										23 07						
Kentish Town a	20 53		21 03	21 08						21 23		21 33		21 38					21 53			22 03	22 08	
West Hampstead Thameslink a	20 59	20 59		21 14			21 21			21 29	21 29			21 44			21 51		21 59		21 59		22 14	
Elstree & Borehamwood a	21 13			21 28			21 35			21 43				21 58			22 05		22 13				22 28	
St Albans City a	21 23	21 11		21 38	21 24		21 45			21 53	21 41			22 08	21 54		22 15		22 23		22 11		22 38	22 24
Harpenden a		21 17			21 31		21 51				21 47				22 01		22 21				22 17			22 31
Luton Airport Parkway ■ ✈ a		21 22			21 36		21 56				21 52				22 06		22 26				22 22			22 36
Luton ■ a		21 26			21 40		22 01				21 56				22 10		22 31				22 26			22 40
Bedford a		21 51			22 05						22 21				22 35						22 51			23 05

Saturdays

26 May to 8 December

Brighton and Gatwick Airport - London, Stevenage, Cambridge, Luton and Bedford

	TL	TL	TL ■	TL	TL ■	TL		TL ■	TL	TL ■	TL	TL	TL ■	TL	TL ■	TL	TL		TL	TL	TL ■	TL ■	TL	TL
Brighton ■ d					20 58			21 08							21 26							21 58		
Horsham d			20 55										21 25								21 55			
Gatwick Airport ■ ✈ d			21 19		21 36			21 46		21 33			21 49		22 06						22 19	22 36		
East Croydon d			21 45		21 51			22 01		22 03			22 15		22 21						22 45	22 51		
Rainham Kt d		20 28										20 58								21 28				
Dartford d		21 15										21 45								22 15				
Abbey Wood d		21 28										21 58								22 28				
Woolwich Arsenal d		21 34										22 04								22 34				
Greenwich d		21 47										22 17								22 47				
Maidstone East d																								
Sevenoaks d	20 52										21 22								21 52					
Swanley d	21 11										21 41								22 11					
St Mary Cray d	21 15										21 45								22 15					
Orpington d						21 33										22 03								22 33
Bromley South d	21 23					21 43					21 53					22 13			22 23					22 43
Catford d	21 35					21 55					22 05					22 25			22 35					22 55
Peckham Rye ■ 195 d	21 44					22 04					22 14					22 34			22 44					23 04
Denmark Hill ■ 195 d	21 47					22 07					22 17					22 37			22 47					23 07
Sutton ■ 179 d				21 19					21 46					21 49			22 18						22 19	
Wimbledon d				21 37										22 07									22 41	
Streatham ■ d				21 48					22 03					22 18			22 35						22 52	
Tulse Hill ■ d				21 53					22 08					22 23			22 40						22 57	
Herne Hill ■ 173,179 d				21 57					22 12					22 27			22 44						23 04	
Loughborough Jn 173,179 d				22 00					22 15					22 30			22 47						23 07	
Elephant & Castle ⊖173,179 d	21 54			22 04		22 14			22 19		22 24			22 34		22 44	22 51		22 54				23 11	23 15
London Bridge d		21 58	22 01		22 05			22 16		22 21		22 28	22 31		22 35					22 58	23 01	23 05		
London Blackfriars a	21 59	22 04	22 06	22 09	22 11	22 19		22 21	22 24	22 26	22 29	22 34	22 36	22 39	22 41	22 49	22 59		22 59	23 04	23 06	23 11	23 16	23 19
London Blackfriars ■ ⊖ d		22 04	22 07	22 09	22 12	22 19		22 22	22 24	22 27		22 34	22 37	22 39	22 42	22 49	22 59			23 04	23 07	23 12	23 17	
City Thameslink ■ d																								
Farringdon ■ ⊖ d		22 09	22 11	22 14	22 16	22 24		22 26	22 29	22 31		22 39	22 41	22 44	22 46	22 54	23 04			23 09	23 11	23 16	23 21	
St Pancras International d		22 13	22 16	22 18	22 21	22 28		22 31	22 33	22 36		22 43	22 46	22 48	22 51	22 58	23 08			23 13	23 16	23 21	23 26	
Finsbury Park a			22 22					22 37					22 52								23 22			
Welwyn Garden City a																								
Stevenage a			22 43					23 01					23 13								23 43			
Hitchin a			22 49					23 08					23 19								23 49			
Letchworth Garden City a								23 14																
Royston a								23 24																
Cambridge a								23 40																
Huntingdon a			23 18										23 48								00 19			
Peterborough a			23 39										00 07								00 37			
Kentish Town a				22 23		22 33			22 38					22 53			23 13						23 30	
West Hampstead Thameslink a		22 21		22 29	22 29				22 44			22 51		23 02	22 59	23 06	23 17			23 21		23 29	23 34	
Elstree & Borehamwood a		22 35		22 43					22 58					23 16			23 31						23 49	
St Albans City a		22 45		22 53	22 41				23 08	22 54				23 26	23 15		23 41					23 46	23 58	
Harpenden a		22 51			22 48				23 15	23 01				23 33	23 22		23 48					23 52	00 06	
Luton Airport Parkway ■ ✈ a		22 57			22 53				23 20	23 06				23 38	23 27		23 53					23 57	00 11	
Luton ■ a		23 02			22 57				23 24	23 10				23 42	23 31		23 57					00 01	00 15	
Bedford a					23 22				23 45	23 35				00 03	23 55		00 18					00 26	00 40	

Table T052-F

Saturdays
26 May to 8 December

Brighton and Gatwick Airport - London, Stevenage, Cambridge, Luton and Bedford

	TL ■	TL	TL	TL	TL ■	TL ■	TL	TL	TL	TL	TL	TL ■	TL	TL ■ A	TL ■ B	TL ■	TL ■
Brighton ■ d	22 08					22 28						22 54				23 24	23 42
Horsham d					22 25									23 11	23 11		
Gatwick Airport ■ ✈ d	22 46				22 49	23 06						23 34		23 35	23 35	00 04	00 21
East Croydon d	23 01				23 15	23 21						23 54		00 10	00 10	00 23	00 40
Rainham Kt d				21 58													
Dartford d				22 45													
Abbey Wood d				22 58													
Woolwich Arsenal d				23 04													
Greenwich d				23 17													
Maidstone East d																	
Sevenoaks d			22 22						22 52				23 22				
Swanley d			22 41						23 11				23 41				
St Mary Cray d			22 45						23 15				23 45				
Orpington d								23 03									
Bromley South d			22 53					23 13	23 23				23 53				
Catford d			23 05					23 25	23 35				00 06				
Peckham Rye ■ 195 d			23 14					23 34	23 44				00 14				
Denmark Hill ■ 195 d			23 17					23 37	23 47				00 17				
Sutton ■ 179 d		22 48					22 49			23 18	23 19						
Wimbledon d							23 11				23 37						
Streatham ■ d		23 05					23 22			23 35	23 48						
Tulse Hill ■ d		23 10					23 27			23 40	23 53						
Herne Hill ■ 173,179 d		23 14					23 34			23 44	23 57						
Loughborough Jn 173,179 d		23 17					23 37			23 47							
Elephant & Castle ⊖173,179 d		23 21	23 24				23 41	23 44	23 55	23 54	00 04		00 24				
London Bridge d	23 16			23 28	23 31	23 35											
London Blackfriars a	23 21	23 26	23 29	23 34	23 36	23 41	23 46	23 49	23 59	00 01	00 08	00 19	00 29	00 36	00 36	00 49	01 06
London Blackfriars ■ ⊖ d	23 22	23 27		23 34	23 37	23 42	23 49			00 02	00 09	00 22		00 37	00 37	00 50	01 06
City Thameslink ■ d																	
Farringdon ■ ⊖ d	23 26	23 31		23 39	23 41	23 46	23 53			00 06	00 13	00 26		00 41	00 41		
St Pancras International d	23 31	23 36		23 43	23 46	23 51	23 58			00 11	00 18	00 31		00 46	00 46	01 01	01 16
Finsbury Park a	23 37				23 52									00 52	00 52		
Welwyn Garden City a														01 12	01 12		
Stevenage a	23 57				00 13									01 21	01 21		
Hitchin a	00 07				00 22									01 30	01 30		
Letchworth Garden City a	00 14																
Royston a	00 24																
Cambridge a	00 41																
Huntingdon a					00 51										01 59		
Peterborough a					01 10										02 17		
Kentish Town a		23 40					00 01				00 22					01 05	
West Hampstead Thameslink a		23 44		23 51		23 59	00 06			00 19	00 26	00 39				01 09	01 24
Elstree & Borehamwood a		23 59					00 21				00 41					01 24	
St Albans City a		00 09				00 16	00 31			00 35	00 51	00 56				01 34	01 40
Harpenden a		00 16				00 22	00 38			00 42	00 57	01 02				01 40	01 47
Luton Airport Parkway ■ ✈ a		00 21				00 27	00 43			00 47	01 02	01 07				01 45	01 52
Luton ■ a		00 25				00 31	00 47			00 51	01 06	01 11				01 49	01 56
Bedford a		00 50				00 56	01 08			01 18	01 32	01 37				02 15	02 21

A from 15 September
B until 8 September

Table T052-F

Sundays
20 May to 2 December

Brighton and Gatwick Airport - London, Stevenage, Cambridge, Luton and Bedford

	TL A	TL A	TL ■ B	TL C	TL ■ D	TL ■ E	TL ■ B	TL ■ B	TL ■	TL ■	TL	TL ■ F	TL ■	TL	TL ■	TL	TL	TL ■ F	TL ■	TL	TL ■	TL
Brighton ■ d									00 04				08 42						09 08			
Horsham d															08 48							
Gatwick Airport ■ ✈ d							00 04	00 21	00 42	08 46		08 49	09 19		09 11			09 19	09 49		09 46	
East Croydon d					00 10	00 10	00 23	00 40	01 10	09 07		09 18	09 34		09 37			09 48	10 04		10 07	
Rainham Kt d																08 30						09 00
Dartford d																09 15						09 45
Abbey Wood d																09 28						09 58
Woolwich Arsenal d																09 34						10 04
Greenwich d																09 47						10 17
Maidstone East d																						
Sevenoaks d											08 28						08 58					
Swanley d											08 47						09 17					
St Mary Cray d											08 51						09 21					
Orpington d																						
Bromley South d											08 59						09 29					
Catford d				00 06							09 11						09 41					
Peckham Rye ■ 195 d				00 14							09 20						09 50					
Denmark Hill ■ 195 d				00 17							09 23						09 53					
Sutton ■ 179 d														09 09						09 39		
Wimbledon d														09 27						09 57		
Streatham ■ d														09 37						10 07		
Tulse Hill ■ d														09 41						10 11		
Herne Hill ■ 173,179 d														09 45						10 15		
Loughborough Jn 173,179 d														09 48						10 18		
Elephant & Castle ⊖173,179 d		00 04		00 24							09 30			09 53			10 00			10 23		
London Bridge d										09 25		09 33	09 49		09 55	09 58		10 03	10 19		10 25	10 28
London Blackfriars a		00 08		00 29	00 36	00 36	00 49	01 06	01 36	09 30	09 34	09 38	09 54	09 57	10 00	10 04	10 04	10 08	10 24	10 27	10 30	10 34
London Blackfriars ■ ⊖ d	00 02	00 09	00 22		00 37	00 37	00 50	01 06	01 36	09 31		09 39	09 55	09 58	10 01	10 05		10 09	10 25	10 28	10 31	10 35
City Thameslink ■ d																						
Farringdon ■ ⊖ d	00 06	00 13	00 26		00 41	00 41				09 35		09 43	09 59	10 02	10 05	10 09		10 13	10 29	10 32	10 35	10 39
St Pancras International d	00 11	00 18	00 31		00 46	00 46	01 01	01 16	01 46	09 40		09 48	10 04	10 07	10 10	10 14		10 18	10 34	10 37	10 40	10 44
Finsbury Park a					00 52	00 52				09 46					10 16						10 45	
Welwyn Garden City a					01 12	01 12																
Stevenage a					01 21	01 21				10 06					10 36						11 06	
Hitchin a					01 30	01 30				10 12					10 42						11 12	
Letchworth Garden City a										10 18											11 18	
Royston a										10 29											11 29	
Cambridge a										10 48											11 48	
Huntingdon a						01 59									11 12							
Peterborough a						02 17									11 28							
Kentish Town a		00 22					01 05		01 50					10 11		10 18				10 41		10 48
West Hampstead Thameslink a	00 19	00 26	00 39				01 09	01 24	01 54				10 12	10 15				10 26	10 42	10 45		
Elstree & Borehamwood a		00 41					01 24		02 09					10 28						10 58		
St Albans City a	00 35	00 51	00 56				01 34	01 40	02 19			10 10	10 28	10 38				10 42	10 58	11 08		
Harpenden a	00 42	00 57	01 02				01 40	01 47	02 27			10 17	10 35	10 45				10 49	11 05	11 15		
Luton Airport Parkway ■ ✈ a	00 47	01 02	01 07				01 45	01 52	02 32			10 22	10 40	10 50				10 54	11 10	11 20		
Luton ■ a	00 51	01 06	01 11				01 49	01 56	02 36			10 26	10 44	10 54				10 58	11 14	11 24		
Bedford a	01 18	01 32	01 37				02 15	02 21	03 01			10 52	11 09					11 24	11 40			

A not 20 May. From Sutton (Surrey)
B not 20 May. From Brighton
C not 20 May. From Sevenoaks
D from 16 September. From Horsham
E from 27 May until 9 September. From Horsham
F From Three Bridges

Table T052-F

Sundays

20 May to 2 December

Brighton and Gatwick Airport - London, Stevenage, Cambridge, Luton and Bedford

		TL	TL ■ A	TL ■	TL	TL ■	TL	TL	TL ■		TL	TL ■	TL	TL ■	TL	TL	TL ■ A	TL	TL ■	TL		TL ■	TL	TL	TL ■
Brighton ■	d			09 42								10 08							10 42						
Horsham	d					09 48																10 48			
Gatwick Airport ■ ✈	d		09 49	10 19		10 11			10 19			10 49		10 46			10 49		11 19			11 11			11 19
East Croydon	d		10 18	10 34		10 37			10 48			11 04		11 07			11 18		11 34			11 37			11 48
Rainham Kt	d						09 30								10 00								10 30		
Dartford	d						10 15								10 46								11 15		
Abbey Wood	d						10 28								10 58								11 28		
Woolwich Arsenal	d						10 34								11 04								11 34		
Greenwich	d						10 47								11 17								11 47		
Maidstone East	d																								
Sevenoaks	d	09 28						09 58								10 28								10 58	
Swanley	d	09 47						10 17								10 47								11 17	
St Mary Cray	d	09 51						10 21								10 51								11 21	
Orpington	d																								
Bromley South	d	09 59						10 29								10 59								11 29	
Catford	d	10 11						10 41								11 11								11 41	
Peckham Rye ■	195 d	10 20						10 50								11 20								11 50	
Denmark Hill ■	195 d	10 23						10 53								11 23								11 53	
Sutton ■	179 d				10 09						10 40		10 39					11 10		11 09					
Wimbledon	d				10 27								10 57							11 27					
Streatham ■	d				10 37						10 55		11 07					11 25		11 37					
Tulse Hill ■	d				10 41						10 59		11 11					11 29		11 41					
Herne Hill ■	173,179 d				10 45						11 03		11 15					11 33		11 45					
Loughborough Jn	173,179 d				10 48						11 06		11 18					11 36		11 48					
Elephant & Castle ⊖	173,179 d	10 30			10 53			11 00			11 11		11 23			11 30		11 41		11 53				12 00	
London Bridge	d		10 33	10 49		10 55	10 58		11 03			11 19		11 25	11 28		11 33		11 49			11 55	11 58		12 03
London Blackfriars	a	10 34	10 38	10 54	10 57	11 00	11 04	11 04	11 08		11 15	11 24	11 27	11 30	11 34	11 34	11 38	11 45	11 54	11 57		12 00	12 04	12 04	12 08
London Blackfriars ■ ⊖	d		10 39	10 55	10 58	11 01	11 05		11 09			11 25	11 28	11 31	11 35		11 39		11 55	11 58		12 01	12 05		12 09
City Thameslink ■	d																								
Farringdon ■ ⊖	d		10 43	10 59	11 02	11 05	11 09		11 13			11 29	11 32	11 35	11 39		11 43		11 59	12 02		12 05	12 09		12 13
St Pancras International	d		10 48	11 04	11 07	11 10	11 14		11 18			11 34	11 37	11 40	11 44		11 48		12 04	12 07		12 10	12 14		12 18
Finsbury Park	a					11 16								11 45								12 16			
Welwyn Garden City	a																								
Stevenage	a					11 36								12 05								12 36			
Hitchin	a					11 42								12 11								12 42			
Letchworth Garden City	a													12 17											
Royston	a													12 29											
Cambridge	a													12 48											
Huntingdon	a					12 12																13 12			
Peterborough	a					12 28																13 28			
Kentish Town	a				11 11		11 18						11 41		11 48					12 11			12 18		
West Hampstead Thameslink	a		10 56	11 12	11 15				11 26			11 42	11 45				11 56		12 12	12 16					12 26
Elstree & Borehamwood	a				11 28								12 00							12 31					
St Albans City	a		11 12	11 28	11 38				11 42			11 58	12 10				12 14		12 28	12 42					12 38
Harpenden	a		11 19	11 35	11 45				11 49			12 05	12 17				12 21		12 34						12 45
Luton Airport Parkway ■ ✈	a		11 24	11 40	11 50				11 54			12 10	12 22				12 26		12 39						12 51
Luton ■	a		11 28	11 44	11 54				11 58			12 14	12 26				12 30		12 43						12 55
Bedford	a		11 54	12 09					12 24			12 39					12 55		13 10						13 20

A From Three Bridges

Table T052-F

Sundays

20 May to 2 December

Brighton and Gatwick Airport - London, Stevenage, Cambridge, Luton and Bedford

		TL	TL ■	TL	TL ■	TL	TL		TL ■ A	TL	TL ■	TL	TL ■	TL	TL	TL ■	TL	TL ■		TL	TL ■	TL	TL	TL ■ A	TL
Brighton ■	d		11 08								11 42							12 08							
Horsham	d												11 48												
Gatwick Airport ■ ✈	d		11 49		11 46				11 49		12 19		12 11			12 19		12 49			12 46			12 49	
East Croydon	d		12 04		12 07				12 18		12 34		12 37			12 48		13 04			13 07			13 18	
Rainham Kt	d					11 00								11 30								12 00			
Dartford	d					11 45								12 15								12 45			
Abbey Wood	d					11 58								12 28								12 58			
Woolwich Arsenal	d					12 04								12 34								13 04			
Greenwich	d					12 17								12 47								13 17			
Maidstone East	d																								
Sevenoaks	d						11 28								11 58								12 28		
Swanley	d						11 47								12 17								12 47		
St Mary Cray	d						11 51								12 21								12 51		
Orpington	d																								
Bromley South	d						11 59								12 29								12 59		
Catford	d						12 11								12 41								13 11		
Peckham Rye ■	195 d						12 20								12 50								13 20		
Denmark Hill ■	195 d						12 23								12 53								13 23		
Sutton ■	179 d	11 40		11 39						12 10		12 09					12 40			12 39					13 10
Wimbledon	d			11 57								12 27								12 57					
Streatham ■	d	11 55		12 07						12 25		12 37					12 55			13 07					13 25
Tulse Hill ■	d	11 59		12 11						12 29		12 41					12 59			13 11					13 29
Herne Hill ■	173,179 d	12 03		12 15						12 33		12 45					13 03			13 15					13 33
Loughborough Jn	173,179 d	12 06		12 18						12 36		12 48					13 06			13 18					13 36
Elephant & Castle ⊖	173,179 d	12 11		12 23			12 30			12 41		12 53			13 00		13 11			13 23			13 30		13 41
London Bridge	d		12 19		12 25	12 28			12 33		12 49		12 55	12 58		13 03		13 19			13 25	13 28		13 33	
London Blackfriars	a	12 15	12 24	12 27	12 30	12 34	12 34		12 38	12 45	12 54	12 57	13 00	13 04	13 04	13 08	13 15	13 24		13 27	13 30	13 34	13 34	13 38	13 45
London Blackfriars ■ ⊖	d	12 16	12 25	12 28	12 31	12 35			12 41	12 46	12 55	12 58	13 01	13 05		13 09	13 16	13 25		13 28	13 31	13 35		13 39	13 46
City Thameslink ■	d																								
Farringdon ■ ⊖	d	12 20	12 29	12 32	12 35	12 39			12 45	12 50	12 59	13 02	13 05	13 09		13 13	13 20	13 29		13 32	13 35	13 39		13 43	13 50
St Pancras International	d	12 25	12 34	12 37	12 40	12 44			12 50	12 55	13 04	13 07	13 10	13 14		13 18	13 25	13 34		13 37	13 40	13 44		13 48	13 55
Finsbury Park	a				12 45								13 16								13 45				
Welwyn Garden City	a																								
Stevenage	a				13 05								13 36								14 05				
Hitchin	a				13 11								13 42								14 11				
Letchworth Garden City	a				13 17																14 17				
Royston	a				13 29																14 29				
Cambridge	a				13 48																14 48				
Huntingdon	a												14 12												
Peterborough	a												14 28												
Kentish Town	a			12 41		12 48						13 11		13 18						13 41		13 48			
West Hampstead Thameslink	a	12 34	12 42	12 46					12 59	13 04	13 12	13 15				13 26	13 34	13 42		13 46				13 56	14 03
Elstree & Borehamwood	a	12 44		13 01						13 14		13 31					13 44			14 01					14 14
St Albans City	a	12 54	12 58	13 12					13 12	13 24	13 28	13 42				13 38	13 54	13 58		14 14				14 10	14 24
Harpenden	a	13 00	13 04						13 18	13 30	13 34					13 45	14 00	14 04						14 16	14 30
Luton Airport Parkway ■ ✈	a	13 05	13 09						13 23	13 35	13 39					13 51	14 05	14 09						14 21	14 35
Luton ■	a	13 10	13 13						13 27	13 40	13 43					13 55	14 10	14 13						14 25	14 40
Bedford	a		13 39						13 52		14 08					14 20		14 38						14 50	

A From Three Bridges

Table T052-F

Sundays

20 May to 2 December

Brighton and Gatwick Airport - London, Stevenage, Cambridge, Luton and Bedford

		TL ■	TL	TL ■	TL	TL	TL ■	TL	TL ■	TL	TL ■	TL	TL	TL ■ A	TL	TL ■	TL	TL ■	TL	TL	TL ■	TL	TL ■
Brighton 10	d	12 42							13 08							13 42							14 08
Horsham	d			12 48														13 48					
Gatwick Airport 10 ✈	d	13 19		13 11			13 19		13 49		13 46			13 49		14 19		14 11			14 19		14 49
East Croydon	d	13 34		13 37			13 48		14 04		14 07			14 18		14 34		14 37			14 48		15 04
Rainham Kt	d				12 30							13 00							13 30				
Dartford	d				13 15							13 45							14 15				
Abbey Wood	d				13 28							13 58							14 28				
Woolwich Arsenal	d				13 34							14 04							14 34				
Greenwich	d				13 47							14 17							14 47				
Maidstone East	d																						
Sevenoaks	d					12 58							13 28							13 58			
Swanley	d					13 17							13 47							14 17			
St Mary Cray	d					13 21							13 51							14 21			
Orpington	d																						
Bromley South	d					13 29							13 59							14 29			
Catford	d					13 41							14 11							14 41			
Peckham Rye 4 195	d					13 50							14 20							14 50			
Denmark Hill 4 195	d					13 53							14 23							14 53			
Sutton 4 179	d		13 09					13 40		13 39					14 10		14 09					14 40	
Wimbledon	d		13 27							13 57							14 27						
Streatham 4	d		13 37					13 55		14 07					14 25		14 37					14 55	
Tulse Hill 3	d		13 41					13 59		14 11					14 29		14 41					14 59	
Herne Hill 4 173,179	d		13 45					14 03		14 15					14 33		14 45					15 03	
Loughborough Jn 173,179	d		13 48					14 06		14 18					14 36		14 48					15 06	
Elephant & Castle ⊖173,179	d		13 53			14 00		14 11		14 23			14 30		14 41		14 53			15 00		15 11	
London Bridge	d	13 49		13 55	13 58		14 03		14 19		14 25	14 28		14 33		14 49		14 55	14 58		15 03		15 19
London Blackfriars	a	13 54	13 57	14 00	14 04	14 04	14 08	14 15	14 24	14 27	14 30	14 34	14 34	14 38	14 45	14 54	14 57	15 00	15 04	15 04	15 08	15 15	15 24
London Blackfriars 3 ⊖	d	13 55	13 58	14 01	14 05		14 09	14 16	14 25	14 28	14 31	14 35		14 39	14 46	14 55	14 58	15 01	15 05		15 09	15 16	15 25
City Thameslink 3	d																						
Farringdon 3 ⊖	d	13 59	14 02	14 05	14 09		14 13	14 20	14 29	14 32	14 35	14 39		14 43	14 50	14 59	15 02	15 05	15 09		15 13	15 20	15 29
St Pancras International	d	14 04	14 07	14 10	14 14		14 18	14 25	14 34	14 37	14 40	14 44		14 48	14 55	15 04	15 07	15 10	15 14		15 18	15 25	15 34
Finsbury Park	a			14 16							14 45							15 16					
Welwyn Garden City	a																						
Stevenage	a			14 36							15 05							15 36					
Hitchin	a			14 42							15 11							15 42					
Letchworth Garden City	a										15 17												
Royston	a										15 29												
Cambridge	a										15 48												
Huntingdon	a			15 12														16 12					
Peterborough	a			15 28														16 28					
Kentish Town	a		14 11		14 18					14 41		14 48					15 11		15 18				
West Hampstead Thameslink	a	14 12	14 16				14 26	14 34	14 42	14 46				14 56	15 03	15 12	15 16				15 26	15 34	15 42
Elstree & Borehamwood	a		14 31					14 44		15 01					15 14		15 31					15 44	
St Albans City	a	14 28	14 44				14 40	14 54	14 58	15 14				15 10	15 24	15 28	15 42				15 38	15 54	15 58
Harpenden	a	14 34					14 46	15 00	15 04					15 16	15 30	15 34					15 45	16 00	16 04
Luton Airport Parkway 7 ✈	a	14 39					14 51	15 05	15 09					15 21	15 35	15 39					15 51	16 05	16 09
Luton 10	a	14 43					14 55	15 10	15 13					15 25	15 40	15 43					15 55	16 10	16 13
Bedford	a	15 08					15 20		15 38					15 50		16 08					16 20		16 38

A From Three Bridges

Table T052-F

Sundays

20 May to 2 December

Brighton and Gatwick Airport - London, Stevenage, Cambridge, Luton and Bedford

		TL	TL ■	TL	TL	TL ■ A	TL	TL ■	TL	TL ■	TL	TL	TL ■	TL	TL ■	TL	TL ■	TL	TL	TL ■ A	TL	TL ■	TL
Brighton 10	d							14 42							15 08							15 42	
Horsham	d									14 48													
Gatwick Airport 10 ✈	d		14 46			14 49		15 19		15 11			15 19		15 49		15 46			15 49		16 19	
East Croydon	d		15 07			15 18		15 34		15 37			15 48		16 04		16 07			16 18		16 34	
Rainham Kt	d			14 00							14 30							15 00					
Dartford	d			14 45							15 15							15 45					
Abbey Wood	d			14 58							15 28							15 58					
Woolwich Arsenal	d			15 04							15 34							16 04					
Greenwich	d			15 17							15 47							16 17					
Maidstone East	d																						
Sevenoaks	d				14 28							14 58							15 28				
Swanley	d				14 47							15 17							15 47				
St Mary Cray	d				14 51							15 21							15 51				
Orpington	d																						
Bromley South	d				14 59							15 29							15 59				
Catford	d				15 11							15 41							16 11				
Peckham Rye 4 195	d				15 20							15 50							16 20				
Denmark Hill 4 195	d				15 23							15 53							16 23				
Sutton 4 179	d	14 39					15 10		15 09					15 40		15 39					16 10		16 09
Wimbledon	d	14 57							15 27							15 57							16 27
Streatham 4	d	15 07					15 25		15 37					15 55		16 07					16 25		16 37
Tulse Hill 3	d	15 11					15 29		15 41					15 59		16 11					16 29		16 41
Herne Hill 4 173,179	d	15 15					15 33		15 45					16 03		16 15					16 33		16 45
Loughborough Jn 173,179	d	15 18					15 36		15 48					16 06		16 18					16 36		16 48
Elephant & Castle ⊖173,179	d	15 23			15 30		15 41		15 53			16 00		16 11		16 23			16 30		16 41		16 53
London Bridge	d		15 25	15 28		15 33		15 49		15 55	15 58		16 03		16 19		16 25	16 28		16 33		16 49	
London Blackfriars	a	15 27	15 30	15 34	15 34	15 38	15 45	15 54	15 57	16 00	16 04	16 04	16 08	16 15	16 24	16 27	16 30	16 34	16 34	16 38	16 45	16 54	16 57
London Blackfriars 3 ⊖	d	15 28	15 31	15 35		15 39	15 46	15 55	15 58	16 01	16 05		16 09	16 16	16 25	16 28	16 31	16 35		16 39	16 46	16 55	16 58
City Thameslink 3	d																						
Farringdon 3 ⊖	d	15 32	15 35	15 39		15 43	15 50	15 59	16 02	16 05	16 09		16 13	16 20	16 29	16 32	16 35	16 39		16 43	16 50	16 59	17 02
St Pancras International	d	15 37	15 40	15 44		15 48	15 55	16 04	16 07	16 10	16 14		16 18	16 25	16 34	16 37	16 40	16 44		16 48	16 55	17 04	17 07
Finsbury Park	a		15 45							16 16							16 45						
Welwyn Garden City	a																						
Stevenage	a		16 05							16 36							17 05						
Hitchin	a		16 11							16 42							17 11						
Letchworth Garden City	a		16 17														17 17						
Royston	a		16 29														17 29						
Cambridge	a		16 48														17 48						
Huntingdon	a									17 12													
Peterborough	a									17 29													
Kentish Town	a	15 41		15 48					16 11		16 18					16 41		16 48					17 11
West Hampstead Thameslink	a	15 46				15 56	16 03	16 12	16 16				16 26	16 34	16 42	16 46				16 56	17 03	17 12	17 16
Elstree & Borehamwood	a	16 01					16 14		16 31					16 44		17 01					17 14		17 31
St Albans City	a	16 14				16 10	16 24	16 28	16 42				16 38	16 54	16 58	17 12				17 08	17 24	17 28	17 44
Harpenden	a					16 16	16 30	16 34					16 45	17 00	17 04					17 15	17 30	17 34	
Luton Airport Parkway 7 ✈	a					16 21	16 35	16 39					16 51	17 05	17 09					17 21	17 35	17 39	
Luton 10	a					16 25	16 40	16 43					16 55	17 10	17 13					17 25	17 40	17 43	
Bedford	a					16 50		17 08					17 20		17 38					17 50		18 08	

A From Three Bridges

Table T052-F

Sundays
20 May to 2 December

Brighton and Gatwick Airport - London, Stevenage, Cambridge, Luton and Bedford

		TL ■	TL	TL	TL ■	TL	TL ■	TL	TL ■	TL	TL	TL ■ A	TL	TL ■	TL	TL ■	TL	TL	TL ■	TL	TL ■	TL
Brighton	d						16 08							16 42							17 08	
Horsham	d	15 48														16 48						
Gatwick Airport	d	16 11			16 19		16 49		16 46			16 49		17 19		17 11			17 19		17 49	
East Croydon	d	16 37			16 48		17 04		17 07			17 18		17 34		17 37			17 48		18 04	
Rainham Kt	d		15 30							16 00							16 30					
Dartford	d		16 15							16 45							17 15					
Abbey Wood	d		16 28							16 58							17 28					
Woolwich Arsenal	d		16 34							17 04							17 34					
Greenwich	d		16 47							17 17							17 47					
Maidstone East	d																					
Sevenoaks	d			15 58							16 28							16 58				
Swanley	d			16 17							16 47							17 17				
St Mary Cray	d			16 21							16 51							17 21				
Orpington	d																					
Bromley South	d			16 29							16 59							17 29				
Catford	d			16 41							17 11							17 41				
Peckham Rye 195	d			16 50							17 20							17 50				
Denmark Hill 195	d			16 53							17 23							17 53				
Sutton 179	d					16 40		16 39					17 10		17 09					17 40		17 39
Wimbledon	d							16 57							17 27							17 57
Streatham	d					16 55		17 07					17 25		17 37					17 55		18 07
Tulse Hill	d					16 59		17 11					17 29		17 41					17 59		18 11
Herne Hill 173,179	d					17 03		17 15					17 33		17 45					18 03		18 15
Loughborough Jn 173,179	d					17 06		17 18					17 36		17 48					18 06		18 18
Elephant & Castle ⊖173,179	d			17 00		17 11		17 23			17 30		17 41		17 53			18 00		18 11		18 23
London Bridge	d	16 55	16 58		17 03		17 19		17 25	17 28		17 33		17 49		17 55	17 58		18 03		18 19	
London Blackfriars	a	17 00	17 04	17 04	17 08	17 15	17 24	17 27	17 30	17 34	17 34	17 38	17 45	17 54	17 57	18 00	18 04	18 04	18 08	18 15	18 24	18 27
London Blackfriars ⊖	d	17 01	17 05		17 09	17 16	17 25	17 28	17 31	17 35		17 39	17 46	17 55	17 58	18 01	18 05		18 09	18 16	18 25	18 28
City Thameslink	d																					
Farringdon ⊖	d	17 05	17 09		17 13	17 20	17 29	17 32	17 35	17 39		17 43	17 50	17 59	18 02	18 05	18 09		18 13	18 20	18 29	18 32
St Pancras International	d	17 10	17 14		17 18	17 25	17 34	17 37	17 40	17 44		17 48	17 55	18 04	18 07	18 10	18 14		18 18	18 25	18 34	18 37
Finsbury Park	a	17 16							17 45							18 16						
Welwyn Garden City	a																					
Stevenage	a	17 36							18 05							18 36						
Hitchin	a	17 42							18 11							18 42						
Letchworth Garden City	a								18 17													
Royston	a								18 29													
Cambridge	a								18 48													
Huntingdon	a	18 12														19 12						
Peterborough	a	18 29														19 29						
Kentish Town	a		17 18					17 41		17 48					18 11		18 18					18 41
West Hampstead Thameslink	a				17 26	17 34	17 42	17 46				17 56	18 03	18 12	18 16				18 26	18 34	18 42	18 46
Elstree & Borehamwood	a					17 44		18 01					18 14		18 31					18 44		19 01
St Albans City	a				17 40	17 54	17 58	18 12				18 08	18 24	18 28	18 42				18 38	18 54	18 58	19 12
Harpenden	a				17 46	18 00	18 04					18 15	18 30	18 34					18 45	19 00	19 04	
Luton Airport Parkway ✈	a				17 51	18 05	18 09					18 21	18 35	18 39					18 51	19 05	19 09	
Luton	a				17 55	18 10	18 13					18 25	18 40	18 43					18 55	19 10	19 13	
Bedford	a				18 20		18 38					18 50		19 08					19 20		19 38	

A From Three Bridges

Table T052-F

Sundays
20 May to 2 December

Brighton and Gatwick Airport - London, Stevenage, Cambridge, Luton and Bedford

		TL ■	TL	TL	TL ■ A	TL	TL ■	TL	TL ■	TL	TL	TL ■	TL	TL ■	TL	TL ■	TL	TL	TL ■ A	TL	TL ■	TL	TL ■
Brighton	d						17 42							18 08							18 42		
Horsham	d								17 48														18 48
Gatwick Airport	d	17 46			17 49		18 19		18 11			18 19		18 49		18 46			18 49		19 19		19 11
East Croydon	d	18 07			18 18		18 34		18 37			18 48		19 04		19 07			19 18		19 34		19 37
Rainham Kt	d		17 00							17 30							18 00						
Dartford	d		17 45							18 15							18 45						
Abbey Wood	d		17 58							18 28							18 58						
Woolwich Arsenal	d		18 04							18 34							19 04						
Greenwich	d		18 17							18 47							19 17						
Maidstone East	d																						
Sevenoaks	d			17 28							17 58							18 28					
Swanley	d			17 47							18 17							18 47					
St Mary Cray	d			17 51							18 21							18 51					
Orpington	d																						
Bromley South	d			17 59							18 29							18 59					
Catford	d			18 11							18 41							19 11					
Peckham Rye 195	d			18 20							18 50							19 20					
Denmark Hill 195	d			18 23							18 53							19 23					
Sutton 179	d					18 10		18 09					18 40		18 39					19 10		19 09	
Wimbledon	d							18 27							18 57							19 27	
Streatham	d					18 25		18 37					18 55		19 07					19 25		19 37	
Tulse Hill	d					18 29		18 41					18 59		19 11					19 29		19 41	
Herne Hill 173,179	d					18 33		18 45					19 03		19 15					19 33		19 45	
Loughborough Jn 173,179	d					18 36		18 48					19 06		19 18					19 36		19 48	
Elephant & Castle ⊖173,179	d			18 30		18 41		18 53			19 00		19 11		19 23			19 30		19 41		19 53	
London Bridge	d	18 25	18 28		18 33		18 49		18 55	18 58		19 03		19 19		19 25	19 28		19 33		19 49		19 55
London Blackfriars	a	18 30	18 34	18 34	18 38	18 45	18 54	18 57	19 00	19 04	19 04	19 08	19 15	19 24	19 27	19 30	19 34	19 34	19 38	19 45	19 54	19 57	20 00
London Blackfriars ⊖	d	18 31	18 35		18 39	18 46	18 55	18 58	19 01	19 05		19 09	19 16	19 25	19 28	19 31	19 35		19 39	19 46	19 55	19 58	20 01
City Thameslink	d																						
Farringdon ⊖	d	18 35	18 39		18 43	18 50	18 59	19 02	19 05	19 09		19 13	19 20	19 29	19 32	19 35	19 39		19 43	19 50	19 59	20 02	20 05
St Pancras International	d	18 40	18 44		18 48	18 55	19 04	19 07	19 10	19 14		19 18	19 25	19 34	19 37	19 40	19 44		19 48	19 55	20 04	20 07	20 10
Finsbury Park	a	18 45							19 16							19 45							20 16
Welwyn Garden City	a																						
Stevenage	a	19 05							19 36							20 05							20 36
Hitchin	a	19 11							19 42							20 11							20 42
Letchworth Garden City	a	19 17														20 17							
Royston	a	19 29														20 29							
Cambridge	a	19 48														20 48							
Huntingdon	a								20 12														21 12
Peterborough	a								20 29														21 29
Kentish Town	a		18 48					19 11		19 18					19 41		19 48					20 11	
West Hampstead Thameslink	a				18 56	19 04	19 12	19 16				19 26	19 34	19 42	19 46				19 56	20 03	20 12	20 16	
Elstree & Borehamwood	a					19 14		19 31					19 44		20 01					20 14		20 31	
St Albans City	a				19 08	19 24	19 28	19 44				19 40	19 54	19 58	20 12				20 08	20 24	20 28	20 42	
Harpenden	a				19 15	19 30	19 34					19 46	20 00	20 04					20 15	20 30	20 34		
Luton Airport Parkway ✈	a				19 21	19 35	19 39					19 51	20 05	20 09					20 21	20 35	20 39		
Luton	a				19 25	19 40	19 43					19 55	20 10	20 13					20 25	20 40	20 43		
Bedford	a				19 51		20 09					20 20		20 38					20 50		21 08		

A From Three Bridges

Table T052-F

Sundays
20 May to 2 December

Brighton and Gatwick Airport - London, Stevenage, Cambridge, Luton and Bedford

		TL	TL	TL ■	TL	TL ■	TL	TL ■	TL	TL	TL ■ A	TL	TL ■	TL	TL ■	TL	TL	TL ■	TL	TL ■	TL	TL ■	TL
Brighton 10	d					19 08							19 42							20 08			
Horsham	d														19 48								
Gatwick Airport 10 ✈	d			19 19		19 49		19 46			19 49		20 19		20 11			20 19		20 49		20 46	
East Croydon	d			19 48		20 04		20 07			20 18		20 34		20 37			20 48		21 04		21 07	
Rainham Kt	d	18 30							19 00							19 30							20 00
Dartford	d	19 15							19 45							20 15							20 45
Abbey Wood	d	19 28							19 58							20 28							20 58
Woolwich Arsenal	d	19 34							20 04							20 34							21 04
Greenwich	d	19 47							20 17							20 47							21 17
Maidstone East	d																						
Sevenoaks	d		18 58							19 28							19 58						
Swanley	d		19 17							19 47							20 17						
St Mary Cray	d		19 21							19 51							20 21						
Orpington	d																						
Bromley South	d		19 29							19 59							20 29						
Catford	d		19 41							20 11							20 41						
Peckham Rye 4 195	d		19 50							20 20							20 50						
Denmark Hill 4 195	d		19 53							20 23							20 53						
Sutton 4 179	d				19 40		19 39					20 10		20 09					20 40		20 39		
Wimbledon	d						19 57							20 27							20 57		
Streatham 4	d				19 55		20 07					20 25		20 37					20 55		21 07		
Tulse Hill 3	d				19 59		20 11					20 29		20 41					20 59		21 11		
Herne Hill 4 173,179	d				20 03		20 15					20 33		20 45					21 03		21 15		
Loughborough Jn 173,179	d				20 06		20 18					20 36		20 48					21 06		21 18		
Elephant & Castle ⊖173,179	d		20 00		20 11		20 23			20 30		20 41		20 53			21 00		21 11		21 23		
London Bridge	d	19 58		20 03		20 19		20 25	20 28		20 33		20 49		20 55	20 58		21 03		21 19		21 25	21 28
London Blackfriars	a	20 04	20 04	20 08	20 15	20 24	20 27	20 30	20 34	20 34	20 38	20 45	20 54	20 57	21 00	21 04	21 04	21 08	21 15	21 24	21 27	21 30	21 34
London Blackfriars 3 ⊖	d	20 05		20 09	20 16	20 25	20 28	20 31	20 35		20 39	20 46	20 55	20 58	21 01	21 05		21 09	21 16	21 25	21 28	21 31	21 35
City Thameslink 3	d																						
Farringdon 3 ⊖	d	20 09		20 13	20 20	20 29	20 32	20 35	20 39		20 43	20 50	20 59	21 02	21 05	21 09		21 13	21 20	21 29	21 32	21 35	21 39
St Pancras International	d	20 14		20 18	20 25	20 34	20 37	20 40	20 44		20 48	20 55	21 04	21 07	21 10	21 14		21 18	21 25	21 34	21 37	21 40	21 44
Finsbury Park	a							20 45							21 16							21 45	
Welwyn Garden City	a																						
Stevenage	a							21 05							21 36							22 05	
Hitchin	a							21 11							21 42							22 11	
Letchworth Garden City	a							21 17														22 17	
Royston	a							21 29														22 29	
Cambridge	a							21 45														22 48	
Huntingdon	a														22 12								
Peterborough	a														22 29								
Kentish Town	a	20 18					20 41		20 48					21 11		21 18					21 41		21 48
West Hampstead Thameslink	a			20 26	20 33	20 42	20 46				20 56	21 04	21 12	21 16				21 26	21 34	21 42	21 46		
Elstree & Borehamwood	a				20 44		21 01					21 14		21 31					21 44		22 01		
St Albans City	a			20 38	20 54	20 58	21 12				21 08	21 24	21 28	21 42				21 38	21 54	21 58	22 12		
Harpenden	a			20 45	21 00	21 04					21 15	21 30	21 34					21 46	22 00	22 04			
Luton Airport Parkway 7 ✈	a			20 51	21 05	21 09					21 21	21 35	21 39					21 51	22 05	22 09			
Luton 10	a			20 55	21 10	21 13					21 25	21 40	21 43					21 55	22 10	22 13			
Bedford	a			21 20		21 38					21 50		22 08					22 20		22 38			

A From Three Bridges

Table T052-F

Sundays
20 May to 2 December

Brighton and Gatwick Airport - London, Stevenage, Cambridge, Luton and Bedford

		TL	TL ■ A	TL	TL ■	TL	TL ■	TL	TL	TL ■	TL	TL ■	TL ■	TL	TL	TL	TL ■	TL	TL	TL	TL ■	TL	TL ■
Brighton 10	d				20 42							21 08					21 42						22 08
Horsham	d						20 48														21 48		
Gatwick Airport 10 ✈	d		20 49		21 19		21 11			21 19		21 49	21 46				22 19				22 11		22 49
East Croydon	d		21 18		21 34		21 37			21 48		22 04	22 07				22 34				22 47		23 04
Rainham Kt	d							20 30						21 00					21 30				
Dartford	d							21 15						21 45					22 15				
Abbey Wood	d							21 28						21 58					22 28				
Woolwich Arsenal	d							21 34						22 04					22 34				
Greenwich	d							21 47						22 17					22 47				
Maidstone East	d																						
Sevenoaks	d	20 28							20 58						21 28					21 58			
Swanley	d	20 47							21 17						21 47					22 17			
St Mary Cray	d	20 51							21 21						21 51					22 21			
Orpington	d																						
Bromley South	d	20 59							21 29						21 59					22 29			
Catford	d	21 11							21 41						22 11					22 41			
Peckham Rye 4 195	d	21 20							21 50						22 20					22 50			
Denmark Hill 4 195	d	21 23							21 53						22 23					22 53			
Sutton 4 179	d			21 10		21 09					21 40					22 10		22 09				22 40	
Wimbledon	d					21 27												22 27					
Streatham 4	d			21 25		21 37					21 55					22 25		22 37				22 55	
Tulse Hill 3	d			21 29		21 41					21 59					22 29		22 41				22 59	
Herne Hill 4 173,179	d			21 33		21 45					22 03					22 33		22 45				23 03	
Loughborough Jn 173,179	d			21 36		21 48					22 06					22 36		22 48				23 06	
Elephant & Castle ⊖173,179	d	21 30		21 41		21 53			22 00		22 11				22 30	22 41		22 53		23 00		23 11	
London Bridge	d		21 33		21 49		21 55	21 58		22 03		22 19	22 25	22 28			22 49		22 58		23 05		23 19
London Blackfriars	a	21 34	21 38	21 45	21 54	21 57	22 00	22 04	22 04	22 08	22 15	22 24	22 30	22 34	22 34	22 45	22 54	22 57	23 04	23 04	23 10	23 15	23 24
London Blackfriars 3 ⊖	d		21 39	21 46	21 55	21 58	22 01	22 05		22 09	22 16	22 25	22 31	22 35			22 55	22 58	23 05		23 12	23 16	23 27
City Thameslink 3	d																						
Farringdon 3 ⊖	d		21 43	21 50	21 59	22 02	22 05	22 09		22 13	22 20	22 29	22 35	22 39			22 59	23 02	23 09		23 16	23 20	23 31
St Pancras International	d		21 48	21 55	22 04	22 07	22 10	22 14		22 18	22 25	22 34	22 40	22 44			23 04	23 07	23 14		23 21	23 25	23 36
Finsbury Park	a						22 16						22 45								23 27		
Welwyn Garden City	a																						
Stevenage	a						22 36						23 05								23 47		
Hitchin	a						22 42						23 11								23 53		
Letchworth Garden City	a												23 17										
Royston	a												23 29										
Cambridge	a												23 45										
Huntingdon	a						23 15														00 22		
Peterborough	a						23 30														00 41		
Kentish Town	a					22 11		22 18						22 48				23 11	23 18			23 29	
West Hampstead Thameslink	a		21 56	22 04	22 12	22 15				22 26	22 33	22 42					23 12	23 15	23 22			23 33	23 44
Elstree & Borehamwood	a			22 14		22 30												23 30				23 48	
St Albans City	a		22 08	22 24	22 28	22 40				22 38		22 58					23 28	23 40				23 58	00 02
Harpenden	a		22 15	22 30	22 34	22 49				22 45		23 04					23 35	23 47				00 05	00 09
Luton Airport Parkway 7 ✈	a		22 21	22 35	22 39	22 55				22 51		23 09					23 40	23 52				00 10	00 14
Luton 10	a		22 25	22 40	22 43	22 59				22 55		23 13					23 44	23 56				00 14	00 18
Bedford	a		22 50		23 08	23 24				23 20		23 38					00 09	00 21				00 35	00 43

A From Three Bridges

Table T052-F

Sundays
20 May to 2 December

Brighton and Gatwick Airport - London, Stevenage, Cambridge, Luton and Bedford

		TL	TL	TL 1	TL 1	TL 1
Brighton 10	d			22 42	23 08	23 42
Horsham	d					
Gatwick Airport 10 ✈	d			23 21	23 51	00 21
East Croydon	d			23 40	00 10	00 40
Rainham Kt	d	22 00				
Dartford	d	22 45				
Abbey Wood	d	22 58				
Woolwich Arsenal	d	23 04				
Greenwich	d	23 17				
Maidstone East	d					
Sevenoaks	d		22 28			
Swanley	d		22 47			
St Mary Cray	d		22 51			
Orpington	d					
Bromley South	d		22 59			
Catford	d		23 11			
Peckham Rye 4 195	d		23 20			
Denmark Hill 4 195	d		23 23			
Sutton 4 179	d					
Wimbledon	d					
Streatham 4	d					
Tulse Hill 3	d					
Herne Hill 4 173,179	d					
Loughborough Jn 173,179	d					
Elephant & Castle ⊖ 173,179	d		23 30			
London Bridge	d	23 28				
London Blackfriars	a	23 34	23 34	00 06	00 36	01 06
London Blackfriars 3 ⊖	d	23 37		00 06	00 36	01 06
City Thameslink 3	d					
Farringdon 3 ⊖	d	23 41		00 11		
St Pancras International	d	23 46		00 16	00 46	01 16
Finsbury Park	a					
Welwyn Garden City	a					
Stevenage	a					
Hitchin	a					
Letchworth Garden City	a					
Royston	a					
Cambridge	a					
Huntingdon	a					
Peterborough	a					
Kentish Town	a	23 50		00 20	00 50	
West Hampstead Thameslink	a	23 54		00 24	00 54	01 24
Elstree & Borehamwood	a	00 09		00 39	01 09	
St Albans City	a	00 19		00 49	01 19	01 40
Harpenden	a	00 27		00 57	01 27	01 47
Luton Airport Parkway 7 ✈	a	00 32		01 02	01 32	01 52
Luton 10	a	00 36		01 06	01 36	01 56
Bedford	a	01 01		01 31	02 01	02 21

Table T052-R

Mondays to Fridays
21 May to 7 December

Bedford, Luton, Cambridge, Stevenage and London - Gatwick Airport and Brighton

		TL MO 1 A	TL MX 1 A	TL 1 B	TL MO 1 A	TL MX 1 A	TL 1 C	TL 1 C	TL 1 C	TL 1 C	TL 1	TL 1	TL	TL 1	TL	TL	TL	TL 1	TL	TL 1 D	TL	TL E	TL
Bedford	d						00 15	01 15	01 53	02 15	02 53	03 10		03 45				04 13					
Luton 10	d				00 10	00 10	00 40	01 40	02 18	02 40	03 18	03 35		04 10		04 20		04 38					
Luton Airport Parkway 7 ✈	d				00 13	00 13	00 43	01 43	02 21	02 43	03 21	03 38		04 13		04 23		04 41					
Harpenden	d				00 18	00 18	00 48	01 48	02 26	02 48	03 26	03 43		04 18		04 28		04 46					
St Albans City	d				00 25	00 25	00 55	01 55	02 33	02 55	03 33	03 50		04 25		04 35		04 53					
Elstree & Borehamwood	d						01 04	02 04		03 04		03 59				04 44							
West Hampstead Thameslink	d			00 09	00 41	00 42	01 20	02 20	02 50	03 20	03 50	04 15		04 41		04 59		05 09	05 16		05 22		
Kentish Town	d			00 13			01 24	02 24		03 24		04 19				05 04			05 21				
Peterborough	d																						
Huntingdon	d																						
Cambridge	d																						
Royston	d																						
Letchworth Garden City	d																						
Hitchin	d																						
Stevenage	d																						
Welwyn Garden City	d																						
Finsbury Park	d																						
St Pancras International	d			00 21	00 51	00 52	01 32	02 32	03 02	03 32	04 02	04 32		04 51		05 12		05 20	05 27		05 32		
Farringdon 3 ⊖	d			00 26										04 56		05 17		05 24	05 32		05 37		
City Thameslink 3	d													04 58		05 19		05 26	05 34		05 39		
London Blackfriars	a			00 30	01 00	01 01	01 39	02 39	03 09	03 39	04 09	04 39		05 00		05 21		05 28	05 36		05 41		
London Blackfriars 3 ⊖	d	00 01	00 01	00 31	01 01	01 02	01 40	02 40	03 10	03 40	04 10	04 40	04 56	05 01	05 16	05 21	05 26	05 29	05 36		05 41		05 46
London Bridge	d																	05 35		05 37	05 48	05 55	
Elephant & Castle ⊖ 173,179	a												04 59		05 19	05 25	05 29		05 40				05 49
Loughborough Jn 173,179	a															05 30			05 45				
Herne Hill 4 173,179	a															05 34			05 49				
Tulse Hill 3	a															05 39			05 54				
Streatham 4	a															05 44			05 59				
Wimbledon	a															05 54							
Sutton 4 179	a															06 14			06 17			06 28	
Denmark Hill 4 195	a												05 07		05 27		05 37						05 57
Peckham Rye 4 195	a												05 10		05 30		05 40						06 00
Catford	a												05 19		05 39		05 49						06 09
Bromley South	a												05 32		05 52		06 02						06 22
Orpington	a												05 44				06 14						
St Mary Cray	a														06 01								06 31
Swanley	a														06 05								06 35
Sevenoaks	a														06 25								06 55
Maidstone East	a																						
Greenwich	a																				05 57		
Woolwich Arsenal	a																				06 10		
Abbey Wood	a																				06 16		
Dartford	a																				06 27		
Rainham Kt	a																				07 11		
East Croydon	a	00 27	00 27	00 57	01 27	01 28	02 06	03 06	03 36	04 06	04 36	05 06		05 27				05 48		05 54			
Gatwick Airport 10 ✈	a	00 47	00 48	01 20	01 56	01 56	02 30	03 30	03 56	04 30	04 57	05 31		05 47				06 04					
Horsham	a																						
Brighton 10	a	01 24	01 24		02 28	02 28					05 32	06 10		06 26				06 42					

A From Bedford
B From Bedford to Three Bridges
C To Three Bridges
D To East Grinstead
E To Guildford

Table T052-R

Mondays to Fridays
21 May to 7 December

Bedford, Luton, Cambridge, Stevenage and London - Gatwick Airport and Brighton

Station		TL	TL ■	TL	TL ■	TL ■ A	TL	TL ■	TL	TL	TL	TL ■	TL	TL ■	TL ■ A	TL	TL	TL ■	TL B	TL	TL	TL ■	TL
Bedford	d				04 43									05 15	05 25			05 44					
Luton ■	d	04 50			05 08						05 20			05 40	05 48	05 36		06 02					06 00
Luton Airport Parkway ■ ✈	d	04 53			05 11						05 23			05 43	05 51	05 39							06 03
Harpenden	d	04 58			05 16						05 28			05 48	05 56	05 44		06 08					06 09
St Albans City	d	05 05			05 23						05 35			05 55	06 01	05 51		06 13			06 07		06 15
Elstree & Borehamwood	d	05 14									05 44					06 00					06 16		06 24
West Hampstead Thameslink	d	05 31		05 36	05 39	05 43			05 52		05 59		06 06	06 09		06 17	06 21				06 32		06 36
Kentish Town	d	05 36		05 41			05 51				06 04		06 11			06 21					06 36		
Peterborough	d		04 20									04 54										05 24	
Huntingdon	d		04 35									05 11										05 41	
Cambridge	d							04 54															
Royston	d							05 09															
Letchworth Garden City	d							05 21															
Hitchin	d		05 07					05 26				05 41										06 11	
Stevenage	d		05 13					05 32				05 47										06 17	
Welwyn Garden City	d		05 22																				
Finsbury Park	d		05 37					05 52				06 08										06 38	
St Pancras International	d	05 42	05 45	05 47	05 50	05 55	05 57	06 00	06 02		06 12	06 15	06 17	06 20	06 25	06 27	06 32	06 35			06 42	06 45	06 47
Farringdon ■ ⊖	d	05 47	05 49	05 52	05 54	05 59	06 02	06 04	06 07		06 17	06 19	06 22	06 24	06 29	06 32	06 37	06 39			06 47	06 49	06 52
City Thameslink ■	d	05 49	05 51	05 54	05 56	06 01	06 04	06 06	06 09		06 19	06 21	06 24	06 26	06 31	06 34	06 39	06 41			06 49	06 51	06 54
London Blackfriars	a	05 51	05 53	05 56	05 58	06 03	06 06	06 08	06 11		06 21	06 23	06 26	06 28	06 33	06 36	06 41	06 43			06 51	06 53	06 56
London Blackfriars ■ ⊖	d	05 51	05 54	05 56	05 59	06 04	06 06	06 09	06 11	06 16	06 21	06 24	06 26	06 29	06 34	06 36	06 41	06 44		06 46	06 51	06 54	06 56
London Bridge	d		06 00		06 05	06 11		06 15	06 18			06 30		06 35	06 41		06 48	06 51	06 55			07 00	
Elephant & Castle ⊖173,179	a	05 55		06 00			06 10			06 19	06 25		06 30			06 40				06 49	06 55		07 00
Loughborough Jn 173,179	a	06 00					06 15				06 30					06 45					07 00		
Herne Hill ■ 173,179	a	06 04					06 19				06 34					06 49					07 04		
Tulse Hill ■	a	06 09					06 24				06 39					06 54					07 09		
Streatham ■	a	06 14					06 29				06 44					06 59					07 14		
Wimbledon	a	06 24									06 54										07 24		
Sutton ■ 179	a	06 44					06 47				07 14					07 17			07 28		07 44		
Denmark Hill ■ 195	a			06 07						06 27			06 37							06 57			07 07
Peckham Rye ■ 195	a			06 10						06 30			06 40							07 00			07 10
Catford	a			06 19						06 39			06 49							07 09			07 19
Bromley South	a			06 32						06 52			07 02							07 22			07 32
Orpington	a			06 44									07 14										07 45
St Mary Cray	a									07 01										07 32			
Swanley	a									07 05										07 36			
Sevenoaks	a									07 25										07 56			
Maidstone East	a																						
Greenwich	a								06 27								06 57						
Woolwich Arsenal	a								06 40								07 10						
Abbey Wood	a								06 46								07 16						
Dartford	a								06 57								07 29						
Rainham Kt	a								07 42								08 21						
East Croydon 🚋	a		06 16		06 18	06 24		06 28				06 46		06 48	06 54			07 06				07 16	
Gatwick Airport ■ ✈	a		06 50		06 34			06 44				07 19		07 04				07 28				07 46	
Horsham	a		07 13									07 45										08 11	
Brighton ■	a				07 14			07 22						07 44									

A To East Grinstead
B To Epsom

Table T052-R

Mondays to Fridays
21 May to 7 December

Bedford, Luton, Cambridge, Stevenage and London - Gatwick Airport and Brighton

Station		TL ■	TL ■ A	TL	TL ■	TL	TL	TL ■	TL	TL ■	TL	TL ■	TL ■ A	TL	TL	TL B	TL	TL ■	TL	TL ■	TL	TL ■	TL ■ A
Bedford	d	05 48	06 04			06 01		06 22				06 18	06 34		06 31			06 52				06 48	07 04
Luton ■	d	06 12	06 22			06 25		06 39			06 30	06 42	06 52		06 55			07 09			07 00	07 12	07 22
Luton Airport Parkway ■ ✈	d	06 15				06 28					06 33	06 45			06 58						07 03	07 15	
Harpenden	d	06 21	06 28			06 33					06 39	06 51	06 58		07 04						07 09	07 21	07 28
St Albans City	d	06 27	06 33	06 21		06 38		06 48	06 34		06 45	06 57	07 03	06 52	07 10			07 18	07 07		07 15	07 27	07 33
Elstree & Borehamwood	d			06 30					06 43		06 54			07 01					07 16		07 24		
West Hampstead Thameslink	d	06 39		06 47					07 02		07 06	07 09		07 17					07 32		07 36		
Kentish Town	d			06 51					07 06					07 21					07 36				
Peterborough	d									05 54										06 24			
Huntingdon	d									06 11										06 41			
Cambridge	d				05 54																		
Royston	d				06 09																		
Letchworth Garden City	d				06 21																		
Hitchin	d				06 26					06 41										07 11			
Stevenage	d				06 32					06 47										07 17			
Welwyn Garden City	d																						
Finsbury Park	d				06 52					07 08										07 38			
St Pancras International	d	06 50	06 55	06 57	07 00	07 02		07 10	07 12	07 15	07 17	07 20	07 25	07 27	07 32			07 40	07 42	07 45	07 47	07 50	07 55
Farringdon ■ ⊖	d	06 54	06 59	07 02	07 04	07 07		07 14	07 17	07 19	07 22	07 24	07 29	07 32	07 37			07 44	07 47	07 49	07 52	07 54	07 59
City Thameslink ■	d	06 56	07 01	07 04	07 06	07 09		07 16	07 19	07 21	07 24	07 26	07 31	07 34	07 39			07 46	07 49	07 51	07 54	07 56	08 01
London Blackfriars	a	06 58	07 03	07 06	07 08	07 11		07 18	07 21	07 23	07 26	07 28	07 33	07 36	07 41			07 48	07 51	07 53	07 56	07 58	08 03
London Blackfriars ■ ⊖	d	06 59	07 04	07 06	07 09	07 11	07 16	07 19	07 21	07 24	07 26	07 29	07 34	07 36	07 41		07 46	07 49	07 51	07 54	07 56	07 59	08 04
London Bridge	d	07 05	07 11		07 15	07 18		07 25		07 30		07 35	07 41		07 48	07 55		07 55		08 00		08 05	08 11
Elephant & Castle ⊖173,179	a			07 10			07 19		07 25		07 30			07 40			07 49		07 55		08 00		
Loughborough Jn 173,179	a			07 15					07 30					07 45					08 00				
Herne Hill ■ 173,179	a			07 19					07 34					07 49					08 04				
Tulse Hill ■	a			07 24					07 39					07 54					08 09				
Streatham ■	a			07 29					07 44					07 59					08 14				
Wimbledon	a								07 54										08 24				
Sutton ■ 179	a			07 47					08 14					08 17		08 28			08 44				
Denmark Hill ■ 195	a						07 27				07 38						07 57				08 07		
Peckham Rye ■ 195	a						07 30				07 41						08 00				08 10		
Catford	a						07 39				07 50						08 09				08 19		
Bromley South	a						07 52				08 03						08 22				08 32		
Orpington	a										08 18										08 47		
St Mary Cray	a						08 02										08 31						
Swanley	a						08 07										08 36						
Sevenoaks	a						08 26										08 55						
Maidstone East	a																						
Greenwich	a					07 27									07 57								
Woolwich Arsenal	a					07 40									08 10								
Abbey Wood	a					07 46									08 16								
Dartford	a					07 57									08 27								
Rainham Kt	a					08 49									09 11								
East Croydon 🚋	a	07 18	07 24		07 29			07 38		07 46		07 48	07 54					08 08		08 16		08 18	08 24
Gatwick Airport ■ ✈	a	07 34			07 44			07 53		08 15		08 04						08 23		08 45		08 34	
Horsham	a									08 41										09 11			
Brighton ■	a	08 12			08 19							08 44										09 12	

A To East Grinstead
B To Epsom

Table T052-R

Mondays to Fridays

21 May to 7 December

Bedford, Luton, Cambridge, Stevenage and London - Gatwick Airport and Brighton

Station		TL	TL 1	TL 1 A	TL B	TL	TL 1 C	TL	TL 1	TL	TL 1	TL 1	TL	TL	TL 1 D	TL B	TL	TL 1 E	TL	TL 1	TL	TL 1	TL 1
Bedford	d			07 01			07 22				07 18	07 34						07 52				07 48	08 04
Luton 10	d			07 25			07 39			07 30	07 42	07 52		07 46	07 58			08 09			08 02	08 12	08 22
Luton Airport Parkway 7 ✈	d			07 28						07 33	07 45			07 49	08 01						08 05	08 15	
Harpenden	d			07 34						07 39	07 50	07 58		07 55	08 06						08 10	08 20	08 28
St Albans City	d	07 22		07 39			07 48	07 36		07 45	07 56	08 03	07 52	08 00	08 12			08 18	08 07		08 16	08 26	08 33
Elstree & Borehamwood	d	07 31						07 46		07 54			08 01	08 09					08 16		08 24		
West Hampstead Thameslink	d	07 47						08 02		08 06			08 17	08 21					08 32		08 36		
Kentish Town	d	07 51						08 06					08 21						08 36				
Peterborough	d								06 54											07 24			
Huntingdon	d								07 11											07 41			
Cambridge	d		06 54																				
Royston	d		07 09																				
Letchworth Garden City	d		07 21																				
Hitchin	d		07 26						07 41											08 11			
Stevenage	d		07 32						07 47											08 17			
Welwyn Garden City	d																						
Finsbury Park	d		07 52						08 08											08 38			
St Pancras International	d	07 57	08 00	08 03			08 10	08 12	08 15	08 17	08 20	08 25	08 27	08 32	08 35			08 40	08 42	08 45	08 47	08 50	08 55
Farringdon 3 ⊖	d	08 02	08 04	08 07			08 14	08 17	08 19	08 22	08 24	08 29	08 32	08 37	08 39			08 44	08 47	08 49	08 52	08 54	08 59
City Thameslink 3	d	08 04	08 06	08 09			08 16	08 19	08 21	08 24	08 26	08 31	08 34	08 39	08 41			08 46	08 49	08 51	08 54	08 56	09 01
London Blackfriars	a	08 06	08 08	08 11			08 18	08 21	08 23	08 26	08 28	08 33	08 36	08 41	08 43			08 48	08 51	08 53	08 56	08 58	09 03
London Blackfriars 3 ⊖	d	08 06	08 09	08 12		08 16	08 19	08 21	08 24	08 26	08 29	08 34	08 36	08 41	08 44		08 46	08 49	08 51	08 54	08 56	08 59	09 04
London Bridge	d		08 15	08 18	08 25		08 25		08 30		08 35	08 41		08 48	08 51	08 55		08 55		09 00		09 05	09 11
Elephant & Castle ⊖173,179	a	08 10				08 19		08 25		08 30			08 40				08 49		08 55		09 00		
Loughborough Jn 173,179	a	08 15						08 30					08 45						09 00				
Herne Hill 4 173,179	a	08 19						08 34					08 49						09 04				
Tulse Hill 5	a	08 24						08 39					08 54						09 09				
Streatham 4	a	08 30						08 44					09 00						09 14				
Wimbledon	a							08 54											09 24				
Sutton 4 179	a	08 47			08 58			09 14					09 17			09 28			09 44				
Denmark Hill 4 195	a					08 27				08 37							08 57				09 07		
Peckham Rye 4 195	a					08 30				08 40							09 00				09 11		
Catford	a					08 39				08 49							09 09				09 20		
Bromley South	a					08 52				09 02							09 22				09 33		
Orpington	a									09 14											09 46		
St Mary Cray	a					09 01											09 32						
Swanley	a					09 05											09 36						
Sevenoaks	a					09 25											09 56						
Maidstone East	a																						
Greenwich	a			08 27										08 57									
Woolwich Arsenal	a			08 40										09 10									
Abbey Wood	a			08 46										09 16									
Dartford	a			08 57										09 27									
Rainham Kt	a			09 41										10 11									
East Croydon	a		08 30				08 38		08 46		08 48	08 54			09 06			09 08		09 14		09 18	09 24
Gatwick Airport 10 ✈	a		08 45						09 15		09 04	09 19			09 35			09 23		09 42		09 34	09 47
Horsham	a								09 39											10 08			
Brighton 10	a		09 20								09 44											10 12	

A 1 from London Blackfriars
B To Epsom
C To Littlehampton
D From Flitwick to Three Bridges
E To Three Bridges

Table T052-R

Mondays to Fridays

21 May to 7 December

Bedford, Luton, Cambridge, Stevenage and London - Gatwick Airport and Brighton

Station		TL	TL 1	TL	TL 1	TL A	TL	TL 1 B	TL	TL 1	TL	TL 1	TL	TL	TL 1	TL A	TL	TL 1 B	TL	TL 1	TL	TL 1	TL
Bedford	d				08 01			08 22				08 18			08 32			08 52				08 46	
Luton 10	d			08 16	08 26			08 39			08 30	08 42		08 46	08 56			09 09			09 00	09 12	
Luton Airport Parkway 7 ✈	d			08 19	08 29						08 33	08 45		08 49	08 59						09 03	09 15	
Harpenden	d			08 24	08 34						08 39	08 50		08 54	09 04						09 09	09 20	
St Albans City	d	08 22		08 30	08 41			08 48	08 37		08 45	08 56	08 52	09 00	09 11			09 18	09 07		09 15	09 26	09 22
Elstree & Borehamwood	d	08 31		08 39					08 46		08 54		09 01	09 09					09 16		09 24		09 31
West Hampstead Thameslink	d	08 47		08 51					09 02		09 06		09 17	09 21					09 32		09 36		09 47
Kentish Town	d	08 51							09 06				09 21						09 36				09 51
Peterborough	d									07 54										08 23			
Huntingdon	d									08 11										08 38			
Cambridge	d		07 54																				
Royston	d		08 08																				
Letchworth Garden City	d		08 21																				
Hitchin	d		08 26							08 41										09 07			
Stevenage	d		08 32							08 47										09 13			
Welwyn Garden City	d																						
Finsbury Park	d		08 52							09 08										09 38			
St Pancras International	d	08 57	09 00	09 02	09 05			09 10	09 12	09 15	09 17	09 20	09 27	09 32	09 35			09 40	09 42	09 45	09 47	09 50	09 57
Farringdon 3 ⊖	d	09 02	09 04	09 07	09 09			09 14	09 17	09 19	09 22	09 24	09 32	09 37	09 39			09 44	09 47	09 49	09 52	09 54	10 02
City Thameslink 3	d	09 04	09 06	09 09	09 11			09 16	09 19	09 21	09 24	09 26	09 34	09 39	09 41			09 46	09 49	09 51	09 54	09 56	10 04
London Blackfriars	a	09 06	09 08	09 11	09 13			09 18	09 21	09 23	09 26	09 28	09 36	09 41	09 43			09 48	09 51	09 53	09 56	09 58	10 06
London Blackfriars 3 ⊖	d	09 06	09 09	09 11	09 14		09 16	09 19	09 21	09 24	09 26	09 29	09 36	09 41	09 44		09 46	09 49	09 51	09 54	09 56	09 59	10 06
London Bridge	d		09 15	09 18	09 21	09 25		09 25		09 30		09 35		09 48	09 51	09 55		09 55		10 00		10 05	
Elephant & Castle ⊖173,179	a	09 10					09 19		09 25		09 30		09 40				09 49		09 55		10 00		10 10
Loughborough Jn 173,179	a	09 15							09 30				09 45						10 00				10 15
Herne Hill 4 173,179	a	09 19							09 34				09 49						10 04				10 19
Tulse Hill 5	a	09 24							09 39				09 54						10 09				10 24
Streatham 4	a	09 30							09 44				09 59						10 14				10 29
Wimbledon	a								09 54										10 24				
Sutton 4 179	a	09 47				09 58			10 14				10 17			10 28			10 44				10 47
Denmark Hill 4 195	a						09 27				09 37						09 57				10 07		
Peckham Rye 4 195	a						09 30				09 40						10 00				10 10		
Catford	a						09 39				09 49						10 09				10 19		
Bromley South	a						09 52				10 02						10 22				10 32		
Orpington	a										10 14										10 45		
St Mary Cray	a						10 01										10 31						
Swanley	a						10 05										10 35						
Sevenoaks	a						10 25										10 55						
Maidstone East	a																						
Greenwich	a			09 27										09 57									
Woolwich Arsenal	a			09 40										10 10									
Abbey Wood	a			09 46										10 16									
Dartford	a			09 57										10 27									
Rainham Kt	a			10 41										11 11									
East Croydon	a		09 28		09 36			09 38		09 44		09 48			10 06			10 08		10 14		10 18	
Gatwick Airport 10 ✈	a		09 44		10 08			09 53		10 12		10 04			10 38			10 23		10 42		10 34	
Horsham	a									10 38										11 08			
Brighton 10	a		10 20									10 44										11 12	

A To Epsom
B To Three Bridges

Table T052-R

Mondays to Fridays

21 May to 7 December

Bedford, Luton, Cambridge, Stevenage and London - Gatwick Airport and Brighton

		TL ■	TL	TL ■	TL	TL ■	TL	TL	TL ■	TL	TL ■	TL	TL	TL ■	TL	TL	TL	TL ■	TL	TL ■	TL	TL ■
						A	B								B							
Bedford	d			09 02							09 16			09 34						09 48		
Luton ■	d		09 16	09 26							09 41		09 46	09 59						10 12		
Luton Airport Parkway ■ ✈	d		09 19	09 29							09 44		09 51	10 02						10 15		
Harpenden	d		09 24	09 34							09 49		09 56	10 08						10 22		
St Albans City	d		09 30	09 41				09 37			09 55	09 51	10 01	10 13			10 07			10 27	10 22	
Elstree & Borehamwood	d		09 39					09 46				10 01	10 10				10 16				10 31	
West Hampstead Thameslink	d		09 51					10 01			10 09	10 16	10 21				10 31			10 39	10 46	
Kentish Town	d							10 06		10 11		10 21					10 36		10 41		10 51	
Peterborough	d								08 57									09 26				
Huntingdon	d								09 12									09 41				
Cambridge	d	08 54																				09 54
Royston	d	09 09																				10 09
Letchworth Garden City	d	09 20																				10 21
Hitchin	d	09 24							09 41									10 11				10 26
Stevenage	d	09 30							09 47									10 17				10 32
Welwyn Garden City	d																					
Finsbury Park	d	09 52							10 08									10 38				10 52
St Pancras International	d	10 00	10 02	10 05				10 12	10 15	10 17	10 20	10 27	10 32	10 35			10 42	10 45	10 47	10 50	10 57	11 00
Farringdon ■ ⊖	d	10 04	10 07	10 09				10 17	10 19	10 22	10 24	10 32	10 37	10 39			10 47	10 49	10 52	10 54	11 02	11 04
City Thameslink ■	d	10 06	10 09	10 11				10 19	10 21	10 24	10 26	10 34	10 39	10 41			10 49	10 51	10 54	10 56	11 04	11 06
London Blackfriars	a	10 08	10 11	10 13				10 21	10 23	10 26	10 28	10 36	10 41	10 43			10 51	10 53	10 56	10 58	11 06	11 08
London Blackfriars ■ ⊖	d	10 09	10 11	10 14	10 16			10 21	10 24	10 26	10 29	10 36	10 41	10 44		10 46	10 51	10 54	10 56	10 59	11 06	11 09
London Bridge	d	10 15	10 18	10 21		10 22	10 25		10 30		10 35		10 48	10 51	10 55			11 00		11 05		11 15
Elephant & Castle ⊖	173,179 a				10 19			10 25		10 30		10 40				10 49	10 55		11 00		11 10	
Loughborough Jn	173,179 a							10 30				10 45					11 00				11 15	
Herne Hill ■	173,179 a							10 34				10 49					11 04				11 19	
Tulse Hill ■	a							10 39				10 54					11 09				11 24	
Streatham ■	a							10 44				10 59					11 14				11 29	
Wimbledon	a							10 54									11 24					
Sutton ■	179 a						10 58	11 14				11 17			11 28		11 44				11 47	
Denmark Hill ■	195 a				10 27					10 37						10 57			11 07			
Peckham Rye ■	195 a				10 30					10 40						11 00			11 10			
Catford	a				10 39					10 49						11 09			11 19			
Bromley South	a				10 52					11 02						11 22			11 32			
Orpington	a									11 14									11 44			
St Mary Cray	a				11 01											11 31						
Swanley	a				11 05											11 35						
Sevenoaks	a				11 25											11 55						
Maidstone East	a																					
Greenwich	a		10 27										10 57									
Woolwich Arsenal	a		10 40										11 10									
Abbey Wood	a		10 46										11 16									
Dartford	a		10 57										11 27									
Rainham Kt	a		11 41										12 11									
East Croydon 🚌	a	10 28		10 36		10 38			10 44		10 48			11 06				11 14		11 18		11 28
Gatwick Airport ■ ✈	a	10 44		11 08		10 53			11 12		11 04			11 38				11 42		11 34		11 44
Horsham	a								11 38									12 08				
Brighton ■	a	11 19									11 44									12 12		12 19

A To Three Bridges **B** To Epsom

Table T052-R

Mondays to Fridays

21 May to 7 December

Bedford, Luton, Cambridge, Stevenage and London - Gatwick Airport and Brighton

		TL	TL ■	TL	TL	TL	TL ■	TL	TL ■	TL	TL	TL ■	TL	TL	TL	TL ■	TL	TL ■	TL ■	TL	TL ■	TL	TL ■
				A									A					B	C				
Bedford	d		10 04						10 19			10 35						10 49	10 49				11 05
Luton ■	d	10 16	10 28						10 43		10 48	10 59						11 13	11 13			11 18	11 29
Luton Airport Parkway ■ ✈	d	10 21	10 31						10 46		10 51	11 02						11 16	11 16			11 21	11 32
Harpenden	d	10 26	10 38						10 52		10 56	11 08						11 22	11 22			11 26	11 38
St Albans City	d	10 31	10 43			10 37			10 57	10 52	11 01	11 13			11 07			11 27	11 27	11 22		11 31	11 43
Elstree & Borehamwood	d	10 40				10 46				11 01	11 10				11 16					11 31		11 40	
West Hampstead Thameslink	d	10 51				11 01			11 09	11 16	11 21				11 32			11 39	11 39	11 46		11 51	
Kentish Town	d					11 06		11 11		11 21					11 36		11 41			11 51			
Peterborough	d						09 54									10 24							
Huntingdon	d						10 11									10 41							
Cambridge	d																				10 54		
Royston	d																				11 09		
Letchworth Garden City	d																				11 21		
Hitchin	d						10 41									11 11					11 26		
Stevenage	d						10 47									11 17					11 32		
Welwyn Garden City	d																						
Finsbury Park	d						11 08									11 38					11 52		
St Pancras International	d	11 02	11 05			11 12	11 15	11 17	11 20	11 27	11 32	11 35			11 42	11 45	11 47	11 50	11 51	11 57	12 00	12 02	12 05
Farringdon ■ ⊖	d	11 07	11 09			11 17	11 19	11 22	11 24	11 32	11 37	11 39			11 47	11 49	11 52	11 54	11 55	12 02	12 04	12 07	12 09
City Thameslink ■	d	11 09	11 11			11 19	11 21	11 24	11 26	11 34	11 39	11 41			11 49	11 51	11 54	11 56	11 57	12 04	12 06	12 09	12 11
London Blackfriars	a	11 11	11 13			11 21	11 23	11 26	11 28	11 36	11 41	11 43			11 51	11 53	11 56	11 58	11 59	12 06	12 08	12 11	12 13
London Blackfriars ■ ⊖	d	11 11	11 14		11 16	11 21	11 24	11 26	11 29	11 36	11 41	11 44		11 46	11 51	11 54	11 56	11 59	12 00	12 06	12 09	12 11	12 14
London Bridge	d	11 18	11 21	11 25			11 30		11 35		11 48	11 51	11 55			12 00		12 05	12 06		12 15	12 18	12 21
Elephant & Castle ⊖	173,179 a				11 19	11 25		11 30		11 40				11 49	11 55		12 00			12 10			
Loughborough Jn	173,179 a					11 30				11 45					12 00					12 15			
Herne Hill ■	173,179 a					11 34				11 49					12 04					12 19			
Tulse Hill ■	a					11 39				11 54					12 09					12 24			
Streatham ■	a					11 44				11 59					12 14					12 29			
Wimbledon	a					11 54									12 24								
Sutton ■	179 a			11 58		12 14				12 17			12 28		12 44					12 47			
Denmark Hill ■	195 a				11 27			11 37						11 57			12 07						
Peckham Rye ■	195 a				11 30			11 40						12 00			12 10						
Catford	a				11 39			11 49						12 09			12 19						
Bromley South	a				11 52			12 02						12 22			12 32						
Orpington	a							12 14									12 44						
St Mary Cray	a				12 01									12 31									
Swanley	a				12 05									12 35									
Sevenoaks	a				12 25									12 55									
Maidstone East	a																						
Greenwich	a	11 27									11 57											12 27	
Woolwich Arsenal	a	11 40									12 10											12 40	
Abbey Wood	a	11 46									12 16											12 46	
Dartford	a	11 57									12 27											12 57	
Rainham Kt	a	12 41									13 11											13 41	
East Croydon 🚌	a		11 36				11 44		11 48			12 06				12 14		12 18	12 19		12 28		12 36
Gatwick Airport ■ ✈	a		12 08				12 12		12 04			12 38				12 42		12 34	12 34		12 44		13 08
Horsham	a						12 38									13 08							
Brighton ■	a								12 44									13 12	13 12		13 19		

A To Epsom **B** from 23 July until 5 October **C** until 20 July, from 8 October

Table T052-R

Mondays to Fridays

21 May to 7 December

Bedford, Luton, Cambridge, Stevenage and London - Gatwick Airport and Brighton

		TL A	TL	TL	TL 1	TL	TL 1 B	TL 1 C	TL B	TL C	TL	TL 1	TL A	TL	TL	TL 1	TL	TL 1	TL	TL 1	TL	TL 1	TL A
Bedford	d						11 19	11 19				11 35						11 49				12 05	
Luton 10	d						11 42	11 43			11 48	11 59						12 13			12 18	12 29	
Luton Airport Parkway 7	d						11 45	11 46			11 51	12 02						12 16			12 21	12 32	
Harpenden	d						11 50	11 51			11 56	12 08						12 22			12 26	12 38	
St Albans City	d			11 37			11 55	11 57	11 51	11 52	12 01	12 13			12 07			12 27	12 22		12 31	12 43	
Elstree & Borehamwood	d			11 46					12 00	12 01	12 10				12 16				12 31		12 40		
West Hampstead Thameslink	d			12 01			12 09	12 09	12 16	12 16	12 21				12 31			12 39	12 47		12 51		
Kentish Town	d			12 06		12 11			12 21	12 21					12 36		12 41		12 51				
Peterborough	d				10 54											11 23							
Huntingdon	d				11 11											11 41							
Cambridge	d																			11 54			
Royston	d																			12 09			
Letchworth Garden City	d																			12 21			
Hitchin	d				11 41											12 11				12 26			
Stevenage	d				11 47											12 17				12 32			
Welwyn Garden City	d																						
Finsbury Park	d				12 08											12 38				12 52			
St Pancras International	d			12 12	12 15	12 17	12 20	12 20	12 27	12 27	12 32	12 35			12 42	12 45	12 47	12 50	12 57	13 00	13 02	13 05	
Farringdon 3 ⊖	d			12 17	12 19	12 22	12 24	12 24	12 32	12 32	12 37	12 39			12 47	12 49	12 52	12 54	13 02	13 04	13 07	13 09	
City Thameslink 3	d			12 19	12 21	12 24	12 26	12 26	12 34	12 34	12 39	12 41			12 49	12 51	12 54	12 56	13 04	13 06	13 09	13 11	
London Blackfriars	a			12 21	12 23	12 26	12 28	12 28	12 36	12 36	12 41	12 43			12 51	12 53	12 56	12 58	13 06	13 08	13 11	13 13	
London Blackfriars 3 ⊖	d		12 16	12 21	12 24	12 26	12 29	12 29	12 36	12 36	12 41	12 44		12 46	12 51	12 54	12 56	12 59	13 06	13 09	13 11	13 14	
London Bridge	d	12 25			12 30		12 35	12 35			12 48	12 51	12 55			13 00		13 05		13 15	13 18	13 21	13 25
Elephant & Castle ⊖ 173,179	a		12 19	12 25		12 30			12 40	12 40				12 49	12 55		13 00		13 10				
Loughborough Jn 173,179	a			12 30					12 45	12 45					13 00				13 15				
Herne Hill 4 173,179	a			12 34					12 49	12 49					13 04				13 19				
Tulse Hill 3	a			12 39					12 54	12 54					13 09				13 24				
Streatham 4	a			12 44					12 59	12 59					13 14				13 29				
Wimbledon	a			12 54											13 24								
Sutton 4 179	a	12 58		13 14					13 17	13 17			13 28		13 44				13 47				13 58
Denmark Hill 4 195	a		12 27			12 37								12 57			13 07						
Peckham Rye 4 195	a		12 30			12 40								13 00			13 10						
Catford	a		12 39			12 49								13 09			13 19						
Bromley South	a		12 52			13 02								13 22			13 32						
Orpington	a					13 14											13 44						
St Mary Cray	a		13 01											13 31									
Swanley	a		13 05											13 35									
Sevenoaks	a		13 25											13 55									
Maidstone East	a																						
Greenwich	a										12 57										13 27		
Woolwich Arsenal	a										13 10										13 40		
Abbey Wood	a										13 16										13 46		
Dartford	a										13 27										13 57		
Rainham Kt	a										14 11										14 41		
East Croydon	a				12 44		12 48	12 48				13 06				13 14		13 18		13 28		13 36	
Gatwick Airport 10 ✈	a				13 12		13 04	13 04				13 38				13 42		13 34		13 44		14 08	
Horsham	a				13 38											14 08							
Brighton 10	a						13 44	13 44										14 12		14 19			

A To Epsom

B until 20 July, from 8 October

C from 23 July until 5 October

Table T052-R

Mondays to Fridays

21 May to 7 December

Bedford, Luton, Cambridge, Stevenage and London - Gatwick Airport and Brighton

		TL	TL	TL 1	TL	TL 1	TL	TL	TL 1	TL A	TL	TL	TL 1	TL	TL 1 B	TL 1 C	TL	TL 1	TL	TL 1	TL A	TL	TL
Bedford	d					12 19			12 35						12 49	12 49				13 05			
Luton 10	d					12 43		12 48	12 59						13 13	13 13			13 18	13 29			
Luton Airport Parkway 7	d					12 46		12 51	13 02						13 16	13 16			13 21	13 32			
Harpenden	d					12 52		12 56	13 08						13 22	13 22			13 26	13 38			
St Albans City	d		12 37			12 57	12 52	13 01	13 13			13 07			13 27	13 27	13 22		13 31	13 43			13 37
Elstree & Borehamwood	d		12 46				13 01	13 10				13 16					13 31		13 40				13 46
West Hampstead Thameslink	d		13 01			13 09	13 16	13 21				13 31			13 39	13 39	13 46		13 51				14 01
Kentish Town	d		13 06		13 11		13 21					13 36		13 41			13 51						14 06
Peterborough	d			11 54									12 24										
Huntingdon	d			12 11									12 41										
Cambridge	d																	12 54					
Royston	d																	13 09					
Letchworth Garden City	d																	13 21					
Hitchin	d			12 41									13 11					13 26					
Stevenage	d			12 47									13 17					13 32					
Welwyn Garden City	d																						
Finsbury Park	d			13 08									13 38					13 52					
St Pancras International	d		13 12	13 15	13 17	13 20	13 27	13 32	13 35			13 42	13 45	13 47	13 50	13 51	13 57	14 00	14 02	14 05			14 12
Farringdon 3 ⊖	d		13 17	13 19	13 22	13 24	13 32	13 37	13 39			13 47	13 49	13 52	13 54	13 55	14 02	14 04	14 07	14 09			14 17
City Thameslink 3	d		13 19	13 21	13 24	13 26	13 34	13 39	13 41			13 49	13 51	13 54	13 56	13 57	14 04	14 06	14 09	14 11			14 19
London Blackfriars	a		13 21	13 23	13 26	13 28	13 36	13 41	13 43			13 51	13 53	13 56	13 58	13 59	14 06	14 08	14 11	14 13			14 21
London Blackfriars 3 ⊖	d	13 16	13 21	13 24	13 26	13 29	13 36	13 41	13 44		13 46	13 51	13 54	13 56	13 59	14 00	14 06	14 09	14 11	14 14		14 16	14 21
London Bridge	d			13 30		13 35		13 48	13 51	13 55			14 00		14 05	14 06		14 15	14 18	14 21	14 25		
Elephant & Castle ⊖ 173,179	a	13 19	13 25		13 30		13 40				13 49	13 55		14 00			14 10					14 19	14 25
Loughborough Jn 173,179	a		13 30				13 45					14 00					14 15						14 30
Herne Hill 4 173,179	a		13 34				13 49					14 04					14 19						14 34
Tulse Hill 3	a		13 39				13 54					14 09					14 24						14 39
Streatham 4	a		13 44				13 59					14 14					14 29						14 42
Wimbledon	a		13 54									14 24											14 52
Sutton 4 179	a		14 14				14 17			14 28		14 44					14 47				14 58		15 14
Denmark Hill 4 195	a	13 27			13 37						13 57			14 07								14 27	
Peckham Rye 4 195	a	13 30			13 40						14 00			14 10								14 30	
Catford	a	13 39			13 49						14 09			14 19								14 39	
Bromley South	a	13 52			14 02						14 22			14 32								14 52	
Orpington	a				14 14									14 44									
St Mary Cray	a	14 01									14 31											15 01	
Swanley	a	14 05									14 35											15 05	
Sevenoaks	a	14 25									14 55											15 25	
Maidstone East	a																						
Greenwich	a							13 57											14 27				
Woolwich Arsenal	a							14 10											14 40				
Abbey Wood	a							14 16											14 46				
Dartford	a							14 27											14 57				
Rainham Kt	a							15 11											15 41				
East Croydon	a			13 44		13 48			14 06				14 14		14 18	14 19		14 28		14 36			
Gatwick Airport 10 ✈	a			14 12		14 04			14 38				14 42		14 34	14 34		14 44		15 08			
Horsham	a			14 38									15 08										
Brighton 10	a					14 44									15 12	15 12		15 19					

A To Epsom

B from 23 July until 5 October

C until 20 July, from 8 October

Table T052-R

Mondays to Fridays
21 May to 7 December

Bedford, Luton, Cambridge, Stevenage and London - Gatwick Airport and Brighton

	TL ■	TL	TL ■ A	TL ■ B	TL A	TL B	TL	TL ■	TL C	TL	TL	TL ■	TL	TL ■ D	TL ■ E	TL	TL ■	TL	TL ■	TL C	TL	TL
Bedford d			13 19	13 19				13 35						13 49	13 49				14 05			
Luton ■ d			13 42	13 43			13 48	13 59						14 13	14 13			14 18	14 29			
Luton Airport Parkway ■ ✈ d			13 45	13 46			13 51	14 02						14 16	14 16			14 21	14 32			
Harpenden d			13 50	13 51			13 56	14 08						14 22	14 22			14 26	14 38			
St Albans City d			13 55	13 57	13 51	13 52	14 01	14 13			14 07			14 27	14 27	14 22		14 31	14 43			14 37
Elstree & Borehamwood d					14 00	14 01	14 10				14 16					14 31		14 40				14 46
West Hampstead Thameslink d			14 09	14 09	14 16	14 16	14 21				14 31			14 39	14 39	14 46		14 51				15 01
Kentish Town d		14 11			14 21	14 21					14 36		14 41			14 51						15 06
Peterborough d	12 54											13 24										
Huntingdon d	13 11											13 41										
Cambridge d																	13 54					
Royston d																	14 09					
Letchworth Garden City d																	14 21					
Hitchin d	13 41											14 11					14 26					
Stevenage d	13 47											14 17					14 32					
Welwyn Garden City d																						
Finsbury Park d	14 08											14 38					14 52					
St Pancras International d	14 15	14 17	14 20	14 20	14 27	14 27	14 32	14 35			14 42	14 45	14 47	14 50	14 51	14 57	15 00	15 02	15 05			15 12
Farringdon ■ ⊖ d	14 19	14 22	14 24	14 24	14 32	14 32	14 37	14 39			14 47	14 49	14 52	14 54	14 55	15 02	15 04	15 07	15 09			15 17
City Thameslink ■ d	14 21	14 24	14 26	14 26	14 34	14 34	14 39	14 41			14 49	14 51	14 54	14 56	14 57	15 04	15 06	15 09	15 11			15 19
London Blackfriars a	14 23	14 26	14 28	14 28	14 36	14 36	14 41	14 43			14 51	14 53	14 56	14 58	14 59	15 06	15 08	15 11	15 13			15 21
London Blackfriars ■ ⊖ d	14 24	14 26	14 29	14 29	14 36	14 36	14 41	14 44		14 46	14 51	14 54	14 56	14 59	15 00	15 06	15 09	15 11	15 14		15 16	15 21
London Bridge d	14 30		14 35	14 35			14 48	14 51	14 55			15 00		15 05	15 06		15 15	15 18	15 21	15 25		
Elephant & Castle ⊖173,179 a		14 30			14 40	14 40				14 49	14 55		15 00			15 10					15 19	15 25
Loughborough Jn 173,179 a					14 45	14 45					15 00					15 15						15 30
Herne Hill ■ 173,179 a					14 49	14 49					15 04					15 19						15 34
Tulse Hill ■ a					14 54	14 54					15 09					15 24						15 39
Streatham ■ a					14 59	14 59					15 14					15 29						15 44
Wimbledon a											15 24											15 54
Sutton ■ 179 a					15 17	15 17			15 28		15 44					15 47				15 58		16 14
Denmark Hill ■ 195 a		14 37								14 57			15 07								15 27	
Peckham Rye ■ 195 a		14 40								15 00			15 10								15 30	
Catford a		14 49								15 09			15 19								15 39	
Bromley South a		15 02								15 22			15 32								15 52	
Orpington a		15 14											15 44									
St Mary Cray a										15 31											16 01	
Swanley a										15 35											16 05	
Sevenoaks a										15 55											16 25	
Maidstone East a																						
Greenwich a							14 57											15 27				
Woolwich Arsenal a							15 10											15 40				
Abbey Wood a							15 16											15 46				
Dartford a							15 27											15 57				
Rainham Kt a							16 11											16 41				
East Croydon ⇌ a	14 44		14 48	14 48				15 06				15 14		15 18	15 19		15 28		15 36			
Gatwick Airport ■ ✈ a	15 12		15 04	15 04				15 38				15 42		15 34	15 34		15 44		16 08			
Horsham a	15 38											16 08										
Brighton ■ a			15 44	15 44										16 12	16 12		16 19					

A until 20 July, from 8 October
B from 23 July until 5 October
C To Epsom
D from 30 July
E until 27 July

Table T052-R

Mondays to Fridays
21 May to 7 December

Bedford, Luton, Cambridge, Stevenage and London - Gatwick Airport and Brighton

	TL ■	TL	TL ■ A	TL ■ B	TL C	TL D	TL	TL ■	TL E	TL	TL	TL ■	TL	TL ■	TL	TL ■	TL	TL ■	TL E	TL	TL
Bedford d			14 19	14 19				14 35						14 49				15 05			
Luton ■ d			14 42	14 43			14 48	14 59						15 13			15 18	15 29			
Luton Airport Parkway ■ ✈ d			14 45	14 46			14 51	15 02						15 16			15 21	15 32			
Harpenden d			14 50	14 51			14 56	15 08						15 22			15 26	15 38			
St Albans City d			14 55	14 57	14 51	14 52	15 01	15 13			15 07			15 27	15 22		15 31	15 43			15 37
Elstree & Borehamwood d					15 00	15 01	15 10				15 16				15 31		15 40				15 46
West Hampstead Thameslink d			15 09	15 09	15 16	15 16	15 21				15 31			15 39	15 47		15 51				16 01
Kentish Town d		15 11			15 21	15 21					15 36		15 41		15 51						16 06
Peterborough d	13 54											14 24									
Huntingdon d	14 11											14 41									
Cambridge d																14 54					
Royston d																15 09					
Letchworth Garden City d																15 21					
Hitchin d	14 41											15 11				15 26					
Stevenage d	14 47											15 17				15 32					
Welwyn Garden City d																					
Finsbury Park d	15 08											15 38				15 52					
St Pancras International d	15 15	15 17	15 20	15 20	15 27	15 27	15 32	15 35			15 42	15 45	15 47	15 50	15 57	16 00	16 02	16 05			16 12
Farringdon ■ ⊖ d	15 19	15 22	15 24	15 24	15 32	15 32	15 37	15 39			15 47	15 49	15 52	15 54	16 02	16 04	16 07	16 09			16 17
City Thameslink ■ d	15 21	15 24	15 26	15 26	15 34	15 34	15 39	15 41			15 49	15 51	15 54	15 56	16 04	16 06	16 09	16 11			16 19
London Blackfriars a	15 23	15 26	15 28	15 28	15 36	15 36	15 41	15 43			15 51	15 53	15 56	15 58	16 06	16 08	16 11	16 13			16 21
London Blackfriars ■ ⊖ d	15 24	15 26	15 29	15 29	15 36	15 36	15 41	15 44		15 46	15 51	15 54	15 56	15 59	16 06	16 09	16 11	16 14		16 16	16 21
London Bridge d	15 30		15 35	15 35			15 48	15 51	15 55			16 00		16 05		16 15	16 18	16 21	16 25		
Elephant & Castle ⊖173,179 a		15 30			15 40	15 40				15 49	15 55		16 00		16 10					16 19	16 25
Loughborough Jn 173,179 a					15 45	15 45					16 00				16 15						16 30
Herne Hill ■ 173,179 a					15 49	15 49					16 04				16 19						16 34
Tulse Hill ■ a					15 54	15 54					16 09				16 24						16 39
Streatham ■ a					15 59	15 59					16 14				16 29						16 44
Wimbledon a											16 24										16 54
Sutton ■ 179 a					16 17	16 17			16 28		16 44				16 47				16 58		17 14
Denmark Hill ■ 195 a		15 37								15 57			16 07							16 27	
Peckham Rye ■ 195 a		15 41								16 00			16 10							16 30	
Catford a		15 50								16 09			16 19							16 39	
Bromley South a		16 03								16 22			16 32							16 52	
Orpington a		16 14											16 44								
St Mary Cray a										16 31										17 01	
Swanley a										16 35										17 05	
Sevenoaks a										16 55										17 25	
Maidstone East a																					
Greenwich a							15 57										16 27				
Woolwich Arsenal a							16 10										16 40				
Abbey Wood a							16 16										16 46				
Dartford a							16 27										16 57				
Rainham Kt a							17 11										17 42				
East Croydon ⇌ a	15 44		15 48	15 48				16 06				16 14		16 19		16 29		16 36			
Gatwick Airport ■ ✈ a	16 12		16 04	16 04				16 38				16 42		16 35		16 44		17 11			
Horsham a	16 38											17 10									
Brighton ■ a			16 44	16 44										17 13		17 21					

A until 27 July
B from 30 July
C until 20 July, from 8 October
D from 23 July until 5 October
E To Epsom

Table T052-R

Mondays to Fridays

21 May to 7 December

Bedford, Luton, Cambridge, Stevenage and London - Gatwick Airport and Brighton

	TL ■	TL	TL ■	TL ■ A	TL	TL	TL ■	TL B	TL	TL ■ C		TL	TL ■	TL	TL ■	TL ■ A	TL	TL ■	TL	TL ■	TL D		TL	TL
Bedford d			15 19				15 35			15 44					15 48	16 06				16 02				
Luton d			15 43	15 49		15 48	15 59			16 06					16 13	16 23			16 18	16 27				
Luton Airport Parkway d			15 46	15 52		15 51	16 02			16 09					16 16				16 21	16 30				
Harpenden d			15 52			15 56	16 08								16 22				16 26	16 35				
St Albans City d			15 57	16 01	15 52	16 01	16 13			16 18		16 07			16 27	16 33	16 22		16 31	16 41				16 37
Elstree & Borehamwood d					16 01	16 10						16 16					16 31		16 40					16 46
West Hampstead Thameslink d			16 09		16 17	16 21						16 32		16 36	16 39		16 47		16 51	16 54				17 02
Kentish Town d		16 11			16 22							16 37		16 41			16 52							17 07
Peterborough d	14 54												15 24											
Huntingdon d	15 11												15 41											
Cambridge d																		15 54						
Royston d																		16 09						
Letchworth Garden City d																		16 21						
Hitchin d	15 41												16 11					16 26						
Stevenage d	15 47												16 17					16 32						
Welwyn Garden City d																								
Finsbury Park d	16 08												16 38					16 52						
St Pancras International d	16 15	16 17	16 20	16 25	16 27	16 32	16 35			16 40		16 42	16 45	16 47	16 50	16 55	16 57	17 00	17 02	17 05				17 12
Farringdon ⊖ d	16 19	16 22	16 24	16 29	16 32	16 37	16 39			16 44		16 47	16 49	16 52	16 54	16 59	17 02	17 04	17 07	17 09				17 17
City Thameslink d	16 21	16 24	16 26	16 31	16 34	16 39	16 41			16 46		16 49	16 51	16 54	16 56	17 01	17 04	17 06	17 09	17 11				17 19
London Blackfriars a	16 23	16 26	16 28	16 33	16 36	16 41	16 43			16 48		16 51	16 53	16 56	16 58	17 03	17 06	17 08	17 11	17 13				17 21
London Blackfriars ⊖ d	16 24	16 26	16 29	16 34	16 36	16 41	16 44		16 46	16 49		16 51	16 54	16 56	16 59	17 04	17 06	17 09	17 11	17 14			17 16	17 21
London Bridge d	16 30		16 35	16 41		16 48	16 51	16 55		16 55			17 00		17 05	17 11		17 15	17 18	17 21	17 25			
Elephant & Castle ⊖173,179 a		16 30			16 40				16 49			16 55		17 00			17 10						17 19	17 25
Loughborough Jn 173,179 a					16 45							17 00					17 15							17 30
Herne Hill 173,179 a					16 49							17 04					17 19							17 34
Tulse Hill a					16 54							17 09					17 24							17 39
Streatham a					16 59							17 14					17 29							17 44
Wimbledon a												17 24												17 54
Sutton 179 a					17 17			17 28				17 44					17 47				17 59			18 14
Denmark Hill 195 a		16 37							16 57					17 07									17 27	
Peckham Rye 195 a		16 40							17 00					17 10									17 30	
Catford a		16 49							17 09					17 19									17 39	
Bromley South a		17 02							17 22					17 32									17 52	
Orpington a		17 14												17 45										
St Mary Cray a									17 31														18 01	
Swanley a									17 35														18 05	
Sevenoaks a									17 55														18 25	
Maidstone East a																								
Greenwich a						16 57													17 27					
Woolwich Arsenal a						17 10													17 40					
Abbey Wood a						17 16													17 46					
Dartford a						17 27													17 57					
Rainham Kt a						18 19													18 42					
East Croydon a	16 44		16 49	16 54			17 06			17 08			17 14		17 19	17 24		17 29		17 36				
Gatwick Airport a	17 15		17 04				17 41						17 45		17 35			17 44		18 11				
Horsham a	17 42												18 12											
Brighton a			17 46												18 15			18 21						

A To East Grinstead
B To Dorking
C To Littlehampton
D To Guildford

Table T052-R

Mondays to Fridays

21 May to 7 December

Bedford, Luton, Cambridge, Stevenage and London - Gatwick Airport and Brighton

	TL ■	TL	TL ■	TL ■ A	TL	TL	TL ■	TL B		TL	TL ■ C	TL	TL ■	TL	TL ■	TL ■ A	TL	TL ■	TL		TL ■	TL B	TL	TL
Bedford d			16 18	16 32			16 35				16 44				16 48						17 04			
Luton d			16 42	16 51		16 46	16 59				17 04				17 12	17 21			17 16		17 28			
Luton Airport Parkway d			16 45	16 54		16 49	17 02				17 07				17 15	17 24			17 19		17 31			
Harpenden d			16 50			16 54	17 08				17 12				17 21				17 25		17 36			
St Albans City d			16 56	17 03	16 52	17 00	17 13				17 18	17 07			17 27	17 33	17 22		17 30		17 42			17 37
Elstree & Borehamwood d					17 01	17 09						17 16					17 31		17 39					17 46
West Hampstead Thameslink d		17 06			17 17	17 21						17 32		17 36	17 39		17 47		17 51		17 54			18 01
Kentish Town d		17 11			17 22							17 37		17 41			17 52							18 06
Peterborough d	15 54												16 24											
Huntingdon d	16 11												16 41											
Cambridge d																		16 54						
Royston d																		17 09						
Letchworth Garden City d																		17 21						
Hitchin d	16 41												17 11					17 26						
Stevenage d	16 47												17 17					17 32						
Welwyn Garden City d																								
Finsbury Park d	17 08												17 38					17 52						
St Pancras International d	17 15	17 17	17 20	17 25	17 27	17 32	17 35				17 40	17 42	17 45	17 47	17 50	17 55	17 57	18 00	18 02		18 05			18 12
Farringdon ⊖ d	17 19	17 22	17 24	17 29	17 32	17 37	17 39				17 44	17 47	17 49	17 52	17 54	17 59	18 02	18 04	18 07		18 09			18 17
City Thameslink d	17 21	17 24	17 26	17 31	17 34	17 39	17 41				17 46	17 49	17 51	17 54	17 56	18 01	18 04	18 06	18 09		18 11			18 19
London Blackfriars a	17 23	17 26	17 28	17 33	17 36	17 41	17 43				17 48	17 51	17 53	17 56	17 58	18 03	18 06	18 08	18 11		18 13			18 21
London Blackfriars ⊖ d	17 24	17 26	17 29	17 34	17 36	17 41	17 44			17 46	17 49	17 51	17 54	17 56	17 59	18 04	18 06	18 09	18 11		18 14		18 16	18 21
London Bridge d	17 30		17 35	17 41		17 48	17 51	17 55			17 55		18 00		18 05	18 11		18 15	18 18		18 21	18 25		
Elephant & Castle ⊖173,179 a		17 30			17 40					17 50		17 55		18 00			18 10						18 19	18 25
Loughborough Jn 173,179 a					17 45							18 00					18 15							18 30
Herne Hill 173,179 a					17 49							18 04					18 19							18 34
Tulse Hill a					17 54							18 09					18 24							18 39
Streatham a					17 59							18 14					18 29							18 44
Wimbledon a												18 24												18 54
Sutton 179 a					18 17			18 29				18 44					18 47					18 59		19 14
Denmark Hill 195 a		17 37								17 57				18 07									18 27	
Peckham Rye 195 a		17 40								18 00				18 10									18 30	
Catford a		17 49								18 09				18 19									18 39	
Bromley South a		18 02								18 22				18 32									18 52	
Orpington a		18 16												18 48										
St Mary Cray a										18 30													19 01	
Swanley a										18 34													19 05	
Sevenoaks a										18 55													19 25	
Maidstone East a																								
Greenwich a						17 57													18 27					
Woolwich Arsenal a						18 10													18 40					
Abbey Wood a						18 16													18 46					
Dartford a						18 29													18 57					
Rainham Kt a						19 19													19 44					
East Croydon a	17 44		17 49	17 54			18 06				18 08		18 14		18 19	18 24		18 29			18 36			
Gatwick Airport a	18 15		18 05				18 41						18 45		18 35			18 44			19 11			
Horsham a	18 42												19 12											
Brighton a			18 46												19 15			19 21						

A To East Grinstead
B To Dorking
C To Littlehampton

Bedford, Luton, Cambridge, Stevenage and London - Gatwick Airport and Brighton

		TL ■	TL	TL ■	TL ■ A	TL	TL	TL ■	TL B	TL	TL	TL ■	TL	TL ■	TL ■ A	TL	TL ■	TL	TL ■	TL C	TL	TL	TL ■
Bedford	d			17 18	17 28			17 40						17 46	17 56				18 06				
Luton	d		17 32	17 42	17 53		17 46	17 57					18 02	18 12	18 20			18 16	18 27				
Luton Airport Parkway ■	d		17 35	17 45			17 49	18 00					18 05	18 15	18 22			18 19	18 30				
Harpenden	d		17 40	17 50			17 54	18 06					18 10	18 20	18 27			18 24	18 36				
St Albans City	d		17 46	17 56	18 03	17 52	18 00	18 12			18 07		18 16	18 26	18 33	18 22		18 30	18 42			18 37	
Elstree & Borehamwood	d		17 54			18 01	18 09				18 16		18 24			18 31		18 39				18 46	
West Hampstead Thameslink	d		18 06			18 17	18 21	18 24			18 31		18 36			18 47		18 51	18 54			19 00	
Kentish Town	d		18 11			18 22					18 36		18 41			18 52						19 05	
Peterborough	d	16 54										17 24											17 54
Huntingdon	d	17 11										17 41											18 11
Cambridge	d																17 54						
Royston	d																18 09						
Letchworth Garden City	d																18 21						
Hitchin	d	17 41										18 11					18 26						18 41
Stevenage	d	17 47										18 17					18 32						18 47
Welwyn Garden City	d																						
Finsbury Park	d	18 08										18 37					18 52						19 08
St Pancras International	d	18 15	18 17	18 20	18 25	18 27	18 32	18 35			18 42	18 45	18 47	18 50	18 55	18 57	19 00	19 02	19 05			19 12	19 15
Farringdon ■ ⊖	d	18 19	18 22	18 24	18 29	18 32	18 37	18 39			18 47	18 49	18 52	18 54	18 59	19 02	19 04	19 07	19 09			19 17	19 19
City Thameslink ■	d	18 21	18 24	18 26	18 31	18 34	18 39	18 41			18 49	18 51	18 54	18 56	19 01	19 04	19 06	19 09	19 11			19 19	19 21
London Blackfriars	a	18 23	18 26	18 28	18 33	18 36	18 41	18 43			18 51	18 53	18 56	18 58	19 03	19 06	19 08	19 11	19 13			19 21	19 23
London Blackfriars ■ ⊖	d	18 24	18 26	18 29	18 34	18 36	18 41	18 44		18 46	18 51	18 54	18 56	18 59	19 04	19 06	19 09	19 11	19 14		19 16	19 21	19 24
London Bridge	d	18 30		18 35	18 41		18 48	18 51	18 55			19 00		19 05	19 11		19 15	19 18	19 21	19 25			19 30
Elephant & Castle ⊖ 173,179	a		18 30			18 40				18 49	18 55		19 00			19 10					19 19	19 25	
Loughborough Jn 173,179	a					18 45					19 00					19 15						19 30	
Herne Hill ■ 173,179	a					18 49					19 04					19 19						19 34	
Tulse Hill ■	a					18 54					19 09					19 24						19 39	
Streatham ■	a					18 59					19 14					19 29						19 44	
Wimbledon	a										19 24											19 54	
Sutton ■ 179	a					19 17			19 28		19 44					19 47				19 58		20 14	
Denmark Hill ■ 195	a		18 37							18 57			19 07								19 27		
Peckham Rye ■ 195	a		18 40							19 00			19 10								19 30		
Catford	a		18 49							19 09			19 19								19 39		
Bromley South	a		19 02							19 22			19 32								19 52		
Orpington	a		19 14										19 44										
St Mary Cray	a									19 31											20 01		
Swanley	a									19 35											20 05		
Sevenoaks	a									19 55											20 25		
Maidstone East	a																						
Greenwich	a						18 57											19 27					
Woolwich Arsenal	a						19 10											19 40					
Abbey Wood	a						19 16											19 46					
Dartford	a						19 27											19 57					
Rainham Kt	a						20 12											20 41					
East Croydon	a	18 44		18 49	18 54			19 06				19 14		19 19	19 24		19 29		19 36				19 44
Gatwick Airport ■ ✈	a	19 15		19 05				19 41				19 45		19 35			19 44		20 11				20 14
Horsham	a	19 42										20 12											20 39
Brighton ■	a			19 46										20 13			20 19						

A To East Grinstead
B To Guildford
C To Epsom

Table T052-R

Mondays to Fridays

21 May to 7 December

Bedford, Luton, Cambridge, Stevenage and London - Gatwick Airport and Brighton

		TL	TL ■	TL	TL	TL ■	TL A	TL	TL	TL ■	TL	TL ■ B	TL ■ C	TL	TL ■	TL	TL ■	TL	TL ■ D	TL A	TL	TL ■	TL
Bedford	d		18 16			18 32						18 46	18 46				19 02						
Luton	d	18 32	18 42		18 46	18 57					19 02	19 12	19 12			19 18	19 27						19 32
Luton Airport Parkway ■	d	18 35	18 45		18 49	19 00					19 05	19 15	19 15			19 21	19 30						19 35
Harpenden	d	18 40	18 50		18 54	19 06					19 10	19 21	19 21			19 26	19 36						19 40
St Albans City	d	18 46	18 56	18 52	19 00	19 11			19 07		19 16	19 27	19 27	19 22		19 31	19 42				19 37		19 46
Elstree & Borehamwood	d	18 54		19 01	19 09				19 16		19 24			19 31		19 40					19 46		19 54
West Hampstead Thameslink	d	19 07		19 16	19 21				19 31		19 36	19 39	19 39	19 46		19 51					20 01		20 06
Kentish Town	d	19 11		19 21					19 36		19 41			19 51							20 06		20 11
Peterborough	d									18 24												18 52	
Huntingdon	d									18 41												19 10	
Cambridge	d														18 53								
Royston	d														19 09								
Letchworth Garden City	d														19 21								
Hitchin	d									19 11					19 26							19 39	
Stevenage	d									19 17					19 32							19 45	
Welwyn Garden City	d																						
Finsbury Park	d									19 38					19 52							20 08	
St Pancras International	d	19 17	19 20	19 27	19 32	19 35			19 42	19 45	19 47	19 50	19 51	19 57	20 00	20 02	20 05				20 12	20 15	20 17
Farringdon ■ ⊖	d	19 22	19 24	19 32	19 37	19 39			19 47	19 49	19 52	19 54	19 55	20 02	20 04	20 07	20 09				20 17	20 19	20 22
City Thameslink ■	d	19 24	19 26	19 34	19 39	19 41			19 49	19 51	19 54	19 56	19 57	20 04	20 06	20 09	20 11				20 19	20 21	20 24
London Blackfriars	a	19 26	19 28	19 36	19 41	19 43			19 51	19 53	19 56	19 58	19 59	20 06	20 08	20 11	20 13				20 21	20 23	20 26
London Blackfriars ■ ⊖	d	19 26	19 29	19 36	19 41	19 44		19 46	19 51	19 54	19 56	19 59	20 00	20 06	20 09	20 11	20 14	20 16			20 21	20 24	20 26
London Bridge	d		19 35		19 48	19 51	19 55			20 00		20 05	20 06		20 15	20 18	20 21		20 22	20 25		20 30	
Elephant & Castle ⊖ 173,179	a	19 30		19 40				19 49	19 55		20 00			20 10				20 19			20 25		20 30
Loughborough Jn 173,179	a			19 45					20 00					20 15							20 30		
Herne Hill ■ 173,179	a			19 49					20 04					20 19							20 34		
Tulse Hill ■	a			19 54					20 09					20 24							20 39		
Streatham ■	a			19 59					20 14					20 29							20 44		
Wimbledon	a								20 24												20 54		
Sutton ■ 179	a			20 17			20 28		20 44					20 47						20 58	21 14		
Denmark Hill ■ 195	a	19 37						19 57			20 08							20 27					20 37
Peckham Rye ■ 195	a	19 41						20 00			20 11							20 30					20 40
Catford	a	19 50						20 09			20 19							20 39					20 49
Bromley South	a	20 03						20 22			20 32							20 52					21 02
Orpington	a	20 14									20 44												21 14
St Mary Cray	a							20 31										21 01					
Swanley	a							20 35										21 05					
Sevenoaks	a							20 55										21 25					
Maidstone East	a																						
Greenwich	a				19 57											20 27							
Woolwich Arsenal	a				20 10											20 40							
Abbey Wood	a				20 16											20 46							
Dartford	a				20 27											20 57							
Rainham Kt	a				21 11											21 41							
East Croydon	a		19 48			20 06				20 14		20 18	20 19		20 28		20 36		20 38			20 44	
Gatwick Airport ■ ✈	a		20 04			20 38				20 42		20 34	20 34		20 44		21 08		20 53			21 12	
Horsham	a									21 08												21 38	
Brighton ■	a		20 44									21 12	21 12		21 19								

A To Epsom
B from 30 July
C until 27 July
D To Three Bridges

Table T052-R

Mondays to Fridays

21 May to 7 December

Bedford, Luton, Cambridge, Stevenage and London - Gatwick Airport and Brighton

		TL ■ A	TL ■ B	TL C	TL D	TL	TL ■	TL	TL ■ E	TL F	TL	TL ■	TL	TL ■	TL	TL ■	TL	TL ■	TL	TL ■ E	TL F	TL	TL ■
Bedford	d	19 16	19 16				19 32							19 48				20 04					
Luton ■	d	19 41	19 42			19 48	19 57							20 14			20 18	20 29					
Luton Airport Parkway ■ ✈	d	19 44	19 45			19 51	20 00							20 16			20 21	20 32					
Harpenden	d	19 50	19 52			19 56	20 08							20 22			20 26	20 38					
St Albans City	d	19 55	19 57	19 51	19 52	20 01	20 13				20 07			20 27	20 22		20 31	20 43				20 37	
Elstree & Borehamwood	d			20 00	20 01	20 10					20 16				20 31		20 40					20 46	
West Hampstead Thameslink	d	20 09	20 09	20 16	20 16	20 21					20 31			20 39	20 46		20 51					21 01	
Kentish Town	d			20 21	20 21						20 36		20 41		20 51							21 06	
Peterborough	d											19 24											19 54
Huntingdon	d											19 41											20 11
Cambridge	d															19 54							
Royston	d															20 09							
Letchworth Garden City	d															20 21							
Hitchin	d											20 11				20 26							20 41
Stevenage	d											20 17				20 32							20 47
Welwyn Garden City	d																						
Finsbury Park	d											20 38				20 52							21 08
St Pancras International	d	20 20	20 20	20 27	20 27	20 32	20 35				20 42	20 45	20 47	20 50	20 57	21 00	21 02	21 05				21 12	21 15
Farringdon ■ ⊖	d	20 24	20 24	20 32	20 32	20 37	20 39				20 47	20 49	20 52	20 54	21 02	21 04	21 07	21 09				21 17	21 19
City Thameslink ■	d	20 26	20 26	20 34	20 34	20 39	20 41				20 49	20 51	20 54	20 56	21 04	21 06	21 09	21 11				21 19	21 21
London Blackfriars	a	20 28	20 28	20 36	20 36	20 41	20 43				20 51	20 53	20 56	20 58	21 06	21 08	21 11	21 13				21 21	21 23
London Blackfriars ■ ⊖	d	20 29	20 29	20 36	20 36	20 41	20 44	20 46			20 51	20 54	20 56	20 59	21 06	21 09	21 11	21 14	21 16			21 21	21 24
London Bridge	d	20 35	20 35			20 48	20 51		20 52	20 55		21 00		21 05		21 15	21 18	21 21		21 22	21 25		21 30
Elephant & Castle ⊖173,179	a			20 40	20 40			20 49			20 55		21 00		21 10				21 19			21 25	
Loughborough Jn 173,179	a			20 45	20 45						21 00				21 15							21 30	
Herne Hill ■ 173,179	a			20 49	20 49						21 04				21 19							21 34	
Tulse Hill ■	a			20 54	20 54						21 09				21 24							21 39	
Streatham ■	a			20 59	20 59						21 14				21 29							21 44	
Wimbledon	a										21 24											21 54	
Sutton ■ 179	a			21 17	21 17					21 28	21 44				21 47						21 58	22 14	
Denmark Hill ■ 195	a							20 57					21 07						21 27				
Peckham Rye ■ 195	a							21 00					21 10						21 30				
Catford	a							21 09					21 19						21 39				
Bromley South	a							21 22					21 32						21 52				
Orpington	a												21 44										
St Mary Cray	a							21 31											22 01				
Swanley	a							21 35											22 05				
Sevenoaks	a							21 55											22 25				
Maidstone East	a																						
Greenwich	a					20 57											21 27						
Woolwich Arsenal	a					21 10											21 40						
Abbey Wood	a					21 16											21 46						
Dartford	a					21 27											21 57						
Rainham Kt	a					22 12											22 41						
East Croydon 🚌	a	20 48	20 48				21 06		21 08			21 14		21 18		21 28		21 36		21 38			21 44
Gatwick Airport ■ ✈	a	21 04	21 04				21 37		21 23			21 42		21 34		21 44		22 08		21 53			22 12
Horsham	a											22 08											22 38
Brighton ■	a	21 44	21 44											22 12		22 19							

A until 27 July
B from 30 July
C until 20 July, from 8 October
D from 23 July until 5 October
E To Three Bridges
F To Epsom

Table T052-R

Mondays to Fridays

21 May to 7 December

Bedford, Luton, Cambridge, Stevenage and London - Gatwick Airport and Brighton

		TL	TL ■	TL	TL	TL ■	TL A	TL	TL	TL ■	TL	TL ■	TL	TL ■	TL	TL ■	TL A	TL	TL	TL ■	TL	TL ■
Bedford	d		20 18			20 34						20 49				21 05						21 19
Luton ■	d		20 43		20 48	20 59						21 13			21 18	21 29						21 43
Luton Airport Parkway ■ ✈	d		20 46		20 51	21 02						21 16			21 21	21 32						21 46
Harpenden	d		20 52		20 56	21 08						21 22			21 26	21 38						21 52
St Albans City	d		20 57	20 52	21 01	21 13			21 07			21 27	21 22		21 31	21 43			21 37			21 57
Elstree & Borehamwood	d			21 01	21 10				21 16				21 31		21 40				21 46			
West Hampstead Thameslink	d		21 09	21 16	21 21				21 31			21 39	21 46		21 51				22 01			22 09
Kentish Town	d	21 11		21 21					21 36		21 41		21 51						22 06		22 11	
Peterborough	d									20 24										20 54		
Huntingdon	d									20 41										21 11		
Cambridge	d													20 54								
Royston	d													21 08								
Letchworth Garden City	d													21 19								
Hitchin	d									21 11				21 24						21 41		
Stevenage	d									21 17				21 29						21 47		
Welwyn Garden City	d																					
Finsbury Park	d									21 37				21 53						22 07		
St Pancras International	d	21 17	21 20	21 27	21 32	21 35			21 42	21 45	21 47	21 51	21 57	22 00	22 02	22 05			22 12	22 15	22 17	22 20
Farringdon ■ ⊖	d	21 22	21 24	21 32	21 37	21 39			21 47	21 49	21 52	21 55	22 02	22 04	22 07	22 09			22 17	22 19	22 22	22 24
City Thameslink ■	d	21 24	21 26	21 34	21 39	21 41			21 49	21 51	21 54	21 57	22 04	22 06	22 09	22 11			22 19	22 21	22 24	22 26
London Blackfriars	a	21 26	21 28	21 36	21 41	21 43			21 51	21 53	21 56	21 59	22 06	22 08	22 11	22 13			22 21	22 23	22 26	22 28
London Blackfriars ■ ⊖	d	21 26	21 29	21 36	21 41	21 44		21 46	21 51	21 54	21 56	22 00	22 06	22 09	22 11	22 14		22 16	22 21	22 24	22 26	22 29
London Bridge	d		21 35		21 48	21 51	21 55			22 00		22 06		22 15	22 18	22 21	22 25			22 30		22 35
Elephant & Castle ⊖173,179	a	21 30		21 40				21 49	21 55		22 00		22 10					22 19	22 25		22 30	
Loughborough Jn 173,179	a			21 45					22 00				22 15						22 30			
Herne Hill ■ 173,179	a			21 49					22 04				22 19						22 34			
Tulse Hill ■	a			21 54					22 09				22 24						22 39			
Streatham ■	a			21 59					22 14				22 29						22 44			
Wimbledon	a								22 24										22 54			
Sutton ■ 179	a			22 17			22 28		22 44				22 47				22 58		23 14			
Denmark Hill ■ 195	a	21 37						21 57			22 07							22 27			22 37	
Peckham Rye ■ 195	a	21 40						22 00			22 10							22 30			22 40	
Catford	a	21 49						22 09			22 19							22 39			22 49	
Bromley South	a	22 02						22 22			22 32							22 52			23 02	
Orpington	a	22 14									22 44										23 14	
St Mary Cray	a							22 31										23 01				
Swanley	a							22 35										23 05				
Sevenoaks	a							22 55										23 25				
Maidstone East	a																					
Greenwich	a				21 57										22 27							
Woolwich Arsenal	a				22 10										22 40							
Abbey Wood	a				22 16										22 46							
Dartford	a				22 27										22 57							
Rainham Kt	a				23 11										23 41							
East Croydon 🚌	a		21 48			22 06				22 14		22 19		22 28		22 36				22 44		22 48
Gatwick Airport ■ ✈	a		22 04			22 38				22 42		22 34		22 44		23 08				23 12		23 04
Horsham	a									23 08										23 38		
Brighton ■	a		22 44									23 12		23 19								23 44

A To Epsom

Table T052-R

Mondays to Fridays

21 May to 7 December

Bedford, Luton, Cambridge, Stevenage and London - Gatwick Airport and Brighton

		TL	TL A	TL ■ B	TL C	TL	TL	TL ■	TL	TL ■	TL	TL ■	TL A	TL ■	TL	TL	TL ■	TL ■	TL	TL	TL ■	TL ■ B	TL ■
Bedford	d			21 35						21 49				22 05				22 17			22 45	23 05	23 45
Luton ■	d		21 48	21 59						22 13			22 18	22 29				22 41			23 10	23 30	00 10
Luton Airport Parkway ■ ✈	d		21 51	22 02						22 16			22 21	22 32				22 44			23 13	23 33	00 13
Harpenden	d		21 56	22 08						22 22			22 26	22 38				22 49			23 18	23 38	00 18
St Albans City	d	21 52	22 01	22 13			22 08			22 27	22 22		22 31	22 43		22 37		22 55		23 09	23 25	23 45	00 25
Elstree & Borehamwood	d	22 01	22 10				22 17				22 31		22 40			22 46				23 18		23 54	
West Hampstead Thameslink	d	22 16	22 21				22 31			22 39	22 46		22 51			23 01		23 11		23 33	23 41	00 09	00 42
Kentish Town	d	22 21					22 36		22 41		22 51					23 06				23 38		00 13	
Peterborough	d							21 24									21 54						
Huntingdon	d							21 41									22 11						
Cambridge	d											21 54											
Royston	d											22 09											
Letchworth Garden City	d											22 21											
Hitchin	d							22 11				22 26					22 41						
Stevenage	d							22 17				22 32					22 47						
Welwyn Garden City	d																						
Finsbury Park	d							22 37				22 52					23 07						
St Pancras International	d	22 27	22 32	22 35			22 42	22 45	22 47	22 50	22 57	23 00	23 02	23 05		23 12	23 15	23 22		23 44	23 51	00 21	00 52
Farringdon ■ ⊖	d	22 32	22 37	22 39			22 47	22 49	22 52	22 54	23 02	23 04	23 07	23 09		23 17	23 19	23 27		23 49	23 56	00 26	
City Thameslink ■	d	22 34	22 39	22 41			22 49	22 51	22 54	22 56													
London Blackfriars	a	22 36	22 41	22 43			22 51	22 53	22 56	22 58	23 06	23 08	23 11	23 13		23 21	23 23	23 30		23 53	23 59	00 30	01 01
London Blackfriars ■ ⊖	d	22 36	22 41	22 44		22 46	22 51	22 54	22 56	22 59	23 06	23 09	23 11	23 14	23 16	23 21	23 24	23 31	23 46	23 53	00 01	00 31	01 02
London Bridge	d		22 48	22 51	22 55			23 00		23 05		23 15	23 18	23 21			23 30	23 37					
Elephant & Castle ⊖173,179	a	22 40				22 49	22 55		23 00		23 10				23 19	23 25			23 49	23 57			
Loughborough Jn 173,179	a	22 45					23 00				23 15					23 30				00 02			
Herne Hill ■ 173,179	a	22 49					23 04				23 19					23 34				00 06			
Tulse Hill ■	a	22 54					23 09				23 24					23 39				00 10			
Streatham ■	a	22 59					23 14				23 29					23 44				00 14			
Wimbledon	a						23 24									23 54				00 24			
Sutton ■ 179	a	23 17			23 28		23 44				23 47					00 14				00 44			
Denmark Hill ■ 195	a					22 57			23 07						23 27				23 57				
Peckham Rye ■ 195	a					23 00			23 10						23 30				00 01				
Catford	a					23 09			23 19						23 39				00 10				
Bromley South	a					23 22			23 32						23 52				00 22				
Orpington	a								23 44														
St Mary Cray	a					23 31									00 01				00 31				
Swanley	a					23 35									00 06				00 35				
Sevenoaks	a					23 55									00 25				00 55				
Maidstone East	a																						
Greenwich	a		22 57										23 27										
Woolwich Arsenal	a		23 10										23 40										
Abbey Wood	a		23 16										23 46										
Dartford	a		23 27										23 57										
Rainham Kt	a																						
East Croydon	a			23 06				23 14		23 18		23 28		23 36			23 44	23 50			00 27	00 57	01 28
Gatwick Airport ■ ✈	a			23 37				23 41		23 34		23 47		00 01			00 12	00 17			00 48	01 20	01 56
Horsham	a							00 06									00 36						
Brighton ■	a									00 12		00 23						00 56			01 24		02 28

A To Gillingham (Kent)   B To Three Bridges   C To Epsom

Table T052-R

Saturdays

26 May to 8 December

Bedford, Luton, Cambridge, Stevenage and London - Gatwick Airport and Brighton

		TL ■ A	TL ■ B	TL ■ A	TL ■ C	TL ■ C	TL ■ C	TL ■ C	TL ■	TL ■	TL ■	TL	TL	TL ■	TL	TL	TL	TL	TL ■	TL ■	TL	TL ■	TL
Bedford	d				00 15	01 15	01 53	02 15	02 53	03 10	03 45			04 13						04 45			
Luton ■	d			00 10	00 40	01 40	02 18	02 40	03 18	03 35	04 10		04 20	04 38				04 50		05 10			
Luton Airport Parkway ■ ✈	d			00 13	00 43	01 43	02 21	02 43	03 21	03 38	04 13		04 23	04 41				04 53		05 13			
Harpenden	d			00 18	00 48	01 48	02 26	02 48	03 26	03 43	04 18		04 28	04 46				04 58		05 18			
St Albans City	d			00 25	00 55	01 55	02 33	02 55	03 33	03 50	04 25		04 35	04 53				05 05		05 25			
Elstree & Borehamwood	d				01 04	02 04		03 04		03 59			04 44					05 14					
West Hampstead Thameslink	d		00 09	00 42	01 20	02 20	02 50	03 20	03 50	04 15	04 41		04 59	05 09	05 16	05 22		05 29		05 41	05 46		05 52
Kentish Town	d		00 13		01 24	02 24		03 24		04 19			05 04		05 21			05 34			05 51		
Peterborough	d																		04 18				
Huntingdon	d																		04 33				
Cambridge	d																					04 53	
Royston	d																					05 09	
Letchworth Garden City	d																					05 21	
Hitchin	d																		05 05			05 26	
Stevenage	d																		05 11			05 32	
Welwyn Garden City	d																		05 20				
Finsbury Park	d																		05 35			05 52	
St Pancras International	d		00 21	00 52	01 32	02 32	03 02	03 32	04 02	04 32	04 51		05 12	05 20	05 27	05 32		05 42	05 45	05 50	05 57	06 00	06 02
Farringdon ■ ⊖	d		00 26								04 56		05 17	05 24	05 32	05 37		05 47	05 49	05 54	06 02	06 04	06 07
City Thameslink ■	d																						
London Blackfriars	a		00 30	01 01	01 39	02 39	03 09	03 39	04 09	04 39	05 00		05 21	05 28	05 36	05 41		05 51	05 53	05 58	06 06	06 08	06 11
London Blackfriars ■ ⊖	d	00 01	00 31	01 02	01 40	02 40	03 10	03 40	04 10	04 40	05 01	05 16	05 21	05 29	05 36	05 41	05 46	05 51	05 54	05 59	06 06	06 09	06 11
London Bridge	d													05 35		05 48			06 00	06 05		06 15	06 18
Elephant & Castle ⊖173,179	a											05 19	05 25		05 40		05 49	05 55			06 10		
Loughborough Jn 173,179	a												05 30		05 45			06 00			06 15		
Herne Hill ■ 173,179	a												05 34		05 49			06 04			06 19		
Tulse Hill ■	a												05 39		05 54			06 09			06 24		
Streatham ■	a												05 44		05 59			06 14			06 29		
Wimbledon	a												05 54					06 24					
Sutton ■ 179	a												06 14		06 17			06 44			06 47		
Denmark Hill ■ 195	a											05 27					05 57						
Peckham Rye ■ 195	a											05 30					06 00						
Catford	a											05 39					06 09						
Bromley South	a											05 52					06 22						
Orpington	a																						
St Mary Cray	a											06 01					06 31						
Swanley	a											06 05					06 35						
Sevenoaks	a											06 25					06 55						
Maidstone East	a																						
Greenwich	a															05 57							06 27
Woolwich Arsenal	a															06 10							06 40
Abbey Wood	a															06 16							06 46
Dartford	a															06 27							06 57
Rainham Kt	a															07 11							07 41
East Croydon	a	00 27	00 57	01 28	02 06	03 06	03 36	04 06	04 36	05 06	05 27			05 48					06 14	06 18		06 28	
Gatwick Airport ■ ✈	a	00 48	01 20	01 56	02 30	03 30	03 58	04 30	05 02	05 29	05 47			06 04					06 50	06 34		06 44	
Horsham	a																		07 14				
Brighton ■	a	01 24		02 28					05 38	06 07	06 26			06 46						07 06		07 22	

A From Bedford   B From Bedford to Three Bridges   C To Three Bridges

Table T052-R

Saturdays

26 May to 8 December

Bedford, Luton, Cambridge, Stevenage and London - Gatwick Airport and Brighton

		TL	TL	TL ■	TL ■	TL	TL	TL A	TL	TL	TL ■	TL	TL ■	TL	TL ■	TL	TL ■	TL A	TL	TL	TL ■	TL	TL ■
Bedford	d				05 15								05 49			06 00	06 05						06 19
Luton ■	d		05 20		05 40	05 36							06 13			06 18	06 29						06 43
Luton Airport Parkway ■ ✈	d		05 23		05 43	05 39							06 16			06 21	06 32						06 46
Harpenden	d		05 28		05 48	05 44							06 22			06 26	06 38						06 52
St Albans City	d		05 35		05 55	05 51				06 07			06 27	06 22		06 31	06 43			06 37			06 57
Elstree & Borehamwood	d		05 44			06 00				06 16				06 31		06 40				06 46			
West Hampstead Thameslink	d		05 59		06 09	06 17	06 22			06 31			06 39	06 46		06 51				07 01			07 09
Kentish Town	d		06 04			06 21				06 36				06 51						07 06		07 11	
Peterborough	d			04 54							05 24										05 54		
Huntingdon	d			05 11							05 41										06 11		
Cambridge	d														05 54								
Royston	d														06 09								
Letchworth Garden City	d														06 21								
Hitchin	d			05 41							06 11				06 26						06 41		
Stevenage	d			05 47							06 17				06 32						06 47		
Welwyn Garden City	d																						
Finsbury Park	d			06 07							06 37				06 52						07 07		
St Pancras International	d		06 12	06 15	06 20	06 27	06 32			06 42	06 45		06 50	06 57	07 00	07 02	07 05			07 12	07 15	07 17	07 20
Farringdon ■ ⊖	d		06 17	06 19	06 24	06 32	06 37			06 47	06 49		06 54	07 02	07 04	07 07	07 09			07 17	07 19	07 22	07 24
City Thameslink ■	d																						
London Blackfriars	a		06 21	06 23	06 28	06 36	06 41			06 51	06 53		06 58	07 06	07 08	07 11	07 13			07 21	07 23	07 26	07 28
London Blackfriars ■ ⊖	d	06 16	06 21	06 24	06 29	06 36	06 41		06 46	06 51	06 54	06 56	06 59	07 06	07 09	07 11	07 14		07 16	07 21	07 24	07 26	07 29
London Bridge	d			06 30	06 35		06 48	06 55			07 00		07 05		07 15	07 18	07 22	07 25			07 30		07 35
Elephant & Castle ⊖ 173,179	a	06 19	06 25			06 40			06 49	06 55		06 59		07 10					07 19	07 25		07 30	
Loughborough Jn 173,179	a		06 30			06 45				07 00				07 15						07 30			
Herne Hill ■ 173,179	a		06 34			06 49				07 04				07 19						07 34			
Tulse Hill ■	a		06 39			06 54				07 09				07 24						07 39			
Streatham ■	a		06 44			06 59				07 14				07 29						07 44			
Wimbledon	a		06 54							07 24										07 54			
Sutton ■ 179	a		07 14			07 17		07 28		07 44				07 47				07 58		08 14			
Denmark Hill ■ 195	a	06 27							06 57			07 07							07 27			07 37	
Peckham Rye ■ 195	a	06 30							07 00			07 10							07 30			07 40	
Catford	a	06 39							07 09			07 19							07 39			07 49	
Bromley South	a	06 52							07 22			07 32							07 52			08 02	
Orpington	a											07 44										08 14	
St Mary Cray	a	07 01							07 31										08 01				
Swanley	a	07 05							07 35										08 05				
Sevenoaks	a	07 25							07 55										08 25				
Maidstone East	a																						
Greenwich	a						06 57									07 27							
Woolwich Arsenal	a						07 10									07 40							
Abbey Wood	a						07 16									07 46							
Dartford	a						07 27									07 57							
Rainham Kt	a						08 11									08 41							
East Croydon	a			06 44	06 48						07 14		07 18		07 28		07 36				07 44		07 48
Gatwick Airport ■ ✈	a			07 12	07 04						07 42		07 34		07 44		08 08				08 12		08 04
Horsham	a			07 38							08 08										08 38		
Brighton ■	a				07 44								08 12		08 19								08 44

A To Epsom

Table T052-R

Saturdays

26 May to 8 December

Bedford, Luton, Cambridge, Stevenage and London - Gatwick Airport and Brighton

		TL	TL	TL ■	TL A	TL	TL	TL ■	TL	TL ■	TL	TL ■	TL	TL ■	TL A	TL	TL	TL ■	TL	TL ■	TL	TL	TL ■
Bedford	d		06 30	06 35						06 49				07 05						07 19			07 35
Luton ■	d		06 48	06 59						07 13			07 18	07 29						07 43		07 48	07 59
Luton Airport Parkway ■ ✈	d		06 51	07 02						07 16			07 21	07 32						07 46		07 51	08 02
Harpenden	d		06 56	07 08						07 22			07 26	07 38						07 52		07 56	08 08
St Albans City	d	06 52	07 01	07 13			07 07			07 27	07 22		07 31	07 43			07 37			07 57	07 52	08 01	08 13
Elstree & Borehamwood	d	07 01	07 10				07 16				07 31		07 40				07 46				08 01	08 10	
West Hampstead Thameslink	d	07 16	07 21				07 31			07 39	07 46		07 51				08 01			08 09	08 16	08 21	
Kentish Town	d	07 21					07 36		07 41		07 51						08 06		08 11		08 21		
Peterborough	d							06 24										06 54					
Huntingdon	d							06 41										07 11					
Cambridge	d											06 54											
Royston	d											07 09											
Letchworth Garden City	d											07 21											
Hitchin	d							07 11				07 26						07 41					
Stevenage	d							07 17				07 32						07 47					
Welwyn Garden City	d																						
Finsbury Park	d							07 37				07 52						08 08					
St Pancras International	d	07 27	07 32	07 35			07 42	07 45	07 47	07 50	07 57	08 00	08 02	08 05			08 12	08 15	08 17	08 20	08 27	08 32	08 35
Farringdon ■ ⊖	d	07 32	07 37	07 39			07 47	07 49	07 52	07 54	08 02	08 04	08 07	08 09			08 17	08 19	08 22	08 24	08 32	08 37	08 39
City Thameslink ■	d																						
London Blackfriars	a	07 36	07 41	07 43			07 51	07 53	07 56	07 58	08 06	08 08	08 11	08 13			08 21	08 23	08 26	08 28	08 36	08 41	08 43
London Blackfriars ■ ⊖	d	07 36	07 41	07 44		07 46	07 51	07 54	07 56	07 59	08 06	08 09	08 11	08 14		08 16	08 21	08 24	08 26	08 29	08 36	08 41	08 44
London Bridge	d		07 48	07 52	07 55			08 00		08 05		08 15	08 18	08 22	08 25			08 30		08 35		08 48	08 52
Elephant & Castle ⊖ 173,179	a	07 40				07 49	07 55		08 00		08 10					08 19	08 25		08 30		08 40		
Loughborough Jn 173,179	a	07 45					08 00				08 15						08 30				08 45		
Herne Hill ■ 173,179	a	07 49					08 04				08 19						08 34				08 49		
Tulse Hill ■	a	07 54					08 09				08 24						08 39				08 54		
Streatham ■	a	07 59					08 14				08 29						08 44				08 59		
Wimbledon	a						08 24										08 54						
Sutton ■ 179	a	08 17			08 28		08 44				08 47				08 58		09 14				09 17		
Denmark Hill ■ 195	a					07 57			08 07							08 27			08 37				
Peckham Rye ■ 195	a					08 00			08 10							08 30			08 40				
Catford	a					08 09			08 19							08 39			08 49				
Bromley South	a					08 22			08 32							08 52			09 02				
Orpington	a								08 44										09 14				
St Mary Cray	a					08 31										09 01							
Swanley	a					08 35										09 05							
Sevenoaks	a					08 55										09 25							
Maidstone East	a																						
Greenwich	a		07 57										08 27									08 57	
Woolwich Arsenal	a		08 10										08 40									09 10	
Abbey Wood	a		08 16										08 46									09 16	
Dartford	a		08 27										08 57									09 27	
Rainham Kt	a		09 11										09 41									10 11	
East Croydon	a			08 06				08 14		08 18		08 28		08 36				08 44		08 48			09 06
Gatwick Airport ■ ✈	a			08 38				08 42		08 34		08 44		09 08				09 12		09 04			09 38
Horsham	a							09 08										09 38					
Brighton ■	a									09 12		09 19								09 44			

A To Epsom

Table T052-R

Saturdays

26 May to 8 December

Bedford, Luton, Cambridge, Stevenage and London - Gatwick Airport and Brighton

		TL A	TL	TL	TL ■	TL	TL ■	TL	TL ■	TL	TL ■	TL A	TL	TL	TL ■	TL	TL ■	TL	TL	TL ■	TL A	TL	TL
Bedford	d						07 49				08 05						08 19			08 35			
Luton ■	d						08 13			08 18	08 29						08 43		08 48	08 59			
Luton Airport Parkway ■ ✈	d						08 16			08 21	08 32						08 46		08 51	09 02			
Harpenden	d						08 22			08 26	08 38						08 52		08 56	09 08			
St Albans City	d			08 07			08 27	08 22		08 31	08 43			08 37			08 57	08 52	09 01	09 13			09 07
Elstree & Borehamwood	d			08 16				08 31		08 40				08 46				09 01	09 10				09 16
West Hampstead Thameslink	d			08 31			08 39	08 46		08 51				09 01			09 09	09 16	09 21				09 31
Kentish Town	d			08 36		08 41		08 51						09 06		09 11		09 21					09 36
Peterborough	d				07 24										07 54								
Huntingdon	d				07 41										08 11								
Cambridge	d								07 54														
Royston	d								08 09														
Letchworth Garden City	d								08 21														
Hitchin	d				08 11				08 26						08 41								
Stevenage	d				08 17				08 32						08 47								
Welwyn Garden City	d																						
Finsbury Park	d				08 38				08 52						09 08								
St Pancras International	d			08 42	08 45	08 47	08 50	08 57	09 00	09 02	09 05			09 12	09 15	09 17	09 20	09 27	09 32	09 35			09 42
Farringdon ■ ⊖	d			08 47	08 49	08 52	08 54	09 02	09 04	09 07	09 09			09 17	09 19	09 22	09 24	09 32	09 37	09 39			09 47
City Thameslink ■	d							09 04	09 06	09 09	09 11			09 19	09 21	09 24	09 26	09 34	09 39	09 41			09 49
London Blackfriars	a			08 51	08 53	08 56	08 58	09 06	09 08	09 11	09 13			09 21	09 23	09 26	09 28	09 36	09 41	09 43			09 51
London Blackfriars ■ ⊖	d		08 46	08 51	08 54	08 56	08 59	09 06	09 09	09 11	09 14		09 16	09 21	09 24	09 26	09 29	09 36	09 41	09 44		09 46	09 51
London Bridge	d	08 55			09 00		09 05		09 15	09 18	09 22	09 25			09 30		09 35		09 48	09 52	09 55		
Elephant & Castle ⊖173,179	a		08 49	08 55		09 00		09 10					09 19	09 25		09 30		09 40				09 49	09 55
Loughborough Jn 173,179	a			09 00				09 15						09 30				09 45					10 00
Herne Hill ■ 173,179	a			09 04				09 19						09 34				09 49					10 04
Tulse Hill ■	a			09 09				09 24						09 39				09 54					10 09
Streatham ■	a			09 14				09 29						09 44				09 59					10 14
Wimbledon	a			09 24										09 54									10 24
Sutton ■ 179	a	09 28		09 44				09 47				09 58		10 14				10 17			10 28		10 44
Denmark Hill ■ 195	a		08 57			09 07							09 27			09 37						09 57	
Peckham Rye ■ 195	a		09 00			09 10							09 30			09 40						10 00	
Catford	a		09 09			09 19							09 39			09 49						10 09	
Bromley South	a		09 22			09 32							09 52			10 02						10 22	
Orpington	a					09 44										10 14							
St Mary Cray	a		09 32										10 01									10 31	
Swanley	a		09 36										10 05									10 35	
Sevenoaks	a		09 56										10 25									10 55	
Maidstone East	a																						
Greenwich	a									09 27									09 57				
Woolwich Arsenal	a									09 40									10 10				
Abbey Wood	a									09 46									10 16				
Dartford	a									09 57									10 27				
Rainham Kt	a									10 41									11 11				
East Croydon	a				09 14		09 18		09 28		09 36				09 44		09 48			10 06			
Gatwick Airport ■ ✈	a				09 42		09 34		09 44		10 08				10 12		10 04			10 38			
Horsham	a				10 08										10 38								
Brighton ■	a						10 12		10 19								10 44						

A To Epsom

Table T052-R

Saturdays

26 May to 8 December

Bedford, Luton, Cambridge, Stevenage and London - Gatwick Airport and Brighton

		TL ■	TL	TL ■	TL	TL ■	TL	TL ■	TL A	TL	TL	TL ■	TL	TL ■	TL	TL	TL ■	TL A	TL	TL	TL ■	TL	TL ■
Bedford	d			08 49				09 05						09 19			09 35						09 49
Luton ■	d			09 13			09 18	09 29						09 43		09 48	09 59						10 13
Luton Airport Parkway ■ ✈	d			09 16			09 21	09 32						09 46		09 51	10 02						10 16
Harpenden	d			09 22			09 26	09 38						09 52		09 56	10 08						10 22
St Albans City	d			09 27	09 22		09 31	09 43			09 37			09 57	09 52	10 01	10 13			10 07			10 27
Elstree & Borehamwood	d				09 31		09 40				09 46				10 01	10 10				10 16			
West Hampstead Thameslink	d			09 39	09 46		09 51				10 01			10 09	10 16	10 21				10 31			10 39
Kentish Town	d		09 41		09 51						10 06		10 11		10 21					10 36		10 41	
Peterborough	d	08 24										08 54									09 24		
Huntingdon	d	08 41										09 11									09 41		
Cambridge	d					08 54																	
Royston	d					09 09																	
Letchworth Garden City	d					09 21																	
Hitchin	d	09 11				09 26						09 41									10 11		
Stevenage	d	09 17				09 32						09 47									10 17		
Welwyn Garden City	d																						
Finsbury Park	d	09 38				09 52						10 08									10 38		
St Pancras International	d	09 45	09 47	09 50	09 57	10 00	10 02	10 05			10 12	10 15	10 17	10 20	10 27	10 32	10 35			10 42	10 45	10 47	10 50
Farringdon ■ ⊖	d	09 49	09 52	09 54	10 02	10 04	10 07	10 09			10 17	10 19	10 22	10 24	10 32	10 37	10 39			10 47	10 49	10 52	10 54
City Thameslink ■	d	09 51	09 54	09 56	10 04	10 06	10 09	10 11			10 19	10 21	10 24	10 26	10 34	10 39	10 41			10 49	10 51	10 54	10 56
London Blackfriars	a	09 53	09 56	09 58	10 06	10 08	10 11	10 13			10 21	10 23	10 26	10 28	10 36	10 41	10 43			10 51	10 53	10 56	10 58
London Blackfriars ■ ⊖	d	09 54	09 56	09 59	10 06	10 09	10 11	10 14		10 16	10 21	10 24	10 26	10 29	10 36	10 41	10 44		10 46	10 51	10 54	10 56	10 59
London Bridge	d	10 00		10 05		10 15	10 18	10 22	10 25			10 30		10 35		10 48	10 52	10 55			11 00		11 05
Elephant & Castle ⊖173,179	a		10 00		10 10					10 19	10 25		10 30		10 40				10 49	10 55		11 00	
Loughborough Jn 173,179	a				10 15						10 30				10 45					11 00			
Herne Hill ■ 173,179	a				10 19						10 34				10 49					11 04			
Tulse Hill ■	a				10 24						10 39				10 54					11 09			
Streatham ■	a				10 29						10 44				10 59					11 14			
Wimbledon	a										10 54									11 24			
Sutton ■ 179	a				10 47				10 58		11 14				11 17			11 28		11 44			
Denmark Hill ■ 195	a		10 07							10 27			10 37						10 57			11 07	
Peckham Rye ■ 195	a		10 10							10 30			10 40						11 00			11 10	
Catford	a		10 19							10 39			10 49						11 09			11 19	
Bromley South	a		10 32							10 52			11 02						11 22			11 32	
Orpington	a		10 44										11 14									11 44	
St Mary Cray	a									11 01									11 31				
Swanley	a									11 05									11 35				
Sevenoaks	a									11 25									11 55				
Maidstone East	a																						
Greenwich	a						10 27									10 57							
Woolwich Arsenal	a						10 40									11 10							
Abbey Wood	a						10 46									11 16							
Dartford	a						10 57									11 27							
Rainham Kt	a						11 41									12 11							
East Croydon	a	10 14		10 18		10 28		10 36				10 44		10 48			11 06				11 14		11 18
Gatwick Airport ■ ✈	a	10 42		10 34		10 44		11 08				11 12		11 04			11 37				11 42		11 34
Horsham	a	11 08										11 38									12 08		
Brighton ■	a			11 12		11 19								11 44									12 12

A To Epsom

Saturdays

26 May to 8 December

Bedford, Luton, Cambridge, Stevenage and London - Gatwick Airport and Brighton

	TL	TL ■	TL	TL ■	TL A	TL	TL	TL ■	TL	TL ■	TL	TL	TL ■	TL A	TL	TL	TL ■	TL	TL ■	TL	TL ■
Bedford d				10 05						10 19			10 35						10 49		
Luton d			10 18	10 29						10 43		10 48	10 59						11 13		
Luton Airport Parkway ✈ d			10 21	10 32						10 46		10 51	11 02						11 16		
Harpenden d			10 26	10 38						10 52		10 56	11 08						11 22		
St Albans City d	10 22		10 31	10 43			10 37			10 57	10 52	11 01	11 13			11 07			11 27	11 22	
Elstree & Borehamwood d	10 31		10 40				10 46				11 01	11 10				11 16				11 31	
West Hampstead Thameslink d	10 46		10 51				11 01			11 09	11 16	11 21				11 31			11 39	11 46	
Kentish Town d	10 51						11 06		11 11		11 21					11 36		11 41		11 51	
Peterborough d								09 54									10 24				
Huntingdon d								10 11									10 41				
Cambridge d		09 54																			10 54
Royston d		10 09																			11 09
Letchworth Garden City d		10 21																			11 21
Hitchin d		10 26						10 41									11 11				11 25
Stevenage d		10 32						10 47									11 17				11 31
Welwyn Garden City d																					
Finsbury Park d		10 52						11 08									11 38				11 52
St Pancras International d	10 57	11 00	11 02	11 05			11 12	11 15	11 17	11 20	11 27	11 32	11 35			11 42	11 45	11 47	11 50	11 57	12 00
Farringdon ⊖ d	11 02	11 04	11 07	11 09			11 17	11 19	11 22	11 24	11 32	11 37	11 39			11 47	11 49	11 52	11 54	12 02	12 04
City Thameslink d	11 04	11 06	11 09	11 11			11 19	11 21	11 24	11 26	11 34	11 39	11 41			11 49	11 51	11 54	11 56	12 04	12 06
London Blackfriars a	11 06	11 08	11 11	11 13			11 21	11 23	11 26	11 28	11 36	11 41	11 43			11 51	11 53	11 56	11 58	12 06	12 08
London Blackfriars ⊖ d	11 06	11 09	11 11	11 14		11 16	11 21	11 24	11 26	11 29	11 36	11 41	11 44		11 46	11 51	11 54	11 56	11 59	12 06	12 09
London Bridge d		11 15	11 18	11 22	11 25			11 30		11 35		11 48	11 52	11 55			12 00		12 05		12 15
Elephant & Castle ⊖173,179 a	11 10					11 19	11 25		11 30		11 40				11 49	11 55		12 00		12 10	
Loughborough Jn 173,179 a	11 15						11 30				11 45					12 00				12 15	
Herne Hill 173,179 a	11 19						11 34				11 49					12 04				12 19	
Tulse Hill a	11 24						11 39				11 54					12 09				12 24	
Streatham a	11 29						11 44				11 59					12 14				12 29	
Wimbledon a							11 54									12 24					
Sutton 179 a	11 47				11 58		12 14				12 17			12 28		12 44				12 47	
Denmark Hill 195 a						11 27			11 37						11 57			12 07			
Peckham Rye 195 a						11 30			11 40						12 00			12 10			
Catford a						11 39			11 49						12 09			12 19			
Bromley South a						11 52			12 02						12 22			12 32			
Orpington a									12 14									12 44			
St Mary Cray a						12 01									12 31						
Swanley a						12 05									12 35						
Sevenoaks a						12 25									12 55						
Maidstone East a																					
Greenwich a			11 27									11 57									
Woolwich Arsenal a			11 40									12 10									
Abbey Wood a			11 46									12 16									
Dartford a			11 57									12 27									
Rainham Kt a			12 41									13 11									
East Croydon a		11 28		11 36				11 44		11 48			12 06				12 14		12 18		12 28
Gatwick Airport ✈ a		11 44		12 08				12 12		12 04			12 38				12 42		12 34		12 44
Horsham a								12 38									13 08				
Brighton a		12 19								12 44									13 12		13 19

A To Epsom

Table T052-R

Saturdays

26 May to 8 December

Bedford, Luton, Cambridge, Stevenage and London - Gatwick Airport and Brighton

	TL	TL ■	TL A	TL	TL	TL ■	TL	TL ■	TL	TL	TL ■	TL A	TL	TL	TL ■	TL	TL ■	TL	TL ■	TL	TL ■	TL A
Bedford d		11 05						11 19			11 35						11 49				12 05	
Luton d	11 18	11 29						11 43		11 48	11 59						12 13			12 18	12 29	
Luton Airport Parkway ✈ d	11 21	11 32						11 46		11 51	12 02						12 16			12 21	12 32	
Harpenden d	11 26	11 38						11 52		11 56	12 08						12 22			12 26	12 38	
St Albans City d	11 31	11 43			11 37			11 57	11 52	12 01	12 13			12 07			12 27	12 22		12 31	12 43	
Elstree & Borehamwood d	11 40				11 46				12 01	12 10				12 16				12 31		12 40		
West Hampstead Thameslink d	11 51				12 01			12 09	12 16	12 21				12 31			12 39	12 46		12 51		
Kentish Town d					12 06		12 11		12 21					12 36		12 41		12 51				
Peterborough d						10 53									11 24							
Huntingdon d						11 11									11 41							
Cambridge d																			11 54			
Royston d																			12 09			
Letchworth Garden City d																			12 21			
Hitchin d						11 41									12 11				12 26			
Stevenage d						11 47									12 17				12 32			
Welwyn Garden City d																						
Finsbury Park d						12 08									12 37				12 52			
St Pancras International d	12 02	12 05			12 12	12 15	12 17	12 20	12 27	12 32	12 35			12 42	12 45	12 47	12 50	12 57	13 00	13 02	13 05	
Farringdon ⊖ d	12 07	12 09			12 17	12 19	12 22	12 24	12 32	12 37	12 39			12 47	12 49	12 52	12 54	13 02	13 04	13 07	13 09	
City Thameslink d	12 09	12 11			12 19	12 21	12 24	12 26	12 34	12 39	12 41			12 49	12 51	12 54	12 56	13 04	13 06	13 09	13 11	
London Blackfriars a	12 11	12 13			12 21	12 23	12 26	12 28	12 36	12 41	12 43			12 51	12 53	12 56	12 58	13 06	13 08	13 11	13 13	
London Blackfriars ⊖ d	12 11	12 14		12 16	12 21	12 24	12 26	12 29	12 36	12 41	12 44		12 46	12 51	12 54	12 56	12 59	13 06	13 09	13 11	13 14	
London Bridge d	12 18	12 22	12 25			12 30		12 35		12 48	12 52	12 55			13 00		13 05		13 15	13 18	13 22	13 25
Elephant & Castle ⊖173,179 a				12 19	12 25		12 30		12 40				12 49	12 55		13 00		13 10				
Loughborough Jn 173,179 a					12 30				12 45					13 00				13 15				
Herne Hill 173,179 a					12 34				12 49					13 04				13 19				
Tulse Hill a					12 39				12 54					13 09				13 24				
Streatham a					12 44				12 59					13 14				13 29				
Wimbledon a					12 54									13 24								
Sutton 179 a			12 58		13 14				13 17			13 28		13 44				13 47				13 58
Denmark Hill 195 a				12 27			12 37						12 57			13 07						
Peckham Rye 195 a				12 30			12 40						13 00			13 10						
Catford a				12 39			12 49						13 09			13 19						
Bromley South a				12 52			13 02						13 22			13 32						
Orpington a							13 14									13 44						
St Mary Cray a				13 01									13 31									
Swanley a				13 05									13 35									
Sevenoaks a				13 25									13 55									
Maidstone East a																						
Greenwich a	12 27									12 57										13 27		
Woolwich Arsenal a	12 40									13 10										13 40		
Abbey Wood a	12 46									13 16										13 46		
Dartford a	12 57									13 27										13 57		
Rainham Kt a	13 41									14 11										14 41		
East Croydon a		12 36				12 44		12 48			13 06				13 14		13 18		13 28		13 36	
Gatwick Airport ✈ a		13 08				13 12		13 04			13 38				13 42		13 34		13 44		14 08	
Horsham a						13 38									14 08							
Brighton a								13 44									14 12		14 19			

A To Epsom

Table T052-R

Saturdays

26 May to 8 December

Bedford, Luton, Cambridge, Stevenage and London - Gatwick Airport and Brighton

		TL	TL	TL ■	TL	TL ■	TL	TL	TL ■	TL A	TL	TL	TL ■	TL	TL ■	TL	TL ■	TL	TL ■	TL A	TL	TL	TL ■
Bedford	d					12 19			12 35						12 49				13 05				
Luton ■	d					12 43		12 48	12 59						13 13			13 18	13 29				
Luton Airport Parkway ■ ✈	d					12 46		12 51	13 02						13 16			13 21	13 32				
Harpenden	d					12 52		12 56	13 08						13 22			13 26	13 38				
St Albans City	d		12 37			12 57	12 52	13 01	13 13			13 07			13 27	13 22		13 31	13 43			13 37	
Elstree & Borehamwood	d		12 46				13 01	13 10				13 16				13 31		13 40				13 46	
West Hampstead Thameslink	d		13 01			13 09	13 16	13 21				13 31			13 39	13 46		13 51				14 01	
Kentish Town	d		13 06		13 11		13 21					13 36		13 41		13 51						14 06	
Peterborough	d			11 54									12 24										12 54
Huntingdon	d			12 11									12 41										13 11
Cambridge	d																12 54						
Royston	d																13 09						
Letchworth Garden City	d																13 21						
Hitchin	d			12 41									13 11				13 26						13 41
Stevenage	d			12 47									13 17				13 32						13 47
Welwyn Garden City	d																						
Finsbury Park	d			13 08									13 38				13 52						14 07
St Pancras International	d		13 12	13 15	13 17	13 20	13 27	13 32	13 35			13 42	13 45	13 47	13 50	13 57	14 00	14 02	14 05			14 12	14 15
Farringdon ■ ⊖	d		13 17	13 19	13 22	13 24	13 32	13 37	13 39			13 47	13 49	13 52	13 54	14 02	14 04	14 07	14 09			14 17	14 19
City Thameslink ■	d		13 19	13 21	13 24	13 26	13 34	13 39	13 41			13 49	13 51	13 54	13 56	14 04	14 06	14 09	14 11			14 19	14 21
London Blackfriars	a		13 21	13 23	13 26	13 28	13 36	13 41	13 43			13 51	13 53	13 56	13 58	14 06	14 08	14 11	14 13			14 21	14 23
London Blackfriars ■ ⊖	d	13 16	13 21	13 24	13 26	13 29	13 36	13 41	13 44		13 46	13 51	13 54	13 56	13 59	14 06	14 09	14 11	14 14		14 16	14 21	14 24
London Bridge	d			13 30		13 35		13 48	13 52	13 55			14 00		14 05		14 15	14 18	14 22	14 25			14 30
Elephant & Castle ⊖173,179	a	13 19	13 25		13 30		13 40				13 49	13 55		14 00		14 10					14 19	14 25	
Loughborough Jn 173,179	a		13 30				13 45					14 00				14 15						14 30	
Herne Hill ■ 173,179	a		13 34				13 49					14 04				14 19						14 34	
Tulse Hill ■	a		13 39				13 54					14 09				14 24						14 39	
Streatham ■	a		13 44				13 59					14 14				14 29						14 44	
Wimbledon	a		13 54									14 24										14 54	
Sutton ■ 179	a		14 14				14 17			14 28		14 44				14 47				14 58		15 14	
Denmark Hill ■ 195	a	13 27			13 37						13 57			14 07							14 27		
Peckham Rye ■ 195	a	13 30			13 40						14 00			14 11							14 30		
Catford	a	13 39			13 49						14 09			14 20							14 39		
Bromley South	a	13 52			14 02						14 22			14 33							14 52		
Orpington	a				14 14									14 44									
St Mary Cray	a	14 01									14 31										15 01		
Swanley	a	14 05									14 35										15 05		
Sevenoaks	a	14 25									14 55										15 25		
Maidstone East	a																						
Greenwich	a							13 57										14 27					
Woolwich Arsenal	a							14 10										14 40					
Abbey Wood	a							14 16										14 46					
Dartford	a							14 27										14 57					
Rainham Kt	a							15 11										15 41					
East Croydon 🚌	a			13 44		13 48			14 06				14 14		14 18		14 28		14 36				14 44
Gatwick Airport ■ ✈	a			14 12		14 04			14 38				14 42		14 34		14 44		15 08				15 12
Horsham	a			14 38									15 08										15 38
Brighton ■	a					14 44									15 12		15 19						

A To Epsom

Table T052-R

Saturdays

26 May to 8 December

Bedford, Luton, Cambridge, Stevenage and London - Gatwick Airport and Brighton

		TL	TL ■	TL	TL	TL ■	TL A	TL	TL	TL ■	TL	TL ■	TL	TL ■	TL	TL ■	TL A	TL	TL	TL ■	TL	TL ■	TL
Bedford	d		13 19			13 35						13 49				14 05						14 19	
Luton ■	d		13 43		13 48	13 59						14 13			14 18	14 29						14 43	
Luton Airport Parkway ■ ✈	d		13 46		13 51	14 02						14 16			14 21	14 32						14 46	
Harpenden	d		13 52		13 56	14 08						14 22			14 26	14 38						14 52	
St Albans City	d		13 57	13 52	14 01	14 13			14 07			14 27	14 22		14 31	14 43			14 37			14 57	14 52
Elstree & Borehamwood	d			14 01	14 10				14 16				14 31		14 40				14 46				15 01
West Hampstead Thameslink	d		14 09	14 16	14 21				14 31			14 39	14 46		14 51				15 01			15 09	15 16
Kentish Town	d	14 11		14 21					14 36		14 41		14 51						15 06		15 11		15 21
Peterborough	d									13 24										13 54			
Huntingdon	d									13 41										14 11			
Cambridge	d													13 54									
Royston	d													14 09									
Letchworth Garden City	d													14 21									
Hitchin	d									14 11				14 26						14 41			
Stevenage	d									14 17				14 32						14 47			
Welwyn Garden City	d																						
Finsbury Park	d									14 38				14 52						15 07			
St Pancras International	d	14 17	14 20	14 27	14 32	14 35			14 42	14 45	14 47	14 50	14 57	15 00	15 02	15 05			15 12	15 15	15 17	15 20	15 27
Farringdon ■ ⊖	d	14 22	14 24	14 32	14 37	14 39			14 47	14 49	14 52	14 54	15 02	15 04	15 07	15 09			15 17	15 19	15 22	15 24	15 32
City Thameslink ■	d	14 24	14 26	14 34	14 39	14 41			14 49	14 51	14 54	14 56	15 04	15 06	15 09	15 11			15 19	15 21	15 24	15 26	15 34
London Blackfriars	a	14 26	14 28	14 36	14 41	14 43			14 51	14 53	14 56	14 58	15 06	15 08	15 11	15 13			15 21	15 23	15 26	15 28	15 36
London Blackfriars ■ ⊖	d	14 26	14 29	14 36	14 41	14 44		14 46	14 51	14 54	14 56	14 59	15 06	15 09	15 11	15 14		15 16	15 21	15 24	15 26	15 29	15 36
London Bridge	d		14 35		14 48	14 52	14 55			15 00		15 05		15 15	15 18	15 22	15 25			15 30		15 35	
Elephant & Castle ⊖173,179	a	14 30		14 40				14 49	14 55		15 00		15 10					15 19	15 25		15 30		15 40
Loughborough Jn 173,179	a			14 45					15 00				15 15						15 30				15 45
Herne Hill ■ 173,179	a			14 49					15 04				15 19						15 34				15 49
Tulse Hill ■	a			14 54					15 09				15 24						15 39				15 54
Streatham ■	a			14 59					15 14				15 29						15 44				15 59
Wimbledon	a								15 24										15 54				
Sutton ■ 179	a			15 17			15 28		15 44				15 47				15 58		16 14				16 17
Denmark Hill ■ 195	a	14 37						14 57			15 07							15 27			15 37		
Peckham Rye ■ 195	a	14 40						15 00			15 10							15 30			15 40		
Catford	a	14 49						15 09			15 19							15 39			15 49		
Bromley South	a	15 02						15 22			15 32							15 52			16 02		
Orpington	a	15 14									15 44										16 14		
St Mary Cray	a							15 31										16 01					
Swanley	a							15 35										16 05					
Sevenoaks	a							15 55										16 25					
Maidstone East	a																						
Greenwich	a				14 57										15 27								
Woolwich Arsenal	a				15 10										15 40								
Abbey Wood	a				15 16										15 46								
Dartford	a				15 27										15 57								
Rainham Kt	a				16 11										16 41								
East Croydon 🚌	a		14 48			15 06				15 14		15 18		15 28		15 36				15 44		15 48	
Gatwick Airport ■ ✈	a		15 04			15 38				15 42		15 34		15 44		16 08				16 12		16 04	
Horsham	a									16 08										16 38			
Brighton ■	a		15 44									16 12		16 19								16 44	

A To Epsom

Table T052-R

Saturdays
26 May to 8 December

Bedford, Luton, Cambridge, Stevenage and London - Gatwick Airport and Brighton

		TL	TL 1	TL		TL	TL	TL 1	TL	TL 1	TL	TL 1	TL	TL 1	TL		TL	TL	TL 1	TL	TL 1	TL	TL	TL 1	TL
				A											A										A
Bedford	d		14 35							14 49				15 05							15 19			15 35	
Luton 10	d	14 48	14 59							15 13			15 18	15 29							15 43		15 48	15 59	
Luton Airport Parkway 7 ✈	d	14 51	15 02							15 16			15 21	15 32							15 46		15 51	16 02	
Harpenden	d	14 56	15 08							15 22			15 26	15 38							15 52		15 56	16 08	
St Albans City	d	15 01	15 13				15 07			15 27	15 22		15 31	15 43				15 37			15 57	15 52	16 01	16 13	
Elstree & Borehamwood	d	15 10					15 16				15 31		15 40					15 46				16 01	16 10		
West Hampstead Thameslink	d	15 21					15 31			15 39	15 46		15 51					16 01			16 09	16 16	16 21		
Kentish Town	d						15 36		15 41		15 51							16 06		16 11		16 21			
Peterborough	d							14 24											14 54						
Huntingdon	d							14 41											15 11						
Cambridge	d											14 54													
Royston	d											15 09													
Letchworth Garden City	d											15 21													
Hitchin	d							15 11				15 26							15 41						
Stevenage	d							15 17				15 32							15 47						
Welwyn Garden City	d																								
Finsbury Park	d							15 38				15 52							16 08						
St Pancras International	d	15 32	15 35				15 42	15 45	15 47	15 50	15 57	16 00	16 02	16 05				16 12	16 15	16 17	16 20	16 27	16 32	16 35	
Farringdon 3 ⊖	d	15 37	15 39				15 47	15 49	15 52	15 54	16 02	16 04	16 07	16 09				16 17	16 19	16 22	16 24	16 32	16 37	16 39	
City Thameslink 3	d	15 39	15 41				15 49	15 51	15 54	15 56	16 04	16 06	16 09	16 11				16 19	16 21	16 24	16 26	16 34	16 39	16 41	
London Blackfriars	a	15 41	15 43				15 51	15 53	15 56	15 58	16 06	16 08	16 11	16 13				16 21	16 23	16 26	16 28	16 36	16 41	16 43	
London Blackfriars 3 ⊖	d	15 41	15 44			15 46	15 51	15 54	15 56	15 59	16 06	16 09	16 11	16 14			16 16	16 21	16 24	16 26	16 29	16 36	16 41	16 44	
London Bridge	d	15 48	15 52	15 55				16 00		16 05		16 15	16 18	16 22	16 25				16 30		16 35		16 48	16 52	16 55
Elephant & Castle ⊖ 173,179	a					15 49	15 55		16 00		16 10						16 19	16 25		16 30		16 40			
Loughborough Jn 173,179	a						16 00				16 15							16 30				16 45			
Herne Hill 4 173,179	a						16 04				16 19							16 34				16 49			
Tulse Hill 3	a						16 09				16 24							16 39				16 54			
Streatham 4	a						16 14				16 29							16 44				16 59			
Wimbledon	a						16 24											16 54							
Sutton 4 179	a			16 28			16 44				16 47				16 58			17 14				17 17			17 28
Denmark Hill 4 195	a					15 57			16 07								16 27			16 37					
Peckham Rye 4 195	a					16 00			16 10								16 30			16 40					
Catford	a					16 09			16 19								16 39			16 49					
Bromley South	a					16 22			16 32								16 52			17 02					
Orpington	a								16 44											17 14					
St Mary Cray	a					16 31											17 01								
Swanley	a					16 35											17 05								
Sevenoaks	a					16 55											17 25								
Maidstone East	a																								
Greenwich	a	15 57											16 27										16 57		
Woolwich Arsenal	a	16 10											16 40										17 10		
Abbey Wood	a	16 16											16 46										17 16		
Dartford	a	16 27											16 57										17 27		
Rainham Kt	a	17 11											17 41										18 11		
East Croydon	a		16 06					16 14		16 18		16 28		16 36					16 44		16 48			17 06	
Gatwick Airport 10 ✈	a		16 38					16 42		16 34		16 44		17 08					17 12		17 04			17 38	
Horsham	a							17 08											17 38						
Brighton 10	a									17 12		17 19									17 44				

A To Epsom

Table T052-R

Saturdays
26 May to 8 December

Bedford, Luton, Cambridge, Stevenage and London - Gatwick Airport and Brighton

		TL		TL	TL 1	TL	TL 1	TL	TL 1	TL	TL 1	TL	TL		TL	TL 1	TL	TL 1	TL	TL	TL 1	TL	TL	TL	
												A										A			
Bedford	d						15 49				16 05							16 19			16 35				
Luton 10	d						16 13			16 18	16 29							16 43		16 48	16 59				
Luton Airport Parkway 7 ✈	d						16 16			16 21	16 32							16 46		16 51	17 02				
Harpenden	d						16 22			16 26	16 38							16 52		16 56	17 08				
St Albans City	d			16 07			16 27	16 22		16 31	16 43				16 37			16 57	16 52	17 01	17 13			17 07	
Elstree & Borehamwood	d			16 16				16 31		16 40					16 46				17 01	17 10				17 16	
West Hampstead Thameslink	d			16 31			16 39	16 46		16 51					17 01			17 09	17 16	17 21				17 31	
Kentish Town	d			16 36		16 41		16 51							17 06		17 11		17 21					17 36	
Peterborough	d				15 24											15 54									
Huntingdon	d				15 41											16 11									
Cambridge	d								15 54																
Royston	d								16 09																
Letchworth Garden City	d								16 21																
Hitchin	d				16 11				16 26							16 41									
Stevenage	d				16 17				16 32							16 47									
Welwyn Garden City	d																								
Finsbury Park	d				16 37				16 52							17 07									
St Pancras International	d			16 42	16 45	16 47	16 50	16 57	17 00	17 02	17 05				17 12	17 15	17 17	17 20	17 27	17 32	17 35			17 42	
Farringdon 3 ⊖	d			16 47	16 49	16 52	16 54	17 02	17 04	17 07	17 09				17 17	17 19	17 22	17 24	17 32	17 37	17 39			17 47	
City Thameslink 3	d			16 49	16 51	16 54	16 56	17 04	17 06	17 09	17 11				17 19	17 21	17 24	17 26	17 34	17 39	17 41			17 49	
London Blackfriars	a			16 51	16 53	16 56	16 58	17 06	17 08	17 11	17 13				17 21	17 23	17 26	17 28	17 36	17 41	17 43			17 51	
London Blackfriars 3 ⊖	d	16 46		16 51	16 54	16 56	16 59	17 06	17 09	17 11	17 14		17 16		17 21	17 24	17 26	17 29	17 36	17 41	17 44		17 46	17 51	
London Bridge	d				17 00		17 05		17 15	17 18	17 22	17 25				17 30		17 35		17 48	17 52	17 55			
Elephant & Castle ⊖ 173,179	a	16 49		16 55		17 00		17 10					17 19		17 25		17 30		17 40				17 49	17 55	
Loughborough Jn 173,179	a			17 00				17 15							17 30				17 45					18 00	
Herne Hill 4 173,179	a			17 04				17 19							17 34				17 49					18 04	
Tulse Hill 3	a			17 09				17 24							17 39				17 54					18 09	
Streatham 4	a			17 14				17 29							17 44				17 59					18 14	
Wimbledon	a			17 24											17 54									18 24	
Sutton 4 179	a			17 44				17 47				17 58			18 14				18 17			18 28		18 44	
Denmark Hill 4 195	a	16 57				17 07							17 27				17 37						17 57		
Peckham Rye 4 195	a	17 00				17 10							17 30				17 40						18 00		
Catford	a	17 09				17 19							17 39				17 49						18 09		
Bromley South	a	17 22				17 32							17 52				18 02						18 22		
Orpington	a					17 44											18 14								
St Mary Cray	a	17 31											18 01										18 31		
Swanley	a	17 35											18 05										18 35		
Sevenoaks	a	17 55											18 25										18 55		
Maidstone East	a																								
Greenwich	a									17 27										17 57					
Woolwich Arsenal	a									17 40										18 10					
Abbey Wood	a									17 46										18 16					
Dartford	a									17 57										18 27					
Rainham Kt	a									18 41										19 11					
East Croydon	a				17 14		17 18		17 28		17 36					17 44		17 48			18 06				
Gatwick Airport 10 ✈	a				17 42		17 34		17 44		18 08					18 12		18 04			18 38				
Horsham	a				18 08											18 38									
Brighton 10	a						18 12		18 19									18 44							

A To Epsom

Table T052-R

Saturdays

26 May to 8 December

Bedford, Luton, Cambridge, Stevenage and London - Gatwick Airport and Brighton

	TL ■	TL	TL ■	TL	TL ■	TL	TL ■	TL A	TL	TL	TL ■	TL	TL ■	TL	TL	TL ■	TL A	TL	TL	TL ■	TL	TL ■
Bedford d			16 49				17 05						17 19			17 35						17 49
Luton d			17 13			17 18	17 29						17 43		17 48	17 59						18 13
Luton Airport Parkway ✈ d			17 16			17 21	17 32						17 46		17 51	18 02						18 16
Harpenden d			17 22			17 26	17 38						17 52		17 56	18 08						18 22
St Albans City d			17 27	17 22		17 31	17 43			17 37			17 57	17 52	18 01	18 13			18 07			18 27
Elstree & Borehamwood d				17 31		17 40				17 46				18 01	18 10				18 16			
West Hampstead Thameslink d			17 39	17 46		17 51				18 01			18 09	18 16	18 21				18 31			18 39
Kentish Town d		17 41		17 51						18 06		18 11		18 21					18 36		18 41	
Peterborough d	16 24										16 54									17 24		
Huntingdon d	16 41										17 11									17 41		
Cambridge d					16 54																	
Royston d					17 08																	
Letchworth Garden City d					17 20																	
Hitchin d	17 11				17 25						17 41									18 11		
Stevenage d	17 17				17 32						17 47									18 17		
Welwyn Garden City d																						
Finsbury Park d	17 38				17 52						18 08									18 37		
St Pancras International d	17 45	17 47	17 50	17 57	18 00	18 02	18 05			18 12	18 15	18 17	18 20	18 27	18 32	18 35			18 42	18 45	18 47	18 50
Farringdon ⊖ d	17 49	17 52	17 54	18 02	18 04	18 07	18 09			18 17	18 19	18 22	18 24	18 32	18 37	18 39			18 47	18 49	18 52	18 54
City Thameslink d	17 51	17 54	17 56	18 04	18 06	18 09	18 11			18 19	18 21	18 24	18 26	18 34	18 39	18 41			18 49	18 51	18 54	18 56
London Blackfriars a	17 53	17 56	17 58	18 06	18 08	18 11	18 13			18 21	18 23	18 26	18 28	18 36	18 41	18 43			18 51	18 53	18 56	18 58
London Blackfriars ⊖ d	17 54	17 56	17 59	18 06	18 09	18 11	18 14		18 16	18 21	18 24	18 26	18 29	18 36	18 41	18 44		18 46	18 51	18 54	18 56	18 59
London Bridge d	18 00		18 05		18 15	18 18	18 22	18 25			18 30		18 35		18 48	18 52	18 55			19 00		19 05
Elephant & Castle ⊖173,179 a		18 00		18 10					18 19	18 25		18 30		18 40				18 49	18 55		19 00	
Loughborough Jn 173,179 a				18 15						18 30				18 45					19 00			
Herne Hill 173,179 a				18 19						18 34				18 49					19 04			
Tulse Hill a				18 24						18 39				18 54					19 09			
Streatham a				18 29						18 44				18 59					19 14			
Wimbledon a										18 54									19 24			
Sutton 179 a				18 47				18 58		19 14				19 17			19 28		19 44			
Denmark Hill 195 a		18 07							18 27			18 37						18 57			19 07	
Peckham Rye 195 a		18 10							18 30			18 40						19 00			19 10	
Catford a		18 19							18 39			18 49						19 09			19 19	
Bromley South a		18 32							18 52			19 02						19 22			19 32	
Orpington a		18 44										19 14									19 44	
St Mary Cray a									19 01									19 31				
Swanley a									19 05									19 35				
Sevenoaks a									19 25									19 55				
Maidstone East a																						
Greenwich a						18 27									18 57							
Woolwich Arsenal a						18 40									19 10							
Abbey Wood a						18 46									19 16							
Dartford a						18 57									19 27							
Rainham Kt a						19 41									20 11							
East Croydon a	18 14		18 18		18 28		18 36				18 44		18 48			19 06				19 14		19 18
Gatwick Airport ✈ a	18 42		18 34		18 44		19 08				19 12		19 04			19 38				19 42		19 34
Horsham a	19 08										19 38									20 08		
Brighton a			19 12		19 19								19 44									20 12

A To Epsom

Table T052-R

Saturdays

26 May to 8 December

Bedford, Luton, Cambridge, Stevenage and London - Gatwick Airport and Brighton

	TL	TL ■	TL	TL ■	TL A	TL	TL	TL ■	TL	TL ■	TL	TL	TL ■	TL A	TL	TL	TL ■	TL	TL ■	TL	TL ■	TL
Bedford d				18 05						18 19			18 35						18 49			
Luton d			18 18	18 29						18 43		18 48	18 59						19 13			19 18
Luton Airport Parkway ✈ d			18 21	18 32						18 46		18 51	19 02						19 16			19 21
Harpenden d			18 26	18 38						18 52		18 56	19 08						19 22			19 26
St Albans City d	18 22		18 31	18 43			18 37			18 57	18 52	19 01	19 13			19 07			19 27	19 22		19 31
Elstree & Borehamwood d	18 31		18 40				18 46				19 01	19 10				19 16				19 31		19 40
West Hampstead Thameslink d	18 46		18 51				19 01			19 09	19 16	19 21				19 31			19 39	19 46		19 51
Kentish Town d	18 51						19 06		19 11		19 21					19 36		19 41		19 51		
Peterborough d								17 56									18 24					
Huntingdon d								18 12									18 41					
Cambridge d		17 54																			18 54	
Royston d		18 09																			19 09	
Letchworth Garden City d		18 21																			19 21	
Hitchin d		18 26						18 41									19 11				19 26	
Stevenage d		18 32						18 47									19 17				19 32	
Welwyn Garden City d																						
Finsbury Park d		18 52						19 08									19 37				19 52	
St Pancras International d	18 57	19 00	19 02	19 05			19 12	19 15	19 17	19 20	19 27	19 32	19 35			19 42	19 45	19 47	19 50	19 57	20 00	20 02
Farringdon ⊖ d	19 02	19 04	19 07	19 09			19 17	19 19	19 22	19 24	19 32	19 37	19 39			19 47	19 49	19 52	19 54	20 02	20 04	20 07
City Thameslink d	19 04	19 06	19 09	19 11			19 19	19 21	19 24	19 26	19 34	19 39	19 41			19 49	19 51	19 54	19 56	20 04	20 06	20 09
London Blackfriars a	19 06	19 08	19 11	19 13			19 21	19 23	19 26	19 28	19 36	19 41	19 43			19 51	19 53	19 56	19 58	20 06	20 08	20 11
London Blackfriars ⊖ d	19 06	19 09	19 11	19 14		19 16	19 21	19 24	19 26	19 29	19 36	19 41	19 44		19 46	19 51	19 54	19 56	19 59	20 06	20 09	20 11
London Bridge d		19 15	19 18	19 22	19 25			19 30		19 35		19 48	19 52	19 55			20 00		20 05		20 15	20 18
Elephant & Castle ⊖173,179 a	19 10					19 19	19 25		19 30		19 40				19 49	19 55		20 00		20 10		
Loughborough Jn 173,179 a	19 15						19 30				19 45					20 00				20 15		
Herne Hill 173,179 a	19 19						19 34				19 49					20 04				20 19		
Tulse Hill a	19 24						19 39				19 54					20 09				20 24		
Streatham a	19 29						19 44				19 59					20 14				20 29		
Wimbledon a							19 54									20 24						
Sutton 179 a	19 47				19 58		20 14				20 17			20 28		20 44				20 47		
Denmark Hill 195 a						19 27			19 37						19 57			20 07				
Peckham Rye 195 a						19 30			19 40						20 00			20 10				
Catford a						19 39			19 49						20 09			20 19				
Bromley South a						19 52			20 02						20 22			20 32				
Orpington a									20 14									20 44				
St Mary Cray a						20 01									20 31							
Swanley a						20 05									20 35							
Sevenoaks a						20 25									20 55							
Maidstone East a																						
Greenwich a			19 27									19 57										20 27
Woolwich Arsenal a			19 40									20 10										20 40
Abbey Wood a			19 46									20 16										20 46
Dartford a			19 57									20 27										20 57
Rainham Kt a			20 41									21 11										21 41
East Croydon a		19 28		19 36				19 44		19 48			20 06				20 14		20 18		20 28	
Gatwick Airport ✈ a		19 44		20 08				20 12		20 04			20 38				20 42		20 34		20 44	
Horsham a								20 38									21 08					
Brighton a		20 19								20 44									21 12		21 19	

A To Epsom

Table T052-R

Saturdays

26 May to 8 December

Bedford, Luton, Cambridge, Stevenage and London - Gatwick Airport and Brighton

		TL ■	TL A	TL	TL	TL ■	TL	TL ■	TL	TL	TL ■	TL A	TL	TL	TL ■	TL	TL ■	TL	TL ■	TL	TL ■ B	TL A	TL
Bedford	d	19 05						19 19			19 35						19 49				20 05		
Luton [10]	d	19 29						19 43		19 48	19 59						20 13			20 18	20 29		
Luton Airport Parkway [7] ✈	d	19 32						19 46		19 51	20 02						20 16			20 21	20 32		
Harpenden	d	19 38						19 52		19 56	20 08						20 22			20 26	20 38		
St Albans City	d	19 43			19 37			19 57	19 52	20 01	20 13			20 07			20 27	20 22		20 31	20 43		
Elstree & Borehamwood	d				19 46				20 01	20 10				20 16				20 31		20 40			
West Hampstead Thameslink	d				20 01			20 09	20 16	20 21				20 31			20 39	20 46		20 51			
Kentish Town	d				20 06		20 11		20 21					20 36		20 41		20 51					
Peterborough	d					18 54									19 24								
Huntingdon	d					19 11									19 41								
Cambridge	d																		19 54				
Royston	d																		20 09				
Letchworth Garden City	d																		20 21				
Hitchin	d					19 41									20 11				20 26				
Stevenage	d					19 47									20 17				20 32				
Welwyn Garden City	d																						
Finsbury Park	d					20 07									20 37				20 52				
St Pancras International	d	20 05			20 12	20 15	20 17	20 20	20 27	20 32	20 35			20 42	20 45	20 47	20 50	20 57	21 00	21 02	21 05		
Farringdon [3] ⊖	d	20 09			20 17	20 19	20 22	20 24	20 32	20 37	20 39			20 47	20 49	20 52	20 54	21 02	21 04	21 07	21 09		
City Thameslink [3]	d	20 11			20 19	20 21	20 24	20 26	20 34	20 39	20 41			20 49	20 51	20 54	20 56						
London Blackfriars	a	20 13			20 21	20 23	20 26	20 28	20 36	20 41	20 43			20 51	20 53	20 56	20 58	21 06	21 08	21 11	21 13		
London Blackfriars [3] ⊖	d	20 14		20 16	20 21	20 24	20 26	20 29	20 36	20 41	20 44		20 46	20 51	20 54	20 56	20 59	21 06	21 09	21 11	21 14		21 16
London Bridge	d	20 22	20 25			20 30		20 35		20 48	20 52	20 55			21 00		21 05		21 15	21 18	21 22	21 25	
Elephant & Castle ⊖ 173,179	a			20 19	20 25		20 30		20 40				20 49	20 55		21 00		21 10					21 19
Loughborough Jn 173,179	a				20 30				20 45					21 00				21 15					
Herne Hill [4] 173,179	a				20 34				20 49					21 04				21 19					
Tulse Hill [3]	a				20 39				20 54					21 09				21 24					
Streatham [4]	a				20 44				20 59					21 14				21 29					
Wimbledon	a				20 54									21 24									
Sutton [4] 179	a		20 58		21 14				21 17			21 28		21 44				21 47				21 58	
Denmark Hill [4] 195	a			20 27			20 37						20 57			21 07							21 27
Peckham Rye [4] 195	a			20 30			20 40						21 00			21 10							21 30
Catford	a			20 39			20 49						21 09			21 19							21 39
Bromley South	a			20 52			21 02						21 22			21 32							21 52
Orpington	a						21 14									21 44							
St Mary Cray	a			21 01									21 31										22 01
Swanley	a			21 05									21 35										22 05
Sevenoaks	a			21 25									21 55										22 25
Maidstone East	a																						
Greenwich	a									20 57										21 27			
Woolwich Arsenal	a									21 10										21 40			
Abbey Wood	a									21 16										21 46			
Dartford	a									21 27										21 57			
Rainham Kt	a									22 11										22 41			
East Croydon ⇌	a	20 36				20 44		20 48			21 06				21 14		21 18		21 28		21 36		
Gatwick Airport [10] ✈	a	21 08				21 12		21 04			21 38				21 42		21 34		21 44		22 08		
Horsham	a					21 38									22 08								
Brighton [10]	a							21 44									22 12		22 19				

A To Epsom

B To Three Bridges

Table T052-R

Saturdays

26 May to 8 December

Bedford, Luton, Cambridge, Stevenage and London - Gatwick Airport and Brighton

		TL	TL ■	TL	TL ■	TL	TL	TL ■ A	TL B	TL	TL	TL ■	TL	TL ■	TL	TL ■	TL	TL ■ A	TL B	TL	TL	TL ■	TL
Bedford	d				20 19			20 35						20 49				21 05					
Luton [10]	d				20 43		20 48	20 59						21 13			21 18	21 29					
Luton Airport Parkway [7] ✈	d				20 46		20 51	21 02						21 16			21 21	21 32					
Harpenden	d				20 52		20 56	21 08						21 22			21 26	21 38					
St Albans City	d	20 37			20 57	20 52	21 01	21 13			21 07			21 27	21 22		21 31	21 43			21 37		
Elstree & Borehamwood	d	20 46				21 01	21 10				21 16				21 31		21 40				21 46		
West Hampstead Thameslink	d	21 01			21 09	21 16	21 21				21 31			21 39	21 46		21 51				22 01		
Kentish Town	d	21 06		21 11		21 21					21 36		21 41		21 51						22 06		22 11
Peterborough	d		19 54									20 24										20 54	
Huntingdon	d		20 11									20 41										21 11	
Cambridge	d															20 54							
Royston	d															21 09							
Letchworth Garden City	d															21 21							
Hitchin	d		20 41									21 11				21 26						21 41	
Stevenage	d		20 47									21 17				21 32						21 47	
Welwyn Garden City	d																						
Finsbury Park	d		21 08									21 37				21 52						22 07	
St Pancras International	d	21 12	21 15	21 17	21 20	21 27	21 32	21 35			21 42	21 45	21 47	21 50	21 57	22 00	22 02	22 05			22 12	22 15	22 17
Farringdon [3] ⊖	d	21 17	21 19	21 22	21 24	21 32	21 37	21 39			21 47	21 49	21 52	21 54	22 02	22 04	22 07	22 09			22 17	22 19	22 22
City Thameslink [3]	d																						
London Blackfriars	a	21 21	21 23	21 26	21 28	21 36	21 41	21 43			21 51	21 53	21 56	21 58	22 06	22 08	22 11	22 13			22 21	22 23	22 26
London Blackfriars [3] ⊖	d	21 21	21 24	21 26	21 29	21 36	21 41	21 44		21 46	21 51	21 54	21 56	21 59	22 06	22 09	22 11	22 14		22 16	22 21	22 24	22 26
London Bridge	d		21 30		21 35		21 48	21 52	21 55			22 00		22 05		22 15	22 18	22 22	22 25			22 30	
Elephant & Castle ⊖ 173,179	a	21 25		21 30		21 40				21 49	21 55		22 00		22 10					22 19	22 25		22 30
Loughborough Jn 173,179	a	21 30				21 45					22 00				22 15						22 30		
Herne Hill [4] 173,179	a	21 34				21 49					22 04				22 19						22 34		
Tulse Hill [3]	a	21 39				21 54					22 09				22 24						22 39		
Streatham [4]	a	21 44				21 59					22 14				22 29						22 44		
Wimbledon	a	21 54									22 24										22 54		
Sutton [4] 179	a	22 14				22 17			22 28		22 44				22 47				22 58		23 14		
Denmark Hill [4] 195	a			21 37						21 57			22 07							22 27			22 37
Peckham Rye [4] 195	a			21 40						22 00			22 10							22 30			22 40
Catford	a			21 49						22 09			22 19							22 39			22 49
Bromley South	a			22 02						22 22			22 32							22 52			23 02
Orpington	a			22 14									22 44										23 14
St Mary Cray	a									22 31										23 01			
Swanley	a									22 35										23 05			
Sevenoaks	a									22 55										23 25			
Maidstone East	a																						
Greenwich	a						21 57										22 27						
Woolwich Arsenal	a						22 10										22 40						
Abbey Wood	a						22 16										22 46						
Dartford	a						22 27										22 57						
Rainham Kt	a						23 11										23 41						
East Croydon ⇌	a		21 44		21 48			22 06				22 14		22 18		22 28		22 36				22 44	
Gatwick Airport [10] ✈	a		22 12		22 04			22 38				22 42		22 34		22 44		23 08				23 12	
Horsham	a		22 38									23 08										23 38	
Brighton [10]	a				22 44									23 12		23 19							

A To Three Bridges

B To Epsom

Bedford, Luton, Cambridge, Stevenage and London - Gatwick Airport and Brighton

		TL ■	TL		TL ■	TL	TL ■	TL	TL	TL	TL ■	TL	TL ■	TL		TL ■	TL	TL ■	TL	TL	TL ■	TL ■	TL	TL	TL ■
						A	B	C									A								
Bedford	d	21 19					21 35						21 49					22 05				22 17			22 45
Luton ■	d	21 43				21 48	21 59						22 13				22 18	22 29				22 41			23 10
Luton Airport Parkway ■ ✈	d	21 46				21 51	22 02						22 16				22 21	22 32				22 44			23 13
Harpenden	d	21 52				21 56	22 08						22 22				22 26	22 38				22 49			23 18
St Albans City	d	21 57	21 52			22 01	22 13			22 07			22 27	22 22			22 31	22 43		22 37		22 56		23 09	23 25
Elstree & Borehamwood	d		22 01			22 10				22 16				22 31			22 40			22 46				23 18	
West Hampstead Thameslink	d	22 09	22 16			22 21				22 31			22 39	22 46			22 51			23 01		23 12		23 33	23 41
Kentish Town	d		22 21							22 36		22 41		22 51						23 06				23 38	
Peterborough	d										21 24										21 54				
Huntingdon	d										21 41										22 11				
Cambridge	d				21 24											21 54									
Royston	d				21 39											22 09									
Letchworth Garden City	d				21 51											22 21									
Hitchin	d				21 56						22 11					22 26					22 41				
Stevenage	d				22 02						22 17					22 32					22 47				
Welwyn Garden City	d																								
Finsbury Park	d				22 22						22 37					22 52					23 07				
St Pancras International	d	22 20	22 27		22 30	22 32	22 35			22 42	22 45	22 47	22 50	22 57		23 00	23 02	23 05		23 12	23 15	23 22		23 44	23 51
Farringdon ■ ⊖	d	22 24	22 32		22 34	22 37	22 39			22 47	22 49	22 52	22 54	23 02		23 04	23 07	23 09		23 17	23 19	23 27		23 49	23 56
City Thameslink ■	d																								
London Blackfriars	a	22 28	22 36		22 38	22 41	22 43			22 51	22 53	22 56	22 58	23 06		23 08	23 11	23 13		23 21	23 23	23 30		23 53	23 59
London Blackfriars ■ ⊖	d	22 29	22 36		22 39	22 41	22 44		22 46	22 51	22 54	22 56	22 59	23 06		23 09	23 11	23 14	23 16	23 21	23 24	23 31	23 46	23 53	00 01
London Bridge	d	22 35			22 45	22 48	22 52	22 55			23 00		23 05			23 15	23 18	23 21			23 30	23 37			
Elephant & Castle ⊖173,179	a		22 40						22 49	22 55		23 00		23 10					23 19	23 25			23 49	23 57	
Loughborough Jn 173,179	a		22 45							23 00				23 15						23 30				00 02	
Herne Hill ■ 173,179	a		22 49							23 04				23 19						23 34				00 06	
Tulse Hill ■	a		22 54							23 09				23 24						23 39				00 10	
Streatham ■	a		22 59							23 14				23 29						23 44				00 14	
Wimbledon	a									23 24										23 54				00 24	
Sutton ■ 179	a		23 17					23 28		23 44				23 47						00 14				00 44	
Denmark Hill ■ 195	a								22 57			23 07							23 27				23 57		
Peckham Rye ■ 195	a								23 00			23 10							23 30				00 01		
Catford	a								23 09			23 19							23 39				00 10		
Bromley South	a								23 22			23 32							23 52				00 22		
Orpington	a											23 44													
St Mary Cray	a								23 31										00 01				00 31		
Swanley	a								23 35										00 06				00 35		
Sevenoaks	a								23 55										00 25				00 55		
Maidstone East	a																								
Greenwich	a					22 57											23 27								
Woolwich Arsenal	a					23 10											23 40								
Abbey Wood	a					23 16											23 46								
Dartford	a					23 27											23 57								
Rainham Kt	a																								
East Croydon 🚌	a	22 48			22 58		23 06				23 14		23 18			23 28		23 36			23 44	23 50			00 27
Gatwick Airport ■ ✈	a	23 04			23 14		23 37				23 41		23 34			23 47		00 01			00 12	00 17			00 48
Horsham	a										00 06										00 36				
Brighton ■	a	23 44			23 49								00 12			00 23						00 56			01 24

A To Gillingham (Kent) B To Three Bridges C To Epsom

Table T052-R

Saturdays
26 May to 8 December

Bedford, Luton, Cambridge, Stevenage and London - Gatwick Airport and Brighton

		TL ■	TL ■
		A	
Bedford	d	23 05	23 35
Luton ■	d	23 30	23 59
Luton Airport Parkway ■ ✈	d	23 33	00 03
Harpenden	d	23 38	00 08
St Albans City	d	23 45	00 15
Elstree & Borehamwood	d	23 54	00 24
West Hampstead Thameslink	d	00 09	00 39
Kentish Town	d	00 13	00 43
Peterborough	d		
Huntingdon	d		
Cambridge	d		
Royston	d		
Letchworth Garden City	d		
Hitchin	d		
Stevenage	d		
Welwyn Garden City	d		
Finsbury Park	d		
St Pancras International	d	00 21	00 51
Farringdon ■ ⊖	d	00 26	
City Thameslink ■	d		
London Blackfriars	a	00 30	01 00
London Blackfriars ■ ⊖	d	00 31	01 01
London Bridge	d		
Elephant & Castle ⊖173,179	a		
Loughborough Jn 173,179	a		
Herne Hill ■ 173,179	a		
Tulse Hill ■	a		
Streatham ■	a		
Wimbledon	a		
Sutton ■ 179	a		
Denmark Hill ■ 195	a		
Peckham Rye ■ 195	a		
Catford	a		
Bromley South	a		
Orpington	a		
St Mary Cray	a		
Swanley	a		
Sevenoaks	a		
Maidstone East	a		
Greenwich	a		
Woolwich Arsenal	a		
Abbey Wood	a		
Dartford	a		
Rainham Kt	a		
East Croydon 🚌	a	00 57	01 27
Gatwick Airport ■ ✈	a	01 20	01 56
Horsham	a		
Brighton ■	a		02 28

A To Three Bridges

Table T052-R

Sundays
20 May to 2 December

Bedford, Luton, Cambridge, Stevenage and London - Gatwick Airport and Brighton

		TL ■ A	TL ■ B	TL ■ A	TL ■	TL ■	TL ■	TL	TL	TL ■	TL		TL	TL ■	TL	TL	TL ■	TL ■	TL	TL	TL ■	TL		TL ■ C	TL
Bedford	d																	08 19						08 35	
Luton	d																	08 44				08 48		09 00	
Luton Airport Parkway ✈	d			00 03														08 47				08 51		09 03	
Harpenden	d			00 08														08 52				08 56		09 08	
St Albans City	d			00 15														08 59				09 03		09 15	
Elstree & Borehamwood	d			00 24																		09 12			
West Hampstead Thameslink	d		00 09	00 39														09 15	09 20			09 26		09 30	
Kentish Town	d		00 13	00 43															09 26			09 31			
Peterborough	d																								
Huntingdon	d																								
Cambridge	d																				08 28				
Royston	d																				08 42				
Letchworth Garden City	d																				08 53				
Hitchin	d																				08 58				
Stevenage	d																				09 04				
Welwyn Garden City	d																								
Finsbury Park	d																				09 27				
St Pancras International	d		00 21	00 51														09 26	09 32		09 35	09 38		09 41	
Farringdon ⊖	d		00 26															09 30	09 36		09 39	09 42		09 45	
City Thameslink	d																								
London Blackfriars	a		00 30	01 00														09 34	09 40		09 43	09 46		09 49	
London Blackfriars ⊖	d	00 01	00 31	01 01											09 30			09 35	09 41	09 42	09 44	09 47		09 50	10 00
London Bridge	d				07 11	07 41	08 11	08 18	08 30	08 41	08 48		09 00	09 11		09 18	09 27	09 41	09 48		09 51			09 56	
Elephant & Castle ⊖ 173,179	a														09 33					09 45		09 50			10 03
Loughborough Jn 173,179	a														09 39							09 56			10 09
Herne Hill 173,179	a														09 42							09 59			10 12
Tulse Hill	a								08 43				09 13		09 48							10 04			10 18
Streatham	a								08 50				09 20		09 52							10 08			10 22
Wimbledon	a																					10 18			
Sutton 179	a								09 05				09 35		10 07							10 38			10 37
Denmark Hill 195	a																			09 53					
Peckham Rye 195	a																			09 56					
Catford	a																			10 05					
Bromley South	a																			10 18					
Orpington	a																								
St Mary Cray	a																			10 25					
Swanley	a																			10 30					
Sevenoaks	a																			10 49					
Maidstone East	a																								
Greenwich	a							08 27			08 57					09 27			09 57						
Woolwich Arsenal	a							08 40			09 10					09 40			10 10						
Abbey Wood	a							08 46			09 16					09 46			10 16						
Dartford	a							08 57			09 27					09 57			10 27						
Rainham Kt	a							09 41			10 11					10 41			11 11						
East Croydon	a	00 27	00 57	01 27	07 24	07 54	08 24			08 54				09 24			09 41	09 54			10 07			10 10	
Gatwick Airport ✈	a	00 48	01 20	01 56	07 43	08 14	08 43			09 09				09 39			10 09	10 09			10 27			10 41	
Horsham	a																								
Brighton	a	01 24		02 28	08 21	08 52	09 21			09 47				10 15				10 47							

A not 20 May. From Bedford
B not 20 May. From Bedford to Three Bridges
C To Three Bridges

Table T052-R

Sundays
20 May to 2 December

Bedford, Luton, Cambridge, Stevenage and London - Gatwick Airport and Brighton

		TL ■	TL	TL	TL ■	TL	TL ■	TL	TL ■		TL	TL	TL ■	TL	TL ■ A	TL	TL ■	TL	TL	TL ■		TL	TL ■	TL	TL ■
Bedford	d	08 49					09 05		09 19						09 35		09 49						10 05		10 19
Luton	d	09 14				09 18	09 30		09 44					09 48	10 00		10 14					10 18	10 30		10 44
Luton Airport Parkway ✈	d	09 17				09 21	09 33		09 47					09 51	10 03		10 17					10 21	10 33		10 47
Harpenden	d	09 22				09 26	09 38		09 52					09 56	10 08		10 22					10 26	10 38		10 52
St Albans City	d	09 29				09 33	09 45		09 59					10 03	10 15		10 29					10 33	10 45		10 59
Elstree & Borehamwood	d					09 42								10 12								10 42			
West Hampstead Thameslink	d	09 45	09 50			09 56	10 00		10 15					10 26	10 30		10 45					10 56	11 00		11 15
Kentish Town	d		09 56			10 01					10 26			10 31				10 56				11 01			
Peterborough	d				08 45															09 45					
Huntingdon	d				09 00															10 00					
Cambridge	d												09 28												
Royston	d												09 42												
Letchworth Garden City	d												09 53												
Hitchin	d				09 30								09 58							10 30					
Stevenage	d				09 36								10 04							10 36					
Welwyn Garden City	d																								
Finsbury Park	d				09 57								10 27							10 57					
St Pancras International	d	09 56	10 02		10 05	10 08	10 11		10 26		10 32		10 35	10 38	10 41		10 56	11 02		11 05		11 08	11 11		11 26
Farringdon ⊖	d	10 00	10 06		10 09	10 12	10 15		10 30		10 36		10 39	10 42	10 45		11 00	11 06		11 09		11 12	11 15		11 30
City Thameslink	d																								
London Blackfriars	a	10 04	10 10		10 13	10 16	10 19		10 34		10 40		10 43	10 46	10 49		11 04	11 10		11 13		11 16	11 19		11 34
London Blackfriars ⊖	d	10 05	10 11	10 12	10 14	10 17	10 20	10 30	10 35		10 41	10 42	10 44	10 47	10 50	11 00	11 05	11 11	11 12	11 14		11 17	11 20	11 30	11 35
London Bridge	d	10 11	10 18		10 21		10 26		10 41		10 48		10 51		10 56		11 11	11 18		11 21			11 26		11 41
Elephant & Castle ⊖ 173,179	a			10 15		10 20		10 33				10 45		10 50		11 03			11 15			11 20		11 33	
Loughborough Jn 173,179	a					10 26		10 39						10 56		11 09						11 26		11 39	
Herne Hill 173,179	a					10 29		10 42						10 59		11 12						11 29		11 42	
Tulse Hill	a					10 34		10 48						11 04		11 18						11 34		11 48	
Streatham	a					10 38		10 52						11 08		11 22						11 38		11 52	
Wimbledon	a					10 48								11 18								11 48			
Sutton 179	a					11 08		11 07						11 38		11 37						12 08		12 07	
Denmark Hill 195	a			10 23								10 53							11 23						
Peckham Rye 195	a			10 26								10 56							11 26						
Catford	a			10 35								11 05							11 35						
Bromley South	a			10 48								11 18							11 48						
Orpington	a																								
St Mary Cray	a			10 55								11 25							11 55						
Swanley	a			11 00								11 30							12 00						
Sevenoaks	a			11 19								11 49							12 19						
Maidstone East	a																								
Greenwich	a		10 27								10 57							11 27							
Woolwich Arsenal	a		10 40								11 10							11 40							
Abbey Wood	a		10 46								11 16							11 46							
Dartford	a		10 57								11 27							11 57							
Rainham Kt	a		11 41								12 11							12 41							
East Croydon	a	10 24			10 37		10 40		10 54				11 07		11 10		11 24			11 37			11 40		11 54
Gatwick Airport ✈	a	10 39			11 02		11 09		11 09				11 27		11 41		11 39			12 02			12 09		12 09
Horsham	a				11 25															12 25					
Brighton	a	11 15							11 47								12 15								12 47

A To Three Bridges

Table T052-R

Sundays

20 May to 2 December

Bedford, Luton, Cambridge, Stevenage and London - Gatwick Airport and Brighton

	TL	TL	TL ■	TL	TL ■ A	TL	TL ■	TL	TL	TL ■	TL	TL ■	TL	TL ■	TL	TL	TL ■	TL	TL ■ A	TL	TL ■	TL
Bedford d					10 35		10 49					11 05		11 19					11 37		11 51	
Luton ■ d				10 48	11 00		11 14				11 18	11 30		11 44				11 48	12 02	11 58	12 16	
Luton Airport Parkway ■ ✈ d				10 51	11 03		11 17				11 21	11 33		11 47				11 51	12 05	12 01	12 19	
Harpenden d				10 56	11 08		11 22				11 26	11 38		11 52				11 56	12 10	12 06	12 24	
St Albans City d				11 03	11 15		11 29				11 33	11 45		11 59				12 03	12 17	12 16	12 30	
Elstree & Borehamwood d				11 12							11 42							12 12		12 25		
West Hampstead Thameslink d				11 26	11 30		11 45				11 56	12 00		12 15				12 26	12 30	12 39	12 45	
Kentish Town d	11 26			11 31				11 56			12 01				12 26			12 31		12 44		12 56
Peterborough d										10 45												
Huntingdon d										11 00												
Cambridge d			10 28														11 28					
Royston d			10 42														11 42					
Letchworth Garden City d			10 53														11 53					
Hitchin d			10 58							11 30							11 58					
Stevenage d			11 04							11 36							12 04					
Welwyn Garden City d																						
Finsbury Park d			11 27							11 57							12 27					
St Pancras International d	11 32		11 35	11 38	11 41		11 56	12 02		12 05	12 08	12 11	12 21	12 26	12 32		12 35	12 38	12 41	12 51	12 56	13 02
Farringdon ■ ⊖ d	11 36		11 39	11 42	11 45		12 00	12 06		12 09	12 12	12 15	12 25	12 30	12 36		12 39	12 42	12 45	12 55	13 00	13 06
City Thameslink ■ d																						
London Blackfriars a	11 40		11 43	11 46	11 49		12 04	12 10		12 13	12 16	12 19	12 29	12 34	12 40		12 43	12 46	12 49	12 59	13 04	13 10
London Blackfriars ■ ⊖ d	11 41	11 42	11 44	11 47	11 50	12 00	12 05	12 11	12 12	12 14	12 17	12 20	12 30	12 35	12 41	12 42	12 44	12 47	12 50	13 00	13 05	13 11
London Bridge d	11 48		11 51		11 56		12 11	12 18		12 21		12 26		12 41	12 48		12 51		12 56		13 11	13 18
Elephant & Castle ⊖173,179 a		11 45		11 50		12 03			12 15		12 20		12 33			12 45		12 50		13 03		
Loughborough Jn 173,179 a				11 56		12 09					12 26		12 39					12 56		13 09		
Herne Hill ■ 173,179 a				11 59		12 12					12 29		12 42					12 59		13 12		
Tulse Hill ■ a				12 04		12 18					12 34		12 48					13 04		13 18		
Streatham ■ a				12 08		12 22					12 38		12 52					13 08		13 22		
Wimbledon a				12 18							12 48							13 18				
Sutton ■ 179 a				12 38		12 37					13 08		13 07					13 38		13 37		
Denmark Hill ■ 195 a		11 53							12 23							12 53						
Peckham Rye ■ 195 a		11 56							12 26							12 56						
Catford a		12 05							12 35							13 05						
Bromley South a		12 18							12 48							13 18						
Orpington a																						
St Mary Cray a		12 25							12 55							13 25						
Swanley a		12 30							13 00							13 30						
Sevenoaks a		12 49							13 19							13 49						
Maidstone East a																						
Greenwich a	11 57							12 27							12 57							13 27
Woolwich Arsenal a	12 10							12 40							13 10							13 40
Abbey Wood a	12 16							12 46							13 16							13 46
Dartford a	12 27							12 57							13 27							13 57
Rainham Kt a	13 11							13 41							14 11							14 41
East Croydon a			12 07		12 10		12 24			12 37		12 40		12 54			13 07		13 10		13 24	
Gatwick Airport ■ ✈ a			12 27		12 41		12 39			13 02		13 09		13 09			13 27		13 41		13 39	
Horsham a										13 25												
Brighton ■ a							13 15							13 47							14 15	

A To Three Bridges

Table T052-R

Sundays

20 May to 2 December

Bedford, Luton, Cambridge, Stevenage and London - Gatwick Airport and Brighton

	TL	TL ■	TL	TL ■	TL	TL ■	TL	TL	TL ■	TL	TL ■ A	TL	TL ■	TL	TL	TL ■	TL	TL ■	TL	TL ■	TL	TL
Bedford d				12 07		12 21					12 37		12 51					13 05		13 21		
Luton ■ d			12 22	12 32		12 46				12 52	13 02		13 16				13 22	13 29		13 46		
Luton Airport Parkway ■ ✈ d			12 25	12 35		12 49				12 55	13 05		13 19				13 25	13 32		13 49		
Harpenden d			12 30	12 40		12 54				13 00	13 10		13 24				13 30	13 37		13 54		
St Albans City d			12 37	12 47	12 46	13 00				13 07	13 17	13 16	13 30				13 37	13 43	13 47	14 00		
Elstree & Borehamwood d			12 46		12 55					13 16		13 25					13 46		13 56			
West Hampstead Thameslink d			12 56	13 00	13 09	13 15				13 26	13 30	13 39	13 45				13 56	14 00	14 09	14 15		
Kentish Town d					13 14		13 26					13 44		13 56					14 14		14 26	
Peterborough d		11 45														12 45						
Huntingdon d		12 00														13 00						
Cambridge d									12 28													
Royston d									12 42													
Letchworth Garden City d									12 53													
Hitchin d		12 30							12 58							13 30						
Stevenage d		12 36							13 04							13 36						
Welwyn Garden City d																						
Finsbury Park d		12 57							13 27							13 57						
St Pancras International d		13 05	13 08	13 11	13 21	13 26	13 32		13 35	13 38	13 41	13 51	13 56	14 02		14 05	14 08	14 11	14 21	14 26	14 32	
Farringdon ■ ⊖ d		13 09	13 12	13 15	13 25	13 30	13 36		13 39	13 42	13 45	13 55	14 00	14 06		14 09	14 12	14 15	14 25	14 30	14 36	
City Thameslink ■ d																						
London Blackfriars a		13 13	13 16	13 19	13 29	13 34	13 40		13 43	13 46	13 49	13 59	14 04	14 10		14 13	14 16	14 19	14 29	14 34	14 40	
London Blackfriars ■ ⊖ d	13 12	13 14	13 17	13 20	13 30	13 35	13 41	13 42	13 44	13 47	13 50	14 00	14 05	14 11	14 12	14 14	14 17	14 20	14 30	14 35	14 41	14 42
London Bridge d		13 21		13 26		13 41	13 48		13 51		13 56		14 11	14 18		14 21		14 26		14 41	14 48	
Elephant & Castle ⊖173,179 a	13 15		13 20		13 33			13 45		13 50		14 03			14 15		14 20		14 33			14 45
Loughborough Jn 173,179 a			13 26		13 39					13 56		14 09					14 26		14 39			
Herne Hill ■ 173,179 a			13 29		13 42					13 59		14 12					14 29		14 42			
Tulse Hill ■ a			13 34		13 48					14 04		14 18					14 34		14 48			
Streatham ■ a			13 38		13 52					14 08		14 22					14 38		14 52			
Wimbledon a			13 48							14 18							14 48					
Sutton ■ 179 a			14 08		14 07					14 38		14 37					15 08		15 07			
Denmark Hill ■ 195 a	13 23							13 53							14 23							14 53
Peckham Rye ■ 195 a	13 26							13 56							14 26							14 56
Catford a	13 35							14 05							14 35							15 05
Bromley South a	13 48							14 18							14 48							15 18
Orpington a																						
St Mary Cray a	13 55							14 25							14 55							15 25
Swanley a	14 00							14 30							15 00							15 30
Sevenoaks a	14 19							14 49							15 19							15 49
Maidstone East a																						
Greenwich a							13 57							14 27							14 57	
Woolwich Arsenal a							14 10							14 40							15 10	
Abbey Wood a							14 16							14 46							15 16	
Dartford a							14 27							14 57							15 27	
Rainham Kt a							15 11							15 41							16 11	
East Croydon a		13 37		13 40		13 54			14 07		14 10		14 24			14 37		14 40		14 54		
Gatwick Airport ■ ✈ a		14 02		14 09		14 09			14 27		14 41		14 39			15 02		15 09		15 09		
Horsham a		14 25														15 25						
Brighton ■ a						14 47							15 15							15 47		

A To Three Bridges

Table T052-R

Sundays
20 May to 2 December

Bedford, Luton, Cambridge, Stevenage and London - Gatwick Airport and Brighton

		TL ■	TL		TL ■ A	TL	TL ■	TL	TL	TL ■	TL	TL ■	TL	TL ■		TL	TL	TL ■	TL	TL ■ A	TL	TL ■	TL	TL	TL ■
Bedford	d				13 37		13 51					14 05		14 21						14 37		14 51			
Luton	d		13 52		14 02		14 16				14 22	14 29		14 46					14 52	15 02		15 16			
Luton Airport Parkway ✈	d		13 55		14 05		14 19				14 25	14 32		14 49					14 55	15 05		15 19			
Harpenden	d		14 00		14 10		14 24				14 30	14 37		14 54					15 00	15 10		15 24			
St Albans City	d		14 07		14 17	14 16	14 30				14 37	14 43	14 47	15 00					15 07	15 17	15 16	15 30			
Elstree & Borehamwood	d		14 16			14 25					14 46		14 56						15 16		15 25				
West Hampstead Thameslink	d		14 26		14 30	14 39	14 45				14 56	15 00	15 09	15 15					15 26	15 30	15 39	15 45			
Kentish Town	d					14 44		14 56					15 14			15 26					15 44		15 56		
Peterborough	d									13 45															14 45
Huntingdon	d									14 00															15 00
Cambridge	d	13 28																14 28							
Royston	d	13 42																14 42							
Letchworth Garden City	d	13 53																14 53							
Hitchin	d	13 58								14 30								14 58							15 30
Stevenage	d	14 04								14 36								15 06							15 36
Welwyn Garden City	d																								
Finsbury Park	d	14 27								14 57								15 27							15 57
St Pancras International	d	14 35	14 38		14 41	14 51	14 56	15 02		15 05	15 08	15 11	15 21	15 26		15 32		15 35	15 38	15 41	15 51	15 56	16 02		16 05
Farringdon ⊖	d	14 39	14 42		14 45	14 55	15 00	15 06		15 09	15 12	15 15	15 25	15 30		15 36		15 39	15 42	15 45	15 55	16 00	16 06		16 09
City Thameslink	d																								
London Blackfriars	a	14 43	14 46		14 49	14 59	15 04	15 10		15 13	15 16	15 19	15 29	15 34		15 40		15 43	15 46	15 49	15 59	16 04	16 10		16 13
London Blackfriars ⊖	d	14 44	14 47		14 50	15 00	15 05	15 11	15 12	15 14	15 17	15 20	15 30	15 35		15 41	15 42	15 44	15 47	15 50	16 00	16 05	16 11	16 12	16 14
London Bridge	d	14 51			14 56		15 11	15 18		15 21		15 26		15 41		15 48		15 51		15 56		16 11	16 18		16 21
Elephant & Castle ⊖173,179	a		14 50			15 03			15 15		15 20		15 33				15 45		15 50		16 03			16 15	
Loughborough Jn 173,179	a		14 56			15 09					15 26		15 39						15 56		16 09				
Herne Hill 173,179	a		14 59			15 12					15 29		15 42						15 59		16 12				
Tulse Hill	a		15 04			15 18					15 34		15 48						16 04		16 18				
Streatham	a		15 08			15 22					15 38		15 52						16 08		16 22				
Wimbledon	a		15 18								15 48								16 18						
Sutton 179	a		15 38			15 37					16 08		16 07						16 38		16 37				
Denmark Hill 195	a								15 23								15 53							16 23	
Peckham Rye 195	a								15 26								15 56							16 26	
Catford	a								15 35								16 05							16 35	
Bromley South	a								15 48								16 18							16 48	
Orpington	a																								
St Mary Cray	a								15 55								16 25							16 55	
Swanley	a								16 00								16 30							17 00	
Sevenoaks	a								16 19								16 49							17 19	
Maidstone East	a																								
Greenwich	a							15 27								15 57							16 27		
Woolwich Arsenal	a							15 40								16 10							16 40		
Abbey Wood	a							15 46								16 16							16 46		
Dartford	a							15 57								16 27							16 57		
Rainham Kt	a							16 41								17 11							17 41		
East Croydon	a	15 07			15 10		15 24			15 37		15 40		15 54				16 07		16 10		16 24			16 37
Gatwick Airport ✈	a	15 27			15 41		15 39			16 02		16 09		16 09				16 27		16 41		16 39			17 02
Horsham	a									16 25															17 25
Brighton	a						16 15							16 47								17 15			

A To Three Bridges

Table T052-R

Sundays
20 May to 2 December

Bedford, Luton, Cambridge, Stevenage and London - Gatwick Airport and Brighton

			TL	TL ■	TL	TL ■	TL	TL	TL ■	TL	TL ■ A	TL		TL ■	TL	TL	TL ■	TL	TL ■	TL	TL ■	TL	TL		TL ■
Bedford	d			15 05		15 21					15 37			15 51					16 05		16 21				
Luton	d		15 22	15 29		15 46				15 52	16 02			16 16				16 22	16 29		16 46				
Luton Airport Parkway ✈	d		15 25	15 32		15 49				15 55	16 05			16 19				16 25	16 32		16 49				
Harpenden	d		15 30	15 37		15 54				16 00	16 10			16 24				16 30	16 37		16 54				
St Albans City	d		15 37	15 43	15 47	16 00				16 07	16 17	16 16		16 30				16 37	16 43	16 47	17 00				
Elstree & Borehamwood	d		15 46		15 56					16 16		16 25						16 46		16 56					
West Hampstead Thameslink	d		15 56	16 00	16 09	16 15				16 26	16 30	16 39		16 45				16 56	17 00	17 09	17 15				
Kentish Town	d				16 14		16 26					16 44			16 56					17 14		17 26			
Peterborough	d																15 45								
Huntingdon	d																16 00								
Cambridge	d								15 28																16 28
Royston	d								15 42																16 42
Letchworth Garden City	d								15 53																16 53
Hitchin	d								15 58								16 30								16 58
Stevenage	d								16 04								16 36								17 04
Welwyn Garden City	d																								
Finsbury Park	d								16 27								16 57								17 27
St Pancras International	d		16 08	16 11	16 21	16 26	16 32		16 35	16 38	16 41	16 51		16 56	17 02		17 05	17 08	17 11	17 21	17 26	17 32			17 35
Farringdon ⊖	d		16 12	16 15	16 25	16 30	16 36		16 39	16 42	16 45	16 55		17 00	17 06		17 09	17 12	17 15	17 25	17 30	17 36			17 39
City Thameslink	d																								
London Blackfriars	a		16 16	16 19	16 29	16 34	16 40		16 43	16 46	16 49	16 59		17 04	17 10		17 13	17 16	17 19	17 29	17 34	17 40			17 43
London Blackfriars ⊖	d		16 17	16 20	16 30	16 35	16 41	16 42	16 44	16 47	16 50	17 00		17 05	17 11	17 12	17 14	17 17	17 20	17 30	17 35	17 41	17 42		17 44
London Bridge	d			16 26		16 41	16 48		16 51		16 56			17 11	17 18		17 21		17 26		17 41	17 48			17 51
Elephant & Castle ⊖173,179	a		16 20		16 33			16 45		16 50		17 03				17 15		17 20		17 33			17 45		
Loughborough Jn 173,179	a		16 26		16 39					16 56		17 09						17 26		17 39					
Herne Hill 173,179	a		16 29		16 42					16 59		17 12						17 29		17 42					
Tulse Hill	a		16 34		16 48					17 04		17 18						17 34		17 48					
Streatham	a		16 38		16 52					17 08		17 22						17 38		17 52					
Wimbledon	a		16 48							17 18								17 48							
Sutton 179	a		17 08		17 07					17 38		17 37						18 08		18 07					
Denmark Hill 195	a							16 53								17 23							17 53		
Peckham Rye 195	a							16 56								17 26							17 56		
Catford	a							17 05								17 35							18 05		
Bromley South	a							17 18								17 48							18 18		
Orpington	a																								
St Mary Cray	a							17 25								17 55							18 25		
Swanley	a							17 30								18 00							18 30		
Sevenoaks	a							17 49								18 19							18 49		
Maidstone East	a																								
Greenwich	a						16 57								17 27							17 57			
Woolwich Arsenal	a						17 10								17 40							18 10			
Abbey Wood	a						17 16								17 46							18 16			
Dartford	a						17 27								17 57							18 27			
Rainham Kt	a						18 11								18 41							19 11			
East Croydon	a			16 40		16 54			17 07		17 10			17 24			17 37		17 40		17 54				18 07
Gatwick Airport ✈	a			17 09		17 09			17 27		17 41			17 39			18 02		18 09		18 09				18 27
Horsham	a																18 25								
Brighton	a					17 47								18 15							18 47				

A To Three Bridges

Table T052-R

Sundays

20 May to 2 December

Bedford, Luton, Cambridge, Stevenage and London - Gatwick Airport and Brighton

		TL	TL [1] A	TL	TL [1]	TL	TL	TL [1]	TL	TL [1]	TL	TL [1]
Bedford	d		16 37		16 51					17 05		17 21
Luton [10]	d	16 52	17 02		17 16				17 22	17 29		17 46
Luton Airport Parkway [7] ✈	d	16 55	17 05		17 19				17 25	17 32		17 49
Harpenden	d	17 00	17 10		17 24				17 30	17 37		17 54
St Albans City	d	17 07	17 17	17 16	17 30				17 37	17 43	17 47	18 00
Elstree & Borehamwood	d	17 16		17 25					17 46		17 56	
West Hampstead Thameslink	d	17 26	17 30	17 39	17 45				17 56	18 00	18 09	18 15
Kentish Town	d			17 44		17 56					18 14	
Peterborough	d							16 45				
Huntingdon	d							17 00				
Cambridge	d											
Royston	d											
Letchworth Garden City	d											
Hitchin	d							17 30				
Stevenage	d							17 36				
Welwyn Garden City	d											
Finsbury Park	d							17 57				
St Pancras International	d	17 38	17 41	17 51	17 56	18 02		18 05	18 08	18 11	18 21	18 26
Farringdon [3] ⊖	d	17 42	17 45	17 55	18 00	18 06		18 09	18 12	18 15	18 25	18 30
City Thameslink [3]	d											
London Blackfriars	a	17 46	17 49	17 59	18 04	18 10		18 13	18 16	18 19	18 29	18 34
London Blackfriars [3] ⊖	d	17 47	17 50	18 00	18 05	18 11	18 12	18 14	18 17	18 20	18 30	18 35
London Bridge	d		17 56		18 11	18 18		18 21		18 26		18 41
Elephant & Castle ⊖173,179	a	17 50		18 03			18 15		18 20		18 33	
Loughborough Jn 173,179	a	17 56		18 09					18 26		18 39	
Herne Hill [4] 173,179	a	17 59		18 12					18 29		18 42	
Tulse Hill [3]	a	18 04		18 18					18 34		18 48	
Streatham [4]	a	18 08		18 22					18 38		18 52	
Wimbledon	a	18 18							18 48			
Sutton [4] 179	a	18 38		18 37					19 08		19 07	
Denmark Hill [4] 195	a						18 23					
Peckham Rye [4] 195	a						18 26					
Catford	a						18 35					
Bromley South	a						18 48					
Orpington	a											
St Mary Cray	a						18 55					
Swanley	a						19 00					
Sevenoaks	a						19 19					
Maidstone East	a											
Greenwich	a					18 27						
Woolwich Arsenal	a					18 40						
Abbey Wood	a					18 46						
Dartford	a					18 57						
Rainham Kt	a					19 41						
East Croydon	a		18 10		18 24			18 37		18 40		18 54
Gatwick Airport [10] ✈	a		18 41		18 39			19 02		19 09		19 09
Horsham	a							19 25				
Brighton [10]	a				19 15							19 47

		TL	TL	TL [1]	TL	TL [1] A	TL	TL [1]	TL	TL	TL [1]	TL
Bedford	d					17 37		17 51				
Luton [10]	d				17 52	18 02		18 16				18 22
Luton Airport Parkway [7] ✈	d				17 55	18 05		18 19				18 25
Harpenden	d				18 00	18 10		18 24				18 30
St Albans City	d				18 07	18 17	18 16	18 30				18 37
Elstree & Borehamwood	d				18 16		18 25					18 46
West Hampstead Thameslink	d				18 26	18 30	18 39	18 45				18 57
Kentish Town	d	18 26					18 44		18 56			
Peterborough	d										17 45	
Huntingdon	d										18 00	
Cambridge	d			17 28								
Royston	d			17 42								
Letchworth Garden City	d			17 53								
Hitchin	d			17 58							18 30	
Stevenage	d			18 04							18 36	
Welwyn Garden City	d											
Finsbury Park	d			18 27							18 57	
St Pancras International	d	18 32		18 35	18 38	18 41	18 51	18 56	19 02		19 05	19 08
Farringdon [3] ⊖	d	18 36		18 39	18 42	18 45	18 55	19 00	19 06		19 09	19 12
City Thameslink [3]	d											
London Blackfriars	a	18 40		18 43	18 46	18 49	18 59	19 04	19 10		19 13	19 16
London Blackfriars [3] ⊖	d	18 41	18 42	18 44	18 47	18 50	19 00	19 05	19 11	19 12	19 14	19 17
London Bridge	d	18 48		18 51		18 56		19 11	19 18		19 21	
Elephant & Castle ⊖173,179	a		18 45		18 50		19 03			19 15		19 20
Loughborough Jn 173,179	a				18 56		19 09					19 26
Herne Hill [4] 173,179	a				18 59		19 12					19 29
Tulse Hill [3]	a				19 04		19 18					19 34
Streatham [4]	a				19 08		19 22					19 38
Wimbledon	a				19 18							19 48
Sutton [4] 179	a				19 38		19 37					20 08
Denmark Hill [4] 195	a		18 53							19 23		
Peckham Rye [4] 195	a		18 56							19 26		
Catford	a		19 05							19 35		
Bromley South	a		19 18							19 48		
Orpington	a											
St Mary Cray	a		19 25							19 55		
Swanley	a		19 30							20 00		
Sevenoaks	a		19 49							20 19		
Maidstone East	a											
Greenwich	a	18 57							19 27			
Woolwich Arsenal	a	19 10							19 40			
Abbey Wood	a	19 16							19 46			
Dartford	a	19 27							19 57			
Rainham Kt	a	20 11							20 41			
East Croydon	a			19 07		19 10		19 24			19 37	
Gatwick Airport [10] ✈	a			19 27		19 41		19 39			20 02	
Horsham	a										20 25	
Brighton [10]	a							20 15				

A To Three Bridges

Table T052-R

Sundays

20 May to 2 December

Bedford, Luton, Cambridge, Stevenage and London - Gatwick Airport and Brighton

		TL [1]	TL	TL [1]	TL	TL	TL [1]	TL	TL [1] A	TL	TL [1]	TL
Bedford	d	18 07		18 21					18 37		18 51	
Luton [10]	d	18 32		18 46				18 52	19 02		19 16	
Luton Airport Parkway [7] ✈	d	18 35		18 49				18 55	19 05		19 19	
Harpenden	d	18 40		18 54				19 00	19 10		19 24	
St Albans City	d	18 47	18 46	19 00				19 07	19 17	19 16	19 30	
Elstree & Borehamwood	d		18 55					19 16		19 25		
West Hampstead Thameslink	d	19 00	19 09	19 15				19 26	19 30	19 39	19 45	
Kentish Town	d		19 14		19 26					19 44		19 56
Peterborough	d											
Huntingdon	d											
Cambridge	d						18 28					
Royston	d						18 42					
Letchworth Garden City	d						18 53					
Hitchin	d						18 58					
Stevenage	d						19 04					
Welwyn Garden City	d											
Finsbury Park	d						19 27					
St Pancras International	d	19 11	19 21	19 26	19 32		19 35	19 38	19 41	19 51	19 56	20 02
Farringdon [3] ⊖	d	19 15	19 25	19 30	19 36		19 39	19 42	19 45	19 55	20 00	20 06
City Thameslink [3]	d											
London Blackfriars	a	19 19	19 29	19 34	19 40		19 43	19 46	19 49	19 59	20 04	20 10
London Blackfriars [3] ⊖	d	19 20	19 30	19 35	19 41	19 42	19 44	19 47	19 50	20 00	20 05	20 11
London Bridge	d	19 26		19 41	19 48		19 51		19 56		20 11	20 18
Elephant & Castle ⊖173,179	a		19 33			19 45		19 50		20 03		
Loughborough Jn 173,179	a		19 39					19 56		20 09		
Herne Hill [4] 173,179	a		19 42					19 59		20 12		
Tulse Hill [3]	a		19 48					20 04		20 18		
Streatham [4]	a		19 52					20 08		20 22		
Wimbledon	a							20 18				
Sutton [4] 179	a		20 07					20 38		20 37		
Denmark Hill [4] 195	a					19 53						
Peckham Rye [4] 195	a					19 56						
Catford	a					20 05						
Bromley South	a					20 18						
Orpington	a											
St Mary Cray	a					20 25						
Swanley	a					20 30						
Sevenoaks	a					20 49						
Maidstone East	a											
Greenwich	a				19 57							20 27
Woolwich Arsenal	a				20 10							20 40
Abbey Wood	a				20 16							20 46
Dartford	a				20 27							20 57
Rainham Kt	a				21 11							21 41
East Croydon	a	19 40		19 54			20 07		20 10		20 24	
Gatwick Airport [10] ✈	a	20 09		20 09			20 27		20 41		20 39	
Horsham	a											
Brighton [10]	a			20 47							21 15	

		TL	TL [1]	TL	TL [1]	TL	TL [1]	TL	TL	TL [1]	TL	TL [1]
Bedford	d				19 05		19 21					19 35
Luton [10]	d			19 22	19 29		19 46				19 52	19 59
Luton Airport Parkway [7] ✈	d			19 25	19 32		19 49				19 55	20 02
Harpenden	d			19 30	19 37		19 54				20 00	20 07
St Albans City	d			19 37	19 43	19 47	20 00				20 07	20 13
Elstree & Borehamwood	d			19 46		19 56					20 16	
West Hampstead Thameslink	d			19 56	20 00	20 09	20 15				20 26	20 30
Kentish Town	d					20 14		20 26				
Peterborough	d		18 45									
Huntingdon	d		19 00									
Cambridge	d									19 28		
Royston	d									19 42		
Letchworth Garden City	d									19 53		
Hitchin	d		19 30							19 58		
Stevenage	d		19 36							20 04		
Welwyn Garden City	d											
Finsbury Park	d		19 57							20 27		
St Pancras International	d		20 05	20 08	20 11	20 21	20 26	20 32		20 35	20 38	20 41
Farringdon [3] ⊖	d		20 09	20 12	20 15	20 25	20 30	20 36		20 39	20 42	20 45
City Thameslink [3]	d											
London Blackfriars	a		20 13	20 16	20 19	20 29	20 34	20 40		20 43	20 46	20 49
London Blackfriars [3] ⊖	d	20 12	20 14	20 17	20 20	20 30	20 35	20 41	20 42	20 44	20 47	20 50
London Bridge	d		20 21		20 26		20 41	20 48		20 51		20 56
Elephant & Castle ⊖173,179	a	20 15		20 20		20 33			20 45		20 50	
Loughborough Jn 173,179	a			20 26		20 39					20 56	
Herne Hill [4] 173,179	a			20 29		20 42					20 59	
Tulse Hill [3]	a			20 34		20 48					21 04	
Streatham [4]	a			20 38		20 52					21 08	
Wimbledon	a			20 48							21 18	
Sutton [4] 179	a			21 08		21 07					21 38	
Denmark Hill [4] 195	a	20 23							20 53			
Peckham Rye [4] 195	a	20 26							20 56			
Catford	a	20 35							21 05			
Bromley South	a	20 48							21 18			
Orpington	a											
St Mary Cray	a	20 55							21 25			
Swanley	a	21 01							21 30			
Sevenoaks	a	21 20							21 49			
Maidstone East	a											
Greenwich	a							20 57				
Woolwich Arsenal	a							21 10				
Abbey Wood	a							21 16				
Dartford	a							21 27				
Rainham Kt	a							22 11				
East Croydon	a		20 37		20 40		20 54			21 07		21 10
Gatwick Airport [10] ✈	a		21 02		21 09		21 09			21 27		21 39
Horsham	a		21 25									
Brighton [10]	a						21 47					

A To Three Bridges

Table T052-R

Sundays

Bedford, Luton, Cambridge, Stevenage and London - Gatwick Airport and Brighton

	TL	TL ■	TL	TL	TL ■	TL	TL ■ A	TL	TL ■	TL	TL
Bedford d		19 51					20 07		20 21		
Luton ■ d		20 16				20 22	20 32		20 46		
Luton Airport Parkway ■ ✈ d		20 19				20 25	20 35		20 49		
Harpenden d		20 24				20 30	20 40		20 54		
St Albans City d	20 17	20 30				20 37	20 47	20 46	21 00		
Elstree & Borehamwood d	20 26					20 46		20 55			
West Hampstead Thameslink d	20 39	20 45				20 57	21 00	21 09	21 15		
Kentish Town d	20 44		20 56					21 14		21 26	
Peterborough d					19 45						
Huntingdon d					20 00						
Cambridge d											
Royston d											
Letchworth Garden City d											
Hitchin d					20 30						
Stevenage d					20 36						
Welwyn Garden City d											
Finsbury Park d					20 57						
St Pancras International d	20 51	20 56	21 02		21 05	21 08	21 11	21 21	21 26	21 32	
Farringdon ■ ⊖ d	20 55	21 00	21 06		21 09	21 12	21 15	21 25	21 30	21 36	
City Thameslink ■ d											
London Blackfriars a	20 59	21 04	21 10		21 13	21 16	21 19	21 29	21 34	21 40	
London Blackfriars ■ ⊖ d	21 00	21 05	21 11	21 12	21 14	21 17	21 20	21 30	21 35	21 41	21 42
London Bridge d		21 11	21 18		21 21		21 26		21 41	21 48	
Elephant & Castle ⊖173,179 a	21 03			21 15		21 20		21 33			21 45
Loughborough Jn 173,179 a	21 09					21 26		21 39			
Herne Hill ■ 173,179 a	21 12					21 29		21 42			
Tulse Hill ■ a	21 18					21 34		21 48			
Streatham ■ a	21 22					21 38		21 52			
Wimbledon a						21 48					
Sutton ■ 179 a	21 37					22 08		22 07			
Denmark Hill ■ 195 a				21 23							21 53
Peckham Rye ■ 195 a				21 26							21 56
Catford a				21 35							22 05
Bromley South a				21 48							22 18
Orpington a											
St Mary Cray a				21 55							22 25
Swanley a				22 00							22 30
Sevenoaks a				22 19							22 49
Maidstone East a											
Greenwich a			21 27							21 57	
Woolwich Arsenal a			21 40							22 10	
Abbey Wood a			21 46							22 16	
Dartford a			21 57							22 27	
Rainham Kt a			22 41							23 11	
East Croydon a		21 24			21 37		21 40		21 54		
Gatwick Airport ■ ✈ a		21 39			22 02		22 09		22 09		
Horsham a					22 25						
Brighton ■ a		22 15							22 47		

	TL ■ A	TL	TL ■ A	TL ■	TL	TL	TL ■	TL ■	TL ■	TL B	TL
Bedford d			20 37	20 51				21 09	21 21		
Luton ■ d		20 52	21 02	21 16				21 33	21 46		
Luton Airport Parkway ■ ✈ d		20 55	21 05	21 19				21 36	21 49		
Harpenden d		21 00	21 10	21 24				21 41	21 54		
St Albans City d		21 07	21 17	21 31	21 27			21 48	22 01	21 57	
Elstree & Borehamwood d		21 16			21 36					22 06	
West Hampstead Thameslink d		21 26	21 30	21 45	21 50			22 00	22 15	22 20	
Kentish Town d					21 55					22 25	
Peterborough d							20 45				
Huntingdon d							21 00				
Cambridge d	20 28										
Royston d	20 42										
Letchworth Garden City d	20 53										
Hitchin d	20 58						21 30				
Stevenage d	21 04						21 36				
Welwyn Garden City d											
Finsbury Park d	21 27						21 57				
St Pancras International d	21 35	21 38	21 41	21 56	22 02		22 05	22 11	22 26	22 32	
Farringdon ■ ⊖ d	21 39	21 42	21 45	22 00	22 06		22 09	22 15	22 30	22 36	
City Thameslink ■ d											
London Blackfriars a	21 43	21 46	21 49	22 04	22 10		22 13	22 19	22 34	22 40	
London Blackfriars ■ ⊖ d	21 44	21 47	21 50	22 05	22 11	22 12	22 14	22 20	22 35	22 41	22 42
London Bridge d	21 51		21 56	22 11	22 18		22 21	22 26	22 41	22 48	
Elephant & Castle ⊖173,179 a		21 50				22 15					22 45
Loughborough Jn 173,179 a		21 56									
Herne Hill ■ 173,179 a		21 59									
Tulse Hill ■ a		22 04									
Streatham ■ a		22 08									
Wimbledon a		22 18									
Sutton ■ 179 a		22 38									
Denmark Hill ■ 195 a						22 23					22 53
Peckham Rye ■ 195 a						22 26					22 56
Catford a						22 35					23 05
Bromley South a						22 48					23 18
Orpington a											
St Mary Cray a						22 55					23 25
Swanley a						23 00					23 30
Sevenoaks a						23 19					23 49
Maidstone East a											
Greenwich a					22 27					22 57	
Woolwich Arsenal a					22 40					23 10	
Abbey Wood a					22 46					23 16	
Dartford a					22 57					23 27	
Rainham Kt a					23 41						
East Croydon a	22 07		22 10	22 24			22 37	22 40	22 54		
Gatwick Airport ■ ✈ a	22 26		22 39	22 39			23 02	23 09	23 09		
Horsham a							23 25				
Brighton ■ a				23 15					23 47		

	TL ■ A	TL ■	TL B	TL	TL ■	TL	TL ■ A	TL ■	TL ■ A	TL ■
Bedford d		21 51			22 11			22 45	23 05	23 45
Luton ■ d		22 16			22 36			23 10	23 30	00 10
Luton Airport Parkway ■ ✈ d		22 19			22 39			23 13	23 33	00 13
Harpenden d		22 24			22 44			23 18	23 38	00 18
St Albans City d		22 31	22 27		22 51			23 25	23 45	00 25
Elstree & Borehamwood d			22 36		23 00				23 54	
West Hampstead Thameslink d		22 45	22 50		23 14			23 41	00 09	00 41
Kentish Town d			22 55		23 19				00 13	
Peterborough d										
Huntingdon d										
Cambridge d	21 28									
Royston d	21 42									
Letchworth Garden City d	21 53									
Hitchin d	21 58									
Stevenage d	22 04									
Welwyn Garden City d										
Finsbury Park d	22 27									
St Pancras International d	22 35	22 56	23 02		23 26			23 51	00 21	00 51
Farringdon ■ ⊖ d	22 39	23 00	23 06		23 30			23 56	00 26	
City Thameslink ■ d										
London Blackfriars a	22 43	23 04	23 10		23 34			23 59	00 30	01 00
London Blackfriars ■ ⊖ d	22 44	23 05	23 11	23 12	23 35	23 42		00 01	00 31	01 01
London Bridge d	22 51	23 11	23 18		23 41		23 45			
Elephant & Castle ⊖173,179 a				23 15		23 45				
Loughborough Jn 173,179 a										
Herne Hill ■ 173,179 a										
Tulse Hill ■ a										
Streatham ■ a										
Wimbledon a										
Sutton ■ 179 a										
Denmark Hill ■ 195 a				23 23		23 53				
Peckham Rye ■ 195 a				23 26		23 56				
Catford a				23 35		00 05				
Bromley South a				23 48		00 18				
Orpington a										
St Mary Cray a				23 55		00 25				
Swanley a				23 59		00 30				
Sevenoaks a				00 19		00 49				
Maidstone East a										
Greenwich a			23 27							
Woolwich Arsenal a			23 40							
Abbey Wood a			23 46							
Dartford a			23 57							
Rainham Kt a										
East Croydon a	23 07	23 24			23 54		23 59	00 27	00 57	01 27
Gatwick Airport ■ ✈ a	23 35	23 42			00 17		00 29	00 47	01 20	01 56
Horsham a										
Brighton ■ a		00 19			00 54			01 24		02 28

A To Three Bridges
B To Gillingham (Kent)

Table T052MML-F

Mondays to Fridays
21 May to 7 December

Gatwick Airport and London - St Albans, Luton and Bedford

	TL MO A	TL MX ■ B	TL MO A	TL MX A	TL MO ■ B	TL MX A	TL MX ■ B	TL MO C	TL MX A	TL MX A	EM MX ◇■ D
Gatwick Airport d											
Elephant & Castle ⊖173,179 d											
London Bridge d											
London Blackfriars d										00 02	
City Thameslink ■ d											
Farringdon ■ ⊖ d										00 06	
St Pancras International d										00 11	00 15
Kentish Town ⊖ d									00 01		
West Hampstead Thameslink ⊖ d									00 06	00 19	
Cricklewood d									00 10		
Hendon d								00 02	00 14		
Mill Hill Broadway d								00 05	00 17		
Elstree & Borehamwood d								00 09	00 21		
Radlett d						00 03		00 13	00 25		
St Albans City d					00 03	00 10	00 16	00 21	00 32	00 36	
Harpenden d			00 05	00 06	00 09	00 16	00 22	00 27	00 38	00 42	
Luton Airport Parkway ■ ✈ d			00 10	00 11	00 14	00 21	00 28	00 32	00 43	00 48	00 55
Luton ■ d		00 02	00 15	00 16	00 19	00 26	00 32	00 37	00 48	00 52	00 58
Leagrave d	00 01	00 06		00 20	00 23		00 36	00 41		00 56	
Harlington d	00 06	00 11		00 24	00 27		00 41	00 45		01 01	
Flitwick d	00 10	00 15		00 28	00 31		00 45	00 49		01 05	
Bedford ■ a	00 21	00 26	00 35	00 40	00 43	00 46	00 56	01 01	01 10	01 18	01 26

	TL MO ■ B	TL MX A	TL MX ■ B	TL MO ■ B	TL MX ■ B	TL MO ■ B	TL MX ■ B	TL ■ B	TL ■ E	TL ■ E	TL ■ E
Gatwick Airport d					00 04	00 21	00 21	00 42	01 46	02 21	02 46
Elephant & Castle ⊖173,179 d		00 04									
London Bridge d											
London Blackfriars d	00 06	00 09	00 22	00 36	00 50	01 06	01 08	01 36	02 36	03 06	03 36
City Thameslink ■ d											
Farringdon ■ ⊖ d	00 11	00 13	00 25								
St Pancras International d	00 16	00 18	00 30	00 46	01 01	01 16	01 16	01 44	02 44	03 14	03 44
Kentish Town ⊖ d	00 20	00 22		00 50	01 05			01 48	02 48		03 48
West Hampstead Thameslink ⊖ d	00 24	00 26	00 39	00 54	01 09	01 24	01 24	01 52	02 52	03 22	03 52
Cricklewood d	00 28	00 30		00 58	01 13			01 56	02 56		03 56
Hendon d	00 32	00 34		01 02	01 17			02 00	03 00		04 00
Mill Hill Broadway d	00 35	00 37		01 05	01 20			02 03	03 03		04 03
Elstree & Borehamwood d	00 39	00 41		01 09	01 24			02 07	03 07		04 07
Radlett d	00 43	00 45		01 13	01 28			02 11	03 11		04 11
St Albans City d	00 51	00 52	00 56	01 21	01 34	01 41	01 41	02 19	03 19	03 41	04 19
Harpenden d	00 57	00 58	01 02	01 27	01 40	01 47	01 47	02 25	03 25	03 47	04 25
Luton Airport Parkway ■ ✈ d	01 02	01 03	01 08	01 32	01 46	01 52	01 52	02 30	03 30	03 52	04 30
Luton ■ d	01 07	01 08	01 12	01 37	01 50	01 57	01 57	02 35	03 35	03 57	04 35
Leagrave d	01 11	01 12	01 16	01 41	01 54	02 01	02 01	02 39	03 39	04 01	04 39
Harlington d	01 15	01 16	01 21	01 45	01 59	02 05	02 05	02 43	03 43	04 05	04 43
Flitwick d	01 19	01 20	01 25	01 49	02 03	02 09	02 09	02 47	03 47	04 09	04 47
Bedford ■ a	01 31	01 32	01 36	02 01	02 14	02 21	02 21	02 59	03 59	04 21	05 01

	TL ■ E	TL ■ E	TL ■ E	EM ◇■ F	TL G	TL ■ B	TL H	EM ◇■ I	TL G	TL ■ E	TL H
Gatwick Airport d	03 21	03 46	04 21			04 41				05 19	
Elephant & Castle ⊖173,179 d					05 14				05 44		
London Bridge d						05 25				05 55	
London Blackfriars d	04 06	04 36	05 06		05 19	05 31			05 49	06 01	
City Thameslink ■ d			05 08		05 21	05 33			05 51	06 03	
Farringdon ■ ⊖ d			05 11		05 24	05 36			05 54	06 06	
St Pancras International d	04 14	04 44	05 16	05 52	05 28	05 40		06 23	05 58	06 10	
Kentish Town ⊖ d		04 48			05 33				06 03		
West Hampstead Thameslink ⊖ d	04 22	04 52	05 24		05 37	05 49			06 07	06 18	
Cricklewood d		04 56			05 40				06 10		
Hendon d		05 00			05 44				06 14		
Mill Hill Broadway d		05 03			05 47				06 17		
Elstree & Borehamwood d		05 07			05 51		←		06 21		←
Radlett d		05 11			05 55		05 55		06 25		06 25
St Albans City d	04 41	05 19	05 41		→	06 01	06 02		→	06 30	06 32
Harpenden d	04 47	05 25	05 47			06 07	06 11			06 37	06 41
Luton Airport Parkway ■ ✈ d	04 52	05 30	05 52			06 13	06 16			06 42	06 47
Luton ■ d	04 57	05 35	05 57	06 15		06 17	06a20	06 46		06 47	06a51
Leagrave d	05 01	05 39	06 01			06 21				06 51	
Harlington d	05 05	05 43	06 05			06 26				06 55	
Flitwick d	05 09	05 47	06 09			06 30				06 59	
Bedford ■ a	05 21	05 59	06 21	06 28		06 42		06 59		07 12	

	TL J	TL G	TL ■ K	TL A	TL ■ E	TL H	TL L	TL ■ M	TL A	TL ■ B	EM ◇■ N
Gatwick Airport d			05 46		05 33			05 49		06 06	
Elephant & Castle ⊖173,179 d		06 14		06 19					06 34		
London Bridge d	05 58		06 16		06 21		06 28	06 31		06 35	
London Blackfriars d	06 04	06 19	06 22	06 24	06 27		06 34	06 37	06 39	06 42	
City Thameslink ■ d	06 06	06 21	06 24	06 26	06 29		06 36	06 39	06 41	06 44	
Farringdon ■ ⊖ d	06 09	06 24	06 26	06 29	06 31		06 39	06 41	06 44	06 46	
St Pancras International d	06 13	06 28	06a30	06 33	06 36		06 43	06a45	06 48	06 51	07 04
Kentish Town ⊖ d	06 18			06 38					06 53		
West Hampstead Thameslink ⊖ d	06 22	06 37		06 44	06 44		06 52		06 58		
Cricklewood d	06 25			06 47					07 01		
Hendon d	06 29			06 51					07 05		
Mill Hill Broadway d	06 32	06 46		06 54			07 01		07 08		
Elstree & Borehamwood d	06 36	06 50		06 58		←	07 05		07 12		
Radlett d	06 40	06 54		07 02		06 54	07 09		07 16		
St Albans City d	06a46	→		07a08	06 57	07 02	→		07a22	07 10	
Harpenden d					07 03	07 09					
Luton Airport Parkway ■ ✈ d					07 08	07 16				07 18	
Luton ■ d					07 13	07a20				07 22	07 27
Leagrave d					07 16						
Harlington d					07 21						
Flitwick d					07 25						
Bedford ■ a					07 38					07 42	07 41

	TL ■ O	TL J	TL G	TL A	TL ■ E	TL ■ B	TL H	TL P	TL ■ Q	TL A	TL ■ O
Gatwick Airport d					05 56	06 25			06 13		
Elephant & Castle ⊖173,179 d			06 44	06 49						07 04	
London Bridge d	06 41				06 51	06 54		06 58	07 01		07 06
London Blackfriars d	06 47		06 49	06 54	06 57	07 02		07 04	07 07	07 09	07 12
City Thameslink ■ d	06 49		06 51	06 56	06 59	07 04		07 06	07 09	07 11	07 14
Farringdon ■ ⊖ d	06 51		06 54	06 59	07 01	07 06		07 09	07 11	07 14	07 16
St Pancras International d	06 56		06 58	07 03	07 06	07 11		07 13	07a15	07 18	07 21
Kentish Town ⊖ d				07 08						07 23	
West Hampstead Thameslink ⊖ d			07 07	07 14				07 22		07 28	07 29
Cricklewood d				07 17				07 25			
Hendon d				07 21				07 29			
Mill Hill Broadway d			07 16	07 24				07 32		07 36	
Elstree & Borehamwood d		←	07 20	07 28			←	07 36		07 40	
Radlett d		07 09	07 24	07 32			07 24	07 40		07 44	
St Albans City d	07 14	07 17	→	07a38	07 25	07 29	07 32	→		07a51	07 41
Harpenden d	07 21	07 26				07 34	07 39				07 48
Luton Airport Parkway ■ ✈ d	07 26	07 32			07 34	07 40	07 46				07 53
Luton ■ d	07 31	07a36			07 38	07 44	07a50				07 58
Leagrave d	07 34					07 48					08 01
Harlington d	07 39					07 52					08 06
Flitwick d	07 43				07 47	07 56					08 10
Bedford ■ a	07 54				07 58	08 11					08 21

	EM ◇■ N	TL C	EM ◇■ R	TL G	TL ■ K	TL A	TL ■ S	TL ■ B	TL P	TL ■ T	TL A
Gatwick Airport d					06 46		06 29	06 55		06 43	
Elephant & Castle ⊖173,179 d				07 14		07 19					07 34
London Bridge d					07 16		07 21	07 24	07 28	07 31	
London Blackfriars d				07 19	07 22	07 24	07 27	07 32	07 34	07 37	07 39
City Thameslink ■ d				07 21	07 24	07 26	07 29	07 34	07 36	07 39	07 41
Farringdon ■ ⊖ d				07 24	07 26	07 29	07 31	07 36	07 39	07 41	07 44
St Pancras International d	07 35		07 49	07 28	07a30	07 33	07 36	07 41	07 43	07a45	07 48
Kentish Town ⊖ d				07 33					07 48		
West Hampstead Thameslink ⊖ d				07 37		07 43			07 52		07 58
Cricklewood d				07 40					07 55		
Hendon d				07 44					07 59		
Mill Hill Broadway d				07 47		07 52			08 02		08 07
Elstree & Borehamwood d		←		07 51		07 56			08 06		08 11
Radlett d		07 40		07 55		07 59			08 10		08 14
St Albans City d		07 47		→		08a06	07 54	07 59	→		08a21
Harpenden d		07 56						08 07			
Luton Airport Parkway ■ ✈ d		08 02					08 02	08 12			
Luton ■ d	07 56	08a06					08 06	08 15			
Leagrave d								08 19			
Harlington d								08 23			
Flitwick d							08 17	08 27			
Bedford ■ a	08 10		08 24				08 30	08 39			

A From Sutton (Surrey)
B From Brighton
C From Rainham Kt
D To Leicester
E From Three Bridges
F not 23 July. To East Midlands Parkway
G From Orpington to Luton
H From Orpington
I To Sheffield
J From Gillingham (Kent)
K From Brighton to Cambridge
L From Gillingham (Kent) to Luton
M From Horsham to Peterborough
N To Nottingham
O From East Grinstead
P From Rainham Kt to Luton
Q From Three Bridges to Peterborough
R To Corby
S From Horsham
T To Peterborough

Table T052MML-F

Mondays to Fridays
21 May to 7 December

Gatwick Airport and London - St Albans, Luton and Bedford

		SN 1 A	TL B	TL 1 C	EM ◇1 D	TL E	TL F	TL G	TL 1 H	TL 1 I	TL B	TL J	TL 1 K	TL G	TL 1 C	TL E	TL F	TL 1 L	TL G	TL 1 H	EM ◇1 M	TL 1 I	TL B
Gatwick Airport	d								06 59	07 25			07 13					07 46		07 29		07 55	
Elephant & Castle ⊖173,179	d						07 44	07 49						08 04			08 14		08 19				
London Bridge	d	07 35		07 41					07 51	07 54		07 58	08 01		08 11			08 16		08 21		08 24	
London Blackfriars	d	07 42		07 47			07 49	07 54	07 57	08 02		08 04	08 07	08 09	08 17		08 19	08 22	08 24	08 27		08 32	
City Thameslink 3	d	07 44		07 49			07 51	07 56	07 59	08 04		08 06	08 09	08 11	08 19		08 21	08 24	08 26	08 29		08 34	
Farringdon 3 ⊖	d	07 46		07 51			07 54	07 59	08 01	08 06		08 09	08 11	08 14	08 21		08 24	08 26	08 29	08 31		08 36	
St Pancras International	d	07 51		07 56	08 05		07 58	08 03	08 06	08 11		08 13	08a15	08 18	08 26		08 28	08a30	08 33	08 36	08 47	08 41	
Kentish Town ⊖	d						08 03					08 18					08 33						
WestHampsteadThameslink ⊖	d						08 07	08 13				08 22		08 29			08 37		08 43				
Cricklewood	d						08 10					08 25					08 40						
Hendon	d						08 14					08 29					08 44						
Mill Hill Broadway	d						08 17	08 22				08 32		08 37			08 47		08 52				
Elstree & Borehamwood	d		←			←	08 21	08 26			←	08 36		08 41		←	08 51		08 56				←
Radlett	d		07 55			08 10	08 25	08 29			08 25	08 40		08 44		08 40	08 55		08 59				08 55
St Albans City	d		08 02	08 14		08 17	→	08a36	08 25	08 29	08 32	→		08a51	08 44	08 47	→		09a06	08 54		08 59	09 02
Harpenden	d		08 11	08 20		08 24				08 35	08 39				08 51	08 55						09 06	09 10
Luton Airport Parkway 7 ✈	d	08 16	08 17	08 25	08 28	08 30			08 34	08 40	08 46				08 57	09 01				09 03		09 11	09 16
Luton 10	d	08 20	08a20	08 30		08a34			08 38	08 45	08a50				09 01	09a04				09 07	09 12	09 16	09a20
Leagrave	d			08 34						08 49					09 04								
Harlington	d			08 38						08 53					09 09								
Flitwick	d	08 31		08 42					08 47	08 57					09 13					09 16			
Bedford 7	a	08 43		08 54	08 42				09 00	09 09					09 24					09 28	09 26	09 38	

		TL E	TL 1 K	EM ◇1 D	TL G	SN 1 A	TL 1 C	TL F	TL G	TL 1 H	TL B	TL E	TL 1 K	TL G	TL 1 I	TL 1 C	EM ◇1 M	TL F	TL 1 L	TL G	TL 1 H	TL B
Gatwick Airport	d		07 43							07 59			08 13		08 36				08 46		08 29	
Elephant & Castle ⊖173,179	d				08 34			08 44	08 49					09 04				09 14		09 19		
London Bridge	d	08 28	08 31			08 35	08 41			08 51		08 58	09 01		09 05	09 11			09 16		09 21	
London Blackfriars	d	08 34	08 37		08 39	08 42	08 47	08 49	08 54	08 57		09 04	09 07	09 09	09 12	09 17		09 19	09 22	09 24	09 27	
City Thameslink 3	d	08 36	08 39		08 41	08 44	08 49	08 51	08 56	08 59		09 06	09 09	09 11	09 14	09 19		09 21	09 24	09 26	09 29	
Farringdon 3 ⊖	d	08 39	08 41		08 44	08 46	08 51	08 54	08 59	09 01		09 09	09 11	09 14	09 16	09 21		09 24	09 26	09 29	09 31	
St Pancras International	d	08 43	08a45	09 05	08 48	08 51	08 56	08 58	09 03	09 06		09 13	09a15	09 18	09 21	09 26	09 47	09 28	09a30	09 33	09 36	
Kentish Town ⊖	d	08 48						09 03				09 18						09 33				
WestHampsteadThameslink ⊖	d	08a52			08 58			09 07	09 14			09a22		09 28				09 37		09 44	09 44	
Cricklewood	d							09 10										09 40				
Hendon	d							09 14										09 44				
Mill Hill Broadway	d				09 07			09 17	09 22					09 37				09 47		09 51		
Elstree & Borehamwood	d				09 11			09 21	09 26		←			09 41				09 51		09 55		←
Radlett	d				09 14			09 25	09 29		09 25			09 44				09 55		09 59		09 55
St Albans City	d				09a21		09 15	→	09a36	09 25	09 32			09a51		09 45		→		10a06	09 56	10 02
Harpenden	d						09 21			09 31	09 37				09 43	09 51					10 02	10 07
Luton Airport Parkway 7 ✈	d			09 26			09 26			09 36	09 45				09 49	09 56					10 08	10 15
Luton 10	d					09 18	09 31			09 40	09a49				09 53	10 01	10 09				10 12	10a19
Leagrave	d					09 22	09 34			09 44						10 04					10 16	
Harlington	d					09 26	09 39			09 48						10 09					10 20	
Flitwick	d					09 30	09 43			09 52					10 02	10 13					10 24	
Bedford 7	a			09 40		09 42	09 54			10 05					10 16	10 26	10 23				10 36	

		TL J	TL 1 K	TL G	TL 1 I	TL 1 C	EM ◇1 D	TL E	TL G	TL 1 H	TL J	TL 1 N	TL G	TL 1 I	TL E	TL 1 L	EM ◇1 M	TL G	TL 1	TL J	TL 1 N	TL G	TL 1 I
Gatwick Airport	d		08 43		09 06					08 59		09 19		09 36		09 46			09 33		09 49		10 06
Elephant & Castle ⊖173,179	d			09 34					09 49				10 04					10 19				10 34	
London Bridge	d	09 28	09 31		09 35	09 41				09 51	09 58	10 01		10 05		10 16			10 21	10 28	10 31		10 35
London Blackfriars	d	09 34	09 37	09 39	09 42	09 47			09 54	09 57	10 04	10 07	10 09	10 12		10 22		10 24	10 27	10 34	10 37	10 39	10 42
City Thameslink 3	d	09 36	09 39	09 41	09 44	09 49			09 56	09 59	10 06	10 09	10 11	10 14		10 24		10 26	10 29	10 36	10 39	10 41	10 44
Farringdon 3 ⊖	d	09 39	09 41	09 44	09 46	09 51			09 59	10 01	10 09	10 11	10 14	10 16		10 26		10 29	10 31	10 39	10 41	10 44	10 46
St Pancras International	d	09 43	09a45	09 48	09 51	09 56	10 05		10 03	10 06	10 13	10a15	10 18	10 21		10a30	10 47	10 33	10 36	10 43	10a45	10 48	10 51
Kentish Town ⊖	d	09 48		09 53					10 08				10 23					10 38				10 53	
WestHampsteadThameslink ⊖	d	09 52		09 59					10 14		10 22		10 29	10 29				10 44		10 52		10 59	10 59
Cricklewood	d	09 55		10 02					10 17				10 32					10 47				11 02	
Hendon	d	09 59		10 06					10 21				10 36					10 51				11 06	
Mill Hill Broadway	d	10 02		10 09					10 24		10 31		10 39					10 54		11 01		11 09	
Elstree & Borehamwood	d	10 06		10 13				←	10 28		10 35		10 43		←			10 58		11 05		11 13	
Radlett	d	10 14		10 18				10 14	10 32		10 39		10 47		10 39			11 02		11 09		11 17	
St Albans City	d	→		10a23		10 16		10 20	10a38	10 25	→		10a53	10 41	10 45			11a08	10 55	→		11a23	11 11
Harpenden	d				10 13	10 21		10 27		10 31				10 47	10 51				11 02				11 17
Luton Airport Parkway 7 ✈	d				10 19	10 27	10 28	10 32		10 37				10 53	10 57				11 07				11 23
Luton 10	d				10 23	10 31		10a36		10 41				10 57	11a01		11 09		11 12				11 27
Leagrave	d					10 35				10 45				11 01					11 16				11 31
Harlington	d					10 39				10 49				11 05					11 20				11 35
Flitwick	d				10 32	10 43				10 53				11 09					11 24				11 39
Bedford 7	a				10 44	10 55	10 42			11 05				11 21			11 23		11 36				11 51

A From Littlehampton
B From Orpington
C From East Grinstead
D To Nottingham
E From Rainham Kt
F From Orpington to Luton
G From Sutton (Surrey)
H From Horsham
I From Brighton
J From Rainham Kt to Luton
K To Peterborough
L From Brighton to Cambridge
M To Corby
N From Horsham to Peterborough

Table T052MML-F

Mondays to Fridays
21 May to 7 December

Gatwick Airport and London - St Albans, Luton and Bedford

		EM ◇1 A	TL B	TL C	TL D	TL 1	TL E	TL 1 F	TL G	TL 1 H	TL B	TL 1 I	EM ◇1 J	TL C	TL D	TL 1	TL E	TL 1 F	TL G	TL 1 H	EM ◇1 A	TL B	TL G
Gatwick Airport	d					10 03		10 19		10 36		10 46				10 33		10 49		11 06			
Elephant & Castle ⊖173,179	d			10 49	10 49				11 04					11 19	11 19				11 34				11 49
London Bridge	d					10 51	10 58	11 01		11 05		11 16				11 21	11 28	11 31		11 35			
London Blackfriars	d			10 54	10 54	10 57	11 04	11 07	11 09	11 12		11 22		11 24	11 24	11 27	11 34	11 37	11 39	11 42			11 54
City Thameslink 3	d			10 56	10 56	10 59	11 06	11 09	11 11	11 14		11 24		11 26	11 26	11 29	11 36	11 39	11 41	11 44			11 56
Farringdon 3 ⊖	d			10 59	10 59	11 01	11 09	11 11	11 14	11 16		11 26		11 29	11 29	11 31	11 39	11 41	11 44	11 46			11 59
St Pancras International	d	11 05		11 03	11 03	11 06	11 13	11a15	11 18	11 21		11a30	11 47	11 33	11 33	11 36	11 43	11a45	11 48	11 51	12 05		12 03
Kentish Town ⊖	d			11 08	11 08				11 23					11 38	11 38				11 53				12 08
WestHampsteadThameslink ⊖	d			11 14	11 14		11 22		11 29	11 29				11 42	11 44		11 52		11 59	11 59			12 14
Cricklewood	d			11 16	11 17				11 32					11 44	11 47				12 02				12 17
Hendon	d			11 20	11 21				11 36					11 48	11 51				12 06				12 21
Mill Hill Broadway	d			11 23	11 24		11 31		11 39					11 51	11 54		12 01		12 09				12 24
Elstree & Borehamwood	d		←	11 27	11 28		11 35		11 43		←			11 55	11 58		12 05		12 13			←	12 28
Radlett	d		11 09	11 31	11 32		11 39		11 47		11 39			11 59	12 02		12 09		12 17			12 09	12 32
St Albans City	d		11 15	11a37	11a38	11 25	→		11a53	11 41	11 45			12a05	12a08	11 55	→		12a23	12 11		12 15	12a38
Harpenden	d		11 21			11 31				11 47	11 51					12 01				12 17		12 21	
Luton Airport Parkway 7 ✈	d	11 26	11 27			11 36				11 53	11 57					12 06				12 23	12 26	12 27	
Luton 10	d		11a31			11 41				11 57	12a01		12 09			12 11				12 27		12a31	
Leagrave	d					11 45				12 01						12 15				12 31			
Harlington	d					11 49				12 05						12 19				12 35			
Flitwick	d					11 53				12 09						12 23				12 39			
Bedford 7	a	11 40				12 05				12 21			12 23			12 35				12 51	12 40		

		TL 1	TL E	TL 1 F	TL G	TL 1 H	TL B	TL 1 I	EM ◇1 J	TL G	TL 1	TL E	TL 1 F	TL G	TL 1 H	EM ◇1 A	TL B	TL C	TL D	TL 1	TL E	TL 1 F	TL G
Gatwick Airport	d	11 03		11 19		11 36		11 46			11 33		11 49		12 06					12 03		12 19	
Elephant & Castle ⊖173,179	d				12 04					12 19				12 34				12 49	12 49				13 04
London Bridge	d	11 51	11 58	12 01		12 05		12 16			12 21	12 28	12 31		12 35					12 51	12 58	13 01	
London Blackfriars	d	11 57	12 04	12 07	12 09	12 12		12 22		12 24	12 27	12 34	12 37	12 39	12 42			12 54	12 54	12 57	13 04	13 07	13 09
City Thameslink 3	d	11 59	12 06	12 09	12 11	12 14		12 24		12 26	12 29	12 36	12 39	12 41	12 44			12 56	12 56	12 59	13 06	13 09	13 11
Farringdon 3 ⊖	d	12 01	12 09	12 11	12 14	12 16		12 26		12 29	12 31	12 39	12 41	12 44	12 46			12 59	12 59	13 01	13 09	13 11	13 14
St Pancras International	d	12 06	12 13	12a15	12 18	12 21		12a30	12 47	12 33	12 36	12 43	12a45	12 48	12 51	13 05		13 03	13 03	13 06	13 13	13a15	13 18
Kentish Town ⊖	d				12 23					12 38				12 53				13 08	13 08				13 23
WestHampsteadThameslink ⊖	d		12 22		12 29	12 29				12 44		12 52		12 59	12 59			13 14	13 14		13 22		13 29
Cricklewood	d				12 32					12 47				13 02				13 16	13 17				13 32
Hendon	d				12 36					12 51				13 06				13 20	13 21				13 36
Mill Hill Broadway	d		12 31		12 39					12 54		13 01		13 09				13 23	13 24		13 31		13 39
Elstree & Borehamwood	d		12 35		12 43		←			12 58		13 05		13 13			←	13 27	13 28		13 35		13 43
Radlett	d		12 39		12 47		12 39			13 02		13 09		13 17			13 09	13 31	13 32		13 39		13 47
St Albans City	d	12 25	→		12a53	12 41	12 45			13a08	12 55	→		13a23	13 11		13 15	13a37	13a38	13 25	→		13a53
Harpenden	d	12 31				12 47	12 51				13 01				13 17		13 21			13 31			
Luton Airport Parkway 7 ✈	d	12 36				12 53	12 57				13 06				13 23	13 26	13 27			13 36			
Luton 10	d	12 41				12 57	13a01		13 09		13 11				13 27		13a31			13 41			
Leagrave	d	12 45				13 01					13 15				13 31					13 45			
Harlington	d	12 49				13 05					13 19				13 35					13 49			
Flitwick	d	12 53				13 09					13 23				13 39					13 53			
Bedford 7	a	13 05				13 21			13 23		13 35				13 51	13 40				14 05			

		TL 1 H	TL B	TL 1 I	EM ◇1 J	TL C	TL D	TL 1	TL E	TL 1 F	TL G	TL 1 H	EM ◇1 A	TL B	TL K	TL L	TL 1	TL E	TL 1 F	TL G	TL 1 H	TL B
Gatwick Airport	d	12 36		12 46				12 33		12 49		13 06					13 03		13 19		13 36	
Elephant & Castle ⊖173,179	d					13 19	13 19				13 34				13 49	13 49				14 04		
London Bridge	d	13 05		13 16				13 21	13 28	13 31		13 35					13 51	13 58	14 01		14 05	
London Blackfriars	d	13 12		13 22		13 24	13 24	13 27	13 34	13 37	13 39	13 42			13 54	13 54	13 57	14 04	14 07	14 09	14 12	
City Thameslink 3	d	13 14		13 24		13 26	13 26	13 29	13 36	13 39	13 41	13 44			13 56	13 56	13 59	14 06	14 09	14 11	14 14	
Farringdon 3 ⊖	d	13 16		13 26		13 29	13 29	13 31	13 39	13 41	13 44	13 46			13 59	13 59	14 01	14 09	14 11	14 14	14 16	
St Pancras International	d	13 21		13a30	13 47	13 33	13 33	13 36	13 43	13a45	13 48	13 51	14 05		14 03	14 03	14 06	14 13	14a15	14 18	14 21	
Kentish Town ⊖	d					13 38	13 38				13 53				14 08	14 08				14 23		
WestHampsteadThameslink ⊖	d	13 29				13 42	13 44		13 52		13 59	13 59			14 14	14 14		14 22		14 29	14 29	
Cricklewood	d					13 44	13 47				14 02				14 16	14 17				14 32		
Hendon	d					13 48	13 51				14 06				14 20	14 21				14 36		
Mill Hill Broadway	d					13 51	13 54		14 01		14 09				14 23	14 24		14 31		14 39		
Elstree & Borehamwood	d		←			13 55	13 58		14 05		14 13			←	14 27	14 28		14 35		14 43		←
Radlett	d		13 39			13 59	14 02		14 09		14 17			14 09	14 31	14 32		14 39		14 47		14 39
St Albans City	d	13 41	13 45			14a05	14a08	13 55	→		14a23	14 11		14 15	14a37	14a38	14 25	→		14a53	14 41	14 45
Harpenden	d	13 47	13 51					14 01				14 17		14 21			14 31				14 47	14 51
Luton Airport Parkway 7 ✈	d	13 53	13 57					14 06				14 23	14 26	14 27			14 36				14 53	14 57
Luton 10	d	13 57	14a01		14 09			14 11				14 27		14a31			14 41				14 57	15a01
Leagrave	d	14 01						14 15				14 31					14 45				15 01	
Harlington	d	14 05						14 19				14 35					14 49				15 05	
Flitwick	d	14 09						14 23				14 39					14 53				15 09	
Bedford 7	a	14 21			14 23			14 35				14 51	14 40				15 05				15 21	

A To Nottingham
B From Rainham Kt
C until 20 July, from 8 October. From Sutton (Surrey)
D from 23 July until 5 October. From Sutton (Surrey)
E From Rainham Kt to Luton
F From Horsham to Peterborough
G From Sutton (Surrey)
H From Brighton
I From Brighton to Cambridge
J To Corby
K until 27 July. From Sutton (Surrey)
L from 30 July. From Sutton (Surrey)

Gatwick Airport and London - St Albans, Luton and Bedford

	TL ■ A	EM ◇■ B	TL C	TL D	TL ■	TL E	TL ■ F	TL G	TL ■ H	EM ◇■ I	TL J	TL G	TL ■	TL E	TL ■ F	TL G	TL ■ H	TL J	TL ■ A	EM ◇■ B	TL G	TL ■
Gatwick Airport d	13 46				13 33		13 49		14 06				14 03		14 19		14 36		14 46			14 33
Elephant & Castle ⊖173,179 d			14 19	14 19				14 34				14 49				15 04					15 19	
London Bridge d	14 16				14 21	14 28	14 31		14 35				14 51	14 58	15 01		15 05		15 16			15 21
London Blackfriars d	14 22		14 24	14 24	14 27	14 34	14 37	14 39	14 42			14 54	14 57	15 04	15 07	15 09	15 12		15 22		15 24	15 27
City Thameslink ■ d	14 24		14 26	14 26	14 29	14 36	14 39	14 41	14 44			14 56	14 59	15 06	15 09	15 11	15 14		15 24		15 26	15 29
Farringdon ■ ⊖ d	14 26		14 29	14 29	14 31	14 39	14 41	14 44	14 46			14 59	15 01	15 09	15 11	15 14	15 16		15 26		15 29	15 31
St Pancras International d	14a30	14 47	14 33	14 33	14 36	14 43	14a45	14 48	14 51	15 05		15 03	15 06	15 13	15a15	15 18	15 21		15a30	15 47	15 33	15 36
Kentish Town ⊖ d			14 38	14 38				14 53				15 08				15 23					15 38	
WestHampsteadThameslink ⊖ d			14 42	14 44		14 52		14 59	14 59			15 14		15 22		15 29	15 29				15 44	
Cricklewood d			14 44	14 47				15 02				15 17				15 32					15 47	
Hendon d			14 48	14 51				15 06				15 21				15 36					15 51	
Mill Hill Broadway d			14 51	14 54		15 01		15 09				15 24		15 31		15 39					15 54	
Elstree & Borehamwood d			14 55	14 58		15 05		15 13			←	15 28		15 35		15 43		←			15 58	
Radlett d			14 59	15 02		15 09		15 17			15 09	15 32		15 39		15 47		15 39			16 02	
St Albans City d			15a05	15a08	14 55	→		15a23	15 11		15 15	15a38	15 25	→		15a53	15 41	15 45			16a08	15 55
Harpenden d					15 01				15 17		15 21		15 31				15 47	15 51				16 01
Luton Airport Parkway ■ ✈ d					15 06				15 23	15 26	15 27		15 36				15 53	15 57				16 06
Luton ■ d		15 09			15 11				15 27		15a31		15 41				15 57	16a01		16 09		16 11
Leagrave d					15 15				15 31				15 45				16 01					16 15
Harlington d					15 19				15 35				15 49				16 05					16 19
Flitwick d					15 23				15 39				15 53				16 09					16 23
Bedford ■ a		15 23			15 35				15 52	15 40			16 05				16 21			16 23		16 35

	TL E	TL ■ F	TL G	TL ■ H	TL J	TL G	TL ■	TL E	TL ■ F	TL G	TL ■ H	TL ■	TL J	TL K	TL ■ A	TL G	TL ■	TL L	TL E	TL ■ F	TL G	TL ■ H
Gatwick Airport d		14 49		15 06			15 03		15 19		15 36	15 27			15 46		15 33			15 49		16 06
Elephant & Castle ⊖173,179 d			15 34			15 49				16 04				16 14		16 19					16 34	
London Bridge d	15 28	15 31		15 35			15 51	15 58	16 01		16 05	16 11			16 16		16 21		16 28	16 31		16 35
London Blackfriars d	15 34	15 37	15 39	15 42		15 54	15 57	16 04	16 07	16 09	16 12	16 17		16 19	16 22	16 24	16 27		16 34	16 37	16 39	16 42
City Thameslink ■ d	15 36	15 39	15 41	15 44		15 56	15 59	16 06	16 09	16 11	16 14	16 19		16 21	16 24	16 26	16 29		16 36	16 39	16 41	16 44
Farringdon ■ ⊖ d	15 39	15 41	15 44	15 46		15 59	16 01	16 09	16 11	16 14	16 16	16 21		16 24	16 26	16 29	16 31		16 39	16 41	16 44	16 46
St Pancras International d	15 43	15a45	15 48	15 51		16 03	16 06	16 13	16a15	16 18	16 21	16 26		16 28	16a30	16 33	16 36		16 43	16a45	16 48	16 51
Kentish Town ⊖ d			15 53			16 08		16 18						16 33					16 48			
WestHampsteadThameslink ⊖ d	15 52		15 59	15 59		16 14		16 22		16 29				16 37		16 44	16 44		16 52		16 59	
Cricklewood d			16 02			16 18		16 26						16 41					16 56			
Hendon d			16 06			16 21		16 29						16 44					16 59			
Mill Hill Broadway d	16 01		16 09			16 24		16 33		16 37				16 48		16 52			17 03		17 07	
Elstree & Borehamwood d	16 05		16 13		←	16 28		16 37		16 41			←	16 52		16 56		←	17 07		17 11	
Radlett d	16 13		16 17		16 13	16 32		16 40		16 45			16 40	16 56		17 00		16 56	17 10		17 15	
St Albans City d	→		16a23	16 14	16 19	16a38	16 25	→		16a52	16 39	16 44	16 47	→		17a07	16 56	17 02	→		17a22	17 10
Harpenden d				16 20	16 27		16 31					16 51	16 55				17 02	17 08				
Luton Airport Parkway ■ ✈ d				16 25	16 32		16 36					16 56	17 01				17 08	17 14				
Luton ■ d				16 29	16a36		16 41				16 50	17 01	17a05				17 12	17a19				17 21
Leagrave d				16 33			16 46					17 05					17 15					
Harlington d				16 37			16 50					17 09					17 20					
Flitwick d				16 41			16 54					17 13					17 24					
Bedford ■ a				16 53			17 06				17 06	17 26					17 35					17 38

	TL ■	TL J	TL K	TL G	TL ■	TL J	TL L	TL ■ F	TL G	TL ■ H	TL ■	TL K	TL ■ A	TL G	TL ■	TL ■ M	TL L	TL E	TL ■ F	TL G	TL ■ H	TL ■
Gatwick Airport d	15 57				16 03			16 19		16 36	16 27		16 46		16 33	16 54			16 49		17 06	16 57
Elephant & Castle ⊖173,179 d			16 44	16 49					17 04			17 14		17 19						17 34		
London Bridge d	16 41				16 51	16 57		17 01		17 05	17 11		17 16		17 21	17 24		17 28	17 31		17 35	17 41
London Blackfriars d	16 47		16 49	16 54	16 57	17 03		17 07	17 09	17 12	17 17	17 19	17 22	17 24	17 27	17 32		17 34	17 37	17 39	17 42	17 47
City Thameslink ■ d	16 49		16 51	16 56	16 59	17 05		17 09	17 11	17 14	17 19	17 21	17 24	17 26	17 29	17 34		17 36	17 39	17 41	17 44	17 49
Farringdon ■ ⊖ d	16 51		16 54	16 59	17 01	17 07		17 11	17 14	17 16	17 21	17 24	17 26	17 29	17 31	17 36		17 39	17 41	17 44	17 46	17 51
St Pancras International d	16 56		16 58	17 03	17 06	17 12		17a15	17 18	17 21	17 26	17 28	17a30	17 33	17 36	17 41		17 43	17a45	17 48	17 51	17 56
Kentish Town ⊖ d			17 03									17 33						17 48				
WestHampsteadThameslink ⊖ d			17 07	17 14					17 29			17 37		17 44				17 52		17 59		
Cricklewood d			17 11									17 41						17 56				
Hendon d			17 14									17 44						17 59				
Mill Hill Broadway d			17 18	17 22					17 37			17 48		17 52				18 03		18 07		
Elstree & Borehamwood d		←	17 22	17 26			←		17 41			17 52		17 56			←	18 07		18 12		
Radlett d		17 10	17 25	17 30			17 25		17 45			17 55		18 00			17 55	18 14		18 18		
St Albans City d	17 14	17 17	→	17a37	17 24	17 29	17 32		17a52	17 40	17 44	→		18a07	17 54	17 59	18 02	→		18a23	18 09	18 16
Harpenden d	17 21	17 26			17 30	17 36	17 41			17 46	17 51				18 00	18 05	18 10					18 22
Luton Airport Parkway ■ ✈ d	17 26	17 32				17 41	17 47				17 56					18 11	18 16					18 28
Luton ■ d	17 31	17a36			17 37	17 46	17a50			17 52	18 01				18 07	18 15	18a21				18 19	18 32
Leagrave d	17 35					17 49					18 05					18 19						18 36
Harlington d	17 39					17 54					18 09					18 24						18 40
Flitwick d	17 43				17 47	17 58				18 03	18 13				18 17	18 28						18 44
Bedford ■ a	17 55				17 58	18 09				18 15	18 25				18 28	18 41					18 36	18 56

A From Brighton to Cambridge
B To Corby
C until 27 July. From Sutton (Surrey)
D from 30 July. From Sutton (Surrey)
E From Rainham Kt to Luton
F From Horsham to Peterborough
G From Sutton (Surrey)
H From Brighton
I To Nottingham
J From Rainham Kt
K From Orpington to Luton
L From Orpington
M From Three Bridges

Table T052MML-F

Mondays to Fridays

21 May to 7 December

Gatwick Airport and London - St Albans, Luton and Bedford

	TL A	TL B	TL C	TL ■	TL ■ D	TL E	TL F	TL ■ G	TL C	TL ■ H	TL ■	TL A	TL B	TL ■ I	TL C	TL ■ J	TL ■ K	TL E	TL F	TL ■ G	TL C
Gatwick Airport d				17 03	17 24			17 19		17 36	17 27			17 46		17 33	17 33			17 49	
Elephant & Castle ⊖173,179 d		17 44	17 49						18 04				18 14		18 19						18 34
London Bridge d				17 51	17 54		17 58	18 01		18 05	18 11			18 16		18 21	18 21		18 28	18 31	
London Blackfriars d		17 49	17 54	17 57	18 02		18 04	18 07	18 09	18 12	18 17		18 19	18 22	18 24	18 27	18 27		18 34	18 37	18 39
City Thameslink ■ d		17 51	17 56	17 59	18 04		18 06	18 09	18 11	18 14	18 19		18 21	18 24	18 26	18 29	18 29		18 36	18 39	18 41
Farringdon ■ ⊖ d		17 54	17 59	18 01	18 06		18 09	18 11	18 14	18 16	18 21		18 24	18 26	18 29	18 31	18 31		18 39	18 41	18 44
St Pancras International d		17 58	18 03	18 06	18 11		18 13	18a15	18 18	18 21	18 26		18 28	18a30	18 33	18 36	18 36		18 43	18a45	18 48
Kentish Town ⊖ d		18 03					18 18						18 33						18 48		
WestHampsteadThameslink ⊖ d		18 07	18 14				18 22		18 29				18 37		18 44				18 52		18 59
Cricklewood d		18 11					18 26						18 41						18 56		
Hendon d		18 14					18 29						18 44						18 59		
Mill Hill Broadway d		18 18	18 22				18 33		18 37				18 48		18 52				19 03		19 07
Elstree & Borehamwood d	←	18 22	18 26			←	18 37		18 41			←	18 52		18 56			←	19 07		19 11
Radlett d	18 14	18 25	18 30			18 25	18 40		18 45			18 40	18 55		19 00			18 55	19 10		19 15
St Albans City d	18 20	→	18a37	18 24	18 29	18 32	→		18a52	18 39	18 44	18 47	→		19a07	18 55	18 55	19 02	→		19a22
Harpenden d	18 26			18 30	18 36	18 41					18 51	18 55				19 02	19 02	19 10			
Luton Airport Parkway ■ ✈ d	18 31				18 42	18 47					18 56	19 01				19 07	19 07	19 16			
Luton ■ d	18a35			18 37	18 46	18a51				18 50	19 01	19a05				19 12	19 12	19a21			
Leagrave d					18 49						19 05					19 15	19 15				
Harlington d					18 54						19 09					19 20	19 20				
Flitwick d				18 47	18 58						19 13					19 24	19 24				
Bedford ■ a				18 58	19 15					19 06	19 25					19 39	19 42				

	TL ■ H	TL ■ L	EM ◇■ M	TL A	TL B	TL N	TL O	TL ■	TL E	TL F	TL ■ G	TL C	TL ■ H	TL ■ L	TL A	TL ■ I	EM ◇■ P	TL N	TL O	TL ■	TL F	TL ■ G
Gatwick Airport d	18 06							18 03			18 19		18 36			18 46				18 33		18 49
Elephant & Castle ⊖173,179 d					18 44	18 49	18 49					19 04						19 19	19 19			
London Bridge d	18 35	18 41						18 51		18 58	19 01		19 05	19 11		19 16				19 21	19 28	19 31
London Blackfriars d	18 42	18 47			18 49	18 54	18 54	18 57		19 04	19 07	19 09	19 12	19 17		19 22		19 24	19 24	19 27	19 34	19 37
City Thameslink ■ d	18 44	18 49			18 51	18 56	18 56	18 59		19 06	19 09	19 11	19 14	19 19		19 24		19 26	19 26	19 29	19 36	19 39
Farringdon ■ ⊖ d	18 46	18 51			18 54	18 59	18 59	19 01		19 09	19 11	19 14	19 16	19 21		19 26		19 29	19 29	19 31	19 39	19 41
St Pancras International d	18 51	18 56	19 04		18 58	19 03	19 03	19 06		19 13	19a15	19 18	19 21	19 26		19a30	19 47	19 33	19 33	19 36	19 43	19a45
Kentish Town ⊖ d					19 03					19 18								19 38	19 38			
WestHampsteadThameslink ⊖ d					19 07	19 14	19 14			19 22		19 29						19 42	19 44	19 44	19 52	
Cricklewood d					19 11					19 26								19 44	19 47			
Hendon d					19 14					19 29								19 48	19 51			
Mill Hill Broadway d					19 18	19 21	19 22			19 33		19 37						19 51	19 54		20 01	
Elstree & Borehamwood d				←	19 22	19 25	19 26		←	19 37		19 42			←			19 55	19 58		20 05	
Radlett d				19 10	19 25	19 29	19 30		19 25	19 44		19 48			19 44			19 59	20 02		20 09	
St Albans City d	19 09	19 14		19 17	→	19a36	19a37	19 25	19 32	→		19a53	19 40	19 46	19 50			20a05	20a08	19 56	→	
Harpenden d		19 21		19 26				19 31	19 41				19 46	19 52	19 57					20 02		
Luton Airport Parkway ■ ✈ d		19 26	19 28	19 32				19 36	19 47					19 57	20 02					20 08		
Luton ■ d	19 20	19 31		19a36				19 41	19a51				19 52	20 02	20a06		20 10			20 12		
Leagrave d		19 35						19 45						20 05						20 16		
Harlington d		19 39						19 49						20 10						20 21		
Flitwick d		19 43						19 53					20 03	20 14						20 25		
Bedford ■ a	19 36	19 55	19 43					20 05					20 14	20 26			20 23			20 36		

	TL C	TL ■ H	TL ■ L	EM ◇■ Q	TL A	TL C	TL ■	TL F	TL ■ G	TL C	TL ■ H	TL A	TL ■ I	TL C	TL ■	TL F	TL ■ G	TL C	TL ■ H	TL A	TL C	EM ◇■ Q
Gatwick Airport d		19 06					19 03		19 19		19 36		19 46		19 33		19 49		20 06			
Elephant & Castle ⊖173,179 d	19 34					19 49				20 04				20 19				20 34			20 49	
London Bridge d		19 35	19 41				19 51	19 58	20 01		20 05		20 16		20 21	20 28	20 31		20 35			
London Blackfriars d	19 39	19 42	19 47			19 54	19 57	20 04	20 07	20 09	20 12		20 22	20 24	20 27	20 34	20 37	20 39	20 42		20 54	
City Thameslink ■ d	19 41	19 44	19 49			19 56	19 59	20 06	20 09	20 11	20 14		20 24	20 26	20 29	20 36	20 39	20 41	20 44		20 56	
Farringdon ■ ⊖ d	19 44	19 46	19 51			19 59	20 01	20 09	20 11	20 14	20 16		20 26	20 29	20 31	20 39	20 41	20 44	20 46		20 59	
St Pancras International d	19 48	19 51	19 56	20 05		20 03	20 06	20 13	20a15	20 18	20 21		20a30	20 33	20 36	20 43	20a45	20 48	20 51		21 03	21 04
Kentish Town ⊖ d	19 53					20 08				20 23				20 38				20 53			21 08	
WestHampsteadThameslink ⊖ d	19 59					20 14		20 22		20 29	20 29			20 44		20 52		20 59	20 59		21 14	
Cricklewood d	20 02					20 17				20 32				20 47				21 02			21 17	
Hendon d	20 06					20 21				20 36				20 51				21 06			21 21	
Mill Hill Broadway d	20 09					20 24		20 31		20 39				20 54		21 01		21 09			21 24	
Elstree & Borehamwood d	20 13				←	20 28		20 35		20 43		←		20 58		21 05		21 13		←	21 28	
Radlett d	20 17				20 09	20 32		20 39		20 47		20 39		21 02		21 09		21 17		21 09	21 32	
St Albans City d	20a23	20 10	20 14		20 17	20a38	20 25	→		20a53	20 41	20 45		21a08	20 55	→		21a23	21 11	21 15	21a38	
Harpenden d		20 16	20 21		20 27		20 31				20 47	20 51			21 01				21 17	21 21		
Luton Airport Parkway ■ ✈ d			20 26	20 28	20 32		20 36				20 53	20 57			21 06				21 23	21 27		21 27
Luton ■ d		20 22	20 31		20a36		20 41				20 57	21a01			21 11				21 27	21a31		
Leagrave d			20 35				20 45				21 01				21 15				21 31			
Harlington d			20 39				20 49				21 05				21 19				21 35			
Flitwick d		20 33	20 43				20 53				21 09				21 23				21 39			
Bedford ■ a		20 44	20 57	20 42			21 05				21 21				21 35				21 51			21 40

A From Rainham Kt
B From Orpington to Luton
C From Sutton (Surrey)
D From Three Bridges
E From Orpington
F From Rainham Kt to Luton
G From Horsham to Peterborough
H From Brighton
I From Brighton to Cambridge
J from 18 June
K until 15 June
L From East Grinstead
M To Leeds
N until 27 July. From Sutton (Surrey)
O from 30 July. From Sutton (Surrey)
P To Corby
Q To Nottingham

Mondays to Fridays

21 May to 7 December

Gatwick Airport and London - St Albans, Luton and Bedford

Station		TL ■	EM ◇■ A	TL B	TL ■ C	TL ■ D	TL E	TL F	TL ■ G	TL F	TL ■	EM ◇■ A	EM ◇■ H	TL I	TL ■ C	TL F	TL ■ D	TL E	TL F	TL ■	EM ◇■ J	TL B	TL ■ C
Gatwick Airport	d	20 03			20 19	20 36			20 46		20 33				20 49		21 06			21 03			21 19
Elephant & Castle ⊖173,179	d							21 11		21 19						21 34			21 49				
London Bridge	d	20 51		20 58	21 01	21 05			21 16		21 21			21 28	21 31		21 35			21 51		21 58	22 01
London Blackfriars	d	20 57		21 04	21 07	21 12		21 17	21 22	21 24	21 27			21 34	21 37	21 39	21 42		21 54	21 57		22 04	22 07
City Thameslink ■	d	20 59		21 06	21 09	21 14		21 19	21 24	21 26	21 29			21 36	21 39	21 41	21 44		21 56	21 59		22 06	22 09
Farringdon ■ ⊖	d	21 01		21 09	21 11	21 16		21 21	21 26	21 29	21 31			21 39	21 41	21 44	21 46		21 59	22 01		22 09	22 11
St Pancras International	d	21 06	21 30	21 13	21a15	21 21		21 26	21a30	21 33	21 36	21 50	22 00	21 43	21a45	21 48	21 51		22 03	22 06	22 20	22 13	22a15
Kentish Town ⊖	d			21 18						21 38						21 53			22 08				
WestHampsteadThameslink ⊖	d			21 24		21 29		21 34		21 44				21 52		21 59	21 59		22 14			22 22	
Cricklewood	d			21 27						21 47						22 02			22 17				
Hendon	d			21 31						21 51						22 06			22 21				
Mill Hill Broadway	d			21 34				21 40		21 54				22 01		22 09			22 24			22 31	
Elstree & Borehamwood	d			21 38			←	21 44		21 58				22 05		22 13		←	22 28			22 35	
Radlett	d			21 42			21 42	21 48		22 02				22 09		22 17		22 09	22 32			22 39	
St Albans City	d	21 25		→		21 41	21 48	21a54		22a08	21 55			→		22a23	22 11	22 15	22a38	22 25		→	
Harpenden	d	21 31				21 47	21 57				22 01						22 17	22 21		22 31			
Luton Airport Parkway ■ ✈	d	21 36				21 53	22 02				22 06	22 13					22 23	22 27		22 36	22 44		
Luton ■	d	21 41	21 55			21 57	22a06				22 11		22 25				22 27	22 32		22 41			
Leagrave	d	21 45				22 01					22 15						22 31			22 45			
Harlington	d	21 49				22 05					22 19						22 35			22 49			
Flitwick	d	21 53				22 09					22 23						22 39			22 53			
Bedford ■	a	22 05	22 08			22 21					22 35	22 26	22 39				22 51	22 55		23 05	22 57		

Station		TL F	TL ■ D	TL E	TL ■ G	TL K	TL ■	TL F	TL E	TL ■ C	TL K	TL ■ D	TL F	EM ◇■ H	TL F	TL E	TL ■ C	TL ■ D	TL F	TL ■ G	TL F	TL E
Gatwick Airport	d		21 36		21 46		21 33			21 49		22 06					22 19	22 36		22 46		
Elephant & Castle ⊖173,179	d	22 04				22 19					22 34				22 51				23 11		23 21	
London Bridge	d		22 05		22 16		22 21		22 28	22 31		22 35				22 58	23 01	23 05		23 16		23 28
London Blackfriars	d	22 09	22 12		22 22	22 24	22 27		22 34	22 37	22 39	22 42			22 59	23 04	23 07	23 12	23 17	23 22	23 27	23 34
City Thameslink ■	d	22 11	22 14		22 24	22 26	22 29		22 36	22 39	22 41	22 44										
Farringdon ■ ⊖	d	22 14	22 16		22 26	22 29	22 31		22 39	22 41	22 44	22 46			23 04	23 09	23 11	23 16	23 21	23 26	23 31	23 39
St Pancras International	d	22 18	22 21		22a30	22 33	22 36		22 43	22a45	22 48	22 51	←	23 08	23 08	23 13	23a15	23 21	23 26	23a30	23 36	23 43
Kentish Town ⊖	d	22 23				22 38					22 58		22 58		23 13				23 30		23 40	
WestHampsteadThameslink ⊖	d	22 29	22 29			22 44			22a51		→	22 59	23 02		23 17	23a21		23 29	23 34		23 44	23a51
Cricklewood	d	22 32				22 47							23 05		23 20				23 38		23 48	
Hendon	d	22 36				22 51							23 09		23 24				23 42		23 52	
Mill Hill Broadway	d	22 39				22 54							23 12		23 27				23 45		23 55	
Elstree & Borehamwood	d	22 43		←		22 58		←					23 16		23 31				23 49		23 59	
Radlett	d	22 47		22 39		23 02		23 02					23 20		23 35				23 53		00 03	
St Albans City	d	22a53	22 41	22 45		→	22 55	23 09				23 16	23 27		23 42			23 46	23 59		00 10	
Harpenden	d		22 47	22 51			23 01	23 15				23 22	23 33		23 48			23 52	00 06		00 16	
Luton Airport Parkway ■ ✈	d		22 53	22 57			23 06	23 20				23 27	23 39		23 54			23 58	00 11		00 21	
Luton ■	d		22 57	23a01			23 11	23 25				23 31	23 43	23 47	23 58			00 02	00 16		00 26	
Leagrave	d		23 01				23 15					23 35						00 06	00 20			
Harlington	d		23 05				23 19					23 40						00 11	00 24			
Flitwick	d		23 09				23 23					23 44						00 15	00 28			
Bedford ■	a		23 21				23 35	23 48				23 55	00 03	00 08	00 18			00 26	00 40		00 46	

Station		TL ■ C	TL ■ D	TL F	TL F	TL ■ D
Gatwick Airport	d	22 49	23 06			23 34
Elephant & Castle ⊖173,179	d			23 41	23 54	
London Bridge	d	23 31	23 35			
London Blackfriars	d	23 37	23 42	23 49	00 02	00 22
City Thameslink ■	d					
Farringdon ■ ⊖	d	23 41	23 46	23 53	00 06	00 25
St Pancras International	d	23a45	23 51	23 58	00 11	00 30
Kentish Town ⊖	d			00 01		
WestHampsteadThameslink ⊖	d		23 59	00 06	00 19	00 39
Cricklewood	d			00 10		
Hendon	d			00 14		
Mill Hill Broadway	d			00 17		
Elstree & Borehamwood	d			00 21		
Radlett	d			00 25		
St Albans City	d		00 16	00 32	00 36	00 56
Harpenden	d		00 22	00 38	00 42	01 02
Luton Airport Parkway ■ ✈	d		00 28	00 43	00 48	01 08
Luton ■	d		00 32	00 48	00 52	01 12
Leagrave	d		00 36		00 56	01 16
Harlington	d		00 41		01 01	01 21
Flitwick	d		00 45		01 05	01 25
Bedford ■	a		00 56	01 10	01 18	01 36

A To East Midlands Parkway
B From Rainham Kt to Luton
C From Horsham to Peterborough
D From Brighton
E From Rainham Kt
F From Sutton (Surrey)
G From Brighton to Cambridge
H To Nottingham
I From Rainham Kt to Bedford
J To Sheffield
K From Sutton (Surrey) to Bedford

Saturdays

26 May to 8 December

Gatwick Airport and London - St Albans, Luton and Bedford

Station		TL ■ A	TL B	TL B	TL ■ A	TL B	TL B	EM ◇■ C	TL B	TL ■ A	TL ■ A	TL ■ A	TL ■ A	TL ■ D	TL ■ D	TL ■ D	TL ■ D	TL ■ D	TL ■ D	TL	EM ◇■ E	TL ■ A	TL ■ D
Gatwick Airport	d										00 04	00 21	00 42	01 46	02 21	02 46	03 21	03 46	04 21			04 41	05 20
Elephant & Castle ⊖173,179	d								00 04														
London Bridge	d																					05 26	05 55
London Blackfriars	d						00 02		00 09	00 22	00 50	01 08	01 36	02 36	03 06	03 36	04 06	04 36	05 06	05 27		05 32	06 02
City Thameslink ■	d																						
Farringdon ■ ⊖	d						00 06		00 13	00 25									05 11	05 31		05 36	06 06
St Pancras International	d						00 11	00 15	00 18	00 30	01 01	01 16	01 44	02 44	03 14	03 44	04 14	04 44	05 16	05 36	05 48	05 41	06 11
Kentish Town ⊖	d					00 01			00 22		01 05		01 48	02 48		03 48	04 18	04 48		05 40			
WestHampsteadThameslink ⊖	d					00 06	00 19		00 26	00 39	01 09	01 24	01 52	02 52	03 22	03 52	04 22	04 52	05 24	05 44		05 48	06 19
Cricklewood	d					00 10			00 30		01 13		01 56	02 56		03 56	04 26	04 56		05 48			
Hendon	d					00 14			00 34		01 17		02 00	03 00		04 00	04 30	05 00		05 51			
Mill Hill Broadway	d					00 17			00 37		01 20		02 03	03 03		04 03	04 33	05 03		05 54			
Elstree & Borehamwood	d					00 21			00 41		01 24		02 07	03 07		04 07	04 37	05 07		05 58			
Radlett	d			00 03		00 25			00 45		01 28		02 11	03 11		04 11	04 41	05 11		06 02			
St Albans City	d			00 10	00 16	00 32	00 36		00 52	00 56	01 34	01 41	02 19	03 19	03 41	04 19	04 49	05 19	05 41	06a08		06 00	06 31
Harpenden	d		00 06	00 16	00 22	00 38	00 42		00 58	01 02	01 40	01 47	02 25	03 25	03 47	04 25	04 55	05 25	05 47			06 06	06 37
Luton Airport Parkway ■ ✈	d		00 11	00 21	00 28	00 43	00 48	00 53	01 03	01 08	01 46	01 52	02 30	03 30	03 52	04 30	05 00	05 30	05 52			06 12	06 43
Luton ■	d	00 02	00 16	00 26	00 32	00 48	00 52	00 57	01 08	01 12	01 50	01 57	02 35	03 35	03 57	04 35	05 05	05 35	05 57		06 14	06 16	06 47
Leagrave	d	00 06	00 20		00 36		00 56		01 12	01 16	01 54	02 01	02 39	03 39	04 01	04 39	05 09	05 39	06 01			06 20	06 51
Harlington	d	00 11	00 24		00 41		01 01		01 16	01 21	01 59	02 05	02 43	03 43	04 05	04 43	05 13	05 43	06 05			06 24	06 55
Flitwick	d	00 15	00 28		00 45		01 05		01 20	01 25	02 03	02 09	02 47	03 47	04 09	04 47	05 17	05 47	06 09			06 28	06 59
Bedford ■	a	00 26	00 40	00 46	00 56	01 10	01 18	01 25	01 32	01 36	02 14	02 21	02 59	03 59	04 21	05 01	05 33	05 59	06 21		06 27	06 41	07 11

Station		TL F	TL ■ G	TL B	TL ■ D	EM ◇■ H	TL I	TL ■ J	TL B	TL ■ A	TL F	TL B	TL ■	TL K	TL ■ J	TL B	TL ■ A	TL ■ G	EM ◇■ H	TL L	TL B	EM ◇■ M	TL ■
Gatwick Airport	d		05 46		05 33			05 49		06 06			06 03		06 19		06 36	06 46					06 33
Elephant & Castle ⊖173,179	d			06 19					06 34			06 49				07 04					07 19		
London Bridge	d	05 58	06 16		06 21		06 28	06 31		06 35			06 51	06 58	07 01		07 05	07 16					07 21
London Blackfriars	d	06 04	06 22	06 24	06 27		06 34	06 37	06 39	06 42		06 54	06 57	07 04	07 07	07 09	07 12	07 22			07 24		07 27
City Thameslink ■	d																						
Farringdon ■ ⊖	d	06 09	06 26	06 29	06 31		06 39	06 41	06 44	06 46		06 59	07 01	07 09	07 11	07 14	07 16	07 26			07 29		07 31
St Pancras International	d	06 13	06a30	06 33	06 36	07 05	06 43	06a45	06 48	06 51		07 03	07 06	07 13	07a15	07 18	07 21	07a30	07 35		07 33	07 47	07 36
Kentish Town ⊖	d	06 18		06 38					06 53			07 08				07 23					07 38		
WestHampsteadThameslink ⊖	d	06 22		06 44	06 44		06 52		06 59	06 59		07 14		07 22		07 29	07 29				07 44		
Cricklewood	d	06 25		06 47					07 02			07 17				07 32					07 47		
Hendon	d	06 29		06 51					07 06			07 21				07 36					07 51		
Mill Hill Broadway	d	06 32		06 54			07 01		07 09			07 24		07 31		07 39					07 54		
Elstree & Borehamwood	d	06 36		06 58			07 05		07 13		←	07 28		07 35		07 43				←	07 58		
Radlett	d	06 39		07 02			07 09		07 17		07 09	07 32		07 39		07 47				07 39	08 02		
St Albans City	d	06 46		07a08	06 57		→		07a23	07 11	07 15	07a38	07 25	→		07a53	07 41			07 45	08a08		07 55
Harpenden	d	06 51			07 03					07 17	07 21		07 31				07 47			07 51			08 01
Luton Airport Parkway ■ ✈	d	06 57			07 08					07 23	07 27		07 36				07 53		07 56	07 57			08 06
Luton ■	d	07a01			07 13	07 27				07 27	07a31		07 41				07 57			08a01		08 09	08 11
Leagrave	d				07 17					07 31			07 45				08 01						08 15
Harlington	d				07 21					07 35			07 49				08 05						08 19
Flitwick	d				07 25					07 39			07 53				08 09						08 23
Bedford ■	a				07 37	07 40				07 51			08 05				08 21		08 10			08 23	08 35

Station		TL K	TL ■ J	TL B	TL ■ A	EM ◇■ H	TL L	TL B	TL ■	TL K	TL ■ J	TL B	TL ■ A	TL L	TL ■ G	EM ◇■ M	TL B	TL ■	TL K	TL ■ J	TL B	TL ■ A	EM ◇■ H
Gatwick Airport	d		06 49		07 06				07 03		07 19		07 36		07 46			07 33		07 49		08 06	
Elephant & Castle ⊖173,179	d			07 34				07 49				08 04					08 19				08 34		
London Bridge	d	07 28	07 31		07 35				07 51	07 58	08 01		08 05		08 16			08 21	08 28	08 31		08 35	
London Blackfriars	d	07 34	07 37	07 39	07 42			07 54	07 57	08 04	08 07	08 09	08 12		08 22		08 24	08 27	08 34	08 37	08 39	08 42	
City Thameslink ■	d																						
Farringdon ■ ⊖	d	07 39	07 41	07 44	07 46			07 59	08 01	08 09	08 11	08 14	08 16		08 26		08 29	08 31	08 39	08 41	08 44	08 46	
St Pancras International	d	07 43	07a45	07 48	07 51	08 05		08 03	08 06	08 13	08a15	08 18	08 21		08a30	08 47	08 33	08 36	08 43	08a45	08 48	08 51	09 05
Kentish Town ⊖	d			07 53				08 08				08 23					08 38				08 53		
WestHampsteadThameslink ⊖	d	07 52		07 59	07 59			08 14		08 22		08 29	08 29				08 44		08 52		08 59	08 59	
Cricklewood	d			08 02				08 17				08 32					08 47				09 02		
Hendon	d			08 06				08 21				08 36					08 51				09 06		
Mill Hill Broadway	d	08 01		08 09				08 24		08 31		08 39					08 54		09 01		09 09		
Elstree & Borehamwood	d	08 05		08 13			←	08 28		08 35		08 43		←			08 58		09 05		09 13		
Radlett	d	08 09		08 17			08 09	08 32		08 39		08 47		08 39			09 02		09 09		09 17		
St Albans City	d	→		08a23	08 11		08 15	08a38	08 25	→		08a53	08 41	08 45			09a08	08 55	→		09a23	09 11	
Harpenden	d				08 17		08 21		08 31				08 47	08 51				09 01				09 17	
Luton Airport Parkway ■ ✈	d				08 23	08 26	08 27		08 36				08 53	08 57				09 06				09 23	09 26
Luton ■	d				08 27		08a31		08 41				08 57	09a01		09 09		09 11				09 27	
Leagrave	d				08 31				08 45				09 01					09 15				09 31	
Harlington	d				08 35				08 49				09 05					09 19				09 35	
Flitwick	d				08 39				08 53				09 09					09 23				09 39	
Bedford ■	a				08 51	08 39			09 05				09 21			09 23		09 35				09 51	09 40

A From Brighton
B From Sutton (Surrey)
C To Leicester
D From Three Bridges
E To East Midlands Parkway
F From Gillingham (Kent)
G From Brighton to Cambridge
H To Nottingham
I From Gillingham (Kent) to Luton
J From Horsham to Peterborough
K From Rainham Kt to Luton
L From Rainham Kt
M To Corby

Table T052MML-F

Saturdays
26 May to 8 December

Gatwick Airport and London - St Albans, Luton and Bedford

		TL A	TL B	TL ■	TL C	TL ■ D	TL B	TL ■ E	TL A	TL ■ F	EM ◇■ G	TL B	TL ■	TL C	TL ■ D	TL B	TL ■ E	EM ◇■ H	TL A	TL B	TL ■	TL C
Gatwick Airport	d			08 03		08 19		08 36		08 46			08 33		08 49		09 06				09 03	
Elephant & Castle ⊖173,179	d		08 49				09 04					09 19				09 34				09 49		
London Bridge	d			08 51	08 58	09 01		09 05		09 16			09 21	09 28	09 31		09 35				09 51	09 58
London Blackfriars	d		08 54	08 57	09 04	09 07	09 09	09 12		09 22		09 24	09 27	09 34	09 37	09 39	09 42			09 54	09 57	10 04
City Thameslink ■	d				09 06	09 09	09 11	09 14		09 24		09 26	09 29	09 36	09 39	09 41	09 44			09 56	09 59	10 06
Farringdon ■ ⊖	d		08 59	09 01	09 09	09 11	09 14	09 16		09 26		09 29	09 31	09 39	09 41	09 44	09 46			09 59	10 01	10 09
St Pancras International	d		09 03	09 06	09 13	09a15	09 18	09 21		09a30	09 47	09 33	09 36	09 43	09a45	09 48	09 51	10 05		10 03	10 06	10 13
Kentish Town ⊖	d		09 08				09 23					09 38				09 53				10 08		
WestHampsteadThameslink ⊖	d		09 14		09 22		09 29	09 29				09 44		09 52		09 59	09 59			10 14		10 22
Cricklewood	d		09 17				09 32					09 47				10 02				10 17		
Hendon	d		09 21				09 36					09 51				10 06				10 21		
Mill Hill Broadway	d		09 24		09 31		09 39					09 54		10 01		10 09				10 24		10 31
Elstree & Borehamwood	d	←	09 28		09 35		09 43		←			09 58		10 05		10 13			←	10 28		10 35
Radlett	d	09 09	09 32		09 39		09 47		09 39			10 02		10 09		10 17			10 09	10 32		10 39
St Albans City	d	09 15	09a38	09 25	→		09a53	09 41	09 45			10a08	09 55	→		10a23	10 11		10 15	10a38	10 25	→
Harpenden	d	09 21		09 31				09 47	09 51				10 01				10 17		10 21		10 31	
Luton Airport Parkway ■ ✈	d	09 27		09 36				09 53	09 57				10 06				10 23	10 26	10 27		10 36	
Luton ■	d	09a31		09 41				09 57	10a01		10 09		10 11				10 27		10a31		10 41	
Leagrave	d			09 45				10 01					10 15				10 31				10 45	
Harlington	d			09 49				10 05					10 19				10 35				10 49	
Flitwick	d			09 53				10 09					10 23				10 39				10 53	
Bedford ■	a			10 05				10 21			10 23		10 35				10 51	10 40			11 05	

		TL ■ D	TL B	TL ■ E	TL A	TL ■ F	EM ◇■ G	TL B	TL ■	TL C	TL ■ D	TL B	TL ■ E	EM ◇■ H	TL A	TL B	TL ■	TL C	TL ■ D	TL B	TL ■ E	TL A	TL ■ F
Gatwick Airport	d	09 19		09 36		09 46			09 33		09 49		10 06				10 03		10 19		10 36		10 46
Elephant & Castle ⊖173,179	d		10 04					10 19				10 34				10 49				11 04			
London Bridge	d	10 01		10 05		10 16			10 21	10 28	10 31		10 35				10 51	10 58	11 01		11 05		11 16
London Blackfriars	d	10 07	10 09	10 12		10 22		10 24	10 27	10 34	10 37	10 39	10 42			10 54	10 57	11 04	11 07	11 09	11 12		11 22
City Thameslink ■	d	10 09	10 11	10 14		10 24		10 26	10 29	10 36	10 39	10 41	10 44			10 56	10 59	11 06	11 09	11 11	11 14		11 24
Farringdon ■ ⊖	d	10 11	10 14	10 16		10 26		10 29	10 31	10 39	10 41	10 44	10 46			10 59	11 01	11 09	11 11	11 14	11 16		11 26
St Pancras International	d	10a15	10 18	10 21		10a30	10 47	10 33	10 36	10 43	10a45	10 48	10 51	11 05		11 03	11 06	11 13	11a15	11 18	11 21		11a30
Kentish Town ⊖	d		10 23					10 38				10 53				11 08				11 23			
WestHampsteadThameslink ⊖	d		10 29	10 29				10 44		10 52		10 59	10 59			11 14		11 22		11 29	11 29		
Cricklewood	d		10 32					10 47				11 02				11 17				11 32			
Hendon	d		10 36					10 51				11 06				11 21				11 36			
Mill Hill Broadway	d		10 39					10 54		11 01		11 09				11 24		11 31		11 39			
Elstree & Borehamwood	d		10 43		←			10 58		11 05		11 13			←	11 28		11 35		11 43		←	
Radlett	d		10 47		10 39			11 02		11 09		11 17			11 09	11 32		11 39		11 47		11 39	
St Albans City	d		10a53	10 41	10 45			11a08	10 55	→		11a23	11 11		11 15	11a38	11 25	→		11a53	11 41	11 45	
Harpenden	d			10 47	10 51				11 01				11 17		11 21		11 31				11 47	11 51	
Luton Airport Parkway ■ ✈	d			10 53	10 57				11 06				11 23	11 26	11 27		11 36				11 53	11 57	
Luton ■	d			10 57	11a01		11 09		11 11				11 27		11a31		11 41				11 57	12a01	
Leagrave	d			11 01					11 15				11 31				11 45				12 01		
Harlington	d			11 05					11 19				11 35				11 49				12 05		
Flitwick	d			11 09					11 23				11 39				11 53				12 09		
Bedford ■	a			11 21			11 23		11 35				11 51	11 40			12 05				12 21		

		TL B	TL ■	EM ◇■ G	TL C	TL ■ D	TL B	TL ■ E	EM ◇■ H	TL A	TL B	TL ■	TL C	TL ■ D	TL B	TL ■ E	TL A	TL ■ F	EM ◇■ G	TL B	TL ■	TL C	TL ■ D
Gatwick Airport	d		10 33			10 49		11 06				11 03		11 19		11 36		11 46			11 33		11 49
Elephant & Castle ⊖173,179	d	11 19					11 34				11 49				12 04					12 19			
London Bridge	d		11 21		11 28	11 31		11 35				11 51	11 58	12 01		12 05		12 16			12 21	12 28	12 31
London Blackfriars	d	11 24	11 27		11 34	11 37	11 39	11 42			11 54	11 57	12 04	12 07	12 09	12 12		12 22		12 24	12 27	12 34	12 37
City Thameslink ■	d	11 26	11 29		11 36	11 39	11 41	11 44			11 56	11 59	12 06	12 09	12 11	12 14		12 24		12 26	12 29	12 36	12 39
Farringdon ■ ⊖	d	11 29	11 31		11 39	11 41	11 44	11 46			11 59	12 01	12 09	12 11	12 14	12 16		12 26		12 29	12 31	12 39	12 41
St Pancras International	d	11 33	11 36	11 50	11 43	11a45	11 48	11 51	12 05		12 03	12 06	12 13	12a15	12 18	12 21		12a30	12 47	12 33	12 36	12 43	12a45
Kentish Town ⊖	d	11 38					11 53				12 08				12 23					12 38			
WestHampsteadThameslink ⊖	d	11 44			11 52		11 59	11 59			12 14		12 22		12 29	12 29				12 44		12 52	
Cricklewood	d	11 47					12 02				12 17				12 32					12 47			
Hendon	d	11 51					12 06				12 21				12 36					12 51			
Mill Hill Broadway	d	11 54			12 01		12 09				12 24		12 31		12 39					12 54		13 01	
Elstree & Borehamwood	d	11 58			12 05		12 13			←	12 28		12 35		12 43		←			12 58		13 05	
Radlett	d	12 02			12 09		12 17			12 09	12 32		12 39		12 47		12 39			13 02		13 09	
St Albans City	d	12a08	11 55		→		12a23	12 11		12 15	12a38	12 25	→		12a53	12 41	12 45			13a08	12 55	→	
Harpenden	d		12 01					12 17		12 21		12 31				12 47	12 51				13 01		
Luton Airport Parkway ■ ✈	d		12 06					12 23	12 26	12 27		12 36				12 53	12 57				13 06		
Luton ■	d		12 11	12 12				12 27		12a31		12 41				12 57	13a01		13 09		13 11		
Leagrave	d		12 15					12 31				12 45				13 01					13 15		
Harlington	d		12 19					12 35				12 49				13 05					13 19		
Flitwick	d		12 23					12 39				12 53				13 09					13 24		
Bedford ■	a		12 35	12 26				12 51	12 40			13 05				13 21			13 23		13 36		

A From Rainham Kt
B From Sutton (Surrey)
C From Rainham Kt to Luton
D From Horsham to Peterborough
E From Brighton
F From Brighton to Cambridge
G To Corby
H To Nottingham

Table T052MML-F

Saturdays
26 May to 8 December

Gatwick Airport and London - St Albans, Luton and Bedford

		TL A	TL ■ B	EM ◇■ C	TL D	TL A	TL ■	TL E	TL ■ F	TL A	TL ■ B	TL D	TL ■ G	EM ◇■ H	TL A	TL ■	TL E	TL ■ F	TL A	TL ■ B	EM ◇■ C	TL D	TL A
Gatwick Airport	d		12 06				12 03		12 19		12 36		12 46			12 33		12 49		13 06			
Elephant & Castle ⊖173,179	d	12 34				12 49				13 04					13 19				13 34				13 49
London Bridge	d		12 35				12 51	12 58	13 01		13 05		13 16			13 21	13 28	13 31		13 35			
London Blackfriars	d	12 39	12 42			12 54	12 57	13 04	13 07	13 09	13 12		13 22		13 24	13 27	13 34	13 37	13 39	13 42			13 54
City Thameslink ■	d	12 41	12 44			12 56	12 59	13 06	13 09	13 11	13 14		13 24		13 26	13 29	13 36	13 39	13 41	13 44			13 56
Farringdon ■ ⊖	d	12 44	12 46			12 59	13 01	13 09	13 11	13 14	13 16		13 26		13 29	13 31	13 39	13 41	13 44	13 46			13 59
St Pancras International	d	12 48	12 51	13 05		13 03	13 06	13 13	13a15	13 18	13 21		13a30	13 47	13 33	13 36	13 43	13a45	13 48	13 51	14 05		14 03
Kentish Town ⊖	d	12 53				13 08				13 23					13 38				13 53				14 08
WestHampsteadThameslink ⊖	d	12 59	12 59			13 14		13 22		13 29	13 29				13 44		13 52		13 59	13 59			14 14
Cricklewood	d	13 02				13 17				13 32					13 47				14 02				14 17
Hendon	d	13 06				13 21				13 36					13 51				14 06				14 21
Mill Hill Broadway	d	13 09				13 24		13 31		13 39					13 54		14 01		14 09				14 24
Elstree & Borehamwood	d	13 13			←	13 28		13 35		13 43		←			13 58		14 05		14 13			←	14 28
Radlett	d	13 17			13 09	13 32		13 39		13 47		13 39			14 02		14 09		14 17			14 09	14 32
St Albans City	d	13a23	13 11		13 15	13a38	13 24	→		13a53	13 41	13 45			14a08	13 55	→		14a23	14 11		14 15	14a38
Harpenden	d		13 17		13 21		13 30				13 47	13 51				14 01				14 17		14 21	
Luton Airport Parkway ■ ✈	d		13 23	13 26	13 27		13 36				13 53	13 57				14 06				14 23	14 26	14 27	
Luton ■	d		13 27		13a31		13 40				13 57	14a01		14 09		14 11				14 27		14a31	
Leagrave	d		13 31				13 44				14 01					14 15				14 31			
Harlington	d		13 35				13 49				14 05					14 19				14 35			
Flitwick	d		13 39				13 53				14 09					14 23				14 39			
Bedford ■	a		13 51	13 40			14 05				14 21			14 23		14 36				14 51	14 40		

		TL ■	TL E	TL ■ F	TL A	TL ■ B	TL D	TL ■ G	EM ◇■ H	TL A	TL ■	TL E	TL ■ F	TL A	TL ■ B	EM ◇■ C	TL D	TL A	TL ■	TL E	TL ■ F	TL A
Gatwick Airport	d	13 03		13 19		13 36		13 46			13 33		13 49		14 06				14 03		14 19	
Elephant & Castle ⊖173,179	d				14 04					14 19				14 34				14 49				15 04
London Bridge	d	13 51	13 58	14 01		14 05		14 16			14 21	14 28	14 31		14 35				14 51	14 58	15 01	
London Blackfriars	d	13 57	14 04	14 07	14 09	14 12		14 22		14 24	14 27	14 34	14 37	14 39	14 42			14 54	14 57	15 04	15 07	15 09
City Thameslink ■	d	13 59	14 06	14 09	14 11	14 14		14 24		14 26	14 29	14 36	14 39	14 41	14 44			14 56	14 59	15 06	15 09	15 11
Farringdon ■ ⊖	d	14 01	14 09	14 11	14 14	14 16		14 26		14 29	14 31	14 39	14 41	14 44	14 46			14 59	15 01	15 09	15 11	15 14
St Pancras International	d	14 06	14 13	14a15	14 18	14 21		14a30	14 47	14 33	14 36	14 43	14a45	14 48	14 51	15 05		15 03	15 06	15 13	15a15	15 18
Kentish Town ⊖	d				14 23					14 38				14 53				15 08				15 23
WestHampsteadThameslink ⊖	d		14 22		14 29	14 29				14 44		14 52		14 59	14 59			15 14		15 22		15 29
Cricklewood	d				14 32					14 47				15 02				15 17				15 32
Hendon	d				14 36					14 51				15 06				15 21				15 36
Mill Hill Broadway	d		14 31		14 39					14 54		15 01		15 09				15 24		15 31		15 39
Elstree & Borehamwood	d		14 35		14 43		←			14 58		15 05		15 13			←	15 28		15 35		15 43
Radlett	d		14 39		14 47		14 39			15 02		15 09		15 17			15 09	15 32		15 39		15 47
St Albans City	d	14 25	→		14a53	14 41	14 45			15a08	14 55	→		15a23	15 11		15 15	15a38	15 25	→		15a53
Harpenden	d	14 31				14 47	14 51				15 01				15 17		15 21		15 31			
Luton Airport Parkway ■ ✈	d	14 36				14 53	14 57				15 06				15 23	15 26	15 27		15 36			
Luton ■	d	14 41				14 57	15a01		15 09		15 11				15 27		15a31		15 41			
Leagrave	d	14 45				15 01					15 15				15 31				15 45			
Harlington	d	14 49				15 05					15 19				15 35				15 49			
Flitwick	d	14 54				15 09					15 23				15 39				15 54			
Bedford ■	a	15 06				15 21			15 23		15 36				15 51	15 40			16 06			

		TL ■ B	TL D	TL ■ G	EM ◇■ H	TL A	TL ■	TL E	TL ■ F	TL A	TL ■ B	EM ◇■ C	TL D	TL A	TL ■	TL E	TL ■ F	TL A	TL ■ B	TL D	TL ■ G	EM ◇■ H	TL A
Gatwick Airport	d	14 36		14 46			14 33		14 49		15 06				15 03		15 19		15 36		15 46		
Elephant & Castle ⊖173,179	d					15 19				15 34				15 49				16 04					16 19
London Bridge	d	15 05		15 16			15 21	15 28	15 31		15 35				15 51	15 58	16 01		16 05		16 16		
London Blackfriars	d	15 12		15 22		15 24	15 27	15 34	15 37	15 39	15 42			15 54	15 57	16 04	16 07	16 09	16 12		16 22		16 24
City Thameslink ■	d	15 14		15 24		15 26	15 29	15 36	15 39	15 41	15 44			15 56	15 59	16 06	16 09	16 11	16 14		16 24		16 26
Farringdon ■ ⊖	d	15 16		15 26		15 29	15 31	15 39	15 41	15 44	15 46			15 59	16 01	16 09	16 11	16 14	16 16		16 26		16 29
St Pancras International	d	15 21		15a30	15 47	15 33	15 36	15 43	15a45	15 48	15 51	16 05		16 03	16 06	16 13	16a15	16 18	16 21		16a30	16 47	16 33
Kentish Town ⊖	d					15 38				15 53				16 08				16 23					16 38
WestHampsteadThameslink ⊖	d	15 29				15 44		15 52		15 59	15 59			16 14		16 22		16 29	16 29				16 44
Cricklewood	d					15 47				16 02				16 17				16 32					16 47
Hendon	d					15 51				16 06				16 21				16 36					16 51
Mill Hill Broadway	d					15 54		16 01		16 09				16 24		16 31		16 39					16 54
Elstree & Borehamwood	d		←			15 58		16 05		16 13			←	16 28		16 35		16 43		←			16 58
Radlett	d		15 39			16 02		16 09		16 17			16 09	16 32		16 39		16 47		16 39			17 02
St Albans City	d	15 41	15 45			16a08	15 55	→		16a23	16 11		16 15	16a38	16 25	→		16a53	16 41	16 45			17a08
Harpenden	d	15 47	15 51				16 01				16 17		16 21		16 31				16 47	16 51			
Luton Airport Parkway ■ ✈	d	15 53	15 57				16 06				16 23	16 26	16 27		16 36				16 53	16 57			
Luton ■	d	15 57	16a01		16 09		16 11				16 27		16a31		16 41				16 57	17a01		17 09	
Leagrave	d	16 01					16 15				16 31				16 45				17 01				
Harlington	d	16 05					16 19				16 35				16 49				17 05				
Flitwick	d	16 09					16 24				16 39				16 54				17 09				
Bedford ■	a	16 21			16 23		16 36				16 51	16 40			17 06				17 21			17 23	

A From Sutton (Surrey)
B From Brighton
C To Nottingham
D From Rainham Kt
E From Rainham Kt to Luton
F From Horsham to Peterborough
G From Brighton to Cambridge
H To Corby

Table T052MML-F

Saturdays

26 May to 8 December

Gatwick Airport and London - St Albans, Luton and Bedford

		TL ■	TL A	TL ■ B	TL C	TL ■ D	EM ◇■ E	TL F	TL C	TL ■	TL A	TL ■ B	TL C	TL ■ D	TL F	TL ■ G	EM ◇■ H	TL C	TL ■	TL A	TL ■ B	TL C	TL ■ D
Gatwick Airport	d	15 33		15 49		16 06				16 03		16 19		16 36		16 46			16 33		16 49		17 06
Elephant & Castle ⊖173,179	d				16 34				16 49				17 04					17 19				17 34	
London Bridge	d	16 21	16 28	16 31		16 35				16 51	16 58	17 01		17 05		17 16			17 21	17 28	17 31		17 35
London Blackfriars	d	16 27	16 34	16 37	16 39	16 42			16 54	16 57	17 04	17 07	17 09	17 12		17 22		17 24	17 27	17 34	17 37	17 39	17 42
City Thameslink ■	d	16 29	16 36	16 39	16 41	16 44			16 56	16 59	17 06	17 09	17 11	17 14		17 24		17 26	17 29	17 36	17 39	17 41	17 44
Farringdon ■ ⊖	d	16 31	16 39	16 41	16 44	16 46			16 59	17 01	17 09	17 11	17 14	17 16		17 26		17 29	17 31	17 39	17 41	17 44	17 46
St Pancras International	d	16 36	16 43	16a45	16 48	16 51	17 05		17 03	17 06	17 13	17a15	17 18	17 21		17a30	17 47	17 33	17 36	17 43	17a45	17 48	17 51
Kentish Town ⊖	d				16 53				17 08				17 23					17 38				17 53	
WestHampsteadThameslink ⊖	d		16 52		16 59	16 59			17 14		17 22		17 29	17 29				17 44		17 52		17 59	17 59
Cricklewood	d				17 02				17 17				17 32					17 47				18 02	
Hendon	d				17 06				17 21				17 36					17 51				18 06	
Mill Hill Broadway	d		17 01		17 09				17 24		17 31		17 39					17 54		18 01		18 09	
Elstree & Borehamwood	d		17 05		17 13			←	17 28		17 35		17 43		←			17 58		18 05		18 13	
Radlett	d		17 09		17 17			17 09	17 32		17 39		17 47		17 39			18 02		18 09		18 17	
St Albans City	d	16 55	→		17a23	17 11		17 15	17a38	17 25	→		17a53	17 41	17 45			18a08	17 55	→		18a23	18 11
Harpenden	d	17 01				17 17		17 21		17 31				17 47	17 51				18 01				18 17
Luton Airport Parkway ■ ✈	d	17 06				17 23	17 26	17 27		17 36				17 53	17 57				18 06				18 23
Luton ■	d	17 11				17 27		17a31		17 41				17 57	18a01		18 09		18 11				18 27
Leagrave	d	17 15				17 31				17 45				18 01					18 15				18 31
Harlington	d	17 19				17 35				17 49				18 05					18 19				18 35
Flitwick	d	17 23				17 39				17 54				18 09					18 23				18 39
Bedford ■	a	17 35				17 51	17 40			18 06				18 21			18 23		18 35				18 51

		EM ◇■ I	TL F	TL C	TL ■	TL A	TL ■ B	TL C	TL ■ D	TL F	TL ■ G	EM ◇■ H	TL C	TL ■	TL A	TL ■ B	TL C	TL ■ D	EM ◇■ I	TL F	TL C	TL ■	TL A
Gatwick Airport	d				17 03		17 19		17 36		17 46			17 33		17 49		18 06				18 03	
Elephant & Castle ⊖173,179	d			17 49				18 04					18 19				18 34				18 49		
London Bridge	d				17 51	17 58	18 01		18 05		18 16			18 21	18 28	18 31		18 35				18 51	18 58
London Blackfriars	d			17 54	17 57	18 04	18 07	18 09	18 12		18 22		18 24	18 27	18 34	18 37	18 39	18 42			18 54	18 57	19 04
City Thameslink ■	d			17 56	17 59	18 06	18 09	18 11	18 14		18 24		18 26	18 29	18 36	18 39	18 41	18 44			18 56	18 59	19 06
Farringdon ■ ⊖	d			17 59	18 01	18 09	18 11	18 14	18 16		18 26		18 29	18 31	18 39	18 41	18 44	18 46			18 59	19 01	19 09
St Pancras International	d	18 05		18 03	18 06	18 13	18a15	18 18	18 21		18a30	18 47	18 33	18 36	18 43	18a45	18 48	18 51	19 05		19 03	19 06	19 13
Kentish Town ⊖	d			18 08				18 23					18 38				18 53				19 08		
WestHampsteadThameslink ⊖	d			18 14		18 22		18 29	18 29				18 44		18 52		18 59	18 59			19 14		19 22
Cricklewood	d			18 17				18 32					18 47				19 02				19 17		
Hendon	d			18 21				18 36					18 51				19 06				19 21		
Mill Hill Broadway	d			18 24		18 31		18 39					18 54		19 01		19 09				19 24		19 31
Elstree & Borehamwood	d		←	18 28		18 35		18 43		←			18 58		19 05		19 13			←	19 28		19 35
Radlett	d		18 09	18 32		18 39		18 47		18 39			19 02		19 09		19 17			19 09	19 32		19 39
St Albans City	d		18 15	18a38	18 25	→		18a53	18 41	18 45			19a08	18 55	→		19a23	19 11		19 15	19a38	19 25	→
Harpenden	d		18 21		18 31				18 47	18 51				19 01				19 17		19 21		19 31	
Luton Airport Parkway ■ ✈	d	18 26	18 27		18 36				18 53	18 57				19 06				19 23	19 26	19 27		19 36	
Luton ■	d		18a31		18 41				18 57	19a01		19 09		19 11				19 27		19a31		19 41	
Leagrave	d				18 45				19 01					19 15				19 31				19 45	
Harlington	d				18 49				19 05					19 19				19 35				19 49	
Flitwick	d				18 53				19 09					19 23				19 39				19 53	
Bedford ■	a	18 40			19 05				19 21			19 23		19 35				19 51	19 40			20 05	

		TL ■ B	TL C	TL ■ D	TL F	TL ■ G	EM ◇■ H	TL C	TL ■	TL A	TL ■ B	TL C	TL ■ D	EM ◇■ I	TL F	TL C	TL ■	TL A	TL ■ B	TL C	TL ■ D	TL F	TL ■ G
Gatwick Airport	d	18 19		18 36		18 46			18 33		18 49		19 06				19 03		19 19		19 36		19 46
Elephant & Castle ⊖173,179	d		19 04					19 19				19 34				19 49				20 04			
London Bridge	d	19 01		19 05		19 16			19 21	19 28	19 31		19 35				19 51	19 58	20 01		20 05		20 16
London Blackfriars	d	19 07	19 09	19 12		19 22		19 24	19 27	19 34	19 37	19 39	19 42			19 54	19 57	20 04	20 07	20 09	20 12		20 22
City Thameslink ■	d	19 09	19 11	19 14		19 24		19 26	19 29	19 36	19 39	19 41	19 44			19 56	19 59	20 06	20 09	20 11	20 14		20 24
Farringdon ■ ⊖	d	19 11	19 14	19 16		19 26		19 29	19 31	19 39	19 41	19 44	19 46			19 59	20 01	20 09	20 11	20 14	20 16		20 26
St Pancras International	d	19a15	19 18	19 21		19a30	19 47	19 33	19 36	19 43	19a45	19 48	19 51	20 05		20 03	20 06	20 13	20a15	20 18	20 21		20a30
Kentish Town ⊖	d		19 23					19 38				19 53				20 08				20 23			
WestHampsteadThameslink ⊖	d		19 29	19 29				19 44		19 52		19 59	19 59			20 14		20 22		20 29	20 29		
Cricklewood	d		19 32					19 47				20 02				20 17				20 32			
Hendon	d		19 36					19 51				20 06				20 21				20 36			
Mill Hill Broadway	d		19 39					19 54		20 01		20 09				20 24		20 31		20 39			
Elstree & Borehamwood	d		19 43		←			19 58		20 05		20 13			←	20 28		20 35		20 43		←	
Radlett	d		19 47		19 39			20 02		20 09		20 17			20 09	20 32		20 39		20 47		20 39	
St Albans City	d		19a53	19 41	19 45			20a08	19 55	→		20a23	20 11		20 15	20a38	20 25	→		20a53	20 41	20 45	
Harpenden	d			19 47	19 51				20 01				20 17		20 21		20 31				20 47	20 51	
Luton Airport Parkway ■ ✈	d			19 53	19 57				20 06				20 23	20 26	20 27		20 36				20 53	20 57	
Luton ■	d			19 57	20a01		20 10		20 11				20 27		20a31		20 41				20 57	21a01	
Leagrave	d			20 01					20 15				20 31				20 45				21 01		
Harlington	d			20 05					20 19				20 35				20 49				21 05		
Flitwick	d			20 09					20 23				20 39				20 53				21 09		
Bedford ■	a			20 21			20 23		20 35				20 51	20 39			21 05				21 21		

A From Rainham Kt to Luton
B From Horsham to Peterborough
C From Sutton (Surrey)
D From Brighton
E To Lincoln
F From Rainham Kt
G From Brighton to Cambridge
H To Corby
I To Nottingham

Table T052MML-F

Saturdays

26 May to 8 December

Gatwick Airport and London - St Albans, Luton and Bedford

		TL A	TL ■	TL B	TL ■ C	TL A	TL ■ D	TL E	TL A	TL ■	EM ◇■ F	TL B	TL ■ C	TL A	TL ■ D	TL E	TL ■ G	TL A	TL ■	EM ◇■ F	EM ◇■ H	TL B	TL ■ C
Gatwick Airport	d		19 33		19 49		20 06			20 03			20 19		20 36		20 46		20 33				20 49
Elephant & Castle ⊖173,179	d	20 19				20 34			20 49					21 04				21 19					
London Bridge	d		20 21	20 28	20 31		20 35			20 51		20 58	21 01		21 05		21 16		21 21			21 28	21 31
London Blackfriars	d	20 24	20 27	20 34	20 37	20 39	20 42		20 54	20 57		21 04	21 07	21 09	21 12		21 22	21 24	21 27			21 34	21 37
City Thameslink ■	d	20 26	20 29	20 36	20 39	20 41	20 44		20 56	20 59													
Farringdon ■ ⊖	d	20 29	20 31	20 39	20 41	20 44	20 46		20 59	21 01		21 09	21 11	21 14	21 16		21 26	21 29	21 31			21 39	21 41
St Pancras International	d	20 33	20 36	20 43	20a45	20 48	20 51		21 03	21 06	21 30	21 13	21a15	21 18	21 21		21a30	21 33	21 36	21 50	22 00	21 43	21a45
Kentish Town ⊖	d	20 38				20 53			21 08					21 23				21 38					
WestHampsteadThameslink ⊖	d	20 44		20 52		20 59	20 59		21 14			21 22		21 29	21 29			21 44				21 52	
Cricklewood	d	20 47				21 02			21 17					21 32				21 47					
Hendon	d	20 51				21 06			21 21					21 36				21 51					
Mill Hill Broadway	d	20 54		21 01		21 09			21 24			21 31		21 39				21 54				22 01	
Elstree & Borehamwood	d	20 58		21 05		21 13		←	21 28			21 35		21 43		←		21 58				22 05	
Radlett	d	21 02		21 09		21 17		21 09	21 32			21 39		21 47		21 39		22 02				22 09	
St Albans City	d	21a08	20 55	→		21a23	21 11	21 15	21a38	21 25		→		21a53	21 41	21 45		22a08	21 55			→	
Harpenden	d		21 01				21 17	21 21		21 31					21 47	21 51			22 01				
Luton Airport Parkway ■ ✈	d		21 06				21 23	21 27		21 36					21 53	21 57			22 06	22 12			
Luton ■	d		21 11				21 27	21a31		21 41	21 54				21 57	22a01			22 11		22 25		
Leagrave	d		21 15				21 31			21 45					22 01				22 15				
Harlington	d		21 19				21 35			21 49					22 06				22 19				
Flitwick	d		21 23				21 39			21 53					22 10				22 23				
Bedford ■	a		21 35				21 51			22 05	22 10				22 21				22 35	22 27	22 41		

		TL A	TL ■ D	TL E	TL A	TL ■	EM ◇■ I	TL B	TL ■ C	TL A	TL ■ D	TL E	TL ■ G	TL J	TL ■	TL A	TL E	TL ■ C	TL J	TL ■ D	TL A	TL A	TL E
Gatwick Airport	d		21 06			21 03			21 19		21 36		21 46		21 33			21 49		22 06			
Elephant & Castle ⊖173,179	d	21 34			21 49					22 04				22 19					22 34			22 51	
London Bridge	d		21 35			21 51		21 58	22 01		22 05		22 16		22 21		22 28	22 31		22 35			22 58
London Blackfriars	d	21 39	21 42		21 54	21 57		22 04	22 07	22 09	22 12		22 22	22 24	22 27		22 34	22 37	22 39	22 42		22 59	23 04
City Thameslink ■	d																						
Farringdon ■ ⊖	d	21 44	21 46		21 59	22 01		22 09	22 11	22 14	22 16		22 26	22 29	22 31		22 39	22 41	22 44	22 46		23 04	23 09
St Pancras International	d	21 48	21 51		22 03	22 06	22 20	22 13	22a15	22 18	22 21		22a30	22 33	22 36		22 43	22a45	22 48	22 51	←	23 08	23 13
Kentish Town ⊖	d	21 53			22 08					22 23				22 38					22 58		22 58	23 13	
WestHampsteadThameslink ⊖	d	21 59	21 59		22 14			22 22		22 29	22 29			22 44			22a51		→	22 59	23 02	23 17	23a21
Cricklewood	d	22 02			22 17					22 32				22 47							23 05	23 20	
Hendon	d	22 06			22 21					22 36				22 51							23 09	23 24	
Mill Hill Broadway	d	22 09			22 24			22 31		22 39				22 54							23 12	23 27	
Elstree & Borehamwood	d	22 13		←	22 28			22 35		22 43		←		22 58		←					23 16	23 31	
Radlett	d	22 17		22 09	22 32			22 39		22 47		22 39		23 02		23 02					23 20	23 35	
St Albans City	d	22a23	22 11	22 15	22a38	22 25		→		22a53	22 41	22 45		→	22 55	23 09				23 16	23 27	23 42	
Harpenden	d		22 17	22 21		22 31					22 48	22 51			23 01	23 15				23 22	23 33	23 48	
Luton Airport Parkway ■ ✈	d		22 23	22 27		22 36	22 42				22 53	22 57			23 06	23 20				23 27	23 39	23 54	
Luton ■	d		22 27	22a31		22 41					22 58	23a02			23 11	23 25				23 31	23 43	23 58	
Leagrave	d		22 31			22 45					23 02				23 15					23 35			
Harlington	d		22 36			22 49					23 06				23 19					23 40			
Flitwick	d		22 40			22 53					23 10				23 23					23 44			
Bedford ■	a		22 51			23 05	22 57				23 22				23 35	23 45				23 55	00 03	00 18	

		TL ■ C	TL ■ D	TL A	TL ■ G	TL A	TL E	TL ■ C	TL ■ D	TL A	TL A	TL ■ D
Gatwick Airport	d	22 19	22 36		22 46			22 49	23 06			23 34
Elephant & Castle ⊖173,179	d			23 11		23 21				23 41	23 54	
London Bridge	d	23 01	23 05		23 16		23 28	23 31	23 35			
London Blackfriars	d	23 07	23 12	23 17	23 22	23 27	23 34	23 37	23 42	23 49	00 02	00 22
City Thameslink ■	d											
Farringdon ■ ⊖	d	23 11	23 16	23 21	23 26	23 31	23 39	23 41	23 46	23 53	00 06	00 26
St Pancras International	d	23a15	23 21	23 26	23a30	23 36	23 43	23a45	23 51	23 58	00 11	00 31
Kentish Town ⊖	d			23 30		23 40				00 01		
WestHampsteadThameslink ⊖	d		23 29	23 34		23 44	23a51		23 59	00 06	00 19	00 39
Cricklewood	d			23 38		23 48				00 10		
Hendon	d			23 42		23 52				00 14		
Mill Hill Broadway	d			23 45		23 55				00 17		
Elstree & Borehamwood	d			23 49		23 59				00 21		
Radlett	d			23 53		00 03				00 25		
St Albans City	d		23 46	23 59		00 10			00 16	00 32	00 36	00 56
Harpenden	d		23 52	00 06		00 16			00 22	00 38	00 42	01 02
Luton Airport Parkway ■ ✈	d		23 58	00 11		00 21			00 28	00 43	00 48	01 08
Luton ■	d		00 02	00 16		00 26			00 32	00 48	00 52	01 12
Leagrave	d		00 06	00 20		00 30			00 36		00 56	01 16
Harlington	d		00 11	00 24		00 34			00 41		01 01	01 21
Flitwick	d		00 15	00 28		00 39			00 45		01 05	01 25
Bedford ■	a		00 26	00 40		00 50			00 56	01 08	01 18	01 37

A From Sutton (Surrey)
B From Rainham Kt to Luton
C From Horsham to Peterborough
D From Brighton
E From Rainham Kt
F To East Midlands Parkway
G From Brighton to Cambridge
H To Nottingham
I To Derby
J From Sutton (Surrey) to Bedford

Table T052MML-F

Sundays

20 May to 2 December

Gatwick Airport and London - St Albans, Luton and Bedford

		TL 1 A	TL B	TL B	TL 1 A	TL B	TL B	TL B	TL 1 A	TL 1 A	TL 1 A	TL 1 C	TL 1 D	TL 1	TL 1		TL 1	TL 1	EM ◇1 E	TL 1	TL 1	EM ◇1 F
Gatwick Airport	d									00 04	00 21	00 42	08 46									
Elephant & Castle ⊖173,179	d							00 04														
London Bridge	d												09 25									
London Blackfriars	d						00 02	00 09	00 22	00 50	01 06	01 36	09 31									
City Thameslink 3	d																					
Farringdon 3 ⊖	d						00 06	00 13	00 26				09 35									
St Pancras International	d						00 11	00 18	00 31	01 01	01 16	01 46	09a39	06 03	07 03	and	08 33	08 48	09 00	09 03	09 18	09 30
Kentish Town ⊖	d					00 01		00 22		01 05		01 50		06 08	07 08	every 30	08 38			09 11		
WestHampsteadThameslink ⊖	d					00 06	00 19	00 26	00 39	01 09	01 24	01 54		06 12	07 12	minutes	08 42	08 56		09 15	09 25	
Cricklewood	d					00 10		00 30		01 13		01 57		06 16	07 16	until	08 46			09 17		
Hendon	d					00 14		00 34		01 17		02 02		06 20	07 20		08 50			09 20		
Mill Hill Broadway	d					00 17		00 37		01 20		02 05		06 23	07 23		08 53			09 23		
Elstree & Borehamwood	d					00 21		00 41		01 24		02 09		06 27	07 27		08 57			09 27		
Radlett	d			00 03		00 25		00 45		01 28		02 13		06 31	07 31		09 01			09 31		
St Albans City	d			00 10	00 16	00 32	00 36	00 51	00 56	01 34	01 41	02 21		06 39	07 39		09 09	09 13		09 38	09 42	
Harpenden	d		00 06	00 16	00 22	00 38	00 42	00 57	01 02	01 40	01 47	02 27		06 45	07 45		09 15	09 19		09 44	09 48	
Luton Airport Parkway 7 ✈	d		00 11	00 21	00 28	00 43	00 48	01 03	01 08	01 46	01 52	02 32		06 50	07 50		09 20	09 24	09 29	09 49	09 53	
Luton 10	d	00 02	00 16	00 26	00 32	00 48	00 52	01 07	01 12	01 50	01 57	02 37		06 55	07 55		09 25	09 29		09a53	09 57	10 03
Leagrave	d	00 06	00 20	00 30	00 36		00 56	01 11	01 16	01 54	02 01	02 41		06 59	07 59		09 29	09 33			10 01	
Harlington	d	00 11	00 24	00 34	00 41		01 01	01 15	01 21	01 59	02 05	02 45		07 03	08 03		09 33	09 37			10 06	
Flitwick	d	00 15	00 28	00 39	00 45		01 05	01 20	01 25	02 03	02 09	02 49		07 07	08 07		09 37	09 41			10 10	
Bedford 7	a	00 26	00 40	00 50	00 56	01 08	01 18	01 32	01 37	02 15	02 21	03 01		07 19	08 19		09 49	09 53	09 55		10 22	10 23

		TL 1	TL 1 G	EM ◇1 E	TL 1 C	TL H	TL 1 I	TL J	TL 1 G	EM ◇1 F	TL 1 C	TL H	TL 1 D	TL J	TL 1 G	EM ◇1 E	TL 1 C	TL H	TL 1 I	TL J	TL 1	EM ◇1 F	TL 1 C
Gatwick Airport	d		08 49		09 19		09 11		09 19		09 49		09 46		09 49		10 19		10 11		10 19		10 49
Elephant & Castle ⊖173,179	d					09 53						10 23						10 53					
London Bridge	d		09 33		09 49		09 55	09 58	10 03		10 19		10 25	10 28	10 33		10 49		10 55	10 58	11 03		11 19
London Blackfriars	d		09 39		09 55	09 58	10 01	10 05	10 09		10 25	10 28	10 31	10 35	10 39		10 55	10 58	11 01	11 05	11 09		11 25
City Thameslink 3	d																						
Farringdon 3 ⊖	d		09 43		09 59	10 02	10 05	10 09	10 13		10 29	10 32	10 35	10 39	10 43		10 59	11 02	11 05	11 09	11 13		11 29
St Pancras International	d	09 33	09 48	10 00	10 04	10 07	10a09	10 14	10 18	10 30	10 34	10 37	10a39	10 44	10 48	11 00	11 04	11 07	11a09	11 14	11 18	11 30	11 34
Kentish Town ⊖	d	09 38				10 11		10a18				10 41		10a48				11 11		11a18			
WestHampsteadThameslink ⊖	d	09 42			10 12	10 15			10 26		10 42	10 45			10 56		11 12	11 15			11 26		11 42
Cricklewood	d	09 46				10 18						10 48						11 18					
Hendon	d	09 49				10 21						10 51						11 21					
Mill Hill Broadway	d	09 52				10 24						10 54						11 24					
Elstree & Borehamwood	d	09 56				10 28						10 58						11 28					
Radlett	d	10 00				10 32						11 02						11 32					
St Albans City	d	10 07	10 11		10 29	10 39			10 43		10 59	11 09			11 13		11 29	11 39			11 43		11 59
Harpenden	d	10 13	10 17		10 35	10 45			10 49		11 05	11 15			11 19		11 35	11 45			11 49		12 05
Luton Airport Parkway 7 ✈	d	10 18	10 22	10 29	10 40	10 50			10 54		11 10	11 20			11 24	11 29	11 40	11 50			11 54	11 59	12 10
Luton 10	d	10a22	10 27		10 45	10a54			10 59	11 03	11 15	11a24			11 29	11 33	11 45	11a54			11 59	12 03	12 15
Leagrave	d		10 31		10 49				11 03		11 19				11 33		11 49				12 03		12 19
Harlington	d		10 35		10 53				11 07		11 23				11 37		11 53				12 07		12 23
Flitwick	d		10 39		10 57				11 11		11 27				11 42		11 57				12 11		12 27
Bedford 7	a		10 52	10 54	11 09				11 24	11 27	11 40				11 54	11 55	12 09				12 24	12 19	12 39

		TL H	TL 1 D	TL J	TL 1 G	EM ◇1 E	TL 1 C	TL H	TL 1 I	TL J	TL 1 K	EM ◇1 L	TL 1 M	TL H	TL 1 C	TL H	TL 1 D	TL J	TL 1 G	EM ◇1 E	TL H	TL 1 C	TL H
Gatwick Airport	d		10 46		10 49		11 19		11 11		11 19				11 49		11 46		11 49			12 19	
Elephant & Castle ⊖173,179	d	11 23						11 53						12 11		12 23					12 41		12 53
London Bridge	d		11 25	11 28	11 33		11 49		11 55	11 58	12 03				12 19		12 25	12 28	12 33			12 49	
London Blackfriars	d	11 28	11 31	11 35	11 39		11 55	11 58	12 01	12 05	12 09			12 16	12 25	12 28	12 31	12 35	12 41		12 46	12 55	12 58
City Thameslink 3	d																						
Farringdon 3 ⊖	d	11 32	11 35	11 39	11 43		11 59	12 02	12 05	12 09	12 13			12 20	12 29	12 32	12 35	12 39	12 45		12 50	12 59	13 02
St Pancras International	d	11 37	11a39	11 44	11 48	12 10	12 04	12 07	12a09	12 14	12 18	12 30		12 25	12 34	12 37	12a39	12 44	12 50	13 10	12 55	13 04	13 07
Kentish Town ⊖	d	11 41		11a48				12 11		12a18						12 41		12a48					13 11
WestHampsteadThameslink ⊖	d	11 45			11 56		12 12	12 16			12 26			12 34	12 42	12 46			12 59		13 04	13 12	13 16
Cricklewood	d	11 49						12 20								12 50							13 20
Hendon	d	11 53						12 24								12 54							13 24
Mill Hill Broadway	d	11 56						12 27						12 40		12 57					13 10		13 27
Elstree & Borehamwood	d	12 00						12 31						12 44		13 01					13 14		13 31
Radlett	d	12 04						12 35						12 48		13 05					13 18		13 35
St Albans City	d	12 11			12 15		12 29	12a42			12 39			12 55	12 59	13a12			13 13		13 25	13 29	13a42
Harpenden	d	12 17			12 21		12 34				12 46			13 00	13 04				13 18		13 30	13 34	
Luton Airport Parkway 7 ✈	d	12 22			12 26	12 32	12 40				12 51	12 52	←	13 06	13 10				13 24	13 32	13 36	13 40	
Luton 10	d	12a26			12 31	12 35	12 44				12 56	12 54	12 56	13a10	13 14				13 28	13 35	13a40	13 44	
Leagrave	d				12 35		12 48				→		13 00		13 18				13 32			13 48	
Harlington	d				12 39		12 52						13 04		13 22				13 36			13 52	
Flitwick	d				12 43		12 56						13 08		13 26				13 40			13 56	
Bedford 7	a				12 55	12 49	13 10					13 08	13 20		13 39				13 52	13 49		14 08	

A not 20 May. From Brighton
B not 20 May. From Sutton (Surrey)
C From Brighton
D To Cambridge
E To Nottingham
F To Sheffield
G From Three Bridges
H From Sutton (Surrey)
I From Horsham to Peterborough
J From Rainham Kt
K To Bedford
L To Corby
M From Gatwick Airport

Table T052MML-F

Sundays

20 May to 2 December

Gatwick Airport and London - St Albans, Luton and Bedford

		TL 1 A	TL B	TL 1 C	EM ◇1 D	TL 1 E	TL F	TL 1 G	TL F	TL 1 H	TL B	TL 1 I	EM ◇1 J	TL F	TL 1 G	TL F	TL 1 A	EM ◇1 D	TL B	TL 1	TL F	TL 1 G	TL F
Gatwick Airport	d	12 11		12 19				12 49		12 46		12 49			13 19		13 11			13 19		13 49	
Elephant & Castle ⊖173,179	d						13 11		13 23					13 41		13 53					14 11		14 23
London Bridge	d	12 55	12 58	13 03				13 19		13 25	13 28	13 33			13 49		13 55		13 58	14 03		14 19	
London Blackfriars	d	13 01	13 05	13 09			13 16	13 25	13 28	13 31	13 35	13 39		13 46	13 55	13 58	14 01		14 05	14 09	14 16	14 25	14 28
City Thameslink 3	d																						
Farringdon 3 ⊖	d	13 05	13 09	13 13			13 20	13 29	13 32	13 35	13 39	13 43		13 50	13 59	14 02	14 05		14 09	14 13	14 20	14 29	14 32
St Pancras International	d	13a09	13 14	13 18	13 30		13 25	13 34	13 37	13a39	13 44	13 48	14 10	13 55	14 04	14 07	14a09	14 30	14 14	14 18	14 25	14 34	14 37
Kentish Town ⊖	d		13a18						13 41		13a48					14 11			14a18				14 41
WestHampsteadThameslink ⊖	d			13 26			13 34	13 42	13 46			13 56		14 04	14 12	14 16				14 26	14 34	14 42	14 46
Cricklewood	d								13 50							14 20							14 50
Hendon	d								13 54							14 24							14 54
Mill Hill Broadway	d						13 40		13 57					14 10		14 27					14 40		14 57
Elstree & Borehamwood	d						13 44		14 01					14 14		14 31					14 44		15 01
Radlett	d						13 48		14 08					14 18		14 38					14 48		15 08
St Albans City	d			13 39			13 55	13 59	14a14			14 10		14 25	14 29	14a44				14 40	14 55	14 59	15a14
Harpenden	d			13 46			14 00	14 04				14 16		14 30	14 34					14 46	15 00	15 04	
Luton Airport Parkway 7 ✈	d			13 51	13 52	←	14 06	14 10				14 21	14 32	14 36	14 40					14 51	15 06	15 10	
Luton 10	d			13 56	13 54	13 56	14a10	14 14				14 26		14a40	14 44			14 53		14 56	15a10	15 14	
Leagrave	d			→		14 00		14 18				14 30			14 48					15 00		15 18	
Harlington	d					14 04		14 22				14 34			14 52					15 04		15 22	
Flitwick	d					14 08		14 26				14 38			14 56					15 09		15 26	
Bedford 7	a				14 08	14 20		14 38				14 50	14 46		15 08			15 06		15 20		15 38	

		TL 1 H	TL B	TL 1 I	EM ◇1 J	TL F	TL 1 G	TL F	TL 1 A	TL B	TL 1	EM ◇1 K	TL F	TL 1 G	TL F	TL 1 H	TL B	TL 1 I	EM ◇1 J	TL F	TL 1 G	TL F
Gatwick Airport	d	13 46		13 49			14 19		14 11		14 19			14 49		14 46		14 49			15 19	
Elephant & Castle ⊖173,179	d					14 41		14 53					15 11		15 23					15 41		15 53
London Bridge	d	14 25	14 28	14 33			14 49		14 55	14 58	15 03			15 19		15 25	15 28	15 33			15 49	
London Blackfriars	d	14 31	14 35	14 39		14 46	14 55	14 58	15 01	15 05	15 09		15 16	15 25	15 28	15 31	15 35	15 39		15 46	15 55	15 58
City Thameslink 3	d																					
Farringdon 3 ⊖	d	14 35	14 39	14 43		14 50	14 59	15 02	15 05	15 09	15 13		15 20	15 29	15 32	15 35	15 39	15 43		15 50	15 59	16 02
St Pancras International	d	14a39	14 44	14 48	15 10	14 55	15 04	15 07	15a09	15 14	15 18	15 40	15 25	15 34	15 37	15a39	15 44	15 48	16 10	15 55	16 04	16 07
Kentish Town ⊖	d		14a48					15 11		15a18					15 41		15a48					16 11
WestHampsteadThameslink ⊖	d			14 56		15 04	15 12	15 16			15 26		15 34	15 42	15 46			15 56		16 04	16 12	16 16
Cricklewood	d							15 20							15 50							16 20
Hendon	d							15 24							15 54							16 24
Mill Hill Broadway	d					15 10		15 27					15 40		15 57					16 10		16 27
Elstree & Borehamwood	d					15 14		15 31					15 44		16 01					16 14		16 31
Radlett	d					15 18		15 35					15 48		16 08					16 18		16 35
St Albans City	d			15 11		15 25	15 29	15a42			15 39		15 55	15 59	16a14			16 11		16 25	16 29	16a42
Harpenden	d			15 16		15 30	15 34				15 46		16 00	16 04				16 16		16 30	16 34	
Luton Airport Parkway 7 ✈	d			15 22	15 33	15 36	15 40				15 51		16 06	16 10				16 22	16 32	16 36	16 40	
Luton 10	d			15 26		15a40	15 44				15 56	16 03	16a10	16 14				16 26		16a40	16 44	
Leagrave	d			15 30			15 48				16 00			16 18				16 30			16 48	
Harlington	d			15 34			15 52				16 04			16 22				16 34			16 52	
Flitwick	d			15 38			15 56				16 08			16 26				16 38			16 56	
Bedford 7	a			15 50	15 48		16 08				16 20	16 17		16 38				16 50	16 46		17 08	

		TL 1 A	TL B	TL 1	EM ◇1 K	TL F	TL 1 G	TL F	TL 1 H	TL B	TL 1 I	EM ◇1 J	TL F	TL 1 G	TL F	TL 1 A	TL B	TL 1	EM ◇1 K	TL F	TL 1 G	TL F	TL 1 H
Gatwick Airport	d	15 11		15 19			15 49		15 46		15 49			16 19		16 11		16 19			16 49		16 46
Elephant & Castle ⊖173,179	d					16 11		16 23					16 41		16 53					17 11		17 23	
London Bridge	d	15 55	15 58	16 03			16 19		16 25	16 28	16 33			16 49		16 55	16 58	17 03			17 19		17 25
London Blackfriars	d	16 01	16 05	16 09		16 16	16 25	16 28	16 31	16 35	16 39		16 46	16 55	16 58	17 01	17 05	17 09		17 16	17 25	17 28	17 31
City Thameslink 3	d																						
Farringdon 3 ⊖	d	16 05	16 09	16 13		16 20	16 29	16 32	16 35	16 39	16 43		16 50	16 59	17 02	17 05	17 09	17 13		17 20	17 29	17 32	17 35
St Pancras International	d	16a09	16 14	16 18	16 40	16 25	16 34	16 37	16a39	16 44	16 48	17 10	16 55	17 04	17 07	17a09	17 14	17 18	17 40	17 25	17 34	17 37	17a39
Kentish Town ⊖	d		16a18					16 41		16a48					17 11		17a18					17 41	
WestHampsteadThameslink ⊖	d			16 26		16 34	16 42	16 46			16 56		17 04	17 12	17 16			17 26		17 34	17 42	17 46	
Cricklewood	d							16 50							17 20							17 50	
Hendon	d							16 54							17 24							17 54	
Mill Hill Broadway	d					16 40		16 57					17 10		17 27					17 40		17 57	
Elstree & Borehamwood	d					16 44		17 01					17 14		17 31					17 44		18 01	
Radlett	d					16 48		17 05					17 18		17 38					17 48		18 05	
St Albans City	d			16 39		16 55	16 59	17a12			17 09		17 25	17 29	17a44			17 40		17 55	17 59	18a12	
Harpenden	d			16 46		17 00	17 04				17 16		17 30	17 34				17 46		18 00	18 04		
Luton Airport Parkway 7 ✈	d			16 51		17 06	17 10				17 21	17 32	17 36	17 40				17 51		18 06	18 10		
Luton 10	d			16 56	17 03	17a10	17 14				17 26		17a40	17 44				17 56	18 03	18a10	18 14		
Leagrave	d			17 00			17 18				17 30			17 48				18 00			18 18		
Harlington	d			17 04			17 22				17 34			17 52				18 04			18 22		
Flitwick	d			17 08			17 26				17 38			17 56				18 08			18 26		
Bedford 7	a			17 20	17 17		17 38				17 50	17 46		18 08				18 20	18 17		18 38		

A From Horsham to Peterborough
B From Rainham Kt
C To Bedford
D To Corby
E From Gatwick Airport
F From Sutton (Surrey)
G From Brighton
H To Cambridge
I From Three Bridges
J To Nottingham
K To East Midlands Parkway

Table T052MML-F

Sundays

20 May to 2 December

Gatwick Airport and London - St Albans, Luton and Bedford

		TL	TL ■	EM ◇■	TL	TL ■	TL	TL ■	TL	TL ■	EM ◇■	TL	TL ■	TL	TL ■	TL	TL ■	EM ◇■	TL	TL ■	TL	TL ■	TL
		A	B	C	D	E	D	F	A		G	D	E	D	H	A	B	C	D	E	D	F	A
Gatwick Airport	d		16 49			17 19		17 11		17 19			17 49		17 46		17 49			18 19		18 11	
Elephant & Castle ⊖173,179	d				17 41		17 53					18 11		18 23					18 41		18 53		
London Bridge	d	17 28	17 33			17 49		17 55	17 58	18 03			18 19		18 25	18 28	18 33			18 49		18 55	18 58
London Blackfriars	d	17 35	17 39		17 46	17 55	17 58	18 01	18 05	18 09		18 16	18 25	18 28	18 31	18 35	18 39		18 46	18 55	18 58	19 01	19 05
City Thameslink ■	d																						
Farringdon ■ ⊖	d	17 39	17 43		17 50	17 59	18 02	18 05	18 09	18 13		18 20	18 29	18 32	18 35	18 39	18 43		18 50	18 59	19 02	19 05	19 09
St Pancras International	d	17 44	17 48	18 10	17 55	18 04	18 07	18a09	18 14	18 18	18 40	18 25	18 34	18 37	18a39	18 44	18 48	19 10	18 55	19 04	19 07	19a09	19 14
Kentish Town ⊖	d	17a48					18 11		18a18					18 41		18a48					19 11		19a18
WestHampsteadThameslink ⊖	d		17 56		18 04	18 12	18 16			18 26		18 34	18 42	18 46			18 56		19 04	19 12	19 16		
Cricklewood	d						18 20							18 50							19 20		
Hendon	d						18 24							18 54							19 24		
Mill Hill Broadway	d				18 10		18 27					18 40		18 57					19 10		19 27		
Elstree & Borehamwood	d				18 14		18 31					18 44		19 01					19 14		19 31		
Radlett	d				18 18		18 35					18 48		19 05					19 18		19 38		
St Albans City	d		18 09		18 25	18 29	18a42			18 39		18 55	18 59	19a12			19 09		19 25	19 29	19a44		
Harpenden	d		18 16		18 30	18 34				18 46		19 00	19 04				19 16		19 30	19 34			
Luton Airport Parkway ■ ✈	d		18 21	18 32	18 36	18 40				18 51		19 06	19 10				19 21	19 32	19 36	19 40			
Luton ■	d		18 26		18a40	18 44				18 56	19 03	19a10	19 14				19 26		19a40	19 44			
Leagrave	d		18 30			18 48				19 00			19 18				19 30			19 48			
Harlington	d		18 34			18 52				19 04			19 22				19 34			19 52			
Flitwick	d		18 38			18 56				19 08			19 26				19 38			19 56			
Bedford ■	a		18 50	18 46		19 08				19 20	19 17		19 38				19 51	19 46		20 09			

		TL ■	EM ◇■	TL	TL ■	TL	TL ■	TL	TL ■	EM ◇■	TL	TL ■	TL	TL ■	TL	TL ■	EM ◇■	TL	TL ■	TL	TL ■	TL	TL ■
			G	D	E	D	H	A	B	C	D	E	D	F	A		I	D	E	D	H	A	B
Gatwick Airport	d	18 19			18 49		18 46		18 49			19 19		19 11		19 19			19 49		19 46		19 49
Elephant & Castle ⊖173,179	d			19 11		19 23					19 41		19 53					20 11		20 23			
London Bridge	d	19 03			19 19		19 25	19 28	19 33			19 49		19 55	19 58	20 03			20 19		20 25	20 28	20 33
London Blackfriars	d	19 09		19 16	19 25	19 28	19 31	19 35	19 39		19 46	19 55	19 58	20 01	20 05	20 09		20 16	20 25	20 28	20 31	20 35	20 39
City Thameslink ■	d																						
Farringdon ■ ⊖	d	19 13		19 20	19 29	19 32	19 35	19 39	19 43		19 50	19 59	20 02	20 05	20 09	20 13		20 20	20 29	20 32	20 35	20 39	20 43
St Pancras International	d	19 18	19 40	19 25	19 34	19 37	19a39	19 44	19 48	20 10	19 55	20 04	20 07	20a09	20 14	20 18	20 40	20 25	20 34	20 37	20a39	20 44	20 48
Kentish Town ⊖	d					19 41		19a48					20 11		20a18					20 41		20a48	
WestHampsteadThameslink ⊖	d	19 26		19 34	19 42	19 46			19 56		20 04	20 12	20 16			20 26		20 34	20 42	20 46			20 56
Cricklewood	d					19 50							20 20							20 50			
Hendon	d					19 54							20 24							20 54			
Mill Hill Broadway	d			19 40		19 57					20 10		20 27					20 40		20 57			
Elstree & Borehamwood	d			19 44		20 01					20 14		20 31					20 44		21 01			
Radlett	d			19 48		20 05					20 18		20 35					20 48		21 05			
St Albans City	d	19 40		19 55	19 59	20a12			20 09		20 25	20 29	20a42			20 39		20 55	20 59	21a12			21 09
Harpenden	d	19 46		20 00	20 04				20 16		20 30	20 34				20 46		21 00	21 04				21 16
Luton Airport Parkway ■ ✈	d	19 51		20 06	20 10				20 21	20 32	20 36	20 40				20 51		21 06	21 10				21 21
Luton ■	d	19 56	20 03	20a10	20 14				20 26		20a40	20 44				20 56	21 04	21a10	21 14				21 26
Leagrave	d	20 00			20 18				20 30			20 48				21 00			21 18				21 30
Harlington	d	20 04			20 22				20 34			20 52				21 04			21 22				21 34
Flitwick	d	20 08			20 26				20 38			20 56				21 08			21 26				21 38
Bedford ■	a	20 20	20 17		20 38				20 50	20 46		21 08				21 20	21 19		21 38				21 50

		EM ◇■	TL	TL ■	TL	TL ■	EM ◇■	TL	TL ■	TL	TL ■	TL	TL ■	TL	TL ■	TL	TL ■	TL	TL ■	TL	TL ■	EM ◇■
		C	D	E	D	F	J	A		D	E	D	H	A	B	D	E	K	F	A		C
Gatwick Airport	d			20 19		20 11			20 19		20 49		20 46		20 49		21 19		21 11		21 19	
Elephant & Castle ⊖173,179	d		20 41		20 53					21 11		21 23				21 41		21 53				
London Bridge	d			20 49		20 55		20 58	21 03		21 19		21 25	21 28	21 33		21 49		21 55	21 58	22 03	
London Blackfriars	d		20 46	20 55	20 58	21 01		21 05	21 09	21 16	21 25	21 28	21 31	21 35	21 39	21 46	21 55	21 58	22 01	22 05	22 09	
City Thameslink ■	d																					
Farringdon ■ ⊖	d		20 50	20 59	21 02	21 05		21 09	21 13	21 20	21 29	21 32	21 35	21 39	21 43	21 50	21 59	22 02	22 05	22 09	22 13	
St Pancras International	d	21 10	20 55	21 04	21 07	21a09	21 30	21 14	21 18	21 25	21 34	21 37	21a39	21 44	21 48	21 55	22 04	22 07	22a09	22 14	22 18	22 30
Kentish Town ⊖	d				21 11			21a18				21 41		21a48				22 11		22a18		
WestHampsteadThameslink ⊖	d		21 04	21 12	21 16				21 26	21 34	21 42	21 46			21 56	22 04	22 12	22 15			22 26	
Cricklewood	d				21 20							21 50						22 19				
Hendon	d				21 24							21 54						22 23				
Mill Hill Broadway	d		21 10		21 27					21 40		21 57				22 10		22 26				
Elstree & Borehamwood	d		21 14		21 31					21 44		22 01				22 14		22 30				
Radlett	d		21 18		21 35					21 48		22 05				22 18		22 34				
St Albans City	d		21 25	21 29	21a42				21 39	21 55	21 59	22a12			22 09	22 25	22 29	→			22 39	
Harpenden	d		21 30	21 34					21 46	22 00	22 04				22 16	22 30	22 34				22 46	
Luton Airport Parkway ■ ✈	d	21 32	21 36	21 40					21 52	22 06	22 10				22 21	22 36	22 40				22 51	22 52
Luton ■	d		21a40	21 44			21 54		21 56	22a10	22 14				22 26	22a40	22 44				22 56	
Leagrave	d			21 48					22 00		22 18				22 30		22 48				23 00	
Harlington	d			21 52					22 04		22 22				22 34		22 52				23 04	
Flitwick	d			21 56					22 08		22 26				22 38		22 56				23 08	
Bedford ■	a	21 46		22 08			22 07		22 20		22 38				22 50		23 08				23 20	23 11

A From Rainham Kt
B From Three Bridges
C To Nottingham
D From Sutton (Surrey)
E From Brighton
F From Horsham to Peterborough
G To East Midlands Parkway
H To Cambridge
I To Leeds
J To Sheffield
K From Sutton (Surrey) to Bedford

Table T052MML-F

Sundays

20 May to 2 December

Gatwick Airport and London - St Albans, Luton and Bedford

		TL	TL ■	TL ■	EM ◇■	TL	TL ■	TL	TL	TL ■	TL	TL ■	TL	TL ■	TL ■
		A	B	C	D	E	B	A	E	F	A	B	E	B	B
Gatwick Airport	d		21 49	21 46			22 19			22 11		22 49		23 21	23 51
Elephant & Castle ⊖173,179	d							22 53			23 11				
London Bridge	d		22 19	22 25		22 28	22 49		22 58	23 05		23 19	23 28		
London Blackfriars	d		22 25	22 31		22 35	22 55	22 58	23 05	23 12	23 16	23 27	23 37	00 06	00 36
City Thameslink ■	d														
Farringdon ■ ⊖	d		22 29	22 35		22 39	22 59	23 02	23 09	23 16	23 20	23 31	23 41	00 11	
St Pancras International	d		22 34	22a39	23 00	22 44	23 04	23 07	23 14	23a20	23 25	23 36	23 46	00 16	00 46
Kentish Town ⊖	d					22a48		23 11	23 18		23 29		23 50	00 20	00 50
WestHampsteadThameslink ⊖	d		22 42				23 12	23 15	23a22		23 33	23 44	23 54	00 24	00 54
Cricklewood	d							23 19			23 37		23 58	00 28	00 58
Hendon	d							23 23			23 41		00 02	00 32	01 02
Mill Hill Broadway	d							23 26			23 44		00 05	00 35	01 05
Elstree & Borehamwood	d	←						23 30			23 48		00 09	00 39	01 09
Radlett	d	22 34						23 34			23 52		00 13	00 43	01 13
St Albans City	d	22 41	22 59				23 29	23 41			23 59	00 03	00 21	00 51	01 21
Harpenden	d	22 50	23 04				23 35	23 47			00 05	00 09	00 27	00 57	01 27
Luton Airport Parkway ■ ✈	d	22 55	23 10		23 28		23 40	23 52			00 10	00 14	00 32	01 02	01 32
Luton ■	d	23 00	23 14				23 45	23 57			00 15	00 19	00 37	01 07	01 37
Leagrave	d	23 04	23 18				23 49	00 01				00 23	00 41	01 11	01 41
Harlington	d	23 08	23 22				23 53	00 06				00 27	00 45	01 15	01 45
Flitwick	d	23 13	23 26				23 57	00 10				00 31	00 49	01 19	01 49
Bedford ■	a	23 24	23 38		23 53		00 09	00 21			00 35	00 43	01 01	01 31	02 01

A From Sutton (Surrey)
B From Brighton
C To Cambridge
D To East Midlands Parkway
E From Rainham Kt
F From Horsham to Peterborough

Bedford, Luton and St Albans - London and Gatwick Airport

	TL [1] A	TL MO [1] B	TL MX [1] B	TL [1] C	TL [1] C	TL [1] C	TL [1] C	TL [1] D	TL [1] D	TL [1] D	TL E	TL [1] D	TL E	TL F	TL E	TL G	TL [1] D	TL [1] H	TL E	TL F	TL E	TL G
Bedford [7] d				00 15	01 15	01 53	02 15	02 53	03 10	03 45		04 13					04 43					
Flitwick d				00 26	01 26	02 04	02 26	03 04	03 21	03 56		04 24					04 54					
Harlington d		00 01	00 01	00 30	01 30	02 08	02 30	03 08	03 25	04 00		04 28					04 58					
Leagrave d		00 06	00 06	00 35	01 35	02 13	02 35	03 13	03 30	04 05		04 33					05 03					
Luton [10] d		00 10	00 10	00 40	01 40	02 18	02 40	03 18	03 35	04 10	04 20	04 38			04 50		05 08				05 20	
Luton Airport Parkway [7] ✈ d		00 13	00 13	00 43	01 43	02 21	02 43	03 21	03 38	04 13	04 23	04 41			04 53		05 11				05 23	
Harpenden d		00 18	00 18	00 48	01 48	02 26	02 48	03 26	03 43	04 18	04 28	04 46			04 58		05 16				05 28	
St Albans City d		00 25	00 25	00 55	01 55	02 33	02 55	03 33	03 50	04 25	04 35	04 53			05 05		05 23				05 35	
Radlett d				01 00	02 00		03 00		03 55		04 41				05 11						05 41	
Elstree & Borehamwood d				01 04	02 04		03 04		03 59		04 44				05 14						05 44	
Mill Hill Broadway d				01 08	02 08		03 08		04 03		04 48				05 18						05 48	
Hendon d	00 01			01 11	02 11		03 11		04 06		04 52				05 22						05 52	
Cricklewood d	00 06			01 16	02 16		03 16		04 11		04 56				05 28						05 56	
WestHampsteadThameslink ⊖ d	00 09	00 41	00 42	01 20	02 20	02 50	03 20	03 50	04 15	04 41	04 59	05 09	05 16	05 22	05 31	05 36	05 39	05 43		05 52	05 59	06 06
Kentish Town ⊖ d	00 13			01 24	02 24		03 24		04 19		05 04		05 21		05 36	05 41			05 51		06 04	06 11
St Pancras International a	00 19	00 51	00 52	01 30	02 31	03 01	03 31	04 01	04 25	04 51	05 10	05 19	05 27	05 32	05 42	05 47	05 49	05 53	05 57	06 02	06 10	06 17
Farringdon [3] ⊖ a	00 25									04 55	05 16	05 24	05 31	05 36	05 46	05 51	05 54	05 59	06 01	06 06	06 16	06 21
City Thameslink [3] a										04 57	05 18	05 26	05 33	05 38	05 48	05 53	05 56	06 01	06 03	06 08	06 18	06 23
London Blackfriars a	00 30	01 00	01 01	01 39	02 39	03 09	03 39	04 09	04 39	05 00	05 21	05 28	05 36	05 41	05 51	05 56	05 58	06 03	06 06	06 11	06 21	06 26
London Bridge a																						
London Bridge a												05 34		05 47			06 04	06 10		06 17		
Elephant & Castle ⊖173,179 a											05 25		05 40		05 55	06 00			06 10		06 25	06 30
Gatwick Airport a	01 20	01 56	01 56	02 30	03 30	03 56	04 30	04 57	05 31	05 47		06 04					06 34					

	TL E	TL [1] D	TL [1] H	TL I	EM ◇[1] J ⊤	TL F	TL G	TL E	TL [1]	TL K	TL L	TL E	TL [1] D	TL F	TL [1] H	TL K	TL E	TL M	EM ◇[1] N ⊤	TL G	TL [1] D	TL [1]
Bedford [7] d		05 15	05 25		05 38				05 44				05 48	06 01	06 04						06 18	06 22
Flitwick d		05 26	05 35						05 53				05 59	06 12	06 13			←			06 29	
Harlington d		05 30	05 39										06 03	06 16				06 16			→	
Leagrave d		05 35	05 43										06 08	→				06 21				
Luton [10] d	05 36	05 40	05 48				06 00		06 02		←		06 12		06 22			06 25	06 27	06 30		06 39
Luton Airport Parkway [7] ✈ d	05 39	05 43	05 51		05 58		06 03				06 03		06 15					06 28		06 33		
Harpenden d	05 44	05 48	05 56				→		06 08		06 09		06 21		06 28			06 33		06 39		
St Albans City d	05 51	05 55	06 01	←				06 07	06 13	←	06 15	06 21	06 27		06 33	←	06 34	06 38		06 45		06 48
Radlett d	05 57			05 57				06 12		06 12	06 20	06 26				06 26	06 39			06 50		
Elstree & Borehamwood d	→			06 00				→		06 16	06 24	→				06 30	06 43			→		
Mill Hill Broadway d				06 04						06 20	06 28					06 34	→					
Hendon d				06 08						06 23						06 38						
Cricklewood d				06 13						06 28						06 43						
WestHampsteadThameslink ⊖ d		06 09		06 17		06 21				06 32	06 36		06 39			06 47						
Kentish Town ⊖ d				06 21						06 36						06 51						
St Pancras International a		06 19	06 24	06 27	06 24	06 32			06 34		06 47		06 49		06 54	06 57		07 02	06 54			07 09
Farringdon [3] ⊖ a		06 24	06 29	06 31		06 36			06 39	06 46	06 51		06 54		06 59	07 01		07 06				07 14
City Thameslink [3] a		06 26	06 31	06 33		06 38			06 41	06 48	06 53		06 56		07 01	07 03		07 08				07 16
London Blackfriars a		06 28	06 33	06 36		06 41			06 43	06 51	06 56		06 58		07 03	07 06		07 11				07 18
London Bridge a																						
London Bridge a		06 34	06 40			06 47			06 50				07 04		07 10			07 17				07 24
Elephant & Castle ⊖173,179 a				06 40						06 55	07 00					07 10						
Gatwick Airport a		07 04							07 28				07 34									07 53

	TL K	TL L	TL E	TL [1] B	TL F	TL [1] H	TL K	TL E	TL M	TL G	EM ◇[1] O ⊤	TL [1] D	TL [1]	TL K	TL L	TL E	TL [1] B	TL F	TL [1] H	TL K	TL E	TL [1] P
Bedford [7] d				←	06 31	06 34						06 48	06 52				←	07 01	07 04			
Flitwick d				06 29	06 42	06 43			←			06 59					06 59	07 12	07 13			←
Harlington d				06 33	06 46				06 46			→					07 03	07 16				07 16
Leagrave d				06 38	→				06 51								07 08	→				07 21
Luton [10] d				06 42		06 52			06 55	07 00			07 09				07 12		07 22			07 25
Luton Airport Parkway [7] ✈ d				06 45					06 58	07 03	07 05						07 15					07 28
Harpenden d				06 51		06 58			07 04	07 09							07 21		07 28			07 34
St Albans City d		←	06 52	06 57		07 03	←	07 07	07 10	07 15			07 18		←	07 22	07 27		07 33	←	07 36	07 39
Radlett d	←	06 50	06 57				06 57	07 12		07 20				←	07 20	07 27				07 27	07 41	
Elstree & Borehamwood d	06 43	06 54	→				07 01	07 16		→				07 16	07 24	→				07 31	07 46	
Mill Hill Broadway d	06 47	06 58					07 05	→						07 20	07 28					07 35	→	
Hendon d	06 51						07 08							07 23						07 38		
Cricklewood d	06 56						07 13							07 28						07 43		
WestHampsteadThameslink ⊖ d	07 02	07 06		07 09			07 17							07 32	07 36					07 47		
Kentish Town ⊖ d	07 06						07 21							07 36						07 51		
St Pancras International a				07 19		07 24	07 27		07 32		07 36		07 39				07 49		07 54			08 02
Farringdon [3] ⊖ a	07 16	07 21		07 24		07 29	07 31		07 36				07 44	07 46	07 51		07 54		07 59	08 01		08 07
City Thameslink [3] a	07 18	07 23		07 26		07 31	07 33		07 38				07 46	07 48	07 53		07 56		08 01	08 03		08 09
London Blackfriars a	07 21	07 26		07 28		07 33	07 36		07 41				07 48	07 51	07 56		07 58		08 03	08 06		08 11
London Bridge a																						
London Bridge a				07 34		07 40			07 47				07 54				08 04		08 10			08 17
Elephant & Castle ⊖173,179 a	07 25	07 30					07 40							07 55	08 00					08 10		
Gatwick Airport a				08 04									08 23				08 34					

A From Bedford to Three Bridges
B From Bedford to Brighton
C To Three Bridges
D To Brighton
E To Sutton (Surrey)
F To Rainham Kt
G To Orpington
H To East Grinstead
I From Luton to Sutton (Surrey)
J From Leicester
K From St Albans City to Sutton (Surrey)
L From Luton to Orpington
M From Bedford to Rainham Kt
N From Derby
O From Nottingham
P From Bedford to Rainham Kt. [1] from London Blackfriars

Table T052MML-R

Mondays to Fridays

21 May to 7 December

Bedford, Luton and St Albans - London and Gatwick Airport

	TL A	EM ◇[1] B ⊠	EM ◇[1] C ⊠	TL [1] D	TL [1] E	TL F	TL G	TL H	TL [1] I	TL J	TL [1]	TL F	TL K	TL H	TL [1] L	EM ◇[1] M ⊠	EM ◇[1] N ⊠	TL A	EM ◇[1] O ⊠	TL [1] D	TL [1] L
Bedford [7] d				07 18	07 22				←		07 34									07 48	07 52
Flitwick d				07 29					07 29		07 43				07 44					07 59	
Harlington d				→					07 33						07 48					→	
Leagrave d									07 38						07 53						
Luton [10] d	07 30				07 39				07 42	07 46	07 52				07 58			08 02			08 09
Luton Airport Parkway [7] ✈ d	07 33	07 44	07 45						07 45	07 49					08 01	08 03	08 03	08 05	08 10		
Harpenden d	07 39								07 50	07 55	07 58				08 06			08 10			
St Albans City d	07 45				07 48		←	07 52	07 56	08 00	08 03		←	08 07	08 12			08 16			08 18
Radlett d	07 50					←	07 50	07 57		08 05		←	08 05	08 12				08 21			
Elstree & Borehamwood d	→					07 46	07 54	08 01		→		08 01	08 09	08 16				→			
Mill Hill Broadway d						07 50	07 58	→				08 05	08 13	→							
Hendon d						07 53						08 08									
Cricklewood d						07 58						08 13									
WestHampsteadThameslink ⊖ d						08 02	08 06					08 17	08 21								
Kentish Town ⊖ d						08 06						08 21									
St Pancras International a		08 09	08 09		08 09				08 19		08 24				08 34	08 28	08 29		08 39		08 39
Farringdon [3] ⊖ a					08 14	08 16	08 21		08 24		08 29	08 31	08 36		08 39						08 44
City Thameslink [3] a					08 16	08 18	08 23		08 26		08 31	08 33	08 38		08 41						08 46
London Blackfriars a					08 18	08 21	08 26		08 28		08 33	08 36	08 41		08 43						08 48
London Bridge a																					
London Bridge a					08 24				08 34		08 40		08 47		08 50						08 54
Elephant & Castle ⊖173,179 a						08 25	08 30					08 40									
Gatwick Airport a									09 04		09 19				09 35						09 23

	TL F	TL G	TL H	TL [1] I	TL J	TL [1] P	TL [1]	TL F	TL K	TL H	TL [1] Q	TL A	TL [1] D	TL [1] L	TL F	TL G	TL H	TL [1] I	TL F	TL J	TL H	TL [1]
Bedford [7] d				←		08 01	08 04						08 18	08 22				←				08 32
Flitwick d				07 59		08 12	08 13				←		08 29					08 29				08 43
Harlington d				08 03		08 16					08 16		→					08 33				08 47
Leagrave d				08 08		→					08 21							08 38				08 52
Luton [10] d				08 12	08 16		08 22				08 26	08 30		08 39				08 42		08 46		08 56
Luton Airport Parkway [7] ✈ d				08 15	08 19						08 29	08 33						08 45		08 49		08 59
Harpenden d				08 20	08 24		08 28				08 34	08 39						08 50		08 54		09 04
St Albans City d		←	08 22	08 26	08 30		08 33		←	08 37	08 41	08 45		08 48		←	08 52	08 56	←	09 00	09 07	09 11
Radlett d	←	08 21	08 27		08 35			←	08 35	08 42		08 50			←	08 50	08 57		08 57	09 05	09 12	
Elstree & Borehamwood d	08 16	08 24	08 31		→			08 31	08 39	08 46		→			08 46	08 54	→		09 01	09 09	09 16	
Mill Hill Broadway d	08 20	08 28	→					08 35	08 43	→					08 50	08 58			09 05	09 13	→	
Hendon d	08 23							08 38							08 53				09 08			
Cricklewood d	08 28							08 43							08 58				09 13			
WestHampsteadThameslink ⊖ d	08 32	08 36						08 47	08 51						09 02	09 06			09 17	09 21		
Kentish Town ⊖ d	08 36							08 51							09 06				09 21			
St Pancras International a				08 49			08 54				09 04			09 09				09 19		09 32		09 34
Farringdon [3] ⊖ a	08 46	08 51		08 54			08 59	09 01	09 06		09 09			09 14	09 16	09 21		09 24	09 31	09 36		09 39
City Thameslink [3] a	08 48	08 53		08 56			09 01	09 03	09 08		09 11			09 16	09 18	09 23		09 26	09 33	09 38		09 41
London Blackfriars a	08 51	08 56		08 58			09 03	09 06	09 11		09 13			09 18	09 21	09 26		09 28	09 36	09 41		09 43
London Bridge a																						
London Bridge a				09 04			09 10		09 17		09 20			09 24				09 34		09 47		09 50
Elephant & Castle ⊖173,179 a	08 55	09 00						09 10							09 25	09 30			09 40			
Gatwick Airport a				09 34			09 47				10 08			09 53				10 04				10 38

	TL A	TL [1] D	TL [1] L	TL F	TL G	TL H	TL [1] I	TL F	TL J	TL H	TL [1]	TL F	EM ◇[1] R ⊤	TL A	TL H	TL [1] D	TL F	TL J	TL H	TL [1]	TL F	TL A
Bedford [7] d		08 46	08 52				←				09 02					09 16				09 34		
Flitwick d		08 57					08 57				09 13					09 27				09 45		
Harlington d		→					09 01				09 17					09 31				09 49		
Leagrave d							09 06				09 22					09 36				09 54		
Luton [10] d	09 00		09 09				09 12		09 16		09 26					09 41		09 46		09 59		
Luton Airport Parkway [7] ✈ d	09 03						09 15		09 19		09 29		09 31			09 44		09 51		10 02		
Harpenden d	09 09						09 20		09 24		09 34					09 49		09 56		10 08		
St Albans City d	09 15		09 18		←	09 22	09 26	←	09 30	09 37	09 41	←			09 51	09 55	←	10 01	10 07	10 13	←	
Radlett d	09 20			←	09 20	09 27		09 27	09 35	09 42		09 42			09 56		09 56	10 06	10 12		10 12	
Elstree & Borehamwood d	→			09 16	09 24	→		09 31	09 39	→		09 46			→		10 01	10 10	→		10 16	
Mill Hill Broadway d				09 20	09 28			09 35	09 43			09 50					10 05	10 14			10 20	
Hendon d				09 23				09 38				09 53					10 08				10 23	
Cricklewood d				09 28				09 43				09 58					10 13				10 28	
WestHampsteadThameslink ⊖ d				09 32	09 36			09 47	09 51			10 01				10 09	10 16	10 21			10 31	
Kentish Town ⊖ d				09 36				09 51				10 06		10 11			10 21				10 36	10 41
St Pancras International a			09 39				09 49		10 02		10 04		09 55	10 17		10 19	10 27	10 32		10 34		10 47
Farringdon [3] ⊖ a			09 44	09 46	09 51		09 54	10 01	10 06		10 09	10 16		10 21		10 24	10 31	10 36		10 39	10 46	10 51
City Thameslink [3] a			09 46	09 48	09 53		09 56	10 03	10 08		10 11	10 18		10 23		10 26	10 33	10 38		10 41	10 48	10 53
London Blackfriars a			09 48	09 51	09 56		09 58	10 06	10 11		10 13	10 21		10 26		10 28	10 36	10 41		10 43	10 51	10 56
London Bridge a																						
London Bridge a			09 54				10 04		10 17		10 20					10 34		10 47		10 50		
Elephant & Castle ⊖173,179 a				09 55	10 00			10 10				10 25		10 30			10 40				10 55	11 00
Gatwick Airport a			10 23				10 34				11 08					11 04				11 38		

A To Orpington
B until 5 October. From Sheffield
C from 8 October. From Sheffield
D To Brighton
E To Littlehampton
F From St Albans City to Sutton (Surrey)
G From Luton to Orpington
H To Sutton (Surrey)
I From Bedford to Brighton
J To Rainham Kt
K From Luton to Rainham Kt
L To Three Bridges
M from 8 October. From Sheffield. The Sheffield Continental
N until 5 October, not from 13 August until 17 August. From Sheffield. The Sheffield Continental
O from 13 August until 17 August. From Sheffield. The Sheffield Continental
P To Gatwick Airport
Q From Bedford
R From Lincoln

Table T052MML-R

Mondays to Fridays

21 May to 7 December

Bedford, Luton and St Albans - London and Gatwick Airport

	TL A	TL ■ B	TL C	TL D	TL A	TL ■	TL C	EM ◇■ E	TL F	TL ■ B	EM ◇■ G	TL A	TL ■ H	TL C	TL D	TL A	TL ■	TL C	TL F	TL A	TL ■ I	TL ■ J
Bedford ■ d		09 48				10 04		10 13		10 19	10 23		←				10 35				10 49	10 49
Flitwick d		09 59				10 15				10 30			10 30				10 46				11 00	11 00
Harlington d		10 03				10 19				→			10 34				10 50				11 04	11 04
Leagrave d		10 08				10 24							10 39				10 55				11 09	11 09
Luton ■ d		10 12		10 16		10 28		10 28					10 43		10 48		10 59				11 13	11 13
Luton Airport Parkway ■ ✈ d		10 15		10 21		10 31					10 39		10 46		10 51		11 02				11 16	11 16
Harpenden d		10 22		10 26		10 38							10 52		10 56		11 08				11 22	11 22
St Albans City d	10 22	10 27	←	10 31	10 37	10 43	←					10 52	10 57	←	11 01	11 07	11 13	←		11 22	11 27	11 27
Radlett d	10 27		10 27	10 36	10 42		10 42					10 57		10 57	11 06	11 12		11 12		11 27		
Elstree & Borehamwood d	→		10 31	10 40	→		10 46					→		11 01	11 10	→		11 16		→		
Mill Hill Broadway d			10 35	10 44			10 50							11 05	11 14			11 20				
Hendon d			10 38				10 53							11 08				11 23				
Cricklewood d			10 43				10 58							11 13				11 28				
West Hampstead Thameslink ⊖ d		10 39	10 46	10 51			11 01						11 09	11 16	11 21			11 32			11 39	11 39
Kentish Town ⊖ d			10 51				11 06		11 11					11 21				11 36	11 41			
St Pancras International a		10 49	10 57	11 02		11 04		10 51	11 17		11 05		11 19	11 27	11 32		11 34		11 47		11 49	11 50
Farringdon ■ ⊖ a		10 54	11 01	11 06		11 09	11 16		11 21				11 24	11 31	11 36		11 39	11 46	11 51		11 54	11 55
City Thameslink ■ a		10 56	11 03	11 08		11 11	11 18		11 23				11 26	11 33	11 38		11 41	11 48	11 53		11 56	11 57
London Blackfriars a		10 58	11 06	11 11		11 13	11 21		11 26				11 28	11 36	11 41		11 43	11 51	11 56		11 58	11 59
London Bridge a																						
London Bridge a		11 04		11 17		11 20							11 34		11 47		11 50				12 04	12 05
Elephant & Castle ⊖173,179 a			11 10				11 25		11 30					11 40				11 55	12 00			
Gatwick Airport a		11 34				12 08							12 04				12 38				12 34	12 34

	TL C	TL D	TL ■ K	EM ◇■ E	TL A	TL ■ L	TL C	TL F	TL ■ J	TL ■ I	EM ◇■ G	TL M	TL N	TL ■ O	TL ■ P	TL Q	TL R	TL D	TL A	TL ■	TL C
Bedford ■ d			11 05	11 13		←			11 19	11 19	11 23				←					11 35	
Flitwick d			11 16			11 16			11 29	11 30				←	11 30					11 46	
Harlington d			→			11 20			11 33	→				11 33	11 34					11 50	
Leagrave d						11 25			→					11 38	11 39					11 55	
Luton ■ d		11 18		11 28		11 29								11 42	11 43			11 48		11 59	
Luton Airport Parkway ■ ✈ d		11 21				11 32					11 39			11 45	11 46			11 51		12 02	
Harpenden d		11 26				11 38								11 50	11 51			11 56		12 08	
St Albans City d	←	11 31			11 37	11 43	←					11 51	11 52	11 55	11 57		←	12 01	12 07	12 13	←
Radlett d	11 27	11 36			11 42		11 42					11 56	11 57			←	11 57	12 06	12 12		12 12
Elstree & Borehamwood d	11 31	11 40			→		11 46					12 00	→			12 00	12 01	12 10	→		12 16
Mill Hill Broadway d	11 35	11 44					11 50					→				12 04	12 05	12 14			12 20
Hendon d	11 38						11 53									12 08	12 08				12 23
Cricklewood d	11 43						11 58									12 13	12 13				12 28
West Hampstead Thameslink ⊖ d	11 46	11 51					12 01							12 09	12 09	12 16	12 16	12 21			12 31
Kentish Town ⊖ d	11 51						12 06	12 11								12 21	12 21				12 36
St Pancras International a	11 57	12 02		11 52		12 04		12 17			12 08			12 19	12 19	12 27	12 27	12 32		12 34	
Farringdon ■ ⊖ a	12 01	12 06				12 09	12 16	12 21						12 24	12 24	12 31	12 31	12 36		12 39	12 46
City Thameslink ■ a	12 03	12 08				12 11	12 18	12 23						12 26	12 26	12 33	12 33	12 38		12 41	12 48
London Blackfriars a	12 06	12 11				12 13	12 21	12 26						12 28	12 28	12 36	12 36	12 41		12 43	12 51
London Bridge a																					
London Bridge a		12 17				12 20								12 34	12 34			12 47		12 50	
Elephant & Castle ⊖173,179 a	12 10						12 25	12 30								12 40	12 40				12 55
Gatwick Airport a						13 08								13 04	13 04					13 38	

	TL F	TL A	TL ■ B	TL C	TL D	TL ■ K	EM ◇■ E	TL A	TL ■ L	TL C	TL F	TL ■ B	EM ◇■ G	TL A	TL ■ H	TL C	TL D	TL A	TL ■	TL C	TL F	TL A
Bedford ■ d			11 49			12 05	12 13		←			12 19	12 23		←				12 35			
Flitwick d			12 00			12 16			12 16			12 30			12 30				12 46			
Harlington d			12 04			→			12 20			→			12 34				12 50			
Leagrave d			12 09						12 25						12 39				12 55			
Luton ■ d			12 13		12 18		12 28		12 29						12 43		12 48		12 59			
Luton Airport Parkway ■ ✈ d			12 16		12 21				12 32				12 39		12 46		12 51		13 02			
Harpenden d			12 22		12 26				12 38						12 52		12 56		13 08			
St Albans City d		12 22	12 27	←	12 31			12 37	12 43	←				12 52	12 57	←	13 01	13 07	13 13	←		13 22
Radlett d		12 27		12 27	12 36			12 42		12 42				12 57		12 57	13 06	13 12		13 12		13 27
Elstree & Borehamwood d		→		12 31	12 40			→		12 46				→		13 01	13 10	→		13 16		→
Mill Hill Broadway d				12 35	12 44					12 50						13 05	13 14			13 20		
Hendon d				12 38						12 53						13 08				13 23		
Cricklewood d				12 43						12 58						13 13				13 28		
West Hampstead Thameslink ⊖ d			12 39	12 47	12 51					13 01					13 09	13 16	13 21			13 31		
Kentish Town ⊖ d	12 41			12 51						13 06	13 11					13 21				13 36	13 41	
St Pancras International a	12 47		12 49	12 57	13 02		12 51		13 04		13 17		13 06		13 19	13 27	13 32		13 34		13 47	
Farringdon ■ ⊖ a	12 51		12 54	13 01	13 06				13 09	13 16	13 21				13 24	13 31	13 36		13 39	13 46	13 51	
City Thameslink ■ a	12 53		12 56	13 03	13 08				13 11	13 18	13 23				13 26	13 33	13 38		13 41	13 48	13 53	
London Blackfriars a	12 56		12 58	13 06	13 11				13 13	13 21	13 26				13 28	13 36	13 41		13 43	13 51	13 56	
London Bridge a																						
London Bridge a			13 04		13 17				13 20						13 34		13 47		13 50			
Elephant & Castle ⊖173,179 a	13 00			13 10						13 25	13 30					13 40				13 55	14 00	
Gatwick Airport a			13 34						14 08						14 04				14 38			

A To Sutton (Surrey)
B To Brighton
C From St Albans City to Sutton (Surrey)
D To Rainham Kt
E From Corby
F To Orpington
G From Nottingham
H From Bedford to Brighton
I from 23 July until 5 October. To Brighton
J until 20 July, from 8 October. To Brighton
K To Gatwick Airport
L From Bedford
M until 20 July, from 8 October. To Sutton (Surrey)
N from 23 July until 5 October. To Sutton (Surrey)
O until 20 July, from 8 October. From Bedford to Brighton
P from 23 July until 5 October. From Bedford to Brighton
Q until 20 July, from 8 October. From St Albans City to Sutton (Surrey)
R from 23 July until 5 October. From St Albans City to Sutton (Surrey)

Table T052MML-R

Mondays to Fridays

21 May to 7 December

Bedford, Luton and St Albans - London and Gatwick Airport

	TL ■ A	TL ■ B	TL C	TL D	TL ■ E	EM ◇■ F	TL G	TL ■ H	TL C	TL I	TL ■ B	TL ■ A	EM ◇■ J	TL K	TL L	TL ■ M	TL ■ N	TL O	TL P	TL D	TL G	TL ■
Bedford ■ d	12 49	12 49			13 05	13 13		←			13 19	13 19	13 23				←					13 35
Flitwick d	13 00	13 00			13 16			13 16			13 29	13 30				←	13 30					13 46
Harlington d	13 04	13 04			→			13 20			13 33	→				13 33	13 34					13 50
Leagrave d	13 09	13 09						13 25			→					13 38	13 39					13 55
Luton ■ d	13 13	13 13		13 18		13 28		13 29								13 42	13 43			13 48		13 59
Luton Airport Parkway ■ ✈ d	13 16	13 16		13 21				13 32					13 39			13 45	13 46			13 51		14 02
Harpenden d	13 22	13 22		13 26				13 38								13 50	13 51			13 56		14 08
St Albans City d	13 27	13 27	←	13 31			13 37	13 43	←					13 51	13 52	13 55	13 57		←	14 01	14 07	14 13
Radlett d			13 27	13 36			13 42		13 42					13 56	13 57			←	13 57	14 06	14 12	
Elstree & Borehamwood d			13 31	13 40			→		13 46					14 00	→			14 00	14 01	14 10	→	
Mill Hill Broadway d			13 35	13 44					13 50					→				14 04	14 05	14 14		
Hendon d			13 38						13 53									14 08	14 08			
Cricklewood d			13 43						13 58									14 13	14 13			
West Hampstead Thameslink ⊖ d	13 39	13 39	13 46	13 51					14 01							14 09	14 09	14 16	14 16	14 21		
Kentish Town ⊖ d			13 51						14 06	14 11								14 21	14 21			
St Pancras International a	13 49	13 50	13 57	14 02		13 51		14 04		14 17			14 07			14 19	14 19	14 27	14 27	14 32		14 34
Farringdon ■ ⊖ a	13 54	13 55	14 01	14 06				14 09	14 16	14 21						14 24	14 24	14 31	14 31	14 36		14 39
City Thameslink ■ a	13 56	13 57	14 03	14 08				14 11	14 18	14 23						14 26	14 26	14 33	14 33	14 38		14 41
London Blackfriars a	13 58	13 59	14 06	14 11				14 13	14 21	14 26						14 28	14 28	14 36	14 36	14 41		14 43
London Bridge a																						
London Bridge a	14 04	14 05		14 17				14 20								14 34	14 34			14 47		14 50
Elephant & Castle ⊖173,179 a			14 10						14 25	14 30								14 40	14 40			
Gatwick Airport a	14 34	14 34						15 08								15 04	15 04					15 38

	TL C	TL I	TL G	TL ■ Q	TL ■ R	TL C	TL D	TL ■ E	EM ◇■ F	TL G	TL ■ H	TL C	TL I	TL ■ R	TL ■ Q	EM ◇■ J	TL K	TL L	TL ■ S	TL ■ T	TL O	TL P
Bedford ■ d				13 49	13 49			14 05	14 13		←			14 19	14 19	14 23				←		
Flitwick d				14 00	14 00			14 16			14 16			14 29	14 30				←	14 30		
Harlington d				14 04	14 04			→			14 20			14 33	→				14 33	14 34		
Leagrave d				14 09	14 09						14 25			→					14 38	14 39		
Luton ■ d				14 13	14 13		14 18		14 28		14 29								14 42	14 43		
Luton Airport Parkway ■ ✈ d				14 16	14 16		14 21				14 32					14 39			14 45	14 46		
Harpenden d				14 22	14 22		14 26				14 38								14 50	14 51		
St Albans City d	←		14 22	14 27	14 27	←	14 31			14 37	14 43	←					14 51	14 52	14 55	14 57		←
Radlett d	14 12		14 27			14 27	14 36			14 42		14 42					14 56	14 57			←	14 57
Elstree & Borehamwood d	14 16		→			14 31	14 40			→		14 46					15 00	→			15 00	15 01
Mill Hill Broadway d	14 20					14 35	14 44					14 50					→				15 04	15 05
Hendon d	14 23					14 38						14 53									15 08	15 08
Cricklewood d	14 28					14 43						14 58									15 13	15 13
West Hampstead Thameslink ⊖ d	14 31			14 39	14 39	14 46	14 51					15 01							15 09	15 09	15 16	15 16
Kentish Town ⊖ d	14 36	14 41				14 51						15 06	15 11								15 21	15 21
St Pancras International a		14 47		14 49	14 50	14 57	15 02		14 51		15 04		15 17			15 05			15 19	15 19	15 27	15 27
Farringdon ■ ⊖ a	14 46	14 51		14 54	14 55	15 01	15 06				15 09	15 16	15 21						15 24	15 24	15 31	15 31
City Thameslink ■ a	14 48	14 53		14 56	14 57	15 03	15 08				15 11	15 18	15 23						15 26	15 26	15 33	15 33
London Blackfriars a	14 51	14 56		14 58	14 59	15 06	15 11				15 13	15 21	15 26						15 28	15 28	15 36	15 36
London Bridge a																						
London Bridge a				15 04	15 05		15 17				15 20								15 34	15 34		
Elephant & Castle ⊖173,179 a	14 55	15 00				15 10						15 25	15 30								15 40	15 40
Gatwick Airport a				15 34	15 34						16 08								16 04	16 04		

	TL D	TL G	TL ■	TL C	TL I	TL G	TL ■ U	TL C	TL D	TL ■ E	EM ◇■ F	TL G	TL ■ H	TL C	TL I	TL ■ U	EM ◇■ J	TL G	TL ■ V	TL D	TL ■ W	TL C
Bedford ■ d			14 35				14 49			15 05	15 13		←			15 19	15 23		←			
Flitwick d			14 46				15 00			15 16			15 16			15 30			15 30			
Harlington d			14 50				15 04			→			15 20			→			15 34			
Leagrave d			14 55				15 09						15 25						15 39			
Luton ■ d	14 48		14 59				15 13		15 18		15 28		15 29						15 43	15 48	15 49	
Luton Airport Parkway ■ ✈ d	14 51		15 02				15 16		15 21				15 32				15 39		15 46	15 51	15 52	
Harpenden d	14 56		15 08				15 22		15 26				15 38						15 52	15 56		
St Albans City d	15 01	15 07	15 13	←		15 22	15 27	←	15 31			15 37	15 43	←				15 52	15 57	→	16 01	←
Radlett d	15 06	15 12		15 12		15 27		15 27	15 36			15 42		15 42				15 57				15 57
Elstree & Borehamwood d	15 10	→		15 16		→		15 31	15 40			→		15 46				→				16 01
Mill Hill Broadway d	15 14			15 20				15 35	15 44					15 50								16 05
Hendon d				15 23				15 38						15 53								16 08
Cricklewood d				15 28				15 43						15 58								16 13
West Hampstead Thameslink ⊖ d	15 21			15 31			15 39	15 47	15 51					16 01					16 09			16 17
Kentish Town ⊖ d				15 36	15 41			15 51						16 06	16 11							16 22
St Pancras International a	15 32		15 34		15 47		15 49	15 57	16 02		15 51		16 04		16 17		16 11		16 19		16 24	
Farringdon ■ ⊖ a	15 36		15 39	15 46	15 51		15 54	16 01	16 06				16 09	16 16	16 21				16 24		16 29	16 31
City Thameslink ■ a	15 38		15 41	15 48	15 53		15 56	16 03	16 08				16 11	16 18	16 23				16 26		16 31	16 33
London Blackfriars a	15 41		15 43	15 51	15 56		15 58	16 06	16 11				16 13	16 21	16 26				16 28		16 33	16 36
London Bridge a																						
London Bridge a	15 47		15 50				16 04		16 17				16 20						16 34		16 40	
Elephant & Castle ⊖173,179 a				15 55	16 00			16 10						16 25	16 30							16 40
Gatwick Airport a			16 38				16 35						17 11						17 04			

A from 23 July until 5 October. To Brighton
B until 20 July, from 8 October. To Brighton
C From St Albans City to Sutton (Surrey)
D To Rainham Kt
E To Gatwick Airport
F From Corby
G To Sutton (Surrey)
H From Bedford
I To Orpington
J From Nottingham
K until 20 July, from 8 October. To Sutton (Surrey)
L from 23 July until 5 October. To Sutton (Surrey)
M until 20 July, from 8 October. From Bedford to Brighton
N from 23 July until 5 October. From Bedford to Brighton
O until 20 July, from 8 October. From St Albans City to Sutton (Surrey)
P from 23 July until 5 October. From St Albans City to Sutton (Surrey)
Q from 30 July. To Brighton
R until 27 July. To Brighton
S until 27 July. From Bedford to Brighton
T from 30 July. From Bedford to Brighton
U To Brighton
V From Bedford to Brighton
W To East Grinstead

Table T052MML-R

Mondays to Fridays

21 May to 7 December

Bedford, Luton and St Albans - London and Gatwick Airport

Station		TL A	TL B	TL ■	TL ■ C	TL D	TL E	TL B	TL ■ F	TL D		TL G	TL ■ H	TL ■ I	TL D	TL A	EM ◇■ J ⚲	TL B	TL ■ K	TL D	TL E		TL ■ F	EM ◇■ L ⚲	TL B
Bedford 7	d			15 35	15 44				15 48				16 02	16 06			16 11		←				16 18	16 22	
Flitwick	d			15 46					15 59				16 13						16 13				16 29		
Harlington	d			15 50					16 03				→						16 17				→		
Leagrave	d			15 55	16 00				16 08										16 22						
Luton 10	d			15 59	16 06				16 13			16 18		16 23			16 27		16 27						
Luton Airport Parkway 7 ✈	d	←		16 02	16 09				16 16			16 21							16 30					16 38	
Harpenden	d	15 56		16 08					16 22			16 26							16 35						
St Albans City	d	16 01	16 07	16 13	16 18	←		16 22	16 27	←		16 31		16 33		←		16 37	16 41	←					16 52
Radlett	d	16 06	16 12			16 12		16 27		16 27		16 36			←	16 36		16 42		16 42					16 57
Elstree & Borehamwood	d	16 10	→			16 16		→		16 31		→			16 31	16 40		→		16 46					17 01
Mill Hill Broadway	d	16 14				16 20				→					16 35	16 43				16 50					→
Hendon	d					16 23									16 38					16 53					
Cricklewood	d					16 28									16 43					16 58					
WestHampsteadThameslink ⊖	d	16 21				16 32	16 36		16 39						16 47	16 51			16 54	17 02	17 06				
Kentish Town ⊖	d					16 37	16 41								16 52					17 07	17 11				
St Pancras International	a			16 34	16 39		16 47		16 49					16 54			16 55		17 04	17 12	17 17			17 12	
Farringdon 3 ⊖	a	16 36		16 39	16 44	16 46	16 51		16 54					16 59	17 01	17 06			17 09	17 16	17 21				
City Thameslink 3	a	16 38		16 41	16 46	16 48	16 53		16 56					17 01	17 03	17 08			17 11	17 18	17 23				
London Blackfriars	a	16 41		16 43	16 48	16 51	16 56		16 58					17 03	17 06	17 11			17 13	17 21	17 26				
London Bridge	a																								
London Bridge	a	16 47		16 50	16 54				17 04					17 10		17 17			17 20						
Elephant & Castle ⊖173,179	a					16 55	17 00								17 10					17 25	17 30				
Gatwick Airport	a			17 41					17 35										18 11						

Station		TL ■ M	TL G	TL ■ I	TL D	TL A	TL B	TL ■		TL ■ C	TL D	TL E	TL B	TL ■ F	TL D	TL G	TL ■ I	TL D	TL A		TL ■ H	EM ◇■ J ⚲	TL B	TL ■ K	TL D
Bedford 7	d	←		16 32				16 35		16 44				16 48							17 04	17 11		←	
Flitwick	d	16 29						16 46						16 59							17 15			17 15	
Harlington	d	16 33						16 50						17 03							→			17 19	
Leagrave	d	16 38						16 55		17 00				17 08										17 24	
Luton 10	d	16 42	16 46	16 51				16 59		17 04				17 12		17 16	17 21					17 25		17 28	
Luton Airport Parkway 7 ✈	d	16 45	16 49	16 54				17 02		17 07				17 15		17 19	17 24							17 31	
Harpenden	d	16 50	16 54					17 08		17 12				17 21		17 25								17 36	
St Albans City	d	16 56	17 00	17 03		←	17 07	17 13		17 18	←		17 22	17 27	←	17 30	17 33		←				17 37	17 42	←
Radlett	d		17 05		←	17 05	17 12				17 12		17 27		17 27	17 35		←	17 35				17 42		17 42
Elstree & Borehamwood	d		→		17 01	17 09	→				17 16		→		17 31	→		17 31	17 39				→		17 46
Mill Hill Broadway	d				17 05	17 13					17 20				→			17 35	17 43						17 50
Hendon	d				17 08						17 23							17 38							17 53
Cricklewood	d				17 13						17 28							17 43							17 58
WestHampsteadThameslink ⊖	d				17 17	17 21					17 32	17 36		17 39				17 47	17 51					17 54	18 01
Kentish Town ⊖	d				17 22						17 37	17 41						17 52							18 06
St Pancras International	a	17 19		17 24				17 34		17 39		17 47		17 49			17 54					17 55		18 04	18 12
Farringdon 3 ⊖	a	17 24		17 29	17 31	17 36		17 39		17 44	17 46	17 51		17 54			17 59	18 01	18 06					18 09	18 16
City Thameslink 3	a	17 26		17 31	17 33	17 38		17 41		17 46	17 48	17 53		17 56			18 01	18 03	18 08					18 11	18 18
London Blackfriars	a	17 28		17 33	17 36	17 41		17 43		17 48	17 51	17 56		17 58			18 03	18 06	18 11					18 13	18 21
London Bridge	a																								
London Bridge	a	17 34		17 40		17 47		17 50		17 54				18 04			18 10		18 17					18 20	
Elephant & Castle ⊖173,179	a				17 40						17 55	18 00						18 10							18 25
Gatwick Airport	a	18 05						18 41						18 35										19 11	

Station		TL E	TL ■ F	EM ◇■ L ⚲	TL B	TL ■ M		TL G	TL ■ I	TL D	TL A	TL B	TL ■	TL D	TL E	EM ◇■ L ⚲	TL B		TL ■ F	TL G	TL ■ I	TL D	TL A	TL B	TL ■
Bedford 7	d		17 18	17 23		←			17 28				17 40						17 46		17 56				18 06
Flitwick	d		17 29			17 29			17 39										17 57		18 06				
Harlington	d		→			17 33			17 43										18 01		18 10				
Leagrave	d					17 38			17 48										18 06		18 15				18 23
Luton 10	d	17 32				17 42		17 46	17 53				17 57		18 02	18 05			18 12	18 16	18 20				18 27
Luton Airport Parkway 7 ✈	d	17 35		17 38		17 45		17 49					18 00		18 05				18 15	18 19	18 22				18 30
Harpenden	d	17 40				17 50		17 54					18 06		18 10				18 20	18 24	18 27				18 36
St Albans City	d	17 46			17 52	17 56		18 00	18 03		←	18 07	18 12	←	18 16		18 22		18 26	18 30	18 33		←	18 37	18 42
Radlett	d	17 51			17 57			18 05		←	18 05	18 12		18 12	18 21		18 27			18 35		←	18 35	18 42	
Elstree & Borehamwood	d	17 54			18 01			→		18 01	18 09	→		18 16	18 24		18 31			→		18 31	18 39	→	
Mill Hill Broadway	d	17 58			→					18 05	18 13			18 20	18 28		→					18 35	18 43		
Hendon	d									18 08				18 23								18 38			
Cricklewood	d									18 13				18 28								18 43			
WestHampsteadThameslink ⊖	d	18 06								18 17	18 21		18 24	18 31	18 36							18 47	18 51		18 54
Kentish Town ⊖	d	18 11								18 22				18 36	18 41							18 52			
St Pancras International	a	18 17		18 06		18 19			18 24				18 34	18 42	18 47	18 40			18 49		18 54				19 04
Farringdon 3 ⊖	a	18 21				18 24			18 29	18 31	18 36		18 39	18 46	18 51				18 54		18 59	19 01	19 06		19 09
City Thameslink 3	a	18 23				18 26			18 31	18 33	18 38		18 41	18 48	18 53				18 56		19 01	19 03	19 08		19 11
London Blackfriars	a	18 26				18 28			18 33	18 36	18 41		18 43	18 51	18 56				18 58		19 03	19 06	19 11		19 13
London Bridge	a																								
London Bridge	a					18 34			18 40		18 47		18 50						19 04		19 10		19 17		19 20
Elephant & Castle ⊖173,179	a	18 30								18 40				18 55	19 00							19 10			
Gatwick Airport	a					19 05							19 41						19 35						20 11

A From Luton to Rainham Kt
B To Sutton (Surrey)
C To Littlehampton
D From St Albans City to Sutton (Surrey)
E To Orpington
F To Brighton
G To Rainham Kt
H To Gatwick Airport
I To East Grinstead
J From Corby
K From Bedford
L From Nottingham
M From Bedford to Brighton

Table T052MML-R

Mondays to Fridays

21 May to 7 December

Bedford, Luton and St Albans - London and Gatwick Airport

Station		TL A		EM ◇■ B ⚲	TL C	TL ■ D	EM ◇■ E ⚲	TL F	TL ■ G	TL A	TL H	TL F	TL ■		TL A	TL C	TL F	TL ■ I	TL ■ J	TL A	TL H	TL F	TL ■	TL A
Bedford 7	d			18 11		18 16	18 23		←				18 32					18 46	18 46				19 02	
Flitwick	d					18 27			18 27				18 43					18 57	18 57				19 13	
Harlington	d					→			18 31				18 47					19 01	19 01				19 17	
Leagrave	d								18 36				18 52					19 06	19 06				19 22	
Luton 10	d			18 27	18 32				18 42		18 46		18 57			19 02		19 12	19 12		19 18		19 27	
Luton Airport Parkway 7 ✈	d				18 35		18 41		18 45		18 49		19 00			19 05		19 15	19 15		19 21		19 30	
Harpenden	d				18 40				18 50		18 54		19 06			19 10		19 21	19 21		19 26		19 36	
St Albans City	d	←			18 46			18 52	18 56	←	19 00	19 07	19 11		←	19 16	19 22	19 27	19 27	←	19 31	19 37	19 42	←
Radlett	d	18 42			18 51			18 57		18 57	19 05	19 12			19 12	19 21	19 27			19 27	19 36	19 42		19 42
Elstree & Borehamwood	d	18 46			18 54			→		19 01	19 09	→			19 16	19 24	→			19 31	19 40	→		19 46
Mill Hill Broadway	d	18 49			18 58					19 05	19 13				19 20	19 28				19 35	19 44			19 50
Hendon	d	18 53								19 08					19 23					19 38				19 53
Cricklewood	d	18 57								19 13					19 28					19 43				19 58
WestHampsteadThameslink ⊖	d	19 00			19 07					19 16	19 21				19 31	19 36		19 39	19 39	19 46	19 51			20 01
Kentish Town ⊖	d	19 05			19 11					19 21					19 36	19 41				19 51				20 06
St Pancras International	a	19 12		18 55	19 17		19 06		19 19		19 32		19 34			19 47		19 49	19 50	19 57	20 02		20 04	
Farringdon 3 ⊖	a	19 16			19 21				19 24	19 31	19 36		19 39		19 46	19 51		19 54	19 55	20 01	20 06		20 09	20 16
City Thameslink 3	a	19 18			19 23				19 26	19 33	19 38		19 41		19 48	19 53		19 56	19 57	20 03	20 08		20 11	20 18
London Blackfriars	a	19 21			19 26				19 28	19 36	19 41		19 43		19 51	19 56		19 58	19 59	20 06	20 11		20 13	20 21
London Bridge	a																							
London Bridge	a								19 34		19 47		19 50					20 04	20 05		20 17		20 20	
Elephant & Castle ⊖173,179	a	19 25			19 30					19 40					19 55	20 00				20 10				20 25
Gatwick Airport	a								20 04				20 38					20 34	20 34				21 08	

Station		EM ◇■ B ⚲	TL C	TL ■ J	TL ■ I	EM ◇■ E ⚲	TL K	TL L	TL ■ M	TL ■ N	TL O		TL P	TL H	TL F	TL ■	TL A	TL C	TL F	TL ■ D	TL A	TL H		TL ■ Q	EM ◇■ B ⚲
Bedford 7	d	19 12		19 16	19 16	19 25			←	←						19 32				19 48				20 04	20 11
Flitwick	d			19 27	19 27				19 27	19 27						19 43				19 59				20 15	
Harlington	d			→	→				19 31	19 31						19 47				20 03				→	
Leagrave	d								19 36	19 36						19 52				20 08					
Luton 10	d	19 28	19 32						19 41	19 42				19 48		19 57				20 14		20 18			20 27
Luton Airport Parkway 7 ✈	d		19 35			19 42			19 44	19 45				19 51		20 00				20 16		20 21			
Harpenden	d		19 40						19 50	19 52				19 56		20 08				20 22		20 26			
St Albans City	d		19 46				19 51	19 52	19 55	19 57			←	20 01	20 07	20 13	←		20 22	20 27	←	20 31			
Radlett	d		19 51				19 56	19 57			←		19 57	20 06	20 12		20 12		20 27		20 27	20 36			
Elstree & Borehamwood	d		19 54				20 00	→			20 00		20 01	20 10	→		20 16		→		20 31	20 40			
Mill Hill Broadway	d		19 58				→				20 04		20 05	20 14			20 20				20 35	20 44			
Hendon	d										20 08		20 08				20 23				20 38				
Cricklewood	d										20 13		20 13				20 28				20 43				
WestHampsteadThameslink ⊖	d		20 06						20 09	20 09	20 16		20 16	20 21			20 31			20 39	20 46	20 51			
Kentish Town ⊖	d		20 11								20 21		20 21				20 36	20 41			20 51				
St Pancras International	a	19 57	20 17			20 07			20 19	20 19	20 27		20 27	20 32		20 34		20 47		20 49	20 57	21 02			20 51
Farringdon 3 ⊖	a		20 21						20 24	20 24	20 31		20 31	20 36		20 39	20 46	20 51		20 54	21 01	21 06			
City Thameslink 3	a		20 23						20 26	20 26	20 33		20 33	20 38		20 41	20 48	20 53		20 56	21 03	21 08			
London Blackfriars	a		20 26						20 28	20 28	20 36		20 36	20 41		20 43	20 51	20 56		20 58	21 06	21 11			
London Bridge	a																								
London Bridge	a								20 34	20 34				20 47		20 50				21 04		21 17			
Elephant & Castle ⊖173,179	a		20 30								20 40		20 40				20 55	21 00			21 10				
Gatwick Airport	a								21 04	21 04						21 37				21 34					

Station		TL F	TL ■ R	TL A	TL C	TL ■ D	EM ◇■ E ⚲	TL F	TL ■ G		TL A	TL H	TL F	TL ■	TL A	TL C	TL F	TL ■ D	TL A	TL H		TL ■ Q	EM ◇■ B ⚲	TL F	TL ■ R
Bedford 7	d		←			20 18	20 23		←					20 34				20 49				21 05	21 13		←
Flitwick	d		20 15			20 29			20 29					20 45				21 00				21 16			21 16
Harlington	d		20 19			→			20 33					20 49				21 04				→			21 20
Leagrave	d		20 24						20 38					20 54				21 09							21 25
Luton 10	d		20 29						20 43			20 48		20 59				21 13		21 18			21 28		21 29
Luton Airport Parkway 7 ✈	d		20 32				20 38		20 46			20 51		21 02				21 16		21 21					21 32
Harpenden	d		20 38						20 52			20 56		21 08				21 22		21 26					21 38
St Albans City	d	20 37	20 43	←				20 52	20 57		←	21 01	21 07	21 13	←		21 22	21 27	←	21 31				21 37	21 43
Radlett	d	20 42		20 42				20 57			20 57	21 06	21 12		21 12		21 27		21 27	21 36				21 42	
Elstree & Borehamwood	d	→		20 46				→			21 01	21 10	→		21 16		→		21 31	21 40				→	
Mill Hill Broadway	d			20 50							21 05	21 14			21 20				21 35	21 44					
Hendon	d			20 53							21 08				21 23				21 38						
Cricklewood	d			20 58							21 13				21 28				21 43						
WestHampsteadThameslink ⊖	d			21 01					21 09		21 16	21 21			21 31			21 39	21 46	21 51					
Kentish Town ⊖	d			21 06	21 11						21 21				21 36	21 41			21 51						
St Pancras International	a		21 04		21 17		21 06		21 19		21 27	21 32		21 34		21 47		21 50	21 57	22 02			21 55		22 04
Farringdon 3 ⊖	a		21 09	21 16	21 21				21 24		21 31	21 36		21 39	21 46	21 51		21 55	22 01	22 06					22 09
City Thameslink 3	a		21 11	21 18	21 23				21 26		21 33	21 38		21 41	21 48	21 53		21 57	22 03	22 08					22 11
London Blackfriars	a		21 13	21 21	21 26				21 28		21 36	21 41		21 43	21 51	21 56		21 59	22 06	22 11					22 13
London Bridge	a																								
London Bridge	a		21 20						21 34			21 47		21 50				22 05		22 17					22 20
Elephant & Castle ⊖173,179	a			21 25	21 30						21 40				21 55	22 00			22 10						
Gatwick Airport	a		22 08						22 04					22 38				22 34							23 08

A From St Albans City to Sutton (Surrey)
B From Corby
C To Orpington
D To Brighton
E From Nottingham
F To Sutton (Surrey)
G From Bedford to Brighton
H To Rainham Kt
I from 30 July. To Brighton
J until 27 July. To Brighton
K until 20 July, from 8 October. To Sutton (Surrey)
L from 23 July until 5 October. To Sutton (Surrey)
M until 27 July. From Bedford to Brighton
N from 30 July. From Bedford to Brighton
O until 20 July, from 8 October. From St Albans City to Sutton (Surrey)
P from 23 July until 5 October. From St Albans City to Sutton (Surrey)
Q To Gatwick Airport
R From Bedford

Table T052MML-R

Mondays to Fridays

21 May to 7 December

Bedford, Luton and St Albans - London and Gatwick Airport

		TL	TL	TL	EM	TL	TL	TL	TL	TL	TL	TL	TL	TL	TL	TL	TL	TL	EM	TL	TL	TL	TL
				■	◇■		■				■				■			■	◇■		■		■
		A	B	C	D ⚲	E	F	A	G	E	H	A	B	E	C	A	G	I	D ⚲	E	J	A	C
Bedford ■	d			21 19	21 26		←				21 35				21 49			22 05	22 13		←		22 17
Flitwick	d			21 30			21 30				21 46				22 00			22 16			22 16		22 28
Harlington	d			→			21 34				21 50				22 04			→			22 20		22 32
Leagrave	d						21 39				21 55				22 09						22 25		22 37
Luton ■	d						21 43		21 48		21 59				22 13		22 18		22 28		22 29		22 41
Luton Airport Parkway ■ ✈	d				21 43		21 46		21 51		22 02				22 16		22 21		22 31		22 32		22 44
Harpenden	d						21 52		21 56		22 08				22 22		22 26				22 38		22 49
St Albans City	d	←				21 52	21 57	←	22 01	22 08	22 13	←		22 22	22 27	←	22 31			22 37	22 43	←	22 55
Radlett	d	21 42				21 57		21 57	22 06	22 13		22 13		22 27		22 27	22 36			22 42		22 42	
Elstree & Borehamwood	d	21 46				→		22 01	22 10	→		22 17		→		22 31	22 40			→		22 46	
Mill Hill Broadway	d	21 50						22 05	22 14			22 20				22 35	22 44					22 50	
Hendon	d	21 53						22 08				22 24				22 38						22 53	
Cricklewood	d	21 58						22 13				22 28				22 43						22 58	
WestHampsteadThameslink ⊖	d	22 01					22 09	22 16	22 21			22 31			22 39	22 46	22 51					23 01	23 11
Kentish Town ⊖	d	22 06	22 11					22 21				22 36	22 41			22 51						23 06	
St Pancras International	a		22 17		22 07		22 19	22 27	22 32		22 34		22 47		22 49	22 57	23 02		22 57		23 04		23 22
Farringdon ■ ⊖	a	22 16	22 21				22 24	22 31	22 36		22 39	22 46	22 51		22 54	23 01	23 06				23 09	23 16	23 26
City Thameslink ■	a	22 18	22 23				22 26	22 33	22 38		22 41	22 48	22 53		22 56								
London Blackfriars	a	22 21	22 26				22 28	22 36	22 41		22 43	22 51	22 56		22 58	23 06	23 11				23 13	23 21	23 30
London Bridge	a																						
London Bridge	a						22 34		22 47		22 50				23 04		23 17				23 20		23 36
Elephant & Castle ⊖173,179	a	22 25	22 30					22 40				22 55	23 00			23 10						23 25	
Gatwick Airport	a						23 04				23 37				23 34						00 01		00 17

		TL	EM	TL	TL	TL
			◇■	■	■	■
		E	D ⚲	C	H	C
Bedford ■	d		22 40	22 45	23 05	23 45
Flitwick	d			22 56	23 16	23 56
Harlington	d			23 00	23 20	00 01
Leagrave	d			23 05	23 25	00 06
Luton ■	d		22 57	23 10	23 30	00 10
Luton Airport Parkway ■ ✈	d			23 13	23 33	00 13
Harpenden	d			23 18	23 38	00 18
St Albans City	d	23 09		23 25	23 45	00 25
Radlett	d	23 14			23 50	
Elstree & Borehamwood	d	23 18			23 54	
Mill Hill Broadway	d	23 22			23 58	
Hendon	d	23 25			00 01	
Cricklewood	d	23 30			00 06	
WestHampsteadThameslink ⊖	d	23 33		23 41	00 09	00 42
Kentish Town ⊖	d	23 38			00 13	
St Pancras International	a	23 44	23 25	23 51	00 19	00 52
Farringdon ■ ⊖	a	23 48		23 55	00 25	
City Thameslink ■	a					
London Blackfriars	a	23 53		23 59	00 30	01 01
London Bridge	a					
London Bridge	a					
Elephant & Castle ⊖173,179	a	23 57				
Gatwick Airport	a			00 48	01 20	01 56

Saturdays

26 May to 8 December

		TL	TL	TL	TL	TL	TL	TL	TL	TL	TL	TL	TL	TL	TL	TL	TL	TL	TL	TL	TL	TL	EM
		■	■	■	■	■	■	■	■	■		■				■					■		◇■
		K	F	H	H	H	H	C	C	C	E	C	E	L	E	C	E	L	E	E	C	M	N ⚲
Bedford ■	d			00 15	01 15	01 53	02 15	02 53	03 10	03 45		04 13				04 45					05 15		05 34
Flitwick	d			00 26	01 26	02 04	02 26	03 04	03 21	03 56		04 24				04 56					05 26		
Harlington	d		00 01	00 30	01 30	02 08	02 30	03 08	03 25	04 00		04 28				05 00					05 30		
Leagrave	d		00 06	00 35	01 35	02 13	02 35	03 13	03 30	04 05		04 33				05 05					05 35		
Luton ■	d		00 10	00 40	01 40	02 18	02 40	03 18	03 35	04 10	04 20	04 38			04 50	05 10			05 20	05 36	05 40		
Luton Airport Parkway ■ ✈	d		00 13	00 43	01 43	02 21	02 43	03 21	03 38	04 13	04 23	04 41			04 53	05 13			05 23	05 39	05 43		05 52
Harpenden	d		00 18	00 48	01 48	02 26	02 48	03 26	03 43	04 18	04 28	04 46			04 58	05 18			05 28	05 44	05 48		
St Albans City	d		00 25	00 55	01 55	02 33	02 55	03 33	03 50	04 25	04 35	04 53			05 05	05 25			05 35	05 51	05 55	←	
Radlett	d			01 00	02 00		03 00		03 55		04 41				05 11				05 41	05 57		05 57	
Elstree & Borehamwood	d			01 04	02 04		03 04		03 59		04 44				05 14				05 44	→		06 00	
Mill Hill Broadway	d			01 08	02 08		03 08		04 03		04 48				05 18				05 48			06 04	
Hendon	d	00 01		01 11	02 11		03 11		04 06		04 52				05 22				05 52			06 08	
Cricklewood	d	00 06		01 16	02 16		03 16		04 11		04 56				05 26				05 56			06 13	
WestHampsteadThameslink ⊖	d	00 09	00 42	01 20	02 20	02 50	03 20	03 50	04 15	04 41	04 59	05 09	05 16	05 22	05 29	05 41	05 46	05 52	05 59		06 09	06 17	
Kentish Town ⊖	d	00 13		01 24	02 24		03 24		04 19		05 04		05 21		05 34		05 51		06 04			06 21	
St Pancras International	a	00 19	00 52	01 30	02 31	03 01	03 31	04 01	04 25	04 51	05 10	05 19	05 27	05 32	05 40	05 49	05 57	06 02	06 10		06 19	06 27	06 21
Farringdon ■ ⊖	a	00 25								04 55	05 16	05 24	05 31	05 36	05 46	05 54	06 01	06 06	06 16		06 24	06 31	
City Thameslink ■	a																						
London Blackfriars	a	00 30	01 01	01 39	02 39	03 09	03 39	04 09	04 39	05 00	05 21	05 28	05 36	05 41	05 51	05 58	06 06	06 11	06 21		06 28	06 36	
London Bridge	a																						
London Bridge	a											05 34		05 47		06 04		06 17			06 34		
Elephant & Castle ⊖173,179	a										05 25		05 40		05 55		06 10		06 25			06 40	
Gatwick Airport	a	01 20	01 56	02 30	03 30	03 58	04 30	05 02	05 29	05 47		06 04				06 34					07 04		

A From St Albans City to Sutton (Surrey)
B To Orpington
C To Brighton
D From Nottingham
E To Sutton (Surrey)
F From Bedford to Brighton
G To Gillingham (Kent)
H To Three Bridges
I To Gatwick Airport
J From Bedford
K From Bedford to Three Bridges
L To Rainham Kt
M From Luton to Sutton (Surrey)
N From Leicester

Table T052MML-R

Saturdays

26 May to 8 December

Bedford, Luton and St Albans - London and Gatwick Airport

		TL	TL	TL	TL	TL	TL	TL	TL	TL	TL	TL	TL	TL	TL	TL	EM	TL	TL	TL	TL	TL	TL
					■				■				■			■	◇■		■				■
		A	B	B	C	D	A	B		D	E	B	C	D	A	F	G ⚲	B	H	D	E	B	C
Bedford ■	d				05 49		06 00		06 05				06 19		06 30	06 35	06 38		←				06 49
Flitwick	d				06 00				06 16				06 30			06 46			06 46				07 00
Harlington	d				06 04				06 20				06 34			→			06 50				07 04
Leagrave	d				06 09				06 25				06 39						06 55				07 09
Luton ■	d				06 13		06 18		06 29				06 43		06 48		06 53		06 59				07 13
Luton Airport Parkway ■ ✈	d				06 16		06 21		06 32				06 46		06 51				07 02				07 16
Harpenden	d				06 22		06 26		06 38				06 52		06 56				07 08				07 22
St Albans City	d		06 07	06 22	06 27	←	06 31	06 37	06 43	←		06 52	06 57	←	07 01			07 07	07 13	←		07 22	07 27
Radlett	d		06 12	06 27		06 27	06 36	06 42		06 42		06 57		06 57	07 06			07 12		07 12		07 27	
Elstree & Borehamwood	d		06 16	→		06 31	06 40	→		06 46		→		07 01	07 10			→		07 16		→	
Mill Hill Broadway	d		06 20			06 35	06 44			06 50				07 05	07 14					07 20			
Hendon	d		06 23			06 38				06 53				07 08						07 23			
Cricklewood	d		06 28			06 43				06 58				07 13						07 28			
WestHampsteadThameslink ⊖	d	06 22	06 31		06 39	06 46	06 51			07 01			07 09	07 16	07 21					07 31			07 39
Kentish Town ⊖	d		06 36			06 51				07 06	07 11			07 21						07 36	07 41		
St Pancras International	a	06 32	06 42		06 49	06 57	07 02		07 04		07 17		07 19	07 27	07 32		07 21		07 34		07 47		07 49
Farringdon ■ ⊖	a	06 36	06 46		06 54	07 01	07 06		07 09	07 16	07 21		07 24	07 31	07 36				07 39	07 46	07 51		07 54
City Thameslink ■	a																						
London Blackfriars	a	06 41	06 51		06 58	07 06	07 11		07 13	07 21	07 26		07 28	07 36	07 41				07 43	07 51	07 56		07 58
London Bridge	a																						
London Bridge	a	06 47			07 04		07 17		07 21				07 34		07 47				07 51				08 04
Elephant & Castle ⊖173,179	a		06 55			07 10				07 25	07 30			07 40						07 55	08 00		
Gatwick Airport	a				07 34				08 08				08 04						08 38				08 34

		TL	TL	TL	TL	TL	TL	TL	EM	TL	TL	TL	TL	TL	EM	TL	TL	TL	TL	TL	TL	TL	TL
					■			■	◇■		■			■	◇■		■				■		
		D	A	B		D	E	C	I ⚲	B	J	D	A	F	G ⚲	B	H	D	E	B	C	D	A
Bedford ■	d				07 05			07 19	07 23		←			07 35	07 42		←				07 49		
Flitwick	d				07 16			07 30			07 30			07 46			07 46				08 00		
Harlington	d				07 20			→			07 34			→			07 50				08 04		
Leagrave	d				07 25						07 39						07 55				08 09		
Luton ■	d		07 18		07 29						07 43		07 48		07 57		07 59				08 13		08 18
Luton Airport Parkway ■ ✈	d		07 21		07 32				07 39		07 46		07 51				08 02				08 16		08 21
Harpenden	d		07 26		07 38						07 52		07 56				08 08				08 22		08 26
St Albans City	d	←	07 31	07 37	07 43	←				07 52	07 57	←	08 01			08 07	08 13	←		08 22	08 27	←	08 31
Radlett	d	07 27	07 36	07 42		07 42				07 57		07 57	08 06			08 12		08 12		08 27		08 27	08 36
Elstree & Borehamwood	d	07 31	07 40	→		07 46				→		08 01	08 10			→		08 16		→		08 31	08 40
Mill Hill Broadway	d	07 35	07 44			07 50						08 05	08 14					08 20				08 35	08 44
Hendon	d	07 38				07 53						08 08						08 23				08 38	
Cricklewood	d	07 43				07 58						08 13						08 28				08 43	
WestHampsteadThameslink ⊖	d	07 46	07 51			08 01					08 09	08 16	08 21					08 31			08 39	08 46	08 51
Kentish Town ⊖	d	07 51				08 06	08 11					08 21						08 36	08 41			08 51	
St Pancras International	a	07 57	08 02		08 04		08 17		08 06		08 19	08 27	08 32		08 22		08 34		08 47		08 49	08 57	09 02
Farringdon ■ ⊖	a	08 01	08 06		08 09	08 16	08 21				08 24	08 31	08 36				08 39	08 46	08 51		08 54	09 01	09 06
City Thameslink ■	a																					09 03	09 08
London Blackfriars	a	08 06	08 11		08 13	08 21	08 26				08 28	08 36	08 41				08 43	08 51	08 56		08 58	09 06	09 11
London Bridge	a																						
London Bridge	a		08 17		08 21						08 34		08 47				08 51				09 04		09 17
Elephant & Castle ⊖173,179	a	08 10				08 25	08 30					08 40						08 55	09 00			09 10	
Gatwick Airport	a				09 08						09 04						09 38				09 34		

		TL	TL	TL	TL	TL	EM	TL	TL	TL	TL	TL	TL	TL	TL	TL	TL	TL	TL	TL	EM	TL	TL
			■			■	◇■		■				■				■			■	◇■		■
		B		D	E	C	I ⚲	B	J	D	A	B		D	E	B	C	D	A	F	K ⚲	B	H
Bedford ■	d		08 05			08 19	08 24		←				08 35				08 49			09 05	09 12		←
Flitwick	d		08 16			08 30			08 30				08 46				09 00			09 16			09 16
Harlington	d		08 20			→			08 34				08 50				09 04			→			09 20
Leagrave	d		08 25						08 39				08 55				09 09						09 25
Luton ■	d		08 29						08 43		08 48		08 59				09 13		09 18		09 28		09 29
Luton Airport Parkway ■ ✈	d		08 32				08 39		08 46		08 51		09 02				09 16		09 21				09 32
Harpenden	d		08 38						08 52		08 56		09 08				09 22		09 26				09 38
St Albans City	d	08 37	08 43	←				08 52	08 57	←	09 01	09 07	09 13	←		09 22	09 27	←	09 31			09 37	09 43
Radlett	d	08 42		08 42				08 57		08 57	09 06	09 12		09 12		09 27		09 27	09 36			09 42	
Elstree & Borehamwood	d	→		08 46				→		09 01	09 10	→		09 16		→		09 31	09 40			→	
Mill Hill Broadway	d			08 50						09 05	09 14			09 20				09 35	09 44				
Hendon	d			08 53						09 08				09 23				09 38					
Cricklewood	d			08 58						09 13				09 28				09 43					
WestHampsteadThameslink ⊖	d			09 01					09 09	09 16	09 21			09 31			09 39	09 46	09 51				
Kentish Town ⊖	d			09 06	09 11					09 21				09 36	09 41			09 51					
St Pancras International	a		09 04		09 17		09 07		09 19	09 27	09 32		09 34		09 47		09 49	09 57	10 02		09 51		10 04
Farringdon ■ ⊖	a		09 09	09 16	09 21				09 24	09 31	09 36		09 39	09 46	09 51		09 54	10 01	10 06				10 09
City Thameslink ■	a		09 11	09 18	09 23				09 26	09 33	09 38		09 41	09 48	09 53		09 56	10 03	10 08				10 11
London Blackfriars	a		09 13	09 21	09 26				09 28	09 36	09 41		09 43	09 51	09 56		09 58	10 06	10 11				10 13
London Bridge	a																						
London Bridge	a		09 21						09 34		09 47		09 51				10 04		10 17				10 21
Elephant & Castle ⊖173,179	a			09 25	09 30					09 40				09 55	10 00			10 10					
Gatwick Airport	a		10 08						10 04				10 38				10 34						11 08

A To Rainham Kt
B To Sutton (Surrey)
C To Brighton
D From St Albans City to Sutton (Surrey)
E To Orpington
F To Gatwick Airport
G From Derby
H From Bedford
I From Nottingham
J From Bedford to Brighton
K From Corby

Table T052MML-R

Saturdays

26 May to 8 December

Bedford, Luton and St Albans - London and Gatwick Airport

	TL A	TL B	TL ■ C	EM ◇■ D (catering)	TL E	TL ■ F	TL A	TL G	TL E		TL ■	TL A	TL B	TL E	TL ■ C	TL A	TL G	TL ■ H	EM ◇■ I (catering)	TL E		TL ■ J	TL A	TL B
Bedford ■ d			09 19	09 23		←					09 35				09 49			10 05	10 12			←		
Flitwick d			09 30			09 30					09 46				10 00			10 16				10 16		
Harlington d			→			09 34					09 50				10 04			→				10 20		
Leagrave d						09 39					09 55				10 09							10 25		
Luton ■ d						09 43		09 48			09 59				10 13		10 18		10 28			10 29		
Luton Airport Parkway ■ ✈ d				09 38		09 46		09 51			10 02				10 16		10 21					10 32		
Harpenden d						09 52		09 56			10 08				10 22		10 26					10 38		
St Albans City d	←				09 52	09 57	←	10 01	10 07		10 13	←		10 22	10 27	←	10 31			10 37		10 43	←	
Radlett d	09 42				09 57		09 57	10 06	10 12			10 12		10 27		10 27	10 36			10 42			10 42	
Elstree & Borehamwood d	09 46				→		10 01	10 10	→			10 16		→		10 31	10 40			→			10 46	
Mill Hill Broadway d	09 50						10 05	10 14				10 20				10 35	10 44						10 50	
Hendon d	09 53						10 08					10 23				10 38							10 53	
Cricklewood d	09 58						10 13					10 28				10 43							10 58	
WestHampsteadThameslink ⊖ d	10 01					10 09	10 16	10 21				10 31			10 39	10 46	10 51						11 01	
Kentish Town ⊖ d	10 06	10 11					10 21					10 36	10 41			10 51							11 06	11 11
St Pancras International a		10 17		10 07		10 19	10 27	10 32			10 34		10 47		10 49	10 57	11 02		10 51			11 04		11 17
Farringdon ■ ⊖ a	10 16	10 21				10 24	10 31	10 36			10 39	10 46	10 51		10 54	11 01	11 06					11 09	11 16	11 21
City Thameslink ■ a	10 18	10 23				10 26	10 33	10 38			10 41	10 48	10 53		10 56	11 03	11 08					11 11	11 18	11 23
London Blackfriars a	10 21	10 26				10 28	10 36	10 41			10 43	10 51	10 56		10 58	11 06	11 11					11 13	11 21	11 26
London Bridge a																								
London Bridge a						10 34		10 47			10 51				11 04		11 17					11 21		
Elephant & Castle ⊖173,179 a	10 25	10 30					10 40					10 55	11 00			11 10							11 25	11 30
Gatwick Airport a						11 04					11 37				11 34							12 08		

	TL ■ C	EM ◇■ K (catering)	TL E	TL ■ F	TL A	TL G	TL E		TL ■	TL A	TL B	TL E	TL ■ C	TL A	TL G	TL ■ H	EM ◇■ I (catering)	TL E		TL ■ J	TL A	TL B	TL ■ C	EM ◇■ K (catering)
Bedford ■ d	10 19	10 23		←					10 35				10 49			11 05	11 12			←			11 19	11 22
Flitwick d	10 30			10 30					10 46				11 00			11 15				11 15			11 30	
Harlington d	→			10 34					10 50				11 04			→				11 19			→	
Leagrave d				10 39					10 55				11 09							11 25				
Luton ■ d				10 43		10 48			10 59				11 13		11 18		11 28			11 29				
Luton Airport Parkway ■ ✈ d		10 39		10 46		10 51			11 02				11 16		11 21					11 32				11 38
Harpenden d				10 52		10 56			11 08				11 22		11 26					11 38				
St Albans City d			10 52	10 57	←	11 01	11 07		11 13	←		11 22	11 27	←	11 31			11 37		11 43	←			
Radlett d			10 57		10 57	11 06	11 12			11 12		11 27		11 27	11 36			11 42			11 42			
Elstree & Borehamwood d			→		11 01	11 10	→			11 16		→		11 31	11 40			→			11 46			
Mill Hill Broadway d					11 05	11 14				11 20				11 35	11 44						11 50			
Hendon d					11 08					11 23				11 38							11 53			
Cricklewood d					11 13					11 28				11 43							11 58			
WestHampsteadThameslink ⊖ d				11 09	11 16	11 21				11 31			11 39	11 46	11 51						12 01			
Kentish Town ⊖ d					11 21					11 36	11 41			11 51							12 06	12 11		
St Pancras International a		11 08		11 19	11 27	11 32			11 34		11 47		11 49	11 57	12 02		11 50			12 04		12 17		12 07
Farringdon ■ ⊖ a				11 24	11 31	11 36			11 39	11 46	11 51		11 54	12 01	12 06					12 09	12 16	12 21		
City Thameslink ■ a				11 26	11 33	11 38			11 41	11 48	11 53		11 56	12 03	12 08					12 11	12 18	12 23		
London Blackfriars a				11 28	11 36	11 41			11 43	11 51	11 56		11 58	12 06	12 11					12 13	12 21	12 26		
London Bridge a																								
London Bridge a				11 34		11 47			11 51				12 04		12 17					12 21				
Elephant & Castle ⊖173,179 a					11 40					11 55	12 00			12 10							12 25	12 30		
Gatwick Airport a				12 04					12 38				12 34							13 08				

	TL E	TL ■ F	TL A	TL G	TL E		TL ■	TL A	TL B	TL E	TL ■ C	TL A	TL G	TL ■ H	EM ◇■ I (catering)	TL E		TL ■ J	TL A	TL B	TL ■ C	EM ◇■ K (catering)	TL E	TL ■ F
Bedford ■ d		←					11 35				11 49			12 05	12 12			←			12 19	12 23		←
Flitwick d		11 30					11 46				12 00			12 16				12 16			12 30			12 30
Harlington d		11 34					11 50				12 04			→				12 20			→			12 34
Leagrave d		11 39					11 55				12 09							12 25						12 39
Luton ■ d		11 43		11 48			11 59				12 13		12 18		12 28			12 29						12 43
Luton Airport Parkway ■ ✈ d		11 46		11 51			12 02				12 16		12 21					12 32				12 39		12 46
Harpenden d		11 52		11 56			12 08				12 22		12 26					12 38						12 52
St Albans City d	11 52	11 57	←	12 01	12 07		12 13	←		12 22	12 27	←	12 31			12 37		12 43	←				12 52	12 57
Radlett d	11 57		11 57	12 06	12 12			12 12		12 27		12 27	12 36			12 42			12 42				12 57	
Elstree & Borehamwood d	→		12 01	12 10	→			12 16		→		12 31	12 40			→			12 46				→	
Mill Hill Broadway d			12 05	12 14				12 20				12 35	12 44						12 50					
Hendon d			12 08					12 23				12 38							12 53					
Cricklewood d			12 13					12 28				12 43							12 58					
WestHampsteadThameslink ⊖ d		12 09	12 16	12 21				12 31			12 39	12 46	12 51						13 01					13 09
Kentish Town ⊖ d			12 21					12 36	12 41			12 51							13 06	13 11				
St Pancras International a		12 19	12 27	12 32			12 34		12 47		12 49	12 57	13 02		12 51			13 04		13 17		13 08		13 19
Farringdon ■ ⊖ a		12 24	12 31	12 36			12 39	12 46	12 51		12 54	13 01	13 06					13 09	13 16	13 21				13 24
City Thameslink ■ a		12 26	12 33	12 38			12 41	12 48	12 53		12 56	13 03	13 08					13 11	13 18	13 23				13 26
London Blackfriars a		12 28	12 36	12 41			12 43	12 51	12 56		12 58	13 06	13 11					13 13	13 21	13 26				13 28
London Bridge a																								
London Bridge a		12 34		12 47			12 51				13 04		13 17					13 21						13 34
Elephant & Castle ⊖173,179 a			12 40					12 55	13 00			13 10							13 25	13 30				
Gatwick Airport a		13 04					13 38				13 34							14 08						14 04

A From St Albans City to Sutton (Surrey)
B To Orpington
C To Brighton
D From Lincoln
E To Sutton (Surrey)
F From Bedford to Brighton
G To Rainham Kt
H To Gatwick Airport
I From Corby
J From Bedford
K From Nottingham

Table T052MML-R

Saturdays

26 May to 8 December

Bedford, Luton and St Albans - London and Gatwick Airport

	TL A		TL B	TL C	TL ■	TL A	TL D	TL C	TL ■ E	TL A	TL B	TL ■ F		EM ◇■ G (catering)	TL C	TL ■ H	TL A	TL D	TL ■ E	EM ◇■ I (catering)	TL C	TL ■ J	TL A
Bedford ■ d					12 35				12 49			13 05		13 11		←			13 19	13 23		←	
Flitwick d					12 46				13 00			13 16				13 16			13 30			13 30	
Harlington d					12 50				13 04			→				13 20			→			13 34	
Leagrave d					12 55				13 09							13 25						13 39	
Luton ■ d			12 48		12 59				13 13		13 18			13 28		13 29						13 43	
Luton Airport Parkway ■ ✈ d			12 51		13 02				13 16		13 21					13 32				13 39		13 46	
Harpenden d			12 56		13 08				13 22		13 26					13 38						13 52	
St Albans City d	←		13 01	13 07	13 13	←		13 22	13 27	←	13 31				13 37	13 43	←				13 52	13 57	←
Radlett d	12 57		13 06	13 12		13 12		13 27		13 27	13 36				13 42		13 42				13 57		13 57
Elstree & Borehamwood d	13 01		13 10	→		13 16		→		13 31	13 40				→		13 46				→		14 01
Mill Hill Broadway d	13 05		13 14			13 20				13 35	13 44						13 50						14 05
Hendon d	13 08					13 23				13 38							13 53						14 08
Cricklewood d	13 13					13 28				13 43							13 58						14 13
WestHampsteadThameslink ⊖ d	13 16		13 21			13 31			13 39	13 46	13 51						14 01					14 09	14 16
Kentish Town ⊖ d	13 21					13 36	13 41			13 51							14 06	14 11					14 21
St Pancras International a	13 27		13 32		13 34		13 47		13 49	13 57	14 02			13 51		14 04		14 17		14 08		14 19	14 27
Farringdon ■ ⊖ a	13 31		13 36		13 39	13 46	13 51		13 54	14 01	14 06					14 09	14 16	14 21				14 24	14 31
City Thameslink ■ a	13 33		13 38		13 41	13 48	13 53		13 56	14 03	14 08					14 11	14 18	14 23				14 26	14 33
London Blackfriars a	13 36		13 41		13 43	13 51	13 56		13 58	14 06	14 11					14 13	14 21	14 26				14 28	14 36
London Bridge a																							
London Bridge a			13 47		13 51				14 04		14 17					14 21						14 34	
Elephant & Castle ⊖173,179 a	13 40					13 55	14 00			14 10							14 25	14 30					14 40
Gatwick Airport a					14 38				14 34							15 08						15 04	

	TL B	TL C	TL ■	TL A	TL D	TL C	TL ■ E	TL A	TL B	TL ■ F		EM ◇■ G (catering)	TL C	TL ■ H	TL A	TL D	TL ■ E	EM ◇■ I (catering)	TL C	TL ■ J	TL A		TL B	TL C
Bedford ■ d			13 35				13 49			14 05		14 12		←			14 19	14 23		←				
Flitwick d			13 46				14 00			14 16				14 16			14 30			14 30				
Harlington d			13 50				14 04			→				14 20			→			14 34				
Leagrave d			13 55				14 09							14 25						14 39				
Luton ■ d	13 48		13 59				14 13		14 18			14 28		14 29						14 43			14 48	
Luton Airport Parkway ■ ✈ d	13 51		14 02				14 16		14 21					14 32				14 39		14 46			14 51	
Harpenden d	13 56		14 08				14 22		14 26					14 38						14 52			14 56	
St Albans City d	14 01	14 07	14 13	←		14 22	14 27	←	14 31				14 37	14 43	←				14 52	14 57	←		15 01	15 07
Radlett d	14 06	14 12		14 12		14 27		14 27	14 36				14 42		14 42				14 57		14 57		15 06	15 12
Elstree & Borehamwood d	14 10	→		14 16		→		14 31	14 40				→		14 46				→		15 01		15 10	→
Mill Hill Broadway d	14 14			14 20				14 35	14 44						14 50						15 05		15 14	
Hendon d				14 23				14 38							14 53						15 08			
Cricklewood d				14 28				14 43							14 58						15 13			
WestHampsteadThameslink ⊖ d	14 21			14 31			14 39	14 46	14 51						15 01					15 09	15 16		15 21	
Kentish Town ⊖ d				14 36	14 41			14 51							15 06	15 11					15 21			
St Pancras International a	14 32		14 34		14 47		14 49	14 57	15 02			14 50		15 04		15 17		15 08		15 19	15 27		15 32	
Farringdon ■ ⊖ a	14 36		14 39	14 46	14 51		14 54	15 01	15 06					15 09	15 16	15 21				15 24	15 31		15 36	
City Thameslink ■ a	14 38		14 41	14 48	14 53		14 56	15 03	15 08					15 11	15 18	15 23				15 26	15 33		15 38	
London Blackfriars a	14 41		14 43	14 51	14 56		14 58	15 06	15 11					15 13	15 21	15 26				15 28	15 36		15 41	
London Bridge a																								
London Bridge a	14 47		14 51				15 04		15 17					15 21						15 34			15 47	
Elephant & Castle ⊖173,179 a				14 55	15 00			15 10							15 25	15 30					15 40			
Gatwick Airport a			15 38				15 34							16 08						16 04				

	TL ■	TL A	TL D	TL C	TL ■ E	TL A	TL B	TL ■ F		EM ◇■ G (catering)	TL C	TL ■ H	TL A	TL D	TL ■ E	EM ◇■ I (catering)	TL C	TL ■ J	TL A		TL B	TL C	TL ■	TL A
Bedford ■ d	14 35				14 49			15 05		15 11		←			15 19	15 23		←					15 35	
Flitwick d	14 46				15 00			15 16				15 16			15 30			15 30					15 46	
Harlington d	14 50				15 04			→				15 20			→			15 34					15 50	
Leagrave d	14 55				15 09							15 25						15 39					15 55	
Luton ■ d	14 59				15 13		15 18			15 28		15 29						15 43			15 48		15 59	
Luton Airport Parkway ■ ✈ d	15 02				15 16		15 21					15 32				15 38		15 46			15 51		16 02	
Harpenden d	15 08				15 22		15 26					15 38						15 52			15 56		16 08	
St Albans City d	15 13	←		15 22	15 27	←	15 31				15 37	15 43	←				15 52	15 57	←		16 01	16 07	16 13	←
Radlett d		15 12		15 27		15 27	15 36				15 42		15 42				15 57		15 57		16 06	16 12		16 12
Elstree & Borehamwood d		15 16		→		15 31	15 40				→		15 46				→		16 01		16 10	→		16 16
Mill Hill Broadway d		15 20				15 35	15 44						15 50						16 05		16 14			16 20
Hendon d		15 23				15 38							15 53						16 08					16 23
Cricklewood d		15 28				15 43							15 58						16 13					16 28
WestHampsteadThameslink ⊖ d		15 31			15 39	15 46	15 51						16 01					16 09	16 16		16 21			16 31
Kentish Town ⊖ d		15 36	15 41			15 51							16 06	16 11					16 21					16 36
St Pancras International a	15 34		15 47		15 49	15 57	16 02			15 51		16 04		16 17		16 05		16 19	16 27		16 32		16 34	
Farringdon ■ ⊖ a	15 39	15 46	15 51		15 54	16 01	16 06					16 09	16 16	16 21				16 24	16 31		16 36		16 39	16 46
City Thameslink ■ a	15 41	15 48	15 53		15 56	16 03	16 08					16 11	16 18	16 23				16 26	16 33		16 38		16 41	16 48
London Blackfriars a	15 43	15 51	15 56		15 58	16 06	16 11					16 13	16 21	16 26				16 28	16 36		16 41		16 43	16 51
London Bridge a																								
London Bridge a	15 51				16 04		16 17					16 21						16 34			16 47		16 51	
Elephant & Castle ⊖173,179 a		15 55	16 00			16 10							16 25	16 30					16 40					16 55
Gatwick Airport a	16 38				16 34							17 08						17 04					17 38	

A From St Albans City to Sutton (Surrey)
B To Rainham Kt
C To Sutton (Surrey)
D To Orpington
E To Brighton
F To Gatwick Airport
G From Corby
H From Bedford
I From Nottingham
J From Bedford to Brighton

Bedford, Luton and St Albans - London and Gatwick Airport

		TL	TL	TL	TL	TL	TL	EM	TL	TL	TL	TL	TL	EM	TL	TL	TL	TL	TL	TL	TL	TL	TL
				1			1	◇1		1			1	◇1		1				1			
		A	B	C	D	E	F	G ✠	B	H	D	A	C	I ✠	B	J	D	E	B		D	A	B
Bedford 7	d			15 49			16 05	16 12		←			16 19	16 23		←				16 35			
Flitwick	d			16 00			16 16			16 16			16 30			16 30				16 46			
Harlington	d			16 04			→			16 20			→			16 34				16 50			
Leagrave	d			16 09						16 25						16 39				16 55			
Luton 10	d			16 13		16 18		16 28		16 29						16 43		16 48		16 59			
Luton Airport Parkway 7 ✈	d			16 16		16 21				16 32				16 39		16 46		16 51		17 02			
Harpenden	d			16 22		16 26				16 38						16 52		16 56		17 08			
St Albans City	d		16 22	16 27	←	16 31			16 37	16 43	←				16 52	16 57	←	17 01	17 07	17 13	←		17 22
Radlett	d		16 27		16 27	16 36			16 42		16 42				16 57		16 57	17 06	17 12		17 12		17 27
Elstree & Borehamwood	d		→		16 31	16 40			→		16 46				→		17 01	17 10	→		17 16		→
Mill Hill Broadway	d				16 35	16 44					16 50						17 05	17 14			17 20		
Hendon	d				16 38						16 53						17 08				17 23		
Cricklewood	d				16 43						16 58						17 13				17 28		
WestHampsteadThameslink ⊖	d			16 39	16 46	16 51					17 01					17 09	17 16	17 21			17 31		
Kentish Town ⊖	d	16 41			16 51						17 06	17 11					17 21				17 36	17 41	
St Pancras International	a	16 47		16 49	16 57	17 02		16 50		17 04		17 17		17 08		17 19	17 27	17 32		17 34		17 47	
Farringdon 3 ⊖	a	16 51		16 54	17 01	17 06				17 09	17 16	17 21				17 24	17 31	17 36		17 39	17 46	17 51	
City Thameslink 3	a	16 53		16 56	17 03	17 08				17 11	17 18	17 23				17 26	17 33	17 38		17 41	17 48	17 53	
London Blackfriars	a	16 56		16 58	17 06	17 11				17 13	17 21	17 26				17 28	17 36	17 41		17 43	17 51	17 56	
London Bridge	a																						
London Bridge	a			17 04		17 17				17 21						17 34		17 47		17 51			
Elephant & Castle ⊖173,179	a	17 00			17 10						17 25	17 30					17 40				17 55	18 00	
Gatwick Airport	a			17 34						18 08						18 04				18 38			

		TL	TL	TL	TL	EM	TL	TL	TL	TL	TL	EM	TL	TL	TL	TL	TL	TL	TL	TL	TL	TL	TL
		1			1	◇1		1			1	◇1		1				1				1	
		C	D	E	F	G ✠	B	H	D	A	C	I ✠	B	J	D	E	B		D	A	B	C	D
Bedford 7	d	16 49			17 05	17 12		←			17 19	17 23		←				17 35				17 49	
Flitwick	d	17 00			17 16			17 16			17 30			17 30				17 46				18 00	
Harlington	d	17 04			→			17 20			→			17 34				17 50				18 04	
Leagrave	d	17 09						17 25						17 39				17 55				18 09	
Luton 10	d	17 13		17 18		17 28		17 29						17 43		17 48		17 59				18 13	
Luton Airport Parkway 7 ✈	d	17 16		17 21				17 32				17 39		17 46		17 51		18 02				18 16	
Harpenden	d	17 22		17 26				17 38						17 52		17 56		18 08				18 22	
St Albans City	d	17 27	←	17 31			17 37	17 43	←				17 52	17 57	←	18 01	18 07	18 13	←		18 22	18 27	←
Radlett	d		17 27	17 36			17 42		17 42				17 57		17 57	18 06	18 12		18 12		18 27		18 27
Elstree & Borehamwood	d		17 31	17 40			→		17 46				→		18 01	18 10	→		18 16		→		18 31
Mill Hill Broadway	d		17 35	17 44					17 50						18 05	18 14			18 20				18 35
Hendon	d		17 38						17 53						18 08				18 23				18 38
Cricklewood	d		17 43						17 58						18 13				18 28				18 43
WestHampsteadThameslink ⊖	d	17 39	17 46	17 51					18 01					18 09	18 16	18 21			18 31			18 39	18 46
Kentish Town ⊖	d		17 51						18 06	18 11					18 21				18 36	18 41			18 51
St Pancras International	a	17 49	17 57	18 02		17 51		18 04		18 17		18 08		18 19	18 27	18 32		18 34		18 47		18 49	18 57
Farringdon 3 ⊖	a	17 54	18 01	18 06				18 09	18 16	18 21				18 24	18 31	18 36		18 39	18 46	18 51		18 54	19 01
City Thameslink 3	a	17 56	18 03	18 08				18 11	18 18	18 23				18 26	18 33	18 38		18 41	18 48	18 53		18 56	19 03
London Blackfriars	a	17 58	18 06	18 11				18 13	18 21	18 26				18 28	18 36	18 41		18 43	18 51	18 56		18 58	19 06
London Bridge	a																						
London Bridge	a	18 04		18 17				18 21						18 34		18 47		18 51				19 04	
Elephant & Castle ⊖173,179	a		18 10						18 25	18 30					18 40				18 55	19 00			19 10
Gatwick Airport	a	18 34						19 08						19 04				19 38				19 34	

		TL	TL	EM	TL	TL	TL	TL	TL	EM	TL	TL	TL	TL	TL	TL	TL	TL	TL	TL	TL	TL
			1	◇1		1			1	◇1		1				1				1		
		E	F	G ✠	B	H	D	A	C	I ✠	B	J	D	E	B		D	A	B	C	D	E
Bedford 7	d		18 05	18 12		←			18 19	18 23		←				18 35				18 49		
Flitwick	d		18 16			18 16			18 30			18 30				18 46				19 00		
Harlington	d		→			18 20			→			18 34				18 50				19 04		
Leagrave	d					18 25						18 39				18 55				19 09		
Luton 10	d	18 18		18 28		18 29						18 43		18 48		18 59				19 13		19 18
Luton Airport Parkway 7 ✈	d	18 21				18 32				18 39		18 46		18 51		19 02				19 16		19 21
Harpenden	d	18 26				18 38						18 52		18 56		19 08				19 22		19 26
St Albans City	d	18 31			18 37	18 43	←				18 52	18 57	←	19 01	19 07	19 13	←		19 22	19 27	←	19 31
Radlett	d	18 36			18 42		18 42				18 57		18 57	19 06	19 12		19 12		19 27		19 27	19 36
Elstree & Borehamwood	d	18 40			→		18 46				→		19 01	19 10	→		19 16		→		19 31	19 40
Mill Hill Broadway	d	18 44					18 50						19 05	19 14			19 20				19 35	19 44
Hendon	d						18 53						19 08				19 23				19 38	
Cricklewood	d						18 58						19 13				19 28				19 43	
WestHampsteadThameslink ⊖	d	18 51					19 01					19 09	19 16	19 21			19 31			19 39	19 46	19 51
Kentish Town ⊖	d						19 06	19 11					19 21				19 36	19 41			19 51	
St Pancras International	a	19 02		18 50		19 04		19 17		19 08		19 19	19 27	19 32		19 34		19 47		19 49	19 57	20 02
Farringdon 3 ⊖	a	19 06				19 09	19 16	19 21				19 24	19 31	19 36		19 39	19 46	19 51		19 54	20 01	20 06
City Thameslink 3	a	19 08				19 11	19 18	19 23				19 26	19 33	19 38		19 41	19 48	19 53		19 56	20 03	20 08
London Blackfriars	a	19 11				19 13	19 21	19 26				19 28	19 36	19 41		19 43	19 51	19 56		19 58	20 06	20 11
London Bridge	a																					
London Bridge	a	19 17				19 21						19 34		19 47		19 51				20 04		20 17
Elephant & Castle ⊖173,179	a						19 25	19 30					19 40				19 55	20 00			20 10	
Gatwick Airport	a					20 08						20 04				20 38				20 34		

A To Orpington
B To Sutton (Surrey)
C To Brighton
D From St Albans City to Sutton (Surrey)
E To Rainham Kt
F To Gatwick Airport
G From Corby
H From Bedford
I From Nottingham
J From Bedford to Brighton

Bedford, Luton and St Albans - London and Gatwick Airport

		TL	EM	TL	TL	TL	TL	TL	EM	TL	TL	TL	TL	TL	TL	TL	TL	TL	TL	TL	TL	TL	EM
		1	◇1		1			1	◇1		1				1				1			1	◇1
		A	B ✠	C	D	E	F	G	H ✠	C	I	E	J	C		E	F	C	G	E	J	K	B ✠
Bedford 7	d	19 05	19 12		←			19 19	19 23		←				19 35				19 49			20 05	20 12
Flitwick	d	19 16			19 16			19 30			19 30				19 46				20 00			20 16	
Harlington	d	→			19 20			→			19 34				19 50				20 04			→	
Leagrave	d				19 25						19 39				19 55				20 09				
Luton 10	d		19 28		19 29						19 43		19 48		19 59				20 13		20 18		20 28
Luton Airport Parkway 7 ✈	d				19 32				19 39		19 46		19 51		20 02				20 16		20 21		
Harpenden	d				19 38						19 52		19 56		20 08				20 22		20 26		
St Albans City	d			19 37	19 43	←				19 52	19 57	←	20 01	20 07	20 13	←		20 22	20 27	←	20 31		
Radlett	d			19 42		19 42				19 57		19 57	20 06	20 12		20 12		20 27		20 27	20 36		
Elstree & Borehamwood	d			→		19 46				→		20 01	20 10	→		20 16		→		20 31	20 40		
Mill Hill Broadway	d					19 50						20 05	20 14			20 20				20 35	20 44		
Hendon	d					19 53						20 08				20 23				20 38			
Cricklewood	d					19 58						20 13				20 28				20 43			
WestHampsteadThameslink ⊖	d					20 01					20 09	20 16	20 21			20 31			20 39	20 46	20 51		
Kentish Town ⊖	d					20 06	20 11					20 21				20 36	20 41			20 51			
St Pancras International	a		19 51		20 04		20 17		20 08		20 19	20 27	20 32		20 34		20 47		20 49	20 57	21 02		20 51
Farringdon 3 ⊖	a				20 09	20 16	20 21				20 24	20 31	20 36		20 39	20 46	20 51		20 54	21 01	21 06		
City Thameslink 3	a				20 11	20 18	20 23				20 26	20 33	20 38		20 41	20 48	20 53		20 56				
London Blackfriars	a				20 13	20 21	20 26				20 28	20 36	20 41		20 43	20 51	20 56		20 58	21 06	21 11		
London Bridge	a																						
London Bridge	a				20 21						20 34		20 47		20 51				21 04		21 17		
Elephant & Castle ⊖173,179	a					20 25	20 30					20 40				20 55	21 00			21 10			
Gatwick Airport	a				21 08						21 04				21 38				21 34				

		TL	TL	TL	TL	TL	EM	TL	TL	TL	TL	TL	TL	TL	TL	TL	TL	TL	TL	TL	EM	TL	TL
			1			1	◇1		1				1				1			1	◇1		1
		C	L	E	F	G	H ✠	C	I	E	J	C	K	E	F	C	G	E	J	K	B ✠	C	L
Bedford 7	d		←			20 19	20 23		←				20 35				20 49			21 05	21 12		←
Flitwick	d		20 16			20 30			20 30				20 46				21 00			21 16			21 16
Harlington	d		20 20			→			20 34				20 50				21 04			→			21 20
Leagrave	d		20 25						20 39				20 55				21 09						21 25
Luton 10	d		20 29						20 43		20 48		20 59				21 13		21 18		21 28		21 29
Luton Airport Parkway 7 ✈	d		20 32				20 39		20 46		20 51		21 02				21 16		21 21				21 32
Harpenden	d		20 38						20 52		20 56		21 08				21 22		21 26				21 38
St Albans City	d	20 37	20 43	←				20 52	20 57	←	21 01	21 07	21 13	←		21 22	21 27	←	21 31			21 37	21 43
Radlett	d	20 42		20 42				20 57		20 57	21 06	21 12		21 12		21 27		21 27	21 36			21 42	
Elstree & Borehamwood	d	→		20 46				→		21 01	21 10	→		21 16		→		21 31	21 40			→	
Mill Hill Broadway	d			20 50						21 05	21 14			21 20				21 35	21 44				
Hendon	d			20 53						21 08				21 23				21 38					
Cricklewood	d			20 58						21 13				21 28				21 43					
WestHampsteadThameslink ⊖	d			21 01					21 09	21 16	21 21			21 31			21 39	21 46	21 51				
Kentish Town ⊖	d			21 06	21 11					21 21				21 36	21 41			21 51					
St Pancras International	a		21 04		21 17		21 08		21 19	21 27	21 32		21 34		21 47		21 49	21 57	22 02		21 51		22 04
Farringdon 3 ⊖	a		21 09	21 16	21 21				21 24	21 31	21 36		21 39	21 46	21 51		21 54	22 01	22 06				22 09
City Thameslink 3	a																						
London Blackfriars	a		21 13	21 21	21 26				21 28	21 36	21 41		21 43	21 51	21 56		21 58	22 06	22 11				22 13
London Bridge	a																						
London Bridge	a		21 21						21 34		21 47		21 51				22 04		22 17				22 21
Elephant & Castle ⊖173,179	a			21 25	21 30					21 40				21 55	22 00			22 10					
Gatwick Airport	a		22 08						22 04				22 38				22 34						23 08

		TL	TL	TL	EM	TL	TL	TL	TL	TL	TL	TL	TL	TL	TL	TL	TL	TL	TL	TL	TL	EM	TL
				1	◇1		1				1				1				1		1	◇1	1
		E	F	G	H ✠	C	I	E	M	C	K	E	F	C	G	E	M	C		E	G	H ✠	I
Bedford 7	d			21 19	21 26		←				21 35				21 49				22 05		22 17	22 20	←
Flitwick	d			21 30			21 30				21 46				22 00				22 16		22 28		22 28
Harlington	d			→			21 34				21 50				22 04				22 20		→		22 32
Leagrave	d						21 39				21 55				22 09				22 25				22 37
Luton 10	d						21 43		21 48		21 59				22 13		22 18		22 29			22 35	22 41
Luton Airport Parkway 7 ✈	d				21 42		21 46		21 51		22 02				22 16		22 21		22 32			22 38	22 44
Harpenden	d						21 52		21 56		22 08				22 22		22 26		22 38				22 49
St Albans City	d	←				21 52	21 57	←	22 01	22 07	22 13	←		22 22	22 27	←	22 31	22 37	22 43	←			22 56
Radlett	d	21 42				21 57		21 57	22 06	22 12		22 12		22 27		22 27	22 36	22 42		22 42			
Elstree & Borehamwood	d	21 46				→		22 01	22 10	→		22 16		→		22 31	22 40	→		22 46			
Mill Hill Broadway	d	21 50						22 05	22 14			22 20				22 35	22 44			22 50			
Hendon	d	21 53						22 08				22 23				22 38				22 53			
Cricklewood	d	21 58						22 13				22 28				22 43				22 58			
WestHampsteadThameslink ⊖	d	22 01					22 09	22 16	22 21			22 31			22 39	22 46	22 51			23 01			23 12
Kentish Town ⊖	d	22 06	22 11					22 21				22 36	22 41			22 51				23 06			
St Pancras International	a		22 17		22 09		22 19	22 27	22 32		22 34		22 47		22 49	22 57	23 02		23 04			23 11	23 22
Farringdon 3 ⊖	a	22 16	22 21				22 24	22 31	22 36		22 39	22 46	22 51		22 54	23 01	23 06		23 09	23 16			23 26
City Thameslink 3	a																						
London Blackfriars	a	22 21	22 26				22 28	22 36	22 41		22 43	22 51	22 56		22 58	23 06	23 11		23 13	23 21			23 30
London Bridge	a																						
London Bridge	a						22 34		22 47		22 51				23 04		23 17		23 20				23 36
Elephant & Castle ⊖173,179	a	22 25	22 30					22 40				22 55	23 00			23 10				23 25			
Gatwick Airport	a						23 04				23 37				23 34				00 01				00 17

A To Gatwick Airport
B From Corby
C To Sutton (Surrey)
D From Bedford
E From St Albans City to Sutton (Surrey)
F To Orpington
G To Brighton
H From Nottingham
I From Bedford to Brighton
J To Rainham Kt
K To Three Bridges
L From Bedford to Three Bridges
M To Gillingham (Kent)

Table T052MML-R

Saturdays
26 May to 8 December

Bedford, Luton and St Albans - London and Gatwick Airport

Station		TL A	EM ◇ B	TL C	TL D	TL C
Bedford	d		22 39	22 45	23 05	23 35
Flitwick	d			22 56	23 16	23 46
Harlington	d			23 00	23 20	23 50
Leagrave	d			23 05	23 25	23 55
Luton	d		22 56	23 10	23 30	23 59
Luton Airport Parkway ✈	d			23 13	23 33	00 03
Harpenden	d			23 18	23 38	00 08
St Albans City	d	23 09		23 25	23 45	00 15
Radlett	d	23 14			23 50	00 20
Elstree & Borehamwood	d	23 18			23 54	00 24
Mill Hill Broadway	d	23 22			23 58	00 28
Hendon	d	23 25			00 01	00 31
Cricklewood	d	23 30			00 06	00 36
WestHampsteadThameslink ⊖	d	23 33		23 41	00 09	00 39
Kentish Town ⊖	d	23 38			00 13	00 43
St Pancras International	a	23 44	23 29	23 51	00 19	00 49
Farringdon ⊖	a	23 48		23 55	00 25	
City Thameslink	a					
London Blackfriars	a	23 53		23 59	00 30	01 00
London Bridge	a					
London Bridge	a					
Elephant & Castle ⊖173,179	a	23 57				
Gatwick Airport	a			00 48	01 20	01 56

Sundays
20 May to 2 December

Station		TL E	TL F	TL	TL	TL	TL	TL	TL	TL	EM ◇ G	TL C	TL H	TL A	TL D	EM ◇ B	TL C	TL H	TL A	TL	EM ◇ G	TL C	TL H
Bedford	d			05 40	06 05	06 35	07 05	07 35		08 05	08 15	08 19			08 35	08 45	08 49			09 05	09 15	09 19	
Flitwick	d			05 51	06 16	06 46	07 16	07 46		08 16		08 30			08 46		09 00			09 16		09 30	
Harlington	d			05 55	06 20	06 50	07 20	07 50		08 20		08 34			08 50		09 04			09 20		09 34	
Leagrave	d			06 00	06 25	06 55	07 25	07 55		08 25		08 39			08 55		09 09			09 25		09 39	
Luton	d			06 05	06 30	07 00	07 30	08 00	08 04	08 30	08 35	08 44		08 48	09 00		09 14		09 18	09 30	09 35	09 44	
Luton Airport Parkway ✈	d		00 03	06 08	06 33	07 03	07 33	08 03	08 07	08 33		08 47		08 51	09 03	09 06	09 17		09 21	09 33		09 47	
Harpenden	d		00 08	06 13	06 38	07 08	07 38	08 08	08 12	08 38		08 52		08 56	09 08		09 22		09 26	09 38		09 52	
St Albans City	d		00 15	06 20	06 45	07 15	07 45	08 15	08 19	08 45		08 59		09 03	09 15		09 29		09 33	09 45		09 59	
Radlett	d		00 20	06 25	06 50	07 20	07 50		08 24					09 09					09 39				
Elstree & Borehamwood	d		00 24	06 29	06 54	07 24	07 54		08 28					09 12					09 42				
Mill Hill Broadway	d		00 28	06 33	06 58	07 28	07 58		08 32					09 16					09 46				
Hendon	d	00 01	00 31	06 36	07 01	07 31	08 01		08 35					09 19					09 49				
Cricklewood	d	00 06	00 36	06 41	07 06	07 36	08 06		08 40					09 24					09 54				
WestHampsteadThameslink ⊖	d	00 09	00 39	06 44	07 09	07 39	08 09	08 31	08 43	09 01		09 15	09 20	09 26	09 30		09 45	09 50	09 56	10 00		10 15	
Kentish Town ⊖	d	00 13	00 43	06 50	07 15	07 45	08 15		08 49				09 26	09 31				09 56	10 01				10 26
St Pancras International	a	00 19	00 49	06 55	07 20	07 50	08 20	08 40	08 55	09 10	09 13	09 25	09 31	09 37	09 40	09 42	09 55	10 01	10 07	10 10	10 11	10 25	10 31
Farringdon ⊖	a	00 25										09 30	09 36	09 42	09 45		10 00	10 06	10 12	10 15		10 30	10 36
City Thameslink	a																						
London Blackfriars	a	00 30	01 00									09 34	09 40	09 46	09 49		10 04	10 10	10 16	10 19		10 34	10 40
London Bridge	a																						
London Bridge	a											09 40	09 46		09 55		10 10	10 16		10 25		10 40	10 46
Elephant & Castle ⊖173,179	a													09 50					10 20				
Gatwick Airport	a	01 20	01 56									10 09			10 41		10 39			11 09		11 09	

Station		TL A	TL D	EM ◇ B	TL C	TL H	TL A	TL	EM ◇ I	TL C	TL H	TL A	TL D	EM ◇ B	TL C	TL H	TL A	TL	EM ◇ I	TL C	TL H	TL A	TL A
Bedford	d		09 35	09 45	09 49			10 05	10 15	10 19			10 35	10 45	10 49			11 05	11 15	11 19			
Flitwick	d		09 46		10 00			10 16		10 30			10 46		11 00			11 16		11 30			
Harlington	d		09 50		10 04			10 20		10 34			10 50		11 04			11 20		11 34			
Leagrave	d		09 55		10 09			10 25		10 39			10 55		11 09			11 25		11 39			
Luton	d	09 48	10 00		10 14		10 18	10 30	10 34	10 44		10 48	11 00		11 14		11 18	11 30	11 35	11 44		11 48	11 58
Luton Airport Parkway ✈	d	09 51	10 03	10 06	10 17		10 21	10 33		10 47		10 51	11 03	11 06	11 17		11 21	11 33		11 47		11 51	12 01
Harpenden	d	09 56	10 08		10 22		10 26	10 38		10 52		10 56	11 08		11 22		11 26	11 38		11 52		11 56	12 06
St Albans City	d	10 03	10 15		10 29		10 33	10 45		10 59		11 03	11 15		11 29		11 33	11 45		11 59		12 03	12 16
Radlett	d	10 09					10 39					11 09					11 39					12 08	12 21
Elstree & Borehamwood	d	10 12					10 42					11 12					11 42					12 12	→
Mill Hill Broadway	d	10 16					10 46					11 16					11 46					12 16	
Hendon	d	10 19					10 49					11 19					11 49					12 19	
Cricklewood	d	10 24					10 54					11 24					11 54					12 24	
WestHampsteadThameslink ⊖	d	10 26	10 30		10 45		10 56	11 00		11 15		11 26	11 30		11 45		11 56	12 00		12 15		12 26	
Kentish Town ⊖	d	10 31				10 56	11 01				11 26	11 31				11 56	12 01				12 26	12 31	
St Pancras International	a	10 37	10 40	10 42	10 55	11 01	11 07	11 10	11 10	11 25	11 31	11 37	11 40	11 42	11 55	12 01	12 07	12 10	12 12	12 25	12 31	12 37	
Farringdon ⊖	a	10 42	10 45		11 00	11 06	11 12	11 15		11 30	11 36	11 42	11 45		12 00	12 06	12 12	12 15		12 30	12 36	12 42	
City Thameslink	a																						
London Blackfriars	a	10 46	10 49		11 04	11 10	11 16	11 19		11 34	11 40	11 46	11 49		12 04	12 10	12 16	12 19		12 34	12 40	12 46	
London Bridge	a																						
London Bridge	a		10 55		11 10	11 16		11 25		11 40	11 46		11 55		12 10	12 16		12 25		12 40	12 46		
Elephant & Castle ⊖173,179	a	10 50					11 20					11 50					12 20					12 50	
Gatwick Airport	a		11 41		11 39			12 09		12 09			12 41		12 39			13 09		13 09			

A To Sutton (Surrey)
B From Nottingham
C To Brighton
D To Three Bridges
E not 20 May. From Bedford to Three Bridges
F not 20 May. From Bedford to Brighton
G From Derby
H To Rainham Kt
I From Sheffield

Table T052MML-R

Sundays
20 May to 2 December

Bedford, Luton and St Albans - London and Gatwick Airport

Station		TL A	TL B	TL C	EM ◇ D	TL E	TL F	TL G	TL H	EM ◇ I	TL G	TL J	TL K	TL C	TL F	TL G	TL G	TL A	TL K	TL C	EM ◇ L	TL E	TL F
Bedford	d	11 37		11 51	11 57	←			12 07	12 15		←		12 21				12 37		12 51	13 02	←	
Flitwick	d	11 48		12 02		12 02			12 18			12 18		12 32				12 48		13 02		13 02	
Harlington	d	11 52		→		12 06			→			12 22		12 36				12 52		→		13 06	
Leagrave	d	11 57				12 11						12 27		12 41				12 57				13 11	
Luton	d	12 02				12 16		12 22		12 30		12 32		12 46		12 52		13 02				13 16	
Luton Airport Parkway ✈	d	12 05			12 13	12 19		12 25				12 35		12 49		12 55		13 05			13 18	13 19	
Harpenden	d	12 10				12 24		12 30				12 40		12 54		13 00		13 10				13 24	
St Albans City	d	12 17	←			12 30		12 37			12 46	12 47	←	13 00		13 07	13 16	13 17	←			13 30	
Radlett	d		12 21					12 42			12 51		12 51			13 12	13 21		13 21				
Elstree & Borehamwood	d		12 25					12 46			→		12 55			13 16	→		13 25				
Mill Hill Broadway	d		12 29					12 50					12 59			13 20			13 29				
Hendon	d		12 32										13 02						13 32				
Cricklewood	d		12 37										13 07						13 37				
WestHampsteadThameslink ⊖	d	12 30	12 39			12 45		12 56				13 00	13 09	13 15		13 26		13 30	13 39			13 45	
Kentish Town ⊖	d		12 44				12 56						13 14		13 26				13 44				13 56
St Pancras International	a	12 40	12 50		12 41	12 55	13 01	13 07		12 54		13 10	13 20	13 25	13 31	13 37		13 40	13 50		13 44	13 55	14 01
Farringdon ⊖	a	12 45	12 55			13 00	13 06	13 12				13 15	13 25	13 30	13 36	13 42		13 45	13 55			14 00	14 06
City Thameslink	a																						
London Blackfriars	a	12 49	12 59			13 04	13 10	13 16				13 19	13 29	13 34	13 40	13 46		13 49	13 59			14 04	14 10
London Bridge	a																						
London Bridge	a	12 55				13 10	13 16					13 25		13 40	13 46			13 55				14 10	14 16
Elephant & Castle ⊖173,179	a		13 03					13 20					13 33			13 50			14 03				
Gatwick Airport	a	13 41				13 39						14 09		14 09				14 41				14 39	

Station		TL G	TL	TL G	TL C	TL F	TL G	TL A	EM ◇ M	TL G	TL N	TL K	TL C	TL F	TL G	TL H	EM ◇ D	TL J	TL G	TL C	TL F	TL G	TL A
Bedford	d		13 05		13 21			13 37	13 44		←		13 51			14 05	14 15	←		14 21			14 37
Flitwick	d		13 16		13 32			13 47			13 47		14 02			14 16		14 16		14 32			14 48
Harlington	d		13 20		13 36			→			13 52		14 06			→		14 20		14 36			→
Leagrave	d		13 25		13 41						13 57		14 11					14 25		14 41			
Luton	d	13 22	13 29		13 46		13 52		14 01		14 02		14 16		14 22			14 29		14 46		14 52	
Luton Airport Parkway ✈	d	13 25	13 32		13 49		13 55				14 05		14 19		14 25		14 31	14 32		14 49		14 55	
Harpenden	d	13 30	13 37		13 54		14 00				14 10		14 24		14 30			14 37		14 54		15 00	
St Albans City	d	13 37	13 43	13 47	14 00		14 07			14 16	14 17	←	14 30		14 37			14 43	14 47	15 00		15 07	
Radlett	d	13 42		13 52			14 12			14 21		14 21			14 42				14 52			15 12	
Elstree & Borehamwood	d	13 46		13 56			14 16			→		14 25			14 46				14 56			15 16	
Mill Hill Broadway	d	13 50		13 59			14 20					14 29			14 50				14 59			15 20	
Hendon	d			14 03								14 32							15 03				
Cricklewood	d			14 07								14 37							15 07				
WestHampsteadThameslink ⊖	d	13 56	14 00	14 09	14 15		14 26				14 30	14 39	14 45		14 56			15 00	15 09	15 15		15 26	
Kentish Town ⊖	d			14 14		14 26						14 44		14 56					15 14		15 26		
St Pancras International	a	14 07	14 10	14 20	14 25	14 31	14 37		14 24		14 40	14 50	14 55	15 01	15 07		14 59	15 10	15 20	15 25	15 31	15 37	
Farringdon ⊖	a	14 12	14 15	14 25	14 30	14 36	14 42				14 45	14 55	15 00	15 06	15 12			15 15	15 25	15 30	15 36	15 42	
City Thameslink	a																						
London Blackfriars	a	14 16	14 19	14 29	14 34	14 40	14 46				14 49	14 59	15 04	15 10	15 16			15 19	15 29	15 34	15 40	15 46	
London Bridge	a																						
London Bridge	a		14 25		14 40	14 46					14 55		15 10	15 16				15 25		15 40	15 46		
Elephant & Castle ⊖173,179	a	14 20		14 33			14 50					15 03			15 20				15 33			15 50	
Gatwick Airport	a		15 09		15 09						15 41		15 39					16 09		16 09			

Station		EM ◇ M	TL G	TL N	TL K	TL C	TL F	TL G	TL H	EM ◇ D	TL J	TL G	TL C	TL F	TL G	TL A	EM ◇ M	TL G	TL N	TL K	TL C	TL F
Bedford	d	14 46		←		14 51			15 05	15 15	←		15 21			15 37	15 46		←		15 51	
Flitwick	d			14 48		15 02			15 16		15 16		15 32			15 48			15 48		16 02	
Harlington	d			14 52		15 06			→		15 20		15 36			→			15 52		16 06	
Leagrave	d			14 57		15 11					15 25		15 41						15 57		16 11	
Luton	d	15 01		15 02		15 16		15 22			15 29		15 46		15 52		16 01		16 02		16 16	
Luton Airport Parkway ✈	d			15 05		15 19		15 25		15 31	15 32		15 49		15 55				16 05		16 19	
Harpenden	d			15 10		15 24		15 30			15 37		15 54		16 00				16 10		16 24	
St Albans City	d		15 16	15 17	←	15 30		15 37			15 43	15 47	16 00		16 07			16 16	16 17	←	16 30	
Radlett	d		15 21		15 21			15 42				15 52			16 12			16 21		16 21		
Elstree & Borehamwood	d		→		15 25			15 46				15 56			16 16			→		16 25		
Mill Hill Broadway	d				15 29			15 50				15 59			16 20					16 29		
Hendon	d				15 32							16 03								16 32		
Cricklewood	d				15 37							16 07								16 37		
WestHampsteadThameslink ⊖	d			15 30	15 39	15 45		15 56			16 00	16 09	16 15		16 26				16 30	16 39	16 45	
Kentish Town ⊖	d				15 44		15 56					16 14		16 26						16 44		16 56
St Pancras International	a	15 24		15 40	15 50	15 55	16 01	16 07		15 59	16 10	16 20	16 25	16 31	16 37		16 24		16 40	16 50	16 55	17 01
Farringdon ⊖	a			15 45	15 55	16 00	16 06	16 12			16 15	16 25	16 30	16 36	16 42				16 45	16 55	17 00	17 06
City Thameslink	a																					
London Blackfriars	a			15 49	15 59	16 04	16 10	16 16			16 19	16 29	16 34	16 40	16 46				16 49	16 59	17 04	17 10
London Bridge	a																					
London Bridge	a			15 55		16 10	16 16				16 25		16 40	16 46					16 55		17 10	17 16
Elephant & Castle ⊖173,179	a				16 03			16 20				16 33			16 50					17 03		
Gatwick Airport	a			16 41		16 39					17 09		17 09						17 41		17 39	

A To Three Bridges
B From Luton to Sutton (Surrey)
C To Brighton
D From Nottingham
E From Bedford to Brighton
F To Rainham Kt
G To Sutton (Surrey)
H To Gatwick Airport
I From Sheffield
J From Bedford
K From St Albans City to Sutton (Surrey)
L From Leeds
M From Corby
N From Bedford to Three Bridges

Bedford, Luton and St Albans - London and Gatwick Airport

Station		TL A	TL ■ B	EM ◇■ C	TL ■ D	TL A	EM ◇■ E	EM ◇■ F	TL ■ G	TL H	TL A	TL A	TL ■ I	TL J	TL ■ G	TL H	TL A	TL ■ B	EM ◇■ C	TL ■ D	TL A	TL ■ G	EM ◇■ K
Bedford ■	d		16 05	16 09	←				16 21				16 37		16 51			17 05	17 09	←		17 21	17 28
Flitwick	d		16 16		16 16				16 32				16 48		17 02			17 16		17 16		17 32	
Harlington	d		→		16 20				16 36				16 52		17 06			→		17 20		17 36	
Leagrave	d				16 25				16 41				16 57		17 11					17 25		17 41	
Luton ■	d	16 22			16 29		16 41	16 42	16 46		16 52		17 02		17 16		17 22			17 29		17 46	17 46
Luton Airport Parkway ■ ✈	d	16 25		16 25	16 32				16 49		16 55		17 05		17 19		17 25		17 26	17 32		17 49	
Harpenden	d	16 30			16 37				16 54		17 00		17 10		17 24		17 30			17 37		17 54	
St Albans City	d	16 37			16 43	16 47			17 00		17 07	17 16	17 17	←	17 30		17 37			17 43	17 47	18 00	
Radlett	d	16 42				16 52					17 12	17 21		17 21			17 42				17 52		
Elstree & Borehamwood	d	16 46				16 56					17 16	→		17 25			17 46				17 56		
Mill Hill Broadway	d	16 50				16 59					17 20			17 29			17 50				17 59		
Hendon	d					17 03								17 32							18 03		
Cricklewood	d					17 07								17 37							18 07		
WestHampsteadThameslink ⊖	d	16 56			17 00	17 09			17 15		17 26		17 30	17 39	17 45		17 56			18 00	18 09	18 15	
Kentish Town ⊖	d					17 14				17 26				17 44		17 56					18 14		
St Pancras International	a	17 07		16 48	17 10	17 20	17 05	17 06	17 25	17 31	17 37		17 40	17 50	17 55	18 01	18 07		17 50	18 10	18 20	18 25	18 11
Farringdon ■ ⊖	a	17 12			17 15	17 25			17 30	17 36	17 42		17 45	17 55	18 00	18 06	18 12			18 15	18 25	18 30	
City Thameslink ■	a																						
London Blackfriars	a	17 16			17 19	17 29			17 34	17 40	17 46		17 49	17 59	18 04	18 10	18 16			18 19	18 29	18 34	
London Bridge	a																						
London Bridge	a				17 25				17 40	17 46			17 55		18 10	18 16				18 25		18 40	
Elephant & Castle ⊖173,179	a	17 20				17 33					17 50			18 03			18 20				18 33		
Gatwick Airport	a				18 09				18 09				18 41		18 39					19 09		19 09	

Station		TL H	TL A	TL A	TL ■ I	TL J	TL ■ G	TL H	TL A	TL ■ B	EM ◇■ C	EM ◇■ L	TL A	TL ■ D	TL J	TL ■ G	TL H	TL A	TL A	TL ■ I	TL J	TL ■ G	TL H
Bedford ■	d				17 37		17 51			18 07	18 08	18 17		←		18 21				18 37		18 51	
Flitwick	d				17 48		18 02			18 18				18 18		18 32				18 48		19 02	
Harlington	d				17 52		18 06			→				18 22		18 36				18 52		19 06	
Leagrave	d				17 57		18 11							18 27		18 41				18 57		19 11	
Luton ■	d		17 52		18 02		18 16		18 22			18 32		18 32		18 46		18 52		19 02		19 16	
Luton Airport Parkway ■ ✈	d		17 55		18 05		18 19		18 25		18 25			18 35		18 49		18 55		19 05		19 19	
Harpenden	d		18 00		18 10		18 24		18 30					18 40		18 54		19 00		19 10		19 24	
St Albans City	d		18 07	18 16	18 17	←	18 30		18 37				18 46	18 47	←	19 00		19 07	19 16	19 17	←	19 30	
Radlett	d		18 12	18 21		18 21			18 42				18 51		18 51			19 12	19 21		19 21		
Elstree & Borehamwood	d		18 16	→		18 25			18 46				→		18 55			19 16	→		19 25		
Mill Hill Broadway	d		18 20			18 29			18 50						18 59			19 20			19 29		
Hendon	d					18 32									19 02						19 32		
Cricklewood	d					18 37									19 07						19 37		
WestHampsteadThameslink ⊖	d		18 26		18 30	18 39	18 45		18 57					19 00	19 09	19 15		19 26		19 30	19 39	19 45	
Kentish Town ⊖	d	18 26				18 44		18 56							19 14		19 26				19 44		19 56
St Pancras International	a	18 31	18 37		18 40	18 50	18 55	19 01	19 07		18 47	18 55		19 10	19 20	19 25	19 31	19 37		19 40	19 50	19 55	20 01
Farringdon ■ ⊖	a	18 36	18 42		18 45	18 55	19 00	19 06	19 12					19 15	19 25	19 30	19 36	19 42		19 45	19 55	20 00	20 06
City Thameslink ■	a																						
London Blackfriars	a	18 40	18 46		18 49	18 59	19 04	19 10	19 16					19 19	19 29	19 34	19 40	19 46		19 49	19 59	20 04	20 10
London Bridge	a																						
London Bridge	a	18 46			18 55		19 10	19 16						19 25		19 40	19 46			19 55		20 10	20 16
Elephant & Castle ⊖173,179	a		18 50			19 03			19 20						19 33			19 50			20 03		
Gatwick Airport	a				19 41		19 39							20 09		20 09				20 41		20 39	

Station		TL A	TL ■ B	EM ◇■ C	TL ■ D	TL A	TL ■ G	EM ◇■ L	TL ■ M	TL H	TL A	TL ■	TL A	TL ■ G	EM ◇■ C	TL ■ M	TL H	TL A	TL ■ I	EM ◇■ C	TL A	TL ■ N	TL J
Bedford ■	d		19 05	19 09	←		19 21	19 28	←			19 35		19 51	19 59	←			20 07	20 10		←	
Flitwick	d		19 16		19 16		19 32		19 32			19 46		20 02		20 02			20 18			20 18	
Harlington	d		→		19 20		→		19 36			19 50		→		20 06			→			20 22	
Leagrave	d				19 25				19 41			19 55				20 11						20 27	
Luton ■	d	19 22			19 29			19 45	19 46		19 52	19 59			20 15	20 16		20 22				20 32	
Luton Airport Parkway ■ ✈	d	19 25		19 25	19 32				19 49		19 55	20 02				20 19		20 25		20 26		20 35	
Harpenden	d	19 30			19 37				19 54		20 00	20 07				20 24		20 30				20 40	
St Albans City	d	19 37			19 43	19 47			20 00		20 07	20 13	20 17			20 30		20 37			20 46	20 47	←
Radlett	d	19 42				19 52					20 12		20 22					20 42			20 51		20 51
Elstree & Borehamwood	d	19 46				19 56					20 16		20 26					20 46			→		20 55
Mill Hill Broadway	d	19 50				19 59					20 20		20 29					20 50					20 59
Hendon	d					20 03							20 33										21 02
Cricklewood	d					20 07							20 37										21 07
WestHampsteadThameslink ⊖	d	19 56			20 00	20 09			20 15		20 26	20 30	20 39			20 45		20 57				21 00	21 09
Kentish Town ⊖	d					20 14				20 26			20 44				20 56						21 14
St Pancras International	a	20 07		19 50	20 10	20 20		20 08	20 25	20 31	20 37	20 40	20 50		20 39	20 55	21 01	21 07		20 50		21 10	21 20
Farringdon ■ ⊖	a	20 12			20 15	20 25			20 30	20 36	20 42	20 45	20 55			21 00	21 06	21 12				21 15	21 25
City Thameslink ■	a																						
London Blackfriars	a	20 16			20 19	20 29			20 34	20 40	20 46	20 49	20 59			21 04	21 10	21 16				21 19	21 29
London Bridge	a																						
London Bridge	a				20 25				20 40	20 46		20 55				21 10	21 16					21 25	
Elephant & Castle ⊖173,179	a	20 20				20 33					20 50		21 03					21 20					21 33
Gatwick Airport	a				21 09				21 09			21 39				21 39						22 09	

A To Sutton (Surrey)
B To Gatwick Airport
C From Nottingham
D From Bedford
E until 2 September, from 14 October, not 19 August. From Sheffield
F 19 August, 9 September, 16 September, 23 September, 30 September, 7 October. From Sheffield
G To Brighton
H To Rainham Kt
I To Three Bridges
J From St Albans City to Sutton (Surrey)
K From Leeds
L From Derby
M From Bedford to Brighton
N From Bedford to Three Bridges

Table T052MML-R

Sundays

20 May to 2 December

Bedford, Luton and St Albans - London and Gatwick Airport

Station		TL ■ A	TL B	TL C	TL ■ D	EM ◇■ E	EM ◇■ F	TL ■ G	TL B	TL ■ A	TL H	EM ◇■ I	TL ■	TL J	TL ■ A	EM ◇■ K	EM ◇■ L	TL ■ M	TL N	TL J	TL ■ A	TL N	TL ■ A
Bedford ■	d	20 21			20 37	20 40	20 41	←		20 51		21 09	21 09		21 21	21 29	21 29	←			21 51		22 11
Flitwick	d	20 32			20 48			20 48		21 02			21 20		21 32			21 32			22 02		22 22
Harlington	d	20 36			→			20 52		21 06			21 24		→			21 36			22 06		22 26
Leagrave	d	20 41						20 57		21 11			21 29					21 41			22 11		22 31
Luton ■	d	20 46		20 52		20 55	20 56	21 02		21 16		21 24	21 33			21 44	21 45	21 46			22 16		22 36
Luton Airport Parkway ■ ✈	d	20 49		20 55		20 58	20 59	21 05		21 19			21 36					21 49			22 19		22 39
Harpenden	d	20 54		21 00				21 10		21 24			21 41					21 54			22 24		22 44
St Albans City	d	21 00		21 07				21 17	21 27	21 31	←		21 48	21 57				22 01	←	22 27	22 31	←	22 51
Radlett	d			21 12					21 32		21 32			22 02					22 02	22 32		22 32	22 56
Elstree & Borehamwood	d			21 16					→		21 36			→					22 06	→		22 36	23 00
Mill Hill Broadway	d			21 20							21 40								22 10			22 40	23 04
Hendon	d										21 43								22 13			22 43	23 07
Cricklewood	d										21 48								22 18			22 48	23 12
WestHampsteadThameslink ⊖	d	21 15		21 26				21 30		21 45	21 50		22 00					22 15	22 20		22 45	22 50	23 14
Kentish Town ⊖	d		21 26								21 55								22 25			22 55	23 19
St Pancras International	a	21 25	21 31	21 37		21 21	21 22	21 40		21 55	22 01	21 48	22 10			22 11	22 12	22 25	22 31		22 55	23 01	23 25
Farringdon ■ ⊖	a	21 30	21 36	21 42				21 45		22 00	22 06		22 15					22 30	22 36		23 00	23 06	23 30
City Thameslink ■	a																						
London Blackfriars	a	21 34	21 40	21 46				21 49		22 04	22 10		22 19					22 34	22 40		23 04	23 10	23 34
London Bridge	a																						
London Bridge	a	21 40	21 46					21 55		22 10	22 16		22 25					22 40	22 46		23 10	23 16	23 40
Elephant & Castle ⊖173,179	a			21 50																			
Gatwick Airport	a	22 09						22 39		22 39			23 09					23 09			23 42		00 17

Station		EM ◇■ O	EM ◇■ I	TL ■ A	TL ■ D	TL ■ A
Bedford ■	d	22 20	22 39	22 45	23 05	23 45
Flitwick	d			22 56	23 16	23 56
Harlington	d			23 00	23 20	00 01
Leagrave	d			23 05	23 25	00 06
Luton ■	d	22 36	22 54	23 10	23 30	00 10
Luton Airport Parkway ■ ✈	d			23 13	23 33	00 13
Harpenden	d			23 18	23 38	00 18
St Albans City	d			23 25	23 45	00 25
Radlett	d				23 50	
Elstree & Borehamwood	d				23 54	
Mill Hill Broadway	d				23 58	
Hendon	d				00 01	
Cricklewood	d				00 06	
WestHampsteadThameslink ⊖	d			23 41	00 09	00 41
Kentish Town ⊖	d				00 13	
St Pancras International	a	23 00	23 24	23 51	00 19	00 51
Farringdon ■ ⊖	a			23 55	00 25	
City Thameslink ■	a					
London Blackfriars	a			23 59	00 30	01 00
London Bridge	a					
London Bridge	a					
Elephant & Castle ⊖173,179	a					
Gatwick Airport	a			00 47	01 20	01 56

A To Brighton
B To Rainham Kt
C To Sutton (Surrey)
D To Three Bridges
E 19 August, 9 September, 16 September, 23 September, 30 September, 7 October. From York
F until 2 September, from 14 October, not 19 August. From York
G From Bedford to Three Bridges
H From St Albans City to Rainham Kt
I From Nottingham
J To Gillingham (Kent)
K until 2 September, from 14 October, not 19 August. From Sheffield
L 19 August, 9 September, 16 September, 23 September, 30 September, 7 October. From Sheffield
M From Bedford to Brighton
N From St Albans City to Gillingham (Kent)
O From Sheffield

Table T053-F

London - East Midlands - Sheffield

Mondays to Fridays

21 May to 20 July

Miles	Miles	Miles	Miles			EM MX ◇■ A	EM MO ◇■ A	EM MO ◇■ B	EM MO ◇■ C	EM MX ◇■ A	EM MX ◇■	EM ◇ D	XC ◇■ E	NT ◇	EM ◇■	NT ◇	XC ◇■ F	EM ◇ D	EM	XC ◇■ G	EM ◇■	NT ◇	XC ◇■ H
0	0	—	—	**St Pancras International** ⊖52	d						00 15												
29¼	29¼	—	—	Luton Airport Parkway 52 ✈	d						00 55												
30¼	30¼	—	—	Luton 52	d						00 58												
49¾	49¾	—	—	Bedford 52	d					00 09	01 26												
65¼	65¼	—	—	Wellingborough	d			00 15	00 15	00 22	01 36												
72	72	0	—	Kettering	a			00 25	00 25	00 40	01 46												
—	—	—	—		d			00 26	00 26	00 41	01 46												
—	—	7½	—	Corby	d																		
—	—	21¾	—	Oakham 47	a																		
—	—	33¼	0	Melton Mowbray 47	a																		
83	83	—	—	Market Harborough	d			00 36	00 37	00 52	01 58												
99¼	99¼	48½	—	**Leicester**	a			00 50	00 51	01 06	02 13												
—	—	—	—		d		00 11	00 52	00 52	01 08									06 26				
103	103	—	—	Syston	d														06 33				
105¾	105¾	—	12¾	Sileby	d														06 38				
107¾	107¾	—	—	Barrow Upon Soar	d														06 43				
111¾	111¾	—	—	Loughborough	d		00 21	01 02	01 02	01 19									06 48				
117½	117½	—	—	East Midlands Parkway ✈	d	00 02	00 29	01 09	01 10	01 27									06 56				
123¼	—	—	—	Beeston	a		00 34			01 33									07 06				
126½	—	—	—	**Nottingham**	a		00 41			01 41									07 16				
—	—	—	—		d					01 47		05 23				06 17		06 39				07 18	
—	—	—	—	Newark Castle 27	a																		
—	—	—	—	Lincoln 27	a																		
138½	—	—	—	Langley Mill	d											06 36						07 37	
144¾	—	—	—	Alfreton	d											06 44		07 00				07 45	
—	120½	—	—	Long Eaton	a																		
—	128½	—	—	**Derby**	a	00 14		01 21	01 21	02 05													
—	—	—	—		d	00 16							05 56		06 27		06 35			07 13	07 21		07 44
155	152¾	—	—	Chesterfield	d	00 35						05 51	06 17	06 25	06 46	06 54	07 02	07 10		07 32	07 43	07 57	08 06
167¼	165	—	—	**Sheffield**	a	00 51						06 15	06 31	06 42	07 10	07 11	07 15	07 28		07 45	08 00	08 15	08 19
—	—	—	—	Manchester Piccadilly 78	a							07 38						08 37					
—	—	—	—	Doncaster 29	a								07 00							08 14			
—	—	—	—	Wakefield Kirkgate 31,34	a									07 22		07 57						08 57	
—	—	—	—	Wakefield Westgate 31	a												07 47						08 47
—	—	—	—	Leeds 31,34	a									07 43		08 17	08 01					09 17	09 02
—	—	—	—	York 29	a								07 24				08 29			08 40			09 30

		EM ◇■	EM ◇ D	EM	EM ◇■	EM ◇■	XC ◇■ G	NT ◇	EM ◇■	EM I	XC ◇■ J	EM ◇ K	EM ◇■	EM ◇■	EM L	EM ◇■	EM ◇■	EM ◇■	XC ◇■ M	EM ◇■	NT ◇	XC ◇■ N	EM ◇ K
St Pancras International ⊖52	d	05 52			06 23				06 48				07 04	07 32		07 35		07 49		08 02			
Luton Airport Parkway 52 ✈	d								07 10							07 56							
Luton 52	d	06 15			06 46								07 27										
Bedford 52	d	06 29			07 00								07 41			08 10		08 25					
Wellingborough	d	06 41			07 12								07 54			08 23		08 37					
Kettering	a	06 47			07 18								08 03			08 30		08 45					
	d	06 48			07 19	07 38							08 04			08 30	08 32	08 46					
Corby	d					07a47											08a41	08a55					
Oakham 47	a																						
Melton Mowbray 47	a																						
Market Harborough	d	06 58			07 29								08 15	08 27		08 41							
Leicester	a	07 10			07 41				07 54				08 29	08 39		08 54				09 06			
	d	07 12		07 28	07 42				07 55	08 26			08 30	08 40		08 55				09 07			
Syston	d			07 35						08 34													
Sileby	d			07 40						08 40													
Barrow Upon Soar	d			07 45						08 46					←								
Loughborough	d	07 22		07 50	07 52				08 05	08 51			08 41	08 50	08 51	09 04							
East Midlands Parkway ✈	d	07 29		08 00					08 13	→			08 52	08 58	08 59								
Beeston	a			08 09					08 20						09 09	09 14							
Nottingham	a			08 17					08 27				09 12		09 19	09 23							
	d		07 46					08 17				08 47			09 25						09 17		09 47
Newark Castle 27	a														09 50								
Lincoln 27	a														10 17								
Langley Mill	d							08 36													09 36		
Alfreton	d		08 10					08 44				09 08									09 44		10 08
Long Eaton	a	07 33												09 01									
Derby	a	07 45			08 07									09 14						09 29			
	d	07 47			08 09		08 13				08 44			09 15					09 20	09 30		09 44	
Chesterfield	d	08 10	08 20		08 28		08 36	08 55			09 03	09 20		09 33						09 48	09 55	10 03	10 20
Sheffield	a	08 27	08 38		08 45		08 48	09 13			09 17	09 37		09 47					09 50	10 02	10 13	10 18	10 38
Manchester Piccadilly 78	a		09 37									10 37											11 37
Doncaster 29	a						09 16												10 17				
Wakefield Kirkgate 31,34	a							09 56													10 55		
Wakefield Westgate 31	a										09 46											10 46	
Leeds 31,34	a							10 16			10 00										11 15	11 00	
York 29	a						09 40				10 30								10 40			11 30	

A From St Pancras International
B from 25 June. From St Pancras International
C until 18 June. From St Pancras International
D To Liverpool Lime Street
E To Newcastle
F From Birmingham New Street to Glasgow Central
G From Birmingham New Street to Newcastle
H From Birmingham New Street to Edinburgh
I To Lincoln
J From Bath Spa to Glasgow Central
K From Norwich to Liverpool Lime Street
L From Leicester
M From Guildford to Newcastle
N From Plymouth to Edinburgh

For connections from Gatwick Airport refer to Table T052

Table T053-F

London - East Midlands - Sheffield

Mondays to Fridays

21 May to 20 July

		EM ◇■	EM A	EM ◇■	EM ◇■	EM B	XC ◇■ C	EM ◇	EM ◇■	EM ◇■	NT ◇	XC ◇■ D	EM ◇ E	EM ◇■	EM A	EM ◇■	EM ◇■	EM ◇■	XC ◇■ F	EM ◇■	NT ◇	EM B	XC ◇■ G
St Pancras International ⊖52	d	08 05		08 31	08 34				08 47	09 02				09 05		09 31	09 34	09 47		10 02			
Luton Airport Parkway 52 ✈	d	08 28												09 26									
Luton 52	d								09 12									10 09					
Bedford 52	d	08 42							09 27					09 40				10 24					
Wellingborough	d	08 55							09 41					09 53				10 36					
Kettering	a	09 02							09 52					10 00				10 45					
	d	09 02							09 53					10 00				10 46					
Corby	d							09 26	10a02									10a55					
Oakham 47	a							09 47															
Melton Mowbray 47	a							10 00															
Market Harborough	d	09 13			09 32									10 11			10 31						
Leicester	a	09 25		09 37	09 46					10 06				10 23		10 34	10 44			11 04			
	d	09 26	09 30	09 38	09 46					10 06				10 24	10 30	10 35	10 45			11 04			
Syston	d		09 37												10 36								
Sileby	d		09 42												10 42								
Barrow Upon Soar	d		09 48			←									10 48							←	
Loughborough	d	09 35	09 53	09 48		09 53								10 33	10 53	10 45						10 53	
East Midlands Parkway ✈	d		→	09 56	10 03	10 05		10 31							→	10 53	11 02					11 05	
Beeston	a	09 47				10 12								10 43								11 12	
Nottingham	a	09 57			10 16	10 22								10 52			11 14					11 22	
	d					10 29					10 17		10 51								11 17	11 29	
Newark Castle 27	a					10 51																11 51	
Lincoln 27	a					11 26																12 21	
Langley Mill	d										10 36										11 36		
Alfreton	d										10 44		11 12								11 44		
Long Eaton	a			09 59												10 56							
Derby	a			10 11				10 45		10 28						11 09				11 26			
	d			10 12			10 16			10 29		10 44				11 09			11 16	11 28			11 44
Chesterfield	d			10 30						10 47	10 55	11 03	11 22			11 27				11 47	11 55		12 03
Sheffield	a			10 45			10 50			11 01	11 13	11 17	11 38			11 41			11 46	12 01	12 13		12 17
Manchester Piccadilly 78	a												12 37										
Doncaster 29	a						11 16												12 16				
Wakefield Kirkgate 31,34	a										11 55										12 55		
Wakefield Westgate 31	a											11 46											12 46
Leeds 31,34	a										12 15	12 01									13 15		13 00
York 29	a						11 40					12 30							12 40				13 30

		EM ◇ E	EM ◇■	EM A	EM ◇■	EM ◇■	EM ◇■	XC ◇■ C	EM ◇■	NT ◇	EM B	XC ◇■ H	EM ◇ E	EM ◇■	EM A	EM ◇■	EM ◇■	EM ◇■	XC ◇■ I	EM ◇■	NT ◇	EM B
St Pancras International ⊖52	d		10 05		10 31	10 34	10 47		11 02					11 05		11 31	11 34	11 47		12 02		
Luton Airport Parkway 52 ✈	d		10 28											11 26								
Luton 52	d						11 09											12 09				
Bedford 52	d		10 42				11 24							11 40				12 24				
Wellingborough	d		10 56				11 35							11 53				12 36				
Kettering	a		11 03				11 44							12 00				12 44				
	d		11 03				11 45							12 00				12 45				
Corby	d						11a54											12a54				
Oakham 47	a																					
Melton Mowbray 47	a																					
Market Harborough	d		11 15			11 29								12 11			12 29					
Leicester	a		11 29		11 34	11 43			12 05					12 23		12 34	12 42			13 04		
	d		11 30	11 30	11 35	11 44			12 05					12 24	12 30	12 35	12 43			13 04		
Syston	d			11 37											12 37							
Sileby	d			11 42											12 42							
Barrow Upon Soar	d			11 48							←				12 48							←
Loughborough	d		11 40	11 53	11 46						11 53			12 33	12 53	12 45						12 53
East Midlands Parkway ✈	d			→	11 53	12 01					12 03				→	12 52	13 00					13 04
Beeston	a		11 56								12 11			12 43								13 11
Nottingham	a		12 05			12 13					12 22			12 52			13 13					13 21
	d	11 47								12 17	12 29		12 47								13 17	13 29
Newark Castle 27	a										12 51											13 51
Lincoln 27	a										13 23											14 23
Langley Mill	d									12 36											13 36	
Alfreton	d	12 08								12 44			13 10								13 44	
Long Eaton	a				11 57											12 56						
Derby	a				12 09				12 26							13 08				13 26		
	d				12 09			12 16	12 28			12 44				13 09			13 16	13 28		
Chesterfield	d	12 20			12 27				12 47	12 55		13 03	13 21			13 27				13 47	13 55	
Sheffield	a	12 38			12 41			12 46	13 01	13 13		13 17	13 37			13 41			13 46	14 02	14 13	
Manchester Piccadilly 78	a	13 37											14 37									
Doncaster 29	a							13 16											14 16			
Wakefield Kirkgate 31,34	a									13 55											14 55	
Wakefield Westgate 31	a											13 46										
Leeds 31,34	a									14 15		14 00									15 15	
York 29	a							13 40				14 30							14 40			

A To Lincoln
B From Leicester
C From Reading to Newcastle
D From Plymouth to Glasgow Central
E From Norwich to Liverpool Lime Street
F From Winchester to Newcastle
G From Plymouth to Edinburgh
H From Penzance to Glasgow Central
I From Southampton Central to Newcastle

For connections from Gatwick Airport refer to Table T052

Table T053-F

Mondays to Fridays

21 May to 20 July

London - East Midlands - Sheffield

	XC ◇■ A 🍴	EM ◇ B	EM ◇■ 🍴	EM C	EM ◇■ 🍴	EM ◇■ 🍴	EM ◇■ 🍴	XC ◇■ D 🍴	EM ◇■ 🍴	NT ◇	EM E	XC ◇■ F 🍴	EM ◇ B	EM ◇■ 🍴	EM C	EM ◇■ 🍴	EM ◇■ 🍴	EM ◇■ 🍴	XC ■ G 🍴	EM ◇■ 🍴	NT ◇	EM E
St Pancras International ⊖52 d			12 05		12 31	12 34	12 47		13 02					13 05		13 31	13 34	13 47		14 02		
Luton Airport Parkway ■ 52 ✈ d			12 26											13 26								
Luton ■ 52 d							13 09											14 09				
Bedford ■ 52 d			12 40				13 24							13 40				14 24				
Wellingborough d			12 53				13 36							13 53				14 36				
Kettering ■ a			13 00				13 44							14 00				14 44				
d			13 00				13 45							14 00				14 45				
Corby d							13a54											14a54				
Oakham 47 a																						
Melton Mowbray 47 a																						
Market Harborough d			13 11			13 29								14 11			14 29					
Leicester a			13 24		13 34	13 42			14 04					14 23		14 34	14 42			15 04		
d			13 25	13 30	13 35	13 43			14 04					14 24	14 30	14 35	14 43			15 04		
Syston d				13 37											14 37							
Sileby d				13 42											14 42							
Barrow Upon Soar d				13 48							←				14 48							←
Loughborough d			13 34	13 53	13 45						13 53			14 33	14 53	14 45						14 53
East Midlands Parkway ✈ d				→	13 53	14 00					14 03				→	14 52	15 00					15 04
Beeston a			13 44								14 10			14 43								15 11
Nottingham ■ a			13 53			14 12					14 21			14 52			15 12					15 21
d		13 47								14 17	14 29		14 47								15 17	15 29
Newark Castle 27 a											14 52											15 51
Lincoln 27 a											15 22											16 23
Langley Mill d										14 36											15 36	
Alfreton d		14 08								14 44			15 08								15 44	
Long Eaton a					13 56											14 56						
Derby ■ a					14 08				14 26							15 08				15 26		
d	13 44				14 09			14 16	14 28			14 44				15 09			15 16	15 28		
Chesterfield d	14 03	14 20			14 27				14 47	14 55		15 03	15 20			15 27				15 47	15 55	
Sheffield ■ a	14 17	14 38			14 41			14 46	15 01	15 13		15 17	15 37			15 41			15 46	16 01	16 13	
Manchester Piccadilly 78 a		15 37											16 37									
Doncaster ■ 29 a								15 16											16 17			
Wakefield Kirkgate ■ 31,34 a										15 55											16 55	
Wakefield Westgate ■ 31 a	14 46											15 46										
Leeds ■ 31,34 a	15 00									16 15		16 00									17 15	
York ■ 29 a	15 30							15 40				16 30							16 40			

	XC ◇■ H 🍴	EM ◇ B	EM ◇■ 🍴	EM I	EM ◇■ 🍴	EM ◇■ 🍴	EM ◇■ 🍴	XC ◇■ D 🍴	EM ◇■ 🍴	NT ◇	EM J	XC ◇■ K 🍴	EM ◇ B	EM ◇■ 🍴	EM C	EM ◇■ 🍴	EM ◇■ 🍴	EM ◇■ 🍴	XC ◇■ L 🍴	EM ◇■ 🍴	NT ◇
St Pancras International ⊖52 d			14 05		14 31	14 34	14 47		15 02					15 05		15 31	15 34	15 47		16 02	
Luton Airport Parkway ■ 52 ✈ d			14 26											15 26							
Luton ■ 52 d							15 09											16 09			
Bedford ■ 52 d			14 40				15 24							15 40				16 24			
Wellingborough d			14 53				15 36							15 53				16 35			
Kettering ■ a			15 00				15 44							16 00				16 44			
d			15 00				15 45							16 00				16 45			
Corby d							15a54											16a54			
Oakham 47 a																					
Melton Mowbray 47 a																					
Market Harborough d			15 11			15 29								16 11			16 29				
Leicester a			15 23		15 34	15 42			16 04					16 23		16 34	16 42			17 04	
d			15 24	15 30	15 35	15 43			16 05					16 24	16 30	16 35	16 43			17 05	
Syston d				15 36											16 35						
Sileby d				15 41											16 41						
Barrow Upon Soar d				15 48							←				16 48						
Loughborough d			15 33	15 53	15 45						15 53			16 33	16 53	16 45					
East Midlands Parkway ✈ d				→	15 52	16 00					16 02				→	16 52	17 00				
Beeston a			15 43								16 10			16 44							
Nottingham ■ a			15 52			16 12					16 21			16 54			17 12				
d		15 47								16 17	16 27		16 47								17 17
Newark Castle 27 a											16 51										
Lincoln 27 a											17 16										
Langley Mill d										16 36											17 36
Alfreton d		16 10								16 44			17 08								17 44
Long Eaton a					15 56											16 56					
Derby ■ a					16 08				16 27							17 08				17 27	
d	15 44				16 09			16 16	16 29			16 43				17 08			17 18	17 28	
Chesterfield d	16 03	16 20			16 27				16 47	16 55		17 04	17 20			17 27				17 46	17 55
Sheffield ■ a	16 18	16 37			16 41			16 44	17 02	17 13		17 18	17 37			17 44			17 46	18 01	18 13
Manchester Piccadilly 78 a		17 37											18 37								
Doncaster ■ 29 a								17 13													
Wakefield Kirkgate ■ 31,34 a										17 55											18 55
Wakefield Westgate ■ 31 a	16 46											17 46							18 16		
Leeds ■ 31,34 a	17 00									18 15		18 01							18 34		19 15
York ■ 29 a	17 30							17 42				18 30							19 01		

A From Plymouth to Aberdeen
B From Norwich to Liverpool Lime Street
C To Lincoln
D From Reading to Newcastle
E From Leicester
F From Penzance to Glasgow Central
G From Southampton Central to Newcastle
H From Plymouth to Dundee
I To Sleaford
J From Leicester to Sleaford
K From Plymouth to Glasgow Central
L From Southampton Central to Edinburgh

For connections from Gatwick Airport refer to Table T052

Table T053-F

Mondays to Fridays

21 May to 20 July

London - East Midlands - Sheffield

	EM A	XC ◇■ B 🍴	EM ◇ C	EM ◇■ 🍴	EM D	XC ◇■ E 🍴	EM ◇■ 🍴	EM A	EM ◇■ F 🍴	EM ◇■ G 🍴	EM ◇■ 🍴	NT ◇	XC ◇■ H 🍴	EM ◇ C	EM ◇■ 🍴	EM D	XC ◇■ I 🍴	EM ◇■ 🍴	EM A	EM ◇■ 🍴	EM ◇■ 🍴	EM ◇■ 🍴
St Pancras International ⊖52 d				16 05			16 31		16 34	16 47	16 50				17 05					17 19	17 34	17 50
Luton Airport Parkway ■ 52 ✈ d				16 26																17 42		18 15
Luton ■ 52 d																						
Bedford ■ 52 d																						
Wellingborough d				16 50							17 33				17 50					18 06		18 36
Kettering ■ a				16 57							17 44				17 56					18 14		18 48
d				16 58							17 46				17 57			18 10		18 15		18 54
Corby d											17a55											19 04
Oakham 47 a																						19 25
Melton Mowbray 47 a																						19 36
Market Harborough d				17 08					17 34						18 08					18 26	18 32	
Leicester a				17 21			17 39		17 47	17 55					18 21			18 32		18 40	18 45	
d				17 22	17 27		17 40		17 48	17 58					18 22	18 26		18 36		18 41	18 47	
Syston d					17 35											18 33						
Sileby d					17 40											18 38						
Barrow Upon Soar d	←				17 45			←								18 43			←			
Loughborough d	16 53			17 32	17 51		17 50	17 51							18 32	18 48		18 45	18 48	18 52		
East Midlands Parkway ✈ d	17 02				→		17 58	17 59	18 06						18 40	→		18 53	18 56	19 01	19 05	
Beeston a	17 10			17 43				18 07							18 46				19 04		19 11	
Nottingham ■ a	17 21			17 53				18 15	18 20						18 55				19 13	19 16	19 20	
d	17 21		17 47					18 17				18 17		18 47					19 19	19 28		
Newark Castle 27 a	17 52							18 51											19 54			
Lincoln 27 a	18 24							19 22											20 21			
Langley Mill d			18 03									18 36										
Alfreton d			18 11									18 44		19 08								
Long Eaton a							18 01											18 59		19 41		
Derby ■ a							18 13			18 22								19 11		19 56		
d		17 42				18 16	18 20			18 24			18 44				19 09	19 14				
Chesterfield d		18 03	18 20				18 38			18 43		18 55	19 03	19 20			19 28	19 33				
Sheffield ■ a		18 18	18 38			18 44	18 55			19 03		19 13	19 18	19 37			19 40	19 50				
Manchester Piccadilly 78 a			19 37											20 37								
Doncaster ■ 29 a						19 17											20 13					
Wakefield Kirkgate ■ 31,34 a												19 55										
Wakefield Westgate ■ 31 a		18 48											19 46									
Leeds ■ 31,34 a		19 03										20 15	20 02									
York ■ 29 a		19 30				19 40							20 30				20 41					

	EM ◇■ J 🍴	NT ◇	XC ◇■ K 🍴	EM ◇ L	EM ◇■ 🍴	EM ◇■ 🍴	XC ◇■ E	NT ◇	EM	EM ◇■ M 🍴	EM ◇■ 🍴	EM ◇■ 🍴	XC ◇■ K	EM ◇■ N 🍴	XC ◇■ O	EM ◇■ 🍴	EM D	EM ◇■ 🍴	NT ◇	EM A	EM ◇■ 🍴	EM ◇■ 🍴
St Pancras International ⊖52 d	18 02				18 05	18 19				18 34	18 47	19 01				19 04		19 32			19 35	19 47
Luton Airport Parkway ■ 52 ✈ d						18 42										19 28						
Luton ■ 52 d																						20 10
Bedford ■ 52 d																19 43						20 24
Wellingborough d					18 49					19 20	19 29					19 56						20 35
Kettering ■ a					18 55					19 28	19 37										20 26	20 44
d					18 56					19 29	19 39										20 27	20 45
Corby d											19a48											20a54
Oakham 47 a																						
Melton Mowbray 47 a																						
Market Harborough d						19 16						20 00				20 12		20 29			20 39	
Leicester a	19 06				19 17	19 29				19 50		20 12				20 28		20 42			20 53	
d	19 07				19 21	19 30			19 30	19 54		20 12				20 28	20 30	20 43			20 54	
Syston d									19 37								20 36					
Sileby d									19 42								20 42					
Barrow Upon Soar d									19 48								20 48			←		
Loughborough d						19 40			19 53	20 05		20 23				20 38	20 53			20 53	21 05	
East Midlands Parkway ✈ d					19 36				20 02	20 13		20 31					→	20 56		21 02	21 14	
Beeston a					19 45				20 09					←		20 53				21 09		
Nottingham ■ a					19 53				20 19	20 25				20 25		21 02		21 09		21 20		
d		19 17		19 41	20 00			20 17		20 33				20 33		21 08			21 12	21 20		
Newark Castle 27 a					20 24					→										21 50		
Lincoln 27 a					20 52															22 20		
Langley Mill d		19 36						20 36						20 52		21 25			21 36			
Alfreton d		19 44		20 02				20 44						21 00		21 33			21 44			
Long Eaton a						19 48															21 17	
Derby ■ a	19 29					19 59						20 42									21 30	
d	19 30		19 43			19 59	20 09					20 42	20 48		21 19							
Chesterfield d	19 48	19 55	20 04	20 12		20 19		20 55				21 02	21 07	21 11	21 38	21 44			21 55			
Sheffield ■ a	20 04	20 13	20 18	20 28		20 34	20 37	21 13				21 18	21 19	21 27	21 50	21 58			22 13			
Manchester Piccadilly 78 a				21 36																		
Doncaster ■ 29 a							21 19								22 25							
Wakefield Kirkgate ■ 31,34 a		20 55						21 55											22 55			
Wakefield Westgate ■ 31 a			20 47										21 46	22 15		22 33						
Leeds ■ 31,34 a		21 15	21 02					22 15					22 02	22 34		22 49			23 14			
York ■ 29 a							21 40								22 51							

A From Leicester
B From Plymouth to Edinburgh
C From Norwich to Liverpool Lime Street
D To Lincoln
E From Reading to Newcastle
F The Robin Hood
G The Master Cutler
H From Plymouth to Edinburgh. 🍴 to Leeds
I From Southampton Central to Newcastle
J The South Yorkshireman
K From Plymouth
L From Norwich
M To Leeds
N From St Pancras International
O From Southampton Central

For connections from Gatwick Airport refer to Table T052

Table T053-F

London - East Midlands - Sheffield

Mondays to Fridays

21 May to 20 July

	EM	EM	EM	XC	EM	EM	EM	NT	EM	EM	NT	EM	EM	EM	EM	EM	EM	EM
	◇1	◇1		◇1	◇1	◇1	◇1	◇		◇1	◇	◇1	◇1	◇1	◇1	◇1	◇1	◇1
			A	B					C									
	🍴	🍴			🍴	🍴	🍴			🍴		🍴	🍴	🍴	🍴	🍴	🍴	🍴
St Pancras International ⊖52 d	20 01	20 05			20 31	20 34	21 01			21 04			21 30	21 50	22 00		22 20	23 08
Luton Airport Parkway 7 52 ✈ d		20 28								21 27				22 13			22 44	
Luton 10 52 d													21 55		22 25			23 47
Bedford 7 52 d		20 42								21 43			22 09	22 26	22 40		22 58	00 09
Wellingborough d		20 56								21 55			22 21	22 39	22 53		23 12	00 22
Kettering 5 a		21 02								22 02			22 27	22 46	23 01		23 18	00 40
d		21 02								22 03		22 11	22 28	22 47	23 02	23 11	23 19	00 41
Corby d												22a26				23a26		
Oakham 47 a																		
Melton Mowbray 47 a																		
Market Harborough d		21 13				21 29				22 13			22 38	22 57	23 13		23 29	00 52
Leicester a	21 10	21 27			21 35	21 41	22 06			22 25			22 50	23 08	23 29		23 44	01 06
d	21 11	21 27	21 30		21 37	21 41	22 07			22 26			22 52	23 09	23 31		23 45	01 08
Syston d			21 37															
Sileby d			21 42															
Barrow Upon Soar d			21 48						←									
Loughborough d		21 37	21 53		21 48				21 53	22 36			23 02	23 19	23 42		23 55	01 19
East Midlands Parkway ✈ d			→		21 56	22 00			22 03	22 44			23 09	23 28	23 50		00 02	01 27
Beeston a		21 48							22 11						23 58			01 33
Nottingham 8 ⇌ a		21 57				22 14			22 21	22 54					00 06			01 41
d								22 15			23 18							01 47
Newark Castle 27 a																		
Lincoln 27 a																		
Langley Mill d											23 36							
Alfreton d											23 44							
Long Eaton a					22 00									23 31				
Derby 6 a	21 36				22 17		22 32	22 38					23 20	23 43			00 14	02 05
d	21 37			21 46			22 33	22 39									00 16	
Chesterfield d	21 58			22 08			22 55	23 02			23 54						00 35	
Sheffield 7 ⇌ a	22 18			22 22			23 13	23 24			00 16						00 51	
Manchester Piccadilly 78 a																		
Doncaster 7 29 a																		
Wakefield Kirkgate 4 31,34 a																		
Wakefield Westgate 7 31 a	22 48			22 53														
Leeds 10 31,34 a	23 06			23 07														
York 8 29 a																		

Mondays to Fridays

23 July to 31 August

	EM	EM	EM	EM	EM	EM	EM	EM	EM	NT	EM	NT	XC	EM	EM	EM	XC	EM	NT	XC	EM	EM
	MX	MX	MO	MO		MX	MX	MX													MX	
	◇1	◇1	◇1	◇1	◇1	◇1	◇1	◇1	◇	◇	◇1	◇	◇1	◇		◇1	◇1	◇1	◇	◇1	◇1	◇1
	D	E	F	G	H	D	E		I		J		K	I		L	M	J		N	J	O
	🍴	🍴	☕	☕	☕	🍴	🍴	🍴			🍴		🍴			🍴	🍴	🍴		🍴	🍴	🍴
St Pancras International ⊖52 d								00 15								05 52					05 52	05 52
Luton Airport Parkway 7 52 ✈ d								00 55														
Luton 10 52 d								00 58								06 15					06 15	06 15
Bedford 7 52 d						00 09	00 09	01 26								06 29					06 29	06 29
Wellingborough d				00 15	00 15	00 22	00 22	01 36								06 41					06 41	06 41
Kettering 5 a				00 25	00 25	00 40	00 40	01 46								06 47					06 47	06 47
d				00 26	00 26	00 41	00 41	01 46								06 48					06 48	06 48
Corby d																						
Oakham 47 a																						
Melton Mowbray 47 a																						
Market Harborough d				00 36	00 36	00 52	00 52	01 58								06 58					06 58	06 58
Leicester a				00 50	00 50	01 06	01 06	02 13								07 10					07 10	07 10
d			00 11	00 52	00 52	01 08	01 08								06 26	07 12					07 12	07 12
Syston d															06 33							
Sileby d															06 38							
Barrow Upon Soar d															06 43							
Loughborough d			00 21	01 02	01 02	01 19	01 19								06 48	07 22					07 22	07 22
East Midlands Parkway ✈ d	00 02	00 02	00 29	01a09	01 09	01 27	01 27								06 56	07a29					07 29	07 29
Beeston a			00 34			01 33	01 33								07 06							
Nottingham 8 ⇌ a			00 41			01 41	01 41								07 16							
d							01 47		05 23			06 17		06 39					07 18			
Newark Castle 27 a																						
Lincoln 27 a																						
Langley Mill d												06 36							07 37			
Alfreton d												06 44		07 00					07 45			
Long Eaton a																					07 33	07 33
Derby 6 a		00 14			01 21		02 05														07 45	07 48
d		00 16									06 27							07 21			07 47	
Chesterfield d	00 27	00 35							05 51	06 25	06 46	06 54	07 02	07 10			07 32	07 43	07 57	08 06	08 10	
Sheffield 7 ⇌ a	00 43	00 51							06 15	06 42	07 10	07 11	07 15	07 28			07 45	08 00	08 15	08 19	08 27	
Manchester Piccadilly 78 a									07 38					08 37								
Doncaster 7 29 a																	08 14					
Wakefield Kirkgate 4 31,34 a										07 22		07 57							08 57			
Wakefield Westgate 7 31 a													07 47							08 47		
Leeds 10 31,34 a										07 43		08 17	08 01						09 17	09 02		
York 8 29 a													08 29				08 40			09 30		

A To Nottingham
B From Plymouth
C From Leicester
D from 31 July. From St Pancras International
E until 27 July. From St Pancras International
F From St Pancras International
G from 6 August. From St Pancras International
H 23 July, 30 July. From St Pancras International
I To Liverpool Lime Street
J until 27 July
K From Burton-on-Trent to Glasgow Central
L from 13 August until 17 August
M From Birmingham New Street to Newcastle
N From Birmingham New Street to Edinburgh
O 30 July, 6 August

For connections from Gatwick Airport refer to Table T052

Table T053-F

London - East Midlands - Sheffield

Mondays to Fridays

23 July to 31 August

	EM	EM	EM	EM	EM	XC	EM	EM	NT	EM	EM	XC	EM	EM	EM	EM	EM	EM	EM	EM	EM	XC
	MX																					
	◇1	◇1	◇		◇1	◇1	◇1	◇1	◇	◇1		◇1	◇	◇1	◇1	◇1	◇1		◇1	◇1	◇1	◇1
	A	B	C		D	E	F				G	H	I		J	D	K	L				M
	🍴	🍴			🍴	🍴	🍴	🍴		🍴		🍴		🍴	🍴	🍴	🍴		🍴	🍴	🍴	🍴
St Pancras International ⊖52 d	05 52	05 52			06 23		06 23			06 48				07 04	07 32	07 32	07 32		07 35		07 49	
Luton Airport Parkway 7 52 ✈ d										07 10									07 56			
Luton 10 52 d	06 15	06 15			06 46		06 46							07 27								
Bedford 7 52 d	06 29	06 29			07 00		07 00							07 41					08 10		08 25	
Wellingborough d	06 41	06 41			07 12		07 12							07 54					08 23		08 37	
Kettering 5 a	06 47	06 47			07 18		07 18							08 03					08 30		08 45	
d	06 48	06 48			07 19		07 19	07 38						08 04					08 30	08 32	08 46	
Corby d								07a47												08a41	08a55	
Oakham 47 a																						
Melton Mowbray 47 a																						
Market Harborough d	06 58	06 58			07 29		07 29							08 15	08 27	08 27	08 27		08 41			
Leicester a	07 10	07 10			07 41		07 41			07 54				08 29	08 39	08 39	08 39		08 54			
d	07 12	07 12		07 28	07 42		07 42			07 55	08 26			08 30	08 40	08 40	08 40		08 55			
Syston d				07 35							08 34											
Sileby d				07 40							08 40											
Barrow Upon Soar d				07 45							08 46							←				
Loughborough d	07 22	07 22		07 50	07 52		07 52			08 05	08 51			08 41	08 50	08 50	08 50	08 51	09 04			
East Midlands Parkway ✈ d	07 29	07 29		08 00						08 13	→			08 52	08a57	08 58	08 58	08 59				
Beeston a				08 09						08 20								09 09	09 14			
Nottingham 8 ⇌ a				08 17						08 27				09 12				09 19	09 23			
d			07 46						08 17				08 47					09 25				
Newark Castle 27 a																		09 50				
Lincoln 27 a																		10 17				
Langley Mill d									08 36													
Alfreton d			08 10						08 44				09 08									
Long Eaton a	07 33	07 33														09 01	09 01					
Derby 6 a	07 49	07 51			08 07											09 14	09 27					
d					08 09											09 15						
Chesterfield d			08 20		08 28	08 32	08 37		08 55			09 03	09 20			09 33						09 38
Sheffield 7 ⇌ a			08 38		08 45	08 48	08 52		09 13			09 17	09 37			09 47						09 50
Manchester Piccadilly 78 a			09 37										10 37									
Doncaster 7 29 a						09 16																10 17
Wakefield Kirkgate 4 31,34 a									09 56													
Wakefield Westgate 7 31 a												09 46										
Leeds 10 31,34 a									10 16			10 00										
York 8 29 a						09 40						10 30										10 40

	EM	EM	NT	XC	EM	EM	EM	EM	EM	EM	EM	EM	EM	EM	EM	XC	EM	EM	NT	XC	EM
	◇1	◇1	◇	◇1	◇	◇1		◇1	◇1	◇1	◇1		◇	◇	◇1	◇1	◇1	◇1	◇	◇1	◇
	D	F		N	I		G	J	D	K		L	D	F		O	D	F		P	I
	🍴	🍴		🍴		🍴		🍴	🍴	🍴	🍴		🍴	🍴	🍴	🍴	🍴	🍴		🍴	
St Pancras International ⊖52 d	08 02	08 02				08 05		08 31	08 31	08 31	08 34				08 47		09 02	09 02			
Luton Airport Parkway 7 52 ✈ d						08 28															
Luton 10 52 d															09 12						
Bedford 7 52 d						08 42									09 27						
Wellingborough d						08 55									09 41						
Kettering 5 a						09 02									09 52						
d						09 02									09 53						
Corby d													09 26	09 26	10a02						
Oakham 47 a													09 47	09 47							
Melton Mowbray 47 a													10 00	10 02							
Market Harborough d						09 13					09 32										
Leicester a	09 06	09 06				09 25		09 36	09 37	09 37	09 46						10 06	10 06			
d	09 07	09 07				09 26	09 30	09 37	09 38	09 38	09 46						10 06	10 06			
Syston d							09 37														
Sileby d							09 42														
Barrow Upon Soar d							09 48					←									
Loughborough d						09 35	09 53	09 47	09 48	09 48		09 53									
East Midlands Parkway ✈ d							→	09a55	09 56	09 56	10 03	10 05	10 31								
Beeston a						09 47						10 12									
Nottingham 8 ⇌ a						09 57					10 16	10 22									
d			09 19		09 47							10 29							10 17		10 47
Newark Castle 27 a												10 51									
Lincoln 27 a												11 26									
Langley Mill d			09 38																10 36		
Alfreton d			09 46		10 08														10 44		11 09
Long Eaton a									09 59	09 59											
Derby 6 a	09 29								10 11	10 27			10 45				10 28				
d	09 30								10 12								10 29				
Chesterfield d	09 48	09 43	09 56	10 03	10 20				10 30							10 34	10 47	10 47	10 55	11 03	11 21
Sheffield 7 ⇌ a	10 02	10 03	10 13	10 18	10 38				10 45							10 50	11 01	11 01	11 13	11 17	11 37
Manchester Piccadilly 78 a					11 37																12 37
Doncaster 7 29 a																11 16					
Wakefield Kirkgate 4 31,34 a			10 55																11 55		
Wakefield Westgate 7 31 a				10 46																11 46	
Leeds 10 31,34 a			11 15	11 00															12 15	12 01	
York 8 29 a				11 30												11 40				12 30	

A from 31 July until 10 August
B from 20 August
C To Liverpool Lime Street
D until 27 July
E From Birmingham New Street to Newcastle
F from 30 July
G To Lincoln
H From Birmingham New Street to Glasgow Central
I From Norwich to Liverpool Lime Street
J from 13 August until 17 August
K from 30 July, not from 13 August until 17 August
L From Leicester
M From Bath Spa to Newcastle
N From Guildford to Edinburgh
O From Plymouth to Newcastle
P From Reading to Glasgow Central

For connections from Gatwick Airport refer to Table T052

Table T053-F

Mondays to Fridays

23 July to 31 August

London - East Midlands - Sheffield

	EM ◇1	EM A	EM ◇1 B	EM ◇1 C	EM ◇1 D	EM ◇1	EM ◇1	XC ◇1 E	EM ◇1 F	EM ◇1 C	NT ◇	EM G	XC ◇1 H	EM ◇ I	EM ◇1	EM A	EM ◇1 C	EM ◇1 B	EM ◇1 D	EM ◇1	EM ◇1	XC ◇1 E
St Pancras International ⊖52 d	09 05		09 31	09 31	09 31	09 34	09 47		10 02	10 02					10 05		10 31	10 31	10 31	10 34	10 47	
Luton Airport Parkway 52 d	09 26														10 28							
Luton 52 d							10 09														11 09	
Bedford 52 d	09 40						10 24								10 42						11 24	
Wellingborough d	09 53						10 36								10 56						11 35	
Kettering a	10 00						10 45								11 03						11 44	
d	10 00						10 46								11 03						11 45	
Corby d							10a55														11a54	
Oakham 47 a																						
Melton Mowbray 47 a																						
Market Harborough d	10 11					10 31									11 15					11 29		
Leicester a	10 23		10 34	10 34	10 34	10 44			11 04	11 04					11 29		11 34	11 34	11 35	11 43		
d	10 24	10 30	10 35	10 35	10 35	10 45			11 04	11 04					11 30	11 30	11 35	11 35	11 36	11 44		
Syston d		10 36														11 37						
Sileby d		10 42														11 42						
Barrow Upon Soar d		10 48										←				11 48						
Loughborough d	10 33	10 53	10 45	10 45	10 45							10 53			11 40	11 53	11 46	11 46	11 46			
East Midlands Parkway d		→	10a53	10 53	10 53	11 02						11 05				→	11 53	11a54	11 54	12 01		
Beeston a	10 43											11 12			11 56							
Nottingham a	10 52					11 14						11 22			12 05					12 13		
d											11 17	11 29		11 47								
Newark Castle 27 a												11 51										
Lincoln 27 a												12 21										
Langley Mill d											11 36											
Alfreton d											11 44			12 08								
Long Eaton a				10 56	10 56												11 57		11 58			
Derby a				11 08	11 27					11 26							12 09		12 27			
d				11 09						11 28							12 09					
Chesterfield d				11 27				11 32	11 40	11 47	11 55		12 03	12 20			12 27					12 32
Sheffield a				11 41				11 46	11 58	12 01	12 13		12 17	12 38			12 41					12 46
Manchester Piccadilly 78 a														13 37								
Doncaster 29 a								12 16														13 16
Wakefield Kirkgate 31,34 a											12 55											
Wakefield Westgate 31 a													12 46									
Leeds 31,34 a											13 15		13 00									
York 29 a								12 40					13 30									13 40

	EM ◇1 F	EM ◇1 C	NT ◇	EM G	XC ◇1 J	EM ◇ I	EM ◇1	EM A	EM ◇1 B	EM ◇1 C	EM ◇1 D	EM ◇1	EM ◇1	XC ◇1 K	EM ◇1 F	EM ◇1 C	NT ◇	EM G	XC ◇1 L	EM ◇ I	EM ◇1
St Pancras International ⊖52 d	11 02	11 02					11 05		11 31	11 31	11 31	11 34	11 47		12 02	12 02					12 05
Luton Airport Parkway 52 d							11 26														12 26
Luton 52 d													12 09								
Bedford 52 d							11 40						12 24								12 40
Wellingborough d							11 53						12 36								12 53
Kettering a							12 00						12 44								13 00
d							12 00						12 45								13 00
Corby d													12a54								
Oakham 47 a																					
Melton Mowbray 47 a																					
Market Harborough d							12 11					12 29									13 11
Leicester a	12 05	12 05					12 23		12 34	12 34	12 34	12 42			13 04	13 04					13 24
d	12 05	12 05					12 24	12 30	12 35	12 35	12 35	12 43			13 04	13 04					13 25
Syston d								12 37													
Sileby d								12 42													
Barrow Upon Soar d				←				12 48										←			
Loughborough d				11 53			12 33	12 53	12 45	12 45	12 45							12 53			13 34
East Midlands Parkway d				12 03				→	12a52	12 52	12 52	13 00						13 04			
Beeston a				12 11			12 43											13 11			13 44
Nottingham a				12 22			12 52					13 13						13 21			13 53
d			12 17	12 29		12 47											13 17	13 29		13 47	
Newark Castle 27 a				12 51														13 51			
Lincoln 27 a				13 23														14 23			
Langley Mill d			12 36														13 36				
Alfreton d			12 44			13 10											13 44			14 08	
Long Eaton a										12 57	12 57										
Derby a		12 26								13 09	13 27					13 26					
d		12 28								13 09						13 28					
Chesterfield d	12 40	12 47	12 55		13 03	13 21				13 27				13 34	13 40	13 47	13 55		14 03	14 20	
Sheffield a	12 58	13 01	13 13		13 17	13 37				13 41				13 46	13 55	14 02	14 13		14 17	14 38	
Manchester Piccadilly 78 a						14 37														15 37	
Doncaster 29 a														14 16							
Wakefield Kirkgate 31,34 a			13 55														14 55				
Wakefield Westgate 31 a					13 46														14 46		
Leeds 31,34 a			14 15		14 00												15 15		15 00		
York 29 a					14 30									14 40					15 30		

A To Lincoln
B from 13 August until 17 August
C until 27 July
D from 30 July, not from 13 August until 17 August
E From Plymouth to Newcastle
F from 30 July
G From Leicester
H From Winchester to Edinburgh
I From Norwich to Liverpool Lime Street
J From Reading to Glasgow Central
K From Penzance to Newcastle
L From Southampton Central to Aberdeen

For connections from Gatwick Airport refer to Table T052

Table T053-F

Mondays to Fridays

23 July to 31 August

London - East Midlands - Sheffield

	EM A	EM ◇1 B	EM ◇1 C	EM ◇1 D	EM ◇1	EM ◇1	XC ◇1 E	EM ◇1 F	EM ◇1 C	NT ◇	EM G	XC 1 H	EM ◇ I	EM ◇1	EM A	EM ◇1 B	EM ◇1 C	EM ◇1 D	EM ◇1	EM ◇1	XC ◇1 J	EM ◇1 F
St Pancras International ⊖52 d		12 31	12 31	12 31	12 34	12 47		13 02	13 02					13 05		13 31	13 31	13 31	13 34	13 47		14 02
Luton Airport Parkway 52 d														13 26								
Luton 52 d						13 09														14 09		
Bedford 52 d						13 24								13 40						14 24		
Wellingborough d						13 36								13 53						14 36		
Kettering a						13 44								14 00						14 44		
d						13 45								14 00						14 45		
Corby d						13a54														14a54		
Oakham 47 a																						
Melton Mowbray 47 a																						
Market Harborough d					13 29									14 11					14 29			
Leicester a		13 34	13 34	13 34	13 42			14 04	14 04					14 23		14 34	14 34	14 34	14 42			15 04
d	13 30	13 35	13 35	13 35	13 43			14 04	14 04					14 24	14 30	14 35	14 35	14 35	14 43			15 04
Syston d	13 37														14 37							
Sileby d	13 42														14 42							
Barrow Upon Soar d	13 48										←				14 48							
Loughborough d	13 53	13 46	13 46	13 46							13 53			14 33	14 53	14 45	14 45	14 45				
East Midlands Parkway d	→	13a53	13 53	13 53	14 00						14 03				→	14a52	14 52	14 52	15 00			
Beeston a											14 10			14 43								
Nottingham a					14 12						14 21			14 52					15 12			
d										14 17	14 29		14 47									
Newark Castle 27 a											14 52											
Lincoln 27 a											15 22											
Langley Mill d										14 36												
Alfreton d										14 44			15 08									
Long Eaton a			13 57	13 57													14 56	14 57				
Derby a			14 09	14 27					14 26								15 08	15 27				
d			14 09						14 28								15 09					
Chesterfield d			14 27				14 32	14 42	14 47	14 55		15 03	15 20				15 27				15 32	15 40
Sheffield a			14 41				14 46	15 01	15 01	15 13		15 17	15 37				15 41				15 46	15 55
Manchester Piccadilly 78 a													16 37									
Doncaster 29 a							15 16														16 17	
Wakefield Kirkgate 31,34 a										15 55												
Wakefield Westgate 31 a												15 46										
Leeds 31,34 a										16 15		16 00										
York 29 a							15 40					16 30									16 40	

	EM ◇1 C	NT ◇	EM G	XC ◇1 K	EM ◇ I	EM ◇1	EM L	EM ◇1 B	EM ◇1 C	EM ◇1 D	EM ◇1	EM ◇1	XC ◇1 E	EM ◇1 F	EM ◇1 C	NT ◇	EM M	XC ◇1 H	EM ◇ I	EM ◇1	EM A	EM ◇1 C
St Pancras International ⊖52 d	14 02					14 05		14 31	14 31	14 31	14 34	14 47		15 02	15 02					15 05		15 31
Luton Airport Parkway 52 d						14 26														15 26		
Luton 52 d												15 09										
Bedford 52 d						14 40						15 24								15 40		
Wellingborough d						14 53						15 36								15 53		
Kettering a						15 00						15 44								16 00		
d						15 00						15 45								16 00		
Corby d												15a54										
Oakham 47 a																						
Melton Mowbray 47 a																						
Market Harborough d						15 11					15 29									16 11		
Leicester a	15 04					15 23		15 34	15 34	15 34	15 42			16 04	16 04					16 23		16 34
d	15 04					15 24	15 30	15 35	15 35	15 35	15 43			16 05	16 05					16 24	16 30	16 35
Syston d							15 36														16 35	
Sileby d							15 41														16 41	
Barrow Upon Soar d			←				15 48										←				16 48	
Loughborough d			14 53			15 33	15 53	15 45	15 45	15 45							15 53			16 33	16 53	16 45
East Midlands Parkway d			15 04				→	15a52	15 52	15 52	16 00						16 02				→	16 52
Beeston a			15 11			15 43											16 10			16 44		
Nottingham a			15 21			15 52					16 12						16 21			16 54		
d		15 17	15 29		15 47											16 17	16 27		16 47			
Newark Castle 27 a			15 51														16 51					
Lincoln 27 a			16 23														17 16					
Langley Mill d		15 36														16 36						
Alfreton d		15 44			16 10											16 44			17 08			
Long Eaton a									15 56	15 57												16 57
Derby a	15 26								16 08	16 27					16 27							17 09
d	15 28								16 09						16 29							17 09
Chesterfield d	15 47	15 55		16 03	16 20				16 27				16 36	16 40	16 47	16 55		17 04	17 20			17 28
Sheffield a	16 01	16 13		16 18	16 37				16 41				16 48	16 56	17 02	17 13		17 18	17 37			17 44
Manchester Piccadilly 78 a					17 37														18 37			
Doncaster 29 a													17 13									
Wakefield Kirkgate 31,34 a		16 55														17 55						
Wakefield Westgate 31 a				16 46														17 45				
Leeds 31,34 a		17 15		17 00												18 15		18 00				
York 29 a				17 30									17 42					18 30				

A To Lincoln
B from 13 August until 17 August
C until 27 July
D from 30 July, not from 13 August until 17 August
E From Plymouth to Newcastle
F from 30 July
G From Leicester
H From Reading to Glasgow Central
I From Norwich to Liverpool Lime Street
J From Penzance to Newcastle
K From Southampton Central to Dundee
L To Sleaford
M From Leicester to Sleaford

For connections from Gatwick Airport refer to Table T052

Table T053-F

Mondays to Fridays

23 July to 31 August

London - East Midlands - Sheffield

	EM	EM	EM	EM	XC	EM	EM	NT	EM	XC	EM	EM	EM	EM	XC	EM	EM	EM	EM	EM	EM
	◇1	◇1	◇1	◇1	◇1	◇1	◇1	◇		◇1	◇	◇1		◇1	◇1	◇1	◇1		◇1	◇1	◇1
	A	B			C	D	E		F	G	H		I	J	K	E	L	F	M	N	O
	⊼	⊼	⊼	⊼	⊼	⊼	⊼			⊼		⊼		⊼	⊼	⊼	⊼		⊼	⊼	⊼
St Pancras International ⊖52 d	15 31	15 31	15 34	15 47		16 02	16 02					16 05		16 31		16 31	16 31		16 34	16 47	16 47
Luton Airport Parkway 7 52 ✈ d												16 26									
Luton 10 52 d				16 09																	
Bedford 7 52 d				16 24																	
Wellingborough d				16 35								16 50									
Kettering 5 a				16 44								16 57									
d				16 45								16 58									
Corby d				16a54																	
Oakham 47 a																					
Melton Mowbray 47 a																					
Market Harborough d			16 29									17 08							17 34		
Leicester a	16 34	16 34	16 42			17 04	17 04					17 21		17 39		17 39	17 39		17 47	17 55	17 55
d	16 35	16 35	16 43			17 05	17 05					17 22	17 27	17 40		17 40	17 40		17 48	17 58	17 58
Syston d													17 35								
Sileby d													17 40								
Barrow Upon Soar d									←				17 45					←			
Loughborough d	16 45	16 45							16 53			17 32	17 51	17 50		17 50	17 50	17 51			
East Midlands Parkway ✈ d	16 52	16a53	17 00						17 02				→	17a57		17 58	17 58	17 59	18 06		
Beeston a									17 10			17 43						18 07			
Nottingham 8 a			17 12						17 21			17 53						18 15	18 20		
d								17 17	17 21		17 47							18 17			
Newark Castle 27 a									17 52									18 51			
Lincoln 27 a									18 24									19 22			
Langley Mill d								17 36			18 03										
Alfreton d								17 44			18 11										
Long Eaton a	16 57															18 01	18 01				
Derby 6 a	17 27						17 27									18 14	18 27				18 22
d							17 28									18 14					18 24
Chesterfield d					17 34	17 40	17 46	17 55		18 03	18 20				18 30	18 32				18 37	18 43
Sheffield 7 a					17 48	17 55	18 01	18 13		18 18	18 38				18 44	18 46				18 58	19 03
Manchester Piccadilly 78 a											19 37										
Doncaster 7 29 a															19 17						
Wakefield Kirkgate 4 31,34 a								18 55													
Wakefield Westgate 7 31 a					18 16					18 48											
Leeds 10 31,34 a					18 34			19 15		19 03											
York 8 29 a					19 01					19 30					19 41						

	EM	NT	XC	EM	EM	EM	EM	XC	EM	EM	EM	EM	EM	EM	EM	EM	NT	XC	EM	EM	EM	EM
	◇1	◇	◇1	◇	◇1		◇1	◇1	◇1	◇1		◇1	◇1	◇1	◇1	◇1	◇	◇1	◇	◇1	◇1	◇1
			P	H		I	J	K	E	L	F			Q	R			S	T		J	E
	⊼		⊼		⊼		⊼	⊼	⊼	⊼		⊼	⊼	⊼	⊼	⊼		⊼		⊼	⊼	⊼
St Pancras International ⊖52 d	16 50				17 05							17 19	17 34	17 47	17 47	17 50				18 05	18 19	18 19
Luton Airport Parkway 7 52 ✈ d												17 42				18 15					18 42	18 42
Luton 10 52 d																						
Bedford 7 52 d																						
Wellingborough d	17 33				17 50							18 06				18 36				18 49		
Kettering 5 a	17 44				17 56							18 14				18 48				18 55		
d	17 46				17 57		18 10		18 10	18 10		18 15				18 54				18 56		
Corby d	17a55															19 04						
Oakham 47 a																19 25						
Melton Mowbray 47 a																19 36						
Market Harborough d					18 08							18 26	18 32								19 16	19 16
Leicester a					18 21		18 32		18 32	18 32		18 40	18 45	18 59	18 59					19 17	19 29	19 29
d					18 22	18 26	18 36		18 36	18 36		18 41	18 47	19 01	19 01					19 21	19 30	19 30
Syston d						18 33																
Sileby d						18 38																
Barrow Upon Soar d						18 43					←											
Loughborough d					18 32	18 48	18 45		18 45	18 45	18 48	18 52									19 40	19 40
East Midlands Parkway ✈ d					18 40	→	18a53		18 53	18 53	18 56	19 01	19 05							19 36	19a48	
Beeston a					18 46						19 04		19 11							19 45		
Nottingham 8 a					18 55						19 13	19 17	19 20							19 53		
d		18 17		18 47							19 19						19 17		19 41	20 00		
Newark Castle 27 a											19 54									20 24		
Lincoln 27 a											20 21									20 52		
Langley Mill d		18 36															19 36					
Alfreton d		18 44		19 08													19 44		20 02			
Long Eaton a									18 59	18 59												19 48
Derby 6 a									19 11	19 26					19 22							19 59
d									19 14						19 24							19 59
Chesterfield d		18 55	19 03	19 20				19 28	19 33					19 37	19 42		19 55	20 04	20 12			20 19
Sheffield 7 a		19 13	19 18	19 37				19 40	19 50					19 57	19 57		20 13	20 18	20 28			20 34
Manchester Piccadilly 78 a				20 37															21 36			
Doncaster 7 29 a								20 13														
Wakefield Kirkgate 4 31,34 a		19 55															20 55					
Wakefield Westgate 7 31 a			19 46															20 46				
Leeds 10 31,34 a		20 15	20 02														21 15	21 01				
York 8 29 a			20 30					20 41														

A from 30 July until 10 August
B from 13 August
C From Plymouth to Edinburgh
D from 30 July
E until 27 July
F From Leicester
G From Southampton Central to Edinburgh
H From Norwich to Liverpool Lime Street
I To Lincoln
J from 13 August until 17 August
K From Plymouth to Newcastle
L from 30 July, not from 13 August until 17 August
M The Robin Hood
N from 30 July. The Master Cutler
O until 27 July. The Master Cutler
P From Reading to Edinburgh. ⊼ to Leeds
Q from 30 July. The South Yorkshireman
R until 27 July. The South Yorkshireman
S From Southampton Central
T From Norwich

For connections from Gatwick Airport refer to Table T052

Table T053-F

Mondays to Fridays

23 July to 31 August

London - East Midlands - Sheffield

	EM	EM	XC	NT	EM	XC	EM	EM	EM	EM	XC	EM	EM	EM	NT	EM	EM	EM	EM	EM	EM
	◇1	◇1	◇1	◇		◇1	◇1	◇1	◇1	◇1	◇1	◇1		◇1	◇		◇1	◇1	◇1	◇1	◇1
	A	B	C			D			E	F	G		H			I	J	A	K		E
	⊼	⊼	⊼				⊼	⊼	⊼	⊼		⊼		⊼			⊼	⊼	⊼	⊼	⊼
St Pancras International ⊖52 d	18 19	18 19					18 34	18 47	19 01	19 01		19 04		19 32			19 35	19 35	19 35	19 47	20 01
Luton Airport Parkway 7 52 ✈ d	18 42	18 42										19 28									
Luton 10 52 d																				20 10	
Bedford 7 52 d												19 43								20 24	
Wellingborough d							19 20	19 29				19 56								20 35	
Kettering 5 a							19 28	19 37									20 26	20 26	20 26	20 44	
d							19 29	19 39									20 27	20 27	20 27	20 45	
Corby d								19a48												20a54	
Oakham 47 a																					
Melton Mowbray 47 a																					
Market Harborough d	19 16	19 16							20 00	20 00		20 12		20 29			20 39	20 39	20 39		
Leicester a	19 29	19 29					19 50		20 12	20 12		20 28		20 42			20 53	20 53	20 53		21 10
d	19 30	19 30			19 30		19 54		20 12	20 12		20 28	20 30	20 43			20 54	20 54	20 54		21 11
Syston d					19 37								20 36								
Sileby d					19 42								20 42								
Barrow Upon Soar d					19 48								20 48			←					
Loughborough d	19 40	19 40			19 53		20 05		20 23	20 23		20 38	20 53			20 53	21 05	21 05	21 05		
East Midlands Parkway ✈ d					20 02		20 13		20 31	20 31			→	20 56		21 02	21a14	21 14	21 14		
Beeston a					20 09							20 53				21 09					
Nottingham 8 a					20 19		20 25					21 02		21 09		21 20					
d				20 17			20 33					21 08			21 12	21 20					
Newark Castle 27 a																21 50					
Lincoln 27 a																22 20					
Langley Mill d				20 36								21 25			21 36						
Alfreton d				20 44								21 33			21 44						
Long Eaton a	19 48	19 48																21 17	21 17		
Derby 6 a	20 04	20 06								20 42								21 34	21 37		
d										20 42											
Chesterfield d			20 26	20 55		21 01	21 11		21 05	21 06	21 36	21 44			21 55						21 57
Sheffield 7 a			20 38	21 13		21 16	21 27		21 24	21 24	21 50	21 58			22 13						22 18
Manchester Piccadilly 78 a																					
Doncaster 7 29 a			21 19								22 25										
Wakefield Kirkgate 4 31,34 a				21 55											22 55						
Wakefield Westgate 7 31 a						21 46	22 15					22 33									22 48
Leeds 10 31,34 a				22 15		22 02	22 34					22 49			23 14						23 06
York 8 29 a			21 40								22 51										

	EM	EM	EM	EM	EM	EM	XC	EM	EM	NT	EM	EM	NT	EM	EM	EM	EM	EM	EM	EM	EM	EM
	◇1	◇1		◇1	◇1	◇1	◇1	◇1	◇1	◇		◇1	◇	◇1	◇1	◇1	◇1	◇1	◇1	◇1	◇1	◇1
	F		L	E	F		G	E	F		I				F	E	E	F			E	F
	⊼	⊼		⊼	⊼	⊼		⊼	⊼			⊼		⊼	⊼	⊼	⊼	⊼	⊼	⊼	⊼	⊼
St Pancras International ⊖52 d	20 01	20 05		20 31	20 31	20 34		21 01	21 01			21 04			21 30	21 30	21 50	21 50	22 00		22 20	22 20
Luton Airport Parkway 7 52 ✈ d		20 28										21 27					22 13	22 13			22 44	22 44
Luton 10 52 d															21 55	21 55			22 25			
Bedford 7 52 d		20 42										21 43			22 09	22 09	22 26	22 26	22 40		22 58	22 58
Wellingborough d		20 56										21 55			22 21	22 21	22 39	22 39	22 53		23 12	23 12
Kettering 5 a		21 02										22 02			22 27	22 27	22 46	22 46	23 01		23 18	23 18
d		21 02										22 03		22 11	22 28	22 28	22 47	22 47	23 02	23 11	23 19	23 19
Corby d														22a26						23a26		
Oakham 47 a																						
Melton Mowbray 47 a																						
Market Harborough d		21 13				21 29						22 13			22 38	22 38	22 57	22 57	23 13		23 29	23 29
Leicester a	21 10	21 27		21 35	21 35	21 41		22 06	22 06			22 25			22 50	22 50	23 08	23 08	23 29		23 44	23 44
d	21 11	21 27	21 30	21 37	21 37	21 41		22 07	22 07			22 26			22 52	22 52	23 09	23 09	23 31		23 45	23 45
Syston d			21 37																			
Sileby d			21 42																			
Barrow Upon Soar d			21 48								←											
Loughborough d		21 37	21 53	21 48	21 48						21 53	22 36			23 02	23 02	23 19	23 19	23 42		23 55	23 55
East Midlands Parkway ✈ d			→	21a56	21 56	22 00					22 03	22 44			23 09	23a10	23a28	23 28	23 50		00 02	00 02
Beeston a		21 48									22 11								23 58			
Nottingham 8 a		21 57				22 14					22 21	22 54							00 06			
d										22 15			23 18									
Newark Castle 27 a																						
Lincoln 27 a																						
Langley Mill d													23 36									
Alfreton d													23 44									
Long Eaton a					22 00													23 31				
Derby 6 a	21 36				22 14				22 32	22 38					23 20			23 43				00 14
d	21 37								22 33	22 39												00 16
Chesterfield d	21 58						22 27	22 45	22 55	23 02			23 54								00 27	00 35
Sheffield 7 a	22 18						22 44	23 01	23 13	23 24			00 16								00 43	00 51
Manchester Piccadilly 78 a																						
Doncaster 7 29 a																						
Wakefield Kirkgate 4 31,34 a																						
Wakefield Westgate 7 31 a	22 48						23 12															
Leeds 10 31,34 a	23 06						23 26															
York 8 29 a																						

A from 30 July until 10 August
B from 20 August
C From Plymouth to Newcastle
D From Reading
E from 30 July
F until 27 July
G From Plymouth
H To Lincoln
I From Leicester
J from 13 August until 17 August
K until 27 July, from 20 August
L To Nottingham

For connections from Gatwick Airport refer to Table T052

23 July to 31 August

London - East Midlands - Sheffield

	EM ◇■ A	EM ◇■ B
St Pancras International ⊖52 d	23 08	23 08
Luton Airport Parkway 52 ✈ d		
Luton 52 d	23 47	23 47
Bedford 52 d	00 09	00 09
Wellingborough d	00 22	00 22
Kettering a	00 40	00 40
d	00 41	00 41
Corby d		
Oakham 47 a		
Melton Mowbray 47 a		
Market Harborough d	00 52	00 52
Leicester a	01 06	01 06
d	01 08	01 08
Syston d		
Sileby d		
Barrow Upon Soar d		
Loughborough d	01 19	01 19
East Midlands Parkway ✈ d	01 27	01 27
Beeston a	01 33	01 33
Nottingham a	01 41	01 41
d		01 47
Newark Castle 27 a		
Lincoln 27 a		
Langley Mill d		
Alfreton d		
Long Eaton a		
Derby a		02 05
d		
Chesterfield d		
Sheffield a		
Manchester Piccadilly 78 a		
Doncaster 29 a		
Wakefield Kirkgate 31,34 a		
Wakefield Westgate 31 a		
Leeds 31,34 a		
York 29 a		

Mondays to Fridays

3 September to 21 September

	EM MX ◇■ C	EM MO ◇■ C	EM MO ◇■ C	EM MX ◇■ C	EM MX ◇■	EM ◇ D	NT ◇	NT ◇	XC ◇■ E	EM ◇ D	EM	XC ◇■ F	NT ◇	XC ◇■ G	EM ◇■	EM ◇ D	EM	EM ◇■	EM ◇■	XC ◇■ F	NT ◇	EM ◇■
St Pancras International ⊖52 d					00 15										05 52			06 23				06 48
Luton Airport Parkway 52 ✈ d					00 55																	07 10
Luton 52 d					00 58										06 15			06 46				
Bedford 52 d				00 09	01 26										06 29			07 00				
Wellingborough d			00 15	00 22	01 36										06 41			07 12				
Kettering a			00 25	00 40	01 46										06 47			07 18				
d			00 26	00 41	01 46										06 48			07 19	07 38			
Corby d																			07a47			
Oakham 47 a																						
Melton Mowbray 47 a																						
Market Harborough d			00 36	00 52	01 58										06 58			07 29				
Leicester a			00 50	01 06	02 13										07 10			07 41				07 54
d		00 11	00 52	01 08							06 26				07 12		07 28	07 42				07 55
Syston d											06 33						07 35					
Sileby d											06 38						07 40					
Barrow Upon Soar d											06 43						07 45					
Loughborough d		00 21	01 02	01 19							06 48				07 22		07 50	07 52				08 05
East Midlands Parkway ✈ d	00 02	00 29	01 09	01 27							06 56				07 29		08 00					08 13
Beeston a		00 34		01 33							07 06						08 09					08 23
Nottingham a		00 41		01 41							07 16						08 17					08 31
d				01 47		05 23		06 17		06 39			07 18			07 46					08 17	
Newark Castle 27 a																						
Lincoln 27 a																						
Langley Mill d								06 36					07 37								08 36	
Alfreton d								06 44		07 00			07 45			08 10					08 44	
Long Eaton a															07 33							
Derby a			01 21	02 05											07 43							
d									05 56			06 54		07 17						07 48		
Chesterfield d	00 27					05 51	06 25	06 54	07 02	07 10		07 32	07 57	08 06		08 20		08 27		08 36	08 55	
Sheffield a	00 43					06 15	06 42	07 11	07 15	07 28		07 46	08 15	08 19		08 38		08 45		08 48	09 13	
Manchester Piccadilly 78 a						07 38				08 37						09 37						
Doncaster 29 a												08 14								09 16		
Wakefield Kirkgate 31,34 a							07 22	07 57					08 57								09 56	
Wakefield Westgate 31 a									07 47					08 47								
Leeds 31,34 a							07 43	08 17	08 01				09 17	09 02							10 16	
York 29 a									08 29			08 40		09 30						09 40		

A from 30 July
B until 27 July
C From St Pancras International
D To Liverpool Lime Street
E To Glasgow Central
F From Birmingham New Street to Newcastle
G From Birmingham New Street to Edinburgh

For connections from Gatwick Airport refer to Table T052

3 September to 21 September

London - East Midlands - Sheffield

	EM A	XC ◇■ B	EM ◇ C	EM ◇■	EM D	XC ◇■ E	EM ◇■	EM ◇■	EM ◇■	EM ◇■	EM ◇■	NT ◇	XC ◇■ F	EM ◇ C	EM ◇■	EM A	XC ◇■ G	EM ◇■	EM ◇■	EM D	EM ◇	EM ◇■
St Pancras International ⊖52 d				07 04			07 32	07 35		07 49	08 02				08 05			08 31	08 34			08 47
Luton Airport Parkway 52 ✈ d								07 56							08 28							
Luton 52 d				07 27																		09 12
Bedford 52 d				07 41				08 10		08 25					08 42							09 27
Wellingborough d				07 54				08 23		08 37					08 55							09 41
Kettering a				08 03				08 30		08 45					09 02							09 52
d				08 04				08 30	08 32	08 46					09 02							09 53
Corby d									08a41	08a55											09 26	10a02
Oakham 47 a																					09 47	
Melton Mowbray 47 a																					10 00	
Market Harborough d				08 15			08 27	08 41							09 13				09 32			
Leicester a				08 29			08 39	08 54			09 06				09 25			09 37	09 46			
d	08 25			08 30			08 40	08 55			09 07				09 26	09 30		09 38	09 46			
Syston d	08 33															09 37						
Sileby d	08 39															09 42						
Barrow Upon Soar d	08 45				←											09 48				←		
Loughborough d	08 50			08 41	08 50		08 50	09 04							09 35	09 53		09 48		09 53		
East Midlands Parkway ✈ d	→			08 51	08 58		08 58									→		09 56	10 03	10 05	10 37	
Beeston a					09 09			09 14							09 47					10 12		
Nottingham a				09 11	09 19			09 23							09 57				10 18	10 25		
d			08 47		09 25							09 19		09 47						10 29		
Newark Castle 27 a					09 50															10 51		
Lincoln 27 a					10 17															11 26		
Langley Mill d												09 38										
Alfreton d			09 09									09 46		10 08								
Long Eaton a							09 01											09 59				
Derby a							09 13											10 13			10 50	
d		08 19				08 47							09 20				09 53					
Chesterfield d		09 03	09 20			09 38					09 46	09 56	10 03	10 20			10 34					
Sheffield a		09 17	09 37			09 50					10 04	10 13	10 18	10 38			10 48					
Manchester Piccadilly 78 a			10 37											11 37								
Doncaster 29 a						10 17											11 16					
Wakefield Kirkgate 31,34 a												10 55										
Wakefield Westgate 31 a		09 46											10 46									
Leeds 31,34 a		10 00										11 15	11 00									
York 29 a		10 30				10 40							11 30				11 40					

	EM ◇■	NT ◇	XC ◇■ H	EM ◇ C	EM ◇■	EM A	XC ◇■ G	EM ◇■	EM ◇■	EM ◇■	EM ◇■	NT ◇	EM D	EM ◇■	EM A	XC ◇■ I	XC ◇■ G	EM ◇■	EM ◇■	EM ◇■	EM ◇■
St Pancras International ⊖52 d	09 02				09 05			09 31	09 34	09 47	10 02			10 05				10 31	10 34	10 47	11 02
Luton Airport Parkway 52 ✈ d					09 26									10 28							
Luton 52 d										10 09										11 09	
Bedford 52 d					09 40					10 24				10 42						11 24	
Wellingborough d					09 53					10 36				10 56						11 35	
Kettering a					10 00					10 45				11 03						11 44	
d					10 00					10 46				11 03						11 45	
Corby d										10a55										11a54	
Oakham 47 a																					
Melton Mowbray 47 a																					
Market Harborough d					10 11				10 31					11 15					11 29		
Leicester a	10 06				10 23			10 34	10 44		11 04			11 29				11 35	11 43		12 05
d	10 06				10 24	10 30		10 35	10 45		11 04			11 30	11 30			11 36	11 44		12 05
Syston d						10 36									11 37						
Sileby d						10 42									11 42						
Barrow Upon Soar d						10 48							←		11 48						
Loughborough d					10 33	10 53		10 45					10 53	11 40	11 53			11 46			
East Midlands Parkway ✈ d						→		10 53	11 02				11 05		→			11 54	12 01		
Beeston a					10 48								11 14	11 56							
Nottingham a					10 57				11 19				11 25	12 05					12 15		
d		10 17		10 51								11 17	11 29								
Newark Castle 27 a													11 51								
Lincoln 27 a													12 21								
Langley Mill d		10 38										11 37									
Alfreton d		10 46		11 12								11 45									
Long Eaton a								10 56										11 58			
Derby a								11 07										12 13			
d			10 20				10 51									11 19	11 55				
Chesterfield d	10 46	10 56	11 03	11 22			11 32				11 42	11 56				12 03	12 32				12 42
Sheffield a	11 00	11 13	11 17	11 38			11 46				12 00	12 13				12 17	12 46				13 00
Manchester Piccadilly 78 a				12 37																	
Doncaster 29 a							12 16										13 16				
Wakefield Kirkgate 31,34 a		11 55										12 55									
Wakefield Westgate 31 a			11 46													12 46					
Leeds 31,34 a		12 15	12 01									13 15				13 00					
York 29 a			12 30				12 40									13 30	13 40				

A To Lincoln
B From Birmingham New Street to Glasgow Central
C From Norwich to Liverpool Lime Street
D From Leicester
E From Bath Spa to Newcastle
F From Guildford to Edinburgh
G From Plymouth to Newcastle
H From Reading to Glasgow Central
I From Winchester to Edinburgh

For connections from Gatwick Airport refer to Table T052

Table T053-F

London - East Midlands - Sheffield

Mondays to Fridays

3 September to 21 September

	NT ◇	EM A	XC ◇■ B	EM ◇ C	EM ◇■ 🛒	EM D	XC ◇■ E 🛒	EM ◇■ 🛒	EM ◇■ 🛒	EM ◇■ 🛒	EM ◇■ 🛒	NT ◇	EM A	XC ◇■ F 🛒	EM ◇ C	EM ◇■ 🛒	EM D	XC ◇■ G 🛒	EM ◇■ 🛒	EM ◇■ 🛒	EM ◇■ 🛒	EM ◇■ 🛒
St Pancras International ⊖52 d					11 05			11 31	11 34	11 47	12 02					12 05			12 31	12 34	12 47	13 02
Luton Airport Parkway [7] 52 ✈ d					11 26											12 26						
Luton [10] 52 d										12 09											13 09	
Bedford [7] 52 d					11 40					12 24						12 40					13 24	
Wellingborough d					11 53					12 36						12 53					13 36	
Kettering [5] a					12 00					12 44						13 00					13 44	
Kettering d					12 00					12 45						13 00					13 45	
Corby d										12a54											13a54	
Oakham 47 a																						
Melton Mowbray 47 a																						
Market Harborough d					12 11				12 29							13 11				13 29		
Leicester a					12 23			12 34	12 42		13 04					13 24			13 34	13 42		14 04
Leicester d					12 24	12 30		12 35	12 43		13 04					13 25	13 30		13 35	13 43		14 04
Syston d						12 37											13 37					
Sileby d						12 42											13 42					
Barrow Upon Soar d		←				12 48							←				13 48					
Loughborough d		11 53			12 33	12 53		12 45					12 53			13 34	13 53		13 46			
East Midlands Parkway ✈ d		12 03				→		12 52	13 00				13 04				→		13 53	14 00		
Beeston a		12 12			12 43								13 13			13 48						
Nottingham [8] a		12 25			12 54				13 13				13 25			13 57				14 12		
Nottingham d	12 17	12 29		12 47								13 17	13 29		13 47							
Newark Castle 27 a		12 51											13 51									
Lincoln 27 a		13 23											14 23									
Langley Mill d	12 38											13 38										
Alfreton d	12 46			13 10								13 46			14 10							
Long Eaton a								12 57											13 57			
Derby [6] a								13 08											14 08			
Derby d			12 19				12 55							13 20				13 46				
Chesterfield d	12 56		13 03	13 21			13 34				13 43	13 56		14 03	14 20			14 32				14 43
Sheffield [7] a	13 13		13 17	13 37			13 46				14 00	14 13		14 17	14 38			14 46				15 00
Manchester Piccadilly 78 a				14 37											15 37							
Doncaster [7] 29 a							14 16											15 16				
Wakefield Kirkgate [4] 31,34 a	13 55											14 55										
Wakefield Westgate [7] 31 a			13 46											14 46								
Leeds [10] 31,34 a	14 15		14 00									15 15		15 00								
York [8] 29 a			14 30				14 40							15 30				15 40				

	NT ◇	EM A	XC ■ ■ B	EM ◇ C	EM ◇■ 🛒	EM D	XC ◇■ E 🛒	EM ◇■ 🛒	EM ◇■ 🛒	EM ◇■ 🛒	EM ◇■ 🛒	NT ◇	EM A	XC ◇■ H 🛒	EM ◇ C	EM ◇■ 🛒	EM I	XC ◇■ G 🛒	EM ◇■ 🛒	EM ◇■ 🛒	EM ◇■ 🛒
St Pancras International ⊖52 d					13 05			13 31	13 34	13 47	14 02					14 05			14 31	14 34	14 47
Luton Airport Parkway [7] 52 ✈ d					13 26											14 26					
Luton [10] 52 d										14 09											15 09
Bedford [7] 52 d					13 40					14 24						14 40					15 24
Wellingborough d					13 53					14 36						14 53					15 36
Kettering [5] a					14 00					14 44						15 00					15 44
Kettering d					14 00					14 45						15 00					15 45
Corby d										14a54											15a54
Oakham 47 a																					
Melton Mowbray 47 a																					
Market Harborough d					14 11				14 29							15 11				15 29	
Leicester a					14 23			14 34	14 42		15 04					15 23			15 34	15 42	
Leicester d					14 24	14 30		14 35	14 43		15 04					15 24	15 30		15 35	15 43	
Syston d						14 37											15 36				
Sileby d						14 42											15 41				
Barrow Upon Soar d		←				14 48							←				15 48				
Loughborough d		13 53			14 33	14 53		14 45					14 53			15 33	15 53		15 45		
East Midlands Parkway ✈ d		14 03				→		14 52	15 00				15 04				→		15 52	16 00	
Beeston a		14 12			14 43								15 11			15 43					
Nottingham [8] a		14 25			14 54				15 12				15 21			15 54				16 12	
Nottingham d	14 17	14 29		14 47								15 17	15 29		15 47						
Newark Castle 27 a		14 52											15 51								
Lincoln 27 a		15 22											16 23								
Langley Mill d	14 38											15 38									
Alfreton d	14 46			15 08								15 46			16 10						
Long Eaton a								14 57											15 57		
Derby [6] a								15 08											16 08		
Derby d			14 18				14 51							15 22				15 49			
Chesterfield d	14 56		15 03	15 20			15 32				15 46	15 56		16 03	16 20			16 36			
Sheffield [7] a	15 13		15 17	15 37			15 46				16 01	16 13		16 18	16 37			16 48			
Manchester Piccadilly 78 a				16 37											17 37						
Doncaster [7] 29 a							16 17											17 13			
Wakefield Kirkgate [4] 31,34 a	15 55											16 55									
Wakefield Westgate [7] 31 a			15 46											16 46							
Leeds [10] 31,34 a	16 15		16 00									17 15		17 00							
York [8] 29 a			16 30				16 40							17 30				17 42			

A From Leicester
B From Reading to Glasgow Central
C From Norwich to Liverpool Lime Street
D To Lincoln
E From Penzance to Newcastle
F From Southampton Central to Aberdeen
G From Plymouth to Newcastle
H From Southampton Central to Dundee
I To Sleaford

For connections from Gatwick Airport refer to Table T052

Table T053-F

London - East Midlands - Sheffield

Mondays to Fridays

3 September to 21 September

	EM ◇■ 🛒	NT ◇	EM A	XC ◇■ B 🛒	EM ◇ C	EM ◇■ 🛒	EM D	XC ◇■ E 🛒	EM ◇■ 🛒	EM ◇■ 🛒	EM ◇■ 🛒	EM ◇■ 🛒	NT ◇	EM F	XC ◇■ G 🛒	EM ◇ C	EM ◇■ 🛒	EM D	XC ◇■ H 🛒	EM ◇■ 🛒	EM F	EM ◇■ I 🛒
St Pancras International ⊖52 d	15 02					15 05			15 31	15 34	15 47	16 02					16 05			16 31		16 34
Luton Airport Parkway [7] 52 ✈ d						15 26											16 26					
Luton [10] 52 d											16 09											
Bedford [7] 52 d						15 40					16 24											
Wellingborough d						15 53					16 35						16 50					
Kettering [5] a						16 00					16 44						16 57					
Kettering d						16 00					16 45						16 58					
Corby d											16a54											
Oakham 47 a																						
Melton Mowbray 47 a																						
Market Harborough d						16 11				16 29							17 08					17 34
Leicester a	16 04					16 23			16 34	16 42		17 04					17 21			17 39		17 47
Leicester d	16 05					16 24	16 30		16 35	16 43		17 05					17 22	17 27		17 40		17 48
Syston d							16 35											17 35				
Sileby d							16 41											17 40				
Barrow Upon Soar d			←				16 48							←				17 45			←	
Loughborough d			15 53			16 33	16 53		16 45					16 53			17 32	17 51		17 50	17 51	
East Midlands Parkway ✈ d			16 02				→		16 52	17 00				17 02				→		17 58	17 59	18 06
Beeston a			16 10			16 43								17 12			17 43				18 07	
Nottingham [8] a			16 21			16 56				17 15				17 19			17 53				18 15	18 20
Nottingham d		16 17	16 27		16 47								17 17	17 21		17 47					18 17	
Newark Castle 27 a			16 51											17 52							18 51	
Lincoln 27 a			17 16											18 24							19 22	
Langley Mill d		16 38											17 38			18 04						
Alfreton d		16 46			17 08								17 46			18 12						
Long Eaton a									16 57											18 01		
Derby [6] a									17 08											18 13		
Derby d				16 21				16 48							17 18				17 51			
Chesterfield d	16 41	16 56		17 04	17 20			17 34				17 43	17 56		18 03	18 22			18 30			
Sheffield [7] a	16 56	17 13		17 18	17 37			17 48				18 02	18 13		18 18	18 38			18 44			
Manchester Piccadilly 78 a					18 37											19 37						
Doncaster [7] 29 a																			19 17			
Wakefield Kirkgate [4] 31,34 a		17 55											18 55									
Wakefield Westgate [7] 31 a				17 45				18 16							18 48							
Leeds [10] 31,34 a		18 15		18 00				18 34					19 15		19 03							
York [8] 29 a				18 30				19 01							19 30				19 41			

	EM ◇■ J 🛒	EM ◇■ 🛒	NT ◇	XC ◇■ K 🛒	EM ◇ C	EM ◇■ 🛒	EM D	XC ◇■ H 🛒	EM ◇■ 🛒	EM F	EM ◇■ 🛒	EM ◇■ 🛒	EM ◇■ L 🛒	EM ◇■ 🛒	NT ◇	XC ◇■ M 🛒	EM ◇ N	EM ◇■ 🛒	XC ◇■ H 🛒	EM ◇■ 🛒	NT ◇	EM
St Pancras International ⊖52 d	16 47	16 50				17 05					17 19	17 34	17 47	17 50				18 05		18 19		
Luton Airport Parkway [7] 52 ✈ d											17 42			18 15						18 42		
Luton [10] 52 d																						
Bedford [7] 52 d																						
Wellingborough d		17 33				17 50					18 06			18 36				18 49				
Kettering [5] a		17 44				17 56					18 14			18 48				18 55				
Kettering d		17 46				17 57			18 10		18 15			18 54				18 56				
Corby d		17a55												19 04								
Oakham 47 a														19 25								
Melton Mowbray 47 a														19 36								
Market Harborough d						18 08					18 26	18 32								19 16		
Leicester a	17 55					18 21			18 32		18 40	18 45	18 59					19 17		19 29		
Leicester d	17 58					18 22	18 26		18 36		18 41	18 47	19 01					19 21		19 30		19 30
Syston d							18 33															19 37
Sileby d							18 38															19 42
Barrow Upon Soar d							18 43			←												19 48
Loughborough d						18 32	18 48		18 45	18 48	18 52									19 40		19 53
East Midlands Parkway ✈ d						18 40	→		18 53	18 56	19 01	19 05						19 39				20 03
Beeston a						18 46				19 04		19 12						19 48				20 10
Nottingham [8] a						18 55				19 13	19 16	19 23						19 59				20 21
Nottingham d			18 17		18 47					19 19	19 27				19 17		19 40	20 00			20 17	
Newark Castle 27 a										19 54								20 24				
Lincoln 27 a										20 21								20 52				
Langley Mill d			18 38												19 37						20 36	
Alfreton d			18 46		19 08										19 45		20 02				20 44	
Long Eaton a									18 59		19 46									19 51		
Derby [6] a									19 12		19 58									20 03		
Derby d				18 20				18 50								19 19			19 50			
Chesterfield d	18 41		18 56	19 03	19 20			19 28					19 40		19 55	20 04	20 12		20 37		20 54	
Sheffield [7] a	18 57		19 13	19 18	19 37			19 40					19 58		20 13	20 18	20 28		20 49		21 13	
Manchester Piccadilly 78 a					20 37												21 36					
Doncaster [7] 29 a								20 13											21 19			
Wakefield Kirkgate [4] 31,34 a			19 55												20 55						21 55	
Wakefield Westgate [7] 31 a				19 46												20 46						
Leeds [10] 31,34 a			20 15	20 02											21 15	21 01					22 15	
York [8] 29 a				20 30				20 41											21 40			

A From Leicester to Sleaford
B From Reading to Glasgow Central
C From Norwich to Liverpool Lime Street
D To Lincoln
E From Plymouth to Edinburgh
F From Leicester
G From Southampton Central to Edinburgh
H From Plymouth to Newcastle
I The Robin Hood
J The Master Cutler
K From Reading to Edinburgh. 🛒 to Leeds
L The South Yorkshireman
M From Southampton Central
N From Norwich

For connections from Gatwick Airport refer to Table T052

Table T053-F

Mondays to Fridays

3 September to 21 September

London - East Midlands - Sheffield

	XC	EM	EM	EM	XC	EM	EM	EM	NT	EM	EM	EM	EM	EM	EM	XC	EM	EM	EM	NT	EM
	◇■	◇■	◇■	◇■	◇■	◇■		◇■	◇		◇■	◇■	◇■	◇■		◇■	◇■	◇■	◇■	◇	
	A				B		C			D					E	B					D
St Pancras International ⊖52 d		18 34	18 47	19 01		19 04		19 32			19 35	19 47	20 01	20 05			20 31	20 34	21 01		
Luton Airport Parkway 52 d						19 28								20 28							
Luton 52 d												20 10									
Bedford 52 d						19 43						20 24		20 42							
Wellingborough d		19 20	19 29			19 56						20 35		20 56							
Kettering a		19 28	19 37								20 26	20 44		21 02							
Kettering d		19 29	19 39								20 27	20 45		21 02							
Corby d			19a48									20a54									
Oakham 47 a																					
Melton Mowbray 47 a																					
Market Harborough d				20 00		20 12		20 29			20 39			21 13				21 29			
Leicester a		19 50		20 12		20 28		20 42			20 53		21 10	21 27			21 35	21 41	22 06		
Leicester d		19 54		20 12		20 28	20 30	20 43			20 54		21 11	21 27	21 30		21 37	21 41	22 07		
Syston d							20 36								21 37						
Sileby d							20 42								21 42						
Barrow Upon Soar d							20 48			←					21 48						←
Loughborough d		20 05		20 23		20 38	20 53			20 53	21 05			21 37	21 53		21 48				21 53
East Midlands Parkway d		20 13		20 31			→	20 56		21 02	21 14				→		21 56	22 00			22 03
Beeston a						20 53				21 09				21 51							22 11
Nottingham a		20 27				21 02		21 10		21 20				22 00				22 16			22 21
Nottingham d		20 33				21 08			21 12	21 20										22 15	
Newark Castle 27 a										21 50											
Lincoln 27 a										22 20											
Langley Mill d						21 25			21 36												
Alfreton d						21 33			21 44												
Long Eaton a											21 17						22 00				
Derby a											21 30						22 15				
Derby d	20 21				20 50											21 50					
Chesterfield d	21 04	21 10		21 05	21 36	21 44			21 55				22 02			22 27			22 45	23 02	
Sheffield a	21 18	21 27		21 24	21 50	21 58			22 13				22 18			22 44			23 01	23 25	
Manchester Piccadilly 78 a																					
Doncaster 29 a					22 25																
Wakefield Kirkgate 31,34 a									22 55												
Wakefield Westgate 31 a	21 46	22 15				22 33							22 48			23 12					
Leeds 31,34 a	22 02	22 34				22 49			23 14				23 06			23 26					
York 29 a					22 51																

	EM	NT	EM	EM	EM	EM	EM	EM	EM
	◇■	◇	◇■	◇■	◇■	◇■	◇■	◇■	◇■
St Pancras International ⊖52 d	21 04			21 30	21 50	22 00		22 20	23 08
Luton Airport Parkway 52 d	21 27				22 13			22 44	
Luton 52 d				21 55		22 25			23 47
Bedford 52 d	21 43			22 09	22 26	22 40		22 58	00 09
Wellingborough d	21 55			22 21	22 39	22 53		23 12	00 22
Kettering a	22 02			22 27	22 46	23 01		23 18	00 40
Kettering d	22 03		22 11	22 28	22 47	23 02	23 11	23 19	00 41
Corby d			22a26				23a26		
Oakham 47 a									
Melton Mowbray 47 a									
Market Harborough d	22 13			22 38	22 57	23 13		23 29	00 52
Leicester a	22 25			22 50	23 08	23 29		23 44	01 06
Leicester d	22 26			22 52	23 09	23 31		23 45	01 08
Syston d									
Sileby d									
Barrow Upon Soar d									
Loughborough d	22 36			23 02	23 19	23 42		23 55	01 19
East Midlands Parkway d	22 44			23 09	23 28	23 50		00 02	01 27
Beeston a						23 58			01 33
Nottingham a	22 54					00 06			01 41
Nottingham d		23 18							01 47
Newark Castle 27 a									
Lincoln 27 a									
Langley Mill d		23 36							
Alfreton d		23 44							
Long Eaton a					23 31				
Derby a				23 22	23 43				02 05
Derby d									
Chesterfield d		23 54						00 27	
Sheffield a		00 16						00 43	
Manchester Piccadilly 78 a									
Doncaster 29 a									
Wakefield Kirkgate 31,34 a									
Wakefield Westgate 31 a									
Leeds 31,34 a									
York 29 a									

A From Reading
B From Plymouth
C To Lincoln
D From Leicester
E To Nottingham

For connections from Gatwick Airport refer to Table T052

Table T053-F

Mondays to Fridays

24 September to 5 October

London - East Midlands - Sheffield

	EM	EM	EM	EM	EM	EM	NT	NT	XC	EM	EM	XC	NT	XC	EM	EM	EM	EM	EM	XC	NT	EM
	MX	MO	MO	MX	MX																	
	◇■	◇■	◇■	◇■	◇■	◇	◇	◇	◇■	◇		◇■	◇	◇■	◇■	◇		◇■	◇■	◇■	◇	◇■
	A	A	A	A		B			C	B		D		E		B				D		
St Pancras International ⊖52 d					00 15										05 52			06 23				06 48
Luton Airport Parkway 52 d					00 55																	07 10
Luton 52 d					00 58										06 15			06 46				
Bedford 52 d				00 09	01 26										06 29			07 00				
Wellingborough d			00 15	00 22	01 36										06 41			07 12				
Kettering a			00 25	00 40	01 46										06 47			07 18				
Kettering d			00 26	00 41	01 46										06 48			07 19	07 38			
Corby d																			07a47			
Oakham 47 a																						
Melton Mowbray 47 a																						
Market Harborough d			00 36	00 52	01 58										06 58			07 29				
Leicester a			00 50	01 06	02 13										07 10			07 41				07 54
Leicester d		00 11	00 52	01 08							06 26				07 12		07 28	07 42				07 55
Syston d											06 33						07 35					
Sileby d											06 38						07 40					
Barrow Upon Soar d											06 43						07 45					
Loughborough d		00 21	01 02	01 19							06 48				07 22		07 50	07 52				08 05
East Midlands Parkway d	00 02	00 29	01 09	01 27							06 56				07 29		08 00					08 13
Beeston a		00 34		01 33							07 06						08 09					08 23
Nottingham a		00 41		01 41							07 16						08 17					08 31
Nottingham d				01 47		05 23		06 17		06 39			07 18			07 46					08 17	
Newark Castle 27 a																						
Lincoln 27 a																						
Langley Mill d								06 36					07 37								08 36	
Alfreton d								06 44		07 00			07 45			08 10					08 44	
Long Eaton a															07 33							
Derby a			01 21	02 05											07 43							
Derby d									05 56			06 54		07 17						07 48		
Chesterfield d	00 27					05 51	06 25	06 54	07 02	07 10		07 32	07 57	08 06		08 20		08 27		08 36	08 55	
Sheffield a	00 43					06 15	06 42	07 11	07 15	07 28		07 46	08 15	08 19		08 38		08 45		08 48	09 13	
Manchester Piccadilly 78 a						07 38				08 37						09 37						
Doncaster 29 a												08 14								09 16		
Wakefield Kirkgate 31,34 a							07 22	07 57					08 57								09 56	
Wakefield Westgate 31 a									07 47					08 47								
Leeds 31,34 a							07 43	08 17	08 01				09 17	09 02							10 16	
York 29 a									08 29			08 40		09 30						09 40		

	EM	XC	EM	EM	EM	XC	EM	EM	EM	EM	EM	NT	XC	EM	EM	EM	XC	EM	EM	EM	EM	EM
		◇■	◇	◇■		◇■	◇■	◇■	◇■	◇■	◇■	◇	◇■	◇	◇■		◇■	◇■	◇■		◇	◇■
	F	G	H		I	J							K	H		F	L			I		
St Pancras International ⊖52 d				07 04			07 32	07 35		07 49	08 02				08 05			08 31	08 34			08 47
Luton Airport Parkway 52 d								07 56							08 28							
Luton 52 d				07 27																		09 12
Bedford 52 d				07 41				08 10		08 25					08 42							09 27
Wellingborough d				07 54				08 23		08 37					08 55							09 41
Kettering a				08 03				08 30		08 45					09 02							09 52
Kettering d				08 04				08 30	08 32	08 46					09 02							09 53
Corby d									08a41	08a55											09 26	10a02
Oakham 47 a																					09 47	
Melton Mowbray 47 a																					10 00	
Market Harborough d				08 15			08 27	08 41							09 13				09 32			
Leicester a				08 29			08 39	08 54			09 06				09 25			09 37	09 46			
Leicester d	08 25			08 30			08 40	08 55			09 07				09 26	09 30		09 38	09 46			
Syston d	08 33															09 37						
Sileby d	08 39															09 42						
Barrow Upon Soar d	08 45				←											09 48				←		
Loughborough d	08 50			08 41	08 50		08 50	09 04							09 35	09 53		09 48		09 53		
East Midlands Parkway d	→			08 51	08 58		08 58									→		09 56	10 03	10 05	10 37	
Beeston a					09 09			09 14							09 47					10 12		
Nottingham a				09 11	09 20			09 23							09 57				10 18	10 25		
Nottingham d			08 47		09 25							09 19		09 47						10 29		
Newark Castle 27 a					09 50															10 51		
Lincoln 27 a					10 19															11 30		
Langley Mill d												09 38										
Alfreton d			09 09									09 46		10 08								
Long Eaton a							09 01											09 59				
Derby a							09 13											10 13			10 50	
Derby d		08 19				08 47							09 20				09 53					
Chesterfield d		09 03	09 20			09 38					09 46	09 56	10 03	10 20			10 34					
Sheffield a		09 17	09 37			09 50					10 04	10 13	10 18	10 38			10 48					
Manchester Piccadilly 78 a			10 37											11 37								
Doncaster 29 a						10 17											11 16					
Wakefield Kirkgate 31,34 a												10 55										
Wakefield Westgate 31 a		09 46											10 46									
Leeds 31,34 a		10 00										11 15	11 00									
York 29 a		10 30				10 40							11 30				11 40					

A From St Pancras International
B To Liverpool Lime Street
C To Glasgow Central
D From Birmingham New Street to Newcastle
E From Birmingham New Street to Edinburgh
F To Lincoln
G From Birmingham New Street to Glasgow Central
H From Norwich to Liverpool Lime Street
I From Leicester
J From Bath Spa to Newcastle
K From Guildford to Edinburgh
L From Plymouth to Newcastle

For connections from Gatwick Airport refer to Table T052

London - East Midlands - Sheffield

	EM	NT	XC	EM	EM	EM	XC	EM	EM	EM	EM	NT	EM	EM	EM	XC	XC	EM	EM	EM	EM
	◇■ 🍴	◇	◇■ A 🍴	◇ B	◇■ 🍴	C	◇■ D	◇■ 🍴	◇■ 🍴	◇■ 🍴	◇■ 🍴	◇	E	◇■ 🍴	C	◇■ F 🍴	◇■ D 🍴	◇■ 🍴	◇■ 🍴	◇■ 🍴	◇■ 🍴
St Pancras International ⊖52 d	09 02				09 05			09 31	09 34	09 47	10 02			10 05				10 31	10 34	10 47	11 02
Luton Airport Parkway ■ 52 ✈ d					09 26									10 28							
Luton ■ 52 d										10 09										11 09	
Bedford ■ 52 d					09 40					10 24				10 42						11 24	
Wellingborough d					09 53					10 36				10 56						11 35	
Kettering ■ a					10 00					10 45				11 03						11 44	
d					10 00					10 46				11 03						11 45	
Corby d										10a55										11a54	
Oakham 47 a																					
Melton Mowbray 47 a																					
Market Harborough d					10 11				10 31					11 15					11 29		
Leicester a	10 06				10 23			10 34	10 44		11 04			11 29				11 35	11 43		12 05
d	10 06				10 24	10 30		10 35	10 45		11 04			11 30	11 30			11 36	11 44		12 05
Syston d						10 36									11 37						
Sileby d						10 42									11 42						
Barrow Upon Soar d						10 48							←		11 48						
Loughborough d					10 33	10 53		10 45					10 53	11 40	11 53			11 46			
East Midlands Parkway ✈ d						→		10 53	11 02				11 05		→			11 54	12 01		
Beeston a					10 48								11 14	11 56							
Nottingham ■ a					10 57				11 19				11 25	12 05					12 15		
d		10 17		10 51								11 17	11 29								
Newark Castle 27 a													11 51								
Lincoln 27 a													12 23								
Langley Mill d		10 38										11 37									
Alfreton d		10 46		11 12								11 45									
Long Eaton a								10 56										11 58			
Derby ■ a								11 07										12 13			
d			10 20				10 51									11 19	11 55				
Chesterfield d	10 46	10 56	11 03	11 22			11 32				11 42	11 56				12 03	12 32				12 42
Sheffield ■ a	11 00	11 13	11 17	11 38			11 46				12 00	12 13				12 17	12 46				13 00
Manchester Piccadilly 78 a				12 37																	
Doncaster ■ 29 a							12 16										13 16				
Wakefield Kirkgate ■ 31,34 a		11 55										12 55									
Wakefield Westgate ■ 31 a			11 46													12 46					
Leeds ■ 31,34 a		12 15	12 01									13 15				13 00					
York ■ 29 a			12 30				12 40									13 30	13 40				

	NT	EM	XC	EM	EM	EM	XC	EM	EM	EM	EM	NT	EM	XC	EM	EM	EM	XC	EM	EM	EM	EM
	◇	E	◇■ A	◇ B	◇■ 🍴	C	◇■ G 🍴	◇■ 🍴	◇■ 🍴	◇■ 🍴	◇■ 🍴	◇	E	◇■ H 🍴	◇ B	◇■ 🍴	C	◇■ D 🍴	◇■ 🍴	◇■ 🍴	◇■ 🍴	◇■ 🍴
St Pancras International ⊖52 d					11 05			11 31	11 34	11 47	12 02					12 05			12 31	12 34	12 47	13 02
Luton Airport Parkway ■ 52 ✈ d					11 26											12 26						
Luton ■ 52 d										12 09											13 09	
Bedford ■ 52 d					11 40					12 24						12 40					13 24	
Wellingborough d					11 53					12 36						12 53					13 36	
Kettering ■ a					12 00					12 44						13 00					13 44	
d					12 00					12 45						13 00					13 45	
Corby d										12a54											13a54	
Oakham 47 a																						
Melton Mowbray 47 a																						
Market Harborough d					12 11				12 29							13 11				13 29		
Leicester a					12 23			12 34	12 42		13 04					13 24			13 34	13 42		14 04
d					12 24	12 30		12 35	12 43		13 04					13 25	13 30		13 35	13 43		14 04
Syston d						12 37											13 37					
Sileby d						12 42											13 42					
Barrow Upon Soar d		←				12 48							←				13 48					
Loughborough d		11 53			12 33	12 53		12 45					12 53			13 34	13 53		13 46			
East Midlands Parkway ✈ d		12 03				→		12 52	13 00				13 04				→		13 53	14 00		
Beeston a		12 12			12 43								13 13			13 48						
Nottingham ■ a		12 25			12 54				13 13				13 25			13 57				14 12		
d	12 17	12 29		12 47								13 17	13 29		13 47							
Newark Castle 27 a		12 51											13 51									
Lincoln 27 a		13 25											14 25									
Langley Mill d	12 38											13 38										
Alfreton d	12 46			13 10								13 46			14 10							
Long Eaton a								12 57											13 57			
Derby ■ a								13 08											14 08			
d			12 19				12 55							13 20				13 46				
Chesterfield d	12 56		13 03	13 21			13 34				13 43	13 56		14 03	14 20			14 32				14 43
Sheffield ■ a	13 13		13 17	13 37			13 46				14 00	14 13		14 17	14 38			14 46				15 00
Manchester Piccadilly 78 a				14 37											15 37							
Doncaster ■ 29 a							14 16											15 16				
Wakefield Kirkgate ■ 31,34 a	13 55											14 55										
Wakefield Westgate ■ 31 a			13 46											14 46								
Leeds ■ 31,34 a	14 15		14 00									15 15		15 00								
York ■ 29 a			14 30				14 40							15 30				15 40				

A From Reading to Glasgow Central
B From Norwich to Liverpool Lime Street
C To Lincoln
D From Plymouth to Newcastle
E From Leicester
F From Winchester to Edinburgh
G From Penzance to Newcastle
H From Southampton Central to Aberdeen

For connections from Gatwick Airport refer to Table T052

Table T053-F

Mondays to Fridays
24 September to 5 October

London - East Midlands - Sheffield

	NT	EM	XC	EM	EM	EM	XC	EM	EM	EM	EM	NT	EM	XC	EM	EM	EM	XC	EM	EM	EM
	◇	A	■ ■ B	◇ C	◇■ 🍴	D	◇■ E 🍴	◇■ 🍴	◇■ 🍴	◇■ 🍴	◇■ 🍴	◇	A	◇■ F 🍴	◇ C	◇■ 🍴	G	◇■ H 🍴	◇■ 🍴	◇■ 🍴	◇■ 🍴
St Pancras International ⊖52 d					13 05			13 31	13 34	13 47	14 02					14 05			14 31	14 34	14 47
Luton Airport Parkway ■ 52 ✈ d					13 26											14 26					
Luton ■ 52 d										14 09											15 09
Bedford ■ 52 d					13 40					14 24						14 40					15 24
Wellingborough d					13 53					14 36						14 53					15 36
Kettering ■ a					14 00					14 44						15 00					15 44
d					14 00					14 45						15 00					15 45
Corby d										14a54											15a54
Oakham 47 a																					
Melton Mowbray 47 a																					
Market Harborough d					14 11				14 29							15 11				15 29	
Leicester a					14 23			14 34	14 42		15 04					15 23			15 34	15 42	
d					14 24	14 30		14 35	14 43		15 04					15 24	15 30		15 35	15 43	
Syston d						14 37											15 36				
Sileby d						14 42											15 41				
Barrow Upon Soar d		←				14 48							←				15 48				
Loughborough d		13 53			14 33	14 53		14 45					14 53			15 33	15 53		15 45		
East Midlands Parkway ✈ d		14 03				→		14 52	15 00				15 04				→		15 52	16 00	
Beeston a		14 12			14 43								15 11			15 43					
Nottingham ■ a		14 25			14 54				15 12				15 21			15 54				16 12	
d	14 17	14 29		14 47								15 17	15 29		15 47						
Newark Castle 27 a		14 52											15 51								
Lincoln 27 a		15 24											16 25								
Langley Mill d	14 38											15 38									
Alfreton d	14 46			15 08								15 46			16 10						
Long Eaton a								14 57											15 57		
Derby ■ a								15 08											16 08		
d			14 18				14 51							15 22				15 49			
Chesterfield d	14 56		15 03	15 20			15 32				15 46	15 56		16 03	16 20			16 36			
Sheffield ■ a	15 13		15 17	15 37			15 46				16 01	16 13		16 18	16 37			16 48			
Manchester Piccadilly 78 a				16 37											17 37						
Doncaster ■ 29 a							16 17											17 13			
Wakefield Kirkgate ■ 31,34 a	15 55											16 55									
Wakefield Westgate ■ 31 a			15 46											16 46							
Leeds ■ 31,34 a	16 15		16 00									17 15		17 00							
York ■ 29 a			16 30				16 40							17 30				17 42			

	EM	NT	EM	XC	EM	EM	EM	XC	EM	EM	EM	EM	NT	EM	XC	EM	EM	EM	EM	XC	EM	EM
	◇■ 🍴	◇	I	◇■ B 🍴	◇ C	◇■ 🍴	D	◇■ J 🍴	◇■ 🍴	◇■ 🍴	◇■ 🍴	◇■ 🍴	◇	A	◇■ K 🍴	◇ C	◇■ L 🍴	◇■ M 🍴	D	◇■ H 🍴	◇■ 🍴	A
St Pancras International ⊖52 d	15 02					15 05			15 31	15 34	15 47	16 02					16 05	16 05			16 31	
Luton Airport Parkway ■ 52 ✈ d						15 26											16 26	16 26				
Luton ■ 52 d											16 09											
Bedford ■ 52 d						15 40					16 24											
Wellingborough d						15 53					16 35						16 50	16 50				
Kettering ■ a						16 00					16 44						16 57	16 57				
d						16 00					16 45						16 58	16 58				
Corby d											16a54											
Oakham 47 a																						
Melton Mowbray 47 a																						
Market Harborough d						16 11				16 29							17 08	17 08				
Leicester a	16 04					16 23			16 34	16 42		17 04					17 21	17 21			17 39	
d	16 05					16 24	16 30		16 35	16 43		17 05					17 22	17 22	17 27		17 40	
Syston d							16 35												17 35			
Sileby d							16 41												17 40			
Barrow Upon Soar d			←				16 48							←					17 45			←
Loughborough d			15 53			16 33	16 53		16 45					16 53			17 32	17 32	17 51		17 50	17 51
East Midlands Parkway ✈ d			16 02				→		16 52	17 00				17 02					→		17 58	17 59
Beeston a			16 10			16 43								17 12			17 43	17 45				18 07
Nottingham ■ a			16 21			16 56				17 15				17 19			17 53	17 55				18 15
d		16 17	16 27		16 47								17 17	17 21		17 47						18 17
Newark Castle 27 a			16 51											17 52								18 51
Lincoln 27 a			17 18											18 26								19 24
Langley Mill d		16 38											17 38			18 04						
Alfreton d		16 46			17 08								17 46			18 12						
Long Eaton a									16 57												18 01	
Derby ■ a									17 08												18 13	
d				16 21				16 48							17 18					17 51		
Chesterfield d	16 41	16 56		17 04	17 20			17 34				17 43	17 56		18 03	18 22				18 30		
Sheffield ■ a	16 56	17 13		17 18	17 37			17 48				18 02	18 13		18 18	18 38				18 44		
Manchester Piccadilly 78 a					18 37											19 37						
Doncaster ■ 29 a																				19 17		
Wakefield Kirkgate ■ 31,34 a		17 55											18 55									
Wakefield Westgate ■ 31 a				17 45				18 16							18 48							
Leeds ■ 31,34 a		18 15		18 00				18 34					19 15		19 03							
York ■ 29 a				18 30				19 01							19 30					19 41		

A From Leicester
B From Reading to Glasgow Central
C From Norwich to Liverpool Lime Street
D To Lincoln
E From Penzance to Newcastle
F From Southampton Central to Dundee
G To Sleaford
H From Plymouth to Newcastle
I From Leicester to Sleaford
J From Plymouth to Edinburgh
K From Southampton Central to Edinburgh
L not 26 September
M 26 September

For connections from Gatwick Airport refer to Table T052

Table T053-F

London - East Midlands - Sheffield

Mondays to Fridays

24 September to 5 October

		EM	EM	EM	NT	XC	EM	EM	EM	XC	EM	EM	EM	EM	EM	EM	NT	XC	EM	EM	XC	EM	NT
		◇■	◇■	◇■	◇	◇■	◇	◇■		◇■	◇■		◇■	◇■	◇■	◇■	◇	◇■	◇	◇■	◇■	◇■	◇
		A	B			C	D		E	F		G			H			I	J		F		
		🛒	🛒	🛒		🛒		🛒		🛒	🛒		🛒	🛒	🛒	🛒		🛒		🛒	🛒	🛒	
St Pancras International ⊖52	d	16 34	16 47	16 50				17 05					17 19	17 34	17 47	17 50				18 05		18 19	
Luton Airport Parkway ■ 52 ✈	d												17 42			18 15						18 42	
Luton ■ 52	d																						
Bedford ■ 52	d																						
Wellingborough	d			17 33				17 50					18 06			18 36				18 49			
Kettering ■	a			17 44				17 56					18 14			18 48				18 55			
	d			17 46				17 57			18 10		18 15			18 54				18 56			
Corby	d			17a55												19 04							
Oakham 47	a															19 25							
Melton Mowbray 47	a															19 36							
Market Harborough	d	17 34						18 08					18 26	18 32								19 16	
Leicester	a	17 47	17 55					18 21			18 32		18 40	18 45	18 59					19 17		19 29	
	d	17 48	17 58					18 22	18 26		18 36		18 41	18 47	19 01					19 21		19 30	
Syston	d								18 33														
Sileby	d								18 38														
Barrow Upon Soar	d								18 43			←											
Loughborough	d							18 32	18 48		18 45	18 48	18 52									19 40	
East Midlands Parkway ✈	d	18 06						18 40	→		18 53	18 56	19 01	19 05						19 39			
Beeston	a							18 46				19 04		19 12						19 48			
Nottingham ■ 🚢	a	18 20						18 55				19 13	19 16	19 23						19 59			
	d				18 17		18 47					19 19	19 27				19 17		19 40	20 00			20 17
Newark Castle 27	a											19 54								20 24			
Lincoln 27	a											20 23								20 52			
Langley Mill	d				18 38												19 37						20 36
Alfreton	d				18 46		19 08										19 45		20 02				20 44
Long Eaton	a										18 59		19 46									19 51	
Derby ■	a										19 12		19 58									20 03	
	d					18 20				18 50								19 19			19 50		
Chesterfield	d		18 41		18 56	19 03	19 20			19 28					19 40		19 55	20 04	20 12		20 37		20 54
Sheffield ■ 🚢	a		18 57		19 13	19 18	19 37			19 40					19 58		20 13	20 18	20 28		20 49		21 13
Manchester Piccadilly 78	a						20 37												21 36				
Doncaster ■ 29	a									20 13											21 19		
Wakefield Kirkgate ■ 31,34	a				19 55												20 55						21 55
Wakefield Westgate ■ 31	a					19 46												20 46					
Leeds ■ 31,34	a				20 15	20 02											21 15	21 01					22 15
York ■ 29	a					20 30				20 41											21 40		

		EM	XC	EM	EM	EM	XC	EM	EM	EM	NT	EM	EM	EM	EM	EM	EM	XC	EM	EM	EM	NT
			◇■	◇■	◇■	◇■	◇■	◇■		◇■	◇		◇■	◇■	◇■	◇■		◇■	◇■	◇■	◇■	◇
			K				L		E			G					M	L				
				🛒	🛒	🛒		🛒		🛒			🛒	🛒	🛒	🛒			🛒	🛒	🛒	
St Pancras International ⊖52	d			18 34	18 47	19 01		19 04		19 32			19 35	19 47	20 01	20 05			20 31	20 34	21 01	
Luton Airport Parkway ■ 52 ✈	d							19 28								20 28						
Luton ■ 52	d													20 10								
Bedford ■ 52	d							19 43						20 24		20 42						
Wellingborough	d			19 20	19 29			19 56						20 35		20 56						
Kettering ■	a			19 28	19 37								20 26	20 44		21 02						
	d			19 29	19 39								20 27	20 45		21 02						
Corby	d				19a48									20a54								
Oakham 47	a																					
Melton Mowbray 47	a																					
Market Harborough	d					20 00		20 12		20 29			20 39			21 13				21 29		
Leicester	a			19 50		20 12		20 28		20 42			20 53		21 10	21 27			21 35	21 41	22 06	
	d	19 30		19 54		20 12		20 28	20 30	20 43			20 54		21 11	21 27	21 30		21 37	21 41	22 07	
Syston	d	19 37							20 36								21 37					
Sileby	d	19 42							20 42								21 42					
Barrow Upon Soar	d	19 48							20 48			←					21 48					
Loughborough	d	19 53		20 05		20 23		20 38	20 53			20 53	21 05			21 37	21 53		21 48			
East Midlands Parkway ✈	d	20 03		20 13		20 31			→	20 56		21 02	21 14				→		21 56	22 00		
Beeston	a	20 10						20 53				21 09				21 51						
Nottingham ■ 🚢	a	20 21		20 27				21 02		21 10		21 20				22 00				22 16		
	d			20 33				21 08			21 12	21 20										22 15
Newark Castle 27	a											21 50										
Lincoln 27	a											22 22										
Langley Mill	d							21 25			21 36											
Alfreton	d							21 33			21 44											
Long Eaton	a												21 17						22 00			
Derby ■	a												21 30						22 15			
	d		20 21				20 50											21 50				
Chesterfield	d		21 04	21 10		21 05	21 36	21 44			21 55				22 02			22 27			22 45	23 02
Sheffield ■ 🚢	a		21 18	21 27		21 24	21 50	21 58			22 13				22 18			22 44			23 01	23 25
Manchester Piccadilly 78	a																					
Doncaster ■ 29	a						22 25															
Wakefield Kirkgate ■ 31,34	a										22 55											
Wakefield Westgate ■ 31	a		21 46	22 15				22 33							22 48			23 12				
Leeds ■ 31,34	a		22 02	22 34				22 49			23 14				23 06			23 26				
York ■ 29	a						22 51															

A The Robin Hood
B The Master Cutler
C From Reading to Edinburgh. 🛒 to Leeds
D From Norwich to Liverpool Lime Street
E To Lincoln
F From Plymouth to Newcastle
G From Leicester
H The South Yorkshireman
I From Southampton Central
J From Norwich
K From Reading
L From Plymouth
M To Nottingham

For connections from Gatwick Airport refer to Table T052

Table T053-F

London - East Midlands - Sheffield

Mondays to Fridays

24 September to 5 October

		EM	EM	NT	EM	EM	EM	EM	EM	EM	EM
			◇■	◇	◇■	◇■	◇■	◇■	◇■	◇■	◇■
		A									
			🛒		🛒	🛒	🛒	🛒	🛒	🛒	🛒
St Pancras International ⊖52	d		21 04			21 30	21 50	22 00		22 20	23 08
Luton Airport Parkway ■ 52 ✈	d		21 27				22 13			22 44	
Luton ■ 52	d					21 55		22 25			23 47
Bedford ■ 52	d		21 43			22 09	22 26	22 40		22 58	00 09
Wellingborough	d		21 55			22 21	22 39	22 53		23 12	00 22
Kettering ■	a		22 02			22 27	22 46	23 01		23 18	00 40
	d		22 03		22 11	22 28	22 47	23 02	23 11	23 19	00 41
Corby	d				22a26				23a26		
Oakham 47	a										
Melton Mowbray 47	a										
Market Harborough	d		22 13			22 38	22 57	23 13		23 29	00 52
Leicester	a		22 25			22 50	23 08	23 29		23 44	01 06
	d		22 26			22 52	23 09	23 31		23 45	01 08
Syston	d										
Sileby	d										
Barrow Upon Soar	d	←									
Loughborough	d	21 53	22 36			23 02	23 19	23 42		23 55	01 19
East Midlands Parkway ✈	d	22 03	22 44			23 09	23 28	23 50		00 02	01 27
Beeston	a	22 11						23 58			01 33
Nottingham ■ 🚢	a	22 21	22 54					00 06			01 41
	d			23 18							01 47
Newark Castle 27	a										
Lincoln 27	a										
Langley Mill	d			23 36							
Alfreton	d			23 44							
Long Eaton	a						23 31				
Derby ■	a					23 22	23 43				02 05
	d										
Chesterfield	d			23 54						00 27	
Sheffield ■ 🚢	a			00 16						00 43	
Manchester Piccadilly 78	a										
Doncaster ■ 29	a										
Wakefield Kirkgate ■ 31,34	a										
Wakefield Westgate ■ 31	a										
Leeds ■ 31,34	a										
York ■ 29	a										

Mondays to Fridays

8 October to 7 December

		EM	EM	EM	EM	EM	EM	XC	NT	EM	NT	XC	EM	EM	XC	EM	NT	XC	EM	EM	EM	EM	EM
		MX	MO	MO	MX	MX																	
		◇■	◇■	◇■	◇■	◇■	◇	◇■	◇	◇■	◇	◇■	◇		◇■	◇■	◇	◇■	◇■	◇		◇■	◇■
		B	B	B	B		C	D				E	C		F			G		C			
		🛒	🚌	🚌	🛒	🛒				🛒		🛒			🛒	🛒		🛒	🛒			🛒	🛒
St Pancras International ⊖52	d					00 15													05 52			06 23	
Luton Airport Parkway ■ 52 ✈	d					00 55																	
Luton ■ 52	d					00 58													06 15			06 46	
Bedford ■ 52	d				00 09	01 26													06 29			07 00	
Wellingborough	d			00 15	00 22	01 36													06 41			07 12	
Kettering ■	a			00 25	00 40	01 46													06 47			07 18	
	d			00 26	00 41	01 46													06 48			07 19	07 38
Corby	d																						07a47
Oakham 47	a																						
Melton Mowbray 47	a																						
Market Harborough	d			00 36	00 52	01 58													06 58			07 29	
Leicester	a			00 50	01 06	02 13													07 10			07 41	
	d		00 11	00 52	01 08									06 26					07 12		07 28	07 42	
Syston	d													06 33							07 35		
Sileby	d													06 38							07 40		
Barrow Upon Soar	d													06 43							07 45		
Loughborough	d		00 21	01 02	01 19									06 48					07 22		07 50	07 52	
East Midlands Parkway ✈	d	00 02	00 29	01 09	01 27									06 56					07 29		08 00		
Beeston	a		00 34		01 33									07 06							08 09		
Nottingham ■ 🚢	a		00 41		01 41									07 16							08 17		
	d				01 47		05 23				06 17		06 39				07 18			07 46			
Newark Castle 27	a																						
Lincoln 27	a																						
Langley Mill	d										06 36						07 37						
Alfreton	d										06 44		07 00				07 45			08 10			
Long Eaton	a																		07 33				
Derby ■	a	00 14		01 21	02 05														07 43			08 06	
	d	00 17						05 56		06 27		06 35			07 13	07 17		07 44	07 47			08 09	
Chesterfield	d	00 36					05 51	06 17	06 25	06 45	06 54	07 02	07 10		07 32	07 42	07 57	08 06	08 11	08 20		08 28	
Sheffield ■ 🚢	a	00 51					06 15	06 31	06 42	07 09	07 11	07 15	07 28		07 45	08 00	08 15	08 19	08 27	08 38		08 45	
Manchester Piccadilly 78	a						07 38						08 37							09 37			
Doncaster ■ 29	a							07 00							08 14								
Wakefield Kirkgate ■ 31,34	a								07 22		07 57						08 57						
Wakefield Westgate ■ 31	a											07 47						08 47					
Leeds ■ 31,34	a								07 43		08 17	08 01					09 17	09 02					
York ■ 29	a							07 24				08 29			08 40			09 30					

A From Leicester
B From St Pancras International
C To Liverpool Lime Street
D To Newcastle
E From Birmingham New Street to Glasgow Central
F From Birmingham New Street to Newcastle
G From Birmingham New Street to Edinburgh

For connections from Gatwick Airport refer to Table T052

Table T053-F

Mondays to Fridays

8 October to 7 December

London - East Midlands - Sheffield

	XC	NT	EM	EM	XC	EM	EM	EM	EM	EM	EM	EM	XC	EM	NT	XC	EM	EM	EM	EM	EM	EM
	◇■	◇	◇■		◇■	◇	◇■		◇■	◇■	◇■	◇■	◇■	◇■	◇	◇■	◇	◇■		◇■	◇■	
	A			B	C	D		E					F			G	D		B			E
	🍴		🍴		🍴		🍴		🍴	🍴	🍴	🍴	🍴	🍴		🍴		🍴		🍴	🍴	
St Pancras International ⊖52 d			06 48				07 04		07 32	07 35		07 49		08 02				08 05		08 31	08 34	
Luton Airport Parkway ■ 52 ✈ d			07 10							07 56								08 28				
Luton ■ 52 d							07 27															
Bedford ■ 52 d							07 41			08 10		08 25						08 42				
Wellingborough d							07 54			08 23		08 37						08 55				
Kettering ■ a							08 03			08 30		08 45						09 02				
d							08 04			08 30	08 32	08 46						09 02				
Corby d											08a41	08a55										
Oakham 47 a																						
Melton Mowbray 47 a																						
Market Harborough d							08 15		08 27	08 41								09 13			09 32	
Leicester a			07 54				08 29		08 39	08 54				09 06				09 25		09 37	09 46	
d			07 55	08 25			08 30		08 40	08 55				09 07				09 26	09 30	09 38	09 46	
Syston d				08 33															09 37			
Sileby d				08 39															09 42			
Barrow Upon Soar d				08 45				←											09 48			←
Loughborough d			08 05	08 50			08 41	08 50	08 50	09 04								09 35	09 53	09 48		09 53
East Midlands Parkway ✈ d			08 13	→			08 52	08 58	08 58										→	09 56	10 03	10 05
Beeston a			08 20					09 09		09 14								09 47				10 12
Nottingham ■ a			08 27				09 11	09 20		09 23								09 57			10 16	10 22
d		08 17				08 47		09 25							09 17		09 47					10 29
Newark Castle 27 a								09 50														10 51
Lincoln 27 a								10 19														11 30
Langley Mill d		08 36													09 36							
Alfreton d		08 44				09 08									09 44		10 08					
Long Eaton a									09 01											09 59		
Derby ■ a									09 14					09 28						10 10		
d	08 13				08 44				09 15				09 20	09 29		09 44				10 11		
Chesterfield d	08 36	08 55			09 03	09 20			09 33					09 47	09 55	10 03	10 20			10 28		
Sheffield ■ a	08 48	09 13			09 17	09 37			09 47				09 50	10 01	10 13	10 18	10 38			10 45		
Manchester Piccadilly 78 a						10 37											11 37					
Doncaster ■ 29 a	09 16												10 17									
Wakefield Kirkgate ■ 31,34 a		09 56													10 55							
Wakefield Westgate ■ 31 a					09 46											10 46						
Leeds ■ 31,34 a		10 16			10 00										11 15	11 00						
York ■ 29 a	09 40				10 30								10 40			11 30						

	XC	EM	EM	EM	NT	XC	EM	EM	EM	EM	EM	EM	XC	EM	NT	EM	XC	EM	EM	EM	EM
	◇■	◇	◇■	◇■	◇	◇■	◇	◇■		◇■	◇■	◇■	◇■	◇■	◇		◇■	◇	◇■		◇■
	H					I	D		B				J			E	G	D		B	
	🍴	🍴	🍴	🍴		🍴		🍴		🍴	🍴	🍴	🍴	🍴			🍴		🍴		🍴
St Pancras International ⊖52 d			08 47	09 02				09 05		09 31	09 34	09 47		10 02					10 05		10 31
Luton Airport Parkway ■ 52 ✈ d								09 26											10 28		
Luton ■ 52 d			09 12									10 09									
Bedford ■ 52 d			09 27					09 40				10 24							10 42		
Wellingborough d			09 41					09 53				10 36							10 56		
Kettering ■ a			09 52					10 00				10 45							11 03		
d			09 53					10 00				10 46							11 03		
Corby d		09 26	10a02									10a55									
Oakham 47 a		09 47																			
Melton Mowbray 47 a		10 00																			
Market Harborough d								10 11			10 31								11 15		
Leicester a				10 06				10 23		10 34	10 44			11 04					11 29		11 35
d				10 06				10 24	10 30	10 35	10 45			11 04					11 30	11 30	11 36
Syston d									10 36											11 37	
Sileby d									10 42											11 42	
Barrow Upon Soar d									10 48							←				11 48	
Loughborough d								10 33	10 53	10 45						10 53			11 40	11 53	11 46
East Midlands Parkway ✈ d		10 40							→	10 53	11 02					11 05				→	11 54
Beeston a								10 43								11 12			11 56		
Nottingham ■ a								10 52			11 14					11 22			12 05		
d					10 17		10 51								11 17	11 29		11 47			
Newark Castle 27 a																11 51					
Lincoln 27 a																12 23					
Langley Mill d					10 36										11 36						
Alfreton d					10 44		11 12								11 44			12 08			
Long Eaton a										10 56											11 57
Derby ■ a		10 54		10 27						11 07				11 25							12 08
d	10 16			10 29		10 44				11 09			11 16	11 30			11 44				12 09
Chesterfield d				10 47	10 55	11 03	11 22			11 27				11 47	11 55		12 03	12 20			12 27
Sheffield ■ a	10 48			11 01	11 13	11 17	11 38			11 41			11 46	12 01	12 13		12 17	12 38			12 41
Manchester Piccadilly 78 a							12 37											13 37			
Doncaster ■ 29 a	11 16												12 16								
Wakefield Kirkgate ■ 31,34 a					11 55										12 55						
Wakefield Westgate ■ 31 a						11 46											12 46				
Leeds ■ 31,34 a					12 15	12 01									13 15		13 00				
York ■ 29 a	11 40					12 30							12 40				13 30				

A From Birmingham New Street to Newcastle
B To Lincoln
C From Bath Spa to Glasgow Central
D From Norwich to Liverpool Lime Street
E From Leicester
F From Guildford to Newcastle
G From Plymouth to Edinburgh
H From Reading to Newcastle
I From Plymouth to Glasgow Central
J From Winchester to Newcastle

For connections from Gatwick Airport refer to Table T052

Table T053-F

Mondays to Fridays

8 October to 7 December

London - East Midlands - Sheffield

	EM	EM	XC	EM	NT	EM	XC	EM	EM	EM	EM	EM	EM	XC	EM	NT	EM	XC	EM	EM	EM	EM
	◇■	◇■	◇■	◇■	◇		◇■	◇	◇■		◇■	◇■	◇■	◇■	◇■	◇		◇■	◇	◇■		◇■
			A			B	C	D		E				F			B	G	D		E	
	🍴	🍴	🍴	🍴			🍴		🍴		🍴	🍴	🍴	🍴	🍴			🍴		🍴		🍴
St Pancras International ⊖52 d	10 34	10 47		11 02					11 05		11 31	11 34	11 47		12 02					12 05		12 31
Luton Airport Parkway ■ 52 ✈ d									11 26											12 26		
Luton ■ 52 d		11 09											12 09									
Bedford ■ 52 d		11 24							11 40				12 24							12 40		
Wellingborough d		11 35							11 53				12 36							12 53		
Kettering ■ a		11 44							12 00				12 44							13 00		
d		11 45							12 00				12 45							13 00		
Corby d		11a54											12a54									
Oakham 47 a																						
Melton Mowbray 47 a																						
Market Harborough d	11 29								12 11			12 29								13 11		
Leicester a	11 43			12 05					12 23		12 34	12 42			13 04					13 24		13 34
d	11 44			12 05					12 24	12 30	12 35	12 43			13 04					13 25	13 30	13 35
Syston d										12 37											13 37	
Sileby d										12 42											13 42	
Barrow Upon Soar d						←				12 48							←				13 48	
Loughborough d						11 53			12 33	12 53	12 45						12 53			13 34	13 53	13 46
East Midlands Parkway ✈ d	12 01					12 04				→	12 52	13 00					13 04				→	13 53
Beeston a						12 11			12 43								13 11			13 44		
Nottingham ■ a	12 13					12 23			12 52			13 13					13 21			13 53		
d					12 17	12 29		12 47								13 17	13 29		13 47			
Newark Castle 27 a						12 51											13 51					
Lincoln 27 a						13 25											14 25					
Langley Mill d					12 36											13 36						
Alfreton d					12 44			13 10								13 44			14 10			
Long Eaton a											12 57											13 57
Derby ■ a				12 25							13 08				13 25							14 08
d			12 16	12 28			12 44				13 10			13 16	13 28			13 44				14 09
Chesterfield d				12 47	12 55		13 03	13 21			13 27				13 47	13 55		14 03	14 20			14 27
Sheffield ■ a			12 46	13 01	13 13		13 17	13 37			13 41			13 46	14 02	14 13		14 17	14 38			14 41
Manchester Piccadilly 78 a								14 37											15 37			
Doncaster ■ 29 a			13 16											14 16								
Wakefield Kirkgate ■ 31,34 a					13 55											14 55						
Wakefield Westgate ■ 31 a							13 46											14 46				
Leeds ■ 31,34 a					14 15		14 00									15 15		15 00				
York ■ 29 a			13 40				14 30							14 40				15 30				

	EM	EM	XC	EM	NT	EM	XC	EM	EM	EM	EM	EM	EM	XC	EM	NT	EM	XC	EM	EM	EM
	◇■	◇■	◇■	◇■	◇		◇■	◇	◇■		◇■	◇■	◇■	■ ■	◇■	◇		◇■	◇	◇■	
			A			B	C	D		E				F			B	H	D		I
	🍴	🍴	🍴	🍴			🍴		🍴		🍴	🍴	🍴	🍴	🍴			🍴		🍴	
St Pancras International ⊖52 d	12 34	12 47		13 02					13 05		13 31	13 34	13 47		14 02					14 05	
Luton Airport Parkway ■ 52 ✈ d									13 26											14 26	
Luton ■ 52 d		13 09											14 09								
Bedford ■ 52 d		13 24							13 40				14 24							14 40	
Wellingborough d		13 36							13 53				14 36							14 53	
Kettering ■ a		13 44							14 00				14 44							15 00	
d		13 45							14 00				14 45							15 00	
Corby d		13a54											14a54								
Oakham 47 a																					
Melton Mowbray 47 a																					
Market Harborough d	13 29								14 11			14 29								15 11	
Leicester a	13 42			14 04					14 23		14 34	14 42			15 04					15 23	
d	13 43			14 04					14 24	14 30	14 35	14 43			15 04					15 24	15 30
Syston d										14 37											15 36
Sileby d										14 42											15 41
Barrow Upon Soar d						←				14 48							←				15 48
Loughborough d						13 53			14 33	14 53	14 45						14 53			15 33	15 53
East Midlands Parkway ✈ d	14 00					14 03				→	14 52	15 00					15 04				→
Beeston a						14 10			14 43								15 11			15 43	
Nottingham ■ a	14 12					14 21			14 52			15 12					15 21			15 52	
d					14 17	14 29		14 47								15 17	15 29		15 47		
Newark Castle 27 a						14 52											15 51				
Lincoln 27 a						15 24											16 25				
Langley Mill d					14 36											15 36					
Alfreton d					14 44			15 08								15 44			16 10		
Long Eaton a											14 57										
Derby ■ a				14 25							15 08				15 25						
d			14 16	14 28			14 44				15 09			15 16	15 28			15 44			
Chesterfield d				14 47	14 55		15 03	15 20			15 27				15 47	15 55		16 03	16 20		
Sheffield ■ a			14 46	15 01	15 13		15 17	15 37			15 41			15 46	16 01	16 13		16 18	16 37		
Manchester Piccadilly 78 a								16 37											17 37		
Doncaster ■ 29 a			15 16											16 17							
Wakefield Kirkgate ■ 31,34 a					15 55											16 55					
Wakefield Westgate ■ 31 a							15 46											16 46			
Leeds ■ 31,34 a					16 15		16 00									17 15		17 00			
York ■ 29 a			15 40				16 30							16 40				17 30			

A From Reading to Newcastle
B From Leicester
C From Penzance to Glasgow Central
D From Norwich to Liverpool Lime Street
E To Lincoln
F From Southampton Central to Newcastle
G From Plymouth to Aberdeen
H From Plymouth to Dundee
I To Sleaford

For connections from Gatwick Airport refer to Table T052

London - East Midlands - Sheffield

Station		EM ◇1 🛒	EM ◇1 🛒	EM ◇1 🛒	XC ◇1 A 🛒	EM ◇1 🛒	NT ◇	EM B	XC ◇1 C 🛒	EM ◇ D	EM ◇1 🛒	EM E	EM ◇1 🛒	EM ◇1 🛒	EM ◇1 🛒	XC ◇1 F 🛒	EM ◇1 🛒	NT ◇	EM G	XC ◇1 H 🛒	EM ◇ D	EM ◇1 🛒	EM
St Pancras International ⊖52	d	14 31	14 34	14 47		15 02					15 05		15 31	15 34	15 47		16 02					16 05	
Luton Airport Parkway [7] 52 ✈	d										15 26											16 26	
Luton [10] 52	d			15 09											16 09								
Bedford [7] 52	d			15 24							15 40				16 24								
Wellingborough	d			15 36							15 53				16 35							16 50	
Kettering [5]	a			15 44							16 00				16 44							16 57	
	d			15 45							16 00				16 45							16 58	
Corby	d			15a54											16a54								
Oakham 47	a																						
Melton Mowbray 47	a																						
Market Harborough	d		15 29								16 11			16 29								17 08	
Leicester	a	15 34	15 42			16 04					16 23		16 34	16 42			17 04					17 21	
	d	15 35	15 43			16 05					16 24	16 30	16 35	16 43			17 05					17 22	17 27
Syston	d											16 35											17 35
Sileby	d											16 41											17 40
Barrow Upon Soar	d							←				16 48							←				17 45
Loughborough	d	15 45						15 53			16 33	16 53	16 45						16 53			17 32	17 51
East Midlands Parkway ✈	d	15 52	16 00					16 02				→	16 52	17 00					17 02				17 59
Beeston	a							16 10			16 44								17 10			17 43	18 07
Nottingham [8] 🚢	a		16 12					16 21			16 54			17 12					17 21			17 53	18 15
	d						16 17	16 27		16 47								17 17	17 21		17 47		18 17
Newark Castle 27	a							16 51											17 52				18 51
Lincoln 27	a							17 18											18 26				19 24
Langley Mill	d						16 36											17 36			18 03		
Alfreton	d						16 44			17 08								17 44			18 11		
Long Eaton	a	15 57											16 57										
Derby [6]	a	16 08				16 26							17 08				17 26						
	d	16 09			16 16	16 29			16 43				17 09			17 18	17 28			17 42			
Chesterfield	d	16 27				16 47	16 55		17 04	17 20			17 28				17 46	17 55		18 03	18 20		
Sheffield [7] 🚢	a	16 41			16 44	17 02	17 13		17 18	17 37			17 44			17 46	18 01	18 13		18 18	18 38		
Manchester Piccadilly 78	a									18 37											19 37		
Doncaster [7] 29	a				17 13																		
Wakefield Kirkgate [4] 31,34	a						17 55											18 55					
Wakefield Westgate [7] 31	a								17 46							18 16				18 48			
Leeds [10] 31,34	a						18 15		18 01							18 34		19 15		19 03			
York [8] 29	a				17 42				18 30							19 01				19 30			

Station		XC ◇1 A 🛒	EM ◇1 🛒	EM ◇1 I 🛒	EM ◇1 J 🛒	EM ◇1 🛒	NT ◇	XC ◇1 K 🛒	EM ◇ D	EM ◇1 🛒	EM E	XC ◇1 L 🛒	EM ◇1 🛒	EM G	EM ◇1 🛒	EM ◇1 🛒	EM ◇1 M 🛒	EM ◇1 🛒	NT ◇	XC ◇1 N 🛒	EM ◇ O	EM ◇1 🛒	EM ◇1 🛒
St Pancras International ⊖52	d		16 31	16 34	16 47	16 50				17 05					17 19	17 34	17 47	17 50				18 05	18 19
Luton Airport Parkway [7] 52 ✈	d														17 42			18 15					18 42
Luton [10] 52	d																						
Bedford [7] 52	d																						
Wellingborough	d					17 33				17 50					18 06			18 36				18 49	
Kettering [5]	a					17 44				17 56					18 14			18 48				18 55	
	d					17 46				17 57			18 10		18 15			18 54				18 56	
Corby	d					17a55												19 04					
Oakham 47	a																	19 25					
Melton Mowbray 47	a																	19 36					
Market Harborough	d			17 34						18 08					18 26	18 32							19 16
Leicester	a		17 39	17 47	17 55					18 21			18 32		18 40	18 45	18 59					19 17	19 29
	d		17 40	17 48	17 58					18 22	18 26		18 36		18 41	18 47	19 01					19 21	19 30
Syston	d										18 33												
Sileby	d										18 38												
Barrow Upon Soar	d										18 43			←									
Loughborough	d		17 50							18 32	18 48		18 45	18 48	18 52								19 40
East Midlands Parkway ✈	d		17 59	18 06						18 40	→		18 53	18 56	19 01	19 05						19 36	
Beeston	a									18 46				19 04		19 11						19 45	
Nottingham [8] 🚢	a			18 20						18 57				19 13	19 16	19 20						19 53	
	d						18 17		18 47					19 20	19 24				19 17		19 39	20 00	
Newark Castle 27	a													19 55								20 24	
Lincoln 27	a													20 24								20 52	
Langley Mill	d						18 36												19 36				
Alfreton	d						18 44		19 08										19 44		20 01		
Long Eaton	a		18 03										18 59		19 43								19 48
Derby [6]	a		18 14		18 21								19 13		19 55		19 21						19 58
	d	18 10	18 15		18 25			18 44				19 09	19 15				19 27			19 44			19 59
Chesterfield	d		18 36		18 44		18 55	19 03	19 20			19 28	19 33				19 44		19 55	20 04	20 11		20 22
Sheffield [7] 🚢	a	18 44	18 55		19 03		19 13	19 18	19 37			19 40	19 50				19 59		20 13	20 18	20 28		20 41
Manchester Piccadilly 78	a								20 37												21 36		
Doncaster [7] 29	a	19 17										20 13											
Wakefield Kirkgate [4] 31,34	a						19 55												20 55				
Wakefield Westgate [7] 31	a							19 46												20 47			
Leeds [10] 31,34	a						20 15	20 02											21 15	21 02			
York [8] 29	a	19 40						20 30				20 41											

A From Reading to Newcastle
B From Leicester to Sleaford
C From Plymouth to Glasgow Central
D From Norwich to Liverpool Lime Street
E To Lincoln
F From Southampton Central to Edinburgh
G From Leicester
H From Plymouth to Edinburgh
I The Robin Hood
J The Master Cutler
K From Plymouth to Edinburgh. 🛒 to Leeds
L From Southampton Central to Newcastle
M The South Yorkshireman
N From Plymouth
O From Norwich

For connections from Gatwick Airport refer to Table T052

Table T053-F

Mondays to Fridays

8 October to 7 December

London - East Midlands - Sheffield

Station		XC ◇1 A	NT ◇	EM	XC ◇1 B	EM ◇1 🛒	EM ◇1 🛒	EM ◇1 🛒	XC ◇1 C	EM ◇1 🛒	EM D	EM ◇1 🛒	NT ◇	EM E	EM ◇1 🛒	EM ◇1 🛒	EM ◇1 🛒	EM ◇1 🛒	EM F	XC ◇1 B	EM ◇1 🛒	EM ◇1 🛒
St Pancras International ⊖52	d					18 34	18 47	19 01		19 04		19 32			19 35	19 47	20 01	20 05			20 31	20 34
Luton Airport Parkway [7] 52 ✈	d									19 28								20 28				
Luton [10] 52	d															20 10						
Bedford [7] 52	d									19 43						20 24		20 42				
Wellingborough	d					19 20	19 29			19 56						20 35		20 56				
Kettering [5]	a					19 28	19 37								20 26	20 44		21 02				
	d					19 29	19 39								20 27	20 45		21 02				
Corby	d						19a48									20a54						
Oakham 47	a																					
Melton Mowbray 47	a																					
Market Harborough	d							20 00		20 12		20 29			20 39			21 13				21 29
Leicester	a					19 50		20 12		20 28		20 42			20 53		21 10	21 27			21 35	21 41
	d			19 30		19 54		20 12		20 28	20 30	20 43			20 54		21 11	21 27	21 30		21 37	21 41
Syston	d			19 37							20 36								21 37			
Sileby	d			19 42							20 42								21 42			
Barrow Upon Soar	d			19 48							20 48			←					21 48			
Loughborough	d			19 53		20 05		20 23		20 38	20 53			20 53	21 05			21 37	21 53		21 48	
East Midlands Parkway ✈	d			20 02		20 13		20 31			→	20 56		21 02	21 14				→		21 56	22 00
Beeston	a			20 09						20 53				21 09				21 50				
Nottingham [8] 🚢	a			20 18		20 25				21 02		21 10		21 19				21 59				22 22
	d		20 17			20 33				21 08			21 12	21 20								
Newark Castle 27	a													21 50								
Lincoln 27	a													22 22								
Langley Mill	d		20 36			20 52				21 25			21 36									
Alfreton	d		20 44			21 00				21 33			21 44									
Long Eaton	a														21 17						22 00	
Derby [6]	a							20 45							21 30		21 35				22 14	
	d	20 09			20 45			20 45	21 19								21 37			21 46		
Chesterfield	d		20 54		21 03	21 11		21 09	21 38	21 44			21 55				21 59			22 08		
Sheffield [7] 🚢	a	20 44	21 13		21 17	21 27		21 24	21 50	21 58			22 13				22 18			22 22		
Manchester Piccadilly 78	a																					
Doncaster [7] 29	a	21 19							22 25													
Wakefield Kirkgate [4] 31,34	a		21 55										22 55									
Wakefield Westgate [7] 31	a				21 46	22 15				22 33							22 48			22 53		
Leeds [10] 31,34	a		22 15		22 02	22 34				22 49			23 14				23 06			23 07		
York [8] 29	a	21 40							22 51													

Station		EM ◇1 🛒	NT ◇	EM E	EM ◇1 🛒	NT ◇	EM ◇1 🛒	EM ◇1 🛒	EM ◇1 🛒	EM ◇1 🛒	EM ◇1 🛒	EM ◇1 🛒	EM ◇1 🛒
St Pancras International ⊖52	d	21 01			21 04			21 30	21 50	22 00		22 20	23 08
Luton Airport Parkway [7] 52 ✈	d				21 27				22 13			22 44	
Luton [10] 52	d							21 55		22 25			23 47
Bedford [7] 52	d				21 43			22 09	22 26	22 40		22 58	00 09
Wellingborough	d				21 55			22 21	22 39	22 53		23 12	00 22
Kettering [5]	a				22 02			22 27	22 46	23 01		23 18	00 40
	d				22 03		22 11	22 28	22 47	23 02	23 11	23 19	00 41
Corby	d						22a26				23a26		
Oakham 47	a												
Melton Mowbray 47	a												
Market Harborough	d				22 13			22 38	22 57	23 13		23 29	00 52
Leicester	a	22 06			22 25			22 50	23 08	23 29		23 44	01 06
	d	22 07			22 26			22 52	23 09	23 31		23 45	01 08
Syston	d												
Sileby	d												
Barrow Upon Soar	d			←									
Loughborough	d			21 53	22 36			23 02	23 19	23 42		23 55	01 19
East Midlands Parkway ✈	d			22 03	22 44			23 09	23 28	23 50		00 02	01 27
Beeston	a			22 14						23 58			01 33
Nottingham [8] 🚢	a			22 27	22 54					00 06			01 41
	d		22 15			23 18							01 47
Newark Castle 27	a												
Lincoln 27	a												
Langley Mill	d					23 36							
Alfreton	d					23 44							
Long Eaton	a								23 31				
Derby [6]	a	22 30	22 37					23 19	23 43			00 14	02 05
	d	22 31	22 39									00 17	
Chesterfield	d	22 52	23 02			23 54						00 36	
Sheffield [7] 🚢	a	23 05	23 25			00 16						00 51	
Manchester Piccadilly 78	a												
Doncaster [7] 29	a												
Wakefield Kirkgate [4] 31,34	a												
Wakefield Westgate [7] 31	a												
Leeds [10] 31,34	a												
York [8] 29	a												

A From Reading to Newcastle
B From Plymouth
C From Southampton Central
D To Lincoln
E From Leicester
F To Nottingham

For connections from Gatwick Airport refer to Table T052

Saturdays
26 May to 28 July

London - East Midlands - Sheffield

		EM ◇1 A	EM ◇1 A	EM ◇1	EM ◇ B	NT ◇	XC ◇1 C	EM ◇1	NT ◇	XC ◇1 D	XC ◇1 E	EM ◇ F	EM ◇ G	EM	XC ◇1 H	XC ◇1 I	EM ◇1	NT ◇	XC ◇1 J	XC ◇1 K	EM ◇1 L	EM ◇1 M	EM ◇ B
St Pancras International ⊖52	d			00 15																	05 48	05 48	
Luton Airport Parkway 52	d			00 53																			
Luton 52	d			00 57																	06 14	06 14	
Bedford 52	d		00 09	01 25																	06 28	06 28	
Wellingborough	d		00 22	01 36																	06 40	06 40	
Kettering	a		00 40	01 46																	06 47	06 47	
	d		00 41	01 46																	06 48	06 48	
Corby	d																						
Oakham 47	a																						
Melton Mowbray 47	a																						
Market Harborough	d		00 52	01 58																	06 58	06 58	
Leicester	a		01 06	02 13																	07 10	07 10	
	d		01 08											06 26							07 12	07 12	
Syston	d													06 33									
Sileby	d													06 38									
Barrow Upon Soar	d													06 43									
Loughborough	d		01 19											06 48							07 23	07 23	
East Midlands Parkway	d	00 02	01 27											06 56									
Beeston	a		01 33											07 06									
Nottingham	a		01 41											07 15									
	d		01 47		05 20				06 17			06 40	06 40					07 18					07 46
Newark Castle 27	a																						
Lincoln 27	a																						
Langley Mill	d								06 36									07 37					
Alfreton	d								06 44			07 01	07 01					07 45					08 09
Long Eaton	a																				07 31	07 31	
Derby	a	00 14	02 05																		07 45	07 45	
	d	00 16					05 56	06 27		06 38						07 13	07 21		07 44			07 48	
Chesterfield	d	00 35			05 49	06 25	06 31	06 46	06 54	07 02	07 02	07 11	07 11		07 32	07 32	07 43	07 57	08 03	08 03		08 10	08 20
Sheffield	a	00 51			06 15	06 42	06 45	07 08	07 11	07 15	07 15	07 28	07 29		07 44	07 46	07 59	08 15	08 19	08 19		08 26	08 37
Manchester Piccadilly 78	a				07 39							08 37	08 37										09 37
Doncaster 29	a						07 13								08 13	08 13							
Wakefield Kirkgate 31,34	a					07 22			07 57									08 57					
Wakefield Westgate 31	a									07 45	07 45								08 46	08 46			
Leeds 31,34	a					07 43			08 17	08 00	08 00							09 17	09 01	09 01			
York 29	a						07 40			08 30	08 30				08 40	08 40			09 30	09 30			

		EM N	EM O	XC ◇1 I	XC ◇1 H	EM ◇1 P	EM ◇1 Q	EM ◇1	NT ◇	EM ◇1 L	EM ◇1 M	XC ◇1 R	XC ◇1 S	EM ◇ T	EM ◇1	EM U	EM ◇1 L	EM ◇1 M	EM V	EM ◇1	EM ◇1	XC ◇1 W	XC ◇1 X
St Pancras International ⊖52	d					06 33	06 33			06 48	06 48				07 05					07 35	07 47		
Luton Airport Parkway 52	d									07 10	07 10									07 56			
Luton 52	d					06 56	06 56								07 27						08 09		
Bedford 52	d														07 40					08 10	08 24		
Wellingborough	d														07 52					08 23	08 35		
Kettering	a					07 22	07 22								08 00					08 30	08 43		
	d					07 23	07 23	07 38							08 01					08 30	08 44		
Corby	d							07a47													08a54		
Oakham 47	a																						
Melton Mowbray 47	a																						
Market Harborough	d					07 33	07 33								08 11					08 41			
Leicester	a					07 45	07 45			07 53	07 53				08 23					08 53			
	d	07 28	07 28			07 48	07 48			07 54	07 54				08 25	08 26	08 35	08 35		08 54			
Syston	d	07 35	07 35													08 33							
Sileby	d	07 40	07 40													08 38							
Barrow Upon Soar	d	07 45	07 45													08 43			←				
Loughborough	d	07 50	07 50			07 58	07 58			08 03	08 03				08 35	08 48	08 45	08 45	08 48	09 03			
East Midlands Parkway	d	07 58	07 58			08 05	08 05			08 12	08 12				08 42	→	08 52	08 52	08 56				
Beeston	a	08 06	08 07							08 17	08 18								09 04	09 13			
Nottingham	a	08 15	08 15							08 29	08 26				08 54				09 11	09 22			
	d								08 17					08 47					09 22				
Newark Castle 27	a																		09 49				
Lincoln 27	a																		10 19				
Langley Mill	d								08 36														
Alfreton	d								08 44					09 08									
Long Eaton	a																08 56	08 56					
Derby	a					08 18											09 08	09 09					
	d			08 13		08 22						08 44						09 10				09 16	
Chesterfield	d			08 32	08 32	08 41	08 47		08 55			09 03	09 03	09 20				09 28					09 34
Sheffield	a			08 44	08 44	08 56	09 01		09 13			09 17	09 17	09 37				09 41				09 44	09 46
Manchester Piccadilly 78	a													10 37									
Doncaster 29	a			09 15	09 15	09 53	09 53															10 15	10 15
Wakefield Kirkgate 31,34	a								09 56														
Wakefield Westgate 31	a											09 46	09 46										
Leeds 31,34	a								10 16			10 00	10 00										
York 29	a			09 40	09 40	10 17	10 17					10 30	10 30									10 40	10 40

A From St Pancras International
B To Liverpool Lime Street
C not 28 July. To Newcastle
D not 28 July. From Birmingham New Street to Glasgow Central
E 28 July. From Burton-on-Trent to Glasgow Central
F from 23 June. To Liverpool Lime Street
G until 16 June. To Liverpool Lime Street
H 28 July. From Birmingham New Street to Newcastle
I not 28 July. From Birmingham New Street to Newcastle
J not 28 July. From Birmingham New Street to Edinburgh
K 28 July. From Birmingham New Street to Edinburgh
L 28 July
M not 28 July
N from 23 June
O until 16 June
P not 28 July. To Scarborough
Q 28 July. To Scarborough
R not 28 July. From Bristol Temple Meads to Glasgow Central
S 28 July. From Birmingham New Street to Glasgow Central
T From Norwich to Liverpool Lime Street
U To Lincoln
V From Leicester
W not 28 July. From Guildford to Newcastle
X 28 July. From Bristol Temple Meads to Newcastle

For connections from Gatwick Airport refer to Table T052

Saturdays
26 May to 28 July

London - East Midlands - Sheffield

		EM ◇1 A	EM ◇1 B	NT ◇ A	NT ◇ B	XC ◇1 C	XC ◇1 D	EM ◇ E	EM ◇1 F	EM ◇1 G	EM H	EM ◇1 A	EM ◇1 B	EM I	EM ◇1	EM ◇1	XC ◇1 J	XC ◇1 K	EM ◇1 B	EM ◇1 A	NT ◇ B	NT ◇ A
St Pancras International ⊖52	d	08 02	08 02						08 05	08 05		08 31	08 31		08 34	08 47			09 02	09 02		
Luton Airport Parkway 52	d								08 26	08 26												
Luton 52	d															09 09						
Bedford 52	d								08 40	08 40						09 24						
Wellingborough	d								08 53	08 53						09 35						
Kettering	a								09 00	09 00						09 43						
	d								09 00	09 00						09 44						
Corby	d															09a54						
Oakham 47	a																					
Melton Mowbray 47	a																					
Market Harborough	d								09 11	09 11					09 29							
Leicester	a	09 04	09 04						09 23	09 23		09 34	09 34		09 42				10 04	10 04		
	d	09 05	09 05						09 24	09 24	09 26	09 35	09 35		09 43				10 05	10 05		
Syston	d										09 33											
Sileby	d										09 38											
Barrow Upon Soar	d										09 43			←								
Loughborough	d								09 33	09 33	09 48	09 45	09 45	09 48								
East Midlands Parkway	d										→	09 52	09 52	09 56	10 02							
Beeston	a								09 43	09 44				10 04								
Nottingham	a								09 52	09 53				10 14	10 16							
	d			09 16	09 17			09 47						10 29							10 17	10 17
Newark Castle 27	a													10 51								
Lincoln 27	a													11 25								
Langley Mill	d			09 37	09 36																10 36	10 38
Alfreton	d			09 45	09 44			10 08													10 44	10 46
Long Eaton	a											09 56	09 56									
Derby	a		09 26									10 08	10 09						10 26			
	d		09 28			09 44							10 10				10 16		10 28			
Chesterfield	d	09 46	09 46	09 56	09 55	10 03	10 05	10 20					10 28					10 33	10 46	10 46	10 55	10 56
Sheffield	a	10 00	10 01	10 13	10 13	10 17	10 17	10 37					10 42				10 46	10 47	11 01	11 01	11 13	11 13
Manchester Piccadilly 78	a							11 37														
Doncaster 29	a																11 15	11 15				
Wakefield Kirkgate 31,34	a			10 55	10 55																11 55	11 55
Wakefield Westgate 31	a					10 46	10 46															
Leeds 31,34	a			11 15	11 15	11 00	11 00														12 15	12 15
York 29	a					11 30	11 30										11 40	11 40				

		XC ◇1 L	XC ◇1 M	EM ◇ E	EM ◇1	EM H	EM ◇1 A	EM ◇1 B	EM I	EM ◇1	EM ◇1	XC ◇1 N	XC ◇1 K	EM ◇1 A	EM ◇1 B	NT ◇ B	NT ◇ A	XC ◇1 C	XC ◇1 O	EM ◇ E	EM ◇1	EM H	EM ◇1 A
St Pancras International ⊖52	d				09 05		09 31	09 31		09 34	09 47			10 02	10 02						10 05		10 31
Luton Airport Parkway 52	d				09 26																10 26		
Luton 52	d										10 09												
Bedford 52	d				09 40						10 24										10 40		
Wellingborough	d				09 53						10 35										10 53		
Kettering	a				10 00						10 43										11 00		
	d				10 00						10 44										11 00		
Corby	d										10a54												
Oakham 47	a																						
Melton Mowbray 47	a																						
Market Harborough	d				10 11					10 29											11 11		
Leicester	a				10 23		10 34	10 34		10 42				11 04	11 04						11 23		11 34
	d				10 24	10 26	10 35	10 35		10 43				11 05	11 05						11 24	11 26	11 35
Syston	d					10 33																11 33	
Sileby	d					10 38																11 38	
Barrow Upon Soar	d					10 43			←													11 43	
Loughborough	d				10 33	10 48	10 45	10 45	10 48												11 33	11 48	11 45
East Midlands Parkway	d					→	10 52	10 52	10 56	11 00												→	11 52
Beeston	a				10 43				11 04												11 43		
Nottingham	a				10 52				11 14	11 16											11 52		
	d			10 46					11 29							11 17	11 17			11 47			
Newark Castle 27	a								11 51														
Lincoln 27	a								12 26														
Langley Mill	d															11 36	11 38						
Alfreton	d			11 08												11 44	11 46			12 08			
Long Eaton	a						10 56	10 56															11 56
Derby	a						11 08	11 09							11 27								12 07
	d	10 44						11 10				11 16			11 29			11 44					
Chesterfield	d	11 03	11 03	11 20				11 28					11 33	11 41	11 47	11 55	11 56	12 03	12 03	12 20			
Sheffield	a	11 17	11 17	11 38				11 42				11 44	11 45	12 00	12 01	12 13	12 13	12 17	12 17	12 38			
Manchester Piccadilly 78	a			12 37																13 37			
Doncaster 29	a											12 13	12 13										
Wakefield Kirkgate 31,34	a															12 55	12 55						
Wakefield Westgate 31	a	11 46	11 46															12 46	12 46				
Leeds 31,34	a	12 00	12 00													13 15	13 15	13 00	13 00				
York 29	a	12 30	12 30									12 40	12 40					13 30	13 30				

A 28 July
B not 28 July
C not 28 July. From Plymouth to Edinburgh
D 28 July. From Guildford to Edinburgh
E From Norwich to Liverpool Lime Street
F until 16 June
G from 23 June
H To Lincoln
I From Leicester
J not 28 July. From Bournemouth to Newcastle
K 28 July. From Plymouth to Newcastle
L not 28 July. From Plymouth to Glasgow Central
M 28 July. From Bournemouth to Glasgow Central
N not 28 July. From Southampton Central to Newcastle
O 28 July. From Southampton Central to Edinburgh

For connections from Gatwick Airport refer to Table T052

Table T053-F

Saturdays
26 May to 28 July

London - East Midlands - Sheffield

		EM	EM	EM	EM	XC	XC	EM	NT	NT	XC	XC	EM	EM	EM	EM	EM	EM	EM	EM	XC	XC
		◇■		◇■	◇■	◇■	◇■	◇■	◇	◇	◇■	◇■	◇	◇■		◇■	◇■		◇■	◇■	◇■	◇■
		A	B			C	D		A	E	F	G	H		I	E	A	B			J	K
		🚲		🚲	🚲	🚲	🚲	🚲			🚲			🚲		🚲	🚲		🚲	🚲	🚲	🚲
St Pancras International ⊖ 52	d	10 31		10 34	10 47			11 02						11 05		11 31	11 31		11 34	11 50		
Luton Airport Parkway 52 ✈	d													11 26								
Luton 52	d				11 09															12 12		
Bedford 52	d				11 24									11 40						12 27		
Wellingborough	d				11 35									11 53						12 39		
Kettering	a				11 43									12 00						12 48		
	d				11 44									12 00						12 49		
Corby	d				11a53															12a59		
Oakham 47	a																					
Melton Mowbray 47	a																					
Market Harborough	d			11 29										12 11					12 29			
Leicester	a	11 34		11 42				12 04						12 23		12 34	12 34		12 42			
	d	11 35		11 43				12 05						12 24	12 26	12 35	12 35		12 43			
Syston	d														12 33							
Sileby	d														12 38							
Barrow Upon Soar	d		←												12 43			←				
Loughborough	d	11 45	11 48											12 33	12 48	12 45	12 45	12 48				
East Midlands Parkway ✈	d	11 52	11 56	12 00											→	12 52	12 52	12 56	13 00			
Beeston	a		12 04											12 43				13 04				
Nottingham	a		12 14	12 16										12 52				13 14	13 16			
	d		12 29						12 17	12 17			12 47					13 29				
Newark Castle 27	a		12 51															13 50				
Lincoln 27	a		13 22															14 24				
Langley Mill	d								12 36	12 38												
Alfreton	d								12 44	12 46			13 10									
Long Eaton	a	11 56														12 56	12 56					
Derby	a	12 09														13 08	13 09					
	d	12 10				12 16					12 44						13 10					13 16
Chesterfield	d	12 28					12 33	12 40	12 55	12 56	13 03	13 03	13 21				13 28				13 33	
Sheffield	a	12 42				12 44	12 45	12 55	13 13	13 14	13 17	13 18	13 37				13 42				13 45	13 48
Manchester Piccadilly 78	a												14 37									
Doncaster 29	a					13 15	13 15														14 15	14 15
Wakefield Kirkgate 31,34	a								13 55	13 55												
Wakefield Westgate 31	a										13 46	13 46										
Leeds 31,34	a								14 15	14 15	14 00	14 00										
York 29	a					13 40	13 40				14 30	14 30									14 40	14 40

		EM	EM	NT	NT	XC	XC	EM	EM	EM	EM	EM	EM	EM	EM	XC	XC	EM	EM	NT	NT	XC	XC
		◇■	◇■	◇	◇	◇■	◇■	◇	◇■		◇■	◇■		◇■	◇■	◇■	◇■	◇■	◇■	◇	◇	◇■	◇■
		E	A	A	E	L	M	H		I	E	A	B			C	D	E	A	A	E	F	G
		🚲	🚲			🚲	🚲		🚲		🚲	🚲		🚲	🚲	🚲	🚲	🚲	🚲			🚲	
St Pancras International ⊖ 52	d	12 02	12 02						12 05		12 31	12 31		12 34	12 47			13 02	13 02				
Luton Airport Parkway 52 ✈	d								12 26														
Luton 52	d														13 09								
Bedford 52	d								12 40						13 24								
Wellingborough	d								12 53						13 35								
Kettering	a								13 00						13 43								
	d								13 00						13 44								
Corby	d														13a53								
Oakham 47	a																						
Melton Mowbray 47	a																						
Market Harborough	d								13 11					13 29									
Leicester	a	13 04	13 04						13 23		13 34	13 34		13 42				14 04	14 04				
	d	13 05	13 05						13 24	13 26	13 35	13 35		13 43				14 05	14 05				
Syston	d									13 33													
Sileby	d									13 38													
Barrow Upon Soar	d									13 43			←										
Loughborough	d								13 33	13 48	13 45	13 45	13 48										
East Midlands Parkway ✈	d									→	13 52	13 52	13 56	14 00									
Beeston	a								13 43				14 04										
Nottingham	a								13 52				14 14	14 16									
	d			13 17	13 17			13 47					14 19							14 17	14 17		
Newark Castle 27	a												14 42										
Lincoln 27	a												15 11										
Langley Mill	d			13 36	13 38															14 36	14 38		
Alfreton	d			13 44	13 46			14 08												14 44	14 46		
Long Eaton	a										13 56	13 56											
Derby	a		13 26								14 08	14 09							14 26				
	d		13 28				13 44					14 10				14 16			14 28			14 44	
Chesterfield	d	13 40	13 46	13 55	13 56	14 02	14 03	14 20				14 28					14 33	14 44	14 46	14 55	14 56	15 03	15 03
Sheffield	a	13 55	14 01	14 13	14 13	14 17	14 18	14 37				14 42				14 44	14 45	14 59	15 01	15 13	15 13	15 17	15 17
Manchester Piccadilly 78	a							15 37															
Doncaster 29	a															15 15	15 15						
Wakefield Kirkgate 31,34	a			14 55	14 55															15 55	15 55		
Wakefield Westgate 31	a					14 46	14 46															15 46	15 46
Leeds 31,34	a			15 15	15 15	15 00	15 00													16 15	16 15	16 00	16 00
York 29	a					15 30	15 30									15 40	15 40					16 30	16 30

A not 28 July
B From Leicester
C not 28 July. From Reading to Newcastle
D 28 July. From Plymouth to Newcastle
E 28 July
F not 28 July. From Penzance to Glasgow Central
G 28 July. From Reading to Glasgow Central
H From Norwich to Liverpool Lime Street
I To Lincoln
J 28 July. From Penzance to Newcastle
K not 28 July. From Southampton Central to Newcastle
L 28 July. From Southampton Central to Aberdeen
M not 28 July. From Plymouth to Aberdeen

For connections from Gatwick Airport refer to Table T052

Table T053-F

Saturdays
26 May to 28 July

London - East Midlands - Sheffield

		EM	EM	EM	EM	EM	EM	EM	EM	XC	XC	EM	EM	NT	NT	XC	XC	EM	EM	EM	EM	EM	EM
		◇	◇■		◇■	◇■		◇■	◇■	◇■	◇■	◇■	◇■	◇	◇	◇■	◇■	◇	◇■		◇■	◇■	
		A		B	C	D	E			F	G	C	D	D	C	H	I	A		B	C	D	E
			🚲		🚲	🚲		🚲	🚲	🚲	🚲	🚲	🚲			🚲	🚲		🚲		🚲	🚲	
St Pancras International ⊖ 52	d		13 05		13 31	13 31		13 34	13 47			14 02	14 02						14 05		14 31	14 31	
Luton Airport Parkway 52 ✈	d		13 26																14 26				
Luton 52	d								14 09														
Bedford 52	d		13 40						14 24										14 40				
Wellingborough	d		13 53						14 36										14 53				
Kettering	a		14 00						14 45										15 00				
	d		14 00						14 46										15 00				
Corby	d								14a56														
Oakham 47	a																						
Melton Mowbray 47	a																						
Market Harborough	d		14 11					14 29											15 11				
Leicester	a		14 23		14 34	14 34		14 42				15 04	15 04						15 23		15 34	15 34	
	d		14 24	14 26	14 35	14 35		14 43				15 05	15 05						15 24	15 26	15 35	15 35	
Syston	d			14 33																15 33			
Sileby	d			14 38																15 38			
Barrow Upon Soar	d			14 43			←													15 43			←
Loughborough	d		14 33	14 48	14 45	14 45	14 48												15 33	15 48	15 45	15 45	15 48
East Midlands Parkway ✈	d			→	14 52	14 52	14 56	15 00												→	15 52	15 52	15 56
Beeston	a		14 43				15 04												15 43				16 04
Nottingham	a		14 52				15 14	15 16											15 52				16 14
	d	14 47					15 28							15 17	15 17			15 47					16 21
Newark Castle 27	a						15 49																16 42
Lincoln 27	a						16 25																17 08
Langley Mill	d													15 36	15 38								
Alfreton	d	15 08												15 44	15 46			16 10					
Long Eaton	a				14 56	14 56															15 56	15 56	
Derby	a				15 08	15 09							15 26								16 08	16 09	
	d					15 10				15 16			15 28				15 44					16 10	
Chesterfield	d	15 20				15 28					15 33	15 45	15 46	15 55	15 56	16 03	16 03	16 21				16 28	
Sheffield	a	15 37				15 42				15 44	15 45	16 00	16 01	16 13	16 13	16 17	16 18	16 37				16 42	
Manchester Piccadilly 78	a	16 37																17 37					
Doncaster 29	a									16 16	16 16												
Wakefield Kirkgate 31,34	a													16 55	16 55								
Wakefield Westgate 31	a															16 46	16 46						
Leeds 31,34	a													17 15	17 15	17 00	17 00						
York 29	a									16 40	16 40					17 28	17 29						

		EM	EM	XC	XC	EM	EM	NT	NT	XC	XC	EM	EM	EM	EM	XC	EM	EM	EM	EM	EM	XC
		◇■	◇■	◇■	◇■	◇■	◇■	◇	◇	◇■	◇■	◇	◇■		◇■	◇■	◇■		◇■	◇■	◇■	◇■
				J	K	C	D	D	C	L	M	A		B	C	N	D	E		O	P	F
		🚲	🚲	🚲	🚲	🚲	🚲			🚲	🚲		🚲		🚲	🚲	🚲		🚲	🚲	🚲	🚲
St Pancras International ⊖ 52	d	14 34	14 47			15 02	15 02						15 05		15 31		15 31		15 34	15 47	15 47	
Luton Airport Parkway 52 ✈	d												15 26									
Luton 52	d		15 09																	16 09	16 09	
Bedford 52	d		15 24										15 40							16 24	16 24	
Wellingborough	d		15 36										15 53							16 35	16 35	
Kettering	a		15 44										16 00							16 44	16 45	
	d		15 45										16 00							16 45	16 46	
Corby	d		15a54																	16a55	16a56	
Oakham 47	a																					
Melton Mowbray 47	a																					
Market Harborough	d	15 29											16 11						16 29			
Leicester	a	15 42				16 04	16 04						16 23		16 34		16 34		16 42			
	d	15 43				16 05	16 05						16 24	16 26	16 35		16 35		16 43			
Syston	d													16 33								
Sileby	d													16 38								
Barrow Upon Soar	d													16 43				←				
Loughborough	d												16 33	16 48	16 45		16 45	16 48				
East Midlands Parkway ✈	d	16 00												→	16 52		16 52	16 56	17 00			
Beeston	a												16 43					17 04				
Nottingham	a	16 16											16 52					17 14	17 16			
	d							16 17	16 17			16 44						17 29				
Newark Castle 27	a																	17 50				
Lincoln 27	a																	18 23				
Langley Mill	d							16 36	16 38													
Alfreton	d							16 44	16 46			17 05										
Long Eaton	a														16 56		16 56					
Derby	a						16 26								17 09		17 09					
	d			16 16			16 28				16 43						17 10					17 16
Chesterfield	d				16 33	16 40	16 46	16 55	16 56	17 04	17 04	17 15				17 26	17 28					
Sheffield	a			16 44	16 45	16 55	17 01	17 13	17 13	17 17	17 17	17 34				17 40	17 42					17 45
Manchester Piccadilly 78	a											18 37										
Doncaster 29	a			17 15	17 15																	
Wakefield Kirkgate 31,34	a							17 55	17 55													
Wakefield Westgate 31	a									17 45	17 47					18 16						18 16
Leeds 31,34	a							18 15	18 15	18 01	18 01					18 33						18 33
York 29	a			17 40	17 40					18 29	18 30					19 05						19 05

A From Norwich to Liverpool Lime Street
B To Lincoln
C 28 July
D not 28 July
E From Leicester
F not 28 July. From Southampton Central to Newcastle
G 28 July. From Penzance to Newcastle
H 28 July. From Southampton Central to Dundee
I not 28 July. From Newquay to Dundee
J not 28 July. From Reading to Newcastle
K 28 July. From Newquay to Newcastle
L 28 July. From Reading to Glasgow Central
M not 28 July. From Paignton to Glasgow Central
N 28 July. From Paignton to Edinburgh
O 9 June, 16 June
P not from 9 June until 16 June

For connections from Gatwick Airport refer to Table T052

Table T053-F

London - East Midlands - Sheffield

Saturdays
26 May to 28 July

		EM	EM	NT	NT	XC	XC	EM	EM	EM	EM	EM	EM	EM	EM	EM	XC	XC	EM	EM	NT	NT	XC
		◇■	◇■	◇	◇	◇■	◇■	◇	◇■	◇■		◇■	◇■		◇■	◇■	◇■	◇■	◇■	◇■	◇	◇	◇■
		A	B	B	A	C	D	E	B	A	F	A	B	G			H	I	A	B	B	A	J
		🛒	🛒			🛒	🛒		🛒	🛒		🛒	🛒		🛒	🛒	🛒	🛒	🛒	🛒			🛒
St Pancras International ⊖52	d	16 02	16 02						16 05	16 05		16 31	16 31		16 34	16 47			17 02	17 02			
Luton Airport Parkway ■ 52 ✈	d								16 26	16 26													
Luton ■ 52	d															17 09							
Bedford ■ 52	d								16 40	16 40						17 24							
Wellingborough	d								16 53	16 53						17 34							
Kettering ■	a								17 00	17 00						17 43							
	d								17 00	17 00						17 44							
Corby	d															17a53							
Oakham 47	a																						
Melton Mowbray 47	a																						
Market Harborough	d								17 11	17 11					17 29								
Leicester	a	17 04	17 04						17 23	17 23		17 34	17 34		17 42				18 04	18 04			
	d	17 05	17 05						17 24	17 24	17 26	17 35	17 35		17 43				18 05	18 05			
Syston	d										17 33												
Sileby	d										17 38												
Barrow Upon Soar	d										17 43			←									
Loughborough	d								17 33	17 33	17 48	17 45	17 45	17 48									
East Midlands Parkway ✈	d										→	17 52	17 52	17 56	18 00								
Beeston	a								17 43	17 45				18 04									
Nottingham ■	a								17 55	17 55				18 14	18 16								
	d			17 17	17 17			17 44						18 17							18 17	18 17	
Newark Castle 27	a													18 43									
Lincoln 27	a													19 23									
Langley Mill	d			17 36	17 38			18 00													18 36	18 38	
Alfreton	d			17 44	17 46			18 08													18 44	18 46	
Long Eaton	a											17 56	17 56										
Derby ■	a		17 26									18 08	18 09							18 26			
	d		17 28			17 44							18 10				18 16			18 28			
Chesterfield	d	17 46	17 46	17 55	17 56	18 03	18 05	18 18					18 28					18 33	18 40	18 46	18 55	18 56	19 04
Sheffield ■	a	18 01	18 01	18 13	18 14	18 17	18 17	18 34					18 41				18 44	18 47	18 55	19 01	19 13	19 13	19 17
Manchester Piccadilly 78	a							19 37															
Doncaster ■ 29	a																19 13	19 13					
Wakefield Kirkgate ■ 31,34	a			18 55	18 55																19 55	19 55	
Wakefield Westgate ■ 31	a					18 49	18 49																19 46
Leeds ■ 31,34	a			19 15	19 15	19 03	19 03														20 15	20 15	20 02
York ■ 29	a					19 30	19 30									19 40	19 42						20 30

		XC	EM	EM	EM	EM	EM	EM	EM	EM	XC	XC	EM	EM	NT	NT	XC	XC	EM	EM	EM	EM
		◇■	◇	◇■		◇■	◇■		◇■	◇■	◇■	◇■	◇■	◇■	◇	◇	◇■	◇■	◇	◇■		◇■
		K	E		L	A	B	G			M	I	A	B	B	A	N	O	P		F	A
		🛒		🛒		🛒	🛒		🛒	🛒	🛒	🛒	🛒	🛒			🛒	🛒		🛒		🛒
St Pancras International ⊖52	d			17 05		17 31	17 31		17 34	17 47			18 02	18 02						18 05		18 31
Luton Airport Parkway ■ 52 ✈	d			17 26																18 26		
Luton ■ 52	d									18 09												
Bedford ■ 52	d			17 40						18 24										18 40		
Wellingborough	d			17 53						18 35										18 53		
Kettering ■	a			18 00						18 45										19 00		
	d			18 00						18 46										19 00		
Corby	d									18a56												
Oakham 47	a																					
Melton Mowbray 47	a																					
Market Harborough	d			18 11					18 29											19 11		
Leicester	a			18 23		18 34	18 34		18 42				19 04	19 04						19 23		19 34
	d			18 24	18 26	18 35	18 35		18 43				19 05	19 05						19 24	19 26	19 35
Syston	d				18 33																19 33	
Sileby	d				18 38																19 38	
Barrow Upon Soar	d				18 43			←													19 43	
Loughborough	d			18 33	18 48	18 45	18 45	18 48												19 33	19 48	19 45
East Midlands Parkway ✈	d				→	18 52	18 52	18 56	19 00												→	19 52
Beeston	a			18 43				19 04												19 43		
Nottingham ■	a			18 52				19 15	19 16											19 52		
	d		18 47	19 29											19 17	19 17			19 36			
Newark Castle 27	a			19 52																		
Lincoln 27	a			20 26																		
Langley Mill	d														19 36	19 38						
Alfreton	d		19 08												19 44	19 46			20 01			
Long Eaton	a					18 56	18 56															19 56
Derby ■	a					19 08	19 09							19 26								20 08
	d	18 44					19 10				19 16			19 28			19 43					
Chesterfield	d	19 05	19 20				19 28				19 35	19 35	19 40	19 46	19 55	19 56	20 04	20 06	20 11			
Sheffield ■	a	19 17	19 37				19 41				19 47	19 47	19 55	20 01	20 13	20 13	20 18	20 18	20 30			
Manchester Piccadilly 78	a		20 37																21 29			
Doncaster ■ 29	a										20 13	20 13										
Wakefield Kirkgate ■ 31,34	a														20 55	20 55						
Wakefield Westgate ■ 31	a	19 46															20 47	20 46				
Leeds ■ 31,34	a	20 02													21 15	21 15	21 02	21 01				
York ■ 29	a	20 30									20 40	20 40					21 59	21 59				

A 28 July
B not 28 July
C not 28 July. From Plymouth to Edinburgh
D 28 July. From Southampton Central to Edinburgh
E From Norwich to Liverpool Lime Street
F To Lincoln
G From Leicester
H not 28 July. From Reading to Newcastle
I 28 July. From Plymouth to Newcastle
J 28 July. From Reading to Edinburgh. 🛒 to Leeds
K not 28 July. From Plymouth to Edinburgh. 🛒 to Leeds
L To Nottingham
M not 28 July. From Southampton Central to Newcastle
N not 28 July. From Plymouth. 🛒 to Leeds
O 28 July. From Southampton Central. 🛒 to Leeds
P From Norwich

For connections from Gatwick Airport refer to Table T052

Table T053-F

London - East Midlands - Sheffield

Saturdays
26 May to 28 July

		EM	EM	XC	XC	EM	EM	EM	EM	NT	NT	EM	EM	XC	EM	XC	EM	XC	XC	NT	EM	EM	EM
		◇■		◇■	◇■	◇■	◇■	◇■	◇■	◇	◇	◇■		◇■	◇■	◇■	◇■	◇■	◇■	◇		◇■	◇■
		A	B	C	D	E		F	A	F	A		G	H		I	J	K	L		B		
		🛒			🛒	🛒	🛒	🛒	🛒			🛒			🛒		🛒					🛒	🛒
St Pancras International ⊖52	d	18 31				18 34	18 47	19 02	19 02			19 05			19 31							19 34	19 47
Luton Airport Parkway ■ 52 ✈	d											19 26											
Luton ■ 52	d						19 09																20 10
Bedford ■ 52	d						19 24					19 40											20 24
Wellingborough	d						19 36					19 53											20 35
Kettering ■	a						19 45					20 00											20 43
	d						19 46					20 00											20 44
Corby	d						19a55																20a53
Oakham 47	a																						
Melton Mowbray 47	a																						
Market Harborough	d					19 29						20 11										20 29	
Leicester	a	19 34				19 42		20 04	20 04			20 23			20 34							20 42	
	d	19 35				19 43		20 05	20 05			20 24	20 26		20 35							20 43	
Syston	d												20 33										
Sileby	d												20 38										
Barrow Upon Soar	d		←										20 43								←		
Loughborough	d	19 45	19 48									20 33	20 48		20 45						20 48		
East Midlands Parkway ✈	d	19 52	19 56			20 00							→		20 52						20 56	21 00	
Beeston	a		20 04									20 43									21 04		
Nottingham ■	a		20 13			20 17						20 52									21 14	21 16	
	d		20 30			20 25				20 17	20 17									21 12	21 24		
Newark Castle 27	a		20 58																		21 55		
Lincoln 27	a		21 32														←				22 40		
Langley Mill	d					20 49				20 36	20 36						20 49			21 36			
Alfreton	d					→				20 44	20 44						20 57			21 44			
Long Eaton	a	19 56													20 56								
Derby ■	a	20 09							20 26						21 09								
	d	20 10		20 16					20 28					20 42				21 27					
Chesterfield	d	20 29		20 35	20 35			20 40	20 46	20 54	20 55			21 03		21 05	21 07	21 47	21 47	21 55			
Sheffield ■	a	20 42		20 47	20 49			20 55	21 01	21 13	21 13			21 17		21 17	21 23	21 59	22 01	22 13			
Manchester Piccadilly 78	a																						
Doncaster ■ 29	a			21 21	21 21													22 24	22 24				
Wakefield Kirkgate ■ 31,34	a									21 55	21 55									22 55			
Wakefield Westgate ■ 31	a													21 47		21 46	21 57						
Leeds ■ 31,34	a									22 15	22 15			22 03		22 02	22 17			23 14			
York ■ 29	a			21 42	21 42													22 46	22 47				

		EM	EM	EM	EM	XC	EM	EM	EM	EM	XC	EM	EM	XC	NT	NT	EM	EM	EM	XC	NT	EM	EM
		◇■	◇■	◇■		◇■	◇■		◇■	◇■	◇■	◇■	◇■	◇■	◇	◇	◇■	◇■	◇■	◇■	◇	◇■	◇■
		A	F		M	N		B			O	A	F	P	F	A				Q			
		🛒	🛒	🛒			🛒		🛒	⊐		🛒	🛒				🛒	🛒	🛒			🛒	⊐
St Pancras International ⊖52	d	20 02	20 02	20 05			20 31		20 34			21 02	21 02				21 20	21 30	21 50			22 00	
Luton Airport Parkway ■ 52 ✈	d			20 26															22 12				
Luton ■ 52	d																	21 54				22 25	
Bedford ■ 52	d			20 39														22 10	22 27			22 42	
Wellingborough	d			20 51														22 23	22 40			22 55	
Kettering ■	a			20 58														22 32	22 47			23 02	
	d			20 59						22 06								22 33	22 48			23 03	23 05
Corby	d									22a21													23a19
Oakham 47	a																						
Melton Mowbray 47	a																						
Market Harborough	d			21 09					21 28								22 13	22 44	22 58			23 14	
Leicester	a	21 06	21 06	21 21			21 34		21 41			22 04	22 04				22 25	22 58	23 10			23 29	
	d	21 08	21 08	21 23	21 26		21 35		21 41			22 05	22 05				22 27	22 59	23 11			23 30	
Syston	d				21 33																		
Sileby	d				21 38																		
Barrow Upon Soar	d				21 43			←															
Loughborough	d			21 32	21 48		21 45	21 48									22 37		23 21			23 41	
East Midlands Parkway ✈	d			21 41	→		21 52	21 56	21 58								22 44	23 15	23 29			23 50	
Beeston	a			21 47				22 05														23 58	
Nottingham ■	a			21 54				22 15	22 18								22 56					00 07	
	d														22 17	22 17					23 18		
Newark Castle 27	a																						
Lincoln 27	a																						
Langley Mill	d																				23 36		
Alfreton	d																				23 44		
Long Eaton	a						22 00												23 32				
Derby ■	a	21 32					22 12					22 26			22 38	22 39		23 29	23 45				
	d	21 42				21 46						22 28		22 33	22 39	22 40							
Chesterfield	d	22 03	22 03			22 08					22 24	22 47	22 47	22 55	23 02	23 03				23 16	23 54		
Sheffield ■	a	22 18	22 18			22 21					22 36	23 01	23 01	23 11	23 16	23 17				23 30	00 16		
Manchester Piccadilly 78	a																						
Doncaster ■ 29	a					22 48					23 03												
Wakefield Kirkgate ■ 31,34	a																						
Wakefield Westgate ■ 31	a	22 48	22 48			23 12					23 22												
Leeds ■ 31,34	a	23 06	23 06			23 27					23 37												
York ■ 29	a													23 55						00 10			

A not 28 July
B From Leicester
C not 28 July. From Reading to Newcastle
D 28 July. From Plymouth to Newcastle
E To Leeds
F 28 July
G To Lincoln
H not 28 July. From Paignton
I 28 July. From Reading
J From St Pancras International
K not 28 July. From Southampton Central
L 28 July. From Paignton
M To Nottingham
N not 28 July. From Bournemouth
O 28 July. From Bournemouth
P not 28 July. From Penzance
Q 28 July. From Penzance

For connections from Gatwick Airport refer to Table T052

Table T053-F

Saturdays
26 May to 28 July

London - East Midlands - Sheffield

Station		EM
		◇■ 🛒
St Pancras International ⊖52	d	22 20
Luton Airport Parkway ■ 52 ✈	d	22 42
Luton ■ 52	d	
Bedford ■ 52	d	22 58
Wellingborough	d	23 10
Kettering ■	a	23 17
	d	23 18
Corby	d	
Oakham 47	a	
Melton Mowbray 47	a	
Market Harborough	d	23 28
Leicester	a	23 40
	d	23 41
Syston	d	
Sileby	d	
Barrow Upon Soar	d	
Loughborough	d	23 52
East Midlands Parkway ✈	d	23 59
Beeston	a	
Nottingham ■	a	
	d	
Newark Castle 27	a	
Lincoln 27	a	
Langley Mill	d	
Alfreton	d	
Long Eaton	a	00 03
Derby ■	a	00 15
	d	
Chesterfield	d	
Sheffield ■	a	
Manchester Piccadilly 78	a	
Doncaster ■ 29	a	
Wakefield Kirkgate ■ 31,34	a	
Wakefield Westgate ■ 31	a	
Leeds ■ 31,34	a	
York ■ 29	a	

Saturdays
4 August to 1 September

Station		EM	EM	EM	EM	NT	EM	NT	XC	EM	EM	EM	XC	EM	EM	EM	NT	XC	EM	EM	XC	EM	EM
		◇■ A 🛒	◇■ A 🛒	◇ B	◇■ 🛒	◇	◇■ 🛒	◇	◇■ C 🛒	◇ B		◇■ D 🛒	◇■ E 🛒	◇■ 🛒	◇■ F 🛒	◇■ G 🛒	◇	◇■ H 🛒	◇ B		◇■ E 🛒	◇■ I 🛒	◇■ 🛒
St Pancras International ⊖52	d				00 15							05 48			05 48	05 48						06 33	
Luton Airport Parkway ■ 52 ✈	d				00 53																		
Luton ■ 52	d				00 57							06 14			06 14	06 14						06 56	
Bedford ■ 52	d		00 09		01 25							06 28			06 28	06 28							
Wellingborough	d		00 22		01 36							06 40			06 40	06 40							
Kettering ■	a		00 40		01 46							06 47			06 47	06 47						07 22	
	d		00 41		01 46							06 48			06 48	06 48						07 23	07 38
Corby	d																						07a47
Oakham 47	a																						
Melton Mowbray 47	a																						
Market Harborough	d		00 52		01 58							06 58			06 58	06 58						07 33	
Leicester	a		01 06		02 13							07 10			07 10	07 10						07 45	
	d		01 08								06 26	07 12			07 12	07 12				07 28		07 48	
Syston	d										06 33									07 35			
Sileby	d										06 38									07 40			
Barrow Upon Soar	d										06 43									07 45			
Loughborough	d		01 19								06 48	07 23			07 23	07 23				07 50		07 58	
East Midlands Parkway ✈	d	00 02	01 27								06 56	07a31								07 58		08 05	
Beeston	a		01 33								07 06									08 06			
Nottingham ■	a		01 41								07 15									08 15			
	d			05 20				06 17		06 40							07 18		07 46				
Newark Castle 27	a																						
Lincoln 27	a																						
Langley Mill	d							06 36									07 37						
Alfreton	d							06 44		07 01							07 45		08 09				
Long Eaton	a														07 31	07 31							
Derby ■	a														07 47	07 50							
	d						06 27							07 21									
Chesterfield	d	00 27		05 49		06 25	06 46	06 54	07 02	07 11			07 32	07 43			07 57	08 03	08 20		08 32	08 47	
Sheffield ■	a	00 43		06 15		06 42	07 08	07 11	07 15	07 28			07 44	07 59			08 15	08 19	08 37		08 44	09 01	
Manchester Piccadilly 78	a			07 39						08 37									09 37				
Doncaster ■ 29	a												08 13								09 15	09 53	
Wakefield Kirkgate ■ 31,34	a					07 22		07 57									08 57						
Wakefield Westgate ■ 31	a								07 45									08 46					
Leeds ■ 31,34	a					07 43		08 17	08 00								09 17	09 01					
York ■ 29	a								08 30				08 40					09 30			09 40	10 17	

A From St Pancras International
B To Liverpool Lime Street
C From Burton-on-Trent to Glasgow Central
D 18 August
E From Birmingham New Street to Newcastle
F 4 August, 11 August
G 25 August, 1 September
H From Birmingham New Street to Edinburgh
I To Scarborough

For connections from Gatwick Airport refer to Table T052

Table T053-F

Saturdays
4 August to 1 September

London - East Midlands - Sheffield

Station		NT	EM	XC	EM	EM	EM	EM	EM	EM	EM	EM	EM	XC	EM	NT	XC	EM	EM	EM	EM	EM	EM
		◇	◇■ 🛒	◇■ A 🛒	◇ B	◇■ 🛒	C	◇■ D 🛒	◇■ E 🛒	◇■ F 🛒	G	◇■ 🛒	◇■ 🛒	◇■ H	◇■ 🛒	◇	◇■ I 🛒	◇ B	◇■ 🛒	C	◇■ D 🛒	◇■ J 🛒	G
St Pancras International ⊖52	d		06 48			07 05						07 35	07 47		08 02				08 05		08 31	08 31	
Luton Airport Parkway ■ 52 ✈	d		07 10									07 56							08 26				
Luton ■ 52	d					07 27							08 09										
Bedford ■ 52	d					07 40						08 10	08 24						08 40				
Wellingborough	d					07 52						08 23	08 35						08 53				
Kettering ■	a					08 00						08 30	08 43						09 00				
	d					08 01						08 30	08 44						09 00				
Corby	d												08a54										
Oakham 47	a																						
Melton Mowbray 47	a																						
Market Harborough	d					08 11						08 41							09 11				
Leicester	a		07 53			08 23						08 53			09 04				09 23		09 34	09 34	
	d		07 54			08 25	08 26	08 35	08 35	08 35		08 54			09 05				09 24	09 26	09 35	09 35	
Syston	d						08 33													09 33			
Sileby	d						08 38													09 38			
Barrow Upon Soar	d						08 43				←									09 43			←
Loughborough	d		08 03			08 35	08 48	08 45	08 45	08 45	08 48	09 03							09 33	09 48		09 45	09 48
East Midlands Parkway ✈	d		08 12			08 42	→	08a52	08 52	08 52	08 56									→	09a48	09 52	09 56
Beeston	a		08 17								09 04	09 13							09 44				10 04
Nottingham ■	a		08 29			08 54					09 11	09 22							09 53				10 14
	d	08 17			08 47						09 22					09 16		09 47					10 29
Newark Castle 27	a										09 49												10 51
Lincoln 27	a										10 19												11 25
Langley Mill	d	08 36														09 37							
Alfreton	d	08 44			09 08											09 45		10 08					
Long Eaton	a								08 56	08 56												09 56	
Derby ■	a								09 15	09 27												10 27	
	d																						
Chesterfield	d	08 55		09 03	09 20									09 34	09 46	09 56	10 05	10 20					
Sheffield ■	a	09 13		09 17	09 37									09 46	10 00	10 13	10 17	10 37					
Manchester Piccadilly 78	a				10 37													11 37					
Doncaster ■ 29	a													10 15									
Wakefield Kirkgate ■ 31,34	a	09 56														10 55							
Wakefield Westgate ■ 31	a			09 46													10 46						
Leeds ■ 31,34	a	10 16		10 00												11 15	11 00						
York ■ 29	a			10 30										10 40			11 30						

Station		EM	EM	EM	XC	EM	NT	XC	EM	EM	EM	EM	EM	EM	EM	EM	EM	XC	EM	NT	XC	EM
		◇■ J 🛒	◇■ D 🛒	◇■ 🛒	◇■ K	◇■ 🛒	◇	◇■ L 🛒	◇ B	◇■ 🛒	C	◇■ D 🛒	◇■ J 🛒	G	◇■ J 🛒	◇■ D 🛒	◇■ 🛒	◇■ K	◇■ 🛒	◇	◇■ M 🛒	◇ B
St Pancras International ⊖52	d	08 34	08 34	08 47		09 02				09 05		09 31	09 31		09 34	09 34	09 47		10 02			
Luton Airport Parkway ■ 52 ✈	d									09 26												
Luton ■ 52	d			09 09													10 09					
Bedford ■ 52	d			09 24						09 40							10 24					
Wellingborough	d			09 35						09 53							10 35					
Kettering ■	a			09 43						10 00							10 43					
	d			09 44						10 00							10 44					
Corby	d			09a54													10a54					
Oakham 47	a																					
Melton Mowbray 47	a																					
Market Harborough	d	09 29	09 29							10 11					10 29	10 29						
Leicester	a	09 42	09 42			10 04				10 23		10 34	10 34		10 42	10 42			11 04			
	d	09 43	09 43			10 05				10 24	10 26	10 35	10 35		10 43	10 43			11 05			
Syston	d										10 33											
Sileby	d										10 38											
Barrow Upon Soar	d										10 43			←								
Loughborough	d		09 55							10 33	10 48		10 45	10 48		10 55						
East Midlands Parkway ✈	d	10 02	10 06								→	10a48	10 52	10 56	11 00	11 03						
Beeston	a									10 43				11 04								
Nottingham ■	a	10 16	10 20							10 52				11 14	11 16	11 20						
	d						10 17		10 46					11 29						11 17		11 47
Newark Castle 27	a													11 51								
Lincoln 27	a													12 26								
Langley Mill	d						10 38													11 38		
Alfreton	d						10 46		11 08											11 46		12 08
Long Eaton	a												10 56									
Derby ■	a												11 27									
	d																					
Chesterfield	d				10 33	10 46	10 56	11 03	11 20									11 33	11 41	11 56	12 03	12 20
Sheffield ■	a				10 47	11 01	11 13	11 17	11 38									11 45	12 00	12 13	12 17	12 38
Manchester Piccadilly 78	a								12 37													13 37
Doncaster ■ 29	a				11 15													12 13				
Wakefield Kirkgate ■ 31,34	a						11 55													12 55		
Wakefield Westgate ■ 31	a							11 46													12 46	
Leeds ■ 31,34	a						12 15	12 00												13 15	13 00	
York ■ 29	a				11 40			12 30										12 40			13 30	

A From Birmingham New Street to Glasgow Central
B From Norwich to Liverpool Lime Street
C To Lincoln
D 18 August
E 25 August, 1 September
F 4 August, 11 August
G From Leicester
H From Bristol Temple Meads to Newcastle
I From Guildford to Edinburgh
J not 18 August
K From Plymouth to Newcastle
L From Bournemouth to Glasgow Central
M From Southampton Central to Edinburgh

For connections from Gatwick Airport refer to Table T052

Table T053-F

Saturdays

4 August to 1 September

London - East Midlands - Sheffield

	EM	EM	EM	EM	EM	EM	EM	EM	XC	EM	NT	XC	EM	EM	EM	EM	EM	EM	EM	EM	EM	XC
	◇1		◇1	◇1		◇1	◇1	◇1	◇1	◇1	◇	◇1	◇	◇1		◇1	◇1		◇1	◇1	◇1	◇1
		A	B	C	D	C	B		E			F	G		A	B	C	D	C	B		H
	🍴		🍴	🍴		🍴	🍴	🍴	🍴	🍴				🍴		🍴	🍴		🍴	🍴	🍴	🍴
St Pancras International ⊖52 d	10 05		10 31	10 31		10 34	10 34	10 47		11 02				11 05		11 31	11 31		11 34	11 34	11 50	
Luton Airport Parkway [7] 52 ✈ d	10 26													11 26								
Luton [10] 52 d								11 09													12 12	
Bedford [7] 52 d	10 40							11 24						11 40							12 27	
Wellingborough d	10 53							11 35						11 53							12 39	
Kettering [5] a	11 00							11 43						12 00							12 48	
d	11 00							11 44						12 00							12 49	
Corby d								11a53													12a59	
Oakham 47 a																						
Melton Mowbray 47 a																						
Market Harborough d	11 11					11 29	11 29							12 11					12 29	12 29		
Leicester a	11 23		11 34	11 34		11 42	11 42			12 04				12 23		12 34	12 34		12 42	12 42		
d	11 24	11 26	11 35	11 35		11 43	11 43			12 05				12 24	12 26	12 35	12 35		12 43	12 43		
Syston d		11 33													12 33							
Sileby d		11 38													12 38							
Barrow Upon Soar d		11 43			←										12 43			←				
Loughborough d	11 33	11 48		11 45	11 48		11 55							12 33	12 48		12 45	12 48		12 55		
East Midlands Parkway ✈ d		→	11a47	11 52	11 56	12 00	12 03								→	12a48	12 52	12 56	13 00	13 03		
Beeston a	11 43				12 04									12 43				13 04				
Nottingham [8] a	11 52				12 14	12 16	12 20							12 52				13 14	13 16	13 20		
d					12 29						12 17		12 47					13 29				
Newark Castle 27 a					12 51													13 50				
Lincoln 27 a					13 22													14 24				
Langley Mill d											12 38											
Alfreton d											12 46		13 10									
Long Eaton a				11 56													12 56					
Derby [6] a				12 27													13 27					
d																						
Chesterfield d									12 33	12 40	12 56	13 03	13 21									13 33
Sheffield [7] a									12 45	12 55	13 14	13 18	13 37									13 45
Manchester Piccadilly 78 a													14 37									
Doncaster [7] 29 a									13 15													14 15
Wakefield Kirkgate [4] 31,34 a											13 55											
Wakefield Westgate [7] 31 a												13 46										
Leeds [10] 31,34 a											14 15	14 00										
York [8] 29 a									13 40			14 30										14 40

	EM	NT	XC	EM	EM	EM	EM	EM	EM	EM	EM	EM	XC	EM	NT	XC	EM	EM	EM	EM	EM
	◇1	◇	◇1	◇	◇1		◇1	◇1		◇1	◇1	◇1	◇1	◇1	◇	◇1	◇	◇1		◇1	◇1
			I	G		A	B	C	D	C	B		E			F	G		A	B	C
	🍴		🍴		🍴		🍴	🍴		🍴	🍴	🍴	🍴	🍴				🍴		🍴	🍴
St Pancras International ⊖52 d	12 02				12 05		12 31	12 31		12 34	12 34	12 47		13 02				13 05		13 31	13 31
Luton Airport Parkway [7] 52 ✈ d					12 26													13 26			
Luton [10] 52 d												13 09									
Bedford [7] 52 d					12 40							13 24						13 40			
Wellingborough d					12 53							13 35						13 53			
Kettering [5] a					13 00							13 43						14 00			
d					13 00							13 44						14 00			
Corby d												13a53									
Oakham 47 a																					
Melton Mowbray 47 a																					
Market Harborough d					13 11					13 29	13 29							14 11			
Leicester a	13 04				13 23		13 34	13 34		13 42	13 42			14 04				14 23		14 34	14 34
d	13 05				13 24	13 26	13 35	13 35		13 43	13 43			14 05				14 24	14 26	14 35	14 35
Syston d						13 33													14 33		
Sileby d						13 38													14 38		
Barrow Upon Soar d						13 43			←										14 43		
Loughborough d					13 33	13 48		13 45	13 48		13 55							14 33	14 48		14 45
East Midlands Parkway ✈ d						→	13a48	13 52	13 56	14 00	14 03								→	14a48	14 52
Beeston a					13 43				14 04									14 43			
Nottingham [8] a					13 52				14 14	14 16	14 20							14 52			
d		13 17		13 47					14 19						14 17		14 47				
Newark Castle 27 a									14 42												
Lincoln 27 a									15 11												
Langley Mill d		13 38													14 38						
Alfreton d		13 46		14 08											14 46		15 08				
Long Eaton a								13 56													14 56
Derby [6] a								14 27													15 27
d																					
Chesterfield d	13 40	13 56	14 02	14 20									14 33	14 44	14 56	15 03	15 20				
Sheffield [7] a	13 55	14 13	14 17	14 37									14 45	14 59	15 13	15 17	15 37				
Manchester Piccadilly 78 a				15 37													16 37				
Doncaster [7] 29 a													15 15								
Wakefield Kirkgate [4] 31,34 a		14 55													15 55						
Wakefield Westgate [7] 31 a			14 46													15 46					
Leeds [10] 31,34 a		15 15	15 00												16 15	16 00					
York [8] 29 a			15 30										15 40			16 30					

A To Lincoln
B 18 August
C not 18 August
D From Leicester
E From Plymouth to Newcastle
F From Reading to Glasgow Central
G From Norwich to Liverpool Lime Street
H From Penzance to Newcastle
I From Southampton Central to Aberdeen

For connections from Gatwick Airport refer to Table T052

Table T053-F

Saturdays

4 August to 1 September

London - East Midlands - Sheffield

	EM	EM	EM	EM	XC	EM	NT	XC	EM	EM	EM	EM	EM	EM	EM	EM	EM	XC	EM	NT	XC	EM
		◇1	◇1	◇1	◇1	◇1	◇	◇1	◇	◇1		◇1	◇1		◇1	◇1	◇1	◇1	◇1	◇	◇1	◇
	A	B	C		D			E	F		G	C	B	A	B	C		H			I	F
		🍴	🍴	🍴	🍴	🍴		🍴		🍴		🍴	🍴		🍴	🍴	🍴	🍴	🍴		🍴	
St Pancras International ⊖52 d		13 34	13 34	13 47		14 02				14 05		14 31	14 31		14 34	14 34	14 47		15 02			
Luton Airport Parkway [7] 52 ✈ d										14 26												
Luton [10] 52 d				14 09													15 09					
Bedford [7] 52 d				14 24						14 40							15 24					
Wellingborough d				14 36						14 53							15 36					
Kettering [5] a				14 45						15 00							15 44					
d				14 46						15 00							15 45					
Corby d				14a56													15a54					
Oakham 47 a																						
Melton Mowbray 47 a																						
Market Harborough d		14 29	14 29							15 11					15 29	15 29						
Leicester a		14 42	14 42			15 04				15 23		15 34	15 34		15 42	15 42			16 04			
d		14 43	14 43			15 05				15 24	15 26	15 35	15 35		15 43	15 43			16 05			
Syston d											15 33											
Sileby d											15 38											
Barrow Upon Soar d	←										15 43			←								
Loughborough d	14 48		14 55							15 33	15 48		15 45	15 48		15 55						
East Midlands Parkway ✈ d	14 56	15 00	15 03								→	15a48	15 52	15 56	16 00	16 03						
Beeston a	15 04									15 43				16 04								
Nottingham [8] a	15 14	15 16	15 20							15 52				16 14	16 16	16 20						
d	15 28						15 17		15 47					16 21						16 17		16 44
Newark Castle 27 a	15 49													16 42								
Lincoln 27 a	16 25													17 08								
Langley Mill d							15 38													16 38		
Alfreton d							15 46		16 10											16 46		17 05
Long Eaton a													15 56									
Derby [6] a													16 27									
d																						
Chesterfield d					15 33	15 45	15 56	16 03	16 21									16 33	16 40	16 56	17 04	17 15
Sheffield [7] a					15 45	16 00	16 13	16 17	16 37									16 45	16 55	17 13	17 17	17 34
Manchester Piccadilly 78 a									17 37													18 37
Doncaster [7] 29 a					16 16													17 15				
Wakefield Kirkgate [4] 31,34 a							16 55													17 55		
Wakefield Westgate [7] 31 a								16 46													17 45	
Leeds [10] 31,34 a							17 15	17 00												18 15	18 01	
York [8] 29 a					16 40			17 28										17 40			18 29	

	EM	EM	EM	EM	EM	EM	EM	EM	XC	EM	NT	XC	EM	EM	EM	EM	EM	EM	EM	EM	EM	XC
	◇1		◇1	◇1		◇1	◇1	◇1	◇1	◇1	◇	◇1	◇	◇1		◇1	◇1		◇1	◇1	◇1	◇1
		G	C	B	A	B	C		J			K	F		G	C	B	A	B	C		L
	🍴		🍴	🍴		🍴	🍴	🍴	🍴	🍴		🍴		🍴		🍴	🍴		🍴	🍴	🍴	🍴
St Pancras International ⊖52 d	15 05		15 31	15 31		15 34	15 34	15 47		16 02				16 05		16 31	16 31		16 34	16 34	16 47	
Luton Airport Parkway [7] 52 ✈ d	15 26													16 26								
Luton [10] 52 d								16 09													17 09	
Bedford [7] 52 d	15 40							16 24						16 40							17 24	
Wellingborough d	15 53							16 35						16 53							17 34	
Kettering [5] a	16 00							16 45						17 00							17 43	
d	16 00							16 46						17 00							17 44	
Corby d								16a56													17a53	
Oakham 47 a																						
Melton Mowbray 47 a																						
Market Harborough d	16 11					16 29	16 29							17 11					17 29	17 29		
Leicester a	16 23		16 34	16 34		16 42	16 42			17 04				17 23		17 34	17 34		17 42	17 42		
d	16 24	16 26	16 35	16 35		16 43	16 43			17 05				17 24	17 26	17 35	17 35		17 43	17 43		
Syston d		16 33													17 33							
Sileby d		16 38													17 38							
Barrow Upon Soar d		16 43			←										17 43			←				
Loughborough d	16 33	16 48		16 45	16 48		16 55							17 33	17 48		17 45	17 48		17 55		
East Midlands Parkway ✈ d		→	16a49	16 52	16 56	17 00	17 03								→	17a48	17 52	17 56	18 00	18 03		
Beeston a	16 43				17 04									17 45				18 04				
Nottingham [8] a	16 52				17 14	17 16	17 20							17 55				18 14	18 16	18 20		
d					17 29						17 17		17 44					18 17				
Newark Castle 27 a					17 50													18 43				
Lincoln 27 a					18 23													19 23				
Langley Mill d											17 38		18 00									
Alfreton d											17 46		18 08									
Long Eaton a				16 56													17 56					
Derby [6] a				17 27													18 27					
d																						
Chesterfield d									17 26	17 46	17 56	18 05	18 18									18 33
Sheffield [7] a									17 40	18 01	18 14	18 17	18 34									18 47
Manchester Piccadilly 78 a													19 37									
Doncaster [7] 29 a																						19 13
Wakefield Kirkgate [4] 31,34 a											18 55											
Wakefield Westgate [7] 31 a									18 16			18 49										
Leeds [10] 31,34 a									18 33		19 15	19 03										
York [8] 29 a									19 05			19 30										19 42

A From Leicester
B not 18 August
C 18 August
D From Penzance to Newcastle
E From Southampton Central to Dundee
F From Norwich to Liverpool Lime Street
G To Lincoln
H From Newquay to Newcastle
I From Reading to Glasgow Central
J From Paignton to Edinburgh
K From Southampton Central to Edinburgh
L From Plymouth to Newcastle

For connections from Gatwick Airport refer to Table T052

Table T053-F

London - East Midlands - Sheffield

Saturdays
4 August to 1 September

	EM		NT	XC	EM	EM	EM	EM	EM	EM	EM		EM	EM	EM	XC	EM	NT	XC	EM	EM		EM	EM
	◇1		◇	◇1	◇	◇1		◇1	◇1	◇1			◇1	◇1	◇1	◇1	◇1	◇	◇1	◇	◇1			◇1
				A	B		C	D	E	F	G		H	D		I			J	K			L	D
	⌶			⌶		⌶		⌶	⌶	⌶			⌶	⌶	⌶	⌶	⌶		⌶		⌶			⌶
St Pancras International ⊖52 d	17 02					17 05		17 31	17 31	17 31			17 34	17 34	17 47		18 02				18 05			18 31
Luton Airport Parkway 52 ✈ d						17 26															18 26			
Luton 52 d															18 09									
Bedford 52 d						17 40									18 24						18 40			
Wellingborough d						17 53									18 35						18 53			
Kettering a						18 00									18 45						19 00			
d						18 00									18 46						19 00			
Corby d															18a56									
Oakham 47 a																								
Melton Mowbray 47 a																								
Market Harborough d						18 11							18 29	18 29							19 11			
Leicester a	18 04					18 23		18 34	18 34	18 34			18 42	18 42			19 04				19 23			19 34
d	18 05					18 24	18 26	18 35	18 35	18 35			18 43	18 43			19 05				19 24		19 26	19 35
Syston d							18 33																19 33	
Sileby d							18 38																19 38	
Barrow Upon Soar d							18 43				←												19 43	
Loughborough d						18 33	18 48		18 45	18 45	18 48			18 55							19 33		19 48	
East Midlands Parkway ✈ d							→	18a48	18 52	18 52	18 56		19 00	19 03									→	19a47
Beeston a						18 43					19 04										19 43			
Nottingham ⇌ a						18 52					19 15		19 16	19 20							19 52			
d			18 17		18 47	19 29												19 17		19 36				
Newark Castle 27 a						19 52																		
Lincoln 27 a						20 26																		
Langley Mill d			18 38															19 38						
Alfreton d			18 46		19 08													19 46		20 01				
Long Eaton a									18 56	18 56														
Derby a									19 12	19 16														
d																								
Chesterfield d	18 40		18 56	19 04	19 20											19 35	19 40	19 56	20 06	20 11				
Sheffield ⇌ a	18 55		19 13	19 17	19 37											19 47	19 55	20 13	20 18	20 30				
Manchester Piccadilly 78 a					20 37															21 29				
Doncaster 29 a																20 13								
Wakefield Kirkgate 31,34 a			19 55															20 55						
Wakefield Westgate 31 a				19 46															20 46					
Leeds 31,34 a			20 15	20 02														21 15	21 01					
York 29 a				20 30												20 40			21 59					

	EM	EM	EM	XC	EM	EM	EM		EM	NT	EM	EM	EM	EM	EM	XC	XC		NT	EM	EM	EM	EM	EM
	◇1	◇1		◇1	◇1	◇1	◇1		◇1	◇	◇1		◇1	◇1	◇1	◇1	◇1		◇		◇1	◇1	◇1	◇1
	E	F	G	I	H	D						L	D	E	F	M	N			G	H	D		
	⌶	⌶		⌶	⌶	⌶	⌶		⌶		⌶		⌶	⌶	⌶						⌶	⌶	⌶	⌶
St Pancras International ⊖52 d	18 31	18 31			18 34	18 34	18 47		19 02		19 05		19 31	19 31	19 31						19 34	19 34	19 47	20 02
Luton Airport Parkway 52 ✈ d											19 26													
Luton 52 d							19 09																20 10	
Bedford 52 d							19 24				19 40												20 24	
Wellingborough d							19 36				19 53												20 35	
Kettering a							19 45				20 00												20 43	
d							19 46				20 00												20 44	
Corby d							19a55																20a53	
Oakham 47 a																								
Melton Mowbray 47 a																								
Market Harborough d					19 29	19 29					20 11										20 29	20 29		
Leicester a	19 34	19 34			19 42	19 42			20 04		20 23		20 34	20 34	20 34						20 42	20 42		21 06
d	19 35	19 35			19 43	19 43			20 05		20 24	20 26	20 35	20 35	20 35						20 43	20 43		21 08
Syston d												20 33												
Sileby d												20 38												
Barrow Upon Soar d			←									20 43								←				
Loughborough d	19 45	19 45	19 48			19 55					20 33	20 48		20 45	20 45					20 48		20 55		
East Midlands Parkway ✈ d	19 52	19 52	19 56		20 00	20 03						→	20a48	20 52	20 52					20 56	21 00	21 03		
Beeston a			20 04								20 43									21 04				
Nottingham ⇌ a			20 13		20 17	20 20					20 52									21 14	21 16	21 20		
d			20 30		20 25	20 25				20 17									21 12	21 24				
Newark Castle 27 a			20 58																	21 55				
Lincoln 27 a			21 32																	22 40				
Langley Mill d					20 49	20 49				20 36									21 36					
Alfreton d					20 57	20 57				20 44									21 44					
Long Eaton a	19 56	19 56												20 56	20 56									
Derby a	20 12	20 27												21 13	21 16									
d																								
Chesterfield d				20 35	21 07	21 07			20 40	20 54						21 05	21 47		21 55					22 03
Sheffield ⇌ a				20 49	21 23	21 23			20 55	21 13						21 17	22 01		22 13					22 18
Manchester Piccadilly 78 a																								
Doncaster 29 a				21 21													22 24							
Wakefield Kirkgate 31,34 a										21 55									22 55					
Wakefield Westgate 31 a					21 57	21 57										21 46								22 48
Leeds 31,34 a					22 17	22 17				22 15						22 02			23 14					23 06
York 29 a				21 42													22 47							

A From Reading to Edinburgh. ⌶ to Leeds
B From Norwich to Liverpool Lime Street
C To Nottingham
D 18 August
E 4 August, 11 August
F 25 August, 1 September
G From Leicester
H not 18 August
I From Plymouth to Newcastle
J From Southampton Central. ⌶ to Leeds
K From Norwich
L To Lincoln
M From Reading
N From Paignton

For connections from Gatwick Airport refer to Table T052

Table T053-F

London - East Midlands - Sheffield

Saturdays
4 August to 1 September

	EM	EM	EM		EM	EM	EM	XC	EM	NT	EM	EM	EM		XC	NT	EM	EM	EM
	◇1		◇1		◇1	◇1	◇1	◇1	◇1	◇	◇1	◇1	◇1		◇1	◇	◇1	◇1	◇1
					A	B		C							D				
	⌶		⌶		⌶	⌶	⊡		⌶		⌶	⌶	⌶				⌶	⊡	⌶
St Pancras International ⊖52 d	20 05		20 31		20 34	20 34			21 02		21 20	21 30	21 50				22 00		22 20
Luton Airport Parkway 52 ✈ d	20 26												22 12						22 42
Luton 52 d												21 54					22 25		
Bedford 52 d	20 39											22 10	22 27				22 42		22 58
Wellingborough d	20 51											22 23	22 40				22 55		23 10
Kettering a	20 58											22 32	22 47				23 02		23 17
d	20 59						22 06					22 33	22 48				23 03	23 05	23 18
Corby d							22a21											23a19	
Oakham 47 a																			
Melton Mowbray 47 a																			
Market Harborough d	21 09				21 28	21 28					22 13	22 44	22 58				23 14		23 28
Leicester a	21 21		21 34		21 41	21 41			22 04		22 25	22 58	23 10				23 29		23 40
d	21 23	21 26	21 35		21 41	21 41			22 05		22 27	22 59	23 11				23 30		23 41
Syston d		21 33																	
Sileby d		21 38																	
Barrow Upon Soar d		21 43																	
Loughborough d	21 32	21 48				21 51					22 37		23 21				23 41		23 52
East Midlands Parkway ✈ d	21 41	21 56	21a49		21 58	22 02					22 44	23a16	23a30				23 50		23a59
Beeston a	21 47	22 05															23 58		
Nottingham ⇌ a	21 54	22 15			22 18	22 22					22 56						00 07		
d										22 17						23 18			
Newark Castle 27 a																			
Lincoln 27 a																			
Langley Mill d																23 36			
Alfreton d																23 44			
Long Eaton a																			
Derby a										22 38									
d										22 39									
Chesterfield d								22 24	22 47	23 02					23 16	23 54			
Sheffield ⇌ a								22 36	23 01	23 16					23 30	00 16			
Manchester Piccadilly 78 a																			
Doncaster 29 a								23 03											
Wakefield Kirkgate 31,34 a																			
Wakefield Westgate 31 a								23 22											
Leeds 31,34 a								23 37							00 10				
York 29 a																			

Saturdays
8 September to 6 October

	EM	EM	EM	EM	NT	EM	NT	XC	EM		EM	XC	EM	NT	XC	EM	EM	EM	XC		EM	EM	NT	EM
	◇1	◇1	◇1	◇	◇	◇1	◇	◇1	◇			◇1	◇1	◇	◇1	◇1	◇		◇1		◇1	◇1	◇	◇1
	E	E		F				G	F			H			I		F		H					
	⌶	⌶	⌶			⌶		⌶				⌶	⌶		⌶	⌶			⌶		⌶	⌶		⌶
St Pancras International ⊖52 d			00 15													05 48					06 33			06 48
Luton Airport Parkway 52 ✈ d			00 53																					07 10
Luton 52 d			00 57													06 14					06 56			
Bedford 52 d		00 09	01 25													06 28								
Wellingborough d		00 22	01 36													06 40								
Kettering a		00 40	01 46													06 47					07 22			
d		00 41	01 46													06 48					07 23	07 38		
Corby d																						07a47		
Oakham 47 a																								
Melton Mowbray 47 a																								
Market Harborough d		00 52	01 58													06 58					07 33			
Leicester a		01 06	02 13													07 10					07 45			07 53
d		01 08									06 26					07 12		07 28			07 48			07 54
Syston d											06 33							07 35						
Sileby d											06 38							07 40						
Barrow Upon Soar d											06 43							07 45						
Loughborough d		01 19									06 48					07 23		07 50			07 58			08 03
East Midlands Parkway ✈ d	00 02	01 27									06 56							07 58			08 06			08 12
Beeston a		01 33									07 06							08 06						08 18
Nottingham ⇌ a		01 41									07 15							08 15						08 26
d		01 47		05 20			06 17		06 40					07 18			07 46						08 17	
Newark Castle 27 a																								
Lincoln 27 a																								
Langley Mill d							06 36							07 37									08 36	
Alfreton d							06 44		07 01					07 45			08 09						08 44	
Long Eaton a																								
Derby a		02 05																						
d						06 07		06 20				06 54	07 05		07 17				07 50					
Chesterfield d	00 27			05 49	06 25	06 46	06 54	07 02	07 11			07 32	07 43	07 57	08 03	08 08	08 20		08 32		08 44		08 55	
Sheffield ⇌ a	00 43			06 15	06 42	07 08	07 11	07 15	07 28			07 44	07 59	08 15	08 19	08 25	08 37		08 44		08 59		09 13	
Manchester Piccadilly 78 a				07 39					08 37								09 37							
Doncaster 29 a												08 13							09 15		09 53			
Wakefield Kirkgate 31,34 a					07 22		07 57							08 57									09 56	
Wakefield Westgate 31 a								07 45							08 46									
Leeds 31,34 a					07 43		08 17	08 00						09 17	09 01								10 16	
York 29 a								08 29				08 40			09 30				09 40		10 17			

A not 18 August
B 18 August
C From Bournemouth
D From Penzance
E From St Pancras International
F To Liverpool Lime Street
G To Glasgow Central
H From Birmingham New Street to Newcastle
I From Birmingham New Street to Edinburgh

For connections from Gatwick Airport refer to Table T052

Table T053-F

London - East Midlands - Sheffield

Saturdays

8 September to 6 October

	XC	EM	EM	EM	EM	EM	EM	EM	XC	EM	NT	XC	EM	EM	EM	EM	XC	EM	EM	EM	EM	EM
	◇1 A 🛒	◇ B	◇1 🛒	C	◇1 🛒	D	◇1 🛒	◇1 🛒	◇1 E	◇1 🛒	◇	◇1 F 🛒	◇ B	◇1 🛒	G	H	◇1 I	◇1 🛒	J	K	◇1 🛒	◇1 🛒
St Pancras International ⊖52 d			07 05				07 35	07 47		08 02				08 05				08 31			08 34	08 47
Luton Airport Parkway 7 52 ✈ d							07 56							08 26								
Luton 10 52 d			07 27					08 09														09 09
Bedford 7 52 d			07 40				08 10	08 24						08 40								09 24
Wellingborough d			07 52				08 23	08 35						08 53								09 35
Kettering 5 a			08 00				08 30	08 43						09 00								09 43
d			08 01				08 30	08 44						09 00								09 44
Corby d								08a54														09a54
Oakham 47 a																						
Melton Mowbray 47 a																						
Market Harborough d			08 11				08 41							09 11							09 29	
Leicester a			08 23				08 53			09 04				09 23				09 34			09 42	
d			08 25	08 26	08 35		08 54			09 05				09 24	09 26	09 26		09 35			09 43	
Syston d				08 33											09 33	09 33						
Sileby d				08 38											09 38	09 38						
Barrow Upon Soar d				08 43		←									09 43	09 43			←	←		
Loughborough d			08 35	08 48	08 45	08 48	09 03							09 33	09 48	09 48		09 45	09 48	09 48		
East Midlands Parkway ✈ d			08 42	→	08 52	08 56									→	→		09 52	09 56	09 56	10 02	
Beeston a						09 04	09 13							09 44					10 04	10 04		
Nottingham 8 🚊 a			08 54			09 11	09 22							09 53					10 14	10 14	10 16	
d		08 47				09 22					09 19		09 47						10 29	10 29		
Newark Castle 27 a						09 49													10 51	10 51		
Lincoln 27 a						10 19													11 25	11 27		
Langley Mill d											09 38											
Alfreton d		09 08									09 46		10 08									
Long Eaton a																		09 57				
Derby 6 a																		10 08				
d	08 19								08 47			09 20					09 55					
Chesterfield d	09 04	09 20			09 27				09 37	09 46	09 57	10 03	10 20				10 33					
Sheffield 7 🚊 a	09 17	09 37			09 40				09 49	10 00	10 14	10 17	10 37				10 47					
Manchester Piccadilly 78 a		10 37											11 37									
Doncaster 7 29 a									10 15								11 15					
Wakefield Kirkgate 4 31,34 a											10 55											
Wakefield Westgate 7 31 a	09 46											10 46										
Leeds 10 31,34 a	10 00										11 15	11 02										
York 8 29 a	10 30								10 40			11 30					11 40					

	EM	NT	XC	EM	EM	EM	EM	XC	EM	EM	EM	EM	EM	EM	NT	XC	EM	EM	EM	EM	XC
	◇1 🛒	◇	◇1 L 🛒	◇ B	◇1 🛒	G	H	◇1 I	◇1 🛒	J	K	◇1 🛒	◇1 🛒	◇1 🛒	◇	◇1 M 🛒	◇ B	◇1 🛒	G	H	◇1 I 🛒
St Pancras International ⊖52 d	09 02				09 05				09 31			09 34	09 47	10 02				10 05			
Luton Airport Parkway 7 52 ✈ d					09 26													10 26			
Luton 10 52 d													10 09								
Bedford 7 52 d					09 40								10 24					10 40			
Wellingborough d					09 53								10 35					10 53			
Kettering 5 a					10 00								10 43					11 00			
d					10 00								10 44					11 00			
Corby d													10a54								
Oakham 47 a																					
Melton Mowbray 47 a																					
Market Harborough d					10 11							10 29						11 11			
Leicester a	10 04				10 23				10 34			10 42		11 04				11 23			
d	10 05				10 24	10 26	10 26		10 35			10 43		11 05				11 24	11 26	11 26	
Syston d						10 33	10 33												11 33	11 33	
Sileby d						10 38	10 38												11 38	11 38	
Barrow Upon Soar d						10 43	10 43			←	←								11 43	11 43	
Loughborough d					10 33	10 48	10 48		10 45	10 48	10 48							11 33	11 48	11 48	
East Midlands Parkway ✈ d						→	→		10 52	10 56	10 56	11 00							→	→	
Beeston a					10 43					11 04	11 04							11 43			
Nottingham 8 🚊 a					10 52					11 14	11 14	11 16						11 52			
d		10 17		10 46						11 29	11 29				11 17		11 47				
Newark Castle 27 a										11 51	11 51										
Lincoln 27 a										12 26	12 28										
Langley Mill d		10 36													11 36						
Alfreton d		10 44		11 08											11 44		12 08				
Long Eaton a									10 56												
Derby 6 a									11 07												
d			10 18					10 50								11 19					11 55
Chesterfield d	10 46	10 55	11 03	11 20				11 33						11 46	11 55	12 03	12 20				12 38
Sheffield 7 🚊 a	11 01	11 13	11 17	11 38				11 45						12 00	12 13	12 17	12 38				12 50
Manchester Piccadilly 78 a				12 37													13 37				
Doncaster 7 29 a								12 13													13 15
Wakefield Kirkgate 4 31,34 a		11 55													12 55						
Wakefield Westgate 7 31 a			11 46													12 46					
Leeds 10 31,34 a		12 15	12 00												13 15	13 00					
York 8 29 a			12 30					12 40								13 30					13 40

A From Birmingham New Street to Glasgow Central
B From Norwich to Liverpool Lime Street
C To Lincoln
D From Leicester
E From Bristol Temple Meads to Newcastle
F From Guildford to Edinburgh
G 29 September, 6 October. To Lincoln
H not from 29 September. To Lincoln
I From Plymouth to Newcastle
J not from 29 September. From Leicester
K 29 September, 6 October. From Leicester
L From Bournemouth to Glasgow Central
M From Southampton Central to Edinburgh

For connections from Gatwick Airport refer to Table T052

Table T053-F

London - East Midlands - Sheffield

Saturdays

8 September to 6 October

	EM	EM	EM	EM	EM	EM	NT	XC	EM	EM	EM	EM	XC	EM	EM	EM	EM	EM	EM	NT	XC	XC
	◇1 🛒	A	B	◇1 🛒	◇1 🛒	◇1 🛒	◇	◇1 C	◇ D	◇1 🛒	E	F	◇1 G 🛒	◇1 🛒	A	B	◇1 🛒	◇1 🛒	◇1 🛒	◇	◇1 H 🛒	◇1 I 🛒
St Pancras International ⊖52 d	10 31			10 34	10 47	11 02				11 05				11 31			11 34	11 50	12 02			
Luton Airport Parkway 7 52 ✈ d										11 26												
Luton 10 52 d					11 09													12 12				
Bedford 7 52 d					11 24					11 40								12 27				
Wellingborough d					11 35					11 53								12 39				
Kettering 5 a					11 43					12 00								12 48				
d					11 44					12 00								12 49				
Corby d					11a53													12a59				
Oakham 47 a																						
Melton Mowbray 47 a																						
Market Harborough d				11 29						12 11							12 29					
Leicester a	11 34			11 42		12 04				12 23				12 34			12 42		13 04			
d	11 35			11 43		12 05				12 24	12 26	12 26		12 35			12 43		13 05			
Syston d											12 33	12 33										
Sileby d											12 38	12 38										
Barrow Upon Soar d		←	←								12 43	12 43			←	←						
Loughborough d	11 45	11 48	11 48							12 33	12 48	12 48		12 45	12 48	12 48						
East Midlands Parkway ✈ d	11 52	11 56	11 56	12 00							→	→		12 52	12 56	12 56	13 00					
Beeston a		12 04	12 04							12 43					13 04	13 04						
Nottingham 8 🚊 a		12 14	12 14	12 16						12 52					13 14	13 14	13 16					
d		12 29	12 29				12 17		12 47						13 29	13 29				13 17		
Newark Castle 27 a		12 51	12 51												13 50	13 50						
Lincoln 27 a		13 22	13 24												14 24	14 26						
Langley Mill d							12 36													13 36		
Alfreton d							12 44		13 10											13 44		
Long Eaton a	11 56													12 56								
Derby 6 a	12 07													13 07								
d								12 19					12 55								13 10	13 10
Chesterfield d						12 40	12 55	13 03	13 21				13 33						13 40	13 55	14 02	14 03
Sheffield 7 🚊 a						12 55	13 13	13 17	13 37				13 45						13 55	14 13	14 17	14 18
Manchester Piccadilly 78 a									14 37													
Doncaster 7 29 a													14 15									
Wakefield Kirkgate 4 31,34 a							13 55													14 55		
Wakefield Westgate 7 31 a								13 46													14 46	14 46
Leeds 10 31,34 a							14 15	14 00												15 15	15 00	15 00
York 8 29 a								14 30					14 40								15 30	15 30

	EM	EM	EM	XC	EM	EM	EM	EM	EM	NT	XC	EM	EM	EM	EM	XC	EM	EM	EM	EM	EM
	◇ D	◇1 🛒	J	◇1 K 🛒	◇1 🛒	L	◇1 🛒	◇1 🛒	◇1 🛒	◇	◇1 C	◇ D	◇1 🛒	E	F	◇1 G 🛒	◇1 🛒	A	B	◇1 🛒	◇1 🛒
St Pancras International ⊖52 d		12 05			12 31		12 34	12 47	13 02				13 05				13 31			13 34	13 47
Luton Airport Parkway 7 52 ✈ d		12 26											13 26								
Luton 10 52 d								13 09													14 09
Bedford 7 52 d		12 40						13 24					13 40								14 24
Wellingborough d		12 53						13 35					13 53								14 36
Kettering 5 a		13 00						13 43					14 00								14 45
d		13 00						13 44					14 00								14 46
Corby d								13a53													14a56
Oakham 47 a																					
Melton Mowbray 47 a																					
Market Harborough d		13 11					13 29						14 11							14 29	
Leicester a		13 23			13 34		13 42		14 04				14 23				14 34			14 42	
d		13 24	13 26		13 35		13 43		14 05				14 24	14 26	14 26		14 35			14 43	
Syston d			13 33											14 33	14 33						
Sileby d			13 38											14 38	14 38						
Barrow Upon Soar d			13 43			←								14 43	14 43			←	←		
Loughborough d		13 33	13 48		13 45	13 48							14 33	14 48	14 48		14 45	14 48	14 48		
East Midlands Parkway ✈ d			→		13 52	13 56	14 00							→	→		14 52	14 56	14 56	15 00	
Beeston a		13 43				14 04							14 43					15 04	15 04		
Nottingham 8 🚊 a		13 52				14 14	14 16						14 52					15 14	15 14	15 16	
d	13 47					14 19				14 17		14 47						15 28	15 28		
Newark Castle 27 a						14 42												15 49	15 49		
Lincoln 27 a						15 11												16 25	16 27		
Langley Mill d										14 36											
Alfreton d	14 08									14 44		15 08									
Long Eaton a					13 56												14 56				
Derby 6 a					14 07												15 07				
d				13 43							14 18					14 51					
Chesterfield d	14 20			14 33					14 44	14 55	15 03	15 20				15 33					
Sheffield 7 🚊 a	14 37			14 45					14 59	15 13	15 17	15 37				15 45					
Manchester Piccadilly 78 a	15 37											16 37									
Doncaster 7 29 a				15 15												16 16					
Wakefield Kirkgate 4 31,34 a										15 55											
Wakefield Westgate 7 31 a											15 46										
Leeds 10 31,34 a										16 15	16 00										
York 8 29 a				15 40							16 30					16 40					

A not from 29 September. From Leicester
B 29 September, 6 October. From Leicester
C From Reading to Glasgow Central
D From Norwich to Liverpool Lime Street
E 29 September, 6 October. To Lincoln
F not from 29 September. To Lincoln
G From Penzance to Newcastle
H 8 September. From Southampton Central to Aberdeen
I not 8 September. From Southampton Central to Aberdeen
J To Lincoln
K From Plymouth to Newcastle
L From Leicester

For connections from Gatwick Airport refer to Table T052

Table T053-F

Saturdays

8 September to 6 October

London - East Midlands - Sheffield

	EM ◇1 🍴	NT ◇	XC ◇1 A 🍴	XC ◇1 B 🍴	EM ◇ C	EM ◇1 🍴	EM D	EM E	XC ◇1 F 🍴	EM ◇1 🍴	EM G	EM H	EM ◇1 🍴	EM ◇1 🍴	EM ◇1 🍴	NT ◇	XC ◇1 I 🍴	EM ◇ C	EM ◇1 🍴	EM D	EM E	XC ◇1 J 🍴
St Pancras International ⊖52 d	14 02					14 05				14 31			14 34	14 47	15 02				15 05			
Luton Airport Parkway 7 52 ✈ d						14 26													15 26			
Luton 10 52 d														15 09								
Bedford 7 52 d						14 40								15 24					15 40			
Wellingborough d						14 53								15 36					15 53			
Kettering 5 a						15 00								15 44					16 00			
d						15 00								15 45					16 00			
Corby d														15a54								
Oakham 47 a																						
Melton Mowbray 47 a																						
Market Harborough d						15 11							15 29						16 11			
Leicester a	15 04					15 23				15 34			15 42		16 04				16 23			
d	15 05					15 24	15 26	15 26		15 35			15 43		16 05				16 24	16 26	16 26	
Syston d							15 33	15 33												16 33	16 33	
Sileby d							15 38	15 38												16 38	16 38	
Barrow Upon Soar d							15 43	15 43			←	←								16 43	16 43	
Loughborough d						15 33	15 48	15 48		15 45	15 48	15 48							16 33	16 48	16 48	
East Midlands Parkway ✈ d							→	→		15 52	15 56	15 56	16 00							→	→	
Beeston a						15 43					16 04	16 04							16 43			
Nottingham 8 🚌 a						15 52					16 14	16 14	16 16						16 52			
d		15 17			15 47						16 21	16 21				16 17		16 44				
Newark Castle 27 a											16 42	16 42										
Lincoln 27 a											17 08	17 10										
Langley Mill d		15 36														16 36						
Alfreton d		15 44			16 10											16 44		17 05				
Long Eaton a										15 56												
Derby 6 a										16 07												
d			15 10	15 10					15 50								16 21					16 55
Chesterfield d	15 45	15 55	16 03	16 03	16 21				16 33						16 40	16 55	17 04	17 15				17 32
Sheffield 7 🚌 a	16 00	16 13	16 17	16 18	16 37				16 45						16 55	17 13	17 17	17 34				17 46
Manchester Piccadilly 78 a					17 37													18 37				
Doncaster 7 29 a									17 15													
Wakefield Kirkgate 4 31,34 a		16 55														17 55						
Wakefield Westgate 7 31 a			16 46	16 46													17 45					18 16
Leeds 10 31,34 a		17 15	17 00	17 00												18 15	18 01					18 33
York 8 29 a			17 29	17 29					17 40								18 29					19 05

	EM ◇1 🍴	EM G	EM H	EM ◇1 🍴	EM ◇1 🍴	EM ◇1 🍴	NT ◇	XC ◇1 K 🍴	EM ◇ C	EM ◇1 🍴	EM D	EM E	XC ◇1 L 🍴	EM ◇1 🍴	EM G	EM H	EM ◇1 🍴	EM ◇1 🍴	EM ◇1 🍴	NT ◇	XC ◇1 M 🍴	EM ◇ C
St Pancras International ⊖52 d	15 31			15 34	15 47	16 02				16 05				16 31			16 34	16 47	17 02			
Luton Airport Parkway 7 52 ✈ d										16 26												
Luton 10 52 d					16 09													17 09				
Bedford 7 52 d					16 24					16 40								17 24				
Wellingborough d					16 35					16 53								17 34				
Kettering 5 a					16 45					17 00								17 43				
d					16 46					17 00								17 44				
Corby d					16a56													17a53				
Oakham 47 a																						
Melton Mowbray 47 a																						
Market Harborough d				16 29						17 11							17 29					
Leicester a	16 34			16 42		17 04				17 23				17 34			17 42		18 04			
d	16 35			16 43		17 05				17 24	17 26	17 26		17 35			17 43		18 05			
Syston d											17 33	17 33										
Sileby d											17 38	17 38										
Barrow Upon Soar d		←	←								17 43	17 43			←	←						
Loughborough d	16 45	16 48	16 48							17 33	17 48	17 48		17 45	17 48	17 48						
East Midlands Parkway ✈ d	16 52	16 56	16 56	17 00							→	→		17 52	17 56	17 56	18 00					
Beeston a		17 04	17 04							17 43					18 04	18 04						
Nottingham 8 🚌 a		17 14	17 14	17 16						17 55					18 14	18 14	18 16					
d		17 29	17 29				17 17		17 44						18 17	18 17				18 17		18 47
Newark Castle 27 a		17 50	17 50												18 43	18 43						
Lincoln 27 a		18 23	18 25												19 23	19 25						
Langley Mill d							17 36		18 00											18 36		
Alfreton d							17 44		18 08											18 44		19 08
Long Eaton a	16 56													17 57								
Derby 6 a	17 07													18 08								
d								17 19					17 49								18 20	
Chesterfield d						17 46	17 55	18 04	18 18				18 33						18 40	18 55	19 03	19 20
Sheffield 7 🚌 a						18 01	18 13	18 16	18 34				18 47						18 55	19 13	19 17	19 37
Manchester Piccadilly 78 a									19 37													20 37
Doncaster 7 29 a													19 13									
Wakefield Kirkgate 4 31,34 a							18 55													19 55		
Wakefield Westgate 7 31 a								18 49													19 46	
Leeds 10 31,34 a							19 15	19 03												20 15	20 02	
York 8 29 a								19 30					19 42								20 30	

A 8 September. From Southampton Central to Dundee
B not 8 September. From Southampton Central to Dundee
C From Norwich to Liverpool Lime Street
D 29 September, 6 October. To Lincoln
E not from 29 September. To Lincoln
F From Newquay to Newcastle
G not from 29 September. From Leicester
H 29 September, 6 October. From Leicester
I From Reading to Glasgow Central
J From Plymouth to Edinburgh
K From Southampton Central to Edinburgh
L From Plymouth to Newcastle
M From Reading to Edinburgh. 🍴 to Leeds

For connections from Gatwick Airport refer to Table T052

Table T053-F

Saturdays

8 September to 6 October

London - East Midlands - Sheffield

	EM ◇1 🍴	EM A	XC ◇1 B 🍴	EM ◇1 🍴	EM C	EM ◇1 🍴	EM ◇1 🍴	EM ◇1 🍴	NT ◇	XC ◇1 D 🍴	EM ◇ E	EM ◇1 🍴	EM F	EM G	XC ◇1 B 🍴	EM ◇1 🍴	EM H	EM I	EM ◇1 🍴	EM ◇1 🍴	EM ◇1 🍴
St Pancras International ⊖52 d	17 05			17 31		17 34	17 47	18 02				18 05				18 31			18 34	18 47	19 02
Luton Airport Parkway 7 52 ✈ d	17 26											18 26									
Luton 10 52 d							18 09													19 09	
Bedford 7 52 d	17 40						18 24					18 40								19 24	
Wellingborough d	17 53						18 35					18 53								19 36	
Kettering 5 a	18 00						18 45					19 00								19 45	
d	18 00						18 46					19 00								19 46	
Corby d							18a56													19a55	
Oakham 47 a																					
Melton Mowbray 47 a																					
Market Harborough d	18 11					18 29						19 11							19 29		
Leicester a	18 23			18 34		18 42		19 04				19 23				19 34			19 42		20 04
d	18 24	18 26		18 35		18 43		19 05				19 24	19 26	19 26		19 35			19 43		20 05
Syston d		18 33											19 33	19 33							
Sileby d		18 38											19 38	19 38							
Barrow Upon Soar d		18 43			←								19 43	19 43			←	←			
Loughborough d	18 33	18 48		18 45	18 48							19 33	19 48	19 48		19 45	19 48	19 48			
East Midlands Parkway ✈ d		→		18 52	18 56	19 00							→	→		19 52	19 56	19 56	20 00		
Beeston a	18 43				19 04							19 43					20 04	20 04			
Nottingham 8 🚌 a	18 52				19 15	19 16						19 52					20 13	20 13	20 17		
d	19 29								19 17		19 36						20 30	20 30	20 25		
Newark Castle 27 a	19 52																20 58	20 58			
Lincoln 27 a	20 26																21 32	21 33			
Langley Mill d									19 36										20 49		
Alfreton d									19 44		20 01								20 57		
Long Eaton a				18 56												20 00					
Derby 6 a				19 07												20 14					
d			18 50							19 19					19 52						
Chesterfield d			19 35					19 40	19 55	20 05	20 11				20 35				21 07		20 40
Sheffield 7 🚌 a			19 47					19 55	20 13	20 18	20 30				20 49				21 23		20 55
Manchester Piccadilly 78 a											21 29										
Doncaster 7 29 a			20 13												21 21						
Wakefield Kirkgate 4 31,34 a									20 55												
Wakefield Westgate 7 31 a										20 46									21 57		
Leeds 10 31,34 a									21 15	21 01									22 17		
York 8 29 a			20 40							21 59					21 42						

	NT ◇	EM ◇1 🍴	EM J	XC ◇1 K	XC ◇1 L	EM ◇1 🍴	NT ◇	EM C	EM ◇1 🍴	EM ◇1 🍴	EM ◇1 🍴	EM ◇1 🍴	EM A	XC ◇1 M	XC ◇1 N	EM ◇1 🍴	EM C	EM ◇1 🍴	EM ◇1 🍴	EM ◇1 🛒	NT ◇	EM ◇1 🍴
St Pancras International ⊖52 d		19 05				19 31			19 34	19 47	20 02	20 05				20 31		20 34	21 02			21 20
Luton Airport Parkway 7 52 ✈ d		19 26										20 26										
Luton 10 52 d										20 10												
Bedford 7 52 d		19 40								20 24		20 39										
Wellingborough d		19 53								20 35		20 51										
Kettering 5 a		20 00								20 43		20 58										
d		20 00								20 44		20 59								22 06		
Corby d										20a53										22a21		
Oakham 47 a																						
Melton Mowbray 47 a																						
Market Harborough d		20 11							20 29			21 09						21 28				22 13
Leicester a		20 23				20 34			20 42		21 06	21 21				21 34		21 41	22 04			22 25
d		20 24	20 26			20 35			20 43		21 08	21 23	21 26			21 35		21 41	22 05			22 27
Syston d			20 33										21 33									
Sileby d			20 38										21 38									
Barrow Upon Soar d			20 43					←					21 43				←					
Loughborough d		20 33	20 48			20 45		20 48				21 32	21 48			21 45	21 48					22 37
East Midlands Parkway ✈ d			→			20 52		20 56	21 00			21 41	→			21 52	21 56	21 58				22 44
Beeston a		20 43						21 04				21 47					22 05					
Nottingham 8 🚌 a		20 52						21 14	21 16			21 54					22 15	22 18				22 56
d	20 17						21 12	21 24													22 16	
Newark Castle 27 a								21 55														
Lincoln 27 a								22 40														
Langley Mill d	20 36						21 36															
Alfreton d	20 44						21 44															
Long Eaton a						20 58										22 00						
Derby 6 a						21 10										22 12						
d				20 20	20 47									21 49	21 49							
Chesterfield d	20 55			21 03	21 47		21 55				22 03			22 26	22 26				22 47		23 01	
Sheffield 7 🚌 a	21 13			21 16	22 01		22 13				22 18			22 39	22 40				23 01		23 15	
Manchester Piccadilly 78 a																						
Doncaster 7 29 a					22 24									23 03	23 03							
Wakefield Kirkgate 4 31,34 a	21 55						22 55															
Wakefield Westgate 7 31 a				21 46							22 48			23 22	23 22							
Leeds 10 31,34 a	22 15			22 02			23 14				23 06			23 37	23 37							
York 8 29 a					22 47																	

A To Nottingham
B From Plymouth to Newcastle
C From Leicester
D From Southampton Central. 🍴 to Leeds
E From Norwich
F 29 September, 6 October. To Lincoln
G not from 29 September. To Lincoln
H not from 29 September. From Leicester
I 29 September, 6 October. From Leicester
J To Lincoln
K From Reading
L From Plymouth
M 8 September. From Bournemouth
N not 8 September. From Plymouth

For connections from Gatwick Airport refer to Table T052

Table T053-F

London - East Midlands - Sheffield

Saturdays

8 September to 6 October

		XC	EM	EM	NT	EM	EM	EM
		◇1 A	◇1 ⌶	◇1 ⌶	◇	◇1 ⌶	◇1 ⊏⊐	◇1 ⌶
St Pancras International ⊖52	d		21 30	21 50		22 00		22 20
Luton Airport Parkway 7 52 ✈	d			22 12				22 42
Luton 10 52	d		21 54			22 25		
Bedford 7 52	d		22 10	22 27		22 42		22 58
Wellingborough	d		22 23	22 40		22 55		23 10
Kettering 5	a		22 32	22 47		23 02		23 17
	d		22 33	22 48		23 03	23 05	23 18
Corby	d						23a19	
Oakham 47	a							
Melton Mowbray 47	a							
Market Harborough	d		22 44	22 58		23 14		23 28
Leicester	a		22 58	23 10		23 29		23 40
	d		22 59	23 11		23 30		23 41
Syston	d							
Sileby	d							
Barrow Upon Soar	d							
Loughborough	d			23 21		23 41		23 52
East Midlands Parkway ✈	d		23 15	23 29		23 50		23 59
Beeston	a					23 58		
Nottingham 8	a					00 07		
	d				23 18			
Newark Castle 27	a							
Lincoln 27	a							
Langley Mill	d				23 36			
Alfreton	d				23 44			
Long Eaton	a			23 32				00 03
Derby 6	a		23 27	23 44				00 14
	d	22 36						
Chesterfield	d	23 16			23 54			
Sheffield 7	a	23 30			00 16			
Manchester Piccadilly 78	a							
Doncaster 7 29	a							
Wakefield Kirkgate 4 31,34	a							
Wakefield Westgate 7 31	a							
Leeds 10 31,34	a	00 10						
York 8 29	a							

Saturdays

13 October to 8 December

		EM	EM	EM	EM	NT	XC	EM	NT	XC	EM	EM	XC	EM	NT	XC	EM	EM	EM	XC	EM	EM	NT
		◇1 B ⌶	◇1 B ⌶	◇1 ⌶	◇ C	◇	◇1 D	◇1 ⌶	◇	◇1 E ⌶	◇ C		◇1 F ⌶	◇1 ⌶	◇	◇1 G ⌶	◇1 ⌶	◇ C		◇1 F ⌶	◇1 ⌶	◇1 ⌶	◇
St Pancras International ⊖52	d			00 15													05 48				06 33		
Luton Airport Parkway 7 52 ✈	d			00 53																			
Luton 10 52	d			00 57													06 14				06 56		
Bedford 7 52	d		00 09	01 25													06 28						
Wellingborough	d		00 22	01 36													06 40						
Kettering 5	a		00 40	01 46													06 47				07 22		
	d		00 41	01 46													06 48				07 23	07 38	
Corby	d																					07a47	
Oakham 47	a																						
Melton Mowbray 47	a																						
Market Harborough	d		00 52	01 58													06 58				07 33		
Leicester	a		01 06	02 13													07 10				07 45		
	d		01 08									06 26					07 12		07 28		07 48		
Syston	d											06 33							07 35				
Sileby	d											06 38							07 40				
Barrow Upon Soar	d											06 43							07 45				
Loughborough	d		01 19									06 48					07 23		07 50		07 58		
East Midlands Parkway ✈	d	00 02	01 27									06 56							07 58		08 05		
Beeston	a		01 33									07 06							08 06				
Nottingham 8	a		01 41									07 15							08 15				
	d		01 47		05 20				06 17		06 40				07 18			07 46					08 17
Newark Castle 27	a																						
Lincoln 27	a																						
Langley Mill	d								06 36						07 37								08 36
Alfreton	d								06 44		07 01				07 45			08 09					08 44
Long Eaton	a																07 31						
Derby 6	a	00 14	02 05														07 44				08 18		
	d	00 17					05 56	06 27		06 38			07 13	07 21		07 44	07 48			08 13	08 22		
Chesterfield	d	00 36			05 49	06 25	06 31	06 46	06 54	07 02	07 11		07 32	07 43	07 57	08 03	08 10	08 20		08 32	08 41		08 55
Sheffield 7	a	00 51			06 15	06 42	06 45	07 08	07 11	07 15	07 28		07 46	07 59	08 15	08 19	08 30	08 37		08 44	08 56		09 13
Manchester Piccadilly 78	a				07 39						08 37							09 37					
Doncaster 7 29	a						07 13						08 13							09 15	09 53		
Wakefield Kirkgate 4 31,34	a					07 22			07 57						08 57								09 56
Wakefield Westgate 7 31	a									07 45						08 46							
Leeds 10 31,34	a					07 43			08 17	08 00					09 17	09 01							10 16
York 8 29	a						07 40			08 30			08 43			09 30				09 40	10 17		

A 8 September. From Penzance
B From St Pancras International
C To Liverpool Lime Street
D To Newcastle
E From Birmingham New Street to Glasgow Central
F From Birmingham New Street to Newcastle
G From Birmingham New Street to Edinburgh

For connections from Gatwick Airport refer to Table T052

Table T053-F

London - East Midlands - Sheffield

Saturdays

13 October to 8 December

		EM	XC	EM	EM	EM	EM	EM	EM	EM	XC	EM	NT	XC	EM	EM	EM	EM	EM	EM	EM	XC	EM
		◇1 ⌶	◇1 A ⌶	◇ B	◇1 ⌶	C	◇1 ⌶	D	◇1 ⌶	◇1 ⌶	◇1 E ⌶	◇1 ⌶	◇	◇1 F ⌶	◇ B	◇1 ⌶	C	◇1 ⌶	D	◇1 ⌶	◇1 ⌶	◇1 G ⌶	◇1 ⌶
St Pancras International ⊖52	d	06 48			07 05				07 35	07 47		08 02				08 05		08 31		08 34	08 47		09 02
Luton Airport Parkway 7 52 ✈	d	07 10							07 56							08 26							
Luton 10 52	d				07 27					08 09											09 09		
Bedford 7 52	d				07 40				08 10	08 24						08 40					09 24		
Wellingborough	d				07 52				08 23	08 35						08 53					09 35		
Kettering 5	a				08 00				08 30	08 43						09 00					09 43		
	d				08 01				08 30	08 44						09 00					09 44		
Corby	d									08a54											09a54		
Oakham 47	a																						
Melton Mowbray 47	a																						
Market Harborough	d				08 11				08 41							09 11				09 29			
Leicester	a	07 53			08 23				08 53			09 04				09 23		09 34		09 42			10 04
	d	07 54			08 25	08 26	08 35		08 54			09 05				09 24	09 26	09 35		09 43			10 05
Syston	d					08 33											09 33						
Sileby	d					08 38											09 38						
Barrow Upon Soar	d					08 43		←									09 43		←				
Loughborough	d	08 03			08 35	08 48	08 45	08 48	09 03							09 33	09 48	09 45	09 48				
East Midlands Parkway ✈	d	08 12			08 42	→	08 52	08 56									→	09 52	09 56	10 02			
Beeston	a	08 18						09 04	09 13							09 44			10 04				
Nottingham 8	a	08 26			08 54			09 11	09 22							09 53			10 14	10 16			
	d			08 47				09 22					09 19		09 47				10 29				
Newark Castle 27	a							09 49											10 51				
Lincoln 27	a							10 19											11 27				
Langley Mill	d												09 38										
Alfreton	d			09 08									09 46		10 08								
Long Eaton	a						08 56											09 56					
Derby 6	a						09 08					09 26						10 08					10 26
	d		08 44				09 08				09 16	09 28		09 44				10 09				10 16	10 28
Chesterfield	d		09 03	09 20			09 27					09 45	09 57	10 03	10 20			10 27					10 45
Sheffield 7	a		09 17	09 37			09 40				09 44	10 01	10 14	10 17	10 37			10 41				10 46	11 00
Manchester Piccadilly 78	a			10 37											11 37								
Doncaster 7 29	a										10 15											11 15	
Wakefield Kirkgate 4 31,34	a												10 55										
Wakefield Westgate 7 31	a		09 46											10 46									
Leeds 10 31,34	a		10 00										11 15	11 00									
York 8 29	a		10 30								10 40			11 30								11 40	

		NT	XC	EM	EM	EM	EM	EM	EM	EM	XC	EM	NT	XC	EM	EM	EM	EM	EM	EM	EM	XC
		◇	◇1 H ⌶	◇ B	◇1 ⌶	C	◇1 ⌶	D	◇1 ⌶	◇1 ⌶	◇1 I ⌶	◇1 ⌶	◇	◇1 F ⌶	◇ B	◇1 ⌶	C	◇1 ⌶	D	◇1 ⌶	◇1 ⌶	◇1 J ⌶
St Pancras International ⊖52	d				09 05		09 31		09 34	09 47		10 02				10 05		10 31		10 34	10 47	
Luton Airport Parkway 7 52 ✈	d				09 26											10 26						
Luton 10 52	d									10 09											11 09	
Bedford 7 52	d				09 40					10 24						10 40					11 24	
Wellingborough	d				09 53					10 35						10 53					11 35	
Kettering 5	a				10 00					10 43						11 00					11 43	
	d				10 00					10 44						11 00					11 44	
Corby	d									10a54											11a53	
Oakham 47	a																					
Melton Mowbray 47	a																					
Market Harborough	d				10 11				10 29							11 11				11 29		
Leicester	a				10 23		10 34		10 42			11 04				11 23		11 34		11 42		
	d				10 24	10 26	10 35		10 43			11 05				11 24	11 26	11 35		11 43		
Syston	d					10 33											11 33					
Sileby	d					10 38											11 38					
Barrow Upon Soar	d					10 43		←									11 43		←			
Loughborough	d				10 33	10 48	10 45	10 48								11 33	11 48	11 45	11 48			
East Midlands Parkway ✈	d					→	10 52	10 56	11 00								→	11 52	11 56	12 00		
Beeston	a				10 43			11 04								11 43			12 04			
Nottingham 8	a				10 52			11 14	11 16							11 52			12 14	12 16		
	d	10 17		10 46				11 29					11 17		11 47				12 29			
Newark Castle 27	a							11 51											12 51			
Lincoln 27	a							12 28											13 24			
Langley Mill	d	10 36											11 36									
Alfreton	d	10 44		11 08									11 44		12 08							
Long Eaton	a						10 56											11 56				
Derby 6	a						11 09					11 26						12 09				
	d		10 44				11 09				11 16	11 28		11 44				12 09				12 16
Chesterfield	d	10 55	11 03	11 20			11 27					11 46	11 55	12 03	12 20			12 27				
Sheffield 7	a	11 13	11 17	11 38			11 41				11 44	12 00	12 13	12 17	12 38			12 41				12 44
Manchester Piccadilly 78	a			12 37											13 37							
Doncaster 7 29	a										12 13											13 15
Wakefield Kirkgate 4 31,34	a	11 55											12 55									
Wakefield Westgate 7 31	a		11 46											12 46								
Leeds 10 31,34	a	12 15	12 00										13 15	13 00								
York 8 29	a		12 30								12 40			13 30								13 40

A From Bristol Temple Meads to Glasgow Central
B From Norwich to Liverpool Lime Street
C To Lincoln
D From Leicester
E From Guildford to Newcastle
F From Plymouth to Edinburgh
G From Bournemouth to Newcastle
H From Plymouth to Glasgow Central
I From Southampton Central to Newcastle
J From Reading to Newcastle

For connections from Gatwick Airport refer to Table T052

Table T053-F

Saturdays

13 October to 8 December

London - East Midlands - Sheffield

	EM ◇1 🍴	NT ◇	XC ◇1 A 🍴	EM ◇ B	EM ◇1 🍴	EM C	EM ◇1 🍴	EM D	EM ◇1 🍴	EM ◇1 🍴	XC ◇1 E 🍴	EM ◇1 🍴	NT ◇	XC ◇1 F 🍴	EM ◇ B	EM ◇1 🍴	EM C	EM ◇1 🍴	EM D	EM ◇1 🍴	EM ◇1 🍴	XC ◇1 G 🍴
St Pancras International ⊖52 d	11 02				11 05		11 31		11 34	11 50		12 02				12 05		12 31		12 34	12 47	
Luton Airport Parkway 52 ✈ d					11 26											12 26						
Luton 52 d										12 12											13 09	
Bedford 52 d					11 40					12 27						12 40					13 24	
Wellingborough d					11 53					12 39						12 53					13 35	
Kettering a					12 00					12 48						13 00					13 43	
Kettering d					12 00					12 49						13 00					13 44	
Corby d										12a59											13a53	
Oakham 47 a																						
Melton Mowbray 47 a																						
Market Harborough d					12 11				12 29							13 11				13 29		
Leicester a	12 04				12 23		12 34		12 42			13 04				13 23		13 34		13 42		
Leicester d	12 05				12 24	12 26	12 35		12 43			13 05				13 24	13 26	13 35		13 43		
Syston d						12 33											13 33					
Sileby d						12 38											13 38					
Barrow Upon Soar d						12 43		←									13 43		←			
Loughborough d					12 33	12 48	12 45	12 48								13 33	13 48	13 45	13 48			
East Midlands Parkway ✈ d						→	12 52	12 56	13 00								→	13 52	13 56	14 00		
Beeston a					12 43			13 04								13 43			14 04			
Nottingham 🚌 a					12 52			13 14	13 16							13 52			14 14	14 16		
Nottingham d		12 17		12 47				13 29					13 17		13 47				14 19			
Newark Castle 27 a								13 50											14 42			
Lincoln 27 a								14 26											15 11			
Langley Mill d		12 36											13 36									
Alfreton d		12 44		13 10									13 44		14 08							
Long Eaton a							12 56											13 56				
Derby a	12 26						13 09					13 26						14 08				
Derby d	12 28		12 44				13 09				13 16	13 28		13 44				14 09				14 16
Chesterfield d	12 45	12 55	13 03	13 21			13 27					13 45	13 55	14 03	14 20			14 26				
Sheffield 🚌 a	13 00	13 13	13 17	13 37			13 41				13 48	14 00	14 13	14 18	14 37			14 40				14 44
Manchester Piccadilly 78 a				14 37											15 37							
Doncaster 29 a											14 15											15 15
Wakefield Kirkgate 31,34 a		13 55											14 55									
Wakefield Westgate 31 a			13 46											14 46								
Leeds 31,34 a		14 15	14 00										15 15	15 00								
York 29 a			14 30								14 40			15 30								15 40

	EM ◇1 🍴	NT ◇	XC ◇1 A 🍴	EM ◇ B	EM ◇1 🍴	EM C	EM ◇1 🍴	EM D	EM ◇1 🍴	EM ◇1 🍴	XC ◇1 E 🍴	EM ◇1 🍴	NT ◇	XC ◇1 H 🍴	EM ◇ B	EM ◇1 🍴	EM C	EM ◇1 🍴	EM D	EM ◇1 🍴	EM ◇1 🍴
St Pancras International ⊖52 d	13 02				13 05		13 31		13 34	13 47		14 02				14 05		14 31		14 34	14 47
Luton Airport Parkway 52 ✈ d					13 26											14 26					
Luton 52 d										14 09											15 09
Bedford 52 d					13 40					14 24						14 40					15 24
Wellingborough d					13 53					14 36						14 53					15 36
Kettering a					14 00					14 45						15 00					15 44
Kettering d					14 00					14 46						15 00					15 45
Corby d										14a56											15a54
Oakham 47 a																					
Melton Mowbray 47 a																					
Market Harborough d					14 11				14 29							15 11				15 29	
Leicester a	14 04				14 23		14 34		14 42			15 04				15 23		15 34		15 42	
Leicester d	14 05				14 24	14 26	14 35		14 43			15 05				15 24	15 26	15 35		15 43	
Syston d						14 33											15 33				
Sileby d						14 38											15 38				
Barrow Upon Soar d						14 43		←									15 43		←		
Loughborough d					14 33	14 48	14 45	14 48								15 33	15 48	15 45	15 48		
East Midlands Parkway ✈ d						→	14 52	14 56	15 00								→	15 52	15 56	16 00	
Beeston a					14 43			15 04								15 43			16 04		
Nottingham 🚌 a					14 52			15 14	15 16							15 52			16 14	16 16	
Nottingham d		14 17		14 47				15 28					15 17		15 47				16 21		
Newark Castle 27 a								15 49											16 42		
Lincoln 27 a								16 27											17 10		
Langley Mill d		14 36											15 36								
Alfreton d		14 44		15 08									15 44		16 10						
Long Eaton a							14 56											15 56			
Derby a	14 26						15 08					15 26						16 09			
Derby d	14 28		14 44				15 09				15 16	15 28		15 44				16 09			
Chesterfield d	14 45	14 55	15 03	15 20			15 26					15 45	15 55	16 03	16 21			16 26			
Sheffield 🚌 a	15 00	15 13	15 17	15 37			15 40				15 44	16 00	16 13	16 18	16 37			16 40			
Manchester Piccadilly 78 a				16 37											17 37						
Doncaster 29 a											16 16										
Wakefield Kirkgate 31,34 a		15 55											16 55								
Wakefield Westgate 31 a			15 46											16 46							
Leeds 31,34 a		16 15	16 00										17 15	17 00							
York 29 a			16 30								16 40			17 29							

A From Penzance to Glasgow Central
B From Norwich to Liverpool Lime Street
C To Lincoln
D From Leicester
E From Southampton Central to Newcastle
F From Plymouth to Aberdeen
G From Reading to Newcastle
H From Plymouth to Dundee

For connections from Gatwick Airport refer to Table T052

Table T053-F

Saturdays

13 October to 8 December

London - East Midlands - Sheffield

	XC ◇1 A 🍴	EM ◇1 🍴	NT ◇	XC ◇1 B 🍴	EM ◇ C	EM ◇1 🍴	EM D	EM ◇1 🍴	EM E	EM ◇1 🍴	EM ◇1 🍴	XC ◇1 F 🍴	EM ◇1 🍴	NT ◇	XC ◇1 G 🍴	EM ◇ C	EM ◇1 🍴	EM D	EM ◇1 🍴	EM E	EM ◇1 🍴	EM ◇1 🍴
St Pancras International ⊖52 d		15 02				15 05		15 31		15 34	15 47		16 02				16 05		16 31		16 34	16 47
Luton Airport Parkway 52 ✈ d						15 26											16 26					
Luton 52 d											16 09											17 09
Bedford 52 d						15 40					16 24						16 40					17 24
Wellingborough d						15 53					16 35						16 53					17 34
Kettering a						16 00					16 45						17 00					17 43
Kettering d						16 00					16 46						17 00					17 44
Corby d											16a56											17a53
Oakham 47 a																						
Melton Mowbray 47 a																						
Market Harborough d						16 11				16 29							17 11				17 29	
Leicester a		16 04				16 23		16 34		16 42			17 04				17 23		17 34		17 42	
Leicester d		16 05				16 24	16 26	16 35		16 43			17 05				17 24	17 26	17 35		17 43	
Syston d							16 33											17 33				
Sileby d							16 38											17 38				
Barrow Upon Soar d							16 43		←									17 43		←		
Loughborough d						16 33	16 48	16 45	16 48								17 33	17 48	17 45	17 48		
East Midlands Parkway ✈ d							→	16 52	16 56	17 00								→	17 52	17 56	18 00	
Beeston a						16 43			17 04								17 43			18 04		
Nottingham 🚌 a						16 52			17 14	17 16							17 55			18 14	18 16	
Nottingham d			16 17		16 44				17 29					17 17		17 44				18 17		
Newark Castle 27 a									17 50											18 43		
Lincoln 27 a									18 25											19 25		
Langley Mill d			16 36											17 36		18 00						
Alfreton d			16 44		17 05									17 44		18 08						
Long Eaton a								16 56											17 56			
Derby a		16 26						17 08					17 26						18 09			
Derby d	16 16	16 28		16 43				17 09				17 16	17 28		17 44				18 09			
Chesterfield d		16 45	16 55	17 04	17 15			17 26					17 45	17 55	18 03	18 18			18 27			
Sheffield 🚌 a	16 44	17 00	17 13	17 17	17 34			17 42				17 45	18 00	18 13	18 17	18 34			18 40			
Manchester Piccadilly 78 a					18 37											19 37						
Doncaster 29 a	17 15																					
Wakefield Kirkgate 31,34 a			17 55											18 55								
Wakefield Westgate 31 a				17 47								18 16			18 49							
Leeds 31,34 a			18 15	18 01								18 33		19 15	19 03							
York 29 a	17 40			18 30								19 05			19 30							

	XC ◇1 A 🍴	EM ◇1 🍴	NT ◇	XC ◇1 H 🍴	EM ◇ C	EM ◇1 🍴	EM I	EM ◇1 🍴	EM E	EM ◇1 🍴	EM ◇1 🍴	XC ◇1 F 🍴	EM ◇1 🍴	NT ◇	XC ◇1 J 🍴	EM ◇ K	EM ◇1 🍴	EM D	EM ◇1 🍴	EM E	XC ◇1 A	EM ◇1 L 🍴
St Pancras International ⊖52 d		17 02				17 05		17 31		17 34	17 47		18 02				18 05		18 31			18 34
Luton Airport Parkway 52 ✈ d						17 26											18 26					
Luton 52 d											18 09											
Bedford 52 d						17 40					18 24						18 40					
Wellingborough d						17 53					18 35						18 53					
Kettering a						18 00					18 45						19 00					
Kettering d						18 00					18 46						19 00					
Corby d											18a56											
Oakham 47 a																						
Melton Mowbray 47 a																						
Market Harborough d						18 11				18 29							19 11					19 29
Leicester a		18 04				18 23		18 34		18 42			19 04				19 23		19 34			19 42
Leicester d		18 05				18 24	18 26	18 35		18 43			19 05				19 24	19 26	19 35			19 43
Syston d							18 33											19 33				
Sileby d							18 38											19 38				
Barrow Upon Soar d							18 43		←									19 43		←		
Loughborough d						18 33	18 48	18 45	18 48								19 33	19 48	19 45	19 48		
East Midlands Parkway ✈ d							→	18 52	18 56	19 00								→	19 52	19 56		20 00
Beeston a						18 43			19 04								19 43			20 04		
Nottingham 🚌 a						18 52			19 15	19 16							19 52			20 13		20 17
Nottingham d			18 17		18 47	19 29								19 17		19 36				20 30		20 25
Newark Castle 27 a						19 52														20 58		
Lincoln 27 a						20 26														21 33		
Langley Mill d			18 36											19 36								20 43
Alfreton d			18 44		19 08									19 44		20 01						→
Long Eaton a								18 58											19 56			
Derby a		18 26						19 09					19 26						20 08			
Derby d	18 16	18 28		18 44				19 09				19 16	19 28		19 43				20 09		20 16	
Chesterfield d		18 45	18 55	19 05	19 20			19 26				19 35	19 45	19 55	20 04	20 11			20 27		20 35	
Sheffield 🚌 a	18 44	19 00	19 13	19 17	19 37			19 39				19 47	20 00	20 13	20 18	20 30			20 40		20 47	
Manchester Piccadilly 78 a					20 37											21 29						
Doncaster 29 a	19 13											20 13									21 21	
Wakefield Kirkgate 31,34 a			19 55											20 55								
Wakefield Westgate 31 a				19 46											20 47							
Leeds 31,34 a			20 15	20 02										21 15	21 02							
York 29 a	19 40			20 30								20 40			21 59						21 42	

A From Reading to Newcastle
B From Plymouth to Glasgow Central
C From Norwich to Liverpool Lime Street
D To Lincoln
E From Leicester
F From Southampton Central to Newcastle
G From Plymouth to Edinburgh
H From Plymouth to Edinburgh. 🍴 to Leeds
I To Nottingham
J From Plymouth. 🍴 to Leeds
K From Norwich
L To Leeds

For connections from Gatwick Airport refer to Table T052

Table T053-F

London - East Midlands - Sheffield

Saturdays
13 October to 8 December

	EM ◇■ ⊼	EM ◇■ ⊼	NT ◇	EM ◇■ ⊼	EM A	XC ◇■ B	EM ◇■ C ⊼	EM ◇■ ⊼	XC ◇■ D	NT ◇	EM E	EM ◇■ ⊼	EM ◇■ ⊼	EM ◇■ ⊼	EM ◇■ ⊼	EM F	XC ◇■ B	EM ◇■ ⊼	EM E	EM ◇■ ⊼	EM ◇■ ⊼
St Pancras International ⊖52 d	18 47	19 02		19 05				19 31				19 34	19 47	20 02	20 05			20 31		20 34	21 02
Luton Airport Parkway 52 ✈ d				19 26											20 26						
Luton 52 d	19 09												20 10								
Bedford 52 d	19 24			19 40									20 24		20 39						
Wellingborough d	19 36			19 53									20 35		20 51						
Kettering a	19 45			20 00									20 43		20 58						
d	19 46			20 00									20 44		20 59						
Corby d	19a55												20a53								
Oakham 47 a																					
Melton Mowbray 47 a																					
Market Harborough d				20 11								20 29			21 09					21 28	
Leicester a		20 04		20 23				20 34				20 42		21 06	21 21			21 34		21 41	22 04
d		20 05		20 24	20 26			20 35				20 43		21 08	21 23	21 26		21 35		21 41	22 05
Syston d					20 33											21 33					
Sileby d					20 38											21 38					
Barrow Upon Soar d					20 43						←					21 43			←		
Loughborough d				20 33	20 48			20 45			20 48				21 32	21 48		21 45	21 48		
East Midlands Parkway ✈ d					→			20 52			20 56	21 00			21 41	→		21 52	21 56	21 58	
Beeston a				20 43							21 04				21 47				22 05		
Nottingham a				20 52							21 14	21 16			21 54				22 15	22 18	
d			20 17							21 12	21 24										
Newark Castle 27 a											21 55										
Lincoln 27 a							←				22 40										
Langley Mill d			20 36				20 43			21 36											
Alfreton d			20 44				20 51			21 44											
Long Eaton a								20 58										22 00			
Derby a		20 26						21 12						21 32				22 11			22 26
d		20 28				20 44			21 27					21 42			21 46				22 28
Chesterfield d		20 45	20 55			21 05	21 09		21 47	21 55				22 02			22 08				22 46
Sheffield a		21 00	21 13			21 19	21 23		21 59	22 13				22 18			22 22				23 00
Manchester Piccadilly 78 a																					
Doncaster 29 a									22 24								22 50				
Wakefield Kirkgate 31,34 a			21 55							22 55											
Wakefield Westgate 31 a						21 47	21 57							22 48			23 12				
Leeds 31,34 a			22 15			22 03	22 17			23 14				23 06			23 27				
York 29 a									22 46												

	EM ◇■ ⊐	NT ◇	EM ◇■ ⊼	NT ◇	EM ◇■ ⊼	EM ◇■ ⊼	EM ◇■ ⊼	EM ◇■ ⊐	EM ◇■ ⊼
St Pancras International ⊖52 d			21 20		21 30	21 50	22 00		22 20
Luton Airport Parkway 52 ✈ d						22 12			22 42
Luton 52 d					21 54		22 25		
Bedford 52 d					22 10	22 27	22 42		22 58
Wellingborough d					22 23	22 40	22 55		23 10
Kettering a					22 32	22 47	23 02		23 17
d	22 06				22 33	22 48	23 03	23 05	23 18
Corby d	22a21							23a19	
Oakham 47 a									
Melton Mowbray 47 a									
Market Harborough d			22 13		22 44	22 58	23 14		23 28
Leicester a			22 25		22 58	23 10	23 29		23 40
d			22 27		22 59	23 11	23 30		23 41
Syston d									
Sileby d									
Barrow Upon Soar d									
Loughborough d			22 37			23 21	23 41		23 52
East Midlands Parkway ✈ d			22 44		23 15	23 29	23 50		23 59
Beeston a							23 58		
Nottingham a			22 56				00 07		
d		22 17		23 18					
Newark Castle 27 a									
Lincoln 27 a									
Langley Mill d				23 36					
Alfreton d				23 44					
Long Eaton a						23 32			00 03
Derby a		22 37			23 29	23 45			00 14
d		22 39							
Chesterfield d		23 02		23 54					
Sheffield a		23 16		00 16					
Manchester Piccadilly 78 a									
Doncaster 29 a									
Wakefield Kirkgate 31,34 a									
Wakefield Westgate 31 a									
Leeds 31,34 a									
York 29 a									

A To Lincoln
B From Plymouth
C From St Pancras International
D From Southampton Central
E From Leicester
F To Nottingham

For connections from Gatwick Airport refer to Table T052

Table T053-F

London - East Midlands - Sheffield

Sundays
20 May to 15 July

	NT ◇ A	XC ◇■ B ⊼	EM ◇ C	EM ◇■ ⊐	NT ◇	XC ◇■ D ⊼	EM ◇■ ⊐	EM ◇ C	EM ◇■ ⊐	NT ◇	XC ◇■ E ⊼	EM ◇■ ⊐	EM ◇■ ⊐	EM ◇ C	EM ◇■ ⊐	NT ◇	XC ◇■ F ⊼	EM ◇■ ⊐	EM ◇■ ⊐	EM ◇ G	EM ◇■ ⊐	XC ◇■ H ⊼
St Pancras International ⊖52 d									09 00			09 30			10 00			10 30			11 00	
Luton Airport Parkway 52 ✈ d									09 29						10 29						11 29	
Luton 52 d												10 03						11 03			11 33	
Bedford 52 d									09 55			10 23			10 54			11 28			11 55	
Wellingborough d									10 08			10 36			11 08			11 39			12 08	
Kettering a									10 15			10 42			11 16			11 46			12 14	
d				09 55					10 16			10 42	10 55		11 17			11 46	11 55		12 15	
Corby d				10a05									11a05						12a05			
Oakham 47 a																						
Melton Mowbray 47 a																						
Market Harborough d									10 26			10 53			11 28			11 56			12 25	
Leicester a									10 40			11 08			11 44			12 11			12 40	
d							10 20		10 41			11 10			11 46			12 13			12 42	
Syston d																						
Sileby d																						
Barrow Upon Soar d																						
Loughborough d							10 30		10 51			11 20			11 57			12 23			12 52	
East Midlands Parkway ✈ d							10 37		10 59			11 27			12 05			12 30			12 59	
Beeston a									11 04												13 05	
Nottingham a									11 12						12 17						13 13	
d	09 19		09 47		10 13			10 48		11 16				11 44		12 19				12 40		
Newark Castle 27 a																						
Lincoln 27 a																						
Langley Mill d	09 37				10 31					11 36						12 37				12 56		
Alfreton d	09 45		10 05		10 39			11 09		11 44				12 08		12 45				13 04		
Long Eaton a							10 41					11 31						12 34				
Derby a							10 54					11 43						12 46				
d		09 44				10 44	10 55				11 44	11 50					12 44	12 49				13 11
Chesterfield d	09 55	10 03	10 18		10 50	11 03	11 14	11 19		11 55	12 03	12 10		12 18		12 56	13 03	13 12		13 17		13 30
Sheffield a	10 15	10 18	10 37		11 10	11 17	11 28	11 35		12 14	12 18	12 28		12 35		13 15	13 18	13 28		13 33		13 43
Manchester Piccadilly 78 a			11 37					12 37						13 37						14 37		
Doncaster 29 a							11 52															14 14
Wakefield Kirkgate 31,34 a	10 52				11 51					12 58						13 52						
Wakefield Westgate 31 a		10 45				11 45					12 45						13 44					
Leeds 31,34 a	11 12	10 59			12 11	11 59				13 22	13 00					14 18	14 00					
York 29 a		11 29				12 30	12 15				13 27						14 27					14 40

	NT ◇	XC ◇■ I ⊼	EM ◇■ ⊐	EM ◇■ ⊐	EM ◇ G	EM ◇■ ⊐	EM ◇■ ⊐	XC ◇■ H ⊼	NT ◇	XC ◇■ J ⊼	EM ◇■ ⊐	EM ◇ C	EM ◇■ ⊐	EM ◇■ ⊐	XC ◇■ K ⊼	NT ◇	XC ◇■ L ⊼	EM ◇■ ⊐	EM ◇ M	EM ◇■ ⊐	EM ◇■ ⊐	XC ◇■ N ⊼
St Pancras International ⊖52 d			11 30			12 10	12 30				12 50		13 10	13 30				13 55		14 10	14 30	
Luton Airport Parkway 52 ✈ d			11 59			12 32	12 52						13 32	13 52						14 32		
Luton 52 d			12 03			12 35	12 54						13 35	13 54							14 53	
Bedford 52 d			12 20			12 49	13 09						13 49	14 09						14 46	15 07	
Wellingborough d			12 32			13 02	13 21						14 02	14 21						14 59	15 19	
Kettering a			12 39			13 08	13 32				13 38		14 08	14 31						15 05	15 31	
d			12 40	12 50		13 09	13 34				13 39		14 09	14 32						15 06	15 33	
Corby d				13a00			13a44							14a42							15a43	
Oakham 47 a																						
Melton Mowbray 47 a																						
Market Harborough d			12 50			13 19					13 50		14 19					14 51		15 16		
Leicester a			13 05			13 34					14 07		14 34					15 07		15 31		
d			13 06			13 36					14 08		14 36					15 09		15 33		
Syston d																						
Sileby d																						
Barrow Upon Soar d																						
Loughborough d			13 16			13 46					14 19		14 46					15 20		15 43		
East Midlands Parkway ✈ d			13 24			13 53					14 28		14 53					15 28		15 50		
Beeston a						13 59							14 59							15 58		
Nottingham a						14 07							15 07							16 05		
d	13 19				13 42				14 19			14 47				15 19			15 47			
Newark Castle 27 a																						
Lincoln 27 a																						
Langley Mill d	13 37				13 58				14 37			15 03				15 37						
Alfreton d	13 45				14 06				14 45			15 11				15 45			16 08			
Long Eaton a			13 27								14 31							15 32				
Derby a			13 42								14 44							15 45				
d		13 44	13 52					14 11		14 44	14 48				15 11		15 44	15 48				16 11
Chesterfield d	13 56	14 03	14 11		14 16			14 30	14 56	15 03	15 09	15 21				15 56	16 03	16 09	16 18			
Sheffield a	14 15	14 17	14 26		14 34			14 45	15 15	15 17	15 29	15 39			15 45	16 15	16 18	16 28	16 34			16 42
Manchester Piccadilly 78 a					15 37							16 37							17 38			
Doncaster 29 a								15 18							16 14							17 15
Wakefield Kirkgate 31,34 a	14 52								15 52							16 53						
Wakefield Westgate 31 a		14 45								15 45							16 45					
Leeds 31,34 a	15 17	15 00							16 15	16 00						17 17	16 59					
York 29 a		15 27						15 40		16 27					16 40		17 27					17 40

A To Carlisle
B From Birmingham New Street to Edinburgh
C To Liverpool Lime Street
D From Birmingham New Street to Motherwell
E From Bristol Temple Meads to Edinburgh
F From Bristol Temple Meads to Motherwell
G From Norwich to Liverpool Lime Street
H From Birmingham New Street to Newcastle
I From Plymouth to Aberdeen
J From Plymouth to Motherwell
K From Guildford to Newcastle
L From Penzance to Edinburgh
M From Peterborough to Liverpool Lime Street
N From Reading to Newcastle

For connections from Gatwick Airport refer to Table T052

Table T053-F

London - East Midlands - Sheffield

Sundays
20 May to 15 July

	NT	XC	EM	EM	EM	XC	EM	EM	NT	XC	EM	EM	EM	XC	EM	EM	EM	NT	EM	XC	EM
		A		B		C				D		B		E						F	G
St Pancras International ⊖52 d			14 55		15 10		15 40				15 55		16 10		16 35	16 40			17 05		
Luton Airport Parkway 52 d					15 33								16 32								
Luton 52 d							16 03									17 03					
Bedford 52 d					15 48		16 17						16 46			17 17					
Wellingborough d					16 02		16 30						16 59			17 30					
Kettering a					16 10		16 36						17 05			17 36					
d					16 11		16 37	16 50					17 06			17 37	17 50				
Corby d								17a00									18a00				
Oakham 47 a																					
Melton Mowbray 47 a																					
Market Harborough d			15 51		16 22						16 51		17 16			17 47					
Leicester a			16 06		16 38		17 01				17 07		17 31		17 43	18 02			18 10		
d			16 08		16 38		17 02				17 09		17 33		17 44	18 04			18 11		
Syston d																					
Sileby d																					
Barrow Upon Soar d																					
Loughborough d			16 19		16 51		17 12						17 43			18 14					
East Midlands Parkway d			16 27		16 59		17 20				17 25		17 50		18 00	18 21			18 26		
Beeston a					17 05								17 58								
Nottingham a					17 14								18 05						18 36		
d	16 19			16 42					17 19			17 39						18 19			18 40
Newark Castle 27 a																					
Lincoln 27 a																					
Langley Mill d	16 37			17 03					17 37			17 57						18 37			18 56
Alfreton d	16 45			17 11					17 45			18 05						18 45			19 04
Long Eaton a			16 32								17 30					18 26					
Derby a			16 49				17 34				17 46				18 14	18 37					
d		16 43	16 51			17 12				17 43	17 47			18 12	18 14					18 43	
Chesterfield d	16 56	17 04	17 14	17 22					17 56	18 03	18 09	18 16			18 37			18 56		19 05	19 15
Sheffield a	17 15	17 19	17 28	17 39		17 41			18 15	18 19	18 27	18 33		18 42	18 51			19 14		19 20	19 31
Manchester Piccadilly 78 a				18 37								19 37									20 38
Doncaster 29 a						18 14								19 17							
Wakefield Kirkgate 31,34 a	17 52								18 52									19 52			
Wakefield Westgate 31 a		17 44	18 00			18 32				18 45										19 49	
Leeds 31,34 a	18 17	18 00	18 15			18 47			19 15	19 01								20 15		20 04	
York 29 a		18 27				19 21				19 30				19 46						20 30	

	EM	XC	EM	EM	EM	NT	EM	XC	EM	EM	XC	EM	EM	EM	NT	EM	EM	XC	EM	EM	XC	EM
		H						I	G		C							J			K	
St Pancras International ⊖52 d	17 10		17 35	17 40			18 05			18 10		18 35	18 40			19 05	19 10		19 35	19 40		
Luton Airport Parkway 52 d	17 32									18 32							19 32					
Luton 52 d				18 03									19 03							20 03		
Bedford 52 d	17 46			18 17						18 46			19 17				19 46			20 17		
Wellingborough d	17 58			18 30						18 58			19 30				19 58			20 30		
Kettering a	18 05			18 36						19 05			19 36				20 05			20 36		
d	18 06			18 37	18 55					19 06			19 37	19 50			20 05			20 37		20 50
Corby d					19a05									20a00								21a00
Oakham 47 a																						
Melton Mowbray 47 a																						
Market Harborough d	18 15			18 47						19 16			19 47				20 15			20 47		
Leicester a	18 31		18 41	19 02			19 09			19 30		19 43	20 02			20 18	20 31		20 41	21 02		
d	18 33		18 42	19 04			19 10			19 32		19 45	20 04			20 22	20 33		20 42	21 04		
Syston d																						
Sileby d																						
Barrow Upon Soar d																						
Loughborough d	18 43			19 14						19 42			20 14				20 43			21 14		
East Midlands Parkway d	18 50		18 56	19 21			19 26			19 49		20 01	20 21			20 39	20 50		20 56	21 21		
Beeston a	18 58									19 58							20 58					
Nottingham a	19 05						19 37			20 05						20 51	21 05					
d						19 19			19 43						20 19							
Newark Castle 27 a																						
Lincoln 27 a																						
Langley Mill d						19 37									20 37							
Alfreton d						19 45			20 04						20 45							
Long Eaton a				19 25									20 25							21 25		
Derby a			19 08	19 38								20 13	20 37						21 08	21 37		
d		19 06	19 16					19 42			20 09	20 16						20 43	21 10		21 44	
Chesterfield d			19 34			19 56		20 03	20 14			20 37			20 56			21 04	21 33		22 03	
Sheffield a		19 38	19 50			20 15		20 18	20 31		20 38	20 51			21 15			21 18	21 47		22 18	
Manchester Piccadilly 78 a									21 37													
Doncaster 29 a		20 14									21 20											
Wakefield Kirkgate 31,34 a						20 52									21 52							
Wakefield Westgate 31 a								20 45				21 32						21 48			22 47	
Leeds 31,34 a						21 14		21 02				21 49			22 14			22 02			23 02	
York 29 a		20 40						21 31			21 45											

A From Plymouth to Motherwell
B From Norwich to Liverpool Lime Street
C From Reading to Newcastle
D From Newquay to Edinburgh
E From Reading to Edinburgh
F From Plymouth to Edinburgh
G From Norwich
H From Reading to Newcastle. ⚲ to Sheffield
I From Plymouth. ⚲ to Leeds
J From Plymouth
K From Penzance

For connections from Gatwick Airport refer to Table T052

Table T053-F

London - East Midlands - Sheffield

Sundays
20 May to 15 July

	NT	EM	EM	EM	XC	EM	EM	NT	EM	EM	EM	EM	EM	EM
					A						B	C	B	C
St Pancras International ⊖52 d		20 00	20 10	20 35		20 40			21 10	21 30	22 30	22 30	23 00	23 00
Luton Airport Parkway 52 d			20 32						21 32		22 52	22 52	23 28	23 28
Luton 52 d						21 04				21 54				
Bedford 52 d			20 47			21 20			21 46	22 07	23 11	23 11	23 53	23 53
Wellingborough d			20 58			21 33			21 59	22 20	23 34	23 34	00 15	00 15
Kettering a			21 05			21 40			22 05	22 27	23 44	23 44	00 25	00 25
d			21 06			21 41	21 55		22 06	22 28	23 45	23 45	00 26	00 26
Corby d							22a05							
Oakham 47 a														
Melton Mowbray 47 a														
Market Harborough d			21 16			21 52			22 16	22 38	23 55	23 56	00 36	00 37
Leicester a		21 08	21 31	21 41		22 09			22 31	22 52	00 10	00 10	00 50	00 51
d		21 10	21 33	21 42		22 10			22 33	22 54	00 11	00 11	00 52	00 52
Syston d														
Sileby d														
Barrow Upon Soar d														
Loughborough d		21 21	21 43	21 52					22 47	23 04	00 21	00 21	01 02	01 02
East Midlands Parkway d		21 29	21 50	22 00		22 26			22 58	23 16	00 29	00 29	01 09	01 10
Beeston a			22 04						23 04		00 34	00 34		
Nottingham a		21 45	22 11						23 11		00 41	00 41		
d	21 33							22 33						
Newark Castle 27 a														
Lincoln 27 a														
Langley Mill d	21 57							22 57						
Alfreton d	22 05							23 05						
Long Eaton a										23 23				
Derby a				22 12		22 40				23 35			01 21	01 21
d					22 42	22 48				23 36				
Chesterfield d	22 16				23 03	23 09		23 16		23 55				
Sheffield a	22 34				23 18	23 23		23 35		00 08				
Manchester Piccadilly 78 a														
Doncaster 29 a														
Wakefield Kirkgate 31,34 a	23 31													
Wakefield Westgate 31 a						23 52								
Leeds 31,34 a	00 07				00 09	00 08								
York 29 a														

Sundays
22 July to 2 September

	NT	EM	XC	EM	NT	XC	EM	EM	EM	EM	EM	EM	NT	XC	EM	EM	EM	EM	EM	EM	EM	XC
	D		E	F		G	H	I	J	K	F			E	H	K	I	J		F		L
St Pancras International ⊖52 d												09 00			09 30	09 30	09 30	09 30			10 00	
Luton Airport Parkway 52 d												09 29									10 29	
Luton 52 d															10 03	10 03	10 03	10 03				
Bedford 52 d												09 55			10 23	10 23	10 23	10 23			10 54	
Wellingborough d												10 08			10 36	10 36	10 36	10 36			11 08	
Kettering a												10 15			10 42	10 42	10 42	10 42			11 16	
d		09 55										10 16			10 42	10 42	10 42	10 42	10 55		11 17	
Corby d		10a05																	11a05			
Oakham 47 a																						
Melton Mowbray 47 a																						
Market Harborough d												10 26			10 53	10 53	10 53	10 53			11 28	
Leicester a												10 40			11 08	11 08	11 08	11 08			11 44	
d							10 07	10 10	10 20	10 20		10 41			11 10	11 10	11 10	11 14			11 46	
Syston d																						
Sileby d																						
Barrow Upon Soar d																						
Loughborough d							10 18	10 20	10 30	10 30		10 51			11 20	11 20	11 20	11 26			11 57	
East Midlands Parkway d							10 26	10 27	10 37	10 37		10 59			11 27	11 27	11 27	11 38			12 05	
Beeston a												11 04										
Nottingham a												11 12									12 17	
d	09 19			09 47	10 13						10 48		11 16							11 44		
Newark Castle 27 a																						
Lincoln 27 a																						
Langley Mill d	09 37				10 31								11 36									
Alfreton d	09 45			10 05	10 39						11 09		11 44							12 08		
Long Eaton a							10 29	10 31		10 41					11 31	11 31	11 31					
Derby a							10 46	10 51		10 54					11 46	11 43	11 49					
d							10 49	10 52		10 55					11 48	11 50	11 50					
Chesterfield d	09 55		10 03	10 18	10 50	11 03	11 14	11 14	11 14	11 14	11 19		11 55	12 03	12 10	12 10	12 12	12 09		12 18		12 29
Sheffield a	10 15		10 18	10 37	11 10	11 17	11 28	11 28	11 28	11 28	11 35		12 14	12 18	12 28	12 28	12 34	12 33		12 35		12 42
Manchester Piccadilly 78 a				11 37							12 37									13 37		
Doncaster 29 a							11 52	11 52	11 52	11 52												13 13
Wakefield Kirkgate 31,34 a	10 52				11 51								12 58									
Wakefield Westgate 31 a			10 45			11 45								12 45								13 30
Leeds 31,34 a	11 12		10 59		12 11	11 59							13 22	13 00								13 46
York 29 a			11 29			12 30	12 15	12 15	12 15	12 15				13 27								14 27

A From Plymouth
B from 24 June
C until 17 June
D To Carlisle
E From Birmingham New Street to Edinburgh
F To Liverpool Lime Street
G From Birmingham New Street to Motherwell
H 5 August, 12 August
I 26 August
J 19 August
K 22 July, 29 July, 2 September
L From Bristol Temple Meads to Motherwell

For connections from Gatwick Airport refer to Table T052

London - East Midlands - Sheffield

Sundays
22 July to 2 September

	NT ◇	EM ◇1 A ⊡	EM ◇1 B ⊡	EM ◇1 C ⊡	EM ◇ D	XC ◇1 E ✕	EM ◇1 F ⊡	EM ◇1 ⊡	EM ◇1 ⊡	NT ◇	EM ◇1 F ⊡	EM ◇1 C ⊡	EM ◇1 B ⊡	EM ◇1 A ⊡	EM ◇1 ⊡	EM ◇ D	EM ◇1 ⊡	EM ◇1 ⊡	XC ◇1 G ✕	NT ◇	EM ◇1 A ⊡	EM ◇1 B ⊡
St Pancras International ⊖52 d		10 30	10 30	10 30			10 30		11 00		11 30	11 30	11 30	11 30			12 10	12 30			12 50	12 50
Luton Airport Parkway 52 ✈ d									11 29		11 59	11 59	11 59	11 59			12 32	12 52				
Luton 52 d		11 03	11 03	11 03			11 03		11 33		12 03	12 03	12 03	12 03			12 35	12 54				
Bedford 52 d		11 28	11 28	11 28			11 28		11 55		12 20	12 20	12 20	12 20			12 49	13 09				
Wellingborough d		11 39	11 39	11 39			11 39		12 08		12 32	12 32	12 32	12 32			13 02	13 21				
Kettering a		11 46	11 46	11 46			11 46		12 14		12 39	12 39	12 39	12 39			13 08	13 32			13 38	13 38
d		11 46	11 46	11 46			11 46	11 55	12 15		12 40	12 40	12 40	12 40	12 50		13 09	13 34			13 39	13 39
Corby d								12a05							13a00			13a44				
Oakham 47 a																						
Melton Mowbray 47 a																						
Market Harborough d		11 56	11 56	11 56			11 56		12 25		12 50	12 50	12 50	12 50			13 19				13 50	13 50
Leicester a		12 11	12 11	12 11			12 11		12 40		13 05	13 05	13 05	13 05			13 34				14 07	14 07
d		12 13	12 13	12 13			12 13		12 42		13 06	13 06	13 06	13 06			13 36				14 08	14 08
Syston d																						
Sileby d																						
Barrow Upon Soar d																						
Loughborough d		12 23	12 23	12 23			12 23		12 52		13 16	13 16	13 16	13 16			13 46				14 19	14 19
East Midlands Parkway ✈ d		12 30	12 30	12 30			12 30		12 59		13 24	13 24	13 24	13 26			13 53				14 28	14 28
Beeston a									13 05								13 59					
Nottingham a									13 13								14 07					
d	12 19				12 40					13 19						13 42				14 19		
Newark Castle 27 a																						
Lincoln 27 a																						
Langley Mill d	12 37				12 56					13 37						13 58				14 37		
Alfreton d	12 45				13 04					13 45						14 06				14 45		
Long Eaton a			12 34	12 34			12 34				13 27	13 27	13 27									14 31
Derby a			12 46	12 49			12 52				13 46	13 43	13 42									14 44
d			12 49	12 50			12 53				13 47	13 49	13 52									14 48
Chesterfield d	12 56	13 11	13 12	13 12	13 17	13 30	13 36			13 56	14 11	14 11	14 11	14 10		14 16			14 30	14 56	15 08	15 09
Sheffield a	13 15	13 28	13 28	13 28	13 33	13 43	13 53			14 15	14 26	14 26	14 26	14 27		14 34			14 45	15 15	15 29	15 29
Manchester Piccadilly 78 a					14 37											15 37						
Doncaster 29 a						14 14													15 16			
Wakefield Kirkgate 31,34 a	13 52									14 52										15 52		
Wakefield Westgate 31 a						14 44													15 35			
Leeds 31,34 a	14 18					14 59				15 17									15 53	16 15		
York 29 a						15 27													16 27			

	EM ◇1 C ⊡	EM ◇ H	XC ◇1 I ✕	EM ◇1 F ⊡	EM ◇1 ⊡	NT ◇	EM ◇1 ⊡	EM ◇1 A ⊡	EM ◇1 B ⊡	EM ◇ J	XC ◇1 K ✕	EM ◇1 C ⊡	EM ◇1 F ⊡	EM ◇1 ⊡	NT ◇	EM ◇1 ⊡	EM ◇1 A ⊡	EM ◇1 B ⊡	EM ◇1 C ⊡	EM ◇ D	XC ◇1 I ✕
St Pancras International ⊖52 d	12 50			12 50	13 10		13 30	13 55	13 55			13 55	13 55	14 10		14 30	14 55	14 55	14 55		
Luton Airport Parkway 52 ✈ d					13 32		13 52							14 32							
Luton 52 d					13 35		13 54									14 53					
Bedford 52 d					13 49		14 09							14 46		15 07					
Wellingborough d					14 02		14 21							14 59		15 19					
Kettering a	13 38			13 38	14 08		14 31							15 05		15 31					
d	13 39			13 39	14 09		14 32							15 06		15 33					
Corby d							14a42									15a43					
Oakham 47 a																					
Melton Mowbray 47 a																					
Market Harborough d	13 50			13 50	14 19			14 51	14 51			14 51	14 51	15 16			15 51	15 51	15 51		
Leicester a	14 07			14 07	14 34			15 07	15 07			15 07	15 07	15 31			16 06	16 06	16 06		
d	14 08			14 08	14 36			15 09	15 09			15 09	15 09	15 33			16 08	16 08	16 08		
Syston d																					
Sileby d																					
Barrow Upon Soar d																					
Loughborough d	14 19			14 19	14 46			15 20	15 20			15 20	15 20	15 43			16 19	16 19	16 19		
East Midlands Parkway ✈ d	14 28			14 28	14 53			15 28	15 28			15 28	15 28	15 50			16 27	16 27	16 27		
Beeston a					14 59									15 58							
Nottingham a					15 07									16 05							
d		14 47				15 19				15 47					16 19					16 42	
Newark Castle 27 a																					
Lincoln 27 a																					
Langley Mill d		15 03				15 37									16 37					17 03	
Alfreton d		15 11				15 45				16 08					16 45					17 11	
Long Eaton a	14 31			14 31					15 32			15 32	15 32					16 32	16 32		
Derby a	14 48			14 51					15 45			15 48	15 52					16 49	16 48		
d	14 49			14 52					15 48			15 50	15 55					16 51	16 51		
Chesterfield d	15 14	15 21	15 28	15 34		15 56		16 08	16 09	16 18	16 28	16 34	16 35		16 56		17 12	17 14	17 15	17 22	17 28
Sheffield a	15 29	15 39	15 45	15 50		16 15		16 28	16 28	16 34	16 41	16 55	16 54		17 15		17 28	17 28	17 30	17 39	17 43
Manchester Piccadilly 78 a		16 37								17 38										18 37	
Doncaster 29 a			16 11								17 12										18 11
Wakefield Kirkgate 31,34 a						16 53									17 52						
Wakefield Westgate 31 a			16 40								17 33						18 00	18 00	18 00		18 43
Leeds 31,34 a			16 59			17 17					17 54				18 17		18 15	18 15	18 15		18 59
York 29 a			17 27								18 27										19 30

A 19 August
B 22 July, 29 July, 2 September
C 5 August, 12 August
D From Norwich to Liverpool Lime Street
E From Bristol Temple Meads to Aberdeen
F 26 August
G From Plymouth to Motherwell
H To Liverpool Lime Street
I From Plymouth to Edinburgh
J From Peterborough to Liverpool Lime Street
K From Penzance to Motherwell

For connections from Gatwick Airport refer to Table T052

London - East Midlands - Sheffield

Sundays
22 July to 2 September

	EM ◇1 A ⊡	EM ◇1 ⊡	NT ◇	EM ◇1 B ⊡	EM ◇1 C ⊡	EM ◇1 D ⊡	EM ◇1 A ⊡	EM ◇1 ⊡	EM ◇1 B ⊡	EM ◇1 D ⊡	EM ◇1 C ⊡	EM ◇ E	XC ◇1 F ✕	EM ◇1 A ⊡	EM ◇1 ⊡	EM ◇1 G ⊡	EM ◇1 C ⊡	EM ◇1 B ⊡	EM ◇1 C ⊡	EM ◇1 D ⊡	EM ◇1 A ⊡	EM ◇1 ⊡
St Pancras International ⊖52 d	14 55	15 10		15 40	15 40	15 40	15 40		15 55	15 55	15 55			15 55	16 10	16 35	16 35	16 40	16 40	16 40	16 40	
Luton Airport Parkway 52 ✈ d		15 33													16 32							
Luton 52 d				16 03	16 03	16 03	16 03											17 03	17 03	17 03	17 03	
Bedford 52 d		15 48		16 17	16 17	16 17	16 17								16 46			17 17	17 17	17 17	17 17	
Wellingborough d		16 02		16 30	16 30	16 30	16 30								16 59			17 30	17 30	17 30	17 30	
Kettering a		16 10		16 36	16 36	16 36	16 36								17 05			17 36	17 36	17 36	17 36	
d		16 11		16 37	16 37	16 37	16 37	16 50							17 06			17 37	17 37	17 37	17 37	17 50
Corby d								17a00														18a00
Oakham 47 a																						
Melton Mowbray 47 a																						
Market Harborough d	15 51	16 22							16 51	16 51	16 51			16 51	17 16			17 47	17 47	17 47	17 47	
Leicester a	16 06	16 38		17 01	17 01	17 01	17 01		17 07	17 07	17 07			17 07	17 31	17 43	17 43	18 02	18 02	18 02	18 02	
d	16 08	16 38		17 02	17 02	17 02	17 02		17 09	17 09	17 09			17 09	17 33	17 44	17 44	18 04	18 04	18 04	18 04	
Syston d																						
Sileby d																						
Barrow Upon Soar d																						
Loughborough d	16 19	16 51		17 12	17 12	17 12	17 12								17 43			18 14	18 14	18 14	18 14	
East Midlands Parkway ✈ d	16 27	16 59		17a20	17 20	17 20	17 20		17 25	17 25	17 25			17 25	17 50	18 00	18 00	18a21	18 21	18 21	18 21	
Beeston a		17 05													17 58							
Nottingham a		17 14													18 05							
d			17 19									17 39										
Newark Castle 27 a																						
Lincoln 27 a																						
Langley Mill d			17 37									17 57										
Alfreton d			17 45									18 05										
Long Eaton a	16 32									17 29	17 30			17 30					18 26	18 26	18 26	
Derby a	16 56				17 34	17 38	17 41			17 46	17 46			17 50			18 14		18 37	18 41	18 44	
d	16 58									17 47	17 47			17 51			18 14					
Chesterfield d	17 34		17 56						18 08	18 12	18 09	18 16	18 29	18 45		18 35	18 37					
Sheffield a	17 48		18 15						18 27	18 27	18 27	18 33	18 42	19 05		18 51	18 51					
Manchester Piccadilly 78 a												19 37										
Doncaster 29 a													19 17									
Wakefield Kirkgate 31,34 a			18 52																			
Wakefield Westgate 31 a													19 38									
Leeds 31,34 a			19 15										19 57									
York 29 a													20 30									

	NT ◇	EM ◇1 ⊡	EM ◇ H	EM ◇1 ⊡	XC ◇1 I ✕	EM ◇1 C ⊡	EM ◇1 G ⊡	EM ◇1 B ⊡	EM ◇1 C ⊡	EM ◇1 D ⊡	EM ◇1 A ⊡	EM ◇1 ⊡	NT ◇	EM ◇1 ⊡	EM ◇ H	EM ◇1 ⊡	XC ◇1 I ✕	EM ◇1 G ⊡	EM ◇1 C ⊡	EM ◇1 B ⊡	EM ◇1 C ⊡
St Pancras International ⊖52 d		17 05		17 10		17 35	17 35	17 40	17 40	17 40	17 40			18 05		18 10		18 35	18 35	18 40	18 40
Luton Airport Parkway 52 ✈ d				17 32												18 32					
Luton 52 d								18 03	18 03	18 03	18 03									19 03	19 03
Bedford 52 d				17 46				18 17	18 17	18 17	18 17					18 46				19 17	19 17
Wellingborough d				17 58				18 30	18 30	18 30	18 30					18 58				19 30	19 30
Kettering a				18 05				18 36	18 36	18 36	18 36					19 05				19 36	19 36
d				18 06				18 37	18 37	18 37	18 37	18 55				19 06				19 37	19 37
Corby d												19a05									
Oakham 47 a																					
Melton Mowbray 47 a																					
Market Harborough d				18 15				18 47	18 47	18 47	18 47					19 16				19 47	19 47
Leicester a		18 10		18 31		18 41	18 41	19 02	19 02	19 02	19 02			19 09		19 30		19 43	19 43	20 02	20 02
d		18 11		18 33		18 42	18 42	19 04	19 04	19 04	19 04			19 10		19 32		19 45	19 45	20 04	20 04
Syston d																					
Sileby d																					
Barrow Upon Soar d																					
Loughborough d				18 43				19 14	19 14	19 14	19 14					19 42				20 14	20 14
East Midlands Parkway ✈ d		18 26		18 50		18 56	19 02	19a21	19 21	19 21	19 21			19 26		19 49		20 01	20 01	20a21	20 21
Beeston a				18 58												19 58					
Nottingham a		18 36		19 05										19 37		20 05					
d	18 19		18 40										19 19		19 43						
Newark Castle 27 a																					
Lincoln 27 a																					
Langley Mill d	18 37		18 56										19 37								
Alfreton d	18 45		19 04										19 45		20 04						
Long Eaton a									19 25	19 25	19 25										20 25
Derby a						19 08			19 38	19 41	19 45								20 13		20 37
d						19 16													20 16		
Chesterfield d	18 56		19 15		19 27	19 34	19 34						19 56		20 14		20 22	20 35	20 37		
Sheffield a	19 14		19 31		19 43	19 50	19 50						20 15		20 31		20 38	20 51	20 51		
Manchester Piccadilly 78 a			20 38												21 37						
Doncaster 29 a					20 13																
Wakefield Kirkgate 31,34 a	19 52												20 52								
Wakefield Westgate 31 a					20 32												21 07	21 32	21 32		
Leeds 31,34 a	20 15				20 47								21 14				21 22	21 49	21 49		
York 29 a																					

A 26 August
B 19 August
C 22 July, 29 July, 2 September
D 5 August, 12 August
E From Norwich to Liverpool Lime Street
F From Newquay to Edinburgh
G from 5 August until 26 August
H From Norwich
I From Plymouth

For connections from Gatwick Airport refer to Table T052

Table T053-F

Sundays
22 July to 2 September

London - East Midlands - Sheffield

	EM ◇■ A	EM ◇■ B	EM ◇■	NT ◇	EM ◇■	EM ◇■	XC ◇■ C	EM ◇■ D	EM ◇■ E	EM ◇■ E	EM ◇■ D	EM ◇■	NT ◇	EM ◇■	EM ◇■	EM ◇■ E	EM ◇■ D	XC ◇■ F	EM ◇■ E	EM ◇■ D	EM ◇■	NT ◇
St Pancras International ⊖52 d	18 40	18 40			19 05	19 10		19 35	19 35	19 40	19 40			20 00	20 10	20 35	20 35		20 40	20 40		
Luton Airport Parkway 52 d						19 32									20 32							
Luton 52 d	19 03	19 03								20 03	20 03								21 04	21 04		
Bedford 52 d	19 17	19 17				19 46				20 17	20 17				20 47				21 20	21 20		
Wellingborough d	19 30	19 30				19 58				20 30	20 30				20 58				21 33	21 33		
Kettering a	19 36	19 36				20 05				20 36	20 36				21 05				21 40	21 40		
Kettering d	19 37	19 37	19 50			20 05				20 37	20 37	20 50			21 06				21 41	21 41	21 55	
Corby d			20a00									21a00									22a05	
Oakham 47 a																						
Melton Mowbray 47 a																						
Market Harborough d	19 47	19 47				20 15				20 47	20 47				21 16				21 52	21 52		
Leicester a	20 02	20 02			20 18	20 31		20 41	20 41	21 02	21 02			21 08	21 31	21 41	21 41		22 09	22 09		
Leicester d	20 04	20 04			20 22	20 33		20 42	20 42	21 04	21 04			21 10	21 33	21 42	21 42		22 10	22 10		
Syston d																						
Sileby d																						
Barrow Upon Soar d																						
Loughborough d	20 14	20 14				20 43				21 14	21 14			21 21	21 43	21 52	21 52					
East Midlands Parkway d	20 21	20 21			20 39	20 50		20 56	21 06	21a21	21 21			21 29	21 50	22a00	22 00		22 26	22 26		
Beeston a						20 58									22 04							
Nottingham a					20 51	21 05								21 45	22 11							
Nottingham d				20 19									21 33									22 33
Newark Castle 27 a																						
Lincoln 27 a																						
Langley Mill d				20 37									21 57									22 57
Alfreton d				20 45									22 05									23 05
Long Eaton a	20 25	20 25									21 25											
Derby a	20 41	20 44						21 08			21 37						22 12			22 40		
Derby d								21 10												22 48		
Chesterfield d				20 56			21 27	21 33	21 33				22 16					22 22	23 07	23 09		23 16
Sheffield a				21 15			21 39	21 47	21 46				22 34					22 37	23 23	23 23		23 35
Manchester Piccadilly 78 a																						
Doncaster 29 a																						
Wakefield Kirkgate 31,34 a				21 52									23 31									
Wakefield Westgate 31 a							22 09											23 02	23 52	23 52		
Leeds 31,34 a				22 14			22 24						00 07					23 17	00 08	00 08		
York 29 a																						

	EM ◇■	EM ◇■ E	EM ◇■ D	EM ◇■	EM ◇■ E	EM ◇■ D
St Pancras International ⊖52 d	21 10	21 30	21 30	22 30	23 00	23 00
Luton Airport Parkway 52 d	21 32			22 52	23 28	23 28
Luton 52 d		21 54	21 54			
Bedford 52 d	21 46	22 07	22 07	23 11	23 53	23 53
Wellingborough d	21 59	22 20	22 20	23 34	00 15	00 15
Kettering a	22 05	22 27	22 27	23 44	00 25	00 25
Kettering d	22 06	22 28	22 28	23 45	00 26	00 26
Corby d						
Oakham 47 a						
Melton Mowbray 47 a						
Market Harborough d	22 16	22 38	22 38	23 55	00 36	00 36
Leicester a	22 31	22 52	22 52	00 10	00 50	00 50
Leicester d	22 33	22 54	22 54	00 11	00 52	00 52
Syston d						
Sileby d						
Barrow Upon Soar d						
Loughborough d	22 47	23 04	23 04	00 21	01 02	01 02
East Midlands Parkway d	22 58	23 16	23 16	00 29	01a09	01 09
Beeston a	23 04			00 34		
Nottingham a	23 11			00 41		
Nottingham d						
Newark Castle 27 a						
Lincoln 27 a						
Langley Mill d						
Alfreton d						
Long Eaton a			23 23			
Derby a			23 35			01 21
Derby d			23 36			
Chesterfield d		23 54	23 55			
Sheffield a		00 08	00 08			
Manchester Piccadilly 78 a						
Doncaster 29 a						
Wakefield Kirkgate 31,34 a						
Wakefield Westgate 31 a						
Leeds 31,34 a						
York 29 a						

A 5 August, 12 August
B 26 August
C From Plymouth
D 22 July, 29 July, 2 September
E from 5 August until 26 August
F From Penzance

For connections from Gatwick Airport refer to Table T052

Table T053-F

Sundays
9 September to 7 October

London - East Midlands - Sheffield

	NT ◇ A	XC ◇■ B	EM ◇ C	EM ◇■	NT ◇	XC ◇■ D	EM ◇■	EM ◇ C	EM ◇■	NT ◇	XC ◇■ B	EM ◇■	EM ◇■	EM ◇ C	EM ◇■	XC ◇■ E	NT ◇	EM ◇■	EM ◇■	EM ◇ F	EM ◇■	XC ◇■ G
St Pancras International ⊖52 d									09 00			09 30			10 00			10 30			11 00	
Luton Airport Parkway 52 d									09 29						10 29						11 29	
Luton 52 d												10 03						11 03			11 33	
Bedford 52 d									09 55			10 23			10 54			11 28			11 55	
Wellingborough d									10 08			10 36			11 08			11 39			12 08	
Kettering a									10 15			10 42			11 16			11 46			12 14	
Kettering d				09 55					10 16			10 42	10 55		11 17			11 46	11 55		12 15	
Corby d				10a05									11a05						12a05			
Oakham 47 a																						
Melton Mowbray 47 a																						
Market Harborough d									10 26			10 53			11 28			11 56			12 25	
Leicester a									10 40			11 08			11 44			12 11			12 40	
Leicester d							10 20		10 41			11 14			11 46			12 13			12 42	
Syston d																						
Sileby d																						
Barrow Upon Soar d																						
Loughborough d							10 30		10 51			11 26			11 57			12 23			12 52	
East Midlands Parkway d							10 37		10 59			11 38			12 05			12 30			12 59	
Beeston a									11 04												13 05	
Nottingham a									11 12						12 17						13 13	
Nottingham d	09 19		09 47		10 13			10 48		11 16				11 44			12 19			12 40		
Newark Castle 27 a																						
Lincoln 27 a																						
Langley Mill d	09 37				10 31					11 36							12 37			12 56		
Alfreton d	09 45		10 05		10 39			11 09		11 44				12 08			12 45			13 04		
Long Eaton a																						
Derby a																						
Derby d		09 28				10 27					11 28					11 49						12 43
Chesterfield d	09 55	10 03	10 18		10 50	11 03	11 14	11 19		11 55	12 03	12 09		12 18		12 29	12 56	13 11		13 17		13 30
Sheffield a	10 15	10 18	10 37		11 10	11 17	11 28	11 35		12 14	12 18	12 33		12 35		12 42	13 15	13 28		13 33		13 43
Manchester Piccadilly 78 a			11 37					12 37						13 37						14 37		
Doncaster 29 a							11 52									13 13						14 14
Wakefield Kirkgate 31,34 a	10 52				11 51					12 58							13 52					
Wakefield Westgate 31 a		10 45				11 45					12 45					13 30						14 44
Leeds 31,34 a	11 12	10 59			12 11	11 59				13 22	13 00					13 46	14 18					14 59
York 29 a		11 29				12 30	12 15				13 27					14 27						15 27

	NT ◇	EM ◇■	EM ◇■	EM ◇ F	EM ◇■	EM ◇■	XC ◇■ H	NT ◇	EM ◇■	EM ◇ C	EM ◇■	EM ◇■	XC ◇■ I	NT ◇	EM ◇■	EM ◇ J	EM ◇■	EM ◇■	XC ◇■ K	XC ◇■ L	NT ◇	EM ◇■
St Pancras International ⊖52 d		11 30			12 10	12 30			12 50		13 10	13 30			13 55		14 10	14 30				14 55
Luton Airport Parkway 52 d		11 59			12 32	12 52					13 32	13 52					14 32					
Luton 52 d		12 03			12 35	12 54					13 35	13 54						14 53				
Bedford 52 d		12 20			12 49	13 09					13 49	14 09					14 46	15 07				
Wellingborough d		12 32			13 02	13 21					14 02	14 21					14 59	15 19				
Kettering a		12 39			13 08	13 32			13 38		14 08	14 31					15 05	15 31				
Kettering d		12 40	12 50		13 09	13 34			13 39		14 09	14 32					15 06	15 33				
Corby d			13a00			13a44						14a42						15a43				
Oakham 47 a																						
Melton Mowbray 47 a																						
Market Harborough d		12 50			13 19				13 50		14 19				14 51		15 16					15 51
Leicester a		13 05			13 34				14 07		14 34				15 07		15 31					16 06
Leicester d		13 06			13 36				14 08		14 36				15 09		15 33					16 08
Syston d																						
Sileby d																						
Barrow Upon Soar d																						
Loughborough d		13 16			13 46				14 19		14 46				15 20		15 43					16 19
East Midlands Parkway d		13 26			13 53				14 28		14 53				15 28		15 50					16 27
Beeston a					13 59						14 59						15 58					
Nottingham a					14 07						15 07						16 05					
Nottingham d	13 19			13 42				14 19		14 47				15 19		15 47					16 19	
Newark Castle 27 a																						
Lincoln 27 a																						
Langley Mill d	13 37			13 58				14 37		15 03				15 37							16 37	
Alfreton d	13 45			14 06				14 45		15 11				15 45		16 08					16 45	
Long Eaton a																						
Derby a																						
Derby d							13 47						14 48						15 47	15 47		
Chesterfield d	13 56	14 10		14 16			14 30	14 56	15 08	15 21			15 28	15 56	16 08	16 18			16 28	16 28	16 56	17 12
Sheffield a	14 15	14 27		14 34			14 45	15 15	15 29	15 39			15 45	16 15	16 28	16 34			16 41	16 41	17 15	17 28
Manchester Piccadilly 78 a				15 37						16 37						17 38						
Doncaster 29 a							15 16						16 11						17 12	17 12		
Wakefield Kirkgate 31,34 a	14 52							15 52						16 53							17 52	
Wakefield Westgate 31 a							15 35						16 40						17 33	17 33		18 00
Leeds 31,34 a	15 17						15 53	16 15					17 00	17 17					17 54	17 54	18 17	18 15
York 29 a							16 27						17 27						18 27	18 27		

A To Carlisle
B From Birmingham New Street to Edinburgh
C To Liverpool Lime Street
D From Birmingham New Street to Motherwell
E From Bristol Temple Meads to Motherwell
F From Norwich to Liverpool Lime Street
G From Bristol Temple Meads to Aberdeen
H From Plymouth to Motherwell
I From Plymouth to Edinburgh
J From Peterborough to Liverpool Lime Street
K 9 September. From Penzance to Motherwell
L not 9 September. From Penzance to Glasgow Central

For connections from Gatwick Airport refer to Table T052

Table T053-F

London - East Midlands - Sheffield

Sundays

9 September to 7 October

	EM ◇ A	EM ◇1	XC ◇1 B	EM ◇1	EM ◇1	NT ◇	EM ◇1	EM ◇ A	EM ◇1	XC ◇1 C	EM ◇1	EM ◇1	EM ◇1	NT ◇	EM ◇1	EM ◇ D	EM ◇1	XC ◇1 E	EM ◇1	EM ◇1	EM ◇1
St Pancras International ⊖52 d		15 10		15 40			15 55		16 10		16 35	16 40			17 05		17 10		17 35	17 40	
Luton Airport Parkway 7 52 ✈ d		15 33							16 32								17 32				
Luton 10 52 d				16 03								17 03								18 03	
Bedford 7 52 d		15 48		16 17					16 46			17 17					17 46			18 17	
Wellingborough d		16 02		16 30					16 59			17 30					17 58			18 30	
Kettering 5 a		16 10		16 36					17 05			17 36					18 05			18 36	
d		16 11		16 37	16 50				17 06			17 37	17 50				18 06			18 37	18 55
Corby d					17a00								18a00								19a05
Oakham 47 a																					
Melton Mowbray 47 a																					
Market Harborough d		16 22					16 51		17 16			17 47					18 15			18 47	
Leicester a		16 38		17 01			17 07		17 31		17 43	18 02			18 10		18 31		18 41	19 02	
d		16 38		17 02			17 09		17 33		17 44	18 04			18 11		18 33		18 42	19 04	
Syston d																					
Sileby d																					
Barrow Upon Soar d																					
Loughborough d		16 51		17 12					17 43			18 14					18 43			19 14	
East Midlands Parkway ✈ d		16 59		17 20			17 25		17 50		18 00	18 21			18 26		18 50		19 02	19 21	
Beeston a		17 05							17 58								18 58				
Nottingham 8 a		17 14							18 05						18 36		19 05				
d	16 42					17 19		17 39						18 19		18 40					
Newark Castle 27 a																					
Lincoln 27 a																					
Langley Mill d	17 03					17 37		17 57						18 37		18 56					
Alfreton d	17 11					17 45		18 05						18 45		19 04					
Long Eaton a												18 26								19 25	
Derby 6 a				17 37								18 36								19 37	
d			16 48							17 49								18 51			
Chesterfield d	17 22		17 28			17 56	18 08	18 16		18 29	18 35			18 56		19 15		19 28	19 34		
Sheffield 7 a	17 39		17 43			18 15	18 27	18 33		18 42	18 51			19 14		19 31		19 43	19 50		
Manchester Piccadilly 78 a	18 37							19 37								20 38					
Doncaster 7 29 a			18 11							19 17								20 13			
Wakefield Kirkgate 4 31,34 a						18 52								19 52							
Wakefield Westgate 7 31 a			18 43							19 38								20 32			
Leeds 10 31,34 a			18 59			19 15				19 57				20 15				20 47			
York 8 29 a			19 30							20 30											

	NT ◇	EM ◇1	EM ◇ D	EM ◇1	XC ◇1 E	EM ◇1	EM ◇1	EM ◇1	NT ◇	EM ◇1	EM ◇1	XC ◇1 E	EM ◇1	EM ◇1	EM ◇1	NT ◇	EM ◇1	EM ◇1	XC ◇1 F	EM ◇1	EM ◇1	EM ◇1
St Pancras International ⊖52 d		18 05		18 10		18 35	18 40			19 05	19 10		19 35	19 40			20 00	20 10		20 35	20 40	
Luton Airport Parkway 7 52 ✈ d				18 32							19 32							20 32				
Luton 10 52 d							19 03							20 03							21 04	
Bedford 7 52 d				18 46			19 17				19 46			20 17				20 47			21 20	
Wellingborough d				18 58			19 30				19 58			20 30				20 58			21 33	
Kettering 5 a				19 05			19 36				20 05			20 36				21 05			21 40	
d				19 06			19 37	19 50			20 05			20 37	20 50			21 06			21 41	21 55
Corby d								20a00							21a00							22a05
Oakham 47 a																						
Melton Mowbray 47 a																						
Market Harborough d				19 16			19 47				20 15			20 47				21 16			21 52	
Leicester a		19 09		19 30		19 43	20 02			20 18	20 31		20 41	21 02			21 08	21 31		21 41	22 09	
d		19 10		19 32		19 45	20 04			20 22	20 33		20 42	21 04			21 10	21 33		21 42	22 10	
Syston d																						
Sileby d																						
Barrow Upon Soar d																						
Loughborough d				19 42			20 14				20 43			21 14			21 21	21 43		21 52		
East Midlands Parkway ✈ d		19 26		19 49		20 01	20 21			20 39	20 50		21 06	21 21			21 29	21 50		22 00	22 26	
Beeston a				19 58							20 58							22 04				
Nottingham 8 a		19 37		20 05						20 51	21 05						21 45	22 11				
d	19 19		19 43						20 19							21 33						
Newark Castle 27 a																						
Lincoln 27 a																						
Langley Mill d	19 37								20 37							21 57						
Alfreton d	19 45		20 04						20 45							22 05						
Long Eaton a							20 25							21 25								
Derby 6 a							20 37							21 37						22 12		
d					19 46							20 45							21 45			
Chesterfield d	19 56		20 14		20 22	20 35			20 56			21 24	21 33			22 16			22 23		23 07	
Sheffield 7 a	20 15		20 31		20 38	20 51			21 15			21 38	21 46			22 34			22 37		23 23	
Manchester Piccadilly 78 a			21 37																			
Doncaster 7 29 a																						
Wakefield Kirkgate 4 31,34 a	20 52								21 52							23 31						
Wakefield Westgate 7 31 a					21 07	21 32						22 09							23 02		23 52	
Leeds 10 31,34 a	21 14				21 22	21 49			22 14			22 24				00 07			23 17		00 08	
York 8 29 a																						

A From Norwich to Liverpool Lime Street
B From Plymouth to Edinburgh
C From Newquay to Edinburgh
D From Norwich
E From Plymouth
F From Penzance

For connections from Gatwick Airport refer to Table T052

Table T053-F

London - East Midlands - Sheffield

Sundays

9 September to 7 October

	NT ◇	EM ◇1	EM ◇1	EM ◇1	EM ◇1
St Pancras International ⊖52 d		21 10	21 30	22 30	23 00
Luton Airport Parkway 7 52 ✈ d		21 32		22 52	23 28
Luton 10 52 d			21 54		
Bedford 7 52 d		21 46	22 07	23 11	23 53
Wellingborough d		21 59	22 20	23 34	00 15
Kettering 5 a		22 05	22 27	23 44	00 25
d		22 06	22 28	23 45	00 26
Corby d					
Oakham 47 a					
Melton Mowbray 47 a					
Market Harborough d		22 16	22 38	23 55	00 36
Leicester a		22 31	22 52	00 10	00 50
d		22 33	22 54	00 11	00 52
Syston d					
Sileby d					
Barrow Upon Soar d					
Loughborough d		22 47	23 04	00 21	01 02
East Midlands Parkway ✈ d		22 58	23 16	00 29	01 09
Beeston a		23 04		00 34	
Nottingham 8 a		23 11		00 41	
d	22 33				
Newark Castle 27 a					
Lincoln 27 a					
Langley Mill d	22 57				
Alfreton d	23 05				
Long Eaton a					
Derby 6 a					01 21
d					
Chesterfield d	23 16		23 54		
Sheffield 7 a	23 35		00 08		
Manchester Piccadilly 78 a					
Doncaster 7 29 a					
Wakefield Kirkgate 4 31,34 a					
Wakefield Westgate 7 31 a					
Leeds 10 31,34 a					
York 8 29 a					

Sundays

14 October to 2 December

	NT ◇ A	XC ◇1 B	EM ◇ C	EM ◇1	NT ◇	XC ◇1 D	EM ◇1	EM ◇ C	EM ◇1	NT ◇	XC ◇1 E	EM ◇1	EM ◇1	EM ◇ C	EM ◇1	NT ◇	XC ◇1 F	EM ◇1	EM ◇1	EM ◇ C	EM ◇1	XC ◇1 G
St Pancras International ⊖52 d									09 00			09 30			10 00			10 30			11 00	
Luton Airport Parkway 7 52 ✈ d									09 29						10 29						11 29	
Luton 10 52 d												10 03						11 03			11 33	
Bedford 7 52 d									09 55			10 23			10 54			11 28			11 55	
Wellingborough d									10 08			10 36			11 08			11 39			12 08	
Kettering 5 a									10 15			10 42			11 16			11 46			12 14	
d				09 55					10 16			10 42	10 55		11 17			11 46	11 55		12 15	
Corby d				10a05									11a05						12a05			
Oakham 47 a																						
Melton Mowbray 47 a																						
Market Harborough d									10 26			10 53			11 28			11 56			12 25	
Leicester a									10 40			11 08			11 44			12 11			12 40	
d							10 20		10 41			11 10			11 46			12 13			12 42	
Syston d																						
Sileby d																						
Barrow Upon Soar d																						
Loughborough d							10 30		10 51			11 20			11 57			12 23			12 52	
East Midlands Parkway ✈ d							10 37		10 59			11 27			12 05			12 30			12 59	
Beeston a									11 04												13 05	
Nottingham 8 a									11 12						12 17						13 13	
d	09 19		09 47		10 13			10 48		11 16				11 44		12 19				12 40		
Newark Castle 27 a																						
Lincoln 27 a																						
Langley Mill d	09 37				10 31					11 36						12 37				12 56		
Alfreton d	09 45		10 05		10 39			11 09		11 44				12 08		12 45				13 04		
Long Eaton a							10 41					11 31						12 34				
Derby 6 a							10 53					11 43						12 46				
d		09 44				10 44	10 54				11 44	11 50					12 44	12 49				13 11
Chesterfield d	09 55	10 03	10 18		10 50	11 03	11 14	11 19		11 55	12 03	12 09		12 18		12 56	13 03	13 12		13 17		13 30
Sheffield 7 a	10 15	10 18	10 37		11 10	11 17	11 28	11 35		12 14	12 18	12 23		12 35		13 15	13 18	13 28		13 33		13 43
Manchester Piccadilly 78 a			11 37					12 37						13 37						14 37		
Doncaster 7 29 a							11 52															14 14
Wakefield Kirkgate 4 31,34 a	10 52				11 51					12 58						13 52						
Wakefield Westgate 7 31 a		10 45				11 45					12 45						13 44					
Leeds 10 31,34 a	11 12	10 59			12 11	11 59				13 22	13 00					14 18	14 00					
York 8 29 a		11 29				12 30	12 15				13 27						14 27					14 40

A To Carlisle
B From Birmingham New Street to Edinburgh
C To Liverpool Lime Street
D From Birmingham New Street to Glasgow Central
E From Bristol Temple Meads to Edinburgh
F From Bristol Temple Meads to Glasgow Central
G From Birmingham New Street to Newcastle

For connections from Gatwick Airport refer to Table T052

Table T053-F

Sundays

14 October to 2 December

London - East Midlands - Sheffield

	NT	XC	EM	EM	EM	EM	EM	XC	NT	XC	EM	EM	EM	EM	XC	NT	XC	EM	EM	EM	EM	XC
	◇	◇■	◇■	◇■	◇	◇■	◇■	◇■	◇	◇■	◇■	◇	◇■	◇■	◇■	◇	◇■	◇■	◇	◇■	◇■	◇■
		A			B			C		D		E			F		G		H			I
		🛒	☕	☕		☕	☕	🛒		🛒	☕		☕	☕	🛒		🛒	☕		☕	☕	🛒
St Pancras International ⊖52 d			11 30			12 10	12 30				12 50		13 10	13 30				13 55		14 10	14 30	
Luton Airport Parkway ■ 52 ✈ d			11 59			12 32	12 52						13 32	13 52						14 32		
Luton ■ 52 d			12 03			12 35	12 54						13 35	13 54							14 53	
Bedford ■ 52 d			12 20			12 49	13 09						13 49	14 09						14 46	15 07	
Wellingborough d			12 32			13 02	13 21						14 02	14 21						14 59	15 19	
Kettering ■ a			12 39			13 08	13 32				13 38		14 08	14 31						15 05	15 31	
d			12 40	12 50		13 09	13 34				13 39		14 09	14 32						15 06	15 33	
Corby d				13a00			13a44							14a42							15a43	
Oakham 47 a																						
Melton Mowbray 47 a																						
Market Harborough d			12 50			13 19					13 50		14 19					14 51		15 16		
Leicester a			13 05			13 34					14 07		14 34					15 07		15 31		
d			13 06			13 36					14 08		14 36					15 09		15 33		
Syston d																						
Sileby d																						
Barrow Upon Soar d																						
Loughborough d			13 16			13 46					14 19		14 46					15 20		15 43		
East Midlands Parkway ✈ d			13 24			13 53					14 28		14 53					15 28		15 50		
Beeston a						13 59							14 59							15 58		
Nottingham ■ 🚌 a						14 07							15 07							16 05		
d	13 19				13 42				14 19			14 47				15 19			15 47			
Newark Castle 27 a																						
Lincoln 27 a																						
Langley Mill d	13 37				13 58				14 37			15 03				15 37						
Alfreton d	13 45				14 06				14 45			15 11				15 45			16 08			
Long Eaton a			13 27								14 31							15 32				
Derby ■ a			13 44								14 45							15 44				
d		13 44	13 51					14 11		14 44	14 48				15 11		15 44	15 48				16 11
Chesterfield d	13 56	14 03	14 11		14 16			14 30	14 56	15 03	15 09	15 21				15 56	16 03	16 09	16 18			
Sheffield ■ 🚌 a	14 15	14 17	14 26		14 34			14 45	15 15	15 17	15 29	15 39			15 45	16 15	16 18	16 27	16 34			16 42
Manchester Piccadilly 78 a					15 37							16 37							17 38			
Doncaster ■ 29 a								15 18							16 14							17 15
Wakefield Kirkgate ■ 31,34 a	14 52								15 52							16 53						
Wakefield Westgate ■ 31 a		14 45								15 45							16 45					
Leeds ■ 31,34 a	15 17	15 00							16 15	16 00						17 17	16 59					
York ■ 29 a		15 27						15 40		16 27					16 40		17 27					17 40

	NT	XC	EM	EM	EM	XC	EM	EM	NT	XC	EM	EM	EM	XC	EM	EM	EM	NT	EM	XC	EM
	◇	◇■	◇■	◇	◇■	◇■	◇■	◇■	◇	◇■	◇■	◇	◇■	◇■	◇■	◇■	◇■	◇	◇■	◇■	◇
		D		B		I				J		B		K						J	L
		🛒	☕		☕	🛒	☕	☕		🛒	☕		☕	🛒	☕	☕	☕		☕	🛒	
St Pancras International ⊖52 d			14 55		15 10		15 40				15 55		16 10		16 35	16 40			17 05		
Luton Airport Parkway ■ 52 ✈ d					15 33								16 32								
Luton ■ 52 d							16 03									17 03					
Bedford ■ 52 d					15 48		16 17						16 46			17 17					
Wellingborough d					16 02		16 30						16 59			17 30					
Kettering ■ a					16 10		16 36						17 05			17 36					
d					16 11		16 37	16 50					17 06			17 37	17 50				
Corby d								17a00									18a00				
Oakham 47 a																					
Melton Mowbray 47 a																					
Market Harborough d			15 51		16 22						16 51		17 16			17 47					
Leicester a			16 06		16 38		17 01				17 07		17 31		17 43	18 02			18 10		
d			16 08		16 38		17 02				17 09		17 33		17 44	18 04			18 11		
Syston d																					
Sileby d																					
Barrow Upon Soar d																					
Loughborough d			16 19		16 51		17 12						17 43			18 14					
East Midlands Parkway ✈ d			16 27		16 59		17 20				17 25		17 50		18 00	18 21			18 26		
Beeston a					17 05								17 58								
Nottingham ■ 🚌 a					17 14								18 05						18 36		
d	16 19			16 42					17 19			17 39						18 19			18 40
Newark Castle 27 a																					
Lincoln 27 a																					
Langley Mill d	16 37			17 03					17 37			17 57						18 37			18 56
Alfreton d	16 45			17 11					17 45			18 05						18 45			19 04
Long Eaton a			16 32								17 29					18 26					
Derby ■ a			16 47				17 37				17 44				18 12	18 36					
d		16 44	16 49			17 12				17 44	17 49			18 12	18 14					18 43	
Chesterfield d	16 56	17 03	17 14	17 22					17 56	18 02	18 10	18 16			18 37			18 56		19 05	19 15
Sheffield ■ 🚌 a	17 15	17 18	17 28	17 39		17 41			18 15	18 19	18 27	18 33		18 42	18 51			19 14		19 20	19 31
Manchester Piccadilly 78 a				18 37								19 37									20 38
Doncaster ■ 29 a						18 14								19 17							
Wakefield Kirkgate ■ 31,34 a	17 52								18 52									19 52			
Wakefield Westgate ■ 31 a		17 44	18 00			18 32				18 45										19 49	
Leeds ■ 31,34 a	18 17	18 00	18 15			18 47			19 15	19 01								20 15		20 04	
York ■ 29 a		18 27				19 21				19 30				19 46						20 30	

A From Plymouth to Aberdeen
B From Norwich to Liverpool Lime Street
C From Birmingham New Street to Newcastle
D From Plymouth to Glasgow Central
E To Liverpool Lime Street
F From Guildford to Newcastle
G From Penzance to Edinburgh
H From Peterborough to Liverpool Lime Street
I From Reading to Newcastle
J From Plymouth to Edinburgh
K From Reading to Edinburgh
L From Norwich

For connections from Gatwick Airport refer to Table T052

Table T053-F

Sundays

14 October to 2 December

London - East Midlands - Sheffield

	EM	XC	EM	EM	EM	NT	EM	XC	EM	EM	XC	EM	EM	EM	NT	EM	EM	XC	EM	EM	XC	EM
	◇■	◇■	◇■	◇■	◇■	◇	◇■	◇■	◇	◇■	◇■	◇■	◇■	◇■	◇	◇■	◇■	◇■	◇■	◇■	◇■	◇■
		A						B	C		D							E			F	
	☕	🛒	☕	☕	☕		☕	🛒		☕		☕	☕	☕		☕	☕		☕	☕		☕
St Pancras International ⊖52 d	17 10		17 35	17 40			18 05			18 10		18 35	18 40			19 05	19 10		19 35	19 40		
Luton Airport Parkway ■ 52 ✈ d	17 32									18 32							19 32					
Luton ■ 52 d				18 03									19 03							20 03		
Bedford ■ 52 d	17 46			18 17						18 46			19 17				19 46			20 17		
Wellingborough d	17 58			18 30						18 58			19 30				19 58			20 30		
Kettering ■ a	18 05			18 36						19 05			19 36				20 05			20 36		
d	18 06			18 37	18 55					19 06			19 37	19 50			20 05			20 37		20 50
Corby d					19a05									20a00								21a00
Oakham 47 a																						
Melton Mowbray 47 a																						
Market Harborough d	18 15			18 47						19 16			19 47				20 15			20 47		
Leicester a	18 31		18 41	19 02			19 09			19 30		19 43	20 02			20 18	20 31		20 41	21 02		
d	18 33		18 42	19 04			19 10			19 32		19 45	20 04			20 22	20 33		20 42	21 04		
Syston d																						
Sileby d																						
Barrow Upon Soar d																						
Loughborough d	18 43			19 14						19 42			20 14				20 43			21 14		
East Midlands Parkway ✈ d	18 50		18 56	19 21			19 26			19 49		20 01	20 21			20 39	20 50		20 56	21 21		
Beeston a	18 58									19 58							20 58					
Nottingham ■ 🚌 a	19 05						19 37			20 05						20 51	21 05					
d						19 19			19 43						20 19							
Newark Castle 27 a																						
Lincoln 27 a																						
Langley Mill d						19 37									20 37							
Alfreton d						19 45			20 04						20 45							
Long Eaton a				19 25									20 25							21 25		
Derby ■ a			19 08	19 37								20 11	20 37						21 07	21 37		
d		19 06	19 16					19 42			20 09	20 14						20 43	21 09		21 44	
Chesterfield d			19 34			19 56		20 03	20 14			20 37			20 56			21 04	21 29		22 03	
Sheffield ■ 🚌 a		19 38	19 50			20 15		20 18	20 31		20 38	20 51			21 15			21 18	21 43		22 18	
Manchester Piccadilly 78 a									21 37													
Doncaster ■ 29 a		20 14									21 20											
Wakefield Kirkgate ■ 31,34 a						20 52									21 52							
Wakefield Westgate ■ 31 a								20 45				21 32						21 48			22 47	
Leeds ■ 31,34 a						21 14		21 02				21 49			22 14			22 02			23 02	
York ■ 29 a		20 40						21 31			21 45											

	NT	EM	EM	EM	XC	EM	EM	NT	EM	EM	EM	EM
	◇	◇■	◇■	◇■	◇■	◇■	◇■	◇	◇■	◇■	◇■	◇■
					E							
		☕	☕	☕		☕	☕		☕	☕	☕	☕
St Pancras International ⊖52 d		20 00	20 10	20 35		20 40			21 10	21 30	22 30	23 00
Luton Airport Parkway ■ 52 ✈ d			20 32						21 32		22 52	23 28
Luton ■ 52 d						21 04				21 54		
Bedford ■ 52 d			20 47			21 20			21 46	22 07	23 11	23 53
Wellingborough d			20 58			21 33			21 59	22 20	23 34	00 15
Kettering ■ a			21 05			21 40			22 05	22 27	23 44	00 25
d			21 06			21 41	21 55		22 06	22 28	23 45	00 26
Corby d							22a05					
Oakham 47 a												
Melton Mowbray 47 a												
Market Harborough d			21 16			21 52			22 16	22 38	23 55	00 36
Leicester a		21 08	21 31	21 41		22 09			22 31	22 52	00 10	00 50
d		21 10	21 33	21 42		22 10			22 33	22 54	00 11	00 52
Syston d												
Sileby d												
Barrow Upon Soar d												
Loughborough d		21 21	21 43	21 52					22 47	23 04	00 21	01 02
East Midlands Parkway ✈ d		21 29	21 50	22 00		22 26			22 58	23 16	00 29	01 09
Beeston a			22 04						23 04		00 34	
Nottingham ■ 🚌 a		21 45	22 11						23 11		00 41	
d	21 33							22 33				
Newark Castle 27 a												
Lincoln 27 a												
Langley Mill d	21 57							22 57				
Alfreton d	22 05							23 05				
Long Eaton a										23 23		
Derby ■ a				22 12		22 40				23 35		01 21
d					22 42	22 48				23 36		
Chesterfield d	22 16				23 03	23 09		23 16		23 55		
Sheffield ■ 🚌 a	22 34				23 18	23 23		23 35		00 08		
Manchester Piccadilly 78 a												
Doncaster ■ 29 a												
Wakefield Kirkgate ■ 31,34 a	23 31											
Wakefield Westgate ■ 31 a						23 52						
Leeds ■ 31,34 a	00 07				00 09	00 08						
York ■ 29 a												

A From Reading to Newcastle. 🛒 to Sheffield
B From Plymouth. 🛒 to Leeds
C From Norwich
D From Reading to Newcastle
E From Plymouth
F From Penzance

For connections from Gatwick Airport refer to Table T052

Table T053-R

Mondays to Fridays

21 May to 20 July

Sheffield - East Midlands - London

Miles	Miles	Miles	Miles		EM MO	EM MX	EM	EM	EM	EM	EM	EM	EM	NT	EM	EM	EM	XC	EM	EM	EM	EM
					◇ A	◇ A	◇■ ✠	◇■ ✠	◇■ ✠	🚌	◇■ ✠	🚌		◇	◇■ ✠	◇■ ☒	🚌	◇■ B	◇■ ✠	◇■ ✠	◇■ C ☒	🚌
—	—	—	—	York 29 d																		
—	—	—	—	Leeds 31,34 d																		
—	—	—	—	Wakefield Westgate 31 d																		
—	—	—	—	Wakefield Kirkgate 31,34 d																		
—	—	—	—	Doncaster 29 d																		
—	—	—	—	Manchester Piccadilly 78 d																		
0	0	—	—	**Sheffield** d										05 15		05 31		05 59			06 00	
12¼	12¼	—	—	Chesterfield d		00 02								05 30		05 44		06 26			06 13	
—	36½	—	—	**Derby** a												06 03		06 44			06 33	
—	—	—	—	d				05 02	05 19							06 04					06 34	
—	44	—	—	Long Eaton d					05 28												06 44	
22½	—	—	—	Alfreton d										05 45								
34½	—	—	—	Langley Mill d	00 02									05 53								
—	—	—	—	Lincoln 27 d																		
—	—	—	—	Newark Castle 27 d																		
40¾	—	—	—	**Nottingham** a	00 23	00 45								06 11								
—	—	—	—	d							05 32		05 38							06 31		
44	—	—	—	Beeston d																06 37		
—	—	—	—	East Midlands Parkway a				05 12			05 42					06 16				06 42		
—	—	—	—	d				05 13			05 43					06 17				06 43		
55½	53¼	—	—	Loughborough d				05 20			05 51		05 58			06 26					06 54	
59½	57¼	—	—	Barrow Upon Soar d									06 02									
61½	59¼	—	0	Sileby d									06 07									
64¾	62	—	—	Syston d									06 12									
68	65¾	0	—	**Leicester** a				05 29	05 42		06 03		06 20			06 37				06 56	07 05	
—	—	—	—	d			04 45	05 31	05 44		06 04					06 39				06 59	07 07	
84¾	82	—	—	Market Harborough d				05 44	05 57		06 19					06 54				07 12		
—	—	15¾	12¾	Melton Mowbray 47 d											06 03							
—	—	26¾	—	Oakham 47 d											06 15							
—	—	41	—	Corby d											06 38				07 08			
95¾	93	48¾	—	Kettering a			05 04	05 53	06 06		06 29				06 47	07 04			07 17	07 21	07 28	
—	—	—	—	d			05 05	05 55	06 08		06 31				06 48	07 05				07 23	07 29	
102¾	100	—	—	Wellingborough d			05 17	06 03	06 16	06 26	06 39	06 50			06 57	07 14	07 24			07 31	07 38	07 48
117½	115¾	—	—	Bedford 52 a			05 37			07 11		07 35					08 14					08 43
137	134¾	—	—	Luton 52 a				06 25														
138	135¾	—	—	Luton Airport Parkway 52 a			05 53				07 04					07 44					08 02	
167¼	165	—	—	**St Pancras International** 52 a			06 24	06 54	07 08		07 36				07 55	08 09				08 24	08 29	

	EM	NT	EM	EM	EM	EM	EM	EM	XC	EM	EM	EM	NT	EM	XC	EM	EM	EM	EM	EM	XC	NT
	◇■ ✠	◇		◇■ ☒	🚌	◇■ ☒	◇■ ✠	◇■ C ☒	◇■ D ✠	◇■ ✠	🚌		◇	◇■ ✠	◇■ E ✠	◇■ F ✠	◇■ G ☒	◇■ ✠	◇■ H ✠	◇■ I ✠	◇■ J ✠	◇
York 29 d																					06 45	
Leeds 31,34 d				05 19					06 11						06 16	06 33					07 10	07 03
Wakefield Westgate 31 d				05 32					06 23						06 28	06 47					07 23	
Wakefield Kirkgate 31,34 d																						07 22
Doncaster 29 d				05 57											06 46							
Manchester Piccadilly 78 d																						
Sheffield d		06 03		06 25				06 49	06 53				07 02		07 18	07 24	07 29		07 46		07 53	08 03
Chesterfield d		06 19		06 40				07 01	07 06				07 17		07 30	07 37	07 42		07 59		08 06	08 19
Derby a				07 03				07 21	07 26						07 48		08 00		08 17		08 26	
d				07 05				07 23		07 30							08 02		08 19			
Long Eaton d										07 41									08 29			
Alfreton d		06 29											07 28			07 48						08 33
Langley Mill d		06 36											07 35			07 57						08 41
Lincoln 27 d																		07 05				
Newark Castle 27 d																		07 30				
Nottingham a		07 00											07 53			08 24		07 56				08 59
d	06 52					07 11						07 30		07 56		08 32		08 05				
Beeston d	06 58					07 18						07 36						08 11		←		
East Midlands Parkway a	07 03					07 24		07 33				07 43		08 05		08 42			08 33	08 42		
d	07 04					07 26		07 34				07 44		08 05		08 43			08 34	08 43		
Loughborough d			06 59	07 22				07 42		07 51		07 52				→		08 21	08 42			
Barrow Upon Soar d			07 04									07 57										
Sileby d			07 08									08 01										
Syston d			07 14									08 06										
Leicester a	07 17		07 22	07 33		07 41		07 51		08 02		08 18		08 18			08 24	08 31	08 54	08 58		
d	07 19			07 34		07 43		07 55		08 03				08 21			08 26	08 32	08 55	08 59		
Market Harborough d	07 33					07 58				08 18								08 46		09 13		
Melton Mowbray 47 d																						
Oakham 47 d																						
Corby d							08 02															
Kettering a	07 42			07 55		08 08	08 11	08 16		08 28								08 55				
d	07 43			07 56		08 09		08 17		08 29								08 56				
Wellingborough d	07 51			08 04	08 14			08 25		08 38	08 48							09 03				
Bedford 52 a					09 09						09 38											
Luton 52 a																						
Luton Airport Parkway 52 a																		09 30				
St Pancras International 52 a	08 41			08 55		09 08		09 12		09 27				09 38			09 41	09 55	10 03	10 11		

A From Liverpool Lime Street
B To Reading
C The Sheffield Continental
D To Plymouth
E To Southampton Central
F To St Pancras International
G The Master Cutler
H The South Yorkshireman
I From Leeds
J To Plymouth. ✠ from Leeds

For connections to Gatwick Airport refer to Table T052

Table T053-R

Mondays to Fridays

21 May to 20 July

Sheffield - East Midlands - London

	XC	EM	EM	EM	EM	EM	XC	EM	EM	EM	NT	XC	EM	EM	EM	EM	XC	EM	EM	EM	NT	XC
	■ A ✠	◇■ ✠	B	◇■ ✠	◇■ ✠	◇ C	◇■ D ✠	◇■ ✠		◇■ ✠	◇	◇■ E ✠	◇■ ✠	◇■ ✠	◇■ ✠	◇ C	◇■ F ✠	◇■ ✠		◇■ ✠	◇	◇■ G ✠
York 29 d	07 26						07 43					08 27					08 44					09 35
Leeds 31,34 d							08 11				08 04						09 11				09 04	
Wakefield Westgate 31 d							08 23										09 23					
Wakefield Kirkgate 31,34 d											08 22										09 22	
Doncaster 29 d	07 53											08 53										09 59
Manchester Piccadilly 78 d						07 42										08 43						
Sheffield d	08 18	08 26				08 38	08 54	08 59			09 06	09 24	09 28			09 37	09 55	10 00			10 05	10 24
Chesterfield d	08 30	08 38				08 54	09 07	09 12			09 22		09 41			09 51	10 08	10 13			10 22	
Derby a	08 51	08 57					09 24	09 31				09 51	10 00				10 28	10 33				10 51
d		08 57						09 31					10 02					10 33				
Long Eaton d								09 40										10 42				
Alfreton d						09 05					09 33					10 01					10 32	
Langley Mill d											09 40										10 40	
Lincoln 27 d			07 36						08 36										09 37			
Newark Castle 27 d			08 06						09 08										10 07			
Nottingham a			08 33			09 27			09 30		09 59					10 26			10 30		10 58	
d			08 35		09 12				09 35	09 45					10 12				10 35	10 45		
Beeston d			08 41		09 18				09 41						10 18				10 41			
East Midlands Parkway a			08 49					09 44	09 50	09 55								10 46	10 49	10 55		
d			08 50					09 45	09 51	09 56								10 47	10 50	10 56		
Loughborough d			08 58		09 26			09 52	09 59						10 27			10 54	10 58			
Barrow Upon Soar d			09 03						10 04										11 03			
Sileby d			09 07						10 08										11 07			
Syston d			09 13						10 13										11 12			
Leicester a		09 18	09 20		09 36			10 02	10 20	10 13			10 23		10 37			11 04	11 19	11 13		
d		09 18			09 38			10 03		10 13			10 23		10 38			11 05		11 13		
Market Harborough d					09 51					10 26					10 51					11 26		
Melton Mowbray 47 d																						
Oakham 47 d																						
Corby d				09 32										10 41								
Kettering a				09 41	10 00									10 50	11 00							
d				09 42	10 01									10 51	11 01							
Wellingborough d				09 51	10 08									10 59	11 08							
Bedford 52 a				10 12	10 22									11 12	11 22							
Luton 52 a				10 26										11 27								
Luton Airport Parkway 52 a					10 38										11 38							
St Pancras International 52 a		10 25		10 51	11 05			11 08		11 24			11 35	11 52	12 08			12 09		12 24		

	EM	EM	EM	EM	XC	EM	EM	EM	NT	XC	EM	EM	EM	EM	XC	EM	EM	EM	NT	XC	EM
	◇■ ✠	◇■ ✠	◇■ ✠	◇ C	◇■ H ✠	◇■ ✠		◇■ ✠	◇	◇■ E ✠	◇■ ✠	◇■ ✠	◇■ ✠	◇ C	◇■ I ✠	◇■ ✠		◇■ ✠	◇	◇■ A ✠	◇■ ✠
York 29 d					09 44					10 35					10 44					11 35	
Leeds 31,34 d					10 11				10 04						11 11				11 04		
Wakefield Westgate 31 d					10 23										11 23						
Wakefield Kirkgate 31,34 d									10 22										11 22		
Doncaster 29 d										10 59										11 59	
Manchester Piccadilly 78 d				09 42										10 42							
Sheffield d	10 29			10 37	10 55	11 00			11 05	11 24	11 29			11 38	11 55	12 00			12 05	12 24	12 29
Chesterfield d	10 41			10 54	11 07	11 12			11 22		11 41			11 54	12 08	12 13			12 22		12 41
Derby a	11 00				11 24	11 31				11 51	12 01				12 28	12 33				12 51	13 00
d	11 02					11 31					12 02					12 33					13 02
Long Eaton d						11 40										12 42					
Alfreton d				11 05					11 32					12 05					12 32		
Langley Mill d									11 40										12 40		
Lincoln 27 d							10 36										11 40				
Newark Castle 27 d							11 07										12 07				
Nottingham a				11 26			11 30		11 58					12 29			12 30		12 58		
d			11 12				11 35	11 45					12 12				12 35	12 45			
Beeston d			11 18				11 41						12 18				12 41				
East Midlands Parkway a						11 44	11 49	11 55								12 46	12 49	12 55			
d						11 45	11 50	11 56								12 47	12 50	12 56			
Loughborough d			11 27			11 52	11 58						12 27			12 54	12 58				
Barrow Upon Soar d							12 03										13 03				
Sileby d							12 07										13 07				
Syston d							12 12										13 12				
Leicester a	11 25		11 37			12 02	12 19	12 13			12 25		12 37			13 04	13 23	13 13			13 25
d	11 25		11 38			12 03		12 13			12 26		12 38			13 05		13 13			13 26
Market Harborough d			11 51					12 26					12 51					13 26			
Melton Mowbray 47 d																					
Oakham 47 d																					
Corby d		11 41										12 41									
Kettering a		11 50	12 00									12 50	13 00								
d		11 51	12 01									12 51	13 01								
Wellingborough d		12 00	12 08									13 00	13 08								
Bedford 52 a		12 12	12 22									13 12	13 22								
Luton 52 a		12 27										13 27									
Luton Airport Parkway 52 a			12 38										13 38								
St Pancras International 52 a	12 36	12 51	13 06			13 08		13 25			13 36	13 51	14 07			14 12		14 25			14 38

A From Newcastle to Reading
B From Sleaford
C From Liverpool Lime Street to Norwich
D From Newcastle to Plymouth
E From Newcastle to Southampton Central
F From Edinburgh to Plymouth
G From Edinburgh to Reading
H From Glasgow Central to Plymouth
I From Dundee to Plymouth

For connections to Gatwick Airport refer to Table T052

Sheffield - East Midlands - London

		EM	EM	EM	XC	EM	EM	EM	NT	XC	EM	EM	EM	EM	XC	EM	EM	EM	NT	XC	EM	EM	EM
		◇■ 🛒	◇■ 🛒	◇ A	◇■ B 🛒	◇■ 🛒		◇■ 🛒	◇	◇■ C 🛒	◇■ 🛒	◇■ 🛒	◇■ 🛒	◇ A	◇■ D 🛒	◇■ 🛒		◇■ 🛒	◇	◇■ E 🛒	◇■ 🛒	◇■ 🛒	◇■ 🛒
York	29 d				11 44					12 35					12 44					13 35			
Leeds	31,34 d				12 11				12 04						13 11				13 04				
Wakefield Westgate	31 d				12 23										13 23								
Wakefield Kirkgate	31,34 d								12 22										13 23				
Doncaster	29 d									12 59										13 59			
Manchester Piccadilly	78 d			11 42										12 42									
Sheffield	d			12 38	12 55	13 00			13 05	13 24	13 29			13 37	13 55	13 59			14 05	14 24	14 29		
Chesterfield	d			12 52	13 07	13 12			13 22		13 41			13 52	14 07	14 13			14 22		14 41		
Derby	a				13 25	13 31				13 51	14 00				14 24	14 32				14 51	15 00		
	d					13 32					14 02					14 33					15 02		
Long Eaton	d					13 40										14 43							
Alfreton	d			13 03					13 32					14 03					14 32				
Langley Mill	d								13 40										14 40				
Lincoln	27 d						12 34										13 37						
Newark Castle	27 d						13 05										14 07						
Nottingham	a			13 27			13 30		13 58					14 27			14 30		14 58				
	d		13 12				13 35	13 45					14 12				14 35	14 45					15 12
Beeston	d		13 18				13 41						14 18				14 41						15 18
East Midlands Parkway	a					13 45	13 49	13 55								14 47	14 49	14 55					
	d					13 46	13 50	13 56								14 48	14 50	14 56					
Loughborough	d		13 27			13 52	13 58						14 27			14 55	14 58						15 27
Barrow Upon Soar	d						14 03										15 03						
Sileby	d						14 07										15 07						
Syston	d						14 12										15 12						
Leicester	a		13 37			14 02	14 19	14 13			14 25		14 37			15 07	15 19	15 13			15 25		15 37
	d		13 38			14 03		14 13			14 26		14 38			15 08		15 13			15 26		15 38
Market Harborough	d		13 51					14 26					14 51					15 26					15 51
Melton Mowbray	47 d																						
Oakham	47 d																						
Corby	d	13 41										14 41										15 39	
Kettering	a	13 50	14 00									14 50	15 00									15 48	16 00
	d	13 51	14 01									14 51	15 01									15 49	16 01
Wellingborough	d	14 00	14 09									15 00	15 08									15 58	16 08
Bedford	52 a	14 12	14 22									15 12	15 22									16 10	16 21
Luton	52 a	14 27										15 27										16 26	
Luton Airport Parkway	52 ✈ a		14 38										15 38										16 37
St Pancras International	⊖52 a	14 51	15 05			15 08		15 25			15 39	15 51	16 11			16 25		16 27			16 41	16 55	17 12

		EM	XC	EM	EM	EM	NT	XC	EM	EM	EM	EM	XC	EM	EM	EM	EM	NT	XC	EM	EM	EM
		◇ A	◇■ F 🛒	◇■ 🛒		◇■ 🛒	◇	◇■ G 🛒	◇■ 🛒	◇■ 🛒	◇■ 🛒	◇ A	◇■ D 🛒	◇■ 🛒	◇■ 🛒		◇■ 🛒	◇	◇■ E 🛒	◇■ 🛒	◇■ 🛒	◇■ 🛒
York	29 d		13 44					14 35					14 44						15 35			
Leeds	31,34 d		14 11				14 04						15 11					15 04				
Wakefield Westgate	31 d		14 23										15 23									
Wakefield Kirkgate	31,34 d						14 22											15 22				
Doncaster	29 d							14 59											15 59			
Manchester Piccadilly	78 d	13 42										14 42										
Sheffield	d	14 38	14 55	14 59			15 05	15 24	15 29			15 37	15 55		16 00			16 05	16 24	16 29		
Chesterfield	d	14 52	15 07	15 12			15 22		15 41			15 53	16 07		16 12			16 22		16 41		
Derby	a		15 24	15 31				15 51	16 00				16 24		16 31				16 51	17 00		
	d			15 31					16 02					16 27	16 32					17 01		
Long Eaton	d			15 41											16 40							
Alfreton	d	15 03					15 32					16 05						16 32				
Langley Mill	d						15 40											16 40				
Lincoln	27 d				14 36											15 36						
Newark Castle	27 d				15 06											16 08						
Nottingham	a	15 28			15 30		15 58					16 27				16 30		16 58				
	d				15 35	15 45					16 12					16 33	16 45					17 12
Beeston	d				15 41						16 18					16 39						17 18
East Midlands Parkway	a			15 44	15 50	15 55								16 39	16 45	16 49	16 55					
	d			15 45	15 51	15 56								16 39	16 46	16 49	16 56					
Loughborough	d			15 53	15 59						16 27				16 52	16 58						17 26
Barrow Upon Soar	d				16 04											17 02						
Sileby	d				16 08											17 06						
Syston	d				16 13											17 11						
Leicester	a			16 02	16 20	16 13			16 25		16 37				17 02	17 19	17 13			17 22		17 36
	d			16 03		16 13			16 26		16 38				17 03		17 13			17 23		17 37
Market Harborough	d					16 26					16 51						17 26					17 50
Melton Mowbray	47 d													17 09								
Oakham	47 d													17 23								
Corby	d									16 39				17 51							17 39	
Kettering	a									16 48	17 00			18 00	17 23						17 48	17 59
	d									16 49	17 01				17 24						17 49	18 00
Wellingborough	d									16 57	17 08										17 57	18 08
Bedford	52 a									17 10	17 22										18 10	18 21
Luton	52 a									17 24							18 03				18 26	
Luton Airport Parkway	52 ✈ a										17 37											18 40
St Pancras International	⊖52 a			17 12		17 24			17 39	17 55	18 06				18 14		18 40			18 40	18 55	19 06

A From Liverpool Lime Street to Norwich
B From Glasgow Central to Plymouth
C From Newcastle to Southampton Central
D From Glasgow Central to Penzance
E From Newcastle to Reading
F From Aberdeen to Penzance
G From Newcastle to Guildford

For connections to Gatwick Airport refer to Table T052

Sheffield - East Midlands - London

		EM	XC	EM	EM	EM	NT	XC	EM	EM	EM	EM	XC	EM	EM	EM	NT	XC	EM	EM	EM	EM	XC
		◇ A	◇■ B 🛒	◇■ 🛒		◇■ 🛒	◇	◇■ C 🛒	◇■ 🛒	◇■ 🛒	◇■ 🛒	◇ A	◇■ D 🛒	◇■ 🛒		◇■ 🛒	◇	◇■ C 🛒	◇■ 🛒	◇■ 🛒	◇■ 🛒	◇ E	◇■ B 🛒
York	29 d		15 44					16 05					16 44					17 35					17 45
Leeds	31,34 d		16 11				16 04	16 40					17 10				17 03						18 11
Wakefield Westgate	31 d		16 23					16 52					17 22										18 23
Wakefield Kirkgate	31,34 d						16 22										17 22						
Doncaster	29 d																	17 58					
Manchester Piccadilly	78 d	15 42										16 42										17 42	
Sheffield	d	16 37	16 55	17 00			17 05	17 24	17 29			17 45	17 55	18 00			18 03	18 24	18 29			18 53	18 58
Chesterfield	d	16 53	17 07	17 12			17 22		17 41			18 01	18 07	18 12			18 19		18 41			19 08	19 11
Derby	a		17 24	17 32				17 51	18 04				18 24	18 31				18 51	19 00				19 29
	d			17 32					18 04					18 32					19 04				
Long Eaton	d			17 42										18 41									
Alfreton	d	17 04					17 32					18 11					18 30					19 19	
Langley Mill	d						17 40										18 37						
Lincoln	27 d				16 34										17 26								
Newark Castle	27 d				17 05										17 56								
Nottingham	a	17 27			17 30		17 58					18 31			18 30		18 55					19 39	
	d				17 34	17 45					18 12				18 36	18 45					19 12		
Beeston	d				17 40						18 18				18 42						19 18		
East Midlands Parkway	a			17 45	17 50	17 56								18 45	18 50	18 55							
	d			17 46	17 50	17 57								18 46	18 52	18 56							
Loughborough	d			17 54	17 58						18 26			18 53	19 00						19 27		
Barrow Upon Soar	d				18 03										19 05								
Sileby	d				18 07										19 09								
Syston	d				18 12										19 14								
Leicester	a			18 04	18 19	18 13			18 25		18 36			19 03	19 21	19 13			19 25		19 37		
	d			18 04		18 14			18 26		18 37			19 03		19 13			19 26		19 38		
Market Harborough	d					18 27					18 50					19 26					19 51		
Melton Mowbray	47 d																						
Oakham	47 d																						
Corby	d									18 37										19 39			
Kettering	a					18 38				18 46	18 59									19 48	20 00		
	d					18 39				18 47	19 00									19 49	20 01		
Wellingborough	d									18 56	19 08									19 58	20 08		
Bedford	52 a									19 11	19 23									20 10	20 22		
Luton	52 a									19 27										20 26			
Luton Airport Parkway	52 ✈ a										19 41										20 37		
St Pancras International	⊖52 a			19 11		19 37			19 40	19 57	20 07			20 11		20 25			20 40	20 51	21 06		

		EM	EM	EM	NT	XC	EM	EM	EM	EM	EM	XC	NT	EM	XC	EM	EM	XC	EM	EM	EM	NT	XC
		◇■ 🛒		◇■ 🛒	◇	◇■ F 🛒	◇■ 🛒	◇■ 🛒	◇■ 🛒	◇ A		◇■ G 🛒	◇	◇■ 🛒	◇■ H 🛒	◇ E	◇■ 🛒	◇■ I 🛒	◇■ 🛒	◇■ 🛒		◇	◇■ H 🛒
York	29 d					18 36						18 45			19 36			19 45					20 36
Leeds	31,34 d				18 03							19 11	19 03					20 11				20 03	
Wakefield Westgate	31 d											19 23						20 23					
Wakefield Kirkgate	31,34 d				18 21								19 21									20 21	
Doncaster	29 d					18 59									19 59								21 01
Manchester Piccadilly	78 d									18 42						19 42							
Sheffield	d	19 02			19 05	19 24	19 29			19 37		19 58	20 02		20 24	20 41	20 50	20 56				21 02	21 29
Chesterfield	d	19 15			19 21		19 42			19 52		20 10	20 18			20 56	21 02	21 08				21 18	21 41
Derby	a	19 35				19 51	20 02					20 27			20 51		21 21	21 26				21 39	21 58
	d	19 35					20 02										21 22					21 40	
Long Eaton	d	19 45																					
Alfreton	d				19 31					20 03			20 28			21 08							
Langley Mill	d				19 39								20 36										
Lincoln	27 d		18 35																				
Newark Castle	27 d		19 03																				
Nottingham	a		19 30		19 57					20 27			20 55			21 33						22 06	
	d		19 32	19 45					20 12		20 35			20 55						21 29	22 01		
Beeston	d		19 38						20 18		20 42			21 01							22 07		
East Midlands Parkway	a	19 49	19 49	19 55					20 24		20 50			21 06			21 32				22 15		
	d	19 50	19 50	19 56					20 25		20 50			21 07			21 33				22 16		
Loughborough	d	19 58	19 58						20 32		20 58			21 15			21 39			21 46	22 24		
Barrow Upon Soar	d		20 03								21 03										22 29		
Sileby	d		20 07								21 07										22 33		
Syston	d		20 12								21 12										22 38		
Leicester	a	20 08	20 20	20 12			20 27		20 43		21 23			21 27			21 50			21 55	22 49		
	d	20 08		20 13			20 27		20 43					21 29			21 51			21 56			
Market Harborough	d			20 27					20 56					21 42						22 09			
Melton Mowbray	47 d																						
Oakham	47 d																						
Corby	d							20 41											21 43				
Kettering	a							20 50	21 05					21 51					21 52	22 18			
	d							20 51	21 06					21 52						22 19			
Wellingborough	d							21 00	21 14					21 59						22 26			
Bedford	52 a							21 12	21 26					22 12						22 39			
Luton	52 a							21 27						22 27						22 56			
Luton Airport Parkway	52 ✈ a								21 42					22 30									
St Pancras International	⊖52 a	21 21		21 25			21 38	21 55	22 07					22 57			23 06			23 25			

A From Liverpool Lime Street to Norwich
B From Edinburgh to Plymouth
C From Newcastle to Reading
D From Glasgow Central to Plymouth
E From Liverpool Lime Street
F From Newcastle to Southampton Central
G From Glasgow Central to Bristol Temple Meads
H From Newcastle to Birmingham New Street
I From Edinburgh to Bristol Temple Meads. 🛒 to Leeds

For connections to Gatwick Airport refer to Table T052

Table T053-R

Sheffield - East Midlands - London

Mondays to Fridays

21 May to 20 July

	EM ◇ A	EM ◇■ ⊼	XC ◇■ B ⊼	NT ◇	EM	EM ◇■ ⊼	EM ◇■ ⊼	EM ◇ A
York ■ 29 d			20 45					
Leeds ■ 31,34 d			21 11	21 03				
Wakefield Westgate ■ 31 d			21 23					
Wakefield Kirkgate ■ 31,34 d				21 21				
Doncaster ■ 29 d								
Manchester Piccadilly 78 d	20 42							22 28
Sheffield ■ d	21 37	22 01	22 01	22 03			23 21	23 37
Chesterfield d	21 55	22 13	22 25	22 20			23 45	00 02
Derby ■ a		22 34	22 42				00 06	
d								
Long Eaton d								
Alfreton d	22 05			22 31				
Langley Mill d	22 13			22 38				
Lincoln 27 d								
Newark Castle 27 d								
Nottingham ■ a	22 31			22 57				00 45
d					23 10			
Beeston d					23 15			
East Midlands Parkway a					23 22			
d					23 23			
Loughborough d					23 31			
Barrow Upon Soar d								
Sileby d								
Syston d								
Leicester a					23 47			
d								
Market Harborough d								
Melton Mowbray 47 d								
Oakham 47 d								
Corby d						22 43		
Kettering ■ a						22 52		
d								
Wellingborough d								
Bedford ■ 52 a								
Luton ■ 52 a								
Luton Airport Parkway ■ 52 a								
St Pancras International ⊖52 a								

Mondays to Fridays

23 July to 31 August

	EM MO ◇ A	EM MX ◇ A	EM ◇■ ⊼	EM ◇■ C ⊼	EM ◇■ D ⊼	EM ◇■ C ⊼	EM ◇■ D ⊼	EM 🚌	EM ◇■ ⊼	EM 🚌	EM	NT ◇	EM ◇■ ⊼	EM ◇■ D ⊠	EM ◇■ C ⊠	EM 🚌	XC ◇■ E	EM ◇■ ⊼	EM ◇■ ⊼	EM ◇■ F ⊠	EM ◇■ G ⊠	EM ◇■ H ⊠
York ■ 29 d																						
Leeds ■ 31,34 d																						
Wakefield Westgate ■ 31 d																						
Wakefield Kirkgate ■ 31,34 d																						
Doncaster ■ 29 d																						
Manchester Piccadilly 78 d																						
Sheffield ■ d												05 15		05 31	05 31		05 40			06 00		06 00
Chesterfield d		00 02										05 30		05 44	05 44		06a04			06 13		06 13
Derby ■ a															06 03					06 33		
d				05 02		05 19									06 04					06 34		
Long Eaton d						05 28														06 44		
Alfreton d												05 45										
Langley Mill d	00 02											05 53										
Lincoln 27 d																						
Newark Castle 27 d																						
Nottingham ■ a	00 23	00 45										06 11										
d									05 32		05 38								06 31			
Beeston d																			06 37			
East Midlands Parkway a				05 12					05 42					06 16	06 16				06 42			
d				05 13			05 29		05 43					06 17	06 17				06 43			
Loughborough d				05 20					05 51		05 58			06 26	06 26					06 54	06 54	06 54
Barrow Upon Soar d											06 02											
Sileby d											06 07											
Syston d											06 12											
Leicester a				05 29		05 42	05 42		06 03		06 20			06 37	06 37				06 56	07 05	07 05	07 05
d			04 45	05 31	05 31	05 44	05 44		06 04					06 39	06 39				06 59	07 07	07 07	07 07
Market Harborough d				05 44	05 44	05 57	05 57		06 19					06 54	06 54				07 12			
Melton Mowbray 47 d													06 03									
Oakham 47 d													06 15									
Corby d													06 38					07 08				
Kettering ■ a			05 04	05 53	05 53	06 06	06 06		06 29				06 47	07 04	07 04			07 17	07 21	07 28	07 28	07 28
d			05 05	05 55	05 55	06 08	06 08		06 31				06 48	07 05	07 05				07 23	07 29	07 29	07 29
Wellingborough d			05 17	06 03	06 03	06 16	06 16	06 26	06 39	06 50			06 57	07 14	07 14	07 24			07 31	07 38	07 38	07 38
Bedford ■ 52 a			05 37					07 11		07 35						08 14						
Luton ■ 52 a				06 25	06 25																	
Luton Airport Parkway ■ 52 a			05 53						07 04					07 44	07 44					08 02	08 02	08 09
St Pancras International ⊖52 a			06 24	06 54	06 54	07 08	07 08		07 36				07 55	08 09	08 09				08 24	08 29	08 29	08 39

A From Liverpool Lime Street
B From Glasgow Central to Birmingham New Street. ⊼ to Leeds
C until 27 July
D from 30 July
E To Reading
F until 10 August. The Sheffield Continental
G from 20 August. The Sheffield Continental
H from 13 August until 17 August. The Sheffield Continental

For connections to Gatwick Airport refer to Table T052

Table T053-R

Sheffield - East Midlands - London

Mondays to Fridays

23 July to 31 August

	EM 🚌	EM ◇■ ⊼	NT ◇	EM	EM ◇■ A ⊠	XC ◇■ B ⊼	EM ◇■ C ⊠	EM 🚌	EM ◇■ ⊠	EM ◇■ ⊼	EM ◇■ D ⊠	EM ◇■ E ⊠	EM ◇■ F ⊠	EM ◇■ G ⊠	EM ◇■ H ⊼	EM ◇■ I ⊼	EM ◇■ J ⊼	EM ◇■ A ⊼	EM 🚌	EM	NT ◇	EM ◇■ ⊼
York ■ 29 d																						
Leeds ■ 31,34 d					05 19	05 48	05 19															
Wakefield Westgate ■ 31 d					05 32	06 01	05 32															
Wakefield Kirkgate ■ 31,34 d																						
Doncaster ■ 29 d					05 57		05 57															
Manchester Piccadilly 78 d																						
Sheffield ■ d			06 03		06 25	06 30	06 32				06 49			06 49							07 02	
Chesterfield d			06 19		06 40	06a43	06 49				07 01			07 01							07 17	
Derby ■ a					07 03						07 21											
d					07 05						07 23	07 05	07 05		07 23	07 25		07 30				
Long Eaton d															07 41	07 41		07 41				
Alfreton d			06 29																		07 28	
Langley Mill d			06 36																		07 35	
Lincoln 27 d																						
Newark Castle 27 d																						
Nottingham ■ a			07 00																		07 53	
d		06 52							07 11											07 30		07 56
Beeston d		06 58							07 18											07 36		
East Midlands Parkway a		07 03							07 24		07 33	07 34	07 34	07 34						07 43		08 05
d		07 04							07 26		07 34	07 35	07 35	07 35			07 42			07 44		08 05
Loughborough d				06 59	07 22		07 24				07 42	07 42	07 42	07 42	07 51	07 51	07 51	07 51		07 52		
Barrow Upon Soar d				07 04																07 57		
Sileby d				07 08																08 01		
Syston d				07 14																08 06		
Leicester a		07 17		07 22	07 33		07 35		07 41		07 51	07 51	07 51	07 51	08 02	08 02	08 02	08 02		08 18		08 18
d		07 19			07 34		07 37		07 43		07 55	07 56	07 56	07 56	08 03	08 03	08 03	08 03				08 21
Market Harborough d		07 33							07 58						08 18	08 18	08 18	08 18				
Melton Mowbray 47 d																						
Oakham 47 d																						
Corby d										08 02												
Kettering ■ a		07 42			07 55		07 58		08 08	08 11	08 16	08 16	08 16	08 16	08 28	08 28	08 28	08 28				
d		07 43			07 56		07 59		08 09		08 17	08 17	08 17	08 17	08 29	08 29	08 29	08 29				
Wellingborough d	07 48	07 51			08 04		08 07	08 14			08 25	08 25	08 25	08 25	08 38	08 38	08 38	08 38	08 48			
Bedford ■ 52 a	08 43							09 09											09 38			
Luton ■ 52 a																						
Luton Airport Parkway ■ 52 a																						
St Pancras International ⊖52 a		08 41			08 55		08 55		09 08		09 12	09 12	09 13	09 13	09 27	09 27	09 27	09 27				09 38

	XC ◇■ B ⊼	EM ◇■ K ⊼	EM ◇■ L ⊠	EM ◇■ M ⊠	EM ◇■ ⊼	EM ◇■ N ⊼	EM ◇■ O ⊼	EM ◇■ P ⊼	EM ◇■ Q ⊼	EM ◇■ R ⊼	XC ■ ■ S ⊼	NT ◇	XC ◇■ T ⊼	EM ◇■ C ⊼	EM ◇■ A ⊼	EM U	EM ◇■ ⊼	EM ◇■ ⊼	EM ◇ V	XC ◇■ W ⊼	EM ◇■ J ⊼
York ■ 29 d											06 45		07 26							07 43	
Leeds ■ 31,34 d	06 16	06 33				06 33					07 10	07 03								08 11	
Wakefield Westgate ■ 31 d	06 28	06 47				06 47					07 23									08 23	
Wakefield Kirkgate ■ 31,34 d												07 22									
Doncaster ■ 29 d	06 46												07 53								
Manchester Piccadilly 78 d																			07 42		
Sheffield ■ d	07 18	07 24	07 29	07 29		07 32	07 46	07 46			07 53	08 03	08 18	08 26	08 26				08 38	08 54	
Chesterfield d	07a31	07 37	07 41	07 42		07 46	07 59	07 59			08a04	08 19	08a29	08 38	08 38				08 54	09a06	
Derby ■ a				08 00				08 17							08 57						
d				08 02				08 19							08 57						
Long Eaton d								08 29													
Alfreton d		07 48				07 57						08 33							09 05		
Langley Mill d		07 57				08 05						08 41									
Lincoln 27 d					07 05											07 36					
Newark Castle 27 d					07 30											08 06					
Nottingham ■ a		08 24			07 56	08 24						08 59				08 33			09 27		
d		08 32			08 05	08 32										08 35		09 12			
Beeston d					08 11				←	←						08 41		09 18			
East Midlands Parkway a		08 42				08 42	08 30	08 33	08 42	08 42						08 49					
d		08 43				08 43	08 31	08 34	08 43	08 43						08 50					09 45
Loughborough d		→			08 21	→	08 42	08 42								08 58		09 26			09 51
Barrow Upon Soar d																09 03					
Sileby d																09 07					
Syston d																09 13					
Leicester a			08 24	08 24	08 31		08 54	08 54	08 58	08 58				09 18	09 18	09 20		09 36			10 01
d			08 26	08 26	08 32		08 55	08 55	08 59	08 59				09 18	09 18			09 38			10 03
Market Harborough d					08 46				09 13	09 13								09 51			
Melton Mowbray 47 d																					
Oakham 47 d																					
Corby d																	09 32				
Kettering ■ a					08 55												09 41	10 00			
d					08 56												09 42	10 01			
Wellingborough d					09 03												09 51	10 08			
Bedford ■ 52 a																	10 12	10 22			
Luton ■ 52 a																	10 26				
Luton Airport Parkway ■ 52 a					09 30													10 38			
St Pancras International ⊖52 a			09 41	09 41	09 55		10 03	10 03	10 11	10 11				10 25	10 25		10 51	11 05			11 08

A until 27 July
B To Plymouth
C from 30 July
D until 27 July. The Sheffield Continental
E from 30 July until 10 August. The Sheffield Continental
F from 20 August. The Sheffield Continental
G from 13 August until 17 August. The Sheffield Continental
H from 20 August
I from 30 July until 10 August
J from 13 August until 17 August
K until 27 July. To St Pancras International
L from 30 July. The Master Cutler
M until 27 July. The Master Cutler
N from 30 July. To St Pancras International
O from 30 July. The South Yorkshireman
P until 27 July. The South Yorkshireman
Q until 27 July. From Leeds
R from 30 July. From Leeds
S To Reading
T From Newcastle to Plymouth
U From Sleaford
V From Liverpool Lime Street to Norwich
W From Newcastle to Southampton Central

For connections to Gatwick Airport refer to Table T052

Table T053-R

Mondays to Fridays

23 July to 31 August

Sheffield - East Midlands - London

	EM	EM	EM	EM	NT	XC	EM	EM	EM	EM	EM	XC	EM	EM	EM	EM	EM	NT	XC	EM	EM	EM
	◇■ A	◇■ B		◇■	◇	◇■ C	◇■ B	◇■ D	◇■	◇■	◇ E	◇■ F	◇■ A	◇■ G	◇■ B		◇■	◇	◇■ H	◇■ B	◇■ D	◇■
York 29 d						08 27						08 44							09 36			
Leeds 31,34 d					08 04							09 11						09 04				
Wakefield Westgate 31 d												09 23										
Wakefield Kirkgate 31,34 d					08 22													09 22				
Doncaster 29 d						08 53													10 00			
Manchester Piccadilly 78 d											08 43											
Sheffield d		08 59			09 06	09 24	09 28	09 29			09 37	09 55			10 00			10 05	10 24	10 29	10 29	
Chesterfield d		09 12			09 22	09a35	09 41	09 42			09 51	10a06			10 13			10 22	10a37	10 41	10 43	
Derby a		09 31					10 00								10 33					11 00		
d	09 20	09 31					10 02						10 20		10 33					11 02		
Long Eaton d	09 40	09 40											10 41		10 42							
Alfreton d					09 33						10 01							10 32				
Langley Mill d					09 40													10 40				
Lincoln 27 d			08 36													09 37						
Newark Castle 27 d			09 08													10 07						
Nottingham a			09 30		09 59						10 26					10 30		10 58				
d			09 35	09 45						10 12						10 35	10 45					
Beeston d			09 41							10 18						10 41						
East Midlands Parkway a	09 44	09 44	09 50	09 55									10 44		10 46	10 49	10 55					
d	09 45	09 45	09 51	09 56									10 45	10 45	10 47	10 50	10 56					
Loughborough d	09 52	09 52	09 59							10 27			10 53	10 53	10 54	10 58						
Barrow Upon Soar d			10 04													11 03						
Sileby d			10 08													11 07						
Syston d			10 13													11 12						
Leicester a	10 02	10 02	10 20	10 13			10 23	10 23		10 37			11 02	11 02	11 04	11 19	11 13			11 25	11 25	
d	10 03	10 03		10 13			10 23	10 23		10 38			11 03	11 03	11 05		11 13			11 25	11 25	
Market Harborough d				10 26						10 51							11 26					
Melton Mowbray 47 d																						
Oakham 47 d																						
Corby d									10 41													11 41
Kettering a									10 50	11 00												11 50
d									10 51	11 01												11 51
Wellingborough d									10 59	11 08												12 00
Bedford 52 a									11 12	11 22												12 12
Luton 52 a									11 27													12 27
Luton Airport Parkway 52 a										11 38												
St Pancras International ⊖52 a	11 08	11 08		11 24			11 35	11 36	11 52	12 08			12 09	12 09	12 09		12 24			12 36	12 36	12 51

	EM	EM	XC	EM	EM	EM	EM	EM	NT	XC	EM	EM	EM	EM	EM	XC	EM	EM	EM	EM	EM
	◇■	◇ E	◇■ I	◇■ A	◇■ G	◇■ B		◇■	◇	◇■ C	◇■ B	◇■ D	◇■	◇■	◇ E	◇■ J	◇■ A	◇■ G	◇■ B		◇■
York 29 d			09 44							10 35						10 44					
Leeds 31,34 d			10 11						10 04							11 11					
Wakefield Westgate 31 d			10 23													11 23					
Wakefield Kirkgate 31,34 d									10 22												
Doncaster 29 d										10 59											
Manchester Piccadilly 78 d		09 42													10 42						
Sheffield d		10 37	10 55			11 00			11 05	11 24	11 29	11 29			11 38	11 55			12 00		
Chesterfield d		10 54	11a06			11 12			11 22	11a37	11 41	11 43			11 54	12a06			12 13		
Derby a						11 31					12 01								12 33		
d				11 20		11 31					12 02						12 20		12 33		
Long Eaton d				11 40		11 40											12 40		12 42		
Alfreton d		11 05							11 32						12 05						
Langley Mill d									11 40												
Lincoln 27 d							10 36													11 40	
Newark Castle 27 d							11 07													12 07	
Nottingham a		11 26					11 30		11 58						12 29					12 30	
d	11 12						11 35	11 45						12 12						12 35	12 45
Beeston d	11 18						11 41							12 18						12 41	
East Midlands Parkway a				11 44		11 44	11 49	11 55									12 44		12 46	12 49	12 55
d				11 45	11 45	11 45	11 50	11 56									12 45	12 45	12 47	12 50	12 56
Loughborough d	11 27			11 52	11 52	11 52	11 58							12 27			12 52	12 52	12 54	12 58	
Barrow Upon Soar d							12 03													13 03	
Sileby d							12 07													13 07	
Syston d							12 12													13 12	
Leicester a	11 37			12 02	12 02	12 02	12 19	12 13			12 25	12 25		12 37			13 02	13 02	13 04	13 23	13 13
d	11 38			12 03	12 03	12 03		12 13			12 26	12 26		12 38			13 03	13 03	13 05		13 13
Market Harborough d	11 51							12 26						12 51							13 26
Melton Mowbray 47 d																					
Oakham 47 d																					
Corby d													12 41								
Kettering a	12 00												12 50	13 00							
d	12 01												12 51	13 01							
Wellingborough d	12 08												13 00	13 08							
Bedford 52 a	12 22												13 12	13 22							
Luton 52 a													13 27								
Luton Airport Parkway 52 a	12 38													13 38							
St Pancras International ⊖52 a	13 06			13 08	13 08	13 08		13 25			13 36	13 36	13 51	14 07			14 11	14 11	14 12		14 25

A from 30 July, not from 13 August until 17 August
B until 27 July
C From Newcastle to Plymouth
D from 30 July
E From Liverpool Lime Street to Norwich
F From Edinburgh to Reading
G from 13 August until 17 August
H From Edinburgh to Plymouth
I From Glasgow Central to Southampton Central
J From Dundee to Reading

For connections to Gatwick Airport refer to Table T052

Table T053-R

Mondays to Fridays

23 July to 31 August

Sheffield - East Midlands - London

	NT	XC	EM	EM	EM	EM	EM	XC	EM	EM	EM	EM	EM	NT	XC	EM	EM	EM	EM	EM	XC	EM
	◇	◇■ A	◇■ B	◇■ C	◇■	◇■	◇ D	◇■ E	◇■ F	◇■ G	◇■ C		◇■	◇	◇■ H	◇■ B	◇■ C	◇■	◇■	◇ D	◇■ I	◇■ F
York 29 d		11 35						11 44							12 35						12 44	
Leeds 31,34 d	11 04							12 11						12 04							13 11	
Wakefield Westgate 31 d								12 23													13 23	
Wakefield Kirkgate 31,34 d	11 22													12 22								
Doncaster 29 d		11 59													12 59							
Manchester Piccadilly 78 d							11 42													12 42		
Sheffield d	12 05	12 24	12 29	12 29			12 38	12 55			13 00			13 05	13 24	13 29	13 29			13 37	13 55	
Chesterfield d	12 22	12a35	12 41	12 41			12 52	13a06			13 12			13 22	13a35	13 41	13 41			13 52	14a06	
Derby a				13 00							13 31						14 00					
d				13 02					13 20		13 32						14 02					14 20
Long Eaton d									13 40		13 40											14 43
Alfreton d	12 32						13 03							13 32						14 03		
Langley Mill d	12 40													13 40								
Lincoln 27 d												12 34										
Newark Castle 27 d												13 05										
Nottingham a	12 58						13 27					13 30		13 58						14 27		
d						13 12						13 35	13 45						14 12			
Beeston d						13 18						13 41							14 18			
East Midlands Parkway a									13 45		13 45	13 49	13 55									14 47
d									13 46	13 46	13 46	13 50	13 56									14 48
Loughborough d						13 27			13 52	13 52	13 52	13 58							14 27			14 55
Barrow Upon Soar d												14 03										
Sileby d												14 07										
Syston d												14 12										
Leicester a			13 25	13 25		13 37			14 02	14 02	14 02	14 19	14 13			14 25	14 25		14 37			15 07
d			13 26	13 26		13 38			14 03	14 03	14 03		14 13			14 26	14 26		14 38			15 08
Market Harborough d						13 51							14 26						14 51			
Melton Mowbray 47 d																						
Oakham 47 d																						
Corby d					13 41													14 41				
Kettering a					13 50	14 00												14 50	15 00			
d					13 51	14 01												14 51	15 01			
Wellingborough d					14 00	14 09												15 00	15 08			
Bedford 52 a					14 12	14 22												15 12	15 22			
Luton 52 a					14 27													15 27				
Luton Airport Parkway 52 a						14 38													15 38			
St Pancras International ⊖52 a			14 38	14 38	14 51	15 05			15 08	15 08	15 08		15 25			15 39	15 39	15 51	16 11			16 25

	EM	EM	EM	EM	NT	XC	EM	EM	EM	EM	EM	XC	EM	EM	EM	EM	EM	NT	XC	EM	EM	EM
	◇■ G	◇■ C		◇■	◇	◇■ H	◇■ B	◇■ C	◇■	◇■	◇ D	◇■ J	◇■ F	◇■ G	◇■ C		◇■	◇	◇■ H	◇■ B	◇■ C	◇■
York 29 d						13 35						13 44							14 35			
Leeds 31,34 d					13 04							14 11						14 04				
Wakefield Westgate 31 d												14 23										
Wakefield Kirkgate 31,34 d					13 23													14 22				
Doncaster 29 d						13 59													14 59			
Manchester Piccadilly 78 d											13 42											
Sheffield d		13 59			14 05	14 24	14 29	14 29			14 38	14 55			14 59			15 05	15 24	15 29	15 29	
Chesterfield d		14 13			14 22	14a35	14 41	14 41			14 52	15a06			15 12			15 22	15a35	15 41	15 41	
Derby a		14 32						15 00							15 31						16 00	
d		14 33						15 02					15 20		15 31						16 02	
Long Eaton d		14 43											15 41		15 41							
Alfreton d					14 32						15 03							15 32				
Langley Mill d					14 40													15 40				
Lincoln 27 d			13 37													14 36						
Newark Castle 27 d			14 07													15 06						
Nottingham a			14 30		14 58						15 28					15 30		15 58				
d			14 35	14 45						15 12						15 35	15 45					
Beeston d			14 41							15 18						15 41						
East Midlands Parkway a		14 47	14 49	14 55									15 44		15 44	15 50	15 55					
d	14 48	14 48	14 50	14 56									15 45	15 45	15 45	15 51	15 56					
Loughborough d	14 55	14 55	14 58							15 27			15 53	15 53	15 53	15 59						
Barrow Upon Soar d			15 03													16 04						
Sileby d			15 07													16 08						
Syston d			15 12													16 13						
Leicester a	15 07	15 07	15 19	15 13			15 25	15 25		15 37			16 02	16 02	16 02	16 20	16 13			16 25	16 25	
d	15 08	15 08		15 13			15 26	15 26		15 38			16 03	16 03	16 03		16 13			16 26	16 26	
Market Harborough d				15 26						15 51							16 26					
Melton Mowbray 47 d																						
Oakham 47 d																						
Corby d									15 39													16 39
Kettering a									15 48	16 00												16 48
d									15 49	16 01												16 49
Wellingborough d									15 58	16 08												16 57
Bedford 52 a									16 10	16 21												17 10
Luton 52 a									16 26													17 24
Luton Airport Parkway 52 a										16 37												
St Pancras International ⊖52 a	16 25	16 25		16 27			16 41	16 41	16 55	17 12			17 12	17 12	17 12		17 24			17 39	17 39	17 55

A From Newcastle to Plymouth
B from 30 July
C until 27 July
D From Liverpool Lime Street to Norwich
E From Glasgow Central to Southampton Central
F from 30 July, not from 13 August until 17 August
G from 13 August until 17 August
H From Newcastle to Penzance
I From Glasgow Central to Reading
J From Aberdeen to Guildford

For connections to Gatwick Airport refer to Table T052

Table T053-R

Mondays to Fridays
23 July to 31 August

Sheffield - East Midlands - London

	EM ◇1 ⊥	EM ◇ A	XC ◇1 B ⊥	EM ◇1 C ⊥	EM ◇1 D ⊥	EM ◇1 E ⊥	EM ◇1 C ⊥	EM	EM ◇1 ⊥	NT ◇	XC ◇1 F ⊥	EM ◇1 C ⊥	EM ◇1 G ⊥	EM ◇1 ⊥	EM ◇1 ⊥	EM ◇ A	XC ◇1 H ⊥	EM ◇1 G ⊥	EM ◇1 E ⊥	EM ◇1 D ⊥	EM ◇1 C ⊥
York 29 d			14 44								15 35						15 44				
Leeds 31,34 d			15 11							15 04							16 11				
Wakefield Westgate 31 d			15 23														16 23				
Wakefield Kirkgate 31,34 d										15 22											
Doncaster 29 d											15 59										
Manchester Piccadilly 78 d		14 42														15 42					
Sheffield d		15 37	15 55				16 00			16 05	16 24	16 29	16 29			16 37	16 55				17 00
Chesterfield d		15 53	16a06				16 12			16 22	16a35	16 41	16 41			16 53	17a06				17 12
Derby a							16 31					17 00									17 32
d				16 27		16 20	16 32					17 01							17 20		17 32
Long Eaton d						16 40	16 40												17 42		17 42
Alfreton d		16 05								16 32						17 04					
Langley Mill d										16 40											
Lincoln 27 d								15 36													
Newark Castle 27 d								16 08													
Nottingham a		16 27						16 30		16 58						17 27					
d	16 12							16 33	16 45						17 12						
Beeston d	16 18							16 39							17 18						
East Midlands Parkway a				16 39		16 44	16 45	16 49	16 55										17 45		17 45
d				16 39	16 45	16 45	16 46	16 49	16 56										17 46	17 46	17 46
Loughborough d	16 27				16 52	16 52	16 52	16 58							17 26				17 54	17 54	17 54
Barrow Upon Soar d								17 02													
Sileby d								17 06													
Syston d								17 11													
Leicester a	16 37				17 02	17 02	17 02	17 19	17 13			17 22	17 22		17 36				18 04	18 04	18 04
d	16 38				17 03	17 03	17 03		17 13			17 23	17 23		17 37				18 04	18 04	18 04
Market Harborough d	16 51								17 26						17 50						
Melton Mowbray 47 d				17 09														17 09			
Oakham 47 d				17 23														17 23			
Corby d				17 51										17 39				17 51			
Kettering a	17 00			18 00	17 22	17 22	17 23							17 48	17 59			18 00			
d	17 01				17 24	17 24	17 24							17 49	18 00						
Wellingborough d	17 08													17 57	18 08						
Bedford 52 a	17 22													18 10	18 21						
Luton 52 a									18 03					18 26							
Luton Airport Parkway 52 a	17 37														18 40						
St Pancras International ⊖52 a	18 06				18 14	18 14	18 14		18 40			18 40	18 44	18 55	19 06				19 11	19 11	19 11

	EM	EM ◇1 ⊥	NT ◇	XC ◇1 F ⊥	EM ◇1 C ⊥	EM ◇1 G ⊥	EM ◇1 ⊥	EM ◇1 ⊥	EM ◇ A	XC ◇1 B ⊥	EM ◇1 E ⊥	EM ◇1 D ⊥	EM ◇1 C ⊥	EM	EM ◇1 ⊥	NT ◇	XC ◇1 F ⊥	EM ◇1 C ⊥	EM ◇1 G ⊥	EM ◇1 ⊥	EM ◇1 ⊥	EM ◇ I
York 29 d				16 05						16 44							17 35					
Leeds 31,34 d			16 04	16 40						17 10						17 03						
Wakefield Westgate 31 d				16 52						17 22												
Wakefield Kirkgate 31,34 d			16 22													17 22						
Doncaster 29 d																	17 58					
Manchester Piccadilly 78 d									16 42													17 42
Sheffield d			17 05	17 24	17 29	17 29			17 45	17 55			18 00			18 03	18 24	18 29	18 29			18 53
Chesterfield d			17 22	17a35	17 41	17 42			18 01	18a06			18 12			18 19	18a35	18 41	18 42			19 08
Derby a					18 04								18 31					19 00				
d					18 04						18 20		18 32					19 04				
Long Eaton d											18 41		18 41									
Alfreton d			17 32						18 11							18 30						19 19
Langley Mill d			17 40													18 37						
Lincoln 27 d	16 34													17 26								
Newark Castle 27 d	17 05													17 56								
Nottingham a	17 30		17 58						18 31					18 30		18 55						19 39
d	17 34	17 45						18 12						18 36	18 45						19 12	
Beeston d	17 40							18 18						18 42							19 18	
East Midlands Parkway a	17 50	17 56									18 44		18 45	18 50	18 55							
d	17 50	17 57									18 45	18 45	18 46	18 52	18 56							
Loughborough d	17 58							18 26			18 53	18 53	18 53	19 00							19 27	
Barrow Upon Soar d	18 03													19 05								
Sileby d	18 07													19 09								
Syston d	18 12													19 14								
Leicester a	18 19	18 13			18 25	18 25		18 36			19 03	19 03	19 03	19 21	19 13			19 25	19 25		19 37	
d		18 14			18 26	18 26		18 37			19 03	19 03	19 03		19 13			19 26	19 26		19 38	
Market Harborough d		18 27						18 50							19 26						19 51	
Melton Mowbray 47 d																						
Oakham 47 d																						
Corby d							18 37													19 39		
Kettering a		18 38					18 46	18 59												19 48	20 00	
d		18 39					18 47	19 00												19 49	20 01	
Wellingborough d							18 56	19 08												19 58	20 08	
Bedford 52 a							19 11	19 23												20 10	20 22	
Luton 52 a							19 27													20 26		
Luton Airport Parkway 52 a								19 41													20 37	
St Pancras International ⊖52 a		19 37			19 40	19 40	19 57	20 07			20 11	20 11	20 11		20 25			20 40	20 40	20 51	21 06	

A From Liverpool Lime Street to Norwich
B From Glasgow Central to Reading
C until 27 July
D from 13 August until 17 August
E from 30 July, not from 13 August until 17 August
F From Newcastle to Plymouth
G from 30 July
H From Edinburgh to Reading
I From Liverpool Lime Street

For connections to Gatwick Airport refer to Table T052

Table T053-R

Mondays to Fridays
23 July to 31 August

Sheffield - East Midlands - London

	XC ◇1 A ⊥	EM ◇1 B ⊥	EM ◇1 C ⊥	EM ◇1 D ⊥	EM	EM ◇1 ⊥	NT ◇	XC ◇1 E ⊥	EM ◇1 D ⊥	EM ◇1 F ⊥	EM ◇1 ⊥	EM ◇1 ⊥	EM ◇ G	EM	XC ◇1 H ⊥	EM ◇1 ⊥	NT ◇	XC ◇1 E ⊥	EM ◇ I	EM ◇1 D ⊥	EM ◇1 F ⊥
York 29 d	17 45							18 36							18 45			19 36			
Leeds 31,34 d	18 11						18 03								19 11		19 03				
Wakefield Westgate 31 d	18 23														19 23						
Wakefield Kirkgate 31,34 d							18 21										19 21				
Doncaster 29 d								18 59										19 59			
Manchester Piccadilly 78 d													18 42						19 42		
Sheffield d	18 58			19 02			19 05	19 24	19 29	19 29			19 37		19 58		20 02	20 24	20 41	20 50	20 50
Chesterfield d	19a11			19 15			19 21	19a35	19 42	19 43			19 52		20a09		20 21	20a35	20 56	21 02	21 03
Derby a				19 35					20 02											21 21	
d		19 20		19 35					20 02											21 22	
Long Eaton d		19 45		19 45																	
Alfreton d							19 31						20 03				20 32		21 08		
Langley Mill d							19 39										20 40				
Lincoln 27 d					18 35																
Newark Castle 27 d					19 03																
Nottingham a					19 30		19 57						20 27				20 59		21 33		
d					19 32	19 45						20 12		20 35		20 55					
Beeston d					19 38							20 18		20 42		21 01					
East Midlands Parkway a		19 49		19 49	19 49	19 55						20 24		20 50		21 06				21 32	21 32
d		19 50	19 50	19 50	19 50	19 56						20 25		20 50		21 07				21 33	21 33
Loughborough d		19 58	19 58	19 58	19 58							20 32		20 58		21 15				21 39	21 39
Barrow Upon Soar d					20 03									21 03							
Sileby d					20 07									21 07							
Syston d					20 12									21 12							
Leicester a		20 08	20 08	20 08	20 20	20 12			20 27	20 27		20 43		21 23		21 27				21 50	21 50
d		20 08	20 08	20 08		20 13			20 27	20 27		20 43				21 29				21 51	21 51
Market Harborough d						20 27						20 56				21 42					
Melton Mowbray 47 d																					
Oakham 47 d																					
Corby d											20 41										
Kettering a											20 50	21 05				21 51					
d											20 51	21 06				21 52					
Wellingborough d											21 00	21 14				21 59					
Bedford 52 a											21 12	21 26				22 12					
Luton 52 a											21 27					22 27					
Luton Airport Parkway 52 a												21 42				22 30					
St Pancras International ⊖52 a		21 21	21 21	21 21		21 25			21 38	21 38	21 55	22 07				22 57				23 06	23 06

	XC ◇1 J ⊥	EM ◇1 ⊥	EM ◇1 ⊥	EM	NT ◇	XC ◇1 K ⊥	EM ◇ I	EM ◇1 ⊥	XC ◇1 L ⊥	NT ◇	EM	EM ◇1 ⊥	EM ◇1 ⊥	EM ◇ I
York 29 d	19 45					20 36			20 45					
Leeds 31,34 d	20 11				20 03				21 11	21 03				
Wakefield Westgate 31 d	20 23								21 23					
Wakefield Kirkgate 31,34 d					20 21					21 21				
Doncaster 29 d						21 01								
Manchester Piccadilly 78 d							20 42							22 28
Sheffield d	20 58				21 02	21 27	21 37	22 01	22 01	22 03			23 21	23 37
Chesterfield d	21a09				21 18	21a38	21 55	22 13	22a24	22 20			23 45	00 02
Derby a					21 39			22 34					00 06	
d					21 40									
Long Eaton d														
Alfreton d							22 05			22 31				
Langley Mill d							22 13			22 38				
Lincoln 27 d														
Newark Castle 27 d														
Nottingham a					22 06		22 31			22 57				00 45
d			21 29	22 01							23 10			
Beeston d				22 07							23 15			
East Midlands Parkway a				22 15							23 22			
d				22 16							23 23			
Loughborough d			21 46	22 24							23 31			
Barrow Upon Soar d				22 29										
Sileby d				22 33										
Syston d				22 38										
Leicester a			21 55	22 49							23 47			
d			21 56											
Market Harborough d			22 09											
Melton Mowbray 47 d														
Oakham 47 d														
Corby d		21 43										22 43		
Kettering a		21 52	22 18									22 52		
d			22 19											
Wellingborough d			22 26											
Bedford 52 a			22 39											
Luton 52 a			22 56											
Luton Airport Parkway 52 a														
St Pancras International ⊖52 a			23 25											

A From Edinburgh to Southampton Central
B from 30 July, not from 13 August until 17 August
C from 13 August until 17 August
D until 27 July
E From Newcastle to Bristol Temple Meads
F from 30 July
G From Liverpool Lime Street to Norwich
H From Glasgow Central to Birmingham New Street
I From Liverpool Lime Street
J From Edinburgh to Birmingham New Street. ⊥ to Leeds
K From Newcastle to Birmingham New Street
L From Glasgow Central to Birmingham New Street. ⊥ to Leeds

For connections to Gatwick Airport refer to Table T052

Table T053-R

Mondays to Fridays

3 September to 21 September

Sheffield - East Midlands - London

Station			EM MO	EM MX	EM	EM	EM	EM	EM	EM	EM		NT	EM	EM	EM	XC	EM	EM	EM	EM		EM	NT	XC	EM
			◇	◇	◇1	◇1	◇1		◇1				◇	◇1	◇1		◇1	◇1	◇1	◇1			◇1	◇	◇1	
			A	A													B			C					D	
					🛒	🛒	🛒	🚌	🛒	🚌				🛒	⊠	🚌		🛒	🛒	⊠	🚌		🛒		🛒	
York 8	29	d																								
Leeds 10	31,34	d																							05 48	
Wakefield Westgate 7	31	d																							06 01	
Wakefield Kirkgate 4	31,34	d																								
Doncaster 7	29	d																								
Manchester Piccadilly	78	d																								
Sheffield 7		d											05 15		05 31		05 40			06 00				06 03	06 30	
Chesterfield		d		00 02									05 30		05 45		05 52			06 13				06 19	06 44	
Derby 6		a															06 35								07 21	
		d				05 02	05 18																			
Long Eaton		d					05 28																			
Alfreton		d											05 45											06 29		
Langley Mill		d	00 02										05 53											06 36		
Lincoln	27	d																								
Newark Castle	27	d																								
Nottingham 8		a	00 23	00 45									06 11											07 00		
		d							05 32		05 38								06 31				06 52			
Beeston		d																	06 37				06 58			
East Midlands Parkway		a				05 12			05 42						06 16				06 42				07 03			
		d				05 13			05 43						06 17				06 43				07 04			
Loughborough		d				05 20			05 51		05 58				06 26					06 54						06 59
Barrow Upon Soar		d									06 02															07 04
Sileby		d									06 07															07 08
Syston		d									06 12															07 14
Leicester		a				05 29	05 42		06 03		06 20				06 37				06 56	07 05			07 17			07 22
		d			04 45	05 31	05 44		06 04						06 39				06 59	07 07			07 19			
Market Harborough		d				05 44	05 57		06 19						06 54				07 12				07 33			
Melton Mowbray	47	d												06 03												
Oakham	47	d												06 15												
Corby		d												06 38				07 08								
Kettering 5		a			05 04	05 53	06 06		06 29					06 47	07 04			07 17	07 21	07 28			07 42			
		d			05 05	05 55	06 08		06 31					06 48	07 05				07 23	07 29			07 43			
Wellingborough		d			05 17	06 03	06 16	06 26	06 39	06 50				06 57	07 14	07 24			07 31	07 38	07 48		07 51			
Bedford 7	52	a			05 37			07 11		07 35						08 14					08 43					
Luton 10	52	a				06 25																				
Luton Airport Parkway 7	52	a			05 53				07 04						07 44					08 02						
St Pancras International	⊖52	a			06 24	06 54	07 08		07 36					07 55	08 09				08 24	08 29			08 41			

Station			EM	EM	EM	EM	EM		EM	EM	EM	NT	EM	XC	EM	EM	EM		EM	EM	XC	NT	XC	EM	EM	EM
			◇1		◇1	◇1	◇1		◇1			◇	◇1	◇1	◇1	◇1	◇1		◇1	◇1	R 1	◇	◇1	◇1		◇1
							C							D	E		F		G	H	B		I		J	
			⊠	🚌	⊠	🛒	⊠		🛒	🚌			🛒	🛒	⊠	🛒	🛒		🛒	🛒	🛒		🛒	🛒		🛒
York 8	29	d																			06 45		07 26			
Leeds 10	31,34	d	05 19											06 16			06 33				07 10	07 03				
Wakefield Westgate 7	31	d	05 32											06 28			06 47				07 23					
Wakefield Kirkgate 4	31,34	d																				07 22				
Doncaster 7	29	d	05 57											06 46									07 53			
Manchester Piccadilly	78	d																								
Sheffield 7		d	06 33									07 02		07 18	07 26		07 30		07 46		07 53	08 03	08 18	08 26		
Chesterfield		d	06 49									07 17		07 32	07 41		07 46		07 59		08 06	08 21	08 33	08 38		
Derby 6		a												08 16							08 45		09 18			
		d					07 23		07 31																	
Long Eaton		d							07 41																	
Alfreton		d										07 28					07 57					08 33				
Langley Mill		d										07 35					08 05					08 41				
Lincoln	27	d														07 05									07 36	
Newark Castle	27	d														07 30									08 06	
Nottingham 8		a										07 53				07 56	08 24					08 59			08 33	
		d			07 11						07 30		07 56			08 05	08 32								08 36	
Beeston		d			07 18						07 36					08 11				←					08 42	
East Midlands Parkway		a			07 24		07 33				07 43		08 05				08 42		08 29	08 42					08 49	
		d			07 26		07 34				07 44		08 05				08 43		08 30	08 43					08 50	
Loughborough		d	07 24				07 42		07 51		07 52					08 22	→		08 42						08 58	
Barrow Upon Soar		d									07 57														09 03	
Sileby		d									08 01														09 07	
Syston		d									08 06														09 12	
Leicester		a	07 35		07 41		07 51		08 02		08 18		08 18		08 24	08 32			08 54	08 58				09 18	09 22	
		d	07 37		07 43		07 56		08 03				08 21		08 26	08 33			08 55	08 59				09 18		
Market Harborough		d			07 58				08 18							08 47				09 13						
Melton Mowbray	47	d																								
Oakham	47	d																								
Corby		d				08 02																				09 32
Kettering 5		a	07 58		08 08	08 11	08 16		08 28							08 56										09 41
		d	07 59		08 09		08 17		08 29							08 57										09 42
Wellingborough		d	08 07	08 14			08 25		08 38	08 48						09 04										09 51
Bedford 7	52	a		09 09						09 38																10 12
Luton 10	52	a																								10 26
Luton Airport Parkway 7	52	a														09 30										
St Pancras International	⊖52	a	08 55		09 08		09 12		09 27				09 38		09 41	09 55			10 03	10 11				10 25		10 51

A From Liverpool Lime Street
B To Reading
C The Sheffield Continental
D To Plymouth
E The Master Cutler
F To St Pancras International
G The South Yorkshireman
H From Leeds
I From Newcastle to Plymouth
J From Sleaford

For connections to Gatwick Airport refer to Table T052

Table T053-R

Mondays to Fridays

3 September to 21 September

Sheffield - East Midlands - London

Station			EM		EM	EM	XC	EM	EM	NT	XC	EM	EM		EM	EM	EM	XC	EM	EM	NT	XC	EM		EM	EM
			◇1		◇	◇1	◇1		◇1	◇	◇1	◇1	◇1		◇1	◇	◇1	◇1		◇1	◇	◇1	◇1		◇1	◇1
					A		B				C					A		D				E				
			🛒			🛒	🛒		🛒		🛒	🛒	🛒		🛒		🛒	🛒		🛒		🛒	🛒		🛒	🛒
York 8	29	d					07 43				08 27							08 44				09 36				
Leeds 10	31,34	d					08 11			08 04								09 11			09 04					
Wakefield Westgate 7	31	d					08 23											09 23								
Wakefield Kirkgate 4	31,34	d								08 22											09 22					
Doncaster 7	29	d									08 53											10 00				
Manchester Piccadilly	78	d			07 42											08 43										
Sheffield 7		d			08 38		08 54			09 06	09 24	09 29				09 37		09 55			10 05	10 24	10 33			
Chesterfield		d			08 54		09 08			09 22	09 36	09 42				09 51		10 07			10 22	10 40	10 46			
Derby 6		a					09 44				10 19							10 46				11 18				
		d				09 31											10 31									
Long Eaton		d				09 38											10 40									
Alfreton		d			09 05					09 33						10 02					10 32					
Langley Mill		d								09 40											10 40					
Lincoln	27	d						08 36											09 37							
Newark Castle	27	d						09 08											10 07							
Nottingham 8		a			09 27			09 30		09 59						10 28			10 30		10 58					
		d	09 12					09 35	09 45						10 12				10 35	10 45						11 12
Beeston		d	09 18					09 41							10 18				10 41							11 18
East Midlands Parkway		a				09 43		09 50	09 55								10 44		10 49	10 55						
		d				09 44		09 51	09 56								10 45		10 50	10 56						
Loughborough		d	09 26			09 50		09 59							10 27		10 52		10 58							11 27
Barrow Upon Soar		d						10 04											11 03							
Sileby		d						10 08											11 07							
Syston		d						10 13											11 12							
Leicester		a	09 36			10 00		10 20	10 13			10 25			10 37		11 02		11 19	11 13			11 25			11 37
		d	09 38			10 02			10 13			10 26			10 38		11 03			11 13			11 25			11 38
Market Harborough		d	09 51						10 26						10 51					11 26						11 51
Melton Mowbray	47	d																								
Oakham	47	d																								
Corby		d											10 41												11 41	
Kettering 5		a	10 00										10 50		11 00										11 50	12 00
		d	10 01										10 51		11 01										11 51	12 01
Wellingborough		d	10 08										10 59		11 08										12 00	12 08
Bedford 7	52	a	10 22										11 12		11 22										12 12	12 22
Luton 10	52	a											11 27												12 27	
Luton Airport Parkway 7	52	a	10 38												11 38											12 38
St Pancras International	⊖52	a	11 05			11 08			11 24			11 36	11 52		12 08		12 13			12 24			12 36		12 51	13 06

Station			EM	EM	XC	EM	EM	NT	XC		EM	EM	EM	EM	EM	XC	EM	EM	NT		XC	EM	EM	EM	EM	EM
			◇	◇1	◇1		◇1	◇	◇1		◇1	◇1	◇1	◇	◇1	◇1		◇1	◇		◇1	◇1	◇1	◇1	◇	◇1
			A		F				C					A		G					C				A	
				🛒	🛒		🛒		🛒		🛒	🛒	🛒		🛒	🛒		🛒			🛒	🛒	🛒	🛒		🛒
York 8	29	d			09 44				10 35							10 44					11 35					
Leeds 10	31,34	d			10 11			10 04								11 11			11 04							
Wakefield Westgate 7	31	d			10 23											11 23										
Wakefield Kirkgate 4	31,34	d						10 22											11 22							
Doncaster 7	29	d							10 59												11 59					
Manchester Piccadilly	78	d	09 42											10 42											11 42	
Sheffield 7		d	10 38		10 55			11 05	11 24		11 29			11 38		11 55			12 05		12 24	12 29			12 38	
Chesterfield		d	10 54		11 07			11 22	11 38		11 43			11 54		12 07			12 22		12 36	12 41			12 52	
Derby 6		a			11 46				12 16							12 44					13 17					
		d		11 31											12 31											13 31
Long Eaton		d		11 40											12 40											13 40
Alfreton		d	11 05					11 33						12 05					12 32						13 03	
Langley Mill		d						11 42											12 40							
Lincoln	27	d				10 36											11 40									
Newark Castle	27	d				11 07											12 07									
Nottingham 8		a	11 27			11 30		12 00						12 29			12 30		13 00						13 27	
		d				11 35	11 45						12 12				12 35	12 45						13 12		
Beeston		d				11 41							12 18				12 41							13 18		
East Midlands Parkway		a		11 44		11 49	11 55								12 44		12 49	12 55								13 44
		d		11 45		11 50	11 56								12 45		12 50	12 56								13 45
Loughborough		d		11 52		11 58							12 27		12 52		12 58							13 27		13 52
Barrow Upon Soar		d				12 03											13 03									
Sileby		d				12 07											13 07									
Syston		d				12 12											13 12									
Leicester		a		12 02		12 19	12 13				12 25		12 37		13 02		13 23	13 13				13 25		13 37		14 02
		d		12 03			12 13				12 26		12 38		13 03			13 13				13 26		13 38		14 03
Market Harborough		d					12 26						12 51					13 26						13 51		
Melton Mowbray	47	d																								
Oakham	47	d																								
Corby		d										12 41											13 41			
Kettering 5		a										12 50	13 00										13 50	14 00		
		d										12 51	13 01										13 51	14 01		
Wellingborough		d										13 00	13 08										14 00	14 09		
Bedford 7	52	a										13 12	13 22										14 12	14 22		
Luton 10	52	a										13 27											14 27			
Luton Airport Parkway 7	52	a											13 38											14 38		
St Pancras International	⊖52	a		13 08			13 25				13 36	13 51	14 07		14 10			14 25				14 38	14 51	15 05		15 08

A From Liverpool Lime Street to Norwich
B From Newcastle to Southampton Central
C From Newcastle to Plymouth
D From Edinburgh to Reading
E From Edinburgh to Plymouth
F From Glasgow Central to Southampton Central
G From Dundee to Reading

For connections to Gatwick Airport refer to Table T052

Table T053-R

Mondays to Fridays

3 September to 21 September

Sheffield - East Midlands - London

	XC	EM	EM		NT	XC	EM	EM	EM	EM	EM	XC	EM		EM	NT	XC	EM	EM	EM	EM	EM	XC
	◇■ A ✠		◇■ ✠		◇	◇■ B ✠	◇■ ✠	◇■ ✠	◇■ ✠	◇ C	◇■ ✠	◇■ D ✠			◇■ ✠	◇	◇■ B ✠	◇■ ✠	◇■ ✠	◇■ ✠	◇ C	◇■ ✠	◇■ E ✠
York ■ 29 d	11 44					12 35						12 44					13 35						13 44
Leeds ■ 31,34 d	12 11				12 04							13 11				13 04							14 11
Wakefield Westgate ■ 31 d	12 23											13 23											14 23
Wakefield Kirkgate ■ 31,34 d					12 22											13 23							
Doncaster ■ 29 d						12 59											13 59						
Manchester Piccadilly 78 d										12 42											13 42		
Sheffield ■ ⇌ d	12 55				13 05	13 24	13 29			13 37		13 55				14 05	14 24	14 29			14 38		14 55
Chesterfield d	13 07				13 22	13 36	13 41			13 52		14 07				14 22	14 36	14 41			14 52		15 07
Derby ■ a	13 44					14 17						14 45					15 19						15 45
d											14 31											15 30	
Long Eaton d											14 43											15 40	
Alfreton d					13 32					14 03						14 32					15 03		
Langley Mill d					13 40											14 40							
Lincoln 27 d		12 34											13 37										
Newark Castle 27 d		13 05											14 07										
Nottingham ■ ⇌ a		13 30			13 58					14 27			14 30			14 58					15 28		
d		13 35	13 45						14 12				14 35		14 45					15 12			
Beeston d		13 41							14 18				14 41							15 18			
East Midlands Parkway ✈ a		13 49	13 55								14 47		14 49		14 55							15 43	
d		13 50	13 56								14 48		14 50		14 56							15 44	
Loughborough d		13 58							14 27		14 55		14 58							15 27		15 52	
Barrow Upon Soar d		14 03											15 03										
Sileby d		14 07											15 07										
Syston d		14 12											15 12										
Leicester a		14 19	14 13				14 25		14 37		15 07		15 19		15 13			15 25		15 37		16 01	
d			14 13				14 26		14 38		15 08				15 13			15 26		15 38		16 02	
Market Harborough d			14 26						14 51						15 26					15 51			
Melton Mowbray 47 d																							
Oakham 47 d																							
Corby d								14 41											15 39				
Kettering ■ a								14 50	15 00										15 48	16 00			
d								14 51	15 01										15 49	16 01			
Wellingborough d								15 00	15 08										15 58	16 08			
Bedford ■ 52 a								15 12	15 22										16 10	16 21			
Luton ■ 52 a								15 27											16 26				
Luton Airport Parkway ■ 52 ✈ a									15 38											16 37			
St Pancras International ⊖52 a			15 25				15 39	15 51	16 11		16 25				16 27			16 41	16 55	17 12		17 12	

	EM	EM	NT	XC	EM	EM	EM	EM	EM		EM	XC	EM	EM	NT	XC	EM	EM	EM		EM	EM	XC	EM
		◇■ ✠	◇	◇■ B ✠	◇■ ✠	◇■ ✠	◇■ ✠	◇ C	◇■ ✠		◇■ ✠	◇■ D ✠		◇■ ✠	◇	◇■ F ✠	◇■ ✠	◇■ ✠	◇■ ✠		◇ C	◇■ ✠	◇■ G ✠	
York ■ 29 d				14 35								14 44				15 35							15 44	
Leeds ■ 31,34 d			14 04									15 11			15 04								16 11	
Wakefield Westgate ■ 31 d												15 23											16 23	
Wakefield Kirkgate ■ 31,34 d			14 22												15 22									
Doncaster ■ 29 d				14 59												15 59								
Manchester Piccadilly 78 d								14 42													15 42			
Sheffield ■ ⇌ d			15 05	15 24	15 29			15 37				15 55			16 05	16 24	16 29				16 37		16 55	
Chesterfield d			15 22	15 36	15 41			15 53				16 07			16 22	16 36	16 41				16 53		17 07	
Derby ■ a				16 19								16 45				17 22							17 46	
d									16 28		16 32											17 32		
Long Eaton d											16 40											17 42		
Alfreton d			15 32					16 05							16 32						17 04			
Langley Mill d			15 40												16 40									
Lincoln 27 d	14 36												15 36											16 34
Newark Castle 27 d	15 06												16 08											17 05
Nottingham ■ ⇌ a	15 30		15 58					16 29					16 30		16 58						17 27			17 30
d	15 35	15 45					16 12						16 33	16 45					17 12					17 33
Beeston d	15 41						16 18						16 39						17 18					17 39
East Midlands Parkway ✈ a	15 50	15 55							16 39		16 44		16 49	16 55								17 45		17 50
d	15 51	15 56							16 39		16 45		16 49	16 56								17 46		17 50
Loughborough d	15 59						16 27				16 52		16 57						17 26			17 54		17 58
Barrow Upon Soar d	16 04												17 02											18 03
Sileby d	16 08												17 06											18 07
Syston d	16 13												17 11											18 12
Leicester a	16 20	16 13			16 25		16 37				17 02		17 18	17 13			17 24		17 36			18 04		18 19
d		16 13			16 26		16 38				17 03			17 13			17 25		17 37			18 04		
Market Harborough d		16 26					16 51							17 26					17 50					
Melton Mowbray 47 d									17 09															
Oakham 47 d									17 23															
Corby d						16 39			17 51									17 39						
Kettering ■ a						16 48	17 00		18 00		17 23							17 48	17 59					
d						16 49	17 01				17 24							17 49	18 00					
Wellingborough d						16 57	17 08											17 57	18 08					
Bedford ■ 52 a						17 10	17 22											18 10	18 21					
Luton ■ 52 a						17 24								18 03				18 26						
Luton Airport Parkway ■ 52 ✈ a							17 37												18 40					
St Pancras International ⊖52 a		17 24			17 39	17 55	18 06				18 14			18 40			18 40	18 55	19 06			19 11		

A From Glasgow Central to Southampton Central
B From Newcastle to Penzance
C From Liverpool Lime Street to Norwich
D From Glasgow Central to Reading
E From Aberdeen to Guildford
F From Newcastle to Plymouth
G From Edinburgh to Reading

For connections to Gatwick Airport refer to Table T052

Table T053-R

Mondays to Fridays

3 September to 21 September

Sheffield - East Midlands - London

	EM	NT	XC	EM	EM		EM	EM	EM	EM	EM	XC	NT	XC	EM		EM	EM	EM	EM	EM	EM	XC	NT
	◇■ ✠	◇	◇■ A ✠	◇■ ✠	◇■ ✠		◇■ ✠	◇■ ✠		◇ B	◇■ ✠	◇■ C ✠	◇	◇■ A ✠	◇■ ✠		◇■ ✠	◇■ ✠	◇■ ✠		◇■ ✠	◇ D	◇■ E ✠	◇
York ■ 29 d			16 05									16 44		17 35									17 45	
Leeds ■ 31,34 d		16 04	16 40									17 10	17 03										18 11	18 03
Wakefield Westgate ■ 31 d			16 52									17 22											18 23	
Wakefield Kirkgate ■ 31,34 d		16 22											17 22											18 21
Doncaster ■ 29 d														17 58										
Manchester Piccadilly 78 d										16 42												17 42		
Sheffield ■ ⇌ d		17 05	17 24	17 29						17 45		17 55	18 03	18 24	18 29							18 53	18 58	19 05
Chesterfield d		17 22	17 36	17 42						18 01		18 07	18 19	18 36	18 42							19 15	19 12	19 21
Derby ■ a			18 18									18 48		19 18									19 50	
d								18 30											19 35					
Long Eaton d								18 39											19 45					
Alfreton d		17 32								18 11			18 30									19 27		19 31
Langley Mill d		17 40											18 37											19 39
Lincoln 27 d									17 26											18 35				
Newark Castle 27 d									17 56											19 03				
Nottingham ■ ⇌ a		18 00							18 30	18 33			18 55							19 30		19 50		19 57
d	17 45						18 12		18 36		18 45							19 12		19 32	19 45			
Beeston d							18 18		18 42									19 18		19 38				
East Midlands Parkway ✈ a	17 56							18 44	18 50		18 55								19 49	19 49	19 55			
d	17 57							18 45	18 52		18 56								19 50	19 50	19 56			
Loughborough d							18 26	18 53	19 00									19 27	19 58	19 58				
Barrow Upon Soar d									19 05											20 03				
Sileby d									19 09											20 07				
Syston d									19 14											20 12				
Leicester a	18 13			18 25			18 36	19 03	19 21		19 13				19 25			19 37	20 08	20 20	20 12			
d	18 14			18 26			18 37	19 03			19 13				19 26			19 38	20 08		20 13			
Market Harborough d	18 27						18 50				19 26							19 51			20 27			
Melton Mowbray 47 d																								
Oakham 47 d																								
Corby d					18 37												19 39							
Kettering ■ a	18 38				18 46		18 59										19 48	20 00						
d	18 39				18 47		19 00										19 49	20 01						
Wellingborough d					18 56		19 08										19 58	20 08						
Bedford ■ 52 a					19 11		19 23										20 10	20 22						
Luton ■ 52 a					19 27												20 26							
Luton Airport Parkway ■ 52 ✈ a							19 41											20 37						
St Pancras International ⊖52 a	19 37			19 40	19 57		20 07	20 11			20 25				20 40		20 51	21 06	21 21		21 25			

	XC		EM	EM	EM	EM	EM	XC	NT	EM	XC		EM	EM	XC	EM	EM	NT	EM	XC	EM		EM	XC
	◇■ F ✠		◇■ ✠	◇■ ✠	◇■ ✠	◇ B		◇■ G ✠	◇	◇■ ✠	◇■ F ✠		◇ D	◇■ ✠	◇■ H ✠	◇■ ✠	◇■ ✠	◇		◇■ I ✠	◇ D		◇■ ✠	◇■ J ✠
York ■ 29 d	18 36							18 45			19 36				19 45					20 36				20 45
Leeds ■ 31,34 d								19 11	19 03						20 11			20 03						21 11
Wakefield Westgate ■ 31 d								19 23							20 23									21 23
Wakefield Kirkgate ■ 31,34 d									19 21									20 21						
Doncaster ■ 29 d	18 59										19 59									21 01				
Manchester Piccadilly 78 d						18 42							19 42								20 42			
Sheffield ■ ⇌ d	19 24		19 29			19 37		19 58	20 02		20 24		20 41	20 50	20 58			21 02		21 29	21 37		22 01	22 01
Chesterfield d	19 36		19 43			19 52		20 10	20 18		20 36		20 56	21 03	21 10			21 18		21 41	21 55		22 13	22 25
Derby ■ a	20 16							20 49			21 18				21 56					22 18			22 58	23 09
d																								
Long Eaton d																								
Alfreton d						20 03			20 28				21 08								22 05			
Langley Mill d									20 36												22 13			
Lincoln 27 d																								
Newark Castle 27 d																								
Nottingham ■ ⇌ a						20 27			20 55				21 33					21 59			22 31			
d					20 12		20 35			20 55							21 29		22 01					
Beeston d					20 18		20 42			21 01									22 07					
East Midlands Parkway ✈ a					20 24		20 50			21 06				21 32					22 15					
d					20 25		20 50			21 07				21 33					22 16					
Loughborough d					20 32		20 58			21 15				21 39			21 46		22 24					
Barrow Upon Soar d							21 03												22 29					
Sileby d							21 07												22 33					
Syston d							21 12												22 38					
Leicester a			20 27		20 43		21 23			21 27				21 50			21 55		22 49					
d			20 27		20 43					21 29				21 51			21 56							
Market Harborough d					20 56					21 42							22 09							
Melton Mowbray 47 d																								
Oakham 47 d																								
Corby d				20 41												21 43								
Kettering ■ a				20 50	21 05					21 51						21 52	22 18							
d				20 51	21 06					21 52							22 19							
Wellingborough d				21 00	21 14					21 59							22 26							
Bedford ■ 52 a				21 12	21 26					22 12							22 39							
Luton ■ 52 a				21 27						22 27							22 56							
Luton Airport Parkway ■ 52 ✈ a					21 42					22 30														
St Pancras International ⊖52 a			21 38	21 55	22 07					22 57				23 06			23 25							

A From Newcastle to Plymouth
B From Liverpool Lime Street to Norwich
C From Glasgow Central to Reading
D From Liverpool Lime Street
E From Edinburgh to Southampton Central
F From Newcastle to Bristol Temple Meads
G From Glasgow Central to Birmingham New Street
H From Edinburgh to Birmingham New Street. ✠ to Leeds
I From Newcastle to Birmingham New Street
J From Glasgow Central to Birmingham New Street. ✠ to Leeds

For connections to Gatwick Airport refer to Table T052

3 September to 21 September

Sheffield - East Midlands - London

	NT ◇	EM	EM ◇■ ✠	EM ◇■ ✠	EM ◇ A
York 29 d					
Leeds 31,34 d	21 03				
Wakefield Westgate 31 d					
Wakefield Kirkgate 31,34 d	21 21				
Doncaster 29 d					
Manchester Piccadilly 78 d					22 28
Sheffield d	22 03			23 21	23 37
Chesterfield d	22 20			23 45	00 02
Derby a				00 36	
d					
Long Eaton d					
Alfreton d	22 30				
Langley Mill d	22 38				
Lincoln 27 d					
Newark Castle 27 d					
Nottingham a	22 57				00 45
d		23 10			
Beeston d		23 15			
East Midlands Parkway ✈ a		23 22			
d		23 23			
Loughborough d		23 31			
Barrow Upon Soar d					
Sileby d					
Syston d					
Leicester a		23 47			
d					
Market Harborough d					
Melton Mowbray 47 d					
Oakham 47 d					
Corby d			22 43		
Kettering a			22 52		
d					
Wellingborough d					
Bedford 52 a					
Luton 52 a					
Luton Airport Parkway 52 ✈ a					
St Pancras International ⊖52 a					

24 September to 5 October

	EM MO ◇ A	EM MX ◇ A	EM ◇■ ✠	EM ◇■ ✠	EM ◇■ ✠	EM 🚌	EM ◇■ ✠	EM 🚌	EM	NT ◇	EM ◇■ ✠	EM ◇■ ⊠	EM 🚌	XC ◇■ B	EM ◇■ ✠	EM ◇■ ✠	EM ◇■ C ⊠	EM 🚌	EM ◇■ ✠	NT ◇	XC ◇■ D ✠	EM
York 29 d																						
Leeds 31,34 d																					05 48	
Wakefield Westgate 31 d																					06 01	
Wakefield Kirkgate 31,34 d																						
Doncaster 29 d																						
Manchester Piccadilly 78 d																						
Sheffield d										05 15		05 31		05 40			06 00			06 03	06 30	
Chesterfield d		00 02								05 30		05 45		05 52			06 13			06 19	06 44	
Derby a														06 35							07 21	
d				05 02	05 18																	
Long Eaton d					05 28																	
Alfreton d										05 45										06 29		
Langley Mill d	00 02									05 53										06 36		
Lincoln 27 d																						
Newark Castle 27 d																						
Nottingham a	00 23	00 45								06 11										07 00		
d							05 32		05 38							06 31			06 52			
Beeston d																06 37			06 58			
East Midlands Parkway ✈ a				05 12			05 42					06 16				06 42			07 03			
d				05 13			05 43					06 17				06 43			07 04			
Loughborough d				05 20			05 51		05 58			06 26					06 54					06 59
Barrow Upon Soar d									06 02													07 04
Sileby d									06 07													07 08
Syston d									06 12													07 14
Leicester a				05 29	05 42		06 03		06 20			06 37				06 56	07 05		07 17			07 22
d			04 45	05 31	05 44		06 04					06 39				06 59	07 07		07 19			
Market Harborough d				05 44	05 57		06 19					06 54				07 12			07 33			
Melton Mowbray 47 d											06 03											
Oakham 47 d											06 15											
Corby d											06 38				07 08							
Kettering a			05 04	05 53	06 06		06 29				06 47	07 04			07 17	07 21	07 28		07 42			
d			05 05	05 55	06 08		06 31				06 48	07 05				07 23	07 29		07 43			
Wellingborough d			05 17	06 03	06 16	06 26	06 39	06 50			06 57	07 14	07 24			07 31	07 38	07 48	07 51			
Bedford 52 a			05 37			07 11		07 35					08 14					08 43				
Luton 52 a				06 25																		
Luton Airport Parkway 52 ✈ a			05 53				07 04					07 44					08 02					
St Pancras International ⊖52 a			06 24	06 54	07 08		07 36				07 55	08 09				08 24	08 29		08 41			

A From Liverpool Lime Street
B To Reading
C The Sheffield Continental
D To Plymouth

For connections to Gatwick Airport refer to Table T052

24 September to 5 October

Sheffield - East Midlands - London

	EM ◇■ ⊠	EM 🚌	EM ◇■ ⊠	EM ◇■ ✠	EM ◇■ A ⊠	EM ◇■ ✠	EM 🚌	EM	NT ◇	EM ◇■ ✠	XC ◇■ B ✠	EM ◇■ C ⊠	EM ◇■ ✠	EM ◇■ D ✠	EM ◇■ E ✠	EM ◇■ F ✠	XC ■ G ✠	NT ◇	XC ◇■ H ✠	EM ◇■ ✠	EM I	EM ◇■ ✠
York 29 d																	06 45		07 26			
Leeds 31,34 d	05 19										06 16			06 33			07 10	07 03				
Wakefield Westgate 31 d	05 32										06 28			06 47			07 23					
Wakefield Kirkgate 31,34 d																		07 22				
Doncaster 29 d	05 57										06 46								07 53			
Manchester Piccadilly 78 d																						
Sheffield d	06 33								07 02		07 18	07 26		07 30	07 46		07 53	08 03	08 18	08 26		
Chesterfield d	06 49								07 17		07 32	07 41		07 46	07 59		08 06	08 21	08 33	08 38		
Derby a											08 16						08 45		09 18			
d					07 23	07 31																
Long Eaton d						07 41																
Alfreton d									07 28					07 57				08 33				
Langley Mill d									07 35					08 05				08 41				
Lincoln 27 d													07 05								07 36	
Newark Castle 27 d													07 30								08 06	
Nottingham a									07 53				07 56	08 24				08 59			08 34	
d			07 11					07 30		07 56			08 05	08 32							08 36	
Beeston d			07 18					07 36					08 11			←					08 42	
East Midlands Parkway ✈ a			07 24		07 33			07 43		08 05				08 42	08 29	08 42					08 49	
d			07 26		07 34			07 44		08 05				08 43	08 30	08 43					08 50	
Loughborough d	07 24				07 42	07 51		07 52					08 22	→	08 42						08 58	
Barrow Upon Soar d								07 57													09 03	
Sileby d								08 01													09 07	
Syston d								08 06													09 12	
Leicester a	07 35		07 41		07 51	08 02		08 18		08 18		08 24	08 32		08 54	08 58				09 18	09 26	
d	07 37		07 43		07 56	08 03				08 21		08 26	08 33		08 55	08 59				09 18		
Market Harborough d			07 58			08 18							08 47			09 13						
Melton Mowbray 47 d																						
Oakham 47 d																						
Corby d				08 02																		09 32
Kettering a	07 58		08 08	08 11	08 16	08 28							08 56									09 41
d	07 59		08 09		08 17	08 29							08 57									09 42
Wellingborough d	08 07	08 14			08 25	08 38	08 48						09 04									09 51
Bedford 52 a		09 09					09 38															10 12
Luton 52 a																						10 26
Luton Airport Parkway 52 ✈ a													09 30									
St Pancras International ⊖52 a	08 55		09 08		09 12	09 27				09 38		09 41	09 55		10 03	10 11				10 25		10 51

	EM ◇■ ✠	EM ◇ J	EM ◇■ ✠	XC ◇■ K ✠	EM	EM ◇■ ✠	NT ◇	XC ◇■ H ✠	EM ◇■ ✠	EM ◇■ ✠	EM ◇■ ✠	EM ◇ J	EM ◇■ ✠	XC ◇■ L ✠	EM	EM ◇■ ✠	NT ◇	XC ◇■ M ✠	EM ◇■ ✠	EM ◇■ ✠	EM ◇■ ✠
York 29 d				07 43				08 27						08 44				09 36			
Leeds 31,34 d				08 11			08 04							09 11			09 04				
Wakefield Westgate 31 d				08 23										09 23							
Wakefield Kirkgate 31,34 d							08 22										09 22				
Doncaster 29 d								08 53										10 00			
Manchester Piccadilly 78 d		07 42										08 43									
Sheffield d		08 38		08 54			09 06	09 24	09 29			09 37		09 55			10 05	10 24	10 33		
Chesterfield d		08 54		09 08			09 22	09 36	09 42			09 51		10 07			10 22	10 40	10 46		
Derby a				09 44				10 19						10 46				11 18			
d			09 31										10 31								
Long Eaton d			09 38										10 40								
Alfreton d		09 05					09 33					10 02					10 32				
Langley Mill d							09 40										10 40				
Lincoln 27 d					08 36										09 37						
Newark Castle 27 d					09 08										10 07						
Nottingham a		09 27			09 32		09 59					10 28			10 32		10 58				
d	09 12				09 36	09 45					10 12				10 36	10 45					11 12
Beeston d	09 18				09 42						10 18				10 42						11 18
East Midlands Parkway ✈ a			09 43		09 50	09 55							10 44		10 49	10 55					
d			09 44		09 50	09 56							10 45		10 50	10 56					
Loughborough d	09 26		09 50		09 59						10 27		10 52		10 58						11 27
Barrow Upon Soar d					10 03										11 03						
Sileby d					10 07										11 07						
Syston d					10 12										11 12						
Leicester a	09 36		10 00		10 24	10 13			10 25		10 37		11 02		11 23	11 13			11 25		11 37
d	09 38		10 02			10 13			10 26		10 38		11 03			11 13			11 25		11 38
Market Harborough d	09 51					10 26					10 51					11 26					11 51
Melton Mowbray 47 d																					
Oakham 47 d																					
Corby d										10 41										11 41	
Kettering a	10 00									10 50	11 00									11 50	12 00
d	10 01									10 51	11 01									11 51	12 01
Wellingborough d	10 08									10 59	11 08									12 00	12 08
Bedford 52 a	10 22									11 12	11 22									12 12	12 22
Luton 52 a										11 27										12 27	
Luton Airport Parkway 52 ✈ a	10 38										11 38										12 38
St Pancras International ⊖52 a	11 05		11 08			11 24			11 36	11 52	12 08		12 13			12 24			12 36	12 51	13 06

A The Sheffield Continental
B To Plymouth
C The Master Cutler
D To St Pancras International
E The South Yorkshireman
F From Leeds
G To Reading
H From Newcastle to Plymouth
I From Sleaford
J From Liverpool Lime Street to Norwich
K From Newcastle to Southampton Central
L From Edinburgh to Reading
M From Edinburgh to Plymouth

For connections to Gatwick Airport refer to Table T052

Table T053-R

Mondays to Fridays
24 September to 5 October

Sheffield - East Midlands - London

	EM ◇ A	EM ◇■	XC ◇■ B	EM	EM ◇■	NT ◇	XC ◇■ C	EM ◇■	EM ◇■	EM ◇■	EM ◇ A	EM ◇■	XC ◇■ D	EM	EM ◇■	NT ◇	XC ◇■ C	EM ◇■	EM ◇■	EM ◇■	EM ◇ A	EM ◇■
York 29 d			09 44				10 35						10 44				11 35					
Leeds 31,34 d			10 11			10 04							11 11			11 04						
Wakefield Westgate 31 d			10 23										11 23									
Wakefield Kirkgate 31,34 d						10 22										11 22						
Doncaster 29 d							10 59										11 59					
Manchester Piccadilly 78 d	09 42										10 42										11 42	
Sheffield d	10 38		10 55			11 05	11 24	11 29			11 38		11 55			12 05	12 24	12 29			12 38	
Chesterfield d	10 54		11 07			11 22	11 38	11 43			11 54		12 07			12 22	12 36	12 41			12 52	
Derby a			11 46				12 16						12 44				13 17					
d		11 31										12 31										13 31
Long Eaton d		11 40										12 40										13 40
Alfreton d	11 05					11 33					12 05					12 32					13 03	
Langley Mill d						11 42										12 40						
Lincoln 27 d				10 36										11 40								
Newark Castle 27 d				11 07										12 07								
Nottingham a	11 27			11 32		12 00					12 29			12 30		13 00					13 27	
d				11 35	11 45					12 12				12 35	12 45					13 12		
Beeston d				11 41						12 18				12 41						13 18		
East Midlands Parkway a		11 44		11 49	11 55							12 44		12 49	12 55							13 44
d		11 45		11 50	11 56							12 45		12 50	12 56							13 45
Loughborough d		11 52		11 58						12 27		12 52		12 58						13 27		13 52
Barrow Upon Soar d				12 03										13 03								
Sileby d				12 07										13 07								
Syston d				12 12										13 12								
Leicester a		12 02		12 23	12 13			12 25		12 37		13 02		13 23	13 13			13 25		13 37		14 02
d		12 03			12 13			12 26		12 38		13 03			13 13			13 26		13 38		14 03
Market Harborough d					12 26					12 51					13 26					13 51		
Melton Mowbray 47 d																						
Oakham 47 d																						
Corby d									12 41										13 41			
Kettering a									12 50	13 00									13 50	14 00		
d									12 51	13 01									13 51	14 01		
Wellingborough d									13 00	13 08									14 00	14 09		
Bedford 52 a									13 12	13 22									14 12	14 22		
Luton 52 a									13 27										14 27			
Luton Airport Parkway 52 a										13 38										14 38		
St Pancras International 52 a		13 08			13 25			13 36	13 51	14 07		14 10			14 25			14 38	14 51	15 05		15 08

	XC ◇■ B	EM	EM ◇■	NT ◇	XC ◇■ E	EM ◇■	EM ◇■	EM ◇■	EM ◇ A	EM ◇■	XC ◇■ F	EM	EM ◇■	NT ◇	XC ◇■ E	EM ◇■	EM ◇■	EM ◇■	EM ◇ A	EM ◇■	XC ◇■ G
York 29 d	11 44				12 35						12 44				13 35						13 44
Leeds 31,34 d	12 11			12 04							13 11			13 04							14 11
Wakefield Westgate 31 d	12 23										13 23										14 23
Wakefield Kirkgate 31,34 d				12 22										13 23							
Doncaster 29 d					12 59										13 59						
Manchester Piccadilly 78 d									12 42										13 42		
Sheffield d	12 55			13 05	13 24	13 29			13 37		13 55			14 05	14 24	14 29			14 38		14 55
Chesterfield d	13 07			13 22	13 36	13 41			13 52		14 07			14 22	14 36	14 41			14 52		15 07
Derby a	13 44				14 17						14 45				15 19						15 45
d										14 31										15 30	
Long Eaton d										14 43										15 40	
Alfreton d				13 32					14 03					14 32					15 03		
Langley Mill d				13 40										14 40							
Lincoln 27 d		12 34										13 37									
Newark Castle 27 d		13 05										14 07									
Nottingham a		13 32		13 58					14 27			14 32		14 58					15 28		
d		13 35	13 45					14 12				14 35	14 45					15 12			
Beeston d		13 41						14 18				14 41						15 18			
East Midlands Parkway a		13 49	13 55							14 47		14 49	14 55							15 43	
d		13 50	13 56							14 48		14 50	14 56							15 44	
Loughborough d		13 58						14 27		14 55		14 58						15 27		15 52	
Barrow Upon Soar d		14 03										15 03									
Sileby d		14 07										15 07									
Syston d		14 12										15 12									
Leicester a		14 23	14 13			14 25		14 37		15 07		15 23	15 13			15 25		15 37		16 01	
d			14 13			14 26		14 38		15 08			15 13			15 26		15 38		16 02	
Market Harborough d			14 26					14 51					15 26					15 51			
Melton Mowbray 47 d																					
Oakham 47 d																					
Corby d							14 41										15 39				
Kettering a							14 50	15 00									15 48	16 00			
d							14 51	15 01									15 49	16 01			
Wellingborough d							15 00	15 08									15 58	16 08			
Bedford 52 a							15 12	15 22									16 10	16 21			
Luton 52 a							15 27										16 26				
Luton Airport Parkway 52 a								15 38										16 37			
St Pancras International 52 a			15 25			15 39	15 51	16 11		16 25			16 27			16 41	16 55	17 12		17 12	

A From Liverpool Lime Street to Norwich
B From Glasgow Central to Southampton Central
C From Newcastle to Plymouth
D From Dundee to Reading
E From Newcastle to Penzance
F From Glasgow Central to Reading
G From Aberdeen to Guildford

For connections to Gatwick Airport refer to Table T052

Table T053-R

Mondays to Fridays
24 September to 5 October

Sheffield - East Midlands - London

	EM	EM ◇■	NT ◇	XC ◇■ A	EM ◇■	EM ◇■	EM ◇■	EM ◇ B	EM ◇■	EM ◇■	XC ◇■ C	EM	EM ◇■	NT ◇	XC ◇■ D	EM ◇■	EM ◇■	EM ◇■	EM ◇ B	EM ◇■	XC ◇■ E	EM
York 29 d				14 35							14 44				15 35						15 44	
Leeds 31,34 d			14 04								15 11			15 04							16 11	
Wakefield Westgate 31 d											15 23										16 23	
Wakefield Kirkgate 31,34 d			14 22											15 22								
Doncaster 29 d				14 59											15 59							
Manchester Piccadilly 78 d								14 42											15 42			
Sheffield d			15 05	15 24	15 29			15 37			15 55			16 05	16 24	16 29			16 37		16 55	
Chesterfield d			15 22	15 36	15 41			15 53			16 07			16 22	16 36	16 41			16 53		17 07	
Derby a				16 19							16 45				17 22						17 46	
d									16 28	16 32										17 32		
Long Eaton d										16 40										17 42		
Alfreton d			15 32					16 05						16 32					17 04			
Langley Mill d			15 40											16 40								
Lincoln 27 d	14 36											15 36										16 34
Newark Castle 27 d	15 06											16 08										17 05
Nottingham a	15 32		15 58					16 29				16 32		16 58					17 27			17 32
d	15 35	15 45					16 12					16 33	16 45					17 12				17 33
Beeston d	15 41						16 18					16 39						17 18				17 39
East Midlands Parkway a	15 49	15 55							16 39	16 44		16 49	16 55							17 45		17 50
d	15 50	15 56							16 39	16 45		16 49	16 56							17 46		17 50
Loughborough d	15 58						16 27			16 52		16 57						17 26		17 54		17 58
Barrow Upon Soar d	16 03											17 02										18 03
Sileby d	16 07											17 06										18 07
Syston d	16 12											17 11										18 12
Leicester a	16 22	16 13			16 25		16 37			17 02		17 20	17 13			17 24		17 36		18 04		18 21
d		16 13			16 26		16 38			17 03			17 13			17 25		17 37		18 04		
Market Harborough d		16 26					16 51						17 26					17 50				
Melton Mowbray 47 d									17 09													
Oakham 47 d									17 23													
Corby d						16 39			17 51								17 39					
Kettering a						16 48	17 00		18 00	17 23							17 48	17 59				
d						16 49	17 01			17 24							17 49	18 00				
Wellingborough d						16 57	17 08										17 57	18 08				
Bedford 52 a						17 10	17 22										18 10	18 21				
Luton 52 a						17 24							18 03				18 26					
Luton Airport Parkway 52 a							17 37											18 40				
St Pancras International 52 a		17 24			17 39	17 55	18 06			18 14			18 40			18 40	18 55	19 06		19 11		

	EM ◇■	NT ◇	XC ◇■ D	EM ◇■	EM ◇■	EM ◇■	EM ◇■	EM	EM ◇ B	EM ◇■	XC ◇■ C	NT ◇	XC ◇■ D	EM ◇■	EM ◇■	EM ◇■	EM ◇■	EM	EM ◇■	EM ◇ F	XC ◇■ G	NT ◇
York 29 d			16 05								16 44		17 35								17 45	
Leeds 31,34 d		16 04	16 40								17 10	17 03									18 11	18 03
Wakefield Westgate 31 d			16 52								17 22										18 23	
Wakefield Kirkgate 31,34 d		16 22										17 22										18 21
Doncaster 29 d													17 58									
Manchester Piccadilly 78 d									16 42											17 42		
Sheffield d		17 05	17 24	17 29					17 45		17 55	18 03	18 24	18 29						18 53	18 58	19 05
Chesterfield d		17 22	17 36	17 42					18 01		18 07	18 19	18 36	18 42						19 15	19 12	19 21
Derby a			18 18								18 48		19 18								19 50	
d							18 30										19 35					
Long Eaton d							18 39										19 45					
Alfreton d		17 32							18 11			18 30								19 27		19 31
Langley Mill d		17 40										18 37										19 39
Lincoln 27 d								17 26										18 35				
Newark Castle 27 d								17 56										19 03				
Nottingham a		18 00						18 32	18 33			18 55						19 32		19 50		19 57
d	17 45					18 12		18 36		18 45						19 12		19 32	19 45			
Beeston d						18 18		18 42								19 18		19 38				
East Midlands Parkway a	17 56						18 44	18 49		18 55							19 49	19 49	19 55			
d	17 57						18 45	18 52		18 56							19 50	19 50	19 56			
Loughborough d						18 26	18 53	19 00								19 27	19 58	19 58				
Barrow Upon Soar d								19 05										20 03				
Sileby d								19 09										20 07				
Syston d								19 14										20 12				
Leicester a	18 13			18 25		18 36	19 03	19 23		19 13				19 25		19 37	20 08	20 24	20 12			
d	18 14			18 26		18 37	19 03			19 13				19 26		19 38	20 08		20 13			
Market Harborough d	18 27					18 50				19 26						19 51			20 27			
Melton Mowbray 47 d																						
Oakham 47 d																						
Corby d					18 37										19 39							
Kettering a	18 38				18 46	18 59									19 48	20 00						
d	18 39				18 47	19 00									19 49	20 01						
Wellingborough d					18 56	19 08									19 58	20 08						
Bedford 52 a					19 11	19 23									20 10	20 22						
Luton 52 a					19 27										20 26							
Luton Airport Parkway 52 a						19 41										20 37						
St Pancras International 52 a	19 37			19 40	19 57	20 07	20 11			20 25				20 40	20 51	21 06	21 21		21 25			

A From Newcastle to Penzance
B From Liverpool Lime Street to Norwich
C From Glasgow Central to Reading
D From Newcastle to Plymouth
E From Edinburgh to Reading
F From Liverpool Lime Street
G From Edinburgh to Southampton Central

For connections to Gatwick Airport refer to Table T052

Table T053-R

Sheffield - East Midlands - London

Mondays to Fridays
24 September to 5 October

	XC	EM	EM	EM	EM	EM	XC	NT	EM	XC	EM	EM	XC	EM	EM	NT	EM	XC	EM	EM	XC
	◇■ A 🍴	◇■ 🍴	◇■ 🍴	◇■ 🍴	◇ B		◇■ C 🍴	◇	◇■ 🍴	◇■ A 🍴	◇ D	◇■ 🍴	◇■ E 🍴	◇■ 🍴	◇■ 🍴	◇		◇■ F 🍴	◇ D	◇■ 🍴	◇■ G 🍴
York ■ 29 d	18 36						18 45			19 36			19 45					20 36			20 45
Leeds ■ 31,34 d							19 11	19 03					20 11			20 03					21 11
Wakefield Westgate ■ 31 d							19 23						20 23								21 23
Wakefield Kirkgate ■ 31,34 d								19 21								20 21					
Doncaster ■ 29 d	18 59									19 59								21 01			
Manchester Piccadilly 78 d					18 42						19 42								20 42		
Sheffield ■ ⇌ d	19 24	19 29			19 37		19 58	20 02		20 24	20 41	20 50	20 58			21 02		21 29	21 37	22 01	22 01
Chesterfield d	19 36	19 43			19 52		20 10	20 18		20 36	20 56	21 03	21 10			21 18		21 41	21 55	22 13	22 25
Derby ■ a	20 16						20 49			21 18			21 56					22 18		22 58	23 09
d																					
Long Eaton d																					
Alfreton d					20 03			20 28			21 08								22 05		
Langley Mill d								20 36											22 13		
Lincoln 27 d																					
Newark Castle 27 d																					
Nottingham ■ ⇌ a					20 27			20 55			21 33					21 59			22 31		
d				20 12		20 35			20 55						21 29		22 01				
Beeston d				20 18		20 42			21 01								22 07				
East Midlands Parkway ✈ a				20 24		20 50			21 06			21 32					22 15				
d				20 25		20 50			21 07			21 33					22 16				
Loughborough d				20 32		20 58			21 15			21 39			21 46		22 24				
Barrow Upon Soar d						21 03											22 29				
Sileby d						21 07											22 33				
Syston d						21 12											22 38				
Leicester a		20 27		20 43		21 23			21 27			21 50			21 55		22 49				
d		20 27		20 43					21 29			21 51			21 56						
Market Harborough d				20 56					21 42						22 09						
Melton Mowbray 47 d																					
Oakham 47 d																					
Corby d			20 41											21 43							
Kettering ■ a			20 50	21 05					21 51					21 52	22 18						
d			20 51	21 06					21 52						22 19						
Wellingborough d			21 00	21 14					21 59						22 26						
Bedford ■ 52 a			21 12	21 26					22 12						22 39						
Luton ■ 52 a			21 27						22 27						22 56						
Luton Airport Parkway ■ 52 ✈ a				21 42					22 30												
St Pancras International ⊖52 a		21 38	21 55	22 07					22 57			23 06			23 25						

	NT	EM	EM	EM	EM
	◇		◇■ 🍴	◇■ 🍴	◇ D
York ■ 29 d					
Leeds ■ 31,34 d	21 03				
Wakefield Westgate ■ 31 d					
Wakefield Kirkgate ■ 31,34 d	21 21				
Doncaster ■ 29 d					
Manchester Piccadilly 78 d					22 28
Sheffield ■ ⇌ d	22 03			23 21	23 37
Chesterfield d	22 20			23 45	00 02
Derby ■ a				00 36	
d					
Long Eaton d					
Alfreton d	22 30				
Langley Mill d	22 38				
Lincoln 27 d					
Newark Castle 27 d					
Nottingham ■ ⇌ a	22 57				00 45
d		23 10			
Beeston d		23 15			
East Midlands Parkway ✈ a		23 22			
d		23 23			
Loughborough d		23 31			
Barrow Upon Soar d					
Sileby d					
Syston d					
Leicester a		23 47			
d					
Market Harborough d					
Melton Mowbray 47 d					
Oakham 47 d					
Corby d			22 43		
Kettering ■ a			22 52		
d					
Wellingborough d					
Bedford ■ 52 a					
Luton ■ 52 a					
Luton Airport Parkway ■ 52 ✈ a					
St Pancras International ⊖52 a					

A From Newcastle to Bristol Temple Meads
B From Liverpool Lime Street to Norwich
C From Glasgow Central to Birmingham New Street
D From Liverpool Lime Street
E From Edinburgh to Birmingham New Street. 🍴 to Leeds
F From Newcastle to Birmingham New Street
G From Glasgow Central to Birmingham New Street. 🍴 to Leeds

For connections to Gatwick Airport refer to Table T052

Table T053-R

Sheffield - East Midlands - London

Mondays to Fridays
8 October to 7 December

	EM MO	EM MX	EM	EM	EM	EM	EM	EM	EM	NT	EM	EM	EM	XC	EM	EM	EM	EM	EM	NT	EM	EM
	◇ A	◇ A	◇■ 🍴	◇■ 🍴	◇■ 🍴	🚌	◇■ 🍴	🚌		◇	◇■ 🍴	◇■ ⊠	🚌	◇■ B	◇■ 🍴	◇■ 🍴	◇■ C ⊠	🚌	◇■ 🍴	◇		◇■ ⊠
York ■ 29 d																						
Leeds ■ 31,34 d																						05 19
Wakefield Westgate ■ 31 d																						05 32
Wakefield Kirkgate ■ 31,34 d																						
Doncaster ■ 29 d																						05 57
Manchester Piccadilly 78 d																						
Sheffield ■ ⇌ d										05 15		05 31		05 59			06 00			06 03		06 25
Chesterfield d		00 02								05 30		05 44		06 26			06 13			06 19		06 40
Derby ■ a												06 03		06 44			06 33					07 03
d				05 02	05 19							06 05					06 34					07 05
Long Eaton d					05 27												06 44					
Alfreton d										05 45										06 29		
Langley Mill d	00 02									05 53										06 36		
Lincoln 27 d																						
Newark Castle 27 d																						
Nottingham ■ ⇌ a	00 23	00 45								06 11										07 00		
d							05 32		05 38							06 31			06 52			
Beeston d																06 37			06 58			
East Midlands Parkway ✈ a				05 12			05 42					06 16				06 42			07 03			
d				05 13			05 43					06 17				06 43			07 04			
Loughborough d				05 20			05 51		05 58			06 26					06 54				06 59	07 22
Barrow Upon Soar d									06 02												07 04	
Sileby d									06 07												07 08	
Syston d									06 12												07 14	
Leicester a				05 29	05 42		06 03		06 20			06 37				06 56	07 05		07 17		07 22	07 33
d			04 45	05 31	05 44		06 04					06 39				06 59	07 07		07 19			07 36
Market Harborough d				05 44	05 57		06 19					06 54				07 12			07 33			
Melton Mowbray 47 d											06 03											
Oakham 47 d											06 15											
Corby d											06 38				07 08							
Kettering ■ a			05 04	05 53	06 06		06 29				06 47	07 04			07 17	07 21	07 28		07 42			07 57
d			05 05	05 55	06 08		06 31				06 48	07 05				07 23	07 29		07 43			07 59
Wellingborough d			05 17	06 03	06 16	06 26	06 39	06 50			06 57	07 14	07 24			07 31	07 38	07 48	07 51			08 07
Bedford ■ 52 a			05 37			07 11		07 35					08 14					08 43				
Luton ■ 52 a				06 25																		
Luton Airport Parkway ■ 52 ✈ a			05 53				07 04					07 43					08 02					
St Pancras International ⊖52 a			06 24	06 54	07 08		07 36				07 55	08 09				08 24	08 28		08 41			08 55

	EM	EM	EM	EM	XC	EM	EM	EM	NT	EM	XC	EM	EM	EM	EM	EM	XC	NT	XC	EM	EM	EM
	🚌	◇■ ⊠	◇■ 🍴	◇■ C ⊠	◇■ D 🍴	◇■ 🍴	🚌		◇	◇■ 🍴	◇■ E 🍴	◇■ F 🍴	◇■ G ⊠	◇■ 🍴	◇■ H 🍴	◇■ I 🍴	◇■ J 🍴	◇	■ ■ K 🍴	◇■ 🍴	L	◇■ 🍴
York ■ 29 d																	06 45		07 26			
Leeds ■ 31,34 d					06 11						06 16	06 33					07 10	07 03				
Wakefield Westgate ■ 31 d					06 23						06 28	06 47					07 23					
Wakefield Kirkgate ■ 31,34 d																		07 22				
Doncaster ■ 29 d											06 46								07 53			
Manchester Piccadilly 78 d																						
Sheffield ■ ⇌ d				06 49	06 53				07 02		07 18	07 24	07 29		07 46		07 53	08 03	08 18	08 26		
Chesterfield d				07 01	07 06				07 17		07 30	07 37	07 42		07 59		08 06	08 21	08 30	08 38		
Derby ■ a				07 21	07 25						07 48		08 00		08 17		08 26		08 46	08 57		
d				07 23		07 31							08 01		08 19					08 57		
Long Eaton d						07 41									08 29							
Alfreton d									07 28			07 48						08 33				
Langley Mill d									07 35			07 57						08 41				
Lincoln 27 d														07 05							07 36	
Newark Castle 27 d														07 30							08 06	
Nottingham ■ ⇌ a									07 53			08 24		07 56				08 59			08 34	
d		07 11						07 30		07 56		08 32		08 05							08 36	
Beeston d		07 18						07 36						08 11		←					08 42	
East Midlands Parkway ✈ a		07 24		07 33				07 43		08 05		08 42			08 33	08 42					08 49	
d		07 26		07 34				07 44		08 05		08 43			08 34	08 43					08 50	
Loughborough d				07 42		07 51		07 52				→		08 21	08 41						08 58	
Barrow Upon Soar d								07 57													09 03	
Sileby d								08 01													09 07	
Syston d								08 06													09 12	
Leicester a		07 41		07 51		08 02		08 18		08 18			08 24	08 31	08 53	08 58				09 18	09 23	
d		07 43		07 56		08 03				08 21			08 26	08 32	08 55	08 59				09 18		
Market Harborough d		07 58				08 18								08 46		09 13						
Melton Mowbray 47 d																						
Oakham 47 d																						
Corby d			08 02																			09 32
Kettering ■ a		08 08	08 11	08 16		08 28								08 55								09 41
d		08 09		08 17		08 29								08 56								09 42
Wellingborough d	08 14			08 25		08 38	08 48							09 03								09 51
Bedford ■ 52 a	09 09						09 38															10 12
Luton ■ 52 a																						10 26
Luton Airport Parkway ■ 52 ✈ a														09 30								
St Pancras International ⊖52 a		09 08		09 12		09 27				09 38			09 41	09 55	10 03	10 11				10 25		10 51

A From Liverpool Lime Street
B To Reading
C The Sheffield Continental
D To Plymouth
E To Southampton Central
F To St Pancras International
G The Master Cutler
H The South Yorkshireman
I From Leeds
J To Plymouth. 🍴 from Leeds
K From Newcastle to Reading
L From Sleaford

For connections to Gatwick Airport refer to Table T052

Table T053-R

Mondays to Fridays

8 October to 7 December

Sheffield - East Midlands - London

	EM	EM	XC	EM	EM	EM	NT	XC	EM	EM	EM	EM	XC	EM	EM	EM	NT	XC	EM	EM	EM
	◇1	◇	◇1	◇1		◇1	◇	◇1	◇1	◇1	◇1	◇	◇1	◇1		◇1	◇	◇1	◇1	◇1	◇1
		A	B					C				A	D					E			
	☕		☕	☕		☕		☕	☕	☕	☕		☕	☕		☕		☕	☕	☕	☕
York 29 d			07 43					08 27					08 44					09 35			
Leeds 31,34 d			08 11				08 04						09 11				09 04				
Wakefield Westgate 31 d			08 23										09 23								
Wakefield Kirkgate 31,34 d							08 22										09 22				
Doncaster 29 d								08 53										09 59			
Manchester Piccadilly 78 d		07 42										08 43									
Sheffield d		08 38	08 54	08 59			09 06	09 24	09 29			09 37	09 55	10 00			10 05	10 24	10 29		
Chesterfield d		08 54	09 07	09 11			09 22		09 41			09 51	10 08	10 13			10 22		10 41		
Derby a			09 24	09 30				09 51	10 00				10 27	10 32				10 51	11 00		
d				09 30					10 04					10 33					11 02		
Long Eaton d				09 38										10 40							
Alfreton d		09 05					09 33					10 01					10 32				
Langley Mill d							09 40										10 40				
Lincoln 27 d					08 36										09 37						
Newark Castle 27 d					09 08										10 07						
Nottingham a		09 28			09 32		09 59					10 26			10 32		10 58				
d	09 12				09 36	09 45					10 12				10 36	10 45					11 12
Beeston d	09 18				09 42						10 18				10 42						11 18
East Midlands Parkway a				09 43	09 50	09 55								10 45	10 49	10 55					
d				09 44	09 50	09 56								10 46	10 50	10 56					
Loughborough d	09 26			09 50	09 59						10 27			10 52	10 58						11 27
Barrow Upon Soar d					10 03										11 03						
Sileby d					10 07										11 07						
Syston d					10 12										11 12						
Leicester a	09 36			10 00	10 24	10 13			10 25		10 37			11 02	11 23	11 13			11 22		11 37
d	09 38			10 02		10 13			10 26		10 38			11 03		11 13			11 24		11 38
Market Harborough d	09 51					10 26					10 51					11 26					11 51
Melton Mowbray 47 d																					
Oakham 47 d																					
Corby d										10 41										11 41	
Kettering a	10 00									10 50	11 00									11 50	12 00
d	10 01									10 51	11 01									11 51	12 01
Wellingborough d	10 08									10 59	11 08									12 00	12 08
Bedford 52 a	10 22									11 12	11 22									12 12	12 22
Luton 52 a										11 27										12 27	
Luton Airport Parkway 52 a	10 38										11 38										12 38
St Pancras International 52 a	11 05			11 08		11 24			11 36	11 52	12 08			12 09		12 24			12 36	12 51	13 06

	EM	XC	EM	EM	EM	NT	XC	EM	EM	EM	EM	XC	EM	EM	EM	NT	XC	EM	EM	EM	EM	XC
	◇	◇1	◇1		◇1	◇	◇1	◇1	◇1	◇1	◇	◇1	◇1		◇1	◇	◇1	◇1	◇1	◇1	◇	◇1
	A	F					C				A	G					H				A	F
		☕	☕		☕		☕	☕	☕	☕		☕	☕		☕		☕	☕	☕	☕		☕
York 29 d		09 44					10 35					10 44					11 35					11 44
Leeds 31,34 d		10 11				10 04						11 11				11 04						12 11
Wakefield Westgate 31 d		10 23										11 23										12 23
Wakefield Kirkgate 31,34 d						10 22										11 22						
Doncaster 29 d							10 59										11 59					
Manchester Piccadilly 78 d	09 42										10 42										11 42	
Sheffield d	10 37	10 55	11 00			11 05	11 24	11 29			11 38	11 55	12 00			12 05	12 24	12 29			12 38	12 55
Chesterfield d	10 54	11 07	11 12			11 22		11 41			11 54	12 08	12 13			12 22		12 41			12 52	13 07
Derby a		11 24	11 31				11 52	12 00				12 27	12 32				12 51	13 00				13 25
d			11 32					12 04					12 34					13 03				
Long Eaton d			11 40										12 41									
Alfreton d	11 05					11 32					12 05					12 32					13 03	
Langley Mill d						11 40										12 40						
Lincoln 27 d				10 36										11 40								
Newark Castle 27 d				11 07										12 07								
Nottingham a	11 26			11 32		11 58					12 29			12 30		12 58					13 27	
d				11 36	11 45					12 12				12 35	12 45					13 12		
Beeston d				11 42						12 18				12 41						13 18		
East Midlands Parkway a			11 44	11 49	11 55								12 46	12 49	12 55							
d			11 45	11 50	11 56								12 47	12 50	12 56							
Loughborough d			11 52	11 58						12 27			12 53	12 58						13 27		
Barrow Upon Soar d				12 03										13 03								
Sileby d				12 07										13 07								
Syston d				12 12										13 12								
Leicester a			12 02	12 23	12 13			12 25		12 37			13 03	13 23	13 13			13 25		13 37		
d			12 03		12 13			12 26		12 38			13 04		13 13			13 26		13 38		
Market Harborough d					12 26					12 51					13 26					13 51		
Melton Mowbray 47 d																						
Oakham 47 d																						
Corby d									12 41										13 41			
Kettering a									12 50	13 00									13 50	14 00		
d									12 51	13 01									13 51	14 01		
Wellingborough d									13 00	13 08									14 00	14 09		
Bedford 52 a									13 12	13 22									14 12	14 22		
Luton 52 a									13 27										14 27			
Luton Airport Parkway 52 a										13 38										14 38		
St Pancras International 52 a			13 08		13 25			13 36	13 51	14 07			14 11		14 25			14 38	14 51	15 05		

A From Liverpool Lime Street to Norwich
B From Newcastle to Plymouth
C From Newcastle to Southampton Central
D From Edinburgh to Plymouth
E From Edinburgh to Reading
F From Glasgow Central to Plymouth
G From Dundee to Plymouth
H From Newcastle to Reading

For connections to Gatwick Airport refer to Table T052

Table T053-R

Mondays to Fridays

8 October to 7 December

Sheffield - East Midlands - London

	EM	EM	EM	NT	XC	EM	EM	EM	EM	XC	EM	EM	EM	NT	XC	EM	EM	EM	EM	XC	EM
	◇1		◇1	◇	◇1	◇1	◇1	◇1	◇	◇1	◇1		◇1	◇	◇1	◇1	◇1	◇1	◇	◇1	◇1
					A				B	C					D				B	E	
	☕		☕		☕	☕	☕	☕		☕	☕		☕		☕	☕	☕	☕		☕	☕
York 29 d					12 35					12 44					13 35					13 44	
Leeds 31,34 d				12 04						13 11				13 04						14 11	
Wakefield Westgate 31 d										13 23										14 23	
Wakefield Kirkgate 31,34 d				12 22										13 23							
Doncaster 29 d					12 59										13 59						
Manchester Piccadilly 78 d									12 42										13 42		
Sheffield d	13 00			13 05	13 24	13 29			13 37	13 55	13 59			14 05	14 24	14 29			14 38	14 55	15 00
Chesterfield d	13 12			13 22		13 41			13 52	14 07	14 13			14 22		14 41			14 52	15 07	15 12
Derby a	13 29				13 51	14 00				14 24	14 32				14 51	15 00				15 24	15 31
d	13 32					14 03					14 33					15 04					15 31
Long Eaton d	13 40										14 43										15 40
Alfreton d				13 32					14 03					14 32					15 03		
Langley Mill d				13 40										14 40							
Lincoln 27 d		12 34										13 37									
Newark Castle 27 d		13 05										14 07									
Nottingham a		13 32		13 58					14 27			14 32		14 58					15 28		
d		13 36	13 45					14 12				14 36	14 45					15 12			
Beeston d		13 42						14 18				14 42						15 18			
East Midlands Parkway a	13 44	13 49	13 55								14 47	14 49	14 55								15 43
d	13 45	13 50	13 56								14 48	14 50	14 56								15 44
Loughborough d	13 52	13 58						14 27			14 55	14 58						15 27			15 52
Barrow Upon Soar d		14 03										15 03									
Sileby d		14 07										15 07									
Syston d		14 12										15 12									
Leicester a	14 02	14 23	14 13			14 25		14 37			15 07	15 23	15 13			15 25		15 37			16 01
d	14 03		14 13			14 26		14 38			15 08		15 13			15 26		15 38			16 02
Market Harborough d			14 26					14 51					15 26					15 51			
Melton Mowbray 47 d																					
Oakham 47 d																					
Corby d							14 41										15 39				
Kettering a							14 50	15 00									15 48	16 00			
d							14 51	15 01									15 49	16 01			
Wellingborough d							15 00	15 08									15 58	16 08			
Bedford 52 a							15 12	15 22									16 10	16 21			
Luton 52 a							15 27										16 26				
Luton Airport Parkway 52 a								15 38										16 37			
St Pancras International 52 a	15 08		15 25			15 39	15 51	16 11			16 25		16 27			16 41	16 55	17 12			17 12

	EM	EM	NT	XC	EM	EM	EM	EM	XC	EM	EM	EM	EM	NT	XC	EM	EM	EM	EM	XC	EM	EM
		◇1	◇	◇1	◇1	◇1	◇1	◇	◇1	◇1	◇1		◇1	◇	◇1	◇1	◇1	◇1	◇	◇1	◇1	
				F				B	C						D				B	FX G		
		☕		☕	☕	☕	☕		☕	☕	☕		☕		☕	☕	☕	☕		☕	☕	
York 29 d				14 35					14 44						15 35					15 44		
Leeds 31,34 d			14 04						15 11					15 04						16 11		
Wakefield Westgate 31 d									15 23											16 23		
Wakefield Kirkgate 31,34 d			14 22											15 22								
Doncaster 29 d				14 59											15 59							
Manchester Piccadilly 78 d								14 42											15 42			
Sheffield d			15 05	15 24	15 29			15 37	15 55		16 00			16 05	16 24	16 29			16 37	16 55	17 00	
Chesterfield d			15 22		15 41			15 53	16 07		16 12			16 22		16 41			16 53	17 07	17 12	
Derby a				15 51	16 00				16 24		16 31				16 51	17 00				17 24	17 32	
d					16 04					16 25	16 32					17 00					17 32	
Long Eaton d											16 40										17 42	
Alfreton d			15 32					16 05						16 32					17 04			
Langley Mill d			15 40											16 40								
Lincoln 27 d	14 36											15 36										16 34
Newark Castle 27 d	15 06											16 08										17 05
Nottingham a	15 32		15 58					16 27				16 32		16 58					17 27			17 32
d	15 36	15 45					16 12					16 33	16 45					17 12				17 34
Beeston d	15 42						16 18					16 40						17 18				17 40
East Midlands Parkway a	15 50	15 55								16 39	16 44	16 50	16 55								17 45	17 50
d	15 50	15 56								16 39	16 45	16 50	16 56								17 46	17 50
Loughborough d	15 59						16 27				16 52	16 58						17 26			17 54	17 58
Barrow Upon Soar d	16 03											17 03										18 03
Sileby d	16 07											17 07										18 07
Syston d	16 12											17 12										18 12
Leicester a	16 23	16 13			16 25		16 37				17 02	17 23	17 13			17 22		17 36			18 04	18 21
d		16 13			16 26		16 38				17 03		17 13			17 23		17 37			18 04	
Market Harborough d		16 26					16 51						17 26					17 50				
Melton Mowbray 47 d										17 09												
Oakham 47 d										17 23												
Corby d						16 39				17 51							17 39					
Kettering a						16 48	17 00			18 00	17 23						17 48	17 59				
d						16 49	17 01				17 24						17 49	18 00				
Wellingborough d						16 57	17 08										17 57	18 08				
Bedford 52 a						17 10	17 22										18 10	18 21				
Luton 52 a						17 24							18 03				18 26					
Luton Airport Parkway 52 a							17 37											18 40				
St Pancras International 52 a		17 24			17 39	17 55	18 06				18 14		18 40			18 40	18 55	19 06			19 11	

A From Newcastle to Southampton Central
B From Liverpool Lime Street to Norwich
C From Glasgow Central to Penzance
D From Newcastle to Reading
E From Aberdeen to Penzance
F From Newcastle to Guildford
G From Edinburgh to Plymouth

For connections to Gatwick Airport refer to Table T052

Table T053-R

Mondays to Fridays
8 October to 7 December

Sheffield - East Midlands - London

	EM ◇■ ⛾	NT ◇	XC ◇■ A ⛾	EM ◇■ ⛾	EM ◇■ ⛾	EM ◇■ ⛾	EM ◇ B	XC ◇■ C ⛾	EM ◇■ ⛾	EM	EM ◇■ ⛾
York ■ 29 d			16 05					16 44			
Leeds ■ 31,34 d		16 04	16 40					17 10			
Wakefield Westgate ■ 31 d			16 52					17 22			
Wakefield Kirkgate ■ 31,34 d		16 22									
Doncaster ■ 29 d											
Manchester Piccadilly 78 d							16 42				
Sheffield ■ d		17 05	17 24	17 29			17 45	17 55	18 00		
Chesterfield d		17 22		17 41			18 01	18 07	18 12		
Derby ■ a			17 51	18 03				18 24	18 31		
d				18 04					18 31		
Long Eaton d									18 41		
Alfreton d		17 32					18 11				
Langley Mill d		17 40									
Lincoln 27 d										17 26	
Newark Castle 27 d										17 56	
Nottingham ■ a		18 00					18 31			18 32	
d	17 45					18 12				18 36	18 45
Beeston d						18 18				18 42	
East Midlands Parkway ✈ a	17 56								18 44	18 49	18 55
d	17 57								18 45	18 52	18 56
Loughborough d						18 26			18 53	19 00	
Barrow Upon Soar d										19 05	
Sileby d										19 09	
Syston d										19 14	
Leicester a	18 13			18 25		18 36			19 03	19 23	19 13
d	18 14			18 26		18 37			19 03		19 13
Market Harborough d	18 27					18 50					19 26
Melton Mowbray 47 d											
Oakham 47 d											
Corby d					18 37						
Kettering ■ a	18 38				18 46	18 59					
d	18 39				18 47	19 00					
Wellingborough d					18 56	19 08					
Bedford ■ 52 a					19 11	19 23					
Luton ■ 52 a					19 27						
Luton Airport Parkway ■ 52 ✈ a						19 41					
St Pancras International ⊖52 a	19 37			19 39	19 57	20 07			20 11		20 25

	NT ◇	XC ◇■ A ⛾	EM ◇■ ⛾	EM ◇■ ⛾	EM ◇■ ⛾	EM ◇ D	XC ◇■ E ⛾	EM ◇■ ⛾	EM	EM ◇■ ⛾	NT ◇
York ■ 29 d		17 35					17 45				
Leeds ■ 31,34 d	17 03						18 11				18 03
Wakefield Westgate ■ 31 d							18 23				
Wakefield Kirkgate ■ 31,34 d	17 22										18 21
Doncaster ■ 29 d		17 58									
Manchester Piccadilly 78 d						17 42					
Sheffield ■ d	18 03	18 24	18 29			18 52	18 56	19 01			19 05
Chesterfield d	18 19		18 41			19 07	19 11	19 16			19 21
Derby ■ a		18 51	19 00				19 29	19 35			
d			19 04					19 35			
Long Eaton d								19 45			
Alfreton d	18 30					19 19					19 31
Langley Mill d	18 37										19 39
Lincoln 27 d									18 35		
Newark Castle 27 d									19 03		
Nottingham ■ a	18 55					19 40			19 32		19 57
d					19 12				19 32	19 45	
Beeston d					19 18				19 38		
East Midlands Parkway ✈ a								19 49	19 49	19 55	
d								19 50	19 50	19 56	
Loughborough d					19 27			19 58	19 58		
Barrow Upon Soar d									20 03		
Sileby d									20 07		
Syston d									20 12		
Leicester a			19 25		19 37			20 08	20 24	20 12	
d			19 26		19 38			20 08		20 13	
Market Harborough d					19 51					20 27	
Melton Mowbray 47 d											
Oakham 47 d											
Corby d				19 39							
Kettering ■ a				19 48	20 00						
d				19 49	20 01						
Wellingborough d				19 58	20 08						
Bedford ■ 52 a				20 10	20 22						
Luton ■ 52 a				20 26							
Luton Airport Parkway ■ 52 ✈ a					20 37						
St Pancras International ⊖52 a			20 40	20 51	21 06			21 21		21 25	

	XC ◇■ F ⛾	EM ◇■ ⛾	EM ◇■ ⛾	EM ◇■ ⛾	EM ◇ B	EM	XC ◇■ G ⛾	NT ◇	EM ◇■ ⛾	XC ◇■ H ⛾	EM ◇ D
York ■ 29 d	18 36						18 45			19 36	
Leeds ■ 31,34 d							19 11	19 03			
Wakefield Westgate ■ 31 d							19 23				
Wakefield Kirkgate ■ 31,34 d								19 21			
Doncaster ■ 29 d	18 59									19 59	
Manchester Piccadilly 78 d					18 42						19 42
Sheffield ■ d	19 24	19 29			19 37		19 58	20 02		20 24	20 41
Chesterfield d		19 42			19 52		20 10	20 18			20 56
Derby ■ a	19 52	20 02					20 28			20 51	
d		20 02									
Long Eaton d											
Alfreton d					20 03			20 28			21 08
Langley Mill d								20 36			
Lincoln 27 d											
Newark Castle 27 d											
Nottingham ■ a					20 27			20 55			21 34
d				20 12		20 35			20 55		
Beeston d				20 18		20 42			21 01		
East Midlands Parkway ✈ a				20 24		20 50			21 06		
d				20 25		20 50			21 07		
Loughborough d				20 32		20 58			21 15		
Barrow Upon Soar d						21 03					
Sileby d						21 07					
Syston d						21 12					
Leicester a		20 27		20 43		21 23			21 27		
d		20 27		20 43					21 29		
Market Harborough d				20 56					21 42		
Melton Mowbray 47 d											
Oakham 47 d											
Corby d			20 41								
Kettering ■ a			20 50	21 05					21 51		
d			20 51	21 06					21 52		
Wellingborough d			21 00	21 14					21 59		
Bedford ■ 52 a			21 12	21 26					22 12		
Luton ■ 52 a			21 27						22 27		
Luton Airport Parkway ■ 52 ✈ a				21 42					22 30		
St Pancras International ⊖52 a		21 38	21 55	22 07					22 57		

	EM ◇■ ⛾	XC ◇■ I ⛾	EM ◇■ ⛾	EM ◇■ ⛾	NT ◇	EM	XC ◇■ H ⛾	EM ◇ D	EM ◇■ ⛾	XC ◇■ J ⛾
York ■ 29 d		19 45					20 36			20 45
Leeds ■ 31,34 d		20 11			20 03					21 11
Wakefield Westgate ■ 31 d		20 23								21 23
Wakefield Kirkgate ■ 31,34 d					20 21					
Doncaster ■ 29 d							21 01			
Manchester Piccadilly 78 d								20 42		
Sheffield ■ d	20 50	20 58			21 02		21 29	21 37	22 01	22 01
Chesterfield d	21 02	21 10			21 18		21 41	21 55	22 13	22 25
Derby ■ a	21 21	21 28			21 39		21 58		22 34	22 42
d	21 22				21 41					
Long Eaton d										
Alfreton d								22 05		
Langley Mill d								22 13		
Lincoln 27 d										
Newark Castle 27 d										
Nottingham ■ a					22 01			22 31		
d				21 29		22 01				
Beeston d						22 07				
East Midlands Parkway ✈ a	21 32					22 15				
d	21 33					22 16				
Loughborough d	21 39			21 46		22 24				
Barrow Upon Soar d						22 29				
Sileby d						22 33				
Syston d						22 38				
Leicester a	21 50			21 55		22 49				
d	21 51			21 56						
Market Harborough d				22 09						
Melton Mowbray 47 d										
Oakham 47 d										
Corby d			21 43							
Kettering ■ a			21 52	22 18						
d				22 19						
Wellingborough d				22 26						
Bedford ■ 52 a				22 39						
Luton ■ 52 a				22 56						
Luton Airport Parkway ■ 52 ✈ a										
St Pancras International ⊖52 a	23 06			23 25						

A From Newcastle to Reading
B From Liverpool Lime Street to Norwich
C From Glasgow Central to Plymouth
D From Liverpool Lime Street
E From Edinburgh to Plymouth
F From Newcastle to Southampton Central
G From Glasgow Central to Bristol Temple Meads
H From Newcastle to Birmingham New Street
I From Edinburgh to Bristol Temple Meads. ⛾ to Leeds
J From Glasgow Central to Birmingham New Street. ⛾ to Leeds

For connections to Gatwick Airport refer to Table T052

Table T053-R

Mondays to Fridays
8 October to 7 December

Sheffield - East Midlands - London

	NT ◇	EM	EM ◇■ ⛾	EM ◇■ ⛾	EM ◇ A
York ■ 29 d					
Leeds ■ 31,34 d	21 03				
Wakefield Westgate ■ 31 d					
Wakefield Kirkgate ■ 31,34 d	21 21				
Doncaster ■ 29 d					
Manchester Piccadilly 78 d					22 28
Sheffield ■ d	22 03			23 21	23 37
Chesterfield d	22 20			23 45	00 02
Derby ■ a				00 05	
d					
Long Eaton d					
Alfreton d	22 31				
Langley Mill d	22 38				
Lincoln 27 d					
Newark Castle 27 d					
Nottingham ■ a	22 57				00 45
d		23 10			
Beeston d		23 15			
East Midlands Parkway ✈ a		23 22			
d		23 23			
Loughborough d		23 31			
Barrow Upon Soar d					
Sileby d					
Syston d					
Leicester a		23 47			
d					
Market Harborough d					
Melton Mowbray 47 d					
Oakham 47 d					
Corby d			22 43		
Kettering ■ a			22 52		
d					
Wellingborough d					
Bedford ■ 52 a					
Luton ■ 52 a					
Luton Airport Parkway ■ 52 ✈ a					
St Pancras International ⊖52 a					

Saturdays
26 May to 28 July

	EM ◇ A	EM ◇■ ⛾	NT ◇	EM ◇■ ⛾	EM ◇■ B ⛾	EM ◇■ C ⛾	EM ◇■ ⛾	EM ◇■ ⛾	EM ◇■ ⛾	XC ◇■ D	EM ◇■ ⛾
York ■ 29 d											
Leeds ■ 31,34 d											
Wakefield Westgate ■ 31 d											
Wakefield Kirkgate ■ 31,34 d											
Doncaster ■ 29 d											
Manchester Piccadilly 78 d											
Sheffield ■ d			05 15		05 29	05 29				05 45	
Chesterfield d	00 02		05 30		05 41	05 41				05 57	
Derby ■ a					06 00					06 34	
d				05 21	06 01				06 29		
Long Eaton d				05 30					06 38		
Alfreton d			05 45								
Langley Mill d			05 53								
Lincoln 27 d											
Newark Castle 27 d											
Nottingham ■ a	00 45		06 11								
d							06 12				06 45
Beeston d							06 18				
East Midlands Parkway ✈ a				05 34					06 42		06 55
d				05 35					06 43		06 56
Loughborough d				05 42			06 27		06 50		
Barrow Upon Soar d											
Sileby d											
Syston d											
Leicester a				05 52	06 22	06 24	06 37		06 59		07 12
d		04 45		05 53	06 24	06 25	06 38		07 01		07 12
Market Harborough d				06 07			06 52				07 26
Melton Mowbray 47 d											
Oakham 47 d											
Corby d								07 06			
Kettering ■ a		05 04		06 16			07 01	07 15	07 20		
d		05 05		06 17			07 02		07 22		
Wellingborough d		05 17		06 24			07 09		07 29		
Bedford ■ 52 a		05 32		06 37			07 23		07 42		
Luton ■ 52 a				06 52					07 56		
Luton Airport Parkway ■ 52 ✈ a		05 49					07 38				
St Pancras International ⊖52 a		06 21		07 21	07 33	07 33	08 06		08 22		08 26

	NT ◇	EM ◇■ C ⛾	EM	EM ◇■ E ⛾	EM ◇■ F ⛾	XC ◇■ G ⛾	XC ◇■ H ⛾	EM ◇■ ⛾	EM ◇■ ⛾	EM	EM ◇■ ⛾
York ■ 29 d											
Leeds ■ 31,34 d						05 49	06 11				
Wakefield Westgate ■ 31 d						06 01	06 23				
Wakefield Kirkgate ■ 31,34 d											
Doncaster ■ 29 d											
Manchester Piccadilly 78 d											
Sheffield ■ d	06 01	06 27		06 27	06 29	06 30	06 53				
Chesterfield d	06 19	06 39		06 39	06 41	06a43	07 06				
Derby ■ a				06 58	07 00		07 26				
d				07 04	07 03				07 31		
Long Eaton d									07 41		
Alfreton d	06 29										
Langley Mill d	06 36										
Lincoln 27 d											
Newark Castle 27 d											
Nottingham ■ a	07 00										
d								07 12		07 33	07 45
Beeston d								07 18		07 39	
East Midlands Parkway ✈ a									07 44	07 49	07 55
d									07 45	07 50	07 56
Loughborough d			06 59					07 29	07 53	07 58	
Barrow Upon Soar d			07 04							08 03	
Sileby d			07 08							08 07	
Syston d			07 14							08 12	
Leicester a		07 18	07 22	07 24	07 24			07 38	08 02	08 23	08 11
d		07 24		07 24	07 24			07 40	08 03		08 13
Market Harborough d								07 53			08 27
Melton Mowbray 47 d											
Oakham 47 d											
Corby d											
Kettering ■ a								08 02			
d								08 03			
Wellingborough d								08 10			
Bedford ■ 52 a								08 23			
Luton ■ 52 a											
Luton Airport Parkway ■ 52 ✈ a								08 38			
St Pancras International ⊖52 a		08 36		08 36	08 36			09 07	09 11		09 25

A From Liverpool Lime Street
B not 28 July
C 28 July
D not 28 July. To Reading
E from 23 June until 21 July
F until 16 June
G 28 July. To Paignton
H not 28 July. To Paignton

For connections to Gatwick Airport refer to Table T052

Table T053-R

Sheffield - East Midlands - London

Saturdays
26 May to 28 July

Station	NT ◇	XC ◇■ A 🍴	XC ◇■ B	EM ◇■ C ⊠	EM ◇■ D ⊠	EM ◇■ 🍴	EM ◇■ 🍴	EM ◇■ 🍴	EM E	EM F	EM ◇■ ⊠	XC ◇■ G 🍴	XC ◇■ H 🍴	NT ◇	XC ◇■ I 🍴	XC ◇■ J	EM ◇■ C 🍴	EM ◇■ D 🍴	EM ◇■ 🍴	EM ◇■ 🍴	EM ◇■ C 🍴	EM ◇■ K 🍴
York 29 d												06 45	06 45		07 25	07 35						
Leeds 31,34 d		06 17	06 17								06 34	07 11	07 11	07 03								07 40
Wakefield Westgate 31 d		06 29	06 29								06 46	07 23	07 23									07 53
Wakefield Kirkgate 31,34 d														07 22								
Doncaster 29 d		06 51	06 51												07 51	07 58						
Manchester Piccadilly 78 d																						
Sheffield d	07 02	07 18	07 18	07 29	07 29						07 37	07 56	07 56	08 03	08 22	08 22	08 29	08 29				08 34
Chesterfield d	07 17	07 30	07a31	07 41	07 41						07 50	08a07	08 08	08 19	08 34	08a34	08 41	08 41				08 47
Derby a		07 48			07 59								08 25		08 51			08 59				
d					08 04			08 31										09 04				
Long Eaton d								08 41														
Alfreton d	07 28										08 01			08 29								08 57
Langley Mill d	07 35										08 09			08 37								
Lincoln 27 d							07 04		07 36	07 36												
Newark Castle 27 d							07 29		08 04	08 04												
Nottingham a	07 53						07 57		08 28	08 29	08 25			08 55								09 22
d							08 12		08 36	08 35	08 45									09 12		09 45
Beeston d							08 18		08 42	08 41										09 18		
East Midlands Parkway a								08 44	08 49	08 49	08 55											09 55
d								08 45	08 50	08 50	08 56										09 45	09 56
Loughborough d							08 28	08 53	08 58	08 58										09 28	09 53	→
Barrow Upon Soar d									09 03	09 03												
Sileby d									09 07	09 07												
Syston d									09 12	09 12												
Leicester a				08 25	08 25		08 37	09 02	09 25	09 25	09 11						09 24	09 24		09 37	10 02	
d				08 25	08 25		08 39	09 03			09 13						09 25	09 25		09 39	10 03	
Market Harborough d							08 52				09 26									09 52		
Melton Mowbray 47 d																						
Oakham 47 d																						
Corby d						08 41													09 41			
Kettering a						08 50	09 01												09 50	10 01		
d						08 51	09 02												09 51	10 02		
Wellingborough d						09 00	09 09												10 00	10 09		
Bedford 52 a						09 12	09 23												10 12	10 23		
Luton 52 a						09 27													10 27			
Luton Airport Parkway 52 ✈ a							09 37													10 38		
St Pancras International ⊖52 a				09 36	09 36	09 51	10 07	10 10			10 24						10 35	10 35	10 51	11 08	11 11	

Station	EM ◇ L	EM ◇ M	XC ◇■ N 🍴	XC ◇■ O 🍴	EM ◇■ D 🍴	EM	EM ◇■ P 🍴	NT ◇	XC ◇■ Q 🍴	XC ◇■ R 🍴	EM ◇■ D 🍴	EM ◇■ 🍴	EM ◇■ 🍴	EM ◇ S	XC ◇■ T 🍴	XC ◇■ U 🍴	EM ◇■ C 🍴	EM ◇■ D 🍴	EM	EM ◇■ 🍴	NT ◇
York 29 d			07 44	07 45					08 35	08 35					08 45	08 45					
Leeds 31,34 d			08 11	08 11				08 04							09 11	09 11					09 04
Wakefield Westgate 31 d			08 23	08 23											09 23	09 23					
Wakefield Kirkgate 31,34 d								08 22													09 22
Doncaster 29 d									08 58	09 01											
Manchester Piccadilly 78 d	07 42	07 42												08 43							
Sheffield d	08 37	08 37	08 53	08 53	09 00			09 06	09 24	09 24	09 29			09 37	09 53	09 53		10 00			10 05
Chesterfield d	08 52	08 54	09a04	09 05	09 12			09 22	09a37		09 41			09 52	10a04	10 06		10 12			10 22
Derby a				09 26	09 31					09 51	09 59					10 26		10 30			
d					09 31						10 04						10 31	10 31			
Long Eaton d					09 41												10 40	10 40			
Alfreton d	09 03	09 05						09 33						10 03							10 32
Langley Mill d								09 40													10 40
Lincoln 27 d						08 35													09 36		
Newark Castle 27 d						09 04													10 07		
Nottingham a	09 27	09 27				09 31		09 59						10 27					10 30		10 58
d						09 36							10 12						10 36	10 45	
Beeston d						09 42	←						10 18						10 42		
East Midlands Parkway a					09 44	09 49	09 55										10 44	10 44	10 49	10 55	
d					09 45	09 50	09 56										10 44	10 44	10 50	10 56	
Loughborough d					09 53	09 58							10 28				10 53	10 53	10 58		
Barrow Upon Soar d						10 03													11 03		
Sileby d						10 07													11 07		
Syston d						10 12													11 12		
Leicester a					10 02	10 23	10 11				10 24		10 37				11 02	11 02	11 23	11 11	
d					10 03		10 13				10 25		10 39				11 03	11 03		11 13	
Market Harborough d							10 26						10 52							11 26	
Melton Mowbray 47 d																					
Oakham 47 d																					
Corby d												10 41									
Kettering a												10 50	11 01								
d												10 51	11 02								
Wellingborough d												11 00	11 09								
Bedford 52 a												11 12	11 22								
Luton 52 a												11 27									
Luton Airport Parkway 52 ✈ a													11 37								
St Pancras International ⊖52 a					11 11		11 24				11 35	11 50	12 07				12 11	12 11		12 24	

A not 28 July. To Southampton Central
B 28 July. To Plymouth
C 28 July
D not 28 July
E not 28 July. From Sleaford
F 28 July. From Sleaford
G 28 July. To Reading
H not 28 July. To Plymouth. 🍴 from Leeds
I not 28 July. From Newcastle to Reading
J 28 July. To Penzance
K To St Pancras International
L from 23 June. From Liverpool Lime Street to Norwich
M until 16 June. From Liverpool Lime Street to Norwich
N 28 July. From Newcastle to Southampton Central
O not 28 July. To Penzance. 🍴 from Leeds
P From Leeds
Q 28 July. From Newcastle to Plymouth
R not 28 July. From Newcastle to Southampton Central
S From Liverpool Lime Street to Norwich
T 28 July. From Edinburgh to Reading
U not 28 July. From Edinburgh to Plymouth

For connections to Gatwick Airport refer to Table T052

Table T053-R

Sheffield - East Midlands - London

Saturdays
26 May to 28 July

Station	XC ◇■ A 🍴	XC ◇■ B	EM ◇■ C 🍴	EM ◇■ D 🍴	EM ◇■ 🍴	EM ◇■ 🍴	EM ◇ E	XC ◇■ F 🍴	XC ◇■ G 🍴	EM ◇■ C 🍴	EM ◇■ D 🍴	EM	EM ◇■ 🍴	NT ◇	XC ◇■ H 🍴	XC ◇■ I 🍴	EM ◇■ D 🍴	EM ◇■ C 🍴	EM ◇■ 🍴	EM ◇■ 🍴	EM ◇ E	XC ◇■ J 🍴
York 29 d	09 35	09 35						09 45	09 45						10 35	10 35						10 45
Leeds 31,34 d								10 11	10 11					10 04								11 11
Wakefield Westgate 31 d								10 23	10 23													11 23
Wakefield Kirkgate 31,34 d														10 22								
Doncaster 29 d	09 58	09 58													10 59	10 59						
Manchester Piccadilly 78 d							09 42														10 43	
Sheffield d	10 24	10 24	10 29	10 29			10 36	10 53	10 55	11 00				11 05	11 24	11 24	11 29	11 29			11 37	11 55
Chesterfield d		10a36	10 41	10 42			10 52	11 05	11a06	11 12				11 22		11a35	11 41	11 41			11 52	12a06
Derby a	10 51		10 59					11 26		11 30					11 51			11 59				
d			11 04							11 31	11 31							12 04				
Long Eaton d										11 40	11 40											
Alfreton d							11 02							11 32							12 02	
Langley Mill d														11 40								
Lincoln 27 d												10 36										
Newark Castle 27 d												11 04										
Nottingham a							11 27					11 31		11 58							12 27	
d						11 12						11 36	11 45							12 12		
Beeston d						11 18						11 42								12 18		
East Midlands Parkway a										11 44	11 44	11 49	11 55									
d										11 45	11 45	11 50	11 56									
Loughborough d						11 28				11 52	11 52	11 58								12 28		
Barrow Upon Soar d												12 03										
Sileby d												12 07										
Syston d												12 12										
Leicester a			11 24	11 24		11 37				12 02	12 02	12 23	12 12				12 24	12 24		12 37		
d			11 25	11 25		11 39				12 03	12 03		12 12				12 25	12 25		12 39		
Market Harborough d						11 52							12 26							12 52		
Melton Mowbray 47 d																						
Oakham 47 d																						
Corby d					11 41														12 41			
Kettering a					11 50	12 01													12 50	13 01		
d					11 51	12 02													12 51	13 02		
Wellingborough d					12 00	12 09													13 00	13 09		
Bedford 52 a					12 12	12 23													13 11	13 23		
Luton 52 a					12 27														13 27			
Luton Airport Parkway 52 ✈ a						12 38														13 38		
St Pancras International ⊖52 a			12 35	12 35	12 51	13 08				13 11	13 11		13 25				13 35	13 35	13 51	14 08		

Station	XC ◇■ K 🍴	EM ◇■ D 🍴	EM ◇■ C 🍴	EM	EM ◇■ 🍴	NT ◇	XC ◇■ L 🍴	XC ◇■ M 🍴	EM ◇■ D 🍴	EM ◇■ C 🍴	EM ◇■ 🍴	EM ◇■ 🍴	EM ◇ E	XC ◇■ G 🍴	XC ◇■ N 🍴	EM ◇■ D 🍴	EM ◇■ C 🍴	EM	EM ◇■ 🍴	NT ◇	XC ◇■ M 🍴
York 29 d	10 45						11 35	11 35						11 45	11 45						12 35
Leeds 31,34 d	11 11					11 04								12 11	12 11					12 04	
Wakefield Westgate 31 d	11 23													12 23	12 23						
Wakefield Kirkgate 31,34 d						11 22														12 22	
Doncaster 29 d							11 58	11 58													12 59
Manchester Piccadilly 78 d													11 42								
Sheffield d	11 55		12 00			12 05	12 24	12 24	12 29	12 29			12 37	12 55	12 55		13 00			13 05	13 23
Chesterfield d	12 07		12 12			12 22		12a35	12 41	12 41			12 52	13a06	13 07		13 12			13 22	13a36
Derby a	12 25		12 30				12 51			12 59					13 24		13 30				
d		12 31	12 31							13 04						13 31	13 31				
Long Eaton d		12 40	12 40													13 40	13 40				
Alfreton d						12 32							13 02							13 32	
Langley Mill d						12 40														13 40	
Lincoln 27 d				11 40														12 36			
Newark Castle 27 d				12 04														13 06			
Nottingham a				12 27		12 58							13 27					13 29		13 58	
d				12 35	12 45							13 12						13 35	13 45		
Beeston d				12 41								13 18						13 41			
East Midlands Parkway a		12 44	12 44	12 49	12 55											13 44	13 44	13 49	13 55		
d		12 45	12 45	12 50	12 56											13 45	13 45	13 50	13 56		
Loughborough d		12 52	12 52	12 58								13 28				13 52	13 52	13 58			
Barrow Upon Soar d				13 03														14 03			
Sileby d				13 07														14 07			
Syston d				13 12														14 12			
Leicester a		13 02	13 02	13 23	13 11				13 24	13 24		13 37				14 02	14 02	14 23	14 11		
d		13 03	13 03		13 12				13 25	13 25		13 39				14 03	14 03		14 13		
Market Harborough d					13 26							13 52							14 26		
Melton Mowbray 47 d																					
Oakham 47 d																					
Corby d											13 41										
Kettering a											13 50	14 01									
d											13 51	14 02									
Wellingborough d											14 00	14 09									
Bedford 52 a											14 12	14 23									
Luton 52 a											14 27										
Luton Airport Parkway 52 ✈ a												14 38									
St Pancras International ⊖52 a		14 11	14 11		14 24				14 35	14 35	14 50	15 08				15 10	15 10		15 24		

A not 28 July. From Edinburgh to Reading
B 28 July. From Edinburgh to Paignton
C not 28 July
D 28 July
E From Liverpool Lime Street to Norwich
F not 28 July. From Glasgow Central to Paignton
G 28 July. From Glasgow Central to Southampton Central
H not 28 July. From Newcastle to Southampton Central
I 28 July. From Newcastle to Newquay
J 28 July. From Dundee to Reading
K not 28 July. From Dundee to Newquay
L not 28 July. From Newcastle to Reading
M 28 July. From Newcastle to Penzance
N not 28 July. From Glasgow Central to Penzance

For connections to Gatwick Airport refer to Table T052

Sheffield - East Midlands - London

	XC ◇■ A ⏚	EM ◇■ B ⏚	EM ◇■ C ⏚	EM ◇■ ⏚	EM ◇■ ⏚	EM ◇ D	XC ◇■ E ⏚	XC ◇■ F ⏚	EM ◇■ C ⏚	EM ◇■ B ⏚	EM	EM ◇■ ⏚	NT ◇	XC ◇■ G ⏚	XC ◇■ H ⏚	EM ◇■ C ⏚	EM ◇■ B ⏚	EM ◇■ ⏚	EM ◇■ ⏚	EM ◇ D	XC ◇■ I ⏚	XC ◇■ J ⏚
York ■ 29 d	12 35						12 45	12 45						13 35	13 35						13 45	13 45
Leeds ■ 31,34 d							13 11	13 11					13 04								14 11	14 11
Wakefield Westgate ■ 31 d							13 23	13 23													14 23	14 23
Wakefield Kirkgate ■ 31,34 d													13 23									
Doncaster ■ 29 d	12 59													13 58	13 58							
Manchester Piccadilly 78 d						12 42														13 42		
Sheffield ■ d	13 24	13 29	13 29			13 37	13 53	13 54	14 00				14 05	14 25	14 25	14 29	14 29			14 37	14 55	14 55
Chesterfield d		13 41	13 41			13 52	14 06	14a05	14 12				14 22		14a36	14 41	14 42			14 54	15a06	15 07
Derby ■ a	13 51		13 59				14 26		14 30					14 52		14 59						15 24
d			14 04						14 31	14 31						15 04						
Long Eaton d									14 40	14 40												
Alfreton d						14 03							14 32							15 04		
Langley Mill d													14 40									
Lincoln 27 d											13 37											
Newark Castle 27 d											14 05											
Nottingham ■ a						14 27					14 28		14 58							15 28		
d					14 12						14 35	14 45							15 12			
Beeston d					14 18						14 41								15 18			
East Midlands Parkway a									14 44	14 44	14 49	14 55										
d									14 45	14 45	14 50	14 56										
Loughborough d					14 28				14 52	14 52	14 58								15 28			
Barrow Upon Soar d											15 03											
Sileby d											15 07											
Syston d											15 12											
Leicester a		14 24	14 24		14 37				15 02	15 02	15 23	15 11				15 24	15 24		15 37			
d		14 25	14 25		14 39				15 03	15 03		15 13				15 25	15 25		15 39			
Market Harborough d					14 52							15 26							15 52			
Melton Mowbray 47 d																						
Oakham 47 d																						
Corby d				14 41														15 41				
Kettering ■ a				14 50	15 01													15 50	16 01			
d				14 51	15 02													15 51	16 02			
Wellingborough d				15 00	15 09													16 00	16 09			
Bedford ■ 52 a				15 11	15 22													16 12	16 23			
Luton ■ 52 a				15 27														16 27				
Luton Airport Parkway ■ 52 a					15 37														16 38			
St Pancras International ⊖52 a		15 35	15 35	15 51	16 05				16 10	16 10		16 24				16 36	16 36	16 50	17 08			

	EM ◇■ B ⏚	EM ◇■ C ⏚	EM	EM ◇■ ⏚	NT ◇	XC ◇■ K ⏚	XC ◇■ L ⏚	EM ◇■ B ⏚	EM ◇■ C ⏚	EM ◇■ ⏚	EM ◇■ ⏚	EM ◇ D	XC ◇■ F ⏚	XC ◇■ M ⏚	EM ◇■ B ⏚	EM ◇■ C ⏚	EM	EM ◇■ ⏚	NT ◇	XC ◇■ G ⏚	XC ◇■ L ⏚	EM ◇■ B ⏚
York ■ 29 d						14 35	14 35						14 45	14 45						15 35	15 35	
Leeds ■ 31,34 d					14 04								15 11	15 11					15 04			
Wakefield Westgate ■ 31 d													15 23	15 23								
Wakefield Kirkgate ■ 31,34 d					14 22														15 22			
Doncaster ■ 29 d						14 59	14 59													15 58	15 58	
Manchester Piccadilly 78 d												14 42										
Sheffield ■ d		15 00			15 05	15 24	15 24	15 29	15 29			15 37	15 55	15 55		16 00			16 05	16 24	16 24	16 29
Chesterfield d		15 12			15 22		15a35	15 41	15 41			15 52	16a06	16 07		16 12			16 22		16a35	16 41
Derby ■ a		15 30				15 51			15 59					16 24		16 30				16 51		
d	15 31	15 31							16 04						16 31	16 31						
Long Eaton d	15 40	15 40													16 40	16 40						
Alfreton d					15 32							16 03							16 32			
Langley Mill d					15 40														16 40			
Lincoln 27 d			14 32														15 26					
Newark Castle 27 d			15 04														15 59					
Nottingham ■ a			15 30		15 58							16 27					16 27		16 58			
d			15 35	15 45							16 12						16 33	16 45				
Beeston d			15 41								16 18						16 39					
East Midlands Parkway a	15 44	15 44	15 49	15 55											16 44	16 44	16 52	16 55				
d	15 45	15 45	15 50	15 56											16 45	16 45	16 52	16 56				
Loughborough d	15 52	15 52	15 58								16 28				16 52	16 52	17 00					
Barrow Upon Soar d			16 03														17 05					
Sileby d			16 07														17 09					
Syston d			16 12														17 14					
Leicester a	16 02	16 02	16 23	16 11				16 24	16 24		16 37				17 02	17 02	17 23	17 11				17 24
d	16 03	16 03		16 13				16 25	16 25		16 39				17 03	17 03		17 13				17 25
Market Harborough d				16 26							16 52							17 26				
Melton Mowbray 47 d																						
Oakham 47 d																						
Corby d										16 41												
Kettering ■ a										16 50	17 01											
d										16 51	17 02											
Wellingborough d										17 00	17 09											
Bedford ■ 52 a										17 12	17 23											
Luton ■ 52 a										17 27												
Luton Airport Parkway ■ 52 a											17 38											
St Pancras International ⊖52 a	17 11	17 11		17 24				17 35	17 35	17 51	18 08				18 11	18 11		18 24				18 34

- **A** not 28 July. From Newcastle to Southampton Central
- **B** 28 July
- **C** not 28 July
- **D** From Liverpool Lime Street to Norwich
- **E** not 28 July. From Glasgow Central to Penzance
- **F** 28 July. From Glasgow Central to Reading
- **G** not 28 July. From Newcastle to Reading
- **H** 28 July. From Newcastle to Penzance
- **I** 28 July. From Aberdeen to Guildford
- **J** not 28 July. From Aberdeen to Penzance
- **K** not 28 July. From Newcastle to Guildford
- **L** 28 July. From Newcastle to Plymouth
- **M** not 28 July. From Glasgow Central to Plymouth

For connections to Gatwick Airport refer to Table T052

Sheffield - East Midlands - London

	EM ◇■ A ⏚	EM ◇■ ⏚	EM ◇■ ⏚	EM ◇ B	XC ◇■ C ⏚	XC ◇■ D ⏚	EM ◇■ E ⏚	EM ◇■ A ⏚	EM	EM ◇■ ⏚	NT ◇	XC ◇■ F ⏚	XC ◇■ G ⏚	EM ◇■ E ⏚	EM ◇■ A ⏚	EM ◇■ ⏚	EM ◇■ ⏚	EM ◇ B	XC ◇■ H ⏚	XC ◇■ I ⏚	EM ◇■ E ⏚
York ■ 29 d					15 45	15 45						16 04	16 04						16 45	16 45	
Leeds ■ 31,34 d					16 11	16 11					16 04	16 40	16 40						17 10	17 10	
Wakefield Westgate ■ 31 d					16 23	16 23						16 52	16 52						17 22	17 22	
Wakefield Kirkgate ■ 31,34 d											16 22										
Doncaster ■ 29 d																					
Manchester Piccadilly 78 d				15 42														16 42			
Sheffield ■ d	16 29			16 37	16 55	16 55		17 00			17 05	17 24	17 24	17 29	17 29			17 41	17 55	17 55	
Chesterfield d	16 41			16 53	17a06	17 07		17 11			17 22		17a35	17 41	17 41			17 57	18a06	18 07	
Derby ■ a	16 59					17 24		17 30				17 51			17 59					18 24	
d	17 04						17 31	17 31							18 04						18 31
Long Eaton d							17 40	17 40													18 40
Alfreton d				17 04							17 32							18 08			
Langley Mill d											17 40										
Lincoln 27 d									16 35												
Newark Castle 27 d									17 05												
Nottingham ■ a				17 27					17 30		17 58							18 29			
d			17 12						17 33	17 45							18 12				
Beeston d			17 18						17 39								18 18				
East Midlands Parkway a							17 44	17 44	17 52	17 55											18 44
d							17 45	17 45	17 52	17 56											18 45
Loughborough d			17 28				17 52	17 52	18 00								18 28				18 52
Barrow Upon Soar d									18 05												
Sileby d									18 09												
Syston d									18 14												
Leicester a	17 24		17 37				18 02	18 02	18 23	18 11				18 24	18 24		18 37				19 02
d	17 25		17 39				18 03	18 03		18 13				18 25	18 25		18 39				19 02
Market Harborough d			17 52							18 26							18 52				
Melton Mowbray 47 d																					
Oakham 47 d																					
Corby d		17 41														18 41					
Kettering ■ a		17 50	18 01													18 50	19 01				
d		17 51	18 02													18 51	19 02				
Wellingborough d		18 00	18 09													19 00	19 09				
Bedford ■ 52 a		18 12	18 23													19 12	19 23				
Luton ■ 52 a		18 27														19 27					
Luton Airport Parkway ■ 52 a			18 38														19 38				
St Pancras International ⊖52 a	18 34	18 50	19 08				19 11	19 11		19 24				19 35	19 35	19 51	20 08				20 11

	EM ◇■ A ⏚	EM	EM ◇■ ⏚	NT ◇	XC ◇■ F ⏚	XC ◇■ G ⏚	EM ◇■ E ⏚	EM ◇■ A ⏚	EM ◇■ ⏚	EM ◇■ ⏚	EM J	EM ◇ K	XC ◇■ L ⏚	XC ◇■ D ⏚	EM ◇■ M ⏚	EM ◇■ N ⏚	EM A	EM O	EM ◇■ ⏚	NT ◇	XC ◇■ P ⏚	XC ◇■ Q ⏚
York ■ 29 d					17 35	17 35							17 45	17 45	17 50	17 50					18 35	18 35
Leeds ■ 31,34 d				17 03									18 11	18 11						18 03		
Wakefield Westgate ■ 31 d													18 23	18 23								
Wakefield Kirkgate ■ 31,34 d				17 22																18 21		
Doncaster ■ 29 d					17 58	17 58									18 19	18 19					18 58	18 58
Manchester Piccadilly 78 d												17 42										
Sheffield ■ d	18 00			18 03	18 23	18 24	18 29	18 29				18 40	18 55	18 55	19 00	19 00				19 05	19 24	19 24
Chesterfield d	18 12			18 19		18a35	18 41	18 41				18 57	19a06	19 07	19 12	19 12				19 21	19a35	
Derby ■ a	18 30				18 50			18 59						19 24	19 30							19 51
d	18 31							19 04							19 31							
Long Eaton d	18 40														19 40							
Alfreton d				18 30								19 08								19 31		
Langley Mill d				18 37																19 39		
Lincoln 27 d		17 25									18 30						18 30					
Newark Castle 27 d		17 55									18 59						18 59					
Nottingham ■ a		18 30		18 55							19 24	19 29					19 24			19 57		
d		18 35	18 45							19 12	19 30						19 30		19 45			
Beeston d		18 41								19 18	19 36						19 36	←				
East Midlands Parkway a	18 44	18 49	18 55								19 44				19 44	19 44	19 46	19 44	19 55			
d	18 45	18 50	18 56								19 48				19 45	19 45	19 46	19 48	19 56			
Loughborough d	18 52	18 58								19 28	→				19 52	19 52	19 58	19 58				
Barrow Upon Soar d		19 03															20 03	20 03				
Sileby d		19 07															20 07	20 07				
Syston d		19 12															20 12	20 12				
Leicester a	19 02	19 23	19 11				19 24	19 24		19 37					20 02	20 02	20 23	20 23	20 11			
d	19 02		19 13				19 25	19 25		19 39					20 03	20 03			20 13			
Market Harborough d			19 26							19 52									20 26			
Melton Mowbray 47 d																						
Oakham 47 d																						
Corby d									19 41													
Kettering ■ a							19 46	19 46	19 50	20 01												
d							19 47	19 47	19 51	20 02												
Wellingborough d									20 00	20 09												
Bedford ■ 52 a									20 12	20 23												
Luton ■ 52 a									20 27													
Luton Airport Parkway ■ 52 a										20 38												
St Pancras International ⊖52 a	20 11		20 24				20 37	20 37	20 51	21 08					21 10	21 10			21 24			

- **A** not 28 July
- **B** From Liverpool Lime Street to Norwich
- **C** 28 July. From Edinburgh to Reading
- **D** not 28 July. From Edinburgh to Plymouth
- **E** 28 July
- **F** not 28 July. From Newcastle to Reading
- **G** 28 July. From Newcastle to Plymouth
- **H** 28 July. From Glasgow Central to Reading
- **I** not 28 July. From Glasgow Central to Plymouth
- **J** 28 July. To Leicester
- **K** From Liverpool Lime Street
- **L** 28 July. From Edinburgh to Southampton Central
- **M** not 28 July. From Scarborough
- **N** 28 July. From Scarborough
- **O** 28 July. From Lincoln
- **P** 28 July. From Newcastle to Bristol Temple Meads
- **Q** not 28 July. From Newcastle to Southampton Central

For connections to Gatwick Airport refer to Table T052

Table T053-R

Saturdays
26 May to 28 July

Sheffield - East Midlands - London

	EM	EM	EM	EM	EM	EM	XC	XC	NT	XC	XC	EM	EM	EM	EM	EM	EM	EM	XC	XC	NT
	◇■	◇■	◇■	◇■	◇		◇■	◇■	◇	◇■	◇■	◇■	◇■	◇■	◇■	◇■	◇		◇■	◇■	◇
	A	B			C		D	E		F	G	A	B				H		I	J	
	🛒	🛒	🛒	🛒			🛒	🛒		🛒	🛒	🛒	🛒	🚌	🛒	🛒				🛒	
York 29 d							18 45	18 45		19 36	19 36								19 45	19 45	
Leeds 31,34 d							19 11	19 11	19 03										20 11	20 11	20 03
Wakefield Westgate 31 d							19 23	19 23											20 23	20 23	
Wakefield Kirkgate 31,34 d									19 21												20 21
Doncaster 29 d										19 59	19 59										
Manchester Piccadilly 78 d					18 42												19 42				
Sheffield d	19 29	19 29			19 37		19 55	19 55	20 02	20 24	20 24	20 29	20 29				20 39		20 55	20 55	21 02
Chesterfield d	19 41	19 41			19 52		20a06	20 07	20 18		20a35	20 41	20 41				20 54		21a06	21 07	21 18
Derby a		19 59						20 24		20 51			21 00							21 24	21 39
d		20 04											21 01								21 41
Long Eaton d																					
Alfreton d					20 03				20 28								21 05				
Langley Mill d									20 36												
Lincoln 27 d																					
Newark Castle 27 d																					
Nottingham a					20 27				20 55								21 33				22 08
d				20 12		20 33									21 05	21 32		21 34			
Beeston d				20 18		20 39									21 11			21 41			
East Midlands Parkway a				20 23		20 49						21 12	21 12		21 16			21 49			
d				20 24		20 50						21 13	21 13		21 17			21 49			
Loughborough d				20 32		20 58						21 20	21 20		21 25	21 46		21 58			
Barrow Upon Soar d						21 03												22 03			
Sileby d						21 07												22 07			
Syston d						21 12												22 12			
Leicester a	20 24	20 24		20 41		21 23						21 31	21 31		21 35	21 55		22 22			
d	20 25	20 25		20 42											21 36	21 56					
Market Harborough d				20 55											21 49	22 09					
Melton Mowbray 47 d																					
Oakham 47 d																					
Corby d			20 41											21 43							
Kettering a			20 50	21 04										21 52	21 57	22 18					
d			20 51	21 04											21 57	22 19					
Wellingborough d			21 00	21 13											22 06	22 26					
Bedford 52 a			21 12	21 25											22 19	22 39					
Luton 52 a			21 27												22 34	22 55					
Luton Airport Parkway 52 a				21 41											22 37						
St Pancras International 52 a	21 35	21 35	21 51	22 09											23 11	23 29					

	XC	XC	EM	XC	XC	NT	EM	EM	EM	EM	EM
	◇■	◇■	◇	◇■	◇■	◇		◇	◇■	◇■	◇
	G	F	H	K	L			H			H
				🛒	🛒				🚌	🛒	
York 29 d	20 35	20 35		20 45	20 45						
Leeds 31,34 d				21 11	21 11	21 03					
Wakefield Westgate 31 d				21 23	21 23						
Wakefield Kirkgate 31,34 d						21 21					
Doncaster 29 d	20 59	20 59									
Manchester Piccadilly 78 d			20 43					21 41			22 28
Sheffield d	21 25	21 25	21 38	21 55	21 55	22 03		22 42		23 20	23 38
Chesterfield d	21a36	21 37	21 54	22a06	22 07	22 20		22 56		23 32	23 53
Derby a		21 54			22 24					00 06	
d											
Long Eaton d											
Alfreton d			22 05			22 31		23 07			
Langley Mill d			22 13			22 38					
Lincoln 27 d											
Newark Castle 27 d											
Nottingham a			22 34			22 57		23 28			00 30
d							23 05				
Beeston d							23 10				
East Midlands Parkway a							23 17				
d							23 18				
Loughborough d							23 26				
Barrow Upon Soar d											
Sileby d											
Syston d											
Leicester a							23 45				
d											
Market Harborough d											
Melton Mowbray 47 d											
Oakham 47 d											
Corby d									22 43		
Kettering a									22 52		
d											
Wellingborough d											
Bedford 52 a											
Luton 52 a											
Luton Airport Parkway 52 a											
St Pancras International 52 a											

- **A** 28 July
- **B** not 28 July
- **C** From Liverpool Lime Street to Norwich
- **D** 28 July. From Glasgow Central to Birmingham New Street
- **E** not 28 July. From Glasgow Central to Bristol Temple Meads
- **F** not 28 July. From Newcastle to Birmingham New Street
- **G** 28 July. From Newcastle to Birmingham New Street
- **H** From Liverpool Lime Street
- **I** 28 July. From Edinburgh to Birmingham New Street
- **J** not 28 July. From Edinburgh to Birmingham New Street. 🛒 to Leeds
- **K** 28 July. From Glasgow Central to Birmingham New Street. 🛒 to Leeds
- **L** not 28 July. From Glasgow Central to Birmingham New Street. 🛒 to Leeds

For connections to Gatwick Airport refer to Table T052

Table T053-R

Saturdays
4 August to 1 September

Sheffield - East Midlands - London

	EM	EM	NT	EM	EM	EM	EM	EM	EM	NT	EM	XC	EM	EM	EM	EM	EM	EM	NT	XC	EM	EM
	◇	◇■	◇	◇■	◇■	◇■	◇■	◇■	◇■	◇	◇■	◇■		◇■	◇■	◇■		◇■	◇	◇■	◇■	◇■
	A											B			C	D				E		
		🛒		🛒	🛒	🛒	🛒	🛒	🛒		🛒	🛒		🛒	🛒	🛒		🛒			⊠	🛒
York 29 d																						
Leeds 31,34 d												05 49								06 17		
Wakefield Westgate 31 d												06 01								06 29		
Wakefield Kirkgate 31,34 d																						
Doncaster 29 d																				06 51		
Manchester Piccadilly 78 d																						
Sheffield d			05 15		05 29					06 01	06 27	06 30							07 02	07 18	07 29	
Chesterfield d	00 02		05 30		05 41					06 19	06 39	06a43							07 17	07a31	07 41	
Derby a																						
d															07 20							
Long Eaton d															07 41							
Alfreton d			05 45							06 29									07 28			
Langley Mill d			05 53							06 36									07 35			
Lincoln 27 d																						
Newark Castle 27 d																						
Nottingham a	00 45		06 11							07 00									07 53			
d						06 12			06 45					07 12			07 33	07 45				
Beeston d						06 18								07 18			07 39					
East Midlands Parkway a									06 55						07 44		07 49	07 55				
d				05 35				06 43	06 56						07 45	07 45	07 50	07 56				
Loughborough d				05 42		06 27		06 50					06 59	07 29	07 53	07 53	07 58					
Barrow Upon Soar d													07 04				08 03					
Sileby d													07 08				08 07					
Syston d													07 14				08 12					
Leicester a				05 52	06 24	06 37		06 59	07 12		07 18		07 22	07 38	08 02	08 02	08 23	08 11			08 25	
d		04 45		05 53	06 25	06 38		07 01	07 12		07 24			07 40	08 03	08 03		08 13			08 25	
Market Harborough d				06 07		06 52			07 26					07 53				08 27				
Melton Mowbray 47 d																						
Oakham 47 d																						
Corby d							07 06															08 41
Kettering a		05 04		06 16		07 01	07 15	07 20						08 02								08 50
d		05 05		06 17		07 02		07 22						08 03								08 51
Wellingborough d		05 17		06 24		07 09		07 29						08 10								09 00
Bedford 52 a		05 32		06 37		07 23		07 42						08 23								09 12
Luton 52 a				06 52				07 56														09 27
Luton Airport Parkway 52 a		05 49				07 38								08 38								
St Pancras International 52 a		06 21		07 21	07 33	08 06		08 22	08 26		08 36			09 07	09 11	09 11		09 25			09 36	09 51

	EM	EM	EM	EM	EM	XC	NT	XC	EM	EM	EM	EM	EM	EM	EM	EM	XC	NT	XC	EM	EM	EM
	◇■	◇■	◇■		◇■	◇■	◇	◇■	◇■	◇■	◇■	◇■	◇■		◇■	◇	◇■	◇	◇■	◇■	◇■	◇
		C	D	F		G		H				I	J			K	L		M			K
	🛒	🛒	🛒		⊠	🛒			🛒	🛒	🛒	🛒	🛒		🛒		🛒		🛒	🛒	🛒	
York 29 d						06 45		07 35									07 44		08 35			
Leeds 31,34 d					06 34	07 11	07 03								07 40		08 11	08 04				
Wakefield Westgate 31 d					06 46	07 23									07 53		08 23					
Wakefield Kirkgate 31,34 d							07 22											08 22				
Doncaster 29 d								07 58											08 58			
Manchester Piccadilly 78 d																07 42						08 43
Sheffield d					07 37	07 56	08 03	08 22	08 29						08 34	08 37	08 53	09 06	09 24			09 37
Chesterfield d					07 50	08a07	08 19	08a34	08 41						08 47	08 52	09a04	09 22	09a37			09 52
Derby a																						
d		08 20										09 20										
Long Eaton d		08 41										09 41										
Alfreton d					08 01		08 29								08 57	09 03		09 33				10 03
Langley Mill d					08 09		08 37											09 40				
Lincoln 27 d	07 04			07 36										08 35								
Newark Castle 27 d	07 29			08 04										09 04								
Nottingham a	07 57			08 29	08 25		08 55							09 31	09 22	09 27		09 59				10 27
d	08 12			08 35	08 45						09 12			09 36	09 45						10 12	
Beeston d	08 18			08 41							09 18			09 42							10 18	
East Midlands Parkway a		08 44		08 49	08 55							09 44		09 49	09 55							
d		08 45	08 45	08 50	08 56							09 45	09 45	09 50	09 56							
Loughborough d	08 28	08 53	08 53	08 58							09 28	09 53	09 53	09 58							10 28	
Barrow Upon Soar d				09 03										10 03								
Sileby d				09 07										10 07								
Syston d				09 12										10 12								
Leicester a	08 37	09 02	09 02	09 25	09 11				09 24		09 37	10 02	10 02	10 23	10 11						10 37	
d	08 39	09 03	09 03		09 13				09 25		09 39	10 03	10 03		10 13						10 39	
Market Harborough d	08 52				09 26						09 52				10 26						10 52	
Melton Mowbray 47 d																						
Oakham 47 d																						
Corby d										09 41										10 41		
Kettering a	09 01									09 50	10 01									10 50	11 01	
d	09 02									09 51	10 02									10 51	11 02	
Wellingborough d	09 09									10 00	10 09									11 00	11 09	
Bedford 52 a	09 23									10 12	10 23									11 12	11 22	
Luton 52 a										10 27										11 27		
Luton Airport Parkway 52 a	09 37										10 38										11 37	
St Pancras International 52 a	10 07	10 10	10 10		10 24				10 35	10 51	11 08	11 11	11 11		11 24					11 50	12 07	

- **A** From Liverpool Lime Street
- **B** To Paignton
- **C** not 18 August
- **D** 18 August
- **E** To Plymouth
- **F** From Sleaford
- **G** To Reading
- **H** To Penzance
- **I** 4 August, 11 August
- **J** not until 11 August
- **K** From Liverpool Lime Street to Norwich
- **L** From Newcastle to Southampton Central
- **M** From Newcastle to Plymouth

For connections to Gatwick Airport refer to Table T052

NRT MAY 2018 EDITION

Table T053-R

Saturdays

4 August to 1 September

Sheffield - East Midlands - London

	XC A	EM B	EM C	EM	EM	NT	XC D	EM	EM	EM	EM E	XC F	EM B	EM C	EM	EM	NT	XC G	EM	EM	EM
York 29 d	08 45						09 35					09 45						10 35			
Leeds 31,34 d	09 11					09 04						10 11					10 04				
Wakefield Westgate 31 d	09 23											10 23									
Wakefield Kirkgate 31,34 d						09 22											10 22				
Doncaster 29 d							09 58											10 59			
Manchester Piccadilly 78 d											09 42										
Sheffield d	09 53					10 05	10 24	10 29			10 36	10 55					11 05	11 24	11 29		
Chesterfield d	10a04					10 22	10a36	10 42			10 52	11a06					11 22	11a35	11 41		
Derby a																					
d		10 20											11 20								
Long Eaton d		10 40											11 40								
Alfreton d						10 32					11 02						11 32				
Langley Mill d						10 40											11 40				
Lincoln 27 d				09 36											10 36						
Newark Castle 27 d				10 07											11 04						
Nottingham a				10 30		10 58					11 27				11 31		11 58				
d				10 36	10 45					11 12					11 36	11 45					12 12
Beeston d				10 42						11 18					11 42						12 18
East Midlands Parkway a		10 44		10 49	10 55								11 44		11 49	11 55					
d		10 44	10 44	10 50	10 56								11 45	11 45	11 50	11 56					
Loughborough d		10 53	10 53	10 58						11 28			11 52	11 52	11 58						12 28
Barrow Upon Soar d				11 03											12 03						
Sileby d				11 07											12 07						
Syston d				11 12											12 12						
Leicester a		11 02	11 02	11 23	11 11			11 24		11 37			12 02	12 02	12 23	12 12			12 24		12 37
d		11 03	11 03		11 13			11 25		11 39			12 03	12 03		12 12			12 25		12 39
Market Harborough d					11 26					11 52						12 26					12 52
Melton Mowbray 47 d																					
Oakham 47 d																					
Corby d									11 41											12 41	
Kettering a									11 50	12 01										12 50	13 01
d									11 51	12 02										12 51	13 02
Wellingborough d									12 00	12 09										13 00	13 09
Bedford 52 a									12 12	12 23										13 11	13 23
Luton 52 a									12 27											13 27	
Luton Airport Parkway 52 a										12 38											13 38
St Pancras International ⊖52 a		12 11	12 11		12 24			12 35	12 51	13 08			13 11	13 11		13 25			13 35	13 51	14 08

	EM E	XC H	EM B	EM C	EM	EM	NT	XC I	EM	EM	EM	EM E	XC F	EM B	EM C	EM	EM	NT	XC I	EM	EM	EM
York 29 d		10 45						11 35					11 45						12 35			
Leeds 31,34 d		11 11					11 04						12 11					12 04				
Wakefield Westgate 31 d		11 23											12 23									
Wakefield Kirkgate 31,34 d							11 22											12 22				
Doncaster 29 d								11 58											12 59			
Manchester Piccadilly 78 d	10 43											11 42										
Sheffield d	11 37	11 55					12 05	12 24	12 29			12 37	12 55					13 05	13 23	13 29		
Chesterfield d	11 52	12a06					12 22	12a35	12 41			12 52	13a06					13 22	13a36	13 41		
Derby a																						
d			12 20											13 20								
Long Eaton d			12 40											13 40								
Alfreton d	12 02						12 32					13 02						13 32				
Langley Mill d							12 40											13 40				
Lincoln 27 d					11 40											12 36						
Newark Castle 27 d					12 04											13 06						
Nottingham a	12 27				12 27		12 58					13 27				13 29		13 58				
d					12 35	12 45					13 12					13 35	13 45					14 12
Beeston d					12 41						13 18					13 41						14 18
East Midlands Parkway a			12 44		12 49	12 55								13 44		13 49	13 55					
d			12 45	12 45	12 50	12 56								13 45	13 45	13 50	13 56					
Loughborough d			12 52	12 52	12 58						13 28			13 52	13 52	13 58						14 28
Barrow Upon Soar d					13 03											14 03						
Sileby d					13 07											14 07						
Syston d					13 12											14 12						
Leicester a			13 02	13 02	13 23	13 11			13 24		13 37			14 02	14 02	14 23	14 11			14 24		14 37
d			13 03	13 03		13 12			13 25		13 39			14 03	14 03		14 13			14 25		14 39
Market Harborough d						13 26					13 52						14 26					14 52
Melton Mowbray 47 d																						
Oakham 47 d																						
Corby d										13 41											14 41	
Kettering a										13 50	14 01										14 50	15 01
d										13 51	14 02										14 51	15 02
Wellingborough d										14 00	14 09										15 00	15 09
Bedford 52 a										14 12	14 23										15 11	15 22
Luton 52 a										14 27											15 27	
Luton Airport Parkway 52 a											14 38											15 37
St Pancras International ⊖52 a			14 11	14 11		14 24			14 35	14 50	15 08			15 10	15 10		15 24			15 35	15 51	16 05

A From Edinburgh to Reading
B not 18 August
C 18 August
D From Edinburgh to Paignton
E From Liverpool Lime Street to Norwich
F From Glasgow Central to Southampton Central
G From Newcastle to Newquay
H From Dundee to Reading
I From Newcastle to Penzance

For connections to Gatwick Airport refer to Table T052

Table T053-R

Saturdays

4 August to 1 September

Sheffield - East Midlands - London

	EM A	XC B	EM C	EM D	EM	EM	NT	XC E	EM	EM	EM	EM A	XC F	EM C	EM D	EM	EM	NT	XC G	EM	EM
York 29 d		12 45						13 35					13 45						14 35		
Leeds 31,34 d		13 11					13 04						14 11					14 04			
Wakefield Westgate 31 d		13 23											14 23								
Wakefield Kirkgate 31,34 d							13 23											14 22			
Doncaster 29 d								13 58											14 59		
Manchester Piccadilly 78 d	12 42											13 42									
Sheffield d	13 37	13 54					14 05	14 25	14 29			14 37	14 55					15 05	15 24	15 29	
Chesterfield d	13 52	14a05					14 22	14a36	14 42			14 54	15a06					15 22	15a35	15 41	
Derby a																					
d			14 20											15 20							
Long Eaton d			14 40											15 40							
Alfreton d	14 03						14 32					15 04						15 32			
Langley Mill d							14 40											15 40			
Lincoln 27 d					13 37											14 32					
Newark Castle 27 d					14 05											15 04					
Nottingham a	14 27				14 28		14 58					15 28				15 30		15 58			
d					14 35	14 45					15 12					15 35	15 45				
Beeston d					14 41						15 18					15 41					
East Midlands Parkway a			14 44		14 49	14 55								15 44		15 49	15 55				
d			14 45	14 45	14 50	14 56								15 45	15 45	15 50	15 56				
Loughborough d			14 52	14 52	14 58						15 28			15 52	15 52	15 58					
Barrow Upon Soar d					15 03											16 03					
Sileby d					15 07											16 07					
Syston d					15 12											16 12					
Leicester a			15 02	15 02	15 23	15 11			15 24		15 37			16 02	16 02	16 23	16 11			16 24	
d			15 03	15 03		15 13			15 25		15 39			16 03	16 03		16 13			16 25	
Market Harborough d						15 26					15 52						16 26				
Melton Mowbray 47 d																					
Oakham 47 d																					
Corby d										15 41											16 41
Kettering a										15 50	16 01										16 50
d										15 51	16 02										16 51
Wellingborough d										16 00	16 09										17 00
Bedford 52 a										16 12	16 23										17 12
Luton 52 a										16 27											17 27
Luton Airport Parkway 52 a											16 38										
St Pancras International ⊖52 a			16 10	16 10		16 24			16 36	16 50	17 08			17 11	17 11		17 24			17 35	17 51

	EM	EM A	XC B	EM C	EM D	EM	EM	NT	XC G	EM	EM	EM	EM A	XC H	EM C	EM D	EM	EM	NT	XC G	EM	EM
York 29 d			14 45						15 35					15 45						16 04		
Leeds 31,34 d			15 11					15 04						16 11					16 04	16 40		
Wakefield Westgate 31 d			15 23											16 23						16 52		
Wakefield Kirkgate 31,34 d								15 22											16 22			
Doncaster 29 d									15 58													
Manchester Piccadilly 78 d		14 42											15 42									
Sheffield d		15 37	15 55					16 05	16 24	16 29			16 37	16 55					17 05	17 24	17 29	
Chesterfield d		15 52	16a06					16 22	16a35	16 41			16 53	17a06					17 22	17a35	17 41	
Derby a																						
d				16 20											17 20							
Long Eaton d				16 40											17 40							
Alfreton d		16 03						16 32					17 04						17 32			
Langley Mill d								16 40											17 40			
Lincoln 27 d						15 26											16 35					
Newark Castle 27 d						15 59											17 05					
Nottingham a		16 27				16 27		16 58					17 27				17 30		17 58			
d	16 12					16 33	16 45					17 12					17 33	17 45				
Beeston d	16 18					16 39						17 18					17 39					
East Midlands Parkway a				16 44		16 52	16 55								17 44		17 52	17 55				
d				16 45	16 45	16 52	16 56								17 45	17 45	17 52	17 56				
Loughborough d	16 28			16 52	16 52	17 00						17 28			17 52	17 52	18 00					
Barrow Upon Soar d						17 05											18 05					
Sileby d						17 09											18 09					
Syston d						17 14											18 14					
Leicester a	16 37			17 02	17 02	17 23	17 11			17 24		17 37			18 02	18 02	18 23	18 11			18 24	
d	16 39			17 03	17 03		17 13			17 25		17 39			18 03	18 03		18 13			18 25	
Market Harborough d	16 52						17 26					17 52						18 26				
Melton Mowbray 47 d																						
Oakham 47 d																						
Corby d											17 41											18 41
Kettering a	17 01										17 50	18 01										18 50
d	17 02										17 51	18 02										18 51
Wellingborough d	17 09										18 00	18 09										19 00
Bedford 52 a	17 23										18 12	18 23										19 12
Luton 52 a											18 27											19 27
Luton Airport Parkway 52 a	17 38											18 38										
St Pancras International ⊖52 a	18 08			18 11	18 11		18 24			18 34	18 50	19 08			19 11	19 11		19 24			19 35	19 51

A From Liverpool Lime Street to Norwich
B From Glasgow Central to Reading
C not 18 August
D 18 August
E From Newcastle to Penzance
F From Aberdeen to Guildford
G From Newcastle to Plymouth
H From Edinburgh to Reading

For connections to Gatwick Airport refer to Table T052

Sheffield - East Midlands - London

Saturdays
4 August to 1 September

Station	Table		EM	EM	XC	EM	EM	EM	EM	NT	XC	EM	EM	EM	EM	XC	EM	EM	EM	NT	XC	EM	EM	EM
			◇1 ⌶	◇ A	◇1 B ⌶	◇1 C ⌶	◇1 D ⌶		◇1 ⌶	◇	◇1 E ⌶	◇1 ⌶	◇1 ⌶	◇1 ⌶	◇ F	◇1 G ⌶	◇1 H ⌶		◇1 ⌶	◇	◇1 I ⌶	◇1 ⌶	◇1 ⌶	◇1 ⌶
York 8	29	d			16 45						17 35					17 45	17 50				18 35			
Leeds 10	31,34	d			17 10					17 03						18 11				18 03				
Wakefield Westgate 7	31	d			17 22											18 23								
Wakefield Kirkgate 4	31,34	d								17 22										18 21				
Doncaster 7	29	d									17 58						18 19				18 58			
Manchester Piccadilly	78	d		16 42											17 42									
Sheffield 7		d		17 41	17 55					18 03	18 24	18 29			18 40	18 55	19 00			19 05	19 24	19 29		
Chesterfield		d		17 57	18a06					18 19	18a35	18 41			18 57	19a06	19 12			19 21	19a35	19 41		
Derby 6		a																						
		d				18 20																		
Long Eaton		d				18 40																		
Alfreton		d		18 08						18 30					19 08					19 31				
Langley Mill		d								18 37										19 39				
Lincoln	27	d						17 25										18 30						
Newark Castle	27	d						17 55										18 59						
Nottingham 8		a		18 29				18 30		18 55					19 29			19 24		19 57				
		d	18 12					18 35	18 45					19 12				19 30	19 45					20 12
Beeston		d	18 18					18 41						19 18				19 36						20 18
East Midlands Parkway		a				18 44		18 49	18 55								19 44	19 44	19 55					20 23
		d				18 45	18 45	18 50	18 56								19 45	19 48	19 56					20 24
Loughborough		d	18 28			18 52	18 52	18 58						19 28			19 52	19 58						20 32
Barrow Upon Soar		d						19 03										20 03						
Sileby		d						19 07										20 07						
Syston		d						19 12										20 12						
Leicester		a	18 37			19 02	19 02	19 23	19 11			19 24		19 37			20 02	20 23	20 11			20 24		20 41
		d	18 39			19 02	19 02		19 13			19 25		19 39			20 03		20 13			20 25		20 42
Market Harborough		d	18 52						19 26					19 52					20 26					20 55
Melton Mowbray	47	d																						
Oakham	47	d																						
Corby		d											19 41										20 41	
Kettering 5		a	19 01									19 46	19 50	20 01									20 50	21 04
		d	19 02									19 47	19 51	20 02									20 51	21 04
Wellingborough		d	19 09										20 00	20 09									21 00	21 13
Bedford 7	52	a	19 23										20 12	20 23									21 12	21 25
Luton 10	52	a											20 27										21 27	
Luton Airport Parkway 7	52	a	19 38											20 38										21 41
St Pancras International	⊖52	a	20 08			20 11	20 11		20 24			20 37	20 51	21 08			21 10		21 24			21 35	21 51	22 09

Station	Table		EM	EM	XC	NT	XC	EM	EM	EM	EM	EM	EM	XC	NT	XC	EM	XC	NT	EM	EM	EM	EM
			◇ A		◇1 J ⌶	◇	◇1 K ⌶	◇1 ⌶	◇1 ⊡	◇1 ⌶	◇1 ⌶	◇ F		◇1 L	◇	◇1 K	◇ F	◇1 M ⌶	◇		◇ F	◇1 ⊡	◇1 ⌶
York 8	29	d			18 45		19 36							19 45		20 35		20 45					
Leeds 10	31,34	d			19 11	19 03								20 11	20 03			21 11	21 03				
Wakefield Westgate 7	31	d			19 23									20 23				21 23					
Wakefield Kirkgate 4	31,34	d				19 21									20 21				21 21				
Doncaster 7	29	d					19 59									20 59							
Manchester Piccadilly	78	d	18 42									19 42					20 43				21 41		
Sheffield 7		d	19 37		19 55	20 02	20 24	20 29				20 39		20 55	21 02	21 25	21 38	21 55	22 03		22 42		23 20
Chesterfield		d	19 52		20a06	20 18	20a35	20 41				20 54		21a06	21 18	21a36	21 54	22a06	22 20		22 56		23 32
Derby 6		a													21 39								00 06
		d													21 41								
Long Eaton		d																					
Alfreton		d	20 03			20 28						21 05					22 05		22 31		23 07		
Langley Mill		d				20 36											22 13		22 38				
Lincoln	27	d																					
Newark Castle	27	d																					
Nottingham 8		a	20 27			20 55						21 33			22 08		22 34		22 57		23 28		
		d		20 33						21 05	21 32		21 34							23 05			
Beeston		d		20 39						21 11			21 41							23 10			
East Midlands Parkway		a		20 49				21 12		21 16			21 49							23 17			
		d		20 50				21 13		21 17			21 49							23 18			
Loughborough		d		20 58				21 20		21 25	21 46		21 58							23 26			
Barrow Upon Soar		d		21 03									22 03										
Sileby		d		21 07									22 07										
Syston		d		21 12									22 12										
Leicester		a		21 23				21 31		21 35	21 55		22 22							23 45			
		d								21 36	21 56												
Market Harborough		d								21 49	22 09												
Melton Mowbray	47	d																					
Oakham	47	d																					
Corby		d							21 43													22 43	
Kettering 5		a							21 52	21 57	22 18											22 52	
		d								21 57	22 19												
Wellingborough		d								22 06	22 26												
Bedford 7	52	a								22 19	22 39												
Luton 10	52	a								22 34	22 55												
Luton Airport Parkway 7	52	a								22 37													
St Pancras International	⊖52	a								23 11	23 29												

A From Liverpool Lime Street to Norwich
B From Glasgow Central to Reading
C not 18 August
D 18 August
E From Newcastle to Plymouth
F From Liverpool Lime Street
G From Edinburgh to Southampton Central
H From Scarborough
I From Newcastle to Bristol Temple Meads
J From Glasgow Central to Birmingham New Street
K From Newcastle to Birmingham New Street
L From Edinburgh to Birmingham New Street
M From Glasgow Central to Birmingham New Street. ⌶ to Leeds

For connections to Gatwick Airport refer to Table T052

Table T053-R

Sheffield - East Midlands - London

Saturdays
4 August to 1 September

Station	Table		EM
			◇ A
York 8	29	d	
Leeds 10	31,34	d	
Wakefield Westgate 7	31	d	
Wakefield Kirkgate 4	31,34	d	
Doncaster 7	29	d	
Manchester Piccadilly	78	d	22 28
Sheffield 7		d	23 38
Chesterfield		d	23 53
Derby 6		a	
		d	
Long Eaton		d	
Alfreton		d	
Langley Mill		d	
Lincoln	27	d	
Newark Castle	27	d	
Nottingham 8		a	00 30
		d	
Beeston		d	
East Midlands Parkway		a	
		d	
Loughborough		d	
Barrow Upon Soar		d	
Sileby		d	
Syston		d	
Leicester		a	
		d	
Market Harborough		d	
Melton Mowbray	47	d	
Oakham	47	d	
Corby		d	
Kettering 5		a	
		d	
Wellingborough		d	
Bedford 7	52	a	
Luton 10	52	a	
Luton Airport Parkway 7	52	a	
St Pancras International	⊖52	a	

Saturdays
8 September to 6 October

Station	Table		EM	EM	NT	EM	EM	EM	EM	EM	EM	NT	EM	XC	XC	EM	EM	EM	EM	EM	NT	XC	EM	EM
			◇ A	◇1 ⌶	◇	◇1 ⌶	◇1 ⌶	◇1 ⌶	◇1 ⌶	◇1 ⌶	◇1 ⌶	◇	◇1 ⌶	◇1 B ⌶	◇1 C ⌶		◇1 ⌶	◇1 ⌶		◇1 ⌶	◇	◇1 D	◇1 ⊠	◇1 ⌶
York 8	29	d																						
Leeds 10	31,34	d												05 49	05 49							06 17		
Wakefield Westgate 7	31	d												06 01	06 01							06 29		
Wakefield Kirkgate 4	31,34	d																						
Doncaster 7	29	d																				06 51		
Manchester Piccadilly	78	d																						
Sheffield 7		d			05 15		05 29					06 01	06 27	06 30	06 30						07 02	07 18	07 29	
Chesterfield		d	00 02		05 30		05 41					06 19	06 39	06 44	06 44						07 17	07 32	07 41	
Derby 6		a												07 20	07 21							08 15		
		d				05 21				06 29								07 31						
Long Eaton		d				05 30				06 38								07 41						
Alfreton		d			05 45							06 29									07 28			
Langley Mill		d			05 53							06 36									07 35			
Lincoln	27	d																						
Newark Castle	27	d																						
Nottingham 8		a	00 45		06 11							07 00									07 53			
		d						06 12			06 45						07 12		07 33	07 45				
Beeston		d						06 18									07 18		07 39					
East Midlands Parkway		a				05 34				06 42	06 55							07 44	07 49	07 55				
		d				05 35				06 43	06 56							07 45	07 50	07 56				
Loughborough		d				05 42		06 27		06 50						06 59	07 29	07 53	07 58					
Barrow Upon Soar		d														07 04			08 03					
Sileby		d														07 08			08 07					
Syston		d														07 14			08 12					
Leicester		a				05 52	06 24	06 37		06 59	07 12		07 19			07 22	07 38	08 02	08 23	08 11			08 19	
		d		04 45		05 53	06 25	06 38		07 01	07 12		07 25				07 40	08 03		08 13			08 25	
Market Harborough		d				06 07		06 52			07 26						07 53			08 27				
Melton Mowbray	47	d																						
Oakham	47	d																						
Corby		d							07 06															08 41
Kettering 5		a		05 04		06 16		07 01	07 15	07 20							08 02							08 50
		d		05 05		06 17		07 02		07 22							08 03							08 51
Wellingborough		d		05 17		06 24		07 09		07 29							08 10							09 00
Bedford 7	52	a		05 32		06 37		07 23		07 42							08 23							09 12
Luton 10	52	a				06 52				07 56														09 27
Luton Airport Parkway 7	52	a		05 49				07 38									08 38							
St Pancras International	⊖52	a		06 21		07 21	07 33	08 06		08 22	08 26		08 36				09 07	09 11		09 25			09 36	09 51

A From Liverpool Lime Street
B not 8 September. To Plymouth
C 8 September. To Paignton
D To Plymouth

For connections to Gatwick Airport refer to Table T052

Sheffield - East Midlands - London

Saturdays
8 September to 6 October

	EM	EM	EM	EM	EM	XC	XC	NT	XC	XC	EM	EM	EM	EM	EM	EM	EM	EM	XC	XC	NT	XC
	◇■ 🍴	◇■ 🍴	A	B	◇■ ⊠	◇■ C 🍴	◇■ D 🍴	◇	◇■ E	◇■ F	◇■ 🍴	◇■ 🍴	◇■ 🍴	◇■ 🍴	G	H	◇■ 🍴	◇ I	◇■ J 🍴	◇■ K 🍴	◇	◇■ L 🍴
York 29 d						06 20	06 45		07 25	07 35									07 44	07 44		08 35
Leeds 31,34 d					06 34	07 11	07 11	07 03									07 40		08 11	08 11	08 04	
Wakefield Westgate 31 d					06 46	07 23	07 23										07 53		08 23	08 23		
Wakefield Kirkgate 31,34 d								07 22													08 22	
Doncaster 29 d									07 51	07 58												08 58
Manchester Piccadilly 78 d																		07 42				
Sheffield d					07 37	07 56	07 56	08 03	08 22	08 22	08 29						08 34	08 37	08 53	08 54	09 06	09 24
Chesterfield d					07 50	08 08	08 08	08 19	08 35	08 35	08 41						08 47	08 52	09 06	09 06	09 22	09 37
Derby a						08 45	08 45		09 13	09 13									09 45	09 45		10 16
d		08 31												09 31								
Long Eaton d		08 41												09 40								
Alfreton d					08 01			08 29									08 57	09 03			09 33	
Langley Mill d					08 09			08 37													09 40	
Lincoln 27 d	07 04		07 36	07 36											08 35	08 35						
Newark Castle 27 d	07 29		08 04	08 04											09 04	09 04						
Nottingham a	07 57		08 28	08 30	08 25			08 55							09 31	09 33	09 22	09 27			09 59	
d	08 12		08 36	08 36	08 45								09 12		09 36	09 36	09 45					
Beeston d	08 18		08 42	08 42									09 18		09 42	09 42						
East Midlands Parkway a		08 44	08 49	08 49	08 55									09 44	09 49	09 49	09 55					
d		08 45	08 50	08 50	08 56									09 45	09 50	09 50	09 56					
Loughborough d	08 28	08 53	08 58	08 58									09 28	09 53	09 58	09 58						
Barrow Upon Soar d			09 03	09 03											10 03	10 03						
Sileby d			09 07	09 07											10 07	10 07						
Syston d			09 12	09 12											10 12	10 12						
Leicester a	08 37	09 02	09 25	09 25	09 11						09 24		09 37	10 02	10 23	10 23	10 11					
d	08 39	09 03			09 13						09 25		09 39	10 03			10 13					
Market Harborough d	08 52				09 26								09 52				10 26					
Melton Mowbray 47 d																						
Oakham 47 d																						
Corby d												09 41										
Kettering a	09 01											09 50	10 01									
d	09 02											09 51	10 02									
Wellingborough d	09 09											10 00	10 09									
Bedford 52 a	09 23											10 12	10 23									
Luton 52 a												10 27										
Luton Airport Parkway 52 a	09 37												10 38									
St Pancras International 52 a	10 07	10 10			10 24						10 35	10 51	11 08	11 11			11 24					

	EM	EM	EM	EM	EM	XC	EM	EM	EM	NT	XC	XC	EM	EM	EM	EM	EM	XC	EM	EM	EM
	◇■ 🍴	◇■ 🍴	◇■ 🍴	◇ I	◇■ 🍴	◇■ M 🍴	G	H	◇■ 🍴	◇	◇■ N	◇■ O	◇■ 🍴	◇■ 🍴	◇■ 🍴	◇ I	◇■ 🍴	◇■ P 🍴	G	H	◇■ 🍴
York 29 d						08 45					09 35	09 36						09 45			
Leeds 31,34 d						09 11				09 04								10 11			
Wakefield Westgate 31 d						09 23												10 23			
Wakefield Kirkgate 31,34 d										09 22											
Doncaster 29 d											09 58	09 59									
Manchester Piccadilly 78 d				08 43												09 42					
Sheffield d	09 29			09 37		09 53				10 05	10 24	10 24	10 29			10 36		10 55			
Chesterfield d	09 42			09 52		10 05				10 22	10 37	10 37	10 42			10 52		11 07			
Derby a						10 45					11 18	11 18						11 45			
d					10 31												11 31				
Long Eaton d					10 40												11 40				
Alfreton d				10 03						10 32						11 02					
Langley Mill d										10 40											
Lincoln 27 d							09 36	09 36											10 36	10 36	
Newark Castle 27 d							10 07	10 07											11 04	11 04	
Nottingham a				10 27			10 30	10 32		10 58						11 27			11 31	11 32	
d			10 12				10 36	10 36	10 45						11 12				11 36	11 36	11 45
Beeston d			10 18				10 42	10 42							11 18				11 42	11 42	
East Midlands Parkway a					10 44		10 49	10 49	10 55								11 44		11 49	11 49	11 55
d					10 44		10 50	10 50	10 56								11 45		11 50	11 50	11 56
Loughborough d			10 28		10 53		10 58	10 58							11 28		11 52		11 58	11 58	
Barrow Upon Soar d							11 03	11 03											12 03	12 03	
Sileby d							11 07	11 07											12 07	12 07	
Syston d							11 12	11 12											12 12	12 12	
Leicester a	10 24		10 37		11 02		11 23	11 23	11 11				11 24		11 37		12 02		12 23	12 23	12 12
d	10 25		10 39		11 03				11 13				11 25		11 39		12 03				12 12
Market Harborough d			10 52						11 26						11 52						12 26
Melton Mowbray 47 d																					
Oakham 47 d																					
Corby d		10 41												11 41							
Kettering a		10 50	11 01											11 50	12 01						
d		10 51	11 02											11 51	12 02						
Wellingborough d		11 00	11 09											12 00	12 09						
Bedford 52 a		11 12	11 22											12 12	12 23						
Luton 52 a		11 27												12 27							
Luton Airport Parkway 52 a			11 37												12 38						
St Pancras International 52 a	11 35	11 50	12 07		12 11				12 24				12 35	12 51	13 08		13 11				13 25

A not from 29 September. From Sleaford
B 29 September, 6 October. From Sleaford
C not 8 September. To Reading
D 8 September. To Reading
E not 3 September. To Plymouth
F 8 September. To Penzance
G not from 29 September
H 29 September, 6 October
I From Liverpool Lime Street to Norwich
J not 8 September. From Newcastle to Southampton Central
K 8 September. From Newcastle to Southampton Central
L From Newcastle to Plymouth
M From Edinburgh to Reading
N 8 September. From Edinburgh to Paignton
O not 8 September. From Edinburgh to Plymouth
P From Glasgow Central to Southampton Central

For connections to Gatwick Airport refer to Table T052

Sheffield - East Midlands - London

Saturdays
8 September to 6 October

	NT	XC	XC	EM	EM	EM	EM	EM	XC	EM	EM	EM	NT	XC	EM	EM	EM	EM	EM	XC	EM	EM
	◇	◇■ A 🍴	◇■ B 🍴	◇■ 🍴	◇■ 🍴	◇■ 🍴	◇ C	◇■ 🍴	◇■ D 🍴	E	F	◇■ 🍴	◇	◇■ G 🍴	◇■ 🍴	◇■ 🍴	◇■ 🍴	◇ C	◇■ 🍴	◇■ H 🍴	E	F
York 29 d		10 35	10 37						10 45					11 35						11 45		
Leeds 31,34 d	10 04								11 11				11 04							12 11		
Wakefield Westgate 31 d									11 23											12 23		
Wakefield Kirkgate 31,34 d	10 22												11 22									
Doncaster 29 d		10 59	11 01											11 58								
Manchester Piccadilly 78 d							10 43											11 42				
Sheffield d	11 05	11 24	11 24	11 29			11 37		11 55				12 05	12 24	12 29			12 37		12 55		
Chesterfield d	11 22	11 38	11 38	11 41			11 52		12 07				12 22	12 36	12 41			12 52		13 07		
Derby a		12 17	12 17						12 46					13 15						13 45		
d								12 31											13 31			
Long Eaton d								12 40											13 40			
Alfreton d	11 32						12 02						12 32					13 02				
Langley Mill d	11 40												12 40									
Lincoln 27 d										11 40	11 40										12 36	12 36
Newark Castle 27 d										12 04	12 04										13 06	13 06
Nottingham a	11 58						12 27			12 27	12 29		12 58					13 27			13 29	13 31
d						12 12				12 35	12 36	12 45					13 12				13 35	13 36
Beeston d						12 18				12 41	12 42						13 18				13 41	13 42
East Midlands Parkway a								12 44		12 49	12 49	12 55							13 44		13 49	13 49
d								12 45		12 50	12 50	12 56							13 45		13 50	13 50
Loughborough d						12 28		12 52		12 58	12 58						13 28		13 52		13 58	13 58
Barrow Upon Soar d										13 03	13 03										14 03	14 03
Sileby d										13 07	13 07										14 07	14 07
Syston d										13 12	13 12										14 12	14 12
Leicester a				12 24		12 37		13 02		13 23	13 23	13 11			13 24		13 37		14 02		14 23	14 23
d				12 25		12 39		13 03				13 12			13 25		13 39		14 03			
Market Harborough d						12 52						13 26					13 52					
Melton Mowbray 47 d																						
Oakham 47 d																						
Corby d					12 41											13 41						
Kettering a					12 50	13 01										13 50	14 01					
d					12 51	13 02										13 51	14 02					
Wellingborough d					13 00	13 09										14 00	14 09					
Bedford 52 a					13 11	13 23										14 12	14 23					
Luton 52 a					13 27											14 27						
Luton Airport Parkway 52 a						13 38											14 38					
St Pancras International 52 a				13 35	13 51	14 08		14 11				14 24			14 35	14 50	15 08		15 10			

	EM	NT	XC	EM	EM	EM	EM	EM	XC	EM	EM	EM	NT	XC	EM	EM	EM	EM	EM	XC	EM
	◇■ 🍴	◇	◇■ I 🍴	◇■ 🍴	◇■ 🍴	◇■ 🍴	◇ C	◇■ 🍴	◇■ J 🍴	E	F	◇■ 🍴	◇	◇■ I 🍴	◇■ 🍴	◇■ 🍴	◇■ 🍴	◇ C	◇■ 🍴	◇■ K 🍴	E
York 29 d			12 36						12 45					13 35						13 45	
Leeds 31,34 d		12 04							13 11				13 04							14 11	
Wakefield Westgate 31 d									13 23											14 23	
Wakefield Kirkgate 31,34 d		12 22											13 23								
Doncaster 29 d			12 59											13 58							
Manchester Piccadilly 78 d							12 42											13 42			
Sheffield d		13 05	13 23	13 29			13 37		13 54				14 05	14 25	14 29			14 37		14 55	
Chesterfield d		13 22	13 37	13 41			13 52		14 06				14 22	14 37	14 42			14 54		15 07	
Derby a			14 17						14 44					15 17						15 45	
d								14 31											15 31		
Long Eaton d								14 40											15 40		
Alfreton d		13 32					14 03						14 32					15 04			
Langley Mill d		13 40											14 40								
Lincoln 27 d										13 37	13 37										14 32
Newark Castle 27 d										14 05	14 05										15 04
Nottingham a		13 58					14 27			14 28	14 30		14 58					15 28			15 30
d	13 45					14 12				14 35	14 36	14 45					15 12				15 35
Beeston d						14 18				14 41	14 42						15 18				15 41
East Midlands Parkway a	13 55							14 44		14 49	14 49	14 55							15 44		15 49
d	13 56							14 45		14 50	14 50	14 56							15 45		15 50
Loughborough d						14 28		14 52		14 58	14 58						15 28		15 52		15 58
Barrow Upon Soar d										15 03	15 03										16 03
Sileby d										15 07	15 07										16 07
Syston d										15 12	15 12										16 12
Leicester a	14 11			14 24		14 37		15 02		15 23	15 23	15 11			15 24		15 37		16 02		16 23
d	14 13			14 25		14 39		15 03				15 13			15 25		15 39		16 03		
Market Harborough d	14 26					14 52						15 26					15 52				
Melton Mowbray 47 d																					
Oakham 47 d																					
Corby d					14 41											15 41					
Kettering a					14 50	15 01										15 50	16 01				
d					14 51	15 02										15 51	16 02				
Wellingborough d					15 00	15 09										16 00	16 09				
Bedford 52 a					15 11	15 22										16 12	16 23				
Luton 52 a					15 27											16 27					
Luton Airport Parkway 52 a						15 37											16 38				
St Pancras International 52 a	15 24			15 35	15 51	16 05		16 10				16 24			16 36	16 50	17 08		17 11		

A 8 September. From Newcastle to Newquay
B not 8 September. From Newcastle to Plymouth
C From Liverpool Lime Street to Norwich
D From Dundee to Reading
E not from 29 September
F 29 September, 6 October
G From Newcastle to Plymouth
H From Glasgow Central to Southampton Central
I From Newcastle to Penzance
J From Glasgow Central to Reading
K From Aberdeen to Guildford

For connections to Gatwick Airport refer to Table T052

Sheffield - East Midlands - London

	EM	EM	NT	XC	EM	EM	EM	EM	EM	XC	EM	EM	EM	NT	XC	EM	EM	EM	EM	EM	XC	EM
	A	◇■	◇	◇■ B	◇■	◇■	◇■	◇ C	◇■	◇■ D	E	A	◇■	◇	◇■ B	◇■	◇■	◇■	◇ C	◇■	◇■ F	E
York 29 d				14 35						14 45					15 35						15 45	
Leeds 31,34 d			14 04							15 11				15 04							16 11	
Wakefield Westgate 31 d										15 23											16 23	
Wakefield Kirkgate 31,34 d			14 22											15 22								
Doncaster 29 d				14 59											15 58							
Manchester Piccadilly 78 d								14 42											15 42			
Sheffield d			15 05	15 24	15 29			15 37		15 55				16 05	16 24	16 29			16 37		16 55	
Chesterfield d			15 22	15 36	15 41			15 52		16 07				16 22	16 36	16 41			16 53		17 07	
Derby a				16 14						16 45					17 17						17 45	
d									16 31											17 31		
Long Eaton d									16 40											17 40		
Alfreton d			15 32					16 03						16 32					17 04			
Langley Mill d			15 40											16 40								
Lincoln 27 d	14 32										15 26	15 26										16 35
Newark Castle 27 d	15 04										15 59	15 59										17 05
Nottingham a	15 32		15 58					16 27			16 27	16 29		16 58					17 27			17 30
d	15 36	15 45					16 12				16 33	16 33	16 45					17 12				17 33
Beeston d	15 42						16 18				16 39	16 39						17 18				17 39
East Midlands Parkway a	15 49	15 55							16 44		16 52	16 52	16 55							17 44		17 52
d	15 50	15 56							16 45		16 52	16 52	16 56							17 45		17 52
Loughborough d	15 58						16 28		16 52		17 00	17 00						17 28		17 52		18 00
Barrow Upon Soar d	16 03										17 05	17 05										18 05
Sileby d	16 07										17 09	17 09										18 09
Syston d	16 12										17 14	17 14										18 14
Leicester a	16 23	16 11			16 24		16 37		17 02		17 23	17 23	17 11			17 24		17 37		18 02		18 23
d		16 13			16 25		16 39		17 03				17 13			17 25		17 39		18 03		
Market Harborough d		16 26					16 52						17 26					17 52				
Melton Mowbray 47 d																						
Oakham 47 d																						
Corby d						16 41											17 41					
Kettering a						16 50	17 01										17 50	18 01				
d						16 51	17 02										17 51	18 02				
Wellingborough d						17 00	17 09										18 00	18 09				
Bedford 52 a						17 12	17 23										18 12	18 23				
Luton 52 a						17 27											18 27					
Luton Airport Parkway 52 a							17 38											18 38				
St Pancras International ⊖52 a		17 24			17 35	17 51	18 08		18 11				18 24			18 34	18 50	19 08		19 11		

	EM	EM	NT	XC	EM	EM	EM	EM	EM	XC	EM	EM	EM	NT	XC	EM	EM	EM	EM	XC	EM	EM
	A	◇■	◇	◇■ B	◇■	◇■	◇■	◇ C	◇■	◇■ D	E	A	◇■	◇	◇■ B	◇■	◇■	◇■	◇ G	◇■ H	◇■ I	E
York 29 d				16 04						16 45					17 35					17 45	17 50	
Leeds 31,34 d			16 04	16 40						17 10				17 03						18 11		
Wakefield Westgate 31 d				16 52						17 22										18 23		
Wakefield Kirkgate 31,34 d			16 22											17 22								
Doncaster 29 d															17 58						18 19	
Manchester Piccadilly 78 d								16 42											17 42			
Sheffield d			17 05	17 24	17 29			17 41		17 55				18 03	18 24	18 29			18 40	18 55	19 00	
Chesterfield d			17 22	17 36	17 41			17 57		18 07				18 19	18 36	18 41			18 57	19 07	19 12	
Derby a				18 14						18 45					19 18					19 48		
d									18 31													
Long Eaton d									18 40													
Alfreton d			17 32					18 08						18 30					19 08			
Langley Mill d			17 40											18 37								
Lincoln 27 d	16 35										17 25	17 25										18 30
Newark Castle 27 d	17 05										17 55	17 55										18 59
Nottingham a	17 32		17 58					18 29			18 30	18 32		18 55					19 29			19 24
d	17 33	17 45					18 12				18 35	18 36	18 45					19 12				19 30
Beeston d	17 39						18 18				18 41	18 42						19 18				19 36
East Midlands Parkway a	17 52	17 55							18 44		18 49	18 49	18 55								19 44	19 44
d	17 52	17 56							18 45		18 50	18 50	18 56								19 45	19 48
Loughborough d	18 00						18 28		18 52		18 58	18 58						19 28			19 52	19 58
Barrow Upon Soar d	18 05										19 03	19 03										20 03
Sileby d	18 09										19 07	19 07										20 07
Syston d	18 14										19 12	19 12										20 12
Leicester a	18 23	18 11			18 24		18 37		19 02		19 23	19 23	19 11			19 24		19 37			20 02	20 23
d		18 13			18 25		18 39		19 02				19 13			19 25		19 39			20 03	
Market Harborough d		18 26					18 52						19 26					19 52				
Melton Mowbray 47 d																						
Oakham 47 d																						
Corby d						18 41											19 41					
Kettering a						18 50	19 01									19 46	19 50	20 01				
d						18 51	19 02									19 47	19 51	20 02				
Wellingborough d						19 00	19 09										20 00	20 09				
Bedford 52 a						19 12	19 23										20 12	20 23				
Luton 52 a						19 27											20 27					
Luton Airport Parkway 52 a							19 38											20 38				
St Pancras International ⊖52 a		19 24			19 35	19 51	20 08		20 11				20 24			20 37	20 51	21 08			21 10	

A 29 September, 6 October
B From Newcastle to Plymouth
C From Liverpool Lime Street to Norwich
D From Glasgow Central to Reading
E not from 29 September
F From Edinburgh to Reading
G From Liverpool Lime Street
H From Edinburgh to Southampton Central
I From Scarborough

For connections to Gatwick Airport refer to Table T052

Sheffield - East Midlands - London

	EM	EM	NT	XC	EM	EM	EM	EM	EM	XC	NT	XC	EM	EM	EM	EM	EM	EM	XC	NT	XC
	A	◇■	◇	◇■ B	◇■	◇■	◇■	◇ C		◇■ D	◇	◇■ E	◇■	◇■	◇■	◇■	◇ F		◇■ G	◇	◇■ E
York 29 d				18 35						18 45		19 36							19 45		20 35
Leeds 31,34 d			18 03							19 11	19 03								20 11	20 03	
Wakefield Westgate 31 d										19 23									20 23		
Wakefield Kirkgate 31,34 d			18 21								19 21									20 21	
Doncaster 29 d				18 58								19 59									20 59
Manchester Piccadilly 78 d								18 42									19 42				
Sheffield d			19 05	19 24	19 29			19 37		19 55	20 02	20 24	20 29				20 39		20 55	21 02	21 25
Chesterfield d			19 21	19 36	19 41			19 52		20 07	20 18	20 36	20 41				20 54		21 07	21 18	21 37
Derby a				20 14						20 45		21 18							21 45		22 18
d																					
Long Eaton d																					
Alfreton d			19 31					20 03			20 28						21 05				
Langley Mill d			19 39								20 36										
Lincoln 27 d	18 30																				
Newark Castle 27 d	18 59																				
Nottingham a	19 26		19 57					20 27			20 55						21 33			21 47	
d	19 30	19 45					20 12		20 33						21 05	21 32		21 34			
Beeston d	19 36						20 18		20 39						21 11			21 41			
East Midlands Parkway a	19 44	19 55					20 23		20 49				21 12		21 16			21 49			
d	19 48	19 56					20 24		20 50				21 13		21 17			21 49			
Loughborough d	19 58						20 32		20 58				21 20		21 25	21 46		21 58			
Barrow Upon Soar d	20 03								21 03									22 03			
Sileby d	20 07								21 07									22 07			
Syston d	20 12								21 12									22 12			
Leicester a	20 23	20 11			20 24		20 41		21 23				21 31		21 35	21 55		22 22			
d		20 13			20 25		20 42								21 36	21 56					
Market Harborough d		20 26					20 55								21 49	22 09					
Melton Mowbray 47 d																					
Oakham 47 d																					
Corby d						20 41								21 43							
Kettering a						20 50	21 04							21 52	21 57	22 18					
d						20 51	21 04								21 57	22 19					
Wellingborough d						21 00	21 13								22 06	22 26					
Bedford 52 a						21 12	21 25								22 19	22 39					
Luton 52 a						21 27									22 34	22 55					
Luton Airport Parkway 52 a							21 41								22 37						
St Pancras International ⊖52 a		21 24			21 35	21 51	22 09								23 11	23 29					

	EM	XC	NT	EM	EM	EM	EM	EM
	◇ F	◇■ H	◇		◇ F	◇■	◇■	◇ F
York 29 d		20 45						
Leeds 31,34 d		21 11	21 03					
Wakefield Westgate 31 d		21 23						
Wakefield Kirkgate 31,34 d			21 21					
Doncaster 29 d								
Manchester Piccadilly 78 d	20 43				21 41			22 28
Sheffield d	21 38	21 55	22 03		22 42		23 20	23 38
Chesterfield d	21 54	22 07	22 20		22 56		23 32	23 53
Derby a		22 43					00 05	
d								
Long Eaton d								
Alfreton d	22 05		22 31		23 07			
Langley Mill d	22 13		22 38					
Lincoln 27 d								
Newark Castle 27 d								
Nottingham a	22 34		22 57		23 28			00 30
d				23 05				
Beeston d				23 10				
East Midlands Parkway a				23 17				
d				23 18				
Loughborough d				23 26				
Barrow Upon Soar d								
Sileby d								
Syston d								
Leicester a				23 45				
d								
Market Harborough d								
Melton Mowbray 47 d								
Oakham 47 d								
Corby d						22 43		
Kettering a						22 52		
d								
Wellingborough d								
Bedford 52 a								
Luton 52 a								
Luton Airport Parkway 52 a								
St Pancras International ⊖52 a								

A 29 September, 6 October
B From Newcastle to Bristol Temple Meads
C From Liverpool Lime Street to Norwich
D From Glasgow Central to Birmingham New Street
E From Newcastle to Birmingham New Street
F From Liverpool Lime Street
G From Edinburgh to Birmingham New Street
H From Glasgow Central to Birmingham New Street. ✠ to Leeds

For connections to Gatwick Airport refer to Table T052

Table T053-R

Saturdays

13 October to 8 December

Sheffield - East Midlands - London

Station			EM ◇ A	EM ◇1 🍴	NT ◇	EM ◇1 🍴	EM ◇1 🍴	EM ◇1 🍴	EM ◇1 🍴	EM ◇1 🍴	EM ◇1 🍴	NT ◇	EM	EM ◇1 🍴	XC ◇1 B 🍴	EM ◇1 🍴	EM ◇1 🍴	EM	EM ◇1 🍴	NT ◇	XC ◇1 C 🍴	EM ◇1 ⊠	EM ◇1 🍴	EM ◇1 🍴
York 8	29	d																						
Leeds 10	31,34	d													06 11						06 17			
Wakefield Westgate 7	31	d													06 23						06 29			
Wakefield Kirkgate 4	31,34	d																						
Doncaster 7	29	d																			06 51			
Manchester Piccadilly	78	d																						
Sheffield 7	🚋	d			05 15		05 29					06 01		06 27	06 53					07 02	07 18	07 29		
Chesterfield		d	00 02		05 30		05 41					06 19		06 39	07 06					07 17	07 30	07 41		
Derby 6		a					06 00							07 00	07 25						07 48	07 59		
		d				05 21	06 01			06 29				07 04			07 31					08 04		
Long Eaton		d				05 30				06 38							07 41							
Alfreton		d			05 45							06 29								07 28				
Langley Mill		d			05 53							06 36								07 35				
Lincoln	27	d																						07 04
Newark Castle	27	d																						07 29
Nottingham 8	🚋	a	00 45		06 11							07 00								07 53				07 57
		d						06 12			06 45					07 12		07 33	07 45					08 12
Beeston		d						06 18								07 18		07 39						08 18
East Midlands Parkway	✈	a				05 34				06 42	06 55						07 44	07 49	07 55					
		d				05 35				06 43	06 56						07 45	07 50	07 56					
Loughborough		d				05 42		06 27		06 50			06 59			07 29	07 53	07 58						08 28
Barrow Upon Soar		d											07 04					08 03						
Sileby		d											07 08					08 07						
Syston		d											07 14					08 12						
Leicester		a				05 52	06 22	06 37		06 59	07 12		07 22	07 25		07 38	08 02	08 23	08 11			08 25		08 37
		d		04 45		05 53	06 24	06 38		07 01	07 12			07 25		07 40	08 03		08 13			08 25		08 39
Market Harborough		d				06 07		06 52			07 26					07 53			08 27					08 52
Melton Mowbray	47	d																						
Oakham	47	d																						
Corby		d							07 06														08 41	
Kettering 5		a		05 04		06 16		07 01	07 15	07 20						08 02							08 50	09 01
		d		05 05		06 17		07 02		07 22						08 03							08 51	09 02
Wellingborough		d		05 17		06 24		07 09		07 29						08 10							09 00	09 09
Bedford 7	52	a		05 32		06 37		07 23		07 42						08 23							09 12	09 23
Luton 10	52	a				06 52				07 56													09 27	
Luton Airport Parkway 7	52 ✈	a		05 49				07 38								08 38								09 37
St Pancras International	⊖52	a		06 21		07 21	07 33	08 06		08 22	08 26			08 36		09 07	09 11		09 25			09 36	09 51	10 07

Station			EM ◇1 🍴	EM D	EM ◇1 ⊠	XC ◇1 E 🍴	NT ◇	XC F	EM ◇1 🍴	EM ◇1 🍴	EM ◇1 🍴	EM ◇1 G 🍴	EM ◇ H	XC ◇1 I 🍴	EM ◇1 🍴	EM	EM ◇1 J 🍴	NT ◇	XC ◇1 K 🍴	EM ◇1 🍴	EM ◇1 🍴	EM ◇1 🍴	EM ◇ H	XC ◇1 L 🍴
York 8	29	d				06 20		07 25						07 45					08 35					08 45
Leeds 10	31,34	d			06 34	07 11	07 03					07 40		08 11				08 04						09 11
Wakefield Westgate 7	31	d			06 46	07 23						07 53		08 23										09 23
Wakefield Kirkgate 4	31,34	d					07 22											08 22						
Doncaster 7	29	d						07 51											09 01					
Manchester Piccadilly	78	d											07 42										08 43	
Sheffield 7	🚋	d			07 37	07 56	08 03	08 22	08 29			08 34	08 37	08 54	09 00			09 06	09 24	09 29			09 37	09 53
Chesterfield		d			07 50	08 08	08 19	08 34	08 41			08 47	08 52	09 07	09 12			09 22		09 41			09 52	10 06
Derby 6		a				08 25		08 51	08 59					09 24	09 31				09 52	09 59				10 27
		d	08 31						09 04						09 31					10 04				
Long Eaton		d	08 41												09 41									
Alfreton		d			08 01		08 29					08 57	09 03					09 33					10 03	
Langley Mill		d			08 09		08 37											09 40						
Lincoln	27	d		07 36												08 35								
Newark Castle	27	d		08 04												09 04								
Nottingham 8	🚋	a		08 30	08 25		08 55					09 22	09 27			09 33		09 59					10 27	
		d		08 36	08 45						09 12	09 45				09 36						10 12		
Beeston		d		08 42							09 18					09 42	←					10 18		
East Midlands Parkway	✈	a	08 44	08 49	08 55							09 55			09 44	09 49	09 55							
		d	08 45	08 50	08 56							09 56			09 45	09 50	09 56							
Loughborough		d	08 53	08 58							09 28	→			09 53	09 58						10 28		
Barrow Upon Soar		d		09 03												10 03								
Sileby		d		09 07												10 07								
Syston		d		09 12												10 12								
Leicester		a	09 02	09 25	09 11				09 24		09 37				10 02	10 23	10 11			10 24		10 37		
		d	09 03		09 13				09 25		09 39				10 03		10 13			10 25		10 39		
Market Harborough		d			09 26						09 52						10 26					10 52		
Melton Mowbray	47	d																						
Oakham	47	d																						
Corby		d								09 41											10 41			
Kettering 5		a								09 50	10 01										10 50	11 01		
		d								09 51	10 02										10 51	11 02		
Wellingborough		d								10 00	10 09										11 00	11 09		
Bedford 7	52	a								10 12	10 23										11 12	11 22		
Luton 10	52	a								10 27											11 27			
Luton Airport Parkway 7	52 ✈	a									10 38											11 37		
St Pancras International	⊖52	a	10 10		10 24				10 35	10 51	11 08				11 11		11 24			11 35	11 50	12 07		

A From Liverpool Lime Street
B To Plymouth
C To Southampton Central
D From Sleaford
E To Plymouth. 🍴 from Leeds
F From Newcastle to Reading
G To St Pancras International
H From Liverpool Lime Street to Norwich
I From Newcastle to Plymouth. 🍴 from Leeds
J From Leeds
K From Newcastle to Southampton Central
L From Edinburgh to Plymouth

For connections to Gatwick Airport refer to Table T052

Table T053-R

Saturdays

13 October to 8 December

Sheffield - East Midlands - London

Station			EM ◇1 🍴	EM	EM ◇1 🍴	NT ◇	XC ◇1 A 🍴	EM ◇1 🍴	EM ◇1 🍴	EM ◇1 🍴	EM ◇ B	XC ◇1 C 🍴	EM ◇1 🍴	EM	EM ◇1 🍴	NT ◇	XC ◇1 D 🍴	EM ◇1 🍴	EM ◇1 🍴	EM ◇1 🍴	EM ◇ B	XC ◇1 E 🍴	EM ◇1 🍴
York 8	29	d					09 35					09 45					10 35					10 45	
Leeds 10	31,34	d				09 04						10 11				10 04						11 11	
Wakefield Westgate 7	31	d										10 23										11 23	
Wakefield Kirkgate 4	31,34	d				09 22										10 22							
Doncaster 7	29	d					09 58										10 59						
Manchester Piccadilly	78	d									09 42										10 43		
Sheffield 7	🚋	d	10 00			10 05	10 24	10 29			10 36	10 54	11 00			11 05	11 24	11 29			11 37	11 55	12 00
Chesterfield		d	10 13			10 22		10 41			10 52	11 07	11 13			11 22		11 41			11 52	12 09	12 13
Derby 6		a	10 31				10 51	10 59				11 27	11 31				11 51	11 59				12 28	12 31
		d	10 33					11 03					11 33					12 03					12 33
Long Eaton		d	10 40										11 40										12 40
Alfreton		d				10 32					11 02					11 32					12 02		
Langley Mill		d				10 40										11 40							
Lincoln	27	d		09 36										10 36									
Newark Castle	27	d		10 07										11 04									
Nottingham 8	🚋	a		10 32		10 58					11 27			11 32		11 58					12 27		
		d		10 36	10 45					11 12				11 36	11 45					12 12			
Beeston		d		10 42						11 18				11 42						12 18			
East Midlands Parkway	✈	a	10 45	10 49	10 55								11 45	11 49	11 55								12 45
		d	10 45	10 50	10 56								11 46	11 50	11 56								12 46
Loughborough		d	10 53	10 58						11 28			11 52	11 58						12 28			12 52
Barrow Upon Soar		d		11 03										12 03									
Sileby		d		11 07										12 07									
Syston		d		11 12										12 12									
Leicester		a	11 02	11 23	11 11			11 25		11 37			12 02	12 23	12 12			12 24		12 37			13 02
		d	11 03		11 13			11 25		11 39			12 03		12 12			12 25		12 39			13 03
Market Harborough		d			11 26					11 52					12 26					12 52			
Melton Mowbray	47	d																					
Oakham	47	d																					
Corby		d							11 41										12 41				
Kettering 5		a							11 50	12 01									12 50	13 01			
		d							11 51	12 02									12 51	13 02			
Wellingborough		d							12 00	12 09									13 00	13 09			
Bedford 7	52	a							12 12	12 23									13 11	13 23			
Luton 10	52	a							12 27										13 27				
Luton Airport Parkway 7	52 ✈	a								12 38										13 38			
St Pancras International	⊖52	a	12 11		12 24			12 35	12 51	13 08			13 11		13 25			13 35	13 51	14 08			14 11

Station			EM	EM ◇1 🍴	NT ◇	XC ◇1 F 🍴	EM ◇1 🍴	EM ◇1 🍴	EM ◇1 🍴	EM ◇ B	XC ◇1 C 🍴	EM ◇1 🍴	EM	EM ◇1 🍴	NT ◇	XC ◇1 D 🍴	EM ◇1 🍴	EM ◇1 🍴	EM ◇1 🍴	EM ◇ B	XC ◇1 G 🍴	EM ◇1 🍴	EM	EM ◇1 🍴
York 8	29	d				11 35					11 45					12 35					12 45			
Leeds 10	31,34	d			11 04						12 11				12 04						13 11			
Wakefield Westgate 7	31	d									12 23										13 23			
Wakefield Kirkgate 4	31,34	d			11 22										12 22									
Doncaster 7	29	d				11 58										12 59								
Manchester Piccadilly	78	d								11 42										12 42				
Sheffield 7	🚋	d			12 05	12 24	12 29			12 37	12 55	13 00			13 05	13 24	13 29			13 37	13 53	14 00		
Chesterfield		d			12 22		12 41			12 52	13 07	13 12			13 22		13 41			13 52	14 06	14 13		
Derby 6		a				12 51	12 59				13 24	13 29				13 52	13 59				14 28	14 31		
		d					13 03					13 31					14 03					14 33		
Long Eaton		d										13 40										14 40		
Alfreton		d			12 32					13 02					13 32					14 03				
Langley Mill		d			12 40										13 40									
Lincoln	27	d	11 40										12 36										13 37	
Newark Castle	27	d	12 04										13 06										14 05	
Nottingham 8	🚋	a	12 29		12 58					13 27			13 31		13 58					14 27			14 30	
		d	12 36	12 45					13 12				13 36	13 45					14 12				14 36	14 45
Beeston		d	12 42						13 18				13 42						14 18				14 42	
East Midlands Parkway	✈	a	12 49	12 55								13 44	13 49	13 55								14 45	14 49	14 55
		d	12 50	12 56								13 45	13 50	13 56								14 46	14 50	14 56
Loughborough		d	12 58						13 28			13 52	13 58						14 28			14 52	14 58	
Barrow Upon Soar		d	13 03										14 03										15 03	
Sileby		d	13 07										14 07										15 07	
Syston		d	13 12										14 12										15 12	
Leicester		a	13 23	13 11			13 24		13 37			14 02	14 23	14 11			14 24		14 37			15 02	15 23	15 11
		d		13 12			13 25		13 39			14 03		14 13			14 25		14 39			15 03		15 13
Market Harborough		d		13 26					13 52					14 26					14 52					15 26
Melton Mowbray	47	d																						
Oakham	47	d																						
Corby		d						13 41										14 41						
Kettering 5		a						13 50	14 01									14 50	15 01					
		d						13 51	14 02									14 51	15 02					
Wellingborough		d						14 00	14 09									15 00	15 09					
Bedford 7	52	a						14 12	14 23									15 11	15 22					
Luton 10	52	a						14 27										15 27						
Luton Airport Parkway 7	52 ✈	a							14 38										15 37					
St Pancras International	⊖52	a		14 24			14 35	14 50	15 08			15 10		15 24			15 35	15 51	16 05			16 10		16 24

A From Edinburgh to Reading
B From Liverpool Lime Street to Norwich
C From Glasgow Central to Plymouth
D From Newcastle to Southampton Central
E From Dundee to Plymouth
F From Newcastle to Reading
G From Glasgow Central to Penzance

For connections to Gatwick Airport refer to Table T052

Table T053-R

Sheffield - East Midlands - London

Saturdays

13 October to 8 December

	NT ◇	XC ◇■ A ✕	EM ◇■ ✕	EM ◇■ ✕	EM ◇■ ✕	EM ◇ B	XC ◇■ C ✕	EM ◇■ ✕	EM	EM ◇■ ✕	NT ◇	XC ◇■ D ✕	EM ◇■ ✕	EM ◇■ ✕	EM ◇■ ✕	EM ◇ B	XC ◇■ E ✕	EM ◇■ ✕	EM	EM ◇■ ✕	NT ◇
York 29 d		13 35					13 45					14 35					14 45				
Leeds 31,34 d	13 04						14 11				14 04						15 11				15 04
Wakefield Westgate 31 d							14 23										15 23				
Wakefield Kirkgate 31,34 d	13 23										14 22										15 22
Doncaster 29 d		13 58										14 59									
Manchester Piccadilly 78 d						13 42										14 42					
Sheffield d	14 05	14 25	14 29			14 37	14 55	15 00			15 05	15 24	15 29			15 37	15 55	16 00			16 05
Chesterfield d	14 22		14 41			14 54	15 07	15 12			15 22		15 41			15 52	16 07	16 12			16 22
Derby a		14 52	14 59				15 24	15 29				15 51	15 59				16 24	16 29			
d			15 03					15 31					16 03					16 31			
Long Eaton d								15 40										16 40			
Alfreton d	14 32					15 04					15 32					16 03					16 32
Langley Mill d	14 40										15 40										16 40
Lincoln 27 d									14 32										15 26		
Newark Castle 27 d									15 04										15 59		
Nottingham a	14 58					15 28			15 32		15 58					16 27			16 29		16 58
d					15 12				15 36	15 45					16 12				16 33	16 45	
Beeston d					15 18				15 42						16 18				16 39		
East Midlands Parkway a								15 44	15 49	15 55								16 44	16 52	16 55	
d								15 45	15 50	15 56								16 45	16 52	16 56	
Loughborough d					15 28			15 52	15 58						16 28			16 52	17 00		
Barrow Upon Soar d									16 03										17 05		
Sileby d									16 07										17 09		
Syston d									16 12										17 14		
Leicester a			15 24		15 37			16 02	16 23	16 11			16 24		16 37			17 02	17 23	17 11	
d			15 25		15 39			16 03		16 13			16 25		16 39			17 03		17 13	
Market Harborough d					15 52					16 26					16 52					17 26	
Melton Mowbray 47 d																					
Oakham 47 d																					
Corby d				15 41										16 41							
Kettering a				15 50	16 01									16 50	17 01						
d				15 51	16 02									16 51	17 02						
Wellingborough d				16 00	16 09									17 00	17 09						
Bedford 52 a				16 12	16 23									17 12	17 23						
Luton 52 a				16 27										17 27							
Luton Airport Parkway 52 a					16 38										17 38						
St Pancras International ⊖52 a			16 36	16 50	17 08			17 11		17 24			17 35	17 51	18 08			18 11		18 24	

	XC ◇■ A ✕	EM ◇■ ✕	EM ◇■ ✕	EM ◇■ ✕	EM ◇ B	XC ◇■ F ✕	EM ◇■ ✕	EM	EM ◇■ ✕	NT ◇	XC ◇■ A ✕	EM ◇■ ✕	EM ◇■ ✕	EM ◇■ ✕	EM ◇ B	XC ◇■ G ✕	EM ◇■ ✕	EM	EM ◇■ ✕	NT ◇	XC ◇■ A ✕	EM ◇■ ✕
York 29 d	15 35					15 45					16 04					16 45					17 35	
Leeds 31,34 d						16 11				16 04	16 40					17 10				17 03		
Wakefield Westgate 31 d						16 23					16 52					17 22						
Wakefield Kirkgate 31,34 d										16 22										17 22		
Doncaster 29 d	15 58																				17 58	
Manchester Piccadilly 78 d					15 42										16 42							
Sheffield d	16 24	16 29			16 37	16 55	17 00			17 05	17 24	17 29			17 41	17 55	18 00			18 03	18 23	18 29
Chesterfield d		16 41			16 53	17 07	17 11			17 22		17 41			17 57	18 07	18 12			18 19		18 41
Derby a	16 51	16 59				17 24	17 29				17 51	17 59				18 24	18 29				18 50	18 59
d		17 03					17 31					18 03					18 31					19 03
Long Eaton d							17 40										18 40					
Alfreton d					17 04					17 32					18 08					18 30		
Langley Mill d										17 40										18 37		
Lincoln 27 d								16 35										17 25				
Newark Castle 27 d								17 05										17 55				
Nottingham a					17 27			17 32		17 58					18 29			18 32		18 55		
d				17 12				17 33	17 45					18 12				18 36	18 45			
Beeston d				17 18				17 39						18 18				18 42				
East Midlands Parkway a							17 44	17 52	17 55								18 44	18 49	18 59			
d							17 45	17 52	17 56								18 45	18 50	19 00			
Loughborough d				17 28			17 52	18 00						18 28			18 52	18 58				
Barrow Upon Soar d								18 05										19 03				
Sileby d								18 09										19 07				
Syston d								18 14										19 12				
Leicester a		17 24		17 37			18 02	18 23	18 11			18 24		18 37			19 02	19 23	19 15			19 24
d		17 25		17 39			18 03		18 13			18 25		18 39			19 02		19 17			19 25
Market Harborough d				17 52					18 26					18 52					19 30			
Melton Mowbray 47 d																						
Oakham 47 d																						
Corby d			17 41										18 41									
Kettering a			17 50	18 01									18 50	19 01								19 46
d			17 51	18 02									18 51	19 02								19 47
Wellingborough d			18 00	18 09									19 00	19 09								
Bedford 52 a			18 12	18 23									19 12	19 23								
Luton 52 a			18 27										19 27									
Luton Airport Parkway 52 a				18 38										19 38								
St Pancras International ⊖52 a		18 34	18 50	19 08			19 11		19 24			19 35	19 51	20 08			20 11		20 28			20 37

A From Newcastle to Reading
B From Liverpool Lime Street to Norwich
C From Aberdeen to Penzance
D From Newcastle to Guildford
E From Glasgow Central to Penzance
F From Edinburgh to Plymouth
G From Glasgow Central to Plymouth

For connections to Gatwick Airport refer to Table T052

Table T053-R

Sheffield - East Midlands - London

Saturdays

13 October to 8 December

	EM ◇■ ✕	EM ◇■ ✕	EM ◇ A	XC ◇■ B ✕	EM ◇■ ✕	EM	EM ◇■ ✕	NT ◇	XC ◇■ C ✕	EM ◇■ ✕	EM ◇■ ✕	EM ◇■ ✕	EM ◇ D	EM	XC ◇■ E ✕	NT ◇	XC ◇■ F ✕	EM ◇■ ✕	EM ◇■ 🛒	EM ◇■ ✕	EM ◇■ ✕	EM ◇ A
York 29 d				17 45	17 50				18 35						18 45		19 36					
Leeds 31,34 d				18 11				18 03							19 11	19 03						
Wakefield Westgate 31 d				18 23											19 23							
Wakefield Kirkgate 31,34 d								18 21								19 21						
Doncaster 29 d					18 19				18 58								19 59					
Manchester Piccadilly 78 d			17 42										18 42									19 42
Sheffield d			18 40	18 55	19 00			19 05	19 24	19 29			19 37		19 55	20 02	20 24	20 29				20 39
Chesterfield d			18 57	19 07	19 12			19 21		19 41			19 52		20 07	20 18		20 41				20 54
Derby a				19 24	19 29				19 51	19 59					20 24		20 51	21 00				
d					19 31					20 03								21 01				
Long Eaton d					19 40																	
Alfreton d			19 08					19 31					20 03			20 28						21 05
Langley Mill d								19 39								20 36						
Lincoln 27 d						18 30																
Newark Castle 27 d						18 59																
Nottingham a			19 29			19 26		19 57					20 27			20 55						21 33
d		19 12				19 36	19 45					20 12		20 33						21 05	21 32	
Beeston d		19 18				19 42						20 18		20 39						21 11		
East Midlands Parkway a					19 44	19 49	19 55					20 23		20 49				21 12		21 16		
d					19 45	19 50	19 56					20 24		20 50				21 13		21 17		
Loughborough d		19 28			19 52	19 58						20 32		20 58				21 20		21 25	21 46	
Barrow Upon Soar d						20 03								21 03								
Sileby d						20 07								21 07								
Syston d						20 12								21 12								
Leicester a		19 37			20 02	20 23	20 11			20 24		20 41		21 23				21 31		21 35	21 55	
d		19 39			20 03		20 13			20 25		20 42								21 36	21 56	
Market Harborough d		19 52					20 26					20 55								21 49	22 09	
Melton Mowbray 47 d																						
Oakham 47 d																						
Corby d	19 41										20 41								21 43			
Kettering a	19 50	20 01									20 50	21 04							21 52	21 57	22 18	
d	19 51	20 02									20 51	21 04								21 57	22 19	
Wellingborough d	20 00	20 09									21 00	21 13								22 06	22 26	
Bedford 52 a	20 12	20 23									21 12	21 25								22 19	22 39	
Luton 52 a	20 27										21 27									22 34	22 55	
Luton Airport Parkway 52 a		20 38										21 41								22 37		
St Pancras International ⊖52 a	20 51	21 08			21 10		21 24			21 35	21 51	22 09								23 11	23 29	

	EM	XC ◇■ G ✕	NT ◇	XC ◇■ F	EM ◇ A	XC ◇■ H ✕	NT ◇	EM	EM ◇ A	EM ◇■ 🛒	EM ◇■ ✕	EM ◇ A
York 29 d		19 45		20 35		20 45						
Leeds 31,34 d		20 11	20 03			21 11	21 03					
Wakefield Westgate 31 d		20 23				21 23						
Wakefield Kirkgate 31,34 d			20 21				21 21					
Doncaster 29 d				20 59								
Manchester Piccadilly 78 d					20 43				21 41			22 28
Sheffield d		20 55	21 02	21 25	21 38	21 55	22 03		22 42		23 20	23 38
Chesterfield d		21 07	21 18	21 37	21 54	22 07	22 20		22 56		23 32	23 53
Derby a		21 24	21 39	21 54		22 24					00 05	
d			21 41									
Long Eaton d												
Alfreton d					22 05		22 31		23 07			
Langley Mill d					22 13		22 38					
Lincoln 27 d												
Newark Castle 27 d												
Nottingham a			22 08		22 34		22 57		23 28			00 30
d	21 34							23 05				
Beeston d	21 41							23 10				
East Midlands Parkway a	21 49							23 17				
d	21 49							23 18				
Loughborough d	21 58							23 26				
Barrow Upon Soar d	22 03											
Sileby d	22 07											
Syston d	22 12											
Leicester a	22 22							23 45				
d												
Market Harborough d												
Melton Mowbray 47 d												
Oakham 47 d												
Corby d										22 43		
Kettering a										22 52		
d												
Wellingborough d												
Bedford 52 a												
Luton 52 a												
Luton Airport Parkway 52 a												
St Pancras International ⊖52 a												

A From Liverpool Lime Street
B From Edinburgh to Plymouth
C From Newcastle to Southampton Central
D From Liverpool Lime Street to Norwich
E From Glasgow Central to Bristol Temple Meads
F From Newcastle to Birmingham New Street
G From Edinburgh to Birmingham New Street. ✕ to Leeds
H From Glasgow Central to Birmingham New Street. ✕ to Leeds

For connections to Gatwick Airport refer to Table T052

Table T053-R

Sundays
20 May to 15 July

Sheffield - East Midlands - London

	EM	EM	EM	EM	EM	EM	XC A	EM	NT	EM	EM
York 29 d											
Leeds 31,34 d							08 10				
Wakefield Westgate 31 d							08 23				
Wakefield Kirkgate 31,34 d											
Doncaster 29 d											
Manchester Piccadilly 78 d											
Sheffield d						08 18	08 54		09 05		09 24
Chesterfield d						08 31	09 07		09 21		09 37
Derby a						08 49	09 28				09 56
d	06 50		07 51			08 51					09 58
Long Eaton d			08 01			09 00					10 07
Alfreton d									09 32		
Langley Mill d									09 39		
Lincoln 27 d											
Newark Castle 27 d											
Nottingham a									10 00		
d		07 29		08 22				09 20			
Beeston d				08 28							
East Midlands Parkway a	07 01	07 38	08 04	08 34		09 04		09 30			10 11
d	07 02	07 39	08 05	08 35		09 05		09 31			10 12
Loughborough d			08 13	08 43		09 12		09 40			10 19
Barrow Upon Soar d											
Sileby d											
Syston d											
Leicester a	07 19	07 53	08 23	08 53		09 23		09 52			10 29
d	07 20	07 55	08 25	08 55		09 24		09 54			10 31
Market Harborough d	07 38	08 11	08 41	09 11		09 40		10 11			10 44
Melton Mowbray 47 d											
Oakham 47 d											
Corby d					09 30					10 25	
Kettering a	07 48	08 20	08 50	09 20	09 39	09 49		10 21		10 34	10 53
d	07 49	08 21	08 51	09 21		09 50		10 22			10 54
Wellingborough d	07 57	08 28	08 58	09 28		10 02		10 30			11 01
Bedford 52 a	08 15	08 45	09 15	09 45		10 15		10 45			11 15
Luton 52 a	08 35		09 34			10 33					11 34
Luton Airport Parkway 52 a		09 06		10 06				11 06			
St Pancras International ⊖52 a	09 13	09 42	10 11	10 42		11 10		11 42			12 12

	XC A	EM	NT	EM	EM	EM	EM	EM B	XC A	NT	EM
York 29 d									09 33		
Leeds 31,34 d	09 00		09 08				09 50		09 59	10 08	10 50
Wakefield Westgate 31 d	09 11						10 02		10 12		11 03
Wakefield Kirkgate 31,34 d			09 24							10 24	
Doncaster 29 d	09 31								10 30		
Manchester Piccadilly 78 d											
Sheffield d	09 57		10 06		10 25		10 35	10 48	10 55	11 06	11 43
Chesterfield d	10 09		10 22		10 37		10 48	11 04	11 08	11 22	11 55
Derby a	10 32				10 56				11 28		12 17
d					10 57						12 17
Long Eaton d					11 07						12 29
Alfreton d			10 32					11 14		11 32	
Langley Mill d			10 40							11 40	
Lincoln 27 d											
Newark Castle 27 d											
Nottingham a			11 00				11 21	11 39		12 00	
d		10 30					11 39				
Beeston d		10 37									
East Midlands Parkway a		10 44			11 10		11 49				12 33
d		10 45			11 11		11 50				12 34
Loughborough d		10 53			11 19		11 59				12 42
Barrow Upon Soar d											
Sileby d											
Syston d											
Leicester a		11 06			11 29		12 11				12 54
d		11 08			11 30		12 13				12 56
Market Harborough d		11 22			11 43		12 27				13 10
Melton Mowbray 47 d											
Oakham 47 d											
Corby d				11 25		12 20					
Kettering a		11 32		11 34	11 52	12 29	12 37				
d		11 33			11 53		12 38				
Wellingborough d		11 41			12 01		12 46				
Bedford 52 a		11 57			12 15		13 02				
Luton 52 a					12 29						
Luton Airport Parkway 52 a		12 13					13 18				
St Pancras International ⊖52 a		12 41			12 54		13 44				14 09

	XC C	EM	EM	NT	EM B	EM	XC D	EM	EM	NT	EM
York 29 d	10 33						11 41				
Leeds 31,34 d	11 00			11 08			12 11			12 08	
Wakefield Westgate 31 d	11 12						12 24				
Wakefield Kirkgate 31,34 d				11 24						12 24	
Doncaster 29 d	11 30										
Manchester Piccadilly 78 d											
Sheffield d	11 57			12 06	12 43	12 49	12 57			13 06	13 43
Chesterfield d	12 09			12 22	12 57	13 01	13 09			13 22	13 56
Derby a	12 28					13 20	13 30				14 15
d						13 21					14 16
Long Eaton d						13 31					14 26
Alfreton d				12 32	13 08					13 32	
Langley Mill d				12 40						13 40	
Lincoln 27 d											
Newark Castle 27 d											
Nottingham a				13 00	13 34					14 00	
d			12 49						13 49		
Beeston d			12 56						13 56		
East Midlands Parkway a			13 02			13 34			14 02		14 29
d			13 03			13 35			14 03		14 30
Loughborough d			13 12			13 43			14 12		14 38
Barrow Upon Soar d											
Sileby d											
Syston d											
Leicester a			13 24			13 53			14 24		14 53
d			13 26			13 54			14 26		14 55
Market Harborough d			13 40			14 07			14 40		15 08
Melton Mowbray 47 d											
Oakham 47 d											
Corby d		13 13						14 13			
Kettering a		13 22	13 50					14 22	14 50		
d		13 23	13 51					14 23	14 51		
Wellingborough d		13 32	13 59					14 31	14 59		
Bedford 52 a		13 44	14 15					14 45	15 15		
Luton 52 a		14 00						15 00			
Luton Airport Parkway 52 a			14 31						15 31		
St Pancras International ⊖52 a		14 24	14 59			15 02		15 24	15 59		16 04

	EM B	XC E	EM	EM	NT	XC F	EM G	EM	XC D	EM	EM
York 29 d		12 45							13 43		
Leeds 31,34 d		13 11			13 08				14 11		
Wakefield Westgate 31 d		13 24							14 23		
Wakefield Kirkgate 31,34 d					13 24						
Doncaster 29 d											
Manchester Piccadilly 78 d	12 43						13 43				
Sheffield d	13 48	13 57			14 06	14 22	14 41	14 49	14 55		
Chesterfield d	14 02	14 09			14 22	14 32	14 55	15 01	15 07		
Derby a		14 27				14 50		15 19	15 25		
d								15 21			
Long Eaton d								15 30			
Alfreton d	14 12				14 32		15 08				
Langley Mill d					14 40		15 15				
Lincoln 27 d											
Newark Castle 27 d											
Nottingham a	14 35				15 00		15 32				
d				14 52						15 43	
Beeston d				14 58							
East Midlands Parkway a				15 03				15 34		15 53	
d				15 04				15 35		15 53	
Loughborough d				15 12				15 42			
Barrow Upon Soar d											
Sileby d											
Syston d											
Leicester a				15 22				15 53		16 11	
d				15 24				15 55		16 12	
Market Harborough d				15 37							
Melton Mowbray 47 d											
Oakham 47 d											
Corby d			15 13								16 20
Kettering a			15 22	15 46							16 29
d			15 23	15 47							
Wellingborough d			15 31	15 54							
Bedford 52 a			15 45	16 09							
Luton 52 a			16 00					16 40			
Luton Airport Parkway 52 a				16 25							
St Pancras International ⊖52 a			16 24	16 48				17 05		17 23	

A To Plymouth
B To Norwich
C From Newcastle to Plymouth
D From Edinburgh to Plymouth
E From Edinburgh to Penzance
F To Reading
G From Liverpool Lime Street to Norwich

For connections to Gatwick Airport refer to Table T052

Table T053-R

Sundays
20 May to 15 July

Sheffield - East Midlands - London

	EM	NT	XC A	EM	EM B	EM	XC C	EM	EM	EM	NT
York 29 d			14 35				14 44				
Leeds 31,34 d		14 08		14 34			15 11				15 08
Wakefield Westgate 31 d				14 47			15 23				
Wakefield Kirkgate 31,34 d		14 24									15 24
Doncaster 29 d			15 00								
Manchester Piccadilly 78 d					14 43						
Sheffield d		15 06	15 24	15 29	15 39	15 50	15 55				16 06
Chesterfield d		15 22		15 42	15 53	16 02	16 07				16 22
Derby a			15 52	16 02		16 21	16 25				
d				16 02		16 26					
Long Eaton d											
Alfreton d		15 32			16 03						16 32
Langley Mill d		15 40			16 11						16 40
Lincoln 27 d											
Newark Castle 27 d											
Nottingham a		16 00			16 28						17 00
d	15 52							16 45		16 50	
Beeston d	15 58									16 57	
East Midlands Parkway a	16 04			16 15		16 36		16 54		17 02	
d	16 05			16 16		16 37		16 55		17 03	
Loughborough d	16 12			16 25						17 11	
Barrow Upon Soar d											
Sileby d											
Syston d											
Leicester a	16 23			16 37		16 53		17 09		17 21	
d	16 24			16 39		16 55		17 10		17 23	
Market Harborough d	16 37			16 53						17 36	
Melton Mowbray 47 d											
Oakham 47 d											
Corby d									17 20		
Kettering a	16 46			17 03					17 29	17 45	
d	16 47			17 03						17 46	
Wellingborough d	16 55			17 12						17 54	
Bedford 52 a	17 09			17 28						18 07	
Luton 52 a				17 45							
Luton Airport Parkway 52 a	17 25									18 24	
St Pancras International ⊖52 a	17 50			18 11		18 02		18 17		18 47	

	XC A	EM	EM B	EM	XC D	EM	EM	EM	NT	XC E
York 29 d	15 35				15 42					16 25
Leeds 31,34 d					16 11				16 08	
Wakefield Westgate 31 d					16 23					
Wakefield Kirkgate 31,34 d									16 24	
Doncaster 29 d	15 58									16 51
Manchester Piccadilly 78 d			15 42							
Sheffield d	16 24		16 43	16 49	16 55				17 06	17 24
Chesterfield d			16 57	17 00	17 07				17 22	
Derby a	16 53			17 19	17 25					17 52
d		16 57		17 23						
Long Eaton d		17 07								
Alfreton d			17 07						17 32	
Langley Mill d			17 15						17 40	
Lincoln 27 d										
Newark Castle 27 d										
Nottingham a			17 30						18 00	
d						17 45		17 52		
Beeston d								17 58		
East Midlands Parkway a		17 10		17 36		17 55		18 03		
d		17 11		17 36		17 55		18 04		
Loughborough d		17 19						18 12		
Barrow Upon Soar d										
Sileby d										
Syston d										
Leicester a		17 29		17 54		18 13		18 22		
d		17 31		17 54		18 14		18 25		
Market Harborough d		17 44						18 38		
Melton Mowbray 47 d										
Oakham 47 d										
Corby d							18 20			
Kettering a		17 54					18 29	18 47		
d		17 55						18 48		
Wellingborough d		18 02						18 55		
Bedford 52 a		18 16						19 09		
Luton 52 a		18 31								
Luton Airport Parkway 52 a								19 24		
St Pancras International ⊖52 a		18 55		19 10		19 25		19 50		

	EM	EM B	EM	XC F	EM	EM	EM	NT	XC A	EM G	EM
York 29 d				16 41					17 35		17 48
Leeds 31,34 d				17 11				17 08			
Wakefield Westgate 31 d				17 23							
Wakefield Kirkgate 31,34 d								17 24			
Doncaster 29 d									17 58		18 13
Manchester Piccadilly 78 d		16 42								17 42	
Sheffield d		17 40	17 50	17 55				18 06	18 24	18 40	18 47
Chesterfield d		17 54	18 02	18 07				18 22		18 54	19 00
Derby a			18 21	18 25					18 53		19 19
d	18 06		18 26								19 19
Long Eaton d	18 15										19 30
Alfreton d		18 05						18 32		19 05	
Langley Mill d		18 12						18 40		19 12	
Lincoln 27 d											
Newark Castle 27 d											
Nottingham a		18 34						19 00		19 33	
d						18 45	18 52				
Beeston d							18 58				
East Midlands Parkway a	18 19		18 36			18 54	19 04				19 33
d	18 20		18 37			18 55	19 05				19 34
Loughborough d	18 28					19 02	19 12				19 42
Barrow Upon Soar d											
Sileby d											
Syston d											
Leicester a	18 38		18 53			19 13	19 23				19 53
d	18 40		18 54			19 14	19 25				19 55
Market Harborough d	18 53					19 27	19 38				20 08
Melton Mowbray 47 d											
Oakham 47 d											
Corby d					19 20						
Kettering a	19 02				19 29	19 36	19 47				20 15
d	19 05					19 37	19 48				20 15
Wellingborough d	19 12					19 45	19 55				20 25
Bedford 52 a	19 27					19 58	20 09				20 38
Luton 52 a	19 44					20 14					20 55
Luton Airport Parkway 52 a							20 25				20 58
St Pancras International ⊖52 a	20 08		20 01			20 39	20 50				21 22

	XC D	EM	EM	NT H	XC I	EM	EM B	XC J	NT	XC K	EM
York 29 d	17 44				18 35			18 45		19 24	
Leeds 31,34 d	18 11			18 08				19 11	19 08		
Wakefield Westgate 31 d	18 23							19 24			
Wakefield Kirkgate 31,34 d				18 25					19 24		
Doncaster 29 d					18 58					19 54	
Manchester Piccadilly 78 d							18 42				
Sheffield d	18 55			19 06	19 24	19 28	19 40	19 55	20 06	20 21	
Chesterfield d	19 07			19 22		19 41	19 54	20 07	20 22		
Derby a	19 25				19 52	20 00		20 25		20 49	
d						20 02					
Long Eaton d						20 12					
Alfreton d				19 32			20 05		20 32		
Langley Mill d				19 40			20 12		20 40		
Lincoln 27 d											
Newark Castle 27 d											
Nottingham a				20 00			20 30		21 00		
d			19 52								
Beeston d			19 58								
East Midlands Parkway a			20 04			20 16					
d			20 05			20 17					
Loughborough d			20 12			20 26					
Barrow Upon Soar d											
Sileby d											
Syston d											
Leicester a			20 22			20 38					
d			20 24			20 40					
Market Harborough d			20 37			20 54					
Melton Mowbray 47 d											
Oakham 47 d											
Corby d		20 20									21 25
Kettering a		20 29	20 46			21 04					21 34
d			20 47			21 05					
Wellingborough d			20 54			21 13					
Bedford 52 a			21 08			21 28					
Luton 52 a			21 23			21 44					
Luton Airport Parkway 52 a											
St Pancras International ⊖52 a			21 48			22 11					

A From Newcastle to Reading
B From Liverpool Lime Street to Norwich
C From Motherwell to Penzance
D From Motherwell to Plymouth
E From Edinburgh to Reading
F From Aberdeen to Plymouth
G From Liverpool Lime Street
H From Carlisle
I From Newcastle to Guildford
J From Motherwell to Bristol Temple Meads
K From Newcastle to Birmingham New Street

For connections to Gatwick Airport refer to Table T052

Table T053-R

Sheffield - East Midlands - London

Sundays
20 May to 15 July

Station		EM	EM	EM	XC	NT	XC	EM	XC	NT	EM	EM
		◇■	◇■	◇	◇■	◇	◇■	◇	◇■	◇	◇■	◇
				A	B		C	A	D			A
York	29 d				19 45		20 26		20 45			
Leeds	31,34 d				20 11	20 08			21 11	21 08		
Wakefield Westgate	31 d				20 23				21 23			
Wakefield Kirkgate	31,34 d					20 24				21 29		
Doncaster	29 d						20 51					
Manchester Piccadilly	78 d			19 42				20 43				22 11
Sheffield	d	20 26		20 40	20 54	21 06	21 20	21 40	21 54	22 09	22 36	23 30
Chesterfield	d	20 39		20 54	21 06	21 22	21 32	21 56	22 06	22 25	22 48	23 44
Derby	a	20 59			21 25		21 51		22 24		23 23	
	d	21 01										
Long Eaton	d											
Alfreton	d			21 05		21 32		22 06		22 36		23 55
Langley Mill	d			21 12		21 40		22 14		22 43		00 02
Lincoln	27 d											
Newark Castle	27 d											
Nottingham	a			21 33		22 00		22 36		23 07		00 23
	d		21 21									
Beeston	d											
East Midlands Parkway	a	21 12	21 30									
	d	21 13	21 31									
Loughborough	d		21 39									
Barrow Upon Soar	d											
Sileby	d											
Syston	d											
Leicester	a	21 30	21 53									
	d	21 32	21 54									
Market Harborough	d	21 46	22 08									
Melton Mowbray	47 d											
Oakham	47 d											
Corby	d											
Kettering	a	21 56	22 17									
	d	21 57	22 18									
Wellingborough	d	22 05	22 25									
Bedford	52 a	22 19	22 39									
Luton	52 a	22 35	22 54									
Luton Airport Parkway	52 a											
St Pancras International	⊖52 a	23 00	23 24									

Sundays
22 July to 2 September

Station		EM	EM	EM	EM	EM	EM	EM	EM	EM	EM	EM	EM	EM	EM	XC	EM	EM	EM	NT	EM	EM	EM
		◇■	◇■	◇■	◇■	◇■	◇■	◇■	◇■	◇■	◇■	◇■	◇■	◇■	◇■	◇■	◇■	◇■	◇■	◇	◇■	◇■	◇■
		E	F		G	H	I	E			J	G	K	I	E	L			J		M	G	K
York	29 d																						
Leeds	31,34 d															08 10							
Wakefield Westgate	31 d															08 23							
Wakefield Kirkgate	31,34 d																						
Doncaster	29 d																						
Manchester Piccadilly	78 d																						
Sheffield	d										08 07	08 18			08 18	08 55			09 00	09 05	09 19	09 24	
Chesterfield	d										08 20	08 31			08 31	09a07			09 17	09 21	09 31	09 37	
Derby	a										08 41				08 49				09 48		09 56		
	d	06 50				07 43	07 46	07 51			08 43			08 46	08 51				09 50		09 58		
Long Eaton	d					08 01	08 01	08 01			09 00			09 00	09 00				10 07		10 07		
Alfreton	d																			09 32			
Langley Mill	d																			09 39			
Lincoln	27 d																						
Newark Castle	27 d																						
Nottingham	a																			10 00			
	d			07 29					08 22								09 20						
Beeston	d								08 28				←										←
East Midlands Parkway	a	07 01		07 38		08 04	08 04	08 04	08 34		09 04	08 58	09 04	09 04	09 04		09 30		10 11		10 11	10 08	10 11
	d	07 02	07 02	07 39	08 05	08 05	08 05	08 05	08 35		09 05	09 05	09 05	09 05	09 05		09 31		10 12		10 12	10 12	10 12
Loughborough	d				08 13	08 13	08 13	08 13	08 43		→	09 12	09 12	09 12	09 12		09 40		→		→	10 19	10 19
Barrow Upon Soar	d																						
Sileby	d																						
Syston	d																						
Leicester	a	07 19	07 19	07 53	08 23	08 23	08 23	08 23	08 53			09 23	09 23	09 23	09 23		09 52					10 29	10 29
	d	07 20	07 20	07 55	08 25	08 25	08 25	08 25	08 55			09 24	09 24	09 24	09 24		09 54					10 31	10 31
Market Harborough	d	07 38	07 38	08 11	08 41	08 41	08 41	08 41	09 11			09 40	09 40	09 40	09 40		10 11					10 44	10 44
Melton Mowbray	47 d																						
Oakham	47 d																						
Corby	d									09 30								10 25					
Kettering	a	07 48	07 48	08 20	08 50	08 50	08 50	08 50	09 20	09 39		09 49	09 49	09 49	09 49		10 21	10 34				10 53	10 53
	d	07 49	07 49	08 21	08 51	08 51	08 51	08 51	09 21			09 50	09 50	09 50	09 50		10 22					10 54	10 54
Wellingborough	d	07 57	07 57	08 28	08 58	08 58	08 58	08 58	09 28			10 02	10 02	10 02	10 02		10 30					11 01	11 01
Bedford	52 a	08 15	08 15	08 45	09 15	09 15	09 15	09 15	09 45			10 15	10 15	10 15	10 15		10 45					11 15	11 15
Luton	52 a	08 35	08 35		09 34	09 34	09 34	09 34				10 33	10 33	10 33	10 33							11 34	11 34
Luton Airport Parkway	52 a			09 06					10 06								11 06						
St Pancras International	⊖52 a	09 13	09 13	09 42	10 11	10 11	10 11	10 11	10 42			11 10	11 10	11 10	11 10		11 42					12 12	12 12

A From Liverpool Lime Street
B From Edinburgh to Bristol Temple Meads. ✕ to Leeds
C From Newcastle to Birmingham New Street
D From Motherwell to Birmingham New Street. ✕ to Leeds
E 22 July, 29 July, 2 September
F from 5 August until 26 August
G 19 August
H 26 August
I 5 August, 12 August
J 26 August. To St Pancras International
K 26 August. From Sheffield
L To Plymouth
M 5 August, 12 August. To St Pancras International

For connections to Gatwick Airport refer to Table T052

Table T053-R

Sheffield - East Midlands - London

Sundays
22 July to 2 September

Station		EM	EM	XC	EM	NT	EM	EM	EM	EM	EM	EM	EM	EM	EM	XC	NT	EM	EM	EM	EM	EM	EM
		◇■	◇■	◇■	◇■	◇	◇■	◇■	◇■	◇■	◇■	◇■	◇■	◇■	◇	◇■	◇	◇■	◇■	◇■	◇■	◇■	◇■
		A	B	C				D	E	F	B	G			H	I		D	J	K	L	M	N
York	29 d															09 33							
Leeds	31,34 d			09 00		09 08								09 50		09 59	10 08	10 50	10 50	10 50			
Wakefield Westgate	31 d			09 11										10 02		10 12		11 03	11 03	11 03			
Wakefield Kirkgate	31,34 d					09 24											10 24						
Doncaster	29 d			09 31												10 30							
Manchester Piccadilly	78 d																						
Sheffield	d		09 24	09 57		10 06		10 10	10 25		10 25			10 35	10 48	10 55	11 06	11 33	11 34	11 43			
Chesterfield	d		09 37	10a09		10 22		10 27	10 37		10 37			10 48	11 04	11a07	11 22	11 44	11 46	11 55			
Derby	a		09 56					10 48			10 56							12 08	12 12				
	d		09 58					10 49			10 57	10 57						12 09	12 12				
Long Eaton	d		10 07					11 07			11 07	11 07						12 28	12 29				
Alfreton	d					10 32									11 14		11 32						
Langley Mill	d					10 40											11 40						
Lincoln	27 d																						
Newark Castle	27 d																						
Nottingham	a					11 00								11 21	11 39		12 00						
	d				10 30									11 39									
Beeston	d	←			10 37					←											←	←	←
East Midlands Parkway	a	10 11	10 11		10 44			11 10	11 09	11 10	11 10	11 10		11 49				12 32	12 33	12 25	12 32	12 33	12 25
	d	10 12	10 12		10 45			11 11	11 11	11 11	11 11	11 11		11 50				12 33	12 34	12 34	12 33	12 34	12 34
Loughborough	d	10 19	10 19		10 53			→	11 19	11 19	11 19	11 19		11 59				→	→	→	12 42	12 42	12 42
Barrow Upon Soar	d																						
Sileby	d																						
Syston	d																						
Leicester	a	10 29	10 29		11 06				11 29	11 29	11 29	11 29		12 11							12 54	12 54	12 54
	d	10 31	10 31		11 08				11 30	11 30	11 30	11 30		12 13							12 55	12 56	12 56
Market Harborough	d	10 44	10 44		11 22				11 43	11 43	11 43	11 43		12 27							13 09	13 10	13 10
Melton Mowbray	47 d																						
Oakham	47 d																						
Corby	d						11 25						12 20										
Kettering	a	10 53	10 53		11 32		11 34		11 52	11 52	11 52	11 52	12 29	12 37									
	d	10 54	10 54		11 33				11 53	11 53	11 53	11 53		12 38									
Wellingborough	d	11 01	11 01		11 41				12 01	12 01	12 01	12 01		12 46									
Bedford	52 a	11 15	11 15		11 57				12 15	12 15	12 15	12 15		13 02									
Luton	52 a	11 34	11 34						12 29	12 29	12 29	12 29											
Luton Airport Parkway	52 a				12 13									13 18									
St Pancras International	⊖52 a	12 12	12 12		12 41				12 54	12 54	12 54	12 54		13 44							14 09	14 09	14 09

Station		EM	XC	EM	EM	NT	EM	EM	EM	EM	EM	EM	EM	EM	EM	EM	NT	XC	EM	EM	EM	EM
		◇■	◇■	◇■	◇■	◇	◇■	◇■	◇	◇■	◇■	◇■	◇■	◇■	◇■	◇■	◇	◇■	◇■	◇■	◇■	◇■
		B	O				D	J	H	K	F	A	B	P				Q	J	D	K	A
York	29 d		10 33															11 41				
Leeds	31,34 d	10 50	11 00			11 08											12 08	12 11				
Wakefield Westgate	31 d	11 03	11 12															12 24				
Wakefield Kirkgate	31,34 d					11 24											12 24					
Doncaster	29 d		11 30															12 54				
Manchester Piccadilly	78 d																					
Sheffield	d	11 43	11 57			12 06	12 35	12 35	12 43	12 49			12 49				13 06	13 24	13 32	13 33	13 43	
Chesterfield	d	11 55	12a08			12 22	12 50	12 53	12 57	13 01			13 01				13 22	13a35	13 48	13 46	13 56	
Derby	a	12 17					13 12	13 15					13 20						14 10	14 07		
	d	12 17					13 13	13 16					13 21						14 11	14 08		
Long Eaton	d	12 29					13 31	13 31					13 31						14 26	14 26		
Alfreton	d					12 32			13 08								13 32					
Langley Mill	d					12 40											13 40					
Lincoln	27 d																					
Newark Castle	27 d																					
Nottingham	a					13 00			13 34								14 00					
	d				12 49											13 49						
Beeston	d				12 56						←	←		←		13 56						←
East Midlands Parkway	a	12 33			13 02		13 34	13 34		13 32	13 34	13 34	13 34	13 32		14 02			14 29	14 29	14 24	14 29
	d	12 34			13 03		13 35	13 35		13 36	13 35	13 35	13 35	13 36		14 03			14 30	14 30	14 31	14 30
Loughborough	d	12 42			13 12		→	→		→	13 43	13 43	13 43	13 43		14 12			→	→	→	14 38
Barrow Upon Soar	d																					
Sileby	d																					
Syston	d																					
Leicester	a	12 54			13 24						13 53	13 53	13 53	13 53		14 24						14 53
	d	12 56			13 26						13 54	13 54	13 54	13 55		14 26						14 55
Market Harborough	d	13 10			13 40						14 07	14 07	14 07	14 08		14 40						15 08
Melton Mowbray	47 d																					
Oakham	47 d																					
Corby	d			13 13											14 13							
Kettering	a			13 22	13 50										14 22	14 50						
	d			13 23	13 51										14 23	14 51						
Wellingborough	d			13 32	13 59										14 31	14 59						
Bedford	52 a			13 44	14 15										14 45	15 15						
Luton	52 a			14 00											15 00							
Luton Airport Parkway	52 a				14 31											15 31						
St Pancras International	⊖52 a	14 09		14 24	14 59						15 02	15 02	15 02	15 03	15 24	15 59						16 04

A 5 August, 12 August. From Sheffield
B 22 July, 29 July, 2 September
C To Plymouth
D 26 August. To St Pancras International
E 19 August
F 26 August. From Sheffield
G 5 August, 12 August
H To Norwich
I To Birmingham New Street
J 5 August, 12 August. To St Pancras International
K 19 August. To St Pancras International
L 26 August. From Leeds
M 5 August, 12 August. From Leeds
N 19 August. From Leeds
O From Newcastle to Bristol Temple Meads
P 19 August. From Sheffield
Q From Edinburgh to Penzance

For connections to Gatwick Airport refer to Table T052

Table T053-R

Sundays

22 July to 2 September

Sheffield - East Midlands - London

Station			EM A	EM B	EM C	EM ◇ D	EM	EM	NT ◇	XC E	EM F	EM G	EM ◇ H	EM B	EM I	EM	EM	EM	NT ◇	XC J	EM I	EM F	EM G	EM B
York	29	d								12 42										13 45				
Leeds	31,34	d							13 08	13 11									14 08	14 11	14 34	14 34	14 34	14 34
Wakefield Westgate	31	d								13 24										14 23	14 47	14 47	14 47	14 47
Wakefield Kirkgate	31,34	d							13 24										14 24					
Doncaster	29	d								13 54										14 54				
Manchester Piccadilly	78	d				12 43							13 43											
Sheffield		d		13 43		13 48			14 06	14 22	14 28	14 28	14 41	14 49	14 49				15 06	15 24	15 29			15 29
Chesterfield		d		13 56		14 02			14 22	14a33	14 50	14 50	14 55	15 01	15 01				15 22	15a35	15 42			15 42
Derby		a		14 15							15 11	15 14		15 19								15 54	15 57	16 02
		d		14 16							15 13	15 16		15 21								15 54	15 57	16 02
Long Eaton		d		14 26							15 30	15 30		15 30										
Alfreton		d				14 12			14 32				15 08						15 32					
Langley Mill		d							14 40				15 15						15 40					
Lincoln	27	d																						
Newark Castle	27	d																						
Nottingham		a				14 35			15 00				15 32						16 00					
		d						14 52								15 43		15 52						
Beeston		d	←		←			14 58										15 58						
East Midlands Parkway		a	14 29	14 29	14 24			15 03			15 34	15 34		15 34	15 34	15 53		16 04			16 10	16 15	16 15	16 15
		d	14 30	14 30	14 31			15 04			15 35	15 35		15 35	15 36	15 53		16 05			16 16	16 16	16 16	16 16
Loughborough		d	14 38	14 38	14 38			15 12			15 42	15 42		15 42	15 43			16 12			16 25	16 25	16 25	16 25
Barrow Upon Soar		d																						
Sileby		d																						
Syston		d																						
Leicester		a	14 53	14 53	14 54			15 22			15 53	15 53		15 53	15 54	16 11		16 23			16 37	16 37	16 37	16 37
		d	14 55	14 55	14 55			15 24			15 55	15 55		15 55	15 56	16 12		16 24			16 39	16 39	16 39	16 39
Market Harborough		d	15 08	15 08	15 08			15 37										16 37			16 53	16 53	16 53	16 53
Melton Mowbray	47	d																						
Oakham	47	d																						
Corby		d					15 13										16 20							
Kettering		a					15 22	15 46									16 29	16 46			17 03	17 03	17 03	17 03
		d					15 23	15 47										16 47			17 03	17 03	17 03	17 03
Wellingborough		d					15 31	15 54										16 55			17 12	17 12	17 12	17 12
Bedford	52	a					15 45	16 09										17 09			17 28	17 28	17 28	17 28
Luton	52	a					16 00				16 40	16 40		16 40	16 41						17 45	17 45	17 45	17 45
Luton Airport Parkway	52	a						16 25										17 25						
St Pancras International	⊖52	a	16 04	16 04	16 05		16 24	16 48			17 05	17 05		17 05	17 06	17 23		17 50			18 11	18 11	18 11	18 11

Station			EM	EM K	EM L	EM ◇ H	EM M	EM A	EM N	EM B	EM C	EM	EM	NT ◇	XC O	EM ◇ H	EM F	EM I	EM P	EM Q	EM B	EM	EM
York	29	d													14 44								
Leeds	31,34	d												15 08	15 11								
Wakefield Westgate	31	d													15 23								
Wakefield Kirkgate	31,34	d												15 24									
Doncaster	29	d													15 54								
Manchester Piccadilly	78	d				14 43										15 42							
Sheffield		d		15 30	15 34	15 39	15 50			15 50				16 06	16 24	16 43				16 49	16 49		
Chesterfield		d		15 47	15 46	15 53	16 02			16 02				16 22	16a35	16 57				17 00	17 00		
Derby		a		16 13	16 16					16 21											17 19		
		d		16 18	16 21					16 26							16 49		16 57		17 23		
Long Eaton		d															17 07		17 07				
Alfreton		d				16 03								16 32		17 07							
Langley Mill		d				16 11								16 40		17 15							
Lincoln	27	d																					
Newark Castle	27	d																					
Nottingham		a				16 28								17 00		17 30							
		d										16 45	16 50									17 45	
Beeston		d						←	←				16 57										
East Midlands Parkway		a		16 36	16 36		16 30	16 36	16 36	16 36		16 54	17 02				17 10		17 10	17 32	17 36	17 55	
		d		16 37	16 37		16 37	16 37	16 37	16 37		16 55	17 03				17 11	17 11	17 11	17 36	17 36	17 55	
Loughborough		d		→	→								17 11				17 19	17 19	17 19				
Barrow Upon Soar		d																					
Sileby		d																					
Syston		d									←												
Leicester		a					16 54	16 53	16 53	16 53	16 54	17 09	17 21				17 29	17 29	17 29	17 54	17 54	18 13	
		d					16 55	16 55	16 55	16 55	16 55	17 10	17 23				17 31	17 31	17 31	17 54	17 54	18 14	
Market Harborough		d					→						17 36				17 44	17 44	17 44				
Melton Mowbray	47	d																					
Oakham	47	d																					
Corby		d	17 20																				18 20
Kettering		a	17 29										17 45				17 54	17 54	17 54				18 29
		d											17 46				17 55	17 55	17 55				
Wellingborough		d											17 54				18 02	18 02	18 02				
Bedford	52	a											18 07				18 16	18 16	18 16				
Luton	52	a															18 31	18 31	18 31				
Luton Airport Parkway	52	a											18 24										
St Pancras International	⊖52	a						18 02	18 02	18 02	18 02	18 17	18 47				18 55	18 55	18 55	19 10	19 10	19 25	

A 26 August. From Sheffield
B 22 July, 29 July, 2 September
C 19 August. From Sheffield
D To Norwich
E From Edinburgh to Plymouth
F 26 August
G 5 August, 12 August
H From Liverpool Lime Street to Norwich
I 19 August
J From Edinburgh to Penzance
K 26 August. To St Pancras International
L 5 August, 12 August. To St Pancras International
M 19 August. To St Pancras International
N 5 August, 12 August. From Sheffield
O From Motherwell to Plymouth
P not from 19 August until 26 August
Q from 5 August until 26 August

For connections to Gatwick Airport refer to Table T052

Table T053-R

Sundays

22 July to 2 September

Sheffield - East Midlands - London

Station			EM	NT ◇	XC A	EM ◇ B	EM C	EM D	EM E	EM F	EM G	EM F	EM	EM	EM	NT ◇	XC H	EM I	EM J	EM ◇ K	EM ◇ L	EM D	EM M	EM N
York	29	d			15 42												16 41					17 48		
Leeds	31,34	d		16 08	16 11											17 08	17 11							
Wakefield Westgate	31	d			16 23												17 23							
Wakefield Kirkgate	31,34	d		16 24												17 24								
Doncaster	29	d			16 46												17 46					18 13		
Manchester Piccadilly	78	d				16 42														17 42	17 42			
Sheffield		d		17 06	17 19	17 40					17 50	17 50				18 06	18 24	18 28	18 31	18 40	18 45	18 47		
Chesterfield		d		17 22	17a30	17 54					18 02	18 02				18 22	18a35	18 49	18 47	18 54	18 59	18 59		
Derby		a										18 21						19 11	19 14					
		d					17 58		18 01	18 06		18 26						19 11	19 14					
Long Eaton		d					18 15		18 15	18 15								19 30	19 30					
Alfreton		d		17 32		18 05										18 32				19 05	19 10			
Langley Mill		d		17 40		18 12										18 40				19 12	19 17			
Lincoln	27	d																						
Newark Castle	27	d																						
Nottingham		a		18 00		18 34										19 00				19 33	19 38			
		d	17 52											18 45	18 52									
Beeston		d	17 58												18 58								←	←
East Midlands Parkway		a	18 03				18 19		18 19	18 19	18 33	18 36		18 54	19 04			19 33	19 33			19 32	19 33	19 33
		d	18 04				18 20	18 20	18 20	18 20	18 37	18 37		18 55	19 05			19 34	19 34			19 33	19 34	19 34
Loughborough		d	18 12				18 28	18 28	18 28	18 28				19 02	19 12			→	→			19 41	19 42	19 42
Barrow Upon Soar		d																						
Sileby		d																						
Syston		d																						
Leicester		a	18 22				18 38	18 38	18 38	18 38	18 53	18 53		19 13	19 23							19 52	19 53	19 53
		d	18 25				18 40	18 40	18 40	18 40	18 54	18 54		19 14	19 25							19 54	19 55	19 55
Market Harborough		d	18 38				18 53	18 53	18 53	18 53				19 27	19 38							20 07	20 08	20 08
Melton Mowbray	47	d																						
Oakham	47	d																						
Corby		d											19 20											
Kettering		a	18 47				19 02	19 02	19 02	19 02			19 29	19 36	19 47							20 14	20 15	20 15
		d	18 48				19 05	19 05	19 05	19 05				19 37	19 48							20 14	20 15	20 15
Wellingborough		d	18 55				19 12	19 12	19 12	19 12				19 45	19 55							20 24	20 25	20 25
Bedford	52	a	19 09				19 27	19 27	19 27	19 27				19 58	20 09							20 37	20 38	20 38
Luton	52	a					19 44	19 44	19 44	19 44				20 14								20 54	20 55	20 55
Luton Airport Parkway	52	a	19 24												20 25							20 57	20 58	20 58
St Pancras International	⊖52	a	19 50				20 08	20 08	20 08	20 08	20 01	20 01		20 39	20 50							21 21	21 22	21 22

Station			EM F	EM	EM	NT ◇ O	EM I	EM J	XC P	EM Q	EM M	EM N	EM F	EM R	EM ◇ B	NT ◇	XC P	EM	EM G	EM F	EM	EM ◇ S	XC T	NT ◇
York	29	d	17 48						17 44								18 45						19 45	
Leeds	31,34	d				18 08			18 11							19 08	19 11						20 11	20 08
Wakefield Westgate	31	d							18 23								19 24						20 23	
Wakefield Kirkgate	31,34	d				18 25										19 24								20 24
Doncaster	29	d	18 13						18 58								19 47							
Manchester Piccadilly	78	d													18 42							19 42		
Sheffield		d	18 47			19 06	19 17	19 18	19 24	19 28			19 28		19 40	20 06	20 21		20 26	20 26		20 40	20 54	21 06
Chesterfield		d	19 00			19 22	19 30	19 31	19a35	19 41			19 41		19 54	20 22	20a32		20 39	20 39		20 54	21a05	21 22
Derby		a	19 19				19 52	19 55					20 00							20 59				
		d	19 19				19 54	19 57					20 02							21 01				
Long Eaton		d	19 30				20 12	20 12					20 12											
Alfreton		d				19 32									20 05	20 32						21 05		21 32
Langley Mill		d				19 40									20 12	20 40						21 12		21 40
Lincoln	27	d																						
Newark Castle	27	d																						
Nottingham		a				20 00									20 30	21 00						21 33		22 00
		d			19 52																21 21			
Beeston		d			19 58						←	←		←										
East Midlands Parkway		a	19 33		20 04		20 16	20 16		20 09	20 16	20 16	20 16	20 09					21 07	21 12	21 30			
		d	19 34		20 05		20 17	20 17		20 18	20 17	20 17	20 17	20 18					21 13	21 13	21 31			
Loughborough		d	19 42		20 12		→	→		→	20 26	20 26	20 26	20 26							21 39			
Barrow Upon Soar		d																						
Sileby		d																						
Syston		d																						
Leicester		a	19 53		20 22						20 38	20 38	20 38	20 39					21 30	21 30	21 53			
		d	19 55		20 24						20 40	20 40	20 40	20 40					21 32	21 32	21 54			
Market Harborough		d	20 08		20 37						20 54	20 54	20 54	20 54					21 46	21 46	22 08			
Melton Mowbray	47	d																						
Oakham	47	d																						
Corby		d		20 20														21 25						
Kettering		a	20 15	20 29	20 46						21 04	21 04	21 04	21 04				21 34	21 56	21 56	22 17			
		d	20 15		20 47						21 05	21 05	21 05	21 05					21 57	21 57	22 18			
Wellingborough		d	20 25		20 54						21 13	21 13	21 13	21 13					22 05	22 05	22 25			
Bedford	52	a	20 38		21 08						21 28	21 28	21 28	21 28					22 19	22 19	22 39			
Luton	52	a	20 55		21 23						21 44	21 44	21 44	21 45					22 35	22 35	22 54			
Luton Airport Parkway	52	a	20 58																					
St Pancras International	⊖52	a	21 22		21 48						22 11	22 11	22 11	22 12					23 00	23 00	23 24			

A From Motherwell to Plymouth
B From Liverpool Lime Street to Norwich
C 26 August
D 19 August
E 5 August, 12 August
F 22 July, 29 July, 2 September
G from 5 August until 26 August
H From Aberdeen to Plymouth
I 26 August. To St Pancras International
J 5 August, 12 August. To St Pancras International
K 22 July, 29 July, 19 August, 2 September. From Liverpool Lime Street
L 5 August, 12 August, 26 August. From Liverpool Lime Street
M 26 August. From Sheffield
N 5 August, 12 August. From Sheffield
O From Carlisle
P From Motherwell to Bristol Temple Meads
Q 19 August. To St Pancras International
R 19 August. From Sheffield
S From Liverpool Lime Street
T From Edinburgh to Birmingham New Street

For connections to Gatwick Airport refer to Table T052

Table T053-R

Sundays

22 July to 2 September

Sheffield - East Midlands - London

	EM	XC	NT	EM	EM
	◇ A	◇1 B ⊼	◇	◇1 ⊏	◇ A
York 29 d		20 45			
Leeds 31,34 d		21 11	21 08		
Wakefield Westgate 31 d		21 23			
Wakefield Kirkgate 31,34 d			21 29		
Doncaster 29 d					
Manchester Piccadilly 78 d	20 43				22 11
Sheffield d	21 40	21 54	22 09	22 36	23 30
Chesterfield d	21 56	22a05	22 25	22 48	23 44
Derby a				23 23	
Derby d					
Long Eaton d					
Alfreton d	22 06		22 36		23 55
Langley Mill d	22 14		22 43		00 02
Lincoln 27 d					
Newark Castle 27 d					
Nottingham a	22 36		23 07		00 23
Nottingham d					
Beeston d					
East Midlands Parkway a					
East Midlands Parkway d					
Loughborough d					
Barrow Upon Soar d					
Sileby d					
Syston d					
Leicester a					
Leicester d					
Market Harborough d					
Melton Mowbray 47 d					
Oakham 47 d					
Corby d					
Kettering a					
Kettering d					
Wellingborough d					
Bedford 52 a					
Luton 52 a					
Luton Airport Parkway 52 a					
St Pancras International ⊖52 a					

Sundays

9 September to 7 October

	EM	EM	EM	EM	EM	EM	XC	EM	NT	EM	EM
	◇1 ⊏	◇1 ⊏	◇1 ⊏	◇1 ⊏	◇1 ⊏	◇1 ⊏	◇1 C ⊼	◇1 ⊏	◇	◇1 ⊏	◇1 ⊏
York 29 d											
Leeds 31,34 d							08 10				
Wakefield Westgate 31 d							08 23				
Wakefield Kirkgate 31,34 d											
Doncaster 29 d											
Manchester Piccadilly 78 d											
Sheffield d						08 18	08 55		09 05		09 24
Chesterfield d						08 31	09 08		09 21		09 37
Derby a							09 46				
Derby d	06 50		07 51								
Long Eaton d			08 01								
Alfreton d									09 32		
Langley Mill d									09 39		
Lincoln 27 d											
Newark Castle 27 d											
Nottingham a									10 00		
Nottingham d		07 29		08 22				09 20			
Beeston d				08 28							
East Midlands Parkway a	07 01	07 38	08 04	08 34		08 58		09 30			10 08
East Midlands Parkway d	07 02	07 39	08 05	08 35		09 05		09 31			10 12
Loughborough d			08 13	08 43		09 12		09 40			10 19
Barrow Upon Soar d											
Sileby d											
Syston d											
Leicester a	07 19	07 53	08 23	08 53		09 23		09 52			10 29
Leicester d	07 20	07 55	08 25	08 55		09 24		09 54			10 31
Market Harborough d	07 38	08 11	08 41	09 11		09 40		10 11			10 44
Melton Mowbray 47 d											
Oakham 47 d											
Corby d					09 30					10 25	
Kettering a	07 48	08 20	08 50	09 20	09 39	09 49		10 21		10 34	10 53
Kettering d	07 49	08 21	08 51	09 21		09 50		10 22			10 54
Wellingborough d	07 57	08 28	08 58	09 28		10 02		10 30			11 01
Bedford 52 a	08 15	08 45	09 15	09 45		10 15		10 45			11 15
Luton 52 a	08 35		09 34			10 33					11 34
Luton Airport Parkway 52 a		09 06		10 06				11 06			
St Pancras International ⊖52 a	09 13	09 42	10 11	10 42		11 10		11 42			12 12

	XC	EM	NT	EM	EM	EM	EM	EM	XC	NT	EM
	◇1 C ⊼	◇1 ⊏	◇	◇1 ⊏	◇1 ⊏	◇1 ⊏	◇1 ⊏	◇ D	◇1 E ⊼	◇	◇1 ⊏
York 29 d									09 33		
Leeds 31,34 d	09 00		09 08				09 50		09 59	10 08	10 50
Wakefield Westgate 31 d	09 11						10 02		10 12		11 03
Wakefield Kirkgate 31,34 d			09 24							10 24	
Doncaster 29 d	09 31								10 30		
Manchester Piccadilly 78 d											
Sheffield d	09 58		10 06		10 25		10 35	10 48	10 55	11 06	11 43
Chesterfield d	10 11		10 22		10 37		10 48	11 04	11 08	11 22	11 55
Derby a	10 46								11 46		
Derby d											
Long Eaton d											
Alfreton d			10 32					11 14		11 32	
Langley Mill d			10 40							11 40	
Lincoln 27 d											
Newark Castle 27 d											
Nottingham a			11 00				11 21	11 39		12 00	
Nottingham d		10 30					11 39				
Beeston d		10 37									
East Midlands Parkway a		10 44			11 09		11 49				12 25
East Midlands Parkway d		10 45			11 11		11 50				12 34
Loughborough d		10 53			11 19		11 59				12 42
Barrow Upon Soar d											
Sileby d											
Syston d											
Leicester a		11 06			11 29		12 11				12 54
Leicester d		11 08			11 30		12 13				12 56
Market Harborough d		11 22			11 43		12 27				13 10
Melton Mowbray 47 d											
Oakham 47 d											
Corby d				11 25		12 20					
Kettering a		11 32		11 34	11 52	12 29	12 37				
Kettering d		11 33			11 53		12 38				
Wellingborough d		11 41			12 01		12 46				
Bedford 52 a		11 57			12 15		13 02				
Luton 52 a					12 29						
Luton Airport Parkway 52 a		12 13					13 18				
St Pancras International ⊖52 a		12 41			12 54		13 44				14 09

A From Liverpool Lime Street
B From Motherwell to Birmingham New Street. ⊼ to Leeds
C To Plymouth
D 9 September. To Norwich
E To Birmingham New Street

For connections to Gatwick Airport refer to Table T052

Table T053-R

Sundays

9 September to 7 October

Sheffield - East Midlands - London

	XC	EM	EM	NT	EM	EM	EM	EM	NT	XC	EM
	◇1 A ⊼	◇1 ⊏	◇1 ⊏	◇	◇ B	◇1 ⊏	◇1 ⊏	◇1 ⊏	◇	◇1 C ⊼	◇1 ⊏
York 29 d	10 33									11 41	
Leeds 31,34 d	11 00			11 08					12 08	12 11	
Wakefield Westgate 31 d	11 12									12 24	
Wakefield Kirkgate 31,34 d				11 24					12 24		
Doncaster 29 d	11 30									12 54	
Manchester Piccadilly 78 d											
Sheffield d	11 57			12 06	12 43	12 49			13 06	13 24	13 43
Chesterfield d	12 09			12 22	12 57	13 01			13 22	13 36	13 56
Derby a	12 50									14 14	
Derby d											
Long Eaton d											
Alfreton d				12 32	13 08				13 32		
Langley Mill d				12 40					13 40		
Lincoln 27 d											
Newark Castle 27 d											
Nottingham a				13 00	13 34				14 00		
Nottingham d			12 49					13 49			
Beeston d			12 56					13 56			
East Midlands Parkway a			13 02			13 32		14 02			14 24
East Midlands Parkway d			13 03			13 36		14 03			14 31
Loughborough d			13 12			13 43		14 12			14 38
Barrow Upon Soar d											
Sileby d											
Syston d											
Leicester a			13 24			13 53		14 24			14 54
Leicester d			13 26			13 55		14 26			14 55
Market Harborough d			13 40			14 08		14 40			15 08
Melton Mowbray 47 d											
Oakham 47 d											
Corby d		13 13					14 13				
Kettering a		13 22	13 50				14 22	14 50			
Kettering d		13 23	13 51				14 23	14 51			
Wellingborough d		13 32	13 59				14 31	14 59			
Bedford 52 a		13 44	14 15				14 45	15 15			
Luton 52 a		14 00					15 00				
Luton Airport Parkway 52 a			14 31					15 31			
St Pancras International ⊖52 a		14 24	14 59			15 03	15 24	15 59			16 05

	EM	EM	EM	NT	XC	EM	EM	EM	EM	EM	NT
	◇ B	◇1 ⊏	◇1 ⊏	◇	◇1 D ⊼	◇ E	◇1 ⊏	◇1 ⊏	◇1 ⊏	◇1 ⊏	◇
York 29 d					12 42						
Leeds 31,34 d				13 08	13 11						14 08
Wakefield Westgate 31 d					13 24						
Wakefield Kirkgate 31,34 d				13 24							14 24
Doncaster 29 d					13 54						
Manchester Piccadilly 78 d	12 43					13 43					
Sheffield d	13 48			14 06	14 22	14 41	14 49				15 06
Chesterfield d	14 02			14 22	14 34	14 55	15 01				15 22
Derby a					15 12						
Derby d											
Long Eaton d											
Alfreton d	14 12			14 32		15 08					15 32
Langley Mill d				14 40		15 15					15 40
Lincoln 27 d											
Newark Castle 27 d											
Nottingham a	14 35			15 00		15 32					16 00
Nottingham d			14 52					15 43		15 52	
Beeston d			14 58							15 58	
East Midlands Parkway a			15 03				15 34	15 53		16 04	
East Midlands Parkway d			15 04				15 36	15 53		16 05	
Loughborough d			15 12				15 43			16 12	
Barrow Upon Soar d											
Sileby d											
Syston d											
Leicester a			15 22				15 54	16 11		16 23	
Leicester d			15 24				15 56	16 12		16 24	
Market Harborough d			15 37							16 37	
Melton Mowbray 47 d											
Oakham 47 d											
Corby d		15 13							16 20		
Kettering a		15 22	15 46						16 29	16 46	
Kettering d		15 23	15 47							16 47	
Wellingborough d		15 31	15 54							16 55	
Bedford 52 a		15 45	16 09							17 09	
Luton 52 a		16 00					16 41				
Luton Airport Parkway 52 a			16 25							17 25	
St Pancras International ⊖52 a		16 24	16 48				17 06	17 23		17 50	

	XC	EM	EM	EM	EM	EM	EM	NT	EM	XC
	◇1 C ⊼	◇1 ⊏	◇ E	◇1 ⊏	◇1 ⊏	◇1 ⊏	◇1 ⊏	◇	◇1 ⊏	◇1 F ⊼
York 29 d	13 45									14 44
Leeds 31,34 d	14 11	14 34						15 08		15 11
Wakefield Westgate 31 d	14 23	14 47								15 23
Wakefield Kirkgate 31,34 d								15 24		
Doncaster 29 d	14 54									15 54
Manchester Piccadilly 78 d			14 43							
Sheffield d	15 24	15 29	15 39	15 50				16 06		16 24
Chesterfield d	15 36	15 42	15 53	16 02				16 22		16 36
Derby a	16 14									17 16
Derby d									16 57	
Long Eaton d									17 07	
Alfreton d			16 03					16 32		
Langley Mill d			16 11					16 40		
Lincoln 27 d										
Newark Castle 27 d										
Nottingham a			16 28					17 00		
Nottingham d					16 45		16 50			
Beeston d							16 57			
East Midlands Parkway a		16 10		16 30	16 54		17 02		17 10	
East Midlands Parkway d		16 16		16 37	16 55		17 03		17 11	
Loughborough d		16 25					17 11		17 19	
Barrow Upon Soar d										
Sileby d										
Syston d										
Leicester a		16 37		16 54	17 09		17 21		17 29	
Leicester d		16 39		16 55	17 10		17 23		17 31	
Market Harborough d		16 53					17 36		17 44	
Melton Mowbray 47 d										
Oakham 47 d										
Corby d						17 20				
Kettering a		17 03				17 29	17 45		17 54	
Kettering d		17 03					17 46		17 55	
Wellingborough d		17 12					17 54		18 02	
Bedford 52 a		17 28					18 07		18 16	
Luton 52 a		17 45							18 31	
Luton Airport Parkway 52 a							18 24			
St Pancras International ⊖52 a		18 11		18 02	18 17		18 47		18 55	

	EM	EM	EM	EM	EM	NT	EM	XC	EM	EM	EM
	◇ E	◇1 ⊏	◇1 ⊏	◇1 ⊏	◇1 ⊏	◇	◇1 ⊏	◇1 F	◇ E	◇1 ⊏	◇1 ⊏
York 29 d								15 42			
Leeds 31,34 d						16 08		16 11			
Wakefield Westgate 31 d								16 23			
Wakefield Kirkgate 31,34 d						16 24					
Doncaster 29 d								16 46			
Manchester Piccadilly 78 d	15 42								16 42		
Sheffield d	16 43	16 49				17 06		17 19	17 40	17 50	
Chesterfield d	16 57	17 00				17 22		17 31	17 54	18 02	
Derby a								18 14			
Derby d							18 06				
Long Eaton d							18 15				
Alfreton d	17 07					17 32			18 05		
Langley Mill d	17 15					17 40			18 12		
Lincoln 27 d											
Newark Castle 27 d											
Nottingham a	17 30					18 00			18 34		
Nottingham d			17 45		17 52						
Beeston d					17 58						
East Midlands Parkway a		17 32	17 55		18 03		18 19			18 33	
East Midlands Parkway d		17 36	17 55		18 04		18 20			18 37	
Loughborough d					18 12		18 28				
Barrow Upon Soar d											
Sileby d											
Syston d											
Leicester a		17 54	18 13		18 22		18 38			18 53	
Leicester d		17 54	18 14		18 25		18 40			18 54	
Market Harborough d					18 38		18 53				
Melton Mowbray 47 d											
Oakham 47 d											
Corby d				18 20							19 20
Kettering a				18 29	18 47		19 02				19 29
Kettering d					18 48		19 05				
Wellingborough d					18 55		19 12				
Bedford 52 a					19 09		19 27				
Luton 52 a							19 44				
Luton Airport Parkway 52 a					19 24						
St Pancras International ⊖52 a		19 10	19 25		19 50		20 08			20 01	

A From Newcastle to Bristol Temple Meads
B To Norwich
C From Edinburgh to Penzance
D From Edinburgh to Plymouth
E From Liverpool Lime Street to Norwich
F From Glasgow Central to Plymouth

For connections to Gatwick Airport refer to Table T052

Table T053-R

Sheffield - East Midlands - London

Sundays

9 September to 7 October

	EM	EM	NT	XC	EM	EM	EM	EM	NT	XC	EM	EM	NT	XC	EM	EM	EM	EM	XC	NT	EM	XC
	◇■	◇■	◇	◇■	◇	◇■	◇■	◇■	◇	◇■	◇■	◇	◇	◇■	◇■	◇■	◇■	◇	◇■	◇	◇	◇■
				A	B				C	D		E		D				B	F		B	G
York 29 d				16 41		17 48				17 44				18 45					19 45			20 45
Leeds 31,34 d			17 08	17 11					18 08	18 11			19 08	19 11					20 11	20 08		21 11
Wakefield Westgate 31 d				17 23						18 23				19 24					20 23			21 23
Wakefield Kirkgate 31,34 d			17 24						18 25				19 24							20 24		
Doncaster 29 d				17 46		18 13				18 58				19 54								
Manchester Piccadilly 78 d					17 42							18 42						19 42			20 43	
Sheffield d			18 06	18 24	18 40	18 47			19 06	19 24	19 28	19 40	20 06	20 21		20 26		20 40	20 54	21 06	21 40	21 54
Chesterfield d			18 22	18 36	18 54	18 59			19 22	19 36	19 41	19 54	20 22	20 33		20 39		20 54	21 06	21 22	21 56	22 06
Derby a				19 13						20 13				21 12					21 44			22 44
d																						
Long Eaton d																						
Alfreton d			18 32		19 05				19 32			20 05	20 32					21 05		21 32	22 06	
Langley Mill d			18 40		19 12				19 40			20 12	20 40					21 12		21 40	22 14	
Lincoln 27 d																						
Newark Castle 27 d																						
Nottingham a			19 00		19 33				20 00			20 30	21 00					21 33		22 00	22 36	
d	18 45	18 52						19 52									21 21					
Beeston d		18 58						19 58														
East Midlands Parkway a	18 54	19 04				19 32		20 04			20 09					21 07	21 30					
d	18 55	19 05				19 33		20 05			20 18					21 13	21 31					
Loughborough d	19 02	19 12				19 41		20 12			20 26						21 39					
Barrow Upon Soar d																						
Sileby d																						
Syston d																						
Leicester a	19 13	19 23				19 52		20 22			20 39					21 30	21 53					
d	19 14	19 25				19 54		20 24			20 40					21 32	21 54					
Market Harborough d	19 27	19 38				20 07		20 37			20 54					21 46	22 08					
Melton Mowbray 47 d																						
Oakham 47 d																						
Corby d							20 20								21 25							
Kettering a	19 36	19 47				20 14	20 29	20 46			21 04				21 34	21 56	22 17					
d	19 37	19 48				20 14		20 47			21 05					21 57	22 18					
Wellingborough d	19 45	19 55				20 24		20 54			21 13					22 05	22 25					
Bedford 52 a	19 58	20 09				20 37		21 08			21 28					22 19	22 39					
Luton 52 a	20 14					20 54		21 23			21 45					22 35	22 54					
Luton Airport Parkway 52 a		20 25				20 57																
St Pancras International 52 a	20 39	20 50				21 21		21 48			22 12					23 00	23 24					

	NT	EM	EM
	◇	◇■	◇
			B
York 29 d			
Leeds 31,34 d	21 08		
Wakefield Westgate 31 d			
Wakefield Kirkgate 31,34 d	21 29		
Doncaster 29 d			
Manchester Piccadilly 78 d			22 11
Sheffield d	22 09	22 36	23 30
Chesterfield d	22 25	22 48	23 44
Derby a		23 23	
d			
Long Eaton d			
Alfreton d	22 36		23 55
Langley Mill d	22 43		00 02
Lincoln 27 d			
Newark Castle 27 d			
Nottingham a	23 07		00 23
d			
Beeston d			
East Midlands Parkway a			
d			
Loughborough d			
Barrow Upon Soar d			
Sileby d			
Syston d			
Leicester a			
d			
Market Harborough d			
Melton Mowbray 47 d			
Oakham 47 d			
Corby d			
Kettering a			
d			
Wellingborough d			
Bedford 52 a			
Luton 52 a			
Luton Airport Parkway 52 a			
St Pancras International 52 a			

A From Aberdeen to Plymouth
B From Liverpool Lime Street
C From Carlisle
D From Glasgow Central to Bristol Temple Meads
E From Liverpool Lime Street to Norwich
F From Edinburgh to Birmingham New Street
G From Glasgow Central to Birmingham New Street. to Leeds

For connections to Gatwick Airport refer to Table T052

Table T053-R

Sheffield - East Midlands - London

Sundays

14 October to 2 December

	EM	EM	EM	EM	EM	EM	XC	EM	NT	EM	EM	XC	EM	NT	EM	EM	EM	EM	XC	NT	EM	XC
	◇■	◇■	◇■	◇■	◇■	◇■	◇■	◇■	◇	◇■	◇■	◇■	◇■	◇	◇■	◇■	◇■	◇■	◇■	◇	◇■	◇■
							A					A							A			B
York 29 d																			09 33			10 33
Leeds 31,34 d							08 10					09 00		09 08				09 50	09 59	10 08	10 50	11 00
Wakefield Westgate 31 d							08 23					09 11						10 02	10 12		11 03	11 12
Wakefield Kirkgate 31,34 d														09 24						10 24		
Doncaster 29 d												09 31							10 30			11 30
Manchester Piccadilly 78 d																						
Sheffield d						08 18	08 54		09 05		09 25	09 57		10 06		10 25		10 35	10 55	11 06	11 43	11 57
Chesterfield d						08 31	09 07		09 21		09 37	10 09		10 22		10 37		10 48	11 08	11 22	11 55	12 09
Derby a						08 49	09 28				09 56	10 32				10 56			11 28		12 17	12 28
d	06 50		07 51			08 51					09 58					10 57					12 17	
Long Eaton d			08 01			09 00					10 07					11 07					12 29	
Alfreton d									09 32					10 32						11 32		
Langley Mill d									09 39					10 40						11 40		
Lincoln 27 d																						
Newark Castle 27 d																						
Nottingham a									10 00					11 00				11 21		12 00		
d		07 29		08 22				09 20					10 30					11 39				
Beeston d				08 28									10 37									
East Midlands Parkway a	07 01	07 38	08 04	08 34		09 04		09 30			10 11		10 44			11 10		11 49			12 33	
d	07 02	07 39	08 05	08 35		09 05		09 31			10 12		10 45			11 11		11 50			12 34	
Loughborough d			08 13	08 43		09 12		09 40			10 19		10 53			11 19		11 59			12 42	
Barrow Upon Soar d																						
Sileby d																						
Syston d																						
Leicester a	07 19	07 53	08 23	08 53		09 23		09 52			10 29		11 06			11 29		12 11			12 54	
d	07 20	07 55	08 25	08 55		09 24		09 54			10 31		11 08			11 30		12 13			12 56	
Market Harborough d	07 38	08 11	08 41	09 11		09 40		10 11			10 44		11 22			11 43		12 27			13 10	
Melton Mowbray 47 d																						
Oakham 47 d																						
Corby d					09 30					10 25					11 25		12 20					
Kettering a	07 48	08 20	08 50	09 20	09 39	09 49		10 21		10 34	10 53		11 32		11 34	11 52	12 29	12 37				
d	07 49	08 21	08 51	09 21		09 50		10 22			10 54		11 33			11 53		12 38				
Wellingborough d	07 57	08 28	08 58	09 28		10 02		10 30			11 01		11 41			12 01		12 46				
Bedford 52 a	08 15	08 45	09 15	09 45		10 15		10 45			11 15		11 57			12 15		13 02				
Luton 52 a	08 35		09 34			10 33					11 34					12 29						
Luton Airport Parkway 52 a		09 06		10 06				11 06					12 13					13 18				
St Pancras International 52 a	09 13	09 42	10 11	10 42		11 10		11 42			12 12		12 41			12 54		13 44			14 09	

	EM	EM	NT	EM	EM	XC	EM	EM	NT	EM	EM	XC	EM	EM	NT	XC	EM	EM	XC	EM	EM	EM
	◇■	◇■	◇	◇	◇■	◇■	◇■	◇■	◇	◇■	◇	◇■	◇■	◇■	◇	◇■	◇	◇■	◇■	◇■	◇■	◇■
				C		D					C	E				F	G		D			
York 29 d						11 41						12 45							13 45			
Leeds 31,34 d			11 08			12 11			12 08			13 11			13 08				14 11			
Wakefield Westgate 31 d						12 24						13 24							14 23			
Wakefield Kirkgate 31,34 d			11 24						12 24						13 24							
Doncaster 29 d																						
Manchester Piccadilly 78 d											12 43						13 43					
Sheffield d			12 06	12 43	12 49	12 57			13 06	13 43	13 48	13 57			14 06	14 22	14 41	14 49	14 55			
Chesterfield d			12 22	12 57	13 02	13 09			13 22	13 56	14 02	14 09			14 22	14 32	14 55	15 01	15 07			
Derby a					13 21	13 30				14 15		14 27				14 50		15 19	15 25			
d					13 22					14 16								15 21				
Long Eaton d					13 31					14 26								15 30				
Alfreton d			12 32	13 08					13 32		14 12				14 32		15 08					
Langley Mill d			12 40						13 40						14 40		15 15					
Lincoln 27 d																						
Newark Castle 27 d																						
Nottingham a			13 00	13 34					14 00		14 35				15 00		15 32					
d		12 49						13 49						14 52						15 43		15 52
Beeston d		12 56						13 56						14 58								15 58
East Midlands Parkway a		13 02			13 34			14 02		14 29				15 03				15 34		15 53		16 04
d		13 03			13 35			14 03		14 30				15 04				15 35		15 53		16 05
Loughborough d		13 12			13 43			14 12		14 38				15 12				15 42				16 12
Barrow Upon Soar d																						
Sileby d																						
Syston d																						
Leicester a		13 24			13 53			14 24		14 53				15 22				15 53		16 11		16 23
d		13 26			13 54			14 26		14 55				15 24				15 55		16 12		16 24
Market Harborough d		13 40			14 07			14 40		15 08				15 37								16 37
Melton Mowbray 47 d																						
Oakham 47 d																						
Corby d	13 13						14 13						15 13								16 20	
Kettering a	13 22	13 50					14 22	14 50					15 22	15 46							16 29	16 46
d	13 23	13 51					14 23	14 51					15 23	15 47								16 47
Wellingborough d	13 32	13 59					14 31	14 59					15 31	15 54								16 55
Bedford 52 a	13 44	14 15					14 45	15 15					15 45	16 09								17 09
Luton 52 a	14 00						15 00						16 00					16 40				
Luton Airport Parkway 52 a		14 31						15 31						16 25								17 25
St Pancras International 52 a	14 24	14 59			15 02		15 24	15 59		16 04			16 24	16 48				17 05		17 23		17 50

A To Plymouth
B From Newcastle to Plymouth
C To Norwich
D From Edinburgh to Plymouth
E From Edinburgh to Penzance
F To Reading
G From Liverpool Lime Street to Norwich

For connections to Gatwick Airport refer to Table T052

Sheffield - East Midlands - London

	NT		XC	EM	EM	EM	XC	EM	EM	EM	NT		XC	EM	EM	EM	XC	EM	EM	EM	NT		XC	EM
	◇		◇■	◇■	◇	◇■	◇■	◇■	◇■	◇■	◇		◇■	◇■	◇	◇■	◇■	◇■	◇■	◇■	◇		◇■	◇■
			A		B		C						A		B		D						E	
			🍴	☕		☕	🍴	☕	☕	☕			🍴	☕		☕	🍴	☕	☕	☕			🍴	☕
York [8] 29 d			14 35				14 44						15 35				15 42						16 25	
Leeds [10] 31,34 d	14 08			14 34			15 11				15 08						16 11				16 08			
Wakefield Westgate [7] 31 d				14 47			15 23										16 23							
Wakefield Kirkgate [4] 31,34 d	14 24										15 24										16 24			
Doncaster [7] 29 d			15 00										15 58										16 51	
Manchester Piccadilly 78 d					14 43										15 42									
Sheffield [7] d	15 06		15 24	15 28	15 39	15 50	15 55				16 06		16 24		16 43	16 49	16 55				17 06		17 24	
Chesterfield d	15 22			15 42	15 53	16 02	16 07				16 22				16 57	17 00	17 07				17 22			
Derby [6] a			15 52	16 02		16 21	16 25						16 53			17 19	17 25						17 52	
d				16 02		16 26								16 57		17 23								18 06
Long Eaton d														17 07										18 15
Alfreton d	15 32				16 03						16 32				17 07						17 32			
Langley Mill d	15 40				16 11						16 40				17 15						17 40			
Lincoln 27 d																								
Newark Castle 27 d																								
Nottingham [8] a	16 00				16 28						17 00				17 30						18 00			
d								16 45		16 50								17 45		17 52				
Beeston d										16 57										17 58				
East Midlands Parkway a				16 15		16 36		16 54		17 02				17 10		17 36		17 55		18 03				18 19
d				16 16		16 37		16 55		17 03				17 11		17 36		17 55		18 04				18 20
Loughborough d				16 25						17 11				17 19						18 12				18 28
Barrow Upon Soar d																								
Sileby d																								
Syston d																								
Leicester a				16 37		16 53		17 09		17 21				17 29		17 54		18 13		18 22				18 38
d				16 39		16 55		17 10		17 23				17 31		17 54		18 14		18 25				18 40
Market Harborough d				16 53						17 36				17 44						18 38				18 53
Melton Mowbray 47 d																								
Oakham 47 d																								
Corby d									17 20										18 20					
Kettering [5] a				17 03					17 29	17 45				17 54					18 29	18 47				19 02
d				17 03						17 46				17 55						18 48				19 05
Wellingborough d				17 12						17 54				18 02						18 55				19 12
Bedford [7] 52 a				17 28						18 07				18 16						19 09				19 27
Luton [10] 52 a				17 45										18 31										19 44
Luton Airport Parkway [7] 52 a										18 24										19 24				
St Pancras International ⊖52 a				18 11		18 02		18 17		18 47				18 55		19 09		19 25		19 50				20 08

	EM	EM	XC	EM	EM	EM	NT		XC	EM	EM	XC	EM	EM	NT	XC	EM		EM	XC	NT	XC	EM	EM
	◇	◇■	◇■	◇■	◇■	◇■	◇		◇■	◇	◇■	◇■	◇■	◇■	◇	◇■	◇■		◇	◇■	◇	◇■	◇■	◇■
	B		F						A	G		D			H	I			B	J		K		
		☕	🍴	☕	☕	☕			🍴		☕	🍴	☕	☕		🍴	☕			🍴		🍴	☕	☕
York [8] 29 d			16 41						17 35		17 48	17 44				18 35				18 45		19 24		
Leeds [10] 31,34 d			17 11				17 08					18 11			18 08					19 11	19 08			
Wakefield Westgate [7] 31 d			17 23									18 23								19 24				
Wakefield Kirkgate [4] 31,34 d							17 24								18 25						19 24			
Doncaster [7] 29 d									17 58		18 13					18 58						19 54		
Manchester Piccadilly 78 d	16 42									17 42									18 42					
Sheffield [7] d	17 40	17 50	17 55				18 06		18 24	18 40	18 47	18 55			19 06	19 24	19 28		19 40	19 55	20 06	20 21		20 26
Chesterfield d	17 54	18 02	18 07				18 22			18 54	19 00	19 07			19 22		19 41		19 54	20 07	20 22			20 39
Derby [6] a		18 21	18 25						18 53		19 19	19 25				19 52	20 00			20 25		20 49		20 59
d		18 26									19 19						20 02							21 01
Long Eaton d											19 30						20 12							
Alfreton d	18 05						18 32			19 05					19 32				20 05		20 32			
Langley Mill d	18 12						18 40			19 12					19 40				20 12		20 40			
Lincoln 27 d																								
Newark Castle 27 d																								
Nottingham [8] a	18 34						19 00			19 33					20 00				20 30		21 00			
d					18 45	18 52								19 52										
Beeston d						18 58								19 58										
East Midlands Parkway a		18 36			18 54	19 04					19 33			20 04			20 16							21 12
d		18 37			18 55	19 05					19 34			20 05			20 17							21 13
Loughborough d					19 02	19 12					19 42			20 12			20 26							
Barrow Upon Soar d																								
Sileby d																								
Syston d																								
Leicester a		18 53			19 13	19 23					19 53			20 22			20 38							21 30
d		18 54			19 14	19 25					19 55			20 24			20 40							21 32
Market Harborough d					19 27	19 38					20 08			20 37			20 54							21 46
Melton Mowbray 47 d																								
Oakham 47 d																								
Corby d				19 20									20 20										21 25	
Kettering [5] a				19 29	19 36	19 47					20 15		20 29	20 46			21 04						21 34	21 56
d					19 37	19 48					20 15			20 47			21 05							21 57
Wellingborough d					19 45	19 55					20 25			20 54			21 13							22 05
Bedford [7] 52 a					19 58	20 09					20 38			21 08			21 28							22 19
Luton [10] 52 a					20 14						20 55			21 23			21 44							22 35
Luton Airport Parkway [7] 52 a						20 25					20 58													
St Pancras International ⊖52 a		20 01			20 39	20 50					21 22			21 48			22 11							23 00

A From Newcastle to Reading
B From Liverpool Lime Street to Norwich
C From Glasgow Central to Penzance
D From Glasgow Central to Plymouth
E From Edinburgh to Reading
F From Aberdeen to Plymouth
G From Liverpool Lime Street
H From Carlisle
I From Newcastle to Guildford
J From Glasgow Central to Bristol Temple Meads
K From Newcastle to Birmingham New Street

For connections to Gatwick Airport refer to Table T052

Sheffield - East Midlands - London

	EM	EM	XC		NT	XC	EM	XC	NT	EM	EM
	◇■	◇	◇■		◇	◇■	◇	◇■	◇	◇■	◇
		A	B			C	A	D			A
	☕		🍴					🍴		☕	
York [8] 29 d			19 45			20 26		20 45			
Leeds [10] 31,34 d			20 11		20 08			21 11	21 08		
Wakefield Westgate [7] 31 d			20 23					21 23			
Wakefield Kirkgate [4] 31,34 d					20 24				21 29		
Doncaster [7] 29 d						20 51					
Manchester Piccadilly 78 d		19 42					20 43				22 11
Sheffield [7] d		20 40	20 54		21 06	21 20	21 40	21 54	22 09	22 36	23 30
Chesterfield d		20 54	21 06		21 22	21 32	21 56	22 06	22 25	22 48	23 44
Derby [6] a			21 25			21 51		22 24		23 23	
d											
Long Eaton d											
Alfreton d		21 05			21 32		22 06		22 36		23 55
Langley Mill d		21 12			21 40		22 14		22 43		00 02
Lincoln 27 d											
Newark Castle 27 d											
Nottingham [8] a		21 33			22 00		22 36		23 07		00 23
d	21 21										
Beeston d											
East Midlands Parkway a	21 30										
d	21 31										
Loughborough d	21 39										
Barrow Upon Soar d											
Sileby d											
Syston d											
Leicester a	21 53										
d	21 54										
Market Harborough d	22 08										
Melton Mowbray 47 d											
Oakham 47 d											
Corby d											
Kettering [5] a	22 17										
d	22 18										
Wellingborough d	22 25										
Bedford [7] 52 a	22 39										
Luton [10] 52 a	22 54										
Luton Airport Parkway [7] 52 a											
St Pancras International ⊖52 a	23 24										

A From Liverpool Lime Street
B From Edinburgh to Bristol Temple Meads. 🍴 to Leeds
C From Newcastle to Birmingham New Street
D From Glasgow Central to Birmingham New Street. 🍴 to Leeds

For connections to Gatwick Airport refer to Table T052

Table T055-F

Nottingham - Mansfield - Worksop

Mondays to Fridays

21 May to 7 December

Miles			EM	EM	EM	EM	EM	EM	EM	EM	EM	EM	EM	EM	EM	EM	EM	EM	EM	EM	EM	EM	EM
0	**Nottingham**	d	05 40	06 05	07 01	08 26	08 54	09 26	09 55	10 26	10 55	11 26	11 55	12 26	12 55	13 26	13 55	14 26	14 55	15 26	15 55	16 26	16 55
5½	Bulwell	d	05 49	06 14	07 10	08 36	09 03		10 05		11 05		12 05		13 05		14 05		15 05		16 05		17 06
8¼	Hucknall	d	05 54	06 19	07 16	08 41	09 08	09 39	10 10	10 39	11 10	11 39	12 10	12 39	13 10	13 39	14 10	14 39	15 10	15 39	16 10	16 39	17 11
10¾	Newstead	d	05 59	06 24	07 21	08 46	09 13	09 44		10 44		11 44		12 44		13 44		14 44		15 44		16 44	17 17
13¾	Kirkby In Ashfield	d	06 05	06 30	07 31	08 52	09 19	09 49	10 19	10 49	11 19	11 49	12 19	12 49	13 19	13 49	14 19	14 49	15 19	15 49	16 19	16 49	17 23
14½	Sutton Parkway	d	06 08	06 33	07 34	08 55	09 22	09 52	10 22	10 52	11 22	11 52	12 22	12 52	13 22	13 52	14 22	14 52	15 22	15 52	16 22	16 52	17 26
17¼	**Mansfield**	d	06 13	06 38	07 40	09 00	09 27	09 57	10 27	10 57	11 27	11 57	12 27	12 57	13 27	13 57	14 27	14 57	15 27	15 57	16 27	16 57	17 32
18¾	Mansfield Woodhouse	d	06 18	06 46	07 45	09 04	09a34	10 02	10a34	11 02	11a34	12 02	12a34	13 02	13a34	14 02	14a34	15 02	15a34	16 02	16a34	17 02	17a39
21½	Shirebrook	d	06 24	06 53	07 51	09 11		10 08		11 08		12 08		13 08		14 08		15 08		16 08		17 08	
22¼	Langwith - Whaley Thorns	d	06 28	06 57	07 55	09 15		10 12		11 12		12 12		13 12		14 12		15 12		16 12		17 12	
25½	Creswell (Derbys)	d	06 32	07 01	07 59	09 19		10 16		11 16		12 16		13 16		14 16		15 16		16 16		17 16	
26¾	Whitwell	d	06 36	07 08	08 03	09 22		10 20		11 20		12 20		13 20		14 20		15 20		16 20		17 20	
31½	**Worksop**	a	06 49	07 20	08 18	09 33		10 33		11 33		12 33		13 33		14 33		15 33		16 33		17 33	

		EM	EM	EM	EM A	EM B	EM C	EM B	EM D	EM D	EM B
Nottingham	d	17 26	17 55	18 56	19 55	19 56	19 57	20 55	20 56	22 00	22 02
Bulwell	d	17 38	18 12	19 05	20 05	20 05	20 06	21 05	21 05	22 12	22 12
Hucknall	d	17 44	18 17	19 10	20 17	20 17	20 17	21 17	21 17	22 17	22 17
Newstead	d	17 49	18 22	19 15	20 22	20 22	20 22	21 22	21 22	22 22	22 22
Kirkby In Ashfield	d	17 55	18 28	19 21	20 28	20 28	20 28	21 28	21 28	22 27	22 27
Sutton Parkway	d	17 58	18 31	19 24	20 31	20 31	20 31	21 31	21 31	22 30	22 30
Mansfield	d	18 03	18 36	19 29	20 36	20 36	20 36	21 36	21 36	22 35	22 35
Mansfield Woodhouse	d	18 08	18 41	19 35	20 41	20 41	20 41	21 41	21 41	22 40	22 40
Shirebrook	d	18 14	18 47	19 41	20 47	20 47	20 47	21 47	21 47	22 47	22 47
Langwith - Whaley Thorns	d	18 18	18 51	19 45	20 51	20 51	20 51	21 51	21 51	22 50	22 50
Creswell (Derbys)	d	18 22	18 55	19 49	20 55	20 55	20 55	21 55	21 55	22 54	22 54
Whitwell	d	18 26	18 58	19 52	20 58	20 58	20 58	21 58	21 58	22 57	22 57
Worksop	a	18 37	19 08	20 05	21 09	21 09	21 09	22 08	22 08	23 07	23 07

Saturdays

26 May to 8 December

		EM	EM	EM	EM	EM	EM	EM	EM	EM	EM	EM	EM	EM	EM	EM	EM	EM	EM	EM	EM	EM	EM
Nottingham	d	05 40	06 05	07 03	08 26	08 54	09 26	09 55	10 26	10 55	11 26	11 55	12 26	12 55	13 26	13 55	14 26	14 55	15 26	15 55	16 26	16 55	17 26
Bulwell	d	05 49	06 14	07 12	08 36	09 03		10 05		11 05		12 05		13 05		14 05		15 05		16 05		17 06	17 38
Hucknall	d	05 54	06 19	07 18	08 41	09 08	09 39	10 10	10 39	11 10	11 39	12 10	12 39	13 10	13 39	14 10	14 39	15 10	15 39	16 10	16 39	17 11	17 44
Newstead	d	05 59	06 24	07 23	08 46	09 13	09 44		10 44		11 44		12 44		13 44		14 44		15 44		16 44	17 17	17 49
Kirkby In Ashfield	d	06 05	06 30	07 31	08 52	09 19	09 49	10 19	10 49	11 19	11 49	12 19	12 49	13 19	13 50	14 19	14 49	15 19	15 49	16 19	16 49	17 23	17 55
Sutton Parkway	d	06 08	06 33	07 34	08 55	09 22	09 52	10 22	10 52	11 22	11 52	12 22	12 52	13 22	13 53	14 22	14 52	15 22	15 52	16 22	16 52	17 26	17 58
Mansfield	d	06 13	06 38	07 40	09 00	09 27	09 57	10 27	10 57	11 27	11 57	12 27	12 57	13 27	13 59	14 27	14 57	15 27	15 57	16 27	16 57	17 32	18 03
Mansfield Woodhouse	d	06 18	06 46	07 45	09 04	09a34	10 02	10a34	11 02	11a34	12 02	12a34	13 02	13a34	14 04	14a34	15 02	15a34	16 02	16a34	17 02	17a39	18 08
Shirebrook	d	06 24	06 53	07 51	09 11		10 08		11 08		12 08		13 08		14 10		15 08		16 08		17 08		18 14
Langwith - Whaley Thorns	d	06 28	06 57	07 55	09 15		10 12		11 12		12 12		13 12		14 14		15 12		16 12		17 12		18 18
Creswell (Derbys)	d	06 32	07 01	07 59	09 19		10 16		11 16		12 16		13 16		14 18		15 16		16 16		17 16		18 22
Whitwell	d	06 36	07 04	08 03	09 22		10 20		11 20		12 20		13 20		14 22		15 20		16 20		17 20		18 26
Worksop	a	06 48	07 18	08 14	09 33		10 33		11 33		12 33		13 33		14 35		15 33		16 31		17 32		18 36

		EM	EM	EM	EM	EM	EM
Nottingham	d	17 55	18 55	19 55	20 55	22 00	23 05
Bulwell	d	18 12	19 05	20 05	21 05	22 12	23 19
Hucknall	d	18 17	19 10	20 17	21 17	22 17	23 24
Newstead	d	18 22	19 15	20 22	21 22	22 22	23 29
Kirkby In Ashfield	d	18 28	19 21	20 28	21 28	22 27	23 34
Sutton Parkway	d	18 31	19 24	20 31	21 31	22 30	23 38
Mansfield	d	18 36	19 29	20 36	21 36	22 35	23 43
Mansfield Woodhouse	d	18 41	19 35	20 41	21 41	22 40	23a48
Shirebrook	d	18 47	19 41	20 47	21 47	22 47	
Langwith - Whaley Thorns	d	18 51	19 45	20 51	21 51	22 50	
Creswell (Derbys)	d	18 55	19 49	20 55	21 55	22 54	
Whitwell	d	18 58	19 52	20 58	21 58	22 57	
Worksop	a	19 07	20 03	21 09	22 08	23 07	

Sundays

20 May to 2 December

		EM	EM	EM	EM	EM	EM	EM	EM
Nottingham	d	08 07	09 42	11 28	13 28	15 25	16 53	18 29	20 25
Bulwell	d	08 16	09 51	11 38	13 38	15 35	17 03	18 39	20 35
Hucknall	d	08 21	09 57	11 43	13 43	15 40	17 08	18 44	20 40
Newstead	d	08 26	10 02	11 48	13 48	15 45	17 13	18 49	20 45
Kirkby In Ashfield	d	08 32	10 07	11 54	13 53	15 50	17 18	18 54	20 50
Sutton Parkway	d	08 35	10 10	11 57	13 56	15 53	17 21	18 57	20 53
Mansfield	d	08 40	10 16	12 02	14 01	15 58	17 26	19 02	20 58
Mansfield Woodhouse	d	08a47	10a22	12a08	14a08	16a05	17a33	19a09	21a05
Shirebrook	d								
Langwith - Whaley Thorns	d								
Creswell (Derbys)	d								
Whitwell	d								
Worksop	a								

A from 3 September until 5 October
B from 8 October
C until 31 August
D until 5 October

Table T055-R

Worksop - Mansfield - Nottingham

Mondays to Fridays

21 May to 7 December

Miles			EM	EM ◇	EM	EM	EM A	EM B	EM A	EM B	EM	EM	EM	EM	EM	EM	EM C	EM D	EM	EM	EM	EM	EM
0	**Worksop**	d	05 50		06 52		07 38	07 38	08 38	08 38		09 38		10 38		11 38			12 38		13 38		14 38
4¾	Whitwell	d	05 58		07 04		07 47	07 47	08 47	08 47		09 47		10 47		11 47			12 47		13 47		14 47
6	Creswell (Derbys)	d	06 02		07 08		07 50	07 50	08 50	08 50		09 50		10 50		11 50			12 50		13 50		14 50
9¼	Langwith - Whaley Thorns	d	06 06		07 12		07 53	07 53	08 53	08 53		09 53		10 53		11 53			12 53		13 53		14 53
10	Shirebrook	d	06 10		07 16		07 58	07 58	08 58	08 58		09 58		10 58		11 58			12 58		13 58		14 58
12¾	Mansfield Woodhouse	d	06 17	07 07	07 24	07 39	08 06	08 06	09 06	09 06	09 37	10 06	10 37	11 06	11 37	12 06	12 37	12 37	13 06	13 37	14 06	14 37	15 06
14¼	**Mansfield**	d	06 21	07 11	07 29	07 43	08 10	08 10	09 10	09 10	09 40	10 10	10 40	11 10	11 40	12 10	12 40	12 40	13 10	13 40	14 10	14 40	15 10
17	Sutton Parkway	d	06 27	07 16	07 35	07 48	08 15	08 15	09 15	09 15	09 46	10 16	10 46	11 16	11 46	12 16	12 46	12 46	13 16	13 46	14 16	14 46	15 16
17¾	Kirkby In Ashfield	d	06 30	07 19	07 38	07 52	08 18	08 18	09 18	09 18	09 49	10 19	10 49	11 19	11 49	12 19	12 49	12 49	13 19	13 49	14 19	14 49	15 19
20¾	Newstead	d	06 35	07 26	07 43	07 57	08 23	08 23	09 23	09 23	09 53		10 53		11 53		12 53	12 53		13 53		14 53	
23¼	Hucknall	d	06 40	07 31	07 48	08 02	08 28	08 28	09 27	09 27	09 58	10 26	10 58	11 26	11 58	12 26	12 58	12 58	13 26	13 58	14 26	14 58	15 26
26	Bulwell	d	06 44	07 35	07 53	08 06	08 32	08 32	09 31	09 31		10 30		11 30		12 30			13 30		14 30		15 30
31½	**Nottingham**	a	06 56	07 49	08 04	08 22	08 43	08 45	09 43	09 44	10 15	10 42	11 15	11 43	12 15	12 43	13 15	13 18	13 43	14 15	14 43	15 15	15 43

		EM	EM	EM	EM	EM	EM	EM E	EM F	EM	EM	EM	EM
Worksop	d		15 38		16 38		17 46	18 41	18 41	19 22	20 22	21 22	22 22
Whitwell	d		15 47		16 47		17 54	18 50	18 50	19 30	20 30	21 30	22 30
Creswell (Derbys)	d		15 50		16 50		17 58	18 53	18 53	19 34	20 34	21 34	22 34
Langwith - Whaley Thorns	d		15 53		16 53		18 01	18 56	18 56	19 37	20 37	21 37	22 37
Shirebrook	d		15 58		16 58		18 06	19 01	19 01	19 41	20 41	21 41	22 41
Mansfield Woodhouse	d	15 37	16 06	16 37	17 06	17 42	18 14	19 09	19 09	19 49	20 49	21 49	22 49
Mansfield	d	15 40	16 10	16 40	17 10	17 46	18 18	19 13	19 13	19 53	20 53	21 53	22 53
Sutton Parkway	d	15 46	16 16	16 46	17 16	17 52	18 24	19 18	19 18	19 58	20 58	21 58	22 58
Kirkby In Ashfield	d	15 49	16 19	16 49	17 19	17 55	18 27	19 21	19 21	20 01	21 01	22 01	23 01
Newstead	d	15 53		16 53		17 59	18 32	19 26	19 26	20 06	21 06	22 06	23 06
Hucknall	d	15 58	16 26	16 58	17 26	18 04	18 36	19 30	19 30	20 10	21 10	22 10	23 10
Bulwell	d		16 30		17 30		18 40	19 34	19 34	20 14	21 14	22 14	23 14
Nottingham	a	16 15	16 43	17 15	17 44	18 19	18 52	19 47	19 49	20 32	21 25	22 25	23 26

Saturdays

26 May to 8 December

		EM	EM	EM	EM	EM	EM	EM	EM	EM	EM	EM	EM	EM	EM	EM	EM	EM	EM	EM	EM	EM	EM
Worksop	d	05 50	06 56	07 38	08 38		09 38		10 38		11 38		12 38		13 38		14 38		15 38		16 38		17 46
Whitwell	d	05 59	07 05	07 47	08 47		09 47		10 47		11 47		12 47		13 47		14 47		15 47		16 50		17 54
Creswell (Derbys)	d	06 02	07 08	07 50	08 50		09 50		10 50		11 50		12 50		13 50		14 50		15 50		16 53		17 58
Langwith - Whaley Thorns	d	06 06	07 11	07 53	08 53		09 53		10 53		11 53		12 53		13 53		14 53		15 53		16 56		18 01
Shirebrook	d	06 10	07 16	07 58	08 58		09 58		10 58		11 58		12 58		13 58		14 58		15 58		17 01		18 06
Mansfield Woodhouse	d	06 17	07 24	08 06	09 06	09 37	10 06	10 37	11 06	11 37	12 06	12 37	13 06	13 37	14 06	14 37	15 06	15 37	16 06	16 37	17 09	17 42	18 14
Mansfield	d	06 22	07 29	08 10	09 10	09 40	10 10	10 40	11 10	11 40	12 10	12 40	13 10	13 40	14 10	14 40	15 10	15 40	16 10	16 40	17 13	17 46	18 18
Sutton Parkway	d	06 27	07 35	08 15	09 15	09 46	10 16	10 46	11 16	11 46	12 16	12 46	13 16	13 46	14 16	14 46	15 16	15 46	16 16	16 46	17 18	17 52	18 24
Kirkby In Ashfield	d	06 30	07 38	08 18	09 18	09 49	10 19	10 49	11 19	11 49	12 19	12 49	13 19	13 49	14 19	14 49	15 19	15 49	16 19	16 49	17 21	17 55	18 27
Newstead	d	06 35	07 43	08 23	09 23	09 53		10 53		11 53		12 53		13 53		14 53		15 53		16 53		17 59	18 32
Hucknall	d	06 40	07 48	08 28	09 27	09 58	10 26	10 58	11 26	11 58	12 26	12 58	13 26	13 58	14 26	14 58	15 26	15 58	16 26	16 58	17 28	18 04	18 36
Bulwell	d	06 44	07 53	08 32	09 31		10 30		11 30		12 30		13 30		14 30		15 30		16 30		17 32		18 40
Nottingham	a	06 56	08 05	08 46	09 44	10 15	10 44	11 15	11 43	12 15	12 43	13 15	13 43	14 15	14 43	15 14	15 43	16 15	16 43	17 15	17 45	18 19	18 52

		EM	EM	EM	EM	EM
Worksop	d	18 41	19 22	20 22	21 22	22 22
Whitwell	d	18 50	19 30	20 30	21 30	22 30
Creswell (Derbys)	d	18 53	19 34	20 34	21 34	22 34
Langwith - Whaley Thorns	d	18 56	19 37	20 37	21 37	22 37
Shirebrook	d	19 01	19 41	20 41	21 41	22 41
Mansfield Woodhouse	d	19 09	19 49	20 49	21 49	22 49
Mansfield	d	19 13	19 53	20 53	21 53	22 53
Sutton Parkway	d	19 18	19 58	20 58	21 58	22 58
Kirkby In Ashfield	d	19 21	20 01	21 01	22 01	23 01
Newstead	d	19 26	20 06	21 06	22 06	23 06
Hucknall	d	19 30	20 10	21 10	22 10	23 10
Bulwell	d	19 34	20 14	21 14	22 14	23 14
Nottingham	a	19 48	20 30	21 25	22 26	23 26

Sundays

20 May to 2 December

		EM	EM	EM	EM	EM	EM	EM	EM
Worksop	d								
Whitwell	d								
Creswell (Derbys)	d								
Langwith - Whaley Thorns	d								
Shirebrook	d								
Mansfield Woodhouse	d	08 52	10 29	12 14	14 11	16 09	17 36	19 18	21 07
Mansfield	d	08 55	10 33	12 17	14 15	16 12	17 39	19 21	21 10
Sutton Parkway	d	09 01	10 38	12 23	14 20	16 18	17 45	19 27	21 16
Kirkby In Ashfield	d	09 04	10 41	12 26	14 23	16 21	17 48	19 30	21 19
Newstead	d	09 08	10 46	12 30	14 28	16 25	17 52	19 34	21 23
Hucknall	d	09 13	10 51	12 35	14 33	16 30	17 57	19 39	21 28
Bulwell	d	09 17	10 55	12 39	14 37	16 34	18 01	19 43	21 32
Nottingham	a	09 31	11 07	12 51	14 50	16 46	18 13	19 55	21 44

A from 8 October
B until 5 October
C until 31 August, from 8 October
D from 3 September until 5 October
E from 3 September
F until 31 August

Table T056-F

Nottingham - Derby - Matlock

Mondays to Fridays
21 May to 20 July

Miles	Station		EM MX	EM	XC	EM	XC	XC	EM	XC	XC	EM	XC	XC	EM	XC	XC	EM	XC	XC	EM	XC	XC
			◇1		◇1		◇1	◇1		1	◇1		1	◇1		1	◇1		1	◇1		1	◇1
			A 🍴		B 🍴		C	B	D	E	B	D	E	B 🍴	D	E	B 🍴	D	E	B 🍴	D	E	B 🍴
0	Nottingham	d	01 47		06 00	06 17	06 37	07 04	07 20	07 37	08 09	08 20	08 39	09 07	09 20	09 41	10 07	10 20	10 41	11 07	11 20	11 41	12 07
3¼	Beeston	d			06 06	06 24	06 43	07 09	07 25	07 42	08 14	08 25	08 44	09 12	09 25		10 12	10 25		11 12	11 25		12 12
4¾	Attenborough	d			06 09	06 27		07 13	07 29			08 29			09 29			10 29			11 29		
7¾	Long Eaton	d			06 19	06 36		07 21	07 38	07 52	08 23	08 37	08 53	09 25	09 37		10 24	10 37		11 22	11 37		12 22
13½	Spondon	d			06 26	06 43			07 44			08 44	08 59										
16	Derby	a	02 05		06 32	06 50	06 59	07 32	07 50	08 02	08 34	08 50	09 05	09 35	09 50	10 03	10 34	10 50	11 02	11 33	11 50	12 02	12 33
—		d		05 42		06 51			07 52			08 52			09 52			10 52			11 52		
21¼	Duffield	d		05 49		06 58			07 59			08 59			09 59			10 59			11 59		
23¾	Belper	d		05 54		07 03			08 04			09 04			10 04			11 04			12 04		
26½	Ambergate	d		06 00		07 09			08 10			09 10			10 10			11 10			12 10		
28½	Whatstandwell	d		06 04		07 13			08 14			09 14			10 14			11 14			12 14		
31½	Cromford	d		06 10		07 19			08 20			09 20			10 20			11 20			12 20		
32¼	Matlock Bath	d		06 12		07 21			08 22			09 22			10 22			11 22			12 22		
33¾	Matlock	a		06 15		07 25			08 26			09 26			10 26			11 26			12 26		

Station		EM	XC	XC	EM	XC	XC	EM	XC	XC	EM	XC	XC	EM	XC	EM	XC	EM	XC	XC	EM	XC	XC
			1	◇1		1	◇1		1	◇1		1	◇1		1		◇1		1	◇1		1	◇1
		D	E	B 🍴	D	E 🍴	F 🍴	D	E	B 🍴	D	E 🍴	B	D	E 🍴		B	D	E 🍴	B	D	E 🍴	B
Nottingham	d	12 20	12 41	13 07	13 20	13 41	14 07	14 20	14 41	15 07	15 20	15 41	16 07	16 20	16 41	16 44	17 07	17 20	17 41	18 07	18 20	18 41	19 07
Beeston	d	12 25		13 12	13 25		14 12	14 25		15 12	15 25		16 12	16 25		16 52	17 12	17 25		18 12	18 25		19 12
Attenborough	d	12 29			13 29			14 29			15 29			16 29		16 55		17 29			18 29		
Long Eaton	d	12 37		13 22	13 37		14 22	14 37		15 22	15 37		16 22	16 39		17 04	17 22	17 38		18 21	18 37		19 21
Spondon	d				13 44													17 46	18 01				
Derby	a	12 50	13 02	13 33	13 50	14 02	14 33	14 50	15 02	15 33	15 50	16 02	16 33	16 52	17 02	17 19	17 33	17 51	18 08	18 33	18 50	19 00	19 33
	d	12 52			13 52			14 52			15 52			16 52				17 53			18 52		
Duffield	d	12 59			13 59			14 59			15 59			16 59				18 00			18 59		
Belper	d	13 04			14 04			15 04			16 04			17 04				18 05			19 04		
Ambergate	d	13 10			14 10			15 10			16 10			17 10				18 11			19 10		
Whatstandwell	d	13 14			14 14			15 14			16 14			17 14				18 15			19 14		
Cromford	d	13 20			14 20			15 20			16 20			17 20				18 21			19 20		
Matlock Bath	d	13 22			14 22			15 22			16 22			17 22				18 23			19 22		
Matlock	a	13 26			14 26			15 26			16 26			17 26				18 27			19 26		

Station		EM	EM	XC	EM	XC	EM	XC	EM	NT	EM	EM
			◇1	1		1		1		◇		
			A 🍴	E 🍴	D	E		E		G		
Nottingham	d	19 20	19 28	19 36	20 20	20 40	21 20	21 39		22 15	22 18	23 20
Beeston	d	19 25		19 42	20 25	20 45	21 25	21 44			22 25	23 25
Attenborough	d	19 29		19 45	20 29		21 29	21 48			22 29	23 29
Long Eaton	d	19 37	19 42	19 54	20 37	20 55	21 37	21 56			22 37	23 37
Spondon	d	19 44						22 02				
Derby	a	19 50	19 56	20 04	20 50	21 05	21 50	22 08		22 38	22 48	23 50
	d	19 52			20 52				22 15			
Duffield	d	19 59			20 59				22 22			
Belper	d	20 04			21 04				22 27			
Ambergate	d	20 10			21 10				22 33			
Whatstandwell	d	20 14			21 14				22 37			
Cromford	d	20 20			21 20				22 43			
Matlock Bath	d	20 22			21 22				22 45			
Matlock	a	20 26			21 26				22 50			

Mondays to Fridays
23 July to 27 July

Station		EM	EM	EM	EM	EM	EM	EM	EM	EM	EM	EM	EM	EM	EM	EM	EM	EM	EM	EM	EM	NT	EM
		◇1																				◇	
		H 🍴			D	D	D	D	D	D	D	D	D	D		D	D		D			G	
Nottingham	d	01 47		06 17	07 20	08 20	09 20	10 20	11 20	12 20	13 20	14 20	15 20	16 20	16 44	17 20	18 20	19 20	20 20	21 20		22 15	22 18
Beeston	d			06 24	07 25	08 25	09 25	10 25	11 25	12 25	13 25	14 25	15 25	16 25	16 52	17 25	18 25	19 25	20 25	21 25			22 25
Attenborough	d			06 27	07 29	08 29	09 29	10 29	11 29	12 29	13 29	14 29	15 29	16 29	16 55	17 29	18 29	19 29	20 29	21 29			22 29
Long Eaton	d			06 36	07 38	08 37	09 39	10 37	11 37	12 37	13 37	14 37	15 37	16 39	17 04	17 38	18 37	19 37	20 37	21 37			22 37
Spondon	d			06 43	07 44	08 44					13 44					17 46		19 44					
Derby	a	02 05		06 50	07 50	08 50	09 52	10 50	11 50	12 50	13 50	14 50	15 50	16 52	17 19	17 51	18 50	19 50	20 50	21 50		22 38	22 48
	d		05 42	06 51	07 52	08 52	09 54	10 52	11 52	12 52	13 52	14 52	15 52	16 52		17 53	18 52	19 52	20 52		22 15		
Duffield	d		05 49	06 58	07 59	08 59	10 01	10 59	11 59	12 59	13 59	14 59	15 59	16 59		18 00	18 59	19 59	20 59		22 22		
Belper	d		05 54	07 03	08 04	09 04	10 06	11 04	12 04	13 04	14 04	15 04	16 04	17 04		18 05	19 04	20 04	21 04		22 27		
Ambergate	d		06 00	07 09	08 10	09 10	10 12	11 10	12 10	13 10	14 10	15 10	16 10	17 10		18 11	19 10	20 10	21 10		22 33		
Whatstandwell	d		06 04	07 13	08 14	09 14	10 16	11 14	12 14	13 14	14 14	15 14	16 14	17 14		18 15	19 14	20 14	21 14		22 37		
Cromford	d		06 10	07 19	08 20	09 20	10 22	11 20	12 20	13 20	14 20	15 20	16 20	17 20		18 21	19 20	20 20	21 20		22 43		
Matlock Bath	d		06 12	07 21	08 22	09 22	10 24	11 22	12 22	13 22	14 22	15 22	16 22	17 22		18 23	19 22	20 22	21 22		22 45		
Matlock	a		06 15	07 25	08 26	09 26	10 28	11 26	12 26	13 26	14 26	15 26	16 26	17 26		18 27	19 26	20 26	21 26		22 50		

A From St Pancras International
B To Cardiff Central
C To Bournemouth
D From Newark Castle
E To Birmingham New Street
F To Nottingham
G To Sheffield
H from 24 July. From St Pancras International

For connections from St Pancras International refer to Table T053

Table T056-F

Nottingham - Derby - Matlock

Mondays to Fridays
23 July to 27 July

Station		EM
Nottingham	d	23 20
Beeston	d	23 25
Attenborough	d	23 29
Long Eaton	d	23 37
Spondon	d	
Derby	a	23 50
	d	
Duffield	d	
Belper	d	
Ambergate	d	
Whatstandwell	d	
Cromford	d	
Matlock Bath	d	
Matlock	a	

Mondays to Fridays
30 July to 31 August

Station		EM	EM	EM	EM	EM	EM	EM	EM	EM	EM	EM	EM	EM		EM	EM	EM	EM	EM	EM	EM
				A		A		A		A		A		A			A		A		B	
Nottingham	d			07 20		08 20		09 20		10 20		11 20		12 20	and at the same minutes past each hour until		17 20		18 20		19 20	
Beeston	d			07 25		08 25		09 25		10 25		11 25		12 25			17 25		18 25		19 25	
Attenborough	d			07 29		08 29		09 29		10 29		11 29		12 29			17 29		18 29		19 29	
Long Eaton	d			07a38		08a40		09a40		10a40		11a38		12a40			17a40		18a38		19a38	
Spondon	d																					
Derby	a																					
	d	05 36	06 36		07 36		08 36		09 36		10 36		11 36			16 36		17 36		18 36		19 36
Duffield	d	05 44	06 43		07 43		08 43		09 43		10 43		11 43			16 43		17 43		18 43		19 43
Belper	d	05 49	06 48		07 48		08 48		09 48		10 48		11 48			16 48		17 48		18 48		19 48
Ambergate	d	05 56	06 55		07 55		08 55		09 55		10 55		11 55			16 55		17 55		18 55		19 55
Whatstandwell	d	06 00	06 59		07 59		08 59		09 59		10 59		11 59			16 59		17 59		18 59		19 59
Cromford	d	06 06	07 05		08 05		09 05		10 05		11 05		12 05			17 05		18 05		19 05		20 05
Matlock Bath	d	06 08	07 07		08 07		09 07		10 07		11 07		12 07			17 07		18 07		19 07		20 07
Matlock	a	06 11	07 11		08 11		09 11		10 11		11 10		12 10			17 10		18 10		19 10		20 10

Station		EM	EM	EM	NT	EM
					◇	
		A		B	C	B
Nottingham	d	20 20		21 20	22 15	22 18
Beeston	d	20 25		21 25		22 25
Attenborough	d	20 29		21 29		22 29
Long Eaton	d	20a40		21a39		22a38
Spondon	d					
Derby	a				22 38	
	d		20 36			
Duffield	d		20 43			
Belper	d		20 48			
Ambergate	d		20 55			
Whatstandwell	d		20 59			
Cromford	d		21 05			
Matlock Bath	d		21 07			
Matlock	a		21 10			

Mondays to Fridays
3 September to 5 October

Station		EM MX	XC	EM	XC	XC	EM	XC	XC	EM	XC	XC	EM	XC	XC	EM	XC	XC	EM	XC	XC	EM	XC
		◇1	◇1		◇1	◇1		1	◇1		1	◇1		1	◇1		1	◇1		1	◇1		1
		D 🍴	E 🍴		F	E	G	H	E	G	H	E 🍴	G	H	E 🍴	G	H	E 🍴	G	H	E 🍴	G	H
Nottingham	d	01 47	05 57	06 17	06 37	07 04	07 20	07 37	08 09	08 20	08 41	09 07	09 20	09 41	10 04	10 20	10 41	11 04	11 20	11 41	12 04	12 20	12 41
Beeston	d		06 03	06 24	06 43	07 09	07 25	07 42	08 14	08 25	08 46	09 12	09 25		10 09	10 26		11 09	11 25		12 09	12 25	
Attenborough	d		06 06	06 27		07 13	07 29			08 29			09 33			10 35			11 33			12 29	
Long Eaton	d		06 18	06 39		07 23	07 38	07 52		08 39	08 55	09 22	09 45		10 23	10 45		11 22	11 41		12 22	12 40	
Spondon	d		06 25	06 46			07 44			08 47	09 01												
Derby	a	02 05	06 31	06 52	07 01	07 33	07 53	08 02	08 33	08 52	09 07	09 32	09 58	10 02	10 34	10 58	11 02	11 33	11 52	12 02	12 33	12 51	13 02
	d																						
Duffield	d																						
Belper	d																						
Ambergate	d																						
Whatstandwell	d																						
Cromford	d																						
Matlock Bath	d																						
Matlock	a																						

A until 10 August. From Newark Castle
B until 10 August
C To Sheffield
D From St Pancras International
E To Cardiff Central
F To Bournemouth
G From Newark Castle
H To Birmingham New Street

For connections from St Pancras International refer to Table T053

Table T056-F

Nottingham - Derby - Matlock

Mondays to Fridays

3 September to 5 October

		XC ◇■ A	EM B	XC ■ C	XC ◇■ D	EM B	XC ■ C	XC ◇■ A	EM B	XC ■ C	XC ◇■ A	EM B	XC ■ C	EM	XC ◇■ A	EM B	XC ■ C	XC ◇■ A	EM B	XC ■ C	XC ◇■ A	EM
Nottingham	d	13 04	13 20	13 41	14 04	14 20	14 41	15 04	15 20	15 41	16 04	16 20	16 41	16 49	17 04	17 20	17 41	18 04	18 26	18 41	19 04	19 16
Beeston	d	13 09	13 29		14 09	14 25		15 09	15 25		16 09	16 26		16 54	17 09	17 25		18 09	18 31		19 09	19 21
Attenborough	d		13 36			14 29			15 29			16 29		16 57		17 29			18 35			19 25
Long Eaton	d	13 22	13 47		14 22	14 39		15 22	15 40		16 22	16 40		17 06	17 22	17 40		18 21	18 46		19 22	19 33
Spondon	d		13 54													17 54	18 01					19 40
Derby	a	13 32	13 59	14 03	14 33	14 49	15 02	15 33	15 54	16 03	16 33	16 55	17 02	17 22	17 33	18 00	18 07	18 33	18 59	19 02	19 33	19 45
	d																					
Duffield	d																					
Belper	d																					
Ambergate	d																					
Whatstandwell	d																					
Cromford	d																					
Matlock Bath	d																					
Matlock	a																					

		EM ◇■ E	XC ■ C	EM B	XC ■ C	EM	XC ■ C	EM	EM
Nottingham	d	19 27	19 36	20 20	20 40	21 20	21 39	22 18	23 19
Beeston	d		19 42	20 26	20 45	21 25	21 44	22 25	23 24
Attenborough	d		19 45	20 34		21 29	21 48	22 29	23 28
Long Eaton	d	19 47	19 57	20 45	20 55	21 37	21 56	22 37	23 37
Spondon	d						22 02		
Derby	a	19 58	20 06	20 57	21 05	21 53	22 08	22 48	23 50
	d								
Duffield	d								
Belper	d								
Ambergate	d								
Whatstandwell	d								
Cromford	d								
Matlock Bath	d								
Matlock	a								

Mondays to Fridays

8 October to 7 December

		EM MX ◇■ E	EM	XC ◇■ A	EM	XC ◇■ F	XC ◇■ A	EM B	XC ■ C	XC ◇■ A	EM B	XC ■ C	XC ◇■ A	EM B	XC ■ C	XC ◇■ A	EM B	XC ■ C	XC ◇■ A	EM B	XC ■ C	XC ◇■ A	EM B
Nottingham	d	01 47		06 00	06 17	06 37	07 04	07 20	07 37	08 09	08 20	08 40	09 07	09 20	09 41	10 07	10 20	10 41	11 07	11 20	11 41	12 07	12 20
Beeston	d			06 06	06 24	06 43	07 09	07 25	07 42	08 15	08 25	08 45	09 12	09 25		10 12	10 25		11 12	11 25		12 12	12 25
Attenborough	d			06 09	06 27		07 13	07 29			08 29			09 29			10 29			11 29			12 29
Long Eaton	d			06 18	06 36		07 21	07 38	07 52	08 23	08 37	08 54	09 25	09 37		10 24	10 37		11 22	11 37		12 22	12 37
Spondon	d			06 25	06 43			07 44			08 44	09 00											
Derby	a	02 05		06 32	06 49	06 58	07 31	07 51	08 02	08 34	08 50	09 06	09 35	09 49	10 02	10 34	10 50	11 02	11 33	11 51	12 02	12 33	12 51
	d		05 42		06 51			07 53			08 51			09 51			10 51			11 52			12 52
Duffield	d		05 49		06 58			08 00			08 59			09 59			10 59			11 59			12 59
Belper	d		05 54		07 03			08 05			09 04			10 04			11 04			12 04			13 04
Ambergate	d		06 00		07 09			08 11			09 10			10 10			11 10			12 10			13 10
Whatstandwell	d		06 04		07 13			08 15			09 14			10 14			11 14			12 14			13 14
Cromford	d		06 10		07 19			08 21			09 19			10 19			11 19			12 20			13 20
Matlock Bath	d		06 12		07 21			08 23			09 22			10 22			11 22			12 22			13 22
Matlock	a		06 15		07 26			08 28			09 27			10 27			11 27			12 27			13 27

		XC ■ C	XC ◇■ A	EM B	XC ■ C	XC ◇■ D	EM B	XC ■ C	XC ◇■ A	EM B	XC ■ C	XC ◇■ A	EM B	XC ■ C	EM	XC ◇■ A	EM B	XC ■ C	XC ◇■ A	EM B	XC ■ C	XC ◇■ A	EM
Nottingham	d	12 41	13 07	13 20	13 41	14 07	14 20	14 41	15 07	15 20	15 41	16 07	16 20	16 41	16 49	17 07	17 20	17 41	18 07	18 20	18 41	19 07	19 20
Beeston	d		13 12	13 25		14 12	14 25		15 12	15 25		16 12	16 25		16 54	17 12	17 25		18 12	18 25		19 12	19 25
Attenborough	d			13 29			14 29			15 29			16 29		16 57		17 29			18 29			19 29
Long Eaton	d		13 22	13 37		14 22	14 37		15 22	15 37		16 22	16 37		17 06	17 22	17 38		18 21	18 37		19 21	19 37
Spondon	d			13 44													17 46	18 01					19 44
Derby	a	13 02	13 33	13 50	14 02	14 33	14 50	15 02	15 33	15 50	16 03	16 33	16 51	17 02	17 22	17 33	17 51	18 07	18 33	18 50	19 02	19 32	19 49
	d			13 52			14 51			15 51			16 52				17 52			18 52			19 51
Duffield	d			14 01			14 59			15 59			16 59				18 00			18 59			19 59
Belper	d			14 06			15 04			16 04			17 04				18 05			19 04			20 04
Ambergate	d			14 12			15 10			16 10			17 10				18 11			19 10			20 10
Whatstandwell	d			14 16			15 14			16 14			17 14				18 15			19 14			20 14
Cromford	d			14 21			15 19			16 19			17 20				18 20			19 20			20 19
Matlock Bath	d			14 24			15 22			16 22			17 22				18 23			19 22			20 22
Matlock	a			14 29			15 27			16 27			17 27				18 28			19 27			20 27

A To Cardiff Central
B From Newark Castle
C To Birmingham New Street
D To Nottingham
E From St Pancras International
F To Bournemouth

For connections from St Pancras International refer to Table T053

Table T056-F

Nottingham - Derby - Matlock

Mondays to Fridays

8 October to 7 December

		EM ◇■ A	XC ■ B	EM C	XC ■ B	EM	XC ■ B	EM	NT ◇ D	EM	EM
Nottingham	d	19 24	19 36	20 20	20 40	21 20	21 39		22 15	22 19	23 20
Beeston	d		19 42	20 25	20 46	21 25	21 44			22 25	23 25
Attenborough	d		19 45	20 29		21 29	21 48			22 29	23 29
Long Eaton	d	19 44	19 54	20 39	20 55	21 37	21 56			22 37	23 37
Spondon	d						22 02				
Derby	a	19 55	20 04	20 51	21 05	21 51	22 08		22 37	22 48	23 50
	d			20 51				22 15			
Duffield	d			21 01				22 22			
Belper	d			21 06				22 27			
Ambergate	d			21 12				22 33			
Whatstandwell	d			21 16				22 37			
Cromford	d			21 21				22 43			
Matlock Bath	d			21 24				22 45			
Matlock	a			21 29				22 50			

Saturdays

26 May to 28 July

		EM ◇■ A	EM	XC ◇■ E	EM	XC ◇■ F	XC ◇■ E	EM	XC ■ G	XC ◇■ E	EM C	XC ■ G	XC ◇■ E	EM H	EM I	XC ■ G	XC ◇■ E	EM H	EM I	XC ■ G	XC ◇■ E	EM C	XC ■ G
Nottingham	d	01 47		05 58	06 20	06 37	06 58	07 20	07 37	08 07	08 20	08 41	09 07	09 20	09 20	09 41	10 06	10 20	10 20	10 41	11 06	11 20	11 41
Beeston	d			06 03	06 25	06 43	07 03	07 25	07 42	08 12	08 25		09 12	09 25	09 25		10 11	10 25	10 26		11 11	11 25	
Attenborough	d			06 07	06 29		07 07	07 29			08 29			09 29	09 29			10 29	10 30			11 29	
Long Eaton	d			06 15	06 37		07 16	07 37	07 52	08 21	08 37		09 22	09 37	09 38		10 23	10 37	10 37		11 23	11 37	
Spondon	d			06 22	06 45						08 44	08 56											
Derby	a	02 05		06 30	06 50	06 59	07 30	07 50	08 02	08 32	08 50	09 02	09 32	09 50	09 51	10 02	10 33	10 50	10 50	11 02	11 34	11 50	12 02
	d		05 42		06 52			07 52			08 52			09 52	09 52			10 52	10 52			11 52	
Duffield	d		05 49		06 59			07 59			08 59			09 59	09 59			10 59	10 59			11 59	
Belper	d		05 54		07 04			08 04			09 04			10 04	10 04			11 04	11 04			12 04	
Ambergate	d		06 00		07 10			08 10			09 10			10 10	10 10			11 10	11 10			12 10	
Whatstandwell	d		06 04		07 14			08 14			09 14			10 14	10 14			11 14	11 14			12 14	
Cromford	d		06 10		07 20			08 20			09 20			10 20	10 20			11 20	11 20			12 20	
Matlock Bath	d		06 12		07 22			08 22			09 22			10 22	10 22			11 22	11 22			12 22	
Matlock	a		06 15		07 26			08 26			09 26			10 26	10 26			11 26	11 26			12 26	

		XC ◇■ E	EM H	EM I	XC ■ G	XC ◇■ E	EM C	XC ■ G	EM J	XC ◇■ E	EM H	EM I	XC ■ G	XC ◇■ E	EM C	XC ■ G	XC ◇■ E	EM C	XC ■ G	XC ◇■ E	EM C	XC ■ G	XC ◇■ E
Nottingham	d	12 06	12 20	12 20	12 41	13 06	13 20	13 41	13 50	14 06	14 20	14 20	14 41	15 06	15 20	15 41	16 06	16 20	16 41	17 06	17 20	17 41	18 06
Beeston	d	12 11	12 25	12 25		13 11	13 25		13 57	14 11	14 25	14 25		15 11	15 25		16 11	16 25		17 11	17 25		18 11
Attenborough	d		12 29	12 29			13 29				14 29	14 29			15 29			16 29			17 29		
Long Eaton	d	12 22	12 36	12 39		13 22	13 37		14 07	14 22	14 37	14 41		15 22	15 37		16 22	16 37		17 22	17 38		18 22
Spondon	d						13 44														17 46		
Derby	a	12 33	12 50	12 52	13 02	13 33	13 50	14 02	14 19	14 33	14 50	14 52	15 02	15 33	15 50	16 02	16 33	16 50	17 02	17 33	17 51	18 02	18 33
	d		12 52	12 52			13 52				14 52	14 54			15 52			16 52			17 53		
Duffield	d		12 59	13 00			13 59				14 59	15 01			15 59			16 59			18 00		
Belper	d		13 04	13 05			14 04				15 04	15 06			16 04			17 04			18 05		
Ambergate	d		13 10	13 11			14 10				15 10	15 12			16 10			17 10			18 11		
Whatstandwell	d		13 14	13 15			14 14				15 14	15 16			16 14			17 14			18 15		
Cromford	d		13 20	13 20			14 20				15 20	15 22			16 20			17 20			18 21		
Matlock Bath	d		13 22	13 23			14 22				15 22	15 24			16 22			17 22			18 23		
Matlock	a		13 26	13 27			14 26				15 26	15 28			16 26			17 26			18 27		

		EM C	XC ■ G	XC ◇■ E	EM C	XC ■ G	EM C	XC ■ G	EM	XC ■ G	EM	NT ◇ K	NT ◇ L	EM	EM
Nottingham	d	18 20	18 41	19 06	19 20	19 34	20 20	20 38	21 20	21 39		22 17	22 17	22 20	23 20
Beeston	d	18 25		19 11	19 25	19 40	20 25	20 43	21 25	21 44				22 25	23 25
Attenborough	d	18 29			19 29	19 43	20 29		21 29	21 48				22 29	23 29
Long Eaton	d	18 37		19 22	19 37	19 51	20 38	20 52	21 37	21 56				22 36	23 37
Spondon	d			19 30	19 44					22 02					
Derby	a	18 50	19 02	19 35	19 51	20 02	20 51	21 02	21 50	22 08		22 38	22 39	22 48	23 50
	d	18 52			19 52		20 52				22 16				
Duffield	d	18 59			19 59		20 59				22 23				
Belper	d	19 04			20 04		21 04				22 28				
Ambergate	d	19 10			20 10		21 10				22 35				
Whatstandwell	d	19 14			20 14		21 14				22 39				
Cromford	d	19 20			20 20		21 20				22 45				
Matlock Bath	d	19 22			20 22		21 22				22 47				
Matlock	a	19 26			20 26		21 26				22 50				

A From St Pancras International
B To Birmingham New Street
C From Newark Castle
D To Sheffield
E not 28 July. To Cardiff Central
F not 28 July. To Bournemouth
G not 28 July. To Birmingham New Street
H not 28 July. From Newark Castle
I 28 July. From Newark Castle
J 21 July, 28 July. From Skegness
K 28 July. To Sheffield
L not 28 July. To Sheffield

For connections from St Pancras International refer to Table T053

Table T056-F

Saturdays

4 August to 1 September

Nottingham - Derby - Matlock

		EM	EM	EM A	EM	EM B	EM	EM B	EM	EM B	EM	EM B	EM	EM B	EM	EM B	EM	EM C	EM	EM B
Nottingham ■	d			07 20		08 20		09 20		10 20		11 20		12 20		13 20		13 50		14 20
Beeston	d			07 25		08 25		09 25		10 26		11 25		12 25		13 25		13 57		14 25
Attenborough	d			07 29		08 29		09 29		10 30		11 29		12 29		13 29				14 29
Long Eaton	d			07a37		08a37		09a38		10a39		11a37		12a39		13a39		14 07		14a40
Spondon	d																			
Derby ■	a																	14 19		
	d	06 05	07 05		08 05		09 05		10 05		11 05		12 05		13 05		14 05		15 05	
Duffield	d	06 13	07 13		08 13		09 13		10 13		11 13		12 13		13 13		14 13		15 13	
Belper	d	06 18	07 18		08 18		09 18		10 18		11 18		12 18		13 18		14 18		15 18	
Ambergate	d	06 25	07 25		08 25		09 25		10 25		11 25		12 25		13 25		14 25		15 25	
Whatstandwell	d	06 29	07 29		08 29		09 29		10 29		11 29		12 29		13 29		14 29		15 29	
Cromford	d	06 35	07 35		08 35		09 35		10 35		11 35		12 35		13 35		14 35		15 35	
Matlock Bath	d	06 37	07 37		08 37		09 37		10 37		11 37		12 37		13 37		14 37		15 37	
Matlock	a	06 41	07 41		08 41		09 41		10 41		11 41		12 41		13 41		14 41		15 41	

		EM B	EM		EM B	EM	EM B	EM	EM B	EM	EM A	NT ◇ D	EM A
Nottingham ■	d	15 20		and at the same minutes past each hour until	18 20		19 20		20 20		21 20	22 17	22 20
Beeston	d	15 25			18 25		19 25		20 25		21 25		22 25
Attenborough	d	15 29			18 29		19 29		20 29		21 29		22 29
Long Eaton	d	15a39			18a39		19a37		20a39		21a39		22a39
Spondon	d												
Derby ■	a											22 38	
	d		16 05			19 05		20 05		21 05			
Duffield	d		16 13			19 13		20 13		21 13			
Belper	d		16 18			19 18		20 18		21 18			
Ambergate	d		16 25			19 25		20 25		21 25			
Whatstandwell	d		16 29			19 29		20 29		21 29			
Cromford	d		16 35			19 35		20 35		21 35			
Matlock Bath	d		16 37			19 37		20 37		21 37			
Matlock	a		16 41			19 41		20 41		21 41			

Saturdays

8 September to 6 October

		EM ◇■ E	XC ◇■ F	XC ◇■ G	XC ◇■ F	EM	XC ■ H	XC ◇■ F	EM I	XC ■ H	XC ◇■ F	EM I	XC ■ H	XC ◇■ F	EM I	XC ■ H	XC ◇■ F	EM I	XC ■ H	XC ◇■ F	EM I	XC ■ H	XC ◇■ F
Nottingham ■	d	01 47	05 58	06 37	07 02	07 20	07 37	08 07	08 20	08 41	09 04	09 20	09 41	10 04	10 20	10 41	11 04	11 20	11 41	12 04	12 20	12 41	13 04
Beeston	d		06 03	06 43	07 07	07 25	07 42	08 12	08 25		09 09	09 25		10 09	10 25		11 09	11 25		12 09	12 25		13 09
Attenborough	d		06 07		07 11	07 30			08 29			09 29			10 29			11 29			12 29		
Long Eaton	d		06 17		07 19	07 39	07 52	08 21	08 40		09 19	09 39		10 18	10 37		11 19	11 40		12 22	12 39		13 18
Spondon	d		06 24						08 48	08 56													
Derby ■	a	02 05	06 30	06 59	07 31	07 50	08 02	08 32	08 54	09 02	09 31	09 50	10 02	10 31	10 49	11 02	11 31	11 52	12 02	12 33	12 51	13 02	13 32
	d																						
Duffield	d																						
Belper	d																						
Ambergate	d																						
Whatstandwell	d																						
Cromford	d																						
Matlock Bath	d																						
Matlock	a																						

		EM I	XC ■ H	EM J	XC ◇■ F	EM I	XC ■ H	XC ◇■ F	EM I	XC ■ H	XC ◇■ F	EM I	XC ■ H	XC ◇■ F	EM I	XC ■ H	XC ◇■ F	EM I	XC ■ H	XC ◇■ F	EM I	XC ■ H	EM I
Nottingham ■	d	13 20	13 41	13 50	14 04	14 20	14 41	15 04	15 20	15 41	16 04	16 20	16 41	17 04	17 20	17 41	18 04	18 20	18 41	19 04	19 20	19 34	20 20
Beeston	d	13 25		13 58	14 09	14 25		15 09	15 25		16 09	16 25		17 09	17 25		18 09	18 25		19 09	19 25	19 39	20 25
Attenborough	d	13 29				14 29			15 29			16 29			17 29			18 29			19 29	19 42	20 29
Long Eaton	d	13 39		14 11	14 18	14 39		15 18	15 39		16 19	16 39		17 18	17 39		18 18	18 39		19 18	19 39	19 50	20 39
Spondon	d	13 47													17 47					19 26	19 46		
Derby ■	a	13 52	14 02	14 23	14 30	14 50	15 02	15 32	15 50	16 02	16 33	16 51	17 02	17 33	17 54	18 02	18 33	18 50	19 02	19 33	19 53	20 00	20 51
	d																						
Duffield	d																						
Belper	d																						
Ambergate	d																						
Whatstandwell	d																						
Cromford	d																						
Matlock Bath	d																						
Matlock	a																						

A 4 August, 11 August
B 4 August, 11 August. From Newark Castle
C From Skegness
D To Sheffield
E From St Pancras International
F To Cardiff Central
G To Bournemouth
H To Birmingham New Street
I From Newark Castle
J 8 September. From Skegness

For connections from St Pancras International refer to Table T053

Table T056-F

Saturdays

8 September to 6 October

Nottingham - Derby - Matlock

		XC ■ A	EM	XC ■ A	EM B	EM	EM
Nottingham ■	d	20 40	21 20	21 39		22 20	23 20
Beeston	d	20 45	21 25	21 44		22 25	23 25
Attenborough	d		21 29	21 48		22 29	23 29
Long Eaton	d	20 54	21 39	21 55		22 39	23 37
Spondon	d			22 02			
Derby ■	a	21 04	21 56	22 08		22 51	23 50
	d				22 16		
Duffield	d				22 23		
Belper	d				22 28		
Ambergate	d				22 34		
Whatstandwell	d				22 38		
Cromford	d				22 44		
Matlock Bath	d				22 46		
Matlock	a				22 51		

Saturdays

13 October to 8 December

		EM ◇■ C	EM	XC ◇■ D	EM	XC ◇■ E	XC ◇■ D	EM	XC ■ A	XC ◇■ D	EM F	XC ■ A	XC ◇■ D	EM F	XC ■ A	XC ◇■ D	EM F	XC ■ A	XC ◇■ D	EM F	XC ■ A	XC ◇■ D	EM F
Nottingham ■	d	01 47		05 58	06 20	06 37	06 58	07 20	07 37	08 09	08 20	08 41	09 07	09 20	09 41	10 06	10 20	10 41	11 06	11 20	11 41	12 06	12 20
Beeston	d			06 03	06 25	06 43	07 03	07 25	07 42		08 25		09 12	09 25		10 11	10 25		11 11	11 25		12 11	12 25
Attenborough	d			06 07	06 29		07 07	07 29			08 29			09 29			10 29			11 29			12 29
Long Eaton	d			06 15	06 36		07 16	07 37	07 52		08 37		09 22	09 37		10 22	10 37		11 23	11 37		12 22	12 36
Spondon	d			06 22	06 45						08 44	08 56											
Derby ■	a	02 05		06 30	06 50	06 59	07 29	07 50	08 02	08 29	08 50	09 02	09 32	09 49	10 02	10 32	10 50	11 02	11 34	11 50	12 03	12 33	12 50
	d		05 42		06 52			07 51			08 51			09 51			10 51			11 51			12 51
Duffield	d		05 49		06 59			07 59			08 59			09 59			10 59			11 59			12 59
Belper	d		05 54		07 04			08 04			09 04			10 04			11 04			12 04			13 04
Ambergate	d		06 00		07 10			08 10			09 10			10 10			11 10			12 10			13 10
Whatstandwell	d		06 04		07 14			08 14			09 14			10 14			11 14			12 14			13 14
Cromford	d		06 10		07 20			08 19			09 19			10 19			11 19			12 19			13 19
Matlock Bath	d		06 12		07 22			08 22			09 22			10 22			11 22			12 22			13 22
Matlock	a		06 15		07 27			08 27			09 27			10 27			11 27			12 27			13 27

		XC ■ A	XC ◇■ D	EM F	XC ■ A	XC ◇■ D	EM F	XC ■ A	XC ◇■ D	EM F	XC ■ A	XC ◇■ D	EM F	XC ■ A	XC ◇■ D	EM F	XC ■ A	XC ◇■ D	EM F	XC ■ A	XC ◇■ D	EM F	XC ■ A
Nottingham ■	d	12 41	13 06	13 20	13 41	14 06	14 20	14 41	15 06	15 20	15 41	16 06	16 20	16 41	17 06	17 20	17 41	18 06	18 20	18 41	19 06	19 20	19 29
Beeston	d		13 11	13 25		14 11	14 25		15 11	15 25		16 11	16 25		17 11	17 25		18 11	18 25		19 11	19 25	19 35
Attenborough	d			13 29			14 29			15 29			16 29			17 29			18 29			19 29	19 38
Long Eaton	d		13 22	13 37		14 22	14 37		15 22	15 37		16 22	16 37		17 22	17 38		18 22	18 37		19 22	19 37	19 46
Spondon	d			13 44												17 46					19 30	19 44	
Derby ■	a	13 02	13 33	13 50	14 02	14 33	14 50	15 02	15 33	15 50	16 02	16 33	16 49	17 02	17 33	17 51	18 03	18 33	18 49	19 02	19 35	19 51	20 02
	d			13 51			14 51			15 51			16 51			17 52			18 51			19 51	
Duffield	d			13 59			14 59			15 59			16 59			18 00			18 59			19 59	
Belper	d			14 04			15 04			16 04			17 04			18 05			19 04			20 04	
Ambergate	d			14 10			15 10			16 10			17 10			18 11			19 10			20 10	
Whatstandwell	d			14 14			15 14			16 14			17 14			18 15			19 14			20 14	
Cromford	d			14 19			15 19			16 19			17 19			18 20			19 19			20 19	
Matlock Bath	d			14 22			15 22			16 22			17 22			18 23			19 22			20 22	
Matlock	a			14 27			15 27			16 27			17 27			18 28			19 27			20 27	

		EM F	XC ■ A	EM	XC ■ A	EM	NT ◇ G	EM	EM
Nottingham ■	d	20 20	20 40	21 20	21 39		22 17	22 20	23 20
Beeston	d	20 25	20 45	21 25	21 44			22 25	23 25
Attenborough	d	20 29		21 29	21 48			22 29	23 29
Long Eaton	d	20 37	20 54	21 37	21 56			22 38	23 37
Spondon	d				22 02				
Derby ■	a	20 50	21 04	21 50	22 08		22 37	22 52	23 50
	d	20 51				22 16			
Duffield	d	20 59				22 23			
Belper	d	21 04				22 28			
Ambergate	d	21 10				22 34			
Whatstandwell	d	21 14				22 38			
Cromford	d	21 19				22 44			
Matlock Bath	d	21 22				22 46			
Matlock	a	21 27				22 51			

A To Birmingham New Street
B 29 September, 6 October
C From St Pancras International
D To Cardiff Central
E To Bournemouth
F From Newark Castle
G To Sheffield

For connections from St Pancras International refer to Table T053

Nottingham - Derby - Matlock

Sundays
20 May to 22 July

		EM	EM	XC ◇1 A 🛒	XC ◇1 A	EM	XC ◇1 A	XC ◇1 A	EM	XC ◇1 A 🛒	EM	XC ◇1 A	EM
Nottingham	d		09 26	09 54	11 11	11 27	12 10	13 10	13 23	14 10	14 22	15 10	15 28
Beeston	d		09 32			11 32			13 29		14 28		15 34
Attenborough	d		09 35			11 36			13 32		14 31		15 37
Long Eaton	d		09 43			11 44			13 40		14 39		15 45
Spondon	d												
Derby	a		09 54	10 13	11 32		12 31	13 30	13 51	14 29	14 50	15 30	15 56
	d	07 56	09 56						13 56				15 58
Duffield	d	08 03	10 03			12 04			14 03				16 05
Belper	d	08 08	10 08			12 09			14 08				16 10
Ambergate	d	08 14	10 14			12 15			14 14				16 16
Whatstandwell	d	08 18	10 18			12 19			14 18				16 20
Cromford	d	08 24	10 24			12 24			14 24				16 26
Matlock Bath	d	08 26	10 26			12 27			14 26				16 28
Matlock	a	08 30	10 30			12 30			14 30				16 32

		XC ◇1 A 🛒	EM	XC ◇1 A 🛒	EM	XC ◇1 A 🛒	EM B	XC ◇1 C 🛒	EM	XC ◇1 C	EM
Nottingham	d	16 10	16 23	17 10	17 22	18 10	18 22	19 10	19 22	20 10	20 20
Beeston	d		16 29		17 28		18 28		19 28		20 26
Attenborough	d		16 32		17 31		18 31		19 31		20 29
Long Eaton	d		16 40		17 40		18 39		19 39		20 37
Spondon	d										
Derby	a	16 30	16 51	17 30	17 51	18 30	18 50	19 30	19 50	20 30	20 49
	d		16 56		17 56				19 52		
Duffield	d		17 04		18 03				19 59		
Belper	d		17 09		18 08				20 04		
Ambergate	d		17 15		18 14				20 10		
Whatstandwell	d		17 19		18 18				20 14		
Cromford	d		17 24		18 24				20 20		
Matlock Bath	d		17 27		18 26				20 22		
Matlock	a		17 30		18 30				20 26		

		XC ◇1 C	EM
Nottingham	d	21 10	21 24
Beeston	d		21 30
Attenborough	d		21 33
Long Eaton	d		21 41
Spondon	d		
Derby	a	21 30	21 52
	d		21 55
Duffield	d		22 02
Belper	d		22 07
Ambergate	d		22 13
Whatstandwell	d		22 17
Cromford	d		22 23
Matlock Bath	d		22 25
Matlock	a		22 29

Sundays
29 July to 2 September

		EM D	EM E	EM D	EM E	EM D	EM E	EM D	EM E	EM D
Nottingham	d			09 26		11 27		13 23		14 22
Beeston	d			09 32		11 32		13 29		14 28
Attenborough	d			09 35		11 36		13 32		14 31
Long Eaton	d			09 43		11 44		13 40		14 39
Spondon	d									
Derby	a			09 54				13 51		14 50
	d	07 56	07 56	09 56	10 05		11 57	13 56	14 00	
Duffield	d	08 03	08 04	10 03	10 13	12 04	12 05	14 03	14 08	
Belper	d	08 08	08 09	10 08	10 18	12 09	12 10	14 08	14 13	
Ambergate	d	08 14	08 15	10 14	10 24	12 15	12 16	14 14	14 19	
Whatstandwell	d	08 18	08 19	10 18	10 28	12 19	12 20	14 18	14 23	
Cromford	d	08 24	08 25	10 24	10 34	12 24	12 26	14 24	14 29	
Matlock Bath	d	08 26	08 27	10 26	10 36	12 27	12 28	14 26	14 31	
Matlock	a	08 30	08 31	10 30	10 40	12 30	12 32	14 30	14 35	

		EM D	EM E	EM D	EM E	EM D	EM E	EM F	EM D	EM E	EM D	EM D
Nottingham	d	15 28		16 23		17 22		18 22	19 22		20 20	21 24
Beeston	d	15 34		16 29		17 28		18 28	19 28		20 26	21 30
Attenborough	d	15 37		16 32		17 31		18 31	19 31		20 29	21 33
Long Eaton	d	15 45		16 40		17 40		18 39	19 39		20 37	21 41
Spondon	d											
Derby	a	15 56		16 51		17 51		18 50	19 50		20 49	21 52
	d	15 58	16 00	16 56	17 03	17 56	18 11		19 52	20 00		21 55
Duffield	d	16 05	16 08	17 04	17 12	18 03	18 19		19 59	20 08		22 02
Belper	d	16 10	16 13	17 09	17 17	18 08	18 24		20 04	20 13		22 07
Ambergate	d	16 16	16 19	17 15	17 23	18 14	18 30		20 10	20 19		22 13
Whatstandwell	d	16 20	16 23	17 19	17 27	18 18	18 34		20 14	20 23		22 17
Cromford	d	16 26	16 29	17 24	17 32	18 24	18 40		20 20	20 29		22 23
Matlock Bath	d	16 28	16 31	17 27	17 35	18 26	18 42		20 22	20 31		22 25
Matlock	a	16 32	16 35	17 30	17 38	18 30	18 46		20 26	20 35		22 29

Sundays
9 September to 7 October

		EM	XC ◇1 G 🛒	XC ◇1 G	EM H	XC ◇1 G	XC ◇1 G	EM	XC ◇1 G 🛒	EM	XC ◇1 G
Nottingham	d	09 26	09 54	11 11	11 27	12 10	13 10	13 23	14 10	14 22	15 10
Beeston	d	09 32			11 32			13 29		14 28	
Attenborough	d	09 35			11 36			13 32		14 31	
Long Eaton	d	09 43			11 43			13 40		14 39	
Spondon	d										
Derby	a	09 54	10 12	11 31	11 54	12 30	13 30	13 51	14 29	14 50	15 30
	d										
Duffield	d										
Belper	d										
Ambergate	d										
Whatstandwell	d										
Cromford	d										
Matlock Bath	d										
Matlock	a										

		EM	XC ◇1 G 🛒	EM	XC ◇1 G 🛒	EM	XC ◇1 G 🛒	EM B	XC ◇1 I 🛒	EM	XC ◇1 I	EM	XC ◇1 I
Nottingham	d	15 28	16 10	16 23	17 10	17 22	18 10	18 22	19 10	19 22	20 10	20 20	21 10
Beeston	d	15 34		16 29		17 28		18 28		19 28		20 26	
Attenborough	d	15 37		16 32		17 31		18 31		19 31		20 29	
Long Eaton	d	15 45		16 40		17 40		18 39		19 39		20 37	
Spondon	d												
Derby	a	15 56	16 30	16 54	17 29	17 51	18 30	18 50	19 30	19 50	20 30	20 49	21 30
	d												
Duffield	d												
Belper	d												
Ambergate	d												
Whatstandwell	d												
Cromford	d												
Matlock Bath	d												
Matlock	a												

A not 22 July. To Cardiff Central
B From Skegness
C not 22 July. To Birmingham New Street
D 29 July, 2 September
E not 29 July, 2 September
F 29 July, 2 September. From Skegness
G To Cardiff Central
H From Grantham
I To Birmingham New Street

For connections from St Pancras International refer to Table T053

Nottingham - Derby - Matlock

Sundays
9 September to 7 October

		EM
Nottingham	d	21 24
Beeston	d	21 30
Attenborough	d	21 33
Long Eaton	d	21 41
Spondon	d	
Derby	a	21 52
	d	
Duffield	d	
Belper	d	
Ambergate	d	
Whatstandwell	d	
Cromford	d	
Matlock Bath	d	
Matlock	a	

Sundays
14 October to 2 December

		EM	EM	XC ◇1 A 🛒	XC ◇1 A	EM B	XC ◇1 A	XC ◇1 A	EM	XC ◇1 A 🛒	EM	XC ◇1 A
Nottingham	d		09 26	09 54	11 11	11 27	12 10	13 10	13 23	14 10	14 22	15 10
Beeston	d		09 32			11 32			13 29		14 28	
Attenborough	d		09 35			11 36			13 32		14 31	
Long Eaton	d		09 43			11 43			13 40		14 39	
Spondon	d											
Derby	a		09 54	10 12	11 31		12 30	13 30	13 51	14 29	14 50	15 30
	d	07 56	09 55						13 55			
Duffield	d	08 03	10 03			12 03			14 03			
Belper	d	08 08	10 08			12 08			14 08			
Ambergate	d	08 14	10 14			12 14			14 14			
Whatstandwell	d	08 18	10 18			12 18			14 18			
Cromford	d	08 24	10 23			12 24			14 23			
Matlock Bath	d	08 26	10 26			12 26			14 26			
Matlock	a	08 30	10 30			12 30			14 30			

		EM	XC ◇1 A 🛒	EM	XC ◇1 A 🛒	EM	XC ◇1 A 🛒	EM	XC ◇1 C 🛒	EM	XC ◇1 C	EM
Nottingham	d	15 28	16 10	16 23	17 10	17 22	18 10	18 22	19 10	19 22	20 10	20 20
Beeston	d	15 34		16 29		17 28		18 28		19 28		20 26
Attenborough	d	15 37		16 32		17 31		18 31		19 31		20 29
Long Eaton	d	15 45		16 40		17 40		18 39		19 39		20 37
Spondon	d											
Derby	a	15 56	16 30	16 51	17 29	17 51	18 30	18 50	19 30	19 50	20 30	20 49
	d	15 57		16 55		17 55				19 51		
Duffield	d	16 05		17 04		18 03				19 59		
Belper	d	16 10		17 09		18 08				20 04		
Ambergate	d	16 16		17 14		18 14				20 10		
Whatstandwell	d	16 20		17 18		18 18				20 14		
Cromford	d	16 25		17 24		18 23				20 19		
Matlock Bath	d	16 28		17 26		18 26				20 22		
Matlock	a	16 32		17 30		18 30				20 26		

		XC ◇1 C	EM
Nottingham	d	21 10	21 24
Beeston	d		21 30
Attenborough	d		21 33
Long Eaton	d		21 41
Spondon	d		
Derby	a	21 30	21 52
	d		21 55
Duffield	d		22 02
Belper	d		22 07
Ambergate	d		22 13
Whatstandwell	d		22 17
Cromford	d		22 23
Matlock Bath	d		22 25
Matlock	a		22 29

A To Cardiff Central
B From Grantham
C To Birmingham New Street

For connections from St Pancras International refer to Table T053

Table T056-R

Mondays to Fridays

21 May to 20 July

Matlock - Derby - Nottingham

Miles		XC ◇	EM	EM	EM A	EM ◇■ 🍴	XC ■ B	EM	EM	XC ■ B	EM	XC ■ B 🍴	EM ◇ C	XC ■ B	XC ■ B 🍴	EM C	XC ◇■ D	XC ■ B 🍴	EM C	XC ◇■ D	XC ■ B 🍴	EM C
0	**Matlock** d			06 21									07 37			08 37			09 37			10 37
1	Matlock Bath d			06 23									07 39			08 39			09 39			10 39
1¾	Cromford d			06 26									07 42			08 42			09 42			10 42
4¾	Whatstandwell d			06 31									07 47			08 47			09 47			10 47
6¾	Ambergate d			06 36				06 57					07 52			08 52			09 52			10 52
9½	Belper d			06 42				07 03					07 59			08 59			09 59			10 59
12	Duffield d			06 46				07 07					08 03			09 03			10 03			11 03
17¾	**Derby** ■ a			06 55				07 16					08 11			09 11			10 11			11 12
—	d	06 00	06 27			07 00	07 08		07 36	07 43	07 53	08 10	08 13	08 41	09 08	09 13	09 42	10 08	10 13	10 41	11 08	11 14
19¾	Spondon d		06 32				07 14			07 48			08 18									
25½	Long Eaton d		06 39				07 21		07 46	07 55	08 03	08 19	08 25	08 50		09 24	09 51		10 24	10 50		11 25
28½	Attenborough d		06 47		07 03		07 28		07 54		08 13		08 33	08 58		09 32			10 32			11 32
30	Beeston d	06 16	06 50		07 06		07 32		07 57	08 03	08 16	08 27	08 36	09 01		09 35	09 59		10 35	10 58		11 35
33¼	**Nottingham** ■ a	06 22	06 59		07 16	07 20	07 38		08 06	08 09	08 25	08 34	08 46	09 08	09 28	09 42	10 05	10 28	10 41	11 04	11 28	11 41

	XC ◇■ D	XC ■ B 🍴	EM C	XC ◇■ D 🍴	XC ■ B 🍴	EM C	XC ◇■ D	XC ■ B 🍴	EM C	XC ◇■ D 🍴	XC ■ B	EM C	XC ◇■ D 🍴	XC ■ B	EM C	XC ◇■ D 🍴	XC ■ B	EM	XC ◇■ D 🍴	EM	XC ■ B
Matlock d			11 37			12 37			13 37			14 37			15 37			16 37			
Matlock Bath d			11 39			12 39			13 39			14 39			15 39			16 39			
Cromford d			11 42			12 42			13 42			14 42			15 42			16 42			
Whatstandwell d			11 47			12 47			13 47			14 47			15 47			16 47			
Ambergate d			11 52			12 52			13 52			14 52			15 52			16 52			
Belper d			11 59			12 59			13 59			14 59			15 59			16 59			
Duffield d			12 03			13 03			14 03			15 03			16 03			17 03			
Derby ■ a			12 11			13 11			14 11			15 11			16 11			17 11			
d	11 40	12 08	12 13	12 40	13 08	13 13	13 40	14 08	14 13	14 40	15 08	15 13	15 40	16 08	16 13	16 40	17 08	17 13	17 40	17 52	18 08
Spondon d						13 18												17 18		17 58	
Long Eaton d	11 49		12 24	12 50		13 25	13 49		14 24	14 49		15 24	15 49		16 24	16 49	17 17	17 25	17 50	18 05	18 18
Attenborough d			12 32			13 33			14 32			15 32			16 32			17 33		18 15	
Beeston d	11 59		12 35	12 58		13 36	13 57		14 35	14 57		15 35	15 57		16 35	16 57	17 25	17 36	17 58	18 18	18 25
Nottingham ■ a	12 06	12 28	12 41	13 05	13 28	13 42	14 03	14 28	14 41	15 03	15 28	15 41	16 03	16 28	16 41	17 03	17 31	17 42	18 04	18 25	18 32

	EM C	XC ◇■ D 🍴	XC ■ B	EM	XC ◇■ D	XC ■ B	EM	XC ◇■ E	EM	XC ◇■ D	NT ◇ F	EM	XC ■ B	EM	XC ■ B
Matlock d	17 37			18 37			19 37		20 37			21 41		22 55	
Matlock Bath d	17 39			18 39			19 39		20 39			21 43		22 57	
Cromford d	17 42			18 42			19 42		20 42			21 46		23 00	
Whatstandwell d	17 47			18 47			19 47		20 47			21 51		23 05	
Ambergate d	17 52			18 52			19 52		20 52			21 56		23 10	
Belper d	17 59			18 59			19 59		20 59			22 03		23 17	
Duffield d	18 03			19 03			20 03		21 03			22 07		23 21	
Derby ■ a	18 11			19 11			20 11		21 11			22 15		23 28	
d	18 13	18 40	19 08	19 13	19 40	20 08	20 16	20 40	21 14	21 34	21 40		22 59	23 31	23 57
Spondon d	18 18									21 39			23 04		
Long Eaton d	18 25	18 49	19 17	19 24	19 49		20 26	20 49	21 24	21 46			23 10	23 41	
Attenborough d	18 34			19 32			20 36		21 32	21 55			23 18	23 49	
Beeston d	18 38	18 57	19 24	19 35	19 57		20 39	20 57	21 35	21 58			23 21	23 52	
Nottingham ■ a	18 46	19 03	19 31	19 42	20 04	20 28	20 45	21 03	21 43	22 04	22 06		23 27	00 02	00 16

Mondays to Fridays

23 July to 27 July

	EM	EM	EM A	EM ◇■ 🍴	EM	XC ■ B	EM	EM	EM ◇ C	XC ■ B	EM C	EM C	EM C	EM C	EM C	EM C	EM C	EM C	EM	EM	EM C	EM
Matlock d		06 21							07 37		08 37	09 37	10 37	11 37	12 37	13 37	14 37	15 37	16 37		17 37	18 37
Matlock Bath d		06 23							07 39		08 39	09 39	10 39	11 39	12 39	13 39	14 39	15 39	16 39		17 39	18 39
Cromford d		06 26							07 42		08 42	09 42	10 42	11 42	12 42	13 42	14 42	15 42	16 42		17 42	18 42
Whatstandwell d		06 31							07 47		08 47	09 47	10 47	11 47	12 47	13 47	14 47	15 47	16 47		17 47	18 47
Ambergate d		06 36			06 57				07 52		08 52	09 52	10 52	11 52	12 52	13 52	14 52	15 52	16 52		17 52	18 52
Belper d		06 42			07 03				07 59		08 59	09 59	10 59	11 59	12 59	13 59	14 59	15 59	16 59		17 59	18 59
Duffield d		06 46			07 07				08 03		09 03	10 03	11 03	12 03	13 03	14 03	15 03	16 03	17 03		18 03	19 03
Derby ■ a		06 55			07 16				08 11		09 11	10 11	11 12	12 11	13 11	14 11	15 11	16 11	17 11		18 11	19 11
d	06 27			06 56			07 36	07 53	08 13		09 13	10 13	11 14	12 13	13 13	14 13	15 13	16 13	17 13	17 52	18 13	19 13
Spondon d	06 32								08 18						13 18				17 18	17 58	18 18	
Long Eaton d	06 39						07 46	08 03	08 25		09 24	10 24	11 25	12 24	13 25	14 24	15 24	16 24	17 25	18 05	18 25	19 24
Attenborough d	06 47		07 03			07 28	07 54	08 13	08 33	08 57	09 32	10 32	11 32	12 32	13 33	14 32	15 32	16 32	17 33	18 15	18 34	19 32
Beeston d	06 50		07 06			07 32	07 57	08 16	08 36	09 00	09 35	10 35	11 35	12 35	13 36	14 35	15 35	16 35	17 36	18 18	18 38	19 35
Nottingham ■ a	06 59		07 16	07 18		07 38	08 06	08 25	08 46	09 07	09 42	10 41	11 41	12 41	13 42	14 41	15 41	16 41	17 42	18 25	18 46	19 42

A From Leicester
B From Birmingham New Street
C To Newark Castle
D From Cardiff Central
E From Nottingham
F From Leeds

For connections to St Pancras International refer to Table T053

Table T056-R

Mondays to Fridays

23 July to 27 July

Matlock - Derby - Nottingham

	EM	EM	XC ◇■ A	NT ◇ B	EM	XC ■ C	EM
Matlock d	19 37	20 37			21 41		22 55
Matlock Bath d	19 39	20 39			21 43		22 57
Cromford d	19 42	20 42			21 46		23 00
Whatstandwell d	19 47	20 47			21 51		23 05
Ambergate d	19 52	20 52			21 56		23 10
Belper d	19 59	20 59			22 03		23 17
Duffield d	20 03	21 03			22 07		23 21
Derby ■ a	20 11	21 11			22 15		23 28
d	20 16	21 14		21 40			23 31
Spondon d							
Long Eaton d	20 26	21 24					23 41
Attenborough d	20 36	21 32	21 53			23 18	23 49
Beeston d	20 39	21 35	21 56			23 21	23 52
Nottingham ■ a	20 45	21 43	22 02	22 06		23 27	00 02

Mondays to Fridays

30 July to 31 August

	EM	EM D	XC ■ C	EM	EM ◇ E	EM	XC ■ C	EM E	EM	EM E	EM	EM E	EM	EM E	EM	EM E	EM	EM E	EM	EM E	EM	EM E
Matlock d				07 29		08 29			09 29		10 29		11 29		12 29		13 29		14 29		15 29	
Matlock Bath d				07 31		08 31			09 31		10 31		11 31		12 31		13 31		14 31		15 31	
Cromford d				07 34		08 34			09 34		10 34		11 34		12 34		13 34		14 34		15 34	
Whatstandwell d				07 39		08 39			09 39		10 39		11 39		12 39		13 39		14 39		15 39	
Ambergate d				07 44		08 44			09 44		10 44		11 44		12 44		13 44		14 44		15 44	
Belper d				07 51		08 51			09 51		10 51		11 51		12 51		13 51		14 51		15 51	
Duffield d				07 55		08 55			09 55		10 55		11 55		12 55		13 55		14 55		15 55	
Derby ■ a				08 03		09 03			10 03		11 03		12 03		13 03		14 03		15 03		16 03	
d	06 27																					
Spondon d	06 32																					
Long Eaton d	06 39				08 25			09 24		10 24		11 25		12 24		13 25		14 24		15 24		16 24
Attenborough d	06 47	07 03	07 28		08 33		08 57	09 32		10 32		11 32		12 32		13 33		14 32		15 32		16 32
Beeston d	06 50	07 06	07 32		08 36		09 00	09 35		10 35		11 35		12 35		13 36		14 35		15 35		16 35
Nottingham ■ a	06 59	07 16	07 38		08 46		09 07	09 42		10 41		11 41		12 41		13 42		14 41		15 41		16 41

	EM	EM F	EM	EM E	EM	EM F	EM	EM F	EM	EM F	XC ◇■ A	NT ◇ B	EM	EM G	XC ■ C
Matlock d	16 29		17 29		18 29		19 29		20 29				21 29	21 41	
Matlock Bath d	16 31		17 31		18 31		19 31		20 31				21 31	21 43	
Cromford d	16 34		17 34		18 34		19 34		20 34				21 34	21 46	
Whatstandwell d	16 39		17 39		18 39		19 39		20 39				21 39	21 51	
Ambergate d	16 44		17 44		18 44		19 44		20 44				21 44	21 56	
Belper d	16 51		17 51		18 51		19 51		20 51				21 51	22 03	
Duffield d	16 55		17 55		18 55		19 55		20 55				21 55	22 07	
Derby ■ a	17 03		18 03		19 03		20 03		21 03				22 06	22 15	
d												21 40			
Spondon d															
Long Eaton d		17 25		18 25		19 24		20 26		21 24					
Attenborough d		17 33		18 34		19 32		20 36		21 32	21 53				23 18
Beeston d		17 36		18 38		19 35		20 39		21 35	21 56				23 21
Nottingham ■ a		17 42		18 46		19 41		20 45		21 41	22 02	22 06			23 27

Mondays to Fridays

3 September to 5 October

	XC ◇	EM	EM D	EM ◇■ 🍴	XC ■ C	EM	XC ■ C	EM	XC ■ C 🍴	EM ◇ H	XC ■ C	XC ■ C 🍴	EM H	XC ◇■ A	XC ■ C 🍴	EM H	XC ◇■ A	XC ■ C 🍴	EM H	XC ◇■ A	XC ■ C 🍴	EM H
Matlock d																						
Matlock Bath d																						
Cromford d																						
Whatstandwell d																						
Ambergate d																						
Belper d																						
Duffield d																						
Derby ■ a																						
d	06 00	06 27		07 00	07 08	07 36	07 44	07 54	08 10	08 14	08 40	09 03	09 12	09 41	10 07	10 13	10 41	11 08	11 12	11 41	12 07	12 13
Spondon d		06 32			07 14		07 48			08 18												
Long Eaton d		06 39			07 21	07 46	07 55	08 09	08 19	08 25	08 49		09 24	09 49		10 22	10 49		11 22	11 51		12 22
Attenborough d		06 47	07 03		07 28	07 54		08 16		08 33	08 57		09 32			10 30			11 29			12 30
Beeston d	06 16	06 50	07 06		07 32	07 57	08 04	08 19	08 28	08 36	09 00		09 35	09 57		10 33	10 57		11 32	12 00		12 33
Nottingham ■ a	06 22	06 59	07 16	07 19	07 38	08 06	08 12	08 29	08 35	08 46	09 07	09 28	09 42	10 03	10 31	10 40	11 03	11 29	11 40	12 07	12 30	12 39

A From Cardiff Central
B From Leeds
C From Birmingham New Street
D From Leicester
E until 10 August. To Newark Castle
F until 10 August
G from 13 August
H To Newark Castle

For connections to St Pancras International refer to Table T053

Table T056-R

Matlock - Derby - Nottingham

Mondays to Fridays
3 September to 5 October

	XC ◇1 A ⊤	XC 1 B ⊤	EM C	XC ◇1 A	XC 1 B ⊤	EM C	XC ◇1 A ⊤	XC 1 B	EM C	XC ◇1 A ⊤	XC 1 B	EM C	XC ◇1 A ⊤	XC 1 B	EM	XC ◇1 A ⊤	EM	XC 1 B	EM C	XC ◇1 A ⊤	XC 1 B
Matlock d																					
Matlock Bath d																					
Cromford d																					
Whatstandwell d																					
Ambergate d																					
Belper d																					
Duffield d																					
Derby a																					
Derby d	12 40	13 08	13 12	13 40	14 08	14 12	14 39	15 08	15 13	15 40	16 08	16 12	16 40	17 08	17 12	17 40	17 55	18 08	18 13	18 40	19 08
Spondon d			13 16												17 16		18 00		18 18		
Long Eaton d	12 49		13 23	13 49		14 22	14 49		15 23	15 49		16 23	16 49	17 17	17 23	17 50	18 11	18 17	18 25	18 49	19 17
Attenborough d			13 31			14 30			15 31			16 35			17 31		18 21		18 34		
Beeston d	12 57		13 34	13 57		14 33	14 57		15 34	15 57		16 38	16 57	17 25	17 34	17 58	18 24	18 28	18 38	18 57	19 24
Nottingham a	13 03	13 31	13 40	14 03	14 32	14 40	15 03	15 29	15 40	16 03	16 29	16 44	17 03	17 32	17 40	18 04	18 30	18 35	18 46	19 03	19 31

	EM	XC ◇1 A	XC 1 B	EM	XC ◇1 D	EM	XC ◇1 A	XC 1 B	EM	XC 1 B
Matlock d										
Matlock Bath d										
Cromford d										
Whatstandwell d										
Ambergate d										
Belper d										
Duffield d										
Derby a										
Derby d	19 13	19 40	20 09	20 17	20 40	21 13	21 40	22 59	23 30	23 57
Spondon d							21 45	23 04		
Long Eaton d	19 22	19 49		20 26	20 49	21 29	21 52	23 10	23 41	
Attenborough d	19 30			20 34		21 37	22 01	23 18	23 49	
Beeston d	19 33	19 57		20 37	20 57	21 40	22 04	23 21	23 52	
Nottingham a	19 39	20 04	20 30	20 44	21 04	21 46	22 10	23 27	00 03	00 16

Mondays to Fridays
8 October to 7 December

	XC ◇	EM	EM	EM E	EM ◇1 ⊤	XC 1 B	EM	EM	XC 1 B	EM	XC 1 B ⊤	EM ◇ C	XC 1 B	XC 1 B ⊤	EM C	XC ◇1 A	XC 1 B ⊤	EM C	XC ◇1 A	XC 1 B ⊤	EM C	XC ◇1 A
Matlock d			06 20									07 36			08 36			09 36			10 36	
Matlock Bath d			06 22									07 38			08 38			09 38			10 38	
Cromford d			06 25									07 41			08 41			09 41			10 41	
Whatstandwell d			06 30									07 46			08 46			09 46			10 46	
Ambergate d			06 36				06 57					07 51			08 51			09 51			10 51	
Belper d			06 42				07 02					07 58			08 58			09 58			10 58	
Duffield d			06 47				07 07					08 03			09 03			10 03			11 03	
Derby a			06 56				07 16					08 10			09 10			10 10			11 10	
Derby d	06 00	06 27			07 00	07 08		07 36	07 44	07 53	08 08	08 12	08 40	09 08	09 12	09 41	10 09	10 12	10 41	11 08	11 12	11 41
Spondon d		06 32				07 14			07 48			08 16										
Long Eaton d		06 39				07 21		07 46	07 56	08 05	08 19	08 23	08 49		09 24	09 51		10 22	10 50		11 22	11 51
Attenborough d		06 47		07 03		07 28		07 54		08 13		08 31	08 57		09 32			10 30			11 30	
Beeston d	06 16	06 50		07 06		07 32		07 57	08 06	08 16	08 27	08 34	09 00		09 35	09 59		10 33	10 58		11 33	12 00
Nottingham a	06 22	06 59		07 16	07 19	07 38		08 06	08 12	08 25	08 34	08 45	09 07	09 28	09 42	10 05	10 28	10 39	11 04	11 28	11 39	12 07

	XC 1 B ⊤	EM C	XC ◇1 A ⊤	XC 1 B ⊤	EM C	XC ◇1 A	XC 1 B ⊤	EM C	XC ◇1 A ⊤	XC 1 B	EM C	XC ◇1 A ⊤	XC 1 B	EM C	XC ◇1 A ⊤	XC 1 B	EM	XC ◇1 A ⊤	EM	XC 1 B	EM C	XC ◇1 A ⊤
Matlock d		11 36			12 36			13 36			14 36			15 36			16 37				17 36	
Matlock Bath d		11 38			12 38			13 38			14 38			15 38			16 39				17 38	
Cromford d		11 41			12 41			13 41			14 41			15 41			16 42				17 41	
Whatstandwell d		11 46			12 46			13 46			14 46			15 46			16 47				17 46	
Ambergate d		11 51			12 51			13 51			14 51			15 51			16 52				17 51	
Belper d		11 58			12 58			13 58			14 58			15 58			16 58				17 58	
Duffield d		12 03			13 03			14 03			15 03			16 03			17 03				18 03	
Derby a		12 10			13 10			14 10			15 10			16 10			17 10				18 10	
Derby d	12 08	12 12	12 40	13 08	13 12	13 40	14 08	14 12	14 40	15 08	15 12	15 40	16 08	16 12	16 40	17 08	17 12	17 40	17 55	18 08	18 12	18 40
Spondon d					13 16												17 16		18 00		18 18	
Long Eaton d		12 22	12 49		13 23	13 49		14 22	14 49		15 23	15 49		16 22	16 49	17 17	17 23	17 50	18 07	18 17	18 25	18 49
Attenborough d		12 31			13 31			14 30			15 31			16 30			17 31		18 17		18 34	
Beeston d		12 34	12 57		13 34	13 57		14 33	14 57		15 34	15 57		16 33	16 57	17 25	17 34	17 58	18 20	18 25	18 38	18 57
Nottingham a	12 28	12 40	13 03	13 28	13 40	14 03	14 28	14 39	15 03	15 28	15 40	16 03	16 28	16 39	17 03	17 31	17 40	18 04	18 26	18 31	18 50	19 05

A From Cardiff Central
B From Birmingham New Street
C To Newark Castle
D From Nottingham
E From Leicester

For connections to St Pancras International refer to Table T053

Table T056-R

Matlock - Derby - Nottingham

Mondays to Fridays
8 October to 7 December

	XC 1 A	EM	XC ◇1 B	XC 1 A	EM	XC ◇1 C	EM	NT ◇ D	XC ◇1 B	EM	XC 1 A	EM	XC 1 A
Matlock d		18 37			19 36		20 36			21 40		22 54	
Matlock Bath d		18 39			19 38		20 38			21 42		22 56	
Cromford d		18 42			19 41		20 41			21 45		22 59	
Whatstandwell d		18 47			19 46		20 46			21 50		23 04	
Ambergate d		18 52			19 51		20 51			21 55		23 09	
Belper d		18 58			19 58		20 58			22 02		23 16	
Duffield d		19 03			20 03		21 03			22 07		23 20	
Derby a		19 10			20 10		21 10			22 14		23 27	
Derby d	19 08	19 13	19 44	20 08	20 15	20 40	21 13	21 41	21 43		22 59	23 30	23 57
Spondon d									21 47		23 04		
Long Eaton d	19 17	19 22	19 53		20 24	20 49	21 24		21 54		23 10	23 39	
Attenborough d		19 31			20 32		21 32		22 03		23 18	23 47	
Beeston d	19 25	19 34	20 00		20 35	20 57	21 35		22 06		23 21	23 50	
Nottingham a	19 34	19 44	20 08	20 28	20 41	21 04	21 41	22 01	22 12		23 27	00 01	00 16

Saturdays
26 May to 28 July

	EM	EM	EM E	XC 1 F	XC 1 G	EM H	EM I	XC 1 F	XC 1 F ⊤	EM J	XC 1 G	XC 1 F	XC 1 F ⊤	EM J	XC ◇1 K		XC 1 F ⊤	EM J	XC ◇1 K ⊤	XC 1 F ⊤	EM J
Matlock d		06 21								07 37				08 37		and at the same minutes past each hour until		11 37			12 37
Matlock Bath d		06 23								07 39				08 39				11 39			12 39
Cromford d		06 26								07 42				08 42				11 42			12 42
Whatstandwell d		06 31								07 47				08 47				11 47			12 47
Ambergate d		06 37								07 52				08 52				11 52			12 52
Belper d		06 43								07 59				08 59				11 59			12 59
Duffield d		06 47								08 03				09 03				12 03			13 03
Derby a		06 55								08 11				09 11				12 11			13 11
Derby d	06 12			07 09		07 25	07 25	07 40	08 10	08 13		08 40	09 08	09 13	09 40		12 08	12 13	12 40	13 08	13 13
Spondon d	06 17			07 14				07 45		08 18											13 18
Long Eaton d	06 23			07 21		07 35	07 35	07 52	08 19	08 25		08 49		09 24	09 49			12 24	12 49		13 25
Attenborough d	06 32		07 03	07 28	07 28	07 43	07 43			08 33	08 56	08 57		09 32				12 32			13 33
Beeston d	06 35		07 06	07 32	07 32	07 46	07 47	08 00	08 27	08 36	09 00	09 00		09 35	09 57			12 35	12 57		13 36
Nottingham a	06 45		07 15	07 38	07 38	07 56	07 57	08 06	08 34	08 46	09 06	09 07	09 28	09 41	10 03		12 28	12 41	13 03	13 28	13 42

	XC ◇1 K	XC 1 F ⊤	EM J	XC ◇1 K ⊤	XC 1 F	EM J	XC ◇1 K ⊤	XC 1 F	EM J	XC ◇1 K ⊤	XC 1 F	EM J	XC ◇1 K ⊤	XC 1 F	EM J	XC ◇1 K ⊤	XC 1 F	EM	XC ◇1 K	XC 1 F	EM	XC ◇1 K
Matlock d			13 37			14 37			15 37			16 37			17 37			18 37			19 37	
Matlock Bath d			13 39			14 39			15 39			16 39			17 39			18 39			19 39	
Cromford d			13 42			14 42			15 42			16 42			17 42			18 42			19 42	
Whatstandwell d			13 47			14 47			15 47			16 47			17 47			18 47			19 47	
Ambergate d			13 52			14 52			15 52			16 52			17 52			18 52			19 52	
Belper d			13 59			14 59			15 59			16 59			17 59			18 59			19 59	
Duffield d			14 03			15 03			16 03			17 03			18 03			19 03			20 03	
Derby a			14 11			15 11			16 11			17 11			18 11			19 11			20 11	
Derby d	13 40	14 08	14 13	14 40	15 08	15 13	15 40	16 08	16 13	16 40	17 08	17 12	17 40	18 08	18 13	18 40	19 08	19 13	19 41	20 08	20 13	20 40
Spondon d												17 18			18 18							
Long Eaton d	13 49		14 24	14 49		15 24	15 49		16 24	16 49	17 17	17 25	17 49	18 17	18 25	18 49	19 17	19 24	19 50		20 24	20 49
Attenborough d			14 32			15 32			16 32			17 33			18 33			19 32			20 32	
Beeston d	13 57		14 35	14 57		15 35	15 57		16 35	16 57	17 25	17 36	17 58	18 25	18 36	18 57	19 25	19 35	19 58		20 35	20 57
Nottingham a	14 03	14 28	14 41	15 03	15 28	15 41	16 03	16 28	16 41	17 03	17 31	17 42	18 04	18 31	18 45	19 03	19 31	19 41	20 04	20 28	20 41	21 03

	EM	XC ◇1 K	XC ◇1 L	NT ◇ D	EM	XC ◇1 K	XC ◇1 L	EM
Matlock d	20 37				21 42			22 54
Matlock Bath d	20 39				21 44			22 56
Cromford d	20 42				21 47			22 59
Whatstandwell d	20 47				21 52			23 04
Ambergate d	20 52				21 57			23 09
Belper d	20 59				22 04			23 16
Duffield d	21 03				22 08			23 21
Derby a	21 11				22 16			23 28
Derby d	21 14	21 37		21 41		22 59		23 30
Spondon d		21 42				23 04		
Long Eaton d	21 24	21 48				23 10		23 40
Attenborough d	21 32	21 55	21 55			23 18	23 18	23 48
Beeston d	21 35	21 58	21 58			23 21	23 21	23 51
Nottingham a	21 41	22 04	22 04	22 08		23 27	23 27	23 59

A From Birmingham New Street
B From Cardiff Central
C From Nottingham
D From Leeds
E From Leicester
F not 28 July. From Birmingham New Street
G 28 July. From Birmingham New Street
H not 28 July
I 28 July
J To Newark Castle
K not 28 July. From Cardiff Central
L 28 July. From Cardiff Central

For connections to St Pancras International refer to Table T053

Table T056-R

Matlock - Derby - Nottingham

Saturdays

4 August to 1 September

		EM	EM	XC	EM	EM	XC	EM	EM		EM	EM		EM	EM	EM	EM	EM	EM	EM	EM	EM		EM
				■			■																	
			A	B		C	B		C			C			C		C		C		C			C
Matlock	d	06 59			07 59			08 59		and at the same minutes past each hour until	11 59			12 59		13 59		14 59		15 59		16 59		
Matlock Bath	d	07 01			08 01			09 01			12 01			13 01		14 01		15 01		16 01		17 01		
Cromford	d	07 04			08 04			09 04			12 04			13 04		14 04		15 04		16 04		17 04		
Whatstandwell	d	07 09			08 09			09 09			12 09			13 09		14 09		15 09		16 09		17 09		
Ambergate	d	07 14			08 14			09 14			12 14			13 14		14 14		15 14		16 14		17 14		
Belper	d	07 21			08 21			09 21			12 21			13 21		14 21		15 21		16 21		17 21		
Duffield	d	07 26			08 26			09 26			12 26			13 26		14 26		15 26		16 26		17 26		
Derby ■	a	07 36			08 36			09 36			12 36			13 36		14 36		15 36		16 36		17 36		
	d																							
Spondon	d																							
Long Eaton	d					08 25			09 24			12 24			13 25		14 24		15 24		16 24			17 25
Attenborough	d		07 03	07 28		08 33	08 56		09 32			12 32			13 33		14 32		15 32		16 32			17 33
Beeston	d		07 06	07 32		08 36	09 00		09 35			12 35			13 36		14 35		15 35		16 35			17 36
Nottingham ■	a		07 15	07 38		08 46	09 06		09 41			12 41			13 42		14 41		15 41		16 41			17 42

		EM	EM	EM	EM	EM	EM	EM	EM		XC	NT	EM	XC
											◇■	◇		◇■
			C		D		D		D		E	F		E
Matlock	d	17 59		18 59		19 59		20 59					21 59	
Matlock Bath	d	18 01		19 01		20 01		21 01					22 01	
Cromford	d	18 04		19 04		20 04		21 04					22 04	
Whatstandwell	d	18 09		19 09		20 09		21 09					22 09	
Ambergate	d	18 14		19 14		20 14		21 14					22 14	
Belper	d	18 21		19 21		20 21		21 21					22 21	
Duffield	d	18 26		19 26		20 26		21 26					22 26	
Derby ■	a	18 36		19 36		20 36		21 36					22 36	
	d											21 41		
Spondon	d													
Long Eaton	d		18 25		19 24		20 24		21 24					
Attenborough	d		18 33		19 32		20 32		21 32		21 55			23 18
Beeston	d		18 36		19 35		20 35		21 35		21 58			23 21
Nottingham ■	a		18 45		19 41		20 41		21 41		22 04	22 08		23 27

Saturdays

8 September to 6 October

		EM	EM	XC	EM	XC	EM	XC	EM	XC		XC	EM	XC	XC	EM	XC	XC	EM	XC		XC	EM	XC	XC
				■		■		■		■		■		◇■	■		◇■	■		◇■		■		◇■	■
			A	B		B	G	B ⚲	H	B		B ⚲	H	E	B ⚲	H	E	B ⚲	H	E		B ⚲	H	E ⚲	B ⚲
Matlock	d																								
Matlock Bath	d																								
Cromford	d																								
Whatstandwell	d																								
Ambergate	d																								
Belper	d																								
Duffield	d																								
Derby ■	a																								
	d	06 12		07 08	07 25	07 40	07 54	08 10	08 14	08 40		09 08	09 12	09 40	10 08	10 12	10 40	11 08	11 12	11 40		12 08	12 12	12 40	13 08
Spondon	d	06 16		07 14		07 45			08 18																
Long Eaton	d	06 22		07 21	07 34	07 52	08 04	08 19	08 25	08 49			09 22	09 49		10 22	10 49		11 22	11 49			12 22	12 49	
Attenborough	d	06 31	07 03	07 28	07 42				08 33	08 57			09 30			10 30			11 29				12 30		
Beeston	d	06 34	07 06	07 32	07 45	08 00	08 13	08 27	08 36	09 00			09 33	09 57		10 33	10 57		11 32	11 57			12 33	12 57	
Nottingham ■	a	06 45	07 15	07 38	07 52	08 06	08 20	08 34	08 46	09 07		09 30	09 39	10 03	10 30	10 39	11 03	11 30	11 41	12 03		12 28	12 39	13 03	13 28

		EM	XC	XC	EM	XC		XC	EM	XC	XC	EM	XC	XC	EM	XC		XC	EM	XC	XC	EM	XC	XC	EM
			◇■	■		◇■		■		◇■	■		◇■	■		◇■		■		◇■	■		◇■	■	
		H	E	B ⚲	H	E ⚲		B	H	E ⚲	B	H	E ⚲	B	H	E ⚲		B	H	E ⚲	B		E	B	
Matlock	d																								
Matlock Bath	d																								
Cromford	d																								
Whatstandwell	d																								
Ambergate	d																								
Belper	d																								
Duffield	d																								
Derby ■	a																								
	d	13 12	13 40	14 08	14 12	14 40		15 08	15 12	15 40	16 08	16 12	16 40	17 08	17 11	17 40		18 08	18 13	18 40	19 08	19 13	19 40	20 08	20 14
Spondon	d	13 16													17 16				18 18						
Long Eaton	d	13 23	13 49		14 22	14 49			15 22	15 49		16 22	16 49	17 17	17 23	17 49		18 17	18 25	18 49	19 17	19 22	19 50		20 23
Attenborough	d	13 31			14 30				15 30			16 30			17 31				18 33			19 30			20 30
Beeston	d	13 34	13 57		14 33	14 57			15 33	15 57		16 33	16 57	17 25	17 34	17 57		18 25	18 36	18 57	19 25	19 33	19 58		20 33
Nottingham ■	a	13 40	14 03	14 28	14 39	15 03		15 28	15 39	16 03	16 28	16 39	17 03	17 31	17 40	18 03		18 31	18 45	19 03	19 31	19 39	20 04	20 28	20 39

A From Leicester
B From Birmingham New Street
C 4 August, 11 August. To Newark Castle
D 4 August, 11 August
E From Cardiff Central
F From Leeds
G 8 September. To Skegness
H To Newark Castle

For connections to St Pancras International refer to Table T053

Table T056-R

Matlock - Derby - Nottingham

Saturdays

8 September to 6 October

		XC	EM	XC	EM		XC	EM
		◇■		◇■			◇■	
		A		A	B		A	
Matlock	d				21 42			
Matlock Bath	d				21 44			
Cromford	d				21 47			
Whatstandwell	d				21 52			
Ambergate	d				21 57			
Belper	d				22 03			
Duffield	d				22 08			
Derby ■	a				22 16			
	d	20 40	21 13	21 37			22 59	23 29
Spondon	d			21 41			23 04	
Long Eaton	d	20 49	21 22	21 47			23 10	23 38
Attenborough	d		21 30	21 55			23 18	23 46
Beeston	d	20 56	21 33	21 58			23 21	23 49
Nottingham ■	a	21 03	21 39	22 04			23 27	23 57

Saturdays

13 October to 8 December

		EM	EM	EM	XC	EM	XC	XC	EM	XC		XC	EM	XC	XC	EM	XC	XC	EM	XC		XC	EM	XC	XC
					■		■	■		■		■		◇■	■		◇■	■		◇■		■		◇■	■
				C	D		D	D ⚲	E	D		D ⚲	E	A	D ⚲	E	A	D ⚲	E	A		D ⚲	E	A ⚲	D ⚲
Matlock	d		06 20						07 36				08 36			09 36			10 37				11 36		
Matlock Bath	d		06 22						07 38				08 38			09 38			10 39				11 38		
Cromford	d		06 25						07 41				08 41			09 41			10 42				11 41		
Whatstandwell	d		06 30						07 46				08 46			09 46			10 47				11 46		
Ambergate	d		06 36						07 51				08 51			09 51			10 52				11 51		
Belper	d		06 42						07 58				08 58			09 58			10 58				11 58		
Duffield	d		06 46						08 03				09 02			10 02			11 03				12 03		
Derby ■	a		06 55						08 10				09 10			10 10			11 10				12 10		
	d	06 12			07 09	07 25	07 40	08 10	08 13	08 40		09 08	09 12	09 40	10 08	10 12	10 40	11 08	11 12	11 40		12 08	12 12	12 40	13 08
Spondon	d	06 16			07 14		07 45		08 18																
Long Eaton	d	06 23			07 21	07 37	07 52	08 19	08 25	08 49			09 22	09 49		10 22	10 49		11 22	11 49			12 22	12 48	
Attenborough	d	06 32		07 03	07 28	07 45			08 31	08 57			09 30			10 30			11 30				12 30		
Beeston	d	06 35		07 06	07 32	07 48	08 00	08 27	08 34	09 00			09 33	09 57		10 33	10 57		11 33	11 57			12 33	12 56	
Nottingham ■	a	06 45		07 15	07 38	07 58	08 06	08 34	08 44	09 07		09 28	09 39	10 03	10 28	10 39	11 03	11 28	11 39	12 03		12 28	12 39	13 02	13 28

		EM	XC	XC	EM	XC		XC	EM	XC	XC	EM	XC	XC	EM	XC		XC	EM	XC	XC	EM	XC	XC	EM
			◇■	■		◇■		■		◇■	■		◇■	■		◇■		■		◇■	■		◇■	■	
		E	A	D ⚲	E	A ⚲		D	E	A ⚲	D	E	A ⚲	D	E	A ⚲		D	E	A ⚲	D		A	D	
Matlock	d	12 36			13 36				14 36			15 36			16 36				17 36			18 36			19 36
Matlock Bath	d	12 38			13 38				14 38			15 38			16 38				17 38			18 38			19 38
Cromford	d	12 41			13 41				14 41			15 41			16 41				17 41			18 41			19 41
Whatstandwell	d	12 46			13 46				14 46			15 46			16 46				17 46			18 46			19 46
Ambergate	d	12 51			13 51				14 51			15 51			16 51				17 51			18 52			19 51
Belper	d	12 58			13 58				14 58			15 58			16 58				17 58			18 58			19 58
Duffield	d	13 03			14 03				15 03			16 03			17 03				18 02			19 03			20 03
Derby ■	a	13 10			14 10				15 10			16 10			17 10				18 10			19 10			20 10
	d	13 12	13 40	14 08	14 12	14 40		15 08	15 12	15 40	16 08	16 12	16 40	17 08	17 11	17 40		18 08	18 12	18 40	19 08	19 12	19 40	20 08	20 12
Spondon	d	13 16													17 16				18 18						
Long Eaton	d	13 23	13 49		14 22	14 49			15 22	15 49		16 22	16 49	17 17	17 23	17 49		18 17	18 25	18 49	19 17	19 22	19 49		20 22
Attenborough	d	13 31			14 30				15 30			16 30			17 31				18 33			19 30			20 30
Beeston	d	13 34	13 57		14 33	14 57			15 33	15 57		16 33	16 57	17 25	17 34	17 58		18 25	18 36	18 57	19 25	19 33	19 57		20 33
Nottingham ■	a	13 40	14 03	14 28	14 39	15 03		15 28	15 39	16 03	16 28	16 39	17 03	17 31	17 40	18 04		18 31	18 45	19 03	19 31	19 39	20 04	20 28	20 39

		XC		EM	XC	NT	EM	XC	EM
		◇■			◇■	◇		◇■	
		A			A	F		A	
Matlock	d			20 36			21 41		22 54
Matlock Bath	d			20 38			21 43		22 56
Cromford	d			20 41			21 46		22 59
Whatstandwell	d			20 46			21 51		23 04
Ambergate	d			20 51			21 56		23 09
Belper	d			20 58			22 03		23 15
Duffield	d			21 02			22 08		23 20
Derby ■	a			21 10			22 15		23 27
	d	20 40		21 13	21 37	21 41		22 59	23 29
Spondon	d				21 42			23 04	
Long Eaton	d	20 49		21 22	21 48			23 10	23 38
Attenborough	d			21 30	21 55			23 18	23 46
Beeston	d	20 56		21 33	21 58			23 21	23 49
Nottingham ■	a	21 03		21 39	22 04	22 08		23 27	23 57

A From Cardiff Central
B not from 29 September
C From Leicester
D From Birmingham New Street
E To Newark Castle
F From Leeds

For connections to St Pancras International refer to Table T053

Table T056-R

Matlock - Derby - Nottingham

Sundays

20 May to 22 July

		EM	EM	EM	XC ◇1 A	EM	XC ◇1 B	XC ◇1 B	EM	XC ◇1 B	EM	XC ◇1 B	EM	XC ◇1 B	EM	XC ◇1 C	EM	XC ◇1 B	EM	XC ◇1 B	EM	XC ◇1 B	EM D
Matlock	d		08 38	10 38		12 38			14 41				16 38		17 42		18 38				20 38		
Matlock Bath	d		08 40	10 40		12 40			14 43				16 40		17 44		18 40				20 40		
Cromford	d		08 43	10 43		12 43			14 46				16 43		17 47		18 43				20 43		
Whatstandwell	d		08 48	10 48		12 48			14 51				16 48		17 52		18 48				20 48		
Ambergate	d		08 54	10 54		12 54			14 56				16 54		17 58		18 54				20 54		
Belper	d		09 00	11 00		13 00			15 03				17 01		18 05		19 00				21 00		
Duffield	d		09 05	11 05		13 05			15 07				17 05		18 09		19 05				21 05		
Derby 6	a		09 12	11 12		13 12			15 15				17 12		18 16		19 12				21 12		
	d	08 18	09 14	11 14	12 40	13 14	13 40	14 39	15 16	15 40	16 14	16 40	17 14	17 40	18 18	18 40	19 14	19 40	20 14	20 38	21 14	21 40	22 12
Spondon	d																						
Long Eaton	d	08 28	09 24	11 24		13 24			15 26		16 23		17 24		18 28		19 24		20 23		21 24		22 22
Attenborough	d	08 36	09 31	11 31		13 31			15 34		16 31		17 31		18 35		19 34		20 31		21 31		22 30
Beeston	d	08 39	09 34	11 34		13 34			15 37		16 34		17 34		18 38		19 37		20 34		21 34		22 33
Nottingham 8	a	08 45	09 41	11 41	13 00	13 41	14 00	15 00	15 43	16 00	16 43	17 00	17 44	18 00	18 45	18 58	19 44	20 00	20 41	20 56	21 41	22 00	22 39

		EM E	EM
Matlock	d		22 44
Matlock Bath	d		22 46
Cromford	d		22 49
Whatstandwell	d		22 54
Ambergate	d		23 00
Belper	d		23 07
Duffield	d		23 11
Derby 6	a		23 18
	d	22 21	
Spondon	d		
Long Eaton	d	22 31	
Attenborough	d	22 38	
Beeston	d	22 41	
Nottingham 8	a	22 48	

Sundays

29 July to 2 September

		EM F	EM F	EM G	EM F	EM G	EM F	EM G	EM F	EM G	EM F	EM F	EM G	EM F	EM G	EM F	EM G	EM F	EM F	EM G	EM F	EM F
Matlock	d		08 38	08 38	10 38	10 48	12 38	12 48	14 41	14 47		16 38	16 49	17 42	17 45	18 38	18 52		20 38	20 52		22 44
Matlock Bath	d		08 40	08 40	10 40	10 50	12 40	12 50	14 43	14 49		16 40	16 51	17 44	17 47	18 40	18 54		20 40	20 54		22 46
Cromford	d		08 43	08 43	10 43	10 53	12 43	12 53	14 46	14 52		16 43	16 54	17 47	17 50	18 43	18 57		20 43	20 57		22 49
Whatstandwell	d		08 48	08 48	10 48	10 58	12 48	12 58	14 51	14 57		16 48	16 59	17 52	17 55	18 48	19 02		20 48	21 02		22 54
Ambergate	d		08 54	08 54	10 54	11 04	12 54	13 04	14 56	15 02		16 54	17 04	17 58	18 01	18 54	19 07		20 54	21 07		23 00
Belper	d		09 00	09 00	11 00	11 10	13 00	13 10	15 03	15 09		17 01	17 11	18 05	18 08	19 00	19 13		21 00	21 13		23 07
Duffield	d		09 05	09 05	11 05	11 15	13 05	13 15	15 07	15 13		17 05	17 15	18 09	18 12	19 05	19 18		21 05	21 18		23 11
Derby 6	a		09 12	09 15	11 12	11 25	13 12	13 25	15 15	15 23		17 12	17 25	18 16	18 25	19 12	19 28		21 12	21 28		23 18
	d	08 18	09 14		11 14		13 14		15 16		16 14	17 14		18 18		19 14		20 14	21 14		22 21	
Spondon	d																					
Long Eaton	d	08 28	09 24		11 24		13 24		15 26		16 23	17 24		18 28		19 24		20 23	21 24		22 31	
Attenborough	d	08 36	09 31		11 31		13 31		15 34		16 31	17 31		18 35		19 34		20 31	21 31		22 38	
Beeston	d	08 39	09 34		11 34		13 34		15 37		16 34	17 34		18 38		19 37		20 34	21 34		22 41	
Nottingham 8	a	08 45	09 41		11 41		13 41		15 43		16 43	17 44		18 45		19 44		20 41	21 41		22 48	

Sundays

9 September to 7 October

		EM H	EM	EM	XC ◇1 I	EM	XC ◇1 J	XC ◇1 J	EM	XC ◇1 J	EM	XC ◇1 J	EM	XC ◇1 J	EM	XC ◇1 K	EM	XC ◇1 J	EM	XC ◇1 J	EM	XC ◇1 J	EM
Matlock	d																						
Matlock Bath	d																						
Cromford	d																						
Whatstandwell	d																						
Ambergate	d																						
Belper	d																						
Duffield	d																						
Derby 6	a																						
	d	08 18	09 14	11 13	12 40	13 13	13 40	14 39	15 15	15 40	16 14	16 40	17 15	17 39	18 17	18 40	19 14	19 40	20 14	20 40	21 13	21 40	22 21
Spondon	d																						
Long Eaton	d	08 28	09 24	11 24		13 24			15 24		16 23		17 24		18 28		19 23		20 23		21 22		22 31
Attenborough	d	08 36	09 31	11 31		13 31			15 32		16 31		17 31		18 35		19 32		20 31		21 29		22 38
Beeston	d	08 39	09 34	11 34		13 34			15 35		16 34		17 34		18 38		19 35		20 34		21 32		22 41
Nottingham 8	a	08 45	09 41	11 41	13 00	13 41	14 00	15 00	15 41	16 00	16 43	17 00	17 44	18 00	18 45	18 58	19 42	20 00	20 41	21 00	21 39	22 00	22 48

A not 22 July. From Birmingham New Street
B not 22 July. From Cardiff Central
C not 22 July. From Nottingham
D 3 June
E not 3 June
F 29 July, 2 September
G not 29 July, 2 September
H 9 September
I From Birmingham New Street
J From Cardiff Central
K From Nottingham

For connections to St Pancras International refer to Table T053

Table T056-R

Matlock - Derby - Nottingham

Sundays

14 October to 2 December

		EM	EM	XC ◇1 A	EM	XC ◇1 B	XC ◇1 B	EM	XC ◇1 B	EM	XC ◇1 B	EM	XC ◇1 B	EM	XC ◇1 C	EM	XC ◇1 B	EM	XC ◇1 B	EM	XC ◇1 B	EM	EM
Matlock	d	08 38			12 38			14 41						17 42		18 38				20 38			22 44
Matlock Bath	d	08 40			12 40			14 43						17 44		18 40				20 40			22 46
Cromford	d	08 43			12 43			14 46						17 47		18 43				20 43			22 49
Whatstandwell	d	08 48			12 48			14 51						17 52		18 48				20 48			22 54
Ambergate	d	08 54			12 54			14 56						17 58		18 54				20 54			23 00
Belper	d	08 59			12 59			15 02						18 04		18 59				20 59			23 06
Duffield	d	09 04			13 04			15 07						18 08		19 04				21 04			23 10
Derby 6	a	09 12			13 11			15 14						18 15		19 11				21 11			23 18
	d	09 14	11 13	12 40	13 13	13 40	14 40	15 15	15 40	16 14	16 40	17 15	17 40	18 17	18 40	19 13	19 40	20 14	20 40	21 13	21 40	22 21	
Spondon	d																						
Long Eaton	d	09 24	11 24		13 24			15 24		16 23		17 24		18 28		19 22		20 23		21 22		22 31	
Attenborough	d	09 31	11 31		13 31			15 32		16 31		17 31		18 35		19 32		20 31		21 29		22 38	
Beeston	d	09 34	11 34		13 34			15 35		16 34		17 34		18 38		19 35		20 34		21 32		22 41	
Nottingham 8	a	09 41	11 41	13 00	13 41	14 00	14 59	15 41	16 00	16 43	17 00	17 44	18 00	18 45	18 58	19 42	20 00	20 41	21 00	21 39	22 00	22 48	

A From Birmingham New Street
B From Cardiff Central
C From Nottingham

For connections to St Pancras International refer to Table T053

21 May to 20 July

Nottingham and Derby - Birmingham - Bristol and Cardiff

Miles	Miles		AW A	XC ◇1	XC ◇1	XC ◇1 B ⌶	AW A	XC ◇1 C ⌶	XC ◇1 ⌶	XC ◇1 D	XC ◇1 E ⌶	AW A	XC ◇1 F	XC ◇1 G ⌶	XC ◇1	XC ◇1 H ⌶	XC ◇1 E ⌶	XC 1	XC ◇1 I ⌶	XC ◇1 J ⌶	XC 1 K ⌶	XC ◇1 L ⌶
0	—	**Nottingham** 56 ⇌ d							06 00				06 37		07 04			07 37		08 09		
3¼	—	Beeston 56 d							06 06				06 43		07 09			07 42		08 14		
4¾	—	Attenborough 56 d							06 09						07 13							
8	—	Long Eaton 56 d							06 19						07 21			07 52		08 23		
16	—	**Derby** 56 d						06 10	06 36	06 48			07 06	07 27	07 36	07 50		08 06	08 28	08 38	08 53	
22¾	—	Willington d													07 44							
27	—	Burton-on-Trent d						06 20	06 48	06 58			07 17	07 38	07 50	08 00		08 18	08 38	08 50		
40	—	Tamworth d						06 31	07 01	07 09			07 30	07 50	08 03	08 11		08 30	08 50	09 03		
41½	—	Wilnecote d							07 05						08 07			08 34				
49½	—	Water Orton d																08 42				
57¼	0	**Birmingham New Street** a						06 52	07 25	07 27			07 53	08 08	08 25	08 27		08 55	09 10	09 24	09 27	
—	—	d		05 00	05 37	06 42		07 12	07 30		07 42			08 12	08 30		08 42		09 17	09 30		09 42
58¾	2½	University a							07 36						08 36					09 36		
70¾	14¼	Bromsgrove a																				
95½	40¼	Ashchurch for Tewkesbury d			06 27																	
102¼	48	Cheltenham Spa d	05 37	06 02	06 43	07 23	07 46	07 52	08 11		08 25	08 46		08 52	09 11		09 26		10 00	10 10		10 26
109¼	—	Gloucester 134 a	05 48	06 12	06 53		07 57		08 20			08 58			09 20					10 20		
—	—	d	05 50	06 14	07 01		07 58		08 25			08 58			09 25					10 25		
—	87½	Bristol Parkway 134 a				07 54		08 26			08 54			09 25			09 55		10 30			10 56
—	93¼	**Bristol Temple Meads** 134 a				08 06		08 40			09 11			09 39			10 08		10 43			11 10
128¾	—	Lydney d	06 09	06 33	07 20		08 17					09 17								10 44		
136½	—	Chepstow d	06 19	06 42	07 29		08 27		08 51			09 27			09 51							
143¼	—	Caldicot d	06 26	06 51	07 38		08 35					09 35										
144	—	Severn Tunnel Jn 132 d	06 29	06 55	07 41		08 38					09 38										
154	—	Newport (South Wales) 132 a	06 41	07 06	07 52		08 50		09 13			09 51			10 11					11 11		
165¾	—	**Cardiff Central** 132 a	07 00	07 22	08 08		09 07		09 29			10 11			10 27					11 29		

	AW A	XC 1	XC ◇1 M ⌶	XC ◇1 ⌶	XC ◇1 N ⌶	XC ◇1 E ⌶	AW	XC 1	XC ◇1 O ⌶	XC ◇1 ⌶	XC ◇1 P ⌶	XC ◇1 E ⌶	XC 1	XC ◇1 Q ⌶	XC ◇1 ⌶	XC ◇1 N ⌶	XC ◇1 E ⌶	AW A	XC 1	XC ◇1 R ⌶	XC ◇1 ⌶	AW ◇ S ⌶
Nottingham 56 ⇌ d		08 39		09 07				09 41		10 07			10 41		11 07				11 41		12 07	
Beeston 56 d		08 44		09 12						10 12					11 12						12 12	
Attenborough 56 d																						
Long Eaton 56 d		08 53		09 25						10 24					11 22						12 22	
Derby 56 d		09 10	09 26	09 39	09 53			10 10	10 30	10 38	10 53		11 10	11 28	11 37	11 53			12 10	12 29	12 37	
Willington d				09 46																		
Burton-on-Trent d		09 22	09 38	09 52				10 21		10 49			11 21		11 49				12 21		12 49	
Tamworth d		09 34		10 04				10 33	10 50	11 02			11 33		12 02				12 33	12 49	13 02	
Wilnecote d		09 38						10 37					11 37						12 37			
Water Orton d																						
Birmingham New Street a		09 55	10 08	10 24	10 27			10 55	11 09	11 24	11 27		11 55	12 07	12 24	12 27			12 55	13 08	13 24	
d			10 17	10 30		10 42			11 17	11 30		11 42		12 17	12 30		12 42			13 17	13 30	
University a				10 36						11 36					12 36						13 36	
Bromsgrove a																						
Ashchurch for Tewkesbury d																						
Cheltenham Spa d	10 45		11 00	11 11		11 26	11 46		11 59	12 10		12 26		13 02	13 11		13 26	13 45		14 02	14 10	
Gloucester 134 a	10 57			11 20			11 57			12 20					13 20			13 57			14 22	
d	10 58			11 25			11 59			12 25					13 25			13 58			14 24	14 48
Bristol Parkway 134 a			11 31			11 55			12 28			12 56		13 30			13 56			14 28		
Bristol Temple Meads 134 a			11 42			12 05			12 42			13 10		13 41			14 08			14 43		
Lydney d	11 17						12 18								13 44			14 17				15 07
Chepstow d	11 27			11 51			12 28			12 51								14 27			14 51	15 17
Caldicot d	11 35						12 36											14 35				15 25
Severn Tunnel Jn 132 d	11 38						12 39											14 38				15 28
Newport (South Wales) 132 a	11 50			12 10			12 51			13 09					14 11			14 50			15 12	15 40
Cardiff Central 132 a	12 13			12 26			13 08			13 26					14 26			15 15			15 30	15 58

A To Maesteg
B To Paignton
C To Plymouth. ⌶ from Birmingham New Street
D From Sheffield to Reading
E From Manchester Piccadilly
F To Bournemouth
G From Leeds to Plymouth
H From Leeds to Southampton Central
I From York to Plymouth
J ⌶ from Birmingham New Street
K From Newcastle to Reading
L From Manchester Piccadilly to Paignton
M From Newcastle to Plymouth
N From Newcastle to Southampton Central
O From Edinburgh to Plymouth
P From Edinburgh to Reading
Q From Glasgow Central to Plymouth
R From Dundee to Plymouth
S To Fishguard Harbour

Trains between Gloucester & Cheltenham are shown on Table T058

Trains between Birmingham & Bromsgrove are shown on Table T069

Table T057-F

Mondays to Fridays

21 May to 20 July

Nottingham and Derby - Birmingham - Bristol and Cardiff

	XC ◇1 A ⌶	XC ◇1 B ⌶	XC 1	XC ◇1 C ⌶	XC ◇1 ⌶	XC ◇1 D ⌶	XC ◇1 E ⌶	XC 1 ⌶	XC ◇1 F ⌶	XC ◇1 G ⌶	XC ◇1 A ⌶	XC ◇1 H ⌶	AW I	XC 1	XC ◇1 J ⌶	XC ◇1 ⌶	XC ◇1 K ⌶	XC ◇1 E ⌶	AW I	XC 1 ⌶	XC ◇1 F ⌶	XC ◇1
Nottingham 56 ⇌ d			12 41		13 07			13 41		14 07				14 41		15 07				15 41		16 07
Beeston 56 d					13 12					14 12						15 12						16 12
Attenborough 56 d																						
Long Eaton 56 d					13 22					14 22						15 22						16 22
Derby 56 d	12 53		13 10	13 28	13 37	13 53		14 10	14 28	14 37	14 53			15 10	15 28	15 37	15 53			16 10	16 28	16 37
Willington d			13 18											15 18								
Burton-on-Trent d			13 24	13 38	13 49			14 21		14 50				15 24	15 38	15 49				16 21		16 49
Tamworth d			13 35		14 02			14 33	14 47	15 02				15 35		16 02				16 33	16 47	17 02
Wilnecote d								14 37												16 37		
Water Orton d																						
Birmingham New Street a	13 27		13 55	14 08	14 24	14 27		14 55	15 08	15 25	15 27			15 55	16 03	16 25	16 28			16 55	17 08	17 25
d		13 42		14 17	14 30		14 42		15 17	15 30		15 42			16 12	16 30		16 42			17 12	17 30
University a					14 36					15 36						16 36						17 36
Bromsgrove a																						17 50
Ashchurch for Tewkesbury d																17 05						18 08
Cheltenham Spa d		14 26		15 00	15 11		15 26		16 00	16 11		16 26	16 45		16 51	17 14		17 26	17 45		17 52	18 17
Gloucester 134 a					15 20					16 22			16 56			17 24			17 57			18 28
d					15 25					16 25			16 58			17 25			17 58			18 31
Bristol Parkway 134 a		14 56		15 29			15 56		16 30			16 56			17 25			17 56			18 28	
Bristol Temple Meads 134 a		15 10		15 41			16 11		16 43			17 10			17 40			18 07			18 42	
Lydney d										16 44			17 17			17 44			18 17			
Chepstow d					15 51					16 53			17 27						18 27			
Caldicot d													17 35						18 35			
Severn Tunnel Jn 132 d													17 38						18 38			
Newport (South Wales) 132 a					16 12					17 11			17 50			18 10			18 49			19 14
Cardiff Central 132 a					16 30					17 30			18 10			18 27			19 09			19 33

	XC ◇1 A ⌶	XC ◇1 E ⌶	AW I	XC 1 ⌶	XC ◇1 L ⌶	XC ◇1	XC ◇1 A ⌶	XC ◇1 M ⌶	AW I	XC 1 ⌶	XC ◇1 C ⌶	XC ◇1	XC ◇1 A ⌶	XC ◇1 N ⌶	XC 1 ⌶	XC ◇1 O ⌶	XC FX ◇1	XC FO ◇1	XC ◇1 D ⌶	XC ◇1 E	XC 1 ⌶	XC ◇1 P ⌶
Nottingham 56 ⇌ d				16 41		17 07				17 41		18 07			18 41		19 07	19 07			19 36	
Beeston 56 d						17 12						18 12					19 12	19 12			19 42	
Attenborough 56 d																					19 45	
Long Eaton 56 d						17 22						18 21					19 21	19 21			19 54	
Derby 56 d	16 53			17 10	17 29	17 37	17 53			18 13	18 29	18 37	18 53		19 08	19 30	19 37	19 37	19 54		20 10	20 29
Willington d				17 18						18 21												
Burton-on-Trent d				17 24	17 39	17 49				18 27		18 49			19 21	19 41	19 49	19 49			20 21	
Tamworth d				17 35		18 02				18 38	18 49	19 02			19 33		20 03	20 03			20 33	20 47
Wilnecote d						18 06									19 37						20 37	
Water Orton d																						
Birmingham New Street a	17 28			17 55	18 04	18 23	18 28			18 57	19 08	19 24	19 27		19 55	20 07	20 25	20 25	20 28		20 55	21 07
d		17 42			18 12	18 30		18 42			19 12	19 30		19 42		20 12	20 30	20 30		20 42		21 12
University a						18 36						19 36					20 36	20 36				
Bromsgrove a						18 50																
Ashchurch for Tewkesbury d																						
Cheltenham Spa d		18 25	18 45		18 52	19 13		19 25	19 45		19 52	20 12		20 26		20 54	21 11	21 11		21 26		21 52
Gloucester 134 a			18 58		19 01	19 23			19 56			20 20					21 19	21 19				22 02
d			19 00		19 06	19 25			19 58			20 25					21 21	21 21				22 06
Bristol Parkway 134 a		18 54			19 31			19 56			20 30			20 55		21 25				22 01		22 33
Bristol Temple Meads 134 a		19 06			19 43			20 09			20 42			21 05		21 36				22 14		22 43
Lydney d			19 20						20 17								21 40	21 40				
Chepstow d			19 29						20 27								21 50	21 50				
Caldicot d			19 37						20 35								21 58	21 58				
Severn Tunnel Jn 132 d			19 40					20 37	20 38								22 01	22 01				
Newport (South Wales) 132 a			19 53			20 11		20 47	20 50			21 11					22 12	22 13				
Cardiff Central 132 a			20 12			20 28		21 03	21 10			21 28					22 35	22 30				

A From Newcastle to Reading
B From Manchester Piccadilly to Exeter St Davids
C From Glasgow Central to Plymouth
D From Newcastle to Southampton Central
E From Manchester Piccadilly
F From Glasgow Central to Penzance
G To Nottingham
H From Manchester Piccadilly to Paignton
I To Maesteg
J From Aberdeen to Penzance
K From Newcastle to Guildford
L From Edinburgh to Plymouth
M From Manchester Piccadilly. ⌶ to Bristol Temple Meads
N From Manchester Piccadilly to Plymouth
O From Edinburgh to Plymouth. ⌶ to Birmingham New Street
P From Glasgow Central. ⌶ to Birmingham New Street

Trains between Gloucester & Cheltenham are shown on Table T058

Trains between Birmingham & Bromsgrove are shown on Table T069

21 May to 20 July

Nottingham and Derby - Birmingham - Bristol and Cardiff

	XC ◇■ A 🍴	XC ■	XC ◇■ B	AW FX	XC ◇■ A 🍴	AW FO	LM FO	XC ■	XC ◇■ C
Nottingham ■ 56 ⇌ d		20 40						21 39	
Beeston 56 d		20 45						21 44	
Attenborough 56 d								21 48	
Long Eaton 56 d		20 55						21 56	
Derby ■ 56 d	20 54	21 10	21 28		22 02			22 12	22 45
Willington d		21 18							
Burton-on-Trent d		21 24	21 40					22 23	22 56
Tamworth d		21 34	21 50					22 35	23 07
Wilnecote d		21 38						22 38	
Water Orton d									
Birmingham New Street ■ a	21 29	21 57	22 09		22 51			23 01	23 26
d			22 12				23 00		
University a							23 05		
Bromsgrove a							23 20		
Ashchurch for Tewkesbury d							23 59		
Cheltenham Spa ■ d			22 52	23 00		23 00	00 08		
Gloucester ■ 134 a				23 11		23 11	00 19		
d				23 13		23 13			
Bristol Parkway ■ 134 a			23 21						
Bristol Temple Meads ■ 134 a			23 41						
Lydney d				23 33		23 33			
Chepstow d				23 42		23 42			
Caldicot d				23 51		23 51			
Severn Tunnel Jn 132 d				23 54		23 54			
Newport (South Wales) 132 a				00 05		00 06			
Cardiff Central ■ 132 a				00 34		00 26			

23 July to 31 August

	AW D	XC ◇■	XC ◇■	XC ◇■ E 🍴	AW D	XC ◇■ F 🍴	XC ◇■ 🍴	XC ◇■ G	XC ◇■ H 🍴	AW D	XC ◇■ I	XC ◇■ J 🍴	XC ◇■	EM K	XC ◇■ L 🍴	XC ◇■ H 🍴	XC ■	XC ◇■ J 🍴	XC ◇■ M 🍴	EM K	XC ■ ■ N 🍴	XC ◇■ O 🍴
Nottingham ■ 56 ⇌ d							06 00				06 37		07 04	07 20			07 37		08 12	08 20		
Beeston 56 d							06 06				06 43		07 09	07 25			07 42			08 25		
Attenborough 56 d							06 09						07 13	07 29						08 29		
Long Eaton 56 d														07a38						08a40		
Derby ■ 56 d																						
Willington d													07 44									
Burton-on-Trent d						06 20	06 48	06 58			07 19	07 38	07 50		08 00		08 18	08 38	08 49		09 01	
Tamworth d						06 31	07 01	07 09			07 30	07 50	08 03		08 11		08 30	08 50	09 02			
Wilnecote d							07 05						08 07				08 34					
Water Orton d																	08 42					
Birmingham New Street ■ a						06 52	07 25	07 27			07 53	08 08	08 25		08 27		08 55	09 10	09 24		09 27	
d		05 00	05 37	06 42		07 12	07 30		07 42			08 12	08 30			08 42		09 17	09 30			09 42
University a							07 36						08 36						09 36			
Bromsgrove a																						
Ashchurch for Tewkesbury d			06 27																			
Cheltenham Spa ■ d	05 37	06 02	06 43	07 23	07 46	07 52	08 11		08 25	08 46		08 52	09 11			09 26		10 00	10 10			10 26
Gloucester ■ 134 a	05 48	06 12	06 53		07 57		08 20			08 58			09 20						10 20			
d	05 50	06 14	07 01		07 58		08 25			08 58			09 25						10 25			
Bristol Parkway ■ 134 a				07 54		08 26			08 54			09 25				09 55		10 30				10 56
Bristol Temple Meads ■ 134 a				08 06		08 40			09 11			09 39				10 08		10 43				11 10
Lydney d	06 09	06 33	07 20		08 17					09 17									10 44			
Chepstow d	06 19	06 42	07 29		08 27		08 51			09 27			09 51									
Caldicot d	06 26	06 51	07 38		08 35					09 35												
Severn Tunnel Jn 132 d	06 29	06 55	07 41		08 38					09 38												
Newport (South Wales) 132 a	06 41	07 06	07 52		08 50		09 13			09 51			10 11						11 11			
Cardiff Central ■ 132 a	07 00	07 22	08 08		09 07		09 29			10 11			10 27						11 28			

A From Newcastle
B From Edinburgh
C From Glasgow Central
D To Maesteg
E To Paignton
F To Plymouth. 🍴 from Birmingham New Street
G From Sheffield to Reading
H From Manchester Piccadilly
I To Bournemouth
J From Leeds to Plymouth
K from 30 July until 10 August. From Newark Castle
L To Southampton Central
M 🍴 from Birmingham New Street
N From York to Reading
O From Manchester Piccadilly to Paignton

Trains between Gloucester & Cheltenham are shown on Table T058

Trains between Birmingham & Bromsgrove are shown on Table T069

23 July to 31 August

Nottingham and Derby - Birmingham - Bristol and Cardiff

	AW A	XC ■	XC ◇■ B 🍴	XC ◇■ 🍴	EM C	XC ◇■ D 🍴	XC ◇■ E 🍴	AW	XC ■	XC ◇■ B 🍴	XC ◇■ 🍴	EM C	XC ◇■ F 🍴	XC ◇■ E 🍴	XC ■	XC ◇■ G 🍴	XC ◇■ 🍴	EM C	XC ◇■ H 🍴	XC ◇■ E 🍴	AW A
Nottingham ■ 56 ⇌ d		08 41		09 07	09 20				09 41		10 07	10 20			10 41		11 07	11 20			
Beeston 56 d				09 12	09 25						10 12	10 25					11 12	11 25			
Attenborough 56 d					09 29							10 29						11 29			
Long Eaton 56 d					09a40							10a40						11a38			
Derby ■ 56 d																					
Willington d				09 44																	
Burton-on-Trent d		09 22	09 38	09 50		10 01			10 21	10 39	10 49		11 00		11 21	11 36	11 49		12 02		
Tamworth d		09 34		10 02					10 33	10 50	11 02				11 33		12 02				
Wilnecote d		09 38							10 37						11 37						
Water Orton d																					
Birmingham New Street ■ a		09 55	10 08	10 24		10 27			10 55	11 08	11 24		11 27		11 55	12 09	12 24		12 27		
d			10 17	10 30			10 42			11 17	11 30			11 42		12 17	12 30			12 42	
University a				10 36							11 36						12 36				
Bromsgrove a																					
Ashchurch for Tewkesbury d																					
Cheltenham Spa ■ d	10 45		11 00	11 11			11 26	11 46		12 00	12 10			12 26		13 02	13 11			13 26	13 45
Gloucester ■ 134 a	10 57			11 20				11 57			12 20						13 20				13 57
d	10 58			11 25				11 59			12 25						13 25				13 58
Bristol Parkway ■ 134 a			11 31				11 55			12 28				12 56		13 30				13 56	
Bristol Temple Meads ■ 134 a			11 42				12 05			12 42				13 10		13 42				14 08	
Lydney d	11 17							12 18									13 44				14 17
Chepstow d	11 27			11 51				12 28			12 51										14 27
Caldicot d	11 35							12 36													14 35
Severn Tunnel Jn 132 d	11 38							12 39													14 38
Newport (South Wales) 132 a	11 50			12 10				12 51			13 09						14 11				14 50
Cardiff Central ■ 132 a	12 13			12 26				13 08			13 26						14 26				15 15

	XC ■	XC ◇■ B 🍴	XC ◇■ 🍴	AW ◇ I 🍴	EM C	XC ◇■ J 🍴	XC ◇■ K 🍴	XC ■	XC ◇■ B 🍴	XC ◇■ 🍴	EM C	XC ◇■ H 🍴	XC ◇■ E 🍴	XC ■ 🍴	XC ◇■ L 🍴	XC ◇■ M 🍴	EM C	XC ◇■ N 🍴	XC ◇■ O 🍴	AW A	XC ■	XC ◇■ L 🍴
Nottingham ■ 56 ⇌ d	11 41		12 07		12 20			12 41		13 07	13 20			13 41		14 07	14 20				14 41	
Beeston 56 d			12 12		12 25					13 12	13 25					14 12	14 25					
Attenborough 56 d					12 29						13 29						14 29					
Long Eaton 56 d					12a40						13a40						14a40					
Derby ■ 56 d																						
Willington d								13 18													15 18	
Burton-on-Trent d	12 21	12 38	12 49			13 01		13 24	13 38	13 49		14 02		14 21	14 36	14 50		15 01			15 24	15 38
Tamworth d	12 33	12 49	13 02					13 35		14 02				14 33	14 47	15 02					15 35	
Wilnecote d	12 37													14 37								
Water Orton d																						
Birmingham New Street ■ a	12 55	13 08	13 24			13 27		13 55	14 08	14 24		14 27		14 55	15 08	15 25		15 27			15 54	16 03
d		13 17	13 30				13 42		14 17	14 30			14 42		15 17	15 30			15 42			16 12
University a			13 36							14 36						15 36						
Bromsgrove a																						
Ashchurch for Tewkesbury d																						
Cheltenham Spa ■ d		14 02	14 10				14 26		15 00	15 11			15 26		16 00	16 11			16 26	16 45		16 51
Gloucester ■ 134 a			14 22							15 20						16 22				16 56		
d			14 24	14 48						15 25						16 25				16 58		
Bristol Parkway ■ 134 a		14 28					14 56		15 29				15 56		16 30				16 56			17 25
Bristol Temple Meads ■ 134 a		14 42					15 10		15 41				16 11		16 43				17 10			17 40
Lydney d				15 07												16 44				17 17		
Chepstow d			14 51	15 17						15 51						16 53				17 27		
Caldicot d				15 25																17 35		
Severn Tunnel Jn 132 d				15 28																17 38		
Newport (South Wales) 132 a			15 12	15 40						16 12						17 11				17 50		
Cardiff Central ■ 132 a			15 30	15 58						16 30						17 30				18 10		

A To Maesteg
B From Newcastle to Plymouth
C from 30 July until 10 August. From Newark Castle
D From Newcastle to Southampton Central
E From Manchester Piccadilly
F From Edinburgh to Reading
G From Edinburgh to Plymouth
H From Glasgow Central to Southampton Central
I To Fishguard Harbour
J From Dundee to Reading
K From Manchester Piccadilly to Exeter St Davids
L From Newcastle to Penzance
M To Nottingham
N From Glasgow Central to Reading
O From Manchester Piccadilly to Paignton

Trains between Gloucester & Cheltenham are shown on Table T058

Trains between Birmingham & Bromsgrove are shown on Table T069

Table T057-F

Mondays to Fridays

23 July to 31 August

Nottingham and Derby - Birmingham - Bristol and Cardiff

	XC	EM	XC	XC	AW	XC	XC	XC	EM		XC	XC	AW	XC	XC	XC	EM	XC	XC		AW	XC	XC	XC
	◇1		◇1	◇1		1	◇1	◇1			◇1	◇1		1	◇1	◇1		◇1	◇1			1	◇1	◇1
		A	B	C	D		E		A		F	C	D		G		A	H	I		D		G	
	✠		✠	✠		✠	✠				✠	✠		✠	✠			✠	✠			✠	✠	
Nottingham 8 56 ⇌ d	15 07	15 20				15 41		16 07	16 20					16 41		17 07	17 20					17 41		18 07
Beeston 56 d	15 12	15 25						16 12	16 25							17 12	17 25							18 12
Attenborough 56 d		15 29							16 29								17 29							
Long Eaton 56 d		15a40							16a40								17a40							
Derby 6 56 d																								
Willington d														17 18								18 21		
Burton-on-Trent d	15 49		16 01			16 21	16 36	16 49			17 01			17 24	17 39	17 49		18 01				18 27	18 37	18 49
Tamworth d	16 02					16 33	16 47	17 02						17 35		18 02						18 38	18 49	19 02
Wilnecote d						16 37										18 06								
Water Orton d																								
Birmingham New Street 12 a	16 25		16 28			16 55	17 08	17 25			17 28			17 55	18 05	18 23		18 27				18 57	19 08	19 24
d	16 30			16 42			17 12	17 30				17 42			18 12	18 30			18 42				19 12	19 30
University a	16 36							17 36								18 36								19 36
Bromsgrove a								17 50								18 50								
Ashchurch for Tewkesbury d	17 05							18 08																
Cheltenham Spa 4 d	17 14			17 26	17 45		17 52	18 17				18 25	18 45		18 52	19 13			19 25		19 45		19 52	20 12
Gloucester 7 134 a	17 23				17 57			18 28					18 58		19 01	19 23					19 56			20 20
d	17 25				17 58			18 31					19 00		19 06	19 25					19 58			20 25
Bristol Parkway 7 134 a				17 56			18 28					18 54			19 31				19 56				20 30	
Bristol Temple Meads 10 134 a				18 07			18 42					19 06			19 43				20 09				20 42	
Lydney d	17 44				18 17								19 20								20 17			
Chepstow d					18 27								19 29								20 27			
Caldicot d					18 35								19 37								20 35			
Severn Tunnel Jn 132 d					18 38								19 40						20 37		20 38			
Newport (South Wales) 132 a	18 10				18 49			19 14					19 53			20 11			20 47		20 50			21 11
Cardiff Central 7 132 a	18 27				19 09			19 33					20 12			20 28			21 03		21 10			21 28

	EM	XC	XC	XC	XC		XC FX	XC FO	EM	XC	XC	XC	EM	XC	XC		XC	EM	XC	AW FX	XC FO	XC FX	XC	AW FO
		◇1	◇1	1	◇1		◇1	◇1		◇1	◇1	1		◇1	◇1		1		◇1		◇1	◇1	◇1	
	A	F	J		K				L	M	C		A	N	O			L	P		Q	Q	P	
		✠	✠	✠	✠					✠		✠		✠	✠				✠				✠	
Nottingham 8 56 ⇌ d	18 20			18 41			19 07	19 07	19 20			19 36	20 20				20 40	21 20						
Beeston 56 d	18 25						19 12	19 12	19 25			19 42	20 25				20 45	21 25						
Attenborough 56 d	18 29								19 29			19 45	20 29					21 29						
Long Eaton 56 d	18a38								19a38				20a40					21a39						
Derby 6 56 d																								
Willington d																	21 18							
Burton-on-Trent d		19 01		19 21	19 41		19 49	19 49		20 06		20 21		20 37	21 05		21 24		21 40		22 09	22 10	22 31	
Tamworth d				19 33			20 03	20 03				20 33		20 47			21 34		21 50					
Wilnecote d				19 37								20 37					21 38							
Water Orton d																								
Birmingham New Street 12 a		19 27		19 55	20 07		20 25	20 25		20 28		20 55		21 07	21 29		21 57		22 09		22 36	22 48	22 55	
d			19 42		20 12		20 30	20 30			20 42			21 12					22 12					
University a							20 36	20 36																
Bromsgrove a																								
Ashchurch for Tewkesbury d																								
Cheltenham Spa 4 d			20 26		20 54		21 11	21 11			21 26			21 52					22 52	23 00				23 00
Gloucester 7 134 a							21 19	21 19						22 02						23 11				23 11
d							21 21	21 21						22 06						23 13				23 13
Bristol Parkway 7 134 a			20 55		21 25						22 01			22 33					23 21					
Bristol Temple Meads 10 134 a			21 05		21 36						22 14			22 43					23 41					
Lydney d							21 40	21 40												23 33				23 33
Chepstow d							21 50	21 50												23 42				23 42
Caldicot d							21 58	21 58												23 51				23 51
Severn Tunnel Jn 132 d							22 01	22 01												23 54				23 54
Newport (South Wales) 132 a							22 12	22 13												00 05				00 06
Cardiff Central 7 132 a							22 35	22 30												00 34				00 26

A from 30 July until 10 August. From Newark Castle
B From Aberdeen to Guildford
C From Manchester Piccadilly
D To Maesteg
E From Newcastle to Penzance
F From Glasgow Central to Reading
G From Newcastle to Plymouth
H From Edinburgh to Reading
I From Manchester Piccadilly. ✠ to Bristol Temple Meads
J From Manchester Piccadilly to Plymouth
K From Newcastle to Plymouth. ✠ to Birmingham New Street
L from 30 July until 10 August
M From Edinburgh to Southampton Central
N From Newcastle. ✠ to Birmingham New Street
O From Glasgow Central
P From Newcastle
Q From Edinburgh

Trains between Gloucester & Cheltenham are shown on Table T058

Trains between Birmingham & Bromsgrove are shown on Table T069

Table T057-F

Mondays to Fridays

23 July to 31 August

Nottingham and Derby - Birmingham - Bristol and Cardiff

	LM FO	XC	EM	XC
		1		◇1
			A	B
Nottingham 8 56 ⇌ d		21 39	22 18	
Beeston 56 d		21 44	22 25	
Attenborough 56 d		21 48	22 29	
Long Eaton 56 d			22a38	
Derby 6 56 d				
Willington d				
Burton-on-Trent d		22 23		23 24
Tamworth d		22 35		23 35
Wilnecote d		22 38		
Water Orton d				
Birmingham New Street 12 a		23 01		23 50
d	23 00			
University a	23 05			
Bromsgrove a	23 20			
Ashchurch for Tewkesbury d	23 59			
Cheltenham Spa 4 d	00 08			
Gloucester 7 134 a	00 19			
d				
Bristol Parkway 7 134 a				
Bristol Temple Meads 10 134 a				
Lydney d				
Chepstow d				
Caldicot d				
Severn Tunnel Jn 132 d				
Newport (South Wales) 132 a				
Cardiff Central 7 132 a				

Mondays to Fridays

3 September to 5 October

	AW	XC	XC	XC	AW	XC	XC	XC	XC		AW	XC	XC	XC	XC	XC	XC	XC	XC		XC	XC	AW	XC
		◇1	◇1	◇1		◇1	◇1	◇1	◇1			◇1	◇1	◇1	◇1	◇1	1	◇1	◇1		1	◇1		1
	C			D	C	E		F	G		C	H	I		J	G		I	K		L	M	C	
				✠		✠	✠		✠				✠		✠	✠		✠	✠		✠	✠		
Nottingham 8 56 ⇌ d							05 57					06 37		07 04			07 37		08 09					08 41
Beeston 56 d							06 03					06 43		07 09			07 42		08 14					08 46
Attenborough 56 d							06 06							07 13										
Long Eaton 56 d							06 18							07 23			07 52							08 55
Derby 6 56 d						06 10	06 36	06 44				07 07	07 27	07 36	07 50		08 06	08 28	08 37		08 53			09 11
Willington d														07 44										
Burton-on-Trent d						06 20	06 48	06 58				07 17	07 38	07 50	08 00		08 18	08 38	08 49					09 22
Tamworth d						06 31	07 01	07 09				07 30	07 50	08 03	08 11		08 30	08 50	09 02					09 34
Wilnecote d							07 05							08 07			08 34							09 38
Water Orton d																	08 42							
Birmingham New Street 12 a						06 52	07 25	07 27				07 53	08 08	08 25	08 27		08 55	09 10	09 24		09 27			09 55
d		05 00	05 37	06 42		07 12	07 30		07 42				08 12	08 30		08 42		09 17	09 30			09 42		
University a							07 36							08 36					09 36					
Bromsgrove a																								
Ashchurch for Tewkesbury d			06 27																					
Cheltenham Spa 4 d	05 37	06 02	06 43	07 23	07 46	07 52	08 11		08 25		08 46		08 52	09 11		09 26		10 00	10 10			10 26	10 45	
Gloucester 7 134 a	05 48	06 12	06 53		07 57		08 20				08 58			09 20					10 20				10 57	
d	05 50	06 14	07 01		07 58		08 25				08 58			09 25					10 25				10 58	
Bristol Parkway 7 134 a				07 54		08 26			08 54				09 25			09 55		10 30				10 56		
Bristol Temple Meads 10 134 a				08 06		08 40			09 11				09 39			10 08		10 43				11 10		
Lydney d	06 09	06 33	07 20		08 17						09 17								10 44				11 17	
Chepstow d	06 19	06 42	07 29		08 27		08 51				09 27			09 51									11 27	
Caldicot d	06 26	06 51	07 38		08 35						09 35												11 35	
Severn Tunnel Jn 132 d	06 29	06 55	07 41		08 38						09 38												11 38	
Newport (South Wales) 132 a	06 41	07 06	07 52		08 50		09 13				09 51			10 11					11 11				11 50	
Cardiff Central 7 132 a	07 00	07 22	08 08		09 07		09 29				10 11			10 27					11 28				12 13	

A from 30 July until 10 August
B From Glasgow Central
C To Maesteg
D To Paignton
E To Plymouth. ✠ from Birmingham New Street
F From Sheffield to Reading
G From Manchester Piccadilly
H To Bournemouth
I From Leeds to Plymouth
J To Southampton Central
K ✠ from Birmingham New Street
L From York to Reading
M From Manchester Piccadilly to Paignton

Trains between Gloucester & Cheltenham are shown on Table T058

Trains between Birmingham & Bromsgrove are shown on Table T069

Table T057-F

Mondays to Fridays

3 September to 5 October

Nottingham and Derby - Birmingham - Bristol and Cardiff

Station		XC ◇1 A ✠	XC ◇1 ✠	XC ◇1 B ✠	XC ◇1 C ✠	AW	XC 1	XC ◇1 A ✠	XC ◇1 ✠	XC ◇1 D ✠	XC ◇1 C ✠	XC 1	XC ◇1 E ✠	XC ◇1 ✠	XC ◇1 F ✠	XC ◇1 C ✠	AW G	XC 1	XC ◇1 A ✠	XC ◇1 ✠	AW ◇ H ✠	XC ◇1 I ✠
Nottingham 8 56	d		09 07				09 41		10 04			10 41		11 04				11 41		12 04		
Beeston 56	d		09 12						10 09					11 09						12 09		
Attenborough 56	d																					
Long Eaton 56	d		09 22						10 23					11 22						12 22		
Derby 6 56	d	09 27	09 39	09 51			10 10	10 28	10 37	10 53		11 10	11 29	11 37	11 53			12 10	12 29	12 37		12 53
Willington	d		09 46																			
Burton-on-Trent	d	09 38	09 52				10 21		10 49			11 21		11 49				12 21		12 49		
Tamworth	d		10 03				10 33	10 50	11 02			11 33		12 02				12 33	12 49	13 02		
Wilnecote	d						10 37					11 37						12 37				
Water Orton	d																					
Birmingham New Street 12	a	10 08	10 24	10 27			10 55	11 08	11 24	11 27		11 55	12 07	12 24	12 27			12 55	13 08	13 24		13 27
	d	10 17	10 30		10 42			11 17	11 30		11 42		12 17	12 30		12 42			13 17	13 30		
University	a		10 36						11 36					12 36						13 36		
Bromsgrove	a																					
Ashchurch for Tewkesbury	d																					
Cheltenham Spa 4	d	11 00	11 11		11 26	11 46		12 00	12 10		12 26		13 02	13 11		13 26	13 45		14 02	14 10		
Gloucester 7 134	a		11 20			11 57			12 20					13 20			13 57			14 22		
	d		11 25			11 59			12 25					13 25			13 58			14 24	14 48	
Bristol Parkway 7 134	a	11 31			11 55			12 28			12 56		13 30			13 56			14 28			
Bristol Temple Meads 10 134	a	11 42			12 05			12 42			13 10		13 42			14 08			14 42			
Lydney	d					12 18								13 44			14 17				15 07	
Chepstow	d		11 51			12 28			12 51								14 27			14 51	15 17	
Caldicot	d					12 36											14 35				15 25	
Severn Tunnel Jn 132	d					12 39											14 38				15 28	
Newport (South Wales) 132	a		12 10			12 51			13 09					14 11			14 50			15 12	15 40	
Cardiff Central 7 132	a		12 26			13 08			13 26					14 26			15 15			15 30	15 58	

Station		XC ◇1 J ✠	XC 1	XC ◇1 A ✠	XC ◇1 ✠	XC ◇1 F ✠	XC ◇1 C ✠	XC 1 ✠	XC ◇1 K ✠	XC ◇1 L ✠	XC ◇1 M ✠	XC ◇1 N ✠	AW G	XC 1	XC ◇1 K ✠	XC ◇1 ✠	XC ◇1 O ✠	XC ◇1 C ✠	AW G	XC 1 ✠	XC ◇1 K ✠	XC ◇1	XC ◇1 M ✠
Nottingham 8 56	d		12 41		13 04			13 41		14 04				14 41		15 04				15 41		16 04	
Beeston 56	d				13 09					14 09						15 09						16 09	
Attenborough 56	d																						
Long Eaton 56	d				13 22					14 22						15 22						16 22	
Derby 6 56	d		13 10	13 28	13 36	13 52		14 10	14 28	14 37	14 53			15 10	15 27	15 37	15 53			16 10	16 28	16 37	16 53
Willington	d		13 18											15 18									
Burton-on-Trent	d		13 24	13 38	13 49			14 21		14 50				15 24	15 38	15 49				16 21		16 49	
Tamworth	d		13 35		14 02			14 33	14 47	15 02				15 35		16 02				16 33	16 47	17 02	
Wilnecote	d							14 37												16 37			
Water Orton	d																						
Birmingham New Street 12	a		13 55	14 08	14 24	14 27		14 55	15 08	15 25	15 27			15 54	16 03	16 25	16 28			16 55	17 08	17 25	17 28
	d	13 42		14 17	14 30		14 42		15 17	15 30		15 42			16 12	16 30		16 42			17 12	17 30	
University	a				14 36					15 36						16 36						17 36	
Bromsgrove	a																					17 50	
Ashchurch for Tewkesbury	d															17 05						18 08	
Cheltenham Spa 4	d	14 26		15 00	15 11		15 26		16 00	16 11		16 26	16 45		16 51	17 14		17 26	17 45		17 52	18 17	
Gloucester 7 134	a				15 20					16 22			16 56			17 24			17 57			18 28	
	d				15 25					16 25			16 58			17 25			17 58			18 31	
Bristol Parkway 7 134	a	14 56		15 29			15 56		16 30			16 56			17 25			17 56			18 28		
Bristol Temple Meads 10 134	a	15 10		15 41			16 11		16 43			17 10			17 40			18 07			18 42		
Lydney	d									16 44			17 17			17 44			18 17				
Chepstow	d				15 51					16 53			17 27						18 27				
Caldicot	d												17 35						18 35				
Severn Tunnel Jn 132	d												17 38						18 38				
Newport (South Wales) 132	a				16 12					17 11			17 50			18 10			18 49			19 14	
Cardiff Central 7 132	a				16 30					17 30			18 10			18 27			19 09			19 33	

A From Newcastle to Plymouth
B From Newcastle to Southampton Central
C From Manchester Piccadilly
D From Edinburgh to Reading
E From Edinburgh to Plymouth
F From Glasgow Central to Southampton Central
G To Maesteg
H To Fishguard Harbour
I From Dundee to Reading
J From Manchester Piccadilly to Exeter St Davids
K From Newcastle to Penzance
L To Nottingham
M From Glasgow Central to Reading
N From Manchester Piccadilly to Paignton
O From Aberdeen to Guildford

Trains between Gloucester & Cheltenham are shown on Table T058

Trains between Birmingham & Bromsgrove are shown on Table T069

Table T057-F

Mondays to Fridays

3 September to 5 October

Nottingham and Derby - Birmingham - Bristol and Cardiff

Station		XC ◇1 A ✠	AW B	XC 1 ✠	XC ◇1 C ✠	XC ◇1	XC ◇1 D ✠	XC ◇1 E ✠	AW B	XC 1 ✠	XC ◇1 C ✠	XC ◇1	XC ◇1 F ✠	XC ◇1 G ✠	XC 1 ✠	XC ◇1 H ✠	XC FX ◇1	XC FO ◇1	XC ◇1 I ✠	XC ◇1 A	XC 1 ✠	XC ◇1 J ✠	XC ◇1 K ✠
Nottingham 8 56	d			16 41		17 04				17 41		18 04			18 41		19 04	19 04			19 36		
Beeston 56	d					17 09						18 09					19 09	19 09			19 42		
Attenborough 56	d																				19 45		
Long Eaton 56	d					17 22						18 21					19 22	19 22			19 57		
Derby 6 56	d			17 10	17 29	17 37	17 52			18 13	18 29	18 37	18 53		19 10	19 29	19 37	19 37	19 54		20 10	20 29	20 55
Willington	d			17 18						18 21													
Burton-on-Trent	d			17 24	17 39	17 49				18 27		18 49			19 21	19 41	19 49	19 49			20 21		
Tamworth	d			17 35		18 02				18 38	18 49	19 02			19 33		20 03	20 03			20 33	20 47	
Wilnecote	d					18 06									19 37						20 37		
Water Orton	d																						
Birmingham New Street 12	a			17 55	18 05	18 23	18 27			18 57	19 08	19 24	19 27		19 55	20 07	20 25	20 25	20 28		20 55	21 07	21 29
	d	17 42			18 12	18 30		18 42			19 12	19 30		19 42		20 12	20 30	20 30		20 42		21 12	
University	a					18 36						19 36					20 36	20 36					
Bromsgrove	a					18 50																	
Ashchurch for Tewkesbury	d																						
Cheltenham Spa 4	d	18 25	18 45		18 52	19 13		19 25	19 45		19 52	20 12		20 26		20 54	21 11	21 11		21 26		21 52	
Gloucester 7 134	a		18 58		19 01	19 23			19 56			20 20					21 19	21 19				22 02	
	d		19 00		19 06	19 25			19 58			20 25					21 21	21 21				22 06	
Bristol Parkway 7 134	a	18 54			19 31			19 56			20 30			20 55		21 25				22 01		22 33	
Bristol Temple Meads 10 134	a	19 06			19 43			20 09			20 42			21 05		21 36				22 14		22 43	
Lydney	d		19 20						20 17								21 40	21 40					
Chepstow	d		19 29						20 27								21 50	21 50					
Caldicot	d		19 37						20 35								21 58	21 58					
Severn Tunnel Jn 132	d		19 40					20 37	20 38								22 01	22 01					
Newport (South Wales) 132	a		19 53			20 11		20 47	20 50			21 11					22 12	22 13					
Cardiff Central 7 132	a		20 12			20 28		21 03	21 10			21 28					22 35	22 30					

Station		XC 1	XC ◇1 L ✠	AW FX	XC FO ◇1 M	XC FX ◇1 M	XC 1	XC ◇1 L ✠	AW FO	LM FO	XC ◇1 K
Nottingham 8 56	d	20 40					21 39				
Beeston 56	d	20 45					21 44				
Attenborough 56	d						21 48				
Long Eaton 56	d	20 55					21 56				
Derby 6 56	d	21 10	21 29		22 02	22 02	22 12	22 23			23 14
Willington	d	21 18									
Burton-on-Trent	d	21 24	21 40				22 23				23 24
Tamworth	d	21 34	21 50				22 35				23 35
Wilnecote	d	21 38					22 38				
Water Orton	d										
Birmingham New Street 12	a	21 57	22 09		22 36	22 48	23 01	22 55			23 50
	d		22 12							23 00	
University	a									23 05	
Bromsgrove	a									23 20	
Ashchurch for Tewkesbury	d									23 59	
Cheltenham Spa 4	d		22 52	23 00					23 00	00 08	
Gloucester 7 134	a			23 11					23 11	00 19	
	d			23 13					23 13		
Bristol Parkway 7 134	a		23 21								
Bristol Temple Meads 10 134	a		23 41								
Lydney	d			23 33					23 33		
Chepstow	d			23 42					23 42		
Caldicot	d			23 51					23 51		
Severn Tunnel Jn 132	d			23 54					23 54		
Newport (South Wales) 132	a			00 05					00 06		
Cardiff Central 7 132	a			00 34					00 26		

A From Manchester Piccadilly
B To Maesteg
C From Newcastle to Plymouth
D From Edinburgh to Reading
E From Manchester Piccadilly. ✠ to Bristol Temple Meads
F From Glasgow Central to Reading
G From Manchester Piccadilly to Plymouth
H From Newcastle to Plymouth. ✠ to Birmingham New Street
I From Edinburgh to Southampton Central
J From Newcastle. ✠ to Birmingham New Street
K From Glasgow Central
L From Newcastle
M From Edinburgh

Trains between Gloucester & Cheltenham are shown on Table T058

Trains between Birmingham & Bromsgrove are shown on Table T069

Table T057-F

Mondays to Fridays

8 October to 7 December

Nottingham and Derby - Birmingham - Bristol and Cardiff

	AW A	XC ◇1	XC ◇1	XC ◇1 B ⌶	AW A	XC ◇1 C ⌶	XC ◇1 ⌶	XC ◇1 D	XC ◇1 E ⌶	AW A	XC ◇1 F	XC ◇1 G ⌶	XC ◇1	XC ◇1 H ⌶	XC ◇1 E ⌶	XC 1	XC ◇1 I ⌶	XC ◇1 J ⌶	XC 1 K ⌶	XC ◇1 L ⌶	AW A	XC 1
Nottingham 56 d							06 00				06 37		07 04			07 37		08 09				08 40
Beeston 56 d							06 06				06 43		07 09			07 42		08 15				08 45
Attenborough 56 d							06 09						07 13									
Long Eaton 56 d							06 18						07 21			07 52		08 23				08 54
Derby 56 d						06 10	06 36	06 48			07 06	07 27	07 36	07 50		08 06	08 28	08 38	08 53			09 11
Willington d													07 44									
Burton-on-Trent d						06 20	06 48	06 58			07 17	07 38	07 50	08 00		08 18	08 38	08 50				09 22
Tamworth d						06 31	07 01	07 09			07 30	07 50	08 03	08 11		08 30	08 50	09 03				09 34
Wilnecote d							07 05						08 07			08 34						09 38
Water Orton d																08 42						
Birmingham New Street a						06 52	07 25	07 27			07 53	08 08	08 25	08 27		08 55	09 10	09 24	09 27			09 55
d		05 00	05 37	06 42		07 12	07 30		07 42			08 12	08 30		08 42		09 17	09 30		09 42		
University a							07 36						08 36					09 36				
Bromsgrove a																						
Ashchurch for Tewkesbury d			06 27																			
Cheltenham Spa d	05 37	06 02	06 43	07 23	07 46	07 52	08 11		08 25	08 46		08 52	09 11		09 26		10 00	10 10		10 26	10 45	
Gloucester 134 a	05 48	06 12	06 53		07 57		08 20			08 58			09 20					10 20			10 57	
d	05 50	06 14	07 01		07 58		08 25			08 58			09 25					10 25			10 58	
Bristol Parkway 134 a				07 54		08 26			08 54			09 25			09 55		10 30			10 56		
Bristol Temple Meads 134 a				08 06		08 40			09 11			09 39			10 08		10 43			11 10		
Lydney d	06 09	06 33	07 20		08 17					09 17								10 44			11 17	
Chepstow d	06 19	06 42	07 29		08 27		08 51			09 27			09 51								11 27	
Caldicot d	06 26	06 51	07 38		08 35					09 35											11 35	
Severn Tunnel Jn 132 d	06 29	06 55	07 41		08 38					09 38											11 38	
Newport (South Wales) 132 a	06 41	07 06	07 52		08 50		09 13			09 51			10 11					11 11			11 50	
Cardiff Central 132 a	07 00	07 22	08 08		09 07		09 29			10 11			10 27					11 28			12 13	

	XC ◇1 M ⌶	XC ◇1 ⌶	XC ◇1 N ⌶	XC ◇1 E ⌶	AW	XC 1	XC ◇1 O ⌶	XC ◇1 ⌶	XC ◇1 P ⌶	XC ◇1 E ⌶	XC 1	XC ◇1 Q ⌶	XC ◇1 ⌶	XC ◇1 N ⌶	XC ◇1 E ⌶	AW A	XC 1	XC ◇1 R ⌶	XC ◇1 ⌶	AW ◇ S ⌶	XC ◇1 K ⌶
Nottingham 56 d		09 07				09 41		10 07			10 41		11 07				11 41		12 07		
Beeston 56 d		09 12						10 12					11 12						12 12		
Attenborough 56 d																					
Long Eaton 56 d		09 25						10 24					11 22						12 22		
Derby 56 d	09 26	09 39	09 53			10 10	10 29	10 38	10 53		11 10	11 28	11 37	11 53			12 10	12 29	12 37		12 53
Willington d		09 46																			
Burton-on-Trent d	09 38	09 52				10 21		10 49			11 21		11 49				12 21		12 49		
Tamworth d		10 03				10 33	10 50	11 02			11 33		12 02				12 33	12 49	13 02		
Wilnecote d						10 37					11 37						12 37				
Water Orton d																					
Birmingham New Street a	10 08	10 24	10 27			10 55	11 09	11 24	11 27		11 55	12 07	12 24	12 27			12 55	13 08	13 24		13 27
d	10 17	10 30		10 42			11 17	11 30		11 42		12 17	12 30		12 42			13 17	13 30		
University a		10 36						11 36					12 36						13 36		
Bromsgrove a																					
Ashchurch for Tewkesbury d																					
Cheltenham Spa d	11 00	11 11		11 26	11 46		11 59	12 10		12 26		13 02	13 11		13 26	13 45		14 02	14 10		
Gloucester 134 a		11 20			11 57			12 20					13 20			13 57			14 22		
d		11 25			11 59			12 25					13 25			13 58			14 24	14 48	
Bristol Parkway 134 a	11 31			11 55			12 28			12 56		13 30			13 56			14 28			
Bristol Temple Meads 134 a	11 42			12 05			12 42			13 10		13 41			14 08			14 42			
Lydney d					12 18								13 44			14 17				15 07	
Chepstow d		11 51			12 28			12 51								14 27			14 51	15 17	
Caldicot d					12 36											14 35				15 25	
Severn Tunnel Jn 132 d					12 39											14 38				15 28	
Newport (South Wales) 132 a		12 10			12 51			13 09					14 11			14 50			15 12	15 40	
Cardiff Central 132 a		12 26			13 08			13 26					14 26			15 15			15 30	15 58	

- A To Maesteg
- B To Paignton
- C To Plymouth. ⌶ from Birmingham New Street
- D From Sheffield to Reading
- E From Manchester Piccadilly
- F To Bournemouth
- G From Leeds to Plymouth
- H From Leeds to Southampton Central
- I From York to Plymouth
- J ⌶ from Birmingham New Street
- K From Newcastle to Reading
- L From Manchester Piccadilly to Paignton
- M From Newcastle to Plymouth
- N From Newcastle to Southampton Central
- O From Edinburgh to Plymouth
- P From Edinburgh to Reading
- Q From Glasgow Central to Plymouth
- R From Dundee to Plymouth
- S To Fishguard Harbour

Trains between Gloucester & Cheltenham are shown on Table T058

Trains between Birmingham & Bromsgrove are shown on Table T069

Table T057-F

Mondays to Fridays

8 October to 7 December

Nottingham and Derby - Birmingham - Bristol and Cardiff

	XC ◇1 A ⌶	XC 1	XC ◇1 B ⌶	XC ◇1 ⌶	XC ◇1 C ⌶	XC ◇1 D ⌶	XC 1 ⌶	XC ◇1 E ⌶	XC ◇1 F ⌶	XC ◇1 G ⌶	XC ◇1 H ⌶	AW I	XC 1	XC ◇1 J ⌶	XC ◇1 ⌶	XC ◇1 K ⌶	XC ◇1 D ⌶	AW I	XC 1 ⌶	XC ◇1 E ⌶	XC ◇1
Nottingham 56 d		12 41		13 07			13 41		14 07				14 41		15 07				15 41		16 07
Beeston 56 d				13 12					14 12						15 12						16 12
Attenborough 56 d																					
Long Eaton 56 d				13 22					14 22						15 22						16 22
Derby 56 d		13 10	13 28	13 37	13 53		14 10	14 28	14 37	14 53			15 10	15 28	15 37	15 53			16 10	16 28	16 37
Willington d		13 18											15 18								
Burton-on-Trent d		13 24	13 38	13 49			14 21		14 50				15 24	15 38	15 49				16 21		16 49
Tamworth d		13 35		14 02			14 33	14 47	15 02				15 35		16 02				16 33	16 47	17 02
Wilnecote d							14 37												16 37		
Water Orton d																					
Birmingham New Street a		13 55	14 08	14 24	14 27		14 55	15 08	15 25	15 27			15 54	16 03	16 25	16 28			16 55	17 08	17 25
d	13 42		14 17	14 30		14 42		15 17	15 30		15 42			16 12	16 30		16 42			17 12	17 30
University a				14 36					15 36						16 36						17 36
Bromsgrove a																					17 50
Ashchurch for Tewkesbury d															17 05						18 08
Cheltenham Spa d	14 26		15 00	15 11		15 26		16 00	16 11		16 26	16 45		16 51	17 14		17 26	17 45		17 52	18 17
Gloucester 134 a				15 20					16 22			16 56			17 24			17 57			18 28
d				15 25					16 25			16 58			17 25			17 58			18 31
Bristol Parkway 134 a	14 56		15 29			15 56		16 30			16 56			17 25			17 56			18 28	
Bristol Temple Meads 134 a	15 10		15 41			16 11		16 43			17 10			17 40			18 07			18 42	
Lydney d									16 44			17 17			17 44			18 17			
Chepstow d				15 51					16 53			17 27						18 27			
Caldicot d												17 35						18 35			
Severn Tunnel Jn 132 d												17 38						18 38			
Newport (South Wales) 132 a				16 12					17 11			17 50			18 10			18 49			19 14
Cardiff Central 132 a				16 30					17 30			18 10			18 27			19 09			19 33

	XC ◇1 G ⌶	XC ◇1 D ⌶	AW I	XC 1 ⌶	XC FX ◇1 L ⌶	XC ◇1	XC ◇1 G ⌶	XC ◇1 M ⌶	AW I	XC 1 ⌶	XC ◇1 B ⌶	XC ◇1	XC ◇1 G ⌶	XC ◇1 N ⌶	XC 1 ⌶	XC ◇1 O ⌶	XC FX ◇1	XC FO ◇1	XC ◇1 C ⌶	XC ◇1 D	XC 1 ⌶	XC ◇1 P ⌶
Nottingham 56 d				16 41		17 07				17 41		18 07			18 41		19 07	19 07			19 36	
Beeston 56 d						17 12						18 12					19 12	19 12			19 42	
Attenborough 56 d																					19 45	
Long Eaton 56 d						17 22						18 21					19 21	19 21			19 54	
Derby 56 d	16 53			17 10	17 27	17 37	17 53			18 13	18 29	18 37	18 53		19 10	19 30	19 37	19 37	19 54		20 10	20 29
Willington d				17 18						18 21												
Burton-on-Trent d				17 24	17 39	17 49				18 27		18 49			19 21	19 41	19 49	19 49			20 21	
Tamworth d				17 35		18 02				18 38	18 49	19 02			19 33		20 03	20 03			20 33	20 47
Wilnecote d						18 06									19 37						20 37	
Water Orton d																						
Birmingham New Street a	17 28			17 55	18 04	18 23	18 27			18 57	19 08	19 24	19 27		19 55	20 07	20 25	20 25	20 28		20 55	21 07
d		17 42			18 12	18 30		18 42			19 12	19 30		19 42		20 12	20 30	20 30		20 42		21 12
University a						18 36						19 36					20 36	20 36				
Bromsgrove a						18 50																
Ashchurch for Tewkesbury d																						
Cheltenham Spa d		18 25	18 45		18 52	19 13		19 25	19 45		19 52	20 12		20 26		20 54	21 11	21 11		21 26		21 52
Gloucester 134 a			18 58		19 01	19 23			19 56			20 20					21 19	21 19				22 02
d			19 00		19 06	19 25			19 58			20 25					21 21	21 21				22 06
Bristol Parkway 134 a		18 54			19 31			19 56			20 30			20 55		21 25				22 01		22 33
Bristol Temple Meads 134 a		19 06			19 43			20 09			20 42			21 05		21 36				22 14		22 43
Lydney d			19 20						20 17								21 40	21 40				
Chepstow d			19 29						20 27								21 50	21 50				
Caldicot d			19 37						20 35								21 58	21 58				
Severn Tunnel Jn 132 d			19 40					20 37	20 38								22 01	22 01				
Newport (South Wales) 132 a			19 53			20 11		20 47	20 50			21 11					22 12	22 13				
Cardiff Central 132 a			20 12			20 28		21 03	21 10			21 28					22 35	22 30				

- A From Manchester Piccadilly to Exeter St Davids
- B From Glasgow Central to Plymouth
- C From Newcastle to Southampton Central
- D From Manchester Piccadilly
- E From Glasgow Central to Penzance
- F To Nottingham
- G From Newcastle to Reading
- H From Manchester Piccadilly to Paignton
- I To Maesteg
- J From Aberdeen to Penzance
- K From Newcastle to Guildford
- L From Edinburgh to Plymouth
- M From Manchester Piccadilly. ⌶ to Bristol Temple Meads
- N From Manchester Piccadilly to Plymouth
- O From Edinburgh to Plymouth. ⌶ to Birmingham New Street
- P From Glasgow Central. ⌶ to Birmingham New Street

Trains between Gloucester & Cheltenham are shown on Table T058

Trains between Birmingham & Bromsgrove are shown on Table T069

Table T057-F

Mondays to Fridays
8 October to 7 December

Nottingham and Derby - Birmingham - Bristol and Cardiff

	XC ◇■ A ⚒	XC ■	XC ◇■ B	AW FX	XC ◇■ A ⚒	AW FO	LM FO	XC ■	XC ◇■ C
Nottingham ■ 56 ⇌ d		20 40						21 39	
Beeston 56 d		20 46						21 44	
Attenborough 56 d								21 48	
Long Eaton 56 d		20 55						21 56	
Derby ■ 56 d	20 54	21 10	21 30		22 02			22 12	22 45
Willington d		21 18							
Burton-on-Trent d		21 24	21 40					22 23	22 56
Tamworth d		21 34	21 50					22 35	23 07
Wilnecote d		21 38						22 38	
Water Orton d									
Birmingham New Street ■ a	21 29	21 57	22 09		22 51			23 01	23 26
d			22 12				23 00		
University a							23 05		
Bromsgrove a							23 20		
Ashchurch for Tewkesbury d							23 59		
Cheltenham Spa ■ d			22 52	23 00		23 00	00 08		
Gloucester ■ 134 a				23 11		23 11	00 19		
d				23 13		23 13			
Bristol Parkway ■ 134 a			23 21						
Bristol Temple Meads ■ 134 a			23 41						
Lydney d				23 33		23 33			
Chepstow d				23 42		23 42			
Caldicot d				23 51		23 51			
Severn Tunnel Jn 132 d				23 54		23 54			
Newport (South Wales) 132 a				00 05		00 06			
Cardiff Central ■ 132 a				00 34		00 26			

Saturdays
26 May to 16 June

	AW D	XC ◇■	XC ◇■	XC ◇■ E ⚒	AW	XC ◇■ F ⚒	XC ◇■ G ⚒	XC ◇■ H	XC ◇■ I ⚒
Nottingham ■ 56 ⇌ d							05 58		
Beeston 56 d							06 03		
Attenborough 56 d							06 07		
Long Eaton 56 d							06 15		
Derby ■ 56 d						06 10	06 36	06 47	
Willington d									
Burton-on-Trent d						06 20	06 48	06 58	
Tamworth d						06 31	07 01	07 09	
Wilnecote d							07 05		
Water Orton d									
Birmingham New Street ■ a						06 50	07 24	07 28	
d		05 00	05 42	06 42		07 12	07 30		07 42
University a							07 36		
Bromsgrove a			06 03						
Ashchurch for Tewkesbury d			06 33						
Cheltenham Spa ■ d		06 03	06 42	07 25	07 45	07 52	08 11		08 25
Gloucester ■ 134 a		06 12	06 52		07 57		08 20		
d	05 50	06 14	06 57		07 58		08 22		
Bristol Parkway ■ 134 a				07 53		08 24			08 54
Bristol Temple Meads ■ 134 a				08 05		08 38			09 07
Lydney d	06 09	06 33	07 16		08 17				
Chepstow d	06 19	06 42	07 26		08 27		08 48		
Caldicot d	06 27	06 51	07 34		08 35				
Severn Tunnel Jn 132 d	06 30	06 54	07 37		08 38				
Newport (South Wales) 132 a	06 42	07 05	07 48		08 50		09 06		
Cardiff Central ■ 132 a	07 03	07 21	08 04		09 10		09 23		

	AW D	XC ◇■ J ⚒	XC ◇■ K ⚒	XC ◇■	XC ◇■ L ⚒	XC ◇■ M ⚒	XC ■	XC ◇■ N ⚒	XC ◇■ G ⚒	XC ◇■ O ⚒	XC ◇■ P ⚒	AW D	XC ■
Nottingham ■ 56 ⇌ d		06 37		06 58			07 37		08 07				08 41
Beeston 56 d		06 43		07 03			07 42		08 12				
Attenborough 56 d				07 07									
Long Eaton 56 d				07 16			07 52		08 21				
Derby ■ 56 d		07 06	07 27	07 36	07 51		08 06	08 28	08 37	08 53			09 10
Willington d				07 43									
Burton-on-Trent d		07 17	07 38	07 50	08 00		08 18	08 38	08 49				09 22
Tamworth d		07 30	07 49	08 02	08 12		08 30	08 49	09 02				09 34
Wilnecote d				08 05			08 34						09 38
Water Orton d							08 42						
Birmingham New Street ■ a		07 52	08 08	08 24	08 27		08 55	09 08	09 24	09 27			09 56
d			08 12	08 30		08 42		09 12	09 30		09 42		
University a				08 36					09 36				
Bromsgrove a													
Ashchurch for Tewkesbury d													
Cheltenham Spa ■ d	08 45		08 52	09 11		09 25		09 52	10 11		10 25	10 45	
Gloucester ■ 134 a	08 57			09 20					10 20			10 56	
d	08 58			09 22					10 22			10 58	
Bristol Parkway ■ 134 a			09 24			09 53		10 29			10 54		
Bristol Temple Meads ■ 134 a			09 39			10 04		10 42			11 09		
Lydney d	09 17								10 41			11 17	
Chepstow d	09 27			09 48								11 27	
Caldicot d	09 35											11 35	
Severn Tunnel Jn 132 d	09 38											11 38	
Newport (South Wales) 132 a	09 50			10 05					11 06			11 50	
Cardiff Central ■ 132 a	10 09			10 21					11 24			12 06	

A From Newcastle
B From Edinburgh
C From Glasgow Central
D To Maesteg
E To Paignton
F To Plymouth. ⚒ from Birmingham New Street
G ⚒ from Birmingham New Street
H From Sheffield to Reading
I From Manchester Piccadilly
J To Bournemouth. ⚒ from Derby
K From Leeds to Paignton
L From Leeds to Southampton Central
M From Manchester Piccadilly to Newquay
N From York to Plymouth
O From Newcastle to Reading
P From Manchester Piccadilly to Paignton

Trains between Gloucester & Cheltenham are shown on Table T058

Trains between Birmingham & Bromsgrove are shown on Table T069

Table T057-F

Saturdays
26 May to 16 June

Nottingham and Derby - Birmingham - Bristol and Cardiff

	XC ◇■ A ⚒	XC ◇■ ⚒	XC ◇■ B ⚒	XC ◇■ C ⚒	AW	XC ■	XC ◇■ D ⚒	XC ◇■ ⚒	XC ◇■ E ⚒	XC ◇■ C ⚒
Nottingham ■ 56 ⇌ d		09 07				09 41		10 06		
Beeston 56 d		09 12						10 11		
Attenborough 56 d										
Long Eaton 56 d		09 22						10 23		
Derby ■ 56 d	09 29	09 36	09 53			10 10	10 28	10 37	10 53	
Willington d		09 44								
Burton-on-Trent d	09 41	09 49				10 21		10 49		
Tamworth d		10 02				10 33	10 49	11 02		
Wilnecote d						10 37				
Water Orton d										
Birmingham New Street ■ a	10 06	10 24	10 27			10 55	11 08	11 24	11 27	
d	10 12	10 30		10 42			11 12	11 30		11 42
University a		10 36						11 36		
Bromsgrove a										
Ashchurch for Tewkesbury d										
Cheltenham Spa ■ d	10 52	11 11		11 25	11 46		11 54	12 11		12 25
Gloucester ■ 134 a		11 20			11 56			12 20		
d		11 22			11 58			12 22		
Bristol Parkway ■ 134 a	11 25			11 53			12 29			12 53
Bristol Temple Meads ■ 134 a	11 39			12 04			12 42			13 09
Lydney d					12 17					
Chepstow d		11 48			12 27			12 48		
Caldicot d					12 35					
Severn Tunnel Jn 132 d					12 38					
Newport (South Wales) 132 a		12 05			12 50			13 05		
Cardiff Central ■ 132 a		12 23			13 07			13 21		

	XC ■	XC ◇■ F ⚒	XC ◇■ ⚒	XC ◇■ B ⚒	XC ◇■ C ⚒	AW G	XC ■	XC ◇■ H ⚒	XC ◇■ ⚒	AW ◇ I ⚒	XC ◇■ J ⚒
Nottingham ■ 56 ⇌ d	10 41		11 06				11 41		12 06		
Beeston 56 d			11 11						12 11		
Attenborough 56 d											
Long Eaton 56 d			11 23						12 22		
Derby ■ 56 d	11 10	11 28	11 37	11 53			12 10	12 28	12 37		12 53
Willington d											
Burton-on-Trent d	11 21	11 41	11 49				12 21		12 49		
Tamworth d	11 33		12 02				12 33	12 49	13 02		
Wilnecote d	11 37						12 37				
Water Orton d											
Birmingham New Street ■ a	11 55	12 08	12 24	12 27			12 55	13 08	13 24		13 27
d		12 12	12 30		12 42			13 12	13 30		
University a			12 36						13 36		
Bromsgrove a											
Ashchurch for Tewkesbury d											
Cheltenham Spa ■ d		12 53	13 11		13 25	13 45		13 52	14 11		
Gloucester ■ 134 a			13 20			13 57			14 20		
d			13 22			13 58			14 22	14 42	
Bristol Parkway ■ 134 a		13 24			13 54			14 26			
Bristol Temple Meads ■ 134 a		13 39			14 05			14 40			
Lydney d			13 41			14 17				15 01	
Chepstow d						14 27			14 49	15 11	
Caldicot d						14 35				15 19	
Severn Tunnel Jn 132 d						14 38				15 23	
Newport (South Wales) 132 a			14 06			14 50			15 09	15 35	
Cardiff Central ■ 132 a			14 22			15 09			15 26	15 53	

	XC ◇■ K ⚒	XC ■	XC ◇■ L ⚒	XC ◇■ ⚒	XC ◇■ B ⚒	XC ◇■ C ⚒	XC ■ ⚒	XC ◇■ L ⚒	XC ◇■ ⚒	XC ◇■ J ⚒	XC ◇■ C ⚒	AW G
Nottingham ■ 56 ⇌ d		12 41		13 06			13 41		14 06			
Beeston 56 d				13 11					14 11			
Attenborough 56 d												
Long Eaton 56 d				13 22					14 22			
Derby ■ 56 d		13 10	13 28	13 37	13 53		14 10	14 28	14 37	14 54		
Willington d		13 18										
Burton-on-Trent d		13 24	13 38	13 49			14 21		14 49			
Tamworth d		13 35		14 02			14 33	14 49	15 02			
Wilnecote d							14 37					
Water Orton d												
Birmingham New Street ■ a		13 55	14 03	14 24	14 27		14 55	15 08	15 24	15 27		
d	13 42		14 12	14 30		14 42		15 12	15 30		15 42	
University a				14 36					15 36			
Bromsgrove a												
Ashchurch for Tewkesbury d												
Cheltenham Spa ■ d	14 25		14 52	15 11		15 25		15 52	16 11		16 25	16 45
Gloucester ■ 134 a				15 20					16 20			16 56
d				15 22					16 22			16 58
Bristol Parkway ■ 134 a	14 54					15 54		16 29			16 53	
Bristol Temple Meads ■ 134 a	15 09		16 31			16 07		16 43			17 08	
Lydney d									16 41			17 17
Chepstow d				15 48					16 51			17 27
Caldicot d												17 35
Severn Tunnel Jn 132 d												17 38
Newport (South Wales) 132 a				16 06					17 08			17 50
Cardiff Central ■ 132 a				16 25					17 24			18 10

	XC ■	XC ◇■ M ⚒	XC ◇■ ⚒	XC ◇■ N ⚒	XC ◇■ C ⚒	AW G	XC ■ ⚒	XC ◇■ O ⚒	XC ◇■	XC ◇■ J ⚒
Nottingham ■ 56 ⇌ d	14 41		15 06				15 41		16 06	
Beeston 56 d			15 11						16 11	
Attenborough 56 d										
Long Eaton 56 d			15 22						16 22	
Derby ■ 56 d	15 10	15 28	15 37	15 53			16 10	16 28	16 37	16 53
Willington d	15 18									
Burton-on-Trent d	15 24	15 38	15 49				16 21		16 49	
Tamworth d	15 35		16 02				16 33	16 48	17 02	
Wilnecote d							16 37			
Water Orton d										
Birmingham New Street ■ a	15 55	16 03	16 24	16 27			16 55	17 07	17 24	17 27
d		16 12	16 30		16 42			17 12	17 30	
University a			16 36						17 36	
Bromsgrove a									17 50	
Ashchurch for Tewkesbury d									18 08	
Cheltenham Spa ■ d		16 52	17 10		17 25	17 45		17 52	18 17	
Gloucester ■ 134 a			17 20			17 56			18 25	
d			17 22			17 58			18 28	
Bristol Parkway ■ 134 a		17 25			17 53			18 29		
Bristol Temple Meads ■ 134 a		17 39			18 04			18 43		
Lydney d			17 41			18 17				
Chepstow d						18 27				
Caldicot d						18 35				
Severn Tunnel Jn 132 d						18 38				
Newport (South Wales) 132 a			18 06			18 50			19 10	
Cardiff Central ■ 132 a			18 24			19 12			19 30	

A From York to Penzance
B From Newcastle to Southampton Central
C From Manchester Piccadilly
D From Edinburgh to Plymouth
E From Edinburgh to Reading
F From Glasgow Central to Paignton
G To Maesteg
H From Dundee to Newquay
I To Fishguard Harbour
J From Newcastle to Reading
K From Manchester Piccadilly to Paignton
L From Glasgow Central to Penzance
M From Aberdeen to Penzance
N From Newcastle to Guildford
O From Glasgow Central to Plymouth

Trains between Gloucester & Cheltenham are shown on Table T058

Trains between Birmingham & Bromsgrove are shown on Table T069

Table T057-F

Saturdays
26 May to 16 June

Nottingham and Derby - Birmingham - Bristol and Cardiff

Station		XC ◇1 A 🍴	AW B	XC 1 🍴	XC ◇1 C 🍴	XC ◇1	XC ◇1 D 🍴	XC ◇1 E 🍴	AW B	XC 1 🍴	XC ◇1 F 🍴	XC ◇1	XC ◇1 D 🍴	XC ◇1 A	XC 1 🍴	XC ◇1 G 🍴	XC ◇1	XC ◇1 H 🍴	XC ◇1 A	XC 1 🍴	XC ◇1 I 🍴	XC ◇1 J 🍴	XC 1
Nottingham 8	56 ⇌ d			16 41		17 06				17 41		18 06			18 41		19 06			19 34			20 38
Beeston	56 d					17 11						18 11					19 11			19 40			20 43
Attenborough	56 d																			19 43			
Long Eaton	56 d					17 22						18 22					19 22			19 51			20 52
Derby 8	56 d			17 10	17 28	17 37	17 53			18 10	18 29	18 37	18 53		19 10	19 29	19 39	19 54		20 10	20 28	20 53	21 06
Willington	d			17 18						18 18													21 18
Burton-on-Trent	d			17 24	17 38	17 49				18 24		18 49			19 21	19 39	19 50			20 22			21 24
Tamworth	d			17 35		18 02				18 35	18 47	19 02			19 33		20 02			20 34	20 46		21 35
Wilnecote	d					18 06									19 37					20 38			21 39
Water Orton	d																						
Birmingham New Street 12	a			17 55	18 07	18 24	18 27			18 55	19 07	19 24	19 27		19 55	20 06	20 24	20 27		20 55	21 04	21 25	21 56
	d	17 42			18 12	18 30		18 42			19 12	19 30		19 42		20 12	20 30		20 42		21 12		
University	a					18 36						19 36					20 36						
Bromsgrove	a																						
Ashchurch for Tewkesbury	d																						
Cheltenham Spa 4	d	18 25	18 45		18 52	19 11		19 25	19 45		19 52	20 11		20 25		20 52	21 11		21 25		21 52		
Gloucester 7	134 a		18 56			19 20			19 56			20 20					21 20				22 01		
	d		18 58			19 22			19 58			20 22					21 22				22 06		
Bristol Parkway 7	134 a	18 53			19 24			19 54			20 29			20 53		21 22			21 58		22 32		
Bristol Temple Meads 10	134 a	19 08			19 39			20 05			20 42			21 04		21 34			22 12		22 42		
Lydney	d		19 17						20 17								21 41						
Chepstow	d		19 27						20 27								21 50						
Caldicot	d		19 34						20 35								21 59						
Severn Tunnel Jn	132 d		19 37					20 31	20 38								22 02						
Newport (South Wales)	132 a		19 50			20 03		20 44	20 50			21 09					22 18						
Cardiff Central 7	132 a		20 11			20 20		21 00	21 07			21 26					22 42						

Station		XC ◇1 K	XC ◇1 J	XC 1	XC ◇1 I	AW
Nottingham 8	56 ⇌ d			21 39		
Beeston	56 d			21 44		
Attenborough	56 d			21 48		
Long Eaton	56 d			21 56		
Derby 8	56 d	21 28	21 56	22 12	22 26	
Willington	d					
Burton-on-Trent	d	21 38		22 22	22 37	
Tamworth	d	21 49		22 35	22 47	
Wilnecote	d			22 38		
Water Orton	d					
Birmingham New Street 12	a	22 06	22 44	23 02	23 06	
	d					
University	a					
Bromsgrove	a					
Ashchurch for Tewkesbury	d					
Cheltenham Spa 4	d					
Gloucester 7	134 a					
	d					23 09
Bristol Parkway 7	134 a					
Bristol Temple Meads 10	134 a					
Lydney	d					23 28
Chepstow	d					23 38
Caldicot	d					23 46
Severn Tunnel Jn	132 d					23 49
Newport (South Wales)	132 a					00 11
Cardiff Central 7	132 a					00 38

A From Manchester Piccadilly
B To Maesteg
C From Edinburgh to Plymouth
D From Newcastle to Reading
E From Manchester Piccadilly. 🍴 to Bristol Temple Meads
F From Glasgow Central to Plymouth
G From Edinburgh to Plymouth. 🍴 to Birmingham New Street
H From Newcastle to Southampton Central
I From Glasgow Central
J From Newcastle
K From Edinburgh

Trains between Gloucester & Cheltenham are shown on Table T058

Trains between Birmingham & Bromsgrove are shown on Table T069

Table T057-F

Saturdays
23 June to 21 July

Nottingham and Derby - Birmingham - Bristol and Cardiff

Station		AW A	XC ◇1	XC ◇1	XC ◇1 B 🍴	AW	XC ◇1 C 🍴	XC ◇1 D 🍴	XC ◇1 E	XC ◇1 F 🍴	AW A	XC ◇1 G 🍴	XC ◇1 H 🍴	XC ◇1	XC ◇1 I 🍴	XC ◇1 J 🍴	XC 1	XC ◇1 K 🍴	XC ◇1 D 🍴	XC ◇1 L 🍴	XC ◇1 M 🍴	AW A	XC 1
Nottingham 8	56 ⇌ d							05 58				06 37		06 58			07 37		08 07				08 41
Beeston	56 d							06 03				06 43		07 03			07 42		08 12				
Attenborough	56 d							06 07						07 07									
Long Eaton	56 d							06 15						07 16			07 52		08 21				
Derby 8	56 d						06 10	06 36	06 47			07 06	07 27	07 36	07 51		08 06	08 28	08 37	08 53			09 10
Willington	d													07 43									
Burton-on-Trent	d						06 20	06 48	06 58			07 17	07 38	07 50	08 00		08 18	08 38	08 49				09 22
Tamworth	d						06 31	07 01	07 09			07 30	07 49	08 02	08 12		08 30	08 49	09 02				09 34
Wilnecote	d							07 05						08 05			08 34						09 38
Water Orton	d																08 42						
Birmingham New Street 12	a						06 50	07 24	07 28			07 52	08 08	08 24	08 27		08 55	09 08	09 24	09 27			09 56
	d		05 00	05 42	06 42		07 12	07 30		07 42			08 12	08 30		08 42		09 12	09 30		09 42		
University	a							07 36						08 36					09 36				
Bromsgrove	a			06 03																			
Ashchurch for Tewkesbury	d			06 33																			
Cheltenham Spa 4	d		06 03	06 42	07 25	07 45	07 52	08 11		08 25	08 45		08 52	09 11		09 25		09 52	10 11		10 25	10 45	
Gloucester 7	134 a		06 12	06 52		07 57		08 20			08 57			09 20					10 20			10 56	
	d	05 50	06 14	06 57		07 58		08 22			08 58			09 22					10 22			10 58	
Bristol Parkway 7	134 a				07 53		08 24			08 54			09 24			09 53		10 29			10 54		
Bristol Temple Meads 10	134 a				08 05		08 38			09 07			09 39			10 04		10 42			11 09		
Lydney	d	06 09	06 33	07 16		08 17					09 17								10 41			11 17	
Chepstow	d	06 19	06 42	07 26		08 27		08 48			09 27			09 48								11 27	
Caldicot	d	06 27	06 51	07 34		08 35					09 35											11 35	
Severn Tunnel Jn	132 d	06 30	06 54	07 37		08 38					09 38											11 38	
Newport (South Wales)	132 a	06 42	07 05	07 48		08 50		09 06			09 50			10 05					11 06			11 50	
Cardiff Central 7	132 a	07 03	07 21	08 04		09 10		09 23			10 09			10 21					11 24			12 06	

Station		XC ◇1 N 🍴	XC ◇1 🍴	XC ◇1 O 🍴	XC ◇1 F 🍴	AW	XC 1	XC ◇1 P 🍴	XC ◇1 🍴	XC ◇1 Q 🍴	XC ◇1 F 🍴	XC 1	XC ◇1 R 🍴	XC ◇1 🍴	XC ◇1 O 🍴	XC ◇1 F 🍴	AW A	XC 1	XC ◇1 S 🍴	XC ◇1 🍴	AW ◇ T 🍴	XC ◇1 L 🍴
Nottingham 8	56 ⇌ d		09 07				09 41		10 06			10 41		11 06				11 41		12 06		
Beeston	56 d		09 12						10 11					11 11						12 11		
Attenborough	56 d																					
Long Eaton	56 d		09 22						10 23					11 23						12 22		
Derby 8	56 d	09 29	09 36	09 53			10 10	10 28	10 37	10 53		11 10	11 28	11 37	11 53			12 10	12 28	12 37		12 53
Willington	d		09 44																			
Burton-on-Trent	d	09 41	09 49				10 21		10 49			11 21	11 41	11 49				12 21		12 49		
Tamworth	d		10 02				10 33	10 49	11 02			11 33		12 02				12 33	12 49	13 02		
Wilnecote	d						10 37					11 37						12 37				
Water Orton	d																					
Birmingham New Street 12	a	10 06	10 24	10 27			10 55	11 08	11 24	11 27		11 55	12 08	12 24	12 27			12 55	13 08	13 24		13 27
	d	10 12	10 30		10 42			11 12	11 30		11 42		12 12	12 30		12 42			13 12	13 30		
University	a		10 36						11 36					12 36						13 36		
Bromsgrove	a																					
Ashchurch for Tewkesbury	d																					
Cheltenham Spa 4	d	10 52	11 11		11 25	11 46		11 54	12 11		12 25		12 53	13 11		13 25	13 45		13 52	14 11		
Gloucester 7	134 a		11 20			11 56			12 20					13 20			13 57			14 20		
	d		11 22			11 58			12 22					13 22			13 58			14 22	14 42	
Bristol Parkway 7	134 a	11 25			11 53			12 29			12 53		13 24			13 54			14 26			
Bristol Temple Meads 10	134 a	11 39			12 04			12 42			13 09		13 39			14 05			14 40			
Lydney	d					12 17								13 41			14 17				15 01	
Chepstow	d		11 48			12 27			12 48								14 27			14 49	15 11	
Caldicot	d					12 35											14 35				15 19	
Severn Tunnel Jn	132 d					12 38											14 38				15 23	
Newport (South Wales)	132 a		12 05			12 50			13 05					14 06			14 50			15 09	15 35	
Cardiff Central 7	132 a		12 23			13 07			13 21					14 22			15 09			15 26	15 53	

A To Maesteg
B To Paignton
C To Plymouth. 🍴 from Birmingham New Street
D 🍴 from Birmingham New Street
E From Sheffield to Reading
F From Manchester Piccadilly
G To Bournemouth. 🍴 from Derby
H From Leeds to Paignton
I From Leeds to Southampton Central
J From Manchester Piccadilly to Newquay
K From York to Plymouth
L From Newcastle to Reading
M From Manchester Piccadilly to Paignton
N From York to Penzance
O From Newcastle to Southampton Central
P From Edinburgh to Plymouth
Q From Edinburgh to Reading
R From Glasgow Central to Paignton
S From Dundee to Newquay
T To Fishguard Harbour

Trains between Gloucester & Cheltenham are shown on Table T058

Trains between Birmingham & Bromsgrove are shown on Table T069

Table T057-F

Saturdays
23 June to 21 July

Nottingham and Derby - Birmingham - Bristol and Cardiff

		XC ◇1 A ✠	XC 1	XC ◇1 B ✠	XC ◇1 ✠	XC ◇1 C ✠	XC ◇1 D ✠	XC 1 ✠	XC ◇1 B ✠	XC ◇1 ✠	XC ◇1 E ✠	XC ◇1 D ✠	AW F	XC 1	XC ◇1 G ✠	XC ◇1 ✠	XC ◇1 H ✠	XC ◇1 D ✠	AW F	XC 1 ✠	XC ◇1 I ✠	XC ◇1
Nottingham 8 56 ⇌	d		12 41		13 06			13 41		14 06				14 41		15 06				15 41		16 06
Beeston 56	d				13 11					14 11						15 11						16 11
Attenborough 56	d																					
Long Eaton 56	d				13 22					14 22						15 22						16 22
Derby 6 56	d		13 10	13 28	13 37	13 53		14 10	14 28	14 37	14 54			15 10	15 28	15 37	15 53			16 10	16 28	16 37
Willington	d		13 18											15 18								
Burton-on-Trent	d		13 24	13 38	13 49			14 21		14 49				15 24	15 38	15 49				16 21		16 49
Tamworth	d		13 35		14 02			14 33	14 49	15 02				15 35		16 02				16 33	16 48	17 02
Wilnecote	d							14 37												16 37		
Water Orton	d																					
Birmingham New Street 12	a		13 55	14 03	14 24	14 27		14 55	15 08	15 24	15 27			15 55	16 03	16 24	16 27			16 55	17 07	17 24
	d	13 42		14 12	14 30		14 42		15 12	15 30		15 42			16 12	16 30		16 42			17 12	17 30
University	a				14 36					15 36						16 36						17 36
Bromsgrove	a																					17 50
Ashchurch for Tewkesbury	d																					18 08
Cheltenham Spa 4	d	14 25		14 52	15 11		15 25		15 52	16 11		16 25	16 45		16 52	17 10		17 25	17 45		17 52	18 17
Gloucester 7 134	a				15 20					16 20			16 56			17 20			17 56			18 25
	d				15 22					16 22			16 58			17 22			17 58			18 28
Bristol Parkway 7 134	a	14 54					15 54		16 29			16 53			17 25			17 53			18 29	
Bristol Temple Meads 10 134	a	15 09		16 31			16 07		16 43			17 08			17 39			18 04			18 43	
Lydney	d									16 41			17 17			17 41			18 17			
Chepstow	d				15 48					16 51			17 27						18 27			
Caldicot	d												17 35						18 35			
Severn Tunnel Jn 132	d												17 38						18 38			
Newport (South Wales) 132	a				16 06					17 08			17 50			18 06			18 50			19 10
Cardiff Central 7 132	a				16 25					17 24			18 10			18 24			19 12			19 30

		XC ◇1 E ✠	XC ◇1 D ✠	AW F	XC 1 ✠	XC ◇1 J ✠	XC ◇1	XC ◇1 E ✠	XC ◇1 K ✠	AW F	XC 1 ✠	XC ◇1 I ✠	XC ◇1	XC ◇1 E ✠	XC ◇1 D	XC 1 ✠	XC ◇1 L ✠	XC ◇1	XC ◇1 C ✠	XC ◇1 D	XC 1 ✠	XC ◇1 M ✠	XC ◇1 N ✠
Nottingham 8 56 ⇌	d				16 41		17 06				17 41		18 06			18 41		19 06			19 34		
Beeston 56	d						17 11						18 11					19 11			19 40		
Attenborough 56	d																				19 43		
Long Eaton 56	d						17 22						18 22					19 22			19 51		
Derby 6 56	d	16 53			17 10	17 28	17 37	17 53			18 10	18 29	18 37	18 53		19 10	19 29	19 39	19 54		20 10	20 28	20 53
Willington	d				17 18						18 18												
Burton-on-Trent	d				17 24	17 38	17 49				18 24		18 49			19 21	19 39	19 50			20 22		
Tamworth	d				17 35		18 02				18 35	18 47	19 02			19 33		20 02			20 34	20 46	
Wilnecote	d						18 06									19 37					20 38		
Water Orton	d																						
Birmingham New Street 12	a	17 27			17 55	18 07	18 24	18 27			18 55	19 07	19 24	19 27		19 55	20 06	20 24	20 27		20 55	21 04	21 25
	d		17 42			18 12	18 30		18 42			19 12	19 30		19 42		20 12	20 30		20 42		21 12	
University	a						18 36						19 36					20 36					
Bromsgrove	a																						
Ashchurch for Tewkesbury	d																						
Cheltenham Spa 4	d		18 25	18 45		18 52	19 11		19 25	19 45		19 52	20 11		20 25		20 52	21 11		21 25		21 52	
Gloucester 7 134	a			18 56			19 20			19 56			20 20					21 20				22 01	
	d			18 58			19 22			19 58			20 22					21 22				22 06	
Bristol Parkway 7 134	a		18 53			19 24			19 54			20 29			20 53		21 22			21 58		22 32	
Bristol Temple Meads 10 134	a		19 08			19 39			20 05			20 42			21 04		21 34			22 12		22 42	
Lydney	d			19 17						20 17								21 41					
Chepstow	d			19 27						20 27								21 50					
Caldicot	d			19 34						20 35								21 59					
Severn Tunnel Jn 132	d			19 37					20 31	20 38								22 02					
Newport (South Wales) 132	a			19 50			20 03		20 44	20 50			21 09					22 18					
Cardiff Central 7 132	a			20 11			20 20		21 00	21 07			21 26					22 42					

A From Manchester Piccadilly to Paignton
B From Glasgow Central to Penzance
C From Newcastle to Southampton Central
D From Manchester Piccadilly
E From Newcastle to Reading
F To Maesteg
G From Aberdeen to Penzance
H From Newcastle to Guildford
I From Glasgow Central to Plymouth
J From Edinburgh to Plymouth
K From Manchester Piccadilly. ✠ to Bristol Temple Meads
L From Edinburgh to Plymouth. ✠ to Birmingham New Street
M From Glasgow Central
N From Newcastle

Trains between Gloucester & Cheltenham are shown on Table T058

Trains between Birmingham & Bromsgrove are shown on Table T069

Table T057-F

Saturdays
23 June to 21 July

Nottingham and Derby - Birmingham - Bristol and Cardiff

		XC 1	XC ◇1 A	XC ◇1 B	XC 1	XC ◇1 C	AW
Nottingham 8 56 ⇌	d	20 38			21 39		
Beeston 56	d	20 43			21 44		
Attenborough 56	d				21 48		
Long Eaton 56	d	20 52			21 56		
Derby 6 56	d	21 06	21 28	21 56	22 12	22 26	
Willington	d	21 18					
Burton-on-Trent	d	21 24	21 38		22 22	22 37	
Tamworth	d	21 35	21 49		22 35	22 47	
Wilnecote	d	21 39			22 38		
Water Orton	d						
Birmingham New Street 12	a	21 56	22 06	22 44	23 02	23 06	
	d						
University	a						
Bromsgrove	a						
Ashchurch for Tewkesbury	d						
Cheltenham Spa 4	d						
Gloucester 7 134	a						
	d						23 09
Bristol Parkway 7 134	a						
Bristol Temple Meads 10 134	a						
Lydney	d						23 28
Chepstow	d						23 38
Caldicot	d						23 46
Severn Tunnel Jn 132	d						23 49
Newport (South Wales) 132	a						00 11
Cardiff Central 7 132	a						00 38

Saturdays
28 July to 1 September

		AW D	XC ◇1	XC ◇1	XC ◇1 E ✠	AW	XC ◇1 F ✠	XC ◇1 G ✠	XC ◇1 H	XC ◇1 I ✠	AW D	XC ◇1 J	XC ◇1 K ✠	XC ◇1	EM L	XC ◇1 M ✠	XC ◇1 N ✠	XC 1	XC ◇1 O	XC ◇1 G ✠	EM P	XC ◇1 Q ✠	XC ◇1 R ✠
Nottingham 8 56 ⇌	d							05 58				06 37		06 58	07 20			07 37		08 07	08 20		
Beeston 56	d							06 03				06 43		07 03	07 25			07 42		08 12	08 25		
Attenborough 56	d							06 07						07 07	07 29						08 29		
Long Eaton 56	d														07a37						08a37		
Derby 6 56	d																						
Willington	d													07 43									
Burton-on-Trent	d						06 20	06 48	06 58			07 17	07 38	07 50		08 00		08 18	08 38	08 49		09 02	
Tamworth	d						06 31	07 01	07 09			07 30	07 49	08 02		08 12		08 30	08 49	09 02			
Wilnecote	d							07 05						08 05				08 34					
Water Orton	d																	08 42					
Birmingham New Street 12	a						06 50	07 24	07 28			07 52	08 08	08 24		08 27		08 55	09 08	09 24		09 27	
	d		05 00	05 42	06 42		07 12	07 30		07 42			08 12	08 30			08 42		09 12	09 30			09 42
University	a							07 36						08 36						09 36			
Bromsgrove	a			06 03																			
Ashchurch for Tewkesbury	d			06 33																			
Cheltenham Spa 4	d		06 03	06 42	07 25	07 45	07 52	08 11		08 25	08 45		08 52	09 11			09 25		09 52	10 11			10 25
Gloucester 7 134	a		06 12	06 52		07 57		08 20			08 57			09 20						10 20			
	d	05 50	06 14	06 57		07 58		08 22			08 58			09 22						10 22			
Bristol Parkway 7 134	a				07 53		08 24			08 54			09 24				09 53		10 29				10 54
Bristol Temple Meads 10 134	a				08 05		08 38			09 07			09 39				10 04		10 43				11 09
Lydney	d	06 09	06 33	07 16		08 17					09 17									10 41			
Chepstow	d	06 19	06 42	07 26		08 27		08 48			09 27			09 48									
Caldicot	d	06 27	06 51	07 34		08 35					09 35												
Severn Tunnel Jn 132	d	06 30	06 54	07 37		08 38					09 38												
Newport (South Wales) 132	a	06 42	07 05	07 48		08 50		09 06			09 50			10 05						11 06			
Cardiff Central 7 132	a	07 03	07 21	08 04		09 10		09 23			10 09			10 21						11 24			

A From Edinburgh
B From Newcastle
C From Glasgow Central
D To Maesteg
E To Paignton
F To Plymouth. ✠ from Birmingham New Street
G ✠ from Birmingham New Street
H To Reading
I From Manchester Piccadilly
J To Bournemouth
K From Leeds to Paignton
L 4 August, 11 August
M To Southampton Central
N From Manchester Piccadilly to Newquay
O From Leeds to Plymouth
P 4 August, 11 August. From Newark Castle
Q From York to Reading
R From Manchester Piccadilly to Paignton

Trains between Gloucester & Cheltenham are shown on Table T058

Trains between Birmingham & Bromsgrove are shown on Table T069

Table T057-F

Saturdays
28 July to 1 September

Nottingham and Derby - Birmingham - Bristol and Cardiff

	AW		XC	XC	XC	EM	XC	XC	AW	XC	XC		XC	EM	XC	XC	XC	XC	XC	EM	XC		XC	AW
			■	◇■	◇■		◇■	◇■		■	◇■		◇■		◇■	◇■	■	◇■	◇■		◇■		◇■	
	A			B	⌶	C	D ⌶	E ⌶			F ⌶		⌶	C	G ⌶	E ⌶		H	⌶	C	I ⌶		E ⌶	A
Nottingham ■ 56 d			08 41		09 04	09 20				09 41			10 04	10 20			10 41		11 04	11 20				
Beeston 56 d					09 09	09 25							10 09	10 26					11 09	11 25				
Attenborough 56 d						09 29								10 30						11 29				
Long Eaton 56 d						09a38								10a39						11a37				
Derby ■ 56 d																								
Willington d					09 44																			
Burton-on-Trent d			09 22	09 41	09 49		10 01			10 21	10 37		10 49		11 01		11 21	11 41	11 49		12 03			
Tamworth d			09 34		10 02					10 33	10 49		11 02				11 33		12 02					
Wilnecote d			09 38							10 37							11 37							
Water Orton d																								
Birmingham New Street ■ a			09 56	10 06	10 24		10 27			10 55	11 08		11 24		11 27		11 55	12 08	12 24		12 27			
d				10 12	10 30			10 42			11 12		11 30			11 42		12 12	12 30				12 42	
University a					10 36								11 36						12 36					
Bromsgrove a																								
Ashchurch for Tewkesbury d																								
Cheltenham Spa ■ d	10 45			10 52	11 11			11 25	11 46		11 54		12 11			12 25		12 53	13 11				13 25	13 45
Gloucester ■ 134 a	10 56				11 20				11 56				12 20						13 20					13 57
d	10 58				11 22				11 58				12 22						13 22					13 58
Bristol Parkway ■ 134 a				11 25				11 53			12 29					12 53		13 24					13 54	
Bristol Temple Meads ■ 134 a				11 39				12 04			12 42					13 09		13 39					14 05	
Lydney d	11 17								12 17										13 41					14 17
Chepstow d	11 27				11 48				12 27				12 48											14 27
Caldicot d	11 35								12 35															14 35
Severn Tunnel Jn 132 d	11 38								12 38															14 38
Newport (South Wales) 132 a	11 50				12 05				12 50				13 05						14 06					14 50
Cardiff Central ■ 132 a	12 06				12 23				13 07				13 21						14 22					15 09

	XC	XC	XC	AW	EM	XC	XC		XC	XC	XC	EM	XC	XC	XC	XC	XC		EM	XC	XC	AW	XC	XC
	■	◇■	◇■	◇		◇■	◇■		■	◇■	◇■		◇■	◇■	■	◇■	◇■			◇■	◇■		■	◇■
		J ⌶	⌶	K ⌶	C	L ⌶	M ⌶			N ⌶	⌶	C	I ⌶	E ⌶	⌶	N ⌶	⌶		C	O ⌶	E ⌶	A		N ⌶
Nottingham ■ 56 d	11 41		12 04		12 20				12 41		13 04	13 20			13 41		14 04		14 20				14 41	
Beeston 56 d			12 09		12 25						13 09	13 25					14 09		14 25					
Attenborough 56 d					12 29							13 29							14 29					
Long Eaton 56 d					12a39							13a39							14a40					
Derby ■ 56 d																								
Willington d									13 12														15 12	
Burton-on-Trent d	12 21	12 37	12 49			13 01			13 24	13 38	13 49		14 01		14 21	14 37	14 49			15 01			15 24	15 38
Tamworth d	12 33	12 49	13 02						13 35		14 02				14 33	14 49	15 02						15 35	
Wilnecote d	12 37														14 37									
Water Orton d																								
Birmingham New Street ■ a	12 55	13 08	13 24			13 27			13 55	14 03	14 24		14 27		14 55	15 08	15 24			15 27			15 55	16 03
d		13 12	13 30				13 42			14 12	14 30			14 42		15 12	15 30				15 42			16 12
University a			13 36								14 36						15 36							
Bromsgrove a																								
Ashchurch for Tewkesbury d																								
Cheltenham Spa ■ d		13 52	14 11				14 25			14 52	15 11			15 25		15 52	16 11				16 25	16 45		16 52
Gloucester ■ 134 a			14 20								15 20						16 20					16 56		
d			14 22	14 42							15 22						16 22					16 58		
Bristol Parkway ■ 134 a		14 26					14 54			15 24				15 54		16 29					16 53			17 25
Bristol Temple Meads ■ 134 a		14 40					15 09			15 38				16 07		16 43					17 08			17 39
Lydney d				15 01													16 41					17 17		
Chepstow d			14 49	15 11							15 48						16 51					17 27		
Caldicot d				15 19																		17 35		
Severn Tunnel Jn 132 d				15 23																		17 38		
Newport (South Wales) 132 a			15 09	15 35							16 06						17 08					17 50		
Cardiff Central ■ 132 a			15 26	15 53							16 25						17 24					18 10		

A To Maesteg
B From York to Penzance
C 4 August, 11 August. From Newark Castle
D From Newcastle to Southampton Central
E From Manchester Piccadilly
F From Newcastle to Plymouth
G From Edinburgh to Reading
H From Edinburgh to Paignton
I From Glasgow Central to Southampton Central
J From Newcastle to Newquay
K To Fishguard Harbour
L From Dundee to Reading
M From Manchester Piccadilly to Paignton
N From Newcastle to Penzance
O From Glasgow Central to Reading

Trains between Gloucester & Cheltenham are shown on Table T058

Trains between Birmingham & Bromsgrove are shown on Table T069

Table T057-F

Saturdays
28 July to 1 September

Nottingham and Derby - Birmingham - Bristol and Cardiff

	XC	EM	XC	XC	AW	XC	XC	XC	EM		XC	XC	AW	XC	XC	XC	EM	XC	XC		AW	XC	XC	XC
	◇■		◇■	◇■		■	◇■	◇■			◇■	◇■		■	◇■	◇■		◇■	◇■			■	◇■	◇■
	⌶	A	B ⌶	C ⌶	D	⌶	E ⌶		A		F ⌶	C ⌶	D	⌶	E ⌶		A	G ⌶	H ⌶		D	⌶	E ⌶	
Nottingham ■ 56 d	15 04	15 20				15 41		16 04	16 20					16 41		17 04	17 20					17 41		18 04
Beeston 56 d	15 09	15 25						16 09	16 25							17 09	17 25							18 09
Attenborough 56 d		15 29							16 29								17 29							
Long Eaton 56 d		15a39							16a39								17a39							
Derby ■ 56 d																								
Willington d														17 12								18 12		
Burton-on-Trent d	15 49		16 01			16 21	16 37	16 49			17 01			17 24	17 38	17 49		18 01				18 24	18 37	18 49
Tamworth d	16 02					16 33	16 48	17 02						17 35		18 02						18 35	18 47	19 02
Wilnecote d						16 37										18 06								
Water Orton d																								
Birmingham New Street ■ a	16 24		16 27			16 55	17 07	17 24			17 27			17 55	18 07	18 24		18 27				18 55	19 07	19 24
d	16 30			16 42			17 12	17 30				17 42			18 12	18 30			18 42				19 12	19 30
University a	16 36							17 36								18 36								19 36
Bromsgrove a								17 50																
Ashchurch for Tewkesbury d								18 08																
Cheltenham Spa ■ d	17 10			17 25	17 45		17 52	18 17				18 25	18 45		18 52	19 11			19 25		19 45		19 52	20 11
Gloucester ■ 134 a	17 20				17 56			18 25					18 56			19 20					19 56			20 20
d	17 22				17 58			18 28					18 58			19 22					19 58			20 22
Bristol Parkway ■ 134 a				17 53			18 29					18 53			19 24				19 54				20 29	
Bristol Temple Meads ■ 134 a				18 04			18 43					19 08			19 39				20 05				20 42	
Lydney d	17 41				18 17								19 17								20 17			
Chepstow d					18 27								19 27								20 27			
Caldicot d					18 35								19 34								20 35			
Severn Tunnel Jn 132 d					18 38								19 37						20 31		20 38			
Newport (South Wales) 132 a	18 06				18 50			19 10					19 50			20 03			20 44		20 50			21 09
Cardiff Central ■ 132 a	18 24				19 12			19 30					20 11			20 20			21 00		21 07			21 26

	EM	XC	XC	XC	XC		XC	EM	XC	XC	XC	EM	XC	XC	XC		EM	XC	XC	XC	EM	XC	XC	AW
		◇■	◇■	■	◇■		◇■		◇■	◇■	■		◇■	◇■	■			◇■	◇■	■		◇■	◇■	
	A	F ⌶	C	⌶	I ⌶			A	J ⌶	C	⌶	A	K ⌶	L ⌶			M	K ⌶	N		M	K	L	
Nottingham ■ 56 d	18 20			18 41			19 04	19 20			19 34	20 20			20 37		21 20			21 39	22 20			
Beeston 56 d	18 25						19 09	19 25			19 39	20 25			20 43		21 25			21 44	22 25			
Attenborough 56 d	18 29							19 29			19 42	20 29					21 29			21 48	22 29			
Long Eaton 56 d	18a39							19a37				20a39					21a39				22a39			
Derby ■ 56 d																								
Willington d															21 18									
Burton-on-Trent d		19 01		19 21	19 39		19 50		20 02		20 22		20 36	21 01	21 24			21 38	21 57	22 22		22 29	23 00	
Tamworth d				19 33			20 02				20 34		20 46		21 35			21 49		22 35			23 10	
Wilnecote d				19 37							20 38				21 39					22 38				
Water Orton d																								
Birmingham New Street ■ a		19 27		19 55	20 06		20 24		20 27		20 55		21 04	21 25	21 56			22 06	22 21	23 02		23 05	23 32	
d			19 42		20 12		20 30			20 42			21 12											
University a							20 36																	
Bromsgrove a																								
Ashchurch for Tewkesbury d																								
Cheltenham Spa ■ d			20 25		20 52		21 11			21 25			21 52											
Gloucester ■ 134 a							21 20						22 01											
d							21 22						22 06											23 09
Bristol Parkway ■ 134 a			20 53		21 22					21 58			22 32											
Bristol Temple Meads ■ 134 a			21 04		21 34					22 12			22 42											
Lydney d							21 41																	23 28
Chepstow d							21 50																	23 38
Caldicot d							21 59																	23 46
Severn Tunnel Jn 132 d							22 02																	23 49
Newport (South Wales) 132 a							22 18																	00 11
Cardiff Central ■ 132 a							22 42																	00 38

A 4 August, 11 August. From Newark Castle
B From Aberdeen to Guildford
C From Manchester Piccadilly
D To Maesteg
E From Newcastle to Plymouth
F From Glasgow Central to Reading
G From Edinburgh to Reading
H From Manchester Piccadilly. ⌶ to Bristol Temple Meads
I From Newcastle to Plymouth. ⌶ to Birmingham New Street
J From Edinburgh to Southampton Central
K From Newcastle
L From Glasgow Central
M 4 August, 11 August
N From Edinburgh

Trains between Gloucester & Cheltenham are shown on Table T058

Trains between Birmingham & Bromsgrove are shown on Table T069

Table T057-F

Saturdays

8 September to 6 October

Nottingham and Derby - Birmingham - Bristol and Cardiff

	AW	XC	XC	XC	AW	XC	XC	XC	XC	AW	XC	XC	XC	XC	XC	XC	XC	XC	XC	XC	AW	XC
	A	◇1	◇1	◇1 B trolley		◇1 C trolley	◇1 D trolley	◇1 E	◇1 F trolley	A	◇1 G trolley	◇1 H trolley	◇1	◇1 I trolley	◇1 F trolley	1	◇1 J	◇1 D trolley	◇1 K trolley	◇1 L trolley	A	1
Nottingham 8 56 d							05 58				06 37		07 02			07 37		08 07				08 41
Beeston 56 d							06 03				06 43		07 07			07 42		08 12				
Attenborough 56 d							06 07						07 11									
Long Eaton 56 d							06 17						07 19			07 52		08 21				
Derby 6 56 d						06 10	06 36	06 48			07 06	07 27	07 36	07 50		08 06	08 28	08 37	08 53			09 10
Willington d													07 43									
Burton-on-Trent d						06 20	06 48	06 58			07 17	07 38	07 50	08 00		08 18	08 38	08 49				09 22
Tamworth d						06 31	07 01	07 09			07 30	07 49	08 02	08 12		08 30	08 49	09 02				09 34
Wilnecote d							07 05						08 05			08 34						09 38
Water Orton d																08 42						
Birmingham New Street 12 a						06 50	07 24	07 28			07 52	08 08	08 24	08 27		08 55	09 08	09 24	09 27			09 56
d		05 00	05 42	06 42		07 12	07 30		07 42			08 12	08 30		08 42		09 12	09 30		09 42		
University a							07 36						08 36					09 36				
Bromsgrove a			06 03																			
Ashchurch for Tewkesbury d			06 33																			
Cheltenham Spa 4 d		06 03	06 42	07 25	07 45	07 52	08 11		08 25	08 45		08 52	09 11		09 25		09 52	10 11		10 25	10 45	
Gloucester 7 134 a		06 12	06 52		07 57		08 20			08 57			09 20					10 20			10 56	
d	05 50	06 14	06 57		07 58		08 22			08 58			09 22					10 22			10 58	
Bristol Parkway 7 134 a				07 53		08 24			08 54			09 24			09 53		10 29			10 54		
Bristol Temple Meads 10 134 a				08 05		08 38			09 07			09 39			10 04		10 43			11 09		
Lydney d	06 09	06 33	07 16		08 17					09 17								10 41			11 17	
Chepstow d	06 19	06 42	07 26		08 27		08 48			09 27			09 48								11 27	
Caldicot d	06 27	06 51	07 34		08 35					09 35											11 35	
Severn Tunnel Jn 132 d	06 30	06 54	07 37		08 38					09 38											11 38	
Newport (South Wales) 132 a	06 42	07 05	07 48		08 50		09 06			09 50			10 05					11 06			11 50	
Cardiff Central 7 132 a	07 03	07 21	08 04		09 10		09 23			10 09			10 21					11 24			12 06	

	XC	XC	XC	XC	XC	AW	XC	XC	XC	XC	XC	XC	XC	XC	XC	XC	AW	XC	XC	XC	XC
	◇1 M	◇1 N	◇1 trolley	◇1 O trolley	◇1 F trolley		1	◇1 P trolley	◇1 trolley	◇1 Q trolley	◇1 F trolley	1	◇1 R	◇1 trolley	◇1 S trolley	◇1 F trolley	A	1	◇1 T trolley	◇1 U trolley	◇1 trolley
Nottingham 8 56 d			09 04				09 41		10 04			10 41		11 04				11 41			12 04
Beeston 56 d			09 09						10 09					11 09							12 09
Attenborough 56 d																					
Long Eaton 56 d			09 19						10 18					11 19							12 22
Derby 6 56 d	09 24	09 30	09 37	09 51			10 10	10 28	10 37	10 53		11 10	11 29	11 37	11 53			12 10	12 29	12 29	12 37
Willington d			09 44																		
Burton-on-Trent d	09 34	09 41	09 49				10 21		10 49			11 21	11 41	11 49				12 21			12 49
Tamworth d			10 02				10 33	10 49	11 02			11 33		12 02				12 33	12 49	12 49	13 02
Wilnecote d							10 37					11 37						12 37			
Water Orton d																					
Birmingham New Street 12 a	10 00	10 06	10 24	10 27			10 55	11 08	11 24	11 27		11 55	12 08	12 24	12 27			12 55	13 08	13 08	13 24
d	10 05	10 12	10 30		10 42			11 12	11 30		11 42		12 12	12 30		12 42			13 12	13 12	13 30
University a			10 36						11 36					12 36							13 36
Bromsgrove a																					
Ashchurch for Tewkesbury d																					
Cheltenham Spa 4 d	10 46	10 52	11 11		11 25	11 46		11 54	12 11		12 25		12 53	13 11		13 25	13 45		13 52	13 52	14 11
Gloucester 7 134 a			11 20			11 56			12 20					13 20			13 57				14 20
d			11 22			11 58			12 22					13 22			13 58				14 22
Bristol Parkway 7 134 a	11 19	11 25			11 53			12 29			12 53		13 24			13 54			14 26	14 26	
Bristol Temple Meads 10 134 a	11 33	11 39			12 04			12 42			13 09		13 39			14 05			14 40	14 41	
Lydney d						12 17								13 41			14 17				
Chepstow d			11 48			12 27			12 48								14 27				14 49
Caldicot d						12 35											14 35				
Severn Tunnel Jn 132 d						12 38											14 38				
Newport (South Wales) 132 a			12 05			12 50			13 05					14 06			14 50				15 09
Cardiff Central 7 132 a			12 23			13 07			13 21					14 22			15 09				15 26

- A To Maesteg
- B To Paignton
- C To Plymouth. trolley from Birmingham New Street
- D trolley from Birmingham New Street
- E To Reading
- F From Manchester Piccadilly
- G To Bournemouth. trolley from Derby
- H From Leeds to Paignton
- I To Southampton Central
- J From Leeds to Plymouth
- K From York to Reading
- L From Manchester Piccadilly to Paignton
- M not 8 September. From York to Plymouth
- N 8 September. From York to Penzance
- O From Newcastle to Southampton Central
- P From Newcastle to Plymouth
- Q From Edinburgh to Reading
- R From Edinburgh to Paignton
- S From Glasgow Central to Southampton Central
- T 8 September. From Newcastle to Newquay
- U not 8 September. From Newcastle to Plymouth

Trains between Gloucester & Cheltenham are shown on Table T058

Trains between Birmingham & Bromsgrove are shown on Table T069

Table T057-F

Saturdays

8 September to 6 October

Nottingham and Derby - Birmingham - Bristol and Cardiff

	AW	XC	XC	XC	XC	XC	XC	XC	XC	XC	XC	XC	XC	XC	AW	XC	XC	XC	XC	XC	AW
	◇ A trolley	◇1 B trolley	◇1 C trolley	1	◇1 D trolley	◇1 trolley	◇1 E trolley	◇1 F trolley	1 trolley	◇1 G trolley	◇1 trolley	◇1 H trolley	◇1 I trolley	◇1 J trolley	K	1	◇1 G trolley	◇1 trolley	◇1 L trolley	◇1 F trolley	K
Nottingham 8 56 d				12 41		13 04			13 41		14 04					14 41		15 04			
Beeston 56 d						13 09					14 09							15 09			
Attenborough 56 d																					
Long Eaton 56 d						13 18					14 18							15 18			
Derby 6 56 d		12 53		13 10	13 28	13 37	13 53		14 10	14 26	14 37	14 53				15 10	15 27	15 37	15 53		
Willington d				13 18												15 18					
Burton-on-Trent d				13 24	13 38	13 49			14 21		14 49					15 24	15 38	15 49			
Tamworth d				13 35		14 02			14 33	14 49	15 02					15 35		16 02			
Wilnecote d									14 37												
Water Orton d																					
Birmingham New Street 12 a		13 27		13 55	14 04	14 24	14 27		14 55	15 08	15 24	15 27				15 55	16 03	16 24	16 27		
d			13 42		14 12	14 30		14 42		15 12	15 30		15 42	15 42			16 12	16 30		16 42	
University a						14 36					15 36							16 36			
Bromsgrove a																					
Ashchurch for Tewkesbury d																					
Cheltenham Spa 4 d			14 25		14 52	15 11		15 25		15 52	16 11		16 25	16 25	16 45		16 52	17 10		17 25	17 45
Gloucester 7 134 a						15 20					16 20				16 56			17 20			17 56
d	14 42					15 22					16 22				16 58			17 22			17 58
Bristol Parkway 7 134 a			14 54		15 24			15 54		16 29			16 53	16 53			17 25			17 53	
Bristol Temple Meads 10 134 a			15 09		15 38			16 07		16 43			17 07	17 08			17 39			18 04	
Lydney d	15 01										16 41				17 17			17 41			18 17
Chepstow d	15 11					15 48					16 51				17 27						18 27
Caldicot d	15 19														17 35						18 35
Severn Tunnel Jn 132 d	15 23														17 38						18 38
Newport (South Wales) 132 a	15 35					16 06					17 08				17 50			18 06			18 50
Cardiff Central 7 132 a	15 53					16 25					17 24				18 10			18 24			19 12

	XC	XC	XC	XC	XC	XC	AW	XC	XC	XC	XC	XC	AW	XC	XC	XC	XC	XC	XC	XC	XC	XC
	1 trolley	◇1 D trolley	◇1	◇1 H trolley	◇1 M trolley	◇1 J trolley	K	1 trolley	◇1 D trolley	◇1	◇1 N trolley	◇1 O trolley	K	1 trolley	◇1 D trolley	◇1	◇1 H trolley	◇1 F	1 trolley	◇1 P trolley	◇1	◇1 Q trolley
Nottingham 8 56 d	15 41		16 04					16 41		17 04				17 41		18 04			18 41		19 04	
Beeston 56 d			16 09							17 09						18 09					19 09	
Attenborough 56 d																						
Long Eaton 56 d			16 19							17 18						18 18					19 18	
Derby 6 56 d	16 10	16 28	16 37	16 53				17 10	17 29	17 37	17 53			18 10	18 29	18 37	18 53		19 10	19 29	19 37	19 54
Willington d								17 18						18 18								
Burton-on-Trent d	16 21		16 49					17 24	17 38	17 49				18 24		18 49			19 21	19 39	19 49	
Tamworth d	16 33	16 48	17 02					17 35		18 02				18 35	18 47	19 02			19 33		20 02	
Wilnecote d	16 37									18 06									19 37			
Water Orton d																						
Birmingham New Street 12 a	16 55	17 07	17 24	17 27				17 55	18 07	18 24	18 27			18 55	19 07	19 24	19 27		19 55	20 06	20 24	20 27
d		17 12	17 30		17 42	17 42			18 12	18 30		18 42			19 12	19 30		19 42		20 12	20 30	
University a			17 36							18 36						19 36					20 36	
Bromsgrove a			17 50																			
Ashchurch for Tewkesbury d			18 08																			
Cheltenham Spa 4 d		17 52	18 17		18 25	18 25	18 45		18 52	19 11		19 25	19 45		19 52	20 11		20 25		20 52	21 11	
Gloucester 7 134 a			18 25				18 56			19 20			19 56			20 20					21 20	
d			18 28				18 58			19 22			19 58			20 22					21 22	
Bristol Parkway 7 134 a		18 29			18 53	18 53			19 24			19 54			20 29			20 53		21 22		
Bristol Temple Meads 10 134 a		18 43			19 05	19 08			19 39			20 05			20 42			21 04		21 34		
Lydney d							19 17						20 17								21 41	
Chepstow d							19 27						20 27								21 50	
Caldicot d							19 34						20 35								21 59	
Severn Tunnel Jn 132 d							19 37					20 31	20 38								22 02	
Newport (South Wales) 132 a			19 10				19 50			20 03		20 44	20 50			21 09					22 18	
Cardiff Central 7 132 a			19 30				20 11			20 20		21 00	21 07			21 26					22 42	

- A To Fishguard Harbour
- B From Dundee to Reading
- C From Manchester Piccadilly to Exeter St Davids
- D From Newcastle to Plymouth
- E From Glasgow Central to Southampton Central
- F From Manchester Piccadilly
- G From Newcastle to Penzance
- H From Glasgow Central to Reading
- I not 8 September. From Manchester Piccadilly to Paignton
- J 8 September. From Manchester Piccadilly
- K To Maesteg
- L From Aberdeen to Guildford
- M not 8 September. From Manchester Piccadilly
- N From Edinburgh to Reading
- O From Manchester Piccadilly. trolley to Bristol Temple Meads
- P From Newcastle to Plymouth. trolley to Birmingham New Street
- Q From Edinburgh to Southampton Central

Trains between Gloucester & Cheltenham are shown on Table T058

Trains between Birmingham & Bromsgrove are shown on Table T069

Table T057-F

Saturdays
8 September to 6 October

Nottingham and Derby - Birmingham - Bristol and Cardiff

	XC ◇ A	XC	XC ◇ B	XC ◇ C	XC	XC ◇ B	XC ◇ D	XC	XC ◇ B	XC ◇ C	AW
Nottingham 56 d		19 34			20 40			21 39			
Beeston 56 d		19 39			20 45			21 44			
Attenborough 56 d		19 42						21 48			
Long Eaton 56 d		19 50			20 54			21 55			
Derby 56 d		20 11	20 28	20 53	21 10	21 28	21 50	22 12	22 23	22 50	
Willington d					21 18						
Burton-on-Trent d		20 22			21 24	21 38		22 22		23 00	
Tamworth d		20 34	20 46		21 35	21 49		22 35		23 10	
Wilnecote d		20 38			21 39			22 38			
Water Orton d											
Birmingham New Street a		20 55	21 04	21 25	21 56	22 06	22 21	23 02	23 05	23 32	
d	20 42		21 12								
University a											
Bromsgrove a											
Ashchurch for Tewkesbury d											
Cheltenham Spa d	21 25		21 52								
Gloucester 134 a			22 01								
d			22 06								23 09
Bristol Parkway 134 a	21 58		22 32								
Bristol Temple Meads 134 a	22 12		22 42								
Lydney d											23 28
Chepstow d											23 38
Caldicot d											23 46
Severn Tunnel Jn 132 d											23 49
Newport (South Wales) 132 a											00 11
Cardiff Central 132 a											00 38

Saturdays
13 October to 8 December

	AW E	XC ◇	XC ◇	XC ◇ F	AW	XC ◇ G	XC ◇ H	XC ◇ I	XC ◇ A	AW E	XC ◇ J	XC ◇ K	XC ◇	XC ◇ L	XC ◇ A	XC	XC ◇ M	XC ◇ H	XC N	XC ◇ O	AW E	XC
Nottingham 56 d							05 58				06 37		06 58			07 37		08 09				08 41
Beeston 56 d							06 03				06 43		07 03			07 42						
Attenborough 56 d							06 07						07 07									
Long Eaton 56 d							06 15						07 16			07 52						
Derby 56 d						06 10	06 36	06 48			07 06	07 27	07 36	07 51		08 06	08 28	08 37	08 53			09 10
Willington d													07 43									
Burton-on-Trent d						06 20	06 48	06 58			07 17	07 38	07 50	08 00		08 18	08 38	08 49				09 22
Tamworth d						06 31	07 01	07 09			07 30	07 49	08 02	08 12		08 30	08 49	09 02				09 34
Wilnecote d							07 05						08 05			08 34						09 38
Water Orton d																08 42						
Birmingham New Street a						06 50	07 24	07 28			07 52	08 08	08 24	08 27		08 55	09 08	09 24	09 27			09 56
d		05 00	05 42	06 42		07 12	07 30		07 42			08 12	08 30		08 42		09 12	09 30		09 42		
University a							07 36						08 36					09 36				
Bromsgrove a			06 03																			
Ashchurch for Tewkesbury d			06 33																			
Cheltenham Spa d		06 03	06 42	07 25	07 45	07 52	08 11		08 25	08 45		08 52	09 11		09 25		09 52	10 11		10 25	10 45	
Gloucester 134 a		06 12	06 52		07 57		08 20			08 57			09 20					10 20			10 56	
d	05 50	06 14	06 57		07 58		08 22			08 58			09 22					10 22			10 58	
Bristol Parkway 134 a				07 53		08 24			08 54			09 24			09 53		10 29			10 54		
Bristol Temple Meads 134 a				08 05		08 38			09 07			09 39			10 04		10 42			11 09		
Lydney d	06 09	06 33	07 16		08 17					09 17								10 41			11 17	
Chepstow d	06 19	06 42	07 26		08 27		08 48			09 27			09 48								11 27	
Caldicot d	06 27	06 51	07 34		08 35					09 35											11 35	
Severn Tunnel Jn 132 d	06 30	06 54	07 37		08 38					09 38											11 38	
Newport (South Wales) 132 a	06 42	07 05	07 48		08 50		09 06			09 50			10 05					11 06			11 50	
Cardiff Central 132 a	07 03	07 21	08 04		09 10		09 23			10 09			10 21					11 24			12 06	

A From Manchester Piccadilly
B From Newcastle
C From Glasgow Central
D From Edinburgh
E To Maesteg
F To Paignton
G To Plymouth. from Birmingham New Street
H from Birmingham New Street
I To Reading
J To Bournemouth. from Derby
K From Leeds to Plymouth
L From Leeds to Southampton Central
M From York to Plymouth
N From Newcastle to Reading
O From Manchester Piccadilly to Paignton

Trains between Gloucester & Cheltenham are shown on Table T058

Trains between Birmingham & Bromsgrove are shown on Table T069

Table T057-F

Saturdays
13 October to 8 December

Nottingham and Derby - Birmingham - Bristol and Cardiff

	XC ◇ A	XC ◇	XC ◇ B	XC ◇ C	AW	XC	XC ◇ D	XC ◇	XC ◇ E	XC ◇ C	XC	XC ◇ F	XC ◇	XC ◇ B	XC ◇ C	AW G	XC	XC ◇ H	XC ◇	AW ◇ I	XC ◇ J
Nottingham 56 d		09 07				09 41		10 06			10 41		11 06				11 41		12 06		
Beeston 56 d		09 12						10 11					11 11						12 11		
Attenborough 56 d																					
Long Eaton 56 d		09 22						10 22					11 23						12 22		
Derby 56 d	09 31	09 36	09 53			10 10	10 29	10 37	10 53		11 09	11 30	11 37	11 53			12 10	12 30	12 37		12 53
Willington d		09 44																			
Burton-on-Trent d	09 41	09 49				10 21		10 49			11 21	11 41	11 49				12 21		12 49		
Tamworth d		10 02				10 33	10 49	11 02			11 33		12 02				12 33	12 49	13 02		
Wilnecote d						10 37					11 37						12 37				
Water Orton d																					
Birmingham New Street a	10 06	10 24	10 27			10 55	11 08	11 24	11 27		11 55	12 08	12 24	12 27			12 55	13 08	13 24		13 27
d	10 12	10 30		10 42			11 12	11 30		11 42		12 12	12 30		12 42			13 12	13 30		
University a		10 36						11 36					12 36						13 36		
Bromsgrove a																					
Ashchurch for Tewkesbury d																					
Cheltenham Spa d	10 52	11 11		11 25	11 46		11 54	12 11		12 25		12 53	13 11		13 25	13 45		13 52	14 11		
Gloucester 134 a		11 20			11 56			12 20					13 20			13 57			14 20		
d		11 22			11 58			12 22					13 22			13 58			14 22	14 42	
Bristol Parkway 134 a	11 25			11 53			12 29			12 53		13 24			13 54			14 26			
Bristol Temple Meads 134 a	11 39			12 04			12 42			13 09		13 39			14 05			14 41			
Lydney d					12 17								13 41			14 17				15 01	
Chepstow d		11 48			12 27			12 48								14 27			14 49	15 11	
Caldicot d					12 35											14 35				15 19	
Severn Tunnel Jn 132 d					12 38											14 38				15 23	
Newport (South Wales) 132 a		12 05			12 50			13 05					14 06			14 50			15 09	15 35	
Cardiff Central 132 a		12 23			13 07			13 21					14 22			15 09			15 26	15 53	

	XC ◇ K	XC	XC ◇ F	XC ◇	XC ◇ B	XC ◇ C	XC	XC ◇ L	XC ◇	XC ◇ J	XC ◇ M	AW G	XC	XC ◇ N	XC ◇	XC ◇ O	XC ◇ C	AW G	XC	XC ◇ L	XC ◇	XC ◇ J
Nottingham 56 d		12 41		13 06			13 41		14 06				14 41		15 06				15 41		16 06	
Beeston 56 d				13 11					14 11						15 11						16 11	
Attenborough 56 d																						
Long Eaton 56 d				13 22					14 22						15 22						16 22	
Derby 56 d		13 10	13 28	13 37	13 53		14 10	14 30	14 37	14 54			15 10	15 28	15 37	15 53			16 10	16 28	16 37	16 53
Willington d		13 18											15 18									
Burton-on-Trent d		13 24	13 38	13 49			14 21		14 49				15 24	15 38	15 49				16 21		16 49	
Tamworth d		13 35		14 02			14 33	14 49	15 02				15 35		16 02				16 33	16 48	17 02	
Wilnecote d							14 37												16 37			
Water Orton d																						
Birmingham New Street a		13 55	14 03	14 24	14 27		14 55	15 08	15 24	15 27			15 55	16 03	16 24	16 27			16 55	17 07	17 24	17 27
d	13 42		14 12	14 30		14 42		15 12	15 30		15 42			16 12	16 30		16 42			17 12	17 30	
University a				14 36					15 36						16 36						17 36	
Bromsgrove a																					17 50	
Ashchurch for Tewkesbury d																					18 08	
Cheltenham Spa d	14 25		14 52	15 11		15 25		15 52	16 11		16 25	16 45		16 52	17 10		17 25	17 45		17 52	18 17	
Gloucester 134 a				15 20					16 20			16 56			17 20			17 56			18 25	
d				15 22					16 22			16 58			17 22			17 58			18 28	
Bristol Parkway 134 a	14 54		15 24			15 54		16 29			16 53			17 25			17 53			18 29		
Bristol Temple Meads 134 a	15 09		15 38			16 07		16 43			17 07			17 39			18 04			18 43		
Lydney d									16 41			17 17			17 41			18 17				
Chepstow d				15 48					16 51			17 27						18 27				
Caldicot d												17 35						18 35				
Severn Tunnel Jn 132 d												17 38						18 38				
Newport (South Wales) 132 a				16 06					17 08			17 50			18 06			18 50			19 10	
Cardiff Central 132 a				16 25					17 24			18 10			18 24			19 12			19 30	

A From Newcastle to Plymouth
B From Newcastle to Southampton Central
C From Manchester Piccadilly
D From Edinburgh to Plymouth
E From Edinburgh to Reading
F From Glasgow Central to Plymouth
G To Maesteg
H From Dundee to Plymouth
I To Fishguard Harbour
J From Newcastle to Reading
K From Manchester Piccadilly to Exeter St Davids
L From Glasgow Central to Penzance
M From Manchester Piccadilly to Paignton
N From Aberdeen to Penzance
O From Newcastle to Guildford

Trains between Gloucester & Cheltenham are shown on Table T058

Trains between Birmingham & Bromsgrove are shown on Table T069

Table T057-F

Saturdays
13 October to 8 December

Nottingham and Derby - Birmingham - Bristol and Cardiff

			XC	AW	XC	XC	XC	XC	XC	AW	XC		XC	XC	XC	XC	XC	XC	XC	XC	XC		XC	XC	XC	XC
			◇1		1	◇1	◇1	◇1	◇1		1		◇1	◇1	◇1	◇1	1	◇1	◇1	◇1	◇1		1	◇1	◇1	1
			A	B		C		D	E	B			F		D	G		H		I	A			J	K	
			🛒		🛒	🛒		🛒	🛒		🛒		🛒		🛒		🛒	🛒		🛒			🛒	🛒	🛒	
Nottingham 8	56 ⇌	d			16 41		17 06				17 41			18 06			18 41		19 06				19 29			20 40
Beeston	56	d					17 11							18 11					19 11				19 35			20 45
Attenborough	56	d																					19 38			
Long Eaton	56	d					17 22							18 22					19 22				19 46			20 54
Derby 6	56	d			17 10	17 28	17 37	17 53			18 10		18 29	18 37	18 53		19 10	19 29	19 39	19 54			20 10	20 28	20 53	21 09
Willington		d			17 18						18 18															21 18
Burton-on-Trent		d			17 24	17 38	17 49				18 24			18 49			19 21	19 39	19 50				20 22			21 24
Tamworth		d			17 35		18 02				18 35		18 47	19 02			19 33		20 02				20 34	20 46		21 35
Wilnecote		d					18 06										19 37						20 38			21 39
Water Orton		d																								
Birmingham New Street 12		a			17 55	18 07	18 24	18 27			18 55		19 07	19 24	19 27		19 55	20 06	20 24	20 27			20 55	21 04	21 25	21 56
		d	17 42			18 12	18 30		18 42				19 12	19 30		19 42		20 12	20 30		20 42			21 12		
University		a					18 36							19 36					20 36							
Bromsgrove		a																								
Ashchurch for Tewkesbury		d																								
Cheltenham Spa 4		d	18 25	18 45		18 52	19 11		19 25	19 45			19 52	20 11		20 25		20 52	21 11		21 25			21 52		
Gloucester 7	134	a		18 56			19 20			19 56				20 20					21 20					22 01		
		d		18 58			19 22			19 58				20 22					21 22					22 06		
Bristol Parkway 7	134	a	18 53			19 24			19 54				20 29			20 53		21 22			21 58			22 32		
Bristol Temple Meads 10	134	a	19 05			19 39			20 05				20 42			21 04		21 34			22 12			22 42		
Lydney		d		19 17						20 17									21 41							
Chepstow		d		19 27						20 27									21 50							
Caldicot		d		19 34						20 35									21 59							
Severn Tunnel Jn	132	d		19 37					20 31	20 38									22 02							
Newport (South Wales)	132	a		19 50			20 03		20 44	20 50				21 09					22 18							
Cardiff Central 7	132	a		20 11			20 20		21 00	21 07				21 26					22 42							

			XC	XC	XC	XC	AW
			◇1	◇1	1	◇1	
			L	K		J	
Nottingham 8	56 ⇌	d			21 39		
Beeston	56	d			21 44		
Attenborough	56	d			21 48		
Long Eaton	56	d			21 56		
Derby 6	56	d	21 28	21 56	22 12	22 26	
Willington		d					
Burton-on-Trent		d	21 38		22 22	22 37	
Tamworth		d	21 49		22 35	22 47	
Wilnecote		d			22 38		
Water Orton		d					
Birmingham New Street 12		a	22 06	22 44	23 02	23 06	
		d					
University		a					
Bromsgrove		a					
Ashchurch for Tewkesbury		d					
Cheltenham Spa 4		d					
Gloucester 7	134	a					
		d					23 09
Bristol Parkway 7	134	a					
Bristol Temple Meads 10	134	a					
Lydney		d					23 28
Chepstow		d					23 38
Caldicot		d					23 46
Severn Tunnel Jn	132	d					23 49
Newport (South Wales)	132	a					00 11
Cardiff Central 7	132	a					00 38

A From Manchester Piccadilly
B To Maesteg
C From Edinburgh to Plymouth
D From Newcastle to Reading
E From Manchester Piccadilly. 🛒 to Bristol Temple Meads
F From Glasgow Central to Plymouth
G From Manchester Piccadilly to Plymouth
H From Edinburgh to Plymouth. 🛒 to Birmingham New Street
I From Newcastle to Southampton Central
J From Glasgow Central
K From Newcastle
L From Edinburgh

Trains between Gloucester & Cheltenham are shown on Table T058

Trains between Birmingham & Bromsgrove are shown on Table T069

Table T057-F

Sundays
20 May to 15 July

Nottingham and Derby - Birmingham - Bristol and Cardiff

			XC	AW	XC	XC	XC		XC	AW	XC	XC	EM	XC	XC	AW	XC		XC	XC	XC	XC	XC	XC	XC	AW
			◇1		◇1	◇1	◇1		◇1		◇1	◇1		◇1	◇1		◇1		◇1	◇1	◇1	◇1	◇1	◇1	◇1	
			A			B			B		C	D	E	F	D				G	D	H	I	J		K	
			🛒		🛒	🛒	🛒		🛒		🛒	🛒		🛒	🛒		🛒		🛒	🛒	🛒	🛒	🛒	🛒	🛒	
Nottingham 8	56 ⇌	d					09 54					11 11	11 27		12 10					13 10				14 10		
Beeston	56	d											11 32													
Attenborough	56	d											11 36													
Long Eaton	56	d											11a44													
Derby 6	56	d				09 28	10 18		10 33		11 29	11 36		12 29	12 36				13 32	13 38	13 55		14 29	14 34	14 53	
Willington		d																								
Burton-on-Trent		d					10 30				11 40	11 47			12 47				13 43	13 49				14 47		
Tamworth		d					10 42		10 53			12 00		12 48	13 00					14 00			14 48	15 00		
Wilnecote		d																								
Water Orton		d																								
Birmingham New Street 12		a				10 18	11 03		11 21		12 06	12 21		13 06	13 21				14 09	14 22	14 27		15 05	15 20	15 26	
		d	09 30		10 12	10 30	11 12		11 30		12 12	12 30		13 12	13 30		13 42		14 12	14 30		14 42	15 12	15 30		
University		a			10 18		11 18					12 36			13 36					14 36				15 36		
Bromsgrove		a																								
Ashchurch for Tewkesbury		d																								
Cheltenham Spa 4		d	10 10		10 52	11 11	11 53		12 10	12 21	12 52	13 10		13 52	14 10	14 19	14 25		14 52	15 10		15 26	15 52	16 10		16 19
Gloucester 7	134	a			11 02		12 02			12 31		13 20			14 20	14 32				15 22				16 20		16 33
		d		10 48	11 05		12 05			12 33		13 23			14 24	14 34				15 24				16 23		16 33
Bristol Parkway 7	134	a	10 37			11 39			12 39		13 21			14 20			14 53		15 23			15 55	16 20			
Bristol Temple Meads 10	134	a	10 48			11 51			12 50		13 32			14 31			15 08		15 34			16 09	16 32			
Lydney		d		11 07						12 52						14 53										16 52
Chepstow		d		11 17						13 02						15 03										17 03
Caldicot		d		11 25						13 10						15 11										17 10
Severn Tunnel Jn	132	d		11 27						13 13						15 14										17 13
Newport (South Wales)	132	a		11 39	11 47		12 44			13 25		14 06			15 01	15 26				16 06				17 04		17 26
Cardiff Central 7	132	a		12 06	12 09		13 07			13 50		14 27			15 27	15 50				16 29				17 26		17 49

			XC		XC	XC	XC	XC	XC	XC	XC	XC	AW		XC	XC	XC	XC	XC	XC	XC	AW	XC		XC	XC
			◇1		◇1	◇1	◇1	◇1	◇1	◇1	◇1	◇1			◇1	◇1	◇1	◇1	◇1	◇1	◇1		◇1		◇1	◇1
			L		G		M	L	N	O	M	L			P	O	Q	I	R	O	M		L		P	
			🛒		🛒		🛒	🛒	🛒	🛒	🛒	🛒			🛒	🛒	🛒	🛒	🛒	🛒	🛒				🛒	🛒
Nottingham 8	56 ⇌	d				15 10				16 10						17 10				18 10						19 10
Beeston	56	d																								
Attenborough	56	d																								
Long Eaton	56	d																								
Derby 6	56	d			15 26	15 34	15 53		16 27	16 34	16 54				17 27	17 35	17 54		18 26	18 35	18 54				19 27	19 35
Willington		d																								
Burton-on-Trent		d			15 37	15 47				16 47					17 37	17 47				18 47					19 38	19 47
Tamworth		d				16 00			16 46	17 00						18 00			18 45	19 00						19 59
Wilnecote		d				16 03																				20 03
Water Orton		d																								
Birmingham New Street 12		a			16 01	16 21	16 26		17 03	17 19	17 26				18 01	18 19	18 26		19 03	19 21	19 28				20 02	20 21
		d	15 42		16 12	16 30		16 42	17 12	17 30		17 42			18 12	18 30		18 42	19 12	19 30			19 42		20 12	
University		a				16 36				17 36						18 36				19 36						
Bromsgrove		a																								
Ashchurch for Tewkesbury		d																								
Cheltenham Spa 4		d	16 26		16 52	17 11		17 26	17 52	18 10		18 26	18 35		18 52	19 12		19 26	19 52	20 10		20 19	20 26		20 52	
Gloucester 7	134	a				17 20				18 20			18 46			19 26				20 19		20 30				
		d				17 23				18 23			18 48			19 28				20 22		20 33				
Bristol Parkway 7	134	a	16 54		17 20			18 03	18 20			18 54			19 21			20 03	20 20				20 56		21 20	
Bristol Temple Meads 10	134	a	17 08		17 31			18 14	18 35			19 08			19 32			20 14	20 31				21 06		21 30	
Lydney		d											19 07									20 52				
Chepstow		d											19 17									21 02				
Caldicot		d											19 25									21 10				
Severn Tunnel Jn	132	d											19 31									21 13				
Newport (South Wales)	132	a				18 06				19 05			19 47			20 06				21 06		21 25				
Cardiff Central 7	132	a				18 29				19 27			20 14			20 30				21 27		21 48				

A To Penzance
B From Leeds to Plymouth
C From York to Plymouth
D 🛒 from Birmingham New Street
E To Matlock
F From Newcastle to Plymouth
G From Edinburgh to Plymouth
H To Reading
I From Manchester Piccadilly to Paignton
J From Edinburgh to Penzance
K From Sheffield to Reading
L From Manchester Piccadilly
M From Newcastle to Reading
N From Motherwell to Penzance
O 🛒 to Birmingham New Street
P From Motherwell to Plymouth
Q From Edinburgh to Reading
R From Aberdeen to Plymouth

Trains between Gloucester & Cheltenham are shown on Table T058

Trains between Birmingham & Bromsgrove are shown on Table T069

Table T057-F

Sundays

20 May to 15 July

Nottingham and Derby - Birmingham - Bristol and Cardiff

	XC	XC	XC	XC	XC	XC	XC	XC	XC	XC	AW
	◇1	◇1	◇1	◇1	◇1	◇1	◇1	◇1	◇1	◇1	
	A	B	C		D	B	E		D	F	
	⊥		⊥		⊥						
Nottingham [8] 56 ⇌ d				20 10				21 10			
Beeston 56 d											
Attenborough 56 d											
Long Eaton 56 d											
Derby [6] 56 d	19 56		20 27	20 35	20 54		21 26	21 37	21 53	22 26	
Willington d											
Burton-on-Trent d				20 47			21 37	21 48	22 03	22 37	
Tamworth d			20 46	20 59			21 47	22 00	22 14	22 47	
Wilnecote d								22 03			
Water Orton d											
Birmingham New Street [12] a	20 27		21 03	21 18	21 26		22 05	22 23	22 31	23 05	
d		20 42	21 12			21 42	22 11				
University a											
Bromsgrove a											
Ashchurch for Tewkesbury d											
Cheltenham Spa [4] d		21 26	21 52			22 25	22 53				
Gloucester [7] 134 a			22 04								
d			22 08								22 33
Bristol Parkway [7] 134 a		21 59	22 35			22 52	23 22				
Bristol Temple Meads [10] 134 a		22 10	22 46			23 02	23 33				
Lydney d											22 52
Chepstow d											23 02
Caldicot d											23 10
Severn Tunnel Jn 132 d											23 13
Newport (South Wales) 132 a											23 30
Cardiff Central [7] 132 a											23 51

Sundays

22 July to 2 September

	XC	AW	XC	XC	XC	XC	AW	XC	XC	EM	XC	XC	XC	AW	XC	XC	XC	XC	XC	XC	AW	XC
	◇1		◇1	◇1	◇1	◇1		◇1	◇1		◇1	◇1	◇1		◇1	◇1	◇1	◇1	◇1	◇1		◇1
	G			H		H		I	J	K	L	I	J		D	I	J	M	N			B
	⊥		⊥	⊥	⊥	⊥		⊥	⊥		⊥	⊥	⊥		⊥	⊥	⊥	⊥	⊥	⊥		⊥
Nottingham [8] 56 ⇌ d					09 54				11 11	11§27			12 10				13 10			14 10		
Beeston 56 d										11§32												
Attenborough 56 d										11§36												
Long Eaton 56 d										11a44												
Derby [6] 56 d																						
Willington d																						
Burton-on-Trent d				10 00	10 29	11 00			11 47		12 02		12 47		13 03		13 49		14 37	14 47		
Tamworth d					10 42	11 12			12 00		12 13		13 00		13 13		14 00		14 48	15 00		
Wilnecote d																						
Water Orton d																						
Birmingham New Street [12] a				10 26	11 02	11 30			12 21		12 32		13 21		13 31		14 22		15 05	15 20		
d	09 30		10 12	10 30	11 12	11 30		12 12	12 30			13 12	13 30		13 42	14 12	14 30	14 42	15 12	15 30		15 42
University a			10 18		11 18				12 36				13 36				14 36			15 36		
Bromsgrove a																						
Ashchurch for Tewkesbury d																						
Cheltenham Spa [4] d	10 10		10 52	11 11	11 52	12 10	12 21	12 52	13 10			13 52	14 10	14 19	14 25	14 52	15 10	15 26	15 52	16 10	16 19	16 26
Gloucester [7] 134 a			11 02		12 02		12 31		13 20				14 20	14 32			15 22			16 20	16 33	
d		10 48	11 05		12 05		12 33		13 23				14 24	14 34			15 24			16 23	16 33	
Bristol Parkway [7] 134 a	10 37			11 39		12 39		13 21				14 20			14 53	15 23		15 55	16 20			16 54
Bristol Temple Meads [10] 134 a	10 48			11 51		12 51		13 32				14 31			15 08	15 34		16 09	16 32			17 08
Lydney d		11 07					12 52							14 53							16 52	
Chepstow d		11 17					13 02							15 03							17 03	
Caldicot d		11 25					13 10							15 11							17 10	
Severn Tunnel Jn 132 d		11 27					13 13							15 14							17 13	
Newport (South Wales) 132 a		11 39	11 47		12 44		13 25		14 06				15 01	15 26			16 06			17 04	17 26	
Cardiff Central [7] 132 a		12 06	12 09		13 07		13 50		14 27				15 28	15 50			16 29			17 26	17 49	

A From Newcastle to Guildford
B From Manchester Piccadilly
C From Motherwell. ⊥ to Birmingham New Street
D From Newcastle
E From Edinburgh
F From Motherwell
G To Penzance
H From Leeds to Plymouth
I To Plymouth
J ⊥ from Birmingham New Street
K 22 July, 29 July, 2 September. To Matlock
L From York
M From Manchester Piccadilly to Paignton
N From Edinburgh to Penzance

Trains between Gloucester & Cheltenham are shown on Table T058

Trains between Birmingham & Bromsgrove are shown on Table T069

Table T057-F

Sundays

22 July to 2 September

Nottingham and Derby - Birmingham - Bristol and Cardiff

	XC	XC	XC	XC	XC	XC	AW	XC	XC	XC	XC	XC	AW	XC	XC	XC	XC	XC	XC	XC	XC
	◇1	◇1	◇1	◇1	◇1	◇1		◇1	◇1	◇1	◇1	◇1		◇1	◇1	◇1	◇1	◇1	◇1	◇1	◇1
	A		B	C	D	B		E	D	F	E	D		B	G		B	H		B	I
	⊥		⊥	⊥	⊥	⊥		⊥	⊥	⊥		⊥			⊥	⊥		⊥			⊥
Nottingham [8] 56 ⇌ d		15 10			16 10				17 10			18 10				19 10			20 10		
Beeston 56 d																					
Attenborough 56 d																					
Long Eaton 56 d																					
Derby [6] 56 d																					
Willington d																					
Burton-on-Trent d	15 37	15 47		16 35	16 47			17 37	17 47		18 35	18 47			19 38	19 47		20 35	20 47		21 37
Tamworth d		16 00		16 46	17 00				18 00		18 45	19 00				19 59		20 46	20 59		21 47
Wilnecote d		16 03														20 03					
Water Orton d																					
Birmingham New Street [12] a	16 01	16 21		17 03	17 19			18 01	18 19		19 03	19 21			20 02	20 21		21 03	21 18		22 05
d	16 12	16 30	16 42	17 12	17 30	17 42		18 12	18 30	18 42	19 12	19 30		19 42	20 12		20 42	21 12		21 42	22 12
University a		16 36			17 36				18 36			19 36									
Bromsgrove a																					
Ashchurch for Tewkesbury d																					
Cheltenham Spa [4] d	16 52	17 11	17 26	17 52	18 10	18 26	18 35	18 52	19 12	19 26	19 52	20 10	20 19	20 26	20 52		21 26	21 52		22 25	22 53
Gloucester [7] 134 a		17 20			18 20		18 46		19 26			20 19	20 30					22 04			
d		17 23			18 23		18 48		19 28			20 22	20 33					22 08			
Bristol Parkway [7] 134 a	17 20		18 03	18 20		18 54		19 21		20 03	20 20			20 56	21 20		21 59	22 35		22 52	23 22
Bristol Temple Meads [10] 134 a	17 31		18 14	18 35		19 08		19 32		20 14	20 31			21 06	21 30		22 10	22 46		23 02	23 33
Lydney d							19 07						20 52								
Chepstow d							19 17						21 02								
Caldicot d							19 25						21 10								
Severn Tunnel Jn 132 d							19 31						21 13								
Newport (South Wales) 132 a		18 06			19 05		19 47		20 06			21 06	21 25								
Cardiff Central [7] 132 a		18 29			19 27		20 14		20 30			21 27	21 48								

	XC	XC	AW	XC
	◇1	◇1		◇1
		J		I
Nottingham [8] 56 ⇌ d	21 10			
Beeston 56 d				
Attenborough 56 d				
Long Eaton 56 d				
Derby [6] 56 d				
Willington d				
Burton-on-Trent d	21 48	22 03		22 59
Tamworth d	22 00	22 14		23 10
Wilnecote d	22 03			
Water Orton d				
Birmingham New Street [12] a	22 23	22 31		23 27
d				
University a				
Bromsgrove a				
Ashchurch for Tewkesbury d				
Cheltenham Spa [4] d				
Gloucester [7] 134 a				
d			22 33	
Bristol Parkway [7] 134 a				
Bristol Temple Meads [10] 134 a				
Lydney d			22 52	
Chepstow d			23 02	
Caldicot d			23 10	
Severn Tunnel Jn 132 d			23 13	
Newport (South Wales) 132 a			23 30	
Cardiff Central [7] 132 a			23 51	

A From Edinburgh to Plymouth
B From Manchester Piccadilly
C From Edinburgh to Penzance
D ⊥ to Birmingham New Street
E From Motherwell to Plymouth
F From Manchester Piccadilly to Paignton
G From Aberdeen to Plymouth
H From Motherwell. ⊥ to Birmingham New Street
I From Motherwell
J From Edinburgh

Trains between Gloucester & Cheltenham are shown on Table T058

Trains between Birmingham & Bromsgrove are shown on Table T069

Table T057-F

Sundays
9 September to 7 October

Nottingham and Derby - Birmingham - Bristol and Cardiff

	XC ◇1 A ⌶	AW	XC ◇1 ⌶	XC ◇1 B ⌶	XC ◇1 ⌶	XC ◇1 B ⌶	AW	XC ◇1 C ⌶	XC ◇1 D ⌶	XC ◇1 E ⌶	XC ◇1 C ⌶	XC ◇1 D ⌶	AW	XC ◇1 F ⌶	XC ◇1 C ⌶	XC ◇1 D ⌶	XC ◇1 G ⌶	XC ◇1 H ⌶	XC ◇1 I ⌶	XC ◇1 ⌶	XC ◇1 G ⌶	AW
Nottingham [8] 56 ⇌ d					09 54				11 11			12 10				13 10				14 10		
Beeston 56 d																						
Attenborough 56 d																						
Long Eaton 56 d																						
Derby [6] 56 d				09 52	10 18	10 52			11 36	11 50		12 35		12 54	13 32	13 38	13 55		14 29	14 34	14 53	
Willington d																						
Burton-on-Trent d					10 29				11 47	12 02		12 47			13 43	13 49				14 47		
Tamworth d					10 42	11 12			12 00	12 13		13 00		13 13		14 00			14 48	15 00		
Wilnecote d																						
Water Orton d																						
Birmingham New Street [12] a				10 26	11 02	11 30			12 21	12 32		13 21		13 31	14 09	14 22	14 27		15 05	15 20	15 26	
d	09 30		10 12	10 30	11 12	11 30		12 12	12 30		13 12	13 30		13 42	14 12	14 30		14 42	15 12	15 30		
University a			10 18		11 18				12 36			13 36				14 36				15 36		
Bromsgrove a																						
Ashchurch for Tewkesbury d																						
Cheltenham Spa [4] d	10 10		10 52	11 11	11 52	12 10	12 21	12 52	13 10		13 52	14 10	14 19	14 25	14 52	15 10		15 26	15 52	16 10		16 19
Gloucester [7] 134 a			11 02		12 02		12 31		13 20			14 20	14 32			15 22				16 20		16 33
d		10 48	11 05		12 05		12 33		13 23			14 24	14 34			15 24				16 23		16 33
Bristol Parkway [7] 134 a	10 37			11 39		12 39		13 21			14 20			14 53	15 23			15 55	16 20			
Bristol Temple Meads [10] 134 a	10 48			11 51		12 51		13 32			14 31			15 08	15 34			16 09	16 32			
Lydney d		11 07					12 52						14 53									16 52
Chepstow d		11 17					13 02						15 03									17 03
Caldicot d		11 25					13 10						15 11									17 10
Severn Tunnel Jn 132 d		11 27					13 13						15 14									17 13
Newport (South Wales) 132 a		11 39	11 47		12 44		13 25		14 06			15 01	15 26			16 06				17 04		17 26
Cardiff Central [7] 132 a		12 06	12 09		13 07		13 50		14 27			15 28	15 50			16 29				17 26		17 49

	XC ◇1 J ⌶	XC ◇1 K ⌶	XC ◇1	XC ◇1 G ⌶	XC ◇1 J ⌶	XC ◇1 I ⌶	XC ◇1 L ⌶	XC ◇1 G ⌶	XC ◇1 J ⌶	AW	XC ◇1 M ⌶	XC ◇1 L ⌶	XC ◇1 G ⌶	XC ◇1 H ⌶	XC ◇1 M	XC ◇1 L ⌶	XC ◇1 G ⌶	AW	XC ◇1 J	XC ◇1 N ⌶	XC ◇1 ⌶
Nottingham [8] 56 ⇌ d			15 10				16 10					17 10				18 10					19 10
Beeston 56 d																					
Attenborough 56 d																					
Long Eaton 56 d																					
Derby [6] 56 d		15 26	15 34	15 54		16 27	16 34	16 55			17 26	17 35	17 55		18 26	18 35	18 55			19 27	19 35
Willington d																					
Burton-on-Trent d		15 37	15 47				16 47				17 37	17 47				18 46				19 38	19 46
Tamworth d			16 00			16 46	17 00					18 00			18 45	19 00					19 58
Wilnecote d			16 03																		20 02
Water Orton d																					
Birmingham New Street [12] a		16 01	16 21	16 26		17 03	17 19	17 26			18 01	18 19	18 26		19 03	19 21	19 28			20 02	20 21
d	15 42	16 12	16 30		16 42	17 12	17 30		17 42		18 12	18 30		18 42	19 12	19 30			19 42	20 12	
University a			16 36				17 36					18 36				19 36					
Bromsgrove a																					
Ashchurch for Tewkesbury d																					
Cheltenham Spa [4] d	16 26	16 52	17 11		17 26	17 52	18 10		18 26	18 35	18 52	19 12		19 26	19 52	20 10		20 19	20 26	20 52	
Gloucester [7] 134 a			17 20				18 20			18 46		19 26				20 19		20 30			
d			17 23				18 23			18 48		19 28				20 22		20 33			
Bristol Parkway [7] 134 a	16 54	17 20			18 03	18 20			18 54		19 21			20 03	20 20				20 56	21 20	
Bristol Temple Meads [10] 134 a	17 08	17 31			18 14	18 35			19 08		19 32			20 14	20 31				21 06	21 30	
Lydney d										19 07								20 52			
Chepstow d										19 17								21 02			
Caldicot d										19 25								21 10			
Severn Tunnel Jn 132 d										19 31								21 13			
Newport (South Wales) 132 a			18 06				19 05			19 47		20 06				21 06		21 25			
Cardiff Central [7] 132 a			18 29				19 27			20 14		20 30				21 27		21 48			

A To Penzance
B From Leeds to Plymouth
C To Plymouth
D ⌶ from Birmingham New Street
E From York
F From Newcastle
G To Reading
H From Manchester Piccadilly to Paignton
I From Edinburgh to Penzance
J From Manchester Piccadilly
K From Edinburgh to Plymouth
L ⌶ to Birmingham New Street
M From Glasgow Central to Plymouth
N From Aberdeen to Plymouth

Trains between Gloucester & Cheltenham are shown on Table T058

Trains between Birmingham & Bromsgrove are shown on Table T069

Table T057-F

Sundays
9 September to 7 October

Nottingham and Derby - Birmingham - Bristol and Cardiff

	XC ◇1 A ⌶	XC ◇1 B	XC ◇1 C ⌶	XC ◇1	XC ◇1 ⌶	XC ◇1 B	XC ◇1 D ⌶	XC ◇1	XC ◇1 E	AW	XC ◇1 D
Nottingham [8] 56 ⇌ d				20 10				21 10			
Beeston 56 d											
Attenborough 56 d											
Long Eaton 56 d											
Derby [6] 56 d	19 55		20 27	20 35	20 54		21 26	21 37	21 53		22 48
Willington d											
Burton-on-Trent d				20 46			21 37	21 48	22 03		22 59
Tamworth d			20 46	20 59			21 47	22 00	22 14		23 10
Wilnecote d								22 03			
Water Orton d											
Birmingham New Street [12] a	20 27		21 03	21 18	21 26		22 05	22 23	22 31		23 27
d		20 42	21 12			21 42	22 12				
University a											
Bromsgrove a											
Ashchurch for Tewkesbury d											
Cheltenham Spa [4] d		21 26	21 52			22 25	22 53				
Gloucester [7] 134 a			22 04								
d			22 08							22 33	
Bristol Parkway [7] 134 a		21 59	22 35			22 52	23 22				
Bristol Temple Meads [10] 134 a		22 10	22 46			23 02	23 33				
Lydney d										22 52	
Chepstow d										23 02	
Caldicot d										23 10	
Severn Tunnel Jn 132 d										23 13	
Newport (South Wales) 132 a										23 30	
Cardiff Central [7] 132 a										23 51	

Sundays
14 October to 2 December

	XC ◇1 F ⌶	AW	XC ◇1 ⌶	XC ◇1 G ⌶	XC ◇1 ⌶	XC ◇1 G ⌶	AW	XC ◇1 H ⌶	XC ◇1 I ⌶	EM J	XC ◇1 K ⌶	XC ◇1 I ⌶	AW	XC ◇1 ⌶	XC ◇1 L ⌶	XC ◇1 I ⌶	XC ◇1 M ⌶	XC ◇1 N ⌶	XC ◇1 O ⌶	XC ◇1 ⌶	XC ◇1 P ⌶	AW
Nottingham [8] 56 ⇌ d					09 54				11 11	11 27		12 10				13 10				14 10		
Beeston 56 d										11 32												
Attenborough 56 d										11 36												
Long Eaton 56 d										11a43												
Derby [6] 56 d				09 28	10 18	10 33		11 29	11 36		12 29	12 36			13 32	13 38	13 55		14 29	14 34	14 53	
Willington d																						
Burton-on-Trent d					10 29			11 40	11 47			12 47			13 43	13 49				14 47		
Tamworth d					10 42	10 53			12 00		12 48	13 00				14 00			14 48	15 00		
Wilnecote d																						
Water Orton d																						
Birmingham New Street [12] a				10 18	11 02	11 21		12 06	12 21		13 06	13 21			14 09	14 22	14 27		15 05	15 20	15 26	
d	09 30		10 12	10 30	11 12	11 30		12 12	12 30		13 12	13 30		13 42	14 12	14 30		14 42	15 12	15 30		
University a			10 18		11 18				12 36			13 36				14 36				15 36		
Bromsgrove a																						
Ashchurch for Tewkesbury d																						
Cheltenham Spa [4] d	10 10		10 52	11 11	11 52	12 10	12 21	12 52	13 10		13 52	14 10	14 19	14 25	14 52	15 10		15 26	15 52	16 10		16 19
Gloucester [7] 134 a			11 02		12 02		12 31		13 20			14 20	14 32			15 22				16 20		16 33
d		10 48	11 05		12 05		12 33		13 23			14 24	14 34			15 24				16 23		16 33
Bristol Parkway [7] 134 a	10 37			11 39		12 39		13 21			14 20			14 53	15 23			15 55	16 20			
Bristol Temple Meads [10] 134 a	10 48			11 51		12 50		13 32			14 31			15 08	15 34			16 09	16 32			
Lydney d		11 07					12 52						14 53									16 52
Chepstow d		11 17					13 02						15 03									17 03
Caldicot d		11 25					13 10						15 11									17 10
Severn Tunnel Jn 132 d		11 27					13 13						15 14									17 13
Newport (South Wales) 132 a		11 39	11 47		12 44		13 25		14 06			15 01	15 26			16 06				17 04		17 26
Cardiff Central [7] 132 a		12 06	12 09		13 07		13 50		14 27			15 28	15 50			16 29				17 26		17 49

A To Guildford
B From Manchester Piccadilly
C From Glasgow Central. ⌶ to Birmingham New Street
D From Glasgow Central
E From Edinburgh
F To Penzance
G From Leeds to Plymouth
H From York to Plymouth
I ⌶ from Birmingham New Street
J From Grantham to Matlock
K From Newcastle to Plymouth
L From Edinburgh to Plymouth
M To Reading
N From Manchester Piccadilly to Paignton
O From Edinburgh to Penzance
P From Sheffield to Reading

Trains between Gloucester & Cheltenham are shown on Table T058

Trains between Birmingham & Bromsgrove are shown on Table T069

Table T057-F

Sundays

14 October to 2 December

Nottingham and Derby - Birmingham - Bristol and Cardiff

		XC ◇1 A	XC ◇1 B	XC ◇1	XC ◇1 C	XC ◇1 A	XC ◇1 D	XC ◇1 E	XC ◇1 C	XC ◇1 A	AW	XC ◇1 F	XC ◇1 E	XC ◇1 G	XC ◇1 H	XC ◇1 I	XC ◇1 E	XC ◇1 C	AW	XC ◇1 A	XC ◇1 F	XC ◇1
Nottingham 8 56	d			15 10				16 10					17 10				18 10					19 10
Beeston 56	d																					
Attenborough 56	d																					
Long Eaton 56	d																					
Derby 6 56	d		15 26	15 34	15 53		16 27	16 34	16 54			17 27	17 35	17 54		18 26	18 35	18 54			19 27	19 35
Willington	d																					
Burton-on-Trent	d		15 37	15 47				16 47				17 37	17 47				18 47				19 38	19 46
Tamworth	d			16 00			16 46	17 00					18 00			18 45	19 00					19 58
Wilnecote	d			16 03																		20 02
Water Orton	d																					
Birmingham New Street 12	a		16 01	16 21	16 26		17 03	17 19	17 26			18 01	18 19	18 26		19 03	19 21	19 28			20 02	20 21
	d	15 42	16 12	16 30		16 42	17 12	17 30		17 42		18 12	18 30		18 42	19 12	19 30			19 42	20 12	
University	a			16 36				17 36					18 36				19 36					
Bromsgrove	a																					
Ashchurch for Tewkesbury	d																					
Cheltenham Spa 4	d	16 26	16 52	17 11		17 26	17 52	18 10		18 26	18 35	18 52	19 12		19 26	19 52	20 10		20 19	20 26	20 52	
Gloucester 7 134	a			17 20				18 20			18 46		19 26				20 19		20 30			
	d			17 23				18 23			18 48		19 28				20 22		20 33			
Bristol Parkway 7 134	a	16 54	17 20			18 03	18 20			18 54		19 21			20 03	20 20				20 56	21 20	
Bristol Temple Meads 10 134	a	17 08	17 31			18 14	18 35			19 08		19 32			20 14	20 31				21 06	21 30	
Lydney	d										19 07								20 52			
Chepstow	d										19 17								21 02			
Caldicot	d										19 25								21 10			
Severn Tunnel Jn 132	d										19 31								21 13			
Newport (South Wales) 132	a			18 06				19 05			19 47		20 06				21 06		21 25			
Cardiff Central 7 132	a			18 29				19 27			20 14		20 30				21 27		21 48			

		XC ◇1 J	XC ◇1 A	XC ◇1 K	XC ◇1	XC ◇1 L	XC ◇1 A	XC ◇1 M	XC ◇1	XC ◇1 L	XC ◇1 N	AW
Nottingham 8 56	d				20 10				21 10			
Beeston 56	d											
Attenborough 56	d											
Long Eaton 56	d											
Derby 6 56	d	19 56		20 27	20 35	20 54		21 26	21 37	21 53	22 26	
Willington	d											
Burton-on-Trent	d				20 46			21 37	21 48	22 03	22 37	
Tamworth	d			20 46	20 59			21 47	22 00	22 14	22 47	
Wilnecote	d								22 03			
Water Orton	d											
Birmingham New Street 12	a	20 27		21 03	21 18	21 26		22 05	22 23	22 31	23 05	
	d		20 42	21 12			21 42	22 11				
University	a											
Bromsgrove	a											
Ashchurch for Tewkesbury	d											
Cheltenham Spa 4	d		21 26	21 52			22 25	22 53				
Gloucester 7 134	a			22 04								
	d			22 08								22 33
Bristol Parkway 7 134	a		21 59	22 35			22 52	23 22				
Bristol Temple Meads 10 134	a		22 10	22 46			23 02	23 33				
Lydney	d											22 52
Chepstow	d											23 02
Caldicot	d											23 10
Severn Tunnel Jn 132	d											23 13
Newport (South Wales) 132	a											23 30
Cardiff Central 7 132	a											23 51

A From Manchester Piccadilly
B From Edinburgh to Plymouth
C From Newcastle to Reading
D From Glasgow Central to Penzance
E to Birmingham New Street
F From Glasgow Central to Plymouth
G From Edinburgh to Reading
H From Manchester Piccadilly to Plymouth
I From Aberdeen to Plymouth
J From Newcastle to Guildford
K From Glasgow Central. to Birmingham New Street
L From Newcastle
M From Edinburgh
N From Glasgow Central

Trains between Gloucester & Cheltenham are shown on Table T058

Trains between Birmingham & Bromsgrove are shown on Table T069

Table T057-R

Mondays to Fridays

21 May to 20 July

Cardiff and Bristol - Birmingham - Derby and Nottingham

Miles	Miles			XC ◇1 A	XC 1	XC ◇1 B	XC 1	XC ◇1 C	XC 1	XC ◇1 B	XC 1	XC ◇1 D	XC ◇1 E	XC 1	AW F	XC ◇1 G	XC ◇1 H	XC ◇1	XC ◇1 I	XC 1	AW	XC ◇1 J	XC ◇1 K
0	—	Cardiff Central 7 132	d												06 12			06 40			07 05	07 00	
11¾	—	Newport (South Wales) 132	d												06 28			06 55			07 23	07 14	
21½	—	Severn Tunnel Jn 132	d												06 39			07 05			07 38	07 25	
22¼	—	Caldicot	d												06 41			07 08			07 40		
29	—	Chepstow	d												06 50			07 16			07 49		
37	—	Lydney	d												06 59			07 25			07 58		
—	0	Bristol Temple Meads 10 134	d									06 27				07 00			07 30			08 00	
—	5¾	Bristol Parkway 7 134	d									06 39				07 10			07 40			08 10	
56½	—	Gloucester 7 134	a												07 20			07 44			08 20		
—	—		d										07 10		07 22			07 46			08 21		
63	45¼	Cheltenham Spa 4	a									07 08	07 19		07 34	07 39		07 56	08 09		08 34	08 39	
—	—		d									07 10	07 21			07 41		07 57	08 11			08 41	
70¼	52½	Ashchurch for Tewkesbury	d										07 29					08 05					
97¾	79	Bromsgrove	d										07 49					08 24					
109¾	90¾	University	d										08 10					08 39					
111	93¼	Birmingham New Street 12	a									07 56	08 17			08 26		08 45	08 56			09 26	
—	—		d	06 00	06 19	06 30	06 49	07 03	07 19	07 30	07 49	08 03		08 19			08 30	08 49	09 03	09 19			09 30
116	—	Water Orton	d																				
124	—	Wilnecote	d		06 35				07 35									09 05					
125¾	—	Tamworth	d		06 39		07 07	07 19	07 39		08 07	08 19		08 36				09 09		09 36			
138¾	—	Burton-on-Trent	d		06 51		07 20	07 31	07 50		08 19	08 29		08 48				09 20	09 27	09 48			
143½	—	Willington	d				07 25				08 25												
149¾	—	Derby 6 56	d	06a33	07 08	07a11	07 43	07a42	08 10	08a09	08 41	08a41		09 08			09a07	09 42	09a38	10 08			10a04
157¾	—	Long Eaton 56	d		07 21		07 55		08 19		08 50							09 51					
160	—	Attenborough 56	d		07 28						08 58												
162¼	—	Beeston 56	d		07 32		08 03		08 27		09 01							09 59					
165¾	—	Nottingham 8 56	a		07 38		08 09		08 34		09 08			09 28				10 05		10 28			

		XC ◇1	XC ◇1 L	XC 1	XC ◇1 M	XC ◇1 N	XC ◇1	XC ◇1 I	XC 1	AW	XC ◇1 G	XC ◇1 K	XC ◇1	XC ◇1 O	AW P	XC 1	XC ◇1 G	XC ◇1 Q	XC ◇1	XC ◇1 R	XC 1	XC ◇1 M	XC ◇1 K
Cardiff Central 7 132	d	07 45					08 45			09 12			09 45		10 09				10 45				
Newport (South Wales) 132	d	08 02					09 00			09 28			10 00		10 27				11 00				
Severn Tunnel Jn 132	d									09 38					10 38								
Caldicot	d									09 39					10 40								
Chepstow	d						09 18			09 48			10 18		10 49								
Lydney	d	08 25								09 57					10 58				11 25				
Bristol Temple Meads 10 134	d		08 30		09 00			09 30			10 00			10 30			11 00			11 30		12 00	
Bristol Parkway 7 134	d		08 40		09 10			09 40			10 10			10 40			11 10			11 40		12 10	
Gloucester 7 134	a	08 45					09 44			10 20			10 44		11 20				11 44				
	d	08 49					09 50			10 20			10 50		11 21				11 50				
Cheltenham Spa 4	a	08 58	09 10		09 40		10 00	10 09		10 31	10 40		11 00	11 09	11 32		11 40		12 00	12 09		12 39	
	d	09 00	09 12		09 42		10 01	10 11			10 41		11 01	11 11			11 42		12 01	12 11		12 41	
Ashchurch for Tewkesbury	d																						
Bromsgrove	d																						
University	d	09 39					10 39						11 39						12 39				
Birmingham New Street 12	a	09 45	09 58		10 23		10 45	10 56			11 26		11 45	11 58			12 26		12 45	12 56		13 26	
	d	09 49	10 03	10 19		10 30	10 49	11 03	11 19			11 30	11 49	12 03		12 19		12 30	12 49	13 03	13 19		13 30
Water Orton	d																						
Wilnecote	d						11 05												13 05				
Tamworth	d	10 07	10 19	10 36			11 09		11 36				12 07	12 19		12 36			13 09		13 36		
Burton-on-Trent	d	10 19		10 48			11 21	11 26	11 48				12 19			12 48			13 19	13 28	13 48		
Willington	d	10 25											12 25										
Derby 6 56	d	10 41	10a41	11 08		11a05	11 40	11a38	12 08			12a05	12 40	12a42		13 08		13a05	13 40	13a39	14 08		14a05
Long Eaton 56	d	10 50					11 49						12 50						13 49				
Attenborough 56	d																						
Beeston 56	d	10 58					11 59						12 58						13 57				
Nottingham 8 56	a	11 04		11 28			12 06		12 28				13 05			13 28			14 03		14 28		

A To Glasgow Central
B To Newcastle
C To Edinburgh
D From Bath Spa to Glasgow Central
E To Stansted Airport
F From Cardiff Canton Sidings
G To Manchester Piccadilly
H From Guildford to Newcastle
I From Plymouth to Edinburgh
J To Manchester Piccadilly. from Bristol Temple Meads
K From Reading to Newcastle
L From Plymouth to Glasgow Central
M From Paignton to Manchester Piccadilly
N From Winchester to Newcastle
O From Penzance to Glasgow Central
P From Maesteg
Q From Southampton Central to Newcastle
R From Plymouth to Aberdeen

Trains between Gloucester & Cheltenham are shown on Table T058

Trains between Birmingham & Bromsgrove are shown on Table T069

Table T057-R

Cardiff and Bristol - Birmingham - Derby and Nottingham

Mondays to Fridays

21 May to 20 July

	XC ◇■ ᚹ	XC ◇■ A ᚹ	AW B	XC ■	XC ◇■ C ᚹ	XC ■ D ᚹ	XC ◇■ ᚹ		AW B	XC ◇■ E ᚹ	XC ■	XC ◇■ F ᚹ	XC ◇■ G ᚹ	XC ◇■ ᚹ	XC ◇■ H ᚹ	XC ■	XC ◇■ C ᚹ		XC ◇■ I ᚹ	XC ◇■ ᚹ	XC ◇■ J ᚹ	XC ■	AW B	XC ◇■ K ᚹ
Cardiff Central ■ 132 d	11 45		12 12				12 45		13 12					13 45						14 45			15 12	
Newport (South Wales) 132 d	12 00		12 28				13 01		13 28					14 00						15 00			15 28	
Severn Tunnel Jn. 132 d			12 39						13 39														15 37	
Caldicot d			12 42						13 43														15 41	
Chepstow d	12 18		12 51				13 18		13 52											15 18			15 50	
Lydney d			13 00						14 01					14 25									15 59	
Bristol Temple Meads ■ 134 d		12 30			13 00					13 30		14 00			14 30		15 00				15 30			16 00
Bristol Parkway ■ 134 d		12 40			13 10					13 40		14 10			14 40		15 10				15 40			16 10
Gloucester ■ 134 a	12 44		13 20				13 44		14 22					14 44						15 44			16 21	
d	12 48		13 22				13 50							14 50						15 50			16 22	
Cheltenham Spa ■ a	12 58	13 09	13 33		13 39		14 00			14 09		14 40		15 00	15 10		15 41			16 00	16 10		16 31	16 39
d	12 58	13 11			13 41		14 01			14 11		14 41		15 01	15 11		15 42			16 01	16 11			16 41
Ashchurch for Tewkesbury d	13 07																							
Bromsgrove d																								
University d	13 39						14 39							15 39						16 39				
Birmingham New Street ■ a	13 45	13 56			14 23		14 45			14 56		15 23		15 45	15 56		16 23			16 45	16 56			17 23
d	13 49	14 03		14 19		14 30	14 49			15 03	15 19		15 30	15 49	16 03	16 19			16 30	16 49	17 03	17 19		
Water Orton d																								
Wilnecote d	14 05						15 05							16 05						17 05				
Tamworth d	14 09	14 19		14 36			15 09				15 36			16 09	16 20	16 36				17 09		17 36		
Burton-on-Trent d	14 21			14 48			15 21			15 26	15 48			16 21		16 48				17 21	17 26	17 48		
Willington d							15 26																	
Derby ■ 56 d	14 40	14a41		15 08		15a05	15 40			15a41	16 08		16a05	16 40	16a41	17 08			17a05	17 40	17a40	18 08		
Long Eaton 56 d	14 49						15 49							16 49		17 17				17 50		18 18		
Attenborough 56 d																								
Beeston 56 d	14 57						15 57							16 57		17 25				17 58		18 25		
Nottingham ■ 56 🚊 a	15 03			15 28			16 03				16 28			17 03		17 31				18 04		18 32		

	XC ◇■ G ᚹ	XC ■	XC ◇■ ᚹ		XC ◇■ J ᚹ	AW B	XC ■	XC ◇■ C ᚹ	XC ◇■ D ᚹ	XC ◇■ L ᚹ	XC ◇■ M ᚹ	XC ■	AW B		XC ◇■ N ᚹ	XC ◇■ G	XC ◇■ O ᚹ	XC ◇■ P ᚹ	AW B	XC ◇■ C ᚹ	XC ◇■ Q	XC ◇■ L ᚹ	XC ◇■ P ᚹ
Cardiff Central ■ 132 d			15 45			16 10				16 45			17 12				17 45		18 08			18 45	
Newport (South Wales) 132 d			16 00			16 27				17 00			17 28				18 00		18 24			19 00	
Severn Tunnel Jn. 132 d						16 38							17 39						18 35				
Caldicot d						16 40							17 41						18 37				
Chepstow d			16 18			16 49							17 50				18 18		18 46			19 17	
Lydney d						16 58				17 25			17 59						18 55				
Bristol Temple Meads ■ 134 d					16 30			17 00			17 30				18 00			18 30		19 00			19 30
Bristol Parkway ■ 134 d					16 40			17 10			17 40				18 10			18 40		19 10			19 40
Gloucester ■ 134 a			16 44			17 19				17 44			18 20				18 44		19 17			19 43	
d			16 50			17 23				17 50			18 21				18 46		19 21			19 45	
Cheltenham Spa ■ a			17 00		17 09	17 32		17 41		18 00	18 10		18 30		18 40		18 56	19 09	19 31	19 39		19 56	20 10
d			17 01		17 11			17 42		18 01	18 11				18 41		18 57	19 11		19 41		19 58	20 11
Ashchurch for Tewkesbury d																	19 05						
Bromsgrove d																							
University d			17 39							18 39							19 39					20 34	
Birmingham New Street ■ a			17 45		17 56			18 23		18 45	18 56				19 23		19 45	19 56		20 23		20 40	20 51
d	17 30	17 39	17 49		18 03		18 19		18 30	18 49	19 03	19 19				19 30	19 49	20 03			20 30	20 49	21 03
Water Orton d		17 51																					
Wilnecote d		17 59	18 05							19 05							20 05					21 05	
Tamworth d		18 03	18 09		18 19		18 36			19 09		19 36					20 09	20 19				21 09	21 19
Burton-on-Trent d		18 14	18 21				18 48			19 21	19 29	19 48					20 21					21 21	21 30
Willington d		18 20																					
Derby ■ 56 d	18a05	18a30	18 40		18a39		19 08		19a07	19 40	19a38	20 08				20a08	20 40	20a39			21a09	21 34	21a43
Long Eaton 56 d			18 49				19 17			19 49							20 49					21 46	
Attenborough 56 d																						21 55	
Beeston 56 d			18 57				19 24			19 57							20 57					21 58	
Nottingham ■ 56 🚊 a			19 03				19 31			20 04		20 28					21 03					22 04	

A From Penzance to Glasgow Central
B From Maesteg
C To Manchester Piccadilly
D From Southampton Central to Newcastle
E From Plymouth to Dundee
F From Penzance to Manchester Piccadilly
G From Reading to Newcastle
H From Plymouth to Glasgow Central
I From Southampton Central to Edinburgh
J From Plymouth to Edinburgh
K From Paignton to Manchester Piccadilly
L ᚹ to Birmingham New Street
M From Plymouth to Leeds
N From Exeter St Davids to Manchester Piccadilly
O From Nottingham. ᚹ to Birmingham New Street
P From Plymouth to Leeds. ᚹ to Birmingham New Street
Q From Southampton Central to York

Trains between Gloucester & Cheltenham are shown on Table T058

Trains between Birmingham & Bromsgrove are shown on Table T069

Table T057-R

Cardiff and Bristol - Birmingham - Derby and Nottingham

Mondays to Fridays

21 May to 20 July

	XC ◇■	XC ◇■	XC ◇■ A	XC ■	XC ◇■	XC ■	AW B	XC ◇■ C		XC ◇■ D	AW B
Cardiff Central ■ 132 d		19 50			21 05		21 12			21 50	23 20
Newport (South Wales) 132 d		20 05			21 21		21 27			22 05	23 38
Severn Tunnel Jn. 132 d		20 15					21 38				23 58
Caldicot d		20 18					21 41				00 01
Chepstow d		20 26					21 50				00 10
Lydney d		20 35					21 59				00 19
Bristol Temple Meads ■ 134 d	20 00		20 30					22 00			
Bristol Parkway ■ 134 d	20 10		20 40					22 10			
Gloucester ■ 134 a	20 38	20 54			22 02		22 22			22 46	00 39
d	20 46	20 59			22 04		22 23			22 47	
Cheltenham Spa ■ a	20 55	21 09	21 15		22 14		22 34	22 41		22 56	
d	20 56	21 11	21 17		22 15			22 42		22 58	
Ashchurch for Tewkesbury d					22 23						
Bromsgrove d											
University d		21 45									
Birmingham New Street ■ a	21 37	21 51	22 02		23 05			23 43		23 59	
d				22 03		23 09					
Water Orton d											
Wilnecote d						23 24					
Tamworth d				22 27		23 28					
Burton-on-Trent d				22 39		23 40					
Willington d						23 45					
Derby ■ 56 d				22 59		23 57					
Long Eaton 56 d				23 10							
Attenborough 56 d				23 18							
Beeston 56 d				23 21							
Nottingham ■ 56 🚊 a				23 27		00 16					

Mondays to Fridays

23 July to 31 August

	XC ◇■ E ᚹ	XC ■	XC ◇■ F ᚹ	XC ■	XC ◇■ E ᚹ	XC ■ ᚹ	XC ◇■ G ᚹ	EM ◇ H	XC ■		XC ◇■ I ᚹ	XC ◇■ J	XC ■ ᚹ	AW K	XC ◇■ L ᚹ	XC ◇■ M ᚹ	EM H	XC ◇■	XC ◇■ N ᚹ		XC ■ ᚹ	AW	XC ◇■ O ᚹ	XC ◇■ P ᚹ
Cardiff Central ■ 132 d														06 12				06 40				07 05	07 00	
Newport (South Wales) 132 d														06 28				06 55				07 23	07 14	
Severn Tunnel Jn. 132 d														06 39				07 05				07 38	07 25	
Caldicot d														06 41				07 08				07 40		
Chepstow d														06 50				07 16				07 49		
Lydney d														06 59				07 25				07 58		
Bristol Temple Meads ■ 134 d											06 27				07 00				07 30				08 00	
Bristol Parkway ■ 134 d											06 39				07 10				07 40				08 10	
Gloucester ■ 134 a														07 20				07 44				08 20		
d												07 10		07 22				07 46				08 21		
Cheltenham Spa ■ a											07 08	07 19		07 34	07 39			07 56	08 09			08 34	08 39	
d											07 10	07 21			07 41			07 57	08 11				08 41	
Ashchurch for Tewkesbury d												07 29						08 05						
Bromsgrove d												07 49						08 24						
University d												08 10						08 39						
Birmingham New Street ■ a											07 56	08 17			08 26			08 45	08 56				09 26	
d	06 00	06 19	06 30	06 49	07 03	07 19	07 30		07 49		08 03		08 19			08 30		08 49	09 03		09 19			09 30
Water Orton d																								
Wilnecote d		06 35				07 35												09 05						
Tamworth d		06 39	06 46	07 07	07 19	07 39			08 07		08 20		08 36					09 09			09 36			
Burton-on-Trent d	06a27	06 51	06a56	07 20	07a30	07 50	07a54		08 19		08a30		08 48			08a53		09 21	09a25		09 48			09a51
Willington d				07 25					08 25															
Derby ■ 56 d																								
Long Eaton 56 d								08 25									09 24							
Attenborough 56 d		07 28						08 33	08 57								09 32							
Beeston 56 d		07 32		08 03		08 27		08 36	09 00								09 35	09 57						
Nottingham ■ 56 🚊 a		07 38		08 09		08 34		08 46	09 07				09 25				09 42	10 03			10 25			

A From Plymouth
B From Maesteg
C From Paignton
D From Nottingham
E To Newcastle
F To Edinburgh
G To Glasgow Central
H from 30 July until 10 August. To Newark Castle
I From Bath Spa to Newcastle
J To Stansted Airport
K From Cardiff Canton Sidings
L To Manchester Piccadilly
M From Guildford to Edinburgh
N From Plymouth to Newcastle
O To Manchester Piccadilly. ᚹ from Bristol Temple Meads
P From Reading to Glasgow Central

Trains between Gloucester & Cheltenham are shown on Table T058

Trains between Birmingham & Bromsgrove are shown on Table T069

Table T057-R

Mondays to Fridays

23 July to 31 August

Cardiff and Bristol - Birmingham - Derby and Nottingham

		EM	XC	XC	XC	XC	XC	EM	XC	XC	XC	AW	XC	XC	EM	XC	XC	AW	XC	XC	XC	EM
			◇1	◇1	1	◇1	◇1		◇1	◇1	1		◇1	◇1		◇1	◇1		1	◇1	◇1	
		A		B		C	D	A		B			E	F	A		G	H		E	I	A
					🛒	🛒	🛒			🛒	🛒		🛒			🛒	🛒		🛒	🛒	🛒	
Cardiff Central	132 d		07 45						08 45			09 12				09 45		10 09				
Newport (South Wales)	132 d		08 02						09 00			09 28				10 00		10 27				
Severn Tunnel Jn.	132 d											09 38						10 38				
Caldicot	d											09 39						10 40				
Chepstow	d								09 18			09 48				10 18		10 49				
Lydney	d		08 25									09 57						10 58				
Bristol Temple Meads	134 d			08 30		09 00				09 30			10 00				10 30			11 00		
Bristol Parkway	134 d			08 40		09 10				09 40			10 10				10 40			11 10		
Gloucester	134 a		08 45						09 44			10 20				10 44		11 20				
	d		08 49						09 50			10 20				10 50		11 21				
Cheltenham Spa	a		08 58	09 10		09 40			10 00	10 09		10 31	10 40			11 00	11 09	11 32		11 40		
	d		09 00	09 12		09 42			10 01	10 11			10 41			11 01	11 11			11 42		
Ashchurch for Tewkesbury	d																					
Bromsgrove	d																					
University	d		09 39						10 39							11 39						
Birmingham New Street	a		09 45	09 58		10 23			10 45	10 56			11 26			11 45	11 58			12 26		
	d		09 49	10 03	10 19		10 30		10 49	11 03	11 19			11 30		11 49	12 03		12 19		12 30	
Water Orton	d																					
Wilnecote	d								11 05													
Tamworth	d		10 07	10 19	10 36				11 09		11 36					12 07	12 19		12 36			
Burton-on-Trent	d		10 19	10a28	10 48		10a54		11 21	11a24	11 48			11a51		12 19	12a30		12 48		12a53	
Willington	d		10 25													12 25						
Derby	56 d																					
Long Eaton	56 d	10 24						11 25							12 24							13 25
Attenborough	56 d	10 32						11 32							12 32							13 33
Beeston	56 d	10 35	10 57					11 35	12 00						12 35	12 57						13 36
Nottingham	56 ⇌ a	10 41	11 03		11 25			11 41	12 07		12 25				12 41	13 03			13 25			13 42

		XC	XC	XC	XC	XC	EM	XC	XC	AW	XC	XC	XC	EM	XC	AW	XC	XC	XC	XC	EM	XC	XC
		◇1	◇1	1	◇1	1		◇1	◇1		1	◇1	◇1		◇1		◇1	1	◇1	◇1		◇1	◇1
			B		C	F	A		G	H		E	J	A		H	B		K	F	A		L
			🛒	🛒	🛒			🛒	🛒			🛒	🛒		🛒		🛒		🛒	🛒		🛒	🛒
Cardiff Central	132 d	10 45						11 45		12 12					12 45	13 12						13 45	
Newport (South Wales)	132 d	11 00						12 00		12 28					13 01	13 28						14 00	
Severn Tunnel Jn.	132 d									12 39						13 39							
Caldicot	d									12 42						13 43							
Chepstow	d							12 18		12 51					13 18	13 52							
Lydney	d	11 25								13 00						14 01						14 25	
Bristol Temple Meads	134 d		11 30		12 00				12 30			13 00					13 30		14 00				14 30
Bristol Parkway	134 d		11 40		12 10				12 40			13 10					13 40		14 10				14 40
Gloucester	134 a	11 44						12 44		13 20					13 44	14 22						14 44	
	d	11 50						12 48		13 22					13 50							14 50	
Cheltenham Spa	a	12 00	12 09		12 39			12 58	13 09	13 33		13 39			14 00		14 09		14 40			15 00	15 10
	d	12 01	12 11		12 41			12 58	13 11			13 41			14 01		14 11		14 41			15 01	15 11
Ashchurch for Tewkesbury	d							13 07															
Bromsgrove	d																						
University	d	12 39						13 39							14 39							15 39	
Birmingham New Street	a	12 45	12 56		13 26			13 45	13 56			14 23			14 45		14 56		15 23			15 45	15 56
	d	12 49	13 03	13 19		13 30		13 49	14 03		14 19		14 30		14 49		15 03	15 19		15 30		15 49	16 03
Water Orton	d																						
Wilnecote	d	13 05						14 05							15 05							16 05	
Tamworth	d	13 09		13 36				14 09	14 19		14 36				15 09			15 36				16 09	16 20
Burton-on-Trent	d	13 19	13a25	13 48		13a52		14 21	14a28		14 48		14a52		15 21		15a25	15 48		15a54		16 21	16a31
Willington	d														15 26								
Derby	56 d																						
Long Eaton	56 d						14 24							15 24							16 24		
Attenborough	56 d						14 32							15 32							16 32		
Beeston	56 d	13 57					14 35	14 57						15 35	15 57						16 35	16 57	
Nottingham	56 ⇌ a	14 03		14 25			14 41	15 03			15 25			15 41	16 03			16 25			16 41	17 03	

A from 30 July until 10 August. To Newark Castle
B From Plymouth to Newcastle
C From Paignton to Manchester Piccadilly
D From Winchester to Edinburgh
E To Manchester Piccadilly
F From Reading to Glasgow Central
G From Penzance to Newcastle
H From Maesteg
I From Southampton Central to Aberdeen
J From Southampton Central to Dundee
K From Penzance to Manchester Piccadilly
L From Plymouth to Edinburgh

Trains between Gloucester & Cheltenham are shown on Table T058

Trains between Birmingham & Bromsgrove are shown on Table T069

Table T057-R

Mondays to Fridays

23 July to 31 August

Cardiff and Bristol - Birmingham - Derby and Nottingham

		XC	XC	XC	EM	XC	XC	XC	AW	XC	XC	EM	XC	XC	AW	XC	XC	XC	EM	XC	XC	XC	AW
		1	◇1	◇1		◇1	◇1	1		◇1	◇1		◇1	◇1		1	◇1	◇1		◇1	◇1	1	
			A	B	C		D		E	F	G	H		D	E		A	I	C	J	D		E
			🛒	🛒		🛒	🛒			🛒	🛒		🛒	🛒			🛒	🛒		🛒	🛒		
Cardiff Central	132 d					14 45			15 12				15 45		16 10					16 45			17 12
Newport (South Wales)	132 d					15 00			15 28				16 00		16 27					17 00			17 28
Severn Tunnel Jn.	132 d								15 37						16 38								17 39
Caldicot	d								15 41						16 40								17 41
Chepstow	d					15 18			15 50				16 18		16 49								17 50
Lydney	d								15 59						16 58					17 25			17 59
Bristol Temple Meads	134 d		15 00				15 30			16 00				16 30			17 00				17 30		
Bristol Parkway	134 d		15 10				15 40			16 10				16 40			17 10				17 40		
Gloucester	134 a					15 44			16 21				16 44		17 19					17 44			18 20
	d					15 50			16 22				16 50		17 23					17 50			18 21
Cheltenham Spa	a		15 41			16 00	16 10		16 31	16 39			17 00	17 09	17 32		17 41			18 00	18 10		18 30
	d		15 42			16 01	16 11			16 41			17 01	17 11			17 42			18 01	18 11		
Ashchurch for Tewkesbury	d																						
Bromsgrove	d																						
University	d					16 39							17 39							18 39			
Birmingham New Street	a		16 23			16 45	16 56			17 23			17 45	17 56			18 23			18 45	18 56		
	d	16 19		16 30		16 49	17 03	17 19			17 30		17 49	18 03		18 19		18 30		18 49	19 03	19 19	
Water Orton	d												17 59										
Wilnecote	d					17 05							18 06							19 05			
Tamworth	d	16 36				17 09		17 36					18 10	18 19		18 36				19 09		19 36	
Burton-on-Trent	d	16 48		16a52		17 21	17a25	17 48			17a51		18 21	18a28		18 48		18a51		19 21	19a29	19 48	
Willington	d												18 29										
Derby	56 d																						
Long Eaton	56 d				17 25							18 25							19 24				
Attenborough	56 d				17 33							18 34							19 32				
Beeston	56 d	17 25			17 36	17 57		18 25				18 38	18 57			19 24			19 35	19 57			
Nottingham	56 ⇌ a	17 31			17 42	18 03		18 31				18 46	19 04			19 31			19 41	20 04		20 25	

		XC	XC	EM	XC	XC	AW	XC	EM	XC	XC	XC	XC	XC	XC	XC	XC	AW	XC	XC	AW
		◇1	◇1		◇1	◇1		◇1		◇1	◇1	◇1	◇1	◇1	1	◇1	1		◇1	◇1	
		K	L	C	M	N	E	A	C	J	O			P				E	Q	R	E
		🛒			🛒	🛒		🛒		🛒	🛒										
Cardiff Central	132 d				17 45		18 08			18 45			19 50			21 05		21 12		21 50	23 20
Newport (South Wales)	132 d				18 00		18 24			19 00			20 05			21 21		21 27		22 05	23 38
Severn Tunnel Jn.	132 d						18 35						20 15					21 38			23 58
Caldicot	d						18 37						20 18					21 41			00 01
Chepstow	d				18 18		18 46			19 17			20 26					21 50			00 10
Lydney	d						18 55						20 35					21 59			00 19
Bristol Temple Meads	134 d	18 00				18 30		19 00			19 30	20 00		20 30					22 00		
Bristol Parkway	134 d	18 10				18 40		19 10			19 40	20 10		20 40					22 10		
Gloucester	134 a				18 44		19 17			19 43		20 38	20 54			22 02		22 22		22 46	00 39
	d				18 46		19 21			19 45		20 46	20 59			22 04		22 23		22 47	
Cheltenham Spa	a	18 40			18 56	19 09	19 31	19 39		19 56	20 10	20 55	21 09	21 15		22 14		22 34	22 41	22 56	
	d	18 41			18 57	19 11		19 41		19 58	20 11	20 56	21 11	21 17		22 15			22 42	22 58	
Ashchurch for Tewkesbury	d				19 05											22 23					
Bromsgrove	d																				
University	d				19 39					20 34			21 45								
Birmingham New Street	a	19 23			19 45	19 56		20 23		20 40	20 51	21 37	21 51	22 02		23 05			23 43	23 59	
	d		19 30		19 49	20 03				20 49	21 03				22 03		23 09				
Water Orton	d																				
Wilnecote	d				20 05					21 05							23 24				
Tamworth	d				20 09	20 19				21 09	21 19				22 27		23 28				
Burton-on-Trent	d		19a51		20 21	20a29				21 21	21a29				22 39		23 40				
Willington	d																23 45				
Derby	56 d																				
Long Eaton	56 d			20 26					21 24												
Attenborough	56 d			20 36					21 32	21 53					23 18						
Beeston	56 d			20 39	20 57				21 35	21 56					23 21						
Nottingham	56 ⇌ a			20 45	21 03				21 41	22 02					23 27		00 19				

A To Manchester Piccadilly
B From Southampton Central to Edinburgh
C from 30 July until 10 August
D From Plymouth to Newcastle
E From Maesteg
F From Paignton to Manchester Piccadilly
G From Reading to Edinburgh
H from 30 July until 10 August. To Newark Castle
I From Southampton Central to Leeds
J 🛒 to Birmingham New Street
K From Exeter St Davids to Manchester Piccadilly
L From Reading to Leeds
M From Nottingham. 🛒 to Birmingham New Street
N From Plymouth to York. 🛒 to Birmingham New Street
O From Plymouth to Leeds. 🛒 to Birmingham New Street
P From Plymouth
Q From Paignton
R From Nottingham

Trains between Gloucester & Cheltenham are shown on Table T058

Trains between Birmingham & Bromsgrove are shown on Table T069

Table T057-R

Mondays to Fridays

3 September to 5 October

Cardiff and Bristol - Birmingham - Derby and Nottingham

		XC	XC	XC	XC	XC		XC	XC	XC	XC	XC	XC	AW	XC	XC		XC	XC	XC	AW	XC	XC	XC	XC
		◇[1]	[1]	◇[1]	[1]	◇[1]		[1]	◇[1]	[1]	◇[1]	◇[1]	[1]		◇[1]	◇[1]		◇[1]	◇[1]	[1]		◇[1]	◇[1]	◇[1]	◇[1]
		A		B		A			C		D	E		F	G	H			I			J	K		I
		🍴		🍴		🍴		🍴	🍴		🍴		🍴		🍴	🍴			🍴	🍴		🍴	🍴		
Cardiff Central [7]	132 d													06 12				06 40			07 05	07 00		07 45	
Newport (South Wales)	132 d													06 28				06 55			07 23	07 14		08 02	
Severn Tunnel Jn.	132 d													06 39				07 05			07 38	07 25			
Caldicot	d													06 41				07 08			07 40				
Chepstow	d													06 50				07 16			07 49				
Lydney	d													06 59				07 25			07 58			08 25	
Bristol Temple Meads [10]	134 d										06 27				07 00				07 30			08 00			08 30
Bristol Parkway [7]	134 d										06 39				07 10				07 40			08 10			08 40
Gloucester [7]	134 a													07 20				07 44			08 20			08 45	
	d											07 10		07 22				07 46			08 21			08 49	
Cheltenham Spa [4]	a										07 08	07 19		07 34	07 39			07 56	08 09		08 34	08 39		08 58	09 10
	d										07 10	07 21			07 41			07 57	08 11			08 41		09 00	09 12
Ashchurch for Tewkesbury	d											07 29						08 05							
Bromsgrove	d											07 49						08 24							
University	d											08 10						08 39						09 39	
Birmingham New Street [12]	a										07 56	08 17			08 26			08 45	08 56			09 26		09 45	09 58
	d	06 00	06 19	06 30	06 49	07 03		07 19	07 30	07 49	08 03		08 19			08 30		08 49	09 03	09 19			09 30	09 49	10 03
Water Orton	d																								
Wilnecote	d		06 35					07 35										09 05							
Tamworth	d		06 39		07 07	07 19		07 39		08 07	08 19		08 36					09 09		09 36				10 07	10 19
Burton-on-Trent	d		06 51		07 20	07 31		07 50		08 19	08 29		08 48					09 21	09 27	09 48				10 19	
Willington	d				07 25					08 25														10 25	
Derby [6]	56 d	06a49	07 08	07a11	07 44	07a42		08 10	08a10	08 40	08a42		09 03			09a12		09 41	09a46	10 07			10a12	10 41	10a45
Long Eaton	56 d		07 21		07 55			08 19		08 49								09 49						10 49	
Attenborough	56 d		07 28							08 57															
Beeston	56 d		07 32		08 04			08 28		09 00								09 57						10 57	
Nottingham [6]	56 a		07 38		08 12			08 35		09 07			09 28					10 03		10 31				11 03	

		XC		XC	XC	XC	XC	XC	AW	XC	XC	XC		XC	AW	XC	XC	XC	XC	XC	XC	XC		XC	XC
		[1]		◇[1]	◇[1]	◇[1]	◇[1]	[1]		◇[1]	◇[1]	◇[1]		◇[1]		[1]	◇[1]	◇[1]	◇[1]	◇[1]	[1]	◇[1]		[1] [1]	◇[1]
				L	M		I			G	K			N	O		G	P		I		L		K	
		🍴		🍴	🍴		🍴	🍴		🍴		🍴		🍴		🍴	🍴	🍴		🍴	🍴	🍴			🍴
Cardiff Central [7]	132 d					08 45			09 12			09 45			10 09				10 45						11 45
Newport (South Wales)	132 d					09 00			09 28			10 00			10 27				11 00						12 00
Severn Tunnel Jn.	132 d								09 38						10 38										
Caldicot	d								09 39						10 40										
Chepstow	d					09 18			09 48			10 18			10 49										12 18
Lydney	d								09 57						10 58				11 25						
Bristol Temple Meads [10]	134 d			09 00			09 30			10 00				10 30			11 00			11 30		12 00			
Bristol Parkway [7]	134 d			09 10			09 40			10 10				10 40			11 10			11 40		12 10			
Gloucester [7]	134 a					09 44			10 20			10 44			11 20				11 44						12 44
	d					09 50			10 20			10 50			11 21				11 50						12 48
Cheltenham Spa [4]	a			09 40		10 00	10 09		10 31	10 40		11 00		11 09	11 32		11 40		12 00	12 09		12 39			12 58
	d			09 42		10 01	10 11			10 41		11 01		11 11			11 42		12 01	12 11		12 41			12 58
Ashchurch for Tewkesbury	d																								13 07
Bromsgrove	d																								
University	d					10 39						11 39							12 39						13 39
Birmingham New Street [12]	a			10 23		10 45	10 56			11 26		11 45		11 58			12 26		12 45	12 56		13 26			13 45
	d	10 19			10 30	10 49	11 03	11 19			11 30	11 49		12 03		12 19		12 30	12 49	13 03	13 19			13 30	13 49
Water Orton	d																								
Wilnecote	d					11 05													13 05						14 05
Tamworth	d	10 36				11 09		11 36				12 07		12 19		12 36			13 09		13 36				14 09
Burton-on-Trent	d	10 48				11 21	11 26	11 48				12 19				12 48			13 19	13 28	13 48				14 21
Willington	d											12 25													
Derby [6]	56 d	11 08			11a12	11 41	11a47	12 07			12a12	12 40		12a46		13 08		13a13	13 40	13a39	14 08			14a12	14 39
Long Eaton	56 d					11 51						12 49							13 49						14 49
Attenborough	56 d																								
Beeston	56 d					12 00						12 57							13 57						14 57
Nottingham [6]	56 a	11 29				12 07		12 30				13 03				13 31			14 03		14 32				15 03

A To Newcastle
B To Edinburgh
C To Glasgow Central
D From Bath Spa to Newcastle
E To Stansted Airport
F From Cardiff Canton Sidings
G To Manchester Piccadilly
H From Guildford to Edinburgh
I From Plymouth to Newcastle
J To Manchester Piccadilly. 🍴 from Bristol Temple Meads
K From Reading to Glasgow Central
L From Paignton to Manchester Piccadilly
M From Winchester to Edinburgh
N From Penzance to Newcastle
O From Maesteg
P From Southampton Central to Aberdeen

Trains between Gloucester & Cheltenham are shown on Table T058

Trains between Birmingham & Bromsgrove are shown on Table T069

Table T057-R

Mondays to Fridays

3 September to 5 October

Cardiff and Bristol - Birmingham - Derby and Nottingham

		XC	AW	XC		XC	XC	XC	AW	XC	XC	XC	XC	XC		XC	XC	XC	XC	XC	XC	XC	AW	XC	
		◇[1]		[1]		◇[1]	◇[1]	◇[1]		◇[1]	[1]	◇[1]	◇[1]	◇[1]		◇[1]	[1]	◇[1]	◇[1]	◇[1]	◇[1]	[1]		◇[1]	
		A	B			C	D		B	E		F	G			H		C	I		E		B	J	
		🍴				🍴	🍴	🍴		🍴		🍴	🍴	🍴		🍴		🍴	🍴	🍴	🍴			🍴	
Cardiff Central [7]	132 d		12 12					12 45	13 12					13 45						14 45			15 12		
Newport (South Wales)	132 d		12 28					13 01	13 28					14 00						15 00			15 28		
Severn Tunnel Jn.	132 d		12 39						13 39														15 37		
Caldicot	d		12 42						13 43														15 41		
Chepstow	d		12 51					13 18	13 52											15 18			15 50		
Lydney	d		13 00						14 01					14 25									15 59		
Bristol Temple Meads [10]	134 d	12 30				13 00				13 30		14 00				14 30		15 00			15 30			16 00	
Bristol Parkway [7]	134 d	12 40				13 10				13 40		14 10				14 40		15 10			15 40			16 10	
Gloucester [7]	134 a		13 20					13 44	14 22					14 44						15 44			16 21		
	d		13 22					13 50						14 50						15 50			16 22		
Cheltenham Spa [4]	a	13 09	13 33			13 39		14 00		14 09		14 40		15 00		15 10		15 41		16 00	16 10		16 31	16 39	
	d	13 11				13 41		14 01		14 11		14 41		15 01		15 11		15 42		16 01	16 11			16 41	
Ashchurch for Tewkesbury	d																								
Bromsgrove	d																								
University	d							14 39						15 39						16 39					
Birmingham New Street [12]	a	13 56				14 23		14 45		14 56		15 23		15 45		15 56		16 23		16 45	16 56			17 23	
	d	14 03		14 19			14 30	14 49		15 03	15 19		15 30	15 49		16 03	16 19		16 30	16 49	17 03	17 19			
Water Orton	d																								
Wilnecote	d							15 05						16 05						17 05					
Tamworth	d	14 19		14 36				15 09			15 36			16 09		16 20	16 36			17 09		17 36			
Burton-on-Trent	d			14 48				15 21		15 26	15 48			16 21			16 48			17 21	17 26	17 48			
Willington	d							15 26																	
Derby [6]	56 d	14a43		15 08			15a12	15 40		15a44	16 08		16a14	16 40		16a42	17 08		17a12	17 40	17a44	18 08			
Long Eaton	56 d							15 49						16 49			17 17			17 50		18 17			
Attenborough	56 d																								
Beeston	56 d							15 57						16 57			17 25			17 58		18 28			
Nottingham [6]	56 a			15 29				16 03			16 29			17 03			17 32			18 04		18 35			

		XC	XC	XC	XC	AW	XC	XC	XC	XC		XC	XC	AW	XC	XC	XC	XC	AW	XC		XC	XC	XC	XC
		◇[1]	[1]	◇[1]	◇[1]		[1]	◇[1]	◇[1]	◇[1]		◇[1]	[1]		◇[1]	◇[1]	◇[1]	◇[1]		◇[1]		◇[1]	◇[1]	◇[1]	◇[1]
		K			E	B		C	L	M		E		B	N	O	P	Q	B	C		M	R		
		🍴		🍴	🍴			🍴	🍴	🍴		🍴			🍴		🍴	🍴		🍴		🍴	🍴		
Cardiff Central [7]	132 d			15 45		16 10				16 45				17 12			17 45		18 08			18 45			19 50
Newport (South Wales)	132 d			16 00		16 27				17 00				17 28			18 00		18 24			19 00			20 05
Severn Tunnel Jn.	132 d					16 38								17 39					18 35						20 15
Caldicot	d					16 40								17 41					18 37						20 18
Chepstow	d			16 18		16 49								17 50			18 18		18 46			19 17			20 26
Lydney	d					16 58				17 25				17 59					18 55						20 35
Bristol Temple Meads [10]	134 d				16 30			17 00				17 30			18 00			18 30		19 00			19 30	20 00	
Bristol Parkway [7]	134 d				16 40			17 10				17 40			18 10			18 40		19 10			19 40	20 10	
Gloucester [7]	134 a			16 44		17 19				17 44				18 20			18 44		19 17			19 43		20 38	20 54
	d			16 50		17 23				17 50				18 21			18 46		19 21			19 45		20 46	20 59
Cheltenham Spa [4]	a			17 00	17 09	17 32		17 41		18 00		18 10		18 30	18 40		18 56	19 09	19 31	19 39		19 56	20 10	20 55	21 09
	d			17 01	17 11			17 42		18 01		18 11			18 41		18 57	19 11		19 41		19 58	20 11	20 56	21 11
Ashchurch for Tewkesbury	d																19 05								
Bromsgrove	d																								
University	d			17 39						18 39							19 39					20 34			21 45
Birmingham New Street [12]	a			17 45	17 56			18 23		18 45		18 56			19 23		19 45	19 56		20 23		20 40	20 51	21 37	21 51
	d	17 30	17 39	17 49	18 03		18 19		18 30	18 49		19 03	19 19			19 30	19 49	20 03				20 49	21 03		
Water Orton	d		17 51																						
Wilnecote	d		17 59	18 05						19 05							20 05					21 05			
Tamworth	d		18 03	18 09	18 19		18 36			19 09			19 36				20 09	20 19				21 09	21 19		
Burton-on-Trent	d		18 14	18 21			18 48			19 21		19 29	19 48				20 21	20 30				21 21	21 30		
Willington	d		18 20																						
Derby [6]	56 d	18a12	18a29	18 40	18a41		19 08		19a12	19 40		19a43	20 09			20a13	20 40	20a42				21 40	21a42		
Long Eaton	56 d			18 49			19 17			19 49							20 49					21 52			
Attenborough	56 d																					22 01			
Beeston	56 d			18 57			19 24			19 57							20 57					22 04			
Nottingham [6]	56 a			19 03			19 31			20 04			20 30				21 04					22 10			

A From Penzance to Newcastle
B From Maesteg
C To Manchester Piccadilly
D From Southampton Central to Dundee
E From Plymouth to Newcastle
F From Penzance to Manchester Piccadilly
G From Reading to Glasgow Central
H From Plymouth to Edinburgh
I From Southampton Central to Edinburgh
J From Paignton to Manchester Piccadilly
K From Reading to Edinburgh
L From Southampton Central to Leeds
M 🍴 to Birmingham New Street
N From Exeter St Davids to Manchester Piccadilly
O From Reading to Leeds
P From Nottingham. 🍴 to Birmingham New Street
Q From Plymouth to York. 🍴 to Birmingham New Street
R From Plymouth to Leeds. 🍴 to Birmingham New Street

Trains between Gloucester & Cheltenham are shown on Table T058

Trains between Birmingham & Bromsgrove are shown on Table T069

Table T057-R

Cardiff and Bristol - Birmingham - Derby and Nottingham

Mondays to Fridays
3 September to 5 October

		XC ◇1 A	XC 1	XC ◇1	XC 1	AW B	XC ◇1 C	XC ◇1 D	AW B
Cardiff Central	132 d			21 05		21 12		21 50	23 20
Newport (South Wales)	132 d			21 21		21 27		22 05	23 38
Severn Tunnel Jn.	132 d					21 38			23 58
Caldicot	d					21 41			00 01
Chepstow	d					21 50			00 10
Lydney	d					21 59			00 19
Bristol Temple Meads	134 d	20 30					22 00		
Bristol Parkway	134 d	20 40					22 10		
Gloucester	134 a			22 02		22 22		22 46	00 39
	d			22 04		22 23		22 47	
Cheltenham Spa	a	21 15		22 14		22 34	22 41	22 56	
	d	21 17		22 15			22 42	22 58	
Ashchurch for Tewkesbury	d			22 23					
Bromsgrove	d								
University	d								
Birmingham New Street	a	22 02		23 05			23 43	23 59	
	d		22 03		23 09				
Water Orton	d								
Wilnecote	d				23 24				
Tamworth	d		22 27		23 28				
Burton-on-Trent	d		22 39		23 40				
Willington	d				23 45				
Derby	56 d		22 59		23 57				
Long Eaton	56 d		23 10						
Attenborough	56 d		23 18						
Beeston	56 d		23 21						
Nottingham	56 ⇌ a		23 27		00 16				

Mondays to Fridays
8 October to 7 December

		XC ◇1 E 🍴	XC 1	XC ◇1 F 🍴	XC 1	XC ◇1 G 🍴	XC 1 🍴	XC ◇1 F 🍴	XC 1	XC ◇1 H 🍴	XC ◇1 I	XC 1 🍴	AW J	XC ◇1 K 🍴	XC ◇1 L 🍴	XC ◇1	XC ◇1 M 🍴	XC 1 🍴	AW	XC ◇1 N 🍴	XC ◇1 O 🍴	XC ◇1	XC ◇1 P 🍴
Cardiff Central	132 d												06 12			06 40			07 05	07 00		07 45	
Newport (South Wales)	132 d												06 28			06 55			07 23	07 14		08 02	
Severn Tunnel Jn.	132 d												06 39			07 05			07 38	07 25			
Caldicot	d												06 41			07 08			07 40				
Chepstow	d												06 50			07 16			07 49				
Lydney	d												06 59			07 25			07 58			08 25	
Bristol Temple Meads	134 d									06 27				07 00			07 30			08 00			08 30
Bristol Parkway	134 d									06 39				07 10			07 40			08 10			08 40
Gloucester	134 a												07 20			07 44			08 20			08 45	
	d										07 10		07 22			07 46			08 21			08 49	
Cheltenham Spa	a									07 08	07 19		07 34	07 39		07 56	08 09		08 34	08 39		08 58	09 10
	d									07 10	07 21			07 41		07 57	08 11			08 41		09 00	09 12
Ashchurch for Tewkesbury	d										07 29					08 05							
Bromsgrove	d										07 49					08 24							
University	d										08 10					08 39						09 39	
Birmingham New Street	a									07 56	08 17			08 26		08 45	08 56			09 26		09 45	09 58
	d	06 00	06 19	06 30	06 49	07 03	07 19	07 30	07 49	08 03		08 19			08 30	08 49	09 03	09 19			09 30	09 49	10 03
Water Orton	d																						
Wilnecote	d		06 35				07 35									09 05							
Tamworth	d		06 39		07 07	07 19	07 39		08 07	08 19		08 36				09 09		09 36				10 07	10 19
Burton-on-Trent	d		06 51		07 20	07 31	07 50		08 19	08 29		08 48				09 20	09 27	09 48				10 19	
Willington	d				07 25				08 25													10 25	
Derby	56 d	06a33	07 08	07a11	07 44	07a42	08 08	08a09	08 40	08a41		09 08			09a05	09 41	09a41	10 09			10a05	10 41	10a41
Long Eaton	56 d		07 21		07 56		08 19		08 49							09 51						10 50	
Attenborough	56 d		07 28						08 57														
Beeston	56 d		07 32		08 06		08 27		09 00							09 59						10 58	
Nottingham	56 ⇌ a		07 38		08 12		08 34		09 07			09 28				10 05		10 28				11 04	

A From Plymouth
B From Maesteg
C From Paignton
D From Nottingham
E To Glasgow Central
F To Newcastle
G To Edinburgh
H From Bath Spa to Glasgow Central
I To Stansted Airport
J From Cardiff Canton Sidings
K To Manchester Piccadilly
L From Guildford to Newcastle
M From Plymouth to Edinburgh
N To Manchester Piccadilly. 🍴 from Bristol Temple Meads
O From Reading to Newcastle
P From Plymouth to Glasgow Central

Trains between Gloucester & Cheltenham are shown on Table T058

Trains between Birmingham & Bromsgrove are shown on Table T069

Table T057-R

Cardiff and Bristol - Birmingham - Derby and Nottingham

Mondays to Fridays
8 October to 7 December

		XC 1 🍴	XC ◇1 A 🍴	XC ◇1 B 🍴	XC ◇1	XC ◇1 C 🍴	XC 1 🍴	AW	XC ◇1 D 🍴	XC ◇1 E 🍴	XC ◇1 🍴	XC ◇1 F 🍴	AW G	XC 1 🍴	XC ◇1 D 🍴	XC ◇1 H 🍴	XC ◇1	XC ◇1 I 🍴	XC 1 🍴	XC ◇1 A 🍴	XC ◇1 E 🍴	XC ◇1 🍴
Cardiff Central	132 d				08 45			09 12			09 45		10 09				10 45					11 45
Newport (South Wales)	132 d				09 00			09 28			10 00		10 27				11 00					12 00
Severn Tunnel Jn.	132 d							09 38					10 38									
Caldicot	d							09 39					10 40									
Chepstow	d				09 18			09 48			10 18		10 49									12 18
Lydney	d							09 57					10 58				11 25					
Bristol Temple Meads	134 d		09 00			09 30			10 00			10 30			11 00			11 30		12 00		
Bristol Parkway	134 d		09 10			09 40			10 10			10 40			11 10			11 40		12 10		
Gloucester	134 a				09 44			10 20			10 44		11 20				11 44					12 44
	d				09 50			10 20			10 50		11 21				11 50					12 48
Cheltenham Spa	a		09 40		10 00	10 09		10 31	10 40		11 00	11 09	11 32		11 40		12 00	12 09		12 39		12 58
	d		09 42		10 01	10 11			10 41		11 01	11 11			11 42		12 01	12 11		12 41		12 58
Ashchurch for Tewkesbury	d																					13 07
Bromsgrove	d																					
University	d				10 39						11 39						12 39					13 39
Birmingham New Street	a		10 23		10 45	10 56			11 26		11 45	11 58			12 26		12 45	12 56		13 26		13 45
	d	10 19		10 30	10 49	11 03	11 19			11 30	11 49	12 03		12 19		12 30	12 49	13 03	13 19		13 30	13 49
Water Orton	d																					
Wilnecote	d				11 05												13 05					14 05
Tamworth	d	10 36			11 09		11 36				12 07	12 19		12 36			13 09		13 36			14 09
Burton-on-Trent	d	10 48			11 21	11 26	11 48				12 19			12 48			13 19	13 28	13 48			14 21
Willington	d										12 25											
Derby	56 d	11 08		11a05	11 41	11a40	12 08			12a05	12 40	12a41		13 08		13a05	13 40	13a39	14 08		14a05	14 40
Long Eaton	56 d				11 51						12 49						13 49					14 49
Attenborough	56 d																					
Beeston	56 d				12 00						12 57						13 57					14 57
Nottingham	56 ⇌ a	11 28			12 07		12 28				13 03			13 28			14 03		14 28			15 03

		XC ◇1 F 🍴	AW G	XC 1	XC ◇1 D 🍴	XC 1 H 🍴	XC ◇1 🍴	AW G	XC ◇1 J 🍴	XC 1	XC ◇1 K 🍴	XC ◇1 E 🍴	XC ◇1 🍴	XC ◇1 L 🍴	XC 1	XC ◇1 D 🍴	XC ◇1 M 🍴	XC ◇1 🍴	XC ◇1 C 🍴	XC 1	AW G	XC ◇1 A 🍴	XC ◇1 E 🍴
Cardiff Central	132 d		12 12				12 45	13 12					13 45					14 45			15 12		
Newport (South Wales)	132 d		12 28				13 01	13 28					14 00					15 00			15 28		
Severn Tunnel Jn.	132 d		12 39					13 39													15 37		
Caldicot	d		12 42					13 43													15 41		
Chepstow	d		12 51				13 18	13 52										15 18			15 50		
Lydney	d		13 00					14 01					14 25								15 59		
Bristol Temple Meads	134 d	12 30			13 00				13 30		14 00			14 30		15 00			15 30			16 00	
Bristol Parkway	134 d	12 40			13 10				13 40		14 10			14 40		15 10			15 40			16 10	
Gloucester	134 a		13 20				13 44	14 22					14 44					15 44			16 21		
	d		13 22				13 50						14 50					15 50			16 22		
Cheltenham Spa	a	13 09	13 33		13 39		14 00		14 09		14 40		15 00	15 10		15 41		16 00	16 10		16 31	16 39	
	d	13 11			13 41		14 01		14 11		14 41		15 01	15 11		15 42		16 01	16 11			16 41	
Ashchurch for Tewkesbury	d																						
Bromsgrove	d																						
University	d						14 39						15 39					16 39					
Birmingham New Street	a	13 56			14 23		14 45		14 56		15 23		15 45	15 56		16 23		16 45	16 56			17 23	
	d	14 03		14 19		14 30	14 49		15 03	15 19		15 30	15 49	16 03	16 19		16 30	16 49	17 03	17 19			17 30
Water Orton	d																						
Wilnecote	d						15 05						16 05					17 05					
Tamworth	d	14 19		14 36			15 09			15 36			16 09	16 20	16 36			17 09		17 36			
Burton-on-Trent	d			14 48			15 21		15 26	15 48			16 21		16 48			17 21	17 26	17 48			
Willington	d						15 26																
Derby	56 d	14a41		15 08		15a05	15 40		15a40	16 08		16a06	16 40	16a41	17 08		17a05	17 40	17a40	18 08			18a05
Long Eaton	56 d						15 49						16 49		17 17			17 50		18 17			
Attenborough	56 d																						
Beeston	56 d						15 57						16 57		17 25			17 58		18 25			
Nottingham	56 ⇌ a			15 28			16 03			16 28			17 03		17 31			18 04		18 31			

A From Paignton to Manchester Piccadilly
B From Winchester to Newcastle
C From Plymouth to Edinburgh
D To Manchester Piccadilly
E From Reading to Newcastle
F From Penzance to Glasgow Central
G From Maesteg
H From Southampton Central to Newcastle
I From Plymouth to Aberdeen
J From Plymouth to Dundee
K From Penzance to Manchester Piccadilly
L From Plymouth to Glasgow Central
M From Southampton Central to Edinburgh

Trains between Gloucester & Cheltenham are shown on Table T058

Trains between Birmingham & Bromsgrove are shown on Table T069

8 October to 7 December

Cardiff and Bristol - Birmingham - Derby and Nottingham

		XC	XC	XC	AW	XC	XC	XC	XC	XC	XC	AW	XC	XC	XC	XC	AW	XC	XC	XC	XC	XC	XC
		1	◇1	◇1		1	◇1	◇1	◇1	◇1	1		◇1	◇1	◇1	◇1		◇1	◇1	◇1	◇1	◇1	◇1
				A	B		C	D	E	F		B	G	H	I	J	B	C	K	E	J		
			🛒	🛒			🛒	🛒	🛒	🛒			🛒		🛒	🛒		🛒		🛒	🛒		
Cardiff Central 7	132 d		15 45		16 10				16 45			17 12			17 45		18 08			18 45			19 50
Newport (South Wales)	132 d		16 00		16 27				17 00			17 28			18 00		18 24			19 00			20 05
Severn Tunnel Jn.	132 d				16 38							17 39					18 35						20 15
Caldicot	d				16 40							17 41					18 37						20 18
Chepstow	d		16 18		16 49							17 50			18 18		18 46			19 17			20 26
Lydney	d				16 58				17 25			17 59					18 55						20 35
Bristol Temple Meads 10	134 d			16 30			17 00			17 30			18 00			18 30		19 00			19 30	20 00	
Bristol Parkway 7	134 d			16 40			17 10			17 40			18 10			18 40		19 10			19 40	20 10	
Gloucester 7	134 a		16 44		17 19				17 44			18 20			18 44		19 17			19 43		20 38	20 54
	d		16 50		17 23				17 50			18 21			18 46		19 21			19 45		20 46	20 59
Cheltenham Spa 4	a		17 00	17 09	17 32		17 41		18 00	18 10		18 30	18 40		18 56	19 09	19 31	19 39		19 56	20 10	20 55	21 09
	d		17 01	17 11			17 42		18 01	18 11			18 41		18 57	19 11		19 41		19 58	20 11	20 56	21 11
Ashchurch for Tewkesbury	d														19 05								
Bromsgrove	d																						
University	d		17 39						18 39						19 39					20 34			21 45
Birmingham New Street 12	a		17 45	17 56			18 23		18 45	18 56			19 23		19 45	19 56		20 23		20 40	20 51	21 37	21 51
	d	17 39	17 49	18 03		18 19		18 30	18 49	19 03	19 19			19 30	19 49	20 03			20 30	20 49	21 03		
Water Orton	d	17 51																					
Wilnecote	d	17 59	18 05						19 05						20 05					21 05			
Tamworth	d	18 03	18 09	18 19		18 36			19 09		19 36				20 09	20 19				21 09	21 19		
Burton-on-Trent	d	18 14	18 21			18 48			19 21	19 29	19 48				20 21					21 21	21 30		
Willington	d	18 20																					
Derby 6	56 d	18a29	18 40	18a40		19 08		19a05	19 44	19a42	20 08			20a06	20 40	20a38			21a09	21 43	21a43		
Long Eaton	56 d		18 49			19 17			19 53						20 49					21 54			
Attenborough	56 d																			22 03			
Beeston	56 d		18 57			19 25			20 00						20 57					22 06			
Nottingham 8	56 ⛴ a		19 05			19 34			20 08		20 28				21 04					22 12			

		XC	XC	XC	XC	AW	XC	XC	AW
		◇1	1	◇1	1		◇1	◇1	
		L				B	M	N	B
Cardiff Central 7	132 d			21 05		21 12		21 50	23 20
Newport (South Wales)	132 d			21 21		21 27		22 05	23 38
Severn Tunnel Jn.	132 d					21 38			23 58
Caldicot	d					21 41			00 01
Chepstow	d					21 50			00 10
Lydney	d					21 59			00 19
Bristol Temple Meads 10	134 d	20 30					22 00		
Bristol Parkway 7	134 d	20 40					22 10		
Gloucester 7	134 a			22 02		22 22		22 46	00 39
	d			22 04		22 23		22 47	
Cheltenham Spa 4	a	21 15		22 14		22 34	22 41	22 56	
	d	21 17		22 15			22 42	22 58	
Ashchurch for Tewkesbury	d			22 23					
Bromsgrove	d								
University	d								
Birmingham New Street 12	a	22 02		23 05			23 43	23 59	
	d		22 03		23 09				
Water Orton	d								
Wilnecote	d				23 24				
Tamworth	d		22 27		23 28				
Burton-on-Trent	d		22 39		23 40				
Willington	d				23 45				
Derby 6	56 d		22 59		23 57				
Long Eaton	56 d		23 10						
Attenborough	56 d		23 18						
Beeston	56 d		23 21						
Nottingham 8	56 ⛴ a		23 27		00 16				

A From Plymouth to Edinburgh
B From Maesteg
C To Manchester Piccadilly
D From Southampton Central to Newcastle
E 🛒 to Birmingham New Street
F From Plymouth to Leeds
G From Exeter St Davids to Manchester Piccadilly
H From Reading to Newcastle
I From Nottingham. 🛒 to Birmingham New Street
J From Plymouth to Leeds. 🛒 to Birmingham New Street
K From Southampton Central to York
L From Plymouth
M From Paignton
N From Nottingham

Trains between Gloucester & Cheltenham are shown on Table T058

Trains between Birmingham & Bromsgrove are shown on Table T069

26 May to 16 June

Cardiff and Bristol - Birmingham - Derby and Nottingham

		XC	XC	XC	XC	XC	XC	XC	XC	XC	XC	XC	AW	XC	XC	XC	XC	XC	AW	XC	XC	XC	XC
		◇1	1	◇1	1	◇1	1	◇1	1	◇1	◇1	1		◇1	◇1	◇1	◇1	1		◇1	◇1	◇1	◇1
		A		B		C		B		A	D			E	F		G			H	I		J
		🛒		🛒		🛒	🛒	🛒		🛒		🛒		🛒	🛒		🛒	🛒		🛒	🛒		🛒
Cardiff Central 7	132 d												06 10			06 40			07 07	07 00		07 45	
Newport (South Wales)	132 d												06 26			06 55			07 23	07 15		08 00	
Severn Tunnel Jn.	132 d												06 37			07 05			07 34	07 25			
Caldicot	d												06 39			07 08			07 36				
Chepstow	d												06 48			07 16			07 45				
Lydney	d												06 57			07 25			07 54			08 25	
Bristol Temple Meads 10	134 d									06 15				07 00			07 30			08 00			08 30
Bristol Parkway 7	134 d									06 25				07 10			07 40			08 10			08 40
Gloucester 7	134 a									06 52			07 18			07 44			08 21			08 45	
	d									07 00	07 06		07 21			07 46			08 22			08 50	
Cheltenham Spa 4	a									07 09	07 15		07 34	07 39		07 55	08 09		08 35	08 40		09 00	09 09
	d									07 11	07 17			07 41		07 57	08 11			08 41		09 01	09 11
Ashchurch for Tewkesbury	d										07 24					08 04							
Bromsgrove	d										07 43												
University	d										08 00					08 39						09 39	
Birmingham New Street 12	a									07 56	08 07			08 25		08 45	08 56			09 26		09 45	09 56
	d	05 58	06 19	06 30	06 49	07 03	07 19	07 30	07 49	08 03		08 19			08 30	08 49	09 03	09 19			09 30	09 49	10 03
Water Orton	d																						
Wilnecote	d		06 35				07 35									09 05							
Tamworth	d	06 14	06 39	06 46	07 07	07 19	07 39	07 46	08 07	08 19		08 36				09 09		09 36				10 07	10 19
Burton-on-Trent	d	06 25	06 51	06 56	07 19	07 31	07 50	07 56	08 19	08 29		08 48				09 21	09 28	09 48				10 19	
Willington	d				07 25				08 25													10 25	
Derby 6	56 d	06a35	07 09	07a09	07 40	07a41	08 10	08a08	08 40	08a41		09 08			09a05	09 40	09a39	10 08			10a05	10 40	10a39
Long Eaton	56 d		07 21		07 52		08 19		08 49							09 49						10 49	
Attenborough	56 d		07 28						08 57														
Beeston	56 d		07 32		08 00		08 27		09 00							09 57						10 57	
Nottingham 8	56 ⛴ a		07 38		08 06		08 34		09 07			09 28				10 03		10 28				11 03	

		XC	XC	XC	XC	XC	XC	AW	XC	XC	XC	XC	AW	XC	XC	XC	XC	XC	XC	XC	XC	XC
		1	◇1	◇1	◇1	◇1	1		◇1	◇1	◇1	◇1		1	◇1	◇1	◇1	◇1	1	◇1	◇1	◇1
			K	L		G		M	E	N		O	M		P	L		Q		K	N	
		🛒	🛒	🛒		🛒	🛒		🛒	🛒	🛒	🛒		🛒	🛒	🛒		🛒	🛒	🛒	🛒	🛒
Cardiff Central 7	132 d				08 45			09 10			09 45		10 10				10 45					11 45
Newport (South Wales)	132 d				09 00			09 25			09 59		10 27				11 00					12 00
Severn Tunnel Jn.	132 d							09 35					10 38									
Caldicot	d							09 37					10 40									
Chepstow	d				09 18			09 47			10 18		10 49									12 18
Lydney	d							09 55					10 58				11 25					
Bristol Temple Meads 10	134 d		09 00			09 30			10 00			10 30			11 00			11 30		12 00		
Bristol Parkway 7	134 d		09 10			09 40			10 10			10 40			11 10			11 40		12 10		
Gloucester 7	134 a				09 46			10 19			10 44		11 20				11 44					12 44
	d				09 50			10 21			10 50		11 22				11 50					12 48
Cheltenham Spa 4	a		09 39		10 00	10 09		10 32	10 39		11 00	11 09	11 32		11 40		12 00	12 09		12 39		12 58
	d		09 41		10 01	10 11			10 41		11 01	11 11			11 41		12 01	12 11		12 41		12 59
Ashchurch for Tewkesbury	d																					13 07
Bromsgrove	d																					
University	d				10 39						11 39						12 39					13 39
Birmingham New Street 12	a		10 25		10 45	10 56			11 26		11 45	11 56			12 26		12 45	12 56		13 26		13 45
	d	10 19		10 30	10 49	11 03	11 19			11 30	11 49	12 03		12 19		12 30	12 49	13 03	13 19		13 30	13 49
Water Orton	d																					
Wilnecote	d				11 05												13 05					14 05
Tamworth	d	10 36			11 09		11 36				12 07	12 19		12 36			13 09		13 36			14 09
Burton-on-Trent	d	10 48			11 21	11 28	11 48				12 19			12 48			13 21	13 27	13 48			14 21
Willington	d										12 25											
Derby 6	56 d	11 08		11a05	11 40	11a39	12 08			12a05	12 40	12a39		13 08		13a05	13 40	13a39	14 08		14a05	14 40
Long Eaton	56 d				11 49						12 49						13 49					14 49
Attenborough	56 d																					
Beeston	56 d				11 57						12 57						13 57					14 57
Nottingham 8	56 ⛴ a	11 28			12 03		12 28				13 03			13 28			14 03		14 28			15 03

A To Glasgow Central
B To Newcastle
C To Edinburgh
D To Stansted Airport
E To Manchester Piccadilly
F From Guildford to Newcastle
G From Plymouth to Edinburgh
H To Manchester Piccadilly. 🛒 from Bristol Temple Meads
I From Bournemouth to Newcastle
J From Plymouth to Glasgow Central
K From Paignton to Manchester Piccadilly
L From Southampton Central to Newcastle
M From Maesteg
N From Reading to Newcastle
O From Penzance to Glasgow Central
P From Plymouth to Manchester Piccadilly
Q From Plymouth to Aberdeen

Trains between Gloucester & Cheltenham are shown on Table T058

Trains between Birmingham & Bromsgrove are shown on Table T069

Table T057-R

Saturdays
26 May to 16 June

Cardiff and Bristol - Birmingham - Derby and Nottingham

	XC ◇1 A ☕	AW B	XC 1	XC ◇1 C ☕	XC ◇1 D ☕	XC ◇1 ☕	AW ☕	XC ◇1 E ☕	XC 1	XC ◇1 C ☕	XC ◇1 F ☕	XC ◇1 ☕	XC ◇1 G ☕	XC 1	XC ◇1 C ☕	XC ◇1 D ☕	XC ◇1 ☕	XC ◇1 H ☕	XC 1	AW B	XC ◇1 I ☕
Cardiff Central 7 132 d		12 09				12 45	13 12					13 45					14 45			15 08	
Newport (South Wales) 132 d		12 27				13 00	13 27					14 00					15 00			15 27	
Severn Tunnel Jn. 132 d		12 38					13 38													15 37	
Caldicot d		12 40					13 41													15 38	
Chepstow d		12 49				13 18	13 50										15 18			15 47	
Lydney d		12 58					13 59					14 25								15 56	
Bristol Temple Meads 10 134 d	12 30			13 00				13 30		14 00			14 30		15 00			15 30			16 00
Bristol Parkway 7 134 d	12 40			13 10				13 40		14 10			14 40		15 10			15 40			16 10
Gloucester 7 134 a		13 21				13 44	14 20					14 44					15 44			16 19	
d		13 22				13 50						14 50					15 50			16 21	
Cheltenham Spa 4 a	13 10	13 32		13 39		14 00		14 09		14 39		15 00	15 09		15 39		16 00	16 09		16 32	16 39
d	13 11			13 41		14 01		14 11		14 41		15 01	15 11		15 41		16 01	16 11			16 41
Ashchurch for Tewkesbury d																					
Bromsgrove d																					
University d						14 39						15 39					16 39				
Birmingham New Street 12 a	13 56			14 26		14 45		14 56		15 26		15 45	15 56		16 26		16 45	16 56			17 26
d	14 03		14 19		14 30	14 49		15 03	15 19		15 30	15 49	16 03	16 19		16 30	16 49	17 03	17 19		
Water Orton d																					
Wilnecote d						15 05						16 05					17 05				
Tamworth d	14 19		14 36			15 09			15 36			16 09	16 19	16 36			17 09		17 36		
Burton-on-Trent d			14 48			15 21		15 27	15 48			16 21		16 48		16 54	17 21	17 26	17 48		
Willington d						15 27															
Derby 6 56 d	14a39		15 08		15a05	15 40		15a40	16 08		16a05	16 40	16a40	17 08		17a05	17 40	17a39	18 08		
Long Eaton 56 d						15 49						16 49		17 17			17 49		18 17		
Attenborough 56 d																					
Beeston 56 d						15 57						16 57		17 25			17 58		18 25		
Nottingham 5 56 ⇌ a			15 28			16 03			16 28			17 03		17 31			18 04		18 31		

	XC ◇1 F ☕	XC ◇1 ☕	XC ◇1 H ☕	AW B	XC 1	XC ◇1 C ☕	XC ◇1 D ☕	XC ◇1 J ☕	XC ◇1 K ☕	XC 1	AW B	XC ◇1 C ☕	XC ◇1 F	XC ◇1 J ☕	XC ◇1 L ☕	AW B	XC ◇1 C ☕	XC ◇1 M	XC ◇1 J ☕	XC ◇1 N ☕	XC ◇1 O	XC ◇1 P
Cardiff Central 7 132 d		15 45		16 08				16 45			17 09			17 45		18 08			18 45			
Newport (South Wales) 132 d		16 00		16 24				17 00			17 25			18 00		18 27			19 00			
Severn Tunnel Jn. 132 d				16 35							17 36					18 38						
Caldicot d				16 37							17 38					18 40						
Chepstow d		16 18		16 46							17 47			18 18		18 49			19 18			
Lydney d				16 55				17 25			17 56					18 58						
Bristol Temple Meads 10 134 d			16 30			17 00			17 30			18 00			18 30		19 00			19 30		20 00
Bristol Parkway 7 134 d			16 40			17 10			17 40			18 10			18 39		19 10			19 40		20 10
Gloucester 7 134 a		16 44		17 19				17 44			18 18			18 44		19 20			19 44			
d		16 50		17 23				17 50			18 24			18 46		19 21			19 46			
Cheltenham Spa 4 a		17 00	17 10	17 33		17 39		18 00	18 11		18 33	18 39		18 56	19 10	19 31	19 39		19 56	20 11		20 40
d		17 01	17 12			17 41		18 01	18 13			18 41		18 57	19 11		19 41		19 57	20 12		20 41
Ashchurch for Tewkesbury d														19 05								
Bromsgrove d																						
University d		17 39						18 39						19 39					20 35			
Birmingham New Street 12 a		17 45	17 56			18 26		18 45	18 56			19 26		19 45	19 58		20 26		20 42	20 49		21 38
d	17 30	17 49	18 03		18 19		18 30	18 49	19 03	19 19			19 30	19 49	20 03			20 30	20 49		21 03	
Water Orton d																						
Wilnecote d		18 05						19 05						20 05					21 05			
Tamworth d		18 09	18 19		18 36			19 09		19 36				20 09	20 19				21 09		21 19	
Burton-on-Trent d		18 21			18 48			19 21	19 27	19 48				20 21					21 21		21 30	
Willington d		18 27																				
Derby 6 56 d	18a05	18 40	18a40		19 08		19a05	19 41	19a41	20 08			20a05	20 40	20a40			21a24	21 37		21a42	
Long Eaton 56 d		18 49			19 17			19 50						20 49					21 48			
Attenborough 56 d																			21 55			
Beeston 56 d		18 57			19 25			19 58						20 57					21 58			
Nottingham 5 56 ⇌ a		19 03			19 31			20 04		20 28				21 03					22 04			

A From Penzance to Glasgow Central
B From Maesteg
C To Manchester Piccadilly
D From Southampton Central to Newcastle
E From Newquay to Dundee
F From Reading to Newcastle
G From Paignton to Glasgow Central
H From Plymouth to Edinburgh
I From Paignton to Manchester Piccadilly
J ☕ to Birmingham New Street
K From Plymouth to York
L From Paignton to Leeds. ☕ to Birmingham New Street
M From Southampton Central to York
N From Newquay to Manchester Piccadilly
O From Bournemouth to Leeds
P From Paignton

Trains between Gloucester & Cheltenham are shown on Table T058

Trains between Birmingham & Bromsgrove are shown on Table T069

Table T057-R

Saturdays
26 May to 16 June

Cardiff and Bristol - Birmingham - Derby and Nottingham

	XC ◇1 A	XC ◇1	XC ◇1	XC 1	AW B	AW B
Cardiff Central 7 132 d		20 00	20 50		21 11	23 18
Newport (South Wales) 132 d		20 15	21 05		21 27	23 37
Severn Tunnel Jn. 132 d		20 25			21 38	23 56
Caldicot d		20 28			21 40	23 59
Chepstow d		20 36			21 49	00 08
Lydney d		20 45			21 58	00 17
Bristol Temple Meads 10 134 d	20 30					
Bristol Parkway 7 134 d	20 40					
Gloucester 7 134 a		21 04	21 47		22 19	00 40
d		21 07	21 49			
Cheltenham Spa 4 a	21 10	21 16	21 58			
d	21 11	21 18	21 59			
Ashchurch for Tewkesbury d		21 25				
Bromsgrove d		21 44				
University d		22 01	22 35			
Birmingham New Street 12 a	21 51	22 07	22 42			
d	21 56	22 10		22 49		
Water Orton d						
Wilnecote d				23 04		
Tamworth d		22 27		23 08		
Burton-on-Trent d		22 39		23 20		
Willington d		22 45				
Derby 6 56 d	22a29	22 59		23a33		
Long Eaton 56 d		23 10				
Attenborough 56 d		23 18				
Beeston 56 d		23 21				
Nottingham 5 56 ⇌ a		23 27				

Saturdays
23 June to 21 July

	XC ◇1 C ☕	XC 1	XC ◇1 D ☕	XC 1	XC ◇1 E ☕	XC 1 ☕	XC ◇1 D ☕	XC 1	XC ◇1 C ☕	XC ◇1 F	XC 1 ☕	AW	XC ◇1 G ☕	XC ◇1 H ☕	XC ◇1	XC ◇1 I ☕	XC 1 ☕	AW	XC ◇1 J ☕	XC ◇1 K ☕	XC ◇1	XC ◇1 L ☕
Cardiff Central 7 132 d												06 10			06 40			07 07	07 00		07 45	
Newport (South Wales) 132 d												06 26			06 55			07 23	07 15		08 00	
Severn Tunnel Jn. 132 d												06 37			07 05			07 34	07 25			
Caldicot d												06 39			07 08			07 36				
Chepstow d												06 48			07 16			07 45				
Lydney d												06 57			07 25			07 54			08 25	
Bristol Temple Meads 10 134 d									06 15				07 00			07 30			08 00			08 30
Bristol Parkway 7 134 d									06 25				07 10			07 40			08 10			08 40
Gloucester 7 134 a									06 52			07 18			07 44			08 21			08 45	
d									07 00	07 06		07 21			07 46			08 22			08 50	
Cheltenham Spa 4 a									07 09	07 15		07 34	07 39		07 55	08 09		08 35	08 40		09 00	09 09
d									07 11	07 17			07 41		07 57	08 11			08 41		09 01	09 11
Ashchurch for Tewkesbury d										07 24					08 04							
Bromsgrove d										07 43												
University d										08 00					08 39						09 39	
Birmingham New Street 12 a									07 56	08 07			08 25		08 45	08 56			09 26		09 45	09 56
d	05 58	06 19	06 30	06 49	07 03	07 19	07 30	07 49	08 03		08 19			08 30	08 49	09 03	09 19			09 30	09 49	10 03
Water Orton d																						
Wilnecote d		06 35				07 35									09 05							
Tamworth d	06 14	06 39	06 46	07 07	07 19	07 39	07 46	08 07	08 19		08 36				09 09		09 36				10 07	10 19
Burton-on-Trent d	06 25	06 51	06 56	07 19	07 31	07 50	07 56	08 19	08 29		08 48				09 21	09 28	09 48				10 19	
Willington d				07 25				08 25													10 25	
Derby 6 56 d	06a35	07 09	07a09	07 40	07a41	08 10	08a08	08 40	08a41		09 08			09a05	09 40	09a39	10 08			10a05	10 40	10a39
Long Eaton 56 d		07 21		07 52		08 19		08 49							09 49						10 49	
Attenborough 56 d		07 28						08 57														
Beeston 56 d		07 32		08 00		08 27		09 00							09 57						10 57	
Nottingham 5 56 ⇌ a		07 38		08 06		08 34		09 07			09 28				10 03		10 28				11 03	

A From Penzance to Leeds
B From Maesteg
C To Glasgow Central
D To Newcastle
E To Edinburgh
F To Stansted Airport
G To Manchester Piccadilly
H From Guildford to Newcastle
I From Plymouth to Edinburgh
J To Manchester Piccadilly. ☕ from Bristol Temple Meads
K From Bournemouth to Newcastle
L From Plymouth to Glasgow Central

Trains between Gloucester & Cheltenham are shown on Table T058

Trains between Birmingham & Bromsgrove are shown on Table T069

Table T057-R

Saturdays

23 June to 21 July

Cardiff and Bristol - Birmingham - Derby and Nottingham

	XC 1 ⌶		XC ◇1 A ⌶	XC ◇1 B ⌶	XC ◇1	XC ◇1 C ⌶	XC 1 ⌶	AW D	XC ◇1 E ⌶	XC ◇1 F ⌶	XC ◇1 ⌶		XC ◇1 G ⌶	AW D	XC 1 ⌶	XC ◇1 H ⌶	XC ◇1 B ⌶	XC ◇1	XC ◇1 I ⌶	XC 1 ⌶	XC ◇1 A ⌶		XC ◇1 F ⌶	XC ◇1 ⌶
Cardiff Central 7 132 d					08 45			09 10			09 45			10 10				10 45						11 45
Newport (South Wales) 132 d					09 00			09 25			09 59			10 27				11 00						12 00
Severn Tunnel Jn 132 d								09 35						10 38										
Caldicot d								09 37						10 40										
Chepstow d					09 18			09 47			10 18			10 49										12 18
Lydney d								09 55						10 58				11 25						
Bristol Temple Meads 10 134 d			09 00			09 30			10 00				10 30			11 00			11 30		12 00			
Bristol Parkway 7 134 d			09 10			09 40			10 10				10 40			11 10			11 40		12 10			
Gloucester 7 134 a					09 46			10 19			10 44			11 20				11 44						12 44
d					09 50			10 21			10 50			11 22				11 50						12 48
Cheltenham Spa 4 a			09 39		10 00	10 09		10 32	10 39		11 00		11 09	11 32		11 40		12 00	12 09		12 39			12 58
d			09 41		10 01	10 11			10 41		11 01		11 11			11 41		12 01	12 11		12 41			12 59
Ashchurch for Tewkesbury d																								13 07
Bromsgrove d																								
University d					10 39						11 39							12 39						13 39
Birmingham New Street 12 a			10 25		10 45	10 56			11 26		11 45		11 56			12 26		12 45	12 56		13 26			13 45
d	10 19			10 30	10 49	11 03	11 19			11 30	11 49		12 03		12 19		12 30	12 49	13 03	13 19			13 30	13 49
Water Orton d																								
Wilnecote d					11 05													13 05						14 05
Tamworth d	10 36				11 09		11 36				12 07		12 19		12 36			13 09		13 36				14 09
Burton-on-Trent d	10 48				11 21	11 28	11 48				12 19				12 48			13 21	13 27	13 48				14 21
Willington d											12 25													
Derby 6 56 d	11 08			11a05	11 40	11a39	12 08			12a05	12 40		12a39		13 08		13a05	13 40	13a39	14 08			14a05	14 40
Long Eaton 56 d					11 49						12 49							13 49						14 49
Attenborough 56 d																								
Beeston 56 d					11 57						12 57							13 57						14 57
Nottingham 8 56 ⛴ a	11 28				12 03		12 28				13 03				13 28			14 03		14 28				15 03

	XC ◇1 G ⌶	AW D	XC 1	XC ◇1 E ⌶	XC ◇1 B ⌶	XC ◇1 ⌶	AW ⌶		XC ◇1 J ⌶	XC 1	XC ◇1 E ⌶	XC ◇1 F ⌶	XC ◇1 ⌶	XC ◇1 K ⌶	XC 1	XC ◇1 E ⌶	XC ◇1 B ⌶		XC ◇1 ⌶	XC ◇1 C ⌶	XC 1	AW D	XC ◇1 A ⌶	XC ◇1 F ⌶
Cardiff Central 7 132 d		12 09				12 45	13 12						13 45						14 45			15 08		
Newport (South Wales) 132 d		12 27				13 00	13 27						14 00						15 00			15 27		
Severn Tunnel Jn 132 d		12 38					13 38															15 37		
Caldicot d		12 40					13 41															15 38		
Chepstow d		12 49				13 18	13 50												15 18			15 47		
Lydney d		12 58					13 59						14 25									15 56		
Bristol Temple Meads 10 134 d	12 30			13 00					13 30		14 00			14 30		15 00				15 30			16 00	
Bristol Parkway 7 134 d	12 40			13 10					13 40		14 10			14 40		15 10				15 40			16 10	
Gloucester 7 134 a		13 21				13 44	14 20						14 44						15 44			16 19		
d		13 22				13 50							14 50						15 50			16 21		
Cheltenham Spa 4 a	13 10	13 32		13 39		14 00			14 09		14 39		15 00	15 09		15 39			16 00	16 09		16 32	16 39	
d	13 11			13 41		14 01			14 11		14 41		15 01	15 11		15 41			16 01	16 11			16 41	
Ashchurch for Tewkesbury d																								
Bromsgrove d																								
University d						14 39							15 39						16 39					
Birmingham New Street 12 a	13 56			14 26		14 45			14 56		15 26		15 45	15 56		16 26			16 45	16 56			17 26	
d	14 03		14 19		14 30	14 49			15 03	15 19		15 30	15 49	16 03	16 19		16 30		16 49	17 03	17 19			17 30
Water Orton d																								
Wilnecote d						15 05							16 05						17 05					
Tamworth d	14 19		14 36			15 09				15 36			16 09	16 19	16 36				17 09		17 36			
Burton-on-Trent d			14 48			15 21			15 27	15 48			16 21		16 48		16 54		17 21	17 26	17 48			
Willington d						15 27																		
Derby 6 56 d	14a39		15 08		15a05	15 40			15a40	16 08		16a05	16 40	16a40	17 08		17a05		17 40	17a39	18 08			18a05
Long Eaton 56 d						15 49							16 49		17 17				17 49		18 17			
Attenborough 56 d																								
Beeston 56 d						15 57							16 57		17 25				17 58		18 25			
Nottingham 8 56 ⛴ a			15 28			16 03				16 28			17 03		17 31				18 04		18 31			

A From Paignton to Manchester Piccadilly
B From Southampton Central to Newcastle
C From Plymouth to Edinburgh
D From Maesteg
E To Manchester Piccadilly
F From Reading to Newcastle
G From Penzance to Glasgow Central
H From Plymouth to Manchester Piccadilly
I From Plymouth to Aberdeen
J From Newquay to Dundee
K From Paignton to Glasgow Central

Trains between Gloucester & Cheltenham are shown on Table T058

Trains between Birmingham & Bromsgrove are shown on Table T069

Table T057-R

Saturdays

23 June to 21 July

Cardiff and Bristol - Birmingham - Derby and Nottingham

	XC ◇1 ⌶	XC ◇1 A ⌶	AW B	XC 1	XC ◇1 C ⌶	XC ◇1 D ⌶	XC ◇1 E ⌶	XC ◇1 F ⌶	XC 1		AW B	XC ◇1 C ⌶	XC ◇1 G	XC ◇1 E ⌶	XC ◇1 H ⌶	AW B	XC ◇1 C ⌶	XC ◇1 I	XC ◇1 E ⌶		XC ◇1 J ⌶	XC ◇1 K	XC ◇1 L	XC ◇1 M
Cardiff Central 7 132 d	15 45		16 08				16 45				17 09			17 45		18 08			18 45					
Newport (South Wales) 132 d	16 00		16 24				17 00				17 25			18 00		18 27			19 00					
Severn Tunnel Jn 132 d			16 35								17 36					18 38								
Caldicot d			16 37								17 38					18 40								
Chepstow d	16 18		16 46								17 47			18 18		18 49			19 18					
Lydney d			16 55				17 25				17 56					18 58								
Bristol Temple Meads 10 134 d		16 30			17 00			17 30				18 00			18 30		19 00				19 30		20 00	20 30
Bristol Parkway 7 134 d		16 40			17 10			17 40				18 10			18 39		19 10				19 40		20 10	20 40
Gloucester 7 134 a	16 44		17 19				17 44				18 18			18 44		19 20			19 44					
d	16 50		17 23				17 50				18 24			18 46		19 21			19 46					
Cheltenham Spa 4 a	17 00	17 10	17 33		17 39		18 00	18 11			18 33	18 39		18 56	19 10	19 31	19 39		19 56		20 11		20 40	21 10
d	17 01	17 12			17 41		18 01	18 13				18 41		18 57	19 11		19 41		19 57		20 12		20 41	21 11
Ashchurch for Tewkesbury d														19 05										
Bromsgrove d																								
University d	17 39						18 39							19 39					20 35					
Birmingham New Street 12 a	17 45	17 56			18 26		18 45	18 56				19 26		19 45	19 58		20 26		20 42		20 49		21 38	21 51
d	17 49	18 03		18 19		18 30	18 49	19 03	19 19				19 30	19 49	20 03			20 30	20 49			21 03		21 56
Water Orton d																								
Wilnecote d	18 05						19 05							20 05					21 05					
Tamworth d	18 09	18 19		18 36			19 09		19 36					20 09	20 19				21 09			21 19		
Burton-on-Trent d	18 21			18 48			19 21	19 27	19 48					20 21					21 21			21 30		
Willington d	18 27																							
Derby 6 56 d	18 40	18a40		19 08		19a05	19 41	19a41	20 08				20a05	20 40	20a40			21a24	21 37			21a42		22a29
Long Eaton 56 d	18 49			19 17			19 50							20 49					21 48					
Attenborough 56 d																			21 55					
Beeston 56 d	18 57			19 25			19 58							20 57					21 58					
Nottingham 8 56 ⛴ a	19 03			19 31			20 04		20 28					21 03					22 04					

	XC ◇1	XC ◇1	XC 1	AW B	AW B
Cardiff Central 7 132 d	20 00	20 50		21 11	23 18
Newport (South Wales) 132 d	20 15	21 05		21 27	23 37
Severn Tunnel Jn 132 d	20 25			21 38	23 56
Caldicot d	20 28			21 40	23 59
Chepstow d	20 36			21 49	00 08
Lydney d	20 45			21 58	00 17
Bristol Temple Meads 10 134 d					
Bristol Parkway 7 134 d					
Gloucester 7 134 a	21 04	21 47		22 19	00 40
d	21 07	21 49			
Cheltenham Spa 4 a	21 16	21 58			
d	21 18	21 59			
Ashchurch for Tewkesbury d	21 25				
Bromsgrove d	21 44				
University d	22 01	22 35			
Birmingham New Street 12 a	22 07	22 42			
d	22 10		22 49		
Water Orton d					
Wilnecote d			23 04		
Tamworth d	22 27		23 08		
Burton-on-Trent d	22 39		23 20		
Willington d	22 45				
Derby 6 56 d	22 59		23a33		
Long Eaton 56 d	23 10				
Attenborough 56 d	23 18				
Beeston 56 d	23 21				
Nottingham 8 56 ⛴ a	23 27				

A From Plymouth to Edinburgh
B From Maesteg
C To Manchester Piccadilly
D From Southampton Central to Newcastle
E ⌶ to Birmingham New Street
F From Plymouth to York
G From Reading to Newcastle
H From Paignton to Leeds. ⌶ to Birmingham New Street
I From Southampton Central to York
J From Newquay to Manchester Piccadilly
K From Bournemouth to Leeds
L From Paignton
M From Penzance to Leeds

Trains between Gloucester & Cheltenham are shown on Table T058

Trains between Birmingham & Bromsgrove are shown on Table T069

Table T057-R

Saturdays
28 July to 1 September

Cardiff and Bristol - Birmingham - Derby and Nottingham

			XC ◇1 A ⌶	XC 1	XC ◇1 B ⌶	XC 1	XC ◇1 A ⌶		XC 1 ⌶	XC ◇1 C ⌶	EM D	XC 1	XC ◇1 A	XC ◇1 E	XC 1 ⌶	AW	XC ◇1 F ⌶		XC ◇1 G ⌶	EM D	XC ◇1	XC ◇1 H	XC 1 ⌶	AW	XC ◇1 I ⌶	XC ◇1 J ⌶
Cardiff Central 7	132	d														06 10					06 40			07 07	07 00	
Newport (South Wales)	132	d														06 26					06 55			07 23	07 15	
Severn Tunnel Jn.	132	d														06 37					07 05			07 34	07 25	
Caldicot		d														06 39					07 08			07 36		
Chepstow		d														06 48					07 16			07 45		
Lydney		d														06 57					07 25			07 54		
Bristol Temple Meads 10	134	d											06 15				07 00					07 30			08 00	
Bristol Parkway 7	134	d											06 25				07 10					07 40			08 10	
Gloucester 7	134	a											06 52			07 18					07 44			08 21		
		d											07 00	07 06		07 21					07 46			08 22		
Cheltenham Spa 4		a											07 09	07 15		07 34	07 39				07 55	08 09		08 35	08 40	
		d											07 11	07 17			07 41				07 57	08 11			08 41	
Ashchurch for Tewkesbury		d												07 24							08 04					
Bromsgrove		d												07 43												
University		d												08 00							08 39					
Birmingham New Street 12		a											07 56	08 07			08 25				08 45	08 56			09 26	
		d	05 58	06 19	06 30	06 49	07 03		07 19	07 30		07 49	08 03		08 19				08 30		08 49	09 03	09 19			09 30
Water Orton		d																								
Wilnecote		d		06 35					07 35												09 05					
Tamworth		d	06 14	06 39	06 46	07 07	07 19		07 39	07 46		08 07	08 19		08 36						09 09		09 36			
Burton-on-Trent		d	06a23	06 51	06a55	07 19	07a30		07 50	07a55		08 19	08a28		08 48				08a52		09 21	09a26	09 48			09a54
Willington		d				07 25						08 25														
Derby 6	56	d																								
Long Eaton	56	d									08 25									09 24						
Attenborough	56	d		07 28							08 33	08 56								09 32						
Beeston	56	d		07 32		07 59			08 27		08 36	09 00								09 35	09 57					
Nottingham 6	56	a		07 38		08 06			08 34		08 46	09 06			09 30					09 41	10 03		10 31			

			EM D		XC ◇1	XC ◇1 H	XC 1 ⌶	XC ◇1 K ⌶	XC ◇1 L ⌶	EM D	XC ◇1	XC ◇1 H ⌶	XC 1 ⌶		AW M	XC ◇1 F ⌶	XC ◇1 N	EM D	XC ◇1 ⌶	XC ◇1 O ⌶	AW M	XC 1 ⌶	XC ◇1 P ⌶		XC ◇1 Q ⌶	EM D
Cardiff Central 7	132	d			07 45						08 45				09 10				09 45		10 10					
Newport (South Wales)	132	d			08 00						09 00				09 25				09 59		10 27					
Severn Tunnel Jn.	132	d													09 35						10 38					
Caldicot		d													09 37						10 40					
Chepstow		d									09 18				09 47				10 18		10 49					
Lydney		d			08 25										09 55						10 58					
Bristol Temple Meads 10	134	d				08 30		09 00				09 30				10 00				10 30			11 00			
Bristol Parkway 7	134	d				08 40		09 10				09 40				10 10				10 40			11 10			
Gloucester 7	134	a			08 45						09 46				10 19				10 44		11 20					
		d			08 50						09 50				10 21				10 50		11 22					
Cheltenham Spa 4		a			09 00	09 09		09 39			10 00	10 09			10 32	10 39			11 00	11 09	11 32		11 40			
		d			09 01	09 11		09 41			10 01	10 11				10 41			11 01	11 11			11 41			
Ashchurch for Tewkesbury		d																								
Bromsgrove		d																								
University		d			09 39						10 39								11 39							
Birmingham New Street 12		a			09 45	09 56		10 25			10 45	10 56				11 26			11 45	11 56			12 26			
		d			09 49	10 03	10 19		10 30		10 49	11 03	11 19				11 30		11 49	12 03		12 19			12 30	
Water Orton		d																								
Wilnecote		d									11 05															
Tamworth		d			10 07	10 19	10 36				11 09		11 36						12 07	12 19		12 36				
Burton-on-Trent		d			10 19	10a28	10 48		10a52		11 21	11a26	11 48				11a55		12 19	12a28		12 48			12a56	
Willington		d			10 25														12 25							
Derby 6	56	d																								
Long Eaton	56	d	10 24							11 24								12 24								13 25
Attenborough	56	d	10 32							11 32								12 32								13 33
Beeston	56	d	10 35		10 57					11 35	11 57							12 35	12 57							13 36
Nottingham 6	56	a	10 41		11 03		11 30			11 41	12 03		12 30					12 41	13 03			13 30				13 42

A To Newcastle
B To Edinburgh
C To Glasgow Central
D 4 August, 11 August. To Newark Castle
E To Stansted Airport
F To Manchester Piccadilly
G From Guildford to Edinburgh
H From Plymouth to Newcastle
I To Manchester Piccadilly. ⌶ from Bristol Temple Meads
J From Bournemouth to Glasgow Central
K From Paignton to Manchester Piccadilly
L From Southampton Central to Edinburgh
M From Maesteg
N From Reading to Glasgow Central
O From Penzance to Newcastle
P From Plymouth to Manchester Piccadilly
Q From Southampton Central to Aberdeen

Trains between Gloucester & Cheltenham are shown on Table T058

Trains between Birmingham & Bromsgrove are shown on Table T069

Table T057-R

Saturdays
28 July to 1 September

Cardiff and Bristol - Birmingham - Derby and Nottingham

			XC ◇1	XC ◇1 A ⌶	XC 1 ⌶		XC ◇1 B ⌶	XC ◇1 C	EM D	XC ◇1 ⌶	XC ◇1 E ⌶	AW F	XC 1	XC ◇1 G ⌶	XC ◇1 H ⌶		EM D	XC ◇1 ⌶	AW ⌶	XC ◇1 I ⌶	XC 1	XC ◇1 G ⌶	XC ◇1 C ⌶	EM D	XC ◇1 ⌶	
Cardiff Central 7	132	d	10 45							11 45		12 09						12 45	13 12						13 45	
Newport (South Wales)	132	d	11 00							12 00		12 27						13 00	13 27						14 00	
Severn Tunnel Jn.	132	d										12 38							13 38							
Caldicot		d										12 40							13 41							
Chepstow		d								12 18		12 49						13 18	13 50							
Lydney		d	11 25									12 58							13 59						14 25	
Bristol Temple Meads 10	134	d		11 30			12 00				12 30			13 00						13 30		14 00				
Bristol Parkway 7	134	d		11 40			12 10				12 40			13 10						13 40		14 10				
Gloucester 7	134	a	11 44							12 44		13 21						13 44	14 20						14 44	
		d	11 50							12 48		13 22						13 50							14 50	
Cheltenham Spa 4		a	12 00	12 09			12 39			12 58	13 10	13 32		13 39				14 00		14 09		14 39			15 00	
		d	12 01	12 11			12 41			12 59	13 11			13 41				14 01		14 11		14 41			15 01	
Ashchurch for Tewkesbury		d								13 07																
Bromsgrove		d																								
University		d	12 39							13 39								14 39							15 39	
Birmingham New Street 12		a	12 45	12 56			13 26			13 45	13 56			14 26				14 45		14 56		15 26			15 45	
		d	12 49	13 03	13 19			13 30		13 49	14 03		14 19		14 30			14 49		15 03	15 19		15 30		15 49	
Water Orton		d																								
Wilnecote		d	13 05							14 05								15 05							16 05	
Tamworth		d	13 09		13 36					14 09	14 19		14 36					15 09			15 36				16 09	
Burton-on-Trent		d	13 21	13a25	13 48			13a54		14 21	14a28		14 48		14a54			15 21		15a26	15 48		15a54		16 21	
Willington		d																15 27								
Derby 6	56	d																								
Long Eaton	56	d							14 24								15 24							16 24		
Attenborough	56	d							14 32								15 32							16 32		
Beeston	56	d	13 57						14 35	14 57							15 35	15 57						16 35	16 57	
Nottingham 6	56	a	14 03		14 30				14 41	15 03			15 30				15 41	16 03			16 30			16 41	17 03	

			XC ◇1 J ⌶	XC 1	XC ◇1 G ⌶	XC ◇1 K ⌶	EM D	XC ◇1 ⌶	XC ◇1 A ⌶	XC 1	AW F		XC ◇1 B ⌶	XC ◇1 L ⌶	EM D	XC ◇1 ⌶	XC ◇1 A ⌶	AW F	XC 1	XC ◇1 G ⌶	XC ◇1 M ⌶		EM N	XC ◇1 O ⌶	XC ◇1 A ⌶	XC 1
Cardiff Central 7	132	d						14 45			15 08					15 45		16 08						16 45		
Newport (South Wales)	132	d						15 00			15 27					16 00		16 24						17 00		
Severn Tunnel Jn.	132	d									15 37							16 35								
Caldicot		d									15 38							16 37								
Chepstow		d						15 18			15 47					16 18		16 46								
Lydney		d									15 56							16 55						17 25		
Bristol Temple Meads 10	134	d	14 30		15 00				15 30				16 00				16 30			17 00					17 30	
Bristol Parkway 7	134	d	14 40		15 10				15 40				16 10				16 40			17 10					17 40	
Gloucester 7	134	a						15 44			16 19					16 44		17 19						17 44		
		d						15 50			16 21					16 50		17 23						17 50		
Cheltenham Spa 4		a	15 09		15 39			16 00	16 09		16 32		16 39			17 00	17 10	17 33		17 39				18 00	18 11	
		d	15 11		15 41			16 01	16 11				16 41			17 01	17 12			17 41				18 01	18 13	
Ashchurch for Tewkesbury		d																								
Bromsgrove		d																								
University		d						16 39								17 39								18 39		
Birmingham New Street 12		a	15 56		16 26			16 45	16 56				17 26			17 45	17 56			18 26				18 45	18 55	
		d	16 03	16 19		16 30		16 49	17 03	17 19				17 30		17 49	18 03		18 19		18 30			18 49	19 03	19 19
Water Orton		d																								
Wilnecote		d						17 05								18 05								19 05		
Tamworth		d	16 19	16 36				17 09		17 36						18 09	18 19		18 36					19 09		19 36
Burton-on-Trent		d	16a30	16 48		16a53		17 21	17a25	17 48				17a55		18 21	18a28		18 48		18a55			19 21	19a25	19 48
Willington		d														18 27										
Derby 6	56	d																								
Long Eaton	56	d					17 25								18 25								19 24			
Attenborough	56	d					17 33								18 33								19 32			
Beeston	56	d		17 26			17 36	17 57		18 26					18 36	18 57			19 26				19 35	19 57		
Nottingham 6	56	a		17 32			17 42	18 03		18 32					18 45	19 03			19 32				19 41	20 04		20 30

A From Plymouth to Newcastle
B From Paignton to Manchester Piccadilly
C From Reading to Glasgow Central
D 4 August, 11 August. To Newark Castle
E From Penzance to Newcastle
F From Maesteg
G To Manchester Piccadilly
H From Southampton Central to Dundee
I From Newquay to Newcastle
J From Paignton to Edinburgh
K From Southampton Central to Edinburgh
L From Reading to Edinburgh
M From Southampton Central to York
N 4 August, 11 August
O ⌶ to Birmingham New Street

Trains between Gloucester & Cheltenham are shown on Table T058

Trains between Birmingham & Bromsgrove are shown on Table T069

Table T057-R

Cardiff and Bristol - Birmingham - Derby and Nottingham

Saturdays

28 July to 1 September

	AW	XC	XC	EM	XC	XC	AW	XC	EM	XC	XC	XC	XC	XC	XC	XC	XC	AW	AW
		◇1	◇1		◇1	◇1		◇1		◇1	◇1	◇1	◇1	◇1	◇1	◇1	1		
	A	B	C	D	E	F	A	B	D	E	G	H	I	J				A	A
		🛒			🛒	🛒		🛒		🛒	🛒								
Cardiff Central 7 ... 132 d	17 09				17 45		18 08			18 45					20 00	20 50		21 11	23 18
Newport (South Wales) 132 d	17 25				18 00		18 27			19 00					20 15	21 05		21 27	23 37
Severn Tunnel Jn. 132 d	17 36						18 38								20 25			21 38	23 56
Caldicot d	17 38						18 40								20 28			21 40	23 59
Chepstow d	17 47				18 18		18 49			19 18					20 36			21 49	00 08
Lydney d	17 56						18 58								20 45			21 58	00 17
Bristol Temple Meads 10 134 d		18 00				18 30		19 00			19 30		20 00	20 30					
Bristol Parkway 7 134 d		18 10				18 39		19 10			19 40		20 10	20 40					
Gloucester 7 134 a	18 18				18 44		19 20			19 44					21 04	21 47		22 19	00 40
d	18 24				18 46		19 21			19 46					21 07	21 49			
Cheltenham Spa 4 a	18 33	18 39			18 56	19 10	19 31	19 39		19 56	20 11		20 40	21 10	21 16	21 58			
d		18 41			18 57	19 11		19 41		19 57	20 12		20 41	21 11	21 18	21 59			
Ashchurch for Tewkesbury d					19 05										21 25				
Bromsgrove d															21 44				
University d					19 39					20 35					22 01	22 35			
Birmingham New Street 12 a		19 26			19 45	19 58		20 26		20 42	20 49		21 38	21 51	22 07	22 42			
d			19 30		19 49	20 03				20 49		21 03		21 56	22 10		22 49		
Water Orton d																			
Wilnecote d					20 05					21 05							23 04		
Tamworth d					20 09	20 19				21 09		21 19			22 27		23 08		
Burton-on-Trent d			19a53		20 21	20a29				21 21		21a29		22a19	22 39		23a19		
Willington d															22 45				
Derby 6 56 d																			
Long Eaton 56 d				20 24					21 24										
Attenborough 56 d				20 32					21 32	21 55					23 18				
Beeston 56 d				20 35	20 57				21 35	21 58					23 21				
Nottingham 8 56 ⇌ a				20 41	21 03				21 41	22 04					23 27				

Saturdays

8 September to 6 October

	XC	XC	XC	XC	XC	XC	XC	XC	XC	XC	XC	AW	XC	XC	XC	XC	XC	AW	XC	XC	XC	XC
	◇1	1	◇1	1	◇1	1	◇1	1	◇1	◇1	1		◇1	◇1	◇1	◇1	1		◇1	◇1	◇1	◇1
	K		L		K		M		K	N			B	O		P			Q	R		P
	🛒		🛒		🛒	🛒	🛒				🛒		🛒	🛒			🛒		🛒	🛒		
Cardiff Central 7 ... 132 d												06 10			06 40			07 07	07 00		07 45	
Newport (South Wales) 132 d												06 26			06 55			07 23	07 15		08 00	
Severn Tunnel Jn. 132 d												06 37			07 05			07 34	07 25			
Caldicot d												06 39			07 08			07 36				
Chepstow d												06 48			07 16			07 45				
Lydney d												06 57			07 25			07 54			08 25	
Bristol Temple Meads 10 134 d									06 15				07 00			07 30			08 00			08 30
Bristol Parkway 7 134 d									06 25				07 10			07 40			08 10			08 40
Gloucester 7 134 a									06 52			07 18			07 44			08 21			08 45	
d									07 00	07 06		07 21			07 46			08 22			08 50	
Cheltenham Spa 4 a									07 09	07 15		07 34	07 39		07 55	08 09		08 35	08 40		09 00	09 09
d									07 11	07 17			07 41		07 57	08 11			08 41		09 01	09 11
Ashchurch for Tewkesbury d										07 24					08 04							
Bromsgrove d										07 43												
University d										08 00					08 39						09 39	
Birmingham New Street 12 a									07 56	08 07			08 25		08 45	08 56			09 26		09 45	09 56
d	05 58	06 19	06 30	06 49	07 03	07 19	07 30	07 49	08 03		08 19			08 30	08 49	09 03	09 19			09 30	09 49	10 03
Water Orton d																						
Wilnecote d		06 35				07 35									09 05							
Tamworth d	06 14	06 39	06 46	07 07	07 19	07 39	07 46	08 07	08 19		08 36				09 09		09 36				10 07	10 19
Burton-on-Trent d	06 26	06 51	06 56	07 19	07 31	07 50	07 56	08 19	08 29		08 48				09 21	09 28	09 48				10 19	
Willington d				07 25				08 25													10 25	
Derby 6 56 d	06a49	07 08	07a13	07 40	07a45	08 10	08a11	08 40	08a42		09 08			09a13	09 40	09a45	10 08			10a13	10 40	10a45
Long Eaton 56 d		07 21		07 52		08 19		08 49							09 49						10 49	
Attenborough 56 d		07 28						08 57														
Beeston 56 d		07 32		08 00		08 27		09 00							09 57						10 57	
Nottingham 8 56 ⇌ a		07 38		08 06		08 34		09 07			09 30				10 03		10 30				11 03	

A From Maesteg
B To Manchester Piccadilly
C From Reading to Leeds
D 4 August, 11 August
E 🛒 to Birmingham New Street
F From Paignton to York. 🛒 to Birmingham New Street
G From Newquay to Manchester Piccadilly
H From Bournemouth to Leeds
I From Paignton
J From Penzance to Leeds
K To Newcastle
L To Edinburgh
M To Glasgow Central
N To Stansted Airport
O From Guildford to Edinburgh
P From Plymouth to Newcastle
Q To Manchester Piccadilly. 🛒 from Bristol Temple Meads
R From Bournemouth to Glasgow Central

Trains between Gloucester & Cheltenham are shown on Table T058

Trains between Birmingham & Bromsgrove are shown on Table T069

Table T057-R

Cardiff and Bristol - Birmingham - Derby and Nottingham

Saturdays

8 September to 6 October

	XC	XC	XC	XC	XC	XC	AW	XC	XC	XC	XC	AW	XC	XC	XC	XC	XC	XC	XC	XC	XC
	1	◇1	◇1	◇1	◇1	1		◇1	◇1	◇1	◇1		1	◇1	◇1	◇1	◇1	1	◇1	◇1	◇1
		A	B		C		D	E	F		G	D		H	I		C		A	F	
	🛒	🛒	🛒		🛒	🛒		🛒		🛒	🛒		🛒	🛒	🛒		🛒	🛒	🛒		🛒
Cardiff Central 7 ... 132 d				08 45			09 10			09 45		10 10				10 45					11 45
Newport (South Wales) 132 d				09 00			09 25			09 59		10 27				11 00					12 00
Severn Tunnel Jn. 132 d							09 35					10 38									
Caldicot d							09 37					10 40									
Chepstow d				09 18			09 47			10 18		10 49									12 18
Lydney d							09 55					10 58				11 25					
Bristol Temple Meads 10 134 d		09 00			09 30			10 00			10 30			11 00			11 30		12 00		
Bristol Parkway 7 134 d		09 10			09 40			10 10			10 40			11 10			11 40		12 10		
Gloucester 7 134 a				09 46			10 19			10 44		11 20				11 44					12 44
d				09 50			10 21			10 50		11 22				11 50					12 48
Cheltenham Spa 4 a		09 39		10 00	10 09		10 32	10 39		11 00	11 09	11 32		11 40		12 00	12 09		12 39		12 58
d		09 41		10 01	10 11			10 41		11 01	11 11			11 41		12 01	12 11		12 41		12 59
Ashchurch for Tewkesbury d																					13 07
Bromsgrove d																					
University d				10 39						11 39						12 39					13 39
Birmingham New Street 12 a		10 25		10 45	10 56			11 26		11 45	11 56			12 26		12 45	12 56		13 26		13 45
d	10 19		10 30	10 49	11 03	11 19			11 30	11 49	12 03		12 19		12 30	12 49	13 03	13 19		13 30	13 49
Water Orton d																					
Wilnecote d				11 05												13 05					14 05
Tamworth d	10 36			11 09		11 36				12 07	12 19		12 36			13 09		13 36			14 09
Burton-on-Trent d	10 48			11 21	11 26	11 48				12 19			12 48			13 21	13 27	13 48			14 21
Willington d										12 25											
Derby 6 56 d	11 08		11a13	11 40	11a42	12 08			12a13	12 40	12a42		13 08		13a05	13 40	13a38	14 08		14a13	14 40
Long Eaton 56 d				11 49						12 49						13 49					14 49
Attenborough 56 d																					
Beeston 56 d				11 57						12 57						13 57					14 57
Nottingham 8 56 ⇌ a	11 30			12 03		12 28				13 03			13 28			14 03		14 28			15 03

	XC	AW	XC	XC	XC	XC	AW	XC	XC	XC	XC	XC	XC	XC	XC	XC	XC	XC	XC	AW	XC	XC
	◇1		1	◇1	◇1	◇1		◇1	1	◇1	◇1	◇1	◇1	1	◇1	◇1	◇1	◇1	1		◇1	◇1
	G	D		E	J			K		L	F		M		E	B		C		D	A	N
	🛒			🛒	🛒	🛒	🛒	🛒		🛒	🛒	🛒	🛒		🛒	🛒	🛒	🛒			🛒	🛒
Cardiff Central 7 ... 132 d		12 09				12 45	13 12					13 45					14 45			15 08		
Newport (South Wales) 132 d		12 27				13 00	13 27					14 00					15 00			15 27		
Severn Tunnel Jn. 132 d		12 38					13 38													15 37		
Caldicot d		12 40					13 41													15 38		
Chepstow d		12 49				13 18	13 50										15 18			15 47		
Lydney d		12 58					13 59					14 25								15 56		
Bristol Temple Meads 10 134 d	12 30			13 00				13 30		14 00			14 30		15 00			15 30			16 00	
Bristol Parkway 7 134 d	12 40			13 10				13 40		14 10			14 40		15 10			15 40			16 10	
Gloucester 7 134 a		13 21				13 44	14 20					14 44					15 44			16 19		
d		13 22				13 50						14 50					15 50			16 21		
Cheltenham Spa 4 a	13 10	13 32		13 39		14 00		14 09		14 39		15 00	15 09		15 39		16 00	16 09		16 32	16 39	
d	13 11			13 41		14 01		14 11		14 41		15 01	15 11		15 41		16 01	16 11			16 41	
Ashchurch for Tewkesbury d																						
Bromsgrove d																						
University d						14 39						15 39					16 39					
Birmingham New Street 12 a	13 56			14 26		14 45		14 56		15 26		15 45	15 56		16 26		16 45	16 56			17 26	
d	14 03		14 19		14 30	14 49		15 03	15 19		15 30	15 49	16 03	16 19		16 30	16 49	17 03	17 19			17 30
Water Orton d																						
Wilnecote d						15 05						16 05					17 05					
Tamworth d	14 19		14 36			15 09			15 36			16 09	16 19	16 36			17 09		17 36			
Burton-on-Trent d			14 48			15 21		15 27	15 48			16 21		16 48		16 58	17 21	17 27	17 48			
Willington d						15 27																
Derby 6 56 d	14a42		15 08		15a05	15 40		15a45	16 08		16a13	16 40	16a45	17 08		17a13	17 40	17a42	18 08			18a13
Long Eaton 56 d						15 49						16 49		17 17			17 49		18 17			
Attenborough 56 d																						
Beeston 56 d						15 57						16 57		17 25			17 57		18 25			
Nottingham 8 56 ⇌ a			15 28			16 03			16 28			17 03		17 31			18 03		18 31			

A From Paignton to Manchester Piccadilly
B From Southampton Central to Edinburgh
C From Plymouth to Newcastle
D From Maesteg
E To Manchester Piccadilly
F From Reading to Glasgow Central
G From Penzance to Newcastle
H From Plymouth to Manchester Piccadilly
I From Southampton Central to Aberdeen
J From Southampton Central to Dundee
K From Newquay to Newcastle
L From Penzance to Manchester Piccadilly
M From Plymouth to Edinburgh
N From Reading to Edinburgh

Trains between Gloucester & Cheltenham are shown on Table T058

Trains between Birmingham & Bromsgrove are shown on Table T069

Table T057-R

Saturdays

8 September to 6 October

Cardiff and Bristol - Birmingham - Derby and Nottingham

	XC ◇1 🍴	XC ◇1 A 🍴	AW B	XC 1	XC ◇1 C 🍴	XC ◇1 D 🍴	XC ◇1 E 🍴	XC ◇1 A 🍴	XC 1	AW B
Cardiff Central 7 132 d	15 45		16 08				16 45			17 09
Newport (South Wales) 132 d	16 00		16 24				17 00			17 25
Severn Tunnel Jn. 132 d			16 35							17 36
Caldicot d			16 37							17 38
Chepstow d	16 18		16 46							17 47
Lydney d			16 55				17 25			17 56
Bristol Temple Meads 10 134 d		16 30			17 00			17 30		
Bristol Parkway 7 134 d		16 40			17 10			17 40		
Gloucester 7 134 a	16 44		17 19				17 44			18 18
d	16 50		17 23				17 50			18 24
Cheltenham Spa 4 a	17 00	17 10	17 33		17 39		18 00	18 11		18 33
d	17 01	17 12			17 41		18 01	18 13		
Ashchurch for Tewkesbury d										
Bromsgrove d										
University d	17 39						18 39			
Birmingham New Street 12 a	17 45	17 56			18 26		18 45	18 55		
d	17 49	18 03		18 19		18 30	18 49	19 03	19 19	
Water Orton d										
Wilnecote d	18 05						19 05			
Tamworth d	18 09	18 19		18 36			19 09		19 36	
Burton-on-Trent d	18 21			18 48			19 21	19 29	19 48	
Willington d	18 27									
Derby 6 56 d	18 40	18a42		19 08		19a13	19 40	19a42	20 08	
Long Eaton 56 d	18 49			19 17			19 50			
Attenborough 56 d										
Beeston 56 d	18 57			19 25			19 58			
Nottingham 8 56 ⇌ a	19 03			19 31			20 04		20 28	

	XC ◇1 F 🍴	XC ◇1 G	XC ◇1 E 🍴	XC ◇1 H 🍴	AW B	XC ◇1 C 🍴	XC ◇1 E 🍴	XC ◇1 I 🍴	XC ◇1 J 🍴	XC ◇1 K	XC ◇1 L	XC ◇1 M
Cardiff Central 7 132 d			17 45		18 08		18 45					
Newport (South Wales) 132 d			18 00		18 27		19 00					
Severn Tunnel Jn. 132 d					18 38							
Caldicot d					18 40							
Chepstow d			18 18		18 49		19 18					
Lydney d					18 58							
Bristol Temple Meads 10 134 d	18 00			18 30		19 00		19 30	19 30		20 00	20 00
Bristol Parkway 7 134 d	18 10			18 39		19 10		19 40	19 40		20 10	20 10
Gloucester 7 134 a			18 44		19 20		19 44					
d			18 46		19 21		19 46					
Cheltenham Spa 4 a	18 39		18 56	19 10	19 31	19 39	19 56	20 11	20 11		20 39	20 40
d	18 41		18 57	19 11		19 41	19 57	20 12	20 12		20 41	20 41
Ashchurch for Tewkesbury d			19 05									
Bromsgrove d												
University d			19 39				20 35					
Birmingham New Street 12 a	19 26		19 45	19 58		20 26	20 42	20 49	20 51		21 38	21 38
d		19 30	19 49	20 03			20 49		21 03	21 03		
Water Orton d												
Wilnecote d			20 05				21 05					
Tamworth d			20 09	20 19			21 09		21 19	21 19		
Burton-on-Trent d			20 21				21 21		21 30	21 30		
Willington d												
Derby 6 56 d		20a13	20 40	20a40			21 37		21a42	21a42		
Long Eaton 56 d			20 49				21 47					
Attenborough 56 d							21 55					
Beeston 56 d			20 56				21 58					
Nottingham 8 56 ⇌ a			21 03				22 04					

	XC ◇1 N	XC ◇1 O	XC ◇1	XC ◇1	XC 1	AW B	AW B
Cardiff Central 7 132 d			20 00	20 50		21 11	23 18
Newport (South Wales) 132 d			20 15	21 05		21 27	23 37
Severn Tunnel Jn. 132 d			20 25			21 38	23 56
Caldicot d			20 28			21 40	23 59
Chepstow d			20 36			21 49	00 08
Lydney d			20 45			21 58	00 17
Bristol Temple Meads 10 134 d	20 30	20 30					
Bristol Parkway 7 134 d	20 40	20 40					
Gloucester 7 134 a			21 04	21 47		22 19	00 40
d			21 07	21 49			
Cheltenham Spa 4 a	21 09	21 10	21 16	21 58			
d	21 11	21 11	21 18	21 59			
Ashchurch for Tewkesbury d			21 25				
Bromsgrove d			21 44				
University d			22 01	22 35			
Birmingham New Street 12 a	21 52	21 51	22 07	22 42			
d		21 56	22 10		22 49		
Water Orton d							
Wilnecote d					23 04		
Tamworth d			22 27		23 08		
Burton-on-Trent d			22 39		23 20		
Willington d			22 45				
Derby 6 56 d		22a28	22 59		23a33		
Long Eaton 56 d			23 10				
Attenborough 56 d			23 18				
Beeston 56 d			23 21				
Nottingham 8 56 ⇌ a			23 27				

A From Plymouth to Newcastle
B From Maesteg
C To Manchester Piccadilly
D From Southampton Central to York
E 🍴 to Birmingham New Street
F From Exeter St Davids to Manchester Piccadilly
G From Reading to Leeds
H From Plymouth to York. 🍴 to Birmingham New Street
I 8 September. From Newquay to Manchester Piccadilly
J not 8 September. From Plymouth to Leeds. 🍴 to Birmingham New Street
K 8 September. From Bournemouth to Leeds
L not 8 September
M 8 September. From Paignton
N not 8 September. From Plymouth
O 8 September. From Penzance to Leeds

Trains between Gloucester & Cheltenham are shown on Table T058

Trains between Birmingham & Bromsgrove are shown on Table T069

Table T057-R

Saturdays

13 October to 8 December

Cardiff and Bristol - Birmingham - Derby and Nottingham

	XC ◇1 A 🍴	XC 1	XC ◇1 B 🍴	XC 1	XC ◇1 C 🍴	XC 1 🍴	XC ◇1 B 🍴	XC 1	XC ◇1 A 🍴	XC ◇1 D	XC 1 🍴	AW	XC ◇1 E 🍴	XC ◇1 F 🍴
Cardiff Central 7 132 d												06 10		
Newport (South Wales) 132 d												06 26		
Severn Tunnel Jn. 132 d												06 37		
Caldicot d												06 39		
Chepstow d												06 48		
Lydney d												06 57		
Bristol Temple Meads 10 134 d									06 15				07 00	
Bristol Parkway 7 134 d									06 25				07 10	
Gloucester 7 134 a									06 52			07 18		
d									07 00	07 06		07 21		
Cheltenham Spa 4 a									07 09	07 15		07 34	07 39	
d									07 11	07 17			07 41	
Ashchurch for Tewkesbury d										07 24				
Bromsgrove d										07 43				
University d										08 00				
Birmingham New Street 12 a									07 56	08 07			08 25	
d	05 58	06 19	06 30	06 49	07 03	07 19	07 30	07 49	08 03		08 19			08 30
Water Orton d														
Wilnecote d		06 35				07 35								
Tamworth d	06 14	06 39	06 46	07 07	07 19	07 39	07 46	08 07	08 19		08 36			
Burton-on-Trent d	06 25	06 51	06 56	07 19	07 31	07 50	07 56	08 19	08 29		08 48			
Willington d				07 25				08 25						
Derby 6 56 d	06a35	07 09	07a09	07 40	07a41	08 10	08a08	08 40	08a41		09 08			09a05
Long Eaton 56 d		07 21		07 52		08 19		08 49						
Attenborough 56 d		07 28						08 57						
Beeston 56 d		07 32		08 00		08 27		09 00						
Nottingham 8 56 ⇌ a		07 38		08 06		08 34		09 07			09 28			

	XC ◇1	XC ◇1 G 🍴	XC 1 🍴	AW	XC ◇1 H 🍴	XC ◇1 I 🍴	XC ◇1	XC ◇1 J 🍴
Cardiff Central 7 132 d	06 40			07 07	07 00		07 45	
Newport (South Wales) 132 d	06 55			07 23	07 15		08 00	
Severn Tunnel Jn. 132 d	07 05			07 34	07 25			
Caldicot d	07 08			07 36				
Chepstow d	07 16			07 45				
Lydney d	07 25			07 54			08 25	
Bristol Temple Meads 10 134 d		07 30			08 00			08 30
Bristol Parkway 7 134 d		07 40			08 10			08 40
Gloucester 7 134 a	07 44			08 21			08 45	
d	07 46			08 22			08 50	
Cheltenham Spa 4 a	07 55	08 09		08 35	08 40		09 00	09 09
d	07 57	08 11			08 41		09 01	09 11
Ashchurch for Tewkesbury d	08 04							
Bromsgrove d								
University d	08 39						09 39	
Birmingham New Street 12 a	08 45	08 56			09 26		09 45	09 56
d	08 49	09 03	09 19			09 30	09 49	10 03
Water Orton d								
Wilnecote d	09 05							
Tamworth d	09 09		09 36				10 07	10 19
Burton-on-Trent d	09 21	09 28	09 48				10 19	
Willington d							10 25	
Derby 6 56 d	09 40	09a39	10 08			10a06	10 40	10a38
Long Eaton 56 d	09 49						10 49	
Attenborough 56 d								
Beeston 56 d	09 57						10 57	
Nottingham 8 56 ⇌ a	10 03		10 28				11 03	

	XC 1 🍴	XC ◇1 K 🍴	XC ◇1 L 🍴	XC ◇1	XC ◇1 G 🍴	XC 1 🍴	AW M	XC ◇1 E 🍴	XC ◇1 N 🍴	XC ◇1 🍴	XC ◇1 O 🍴	AW M
Cardiff Central 7 132 d				08 45			09 10			09 45		10 10
Newport (South Wales) 132 d				09 00			09 25			09 59		10 27
Severn Tunnel Jn. 132 d							09 35					10 38
Caldicot d							09 37					10 40
Chepstow d				09 18			09 47			10 18		10 49
Lydney d							09 55					10 58
Bristol Temple Meads 10 134 d		09 00			09 30			10 00			10 30	
Bristol Parkway 7 134 d		09 10			09 40			10 10			10 40	
Gloucester 7 134 a				09 46			10 19			10 44		11 20
d				09 50			10 21			10 50		11 22
Cheltenham Spa 4 a		09 39		10 00	10 09		10 32	10 39		11 00	11 09	11 32
d		09 41		10 01	10 11			10 41		11 01	11 11	
Ashchurch for Tewkesbury d												
Bromsgrove d												
University d				10 39						11 39		
Birmingham New Street 12 a		10 25		10 45	10 56			11 26		11 45	11 56	
d	10 19		10 30	10 49	11 03	11 19			11 30	11 49	12 03	
Water Orton d												
Wilnecote d				11 05								
Tamworth d	10 36			11 09		11 36				12 07	12 19	
Burton-on-Trent d	10 48			11 21	11 28	11 48				12 19		
Willington d										12 25		
Derby 6 56 d	11 08		11a05	11 40	11a38	12 08			12a05	12 40	12a38	
Long Eaton 56 d				11 49						12 48		
Attenborough 56 d												
Beeston 56 d				11 57						12 56		
Nottingham 8 56 ⇌ a	11 28			12 03		12 28				13 02		

	XC 1 🍴	XC ◇1 E 🍴	XC ◇1 L 🍴	XC ◇1	XC ◇1 P 🍴	XC 1 🍴	XC ◇1 K 🍴	XC ◇1 N 🍴	XC ◇1 🍴
Cardiff Central 7 132 d				10 45					11 45
Newport (South Wales) 132 d				11 00					12 00
Severn Tunnel Jn. 132 d									
Caldicot d									
Chepstow d									12 18
Lydney d				11 25					
Bristol Temple Meads 10 134 d		11 00			11 30		12 00		
Bristol Parkway 7 134 d		11 10			11 40		12 10		
Gloucester 7 134 a				11 44					12 44
d				11 50					12 48
Cheltenham Spa 4 a		11 40		12 00	12 09		12 39		12 58
d		11 41		12 01	12 11		12 41		12 59
Ashchurch for Tewkesbury d									13 07
Bromsgrove d									
University d				12 39					13 39
Birmingham New Street 12 a		12 26		12 45	12 56		13 26		13 45
d	12 19		12 30	12 49	13 03	13 19		13 30	13 49
Water Orton d									
Wilnecote d				13 05					14 05
Tamworth d	12 36			13 09		13 36			14 09
Burton-on-Trent d	12 48			13 21	13 27	13 48			14 21
Willington d									
Derby 6 56 d	13 08		13a05	13 40	13a38	14 08		14a05	14 40
Long Eaton 56 d				13 49					14 49
Attenborough 56 d									
Beeston 56 d				13 57					14 57
Nottingham 8 56 ⇌ a	13 28			14 03		14 28			15 03

A To Glasgow Central
B To Newcastle
C To Edinburgh
D To Stansted Airport
E To Manchester Piccadilly
F From Guildford to Newcastle
G From Plymouth to Edinburgh
H To Manchester Piccadilly. 🍴 from Bristol Temple Meads
I From Bournemouth to Newcastle
J From Plymouth to Glasgow Central
K From Paignton to Manchester Piccadilly
L From Southampton Central to Newcastle
M From Maesteg
N From Reading to Newcastle
O From Penzance to Glasgow Central
P From Plymouth to Aberdeen

Trains between Gloucester & Cheltenham are shown on Table T058

Trains between Birmingham & Bromsgrove are shown on Table T069

Cardiff and Bristol - Birmingham - Derby and Nottingham

Saturdays
13 October to 8 December

	XC	AW	XC	XC	XC	XC	AW	XC	XC	XC	XC	XC	XC	XC	XC	XC	XC	XC	XC	AW	XC
	◇1 A 🍴	B	1	◇1 C 🍴	◇1 D 🍴	◇1 🍴	🍴	◇1 E 🍴	1	◇1 F 🍴	◇1 G 🍴	◇1 🍴	◇1 H 🍴	1	◇1 C 🍴	◇1 D 🍴	◇1 🍴	◇1 I 🍴	1	B	◇1 J 🍴
Cardiff Central 7 132 d		12 09				12 45	13 12					13 45					14 45			15 08	
Newport (South Wales) 132 d		12 27				13 00	13 27					14 00					15 00			15 27	
Severn Tunnel Jn. 132 d		12 38					13 38													15 37	
Caldicot d		12 40					13 41													15 38	
Chepstow d		12 49				13 18	13 50										15 18			15 47	
Lydney d		12 58					13 59					14 25								15 56	
Bristol Temple Meads 10 134 d	12 30			13 00				13 30		14 00			14 30		15 00			15 30			16 00
Bristol Parkway 7 134 d	12 40			13 10				13 40		14 10			14 40		15 10			15 40			16 10
Gloucester 7 134 a		13 21				13 44	14 20					14 44					15 44			16 19	
d		13 22				13 50						14 50					15 50			16 21	
Cheltenham Spa 4 a	13 10	13 32		13 39		14 00		14 09		14 39		15 00	15 09		15 39		16 00	16 09		16 32	16 39
d	13 11			13 41		14 01		14 11		14 41		15 01	15 11		15 41		16 01	16 11			16 41
Ashchurch for Tewkesbury d																					
Bromsgrove d																					
University d						14 39						15 39					16 39				
Birmingham New Street 12 a	13 56			14 26		14 45		14 56		15 26		15 45	15 56		16 26		16 45	16 56			17 26
d	14 03		14 19		14 30	14 49		15 03	15 19		15 30	15 49	16 03	16 19		16 30	16 49	17 03	17 19		
Water Orton d																					
Wilnecote d						15 05						16 05					17 05				
Tamworth d	14 19		14 36			15 09			15 36			16 09	16 19	16 36			17 09		17 36		
Burton-on-Trent d			14 48			15 21		15 27	15 48			16 21		16 48		16 54	17 21	17 26	17 48		
Willington d						15 27															
Derby 6 56 d	14a38		15 08		15a05	15 40		15a40	16 08		16a06	16 40	16a40	17 08		17a05	17 40	17a40	18 08		
Long Eaton 56 d						15 49						16 49		17 17			17 49		18 17		
Attenborough 56 d																					
Beeston 56 d						15 57						16 57		17 25			17 58		18 25		
Nottingham 8 56 ⛴ a			15 28			16 03			16 28			17 03		17 31			18 04		18 31		

	XC	XC	XC	AW	XC	XC	XC	XC	XC	XC	AW	XC	XC	XC	XC	AW	XC	XC	XC	XC	XC	XC
	◇1 G 🍴	◇1 🍴	◇1 I 🍴	B	1	◇1 C 🍴	◇1 D 🍴	◇1 K 🍴	◇1 L 🍴	1	B	◇1 M 🍴	◇1 G	◇1 K 🍴	◇1 N 🍴	B	◇1 C 🍴	◇1 O	◇1 K 🍴	◇1 N 🍴	◇1	◇1 P
Cardiff Central 7 132 d		15 45		16 08				16 45			17 09			17 45		18 08			18 45			
Newport (South Wales) 132 d		16 00		16 24				17 00			17 25			18 00		18 27			19 00			
Severn Tunnel Jn. 132 d				16 35							17 36					18 38						
Caldicot d				16 37							17 38					18 40						
Chepstow d		16 18		16 46							17 47			18 18		18 49			19 18			
Lydney d				16 55				17 25			17 56					18 58						
Bristol Temple Meads 10 134 d			16 30			17 00			17 30			18 00			18 30		19 00			19 30	20 00	20 30
Bristol Parkway 7 134 d			16 40			17 10			17 40			18 10			18 39		19 10			19 40	20 10	20 40
Gloucester 7 134 a		16 44		17 19				17 44			18 18			18 44		19 20			19 44			
d		16 50		17 23				17 50			18 24			18 46		19 21			19 46			
Cheltenham Spa 4 a		17 00	17 10	17 33		17 39		18 00	18 11		18 33	18 39		18 56	19 10	19 31	19 39		19 56	20 11	20 39	21 09
d		17 01	17 12			17 41		18 01	18 13			18 41		18 57	19 11		19 41		19 57	20 12	20 41	21 11
Ashchurch for Tewkesbury d														19 05								
Bromsgrove d																						
University d		17 39						18 39						19 39					20 35			
Birmingham New Street 12 a		17 45	17 56			18 26		18 45	18 56			19 26		19 45	19 58		20 26		20 42	20 51	21 38	21 52
d	17 30	17 49	18 03		18 19		18 30	18 49	19 03	19 19			19 30	19 49	20 03			20 30	20 49	21 03		
Water Orton d																						
Wilnecote d		18 05						19 05						20 05					21 05			
Tamworth d		18 09	18 19		18 36			19 09		19 36				20 09	20 19				21 09	21 19		
Burton-on-Trent d		18 21			18 48			19 21	19 27	19 48				20 21					21 21	21 30		
Willington d		18 27																				
Derby 6 56 d	18a05	18 40	18a40		19 08		19a05	19 40	19a39	20 08			20a05	20 40	20a40			21a24	21 37	21a43		
Long Eaton 56 d		18 49			19 17			19 49						20 49					21 48			
Attenborough 56 d																			21 55			
Beeston 56 d		18 57			19 25			19 57						20 56					21 58			
Nottingham 8 56 ⛴ a		19 03			19 31			20 04		20 28				21 03					22 04			

A From Penzance to Glasgow Central
B From Maesteg
C To Manchester Piccadilly
D From Southampton Central to Newcastle
E From Plymouth to Dundee
F From Penzance to Manchester Piccadilly
G From Reading to Newcastle
H From Plymouth to Glasgow Central
I From Plymouth to Edinburgh
J From Paignton to Manchester Piccadilly
K 🍴 to Birmingham New Street
L From Plymouth to York
M From Exeter St Davids to Manchester Piccadilly
N From Plymouth to Leeds. 🍴 to Birmingham New Street
O From Southampton Central to York
P From Plymouth

Trains between Gloucester & Cheltenham are shown on Table T058

Trains between Birmingham & Bromsgrove are shown on Table T069

Table T057-R

Cardiff and Bristol - Birmingham - Derby and Nottingham

Saturdays
13 October to 8 December

	XC	XC	XC	AW	AW
	◇1	◇1	1	A	A
Cardiff Central 7 132 d	20 00	20 50		21 11	23 18
Newport (South Wales) 132 d	20 15	21 05		21 27	23 37
Severn Tunnel Jn. 132 d	20 25			21 38	23 56
Caldicot d	20 28			21 40	23 59
Chepstow d	20 36			21 49	00 08
Lydney d	20 45			21 58	00 17
Bristol Temple Meads 10 134 d					
Bristol Parkway 7 134 d					
Gloucester 7 134 a	21 04	21 47		22 19	00 40
d	21 07	21 49			
Cheltenham Spa 4 a	21 16	21 58			
d	21 18	21 59			
Ashchurch for Tewkesbury d	21 25				
Bromsgrove d	21 44				
University d	22 01	22 35			
Birmingham New Street 12 a	22 07	22 42			
d	22 10		22 49		
Water Orton d					
Wilnecote d			23 04		
Tamworth d	22 27		23 08		
Burton-on-Trent d	22 39		23 20		
Willington d	22 45				
Derby 6 56 d	22 59		23a33		
Long Eaton 56 d	23 10				
Attenborough 56 d	23 18				
Beeston 56 d	23 21				
Nottingham 8 56 ⛴ a	23 27				

Sundays
20 May to 15 July

	XC	XC	XC	XC	XC	AW	XC	XC	XC	XC	XC	XC	XC	XC	AW	XC	XC	XC	XC	XC	XC	XC
	◇1 B 🍴	◇1 C 🍴	◇1 B 🍴	◇1 🍴	◇1 C 🍴		◇1 D 🍴	◇1 E 🍴	◇1 F 🍴	◇1 D 🍴	◇1 E 🍴	◇1 G 🍴	◇1 H 🍴	◇1 I 🍴		◇1 E 🍴	◇1 J 🍴	◇1 K 🍴	◇1 L 🍴	◇1 E 🍴	◇1 G 🍴	◇1 K 🍴
Cardiff Central 7 132 d						10 30		10 45			11 45				12 25	12 45				13 45		
Newport (South Wales) 132 d						10 48		11 06			12 05				12 47	13 05				14 05		
Severn Tunnel Jn. 132 d						10 59									12 58							
Caldicot d						11 01									13 00							
Chepstow d						11 10									13 09							
Lydney d						11 19									13 18							
Bristol Temple Meads 10 134 d			09 15		10 30				11 30			12 30	13 00				13 30	14 00			14 30	15 00
Bristol Parkway 7 134 d			09 25		10 40				11 40			12 40	13 10				13 40	14 10			14 40	15 10
Gloucester 7 134 a			09 52			11 40		11 47			12 46				13 39	13 46				14 46		
d			10 00			11 42		11 50			12 50				13 40	13 50				14 50		
Cheltenham Spa 4 a			10 09		11 09	11 55		12 00	12 09		13 00	13 09	13 39		13 52	14 00	14 09	14 39		15 00	15 10	15 37
d			10 12		11 11			12 01	12 11		13 01	13 11	13 41			14 01	14 11	14 41		15 01	15 11	15 40
Ashchurch for Tewkesbury d																						
Bromsgrove d																						
University d								12 39			13 39					14 39				15 39		
Birmingham New Street 12 a			10 49		11 48			12 45	12 49		13 45	13 48	14 27			14 45	14 48	15 27		15 45	15 49	16 27
d	09 03	10 03	11 03	11 49	12 03		12 30	12 49	13 03	13 30	13 49	14 03		14 30		14 49	15 03		15 30	15 49	16 03	
Water Orton d																						
Wilnecote d																15 04						
Tamworth d	09 19	10 18		12 07	12 19			13 07			14 07	14 19				15 09				16 07	16 19	
Burton-on-Trent d	09 28	10 29	11 25	12 19				13 19	13 26		14 19					15 21	15 25			16 19		
Willington d																						
Derby 6 56 d	09a41	10a40	11a37	12 40	12a38		13a01	13 40	13a37	14a01	14 39	14a39		15a01		15 40	15a37		16a01	16 40	16a40	
Long Eaton 56 d																						
Attenborough 56 d																						
Beeston 56 d																						
Nottingham 8 56 ⛴ a				13 00				14 00			15 00					16 00				17 00		

A From Maesteg
B To Edinburgh
C To Motherwell
D To Newcastle
E 🍴 from Birmingham New Street
F From Plymouth to Aberdeen
G From Plymouth to Motherwell
H From Paignton to Manchester Piccadilly
I From Guildford to Newcastle
J From Penzance to Edinburgh
K From Plymouth to Manchester Piccadilly
L From Reading to Newcastle

Trains between Gloucester & Cheltenham are shown on Table T058

Trains between Birmingham & Bromsgrove are shown on Table T069

Table T057-R

Sundays
20 May to 15 July

Cardiff and Bristol - Birmingham - Derby and Nottingham

	XC ◇1 A ⊥	AW	XC ◇1 ⊥	XC ◇1 B ⊥	XC ◇1 C ⊥	XC ◇1 D ⊥	XC ◇1 E ⊥	XC ◇1 F ⊥	XC ◇1 G ⊥	XC ◇1 A ⊥	AW	XC ◇1 H ⊥	XC ◇1 I ⊥	XC ◇1 C ⊥	XC ◇1 A	XC ◇1 H ⊥	XC ◇1 J ⊥	XC ◇1 C ⊥	AW	XC ◇1 H ⊥	XC ◇1 K ⊥
Cardiff Central 7 132 d		14 25	14 45				15 45				16 25	16 45				17 45			18 24	18 45	
Newport (South Wales) 132 d		14 45	15 05				16 05				16 45	17 03				18 04			18 46	19 03	
Severn Tunnel Jn. 132 d		14 56									16 55								18 57		
Caldicot d		14 58									16 58								18 59		
Chepstow d		15 07									17 07								19 08		
Lydney d		15 16									17 16								19 17		
Bristol Temple Meads 10 134 d				15 30	16 00			16 30	17 00				17 30	18 00			18 30	19 00			19 30
Bristol Parkway 7 134 d				15 40	16 10			16 40	17 10				17 40	18 10			18 40	19 10			19 40
Gloucester 7 134 a		15 37	15 46				16 46				17 37	17 47				18 46			19 38	19 46	
d		15 40	15 50				16 50				17 40	17 50				18 50			19 42	19 50	
Cheltenham Spa 4 a		15 50	16 00	16 09	16 39		17 00	17 09	17 39		17 50	18 00	18 09	18 39		19 00	19 10	19 40	19 55	20 00	20 09
d			16 01	16 11	16 41		17 01	17 12	17 41			18 01	18 11	18 41		19 01	19 11	19 41		20 01	20 11
Ashchurch for Tewkesbury d																					
Bromsgrove d																					
University d			16 39				17 39					18 39				19 39				20 39	
Birmingham New Street 12 a			16 45	16 49	17 26		17 45	17 49	18 27			18 45	18 50	19 26		19 45	19 50	20 27		20 45	20 52
d	16 30		16 49	17 03		17 30	17 49	18 03		18 30		18 49	19 03		19 30	19 49	20 03			20 49	21 03
Water Orton d																					
Wilnecote d												19 04									
Tamworth d			17 07				18 07	18 19				19 09				20 07	20 19			21 06	21 19
Burton-on-Trent d			17 19	17 25			18 19					19 21	19 26			20 19				21 19	21 29
Willington d																					
Derby 6 56 d	17a02		17 40	17a36		18a02	18 40	18a39		19a03		19 40	19a40		20a01	20 38	20a40			21 40	21a41
Long Eaton 56 d																					
Attenborough 56 d																					
Beeston 56 d																					
Nottingham 8 56 a			18 00				18 58					20 00				20 56				22 00	

	XC ◇1 L	XC ◇1 M	AW N	XC ◇1 O	XC ◇1	XC ◇1	AW
Cardiff Central 7 132 d		19 45	20 24		20 45		22 26
Newport (South Wales) 132 d		20 03	20 46		21 05		22 46
Severn Tunnel Jn. 132 d			20 57				22 57
Caldicot d			20 59				22 59
Chepstow d			21 08				23 08
Lydney d			21 17				23 17
Bristol Temple Meads 10 134 d	20 00			20 30		22 10	
Bristol Parkway 7 134 d	20 09			20 40		22 20	
Gloucester 7 134 a		20 48	21 42		21 47		23 42
d		20 50			21 50		
Cheltenham Spa 4 a	20 39	21 00		21 09	22 00	22 48	
d	20 40	21 01		21 11	22 01	22 49	
Ashchurch for Tewkesbury d							
Bromsgrove d							
University d		21 39			22 39		
Birmingham New Street 12 a	21 18	21 45		21 48	22 45	23 40	
d				22 03			
Water Orton d							
Wilnecote d							
Tamworth d				22 19			
Burton-on-Trent d							
Willington d							
Derby 6 56 d				22a40			
Long Eaton 56 d							
Attenborough 56 d							
Beeston 56 d							
Nottingham 8 56 a							

A From Reading to Newcastle
B From Newquay to Edinburgh
C To Manchester Piccadilly
D From Reading to Edinburgh
E From Nottingham. ⊥ to Birmingham New Street
F From Plymouth to Edinburgh
G From Penzance to Manchester Piccadilly
H ⊥ to Birmingham New Street
I From Plymouth to York
J From Plymouth to Leeds. ⊥ to Birmingham New Street
K From Penzance to Leeds. ⊥ to Birmingham New Street
L From Paignton
M To Leicester
N From Cheltenham Spa
O From Plymouth to Leeds

Trains between Gloucester & Cheltenham are shown on Table T058

Trains between Birmingham & Bromsgrove are shown on Table T069

Table T057-R

Sundays
22 July to 2 September

Cardiff and Bristol - Birmingham - Derby and Nottingham

	XC ◇1 A ⊥	XC ◇1 B ⊥	XC ◇1 A ⊥	XC ◇1 B ⊥	XC ◇1 ⊥	XC ◇1 C ⊥	AW	XC ◇1 D ⊥	XC ◇1 E ⊥	XC ◇1 D ⊥	XC ◇1 F ⊥	XC ◇1 G ⊥	AW	XC ◇1 D ⊥	XC ◇1 H ⊥	XC ◇1 I ⊥	XC ◇1 D ⊥	XC ◇1 F ⊥	XC ◇1 I ⊥	AW	XC ◇1 ⊥	XC ◇1 J ⊥
Cardiff Central 7 132 d							10 30	10 45		11 45			12 25	12 45			13 45			14 25	14 45	
Newport (South Wales) 132 d							10 48	11 06		12 05			12 47	13 05			14 05			14 45	15 05	
Severn Tunnel Jn. 132 d							10 59						12 58							14 56		
Caldicot d							11 01						13 00							14 58		
Chepstow d							11 10						13 09							15 07		
Lydney d							11 19						13 18							15 16		
Bristol Temple Meads 10 134 d				09 15		10 30			11 30		12 30	13 00			13 30	14 00		14 30	15 00			15 30
Bristol Parkway 7 134 d				09 25		10 40			11 40		12 40	13 10			13 40	14 10		14 40	15 10			15 40
Gloucester 7 134 a				09 52			11 40	11 47		12 46			13 39	13 46			14 46			15 37	15 46	
d				10 00			11 42	11 50		12 50			13 40	13 50			14 50			15 40	15 50	
Cheltenham Spa 4 a				10 09		11 09	11 55	12 00	12 09	13 00	13 09	13 39	13 52	14 00	14 09	14 39	15 00	15 09	15 37	15 50	16 00	16 09
d				10 12		11 11		12 01	12 11	13 01	13 11	13 41		14 01	14 11	14 41	15 01	15 11	15 40		16 01	16 11
Ashchurch for Tewkesbury d																						
Bromsgrove d																						
University d								12 39		13 39				14 39			15 39				16 39	
Birmingham New Street 12 a				10 49		11 48		12 45	12 49	13 45	13 48	14 27		14 45	14 48	15 27	15 45	15 48	16 27		16 45	16 49
d	08 44	09 44	10 49	11 10	11 49	12 03		12 49	13 03	13 49	14 03			14 49	15 03		15 49	16 03			16 49	17 03
Water Orton d																						
Wilnecote d														15 04								
Tamworth d	09 01	10 00			12 07	12 19		13 07		14 07	14 19			15 09			16 07	16 19			17 07	
Burton-on-Trent d	09a10	10a09	11a10	11a31	12 19	12a28		13 19	13a24	14 19	14a29			15 21	15a24		16 19	16a28			17 19	17a24
Willington d																						
Derby 6 56 d																						
Long Eaton 56 d																						
Attenborough 56 d																						
Beeston 56 d																						
Nottingham 8 56 a					12 56			13 56		14 58				16 00			16 56				17 56	

	XC ◇1 K ⊥	XC ◇1 L ⊥	XC ◇1 M ⊥	XC ◇1 N ⊥	AW	XC ◇1 O ⊥	XC ◇1 M ⊥	XC ◇1 K ⊥	XC ◇1 O ⊥	XC ◇1 P ⊥	XC ◇1 K ⊥	AW	XC ◇1 O ⊥	XC ◇1 Q ⊥	XC ◇1 R	XC ◇1 S	AW T	XC ◇1 U	XC ◇1	XC ◇1	AW
Cardiff Central 7 132 d		15 45			16 25	16 45			17 45			18 24	18 45			19 45	20 24		20 45		22 26
Newport (South Wales) 132 d		16 05			16 45	17 03			18 04			18 46	19 03			20 03	20 46		21 05		22 46
Severn Tunnel Jn. 132 d					16 55							18 57					20 57				22 57
Caldicot d					16 58							18 59					20 59				22 59
Chepstow d					17 07							19 08					21 08				23 08
Lydney d					17 16							19 17					21 17				23 17
Bristol Temple Meads 10 134 d	16 00		16 30	17 00			17 30	18 00		18 30	19 00			19 30	20 00			20 30		22 10	
Bristol Parkway 7 134 d	16 10		16 40	17 10			17 40	18 10		18 40	19 10			19 40	20 09			20 40		22 20	
Gloucester 7 134 a		16 46			17 37	17 47			18 46			19 38	19 46			20 48	21 42		21 47		23 42
d		16 50			17 40	17 50			18 50			19 42	19 50			20 50			21 50		
Cheltenham Spa 4 a	16 39	17 00	17 09	17 39	17 50	18 00	18 09	18 39	19 00	19 10	19 40	19 55	20 00	20 09	20 39	21 00		21 09	22 00	22 48	
d	16 41	17 01	17 12	17 41		18 01	18 11	18 41	19 01	19 11	19 41		20 01	20 11	20 40	21 01		21 11	22 01	22 49	
Ashchurch for Tewkesbury d																					
Bromsgrove d																					
University d		17 39				18 39			19 39				20 39			21 39			22 39		
Birmingham New Street 12 a	17 26	17 45	17 49	18 27		18 45	18 50	19 26	19 45	19 50	20 27		20 45	20 52	21 18	21 45		21 48	22 45	23 40	
d		17 49	18 03			18 49	19 03		19 49	20 03			20 49	21 03				22 03			
Water Orton d																					
Wilnecote d						19 04															
Tamworth d		18 07	18 19			19 09			20 07	20 19			21 06	21 19				22 19			
Burton-on-Trent d		18 19	18a29			19 21	19a25		20 19	20a29			21 19	21a28				22a30			
Willington d																					
Derby 6 56 d																					
Long Eaton 56 d																					
Attenborough 56 d																					
Beeston 56 d																					
Nottingham 8 56 a		18 56				19 58			20 56				21 56								

A To Edinburgh
B To Motherwell
C To Aberdeen
D ⊥ from Birmingham New Street
E From Plymouth to Motherwell
F From Plymouth to Edinburgh
G From Paignton to Manchester Piccadilly
H From Penzance to Motherwell
I From Plymouth to Manchester Piccadilly
J From Newquay to Edinburgh
K To Manchester Piccadilly
L From Nottingham. ⊥ to Birmingham New Street
M From Plymouth to Leeds
N From Penzance to Manchester Piccadilly
O ⊥ to Birmingham New Street
P From Plymouth to Leeds. ⊥ to Birmingham New Street
Q From Penzance to Leeds. ⊥ to Birmingham New Street
R From Paignton
S To Leicester
T From Cheltenham Spa
U From Plymouth

Trains between Gloucester & Cheltenham are shown on Table T058

Trains between Birmingham & Bromsgrove are shown on Table T069

Table T057-R

Sundays
9 September to 7 October

Cardiff and Bristol - Birmingham - Derby and Nottingham

	XC	XC	XC	XC	XC		XC	AW	XC	XC	XC	XC	XC	XC	XC		XC	AW	XC	XC	XC	XC	XC	XC
	◇1	◇1	◇1	◇1	◇1		◇1		◇1	◇1	◇1	◇1	◇1	◇1	◇1		◇1		◇1	◇1	◇1	◇1	◇1	◇1
	A	B	A	B			C			D	E		D	F	G		H		D	I	J	K	L	D
	🍴	🍴	🍴	🍴	🍴		🍴		🍴	🍴	🍴	🍴	🍴	🍴	🍴		🍴		🍴	🍴	🍴	🍴	🍴	🍴
Cardiff Central 132 d								10 30		10 45			11 45					12 25	12 45					13 45
Newport (South Wales) 132 d								10 48		11 06			12 05					12 47	13 05					14 05
Severn Tunnel Jn. 132 d								10 59										12 58						
Caldicot d								11 01										13 00						
Chepstow d								11 10										13 09						
Lydney d								11 19										13 18						
Bristol Temple Meads 134 d				09 15			10 30				11 30			12 30	13 00					13 30	13 30	14 00		
Bristol Parkway 134 d				09 25			10 40				11 40			12 40	13 10					13 40	13 40	14 10		
Gloucester 134 a				09 52				11 40		11 47			12 46					13 39	13 46					14 46
d				10 00				11 42		11 50			12 50					13 40	13 50					14 50
Cheltenham Spa a				10 09			11 09	11 55		12 00	12 09		13 00	13 09	13 39			13 52	14 00	14 09	14 09	14 39		15 00
d				10 12			11 11			12 01	12 11		13 01	13 11	13 41				14 01	14 11	14 11	14 41		15 01
Ashchurch for Tewkesbury d																								
Bromsgrove d																								
University d										12 39			13 39						14 39					15 39
Birmingham New Street a				10 49			11 48			12 45	12 49		13 45	13 48	14 27				14 45	14 48	14 48	15 27		15 45
d	08 44	09 44	10 49	11 10	11 49		12 03		12 30	12 49	13 03	13 30	13 49	14 03			14 30		14 49	15 03	15 03		15 30	15 49
Water Orton d																								
Wilnecote d																			15 04					
Tamworth d	09 01	10 00			12 07		12 19			13 07			14 07	14 19					15 09					16 07
Burton-on-Trent d	09 11	10 10	11 11	11 32	12 19					13 19	13 26		14 19						15 21	15 25	15 25			16 19
Willington d																								
Derby 56 d	09a23	10a23	11a23	11a44	12 40		12a39		13a01	13 40	13a42	14a01	14 39	14a43			15a02		15 40	15a42	15a42		16a02	16 40
Long Eaton 56 d																								
Attenborough 56 d																								
Beeston 56 d																								
Nottingham 56 a					13 00					14 00			15 00						16 00					17 00

	XC		XC	XC	AW	XC	XC	XC	XC	XC	XC		XC	XC	AW	XC	XC	XC	XC	XC	XC		XC	AW
	◇1		◇1	◇1		◇1	◇1	◇1	◇1	◇1	◇1		◇1	◇1		◇1	◇1	◇1	◇1	◇1	◇1		◇1	
	F		K	L			M	N	L	O	P		Q	L		R	P	N	L	R	S		N	
	🍴		🍴	🍴		🍴	🍴	🍴	🍴	🍴	🍴		🍴	🍴		🍴	🍴	🍴		🍴	🍴		🍴	
Cardiff Central 132 d					14 25	14 45				15 45					16 25	16 45				17 45				18 24
Newport (South Wales) 132 d					14 45	15 05				16 05					16 45	17 03				18 04				18 46
Severn Tunnel Jn. 132 d					14 56										16 55									18 57
Caldicot d					14 58										16 58									18 59
Chepstow d					15 07										17 07									19 08
Lydney d					15 16										17 16									19 17
Bristol Temple Meads 134 d	14 30		15 00				15 30	16 00			16 30		17 00				17 30	18 00			18 30		19 00	
Bristol Parkway 134 d	14 40		15 10				15 40	16 10			16 40		17 10				17 40	18 10			18 40		19 10	
Gloucester 134 a					15 37	15 46				16 46					17 37	17 47				18 46				19 38
d					15 40	15 50				16 50					17 40	17 50				18 50				19 42
Cheltenham Spa a	15 09		15 37		15 50	16 00	16 09	16 39		17 00	17 09		17 39		17 50	18 00	18 09	18 39		19 00	19 10		19 40	19 55
d	15 11		15 40			16 01	16 11	16 41		17 01	17 12		17 41			18 01	18 11	18 41		19 01	19 11		19 41	
Ashchurch for Tewkesbury d																								
Bromsgrove d																								
University d						16 39				17 39						18 39				19 39				
Birmingham New Street a	15 48		16 27			16 45	16 49	17 26		17 45	17 49		18 27			18 45	18 50	19 26		19 45	19 50		20 27	
d	16 03			16 30		16 49	17 03		17 30	17 49	18 03			18 30		18 49	19 03		19 30	19 49	20 03			
Water Orton d																								
Wilnecote d																19 04								
Tamworth d	16 19					17 07				18 07	18 19					19 09				20 07	20 19			
Burton-on-Trent d						17 19	17 34			18 19						19 21	19 26			20 19				
Willington d																								
Derby 56 d	16a44			17a03		17 39	17a44		18a03	18 40	18a39			19a04		19 40	19a39		20a03	20 40	20a40			
Long Eaton 56 d																								
Attenborough 56 d																								
Beeston 56 d																								
Nottingham 56 a						18 00				18 58						20 00				21 00				

A To Edinburgh
B To Motherwell
C To Aberdeen
D 🍴 from Birmingham New Street
E From Plymouth to Motherwell
F From Plymouth to Edinburgh
G From Paignton to Manchester Piccadilly
H From Guildford
I 9 September. From Penzance to Motherwell
J not 9 September. From Penzance to Glasgow Central. 🍴 to Birmingham New Street
K From Plymouth to Manchester Piccadilly
L From Reading
M From Newquay to Edinburgh
N To Manchester Piccadilly
O From Nottingham. 🍴 to Birmingham New Street
P From Plymouth to Leeds
Q From Penzance to Manchester Piccadilly
R 🍴 to Birmingham New Street
S From Plymouth to Leeds. 🍴 to Birmingham New Street

Trains between Gloucester & Cheltenham are shown on Table T058

Trains between Birmingham & Bromsgrove are shown on Table T069

Table T057-R

Sundays
9 September to 7 October

Cardiff and Bristol - Birmingham - Derby and Nottingham

	XC	XC	XC	XC	AW	XC	XC		XC	AW
	◇1	◇1	◇1	◇1		◇1	◇1		◇1	
	A	B	C	D	E	F				
	🍴	🍴								
Cardiff Central 132 d	18 45			19 45	20 24		20 45			22 26
Newport (South Wales) 132 d	19 03			20 03	20 46		21 05			22 46
Severn Tunnel Jn. 132 d					20 57					22 57
Caldicot d					20 59					22 59
Chepstow d					21 08					23 08
Lydney d					21 17					23 17
Bristol Temple Meads 134 d		19 30	20 00			20 30			22 10	
Bristol Parkway 134 d		19 40	20 09			20 40			22 20	
Gloucester 134 a	19 46			20 48	21 42		21 47			23 42
d	19 50			20 50			21 50			
Cheltenham Spa a	20 00	20 09	20 39	21 00		21 09	22 00		22 48	
d	20 01	20 11	20 40	21 01		21 11	22 01		22 49	
Ashchurch for Tewkesbury d										
Bromsgrove d										
University d	20 39			21 39			22 39			
Birmingham New Street a	20 45	20 52	21 18	21 45		21 48	22 45		23 40	
d	20 49	21 03				22 03				
Water Orton d										
Wilnecote d										
Tamworth d	21 06	21 19				22 19				
Burton-on-Trent d	21 19	21 29								
Willington d										
Derby 56 d	21 40	21a41				22a40				
Long Eaton 56 d										
Attenborough 56 d										
Beeston 56 d										
Nottingham 56 a	22 00									

Sundays
14 October to 2 December

	XC	XC	XC	XC	XC	AW	XC	XC	XC		XC	XC	XC	XC	XC	AW	XC	XC	XC		XC	XC	XC	XC
	◇1	◇1	◇1	◇1	◇1		◇1	◇1	◇1		◇1	◇1	◇1	◇1	◇1		◇1	◇1	◇1		◇1	◇1	◇1	◇1
	G	H	G		H		I	J	K		I	J	L	M	N		J	O	P		Q	J	L	P
	🍴	🍴	🍴	🍴	🍴		🍴	🍴	🍴		🍴	🍴	🍴	🍴	🍴		🍴	🍴	🍴		🍴	🍴	🍴	🍴
Cardiff Central 132 d						10 30		10 45				11 45				12 25	12 45					13 45		
Newport (South Wales) 132 d						10 48		11 06				12 05				12 47	13 05					14 05		
Severn Tunnel Jn. 132 d						10 59										12 58								
Caldicot d						11 01										13 00								
Chepstow d						11 10										13 09								
Lydney d						11 19										13 18								
Bristol Temple Meads 134 d			09 15		10 30				11 30				12 30	13 00				13 30	14 00				14 30	15 00
Bristol Parkway 134 d			09 25		10 40				11 40				12 40	13 10				13 40	14 10				14 40	15 10
Gloucester 134 a			09 52			11 40		11 47				12 46				13 39	13 46					14 46		
d			10 00			11 42		11 50				12 50				13 40	13 50					14 50		
Cheltenham Spa a			10 09		11 09	11 55		12 00	12 09			13 00	13 09	13 39		13 52	14 00	14 09	14 39			15 00	15 09	15 37
d			10 12		11 11			12 01	12 11			13 01	13 11	13 41			14 01	14 11	14 41			15 01	15 11	15 40
Ashchurch for Tewkesbury d																								
Bromsgrove d																								
University d								12 39				13 39					14 39					15 39		
Birmingham New Street a			10 49		11 48			12 45	12 49			13 45	13 48	14 27			14 45	14 48	15 27			15 45	15 48	16 27
d	09 03	10 03	11 03	11 49	12 03		12 30	12 49	13 03		13 30	13 49	14 03		14 30		14 49	15 03			15 30	15 49	16 03	
Water Orton d																								
Wilnecote d																	15 04							
Tamworth d	09 19	10 18		12 07	12 19			13 07				14 07	14 19				15 09					16 07	16 19	
Burton-on-Trent d	09 28	10 29	11 25	12 19				13 19	13 26			14 19					15 21	15 25				16 19		
Willington d																								
Derby 56 d	09a41	10a40	11a37	12 40	12a38		13a01	13 40	13a37		14a01	14 40	14a39		15a01		15 40	15a37			16a01	16 40	16a38	
Long Eaton 56 d																								
Attenborough 56 d																								
Beeston 56 d																								
Nottingham 56 a				13 00				14 00				14 59					16 00					17 00		

A 🍴 to Birmingham New Street
B From Penzance to Leeds. 🍴 to Birmingham New Street
C From Paignton
D To Leicester
E From Cheltenham Spa
F From Plymouth
G To Edinburgh
H To Glasgow Central
I To Newcastle
J 🍴 from Birmingham New Street
K From Plymouth to Aberdeen
L From Plymouth to Glasgow Central
M From Paignton to Manchester Piccadilly
N From Guildford to Newcastle
O From Penzance to Edinburgh
P From Plymouth to Manchester Piccadilly
Q From Reading to Newcastle

Trains between Gloucester & Cheltenham are shown on Table T058

Trains between Birmingham & Bromsgrove are shown on Table T069

Table T057-R

Sundays

14 October to 2 December

Cardiff and Bristol - Birmingham - Derby and Nottingham

		XC	AW	XC	XC	XC	XC	XC	XC	XC	XC	AW	XC	XC	XC	XC	XC	XC	XC	AW	XC	XC
		◇■ A		◇■	◇■ B	◇■ C	◇■ D	◇■ E	◇■ B	◇■ F	◇■ A		◇■ G	◇■ H	◇■ C	◇■ A	◇■ G	◇■ I	◇■ C		◇■ G	◇■ J
Cardiff Central	132 d		14 25	14 45				15 45				16 25	16 45				17 45			18 24	18 45	
Newport (South Wales)	132 d		14 45	15 05				16 05				16 45	17 03				18 04			18 46	19 03	
Severn Tunnel Jn.	132 d		14 56									16 55								18 57		
Caldicot	d		14 58									16 58								18 59		
Chepstow	d		15 07									17 07								19 08		
Lydney	d		15 16									17 16								19 17		
Bristol Temple Meads	134 d				15 30	16 00			16 30	17 00				17 30	18 00			18 30	19 00			19 30
Bristol Parkway	134 d				15 40	16 10			16 40	17 10				17 40	18 10			18 40	19 10			19 40
Gloucester	134 a		15 37	15 46				16 46				17 37	17 47				18 46			19 38	19 46	
	d		15 40	15 50				16 50				17 40	17 50				18 50			19 42	19 50	
Cheltenham Spa	a		15 50	16 00	16 09	16 39		17 00	17 09	17 39		17 50	18 00	18 09	18 39		19 00	19 10	19 40	19 55	20 00	20 09
	d			16 01	16 11	16 41		17 01	17 12	17 41			18 01	18 11	18 41		19 01	19 11	19 41		20 01	20 11
Ashchurch for Tewkesbury	d																					
Bromsgrove	d																					
University	d			16 39				17 39					18 39				19 39				20 39	
Birmingham New Street	a			16 45	16 49	17 26		17 45	17 49	18 27			18 45	18 50	19 26		19 45	19 50	20 27		20 45	20 52
	d	16 30		16 49	17 03		17 30	17 49	18 03		18 30		18 49	19 03		19 30	19 49	20 03			20 49	21 03
Water Orton	d																					
Wilnecote	d												19 04									
Tamworth	d			17 07				18 07	18 19				19 09				20 07	20 19			21 06	21 19
Burton-on-Trent	d			17 19	17 25			18 19					19 21	19 26			20 19				21 19	21 29
Willington	d																					
Derby	56 d	17a02		17 40	17a36		18a02	18 40	18a39		19a03		19 40	19a40		20a01	20 40	20a40			21 40	21a41
Long Eaton	56 d																					
Attenborough	56 d																					
Beeston	56 d																					
Nottingham	56 a			18 00				18 58					20 00				21 00				22 00	

		XC	XC	AW	XC	XC	XC	AW
		◇■ K	◇■ L	M	◇■ N	◇■	◇■	
Cardiff Central	132 d		19 45	20 24		20 45		22 26
Newport (South Wales)	132 d		20 03	20 46		21 05		22 46
Severn Tunnel Jn.	132 d			20 57				22 57
Caldicot	d			20 59				22 59
Chepstow	d			21 08				23 08
Lydney	d			21 17				23 17
Bristol Temple Meads	134 d	20 00			20 30		22 10	
Bristol Parkway	134 d	20 09			20 40		22 20	
Gloucester	134 a		20 48	21 42		21 47		23 42
	d		20 50			21 50		
Cheltenham Spa	a	20 39	21 00		21 09	22 00	22 48	
	d	20 40	21 01		21 11	22 01	22 49	
Ashchurch for Tewkesbury	d							
Bromsgrove	d							
University	d		21 39			22 39		
Birmingham New Street	a	21 18	21 45		21 48	22 45	23 40	
	d				22 03			
Water Orton	d							
Wilnecote	d							
Tamworth	d				22 19			
Burton-on-Trent	d							
Willington	d							
Derby	56 d				22a40			
Long Eaton	56 d							
Attenborough	56 d							
Beeston	56 d							
Nottingham	56 a							

A From Reading to Newcastle
B From Plymouth to Edinburgh
C To Manchester Piccadilly
D From Reading to Edinburgh
E From Nottingham. ✕ to Birmingham New Street
F From Penzance to Manchester Piccadilly
G ✕ to Birmingham New Street
H From Plymouth to York
I From Plymouth to Leeds. ✕ to Birmingham New Street
J From Penzance to Leeds. ✕ to Birmingham New Street
K From Paignton
L To Leicester
M From Cheltenham Spa
N From Plymouth to Leeds

Trains between Gloucester & Cheltenham are shown on Table T058

Trains between Birmingham & Bromsgrove are shown on Table T069

Table T058-F

Mondays to Fridays

21 May to 31 August

Worcester Shrub Hill - Cheltenham Spa - Gloucester

Miles			AW	GW	XC	GW	GW	GW	XC	GW	GW	GW	AW	XC	GW	GW	AW	XC	GW	GW	XC	XC	GW
			A	◇■ B	◇■ C	D	E	◇■ B	◇■ C	F	◇ G	◇■ B	A	◇■ H	◇■ B	◇ G	A	◇■ H	F	◇ I	◇■ J	◇■ K	◇ G
0	Worcester Shrub Hill	d		05 28							06 49	07 08								09 06			
12	Ashchurch for Tewkesbury	d		05 44					06 27		07 05									09 24			
19¼	**Cheltenham Spa**	d	05 37	05 54	06 02		06 24	06 30	06 43		07 16	07 31	07 46	08 11	08 31		08 46	09 11	09 18	09 33	10 10	10 10	
25¾	**Gloucester**	a	05 48	06 03	06 12		06 34	06 39	06 53		07 26	07 40	07 57	08 20	08 40		08 58	09 20	09 28	09 42	10 20	10 20	
—		d	05 50		06 14	06 16	06 42		07 01	07 05	07 41		07 58	08 25		08 41	08 58	09 25		09 44	10 25	10 25	10 41
—	Bristol Parkway	d				06 57	07 24			07 49	08 20					09 19				10 22			11 19
—	Bristol Temple Meads	a				07 13	07 40			08 00	08 36					09 35				10 39			11 34
—	Cardiff Central	a	07 00		07 22				08 08				09 07	09 29			10 11	10 27			11 28	11 29	

		GW	AW	XC	GW	GW	AW	XC	GW	GW	XC	GW	GW	AW	XC	GW	GW	AW	XC	GW	GW	XC	GW
		◇■ B	A	◇■ H	F	■ L		◇■ H	M	◇■ B	◇■ H	F	◇ N	A	◇■ H	E	◇■ O	◇ P	◇■ H	F	◇ N	◇■ Q	◇■ B
Worcester Shrub Hill	d					11 06							13 06								15 06		
Ashchurch for Tewkesbury	d					11 24							13 24								15 24		
Cheltenham Spa	d	10 36	10 45	11 11	11 20	11 33	11 46	12 10		12 36	13 11	13 20	13 33	13 45	14 10		14 36		15 11	15 20	15 33	16 11	16 20
Gloucester	a	10 45	10 57	11 20	11 30	11 44	11 57	12 20		12 45	13 20	13 30	13 43	13 57	14 22		14 45		15 20	15 30	15 43	16 22	16 30
	d		10 58	11 25		11 47	11 59	12 25	12 42		13 25		13 46	13 58	14 24	14 41		14 48	15 25		15 46	16 25	
Bristol Parkway	d					12 23			13 19				14 23			15 20					16 24		
Bristol Temple Meads	a					12 35			13 36				14 39			15 38					16 39		
Cardiff Central	a		12 13	12 26			13 08	13 26			14 26			15 15	15 30			15 58	16 30			17 30	

		GW	AW	XC	XC	GW	GW	AW	XC	GW	GW	AW	XC	XC	GW	AW	GW	XC	GW	GW	XC FO	XC FX
		◇ G	A	◇■ J	◇■ K	I	◇ R	A	◇■ H		◇■ B	A	◇■ H	◇■ S	T	A	F	◇■ H		F	◇■ H	◇■ H
Worcester Shrub Hill	d					17 06									19 07							
Ashchurch for Tewkesbury	d			17 05	17 05	17 24			18 08						19 24							
Cheltenham Spa	d		16 45	17 14	17 14	17 33	17 41	17 45	18 17		18 33	18 45	19 13	19 25	19 34	19 45	20 01	20 12	20 20	21 02	21 11	21 11
Gloucester	a		16 56	17 23	17 24	17 42	17 51	17 57	18 28		18 43	18 58	19 23		19 42	19 56	20 11	20 20	20 29	21 11	21 19	21 19
	d	16 40	16 58	17 25	17 25	17 46		17 58	18 31	18 42		19 00	19 25		19 45	19 58		20 25	20 39		21 21	21 21
Bristol Parkway	d	17 20				18 23				19 19				19 57	20 27				21 19			
Bristol Temple Meads	a	17 35				18 38				19 34				20 09	20 38				21 31			
Cardiff Central	a		18 10	18 27	18 27			19 09	19 33			20 12	20 28	21 03		21 10		21 28			22 30	22 35

		GW	GW	GW	AW FO	AW FX	GW	LM FO
		■	F	T				C
Worcester Shrub Hill	d			21 52			22 28	23 46
Ashchurch for Tewkesbury	d			22 08			22 51	23 59
Cheltenham Spa	d	21 20	22 01	22 18	23 00	23 00	23 05	00 08
Gloucester	a	21 29	22 11	22 28	23 11	23 11	23 17	00 19
	d	21 35		22 32	23 13	23 13		
Bristol Parkway	d	22 11		23 04				
Bristol Temple Meads	a	22 24		23 14				
Cardiff Central	a				00 26	00 34		

Mondays to Fridays

3 September to 5 October

		AW	GW	XC	GW	GW	GW	XC	GW	GW	GW	AW	XC	GW	GW	AW	XC	GW	GW	XC	GW	GW	AW
		A	◇■ B	◇■ C	D	E	◇■ B	◇■ C	F	◇ G	◇■ B	A	◇■ H	◇■ B	◇ G	A	◇■ H	F	◇ I	◇■ H	◇ G	◇■ B	A
Worcester Shrub Hill	d		05 28							06 49	07 08								09 06				
Ashchurch for Tewkesbury	d		05 44					06 27		07 05									09 24				
Cheltenham Spa	d	05 37	05 54	06 02		06 24	06 30	06 43		07 16	07 31	07 46	08 11	08 31		08 46	09 11	09 18	09 33	10 10		10 36	10 45
Gloucester	a	05 48	06 03	06 12		06 34	06 39	06 53		07 26	07 40	07 57	08 20	08 40		08 58	09 20	09 28	09 42	10 20		10 45	10 57
	d	05 50		06 14	06 16	06 42		07 01	07 05	07 41		07 58	08 25		08 41	08 58	09 25		09 44	10 25	10 41		10 58
Bristol Parkway	d				06 57	07 24			07 49	08 20					09 19				10 22		11 19		
Bristol Temple Meads	a				07 13	07 40			08 00	08 36					09 35				10 39		11 34		
Cardiff Central	a	07 00		07 22				08 08				09 07	09 29			10 11	10 27			11 28			12 13

A To Maesteg
B To London Paddington
C From Birmingham New Street
D To Taunton
E To Westbury
F To Swindon
G To Weymouth
H From Nottingham
I From Great Malvern to Westbury
J from 23 July. From Nottingham
K until 20 July. From Nottingham
L From Great Malvern to Brighton
M To Frome
N From Great Malvern to Weymouth
O To London Paddington. The Cheltenham Spa Express
P To Fishguard Harbour
Q From Nottingham to Cardiff Central continues to Nottingham
R To Southampton Central
S From Manchester Piccadilly. ✕ to Bristol Temple Meads
T From Great Malvern

Table T058-F

Worcester Shrub Hill - Cheltenham Spa - Gloucester

Mondays to Fridays

3 September to 5 October

		XC	GW	GW	AW	XC	GW	GW	XC	GW	GW	AW	XC	GW	GW	AW	XC	GW	GW	XC	GW	GW
		◇■ A 🍴	B	■ C		◇■ A 🍴	D	◇■ E ⊐	◇■ A 🍴	B	◇ F	G	◇■ A 🍴	H	◇■ I ⊐	◇ J 🍴	◇■ A 🍴	B	◇ F	◇■ K 🍴	◇■ E ⊐	◇ L
Worcester Shrub Hill ■	d			11 06							13 06								15 06			
Ashchurch for Tewkesbury	d			11 24							13 24								15 24			
Cheltenham Spa ■	d	11 11	11 20	11 33	11 46	12 10		12 36	13 11	13 20	13 33	13 45	14 10		14 36		15 11	15 20	15 33	16 11	16 20	
Gloucester ■	a	11 20	11 30	11 44	11 57	12 20		12 45	13 20	13 30	13 43	13 57	14 22		14 45		15 20	15 30	15 43	16 22	16 30	
	d	11 25		11 47	11 59	12 25	12 42		13 25		13 46	13 58	14 24	14 41		14 48	15 25		15 46	16 25		16 40
Bristol Parkway ■	d			12 23			13 19				14 23			15 20					16 24			17 20
Bristol Temple Meads ■	a			12 35			13 36				14 39			15 38					16 39			17 35
Cardiff Central ■	a	12 26			13 08	13 26			14 26			15 15	15 30			15 58	16 30			17 30		

		AW	XC	GW	GW	AW	XC	GW	GW	AW	XC	XC	GW	AW	GW	XC	GW	GW	XC FO	XC FX	GW	GW	GW
		G	◇■ A 🍴	M	◇ N	G	◇■ A		◇■ E ⊐	G	◇■ A	◇■ O 🍴	P	G	B	◇■ A		B	◇■ A	◇■ A	■	B	P
Worcester Shrub Hill ■	d			17 06									19 07										21 52
Ashchurch for Tewkesbury	d		17 05	17 24			18 08						19 24										22 08
Cheltenham Spa ■	d	16 45	17 14	17 33	17 41	17 45	18 17		18 33	18 45	19 13	19 25	19 34	19 45	20 01	20 12	20 20	21 02	21 11	21 11	21 20	22 01	22 18
Gloucester ■	a	16 56	17 24	17 42	17 51	17 57	18 28		18 43	18 58	19 23		19 42	19 56	20 11	20 20	20 29	21 11	21 19	21 19	21 29	22 11	22 28
	d	16 58	17 25	17 46		17 58	18 31	18 42		19 00	19 25		19 45	19 58		20 25	20 39		21 21	21 21	21 35		22 32
Bristol Parkway ■	d			18 23				19 19				19 57	20 27				21 19				22 11		23 04
Bristol Temple Meads ■	a			18 38				19 34				20 09	20 38				21 31				22 24		23 14
Cardiff Central ■	a	18 10	18 27			19 09	19 33			20 12	20 28	21 03		21 10		21 28			22 30	22 35			

		AW FO	AW FX	GW	LM FO Q
Worcester Shrub Hill ■	d			22 28	23 46
Ashchurch for Tewkesbury	d			22 51	23 59
Cheltenham Spa ■	d	23 00	23 00	23 05	00 08
Gloucester ■	a	23 11	23 11	23 17	00 19
	d	23 13	23 13		
Bristol Parkway ■	d				
Bristol Temple Meads ■	a				
Cardiff Central ■	a	00 26	00 34		

Mondays to Fridays

8 October to 7 December

		AW	GW	XC	GW	GW	GW	XC	GW	GW	GW	AW	XC	GW	GW	AW	XC	GW	GW	XC	GW	GW	AW
		G	◇■ E ⊐	◇■ Q	R	H	◇■ E ⊐	◇■ Q	B	◇ L	◇■ E ⊐	G	◇■ A 🍴	◇■ E ⊐	◇ L	G	◇■ A	B	◇ M	◇■ A 🍴	◇ L	◇■ E ⊐	G
Worcester Shrub Hill ■	d		05 28							06 49	07 08								09 06				
Ashchurch for Tewkesbury	d		05 44					06 27		07 05									09 24				
Cheltenham Spa ■	d	05 37	05 54	06 02		06 24	06 30	06 43		07 16	07 31	07 46	08 11	08 31		08 46	09 11	09 18	09 33	10 10		10 36	10 45
Gloucester ■	a	05 48	06 03	06 12		06 34	06 39	06 53		07 26	07 40	07 57	08 20	08 40		08 58	09 20	09 28	09 42	10 20		10 45	10 57
	d	05 50		06 14	06 16	06 42		07 01	07 05	07 41		07 58	08 25		08 41	08 58	09 25		09 44	10 25	10 41		10 58
Bristol Parkway ■	d				06 57	07 24			07 49	08 20					09 19				10 22		11 19		
Bristol Temple Meads ■	a				07 13	07 40			08 00	08 36					09 35				10 39		11 34		
Cardiff Central ■	a	07 00		07 22				08 08				09 07	09 29			10 11	10 27			11 28			12 13

		XC	GW	GW	AW	XC	GW	GW	XC	GW	GW	AW	XC	GW	GW	AW	XC	GW	GW	XC	GW	GW	AW
		◇■ A 🍴	B	■ C		◇■ A 🍴	D	◇■ E ⊐	◇■ A 🍴	B	◇ F	G	◇■ A 🍴	H	◇■ I ⊐	◇ J 🍴	◇■ A 🍴	B	◇ F	◇■ K 🍴	◇■ E ⊐	◇ L	G
Worcester Shrub Hill ■	d			11 06							13 06								15 06				
Ashchurch for Tewkesbury	d			11 24							13 24								15 24				
Cheltenham Spa ■	d	11 11	11 20	11 33	11 46	12 10		12 36	13 11	13 20	13 33	13 45	14 10		14 36		15 11	15 20	15 33	16 11	16 20		16 45
Gloucester ■	a	11 20	11 30	11 44	11 57	12 20		12 45	13 20	13 30	13 43	13 57	14 22		14 45		15 20	15 30	15 43	16 22	16 30		16 56
	d	11 25		11 47	11 59	12 25	12 42		13 25		13 46	13 58	14 24	14 41		14 48	15 25		15 46	16 25		16 40	16 58
Bristol Parkway ■	d			12 23			13 19				14 23			15 20					16 24			17 20	
Bristol Temple Meads ■	a			12 35			13 36				14 39			15 38					16 39			17 35	
Cardiff Central ■	a	12 26			13 08	13 26			14 26			15 15	15 30			15 58	16 30			17 30			18 10

		XC	GW	GW	AW	XC	GW	GW	AW	XC	XC	GW	AW	GW	XC	GW	GW	XC FO	XC FX	GW	GW	GW
		◇■ A 🍴	M	◇ N	G	◇■ A		◇■ E ⊐	G	◇■ A	◇■ O 🍴	P	G	B	◇■ A		B	◇■ A	◇■ A	■	B	P
Worcester Shrub Hill ■	d		17 06									19 07										21 52
Ashchurch for Tewkesbury	d	17 05	17 24			18 08						19 24										22 08
Cheltenham Spa ■	d	17 14	17 33	17 41	17 45	18 17		18 33	18 45	19 13	19 25	19 34	19 45	20 01	20 12	20 20	21 02	21 11	21 11	21 20	22 01	22 18
Gloucester ■	a	17 24	17 42	17 51	17 57	18 28		18 43	18 58	19 23		19 42	19 56	20 11	20 20	20 29	21 11	21 19	21 19	21 29	22 11	22 28
	d	17 25	17 46		17 58	18 31	18 42		19 00	19 25		19 45	19 58		20 25	20 39		21 21	21 21	21 35		22 32
Bristol Parkway ■	d		18 23				19 19				19 57	20 27				21 19				22 11		23 04
Bristol Temple Meads ■	a		18 38				19 34				20 09	20 38				21 31				22 24		23 14
Cardiff Central ■	a	18 27			19 09	19 33			20 12	20 28	21 03		21 10		21 28			22 30	22 35			

A From Nottingham
B To Swindon
C From Great Malvern to Brighton
D To Frome
E To London Paddington
F From Great Malvern to Weymouth
G To Maesteg
H To Westbury
I To London Paddington. The Cheltenham Spa Express
J To Fishguard Harbour
K From Nottingham to Cardiff Central continues to Nottingham
L To Weymouth
M From Great Malvern to Westbury
N To Southampton Central
O From Manchester Piccadilly. 🍴 to Bristol Temple Meads
P From Great Malvern
Q From Birmingham New Street
R To Taunton

Table T058-F

Worcester Shrub Hill - Cheltenham Spa - Gloucester

Mondays to Fridays

8 October to 7 December

		AW FO	AW FX	GW	LM FO A
Worcester Shrub Hill ■	d			22 28	23 46
Ashchurch for Tewkesbury	d			22 51	23 59
Cheltenham Spa ■	d	23 00	23 00	23 05	00 08
Gloucester ■	a	23 11	23 11	23 17	00 19
	d	23 13	23 13		
Bristol Parkway ■	d				
Bristol Temple Meads ■	a				
Cardiff Central ■	a	00 26	00 34		

Saturdays

26 May to 8 September

		GW	AW	XC	GW	XC	GW	GW	GW	AW	XC	GW	AW	GW	XC	GW	GW	XC	GW	AW	GW	XC	GW
		B	C	◇■ A	D	◇■ A	E	◇ F	◇■ G ⊐		◇■ H 🍴	◇ F	C	◇■ G ⊐	◇■ H	I	B	◇■ H 🍴	◇ F	C	◇■ G ⊐	◇■ H 🍴	■ J
Worcester Shrub Hill ■	d							06 49						08 37		09 10							11 13
Ashchurch for Tewkesbury	d					06 33		07 05								09 27							11 29
Cheltenham Spa ■	d	05 30		06 03		06 42	06 48	07 16	07 31	07 45	08 11		08 45	09 00	09 11	09 36	10 01	10 11		10 45	11 00	11 11	11 38
Gloucester ■	a	05 41		06 12		06 52	06 58	07 25	07 40	07 57	08 20		08 57	09 09	09 20	09 45	10 12	10 20		10 56	11 09	11 20	11 47
	d		05 50	06 14	06 21	06 57	07 02	07 41		07 58	08 22	08 41	08 58		09 22	09 48		10 22	10 41	10 58		11 22	11 50
Bristol Parkway ■	d				07 01		07 43	08 20				09 19				10 23			11 20				12 25
Bristol Temple Meads ■	a				07 13		07 55	08 34				09 34				10 39			11 35				12 38
Cardiff Central ■	a		07 03	07 21		08 04				09 10	09 23		10 09		10 21			11 24		12 06		12 23	

		AW	GW	XC	GW	GW	XC	GW	AW	GW	XC	GW	AW	GW	XC	GW	GW	XC	GW	AW	GW	XC	GW
			B	◇■ H 🍴	K	◇■ G ⊐	◇■ H 🍴	◇ L	C	B	◇■ H 🍴	I	◇ M 🍴	◇■ G ⊐	◇■ H 🍴	◇ N	B	◇■ H 🍴	◇ F	C	◇■ G ⊐	◇■ H 🍴	O
Worcester Shrub Hill ■	d							12 54								15 07							17 08
Ashchurch for Tewkesbury	d							13 11								15 24							17 24
Cheltenham Spa ■	d	11 46	12 01	12 11		13 00	13 11	13 20	13 45	14 01	14 11			15 00	15 11	15 34	16 01	16 11		16 45	17 00	17 10	17 34
Gloucester ■	a	11 56	12 12	12 20		13 10	13 20	13 35	13 57	14 12	14 20			15 09	15 20	15 43	16 12	16 20		16 56	17 10	17 20	17 44
	d	11 58		12 22	12 42		13 22	13 42	13 58		14 22	14 41	14 42		15 22	15 47		16 22	16 42	16 58		17 22	17 47
Bristol Parkway ■	d				13 19			14 20				15 19				16 24			17 20				18 25
Bristol Temple Meads ■	a				13 35			14 36				15 34				16 39			17 36				18 39
Cardiff Central ■	a	13 07		13 21			14 22		15 09		15 26		15 53		16 25			17 24		18 10		18 24	

		AW	GW	XC	GW	AW	GW	XC	XC	GW	AW	GW	XC	GW	XC	GW	GW	GW	AW
		C	B	◇■ H	K	C	◇■ G ⊐	◇■ H	◇■ P 🍴	Q	C	I	◇■ H		◇■ H	B	Q		
Worcester Shrub Hill ■	d									19 08							21 32	22 25	
Ashchurch for Tewkesbury	d			18 08						19 24							21 51	22 41	
Cheltenham Spa ■	d	17 45	18 01	18 17		18 45	19 00	19 11	19 25	19 34	19 45	20 02	20 11	21 02	21 11	21 20	22 02	22 51	
Gloucester ■	a	17 56	18 12	18 25		18 56	19 10	19 20		19 44	19 56	20 12	20 20	21 12	21 20	21 30	22 12	23 01	
	d	17 58		18 28	18 41	18 58		19 22		19 47	19 58		20 22	21 14	21 22				23 09
Bristol Parkway ■	d				19 20				19 56	20 26				21 52					
Bristol Temple Meads ■	a				19 35				20 05	20 40				22 07					
Cardiff Central ■	a	19 12		19 30		20 11		20 20	21 00		21 07		21 26		22 42				00 38

Saturdays

15 September to 8 December

		GW	AW	XC	GW	XC	GW	GW	GW	AW	XC	GW	AW	GW	XC	GW	GW	XC	GW	AW	GW	XC	GW
		B	C	◇■ A	D	◇■ A	E	◇ F	◇■ G ⊐		◇■ H 🍴	◇ F	C	◇■ G ⊐	◇■ H	I	B	◇■ H 🍴	◇ F	C	◇■ G ⊐	◇■ H 🍴	■ J
Worcester Shrub Hill ■	d							06 49						08 37		09 10							11 13
Ashchurch for Tewkesbury	d					06 33		07 05								09 27							11 29
Cheltenham Spa ■	d	05 30		06 03		06 42	06 48	07 16	07 31	07 45	08 11		08 45	09 00	09 11	09 36	10 01	10 11		10 45	11 00	11 11	11 38
Gloucester ■	a	05 41		06 12		06 52	06 58	07 25	07 40	07 57	08 20		08 57	09 09	09 20	09 45	10 12	10 20		10 56	11 09	11 20	11 47
	d		05 50	06 14	06 21	06 57	07 02	07 41		07 58	08 22	08 41	08 58		09 22	09 48		10 22	10 41	10 58		11 22	11 50
Bristol Parkway ■	d				07 01		07 43	08 20				09 19				10 23			11 20				12 25
Bristol Temple Meads ■	a				07 13		07 55	08 34				09 34				10 39			11 35				12 38
Cardiff Central ■	a		07 03	07 21		08 04				09 10	09 23		10 09		10 21			11 24		12 06		12 23	

		AW	GW	XC	GW	GW	XC	GW	AW	GW	XC	GW	AW	GW	XC	GW	GW	XC	GW	AW	GW	XC	GW
			B	◇■ H 🍴	K	◇■ G ⊐	◇■ H 🍴	◇ L	C	B	◇■ H 🍴	I	◇ M 🍴	◇■ G ⊐	◇■ H 🍴	◇ N	B	◇■ H 🍴	◇ F	C	◇■ G ⊐	◇■ H 🍴	O
Worcester Shrub Hill ■	d							12 54								15 07							17 08
Ashchurch for Tewkesbury	d							13 11								15 24							17 24
Cheltenham Spa ■	d	11 46	12 01	12 11		13 00	13 11	13 20	13 45	14 01	14 11			15 00	15 11	15 34	16 01	16 11		16 45	17 00	17 10	17 34
Gloucester ■	a	11 56	12 12	12 20		13 10	13 20	13 35	13 57	14 12	14 20			15 09	15 20	15 43	16 12	16 20		16 56	17 10	17 20	17 44
	d	11 58		12 22	12 42		13 22	13 42	13 58		14 22	14 41	14 42		15 22	15 47		16 22	16 42	16 58		17 22	17 47
Bristol Parkway ■	d				13 19			14 20				15 19				16 24			17 20				18 25
Bristol Temple Meads ■	a				13 35			14 37				15 34				16 39			17 36				18 39
Cardiff Central ■	a	13 07		13 21			14 22		15 09		15 26		15 53		16 25			17 24		18 10		18 24	

A From Birmingham New Street
B To Swindon
C To Maesteg
D To Taunton
E To Weston-super-Mare
F To Weymouth
G To London Paddington
H From Nottingham
I To Westbury
J From Great Malvern to Brighton
K To Frome
L From Worcester Foregate Street to Weymouth
M To Fishguard Harbour
N From Great Malvern to Weymouth
O From Great Malvern to Westbury
P From Manchester Piccadilly. 🍴 to Bristol Temple Meads
Q From Great Malvern

Table T058-F

Saturdays
15 September to 8 December

Worcester Shrub Hill - Cheltenham Spa - Gloucester

		AW A	GW B	XC ◇1 C	GW D	AW A	GW ◇1 E ☕	XC ◇1 C	XC ◇1 F 🛒	GW G	AW A	GW H	XC ◇1 C	GW	XC ◇1 C	GW B	GW G	GW	AW
Worcester Shrub Hill 7	d									19 08							21 32	22 25	
Ashchurch for Tewkesbury	d			18 08						19 24							21 51	22 41	
Cheltenham Spa 4	d	17 45	18 01	18 17		18 45	19 00	19 11	19 25	19 34	19 45	20 02	20 11	21 02	21 11	21 20	22 02	22 51	
Gloucester 7	a	17 56	18 12	18 25		18 56	19 10	19 20		19 44	19 56	20 12	20 20	21 12	21 20	21 30	22 12	23 01	
	d	17 58		18 28	18 41	18 58		19 22		19 47	19 58		20 22	21 14	21 22				23 09
Bristol Parkway 10	d				19 20				19 56	20 26				21 52					
Bristol Temple Meads 10	a				19 35				20 05	20 40				22 07					
Cardiff Central 7	a	19 12		19 30		20 11		20 20	21 00		21 07		21 26		22 42				00 38

Sundays
20 May to 15 July

		GW B	GW I	AW	XC ◇1 J 🛒	GW ◇1 E ☕	XC ◇1 C 🛒	GW	AW	GW B	XC ◇1 C 🛒	GW ◇1 E ☕	XC ◇1 C 🛒	AW	GW K	XC ◇1 C 🛒	GW ◇1 E ☕	XC ◇1 C 🛒	AW	GW B	GW	XC ◇1 C	GW ◇1 E ☕
Worcester Shrub Hill 7	d							11 38							14 36						16 40		
Ashchurch for Tewkesbury	d							11 53							14 51						16 56		
Cheltenham Spa 4	d	09 24	10 04		10 52	11 18	11 53	12 03	12 21	12 32	13 10	13 33	14 10	14 19	15 01	15 10	15 33	16 10	16 19	16 32	17 06	17 11	17 33
Gloucester 7	a	09 35	10 14		11 02	11 27	12 02	12 14	12 31	12 42	13 20	13 45	14 20	14 32	15 11	15 22	15 42	16 20	16 33	16 43	17 16	17 20	17 42
	d		10 16	10 48	11 05		12 05	12 18	12 33		13 23		14 24	14 34	15 13	15 24		16 23	16 33		17 19	17 23	
Bristol Parkway 10	d		10 55					12 58							16 01						17 57		
Bristol Temple Meads 10	a		11 06					13 09							16 13						18 09		
Cardiff Central 7	a			12 06	12 09		13 07		13 50		14 27		15 27	15 50		16 29		17 26	17 49			18 29	

		XC ◇1 C	AW	GW	XC ◇1 C	GW ◇1 E ☕	XC ◇1 C	AW	GW	GW B	GW	AW
Worcester Shrub Hill 7	d			18 40					20 38			
Ashchurch for Tewkesbury	d			18 56					20 54			
Cheltenham Spa 4	d	18 10	18 35	19 06	19 12	19 32	20 10	20 19	21 03	21 47	22 01	
Gloucester 7	a	18 20	18 46	19 16	19 26	19 41	20 19	20 30	21 13	21 56	22 11	
	d	18 23	18 48	19 19	19 28		20 22	20 33	21 15			22 33
Bristol Parkway 10	d			19 58					21 54			
Bristol Temple Meads 10	a			20 10					22 06			
Cardiff Central 7	a	19 27	20 14		20 30		21 27	21 48				23 51

Sundays
22 July to 9 September

		GW B	GW I	AW	XC ◇1 J 🛒	GW ◇1 E ☕	XC ◇1 C 🛒	GW	AW	GW B	XC ◇1 C 🛒	GW ◇1 E ☕	XC ◇1 C 🛒	AW	GW K	XC ◇1 C 🛒	GW ◇1 E ☕	XC ◇1 C 🛒	AW	GW B	GW	XC ◇1 C	GW ◇1 E ☕
Worcester Shrub Hill 7	d							11 38							14 36						16 40		
Ashchurch for Tewkesbury	d							11 53							14 51						16 56		
Cheltenham Spa 4	d	09 24	10 04		10 52	11 18	11 52	12 03	12 21	12 32	13 10	13 33	14 10	14 19	15 01	15 10	15 33	16 10	16 19	16 32	17 06	17 11	17 33
Gloucester 7	a	09 35	10 14		11 02	11 27	12 02	12 14	12 31	12 42	13 20	13 45	14 20	14 32	15 11	15 22	15 42	16 20	16 33	16 43	17 16	17 20	17 42
	d		10 16	10 48	11 05		12 05	12 18	12 33		13 23		14 24	14 34	15 13	15 24		16 23	16 33		17 19	17 23	
Bristol Parkway 10	d		10 55					12 58							16 01						17 57		
Bristol Temple Meads 10	a		11 06					13 09							16 13						18 09		
Cardiff Central 7	a			12 06	12 09		13 07		13 50		14 27		15 28	15 50		16 29		17 26	17 49			18 29	

		XC ◇1 C	AW	GW	XC ◇1 C	GW ◇1 E ☕	XC ◇1 C	AW	GW	GW B	GW	AW
Worcester Shrub Hill 7	d			18 40					20 38			
Ashchurch for Tewkesbury	d			18 56					20 54			
Cheltenham Spa 4	d	18 10	18 35	19 06	19 12	19 32	20 10	20 19	21 03	21 47	22 01	
Gloucester 7	a	18 20	18 46	19 16	19 26	19 41	20 19	20 30	21 13	21 56	22 11	
	d	18 23	18 48	19 19	19 28		20 22	20 33	21 15			22 33
Bristol Parkway 10	d			19 58					21 54			
Bristol Temple Meads 10	a			20 10					22 06			
Cardiff Central 7	a	19 27	20 14		20 30		21 27	21 48				23 51

A To Maesteg
B To Swindon
C From Nottingham
D To Frome
E To London Paddington
F From Manchester Piccadilly. 🛒 to Bristol Temple Meads
G From Great Malvern
H To Westbury
I To Taunton
J From Birmingham New Street
K To Weston-super-Mare

Table T058-F

Sundays
16 September to 2 December

Worcester Shrub Hill - Cheltenham Spa - Gloucester

		GW A	GW B	AW	XC ◇1 C 🛒	GW ◇1 D ☕	XC ◇1 E 🛒	GW	AW	GW A	XC ◇1 E 🛒	GW ◇1 D ☕	XC ◇1 E 🛒	AW	GW F	XC ◇1 E 🛒	GW ◇1 D ☕	XC ◇1 E 🛒	AW	GW A	GW	XC ◇1 E	GW ◇1 D ☕
Worcester Shrub Hill 7	d							11 38							14 36						16 40		
Ashchurch for Tewkesbury	d							11 53							14 51						16 56		
Cheltenham Spa 4	d	09 24	10 04		10 52	11 18	11 52	12 03	12 21	12 46	13 10	13 46	14 10	14 19	15 01	15 10	15 46	16 10	16 19	16 46	17 06	17 11	17 46
Gloucester 7	a	09 35	10 14		11 02	11 27	12 02	12 14	12 31	12 56	13 20	13 58	14 20	14 32	15 11	15 22	15 57	16 20	16 33	16 57	17 16	17 20	17 55
	d		10 16	10 48	11 05		12 05	12 18	12 33		13 23		14 24	14 34	15 13	15 24		16 23	16 33		17 19	17 23	
Bristol Parkway 10	d		10 55					12 58							16 01						17 57		
Bristol Temple Meads 10	a		11 07					13 09							16 13						18 09		
Cardiff Central 7	a			12 06	12 09		13 07		13 50		14 27		15 28	15 50		16 29		17 26	17 49			18 29	

		XC ◇1 E	AW	GW	XC ◇1 E	GW ◇1 D ☕	XC ◇1 E	AW	GW G	GW H	GW A	GW	AW
Worcester Shrub Hill 7	d			18 40					20 38	20 38			
Ashchurch for Tewkesbury	d			18 56					20 54	20 54			
Cheltenham Spa 4	d	18 10	18 35	19 06	19 12	19 46	20 10	20 19	21 03	21 03	21 47	22 01	
Gloucester 7	a	18 20	18 46	19 16	19 26	19 55	20 19	20 30	21 13	21 13	21 56	22 11	
	d	18 23	18 48	19 19	19 28		20 22	20 33	21 14	21 15			22 33
Bristol Parkway 10	d			19 58					21 54	21 54			
Bristol Temple Meads 10	a			20 10					22 06	22 06			
Cardiff Central 7	a	19 27	20 14		20 30		21 27	21 48					23 51

A To Swindon
B To Taunton
C From Birmingham New Street
D To London Paddington
E From Nottingham
F To Weston-super-Mare
G until 21 October
H from 28 October

Table T058-R

Mondays to Fridays
21 May to 31 August

Gloucester - Cheltenham Spa - Worcester Shrub Hill

Miles			GW MX A	GW	XC ◇1 B	GW C	AW D	GW ◇1 A ☕	XC ◇1 E	GW F	XC ◇1 G ⊼	AW	XC ◇1 E	GW H	GW I	GW ◇1 J ☕	XC ◇1 E	AW	GW H	GW A	XC ◇1 E ⊼	AW K	GW ◇ L
—	Cardiff Central [7]	d					06 12		06 40		07 00	07 05	07 45				08 45	09 12			09 45	10 09	
—	Bristol Temple Meads [10]	d								07 34	08 00				08 41				09 41				10 41
—	Bristol Parkway [10]	d								07 49	08 10				08 55				09 52				10 53
0	Gloucester [7]	a					07 20		07 44	08 30		08 20	08 45		09 35		09 44	10 20	10 32		10 44	11 20	11 33
—		d	00 30	06 00	07 10	07 14	07 22	07 37	07 46			08 21	08 49	08 52	09 38	09 43	09 50	10 20		10 33	10 50	11 21	11 37
6½	Cheltenham Spa [4]	a	00 40	06 10	07 19	07 24	07 34	07 47	07 56		08 39	08 34	08 58	09 05	09 46	09 52	10 00	10 31		10 46	11 00	11 32	11 46
13¼	Ashchurch for Tewkesbury	a		06 19	07 28	07 33			08 04						09 55								11 56
25¾	Worcester Shrub Hill [7]	a		06 39		07 53									10 14								12 13

		GW ◇1 J ☕	XC ◇1 E	GW ◇ M	GW A	XC ◇1 E ⊼	AW K	GW ◇ N	GW ◇1 J ☕	XC ◇1 E ⊼	AW K	GW ◇ M	GW A	XC ◇1 E ⊼	GW ◇ L	GW ◇1 J ☕	XC ◇1 E ⊼	AW K	GW ◇ M	GW A	XC ◇1 E ⊼	AW K
Cardiff Central [7]	d		10 45			11 45	12 12			12 45	13 12			13 45			14 45	15 12			15 45	16 10
Bristol Temple Meads [10]	d			11 41				12 41				13 41			14 41				15 41			
Bristol Parkway [10]	d			11 52				12 52				13 52			14 53				15 52			
Gloucester [7]	a		11 44	12 33		12 44	13 20	13 33		13 44	14 22	14 31		14 44	15 33		15 44	16 21	16 34		16 44	17 19
	d	11 43	11 50		12 33	12 48	13 22	13 37	13 41	13 50			14 33	14 50	15 37	15 41	15 50	16 22		16 35	16 50	17 23
Cheltenham Spa [4]	a	11 52	12 00		12 46	12 58	13 33	13 46	13 52	14 00			14 45	15 00	15 46	15 52	16 00	16 31		16 45	17 00	17 32
Ashchurch for Tewkesbury	a					13 06		13 55							15 56							
Worcester Shrub Hill [7]	a							14 12							16 14							

		GW I	GW ◇1 J ☕	XC ◇1 E ⊼	AW K	GW ◇ M	XC ◇1 O ⊼	GW ◇ A	AW K	GW I	GW ◇1 P ☕	XC ◇1 E ⊼	GW ◇1 J ☕	GW Q	XC ◇1 R	GW ◇ H	GW	GW ◇1 J ☕	XC ◇1 R	AW K	GW S	XC ◇1 T	GW A
Cardiff Central [7]	d			16 45	17 12		17 45		18 08			18 45			19 50				21 05	21 12		21 50	
Bristol Temple Meads [10]	d	16 41				17 41				18 36				19 41			20 41				21 41		
Bristol Parkway [10]	d	16 52				17 53				18 48				19 52			20 52				21 56		
Gloucester [7]	a	17 34		17 44	18 20	18 33	18 44		19 17	19 27		19 43		20 33	20 54		21 32		22 02	22 22	22 38	22 46	
	d	17 37	17 43	17 50	18 21		18 46	18 54	19 21	19 35	19 39	19 45	20 33	20 37	20 59	21 23	21 33	21 51	22 04	22 23		22 47	22 51
Cheltenham Spa [4]	a	17 46	17 52	18 00	18 30		18 56	19 03	19 31	19 45	19 49	19 56	20 43	20 48	21 09	21 33	21 44	22 00	22 14	22 34		22 56	23 02
Ashchurch for Tewkesbury	a	17 56					19 04			19 54							21 53		22 22				
Worcester Shrub Hill [7]	a	18 16								20 18							22 11	22 22					

		GW	AW K
Cardiff Central [7]	d		23 20
Bristol Temple Meads [10]	d	22 42	
Bristol Parkway [10]	d	22 53	
Gloucester [7]	a	23 38	00 39
	d		
Cheltenham Spa [4]	a		
Ashchurch for Tewkesbury	a		
Worcester Shrub Hill [7]	a		

Mondays to Fridays
3 September to 5 October

		GW MX A	GW	XC ◇1 B	GW C	AW D	GW ◇1 A ☕	XC ◇1 E	GW F	XC ◇1 G ⊼	AW	XC ◇1 E	GW H	GW I	GW ◇1 J ☕	XC ◇1 E	AW	GW H	GW A	XC ◇1 E ⊼	AW K	GW ◇ L	GW ◇1 J ☕
Cardiff Central [7]	d					06 12		06 40		07 00	07 05	07 45				08 45	09 12			09 45	10 09		
Bristol Temple Meads [10]	d								07 34	08 00				08 41				09 41				10 41	
Bristol Parkway [10]	d								07 49	08 10				08 55				09 52				10 53	
Gloucester [7]	a					07 20		07 44	08 30		08 20	08 45		09 35		09 44	10 20	10 32		10 44	11 20	11 33	
	d	00 30	06 00	07 10	07 14	07 22	07 37	07 46			08 21	08 49	08 52	09 38	09 43	09 50	10 20		10 33	10 50	11 21	11 37	11 43
Cheltenham Spa [4]	a	00 40	06 10	07 19	07 24	07 34	07 47	07 56		08 39	08 34	08 58	09 05	09 46	09 52	10 00	10 31		10 46	11 00	11 32	11 46	11 52
Ashchurch for Tewkesbury	a		06 19	07 28	07 33			08 04						09 55								11 56	
Worcester Shrub Hill [7]	a		06 39		07 53									10 14								12 13	

		XC ◇1 E	GW ◇ M	GW A	XC ◇1 E ⊼	AW K	GW ◇ N	GW ◇1 J ☕	XC ◇1 E ⊼	AW K	GW ◇ M	GW A	XC ◇1 E ⊼	GW ◇ L	GW ◇1 J ☕	XC ◇1 E ⊼	AW K	GW ◇ M	GW A	XC ◇1 E ⊼	AW K	GW I	GW ◇1 J ☕
Cardiff Central [7]	d	10 45			11 45	12 12			12 45	13 12			13 45			14 45	15 12			15 45	16 10		
Bristol Temple Meads [10]	d		11 41				12 41				13 41			14 41				15 41				16 41	
Bristol Parkway [10]	d		11 52				12 52				13 52			14 53				15 52				16 52	
Gloucester [7]	a	11 44	12 33		12 44	13 20	13 33		13 44	14 22	14 31		14 44	15 33		15 44	16 21	16 34		16 44	17 19	17 34	
	d	11 50		12 33	12 48	13 22	13 37	13 41	13 50			14 33	14 50	15 37	15 41	15 50	16 22		16 35	16 50	17 23	17 37	17 43
Cheltenham Spa [4]	a	12 00		12 46	12 58	13 33	13 46	13 52	14 00			14 45	15 00	15 46	15 52	16 00	16 31		16 45	17 00	17 32	17 46	17 52
Ashchurch for Tewkesbury	a				13 06		13 55							15 56								17 56	
Worcester Shrub Hill [7]	a						14 12							16 14								18 16	

A From Swindon
B To Stansted Airport
C To Great Malvern
D From Cardiff Canton Sidings
E To Nottingham
F From Salisbury
G To Manchester Piccadilly. ⊼ from Bristol Temple Meads
H From Westbury
I From Warminster to Great Malvern
J From London Paddington
K From Maesteg
L From Southampton Central to Great Malvern
M From Weymouth
N From Brighton to Great Malvern
O From Nottingham to Ashchurch for Tewkesbury continues to Nottingham
P From London Paddington. The Cheltenham Spa Express
Q From Warminster
R To Birmingham New Street
S From Taunton
T From Nottingham to Birmingham New Street

Table T058-R

Mondays to Fridays
3 September to 5 October

Gloucester - Cheltenham Spa - Worcester Shrub Hill

		XC ◇1 A ⊼	AW B	GW ◇ C	XC ◇1 D ⊼	GW ◇ E	AW B	GW F	GW ◇1 G ☕	XC ◇1 A ⊼	GW ◇1 H ☕	GW I	XC ◇1 J	GW ◇ K	GW	GW ◇1 H ☕	XC ◇1 J	AW B	GW L	XC ◇1 M	GW E	GW	AW B
Cardiff Central [7]	d	16 45	17 12		17 45		18 08			18 45			19 50				21 05	21 12		21 50			23 20
Bristol Temple Meads [10]	d			17 41				18 36				19 41			20 41				21 41			22 42	
Bristol Parkway [10]	d			17 53				18 48				19 52			20 52				21 56			22 53	
Gloucester [7]	a	17 44	18 20	18 33	18 44		19 17	19 27		19 43		20 33	20 54		21 32		22 02	22 22	22 38	22 46		23 38	00 39
	d	17 50	18 21		18 46	18 54	19 21	19 35	19 39	19 45	20 33	20 37	20 59	21 23	21 33	21 51	22 04	22 23		22 47	22 51		
Cheltenham Spa [4]	a	18 00	18 30		18 56	19 03	19 31	19 45	19 49	19 56	20 43	20 48	21 09	21 33	21 44	22 00	22 14	22 34		22 56	23 02		
Ashchurch for Tewkesbury	a				19 04			19 54							21 53		22 22						
Worcester Shrub Hill [7]	a							20 18							22 11	22 22							

Mondays to Fridays
8 October to 7 December

		GW MX E	GW	XC ◇1 N	GW O	AW P	GW ◇1 E ☕	XC ◇1 A	GW Q	XC ◇1 R ⊼	AW	XC ◇1 A	GW K	GW F	GW ◇1 H ☕	XC ◇1 A	AW	GW K	GW E	XC ◇1 A ⊼	AW B	GW ◇ S	GW ◇1 H ☕
Cardiff Central [7]	d					06 12		06 40		07 00	07 05	07 45				08 45	09 12			09 45	10 09		
Bristol Temple Meads [10]	d								07 34	08 00				08 41				09 41				10 41	
Bristol Parkway [10]	d								07 49	08 10				08 55				09 52				10 53	
Gloucester [7]	a					07 20		07 44	08 30		08 20	08 45		09 35		09 44	10 20	10 32		10 44	11 20	11 33	
	d	00 30	06 00	07 10	07 14	07 22	07 37	07 46			08 21	08 49	08 52	09 38	09 43	09 50	10 20		10 33	10 50	11 21	11 37	11 43
Cheltenham Spa [4]	a	00 40	06 10	07 19	07 24	07 34	07 47	07 56		08 39	08 34	08 58	09 05	09 46	09 52	10 00	10 31		10 46	11 00	11 32	11 46	11 52
Ashchurch for Tewkesbury	a		06 19	07 28	07 33			08 04						09 55								11 56	
Worcester Shrub Hill [7]	a		06 39		07 53									10 14								12 13	

		XC ◇1 A	GW ◇ C	GW E	XC ◇1 A ⊼	AW B	GW ◇ T	GW ◇1 H ☕	XC ◇1 A ⊼	AW B	GW ◇ C	GW E	XC ◇1 A ⊼	GW ◇ S	GW ◇1 H ☕	XC ◇1 A ⊼	AW B	GW ◇ C	GW E	XC ◇1 A ⊼	AW B	GW F	GW ◇1 H ☕
Cardiff Central [7]	d	10 45			11 45	12 12			12 45	13 12			13 45			14 45	15 12			15 45	16 10		
Bristol Temple Meads [10]	d		11 41				12 41				13 41			14 41				15 41				16 41	
Bristol Parkway [10]	d		11 52				12 52				13 52			14 53				15 52				16 52	
Gloucester [7]	a	11 44	12 33		12 44	13 20	13 33		13 44	14 22	14 31		14 44	15 33		15 44	16 21	16 34		16 44	17 19	17 34	
	d	11 50		12 33	12 48	13 22	13 37	13 41	13 50			14 33	14 50	15 37	15 41	15 50	16 22		16 35	16 50	17 23	17 37	17 43
Cheltenham Spa [4]	a	12 00		12 46	12 58	13 33	13 46	13 52	14 00			14 45	15 00	15 46	15 52	16 00	16 31		16 45	17 00	17 32	17 46	17 52
Ashchurch for Tewkesbury	a				13 06		13 55							15 56								17 56	
Worcester Shrub Hill [7]	a						14 12							16 14								18 16	

		XC ◇1 A ⊼	AW B	GW ◇ C	XC ◇1 D ⊼	GW ◇ E	AW B	GW F	GW ◇1 G ☕	XC ◇1 A ⊼	GW ◇1 H ☕	GW I	XC ◇1 J	GW ◇ K	GW	GW ◇1 H ☕	XC ◇1 J	AW B	GW L	XC ◇1 M	GW E	GW
Cardiff Central [7]	d	16 45	17 12		17 45		18 08			18 45			19 50				21 05	21 12		21 50		
Bristol Temple Meads [10]	d			17 41				18 36				19 41			20 41				21 41			22 42
Bristol Parkway [10]	d			17 53				18 48				19 52			20 52				21 56			22 53
Gloucester [7]	a	17 44	18 20	18 33	18 44		19 17	19 27		19 43		20 33	20 54		21 32		22 02	22 22	22 38	22 46		23 38
	d	17 50	18 21		18 46	18 54	19 21	19 35	19 39	19 45	20 33	20 37	20 59	21 23	21 33	21 51	22 04	22 23		22 47	22 51	
Cheltenham Spa [4]	a	18 00	18 30		18 56	19 03	19 31	19 45	19 49	19 56	20 43	20 48	21 09	21 33	21 44	22 00	22 14	22 34		22 56	23 02	
Ashchurch for Tewkesbury	a				19 04			19 54							21 53		22 22					
Worcester Shrub Hill [7]	a							20 18							22 11	22 22						

		AW B
Cardiff Central [7]	d	23 20
Bristol Temple Meads [10]	d	
Bristol Parkway [10]	d	
Gloucester [7]	a	00 39
	d	
Cheltenham Spa [4]	a	
Ashchurch for Tewkesbury	a	
Worcester Shrub Hill [7]	a	

Saturdays
26 May to 8 September

		GW E	GW	XC ◇1 N	GW	AW	XC ◇1 A	GW E	GW Q	XC ◇1 R ⊼	AW	XC ◇1 A	GW F	XC ◇1 A	GW ◇1 H ☕	AW B	GW K	XC ◇1 A ⊼	GW E	AW B	GW ◇ U	XC ◇1 A	GW ◇1 H ☕
Cardiff Central [7]	d					06 10	06 40			07 00	07 07	07 45		08 45		09 10		09 45		10 10		10 45	
Bristol Temple Meads [10]	d								07 41	08 00			08 40				09 41				10 41		
Bristol Parkway [10]	d								07 53	08 10			08 53				09 52				10 52		
Gloucester [7]	a					07 18	07 44		08 32		08 21	08 45	09 30	09 46		10 19	10 33	10 44		11 20	11 32	11 44	
	d	00 33	06 00	07 06	07 15	07 21	07 46	08 09			08 22	08 50	09 38	09 50	10 13	10 21		10 50	11 08	11 22	11 37	11 50	12 13
Cheltenham Spa [4]	a	00 43	06 10	07 15	07 24	07 34	07 55	08 20		08 40	08 35	09 00	09 46	10 00	10 22	10 32		11 00	11 20	11 32	11 47	12 00	12 22
Ashchurch for Tewkesbury	a		06 19	07 24	07 33		08 03						09 55								11 56		
Worcester Shrub Hill [7]	a		06 40		07 53								10 14								12 14		

A To Nottingham
B From Maesteg
C From Weymouth
D From Nottingham to Ashchurch for Tewkesbury continues to Nottingham
E From Swindon
F From Warminster to Great Malvern
G From London Paddington. The Cheltenham Spa Express
H From London Paddington
I From Warminster
J To Birmingham New Street
K From Westbury
L From Taunton
M From Nottingham to Birmingham New Street
N To Stansted Airport
O To Great Malvern
P From Cardiff Canton Sidings
Q From Salisbury
R To Manchester Piccadilly. ⊼ from Bristol Temple Meads
S From Southampton Central to Great Malvern
T From Brighton to Great Malvern
U From Southampton Central to Worcester Foregate Street

Table T058-R

Gloucester - Cheltenham Spa - Worcester Shrub Hill

Saturdays
26 May to 8 September

		GW	XC	GW	AW	GW	XC	GW	AW	GW	XC	GW	GW	XC	GW	AW	GW	XC	GW	AW	GW	XC
		◇ A	◇1 B ✠	C	D	◇ E	◇1 B ✠	◇1 F ⊏	✠	◇ A	◇1 B ✠	C	◇ G	◇1 B ✠	◇1 F ⊏	D	◇ A	◇1 B ✠	C	D	H	◇1 B ✠
Cardiff Central 7	d		11 45		12 09		12 45		13 12		13 45			14 45		15 08		15 45		16 08		16 45
Bristol Temple Meads 10	d	11 41				12 41				13 41			14 41				15 41				16 41	
Bristol Parkway 10	d	11 52				12 55				13 52			14 53				15 52				16 52	
Gloucester 7	a	12 31	12 44		13 21	13 32	13 44		14 20	14 34	14 44		15 33	15 44		16 19	16 33	16 44		17 19	17 33	17 44
	d		12 48	13 08	13 22	13 37	13 50	14 13			14 50	15 08	15 37	15 50	16 13	16 21		16 50	17 08	17 23	17 37	17 50
Cheltenham Spa 4	a		12 58	13 20	13 32	13 46	14 00	14 22			15 00	15 20	15 47	16 00	16 22	16 32		17 00	17 20	17 33	17 47	18 00
Ashchurch for Tewkesbury	a		13 06			13 55							15 56								17 56	
Worcester Shrub Hill 7	a					14 13							16 14								18 16	

		GW	AW	GW	XC	GW	AW	GW	XC	GW	GW	GW	XC	GW	XC	GW	AW	GW	AW
		◇1 F ⊏	D	◇ I	◇1 B ✠	C	D	J	◇1 B ✠	◇1 F ⊏	K	C	◇1 B		◇1 L	◇1 F ⊏	D		D
Cardiff Central 7	d		17 09		17 45		18 08		18 45				20 00		20 50		21 11		23 18
Bristol Temple Meads 10	d			17 41				18 41			19 41			20 41				22 11	
Bristol Parkway 10	d			17 52				18 52			19 52			20 52				22 23	
Gloucester 7	a		18 18	18 32	18 44		19 20	19 32	19 44		20 32		21 04	21 32	21 47		22 19	23 03	00 40
	d	18 13	18 24		18 46	19 08	19 21	19 38	19 46	20 13	20 38	20 52	21 07	21 38	21 49	22 13			
Cheltenham Spa 4	a	18 22	18 33		18 56	19 20	19 31	19 47	19 56	20 22	20 48	21 04	21 16	21 48	21 58	22 22			
Ashchurch for Tewkesbury	a				19 04			19 56					21 25	21 57					
Worcester Shrub Hill 7	a							20 14						22 18					

Saturdays
15 September to 8 December

		GW	GW	XC	GW	AW	XC	GW	GW	XC	AW	XC	GW	XC	GW	AW	GW	XC	GW	AW	GW	XC	GW
		C		◇1 M			◇1 B	C	N	◇1 O ✠		◇1 B	H	◇1 B	◇1 F ⊏	D	K	◇1 B ✠	C	D	◇ P	◇1 B	◇1 F ⊏
Cardiff Central 7	d					06 10	06 40			07 00	07 07	07 45		08 45		09 10		09 45		10 10		10 45	
Bristol Temple Meads 10	d								07 41	08 00			08 40				09 41				10 41		
Bristol Parkway 10	d								07 53	08 10			08 53				09 52				10 52		
Gloucester 7	a					07 18	07 44		08 32		08 21	08 45	09 30	09 46		10 19	10 33	10 44		11 20	11 32	11 44	
	d	00 33	06 00	07 06	07 15	07 21	07 46	08 09			08 22	08 50	09 38	09 50	10 13	10 21		10 50	11 08	11 22	11 37	11 50	12 13
Cheltenham Spa 4	a	00 43	06 10	07 15	07 24	07 34	07 55	08 20		08 40	08 35	09 00	09 46	10 00	10 22	10 32		11 00	11 20	11 32	11 47	12 00	12 22
Ashchurch for Tewkesbury	a		06 19	07 24	07 33		08 03						09 55								11 56		
Worcester Shrub Hill 7	a		06 40		07 53								10 14								12 14		

		GW	XC	GW	AW	GW	XC	GW	AW	GW	XC	GW	GW	XC	GW	AW	GW	XC	GW	AW	GW	XC	GW
		◇ A	◇1 B ✠	C	D	◇ E	◇1 B ✠	◇1 F ⊏	✠	◇ A	◇1 B ✠	C	◇ G	◇1 B ✠	◇1 F ⊏	D	◇ A	◇1 B ✠	C	D	H	◇1 B ✠	◇1 F ⊏
Cardiff Central 7	d		11 45		12 09		12 45		13 12		13 45			14 45		15 08		15 45		16 08		16 45	
Bristol Temple Meads 10	d	11 41				12 41				13 41			14 41				15 41				16 41		
Bristol Parkway 10	d	11 52				12 55				13 52			14 53				15 52				16 52		
Gloucester 7	a	12 31	12 44		13 21	13 32	13 44		14 20	14 34	14 44		15 33	15 44		16 19	16 33	16 44		17 19	17 33	17 44	
	d		12 48	13 08	13 22	13 37	13 50	14 13			14 50	15 08	15 37	15 50	16 13	16 21		16 50	17 08	17 23	17 37	17 50	18 13
Cheltenham Spa 4	a		12 58	13 20	13 32	13 46	14 00	14 22			15 00	15 20	15 47	16 00	16 22	16 32		17 00	17 20	17 33	17 47	18 00	18 22
Ashchurch for Tewkesbury	a		13 06			13 55							15 56								17 56		
Worcester Shrub Hill 7	a					14 13							16 14								18 16		

		AW	GW	XC	GW	AW	GW	XC	GW	GW	GW	XC	GW	XC	GW	AW	GW	AW
		D	◇ A	◇1 B ✠	C	D	H	◇1 B ✠	◇1 F ⊏	K	C	◇1 B		◇1 L	◇1 F ⊏	D		D
Cardiff Central 7	d	17 09		17 45		18 08		18 45				20 00		20 50		21 11		23 18
Bristol Temple Meads 10	d		17 41				18 41			19 41			20 41				22 11	
Bristol Parkway 10	d		17 52				18 52			19 52			20 52				22 23	
Gloucester 7	a	18 18	18 32	18 44		19 20	19 32	19 44		20 32		21 04	21 32	21 47		22 19	23 03	00 40
	d	18 24		18 46	19 08	19 21	19 38	19 46	20 13	20 38	20 52	21 07	21 38	21 49	22 13			
Cheltenham Spa 4	a	18 33		18 56	19 20	19 31	19 47	19 56	20 22	20 48	21 04	21 16	21 48	21 58	22 22			
Ashchurch for Tewkesbury	a			19 04			19 56					21 25	21 57					
Worcester Shrub Hill 7	a						20 14						22 18					

Sundays
20 May to 15 July

		GW	GW	GW	AW	XC	GW	XC	GW	AW	XC	GW	XC	GW	GW	AW	XC	GW	XC	GW	AW	XC	GW
			◇1 F ⊏	C		◇1 B	◇1 F ⊏	◇1 B			◇1 B	◇1 F ⊏	◇1 B	C			◇1 B ✠	◇1 F ⊏	◇1 Q ✠			◇1 B ✠	◇1 F ⊏
Cardiff Central 7	d				10 30	10 45		11 45		12 25	12 45		13 45			14 25	14 45		15 45		16 25	16 45	
Bristol Temple Meads 10	d	09 20							12 11						14 39					16 41			
Bristol Parkway 10	d	09 29							12 22						14 51					16 51			
Gloucester 7	a	10 10			11 40	11 47		12 46	13 04	13 39	13 46		14 46		15 33	15 37	15 46		16 46	17 33	17 37	17 47	
	d	10 12	10 33	11 38	11 42	11 50	12 33	12 50	13 05	13 40	13 50	14 33	14 50	15 23	15 35	15 40	15 50	16 33	16 50	17 35	17 40	17 50	18 29
Cheltenham Spa 4	a	10 21	10 43	11 47	11 55	12 00	12 45	13 00	13 16	13 52	14 00	14 46	15 00	15 33	15 45	15 50	16 00	16 47	17 00	17 45	17 50	18 00	18 40
Ashchurch for Tewkesbury	a	10 30							13 25						15 55					17 55			
Worcester Shrub Hill 7	a	10 51							13 42						16 12					18 15			

A From Weymouth
B To Nottingham
C From Swindon
D From Maesteg
E From Brighton to Great Malvern
F From London Paddington
G From Southampton Central to Great Malvern
H From Warminster to Great Malvern
I From Warminster
J From Weymouth to Great Malvern
K From Westbury
L To Birmingham New Street
M To Stansted Airport
N From Salisbury
O To Manchester Piccadilly. ✠ from Bristol Temple Meads
P From Southampton Central to Worcester Foregate Street
Q From Nottingham to Cheltenham Spa continues to Nottingham

Table T058-R

Gloucester - Cheltenham Spa - Worcester Shrub Hill

Sundays
20 May to 15 July

		XC	GW	AW	XC	GW	XC	GW	GW	AW	XC	GW	GW	AW	GW
		◇1 A ✠			◇1 A ✠	◇1 B ⊏	◇1 C	D		E	◇1 F	◇1 B ⊏			G
Cardiff Central 7	d	17 45		18 24	18 45		19 45			20 24	20 45			22 26	
Bristol Temple Meads 10	d		18 37						20 41				22 30		
Bristol Parkway 10	d		18 46						20 51				22 39		
Gloucester 7	a	18 46	19 30	19 38	19 46		20 48		21 34	21 42	21 47		23 21	23 42	
	d	18 50	19 34	19 42	19 50	20 33	20 50	21 20	21 38		21 50	22 26			23 56
Cheltenham Spa 4	a	19 00	19 46	19 55	20 00	20 45	21 00	21 28	21 47		22 00	22 35			00 05
Ashchurch for Tewkesbury	a		19 55												
Worcester Shrub Hill 7	a		20 20												

Sundays
22 July to 9 September

		GW	GW	GW	AW	XC	GW	XC	GW	AW	XC	GW	XC	GW	GW	AW	XC	GW	XC	GW	AW	XC	GW
			◇1 B ⊏	G		◇1 A	◇1 B ⊏	◇1 A			◇1 A	◇1 B ⊏	◇1 A	G			◇1 A ✠	◇1 B ⊏	◇1 H ✠			◇1 A ✠	◇1 B ⊏
Cardiff Central 7	d				10 30	10 45		11 45		12 25	12 45		13 45			14 25	14 45		15 45		16 25	16 45	
Bristol Temple Meads 10	d	09 20							12 11						14 39					16 41			
Bristol Parkway 10	d	09 29							12 22						14 51					16 51			
Gloucester 7	a	10 10			11 40	11 47		12 46	13 04	13 39	13 46		14 46		15 33	15 37	15 46		16 46	17 33	17 37	17 47	
	d	10 12	10 33	11 38	11 42	11 50	12 33	12 50	13 05	13 40	13 50	14 33	14 50	15 23	15 35	15 40	15 50	16 33	16 50	17 35	17 40	17 50	18 29
Cheltenham Spa 4	a	10 21	10 43	11 47	11 55	12 00	12 45	13 00	13 16	13 52	14 00	14 46	15 00	15 33	15 45	15 50	16 00	16 47	17 00	17 45	17 50	18 00	18 40
Ashchurch for Tewkesbury	a	10 30							13 25						15 55					17 55			
Worcester Shrub Hill 7	a	10 51							13 42						16 12					18 15			

		XC	GW	AW	XC	GW	XC	GW	GW	AW	XC	GW	GW	AW	GW
		◇1 A ✠			◇1 A ✠	◇1 B ⊏	◇1 C	D		E	◇1 F	◇1 B ⊏			G
Cardiff Central 7	d	17 45		18 24	18 45		19 45			20 24	20 45			22 26	
Bristol Temple Meads 10	d		18 37						20 41				22 30		
Bristol Parkway 10	d		18 46						20 51				22 39		
Gloucester 7	a	18 46	19 30	19 38	19 46		20 48		21 34	21 42	21 47		23 21	23 42	
	d	18 50	19 34	19 42	19 50	20 33	20 50	21 20	21 38		21 50	22 26			23 56
Cheltenham Spa 4	a	19 00	19 46	19 55	20 00	20 45	21 00	21 28	21 47		22 00	22 35			00 05
Ashchurch for Tewkesbury	a		19 55												
Worcester Shrub Hill 7	a		20 20												

Sundays
16 September to 2 December

		GW	GW	GW	AW	XC	GW	XC	GW	AW	XC	GW	XC	GW	GW	AW	XC	GW	XC	GW	AW	XC	GW
			◇1 B ⊏	G		◇1 A	◇1 B ⊏	◇1 A			◇1 A	◇1 B ⊏	◇1 A	G			◇1 A ✠	◇1 B ⊏	◇1 H ✠			◇1 A ✠	◇1 B ⊏
Cardiff Central 7	d				10 30	10 45		11 45		12 25	12 45		13 45			14 25	14 45		15 45		16 25	16 45	
Bristol Temple Meads 10	d	09 20							12 11						14 39					16 41			
Bristol Parkway 10	d	09 29							12 22						14 51					16 51			
Gloucester 7	a	10 10			11 40	11 47		12 46	13 04	13 39	13 46		14 46		15 33	15 37	15 46		16 46	17 33	17 37	17 47	
	d	10 12	10 33	11 38	11 42	11 50	12 33	12 50	13 05	13 40	13 50	14 33	14 50	15 23	15 35	15 40	15 50	16 33	16 50	17 35	17 40	17 50	18 33
Cheltenham Spa 4	a	10 21	10 43	11 47	11 55	12 00	12 45	13 00	13 16	13 52	14 00	14 45	15 00	15 33	15 45	15 50	16 00	16 47	17 00	17 45	17 50	18 00	18 46
Ashchurch for Tewkesbury	a	10 30							13 25						15 55					17 55			
Worcester Shrub Hill 7	a	10 51							13 42						16 12					18 15			

		XC	GW	GW	AW	XC	GW	XC	GW	GW	AW	XC	GW	GW	AW	GW	GW
		◇1 A ✠	I	J		◇1 A ✠	◇1 B ⊏	◇1 C	D		E	◇1 F	◇1 B ⊏			K	L
Cardiff Central 7	d	17 45			18 24	18 45		19 45			20 24	20 45			22 26		
Bristol Temple Meads 10	d		18 37	18 37						20 41				22 30			
Bristol Parkway 10	d		18 46	18 46						20 51				22 39			
Gloucester 7	a	18 46	19 30	19 31	19 38	19 46		20 48		21 34	21 42	21 47		23 21	23 42		
	d	18 50	19 34	19 34	19 42	19 50	20 33	20 50	21 26	21 38		21 50	22 29			23 56	23 57
Cheltenham Spa 4	a	19 00	19 46	19 46	19 55	20 00	20 45	21 00	21 34	21 47		22 00	22 38			00 07	00 06
Ashchurch for Tewkesbury	a		19 55	19 56													
Worcester Shrub Hill 7	a		20 21	20 21													

A To Nottingham
B From London Paddington
C To Leicester
D From Westbury
E From Cheltenham Spa
F To Birmingham New Street
G From Swindon
H From Nottingham to Cheltenham Spa continues to Nottingham
I from 28 October
J until 21 October
K from 28 October. From Swindon
L until 21 October. From Swindon

Table T059-F

Mondays to Fridays
21 May to 7 December

Stratford - Highbury & Islington, West Hampstead, Willesden Junction, Clapham Junction and Richmond

Miles	Miles		LO MX	LO MO	LO MX	LO MX	LO MX	LO	LO MX	LO MX	LO	LO	LO	LO	LO	LO	LO	LO	LO	LO	LO	LO	LO
0	—	**Stratford** 7 ⊖ d								00 15			05 47		05 58	06 07	06 17	06 22	06 27	06 35	06 47	06 53	06 59
1	—	Hackney Wick d							00 03	00 18			05 50		06 01	06 10	06 20	06 27	06 31	06 39	06 50	06 56	07 02
1¾	—	Homerton d							00 05	00 21			05 53		06 04	06 13	06 23	06 30	06 34	06 42	06 53	06 59	07 05
2½	—	Hackney Central d							00 07	00 23			05 55		06 06	06 15	06 25	06 32	06 36	06 44	06 55	07 01	07 07
3¼	—	Dalston Kingsland d							00 09	00 25			05 57		06 08	06 17	06 27	06 34	06 38	06 46	06 57	07 03	07 09
4¼	—	Canonbury 178 d							00 11	00 27			05 59		06 10	06 19	06 29	06 36	06 40	06 48	06 59	07 06	07 11
4¾	—	**Highbury & Islington** ⊖178 d							00 14	00 29			06 01		06 12	06 21	06 31	06 38	06 42	06 50	07 02	07 09	07 14
5¾	—	Caledonian Rd & Barnsbury d					00 01		00 16	00 31			06 03		06 14	06 24	06 33	06 40	06 44	06 52	07 04	07 12	07 16
6¼	—	Camden Road d					00 03		00 19	00 34			06 06		06 17	06 27	06 36	06 43	06 47	06 55	07 09	07 16	07 20
6¾	—	Kentish Town West d					00 06		00 21	00 37			06 09		06 20	06 29	06 39	06 46	06 50	06 58	07 11	07 18	07 22
7½	—	**Gospel Oak** d					00 08		00 23	00 39			06 11		06 22	06 31	06 43	06 48	06 52	07 02	07 13	07 20	07 25
8	—	Hampstead Heath d					00 10		00 25	00 41			06 13		06 24	06 33	06 45	06 50	06 54	07 04	07 15	07 22	07 27
9	—	Finchley Road & Frognal d					00 12		00 27	00 43			06 15		06 26	06 35	06 47	06 52	06 56	07 06	07 17	07 24	07 29
9½	—	West Hampstead ⊖ d					00 14		00 29	00 45			06 17		06 28	06 37	06 49	06 54	06 58	07 08	07 19	07 26	07 31
10	—	Brondesbury d					00 15		00 31	00 46			06 18		06 29	06 39	06 50	06 55	06 59	07 09	07 21	07 28	07 33
10¾	—	Brondesbury Park d				00 01	00 17		00 32	00 48			06 20		06 31	06 40	06 52	06 57	07 01	07 11	07 22	07 29	07 34
11	—	Kensal Rise d				00 02	00 19		00 34	00 50			06 22		06 33	06 42	06 54	06 59	07 03	07 13	07 24	07 31	07 36
12	0	**Willesden Jn. High Level** ⊖ a				00 08	00 25						06 27		06 38	06 46	06 58	07 02	07 07	07 16	07 29	07 34	07 41
—	—	d			00 01			05 58			06 02	06 10	06 28	06 35	06 40	06 47	06 59	07 03	07 08	07 17	07 30	07 35	07 42
12	—	**Willesden Jn Low Level** ⊖ a							00 44	00 58													
—	2	**Shepherd's Bush** ⊖66,176 d		00 05	00 09			06 05				06 16		06 41		06 53	07 05		07 17			07 42	
—	2¾	**Kensington (Olympia)** ⊖176 d		00 07	00 11			06 07				06 18		06 43		06 55	07 07		07 19			07 44	
—	3½	West Brompton ⊖176 d		00 10	00 14			06 10				06 21		06 46		06 58	07 10		07 22			07 46	
—	4½	Imperial Wharf 176 d		00a13	00 17			06 13				06 24		06 49		07 01	07 13		07 25			07 49	
—	6	**Clapham Junction** 10 66,176 a			00 22			06 19				06 31		06 56		07 09	07 22		07 32			07 55	
13¾	—	Acton Central d	00 02								06 07		06 37		06 46			07 09		07 24	07 35		07 47
14½	—	South Acton d	00 04								06 09		06 40		06 49			07 12		07 26	07 38		07 50
15¼	—	Gunnersbury ⊖ d	00 08								06 13		06 44		06 52			07 19		07 29	07 41		07 55
16¾	—	Kew Gardens ⊖ d	00 11								06 16		06 47		06 55			07 22		07 32	07 44		07 58
17¾	—	**Richmond** ⊖ a	00 15								06 23		06 51		07 00			07 26		07 38	07 49		08 03

	LO	LO	LO	LO	LO	LO	LO	LO	LO	LO	LO	LO	LO	LO	LO	LO	LO	LO	LO	LO	LO	LO
Stratford 7 ⊖ d	07 05	07 18	07 23	07 29	07 35	07 47	07 54	07 59	08 06	08 11	08 17	08 29	08 37	08 47	08 53	08 57	09 06	09 12	09 15	09 28	09 35	09 45
Hackney Wick d	07 08	07 21	07 26	07 32	07 38	07 50	07 57	08 02	08 09	08 14	08 20	08 32	08 40	08 50	08 56	09 00	09 08	09 16	09 20	09 31	09 38	09 49
Homerton d	07 11	07 24	07 29	07 35	07 41	07 53	08 00	08 05	08 12	08 17	08 23	08 35	08 43	08 53	08 59	09 03	09 11	09 18	09 23	09 34	09 41	09 52
Hackney Central d	07 13	07 26	07 31	07 37	07 43	07 55	08 02	08 07	08 14	08 19	08 25	08 37	08 45	08 55	09 01	09 05	09 13	09 20	09 25	09 36	09 43	09 54
Dalston Kingsland d	07 15	07 28	07 33	07 39	07 45	07 57	08 04	08 09	08 16	08 21	08 27	08 39	08 47	08 57	09 03	09 07	09 15	09 22	09 27	09 38	09 45	09 56
Canonbury 178 d	07 17	07 30	07 35	07 41	07 47	07 59	08 06	08 11	08 18	08 23	08 29	08 41	08 49	08 59	09 05	09 09	09 17	09 24	09 29	09 40	09 47	09 58
Highbury & Islington ⊖178 d	07 20	07 33	07 38	07 44	07 50	08 02	08 09	08 14	08 21	08 26	08 32	08 43	08 52	09 01	09 07	09 11	09 19	09 27	09 31	09 44	09 49	10 00
Caledonian Rd & Barnsbury d	07 22	07 35	07 40	07 46	07 52	08 04	08 11	08 16	08 23	08 28	08 34	08 45	08 54	09 03	09 09	09 13	09 21	09 29	09 33	09 46	09 51	10 02
Camden Road d	07 25	07 38	07 43	07 49	07 55	08 10	08 14	08 19	08 26	08 31	08 37	08 48	08 57	09 06	09 12	09 16	09 24	09 32	09 36	09 49	09 54	10 05
Kentish Town West d	07 27	07 41	07 45	07 51	07 57	08 12	08 16	08 21	08 28	08 33	08 39	08 51	08 59	09 09	09 15	09 19	09 27	09 34	09 39	09 52	09 57	10 08
Gospel Oak d	07 31	07 43	07 49	07 55	08 01	08 14	08 19	08 25	08 31	08 37	08 43	08 53	09 01	09 15	09 20	09 24	09 32	09 36	09 41	09 54	09 59	10 10
Hampstead Heath d	07 33	07 45	07 51	07 57	08 03	08 16	08 21	08 27	08 33	08 39	08 45	08 55	09 03	09 17	09 22	09 26	09 34	09 38	09 43	09 57	10 01	10 12
Finchley Road & Frognal d	07 35	07 47	07 53	07 59	08 05	08 18	08 23	08 29	08 35	08 41	08 47	08 57	09 05	09 19	09 24	09 28	09 36	09 40	09 45	09 59	10 03	10 14
West Hampstead ⊖ d	07 37	07 49	07 55	08 01	08 07	08 20	08 25	08 31	08 37	08 43	08 49	08 59	09 07	09 21	09 26	09 30	09 38	09 42	09 47	10 01	10 05	10 16
Brondesbury d	07 39	07 51	07 57	08 03	08 09	08 22	08 27	08 33	08 39	08 45	08 51	09 00	09 09	09 23	09 27	09 32	09 39	09 44	09 48	10 02	10 07	10 17
Brondesbury Park d	07 40	07 52	07 58	08 04	08 10	08 23	08 28	08 34	08 40	08 46	08 52	09 02	09 10	09 24	09 29	09 33	09 41	09 45	09 50	10 04	10 08	10 19
Kensal Rise d	07 42	07 54	08 00	08 06	08 12	08 25	08 30	08 36	08 42	08 48	08 54	09 04	09 12	09 26	09 31	09 35	09 43	09 47	09 52	10 06	10 10	10 21
Willesden Jn. High Level ⊖ a	07 46	07 58	08 05	08 10	08 17	08 29	08 34	08 41	08 46	08 53	08 58	09 08	09 17	09 29	09 34	09 38	09 46	09 50	09 55	10 09	10 13	10 24
d	07 47	07 59	08 06	08 11	08 18	08 30	08 35	08 42	08 47	08 54	08 59	09 09	09 18	09 30	09 35	09 39	09 47	09 51	09 56	10 10	10 14	10 25
Willesden Jn Low Level ⊖ a																						
Shepherd's Bush ⊖66,176 d	07 54	08 06		08 17			08 41		08 54		09 06	09 17			09 41		09 56		10 05	10 17		
Kensington (Olympia) ⊖176 d	07 56	08 08		08 19			08 43		08 56		09 08	09 19			09 43		09 58		10 07	10 19		
West Brompton ⊖176 d	07 59	08 10		08 22			08 46		08 58		09 10	09 22			09 46		10 01		10 10	10 22		
Imperial Wharf 176 d	08 02	08 13		08 25			08 49		09 01		09 13	09 25			09 49		10 04		10 13	10 25		
Clapham Junction 10 66,176 a	08 07	08 23		08 31			08 56		09 11		09 22	09 34			09 55		10 11		10 20	10 33		
Acton Central d			08 11		08 23	08 35		08 47		08 59			09 24	09 35		09 45		09 58			10 19	10 32
South Acton d			08 14		08 26	08 38		08 50		09 02			09 27	09 38		09 47		10 01			10 22	10 37
Gunnersbury ⊖ d			08 19		08 29	08 41		08 53		09 05			09 30	09 42		09 55		10 06			10 26	10 42
Kew Gardens ⊖ d			08 22		08 32	08 44		08 56		09 08			09 33	09 45		09 58		10 09			10 29	10 45
Richmond ⊖ a			08 27		08 37	08 52		09 01		09 13			09 37	09 53		10 02		10 15			10 37	10 52

For services between Shepherds Bush and Clapham Junction refer to Table T066 and T176

Table T059-F

Mondays to Fridays
21 May to 7 December

Stratford - Highbury & Islington, West Hampstead, Willesden Junction, Clapham Junction and Richmond

	LO	LO	LO	LO	LO	LO	LO	LO	LO	LO	LO	LO	LO	LO	LO	LO	LO	LO	LO	LO	LO	LO
Stratford 7 ⊖ d	09 53	09 57	10 08	10 15	10 23	10 30	10 38	10 45	10 53	11 00	11 08	11 15	11 23	11 28	11 38	11 45	11 53	12 00	12 08	12 15	12 23	12 30
Hackney Wick d	09 56	10 00	10 13	10 18	10 26	10 33	10 42	10 49	10 56	11 03	11 11	11 18	11 26	11 31	11 41	11 48	11 56	12 03	12 11	12 18	12 26	12 33
Homerton d	09 59	10 03	10 15	10 21	10 29	10 36	10 45	10 51	10 59	11 06	11 14	11 21	11 29	11 34	11 44	11 51	11 59	12 06	12 14	12 21	12 29	12 36
Hackney Central d	10 01	10 05	10 17	10 23	10 31	10 38	10 47	10 53	11 01	11 08	11 16	11 23	11 31	11 36	11 46	11 53	12 01	12 08	12 16	12 23	12 31	12 38
Dalston Kingsland d	10 03	10 07	10 19	10 25	10 33	10 40	10 49	10 56	11 03	11 10	11 18	11 25	11 33	11 38	11 48	11 55	12 03	12 10	12 18	12 25	12 33	12 40
Canonbury 178 d	10 05	10 09	10 21	10 27	10 35	10 42	10 51	10 58	11 05	11 12	11 20	11 27	11 35	11 40	11 50	11 57	12 05	12 12	12 20	12 27	12 35	12 42
Highbury & Islington ⊖178 d	10 07	10 11	10 24	10 29	10 37	10 44	10 53	11 00	11 07	11 14	11 22	11 29	11 37	11 42	11 52	11 59	12 07	12 15	12 22	12 29	12 37	12 44
Caledonian Rd & Barnsbury d	10 09	10 13	10 26	10 31	10 39	10 46	10 55	11 02	11 09	11 16	11 24	11 31	11 39	11 45	11 54	12 01	12 09	12 17	12 24	12 31	12 39	12 46
Camden Road d	10 12	10 16	10 29	10 34	10 43	10 49	10 58	11 06	11 12	11 19	11 27	11 34	11 42	11 49	11 57	12 04	12 12	12 20	12 27	12 34	12 42	12 49
Kentish Town West d	10 15	10 19	10 31	10 37	10 46	10 52	11 01	11 09	11 15	11 22	11 30	11 37	11 45	11 52	12 00	12 07	12 15	12 23	12 30	12 37	12 45	12 52
Gospel Oak d	10 17	10 21	10 35	10 40	10 49	10 54	11 03	11 11	11 19	11 24	11 34	11 40	11 49	11 56	12 02	12 10	12 17	12 26	12 34	12 39	12 49	12 56
Hampstead Heath d	10 19	10 24	10 37	10 42	10 52	10 56	11 05	11 13	11 22	11 26	11 36	11 42	11 51	11 59	12 04	12 12	12 19	12 28	12 36	12 41	12 51	12 59
Finchley Road & Frognal d	10 21	10 26	10 39	10 44	10 54	10 58	11 07	11 15	11 24	11 28	11 38	11 44	11 53	12 01	12 06	12 14	12 21	12 30	12 38	12 43	12 53	13 01
West Hampstead ⊖ d	10 23	10 28	10 41	10 46	10 56	11 00	11 09	11 17	11 26	11 30	11 40	11 46	11 55	12 03	12 08	12 16	12 23	12 32	12 40	12 45	12 55	13 03
Brondesbury d	10 25	10 29	10 42	10 48	10 57	11 01	11 10	11 19	11 27	11 32	11 41	11 48	11 56	12 05	12 09	12 18	12 24	12 34	12 41	12 47	12 56	13 05
Brondesbury Park d	10 26	10 31	10 44	10 49	10 59	11 03	11 12	11 20	11 29	11 33	11 43	11 49	11 58	12 06	12 11	12 19	12 26	12 35	12 43	12 48	12 58	13 06
Kensal Rise d	10 28	10 33	10 46	10 51	11 01	11 05	11 14	11 22	11 31	11 35	11 45	11 51	12 00	12 08	12 13	12 21	12 28	12 37	12 45	12 50	13 00	13 08
Willesden Jn. High Level ⊖ a	10 32	10 37	10 49	10 54	11 04	11 08	11 18	11 25	11 34	11 38	11 49	11 55	12 04	12 11	12 16	12 24	12 31	12 42	12 48	12 53	13 04	13 12
d	10 33	10 38	10 50	10 55	11 05	11 09	11 19	11 26	11 35	11 39	11 50	11 56	12 05	12 12	12 17	12 25	12 32	12 43	12 49	12 55	13 05	13 13
Willesden Jn Low Level ⊖ a																						
Shepherd's Bush ⊖66,176 d	10 41		10 56		11 11		11 26		11 41		11 56		12 11		12 27		12 41		12 55		13 11	
Kensington (Olympia) ⊖176 d	10 43		10 58		11 13		11 29		11 43		11 58		12 13		12 29		12 43		12 57		13 13	
West Brompton ⊖176 d	10 46		11 01		11 16		11 32		11 46		12 01		12 16		12 32		12 46		13 00		13 16	
Imperial Wharf 176 d	10 49		11 04		11 19		11 35		11 49		12 04		12 19		12 35		12 49		13 03		13 19	
Clapham Junction 10 66,176 a	10 55		11 10		11 25		11 40		11 55		12 10		12 25		12 40		12 55		13 10		13 25	
Acton Central d		10 45		11 04		11 14		11 31		11 44		12 03		12 17		12 30		12 48		13 00		13 20
South Acton d		10 47		11 06		11 17		11 35		11 47		12 06		12 20		12 33		12 51		13 02		13 22
Gunnersbury ⊖ d		10 53		11 09		11 20		11 38		11 50		12 09		12 23		12 38		12 54		13 08		13 25
Kew Gardens ⊖ d		10 56		11 12		11 23		11 41		11 53		12 12		12 26		12 41		12 57		13 11		13 28
Richmond ⊖ a		11 01		11 18		11 29		11 46		11 59		12 17		12 31		12 47		13 02		13 17		13 33

	LO	LO	LO	LO	LO	LO	LO	LO	LO	LO	LO	LO	LO	LO	LO	LO	LO	LO	LO	LO	LO	LO
Stratford 7 ⊖ d	12 38	12 45	12 53	13 00	13 08	13 15	13 23	13 30	13 39	13 45	13 53	14 00	14 07	14 15	14 23	14 30	14 38	14 45	14 53	14 59	15 05	15 12
Hackney Wick d	12 41	12 48	12 56	13 03	13 11	13 18	13 26	13 33	13 42	13 48	13 56	14 03	14 10	14 18	14 26	14 33	14 41	14 48	14 56	15 02	15 08	15 16
Homerton d	12 44	12 51	12 59	13 06	13 14	13 21	13 29	13 36	13 45	13 51	13 59	14 06	14 13	14 21	14 29	14 36	14 44	14 51	14 59	15 05	15 11	15 18
Hackney Central d	12 46	12 53	13 01	13 08	13 16	13 23	13 31	13 38	13 48	13 53	14 01	14 08	14 15	14 23	14 31	14 38	14 46	14 53	15 01	15 07	15 13	15 20
Dalston Kingsland d	12 48	12 55	13 03	13 10	13 18	13 25	13 33	13 40	13 51	13 55	14 03	14 10	14 17	14 25	14 33	14 40	14 48	14 55	15 03	15 09	15 15	15 22
Canonbury 178 d	12 50	12 57	13 05	13 12	13 20	13 27	13 35	13 42	13 53	13 57	14 05	14 12	14 19	14 27	14 35	14 42	14 50	14 57	15 05	15 11	15 17	15 24
Highbury & Islington ⊖178 d	12 52	12 59	13 07	13 14	13 22	13 29	13 37	13 44	13 55	13 59	14 07	14 14	14 21	14 29	14 37	14 44	14 52	14 59	15 07	15 13	15 19	15 27
Caledonian Rd & Barnsbury d	12 54	13 01	13 09	13 16	13 24	13 31	13 39	13 46	13 57	14 01	14 09	14 16	14 23	14 31	14 39	14 46	14 54	15 01	15 09	15 15	15 21	15 29
Camden Road d	12 57	13 06	13 12	13 19	13 27	13 34	13 42	13 49	14 00	14 04	14 12	14 19	14 26	14 34	14 42	14 49	14 57	15 04	15 12	15 18	15 24	15 32
Kentish Town West d	13 00	13 08	13 15	13 22	13 30	13 37	13 45	13 52	14 03	14 07	14 15	14 22	14 29	14 37	14 45	14 52	15 00	15 07	15 15	15 21	15 27	15 34
Gospel Oak d	13 03	13 11	13 19	13 24	13 34	13 41	13 49	13 56	14 05	14 11	14 19	14 25	14 33	14 41	14 50	14 56	15 04	15 11	15 20	15 24	15 31	15 37
Hampstead Heath d	13 05	13 13	13 21	13 26	13 36	13 43	13 51	13 58	14 07	14 13	14 22	14 27	14 35	14 43	14 52	14 58	15 07	15 13	15 22	15 26	15 34	15 39
Finchley Road & Frognal d	13 07	13 15	13 23	13 28	13 38	13 45	13 53	14 00	14 09	14 15	14 24	14 29	14 37	14 45	14 54	15 00	15 09	15 15	15 24	15 28	15 36	15 41
West Hampstead ⊖ d	13 09	13 17	13 25	13 30	13 40	13 47	13 55	14 02	14 11	14 17	14 26	14 31	14 39	14 47	14 56	15 02	15 11	15 17	15 26	15 30	15 38	15 43
Brondesbury d	13 10	13 18	13 27	13 31	13 41	13 49	13 56	14 04	14 12	14 19	14 27	14 32	14 40	14 49	14 57	15 04	15 12	15 18	15 27	15 31	15 39	15 45
Brondesbury Park d	13 12	13 20	13 28	13 33	13 43	13 50	13 58	14 05	14 14	14 20	14 29	14 34	14 42	14 50	14 59	15 05	15 14	15 20	15 29	15 33	15 41	15 46
Kensal Rise d	13 14	13 22	13 30	13 35	13 45	13 52	14 00	14 07	14 16	14 22	14 31	14 36	14 44	14 52	15 01	15 07	15 16	15 22	15 31	15 35	15 43	15 48
Willesden Jn. High Level ⊖ a	13 18	13 25	13 33	13 38	13 49	13 57	14 03	14 12	14 20	14 26	14 34	14 39	14 48	14 57	15 04	15 10	15 20	15 25	15 34	15 38	15 47	15 51
d	13 19	13 26	13 34	13 39	13 50	13 58	14 04	14 13	14 21	14 28	14 35	14 40	14 49	14 58	15 05	15 11	15 21	15 26	15 35	15 39	15 48	15 52
Willesden Jn Low Level ⊖ a																						
Shepherd's Bush ⊖66,176 d	13 27		13 41		13 56		14 11		14 28		14 41		14 56		15 11		15 27		15 41		15 54	
Kensington (Olympia) ⊖176 d	13 29		13 43		13 58		14 13		14 30		14 43		14 58		15 13		15 30		15 43		15 56	
West Brompton ⊖176 d	13 32		13 46		14 01		14 16		14 32		14 46		15 01		15 16		15 33		15 46		15 59	
Imperial Wharf 176 d	13 35		13 49		14 04		14 19		14 35		14 49		15 04		15 19		15 36		15 49		16 02	
Clapham Junction 10 66,176 a	13 40		13 55		14 10		14 25		14 41		14 55		15 09		15 28		15 43		15 55		16 07	
Acton Central d		13 31		13 44		14 03		14 18		14 33		14 46		15 03		15 16		15 31		15 44		15 57
South Acton d		13 33		13 46		14a09		14 21		14a39		14 49		15 06		15 19		15a36		15 47		16 00
Gunnersbury ⊖ d		13 38		13 49				14 24				14 52		15 09		15 22				15 50		16 04
Kew Gardens ⊖ d		13 41		13 52				14 27				14 55		15 12		15 25				15 53		16 07
Richmond ⊖ a		13 47		14 02				14 32				15 02		15 16		15 32				16 01		16 14

For services between Shepherds Bush and Clapham Junction refer to Table T066 and T176

21 May to 7 December

Stratford - Highbury & Islington, West Hampstead, Willesden Junction, Clapham Junction and Richmond

		LO	LO	LO	LO	LO	LO	LO	LO	LO	LO	LO	LO	LO	LO	LO	LO	LO	LO	LO	LO	LO	LO
Stratford 7 ⊖ ⇌	d	15 23	15 29	15 36	15 42	15 53	15 59	16 05	16 11	16 23	16 29	16 35	16 41	16 53	16 59	17 06	17 11	17 23	17 31	17 35	17 41	17 54	17 59
Hackney Wick	d	15 26	15 32	15 39	15 45	15 56	16 02	16 08	16 14	16 26	16 32	16 39	16 44	16 56	17 02	17 09	17 14	17 26	17 34	17 39	17 44	17 57	18 03
Homerton	d	15 29	15 35	15 42	15 48	15 59	16 05	16 11	16 17	16 29	16 35	16 41	16 47	16 59	17 05	17 12	17 17	17 29	17 37	17 41	17 47	18 00	18 06
Hackney Central	d	15 31	15 37	15 44	15 50	16 01	16 07	16 13	16 19	16 31	16 37	16 43	16 49	17 01	17 07	17 14	17 19	17 31	17 39	17 44	17 49	18 02	18 08
Dalston Kingsland	d	15 33	15 39	15 46	15 52	16 03	16 10	16 15	16 21	16 33	16 39	16 46	16 51	17 03	17 09	17 16	17 21	17 33	17 41	17 46	17 51	18 04	18 11
Canonbury 178	d	15 35	15 41	15 48	15 54	16 05	16 12	16 17	16 23	16 35	16 41	16 48	16 53	17 05	17 11	17 18	17 23	17 35	17 43	17 48	17 53	18 06	18 13
Highbury & Islington ⊖178	d	15 37	15 43	15 50	15 56	16 07	16 15	16 19	16 25	16 38	16 44	16 51	16 56	17 08	17 14	17 21	17 26	17 38	17 46	17 52	17 56	18 09	18 17
Caledonian Rd & Barnsbury	d	15 39	15 45	15 52	15 58	16 09	16 17	16 21	16 27	16 40	16 46	16 53	16 58	17 10	17 16	17 23	17 28	17 40	17 48	17 54	17 58	18 11	18 19
Camden Road	d	15 42	15 48	15 55	16 01	16 12	16 20	16 24	16 30	16 43	16 49	16 56	17 01	17 13	17 19	17 26	17 31	17 43	17 51	17 57	18 01	18 14	18 22
Kentish Town West	d	15 45	15 51	15 58	16 04	16 15	16 23	16 27	16 33	16 45	16 51	16 59	17 03	17 15	17 21	17 28	17 33	17 45	17 53	17 59	18 03	18 16	18 24
Gospel Oak	d	15 48	15 53	16 02	16 07	16 17	16 25	16 30	16 37	16 49	16 55	17 01	17 07	17 19	17 25	17 31	17 37	17 49	17 55	18 03	18 07	18 18	18 26
Hampstead Heath	d	15 50	15 55	16 04	16 09	16 19	16 27	16 32	16 39	16 51	16 57	17 03	17 09	17 21	17 27	17 33	17 39	17 52	17 57	18 05	18 09	18 20	18 29
Finchley Road & Frognal	d	15 52	15 57	16 06	16 11	16 21	16 29	16 34	16 41	16 53	16 59	17 05	17 11	17 23	17 29	17 35	17 41	17 54	17 59	18 07	18 11	18 22	18 31
West Hampstead ⊖	d	15 54	15 59	16 08	16 13	16 23	16 31	16 36	16 43	16 55	17 01	17 07	17 13	17 25	17 31	17 37	17 43	17 56	18 01	18 09	18 13	18 24	18 33
Brondesbury	d	15 56	16 00	16 10	16 14	16 24	16 33	16 37	16 45	16 57	17 03	17 09	17 15	17 27	17 33	17 39	17 45	17 57	18 03	18 10	18 15	18 26	18 35
Brondesbury Park	d	15 57	16 02	16 11	16 16	16 26	16 34	16 39	16 46	16 58	17 04	17 10	17 16	17 28	17 34	17 40	17 46	17 59	18 04	18 12	18 16	18 27	18 36
Kensal Rise	d	15 59	16 04	16 13	16 18	16 28	16 36	16 41	16 48	17 00	17 06	17 12	17 18	17 30	17 36	17 42	17 48	18 01	18 06	18 14	18 18	18 29	18 38
Willesden Jn. High Level ⊖	a	16 02	16 07	16 17	16 22	16 31	16 41	16 46	16 53	17 04	17 10	17 17	17 22	17 34	17 41	17 46	17 53	18 05	18 10	18 18	18 22	18 32	18 42
	d	16 03	16 08	16 18	16 23	16 35	16 42	16 47	16 54	17 05	17 11	17 18	17 23	17 35	17 42	17 47	17 54	18 06	18 11	18 19	18 23	18 33	18 43
Willesden Jn Low Level ⊖	a																						
Shepherd's Bush ⊖66,176	d		16 15		16 29	16 41		16 54			17 17		17 30	17 42		17 54			18 17		18 30	18 41	
Kensington (Olympia) ⊖176	d		16 17		16 31	16 43		16 56			17 19		17 32	17 44		17 56			18 19		18 32	18 43	
West Brompton ⊖176	d		16 20		16 34	16 46		16 59			17 22		17 34	17 46		17 58			18 22		18 34	18 45	
Imperial Wharf 176	d		16 24		16 37	16 49		17 02			17 25		17 37	17 49		18 01			18 25		18 37	18 48	
Clapham Junction 10 66,176	a		16 31		16 44	16 58		17 10			17 31		17 43	17 58		18 08			18 36		18 46	18 59	
Acton Central	d	16 08		16 24			16 47		16 59	17 10		17 23			17 47		17 59	18 11		18 24			18 48
South Acton	d	16 11		16 27			16 49		17 02	17 13		17 26			17 50		18 02	18 14		18 26			18 50
Gunnersbury ⊖	d	16 14		16 30			16 52		17 05	17 18		17 29			17 53		18 06	18 18		18 30			18 53
Kew Gardens ⊖	d	16 17		16 33			16 55		17 08	17 21		17 32			17 56		18 09	18 21		18 33			18 56
Richmond ⊖	a	16 25		16 38			17 01		17 13	17 28		17 37			18 01		18 14	18 29		18 37			19 01

		LO	LO	LO	LO	LO	LO	LO	LO	LO	LO	LO	LO	LO	LO	LO	LO	LO	LO	LO	LO	LO	LO
Stratford 7 ⊖ ⇌	d	18 06	18 14	18 23	18 29	18 35	18 41	18 53	18 57	19 05	19 11	19 17	19 22	19 29	19 42	19 53	19 59	20 05	20 13	20 20	20 25	20 35	20 42
Hackney Wick	d	18 09	18 17	18 26	18 32	18 38	18 44	18 56	19 00	19 08	19 15	19 20	19 25	19 32	19 45	19 56	20 03	20 08	20 16	20 24	20 28	20 39	20 45
Homerton	d	18 12	18 20	18 29	18 35	18 41	18 47	18 59	19 03	19 11	19 17	19 23	19 28	19 35	19 48	19 59	20 05	20 11	20 19	20 27	20 31	20 41	20 48
Hackney Central	d	18 14	18 22	18 31	18 37	18 43	18 49	19 01	19 05	19 13	19 19	19 25	19 30	19 37	19 50	20 01	20 07	20 13	20 21	20 29	20 33	20 43	20 50
Dalston Kingsland	d	18 16	18 24	18 33	18 39	18 45	18 51	19 03	19 07	19 15	19 21	19 27	19 32	19 39	19 52	20 03	20 10	20 15	20 23	20 31	20 35	20 45	20 52
Canonbury 178	d	18 18	18 26	18 35	18 41	18 47	18 53	19 05	19 09	19 17	19 23	19 29	19 34	19 41	19 54	20 05	20 12	20 17	20 25	20 33	20 37	20 47	20 54
Highbury & Islington ⊖178	d	18 21	18 29	18 38	18 44	18 50	18 56	19 07	19 11	19 19	19 26	19 31	19 36	19 43	19 56	20 07	20 14	20 19	20 27	20 35	20 39	20 50	20 56
Caledonian Rd & Barnsbury	d	18 23	18 31	18 40	18 46	18 52	18 58	19 09	19 13	19 21	19 28	19 33	19 38	19 45	19 58	20 09	20 17	20 21	20 29	20 37	20 41	20 52	20 58
Camden Road	d	18 26	18 34	18 43	18 49	18 56	19 01	19 12	19 17	19 24	19 32	19 36	19 41	19 48	20 01	20 12	20 20	20 24	20 32	20 40	20 44	20 55	21 01
Kentish Town West	d	18 28	18 36	18 45	18 51	18 58	19 03	19 15	19 20	19 27	19 35	19 39	19 44	19 51	20 04	20 15	20 22	20 27	20 35	20 43	20 47	20 57	21 04
Gospel Oak	d	18 31	18 38	18 50	18 55	19 02	19 07	19 17	19 25	19 30	19 39	19 43	19 49	19 55	20 07	20 19	20 25	20 30	20 38	20 45	20 49	21 00	21 06
Hampstead Heath	d	18 33	18 40	18 53	18 57	19 06	19 09	19 19	19 28	19 32	19 41	19 46	19 51	19 57	20 09	20 22	20 27	20 32	20 41	20 47	20 51	21 02	21 08
Finchley Road & Frognal	d	18 35	18 42	18 55	18 59	19 08	19 11	19 21	19 30	19 34	19 43	19 48	19 53	19 59	20 11	20 24	20 29	20 34	20 43	20 49	20 53	21 04	21 10
West Hampstead ⊖	d	18 37	18 44	18 57	19 01	19 10	19 13	19 23	19 32	19 36	19 45	19 50	19 55	20 01	20 13	20 26	20 31	20 36	20 45	20 51	20 55	21 06	21 12
Brondesbury	d	18 39	18 46	18 59	19 03	19 11	19 15	19 25	19 33	19 38	19 47	19 51	19 57	20 02	20 14	20 27	20 33	20 37	20 46	20 52	20 57	21 08	21 13
Brondesbury Park	d	18 40	18 47	19 00	19 04	19 13	19 16	19 26	19 35	19 39	19 48	19 53	19 58	20 04	20 16	20 29	20 34	20 39	20 48	20 54	20 58	21 09	21 15
Kensal Rise	d	18 42	18 49	19 02	19 06	19 15	19 18	19 28	19 37	19 41	19 50	19 55	20 00	20 06	20 18	20 31	20 36	20 41	20 50	20 56	21 00	21 11	21 17
Willesden Jn. High Level ⊖	a	18 46	18 52	19 05	19 10	19 18	19 22	19 31	19 40	19 44	19 53	19 58	20 05	20 10	20 22	20 34	20 39	20 44	20 53	21 00	21 05	21 15	21 20
	d	18 47	18 53	19 06	19 11	19 19	19 23	19 32	19 41	19 47	19 54	19 59	20 06	20 11	20 27	20 35	20 40	20 45	20 54	21 01	21 06	21 16	21 21
Willesden Jn Low Level ⊖	a																						
Shepherd's Bush ⊖66,176	d	18 54			19 17		19 30	19 40		19 53		20 05		20 17		20 41		20 53		21 07		21 23	
Kensington (Olympia) ⊖176	d	18 56			19 19		19 32	19 42		19 55		20 07		20 19		20 43		20 55		21 09		21 26	
West Brompton ⊖176	d	18 58			19 22		19 34	19 45		19 58		20 10		20 22		20 46		20 57		21 12		21 29	
Imperial Wharf 176	d	19 01			19 25		19 37	19 49		20 01		20 13		20 25		20 49		21 01		21 15		21 32	
Clapham Junction 10 66,176	a	19 11			19 34		19 46	19 58		20 07		20 19		20 31		20 55		21 07		21 22		21 37	
Acton Central	d		18 59	19 11		19 25			19 47		19 59		20 12		20 32		20 45		21 00		21 11		21 26
South Acton	d		19 02	19 14		19 28			19 49		20 02		20 15		20 35		20 48		21 03		21 14		21 28
Gunnersbury ⊖	d		19 07	19 17		19 31			19 54		20 05		20 19		20 39		20 51		21 07		21 18		21 31
Kew Gardens ⊖	d		19 10	19 20		19 34			19 57		20 08		20 22		20 43		20 55		21 10		21 21		21 34
Richmond ⊖	a		19 16	19 28		19 38			20 02		20 13		20 27		20 47		21 01		21 15		21 27		21 44

For services between Shepherds Bush and Clapham Junction refer to Table T066 and T176

Table T059-F

Mondays to Fridays

21 May to 7 December

Stratford - Highbury & Islington, West Hampstead, Willesden Junction, Clapham Junction and Richmond

		LO	LO	LO	LO	LO	LO	LO	LO	LO	LO	LO	LO	LO	LO	LO	LO	LO	LO	LO	LO	LO	LO
Stratford 7 ⊖ ⇌	d	20 46	20 58	21 07	21 14	21 19	21 26	21 34	21 41	21 49	21 57	22 04	22 10	22 14	22 36	22 42		23 02		23 12	23 27	23 44	23 59
Hackney Wick	d	20 49	21 01	21 10	21 17	21 22	21 29	21 37	21 44	21 52	22 00	22 07	22 13	22 17	22 39	22 45		23 05		23 16	23 30	23 47	00 03
Homerton	d	20 52	21 04	21 13	21 20	21 25	21 32	21 40	21 47	21 55	22 03	22 10	22 16	22 20	22 42	22 48		23 08		23 18	23 33	23 50	00 05
Hackney Central	d	20 54	21 06	21 15	21 22	21 27	21 34	21 42	21 49	21 57	22 05	22 12	22 18	22 22	22 44	22 50		23 10		23 20	23 35	23 52	00 07
Dalston Kingsland	d	20 56	21 08	21 17	21 24	21 29	21 36	21 44	21 51	21 59	22 07	22 14	22 20	22 24	22 46	22 52		23 12		23 22	23 37	23 54	00 09
Canonbury 178	d	20 58	21 10	21 19	21 26	21 31	21 38	21 46	21 53	22 01	22 09	22 16	22 22	22 26	22 48	22 54		23 14		23 24	23 39	23 56	00 11
Highbury & Islington ⊖178	d	21 00	21 12	21 21	21 28	21 33	21 40	21 48	21 55	22 03	22 11	22 18	22 24	22 28	22 50	22 56		23 16		23 27	23 41	23 58	00 14
Caledonian Rd & Barnsbury	d	21 02	21 14	21 23	21 30	21 35	21 42	21 50	21 57	22 05	22 13	22 20	22 26	22 30	22 52	22 58		23 18		23 29	23 43	00 01	00 16
Camden Road	d	21 05	21 17	21 26	21 34	21 38	21 45	21 53	22 00	22 08	22 16	22 23	22 29	22 33	22 55	23 01		23 21		23 32	23 47	00 03	00 19
Kentish Town West	d	21 08	21 20	21 29	21 37	21 41	21 48	21 56	22 03	22 11	22 19	22 26	22 32	22 36	22 58	23 04		23 24		23 34	23 50	00 06	00 21
Gospel Oak	d	21 12	21 23	21 31	21 39	21 43	21 50	22 00	22 08	22 15	22 23	22 30	22 36	22 40	23 02	23 08		23 26		23 37	23 52	00 08	00 23
Hampstead Heath	d	21 15	21 25	21 34	21 42	21 47	21 52	22 02	22 10	22 17	22 25	22 32	22 38	22 43	23 06	23 10		23 28		23 39	23 54	00 10	00 25
Finchley Road & Frognal	d	21 17	21 27	21 36	21 44	21 49	21 54	22 04	22 12	22 19	22 27	22 34	22 40	22 45	23 08	23 12		23 30		23 41	23 56	00 12	00 27
West Hampstead ⊖	d	21 19	21 29	21 38	21 46	21 51	21 56	22 06	22 14	22 21	22 29	22 36	22 42	22 47	23 10	23 14		23 32		23 43	23 58	00 14	00 29
Brondesbury	d	21 20	21 31	21 39	21 48	21 52	21 57	22 07	22 16	22 22	22 31	22 37	22 44	22 49	23 11	23 16		23 33		23 45	23 59	00 15	00 31
Brondesbury Park	d	21 22	21 32	21 41	21 49	21 54	21 59	22 09	22 17	22 24	22 32	22 39	22 45	22 50	23 13	23 17		23 35		23 46	00 01	00 17	00 32
Kensal Rise	d	21 24	21 34	21 43	21 51	21 56	22 01	22 11	22 19	22 26	22 34	22 41	22 47	22 52	23 15	23 19		23 37		23 48	00 02	00 19	00 34
Willesden Jn. High Level ⊖	a	21 27	21 39	21 47	21 55	22 00	22 04	22 15	22 24	22 30	22 39	22 45	22 51	22 58	23 18	23 24		23 40		23 53	00 08	00 25	
	d	21 28	21 40	21 48	21 56	22 01	22 07	22 16	22 25	22 31	22 40	22 46	22 54	22 59	23 19	23 25	23 30	23 41	23 44	23 54			
Willesden Jn Low Level ⊖	a																						00 44
Shepherd's Bush ⊖66,176	d	21 36		21 55		22 07		22 23		22 37		22 52		23 07	23 26		23 36		23 50				
Kensington (Olympia) ⊖176	d	21 38		21 57		22 09		22 25		22 39		22 54		23 09	23 28		23 38		23 52				
West Brompton ⊖176	d	21 41		21 59		22 12		22 28		22 42		22 57		23 12	23 31		23 41		23 55				
Imperial Wharf 176	d	21 45		22 02		22 15		22 31		22 45		23 00		23 15	23a34		23 44		23 58				
Clapham Junction 10 66,176	a	21 51		22 09		22 21		22 36		22 51		23 06		23 21			23 51		00 05				
Acton Central	d		21 45		22 01		22 13		22 30		22 45		23 00			23 30		23 46		00 02			
South Acton	d		21 48		22 04		22 15		22 33		22 48		23 03			23 33		23 48		00 04			
Gunnersbury ⊖	d		21 51		22 07		22 21		22 37		22 52		23 08			23 37		23 51		00 08			
Kew Gardens ⊖	d		21 54		22 10		22 24		22 40		22 55		23 11			23 40		23 54		00 11			
Richmond ⊖	a		22 00		22 16		22 29		22 45		22 59		23 16			23 45		00 04		00 15			

Saturdays

26 May to 8 December

		LO	LO	LO	LO	LO	LO	LO	LO	LO	LO	LO	LO	LO	LO	LO	LO	LO	LO	LO	LO	LO	LO
Stratford 7 ⊖ ⇌	d							00 15			05 43	05 55	06 01	06 08	06 14	06 23	06 30	06 38	06 47	06 53	07 00	07 08	07 15
Hackney Wick	d						00 03	00 18			05 46	05 58	06 04	06 11	06 17	06 27	06 33	06 42	06 50	06 56	07 03	07 11	07 18
Homerton	d						00 05	00 21			05 49	06 01	06 07	06 14	06 20	06 30	06 36	06 45	06 53	06 59	07 06	07 14	07 21
Hackney Central	d						00 07	00 23			05 51	06 03	06 09	06 16	06 22	06 32	06 38	06 47	06 55	07 01	07 08	07 16	07 23
Dalston Kingsland	d						00 09	00 25			05 53	06 05	06 11	06 18	06 24	06 34	06 40	06 49	06 57	07 03	07 10	07 18	07 25
Canonbury 178	d						00 11	00 27			05 55	06 07	06 13	06 20	06 26	06 36	06 42	06 51	06 59	07 05	07 12	07 20	07 27
Highbury & Islington ⊖178	d						00 14	00 29			05 57	06 09	06 15	06 22	06 28	06 38	06 44	06 53	07 01	07 07	07 14	07 22	07 29
Caledonian Rd & Barnsbury	d			00 01			00 16	00 31			05 59	06 11	06 17	06 24	06 30	06 40	06 46	06 55	07 03	07 09	07 16	07 24	07 31
Camden Road	d			00 03			00 19	00 34			06 02	06 14	06 20	06 27	06 33	06 43	06 49	06 58	07 06	07 12	07 19	07 27	07 34
Kentish Town West	d			00 06			00 21	00 37			06 05	06 17	06 23	06 30	06 36	06 46	06 52	07 01	07 09	07 15	07 22	07 30	07 37
Gospel Oak	d			00 08			00 23	00 39			06 07	06 21	06 27	06 34	06 40	06 49	06 56	07 04	07 11	07 19	07 26	07 34	07 41
Hampstead Heath	d			00 10			00 25	00 41			06 09	06 23	06 29	06 36	06 42	06 51	06 58	07 06	07 13	07 21	07 28	07 36	07 43
Finchley Road & Frognal	d			00 12			00 27	00 43			06 11	06 25	06 31	06 38	06 44	06 53	07 00	07 08	07 15	07 23	07 30	07 38	07 45
West Hampstead ⊖	d			00 14			00 29	00 45			06 13	06 27	06 33	06 40	06 46	06 55	07 02	07 10	07 17	07 25	07 32	07 40	07 47
Brondesbury	d			00 15			00 31	00 46			06 15	06 28	06 35	06 41	06 48	06 56	07 04	07 11	07 19	07 26	07 34	07 41	07 49
Brondesbury Park	d		00 01	00 17			00 32	00 48			06 16	06 30	06 36	06 43	06 49	06 58	07 05	07 13	07 20	07 28	07 35	07 43	07 50
Kensal Rise	d		00 02	00 19			00 34	00 50			06 18	06 32	06 38	06 45	06 51	07 00	07 07	07 15	07 22	07 30	07 37	07 45	07 52
Willesden Jn. High Level ⊖	a		00 08	00 25							06 23	06 36	06 42	06 49	06 56	07 04	07 12	07 19	07 27	07 34	07 42	07 49	07 57
	d	00 01			06 05				06 10	06 20	06 24	06 37	06 43	06 50	06 57	07 05	07 13	07 20	07 28	07 35	07 43	07 50	07 58
Willesden Jn Low Level ⊖	a						00 44	00 58															
Shepherd's Bush ⊖66,176	d	00 09			06 11					06 26		06 43		06 56		07 11		07 26		07 41		07 56	
Kensington (Olympia) ⊖176	d	00 11			06 13					06 28		06 45		06 58		07 13		07 28		07 43		07 58	
West Brompton ⊖176	d	00 14			06 16					06 31		06 48		07 01		07 16		07 31		07 46		08 01	
Imperial Wharf 176	d	00 17			06 19					06 34		06 51		07 04		07 19		07 34		07 49		08 04	
Clapham Junction 10 66,176	a	00 22			06 26					06 41		06 57		07 10		07 25		07 40		07 55		08 10	
Acton Central	d					00 02			06 15		06 29		06 48		07 02		07 18		07 33		07 48		08 03
South Acton	d					00 04			06 17		06 32		06 50		07 05		07 21		07 36		07 51		08 06
Gunnersbury ⊖	d					00 08			06 20		06 35		06 53		07 09		07 24		07 39		07 54		08 09
Kew Gardens ⊖	d					00 11			06 23		06 38		06 56		07 12		07 27		07 42		07 57		08 12
Richmond ⊖	a					00 15			06 32		06 45		07 03		07 16		07 32		07 49		08 02		08 17

For services between Shepherds Bush and Clapham Junction refer to Table T066 and T176

Table T059-F

Saturdays

26 May to 8 December

Stratford - Highbury & Islington, West Hampstead, Willesden Junction, Clapham Junction and Richmond

		LO	LO	LO	LO	LO	LO	LO	LO	LO	LO	LO	LO	LO	LO	LO	LO	LO	LO	LO	LO	LO	LO
Stratford 7 ⊖	d	07 23	07 30	07 38	07 45	07 53	08 00	08 08	08 15	08 23	08 30	08 38	08 45	08 53	09 00	09 08	09 15	09 23	09 30	09 38	09 45	09 53	10 00
Hackney Wick	d	07 26	07 33	07 42	07 48	07 56	08 03	08 11	08 18	08 27	08 33	08 41	08 48	08 56	09 03	09 11	09 18	09 26	09 34	09 41	09 48	09 57	10 03
Homerton	d	07 29	07 36	07 44	07 51	07 59	08 06	08 14	08 21	08 30	08 36	08 44	08 51	08 59	09 06	09 14	09 21	09 29	09 37	09 44	09 51	10 00	10 06
Hackney Central	d	07 31	07 38	07 46	07 53	08 01	08 08	08 16	08 23	08 32	08 38	08 46	08 53	09 01	09 08	09 16	09 23	09 31	09 39	09 46	09 53	10 02	10 08
Dalston Kingsland	d	07 33	07 40	07 48	07 55	08 03	08 10	08 18	08 25	08 34	08 40	08 48	08 55	09 03	09 10	09 18	09 25	09 33	09 41	09 48	09 55	10 04	10 10
Canonbury 178	d	07 35	07 42	07 50	07 57	08 05	08 12	08 20	08 27	08 36	08 42	08 50	08 57	09 05	09 12	09 20	09 27	09 35	09 43	09 50	09 57	10 06	10 12
Highbury & Islington ⊖178	d	07 37	07 44	07 53	07 59	08 07	08 14	08 22	08 29	08 38	08 44	08 52	08 59	09 07	09 14	09 22	09 29	09 37	09 45	09 52	09 59	10 08	10 14
Caledonian Rd & Barnsbury	d	07 39	07 46	07 55	08 02	08 09	08 16	08 24	08 31	08 40	08 46	08 54	09 01	09 09	09 16	09 24	09 31	09 39	09 47	09 54	10 01	10 10	10 16
Camden Road	d	07 42	07 49	07 58	08 05	08 12	08 19	08 27	08 34	08 43	08 49	08 57	09 04	09 12	09 19	09 27	09 34	09 42	09 52	09 57	10 04	10 13	10 19
Kentish Town West	d	07 45	07 52	08 00	08 09	08 15	08 22	08 30	08 37	08 46	08 52	09 00	09 07	09 15	09 22	09 30	09 37	09 45	09 54	10 00	10 07	10 16	10 22
Gospel Oak	d	07 49	07 56	08 03	08 12	08 19	08 26	08 34	08 41	08 49	08 56	09 04	09 11	09 19	09 26	09 34	09 41	09 49	09 58	10 04	10 11	10 21	10 26
Hampstead Heath	d	07 51	07 58	08 05	08 14	08 21	08 28	08 36	08 43	08 51	08 58	09 06	09 13	09 21	09 28	09 36	09 43	09 51	10 00	10 06	10 13	10 23	10 28
Finchley Road & Frognal	d	07 53	08 00	08 07	08 16	08 23	08 30	08 38	08 45	08 53	09 00	09 08	09 15	09 23	09 30	09 38	09 45	09 53	10 02	10 08	10 15	10 25	10 30
West Hampstead ⊖	d	07 55	08 02	08 09	08 18	08 25	08 32	08 40	08 47	08 55	09 02	09 10	09 17	09 25	09 32	09 40	09 47	09 55	10 04	10 10	10 17	10 27	10 32
Brondesbury	d	07 56	08 04	08 11	08 20	08 26	08 34	08 41	08 49	08 56	09 04	09 11	09 19	09 26	09 34	09 41	09 49	09 56	10 05	10 11	10 19	10 28	10 34
Brondesbury Park	d	07 58	08 05	08 12	08 21	08 28	08 35	08 43	08 50	08 58	09 05	09 13	09 20	09 28	09 35	09 43	09 50	09 58	10 07	10 13	10 20	10 30	10 35
Kensal Rise	d	08 00	08 07	08 14	08 23	08 30	08 37	08 45	08 52	09 00	09 07	09 15	09 22	09 30	09 37	09 45	09 52	10 00	10 09	10 15	10 22	10 32	10 37
Willesden Jn. High Level ⊖	a	08 04	08 12	08 19	08 27	08 34	08 42	08 49	08 57	09 04	09 12	09 19	09 27	09 34	09 42	09 49	09 57	10 03	10 12	10 19	10 25	10 35	10 42
	d	08 05	08 13	08 20	08 28	08 35	08 43	08 50	08 58	09 05	09 13	09 20	09 28	09 35	09 43	09 50	09 58	10 04	10 13	10 20	10 26	10 36	10 43
Willesden Jn Low Level ⊖	a																						
Shepherd's Bush ⊖66,176	d	08 11		08 27		08 41		08 56		09 11		09 26		09 41		09 56		10 11		10 26		10 42	
Kensington (Olympia) ⊖176	d	08 13		08 29		08 43		08 58		09 13		09 28		09 43		09 58		10 13		10 28		10 44	
West Brompton ⊖176	d	08 16		08 31		08 46		09 01		09 16		09 31		09 46		10 01		10 16		10 31		10 47	
Imperial Wharf 176	d	08 19		08 34		08 49		09 04		09 19		09 34		09 49		10 04		10 19		10 34		10 50	
Clapham Junction 10 66,176	a	08 25		08 40		08 55		09 10		09 25		09 40		09 55		10 10		10 25		10 40		10 55	
Acton Central	d		08 18		08 33		08 48		09 03		09 18		09 33		09 48		10 03		10 18		10 33		10 48
South Acton	d		08 21		08 36		08 51		09 06		09 21		09 36		09 51		10 06		10 21		10 36		10 51
Gunnersbury ⊖	d		08 24		08 39		08 54		09 09		09 24		09 39		09 54		10 09		10 24		10 39		10 54
Kew Gardens ⊖	d		08 27		08 42		08 57		09 12		09 27		09 42		09 57		10 12		10 27		10 42		10 57
Richmond ⊖	a		08 32		08 47		09 02		09 17		09 32		09 47		10 02		10 17		10 32		10 47		11 02

		LO	LO	LO	LO	LO	LO	LO	LO	LO	LO	LO	LO	LO	LO	LO	LO	LO	LO	LO	LO	LO	LO
Stratford 7 ⊖	d	10 08	10 15	10 23	10 30	10 38	10 45	10 53	11 00	11 08	11 15	11 23	11 30	11 38	11 45	11 53	12 00	12 08	12 15	12 23	12 30	12 38	12 45
Hackney Wick	d	10 11	10 18	10 26	10 33	10 42	10 48	10 56	11 03	11 11	11 19	11 26	11 33	11 41	11 48	11 56	12 03	12 12	12 18	12 26	12 33	12 41	12 48
Homerton	d	10 14	10 21	10 29	10 36	10 44	10 51	10 59	11 06	11 14	11 22	11 29	11 36	11 44	11 51	11 59	12 06	12 15	12 21	12 29	12 36	12 44	12 51
Hackney Central	d	10 16	10 23	10 31	10 38	10 46	10 53	11 01	11 08	11 16	11 24	11 31	11 38	11 46	11 53	12 01	12 08	12 17	12 23	12 31	12 38	12 46	12 53
Dalston Kingsland	d	10 18	10 25	10 33	10 40	10 48	10 55	11 03	11 10	11 18	11 26	11 33	11 40	11 48	11 55	12 03	12 10	12 19	12 25	12 33	12 40	12 48	12 55
Canonbury 178	d	10 20	10 27	10 35	10 42	10 50	10 57	11 05	11 12	11 20	11 28	11 35	11 42	11 50	11 57	12 05	12 12	12 21	12 27	12 35	12 42	12 50	12 57
Highbury & Islington ⊖178	d	10 22	10 29	10 37	10 44	10 53	10 59	11 07	11 14	11 22	11 30	11 37	11 44	11 52	11 59	12 07	12 14	12 23	12 29	12 37	12 44	12 53	12 59
Caledonian Rd & Barnsbury	d	10 24	10 31	10 39	10 46	10 55	11 01	11 09	11 16	11 24	11 33	11 39	11 46	11 54	12 01	12 09	12 16	12 25	12 31	12 39	12 46	12 55	13 01
Camden Road	d	10 27	10 34	10 42	10 49	10 58	11 04	11 12	11 19	11 27	11 36	11 42	11 49	11 58	12 06	12 12	12 19	12 28	12 34	12 42	12 49	12 58	13 04
Kentish Town West	d	10 30	10 37	10 45	10 52	11 00	11 07	11 15	11 22	11 30	11 39	11 45	11 52	12 01	12 09	12 15	12 22	12 31	12 37	12 45	12 52	13 01	13 07
Gospel Oak	d	10 34	10 41	10 49	10 56	11 04	11 11	11 19	11 25	11 34	11 43	11 49	11 56	12 04	12 11	12 19	12 25	12 35	12 41	12 49	12 56	13 04	13 11
Hampstead Heath	d	10 36	10 43	10 51	10 58	11 06	11 13	11 22	11 27	11 36	11 45	11 51	11 58	12 06	12 13	12 21	12 27	12 37	12 43	12 51	12 58	13 06	13 13
Finchley Road & Frognal	d	10 38	10 45	10 53	11 00	11 08	11 15	11 24	11 29	11 38	11 47	11 53	12 00	12 08	12 15	12 23	12 29	12 39	12 45	12 53	13 00	13 08	13 15
West Hampstead ⊖	d	10 40	10 47	10 55	11 02	11 10	11 17	11 26	11 31	11 40	11 49	11 55	12 02	12 10	12 17	12 25	12 31	12 41	12 47	12 55	13 02	13 10	13 17
Brondesbury	d	10 41	10 49	10 56	11 04	11 11	11 19	11 27	11 32	11 41	11 51	11 56	12 04	12 11	12 19	12 26	12 33	12 42	12 49	12 56	13 04	13 11	13 19
Brondesbury Park	d	10 43	10 50	10 58	11 05	11 13	11 20	11 29	11 34	11 43	11 52	11 58	12 05	12 13	12 20	12 28	12 34	12 44	12 50	12 58	13 05	13 13	13 20
Kensal Rise	d	10 45	10 52	11 00	11 07	11 15	11 22	11 31	11 36	11 45	11 54	12 00	12 07	12 15	12 22	12 30	12 36	12 46	12 52	13 00	13 07	13 15	13 22
Willesden Jn. High Level ⊖	a	10 49	10 57	11 04	11 12	11 19	11 25	11 34	11 40	11 49	11 57	12 04	12 12	12 19	12 27	12 34	12 41	12 50	12 57	13 04	13 12	13 19	13 27
	d	10 50	10 58	11 05	11 13	11 20	11 26	11 35	11 41	11 50	11 58	12 05	12 13	12 20	12 28	12 35	12 42	12 51	12 58	13 05	13 13	13 20	13 28
Willesden Jn Low Level ⊖	a																						
Shepherd's Bush ⊖66,176	d	10 56		11 11		11 26		11 41		11 56		12 11		12 26		12 41		12 57		13 11		13 26	
Kensington (Olympia) ⊖176	d	10 58		11 13		11 28		11 43		11 58		12 13		12 28		12 43		12 59		13 13		13 28	
West Brompton ⊖176	d	11 01		11 16		11 31		11 46		12 01		12 16		12 31		12 46		13 02		13 16		13 31	
Imperial Wharf 176	d	11 04		11 19		11 34		11 49		12 04		12 19		12 34		12 49		13 05		13 19		13 34	
Clapham Junction 10 66,176	a	11 10		11 25		11 40		11 55		12 10		12 25		12 40		12 55		13 13		13 25		13 40	
Acton Central	d		11 03		11 18		11 33		11 47		12 03		12 18		12 33		12 47		13 03		13 18		13 33
South Acton	d		11 06		11 21		11 36		11 50		12 06		12 21		12 36		12 50		13 06		13 21		13 36
Gunnersbury ⊖	d		11 09		11 24		11 39		11 53		12 09		12 24		12 39		12 53		13 09		13 24		13 39
Kew Gardens ⊖	d		11 12		11 27		11 42		11 56		12 12		12 27		12 42		12 56		13 12		13 27		13 42
Richmond ⊖	a		11 17		11 32		11 47		12 02		12 17		12 32		12 47		13 02		13 17		13 32		13 47

For services between Shepherds Bush and Clapham Junction refer to Table T066 and T176

Table T059-F

Saturdays

26 May to 8 December

Stratford - Highbury & Islington, West Hampstead, Willesden Junction, Clapham Junction and Richmond

		LO	LO	LO	LO	LO	LO	LO	LO	LO	LO	LO	LO	LO	LO	LO	LO	LO	LO	LO	LO	LO	LO
Stratford 7 ⊖	d	12 53	13 00	13 07	13 15	13 23	13 30	13 38	13 45	13 53	14 00	14 08	14 15	14 23	14 33	14 38	14 45	14 53	15 00	15 08	15 15	15 23	15 30
Hackney Wick	d	12 56	13 03	13 10	13 18	13 26	13 33	13 41	13 48	13 56	14 03	14 11	14 18	14 26	14 36	14 41	14 48	14 56	15 03	15 11	15 18	15 26	15 33
Homerton	d	12 59	13 06	13 13	13 21	13 29	13 36	13 44	13 51	13 59	14 06	14 14	14 21	14 29	14 39	14 44	14 51	14 59	15 06	15 14	15 21	15 29	15 36
Hackney Central	d	13 01	13 08	13 15	13 23	13 31	13 38	13 46	13 53	14 01	14 08	14 16	14 23	14 31	14 41	14 46	14 53	15 01	15 08	15 16	15 23	15 31	15 38
Dalston Kingsland	d	13 03	13 10	13 17	13 25	13 33	13 40	13 48	13 55	14 03	14 10	14 18	14 25	14 33	14 43	14 48	14 55	15 03	15 10	15 18	15 25	15 33	15 40
Canonbury 178	d	13 05	13 12	13 19	13 27	13 35	13 42	13 50	13 57	14 05	14 12	14 20	14 27	14 35	14 45	14 50	14 57	15 05	15 12	15 20	15 27	15 35	15 42
Highbury & Islington ⊖178	d	13 07	13 14	13 21	13 29	13 37	13 44	13 52	13 59	14 07	14 14	14 22	14 29	14 37	14 47	14 52	14 59	15 07	15 14	15 22	15 29	15 37	15 44
Caledonian Rd & Barnsbury	d	13 09	13 16	13 23	13 31	13 39	13 46	13 54	14 01	14 09	14 16	14 24	14 31	14 39	14 49	14 54	15 01	15 09	15 16	15 24	15 31	15 39	15 46
Camden Road	d	13 12	13 19	13 26	13 34	13 42	13 49	13 57	14 04	14 12	14 19	14 27	14 34	14 42	14 52	14 57	15 04	15 12	15 19	15 27	15 34	15 42	15 49
Kentish Town West	d	13 15	13 22	13 29	13 37	13 45	13 52	14 00	14 07	14 15	14 22	14 30	14 37	14 45	14 55	15 00	15 07	15 15	15 22	15 30	15 37	15 45	15 52
Gospel Oak	d	13 19	13 26	13 33	13 41	13 49	13 56	14 04	14 11	14 19	14 26	14 34	14 41	14 49	14 57	15 04	15 11	15 19	15 26	15 34	15 41	15 49	15 56
Hampstead Heath	d	13 21	13 28	13 35	13 44	13 51	13 58	14 06	14 13	14 21	14 28	14 36	14 43	14 51	14 59	15 06	15 13	15 21	15 28	15 36	15 43	15 51	15 58
Finchley Road & Frognal	d	13 23	13 30	13 37	13 46	13 53	14 00	14 08	14 15	14 23	14 30	14 38	14 45	14 53	15 01	15 08	15 15	15 23	15 30	15 38	15 45	15 53	16 00
West Hampstead ⊖	d	13 25	13 32	13 39	13 48	13 55	14 02	14 10	14 17	14 25	14 32	14 40	14 47	14 55	15 03	15 10	15 17	15 25	15 32	15 40	15 47	15 55	16 02
Brondesbury	d	13 26	13 34	13 40	13 49	13 56	14 04	14 11	14 19	14 26	14 34	14 41	14 49	14 56	15 04	15 11	15 19	15 26	15 34	15 41	15 49	15 56	16 04
Brondesbury Park	d	13 28	13 35	13 42	13 51	13 58	14 05	14 13	14 20	14 28	14 35	14 43	14 50	14 58	15 06	15 13	15 20	15 28	15 35	15 43	15 50	15 58	16 05
Kensal Rise	d	13 30	13 37	13 44	13 53	14 00	14 07	14 15	14 22	14 30	14 37	14 45	14 52	15 00	15 08	15 15	15 22	15 30	15 37	15 45	15 52	16 00	16 07
Willesden Jn. High Level ⊖	a	13 34	13 42	13 48	13 57	14 04	14 12	14 19	14 27	14 34	14 42	14 49	14 57	15 04	15 12	15 19	15 27	15 34	15 42	15 49	15 57	16 04	16 12
	d	13 35	13 43	13 49	13 58	14 05	14 13	14 20	14 28	14 35	14 43	14 50	14 58	15 05	15 13	15 20	15 28	15 35	15 43	15 50	15 58	16 05	16 13
Willesden Jn Low Level ⊖	a																						
Shepherd's Bush ⊖66,176	d	13 41		13 56		14 11		14 26		14 41		14 56		15 11		15 26		15 41		15 56		16 11	
Kensington (Olympia) ⊖176	d	13 43		13 58		14 13		14 28		14 43		14 58		15 13		15 28		15 43		15 58		16 13	
West Brompton ⊖176	d	13 46		14 01		14 16		14 31		14 46		15 01		15 16		15 31		15 46		16 01		16 16	
Imperial Wharf 176	d	13 49		14 04		14 19		14 34		14 49		15 04		15 19		15 34		15 49		16 04		16 19	
Clapham Junction 10 66,176	a	13 55		14 12		14 25		14 40		14 55		15 10		15 25		15 40		15 55		16 10		16 25	
Acton Central	d		13 48		14 03		14 18		14 33		14 48		15 03		15 18		15 33		15 48		16 03		16 18
South Acton	d		13 51		14 06		14 21		14 36		14 51		15 06		15 21		15 36		15 51		16 06		16 21
Gunnersbury ⊖	d		13 54		14 09		14 24		14 39		14 54		15 09		15 24		15 39		15 54		16 09		16 24
Kew Gardens ⊖	d		13 57		14 12		14 27		14 42		14 57		15 12		15 27		15 42		15 57		16 12		16 27
Richmond ⊖	a		14 02		14 17		14 32		14 47		15 02		15 17		15 35		15 47		16 02		16 17		16 32

		LO	LO	LO	LO	LO	LO	LO	LO	LO	LO	LO	LO	LO	LO	LO	LO	LO	LO	LO	LO	LO	LO
Stratford 7 ⊖	d	15 38	15 45	15 53	16 00	16 08	16 15	16 23	16 30	16 38	16 45	16 53	17 00	17 08	17 15	17 23	17 30	17 38	17 45	17 53	18 00	18 08	18 15
Hackney Wick	d	15 41	15 48	15 56	16 03	16 11	16 18	16 26	16 33	16 41	16 48	16 56	17 03	17 11	17 18	17 26	17 33	17 41	17 48	17 56	18 03	18 11	18 18
Homerton	d	15 44	15 51	15 59	16 06	16 14	16 21	16 29	16 36	16 44	16 51	16 59	17 06	17 14	17 21	17 29	17 36	17 44	17 51	17 59	18 06	18 14	18 21
Hackney Central	d	15 46	15 53	16 01	16 08	16 16	16 23	16 31	16 38	16 46	16 53	17 01	17 08	17 16	17 23	17 31	17 38	17 46	17 53	18 01	18 08	18 16	18 23
Dalston Kingsland	d	15 48	15 55	16 03	16 10	16 18	16 25	16 33	16 40	16 48	16 55	17 03	17 10	17 18	17 25	17 33	17 40	17 48	17 55	18 03	18 10	18 18	18 25
Canonbury 178	d	15 50	15 57	16 05	16 12	16 20	16 27	16 35	16 42	16 50	16 57	17 05	17 12	17 20	17 27	17 35	17 42	17 50	17 57	18 05	18 12	18 20	18 27
Highbury & Islington ⊖178	d	15 52	15 59	16 07	16 14	16 22	16 29	16 37	16 44	16 52	16 59	17 07	17 14	17 22	17 29	17 37	17 44	17 52	17 59	18 07	18 14	18 22	18 29
Caledonian Rd & Barnsbury	d	15 54	16 01	16 09	16 16	16 24	16 31	16 39	16 46	16 54	17 01	17 09	17 16	17 24	17 31	17 39	17 46	17 54	18 01	18 09	18 16	18 24	18 31
Camden Road	d	15 57	16 04	16 12	16 19	16 27	16 34	16 42	16 49	16 57	17 04	17 12	17 19	17 27	17 34	17 42	17 49	17 57	18 04	18 12	18 19	18 27	18 34
Kentish Town West	d	16 00	16 07	16 15	16 22	16 30	16 37	16 45	16 52	17 00	17 07	17 15	17 22	17 30	17 37	17 45	17 52	18 00	18 07	18 15	18 22	18 30	18 37
Gospel Oak	d	16 04	16 11	16 19	16 26	16 34	16 41	16 49	16 56	17 04	17 11	17 19	17 26	17 34	17 41	17 49	17 56	18 04	18 11	18 19	18 26	18 34	18 41
Hampstead Heath	d	16 06	16 13	16 21	16 28	16 36	16 43	16 51	16 58	17 06	17 13	17 21	17 28	17 36	17 43	17 51	17 58	18 06	18 13	18 21	18 28	18 36	18 43
Finchley Road & Frognal	d	16 08	16 15	16 23	16 30	16 38	16 45	16 53	17 00	17 08	17 15	17 23	17 30	17 38	17 45	17 53	18 00	18 08	18 15	18 23	18 30	18 38	18 45
West Hampstead ⊖	d	16 10	16 17	16 25	16 32	16 40	16 47	16 55	17 02	17 10	17 17	17 25	17 32	17 40	17 47	17 55	18 02	18 10	18 17	18 25	18 32	18 40	18 47
Brondesbury	d	16 11	16 19	16 26	16 34	16 41	16 49	16 56	17 04	17 11	17 19	17 26	17 34	17 41	17 49	17 56	18 04	18 11	18 19	18 26	18 34	18 41	18 49
Brondesbury Park	d	16 13	16 20	16 28	16 35	16 43	16 50	16 58	17 05	17 13	17 20	17 28	17 35	17 43	17 50	17 58	18 05	18 13	18 20	18 28	18 35	18 43	18 50
Kensal Rise	d	16 15	16 22	16 30	16 37	16 45	16 52	17 00	17 07	17 15	17 22	17 30	17 37	17 45	17 52	18 00	18 07	18 15	18 22	18 30	18 37	18 45	18 52
Willesden Jn. High Level ⊖	a	16 19	16 27	16 34	16 42	16 49	16 57	17 04	17 12	17 19	17 27	17 34	17 42	17 49	17 57	18 04	18 12	18 19	18 27	18 34	18 42	18 49	18 57
	d	16 20	16 28	16 35	16 43	16 50	16 58	17 05	17 13	17 20	17 28	17 35	17 43	17 50	17 58	18 05	18 13	18 20	18 28	18 35	18 43	18 50	18 58
Willesden Jn Low Level ⊖	a																						
Shepherd's Bush ⊖66,176	d	16 26		16 41		16 56		17 11		17 26		17 41		17 56		18 11		18 26		18 41		18 56	
Kensington (Olympia) ⊖176	d	16 28		16 43		16 58		17 13		17 28		17 43		17 58		18 13		18 28		18 43		18 58	
West Brompton ⊖176	d	16 31		16 46		17 01		17 16		17 31		17 46		18 01		18 16		18 31		18 46		19 01	
Imperial Wharf 176	d	16 34		16 49		17 04		17 19		17 34		17 49		18 04		18 19		18 34		18 49		19 04	
Clapham Junction 10 66,176	a	16 40		16 55		17 10		17 25		17 40		17 55		18 13		18 28		18 43		18 58		19 10	
Acton Central	d		16 33		16 48		17 03		17 18		17 33		17 48		18 03		18 18		18 33		18 48		19 03
South Acton	d		16 36		16 51		17 06		17 21		17 36		17 51		18 06		18 21		18 36		18 51		19 06
Gunnersbury ⊖	d		16 39		16 54		17 09		17 24		17 39		17 54		18 09		18 24		18 39		18 54		19 09
Kew Gardens ⊖	d		16 42		16 57		17 12		17 27		17 42		17 57		18 12		18 27		18 42		18 57		19 12
Richmond ⊖	a		16 47		17 02		17 17		17 32		17 47		18 02		18 17		18 32		18 47		19 02		19 17

For services between Shepherds Bush and Clapham Junction refer to Table T066 and T176

Table T059-F

Saturdays
26 May to 8 December

Stratford - Highbury & Islington, West Hampstead, Willesden Junction, Clapham Junction and Richmond

Station		LO	LO	LO	LO	LO	LO	LO	LO	LO	LO	LO	LO	LO	LO	LO	LO	LO	LO	LO	LO	LO	LO
Stratford ⊖ ⇌	d	18 23	18 30	18 38	18 45	18 53	19 00	19 08	19 15	19 23	19 30	19 38	19 45	19 53	20 00	20 08	20 15	20 23	20 30	20 38	20 45	20 53	21 00
Hackney Wick	d	18 26	18 33	18 41	18 48	18 56	19 03	19 11	19 18	19 26	19 33	19 41	19 48	19 56	20 03	20 11	20 18	20 26	20 33	20 41	20 48	20 56	21 03
Homerton	d	18 29	18 36	18 44	18 51	18 59	19 06	19 14	19 21	19 29	19 36	19 44	19 51	19 59	20 06	20 14	20 21	20 29	20 36	20 44	20 51	20 59	21 06
Hackney Central	d	18 31	18 38	18 46	18 53	19 01	19 08	19 16	19 23	19 31	19 38	19 46	19 53	20 01	20 08	20 16	20 23	20 31	20 38	20 46	20 53	21 01	21 08
Dalston Kingsland	d	18 33	18 40	18 48	18 55	19 03	19 10	19 18	19 25	19 33	19 40	19 48	19 55	20 03	20 10	20 18	20 25	20 33	20 40	20 48	20 55	21 03	21 10
Canonbury 178	d	18 35	18 42	18 50	18 57	19 05	19 12	19 20	19 27	19 35	19 42	19 50	19 57	20 05	20 12	20 20	20 27	20 35	20 42	20 50	20 57	21 05	21 12
Highbury & Islington ⊖178	d	18 37	18 44	18 52	18 59	19 07	19 14	19 22	19 29	19 37	19 44	19 52	19 59	20 07	20 14	20 22	20 29	20 37	20 44	20 52	20 59	21 07	21 14
Caledonian Rd & Barnsbury	d	18 39	18 46	18 54	19 01	19 09	19 16	19 24	19 31	19 39	19 46	19 54	20 01	20 09	20 16	20 24	20 31	20 39	20 46	20 54	21 01	21 09	21 16
Camden Road	d	18 42	18 49	18 57	19 04	19 12	19 19	19 27	19 34	19 42	19 49	19 57	20 04	20 12	20 19	20 27	20 34	20 42	20 49	20 57	21 04	21 12	21 22
Kentish Town West	d	18 45	18 52	19 00	19 07	19 15	19 22	19 30	19 37	19 45	19 52	20 00	20 07	20 15	20 22	20 30	20 37	20 45	20 52	21 00	21 07	21 15	21 25
Gospel Oak	d	18 49	18 56	19 04	19 11	19 19	19 26	19 32	19 41	19 49	19 56	20 04	20 11	20 19	20 26	20 34	20 41	20 49	20 56	21 04	21 11	21 18	21 27
Hampstead Heath	d	18 51	18 58	19 06	19 13	19 21	19 28	19 34	19 43	19 51	19 58	20 06	20 13	20 21	20 28	20 36	20 43	20 51	20 58	21 06	21 13	21 20	21 29
Finchley Road & Frognal	d	18 53	19 00	19 08	19 15	19 23	19 30	19 36	19 45	19 53	20 00	20 08	20 15	20 23	20 30	20 38	20 45	20 53	21 00	21 08	21 15	21 22	21 31
West Hampstead ⊖	d	18 55	19 02	19 10	19 17	19 25	19 32	19 38	19 47	19 55	20 02	20 10	20 17	20 25	20 32	20 40	20 47	20 55	21 02	21 10	21 17	21 24	21 33
Brondesbury	d	18 56	19 04	19 11	19 19	19 26	19 34	19 39	19 49	19 56	20 04	20 11	20 19	20 26	20 34	20 41	20 49	20 56	21 04	21 11	21 19	21 25	21 35
Brondesbury Park	d	18 58	19 05	19 13	19 20	19 28	19 35	19 41	19 50	19 58	20 05	20 13	20 20	20 28	20 35	20 43	20 50	20 58	21 05	21 13	21 20	21 27	21 36
Kensal Rise	d	19 00	19 07	19 15	19 22	19 30	19 37	19 43	19 52	20 00	20 07	20 15	20 22	20 30	20 37	20 45	20 52	21 00	21 07	21 15	21 22	21 29	21 38
Willesden Jn. High Level ⊖	a	19 04	19 12	19 19	19 27	19 34	19 42	19 47	19 57	20 04	20 12	20 19	20 27	20 34	20 42	20 49	20 57	21 04	21 12	21 19	21 27	21 34	21 45
	d	19 05	19 13	19 20	19 28	19 35	19 43	19 50	19 58	20 05	20 13	20 20	20 28	20 35	20 43	20 50	20 58	21 05	21 13	21 20	21 28	21 35	21 46
Willesden Jn Low Level ⊖	a																						
Shepherd's Bush ⊖66,176	d	19 11		19 26		19 41		19 56		20 11		20 26		20 41		20 56		21 11		21 26		21 41	
Kensington (Olympia) ⊖176	d	19 13		19 28		19 43		19 58		20 13		20 28		20 43		20 58		21 13		21 28		21 43	
West Brompton ⊖176	d	19 16		19 31		19 46		20 01		20 16		20 31		20 46		21 01		21 16		21 31		21 46	
Imperial Wharf 176	d	19 19		19 34		19 49		20 04		20 19		20 34		20 49		21 04		21 19		21 34		21 49	
Clapham Junction 10 66,176	a	19 25		19 40		19 55		20 10		20 25		20 40		20 55		21 10		21 25		21 40		21 55	
Acton Central	d		19 18		19 33		19 48		20 03		20 18		20 33		20 48		21 03		21 18		21 33		21 52
South Acton	d		19 21		19 36		19 51		20 06		20 21		20 36		20 51		21 06		21 21		21 36		21 55
Gunnersbury ⊖	d		19 24		19 39		19 54		20 09		20 24		20 39		20 54		21 09		21 24		21 39		22 00
Kew Gardens ⊖	d		19 27		19 42		19 57		20 12		20 27		20 42		20 57		21 12		21 27		21 42		22 03
Richmond ⊖	a		19 32		19 47		20 02		20 17		20 32		20 47		21 02		21 17		21 32		21 47		22 07

Station		LO	LO	LO	LO	LO	LO	LO	LO	LO	LO	LO	LO	LO	LO	LO	LO	LO	LO	LO	LO	LO	
Stratford ⊖ ⇌	d	21 08	21 15	21 23	21 30	21 38	21 45	21 53	22 00	22 08	22 15		22 30	22 38	22 45		23 00	23 08	23 15	23 30	23 45	23 59	
Hackney Wick	d	21 11	21 18	21 26	21 33	21 41	21 48	21 56	22 03	22 11	22 18		22 33	22 41	22 48		23 03	23 11	23 18	23 33	23 48	00 02	
Homerton	d	21 14	21 21	21 29	21 36	21 44	21 51	21 59	22 06	22 14	22 21		22 36	22 44	22 51		23 06	23 14	23 21	23 36	23 51	00 05	
Hackney Central	d	21 16	21 23	21 31	21 38	21 46	21 53	22 01	22 08	22 16	22 23		22 38	22 46	22 53		23 08	23 16	23 23	23 38	23 53	00 07	
Dalston Kingsland	d	21 18	21 25	21 33	21 40	21 48	21 55	22 03	22 10	22 18	22 25		22 40	22 48	22 55		23 10	23 18	23 25	23 40	23 55	00 09	
Canonbury 178	d	21 20	21 27	21 35	21 42	21 50	21 57	22 05	22 12	22 20	22 27		22 42	22 50	22 57		23 12	23 20	23 27	23 42	23 57	00 11	
Highbury & Islington ⊖178	d	21 22	21 29	21 37	21 44	21 52	21 59	22 07	22 14	22 22	22 29		22 44	22 52	22 59		23 14	23 22	23 29	23 44	23 59	00 13	
Caledonian Rd & Barnsbury	d	21 24	21 31	21 39	21 46	21 54	22 01	22 09	22 16	22 24	22 31		22 46	22 54	23 01		23 16	23 24	23 31	23 46	00 02	00 15	
Camden Road	d	21 27	21 34	21 42	21 50	21 57	22 04	22 12	22 19	22 27	22 34		22 49	22 57	23 04		23 19	23 27	23 34	23 49	00 04	00 18	
Kentish Town West	d	21 30	21 37	21 45	21 53	22 00	22 07	22 15	22 22	22 30	22 37		22 52	23 00	23 07		23 22	23 30	23 37	23 52	00 07	00 21	
Gospel Oak	d	21 34	21 41	21 49	21 57	22 04	22 11	22 19	22 26	22 34	22 41		22 56	23 04	23 11		23 25	23 34	23 41	23 56	00 11	00 25	
Hampstead Heath	d	21 36	21 43	21 51	22 01	22 06	22 13	22 21	22 28	22 36	22 43		22 58	23 07	23 13		23 27	23 36	23 43	23 58	00 13	00 27	
Finchley Road & Frognal	d	21 38	21 45	21 53	22 03	22 08	22 15	22 23	22 30	22 38	22 45		23 00	23 09	23 15		23 29	23 38	23 45	00 01	00 15	00 29	
West Hampstead ⊖	d	21 40	21 47	21 55	22 05	22 10	22 17	22 25	22 32	22 40	22 47		23 02	23 11	23 17		23 31	23 40	23 47	00 02	00 17	00 31	
Brondesbury	d	21 41	21 49	21 56	22 06	22 11	22 19	22 26	22 34	22 41	22 49		23 04	23 12	23 19		23 33	23 41	23 49	00 04	00 19	00 33	
Brondesbury Park	d	21 43	21 50	21 58	22 08	22 13	22 20	22 28	22 35	22 43	22 50		23 05	23 14	23 20		23 34	23 43	23 50	00 05	00 20	00 34	
Kensal Rise	d	21 45	21 52	22 00	22 10	22 15	22 22	22 30	22 37	22 45	22 52		23 07	23 16	23 22		23 36	23 45	23 52	00 07	00 22	00 36	
Willesden Jn. High Level ⊖	a	21 49	21 57	22 04	22 13	22 19	22 27	22 34	22 42	22 49	22 57		23 11	23 19	23 27		23 39	23 49	23 57	00 13		00 42	
	d	21 50	21 58	22 05	22 14	22 20	22 28	22 35	22 43	22 50	22 58	23 05	23 13	23 20	23 28	23 35	23 40	23 50	23 58				
Willesden Jn Low Level ⊖	a																				00 32		
Shepherd's Bush ⊖66,176	d	21 57		22 11		22 26		22 41		22 56		23 11		23 26		23 41		23 56					
Kensington (Olympia) ⊖176	d	21 59		22 13		22 28		22 43		22 58		23 13		23 28		23 43		23 58					
West Brompton ⊖176	d	22 01		22 16		22 31		22 46		23 01		23 16		23 31		23 46		00 02					
Imperial Wharf 176	d	22 04		22 19		22 34		22 49		23 04		23 19		23 34		23 49		00 05					
Clapham Junction 10 66,176	a	22 10		22 25		22 40		22 55		23 10		23 26		23 40		23 56		00 10					
Acton Central	d		22 03		22 19		22 33		22 48		23 03		23 18		23 33		23 45		00 03				
South Acton	d		22 06		22 22		22 36		22 51		23 06		23 21		23 36		23 48		00 06				
Gunnersbury ⊖	d		22 09		22 25		22 39		22 54		23 09		23 24		23 39		23 51		00 09				
Kew Gardens ⊖	d		22 12		22 28		22 42		22 57		23 12		23 27		23 42		23 54		00 12				
Richmond ⊖	a		22 17		22 32		22 47		23 02		23 17		23 32		23 47		23 58		00 17				

For services between Shepherds Bush and Clapham Junction refer to Table T066 and T176

Table T059-F

Sundays
20 May to 2 December

Stratford - Highbury & Islington, West Hampstead, Willesden Junction, Clapham Junction and Richmond

Station		LO	LO	LO	LO	LO	LO	LO	LO	LO	LO	LO	LO	LO	LO	LO	LO	LO	LO	LO	LO	LO	LO
Stratford ⊖ ⇌	d								00 15								09 05	09 13		09 28	09 35	09 43	09 50
Hackney Wick	d						00 02		00 18								09 08	09 16		09 31	09 38	09 46	09 53
Homerton	d						00 05		00 21								09 11	09 19		09 34	09 41	09 49	09 56
Hackney Central	d						00 07		00 23								09 13	09 21		09 36	09 43	09 51	09 58
Dalston Kingsland	d						00 09		00 25								09 15	09 23		09 38	09 45	09 53	10 00
Canonbury 178	d						00 11		00 27								09 17	09 25		09 40	09 47	09 55	10 02
Highbury & Islington ⊖178	d						00 13		00 29								09 19	09 27		09 42	09 49	09 57	10 04
Caledonian Rd & Barnsbury	d					00 02	00 15		00 31								09 21	09 29		09 44	09 51	09 59	10 06
Camden Road	d					00 04	00 18		00 34								09 24	09 32		09 47	09 54	10 02	10 09
Kentish Town West	d					00 07	00 21		00 37								09 27	09 35		09 50	09 57	10 05	10 12
Gospel Oak	d					00 11	00 25		00 40								09 31	09 39		09 54	10 01	10 09	10 16
Hampstead Heath	d					00 13	00 27		00 42								09 33	09 41		09 56	10 03	10 11	10 18
Finchley Road & Frognal	d				00 01	00 15	00 29		00 44								09 35	09 43		09 58	10 05	10 13	10 20
West Hampstead ⊖	d				00 02	00 17	00 31		00 46								09 37	09 45		10 00	10 07	10 15	10 22
Brondesbury	d				00 04	00 19	00 33		00 48								09 38	09 46		10 01	10 08	10 16	10 23
Brondesbury Park	d				00 05	00 20	00 34		00 49								09 40	09 48		10 03	10 10	10 18	10 25
Kensal Rise	d				00 07	00 22	00 36		00 51								09 42	09 50		10 05	10 12	10 20	10 27
Willesden Jn. High Level ⊖	a				00 13		00 42										09 47	09 55		10 10	10 16	10 25	10 31
	d			00 05				08 35		08 47	08 56	09 05	09 20	09 26	09 32	09 43	09 48	09 56	10 02	10 11	10 17	10 26	10 32
Willesden Jn Low Level ⊖	a					00 32			01 02														
Shepherd's Bush ⊖66,176	d			00 11				08 41		08 53		09 11	09 26		09 38		09 54		10 08		10 23		10 38
Kensington (Olympia) ⊖176	d			00 13				08 43		08 55		09 13	09 28		09 40		09 56		10 10		10 25		10 40
West Brompton ⊖176	d	00 02		00 16				08 46		08 58		09 16	09 31		09 43		09 59		10 13		10 28		10 43
Imperial Wharf 176	d	00 05		00 19				08 49		09 01		09 19	09 34		09 46		10 02		10 16		10 31		10 46
Clapham Junction 10 66,176	a	00 10		00 26				08 56		09 08		09 26	09 41		09 53		10 08		10 24		10 37		10 52
Acton Central	d		00 03								09 01			09 31		09 48		10 01		10 16		10 31	
South Acton	d		00 06								09 05			09 35		09 50		10 05		10 19		10 35	
Gunnersbury ⊖	d		00 09								09 08			09 38		09 53		10 08		10 22		10 38	
Kew Gardens ⊖	d		00 12								09 11			09 41		09 56		10 11		10 25		10 41	
Richmond ⊖	a		00 17								09 20			09 50		10 05		10 16		10 30		10 46	

Station		LO	LO	LO	LO		LO	LO	LO	LO	LO	LO	LO	LO	LO	LO	LO	LO	LO	LO	LO	LO	LO
Stratford ⊖ ⇌	d	09 58	10 05	10 13	10 20		12 28	12 35	12 43	12 50	12 58	13 05	13 13	13 20	13 28	13 35	13 43	13 50	13 58	14 05	14 13	14 20	14 28
Hackney Wick	d	10 01	10 08	10 16	10 23		12 31	12 38	12 46	12 53	13 01	13 08	13 16	13 23	13 31	13 38	13 46	13 53	14 01	14 08	14 16	14 23	14 31
Homerton	d	10 04	10 11	10 19	10 26		12 34	12 41	12 49	12 56	13 04	13 11	13 19	13 26	13 34	13 41	13 49	13 56	14 04	14 11	14 19	14 26	14 34
Hackney Central	d	10 06	10 13	10 21	10 28		12 36	12 43	12 51	12 58	13 06	13 13	13 21	13 28	13 36	13 43	13 51	13 58	14 06	14 13	14 21	14 28	14 36
Dalston Kingsland	d	10 08	10 15	10 23	10 30		12 38	12 45	12 53	13 00	13 08	13 15	13 23	13 30	13 38	13 45	13 53	14 00	14 08	14 15	14 23	14 30	14 38
Canonbury 178	d	10 10	10 17	10 25	10 32		12 40	12 47	12 55	13 02	13 10	13 17	13 25	13 32	13 40	13 47	13 55	14 02	14 10	14 17	14 26	14 32	14 40
Highbury & Islington ⊖178	d	10 12	10 19	10 27	10 34		12 42	12 49	12 57	13 04	13 12	13 19	13 27	13 34	13 42	13 49	13 57	14 04	14 12	14 19	14 29	14 34	14 42
Caledonian Rd & Barnsbury	d	10 14	10 21	10 29	10 36		12 44	12 51	12 59	13 06	13 14	13 21	13 29	13 36	13 44	13 51	13 59	14 06	14 14	14 21	14 31	14 36	14 44
Camden Road	d	10 17	10 24	10 32	10 39		12 47	12 54	13 02	13 09	13 17	13 24	13 32	13 39	13 47	13 54	14 02	14 09	14 17	14 24	14 34	14 39	14 47
Kentish Town West	d	10 20	10 27	10 35	10 42		12 50	12 57	13 05	13 12	13 20	13 27	13 35	13 42	13 50	13 57	14 05	14 12	14 20	14 27	14 36	14 42	14 50
Gospel Oak	d	10 24	10 31	10 39	10 46	and at	12 54	13 01	13 09	13 16	13 24	13 31	13 39	13 46	13 54	14 01	14 09	14 16	14 24	14 31	14 39	14 46	14 54
Hampstead Heath	d	10 26	10 33	10 41	10 48	the same	12 56	13 03	13 11	13 18	13 26	13 33	13 41	13 48	13 56	14 03	14 11	14 18	14 26	14 33	14 41	14 48	14 56
Finchley Road & Frognal	d	10 28	10 35	10 43	10 50	minutes	12 58	13 05	13 13	13 20	13 28	13 35	13 43	13 50	13 58	14 05	14 13	14 20	14 28	14 35	14 43	14 50	14 58
West Hampstead ⊖	d	10 30	10 37	10 45	10 52	past	13 00	13 07	13 15	13 22	13 30	13 37	13 45	13 52	14 00	14 07	14 15	14 22	14 30	14 37	14 45	14 52	15 00
Brondesbury	d	10 31	10 38	10 46	10 53	each	13 01	13 08	13 16	13 23	13 31	13 38	13 46	13 53	14 01	14 08	14 16	14 23	14 31	14 38	14 46	14 53	15 01
Brondesbury Park	d	10 33	10 40	10 48	10 55	hour until	13 03	13 10	13 18	13 25	13 33	13 40	13 48	13 55	14 03	14 10	14 18	14 25	14 33	14 40	14 48	14 55	15 03
Kensal Rise	d	10 35	10 42	10 50	10 57		13 05	13 12	13 20	13 27	13 35	13 42	13 50	13 57	14 05	14 12	14 20	14 27	14 35	14 42	14 50	14 57	15 05
Willesden Jn. High Level ⊖	a	10 40	10 46	10 55	11 01		13 10	13 16	13 25	13 31	13 40	13 46	13 55	14 01	14 10	14 16	14 25	14 31	14 40	14 46	14 55	15 01	15 10
	d	10 41	10 47	10 56	11 02		13 11	13 17	13 26	13 32	13 41	13 47	13 56	14 02	14 11	14 17	14 26	14 32	14 41	14 47	14 56	15 02	15 11
Willesden Jn Low Level ⊖	a																						
Shepherd's Bush ⊖66,176	d		10 53		11 08			13 23		13 38		13 53		14 08		14 23		14 38		14 53		15 08	
Kensington (Olympia) ⊖176	d		10 55		11 10			13 25		13 40		13 55		14 10		14 25		14 40		14 55		15 10	
West Brompton ⊖176	d		10 58		11 13			13 28		13 43		13 58		14 13		14 28		14 43		14 58		15 13	
Imperial Wharf 176	d		11 01		11 16			13 31		13 46		14 01		14 16		14 31		14 46		15 01		15 16	
Clapham Junction 10 66,176	a		11 07		11 22			13 37		13 52		14 07		14 22		14 37		14 52		15 07		15 22	
Acton Central	d	10 46		11 01			13 16		13 31		13 46		14 01		14 16		14 31		14 46		15 01		15 16
South Acton	d	10 49		11 05			13 19		13 35		13 49		14 05		14 19		14 35		14 49		15 05		15 19
Gunnersbury ⊖	d	10 52		11 08			13 22		13 38		13 52		14 08		14 22		14 38		14 52		15 08		15 22
Kew Gardens ⊖	d	10 55		11 11			13 25		13 41		13 55		14 11		14 25		14 41		14 55		15 11		15 25
Richmond ⊖	a	11 00		11 16			13 30		13 46		14 00		14 16		14 30		14 46		15 00		15 16		15 30

For services between Shepherds Bush and Clapham Junction refer to Table T066 and T176

Table T059-F

Sundays

20 May to 2 December

Stratford - Highbury & Islington, West Hampstead, Willesden Junction, Clapham Junction and Richmond

	LO	LO	LO	LO	LO	LO	LO	LO	LO	LO	LO	LO	LO	LO	LO	LO	LO	LO	LO	LO	LO	LO
Stratford 7 ⊖ d	14 35	14 43	14 50	14 58	15 05	15 13	15 20	15 28	15 35	15 43	15 50	15 58	16 05	16 13	16 20	16 28	16 35	16 43	16 50	16 58	17 05	17 13
Hackney Wick d	14 38	14 46	14 53	15 01	15 08	15 16	15 23	15 31	15 38	15 46	15 53	16 01	16 08	16 16	16 23	16 31	16 38	16 46	16 53	17 01	17 08	17 16
Homerton d	14 41	14 49	14 56	15 04	15 11	15 19	15 26	15 34	15 41	15 49	15 56	16 04	16 11	16 19	16 26	16 34	16 41	16 49	16 56	17 04	17 11	17 19
Hackney Central d	14 43	14 51	14 58	15 06	15 13	15 21	15 28	15 36	15 43	15 51	15 58	16 06	16 13	16 21	16 28	16 36	16 43	16 51	16 58	17 06	17 13	17 21
Dalston Kingsland d	14 45	14 53	15 00	15 08	15 15	15 23	15 30	15 38	15 45	15 53	16 00	16 08	16 15	16 23	16 30	16 38	16 45	16 53	17 00	17 08	17 15	17 23
Canonbury 178 d	14 47	14 55	15 02	15 10	15 17	15 25	15 32	15 40	15 47	15 55	16 02	16 10	16 17	16 25	16 32	16 40	16 47	16 55	17 02	17 10	17 17	17 25
Highbury & Islington ⊖178 d	14 49	14 57	15 04	15 12	15 19	15 27	15 34	15 42	15 49	15 57	16 04	16 12	16 19	16 27	16 34	16 42	16 49	16 57	17 04	17 12	17 19	17 27
Caledonian Rd & Barnsbury d	14 51	14 59	15 06	15 14	15 21	15 29	15 36	15 44	15 51	15 59	16 06	16 14	16 21	16 29	16 36	16 44	16 51	16 59	17 06	17 14	17 21	17 29
Camden Road d	14 54	15 02	15 09	15 17	15 24	15 32	15 39	15 47	15 54	16 02	16 09	16 17	16 24	16 32	16 39	16 47	16 54	17 02	17 09	17 17	17 24	17 32
Kentish Town West d	14 57	15 05	15 12	15 20	15 27	15 35	15 42	15 50	15 57	16 05	16 12	16 20	16 27	16 35	16 42	16 50	16 57	17 05	17 12	17 20	17 27	17 35
Gospel Oak d	15 01	15 09	15 16	15 24	15 31	15 39	15 46	15 54	16 01	16 09	16 16	16 24	16 31	16 39	16 46	16 54	17 01	17 09	17 16	17 24	17 31	17 39
Hampstead Heath d	15 03	15 11	15 18	15 26	15 33	15 41	15 48	15 56	16 03	16 11	16 18	16 26	16 33	16 41	16 48	16 56	17 03	17 11	17 18	17 26	17 33	17 41
Finchley Road & Frognal d	15 05	15 13	15 20	15 28	15 35	15 43	15 50	15 58	16 05	16 13	16 20	16 28	16 35	16 43	16 50	16 58	17 05	17 13	17 20	17 28	17 35	17 43
West Hampstead ⊖ d	15 07	15 15	15 22	15 30	15 37	15 45	15 52	16 00	16 07	16 15	16 22	16 30	16 37	16 45	16 52	17 00	17 07	17 15	17 22	17 30	17 37	17 45
Brondesbury d	15 08	15 16	15 23	15 31	15 38	15 46	15 53	16 01	16 08	16 16	16 23	16 31	16 38	16 46	16 53	17 01	17 08	17 16	17 23	17 31	17 38	17 46
Brondesbury Park d	15 10	15 18	15 25	15 33	15 40	15 48	15 55	16 03	16 10	16 18	16 25	16 33	16 40	16 48	16 55	17 03	17 10	17 18	17 25	17 33	17 40	17 48
Kensal Rise d	15 12	15 20	15 27	15 35	15 42	15 50	15 57	16 05	16 12	16 20	16 27	16 35	16 42	16 50	16 57	17 05	17 12	17 20	17 27	17 35	17 42	17 50
Willesden Jn. High Level ⊖ a	15 16	15 25	15 31	15 40	15 46	15 55	16 01	16 10	16 16	16 25	16 31	16 40	16 46	16 55	17 01	17 10	17 16	17 25	17 31	17 40	17 46	17 55
d	15 17	15 26	15 32	15 41	15 47	15 56	16 02	16 11	16 17	16 26	16 32	16 41	16 47	16 56	17 02	17 11	17 17	17 26	17 32	17 41	17 47	17 56
Willesden Jn Low Level ⊖ a																						
Shepherd's Bush ⊖66,176 d	15 23		15 38		15 53		16 08		16 23		16 38		16 53		17 08		17 23		17 38		17 53	
Kensington (Olympia) ⊖176 d	15 25		15 40		15 55		16 10		16 25		16 40		16 55		17 10		17 25		17 40		17 55	
West Brompton ⊖176 d	15 28		15 43		15 58		16 13		16 28		16 43		16 58		17 13		17 28		17 43		17 58	
Imperial Wharf 176 d	15 31		15 46		16 01		16 16		16 31		16 46		17 01		17 16		17 31		17 46		18 01	
Clapham Junction 10 66,176 a	15 37		15 52		16 07		16 22		16 37		16 52		17 10		17 25		17 40		17 55		18 10	
Acton Central d		15 31		15 46		16 01		16 16		16 31		16 46		17 01		17 16		17 31		17 46		18 01
South Acton d		15 35		15 49		16 05		16 19		16 35		16 49		17 05		17 19		17 35		17 49		18 05
Gunnersbury ⊖ d		15 38		15 52		16 08		16 22		16 38		16 52		17 08		17 22		17 38		17 52		18 08
Kew Gardens ⊖ d		15 41		15 55		16 11		16 25		16 41		16 55		17 11		17 25		17 41		17 55		18 11
Richmond ⊖ a		15 46		16 00		16 16		16 30		16 46		17 00		17 16		17 30		17 46		18 00		18 16

	LO	LO	LO	LO	LO	LO	LO	LO	LO	LO	LO	LO	LO	LO	LO	LO	LO	LO	LO	LO	LO	LO
Stratford 7 ⊖ d	17 20	17 28	17 35	17 43	17 50	17 58	18 05	18 13	18 20	18 28	18 35	18 43	18 50	18 58	19 05	19 13	19 20	19 28	19 35	19 43	19 50	19 58
Hackney Wick d	17 23	17 31	17 38	17 46	17 53	18 01	18 08	18 16	18 23	18 31	18 38	18 46	18 53	19 01	19 08	19 16	19 23	19 31	19 38	19 46	19 53	20 01
Homerton d	17 26	17 34	17 41	17 49	17 56	18 04	18 11	18 19	18 26	18 34	18 41	18 49	18 56	19 04	19 11	19 19	19 26	19 34	19 41	19 49	19 56	20 04
Hackney Central d	17 28	17 36	17 43	17 51	17 58	18 06	18 13	18 21	18 28	18 36	18 43	18 51	18 58	19 06	19 13	19 21	19 28	19 36	19 43	19 51	19 58	20 06
Dalston Kingsland d	17 30	17 38	17 45	17 53	18 00	18 08	18 15	18 23	18 30	18 38	18 45	18 53	19 00	19 08	19 15	19 23	19 30	19 38	19 45	19 53	20 00	20 08
Canonbury 178 d	17 32	17 40	17 47	17 55	18 02	18 10	18 17	18 25	18 32	18 40	18 47	18 55	19 02	19 10	19 17	19 25	19 32	19 40	19 47	19 55	20 02	20 10
Highbury & Islington ⊖178 d	17 34	17 42	17 49	17 57	18 04	18 12	18 19	18 27	18 34	18 42	18 49	18 57	19 04	19 12	19 19	19 27	19 34	19 42	19 49	19 57	20 04	20 12
Caledonian Rd & Barnsbury d	17 36	17 44	17 51	17 59	18 06	18 14	18 21	18 29	18 36	18 44	18 51	18 59	19 06	19 14	19 21	19 29	19 36	19 44	19 51	19 59	20 06	20 14
Camden Road d	17 39	17 47	17 54	18 02	18 09	18 17	18 24	18 32	18 39	18 47	18 54	19 02	19 09	19 17	19 24	19 32	19 39	19 49	19 54	20 02	20 09	20 17
Kentish Town West d	17 42	17 50	17 57	18 05	18 12	18 20	18 27	18 35	18 42	18 50	18 57	19 05	19 12	19 20	19 27	19 35	19 42	19 51	19 57	20 05	20 12	20 20
Gospel Oak d	17 46	17 54	18 01	18 09	18 16	18 24	18 31	18 39	18 46	18 54	19 01	19 09	19 16	19 24	19 31	19 39	19 45	19 55	20 01	20 09	20 16	20 24
Hampstead Heath d	17 48	17 56	18 03	18 11	18 18	18 26	18 33	18 41	18 48	18 56	19 03	19 11	19 18	19 26	19 33	19 41	19 47	19 57	20 03	20 11	20 18	20 26
Finchley Road & Frognal d	17 50	17 58	18 05	18 13	18 20	18 28	18 35	18 43	18 50	18 58	19 05	19 13	19 20	19 28	19 35	19 43	19 49	19 59	20 05	20 13	20 20	20 28
West Hampstead ⊖ d	17 52	18 00	18 07	18 15	18 22	18 30	18 37	18 45	18 52	19 00	19 07	19 15	19 22	19 30	19 37	19 45	19 51	20 01	20 07	20 15	20 22	20 30
Brondesbury d	17 53	18 01	18 08	18 16	18 23	18 31	18 38	18 46	18 53	19 01	19 08	19 16	19 23	19 31	19 38	19 46	19 52	20 02	20 08	20 16	20 23	20 31
Brondesbury Park d	17 55	18 03	18 10	18 18	18 25	18 33	18 40	18 48	18 55	19 03	19 10	19 18	19 25	19 33	19 40	19 48	19 54	20 04	20 10	20 18	20 25	20 33
Kensal Rise d	17 57	18 05	18 12	18 20	18 27	18 35	18 42	18 50	18 57	19 05	19 12	19 20	19 27	19 35	19 42	19 50	19 56	20 06	20 12	20 20	20 27	20 35
Willesden Jn. High Level ⊖ a	18 01	18 10	18 16	18 25	18 31	18 40	18 46	18 55	19 01	19 10	19 16	19 25	19 31	19 40	19 46	19 55	20 00	20 10	20 16	20 25	20 31	20 40
d	18 02	18 11	18 17	18 26	18 32	18 41	18 47	18 56	19 02	19 11	19 17	19 26	19 32	19 41	19 47	19 56	20 01	20 11	20 17	20 26	20 32	20 41
Willesden Jn Low Level ⊖ a																						
Shepherd's Bush ⊖66,176 d	18 08		18 23		18 38		18 53		19 08		19 23		19 38		19 53		20 08		20 23		20 38	
Kensington (Olympia) ⊖176 d	18 10		18 25		18 40		18 55		19 10		19 25		19 40		19 55		20 10		20 25		20 40	
West Brompton ⊖176 d	18 13		18 28		18 43		18 58		19 13		19 28		19 43		19 58		20 13		20 28		20 43	
Imperial Wharf 176 d	18 16		18 31		18 46		19 01		19 16		19 31		19 46		20 01		20 16		20 31		20 46	
Clapham Junction 10 66,176 a	18 22		18 37		18 52		19 07		19 22		19 37		19 52		20 07		20 22		20 37		20 52	
Acton Central d		18 16		18 31		18 46		19 01		19 16		19 31		19 46		20 01		20 16		20 31		20 46
South Acton d		18 19		18 35		18 49		19 05		19 19		19 35		19 49		20 05		20 19		20 35		20 49
Gunnersbury ⊖ d		18 22		18 38		18 52		19 08		19 22		19 38		19 52		20 08		20 22		20 38		20 52
Kew Gardens ⊖ d		18 25		18 41		18 55		19 11		19 25		19 41		19 55		20 11		20 25		20 41		20 55
Richmond ⊖ a		18 30		18 46		19 00		19 16		19 30		19 46		20 00		20 16		20 30		20 46		21 00

For services between Shepherds Bush and Clapham Junction refer to Table T066 and T176

Table T059-F

Sundays

20 May to 2 December

Stratford - Highbury & Islington, West Hampstead, Willesden Junction, Clapham Junction and Richmond

	LO	LO	LO	LO	LO	LO	LO	LO	LO	LO	LO	LO	LO	LO	LO	LO	LO	LO	LO	LO	LO	LO
Stratford 7 ⊖ d	20 05	20 13	20 20	20 28	20 35	20 43	20 50	20 58	21 05	21 13		21 28	21 35	21 44		21 58	22 05	22 15		22 30		22 45
Hackney Wick d	20 08	20 16	20 23	20 31	20 38	20 46	20 53	21 01	21 08	21 16		21 31	21 38	21 47		22 01	22 08	22 18		22 33		22 48
Homerton d	20 11	20 19	20 26	20 34	20 41	20 49	20 56	21 04	21 11	21 19		21 34	21 41	21 50		22 04	22 11	22 21		22 36		22 51
Hackney Central d	20 13	20 21	20 28	20 36	20 43	20 51	20 58	21 06	21 13	21 21		21 36	21 43	21 52		22 06	22 13	22 23		22 38		22 53
Dalston Kingsland d	20 15	20 23	20 30	20 38	20 45	20 53	21 00	21 08	21 15	21 23		21 38	21 45	21 54		22 08	22 15	22 25		22 40		22 55
Canonbury 178 d	20 17	20 25	20 32	20 40	20 47	20 55	21 02	21 10	21 17	21 25		21 40	21 47	21 56		22 10	22 17	22 27		22 42		22 57
Highbury & Islington ⊖178 d	20 19	20 27	20 34	20 42	20 49	20 57	21 04	21 12	21 19	21 27		21 42	21 49	21 58		22 12	22 19	22 31		22 44		22 59
Caledonian Rd & Barnsbury d	20 21	20 29	20 36	20 44	20 51	20 59	21 06	21 14	21 21	21 29		21 44	21 51	22 00		22 14	22 21	22 33		22 46		23 01
Camden Road d	20 24	20 32	20 39	20 47	20 54	21 02	21 09	21 17	21 24	21 32		21 47	21 54	22 03		22 17	22 24	22 36		22 49		23a07
Kentish Town West d	20 27	20 35	20 42	20 50	20 57	21 05	21 12	21 20	21 27	21 35		21 50	21 57	22 06		22 20	22 27	22 39		22 52		
Gospel Oak d	20 31	20 39	20 46	20 54	21 01	21 09	21 16	21 24	21 30	21 39		21 54	22 01	22 10		22 24	22 31	22 41		22 56		
Hampstead Heath d	20 33	20 41	20 48	20 56	21 03	21 11	21 18	21 26	21 32	21 41		21 56	22 03	22 12		22 26	22 33	22 43		22 58		
Finchley Road & Frognal d	20 35	20 43	20 50	20 58	21 05	21 13	21 20	21 28	21 34	21 43		21 58	22 05	22 14		22 28	22 35	22 45		23 00		
West Hampstead ⊖ d	20 37	20 45	20 52	21 00	21 07	21 15	21 22	21 30	21 36	21 45		22 00	22 07	22 16		22 30	22 37	22 47		23 02		
Brondesbury d	20 38	20 46	20 53	21 01	21 08	21 16	21 23	21 31	21 37	21 46		22 01	22 08	22 17		22 31	22 38	22 48		23 03		
Brondesbury Park d	20 40	20 48	20 55	21 03	21 10	21 18	21 25	21 33	21 39	21 48		22 03	22 10	22 19		22 33	22 40	22 50		23 05		
Kensal Rise d	20 42	20 50	20 57	21 05	21 12	21 20	21 27	21 35	21 41	21 50		22 05	22 12	22 21		22 35	22 42	22 52		23 07		
Willesden Jn. High Level ⊖ a	20 46	20 55	21 01	21 10	21 16	21 25	21 31	21 40	21 45	21 55		22 10	22 16	22 26		22 40	22 46	22 57		23 11		
d	20 47	20 56	21 02	21 11	21 17	21 26	21 32	21 41	21 46	21 56	22 02	22 11	22 17	22 27	22 32	22 41	22 47	22 58	23 02	23 12	23 17	
Willesden Jn Low Level ⊖ a																						
Shepherd's Bush ⊖66,176 d	20 53		21 08		21 23		21 38		21 53		22 08		22 23		22 38		22 53		23 08		23 23	
Kensington (Olympia) ⊖176 d	20 55		21 10		21 25		21 40		21 55		22 10		22 25		22 40		22 55		23 10		23 25	
West Brompton ⊖176 d	20 58		21 13		21 28		21 43		21 58		22 13		22 28		22 43		22 58		23 13		23 28	
Imperial Wharf 176 d	21 01		21 16		21 31		21 46		22 01		22 16		22 31		22 46		23 01		23 16		23 31	
Clapham Junction 10 66,176 a	21 07		21 22		21 37		21 52		22 07		22 23		22 37		22 53		23 07		23 23		23 38	
Acton Central d		21 01		21 16		21 31		21 46		22 01		22 16		22 32		22 46		23 03		23 18		
South Acton d		21 05		21 19		21 35		21 49		22 05		22 19		22 35		22 49		23 06		23 21		
Gunnersbury ⊖ d		21 08		21 22		21 38		21 52		22 08		22 22		22 38		22 52		23 09		23 24		
Kew Gardens ⊖ d		21 11		21 25		21 41		21 55		22 11		22 25		22 41		22 55		23 12		23 27		
Richmond ⊖ a		21 16		21 30		21 46		22 00		22 16		22 30		22 46		23 00		23 17		23 32		

	LO	LO	LO	LO
Stratford 7 ⊖ d	23 00			
Hackney Wick d	23 03			
Homerton d	23 06			
Hackney Central d	23 08			
Dalston Kingsland d	23 10			
Canonbury 178 d	23 12			
Highbury & Islington ⊖178 d	23 14			
Caledonian Rd & Barnsbury d	23 16			
Camden Road d	23 19			
Kentish Town West d	23 22			
Gospel Oak d	23 26			
Hampstead Heath d	23 28			
Finchley Road & Frognal d	23 30			
West Hampstead ⊖ d	23 32			
Brondesbury d	23 34			
Brondesbury Park d	23 35			
Kensal Rise d	23 37			
Willesden Jn. High Level ⊖ a				
d		23 32	23 47	23 59
Willesden Jn Low Level ⊖ a	23 50			
Shepherd's Bush ⊖66,176 d		23 38	23 53	00 05
Kensington (Olympia) ⊖176 d		23 40	23 55	00 07
West Brompton ⊖176 d		23 43	23 58	00 10
Imperial Wharf 176 d		23 46	00a01	00a13
Clapham Junction 10 66,176 a		23 53		
Acton Central d				
South Acton d				
Gunnersbury ⊖ d				
Kew Gardens ⊖ d				
Richmond ⊖ a				

For services between Shepherds Bush and Clapham Junction refer to Table T066 and T176

Table T059-R

Mondays to Fridays

21 May to 7 December

Richmond and Clapham Junction - Willesden Junction, West Hampstead, Highbury & Islington and Stratford

Miles	Miles	Station		LO MX	LO	LO	LO	LO	LO	LO	LO	LO	LO	LO	LO	LO	LO	LO	LO	LO	LO	LO	LO
0	—	**Richmond** ⊖	d				05 54		06 08			06 34		06 45	06 57		07 09			07 34		07 45	07 57
1½	—	Kew Gardens ⊖	d				05 57		06 11			06 37		06 48	07 00		07 13			07 37		07 48	08 00
2½	—	Gunnersbury ⊖	d				06 00		06 14			06 40		06 51	07 03		07 16			07 40		07 51	08 03
3	—	South Acton	d				06 03		06 17			06 43		06 54	07 06		07 19			07 43		07 54	08 06
3¾	—	Acton Central	d				06 06		06 20			06 46		06 57	07 09		07 22			07 46		07 57	08 09
—	0	**Clapham Junction** 10 66,176	d							06 12	06 25		06 36			07 01		07 13	07 25		07 36		
—	1½	Imperial Wharf 176	d					06 04		06 16	06 29		06 40			07 05		07 17	07 29		07 40		
—	2½	West Brompton ⊖176	d					06 07		06 19	06 32		06 43			07 08		07 20	07 32		07 43		
—	3¼	**Kensington (Olympia)** ⊖176	d					06 10		06 22	06 35		06 46			07 11		07 23	07 35		07 46		
—	4	**Shepherd's Bush** ⊖66,176	d					06 12		06 24	06 37		06 49			07 13		07 25	07 37		07 48		
5½	—	**Willesden Jn Low Level** ⊖	d			05 51																	
5½	6	**Willesden Jn. High Level** ⊖	a				06 13	06 21	06 26	06 34	06 45	06 53	06 57	07 03	07 16	07 21	07 27	07 34	07 45	07 51	07 55	08 03	08 15
—	—		d				06 14	06 22	06 27	06 35	06 46	06 54	06 58	07 04	07 17	07 22	07 28	07 35	07 46	07 52	07 58	08 04	08 16
6½	—	Kensal Rise	d			06 00	06 17	06 25	06 29	06 37	06 48	06 57	07 00	07 06	07 19	07 26	07 32	07 36	07 48	07 54	08 00	08 06	08 18
7¼	—	Brondesbury Park	d			06 02	06 19	06 27	06 31	06 39	06 50	06 59	07 02	07 08	07 21	07 28	07 34	07 38	07 50	07 56	08 02	08 08	08 20
7½	—	Brondesbury	d			06 04	06 21	06 28	06 33	06 41	06 52	07 01	07 04	07 10	07 23	07 29	07 35	07 40	07 52	07 58	08 04	08 10	08 22
8	—	West Hampstead ⊖	d			06 06	06 23	06 30	06 35	06 43	06 54	07 03	07 06	07 12	07 25	07 32	07 37	07 42	07 54	08 00	08 06	08 12	08 24
8½	—	Finchley Road & Frognal	d			06 07	06 24	06 32	06 36	06 44	06 55	07 04	07 07	07 13	07 26	07 34	07 39	07 43	07 55	08 01	08 07	08 13	08 25
9¼	—	Hampstead Heath	d			06 10	06 27	06 34	06 39	06 47	06 58	07 07	07 10	07 16	07 29	07 36	07 41	07 46	07 58	08 04	08 10	08 16	08 28
10	—	**Gospel Oak**	d			06 14	06 29	06 37	06 41	06 49	07 00	07 10	07 13	07 18	07 31	07 39	07 44	07 48	08 00	08 06	08 13	08 19	08 30
10¾	—	Kentish Town West	d			06 16	06 31	06 39	06 43	06 51	07 02	07 12	07 15	07 20	07 33	07 41	07 46	07 50	08 02	08 08	08 15	08 21	08 32
11¼	—	Camden Road	d		06 02	06 20	06 34	06 42	06 46	06 56	07 08	07 15	07 18	07 25	07 36	07 44	07 49	07 54	08 08	08 13	08 19	08 25	08 37
12¼	—	Caledonian Rd & Barnsbury	d		06 05	06 23	06 37	06 45	06 49	06 59	07 12	07 18	07 21	07 28	07 39	07 47	07 52	07 57	08 11	08 16	08 22	08 28	08 40
12¾	—	**Highbury & Islington** ⊖178	d		06 07	06 25	06 39	06 47	06 52	07 02	07 15	07 21	07 24	07 31	07 42	07 50	07 55	08 00	08 14	08 19	08 25	08 31	08 43
13¼	—	Canonbury ⊖178	d		06 09	06 27	06 41	06 49	06 54	07 04	07 17	07 23	07 26	07 33	07 44	07 52	07 57	08 02	08 16	08 21	08 27	08 33	08 45
14¼	—	Dalston Kingsland	d		06 11	06 29	06 43	06 51	06 56	07 06	07 19	07 25	07 28	07 35	07 46	07 54	07 59	08 04	08 18	08 23	08 29	08 35	08 47
15	—	Hackney Central	d		06 13	06 31	06 45	06 53	06 58	07 08	07 21	07 27	07 30	07 37	07 48	07 56	08 01	08 06	08 20	08 25	08 31	08 37	08 49
15¾	—	Homerton	d	00 01	06 15	06 33	06 47	06 55	07 00	07 10	07 23	07 29	07 32	07 39	07 50	07 58	08 03	08 08	08 22	08 27	08 33	08 39	08 51
16½	—	Hackney Wick	d	00 04	06 18	06 36	06 50	06 58	07 02	07 12	07 25	07 31	07 35	07 41	07 53	08 00	08 05	08 10	08 25	08 29	08 35	08 41	08 53
17½	—	**Stratford** 7 ⊖	a	00 10	06 28	06 44	06 56	07 04	07 10	07 21	07 32	07 38	07 41	07 50	08 01	08 05	08 11	08 17	08 31	08 36	08 41	08 50	09 02

Station		LO	LO	LO	LO	LO	LO	LO	LO	LO	LO	LO	LO	LO	LO	LO	LO	LO	LO	LO	LO	LO	LO
Richmond ⊖	d		08 09			08 34		08 45	08 57		09 09		09 26		09 43		09 57		10 08		10 26		10 40
Kew Gardens ⊖	d		08 12			08 37		08 48	09 00		09 13		09 29		09 46		10 00		10 11		10 30		10 43
Gunnersbury ⊖	d		08 15			08 40		08 51	09 03		09 16		09 32		09 49		10 03		10 14		10 33		10 46
South Acton	d		08 18			08 43		08 54	09 06		09 19		09 35		09 52		10 06		10 17		10 36		10 49
Acton Central	d		08 21			08 46		08 57	09 09		09 22		09 38		09 55		10 09		10 21		10 39		10 53
Clapham Junction 10 66,176	d	08 01		08 13	08 25		08 36			09 01		09 14		09 29		09 46		10 01		10 17		10 30	
Imperial Wharf 176	d	08 05		08 17	08 29		08 40			09 05		09 18		09 33		09 50		10 05		10 21		10 34	
West Brompton ⊖176	d	08 08		08 20	08 32		08 43			09 08		09 21		09 36		09 53		10 08		10 24		10 37	
Kensington (Olympia) ⊖176	d	08 11		08 23	08 35		08 46			09 11		09 24		09 39		09 56		10 11		10 27		10 42	
Shepherd's Bush ⊖66,176	d	08 13		08 25	08 37		08 48			09 13		09 26		09 41		09 58		10 13		10 29		10 44	
Willesden Jn Low Level ⊖	d																						
Willesden Jn. High Level ⊖	a	08 21	08 26	08 33	08 44	08 51	08 55	09 03	09 16	09 21	09 29	09 34	09 43	09 49	10 00	10 07	10 15	10 21	10 26	10 36	10 45	10 52	10 59
	d	08 22	08 27	08 34	08 45	08 52	08 58	09 04	09 17	09 24	09 30	09 35	09 44	09 50	10 01	10 08	10 16	10 22	10 27	10 37	10 46	10 53	11 00
Kensal Rise	d	08 24	08 30	08 37	08 47	08 54	09 00	09 06	09 20	09 27	09 32	09 37	09 46	09 52	10 03	10 10	10 18	10 24	10 31	10 39	10 48	10 55	11 03
Brondesbury Park	d	08 26	08 32	08 39	08 49	08 56	09 02	09 08	09 22	09 29	09 34	09 39	09 48	09 54	10 05	10 12	10 20	10 26	10 33	10 41	10 50	10 57	11 05
Brondesbury	d	08 28	08 33	08 40	08 51	08 58	09 04	09 10	09 23	09 30	09 36	09 41	09 50	09 56	10 07	10 14	10 22	10 28	10 34	10 43	10 52	10 59	11 06
West Hampstead ⊖	d	08 30	08 35	08 42	08 53	09 00	09 06	09 12	09 25	09 32	09 38	09 43	09 52	09 58	10 09	10 16	10 24	10 30	10 36	10 45	10 54	11 01	11 08
Finchley Road & Frognal	d	08 31	08 37	08 44	08 54	09 01	09 07	09 13	09 27	09 34	09 39	09 44	09 53	09 59	10 10	10 17	10 25	10 31	10 38	10 46	10 55	11 02	11 10
Hampstead Heath	d	08 34	08 39	08 46	08 57	09 04	09 10	09 16	09 29	09 36	09 42	09 47	09 56	10 02	10 13	10 20	10 28	10 34	10 40	10 49	10 58	11 05	11 12
Gospel Oak	d	08 36	08 42	08 49	08 59	09 06	09 13	09 18	09 32	09 39	09 44	09 49	09 58	10 04	10 15	10 22	10 30	10 38	10 43	10 51	11 01	11 07	11 15
Kentish Town West	d	08 38	08 44	08 51	09 01	09 08	09 15	09 20	09 34	09 41	09 46	09 51	10 00	10 06	10 17	10 24	10 32	10 40	10 45	10 53	11 03	11 09	11 17
Camden Road	d	08 43	08 49	08 55	09 05	09 11	09 18	09 25	09 37	09 44	09 51	09 55	10 05	10 11	10 21	10 28	10 35	10 43	10 48	10 58	11 06	11 14	11 21
Caledonian Rd & Barnsbury	d	08 46	08 52	08 59	09 08	09 14	09 21	09 29	09 40	09 47	09 55	09 58	10 08	10 14	10 24	10 31	10 38	10 46	10 51	11 01	11 09	11 17	11 24
Highbury & Islington ⊖178	d	08 49	08 55	09 03	09 10	09 16	09 24	09 32	09 42	09 50	09 58	10 01	10 10	10 16	10 26	10 33	10 40	10 48	10 53	11 03	11 11	11 19	11 26
Canonbury ⊖178	d	08 51	08 57	09 05	09 12	09 18	09 26	09 34	09 44	09 52	10 00	10 03	10 12	10 18	10 28	10 35	10 42	10 50	10 55	11 06	11 13	11 21	11 29
Dalston Kingsland	d	08 53	08 59	09 07	09 14	09 20	09 28	09 36	09 46	09 54	10 02	10 05	10 14	10 20	10 30	10 37	10 44	10 52	10 57	11 08	11 15	11 23	11 31
Hackney Central	d	08 55	09 01	09 09	09 16	09 22	09 30	09 38	09 48	09 56	10 04	10 07	10 16	10 22	10 32	10 39	10 46	10 54	10 59	11 10	11 17	11 25	11 33
Homerton	d	08 57	09 03	09 11	09 18	09 24	09 32	09 40	09 50	09 58	10 06	10 09	10 18	10 24	10 34	10 41	10 48	10 56	11 01	11 12	11 19	11 27	11 35
Hackney Wick	d	08 59	09 05	09 13	09 21	09 27	09 34	09 43	09 53	10 00	10 09	10 13	10 21	10 27	10 37	10 44	10 51	10 59	11 04	11 15	11 22	11 30	11 38
Stratford 7 ⊖	a	09 06	09 11	09 18	09 30	09 36	09 41	09 48	10 02	10 07	10 14	10 18	10 28	10 33	10 45	10 51	10 59	11 05	11 11	11 21	11 28	11 36	11 42

For services between Shepherds Bush and Clapham Junction refer to Table T066 and T176

Table T059-R

Mondays to Fridays

21 May to 7 December

Richmond and Clapham Junction - Willesden Junction, West Hampstead, Highbury & Islington and Stratford

Station		LO	LO	LO	LO	LO	LO	LO	LO	LO	LO	LO	LO	LO	LO	LO	LO	LO	LO	LO	LO	LO	LO
Richmond ⊖	d		10 56		11 08		11 26		11 40		11 56		12 10		12 28		12 40		12 56		13 10		13 26
Kew Gardens ⊖	d		11 00		11 11		11 30		11 43		12 00		12 13		12 31		12 43		13 00		13 13		13 30
Gunnersbury ⊖	d		11 03		11 14		11 33		11 46		12 03		12 16		12 35		12 46		13 03		13 16		13 33
South Acton	d		11 06		11 17		11 36		11 49		12 06		12 19		12 38		12 49		13 06		13 19		13 36
Acton Central	d		11 09		11 20		11 39		11 53		12 09		12 23		12 41		12 53		13 09		13 23		13 39
Clapham Junction 10 66,176	d	10 48		11 02		11 17		11 32		11 47		12 02		12 17		12 32		12 47		13 02		13 17	
Imperial Wharf 176	d	10 52		11 06		11 21		11 36		11 51		12 06		12 21		12 36		12 51		13 06		13 21	
West Brompton ⊖176	d	10 55		11 09		11 24		11 39		11 54		12 09		12 24		12 39		12 54		13 09		13 24	
Kensington (Olympia) ⊖176	d	10 58		11 12		11 27		11 42		11 57		12 12		12 27		12 42		12 57		13 12		13 27	
Shepherd's Bush ⊖66,176	d	11 00		11 14		11 29		11 44		11 59		12 14		12 29		12 44		12 59		13 14		13 29	
Willesden Jn Low Level ⊖	d																						
Willesden Jn. High Level ⊖	a	11 08	11 14	11 21	11 25	11 39	11 44	11 52	11 58	12 07	12 14	12 22	12 28	12 36	12 46	12 52	12 59	13 07	13 14	13 21	13 30	13 37	13 44
	d	11 09	11 15	11 22	11 26	11 40	11 45	11 53	11 59	12 08	12 15	12 23	12 29	12 37	12 47	12 53	13 00	13 08	13 15	13 22	13 32	13 38	13 45
Kensal Rise	d	11 11	11 17	11 24	11 29	11 42	11 47	11 55	12 02	12 10	12 18	12 25	12 32	12 39	12 50	12 56	13 02	13 10	13 17	13 24	13 34	13 40	13 47
Brondesbury Park	d	11 13	11 19	11 26	11 31	11 44	11 49	11 57	12 04	12 12	12 20	12 27	12 34	12 41	12 52	12 58	13 04	13 12	13 19	13 26	13 36	13 42	13 49
Brondesbury	d	11 15	11 21	11 28	11 32	11 46	11 51	11 59	12 05	12 14	12 21	12 29	12 36	12 43	12 53	12 59	13 06	13 14	13 21	13 28	13 38	13 44	13 51
West Hampstead ⊖	d	11 17	11 23	11 31	11 35	11 48	11 53	12 01	12 07	12 16	12 24	12 31	12 38	12 45	12 55	13 01	13 08	13 16	13 23	13 30	13 40	13 46	13 53
Finchley Road & Frognal	d	11 18	11 24	11 32	11 37	11 49	11 54	12 02	12 09	12 17	12 25	12 32	12 39	12 46	12 57	13 03	13 09	13 17	13 24	13 31	13 41	13 47	13 54
Hampstead Heath	d	11 21	11 27	11 35	11 39	11 52	11 57	12 05	12 11	12 20	12 28	12 35	12 42	12 49	12 59	13 05	13 12	13 20	13 27	13 34	13 44	13 50	13 57
Gospel Oak	d	11 23	11 29	11 37	11 42	11 57	12 01	12 07	12 14	12 22	12 31	12 38	12 44	12 51	13 02	13 08	13 14	13 22	13 31	13 36	13 46	13 52	13 59
Kentish Town West	d	11 25	11 31	11 39	11 44	11 59	12 03	12 09	12 16	12 24	12 33	12 40	12 46	12 53	13 04	13 10	13 16	13 24	13 33	13 38	13 48	13 54	14 01
Camden Road	d	11 30	11 36	11 44	11 48	12 01	12 07	12 14	12 20	12 28	12 35	12 44	12 51	12 58	13 06	13 14	13 21	13 29	13 36	13 43	13 51	13 59	14 06
Caledonian Rd & Barnsbury	d	11 33	11 39	11 47	11 51	12 04	12 10	12 17	12 23	12 31	12 39	12 47	12 54	13 01	13 09	13 17	13 24	13 32	13 39	13 46	13 54	14 02	14 09
Highbury & Islington ⊖178	d	11 35	11 41	11 49	11 54	12 07	12 13	12 19	12 26	12 34	12 42	12 49	12 57	13 03	13 12	13 20	13 26	13 34	13 41	13 48	13 56	14 04	14 11
Canonbury ⊖178	d	11 37	11 43	11 51	11 56	12 09	12 15	12 21	12 28	12 36	12 44	12 51	12 59	13 05	13 14	13 22	13 28	13 36	13 43	13 50	13 58	14 06	14 13
Dalston Kingsland	d	11 39	11 45	11 53	11 58	12 11	12 17	12 23	12 30	12 38	12 46	12 53	13 01	13 07	13 16	13 24	13 30	13 38	13 45	13 52	14 00	14 08	14 15
Hackney Central	d	11 41	11 48	11 55	12 00	12 13	12 19	12 25	12 32	12 40	12 48	12 55	13 03	13 09	13 18	13 26	13 32	13 40	13 47	13 54	14 02	14 10	14 17
Homerton	d	11 43	11 50	11 57	12 02	12 15	12 21	12 27	12 34	12 42	12 50	12 57	13 05	13 11	13 20	13 28	13 34	13 42	13 49	13 56	14 04	14 12	14 19
Hackney Wick	d	11 46	11 52	12 00	12 04	12 17	12 23	12 30	12 36	12 45	12 52	13 00	13 08	13 14	13 22	13 30	13 37	13 45	13 52	13 59	14 07	14 15	14 22
Stratford 7 ⊖	a	11 52	11 58	12 06	12 11	12 21	12 28	12 36	12 42	12 51	12 58	13 06	13 12	13 21	13 30	13 37	13 42	13 51	13 58	14 06	14 12	14 21	14 28

Station		LO	LO	LO	LO	LO	LO	LO	LO	LO	LO	LO	LO	LO	LO	LO	LO	LO	LO	LO	LO	LO	LO
Richmond ⊖	d		13 40		13 56				14 21			14 45			15 09		15 20			15 45			16 09
Kew Gardens ⊖	d		13 43		13 59				14 24			14 49			15 12		15 23			15 49			16 13
Gunnersbury ⊖	d		13 46		14 02				14 27			14 52			15 15		15 26			15 52			16 16
South Acton	d		13 49		14 05		14 14		14 30	14 42		14 55			15 18		15 29	15 41		15 55			16 19
Acton Central	d		13 52		14 08		14 24		14 33	14 45		14 59			15 21		15 33	15 45		15 59			16 22
Clapham Junction 10 66,176	d	13 32		13 47		14 02		14 14			14 36		14 49	15 01		15 14			15 36		15 49	16 01	
Imperial Wharf 176	d	13 36		13 51		14 06		14 18			14 40		14 53	15 05		15 18			15 40		15 53	16 05	
West Brompton ⊖176	d	13 39		13 54		14 09		14 21			14 43		14 56	15 08		15 21			15 43		15 56	16 08	
Kensington (Olympia) ⊖176	d	13 42		13 57		14 12		14 24			14 46		14 59	15 11		15 24			15 46		15 59	16 11	
Shepherd's Bush ⊖66,176	d	13 44		13 59		14 14		14 27			14 48		15 01	15 13		15 26			15 48		16 01	16 13	
Willesden Jn Low Level ⊖	d																						
Willesden Jn. High Level ⊖	a	13 52	13 59	14 06	14 16	14 21	14 30	14 35	14 39	14 51	14 55	15 05	15 08	15 21	15 27	15 33	15 39	15 51	15 54	16 04	16 08	16 22	16 27
	d	13 53	14 00	14 07	14 18	14 22	14 31	14 36	14 40	14 52	14 56	15 06	15 10	15 22	15 28	15 34	15 41	15 52	15 55	16 05	16 10	16 23	16 28
Kensal Rise	d	13 55	14 02	14 10	14 20	14 25	14 34	14 38	14 43	14 55	14 58	15 08	15 12	15 24	15 30	15 36	15 44	15 54	15 58	16 08	16 12	16 25	16 31
Brondesbury Park	d	13 57	14 04	14 12	14 22	14 27	14 36	14 40	14 45	14 58	15 01	15 10	15 14	15 26	15 32	15 38	15 46	15 56	16 00	16 10	16 14	16 27	16 33
Brondesbury	d	13 59	14 06	14 13	14 24	14 28	14 37	14 42	14 46	15 00	15 04	15 12	15 16	15 28	15 34	15 40	15 47	15 58	16 01	16 11	16 16	16 29	16 34
West Hampstead ⊖	d	14 01	14 08	14 15	14 26	14 30	14 39	14 44	14 48	15 02	15 06	15 14	15 18	15 30	15 36	15 42	15 50	16 00	16 03	16 13	16 18	16 31	16 36
Finchley Road & Frognal	d	14 02	14 09	14 17	14 27	14 32	14 41	14 45	14 50	15 04	15 07	15 16	15 19	15 31	15 37	15 43	15 52	16 01	16 05	16 15	16 19	16 32	16 38
Hampstead Heath	d	14 05	14 12	14 19	14 30	14 34	14 43	14 48	14 52	15 06	15 10	15 18	15 22	15 34	15 40	15 46	15 54	16 04	16 07	16 17	16 22	16 35	16 40
Gospel Oak	d	14 07	14 14	14 22	14 32	14 37	14 46	14 50	14 55	15 09	15 12	15 21	15 24	15 36	15 42	15 48	15 57	16 06	16 10	16 20	16 24	16 37	16 43
Kentish Town West	d	14 09	14 16	14 24	14 34	14 39	14 48	14 52	14 57	15 11	15 14	15 23	15 26	15 38	15 44	15 50	15 59	16 08	16 12	16 22	16 26	16 39	16 45
Camden Road	d	14 14	14 21	14 26	14 37	14 42	14 50	14 55	15 00	15 13	15 18	15 26	15 31	15 43	15 47	15 56	16 01	16 13	16 17	16 25	16 31	16 44	16 49
Caledonian Rd & Barnsbury	d	14 17	14 24	14 30	14 40	14 45	14 53	14 58	15 03	15 16	15 21	15 29	15 34	15 46	15 50	15 59	16 04	16 16	16 20	16 28	16 34	16 47	16 52
Highbury & Islington ⊖178	d	14 19	14 26	14 33	14 42	14 48	14 56	15 00	15 05	15 19	15 23	15 31	15 36	15 48	15 52	16 01	16 07	16 18	16 22	16 31	16 37	16 50	16 55
Canonbury ⊖178	d	14 21	14 28	14 35	14 44	14 50	14 58	15 02	15 07	15 21	15 25	15 33	15 38	15 50	15 54	16 03	16 09	16 20	16 24	16 33	16 39	16 52	16 57
Dalston Kingsland	d	14 23	14 30	14 38	14 46	14 52	15 00	15 04	15 09	15 23	15 27	15 35	15 40	15 52	15 56	16 05	16 11	16 22	16 26	16 35	16 41	16 54	16 59
Hackney Central	d	14 25	14 32	14 40	14 48	14 54	15 02	15 06	15 11	15 25	15 29	15 37	15 42	15 55	15 58	16 07	16 13	16 24	16 28	16 37	16 43	16 56	17 01
Homerton	d	14 27	14 34	14 43	14 50	14 56	15 04	15 08	15 13	15 27	15 31	15 39	15 44	15 57	16 00	16 09	16 15	16 26	16 30	16 39	16 45	16 58	17 03
Hackney Wick	d	14 30	14 37	14 45	14 53	14 58	15 06	15 11	15 16	15 29	15 34	15 42	15 47	15 59	16 03	16 12	16 17	16 29	16 33	16 41	16 47	17 00	17 06
Stratford 7 ⊖	a	14 36	14 42	14 51	14 58	15 06	15 12	15 18	15 26	15 37	15 40	15 47	15 56	16 05	16 11	16 18	16 26	16 37	16 40	16 47	16 56	17 07	17 11

For services between Shepherds Bush and Clapham Junction refer to Table T066 and T176

Richmond and Clapham Junction - Willesden Junction, West Hampstead, Highbury & Islington and Stratford

		LO	LO	LO	LO	LO	LO	LO	LO	LO	LO	LO	LO	LO	LO	LO	LO	LO	LO	LO	LO	LO	LO
Richmond ⊖	d		16 20	16 33		16 45			17 10		17 20	17 33		17 45			18 07		18 20	18 32		18 45	
Kew Gardens ⊖	d		16 24	16 36		16 48			17 14		17 24	17 36		17 48			18 10		18 23	18 35		18 48	
Gunnersbury ⊖	d		16 27	16 39		16 51			17 17		17 27	17 39		17 51			18 13		18 26	18 38		18 51	
South Acton	d		16 30	16 42		16 54			17 20		17 30	17 42		17 54			18 16		18 29	18 41		18 54	
Acton Central	d		16 33	16 45		16 57			17 23		17 33	17 45		17 57			18 21		18 33	18 45		18 57	
Clapham Junction [10] 66,176	d	16 13			16 36		16 49	17 02		17 13			17 36		17 49	18 01		18 13			18 36		18 49
Imperial Wharf 176	d	16 17			16 40		16 53	17 06		17 17			17 40		17 53	18 05		18 17			18 40		18 53
West Brompton ⊖176	d	16 20			16 43		16 56	17 10		17 20			17 43		17 56	18 08		18 20			18 43		18 56
Kensington (Olympia) ⊖176	d	16 23			16 46		16 59	17 13		17 23			17 46		17 59	18 11		18 23			18 46		18 59
Shepherd's Bush ⊖66,176	d	16 25			16 48		17 01	17 16		17 26			17 48		18 01	18 13		18 25			18 48		19 01
Willesden Jn Low Level ⊖	d																						
Willesden Jn. High Level ⊖	a	16 33	16 39	16 51	16 54	17 03	17 09	17 23	17 29	17 33	17 39	17 51	17 55	18 03	18 09	18 21	18 27	18 33	18 39	18 51	18 56	19 03	19 09
	d	16 35	16 40	16 52	16 55	17 04	17 10	17 24	17 30	17 34	17 40	17 52	17 57	18 04	18 10	18 22	18 28	18 34	18 40	18 52	18 57	19 04	19 10
Kensal Rise	d	16 37	16 43	16 54	16 58	17 06	17 12	17 27	17 32	17 36	17 42	17 54	17 59	18 06	18 12	18 24	18 30	18 36	18 42	18 55	18 59	19 06	19 12
Brondesbury Park	d	16 39	16 45	16 56	17 00	17 08	17 14	17 29	17 34	17 38	17 44	17 56	18 01	18 08	18 14	18 26	18 32	18 38	18 44	18 57	19 01	19 08	19 14
Brondesbury	d	16 41	16 46	16 58	17 01	17 10	17 16	17 30	17 36	17 40	17 46	17 58	18 03	18 10	18 16	18 28	18 34	18 40	18 46	18 58	19 03	19 10	19 16
West Hampstead ⊖	d	16 43	16 48	17 00	17 03	17 12	17 18	17 32	17 38	17 42	17 48	18 00	18 05	18 12	18 18	18 30	18 36	18 42	18 48	19 00	19 05	19 12	19 18
Finchley Road & Frognal	d	16 44	16 50	17 01	17 05	17 13	17 19	17 34	17 39	17 43	17 49	18 01	18 06	18 13	18 19	18 31	18 37	18 43	18 49	19 02	19 06	19 13	19 19
Hampstead Heath	d	16 47	16 52	17 04	17 07	17 16	17 22	17 36	17 42	17 46	17 52	18 04	18 09	18 16	18 22	18 34	18 40	18 46	18 52	19 04	19 09	19 16	19 22
Gospel Oak	d	16 49	16 55	17 06	17 10	17 18	17 24	17 39	17 44	17 48	17 54	18 06	18 11	18 18	18 24	18 36	18 42	18 48	18 54	19 07	19 11	19 18	19 24
Kentish Town West	d	16 51	16 57	17 08	17 12	17 20	17 26	17 41	17 46	17 50	17 56	18 08	18 13	18 20	18 26	18 38	18 44	18 50	18 56	19 09	19 13	19 20	19 26
Camden Road	d	16 55	17 01	17 13	17 17	17 23	17 30	17 45	17 50	17 55	18 01	18 13	18 18	18 25	18 31	18 43	18 47	18 55	19 01	19 13	19 17	19 25	19 31
Caledonian Rd & Barnsbury	d	16 58	17 04	17 16	17 20	17 28	17 33	17 48	17 53	17 58	18 04	18 16	18 21	18 28	18 34	18 46	18 50	18 58	19 04	19 16	19 20	19 28	19 34
Highbury & Islington ⊖178	d	17 01	17 07	17 20	17 24	17 31	17 36	17 51	17 56	18 01	18 07	18 19	18 24	18 31	18 37	18 49	18 53	19 01	19 06	19 18	19 22	19 30	19 36
Canonbury ⊖178	d	17 03	17 09	17 22	17 26	17 33	17 38	17 53	17 58	18 03	18 09	18 21	18 26	18 33	18 39	18 51	18 55	19 03	19 08	19 20	19 24	19 32	19 38
Dalston Kingsland	d	17 05	17 11	17 24	17 28	17 35	17 40	17 55	18 00	18 05	18 11	18 23	18 28	18 35	18 41	18 53	18 57	19 05	19 10	19 22	19 26	19 34	19 40
Hackney Central	d	17 07	17 13	17 26	17 30	17 37	17 42	17 58	18 02	18 07	18 13	18 25	18 30	18 37	18 43	18 55	18 59	19 07	19 12	19 24	19 28	19 36	19 42
Homerton	d	17 09	17 15	17 28	17 32	17 39	17 44	18 00	18 04	18 09	18 15	18 27	18 32	18 39	18 45	18 57	19 01	19 09	19 14	19 26	19 30	19 38	19 44
Hackney Wick	d	17 11	17 17	17 30	17 34	17 41	17 46	18 03	18 07	18 11	18 17	18 29	18 34	18 41	18 47	18 59	19 04	19 11	19 17	19 29	19 33	19 41	19 47
Stratford [7] ⊖ ⇌	a	17 17	17 26	17 38	17 40	17 47	17 57	18 12	18 12	18 18	18 26	18 38	18 41	18 47	18 56	19 06	19 09	19 18	19 23	19 38	19 41	19 47	19 56

		LO	LO	LO	LO	LO	LO	LO	LO	LO	LO	LO	LO	LO	LO	LO	LO	LO	LO	LO	LO	LO	LO
Richmond ⊖	d		19 09		19 22	19 32		19 47			20 09		20 22		20 38		20 52		21 07		21 29		21 38
Kew Gardens ⊖	d		19 13		19 25	19 35		19 50			20 12		20 25		20 41		20 55		21 10		21 32		21 41
Gunnersbury ⊖	d		19 16		19 29	19 38		19 54			20 15		20 28		20 44		20 58		21 13		21 35		21 44
South Acton	d		19 19		19 31	19 41		19 56			20 18		20 31		20 47		21 01		21 16		21 39		21 47
Acton Central	d		19 22		19 36	19 45		20 01			20 21		20 35		20 50		21 04		21 19		21 42		21 50
Clapham Junction [10] 66,176	d	19 01		19 13			19 36		19 49	20 01		20 13		20 28		20 44		21 00		21 17		21 30	
Imperial Wharf 176	d	19 05		19 17			19 40		19 53	20 05		20 17		20 32		20 48		21 04		21 22		21 35	
West Brompton ⊖176	d	19 08		19 20			19 43		19 56	20 08		20 20		20 35		20 51		21 07		21 26		21 38	
Kensington (Olympia) ⊖176	d	19 11		19 23			19 46		19 59	20 11		20 23		20 38		20 54		21 10		21 29		21 42	
Shepherd's Bush ⊖66,176	d	19 13		19 25			19 48		20 01	20 13		20 25		20 40		20 56		21 12		21a34		21 44	
Willesden Jn Low Level ⊖	d																						
Willesden Jn. High Level ⊖	a	19 20	19 27	19 33	19 43	19 53	19 56	20 06	20 09	20 22	20 28	20 33	20 41	20 48	20 56	21 04	21 09	21 19	21 24		21 47	21 51	21 56
	d	19 21	19 28	19 34	19 44	19 54	19 57	20 07	20 10	20 23	20 29	20 34	20 42	20 49	20 57	21 05	21 10	21 20	21 25		21 48	21 52	21 57
Kensal Rise	d	19 23	19 30	19 36	19 46	19 56	20 00	20 09	20 13	20 26	20 31	20 36	20 44	20 51	20 59	21 07	21 13	21 22	21 27		21 50	21 55	21 59
Brondesbury Park	d	19 25	19 32	19 38	19 48	19 58	20 02	20 11	20 15	20 28	20 33	20 38	20 46	20 53	21 01	21 09	21 15	21 24	21 29		21 52	21 57	22 01
Brondesbury	d	19 27	19 34	19 40	19 50	20 00	20 03	20 13	20 16	20 29	20 35	20 40	20 48	20 55	21 03	21 11	21 17	21 26	21 31		21 54	21 58	22 03
West Hampstead ⊖	d	19 29	19 36	19 43	19 52	20 02	20 05	20 15	20 18	20 31	20 37	20 43	20 50	20 57	21 05	21 13	21 19	21 28	21 33		21 56	22 00	22 05
Finchley Road & Frognal	d	19 30	19 37	19 44	19 53	20 03	20 07	20 16	20 20	20 33	20 38	20 45	20 51	20 58	21 06	21 14	21 20	21 29	21 34		21 57	22 02	22 06
Hampstead Heath	d	19 33	19 40	19 47	19 56	20 06	20 09	20 19	20 22	20 35	20 41	20 47	20 54	21 01	21 09	21 17	21 23	21 32	21 37		22 00	22 04	22 09
Gospel Oak	d	19 35	19 42	19 49	19 58	20 08	20 12	20 21	20 25	20 38	20 43	20 50	20 56	21 03	21 11	21 19	21 25	21 34	21 39		22 02	22 07	22 11
Kentish Town West	d	19 37	19 44	19 51	20 00	20 10	20 14	20 23	20 27	20 40	20 45	20 53	20 58	21 05	21 13	21 21	21 27	21 36	21 41		22 04	22 09	22 13
Camden Road	d	19 41	19 49	19 55	20 03	20 13	20 17	20 26	20 30	20 44	20 49	20 57	21 03	21 10	21 18	21 26	21 32	21 41	21 45		22 09	22 13	22 18
Caledonian Rd & Barnsbury	d	19 44	19 52	19 58	20 06	20 16	20 20	20 29	20 33	20 48	20 52	21 00	21 06	21 13	21 21	21 29	21 36	21 44	21 48		22 12	22 16	22 21
Highbury & Islington ⊖178	d	19 46	19 54	20 01	20 08	20 18	20 23	20 31	20 36	20 50	20 54	21 03	21 08	21 15	21 23	21 31	21 38	21 46	21 50		22 15	22 19	22 23
Canonbury ⊖178	d	19 48	19 56	20 03	20 10	20 20	20 25	20 34	20 38	20 53	20 57	21 05	21 10	21 17	21 25	21 33	21 40	21 48	21 52		22 17	22 21	22 25
Dalston Kingsland	d	19 50	19 58	20 05	20 12	20 22	20 27	20 36	20 40	20 55	20 59	21 07	21 12	21 19	21 27	21 35	21 42	21 50	21 54		22 19	22 23	22 27
Hackney Central	d	19 52	20 00	20 07	20 14	20 24	20 29	20 38	20 42	20 57	21 01	21 09	21 14	21 21	21 29	21 37	21 44	21 52	21 56		22 21	22 25	22 29
Homerton	d	19 54	20 02	20 09	20 16	20 26	20 31	20 40	20 44	20 59	21 03	21 11	21 16	21 23	21 31	21 39	21 46	21 54	21 58		22 23	22 27	22 31
Hackney Wick	d	19 57	20 05	20 11	20 19	20 29	20 33	20 43	20 47	21 01	21 05	21 13	21 19	21 26	21 34	21 42	21 49	21 57	22 01		22 25	22 29	22 34
Stratford [7] ⊖ ⇌	a	20 06	20 11	20 17	20 24	20 38	20 40	20 49	20 53	21 08	21 11	21 17	21 25	21 32	21 40	21 48	21 58	22 04	22 09		22 31	22 34	22 40

For services between Shepherds Bush and Clapham Junction refer to Table T066 and T176

Richmond and Clapham Junction - Willesden Junction, West Hampstead, Highbury & Islington and Stratford

		LO	LO	LO	LO	LO	LO	LO	LO	LO	LO	LO	LO	LO	LO	LO	LO
Richmond ⊖	d		21 50		22 08		22 22		22 38		22 52		23 07		23 25		
Kew Gardens ⊖	d		21 53		22 11		22 25		22 41		22 55		23 10		23 29		
Gunnersbury ⊖	d		21 57		22 14		22 28		22 44		22 58		23 13		23 32		
South Acton	d		22 00		22 17		22 31		22 47		23 01		23 16		23 35		
Acton Central	d		22 07		22 21		22 35		22 50		23 05		23 19		23 38		
Clapham Junction [10] 66,176	d	21 44		21 59		22 14		22 29		22 44		23 00		23 15		23 30	
Imperial Wharf 176	d	21 48		22 03		22 18		22 33		22 48		23 04		23 19		23 34	23 51
West Brompton ⊖176	d	21 51		22 06		22 21		22 36		22 51		23 07		23 22		23 37	23 54
Kensington (Olympia) ⊖176	d	21 54		22 09		22 24		22 39		22 54		23 10		23 25		23 40	23 57
Shepherd's Bush ⊖66,176	d	21 56		22 11		22 26		22 41		22 56		23 12		23 27		23 42	23 59
Willesden Jn Low Level ⊖	d																
Willesden Jn. High Level ⊖	a	22 05	22 13	22 19	22 27	22 34	22 41	22 49	22 57	23 03	23 10	23 21	23 24	23 36	23 46	23 51	00 06
	d		22 15	22 21	22 28	22 35	22 42	22 50	22 58	23 04	23 11		23 25				
Kensal Rise	d		22 18	22 24	22 31	22 37	22 44	22 52	23 01	23 06	23 13		23 27				
Brondesbury Park	d		22 20	22 26	22 33	22 39	22 46	22 54	23 03	23 08	23 15		23 29				
Brondesbury	d		22 21	22 27	22 34	22 41	22 48	22 56	23 04	23 10	23 17		23 31				
West Hampstead ⊖	d		22 25	22 29	22 36	22 43	22 50	22 58	23 06	23 12	23 19		23 33				
Finchley Road & Frognal	d		22 26	22 31	22 38	22 44	22 51	22 59	23 08	23 13	23 20		23 34				
Hampstead Heath	d		22 29	22 33	22 40	22 47	22 54	23 02	23 10	23 16	23 23		23 37				
Gospel Oak	d		22 31	22 36	22 43	22 49	22 56	23 04	23 13	23 22	23 26		23 40				
Kentish Town West	d		22 33	22 38	22 45	22 51	22 58	23 06	23 15	23 24	23 28		23 42				
Camden Road	d		22 36	22 42	22 48	22 56	23 03	23 11	23 19	23 29	23 33		23 47				
Caledonian Rd & Barnsbury	d		22 39	22 46	22 51	22 59	23 06	23 14	23 22	23 32	23 36		23 50				
Highbury & Islington ⊖178	d		22 41	22 49	22 53	23 01	23 09	23 16	23 25	23 34	23 38		23 52				
Canonbury ⊖178	d		22 43	22 51	22 55	23 03	23 11	23 18	23 27	23 38	23 42		23 55				
Dalston Kingsland	d		22 45	22 53	22 57	23 05	23 13	23 20	23 29	23 40	23 44		23 57				
Hackney Central	d		22 47	22 55	22 59	23 07	23 15	23 22	23 31	23 42	23 46		23 59				
Homerton	d		22 49	22 57	23 01	23 09	23 17	23 24	23 33	23 44	23 48		00 01				
Hackney Wick	d		22 52	23 00	23 04	23 12	23 19	23 27	23 35	23 46	23 50		00 04				
Stratford [7] ⊖ ⇌	a		22 56	23 04	23 10	23 18	23 25	23 33	23 40	23 50	23 55		00 10				

Saturdays

26 May to 8 December

		LO	LO	LO	LO	LO	LO	LO	LO	LO	LO	LO	LO	LO	LO	LO	LO	LO	LO	LO	LO	LO	LO
Richmond ⊖	d				05 56		06 10		06 27		06 40		06 56		07 10		07 27		07 40		07 57		08 10
Kew Gardens ⊖	d				05 59		06 13		06 30		06 43		07 00		07 13		07 30		07 43		08 00		08 13
Gunnersbury ⊖	d				06 02		06 16		06 33		06 46		07 03		07 16		07 33		07 46		08 03		08 16
South Acton	d				06 05		06 19		06 36		06 49		07 06		07 19		07 36		07 49		08 06		08 19
Acton Central	d				06 08		06 23		06 39		06 53		07 09		07 23		07 39		07 53		08 09		08 23
Clapham Junction [10] 66,176	d							06 17		06 32		06 47		07 02		07 17		07 32		07 47		08 02	
Imperial Wharf 176	d		05 54			06 06		06 21		06 36		06 51		07 06		07 21		07 36		07 51		08 06	
West Brompton ⊖176	d		05 57			06 09		06 24		06 39		06 54		07 09		07 24		07 39		07 54		08 09	
Kensington (Olympia) ⊖176	d		06 00			06 12		06 27		06 42		06 57		07 12		07 27		07 42		07 57		08 12	
Shepherd's Bush ⊖66,176	d		06 02			06 14		06 29		06 44		06 59		07 14		07 29		07 44		07 59		08 14	
Willesden Jn Low Level ⊖	d			06 00																			
Willesden Jn. High Level ⊖	a		06 11		06 14	06 22	06 29	06 37	06 44	06 52	06 59	07 07	07 14	07 22	07 29	07 37	07 44	07 52	07 59	08 07	08 14	08 22	08 29
	d				06 15	06 23	06 30	06 38	06 45	06 53	07 00	07 08	07 15	07 23	07 30	07 38	07 45	07 53	08 00	08 08	08 15	08 23	08 30
Kensal Rise	d			06 07	06 17	06 25	06 33	06 40	06 47	06 55	07 02	07 10	07 18	07 25	07 32	07 40	07 47	07 55	08 02	08 10	08 17	08 25	08 32
Brondesbury Park	d			06 09	06 19	06 27	06 35	06 42	06 49	06 57	07 04	07 12	07 20	07 27	07 34	07 42	07 49	07 57	08 04	08 12	08 19	08 27	08 34
Brondesbury	d			06 10	06 21	06 29	06 37	06 44	06 51	06 59	07 06	07 14	07 21	07 29	07 36	07 44	07 51	07 59	08 06	08 14	08 21	08 29	08 36
West Hampstead ⊖	d			06 12	06 23	06 31	06 39	06 46	06 53	07 01	07 08	07 16	07 23	07 31	07 38	07 46	07 53	08 01	08 08	08 16	08 23	08 31	08 38
Finchley Road & Frognal	d			06 14	06 24	06 32	06 40	06 47	06 54	07 02	07 09	07 17	07 25	07 32	07 39	07 47	07 54	08 02	08 09	08 17	08 24	08 32	08 39
Hampstead Heath	d			06 16	06 27	06 35	06 43	06 50	06 57	07 05	07 12	07 20	07 27	07 35	07 42	07 50	07 57	08 05	08 12	08 20	08 27	08 35	08 42
Gospel Oak	d			06 19	06 29	06 37	06 45	06 52	06 59	07 07	07 14	07 22	07 30	07 37	07 44	07 52	07 59	08 07	08 14	08 22	08 29	08 37	08 44
Kentish Town West	d			06 21	06 31	06 39	06 47	06 54	07 01	07 09	07 16	07 24	07 32	07 39	07 46	07 54	08 01	08 09	08 16	08 24	08 31	08 39	08 46
Camden Road	d			06 23	06 36	06 44	06 51	06 59	07 06	07 13	07 21	07 29	07 36	07 44	07 50	07 59	08 06	08 14	08 21	08 29	08 36	08 43	08 51
Caledonian Rd & Barnsbury	d			06 26	06 39	06 47	06 54	07 02	07 09	07 16	07 25	07 32	07 39	07 47	07 53	08 03	08 09	08 17	08 24	08 32	08 39	08 46	08 54
Highbury & Islington ⊖178	d			06 29	06 43	06 49	06 56	07 04	07 11	07 19	07 28	07 34	07 41	07 49	07 56	08 05	08 11	08 19	08 26	08 34	08 41	08 48	08 57
Canonbury ⊖178	d			06 31	06 45	06 51	06 58	07 06	07 13	07 21	07 30	07 36	07 43	07 51	07 58	08 07	08 13	08 21	08 28	08 36	08 43	08 50	08 59
Dalston Kingsland	d			06 33	06 47	06 53	07 00	07 08	07 15	07 23	07 32	07 38	07 45	07 53	08 00	08 09	08 15	08 23	08 30	08 38	08 45	08 52	09 01
Hackney Central	d			06 35	06 49	06 55	07 02	07 10	07 17	07 25	07 34	07 40	07 47	07 55	08 02	08 11	08 17	08 25	08 32	08 40	08 47	08 54	09 03
Homerton	d	00 01		06 37	06 51	06 57	07 04	07 12	07 19	07 27	07 36	07 42	07 49	07 57	08 04	08 13	08 19	08 27	08 34	08 42	08 49	08 56	09 05
Hackney Wick	d	00 04		06 39	06 54	07 00	07 07	07 15	07 22	07 30	07 38	07 45	07 52	08 00	08 06	08 16	08 22	08 30	08 37	08 45	08 52	08 59	09 08
Stratford [7] ⊖ ⇌	a	00 10		06 47	06 58	07 06	07 12	07 21	07 28	07 36	07 44	07 51	07 58	08 06	08 12	08 22	08 29	08 37	08 42	08 52	08 59	09 07	09 12

For services between Shepherds Bush and Clapham Junction refer to Table T066 and T176

Richmond and Clapham Junction - Willesden Junction, West Hampstead, Highbury & Islington and Stratford

		LO	LO	LO	LO	LO	LO	LO	LO	LO	LO	LO	LO	LO	LO	LO	LO	LO	LO	LO	LO	LO	LO
Richmond	⊖ d		08 27		08 40		08 56		09 10		09 27		09 40		09 57		10 10		10 26		10 40		10 57
Kew Gardens	⊖ d		08 30		08 43		09 00		09 13		09 30		09 43		10 00		10 13		10 30		10 43		11 00
Gunnersbury	⊖ d		08 33		08 46		09 03		09 16		09 33		09 46		10 03		10 16		10 33		10 46		11 03
South Acton	d		08 36		08 49		09 06		09 19		09 36		09 49		10 06		10 19		10 36		10 49		11 06
Acton Central	d		08 39		08 53		09 09		09 23		09 39		09 53		10 10		10 22		10 39		10 53		11 09
Clapham Junction 10 66,176	d	08 17		08 32		08 47		09 02		09 17		09 32		09 47		10 02		10 17		10 32		10 47	
Imperial Wharf 176	d	08 21		08 36		08 51		09 06		09 21		09 36		09 51		10 06		10 21		10 36		10 51	
West Brompton ⊖176	d	08 24		08 39		08 54		09 09		09 24		09 39		09 54		10 09		10 24		10 39		10 54	
Kensington (Olympia) ⊖176	d	08 27		08 42		08 57		09 12		09 27		09 42		09 57		10 12		10 27		10 42		10 57	
Shepherd's Bush ⊖66,176	d	08 29		08 44		08 59		09 14		09 29		09 44		09 59		10 14		10 29		10 44		10 59	
Willesden Jn Low Level	⊖ d																						
Willesden Jn. High Level	⊖ a	08 37	08 44	08 52	08 59	09 07	09 14	09 22	09 29	09 37	09 44	09 52	09 58	10 07	10 16	10 22	10 29	10 37	10 44	10 52	10 59	11 07	11 14
	d	08 38	08 45	08 53	09 00	09 08	09 15	09 23	09 30	09 38	09 45	09 53	09 59	10 08	10 17	10 23	10 31	10 38	10 45	10 53	11 00	11 08	11 15
Kensal Rise	d	08 40	08 47	08 55	09 02	09 10	09 17	09 25	09 32	09 40	09 47	09 55	10 01	10 10	10 19	10 25	10 34	10 40	10 47	10 55	11 02	11 10	11 17
Brondesbury Park	d	08 42	08 49	08 57	09 04	09 12	09 19	09 27	09 34	09 42	09 49	09 57	10 03	10 12	10 21	10 27	10 36	10 42	10 49	10 57	11 04	11 12	11 19
Brondesbury	d	08 44	08 51	08 59	09 06	09 14	09 21	09 29	09 36	09 44	09 51	09 59	10 05	10 14	10 23	10 29	10 37	10 44	10 51	10 59	11 06	11 14	11 21
West Hampstead	⊖ d	08 46	08 53	09 01	09 08	09 16	09 23	09 31	09 38	09 46	09 53	10 01	10 07	10 16	10 25	10 31	10 39	10 46	10 53	11 01	11 08	11 16	11 23
Finchley Road & Frognal	d	08 47	08 54	09 02	09 09	09 17	09 24	09 32	09 39	09 47	09 54	10 02	10 08	10 17	10 26	10 32	10 41	10 47	10 54	11 02	11 09	11 17	11 24
Hampstead Heath	d	08 50	08 57	09 05	09 12	09 20	09 27	09 35	09 42	09 50	09 57	10 05	10 11	10 20	10 29	10 35	10 43	10 50	10 57	11 05	11 12	11 20	11 27
Gospel Oak	d	08 52	08 59	09 07	09 14	09 22	09 29	09 37	09 44	09 52	09 59	10 07	10 13	10 22	10 31	10 37	10 46	10 52	10 59	11 07	11 14	11 23	11 29
Kentish Town West	d	08 54	09 01	09 09	09 16	09 24	09 31	09 39	09 46	09 54	10 01	10 09	10 15	10 24	10 33	10 39	10 48	10 54	11 01	11 09	11 16	11 25	11 31
Camden Road	d	08 59	09 06	09 14	09 21	09 29	09 36	09 44	09 51	09 59	10 06	10 14	10 20	10 29	10 37	10 44	10 51	10 59	11 06	11 14	11 21	11 30	11 36
Caledonian Rd & Barnsbury	d	09 02	09 09	09 17	09 24	09 32	09 39	09 47	09 54	10 02	10 09	10 17	10 23	10 32	10 40	10 47	10 54	11 02	11 09	11 17	11 24	11 33	11 39
Highbury & Islington ⊖178	d	09 04	09 11	09 19	09 26	09 34	09 41	09 50	09 56	10 04	10 11	10 19	10 25	10 34	10 42	10 49	10 56	11 04	11 11	11 19	11 26	11 36	11 41
Canonbury ⊖178	d	09 06	09 13	09 21	09 28	09 36	09 43	09 52	09 58	10 06	10 13	10 21	10 27	10 36	10 44	10 51	10 58	11 06	11 13	11 21	11 28	11 38	11 43
Dalston Kingsland	d	09 08	09 15	09 23	09 30	09 38	09 45	09 54	10 00	10 08	10 15	10 23	10 29	10 38	10 46	10 53	11 00	11 08	11 15	11 23	11 30	11 40	11 45
Hackney Central	d	09 10	09 17	09 25	09 32	09 40	09 47	09 56	10 02	10 10	10 17	10 25	10 31	10 40	10 48	10 55	11 02	11 10	11 17	11 25	11 32	11 42	11 47
Homerton	d	09 12	09 19	09 27	09 34	09 42	09 49	09 58	10 04	10 12	10 19	10 27	10 33	10 42	10 50	10 57	11 04	11 12	11 19	11 27	11 34	11 44	11 49
Hackney Wick	d	09 15	09 22	09 30	09 37	09 45	09 52	10 01	10 07	10 15	10 22	10 30	10 36	10 45	10 53	11 00	11 07	11 15	11 22	11 30	11 37	11 46	11 52
Stratford 7	⊖ ⇌ a	09 22	09 29	09 37	09 42	09 52	09 58	10 07	10 12	10 22	10 29	10 37	10 42	10 51	10 59	11 06	11 12	11 21	11 28	11 36	11 42	11 51	11 59

		LO	LO	LO	LO	LO	LO	LO	LO	LO	LO	LO	LO	LO	LO	LO	LO	LO	LO	LO	LO	LO	LO
Richmond	⊖ d		11 10		11 27		11 40		11 57		12 10		12 27		12 40		12 57		13 10		13 27		13 40
Kew Gardens	⊖ d		11 13		11 30		11 43		12 00		12 13		12 30		12 43		13 00		13 13		13 30		13 43
Gunnersbury	⊖ d		11 16		11 33		11 46		12 03		12 16		12 33		12 46		13 03		13 16		13 33		13 46
South Acton	d		11 19		11 36		11 49		12 06		12 19		12 36		12 49		13 06		13 19		13 36		13 49
Acton Central	d		11 23		11 39		11 53		12 09		12 23		12 39		12 53		13 09		13 23		13 39		13 53
Clapham Junction 10 66,176	d	11 02		11 17		11 32		11 47		12 02		12 17		12 32		12 47		13 02		13 17		13 32	
Imperial Wharf 176	d	11 06		11 21		11 36		11 51		12 06		12 21		12 36		12 51		13 06		13 21		13 36	
West Brompton ⊖176	d	11 09		11 24		11 39		11 54		12 09		12 24		12 39		12 54		13 09		13 24		13 39	
Kensington (Olympia) ⊖176	d	11 12		11 27		11 42		11 57		12 12		12 27		12 42		12 57		13 12		13 27		13 42	
Shepherd's Bush ⊖66,176	d	11 14		11 29		11 44		11 59		12 14		12 29		12 44		12 59		13 14		13 29		13 44	
Willesden Jn Low Level	⊖ d																						
Willesden Jn. High Level	⊖ a	11 22	11 29	11 36	11 46	11 53	11 59	12 07	12 16	12 22	12 30	12 37	12 46	12 52	12 59	13 06	13 16	13 22	13 29	13 37	13 44	13 51	13 59
	d	11 23	11 30	11 37	11 47	11 54	12 00	12 08	12 17	12 23	12 31	12 38	12 47	12 53	13 00	13 07	13 17	13 23	13 30	13 38	13 45	13 53	14 00
Kensal Rise	d	11 25	11 32	11 39	11 50	11 56	12 02	12 10	12 19	12 25	12 34	12 40	12 49	12 55	13 02	13 09	13 19	13 25	13 32	13 40	13 47	13 55	14 02
Brondesbury Park	d	11 27	11 34	11 41	11 52	11 58	12 04	12 12	12 21	12 27	12 36	12 42	12 51	12 57	13 04	13 11	13 21	13 27	13 34	13 42	13 49	13 57	14 04
Brondesbury	d	11 29	11 36	11 43	11 53	12 00	12 06	12 14	12 23	12 29	12 37	12 44	12 53	12 59	13 06	13 13	13 23	13 29	13 36	13 44	13 51	13 59	14 06
West Hampstead	⊖ d	11 31	11 38	11 45	11 55	12 02	12 08	12 16	12 25	12 31	12 39	12 46	12 55	13 01	13 08	13 15	13 25	13 31	13 38	13 46	13 53	14 01	14 08
Finchley Road & Frognal	d	11 32	11 39	11 46	11 57	12 03	12 09	12 17	12 26	12 32	12 41	12 47	12 56	13 02	13 09	13 16	13 26	13 32	13 39	13 47	13 54	14 02	14 09
Hampstead Heath	d	11 35	11 42	11 49	11 59	12 06	12 12	12 20	12 29	12 35	12 43	12 50	12 59	13 05	13 12	13 19	13 29	13 35	13 42	13 50	13 57	14 05	14 12
Gospel Oak	d	11 37	11 44	11 51	12 02	12 08	12 14	12 22	12 32	12 37	12 46	12 52	13 01	13 07	13 14	13 21	13 31	13 37	13 44	13 52	13 59	14 07	14 14
Kentish Town West	d	11 39	11 46	11 53	12 04	12 10	12 16	12 24	12 34	12 39	12 48	12 54	13 03	13 09	13 16	13 23	13 33	13 39	13 46	13 54	14 01	14 09	14 16
Camden Road	d	11 44	11 51	11 58	12 06	12 14	12 21	12 29	12 37	12 44	12 51	12 59	13 06	13 14	13 20	13 28	13 36	13 44	13 51	13 57	14 06	14 14	14 21
Caledonian Rd & Barnsbury	d	11 47	11 54	12 01	12 09	12 17	12 24	12 32	12 40	12 47	12 54	13 02	13 09	13 17	13 23	13 31	13 39	13 47	13 54	14 00	14 09	14 17	14 24
Highbury & Islington ⊖178	d	11 49	11 56	12 04	12 12	12 19	12 26	12 34	12 42	12 49	12 56	13 04	13 11	13 19	13 25	13 34	13 41	13 49	13 56	14 02	14 11	14 19	14 26
Canonbury ⊖178	d	11 51	11 58	12 06	12 14	12 21	12 28	12 36	12 44	12 51	12 58	13 06	13 13	13 21	13 27	13 36	13 43	13 51	13 58	14 04	14 13	14 21	14 28
Dalston Kingsland	d	11 53	12 00	12 08	12 16	12 23	12 30	12 38	12 46	12 53	13 00	13 08	13 15	13 23	13 29	13 38	13 45	13 53	14 00	14 06	14 15	14 23	14 30
Hackney Central	d	11 55	12 02	12 10	12 18	12 25	12 32	12 40	12 48	12 55	13 02	13 10	13 17	13 25	13 31	13 40	13 47	13 55	14 02	14 08	14 17	14 25	14 32
Homerton	d	11 57	12 04	12 12	12 20	12 27	12 34	12 42	12 50	12 57	13 04	13 12	13 19	13 27	13 33	13 42	13 49	13 57	14 04	14 10	14 19	14 27	14 34
Hackney Wick	d	12 00	12 07	12 15	12 22	12 30	12 37	12 45	12 53	13 00	13 07	13 15	13 22	13 30	13 36	13 45	13 52	14 00	14 07	14 13	14 22	14 30	14 37
Stratford 7	⊖ ⇌ a	12 06	12 12	12 21	12 29	12 36	12 42	12 51	12 59	13 06	13 12	13 21	13 29	13 36	13 42	13 51	13 59	14 06	14 12	14 21	14 29	14 36	14 42

For services between Shepherds Bush and Clapham Junction refer to Table T066 and T176

Table T059-R

Saturdays
26 May to 8 December

Richmond and Clapham Junction - Willesden Junction, West Hampstead, Highbury & Islington and Stratford

		LO	LO	LO	LO	LO	LO	LO	LO	LO	LO	LO	LO	LO	LO	LO	LO	LO	LO	LO	LO	LO	LO
Richmond	⊖ d		13 57		14 10		14 27		14 40		14 57		15 10		15 27		15 40		15 57		16 10		16 27
Kew Gardens	⊖ d		14 00		14 13		14 30		14 43		15 00		15 13		15 30		15 43		16 00		16 13		16 30
Gunnersbury	⊖ d		14 03		14 16		14 33		14 46		15 03		15 16		15 33		15 46		16 03		16 16		16 33
South Acton	d		14 06		14 19		14 36		14 49		15 06		15 19		15 36		15 49		16 06		16 19		16 36
Acton Central	d		14 09		14 23		14 39		14 53		15 09		15 23		15 39		15 53		16 09		16 23		16 39
Clapham Junction 10 66,176	d	13 47		14 02		14 17		14 32		14 47		15 02		15 17		15 32		15 47		16 02		16 17	
Imperial Wharf 176	d	13 51		14 06		14 21		14 36		14 51		15 06		15 21		15 36		15 51		16 06		16 21	
West Brompton ⊖176	d	13 54		14 09		14 24		14 39		14 54		15 09		15 24		15 39		15 54		16 09		16 24	
Kensington (Olympia) ⊖176	d	13 57		14 12		14 27		14 42		14 57		15 12		15 27		15 42		15 57		16 12		16 27	
Shepherd's Bush ⊖66,176	d	13 59		14 14		14 29		14 44		14 59		15 14		15 29		15 44		15 59		16 14		16 29	
Willesden Jn Low Level	⊖ d																						
Willesden Jn. High Level	⊖ a	14 06	14 15	14 22	14 28	14 37	14 44	14 52	14 59	15 07	15 14	15 22	15 29	15 37	15 44	15 52	15 58	16 07	16 14	16 22	16 29	16 37	16 44
	d	14 07	14 16	14 23	14 29	14 38	14 45	14 53	15 00	15 08	15 15	15 23	15 30	15 38	15 45	15 53	15 59	16 08	16 15	16 23	16 30	16 38	16 45
Kensal Rise	d	14 09	14 19	14 25	14 31	14 40	14 47	14 55	15 02	15 10	15 17	15 25	15 32	15 40	15 47	15 55	16 01	16 10	16 17	16 25	16 32	16 40	16 47
Brondesbury Park	d	14 11	14 21	14 27	14 33	14 42	14 49	14 57	15 04	15 12	15 19	15 27	15 34	15 42	15 49	15 57	16 03	16 12	16 19	16 27	16 34	16 42	16 49
Brondesbury	d	14 13	14 22	14 29	14 35	14 44	14 51	14 59	15 06	15 14	15 21	15 29	15 36	15 44	15 51	15 59	16 05	16 14	16 21	16 29	16 36	16 44	16 51
West Hampstead	⊖ d	14 15	14 24	14 31	14 37	14 46	14 53	15 01	15 08	15 16	15 23	15 31	15 38	15 46	15 53	16 01	16 07	16 16	16 23	16 31	16 38	16 46	16 53
Finchley Road & Frognal	d	14 16	14 26	14 32	14 38	14 47	14 54	15 02	15 09	15 17	15 24	15 32	15 40	15 47	15 54	16 02	16 08	16 17	16 24	16 32	16 39	16 47	16 54
Hampstead Heath	d	14 19	14 28	14 35	14 41	14 50	14 57	15 05	15 12	15 20	15 27	15 35	15 42	15 50	15 57	16 05	16 11	16 20	16 27	16 35	16 42	16 50	16 57
Gospel Oak	d	14 21	14 31	14 37	14 44	14 52	14 59	15 07	15 14	15 22	15 29	15 37	15 45	15 52	15 59	16 07	16 13	16 22	16 29	16 37	16 44	16 52	16 59
Kentish Town West	d	14 23	14 33	14 39	14 46	14 54	15 01	15 09	15 16	15 24	15 31	15 39	15 47	15 54	16 01	16 09	16 15	16 24	16 31	16 39	16 46	16 54	17 01
Camden Road	d	14 26	14 36	14 44	14 51	14 59	15 06	15 14	15 21	15 29	15 36	15 44	15 52	15 59	16 06	16 14	16 20	16 27	16 36	16 44	16 51	16 57	17 06
Caledonian Rd & Barnsbury	d	14 29	14 39	14 47	14 54	15 02	15 09	15 17	15 24	15 32	15 39	15 47	15 55	16 02	16 09	16 17	16 23	16 30	16 39	16 47	16 54	17 00	17 09
Highbury & Islington ⊖178	d	14 32	14 41	14 49	14 56	15 04	15 11	15 19	15 26	15 34	15 41	15 49	15 57	16 04	16 11	16 19	16 25	16 32	16 41	16 49	16 56	17 02	17 11
Canonbury ⊖178	d	14 34	14 43	14 51	14 58	15 06	15 13	15 21	15 28	15 36	15 43	15 51	15 59	16 06	16 13	16 21	16 27	16 34	16 43	16 51	16 58	17 04	17 13
Dalston Kingsland	d	14 37	14 45	14 53	15 00	15 08	15 15	15 23	15 30	15 38	15 45	15 53	16 01	16 08	16 15	16 23	16 29	16 36	16 45	16 53	17 00	17 06	17 15
Hackney Central	d	14 39	14 47	14 55	15 02	15 10	15 17	15 25	15 32	15 40	15 47	15 55	16 03	16 10	16 17	16 25	16 31	16 38	16 47	16 55	17 02	17 08	17 17
Homerton	d	14 42	14 49	14 57	15 04	15 12	15 19	15 27	15 34	15 42	15 49	15 57	16 05	16 12	16 19	16 27	16 33	16 40	16 49	16 57	17 04	17 10	17 19
Hackney Wick	d	14 45	14 52	15 00	15 07	15 15	15 22	15 30	15 37	15 45	15 52	16 00	16 08	16 15	16 22	16 30	16 36	16 43	16 52	17 00	17 07	17 13	17 22
Stratford 7	⊖ ⇌ a	14 51	14 59	15 06	15 12	15 21	15 29	15 36	15 42	15 51	15 59	16 06	16 12	16 21	16 29	16 36	16 42	16 51	16 59	17 07	17 12	17 22	17 29

		LO	LO	LO	LO	LO	LO	LO	LO	LO	LO	LO	LO	LO	LO	LO	LO	LO	LO	LO	LO	LO	LO
Richmond	⊖ d		16 40		16 57		17 10		17 27		17 39		17 57		18 10		18 27		18 40		18 57		19 10
Kew Gardens	⊖ d		16 43		17 00		17 13		17 30		17 42		18 00		18 13		18 30		18 43		19 00		19 13
Gunnersbury	⊖ d		16 46		17 03		17 16		17 33		17 45		18 03		18 16		18 33		18 46		19 03		19 16
South Acton	d		16 49		17 06		17 19		17 36		17 48		18 06		18 19		18 36		18 49		19 06		19 19
Acton Central	d		16 53		17 09		17 23		17 39		17 52		18 09		18 23		18 39		18 53		19 09		19 23
Clapham Junction 10 66,176	d	16 32		16 47		17 02		17 17		17 32		17 47		18 02		18 17		18 32		18 47		19 02	
Imperial Wharf 176	d	16 36		16 51		17 06		17 21		17 36		17 51		18 06		18 21		18 36		18 51		19 06	
West Brompton ⊖176	d	16 39		16 54		17 09		17 24		17 39		17 54		18 09		18 24		18 39		18 54		19 09	
Kensington (Olympia) ⊖176	d	16 42		16 57		17 12		17 27		17 42		17 57		18 12		18 27		18 42		18 57		19 12	
Shepherd's Bush ⊖66,176	d	16 44		16 59		17 14		17 29		17 44		17 59		18 14		18 29		18 44		18 59		19 14	
Willesden Jn Low Level	⊖ d																						
Willesden Jn. High Level	⊖ a	16 52	16 59	17 07	17 14	17 22	17 29	17 37	17 44	17 51	17 57	18 06	18 14	18 22	18 29	18 37	18 44	18 52	18 59	19 07	19 14	19 22	19 29
	d	16 53	17 00	17 08	17 15	17 23	17 30	17 38	17 45	17 52	17 58	18 07	18 15	18 23	18 30	18 38	18 45	18 53	19 00	19 08	19 15	19 23	19 30
Kensal Rise	d	16 55	17 02	17 10	17 17	17 25	17 32	17 40	17 47	17 54	18 00	18 09	18 18	18 25	18 32	18 40	18 47	18 55	19 02	19 10	19 17	19 25	19 32
Brondesbury Park	d	16 57	17 04	17 12	17 19	17 27	17 34	17 42	17 49	17 56	18 02	18 11	18 20	18 27	18 34	18 42	18 49	18 57	19 04	19 12	19 19	19 27	19 34
Brondesbury	d	16 59	17 06	17 14	17 21	17 29	17 36	17 44	17 51	17 58	18 04	18 13	18 21	18 29	18 36	18 44	18 51	18 59	19 06	19 14	19 21	19 29	19 36
West Hampstead	⊖ d	17 01	17 08	17 16	17 23	17 31	17 38	17 46	17 53	18 00	18 06	18 15	18 23	18 31	18 38	18 46	18 53	19 01	19 08	19 16	19 23	19 31	19 38
Finchley Road & Frognal	d	17 02	17 09	17 17	17 24	17 32	17 39	17 47	17 55	18 01	18 07	18 16	18 25	18 32	18 39	18 47	18 54	19 02	19 09	19 17	19 24	19 32	19 39
Hampstead Heath	d	17 05	17 12	17 20	17 27	17 35	17 42	17 50	17 57	18 04	18 10	18 19	18 27	18 35	18 42	18 50	18 57	19 05	19 12	19 20	19 27	19 35	19 42
Gospel Oak	d	17 07	17 14	17 22	17 29	17 37	17 44	17 52	18 00	18 06	18 12	18 21	18 30	18 37	18 44	18 52	18 59	19 07	19 14	19 22	19 29	19 39	19 44
Kentish Town West	d	17 09	17 16	17 24	17 31	17 39	17 46	17 54	18 02	18 08	18 14	18 23	18 32	18 39	18 46	18 54	19 01	19 09	19 16	19 24	19 31	19 41	19 46
Camden Road	d	17 14	17 21	17 29	17 36	17 44	17 51	17 59	18 06	18 11	18 17	18 26	18 36	18 44	18 51	18 59	19 06	19 14	19 21	19 29	19 36	19 44	19 51
Caledonian Rd & Barnsbury	d	17 17	17 24	17 32	17 39	17 47	17 54	18 02	18 09	18 14	18 20	18 29	18 39	18 47	18 54	19 02	19 09	19 17	19 24	19 32	19 39	19 47	19 54
Highbury & Islington ⊖178	d	17 19	17 26	17 34	17 41	17 49	17 56	18 04	18 11	18 17	18 23	18 31	18 41	18 49	18 56	19 04	19 11	19 19	19 26	19 34	19 41	19 49	19 56
Canonbury ⊖178	d	17 21	17 28	17 36	17 43	17 51	17 58	18 06	18 13	18 19	18 25	18 33	18 43	18 51	18 58	19 06	19 13	19 21	19 28	19 36	19 43	19 51	19 58
Dalston Kingsland	d	17 23	17 30	17 38	17 45	17 53	18 00	18 08	18 15	18 22	18 28	18 35	18 45	18 53	19 00	19 08	19 15	19 23	19 30	19 38	19 45	19 53	20 00
Hackney Central	d	17 25	17 32	17 40	17 47	17 55	18 02	18 10	18 17	18 24	18 30	18 37	18 47	18 55	19 02	19 10	19 17	19 25	19 32	19 40	19 47	19 55	20 02
Homerton	d	17 27	17 34	17 42	17 49	17 57	18 04	18 12	18 19	18 27	18 33	18 39	18 49	18 57	19 04	19 12	19 19	19 27	19 34	19 42	19 49	19 57	20 04
Hackney Wick	d	17 30	17 37	17 45	17 52	18 00	18 07	18 15	18 22	18 30	18 36	18 42	18 52	19 00	19 07	19 15	19 22	19 30	19 37	19 45	19 52	20 00	20 07
Stratford 7	⊖ ⇌ a	17 37	17 42	17 52	17 59	18 07	18 12	18 22	18 29	18 37	18 42	18 52	18 59	19 07	19 12	19 22	19 29	19 37	19 42	19 51	19 59	20 06	20 12

For services between Shepherds Bush and Clapham Junction refer to Table T066 and T176

Table T059-R

Saturdays
26 May to 8 December

Richmond and Clapham Junction - Willesden Junction, West Hampstead, Highbury & Islington and Stratford

	LO	LO	LO	LO	LO	LO	LO	LO	LO	LO	LO	LO	LO	LO	LO	LO	LO	LO	LO	LO	LO	LO
Richmond ⊖ d		19 27		19 40		19 57		20 10		20 27		20 40		20 57		21 10		21 27		21 40		21 57
Kew Gardens ⊖ d		19 30		19 43		20 00		20 13		20 30		20 43		21 00		21 13		21 30		21 43		22 00
Gunnersbury ⊖ d		19 33		19 46		20 03		20 16		20 33		20 46		21 03		21 16		21 33		21 46		22 03
South Acton d		19 36		19 49		20 06		20 19		20 36		20 49		21 06		21 19		21 36		21 49		22 06
Acton Central d		19 39		19 52		20 09		20 23		20 39		20 53		21 09		21 23		21 39		21 53		22 09
Clapham Junction [10] 66,176 d	19 17		19 32		19 47		20 02		20 17		20 32		20 47		21 02		21 17		21 32		21 47	
Imperial Wharf 176 d	19 21		19 36		19 51		20 06		20 21		20 36		20 51		21 06		21 21		21 36		21 51	
West Brompton ⊖176 d	19 24		19 39		19 54		20 09		20 24		20 39		20 54		21 09		21 24		21 39		21 54	
Kensington (Olympia) ⊖176 d	19 27		19 42		19 57		20 12		20 27		20 42		20 57		21 12		21 27		21 42		21 57	
Shepherd's Bush ⊖66,176 d	19 29		19 44		19 59		20 14		20 29		20 44		20 59		21 14		21 29		21 44		21 59	
Willesden Jn Low Level ⊖ d																						
Willesden Jn. High Level ⊖ a	19 37	19 44	19 52	19 58	20 07	20 14	20 22	20 29	20 37	20 44	20 52	20 59	21 07	21 14	21 22	21 29	21 37	21 44	21 52	21 59	22 07	22 14
d	19 38	19 45	19 53	20 00	20 08	20 15	20 23	20 31	20 38	20 45	20 53	21 00	21 08	21 15	21 23	21 30	21 38	21 45	21 53	22 00	22 08	22 15
Kensal Rise d	19 40	19 47	19 55	20 02	20 10	20 17	20 25	20 33	20 40	20 47	20 55	21 02	21 10	21 17	21 25	21 32	21 40	21 47	21 55	22 02	22 10	22 17
Brondesbury Park d	19 42	19 49	19 57	20 04	20 12	20 19	20 27	20 35	20 42	20 49	20 57	21 04	21 12	21 19	21 27	21 34	21 42	21 49	21 57	22 04	22 12	22 19
Brondesbury d	19 44	19 51	19 59	20 06	20 14	20 21	20 29	20 37	20 44	20 51	20 59	21 06	21 14	21 21	21 29	21 36	21 44	21 51	21 59	22 06	22 14	22 21
West Hampstead ⊖ d	19 46	19 53	20 01	20 08	20 16	20 23	20 31	20 39	20 46	20 53	21 01	21 08	21 16	21 23	21 31	21 38	21 46	21 53	22 01	22 08	22 16	22 23
Finchley Road & Frognal d	19 47	19 54	20 02	20 09	20 17	20 24	20 32	20 41	20 47	20 54	21 02	21 09	21 17	21 24	21 32	21 39	21 47	21 54	22 02	22 09	22 17	22 24
Hampstead Heath d	19 50	19 57	20 05	20 12	20 20	20 27	20 35	20 43	20 50	20 57	21 05	21 12	21 20	21 27	21 35	21 42	21 50	21 57	22 05	22 12	22 20	22 27
Gospel Oak d	19 52	19 59	20 07	20 14	20 22	20 29	20 37	20 46	20 52	20 59	21 07	21 14	21 22	21 29	21 37	21 44	21 52	21 59	22 07	22 14	22 22	22 29
Kentish Town West d	19 54	20 01	20 09	20 16	20 24	20 31	20 39	20 48	20 54	21 01	21 09	21 16	21 24	21 31	21 39	21 46	21 54	22 01	22 09	22 16	22 24	22 31
Camden Road d	19 59	20 06	20 14	20 21	20 29	20 36	20 44	20 53	20 59	21 06	21 14	21 21	21 29	21 36	21 44	21 51	21 59	22 06	22 14	22 21	22 29	22 36
Caledonian Rd & Barnsbury d	20 02	20 09	20 17	20 24	20 32	20 39	20 47	20 56	21 02	21 09	21 17	21 24	21 32	21 39	21 47	21 54	22 02	22 09	22 17	22 24	22 32	22 39
Highbury & Islington ⊖178 d	20 04	20 11	20 19	20 26	20 34	20 41	20 49	20 58	21 04	21 11	21 19	21 26	21 34	21 41	21 49	21 56	22 04	22 11	22 19	22 26	22 34	22 41
Canonbury ⊖178 d	20 06	20 13	20 21	20 28	20 36	20 43	20 51	21 00	21 06	21 13	21 21	21 28	21 36	21 43	21 51	21 58	22 06	22 13	22 21	22 28	22 36	22 43
Dalston Kingsland d	20 08	20 15	20 23	20 30	20 38	20 45	20 53	21 02	21 08	21 15	21 23	21 30	21 38	21 45	21 53	22 00	22 08	22 15	22 23	22 30	22 38	22 45
Hackney Central d	20 10	20 17	20 25	20 32	20 40	20 47	20 55	21 04	21 10	21 17	21 25	21 32	21 40	21 47	21 55	22 02	22 10	22 17	22 25	22 32	22 40	22 47
Homerton d	20 12	20 19	20 27	20 34	20 42	20 49	20 57	21 06	21 12	21 19	21 27	21 34	21 42	21 49	21 57	22 04	22 12	22 19	22 27	22 34	22 42	22 49
Hackney Wick d	20 15	20 22	20 30	20 37	20 45	20 52	21 00	21 09	21 15	21 22	21 30	21 37	21 45	21 52	22 00	22 07	22 15	22 22	22 30	22 37	22 45	22 52
Stratford [7] ⊖ a	20 21	20 29	20 36	20 42	20 51	20 59	21 06	21 14	21 21	21 29	21 36	21 42	21 51	21 59	22 06	22 12	22 21	22 29	22 36	22 42	22 51	22 59

	LO	LO	LO	LO	LO	LO	LO	LO	LO	LO	LO	LO	LO	LO
Richmond ⊖ d		22 18		22 27		22 40		22 57		23 08		23 27		
Kew Gardens ⊖ d		22 21		22 30		22 43		23 00		23 11		23 30		
Gunnersbury ⊖ d		22 24		22 33		22 46		23 03		23 14		23 33		
South Acton d		22 27		22 36		22 49		23 06		23 17		23 36		
Acton Central d		22 30		22 39		22 53		23 09		23 20		23 39		
Clapham Junction [10] 66,176 d	22 02		22 17		22 32		22 47		23 02		23 17		23 32	23 47
Imperial Wharf 176 d	22 06		22 21		22 36		22 51		23 06		23 21		23 36	23 51
West Brompton ⊖176 d	22 09		22 24		22 39		22 54		23 09		23 24		23 39	23 54
Kensington (Olympia) ⊖176 d	22 12		22 27		22 42		22 57		23 12		23 27		23 42	23 57
Shepherd's Bush ⊖66,176 d	22 14		22 29		22 44		22 59		23 14		23 29		23 44	23 59
Willesden Jn Low Level ⊖ d														
Willesden Jn. High Level ⊖ a	22 22	22 35	22 39	22 44	22 52	22 58	23 08	23 14	23 21	23 25	23 38	23 47	23 55	00 09
d	22 23	22 36		22 45	22 53	22 59		23 15	23 22	23 26				
Kensal Rise d	22 25	22 38		22 47	22 55	23 01		23 17	23 24	23 28				
Brondesbury Park d	22 27	22 40		22 49	22 57	23 03		23 19	23 26	23 30				
Brondesbury d	22 29	22 42		22 51	22 59	23 05		23 21	23 28	23 32				
West Hampstead ⊖ d	22 31	22 44		22 53	23 01	23 07		23 23	23 30	23 34				
Finchley Road & Frognal d	22 32	22 45		22 54	23 02	23 08		23 24	23 31	23 36				
Hampstead Heath d	22 35	22 48		22 57	23 05	23 11		23 27	23 34	23 38				
Gospel Oak d	22 37	22 50		22 59	23 07	23 14		23 29	23 36	23 41				
Kentish Town West d	22 39	22 52		23 01	23 09	23 16		23 31	23 38	23 43				
Camden Road d	22 44	22 55		23 06	23 14	23 21		23 36	23 43	23 47				
Caledonian Rd & Barnsbury d	22 47	22 58		23 09	23 17	23 24		23 39	23 46	23 50				
Highbury & Islington ⊖178 d	22 49	23 00		23 11	23 19	23 26		23 41	23 48	23 53				
Canonbury ⊖178 d	22 51	23 02		23 13	23 21	23 28		23 43	23 50	23 55				
Dalston Kingsland d	22 53	23 04		23 15	23 23	23 30		23 45	23 52	23 57				
Hackney Central d	22 55	23 06		23 17	23 25	23 32		23 47	23 54	23 59				
Homerton d	22 57	23 08		23 19	23 27	23 34		23 49	23 56	00 01				
Hackney Wick d	23 00	23 11		23 22	23 30	23 37		23 52	23 59	00 04				
Stratford [7] ⊖ a	23 06	23 20		23 28	23 36	23 42		23 59	00 06	00 10				

For services between Shepherds Bush and Clapham Junction refer to Table T066 and T176

Table T059-R

Sundays
20 May to 2 December

Richmond and Clapham Junction - Willesden Junction, West Hampstead, Highbury & Islington and Stratford

	LO	LO	LO	LO	LO	LO	LO	LO	LO	LO	LO	LO	LO	LO	LO	LO	LO	LO	LO	LO	LO	LO
Richmond ⊖ d					08 59		09 10		09 27		09 40		09 58		10 10		10 26		10 40		10 56	
Kew Gardens ⊖ d					09 02		09 13		09 30		09 43		10 01		10 13		10 30		10 43		11 00	
Gunnersbury ⊖ d					09 05		09 16		09 33		09 46		10 04		10 16		10 33		10 46		11 03	
South Acton d					09 08		09 19		09 36		09 49		10 07		10 19		10 36		10 49		11 06	
Acton Central d					09 11		09 22		09 39		09 52		10 10		10 22		10 39		10 52		11 09	
Clapham Junction [10] 66,176 d		08 31		08 51		09 01		09 21		09 31		09 50		10 01		10 13		10 29		10 44		10 59
Imperial Wharf 176 d		08 35		08 55		09 05		09 25		09 35		09 54		10 05		10 17		10 33		10 48		11 03
West Brompton ⊖176 d		08 38		08 58		09 08		09 28		09 38		09 57		10 08		10 20		10 36		10 51		11 06
Kensington (Olympia) ⊖176 d		08 41		09 01		09 11		09 31		09 41		10 00		10 11		10 23		10 39		10 54		11 09
Shepherd's Bush ⊖66,176 d		08 43		09 03		09 13		09 33		09 43		10 02		10 13		10 25		10 41		10 56		11 11
Willesden Jn Low Level ⊖ d			09 01																			
Willesden Jn. High Level ⊖ a		08 52		09 10	09 17	09 22	09 28	09 41	09 46	09 51	09 59	10 10	10 16	10 21	10 28	10 33	10 44	10 50	10 58	11 05	11 15	11 20
d				09 11	09 18		09 29	09 42	09 47	09 52	10 00	10 11	10 17	10 22	10 29	10 34	10 45	10 51	10 59	11 06	11 16	11 21
Kensal Rise d			09 05	09 13	09 20		09 31	09 45	09 49	09 55	10 02	10 13	10 19	10 24	10 31	10 36	10 47	10 53	11 01	11 08	11 18	11 23
Brondesbury Park d			09 07	09 15	09 22		09 33	09 47	09 51	09 57	10 04	10 15	10 21	10 26	10 33	10 38	10 49	10 55	11 03	11 10	11 20	11 25
Brondesbury d			09 09	09 17	09 24		09 35	09 48	09 53	09 58	10 06	10 17	10 23	10 28	10 35	10 40	10 51	10 57	11 05	11 12	11 22	11 27
West Hampstead ⊖ d			09 11	09 19	09 26		09 37	09 50	09 55	10 00	10 08	10 19	10 25	10 30	10 37	10 42	10 53	10 59	11 07	11 14	11 24	11 29
Finchley Road & Frognal d			09 12	09 20	09 27		09 38	09 52	09 56	10 02	10 09	10 20	10 26	10 31	10 38	10 43	10 54	11 00	11 08	11 15	11 25	11 30
Hampstead Heath d			09 15	09 23	09 30		09 41	09 54	09 59	10 04	10 12	10 23	10 29	10 34	10 41	10 46	10 57	11 03	11 11	11 18	11 28	11 33
Gospel Oak d			09 17	09 25	09 32		09 43	09 57	10 01	10 07	10 14	10 25	10 31	10 36	10 43	10 48	10 59	11 05	11 13	11 20	11 30	11 35
Kentish Town West d			09 19	09 27	09 34		09 45	09 59	10 03	10 09	10 16	10 27	10 33	10 38	10 45	10 50	11 01	11 07	11 15	11 22	11 32	11 37
Camden Road d			09 24	09 32	09 39		09 50	10 01	10 07	10 12	10 20	10 31	10 38	10 43	10 50	10 55	11 06	11 12	11 20	11 27	11 36	11 42
Caledonian Rd & Barnsbury d			09 27	09 35	09 42		09 53	10 04	10 10	10 15	10 23	10 34	10 41	10 46	10 53	10 58	11 09	11 15	11 23	11 30	11 39	11 45
Highbury & Islington ⊖178 d			09 29	09 37	09 44		09 55	10 07	10 12	10 18	10 25	10 36	10 43	10 48	10 55	11 00	11 11	11 17	11 25	11 32	11 41	11 47
Canonbury ⊖178 d			09 31	09 39	09 46		09 57	10 09	10 14	10 20	10 27	10 38	10 45	10 50	10 57	11 02	11 13	11 19	11 27	11 34	11 43	11 49
Dalston Kingsland d			09 33	09 41	09 48		09 59	10 11	10 16	10 22	10 29	10 40	10 47	10 52	10 59	11 04	11 15	11 21	11 29	11 36	11 45	11 51
Hackney Central d			09 35	09 43	09 50		10 01	10 13	10 18	10 24	10 31	10 42	10 49	10 54	11 01	11 06	11 17	11 23	11 31	11 38	11 47	11 53
Homerton d	00 01		09 37	09 45	09 52		10 03	10 15	10 20	10 26	10 33	10 44	10 51	10 56	11 03	11 08	11 19	11 25	11 33	11 40	11 49	11 55
Hackney Wick d	00 04		09 40	09 48	09 55		10 06	10 17	10 23	10 28	10 36	10 47	10 54	10 59	11 06	11 11	11 22	11 28	11 36	11 43	11 52	11 58
Stratford [7] ⊖ a	00 10		09 49	09 55	10 01		10 12	10 25	10 29	10 35	10 42	10 54	11 00	11 05	11 12	11 17	11 28	11 34	11 42	11 49	11 58	12 04

	LO	LO	LO	LO	LO	LO	LO	LO	LO	LO	LO	LO	LO	LO	LO	LO	LO	LO	LO	LO	LO	LO
Richmond ⊖ d	11 10		11 26		11 40		11 56		12 10		12 26		12 40		12 56		13 10		13 26		13 40	
Kew Gardens ⊖ d	11 13		11 30		11 43		12 00		12 13		12 30		12 43		13 00		13 13		13 30		13 43	
Gunnersbury ⊖ d	11 16		11 33		11 46		12 03		12 16		12 33		12 46		13 03		13 16		13 33		13 46	
South Acton d	11 19		11 36		11 49		12 06		12 19		12 36		12 49		13 06		13 19		13 36		13 49	
Acton Central d	11 22		11 39		11 52		12 09		12 22		12 39		12 52		13 09		13 22		13 39		13 52	
Clapham Junction [10] 66,176 d		11 12		11 29		11 44		11 59		12 14		12 29		12 44		12 59		13 14		13 29		13 43
Imperial Wharf 176 d		11 16		11 33		11 48		12 03		12 18		12 33		12 48		13 03		13 18		13 33		13 47
West Brompton ⊖176 d		11 19		11 36		11 51		12 06		12 21		12 36		12 51		13 06		13 21		13 36		13 50
Kensington (Olympia) ⊖176 d		11 22		11 39		11 54		12 09		12 24		12 39		12 54		13 09		13 24		13 39		13 53
Shepherd's Bush ⊖66,176 d		11 24		11 41		11 56		12 11		12 26		12 41		12 56		13 11		13 26		13 41		13 55
Willesden Jn Low Level ⊖ d																						
Willesden Jn. High Level ⊖ a	11 28	11 33	11 44	11 50	11 58	12 05	12 14	12 20	12 28	12 35	12 44	12 50	12 58	13 05	13 14	13 20	13 28	13 35	13 44	13 50	13 58	14 03
d	11 29	11 34	11 45	11 51	11 59	12 06	12 15	12 21	12 29	12 36	12 45	12 51	12 59	13 06	13 15	13 21	13 29	13 36	13 45	13 51	13 59	14 04
Kensal Rise d	11 31	11 36	11 47	11 53	12 01	12 08	12 17	12 23	12 31	12 38	12 47	12 53	13 01	13 08	13 17	13 23	13 31	13 38	13 47	13 53	14 01	14 06
Brondesbury Park d	11 33	11 38	11 49	11 55	12 03	12 10	12 19	12 25	12 33	12 40	12 49	12 55	13 03	13 10	13 19	13 25	13 33	13 40	13 49	13 55	14 03	14 08
Brondesbury d	11 35	11 40	11 51	11 57	12 05	12 12	12 21	12 27	12 35	12 42	12 51	12 57	13 05	13 12	13 21	13 27	13 35	13 42	13 51	13 57	14 05	14 10
West Hampstead ⊖ d	11 37	11 42	11 53	11 59	12 07	12 14	12 23	12 29	12 37	12 44	12 53	12 59	13 07	13 14	13 23	13 29	13 37	13 44	13 53	13 59	14 07	14 13
Finchley Road & Frognal d	11 38	11 43	11 54	12 00	12 08	12 15	12 24	12 30	12 38	12 45	12 54	13 00	13 08	13 15	13 24	13 30	13 38	13 45	13 54	14 00	14 08	14 14
Hampstead Heath d	11 41	11 46	11 57	12 03	12 11	12 18	12 27	12 33	12 41	12 48	12 57	13 03	13 11	13 18	13 27	13 33	13 41	13 48	13 57	14 03	14 11	14 17
Gospel Oak d	11 43	11 48	11 59	12 05	12 13	12 20	12 29	12 35	12 43	12 50	12 59	13 05	13 13	13 20	13 29	13 35	13 43	13 50	13 59	14 05	14 13	14 19
Kentish Town West d	11 45	11 50	12 01	12 07	12 15	12 22	12 31	12 37	12 45	12 52	13 01	13 07	13 15	13 22	13 31	13 37	13 45	13 52	14 01	14 07	14 15	14 21
Camden Road d	11 50	11 55	12 06	12 12	12 20	12 27	12 36	12 42	12 50	12 57	13 06	13 12	13 20	13 27	13 36	13 42	13 50	13 57	14 06	14 12	14 20	14 25
Caledonian Rd & Barnsbury d	11 53	11 58	12 09	12 15	12 23	12 30	12 39	12 45	12 53	13 00	13 09	13 15	13 23	13 30	13 39	13 45	13 53	14 00	14 09	14 15	14 23	14 28
Highbury & Islington ⊖178 d	11 55	12 00	12 11	12 17	12 25	12 32	12 41	12 47	12 55	13 02	13 11	13 17	13 25	13 32	13 41	13 47	13 55	14 02	14 11	14 17	14 25	14 31
Canonbury ⊖178 d	11 57	12 02	12 13	12 19	12 27	12 34	12 43	12 49	12 57	13 04	13 13	13 19	13 27	13 34	13 43	13 49	13 57	14 04	14 13	14 19	14 27	14 33
Dalston Kingsland d	11 59	12 04	12 15	12 21	12 29	12 36	12 45	12 51	12 59	13 06	13 15	13 21	13 29	13 36	13 45	13 51	13 59	14 06	14 15	14 21	14 29	14 35
Hackney Central d	12 01	12 06	12 17	12 23	12 31	12 38	12 47	12 53	13 01	13 08	13 17	13 23	13 31	13 38	13 47	13 53	14 01	14 08	14 17	14 23	14 31	14 37
Homerton d	12 03	12 08	12 19	12 25	12 33	12 40	12 49	12 55	13 03	13 10	13 19	13 25	13 33	13 40	13 49	13 55	14 03	14 10	14 19	14 25	14 33	14 39
Hackney Wick d	12 06	12 11	12 22	12 28	12 36	12 43	12 52	12 58	13 06	13 13	13 22	13 28	13 36	13 43	13 52	13 58	14 06	14 13	14 22	14 28	14 36	14 42
Stratford [7] ⊖ a	12 12	12 17	12 28	12 33	12 42	12 48	12 58	13 03	13 12	13 18	13 28	13 33	13 42	13 48	13 58	14 03	14 12	14 18	14 28	14 33	14 42	14 47

For services between Shepherds Bush and Clapham Junction refer to Table T066 and T176

Table T059-R

Sundays
20 May to 2 December

Richmond and Clapham Junction - Willesden Junction, West Hampstead, Highbury & Islington and Stratford

		LO	LO	LO	LO	LO	LO	LO	LO	LO	LO	LO	LO	LO	LO	LO	LO	LO	LO	LO	LO	LO	LO
Richmond ⊖	d	13 56		14 10		14 26		14 40		14 56		15 10		15 26		15 40		15 56		16 09		16 26	
Kew Gardens ⊖	d	14 00		14 13		14 30		14 43		15 00		15 13		15 30		15 43		16 00		16 12		16 30	
Gunnersbury ⊖	d	14 03		14 16		14 33		14 46		15 03		15 16		15 33		15 46		16 03		16 15		16 33	
South Acton	d	14 06		14 19		14 36		14 49		15 06		15 19		15 36		15 49		16 06		16 18		16 36	
Acton Central	d	14 09		14 22		14 39		14 52		15 09		15 22		15 39		15 52		16 09		16 21		16 39	
Clapham Junction 10 66,176	d		13 59		14 14		14 29		14 44		14 59		15 14		15 29		15 44		15 59		16 14		16 29
Imperial Wharf 176	d		14 03		14 18		14 33		14 49		15 03		15 18		15 33		15 48		16 03		16 19		16 33
West Brompton ⊖176	d		14 06		14 21		14 36		14 52		15 06		15 21		15 36		15 51		16 06		16 22		16 36
Kensington (Olympia) ⊖176	d		14 09		14 24		14 39		14 55		15 09		15 24		15 39		15 54		16 09		16 25		16 39
Shepherd's Bush ⊖66,176	d		14 11		14 26		14 41		14 58		15 11		15 26		15 41		15 56		16 11		16 28		16 41
Willesden Jn Low Level ⊖	d																						
Willesden Jn. High Level ⊖	a	14 14	14 20	14 28	14 35	14 44	14 50	14 57	15 07	15 14	15 20	15 28	15 35	15 44	15 50	15 58	16 05	16 14	16 20	16 27	16 37	16 44	16 50
	d	14 15	14 21	14 29	14 36	14 45	14 51	14 58	15 08	15 15	15 21	15 29	15 36	15 45	15 51	15 59	16 06	16 15	16 21	16 28	16 38	16 45	16 51
Kensal Rise	d	14 17	14 23	14 31	14 38	14 47	14 53	15 00	15 10	15 17	15 23	15 31	15 38	15 47	15 53	16 01	16 08	16 17	16 23	16 30	16 40	16 47	16 53
Brondesbury Park	d	14 19	14 25	14 33	14 40	14 49	14 55	15 02	15 12	15 19	15 25	15 33	15 40	15 49	15 55	16 03	16 10	16 19	16 25	16 32	16 42	16 49	16 55
Brondesbury	d	14 21	14 27	14 35	14 42	14 51	14 57	15 04	15 14	15 21	15 27	15 35	15 42	15 51	15 57	16 05	16 12	16 21	16 27	16 34	16 44	16 51	16 57
West Hampstead ⊖	d	14 23	14 29	14 37	14 44	14 53	14 59	15 06	15 16	15 23	15 29	15 37	15 44	15 53	15 59	16 07	16 14	16 23	16 29	16 36	16 46	16 53	16 59
Finchley Road & Frognal	d	14 24	14 30	14 38	14 45	14 54	15 00	15 07	15 17	15 24	15 30	15 38	15 45	15 54	16 00	16 08	16 15	16 24	16 30	16 37	16 47	16 54	17 00
Hampstead Heath	d	14 27	14 33	14 41	14 48	14 57	15 03	15 10	15 20	15 27	15 33	15 41	15 48	15 57	16 03	16 11	16 18	16 27	16 33	16 40	16 50	16 57	17 03
Gospel Oak	d	14 29	14 35	14 43	14 50	14 59	15 05	15 12	15 22	15 29	15 35	15 43	15 50	15 59	16 05	16 13	16 20	16 29	16 35	16 42	16 52	16 59	17 05
Kentish Town West	d	14 31	14 37	14 45	14 52	15 01	15 07	15 14	15 24	15 31	15 37	15 45	15 52	16 01	16 07	16 15	16 22	16 31	16 37	16 44	16 54	17 01	17 07
Camden Road	d	14 36	14 42	14 50	14 57	15 06	15 12	15 19	15 28	15 36	15 42	15 50	15 57	16 06	16 12	16 20	16 27	16 36	16 42	16 49	16 58	17 06	17 12
Caledonian Rd & Barnsbury	d	14 39	14 45	14 53	15 00	15 09	15 15	15 22	15 31	15 39	15 45	15 53	16 00	16 09	16 15	16 23	16 30	16 39	16 45	16 52	17 01	17 09	17 15
Highbury & Islington ⊖178	d	14 41	14 47	14 55	15 02	15 11	15 17	15 24	15 33	15 41	15 47	15 55	16 02	16 11	16 17	16 25	16 32	16 41	16 47	16 54	17 03	17 11	17 17
Canonbury ⊖178	d	14 43	14 49	14 57	15 04	15 13	15 19	15 26	15 35	15 43	15 49	15 57	16 04	16 13	16 19	16 27	16 34	16 43	16 49	16 56	17 05	17 13	17 19
Dalston Kingsland	d	14 45	14 51	14 59	15 06	15 15	15 21	15 28	15 37	15 45	15 51	15 59	16 06	16 15	16 21	16 29	16 36	16 45	16 51	16 58	17 07	17 15	17 21
Hackney Central	d	14 47	14 53	15 01	15 08	15 17	15 23	15 30	15 39	15 47	15 53	16 01	16 08	16 17	16 23	16 31	16 38	16 47	16 53	17 00	17 09	17 17	17 23
Homerton	d	14 49	14 55	15 03	15 10	15 19	15 25	15 32	15 41	15 49	15 55	16 03	16 10	16 19	16 25	16 33	16 40	16 49	16 55	17 02	17 11	17 19	17 25
Hackney Wick	d	14 52	14 58	15 06	15 13	15 22	15 28	15 35	15 44	15 52	15 58	16 06	16 13	16 22	16 28	16 36	16 43	16 52	16 58	17 05	17 14	17 22	17 28
Stratford 7 ⊖ ⛴	a	14 58	15 03	15 12	15 18	15 28	15 33	15 42	15 48	15 58	16 03	16 12	16 18	16 28	16 33	16 42	16 48	16 58	17 03	17 11	17 18	17 28	17 33

		LO	LO	LO	LO	LO	LO	LO	LO	LO	LO	LO	LO	LO	LO	LO	LO	LO	LO	LO	LO	LO	LO
Richmond ⊖	d	16 40		16 56		17 10		17 26		17 40		17 56		18 10		18 26		18 40		18 56		19 10	
Kew Gardens ⊖	d	16 43		17 00		17 13		17 30		17 43		18 00		18 13		18 30		18 43		19 00		19 13	
Gunnersbury ⊖	d	16 46		17 03		17 16		17 33		17 46		18 03		18 16		18 33		18 46		19 03		19 16	
South Acton	d	16 49		17 06		17 19		17 36		17 49		18 06		18 19		18 36		18 49		19 06		19 19	
Acton Central	d	16 52		17 09		17 22		17 39		17 52		18 09		18 22		18 39		18 52		19 09		19 22	
Clapham Junction 10 66,176	d		16 44		16 59		17 14		17 29		17 44		17 59		18 14		18 29		18 44		18 59		19 14
Imperial Wharf 176	d		16 48		17 03		17 18		17 33		17 48		18 03		18 18		18 33		18 48		19 03		19 18
West Brompton ⊖176	d		16 51		17 06		17 21		17 36		17 51		18 06		18 21		18 36		18 51		19 06		19 21
Kensington (Olympia) ⊖176	d		16 54		17 09		17 24		17 39		17 54		18 09		18 24		18 39		18 54		19 09		19 24
Shepherd's Bush ⊖66,176	d		16 56		17 11		17 26		17 41		17 56		18 11		18 26		18 41		18 56		19 11		19 26
Willesden Jn Low Level ⊖	d																						
Willesden Jn. High Level ⊖	a	16 58	17 05	17 14	17 20	17 28	17 35	17 44	17 50	17 58	18 05	18 14	18 20	18 28	18 35	18 44	18 50	18 58	19 05	19 14	19 20	19 28	19 35
	d	16 59	17 06	17 15	17 21	17 29	17 36	17 45	17 51	17 59	18 06	18 15	18 21	18 29	18 36	18 45	18 51	18 59	19 06	19 15	19 21	19 29	19 36
Kensal Rise	d	17 01	17 08	17 17	17 23	17 31	17 38	17 47	17 53	18 01	18 08	18 17	18 23	18 31	18 38	18 47	18 53	19 01	19 08	19 17	19 23	19 31	19 38
Brondesbury Park	d	17 03	17 10	17 19	17 25	17 33	17 40	17 49	17 55	18 03	18 10	18 19	18 25	18 33	18 40	18 49	18 55	19 03	19 10	19 19	19 25	19 33	19 40
Brondesbury	d	17 05	17 12	17 21	17 27	17 35	17 42	17 51	17 57	18 05	18 12	18 21	18 27	18 35	18 42	18 51	18 57	19 05	19 12	19 21	19 27	19 35	19 42
West Hampstead ⊖	d	17 07	17 14	17 23	17 29	17 37	17 44	17 53	17 59	18 07	18 14	18 23	18 29	18 37	18 44	18 53	18 59	19 07	19 14	19 23	19 29	19 37	19 44
Finchley Road & Frognal	d	17 08	17 15	17 24	17 30	17 38	17 45	17 54	18 00	18 08	18 15	18 24	18 30	18 38	18 45	18 54	19 00	19 08	19 15	19 24	19 30	19 38	19 45
Hampstead Heath	d	17 11	17 18	17 27	17 33	17 41	17 48	17 57	18 03	18 11	18 18	18 27	18 33	18 41	18 48	18 57	19 03	19 11	19 18	19 27	19 33	19 41	19 48
Gospel Oak	d	17 13	17 20	17 29	17 35	17 43	17 50	17 59	18 05	18 13	18 20	18 29	18 35	18 43	18 50	18 59	19 05	19 13	19 20	19 29	19 35	19 43	19 50
Kentish Town West	d	17 15	17 22	17 31	17 37	17 45	17 52	18 01	18 07	18 15	18 22	18 31	18 37	18 45	18 52	19 01	19 07	19 15	19 22	19 31	19 37	19 45	19 52
Camden Road	d	17 20	17 27	17 36	17 42	17 50	17 57	18 06	18 12	18 20	18 27	18 36	18 42	18 50	18 57	19 06	19 12	19 20	19 27	19 36	19 42	19 50	19 57
Caledonian Rd & Barnsbury	d	17 23	17 30	17 39	17 45	17 53	18 00	18 09	18 15	18 23	18 30	18 39	18 45	18 53	19 00	19 09	19 15	19 23	19 30	19 39	19 45	19 53	20 00
Highbury & Islington ⊖178	d	17 25	17 32	17 41	17 47	17 55	18 02	18 11	18 17	18 25	18 32	18 41	18 47	18 55	19 02	19 11	19 17	19 25	19 32	19 41	19 47	19 55	20 02
Canonbury ⊖178	d	17 27	17 34	17 43	17 49	17 57	18 04	18 13	18 19	18 27	18 34	18 43	18 49	18 57	19 04	19 13	19 19	19 27	19 34	19 43	19 49	19 57	20 04
Dalston Kingsland	d	17 29	17 36	17 45	17 51	17 59	18 06	18 15	18 21	18 29	18 36	18 45	18 51	18 59	19 06	19 15	19 21	19 29	19 36	19 45	19 51	19 59	20 06
Hackney Central	d	17 31	17 38	17 47	17 53	18 01	18 08	18 17	18 23	18 31	18 38	18 47	18 53	19 01	19 08	19 17	19 23	19 31	19 38	19 47	19 53	20 01	20 08
Homerton	d	17 33	17 40	17 49	17 55	18 03	18 10	18 19	18 25	18 33	18 40	18 49	18 55	19 03	19 10	19 19	19 25	19 33	19 40	19 49	19 55	20 03	20 10
Hackney Wick	d	17 36	17 43	17 52	17 58	18 06	18 13	18 22	18 28	18 36	18 43	18 52	18 58	19 06	19 13	19 22	19 28	19 36	19 43	19 52	19 58	20 06	20 13
Stratford 7 ⊖ ⛴	a	17 42	17 48	17 58	18 03	18 12	18 18	18 28	18 33	18 42	18 48	18 58	19 03	19 12	19 18	19 28	19 33	19 42	19 48	19 58	20 03	20 12	20 18

For services between Shepherds Bush and Clapham Junction refer to Table T066 and T176

Table T059-R

Sundays
20 May to 2 December

Richmond and Clapham Junction - Willesden Junction, West Hampstead, Highbury & Islington and Stratford

		LO	LO	LO	LO	LO	LO	LO	LO	LO	LO	LO	LO	LO	LO	LO	LO	LO	LO	LO	LO	LO	LO
Richmond ⊖	d	19 26		19 40		19 56		20 10		20 26		20 40		20 56		21 10		21 26		21 40		21 56	
Kew Gardens ⊖	d	19 30		19 43		20 00		20 13		20 30		20 43		21 00		21 13		21 30		21 43		22 00	
Gunnersbury ⊖	d	19 33		19 46		20 03		20 16		20 33		20 46		21 03		21 16		21 33		21 46		22 03	
South Acton	d	19 36		19 49		20 06		20 19		20 36		20 49		21 06		21 19		21 36		21 49		22 06	
Acton Central	d	19 39		19 52		20 09		20 22		20 39		20 52		21 09		21 22		21 39		21 52		22 09	
Clapham Junction 10 66,176	d		19 29		19 44		19 59		20 14		20 29		20 44		20 59		21 14		21 29		21 44		22 00
Imperial Wharf 176	d		19 33		19 48		20 03		20 18		20 33		20 48		21 03		21 18		21 33		21 48		22 04
West Brompton ⊖176	d		19 36		19 51		20 06		20 21		20 36		20 51		21 06		21 21		21 36		21 51		22 07
Kensington (Olympia) ⊖176	d		19 39		19 54		20 09		20 24		20 39		20 54		21 09		21 24		21 39		21 54		22 10
Shepherd's Bush ⊖66,176	d		19 41		19 56		20 11		20 26		20 41		20 56		21 11		21 26		21 41		21 56		22 12
Willesden Jn Low Level ⊖	d																						
Willesden Jn. High Level ⊖	a	19 44	19 50	19 58	20 05	20 14	20 20	20 28	20 35	20 44	20 50	20 58	21 05	21 14	21 20	21 28	21 35	21 44	21 50	21 58	22 05	22 14	22 21
	d	19 45	19 51	19 59	20 06	20 15	20 21	20 29		20 45	20 51	20 59		21 15	21 21	21 29		21 45	21 51	21 59		22 15	22 22
Kensal Rise	d	19 47	19 53	20 01	20 08	20 17	20 23	20 31		20 47	20 53	21 01		21 17	21 23	21 31		21 47	21 53	22 01		22 17	22 24
Brondesbury Park	d	19 49	19 55	20 03	20 10	20 19	20 25	20 33		20 49	20 55	21 03		21 19	21 25	21 33		21 49	21 55	22 03		22 19	22 26
Brondesbury	d	19 51	19 57	20 05	20 12	20 21	20 27	20 35		20 51	20 57	21 05		21 21	21 27	21 35		21 51	21 57	22 05		22 21	22 28
West Hampstead ⊖	d	19 53	19 59	20 07	20 14	20 23	20 29	20 37		20 53	20 59	21 07		21 23	21 29	21 37		21 53	21 59	22 07		22 23	22 30
Finchley Road & Frognal	d	19 54	20 00	20 08	20 15	20 24	20 30	20 38		20 54	21 00	21 08		21 24	21 30	21 38		21 54	22 00	22 08		22 24	22 31
Hampstead Heath	d	19 57	20 03	20 11	20 18	20 27	20 33	20 41		20 57	21 03	21 11		21 27	21 33	21 41		21 57	22 03	22 11		22 27	22 34
Gospel Oak	d	19 59	20 05	20 13	20 20	20 29	20 35	20 43		20 59	21 05	21 13		21 29	21 37	21 43		21 59	22 05	22 13		22 29	22 36
Kentish Town West	d	20 01	20 07	20 15	20 22	20 31	20 37	20 45		21 01	21 07	21 15		21 31	21 39	21 45		22 01	22 07	22 15		22 31	22 38
Camden Road	d	20 06	20 12	20 20	20 27	20 36	20 42	20 50		21 06	21 12	21 20		21 36	21 42	21 50		22 06	22 12	22 20		22 36	22 43
Caledonian Rd & Barnsbury	d	20 09	20 15	20 23	20 30	20 39	20 45	20 53		21 09	21 15	21 23		21 39	21 45	21 53		22 09	22 15	22 23		22 39	22 46
Highbury & Islington ⊖178	d	20 11	20 17	20 25	20 32	20 41	20 47	20 55		21 11	21 17	21 25		21 41	21 47	21 55		22 11	22 17	22 25		22 41	22 48
Canonbury ⊖178	d	20 13	20 19	20 27	20 34	20 43	20 49	20 57		21 13	21 19	21 27		21 43	21 49	21 57		22 13	22 19	22 27		22 43	22 50
Dalston Kingsland	d	20 15	20 21	20 29	20 36	20 45	20 51	20 59		21 15	21 21	21 29		21 45	21 51	21 59		22 15	22 21	22 29		22 45	22 52
Hackney Central	d	20 17	20 23	20 31	20 38	20 47	20 53	21 01		21 17	21 23	21 31		21 47	21 53	22 01		22 17	22 23	22 31		22 47	22 54
Homerton	d	20 19	20 25	20 33	20 40	20 49	20 55	21 03		21 19	21 25	21 33		21 49	21 55	22 03		22 19	22 25	22 33		22 49	22 56
Hackney Wick	d	20 22	20 28	20 36	20 43	20 52	20 58	21 06		21 22	21 28	21 36		21 52	21 58	22 06		22 22	22 28	22 36		22 52	22 59
Stratford 7 ⊖ ⛴	a	20 28	20 33	20 42	20 48	20 58	21 03	21 12		21 28	21 33	21 42		21 58	22 03	22 12		22 28	22 33	22 42		22 58	23 04

		LO	LO	LO	LO	LO	LO	LO	LO	LO	LO	LO
Richmond ⊖	d	22 10		22 26		22 40		23 01				
Kew Gardens ⊖	d	22 13		22 30		22 43		23 04				
Gunnersbury ⊖	d	22 16		22 33		22 46		23 07				
South Acton	d	22 19		22 36		22 49		23 10				
Acton Central	d	22 22		22 39		22 52		23 13				
Clapham Junction 10 66,176	d		22 15		22 31		22 46		23 01	23 16	23 31	23 46
Imperial Wharf 176	d		22 19		22 35		22 50		23 05	23 20	23 35	23 50
West Brompton ⊖176	d		22 22		22 38		22 53		23 08	23 23	23 38	23 53
Kensington (Olympia) ⊖176	d		22 25		22 41		22 56		23 11	23 26	23 41	23 56
Shepherd's Bush ⊖66,176	d		22 27		22 43		22 58		23 13	23 28	23 43	23 58
Willesden Jn Low Level ⊖	d											
Willesden Jn. High Level ⊖	a	22 28	22 37	22 45	22 52	22 58	23 07	23 18	23 22	23 37	23 52	00 05
	d	22 29		22 46		22 59		23 19				
Kensal Rise	d	22 31		22 48		23 01		23 22				
Brondesbury Park	d	22 33		22 50		23 03		23 24				
Brondesbury	d	22 35		22 52		23 05		23 26				
West Hampstead ⊖	d	22 37		22 54		23 07		23 28				
Finchley Road & Frognal	d	22 38		22 55		23 08		23 29				
Hampstead Heath	d	22 41		22 58		23 11		23 32				
Gospel Oak	d	22 43		23 00		23 13		23 34				
Kentish Town West	d	22 45		23 02		23 15		23 36				
Camden Road	d	22 50		23 07		23 20		23 41				
Caledonian Rd & Barnsbury	d	22 53		23 10		23 23		23 44				
Highbury & Islington ⊖178	d	22 55		23 12		23 25		23 46				
Canonbury ⊖178	d	22 57		23 14		23 27		23 48				
Dalston Kingsland	d	22 59		23 16		23 29		23 50				
Hackney Central	d	23 01		23 18		23 31		23 52				
Homerton	d	23 03		23 20		23 33		23 54				
Hackney Wick	d	23 06		23 23		23 36		23 57				
Stratford 7 ⊖ ⛴	a	23 12		23 29		23 42		00 03				

For services between Shepherds Bush and Clapham Junction refer to Table T066 and T176

Table T060-F

Mondays to Fridays

21 May to 7 December

London, Queen's Park and Harrow & Wealdstone - Watford Junction

Miles			LO	LO	LO	LO	LO	LO	LO	LO	LO	LO	LO	LO	LO	LO	LO		LO	LO	LO	LO
0	**London Euston** [15]	⊖66 d			05 37	06 07	06 37	06 57	07 17	07 37	07 57	08 17	08 37	08 57	09 17	09 37	09 57		15 17	15 37	15 57	16 17
2½	South Hampstead	d		00 03	05 43	06 13	06 43	07 03	07 23	07 43	08 03	08 23	08 43	09 03	09 23	09 43	10 03		15 23	15 43	16 03	16 23
3	Kilburn High Road	d		00 04	05 44	06 14	06 44	07 04	07 24	07 44	08 04	08 24	08 44	09 04	09 24	09 44	10 04		15 24	15 44	16 04	16 24
3¾	**Queen's Park (London)**	⊖ d		00 06	05 46	06 16	06 46	07 06	07 26	07 46	08 06	08 26	08 46	09 06	09 26	09 46	10 06		15 26	15 46	16 06	16 27
4½	Kensal Green	d		00 08	05 48	06 18	06 48	07 08	07 28	07 48	08 08	08 28	08 48	09 08	09 28	09 48	10 08		15 28	15 48	16 08	16 29
5½	**Willesden Jn Low Level**	d		00 11	05 51	06 21	06 51	07 11	07 31	07 51	08 11	08 31	08 51	09 11	09 31	09 51	10 11	and at the same minutes past each hour until	15 31	15 51	16 11	16 32
6	Harlesden	d		00 13	05 53	06 23	06 53	07 13	07 33	07 53	08 13	08 33	08 53	09 13	09 33	09 53	10 13		15 33	15 53	16 13	16 34
7	Stonebridge Park	d		00 15	05 55	06 25	06 55	07 15	07 35	07 55	08 15	08 35	08 55	09 15	09 35	09 55	10 15		15 35	15 55	16 15	16 36
8	Wembley Central	66 d		00 18	05 58	06 28	06 58	07 18	07 38	07 58	08 18	08 38	08 58	09 18	09 38	09 58	10 18		15 38	15 58	16 18	16 39
9	North Wembley	d		00 20	06 00	06 30	07 00	07 20	07 40	08 00	08 20	08 40	09 00	09 20	09 40	10 00	10 20		15 40	16 00	16 20	16 41
9½	South Kenton	d	00 02	00 22	06 02	06 32	07 02	07 22	07 42	08 02	08 22	08 42	09 02	09 22	09 42	10 02	10 22		15 42	16 02	16 22	16 43
10¼	Kenton	d	00 04	00 24	06 04	06 34	07 04	07 24	07 44	08 04	08 24	08 44	09 04	09 24	09 44	10 04	10 24		15 44	16 04	16 24	16 45
11¼	**Harrow & Wealdstone**	66 d	00 06	00 26	06 06	06 36	07 06	07 26	07 46	08 06	08 26	08 46	09 06	09 26	09 46	10 06	10 26		15 46	16 06	16 26	16 48
12½	Headstone Lane	d	00 09	00 29	06 09	06 39	07 09	07 29	07 49	08 09	08 29	08 49	09 09	09 29	09 49	10 09	10 29		15 49	16 09	16 29	16 51
13¼	Hatch End	d	00 11	00 31	06 11	06 41	07 11	07 31	07 51	08 11	08 31	08 51	09 11	09 31	09 51	10 11	10 31		15 51	16 11	16 31	16 53
14¾	Carpenders Park	d	00 14	00 34	06 14	06 44	07 14	07 34	07 54	08 14	08 34	08 54	09 14	09 34	09 54	10 14	10 34		15 54	16 14	16 34	16 56
16	Bushey	66 d	00 17	00 37	06 17	06 47	07 17	07 37	07 57	08 17	08 37	08 57	09 17	09 37	09 57	10 17	10 37		15 57	16 17	16 37	16 59
16¾	Watford High Street	d	00 20	00 40	06 20	06 50	07 20	07 40	08 00	08 20	08 40	09 00	09 20	09 40	10 00	10 20	10 40		16 00	16 20	16 40	17 01
17¾	**Watford Junction**	66 a	00 24	00 44	06 24	06 54	07 24	07 48	08 04	08 24	08 44	09 04	09 24	09 48	10 04	10 24	10 44		16 04	16 24	16 44	17 08

		LO	LO	LO	LO	LO	LO	LO	LO	LO	LO	LO	LO	LO	LO	LO	LO	LO	LO	LO	LO	LO	LO
London Euston [15]	⊖66 d	16 37	16 57	17 17	17 37	17 57	18 17	18 37	18 57	19 17	19 37	19 57	20 17	20 37	20 57	21 17	21 37	21 57	22 17	22 37	22 57	23 17	23 37
South Hampstead	d	16 43	17 03	17 23	17 43	18 03	18 23	18 43	19 03	19 23	19 43	20 03	20 23	20 43	21 03	21 23	21 43	22 03	22 23	22 43	23 03	23 23	23 43
Kilburn High Road	d	16 44	17 04	17 24	17 44	18 04	18 24	18 44	19 04	19 24	19 44	20 04	20 24	20 44	21 04	21 24	21 44	22 04	22 24	22 44	23 04	23 24	23 44
Queen's Park (London)	⊖ d	16 47	17 07	17 27	17 47	18 07	18 27	18 47	19 07	19 26	19 46	20 06	20 26	20 46	21 06	21 26	21 46	22 06	22 26	22 46	23 06	23 26	23 46
Kensal Green	d	16 49	17 09	17 29	17 49	18 09	18 29	18 49	19 09	19 28	19 48	20 08	20 28	20 48	21 08	21 28	21 48	22 08	22 28	22 48	23 08	23 28	23 48
Willesden Jn Low Level	d	16 52	17 12	17 32	17 52	18 12	18 32	18 52	19 12	19 31	19 51	20 11	20 31	20 51	21 11	21 31	21 51	22 11	22 31	22 51	23 11	23 31	23 51
Harlesden	d	16 54	17 14	17 34	17 54	18 14	18 34	18 54	19 14	19 33	19 53	20 13	20 33	20 53	21 13	21 33	21 53	22 13	22 33	22 53	23 13	23 33	23 53
Stonebridge Park	d	16 56	17 16	17 36	17 56	18 16	18 36	18 56	19 16	19 35	19 55	20 15	20 35	20 55	21 15	21 35	21 55	22 15	22 35	22 55	23 15	23 35	23 55
Wembley Central	66 d	16 59	17 19	17 39	17 59	18 19	18 39	18 59	19 19	19 38	19 58	20 18	20 38	20 58	21 18	21 38	21 58	22 18	22 38	22 58	23 18	23 38	23 58
North Wembley	d	17 01	17 21	17 41	18 01	18 21	18 41	19 01	19 21	19 40	20 00	20 20	20 40	21 00	21 20	21 40	22 00	22 20	22 40	23 00	23 20	23 40	23 59
South Kenton	d	17 03	17 23	17 43	18 03	18 23	18 43	19 03	19 23	19 42	20 02	20 22	20 42	21 02	21 22	21 42	22 02	22 22	22 42	23 02	23 22	23 42	00 02
Kenton	d	17 05	17 25	17 45	18 05	18 25	18 45	19 05	19 25	19 44	20 04	20 24	20 44	21 04	21 24	21 44	22 04	22 24	22 44	23 04	23 24	23 44	00 04
Harrow & Wealdstone	66 d	17 08	17 28	17 48	18 08	18 28	18 48	19 08	19 28	19 46	20 06	20 26	20 46	21 06	21 26	21 46	22 06	22 26	22 46	23 06	23 26	23 46	00 06
Headstone Lane	d	17 11	17 31	17 51	18 11	18 31	18 51	19 11	19 31	19 49	20 09	20 29	20 49	21 09	21 29	21 49	22 09	22 29	22 49	23 09	23 29	23 49	00 09
Hatch End	d	17 13	17 33	17 53	18 13	18 33	18 53	19 13	19 33	19 51	20 11	20 31	20 51	21 11	21 31	21 51	22 11	22 31	22 51	23 11	23 31	23 51	00 11
Carpenders Park	d	17 16	17 36	17 56	18 16	18 36	18 56	19 16	19 36	19 54	20 14	20 34	20 54	21 14	21 34	21 54	22 14	22 34	22 54	23 14	23 34	23 54	00 14
Bushey	66 d	17 19	17 39	17 59	18 19	18 39	18 59	19 19	19 39	19 57	20 17	20 37	20 57	21 17	21 37	21 57	22 17	22 37	22 57	23 17	23 37	23 57	00 17
Watford High Street	d	17 21	17 41	18 01	18 21	18 41	19 01	19 21	19 41	20 00	20 20	20 40	21 00	21 20	21 40	22 00	22 20	22 40	23 00	23 20	23 40	23 59	00 20
Watford Junction	66 a	17 28	17 48	18 08	18 32	18 48	19 08	19 28	19 48	20 08	20 28	20 48	21 04	21 28	21 44	22 04	22 24	22 44	23 08	23 24	23 44	00 04	00 24

		LO
London Euston [15]	⊖66 d	23 57
South Hampstead	d	00 03
Kilburn High Road	d	00 04
Queen's Park (London)	⊖ d	00 06
Kensal Green	d	00 08
Willesden Jn Low Level	d	00 11
Harlesden	d	00 13
Stonebridge Park	d	00 15
Wembley Central	66 d	00 18
North Wembley	d	00 20
South Kenton	d	00 22
Kenton	d	00 24
Harrow & Wealdstone	66 d	00 26
Headstone Lane	d	00 29
Hatch End	d	00 31
Carpenders Park	d	00 34
Bushey	66 d	00 37
Watford High Street	d	00 40
Watford Junction	66 a	00 44

Saturdays

26 May to 8 December

		LO	LO	LO	LO	LO	LO	LO	LO	LO		LO	LO	LO	LO	LO	LO	LO	LO	LO
London Euston [15]	⊖66 d			05 37	06 07	06 37	06 57	07 17	07 37	07 57		21 17	21 37	21 57	22 17	22 37	22 57	23 17	23 37	23 57
South Hampstead	d		00 03	05 43	06 13	06 43	07 03	07 23	07 43	08 03		21 23	21 43	22 03	22 23	22 43	23 03	23 23	23 43	00 03
Kilburn High Road	d		00 04	05 44	06 14	06 44	07 04	07 24	07 44	08 04		21 24	21 44	22 04	22 24	22 44	23 04	23 24	23 44	00 04
Queen's Park (London)	⊖ d		00 06	05 46	06 16	06 46	07 06	07 26	07 46	08 06		21 26	21 46	22 06	22 26	22 46	23 06	23 26	23 46	00 06
Kensal Green	d		00 08	05 48	06 18	06 48	07 08	07 28	07 48	08 08		21 28	21 48	22 08	22 28	22 48	23 08	23 28	23 48	00 08
Willesden Jn Low Level	d		00 11	05 51	06 21	06 51	07 11	07 31	07 51	08 11	and at the same minutes past each hour until	21 31	21 51	22 11	22 31	22 51	23 11	23 31	23 51	00 11
Harlesden	d		00 13	05 53	06 23	06 53	07 13	07 33	07 53	08 13		21 33	21 53	22 13	22 33	22 53	23 13	23 33	23 53	00 13
Stonebridge Park	d		00 15	05 55	06 25	06 55	07 15	07 35	07 55	08 15		21 35	21 55	22 15	22 35	22 55	23 15	23 35	23 55	00 15
Wembley Central	66 d		00 18	05 58	06 28	06 58	07 18	07 38	07 58	08 18		21 38	21 58	22 18	22 38	22 58	23 18	23 38	23 58	00 18
North Wembley	d		00 20	06 00	06 30	07 00	07 20	07 40	08 00	08 20		21 40	22 00	22 20	22 40	23 00	23 20	23 40	23 59	00 20
South Kenton	d	00 02	00 22	06 02	06 32	07 02	07 22	07 42	08 02	08 22		21 42	22 02	22 22	22 42	23 02	23 22	23 42	00 02	00 22
Kenton	d	00 04	00 24	06 04	06 34	07 04	07 24	07 44	08 04	08 24		21 44	22 04	22 24	22 44	23 04	23 24	23 44	00 04	00 24
Harrow & Wealdstone	66 d	00 06	00 26	06 06	06 36	07 06	07 26	07 46	08 06	08 26		21 46	22 06	22 26	22 46	23 06	23 26	23 46	00 06	00 26
Headstone Lane	d	00 09	00 29	06 09	06 39	07 09	07 29	07 49	08 09	08 29		21 49	22 09	22 29	22 49	23 09	23 29	23 49	00 09	00 29
Hatch End	d	00 11	00 31	06 11	06 41	07 11	07 31	07 51	08 11	08 31		21 51	22 11	22 31	22 51	23 11	23 31	23 51	00 11	00 31
Carpenders Park	d	00 14	00 34	06 14	06 44	07 14	07 34	07 54	08 14	08 34		21 54	22 14	22 34	22 54	23 14	23 34	23 54	00 14	00 34
Bushey	66 d	00 17	00 37	06 17	06 47	07 17	07 37	07 57	08 17	08 37		21 57	22 17	22 37	22 57	23 17	23 37	23 57	00 17	00 37
Watford High Street	d	00 20	00 40	06 20	06 50	07 20	07 40	08 00	08 20	08 40		22 00	22 20	22 40	23 00	23 20	23 40	23 59	00 20	00 40
Watford Junction	66 a	00 24	00 44	06 28	06 58	07 24	07 48	08 08	08 24	08 44		22 08	22 24	22 44	23 04	23 24	23 44	00 04	00 28	00 44

Stations Queen's Park to Harrow & Wealdstone inclusive are also served by London Underground Bakerloo Line Services

Table T060-F

Sundays

20 May to 2 December

London, Queen's Park and Harrow & Wealdstone - Watford Junction

		LO	LO	LO	LO	LO	LO	LO	LO	LO	LO	LO	LO	LO	LO	LO	LO	LO	LO	LO	LO	LO	LO
London Euston [15]	⊖66 d			06 47	07 17	07 47	08 17	08 47	09 17	09 37	09 57	10 17	10 37	10 57	11 17	11 37	11 57	12 17	12 37	12 57	13 17	13 37	13 57
South Hampstead	d		00 03	06 53	07 23	07 53	08 23	08 53	09 23	09 43	10 03	10 23	10 43	11 03	11 23	11 43	12 03	12 23	12 43	13 03	13 23	13 43	14 03
Kilburn High Road	d		00 04	06 54	07 24	07 54	08 24	08 54	09 24	09 44	10 04	10 24	10 44	11 04	11 24	11 44	12 04	12 24	12 44	13 04	13 24	13 44	14 04
Queen's Park (London)	⊖ d		00 06	06 56	07 26	07 56	08 26	08 56	09 26	09 46	10 06	10 26	10 46	11 06	11 26	11 46	12 06	12 26	12 46	13 06	13 26	13 46	14 06
Kensal Green	d		00 08	06 58	07 28	07 58	08 28	08 58	09 28	09 48	10 08	10 28	10 48	11 08	11 28	11 48	12 08	12 28	12 48	13 08	13 28	13 48	14 08
Willesden Jn Low Level	d		00 11	07 01	07 31	08 01	08 31	09 01	09 31	09 51	10 11	10 31	10 51	11 11	11 31	11 51	12 11	12 31	12 51	13 11	13 31	13 51	14 11
Harlesden	d		00 13	07 03	07 33	08 03	08 33	09 03	09 33	09 53	10 13	10 33	10 53	11 13	11 33	11 53	12 13	12 33	12 53	13 13	13 33	13 53	14 13
Stonebridge Park	d		00 15	07 05	07 35	08 05	08 35	09 05	09 35	09 55	10 15	10 35	10 55	11 15	11 35	11 55	12 15	12 35	12 55	13 15	13 35	13 55	14 15
Wembley Central	66 d		00 18	07 08	07 38	08 08	08 38	09 08	09 38	09 58	10 18	10 38	10 58	11 18	11 38	11 58	12 18	12 38	12 58	13 18	13 38	13 58	14 18
North Wembley	d		00 20	07 10	07 40	08 10	08 40	09 10	09 40	10 00	10 20	10 40	11 00	11 20	11 40	12 00	12 20	12 40	13 00	13 20	13 40	14 00	14 20
South Kenton	d	00 02	00 22	07 12	07 42	08 12	08 42	09 12	09 42	10 02	10 22	10 42	11 02	11 22	11 42	12 02	12 22	12 42	13 02	13 22	13 42	14 02	14 22
Kenton	d	00 04	00 24	07 14	07 44	08 14	08 44	09 14	09 44	10 04	10 24	10 44	11 04	11 24	11 44	12 04	12 24	12 44	13 04	13 24	13 44	14 04	14 24
Harrow & Wealdstone	66 d	00 06	00 26	07 16	07 46	08 16	08 46	09 16	09 46	10 06	10 26	10 46	11 06	11 26	11 46	12 06	12 26	12 46	13 06	13 26	13 46	14 06	14 26
Headstone Lane	d	00 09	00 29	07 19	07 49	08 19	08 49	09 19	09 49	10 09	10 29	10 49	11 09	11 29	11 49	12 09	12 29	12 49	13 09	13 29	13 49	14 09	14 29
Hatch End	d	00 11	00 31	07 21	07 51	08 21	08 51	09 21	09 51	10 11	10 31	10 51	11 11	11 31	11 51	12 11	12 31	12 51	13 11	13 31	13 51	14 11	14 31
Carpenders Park	d	00 14	00 34	07 24	07 54	08 24	08 54	09 24	09 54	10 14	10 34	10 54	11 14	11 34	11 54	12 14	12 34	12 54	13 14	13 34	13 54	14 14	14 34
Bushey	66 d	00 17	00 37	07 27	07 57	08 27	08 57	09 27	09 57	10 17	10 37	10 57	11 17	11 37	11 57	12 17	12 37	12 57	13 17	13 37	13 57	14 17	14 37
Watford High Street	d	00 20	00 40	07 30	08 00	08 30	09 00	09 30	10 00	10 20	10 40	11 00	11 20	11 40	12 00	12 20	12 40	13 00	13 20	13 40	14 00	14 20	14 40
Watford Junction	66 a	00 28	00 44	07 38	08 08	08 34	09 04	09 38	10 04	10 24	10 48	11 04	11 24	11 44	12 08	12 24	12 44	13 04	13 28	13 44	14 04	14 24	14 44

		LO	LO	LO	LO	LO	LO	LO	LO	LO	LO	LO	LO	LO	LO	LO	LO	LO	LO	LO	LO	LO	LO
London Euston [15]	⊖66 d	14 17	14 37	14 57	15 17	15 37	15 57	16 17	16 37	16 57	17 17	17 37	17 57	18 17	18 37	18 57	19 17	19 37	19 57	20 17	20 37	20 57	21 17
South Hampstead	d	14 23	14 43	15 03	15 23	15 43	16 03	16 23	16 43	17 03	17 23	17 43	18 03	18 23	18 43	19 03	19 23	19 43	20 03	20 23	20 43	21 03	21 23
Kilburn High Road	d	14 24	14 44	15 04	15 24	15 44	16 04	16 24	16 44	17 04	17 24	17 44	18 04	18 24	18 44	19 04	19 24	19 44	20 04	20 24	20 44	21 04	21 24
Queen's Park (London)	⊖ d	14 26	14 46	15 06	15 26	15 46	16 06	16 26	16 46	17 06	17 26	17 46	18 06	18 26	18 46	19 06	19 26	19 46	20 06	20 26	20 46	21 06	21 26
Kensal Green	d	14 28	14 48	15 08	15 28	15 48	16 08	16 28	16 48	17 08	17 28	17 48	18 08	18 28	18 48	19 08	19 28	19 48	20 08	20 28	20 48	21 08	21 28
Willesden Jn Low Level	d	14 31	14 51	15 11	15 31	15 51	16 11	16 31	16 51	17 11	17 31	17 51	18 11	18 31	18 51	19 11	19 31	19 51	20 11	20 31	20 51	21 11	21 31
Harlesden	d	14 33	14 53	15 13	15 33	15 53	16 13	16 33	16 53	17 13	17 33	17 53	18 13	18 33	18 53	19 13	19 33	19 53	20 13	20 33	20 53	21 13	21 33
Stonebridge Park	d	14 35	14 55	15 15	15 35	15 55	16 15	16 35	16 55	17 15	17 35	17 55	18 15	18 35	18 55	19 15	19 35	19 55	20 15	20 35	20 55	21 15	21 35
Wembley Central	66 d	14 38	14 58	15 18	15 38	15 58	16 18	16 38	16 58	17 18	17 38	17 58	18 18	18 38	18 58	19 18	19 38	19 58	20 18	20 38	20 58	21 18	21 38
North Wembley	d	14 40	15 00	15 20	15 40	16 00	16 20	16 40	17 00	17 20	17 40	18 00	18 20	18 40	19 00	19 20	19 40	20 00	20 20	20 40	21 00	21 20	21 40
South Kenton	d	14 42	15 02	15 22	15 42	16 02	16 22	16 42	17 02	17 22	17 42	18 02	18 22	18 42	19 02	19 22	19 42	20 02	20 22	20 42	21 02	21 22	21 42
Kenton	d	14 44	15 04	15 24	15 44	16 04	16 24	16 44	17 04	17 24	17 44	18 04	18 24	18 44	19 04	19 24	19 44	20 04	20 24	20 44	21 04	21 24	21 44
Harrow & Wealdstone	66 d	14 46	15 06	15 26	15 46	16 06	16 26	16 46	17 06	17 26	17 46	18 06	18 26	18 46	19 06	19 26	19 46	20 06	20 26	20 46	21 06	21 26	21 46
Headstone Lane	d	14 49	15 09	15 29	15 49	16 09	16 29	16 49	17 09	17 29	17 49	18 09	18 29	18 49	19 09	19 29	19 49	20 09	20 29	20 49	21 09	21 29	21 49
Hatch End	d	14 51	15 11	15 31	15 51	16 11	16 31	16 51	17 11	17 31	17 51	18 11	18 31	18 51	19 11	19 31	19 51	20 11	20 31	20 51	21 11	21 31	21 51
Carpenders Park	d	14 54	15 14	15 34	15 54	16 14	16 34	16 54	17 14	17 34	17 54	18 14	18 34	18 54	19 14	19 34	19 54	20 14	20 34	20 54	21 14	21 34	21 54
Bushey	66 d	14 57	15 17	15 37	15 57	16 17	16 37	16 57	17 17	17 37	17 57	18 17	18 37	18 57	19 17	19 37	19 57	20 17	20 37	20 57	21 17	21 37	21 57
Watford High Street	d	15 00	15 20	15 40	16 00	16 20	16 40	17 00	17 20	17 40	18 00	18 20	18 40	19 00	19 20	19 40	20 00	20 20	20 40	21 00	21 20	21 40	22 00
Watford Junction	66 a	15 04	15 24	15 44	16 04	16 24	16 44	17 04	17 28	17 44	18 04	18 24	18 44	19 08	19 28	19 48	20 08	20 28	20 44	21 08	21 28	21 48	22 04

		LO	LO	LO	LO	LO	LO	LO	LO
London Euston [15]	⊖66 d	21 37	21 57	22 17	22 37	22 57	23 17	23 37	23 57
South Hampstead	d	21 43	22 03	22 23	22 43	23 03	23 23	23 43	00 03
Kilburn High Road	d	21 44	22 04	22 24	22 44	23 04	23 24	23 44	00 04
Queen's Park (London)	⊖ d	21 46	22 06	22 26	22 46	23 06	23 26	23 46	00 06
Kensal Green	d	21 48	22 08	22 28	22 48	23 08	23 28	23 48	00 08
Willesden Jn Low Level	d	21 51	22 11	22 31	22 51	23 11	23 31	23 51	00 11
Harlesden	d	21 53	22 13	22 33	22 53	23 13	23 33	23 53	00 13
Stonebridge Park	d	21 55	22 15	22 35	22 55	23 15	23 35	23 55	00 15
Wembley Central	66 d	21 58	22 18	22 38	22 58	23 18	23 38	23 58	00 18
North Wembley	d	22 00	22 20	22 40	23 00	23 20	23 40	23 59	00 20
South Kenton	d	22 02	22 22	22 42	23 02	23 22	23 42	00 02	00 22
Kenton	d	22 04	22 24	22 44	23 04	23 24	23 44	00 04	00 24
Harrow & Wealdstone	66 d	22 06	22 26	22 46	23 06	23 26	23 46	00 06	00 26
Headstone Lane	d	22 09	22 29	22 49	23 09	23 29	23 49	00 09	00 29
Hatch End	d	22 11	22 31	22 51	23 11	23 31	23 51	00 11	00 31
Carpenders Park	d	22 14	22 34	22 54	23 14	23 34	23 54	00 14	00 34
Bushey	66 d	22 17	22 37	22 57	23 17	23 37	23 57	00 17	00 37
Watford High Street	d	22 20	22 40	23 00	23 20	23 40	23 59	00 20	00 40
Watford Junction	66 a	22 24	22 48	23 04	23 24	23 44	00 04	00 24	00 44

Stations Queen's Park to Harrow & Wealdstone inclusive are also served by London Underground Bakerloo Line Services

Table T060-R

Mondays to Fridays

21 May to 7 December

Watford Junction - Harrow & Wealdstone, Queen's Park and London

Miles	Station		LO MO	LO MX	LO	LO	LO	LO	LO	LO	LO	LO	LO	LO	LO	LO	LO	LO	and at the same minutes past each hour until	LO	LO	LO
0	**Watford Junction**	66 d			05 11	05 41	06 11	06 40	07 00	07 20	07 40	08 00	08 20	08 40	09 00	09 21	09 41	10 01		15 21	15 41	16 01
1	Watford High Street	d			05 14	05 44	06 14	06 43	07 03	07 23	07 43	08 03	08 23	08 43	09 03	09 24	09 44	10 04		15 24	15 44	16 04
1¾	Bushey	66 d			05 16	05 46	06 16	06 45	07 05	07 25	07 45	08 05	08 25	08 45	09 05	09 26	09 46	10 06		15 26	15 46	16 06
3	Carpenders Park	d			05 19	05 49	06 19	06 48	07 08	07 28	07 48	08 08	08 28	08 48	09 08	09 29	09 49	10 09		15 29	15 49	16 09
4½	Hatch End	d			05 22	05 52	06 22	06 51	07 11	07 31	07 51	08 11	08 31	08 51	09 11	09 32	09 52	10 12		15 32	15 52	16 12
5¼	Headstone Lane	d			05 24	05 54	06 24	06 53	07 13	07 33	07 53	08 13	08 33	08 53	09 13	09 34	09 54	10 14		15 34	15 54	16 14
6½	**Harrow & Wealdstone**	66 d			05 27	05 57	06 27	06 56	07 16	07 36	07 56	08 16	08 36	08 56	09 16	09 37	09 57	10 17		15 37	15 57	16 17
7½	Kenton	d			05 29	05 59	06 29	06 59	07 19	07 39	07 59	08 19	08 39	08 59	09 19	09 39	09 59	10 19		15 39	15 59	16 19
8¼	South Kenton	d			05 31	06 01	06 31	07 01	07 21	07 41	08 01	08 21	08 41	09 01	09 21	09 41	10 01	10 21		15 41	16 01	16 21
8¾	North Wembley	d			05 33	06 03	06 33	07 03	07 23	07 43	08 03	08 23	08 43	09 03	09 23	09 43	10 03	10 23		15 43	16 03	16 23
9¾	Wembley Central	66 d			05 35	06 05	06 35	07 05	07 25	07 45	08 05	08 25	08 45	09 05	09 25	09 45	10 05	10 25		15 45	16 05	16 25
10¾	Stonebridge Park	d			05 38	06 08	06 38	07 08	07 28	07 48	08 08	08 28	08 48	09 08	09 28	09 48	10 08	10 28		15 48	16 08	16 28
11¾	Harlesden	d			05 40	06 10	06 40	07 10	07 30	07 50	08 10	08 30	08 50	09 10	09 30	09 50	10 10	10 30		15 50	16 10	16 30
12¼	**Willesden Jn Low Level**	d			05 42	06 12	06 42	07 13	07 33	07 53	08 13	08 33	08 53	09 13	09 33	09 52	10 12	10 32		15 52	16 12	16 32
13¼	Kensal Green	d			05 45	06 15	06 45	07 15	07 35	07 55	08 15	08 35	08 55	09 15	09 35	09 55	10 15	10 35		15 55	16 15	16 35
14	**Queen's Park (London)**	⊖ d			05 47	06 17	06 47	07 18	07 38	07 58	08 18	08 38	08 58	09 18	09 38	09 57	10 17	10 37		15 57	16 17	16 37
14¾	Kilburn High Road	d			05 49	06 19	06 49	07 20	07 40	08 00	08 20	08 40	09 00	09 20	09 40	09 59	10 19	10 39		15 59	16 19	16 39
15¼	South Hampstead	d	00 01	00 01	05 51	06 21	06 51	07 22	07 42	08 02	08 22	08 42	09 02	09 22	09 42	10 01	10 21	10 41		16 01	16 21	16 41
17¾	**London Euston** 15	⊖66 a	00 10	00 13	06 01	06 31	07 03	07 32	07 52	08 12	08 32	08 52	09 12	09 30	09 52	10 11	10 31	10 51		16 11	16 31	16 51

Station		LO	LO	LO	LO	LO	LO	LO	LO	LO	LO	LO	LO	LO	LO	LO	LO	LO	LO	LO	LO	LO	LO
Watford Junction	66 d	16 21	16 41	17 01	17 21	17 41	18 01	18 21	18 41	19 01	19 21	19 41	20 01	20 21	20 41	21 01	21 21	21 41	22 01	22 21	22 41	23 01	23 21
Watford High Street	d	16 24	16 44	17 04	17 24	17 44	18 04	18 24	18 44	19 04	19 24	19 44	20 04	20 24	20 44	21 04	21 24	21 44	22 04	22 24	22 44	23 04	23 24
Bushey	66 d	16 26	16 46	17 06	17 26	17 46	18 06	18 26	18 46	19 06	19 26	19 46	20 06	20 26	20 46	21 06	21 26	21 46	22 06	22 26	22 46	23 06	23 26
Carpenders Park	d	16 29	16 49	17 09	17 29	17 49	18 09	18 29	18 49	19 09	19 29	19 49	20 09	20 29	20 49	21 09	21 29	21 49	22 09	22 29	22 49	23 09	23 29
Hatch End	d	16 32	16 52	17 12	17 32	17 52	18 12	18 32	18 52	19 12	19 32	19 52	20 12	20 32	20 52	21 12	21 32	21 52	22 12	22 32	22 52	23 12	23 32
Headstone Lane	d	16 34	16 54	17 14	17 34	17 54	18 14	18 34	18 54	19 14	19 34	19 54	20 14	20 34	20 54	21 14	21 34	21 54	22 14	22 34	22 54	23 14	23 34
Harrow & Wealdstone	66 d	16 37	16 57	17 17	17 37	17 57	18 17	18 37	18 57	19 17	19 37	19 57	20 17	20 37	20 57	21 17	21 37	21 57	22 17	22 37	22 57	23 17	23 37
Kenton	d	16 39	16 59	17 19	17 39	17 59	18 19	18 39	18 59	19 19	19 39	19 59	20 19	20 39	20 59	21 19	21 39	21 59	22 19	22 39	22 59	23 19	23 39
South Kenton	d	16 41	17 01	17 21	17 41	18 01	18 21	18 41	19 01	19 21	19 41	20 01	20 21	20 41	21 01	21 21	21 41	22 01	22 21	22 41	23 01	23 21	23 41
North Wembley	d	16 43	17 03	17 23	17 43	18 03	18 23	18 43	19 03	19 23	19 43	20 03	20 23	20 43	21 03	21 23	21 43	22 03	22 23	22 43	23 03	23 23	23 43
Wembley Central	66 d	16 45	17 05	17 25	17 45	18 05	18 25	18 45	19 05	19 25	19 45	20 05	20 25	20 45	21 05	21 25	21 45	22 05	22 25	22 45	23 05	23 25	23 45
Stonebridge Park	d	16 48	17 08	17 28	17 48	18 08	18 28	18 48	19 08	19 28	19 48	20 08	20 28	20 48	21 08	21 28	21 48	22 08	22 28	22 48	23 08	23 28	23 48
Harlesden	d	16 50	17 10	17 30	17 50	18 10	18 30	18 50	19 10	19 30	19 50	20 10	20 30	20 50	21 10	21 30	21 50	22 10	22 30	22 50	23 10	23 30	23 50
Willesden Jn Low Level	d	16 52	17 12	17 32	17 52	18 12	18 32	18 52	19 12	19 32	19 52	20 12	20 32	20 52	21 12	21 32	21 52	22 12	22 32	22 52	23 12	23 32	23 52
Kensal Green	d	16 55	17 15	17 35	17 55	18 15	18 35	18 55	19 15	19 35	19 55	20 15	20 35	20 55	21 15	21 35	21 55	22 15	22 35	22 55	23 15	23 35	23 55
Queen's Park (London)	⊖ d	16 57	17 17	17 37	17 57	18 17	18 37	18 57	19 17	19 37	19 57	20 17	20 37	20 57	21 17	21 37	21 57	22 17	22 37	22 57	23 17	23 37	23 57
Kilburn High Road	d	16 59	17 19	17 39	17 59	18 19	18 39	18 59	19 19	19 39	19 59	20 19	20 39	20 59	21 19	21 39	21 59	22 19	22 39	22 59	23 19	23 39	23 59
South Hampstead	d	17 01	17 21	17 41	18 01	18 21	18 41	19 01	19 21	19 41	20 01	20 21	20 41	21 01	21 21	21 41	22 01	22 21	22 41	23 01	23 21	23 41	00 01
London Euston 15	⊖66 a	17 13	17 33	17 51	18 13	18 31	18 51	19 11	19 31	19 53	20 11	20 31	20 53	21 13	21 31	21 53	22 11	22 33	22 51	23 11	23 31	23 51	00 13

Saturdays

26 May to 8 December

Station		LO	LO	LO	LO	LO	LO	LO	and at the same minutes past each hour until	LO	LO	LO	LO	LO	LO	LO	LO	LO	LO	LO	LO	LO
Watford Junction	66 d		05 11	05 41	06 11	06 41	07 01	07 21		16 41	17 01	17 21	17 41	18 01	18 21	18 41	19 01	19 21	19 41	20 01	20 21	20 41
Watford High Street	d		05 14	05 44	06 14	06 44	07 04	07 24		16 44	17 04	17 24	17 44	18 04	18 24	18 44	19 04	19 24	19 44	20 04	20 24	20 44
Bushey	66 d		05 16	05 46	06 16	06 46	07 06	07 26		16 46	17 06	17 26	17 46	18 06	18 26	18 46	19 06	19 26	19 46	20 06	20 26	20 46
Carpenders Park	d		05 19	05 49	06 19	06 49	07 09	07 29		16 49	17 09	17 29	17 49	18 09	18 29	18 49	19 09	19 29	19 49	20 09	20 29	20 49
Hatch End	d		05 22	05 52	06 22	06 52	07 12	07 32		16 52	17 12	17 32	17 52	18 12	18 32	18 52	19 12	19 32	19 52	20 12	20 32	20 52
Headstone Lane	d		05 24	05 54	06 24	06 54	07 14	07 34		16 54	17 14	17 34	17 54	18 14	18 34	18 54	19 14	19 34	19 54	20 14	20 34	20 54
Harrow & Wealdstone	66 d		05 27	05 57	06 27	06 57	07 17	07 37		16 57	17 17	17 37	17 57	18 17	18 37	18 57	19 17	19 37	19 57	20 17	20 37	20 57
Kenton	d		05 29	05 59	06 29	06 59	07 19	07 39		16 59	17 19	17 39	17 59	18 19	18 39	18 59	19 19	19 39	19 59	20 19	20 39	20 59
South Kenton	d		05 31	06 01	06 31	07 01	07 21	07 41		17 01	17 21	17 41	18 01	18 21	18 41	19 01	19 21	19 41	20 01	20 21	20 41	21 01
North Wembley	d		05 33	06 03	06 33	07 03	07 23	07 43		17 03	17 23	17 43	18 03	18 23	18 43	19 03	19 23	19 43	20 03	20 23	20 43	21 03
Wembley Central	66 d		05 35	06 05	06 35	07 05	07 25	07 45		17 05	17 25	17 45	18 05	18 25	18 45	19 05	19 25	19 45	20 05	20 25	20 45	21 05
Stonebridge Park	d		05 38	06 08	06 38	07 08	07 28	07 48		17 08	17 28	17 48	18 08	18 28	18 48	19 08	19 28	19 48	20 08	20 28	20 48	21 08
Harlesden	d		05 40	06 10	06 40	07 10	07 30	07 50		17 10	17 30	17 50	18 10	18 30	18 50	19 10	19 30	19 50	20 10	20 30	20 50	21 10
Willesden Jn Low Level	d		05 42	06 12	06 42	07 12	07 32	07 52		17 12	17 32	17 52	18 12	18 32	18 52	19 12	19 32	19 52	20 12	20 32	20 52	21 12
Kensal Green	d		05 45	06 15	06 45	07 15	07 35	07 55		17 15	17 35	17 55	18 15	18 35	18 55	19 15	19 35	19 55	20 15	20 35	20 55	21 15
Queen's Park (London)	⊖ d		05 47	06 17	06 47	07 17	07 37	07 57		17 17	17 37	17 57	18 17	18 37	18 57	19 17	19 37	19 57	20 17	20 37	20 57	21 17
Kilburn High Road	d		05 49	06 19	06 49	07 19	07 39	07 59		17 19	17 39	17 59	18 19	18 39	18 59	19 19	19 39	19 59	20 19	20 39	20 59	21 19
South Hampstead	d	00 01	05 51	06 21	06 51	07 21	07 41	08 01		17 21	17 41	18 01	18 21	18 41	19 01	19 21	19 41	20 01	20 21	20 41	21 01	21 21
London Euston 15	⊖66 a	00 13	06 00	06 30	07 00	07 30	07 50	08 13		17 30	17 50	18 13	18 30	18 52	19 13	19 30	19 50	20 13	20 33	20 50	21 13	21 33

Station		LO	LO	LO	LO	LO	LO	LO	LO
Watford Junction	66 d	21 01	21 21	21 41	22 01	22 21	22 41	23 01	23 21
Watford High Street	d	21 04	21 24	21 44	22 04	22 24	22 44	23 04	23 24
Bushey	66 d	21 06	21 26	21 46	22 06	22 26	22 46	23 06	23 26
Carpenders Park	d	21 09	21 29	21 49	22 09	22 29	22 49	23 09	23 29
Hatch End	d	21 12	21 32	21 52	22 12	22 32	22 52	23 12	23 32
Headstone Lane	d	21 14	21 34	21 54	22 14	22 34	22 54	23 14	23 34
Harrow & Wealdstone	66 d	21 17	21 37	21 57	22 17	22 37	22 57	23 17	23 37
Kenton	d	21 19	21 39	21 59	22 19	22 39	22 59	23 19	23 39
South Kenton	d	21 21	21 41	22 01	22 21	22 41	23 01	23 21	23 41
North Wembley	d	21 23	21 43	22 03	22 23	22 43	23 03	23 23	23 43
Wembley Central	66 d	21 25	21 45	22 05	22 25	22 45	23 05	23 25	23 45
Stonebridge Park	d	21 28	21 48	22 08	22 28	22 48	23 08	23 28	23 48
Harlesden	d	21 30	21 50	22 10	22 30	22 50	23 10	23 30	23 50
Willesden Jn Low Level	d	21 32	21 52	22 12	22 32	22 52	23 12	23 32	23 52
Kensal Green	d	21 35	21 55	22 15	22 35	22 55	23 15	23 35	23 55
Queen's Park (London)	⊖ d	21 37	21 57	22 17	22 37	22 57	23 17	23 37	23 57
Kilburn High Road	d	21 39	21 59	22 19	22 39	22 59	23 19	23 39	23 59
South Hampstead	d	21 41	22 01	22 21	22 41	23 01	23 21	23 41	00 01
London Euston 15	⊖66 a	21 50	22 13	22 33	22 53	23 10	23 30	23 50	00 10

Stations Harrow & Wealdstone to Queen's Park inclusive are also served by London Underground Bakerloo Line Services

Table T060-R

Sundays

20 May to 2 December

Watford Junction - Harrow & Wealdstone, Queen's Park and London

Station		LO	LO	LO	LO	LO	LO	LO	LO	LO	LO	LO	LO	LO	LO	LO	LO	and at the same minutes past each hour until	LO	LO	LO	LO
Watford Junction	66 d		06 51	07 21	07 51	08 21	08 51	09 21	09 41	10 01	10 21	10 41	11 01	11 21	11 41	12 01	12 21		18 41	19 01	19 21	19 41
Watford High Street	d		06 54	07 24	07 54	08 24	08 54	09 24	09 44	10 04	10 24	10 44	11 04	11 24	11 44	12 04	12 24		18 44	19 04	19 24	19 44
Bushey	66 d		06 56	07 26	07 56	08 26	08 56	09 26	09 46	10 06	10 26	10 46	11 06	11 26	11 46	12 06	12 26		18 46	19 06	19 26	19 46
Carpenders Park	d		06 59	07 29	07 59	08 29	08 59	09 29	09 49	10 09	10 29	10 49	11 09	11 29	11 49	12 09	12 29		18 49	19 09	19 29	19 49
Hatch End	d		07 02	07 32	08 02	08 32	09 02	09 32	09 52	10 12	10 32	10 52	11 12	11 32	11 52	12 12	12 32		18 52	19 12	19 32	19 52
Headstone Lane	d		07 04	07 34	08 04	08 34	09 04	09 34	09 54	10 14	10 34	10 54	11 14	11 34	11 54	12 14	12 34		18 54	19 14	19 34	19 54
Harrow & Wealdstone	66 d		07 07	07 37	08 07	08 37	09 07	09 37	09 57	10 17	10 37	10 57	11 17	11 37	11 57	12 17	12 37		18 57	19 17	19 37	19 57
Kenton	d		07 09	07 39	08 09	08 39	09 09	09 39	09 59	10 19	10 39	10 59	11 19	11 39	11 59	12 19	12 39		18 59	19 19	19 39	19 59
South Kenton	d		07 11	07 41	08 11	08 41	09 11	09 41	10 01	10 21	10 41	11 01	11 21	11 41	12 01	12 21	12 41		19 01	19 21	19 41	20 01
North Wembley	d		07 13	07 43	08 13	08 43	09 13	09 43	10 03	10 23	10 43	11 03	11 23	11 43	12 03	12 23	12 43		19 03	19 23	19 43	20 03
Wembley Central	66 d		07 15	07 45	08 15	08 45	09 15	09 45	10 05	10 25	10 45	11 05	11 25	11 45	12 05	12 25	12 45		19 05	19 25	19 45	20 05
Stonebridge Park	d		07 18	07 48	08 18	08 48	09 18	09 48	10 08	10 28	10 48	11 08	11 28	11 48	12 08	12 28	12 48		19 08	19 28	19 48	20 08
Harlesden	d		07 20	07 50	08 20	08 50	09 20	09 50	10 10	10 30	10 50	11 10	11 30	11 50	12 10	12 30	12 50		19 10	19 30	19 50	20 10
Willesden Jn Low Level	d		07 22	07 52	08 22	08 52	09 22	09 52	10 12	10 32	10 52	11 12	11 32	11 52	12 12	12 32	12 52		19 12	19 32	19 52	20 12
Kensal Green	d		07 25	07 55	08 25	08 55	09 25	09 55	10 15	10 35	10 55	11 15	11 35	11 55	12 15	12 35	12 55		19 15	19 35	19 55	20 15
Queen's Park (London)	⊖ d		07 27	07 57	08 27	08 57	09 27	09 57	10 17	10 37	10 57	11 17	11 37	11 57	12 17	12 37	12 57		19 17	19 37	19 57	20 17
Kilburn High Road	d		07 29	07 59	08 29	08 59	09 29	09 59	10 19	10 39	10 59	11 19	11 39	11 59	12 19	12 39	12 59		19 19	19 39	19 59	20 19
South Hampstead	d	00 01	07 31	08 01	08 31	09 01	09 31	10 01	10 21	10 41	11 01	11 21	11 41	12 01	12 21	12 41	13 01		19 21	19 41	20 01	20 21
London Euston 15	⊖66 a	00 10	07 40	08 10	08 40	09 10	09 40	10 10	10 33	10 50	11 10	11 30	11 50	12 13	12 33	12 50	13 10		19 33	19 50	20 10	20 33

Station		LO	LO	LO	LO	LO	LO	LO	LO	LO	LO	LO
Watford Junction	66 d	20 01	20 21	20 41	21 01	21 21	21 41	22 01	22 21	22 41	23 01	23 21
Watford High Street	d	20 04	20 24	20 44	21 04	21 24	21 44	22 04	22 24	22 44	23 04	23 24
Bushey	66 d	20 06	20 26	20 46	21 06	21 26	21 46	22 06	22 26	22 46	23 06	23 26
Carpenders Park	d	20 09	20 29	20 49	21 09	21 29	21 49	22 09	22 29	22 49	23 09	23 29
Hatch End	d	20 12	20 32	20 52	21 12	21 32	21 52	22 12	22 32	22 52	23 12	23 32
Headstone Lane	d	20 14	20 34	20 54	21 14	21 34	21 54	22 14	22 34	22 54	23 14	23 34
Harrow & Wealdstone	66 d	20 17	20 37	20 57	21 17	21 37	21 57	22 17	22 37	22 57	23 17	23 37
Kenton	d	20 19	20 39	20 59	21 19	21 39	21 59	22 19	22 39	22 59	23 19	23 39
South Kenton	d	20 21	20 41	21 01	21 21	21 41	22 01	22 21	22 41	23 01	23 21	23 41
North Wembley	d	20 23	20 43	21 03	21 23	21 43	22 03	22 23	22 43	23 03	23 23	23 43
Wembley Central	66 d	20 25	20 45	21 05	21 25	21 45	22 05	22 25	22 45	23 05	23 25	23 45
Stonebridge Park	d	20 28	20 48	21 08	21 28	21 48	22 08	22 28	22 48	23 08	23 28	23 48
Harlesden	d	20 30	20 50	21 10	21 30	21 50	22 10	22 30	22 50	23 10	23 30	23 50
Willesden Jn Low Level	d	20 32	20 52	21 12	21 32	21 52	22 12	22 32	22 52	23 12	23 32	23 52
Kensal Green	d	20 35	20 55	21 15	21 35	21 55	22 15	22 35	22 55	23 15	23 35	23 55
Queen's Park (London)	⊖ d	20 37	20 57	21 17	21 37	21 57	22 17	22 37	22 57	23 17	23 37	23 57
Kilburn High Road	d	20 39	20 59	21 19	21 39	21 59	22 19	22 39	22 59	23 19	23 39	23 59
South Hampstead	d	20 41	21 01	21 21	21 41	22 01	22 21	22 41	23 01	23 21	23 41	00 01
London Euston 15	⊖66 a	20 53	21 13	21 30	21 53	22 10	22 30	22 50	23 10	23 33	23 53	00 10

Stations Harrow & Wealdstone to Queen's Park inclusive are also served by London Underground Bakerloo Line Services

Table T061-F

Mondays to Fridays

21 May to 7 December

Watford Junction - St. Albans Abbey

Miles			LM	LM	LM	LM	LM	LM	LM	LM	LM	LM	LM
0	**Watford Junction**	d	05 54	06 38	07 21	08 04	08 54	09 39	10 24	11 09	11 54	12 46	13 33
0¾	Watford North	d	05 56	06 40	07 23	08 06	08 56	09 41	10 26	11 11	11 56	12 48	13 35
1¾	Garston (Hertfordshire)	d	05 59	06 43	07 26	08 09	08 59	09 44	10 29	11 14	11 59	12 51	13 38
3¼	Bricket Wood	d	06 02	06 46	07 29	08 12	09 02	09 47	10 32	11 17	12 02	12 54	13 41
4½	How Wood	d	06 04	06 48	07 31	08 14	09 04	09 49	10 34	11 19	12 04	12 56	13 43
5	Park Street	d	06 06	06 50	07 33	08 16	09 06	09 51	10 36	11 21	12 06	12 58	13 45
6½	**St Albans Abbey**	a	06 10	06 54	07 37	08 20	09 10	09 55	10 40	11 25	12 10	13 02	13 49

Miles			LM	LM	LM	LM	LM	LM	LM	LM	LM	LM
0	**Watford Junction**	d	14 16	15 01	15 46	16 33	17 24	18 11	18 56	19 39	20 33	21 33
0¾	Watford North	d	14 18	15 03	15 48	16 35	17 26	18 13	18 58	19 41	20 35	21 35
1¾	Garston (Hertfordshire)	d	14 21	15 06	15 51	16 38	17 29	18 16	19 01	19 44	20 38	21 38
3¼	Bricket Wood	d	14 24	15 09	15 54	16 41	17 32	18 19	19 04	19 47	20 41	21 41
4½	How Wood	d	14 26	15 11	15 56	16 43	17 34	18 21	19 06	19 49	20 43	21 43
5	Park Street	d	14 28	15 13	15 58	16 45	17 36	18 23	19 08	19 51	20 45	21 45
6½	**St Albans Abbey**	a	14 32	15 17	16 02	16 49	17 40	18 27	19 12	19 55	20 49	21 49

		LM
Watford Junction	d	22 21
Watford North	d	22 23
Garston (Hertfordshire)	d	22 26
Bricket Wood	d	22 29
How Wood	d	22 31
Park Street	d	22 33
St Albans Abbey	a	22 37

Saturdays

26 May to 8 December

		LM	LM	LM	LM	LM	LM	LM	LM	LM	LM	LM
Watford Junction	d	06 01	06 45	07 33	08 16	09 01	09 46	10 31	11 14	11 56	12 46	13 46
Watford North	d	06 03	06 47	07 35	08 18	09 03	09 48	10 33	11 16	11 58	12 48	13 48
Garston (Hertfordshire)	d	06 06	06 50	07 38	08 21	09 06	09 51	10 36	11 19	12 01	12 51	13 51
Bricket Wood	d	06 09	06 53	07 41	08 24	09 09	09 54	10 39	11 22	12 04	12 54	13 54
How Wood	d	06 11	06 55	07 43	08 26	09 11	09 56	10 41	11 24	12 06	12 56	13 56
Park Street	d	06 13	06 57	07 45	08 28	09 13	09 58	10 43	11 26	12 08	12 58	13 58
St Albans Abbey	a	06 17	07 01	07 49	08 32	09 17	10 02	10 47	11 30	12 12	13 02	14 02

		LM	LM	LM	LM	LM	LM	LM	LM	LM	LM	LM
Watford Junction	d	14 33	15 16	15 58	16 46	17 33	18 16	18 59	19 46	20 33	21 33	22 21
Watford North	d	14 35	15 18	16 00	16 48	17 35	18 18	19 01	19 48	20 35	21 35	22 23
Garston (Hertfordshire)	d	14 38	15 21	16 03	16 51	17 38	18 21	19 04	19 51	20 38	21 38	22 26
Bricket Wood	d	14 41	15 24	16 06	16 54	17 41	18 24	19 07	19 54	20 41	21 41	22 29
How Wood	d	14 43	15 26	16 08	16 56	17 43	18 26	19 09	19 56	20 43	21 43	22 31
Park Street	d	14 45	15 28	16 10	16 58	17 45	18 28	19 11	19 58	20 45	21 45	22 33
St Albans Abbey	a	14 49	15 32	16 14	17 02	17 49	18 32	19 15	20 02	20 49	21 49	22 37

Sundays

20 May to 2 December

		LM	LM	LM	LM	LM		LM	LM
Watford Junction	d	08 07	09 07	10 20	11 20	12 07	and	22 07	23 04
Watford North	d	08 09	09 09	10 22	11 22	12 09	hourly	22 09	23 06
Garston (Hertfordshire)	d	08 12	09 12	10 25	11 25	12 12	until	22 12	23 09
Bricket Wood	d	08 15	09 15	10 28	11 28	12 15		22 15	23 12
How Wood	d	08 17	09 17	10 30	11 30	12 17		22 17	23 14
Park Street	d	08 19	09 19	10 32	11 32	12 19		22 19	23 16
St Albans Abbey	a	08 23	09 23	10 36	11 36	12 23		22 23	23 20

For connections from London Euston refer to Table T66

Table T061-R

Mondays to Fridays

21 May to 7 December

St. Albans Abbey- Watford Junction

Miles			LM	LM	LM	LM	LM	LM	LM	LM	LM	LM	LM
0	**St Albans Abbey**	d	06 14	06 58	07 42	08 25	09 15	10 00	10 45	11 30	12 15	13 07	13 54
1½	Park Street	d	06 17	07 01	07 45	08 28	09 18	10 03	10 48	11 33	12 18	13 10	13 57
2¼	How Wood	d	06 19	07 03	07 47	08 30	09 20	10 05	10 50	11 35	12 20	13 12	13 59
3	Bricket Wood	d	06 22	07 06	07 50	08 33	09 23	10 08	10 53	11 38	12 23	13 15	14 02
4¾	Garston (Hertfordshire)	d	06 25	07 09	07 53	08 36	09 26	10 11	10 56	11 41	12 26	13 18	14 05
5½	Watford North	d	06 27	07 11	07 55	08 38	09 28	10 13	10 58	11 43	12 28	13 20	14 07
6½	**Watford Junction**	a	06 30	07 14	07 58	08 41	09 31	10 16	11 01	11 46	12 31	13 23	14 10

Miles			LM	LM	LM	LM	LM	LM	LM	LM	LM	LM
0	**St Albans Abbey**	d	14 37	15 22	16 07	16 54	17 45	18 32	19 17	20 00	20 54	21 54
1½	Park Street	d	14 40	15 25	16 10	16 57	17 48	18 35	19 20	20 03	20 57	21 57
2¼	How Wood	d	14 42	15 27	16 12	16 59	17 50	18 37	19 22	20 05	20 59	21 59
3	Bricket Wood	d	14 45	15 30	16 15	17 02	17 53	18 40	19 25	20 08	21 02	22 02
4¾	Garston (Hertfordshire)	d	14 48	15 33	16 18	17 05	17 56	18 43	19 28	20 11	21 05	22 05
5½	Watford North	d	14 50	15 35	16 20	17 07	17 58	18 45	19 30	20 13	21 07	22 07
6½	**Watford Junction**	a	14 53	15 38	16 23	17 10	18 01	18 48	19 33	20 16	21 10	22 10

		LM
St Albans Abbey	d	22 42
Park Street	d	22 45
How Wood	d	22 47
Bricket Wood	d	22 50
Garston (Hertfordshire)	d	22 53
Watford North	d	22 55
Watford Junction	a	22 58

Saturdays

26 May to 8 December

		LM	LM	LM	LM	LM	LM	LM	LM	LM	LM	LM
St Albans Abbey	d	06 22	07 06	07 54	08 37	09 22	10 07	10 52	11 35	12 17	13 07	14 07
Park Street	d	06 25	07 09	07 57	08 40	09 25	10 10	10 55	11 38	12 20	13 10	14 10
How Wood	d	06 27	07 11	07 59	08 42	09 27	10 12	10 57	11 40	12 22	13 12	14 12
Bricket Wood	d	06 30	07 14	08 02	08 45	09 30	10 15	11 00	11 43	12 25	13 15	14 15
Garston (Hertfordshire)	d	06 33	07 17	08 05	08 48	09 33	10 18	11 03	11 46	12 28	13 18	14 18
Watford North	d	06 35	07 19	08 07	08 50	09 35	10 20	11 05	11 48	12 30	13 20	14 20
Watford Junction	a	06 38	07 22	08 10	08 53	09 38	10 23	11 08	11 51	12 33	13 23	14 23

		LM	LM	LM	LM	LM	LM	LM	LM	LM	LM	LM
St Albans Abbey	d	14 54	15 37	16 19	17 07	17 54	18 37	19 20	20 07	20 54	21 54	22 42
Park Street	d	14 57	15 40	16 22	17 10	17 57	18 40	19 23	20 10	20 57	21 57	22 45
How Wood	d	14 59	15 42	16 24	17 12	17 59	18 42	19 25	20 12	20 59	21 59	22 47
Bricket Wood	d	15 02	15 45	16 27	17 15	18 02	18 45	19 28	20 15	21 02	22 02	22 50
Garston (Hertfordshire)	d	15 05	15 48	16 30	17 18	18 05	18 48	19 31	20 18	21 05	22 05	22 53
Watford North	d	15 07	15 50	16 32	17 20	18 07	18 50	19 33	20 20	21 07	22 07	22 55
Watford Junction	a	15 10	15 53	16 35	17 23	18 10	18 53	19 36	20 23	21 10	22 10	22 58

Sundays

20 May to 2 December

		LM	LM	LM	LM	LM		LM	LM
St Albans Abbey	d	08 28	09 28	10 42	11 42	12 28	and	22 28	23 26
Park Street	d	08 31	09 31	10 45	11 45	12 31	hourly	22 31	23 29
How Wood	d	08 33	09 33	10 47	11 47	12 33	until	22 33	23 31
Bricket Wood	d	08 36	09 36	10 50	11 50	12 36		22 36	23 34
Garston (Hertfordshire)	d	08 39	09 39	10 53	11 53	12 39		22 39	23 37
Watford North	d	08 41	09 41	10 55	11 55	12 41		22 41	23 39
Watford Junction	a	08 44	09 44	10 58	11 58	12 44		22 44	23 42

For connections to London Euston refer to Table T66

Table T062-F

Mondays to Fridays

21 May to 7 December

Gospel Oak - Barking

Miles			LO MX A	LO	LO	LO	LO		LO	LO	LO	LO	LO	LO	LO	LO	LO	LO	LO	LO	LO	LO
0	**Gospel Oak**	d		06 20	06 35	06 50	07 05	and at the same minutes past each hour until	09 20	09 35	09 50	10 05	10 20	10 36	10 50	11 05	11 20	11 36	11 50	12 05	12 20	12 37
1¼	Upper Holloway	d		06 24	06 39	06 54	07 09		09 24	09 39	09 54	10 09	10 24	10 39	10 54	11 09	11 24	11 41	11 54	12 09	12 27	12 43
2	Crouch Hill	d		06 26	06 41	06 56	07 11		09 26	09 41	09 56	10 11	10 26	10 42	10 56	11 11	11 26	11 43	11 56	12 11	12 29	12 45
3	Harringay Green Lanes	d		06 29	06 44	06 59	07 14		09 29	09 44	09 59	10 14	10 29	10 45	10 59	11 14	11 29	11 46	11 59	12 14	12 32	12 48
4	South Tottenham	d		06 33	06 48	07 03	07 18		09 33	09 48	10 03	10 18	10 33	10 49	11 03	11 18	11 33	11 50	12 03	12 18	12 36	12 52
5½	Blackhorse Road ⊖	d		06 37	06 52	07 07	07 22		09 37	09 52	10 07	10 22	10 37	10 53	11 07	11 22	11 37	11 54	12 07	12 22	12 39	12 55
6¼	Walthamstow Queen's Road	d	00 01	06 39	06 54	07 09	07 24		09 39	09 54	10 09	10 24	10 39	10 55	11 09	11 24	11 39	11 56	12 09	12 24	12 41	12 57
7½	Leyton Midland Road	d	00 02	06 42	06 57	07 12	07 27		09 42	09 57	10 12	10 27	10 42	10 58	11 12	11 27	11 42	11 59	12 12	12 27	12 44	13 00
8¼	Leytonstone High Road	d	00 04	06 44	06 59	07 14	07 29		09 44	09 59	10 14	10 29	10 44	11 00	11 14	11 29	11 44	12 01	12 14	12 29	12 46	13 02
9¼	Wanstead Park	d	00 07	06 46	07 01	07 16	07 31		09 46	10 01	10 16	10 31	10 46	11 03	11 16	11 31	11 46	12 03	12 16	12 31	12 48	13 05
10¼	Woodgrange Park	d	00 09	06 49	07 04	07 19	07 34		09 49	10 04	10 19	10 34	10 50	11 06	11 19	11 34	11 49	12 06	12 19	12 34	12 51	13 07
12	**Barking** ⊖	a	00 16	06 54	07 09	07 24	07 39		09 54	10 09	10 24	10 39	10 54	11 10	11 24	11 39	11 54	12 10	12 24	12 39	12 54	13 11

		LO	LO	LO	LO	LO	LO	LO	LO	LO	LO	LO	LO	LO	LO	LO	LO	LO	LO	LO	LO	LO	LO
Gospel Oak	d	12 50	13 05	13 20	13 35	13 50	14 05	14 20	14 35	14 50	15 05	15 20	15 35	15 50	16 05	16 20	16 35	16 50	17 05	17 20	17 35	17 50	18 05
Upper Holloway	d	12 54	13 09	13 24	13 39	13 54	14 09	14 24	14 39	14 54	15 09	15 25	15 39	15 54	16 09	16 24	16 39	16 55	17 09	17 24	17 39	17 54	18 09
Crouch Hill	d	12 56	13 11	13 26	13 41	13 56	14 11	14 26	14 41	14 56	15 11	15 27	15 41	15 57	16 11	16 26	16 41	16 57	17 11	17 26	17 41	17 56	18 11
Harringay Green Lanes	d	12 59	13 14	13 29	13 44	13 59	14 14	14 29	14 44	14 59	15 14	15 30	15 44	16 00	16 14	16 29	16 44	17 00	17 14	17 29	17 44	17 59	18 14
South Tottenham	d	13 03	13 18	13 33	13 48	14 03	14 18	14 33	14 48	15 03	15 18	15 34	15 48	16 04	16 18	16 33	16 49	17 04	17 18	17 33	17 48	18 03	18 18
Blackhorse Road ⊖	d	13 07	13 22	13 37	13 52	14 07	14 22	14 37	14 52	15 07	15 22	15 38	15 52	16 08	16 22	16 37	16 52	17 08	17 22	17 37	17 52	18 07	18 22
Walthamstow Queen's Road	d	13 09	13 24	13 39	13 54	14 09	14 24	14 39	14 54	15 09	15 24	15 40	15 54	16 10	16 24	16 39	16 54	17 10	17 24	17 39	17 54	18 09	18 24
Leyton Midland Road	d	13 12	13 27	13 42	13 57	14 12	14 27	14 42	14 57	15 12	15 27	15 43	15 57	16 13	16 27	16 42	16 57	17 13	17 27	17 42	17 57	18 12	18 27
Leytonstone High Road	d	13 14	13 29	13 44	13 59	14 14	14 29	14 44	14 59	15 14	15 29	15 45	15 59	16 15	16 29	16 44	16 59	17 15	17 29	17 44	17 59	18 14	18 29
Wanstead Park	d	13 16	13 31	13 46	14 01	14 16	14 31	14 46	15 01	15 16	15 31	15 47	16 01	16 17	16 31	16 46	17 02	17 17	17 31	17 46	18 01	18 16	18 31
Woodgrange Park	d	13 20	13 34	13 49	14 04	14 19	14 34	14 49	15 04	15 19	15 34	15 50	16 04	16 20	16 34	16 49	17 05	17 20	17 34	17 49	18 04	18 19	18 34
Barking ⊖	a	13 24	13 39	13 54	14 09	14 24	14 39	14 54	15 09	15 24	15 42	15 54	16 09	16 24	16 42	16 57	17 12	17 27	17 42	17 57	18 12	18 27	18 42

		LO	LO	LO	LO	LO	LO	LO	LO	LO	LO	LO	LO	LO	LO	LO	LO	LO	LO	LO	LO	LO
Gospel Oak	d	18 20	18 35	18 50	19 05	19 19	19 35	19 50	20 05	20 20	20 33	20 50	21 05	21 20	21 35	21 51	22 06	22 22	22 48	23 05	23 25	23 42
Upper Holloway	d	18 24	18 39	18 54	19 09	19 24	19 39	19 54	20 09	20 24	20 37	20 55	21 09	21 24	21 39	21 55	22 10	22 26	22 51	23 09	23 29	23 45
Crouch Hill	d	18 26	18 41	18 56	19 11	19 27	19 41	19 56	20 11	20 26	20 40	20 57	21 11	21 26	21 42	21 58	22 12	22 28	22 54	23 11	23 31	23 48
Harringay Green Lanes	d	18 29	18 44	18 59	19 14	19 30	19 44	19 59	20 14	20 29	20 44	21 01	21 14	21 29	21 45	22 01	22 15	22 31	22 57	23 14	23 34	23 51
South Tottenham	d	18 33	18 48	19 03	19 18	19 35	19 48	20 03	20 18	20 33	20 48	21 05	21 18	21 33	21 49	22 05	22 19	22 36	23 00	23 18	23 38	23 54
Blackhorse Road ⊖	d	18 37	18 52	19 07	19 22	19 38	19 52	20 07	20 22	20 37	20 52	21 09	21 22	21 37	21 53	22 08	22 23	22 39	23 04	23 22	23 42	23 58
Walthamstow Queen's Road	d	18 39	18 54	19 09	19 24	19 40	19 54	20 09	20 24	20 39	20 54	21 11	21 24	21 39	21 55	22 10	22 25	22 41	23 06	23 24	23 44	00 01
Leyton Midland Road	d	18 42	18 57	19 12	19 27	19 43	19 57	20 12	20 27	20 42	20 57	21 14	21 27	21 42	21 58	22 13	22 28	22 45	23 08	23 27	23 47	00 02
Leytonstone High Road	d	18 44	18 59	19 14	19 29	19 45	19 59	20 14	20 29	20 44	20 59	21 16	21 29	21 44	22 00	22 16	22 30	22 47	23 10	23 29	23 49	00 04
Wanstead Park	d	18 46	19 01	19 16	19 31	19 47	20 01	20 16	20 31	20 46	21 01	21 18	21 31	21 46	22 03	22 19	22 32	22 49	23 13	23 31	23 51	00 07
Woodgrange Park	d	18 49	19 04	19 19	19 34	19 50	20 04	20 19	20 34	20 49	21 04	21 21	21 34	21 49	22 07	22 22	22 35	22 53	23 15	23 34	23 54	00 09
Barking ⊖	a	18 57	19 09	19 24	19 42	19 56	20 09	20 27	20 39	20 54	21 10	21 27	21 39	21 54	22 11	22 28	22 43	22 59	23 22	23 39	23 59	00 16

Saturdays

26 May to 8 December

		LO A	LO	LO	LO	LO	LO	LO	LO	LO	LO	LO	LO	LO	LO	LO	LO	LO	LO	LO	LO	LO	LO
Gospel Oak	d		06 20	06 35	06 50	07 05	07 20	07 35	07 50	08 05	08 20	08 35	08 50	09 05	09 20	09 35	09 50	10 05	10 20	10 35	10 50	11 05	11 20
Upper Holloway	d		06 24	06 39	06 54	07 09	07 24	07 39	07 54	08 09	08 24	08 39	08 54	09 09	09 24	09 39	09 54	10 09	10 24	10 39	10 54	11 09	11 24
Crouch Hill	d		06 26	06 41	06 56	07 11	07 26	07 41	07 56	08 11	08 26	08 41	08 56	09 11	09 26	09 41	09 56	10 11	10 26	10 41	10 56	11 11	11 26
Harringay Green Lanes	d		06 29	06 44	06 59	07 14	07 29	07 44	07 59	08 14	08 29	08 44	08 59	09 14	09 29	09 44	09 59	10 14	10 29	10 44	10 59	11 14	11 29
South Tottenham	d		06 33	06 48	07 03	07 18	07 33	07 48	08 03	08 18	08 33	08 48	09 03	09 18	09 33	09 48	10 03	10 18	10 33	10 48	11 03	11 18	11 33
Blackhorse Road ⊖	d		06 37	06 52	07 07	07 22	07 37	07 52	08 07	08 22	08 37	08 52	09 07	09 22	09 37	09 52	10 07	10 22	10 37	10 52	11 07	11 22	11 37
Walthamstow Queen's Road	d	00 01	06 39	06 54	07 09	07 24	07 39	07 54	08 09	08 24	08 39	08 54	09 09	09 24	09 39	09 54	10 09	10 24	10 39	10 54	11 09	11 24	11 39
Leyton Midland Road	d	00 02	06 42	06 57	07 12	07 27	07 42	07 57	08 12	08 27	08 42	08 57	09 12	09 27	09 42	09 57	10 12	10 27	10 42	10 57	11 12	11 27	11 42
Leytonstone High Road	d	00 04	06 44	06 59	07 14	07 29	07 44	07 59	08 14	08 29	08 44	08 59	09 14	09 29	09 44	09 59	10 14	10 29	10 44	10 59	11 14	11 29	11 44
Wanstead Park	d	00 07	06 46	07 01	07 16	07 31	07 46	08 01	08 16	08 31	08 46	09 01	09 16	09 31	09 46	10 01	10 16	10 31	10 46	11 01	11 16	11 31	11 46
Woodgrange Park	d	00 09	06 49	07 04	07 19	07 34	07 49	08 04	08 20	08 34	08 50	09 04	09 20	09 34	09 50	10 04	10 20	10 34	10 49	11 04	11 20	11 34	11 50
Barking ⊖	a	00 16	06 54	07 09	07 24	07 39	07 54	08 09	08 24	08 39	08 54	09 09	09 24	09 39	09 54	10 09	10 24	10 39	10 54	11 09	11 24	11 39	11 54

		LO	LO	LO	LO	LO	LO	LO	LO	LO	LO	LO	LO	LO	LO	LO	LO	LO	LO	LO	LO	LO	LO
Gospel Oak	d	11 35	11 50	12 05	12 20	12 35	12 50	13 05	13 20	13 35	13 50	14 05	14 20	14 35	14 50	15 05	15 20	15 35	15 50	16 05	16 20	16 35	16 50
Upper Holloway	d	11 39	11 54	12 09	12 24	12 39	12 54	13 09	13 24	13 39	13 54	14 09	14 24	14 39	14 54	15 09	15 24	15 39	15 54	16 09	16 25	16 39	16 54
Crouch Hill	d	11 41	11 56	12 11	12 26	12 41	12 56	13 11	13 26	13 41	13 56	14 11	14 26	14 41	14 56	15 11	15 26	15 41	15 56	16 11	16 27	16 41	16 56
Harringay Green Lanes	d	11 44	11 59	12 14	12 29	12 45	12 59	13 14	13 29	13 44	13 59	14 14	14 29	14 44	14 59	15 14	15 29	15 44	15 59	16 14	16 30	16 44	16 59
South Tottenham	d	11 48	12 03	12 18	12 33	12 49	13 03	13 18	13 33	13 48	14 03	14 18	14 33	14 48	15 03	15 18	15 33	15 48	16 03	16 18	16 35	16 48	17 03
Blackhorse Road ⊖	d	11 52	12 07	12 22	12 37	12 53	13 07	13 22	13 37	13 52	14 07	14 22	14 37	14 52	15 07	15 22	15 37	15 52	16 07	16 22	16 39	16 52	17 07
Walthamstow Queen's Road	d	11 54	12 09	12 24	12 39	12 55	13 09	13 24	13 39	13 54	14 09	14 24	14 39	14 54	15 10	15 24	15 39	15 54	16 09	16 24	16 41	16 54	17 09
Leyton Midland Road	d	11 57	12 12	12 27	12 42	12 58	13 12	13 27	13 42	13 57	14 12	14 27	14 42	14 57	15 13	15 27	15 42	15 57	16 12	16 27	16 44	16 57	17 12
Leytonstone High Road	d	11 59	12 14	12 29	12 44	13 00	13 14	13 29	13 44	13 59	14 14	14 29	14 44	14 59	15 15	15 29	15 44	15 59	16 14	16 29	16 46	16 59	17 14
Wanstead Park	d	12 01	12 16	12 31	12 46	13 03	13 16	13 31	13 46	14 01	14 16	14 31	14 46	15 01	15 17	15 31	15 46	16 01	16 16	16 31	16 48	17 01	17 16
Woodgrange Park	d	12 04	12 20	12 34	12 50	13 06	13 20	13 34	13 50	14 04	14 20	14 34	14 50	15 04	15 22	15 34	15 50	16 04	16 21	16 34	16 51	17 04	17 20
Barking ⊖	a	12 09	12 24	12 39	12 54	13 12	13 24	13 39	13 54	14 09	14 24	14 39	14 54	15 09	15 27	15 39	15 54	16 09	16 27	16 39	16 57	17 09	17 24

		LO	LO	LO	LO	LO	LO	LO	LO	LO	LO	LO	LO	LO	LO	LO	LO	LO	LO	LO	LO	LO
Gospel Oak	d	17 05	17 20	17 35	17 50	18 05	18 20	18 35	18 50	19 05	19 20	19 38	19 50	20 05	20 20	20 35	20 50	21 05	21 20	21 35	21 50	22 05
Upper Holloway	d	17 09	17 24	17 39	17 54	18 09	18 24	18 39	18 54	19 09	19 24	19 42	19 54	20 09	20 24	20 39	20 54	21 09	21 24	21 39	21 54	22 09
Crouch Hill	d	17 11	17 26	17 41	17 56	18 11	18 26	18 41	18 56	19 11	19 26	19 44	19 56	20 11	20 26	20 41	20 56	21 11	21 26	21 41	21 56	22 11
Harringay Green Lanes	d	17 14	17 29	17 44	17 59	18 14	18 29	18 44	18 59	19 14	19 29	19 47	19 59	20 14	20 29	20 44	20 59	21 14	21 29	21 44	21 59	22 14
South Tottenham	d	17 18	17 33	17 48	18 03	18 18	18 33	18 48	19 03	19 18	19 33	19 51	20 03	20 18	20 33	20 48	21 03	21 18	21 33	21 48	22 03	22 18
Blackhorse Road ⊖	d	17 22	17 37	17 52	18 07	18 22	18 37	18 52	19 07	19 22	19 37	19 55	20 07	20 22	20 37	20 52	21 07	21 22	21 37	21 52	22 07	22 22
Walthamstow Queen's Road	d	17 24	17 39	17 54	18 09	18 24	18 39	18 54	19 09	19 24	19 39	19 57	20 09	20 24	20 39	20 54	21 09	21 24	21 39	21 54	22 09	22 24
Leyton Midland Road	d	17 27	17 42	17 57	18 12	18 27	18 42	18 57	19 12	19 27	19 42	20 00	20 12	20 27	20 42	20 57	21 12	21 27	21 42	21 57	22 12	22 27
Leytonstone High Road	d	17 29	17 44	17 59	18 14	18 29	18 44	18 59	19 14	19 29	19 44	20 02	20 14	20 29	20 44	20 59	21 14	21 29	21 44	21 59	22 14	22 29
Wanstead Park	d	17 31	17 46	18 01	18 16	18 31	18 46	19 01	19 16	19 31	19 46	20 04	20 16	20 31	20 46	21 01	21 16	21 31	21 46	22 01	22 16	22 31
Woodgrange Park	d	17 34	17 50	18 04	18 20	18 35	18 50	19 04	19 20	19 34	19 50	20 07	20 20	20 34	20 50	21 04	21 20	21 34	21 50	22 04	22 21	22 34
Barking ⊖	a	17 39	17 54	18 09	18 24	18 39	18 54	19 09	19 24	19 39	19 54	20 12	20 24	20 39	20 54	21 09	21 24	21 39	21 54	22 09	22 24	22 39

A From Gospel Oak

Table T062-F

Saturdays

26 May to 8 December

Gospel Oak - Barking

		LO	LO	LO	LO	LO
Gospel Oak	d	22 22	22 45	23 05	23 25	23 48
Upper Holloway	d	22 26	22 49	23 09	23 29	23 53
Crouch Hill	d	22 29	22 51	23 11	23 31	23 55
Harringay Green Lanes	d	22 32	22 54	23 14	23 34	23 58
South Tottenham	d	22 36	22 58	23 18	23 38	00 02
Blackhorse Road ⊖	d	22 40	23 02	23 22	23 42	00 06
Walthamstow Queen's Road	d	22 42	23 04	23 24	23 44	00 08
Leyton Midland Road	d	22 45	23 07	23 27	23 47	00 11
Leytonstone High Road	d	22 47	23 09	23 29	23 49	00 13
Wanstead Park	d	22 50	23 11	23 31	23 51	00 15
Woodgrange Park	d	22 53	23 14	23 34	23 54	00 22
Barking ⊖	a	22 59	23 19	23 38	23 59	00 25

Sundays

20 May to 2 December

		LO A	LO	LO	LO	LO		LO	LO	LO	LO	LO	LO	LO	LO	LO
Gospel Oak	d		08 55	09 10	09 25	09 40	and at the same minutes past each hour until	20 55	21 10	21 25	21 40	21 55	22 10	22 30	22 50	23 10
Upper Holloway	d		08 59	09 14	09 29	09 44		20 59	21 14	21 29	21 44	21 59	22 14	22 34	22 54	23 14
Crouch Hill	d		09 01	09 16	09 31	09 46		21 01	21 16	21 31	21 46	22 01	22 16	22 36	22 56	23 16
Harringay Green Lanes	d		09 04	09 19	09 34	09 49		21 04	21 19	21 34	21 49	22 04	22 19	22 39	22 59	23 19
South Tottenham	d	00 02	09 08	09 23	09 38	09 53		21 08	21 23	21 38	21 53	22 08	22 23	22 43	23 03	23 23
Blackhorse Road ⊖	d	00 06	09 12	09 27	09 42	09 57		21 12	21 27	21 42	21 57	22 12	22 27	22 47	23 07	23 27
Walthamstow Queen's Road	d	00 08	09 14	09 29	09 44	09 59		21 14	21 29	21 44	21 59	22 14	22 29	22 49	23 09	23 29
Leyton Midland Road	d	00 11	09 17	09 32	09 47	10 02		21 17	21 32	21 47	22 02	22 17	22 32	22 52	23 12	23 32
Leytonstone High Road	d	00 13	09 19	09 34	09 49	10 04		21 19	21 34	21 49	22 04	22 19	22 34	22 54	23 14	23 34
Wanstead Park	d	00 15	09 21	09 36	09 51	10 06		21 21	21 36	21 51	22 06	22 21	22 36	22 56	23 16	23 36
Woodgrange Park	d	00 22	09 24	09 39	09 54	10 09		21 24	21 39	21 54	22 09	22 24	22 39	22 59	23 19	23 39
Barking ⊖	a	00 25	09 29	09 44	09 59	10 14		21 29	21 44	21 59	22 14	22 29	22 44	23 04	23 24	23 44

A From Gospel Oak

Table T062-R

Saturdays

26 May to 8 December

Barking - Gospel Oak

		LO	LO	LO	LO	LO	LO	LO	LO	LO	LO
Barking ⊖	d	21 18	21 33	21 48	22 03	22 18	22 33	22 53	23 13	23 33	23 53
Woodgrange Park	d	21 22	21 37	21 52	22 07	22 22	22 37	22 57	23 17	23 37	23 56
Wanstead Park	d	21 25	21 40	21 55	22 10	22 25	22 40	23 00	23 19	23 40	23 59
Leytonstone High Road	d	21 27	21 42	21 57	22 12	22 27	22 42	23 02	23 22	23 42	00 01
Leyton Midland Road	d	21 30	21 45	22 00	22 15	22 30	22 45	23 05	23 25	23 45	00 03
Walthamstow Queen's Road	d	21 32	21 47	22 02	22 17	22 32	22 47	23 07	23 27	23 47	00 06
Blackhorse Road ⊖	d	21 34	21 49	22 04	22 19	22 34	22 49	23 09	23 29	23 49	00 08
South Tottenham	d	21 39	21 54	22 09	22 24	22 39	22 54	23 14	23 34	23 54	00 11
Harringay Green Lanes	d	21 42	21 57	22 12	22 27	22 42	22 57	23 17	23 37	23 57	00 14
Crouch Hill	d	21 45	22 00	22 15	22 30	22 45	23 00	23 20	23 40	00 01	00 17
Upper Holloway	d	21 48	22 03	22 18	22 33	22 48	23 03	23 23	23 44	00 04	00 20
Gospel Oak	a	21 53	22 08	22 26	22 38	22 53	23 08	23 28	23 51	00 08	00 28

Sundays

20 May to 2 December

		LO A	LO A	LO	LO	LO	LO		LO	LO	LO	LO	LO	LO	LO	LO	LO	LO	LO
Barking ⊖	d			08 53	09 08	09 23	09 38	and at the same minutes past each hour until	20 53	21 08	21 23	21 38	21 53	22 08	22 23	22 38	22 58	23 18	23 38
Woodgrange Park	d			08 57	09 12	09 27	09 42		20 57	21 12	21 27	21 42	21 57	22 12	22 27	22 42	23 01	23 22	23 42
Wanstead Park	d			09 00	09 15	09 30	09 45		21 00	21 15	21 30	21 45	22 00	22 15	22 30	22 45	23 04	23 25	23 45
Leytonstone High Road	d		00 01	09 02	09 17	09 32	09 47		21 02	21 17	21 32	21 47	22 02	22 17	22 32	22 47	23 06	23 27	23 47
Leyton Midland Road	d		00 03	09 05	09 20	09 35	09 50		21 05	21 20	21 35	21 50	22 05	22 20	22 35	22 50	23 10	23 30	23 50
Walthamstow Queen's Road	d		00 06	09 07	09 22	09 37	09 52		21 07	21 22	21 37	21 52	22 07	22 22	22 37	22 52	23 12	23 32	23 52
Blackhorse Road ⊖	d		00 08	09 09	09 24	09 39	09 54		21 09	21 24	21 39	21 54	22 09	22 24	22 39	22 54	23 14	23 34	23 54
South Tottenham	d		00 11	09 14	09 29	09 44	09 59		21 14	21 29	21 44	21 59	22 14	22 29	22 44	22 59	23 19	23 39	23 59
Harringay Green Lanes	d		00 14	09 17	09 32	09 47	10 02		21 17	21 32	21 47	22 02	22 17	22 32	22 47	23 02	23 22	23 42	00 02
Crouch Hill	d	00 01	00 17	09 20	09 35	09 50	10 05		21 20	21 35	21 50	22 05	22 20	22 35	22 50	23 05	23 25	23 45	00 05
Upper Holloway	d	00 04	00 20	09 23	09 38	09 53	10 08		21 23	21 38	21 53	22 08	22 24	22 38	22 53	23 08	23 28	23 48	00 08
Gospel Oak	a	00 08	00 28	09 28	09 43	09 58	10 13		21 28	21 43	21 58	22 13	22 33	22 43	22 58	23 13	23 33	23 53	00 13

A From Barking

Table T062-R

Mondays to Fridays

21 May to 7 December

Barking - Gospel Oak

Miles			LO MX A	LO MO A	LO MX A	LO	LO	LO	LO	LO	LO	LO	LO	LO	LO	LO	LO	LO	LO	LO	LO	LO	LO
0	**Barking** ⊖	d				06 06	06 18	06 33	06 48	07 03	07 18	07 33	07 48	08 03	08 18	08 33	08 48	09 03	09 18	09 33	09 48	10 03	10 18
1¾	Woodgrange Park	d				06 10	06 22	06 37	06 52	07 07	07 22	07 37	07 52	08 07	08 22	08 37	08 52	09 07	09 22	09 37	09 52	10 07	10 22
2¾	Wanstead Park	d				06 12	06 25	06 40	06 55	07 10	07 25	07 40	07 55	08 10	08 25	08 40	08 55	09 10	09 25	09 40	09 55	10 10	10 25
3¼	Leytonstone High Road	d			00 02	06 15	06 27	06 42	06 57	07 12	07 27	07 42	07 57	08 12	08 27	08 42	08 57	09 12	09 27	09 42	09 57	10 12	10 27
4½	Leyton Midland Road	d			00 04	06 17	06 30	06 45	07 00	07 15	07 30	07 45	08 00	08 15	08 30	08 45	09 00	09 15	09 30	09 45	10 00	10 15	10 30
5¾	Walthamstow Queen's Road	d			00 06	06 19	06 32	06 47	07 02	07 17	07 32	07 47	08 02	08 17	08 32	08 47	09 02	09 17	09 32	09 47	10 02	10 17	10 32
6½	Blackhorse Road ⊖	d			00 08	06 21	06 34	06 49	07 04	07 20	07 35	07 50	08 05	08 20	08 35	08 50	09 04	09 19	09 34	09 49	10 04	10 20	10 34
8	South Tottenham	d			00 12	06 26	06 39	06 54	07 09	07 24	07 39	07 54	08 09	08 24	08 39	08 54	09 09	09 24	09 39	09 54	10 09	10 26	10 39
9	Harringay Green Lanes	d		00 02	00 15	06 29	06 42	06 57	07 12	07 27	07 42	07 57	08 12	08 27	08 42	08 57	09 12	09 27	09 42	09 57	10 12	10 29	10 43
10	Crouch Hill	d		00 05	00 18	06 32	06 45	07 00	07 15	07 30	07 45	08 00	08 15	08 30	08 45	09 00	09 15	09 30	09 45	10 00	10 15	10 32	10 46
10¾	Upper Holloway	d	00 01	00 08	00 20	06 35	06 48	07 03	07 19	07 33	07 48	08 03	08 18	08 33	08 48	09 03	09 18	09 33	09 48	10 03	10 18	10 35	10 49
12	**Gospel Oak**	a	00 08	00 13	00 28	06 41	06 53	07 11	07 26	07 38	07 53	08 11	08 26	08 41	08 56	09 08	09 23	09 38	09 53	10 08	10 23	10 41	10 53

		LO	LO	LO	LO	LO	LO	LO	LO	LO	LO	LO	LO	LO	LO	LO	LO	LO	LO	LO	LO	LO
Barking ⊖	d	10 33	10 48	11 03	11 18	11 33	11 48	12 03	12 18	12 33	12 48	13 03	13 17	13 33	13 48	14 03	14 18	14 33	14 48	15 03	15 18	15 33
Woodgrange Park	d	10 37	10 52	11 07	11 22	11 37	11 52	12 07	12 22	12 37	12 52	13 07	13 21	13 37	13 52	14 07	14 22	14 37	14 52	15 07	15 22	15 37
Wanstead Park	d	10 40	10 55	11 10	11 25	11 40	11 55	12 10	12 25	12 40	12 55	13 10	13 24	13 40	13 55	14 10	14 25	14 40	14 55	15 10	15 25	15 40
Leytonstone High Road	d	10 42	10 58	11 12	11 27	11 42	11 57	12 12	12 27	12 42	12 57	13 12	13 26	13 42	13 57	14 12	14 27	14 42	14 57	15 12	15 27	15 42
Leyton Midland Road	d	10 45	11 00	11 15	11 30	11 45	12 00	12 15	12 30	12 45	13 00	13 15	13 29	13 45	14 00	14 15	14 30	14 45	15 00	15 15	15 30	15 45
Walthamstow Queen's Road	d	10 47	11 02	11 17	11 32	11 47	12 02	12 17	12 32	12 47	13 02	13 17	13 31	13 47	14 02	14 17	14 32	14 47	15 02	15 17	15 32	15 47
Blackhorse Road ⊖	d	10 49	11 04	11 19	11 34	11 49	12 04	12 19	12 34	12 49	13 04	13 19	13 33	13 49	14 04	14 19	14 34	14 49	15 04	15 19	15 34	15 49
South Tottenham	d	10 54	11 09	11 24	11 39	11 54	12 09	12 24	12 39	12 54	13 09	13 24	13 38	13 54	14 09	14 24	14 39	14 54	15 09	15 24	15 39	15 54
Harringay Green Lanes	d	10 57	11 12	11 27	11 42	11 57	12 12	12 27	12 42	12 57	13 12	13 27	13 41	13 57	14 12	14 27	14 42	14 57	15 12	15 27	15 42	15 57
Crouch Hill	d	11 00	11 15	11 30	11 45	12 00	12 15	12 30	12 45	13 00	13 15	13 30	13 44	14 00	14 15	14 30	14 45	15 00	15 15	15 30	15 45	16 00
Upper Holloway	d	11 03	11 18	11 33	11 48	12 03	12 18	12 33	12 48	13 03	13 18	13 33	13 47	14 03	14 18	14 33	14 48	15 03	15 18	15 33	15 48	16 03
Gospel Oak	a	11 08	11 23	11 41	11 53	12 08	12 23	12 41	12 53	13 08	13 23	13 38	13 55	14 08	14 23	14 38	14 53	15 08	15 23	15 38	15 53	16 08

		LO	LO	LO	LO	LO	LO	LO	LO	LO	LO	LO	LO	LO	LO	LO	LO	LO	LO	LO	LO	LO	LO
Barking ⊖	d	15 48	16 03	16 18	16 33	16 48	17 03	17 18	17 33	17 48	18 03	18 18	18 33	18 48	19 03	19 18	19 33	19 48	20 03	20 18	20 33	20 48	21 03
Woodgrange Park	d	15 52	16 07	16 23	16 37	16 52	17 07	17 22	17 37	17 52	18 07	18 22	18 37	18 52	19 07	19 22	19 37	19 52	20 07	20 22	20 37	20 52	21 07
Wanstead Park	d	15 55	16 10	16 26	16 40	16 55	17 10	17 25	17 40	17 55	18 10	18 25	18 40	18 55	19 10	19 25	19 40	19 55	20 10	20 25	20 40	20 55	21 10
Leytonstone High Road	d	15 57	16 12	16 28	16 42	16 57	17 12	17 27	17 42	17 57	18 12	18 27	18 42	18 57	19 12	19 27	19 42	19 57	20 12	20 27	20 42	20 57	21 12
Leyton Midland Road	d	16 00	16 15	16 31	16 45	17 00	17 15	17 30	17 45	18 00	18 15	18 30	18 45	19 00	19 15	19 30	19 45	20 00	20 15	20 30	20 45	21 00	21 15
Walthamstow Queen's Road	d	16 02	16 17	16 33	16 47	17 02	17 17	17 32	17 47	18 02	18 17	18 32	18 47	19 02	19 17	19 32	19 47	20 02	20 17	20 32	20 47	21 02	21 17
Blackhorse Road ⊖	d	16 04	16 19	16 35	16 49	17 04	17 19	17 34	17 49	18 04	18 19	18 34	18 49	19 04	19 19	19 34	19 49	20 04	20 19	20 34	20 49	21 04	21 19
South Tottenham	d	16 09	16 24	16 40	16 54	17 09	17 24	17 39	17 54	18 09	18 24	18 39	18 54	19 09	19 24	19 39	19 54	20 09	20 24	20 39	20 54	21 09	21 24
Harringay Green Lanes	d	16 12	16 27	16 43	16 57	17 12	17 27	17 42	17 57	18 12	18 27	18 42	18 57	19 13	19 27	19 42	19 57	20 12	20 27	20 42	20 57	21 12	21 27
Crouch Hill	d	16 15	16 30	16 46	17 00	17 15	17 30	17 45	18 00	18 15	18 30	18 45	19 00	19 16	19 30	19 45	20 00	20 15	20 30	20 45	21 00	21 15	21 30
Upper Holloway	d	16 18	16 33	16 49	17 03	17 18	17 33	17 48	18 03	18 18	18 33	18 48	19 03	19 20	19 33	19 48	20 03	20 18	20 33	20 48	21 03	21 18	21 33
Gospel Oak	a	16 23	16 41	16 53	17 08	17 26	17 38	17 53	18 11	18 26	18 41	18 53	19 11	19 25	19 41	19 53	20 08	20 23	20 38	20 53	21 08	21 23	21 38

		LO	LO	LO	LO	LO	LO	LO	LO	LO	LO
Barking ⊖	d	21 20	21 33	21 48	22 03	22 18	22 36	22 53	23 13	23 33	23 53
Woodgrange Park	d	21 24	21 37	21 52	22 07	22 22	22 40	22 57	23 17	23 37	23 57
Wanstead Park	d	21 27	21 40	21 55	22 10	22 25	22 43	23 00	23 19	23 39	23 59
Leytonstone High Road	d	21 29	21 42	21 57	22 12	22 27	22 45	23 02	23 22	23 42	00 02
Leyton Midland Road	d	21 32	21 45	22 00	22 14	22 30	22 47	23 05	23 24	23 44	00 04
Walthamstow Queen's Road	d	21 34	21 47	22 02	22 17	22 32	22 50	23 07	23 26	23 46	00 06
Blackhorse Road ⊖	d	21 36	21 49	22 04	22 19	22 34	22 52	23 09	23 28	23 48	00 08
South Tottenham	d	21 41	21 54	22 09	22 23	22 38	22 56	23 14	23 32	23 52	00 12
Harringay Green Lanes	d	21 44	21 57	22 12	22 26	22 41	22 59	23 17	23 35	23 55	00 15
Crouch Hill	d	21 47	22 00	22 15	22 29	22 44	23 02	23 20	23 38	23 58	00 18
Upper Holloway	d	21 50	22 03	22 18	22 31	22 46	23 05	23 23	23 40	00 01	00 20
Gospel Oak	a	21 58	22 11	22 26	22 38	22 53	23 11	23 28	23 48	00 08	00 28

Saturdays

26 May to 8 December

		LO A	LO A	LO	LO	LO	LO	LO	LO	LO	LO		LO	LO	LO	LO	LO	LO	LO	LO
Barking ⊖	d			06 20	06 34	06 48	07 03	07 18	07 33	07 48	08 03	and at the same minutes past each hour until	11 18	11 33	11 48	12 03	12 18	12 33	12 48	13 03
Woodgrange Park	d			06 24	06 37	06 52	07 07	07 22	07 37	07 52	08 07		11 22	11 37	11 52	12 07	12 22	12 37	12 52	13 08
Wanstead Park	d			06 27	06 40	06 55	07 10	07 25	07 40	07 55	08 10		11 25	11 40	11 55	12 10	12 25	12 40	12 55	13 10
Leytonstone High Road	d		00 02	06 29	06 42	06 57	07 12	07 27	07 42	07 57	08 12		11 27	11 42	11 57	12 12	12 27	12 42	12 57	13 13
Leyton Midland Road	d		00 04	06 32	06 45	07 00	07 15	07 30	07 45	08 00	08 15		11 30	11 45	12 00	12 15	12 30	12 45	13 00	13 15
Walthamstow Queen's Road	d		00 06	06 34	06 47	07 02	07 17	07 32	07 47	08 02	08 17		11 32	11 47	12 02	12 17	12 32	12 47	13 02	13 18
Blackhorse Road ⊖	d		00 08	06 36	06 49	07 04	07 19	07 34	07 49	08 04	08 19		11 34	11 49	12 04	12 19	12 34	12 49	13 04	13 20
South Tottenham	d		00 12	06 41	06 53	07 09	07 24	07 39	07 54	08 09	08 24		11 39	11 54	12 09	12 24	12 39	12 54	13 09	13 24
Harringay Green Lanes	d		00 15	06 44	06 56	07 12	07 27	07 42	07 57	08 12	08 27		11 42	11 57	12 12	12 27	12 42	12 57	13 12	13 27
Crouch Hill	d		00 18	06 47	06 59	07 15	07 30	07 45	08 00	08 15	08 30		11 45	12 00	12 15	12 30	12 45	13 00	13 15	13 30
Upper Holloway	d	00 01	00 20	06 50	07 02	07 18	07 33	07 48	08 03	08 18	08 33		11 48	12 03	12 18	12 33	12 48	13 03	13 18	13 33
Gospel Oak	a	00 08	00 28	06 53	07 08	07 23	07 41	07 53	08 08	08 23	08 38		11 53	12 08	12 23	12 38	12 53	13 08	13 23	13 38

		LO	LO	LO	LO		LO	LO	LO	LO	LO	LO	LO	LO	LO	LO	LO	LO	LO	LO	LO	LO
Barking ⊖	d	13 18	13 33	13 48	14 03	and at the same minutes past each hour until	17 18	17 33	17 48	18 03	18 18	18 33	18 48	19 04	19 18	19 33	19 48	20 03	20 18	20 33	20 48	21 03
Woodgrange Park	d	13 22	13 37	13 52	14 07		17 22	17 37	17 52	18 07	18 22	18 37	18 52	19 08	19 22	19 37	19 52	20 07	20 22	20 37	20 52	21 07
Wanstead Park	d	13 25	13 40	13 55	14 10		17 25	17 40	17 55	18 10	18 25	18 40	18 55	19 11	19 25	19 40	19 55	20 10	20 25	20 40	20 55	21 10
Leytonstone High Road	d	13 27	13 42	13 57	14 12		17 27	17 42	17 57	18 12	18 27	18 42	18 57	19 13	19 27	19 42	19 57	20 12	20 27	20 42	20 57	21 12
Leyton Midland Road	d	13 30	13 45	14 00	14 15		17 30	17 45	18 00	18 15	18 30	18 45	19 00	19 16	19 30	19 45	20 00	20 15	20 30	20 45	21 00	21 15
Walthamstow Queen's Road	d	13 32	13 47	14 02	14 17		17 32	17 47	18 02	18 17	18 32	18 47	19 02	19 18	19 32	19 47	20 02	20 17	20 32	20 47	21 02	21 17
Blackhorse Road ⊖	d	13 34	13 49	14 04	14 19		17 34	17 49	18 04	18 19	18 34	18 49	19 04	19 20	19 34	19 49	20 04	20 19	20 34	20 49	21 04	21 19
South Tottenham	d	13 39	13 54	14 09	14 24		17 39	17 54	18 09	18 24	18 39	18 54	19 09	19 25	19 39	19 54	20 09	20 24	20 39	20 54	21 09	21 24
Harringay Green Lanes	d	13 42	13 57	14 12	14 27		17 42	17 57	18 12	18 27	18 42	18 57	19 12	19 28	19 42	19 57	20 12	20 27	20 42	20 57	21 12	21 27
Crouch Hill	d	13 45	14 00	14 15	14 30		17 45	18 00	18 15	18 30	18 45	19 00	19 15	19 32	19 45	20 00	20 15	20 30	20 45	21 00	21 15	21 30
Upper Holloway	d	13 48	14 03	14 18	14 33		17 48	18 03	18 18	18 33	18 48	19 03	19 18	19 35	19 48	20 03	20 18	20 33	20 48	21 03	21 18	21 33
Gospel Oak	a	13 53	14 08	14 23	14 38		17 53	18 08	18 23	18 38	18 53	19 11	19 23	19 42	19 53	20 08	20 26	20 38	20 53	21 11	21 23	21 38

A From Barking

Table T063-F

Mondays to Fridays

21 May to 7 December

Coventry - Nuneaton

Miles			LM		LM	LM		LM
0	**Coventry**	d	06 04	and hourly until	09 04	10 42	and hourly until	21 42
4	Coventry Arena	d	06 11		09 11	10 49		21 49
6½	Bedworth	d	06 17		09 17	10 55		21 55
8¼	Bermuda Park	d	06 21		09 21	10 59		21 59
10¼	**Nuneaton**	a	06 26		09 26	11 04		22 04

Saturdays

26 May to 8 December

		LM	LM	LM		LM	LM	LM
Coventry	d	06 15	07 15	08 42	and hourly until	18 42	20 15	21 42
Coventry Arena	d	06 22	07 22	08 49		18 49	20 22	21 49
Bedworth	d	06 28	07 28	08 55		18 55	20 28	21 55
Bermuda Park	d	06 32	07 32	08 59		18 59	20 32	21 59
Nuneaton	a	06 37	07 37	09 04		19 04	20 37	22 04

Sundays

20 May to 2 December

		LM	LM		LM	LM	LM
Coventry	d	11 46	13 39	and hourly until	17 39	19 39	21 32
Coventry Arena	d	11 53	13 46		17 46	19 46	21 39
Bedworth	d	11 59	13 52		17 52	19 52	21 45
Bermuda Park	d	12 03	13 56		17 56	19 56	21 49
Nuneaton	a	12 08	14 01		18 01	20 01	21 54

Table T063-R

Mondays to Fridays

21 May to 7 December

Nuneaton - Coventry

Miles			LM	LM	LM	LM	LM	LM	LM	LM	LM		LM	LM
0	**Nuneaton**	d	06 33	07 37	08 33	10 14	11 14	12 14	13 14	14 13	15 14	and hourly until	21 14	22 20
2	Bermuda Park	d	06 37	07 41	08 37	10 18	11 18	12 18	13 18	14 17	15 18		21 18	22 24
3½	Bedworth	d	06 41	07 45	08 41	10 22	11 22	12 22	13 22	14 21	15 22		21 22	22 28
6¼	Coventry Arena	d	06 47	07 51	08 47	10 28	11 28	12 28	13 28	14 26	15 28		21 28	22 34
10¼	**Coventry**	a	06 55	07 59	08 55	10 36	11 36	12 37	13 36	14 36	15 36		21 36	22 42

Saturdays

26 May to 8 December

		LM	LM		LM	LM	LM		LM	LM	LM	LM
Nuneaton	d	06 44	08 14	and hourly until	12 14	13 14	14 14	and hourly until	18 14	19 44	21 14	22 20
Bermuda Park	d	06 48	08 18		12 18	13 18	14 18		18 18	19 48	21 18	22 24
Bedworth	d	06 52	08 22		12 22	13 22	14 22		18 22	19 52	21 22	22 28
Coventry Arena	d	06 58	08 28		12 28	13 28	14 28		18 28	19 58	21 28	22 34
Coventry	a	07 06	08 36		12 36	13 37	14 36		18 36	20 06	21 36	22 42

Sundays

20 May to 2 December

		LM	LM		LM	LM	LM
Nuneaton	d	12 36	14 11	and hourly until	18 11	20 11	22 00
Bermuda Park	d	12 40	14 15		18 15	20 15	22 04
Bedworth	d	12 44	14 19		18 19	20 19	22 08
Coventry Arena	d	12 50	14 25		18 25	20 25	22 14
Coventry	a	12 58	14 33		18 33	20 33	22 22

Table T064-F

Mondays to Saturdays

21 May to 8 December

Bletchley - Bedford

Miles			LM SX	LM SO	LM SX	LM SO	LM	LM SX	LM SO	LM	LM	LM	LM	LM	LM	LM SX	LM SO	LM SX	LM SO	LM SX	LM SO	LM SX	LM SO
0	**Bletchley**	d	05 16	05 34	06 24	06 34	07 31	08 22	08 34	10 01	11 01	12 01	13 01	14 01	15 01	15 51	16 01	16 51	17 01	17 36	17 50	18 31	18 47
1	Fenny Stratford	d	05 19	05 37	06 28	06 37	07 34	08 26	08 37	10 04	11 04	12 04	13 04	14 04	15 04	15 54	16 04	16 54	17 04	17 39	17 53	18 34	18 50
2	Bow Brickhill	d	05 23	05 41	06 32	06 41	07 38	08 30	08 41	10 08	11 08	12 08	13 08	14 08	15 08	15 58	16 08	16 58	17 08	17 43	17 57	18 38	18 54
4	Woburn Sands	d	05 27	05 45	06 36	06 45	07 42	08 34	08 45	10 12	11 12	12 12	13 12	14 12	15 12	16 02	16 12	17 02	17 12	17 48	18 01	18 42	18 58
5	Aspley Guise	d	05 30	05 48	06 39	06 48	07 45	08 37	08 48	10 15	11 15	12 15	13 15	14 15	15 15	16 05	16 15	17 05	17 15	17 50	18 04	18 45	19 01
6¾	Ridgmont	d	05 34	05 52	06 43	06 52	07 49	08 41	08 52	10 19	11 19	12 19	13 19	14 19	15 19	16 09	16 19	17 09	17 19	17 54	18 08	18 49	19 05
8½	Lidlington	d	05 38	05 56	06 47	06 56	07 53	08 45	08 56	10 23	11 23	12 23	13 23	14 23	15 23	16 13	16 23	17 13	17 23	17 58	18 12	18 53	19 09
10	Millbrook (Bedfordshire)	d	05 41	05 59	06 50	06 59	07 56	08 48	08 59	10 26	11 26	12 26	13 26	14 26	15 26	16 16	16 26	17 16	17 26	18 01	18 15	18 56	19 12
11¼	Stewartby	d	05 44	06 02	06 54	07 02	07 59	08 52	09 02	10 29	11 29	12 29	13 29	14 29	15 29	16 19	16 29	17 19	17 29	18 04	18 18	18 59	19 15
13	Kempston Hardwick	d	05 48	06 06	06 57	07 06	08 03	08 55	09 06	10 33	11 33	12 33	13 33	14 33	15 33	16 23	16 33	17 23	17 33	18 08	18 22	19 03	19 19
16	Bedford St Johns	d	05 54	06 12	07 04	07 12	08 09	09 02	09 12	10 39	11 39	12 39	13 39	14 39	15 39	16 29	16 39	17 29	17 39	18 14	18 28	19 09	19 25
16¾	**Bedford** 7	a	06 00	06 18	07 08	07 18	08 15	09 06	09 18	10 45	11 45	12 45	13 45	14 45	15 45	16 35	16 45	17 35	17 45	18 20	18 34	19 15	19 31

		LM SX	LM SO	LM
Bletchley	d	20 01	20 04	21 01
Fenny Stratford	d	20 04	20 07	21 04
Bow Brickhill	d	20 08	20 11	21 08
Woburn Sands	d	20 12	20 15	21 12
Aspley Guise	d	20 15	20 18	21 15
Ridgmont	d	20 19	20 22	21 19
Lidlington	d	20 23	20 26	21 23
Millbrook (Bedfordshire)	d	20 26	20 29	21 26
Stewartby	d	20 29	20 32	21 29
Kempston Hardwick	d	20 33	20 36	21 33
Bedford St Johns	d	20 39	20 42	21 39
Bedford 7	a	20 45	20 48	21 45

No Sunday Service

For connections from Milton Keynes Central refer to Table T66

Table T064-R

Mondays to Saturdays

21 May to 8 December

Bedford - Bletchley

Miles			LM SX	LM SO	LM	LM	LM	LM	LM	LM	LM	LM	LM	LM SX	LM SO	LM SX	LM SO	LM SX	LM SO	LM SX	LM SO	LM	LM
0	**Bedford** 7	d	06 10	06 29	07 29	08 29	09 29	10 55	11 55	12 55	13 55	14 55	15 55	16 40	17 00	17 40	17 55	18 26	18 39	19 29	19 36	21 00	22 00
0¾	Bedford St Johns	d	06 13	06 32	07 32	08 32	09 32	10 58	11 58	12 58	13 58	14 58	15 58	16 43	17 03	17 43	17 58	18 29	18 42	19 32	19 39	21 03	22 03
3¾	Kempston Hardwick	d	06 20	06 39	07 39	08 39	09 39	11 05	12 05	13 05	14 05	15 05	16 05	16 50	17 10	17 50	18 05	18 36	18 49	19 39	19 46	21 10	22 10
5½	Stewartby	d	06 24	06 43	07 43	08 43	09 43	11 08	12 08	13 08	14 08	15 08	16 08	16 54	17 13	17 54	18 08	18 39	18 52	19 43	19 49	21 13	22 14
6¾	Millbrook (Bedfordshire)	d	06 27	06 46	07 46	08 46	09 46	11 12	12 12	13 12	14 12	15 12	16 12	16 57	17 17	17 57	18 12	18 43	18 56	19 46	19 53	21 17	22 17
8¼	Lidlington	d	06 31	06 50	07 50	08 50	09 50	11 15	12 15	13 15	14 15	15 15	16 15	17 01	17 20	18 01	18 15	18 46	18 59	19 50	19 56	21 20	22 21
10	Ridgmont	d	06 35	06 54	07 54	08 54	09 54	11 20	12 20	13 20	14 20	15 20	16 20	17 05	17 25	18 05	18 20	18 51	19 04	19 54	20 01	21 25	22 25
11¾	Aspley Guise	d	06 39	06 58	07 58	08 58	09 58	11 23	12 23	13 23	14 23	15 23	16 23	17 09	17 28	18 09	18 23	18 54	19 07	19 58	20 04	21 28	22 29
12¾	Woburn Sands	d	06 42	07 01	08 01	09 01	10 01	11 26	12 26	13 26	14 26	15 26	16 26	17 12	17 31	18 12	18 26	18 57	19 10	20 01	20 07	21 31	22 32
14¾	Bow Brickhill	d	06 47	07 06	08 06	09 06	10 06	11 30	12 30	13 30	14 30	15 30	16 30	17 16	17 35	18 16	18 30	19 01	19 14	20 06	20 11	21 35	22 37
15¾	Fenny Stratford	d	06 50	07 09	08 09	09 09	10 09	11 33	12 33	13 33	14 33	15 33	16 33	17 19	17 38	18 19	18 33	19 04	19 17	20 09	20 14	21 38	22 40
16¾	**Bletchley**	a	06 53	07 12	08 12	09 12	10 12	11 38	12 38	13 38	14 38	15 38	16 38	17 22	17 43	18 22	18 38	19 09	19 22	20 12	20 19	21 43	22 43

No Sunday Service

For connections to Milton Keynes Central refer to Table T66

Table T065-F

Mondays to Fridays

21 May to 22 June

London & West Midlands to North West England. London, West Midlands & Manchester to Scotland via the West Coast

Miles	Miles	Miles	Miles	Miles		AW MO	NT MX	CS MX	AW MX	CS WThFO	CS TO	CS MX	CS MX	NT		NT	TP	VT	NT	VT	XC	LM	TP	VT
						◇ A	◇ B	C	◇ D	C	C	C	C				◇1	◇1		◇1	◇1	1	◇1	◇1
0	—	—	—	—	**London Euston** 15 ⊖66 d																			
17½	—	—	—	—	Watford Junction 66 d			00u10																
49¾	—	—	—	—	Milton Keynes Central 66 d																			
82½	0	—	—	—	Rugby 66 d																			
97	—	—	—	—	Nuneaton d																			
110	—	—	—	—	Tamworth Low Level d																			
116¼	—	0	—	—	Lichfield Trent Valley d																			
—	11½	—	—	—	Coventry 68 d																			
—	22	—	—	—	Birmingham International 68 ✈ d																			
—	30½	—	—	—	**BirminghamNewSt** 12 68 d															05 30	05 57	06 01		06 15
—	43¾	—	—	—	**Wolverhampton** 7 d															05 48	06 15	06 21		06 37
—	53¾	—	—	—	Penkridge d																	06 31		
133½	59½	—	—	—	**Stafford** d															06 01	06 28	06 37		
—	75¾	30¼	—	—	**Stoke-on-Trent** 84 a																06 44			
—	95¼	50¼	—	—	Macclesfield a																07 05			
158	—	—	0	—	**Crewe** 10 81,91 a															06 20		06 57		07 08
—	—	—	—	—	d	00 01			00 15									05 57		06 23		06 59		07 09
—	—	—	—	—	**Chester** 81 a	00 22			00 37											06 43				
—	—	—	—	—	Wrexham General 75 a																			
—	—	—	—	—	Llandudno Junction 81 a	01 27			01 28											07 32				
—	—	—	—	—	Bangor (Gwynedd) 81 a	01 44			01 46											07 49				
—	—	—	—	—	**Holyhead** 81 a	02 20			02 15											08 20				
—	—	—	—	—	Wilmslow 84 a																			
—	107¼	62¼	—	—	Stockport 84 a																07 19			
—	113	68	—	—	**Manchester Piccadilly** 10 a																07 28			
—	—	—	22½	—	Runcorn 91 a																	07 24		
—	—	—	30	—	Liverpool South Pkwy 7 91 ✈ a																	07 33		
—	—	—	35½	—	**Liverpool Lime Street** 10 91 a																	07 46		
—	—	—	—	—	d																			
—	—	—	—	—	Manchester Airport 82 ✈ d																		06 10	
—	—	—	—	—	**Manchester Picc.** 10 82 d		00 09										05 00		05 00				06 26	
—	—	79¾	—	—	Bolton 82 d														05 25					
182	—	—	—	—	Warrington Bank Quay d													06 15						07 27
193¾	—	—	—	—	Wigan North Western 90 d													06 25						07 38
209	—	99¾	—	—	**Preston** 8 90 a		00 59										05 35	06 38	06 41				07 01	07 51
—	—	117½	—	—	**Blackpool North** 97 a		01 29																	
—	—	—	—	—	**Preston** 8 90 d					00u58	00u58	00u58	00u58	05 16			05 40	06 40					07 03	07 53
230	—	—	—	—	**Lancaster** 6 d									05 36		05 40	05 56	06 54					07 18	08 08
—	—	—	—	—	Barrow-in-Furness 82 a																			
249	—	—	—	—	Oxenholme Lake District 83 d											06 19	06 10	07 10					07 32	08 22
—	—	—	—	—	**Windermere** 83 a											06 39								
281¼	—	—	—	—	Penrith North Lakes d												06 35	07 34						
299	—	—	—	—	**Carlisle** 8 216 a			05s13						09 24			06 51	07 49					08 10	09 00
—	—	—	—	—	d												06 52	07 52					08 12	09 01
324¼	—	—	0	—	Lockerbie 225,226 d												07 11	08 10					08 30	
372½	—	—	—	0	Carstairs 226,225 a			06s22									07 44							
388½	—	—	—	—	Motherwell 226 a			06s55									07 59							
401¼	—	—	—	—	**Glasgow Central** 15 216,226,225 a			07 22									08 20	09 16						
—	—	—	75	26¼	Haymarket a																		09s31	10 12
—	—	—	76¼	27½	**Edinburgh** 10 a																		09 38	10 18
—	—	—	—	—	**Fort William** 227,400 a								09 57											
—	—	—	—	97¼	Perth 229 a							05s41												
—	—	—	135½	—	Dundee 229 a					06s07	06s08													
—	—	—	206¾	—	**Aberdeen** 229 a					07 39	07 39													
—	—	—	—	215¼	**Inverness** 229 a							08 41												

A From Birmingham International
B From Manchester Airport
C From London Euston
D From Birmingham New Street

Refer to Operator websites for full information about Sleeper Services. Contact details for train operators available at National Rail Enquiries

London & West Midlands to North West England. London, West Midlands & Manchester to Scotland via the West Coast

		XC	VT	TP	VT	LM	LM	XC	VT	LM	VT	LM	VT	XC	LM	LM	XC	TP	NT	LM	VT	VT
		◇■	◇■	◇■	◇■	■	■	◇■	◇■	■	◇■	■	◇■	◇■	■	■	◇■	◇■	◇	■	◇■	◇■
							A								B	A	C			D	E	F
		⊥	⊠	⊥	⊠			⊥	⊠		⊠		⊠	⊥			⊥	⊥			⊠	⊠⊥
London Euston ⊖66	d		05 27		05 31				06 16			06 24	06 36								06 43	06 46
Watford Junction 66	d		05u45		05u50							06 41	06u51									
Milton Keynes Central 66	d		06 15		06 23				06 46			07 24									07 13	
Rugby 66	d				06 45		06 06					08 04				06 59						07 40
Nuneaton	d		06 45				06 20					08 16				07 12						
Tamworth Low Level	d						06 35					08 29				07 29						
Lichfield Trent Valley	d						06 41					08 35				07 35						
Coventry 68	d																07 27				07 42	
Birmingham International 68 ✈	d					06 18											07 38				07 53	
Birmingham New St 68	d	06 30				06 36		06 51		07 01	07 15			07 31	07 36		07 57			08 01	08 15	
Wolverhampton	d	06 48				06 54		07 10		07 20	07 37			07 49	07 54		08 15			→	→	
Penkridge	d					07 04				07 29					08 04							
Stafford	d	07 02	07 08			07 10	06 59	07 22		07 36		08 55		08 03	08 10	07 55	08 28					
Stoke-on-Trent 84	a	07 19					07 15		07 45			09 12		08 18		08 11	08 43					
Macclesfield	a	07 37							08 01					08 36			09 01					
Crewe 81,91	a		07 27		07 30	07 32	07 38	07 42		07 56	08 08	09 34	08 10		08 30	08 34						
	d		07 28		07 32	07 33		07 44		07 59	08 09		08 11		08 32							
Chester 81	a																					
Wrexham General 75	a																					
Llandudno Junction 81	a																					
Bangor (Gwynedd) 81	a																					
Holyhead 81	a																					
Wilmslow 84	a							08 00					08 27									
Stockport 84	a	07 49						08 13	08 17				08 35	08 49			09 13					
Manchester Piccadilly	a	07 59						08 24	08 27				08 46	08 59			09 25					
Runcorn 91	a		07 45			07 59				08 24					08 52							
Liverpool South Pkwy 91 ✈	a					08 09				08 32					09 01							
Liverpool Lime Street 91	a		08 03			08 21				08 44					09 11							
	d																					
Manchester Airport 82 ✈	d			07 10														08 10				
Manchester Picc. 82	d			07 26														08 26				
Bolton 82	d																					
Warrington Bank Quay	d				07 49						08 27											08 45
Wigan North Western 90	d				08 00						08 38											08 59
Preston 90	a			08 02	08 13						08 51							09 02				09 14
Blackpool North 97	a																					09 37
Preston 90	d			08 03	08 15						08 53							09 04	09 29			
Lancaster	d			08 19	08 29						09 08							09 19	09 59			
Barrow-in-Furness 82	a																					
Oxenholme Lake District 83	d				08 42													09 33	10 19			
Windermere 83	a																		10 41			
Penrith North Lakes	d			08 54							09 44											
Carlisle 216	a			09 10	09 20						09 59							10 10				
	d			09 11	09 21						10 02							10 12				
Lockerbie 225,226	d			09 30														10 30				
Carstairs 226,225	a																					
Motherwell 226	a			10 14																		
Glasgow Central 216,226,225	a			10 33	10 38						11 15											
Haymarket	a																	11s28				
Edinburgh	a																	11 35				
Fort William 227,400	a																					
Perth 229	a																					
Dundee 229	a																					
Aberdeen 229	a																					
Inverness 229	a																					

A From Northampton
B From Walsall
C From Southampton Central
D From Walsall to Liverpool Lime Street
E To Edinburgh
F ⊥ from Preston ⊠ to Preston

Refer to Operator websites for full information about Sleeper Services. Contact details for train operators available at National Rail Enquiries

Table T065-F

Mondays to Fridays

21 May to 22 June

London & West Midlands to North West England. London, West Midlands & Manchester to Scotland via the West Coast

		VT	VT	VT	LM	VT	VT	NT	VT	NT	VT	XC	LM	XC	TP	LM	VT	LM	VT	VT	VT	LM	VT
		◇■	◇■	◇■	■	◇■	◇■	◇	◇■	◇	◇■	◇■	■	◇■	◇■	■	◇■	■	◇■	◇■	◇■	■	◇■
					A			B	C	D		E		F		G	H					I	
		⊠	⊠	⊠		⊠	⊠		⊠		⊠	⊥		⊥	⊥		⊠		⊠	⊠	⊠		⊠
London Euston ⊖66	d	06 55	07 07	07 10		07 20	07 30				07 35						07 43	07 46	08 00	08 07	08 10		08 20
Watford Junction 66	d																						
Milton Keynes Central 66	d	07 27		07 41		07 50					08 06						08 13	08 19		08 38	08 43		08 50
Rugby 66	d																	08 42					
Nuneaton	d																	08 54					
Tamworth Low Level	d																	09 09					
Lichfield Trent Valley	d																	09 17					
Coventry 68	d													08 27			08 42						
Birmingham International 68 ✈	d				←				←					08 38			08 53						
Birmingham New St 68	d				08 01				08 15			08 31	08 36	08 57		09 01	09 15						
Wolverhampton	d				08 20				08 37			08 49	08 54	09 15		09 20	09 37						
Penkridge	d				08 29								09 04										
Stafford	d		08 24		08 36							09 03	09 10	09 28		09 35		09 42		09 27			
Stoke-on-Trent 84	a	08 24				08 48						09 18		09 43				10 02	09 24				09 48
Macclesfield	a	08 41										09 36		10 01					09 41			←	
Crewe 81,91	a		08 41	08 47	08 56				09 07		09 10		09 30			09 55	10 08	10 24			09 51	09 55	
	d		08 43	08 49	08 57				09 09		09 11		09 32			09 57	10 09				09 53	09 57	
Chester 81	a			09 11												→	→				10 13		
Wrexham General 75	a																						
Llandudno Junction 81	a																				11 04		
Bangor (Gwynedd) 81	a																				11 24		
Holyhead 81	a																				11 55		
Wilmslow 84	a										09 27												
Stockport 84	a	08 54				09 16					09 36	09 49		10 13					09 54				10 16
Manchester Piccadilly	a	09 04				09 27					09 45	09 59		10 25					10 05				10 28
Runcorn 91	a		09 00		09 21								09 52							10 01		10 24	
Liverpool South Pkwy 91 ✈	a				09 30								10 01									10 32	
Liverpool Lime Street 91	a		09 20		09 42								10 11							10 19		10 44	
	d																						
Manchester Airport 82 ✈	d							08 41							09 10								
Manchester Picc. 82	d							09 01							09 26								
Bolton 82	d							09 22															
Warrington Bank Quay	d						09 14		09 27														
Wigan North Western 90	d						09 25		09 38														
Preston 90	a						09 38	09 49	09 51						10 02								
Blackpool North 97	a									←													
Preston 90	d						09 41	09 57	09 54	09 57					10 04								
Lancaster	d						09 55	→	10 08	10 14					10 20								
Barrow-in-Furness 82	a									11 15													
Oxenholme Lake District 83	d								10 22						10 33								
Windermere 83	a																						
Penrith North Lakes	d						10 31								10 58								
Carlisle 216	a						10 46		10 59						11 14								
	d						10 47		11 01						11 16								
Lockerbie 225,226	d														11 37								
Carstairs 226,225	a																						
Motherwell 226	a														12 22								
Glasgow Central 216,226,225	a						11 59								12 39								
Haymarket	a								12 16														
Edinburgh	a								12 22														
Fort William 227,400	a																						
Perth 229	a																						
Dundee 229	a																						
Aberdeen 229	a																						
Inverness 229	a																						

A From Walsall
B To Barrow-in-Furness
C From London Euston
D From Manchester Airport
E From Bristol Temple Meads
F From Southampton Central
G To Liverpool Lime Street
H To Glasgow Central
I From Birmingham New Street

Refer to Operator websites for full information about Sleeper Services. Contact details for train operators available at National Rail Enquiries

Table T065-F

Mondays to Fridays
21 May to 22 June

London & West Midlands to North West England. London, West Midlands & Manchester to Scotland via the West Coast

	VT	VT	VT	XC	LM	XC	TP	LM	VT	LM	VT MO	VT MX	VT	VT MO	VT MX	VT	LM	VT	VT	NT	VT
	◇1	◇1	◇1	◇1	1	◇1	◇1	1	◇1	1	◇1	◇1	◇1	◇1	◇1	◇1	1	◇1	◇1		◇1
		A		B		C		D	E		F	F					G				A
	⊠	⊠	⊠	⌶		⌶	⌶		⊠		⊠🛏	⊠🛏	⊠	⊠	⊠	⊠		⊠	⊠		⊠
London Euston [15] ⊖66 d	08 30		08 40						08 43	08 46	08 53	08 53	09 00	09 07	09 07	09 10		09 20	09 30		
Watford Junction 66 d																					
Milton Keynes Central 66 d									09 13	09 19						09 41		09 50			
Rugby 66 d										09 42	09 46	09 46									
Nuneaton d										09 54											
Tamworth Low Level d										10 09											
Lichfield Trent Valley d										10 17											
Coventry 68 d						09 27			09 42												
Birmingham International 68 ✈ d						09 38			09 53												
BirminghamNewSt [12] 68 d				09 31	09 36	09 57		10 01	10 15												
Wolverhampton [7] d				09 49	09 54	10 15		10 20	10 37												
Penkridge d					10 04																
Stafford d				10 02	10 10	10 28		10 35		10 42				10 24	10 24						
Stoke-on-Trent 84 a				10 17		10 43				11 02			10 24					10 48			
Macclesfield a		←		10 36		11 01							10 41				←				←
Crewe [10] 81,91 a		10 08	10 11		10 31			10 56	11 08	11 24				10 41	10 41	10 47	10 56				11 08
d		10 09	10 12		10 33			10 57	11 09					10 43	10 43	10 49	10 57				11 09
Chester 81 a								→	→							11 13					
Wrexham General 75 a																					
Llandudno Junction 81 a																12 00					
Bangor (Gwynedd) 81 a																12 17					
Holyhead 81 ⛴ a																12 50					
Wilmslow 84 a			10 27																		
Stockport 84 a			10 36	10 49		11 13							10 54					11 16			
Manchester Piccadilly [10] a			10 46	11 00		11 24							11 05					11 28			
Runcorn 91 a					10 51									11 01	11 03		11 21				
Liverpool South Pkwy [7] 91 ✈ a					11 00												11 30				
Liverpool Lime Street [10] 91 a					11 10									11 19	11 21		11 42				
d																					
Manchester Airport 82 ✈ d							10 10														
Manchester Picc. [10] 82 d							10 26														
Bolton 82 d																					
Warrington Bank Quay d	10 14	10 27									10 56	11 00							11 14		11 27
Wigan North Western 90 d	10 25	10 38									11 12	11 12							11 25		11 38
Preston [8] 90 a	10 38	10 51					11 02				11 25	11 25							11 38		11 51
Blackpool North 97 a											11 56	11 56									
Preston [8] 90 d	10 41	10 53					11 03												11 41		11 53
Lancaster [6] d	10 55	11 08																	11 55	12 02	12 08
Barrow-in-Furness 82 a																				13 11	
Oxenholme Lake District 83 d	11 08																				12 21
Windermere 83 a																					
Penrith North Lakes d		11 45																	12 30		
Carlisle [8] 216 a	11 46	12 00					12 05												12 46	15 46	12 59
d	11 47	12 02					12 06												12 47		13 01
Lockerbie 225,226 d																					
Carstairs 226,225 a																					
Motherwell 226 a																					
Glasgow Central [15] 216,226,225 a	12 59	13 15																	13 59		
Haymarket a							13s19														14 12
Edinburgh [10] a							13 26														14 19
Fort William 227,400 a																					
Perth 229 a																					
Dundee 229 a																					
Aberdeen 229 a																					
Inverness 229 a																					

A From London Euston
B From Cardiff Central
C From Bournemouth
D To Liverpool Lime Street
E To Edinburgh
F 🛏 from Preston ⊠ to Preston
G From Birmingham New Street

Refer to Operator websites for full information about Sleeper Services. Contact details for train operators available at National Rail Enquiries

Table T065-F

Mondays to Fridays
21 May to 22 June

London & West Midlands to North West England. London, West Midlands & Manchester to Scotland via the West Coast

	VT	XC	LM	XC	TP	NT	LM	VT	LM	VT	VT	VT	LM	VT	VT	NT	VT	NT	VT	VT	XC	LM
	◇1	◇1	1	◇1	◇1	◇	1	◇1	1	◇1	◇1	◇1	1	◇1	◇1	◇	◇1	◇	◇1	◇1	◇1	1
		A		B			C	D					E			F	G	H	I		J	
	⊠	⌶		⌶	⌶			⊠		⊠	⊠	⊠		⊠	⊠		⊠		⊠🛏	⊠	⌶	
London Euston [15] ⊖66 d	09 40							09 43	09 46	10 00	10 07	10 10		10 20	10 30				10 36	10 40		
Watford Junction 66 d																						
Milton Keynes Central 66 d								10 13	10 19			10 41		10 50								
Rugby 66 d									10 42										11 25			
Nuneaton d									10 54													
Tamworth Low Level d									11 09													
Lichfield Trent Valley d									11 17													
Coventry 68 d				10 27				10 42														
Birmingham International 68 ✈ d				10 38				10 53														
BirminghamNewSt [12] 68 d		10 31	10 36	10 57			11 01	11 15													11 31	11 36
Wolverhampton [7] d		10 49	10 54	11 15			11 20	11 37													11 49	11 54
Penkridge d			11 04																			12 04
Stafford d		11 03	11 10	11 28			11 35		11 42		11 24										12 03	12 10
Stoke-on-Trent 84 a		11 18		11 43					12 02	11 24				11 48							12 18	
Macclesfield a		11 36		12 01						11 41			←				←				12 36	
Crewe [10] 81,91 a	11 11		11 31				11 55	12 07	12 24		11 41	11 47	11 55				12 07			12 11		12 31
d	11 12		11 33				11 57	12 09			11 43	11 49	11 57				12 09			12 12		12 33
Chester 81 a							→	→				12 11										
Wrexham General 75 a																						
Llandudno Junction 81 a																						
Bangor (Gwynedd) 81 a																						
Holyhead 81 ⛴ a																						
Wilmslow 84 a	11 27																			12 27		
Stockport 84 a	11 35	11 49		12 13						11 54				12 16						12 35	12 49	
Manchester Piccadilly [10] a	11 46	11 59		12 25						12 05				12 28						12 46	12 59	
Runcorn 91 a			11 51								12 00		12 25									12 51
Liverpool South Pkwy [7] 91 ✈ a			12 00										12 33									13 00
Liverpool Lime Street [10] 91 a			12 10								12 19		12 44									13 10
d																						
Manchester Airport 82 ✈ d					10 59											11 41						
Manchester Picc. [10] 82 d					11 22											12 01						
Bolton 82 d																12 22						
Warrington Bank Quay d															12 14		12 27		12 34			
Wigan North Western 90 d															12 25		12 38		12 45			
Preston [8] 90 a					11 59										12 38	12 48	12 51		12 57			
Blackpool North 97 a																		←	13 20			
Preston [8] 90 d					12 04	12 17									12 41	12 57	12 53	12 57				
Lancaster [6] d					12 20	12 37										→	13 08	13 14				
Barrow-in-Furness 82 a																		14 14				
Oxenholme Lake District 83 d					12 33	13 02											13 22					
Windermere 83 a						13 24																
Penrith North Lakes d					12 58										13 28							
Carlisle [8] 216 a					13 14										13 44		13 59					
d					13 16										13 45		14 00					
Lockerbie 225,226 d																						
Carstairs 226,225 a																						
Motherwell 226 a					14 21												14 58					
Glasgow Central [15] 216,226,225 a					14 40										14 59		15 15					
Haymarket a																						
Edinburgh [10] a																						
Fort William 227,400 a																						
Perth 229 a																						
Dundee 229 a																						
Aberdeen 229 a																						
Inverness 229 a																						

A From Paignton
B From Bournemouth
C To Liverpool Lime Street
D To Glasgow Central
E From Birmingham New Street
F To Barrow-in-Furness
G From London Euston
H From Manchester Airport
I 🛏 from Preston ⊠ to Preston
J From Bristol Temple Meads

Refer to Operator websites for full information about Sleeper Services. Contact details for train operators available at National Rail Enquiries

Table T065-F

Mondays to Fridays
21 May to 22 June

London & West Midlands to North West England. London, West Midlands & Manchester to Scotland via the West Coast

	XC	TP	LM	VT	LM	VT	VT	VT	LM	VT	VT	VT	VT	XC	LM	XC	TP	NT	LM	VT	LM	VT
	■ 1	◇1	1	◇1	1	◇1	◇1	◇1	1	◇1	■ 1	◇1	◇1	◇1	1	◇1	◇1	◇	1	◇1	1	◇1
	A		B	C					D			E		F		A			B	G		
	🛒	🛒		☕		⊠	⊠	⊠		⊠	⊠	☕	⊠	🛒		🛒	🛒			⊠		⊠
London Euston ⊖66 d				10 43	10 46	11 00	11 07	11 10		11 20	11 30		11 40							11 43	11 46	12 00
Watford Junction 66 d																						
Milton Keynes Central 66 d				11 13	11 19			11 41		11 50										12 13	12 19	
Rugby 66 d					11 42																12 42	
Nuneaton d					11 54																12 54	
Tamworth Low Level d					12 09																13 09	
Lichfield Trent Valley d					12 17																13 17	
Coventry 68 d	11 27			11 42												12 27				12 42		
Birmingham International 68 ✈ d	11 38			11 53												12 38				12 53		
BirminghamNewSt 68 d	11 57		12 01	12 15										12 31	12 36	12 57			13 01	13 15		
Wolverhampton d	12 15		12 20	12 37										12 49	12 54	13 15			13 20	13 37		
Penkridge d															13 04							
Stafford d	12 28		12 35		12 42		12 24							13 03	13 10	13 28			13 35		13 42	
Stoke-on-Trent 84 a	12 43				13 02	12 24				12 48				13 18		13 43					14 02	13 24
Macclesfield a	13 01					12 41			←			←		13 36		14 01						13 41
Crewe 81,91 a			12 55	13 08	13 24		12 41	12 47	12 55			13 08	13 11		13 31				13 56	14 07	14 24	
d			12 57	13 09			12 43	12 49	12 57			13 09	13 12		13 33				13 57	14 09		
Chester 81 a			→	→				13 11											→	→		
Wrexham General 75 a																						
Llandudno Junction 81 a																						
Bangor (Gwynedd) 81 a																						
Holyhead 81 ⛴ a																						
Wilmslow 84 a													13 27									
Stockport 84 a	13 12					12 55				13 16			13 35	13 49		14 13						13 54
Manchester Piccadilly a	13 25					13 05				13 28			13 46	13 59		14 25						14 05
Runcorn 91 a							13 00		13 21						13 51							
Liverpool South Pkwy 91 ✈ a									13 30						14 00							
Liverpool Lime Street 91 a							13 19		13 42						14 10							
d																						
Manchester Airport 82 ✈ d		12 10															13 10					
Manchester Picc. 82 d		12 26															13 26					
Bolton 82 d																						
Warrington Bank Quay d											13 14	13 27										
Wigan North Western 90 d											13 25	13 38										
Preston 90 a		13 02									13 38	13 51					14 02					
Blackpool North 97 a																						
Preston 90 d		13 03									13 41	13 53					14 04	14 10				
Lancaster d		13 19									13 55	14 08					14 19	14 30				
Barrow-in-Furness 82 a																						
Oxenholme Lake District 83 d		13 32									14 08						14 33	14 51				
Windermere 83 a																		15 09				
Penrith North Lakes d												14 43					14 58					
Carlisle 216 a		14 11									14 46	14 59					15 13					
d		14 12									14 47	15 01					15 14					
Lockerbie 225,226 d		14 31															15 37					
Carstairs 226,225 a																						
Motherwell 226 a																	16 21					
Glasgow Central 216,226,225 a											15 59						16 41					
Haymarket a		15s29										16 13										
Edinburgh a		15 34										16 20										
Fort William 227,400 a																						
Perth 229 a																						
Dundee 229 a																						
Aberdeen 229 a																						
Inverness 229 a																						

A From Bournemouth
B To Liverpool Lime Street
C To Edinburgh
D From Birmingham New Street
E From London Euston
F From Bristol Temple Meads
G To Glasgow Central

Refer to Operator websites for full information about Sleeper Services. Contact details for train operators available at National Rail Enquiries

Table T065-F

Mondays to Fridays
21 May to 22 June

London & West Midlands to North West England. London, West Midlands & Manchester to Scotland via the West Coast

	VT	VT	LM	VT	VT	VT	VT	XC	LM	XC	TP	LM	VT	LM	VT	VT	VT	LM	VT	VT	VT
	◇1	◇1	1	◇1	◇1	◇1	◇1	◇1	1	◇1	◇1	1	◇1	1	◇1	◇1	◇1	1	◇1	◇1	◇1
			A			B		C		D		E	F					A			B
	⊠	⊠		⊠	⊠	⊠	⊠	🛒		🛒	🛒		⊠		☕	☕	☕		☕	☕	⊠
London Euston ⊖66 d	12 07	12 10		12 20	12 30		12 40						12 43	12 46	13 00	13 07	13 10		13 20	13 30	
Watford Junction 66 d																					
Milton Keynes Central 66 d		12 41		12 50									13 13	13 19			13 41		13 50		
Rugby 66 d		13 04												13 42							
Nuneaton d														13 54							
Tamworth Low Level d														14 09							
Lichfield Trent Valley d														14 17							
Coventry 68 d										13 27			13 42								
Birmingham International 68 ✈ d										13 38			13 53								
BirminghamNewSt 68 d								13 31	13 36	13 57		14 01	14 15								
Wolverhampton d								13 49	13 54	14 15		14 20	14 37								
Penkridge d									14 04												
Stafford d	13 24							14 03	14 10	14 28		14 35		14 42		14 24					
Stoke-on-Trent 84 a				13 48				14 18		14 43				15 02	14 24				14 48		
Macclesfield a			←			←		14 36		15 01					14 41			←			←
Crewe 81,91 a	13 41	13 50	13 56			14 07	14 11		14 31			14 54	15 07	15 24		14 41	14 47	14 54			15 07
d	13 43	13 52	13 57			14 09	14 12		14 33			14 57	15 09			14 43	14 49	14 57			15 09
Chester 81 a		14 13										→	→				15 10				
Wrexham General 75 a																					
Llandudno Junction 81 a																					
Bangor (Gwynedd) 81 a																					
Holyhead 81 ⛴ a																					
Wilmslow 84 a							14 27														
Stockport 84 a				14 16			14 35	14 49		15 13					14 54				15 16		
Manchester Piccadilly a				14 28			14 46	14 59		15 25					15 05				15 28		
Runcorn 91 a	14 00		14 21						14 53							15 00		15 22			
Liverpool South Pkwy 91 ✈ a			14 30						15 02									15 31			
Liverpool Lime Street 91 a	14 19		14 42						15 12							15 19		15 42			
d																					
Manchester Airport 82 ✈ d											14 10										
Manchester Picc. 82 d											14 26										
Bolton 82 d																					
Warrington Bank Quay d					14 14	14 27														15 14	15 27
Wigan North Western 90 d					14 25	14 38														15 25	15 38
Preston 90 a					14 38	14 51					15 03									15 38	15 51
Blackpool North 97 a																					
Preston 90 d					14 41	14 53					15 04									15 41	15 53
Lancaster d					14 55	15 08					15 20										16 08
Barrow-in-Furness 82 a																					
Oxenholme Lake District 83 d						15 22														16 06	
Windermere 83 a																					
Penrith North Lakes d					15 30						15 55									16 31	16 45
Carlisle 216 a					15 45	16 00					16 11									16 46	17 00
d					15 46	16 02					16 12									16 48	17 01
Lockerbie 225,226 d											16 31										
Carstairs 226,225 a																					
Motherwell 226 a																					
Glasgow Central 216,226,225 a					16 59	17 15														17 59	
Haymarket a											17s31										18 14
Edinburgh a											17 36										18 22
Fort William 227,400 a																					
Perth 229 a																					
Dundee 229 a																					
Aberdeen 229 a																					
Inverness 229 a																					

A From Birmingham New Street
B From London Euston
C From Paignton
D From Bournemouth
E To Liverpool Lime Street
F To Edinburgh

Refer to Operator websites for full information about Sleeper Services. Contact details for train operators available at National Rail Enquiries

Table T065-F

Mondays to Fridays

21 May to 22 June

London & West Midlands to North West England. London, West Midlands & Manchester to Scotland via the West Coast

	NT	VT	XC	LM	XC	TP	LM	VT	LM	VT	VT	VT	LM	VT	VT	NT	VT	VT	XC	LM	XC	TP
			A		B		C	D					E				F		G		B	
London Euston ⊖66 d		13 40						13 43	13 46	14 00	14 07	14 10		14 20	14 30			14 40				
Watford Junction 66 d																						
Milton Keynes Central 66 d								14 13	14 19			14 41		14 50								
Rugby 66 d									14 42													
Nuneaton d									14 54													
Tamworth Low Level d									15 09													
Lichfield Trent Valley d									15 17													
Coventry 68 d					14 27			14 42													15 27	
Birmingham International 68 d					14 38			14 53													15 38	
BirminghamNewSt 68 d			14 31	14 36	14 57		15 01	15 15											15 31	15 36	15 57	
Wolverhampton d			14 49	14 54	15 15		15 20	15 37											15 49	15 54	16 15	
Penkridge d				15 04																16 04		
Stafford d			15 03	15 10	15 28		15 35		15 42		15 24								16 03	16 10	16 28	
Stoke-on-Trent 84 a			15 18		15 43				16 02	15 24				15 48					16 18		16 43	
Macclesfield a			15 36		16 01					15 41			←				←		16 36		17 01	
Crewe 81,91 a		15 10		15 30			15 55	16 07	16 24		15 41	15 47	15 55				16 07	16 11		16 31		
d		15 11		15 33			15 57	16 09			15 43	15 49	15 57				16 09	16 12		16 33		
Chester 81 a							→	→				16 10										
Wrexham General 75 a																						
Llandudno Junction 81 a																						
Bangor (Gwynedd) 81 a																						
Holyhead 81 a																						
Wilmslow 84 a		15 27																16 27				
Stockport 84 a		15 35	15 49		16 13					15 54				16 16				16 35	16 49		17 13	
Manchester Piccadilly a		15 46	15 59		16 25					16 05				16 28				16 46	16 59		17 25	
Runcorn 91 a				15 51							16 00		16 24							16 51		
Liverpool South Pkwy 91 a				16 00									16 32							17 00		
Liverpool Lime Street 91 a				16 10							16 20		16 44							17 11		
d																						
Manchester Airport 82 d						15 10																16 10
Manchester Picc. 82 d						15 26																16 26
Bolton 82 d																						
Warrington Bank Quay d															16 14		16 27					
Wigan North Western 90 d															16 25		16 38					
Preston 90 a						16 02									16 38		16 51					17 02
Blackpool North 97 a																						
Preston 90 d						16 04									16 41		16 53					17 03
Lancaster d	16 13					16 19									16 55	17 01	17 08					17 19
Barrow-in-Furness 82 a	17 16															17 59						
Oxenholme Lake District 83 d						16 33									17 09		17 22					17 32
Windermere 83 a																						
Penrith North Lakes d						16 58									17 35		17 47					17 57
Carlisle 216 a	19 43					17 13									17 50	20 31	18 03					18 12
d						17 15									17 51		18 05					18 13
Lockerbie 225,226 d						17 33																18 32
Carstairs 226,225 a																						
Motherwell 226 a						18 21																
Glasgow Central 216,226,225 a						18 41									19 15		19 23					
Haymarket a																						19s34
Edinburgh a																						19 40
Fort William 227,400 a																						
Perth 229 a																						
Dundee 229 a																						
Aberdeen 229 a																						
Inverness 229 a																						

A From Bristol Temple Meads
B From Bournemouth
C From Walsall to Liverpool Lime Street
D To Glasgow Central
E From Walsall
F From London Euston
G From Penzance

Refer to Operator websites for full information about Sleeper Services. Contact details for train operators available at National Rail Enquiries

Table T065-F

Mondays to Fridays

21 May to 22 June

London & West Midlands to North West England. London, West Midlands & Manchester to Scotland via the West Coast

	LM	VT	LM	VT	VT	VT	LM	VT	VT	VT	VT	XC	LM	XC	TP	NT	LM	VT	LM	VT	VT
	A	B					C			D		E		F			A	G			
London Euston ⊖66 d		14 43	14 46	15 00	15 07	15 10		15 20	15 30		15 40							15 43	15 46	16 00	16 07
Watford Junction 66 d																					
Milton Keynes Central 66 d		15 13	15 19			15 41		15 50										16 13	16 19		
Rugby 66 d			15 42																16 42		
Nuneaton d			15 54																16 54		
Tamworth Low Level d			16 09																17 09		
Lichfield Trent Valley d			16 17																17 17		
Coventry 68 d		15 42												16 27				16 42			
Birmingham International 68 d		15 53												16 38				16 53			
BirminghamNewSt 68 d	16 01	16 15										16 31	16 36	16 57			17 01	17 15			
Wolverhampton d	16 20	16 37										16 49	16 54	17 15			17 20	17 37			
Penkridge d	16 29												17 04				17 29				
Stafford d	16 36		16 42		16 24							17 03	17 10	17 28			17 36		17 42		17 24
Stoke-on-Trent 84 a			17 02	16 24				16 48				17 18		17 43					18 02	17 24	
Macclesfield a				16 41			←	17 05		←		17 36		18 01						17 41	
Crewe 81,91 a	16 56	17 08	17 24		16 41	16 47	16 56			17 08	17 11		17 30				17 56	18 08	18 24		17 41
d	16 57	17 09			16 43	16 49	16 57			17 09	17 12		17 32				17 57	18 09			17 43
Chester 81 a	→	→				17 11											→	→			
Wrexham General 75 a																					
Llandudno Junction 81 a																					
Bangor (Gwynedd) 81 a																					
Holyhead 81 a																					
Wilmslow 84 a											17 27										
Stockport 84 a				16 54				17 17			17 36	17 49		18 13						17 54	
Manchester Piccadilly a				17 05				17 28			17 46	17 59		18 25						18 05	
Runcorn 91 a					17 00		17 24						17 52								18 00
Liverpool South Pkwy 91 a							17 33						18 01								
Liverpool Lime Street 91 a					17 20		17 44						18 11								18 19
d																					
Manchester Airport 82 d															17 10						
Manchester Picc. 82 d															17 27						
Bolton 82 d																					
Warrington Bank Quay d									17 14	17 27											
Wigan North Western 90 d									17 25	17 38											
Preston 90 a									17 38	17 52					18 02						
Blackpool North 97 a																					
Preston 90 d									17 41	17 54					18 03	18 20					
Lancaster d									17 55	18 09					18 19	18 40					
Barrow-in-Furness 82 a																					
Oxenholme Lake District 83 d									18 08	18 24					18 33	19 00					
Windermere 83 a																19 22					
Penrith North Lakes d										18 48					18 58						
Carlisle 216 a									18 45	19 04					19 13						
d									18 47	19 04					19 15						
Lockerbie 225,226 d															19 35						
Carstairs 226,225 a																					
Motherwell 226 a															20 21						
Glasgow Central 216,226,225 a									19 59						20 42						
Haymarket a										20 14											
Edinburgh a										20 23											
Fort William 227,400 a																					
Perth 229 a																					
Dundee 229 a																					
Aberdeen 229 a																					
Inverness 229 a																					

A To Liverpool Lime Street
B To Edinburgh
C From Birmingham New Street
D From London Euston
E From Bristol Temple Meads
F From Bournemouth
G To Glasgow Central

Refer to Operator websites for full information about Sleeper Services. Contact details for train operators available at National Rail Enquiries

Table T065-F

Mondays to Fridays

21 May to 22 June

London & West Midlands to North West England. London, West Midlands & Manchester to Scotland via the West Coast

	VT	LM	VT	VT	NT	VT	NT	VT	VT	VT	XC	LM	XC	TP	LM	VT	LM	VT	VT	VT	VT	VT
	◇1	1	◇1	◇1	◇	1	◇	◇1	◇1	◇1	◇1	1	◇1	◇1	1	◇1	1	◇1	◇1	◇1	◇1	◇1
		A			B	C	D	E		C	F		G		H	I						
	⊐		⊐	⊠		⊐		⊐	⊐	⊐	⫪		⫪	⫪		⊐		⊠	⊠	⊠	⊠	⊠
London Euston 15 ⊖66 d	16 10		16 20	16 30				16 33	16 40							16 43	16 46	16 57	17 00	17 07	17 10	17 10
Watford Junction 66 d																						
Milton Keynes Central 66 d	16u41		16 50							←						17 13	17 19				17u41	17u41
Rugby 66 d								17 23		17 23							17 47					
Nuneaton d								→									18 00				18 12	18 12
Tamworth Low Level d																	18 15	18 00				
Lichfield Trent Valley d																	18 22	18 08				
Coventry 68 d													17 27			17 42						
Birmingham International 68 ✈ d													17 38			17 53						
BirminghamNewSt 12 68 ⛴ d											17 31	17 36	17 57		18 01	18 15						
Wolverhampton 7 ⛴ d											17 49	17 54	18 15		18 20	18 37						
Penkridge d												18 04			18 29							
Stafford d										17 58	18 03	18 10	18 28		18 36		18 42			18 24		
Stoke-on-Trent 84 a			17 48								18 18		18 43				19 02		18 24			
Macclesfield a		←				←					18 36		19 01						18 41			
Crewe 10 81,91 a	17 47	17 56				18 08			18 10	18 17		18 30			18 57	19 07	19 26			18 42	18 55	18 55
d	17 49	17 57				18 09			18 11	18 20		18 32			18 59	19 09				18 44	18 57	18 57
Chester 81 a	18 08														→	→					19 16	19 16
Wrexham General 75 a																						
Llandudno Junction 81 a	18 58																					20 11
Bangor (Gwynedd) 81 a	19 18																					20 28
Holyhead 81 ⛴ a																						21 00
Wilmslow 84 a									18 27													
Stockport 84 a			18 16						18 36		18 49		19 13						18 54			
Manchester Piccadilly 10 ⛴ a			18 27						18 48		18 59		19 24						19 05			
Runcorn 91 a		18 24										18 56								19 00		
Liverpool South Pkwy 7 91 ✈ a		18 32										19 05										
Liverpool Lime Street 10 91 a		18 44										19 17								19 20		
d																						
Manchester Airport 82 ✈⛴ d					17 42									18 10								
Manchester Picc. 10 82 ⛴ d					18 01									18 26								
Bolton 82 d					18 21																	
Warrington Bank Quay d				18 15		18 27				18 37								18 50				
Wigan North Western 90 d				18 26		18 38				18 48								19 01				
Preston 8 90 a				18 40	18 50	18 51				19 01				19 02				19 14				
Blackpool North 97 a							←			19 30												
Preston 8 90 d				18 43	18 58	18 53	18 58							19 04				19 15				
Lancaster 8 d				18 58	→	19 08	19 14							19 21				19 30				
Barrow-in-Furness 82 a							20 14															
Oxenholme Lake District 83 d						19 21								19 34				19 45				
Windermere 83 a																						
Penrith North Lakes d				19 32										19 59				20 10				
Carlisle 8 216 a				19 47		20 00								20 15				20 25				
d				19 48		20 01								20 16				20 25				
Lockerbie 225,226 d														20 35				20 44				
Carstairs 226,225 a																						
Motherwell 226 a																		21 27				
Glasgow Central 15 216,226,225 a				20 59		21 15												21 44				
Haymarket ⛴ a														21s32								
Edinburgh 10 ⛴ a														21 39								
Fort William 227,400 a																						
Perth 229 a																						
Dundee 229 a																						
Aberdeen 229 a																						
Inverness 229 a																						

A From Birmingham New Street
B To Barrow-in-Furness
C From London Euston
D From Manchester Airport
E To Blackpool North
F From Paignton
G From Bournemouth
H To Liverpool Lime Street
I To Edinburgh

Refer to Operator websites for full information about Sleeper Services. Contact details for train operators available at National Rail Enquiries

Table T065-F

Mondays to Fridays

21 May to 22 June

London & West Midlands to North West England. London, West Midlands & Manchester to Scotland via the West Coast

	LM	VT	VT	VT	TP	VT	VT	VT	XC	LM	XC	LM	VT	LM	VT	VT	VT	VT	VT	VT	VT
	1	◇1	◇1	◇1	◇1	◇1	◇1	◇1	◇1	1	◇1	1	◇1	1	◇1	◇1	◇1	◇1	◇1	◇1	◇1
	A			B		C		B	D		E		F								B
		⊠	⊠	⊐	⫪	⊠	⊠	⊠	⫪		⫪		⊐		⊠	⊠	⊠	⊠	⊠	⊠	⊐
London Euston 15 ⊖66 d		17 20	17 30			17 33	17 40						17 43	17 46	17 57	18 00	18 07	18 10	18 20	18 30	
Watford Junction 66 d																					
Milton Keynes Central 66 d		17u50						←					18u13	18 19				18u41	18u50		
Rugby 66 d						18 23		18 23						18 47							
Nuneaton d						→								19 00				19 13			
Tamworth Low Level d														19 15	19 00						
Lichfield Trent Valley d														19 22	19 08						
Coventry 68 d											18 27		18 42								
Birmingham International 68 ✈ d											18 38		18 53								
BirminghamNewSt 12 68 ⛴ d									18 31	18 36	18 57	19 01	19 15								
Wolverhampton 7 ⛴ d									18 49	18 54	19 15	19 20	19 37								
Penkridge d										19 04		19 29									
Stafford d								18 56	19 03	19 10	19 28	19 45		19 42			19 24				
Stoke-on-Trent 84 a		18 48							19 18		19 43	20 06		20 02		19 24			19 48		
Macclesfield a	←			←					19 36		20 01					19 41					←
Crewe 10 81,91 a	18 57			19 07			19 11	19 14		19 31		20 32	20 07	20 25			19 41	19 53			20 07
d	18 59			19 09			19 12	19 16		19 33			20 09				19 43	19 56			20 09
Chester 81 a													→					20 15			
Wrexham General 75 a																		20 38			
Llandudno Junction 81 a																		21 09			
Bangor (Gwynedd) 81 a																		21 25			
Holyhead 81 ⛴ a																		21 56			
Wilmslow 84 a							19 27														
Stockport 84 a		19 16					19 36		19 49		20 13					19 54			20 16		
Manchester Piccadilly 10 ⛴ a		19 28					19 45		19 59		20 25					20 05			20 28		
Runcorn 91 a	19 21							19 33		19 56							20 00				
Liverpool South Pkwy 7 91 ✈ a	19 30									20 05											
Liverpool Lime Street 10 91 a	19 42							19 52		20 17							20 20				
d																					
Manchester Airport 82 ✈⛴ d					19 10																
Manchester Picc. 10 82 ⛴ d					19 26																
Bolton 82 d																					
Warrington Bank Quay d			19 14	19 27											19 50					20 14	20 27
Wigan North Western 90 d			19 25	19 38											20 01					20 25	20 38
Preston 8 90 a			19 38	19 51	20 02										20 14					20 38	20 51
Blackpool North 97 a																					
Preston 8 90 d			19 41	19 53	20 04										20 15					20 41	20 53
Lancaster 8 d			19 55	20 08	20 20										20a30					20 55	21 08
Barrow-in-Furness 82 a																					
Oxenholme Lake District 83 d			20 08		20 33															21 10	21 23
Windermere 83 a																					
Penrith North Lakes d				20 45	20 58															21 35	
Carlisle 8 216 a			20 46	21 00	21 14															21 50	22 00
d			20 47	21 02	21 18															21 50	22 02
Lockerbie 225,226 d					21 37															22 09	
Carstairs 226,225 a																					
Motherwell 226 a			21 44		22 21															22 53	
Glasgow Central 15 216,226,225 a			22 02		22 38															23 09	23 17
Haymarket ⛴ a				22 13																	
Edinburgh 10 ⛴ a				22 19																	
Fort William 227,400 a																					
Perth 229 a																					
Dundee 229 a																					
Aberdeen 229 a																					
Inverness 229 a																					

A From Birmingham New Street
B From London Euston
C To Liverpool Lime Street
D From Bristol Temple Meads
E From Bournemouth
F To Glasgow Central

Refer to Operator websites for full information about Sleeper Services. Contact details for train operators available at National Rail Enquiries

Table T065-F

Mondays to Fridays

21 May to 22 June

London & West Midlands to North West England. London, West Midlands & Manchester to Scotland via the West Coast

	VT	VT	XC	LM	XC	VT	TP	VT FO	LM	VT ThFO	VT FO	VT	VT	VT	VT	VT	VT	XC	LM	XC	VT
	◇■	◇■	◇■	■	◇■	◇■	◇■	◇■	■	◇	◇■	■	■	■	■	■	◇■	◇■	■	◇■	◇■
			A		B			C			D							E		F	
	☒	☒	⚒		⚒	☒	⚒	⊐		⊐	⊐	⊐	⊐	⊐	⊐	⊐	⊐	⚒		⚒	⊐
London Euston ⊖66 d	18 33	18 40				18 43		18 46	18 49	18 57		19 00	19 10	19 10	19 20	19 30	19 40				19 43
Watford Junction 66 d																					
Milton Keynes Central 66 d						19 13		19 19	19 23				19u41	19u41	19u50						20 13
Rugby 66 d	19 23							19 41	20 06												
Nuneaton d									20 19				20 12	20 12							
Tamworth Low Level d		19 44							20 32								20 43				
Lichfield Trent Valley d		19 51							20 38								20 50				
Coventry 68 d					19 27	19 42														20 27	20 42
Birmingham International 68 ✈ d					19 38	19 53														20 38	20 53
BirminghamNewSt 68 d			19 31	19 36	19 57	20 15												20 31	20 36	20 57	21 15
Wolverhampton d			19 49	19 54	20 15	20 37												20 49	20 54	21 15	21 37
Penkridge d				20 04															21 04		
Stafford d	19 54		20 03	20 10	20 28	20 51		20 24	20 55				20 37	20 37			21 04	21 03	21 10	21 29	21 55
Stoke-on-Trent 84 a			20 19		20 43				21 11			20 24			20 49			21 18		21 45	22 10
Macclesfield a			20 36		21 01						←				21 06			21 36		22 02	
Crewe 81,91 a	20 13	20 17		20 30		21 15		20 42	21 34	20s33	20 42		20 53	20 53			21 21		21 32		22 30
d	20 16	20 18		20 33				20 43			20 43		20 55	20 55			21 23		21 33		
Chester 81 a								→					21 17	21 20							
Wrexham General 75 a																					
Llandudno Junction 81 a														22 14							
Bangor (Gwynedd) 81 a														22 30							
Holyhead 81 ⛴ a														23 01							
Wilmslow 84 a		20 33															21 38				
Stockport 84 a		20 42	20 48		21 13							20 53			21 19			21 49		22 15	
Manchester Piccadilly a		20 52	20 59		21 25					21 09		21 05			21 28		21 54	21 59		22 25	
Runcorn 91 a	20 33			20 56															21 55		
Liverpool South Pkwy 91 ✈ a				21 05															22 04		
Liverpool Lime Street 91 a	20 53			21 18															22 16		
d																					
Manchester Airport 82 ✈ d							20 10														
Manchester Picc. 82 d							20 26														
Bolton 82 d																					
Warrington Bank Quay d											21 03					21 16					
Wigan North Western 90 d											21 14					21 27					
Preston 90 a							21 02				21 31					21 39					
Blackpool North 97 a																					
Preston 90 d							21 04									21 42					
Lancaster d							21 20									21 57					
Barrow-in-Furness 82 a																					
Oxenholme Lake District 83 d							21 33									22 10					
Windermere 83 a																					
Penrith North Lakes d							21 58									22 35					
Carlisle 216 a							22 14									22 50					
d							22 15									22 51					
Lockerbie 225,226 d							22 34														
Carstairs 226,225 a																					
Motherwell 226 a																					
Glasgow Central 216,226,225 a																00 05					
Haymarket a							23s31														
Edinburgh a							23 38														
Fort William 227,400 a																					
Perth 229 a																					
Dundee 229 a																					
Aberdeen 229 a																					
Inverness 229 a																					

A From Exeter St Davids
B From Bournemouth
C To Preston
D From London Euston
E From Bristol Temple Meads
F From Bournemouth. ⚒ to BirminghamNewSt

Refer to Operator websites for full information about Sleeper Services. Contact details for train operators available at National Rail Enquiries

Table T065-F

Mondays to Fridays

21 May to 22 June

London & West Midlands to North West England. London, West Midlands & Manchester to Scotland via the West Coast

	LM	VT	VT	VT	TP	VT	VT	VT	LM	XC	LM	NT	XC	NT FX	LM	AW	LM	VT	VT	VT	CS TW ThO	CS MFO
	■	◇■	◇■	◇■	◇■	◇■	◇■	◇■	■	◇■	■		◇■		■	◇	■	◇■	◇■	◇■	R	R
						A		B		C						D						
		⊐	⊐	⊐	⚒	⊐	⊐	⊐						🚌				⊐	⊐	⊐	✕	✕
London Euston ⊖66 d	19 46	20 00	20 07	20 10		20 30	20 40				20 46						20 49	21 00	21 07	21 10	21 15	21 15
Watford Junction 66 d																				21u25	21u33	21u33
Milton Keynes Central 66 d	20 19			20 41							21 19						21 29	21 31	21 39			
Rugby 66 d	20 42										21 45						22 17			22 05		
Nuneaton d	21 00		21 03								22 00								22 08			
Tamworth Low Level d	21 15					21 35		←			22 15											
Lichfield Trent Valley d	21 22					21 42		21 42			22 22											
Coventry 68 d						→				21 27							22 30					
Birmingham International 68 ✈ d										21 38							22 46					
BirminghamNewSt 68 d									21 36	21 57			22 30		22 39	22 52	23 09					
Wolverhampton d									21 54	22 15			22 48		23 05	23 27	23 36					
Penkridge d									22 04						23 15		23 46					
Stafford d	21 42		21 27					22 00	22 10	22 28			23 01		23 21	23 43	23 53			22 37		
Stoke-on-Trent 84 a	22 01	21 25								22 43	22 50		23 17					22 28				
Macclesfield a		21 41								23 01								22 44				
Crewe 81,91 a	22 24		21 46	21 47			22 10	22 17	22 34		23 10				23 49	00 10	00 22		22 53	22 58		
d			21 48	21 49			22 11	22 19	22 36							00 15			22 53	22 59	23u50	23u50
Chester 81 a				22 13												→						
Wrexham General 75 a																						
Llandudno Junction 81 a																						
Bangor (Gwynedd) 81 a																						
Holyhead 81 ⛴ a																						
Wilmslow 84 a							22 27															
Stockport 84 a		21 54					22 36			23 13								22 58				
Manchester Piccadilly a		22 04					22 46			23 25			00 11					23 08				
Runcorn 91 a			22 05						22 59										23 11			
Liverpool South Pkwy 91 ✈ a									23 08													
Liverpool Lime Street 91 a			22 22						23 20										23 34			
d																						
Manchester Airport 82 ✈ d					21 05							22 10										
Manchester Picc. 82 d					21 22							22 26										
Bolton 82 d														22 30								
Warrington Bank Quay d								22 36												23 21		
Wigan North Western 90 d								22 47				22 57								23 32		
Preston 90 a					22 02			23 00				23 14		23 46						23 50		
Blackpool North 97 a																						
Preston 90 d					22 03							23 15									00u58	00u58
Lancaster d					22 19							23 33										
Barrow-in-Furness 82 a												00 37										
Oxenholme Lake District 83 d					22 33																	
Windermere 83 a																						
Penrith North Lakes d					22 58																	
Carlisle 216 a					23 16																	
d					23 18																	
Lockerbie 225,226 d					23 37																	
Carstairs 226,225 a																						
Motherwell 226 a																						
Glasgow Central 216,226,225 a					00 53																	
Haymarket a																						
Edinburgh a																						
Fort William 227,400 a																						
Perth 229 a																						
Dundee 229 a																					06s07	06s08
Aberdeen 229 a																					07 39	07 39
Inverness 229 a																						

A To Preston
B From London Euston
C From Bournemouth
D To Holyhead

Refer to Operator websites for full information about Sleeper Services. Contact details for train operators available at National Rail Enquiries

Table T065-F

Mondays to Fridays

21 May to 22 June

London & West Midlands to North West England. London, West Midlands & Manchester to Scotland via the West Coast

		CS		AW	VT	VT	VT	NT FX	CS FO	CS FX
				◇ A	◇1	◇1	◇1			
London Euston	⊖66 d	21 15			21 40	22 00	23 00		23 50	23 50
Watford Junction	66 d	21u33					23u15		00u10	00u10
Milton Keynes Central	66 d					22 40				
Rugby	66 d					23 03				
Nuneaton	d					23 14				
Tamworth Low Level	d					23s26				
Lichfield Trent Valley	d					23s33				
Coventry	68 d									
Birmingham International	68 d									
Birmingham New St	68 d									
Wolverhampton	d									
Penkridge	d									
Stafford	d					23s48				
Stoke-on-Trent	84 a				23 07		01s18			
Macclesfield	a			←	23 24		01s34			
Crewe	81,91 a			00 10		00 17				
	d	23u50		00 15						
Chester	81 a			00 37						
Wrexham General	75 a									
Llandudno Junction	81 a			01 28						
Bangor (Gwynedd)	81 a			01 46						
Holyhead	81 a			02 15						
Wilmslow	84 a									
Stockport	84 a				23 38		01s48			
Manchester Piccadilly	a				23 49		01 59			
Runcorn	91 a									
Liverpool South Pkwy	91 a									
Liverpool Lime Street	91 a									
	d									
Manchester Airport	82 d									
Manchester Picc.	82 d							23 05		
Bolton	82 d							23 30		
Warrington Bank Quay	d									
Wigan North Western	90 d									
Preston	90 a							00 46		
Blackpool North	97 a									
Preston	90 d	00u58	00u58							
Lancaster	d									
Barrow-in-Furness	82 a									
Oxenholme Lake District	83 d									
Windermere	83 a									
Penrith North Lakes	d									
Carlisle	216 a								05s13	05s13
	d									
Lockerbie	225,226 d									
Carstairs	226,225 a								06s21	06s22
Motherwell	226 a								06s55	06s55
Glasgow Central	216,226,225 a								07 22	07 22
Haymarket	a									
Edinburgh	a									
Fort William	227,400 a		09 57							
Perth	229 a	05s41								
Dundee	229 a									
Aberdeen	229 a									
Inverness	229 a	08 41								

A From Birmingham New Street

Refer to Operator websites for full information about Sleeper Services. Contact details for train operators available at National Rail Enquiries

Table T065-F

Mondays to Fridays

25 June to 7 December

London & West Midlands to North West England. London, West Midlands & Manchester to Scotland via the West Coast

		AW MO	NT MX	CS MX	AW MX	CS MO	CS MO	CS MO	CS WTh FO	CS TO		CS MX	CS MX	NT	NT	TP	VT	NT	VT	XC		LM	TP	VT	XC
		◇ A	◇ B	C	◇ D	C	C	C	C	C		C	C			◇1	◇1		◇1	◇1		1	◇1	◇1	◇1
London Euston	⊖66 d																								
Watford Junction	66 d			00u10																					
Milton Keynes Central	66 d																								
Rugby	66 d																								
Nuneaton	d																								
Tamworth Low Level	d																								
Lichfield Trent Valley	d																								
Coventry	68 d																								
Birmingham International	68 d																								
Birmingham New St	68 d																		05 30	05 57		06 01		06 15	06 30
Wolverhampton	d																		05 48	06 15		06 21		06 37	06 48
Penkridge	d																					06 31			
Stafford	d																		06 01	06 28		06 37			07 02
Stoke-on-Trent	84 a																			06 44					07 19
Macclesfield	a																			07 05					07 37
Crewe	81,91 a																		06 20			06 57		07 08	
	d	00 01			00 15												05 57		06 23			06 59		07 09	
Chester	81 a	00 22			00 37														06 43						
Wrexham General	75 a																								
Llandudno Junction	81 a	01 27			01 28														07 32						
Bangor (Gwynedd)	81 a	01 44			01 46														07 49						
Holyhead	81 a	02 20			02 15														08 20						
Wilmslow	84 a																								
Stockport	84 a																			07 19					07 49
Manchester Piccadilly	a																			07 28					07 59
Runcorn	91 a																					07 24			
Liverpool South Pkwy	91 a																					07 33			
Liverpool Lime Street	91 a																					07 46			
	d																								
Manchester Airport	82 d																						06 10		
Manchester Picc.	82 d		00 09													05 00		05 00					06 26		
Bolton	82 d																	05 25							
Warrington Bank Quay	d																06 15							07 27	
Wigan North Western	90 d																06 25							07 38	
Preston	90 a		00 59													05 35	06 38	06 41					07 01	07 51	
Blackpool North	97 a		01 29																						
Preston	90 d					00u35	00u35	00u35	00u58	00u58		00u58	00u58	05 16		05 40	06 40						07 03	07 53	
Lancaster	d													05 36	05 40	05 56	06 54						07 18	08 08	
Barrow-in-Furness	82 a																								
Oxenholme Lake District	83 d														06 19	06 10	07 10						07 32	08 22	
Windermere	83 a														06 39										
Penrith North Lakes	d															06 35	07 34								
Carlisle	216 a			05s13										09 24		06 51	07 49						08 10	09 00	
	d															06 52	07 52						08 12	09 01	
Lockerbie	225,226 d															07 11	08 10						08 30		
Carstairs	226,225 a			06s22												07 44									
Motherwell	226 a			06s55												07 59									
Glasgow Central	216,226,225 a			07 22												08 20	09 16								
Haymarket	a																						09s31	10 12	
Edinburgh	a																						09 38	10 18	
Fort William	227,400 a							09 57					09 57												
Perth	229 a						05s41					05s41													
Dundee	229 a					06s08			06s07	06s08															
Aberdeen	229 a					07 39			07 39	07 39															
Inverness	229 a						08 41					08 41													

A From Birmingham International

B From Manchester Airport

C From London Euston

D From Birmingham New Street

Refer to Operator websites for full information about Sleeper Services. Contact details for train operators available at National Rail Enquiries

Table T065-F

Mondays to Fridays
25 June to 7 December

London & West Midlands to North West England. London, West Midlands & Manchester to Scotland via the West Coast

	VT	TP	VT	LM	LM	XC	VT	LM	VT	LM	VT	XC	LM	LM	XC	TP	NT	LM	VT	VT	VT	VT
	◇■	◇■	◇■	■	■	◇■	◇■	■	◇■	■	◇■	◇■	■	■	◇■	◇■	◇	■	◇■	◇■	◇■	◇■
					A								B	A	C			D	E	F		
	⊠	⌶	⊠			⌶	⊠		⊠		⊠	⌶			⌶	⌶			⊠	⊠ ⊏P	⊠	⊠
London Euston ■ ⊖66 d	05 27		05 31				06 16			06 24	06 36								06 43	06 46	06 55	07 07
Watford Junction 66 d	05u45		05u50							06 41	06u51											
Milton Keynes Central 66 d	06 15		06 23				06 46			07 24									07 13		07 27	
Rugby 66 d			06 45		06 06					08 04				06 59						07 40		
Nuneaton d	06 45				06 20					08 16				07 12								
Tamworth Low Level d					06 35					08 29				07 29								
Lichfield Trent Valley d					06 41					08 35				07 35								
Coventry 68 d															07 27				07 42			
Birmingham International 68 ✈ d				06 18											07 38				07 53			
BirminghamNewSt ■ 68 ⛴ d				06 36		06 51		07 01	07 15			07 31	07 36		07 57			08 01	08 15			
Wolverhampton ■ ⛴ d				06 54		07 10		07 20	07 37			07 49	07 54		08 15			→	→			
Penkridge d				07 04				07 29					08 04									
Stafford d	07 08			07 10	06 59	07 22		07 36		08 55		08 03	08 10	07 55	08 28							08 24
Stoke-on-Trent 84 a					07 15		07 45			09 12		08 18		08 11	08 43						08 24	
Macclesfield a							08 01					08 36			09 01						08 41	
Crewe ■ 81,91 a	07 27		07 30	07 32	07 38	07 42		07 56	08 08	09 34	08 10		08 30	08 34								08 41
d	07 28		07 32	07 33		07 44		07 59	08 09		08 11		08 32									08 43
Chester 81 a																						
Wrexham General 75 a																						
Llandudno Junction 81 a																						
Bangor (Gwynedd) 81 a																						
Holyhead 81 ⛴ a																						
Wilmslow 84 a						08 00					08 27											
Stockport 84 a						08 13	08 17				08 35	08 49			09 13						08 54	
Manchester Piccadilly ■ ⛴ a						08 24	08 27				08 46	08 59			09 25						09 04	
Runcorn 91 a	07 45			07 59				08 24					08 52									09 00
Liverpool South Pkwy ■ 91 ✈ a				08 09				08 32					09 01									
Liverpool Lime Street ■ 91 a	08 03			08 21				08 44					09 11									09 20
d																						
Manchester Airport 82 ✈⛴ d		07 10														08 10						
Manchester Picc. ■ 82 ⛴ d		07 26														08 26						
Bolton 82 d																						
Warrington Bank Quay d			07 49						08 27											08 45		
Wigan North Western 90 d			08 00						08 38											08 59		
Preston ■ 90 a		08 02	08 13						08 51							09 02				09 14		
Blackpool North 97 a																				09 37		
Preston ■ 90 d		08 03	08 15						08 53							09 04	09 29					
Lancaster ■ d		08 19	08 29						09 08							09 19	09 59					
Barrow-in-Furness 82 a																						
Oxenholme Lake District 83 d			08 42													09 33	10 19					
Windermere 83 a																	10 41					
Penrith North Lakes d		08 54							09 44													
Carlisle ■ 216 a		09 10	09 20						09 59							10 10						
d		09 11	09 21						10 02							10 12						
Lockerbie 225,226 d		09 30														10 30						
Carstairs 226,225 a																						
Motherwell 226 a		10 14																				
Glasgow Central ■ 216,226,225 a		10 33	10 38						11 15													
Haymarket ⛴ a																11s28						
Edinburgh ■ ⛴ a																11 35						
Fort William 227,400 a																						
Perth 229 a																						
Dundee 229 a																						
Aberdeen 229 a																						
Inverness 229 a																						

A From Northampton
B From Walsall
C From Southampton Central
D From Walsall to Liverpool Lime Street
E To Edinburgh
F ⊏P from Preston ⊠ to Preston

Refer to Operator websites for full information about Sleeper Services. Contact details for train operators available at National Rail Enquiries

Table T065-F

Mondays to Fridays
25 June to 7 December

London & West Midlands to North West England. London, West Midlands & Manchester to Scotland via the West Coast

	VT	LM	VT	VT	NT	VT	NT	VT	XC	LM	XC	TP	LM	VT	LM	VT	VT	VT	LM	VT	VT
	◇■	■	◇■	◇■	◇	◇■	◇	◇■	◇■	■	◇■	◇■	■	◇■	■	◇■	◇■	◇■	■	◇■	◇■
		A			B	C	D		E		F		G	H					I		
	⊠		⊠	⊠		⊠		⊠	⌶		⌶	⌶		⊠		⊠	⊠	⊠		⊠	⊠
London Euston ■ ⊖66 d	07 10		07 20	07 30				07 35						07 43	07 46	08 00	08 07	08 10		08 20	08 30
Watford Junction 66 d																					
Milton Keynes Central 66 d	07 41		07 50					08 06						08 13	08 19		08 38	08 43		08 50	
Rugby 66 d															08 42						
Nuneaton d															08 54						
Tamworth Low Level d															09 09						
Lichfield Trent Valley d															09 17						
Coventry 68 d											08 27			08 42							
Birmingham International 68 ✈ d		←				←					08 38			08 53							
BirminghamNewSt ■ 68 ⛴ d		08 01				08 15			08 31	08 36	08 57		09 01	09 15							
Wolverhampton ■ ⛴ d		08 20				08 37			08 49	08 54	09 15		09 20	09 37							
Penkridge d		08 29								09 04											
Stafford d		08 36							09 03	09 10	09 28		09 35		09 42		09 27				
Stoke-on-Trent 84 a			08 48						09 18		09 43				10 02	09 24				09 48	
Macclesfield a									09 36		10 01					09 41			←		
Crewe ■ 81,91 a	08 47	08 56				09 07		09 10		09 30			09 55	10 08	10 24			09 51	09 55		
d	08 49	08 57				09 09		09 11		09 32			09 57	10 09				09 53	09 57		
Chester 81 a	09 11												→	→				10 13			
Wrexham General 75 a																					
Llandudno Junction 81 a																		11 04			
Bangor (Gwynedd) 81 a																		11 24			
Holyhead 81 ⛴ a																		11 55			
Wilmslow 84 a								09 27													
Stockport 84 a			09 16					09 36	09 49		10 13					09 54				10 16	
Manchester Piccadilly ■ ⛴ a			09 27					09 45	09 59		10 25					10 05				10 28	
Runcorn 91 a		09 21								09 52							10 01		10 24		
Liverpool South Pkwy ■ 91 ✈ a		09 30								10 01									10 32		
Liverpool Lime Street ■ 91 a		09 42								10 11							10 19		10 44		
d																					
Manchester Airport 82 ✈⛴ d					08 41							09 10									
Manchester Picc. ■ 82 ⛴ d					09 01							09 26									
Bolton 82 d					09 22																
Warrington Bank Quay d				09 14		09 27															10 14
Wigan North Western 90 d				09 25		09 38															10 25
Preston ■ 90 a				09 38	09 49	09 51						10 02									10 38
Blackpool North 97 a							←														
Preston ■ 90 d				09 41	09 57	09 54	09 57					10 04									10 41
Lancaster ■ d				09 55	→	10 08	10 14					10 20									10 55
Barrow-in-Furness 82 a							11 15														
Oxenholme Lake District 83 d						10 22						10 33									11 08
Windermere 83 a																					
Penrith North Lakes d				10 31								10 58									
Carlisle ■ 216 a				10 46		10 59						11 14									11 46
d				10 47		11 01						11 16									11 47
Lockerbie 225,226 d												11 37									
Carstairs 226,225 a																					
Motherwell 226 a												12 22									
Glasgow Central ■ 216,226,225 a				11 59								12 39									12 59
Haymarket ⛴ a						12 16															
Edinburgh ■ ⛴ a						12 22															
Fort William 227,400 a																					
Perth 229 a																					
Dundee 229 a																					
Aberdeen 229 a																					
Inverness 229 a																					

A From Walsall
B To Barrow-in-Furness
C From London Euston
D From Manchester Airport
E From Bristol Temple Meads
F From Southampton Central
G To Liverpool Lime Street
H To Glasgow Central
I From Birmingham New Street

Refer to Operator websites for full information about Sleeper Services. Contact details for train operators available at National Rail Enquiries

Table T065-F

Mondays to Fridays
25 June to 7 December

London & West Midlands to North West England. London, West Midlands & Manchester to Scotland via the West Coast

	VT ◇■ A ⊠	VT ◇■ ⊠	XC ◇■ B 🛒	LM ■	XC ◇■ C 🛒	TP ◇■ 🛒	LM ■ D	VT ◇■ E ⊠	LM ■	VT MO ◇■ F ⊠⊐	VT MX ◇■ F ⊠⊐	VT ◇■ ⊠	VT MO ◇■ ⊠	VT MX ◇■ ⊠	VT ◇■ ⊠	LM ■ G	VT ◇■ ⊠	VT ◇■ ⊠	NT	VT ◇■ A ⊠	VT ◇■ ⊠	XC ◇■ H 🛒
London Euston 15 ⊖66 d		08 40						08 43	08 46	08 53	08 53	09 00	09 07	09 07	09 10		09 20	09 30			09 40	
Watford Junction 66 d																						
Milton Keynes Central 66 d								09 13	09 19						09 41		09 50					
Rugby 66 d									09 42	09 46	09 46											
Nuneaton d									09 54													
Tamworth Low Level d									10 09													
Lichfield Trent Valley d									10 17													
Coventry 68 d					09 27			09 42														
Birmingham International 68 ✈ d					09 38			09 53														
BirminghamNewSt 12 68 ⛴ d			09 31	09 36	09 57		10 01	10 15														10 31
Wolverhampton 7 ⛴ d			09 49	09 54	10 15		10 20	10 37														10 49
Penkridge d				10 04																		
Stafford d			10 02	10 10	10 28		10 35		10 42				10 24	10 24								11 03
Stoke-on-Trent 84 a			10 17		10 43				11 02			10 24					10 48					11 18
Macclesfield a	←		10 36		11 01							10 41				←				←		11 36
Crewe 10 81,91 a	10 08	10 11		10 31			10 56	11 08	11 24				10 41	10 41	10 47	10 56				11 08	11 11	
d	10 09	10 12		10 33			10 57	11 09					10 43	10 43	10 49	10 57				11 09	11 12	
Chester 81 a							→	→							11 13							
Wrexham General 75 a																						
Llandudno Junction 81 a															12 00							
Bangor (Gwynedd) 81 a															12 17							
Holyhead 81 ⛴ a															12 50							
Wilmslow 84 a		10 27																			11 27	
Stockport 84 a		10 36	10 49		11 13							10 54					11 16				11 35	11 49
Manchester Piccadilly 10 ⛴ a		10 46	11 00		11 24							11 05					11 28				11 46	11 59
Runcorn 91 a				10 51									11 01	11 03		11 21						
Liverpool South Pkwy 7 91 ✈ a				11 00												11 30						
Liverpool Lime Street 10 91 a				11 10									11 19	11 21		11 42						
d																						
Manchester Airport 82 ✈⛴ d						10 10																
Manchester Picc. 10 82 ⛴ d						10 26																
Bolton 82 d																						
Warrington Bank Quay d	10 27									10 56	11 00							11 14		11 27		
Wigan North Western 90 d	10 38									11 12	11 12							11 25		11 38		
Preston 8 90 a	10 51					11 02				11 25	11 25							11 38		11 51		
Blackpool North 97 a										11 56	11 56											
Preston 8 90 d	10 53					11 03												11 41		11 53		
Lancaster 6 d	11 08																	11 55	12 02	12 08		
Barrow-in-Furness 82 a																			13 11			
Oxenholme Lake District 83 d																				12 21		
Windermere 83 a																						
Penrith North Lakes d	11 45																	12 30				
Carlisle 8 216 a	12 00					12 05												12 46	15 46	12 59		
d	12 02					12 06												12 47		13 01		
Lockerbie 225,226 d																						
Carstairs 226,225 a																						
Motherwell 226 a																						
Glasgow Central 15 216,226,225 a	13 15																	13 59				
Haymarket ⛴ a						13s19														14 12		
Edinburgh 10 ⛴ a						13 26														14 19		
Fort William 227,400 a																						
Perth 229 a																						
Dundee 229 a																						
Aberdeen 229 a																						
Inverness 229 a																						

A From London Euston
B From Cardiff Central
C From Bournemouth
D To Liverpool Lime Street
E To Edinburgh
F ⊐ from Preston ⊠ to Preston
G From Birmingham New Street
H From Paignton

Refer to Operator websites for full information about Sleeper Services. Contact details for train operators available at National Rail Enquiries

Table T065-F

Mondays to Fridays
25 June to 7 December

London & West Midlands to North West England. London, West Midlands & Manchester to Scotland via the West Coast

	LM ■	XC ◇■ A 🛒	TP ◇■ 🛒	NT ◇	LM ■ B	VT ◇■ C ⊠	LM ■	VT ◇■ ⊠	VT ◇■ ⊠	VT ◇■ ⊠	LM ■ D	VT ◇■ ⊠	VT ◇■ ⊠	NT ◇ E	VT ◇■ F ⊠	NT ◇ G	VT ◇■ H ⊠⊐	VT ◇■ ⊠	XC ◇■ I 🛒	LM ■	XC ■ A 🛒
London Euston 15 ⊖66 d						09 43	09 46	10 00	10 07	10 10		10 20	10 30				10 36	10 40			
Watford Junction 66 d																					
Milton Keynes Central 66 d						10 13	10 19			10 41		10 50									
Rugby 66 d							10 42										11 25				
Nuneaton d							10 54														
Tamworth Low Level d							11 09														
Lichfield Trent Valley d							11 17														
Coventry 68 d		10 27				10 42															11 27
Birmingham International 68 ✈ d		10 38				10 53															11 38
BirminghamNewSt 12 68 ⛴ d	10 36	10 57			11 01	11 15													11 31	11 36	11 57
Wolverhampton 7 ⛴ d	10 54	11 15			11 20	11 37													11 49	11 54	12 15
Penkridge d	11 04																			12 04	
Stafford d	11 10	11 28			11 35		11 42		11 24										12 03	12 10	12 28
Stoke-on-Trent 84 a		11 43					12 02	11 24				11 48							12 18		12 43
Macclesfield a		12 01						11 41			←				←				12 36		13 01
Crewe 10 81,91 a	11 31				11 55	12 07	12 24		11 41	11 47	11 55				12 07			12 11		12 31	
d	11 33				11 57	12 09			11 43	11 49	11 57				12 09			12 12		12 33	
Chester 81 a					→	→				12 11											
Wrexham General 75 a																					
Llandudno Junction 81 a																					
Bangor (Gwynedd) 81 a																					
Holyhead 81 ⛴ a																					
Wilmslow 84 a																		12 27			
Stockport 84 a		12 13						11 54				12 16						12 35	12 49		13 12
Manchester Piccadilly 10 ⛴ a		12 25						12 05				12 28						12 46	12 59		13 25
Runcorn 91 a	11 51								12 00		12 25									12 51	
Liverpool South Pkwy 7 91 ✈ a	12 00										12 33									13 00	
Liverpool Lime Street 10 91 a	12 10								12 19		12 44									13 10	
d																					
Manchester Airport 82 ✈⛴ d			10 59											11 41							
Manchester Picc. 10 82 ⛴ d			11 22											12 01							
Bolton 82 d														12 22							
Warrington Bank Quay d													12 14		12 27		12 34				
Wigan North Western 90 d													12 25		12 38		12 45				
Preston 8 90 a			11 59										12 38	12 48	12 51		12 57				
Blackpool North 97 a																←	13 20				
Preston 8 90 d			12 04	12 17									12 41	12 57	12 53	12 57					
Lancaster 6 d			12 20	12 37										→	13 08	13 14					
Barrow-in-Furness 82 a																14 14					
Oxenholme Lake District 83 d			12 33	13 02											13 22						
Windermere 83 a				13 24																	
Penrith North Lakes d			12 58										13 28								
Carlisle 8 216 a			13 14										13 44		13 59						
d			13 16										13 45		14 00						
Lockerbie 225,226 d																					
Carstairs 226,225 a																					
Motherwell 226 a			14 21												14 58						
Glasgow Central 15 216,226,225 a			14 40										14 59		15 15						
Haymarket ⛴ a																					
Edinburgh 10 ⛴ a																					
Fort William 227,400 a																					
Perth 229 a																					
Dundee 229 a																					
Aberdeen 229 a																					
Inverness 229 a																					

A From Bournemouth
B To Liverpool Lime Street
C To Glasgow Central
D From Birmingham New Street
E To Barrow-in-Furness
F From London Euston
G From Manchester Airport
H ⊐ from Preston ⊠ to Preston
I From Bristol Temple Meads

Refer to Operator websites for full information about Sleeper Services. Contact details for train operators available at National Rail Enquiries

Table T065-F

Mondays to Fridays
25 June to 7 December

London & West Midlands to North West England. London, West Midlands & Manchester to Scotland via the West Coast

	TP	LM	VT	LM	VT	VT	VT	LM	VT	VT	VT	VT	XC	LM	XC	TP	NT	LM	VT	LM	VT	VT
	◇1	1	◇1	1	◇1	◇1	◇1	1	◇1	R 1	◇1	◇1	◇1	1	◇1	◇1	◇	1	◇1	1	◇1	◇1
		A	B					C			D		E		F			A	G			
	⊥		⊏		⊠	⊠	⊠		⊠	⊠	⊏	⊠	⊥		⊥	⊥			⊠		⊠	⊠
London Euston 15 ⊖66 d			10 43	10 46	11 00	11 07	11 10		11 20	11 30		11 40							11 43	11 46	12 00	12 07
Watford Junction 66 d																						
Milton Keynes Central 66 d			11 13	11 19			11 41		11 50										12 13	12 19		
Rugby 66 d				11 42																12 42		
Nuneaton d				11 54																12 54		
Tamworth Low Level d				12 09																13 09		
Lichfield Trent Valley d				12 17																13 17		
Coventry 68 d			11 42												12 27				12 42			
Birmingham International 68 ✈ d			11 53												12 38				12 53			
BirminghamNewSt 12 68 ⇌ d		12 01	12 15										12 31	12 36	12 57			13 01	13 15			
Wolverhampton 7 ⇌ d		12 20	12 37										12 49	12 54	13 15			13 20	13 37			
Penkridge d														13 04								
Stafford d		12 35		12 42		12 24							13 03	13 10	13 28			13 35		13 42		13 24
Stoke-on-Trent 84 a				13 02	12 24				12 48				13 18		13 43					14 02	13 24	
Macclesfield a					12 41			←			←		13 36		14 01						13 41	
Crewe 10 81,91 a		12 55	13 08	13 24		12 41	12 47	12 55			13 08	13 11		13 31				13 56	14 07	14 24		13 41
d		12 57	13 09			12 43	12 49	12 57			13 09	13 12		13 33				13 57	14 09			13 43
Chester 81 a		→	→				13 11											→	→			
Wrexham General 75 a																						
Llandudno Junction 81 a																						
Bangor (Gwynedd) 81 a																						
Holyhead 81 ⛴ a																						
Wilmslow 84 a												13 27										
Stockport 84 a					12 55				13 16			13 35	13 49		14 13						13 54	
Manchester Piccadilly 10 ⇌ a					13 05				13 28			13 46	13 59		14 25						14 05	
Runcorn 91 a						13 00		13 21						13 51								14 00
Liverpool South Pkwy 7 91 ✈ a								13 30						14 00								
Liverpool Lime Street 10 91 a						13 19		13 42						14 10								14 19
d																						
Manchester Airport 82 ✈⇌ d	12 10															13 10						
Manchester Picc. 10 82 ⇌ d	12 26															13 26						
Bolton 82 d																						
Warrington Bank Quay d										13 14	13 27											
Wigan North Western 90 d										13 25	13 38											
Preston 8 90 a	13 02									13 38	13 51					14 02						
Blackpool North 97 a																						
Preston 8 90 d	13 03									13 41	13 53					14 04	14 10					
Lancaster 6 d	13 19									13 55	14 08					14 19	14 30					
Barrow-in-Furness 82 a																						
Oxenholme Lake District 83 d	13 32									14 08						14 33	14 51					
Windermere 83 a																	15 09					
Penrith North Lakes d											14 43					14 58						
Carlisle 8 216 a	14 11									14 46	14 59					15 13						
d	14 12									14 47	15 01					15 14						
Lockerbie 225,226 d	14 31															15 37						
Carstairs 226,225 a																						
Motherwell 226 a																16 21						
Glasgow Central 15 216,226,225 a										15 59						16 41						
Haymarket ⇌ a	15s29										16 13											
Edinburgh 10 ⇌ a	15 34										16 20											
Fort William 227,400 a																						
Perth 229 a																						
Dundee 229 a																						
Aberdeen 229 a																						
Inverness 229 a																						

A To Liverpool Lime Street
B To Edinburgh
C From Birmingham New Street
D From London Euston
E From Bristol Temple Meads
F From Bournemouth
G To Glasgow Central

Refer to Operator websites for full information about Sleeper Services. Contact details for train operators available at National Rail Enquiries

Table T065-F

Mondays to Fridays
25 June to 7 December

London & West Midlands to North West England. London, West Midlands & Manchester to Scotland via the West Coast

	VT	LM	VT	VT	VT	VT	XC	LM	XC	TP	LM	VT	LM	VT	VT	VT	LM	VT	VT	VT	NT	VT
	◇1	1	◇1	◇1	◇1	◇1	◇1	1	◇1	◇1	1	◇1	1	◇1	◇1	◇1	1	◇1	◇1	◇1		◇1
		A			B		C		D		E	F					A			B		
	⊠		⊠	⊠	⊠	⊠	⊥		⊥	⊥		⊠		⊏	⊏	⊏		⊏	⊏	⊠		⊏
London Euston 15 ⊖66 d	12 10		12 20	12 30		12 40						12 43	12 46	13 00	13 07	13 10		13 20	13 30			13 40
Watford Junction 66 d																						
Milton Keynes Central 66 d	12 41		12 50									13 13	13 19			13 41		13 50				
Rugby 66 d	13 04												13 42									
Nuneaton d													13 54									
Tamworth Low Level d													14 09									
Lichfield Trent Valley d													14 17									
Coventry 68 d									13 27			13 42										
Birmingham International 68 ✈ d									13 38			13 53										
BirminghamNewSt 12 68 ⇌ d							13 31	13 36	13 57		14 01	14 15										
Wolverhampton 7 ⇌ d							13 49	13 54	14 15		14 20	14 37										
Penkridge d								14 04														
Stafford d							14 03	14 10	14 28		14 35		14 42		14 24							
Stoke-on-Trent 84 a			13 48				14 18		14 43				15 02	14 24				14 48				
Macclesfield a		←			←		14 36		15 01					14 41			←			←		
Crewe 10 81,91 a	13 50	13 56			14 07	14 11		14 31			14 54	15 07	15 24		14 41	14 47	14 54			15 07		15 10
d	13 52	13 57			14 09	14 12		14 33			14 57	15 09			14 43	14 49	14 57			15 09		15 11
Chester 81 a	14 13										→	→				15 10						
Wrexham General 75 a																						
Llandudno Junction 81 a																						
Bangor (Gwynedd) 81 a																						
Holyhead 81 ⛴ a																						
Wilmslow 84 a						14 27																15 27
Stockport 84 a			14 16			14 35	14 49		15 13					14 54				15 16				15 35
Manchester Piccadilly 10 ⇌ a			14 28			14 46	14 59		15 25					15 05				15 28				15 46
Runcorn 91 a		14 21						14 53							15 00		15 22					
Liverpool South Pkwy 7 91 ✈ a		14 30						15 02									15 31					
Liverpool Lime Street 10 91 a		14 42						15 12							15 19		15 42					
d																						
Manchester Airport 82 ✈⇌ d										14 10												
Manchester Picc. 10 82 ⇌ d										14 26												
Bolton 82 d																						
Warrington Bank Quay d				14 14	14 27														15 14	15 27		
Wigan North Western 90 d				14 25	14 38														15 25	15 38		
Preston 8 90 a				14 38	14 51					15 03									15 38	15 51		
Blackpool North 97 a																						
Preston 8 90 d				14 41	14 53					15 04									15 41	15 53		
Lancaster 6 d				14 55	15 08					15 20										16 08	16 13	
Barrow-in-Furness 82 a																					17 16	
Oxenholme Lake District 83 d					15 22														16 06			
Windermere 83 a																						
Penrith North Lakes d				15 30						15 55									16 31	16 45		
Carlisle 8 216 a				15 45	16 00					16 11									16 46	17 00	19 43	
d				15 46	16 02					16 12									16 48	17 01		
Lockerbie 225,226 d										16 31												
Carstairs 226,225 a																						
Motherwell 226 a																						
Glasgow Central 15 216,226,225 a				16 59	17 15														17 59			
Haymarket ⇌ a										17s31										18 14		
Edinburgh 10 ⇌ a										17 36										18 22		
Fort William 227,400 a																						
Perth 229 a																						
Dundee 229 a																						
Aberdeen 229 a																						
Inverness 229 a																						

A From Birmingham New Street
B From London Euston
C From Paignton
D From Bournemouth
E To Liverpool Lime Street
F To Edinburgh

Refer to Operator websites for full information about Sleeper Services. Contact details for train operators available at National Rail Enquiries

London & West Midlands to North West England. London, West Midlands & Manchester to Scotland via the West Coast

	XC	LM	XC	TP	LM	VT	LM	VT	VT	VT	LM	VT	VT	NT	VT	VT	XC	LM	XC	TP	LM
	◇1 A 🛒	1	◇1 B 🛒	◇1 🛒	1 C	◇1 D ☕	1	◇1 ☕	◇1 ☕	◇1 ☕	1 E	◇1 ☕	■ 1 ☕		◇1 F ☕	◇1 ☕	◇1 G 🛒	1	◇1 B 🛒	◇1 🛒	1 H
London Euston ⊖66 d						13 43	13 46	14 00	14 07	14 10		14 20	14 30			14 40					
Watford Junction 66 d																					
Milton Keynes Central 66 d						14 13	14 19			14 41		14 50									
Rugby 66 d							14 42														
Nuneaton d							14 54														
Tamworth Low Level d							15 09														
Lichfield Trent Valley d							15 17														
Coventry 68 d			14 27			14 42													15 27		
Birmingham International 68 ✈ d			14 38			14 53													15 38		
BirminghamNewSt 68 d	14 31	14 36	14 57		15 01	15 15											15 31	15 36	15 57		16 01
Wolverhampton d	14 49	14 54	15 15		15 20	15 37											15 49	15 54	16 15		16 20
Penkridge d		15 04																16 04			16 29
Stafford d	15 03	15 10	15 28		15 35		15 42		15 24								16 03	16 10	16 28		16 36
Stoke-on-Trent 84 a	15 18		15 43				16 02	15 24				15 48					16 18		16 43		
Macclesfield a	15 36		16 01					15 41			←				←		16 36		17 01		
Crewe 81,91 a		15 30			15 55	16 07	16 24		15 41	15 47	15 55				16 07	16 11		16 31			16 56
d		15 33			15 57	16 09			15 43	15 49	15 57				16 09	16 12		16 33			16 57
Chester 81 a					→	→				16 10											→
Wrexham General 75 a																					
Llandudno Junction 81 a																					
Bangor (Gwynedd) 81 a																					
Holyhead 81 ⛴ a																					
Wilmslow 84 a																16 27					
Stockport 84 a	15 49		16 13					15 54				16 16				16 35	16 49		17 13		
Manchester Piccadilly a	15 59		16 25					16 05				16 28				16 46	16 59		17 25		
Runcorn 91 a		15 51							16 00		16 24							16 51			
Liverpool South Pkwy 91 ✈ a		16 00									16 32							17 00			
Liverpool Lime Street 91 a		16 10							16 20		16 44							17 11			
d																					
Manchester Airport 82 ✈ d				15 10																16 10	
Manchester Picc. 82 d				15 26																16 26	
Bolton 82 d																					
Warrington Bank Quay d													16 14		16 27						
Wigan North Western 90 d													16 25		16 38						
Preston 90 a				16 02									16 38		16 51					17 02	
Blackpool North 97 a																					
Preston 90 d				16 04									16 41		16 53					17 03	
Lancaster d				16 19									16 55	17 01	17 08					17 19	
Barrow-in-Furness 82 a														17 59							
Oxenholme Lake District 83 d				16 33									17 09		17 22					17 32	
Windermere 83 a																					
Penrith North Lakes d				16 58									17 35		17 47					17 57	
Carlisle 216 a				17 13									17 50	20 31	18 03					18 12	
d				17 15									17 51		18 05					18 13	
Lockerbie 225,226 d				17 33																18 32	
Carstairs 226,225 a																					
Motherwell 226 a				18 21																	
Glasgow Central 216,226,225 a				18 41									19 15		19 23						
Haymarket a																				19s34	
Edinburgh a																				19 40	
Fort William 227,400 a																					
Perth 229 a																					
Dundee 229 a																					
Aberdeen 229 a																					
Inverness 229 a																					

A From Bristol Temple Meads
B From Bournemouth
C From Walsall to Liverpool Lime Street
D To Glasgow Central
E From Walsall
F From London Euston
G From Penzance
H To Liverpool Lime Street

Refer to Operator websites for full information about Sleeper Services. Contact details for train operators available at National Rail Enquiries

London & West Midlands to North West England. London, West Midlands & Manchester to Scotland via the West Coast

	VT	LM	VT	VT	VT	LM	VT	VT	VT	VT	XC	LM	XC	TP	NT	LM	VT	LM	VT	VT	VT	LM
	■ 1 A ☕	1	◇1 ☕	◇1 ☕	◇1 ☕	1 B	◇1 ☕	◇1 ☕	■ 1 C ☕	◇1 ☕	◇1 D 🛒	1	◇1 E 🛒	◇1 🛒	◇	1 F	■ 1 G ☕	1	◇1 ☕	◇1 ☕	◇1 ☕	1 B
London Euston ⊖66 d	14 43	14 46	15 00	15 07	15 10		15 20	15 30		15 40							15 43	15 46	16 00	16 07	16 10	
Watford Junction 66 d																						
Milton Keynes Central 66 d	15 13	15 19			15 41		15 50										16 13	16 19			16u41	
Rugby 66 d		15 42																16 42				
Nuneaton d		15 54																16 54				
Tamworth Low Level d		16 09																17 09				
Lichfield Trent Valley d		16 17																17 17				
Coventry 68 d	15 42												16 27				16 42					
Birmingham International 68 ✈ d	15 53												16 38				16 53					
BirminghamNewSt 68 d	16 15										16 31	16 36	16 57			17 01	17 15					
Wolverhampton d	16 37										16 49	16 54	17 15			17 20	17 37					
Penkridge d												17 04				17 29						
Stafford d		16 42		16 24							17 03	17 10	17 28			17 36		17 42		17 24		
Stoke-on-Trent 84 a		17 02	16 24				16 48				17 18		17 43					18 02	17 24			
Macclesfield a			16 41			←	17 05		←		17 36		18 01						17 41			←
Crewe 81,91 a	17 08	17 24		16 41	16 47	16 56			17 08	17 11		17 30				17 56	18 08	18 24		17 41	17 47	17 56
d	17 09			16 43	16 49	16 57			17 09	17 12		17 32				17 57	18 09			17 43	17 49	17 57
Chester 81 a	→				17 11											→	→				18 08	
Wrexham General 75 a																						
Llandudno Junction 81 a																					18 58	
Bangor (Gwynedd) 81 a																					19 18	
Holyhead 81 ⛴ a																						
Wilmslow 84 a										17 27												
Stockport 84 a			16 54				17 17			17 36	17 49		18 13						17 54			
Manchester Piccadilly a			17 05				17 28			17 46	17 59		18 25						18 05			
Runcorn 91 a				17 00		17 24						17 52								18 00		18 24
Liverpool South Pkwy 91 ✈ a						17 33						18 01										18 32
Liverpool Lime Street 91 a				17 20		17 44						18 11								18 19		18 44
d																						
Manchester Airport 82 ✈ d														17 10								
Manchester Picc. 82 d														17 27								
Bolton 82 d																						
Warrington Bank Quay d								17 14	17 27													
Wigan North Western 90 d								17 25	17 38													
Preston 90 a								17 38	17 52					18 02								
Blackpool North 97 a																						
Preston 90 d								17 41	17 54					18 03	18 20							
Lancaster d								17 55	18 09					18 19	18 40							
Barrow-in-Furness 82 a																						
Oxenholme Lake District 83 d								18 08	18 24					18 33	19 00							
Windermere 83 a															19 22							
Penrith North Lakes d									18 48					18 58								
Carlisle 216 a								18 45	19 04					19 13								
d								18 47	19 04					19 15								
Lockerbie 225,226 d														19 35								
Carstairs 226,225 a																						
Motherwell 226 a														20 21								
Glasgow Central 216,226,225 a								19 59						20 42								
Haymarket a									20 14													
Edinburgh a									20 23													
Fort William 227,400 a																						
Perth 229 a																						
Dundee 229 a																						
Aberdeen 229 a																						
Inverness 229 a																						

A To Edinburgh
B From Birmingham New Street
C From London Euston
D From Bristol Temple Meads
E From Bournemouth
F To Liverpool Lime Street
G To Glasgow Central

Refer to Operator websites for full information about Sleeper Services. Contact details for train operators available at National Rail Enquiries

Table T065-F

Mondays to Fridays

25 June to 7 December

London & West Midlands to North West England. London, West Midlands & Manchester to Scotland via the West Coast

	VT	VT	NT	VT	NT	VT	VT	VT	XC	LM	XC	TP	LM	VT	LM	VT	VT	VT	VT	VT	LM
	◇1	◇1	◇	1	◇	◇1	◇1	◇1	◇1	1	◇1	◇1	1	◇1	1	◇1	◇1	◇1	◇1	◇1	1
			A	B	C	D		B	E		F		G	H							I
	⊏	⊠		⊏		⊏	⊏	⊏	⌶		⌶	⌶		⊏		⊠	⊠	⊠	⊠	⊠	
London Euston 15 ⊖66 d	16 20	16 30				16 33	16 40							16 43	16 46	16 57	17 00	17 07	17 10	17 10	
Watford Junction 66 d																					
Milton Keynes Central 66 d	16 50							←						17 13	17 19				17u41	17u41	
Rugby 66 d						17 23		17 23							17 47						
Nuneaton d						→									18 00				18 12	18 12	
Tamworth Low Level d															18 15	18 00					
Lichfield Trent Valley d															18 22	18 08					
Coventry 68 d											17 27			17 42							
Birmingham International 68 ✈ d											17 38			17 53							
BirminghamNewSt 12 68 ⇌ d									17 31	17 36	17 57		18 01	18 15							
Wolverhampton 7 ⇌ d									17 49	17 54	18 15		18 20	18 37							
Penkridge d										18 04			18 29								
Stafford d								17 58	18 03	18 10	18 28		18 36		18 42			18 24			
Stoke-on-Trent 84 a	17 48								18 18		18 43				19 02		18 24				
Macclesfield a				←					18 36		19 01						18 41				←
Crewe 10 81,91 a				18 08			18 10	18 17		18 30			18 57	19 07	19 26			18 42	18 55	18 55	18 57
d				18 09			18 11	18 20		18 32			18 59	19 09				18 44	18 57	18 57	18 59
Chester 81 a													→	→					19 16	19 16	
Wrexham General 75 a																					
Llandudno Junction 81 a																				20 11	
Bangor (Gwynedd) 81 a																				20 28	
Holyhead 81 ⛴ a																				21 00	
Wilmslow 84 a							18 27														
Stockport 84 a	18 16						18 36		18 49		19 13						18 54				
Manchester Piccadilly 10 ⇌ a	18 27						18 48		18 59		19 24						19 05				
Runcorn 91 a										18 56								19 00			19 21
Liverpool South Pkwy 7 91 ✈ a										19 05											19 30
Liverpool Lime Street 10 91 a										19 17								19 20			19 42
d																					
Manchester Airport 82 ✈⇌ d			17 42									18 10									
Manchester Picc. 10 82 ⇌ d			18 01									18 26									
Bolton 82 d			18 21																		
Warrington Bank Quay d		18 15		18 27				18 37								18 50					
Wigan North Western 90 d		18 26		18 38				18 48								19 01					
Preston 8 90 a		18 40	18 50	18 51				19 01				19 02				19 14					
Blackpool North 97 a					←			19 30													
Preston 8 90 d		18 43	18 58	18 53	18 58							19 04				19 15					
Lancaster 8 d		18 58	→	19 08	19 14							19 21				19 30					
Barrow-in-Furness 82 a					20 14																
Oxenholme Lake District 83 d				19 21								19 34				19 45					
Windermere 83 a																					
Penrith North Lakes d		19 32										19 59				20 10					
Carlisle 8 216 a		19 47		20 00								20 15				20 25					
d		19 48		20 01								20 16				20 25					
Lockerbie 225,226 d												20 35				20 44					
Carstairs 226,225 a																					
Motherwell 226 a																21 27					
Glasgow Central 15 216,226,225 a		20 59		21 15												21 44					
Haymarket ⇌ a												21s32									
Edinburgh 10 ⇌ a												21 39									
Fort William 227,400 a																					
Perth 229 a																					
Dundee 229 a																					
Aberdeen 229 a																					
Inverness 229 a																					

A To Barrow-in-Furness
B From London Euston
C From Manchester Airport
D To Blackpool North
E From Paignton
F From Bournemouth
G To Liverpool Lime Street
H To Edinburgh
I From Birmingham New Street

Refer to Operator websites for full information about Sleeper Services. Contact details for train operators available at National Rail Enquiries

Table T065-F

Mondays to Fridays

25 June to 7 December

London & West Midlands to North West England. London, West Midlands & Manchester to Scotland via the West Coast

	VT	VT	VT	TP	VT	VT	VT	XC	LM	XC	LM	VT	LM	VT	VT	VT	VT	VT	VT	VT	VT
	◇1	◇1	◇1	◇1	◇1	◇1	◇1	◇1	1	◇1	1	◇1	1	◇1	◇1	◇1	◇1	◇1	◇1	◇1	◇1
			A		B		A	C		D		E								A	
	⊠	⊠	⊏	⌶	⊠	⊠	⊠	⌶		⌶		⊏		⊠	⊠	⊠	⊠	⊠	⊠	⊏	⊠
London Euston 15 ⊖66 d	17 20	17 30			17 33	17 40						17 43	17 46	17 57	18 00	18 07	18 10	18 20	18 30		18 33
Watford Junction 66 d																					
Milton Keynes Central 66 d	17u50						←					18u13	18 19				18u41	18u50			
Rugby 66 d					18 23		18 23						18 47								19 23
Nuneaton d					→								19 00				19 13				
Tamworth Low Level d													19 15	19 00							
Lichfield Trent Valley d													19 22	19 08							
Coventry 68 d										18 27		18 42									
Birmingham International 68 ✈ d										18 38		18 53									
BirminghamNewSt 12 68 ⇌ d								18 31	18 36	18 57	19 01	19 15									
Wolverhampton 7 ⇌ d								18 49	18 54	19 15	19 20	19 37									
Penkridge d									19 04		19 29										
Stafford d							18 56	19 03	19 10	19 28	19 45		19 42			19 24					19 54
Stoke-on-Trent 84 a	18 48							19 18		19 43	20 06		20 02		19 24			19 48			
Macclesfield a			←					19 36		20 01					19 41					←	
Crewe 10 81,91 a			19 07			19 11	19 14		19 31		20 32	20 07	20 25			19 41	19 53			20 07	20 13
d			19 09			19 12	19 16		19 33			20 09				19 43	19 56			20 09	20 16
Chester 81 a												→					20 15				
Wrexham General 75 a																	20 38				
Llandudno Junction 81 a																	21 09				
Bangor (Gwynedd) 81 a																	21 25				
Holyhead 81 ⛴ a																	21 56				
Wilmslow 84 a						19 27															
Stockport 84 a	19 16					19 36		19 49		20 13					19 54			20 16			
Manchester Piccadilly 10 ⇌ a	19 28					19 45		19 59		20 25					20 05			20 28			
Runcorn 91 a							19 33		19 56							20 00					20 33
Liverpool South Pkwy 7 91 ✈ a									20 05												
Liverpool Lime Street 10 91 a							19 52		20 17							20 20					20 53
d																					
Manchester Airport 82 ✈⇌ d				19 10																	
Manchester Picc. 10 82 ⇌ d				19 26																	
Bolton 82 d																					
Warrington Bank Quay d		19 14	19 27											19 50					20 14	20 27	
Wigan North Western 90 d		19 25	19 38											20 01					20 25	20 38	
Preston 8 90 a		19 38	19 51	20 02										20 14					20 38	20 51	
Blackpool North 97 a																					
Preston 8 90 d		19 41	19 53	20 04										20 15					20 41	20 53	
Lancaster 8 d		19 55	20 08	20 20										20a30					20 55	21 08	
Barrow-in-Furness 82 a																					
Oxenholme Lake District 83 d		20 08		20 33															21 10	21 23	
Windermere 83 a																					
Penrith North Lakes d			20 45	20 58															21 35		
Carlisle 8 216 a		20 46	21 00	21 14															21 50	22 00	
d		20 47	21 02	21 18															21 50	22 02	
Lockerbie 225,226 d				21 37															22 09		
Carstairs 226,225 a																					
Motherwell 226 a		21 44		22 21															22 53		
Glasgow Central 15 216,226,225 a		22 02		22 38															23 09	23 17	
Haymarket ⇌ a			22 13																		
Edinburgh 10 ⇌ a			22 19																		
Fort William 227,400 a																					
Perth 229 a																					
Dundee 229 a																					
Aberdeen 229 a																					
Inverness 229 a																					

A From London Euston
B To Liverpool Lime Street
C From Bristol Temple Meads
D From Bournemouth
E To Glasgow Central

Refer to Operator websites for full information about Sleeper Services. Contact details for train operators available at National Rail Enquiries

London & West Midlands to North West England. London, West Midlands & Manchester to Scotland via the West Coast

	VT	XC	LM	XC	VT	TP	VT	LM	VT	VT	VT	VT	VT	VT	VT	VT	XC	LM	XC	VT	LM	VT
							FO		ThFO	FO												
		A		B			C			D							E		F			
London Euston ⊖66 d	18 40				18 43		18 46	18 49	18 57		19 00	19 10	19 10	19 20	19 30	19 40				19 43	19 46	20 00
Watford Junction 66 d																						
Milton Keynes Central 66 d					19 13		19 19	19 23				19u41	19u41	19u50						20 13	20 19	
Rugby 66 d							19 41	20 06													20 42	
Nuneaton d								20 19				20 12	20 12								21 00	
Tamworth Low Level d	19 44							20 32								20 43					21 15	
Lichfield Trent Valley d	19 51							20 38								20 50					21 22	
Coventry 68 d				19 27	19 42														20 27	20 42		
Birmingham International 68 ✈ d				19 38	19 53														20 38	20 53		
BirminghamNewSt 68 d		19 31	19 36	19 57	20 15												20 31	20 36	20 57	21 15		
Wolverhampton d		19 49	19 54	20 15	20 37												20 49	20 54	21 15	21 37		
Penkridge d			20 04															21 04				
Stafford d		20 03	20 10	20 28	20 51		20 24	20 55				20 37	20 37			21 04	21 03	21 10	21 29	21 55	21 42	
Stoke-on-Trent 84 a		20 19		20 43				21 11			20 24			20 49			21 18		21 45	22 10	22 01	21 25
Macclesfield a		20 36		21 01						←				21 06			21 36		22 02			21 41
Crewe 81,91 a	20 17		20 30		21 15		20 42	21 34	20s33	20 42		20 53	20 53			21 21		21 32		22 30	22 24	
d	20 18		20 33				20 43			20 43		20 55	20 55			21 23		21 33				
Chester 81 a							→					21 17	21 20									
Wrexham General 75 a																						
Llandudno Junction 81 a													22 14									
Bangor (Gwynedd) 81 a													22 30									
Holyhead 81 ⛴ a													23 01									
Wilmslow 84 a	20 33															21 38						
Stockport 84 a	20 42	20 48		21 13							20 53			21 19			21 49		22 15			21 54
Manchester Piccadilly a	20 52	20 59		21 25					21 09		21 05			21 28		21 54	21 59		22 25			22 04
Runcorn 91 a			20 56															21 55				
Liverpool South Pkwy 91 ✈ a			21 05															22 04				
Liverpool Lime Street 91 a			21 18															22 16				
d																						
Manchester Airport 82 ✈ d						20 10																
Manchester Picc. 82 d						20 26																
Bolton 82 d																						
Warrington Bank Quay d										21 03					21 16							
Wigan North Western 90 d										21 14					21 27							
Preston 90 a						21 02				21 31					21 39							
Blackpool North 97 a																						
Preston 90 d						21 04									21 42							
Lancaster d						21 20									21 57							
Barrow-in-Furness 82 a																						
Oxenholme Lake District 83 d						21 33									22 10							
Windermere 83 a																						
Penrith North Lakes d						21 58									22 35							
Carlisle 216 a						22 14									22 50							
d						22 15									22 51							
Lockerbie 225,226 d						22 34																
Carstairs 226,225 a																						
Motherwell 226 a																						
Glasgow Central 216,226,225 a															00 05							
Haymarket a						23s31																
Edinburgh a						23 38																
Fort William 227,400 a																						
Perth 229 a																						
Dundee 229 a																						
Aberdeen 229 a																						
Inverness 229 a																						

A From Exeter St Davids
B From Bournemouth
C To Preston
D From London Euston
E From Bristol Temple Meads
F From Bournemouth. ✂ to BirminghamNewSt

Refer to Operator websites for full information about Sleeper Services. Contact details for train operators available at National Rail Enquiries

Table T065-F

Mondays to Fridays

25 June to 7 December

London & West Midlands to North West England. London, West Midlands & Manchester to Scotland via the West Coast

	VT	VT	TP	VT	VT	VT	LM	XC	LM	NT	XC	NT	LM	AW	LM	VT	VT	VT	CS	CS
												FX							TW ThO	MFO
				A		B		C						D						
London Euston ⊖66 d	20 07	20 10		20 30	20 40				20 46						20 49	21 00	21 07	21 10	21 15	21 15
Watford Junction 66 d																		21u25	21u33	21u33
Milton Keynes Central 66 d		20 41							21 19						21 29	21 31	21 39			
Rugby 66 d									21 45						22 17			22 05		
Nuneaton d	21 03								22 00								22 08			
Tamworth Low Level d				21 35		←			22 15											
Lichfield Trent Valley d				21 42		21 42			22 22											
Coventry 68 d				→				21 27							22 30					
Birmingham International 68 ✈ d								21 38							22 46					
BirminghamNewSt 68 d							21 36	21 57			22 30		22 39	22 52	23 09					
Wolverhampton d							21 54	22 15			22 48		23 05	23 27	23 36					
Penkridge d							22 04						23 15		23 46					
Stafford d	21 27					22 00	22 10	22 28			23 01		23 21	23 43	23 53			22 37		
Stoke-on-Trent 84 a								22 43	22 50		23 17					22 28				
Macclesfield a								23 01								22 44				
Crewe 81,91 a	21 46	21 47			22 10	22 17	22 34		23 10				23 49	00 10	00 22		22 53	22 58		
d	21 48	21 49			22 11	22 19	22 36							00 15			22 53	22 59	23u50	23u50
Chester 81 a		22 13												→						
Wrexham General 75 a																				
Llandudno Junction 81 a																				
Bangor (Gwynedd) 81 a																				
Holyhead 81 ⛴ a																				
Wilmslow 84 a					22 27															
Stockport 84 a					22 36			23 13								22 58				
Manchester Piccadilly a					22 46			23 25			00 11					23 08				
Runcorn 91 a	22 05						22 59										23 11			
Liverpool South Pkwy 91 ✈ a							23 08													
Liverpool Lime Street 91 a	22 22						23 20										23 34			
d																				
Manchester Airport 82 ✈ d			21 05							22 10										
Manchester Picc. 82 d			21 22							22 26										
Bolton 82 d												22 30								
Warrington Bank Quay d						22 36												23 21		
Wigan North Western 90 d						22 47				22 57								23 32		
Preston 90 a			22 02			23 00				23 14		23 46						23 50		
Blackpool North 97 a																				
Preston 90 d			22 03							23 15									00u58	00u58
Lancaster d			22 19							23 33										
Barrow-in-Furness 82 a										00 37										
Oxenholme Lake District 83 d			22 33																	
Windermere 83 a																				
Penrith North Lakes d			22 58																	
Carlisle 216 a			23 16																	
d			23 18																	
Lockerbie 225,226 d			23 37																	
Carstairs 226,225 a																				
Motherwell 226 a																				
Glasgow Central 216,226,225 a			00 53																	
Haymarket a																				
Edinburgh a																				
Fort William 227,400 a																				
Perth 229 a																				
Dundee 229 a																			06s07	06s08
Aberdeen 229 a																			07 39	07 39
Inverness 229 a																				

A To Preston
B From London Euston
C From Bournemouth
D To Holyhead

Refer to Operator websites for full information about Sleeper Services. Contact details for train operators available at National Rail Enquiries

London & West Midlands to North West England. London, West Midlands & Manchester to Scotland via the West Coast

	CS		AW	VT	VT	VT	NT	CS	CS
							FX	FO	FX
	R							R	R
			◇	◇1	◇1	◇1			
			A						
	🛏 ✕			🍴	🍴	🍴	🚌	🛏 ✕	🛏 ✕
London Euston 15 ⊖66 d	21 15			21 40	22 00	23 00		23 50	23 50
Watford Junction 66 d	21u33					23u15		00u10	00u10
Milton Keynes Central 66 d					22 40				
Rugby 66 d					23 03				
Nuneaton d					23 14				
Tamworth Low Level d					23s26				
Lichfield Trent Valley d					23s33				
Coventry 68 d									
Birmingham International 68 ✈ d									
BirminghamNewSt 12 68 ⛴ d									
Wolverhampton 7 ⛴ d									
Penkridge d									
Stafford d					23s48				
Stoke-on-Trent 84 a				23 07		01s18			
Macclesfield a			←	23 24		01s34			
Crewe 10 81,91 a			00 10		00 17				
d	23u50		00 15						
Chester 81 a			00 37						
Wrexham General 75 a									
Llandudno Junction 81 a			01 28						
Bangor (Gwynedd) 81 a			01 46						
Holyhead 81 ⛴ a			02 15						
Wilmslow 84 a									
Stockport 84 a				23 38		01s48			
Manchester Piccadilly 10 ⛴ a				23 49		01 59			
Runcorn 91 a									
Liverpool South Pkwy 7 91 ✈ a									
Liverpool Lime Street 10 91 a									
d									
Manchester Airport 82 ✈⛴ d									
Manchester Picc. 10 82 ⛴ d							23 05		
Bolton 82 d							23 30		
Warrington Bank Quay d									
Wigan North Western 90 d									
Preston 8 90 a							00 46		
Blackpool North 97 a									
Preston 8 90 d	00u58	00u58							
Lancaster 8 d									
Barrow-in-Furness 82 a									
Oxenholme Lake District 83 d									
Windermere 83 a									
Penrith North Lakes d									
Carlisle 8 216 a								05s13	05s13
d									
Lockerbie 225,226 d									
Carstairs 226,225 a								06s21	06s22
Motherwell 226 a								06s55	06s55
Glasgow Central 15 216,226,225 a								07 22	07 22
Haymarket ⛴ a									
Edinburgh 10 ⛴ a									
Fort William 227,400 a		09 57							
Perth 229 a	05s41								
Dundee 229 a									
Aberdeen 229 a									
Inverness 229 a	08 41								

A From Birmingham New Street

Refer to Operator websites for full information about Sleeper Services. Contact details for train operators available at National Rail Enquiries

London & West Midlands to North West England. London, West Midlands & Manchester to Scotland via the West Coast

	NT	CS	AW	NT	CS	CS	CS	NT	NT	TP	VT	VT	XC	LM	TP	VT	XC	LM	LM	XC	TP	VT
		R			R	R	R															
	◇		◇	◇						◇1	◇1	◇1	◇1	1	◇1	◇1	◇1	1	1	◇1	◇1	◇1
	A	B	C	D	B	B	B												E			
		🛏 ✕			🛏 ✕	🛏 ✕	🛏 ✕			🍴	🍴	🍴			🍴	🍴	🍴			🍴	🍴	🍴
London Euston 15 ⊖66 d																						06 05
Watford Junction 66 d		00u10																				06u20
Milton Keynes Central 66 d																						06 41
Rugby 66 d																			06 02			07 03
Nuneaton d																			06 16			
Tamworth Low Level d																			06 29			
Lichfield Trent Valley d																			06 35			
Coventry 68 d																						
Birmingham International 68 ✈ d																		06 18				
BirminghamNewSt 12 68 ⛴ d												05 30	05 57	06 01		06 15	06 31	06 36		06 57		
Wolverhampton 7 ⛴ d												05 48	06 15	06 20		06 37	06 49	06 54		07 15		
Penkridge d														06 29				07 04				
Stafford d												06 01	06 28	06 36			07 03	07 10	06 58	07 31		07 34
Stoke-on-Trent 84 a													06 44				07 18		07 14			
Macclesfield a													07 05				07 36					
Crewe 10 81,91 a												06 20		06 56		07 08		07 29	07 37	07 50		07 53
d			00 15								05 57	06 23		06 59		07 09		07 33		07 52		07 55
Chester 81 a			00 37									06 43										
Wrexham General 75 a																						
Llandudno Junction 81 a			01 28									07 32										
Bangor (Gwynedd) 81 a			01 46									07 49										
Holyhead 81 ⛴ a			02 15									08 20										
Wilmslow 84 a																				08 07		
Stockport 84 a													07 18				07 49			08 16		
Manchester Piccadilly 10 ⛴ a													07 28				07 59			08 29		
Runcorn 91 a														07 24				07 59				
Liverpool South Pkwy 7 91 ✈ a														07 33				08 09				
Liverpool Lime Street 10 91 a														07 44				08 21				
d																						
Manchester Airport 82 ✈⛴ d															06 10						07 10	
Manchester Picc. 10 82 ⛴ d	00 09									04 54					06 26						07 26	
Bolton 82 d				00 41																		
Warrington Bank Quay d											06 15					07 27						08 12
Wigan North Western 90 d											06 25					07 38						08 23
Preston 8 90 a	00 59			01 06						05 30	06 38				07 01	07 51					08 01	08 36
Blackpool North 97 a	01 29																					
Preston 8 90 d					00u58	00u58	00u58	05 16		05 40	06 40				07 03	07 53					08 03	08 37
Lancaster 8 d								05 36	05 40	05 56	06 54				07 18	08 08					08 18	08 52
Barrow-in-Furness 82 a																						
Oxenholme Lake District 83 d									06 19	06 10	07 09				07 32	08 22					08 32	09 06
Windermere 83 a									06 39													
Penrith North Lakes d										06 35	07 34										08 57	09 32
Carlisle 8 216 a		05s13						09 24		06 51	07 49				08 10	09 00					09 12	09 47
d										06 52	07 51				08 12	09 01					09 14	09 48
Lockerbie 225,226 d										07 11	08 10				08 30						09 33	
Carstairs 226,225 a		06s21								07 44												
Motherwell 226 a		06s55								07 59											10 20	
Glasgow Central 15 216,226,225 a		07 22								08 20	09 12										10 39	10 59
Haymarket ⛴ a															09s30	10 13						
Edinburgh 10 ⛴ a															09 37	10 18						
Fort William 227,400 a							09 57															
Perth 229 a						05s41																
Dundee 229 a					06s08																	
Aberdeen 229 a					07 39																	
Inverness 229 a						08 41																

A From Manchester Airport
B From London Euston
C From Birmingham New Street
D From Manchester Victoria
E From Northampton

Refer to Operator websites for full information about Sleeper Services. Contact details for train operators available at National Rail Enquiries

Table T065-F

Saturdays
26 May to 16 June

London & West Midlands to North West England. London, West Midlands & Manchester to Scotland via the West Coast

		LM ■	VT ◇■	LM ■	VT ◇■	TP ◇■	VT ◇■	XC ◇■	LM ■	LM ■ A	VT ◇■	VT ◇■	XC ◇■ B	VT ◇■	LM ■	NT ◇	VT ◇■	NT ◇ C	VT ◇■	NT ◇ D	VT ◇■	XC ◇■ E	LM ■
London Euston ⊖66	d			06 24	06 36						06 55	07 07		07 20			07 30				07 35		
Watford Junction 66	d			06 41	06u51																		
Milton Keynes Central 66	d			07 24							07 27			07 50							08 06		
Rugby 66	d			08 04						06 58													
Nuneaton	d			08 16						07 12													
Tamworth Low Level	d			08 29						07 29													
Lichfield Trent Valley	d			08 35						07 35													
Coventry 68	d												07 27										
Birmingham International 68	d												07 38										
BirminghamNewSt 68	d	07 01	07 15				07 21	07 31	07 36				07 57		08 01				08 15			08 31	08 36
Wolverhampton	d	07 20	07 37				07 41	07 49	07 54				08 15		08 20				08 37			08 49	08 54
Penkridge	d	07 29							08 04						08 29								09 04
Stafford	d	07 36		08 55			07 59	08 03	08 10	07 55		08 24	08 28		08 36							09 03	09 10
Stoke-on-Trent 84	a			09 12				08 18		08 12	08 24		08 43	08 48								09 18	
Macclesfield	a							08 36			08 41		09 01									09 36	
Crewe 81,91	a	07 58	08 06	09 37	08 10		08 18		08 30	08 37		08 41			08 56				09 08		09 11		09 30
	d	07 59	08 09		08 11		08 19		08 32			08 43			08 57				09 09		09 12		09 32
Chester 81	a																						
Wrexham General 75	a																						
Llandudno Junction 81	a																						
Bangor (Gwynedd) 81	a																						
Holyhead 81	a																						
Wilmslow 84	a				08 27																09 28		
Stockport 84	a				08 35			08 50			08 54		09 13	09 16							09 36	09 49	
Manchester Piccadilly	a				08 46			08 59			09 04		09 25	09 28							09 44	09 59	
Runcorn 91	a	08 24							08 52			09 00			09 21								09 52
Liverpool South Pkwy 91	a	08 32							09 01						09 30								10 01
Liverpool Lime Street 91	a	08 44							09 11			09 20			09 42								10 11
	d																						
Manchester Airport 82	d					08 10												08 41					
Manchester Picc. 82	d					08 26												09 01					
Bolton 82	d																	09 22					
Warrington Bank Quay	d		08 27				08 41										09 14		09 27				
Wigan North Western 90	d		08 38				08 52										09 25		09 38				
Preston 90	a		08 51			09 02	09 09										09 38	09 49	09 51				
Blackpool North 97	a						09 32													←			
Preston 90	d		08 53			09 04										09 29	09 41	09 57	09 53	09 57			
Lancaster	d		09 09			09 19										09 59	09 55	→	10 08	10 14			
Barrow-in-Furness 82	a																			11 15			
Oxenholme Lake District 83	d															10 19			10 22				
Windermere 83	a															10 41							
Penrith North Lakes	d		09 46														10 31						
Carlisle 216	a		10 01			10 07											10 46		10 59				
	d		10 01			10 09											10 47		11 01				
Lockerbie 225,226	d					10 27																	
Carstairs 226,225	a																						
Motherwell 226	a																						
Glasgow Central 216,226,225	a		11 15														11 59						
Haymarket	a					11s27													12 17				
Edinburgh	a					11 34													12 22				
Fort William 227,400	a																						
Perth 229	a																						
Dundee 229	a																						
Aberdeen 229	a																						
Inverness 229	a																						

A From Northampton
B From Southampton Central
C To Barrow-in-Furness
D From Manchester Airport
E From Bristol Temple Meads

Refer to Operator websites for full information about Sleeper Services. Contact details for train operators available at National Rail Enquiries

Table T065-F

Saturdays
26 May to 16 June

London & West Midlands to North West England. London, West Midlands & Manchester to Scotland via the West Coast

		XC ◇■ A	TP ◇■	LM ■ B	VT ◇■ C	LM ■	VT ◇■	VT ◇■	VT ◇■	LM ■ D	VT ◇■	VT ◇■	VT ◇■ E	VT ◇■	XC ◇■ F	LM ■	XC ◇■ G	TP ◇■	LM ■ B	VT ◇■ H	LM ■	VT ◇■
London Euston ⊖66	d				07 43	07 46	08 00	08 07	08 10		08 20	08 30		08 40						08 43	08 46	08 53
Watford Junction 66	d																					
Milton Keynes Central 66	d				08 13	08 19			08 41		08 50									09 13	09 19	
Rugby 66	d					08 42															09 42	09 46
Nuneaton	d					08 54															09 54	
Tamworth Low Level	d					09 09															10 09	
Lichfield Trent Valley	d					09 17															10 17	
Coventry 68	d	08 27			08 42												09 27			09 42		
Birmingham International 68	d	08 38			08 53												09 38			09 53		
BirminghamNewSt 68	d	08 57		09 01	09 15										09 31	09 36	09 57		10 01	10 15		
Wolverhampton	d	09 15		09 20	09 37										09 49	09 54	10 15		10 20	10 37		
Penkridge	d															10 04						
Stafford	d	09 28		09 35		09 42		09 24							10 03	10 10	10 28		10 35		10 42	
Stoke-on-Trent 84	a	09 43				10 02	09 24				09 48				10 18		10 43				11 02	
Macclesfield	a	10 01					09 41			←			←		10 36		11 01					
Crewe 81,91	a			09 55	10 08	10 24		09 41	09 47	09 55			10 08	10 11		10 30			10 55	11 08	11 24	
	d			09 57	10 09			09 43	09 49	09 57			10 09	10 12		10 32			10 57	11 09		
Chester 81	a			→	→				10 10										→	→		
Wrexham General 75	a																					
Llandudno Junction 81	a																					
Bangor (Gwynedd) 81	a																					
Holyhead 81	a																					
Wilmslow 84	a													10 27								
Stockport 84	a	10 13					09 54				10 16			10 36	10 49		11 13					
Manchester Piccadilly	a	10 24					10 04				10 28			10 46	11 00		11 25					
Runcorn 91	a							10 00		10 24						10 52						
Liverpool South Pkwy 91	a									10 32						11 01						
Liverpool Lime Street 91	a							10 19		10 44						11 11						
	d																					
Manchester Airport 82	d		09 10															10 10				
Manchester Picc. 82	d		09 26															10 26				
Bolton 82	d																					
Warrington Bank Quay	d											10 14	10 27									10 59
Wigan North Western 90	d											10 25	10 38									11 12
Preston 90	a		10 03									10 38	10 51					11 02				11 24
Blackpool North 97	a																					11 56
Preston 90	d		10 04									10 41	10 53					11 03				
Lancaster	d		10 20									10 55	11 08									
Barrow-in-Furness 82	a																					
Oxenholme Lake District 83	d		10 35									11 08										
Windermere 83	a																					
Penrith North Lakes	d		11 00										11 45									
Carlisle 216	a		11 16									11 46	12 00					12 05				
	d		11 17									11 47	12 02					12 06				
Lockerbie 225,226	d		11 37																			
Carstairs 226,225	a																					
Motherwell 226	a		12 22																			
Glasgow Central 216,226,225	a		12 44									12 59	13 15									
Haymarket	a																	13s19				
Edinburgh	a																	13 26				
Fort William 227,400	a																					
Perth 229	a																					
Dundee 229	a																					
Aberdeen 229	a																					
Inverness 229	a																					

A From Southampton Central
B To Liverpool Lime Street
C To Glasgow Central
D From Birmingham New Street
E From London Euston
F From Cardiff Central
G From Bournemouth
H To Edinburgh

Refer to Operator websites for full information about Sleeper Services. Contact details for train operators available at National Rail Enquiries

Table T065-F

Saturdays
26 May to 16 June

London & West Midlands to North West England. London, West Midlands & Manchester to Scotland via the West Coast

	VT ◇■	VT ◇■	VT ◇■	LM ■ A	VT ◇■	VT ◇■	VT ◇■ B	VT ◇■	XC ◇■ C	LM ■	XC ◇■ D	TP ◇■	NT ◇	LM ■ E	VT ◇■ F	LM ■	VT ◇■	VT ◇■	VT ◇■	LM ■ A	VT ◇■	VT ◇■
London Euston ⊖66 d	09 00	09 07	09 10		09 20	09 30		09 40							09 43	09 46	10 00	10 07	10 10		10 20	10 30
Watford Junction 66 d																						
Milton Keynes Central 66 d			09 41		09 50										10 13	10 19			10 41		10 50	
Rugby 66 d																10 42						
Nuneaton d																10 54						
Tamworth Low Level d																11 09						
Lichfield Trent Valley d																11 17			11 24			
Coventry 68 d											10 27				10 42							
Birmingham International 68 d											10 38				10 53							
BirminghamNewSt 68 d									10 31	10 36	10 57			11 01	11 15							
Wolverhampton d									10 49	10 54	11 15			11 20	11 37							
Penkridge d										11 04												
Stafford d		10 26							11 03	11 10	11 28			11 35		11 42		11 24				
Stoke-on-Trent 84 a	10 24				10 48				11 18		11 43					12 02	11 24				11 48	
Macclesfield a	10 41			←			←		11 36		12 01						11 41			←		
Crewe 81,91 a		10 44	10 47	10 55			11 08	11 11		11 30				11 54	12 07	12 24		11 41	11 53	11 54		
d		10 46	10 49	10 57			11 09	11 12		11 32				11 57	12 09			11 43	11 56	11 57		
Chester 81 a			11 13											→	→				12 17			
Wrexham General 75 a																						
Llandudno Junction 81 a			12 00																			
Bangor (Gwynedd) 81 a			12 16																			
Holyhead 81 a			12 47																			
Wilmslow 84 a								11 27														
Stockport 84 a	10 54				11 16			11 35	11 49		12 13						11 54				12 16	
Manchester Piccadilly a	11 04				11 28			11 46	11 59		12 25						12 04				12 28	
Runcorn 91 a		11 03		11 21						11 52								12 00		12 24		
Liverpool South Pkwy 91 a				11 30						12 01										12 32		
Liverpool Lime Street 91 a		11 20		11 42						12 11								12 19		12 44		
d																						
Manchester Airport 82 d												10 59										
Manchester Picc. 82 d												11 14										
Bolton 82 d																						
Warrington Bank Quay d						11 14	11 27															12 14
Wigan North Western 90 d						11 25	11 38															12 25
Preston 90 a						11 38	11 51					11 58										12 38
Blackpool North 97 a																						
Preston 90 d						11 41	11 53					12 04	12 17									12 41
Lancaster d						11 55	12 08					12 20	12 37									12 55
Barrow-in-Furness 82 a																						
Oxenholme Lake District 83 d							12 21					12 33	13 02									13 08
Windermere 83 a													13 24									
Penrith North Lakes d						12 30						12 58										
Carlisle 216 a						12 46	12 59					13 14										13 46
d						12 47	13 01					13 17										13 47
Lockerbie 225,226 d												13 37										
Carstairs 226,225 a																						
Motherwell 226 a												14 21										
Glasgow Central 216,226,225 a						13 59						14 40										14 59
Haymarket a							14 11															
Edinburgh a							14 17															
Fort William 227,400 a																						
Perth 229 a																						
Dundee 229 a																						
Aberdeen 229 a																						
Inverness 229 a																						

A From Birmingham New Street
B From London Euston
C From Paignton
D From Bournemouth
E To Liverpool Lime Street
F To Glasgow Central

Refer to Operator websites for full information about Sleeper Services. Contact details for train operators available at National Rail Enquiries

Table T065-F

Saturdays
26 May to 16 June

London & West Midlands to North West England. London, West Midlands & Manchester to Scotland via the West Coast

	NT ◇ A	VT ◇■ B	NT ◇ C	VT ◇■	VT ◇■	XC ◇■ D	LM ■	XC ◇■ E	TP ◇■	LM ■ F	VT ◇■ G	LM ■	VT ◇■	VT ◇■	VT ◇■	LM ■ H	VT ◇■	VT ◇■	VT ◇■ B	VT ◇■	XC ◇■ I
London Euston ⊖66 d				10 36	10 40						10 43	10 46	11 00	11 07	11 10		11 20	11 30		11 40	
Watford Junction 66 d																					
Milton Keynes Central 66 d											11 13	11 19			11 41		11 50				
Rugby 66 d				11 28								11 42									
Nuneaton d												11 54									
Tamworth Low Level d												12 09									
Lichfield Trent Valley d												12 17									
Coventry 68 d								11 27			11 42										
Birmingham International 68 d								11 38			11 53										
BirminghamNewSt 68 d						11 31	11 36	11 57		12 01	12 15										12 31
Wolverhampton d						11 49	11 54	12 15		12 20	12 37										12 49
Penkridge d							12 04														
Stafford d						12 03	12 10	12 28		12 35		12 42		12 24							13 03
Stoke-on-Trent 84 a						12 18		12 43				13 02	12 24				12 48				13 18
Macclesfield a		←				12 36		13 01					12 41			←			←		13 36
Crewe 81,91 a		12 07			12 11		12 30			12 54	13 08	13 24		12 42	12 47	12 54			13 08	13 11	
d		12 09			12 12		12 32			12 57	13 09			12 43	12 49	12 57			13 09	13 12	
Chester 81 a										→	→				13 11						
Wrexham General 75 a																					
Llandudno Junction 81 a																					
Bangor (Gwynedd) 81 a																					
Holyhead 81 a																					
Wilmslow 84 a					12 27															13 27	
Stockport 84 a					12 35	12 49		13 13					12 55				13 16			13 35	13 49
Manchester Piccadilly a					12 46	12 59		13 25					13 04				13 28			13 46	13 59
Runcorn 91 a							12 52							13 00		13 22					
Liverpool South Pkwy 91 a							13 01									13 31					
Liverpool Lime Street 91 a							13 11							13 19		13 42					
d																					
Manchester Airport 82 d	11 41								12 10												
Manchester Picc. 82 d	12 01								12 26												
Bolton 82 d	12 22																				
Warrington Bank Quay d		12 27		12 34														13 14	13 27		
Wigan North Western 90 d		12 38		12 45														13 25	13 38		
Preston 90 a	12 48	12 52		12 57					13 02									13 38	13 51		
Blackpool North 97 a			←	13 20																	
Preston 90 d	12 57	12 53	12 57						13 03									13 41	13 53		
Lancaster d	→	13 08	13 14						13 20									13 55	14 08		
Barrow-in-Furness 82 a			14 14																		
Oxenholme Lake District 83 d		13 23							13 33									14 08			
Windermere 83 a																					
Penrith North Lakes d																			14 43		
Carlisle 216 a		14 00							14 12									14 46	14 59		
d		14 01							14 13									14 47	14 59		
Lockerbie 225,226 d									14 32												
Carstairs 226,225 a																					
Motherwell 226 a		14 58																			
Glasgow Central 216,226,225 a		15 15																15 59			
Haymarket a									15s29										16 16		
Edinburgh a									15 36										16 23		
Fort William 227,400 a																					
Perth 229 a																					
Dundee 229 a																					
Aberdeen 229 a																					
Inverness 229 a																					

A To Barrow-in-Furness
B From London Euston
C From Manchester Airport
D From Bristol Temple Meads
E From Bournemouth
F To Liverpool Lime Street
G To Edinburgh
H From Birmingham New Street
I From Plymouth

Refer to Operator websites for full information about Sleeper Services. Contact details for train operators available at National Rail Enquiries

Table T065-F

Saturdays
26 May to 16 June

London & West Midlands to North West England. London, West Midlands & Manchester to Scotland via the West Coast

Station	LM	XC A	TP	NT	LM B	VT C	LM	VT	VT	VT	LM D	VT	VT	NT	VT E	VT	XC F	LM	XC A	TP	LM B	VT G
London Euston ⊖66 d						11 43	11 46	12 00	12 07	12 10		12 20	12 30			12 40						12 43
Watford Junction 66 d																						
Milton Keynes Central 66 d						12 13	12 19			12 41		12 50										13 13
Rugby 66 d							12 42			13 04												
Nuneaton d							12 54															
Tamworth Low Level d							13 09															
Lichfield Trent Valley d							13 17															
Coventry 68 d		12 27				12 42													13 27			13 42
Birmingham International 68 d		12 38				12 53													13 38			13 53
BirminghamNewSt 68 d	12 36	12 57			13 01	13 15											13 31	13 36	13 57		14 01	14 15
Wolverhampton d	12 54	13 15			13 20	13 37											13 49	13 54	14 15		14 20	14 37
Penkridge d	13 04																	14 04				
Stafford d	13 10	13 28			13 35		13 42		13 24								14 03	14 10	14 28		14 35	
Stoke-on-Trent 84 a		13 43					14 02	13 24				13 48					14 18		14 43			
Macclesfield a		14 01						13 41			←				←		14 36		15 01			
Crewe 81,91 a	13 30				13 56	14 08	14 24		13 41	13 50	13 56				14 08	14 11		14 30			14 55	15 07
d	13 32				13 57	14 09			13 43	13 52	13 57				14 09	14 12		14 32			14 57	15 09
Chester 81 a					→	→				14 15											→	→
Wrexham General 75 a																						
Llandudno Junction 81 a																						
Bangor (Gwynedd) 81 a																						
Holyhead 81 a																						
Wilmslow 84 a																14 27						
Stockport 84 a		14 13						13 54				14 16				14 35	14 49		15 13			
Manchester Piccadilly a		14 25						14 05				14 28				14 46	14 59		15 25			
Runcorn 91 a	13 52								14 00		14 21							14 52				
Liverpool South Pkwy 91 a	14 01										14 30							15 01				
Liverpool Lime Street 91 a	14 11								14 20		14 42							15 11				
d																						
Manchester Airport 82 d			13 10																	14 10		
Manchester Picc. 82 d			13 26																	14 26		
Bolton 82 d																						
Warrington Bank Quay d													14 14		14 27							
Wigan North Western 90 d													14 25		14 38							
Preston 90 a			14 02										14 38		14 51					15 03		
Blackpool North 97 a																						
Preston 90 d			14 04	14 10									14 41		14 53					15 04		
Lancaster d			14 19	14 30									14 55	15 03	15 09					15 20		
Barrow-in-Furness 82 a														16 07								
Oxenholme Lake District 83 d			14 33	14 51											15 22							
Windermere 83 a				15 09																		
Penrith North Lakes d			14 58										15 30							15 55		
Carlisle 216 a			15 13										15 45	18 41	16 00					16 11		
d			15 14										15 46		16 02					16 13		
Lockerbie 225,226 d			15 33																	16 32		
Carstairs 226,225 a																						
Motherwell 226 a			16 21																			
Glasgow Central 216,226,225 a			16 40										16 59		17 15							
Haymarket a																				17s31		
Edinburgh a																				17 36		
Fort William 227,400 a																						
Perth 229 a																						
Dundee 229 a																						
Aberdeen 229 a																						
Inverness 229 a																						

A From Bournemouth
B To Liverpool Lime Street
C To Glasgow Central
D From Birmingham New Street
E From London Euston
F From Paignton
G To Edinburgh

Refer to Operator websites for full information about Sleeper Services. Contact details for train operators available at National Rail Enquiries

Table T065-F

Saturdays
26 May to 16 June

London & West Midlands to North West England. London, West Midlands & Manchester to Scotland via the West Coast

Station	LM	VT	VT	VT	LM A	VT	VT	VT B	NT	VT	XC C	LM	XC D	TP	LM E	VT F	LM	VT	VT	VT	LM A	VT
London Euston ⊖66 d	12 46	13 00	13 07	13 10		13 20	13 30			13 40						13 43	13 46	14 00	14 07	14 10		14 20
Watford Junction 66 d																						
Milton Keynes Central 66 d	13 19			13 41		13 50										14 13	14 19			14 41		14 50
Rugby 66 d	13 42																14 42					
Nuneaton d	13 54																14 54					
Tamworth Low Level d	14 09																15 09					
Lichfield Trent Valley d	14 17																15 17					
Coventry 68 d													14 27			14 42						
Birmingham International 68 d													14 38			14 53						
BirminghamNewSt 68 d											14 31	14 36	14 57		15 01	15 15						
Wolverhampton d											14 49	14 54	15 15		15 20	15 37						
Penkridge d												15 04										
Stafford d	14 42		14 24								15 03	15 10	15 28		15 35		15 42		15 24			
Stoke-on-Trent 84 a	15 02	14 24				14 48					15 18		15 43				16 02	15 24				15 48
Macclesfield a		14 41			←			←			15 36		16 01					15 41			←	
Crewe 81,91 a	15 24		14 41	14 47	14 55			15 07		15 10		15 30			15 55	16 08	16 24		15 41	15 47	15 55	
d			14 43	14 49	14 57			15 09		15 11		15 32			15 57	16 09			15 43	15 49	15 57	
Chester 81 a				15 09											→	→				16 10		
Wrexham General 75 a																						
Llandudno Junction 81 a																				17 01		
Bangor (Gwynedd) 81 a																				17 17		
Holyhead 81 a																				17 48		
Wilmslow 84 a										15 27												
Stockport 84 a		14 54				15 16				15 35	15 49		16 13					15 54				16 16
Manchester Piccadilly a		15 05				15 28				15 46	15 59		16 25					16 05				16 28
Runcorn 91 a			15 00		15 21							15 52							16 00		16 25	
Liverpool South Pkwy 91 a					15 30							16 01									16 33	
Liverpool Lime Street 91 a			15 19		15 42							16 11							16 20		16 44	
d																						
Manchester Airport 82 d														15 10								
Manchester Picc. 82 d														15 26								
Bolton 82 d																						
Warrington Bank Quay d							15 14	15 27														
Wigan North Western 90 d							15 25	15 38														
Preston 90 a							15 38	15 51						16 02								
Blackpool North 97 a																						
Preston 90 d							15 40	15 53						16 03								
Lancaster d							15 54	16 08	16 13					16 19								
Barrow-in-Furness 82 a									17 16													
Oxenholme Lake District 83 d							16 10							16 32								
Windermere 83 a																						
Penrith North Lakes d								16 44						16 57								
Carlisle 216 a							16 48	17 00	19 43					17 13								
d							16 48	17 01						17 14								
Lockerbie 225,226 d																						
Carstairs 226,225 a																						
Motherwell 226 a																						
Glasgow Central 216,226,225 a							17 59							18 31								
Haymarket a								18 14														
Edinburgh a								18 22														
Fort William 227,400 a																						
Perth 229 a																						
Dundee 229 a																						
Aberdeen 229 a																						
Inverness 229 a																						

A From Birmingham New Street
B From London Euston
C From Bristol Temple Meads
D From Bournemouth
E To Liverpool Lime Street
F To Glasgow Central

Refer to Operator websites for full information about Sleeper Services. Contact details for train operators available at National Rail Enquiries

Table T065-F

Saturdays
26 May to 16 June

London & West Midlands to North West England. London, West Midlands & Manchester to Scotland via the West Coast

	VT ◇■ ⊡	NT	VT ◇■ A ⊡	VT ◇■ ⊡	XC ◇■ B ✕	LM ■	XC ◇■ C ✕	TP ◇■ ✕	LM ■ D	VT ■ ■ E ⊡	LM ■	VT ◇■ ⊡	VT ◇■ ⊡	VT ◇■ ⊡	LM ■ F	VT ◇■ ⊡	VT ◇■ ⊡	VT ■ ■ A ⊡	VT ◇■ ⊡	XC ◇■ B ✕	LM ■
London Euston ■ ⊖66 d	14 30			14 40						14 43	14 46	15 00	15 07	15 10		15 20	15 30		15 40		
Watford Junction 66 d																					
Milton Keynes Central 66 d										15 13	15 19			15 41		15 50					
Rugby 66 d											15 42										
Nuneaton d											15 54										
Tamworth Low Level d											16 09										
Lichfield Trent Valley d											16 17										
Coventry 68 d							15 27			15 42											
Birmingham International 68 ✈ d							15 38			15 53											
BirminghamNewSt ■ 68 ⛴ d					15 31	15 36	15 57		16 01	16 15										16 31	16 36
Wolverhampton ■ ⛴ d					15 49	15 54	16 15		16 20	16 37										16 49	16 54
Penkridge d						16 04			16 29												17 04
Stafford d					16 03	16 10	16 28		16 36		16 42		16 24							17 03	17 10
Stoke-on-Trent 84 a					16 18		16 43				17 02	16 24				16 48				17 18	
Macclesfield a			←		16 36		17 01					16 41			←			←		17 36	
Crewe ■ 81,91 a			16 08	16 10		16 30			16 55	17 08	17 24		16 41	16 47	16 55			17 08	17 11		17 30
d			16 09	16 11		16 32			16 57	17 09			16 43	16 49	16 57			17 09	17 12		17 32
Chester 81 a									→	→				17 11							
Wrexham General 75 a																					
Llandudno Junction 81 a																					
Bangor (Gwynedd) 81 a																					
Holyhead 81 ⛴ a																					
Wilmslow 84 a				16 27															17 27		
Stockport 84 a				16 36	16 49		17 13					16 54				17 16			17 36	17 49	
Manchester Piccadilly ■ ⛴ a				16 46	16 59		17 25					17 04				17 28			17 46	17 59	
Runcorn 91 a						16 52							17 00		17 24						17 52
Liverpool South Pkwy ■ 91 ✈ a						17 01									17 33						18 01
Liverpool Lime Street ■ 91 a						17 11							17 20		17 44						18 11
d																					
Manchester Airport 82 ✈⛴ d								16 10													
Manchester Picc. ■ 82 ⛴ d								16 26													
Bolton 82 d																					
Warrington Bank Quay d	16 14		16 27														17 14	17 27			
Wigan North Western 90 d	16 25		16 38														17 25	17 38			
Preston ■ 90 a	16 38		16 51					17 02									17 38	17 51			
Blackpool North 97 a																					
Preston ■ 90 d	16 41		16 53					17 03									17 41	17 53			
Lancaster ■ d	16 55	17 01	17 08					17 19									17 55	18 08			
Barrow-in-Furness 82 a		17 59																			
Oxenholme Lake District 83 d			17 22					17 32									18 08	18 23			
Windermere 83 a																					
Penrith North Lakes d	17 30							17 57										18 48			
Carlisle ■ 216 a	17 46	20 31	18 00					18 12									18 46	19 04			
d	17 47		18 02					18 13									18 47	19 04			
Lockerbie 225,226 d								18 32													
Carstairs 226,225 a																					
Motherwell 226 a																					
Glasgow Central ■ 216,226,225 a	18 59		19 15														19 59				
Haymarket ⛴ a								19s29										20 14			
Edinburgh ■ ⛴ a								19 34										20 21			
Fort William 227,400 a																					
Perth 229 a																					
Dundee 229 a																					
Aberdeen 229 a																					
Inverness 229 a																					

A From London Euston
B From Bristol Temple Meads
C From Bournemouth
D To Liverpool Lime Street
E To Edinburgh
F From Birmingham New Street

Refer to Operator websites for full information about Sleeper Services. Contact details for train operators available at National Rail Enquiries

Table T065-F

Saturdays
26 May to 16 June

London & West Midlands to North West England. London, West Midlands & Manchester to Scotland via the West Coast

	XC ◇■ A ✕	TP ◇■ ✕	NT ◇	LM ■ B	VT ■ ■ C ⊡	LM ■	VT ◇■ ⊡	VT ◇■ ⊡	VT ◇■ ⊡	LM ■ D	VT ◇■ ⊡	VT ◇■ ⊡	VT ◇■ ⊡	NT ◇ E	VT ■ ■ F ⊡	NT ◇ G	VT ◇■ ⊡	XC ◇■ H ✕	LM ■	XC ◇■ A ✕	TP ◇■ ✕	LM ■ B
London Euston ■ ⊖66 d					15 43	15 46	16 00	16 07	16 10		16 20	16 30	16 33				16 40					
Watford Junction 66 d																						
Milton Keynes Central 66 d					16 13	16 19			16 41		16 50											
Rugby 66 d						16 42																
Nuneaton d						16 54																
Tamworth Low Level d						17 09							17 38									
Lichfield Trent Valley d						17 17							17 45									
Coventry 68 d	16 27				16 42															17 27		
Birmingham International 68 ✈ d	16 38				16 53															17 38		
BirminghamNewSt ■ 68 ⛴ d	16 57			17 01	17 15													17 31	17 36	17 57		18 01
Wolverhampton ■ ⛴ d	17 15			17 20	17 37													17 49	17 54	18 15		18 20
Penkridge d				17 29															18 04			18 29
Stafford d	17 28			17 36		17 42		17 24					17 59					18 03	18 10	18 28		18 36
Stoke-on-Trent 84 a	17 43					18 02	17 24				17 48							18 18		18 43		
Macclesfield a	18 01						17 41			←					←			18 36		19 01		
Crewe ■ 81,91 a				17 55	18 07	18 24		17 41	17 47	17 55					18 07		18 10		18 30			18 55
d				17 57	18 09			17 43	17 49	17 57					18 09		18 11		18 32			18 57
Chester 81 a				→	→				18 10													→
Wrexham General 75 a																						
Llandudno Junction 81 a									19 05													
Bangor (Gwynedd) 81 a									19 21													
Holyhead 81 ⛴ a									19 52													
Wilmslow 84 a																	18 27					
Stockport 84 a	18 13						17 54				18 16						18 36	18 49		19 13		
Manchester Piccadilly ■ ⛴ a	18 25						18 04				18 27						18 45	18 59		19 24		
Runcorn 91 a								18 00		18 24			18 32						18 52			
Liverpool South Pkwy ■ 91 ✈ a										18 32									19 01			
Liverpool Lime Street ■ 91 a								18 19		18 44			18 52						19 11			
d																						
Manchester Airport 82 ✈⛴ d		17 10												17 42							18 10	
Manchester Picc. ■ 82 ⛴ d		17 27												18 01							18 26	
Bolton 82 d														18 21								
Warrington Bank Quay d												18 14			18 27							
Wigan North Western 90 d												18 25			18 38							
Preston ■ 90 a		18 02										18 38		18 50	18 51						19 03	
Blackpool North 97 a																←						
Preston ■ 90 d		18 03	18 20									18 41		18 58	18 54	18 58					19 05	
Lancaster ■ d		18 19	18 40									18 55		→	19 09	19 14					19 21	
Barrow-in-Furness 82 a																20 14						
Oxenholme Lake District 83 d		18 33	19 00									19 08			19 23						19 34	
Windermere 83 a			19 22																			
Penrith North Lakes d		18 58										19 34									19 59	
Carlisle ■ 216 a		19 13										19 49			20 01						20 15	
d		19 15										19 51			20 02						20 16	
Lockerbie 225,226 d		19 35																			20 35	
Carstairs 226,225 a																						
Motherwell 226 a		20 21																				
Glasgow Central ■ 216,226,225 a		20 42										21 02			21 15							
Haymarket ⛴ a																					21s31	
Edinburgh ■ ⛴ a																					21 36	
Fort William 227,400 a																						
Perth 229 a																						
Dundee 229 a																						
Aberdeen 229 a																						
Inverness 229 a																						

A From Bournemouth
B To Liverpool Lime Street
C To Glasgow Central
D From Birmingham New Street
E To Barrow-in-Furness
F From London Euston
G From Manchester Airport
H From Paignton

Refer to Operator websites for full information about Sleeper Services. Contact details for train operators available at National Rail Enquiries

Table T065-F

Saturdays
26 May to 16 June

London & West Midlands to North West England. London, West Midlands & Manchester to Scotland via the West Coast

	VT	LM	VT	VT	VT	VT	LM	VT	VT	VT	VT	XC	LM	XC	TP	LM	VT	LM	VT	VT	VT
	◇■	■	◇■	◇■	◇■	◇■	■	◇■	◇■	◇■	◇■	◇■	■	◇■	◇■	■	◇■	■	◇■	◇■	◇■
	A						B			C		D		E		F	A				
	⊡		⊡	⊡	⊡	⊡		⊡	⊡	⊡	⊡	⊼		⊼	⊼		⊡		⊡	⊡	⊡
London Euston ■ ⊖66 d	16 43	16 46	17 00	17 07	17 10	17 10		17 20	17 30		17 40						17 43	17 46	18 00	18 07	18 10
Watford Junction 66 d																					
Milton Keynes Central 66 d	17 13	17 19			17 40	17 41		17 50									18 13	18 19			18 41
Rugby 66 d		17 42																18 42			
Nuneaton d		17 54		18 03														18 54			
Tamworth Low Level d		18 09																19 09			
Lichfield Trent Valley d		18 17																19 17			
Coventry 68 d	17 42													18 27			18 42				
Birmingham International 68 ✈ d	17 53													18 38			18 53				
BirminghamNewSt ■ 68 ⇌ d	18 15											18 31	18 36	18 57		19 01	19 15				
Wolverhampton ■ ⇌ d	18 37											18 49	18 54	19 15		19 20	19 37				
Penkridge d													19 04			19 30					
Stafford d		18 44		18 27								19 03	19 10	19 28		19 36		19 42		19 24	
Stoke-on-Trent 84 a		19 02	18 24					18 48				19 18		19 43				20 02	19 24		
Macclesfield a			18 41				←			←		19 36		20 01					19 41		
Crewe ■ 81,91 a	19 08	19 27		18 45	18 49	18 49	18 55			19 08	19 11		19 30			19 56	20 09	20 24		19 41	19 47
d	19 09			18 47	18 52	18 52	18 57			19 09	19 12					19 57	20 09			19 43	19 49
Chester 81 a	→				19 11	19 11										→	→				20 09
Wrexham General 75 a																					
Llandudno Junction 81 a						20 07															
Bangor (Gwynedd) 81 a						20 23															
Holyhead 81 ⛴ a						20 54															
Wilmslow 84 a											19 27										
Stockport 84 a			18 54					19 16			19 36	19 49		20 13					19 54		
Manchester Piccadilly ■ ⇌ a			19 05					19 28			19 45	19 59		20 25					20 04		
Runcorn 91 a				19 04			19 21													20 00	
Liverpool South Pkwy ■ 91 ✈ a							19 30														
Liverpool Lime Street ■ 91 a				19 22			19 42													20 18	
d																					
Manchester Airport 82 ✈⇌ d															19 10						
Manchester Picc. ■ 82 ⇌ d															19 26						
Bolton 82 d																					
Warrington Bank Quay d									19 14	19 27											
Wigan North Western 90 d									19 25	19 38											
Preston ■ 90 a									19 38	19 54					20 02						
Blackpool North 97 a																					
Preston ■ 90 d									19 41						20 04						
Lancaster ■ d									19 55						20 19						
Barrow-in-Furness 82 a																					
Oxenholme Lake District 83 d									20 08						20 33						
Windermere 83 a																					
Penrith North Lakes d									20 34						20 58						
Carlisle ■ 216 a									20 48						21 13						
d									20 50						21 15						
Lockerbie 225,226 d															21 33						
Carstairs 226,225 a																					
Motherwell 226 a																					
Glasgow Central ■ 216,226,225 a									22 01												
Haymarket ⇌ a															22s31						
Edinburgh ■ ⇌ a															22 38						
Fort William 227,400 a																					
Perth 229 a																					
Dundee 229 a																					
Aberdeen 229 a																					
Inverness 229 a																					

A To Preston
B From Birmingham New Street
C From London Euston
D From Bristol Temple Meads
E From Bournemouth
F To Liverpool Lime Street

Refer to Operator websites for full information about Sleeper Services. Contact details for train operators available at National Rail Enquiries

Table T065-F

Saturdays
26 May to 16 June

London & West Midlands to North West England. London, West Midlands & Manchester to Scotland via the West Coast

	LM	VT	VT	VT	VT	VT	XC	XC	LM	VT	LM	VT	VT	LM	VT	VT	VT	XC	LM	XC	VT	VT
	■	◇■	◇■	◇■	◇■	◇■	◇■	◇■	■	◇■	■	◇■	◇■	■	◇■	◇■	◇■	◇■	■	◇■	◇■	◇■
	A			B			C	D	E					A				C		F		
		⊡	⊡	⊡	⊡	⊡	⊼	⊼		⊡		⊡	⊡		⊡	⊡	⊡				⊡	⊡
London Euston ■ ⊖66 d		18 20	18 30		18 33	18 40				18 43	18 46	19 00	19 07		19 20	19 30	19 40				20 11	20 20
Watford Junction 66 d																						
Milton Keynes Central 66 d		18 50								19 13	19 19				19 50							21 05
Rugby 66 d											19 42										21 15	
Nuneaton d											19 58		20 03									21 33
Tamworth Low Level d					19 38						20 14											
Lichfield Trent Valley d					19 45						20 21											
Coventry 68 d								19 27		19 42												
Birmingham International 68 ✈ d								19 38		19 53												
BirminghamNewSt ■ 68 ⇌ d							19 31	19 57	20 01	20 15								20 31	20 36	20 57		
Wolverhampton ■ ⇌ d							19 49	20 15	20 22	20 37								20 49	20 54	21 17		
Penkridge d									20 31										21 04			
Stafford d					19 59		20 03	20 28	20 38	20 51	20 44		20 27					21 03	21 10	21 30	21 46	
Stoke-on-Trent 84 a		19 48					20 18	20 43			21 02	20 24			20 48			21 18	21 27	21 46		22 05
Macclesfield a	←			←			20 36	21 01				20 41		←				21 36		22 04		22 21
Crewe ■ 81,91 a	19 56			20 09		20 12			20 57	21 10	21 22		20 45	20 57		21 02	21 18		21 49		22 05	
d	19 57			20 09		20 12			20 59				20 47	20 59		21 05	21 19				22 06	
Chester 81 a									→													
Wrexham General 75 a																						
Llandudno Junction 81 a																						
Bangor (Gwynedd) 81 a																						
Holyhead 81 ⛴ a																						
Wilmslow 84 a						20 28											21 34					
Stockport 84 a		20 16				20 36	20 49	21 13				20 54			21 20		21 44	21 49		22 16		22 35
Manchester Piccadilly ■ ⇌ a		20 28				20 45	20 59	21 24				21 04			21 32		21 53	21 59		22 33		22 50
Runcorn 91 a	20 25				20 31								21 05	21 20							22 24	
Liverpool South Pkwy ■ 91 ✈ a	20 33													21 29								
Liverpool Lime Street ■ 91 a	20 44				20 51								21 27	21 40							22 42	
d																						
Manchester Airport 82 ✈⇌ d																						
Manchester Picc. ■ 82 ⇌ d																						
Bolton 82 d																						
Warrington Bank Quay d			20 14	20 27												21 22						
Wigan North Western 90 d			20 25	20 38												21 33						
Preston ■ 90 a			20 38	20 52												21 47						
Blackpool North 97 a																						
Preston ■ 90 d			20 41																			
Lancaster ■ d			20 55																			
Barrow-in-Furness 82 a																						
Oxenholme Lake District 83 d			21 10																			
Windermere 83 a																						
Penrith North Lakes d			21 35																			
Carlisle ■ 216 a			21 50																			
d			21 50																			
Lockerbie 225,226 d			22 09																			
Carstairs 226,225 a																						
Motherwell 226 a			22 52																			
Glasgow Central ■ 216,226,225 a			23 09																			
Haymarket ⇌ a																						
Edinburgh ■ ⇌ a																						
Fort William 227,400 a																						
Perth 229 a																						
Dundee 229 a																						
Aberdeen 229 a																						
Inverness 229 a																						

A From Birmingham New Street
B From London Euston
C From Bristol Temple Meads
D From Bournemouth. ⊼ to BirminghamNewSt
E To Liverpool Lime Street
F From Newquay

Refer to Operator websites for full information about Sleeper Services. Contact details for train operators available at National Rail Enquiries

Table T065-F

Saturdays
26 May to 16 June

London & West Midlands to North West England. London, West Midlands & Manchester to Scotland via the West Coast

		VT	LM	XC	VT	XC	LM
		◇1	1	◇1	◇1	◇1	1
				A			
London Euston 15 ⊖66	d	20 31			21 00		
Watford Junction 66	d	20u46					
Milton Keynes Central 66	d				21 45		
Rugby 66	d	21 36					
Nuneaton	d						
Tamworth Low Level	d	21 53					
Lichfield Trent Valley	d	22 00					
Coventry 68	d			21 27			
Birmingham International 68 ✈	d			21 38			
BirminghamNewSt 12 68	d		21 36	21 57		22 31	22 39
Wolverhampton 7	d		21 59	22 15		22 49	23 06
Penkridge	d		22 09				23 16
Stafford	d		22 16	22 28	22 34	23 02	23 22
Stoke-on-Trent 84	a			22 43		23 19	
Macclesfield	a			23 01		23 38	
Crewe 10 81,91	a	22 29	22 36		22 58		23 42
	d	22 31			22 59		
Chester 81	a						
Wrexham General 75	a						
Llandudno Junction 81	a						
Bangor (Gwynedd) 81	a						
Holyhead 81	a						
Wilmslow 84	a				23 14		
Stockport 84	a			23 13	23 26	23 53	
Manchester Piccadilly 10	a			23 29	23 39	00 10	
Runcorn 91	a						
Liverpool South Pkwy 7 91 ✈	a						
Liverpool Lime Street 10 91	a						
	d						
Manchester Airport 82 ✈	d						
Manchester Picc. 10 82	d						
Bolton 82	d						
Warrington Bank Quay	d	22 48					
Wigan North Western 90	d	23 02					
Preston 8 90	a	23 18					
Blackpool North 97	a						
Preston 8 90	d						
Lancaster 8	d						
Barrow-in-Furness 82	a						
Oxenholme Lake District 83	d						
Windermere 83	a						
Penrith North Lakes	d						
Carlisle 8 216	a						
	d						
Lockerbie 225,226	d						
Carstairs 226,225	a						
Motherwell 226	a						
Glasgow Central 15 216,226,225	a						
Haymarket	a						
Edinburgh 10	a						
Fort William 227,400	a						
Perth 229	a						
Dundee 229	a						
Aberdeen 229	a						
Inverness 229	a						

A From Bournemouth

Refer to Operator websites for full information about Sleeper Services. Contact details for train operators available at National Rail Enquiries

Table T065-F

Saturdays
23 June to 8 September

London & West Midlands to North West England. London, West Midlands & Manchester to Scotland via the West Coast

		NT	CS	AW	NT	CS	CS	CS	NT	NT	TP	VT	VT	XC	LM	TP	VT	XC	LM	LM	XC	TP	VT
		◇		◇	◇						◇1	◇1	◇1	◇1	1	◇1	◇1	◇1	1	1	◇1	◇1	◇1
		A	B	C	D	B	B	B												E			
London Euston 15 ⊖66	d																						06 05
Watford Junction 66	d		00u10																				06u20
Milton Keynes Central 66	d																						06 41
Rugby 66	d																			06 02			07 03
Nuneaton	d																			06 16			
Tamworth Low Level	d																			06 29			
Lichfield Trent Valley	d																			06 35			
Coventry 68	d																						
Birmingham International 68 ✈	d																		06 18				
BirminghamNewSt 12 68	d												05 30	05 57	06 01		06 15	06 31	06 36		06 57		
Wolverhampton 7	d												05 48	06 15	06 20		06 37	06 49	06 54		07 15		
Penkridge	d														06 29				07 04				
Stafford	d												06 01	06 28	06 36			07 03	07 10	06 58	07 31		07 34
Stoke-on-Trent 84	a													06 44				07 18		07 14			
Macclesfield	a													07 05				07 36					
Crewe 10 81,91	a												06 20		06 56		07 08		07 29	07 37	07 50		07 53
	d			00 15								05 57	06 23		06 59		07 09		07 33		07 52		07 55
Chester 81	a			00 37									06 43										
Wrexham General 75	a																						
Llandudno Junction 81	a			01 28									07 32										
Bangor (Gwynedd) 81	a			01 46									07 49										
Holyhead 81	a			02 15									08 20										
Wilmslow 84	a																				08 07		
Stockport 84	a													07 18				07 49			08 16		
Manchester Piccadilly 10	a													07 28				07 59			08 29		
Runcorn 91	a														07 24				07 59				
Liverpool South Pkwy 7 91 ✈	a														07 33				08 09				
Liverpool Lime Street 10 91	a														07 44				08 21				
	d																						
Manchester Airport 82 ✈	d															06 10						07 10	
Manchester Picc. 10 82	d	00 09									04 54					06 26						07 26	
Bolton 82	d				00 41																		
Warrington Bank Quay	d											06 15					07 27						08 12
Wigan North Western 90	d											06 25					07 38						08 23
Preston 8 90	a	00 59			01 06						05 30	06 38				07 01	07 51					08 01	08 36
Blackpool North 97	a	01 29																					
Preston 8 90	d					00u58	00u58	00u58	05 16		05 40	06 40				07 03	07 53					08 03	08 37
Lancaster 8	d								05 36	05 40	05 56	06 54				07 18	08 08					08 18	08 52
Barrow-in-Furness 82	a																						
Oxenholme Lake District 83	d									06 19	06 10	07 09				07 32	08 22					08 32	09 06
Windermere 83	a									06 39													
Penrith North Lakes	d										06 35	07 34										08 57	09 32
Carlisle 8 216	a		05s13						09 24		06 51	07 49				08 10	09 00					09 12	09 47
	d										06 52	07 51				08 12	09 01					09 14	09 48
Lockerbie 225,226	d										07 11	08 10				08 30						09 33	
Carstairs 226,225	a		06s21								07 44												
Motherwell 226	a		06s55								07 59											10 20	
Glasgow Central 15 216,226,225	a		07 22								08 20	09 12										10 39	10 59
Haymarket	a															09s30	10 13						
Edinburgh 10	a															09 37	10 18						
Fort William 227,400	a							09 57															
Perth 229	a						05s41																
Dundee 229	a					06s08																	
Aberdeen 229	a					07 39																	
Inverness 229	a						08 41																

A From Manchester Airport
B From London Euston
C From Birmingham New Street
D From Manchester Victoria
E From Northampton

Refer to Operator websites for full information about Sleeper Services. Contact details for train operators available at National Rail Enquiries

Table T065-F

Saturdays

23 June to 8 September

London & West Midlands to North West England. London, West Midlands & Manchester to Scotland via the West Coast

	LM	VT	LM	VT	TP	VT	XC	LM	LM A	VT	VT	XC B	VT	LM	NT	VT	NT C	VT	NT D	VT	XC E	LM
London Euston ⊖66 d			06 24	06 36						06 55	07 07		07 20			07 30				07 35		
Watford Junction 66 d			06 41	06u51																		
Milton Keynes Central 66 d			07 24							07 27			07 50							08 06		
Rugby 66 d			08 04						06 58													
Nuneaton d			08 16						07 12													
Tamworth Low Level d			08 29						07 29													
Lichfield Trent Valley d			08 35						07 35													
Coventry 68 d												07 27										
Birmingham International 68 d												07 38										
BirminghamNewSt 68 d	07 01	07 15				07 21	07 31	07 36				07 57		08 01				08 15			08 31	08 36
Wolverhampton d	07 20	07 37				07 41	07 49	07 54				08 15		08 20				08 37			08 49	08 54
Penkridge d	07 29							08 04						08 29								09 04
Stafford d	07 36		08 55			07 59	08 03	08 10	07 55		08 24	08 28		08 36							09 03	09 10
Stoke-on-Trent 84 a			09 12				08 18		08 12	08 24		08 43	08 48								09 18	
Macclesfield a							08 36			08 41		09 01									09 36	
Crewe 81,91 a	07 58	08 06	09 37	08 10		08 18		08 30	08 37		08 41			08 56				09 08		09 11		09 30
d	07 59	08 09		08 11		08 19		08 32			08 43			08 57				09 09		09 12		09 32
Chester 81 a																						
Wrexham General 75 a																						
Llandudno Junction 81 a																						
Bangor (Gwynedd) 81 a																						
Holyhead 81 a																						
Wilmslow 84 a				08 27																09 28		
Stockport 84 a				08 35			08 50			08 54		09 13	09 16							09 36	09 49	
Manchester Piccadilly a				08 46			08 59			09 04		09 25	09 28							09 44	09 59	
Runcorn 91 a	08 24							08 52			09 00			09 21								09 52
Liverpool South Pkwy 91 a	08 32							09 01						09 30								10 01
Liverpool Lime Street 91 a	08 44							09 11			09 20			09 42								10 11
d																						
Manchester Airport 82 d					08 10												08 41					
Manchester Picc. 82 d					08 26												09 01					
Bolton 82 d																	09 22					
Warrington Bank Quay d		08 27				08 41										09 14		09 27				
Wigan North Western 90 d		08 38				08 52										09 25		09 38				
Preston 90 a		08 51			09 02	09 09										09 38	09 49	09 51	←			
Blackpool North 97 a						09 32																
Preston 90 d		08 53			09 04										09 29	09 41	09 57	09 53	09 57			
Lancaster d		09 09			09 19										09 59	09 55	→	10 08	10 14			
Barrow-In-Furness 82 a																			11 15			
Oxenholme Lake District 83 d															10 19			10 22				
Windermere 83 a															10 41							
Penrith North Lakes d		09 46														10 31						
Carlisle 216 a		10 01			10 07											10 46		10 59				
d		10 01			10 09											10 47		11 01				
Lockerbie 225,226 d					10 27																	
Carstairs 226,225 a																						
Motherwell 226 a																						
Glasgow Central 216,226,225 a		11 15														11 59						
Haymarket a					11s27													12 17				
Edinburgh a					11 34													12 22				
Fort William 227,400 a																						
Perth 229 a																						
Dundee 229 a																						
Aberdeen 229 a																						
Inverness 229 a																						

A From Northampton
B From Southampton Central
C To Barrow-In-Furness
D From Manchester Airport
E From Bristol Temple Meads

Refer to Operator websites for full information about Sleeper Services. Contact details for train operators available at National Rail Enquiries

Table T065-F

Saturdays

23 June to 8 September

London & West Midlands to North West England. London, West Midlands & Manchester to Scotland via the West Coast

	XC A	TP	LM B	VT C	LM	VT	VT	VT	LM D	VT	VT	VT E	VT	XC F	LM	XC G	TP	LM B	VT H	LM	VT
London Euston ⊖66 d				07 43	07 46	08 00	08 07	08 10		08 20	08 30		08 40						08 43	08 46	08 53
Watford Junction 66 d																					
Milton Keynes Central 66 d				08 13	08 19			08 41		08 50									09 13	09 19	
Rugby 66 d					08 42															09 42	09 46
Nuneaton d					08 54															09 54	
Tamworth Low Level d					09 09															10 09	
Lichfield Trent Valley d					09 17															10 17	
Coventry 68 d	08 27			08 42												09 27			09 42		
Birmingham International 68 d	08 38			08 53												09 38			09 53		
BirminghamNewSt 68 d	08 57		09 01	09 15										09 31	09 36	09 57		10 01	10 15		
Wolverhampton d	09 15		09 20	09 37										09 49	09 54	10 15		10 20	10 37		
Penkridge d															10 04						
Stafford d	09 28		09 35		09 42		09 24							10 03	10 10	10 28		10 35		10 42	
Stoke-on-Trent 84 a	09 43				10 02	09 24				09 48				10 18		10 43				11 02	
Macclesfield a	10 01					09 41			←			←		10 36		11 01					
Crewe 81,91 a			09 55	10 08	10 24		09 41	09 47	09 55			10 08	10 11		10 30			10 55	11 08	11 24	
d			09 57	10 09			09 43	09 49	09 57			10 09	10 12		10 32			10 57	11 09		
Chester 81 a			→	→				10 10										→	→		
Wrexham General 75 a																					
Llandudno Junction 81 a																					
Bangor (Gwynedd) 81 a																					
Holyhead 81 a																					
Wilmslow 84 a													10 27								
Stockport 84 a	10 13					09 54				10 16			10 36	10 49		11 13					
Manchester Piccadilly a	10 24					10 04				10 28			10 46	11 00		11 25					
Runcorn 91 a							10 00		10 24						10 52						
Liverpool South Pkwy 91 a									10 32						11 01						
Liverpool Lime Street 91 a							10 19		10 44						11 11						
d																					
Manchester Airport 82 d		09 10															10 10				
Manchester Picc. 82 d		09 26															10 26				
Bolton 82 d																					
Warrington Bank Quay d											10 14	10 27									10 59
Wigan North Western 90 d											10 25	10 38									11 12
Preston 90 a		10 03									10 38	10 51					11 02				11 24
Blackpool North 97 a																					11 56
Preston 90 d		10 04									10 41	10 53					11 03				
Lancaster d		10 20									10 55	11 08									
Barrow-in-Furness 82 a																					
Oxenholme Lake District 83 d		10 35									11 08										
Windermere 83 a																					
Penrith North Lakes d		11 00										11 45									
Carlisle 216 a		11 16									11 46	12 00					12 05				
d		11 17									11 47	12 02					12 06				
Lockerbie 225,226 d		11 37																			
Carstairs 226,225 a																					
Motherwell 226 a		12 22																			
Glasgow Central 216,226,225 a		12 42									12 59	13 15									
Haymarket a																	13s19				
Edinburgh a																	13 26				
Fort William 227,400 a																					
Perth 229 a																					
Dundee 229 a																					
Aberdeen 229 a																					
Inverness 229 a																					

A From Southampton Central
B To Liverpool Lime Street
C To Glasgow Central
D From Birmingham New Street
E From London Euston
F From Cardiff Central
G From Bournemouth
H To Edinburgh

Refer to Operator websites for full information about Sleeper Services. Contact details for train operators available at National Rail Enquiries

Table T065-F

London & West Midlands to North West England. London, West Midlands & Manchester to Scotland via the West Coast

	VT	VT	VT	LM A	VT	VT	VT B	VT	XC C	LM	XC D	TP	NT	LM E	VT F	LM	VT	VT	VT	LM A	VT	VT
London Euston ⊖66 d	09 00	09 07	09 10		09 20	09 30		09 40							09 43	09 46	10 00	10 07	10 10		10 20	10 30
Watford Junction 66 d																						
Milton Keynes Central 66 d			09 41		09 50										10 13	10 19			10 41		10 50	
Rugby 66 d																10 42						
Nuneaton d																10 54						
Tamworth Low Level d																11 09						
Lichfield Trent Valley d																11 17			11 24			
Coventry 68 d											10 27				10 42							
Birmingham International 68 d											10 38				10 53							
BirminghamNewSt 68 d									10 31	10 36	10 57			11 01	11 15							
Wolverhampton d									10 49	10 54	11 15			11 20	11 37							
Penkridge d										11 04												
Stafford d		10 26							11 03	11 10	11 28			11 35		11 42		11 24				
Stoke-on-Trent 84 a	10 24				10 48				11 18		11 43					12 02	11 24				11 48	
Macclesfield a	10 41			←			←		11 36		12 01						11 41			←		
Crewe 81,91 a		10 44	10 47	10 55			11 08	11 11		11 30				11 54	12 07	12 24		11 41	11 53	11 54		
d		10 46	10 49	10 57			11 09	11 12		11 32				11 57	12 09			11 43	11 56	11 57		
Chester 81 a			11 13											→	→				12 17			
Wrexham General 75 a																						
Llandudno Junction 81 a			12 00																			
Bangor (Gwynedd) 81 a			12 16																			
Holyhead 81 a			12 47																			
Wilmslow 84 a								11 27														
Stockport 84 a	10 54				11 16			11 35	11 49		12 13						11 54				12 16	
Manchester Piccadilly a	11 04				11 28			11 46	11 59		12 25						12 04				12 28	
Runcorn 91 a		11 03		11 21						11 52								12 00		12 24		
Liverpool South Pkwy 91 a				11 30						12 01										12 32		
Liverpool Lime Street 91 a		11 20		11 42						12 11								12 19		12 44		
d																						
Manchester Airport 82 d												10 59										
Manchester Picc. 82 d												11 14										
Bolton 82 d																						
Warrington Bank Quay d						11 14	11 27															12 14
Wigan North Western 90 d						11 25	11 38															12 25
Preston 90 a						11 38	11 51					11 58										12 38
Blackpool North 97 a																						
Preston 90 d						11 41	11 53					12 04	12 17									12 41
Lancaster d						11 55	12 08					12 20	12 37									12 55
Barrow-in-Furness 82 a																						
Oxenholme Lake District 83 d							12 21					12 33	13 02									13 08
Windermere 83 a													13 24									
Penrith North Lakes d						12 30						12 58										
Carlisle 216 a						12 46	12 59					13 14										13 46
d						12 47	13 01					13 17										13 47
Lockerbie 225,226 d												13 37										
Carstairs 226,225 a																						
Motherwell 226 a												14 21										
Glasgow Central 216,226,225 a						13 59						14 40										14 59
Haymarket a							14 11															
Edinburgh a							14 17															
Fort William 227,400 a																						
Perth 229 a																						
Dundee 229 a																						
Aberdeen 229 a																						
Inverness 229 a																						

A From Birmingham New Street
B From London Euston
C From Paignton
D From Bournemouth
E To Liverpool Lime Street
F To Glasgow Central

Refer to Operator websites for full information about Sleeper Services. Contact details for train operators available at National Rail Enquiries

Table T065-F

London & West Midlands to North West England. London, West Midlands & Manchester to Scotland via the West Coast

	NT A	VT B	NT C	VT	VT	XC D	LM	XC E	TP	LM F	VT G	LM	VT	VT	VT	LM H	VT	VT	VT B	VT	XC I
London Euston ⊖66 d				10 36	10 40						10 43	10 46	11 00	11 07	11 10		11 20	11 30		11 40	
Watford Junction 66 d																					
Milton Keynes Central 66 d											11 13	11 19			11 41		11 50				
Rugby 66 d				11 28								11 42									
Nuneaton d												11 54									
Tamworth Low Level d												12 09									
Lichfield Trent Valley d												12 17									
Coventry 68 d								11 27			11 42										
Birmingham International 68 d								11 38			11 53										
BirminghamNewSt 68 d						11 31	11 36	11 57		12 01	12 15										12 31
Wolverhampton d						11 49	11 54	12 15		12 20	12 37										12 49
Penkridge d							12 04														
Stafford d						12 03	12 10	12 28		12 35		12 42		12 24							13 03
Stoke-on-Trent 84 a						12 18		12 43				13 02	12 24				12 48				13 18
Macclesfield a		←				12 36		13 01					12 41			←			←		13 36
Crewe 81,91 a		12 07			12 11		12 30			12 54	13 08	13 24		12 42	12 47	12 54			13 08	13 11	
d		12 09			12 12		12 32			12 57	13 09			12 43	12 49	12 57			13 09	13 12	
Chester 81 a										→	→				13 11						
Wrexham General 75 a																					
Llandudno Junction 81 a																					
Bangor (Gwynedd) 81 a																					
Holyhead 81 a																					
Wilmslow 84 a					12 27															13 27	
Stockport 84 a					12 35	12 49		13 13					12 55				13 16			13 35	13 49
Manchester Piccadilly a					12 46	12 59		13 25					13 04				13 28			13 46	13 59
Runcorn 91 a							12 52							13 00		13 22					
Liverpool South Pkwy 91 a							13 01									13 31					
Liverpool Lime Street 91 a							13 11							13 19		13 42					
d																					
Manchester Airport 82 d	11 41								12 10												
Manchester Picc. 82 d	12 01								12 26												
Bolton 82 d	12 22																				
Warrington Bank Quay d		12 27		12 34														13 14	13 27		
Wigan North Western 90 d		12 38		12 45														13 25	13 38		
Preston 90 a	12 48	12 52		12 57					13 02									13 38	13 51		
Blackpool North 97 a			←	13 20																	
Preston 90 d	12 57	12 53	12 57						13 03									13 41	13 53		
Lancaster d	→	13 08	13 14						13 20									13 55	14 08		
Barrow-in-Furness 82 a			14 14																		
Oxenholme Lake District 83 d		13 23							13 33									14 08			
Windermere 83 a																					
Penrith North Lakes d																			14 43		
Carlisle 216 a		14 00							14 12									14 46	14 59		
d		14 01							14 13									14 47	14 59		
Lockerbie 225,226 d									14 32												
Carstairs 226,225 a																					
Motherwell 226 a		14 58																			
Glasgow Central 216,226,225 a		15 15																15 59			
Haymarket a									15s29										16 16		
Edinburgh a									15 36										16 23		
Fort William 227,400 a																					
Perth 229 a																					
Dundee 229 a																					
Aberdeen 229 a																					
Inverness 229 a																					

A To Barrow-in-Furness
B From London Euston
C From Manchester Airport
D From Bristol Temple Meads
E From Bournemouth
F To Liverpool Lime Street
G To Edinburgh
H From Birmingham New Street
I From Plymouth

Refer to Operator websites for full information about Sleeper Services. Contact details for train operators available at National Rail Enquiries

Table T065-F

Saturdays

23 June to 8 September

London & West Midlands to North West England. London, West Midlands & Manchester to Scotland via the West Coast

	LM	XC A	TP	NT	LM B	VT C	LM	VT	VT	VT	LM D	VT	VT	NT	VT E	VT	XC F	LM	XC A	TP	LM B	VT G
London Euston ⊖66 d						11 43	11 46	12 00	12 07	12 10		12 20	12 30			12 40						12 43
Watford Junction 66 d																						
Milton Keynes Central 66 d						12 13	12 19			12 41		12 50										13 13
Rugby 66 d							12 42			13 04												
Nuneaton d							12 54															
Tamworth Low Level d							13 09															
Lichfield Trent Valley d							13 17															
Coventry 68 d		12 27				12 42													13 27			13 42
Birmingham International 68 d		12 38				12 53													13 38			13 53
BirminghamNewSt 68 d	12 36	12 57			13 01	13 15											13 31	13 36	13 57		14 01	14 15
Wolverhampton d	12 54	13 15			13 20	13 37											13 49	13 54	14 15		14 20	14 37
Penkridge d	13 04																	14 04				
Stafford d	13 10	13 28			13 35		13 42		13 24								14 03	14 10	14 28		14 35	
Stoke-on-Trent 84 a		13 43					14 02	13 24				13 48					14 18		14 43			
Macclesfield a		14 01						13 41			←				←		14 36		15 01			
Crewe 81,91 a	13 30				13 56	14 08	14 24		13 41	13 50	13 56				14 08	14 11		14 30			14 55	15 07
d	13 32				13 57	14 09			13 43	13 52	13 57				14 09	14 12		14 32			14 57	15 09
Chester 81 a					→	→				14 15											→	→
Wrexham General 75 a																						
Llandudno Junction 81 a																						
Bangor (Gwynedd) 81 a																						
Holyhead 81 a																						
Wilmslow 84 a																14 27						
Stockport 84 a		14 13						13 54				14 16				14 35	14 49		15 13			
Manchester Piccadilly a		14 25						14 05				14 28				14 46	14 59		15 25			
Runcorn 91 a	13 52								14 00		14 21							14 52				
Liverpool South Pkwy 91 a	14 01										14 30							15 01				
Liverpool Lime Street 91 a	14 11								14 20		14 42							15 11				
d																						
Manchester Airport 82 d			13 10																	14 10		
Manchester Picc. 82 d			13 26																	14 26		
Bolton 82 d																						
Warrington Bank Quay d													14 14		14 27							
Wigan North Western 90 d													14 25		14 38							
Preston 90 a			14 02										14 38		14 51					15 03		
Blackpool North 97 a																						
Preston 90 d			14 04	14 10									14 41		14 53					15 04		
Lancaster d			14 19	14 30									14 55	15 03	15 09					15 20		
Barrow-in-Furness 82 a														16 07								
Oxenholme Lake District 83 d			14 33	14 51											15 22							
Windermere 83 a				15 09																		
Penrith North Lakes d			14 58										15 30							15 55		
Carlisle 216 a			15 13										15 45	18 41	16 00					16 11		
d			15 14										15 46		16 02					16 13		
Lockerbie 225,226 d			15 33																	16 32		
Carstairs 226,225 a																						
Motherwell 226 a			16 21																			
Glasgow Central 216,226,225 a			16 40										16 59		17 15							
Haymarket a																				17s31		
Edinburgh a																				17 36		
Fort William 227,400 a																						
Perth 229 a																						
Dundee 229 a																						
Aberdeen 229 a																						
Inverness 229 a																						

A From Bournemouth
B To Liverpool Lime Street
C To Glasgow Central
D From Birmingham New Street
E From London Euston
F From Paignton
G To Edinburgh

Refer to Operator websites for full information about Sleeper Services. Contact details for train operators available at National Rail Enquiries

Table T065-F

Saturdays

23 June to 8 September

London & West Midlands to North West England. London, West Midlands & Manchester to Scotland via the West Coast

	LM	VT	VT	VT	LM A	VT	VT	VT B	NT	VT	XC C	LM	XC D	TP	LM E	VT F	LM	VT	VT	VT	LM A	VT
London Euston ⊖66 d	12 46	13 00	13 07	13 10		13 20	13 30			13 40						13 43	13 46	14 00	14 07	14 10		14 20
Watford Junction 66 d																						
Milton Keynes Central 66 d	13 19			13 41		13 50										14 13	14 19			14 41		14 50
Rugby 66 d	13 42																14 42					
Nuneaton d	13 54																14 54					
Tamworth Low Level d	14 09																15 09					
Lichfield Trent Valley d	14 17																15 17					
Coventry 68 d													14 27			14 42						
Birmingham International 68 d													14 38			14 53						
BirminghamNewSt 68 d											14 31	14 36	14 57		15 01	15 15						
Wolverhampton d											14 49	14 54	15 15		15 20	15 37						
Penkridge d												15 04										
Stafford d	14 42		14 24								15 03	15 10	15 28		15 35		15 42		15 24			
Stoke-on-Trent 84 a	15 02	14 24				14 48					15 18		15 43				16 02	15 24				15 48
Macclesfield a		14 41			←			←			15 36		16 01					15 41			←	
Crewe 81,91 a	15 24		14 41	14 47	14 55			15 07		15 10		15 30			15 55	16 08	16 24		15 41	15 47	15 55	
d			14 43	14 49	14 57			15 09		15 11		15 32			15 57	16 09			15 43	15 49	15 57	
Chester 81 a				15 09											→	→				16 10		
Wrexham General 75 a																						
Llandudno Junction 81 a																				17 01		
Bangor (Gwynedd) 81 a																				17 17		
Holyhead 81 a																				17 48		
Wilmslow 84 a										15 27												
Stockport 84 a		14 54				15 16				15 35	15 49		16 13					15 54				16 16
Manchester Piccadilly a		15 05				15 28				15 46	15 59		16 25					16 05				16 28
Runcorn 91 a			15 00		15 21							15 52							16 00		16 25	
Liverpool South Pkwy 91 a					15 30							16 01									16 33	
Liverpool Lime Street 91 a			15 19		15 42							16 11							16 20		16 44	
d																						
Manchester Airport 82 d														15 10								
Manchester Picc. 82 d														15 26								
Bolton 82 d																						
Warrington Bank Quay d							15 14	15 27														
Wigan North Western 90 d							15 25	15 38														
Preston 90 a							15 38	15 51						16 02								
Blackpool North 97 a																						
Preston 90 d							15 40	15 53						16 03								
Lancaster d							15 54	16 08	16 13					16 19								
Barrow-in-Furness 82 a									17 16													
Oxenholme Lake District 83 d							16 10							16 32								
Windermere 83 a																						
Penrith North Lakes d								16 44						16 57								
Carlisle 216 a							16 48	17 00	19 43					17 13								
d							16 48	17 01						17 14								
Lockerbie 225,226 d																						
Carstairs 226,225 a																						
Motherwell 226 a																						
Glasgow Central 216,226,225 a							17 59							18 31								
Haymarket a								18 14														
Edinburgh a								18 22														
Fort William 227,400 a																						
Perth 229 a																						
Dundee 229 a																						
Aberdeen 229 a																						
Inverness 229 a																						

A From Birmingham New Street
B From London Euston
C From Bristol Temple Meads
D From Bournemouth
E To Liverpool Lime Street
F To Glasgow Central

Refer to Operator websites for full information about Sleeper Services. Contact details for train operators available at National Rail Enquiries

Table T065-F

Saturdays
23 June to 8 September

London & West Midlands to North West England. London, West Midlands & Manchester to Scotland via the West Coast

	VT	NT	VT	VT	XC	LM	XC	TP	LM	VT
	◇■		◇■	◇■	◇■	■	◇■	◇■	■	■
			A		B		C		D	E
London Euston ⊖66 d	14 30			14 40						14 43
Watford Junction 66 d										
Milton Keynes Central 66 d										15 13
Rugby 66 d										
Nuneaton d										
Tamworth Low Level d										
Lichfield Trent Valley d										
Coventry 68 d							15 27			15 42
Birmingham International 68 d							15 38			15 53
BirminghamNewSt 68 d					15 31	15 36	15 57		16 01	16 15
Wolverhampton d					15 49	15 54	16 15		16 20	16 37
Penkridge d						16 04			16 29	
Stafford d					16 03	16 10	16 28		16 36	
Stoke-on-Trent 84 a					16 18		16 43			
Macclesfield a			←		16 36		17 01			
Crewe 81,91 a			16 08	16 10		16 30			16 55	17 08
d			16 09	16 11		16 32			16 57	17 09
Chester 81 a									→	→
Wrexham General 75 a										
Llandudno Junction 81 a										
Bangor (Gwynedd) 81 a										
Holyhead 81 a										
Wilmslow 84 a				16 27						
Stockport 84 a				16 36	16 49		17 13			
Manchester Piccadilly a				16 46	16 59		17 25			
Runcorn 91 a						16 52				
Liverpool South Pkwy 91 a						17 01				
Liverpool Lime Street 91 a						17 11				
d										
Manchester Airport 82 d								16 10		
Manchester Picc. 82 d								16 26		
Bolton 82 d										
Warrington Bank Quay d	16 14		16 27							
Wigan North Western 90 d	16 25		16 38							
Preston 90 a	16 38		16 51					17 02		
Blackpool North 97 a										
Preston 90 d	16 41		16 53					17 03		
Lancaster d	16 55	17 01	17 08					17 19		
Barrow-in-Furness 82 a		17 59								
Oxenholme Lake District 83 d			17 22					17 32		
Windermere 83 a										
Penrith North Lakes d	17 30							17 57		
Carlisle 216 a	17 46	20 31	18 00					18 12		
d	17 47		18 02					18 13		
Lockerbie 225,226 d								18 32		
Carstairs 226,225 a										
Motherwell 226 a										
Glasgow Central 216,226,225 a	18 59		19 15							
Haymarket a								19s29		
Edinburgh a								19 34		
Fort William 227,400 a										
Perth 229 a										
Dundee 229 a										
Aberdeen 229 a										
Inverness 229 a										

	LM	VT	VT	VT	LM	VT	VT	VT	VT	XC	LM
	■	◇■	◇■	◇■	■	◇■	◇■	■	◇■	◇■	■
					F			A		B	
London Euston ⊖66 d	14 46	15 00	15 07	15 10		15 20	15 30		15 40		
Watford Junction 66 d											
Milton Keynes Central 66 d	15 19			15 41		15 50					
Rugby 66 d	15 42										
Nuneaton d	15 54										
Tamworth Low Level d	16 09										
Lichfield Trent Valley d	16 17										
Coventry 68 d											
Birmingham International 68 d											
BirminghamNewSt 68 d										16 31	16 36
Wolverhampton d										16 49	16 54
Penkridge d											17 04
Stafford d	16 42		16 24							17 03	17 10
Stoke-on-Trent 84 a	17 02	16 24				16 48				17 18	
Macclesfield a		16 41			←			←		17 36	
Crewe 81,91 a	17 24		16 41	16 47	16 55			17 08	17 11		17 30
d			16 43	16 49	16 57			17 09	17 12		17 32
Chester 81 a				17 11							
Wrexham General 75 a											
Llandudno Junction 81 a											
Bangor (Gwynedd) 81 a											
Holyhead 81 a											
Wilmslow 84 a									17 27		
Stockport 84 a		16 54				17 16			17 36	17 49	
Manchester Piccadilly a		17 04				17 28			17 46	17 59	
Runcorn 91 a			17 00		17 24						17 52
Liverpool South Pkwy 91 a					17 33						18 01
Liverpool Lime Street 91 a			17 20		17 44						18 11
d											
Manchester Airport 82 d											
Manchester Picc. 82 d											
Bolton 82 d											
Warrington Bank Quay d							17 14	17 27			
Wigan North Western 90 d							17 25	17 38			
Preston 90 a							17 38	17 51			
Blackpool North 97 a											
Preston 90 d							17 41	17 53			
Lancaster d							17 55	18 08			
Barrow-in-Furness 82 a											
Oxenholme Lake District 83 d							18 08	18 23			
Windermere 83 a											
Penrith North Lakes d								18 48			
Carlisle 216 a							18 46	19 04			
d							18 47	19 04			
Lockerbie 225,226 d											
Carstairs 226,225 a											
Motherwell 226 a											
Glasgow Central 216,226,225 a							19 59				
Haymarket a								20 14			
Edinburgh a								20 21			
Fort William 227,400 a											
Perth 229 a											
Dundee 229 a											
Aberdeen 229 a											
Inverness 229 a											

A From London Euston
B From Bristol Temple Meads
C From Bournemouth
D To Liverpool Lime Street
E To Edinburgh
F From Birmingham New Street

Refer to Operator websites for full information about Sleeper Services. Contact details for train operators available at National Rail Enquiries

Table T065-F

Saturdays
23 June to 8 September

London & West Midlands to North West England. London, West Midlands & Manchester to Scotland via the West Coast

	XC	TP	NT	LM	VT	LM	VT	VT	VT	LM	VT
	◇■	◇■	◇	■	■	■	◇■	◇■	◇■	■	◇■
	A			B	C					D	
London Euston ⊖66 d					15 43	15 46	16 00	16 07	16 10		16 20
Watford Junction 66 d											
Milton Keynes Central 66 d					16 13	16 19			16 41		16 50
Rugby 66 d						16 42					
Nuneaton d						16 54					
Tamworth Low Level d						17 09					
Lichfield Trent Valley d						17 17					
Coventry 68 d	16 27				16 42						
Birmingham International 68 d	16 38				16 53						
BirminghamNewSt 68 d	16 57			17 01	17 15						
Wolverhampton d	17 15			17 20	17 37						
Penkridge d				17 29							
Stafford d	17 28			17 36		17 42		17 24			
Stoke-on-Trent 84 a	17 43					18 02	17 24				17 48
Macclesfield a	18 01						17 41			←	
Crewe 81,91 a				17 55	18 07	18 24		17 41	17 47	17 55	
d				17 57	18 09			17 43	17 49	17 57	
Chester 81 a				→	→				18 10		
Wrexham General 75 a											
Llandudno Junction 81 a									19 05		
Bangor (Gwynedd) 81 a									19 21		
Holyhead 81 a									19 52		
Wilmslow 84 a											
Stockport 84 a	18 13						17 54				18 16
Manchester Piccadilly a	18 25						18 04				18 27
Runcorn 91 a								18 00		18 24	
Liverpool South Pkwy 91 a										18 32	
Liverpool Lime Street 91 a								18 19		18 44	
d											
Manchester Airport 82 d		17 10									
Manchester Picc. 82 d		17 27									
Bolton 82 d											
Warrington Bank Quay d											
Wigan North Western 90 d											
Preston 90 a		18 02									
Blackpool North 97 a											
Preston 90 d		18 03	18 20								
Lancaster d		18 19	18 40								
Barrow-in-Furness 82 a											
Oxenholme Lake District 83 d		18 33	19 00								
Windermere 83 a			19 22								
Penrith North Lakes d		18 58									
Carlisle 216 a		19 13									
d		19 15									
Lockerbie 225,226 d		19 35									
Carstairs 226,225 a											
Motherwell 226 a		20 21									
Glasgow Central 216,226,225 a		20 42									
Haymarket a											
Edinburgh a											
Fort William 227,400 a											
Perth 229 a											
Dundee 229 a											
Aberdeen 229 a											
Inverness 229 a											

	VT	VT	NT	VT	NT	VT	XC	LM	XC	TP	LM
	◇■	◇■	◇	■	◇	◇■	◇■	■	◇■	◇■	■
			E	F	G		H		A		B
London Euston ⊖66 d	16 30	16 33				16 40					
Watford Junction 66 d											
Milton Keynes Central 66 d											
Rugby 66 d											
Nuneaton d											
Tamworth Low Level d		17 38									
Lichfield Trent Valley d		17 45									
Coventry 68 d									17 27		
Birmingham International 68 d									17 38		
BirminghamNewSt 68 d							17 31	17 36	17 57		18 01
Wolverhampton d							17 49	17 54	18 15		18 20
Penkridge d								18 04			18 29
Stafford d		17 59					18 03	18 10	18 28		18 36
Stoke-on-Trent 84 a							18 18		18 43		
Macclesfield a				←			18 36		19 01		
Crewe 81,91 a				18 07		18 10		18 30			18 55
d				18 09		18 11		18 32			18 57
Chester 81 a											→
Wrexham General 75 a											
Llandudno Junction 81 a											
Bangor (Gwynedd) 81 a											
Holyhead 81 a											
Wilmslow 84 a						18 27					
Stockport 84 a						18 36	18 49		19 13		
Manchester Piccadilly a						18 45	18 59		19 24		
Runcorn 91 a		18 32						18 52			
Liverpool South Pkwy 91 a								19 01			
Liverpool Lime Street 91 a		18 52						19 11			
d											
Manchester Airport 82 d			17 42							18 10	
Manchester Picc. 82 d			18 01							18 26	
Bolton 82 d			18 21								
Warrington Bank Quay d	18 14			18 27							
Wigan North Western 90 d	18 25			18 38							
Preston 90 a	18 38		18 50	18 51						19 03	
Blackpool North 97 a					←						
Preston 90 d	18 41		18 58	18 54	18 58					19 05	
Lancaster d	18 55		→	19 09	19 14					19 21	
Barrow-in-Furness 82 a					20 14						
Oxenholme Lake District 83 d	19 08			19 23						19 34	
Windermere 83 a											
Penrith North Lakes d	19 34									19 59	
Carlisle 216 a	19 49			20 01						20 15	
d	19 51			20 02						20 16	
Lockerbie 225,226 d										20 35	
Carstairs 226,225 a											
Motherwell 226 a											
Glasgow Central 216,226,225 a	21 02			21 15							
Haymarket a										21s31	
Edinburgh a										21 36	
Fort William 227,400 a											
Perth 229 a											
Dundee 229 a											
Aberdeen 229 a											
Inverness 229 a											

A From Bournemouth
B To Liverpool Lime Street
C To Glasgow Central
D From Birmingham New Street
E To Barrow-in-Furness
F From London Euston
G From Manchester Airport
H From Paignton

Refer to Operator websites for full information about Sleeper Services. Contact details for train operators available at National Rail Enquiries

Table T065-F

Saturdays

23 June to 8 September

London & West Midlands to North West England. London, West Midlands & Manchester to Scotland via the West Coast

	VT	LM	VT	VT	VT	VT	LM	VT	VT	VT	VT	XC	LM	XC	TP	LM	VT	LM	VT	VT	VT
	A						B			C		D		E		F	A				
London Euston 15 ⊖66 d	16 43	16 46	17 00	17 07	17 10	17 10		17 20	17 30		17 40						17 43	17 46	18 00	18 07	18 10
Watford Junction 66 d																					
Milton Keynes Central 66 d	17 13	17 19			17 40	17 41		17 50									18 13	18 19			18 41
Rugby 66 d		17 42																18 42			
Nuneaton d		17 54		18 03														18 54			
Tamworth Low Level d		18 09																19 09			
Lichfield Trent Valley d		18 17																19 17			
Coventry 68 d	17 42													18 27			18 42				
Birmingham International 68 ✈ d	17 53													18 38			18 53				
BirminghamNewSt 12 68 d	18 15											18 31	18 36	18 57		19 01	19 15				
Wolverhampton 7 d	18 37											18 49	18 54	19 15		19 20	19 37				
Penkridge d													19 04			19 30					
Stafford d		18 44		18 27								19 03	19 10	19 28		19 36		19 42		19 24	
Stoke-on-Trent 84 a		19 02	18 24					18 48				19 18		19 43				20 02	19 24		
Macclesfield a			18 41				←			←		19 36		20 01					19 41		
Crewe 10 81,91 a	19 08	19 27		18 45	18 49	18 49	18 55			19 08	19 11		19 30			19 56	20 09	20 24		19 41	19 47
d	19 09			18 47	18 52	18 52	18 57			19 09	19 12					19 57	20 09			19 43	19 49
Chester 81 a	→				19 11	19 11										→	→				20 09
Wrexham General 75 a																					
Llandudno Junction 81 a						20 07															
Bangor (Gwynedd) 81 a						20 23															
Holyhead 81 ⛴ a						20 54															
Wilmslow 84 a											19 27										
Stockport 84 a			18 54					19 16			19 36	19 49		20 13					19 54		
Manchester Piccadilly 10 a			19 05					19 28			19 45	19 59		20 25					20 04		
Runcorn 91 a				19 04			19 21													20 00	
Liverpool South Pkwy 7 91 ✈ a							19 30														
Liverpool Lime Street 10 91 a				19 22			19 42													20 18	
d																					
Manchester Airport 82 ✈ d															19 10						
Manchester Picc. 10 82 d															19 26						
Bolton 82 d																					
Warrington Bank Quay d									19 14	19 27											
Wigan North Western 90 d									19 25	19 38											
Preston 8 90 a									19 38	19 54					20 02						
Blackpool North 97 a																					
Preston 8 90 d									19 41						20 04						
Lancaster 6 d									19 55						20 19						
Barrow-in-Furness 82 a																					
Oxenholme Lake District 83 d									20 08						20 33						
Windermere 83 a																					
Penrith North Lakes d									20 34						20 58						
Carlisle 8 216 a									20 48						21 13						
d									20 50						21 15						
Lockerbie 225,226 d															21 33						
Carstairs 226,225 a																					
Motherwell 226 a																					
Glasgow Central 15 216,226,225 a									22 01												
Haymarket ⛴ a															22s31						
Edinburgh 10 ⛴ a															22 38						
Fort William 227,400 a																					
Perth 229 a																					
Dundee 229 a																					
Aberdeen 229 a																					
Inverness 229 a																					

A To Preston
B From Birmingham New Street
C From London Euston
D From Bristol Temple Meads
E From Bournemouth
F To Liverpool Lime Street

Refer to Operator websites for full information about Sleeper Services. Contact details for train operators available at National Rail Enquiries

Table T065-F

Saturdays

23 June to 8 September

London & West Midlands to North West England. London, West Midlands & Manchester to Scotland via the West Coast

	LM	VT	VT	VT	VT	VT	XC	XC	LM	VT	LM	VT	VT	LM	VT	VT	VT	XC	LM	XC	VT	VT
	A			B			C	D	E					A				C		F		
London Euston 15 ⊖66 d		18 20	18 30		18 33	18 40				18 43	18 46	19 00	19 07		19 20	19 30	19 40				20 11	20 20
Watford Junction 66 d																						
Milton Keynes Central 66 d		18 50								19 13	19 19				19 50							21 05
Rugby 66 d											19 42										21 15	
Nuneaton d											19 58		20 03									21 33
Tamworth Low Level d					19 38						20 14											
Lichfield Trent Valley d					19 45						20 21											
Coventry 68 d								19 27		19 42												
Birmingham International 68 ✈ d								19 38		19 53												
BirminghamNewSt 12 68 d							19 31	19 57	20 01	20 15								20 31	20 36	20 57		
Wolverhampton 7 d							19 49	20 15	20 22	20 37								20 49	20 54	21 17		
Penkridge d									20 31										21 04			
Stafford d					19 59		20 03	20 28	20 38	20 51	20 44		20 27					21 03	21 10	21 30	21 46	
Stoke-on-Trent 84 a		19 48					20 18	20 43			21 02	20 24			20 48			21 18	21 27	21 46		22 05
Macclesfield a	←			←			20 36	21 01				20 41		←				21 36		22 04		22 21
Crewe 10 81,91 a	19 56			20 09		20 12			20 57	21 10	21 22		20 45	20 57		21 02	21 18		21 49		22 05	
d	19 57			20 09		20 12			20 59				20 47	20 59		21 05	21 19				22 06	
Chester 81 a									→													
Wrexham General 75 a																						
Llandudno Junction 81 a																						
Bangor (Gwynedd) 81 a																						
Holyhead 81 ⛴ a																						
Wilmslow 84 a						20 28											21 34					
Stockport 84 a		20 16				20 36	20 49	21 13				20 54			21 20		21 44	21 49		22 16		22 35
Manchester Piccadilly 10 a		20 28				20 45	20 59	21 24				21 04			21 32		21 53	21 59		22 33		22 50
Runcorn 91 a	20 25				20 31								21 05	21 20							22 24	
Liverpool South Pkwy 7 91 ✈ a	20 33													21 29								
Liverpool Lime Street 10 91 a	20 44				20 51								21 27	21 40							22 42	
d																						
Manchester Airport 82 ✈ d																						
Manchester Picc. 10 82 d																						
Bolton 82 d																						
Warrington Bank Quay d			20 14	20 27												21 22						
Wigan North Western 90 d			20 25	20 38												21 33						
Preston 8 90 a			20 38	20 52												21 47						
Blackpool North 97 a																						
Preston 8 90 d			20 41																			
Lancaster 6 d			20 55																			
Barrow-in-Furness 82 a																						
Oxenholme Lake District 83 d			21 10																			
Windermere 83 a																						
Penrith North Lakes d			21 35																			
Carlisle 8 216 a			21 50																			
d			21 50																			
Lockerbie 225,226 d			22 09																			
Carstairs 226,225 a																						
Motherwell 226 a			22 52																			
Glasgow Central 15 216,226,225 a			23 09																			
Haymarket ⛴ a																						
Edinburgh 10 ⛴ a																						
Fort William 227,400 a																						
Perth 229 a																						
Dundee 229 a																						
Aberdeen 229 a																						
Inverness 229 a																						

A From Birmingham New Street
B From London Euston
C From Bristol Temple Meads
D From Bournemouth. ✕ to BirminghamNewSt
E To Liverpool Lime Street
F From Newquay

Refer to Operator websites for full information about Sleeper Services. Contact details for train operators available at National Rail Enquiries

Table T065-F

Saturdays
23 June to 8 September

London & West Midlands to North West England. London, West Midlands & Manchester to Scotland via the West Coast

	NT	VT	LM	XC	VT	XC	LM
	◇	◇1	1	◇1	◇1	◇1	1
				A			
London Euston 15 ⊖66 d		20 31			21 00		
Watford Junction 66 d		20u46					
Milton Keynes Central 66 d					21 45		
Rugby 66 d		21 36					
Nuneaton d							
Tamworth Low Level d		21 53					
Lichfield Trent Valley d		22 00					
Coventry 68 d				21 27			
Birmingham International 68 ✈ d				21 38			
BirminghamNewSt 12 68 d			21 36	21 57		22 31	22 39
Wolverhampton 7 d			21 59	22 15		22 49	23 06
Penkridge d			22 09				23 16
Stafford d			22 16	22 28	22 34	23 02	23 22
Stoke-on-Trent 84 a				22 43		23 19	
Macclesfield a				23 01		23 38	
Crewe 10 81,91 a		22 29	22 36		22 58		23 42
d		22 31			22 59		
Chester 81 a							
Wrexham General 75 a							
Llandudno Junction 81 a							
Bangor (Gwynedd) 81 a							
Holyhead 81 ⛴ a							
Wilmslow 84 a					23 14		
Stockport 84 a				23 13	23 26	23 53	
Manchester Piccadilly 10 a				23 29	23 39	00 10	
Runcorn 91 a							
Liverpool South Pkwy 7 91 ✈ a							
Liverpool Lime Street 10 91 a							
d							
Manchester Airport 82 ✈ d	22 10						
Manchester Picc. 10 82 d	22 26						
Bolton 82 d							
Warrington Bank Quay d		22 48					
Wigan North Western 90 d		23 02					
Preston 8 90 a	23 09	23 18					
Blackpool North 97 a							
Preston 8 90 d	23 10						
Lancaster 6 d	23 28						
Barrow-in-Furness 82 a	00 32						
Oxenholme Lake District 83 d							
Windermere 83 a							
Penrith North Lakes d							
Carlisle 8 216 a							
d							
Lockerbie 225,226 d							
Carstairs 226,225 a							
Motherwell 226 a							
Glasgow Central 15 216,226,225 a							
Haymarket a							
Edinburgh 10 a							
Fort William 227,400 a							
Perth 229 a							
Dundee 229 a							
Aberdeen 229 a							
Inverness 229 a							

A From Bournemouth

Refer to Operator websites for full information about Sleeper Services. Contact details for train operators available at National Rail Enquiries

Table T065-F

Saturdays
15 September to 8 December

London & West Midlands to North West England. London, West Midlands & Manchester to Scotland via the West Coast

	NT	CS	AW	NT	CS	CS	CS	NT	NT	TP	VT	VT	XC	LM	TP	VT	XC	LM	LM	XC	TP	VT
		R			R	R	R															
	◇		◇	◇						◇1	◇1	◇1	◇1	1	◇1	◇1	◇1	1	1	◇1	◇1	◇1
	A	B	C	D	B	B	B												E			
London Euston 15 ⊖66 d																						06 05
Watford Junction 66 d		00u10																				06u20
Milton Keynes Central 66 d																						06 41
Rugby 66 d																			06 02			07 03
Nuneaton d																			06 16			
Tamworth Low Level d																			06 29			
Lichfield Trent Valley d																			06 35			
Coventry 68 d																						
Birmingham International 68 ✈ d																		06 18				
BirminghamNewSt 12 68 d												05 30	05 57	06 01		06 15	06 31	06 36		06 57		
Wolverhampton 7 d												05 48	06 15	06 20		06 37	06 49	06 54		07 15		
Penkridge d														06 29				07 04				
Stafford d												06 01	06 28	06 36			07 03	07 10	06 58	07 31		07 34
Stoke-on-Trent 84 a													06 44				07 18		07 14			
Macclesfield a													07 05				07 36					
Crewe 10 81,91 a												06 20		06 56		07 08		07 29	07 37	07 50		07 53
d			00 15								05 57	06 23		06 59		07 09		07 33		07 52		07 55
Chester 81 a			00 37									06 43										
Wrexham General 75 a																						
Llandudno Junction 81 a			01 28									07 32										
Bangor (Gwynedd) 81 a			01 46									07 49										
Holyhead 81 ⛴ a			02 15									08 20										
Wilmslow 84 a																				08 07		
Stockport 84 a													07 18				07 49			08 16		
Manchester Piccadilly 10 a													07 28				07 59			08 29		
Runcorn 91 a														07 24				07 59				
Liverpool South Pkwy 7 91 ✈ a														07 33				08 09				
Liverpool Lime Street 10 91 a														07 44				08 21				
d																						
Manchester Airport 82 ✈ d															06 10						07 10	
Manchester Picc. 10 82 d	00 09									04 54					06 26						07 26	
Bolton 82 d				00 41																		
Warrington Bank Quay d											06 15					07 27						08 12
Wigan North Western 90 d											06 25					07 38						08 23
Preston 8 90 a	00 59			01 06						05 30	06 38				07 01	07 51					08 01	08 36
Blackpool North 97 a	01 29																					
Preston 8 90 d					00u58	00u58	00u58	05 16		05 40	06 40				07 03	07 53					08 03	08 37
Lancaster 6 d								05 36	05 40	05 56	06 54				07 18	08 08					08 18	08 52
Barrow-in-Furness 82 a																						
Oxenholme Lake District 83 d									06 19	06 10	07 09				07 32	08 22					08 32	09 06
Windermere 83 a									06 39													
Penrith North Lakes d										06 35	07 34										08 57	09 32
Carlisle 8 216 a		05s13						09 24		06 51	07 49				08 10	09 00					09 12	09 47
d										06 52	07 51				08 12	09 01					09 14	09 48
Lockerbie 225,226 d										07 11	08 10				08 30						09 33	
Carstairs 226,225 a		06s21								07 44												
Motherwell 226 a		06s55								07 59											10 20	
Glasgow Central 15 216,226,225 a		07 22								08 20	09 12										10 39	10 59
Haymarket a															09s30	10 13						
Edinburgh 10 a															09 37	10 18						
Fort William 227,400 a							09 57															
Perth 229 a						05s41																
Dundee 229 a					06s08																	
Aberdeen 229 a					07 39																	
Inverness 229 a						08 41																

A From Manchester Airport
B From London Euston
C From Birmingham New Street
D From Manchester Victoria
E From Northampton

Refer to Operator websites for full information about Sleeper Services. Contact details for train operators available at National Rail Enquiries

Table T065-F

Saturdays

15 September to 8 December

London & West Midlands to North West England. London, West Midlands & Manchester to Scotland via the West Coast

	LM	VT	LM	VT	TP		VT	XC	LM	LM A	VT	VT	XC B	VT	LM		NT	VT	NT C	VT	NT D	VT	XC E	LM
London Euston ⊖66 d			06 24	06 36							06 55	07 07		07 20				07 30				07 35		
Watford Junction 66 d			06 41	06u51																				
Milton Keynes Central 66 d			07 24								07 27			07 50								08 06		
Rugby 66 d			08 04							06 58														
Nuneaton d			08 16							07 12														
Tamworth Low Level d			08 29							07 29														
Lichfield Trent Valley d			08 35							07 35														
Coventry 68 d													07 27											
Birmingham International 68 d													07 38											
Birmingham New St 68 d	07 01	07 15					07 21	07 31	07 36				07 57		08 01					08 15			08 31	08 36
Wolverhampton d	07 20	07 37					07 41	07 49	07 54				08 15		08 20					08 37			08 49	08 54
Penkridge d	07 29								08 04						08 29									09 04
Stafford d	07 36		08 55				07 59	08 03	08 10	07 55		08 24	08 28		08 36								09 03	09 10
Stoke-on-Trent 84 a			09 12					08 18		08 12	08 24		08 43	08 48									09 18	
Macclesfield a								08 36			08 41		09 01										09 36	
Crewe 81,91 a	07 58	08 06	09 37	08 10			08 18		08 30	08 37		08 41			08 56					09 08		09 11		09 30
d	07 59	08 09		08 11			08 19		08 32			08 43			08 57					09 09		09 12		09 32
Chester 81 a																								
Wrexham General 75 a																								
Llandudno Junction 81 a																								
Bangor (Gwynedd) 81 a																								
Holyhead 81 a																								
Wilmslow 84 a				08 27																		09 28		
Stockport 84 a				08 35				08 50			08 54		09 13	09 16								09 36	09 49	
Manchester Piccadilly a				08 46				08 59			09 04		09 25	09 28								09 44	09 59	
Runcorn 91 a	08 24								08 52			09 00			09 21									09 52
Liverpool South Pkwy 91 a	08 32								09 01						09 30									10 01
Liverpool Lime Street 91 a	08 44								09 11			09 20			09 42									10 11
d																								
Manchester Airport 82 d					08 10														08 41					
Manchester Picc. 82 d					08 26														09 01					
Bolton 82 d																			09 22					
Warrington Bank Quay d		08 27					08 41											09 14		09 27				
Wigan North Western 90 d		08 38					08 52											09 25		09 38				
Preston 90 a		08 51			09 02		09 09											09 38	09 49	09 51				
Blackpool North 97 a							09 32														←			
Preston 90 d		08 53			09 04												09 29	09 41	09 57	09 53	09 57			
Lancaster d		09 09			09 19												09 59	09 55	→	10 08	10 14			
Barrow-in-Furness 82 a																					11 15			
Oxenholme Lake District 83 d																	10 19			10 22				
Windermere 83 a																	10 41							
Penrith North Lakes d		09 46																10 31						
Carlisle 216 a		10 01			10 07													10 46		10 59				
d		10 01			10 09													10 47		11 01				
Lockerbie 225,226 d					10 27																			
Carstairs 226,225 a																								
Motherwell 226 a																								
Glasgow Central 216,226,225 a		11 15																11 59						
Haymarket a					11s27															12 17				
Edinburgh a					11 34															12 22				
Fort William 227,400 a																								
Perth 229 a																								
Dundee 229 a																								
Aberdeen 229 a																								
Inverness 229 a																								

A From Northampton
B From Southampton Central
C To Barrow-in-Furness
D From Manchester Airport
E From Bristol Temple Meads

Refer to Operator websites for full information about Sleeper Services. Contact details for train operators available at National Rail Enquiries

Table T065-F

Saturdays

15 September to 8 December

London & West Midlands to North West England. London, West Midlands & Manchester to Scotland via the West Coast

	XC A		TP	LM B	VT C	LM	VT	VT	VT	LM D	VT		VT	VT E	VT	XC F	LM	XC G	TP	LM B	VT H		LM	VT
London Euston ⊖66 d					07 43	07 46	08 00	08 07	08 10		08 20		08 30		08 40						08 43		08 46	08 53
Watford Junction 66 d																								
Milton Keynes Central 66 d					08 13	08 19			08 41		08 50										09 13		09 19	
Rugby 66 d						08 42																	09 42	09 46
Nuneaton d						08 54																	09 54	
Tamworth Low Level d						09 09																	10 09	
Lichfield Trent Valley d						09 17																	10 17	
Coventry 68 d	08 27				08 42													09 27			09 42			
Birmingham International 68 d	08 38				08 53													09 38			09 53			
Birmingham New St 68 d	08 57			09 01	09 15											09 31	09 36	09 57		10 01	10 15			
Wolverhampton d	09 15			09 20	09 37											09 49	09 54	10 15		10 20	10 37			
Penkridge d																	10 04							
Stafford d	09 28			09 35		09 42		09 24								10 03	10 10	10 28		10 35			10 42	
Stoke-on-Trent 84 a	09 43					10 02	09 24				09 48					10 18		10 43					11 02	
Macclesfield a	10 01						09 41			←				←		10 36		11 01						
Crewe 81,91 a				09 55	10 08	10 24		09 41	09 47	09 55				10 08	10 11		10 30			10 55	11 08		11 24	
d				09 57	10 09			09 43	09 49	09 57				10 09	10 12		10 32			10 57	11 09			
Chester 81 a				→	→				10 10											→	→			
Wrexham General 75 a																								
Llandudno Junction 81 a																								
Bangor (Gwynedd) 81 a																								
Holyhead 81 a																								
Wilmslow 84 a															10 27									
Stockport 84 a	10 13						09 54				10 16				10 36	10 49		11 13						
Manchester Piccadilly a	10 24						10 04				10 28				10 46	11 00		11 25						
Runcorn 91 a								10 00		10 24							10 52							
Liverpool South Pkwy 91 a										10 32							11 01							
Liverpool Lime Street 91 a								10 19		10 44							11 11							
d																								
Manchester Airport 82 d			09 10																10 10					
Manchester Picc. 82 d			09 26																10 26					
Bolton 82 d																								
Warrington Bank Quay d													10 14	10 27										10 59
Wigan North Western 90 d													10 25	10 38										11 12
Preston 90 a			10 03										10 38	10 51					11 02					11 24
Blackpool North 97 a																								11 56
Preston 90 d			10 04										10 41	10 53					11 03					
Lancaster d			10 20										10 55	11 08										
Barrow-in-Furness 82 a																								
Oxenholme Lake District 83 d			10 35										11 08											
Windermere 83 a																								
Penrith North Lakes d			11 00											11 45										
Carlisle 216 a			11 16										11 46	12 00					12 05					
d			11 17										11 47	12 02					12 06					
Lockerbie 225,226 d			11 37																					
Carstairs 226,225 a																								
Motherwell 226 a			12 22																					
Glasgow Central 216,226,225 a			12 42										12 59	13 15										
Haymarket a																			13s19					
Edinburgh a																			13 26					
Fort William 227,400 a																								
Perth 229 a																								
Dundee 229 a																								
Aberdeen 229 a																								
Inverness 229 a																								

A From Southampton Central
B To Liverpool Lime Street
C To Glasgow Central
D From Birmingham New Street
E From London Euston
F From Cardiff Central
G From Bournemouth
H To Edinburgh

Refer to Operator websites for full information about Sleeper Services. Contact details for train operators available at National Rail Enquiries

Table T065-F

Saturdays
15 September to 8 December

London & West Midlands to North West England. London, West Midlands & Manchester to Scotland via the West Coast

	VT ◇■	VT ◇■	VT ◇■	LM ■ A	VT ◇■	VT ◇■	VT ◇■ B	VT ◇■	XC ◇■ C	LM ■	XC ◇■ D	TP ◇■	NT ◇	LM ■ E	VT ◇■ F	LM ■	VT ◇■	VT ◇■	VT ◇■	LM ■ A	VT ◇■	VT ◇■
London Euston 15 ⊖66 d	09 00	09 07	09 10		09 20	09 30		09 40							09 43	09 46	10 00	10 07	10 10		10 20	10 30
Watford Junction 66 d																						
Milton Keynes Central 66 d			09 41		09 50										10 13	10 19			10 41		10 50	
Rugby 66 d																10 42						
Nuneaton d																10 54						
Tamworth Low Level d																11 09						
Lichfield Trent Valley d																11 17			11 24			
Coventry 68 d											10 27				10 42							
Birmingham International 68 ✈ d											10 38				10 53							
BirminghamNewSt 12 68 ⇌ d									10 31	10 36	10 57			11 01	11 15							
Wolverhampton 7 ⇌ d									10 49	10 54	11 15			11 20	11 37							
Penkridge d										11 04												
Stafford d		10 26							11 03	11 10	11 28			11 35		11 42		11 24				
Stoke-on-Trent 84 a	10 24				10 48				11 18		11 43					12 02	11 24				11 48	
Macclesfield a	10 41			←			←		11 36		12 01						11 41			←		
Crewe 10 81,91 a		10 44	10 47	10 55			11 08	11 11		11 30				11 54	12 07	12 24		11 41	11 53	11 54		
d		10 46	10 49	10 57			11 09	11 12		11 32				11 57	12 09			11 43	11 56	11 57		
Chester 81 a			11 13											→	→				12 17			
Wrexham General 75 a																						
Llandudno Junction 81 a			12 00																			
Bangor (Gwynedd) 81 a			12 16																			
Holyhead 81 ⛴ a			12 47																			
Wilmslow 84 a								11 27														
Stockport 84 a	10 54				11 16			11 35	11 49		12 13						11 54				12 16	
Manchester Piccadilly 10 ⇌ a	11 04				11 28			11 46	11 59		12 25						12 04				12 28	
Runcorn 91 a		11 03		11 21						11 52								12 00		12 24		
Liverpool South Pkwy 7 91 ✈ a				11 30						12 01										12 32		
Liverpool Lime Street 10 91 a		11 20		11 42						12 11								12 19		12 44		
d																						
Manchester Airport 82 ✈⇌ d												10 59										
Manchester Picc. 10 82 ⇌ d												11 14										
Bolton 82 d																						
Warrington Bank Quay d						11 14	11 27															12 14
Wigan North Western 90 d						11 25	11 38															12 25
Preston 8 90 a						11 38	11 51					11 58										12 38
Blackpool North 97 a																						
Preston 8 90 d						11 41	11 53					12 04	12 17									12 41
Lancaster 8 d						11 55	12 08					12 20	12 37									12 55
Barrow-in-Furness 82 a																						
Oxenholme Lake District 83 d							12 21					12 33	13 02									13 08
Windermere 83 a													13 24									
Penrith North Lakes d						12 30						12 58										
Carlisle 8 216 a						12 46	12 59					13 14										13 46
d						12 47	13 01					13 17										13 47
Lockerbie 225,226 d												13 37										
Carstairs 226,225 a																						
Motherwell 226 a												14 21										
Glasgow Central 15 216,226,225 a						13 59						14 40										14 59
Haymarket ⇌ a							14 11															
Edinburgh 10 ⇌ a							14 17															
Fort William 227,400 a																						
Perth 229 a																						
Dundee 229 a																						
Aberdeen 229 a																						
Inverness 229 a																						

A From Birmingham New Street
B From London Euston
C From Paignton
D From Bournemouth
E To Liverpool Lime Street
F To Glasgow Central

Refer to Operator websites for full information about Sleeper Services. Contact details for train operators available at National Rail Enquiries

Table T065-F

Saturdays
15 September to 8 December

London & West Midlands to North West England. London, West Midlands & Manchester to Scotland via the West Coast

	NT ◇ A	VT ◇■ B	NT ◇ C	VT ◇■	VT ◇■	XC ◇■ D	LM ■	XC ◇■ E	TP ◇■	LM ■ F	VT ◇■ G	LM ■	VT ◇■	VT ◇■	VT ◇■	LM ■ H	VT ◇■	VT ◇■	VT ◇■ B	VT ◇■	XC ◇■ D
London Euston 15 ⊖66 d				10 36	10 40						10 43	10 46	11 00	11 07	11 10		11 20	11 30		11 40	
Watford Junction 66 d																					
Milton Keynes Central 66 d											11 13	11 19			11 41		11 50				
Rugby 66 d				11 28								11 42									
Nuneaton d												11 54									
Tamworth Low Level d												12 09									
Lichfield Trent Valley d												12 17									
Coventry 68 d								11 27			11 42										
Birmingham International 68 ✈ d								11 38			11 53										
BirminghamNewSt 12 68 ⇌ d						11 31	11 36	11 57		12 01	12 15										12 31
Wolverhampton 7 ⇌ d						11 49	11 54	12 15		12 20	12 37										12 49
Penkridge d							12 04														
Stafford d						12 03	12 10	12 28		12 35		12 42		12 24							13 03
Stoke-on-Trent 84 a						12 18		12 43				13 02	12 24				12 48				13 18
Macclesfield a		←				12 36		13 01					12 41			←			←		13 36
Crewe 10 81,91 a		12 07			12 11		12 30			12 54	13 08	13 24		12 42	12 47	12 54			13 08	13 11	
d		12 09			12 12		12 32			12 57	13 09			12 43	12 49	12 57			13 09	13 12	
Chester 81 a										→	→				13 11						
Wrexham General 75 a																					
Llandudno Junction 81 a																					
Bangor (Gwynedd) 81 a																					
Holyhead 81 ⛴ a																					
Wilmslow 84 a					12 27															13 27	
Stockport 84 a					12 35	12 49		13 13					12 55				13 16			13 35	13 49
Manchester Piccadilly 10 ⇌ a					12 46	12 59		13 25					13 04				13 28			13 46	13 59
Runcorn 91 a							12 52							13 00		13 22					
Liverpool South Pkwy 7 91 ✈ a							13 01									13 31					
Liverpool Lime Street 10 91 a							13 11							13 19		13 42					
d																					
Manchester Airport 82 ✈⇌ d	11 41								12 10												
Manchester Picc. 10 82 ⇌ d	12 01								12 26												
Bolton 82 d	12 22																				
Warrington Bank Quay d		12 27		12 34														13 14	13 27		
Wigan North Western 90 d		12 38		12 45														13 25	13 38		
Preston 8 90 a	12 48	12 52		12 57					13 02									13 38	13 51		
Blackpool North 97 a			←	13 20																	
Preston 8 90 d	12 57	12 53	12 57						13 03									13 41	13 53		
Lancaster 8 d	→	13 08	13 14						13 20									13 55	14 08		
Barrow-in-Furness 82 a			14 14																		
Oxenholme Lake District 83 d		13 23							13 33									14 08			
Windermere 83 a																					
Penrith North Lakes d																			14 43		
Carlisle 8 216 a		14 00							14 12									14 46	14 59		
d		14 01							14 13									14 47	14 59		
Lockerbie 225,226 d									14 32												
Carstairs 226,225 a																					
Motherwell 226 a		14 58																			
Glasgow Central 15 216,226,225 a		15 15																15 59			
Haymarket ⇌ a									15s29										16 16		
Edinburgh 10 ⇌ a									15 36										16 23		
Fort William 227,400 a																					
Perth 229 a																					
Dundee 229 a																					
Aberdeen 229 a																					
Inverness 229 a																					

A To Barrow-in-Furness
B From London Euston
C From Manchester Airport
D From Bristol Temple Meads
E From Bournemouth
F To Liverpool Lime Street
G To Edinburgh
H From Birmingham New Street

Refer to Operator websites for full information about Sleeper Services. Contact details for train operators available at National Rail Enquiries

Table T065-F

Saturdays

15 September to 8 December

London & West Midlands to North West England. London, West Midlands & Manchester to Scotland via the West Coast

	LM	XC	TP	NT	LM	VT	LM	VT	VT	VT	LM	VT	VT	NT	VT	VT	XC	LM	XC	TP	LM	VT
		A			B	C					D				E		F		A		B	G
London Euston ⊖66 d						11 43	11 46	12 00	12 07	12 10		12 20	12 30			12 40						12 43
Watford Junction 66 d																						
Milton Keynes Central 66 d						12 13	12 19			12 41		12 50										13 13
Rugby 66 d							12 42			13 04												
Nuneaton d							12 54															
Tamworth Low Level d							13 09															
Lichfield Trent Valley d							13 17															
Coventry 68 d		12 27				12 42													13 27			13 42
Birmingham International 68 d		12 38				12 53													13 38			13 53
BirminghamNewSt 68 d	12 36	12 57			13 01	13 15											13 31	13 36	13 57		14 01	14 15
Wolverhampton d	12 54	13 15			13 20	13 37											13 49	13 54	14 15		14 20	14 37
Penkridge d	13 04																	14 04				
Stafford d	13 10	13 28			13 35		13 42		13 24								14 03	14 10	14 28		14 35	
Stoke-on-Trent 84 a		13 43					14 02	13 24				13 48					14 18		14 43			
Macclesfield a		14 01						13 41			←				←		14 36		15 01			
Crewe 81,91 a	13 30				13 56	14 08	14 24		13 41	13 50	13 56				14 08	14 11		14 30			14 55	15 07
d	13 32				13 57	14 09			13 43	13 52	13 57				14 09	14 12		14 32			14 57	15 09
Chester 81 a					→	→				14 15											→	→
Wrexham General 75 a																						
Llandudno Junction 81 a																						
Bangor (Gwynedd) 81 a																						
Holyhead 81 a																						
Wilmslow 84 a																14 27						
Stockport 84 a		14 13						13 54				14 16				14 35	14 49		15 13			
Manchester Piccadilly a		14 25						14 05				14 28				14 46	14 59		15 25			
Runcorn 91 a	13 52								14 00		14 21							14 52				
Liverpool South Pkwy 91 a	14 01										14 30							15 01				
Liverpool Lime Street 91 a	14 11								14 20		14 42							15 11				
d																						
Manchester Airport 82 d			13 10																	14 10		
Manchester Picc. 82 d			13 26																	14 26		
Bolton 82 d																						
Warrington Bank Quay d													14 14		14 27							
Wigan North Western 90 d													14 25		14 38							
Preston 90 a			14 02										14 38		14 51					15 03		
Blackpool North 97 a																						
Preston 90 d			14 04	14 10									14 41		14 53					15 04		
Lancaster d			14 19	14 30									14 55	15 03	15 09					15 20		
Barrow-in-Furness 82 a														16 07								
Oxenholme Lake District 83 d			14 33	14 51											15 22							
Windermere 83 a				15 09																		
Penrith North Lakes d			14 58										15 30							15 55		
Carlisle 216 a			15 13										15 45	18 41	16 00					16 11		
d			15 14										15 46		16 02					16 13		
Lockerbie 225,226 d			15 33																	16 32		
Carstairs 226,225 a																						
Motherwell 226 a			16 21																			
Glasgow Central 216,226,225 a			16 40										16 59		17 15							
Haymarket a																				17s31		
Edinburgh a																				17 36		
Fort William 227,400 a																						
Perth 229 a																						
Dundee 229 a																						
Aberdeen 229 a																						
Inverness 229 a																						

A From Bournemouth
B To Liverpool Lime Street
C To Glasgow Central
D From Birmingham New Street
E From London Euston
F From Paignton
G To Edinburgh

Refer to Operator websites for full information about Sleeper Services. Contact details for train operators available at National Rail Enquiries

Table T065-F

Saturdays

15 September to 8 December

London & West Midlands to North West England. London, West Midlands & Manchester to Scotland via the West Coast

	LM	VT	VT	VT	LM	VT	VT	VT	NT	VT	XC	LM	XC	TP	LM	VT	LM	VT	VT	VT	LM	VT
					A			B			C		D		E	F					A	
London Euston ⊖66 d	12 46	13 00	13 07	13 10		13 20	13 30			13 40						13 43	13 46	14 00	14 07	14 10		14 20
Watford Junction 66 d																						
Milton Keynes Central 66 d	13 19			13 41		13 50										14 13	14 19			14 41		14 50
Rugby 66 d	13 42																14 42					
Nuneaton d	13 54																14 54					
Tamworth Low Level d	14 09																15 09					
Lichfield Trent Valley d	14 17																15 17					
Coventry 68 d													14 27			14 42						
Birmingham International 68 d													14 38			14 53						
BirminghamNewSt 68 d											14 31	14 36	14 57		15 01	15 15						
Wolverhampton d											14 49	14 54	15 15		15 20	15 37						
Penkridge d												15 04										
Stafford d	14 42		14 24								15 03	15 10	15 28		15 35		15 42		15 24			
Stoke-on-Trent 84 a	15 02	14 24				14 48					15 18		15 43				16 02	15 24				15 48
Macclesfield a		14 41			←			←			15 36		16 01					15 41			←	
Crewe 81,91 a	15 24		14 41	14 47	14 55			15 07		15 10		15 30			15 55	16 08	16 24		15 41	15 47	15 55	
d			14 43	14 49	14 57			15 09		15 11		15 32			15 57	16 09			15 43	15 49	15 57	
Chester 81 a				15 09											→	→				16 10		
Wrexham General 75 a																						
Llandudno Junction 81 a																				17 01		
Bangor (Gwynedd) 81 a																				17 17		
Holyhead 81 a																				17 48		
Wilmslow 84 a										15 27												
Stockport 84 a		14 54				15 16				15 35	15 49		16 13					15 54				16 16
Manchester Piccadilly a		15 05				15 28				15 46	15 59		16 25					16 05				16 28
Runcorn 91 a			15 00		15 21							15 52							16 00		16 25	
Liverpool South Pkwy 91 a					15 30							16 01									16 33	
Liverpool Lime Street 91 a			15 19		15 42							16 11							16 20		16 44	
d																						
Manchester Airport 82 d														15 10								
Manchester Picc. 82 d														15 26								
Bolton 82 d																						
Warrington Bank Quay d							15 14	15 27														
Wigan North Western 90 d							15 25	15 38														
Preston 90 a							15 38	15 51						16 02								
Blackpool North 97 a																						
Preston 90 d							15 40	15 53						16 03								
Lancaster d							15 54	16 08	16 13					16 19								
Barrow-in-Furness 82 a									17 16													
Oxenholme Lake District 83 d							16 10							16 32								
Windermere 83 a																						
Penrith North Lakes d								16 44						16 57								
Carlisle 216 a							16 48	17 00	19 43					17 13								
d							16 48	17 01						17 14								
Lockerbie 225,226 d																						
Carstairs 226,225 a																						
Motherwell 226 a																						
Glasgow Central 216,226,225 a							17 59							18 31								
Haymarket a								18 14														
Edinburgh a								18 22														
Fort William 227,400 a																						
Perth 229 a																						
Dundee 229 a																						
Aberdeen 229 a																						
Inverness 229 a																						

A From Birmingham New Street
B From London Euston
C From Bristol Temple Meads
D From Bournemouth
E To Liverpool Lime Street
F To Glasgow Central

Refer to Operator websites for full information about Sleeper Services. Contact details for train operators available at National Rail Enquiries

Table T065-F

Saturdays
15 September to 8 December

London & West Midlands to North West England. London, West Midlands & Manchester to Scotland via the West Coast

	VT	NT	VT	VT	XC	LM	XC	TP	LM	VT	LM	VT	VT	VT	LM	VT	VT	VT	VT	XC	LM
	◇■		◇■ A	◇■	◇■ B	■	◇■ C	◇■	■ D	■ E	■	◇■	◇■	◇■	■ F	◇■	◇■	■ A	◇■	◇■ G	■
London Euston ⊖66 d	14 30			14 40						14 43	14 46	15 00	15 07	15 10		15 20	15 30		15 40		
Watford Junction 66 d																					
Milton Keynes Central 66 d										15 13	15 19			15 41		15 50					
Rugby 66 d											15 42										
Nuneaton d											15 54										
Tamworth Low Level d											16 09										
Lichfield Trent Valley d											16 17										
Coventry 68 d							15 27			15 42											
Birmingham International 68 ✈ d							15 38			15 53											
BirminghamNewSt 68 d					15 31	15 36	15 57		16 01	16 15										16 31	16 36
Wolverhampton d					15 49	15 54	16 15		16 20	16 37										16 49	16 54
Penkridge d						16 04			16 29												17 04
Stafford d					16 03	16 10	16 28		16 36		16 42		16 24							17 03	17 10
Stoke-on-Trent 84 a					16 18		16 43				17 02	16 24				16 48				17 18	
Macclesfield a			←		16 36		17 01					16 41			←			←		17 36	
Crewe 81,91 a			16 08	16 10		16 30			16 55	17 08	17 24		16 41	16 47	16 55			17 08	17 11		17 30
d			16 09	16 11		16 32			16 57	17 09			16 43	16 49	16 57			17 09	17 12		17 32
Chester 81 a									→	→				17 11							
Wrexham General 75 a																					
Llandudno Junction 81 a																					
Bangor (Gwynedd) 81 a																					
Holyhead 81 ⛴ a																					
Wilmslow 84 a				16 27															17 27		
Stockport 84 a				16 36	16 49		17 13					16 54				17 16			17 36	17 49	
Manchester Piccadilly a				16 46	16 59		17 25					17 04				17 28			17 46	17 59	
Runcorn 91 a						16 52							17 00		17 24						17 52
Liverpool South Pkwy 91 ✈ a						17 01									17 33						18 01
Liverpool Lime Street 91 a						17 11							17 20		17 44						18 11
d																					
Manchester Airport 82 ✈ d								16 10													
Manchester Picc. 82 d								16 26													
Bolton 82 d																					
Warrington Bank Quay d	16 14		16 27														17 14	17 27			
Wigan North Western 90 d	16 25		16 38														17 25	17 38			
Preston 90 a	16 38		16 51					17 02									17 38	17 51			
Blackpool North 97 a																					
Preston 90 d	16 41		16 53					17 03									17 41	17 53			
Lancaster d	16 55	17 01	17 08					17 19									17 55	18 08			
Barrow-in-Furness 82 a		17 59																			
Oxenholme Lake District 83 d			17 22					17 32									18 08	18 23			
Windermere 83 a																					
Penrith North Lakes d	17 30							17 57										18 48			
Carlisle 216 a	17 46	20 31	18 00					18 12									18 46	19 04			
d	17 47		18 02					18 13									18 47	19 04			
Lockerbie 225,226 d								18 32													
Carstairs 226,225 a																					
Motherwell 226 a																					
Glasgow Central 216,226,225 a	18 59		19 15														19 59				
Haymarket a								19s29										20 14			
Edinburgh a								19 34										20 21			
Fort William 227,400 a																					
Perth 229 a																					
Dundee 229 a																					
Aberdeen 229 a																					
Inverness 229 a																					

A From London Euston
B From Penzance
C From Bournemouth
D To Liverpool Lime Street
E To Edinburgh
F From Birmingham New Street
G From Bristol Temple Meads

Refer to Operator websites for full information about Sleeper Services. Contact details for train operators available at National Rail Enquiries

Table T065-F

Saturdays
15 September to 8 December

London & West Midlands to North West England. London, West Midlands & Manchester to Scotland via the West Coast

	XC	TP	NT	LM	VT	LM	VT	VT	VT	LM	VT	VT	VT	NT	VT	NT	VT	XC	LM	XC	TP	LM
	◇■ A	◇■	◇	■ B	■ C	■	◇■	◇■	◇■	■ D	◇■	◇■	◇■	◇ E	■ F	◇ G	◇■	◇■ H	■	◇■ A	◇■	■ B
London Euston ⊖66 d					15 43	15 46	16 00	16 07	16 10		16 20	16 30	16 33				16 40					
Watford Junction 66 d																						
Milton Keynes Central 66 d					16 13	16 19			16 41		16 50											
Rugby 66 d						16 42																
Nuneaton d						16 54																
Tamworth Low Level d						17 09							17 38									
Lichfield Trent Valley d						17 17							17 45									
Coventry 68 d	16 27				16 42															17 27		
Birmingham International 68 ✈ d	16 38				16 53															17 38		
BirminghamNewSt 68 d	16 57			17 01	17 15													17 31	17 36	17 57		18 01
Wolverhampton d	17 15			17 20	17 37													17 49	17 54	18 15		18 20
Penkridge d				17 29															18 04			18 29
Stafford d	17 28			17 36		17 42		17 24					17 59					18 03	18 10	18 28		18 36
Stoke-on-Trent 84 a	17 43					18 02	17 24				17 48							18 18		18 43		
Macclesfield a	18 01						17 41			←					←			18 36		19 01		
Crewe 81,91 a				17 55	18 07	18 24		17 41	17 47	17 55					18 07		18 10		18 30			18 55
d				17 57	18 09			17 43	17 49	17 57					18 09		18 11		18 32			18 57
Chester 81 a				→	→				18 10													→
Wrexham General 75 a																						
Llandudno Junction 81 a									19 05													
Bangor (Gwynedd) 81 a									19 21													
Holyhead 81 ⛴ a									19 52													
Wilmslow 84 a																	18 27					
Stockport 84 a	18 13						17 54				18 16						18 36	18 49		19 13		
Manchester Piccadilly a	18 25						18 04				18 27						18 45	18 59		19 24		
Runcorn 91 a								18 00		18 24			18 32						18 52			
Liverpool South Pkwy 91 ✈ a										18 32									19 01			
Liverpool Lime Street 91 a								18 19		18 44			18 52						19 11			
d																						
Manchester Airport 82 ✈ d		17 10												17 42							18 10	
Manchester Picc. 82 d		17 27												18 01							18 26	
Bolton 82 d														18 21								
Warrington Bank Quay d												18 14			18 27							
Wigan North Western 90 d												18 25			18 38							
Preston 90 a		18 02										18 38		18 50	18 51						19 03	
Blackpool North 97 a																←						
Preston 90 d		18 03	18 20									18 41		18 58	18 54	18 58					19 05	
Lancaster d		18 19	18 40									18 55		→	19 09	19 14					19 21	
Barrow-in-Furness 82 a																20 14						
Oxenholme Lake District 83 d		18 33	19 00									19 08			19 23						19 34	
Windermere 83 a			19 22																			
Penrith North Lakes d		18 58										19 34									19 59	
Carlisle 216 a		19 13										19 49			20 01						20 15	
d		19 15										19 51			20 02						20 16	
Lockerbie 225,226 d		19 35																			20 35	
Carstairs 226,225 a																						
Motherwell 226 a		20 21																				
Glasgow Central 216,226,225 a		20 42										21 02			21 15							
Haymarket a																					21s31	
Edinburgh a																					21 36	
Fort William 227,400 a																						
Perth 229 a																						
Dundee 229 a																						
Aberdeen 229 a																						
Inverness 229 a																						

A From Bournemouth
B To Liverpool Lime Street
C To Glasgow Central
D From Birmingham New Street
E To Barrow-in-Furness
F From London Euston
G From Manchester Airport
H From Paignton

Refer to Operator websites for full information about Sleeper Services. Contact details for train operators available at National Rail Enquiries

Table T065-F

Saturdays
15 September to 8 December

London & West Midlands to North West England. London, West Midlands & Manchester to Scotland via the West Coast

	VT A	LM	VT	VT	VT	VT	LM B	VT	VT	VT C	VT	XC D	LM	XC E	TP	LM F	VT A	LM	VT	VT	VT
London Euston ⊖66 d	16 43	16 46	17 00	17 07	17 10	17 10		17 20	17 30		17 40						17 43	17 46	18 00	18 07	18 10
Watford Junction 66 d																					
Milton Keynes Central 66 d	17 13	17 19			17 40	17 41		17 50									18 13	18 19			18 41
Rugby 66 d		17 42																18 42			
Nuneaton d		17 54		18 03														18 54			
Tamworth Low Level d		18 09																19 09			
Lichfield Trent Valley d		18 17																19 17			
Coventry 68 d	17 42													18 27			18 42				
Birmingham International 68 d	17 53													18 38			18 53				
BirminghamNewSt 68 d	18 15											18 31	18 36	18 57		19 01	19 15				
Wolverhampton d	18 37											18 49	18 54	19 15		19 20	19 37				
Penkridge d													19 04			19 30					
Stafford d		18 44		18 27								19 03	19 10	19 28		19 36		19 42		19 24	
Stoke-on-Trent 84 a		19 02	18 24					18 48				19 18		19 43				20 02	19 24		
Macclesfield a			18 41				←			←		19 36		20 01					19 41		
Crewe 81,91 a	19 08	19 27		18 45	18 49	18 49	18 55			19 08	19 11		19 30			19 56	20 09	20 24		19 41	19 47
d	19 09			18 47	18 52	18 52	18 57			19 09	19 12					19 57	20 09			19 43	19 49
Chester 81 a	→				19 11	19 11										→	→				20 09
Wrexham General 75 a																					
Llandudno Junction 81 a						20 07															
Bangor (Gwynedd) 81 a						20 23															
Holyhead 81 a						20 54															
Wilmslow 84 a											19 27										
Stockport 84 a			18 54					19 16			19 36	19 49		20 13					19 54		
Manchester Piccadilly a			19 05					19 28			19 45	19 59		20 25					20 04		
Runcorn 91 a				19 04			19 21													20 00	
Liverpool South Pkwy 91 a							19 30														
Liverpool Lime Street 91 a				19 22			19 42													20 18	
d																					
Manchester Airport 82 d															19 10						
Manchester Picc. 82 d															19 26						
Bolton 82 d																					
Warrington Bank Quay d									19 14	19 27											
Wigan North Western 90 d									19 25	19 38											
Preston 90 a									19 38	19 54					20 02						
Blackpool North 97 a																					
Preston 90 d									19 41						20 04						
Lancaster d									19 55						20 19						
Barrow-in-Furness 82 a																					
Oxenholme Lake District 83 d									20 08						20 33						
Windermere 83 a																					
Penrith North Lakes d									20 34						20 58						
Carlisle 216 a									20 48						21 13						
d									20 50						21 15						
Lockerbie 225,226 d															21 33						
Carstairs 226,225 a																					
Motherwell 226 a																					
Glasgow Central 216,226,225 a									22 01												
Haymarket a															22s31						
Edinburgh a															22 38						
Fort William 227,400 a																					
Perth 229 a																					
Dundee 229 a																					
Aberdeen 229 a																					
Inverness 229 a																					

A To Preston
B From Birmingham New Street
C From London Euston
D From Bristol Temple Meads
E From Bournemouth
F To Liverpool Lime Street

Refer to Operator websites for full information about Sleeper Services. Contact details for train operators available at National Rail Enquiries

Table T065-F

Saturdays
15 September to 8 December

London & West Midlands to North West England. London, West Midlands & Manchester to Scotland via the West Coast

	LM A	VT	VT	VT B	VT	VT	XC C	XC D	LM E	VT	LM	VT	VT	LM A	VT	VT	VT	XC F	LM	XC D	VT	VT
London Euston ⊖66 d		18 20	18 30		18 33	18 40				18 43	18 46	19 00	19 07		19 20	19 30	19 40				20 11	20 20
Watford Junction 66 d																						
Milton Keynes Central 66 d		18 50								19 13	19 19				19 50							21 05
Rugby 66 d											19 42										21 15	
Nuneaton d											19 58		20 03									21 33
Tamworth Low Level d					19 38						20 14											
Lichfield Trent Valley d					19 45						20 21											
Coventry 68 d								19 27		19 42										20 27		
Birmingham International 68 d								19 38		19 53										20 38		
BirminghamNewSt 68 d							19 31	19 57	20 01	20 15								20 31	20 36	20 57		
Wolverhampton d							19 49	20 15	20 22	20 37								20 49	20 54	21 17		
Penkridge d									20 31										21 04			
Stafford d					19 59		20 03	20 28	20 38	20 51	20 44		20 27					21 03	21 10	21 30	21 46	
Stoke-on-Trent 84 a		19 48					20 18	20 43			21 02	20 24			20 48			21 18	21 27	21 46		22 05
Macclesfield a	←			←			20 36	21 01				20 41		←				21 36		22 04		22 21
Crewe 81,91 a	19 56			20 09		20 12			20 57	21 10	21 22		20 45	20 57		21 02	21 18		21 49		22 05	
d	19 57			20 09		20 12			20 59				20 47	20 59		21 05	21 19				22 06	
Chester 81 a									→													
Wrexham General 75 a																						
Llandudno Junction 81 a																						
Bangor (Gwynedd) 81 a																						
Holyhead 81 a																						
Wilmslow 84 a						20 28											21 34					
Stockport 84 a		20 16				20 36	20 49	21 13				20 54			21 20		21 44	21 49		22 16		22 35
Manchester Piccadilly a		20 28				20 45	20 59	21 24				21 04			21 32		21 53	21 59		22 33		22 50
Runcorn 91 a	20 25				20 31								21 05	21 20							22 24	
Liverpool South Pkwy 91 a	20 33													21 29								
Liverpool Lime Street 91 a	20 44				20 51								21 27	21 40							22 42	
d																						
Manchester Airport 82 d																						
Manchester Picc. 82 d																						
Bolton 82 d																						
Warrington Bank Quay d			20 14	20 27												21 22						
Wigan North Western 90 d			20 25	20 38												21 33						
Preston 90 a			20 38	20 52												21 47						
Blackpool North 97 a																						
Preston 90 d			20 41																			
Lancaster d			20 55																			
Barrow-in-Furness 82 a																						
Oxenholme Lake District 83 d			21 10																			
Windermere 83 a																						
Penrith North Lakes d			21 35																			
Carlisle 216 a			21 50																			
d			21 50																			
Lockerbie 225,226 d			22 09																			
Carstairs 226,225 a																						
Motherwell 226 a			22 52																			
Glasgow Central 216,226,225 a			23 09																			
Haymarket a																						
Edinburgh a																						
Fort William 227,400 a																						
Perth 229 a																						
Dundee 229 a																						
Aberdeen 229 a																						
Inverness 229 a																						

A From Birmingham New Street
B From London Euston
C From Exeter St Davids
D From Bournemouth. ⚒ to BirminghamNewSt
E To Liverpool Lime Street
F From Bristol Temple Meads

Refer to Operator websites for full information about Sleeper Services. Contact details for train operators available at National Rail Enquiries

Table T065-F

Saturdays
15 September to 8 December

London & West Midlands to North West England. London, West Midlands & Manchester to Scotland via the West Coast

		VT	LM	XC	VT	XC	LM
		◇■	■	◇■	◇■	◇■	■
				A			
London Euston	⊖66 d	20 31			21 00		
Watford Junction	66 d	20u46					
Milton Keynes Central	66 d				21 45		
Rugby	66 d	21 36					
Nuneaton	d						
Tamworth Low Level	d	21 53					
Lichfield Trent Valley	d	22 00					
Coventry	68 d			21 27			
Birmingham International	68 ✈ d			21 38			
BirminghamNewSt	68 d		21 36	21 57		22 31	22 39
Wolverhampton	d		21 59	22 15		22 49	23 06
Penkridge	d		22 09				23 16
Stafford	d		22 16	22 28	22 34	23 02	23 22
Stoke-on-Trent	84 a			22 43		23 19	
Macclesfield	a			23 01		23 38	
Crewe	81,91 a	22 29	22 36		22 58		23 42
	d	22 31			22 59		
Chester	81 a						
Wrexham General	75 a						
Llandudno Junction	81 a						
Bangor (Gwynedd)	81 a						
Holyhead	81 a						
Wilmslow	84 a				23 14		
Stockport	84 a			23 13	23 26	23 53	
Manchester Piccadilly	a			23 29	23 39	00 10	
Runcorn	91 a						
Liverpool South Pkwy	91 ✈ a						
Liverpool Lime Street	91 a						
	d						
Manchester Airport	82 ✈ d						
Manchester Picc.	82 d						
Bolton	82 d						
Warrington Bank Quay	d	22 48					
Wigan North Western	90 d	23 02					
Preston	90 a	23 18					
Blackpool North	97 a						
Preston	90 d						
Lancaster	d						
Barrow-in-Furness	82 a						
Oxenholme Lake District	83 d						
Windermere	83 a						
Penrith North Lakes	d						
Carlisle	216 a						
	d						
Lockerbie	225,226 d						
Carstairs	226,225 a						
Motherwell	226 a						
Glasgow Central	216,226,225 a						
Haymarket	a						
Edinburgh	a						
Fort William	227,400 a						
Perth	229 a						
Dundee	229 a						
Aberdeen	229 a						
Inverness	229 a						

A From Bournemouth

Refer to Operator websites for full information about Sleeper Services. Contact details for train operators available at National Rail Enquiries

Table T065-F

Sundays
20 May to 17 June

London & West Midlands to North West England. London, West Midlands & Manchester to Scotland via the West Coast

		NT	TP	VT	XC	NT	VT	VT	TP	VT	VT	VT	LM	VT	XC	VT	VT	LM	LM	VT	XC	NT	TP
		◇	◇■	◇■	◇■		◇■	◇■	◇■	◇■	◇■	◇■	■	◇■	◇■	◇■	◇■	■	■	◇■	◇■	◇	◇■
		A																	B		C	D	
London Euston	⊖66 d							08 10			08 15	08 20		08 45			09 14			09 20			
Watford Junction	66 d																						
Milton Keynes Central	66 d							08 56				09 06		09 33						10 07			
Rugby	66 d												08 52	10 09					10 03				
Nuneaton	d										09 44						10 45		10 16				
Tamworth Low Level	d																		10 30				
Lichfield Trent Valley	d																11 02		10 37				
Coventry	68 d												09 07								10 29		
Birmingham International	68 ✈ d												09 20								10 40		
BirminghamNewSt	68 d			08 45	09 01		09 20						09 42		10 01	10 20		10 42			11 01		
Wolverhampton	d			09 04	09 19		09 37						10 00		10 19	10 37		11 00			11 19		
Penkridge	d												10 10					11 10					
Stafford	d			09 17	09 33						10 08		10 17		10 33		11 15	11 17	11 00		11 32		
Stoke-on-Trent	84 a				09 51							10 19			10 48				11 16	11 21	11 48		
Macclesfield	a				10 09							10 36			11 08					11 38	12 09		
Crewe	81,91 a			09 35			10 07	10 17			10 28		10 37	10 55		11 10	11 34	11 37	11 41				
	d			09 37			10 09	10 19		10 27	10 30		10 38	10 57		11 11	11 36	11 38					
Chester	81 a																						
Wrexham General	75 a																						
Llandudno Junction	81 a																						
Bangor (Gwynedd)	81 a																						
Holyhead	81 a																						
Wilmslow	84 a							10 33															
Stockport	84 a				10 22			10 43				10 50			11 22					11 52	12 24		
Manchester Piccadilly	a				10 38			10 53				11 02			11 33					12 04	12 41		
Runcorn	91 a										10 48		11 00				11 53	12 00					
Liverpool South Pkwy	91 ✈ a												11 09					12 09					
Liverpool Lime Street	91 a										11 06		11 21				12 11	12 21					
	d																						
Manchester Airport	82 ✈ d		09 05						10 10														11 10
Manchester Picc.	82 d		09 22						10 26														11 26
Bolton	82 d																					11 24	
Warrington Bank Quay	d			09 54			10 27			10 43				11 13		11 29							
Wigan North Western	90 d			10 06			10 38			10 54				11 24		11 40							
Preston	90 a		10 01	10 20			10 51		11 04	11 12				11 38		11 53						12 01	12 02
Blackpool North	97 a																						
Preston	90 d	09 07	10 24			10 36	11 02		11 09	11 19				11 39		11 54							12 04
Lancaster	d		10 40			10 57	11 18		11 25	11a36				11 54		12 09							12 20
Barrow-in-Furness	82 a																						
Oxenholme Lake District	83 d		10 53			11 19	11 33		11 38					12 08		12 24							12 33
Windermere	83 a					11 36																	
Penrith North Lakes	d								12 03					12 34									12 58
Carlisle	216 a	12 16	11 31				12 11		12 19					12 49		13 01							13 14
	d		11 31						12 20					12 49		13 03							13 16
Lockerbie	225,226 d								12 39														13 37
Carstairs	226,225 a																						
Motherwell	226 a																						14 21
Glasgow Central	216,226,225 a		12 55											14 05									14 44
Haymarket	a								13s42							14 16							
Edinburgh	a								13 49							14 21							
Fort William	227,400 a																						
Perth	229 a																						
Dundee	229 a																						
Aberdeen	229 a																						
Inverness	229 a																						

A From Blackpool North
B From Northampton
C From Reading
D From Manchester Oxford Road

Refer to Operator websites for full information about Sleeper Services. Contact details for train operators available at National Rail Enquiries

Table T065-F

Sundays
20 May to 17 June

London & West Midlands to North West England. London, West Midlands & Manchester to Scotland via the West Coast

	VT	VT	NT	LM	VT	VT	LM	XC	LM	NT	TP	VT	VT	VT	VT	LM	VT	XC	VT	NT	TP	VT
	◇■	◇■		■	◇■	◇■	■	◇■	■	◇	◇■	◇■	◇■	◇■	◇■	■	◇■	◇■	◇■	◇	◇■	◇■
								A		B	C							D		B		
London Euston 15 ⊖66 d	09 45			09 54	10 15	10 20			10 24			10 45		11 15	11 20		12 05		12 17			12 28
Watford Junction 66 d				10 10					10 40													
Milton Keynes Central 66 d	10 33			10 50		11 07			11 20			11 33		12 04	12 08				12 50			
Rugby 66 d	11 09			11 30					12 03			12 09										
Nuneaton d				11 43	11 47				12 16													
Tamworth Low Level d				11 57					12 30													
Lichfield Trent Valley d				12 04					12 37													
Coventry 68 d								11 29										12 28				
Birmingham International 68 ✈ d								11 41										12 40				
BirminghamNewSt 12 68 d		11 20					11 42	11 57					12 20			12 35		12 57				
Wolverhampton 7 d		11 37					12 00	12 16					12 37			12 53		13 16				
Penkridge d							12 10									13 03						
Stafford d				12 21	12 14		12 17	12 29	13 00					12 53		13 09	13 25	13 29				
Stoke-on-Trent 84 a				12 37		12 24		12 45	13 16						13 09			13 44	13 50			
Macclesfield a						12 40		13 04							13 26			14 04				
Crewe 10 81,91 a	11 55	12 07		13 03	12 32		12 37		13 41			12 56	13 07	13 12		13 30	13 43					
d	11 57	12 09			12 34		12 38					12 58	13 09	13 15		13 31	13 45					
Chester 81 a																						
Wrexham General 75 a																						
Llandudno Junction 81 a																						
Bangor (Gwynedd) 81 a																						
Holyhead 81 ⛴ a																						
Wilmslow 84 a																						
Stockport 84 a						12 55		13 16							13 41			14 16	14 22			
Manchester Piccadilly 10 a						13 05		13 29							13 50			14 29	14 32			
Runcorn 91 a					12 51		13 01							13 32		13 54	14 02					
Liverpool South Pkwy 7 91 ✈ a							13 10									14 03						
Liverpool Lime Street 10 91 a					13 08		13 21							13 54		14 14	14 20					
d																						
Manchester Airport 82 ✈ d																					13 10	
Manchester Picc. 10 82 d																					13 26	
Bolton 82 d										12 24										13 24		
Warrington Bank Quay d	12 14	12 27										13 15	13 27									14 16
Wigan North Western 90 d	12 25	12 38										13 26	13 38									14 27
Preston 8 90 a	12 38	12 51								12 58		13 40	13 51							13 58	14 03	14 40
Blackpool North 97 a																						
Preston 8 90 d	12 40	12 53									13 04	13 41	13 53								14 04	14 42
Lancaster 6 d	12 55	13 08	13 13								13 19	13 56	14 08								14 20	14 58
Barrow-in-Furness 82 a			14 16																			
Oxenholme Lake District 83 d	13 08	13 22									13 33	14 10									14 35	
Windermere 83 a																						
Penrith North Lakes d	13 34											14 36	14 45								15 00	15 32
Carlisle 8 216 a	13 49	14 00	16 35								14 11	14 51	15 00								15 16	15 47
d		14 02									14 13	14 51	15 03								15 17	
Lockerbie 225,226 d											14 31										15 37	
Carstairs 226,225 a																						
Motherwell 226 a																					16 22	
Glasgow Central 15 216,226,225 a		15 19										16 07									16 45	
Haymarket a											15s29		16 14									
Edinburgh 10 a											15 36		16 20									
Fort William 227,400 a																						
Perth 229 a																						
Dundee 229 a																						
Aberdeen 229 a																						
Inverness 229 a																						

A From Southampton Central
B From Manchester Oxford Road
C From Manchester Victoria
D From Bournemouth

Refer to Operator websites for full information about Sleeper Services. Contact details for train operators available at National Rail Enquiries

Table T065-F

Sundays
20 May to 17 June

London & West Midlands to North West England. London, West Midlands & Manchester to Scotland via the West Coast

	VT	VT	XC	LM	XC	TP	VT	LM	VT	VT	LM	VT	VT	VT	NT	VT	XC	LM	XC	TP	VT
	◇■	◇■	◇■	■	◇■	◇■	◇■	■	◇■	◇■	■	◇■	◇■	◇■		◇■	◇■	■	◇■	◇■	◇■
					A		B				C			D			E		A		F
London Euston 15 ⊖66 d		12 37					12 40	12 50	12 57	13 05		13 17	13 28			13 37					13 40
Watford Junction 66 d								13 06													
Milton Keynes Central 66 d							13 13	13 37				13 50									14 13
Rugby 66 d								14 26			13 26										
Nuneaton d								14 40			13 40										
Tamworth Low Level d								14 55			13 55										
Lichfield Trent Valley d								15 01			14 01										
Coventry 68 d					13 27		13 42												14 27		14 42
Birmingham International 68 ✈ d					13 38		13 53												14 38		14 53
BirminghamNewSt 12 68 d	13 20		13 30	13 35	13 57		14 15										14 31	14 35	14 57		15 15
Wolverhampton 7 d	13 37		13 49	13 53	14 15		14 37										14 49	14 53	15 15		15 37
Penkridge d				14 03														15 03			
Stafford d			14 03	14 09	14 28			15 21		14 25	14 21						15 03	15 09	15 28		
Stoke-on-Trent 84 a			14 18		14 44			15 37	14 24		14 37	14 50					15 18		15 44		
Macclesfield a			14 36		15 01				14 42					←			15 36		16 04		
Crewe 10 81,91 a	14 07	14 12		14 30			15 07	16 05		14 43	15 03			15 07		15 12		15 30			16 08
d	14 09	14 13		14 31			15 09			14 45				15 09		15 13		15 31			16 09
Chester 81 a							→														→
Wrexham General 75 a																					
Llandudno Junction 81 a																					
Bangor (Gwynedd) 81 a																					
Holyhead 81 ⛴ a																					
Wilmslow 84 a		14 28														15 29					
Stockport 84 a		14 38	14 50		15 14				14 55			15 20				15 38	15 50		16 16		
Manchester Piccadilly 10 a		14 48	14 59		15 24				15 06			15 31				15 48	15 59		16 29		
Runcorn 91 a				14 53						15 02								15 53			
Liverpool South Pkwy 7 91 ✈ a				15 02														16 02			
Liverpool Lime Street 10 91 a				15 14						15 20								16 14			
d																					
Manchester Airport 82 ✈ d						14 10														15 10	
Manchester Picc. 10 82 d						14 26														15 26	
Bolton 82 d																					
Warrington Bank Quay d	14 27												15 16	15 27							
Wigan North Western 90 d	14 38												15 27	15 38							
Preston 8 90 a	14 50					15 03							15 40	15 51						16 03	
Blackpool North 97 a																					
Preston 8 90 d	14 53					15 04							15 42	15 53						16 04	
Lancaster 6 d	15 09					15 20							15 58	16 08	16 13					16 20	
Barrow-in-Furness 82 a															17 16						
Oxenholme Lake District 83 d	15 24												16 11							16 35	
Windermere 83 a																					
Penrith North Lakes d						15 55								16 45						17 00	
Carlisle 8 216 a	16 01					16 12							16 48	17 00	19 47					17 16	
d	16 03					16 13							16 49	17 02						17 18	
Lockerbie 225,226 d						16 32														17 37	
Carstairs 226,225 a																					
Motherwell 226 a																				18 22	
Glasgow Central 15 216,226,225 a	17 19												18 07							18 44	
Haymarket a						17s28								18 11							
Edinburgh 10 a						17 34								18 20							
Fort William 227,400 a																					
Perth 229 a																					
Dundee 229 a																					
Aberdeen 229 a																					
Inverness 229 a																					

A From Bournemouth
B To Edinburgh
C From Northampton
D From London Euston
E From Paignton
F To Glasgow Central

Refer to Operator websites for full information about Sleeper Services. Contact details for train operators available at National Rail Enquiries

Table T065-F

Sundays
20 May to 17 June

London & West Midlands to North West England. London, West Midlands & Manchester to Scotland via the West Coast

Station	LM	VT	VT	VT	VT	VT A	VT	XC B	LM	XC C	TP	VT D	LM	VT	VT	VT	VT	VT	VT A	VT	XC B	LM
London Euston ⊖66 d	13 50	13 57	14 05	14 17	14 28		14 37					14 40	14 50	14 57	15 05	15 08	15 17	15 28		15 37		
Watford Junction 66 d	14 06												15 06									
Milton Keynes Central 66 d	14 37			14 50								15 13	15 37			15 42	15 50					
Rugby 66 d	15 26												16 26									
Nuneaton d	15 40												16 40									
Tamworth Low Level d	15 55												16 55									
Lichfield Trent Valley d	16 01												17 01									
Coventry 68 d										15 27		15 42										
Birmingham International 68 ✈ d										15 38		15 53										
BirminghamNewSt 68 d								15 31	15 35	15 57		16 15									16 31	16 35
Wolverhampton d								15 49	15 53	16 15		16 37									16 49	16 53
Penkridge d									16 03													17 03
Stafford d	16 21		15 25					16 03	16 09	16 28			17 21		16 25						17 03	17 09
Stoke-on-Trent 84 a	16 37	15 25		15 50				16 18		16 44			17 37	16 26			16 52				17 18	
Macclesfield a		15 42				←		16 36		17 04				16 42					←		17 36	
Crewe 81,91 a	17 05		15 43			16 08	16 11		16 30			17 07	18 05		16 43	16 50			17 07	17 12		17 30
d			15 45			16 09	16 12		16 31			17 09			16 45	16 52			17 09	17 13		17 31
Chester 81 a												→				17 11						
Wrexham General 75 a																						
Llandudno Junction 81 a																						
Bangor (Gwynedd) 81 a																						
Holyhead 81 ⛴ a																						
Wilmslow 84 a							16 29													17 29		
Stockport 84 a		15 55		16 23			16 35	16 50		17 16				16 56			17 23			17 38	17 50	
Manchester Piccadilly a		16 05		16 32			16 48	16 59		17 29				17 06			17 32			17 48	17 59	
Runcorn 91 a			16 02						16 54						17 02							17 54
Liverpool South Pkwy 91 ✈ a									17 03													18 03
Liverpool Lime Street 91 a			16 23						17 14						17 21							18 14
d																						
Manchester Airport 82 ✈ d											16 10											
Manchester Picc. 82 d											16 26											
Bolton 82 d																						
Warrington Bank Quay d					16 16	16 27												17 16	17 27			
Wigan North Western 90 d					16 27	16 38												17 27	17 38			
Preston 90 a					16 40	16 51					17 02							17 40	17 51			
Blackpool North 97 a																						
Preston 90 d					16 42	16 53					17 03							17 42	17 53			
Lancaster d					16 57	17 08					17 19							17 57	18 09			
Barrow-in-Furness 82 a																						
Oxenholme Lake District 83 d						17 22					17 32							18 11	18 23			
Windermere 83 a																						
Penrith North Lakes d					17 32						17 57								18 48			
Carlisle 216 a					17 47	18 01					18 12							18 48	19 03			
d					17 48	18 03					18 13							18 49	19 04			
Lockerbie 225,226 d											18 32											
Carstairs 226,225 a																						
Motherwell 226 a																						
Glasgow Central 216,226,225 a					19 06	19 20												20 09				
Haymarket ⇌ a											19s30								20 16			
Edinburgh ⇌ a											19 35								20 22			
Fort William 227,400 a																						
Perth 229 a																						
Dundee 229 a																						
Aberdeen 229 a																						
Inverness 229 a																						

A From London Euston
B From Plymouth
C From Bournemouth
D To Edinburgh

Refer to Operator websites for full information about Sleeper Services. Contact details for train operators available at National Rail Enquiries

Table T065-F

Sundays
20 May to 17 June

London & West Midlands to North West England. London, West Midlands & Manchester to Scotland via the West Coast

Station	XC A	TP	VT B	LM	VT	VT	VT	VT	VT	VT C	VT	TP	XC D	XC E	LM	XC A	VT F	LM	VT	VT	VT
London Euston ⊖66 d			15 40	15 50	15 57	16 05	16 08	16 17	16 28		16 37						16 40	16 50	16 57	17 05	17 08
Watford Junction 66 d				16 06														17 06			
Milton Keynes Central 66 d			16 13	16 37			16 42	16 50									17 13	17 37			17 42
Rugby 66 d				17 26														18 26			
Nuneaton d				17 40														18 40		18 04	
Tamworth Low Level d				17 55														18 55			
Lichfield Trent Valley d				18 01														19 01			18 24
Coventry 68 d	16 27		16 42										16 54			17 27	17 45				
Birmingham International 68 ✈ d	16 38		16 53										17 04			17 38	17 55				
BirminghamNewSt 68 d	16 57		17 15										17 30	17 31	17 35	17 57	18 15				
Wolverhampton d	17 15		17 37											17 49	17 53	18 15	18 37				
Penkridge d															18 03						
Stafford d	17 29			18 21		17 26								18 03	18 09	18 28		19 21			18 41
Stoke-on-Trent 84 a	17 45			18 37	17 25			17 50						18 18		18 44		19 37	18 25		
Macclesfield a	18 04				17 42					←				18 36		19 04			18 42		
Crewe 81,91 a			18 07	19 06		17 44	17 50			18 07	18 12				18 30		19 07	20 06		18 44	18 59
d			18 09			17 46	17 52			18 09	18 13				18 31		19 09			18 46	19 01
Chester 81 a			→				18 12										→				19 19
Wrexham General 75 a																					
Llandudno Junction 81 a																					20 18
Bangor (Gwynedd) 81 a																					20 34
Holyhead 81 ⛴ a																					21 03
Wilmslow 84 a											18 29										
Stockport 84 a	18 16				17 55			18 23			18 38			18 50		19 17			18 56		
Manchester Piccadilly a	18 29				18 05			18 32			18 48			18 59		19 28			19 06		
Runcorn 91 a						18 02									18 54					19 02	
Liverpool South Pkwy 91 ✈ a															19 03						
Liverpool Lime Street 91 a						18 21									19 14					19 21	
d																					
Manchester Airport 82 ✈ d		17 10										18 10									
Manchester Picc. 82 d		17 27										18 26									
Bolton 82 d																					
Warrington Bank Quay d									18 16	18 27											
Wigan North Western 90 d									18 27	18 38											
Preston 90 a		18 03							18 41	18 51		19 02									
Blackpool North 97 a																					
Preston 90 d		18 04							18 42	18 53		19 04									
Lancaster d		18 20							18 57	19 08		19 19									
Barrow-in-Furness 82 a																					
Oxenholme Lake District 83 d		18 35							19 12	19 22		19 33									
Windermere 83 a																					
Penrith North Lakes d		19 00							19 37			19 58									
Carlisle 216 a		19 16							19 52	20 00		20 13									
d		19 17							19 53	20 01		20 15									
Lockerbie 225,226 d		19 37										20 33									
Carstairs 226,225 a																					
Motherwell 226 a		20 22																			
Glasgow Central 216,226,225 a		20 48							21 07	21 22											
Haymarket ⇌ a												21s30									
Edinburgh ⇌ a												21 35	22 18								
Fort William 227,400 a																					
Perth 229 a																					
Dundee 229 a																					
Aberdeen 229 a																					
Inverness 229 a																					

A From Bournemouth
B To Glasgow Central
C From London Euston
D From Reading. 🍴 to BirminghamNewSt
E From Bristol Temple Meads
F To Edinburgh

Refer to Operator websites for full information about Sleeper Services. Contact details for train operators available at National Rail Enquiries

Table T065-F

Sundays
20 May to 17 June

London & West Midlands to North West England. London, West Midlands & Manchester to Scotland via the West Coast

	VT	VT	VT	VT	VT	XC	LM	XC	TP	VT	LM	VT	VT	VT	VT	VT	VT	VT	VT	XC	LM	XC
				A		B		C		D								A		E		F
London Euston ⊖66 d	17 08	17 17	17 28		17 37					17 40	17 50	17 57	18 05	18 08	18 08	18 17	18 28		18 37			
Watford Junction 66 d											18 06											
Milton Keynes Central 66 d	17 42	17 50								18 13	18 37			18 42	18 42	18 50						
Rugby 66 d											19 26											
Nuneaton d											19 40											
Tamworth Low Level d											19 55											
Lichfield Trent Valley d	18 24										20 01											
Coventry 68 d								18 27		18 45												19 27
Birmingham International 68 d								18 38		18 55												19 38
BirminghamNewSt 68 d						18 31	18 35	18 57		19 15										19 31	19 35	19 57
Wolverhampton d						18 49	18 53	19 15		19 37										19 49	19 53	20 15
Penkridge d							19 03														20 03	
Stafford d	18 41					19 03	19 09	19 28			20 21		19 25							20 03	20 09	20 28
Stoke-on-Trent 84 a		18 50				19 18		19 44			20 37	19 25				19 50				20 18		20 44
Macclesfield a				←		19 36		20 04				19 42						←		20 36		21 02
Crewe 81,91 a	18 59			19 07	19 12		19 30			20 07	21 06		19 43	19 50	19 50			20 07	20 12		20 31	
d	19 01			19 09	19 13		19 31			20 09			19 45	19 52	19 52			20 09	20 13		20 31	
Chester 81 a	19 20									→				20 11	20 13							
Wrexham General 75 a																						
Llandudno Junction 81 a															21 07							
Bangor (Gwynedd) 81 a															21 23							
Holyhead 81 a															21 54							
Wilmslow 84 a					19 29														20 29			
Stockport 84 a		19 23			19 38	19 50		20 16				19 56				20 23			20 38	20 50		21 15
Manchester Piccadilly a		19 32			19 48	19 59		20 28				20 06				20 32			20 48	20 59		21 29
Runcorn 91 a							19 54						20 02								20 54	
Liverpool South Pkwy 91 a							20 03														21 03	
Liverpool Lime Street 91 a							20 14						20 20								21 14	
d																						
Manchester Airport 82 d									19 10													
Manchester Picc. 82 d									19 26													
Bolton 82 d																						
Warrington Bank Quay d			19 17	19 27													20 16	20 27				
Wigan North Western 90 d			19 28	19 38													20 27	20 38				
Preston 90 a			19 41	19 51					20 02								20 40	20 51				
Blackpool North 97 a																						
Preston 90 d			19 42	19 53					20 04								20 42	20 53				
Lancaster d			19 57	20 08					20 20								20 57	21 08				
Barrow-in-Furness 82 a																						
Oxenholme Lake District 83 d			20 12						20 33								21 11	21 23				
Windermere 83 a																						
Penrith North Lakes d			20 37	20 45					20 58								21 36					
Carlisle 216 a			20 51	20 59					21 14								21 51	22 01				
d			20 51	21 02					21 15								21 52	22 02				
Lockerbie 225,226 d									21 34									22 21				
Carstairs 226,225 a																						
Motherwell 226 a									22 21								22 52	23 04				
Glasgow Central 216,226,225 a			22 06						22 46								23 15	23 24				
Haymarket a				22 14																		
Edinburgh a				22 19																		
Fort William 227,400 a																						
Perth 229 a																						
Dundee 229 a																						
Aberdeen 229 a																						
Inverness 229 a																						

A From London Euston
B From Penzance
C From Bournemouth
D To Glasgow Central
E From Bristol Temple Meads
F From Bournemouth. ⚲ to BirminghamNewSt

Refer to Operator websites for full information about Sleeper Services. Contact details for train operators available at National Rail Enquiries

Table T065-F

Sundays
20 May to 17 June

London & West Midlands to North West England. London, West Midlands & Manchester to Scotland via the West Coast

	VT	LM	VT	VT	VT	VT	TP	VT	VT	XC	XC	VT	LM	VT	VT	VT	VT	VT	VT	CS	VT	LM
										A	B	C							D			
London Euston ⊖66 d	18 40	18 50	18 57	19 05	19 08	19 17		19 28	19 37			19 40	19 50	19 57	20 05	20 08	20 15	20 25		20 28	20 35	
Watford Junction 66 d		19 06											20 06									
Milton Keynes Central 66 d	19 13	19 37			19 42	19 50						20 13	20 37			20 41	20 48					
Rugby 66 d		20 26											21 30									
Nuneaton d		20 40		20 04									21 43		21 04							
Tamworth Low Level d		20 55											21 58					21 32				
Lichfield Trent Valley d		21 01											22 04					21 39				
Coventry 68 d	19 42										20 27	20 42										
Birmingham International 68 d	19 53										20 38	20 53										
BirminghamNewSt 68 d	20 15									20 31	20 57	21 15										21 42
Wolverhampton d	20 37									20 52	21 17	21 37										22 00
Penkridge d																						22 10
Stafford d	20 52	21 21		20 29						21 06	21 30	21 56	22 23			21 33					22 00	22 17
Stoke-on-Trent 84 a		21 37	20 25			20 50				21 21	21 45		22 40	21 25			21 50					
Macclesfield a			20 42							21 39	22 03			21 43					←			
Crewe 81,91 a	21 10	22 06		20 47	20 50				21 12			22 16	23 03		21 44	21 53		22 10	22 16		22 20	22 36
d				20 49	20 55				21 13			22 17			21 46	21 55		22 13	22 17		22 21	22 38
Chester 81 a					21 13							→										
Wrexham General 75 a																						
Llandudno Junction 81 a					22 06																	
Bangor (Gwynedd) 81 a					22 22																	
Holyhead 81 a					22 53																	
Wilmslow 84 a									21 28												22 36	
Stockport 84 a			20 56			21 19			21 38	21 52	22 15			21 59			22 21				22 45	
Manchester Piccadilly a			21 06			21 31			21 49	22 02	22 26			22 09			22 31				22 54	
Runcorn 91 a				21 06											22 03	22 12						22 59
Liverpool South Pkwy 91 a																						23 10
Liverpool Lime Street 91 a				21 23											22 20	22 29						23 24
d																						
Manchester Airport 82 d							20 10															
Manchester Picc. 82 d							20 26															
Bolton 82 d																						
Warrington Bank Quay d								21 16										22 30	22 36			
Wigan North Western 90 d								21 27										22 41	22 47			
Preston 90 a							21 02	21 40										22 55	23 01			
Blackpool North 97 a																						
Preston 90 d							21 04	21 42														
Lancaster d							21 20	21 57														
Barrow-in-Furness 82 a																						
Oxenholme Lake District 83 d							21 33	22 11														
Windermere 83 a																						
Penrith North Lakes d							21 58	22 36														
Carlisle 216 a							22 14	22 51														
d							22 15	22 52														
Lockerbie 225,226 d																						
Carstairs 226,225 a																						
Motherwell 226 a																						
Glasgow Central 216,226,225 a								00 07														
Haymarket a							23s28															
Edinburgh a							23 34															
Fort William 227,400 a																				09 57		
Perth 229 a																						
Dundee 229 a																						
Aberdeen 229 a																						
Inverness 229 a																						

A From Bristol Temple Meads
B From Bournemouth. ⚲ to BirminghamNewSt
C To Preston
D From London Euston

Refer to Operator websites for full information about Sleeper Services. Contact details for train operators available at National Rail Enquiries

Table T065-F

Sundays
20 May to 17 June

London & West Midlands to North West England. London, West Midlands & Manchester to Scotland via the West Coast

	VT	XC	VT	VT	CS	AW	VT
	◇	◇	◇	◇		◇	◇
		A			B		
London Euston ⊖66 d	20 50		21 21	21 25	21 34		21 51
Watford Junction 66 d							
Milton Keynes Central 66 d	21 37			22 17			22 39
Rugby 66 d	22 01						23 19
Nuneaton d			22 57				23 30
Tamworth Low Level d							
Lichfield Trent Valley d							
Coventry 68 d		21 27					
Birmingham International 68 d		21 38				22 40	
BirminghamNewSt 68 d		21 57				22 55	
Wolverhampton d		22 15				23 15	
Penkridge d							
Stafford d		22 28	23 23			23 31	23s54
Stoke-on-Trent 84 a		22 44		23 33			
Macclesfield a		23 01		23 49			
Crewe 81,91 a	22 49		23 44			23 57	00s16
d	22 51		23 46			00 01	
Chester 81 a						00 22	
Wrexham General 75 a							
Llandudno Junction 81 a						01 27	
Bangor (Gwynedd) 81 a						01 44	
Holyhead 81 a						02 20	
Wilmslow 84 a							
Stockport 84 a		23 14		00 03			00s38
Manchester Piccadilly a		23 24		00 13			00 48
Runcorn 91 a			00 04				
Liverpool South Pkwy 91 a							
Liverpool Lime Street 91 a			00 28				
d							
Manchester Airport 82 d							
Manchester Picc. 82 d							
Bolton 82 d							
Warrington Bank Quay d	23 08						
Wigan North Western 90 d	23 19						
Preston 90 a	23 38						
Blackpool North 97 a							
Preston 90 d							
Lancaster d							
Barrow-in-Furness 82 a							
Oxenholme Lake District 83 d							
Windermere 83 a							
Penrith North Lakes d							
Carlisle 216 a							
d							
Lockerbie 225,226 d							
Carstairs 226,225 a							
Motherwell 226 a							
Glasgow Central 216,226,225 a							
Haymarket a							
Edinburgh a					05s20		
Fort William 227,400 a							
Perth 229 a							
Dundee 229 a							
Aberdeen 229 a							
Inverness 229 a							

A From Bournemouth
B To Glasgow Central

Refer to Operator websites for full information about Sleeper Services. Contact details for train operators available at National Rail Enquiries

Table T065-F

Sundays
24 June to 9 September

London & West Midlands to North West England. London, West Midlands & Manchester to Scotland via the West Coast

	NT	TP	NT	NT	TP	VT	XC	VT	VT	TP	VT
	◇	◇	◇		◇	◇	◇	◇	◇	◇	◇
	A										
London Euston ⊖66 d									08 10		
Watford Junction 66 d											
Milton Keynes Central 66 d									08 56		
Rugby 66 d											
Nuneaton d											
Tamworth Low Level d											
Lichfield Trent Valley d											
Coventry 68 d											
Birmingham International 68 d											
BirminghamNewSt 68 d						08 45	09 01	09 20			
Wolverhampton d						09 04	09 19	09 37			
Penkridge d											
Stafford d						09 17	09 33				
Stoke-on-Trent 84 a							09 51				
Macclesfield a							10 09				
Crewe 81,91 a						09 35		10 07	10 17		
d						09 37		10 09	10 19		10 27
Chester 81 a											
Wrexham General 75 a											
Llandudno Junction 81 a											
Bangor (Gwynedd) 81 a											
Holyhead 81 a											
Wilmslow 84 a									10 33		
Stockport 84 a							10 22		10 43		
Manchester Piccadilly a							10 38		10 53		
Runcorn 91 a											
Liverpool South Pkwy 91 a											
Liverpool Lime Street 91 a											
d											
Manchester Airport 82 d					09 05					10 10	
Manchester Picc. 82 d		08 43			09 22					10 26	
Bolton 82 d											
Warrington Bank Quay d						09 54		10 27			10 43
Wigan North Western 90 d						10 06		10 38			10 54
Preston 90 a		09 22			10 02	10 20		10 51		11 04	11 12
Blackpool North 97 a											
Preston 90 d	09 07	09 23	09 38		10 03			11 02		11 09	11 19
Lancaster d		09 39	09 59	10 11	10 19			11 18		11 25	11a36
Barrow-in-Furness 82 a				11 14							
Oxenholme Lake District 83 d			10 30		10 33			11 33		11 38	
Windermere 83 a			10 52								
Penrith North Lakes d					10 58					12 03	
Carlisle 216 a	12 16	10 28		13 42	11 13			12 11		12 19	
d		10 29			11 16					12 20	
Lockerbie 225,226 d		10 48			11 36					12 39	
Carstairs 226,225 a											
Motherwell 226 a					12 21						
Glasgow Central 216,226,225 a					12 44						
Haymarket a		11s48								13s42	
Edinburgh a		11 53								13 49	
Fort William 227,400 a											
Perth 229 a											
Dundee 229 a											
Aberdeen 229 a											
Inverness 229 a											

	VT	VT	LM	VT	XC	VT	VT	LM	LM	VT	XC
	◇	◇		◇	◇	◇	◇			◇	◇
									B		C
London Euston ⊖66 d	08 15	08 20		08 45			09 14			09 20	
Watford Junction 66 d											
Milton Keynes Central 66 d		09 06		09 33						10 07	
Rugby 66 d			08 52	10 09					10 03		
Nuneaton d	09 44						10 45		10 16		
Tamworth Low Level d									10 30		
Lichfield Trent Valley d							11 02		10 37		
Coventry 68 d			09 07								10 29
Birmingham International 68 d			09 20								10 40
BirminghamNewSt 68 d			09 42		10 01	10 20		10 42			11 01
Wolverhampton d			10 00		10 19	10 37		11 00			11 19
Penkridge d			10 10					11 10			
Stafford d	10 08		10 17		10 33		11 15	11 17	11 00		11 32
Stoke-on-Trent 84 a		10 19			10 48				11 16	11 21	11 48
Macclesfield a		10 36			11 08					11 38	12 09
Crewe 81,91 a	10 28		10 37	10 55		11 10	11 34	11 37	11 41		
d	10 30		10 38	10 57		11 11	11 36	11 38			
Chester 81 a											
Wrexham General 75 a											
Llandudno Junction 81 a											
Bangor (Gwynedd) 81 a											
Holyhead 81 a											
Wilmslow 84 a											
Stockport 84 a		10 50			11 22					11 52	12 24
Manchester Piccadilly a		11 02			11 33					12 04	12 41
Runcorn 91 a	10 48		11 00				11 53	12 00			
Liverpool South Pkwy 91 a			11 09					12 09			
Liverpool Lime Street 91 a	11 06		11 21				12 11	12 21			
d											
Manchester Airport 82 d											
Manchester Picc. 82 d											
Bolton 82 d											
Warrington Bank Quay d				11 13		11 29					
Wigan North Western 90 d				11 24		11 40					
Preston 90 a				11 38		11 53					
Blackpool North 97 a											
Preston 90 d				11 39		11 54					
Lancaster d				11 54		12 09					
Barrow-in-Furness 82 a											
Oxenholme Lake District 83 d				12 08		12 24					
Windermere 83 a											
Penrith North Lakes d				12 34							
Carlisle 216 a				12 49		13 01					
d				12 49		13 03					
Lockerbie 225,226 d											
Carstairs 226,225 a											
Motherwell 226 a											
Glasgow Central 216,226,225 a				14 05							
Haymarket a						14 16					
Edinburgh a						14 21					
Fort William 227,400 a											
Perth 229 a											
Dundee 229 a											
Aberdeen 229 a											
Inverness 229 a											

A From Blackpool North
B From Northampton
C From Reading

Refer to Operator websites for full information about Sleeper Services. Contact details for train operators available at National Rail Enquiries

Table T065-F

Sundays
24 June to 9 September

London & West Midlands to North West England. London, West Midlands & Manchester to Scotland via the West Coast

	NT ◇ A	TP ◇1	VT ◇1	VT ◇1	NT	LM 1	VT ◇1	VT ◇1	LM 1	XC ◇1 B	LM 1	NT ◇ A	TP ◇1 C	VT ◇1	VT ◇1	VT ◇1	VT ◇1	LM 1	VT ◇1	XC ◇1 D	VT ◇1	NT ◇ A
London Euston ⊖66 d			09 45			09 54	10 15	10 20			10 24			10 45		11 15	11 20		12 05		12 17	
Watford Junction 66 d						10 10					10 40											
Milton Keynes Central 66 d			10 33			10 50		11 07			11 20			11 33		12 04	12 08				12 50	
Rugby 66 d			11 09			11 30					12 03			12 09								
Nuneaton d						11 43	11 47				12 16											
Tamworth Low Level d						11 57					12 30											
Lichfield Trent Valley d						12 04					12 37											
Coventry 68 d										11 29										12 28		
Birmingham International 68 d										11 41										12 40		
BirminghamNewSt 68 d				11 20					11 42	11 57					12 20			12 35		12 57		
Wolverhampton d				11 37					12 00	12 16					12 37			12 53		13 16		
Penkridge d									12 10									13 03				
Stafford d						12 21	12 14		12 17	12 29	13 00					12 53		13 09	13 25	13 29		
Stoke-on-Trent 84 a						12 37		12 24		12 45	13 16						13 09			13 44	13 50	
Macclesfield a								12 40		13 04							13 26			14 04		
Crewe 81,91 a			11 55	12 07		13 03	12 32		12 37		13 41			12 56	13 07	13 12		13 30	13 43			
d			11 57	12 09			12 34		12 38					12 58	13 09	13 15		13 31	13 45			
Chester 81 a																						
Wrexham General 75 a																						
Llandudno Junction 81 a																						
Bangor (Gwynedd) 81 a																						
Holyhead 81 a																						
Wilmslow 84 a																						
Stockport 84 a								12 55		13 16							13 41			14 16	14 22	
Manchester Piccadilly a								13 05		13 29							13 50			14 29	14 32	
Runcorn 91 a							12 51		13 01							13 32		13 54	14 02			
Liverpool South Pkwy 91 a									13 10									14 03				
Liverpool Lime Street 91 a							13 08		13 21							13 54		14 14	14 20			
d																						
Manchester Airport 82 d		11 10																				
Manchester Picc. 82 d		11 26																				
Bolton 82 d	11 24											12 24										13 24
Warrington Bank Quay d			12 14	12 27										13 15	13 27							
Wigan North Western 90 d			12 25	12 38										13 26	13 38							
Preston 90 a	12 01	12 02	12 38	12 51								12 58		13 40	13 51							13 58
Blackpool North 97 a																						
Preston 90 d		12 04	12 40	12 53									13 04	13 41	13 53							
Lancaster d		12 20	12 55	13 08	13 13								13 19	13 56	14 08							
Barrow-in-Furness 82 a					14 16																	
Oxenholme Lake District 83 d		12 33	13 08	13 22									13 33	14 10								
Windermere 83 a																						
Penrith North Lakes d		12 58	13 34											14 36	14 45							
Carlisle 216 a		13 14	13 49	14 00	16 35								14 11	14 51	15 00							
d		13 16		14 02									14 13	14 51	15 03							
Lockerbie 225,226 d		13 37											14 31									
Carstairs 226,225 a																						
Motherwell 226 a		14 21																				
Glasgow Central 216,226,225 a		14 44		15 19										16 07								
Haymarket a													15s29		16 14							
Edinburgh a													15 36		16 20							
Fort William 227,400 a																						
Perth 229 a																						
Dundee 229 a																						
Aberdeen 229 a																						
Inverness 229 a																						

A From Manchester Oxford Road
B From Southampton Central
C From Manchester Victoria
D From Bournemouth

Refer to Operator websites for full information about Sleeper Services. Contact details for train operators available at National Rail Enquiries

Table T065-F

Sundays
24 June to 9 September

London & West Midlands to North West England. London, West Midlands & Manchester to Scotland via the West Coast

	TP ◇1	VT ◇1	VT ◇1	VT ◇1	XC ◇1	LM 1	XC ◇1 A	TP ◇1	VT ◇1 B	LM 1	VT ◇1	VT ◇1	LM 1 C	VT ◇1	VT ◇1	VT ◇1 D	NT	VT ◇1	XC ◇1 E	LM 1	XC ◇1 A
London Euston ⊖66 d		12 28		12 37					12 40	12 50	12 57	13 05		13 17	13 28			13 37			
Watford Junction 66 d										13 06											
Milton Keynes Central 66 d									13 13	13 37				13 50							
Rugby 66 d										14 26			13 26								
Nuneaton d										14 40			13 40								
Tamworth Low Level d										14 55			13 55								
Lichfield Trent Valley d										15 01			14 01								
Coventry 68 d							13 27		13 42												14 27
Birmingham International 68 d							13 38		13 53												14 38
BirminghamNewSt 68 d			13 20		13 30	13 35	13 57		14 15										14 31	14 35	14 57
Wolverhampton d			13 37		13 49	13 53	14 15		14 37										14 49	14 53	15 15
Penkridge d						14 03														15 03	
Stafford d					14 03	14 09	14 28			15 21		14 25	14 21						15 03	15 09	15 28
Stoke-on-Trent 84 a					14 18		14 44			15 37	14 24		14 37	14 50					15 18		15 44
Macclesfield a					14 36		15 01				14 42					←			15 36		16 04
Crewe 81,91 a			14 07	14 12		14 30			15 07	16 05		14 43	15 03			15 07		15 12		15 30	
d			14 09	14 13		14 31			15 09			14 45				15 09		15 13		15 31	
Chester 81 a									→												
Wrexham General 75 a																					
Llandudno Junction 81 a																					
Bangor (Gwynedd) 81 a																					
Holyhead 81 a																					
Wilmslow 84 a				14 28														15 29			
Stockport 84 a				14 38	14 50		15 14				14 55			15 20				15 38	15 50		16 16
Manchester Piccadilly a				14 48	14 59		15 24				15 06			15 31				15 48	15 59		16 29
Runcorn 91 a						14 53						15 02								15 53	
Liverpool South Pkwy 91 a						15 02														16 02	
Liverpool Lime Street 91 a						15 14						15 20								16 14	
d																					
Manchester Airport 82 d	13 10							14 10													
Manchester Picc. 82 d	13 26							14 26													
Bolton 82 d																					
Warrington Bank Quay d		14 16	14 27												15 16	15 27					
Wigan North Western 90 d		14 27	14 38												15 27	15 38					
Preston 90 a	14 03	14 40	14 50					15 03							15 40	15 51					
Blackpool North 97 a																					
Preston 90 d	14 04	14 42	14 53					15 04							15 42	15 53					
Lancaster d	14 20	14 58	15 09					15 20							15 58	16 08	16 13				
Barrow-in-Furness 82 a																	17 16				
Oxenholme Lake District 83 d	14 35		15 24												16 11						
Windermere 83 a																					
Penrith North Lakes d	15 00	15 32						15 55								16 45					
Carlisle 216 a	15 16	15 47	16 01					16 12							16 48	17 00	19 47				
d	15 17		16 03					16 13							16 49	17 02					
Lockerbie 225,226 d	15 37							16 32													
Carstairs 226,225 a																					
Motherwell 226 a	16 22																				
Glasgow Central 216,226,225 a	16 45		17 19												18 07						
Haymarket a								17s28								18 11					
Edinburgh a								17 34								18 20					
Fort William 227,400 a																					
Perth 229 a																					
Dundee 229 a																					
Aberdeen 229 a																					
Inverness 229 a																					

A From Bournemouth
B To Edinburgh
C From Northampton
D From London Euston
E From Paignton

Refer to Operator websites for full information about Sleeper Services. Contact details for train operators available at National Rail Enquiries

Table T065-F

Sundays

24 June to 9 September

London & West Midlands to North West England. London, West Midlands & Manchester to Scotland via the West Coast

	TP	VT A	LM	VT	VT	VT	VT	VT B	VT	XC C	LM	XC D	TP	VT E	LM	VT	VT	VT	VT	VT	VT B	VT
London Euston ⊖66 d		13 40	13 50	13 57	14 05	14 17	14 28		14 37					14 40	14 50	14 57	15 05	15 08	15 17	15 28		15 37
Watford Junction 66 d			14 06												15 06							
Milton Keynes Central 66 d		14 13	14 37			14 50								15 13	15 37			15 42	15 50			
Rugby 66 d			15 26												16 26							
Nuneaton d			15 40												16 40							
Tamworth Low Level d			15 55												16 55							
Lichfield Trent Valley d			16 01												17 01							
Coventry 68 d		14 42										15 27		15 42								
Birmingham International 68 ✈ d		14 53										15 38		15 53								
BirminghamNewSt 68 ⛴ d		15 15								15 31	15 35	15 57		16 15								
Wolverhampton ⛴ d		15 37								15 49	15 53	16 15		16 37								
Penkridge d											16 03											
Stafford d			16 21		15 25					16 03	16 09	16 28			17 21		16 25					
Stoke-on-Trent 84 a			16 37	15 25		15 50				16 18		16 44			17 37	16 26			16 52			
Macclesfield a				15 42				←		16 36		17 04				16 42					←	
Crewe 81,91 a		16 08	17 05		15 43			16 08	16 11		16 30			17 07	18 05		16 43	16 50			17 07	17 12
d		16 09			15 45			16 09	16 12		16 31			17 09			16 45	16 52			17 09	17 13
Chester 81 a		→												→				17 11				
Wrexham General 75 a																						
Llandudno Junction 81 a																						
Bangor (Gwynedd) 81 a																						
Holyhead 81 ⛴ a																						
Wilmslow 84 a									16 29													17 29
Stockport 84 a				15 55		16 23			16 35	16 50		17 16				16 56			17 23			17 38
Manchester Piccadilly ⛴ a				16 05		16 32			16 48	16 59		17 29				17 06			17 32			17 48
Runcorn 91 a					16 02						16 54						17 02					
Liverpool South Pkwy 91 ✈ a											17 03											
Liverpool Lime Street 91 a					16 23						17 14						17 21					
d																						
Manchester Airport 82 ✈⛴ d	15 10												16 10									
Manchester Picc. 82 ⛴ d	15 26												16 26									
Bolton 82 d																						
Warrington Bank Quay d							16 16	16 27												17 16	17 27	
Wigan North Western 90 d							16 27	16 38												17 27	17 38	
Preston 90 a	16 03						16 40	16 51					17 02							17 40	17 51	
Blackpool North 97 a																						
Preston 90 d	16 04						16 42	16 53					17 03							17 42	17 53	
Lancaster d	16 20						16 57	17 08					17 19							17 57	18 09	
Barrow-in-Furness 82 a																						
Oxenholme Lake District 83 d	16 35							17 22					17 32							18 11	18 23	
Windermere 83 a																						
Penrith North Lakes d	17 00						17 32						17 57								18 48	
Carlisle 216 a	17 16						17 47	18 01					18 12							18 48	19 03	
d	17 18						17 48	18 03					18 13							18 49	19 04	
Lockerbie 225,226 d	17 37												18 32									
Carstairs 226,225 a																						
Motherwell 226 a	18 22																					
Glasgow Central 216,226,225 a	18 44						19 06	19 20												20 09		
Haymarket ⛴ a													19s30								20 16	
Edinburgh ⛴ a													19 35								20 22	
Fort William 227,400 a																						
Perth 229 a																						
Dundee 229 a																						
Aberdeen 229 a																						
Inverness 229 a																						

A To Glasgow Central
B From London Euston
C From Plymouth
D From Bournemouth
E To Edinburgh

Refer to Operator websites for full information about Sleeper Services. Contact details for train operators available at National Rail Enquiries

Table T065-F

Sundays

24 June to 9 September

London & West Midlands to North West England. London, West Midlands & Manchester to Scotland via the West Coast

	XC A	LM	XC B	TP	VT C	LM	VT	VT	VT	VT	VT	VT D	VT	TP	XC E	XC F	LM	XC B	VT G	LM	VT
London Euston ⊖66 d					15 40	15 50	15 57	16 05	16 08	16 17	16 28		16 37						16 40	16 50	16 57
Watford Junction 66 d						16 06														17 06	
Milton Keynes Central 66 d					16 13	16 37			16 42	16 50									17 13	17 37	
Rugby 66 d						17 26														18 26	
Nuneaton d						17 40														18 40	
Tamworth Low Level d						17 55														18 55	
Lichfield Trent Valley d						18 01														19 01	
Coventry 68 d			16 27		16 42										16 54			17 27	17 45		
Birmingham International 68 ✈ d			16 38		16 53										17 04			17 38	17 55		
BirminghamNewSt 68 ⛴ d	16 31	16 35	16 57		17 15										17 30	17 31	17 35	17 57	18 15		
Wolverhampton ⛴ d	16 49	16 53	17 15		17 37											17 49	17 53	18 15	18 37		
Penkridge d		17 03															18 03				
Stafford d	17 03	17 09	17 29			18 21		17 26								18 03	18 09	18 28		19 21	
Stoke-on-Trent 84 a	17 18		17 45			18 37	17 25			17 50						18 18		18 44		19 37	18 25
Macclesfield a	17 36		18 04				17 42					←				18 36		19 04			18 42
Crewe 81,91 a		17 30			18 07	19 06		17 44	17 50			18 07	18 12				18 30		19 07	20 06	
d		17 31			18 09			17 46	17 52			18 09	18 13				18 31		19 09		
Chester 81 a					→				18 12										→		
Wrexham General 75 a																					
Llandudno Junction 81 a																					
Bangor (Gwynedd) 81 a																					
Holyhead 81 ⛴ a																					
Wilmslow 84 a													18 29								
Stockport 84 a	17 50		18 16				17 55			18 23			18 38			18 50		19 17			18 56
Manchester Piccadilly ⛴ a	17 59		18 29				18 05			18 32			18 48			18 59		19 28			19 06
Runcorn 91 a		17 54						18 02									18 54				
Liverpool South Pkwy 91 ✈ a		18 03															19 03				
Liverpool Lime Street 91 a		18 14						18 21									19 14				
d																					
Manchester Airport 82 ✈⛴ d				17 10										18 10							
Manchester Picc. 82 ⛴ d				17 27										18 26							
Bolton 82 d																					
Warrington Bank Quay d											18 16	18 27									
Wigan North Western 90 d											18 27	18 38									
Preston 90 a				18 03							18 41	18 51		19 02							
Blackpool North 97 a																					
Preston 90 d				18 04							18 42	18 53		19 04							
Lancaster d				18 20							18 57	19 08		19 19							
Barrow-in-Furness 82 a																					
Oxenholme Lake District 83 d				18 35							19 12	19 22		19 33							
Windermere 83 a																					
Penrith North Lakes d				19 00							19 37			19 58							
Carlisle 216 a				19 16							19 52	20 00		20 13							
d				19 17							19 53	20 01		20 15							
Lockerbie 225,226 d				19 37										20 33							
Carstairs 226,225 a																					
Motherwell 226 a				20 22																	
Glasgow Central 216,226,225 a				20 48							21 07	21 22									
Haymarket ⛴ a														21s30							
Edinburgh ⛴ a														21 35	22 18						
Fort William 227,400 a																					
Perth 229 a																					
Dundee 229 a																					
Aberdeen 229 a																					
Inverness 229 a																					

A From Plymouth
B From Bournemouth
C To Glasgow Central
D From London Euston
E until 15 July. From Reading. ✕ to BirminghamNewSt
F From Bristol Temple Meads
G To Edinburgh

Refer to Operator websites for full information about Sleeper Services. Contact details for train operators available at National Rail Enquiries

Table T065-F

Sundays
24 June to 9 September

London & West Midlands to North West England. London, West Midlands & Manchester to Scotland via the West Coast

	VT	VT	VT	VT	VT	VT	VT	XC	LM	XC	TP	VT	LM	VT	VT	VT	VT	VT	VT	VT	VT	XC
						A		B		C		D								A		E
London Euston ⊖66 d	17 05	17 08	17 08	17 17	17 28		17 37					17 40	17 50	17 57	18 05	18 08	18 08	18 17	18 28		18 37	
Watford Junction 66 d													18 06									
Milton Keynes Central 66 d		17 42	17 42	17 50								18 13	18 37			18 42	18 42	18 50				
Rugby 66 d													19 26									
Nuneaton d	18 04												19 40									
Tamworth Low Level d													19 55									
Lichfield Trent Valley d		18 24	18 24										20 01									
Coventry 68 d										18 27		18 45										
Birmingham International 68 ✈ d										18 38		18 55										
BirminghamNewSt 68 d								18 31	18 35	18 57		19 15										19 31
Wolverhampton d								18 49	18 53	19 15		19 37										19 49
Penkridge d									19 03													
Stafford d		18 41	18 41					19 03	19 09	19 28			20 21		19 25							20 03
Stoke-on-Trent 84 a				18 50				19 18		19 44			20 37	19 25				19 50				20 18
Macclesfield a						←		19 36		20 04				19 42						←		20 36
Crewe 81,91 a	18 44	18 59	18 59			19 07	19 12		19 30			20 07	21 06		19 43	19 50	19 50			20 07	20 12	
d	18 46	19 01	19 01			19 09	19 13		19 31			20 09			19 45	19 52	19 52			20 09	20 13	
Chester 81 a		19 19	19 20									→				20 11	20 13					
Wrexham General 75 a																						
Llandudno Junction 81 a		20 18															21 07					
Bangor (Gwynedd) 81 a		20 34															21 23					
Holyhead 81 ⛴ a		21 03															21 54					
Wilmslow 84 a							19 29														20 29	
Stockport 84 a				19 23			19 38	19 50		20 16				19 56				20 23			20 38	20 50
Manchester Piccadilly ⇌ a				19 32			19 48	19 59		20 28				20 06				20 32			20 48	20 59
Runcorn 91 a	19 02								19 54						20 02							
Liverpool South Pkwy 91 ✈ a									20 03													
Liverpool Lime Street 91 a	19 21								20 14						20 20							
d																						
Manchester Airport 82 ✈ d											19 10											
Manchester Picc. 82 ⇌ d											19 26											
Bolton 82 d																						
Warrington Bank Quay d					19 17	19 27													20 16	20 27		
Wigan North Western 90 d					19 28	19 38													20 27	20 38		
Preston 90 a					19 41	19 51					20 02								20 40	20 51		
Blackpool North 97 a																						
Preston 90 d					19 42	19 53					20 04								20 42	20 53		
Lancaster d					19 57	20 08					20 20								20 57	21 08		
Barrow-in-Furness 82 a																						
Oxenholme Lake District 83 d					20 12						20 33								21 11	21 23		
Windermere 83 a																						
Penrith North Lakes d					20 37	20 45					20 58								21 36			
Carlisle 216 a					20 51	20 59					21 14								21 51	22 01		
d					20 51	21 02					21 15								21 52	22 02		
Lockerbie 225,226 d											21 34									22 21		
Carstairs 226,225 a																						
Motherwell 226 a											22 21								22 52	23 04		
Glasgow Central 216,226,225 a					22 06						22 46								23 15	23 24		
Haymarket ⇌ a						22 14																
Edinburgh ⇌ a						22 19																
Fort William 227,400 a																						
Perth 229 a																						
Dundee 229 a																						
Aberdeen 229 a																						
Inverness 229 a																						

A From London Euston
B From Penzance
C From Bournemouth
D To Glasgow Central
E From Bristol Temple Meads

Refer to Operator websites for full information about Sleeper Services. Contact details for train operators available at National Rail Enquiries

Table T065-F

Sundays
24 June to 9 September

London & West Midlands to North West England. London, West Midlands & Manchester to Scotland via the West Coast

	LM	XC	VT	LM	VT	VT	VT	VT	TP	VT	VT	XC	XC	VT	LM	VT	VT	VT	VT	VT	VT	VT
		A										B	A	C							D	
London Euston ⊖66 d			18 40	18 50	18 57	19 05	19 08	19 17		19 28	19 37			19 40	19 50	19 57	20 05	20 08	20 15	20 25		20 35
Watford Junction 66 d				19 06											20 06							
Milton Keynes Central 66 d			19 13	19 37			19 42	19 50						20 13	20 37			20 41	20 48			
Rugby 66 d				20 26											21 30							
Nuneaton d				20 40		20 04									21 43		21 04					
Tamworth Low Level d				20 55											21 58					21 32		
Lichfield Trent Valley d				21 01											22 04					21 39		
Coventry 68 d		19 27	19 42										20 27	20 42								
Birmingham International 68 ✈ d		19 38	19 53										20 38	20 53								
BirminghamNewSt 68 ⇌ d	19 35	19 57	20 15									20 31	20 57	21 15								
Wolverhampton ⇌ d	19 53	20 15	20 37									20 52	21 17	21 37								
Penkridge d	20 03																					
Stafford d	20 09	20 28	20 52	21 21		20 29						21 06	21 30	21 56	22 23			21 33				22 00
Stoke-on-Trent 84 a		20 44		21 37	20 25			20 50				21 21	21 45		22 40	21 25			21 50			
Macclesfield a		21 02			20 42							21 39	22 03			21 43					←	
Crewe 81,91 a	20 31		21 10	22 06		20 47	20 50				21 12			22 16	23 03		21 44	21 53		22 10	22 16	22 20
d	20 31					20 49	20 55				21 13			22 17			21 46	21 55		22 13	22 17	22 21
Chester 81 a							21 13							→								
Wrexham General 75 a																						
Llandudno Junction 81 a							22 06															
Bangor (Gwynedd) 81 a							22 22															
Holyhead 81 ⛴ a							22 53															
Wilmslow 84 a											21 28											22 36
Stockport 84 a		21 15			20 56			21 19			21 38	21 52	22 15			21 59			22 21			22 45
Manchester Piccadilly ⇌ a		21 29			21 06			21 31			21 49	22 02	22 26			22 09			22 31			22 54
Runcorn 91 a	20 54					21 06											22 03	22 12				
Liverpool South Pkwy 91 ✈ a	21 03																					
Liverpool Lime Street 91 a	21 14					21 23											22 20	22 29				
d																						
Manchester Airport 82 ✈ d									20 10													
Manchester Picc. 82 ⇌ d									20 26													
Bolton 82 d																						
Warrington Bank Quay d										21 16										22 30	22 36	
Wigan North Western 90 d										21 27										22 41	22 47	
Preston 90 a									21 02	21 40										22 55	23 01	
Blackpool North 97 a																						
Preston 90 d									21 04	21 42												
Lancaster d									21 20	21 57												
Barrow-in-Furness 82 a																						
Oxenholme Lake District 83 d									21 33	22 11												
Windermere 83 a																						
Penrith North Lakes d									21 58	22 36												
Carlisle 216 a									22 14	22 51												
d									22 15	22 52												
Lockerbie 225,226 d																						
Carstairs 226,225 a																						
Motherwell 226 a																						
Glasgow Central 216,226,225 a										00 07												
Haymarket ⇌ a									23s28													
Edinburgh ⇌ a									23 34													
Fort William 227,400 a																						
Perth 229 a																						
Dundee 229 a																						
Aberdeen 229 a																						
Inverness 229 a																						

A From Bournemouth. ⚒ to BirminghamNewSt
B From Bristol Temple Meads
C To Preston
D From London Euston

Refer to Operator websites for full information about Sleeper Services. Contact details for train operators available at National Rail Enquiries

Table T065-F

Sundays
24 June to 9 September

London & West Midlands to North West England. London, West Midlands & Manchester to Scotland via the West Coast

Station		LM	VT	CS		CS	XC	VT	VT	AW	VT	CS
		■	◇■				◇■ A	◇■	◇■	◇	◇■	
London Euston ⊖66	d		20 50	21 00		21 00		21 21	21 25		21 51	23 28
Watford Junction 66	d			21u20		21u20						23u49
Milton Keynes Central 66	d		21 37						22 17		22 39	
Rugby 66	d		22 01								23 19	
Nuneaton	d							22 57			23 30	
Tamworth Low Level	d											
Lichfield Trent Valley	d											
Coventry 68	d						21 27					
Birmingham International 68	d						21 38			22 40		
BirminghamNewSt 68	d	21 42					21 57			22 55		
Wolverhampton	d	22 00					22 15			23 15		
Penkridge	d	22 10										
Stafford	d	22 17					22 28	23 23		23 31	23s54	
Stoke-on-Trent 84	a						22 44		23 33			
Macclesfield	a						23 01		23 49			
Crewe 81,91	a	22 36	22 49					23 44		23 57	00s16	
	d	22 38	22 51	23u36		23u36		23 46		00 01		
Chester 81	a									00 22		
Wrexham General 75	a											
Llandudno Junction 81	a									01 27		
Bangor (Gwynedd) 81	a									01 44		
Holyhead 81	a									02 20		
Wilmslow 84	a											
Stockport 84	a						23 14		00 03		00s38	
Manchester Piccadilly	a						23 24		00 13		00 48	
Runcorn 91	a	22 59						00 04				
Liverpool South Pkwy 91	a	23 10										
Liverpool Lime Street 91	a	23 24						00 28				
	d											
Manchester Airport 82	d											
Manchester Picc. 82	d											
Bolton 82	d											
Warrington Bank Quay	d		23 08									
Wigan North Western 90	d		23 19									
Preston 90	a		23 38									
Blackpool North 97	a											
Preston 90	d			00u35	00u35	00u35						
Lancaster	d											
Barrow-In-Furness 82	a											
Oxenholme Lake District 83	d											
Windermere 83	a											
Penrith North Lakes	d											
Carlisle 216	a											04s43
	d											
Lockerbie 225,226	d											
Carstairs 226,225	a											06s20
Motherwell 226	a											06s55
Glasgow Central 216,226,225	a											07 22
Haymarket	a											
Edinburgh	a											
Fort William 227,400	a					09 57						
Perth 229	a				05s41							
Dundee 229	a			06s08								
Aberdeen 229	a			07 39								
Inverness 229	a				08 41							

A From Bournemouth

Refer to Operator websites for full information about Sleeper Services. Contact details for train operators available at National Rail Enquiries

Table T065-F

Sundays
16 September to 2 December

London & West Midlands to North West England. London, West Midlands & Manchester to Scotland via the West Coast

Station		NT	TP	NT	NT	TP	VT	XC	VT	VT	TP	VT	VT	VT	LM	VT	XC	VT	VT	LM	LM	VT	XC
		◇ A	◇■	◇		◇■	◇■	◇■	◇■	◇■	◇■	◇■	◇■	◇■	■	◇■	◇■	◇■	◇■	■	■ B	◇■	◇■ C
London Euston ⊖66	d									08 10			08 15	08 20		08 45			09 14			09 20	
Watford Junction 66	d																						
Milton Keynes Central 66	d									08 56				09 06		09 33						10 07	
Rugby 66	d														08 52	10 09					10 03		
Nuneaton	d												09 44						10 45		10 16		
Tamworth Low Level	d																				10 30		
Lichfield Trent Valley	d																		11 02		10 37		
Coventry 68	d														09 07								10 29
Birmingham International 68	d														09 20								10 40
BirminghamNewSt 68	d						08 45	09 01	09 20						09 42		10 01	10 20		10 42			11 01
Wolverhampton	d						09 04	09 19	09 37						10 00		10 19	10 37		11 00			11 19
Penkridge	d														10 10					11 10			
Stafford	d						09 17	09 33					10 08		10 17		10 33		11 15	11 17	11 00		11 32
Stoke-on-Trent 84	a							09 51						10 19			10 48				11 16	11 21	11 48
Macclesfield	a							10 09						10 36			11 08					11 38	12 09
Crewe 81,91	a						09 35		10 07	10 17			10 28		10 37	10 55		11 10	11 34	11 37	11 41		
	d						09 37		10 09	10 19		10 27	10 30		10 38	10 57		11 11	11 36	11 38			
Chester 81	a																						
Wrexham General 75	a																						
Llandudno Junction 81	a																						
Bangor (Gwynedd) 81	a																						
Holyhead 81	a																						
Wilmslow 84	a									10 33													
Stockport 84	a							10 22		10 43				10 50			11 22					11 52	12 24
Manchester Piccadilly	a							10 38		10 53				11 02			11 33					12 04	12 41
Runcorn 91	a												10 48		11 00				11 53	12 00			
Liverpool South Pkwy 91	a														11 09					12 09			
Liverpool Lime Street 91	a												11 06		11 21				12 11	12 21			
	d																						
Manchester Airport 82	d					09 05					10 10												
Manchester Picc. 82	d		08 43			09 22					10 26												
Bolton 82	d																						
Warrington Bank Quay	d						09 54		10 27			10 43				11 13		11 29					
Wigan North Western 90	d						10 06		10 38			10 54				11 24		11 40					
Preston 90	a		09 22			10 02	10 20		10 51		11 04	11 12				11 38		11 53					
Blackpool North 97	a																						
Preston 90	d	09 07	09 23	09 38		10 03			11 02		11 09	11 19				11 39		11 54					
Lancaster	d		09 39	09 59	10 11	10 19			11 18		11 25	11a36				11 54		12 09					
Barrow-in-Furness 82	a				11 14																		
Oxenholme Lake District 83	d			10 30		10 33			11 33		11 38					12 08		12 24					
Windermere 83	a			10 52																			
Penrith North Lakes	d					10 58					12 03					12 34							
Carlisle 216	a	12 16	10 28		13 42	11 13			12 10		12 19					12 49		13 01					
	d		10 29			11 16			12 12		12 20					12 49		13 03					
Lockerbie 225,226	d		10 48			11 36					12 39												
Carstairs 226,225	a																						
Motherwell 226	a					12 22																	
Glasgow Central 216,226,225	a					12 46			13 27							14 04							
Haymarket	a		11s48								13s42							14 16					
Edinburgh	a		11 53								13 49							14 21					
Fort William 227,400	a																						
Perth 229	a																						
Dundee 229	a																						
Aberdeen 229	a																						
Inverness 229	a																						

A From Blackpool North
B From Northampton
C From Reading

Refer to Operator websites for full information about Sleeper Services. Contact details for train operators available at National Rail Enquiries

London & West Midlands to North West England. London, West Midlands & Manchester to Scotland via the West Coast

	NT	TP	VT	NT	VT	NT	LM	VT	VT	LM	XC	LM	NT	TP	VT	VT	VT	VT	LM	VT	XC	VT
	◇	◇1	◇1	◇	◇1		1	◇1	◇1	1	◇1	1	◇	◇1	◇1	◇1	◇1	◇1	1	◇1	◇1	◇1
	A			A							B		A	C							D	
London Euston 15 ⊖66 d			09 45				09 54	10 15	10 20			10 24			10 45		11 15	11 20		12 05		12 17
Watford Junction 66 d							10 10					10 40										
Milton Keynes Central 66 d			10 33				10 50		11 07			11 20			11 33		12 04	12 08				12 50
Rugby 66 d			11 09				11 30					12 03			12 09							
Nuneaton d							11 43	11 47				12 16										
Tamworth Low Level d							11 57					12 30										
Lichfield Trent Valley d							12 04					12 37										
Coventry 68 d											11 29										12 28	
Birmingham International 68 ✈ d											11 41										12 40	
BirminghamNewSt 12 68 ⇌ d					11 20					11 42	11 57					12 20			12 35		12 57	
Wolverhampton 7 ⇌ d					11 37					12 00	12 16					12 37			12 53		13 16	
Penkridge d										12 10									13 03			
Stafford d							12 21	12 14		12 17	12 29	13 00					12 53		13 09	13 25	13 29	
Stoke-on-Trent 84 a							12 37		12 24		12 45	13 16						13 09			13 44	13 50
Macclesfield a									12 40		13 04							13 26			14 04	
Crewe 10 81,91 a			11 55		12 07		13 03	12 32		12 37		13 41			12 56	13 07	13 12		13 30	13 43		
d			11 57		12 09			12 34		12 38					12 58	13 09	13 15		13 31	13 45		
Chester 81 a																						
Wrexham General 75 a																						
Llandudno Junction 81 a																						
Bangor (Gwynedd) 81 a																						
Holyhead 81 ⛴ a																						
Wilmslow 84 a																						
Stockport 84 a									12 55		13 16							13 41			14 16	14 22
Manchester Piccadilly 10 ⇌ a									13 05		13 29							13 50			14 29	14 32
Runcorn 91 a								12 51		13 01							13 32		13 54	14 02		
Liverpool South Pkwy 7 91 ✈ a										13 10									14 03			
Liverpool Lime Street 10 91 a								13 08		13 21							13 54		14 14	14 20		
d																						
Manchester Airport 82 ✈⇌ d		11 10																				
Manchester Picc. 10 82 ⇌ d		11 26																				
Bolton 82 d	11 24												12 24									
Warrington Bank Quay d			12 14		12 27										13 15	13 27						
Wigan North Western 90 d			12 25	12 33	12 38										13 26	13 38						
Preston 8 90 a	12 01	12 02	12 38	12 51	12 51								12 58		13 40	13 51						
Blackpool North 97 a				13 16																		
Preston 8 90 d		12 04	12 40		12 53									13 04	13 41	13 53						
Lancaster 6 d		12 20	12 55		13 08	13 13								13 19	13 56	14 08						
Barrow-in-Furness 82 a						14 16																
Oxenholme Lake District 83 d		12 33	13 08		13 22									13 33	14 10							
Windermere 83 a																						
Penrith North Lakes d		12 58	13 34												14 36	14 45						
Carlisle 8 216 a		13 14	13 49		14 00	16 35								14 11	14 51	15 00						
d		13 16	13 50		14 02									14 13	14 51	15 03						
Lockerbie 225,226 d		13 37												14 31								
Carstairs 226,225 a																						
Motherwell 226 a		14 21																				
Glasgow Central 15 216,226,225 a		14 42	15 04		15 16										16 06							
Haymarket ⇌ a														15s29		16 14						
Edinburgh 10 ⇌ a														15 36		16 20						
Fort William 227,400 a																						
Perth 229 a																						
Dundee 229 a																						
Aberdeen 229 a																						
Inverness 229 a																						

A From Manchester Oxford Road
B From Southampton Central
C From Manchester Victoria
D From Bournemouth

Refer to Operator websites for full information about Sleeper Services. Contact details for train operators available at National Rail Enquiries

London & West Midlands to North West England. London, West Midlands & Manchester to Scotland via the West Coast

	NT	TP	VT	VT	VT	XC	LM	XC	TP	VT	LM	VT	VT	LM	VT	VT	VT	NT	VT	XC	LM
	◇	◇1	◇1	◇1	◇1	◇1	1	◇1	◇1	◇1	1	◇1	◇1	1	◇1	◇1	◇1		◇1	◇1	1
	A							B		C				D			E			F	
London Euston 15 ⊖66 d			12 28		12 37					12 40	12 50	12 57	13 05		13 17	13 28			13 37		
Watford Junction 66 d											13 06										
Milton Keynes Central 66 d										13 13	13 37				13 50						
Rugby 66 d											14 26			13 26							
Nuneaton d											14 40			13 40							
Tamworth Low Level d											14 55			13 55							
Lichfield Trent Valley d											15 01			14 01							
Coventry 68 d								13 27		13 42											
Birmingham International 68 ✈ d								13 38		13 53											
BirminghamNewSt 12 68 ⇌ d				13 20		13 30	13 35	13 57		14 15										14 31	14 35
Wolverhampton 7 ⇌ d				13 37		13 49	13 53	14 15		14 37										14 49	14 53
Penkridge d							14 03														15 03
Stafford d						14 03	14 09	14 28			15 21		14 25	14 21						15 03	15 09
Stoke-on-Trent 84 a						14 18		14 44			15 37	14 24		14 37	14 50					15 18	
Macclesfield a						14 36		15 01				14 42					←			15 36	
Crewe 10 81,91 a				14 07	14 12		14 30			15 07	16 05		14 43	15 03			15 07		15 12		15 30
d				14 09	14 13		14 31			15 09			14 45				15 09		15 13		15 31
Chester 81 a										→											
Wrexham General 75 a																					
Llandudno Junction 81 a																					
Bangor (Gwynedd) 81 a																					
Holyhead 81 ⛴ a																					
Wilmslow 84 a					14 28														15 29		
Stockport 84 a					14 38	14 50		15 14				14 55			15 20				15 38	15 50	
Manchester Piccadilly 10 ⇌ a					14 48	14 59		15 24				15 06			15 31				15 48	15 59	
Runcorn 91 a							14 53						15 02								15 53
Liverpool South Pkwy 7 91 ✈ a							15 02														16 02
Liverpool Lime Street 10 91 a							15 14						15 20								16 14
d																					
Manchester Airport 82 ✈⇌ d		13 10							14 10												
Manchester Picc. 10 82 ⇌ d		13 26							14 26												
Bolton 82 d	13 24																				
Warrington Bank Quay d			14 16	14 27												15 16	15 27				
Wigan North Western 90 d			14 27	14 38												15 27	15 38				
Preston 8 90 a	13 58	14 03	14 40	14 50					15 03							15 40	15 51				
Blackpool North 97 a																					
Preston 8 90 d		14 04	14 42	14 53					15 04							15 42	15 53				
Lancaster 6 d		14 20	14 58	15 09					15 20							15 58	16 08	16 13			
Barrow-in-Furness 82 a																		17 16			
Oxenholme Lake District 83 d		14 33		15 24												16 11					
Windermere 83 a																					
Penrith North Lakes d		14 58	15 32						15 55								16 45				
Carlisle 8 216 a		15 14	15 47	16 01					16 12							16 48	17 00	19 47			
d		15 16	15 48	16 03					16 13							16 49	17 02				
Lockerbie 225,226 d		15 37							16 32												
Carstairs 226,225 a																					
Motherwell 226 a		16 21																			
Glasgow Central 15 216,226,225 a		16 42	17 02	17 15												18 02					
Haymarket ⇌ a									17s28								18 11				
Edinburgh 10 ⇌ a									17 34								18 20				
Fort William 227,400 a																					
Perth 229 a																					
Dundee 229 a																					
Aberdeen 229 a																					
Inverness 229 a																					

A From Manchester Oxford Road
B From Bournemouth
C To Edinburgh
D From Northampton
E From London Euston
F From Paignton

Refer to Operator websites for full information about Sleeper Services. Contact details for train operators available at National Rail Enquiries

Table T065-F

Sundays

16 September to 2 December

London & West Midlands to North West England. London, West Midlands & Manchester to Scotland via the West Coast

		XC	TP	VT	LM	VT	VT	VT	VT	VT	VT	XC	LM	XC	TP	VT	LM	VT	VT	VT	VT	VT	VT
		A		B						C		D		A		E							C
London Euston	⊖66 d			13 40	13 50	13 57	14 05	14 17	14 28		14 37					14 40	14 50	14 57	15 05	15 08	15 17	15 28	
Watford Junction	66 d				14 06												15 06						
Milton Keynes Central	66 d			14 13	14 37			14 50								15 13	15 37			15 42	15 50		
Rugby	66 d				15 26												16 26						
Nuneaton	d				15 40												16 40						
Tamworth Low Level	d				15 55												16 55						
Lichfield Trent Valley	d				16 01												17 01						
Coventry	68 d	14 27		14 42										15 27		15 42							
Birmingham International	68 ✈ d	14 38		14 53										15 38		15 53							
BirminghamNewSt	68 d	14 57		15 15								15 31	15 35	15 57		16 15							
Wolverhampton	d	15 15		15 37								15 49	15 53	16 15		16 37							
Penkridge	d												16 03										
Stafford	d	15 28			16 21		15 25					16 03	16 09	16 28			17 21		16 25				
Stoke-on-Trent	84 a	15 44			16 37	15 25		15 50				16 18		16 44			17 37	16 26			16 52		
Macclesfield	a	16 04				15 42				←		16 36		17 04				16 42					←
Crewe	81,91 a			16 08	17 05		15 43			16 08	16 11		16 30			17 07	18 05		16 43	16 50			17 07
	d			16 09			15 45			16 09	16 12		16 31			17 09			16 45	16 52			17 09
Chester	81 a			→												→				17 11			
Wrexham General	75 a																						
Llandudno Junction	81 a																						
Bangor (Gwynedd)	81 a																						
Holyhead	81 ⛴ a																						
Wilmslow	84 a										16 29												
Stockport	84 a	16 16				15 55		16 23			16 35	16 50		17 16				16 56			17 23		
Manchester Piccadilly	a	16 29				16 05		16 32			16 48	16 59		17 29				17 06			17 32		
Runcorn	91 a						16 02						16 54						17 02				
Liverpool South Pkwy	91 ✈ a												17 03										
Liverpool Lime Street	91 a						16 23						17 14						17 21				
	d																						
Manchester Airport	82 ✈ d		15 10												16 10								
Manchester Picc.	82 d		15 26												16 26								
Bolton	82 d																						
Warrington Bank Quay	d								16 16	16 27												17 16	17 27
Wigan North Western	90 d								16 27	16 38												17 27	17 38
Preston	90 a		16 03						16 40	16 51					17 02							17 40	17 51
Blackpool North	97 a																						
Preston	90 d		16 04						16 42	16 53					17 03							17 42	17 53
Lancaster	d		16 20						16 57	17 08					17 19							17 57	18 09
Barrow-in-Furness	82 a																						
Oxenholme Lake District	83 d		16 35							17 23					17 32							18 11	18 23
Windermere	83 a																						
Penrith North Lakes	d		17 00						17 32						17 57								18 48
Carlisle	216 a		17 16						17 47	18 01					18 12							18 48	19 03
	d		17 18						17 48	18 02					18 13							18 49	19 04
Lockerbie	225,226 d		17 37												18 32								
Carstairs	226,225 a																						
Motherwell	226 a		18 22																				
Glasgow Central	216,226,225 a		18 44						19 02	19 13												20 02	
Haymarket	a														19s30								20 16
Edinburgh	a														19 35								20 22
Fort William	227,400 a																						
Perth	229 a																						
Dundee	229 a																						
Aberdeen	229 a																						
Inverness	229 a																						

A From Bournemouth
B To Glasgow Central
C From London Euston
D From Plymouth
E To Edinburgh

Refer to Operator websites for full information about Sleeper Services. Contact details for train operators available at National Rail Enquiries

Table T065-F

Sundays

16 September to 2 December

London & West Midlands to North West England. London, West Midlands & Manchester to Scotland via the West Coast

		VT	XC	LM	XC	TP	VT	LM	VT	VT	VT	VT	VT	VT	VT	TP	XC	XC	LM	XC	VT	LM
			A		B		C							D			E	F		B	G	
London Euston	⊖66 d	15 37					15 40	15 50	15 57	16 05	16 08	16 17	16 28		16 37						16 40	16 50
Watford Junction	66 d							16 06														17 06
Milton Keynes Central	66 d						16 13	16 37			16 42	16 50									17 13	17 37
Rugby	66 d							17 26														18 26
Nuneaton	d							17 40														18 40
Tamworth Low Level	d							17 55														18 55
Lichfield Trent Valley	d							18 01														19 01
Coventry	68 d				16 27		16 42										16 54			17 27	17 45	
Birmingham International	68 ✈ d				16 38		16 53										17 04			17 38	17 55	
BirminghamNewSt	68 d		16 31	16 35	16 57		17 15										17 30	17 31	17 35	17 57	18 15	
Wolverhampton	d		16 49	16 53	17 15		17 37											17 49	17 53	18 15	18 37	
Penkridge	d			17 03															18 03			
Stafford	d		17 03	17 09	17 29			18 21		17 26								18 03	18 09	18 28		19 21
Stoke-on-Trent	84 a		17 18		17 45			18 37	17 25			17 50						18 18		18 44		19 37
Macclesfield	a		17 36		18 04				17 42					←				18 36		19 04		
Crewe	81,91 a	17 12		17 30			18 07	19 06		17 44	17 50			18 07	18 12				18 30		19 07	20 06
	d	17 13		17 31			18 09			17 46	17 52			18 09	18 13				18 31		19 09	
Chester	81 a						→				18 12										→	
Wrexham General	75 a																					
Llandudno Junction	81 a																					
Bangor (Gwynedd)	81 a																					
Holyhead	81 ⛴ a																					
Wilmslow	84 a	17 29													18 29							
Stockport	84 a	17 38	17 50		18 16				17 55			18 23			18 38			18 50		19 17		
Manchester Piccadilly	a	17 48	17 59		18 29				18 05			18 32			18 48			18 59		19 28		
Runcorn	91 a			17 54						18 02									18 54			
Liverpool South Pkwy	91 ✈ a			18 03															19 03			
Liverpool Lime Street	91 a			18 14						18 21									19 14			
	d																					
Manchester Airport	82 ✈ d					17 10										18 10						
Manchester Picc.	82 d					17 26										18 26						
Bolton	82 d																					
Warrington Bank Quay	d												18 16	18 27								
Wigan North Western	90 d												18 27	18 38								
Preston	90 a					18 04							18 41	18 51		19 02						
Blackpool North	97 a																					
Preston	90 d					18 06							18 42	18 53		19 04						
Lancaster	d					18 21							18 57	19 08		19 19						
Barrow-in-Furness	82 a																					
Oxenholme Lake District	83 d					18 35							19 12	19 22		19 33						
Windermere	83 a																					
Penrith North Lakes	d					19 00							19 37			19 58						
Carlisle	216 a					19 15							19 52	20 00		20 13						
	d					19 17							19 53	20 01		20 15						
Lockerbie	225,226 d					19 37										20 33						
Carstairs	226,225 a																					
Motherwell	226 a					20 21																
Glasgow Central	216,226,225 a					20 40							21 04	21 12								
Haymarket	a															21s30						
Edinburgh	a															21 35	22 18					
Fort William	227,400 a																					
Perth	229 a																					
Dundee	229 a																					
Aberdeen	229 a																					
Inverness	229 a																					

A From Plymouth
B From Bournemouth
C To Glasgow Central
D From London Euston
E from 14 October. From Reading. to BirminghamNewSt
F From Bristol Temple Meads
G To Edinburgh

Refer to Operator websites for full information about Sleeper Services. Contact details for train operators available at National Rail Enquiries

London & West Midlands to North West England. London, West Midlands & Manchester to Scotland via the West Coast

Station		VT	VT	VT	VT	VT	VT	VT	VT	XC	LM	XC	TP	VT	LM	VT	VT	VT	VT	VT	VT	VT	VT
								A		B		C		D								A	
London Euston	⊖66 d	16 57	17 05	17 08	17 08	17 17	17 28		17 37					17 40	17 50	17 57	18 05	18 08	18 08	18 17	18 28		18 37
Watford Junction	66 d														18 06								
Milton Keynes Central	66 d			17 42	17 42	17 50								18 13	18 37			18 42	18 42	18 50			
Rugby	66 d														19 26								
Nuneaton	d		18 04												19 40								
Tamworth Low Level	d														19 55								
Lichfield Trent Valley	d			18 24	18 24										20 01								
Coventry	68 d											18 27		18 45									
Birmingham International	68 ✈ d											18 38		18 55									
BirminghamNewSt	68 d									18 31	18 35	18 57		19 15									
Wolverhampton	d									18 49	18 53	19 15		19 37									
Penkridge	d										19 03												
Stafford	d			18 41	18 41					19 03	19 09	19 28			20 21		19 25						
Stoke-on-Trent	84 a	18 25				18 50				19 18		19 44			20 37	19 25				19 50			
Macclesfield	a	18 42						←		19 36		20 04				19 42						←	
Crewe	81,91 a		18 44	18 59	18 59			19 07	19 12		19 30			20 07	21 06		19 43	19 50	19 50			20 07	20 12
	d		18 46	19 01	19 01			19 09	19 13		19 31			20 09			19 45	19 52	19 52			20 09	20 13
Chester	81 a			19 19	19 20									→				20 11	20 13				
Wrexham General	75 a																						
Llandudno Junction	81 a			20 18															21 07				
Bangor (Gwynedd)	81 a			20 34															21 23				
Holyhead	81 ⛴ a			21 03															21 54				
Wilmslow	84 a								19 29														20 29
Stockport	84 a	18 56				19 23			19 38	19 50		20 16				19 56				20 23			20 38
Manchester Piccadilly	a	19 06				19 32			19 48	19 59		20 28				20 06				20 32			20 48
Runcorn	91 a		19 02								19 54						20 02						
Liverpool South Pkwy	91 ✈ a										20 03												
Liverpool Lime Street	91 a		19 21								20 14						20 20						
	d																						
Manchester Airport	82 ✈ d												19 10										
Manchester Picc.	82 d												19 26										
Bolton	82 d																						
Warrington Bank Quay	d						19 17	19 27													20 16	20 27	
Wigan North Western	90 d						19 28	19 38													20 27	20 38	
Preston	90 a						19 41	19 51					20 02								20 40	20 51	
Blackpool North	97 a																						
Preston	90 d						19 42	19 53					20 04								20 42	20 53	
Lancaster	d						19 57	20 08					20 20								20 57	21 08	
Barrow-in-Furness	82 a																						
Oxenholme Lake District	83 d						20 12						20 33								21 11	21 23	
Windermere	83 a																						
Penrith North Lakes	d						20 37	20 45					20 58								21 36		
Carlisle	216 a						20 51	20 59					21 14								21 51	22 01	
	d						20 51	21 02					21 15								21 52	22 02	
Lockerbie	225,226 d												21 34									22 21	
Carstairs	226,225 a																						
Motherwell	226 a												22 20								22 49	23 04	
Glasgow Central	216,226,225 a						22 03						22 42								23 07	23 21	
Haymarket	a							22 14															
Edinburgh	a							22 19															
Fort William	227,400 a																						
Perth	229 a																						
Dundee	229 a																						
Aberdeen	229 a																						
Inverness	229 a																						

A From London Euston
B From Penzance
C From Bournemouth
D To Glasgow Central

Refer to Operator websites for full information about Sleeper Services. Contact details for train operators available at National Rail Enquiries

London & West Midlands to North West England. London, West Midlands & Manchester to Scotland via the West Coast

Station		XC	LM	XC	VT	LM	VT	VT	VT	VT	TP	VT	VT	XC	XC	VT	LM	VT	VT	VT	VT	VT	VT
		A		B										A	B	C							D
London Euston	⊖66 d				18 40	18 50	18 57	19 05	19 08	19 17		19 28	19 37			19 40	19 50	19 57	20 05	20 08	20 15	20 25	
Watford Junction	66 d					19 06											20 06						
Milton Keynes Central	66 d				19 13	19 37			19 42	19 50						20 13	20 37			20 41	20 48		
Rugby	66 d					20 26											21 30						
Nuneaton	d					20 40		20 04									21 43		21 04				
Tamworth Low Level	d					20 55											21 58					21 32	
Lichfield Trent Valley	d					21 01											22 04					21 39	
Coventry	68 d			19 27	19 42										20 27	20 42							
Birmingham International	68 ✈ d			19 38	19 53										20 38	20 53							
BirminghamNewSt	68 d	19 31	19 35	19 57	20 15									20 31	20 57	21 15							
Wolverhampton	d	19 49	19 53	20 15	20 37									20 52	21 17	21 37							
Penkridge	d		20 03																				
Stafford	d	20 03	20 09	20 28	20 52	21 21		20 29						21 06	21 30	21 56	22 23			21 33			
Stoke-on-Trent	84 a	20 18		20 44		21 37	20 25			20 50				21 21	21 45		22 40	21 25			21 50		
Macclesfield	a	20 36		21 02			20 42							21 39	22 03			21 43					←
Crewe	81,91 a		20 31		21 10	22 06		20 47	20 50				21 12			22 16	23 03		21 44	21 53		22 10	22 16
	d		20 31					20 49	20 55				21 13			22 17			21 46	21 55		22 13	22 17
Chester	81 a								21 13							→							
Wrexham General	75 a																						
Llandudno Junction	81 a								22 06														
Bangor (Gwynedd)	81 a								22 22														
Holyhead	81 ⛴ a								22 53														
Wilmslow	84 a												21 28										
Stockport	84 a	20 50		21 15			20 56			21 19			21 38	21 52	22 15			21 59			22 21		
Manchester Piccadilly	a	20 59		21 29			21 06			21 31			21 49	22 02	22 26			22 09			22 31		
Runcorn	91 a		20 54					21 06											22 03	22 12			
Liverpool South Pkwy	91 ✈ a		21 03																				
Liverpool Lime Street	91 a		21 14					21 23											22 20	22 29			
	d																						
Manchester Airport	82 ✈ d										20 10												
Manchester Picc.	82 d										20 26												
Bolton	82 d																						
Warrington Bank Quay	d											21 16										22 30	22 36
Wigan North Western	90 d											21 27										22 41	22 47
Preston	90 a										21 02	21 40										22 55	23 01
Blackpool North	97 a																						
Preston	90 d										21 04	21 42											
Lancaster	d										21 20	21 57											
Barrow-in-Furness	82 a																						
Oxenholme Lake District	83 d										21 33	22 11											
Windermere	83 a																						
Penrith North Lakes	d										21 58	22 36											
Carlisle	216 a										22 14	22 51											
	d										22 15	22 52											
Lockerbie	225,226 d																						
Carstairs	226,225 a																						
Motherwell	226 a																						
Glasgow Central	216,226,225 a											00 04											
Haymarket	a										23s28												
Edinburgh	a										23 34												
Fort William	227,400 a																						
Perth	229 a																						
Dundee	229 a																						
Aberdeen	229 a																						
Inverness	229 a																						

A From Bristol Temple Meads
B From Bournemouth. 🍴 to BirminghamNewSt
C To Preston
D From London Euston

Refer to Operator websites for full information about Sleeper Services. Contact details for train operators available at National Rail Enquiries

Table T065-F

Sundays

16 September to 2 December

London & West Midlands to North West England. London, West Midlands & Manchester to Scotland via the West Coast

	VT		LM	VT	CS		CS	XC	VT	VT	AW		VT	CS
	◇■		■	◇■				◇■	◇■	◇■	◇		◇■	
								A						
London Euston ⊖66 d	20 35			20 50	21 00		21 00		21 21	21 25			21 51	23 28
Watford Junction 66 d					21u20		21u20							23u49
Milton Keynes Central 66 d				21 37						22 17			22 39	
Rugby 66 d				22 01									23 19	
Nuneaton d									22 57				23 30	
Tamworth Low Level d														
Lichfield Trent Valley d														
Coventry 68 d								21 27						
Birmingham International 68 d								21 38			22 40			
BirminghamNewSt 68 d			21 42					21 57			22 55			
Wolverhampton d			22 00					22 15			23 15			
Penkridge d			22 10											
Stafford d	22 00		22 17					22 28	23 23		23 31		23s54	
Stoke-on-Trent 84 a								22 44		23 33				
Macclesfield a								23 01		23 49				
Crewe 81,91 a	22 20		22 36	22 49					23 44		23 57		00s16	
d	22 21		22 38	22 51	23u36		23u36		23 46		00 01			
Chester 81 a											00 22			
Wrexham General 75 a														
Llandudno Junction 81 a											01 27			
Bangor (Gwynedd) 81 a											01 44			
Holyhead 81 a											02 20			
Wilmslow 84 a	22 36													
Stockport 84 a	22 45							23 14		00 03			00s38	
Manchester Piccadilly a	22 54							23 24		00 13			00 48	
Runcorn 91 a			22 59						00 04					
Liverpool South Pkwy 91 a			23 10											
Liverpool Lime Street 91 a			23 24						00 28					
d														
Manchester Airport 82 d														
Manchester Picc. 82 d														
Bolton 82 d														
Warrington Bank Quay d				23 08										
Wigan North Western 90 d				23 19										
Preston 90 a				23 38										
Blackpool North 97 a														
Preston 90 d					00u35	00u35	00u35							
Lancaster d														
Barrow-in-Furness 82 a														
Oxenholme Lake District 83 d														
Windermere 83 a														
Penrith North Lakes d														
Carlisle 216 a														04s43
d														
Lockerbie 225,226 d														
Carstairs 226,225 a														06s20
Motherwell 226 a														06s55
Glasgow Central 216,226,225 a														07 22
Haymarket a														
Edinburgh a														
Fort William 227,400 a							09 57							
Perth 229 a						05s41								
Dundee 229 a					06s08									
Aberdeen 229 a					07 39									
Inverness 229 a						08 41								

A From Bournemouth

Refer to Operator websites for full information about Sleeper Services. Contact details for train operators available at National Rail Enquiries

Table T065-R

Mondays to Fridays

21 May to 7 December

Scotland to Manchester, West Midlands & London via the West Coast. North West England to West Midlands & London

Miles	Miles	Miles	Miles	Miles		NT MX	TP ThO	TP TW FO	CS MO	CS MX	CS MX	AW	LM	VT		XC	VT	XC	VT	LM	VT	VT	LM	XC
							◇■	◇■					■	◇■		◇■	◇■	◇■	◇■	■	◇■	◇■	■	◇■
						A	B	B	C	D	B					E		F		G			H	I
—	0	—	—	—	**Inverness** 229 d																			
—	—	0	—	—	**Aberdeen** 229 d																			
—	—	71¼	—	—	Dundee 229 d																			
—	118	—	—	—	Perth 229 d																			
—	—	—	—	—	**Fort William** 400,227 d																			
—	130¾	187¾	—	—	**Edinburgh** d																			
—	131½	188½	—	—	Haymarket d																			
0	—	—	—	—	**Glasgow Central** 226,216,225 d																			
12¾	—	—	—	—	Motherwell 226 d																			
28¾	158	—	—	—	Carstairs 226,225 d					00u19														
77	—	263½	—	—	Lockerbie 225,226 d																			
102¼	—	—	—	—	**Carlisle** 216 a																			
—	—	—	—	—	d				01u45	01u49	01u49													
120	—	—	—	—	Penrith North Lakes d																			
—	—	—	—	—	**Windermere** 83 d																			
152¼	—	—	—	—	Oxenholme Lake District 83 d																			
—	—	—	—	—	Barrow-in-Furness 82 d																			
171¼	—	—	—	—	Lancaster d														05 13					
174½	—	—	—	—	**Blackpool North** 97 d																			
192¼	—	—	—	—	**Preston** 90 a														05 30					
—	—	—	0	—	**Preston** 90 d		00 57	00 57											05 33					
207½	—	—	—	—	Wigan North Western 90 d														05 45					
219¼	—	—	—	—	Warrington Bank Quay d														05 56					
—	—	—	20	—	Bolton 82 a																			
—	—	—	31¼	—	**Manchester Picc.** 82 a		01 43	01 43																
—	—	—	—	—	Manchester Airport a			01 58																
—	0	—	—	—	**Liverpool Lime Street** 91 a																			
—	—	—	—	—	d												05 26					06 05		
—	5½	—	—	—	Liverpool South Pkwy 91 d																			
—	13	—	—	—	Runcorn 91 d												05 43					06 21		
—	—	—	—	0	**Manchester Picc.** 84 d									05 05		05 11					05 55			06 00
—	—	—	37	5¾	Stockport 84 d									05 13							06 03			06 08
—	—	—	—	—	Wilmslow 84 d	00 02															06 11			06 16
—	—	—	—	—	**Holyhead** 81 d																			
—	—	—	—	—	Bangor (Gwynedd) 81 d																			
—	—	—	—	—	Llandudno Junction 81 d																			
—	—	—	—	—	Wrexham General 75 d																			
—	—	—	—	—	**Chester** 81 d							04 22												
243½	35½	—	—	—	**Crewe** 81,91 a	00 34						04 44		05 33		05 43	06 00				06 27			06 37
—	—	—	—	—	d							04 59	05 21	05 36		05 47	06 02			06 19	06 28		06 35	06 39
—	—	—	49	17¾	Macclesfield d																			
—	—	—	68¾	37¼	**Stoke-on-Trent** 84 d											06 07		←					06 56	
267¾	—	—	—	53½	**Stafford** a							05 23		05 54		06 24	06 20	06 24		06 40		06 52	07 14	06 59
—	—	—	—	—	d							05 24		05 55		06 25	06 22	06 25		06 40		06 54	07 15	07 01
—	—	—	—	59¾	Penkridge a											→				06 46			→	
—	—	—	—	69¾	**Wolverhampton** a							05 39						06 38		06 57				07 12
—	—	—	—	82½	**BirminghamNewSt** 68 a							06 09						06 57		07 20				07 33
—	—	—	—	91	Birmingham International 68 a													07 13						
—	—	—	—	101½	Coventry 68 a													07 24						
285	—	—	99¼	—	Lichfield Trent Valley a								06 07						06 40			07 08		
291¼	—	—	—	—	Tamworth Low Level a								06 14						06 47			07 15		
304¼	—	—	—	—	Nuneaton a								06 30	06 17							07 06			
318¾	—	—	—	113	Rugby 66 a								06 46	06 31			06 52		07 07					
351½	—	—	—	—	Milton Keynes Central 66 a									06 51			07 13							
383½	—	—	—	—	Watford Junction 66 a				06s42	06s43	06s43													
401¼	—	—	—	—	**London Euston** ⊖66 a				07 07	07 07	07 07		08 05	07 26			07 50		07 58		08 08	08 23		

A From Manchester Piccadilly
B From Edinburgh
C from 25 June. From Glasgow Central
D From Glasgow Central
E To Bournemouth
F From Manchester Piccadilly to Bournemouth
G To Walsall
H To Birmingham New Street
I To Bristol Temple Meads

Refer to Operator websites for full information about Sleeper Services. Contact details for train operators available at National Rail Enquiries

Scotland to Manchester, West Midlands & London via the West Coast. North West England to West Midlands & London

	VT	LM	LM	VT	LM	VT	VT	VT	TP	VT	VT	VT	LM	LM	VT	VT	XC	LM	VT	XC	LM
	◇■	■	■	◇■	■	◇■	◇■	◇■	◇■	◇■	◇■	◇■	■	■	◇■	◇■	◇■	■	◇■	■	■
			A		B								A				C			D	
	⊠			⊠		⊠	⊠	⊠		⊠	⊠	⊠			⊠	⊠	⊥		⊠	⊥	
Inverness 229 d																					
Aberdeen 229 d																					
Dundee 229 d																					
Perth 229 d																					
Fort William 400,227 d																					
Edinburgh ■ d																					
Haymarket d																					
Glasgow Central ■ 226,216,225 d																04 28					
Motherwell 226 d																					
Carstairs 226,225 d																					
Lockerbie 225,226 d																					
Carlisle ■ 216 a																05 42					
d																05 44					
Penrith North Lakes d																05 58					
Windermere 83 d																					
Oxenholme Lake District 83 d																06 21					
Barrow-in-Furness 82 d																					
Lancaster ■ d									06 20							06 36					
Blackpool North 97 d						05 30															
Preston ■ 90 a						05 57			06 38							06 54					
Preston ■ 90 d						06 00		06 17	06 47							06 57					
Wigan North Western 90 d						06 11		06 28								07 09					
Warrington Bank Quay d						06 22		06 39								07 19					
Bolton 82 a																					
Manchester Picc. ■ 82 a									07 27												
Manchester Airport ✈ a									07 47												
Liverpool Lime Street ■ 91 a																					
d														06 30	07 00			07 04			
Liverpool South Pkwy ■ 91 ✈ d														06 40				07 15			
Runcorn 91 d														06 48	07u15			07 23			
Manchester Picc. ■ 84 d	06 10			06 27						06 35	06 43	06 58					07 05		07 15	07 27	
Stockport 84 d	06 18			06 35						06 43	06 51	07u05					07 13		07 23	07 36	
Wilmslow 84 d											06 59										
Holyhead 81 d							04 48														
Bangor (Gwynedd) 81 d							05 14														
Llandudno Junction 81 d							05 32														
Wrexham General 75 d																					
Chester 81 d							06 26														
Crewe ■ 81,91 a						06 42	06 47	06 59			07 15			07 15				07 48			
d		06 49			06 52	06 53		07 01			07 17			07 17				07 49			07 55
Macclesfield d	06 31			06 48						06 56							07 26			07 49	
Stoke-on-Trent 84 d	06 48		←	07 06	07 17					07 12			←				07 44		07 50	08 07	08 17
Stafford a		07 08	07 14	07 22	07 34						07 35		07 34	07 39			08 00	08 10		08 23	08 37
d		07 10	07 15	07 24	07 39						07 36		07 39	07 40			08 01	08 10		08 25	08 37
Penkridge a		07 15			→									07 46				08 16			
Wolverhampton ■ a		07 26	07 29	07 40				07 35						07 58			08 13	08 28		08 39	
BirminghamNewSt ■ 68 a		07 50	08 05	08 07				07 56						08 18			08 33	08 48		08 58	
Birmingham International 68 ✈ a		08 05		08 20																09 13	
Coventry 68 a		08 21		08 31																09 24	
Lichfield Trent Valley a													07 56								08 54
Tamworth Low Level a													08 03								09 00
Nuneaton a						07 33							08 18								09 16
Rugby 66 a	07 28	08 36								07 52			08 34								09 32
Milton Keynes Central 66 a		09 21											08 55						08 46		09 53
Watford Junction 66 a		09 58		09s16																	
London Euston ■ ⊖66 a	08 20	10 19		09 33		08 34				08 46	08 54	09 00	09 37		09 04	09 07			09 21		10 29

A From Crewe
B To London Euston
C To Bristol Temple Meads
D To Bournemouth

Refer to Operator websites for full information about Sleeper Services. Contact details for train operators available at National Rail Enquiries

Table T065-R

Mondays to Fridays

21 May to 7 December

Scotland to Manchester, West Midlands & London via the West Coast. North West England to West Midlands & London

	VT	VT	VT	VT	NT	TP	LM	VT	VT	VT	XC	LM	VT	VT	XC	VT	VT	LM	TP	LM	VT	VT
	◇■	◇■	◇■	◇■	◇	◇■	■	◇■	◇■	◇■	◇■	■	◇■	◇■	◇■	◇■	◇■	■	◇■	■	◇■	◇■
		A									B				C			D				
	⊠	⊠	⊠	⊠		⊥		⊠	⊠	⊠	⊥		⊠	⊠	⊥	⊠	⊠		⊥		⊠	⊠
Inverness 229 d																						
Aberdeen 229 d																						
Dundee 229 d																						
Perth 229 d																						
Fort William 400,227 d																						
Edinburgh ■ d																			06 14			
Haymarket d																			06u20			
Glasgow Central ■ 226,216,225 d						04 22			05 40								05 49					
Motherwell 226 d																	06 04					
Carstairs 226,225 d																						
Lockerbie 225,226 d						05 50													07 14			
Carlisle ■ 216 a						06 13			06 48								07 01		07 34			
d						06 22			06 50								07 03		07 36			
Penrith North Lakes d						06 42											07 18		07 50			
Windermere 83 d																						
Oxenholme Lake District 83 d						07 09			07 25								07 42		08 14			
Barrow-in-Furness 82 d					06 11																	
Lancaster ■ d				06 58	07 03	07 25			07 39								07 57		08 28			
Blackpool North 97 d																						
Preston ■ 90 a				07 15	07 22	07 45			07 57								08 15		08 46			
Preston ■ 90 d				07 17	07 28	07 47			07 59								08 17		08 47			
Wigan North Western 90 d				07 28					08 10								08 28					
Warrington Bank Quay d				07 39					08 21								08 39					
Bolton 82 a					07 54																	
Manchester Picc. ■ 82 a					08 15	08 27													09 27			
Manchester Airport ✈ a					08 35	08 47													09 47			
Liverpool Lime Street ■ 91 a																						
d							07 34	07 47				08 04								08 34	08 47	
Liverpool South Pkwy ■ 91 ✈ d							07 44					08 15								08 44		
Runcorn 91 d							07 52	08 03				08 23								08 52	09 03	
Manchester Picc. ■ 84 d			07 36							07 55	08 05		08 15		08 27	08 35						08 55
Stockport 84 d			07 43							08 04	08 13		08 23		08 36	08 43						09 04
Wilmslow 84 d										08 11												09 11
Holyhead 81 d	05 51													06 55								
Bangor (Gwynedd) 81 d	06 18													07 22								
Llandudno Junction 81 d	06 36													07 40								
Wrexham General 75 d		07 00																				
Chester 81 d	07 35													08 35								
Crewe ■ 81,91 a	07 54			07 57			08 16	08 21		08 27		08 46		08 54			08 57			09 18	09 22	09 29
d	07 57			08 01			08 18	08 23		08 29		08 49		08 56			09 01	09 02		09 19	09 24	09 30
Macclesfield d			07 56								08 26				08 49	08 56						
Stoke-on-Trent 84 d			08 12								08 44		08 50		09 07	09 12		09 28				
Stafford a							08 39	08 40			09 00	09 09			09 23			09 51		09 39	09 42	
d							08 40	08 43			09 01	09 10			09 25			09 55		09 40	09 43	
Penkridge a							08 46					09 15						→		09 46		
Wolverhampton ■ a				08 33			08 58				09 13	09 27			09 41		09 33			09 57		
BirminghamNewSt ■ 68 a				09 05			09 18				09 33	09 48			09 58		10 05			10 18		
Birmingham International 68 ✈ a				09 19											10 13		10 19					
Coventry 68 a				09 30											10 24		10 30					
Lichfield Trent Valley a										09 00												
Tamworth Low Level a										09 06												
Nuneaton a			08 44													09 44						
Rugby 66 a	08 45																					
Milton Keynes Central 66 a				09 58									09 49	10 02			10 58					
Watford Junction 66 a			09s32																			
London Euston ■ ⊖66 a	09 41		09 49	10 32				10 00	10 09	10 16			10 26	10 37		10 51	11 34				11 02	11 08

A ⊠ from Chester
B To Paignton
C To Bournemouth
D To London Euston

Refer to Operator websites for full information about Sleeper Services. Contact details for train operators available at National Rail Enquiries

Scotland to Manchester, West Midlands & London via the West Coast. North West England to West Midlands & London

	VT	LM		XC	LM	VT	XC	VT	VT	VT	LM	TP		LM	VT	VT	VT FO	VT	LM	XC	LM	VT		VT
	◇1 ⊠	1 A		◇1 B 🍴	1	◇1 ⊠	◇1 C 🍴	◇1 ⊠	◇1 ⊠	◇1 ⊠	1 D	◇1 🍴		1	◇1 ⊠	◇1 ⊠	◇1 ⊐	◇1 ⊠	1 A	◇1 B 🍴	1	◇1 ⊠		◇1 ⊠
Inverness 229 d																								
Aberdeen 229 d																								
Dundee 229 d																								
Perth 229 d																								
Fort William 400,227 d																								
Edinburgh 10 ⇌ d										06 52														
Haymarket ⇌ d										06 57														
Glasgow Central 15 226,216,225 d	06 30											07 10						07 37						
Motherwell 226 d	06 45											07 25						07 53						
Carstairs 226,225 d																								
Lockerbie 225,226 d	07 26											08 09												
Carlisle 8 216 a	07 44									08 06		08 30						08 49						
d	07 46									08 08		08 34						08 50						
Penrith North Lakes d	08 00									08 22		08 49												
Windermere 83 d																								
Oxenholme Lake District 83 d	08 23											09 13						09 24						
Barrow-in-Furness 82 d																								
Lancaster 6 d	08 38									08 57		09 28						09 39						
Blackpool North 97 d																								
Preston 8 90 a	08 56									09 15		09 45						09 57						
Preston 8 90 d	08 59									09 17		09 47					09 51	10 00						
Wigan North Western 90 d	09 10									09 28							10 04	10 11						
Warrington Bank Quay d	09 20									09 39							10 16	10 20						
Bolton 82 a																								
Manchester Picc. 10 82 ⇌ a												10 27												
Manchester Airport ✈⇌ a												10 47												
Liverpool Lime Street 10 91 a																								
d					09 04									09 34	09 47						10 04			
Liverpool South Pkwy 7 91 ✈ d					09 16									09 44							10 16			
Runcorn 91 d					09 25									09 52	10 03						10 25			
Manchester Picc. 10 84 ⇌ d				09 05		09 15	09 27		09 35							09 55				10 05		10 15		
Stockport 84 d				09 13		09 23	09 36		09 44							10 04				10 13		10 23		
Wilmslow 84 d																10 11								
Holyhead 81 ⛴ d																								08 55
Bangor (Gwynedd) 81 d																								09 22
Llandudno Junction 81 d																								09 40
Wrexham General 75 d																								
Chester 81 d								09 35																10 35
Crewe 10 81,91 a					09 46			09 54		09 57				10 17	10 21	10 27	10 38				10 46			10 54
d					09 49			09 56		10 01	10 02			10 19	10 22	10 29	10 41				10 49			10 56
Macclesfield d				09 26			09 49		09 56											10 26				
Stoke-on-Trent 84 d		←		09 44		09 50	10 07		10 13		10 28								←	10 44		10 50		
Stafford a		09 51		10 00	10 09		10 23				10 50			10 38	10 40				10 50	11 00	11 10			
d		09 55		10 01	10 10		10 25				10 55			10 40	10 42				10 55	11 01	11 10			
Penkridge a					10 15						→			10 45							11 16			
Wolverhampton 7 ⇌ a				10 13	10 27		10 39			10 33				10 57						11 13	11 27			
BirminghamNewSt 12 68 ⇌ a				10 33	10 48		10 58			11 05				11 18						11 33	11 48			
Birmingham International 68 ✈ a							11 13			11 19														
Coventry 68 a							11 24			11 30														
Lichfield Trent Valley a		10 12																	11 12					
Tamworth Low Level a		10 19																	11 19					
Nuneaton a		10 35																	11 35					
Rugby 66 a		10 51																	11 52					
Milton Keynes Central 66 a		11 14				10 46		11 02		11 58									12 14			11 47		12 02
Watford Junction 66 a																								
London Euston 15 ⊖66 a	11 11	11 50				11 20		11 37	11 40	12 33					11 59	12 02	12 30	12 10	12 50			12 20		12 37

A From Crewe
B To Bristol Temple Meads
C To Bournemouth
D To London Euston

Refer to Operator websites for full information about Sleeper Services. Contact details for train operators available at National Rail Enquiries

Scotland to Manchester, West Midlands & London via the West Coast. North West England to West Midlands & London

	XC	VT	VT	LM	NT	TP	LM	VT		VT	VT	LM	XC	LM	VT	XC	VT	VT		VT	LM	VT	TP	LM
	◇1 A 🍴	◇1 ⊠	◇1 ⊠	1 B	◇ C	◇1 🍴	1	◇1 ⊠		◇1 ⊠	◇1 ⊠	1 D	◇1 E 🍴	1	◇1 ⊐	◇1 A 🍴	◇1 ⊐	◇1 ⊐		◇1 ⊠	1 B	◇1 F ⊠⊐	◇1 🍴	1
Inverness 229 d																								
Aberdeen 229 d																								
Dundee 229 d																								
Perth 229 d																								
Fort William 400,227 d																								
Edinburgh 10 ⇌ d						08 11														08 51				
Haymarket ⇌ d						08u16														08 57				
Glasgow Central 15 226,216,225 d			08 00								08 40												09 06	
Motherwell 226 d																							09 23	
Carstairs 226,225 d																								
Lockerbie 225,226 d						09 10																	10 08	
Carlisle 8 216 a			09 08			09 31					09 48									10 06			10 31	
d			09 11			09 34					09 49									10 08			10 34	
Penrith North Lakes d						09 49					10 03												10 49	
Windermere 83 d					09 34																			
Oxenholme Lake District 83 d					09 55	10 13														10 42			11 13	
Barrow-in-Furness 82 d																								
Lancaster 6 d			09 56		10 14	10 30					10 38									10 57			11 30	
Blackpool North 97 d																						10 53		
Preston 8 90 a			10 14		10 37	10 47					10 56									11 15		11 17	11 47	
Preston 8 90 d			10 17		10 44	10 49					10 58									11 17		11 20	11 49	
Wigan North Western 90 d			10 28								11 09									11 28		11 35		
Warrington Bank Quay d			10 39								11 20									11 39		11 48		
Bolton 82 a					11 23																			
Manchester Picc. 10 82 ⇌ a					11 45	11 27																	12 27	
Manchester Airport ✈⇌ a						11 47																	12 48	
Liverpool Lime Street 10 91 a																								
d							10 34	10 47						11 04										11 34
Liverpool South Pkwy 7 91 ✈ d							10 44							11 16										11 44
Runcorn 91 d							10 52	11 03						11 25										11 52
Manchester Picc. 10 84 ⇌ d	10 27	10 35								10 55			11 05		11 15	11 27		11 35						
Stockport 84 d	10 36	10 43								11 04			11 13		11 23	11 36		11 43						
Wilmslow 84 d										11 11														
Holyhead 81 ⛴ d																								
Bangor (Gwynedd) 81 d																								
Llandudno Junction 81 d																								
Wrexham General 75 d																								
Chester 81 d																	11 35							
Crewe 10 81,91 a			10 57				11 16	11 21		11 27				11 46			11 54			11 57				12 17
d			11 01	11 02			11 19	11 22		11 29				11 49			11 56			12 01	12 02			12 19
Macclesfield d	10 49	10 56											11 26			11 49		11 56						
Stoke-on-Trent 84 d	11 07	11 12		11 28								←	11 44		11 50	12 07		12 12			12 28			
Stafford a	11 24			11 50			11 39	11 40				11 50	12 00	12 10		12 23					12 50			12 39
d	11 25			11 55			11 40	11 42				11 55	12 01	12 10		12 25					12 55			12 40
Penkridge a				→			11 45							12 16							→			12 46
Wolverhampton 7 ⇌ a	11 39		11 33				11 57						12 13	12 27		12 39				12 32				12 57
BirminghamNewSt 12 68 ⇌ a	11 58		12 05				12 18						12 33	12 48		12 58				13 05				13 18
Birmingham International 68 ✈ a	12 13		12 19													13 13				13 19				
Coventry 68 a	12 24		12 30													13 24				13 30				
Lichfield Trent Valley a												12 12												
Tamworth Low Level a												12 19												
Nuneaton a												12 35												
Rugby 66 a												12 52										12 59		
Milton Keynes Central 66 a			12 58									13 14			12 46		13 02			13 58				
Watford Junction 66 a																								
London Euston 15 ⊖66 a		12 40	13 33					12 59		13 02	13 10	13 50			13 20		13 37	13 40		14 33		13 53		

A To Bournemouth
B To London Euston
C ◇ to Preston
D From Crewe
E To Bristol Temple Meads
F ⊐ from Preston ⊠ to Preston

Refer to Operator websites for full information about Sleeper Services. Contact details for train operators available at National Rail Enquiries

Table T065-R

Mondays to Fridays

21 May to 7 December

Scotland to Manchester, West Midlands & London via the West Coast. North West England to West Midlands & London

	VT	VT	VT	LM	XC	LM	VT	XC	VT	VT	VT	LM	TP	LM	VT	VT	VT	LM	XC	LM	VT	XC
	◇1	◇1	◇1	1	◇1	1	◇1	◇1	◇1	◇1	◇1	1	◇1	1	◇1	◇1	◇1	1	◇1	1	◇1	◇1
			⊠	A	B			C			⊠	D					⊠	A	E			C
Inverness 229 d																						
Aberdeen 229 d																						
Dundee 229 d																						
Perth 229 d																						
Fort William 400,227 d																						
Edinburgh d													10 13									
Haymarket d													10u17									
Glasgow Central 226,216,225 d			09 40								10 00						10 40					
Motherwell 226 d																						
Carstairs 226,225 d																						
Lockerbie 225,226 d													11 11									
Carlisle 216 a			10 47								11 11		11 31				11 47					
d			10 49								11 12		11 34				11 49					
Penrith North Lakes d											11 27		11 49									
Windermere 83 d																						
Oxenholme Lake District 83 d			11 23										12 13				12 23					
Barrow-in-Furness 82 d																						
Lancaster d			11 38										12 28				12 38					
Blackpool North 97 d																						
Preston 90 a			11 56								12 16		12 45				12 56					
Preston 90 d			11 58								12 18		12 47				12 58					
Wigan North Western 90 d			12 09								12 29						13 09					
Warrington Bank Quay d			12 20								12 40						13 20					
Bolton 82 a																						
Manchester Picc. 82 a													13 27									
Manchester Airport a													13 47									
Liverpool Lime Street 91 a																						
d	11 47					12 04								12 34	12 47					13 04		
Liverpool South Pkwy 91 d						12 16								12 44						13 16		
Runcorn 91 d	12 03					12 25								12 52	13 03					13 25		
Manchester Picc. 84 d		11 55			12 05		12 15	12 27		12 35						12 55			13 05		13 15	13 27
Stockport 84 d		12 04			12 13		12 23	12 36		12 43						13 04			13 13		13 23	13 36
Wilmslow 84 d		12 11														13 11						
Holyhead 81 d																						
Bangor (Gwynedd) 81 d																						
Llandudno Junction 81 d																						
Wrexham General 75 d																						
Chester 81 d									12 35													
Crewe 81,91 a	12 21	12 27				12 46			12 54		12 59			13 18	13 23	13 29				13 46		
d	12 22	12 29				12 49			12 56		13 01	13 02		13 19	13 25	13 30				13 49		
Macclesfield d					12 26			12 49		12 56									13 26			13 49
Stoke-on-Trent 84 d				←	12 44		12 50	13 07		13 12		13 28						←	13 44		13 50	14 07
Stafford a	12 40			12 50	13 00	13 09		13 25				13 55		13 39	13 43			13 55	14 00	14 09		14 23
d	12 42			12 55	13 01	13 10		13 26				13 55		13 40	13 44			13 55	14 01	14 10		14 25
Penkridge a						13 15						→		13 46						14 15		
Wolverhampton a					13 13	13 27		13 39			13 33			13 57					14 13	14 27		14 39
BirminghamNewSt 68 a					13 33	13 48		13 58			14 05			14 18					14 34	14 48		14 58
Birmingham International 68 a								14 13			14 19											15 13
Coventry 68 a								14 24			14 29											15 24
Lichfield Trent Valley a				13 12														14 12				
Tamworth Low Level a				13 19														14 20				
Nuneaton a				13 35														14 35				
Rugby 66 a				13 51													14 23	14 51				
Milton Keynes Central 66 a				14 14			13 46		14 02		14 58							15 14			14 48	
Watford Junction 66 a																						
London Euston ⊖66 a	14 02	14 05	14 10	14 50			14 20		14 38	14 41	15 33				15 04	15 09	15 13	15 50			15 28	

A From Crewe
B To Exeter St Davids
C To Bournemouth
D To London Euston
E To Bristol Temple Meads

Refer to Operator websites for full information about Sleeper Services. Contact details for train operators available at National Rail Enquiries

Table T065-R

Mondays to Fridays

21 May to 7 December

Scotland to Manchester, West Midlands & London via the West Coast. North West England to West Midlands & London

	VT	VT	NT	VT	NT	NT	VT	VT	TP	LM	LM	VT	VT	VT	VT	VT	VT	LM	XC	LM	VT
							MO	MX				FX	FO	FX	FO	FX	FO				FO
	◇1	◇1	◇	◇1	◇		◇1	◇1	◇1	1	1	◇1	◇1	◇1	◇1	◇1	◇1	1	◇1	1	◇1
			A		B					C						⊠	⊠	D	E		
Inverness 229 d																					
Aberdeen 229 d																					
Dundee 229 d																					
Perth 229 d																					
Fort William 400,227 d																					
Edinburgh d				10 52																	
Haymarket d				10 57																	
Glasgow Central 226,216,225 d									11 09							11 40	11 40				
Motherwell 226 d									11 24												
Carstairs 226,225 d																					
Lockerbie 225,226 d									12 08												
Carlisle 216 a				12 06					12 28							12 47	12 47				
d				12 08					12 34							12 49	12 49				
Penrith North Lakes d									12 49							13 03	13 03				
Windermere 83 d						12 32															
Oxenholme Lake District 83 d				12 43		12 53			13 13												
Barrow-in-Furness 82 d			11 53																		
Lancaster d			12 52	12 57		13a14			13 28							13 38	13 38				
Blackpool North 97 d					←		13 02	13 02													
Preston 90 a			13 11	13 15	13 11		13 24	13 24	13 45							13 56	13 56				
Preston 90 d			13 25	13 17	13 25		13 29	13 29	13 47							13 58	13 58				
Wigan North Western 90 d			→	13 28			13 41	13 41								14 09	14 09				
Warrington Bank Quay d				13 39			13 52	13 54								14 20	14 20				
Bolton 82 a					13 52																
Manchester Picc. 82 a					14 15				14 27												
Manchester Airport a					14 35				14 47												
Liverpool Lime Street 91 a																					
d											13 34	13 47	13 47							14 04	
Liverpool South Pkwy 91 d											13 44									14 16	
Runcorn 91 d											13 52	14 03	14 03							14 25	
Manchester Picc. 84 d		13 35												13 55	13 55				14 05		14 15
Stockport 84 d		13 43												14 04	14 04				14 13		14 23
Wilmslow 84 d														14 11	14 11						
Holyhead 81 d																					
Bangor (Gwynedd) 81 d																					
Llandudno Junction 81 d																					
Wrexham General 75 d																					
Chester 81 d	13 35																				
Crewe 81,91 a	13 54			13 57							14 17	14 24	14 24	14 29	14 29					14 46	
d	13 56			14 01						14 02	14 19	14 25	14 25	14 31	14 31					14 49	
Macclesfield d		13 56																	14 26		
Stoke-on-Trent 84 d		14 12								14 28								←	14 44		14 50
Stafford a										14 51	14 38	14 43	14 43					14 51	15 00	15 09	
d										14 55	14 40	14 45	14 45					14 55	15 01	15 10	
Penkridge a										→	14 45									15 15	
Wolverhampton a				14 33							14 57								15 13	15 27	
BirminghamNewSt 68 a				15 05							15 18								15 33	15 48	
Birmingham International 68 a				15 19																	
Coventry 68 a				15 30																	
Lichfield Trent Valley a																		15 13			
Tamworth Low Level a																		15 19			
Nuneaton a																		15 35			
Rugby 66 a							15 08	15 06										15 51			
Milton Keynes Central 66 a	15 02			15 58														16 14			15 46
Watford Junction 66 a																					
London Euston ⊖66 a	15 36	15 39		16 32			15 59	15 59				16 02	16 05	16 05	16 08	16 09	16 11	16 50			16 22

A To Manchester Airport
B From Barrow-in-Furness
C To London Euston
D From Crewe
E To Paignton

Refer to Operator websites for full information about Sleeper Services. Contact details for train operators available at National Rail Enquiries

Table T065-R

Scotland to Manchester, West Midlands & London via the West Coast. North West England to West Midlands & London

	VT FX	VT	VT	XC A	VT	VT	LM B	TP	LM	VT	VT	VT	LM C	XC D	LM	VT	VT	XC A	VT	VT	LM B	VT
Inverness 229 d																						
Aberdeen 229 d																						
Dundee 229 d																						
Perth 229 d																						
Fort William 400,227 d																						
Edinburgh 10 d								12 13												12 52		
Haymarket d								12u17												12 57		
Glasgow Central 15 226,216,225 d						12 00						12 40										
Motherwell 226 d																						
Carstairs 226,225 d																						
Lockerbie 225,226 d								13 11														
Carlisle 8 216 a						13 11		13 31				13 47								14 06		
d						13 11		13 34				13 49								14 08		
Penrith North Lakes d								13 49												14 22		
Windermere 83 d																						
Oxenholme Lake District 83 d								14 13				14 24										
Barrow-in-Furness 82 d																						
Lancaster 6 d						13 57		14 28				14 39								14 57		
Blackpool North 97 d																						15 00
Preston 8 90 a						14 15		14 45				14 56								15 15		15 24
Preston 8 90 d						14 17		14 47				14 58								15 17		15 29
Wigan North Western 90 d						14 29						15 09								15 28		15 45
Warrington Bank Quay d						14 40						15 20								15 39		16 01
Bolton 82 a																						
Manchester Picc. 10 82 a								15 27														
Manchester Airport a								15 47														
Liverpool Lime Street 10 91 a																						
d									14 34	14 47					15 04							
Liverpool South Pkwy 7 91 d									14 44						15 16							
Runcorn 91 d									14 52	15 03					15 25							
Manchester Picc. 10 84 d	14 15			14 27	14 35						14 55			15 05		15 15		15 27	15 35			
Stockport 84 d	14 23			14 36	14 43						15 04			15 13		15 23		15 36	15 43			
Wilmslow 84 d											15 11											
Holyhead 81 d		12 53															13 58					
Bangor (Gwynedd) 81 d		13 21															14 25					
Llandudno Junction 81 d		13 39															14 43					
Wrexham General 75 d																						
Chester 81 d		14 35	14 35														15 35					
Crewe 10 81,91 a		14 54	14 54			14 57			15 17	15 21	15 27				15 46		15 54			15 57		
d		14 56	14 56			15 01	15 02		15 19	15 22	15 29				15 49		15 56			16 01	16 02	
Macclesfield d				14 49	14 56									15 26				15 49	15 56			
Stoke-on-Trent 84 d	14 50			15 07	15 12		15 28						←	15 44		15 50		16 07	16 12		16 28	
Stafford a				15 24			15 50		15 39	15 40			15 50	16 00	16 09			16 24			16 51	
d				15 25			15 55		15 40	15 42			15 55	16 01	16 10			16 25			16 55	
Penkridge a							→		15 46						16 15						→	
Wolverhampton 7 a				15 39		15 33			15 57					16 13	16 27			16 39		16 33		
BirminghamNewSt 12 68 a				15 58		16 05			16 18					16 33	16 48			16 58		17 05		
Birmingham International 68 a				16 13		16 19												17 13		17 19		
Coventry 68 a				16 24		16 30												17 24		17 30		
Lichfield Trent Valley a													16 12									
Tamworth Low Level a													16 19									
Nuneaton a													16 35									
Rugby 66 a													16 51									17 06
Milton Keynes Central 66 a	15 46	16 02	16 02			16 58							17 14			16 46	17 02			17 58		
Watford Junction 66 a																						
London Euston 15 ⊖66 a	16 24	16 37	16 37		16 40	17 33				16 59	17 02	17 09	17 50			17 21	17 37		17 40	18 34		17 59

A To Bournemouth
B To London Euston
C From Crewe
D To Bristol Temple Meads

Refer to Operator websites for full information about Sleeper Services. Contact details for train operators available at National Rail Enquiries

Table T065-R

Scotland to Manchester, West Midlands & London via the West Coast. North West England to West Midlands & London

	NT	TP	LM	VT	VT	VT	LM A	XC B	LM	VT	XC C	VT	VT	VT	LM D	NT	TP	LM E	VT	LM F	VT
Inverness 229 d																					
Aberdeen 229 d																					
Dundee 229 d																					
Perth 229 d																					
Fort William 400,227 d																					
Edinburgh 10 d																	14 18				
Haymarket d																	14u22				
Glasgow Central 15 226,216,225 d		13 09				13 40								14 00							
Motherwell 226 d		13 24																			
Carstairs 226,225 d																					
Lockerbie 225,226 d		14 08															15 16				
Carlisle 8 216 a		14 29				14 47								15 09			15 36				
d		14 34				14 49								15 11			15 38				
Penrith North Lakes d		14 49																			
Windermere 83 d	14 25																				
Oxenholme Lake District 83 d	14 47	15 13				15 24								15 45			16 13				
Barrow-in-Furness 82 d																14 48					
Lancaster 6 d	15 09	15 28				15 39										15 47	16 28				
Blackpool North 97 d																					
Preston 8 90 a	15 33	15 46				15 56								16 14		16 06	16 46				
Preston 8 90 d		15 47				15 58								16 17		16 24	16 47				
Wigan North Western 90 d						16 09								16 28							
Warrington Bank Quay d						16 20								16 39							
Bolton 82 a																16 51					
Manchester Picc. 10 82 a		16 27														17 15	17 29				
Manchester Airport a		16 47														17 35	17 48				
Liverpool Lime Street 10 91 a																					
d			15 34	15 47					16 04									16 34	16 47		
Liverpool South Pkwy 7 91 d			15 44						16 16									16 44			
Runcorn 91 d			15 52	16 03					16 25									16 52	17 03		
Manchester Picc. 10 84 d					15 55			16 05		16 15	16 27		16 35								16 55
Stockport 84 d					16 04			16 13		16 23	16 36		16 43								17 04
Wilmslow 84 d					16 11																17 11
Holyhead 81 d																					
Bangor (Gwynedd) 81 d																					
Llandudno Junction 81 d																					
Wrexham General 75 d																					
Chester 81 d												16 35									
Crewe 10 81,91 a			16 17	16 24	16 29				16 46			16 54		16 57				17 19			17 27
d			16 19	16 25	16 31				16 49			16 56		17 01	17 02			17 19			17 29
Macclesfield d								16 26			16 49		16 56								
Stoke-on-Trent 84 d							←	16 44		16 50	17 07		17 12		17 28					←	
Stafford a			16 40	16 43			16 51	17 00	17 09		17 24				17 50			17 39	17 34	17 39	
d			16 40	16 45			16 55	17 01	17 10		17 25				17 55			17 40	17 36	17 40	
Penkridge a			16 46						17 15						→			→		17 46	
Wolverhampton 7 a			16 58					17 13	17 27		17 39			17 33						17 58	
BirminghamNewSt 12 68 a			17 18					17 33	17 48		17 58			18 05						18 18	
Birmingham International 68 a											18 13			18 19							
Coventry 68 a											18 24			18 30							
Lichfield Trent Valley a							17 13														
Tamworth Low Level a							17 19														
Nuneaton a							17 35														
Rugby 66 a							17 51														
Milton Keynes Central 66 a							18 15			17 46		18 02		18 58					18 23		
Watford Junction 66 a																					18s49
London Euston 15 ⊖66 a				18 02	18 05	18 10	18 52			18 20		18 37	18 40	19 33					19 03		19 06

A From Crewe
B To Bristol Temple Meads
C To Bournemouth
D To London Euston
E To Birmingham New Street
F From Liverpool Lime Street

Refer to Operator websites for full information about Sleeper Services. Contact details for train operators available at National Rail Enquiries

21 May to 7 December

Scotland to Manchester, West Midlands & London via the West Coast. North West England to West Midlands & London

	VT	LM	XC	LM	VT	VT	VT	LM	TP	XC	VT	VT	LM	VT	VT	VT	LM	XC	LM	VT	XC	VT
	◇1 ⊠	1 A	◇1 B	1	◇1 ⊠	◇1 ⊠	1 C	1 C	◇1	◇1 D	◇1 ⊠	1 E	1	◇1 ⊠	◇1 ⊠	◇1 ⊠	1 A	◇1 F	1	◇1 ⊠	◇1 G	◇1 ⊠
Inverness 229 d																						
Aberdeen 229 d																						
Dundee 229 d																						
Perth 229 d																						
Fort William 400,227 d																						
Edinburgh 10 d							14 52															
Haymarket d							14 58															
Glasgow Central 15 226,216,225 d	14 40								15 09							15 40						
Motherwell 226 d									15 24													
Carstairs 226,225 d																						
Lockerbie 225,226 d									16 08													
Carlisle 8 216 a	15 47						16 06		16 28							16 47						
d	15 49						16 08		16 31							16 49						
Penrith North Lakes d							16 21		16 46							17 03						
Windermere 83 d																						
Oxenholme Lake District 83 d	16 24								17 10													
Barrow-in-Furness 82 d																						
Lancaster 6 d	16 38						16 57		17 28							17 37						
Blackpool North 97 d																						
Preston 8 90 a	16 56						17 15		17 46							17 55						
Preston 8 90 d	16 58						17 17		17 47							17 58						
Wigan North Western 90 d	17 09						17 28									18 09						
Warrington Bank Quay d	17 20						17 39									18 20						
Bolton 82 a																						
Manchester Picc. 10 82 a									18 23													
Manchester Airport a									18 43													
Liverpool Lime Street 10 91 a																						
d				17 04									17 34	17 47					18 04			
Liverpool South Pkwy 7 91 d				17 16									17 44						18 15			
Runcorn 91 d				17 25									17 52	18 03					18 25			
Manchester Picc. 10 84 d			17 05		17 15					17 27	17 35				17 55			18 05		18 15	18 27	18 35
Stockport 84 d			17 13		17 23					17 35	17 43				18 04			18 13		18 23	18 36	18 43
Wilmslow 84 d										17 45					18 10							
Holyhead 81 d																						
Bangor (Gwynedd) 81 d																						
Llandudno Junction 81 d																						
Wrexham General 75 d																						
Chester 81 d						17 35																
Crewe 10 81,91 a				17 46		17 54	17 57			18 04			18 18	18 22	18 27				18 48			
d				17 49		17 56	18 01	18 02		18 07			18 19	18 24	18 29				18 49			
Macclesfield d			17 26								17 56							18 26				18 55
Stoke-on-Trent 84 d		←	17 44		17 50			18 28			18 12						←	18 44		18 50	19 07	19 12
Stafford a		17 50	18 00	18 09				18 50		18 25			18 40	18 42			18 50	19 00	19 10		19 24	
d		17 55	18 01	18 10				18 55		18 25			18 40	18 43			18 55	19 01	19 10		19 25	
Penkridge a				18 16				→					18 46						19 16			
Wolverhampton 7 a			18 13	18 27			18 33			18 39		←	18 59					19 13	19 28		19 39	
BirminghamNewSt 12 68 a			18 33	18 48			19 05			18 58		19 05	19 18					19 33	19 48		19 58	
Birmingham International 68 a							→			19 13		19 19									20 13	
Coventry 68 a										19 24		19 30									20 24	
Lichfield Trent Valley a		18 12															19 12					
Tamworth Low Level a		18 19															19 19					
Nuneaton a		18 35															19 35					
Rugby 66 a		18 51															19 50					
Milton Keynes Central 66 a		19 14			18 48	19 01						19 58			19 33		20 14			19 46		
Watford Junction 66 a														19s47								
London Euston 15 ⊖66 a	19 09	19 50			19 24	19 38					19 41	20 32		20 04	20 08	20 12	20 51			20 21		20 39

A From Crewe
B To Cardiff Central
C To London Euston
D To Bournemouth
E From Edinburgh
F To Plymouth
G To Bournemouth. to BirminghamNewSt

Refer to Operator websites for full information about Sleeper Services. Contact details for train operators available at National Rail Enquiries

21 May to 7 December

Scotland to Manchester, West Midlands & London via the West Coast. North West England to West Midlands & London

	VT	LM	TP	LM	VT	LM	VT	VT	XC	LM	VT	XC	VT	VT	LM	NT	TP	LM	VT	VT	VT	LM
	◇1 ⊠	1 A	◇1	1	◇1 ⊠	1 B	◇1 ⊠	◇1 ⊠	◇1 C	1	◇1	◇1 D	◇1	1 ⊠	1 A	◇	◇1	1	◇1	◇1	◇1	1 B
Inverness 229 d																						
Aberdeen 229 d																						
Dundee 229 d																						
Perth 229 d																						
Fort William 400,227 d																						
Edinburgh 10 d			16 13											16 52								
Haymarket d			16u17											16 57								
Glasgow Central 15 226,216,225 d	16 00							16 40									17 10				17 30	
Motherwell 226 d								16 55									17 25					
Carstairs 226,225 d																						
Lockerbie 225,226 d			17 11														18 09					
Carlisle 8 216 a	17 09		17 32					17 51						18 06			18 29				18 45	
d	17 11		17 34					17 53						18 08			18 34				18 46	
Penrith North Lakes d			17 49					18 07									18 49				19 01	
Windermere 83 d																18 30						
Oxenholme Lake District 83 d	17 45		18 13					18 31						18 42		18 49	19 13				19 25	
Barrow-in-Furness 82 d																						
Lancaster 6 d			18 28					18 45						18 59		19 09	19 28				19 39	
Blackpool North 97 d																						
Preston 8 90 a	18 13		18 46					19 03						19 15		19 32	19 46				19 57	
Preston 8 90 d	18 17		18 47					19 05						19 17			19 47				19 59	
Wigan North Western 90 d	18 28							19 16						19 31							20 10	
Warrington Bank Quay d	18 39							19 27						19 41							20 21	
Bolton 82 a																						
Manchester Picc. 10 82 a			19 27														20 27					
Manchester Airport a			19 46														20 47					
Liverpool Lime Street 10 91 a																						
d				18 34	18 47					19 12								19 34	19 47			
Liverpool South Pkwy 7 91 d				18 44						19 22								19 44				
Runcorn 91 d				18 52	19 03					19 30								19 52	20 03			
Manchester Picc. 10 84 d							18 55		19 05		19 15	19 27								19 55		
Stockport 84 d							19 04		19 13		19 23	19 36								20 04		
Wilmslow 84 d							19 11													20 11		
Holyhead 81 d																						
Bangor (Gwynedd) 81 d																						
Llandudno Junction 81 d																						
Wrexham General 75 d																						
Chester 81 d													19 35									
Crewe 10 81,91 a	18 57			19 17	19 21		19 27			19 53			19 54	20 00				20 16	20 22	20 27	20 40	
d	19 01	19 02		19 19	19 22		19 29			19 55			19 56	20 03	20 10			20 19	20 24	20 29	20 42	
Macclesfield d									19 26		19 36	19 49										
Stoke-on-Trent 84 d		19 28				←			19 44		19 53	20 07			20 33							←
Stafford a		19 50		19 39	19 40	19 50			20 00	20 15		20 24			20 54			20 38		20 47		20 54
d		19 50		19 40	19 42	19 50			20 01	20 16		20 25			21 00			20 40		20 48		21 00
Penkridge a		→		19 45						20 21					→			20 45				
Wolverhampton 7 a	19 33			19 57					20 13	20 32		20 42		20 38				20 57				
BirminghamNewSt 12 68 a	20 05			20 18					20 33	20 50		21 00		21 05				21 18				
Birmingham International 68 a	20 19											21 13		21 19								
Coventry 68 a	20 30											21 24		21 30								
Lichfield Trent Valley a						20 07																21 17
Tamworth Low Level a						20 14																21 24
Nuneaton a						20 30													21 02			21 40
Rugby 66 a						20 46															21 28	21 55
Milton Keynes Central 66 a	20 58						20 31	20 45			20 49		21 04	21 58						21 35	21 49	
Watford Junction 66 a	21s19				20s45									22s20					21s49			
London Euston 15 ⊖66 a	21 37				21 02		21 06	21 20			21 23		21 40	22 41					22 06	22 10	22 26	

A To Northampton
B From Crewe to Northampton
C To Bristol Temple Meads
D To Southampton Central. to BirminghamNewSt

Refer to Operator websites for full information about Sleeper Services. Contact details for train operators available at National Rail Enquiries

Table T065-R

Mondays to Fridays
21 May to 7 December

Scotland to Manchester, West Midlands & London via the West Coast. North West England to West Midlands & London

Station		XC	LM	VT	TP	VT	VT	NT	XC	LM	VT	VT	VT	TP	VT	XC	LM	XC	LM	VT	TP	NT
		◇■	■	◇■ ⊠	◇■ trolley	◇■ ☕	◇■ ⊠	◇	◇■	■	◇■ ☕	◇■ ☕	◇■ ⊠	◇■ trolley	◇■ ☕	◇■	■	◇■	■	◇■ ☕	◇■ trolley	
Inverness 229	d																					
Aberdeen 229	d																					
Dundee 229	d																					
Perth 229	d																					
Fort William 400,227	d																					
Edinburgh ■	d				18 13								18 52								20 14	
Haymarket	d				18u18								18 56								20u18	
Glasgow Central ■ 226,216,225	d			17 40			18 40							19 08						20 10		
Motherwell 226	d																					
Carstairs 226,225	d																					
Lockerbie 225,226	d			18 33	19 14									20 08						21 04	21 12	
Carlisle ■ 216	a			18 56	19 34		19 47						20 05	20 29						21 23	21 33	
	d			18 57	19 36		19 49						20 07	20 31						21 25	21 35	
Penrith North Lakes	d				19 50									20 45						21 40		
Windermere 83	d																					22 45
Oxenholme Lake District 83	d			19 33	20 14		20 24						20 42	21 09						22 04	22 11	23 06
Barrow-in-Furness 82	d							19 43														
Lancaster ■	d			19 47	20 28		20 38	20 43					20 56	21 24						22 19	22 26	23 24
Blackpool North 97	d																					
Preston ■ 90	a			20 05	20 46		20 56	21 03					21 14	21 41						22 36	22 44	23 45
Preston ■ 90	d			20 08	20 47		20 58	21 05					21 17	21 43						22 39	22 45	
Wigan North Western 90	d			20 19			21 09						21 28							22 53		
Warrington Bank Quay	d			20 32			21 20						21 39							23 04		
Bolton 82	a																					
Manchester Picc. ■ 82	a				21 27			21 47						22 22							23 24	
Manchester Airport	a				21 44			22 05						22 40							23 41	
Liverpool Lime Street ■ 91	a																					
	d		20 04							20 34	20 48						21 34		22 34			
Liverpool South Pkwy ■ 91	d		20 15							20 44							21 44		22 46			
Runcorn 91	d		20 25							20 52	21 04						21 52		22 55			
Manchester Picc. ■ 84	d	20 05				20 15			20 27						21 15	21 27		22 07				
Stockport 84	d	20 13				20 23			20 36						21 23	21 36		22 16				
Wilmslow 84	d																					
Holyhead 81	d																					
Bangor (Gwynedd) 81	d											20 20										
Llandudno Junction 81	d											20 38										
Wrexham General 75	d																					
Chester 81	d											21 35										
Crewe ■ 81,91	a		20 44	20 51						21 16	21 22	21 54	21 59				22 16		23 24	23 26		
	d		20 47	20 53						21 19	21 24	21 56	22 01				22 19					
Macclesfield	d	20 26				20 36			20 49						21 36	21 49		22 29				
Stoke-on-Trent 84	d	20 44				20 52			21 07						21 53	22 08		22 47				
Stafford	a	21 00	21 09	21 13					21 23	21 39	21 43					22 24	22 39	23 03				
	d	21 01	21 10	21 14					21 25	21 40	21 44					22 26	22 40	23 04				
Penkridge	a		21 15							21 45							22 45					
Wolverhampton ■	a	21 13	21 27	21 30					21 39	21 57		22 27	22 32			22 41	22 59	23 17				
BirminghamNewSt ■ 68	a	21 33	21 48	21 54					22 00	22 18		22 48	22 52			22 59	23 26	23 35				
Birmingham International 68	a																					
Coventry 68	a																					
Lichfield Trent Valley	a										21 57											
Tamworth Low Level	a										22 04											
Nuneaton	a										22 17											
Rugby 66	a										22 31											
Milton Keynes Central 66	a					21 52	22 40				22 54				23 00							
Watford Junction 66	a					22s13	23s15				23s25				23s30							
London Euston ■ ⊖66	a					22 29	23 34				23 43				23 48							

Refer to Operator websites for full information about Sleeper Services. Contact details for train operators available at National Rail Enquiries

Table T065-R

Mondays to Fridays
21 May to 7 December

Scotland to Manchester, West Midlands & London via the West Coast. North West England to West Midlands & London

Station		TP WO	TP WX	LM	CS FX	CS FO	CS	CS MX	CS	CS	CS MO
		◇■ trolley	◇■ trolley	■	✕	✕	✕	✕	✕	✕	✕
Inverness 229	d							20 45			20 45
Aberdeen 229	d									21 43	
Dundee 229	d									23u09	
Perth 229	d							23u26			23u30
Fort William 400,227	d								19 50		
Edinburgh ■	d	22 13	22 13				23 40				
Haymarket	d	22u17	22u17								
Glasgow Central ■ 226,216,225	d				23 40	23 40					
Motherwell 226	d				23u59	23u59					
Carstairs 226,225	d				00u19	00u21					
Lockerbie 225,226	d	23 16	23 16								
Carlisle ■ 216	a	23 42	23 42								
	d	23 44	23 44		01u49	01u49	01u49				
Penrith North Lakes	d										
Windermere 83	d										
Oxenholme Lake District 83	d										
Barrow-in-Furness 82	d										
Lancaster ■	d										
Blackpool North 97	d										
Preston ■ 90	a	00 56	00 56					04s33	04s33	04s33	04s33
Preston ■ 90	d	00 57	00 57								
Wigan North Western 90	d										
Warrington Bank Quay	d										
Bolton 82	a										
Manchester Picc. ■ 82	a	01 43	01 43								
Manchester Airport	a		01 58								
Liverpool Lime Street ■ 91	a										
	d			23 34							
Liverpool South Pkwy ■ 91	d			23 46							
Runcorn 91	d			23 55							
Manchester Picc. ■ 84	d										
Stockport 84	d										
Wilmslow 84	d										
Holyhead 81	d										
Bangor (Gwynedd) 81	d										
Llandudno Junction 81	d										
Wrexham General 75	d										
Chester 81	d										
Crewe ■ 81,91	a			00 26				05s36	05s36		05s36
	d										
Macclesfield	d										
Stoke-on-Trent 84	d										
Stafford	a										
	d										
Penkridge	a										
Wolverhampton ■	a										
BirminghamNewSt ■ 68	a										
Birmingham International 68	a										
Coventry 68	a										
Lichfield Trent Valley	a										
Tamworth Low Level	a										
Nuneaton	a										
Rugby 66	a										
Milton Keynes Central 66	a										
Watford Junction 66	a				06s43	06s43	06s43				
London Euston ■ ⊖66	a				07 07	07 07	07 07	07 49	07 49		07 49

Refer to Operator websites for full information about Sleeper Services. Contact details for train operators available at National Rail Enquiries

Table T065-R

Saturdays
26 May to 8 December

Scotland to Manchester, West Midlands & London via the West Coast. North West England to West Midlands & London

	NT	CS	CS	TP	AW	XC	VT	XC	LM	LM	VT	VT	VT	LM	XC	VT	VT	LM	LM	VT	LM	TP
	A	B	C	C		D		E	F					G	H				F		F	
Inverness 229 d																						
Aberdeen 229 d																						
Dundee 229 d																						
Perth 229 d																						
Fort William 400,227 d																						
Edinburgh d																						
Haymarket d																						
Glasgow Central 226,216,225 d																						
Motherwell 226 d																						
Carstairs 226,225 d		00u21																				
Lockerbie 225,226 d																						
Carlisle 216 a																						
d		01u49	01u49																			
Penrith North Lakes d																						
Windermere 83 d																						
Oxenholme Lake District 83 d																						
Barrow-in-Furness 82 d																						
Lancaster d													05 38									06 29
Blackpool North 97 d																						
Preston 90 a													05 55									06 47
Preston 90 d				00 57									05 58							06 17		06 48
Wigan North Western 90 d													06 09							06 28		
Warrington Bank Quay d													06 20							06 39		
Bolton 82 a																						
Manchester Picc. 82 a				01 43																		07 27
Manchester Airport a				01 58																		07 47
Liverpool Lime Street 91 a																						
d											05 46											
Liverpool South Pkwy 91 d																						
Runcorn 91 d											06 03											
Manchester Picc. 84 d						05 11	05 25					05 55			06 00	06 10	06 35					
Stockport 84 d							05 34					06 03			06 08	06 19	06 43					
Wilmslow 84 d	00 02						05 41					06 11										
Holyhead 81 d																						
Bangor (Gwynedd) 81 d																						
Llandudno Junction 81 d																						
Wrexham General 75 d																						
Chester 81 d					04 22																	
Crewe 81,91 a	00 34				04 43	05 42	05 57					06 27								06 57		
d					04 59	05 47	06 00		06 01	06 11		06 29						06 49	07 00	07 01	07 18	
Macclesfield d															06 21	06 31	06 56					
Stoke-on-Trent 84 d						06 08		←	06 24					←	06 39	06 48	07 12		07 22		07 38	
Stafford a					05 24	06 25	06 18	06 25	06 43	06 30	06 34			06 43	06 55			07 08	07 43		07 57	
d					05 25	06 26	06 19	06 26	06 48	06 31	06 36			06 48	07 01			07 10	07 48		08 08	
Penkridge a						→			→	06 36								07 15	→		→	
Wolverhampton a					05 39			06 38		06 47					07 12			07 27		07 32		
BirminghamNewSt 68 a					05 58			06 57		07 15					07 33			07 50		08 05		
Birmingham International 68 a								07 13												08 20		
Coventry 68 a								07 24												08 30		
Lichfield Trent Valley a														07 04		07 11						
Tamworth Low Level a														07 11		07 17						
Nuneaton a											06 58			07 26								
Rugby 66 a							06 50							07 42			07 52					
Milton Keynes Central 66 a							07 11					07 31	07 38	08 04						08 58		
Watford Junction 66 a		06s43	06s43				07s33				07s45											
London Euston 66 a		07 07	07 07				07 50				08 02	08 07	08 14	08 40		08 25	08 45			09 34		

A From Manchester Piccadilly
B From Glasgow Central
C From Edinburgh
D To Bournemouth
E From Manchester Piccadilly to Bournemouth
F To London Euston
G From Crewe
H To Bristol Temple Meads

Refer to Operator websites for full information about Sleeper Services. Contact details for train operators available at National Rail Enquiries

Table T065-R

Saturdays
26 May to 8 December

Scotland to Manchester, West Midlands & London via the West Coast. North West England to West Midlands & London

	LM	VT	LM	VT	VT	LM	XC	VT	VT	LM	LM	VT	XC	VT	NT	TP	VT	LM	LM	VT	VT	VT
	A		B			C	D			C			E					F				
Inverness 229 d																						
Aberdeen 229 d																						
Dundee 229 d																						
Perth 229 d																						
Fort William 400,227 d																						
Edinburgh d																						
Haymarket d																						
Glasgow Central 226,216,225 d					04 26											04 22						05 40
Motherwell 226 d																						
Carstairs 226,225 d																						
Lockerbie 225,226 d																05 50						
Carlisle 216 a					05 42											06 13						06 47
d					05 44											06 22						06 49
Penrith North Lakes d					05 58											06 42						
Windermere 83 d																						
Oxenholme Lake District 83 d					06 21											07 09						07 24
Barrow-in-Furness 82 d															06 11							
Lancaster d					06 36									06 58	07 03	07 24						07 38
Blackpool North 97 d																						
Preston 90 a					06 54									07 15	07 22	07 44						07 56
Preston 90 d					06 57									07 17	07 28	07 45						07 58
Wigan North Western 90 d					07 09									07 28								08 09
Warrington Bank Quay d					07 19									07 39								08 20
Bolton 82 a															07 54							
Manchester Picc. 82 a															08 15	08 27						
Manchester Airport a															08 35	08 47						
Liverpool Lime Street 91 a																						
d	06 32	06 44									07 04	07 16							07 34	07 47		
Liverpool South Pkwy 91 d	06 42										07 15								07 44			
Runcorn 91 d	06 50	07 01									07 23	07 33							07 52	08 03		
Manchester Picc. 84 d				06 55			07 05	07 15					07 27				07 35				07 55	
Stockport 84 d				07 04			07 13	07 23					07 36				07 43				08 04	
Wilmslow 84 d				07 11																	08 11	
Holyhead 81 d																						
Bangor (Gwynedd) 81 d																						
Llandudno Junction 81 d																						
Wrexham General 75 d																						
Chester 81 d									07 17													
Crewe 81,91 a	07 15	07 19		07 27					07 36		07 47	07 54		07 57					08 17	08 21	08 27	
d	07 19	07 20		07 29					07 41		07 49	07 56		08 01				08 02	08 19	08 22	08 29	
Macclesfield d							07 26						07 49				07 56					
Stoke-on-Trent 84 d			←			←	07 44	07 50		←			08 07				08 12	08 28				
Stafford a	07 38	07 38	07 38			07 43	08 00			07 57	08 09	08 14	08 24					08 51	08 39	08 40		
d	07 40	07 39	07 40			07 48	08 01			08 08	08 10	08 15	08 25					08 55	08 40	08 42		
Penkridge a	→		07 45								08 15							→	08 46			
Wolverhampton a			07 57				08 13				08 27		08 39	08 33					08 58			
BirminghamNewSt 68 a			08 18				08 33				08 48		08 58	09 05					09 18			
Birmingham International 68 a													09 13									
Coventry 68 a													09 24									
Lichfield Trent Valley a						08 04				08 24		08 29										
Tamworth Low Level a						08 11				08 31		08 36										
Nuneaton a						08 26				08 46										09 04		
Rugby 66 a						08 42				09 02												
Milton Keynes Central 66 a						09 05		08 46	08 52	09 24												
Watford Junction 66 a																						
London Euston 66 a		08 57		09 02	09 08	09 52		09 21	09 30	10 00		09 43					09 40			10 04	10 08	10 11

A To Birmingham New Street
B From Liverpool Lime Street
C From Crewe
D To Bristol Temple Meads
E To Bournemouth
F To London Euston

Refer to Operator websites for full information about Sleeper Services. Contact details for train operators available at National Rail Enquiries

Table T065-R

Saturdays
26 May to 8 December

Scotland to Manchester, West Midlands & London via the West Coast. North West England to West Midlands & London

	LM	XC	LM	VT	VT	XC	VT	VT	LM	TP	LM	VT	VT	VT	LM	XC	LM	VT	VT	XC	VT
	■	◇■	■	◇■	◇■	◇■	◇■	◇■	■	◇■	■	◇■	◇■	◇■	■	◇■	■	◇■	◇■	◇■	◇■
	A	B				C			D						A	E				C	
		🍴		☕	☕	🍴	☕	☕		🍴		☕	☕	☕		🍴		☕	☕	🍴	☕
Inverness 229 d																					
Aberdeen 229 d																					
Dundee 229 d																					
Perth 229 d																					
Fort William 400,227 d																					
Edinburgh ■ d										06 15											
Haymarket d										06u19											
Glasgow Central ■ 226,216,225 d								05 50						06 30							
Motherwell 226 d								06 05						06 45							
Carstairs 226,225 d																					
Lockerbie 225,226 d										07 13				07 26							
Carlisle ■ 216 a								07 01		07 33				07 45							
d								07 02		07 35				07 47							
Penrith North Lakes d								07 17		07 49				08 01							
Windermere 83 d																					
Oxenholme Lake District 83 d								07 41		08 13				08 24							
Barrow-in-Furness 82 d																					
Lancaster ■ d								07 56		08 28				08 39							
Blackpool North 97 d																					
Preston ■ 90 a								08 14		08 45				08 57							
Preston ■ 90 d								08 17		08 47				08 59							
Wigan North Western 90 d								08 28						09 10							
Warrington Bank Quay d								08 39						09 21							
Bolton 82 a																					
Manchester Picc. ■ 82 a										09 27											
Manchester Airport a										09 47											
Liverpool Lime Street ■ 91 a																					
d			08 04								08 34	08 47					09 04				
Liverpool South Pkwy ■ 91 d			08 15								08 44						09 16				
Runcorn 91 d			08 25								08 52	09 03					09 25				
Manchester Picc. ■ 84 d		08 05		08 15		08 27	08 35						08 55			09 05		09 15		09 27	09 35
Stockport 84 d		08 13		08 23		08 36	08 43						09 04			09 13		09 23		09 37	09 43
Wilmslow 84 d													09 11								
Holyhead 81 d					06 52														07 55		
Bangor (Gwynedd) 81 d					07 20														08 22		
Llandudno Junction 81 d					07 38														08 40		
Wrexham General 75 d																					
Chester 81 d					08 35														09 35		
Crewe ■ 81,91 a			08 47		08 54			08 57			09 18	09 22	09 29				09 46		09 54		
d			08 49		08 56			09 01	09 02		09 19	09 24	09 30				09 49		09 56		
Macclesfield d		08 26				08 49	08 56									09 26				09 50	09 56
Stoke-on-Trent 84 d	←	08 44		08 50		09 07	09 12		09 28						←	09 44		09 50		10 08	10 12
Stafford a	08 51	09 00	09 10			09 23			09 51		09 39	09 42			09 51	10 00	10 09			10 24	
d	08 55	09 01	09 10			09 25			09 55		09 40	09 43			09 55	10 01	10 10			10 25	
Penkridge a			09 16						→		09 46						10 15				
Wolverhampton ■ a		09 15	09 27			09 38		09 33			09 58					10 13	10 27			10 39	
BirminghamNewSt ■ 68 a		09 33	09 48			09 58		10 05			10 18					10 33	10 48			10 58	
Birmingham International 68 a						10 13		10 19												11 13	
Coventry 68 a						10 24		10 30												11 24	
Lichfield Trent Valley a	09 12														10 12						
Tamworth Low Level a	09 19														10 19						
Nuneaton a	09 35														10 35						
Rugby 66 a	09 51														10 51						
Milton Keynes Central 66 a	10 14			09 46	10 02			10 58							11 14			10 46	11 02		
Watford Junction 66 a																					
London Euston ■ ⊖66 a	10 50			10 21	10 36		10 41	11 33				11 02	11 07	11 11	11 50			11 21	11 36		11 41

A From Crewe
B To Paignton
C To Bournemouth
D To London Euston
E To Bristol Temple Meads

Refer to Operator websites for full information about Sleeper Services. Contact details for train operators available at National Rail Enquiries

Table T065-R

Saturdays
26 May to 8 December

Scotland to Manchester, West Midlands & London via the West Coast. North West England to West Midlands & London

	VT	LM	TP	LM	VT	VT	VT	LM	XC	LM	VT	VT	XC	VT	VT	LM	NT	TP	LM	VT	VT	VT
	◇■	■	◇■	■	◇■	◇■	◇■	■	◇■	■	◇■	◇■	◇■	◇■	◇■	■	◇	◇■	■	◇■	◇■	◇■
		A						B	C				D			A	E					
	☕		🍴		☕	☕	☕		🍴		☕	☕	🍴	☕	☕			🍴		☕	☕	☕
Inverness 229 d																						
Aberdeen 229 d																						
Dundee 229 d																						
Perth 229 d																						
Fort William 400,227 d																						
Edinburgh ■ d	06 52																	08 12				
Haymarket d	06 56																	08u16				
Glasgow Central ■ 226,216,225 d			07 10				07 35								08 00							08 40
Motherwell 226 d			07 25				07 52															
Carstairs 226,225 d																						
Lockerbie 225,226 d			08 09															09 10				
Carlisle ■ 216 a	08 06		08 30				08 48								09 10			09 31				09 48
d	08 07		08 35				08 49								09 11			09 35				09 49
Penrith North Lakes d	08 22		08 50															09 50				10 03
Windermere 83 d																	09 34					
Oxenholme Lake District 83 d			09 14				09 23										09 55	10 14				
Barrow-in-Furness 82 d																						
Lancaster ■ d	08 57		09 29				09 38								09 58		10 14	10 29				10 38
Blackpool North 97 d																						
Preston ■ 90 a	09 15		09 46				09 56								10 16		10 37	10 46				10 56
Preston ■ 90 d	09 17		09 48				09 59								10 17		10 44	10 48				10 58
Wigan North Western 90 d	09 28						10 10								10 29							11 09
Warrington Bank Quay d	09 39						10 21								10 41							11 20
Bolton 82 a																	11 23					
Manchester Picc. ■ 82 a			10 27														11 45	11 27				
Manchester Airport a			10 47															11 47				
Liverpool Lime Street ■ 91 a																						
d				09 34	09 47					10 04									10 34	10 47		
Liverpool South Pkwy ■ 91 d				09 44						10 16									10 44			
Runcorn 91 d				09 52	10 03					10 25									10 52	11 03		
Manchester Picc. ■ 84 d						09 55			10 05		10 15		10 27	10 35							10 55	
Stockport 84 d						10 04			10 13		10 23		10 36	10 43							11 04	
Wilmslow 84 d						10 11															11 11	
Holyhead 81 d												08 55										
Bangor (Gwynedd) 81 d												09 22										
Llandudno Junction 81 d												09 40										
Wrexham General 75 d																						
Chester 81 d												10 35										
Crewe ■ 81,91 a	09 58			10 17	10 21	10 27				10 46		10 54			10 58				11 17	11 21	11 27	
d	10 01	10 02		10 19	10 22	10 29				10 49		10 56			11 02	11 02			11 19	11 22	11 29	
Macclesfield d									10 26				10 49	10 57								
Stoke-on-Trent 84 d		10 28						←	10 44		10 50		11 07	11 13		11 28						
Stafford a		10 50		10 38	10 40			10 50	11 00	11 09			11 24			11 50			11 38	11 40		
d		10 55		10 40	10 42			10 55	11 01	11 10			11 25			11 55			11 40	11 42		
Penkridge a		→		10 45						11 15						→			11 45			
Wolverhampton ■ a	10 32			10 57					11 13	11 27			11 39		11 33				11 57			
BirminghamNewSt ■ 68 a	11 05			11 18					11 33	11 48			11 59		12 05				12 18			
Birmingham International 68 a	11 19												12 13		12 19							
Coventry 68 a	11 30												12 24		12 30							
Lichfield Trent Valley a								11 12														
Tamworth Low Level a								11 19														
Nuneaton a								11 35														
Rugby 66 a								11 51														
Milton Keynes Central 66 a	11 58							12 14			11 46	12 02			12 58							
Watford Junction 66 a																						
London Euston ■ ⊖66 a	12 33				11 59	12 02	12 08	12 50			12 21	12 36		12 42	13 33					12 59	13 02	13 08

A To London Euston
B From Crewe
C To Bristol Temple Meads
D To Bournemouth
E ◇ to Preston

Refer to Operator websites for full information about Sleeper Services. Contact details for train operators available at National Rail Enquiries

Table T065-R

Saturdays
26 May to 8 December

Scotland to Manchester, West Midlands & London via the West Coast. North West England to West Midlands & London

	LM A	XC B	LM	VT	XC C	VT	VT	VT	LM D	VT	TP	LM	VT	VT	VT	LM A	XC E	LM	VT	XC C	VT
Inverness 229 d																					
Aberdeen 229 d																					
Dundee 229 d																					
Perth 229 d																					
Fort William 400,227 d																					
Edinburgh d								08 53													
Haymarket d								08 58													
Glasgow Central 226,216,225 d											09 07				09 40						
Motherwell 226 d											09 22										
Carstairs 226,225 d																					
Lockerbie 225,226 d											10 08										
Carlisle 216 a								10 07			10 29				10 48						
Carlisle d								10 08			10 33				10 50						
Penrith North Lakes d											10 48										
Windermere 83 d																					
Oxenholme Lake District 83 d								10 42			11 12				11 24						
Barrow-in-Furness 82 d																					
Lancaster d								10 57			11 27				11 39						
Blackpool North 97 d										10 53											
Preston 90 a								11 15		11 17	11 45				11 57						
Preston 90 d								11 16		11 20	11 47				11 59						
Wigan North Western 90 d								11 29		11 35					12 10						
Warrington Bank Quay d								11 40		11 48					12 21						
Bolton 82 a																					
Manchester Picc. 82 a											12 27										
Manchester Airport a											12 47										
Liverpool Lime Street 91 a																					
Liverpool Lime Street d			11 04									11 34	11 47					12 04			
Liverpool South Pkwy 91 d			11 16									11 44						12 16			
Runcorn 91 d			11 25									11 52	12 03					12 25			
Manchester Picc. 84 d		11 05		11 15	11 27		11 35							11 55			12 05		12 15	12 27	
Stockport 84 d		11 13		11 23	11 36		11 43							12 04			12 13		12 23	12 36	
Wilmslow 84 d														12 11							
Holyhead 81 d																					
Bangor (Gwynedd) 81 d																					
Llandudno Junction 81 d																					
Wrexham General 75 d																					
Chester 81 d						11 35															12 35
Crewe 81,91 a			11 46			11 54		11 56				12 18	12 22	12 27				12 46			12 54
Crewe d			11 49			11 56		12 00	12 02			12 19	12 23	12 29				12 49			12 56
Macclesfield d		11 26			11 49		11 56										12 26			12 49	
Stoke-on-Trent 84 d	←	11 44		11 50	12 07		12 12		12 28							←	12 44		12 50	13 07	
Stafford a	11 50	12 00	12 09		12 23				12 50			12 39	12 41			12 50	13 00	13 09		13 24	
Stafford d	11 55	12 01	12 10		12 25				12 55			12 40	12 43			12 55	13 01	13 10		13 25	
Penkridge a			12 15						→			12 46						13 15			
Wolverhampton a		12 13	12 27		12 39			12 33				12 58					13 14	13 27		13 39	
BirminghamNewSt 68 a		12 34	12 48		12 58			13 05				13 18					13 34	13 48		13 58	
Birmingham International 68 a					13 13			13 19												14 13	
Coventry 68 a					13 24			13 30												14 24	
Lichfield Trent Valley a	12 12															13 12					
Tamworth Low Level a	12 19															13 19					
Nuneaton a	12 35															13 35					
Rugby 66 a	12 51									12 55						13 51					
Milton Keynes Central 66 a	13 14			12 46		13 02		13 58								14 14			13 46		14 02
Watford Junction 66 a																					
London Euston ⊖66 a	13 50			13 21		13 36	13 39	14 33		13 53			14 01	14 04	14 08	14 50			14 20		14 36

A From Crewe
B To Bristol Temple Meads
C To Bournemouth
D To London Euston
E To Exeter St Davids

Refer to Operator websites for full information about Sleeper Services. Contact details for train operators available at National Rail Enquiries

Table T065-R

Saturdays
26 May to 8 December

Scotland to Manchester, West Midlands & London via the West Coast. North West England to West Midlands & London

	VT	VT	LM A	TP	LM	VT	VT	VT	LM B	XC C	LM	VT	XC D	VT	VT	NT E	VT	NT F	NT	VT	TP	LM A
Inverness 229 d																						
Aberdeen 229 d																						
Dundee 229 d																						
Perth 229 d																						
Fort William 400,227 d																						
Edinburgh d				10 12													10 52					
Haymarket d				10u16													10 57					
Glasgow Central 226,216,225 d		10 00						10 40													11 09	
Motherwell 226 d																					11 24	
Carstairs 226,225 d																						
Lockerbie 225,226 d				11 10																	12 08	
Carlisle 216 a		11 08		11 30				11 47									12 04				12 29	
Carlisle d		11 11		11 35				11 49									12 08				12 35	
Penrith North Lakes d		11 25		11 50																	12 50	
Windermere 83 d																			12 31			
Oxenholme Lake District 83 d				12 14				12 23									12 43		12 52		13 14	
Barrow-in-Furness 82 d																11 53						
Lancaster d				12 29				12 38								12 52	12 57		13a12		13 29	
Blackpool North 97 d																		←		13 02		
Preston 90 a		12 14		12 46				12 56								13 11	13 15	13 11		13 26	13 47	
Preston 90 d		12 17		12 48				12 58								13 25	13 17	13 25		13 29	13 48	
Wigan North Western 90 d		12 28						13 09								→	13 28			13 41		
Warrington Bank Quay d		12 39						13 20									13 39			13 54		
Bolton 82 a																		13 52				
Manchester Picc. 82 a				13 27														14 15			14 27	
Manchester Airport a				13 47														14 35			14 47	
Liverpool Lime Street 91 a																						
Liverpool Lime Street d					12 34	12 47					13 04											
Liverpool South Pkwy 91 d					12 44						13 16											
Runcorn 91 d					12 52	13 03					13 25											
Manchester Picc. 84 d	12 35						12 55			13 05		13 15	13 27		13 35							
Stockport 84 d	12 43						13 04			13 13		13 23	13 36		13 43							
Wilmslow 84 d							13 11															
Holyhead 81 d																						
Bangor (Gwynedd) 81 d																						
Llandudno Junction 81 d																						
Wrexham General 75 d																						
Chester 81 d														13 35								
Crewe 81,91 a		12 57			13 18	13 22	13 29				13 46			13 54			13 57					
Crewe d		13 01	13 02		13 19	13 24	13 30				13 49			13 56			14 01					14 02
Macclesfield d	12 56									13 26			13 49		13 56							
Stoke-on-Trent 84 d	13 12		13 28						←	13 44		13 50	14 07		14 12							14 28
Stafford a			13 50		13 38	13 42			13 50	14 00	14 09		14 24									14 50
Stafford d			13 55		13 40	13 43			13 55	14 01	14 10		14 25									14 55
Penkridge a			→		13 46						14 15											→
Wolverhampton a		13 33			13 58					14 15	14 27		14 39				14 33					
BirminghamNewSt 68 a		14 05			14 18					14 35	14 48		14 58				15 05					
Birmingham International 68 a		14 19											15 13				15 19					
Coventry 68 a		14 29											15 24				15 30					
Lichfield Trent Valley a									14 12													
Tamworth Low Level a									14 19													
Nuneaton a									14 35													
Rugby 66 a								14 22	14 51											15 04		
Milton Keynes Central 66 a		14 58							15 14			14 48		15 02			15 58					
Watford Junction 66 a																						
London Euston ⊖66 a	14 41	15 32				15 00	15 07	15 13	15 50			15 28		15 36	15 41		16 32			15 58		

A To London Euston
B From Crewe
C To Bristol Temple Meads
D To Bournemouth
E To Manchester Airport
F From Barrow-in-Furness

Refer to Operator websites for full information about Sleeper Services. Contact details for train operators available at National Rail Enquiries

Table T065-R

Saturdays
26 May to 8 December

Scotland to Manchester, West Midlands & London via the West Coast. North West England to West Midlands & London

	LM ■	VT ◇■	VT ◇■	VT ◇■	LM ■ A		XC ◇■ B	LM ■	VT ◇■	XC ◇■ C	VT ◇■	VT ◇■	LM ■ D	VT ◇■	TP ◇■		LM ■	VT ◇■	VT ◇■	VT ◇■	LM ■ A	XC ◇■ B	LM ■	VT ◇■
Inverness 229 d																								
Aberdeen 229 d																								
Dundee 229 d																								
Perth 229 d																								
Fort William 400,227 d																								
Edinburgh ■ d															12 12									
Haymarket d															12u16									
Glasgow Central ■ 226,216,225 d				11 40										12 00						12 40				
Motherwell 226 d																								
Carstairs 226,225 d																								
Lockerbie 225,226 d															13 10									
Carlisle ■ 216 a				12 47										13 11	13 30					13 47				
d				12 49										13 13	13 35					13 49				
Penrith North Lakes d				13 03											13 50									
Windermere 83 d																								
Oxenholme Lake District 83 d															14 14					14 24				
Barrow-in-Furness 82 d																								
Lancaster ■ d				13 38										14 00	14 29					14 39				
Blackpool North 97 d																								
Preston ■ 90 a				13 56										14 17	14 46					14 56				
Preston ■ 90 d				13 58										14 20	14 48					14 58				
Wigan North Western 90 d				14 09										14 32						15 09				
Warrington Bank Quay d				14 20										14 43						15 20				
Bolton 82 a																								
Manchester Picc. ■ 82 a															15 27									
Manchester Airport a															15 47									
Liverpool Lime Street ■ 91 a																								
d	13 34	13 47						14 04									14 34	14 47					15 04	
Liverpool South Pkwy ■ 91 d	13 44							14 16									14 44						15 16	
Runcorn 91 d	13 52	14 03						14 25									14 52	15 03					15 25	
Manchester Picc. ■ 84 d			13 55				14 05		14 15	14 27		14 35							14 55			15 05		15 15
Stockport 84 d			14 04				14 13		14 23	14 36		14 43							15 04			15 13		15 23
Wilmslow 84 d			14 11																15 11					
Holyhead 81 d																								
Bangor (Gwynedd) 81 d																								
Llandudno Junction 81 d																								
Wrexham General 75 d																								
Chester 81 d											14 35													
Crewe ■ 81,91 a	14 17	14 23	14 28					14 46			14 54			14 59			15 17	15 21	15 27				15 46	
d	14 19	14 24	14 30					14 49			14 56		15 02	15 03			15 19	15 22	15 29				15 49	
Macclesfield d							14 26			14 49		14 56										15 26		
Stoke-on-Trent 84 d					←		14 44		14 50	15 07		15 12	15 28								←	15 44		15 50
Stafford a	14 39	14 42			14 50		15 00	15 09		15 25			15 51				15 39	15 40			15 51	16 00	16 09	
d	14 40	14 44			14 55		15 01	15 10		15 26			15 55				15 40	15 42			15 55	16 01	16 10	
Penkridge a	14 46							15 15					→				15 45						16 15	
Wolverhampton ■ a	14 57						15 13	15 27		15 39				15 33			15 58					16 13	16 27	
BirminghamNewSt ■ 68 a	15 18						15 33	15 48		15 58				16 05			16 18					16 33	16 48	
Birmingham International 68 a										16 13				16 19										
Coventry 68 a										16 24				16 30										
Lichfield Trent Valley a					15 12																16 12			
Tamworth Low Level a					15 19																16 19			
Nuneaton a					15 35																16 35			
Rugby 66 a					15 51																16 51			
Milton Keynes Central 66 a					16 14				15 46		16 02			16 58							17 14			16 46
Watford Junction 66 a																								
London Euston ■ 66 a		16 01	16 04	16 08	16 50				16 21		16 36	16 40		17 33				16 59	17 03	17 08	17 50			17 21

A From Crewe
B To Bristol Temple Meads
C To Bournemouth
D To London Euston

Refer to Operator websites for full information about Sleeper Services. Contact details for train operators available at National Rail Enquiries

Table T065-R

Saturdays
26 May to 8 December

Scotland to Manchester, West Midlands & London via the West Coast. North West England to West Midlands & London

	VT ◇■		XC ◇■ A	VT ◇■	VT ◇■	LM ■ B	NT ◇	TP ◇■	LM ■	VT ◇■	VT ◇■		VT ◇■	LM ■ C	XC ◇■ D	LM ■	VT ◇■	XC ◇■ A	VT ◇■	VT ◇■	VT ◇■		LM ■ B	VT ◇■
Inverness 229 d																								
Aberdeen 229 d																								
Dundee 229 d																								
Perth 229 d																								
Fort William 400,227 d																								
Edinburgh ■ d					12 52																			
Haymarket d					12 58																			
Glasgow Central ■ 226,216,225 d								13 09					13 40								14 00			
Motherwell 226 d								13 24																
Carstairs 226,225 d																								
Lockerbie 225,226 d								14 09																
Carlisle ■ 216 a					14 05			14 30					14 47								15 09			
d					14 08			14 32					14 49								15 11			
Penrith North Lakes d					14 22			14 47																
Windermere 83 d							14 25																	
Oxenholme Lake District 83 d							14 47	15 12					15 23								15 45			
Barrow-in-Furness 82 d																								
Lancaster ■ d					14 56		15 09	15 27					15 38											
Blackpool North 97 d																								15 54
Preston ■ 90 a					15 15		15 32	15 46					15 56								16 15			16 17
Preston ■ 90 d					15 17			15 47					15 58								16 17			16 20
Wigan North Western 90 d					15 28								16 09								16 28			16 35
Warrington Bank Quay d					15 39								16 20								16 39			16 47
Bolton 82 a																								
Manchester Picc. ■ 82 a								16 27																
Manchester Airport a								16 47																
Liverpool Lime Street ■ 91 a																								
d									15 34	15 47						16 04								
Liverpool South Pkwy ■ 91 d									15 44							16 16								
Runcorn 91 d									15 52	16 03						16 25								
Manchester Picc. ■ 84 d			15 27	15 35							15 55				16 05		16 15	16 27		16 35				
Stockport 84 d			15 36	15 43							16 04				16 13		16 23	16 36		16 43				
Wilmslow 84 d											16 11													
Holyhead 81 d	13 58																							
Bangor (Gwynedd) 81 d	14 25																							
Llandudno Junction 81 d	14 43																							
Wrexham General 75 d																								
Chester 81 d	15 35																		16 35					
Crewe ■ 81,91 a	15 54				15 57				16 17	16 21	16 27					16 46			16 54		16 57			
d	15 56				16 01	16 02			16 19	16 22	16 29					16 49			16 56		17 01		17 02	
Macclesfield d			15 49	15 56											16 26			16 49		16 56				
Stoke-on-Trent 84 d			16 07	16 12		16 28								←	16 44		16 50	17 07		17 12			17 28	
Stafford a			16 23			16 50			16 38	16 40				16 50	17 00	17 09		17 23					17 50	
d			16 25			16 55			16 40	16 42				16 55	17 01	17 10		17 25					17 55	
Penkridge a						→			16 45							17 15							→	
Wolverhampton ■ a			16 39		16 33				16 57						17 13	17 27		17 39			17 33			
BirminghamNewSt ■ 68 a			16 58		17 05				17 18						17 33	17 48		17 58			18 05			
Birmingham International 68 a			17 13		17 19													18 13			18 19			
Coventry 68 a			17 24		17 30													18 24			18 30			
Lichfield Trent Valley a														17 12										
Tamworth Low Level a														17 19										
Nuneaton a														17 35										
Rugby 66 a														17 51										17 56
Milton Keynes Central 66 a	17 02				17 58									18 14			17 46		18 02		18 58			
Watford Junction 66 a																								
London Euston ■ 66 a	17 36			17 41	18 33					17 59	18 02		18 08	18 50			18 21		18 37	18 41	19 32			18 53

A To Bournemouth
B To London Euston
C From Crewe
D To Bristol Temple Meads

Refer to Operator websites for full information about Sleeper Services. Contact details for train operators available at National Rail Enquiries

Scotland to Manchester, West Midlands & London via the West Coast. North West England to West Midlands & London

Station	NT ◇	TP ◇■	LM ■	VT ◇■	VT ◇■	VT ◇■	LM ■ A	XC ◇■ B	LM ■	VT ◇■	XC ◇■ C	VT ◇■	VT ◇■	LM ■ D	TP ◇■	LM ■ E	VT ◇■	LM ■ F	LM ■ G	VT ◇■	VT ◇■	XC ◇■ H
Inverness 229 d																						
Aberdeen 229 d																						
Dundee 229 d																						
Perth 229 d																						
Fort William 400,227 d																						
Edinburgh d		14 17											14 52									
Haymarket d		14u23											14 57									
Glasgow Central 226,216,225 d						14 40									15 09						15 40	
Motherwell 226 d															15 24							
Carstairs 226,225 d																						
Lockerbie 225,226 d		15 17													16 08							
Carlisle 216 a		15 38				15 47							16 06		16 28						16 47	
d		15 39				15 49							16 08		16 35						16 49	
Penrith North Lakes d													16 22		16 50						17 03	
Windermere 83 d																						
Oxenholme Lake District 83 d		16 15				16 24									17 14							
Barrow-in-Furness 82 d	14 57																					
Lancaster d	16 03	16 30				16 38							16 57		17 29						17 38	
Blackpool North 97 d																						
Preston 90 a	16 22	16 47				16 56							17 15		17 47						17 56	
Preston 90 d	16 28	16 49				16 58							17 17		17 48						17 58	
Wigan North Western 90 d						17 09							17 28								18 09	
Warrington Bank Quay d						17 20							17 39								18 20	
Bolton 82 a	16 54																					
Manchester Picc. 82 a	17 15	17 29													18 27							
Manchester Airport a	17 35	17 47													18 47							
Liverpool Lime Street 91 a																						
d			16 34	16 47					17 04							17 34	17 47					
Liverpool South Pkwy 91 d			16 44						17 16							17 44						
Runcorn 91 d			16 52	17 03					17 25							17 52	18 03					
Manchester Picc. 84 d					16 55			17 05		17 15	17 27	17 35								17 55		18 05
Stockport 84 d					17 04			17 13		17 23	17 36	17 43								18 04		18 13
Wilmslow 84 d					17 11															18 11		
Holyhead 81 d																						
Bangor (Gwynedd) 81 d																						
Llandudno Junction 81 d																						
Wrexham General 75 d																						
Chester 81 d																						
Crewe 81,91 a			17 17	17 22	17 27				17 49				17 57			18 19				18 27		
d			17 19	17 23	17 29				17 49				18 01	18 02		18 19				18 29		
Macclesfield d								17 26				17 56										18 26
Stoke-on-Trent 84 d							←	17 44		17 50	18 07	18 12		18 28				←	←			18 44
Stafford a			17 38	17 41			17 50	18 00	18 09		18 24			18 50		18 39	18 36	18 39	18 50			19 00
d			17 40	17 43			17 55	18 01	18 10		18 25			18 55		18 40	18 36	18 40	18 55			19 01
Penkridge a			17 45						18 15					↪		↪		18 45				
Wolverhampton a			17 57					18 14	18 28		18 39		18 32					18 57				19 13
BirminghamNewSt 68 a			18 18					18 33	18 48		18 58		19 05					19 18				19 33
Birmingham International 68 a											19 13		19 19									
Coventry 68 a											19 24		19 30									
Lichfield Trent Valley a				17 57			18 12												19 12			
Tamworth Low Level a							18 19												19 19			
Nuneaton a							18 35												19 35			
Rugby 66 a							18 51						19 42						19 51			
Milton Keynes Central 66 a							19 14			18 48			20 05									
Watford Junction 66 a													20s34									
London Euston ⊖66 a				19 07	19 03	19 10	19 50			19 22		19 39	20 53				19 59			20 02	20 15	

A From Crewe
B To Cardiff Central
C To Bournemouth
D To Northampton
E To Birmingham New Street
F From Liverpool Lime Street
G From Crewe to Northampton
H To Bristol Temple Meads

Refer to Operator websites for full information about Sleeper Services. Contact details for train operators available at National Rail Enquiries

Table T065-R

Saturdays
26 May to 8 December

Scotland to Manchester, West Midlands & London via the West Coast. North West England to West Midlands & London

Station	LM ■	VT ◇■	XC ◇■ A	VT ◇■	LM ■ B	VT ◇■	TP ◇■	LM ■	VT ◇■	VT ◇■	VT ◇■	LM ■ C	XC ◇■ D	LM ■	XC ◇■ E	VT ◇■	VT ◇■	NT ◇	TP ◇■	LM ■	VT ◇■
Inverness 229 d																					
Aberdeen 229 d																					
Dundee 229 d																					
Perth 229 d																					
Fort William 400,227 d																					
Edinburgh d							16 11										16 52				
Haymarket d							16u15										16 58				
Glasgow Central 226,216,225 d						16 00					16 40								17 09		
Motherwell 226 d											16 55								17 24		
Carstairs 226,225 d																					
Lockerbie 225,226 d							17 09												18 08		
Carlisle 216 a						17 09	17 30				17 51						18 06		18 28		
d						17 11	17 35				17 52						18 07		18 35		
Penrith North Lakes d							17 50												18 50		
Windermere 83 d																		18 30			
Oxenholme Lake District 83 d						17 45	18 14				18 26						18 43	18 49	19 14		
Barrow-in-Furness 82 d																					
Lancaster d							18 29				18 41						18 58	19 09	19 29		
Blackpool North 97 d																					
Preston 90 a						18 16	18 47				18 59						19 15	19 32	19 47		
Preston 90 d						18 19	18 48				19 02						19 18		19 48		
Wigan North Western 90 d						18 30					19 13						19 29				
Warrington Bank Quay d						18 41					19 24						19 40				
Bolton 82 a																					
Manchester Picc. 82 a							19 27												20 27		
Manchester Airport a							19 47												20 47		
Liverpool Lime Street 91 a																					
d	18 04							18 34	18 47					19 04						19 34	19 48
Liverpool South Pkwy 91 d	18 15							18 44						19 14						19 44	
Runcorn 91 d	18 24							18 52	19 03					19 25						19 52	20 04
Manchester Picc. 84 d		18 15	18 27	18 35						18 55			19 05		19 27	19 35					
Stockport 84 d		18 23	18 36	18 43						19 04			19 13		19 36	19 43					
Wilmslow 84 d										19 11											
Holyhead 81 d																					
Bangor (Gwynedd) 81 d																					
Llandudno Junction 81 d																					
Wrexham General 75 d																					
Chester 81 d																					
Crewe 81,91 a	18 48					19 00		19 18	19 21	19 27				19 49			19 59			20 17	20 22
d	18 49				19 02	19 03		19 19	19 23	19 29				19 49			20 01			20 19	20 23
Macclesfield d				18 56									19 26		19 49	19 57					
Stoke-on-Trent 84 d		18 49	19 07	19 12	19 28							←	19 44		20 07	20 12					
Stafford a	19 09		19 24		19 50			19 39	19 41			19 50	20 00	20 10	20 23					20 40	20 41
d	19 10		19 25		19 51			19 40	19 42			19 51	20 01	20 10	20 25					20 40	20 43
Penkridge a	19 15				↪			19 45						20 16						20 46	
Wolverhampton a	19 28		19 40			19 34		19 58					20 13	20 29	20 39		20 34			20 57	
BirminghamNewSt 68 a	19 48		19 59			20 05		20 18					20 33	20 48	20 58		21 05			21 18	
Birmingham International 68 a			20 13			20 19									21 13		21 19				
Coventry 68 a			20 24			20 30									21 24		21 30				
Lichfield Trent Valley a												20 08									
Tamworth Low Level a												20 14									
Nuneaton a												20 30									
Rugby 66 a						20 42						20 46					21 42				
Milton Keynes Central 66 a		19 45				21 04					20 42	21 35				21 10	22 04				
Watford Junction 66 a						21s35					21s15	22 19					22s34				
London Euston ⊖66 a		20 34		20 57		21 56			21 17	21 20	21 33	22 38				21 59	22 53				22 15

A To Bournemouth. ⊼ to BirminghamNewSt
B To London Euston
C From Crewe
D To Bristol Temple Meads
E To Southampton Central. ⊼ to BirminghamNewSt

Refer to Operator websites for full information about Sleeper Services. Contact details for train operators available at National Rail Enquiries

Table T065-R

Saturdays
26 May to 8 December

Scotland to Manchester, West Midlands & London via the West Coast. North West England to West Midlands & London

	VT	XC	VT	TP	XC	LM	VT	XC	NT	VT	NT	XC	VT	XC	TP	NT	LM	LM	NT	NT
	◇1	◇1	◇1	◇1	◇1	1	◇1	◇1	◇	◇1	◇	◇1	◇1	◇1	◇1		1	1		
									A		B	C		D		E			F	E
	⊡		⊡	⊼			⊡			⊡			⊡		⊼					
Inverness 229 d																				
Aberdeen 229 d																				
Dundee 229 d																				
Perth 229 d																				
Fort William 400,227 d																				
Edinburgh 10 d				18 12									18 52							
Haymarket d				18u16									18 56							
Glasgow Central 15 226,216,225 d	17 40		18 00							18 40					18 47					
Motherwell 226 d																				
Carstairs 226,225 d																				
Lockerbie 225,226 d	18 33			19 10											19 55					
Carlisle 8 216 a	18 51		19 10	19 30						19 47			20 03		20 15					
d	18 53		19 11	19 36						19 49			20 09		20 17					
Penrith North Lakes d	19 07			19 50						20 03			20 23		20 31					
Windermere 83 d																20 43			22 26	22 25
Oxenholme Lake District 83 d	19 30			20 14						20 26			20 47		20 55	21 02			22 47	23 10
Barrow-in-Furness 82 d									19 34											
Lancaster 8 d	19 44		19 58	20 29					20 34	20 41			21 02		21 09	21a21			23 06	23 55
Blackpool North 97 d											←									
Preston 8 90 a	20 02		20 15	20 46					20 54	20 59	20 54		21 19		21 27				23 29	00 35
Preston 8 90 d	20 05		20 17	20 48					21 05	21 01	21 05		21 22		21 28					
Wigan North Western 90 d	20 16		20 28						→	21 12			21 33							
Warrington Bank Quay d	20 27		20 39							21 23			21 44							
Bolton 82 a																				
Manchester Picc. 10 82 a				21 27							21 49				22 09					
Manchester Airport ✈ a				21 47							22 05				22 26					
Liverpool Lime Street 10 91 a																				
d						20 34											21 34	22 04		
Liverpool South Pkwy 7 91 ✈ d						20 44											21 44	22 15		
Runcorn 91 d						20 52											21 52	22 23		
Manchester Picc. 10 84 d		20 05			20 27		20 35	21 05				21 27								
Stockport 84 d		20 13			20 36		20 43	21 13				21 35								
Wilmslow 84 d																				
Holyhead 81 d																				
Bangor (Gwynedd) 81 d																				
Llandudno Junction 81 d																				
Wrexham General 75 d																				
Chester 81 d																				
Crewe 10 81,91 a	20 46		20 59			21 16				21 42			22 04				22 17	22 47		
d	20 47		21 01			21 19				21 44			22 06				22 19			
Macclesfield d		20 26			20 49		20 56	21 26				21 49								
Stoke-on-Trent 84 d		20 44			21 08		21 12	21 44				22 07		←						
Stafford a		21 00			21 24	21 39		22 00		22 07		22 23	22 24	22 23			22 40			
d		21 01			21 25	21 40		22 01		22 08		22 30	22 25	22 30			22 40			
Penkridge a						21 45						→					22 46			
Wolverhampton 7 a		21 13	21 32		21 40	21 58		22 13		22 22			22 39	22 42			22 58			
BirminghamNewSt 12 68 a		21 33	21 51		21 59	22 18		22 33		22 48			22 58	23 01			23 18			
Birmingham International 68 ✈ a																				
Coventry 68 a																				
Lichfield Trent Valley a																				
Tamworth Low Level a																				
Nuneaton a																				
Rugby 66 a																				
Milton Keynes Central 66 a	21 51						22 10													
Watford Junction 66 a							22s40													
London Euston 15 ⊖66 a	22 42						22 59													

A To Manchester Airport
B From Barrow-in-Furness
C To Birmingham New Street
D From Manchester Piccadilly
E until 16 June, from 15 September
F from 23 June until 8 September

Refer to Operator websites for full information about Sleeper Services. Contact details for train operators available at National Rail Enquiries

Table T065-R

Sundays
20 May to 17 June

Scotland to Manchester, West Midlands & London via the West Coast. North West England to West Midlands & London

	VT	VT	VT	XC	VT	LM	VT	VT	XC	VT	LM	LM	VT	VT	VT	XC	VT	VT	VT	VT	LM	VT
	◇1	◇1	◇1	◇1	◇1	1	◇1	◇1	◇1	◇1	1	1	◇1	◇1	◇1	◇1	◇1	◇1	◇1	◇1	1	◇1
				A					A							A						
	⊡	⊡	⊡	⊼	⊡		⊡	⊡	⊼	⊡			⊡	⊡	⊡	⊼	⊡	⊡	⊡	⊡		⊡
Inverness 229 d																						
Aberdeen 229 d																						
Dundee 229 d																						
Perth 229 d																						
Fort William 400,227 d																						
Edinburgh 10 d																						
Haymarket d																						
Glasgow Central 15 226,216,225 d																						
Motherwell 226 d																						
Carstairs 226,225 d																						
Lockerbie 225,226 d																						
Carlisle 8 216 a																						
d																						
Penrith North Lakes d																						
Windermere 83 d																						
Oxenholme Lake District 83 d																						
Barrow-in-Furness 82 d																						
Lancaster 8 d																						
Blackpool North 97 d																						
Preston 8 90 a																						
Preston 8 90 d							09 00						10 00		10 17				10 58			
Wigan North Western 90 d							09 11						10 12		10 28				11 09			
Warrington Bank Quay d							09 22						10 22		10 39				11 20			
Bolton 82 a																						
Manchester Picc. 10 82 a																						
Manchester Airport ✈ a																						
Liverpool Lime Street 10 91 a																						
d			08 18		08 38					09 38								10 38				
Liverpool South Pkwy 7 91 ✈ d																						
Runcorn 91 d			08 35		08 54					09 54								10 54				
Manchester Picc. 10 84 d	08 05	08 20		08 27				09 20	09 27					10 20		10 26	10 35			11 15		
Stockport 84 d	08 14	08 28		08 36				09 28	09 36					10 29		10 36	10 46			11 24		
Wilmslow 84 d	08 22			08 43										10 37								
Holyhead 81 d																						
Bangor (Gwynedd) 81 d																						
Llandudno Junction 81 d																						
Wrexham General 75 d																						
Chester 81 d																						11 28
Crewe 10 81,91 a	08 39		08 52	09 01	09 11		09 41			10 12			10 41	10 53	10 59			11 12				11 47
d	08 43		08 53	09 05	09 13	09 32	09 43			10 14	10 21	10 37	10 43	10 55	11 02			11 14			11 37	11 49
Macclesfield d		08 41						09 40	09 49							10 49	10 57					
Stoke-on-Trent 84 d		08 57				09 53		10 00	10 07			10 59				11 07	11 15			11 52	11 59	
Stafford a	09 01			09 25	09 31	10 15			10 25	10 32	10 41	11 18				11 26		11 35			12 18	
d	09 03			09 26	09 33	10 19			10 25	10 34	10 42	11 19				11 27		11 36			12 19	
Penkridge a											10 48											
Wolverhampton 7 a				09 40					10 38		11 01				11 31	11 41						
BirminghamNewSt 12 68 a				09 57					10 57		11 19				11 50	11 58						
Birmingham International 68 ✈ a				10 13					11 13							12 13						
Coventry 68 a				10 24					11 24							12 24						
Lichfield Trent Valley a			09 24			10 35						11 35									12 35	
Tamworth Low Level a						10 42						11 42									12 42	
Nuneaton a					09 55	10 58				10 56		11 58						11 58			12 58	12 31
Rugby 66 a						11 17	10 32					12 13	11 31								13 13	
Milton Keynes Central 66 a			10 19			12 04	11 07	11 16		11 45		13 04	12 07				12 21			12 50	14 04	13 04
Watford Junction 66 a	10s34	10s39			11s16	12 40	11s43					13 34		12s37				12s52			14 34	
London Euston 15 ⊖66 a	10 55	10 59	11 05		11 34	13 01	12 03	12 06		12 29		13 53	12 44	12 54			12 57	13 10	13 21	13 28	14 53	13 43

A To Bournemouth

Refer to Operator websites for full information about Sleeper Services. Contact details for train operators available at National Rail Enquiries

Table T065-R

Sundays
20 May to 17 June

Scotland to Manchester, West Midlands & London via the West Coast. North West England to West Midlands & London

	VT	TP	XC	LM	VT	VT	VT	VT	VT	LM	VT	XC	VT	VT	TP	LM	VT	VT	VT	XC	VT	LM
	◇1	◇1	◇1	1	◇1	◇1	◇1	◇1	◇1	1	◇1	◇1	◇1	◇1	◇1	1	◇1	◇1	◇1	◇1	◇1	1
			A									A								B		
Inverness 229 d																						
Aberdeen 229 d																						
Dundee 229 d																						
Perth 229 d																						
Fort William 400,227 d																						
Edinburgh 10 d		09 16													10 17							
Haymarket d		09 20																				
Glasgow Central 15 226,216,225 d								09 32											10 26			
Motherwell 226 d																			10 52			
Carstairs 226,225 d																						
Lockerbie 225,226 d		10 21													11 13							
Carlisle 8 216 a		10 45						10 48							11 33				11 51			
d		10 46						10 51							11 35				11 53			
Penrith North Lakes d								11 05							11 49				12 07			
Windermere 83 d																						
Oxenholme Lake District 83 d		11 23						11 28							12 13				12 31			
Barrow-in-Furness 82 d																						
Lancaster 6 d		11 38						11 43						11 58	12 28				12 45			
Blackpool North 97 d																						
Preston 8 90 a		11 56						12 01						12 15	12 45				13 03			
Preston 8 90 d	11 17	11 58						12 03						12 17	12 47				13 05			
Wigan North Western 90 d	11 28							12 14						12 28					13 16			
Warrington Bank Quay d	11 40							12 25						12 39					13 27			
Bolton 82 a																						
Manchester Picc. 10 82 a		12 41													13 27							
Manchester Airport a		13 00													13 47							
Liverpool Lime Street 10 91 a																						
d				11 34		11 47										12 34	12 47					
Liverpool South Pkwy 7 91 d				11 44												12 44						
Runcorn 91 d				11 52		12 03										12 52	13 03					
Manchester Picc. 10 84 d			11 27		11 35		11 55		12 15			12 26	12 35					12 55		13 05	13 15	
Stockport 84 d			11 36		11 44		12 05		12 23			12 35	12 43					13 05		13 13	13 23	
Wilmslow 84 d							12 12											13 13				
Holyhead 81 d											10 55											
Bangor (Gwynedd) 81 d											11 22											
Llandudno Junction 81 d											11 40											
Wrexham General 75 d																						
Chester 81 d											12 33											
Crewe 10 81,91 a	11 59			12 18		12 21	12 28				12 53			12 59		13 18	13 21	13 29				
d	12 02			12 19		12 23	12 30			12 37	12 55			13 01		13 19	13 23	13 30				13 37
Macclesfield d			11 49		11 57							12 49	12 57							13 26		
Stoke-on-Trent 84 d			12 07		12 14				12 50	12 59		13 07	13 14							13 45	13 51	13 59
Stafford a			12 24	12 39		12 42				13 18		13 24				13 39	13 42			14 01		14 18
d			12 25	12 40		12 44				13 19		13 25				13 40	13 44			14 02		14 19
Penkridge a				12 45												13 45						
Wolverhampton 7 a	12 32		12 38	12 56								13 37		13 32		13 57				14 15		
BirminghamNewSt 12 68 a	12 50		12 57	13 15								13 57		14 06		14 15				14 33		
Birmingham International 68 a			13 13									14 13		14 19								
Coventry 68 a			13 24									14 24		14 30								
Lichfield Trent Valley a										13 35												14 35
Tamworth Low Level a										13 42												14 42
Nuneaton a										13 58												14 58
Rugby 66 a										14 13												15 13
Milton Keynes Central 66 a									13 47	15 04	14 03			14 58							14 49	16 04
Watford Junction 66 a										15 34												16 34
London Euston 15 ⊖66 a					13 47	14 03	14 10	14 15	14 28	15 53	14 41		14 48	15 37			15 03	15 07	15 18		15 26	16 53

A To Bournemouth
B To Paignton

Refer to Operator websites for full information about Sleeper Services. Contact details for train operators available at National Rail Enquiries

Table T065-R

Sundays
20 May to 17 June

Scotland to Manchester, West Midlands & London via the West Coast. North West England to West Midlands & London

	XC	VT	VT	VT	VT	TP	LM	VT	VT	VT	XC	VT	LM	VT	VT	XC	VT	VT	TP	LM	VT
	◇1	◇1	◇1	◇1	◇1	◇1	1	◇1	◇1	◇1	◇1	◇1	1	◇1	◇1	◇1	◇1	◇1	◇1	1	◇1
	A										B					A					
Inverness 229 d																					
Aberdeen 229 d																					
Dundee 229 d																					
Perth 229 d																					
Fort William 400,227 d																					
Edinburgh 10 d					10 51														12 12		
Haymarket d					10 55														12u17		
Glasgow Central 15 226,216,225 d						11 01				11 33											
Motherwell 226 d						11 25															
Carstairs 226,225 d																					
Lockerbie 225,226 d						12 11													13 11		
Carlisle 8 216 a					12 05	12 32				12 47									13 31		
d					12 07	12 34				12 49								13 07	13 33		
Penrith North Lakes d						12 49													13 48		
Windermere 83 d																					
Oxenholme Lake District 83 d					12 43	13 13				13 23									14 12		
Barrow-in-Furness 82 d																					
Lancaster 6 d					12 57	13 28				13 38								13 56	14 27		
Blackpool North 97 d																					
Preston 8 90 a					13 15	13 47				13 56								14 13	14 45		
Preston 8 90 d					13 17	13 48				13 58								14 17	14 46		
Wigan North Western 90 d					13 28					14 09								14 28			
Warrington Bank Quay d					13 39					14 20								14 39			
Bolton 82 a																					
Manchester Picc. 10 82 a						14 27													15 26		
Manchester Airport a						14 47													15 47		
Liverpool Lime Street 10 91 a																					
d							13 34	13 47												14 34	14 47
Liverpool South Pkwy 7 91 d							13 44													14 44	
Runcorn 91 d							13 52	14 03												14 52	15 03
Manchester Picc. 10 84 d	13 27			13 35					13 55		14 05	14 15				14 27	14 35				
Stockport 84 d	13 36			13 42					14 05		14 13	14 22				14 36	14 42				
Wilmslow 84 d									14 12												
Holyhead 81 d			11 50											12 50							
Bangor (Gwynedd) 81 d			12 17											13 18							
Llandudno Junction 81 d			12 35											13 36							
Wrexham General 75 d																					
Chester 81 d		13 30	13 30											14 33	14 33						
Crewe 10 81,91 a		13 50	13 50		13 59		14 17	14 21	14 28					14 54	14 54			14 58		15 18	15 21
d		13 52	13 53		14 01		14 19	14 23	14 30				14 32	14 55	14 56			15 01		15 19	15 23
Macclesfield d	13 49			13 55							14 26					14 49	14 55				
Stoke-on-Trent 84 d	14 07			14 12							14 44	14 50	14 53			15 07	15 12				
Stafford a	14 24						14 39	14 42			15 00		15 14			15 23				15 40	15 42
d	14 25						14 40	14 44			15 01		15 19			15 25				15 40	15 44
Penkridge a							14 45													15 46	
Wolverhampton 7 a	14 39				14 32		14 57				15 14					15 38		15 33		15 57	
BirminghamNewSt 12 68 a	14 57				15 06		15 15				15 33					15 57		16 06		16 15	
Birmingham International 68 a	15 13				15 19											16 13		16 19			
Coventry 68 a	15 24				15 30											16 24		16 30			
Lichfield Trent Valley a													15 35								
Tamworth Low Level a													15 42								
Nuneaton a		14 32	14 32										15 58								
Rugby 66 a													16 13								
Milton Keynes Central 66 a		15 03	15 03		15 58							15 48	17 04	16 03	16 03			16 58			
Watford Junction 66 a													17 34								
London Euston 15 ⊖66 a		15 42	15 42	15 46	16 37			16 03	16 06	16 12		16 26	17 53	16 41	16 41		16 46	17 36			17 04

A To Bournemouth
B To Bristol Temple Meads

Refer to Operator websites for full information about Sleeper Services. Contact details for train operators available at National Rail Enquiries

Table T065-R

Sundays

20 May to 17 June

Scotland to Manchester, West Midlands & London via the West Coast. North West England to West Midlands & London

	VT	VT	XC	VT	LM	VT	XC	VT	VT	TP	LM	VT	VT	VT	XC	VT	LM	VT	XC	VT	VT	TP
	◇■	◇■	◇■	◇■	■	◇■	◇■	◇■	◇■	◇■	■	◇■	◇■	◇■	◇■	◇■	■	◇■	◇■	◇■	◇■	◇■
			A				B								A				B			
Inverness 229 d																						
Aberdeen 229 d																						
Dundee 229 d																						
Perth 229 d																						
Fort William 400,227 d																						
Edinburgh ■ d									12 51													14 12
Haymarket d									12 55													14u16
Glasgow Central ■ 226,216,225 d		12 27								13 08				13 32								
Motherwell 226 d										13 31												
Carstairs 226,225 d																						
Lockerbie 225,226 d										14 15												15 10
Carlisle ■ 216 a		13 47							14 04	14 35				14 47								15 30
d		13 49							14 07	14 37				14 49							15 05	15 33
Penrith North Lakes d									14 22	14 51												15 48
Windermere 83 d																						
Oxenholme Lake District 83 d		14 23								15 15				15 23							15 45	16 12
Barrow-in-Furness 82 d																						
Lancaster ■ d		14 38							14 57	15 29				15 38								16 27
Blackpool North 97 d																						
Preston ■ 90 a		14 56							15 15	15 47				15 56							16 14	16 44
Preston ■ 90 d		14 58							15 17	15 48				15 58							16 17	16 46
Wigan North Western 90 d		15 09							15 28					16 09							16 29	
Warrington Bank Quay d		15 20							15 39					16 20							16 40	
Bolton 82 a																						
Manchester Picc. ■ 82 a										16 26												17 26
Manchester Airport a										16 47												17 43
Liverpool Lime Street ■ 91 a																						
d											15 34	15 47						16 16				
Liverpool South Pkwy ■ 91 d											15 44											
Runcorn 91 d											15 52	16 03						16 32				
Manchester Picc. ■ 84 d	14 55		15 05	15 15			15 27	15 35					15 55		16 05	16 15			16 27	16 35		
Stockport 84 d	15 04		15 13	15 22			15 36	15 42					16 03		16 13	16 23			16 36	16 42		
Wilmslow 84 d	15 12												16 11									
Holyhead 81 d						13 55																
Bangor (Gwynedd) 81 d						14 22																
Llandudno Junction 81 d						14 40																
Wrexham General 75 d																						
Chester 81 d						15 33																
Crewe ■ 81,91 a	15 28					15 52			15 59		16 18	16 21	16 27					16 51			16 59	
d	15 30				15 37	15 54			16 01		16 19	16 23	16 30				16 37	16 54			17 01	
Macclesfield d			15 26				15 49	15 55							16 26				16 49	16 55		
Stoke-on-Trent 84 d			15 44	15 50	15 59		16 07	16 12							16 44	16 50	16 59		17 07	17 12		
Stafford a			16 00		16 18		16 24				16 39	16 42			17 00		17 18		17 24			
d			16 01		16 19		16 25				16 40	16 44			17 01		17 19		17 25			
Penkridge a											16 45											
Wolverhampton ■ a			16 14				16 39		16 32		16 57				17 14				17 39		17 34	
BirminghamNewSt ■ 68 a			16 33				16 57		17 06		17 15				17 32				17 57		18 05	
Birmingham International 68 a							17 13		17 19										18 13		18 19	
Coventry 68 a							17 24		17 29										18 24		18 30	
Lichfield Trent Valley a					16 35												17 35	17 26				
Tamworth Low Level a					16 42												17 42					
Nuneaton a					16 58												17 58					
Rugby 66 a					17 13												18 13					
Milton Keynes Central 66 a				16 50	18 04	17 03			17 58							17 49	19 04	18 04			18 58	
Watford Junction 66 a					18 34												19 34					
London Euston ■ ⊖66 a	17 08	17 11		17 27	18 53	17 41		17 44	18 36			18 03	18 08	18 13		18 27	19 53	18 41		18 46	19 37	

A To Bristol Temple Meads
B To Bournemouth

Refer to Operator websites for full information about Sleeper Services. Contact details for train operators available at National Rail Enquiries

Table T065-R

Sundays

20 May to 17 June

Scotland to Manchester, West Midlands & London via the West Coast. North West England to West Midlands & London

	LM	VT	VT	VT	XC	VT	LM	XC	VT	VT	VT	TP	LM	VT	VT	VT	XC	VT	LM	XC	VT
	■	◇■	◇■	◇■	◇■	◇■	■	◇■	◇■	◇■	◇■	◇■	■	◇■	◇■	◇■	◇■	◇■	■	◇■	◇■
					A			B									C			D	
Inverness 229 d																					
Aberdeen 229 d																					
Dundee 229 d																					
Perth 229 d																					
Fort William 400,227 d																					
Edinburgh ■ d											14 51										
Haymarket d											14 56										
Glasgow Central ■ 226,216,225 d				14 32								15 00				15 33					
Motherwell 226 d												15 24									
Carstairs 226,225 d																					
Lockerbie 225,226 d												16 14									
Carlisle ■ 216 a				15 47							16 02	16 34				16 47					
d				15 49							16 07	16 36				16 49					
Penrith North Lakes d											16 22	16 51				17 03					
Windermere 83 d																					
Oxenholme Lake District 83 d				16 23								17 14									
Barrow-in-Furness 82 d																					
Lancaster ■ d				16 38							16 57	17 29				17 38					
Blackpool North 97 d																					
Preston ■ 90 a				16 56							17 15	17 47				17 56					
Preston ■ 90 d				16 58							17 17	17 48				17 58					
Wigan North Western 90 d				17 09							17 29					18 09					
Warrington Bank Quay d				17 20							17 40					18 20					
Bolton 82 a																					
Manchester Picc. ■ 82 a												18 27									
Manchester Airport a												18 47									
Liverpool Lime Street ■ 91 a																					
d	16 34	16 47											17 34	17 47							
Liverpool South Pkwy ■ 91 d	16 44												17 44								
Runcorn 91 d	16 52	17 03											17 52	18 03							
Manchester Picc. ■ 84 d			16 55		17 05	17 15		17 27		17 35					17 55		18 05	18 15		18 27	
Stockport 84 d			17 03		17 13	17 22		17 36		17 42					18 03		18 13	18 22		18 36	
Wilmslow 84 d			17 11												18 11						
Holyhead 81 d																					
Bangor (Gwynedd) 81 d																					
Llandudno Junction 81 d																					
Wrexham General 75 d																					
Chester 81 d									17 35												18 35
Crewe ■ 81,91 a	17 18	17 21	17 27						17 53		17 59		18 18	18 21	18 27						18 53
d	17 19	17 23	17 30				17 37		17 55		18 01		18 19	18 23	18 29				18 37		18 55
Macclesfield d					17 26			17 49		17 55							18 26			18 49	
Stoke-on-Trent 84 d					17 45	17 50	17 59	18 07		18 12							18 45	18 51	18 59	19 07	
Stafford a	17 39	17 42			18 01		18 18	18 24					18 39	18 42			19 01		19 18	19 24	
d	17 40	17 44			18 02		18 19	18 25					18 40	18 44			19 02		19 22	19 25	
Penkridge a	17 45												18 45								
Wolverhampton ■ a	17 57				18 15			18 37			18 33		18 57				19 15			19 38	
BirminghamNewSt ■ 68 a	18 15				18 33			18 57			19 06		19 15				19 33			19 57	
Birmingham International 68 a								19 13			19 19									20 13	
Coventry 68 a								19 24			19 30									20 24	
Lichfield Trent Valley a							18 35												19 39		
Tamworth Low Level a							18 42												19 45		
Nuneaton a							18 58												20 01		
Rugby 66 a							19 13												20 16		
Milton Keynes Central 66 a						18 49	20 06		19 04		19 58							19 48	21 07		20 03
Watford Junction 66 a							20 35												21 39		
London Euston ■ ⊖66 a		19 03	19 06	19 10		19 27	20 54		19 42	19 46	20 37			20 04	20 07	20 12		20 27	21 58		20 41

A To Paignton
B To Bournemouth
C To Bristol Temple Meads
D To Southampton Central

Refer to Operator websites for full information about Sleeper Services. Contact details for train operators available at National Rail Enquiries

Scotland to Manchester, West Midlands & London via the West Coast. North West England to West Midlands & London

	VT	VT	TP	NT	LM	VT	VT	VT	XC		VT	LM	VT	TP	XC	LM	VT	VT	XC		LM	VT	TP	AW
	◇■	◇■	◇■	◇	■	◇■	◇■	◇■	◇■		◇■	■	◇■	◇■	◇■	■	◇■	◇■	◇■		■	◇■	◇■	◇
				A					B						C				B		D			
	⊡	⊡	🛒	🛒		⊡	⊡	⊡	🛒		⊡		⊡	🛒	🛒		⊡	⊡				⊡	🛒	
Inverness 229 d																								
Aberdeen 229 d																								
Dundee 229 d																								
Perth 229 d																								
Fort William 400,227 d																								
Edinburgh ■ ⛴ d			16 14										16 51										18 14	
Haymarket ⛴ d			16u18										16 55										18u18	
Glasgow Central ■ 226,216,225 d								16 31						17 00								17 31		
Motherwell 226 d								16 53						17 24										
Carstairs 226,225 d																								
Lockerbie 225,226 d			17 12											18 13								18 32	19 12	
Carlisle ■ 216 a			17 32					17 49					18 05	18 34								18 50	19 32	
d		17 05	17 35	17 48				17 51					18 07	18 35								18 52	19 35	
Penrith North Lakes d			17 50					18 05						18 50								19 06	19 49	
Windermere 83 d																								
Oxenholme Lake District 83 d		17 44	18 14					18 28					18 42	19 14								19 29	20 13	
Barrow-in-Furness 82 d																								
Lancaster ■ d			18 29					18 43					18 57	19 29								19 44	20 28	
Blackpool North 97 d																								
Preston ■ 90 a		18 13	18 46	20 46				19 01					19 15	19 48								20 02	20 45	
Preston ■ 90 d		18 17	18 48					19 03					19 17	19 49								20 04	20 47	
Wigan North Western 90 d		18 28						19 14					19 28									20 15		
Warrington Bank Quay d		18 39						19 25					19 39									20 26		
Bolton 82 a																								
Manchester Picc. ■ 82 ⛴ a			19 26											20 26									21 25	
Manchester Airport ✈⛴ a			19 47											20 47									21 42	
Liverpool Lime Street ■ 91 a																								
d					18 34	18 47										19 34		19 47						
Liverpool South Pkwy ■ 91 ✈ d					18 44											19 44								
Runcorn 91 d					18 52	19 03										19 52		20 03						
Manchester Picc. ■ 84 ⛴ d	18 35						18 55		19 05		19 15				19 27		19 35		20 05					
Stockport 84 d	18 42						19 03		19 13		19 22				19 36		19 41		20 14					
Wilmslow 84 d							19 11																	
Holyhead 81 ⛴ d																								18 25
Bangor (Gwynedd) 81 d																								19 04
Llandudno Junction 81 d																								19 24
Wrexham General 75 d																								
Chester 81 d																								20 27
Crewe ■ 81,91 a		18 58			19 17	19 21	19 27						19 59			20 17		20 22				20 45		20 48
d		19 01			19 19	19 23	19 29					19 37	20 01			20 19		20 24			20 42	20 47		20 52
Macclesfield d	18 55								19 26						19 49		19 54		20 27					
Stoke-on-Trent 84 d	19 12								19 45		19 50	19 59			20 06		20 11		20 45		21 07			
Stafford a					19 39	19 42			20 01			20 18			20 24	20 38		20 42	21 01		21 27			21 13
d					19 40	19 44			20 02			20 19			20 26	20 40		20 43	21 02		21 27			21 13
Penkridge a					19 45											20 45					→			
Wolverhampton ■ ⛴ a		19 34			19 57				20 15				20 33		20 38	20 57			21 15					21 29
BirminghamNewSt ■ 68 ⛴ a		20 06			20 15				20 33				20 51		20 57	21 15			21 33					21 53
Birmingham International 68 ✈ a		20 19													21 13									22 08
Coventry 68 a		20 30													21 23									
Lichfield Trent Valley a	19 34											20 35												
Tamworth Low Level a												20 42												
Nuneaton a												20 58												
Rugby 66 a												21 13												
Milton Keynes Central 66 a		20 59									20 46	22 11						21 36				21 52		
Watford Junction 66 a												22 54										22s30		
London Euston ■ ⊖66 a	20 45	21 46				21 03	21 08	21 19			21 31	23 17					22 01	22 25				22 53		

A To Blackpool North
B To Bristol Temple Meads
C To Reading. 🛒 to BirminghamNewSt
D To Northampton

Refer to Operator websites for full information about Sleeper Services. Contact details for train operators available at National Rail Enquiries

Table T065-R

Sundays
20 May to 17 June

Scotland to Manchester, West Midlands & London via the West Coast. North West England to West Midlands & London

	LM	VT	LM	VT	VT		VT	XC	VT	TP	LM	VT	TP	CS	CS		CS	CS	NT	XC	LM
	■	◇■	■	◇■	◇■		◇■	◇■	◇■	◇■	■	◇■	◇■	🛏	🛏		🛏	🛏		◇■	■
	A																				
		⊡		⊡	⊡		⊡		⊡	🛒		⊡	🛒	✕	✕		✕	✕			
Inverness 229 d																	20 26				
Aberdeen 229 d																		21 43			
Dundee 229 d																		23u07			
Perth 229 d																	23u06				
Fort William 400,227 d															19 00						
Edinburgh ■ ⛴ d									18 51				20 15								
Haymarket ⛴ d									18 56				20u20								
Glasgow Central ■ 226,216,225 d							18 31			19 00		20 02		21 44							
Motherwell 226 d										19 25				22u07							
Carstairs 226,225 d														22u26							
Lockerbie 225,226 d										20 09		21 04	21 14								
Carlisle ■ 216 a							19 46		20 02	20 34		21 23	21 34								
d							19 48		20 07	20 36		21 25	21 36								
Penrith North Lakes d									20 22	20 51		21 40									
Windermere 83 d																			21 44		
Oxenholme Lake District 83 d							20 23			21 15		22 04	22 12						22 16		
Barrow-in-Furness 82 d																					
Lancaster ■ d							20 37		20 57	21 31		22 19	22 27						22 35		
Blackpool North 97 d																					
Preston ■ 90 a							20 55		21 15	21 49		22 36	22 44						22 57		
Preston ■ 90 d							20 57		21 17	21 51		22 39	22 46								
Wigan North Western 90 d							21 08		21 29			22 53									
Warrington Bank Quay d							21 19		21 39			23 04									
Bolton 82 a																					
Manchester Picc. ■ 82 ⛴ a										22 27			23 27								
Manchester Airport ✈⛴ a										22 44			23 44								
Liverpool Lime Street ■ 91 a																					
d			20 34		20 47						21 34										23 30
Liverpool South Pkwy ■ 91 ✈ d			20 44								21 44										23 42
Runcorn 91 d			20 52		21 03						21 52										23 52
Manchester Picc. ■ 84 ⛴ d		20 21		20 55				21 05												22 05	
Stockport 84 d		20 27		21 03				21 13												22 13	
Wilmslow 84 d																					
Holyhead 81 ⛴ d																					
Bangor (Gwynedd) 81 d																					
Llandudno Junction 81 d																					
Wrexham General 75 d																					
Chester 81 d																					
Crewe ■ 81,91 a			21 17		21 22		21 39		21 59		22 17	23 22									00 20
d			21 19		21 24		21 41		22 01		22 19										
Macclesfield d		20 40		21 16				21 26												22 26	
Stoke-on-Trent 84 d	←	20 58		21 33				21 45												22 45	
Stafford a	21 27		21 39		21 42		22 00	22 04			22 39									23 01	
d	21 27		21 40		21 44		22 01	22 05			22 40									23 02	
Penkridge a			21 45								22 45										
Wolverhampton ■ ⛴ a			21 57				22 14	22 18	22 32		22 57									23 15	
BirminghamNewSt ■ 68 ⛴ a			22 15				22 33	22 36	22 53		23 16									23 33	
Birmingham International 68 ✈ a																					
Coventry 68 a																					
Lichfield Trent Valley a	21 44				22 00																
Tamworth Low Level a	21 50				22 06																
Nuneaton a	22 06				22 18																
Rugby 66 a	22 21				22 31																
Milton Keynes Central 66 a		22 03		22 46	23 04																
Watford Junction 66 a				23s28	23s34																
London Euston ■ ⊖66 a		22 56		23 46	23 52									07 07	09 17		09 17	09 17			

A From Crewe to Northampton

Refer to Operator websites for full information about Sleeper Services. Contact details for train operators available at National Rail Enquiries

Table T065-R

Sundays
24 June to 9 September

Scotland to Manchester, West Midlands & London via the West Coast. North West England to West Midlands & London

	VT	VT	VT	XC	VT	LM	VT	VT	XC		VT	LM	LM	VT	VT	VT	XC	VT	VT		VT	VT	LM	VT
				A					A								A							
Inverness 229 d																								
Aberdeen 229 d																								
Dundee 229 d																								
Perth 229 d																								
Fort William 400,227 d																								
Edinburgh d																								
Haymarket d																								
Glasgow Central 226,216,225 d																								
Motherwell 226 d																								
Carstairs 226,225 d																								
Lockerbie 225,226 d																								
Carlisle 216 a																								
d																								
Penrith North Lakes d																								
Windermere 83 d																								
Oxenholme Lake District 83 d																								
Barrow-in-Furness 82 d																								
Lancaster d																								
Blackpool North 97 d																								
Preston 90 a																								
Preston 90 d							09 00							10 00		10 17					10 58			
Wigan North Western 90 d							09 11							10 12		10 28					11 09			
Warrington Bank Quay d							09 22							10 22		10 39					11 20			
Bolton 82 a																								
Manchester Picc. 82 a																								
Manchester Airport a																								
Liverpool Lime Street 91 a																								
d			08 18		08 38						09 38								10 38					
Liverpool South Pkwy 91 d																								
Runcorn 91 d			08 35		08 54						09 54								10 54					
Manchester Picc. 84 d	08 05	08 20		08 27				09 20	09 27						10 20		10 26	10 35				11 15		
Stockport 84 d	08 14	08 28		08 36				09 28	09 36						10 29		10 36	10 46				11 24		
Wilmslow 84 d	08 22			08 43											10 37									
Holyhead 81 d																								
Bangor (Gwynedd) 81 d																								
Llandudno Junction 81 d																								
Wrexham General 75 d																								
Chester 81 d																								11 28
Crewe 81,91 a	08 39		08 52	09 01	09 11		09 41				10 12			10 41	10 53	10 59			11 12					11 47
d	08 43		08 53	09 05	09 13	09 32	09 43				10 14	10 21	10 37	10 43	10 55	11 02			11 14				11 37	11 49
Macclesfield d		08 41						09 40	09 49								10 49	10 57						
Stoke-on-Trent 84 d		08 57				09 53		10 00	10 07				10 59				11 07	11 15				11 52	11 59	
Stafford a	09 01			09 25	09 31	10 15			10 25		10 32	10 41	11 18				11 26		11 35				12 18	
d	09 03			09 26	09 33	10 19			10 25		10 34	10 42	11 19				11 27		11 36				12 19	
Penkridge a												10 48												
Wolverhampton a				09 40					10 38			11 01				11 31	11 41							
BirminghamNewSt 68 a				09 57					10 57			11 19				11 50	11 58							
Birmingham International 68 a				10 13					11 13								12 13							
Coventry 68 a				10 24					11 24								12 24							
Lichfield Trent Valley a			09 24			10 35							11 35										12 35	
Tamworth Low Level a						10 42							11 42										12 42	
Nuneaton a					09 55	10 58					10 56		11 58						11 58				12 58	12 31
Rugby 66 a						11 17	10 32						12 13	11 31									13 13	
Milton Keynes Central 66 a			10 19			12 04	11 07	11 16			11 45		13 04	12 07				12 21				12 50	14 04	13 04
Watford Junction 66 a	10s34	10s39			11s16	12 40	11s43						13 34		12s37				12s52				14 34	
London Euston 66 a	10 55	10 59	11 05		11 34	13 01	12 03	12 06			12 29		13 53	12 44	12 54			12 57	13 10		13 21	13 28	14 53	13 43

A To Bournemouth

Refer to Operator websites for full information about Sleeper Services. Contact details for train operators available at National Rail Enquiries

Table T065-R

Sundays
24 June to 9 September

Scotland to Manchester, West Midlands & London via the West Coast. North West England to West Midlands & London

	VT	TP	XC	LM	VT		VT	VT	VT	VT	LM	VT	XC	VT	VT		TP	LM	VT	VT	VT	XC	VT	LM
			A										A									B		
Inverness 229 d																								
Aberdeen 229 d																								
Dundee 229 d																								
Perth 229 d																								
Fort William 400,227 d																								
Edinburgh d		09 16															10 17							
Haymarket d		09 20																						
Glasgow Central 226,216,225 d									09 32												10 26			
Motherwell 226 d																					10 52			
Carstairs 226,225 d																								
Lockerbie 225,226 d		10 14															11 13							
Carlisle 216 a		10 34							10 48								11 33				11 51			
d		10 36							10 51								11 35				11 53			
Penrith North Lakes d									11 05								11 49				12 07			
Windermere 83 d																								
Oxenholme Lake District 83 d		11 11							11 28								12 13				12 31			
Barrow-in-Furness 82 d																								
Lancaster d		11 26							11 43						11 58		12 28				12 45			
Blackpool North 97 d																								
Preston 90 a		11 41							12 01						12 15		12 45				13 03			
Preston 90 d	11 17	11 43							12 03						12 17		12 47				13 05			
Wigan North Western 90 d	11 28								12 14						12 28						13 16			
Warrington Bank Quay d	11 40								12 25						12 39						13 27			
Bolton 82 a																								
Manchester Picc. 82 a		12 23															13 27							
Manchester Airport a		12 40															13 47							
Liverpool Lime Street 91 a																								
d				11 34			11 47											12 34	12 47					
Liverpool South Pkwy 91 d				11 44														12 44						
Runcorn 91 d				11 52			12 03											12 52	13 03					
Manchester Picc. 84 d			11 27		11 35			11 55		12 15			12 26	12 35						12 55		13 05	13 15	
Stockport 84 d			11 36		11 44			12 05		12 23			12 35	12 43						13 05		13 13	13 23	
Wilmslow 84 d								12 12												13 13				
Holyhead 81 d												10 55												
Bangor (Gwynedd) 81 d												11 22												
Llandudno Junction 81 d												11 40												
Wrexham General 75 d																								
Chester 81 d												12 33												
Crewe 81,91 a	11 59			12 18			12 21	12 28				12 53			12 59			13 18	13 21	13 29				
d	12 02			12 19			12 23	12 30			12 37	12 55			13 01			13 19	13 23	13 30				13 37
Macclesfield d			11 49		11 57								12 49	12 57								13 26		
Stoke-on-Trent 84 d			12 07		12 14					12 50	12 59		13 07	13 14								13 45	13 51	13 59
Stafford a			12 24	12 39			12 42				13 18		13 24					13 39	13 42			14 01		14 18
d			12 25	12 40			12 44				13 19		13 25					13 40	13 44			14 02		14 19
Penkridge a				12 45														13 45						
Wolverhampton a	12 32		12 38	12 56									13 37		13 32			13 57				14 15		
BirminghamNewSt 68 a	12 50		12 57	13 15									13 57		14 06			14 15				14 33		
Birmingham International 68 a			13 13										14 13		14 19									
Coventry 68 a			13 24										14 24		14 30									
Lichfield Trent Valley a											13 35													14 35
Tamworth Low Level a											13 42													14 42
Nuneaton a											13 58													14 58
Rugby 66 a											14 13													15 13
Milton Keynes Central 66 a										13 47	15 04	14 03			14 58								14 49	16 04
Watford Junction 66 a											15 34													16 34
London Euston 66 a					13 47		14 03	14 10	14 15	14 28	15 53	14 41		14 48	15 37				15 03	15 07	15 18		15 26	16 53

A To Bournemouth
B To Paignton

Refer to Operator websites for full information about Sleeper Services. Contact details for train operators available at National Rail Enquiries

Scotland to Manchester, West Midlands & London via the West Coast. North West England to West Midlands & London

	XC	VT	VT	VT	VT	TP	LM	VT	VT	VT	XC	VT	LM	VT	VT	XC	VT	VT	TP	LM	VT
	◇■	◇■	◇■	◇■	◇■	◇■	■	◇■	◇■	◇■	◇■	◇■	■	◇■	◇■	◇■	◇■	◇■	◇■	■	◇■
	A										B					A					
Inverness 229 d																					
Aberdeen 229 d																					
Dundee 229 d																					
Perth 229 d																					
Fort William 400,227 d																					
Edinburgh d					10 51														12 12		
Haymarket d					10 55														12u17		
Glasgow Central 226,216,225 d						11 01				11 33											
Motherwell 226 d						11 25															
Carstairs 226,225 d																					
Lockerbie 225,226 d						12 11													13 11		
Carlisle 216 a					12 05	12 32				12 47									13 31		
Carlisle d					12 07	12 34				12 49								13 07	13 33		
Penrith North Lakes d						12 49													13 48		
Windermere 83 d																					
Oxenholme Lake District 83 d					12 43	13 13				13 23									14 12		
Barrow-in-Furness 82 d																					
Lancaster d					12 57	13 28				13 38								13 56	14 27		
Blackpool North 97 d																					
Preston 90 a					13 15	13 47				13 56								14 13	14 45		
Preston 90 d					13 17	13 48				13 58								14 17	14 46		
Wigan North Western 90 d					13 28					14 09								14 28			
Warrington Bank Quay d					13 39					14 20								14 39			
Bolton 82 a																					
Manchester Picc. 82 a						14 27													15 26		
Manchester Airport a						14 47													15 47		
Liverpool Lime Street 91 a																					
Liverpool Lime Street d							13 34	13 47												14 34	14 47
Liverpool South Pkwy 91 d							13 44													14 44	
Runcorn 91 d							13 52	14 03												14 52	15 03
Manchester Picc. 84 d	13 27			13 35					13 55		14 05	14 15				14 27	14 35				
Stockport 84 d	13 36			13 42					14 05		14 13	14 22				14 36	14 42				
Wilmslow 84 d									14 12												
Holyhead 81 d			11 50											12 50							
Bangor (Gwynedd) 81 d			12 17											13 18							
Llandudno Junction 81 d			12 35											13 36							
Wrexham General 75 d																					
Chester 81 d		13 30	13 30											14 33	14 33						
Crewe 81,91 a		13 50	13 50		13 59		14 17	14 21	14 28					14 54	14 54			14 58		15 18	15 21
Crewe d		13 52	13 53		14 01		14 19	14 23	14 30				14 32	14 55	14 56			15 01		15 19	15 23
Macclesfield d	13 49			13 55							14 26					14 49	14 55				
Stoke-on-Trent 84 d	14 07			14 12							14 44	14 50	14 53			15 07	15 12				
Stafford a	14 24						14 39	14 42			15 00		15 14			15 23				15 40	15 42
Stafford d	14 25						14 40	14 44			15 01		15 19			15 25				15 40	15 44
Penkridge a							14 45													15 46	
Wolverhampton a	14 39				14 32		14 57				15 14					15 38		15 33		15 57	
BirminghamNewSt 68 a	14 57				15 06		15 15				15 33					15 57		16 06		16 15	
Birmingham International 68 a	15 13				15 19											16 13		16 19			
Coventry 68 a	15 24				15 30											16 24		16 30			
Lichfield Trent Valley a													15 35								
Tamworth Low Level a													15 42								
Nuneaton a		14 32	14 32										15 58								
Rugby 66 a													16 13								
Milton Keynes Central 66 a		15 03	15 03		15 58							15 48	17 04	16 03	16 03			16 58			
Watford Junction 66 a													17 34								
London Euston ⊖66 a		15 42	15 42	15 46	16 37			16 03	16 06	16 12		16 26	17 53	16 41	16 41		16 46	17 36			17 04

A To Bournemouth

B To Bristol Temple Meads

Refer to Operator websites for full information about Sleeper Services. Contact details for train operators available at National Rail Enquiries

Scotland to Manchester, West Midlands & London via the West Coast. North West England to West Midlands & London

	VT	VT	XC	VT	LM	VT	XC	VT	VT	TP	LM	VT	VT	VT	XC	VT	LM	VT	XC	VT	VT	TP
	◇■	◇■	◇■	◇■	■	◇■	◇■	◇■	◇■	◇■	■	◇■	◇■	◇■	◇■	◇■	■	◇■	◇■	◇■	◇■	◇■
			A				B								A				B			
Inverness 229 d																						
Aberdeen 229 d																						
Dundee 229 d																						
Perth 229 d																						
Fort William 400,227 d																						
Edinburgh d									12 51													14 12
Haymarket d									12 55													14u16
Glasgow Central 226,216,225 d		12 27								13 08				13 32								
Motherwell 226 d										13 31												
Carstairs 226,225 d																						
Lockerbie 225,226 d										14 15												15 10
Carlisle 216 a		13 47							14 04	14 35				14 47								15 30
Carlisle d		13 49							14 07	14 37				14 49							15 05	15 33
Penrith North Lakes d									14 22	14 51												15 48
Windermere 83 d																						
Oxenholme Lake District 83 d		14 23								15 15				15 23							15 45	16 12
Barrow-in-Furness 82 d																						
Lancaster d		14 38							14 57	15 29				15 38								16 27
Blackpool North 97 d																						
Preston 90 a		14 56							15 15	15 47				15 56							16 14	16 44
Preston 90 d		14 58							15 17	15 48				15 58							16 17	16 46
Wigan North Western 90 d		15 09							15 28					16 09							16 29	
Warrington Bank Quay d		15 20							15 39					16 20							16 40	
Bolton 82 a																						
Manchester Picc. 82 a										16 26												17 26
Manchester Airport a										16 47												17 43
Liverpool Lime Street 91 a																						
Liverpool Lime Street d											15 34	15 47						16 16				
Liverpool South Pkwy 91 d											15 44											
Runcorn 91 d											15 52	16 03						16 32				
Manchester Picc. 84 d	14 55		15 05	15 15			15 27	15 35					15 55		16 05	16 15			16 27	16 35		
Stockport 84 d	15 04		15 13	15 22			15 36	15 42					16 03		16 13	16 23			16 36	16 42		
Wilmslow 84 d	15 12												16 11									
Holyhead 81 d						13 55																
Bangor (Gwynedd) 81 d						14 22																
Llandudno Junction 81 d						14 40																
Wrexham General 75 d																						
Chester 81 d						15 33																
Crewe 81,91 a	15 28					15 52			15 59		16 18	16 21	16 27					16 51			16 59	
Crewe d	15 30				15 37	15 54			16 01		16 19	16 23	16 30				16 37	16 54			17 01	
Macclesfield d			15 26				15 49	15 55							16 26				16 49	16 55		
Stoke-on-Trent 84 d			15 44	15 50	15 59		16 07	16 12							16 44	16 50	16 59		17 07	17 12		
Stafford a			16 00		16 18		16 24				16 39	16 42			17 00		17 18		17 24			
Stafford d			16 01		16 19		16 25				16 40	16 44			17 01		17 19		17 25			
Penkridge a											16 45											
Wolverhampton a			16 14				16 39		16 32		16 57				17 14				17 39		17 34	
BirminghamNewSt 68 a			16 33				16 57		17 06		17 15				17 32				17 57		18 05	
Birmingham International 68 a							17 13		17 19										18 13		18 19	
Coventry 68 a							17 24		17 29										18 24		18 30	
Lichfield Trent Valley a					16 35												17 35	17 26				
Tamworth Low Level a					16 42												17 42					
Nuneaton a					16 58												17 58					
Rugby 66 a					17 13												18 13					
Milton Keynes Central 66 a				16 50	18 04	17 03			17 58							17 49	19 04	18 04			18 58	
Watford Junction 66 a					18 34												19 34					
London Euston ⊖66 a	17 08	17 11		17 27	18 53	17 41		17 44	18 36			18 03	18 08	18 13		18 27	19 53	18 41		18 46	19 37	

A To Bristol Temple Meads

B To Bournemouth

Refer to Operator websites for full information about Sleeper Services. Contact details for train operators available at National Rail Enquiries

Table T065-R

Sundays
24 June to 9 September

Scotland to Manchester, West Midlands & London via the West Coast. North West England to West Midlands & London

		LM	VT	VT	VT	XC	VT	LM	XC	VT	VT	VT	TP	LM	VT	VT	VT	XC	VT	LM	XC	VT
		■	◇■	◇■	◇■	◇■	◇■	■	◇■	◇■	◇■	◇■	◇■	■	◇■	◇■	◇■	◇■	◇■	■	◇■	◇■
						A			B									C			D	
			🍽	🍽	🍽	🛒	🍽		🛒	🍽	🍽	🍽	🛒		🍽	🍽	🍽	🛒	🍽		🛒	🍽
Inverness 229	d																					
Aberdeen 229	d																					
Dundee 229	d																					
Perth 229	d																					
Fort William 400,227	d																					
Edinburgh ■ ⇌	d											14 51										
Haymarket ⇌	d											14 56										
Glasgow Central ■ 226,216,225	d				14 32								15 00				15 33					
Motherwell 226	d												15 24									
Carstairs 226,225	d																					
Lockerbie 225,226	d												16 14									
Carlisle ■ 216	a				15 47							16 02	16 34				16 47					
	d				15 49							16 07	16 36				16 49					
Penrith North Lakes	d											16 22	16 51				17 03					
Windermere 83	d																					
Oxenholme Lake District 83	d				16 23								17 14									
Barrow-in-Furness 82	d																					
Lancaster ■	d				16 38							16 57	17 29				17 38					
Blackpool North 97	d																					
Preston ■ 90	a				16 56							17 15	17 47				17 56					
Preston ■ 90	d				16 58							17 17	17 48				17 58					
Wigan North Western 90	d				17 09							17 29					18 09					
Warrington Bank Quay	d				17 20							17 40					18 20					
Bolton 82	a																					
Manchester Picc. ■ 82 ⇌	a												18 27									
Manchester Airport ✈⇌	a												18 47									
Liverpool Lime Street ■ 91	a																					
	d	16 34	16 47											17 34	17 47							
Liverpool South Pkwy ■ 91 ✈	d	16 44												17 44								
Runcorn 91	d	16 52	17 03											17 52	18 03							
Manchester Picc. ■ 84 ⇌	d			16 55		17 05	17 15		17 27		17 35					17 55		18 05	18 15		18 27	
Stockport 84	d			17 03		17 13	17 22		17 36		17 42					18 03		18 13	18 22		18 36	
Wilmslow 84	d			17 11												18 11						
Holyhead 81 ⛴	d																					
Bangor (Gwynedd) 81	d																					
Llandudno Junction 81	d																					
Wrexham General 75	d																					
Chester 81	d									17 35												18 35
Crewe ■ 81,91	a	17 18	17 21	17 27						17 53		17 59		18 18	18 21	18 27						18 53
	d	17 19	17 23	17 30				17 37		17 55		18 01		18 19	18 23	18 29				18 37		18 55
Macclesfield	d					17 26			17 49		17 55							18 26			18 49	
Stoke-on-Trent 84	d					17 45	17 50	17 59	18 07		18 12							18 45	18 51	18 59	19 07	
Stafford	a	17 39	17 42			18 01		18 18	18 24					18 39	18 42			19 01		19 18	19 24	
	d	17 40	17 44			18 02		18 19	18 25					18 40	18 44			19 02		19 22	19 25	
Penkridge	a	17 45												18 45								
Wolverhampton ■ ⇌	a	17 57				18 15			18 37			18 33		18 57				19 15			19 38	
BirminghamNewSt ■ 68 ⇌	a	18 15				18 33			18 57			19 06		19 15				19 33			19 57	
Birmingham International 68 ✈	a								19 13			19 19									20 13	
Coventry 68	a								19 24			19 30									20 24	
Lichfield Trent Valley	a							18 35												19 39		
Tamworth Low Level	a							18 42												19 45		
Nuneaton	a							18 58												20 01		
Rugby 66	a							19 13												20 16		
Milton Keynes Central 66	a						18 49	20 06		19 04		19 58							19 48	21 07		20 03
Watford Junction 66	a							20 35												21 39		
London Euston ■ ⊖66	a		19 03	19 06	19 10		19 27	20 54		19 42	19 46	20 37			20 04	20 07	20 12		20 27	21 58		20 41

A To Paignton
B To Bournemouth
C To Bristol Temple Meads
D To Southampton Central

Refer to Operator websites for full information about Sleeper Services. Contact details for train operators available at National Rail Enquiries

Table T065-R

Sundays
24 June to 9 September

Scotland to Manchester, West Midlands & London via the West Coast. North West England to West Midlands & London

		VT	VT	TP	NT	LM	VT	VT	VT	XC	VT	LM	VT	TP	XC	LM	VT	VT	XC	LM	VT	TP	AW
		◇■	◇■	◇■	◇	■	◇■	◇■	◇■	◇■	◇■	■	◇■	◇■	◇■	■	◇■	◇■	◇■	■	◇■	◇■	◇
					A					B					C				B	D			
		🍽	🍽	🛒	🛒		🍽	🍽	🍽	🛒	🍽		🍽	🛒	🛒		🍽	🍽			🍽	🛒	
Inverness 229	d																						
Aberdeen 229	d																						
Dundee 229	d																						
Perth 229	d																						
Fort William 400,227	d																						
Edinburgh ■ ⇌	d			16 14									16 51									18 14	
Haymarket ⇌	d			16u18									16 55									18u18	
Glasgow Central ■ 226,216,225	d								16 31					17 00							17 31		
Motherwell 226	d								16 53					17 24									
Carstairs 226,225	d																						
Lockerbie 225,226	d			17 12										18 13							18 32	19 12	
Carlisle ■ 216	a			17 32					17 49				18 05	18 34							18 50	19 32	
	d		17 05	17 35	17 48				17 51				18 07	18 35							18 52	19 35	
Penrith North Lakes	d			17 50					18 05					18 50							19 06	19 49	
Windermere 83	d																						
Oxenholme Lake District 83	d		17 44	18 14					18 28				18 42	19 14							19 29	20 13	
Barrow-in-Furness 82	d																						
Lancaster ■	d			18 29					18 43				18 57	19 29							19 44	20 28	
Blackpool North 97	d																						
Preston ■ 90	a		18 13	18 46	20 46				19 01				19 15	19 48							20 02	20 45	
Preston ■ 90	d		18 17	18 48					19 03				19 17	19 49							20 04	20 47	
Wigan North Western 90	d		18 28						19 14				19 28								20 15		
Warrington Bank Quay	d		18 39						19 25				19 39								20 26		
Bolton 82	a																						
Manchester Picc. ■ 82 ⇌	a			19 26										20 26								21 25	
Manchester Airport ✈⇌	a			19 47										20 47								21 42	
Liverpool Lime Street ■ 91	a																						
	d					18 34	18 47									19 34		19 47					
Liverpool South Pkwy ■ 91 ✈	d					18 44										19 44							
Runcorn 91	d					18 52	19 03									19 52		20 03					
Manchester Picc. ■ 84 ⇌	d	18 35						18 55		19 05	19 15				19 27		19 35		20 05				
Stockport 84	d	18 42						19 03		19 13	19 22				19 36		19 41		20 14				
Wilmslow 84	d							19 11															
Holyhead 81 ⛴	d																						18 25
Bangor (Gwynedd) 81	d																						19 04
Llandudno Junction 81	d																						19 24
Wrexham General 75	d																						
Chester 81	d																						20 27
Crewe ■ 81,91	a		18 58			19 17	19 21	19 27					19 59			20 17		20 22			20 45		20 48
	d		19 01			19 19	19 23	19 29				19 37	20 01			20 19		20 24		20 42	20 47		20 52
Macclesfield	d	18 55								19 26					19 49		19 54		20 27				
Stoke-on-Trent 84	d	19 12								19 45	19 50	19 59			20 06		20 11		20 45	21 07			
Stafford	a					19 39	19 42			20 01		20 18			20 24	20 38		20 42	21 01	21 27			21 13
	d					19 40	19 44			20 02		20 19			20 26	20 40		20 43	21 02	21 27			21 13
Penkridge	a					19 45										20 45				↦			
Wolverhampton ■ ⇌	a		19 34			19 57				20 15			20 33		20 38	20 57			21 15				21 29
BirminghamNewSt ■ 68 ⇌	a		20 06			20 15				20 33			20 51		20 57	21 15			21 33				21 53
Birmingham International 68 ✈	a		20 19												21 13								22 08
Coventry 68	a		20 30												21 23								
Lichfield Trent Valley	a	19 34										20 35											
Tamworth Low Level	a											20 42											
Nuneaton	a											20 58											
Rugby 66	a											21 13											
Milton Keynes Central 66	a		20 59								20 46	22 11						21 36			21 52		
Watford Junction 66	a											22 54									22s30		
London Euston ■ ⊖66	a	20 45	21 46				21 03	21 08	21 19		21 31	23 17					22 01	22 25			22 53		

A To Blackpool North
B To Bristol Temple Meads
C To Reading. 🛒 to BirminghamNewSt
D To Northampton

Refer to Operator websites for full information about Sleeper Services. Contact details for train operators available at National Rail Enquiries

Table T065-R

Sundays

24 June to 9 September

Scotland to Manchester, West Midlands & London via the West Coast. North West England to West Midlands & London

	LM	VT	LM	VT	VT	VT	XC	VT	TP	LM	VT	TP	NT	XC	CS	LM	CS	CS	CS
	■ A	◇■ 🍴	■	◇■ 🍴	◇■ 🍴	◇■ 🍴	◇■	◇■ 🍴	◇■ ☕	■	◇■ 🍴	◇■ ☕		◇■	R 🛏 ✕	■	R 🛏 ✕	R 🛏 ✕	R 🛏 ✕
Inverness 229 d																		20 26	
Aberdeen 229 d																			21 43
Dundee 229 d																			23u07
Perth 229 d																		23u06	
Fort William 400,227 d																	19 00		
Edinburgh ■ d								18 51				20 15							
Haymarket d								18 56				20u20							
Glasgow Central ■ 226,216,225 d						18 31			19 00		20 02				23 05				
Motherwell 226 d									19 25						23u30				
Carstairs 226,225 d															23u48				
Lockerbie 225,226 d									20 09		21 04	21 14							
Carlisle ■ 216 a						19 46		20 02	20 34		21 23	21 34							
d						19 48		20 07	20 36		21 25	21 36			01u45				
Penrith North Lakes d								20 22	20 51		21 40								
Windermere 83 d													21 44						
Oxenholme Lake District 83 d						20 23			21 15		22 04	22 12	22 16						
Barrow-in-Furness 82 d																			
Lancaster ■ d						20 37		20 57	21 31		22 19	22 27	22 35						
Blackpool North 97 d																			
Preston ■ 90 a						20 55		21 15	21 49		22 36	22 44	22 57				04s32	04s32	04s32
Preston ■ 90 d						20 57		21 17	21 51		22 39	22 46							
Wigan North Western 90 d						21 08		21 29			22 53								
Warrington Bank Quay d						21 19		21 39			23 04								
Bolton 82 a																			
Manchester Picc. ■ 82 a									22 27			23 27							
Manchester Airport a									22 44			23 44							
Liverpool Lime Street ■ 91 a																			
d			20 34		20 47					21 34						23 30			
Liverpool South Pkwy ■ 91 d			20 44							21 44						23 42			
Runcorn 91 d			20 52		21 03					21 52						23 52			
Manchester Picc. ■ 84 d		20 21		20 55			21 05							22 05					
Stockport 84 d		20 27		21 03			21 13							22 13					
Wilmslow 84 d																			
Holyhead 81 d																			
Bangor (Gwynedd) 81 d																			
Llandudno Junction 81 d																			
Wrexham General 75 d																			
Chester 81 d																			
Crewe ■ 81,91 a			21 17		21 22	21 39		21 59		22 17	23 22					00 20	05s36		05s36
d			21 19		21 24	21 41		22 01		22 19									
Macclesfield d		20 40		21 16			21 26							22 26					
Stoke-on-Trent 84 d	←	20 58		21 33			21 45							22 45					
Stafford a	21 27		21 39		21 42	22 00	22 04			22 39				23 01					
d	21 27		21 40		21 44	22 01	22 05			22 40				23 02					
Penkridge a			21 45							22 45									
Wolverhampton ■ a			21 57			22 14	22 18	22 32		22 57				23 15					
BirminghamNewSt ■ 68 a			22 15			22 33	22 36	22 53		23 16				23 33					
Birmingham International 68 a																			
Coventry 68 a																			
Lichfield Trent Valley a	21 44				22 00														
Tamworth Low Level a	21 50				22 06														
Nuneaton a	22 06				22 18														
Rugby 66 a	22 21				22 31														
Milton Keynes Central 66 a		22 03		22 46	23 04														
Watford Junction 66 a				23s28	23s34										06s42				
London Euston ■ 66 a		22 56		23 46	23 52										07 07		07 49		07 49

A From Crewe to Northampton

Refer to Operator websites for full information about Sleeper Services. Contact details for train operators available at National Rail Enquiries

Table T065-R

Sundays

16 September to 2 December

Scotland to Manchester, West Midlands & London via the West Coast. North West England to West Midlands & London

	VT	VT	VT	XC	VT	LM	VT	VT	XC	VT	LM	LM	VT	VT	VT	XC	VT	VT	VT	VT	LM	VT
	◇■ 🍴	◇■ 🍴	◇■ 🍴	◇■ A ☕	◇■ 🍴	■	◇■ 🍴	◇■ 🍴	◇■ A ☕	◇■ 🍴	■	■	◇■ 🍴	◇■ 🍴	◇■ 🍴	◇■ A ☕	◇■ 🍴	◇■ 🍴	◇■ 🍴	◇■ 🍴	■	◇■ 🍴
Inverness 229 d																						
Aberdeen 229 d																						
Dundee 229 d																						
Perth 229 d																						
Fort William 400,227 d																						
Edinburgh ■ d																						
Haymarket d																						
Glasgow Central ■ 226,216,225 d																						
Motherwell 226 d																						
Carstairs 226,225 d																						
Lockerbie 225,226 d																						
Carlisle ■ 216 a																						
d																						
Penrith North Lakes d																						
Windermere 83 d																						
Oxenholme Lake District 83 d																						
Barrow-in-Furness 82 d																						
Lancaster ■ d																						
Blackpool North 97 d																						
Preston ■ 90 a																						
Preston ■ 90 d							09 00						10 00		10 17				10 58			
Wigan North Western 90 d							09 11						10 12		10 28				11 09			
Warrington Bank Quay d							09 22						10 22		10 39				11 20			
Bolton 82 a																						
Manchester Picc. ■ 82 a																						
Manchester Airport a																						
Liverpool Lime Street ■ 91 a																						
d			08 18		08 38					09 38								10 38				
Liverpool South Pkwy ■ 91 d																						
Runcorn 91 d			08 35		08 54					09 54								10 54				
Manchester Picc. ■ 84 d	08 05	08 20		08 27				09 20	09 27					10 20		10 26	10 35			11 15		
Stockport 84 d	08 14	08 28		08 36				09 28	09 36					10 29		10 36	10 46			11 24		
Wilmslow 84 d	08 22			08 43										10 37								
Holyhead 81 d																						
Bangor (Gwynedd) 81 d																						
Llandudno Junction 81 d																						
Wrexham General 75 d																						
Chester 81 d																						11 28
Crewe ■ 81,91 a	08 39		08 52	09 01	09 11		09 41			10 12			10 41	10 53	10 59			11 12				11 47
d	08 43		08 53	09 05	09 13	09 32	09 43			10 14	10 21	10 37	10 43	10 55	11 02			11 14			11 37	11 49
Macclesfield d		08 41						09 40	09 49							10 49	10 57					
Stoke-on-Trent 84 d		08 57				09 53		10 00	10 07			10 59				11 07	11 15			11 52	11 59	
Stafford a	09 01			09 25	09 31	10 15			10 25	10 32	10 41	11 18				11 26		11 35			12 18	
d	09 03			09 26	09 33	10 19			10 25	10 34	10 42	11 19				11 27		11 36			12 19	
Penkridge a											10 48											
Wolverhampton ■ a				09 40					10 38		11 01				11 31	11 41						
BirminghamNewSt ■ 68 a				09 57					10 57		11 19				11 50	11 58						
Birmingham International 68 a				10 13					11 13							12 13						
Coventry 68 a				10 24					11 24							12 24						
Lichfield Trent Valley a			09 24			10 35						11 35									12 35	
Tamworth Low Level a						10 42						11 42									12 42	
Nuneaton a					09 55	10 58				10 56		11 58						11 58			12 58	12 31
Rugby 66 a						11 17	10 32					12 13	11 31								13 13	
Milton Keynes Central 66 a			10 19			12 04	11 07	11 16		11 45		13 04	12 07				12 21			12 50	14 04	13 04
Watford Junction 66 a	10s34	10s39			11s16	12 40	11s43					13 34		12s37				12s52			14 34	
London Euston ■ 66 a	10 55	10 59	11 05		11 34	13 01	12 03	12 06		12 29		13 53	12 44	12 54			12 57	13 10	13 21	13 28	14 53	13 43

A To Bournemouth

Refer to Operator websites for full information about Sleeper Services. Contact details for train operators available at National Rail Enquiries

Table T065-R

Sundays

16 September to 2 December

Scotland to Manchester, West Midlands & London via the West Coast. North West England to West Midlands & London

	VT	TP	XC	LM	VT		VT	VT	VT	VT	LM	VT	XC	VT	VT		TP	LM	VT	VT	VT	XC	VT	LM
	◇1		◇1	1	◇1		◇1	◇1	◇1	◇1	1	◇1	◇1	◇1	◇1		◇1	1	◇1	◇1	◇1	◇1	◇1	1
			A										A									B		
	⊡		✕		⊡		⊡	⊡	⊡	⊡		⊡	✕	⊡	⊡		✕		⊡	⊡	⊡	✕	⊡	
Inverness 229 d																								
Aberdeen 229 d																								
Dundee 229 d																								
Perth 229 d																								
Fort William 400,227 d																								
Edinburgh d		09 16															10 17							
Haymarket d		09 20																						
Glasgow Central 226,216,225 d									09 38												10 38			
Motherwell 226 d																					10 54			
Carstairs 226,225 d																								
Lockerbie 225,226 d		10 14															11 13							
Carlisle 216 a		10 34							10 48								11 33				11 51			
d		10 36							10 51								11 35				11 53			
Penrith North Lakes d									11 05								11 49				12 07			
Windermere 83 d																								
Oxenholme Lake District 83 d		11 11							11 28								12 13				12 31			
Barrow-in-Furness 82 d																								
Lancaster d		11 26							11 43						11 58		12 28				12 45			
Blackpool North 97 d																								
Preston 90 a		11 41							12 01						12 15		12 45				13 03			
Preston 90 d	11 17	11 43							12 03						12 17		12 47				13 05			
Wigan North Western 90 d	11 28								12 14						12 28						13 16			
Warrington Bank Quay d	11 40								12 25						12 39						13 27			
Bolton 82 a																								
Manchester Picc. 82 a		12 21															13 27							
Manchester Airport ✈ a		12 40															13 47							
Liverpool Lime Street 91 a																								
d				11 34			11 47											12 34	12 47					
Liverpool South Pkwy 91 ✈ d				11 44														12 44						
Runcorn 91 d				11 52			12 03											12 52	13 03					
Manchester Picc. 84 d			11 27		11 35			11 55		12 15			12 26	12 35						12 55		13 05	13 15	
Stockport 84 d			11 36		11 44			12 05		12 23			12 35	12 43						13 05		13 13	13 23	
Wilmslow 84 d								12 12												13 13				
Holyhead 81 ⛴ d												10 55												
Bangor (Gwynedd) 81 d												11 22												
Llandudno Junction 81 d												11 40												
Wrexham General 75 d																								
Chester 81 d												12 33												
Crewe 81,91 a	11 59			12 18			12 21	12 28				12 53			12 59			13 18	13 21	13 29				
d	12 02			12 19			12 23	12 30			12 37	12 55			13 01			13 19	13 23	13 30				13 37
Macclesfield d			11 49		11 57								12 49	12 57								13 26		
Stoke-on-Trent 84 d			12 07		12 14					12 50	12 59		13 07	13 14								13 45	13 51	13 59
Stafford a			12 24	12 39			12 42				13 18		13 24					13 39	13 42			14 01		14 18
d			12 25	12 40			12 44				13 19		13 25					13 40	13 44			14 02		14 19
Penkridge a				12 45														13 45						
Wolverhampton a	12 32		12 38	12 56									13 37		13 32			13 57				14 15		
BirminghamNewSt 68 a	12 50		12 57	13 15									13 57		14 06			14 15				14 33		
Birmingham International 68 ✈ a			13 13										14 13		14 19									
Coventry 68 a			13 24										14 24		14 30									
Lichfield Trent Valley a											13 35													14 35
Tamworth Low Level a											13 42													14 42
Nuneaton a											13 58													14 58
Rugby 66 a											14 13													15 13
Milton Keynes Central 66 a										13 47	15 04	14 03			14 58								14 49	16 04
Watford Junction 66 a											15 34													16 34
London Euston ⊖66 a					13 47		14 03	14 10	14 15	14 28	15 53	14 41		14 48	15 37				15 03	15 07	15 18		15 26	16 53

A To Bournemouth

B To Paignton

Refer to Operator websites for full information about Sleeper Services. Contact details for train operators available at National Rail Enquiries

Table T065-R

Sundays

16 September to 2 December

Scotland to Manchester, West Midlands & London via the West Coast. North West England to West Midlands & London

	XC		VT	VT	VT	VT	TP	LM	VT	VT	VT		XC	VT	LM	VT	VT	XC	VT	VT	TP		LM	VT
	◇1		◇1	◇1	◇1	◇1	◇1	1	◇1	◇1	◇1		◇1	◇1	1	◇1	◇1	◇1	◇1	◇1	◇1		1	◇1
	A												B					A						
	✕		⊡	⊡	⊡	⊡	✕		⊡	⊡	⊡		✕	⊡		⊡	⊡	✕	⊡	⊡	✕			⊡
Inverness 229 d																								
Aberdeen 229 d																								
Dundee 229 d																								
Perth 229 d																								
Fort William 400,227 d																								
Edinburgh d						10 51															12 12			
Haymarket d						10 55															12u17			
Glasgow Central 226,216,225 d							11 08				11 38									11 55				
Motherwell 226 d							11 25																	
Carstairs 226,225 d																								
Lockerbie 225,226 d							12 11														13 11			
Carlisle 216 a						12 05	12 32				12 47									13 06	13 31			
d						12 07	12 34				12 49									13 07	13 33			
Penrith North Lakes d							12 49														13 48			
Windermere 83 d																								
Oxenholme Lake District 83 d						12 43	13 13				13 23										14 12			
Barrow-in-Furness 82 d																								
Lancaster d						12 57	13 28				13 38									13 56	14 27			
Blackpool North 97 d																								
Preston 90 a						13 15	13 47				13 56									14 13	14 45			
Preston 90 d						13 17	13 48				13 58									14 17	14 46			
Wigan North Western 90 d						13 28					14 09									14 28				
Warrington Bank Quay d						13 39					14 20									14 39				
Bolton 82 a																								
Manchester Picc. 82 a							14 27														15 26			
Manchester Airport ✈ a							14 47														15 47			
Liverpool Lime Street 91 a																								
d								13 34	13 47														14 34	14 47
Liverpool South Pkwy 91 ✈ d								13 44															14 44	
Runcorn 91 d								13 52	14 03														14 52	15 03
Manchester Picc. 84 d	13 27				13 35					13 55			14 05	14 15				14 27	14 35					
Stockport 84 d	13 36				13 42					14 05			14 13	14 22				14 36	14 42					
Wilmslow 84 d										14 12														
Holyhead 81 ⛴ d				11 50												12 50								
Bangor (Gwynedd) 81 d				12 17												13 18								
Llandudno Junction 81 d				12 35												13 36								
Wrexham General 75 d																								
Chester 81 d			13 30	13 30												14 33	14 33							
Crewe 81,91 a			13 50	13 50		13 59		14 17	14 21	14 28						14 54	14 54			14 58			15 18	15 21
d			13 52	13 53		14 01		14 19	14 23	14 30					14 32	14 55	14 56			15 01			15 19	15 23
Macclesfield d	13 49				13 55								14 26					14 49	14 55					
Stoke-on-Trent 84 d	14 07				14 12								14 44	14 50	14 53			15 07	15 12					
Stafford a	14 24							14 39	14 42				15 00		15 14			15 23					15 40	15 42
d	14 25							14 40	14 44				15 01		15 19			15 25					15 40	15 44
Penkridge a								14 45															15 46	
Wolverhampton a	14 39					14 32		14 57					15 14					15 38		15 34			15 57	
BirminghamNewSt 68 a	14 57					15 06		15 15					15 33					15 57		16 06			16 15	
Birmingham International 68 ✈ a	15 13					15 19												16 13		16 19				
Coventry 68 a	15 24					15 30												16 24		16 30				
Lichfield Trent Valley a															15 35									
Tamworth Low Level a															15 42									
Nuneaton a			14 32	14 32											15 58									
Rugby 66 a															16 13									
Milton Keynes Central 66 a			15 03	15 03		15 58								15 48	17 04	16 03	16 03			16 58				
Watford Junction 66 a															17 34									
London Euston ⊖66 a			15 42	15 42	15 46	16 37			16 03	16 06	16 12			16 26	17 53	16 41	16 41		16 46	17 36				17 04

A To Bournemouth

B To Bristol Temple Meads

Refer to Operator websites for full information about Sleeper Services. Contact details for train operators available at National Rail Enquiries

Sundays
16 September to 2 December

Scotland to Manchester, West Midlands & London via the West Coast. North West England to West Midlands & London

	VT	VT	XC	VT	LM	VT	XC	VT	VT	TP	LM	VT	VT	VT	XC	VT	LM	VT	XC	VT	VT	TP
	◇1	◇1	◇1	◇1	1	◇1	◇1	◇1	◇1	◇1	1	◇1	◇1	◇1	◇1	◇1	1	◇1	◇1	◇1	◇1	◇1
			A				B								A				B			
Inverness 229 d																						
Aberdeen 229 d																						
Dundee 229 d																						
Perth 229 d																						
Fort William 400,227 d																						
Edinburgh 10 d									12 51													14 12
Haymarket d									12 55													14u16
Glasgow Central 15 226,216,225 d		12 38								13 14				13 38							13 55	
Motherwell 226 d										13 30												
Carstairs 226,225 d																						
Lockerbie 225,226 d										14 15												15 10
Carlisle 8 216 a		13 47							14 04	14 35				14 47							15 08	15 30
Carlisle d		13 49							14 07	14 37				14 49							15 11	15 33
Penrith North Lakes d									14 22	14 51												15 48
Windermere 83 d																						
Oxenholme Lake District 83 d		14 23								15 15				15 23							15 45	16 12
Barrow-in-Furness 82 d																						
Lancaster 6 d		14 38							14 57	15 29				15 38								16 27
Blackpool North 97 d																						
Preston 8 90 a		14 56							15 15	15 47				15 56							16 14	16 44
Preston 8 90 d		14 58							15 17	15 48				15 58							16 17	16 46
Wigan North Western 90 d		15 09							15 28					16 09							16 29	
Warrington Bank Quay d		15 20							15 39					16 20							16 40	
Bolton 82 a																						
Manchester Picc. 10 82 a										16 26												17 26
Manchester Airport a										16 47												17 43
Liverpool Lime Street 10 91 a																						
Liverpool Lime Street d											15 34	15 47						16 16				
Liverpool South Pkwy 7 91 d											15 44											
Runcorn 91 d											15 52	16 03						16 32				
Manchester Picc. 10 84 d	14 55		15 05	15 15			15 27	15 35					15 55		16 05	16 15			16 27	16 35		
Stockport 84 d	15 04		15 13	15 22			15 36	15 42					16 03		16 13	16 23			16 36	16 42		
Wilmslow 84 d	15 12												16 11									
Holyhead 81 d						13 55																
Bangor (Gwynedd) 81 d						14 22																
Llandudno Junction 81 d						14 40																
Wrexham General 75 d																						
Chester 81 d						15 33																
Crewe 10 81,91 a	15 28					15 52			15 59		16 18	16 21	16 27					16 51			16 59	
Crewe d	15 30				15 37	15 54			16 01		16 19	16 23	16 30				16 37	16 54			17 01	
Macclesfield d			15 26				15 49	15 55							16 26				16 49	16 55		
Stoke-on-Trent 84 d			15 44	15 50	15 59		16 07	16 12							16 44	16 50	16 59		17 07	17 12		
Stafford a			16 00		16 18		16 24				16 39	16 42			17 00		17 18		17 24			
Stafford d			16 01		16 19		16 25				16 40	16 44			17 01		17 19		17 25			
Penkridge a											16 45											
Wolverhampton 7 a			16 14				16 39		16 32		16 57				17 14				17 39		17 32	
BirminghamNewSt 12 68 a			16 33				16 57		17 06		17 15				17 32				17 57		18 05	
Birmingham International 68 a							17 13		17 19										18 13		18 19	
Coventry 68 a							17 24		17 29										18 24		18 30	
Lichfield Trent Valley a					16 35												17 35	17 26				
Tamworth Low Level a					16 42												17 42					
Nuneaton a					16 58												17 58					
Rugby 66 a					17 13												18 13					
Milton Keynes Central 66 a				16 50	18 04	17 03			17 58							17 49	19 04	18 04			18 58	
Watford Junction 66 a					18 34												19 34					
London Euston 15 ⊖66 a	17 08	17 11		17 27	18 53	17 41		17 44	18 36			18 03	18 08	18 13		18 27	19 53	18 41		18 46	19 37	

A To Bristol Temple Meads
B To Bournemouth

Refer to Operator websites for full information about Sleeper Services. Contact details for train operators available at National Rail Enquiries

Table T065-R

Sundays
16 September to 2 December

Scotland to Manchester, West Midlands & London via the West Coast. North West England to West Midlands & London

	LM	VT	VT	VT	XC	VT	LM	XC	VT	VT	VT	TP	LM	VT	VT	VT	XC	VT	LM	XC	VT
	1	◇1	◇1	◇1	◇1	◇1	1	◇1	◇1	◇1	◇1	◇1	1	◇1	◇1	◇1	◇1	◇1	1	◇1	◇1
					A			B									C			D	
Inverness 229 d																					
Aberdeen 229 d																					
Dundee 229 d																					
Perth 229 d																					
Fort William 400,227 d																					
Edinburgh 10 d											14 51										
Haymarket d											14 56										
Glasgow Central 15 226,216,225 d				14 38								15 14				15 38					
Motherwell 226 d												15 30									
Carstairs 226,225 d																					
Lockerbie 225,226 d												16 14									
Carlisle 8 216 a				15 47							16 02	16 35				16 47					
Carlisle d				15 49							16 07	16 36				16 49					
Penrith North Lakes d											16 22	16 51				17 03					
Windermere 83 d																					
Oxenholme Lake District 83 d				16 23								17 14									
Barrow-in-Furness 82 d																					
Lancaster 6 d				16 38							16 57	17 29				17 38					
Blackpool North 97 d																					
Preston 8 90 a				16 56							17 15	17 47				17 56					
Preston 8 90 d				16 58							17 17	17 48				17 58					
Wigan North Western 90 d				17 09							17 29					18 09					
Warrington Bank Quay d				17 20							17 40					18 20					
Bolton 82 a																					
Manchester Picc. 10 82 a												18 27									
Manchester Airport a												18 47									
Liverpool Lime Street 10 91 a																					
Liverpool Lime Street d	16 34	16 47											17 34	17 47							
Liverpool South Pkwy 7 91 d	16 44												17 44								
Runcorn 91 d	16 52	17 03											17 52	18 03							
Manchester Picc. 10 84 d			16 55		17 05	17 15		17 27		17 35					17 55		18 05	18 15		18 27	
Stockport 84 d			17 03		17 13	17 22		17 36		17 42					18 03		18 13	18 22		18 36	
Wilmslow 84 d			17 11												18 11						
Holyhead 81 d																					
Bangor (Gwynedd) 81 d																					
Llandudno Junction 81 d																					
Wrexham General 75 d																					
Chester 81 d									17 35												18 35
Crewe 10 81,91 a	17 18	17 21	17 27						17 53		17 59		18 18	18 21	18 27						18 53
Crewe d	17 19	17 23	17 30				17 37		17 55		18 01		18 19	18 23	18 29				18 37		18 55
Macclesfield d					17 26			17 49		17 55							18 26			18 49	
Stoke-on-Trent 84 d					17 45	17 50	17 59	18 07		18 12							18 45	18 51	18 59	19 07	
Stafford a	17 39	17 42			18 01		18 18	18 24					18 39	18 42			19 01		19 18	19 24	
Stafford d	17 40	17 44			18 02		18 19	18 25					18 40	18 44			19 02		19 22	19 25	
Penkridge a	17 45												18 45								
Wolverhampton 7 a	17 57				18 15			18 37			18 33		18 57				19 15			19 38	
BirminghamNewSt 12 68 a	18 15				18 33			18 57			19 06		19 15				19 33			19 57	
Birmingham International 68 a								19 13			19 19									20 13	
Coventry 68 a								19 24			19 30									20 24	
Lichfield Trent Valley a							18 35												19 39		
Tamworth Low Level a							18 42												19 45		
Nuneaton a							18 58												20 01		
Rugby 66 a							19 13												20 16		
Milton Keynes Central 66 a						18 49	20 06		19 04		19 58							19 48	21 07		20 03
Watford Junction 66 a							20 35												21 39		
London Euston 15 ⊖66 a		19 03	19 06	19 10		19 27	20 54		19 42	19 46	20 37			20 04	20 07	20 12		20 27	21 58		20 41

A To Plymouth
B To Bournemouth
C To Bristol Temple Meads
D To Southampton Central

Refer to Operator websites for full information about Sleeper Services. Contact details for train operators available at National Rail Enquiries

Table T065-R

Sundays

16 September to 2 December

Scotland to Manchester, West Midlands & London via the West Coast. North West England to West Midlands & London

	VT	VT	TP	NT	LM	VT	VT	VT	XC	VT	LM	VT	TP	XC	LM	VT	VT	XC	LM	VT	TP	AW
	◇	◇	◇	◇ A		◇	◇	◇	◇ B	◇		◇	◇	◇ C		◇	◇	◇ B	D	◇	◇	◇
Inverness 229 d																						
Aberdeen 229 d																						
Dundee 229 d																						
Perth 229 d																						
Fort William 400,227 d																						
Edinburgh d			16 14									16 51									18 14	
Haymarket d			16u18									16 55									18u18	
Glasgow Central 226,216,225 d		15 57						16 38					17 15							17 38		
Motherwell 226 d								16 53					17 30									
Carstairs 226,225 d																						
Lockerbie 225,226 d			17 12										18 14							18 32	19 12	
Carlisle 216 a		17 08	17 32					17 49				18 05	18 34							18 50	19 32	
Carlisle d		17 10	17 35	17 48				17 51				18 07	18 36							18 52	19 35	
Penrith North Lakes d			17 50					18 05					18 50							19 06	19 49	
Windermere 83 d																						
Oxenholme Lake District 83 d		17 44	18 14					18 28				18 42	19 14							19 29	20 13	
Barrow-in-Furness 82 d																						
Lancaster d			18 29					18 43				18 57	19 29							19 44	20 28	
Blackpool North 97 d																						
Preston 90 a		18 13	18 46	20 46				19 01				19 15	19 47							20 02	20 45	
Preston 90 d		18 17	18 48					19 03				19 17	19 48							20 04	20 47	
Wigan North Western 90 d		18 28						19 14				19 28								20 15		
Warrington Bank Quay d		18 39						19 25				19 39								20 26		
Bolton 82 a																						
Manchester Picc. 82 a			19 26										20 26								21 25	
Manchester Airport a			19 47										20 47								21 42	
Liverpool Lime Street 91 a																						
Liverpool Lime Street d					18 34	18 47									19 34		19 47					
Liverpool South Pkwy 91 d					18 44										19 44							
Runcorn 91 d					18 52	19 03									19 52		20 03					
Manchester Picc. 84 d	18 35						18 55		19 05	19 15				19 27		19 35		20 05				
Stockport 84 d	18 42						19 03		19 13	19 22				19 36		19 41		20 14				
Wilmslow 84 d							19 11															
Holyhead 81 d																						18 25
Bangor (Gwynedd) 81 d																						19 04
Llandudno Junction 81 d																						19 24
Wrexham General 75 d																						
Chester 81 d																						20 27
Crewe 81,91 a		18 58			19 17	19 21	19 27					19 59			20 17		20 22			20 45		20 48
Crewe d		19 01			19 19	19 23	19 29				19 37	20 01			20 19		20 24		20 42	20 47		20 52
Macclesfield d	18 55								19 26					19 49		19 54		20 27				
Stoke-on-Trent 84 d	19 12								19 45	19 50	19 59			20 06		20 11		20 45	21 07			
Stafford a					19 39	19 42			20 01		20 18			20 24	20 38		20 42	21 01	21 27			21 13
Stafford d					19 40	19 44			20 02		20 19			20 26	20 40		20 43	21 02	21 27			21 13
Penkridge a					19 45										20 45				→			
Wolverhampton a		19 34			19 57				20 15			20 33		20 38	20 57			21 15				21 29
BirminghamNewSt 68 a		20 06			20 15				20 33			20 51		20 57	21 15			21 33				21 53
Birmingham International 68 a		20 19												21 13								22 08
Coventry 68 a		20 30												21 23								
Lichfield Trent Valley a	19 34										20 35											
Tamworth Low Level a											20 42											
Nuneaton a											20 58											
Rugby 66 a											21 13											
Milton Keynes Central 66 a		20 59								20 46	22 11						21 36			21 52		
Watford Junction 66 a											22 54									22s30		
London Euston ⊖66 a	20 45	21 46				21 03	21 08	21 19		21 31	23 17					22 01	22 25			22 53		

A To Blackpool North
B To Bristol Temple Meads
C To Reading. to BirminghamNewSt
D To Northampton

Refer to Operator websites for full information about Sleeper Services. Contact details for train operators available at National Rail Enquiries

Table T065-R

Sundays

16 September to 2 December

Scotland to Manchester, West Midlands & London via the West Coast. North West England to West Midlands & London

	LM	VT	LM	VT	VT	VT	XC	VT	TP	LM	VT	TP	NT	XC	CS	CS	LM	CS	CS	CS
	A	◇		◇	◇	◇	◇	◇	◇		◇	◇		◇						
Inverness 229 d																			20 26	
Aberdeen 229 d																				21 43
Dundee 229 d																				23u07
Perth 229 d																			23u06	
Fort William 400,227 d																		19 00		
Edinburgh d								18 51				20 15				23 15				
Haymarket d								18 56				20u20								
Glasgow Central 226,216,225 d						18 37			19 14		20 08				23 15					
Motherwell 226 d									19 30						23u30					
Carstairs 226,225 d															23u48					
Lockerbie 225,226 d									20 15		21 04	21 14								
Carlisle 216 a						19 46		20 02	20 36		21 23	21 34								
Carlisle d						19 48		20 07	20 36		21 25	21 36			01u45					
Penrith North Lakes d								20 22	20 51		21 40									
Windermere 83 d													21 44							
Oxenholme Lake District 83 d						20 23			21 16		22 04	22 12	22 16							
Barrow-in-Furness 82 d																				
Lancaster d						20 37		20 57	21 31		22 19	22 27	22 35							
Blackpool North 97 d																				
Preston 90 a						20 55		21 15	21 50		22 36	22 44	22 57					04s32	04s32	04s32
Preston 90 d						20 57		21 17	21 51		22 39	22 46								
Wigan North Western 90 d						21 08		21 29			22 53									
Warrington Bank Quay d						21 19		21 39			23 04									
Bolton 82 a									22s10											
Manchester Picc. 82 a									22 26			23 27								
Manchester Airport a									22 44			23 44								
Liverpool Lime Street 91 a																				
Liverpool Lime Street d			20 34		20 47					21 34							23 30			
Liverpool South Pkwy 91 d			20 44							21 44							23 42			
Runcorn 91 d			20 52		21 03					21 52							23 52			
Manchester Picc. 84 d		20 21		20 55			21 05							22 05						
Stockport 84 d		20 27		21 03			21 13							22 13						
Wilmslow 84 d																				
Holyhead 81 d																				
Bangor (Gwynedd) 81 d																				
Llandudno Junction 81 d																				
Wrexham General 75 d																				
Chester 81 d																				
Crewe 81,91 a			21 17		21 22	21 39		21 59		22 17	23 22						00 20	05s36		05s36
Crewe d			21 19		21 24	21 41		22 01		22 19										
Macclesfield d		20 40		21 16			21 26							22 26						
Stoke-on-Trent 84 d	←	20 58		21 33			21 45							22 45						
Stafford a	21 27		21 39		21 42	22 00	22 04			22 39				23 01						
Stafford d	21 27		21 40		21 44	22 01	22 05			22 40				23 02						
Penkridge a			21 45							22 45										
Wolverhampton a			21 57			22 14	22 18	22 32		22 57				23 15						
BirminghamNewSt 68 a			22 15			22 33	22 36	22 53		23 16				23 33						
Birmingham International 68 a																				
Coventry 68 a																				
Lichfield Trent Valley a	21 44				22 00															
Tamworth Low Level a	21 50				22 06															
Nuneaton a	22 06				22 18															
Rugby 66 a	22 21				22 31															
Milton Keynes Central 66 a		22 03		22 46	23 04															
Watford Junction 66 a				23s28	23s34										06s42					
London Euston ⊖66 a		22 56		23 46	23 52										07 07			07 49		07 49

A From Crewe to Northampton

Refer to Operator websites for full information about Sleeper Services. Contact details for train operators available at National Rail Enquiries

21 May to 7 December

London - Watford Junction, Milton Keynes, Northampton and West Midlands

Miles	Miles	Miles		LM	VT	LM	LM	VT	LM	LM	LM	LM	LM	LM	LM	LM	SN	VT	VT	LM	VT	SN
				MO	MO	MX	MX	MX	MO	MX	MX	MO	MX	MO								
				A	A	A	A	A	A	A								B	C	D	E	F
0	0	—	London Euston ⊖60 d								00 05	00 05	00 34	00 34	01 34			05 27	05 31	05 34	06 16	
—	—	0	East Croydon 176 d																			
—	—	7¾	Clapham Junction 176 d														05 03					05 32
—	—	8¾	Imperial Wharf 176 d														05 07					05 37
—	—	9¾	West Brompton ⊖176 d														05 10					05 40
—	—	11¼	Kensington (Olympia) ⊖176 d														05 14					05 44
—	—	12½	Shepherd's Bush ⊖176 d														05 17					05 47
8	—	16¾	Wembley Central ⊖60,176 d										00 44	00 44	01 45							06 02
11½	—	—	Harrow & Wealdstone ⊖60 d								00 17	00 17	00 49	00 49	01 50		05 33			05 46		06 07
16	—	—	Bushey 60 d								00 22	00s22	00 54	00s54								
17½	17½	—	Watford Junction 60 a								00 25	00 25	00 56	00 57	01 56		05 40			05 54		06 14
—	—	—	d							00 04	00 25	00 25	00 57	00 57	01 57			05u45	05u50	05 55		06 14
21	—	—	Kings Langley d							00 09			01 02	01 02						05 59		
23	—	—	Apsley d						00 03	00 12			01 05	01 05						06 03		
24½	—	—	Hemel Hempstead d						00 06	00 15	00 32	00 32	01 08	01 08	02 04					06 06		06 22
28	—	—	Berkhamsted d						00 11	00 20	00 37	00 37	01 13	01 13	02 09					06 10		06 26
31¾	—	—	Tring d						00 16	00 25	00 42	00 42	01 18	01 18	02 13					06 18		06 33
36	—	—	Cheddington d						00 21		00 47	00 47	01 24	01 24						06 23		
40¼	—	—	Leighton Buzzard d			00 01	00 07		00 28	00 35	00 54	00 54	01 30	01 30	02 22					06 28		06 42
46¾	—	—	Bletchley d			00 08	00 14		00 35	00 42	01 01	01 01	01 37	01 37	02 29					06 35		06 49
49¾	49¾	—	Milton Keynes Central a			00 16	00 22		00 43	00 50	01 09	01 09	01 45	01 46	02 37			06 13	06 22	06 40	06 46	06 55
—	—	—	d	00 06	00 12	00 17	00 22	00 28	00 43		01 09	01 09	01 46	01 46		05 37		06 15	06 23	06 40		
52½	52½	—	Wolverton d	00 10		00 21	00 26		00 47		01 13	01 13	01 49	01 49		05 40				06 44		
65¾	—	—	Northampton 68 a	00 24		00 34	00 40		01 00		01 26	01 26	02 03	02 03		05 53				06 56		
—	—	—	d													05 55				06 58		
75¼	—	—	Long Buckby 68 a													06 06				→		
84½	82½	—	Rugby 68 a		00s46			01 00								06 17			06 45			
96	—	—	Coventry 68 a		00s58			01 13								06 29						
—	—	—	Nuneaton 65 a															06 44				
106¾	—	—	Birmingham International 68 a		01s09			01 24								06 45						
115¼	—	—	Birmingham New Street 68 a		01s22			01 36								07 01						
120½	—	—	Sandwell & Dudley 68 a																			
128	—	—	Wolverhampton 68 a		01 42			02 05														

	LM	VT	LM	SN	VT	VT	VT	LM	VT	LM	SN	VT	LM	VT	LM	SN	LM	VT	VT	VT	LM	LM
			A		G	H		I	E			J		E		K			E	C	I	
London Euston ⊖60 d	06 04	06 20			06 43	06 46	07 03	06 24	06 55	06 34		07 10	06 54	07 20	07 13		07 05	07 23	07 35	07 43	07 46	07 24
East Croydon 176 d																						
Clapham Junction 176 d				05 53							06 20					06 40						
Imperial Wharf 176 d				05 58							06 24					06 44						
West Brompton ⊖176 d				06 01							06 27					06 47						
Kensington (Olympia) ⊖176 d				06 05							06 31					06 51						
Shepherd's Bush ⊖176 d				06 08							06 34					06 54						
Wembley Central ⊖60,176 d				06 24							06 47					07 07						
Harrow & Wealdstone ⊖60 d	06 16			06 29						06 46						07 12	07 18					
Bushey 60 d																						
Watford Junction 60 a	06 24			06 36				06 40		06 53	06 57		07 09			07 19	07 24					07 41
d	06 25	06u34						06 41		06 54			07 11			07 20	07 25	07u37				07 41
Kings Langley d	06 29									06 59							07 29					
Apsley d	06 33									07 02							07 33					
Hemel Hempstead d	06 36							06 48		07 05			07 18			07 27	07 36					07 48
Berkhamsted d	06 40							06 53		07 10			07 23			07 32	07 41					07 53
Tring d	06a47							06 59		07 15						07 39	07a48					07 59
Cheddington d								07 04		07 20												08 04
Leighton Buzzard d								07 09		07 25			07 36		07 42	07 51						08 09
Bletchley d								07 16		07 32			07 43		07 50	07 58						08 19
Milton Keynes Central a					07 13			07 22	07 25	07 37		07 40	07 48	07 50	07 54	08 03			08 05	08 13	08 18	08 24
d					07 13			07 24		07 37					07 54					08 13	08 19	
Wolverton d			←					07 28		07 41					07 58							
Northampton 68 a			06 56					07 40		07 53					08 10							
d			06 58					07 45		07 55					08 13							
Long Buckby 68 a			07 09							08 06					08 24							
Rugby 68 a		07 12	07 20			07 39	07 51	08 04		08 17					08 35						08 41	
Coventry 68 a		07 22	07 31		07 42		08 02			08 29					08 46			08 22		08 42		
Nuneaton 65 a								08 16													08 53	
Birmingham International 68 a		07 33	07 47		07 53		08 13			08 45					09 04			08 33		08 53		
Birmingham New Street 68 a		07 45	08 05		08 09		08 26			09 02					09 18			08 45		09 05		
Sandwell & Dudley 68 a					08 24															09 24		
Wolverhampton 68 a					08 37															09 37		

A From London Euston
B To Liverpool Lime Street
C To Glasgow Central
D To Birmingham New Street
E To Manchester Piccadilly
F From Balham
G To Edinburgh
H To Blackpool North
I To Crewe
J To Chester
K From Selhurst

Table T066-F

Mondays to Fridays

21 May to 7 December

London - Watford Junction, Milton Keynes, Northampton and West Midlands

	LM	VT	LM	VT	VT	LM	VT	LM	SN	LM	VT	VT	LM	LM	LM	SN	VT	VT	LM	VT	LM	VT
				A	B		C					D	E				F			B		C
London Euston ⊖60 d	07 34	08 03	07 49	08 07	08 10	07 54	08 20	08 13		08 07	08 23	08 43	08 46	08 24	08 34		08 53	09 03	08 49	09 10	08 54	09 20
East Croydon 176 d									07 10							07 40						
Clapham Junction 176 d									07 40							08 18						
Imperial Wharf 176 d									07 44							08 23						
West Brompton ⊖176 d									07 47							08 26						
Kensington (Olympia) ⊖176 d									07 51							08 29						
Shepherd's Bush ⊖176 d									07 53							08 32						
Wembley Central ⊖60,176 d									08 08							08 47						
Harrow & Wealdstone ⊖60 d	07 46								08 13	08 21				08 37	08 46	08 53						
Bushey 60 d										08 26					08 52							
Watford Junction 60 a	07 52		08 03			08 11			08 20	08 29				08 43	08 54	09 01			09 03		09 09	
d	07 54		08 03			08 11			08 20	08 29	08u37			08 43	08 55				09 03		09 11	
Kings Langley d	07 58									08 34					08 59							
Apsley d	08 02									08 37					09 03							
Hemel Hempstead d	08 05					08 18			08 28	08 40				08 51	09 06						09 18	
Berkhamsted d	08 10					08 23			08 32	08 45				08 56	09 10						09 23	
Tring d	08a17								08 38	08a52				09 02	09a17							
Cheddington d														09 07								
Leighton Buzzard d						08 36		08 42	08 46					09 12							09 36	
Bletchley d						08 43		08 50	08 54					09 19					09 24		09 43	
Milton Keynes Central a			08 24	08 37	08 42	08 48	08 50	08 54	09 00			09 13	09 18	09 24					09 29	09 40	09 48	09 50
d			08 25			08 49		08 54				09 13	09 19						09 29		09 49	
Wolverton d						08 53		08 58													09 53	
Northampton 68 a			08 40			09 05		09 11											09 44		10 06	
d			08 55			09 16													09 55			
Long Buckby 68 a			09 06			09 27													10 06			
Rugby 68 a		08 51	09 17			09 37							09 41				09 44	09 51	10 17			
Coventry 68 a		09 02	09 29			09 49					09 22	09 42						10 02	10 29			
Nuneaton 65 a													09 53									
Birmingham International 68 a		09 13	09 45			10 04					09 33	09 53						10 13	10 45			
Birmingham New Street 68 a		09 26	10 01			10 17					09 45	10 04						10 27	11 01			
Sandwell & Dudley 68 a												10 24										
Wolverhampton 68 a												10 37										

	LM	SN	LM	VT	VT	LM	LM	LM	VT	LM	VT	LM	VT	VT	LM	SN	LM	VT	VT	VT	LM
					G	E					H		C	F					I	D	E
London Euston ⊖60 d	09 13		09 05	09 23	09 43	09 46	09 24	09 34	10 03	09 49	10 10	09 54	10 20	10 36	10 13		10 04	10 23	10 23	10 43	10 46
East Croydon 176 d		08 11														09 10					
Clapham Junction 176 d		08 40														09 39					
Imperial Wharf 176 d		08 44														09 44					
West Brompton ⊖176 d		08 47														09 47					
Kensington (Olympia) ⊖176 d		08 51														09 50					
Shepherd's Bush ⊖176 d		08 53														09 53					
Wembley Central ⊖60,176 d		09 08														10 08	10 14				
Harrow & Wealdstone ⊖60 d		09 13	09 17					09 46								10 13	10 19				
Bushey 60 d			09 22					09 52									10 24				
Watford Junction 60 a		09 20	09 25				09 39	09 54		10 03		10 09				10 20	10 26				
d		09 20	09 26	09u37			09 41	09 55		10 03		10 11				10 20	10 27	10u37	10u37		
Kings Langley d			09 30					09 59									10 31				
Apsley d			09 34					10 03									10 35				
Hemel Hempstead d		09 28	09 37				09 48	10 06				10 18				10 28	10 38				
Berkhamsted d		09 32	09 41				09 53	10 10				10 23				10 32	10 43				
Tring d		09 39	09a49				09 59	10a17								10 39	10a49				
Cheddington d							10 04														
Leighton Buzzard d	09 42	09 48					10 09					10 36			10 42	10 48					
Bletchley d	09 50	09 55					10 16			10 24		10 43			10 50	10 57					
Milton Keynes Central a	09 54	10 01			10 13	10 18	10 21			10 29	10 40	10 48	10 50		10 54	11 02				11 13	11 18
d	09 54				10 13	10 19				10 29		10 49			10 54					11 13	11 19
Wolverton d	09 58											10 53			10 58						
Northampton 68 a	10 10									10 45		11 06			11 12						
d	10 16									10 55					11 16						
Long Buckby 68 a	10 27									11 06					11 27						
Rugby 68 a	10 37					10 41			10 51	11 17				11 24	11 37						11 41
Coventry 68 a	10 49			10 22	10 42				11 02	11 29					11 49			11 22	11 22	11 42	
Nuneaton 65 a						10 53															11 53
Birmingham International 68 a	11 04			10 33	10 53				11 13	11 45					12 04			11 33	11 33	11 53	
Birmingham New Street 68 a	11 17			10 45	11 04				11 25	12 02					12 17			11 45	11 45	12 05	
Sandwell & Dudley 68 a					11 24															12 24	
Wolverhampton 68 a					11 37														12 10	12 37	

A To Liverpool Lime Street
B To Holyhead
C To Manchester Piccadilly
D To Edinburgh
E To Crewe
F To Blackpool North
G To Glasgow Central
H To Chester
I To Shrewsbury

London - Watford Junction, Milton Keynes, Northampton and West Midlands

	LM	LM	VT	LM	VT	LM	VT	LM	SN	LM	VT	VT	LM	LM	LM	VT	LM	VT	LM	VT	LM	SN
	■	■	◇■ ⊠	■	◇■ A ⊠	■	◇■ B ⊠	■	■	■	◇■ ⊠	◇■ C ⊠	■ D	■	■	◇■ ⊠	■	◇■ A ⊠	■	◇■ B ⊠	■	■
London Euston ⊖60 d	10 24	10 34	11 03	10 49	11 10	10 54	11 20	11 13		11 04	11 23	11 43	11 46	11 24	11 34	12 03	11 49	12 10	11 54	12 20	12 13	
East Croydon 176 d									10 10													11 10
Clapham Junction 176 d									10 41													11 39
Imperial Wharf 176 d									10 45													11 44
West Brompton ⊖176 d									10 48													11 47
Kensington (Olympia) ⊖176 d									10 51													11 50
Shepherd's Bush ⊖176 d									10 54													11 53
Wembley Central ⊖60,176 d									11 09	11 14												12 09
Harrow & Wealdstone ⊖60 d		10 46							11 14	11 19					11 46							12 14
Bushey 60 d		10 52								11 24					11 52							
Watford Junction 60 a	10 39	10 54		11 03		11 09			11 21	11 26				11 39	11 54		12 03		12 09			12 21
d	10 41	10 55		11 03		11 11			11 21	11 27	11u37			11 41	11 55		12 03		12 11			12 21
Kings Langley d		10 59								11 31					11 59							
Apsley d		11 03								11 35					12 03							
Hemel Hempstead d	10 48	11 06				11 18			11 29	11 38				11 48	12 06				12 18			12 29
Berkhamsted d	10 53	11 10				11 23			11 33	11 43				11 53	12 10				12 23			12 33
Tring d	10 59	11a17							11 39	11a49				11 59	12a17							12 39
Cheddington d	11 04													12 04								
Leighton Buzzard d	11 09					11 36		11 42	11 48					12 09					12 36		12 42	12 48
Bletchley d	11 16					11 43		11 50	11 55					12 16					12 43		12 50	12 55
Milton Keynes Central a	11 21			11 24	11 40	11 48	11 50	11 54	12 00			12 13	12 18	12 21			12 24	12 40	12 48	12 50	12 54	13 00
d				11 25		11 49		11 54				12 13	12 19				12 25	12 41	12 49		12 54	
Wolverton d						11 53		11 58											12 53		12 58	
Northampton 68 a				11 40		12 06		12 11									12 40		13 06		13 11	
d				11 55				12 16									12 55				13 16	
Long Buckby 68 a				12 06				12 27									13 06				13 27	
Rugby 68 a			11 51	12 17				12 37					12 41			12 51	13 17	13 03			13 37	
Coventry 68 a			12 02	12 29				12 49			12 22	12 42				13 02	13 29				13 49	
Nuneaton 65 a													12 53									
Birmingham International 68 a			12 13	12 45				13 04			12 33	12 53				13 13	13 45				14 04	
Birmingham New Street 68 a			12 26	13 01				13 17			12 45	13 05				13 26	14 02				14 17	
Sandwell & Dudley 68 a												13 24										
Wolverhampton 68 a												13 37										

	LM	VT	VT	LM	LM	LM	VT	LM	VT	LM	VT	LM	SN	LM	VT	VT	LM	LM	LM	VT	LM
	■	◇■ ⊠	◇■ E ⊠	■ D	■	■	◇■ ☕	■	◇■ A ☕	■	◇■ B ☕	■	■	■	◇■ ☕	◇■ C ☕	■ D	■	■	◇■ ☕	■
London Euston ⊖60 d	12 04	12 23	12 43	12 46	12 24	12 34	13 03	12 49	13 10	12 54	13 20	13 13		13 04	13 23	13 43	13 46	13 24	13 34	14 03	13 49
East Croydon 176 d													12 10								
Clapham Junction 176 d													12 39								
Imperial Wharf 176 d													12 44								
West Brompton ⊖176 d													12 47								
Kensington (Olympia) ⊖176 d													12 50								
Shepherd's Bush ⊖176 d													12 53								
Wembley Central ⊖60,176 d	12 14												13 09	13 14							
Harrow & Wealdstone ⊖60 d	12 19					12 46							13 14	13 19					13 46		
Bushey 60 d	12 24					12 52								13 24					13 52		
Watford Junction 60 a	12 26				12 40	12 54		13 03		13 09			13 21	13 26				13 42	13 54		14 03
d	12 27	12u37			12 41	12 55		13 03		13 11			13 21	13 27	13u37			13 43	13 55		14 03
Kings Langley d	12 31					12 59								13 31					13 59		
Apsley d	12 35					13 03								13 35					14 03		
Hemel Hempstead d	12 38				12 48	13 06				13 18			13 29	13 38				13 51	14 06		
Berkhamsted d	12 43				12 53	13 10				13 23			13 33	13 43				13 56	14 10		
Tring d	12a49				12 59	13a17							13 39	13a49				14 01	14a17		
Cheddington d					13 04													14 07			
Leighton Buzzard d					13 09					13 36		13 42	13 48					14 12			
Bletchley d					13 16					13 43		13 50	13 55					14 19			
Milton Keynes Central a			13 13	13 18	13 21			13 24	13 40	13 48	13 50	13 54	14 00			14 13	14 18	14 24			14 24
d			13 13	13 19				13 25		13 49		13 54				14 13	14 19				14 25
Wolverton d										13 53		13 58									
Northampton 68 a								13 40		14 06		14 10									14 40
d								13 55				14 16									14 55
Long Buckby 68 a								14 06				14 27									15 06
Rugby 68 a				13 41			13 51	14 17				14 37					14 41			14 51	15 17
Coventry 68 a		13 22	13 42				14 02	14 29				14 49			14 22	14 42				15 02	15 29
Nuneaton 65 a				13 53													14 53				
Birmingham International 68 a		13 33	13 53				14 13	14 45				15 04			14 33	14 53				15 13	15 45
Birmingham New Street 68 a		13 45	14 05				14 26	15 01				15 17			14 45	15 05				15 26	16 01
Sandwell & Dudley 68 a			14 24													15 24					
Wolverhampton 68 a			14 37													15 37					

A To Chester
B To Manchester Piccadilly
C To Glasgow Central
D To Crewe
E To Edinburgh

Table T066-F

Mondays to Fridays
21 May to 7 December

London - Watford Junction, Milton Keynes, Northampton and West Midlands

	VT	LM	VT	LM	SN	SN	LM	VT	VT	LM	LM	LM	VT	LM	VT	LM	VT	LM	SN	LM	VT	VT
					MWFO	TThO																
	◇■ A ☕	■	◇■ B ☕	■	■	■ C	■	◇■ ☕	■ D ☕	■ E	■	■	◇■ ☕	■	◇■ A ☕	■	◇■ B ☕	■	■	■	◇■ ☕	■ F ☕
London Euston ⊖60 d	14 10	13 54	14 20	14 13			14 04	14 23	14 43	14 46	14 24	14 34	15 03	14 49	15 10	14 54	15 20	15 13		15 04	15 23	15 43
East Croydon 176 d					13 10														14 10			
Clapham Junction 176 d					13 39	13 39													14 40			
Imperial Wharf 176 d					13 44	13 44													14 45			
West Brompton ⊖176 d					13 47	13 47													14 48			
Kensington (Olympia) ⊖176 d					13 50	13 50													14 51			
Shepherd's Bush ⊖176 d					13 53	13 53													14 54			
Wembley Central ⊖60,176 d					14 09	14 09	14 14												15 09	15 14		
Harrow & Wealdstone ⊖60 d					14 14	14 14	14 19					14 46							15 14	15 19		
Bushey 60 d							14 24					14 52								15 24		
Watford Junction 60 a		14 10			14 21	14 21	14 26				14 40	14 54		15 03		15 09			15 21	15 26		
d		14 11			14 21	14 21	14 27	14u37			14 41	14 55		15 03		15 11			15 21	15 27	15u37	
Kings Langley d							14 31					14 59								15 31		
Apsley d							14 35					15 03								15 35		
Hemel Hempstead d		14 18			14 29	14 29	14 38				14 48	15 06				15 18			15 29	15 38		
Berkhamsted d		14 23			14 33	14 33	14 43				14 53	15 10				15 23			15 33	15 43		
Tring d					14 39	14 39	14a49				14 59	15a17							15 39	15a49		
Cheddington d											15 04											
Leighton Buzzard d		14 36		14 42	14 48	14 48					15 09					15 36		15 42	15 48			
Bletchley d		14 43		14 50	14 55	14 55					15 16					15 43		15 50	15 55			
Milton Keynes Central a	14 40	14 48	14 50	14 54	15 00	15 00			15 13	15 18	15 22			15 24	15 40	15 48	15 50	15 54	16 00			16 13
d		14 49		14 54					15 13	15 19				15 25		15 49		15 54				16 13
Wolverton d		14 53		14 58												15 53		15 58				
Northampton 68 a		15 06		15 10										15 44		16 06		16 10				
d				15 16										15 55				16 16				
Long Buckby 68 a				15 27										16 06				16 27				
Rugby 68 a				15 37						15 41			15 51	16 17				16 37				
Coventry 68 a				15 49				15 22	15 42				16 02	16 29				16 49			16 22	16 42
Nuneaton 65 a										15 53												
Birmingham International 68 a				16 04				15 33	15 53				16 13	16 45				17 04			16 33	16 53
Birmingham New Street 68 a				16 17				15 45	16 05				16 27	17 02				17 17			16 45	17 05
Sandwell & Dudley 68 a									16 24													17 24
Wolverhampton 68 a									16 37													17 37

	LM	LM	LM	VT	LM	SN	VT	LM	VT	LM	SN	LM	VT	VT	VT	LM	LM	LM	VT	LM	LM	VT
	■ E	■	■	◇■ ☕	■	■	◇■ G ☕	■	◇■ B ☕	■	■	■	◇■ ☕	◇■ ☕	◇■ D ☕	■ E	■	■	◇■ ⊠	■	■	◇■ A ⊠
London Euston ⊖60 d	15 46	15 24	15 34	16 03	15 49		16 33	15 54	16 20	16 13		16 05	16 23	16 43	16 43	16 46	16 30	16 34	17 03	16 50	16 54	17 10
East Croydon 176 d											15 10											
Clapham Junction 176 d						15 19					15 39											
Imperial Wharf 176 d						15 24					15 44											
West Brompton ⊖176 d						15 27					15 47											
Kensington (Olympia) ⊖176 d						15 30					15 51											
Shepherd's Bush ⊖176 d						15 33					15 53											
Wembley Central ⊖60,176 d						15 52					16 08											
Harrow & Wealdstone ⊖60 d			15 46			15 57					16 13	16 18						16 46			17 06	
Bushey 60 d			15 52									16 23						16 52			17 11	
Watford Junction 60 a		15 39	15 54		16 03	16 05		16 09			16 20	16 26					16 46	16 54			17 14	
d		15 41	15 55		16 03			16 11			16 20	16 26	16u37				16 47	16 55			17 14	
Kings Langley d			15 59									16 31						16 59				
Apsley d			16 03									16 34						17 03			17 20	
Hemel Hempstead d		15 48	16 06					16 18			16 28	16 37					16 54	17 06			17 23	
Berkhamsted d		15 53	16 10					16 23			16 32	16 42					16 59	17 10			17 28	
Tring d		15 59	16a17								16 38	16a49					17 05	17a17			17a37	
Cheddington d		16 04															17 10					
Leighton Buzzard d		16 09						16 36		16 42	16 48						17 15			17 20		
Bletchley d		16 16						16 43		16 50	16 55						17 22			17 27		
Milton Keynes Central a	16 18	16 23			16 24			16 48	16 50	16 54	17 00			17 13	17 13	17 18	17 29			17 32		
d	16 19				16 25			16 49		16 54				17 13	17 13	17 19				17 32		17u41
Wolverton d								16 53		16 58										17 36		
Northampton 68 a					16 40			17 06		17 14										17 48		
d					16 55			17 16												17 55		
Long Buckby 68 a					17 06			17 27												18 06		
Rugby 68 a	16 41			16 51	17 17		17 22	17 37								17 41			17 51	18 17		
Coventry 68 a				17 02	17 29			17 49					17 22	17 42	17 42				18 02	18 30		
Nuneaton 65 a	16 53															17 59						18 11
Birmingham International 68 a				17 13	17 45			18 04					17 33	17 53	17 53				18 13	18 46		
Birmingham New Street 68 a				17 26	18 01			18 17					17 45	18 05	18 05				18 27	19 01		
Sandwell & Dudley 68 a															18 24							
Wolverhampton 68 a															18 37							

A To Chester
B To Manchester Piccadilly
C From Selhurst
D To Edinburgh
E To Crewe
F To Glasgow Central
G To Blackpool North

Table T066-F

Mondays to Fridays

21 May to 7 December

London - Watford Junction, Milton Keynes, Northampton and West Midlands

	VT A	LM	LM	SN	LM	LM	VT	VT B	LM C	VT	LM	LM	LM	LM	LM	VT D	VT A	LM	LM	LM	SN
London Euston ⊖60 d	17 33	17 13	17 16		17 05	17 12	17 23	17 43	17 46	18 03	17 24	17 30	17 34	17 41	17 49	18 10	18 33	18 13	17 52	18 16	
East Croydon 176 d				16 10																	17 10
Clapham Junction 176 d				16 39																	17 39
Imperial Wharf 176 d				16 44																	17 44
West Brompton ⊖176 d				16 47																	17 47
Kensington (Olympia) ⊖176 d				16 51																	17 51
Shepherd's Bush ⊖176 d				16 53																	17 53
Wembley Central ⊖60,176 d				17 07																	18 09
Harrow & Wealdstone ⊖60 d				17 12	17 18	17 24								17 53					18 04		18 14
Bushey 60 d						17 30							17 50	17 59							
Watford Junction 60 a				17 19	17 24	17 32					17 43	17 48	17 52	18 04					18 10		18 21
d				17 20	17 25	17 33	17u37				17 43	17 48	17 54						18 11		18 21
Kings Langley d					17 30	17 38							17 59								
Apsley d						17 42						17 55									
Hemel Hempstead d				17 27	17 35						17 51	17 58	18 04						18 19		18 29
Berkhamsted d				17 32	17 40						17 56		18 09						18 24		18 33
Tring d				17 39	17 46	17a51						18 06	18a16								18 39
Cheddington d					17 51							18 11									
Leighton Buzzard d			17 44	17 48							18 09				18 20					18 44	18 48
Bletchley d				17 55	18 01						18 16	18 21							18 41		18 55
Milton Keynes Central a		17 46	17 53	18 00	18 07				18 18		18 21	18 27			18 30			18 45	18 46	18 53	19 00
d		17 48	17 54					18u13	18 19		18 22				18 31	18u41		18 46	18 46	18 54	
Wolverton d			17 58								18 25				18 35				18 50	18 58	
Northampton 68 a		18 10	18 15								18 38				18 48			19 00	19 05	19 18	
d		18 19									18 39				18 57			19 20		19 31	
Long Buckby 68 a		18 30									18 50				19 08			19 31		19 42	
Rugby 68 a	18 21	18 41							18 41	18 51	19 01				19 19		19 22	19 42		19 56	
Coventry 68 a		18 52					18 22	18 42		19 02	19 11				19 30			19 53		20 08	
Nuneaton 65 a									18 59							19 12					
Birmingham International 68 ✈ a		19 07					18 33	18 53		19 13	19 29				19 47			20 08		20 28	
Birmingham New Street 68 a		19 20					18 45	19 05		19 26	19 42				20 03			20 20		20 42	
Sandwell & Dudley 68 a								19 24													
Wolverhampton 68 a								19 37		19 59											

	LM	LM	VT	VT C	VT FO E	LM	VT	LM C	LM	LM	LM	LM	VT ThFO F	VT MTWO F	VT MTWO G	LM	LM	SN	LM	VT	VT C	LM C
London Euston ⊖60 d	18 05	18 12	18 23	18 43	18 46	18 21	19 03	18 49	18 30	18 34	18 41	18 52	19 10	19 10	19 20	18 54	19 13		19 05	19 23	19 43	19 46
East Croydon 176 d																		18 10				
Clapham Junction 176 d																		18 39				
Imperial Wharf 176 d																		18 44				
West Brompton ⊖176 d																		18 47				
Kensington (Olympia) ⊖176 d																		18 51				
Shepherd's Bush ⊖176 d																		18 53				
Wembley Central ⊖60,176 d																		19 09				
Harrow & Wealdstone ⊖60 d	18 18					18 34				18 46						19 06		19 14	19 18			
Bushey 60 d		18 28								18 51	18 56								19 23			
Watford Junction 60 a	18 24	18 30				18 40			18 46	18 54	18 59					19 12		19 21	19 26			
d	18 26	18 32	18u37			18 41			18 47	18 55	19 00					19 13		19 21	19 26	19u37		
Kings Langley d	18 31					18 46					19 04								19 31			
Apsley d	18 35								18 53		19 08								19 35			
Hemel Hempstead d		18 39				18 51				19 04	19 11					19 20		19 29	19 37			
Berkhamsted d		18 45							19 00		19 16					19 25		19 33	19 42			
Tring d	18 44	18a52				18 59				19 13	19a23					19 31		19 39	19a49			
Cheddington d	18 49								19 09	19 18												
Leighton Buzzard d	18 54					19 07				19 24		19 20				19 39	19 42	19 48				
Bletchley d	19 01								19 18	19a34		19 27				19 46		19 55				
Milton Keynes Central a	19 06			19 13	19 18	19 21		19 22	19 24			19 32		19 40	19 50	19 52	19 55	20 00			20 13	20 18
d	19 07			19 13	19 19			19 23	19 27			19 32	19u41	19 41			19 56				20 13	20 19
Wolverton d	19 11								19 31			19 36					19 58					
Northampton 68 a	19 25							19 38	19 43			19 53					20 11					
d								19 47				19 55					20 19					
Long Buckby 68 a												20 06					20 30					
Rugby 68 a					19 40		19 51	20 06				20 17					20 40					20 41
Coventry 68 a			19 22	19 42			20 02					20 29					20 52			20 22	20 42	
Nuneaton 65 a								20 18					20 11	20 11								20 53
Birmingham International 68 ✈ a			19 33	19 53			20 13					20 45					21 07			20 33	20 53	
Birmingham New Street 68 a			19 45	20 06			20 27					21 02					21 20			20 45	21 04	
Sandwell & Dudley 68 a			19 58	20 24																20 58	21 24	
Wolverhampton 68 a			20 11	20 37																21 10	21 37	

A To Liverpool Lime Street
B To Glasgow Central
C To Crewe
D To Wrexham General
E To Preston
F To Chester
G To Manchester Piccadilly

Table T066-F

Mondays to Fridays

21 May to 7 December

London - Watford Junction, Milton Keynes, Northampton and West Midlands

	LM	LM	VT	LM	VT A	LM	LM	SN	LM	VT B	VT	VT	LM C	LM	LM	LM C	VT D	VT	VT B	LM	LM
London Euston ⊖60 d	19 24	19 34	20 03	19 49	20 10	19 54	20 13		20 05	20 07	20 23	20 43	20 46	20 24	20 34	20 49	21 00	21 03	21 07	20 54	21 13
East Croydon 176 d								19 10													
Clapham Junction 176 d								19 40													
Imperial Wharf 176 d								19 45													
West Brompton ⊖176 d								19 48													
Kensington (Olympia) ⊖176 d								19 51													
Shepherd's Bush ⊖176 d								19 54													
Wembley Central ⊖60,176 d								20 08													
Harrow & Wealdstone ⊖60 d		19 46						20 13	20 18						20 48						
Bushey 60 d		19 52							20 23						20 53						
Watford Junction 60 a	19 40	19 54				20 09		20 20	20 25					20 42	20 55					21 11	
d	19 43	19 55				20 11		20 20	20 26		20u37			20 43	20 56					21 12	
Kings Langley d		19 59							20 31						21 01						
Apsley d		20 03							20 35						21 05						
Hemel Hempstead d	19 51	20 06				20 18		20 28	20 37					20 51	21 07					21 19	
Berkhamsted d	19 56	20 10				20 23		20 33	20 42					20 56	21 13					21 24	
Tring d	20 02	20a17						20 39	20a49					21 02	21a19						
Cheddington d	20 07													21 07							
Leighton Buzzard d	20 12			20 18		20 36	20 42	20 48						21 12		21 18				21 37	21 44
Bletchley d	20 19					20 43	20 49	20 55						21 19						21 44	21 52
Milton Keynes Central a	20 24			20 28	20 40	20 48	20 54	21 00				21 13	21 18	21 24		21 28	21 30	21 34	21 38	21 49	21 56
d				20 29		20 49	20 54					21 13	21 19			21 29		21 35	21 39	21 50	21 57
Wolverton d				20 33		20 53	20 58									21 33				21 54	22 01
Northampton 68 a				20 45		21 06	21 11									21 46				22 07	22 15
d				20 55			21 16									21 55					22 19
Long Buckby 68 a				21 06			21 27									22 06					22 30
Rugby 68 a			20 51	21 17			21 38						21 41			22 17		21 56			22 41
Coventry 68 a			21 02	21 29			21 49				21 24	21 42				→		22 07			22 52
Nuneaton 65 a										21 02			21 57						22 07		
Birmingham International 68 ✈ a			21 13	21 45			22 04				21 34	21 53						22 18			23 10
Birmingham New Street 68 a			21 26	22 02			22 18				21 46	22 05						22 30			23 22
Sandwell & Dudley 68 a											21 59	22 16						22 41			
Wolverhampton 68 a			21 57								22 10	22 28						22 53			

	SN	VT E	LM F	LM	LM	LM	VT	LM G	VT C	LM H	LM	SN	LM	LM	VT	LM	LM	SN I	LM	VT FX	VT FO	LM
London Euston ⊖60 d		21 10		21 05	21 24	21 34	21 43	21 49	22 00		21 54		22 07	22 24	22 30	22 44	23 04		23 24	23 30	23 30	23 44
East Croydon 176 d	20 10											21 10										
Clapham Junction 176 d	20 36											21 36						22 36				
Imperial Wharf 176 d	20 41											21 41						22 41				
West Brompton ⊖176 d	20 44											21 44						22 44				
Kensington (Olympia) ⊖176 d	20 47											21 47						22 47				
Shepherd's Bush ⊖176 d	20 50											21 50						22 50				
Wembley Central ⊖60,176 d	21 08																					
Harrow & Wealdstone ⊖60 d	21 13			21 18		21 46					22 06	22 16	22 20			22 59	23 20	23 24				23 58
Bushey 60 d				21 23		21 52					22 12		22 25				23 25					
Watford Junction 60 a	21 20			21 26	21 40	21 54					22 14	22 23	22 28	22 39		23 05	23 28	23 32	23 39			00 04
d	21 20	21u25		21 26	21 41	21 55	21u58				22 15		22 28	22 41	22u45	23 06	23 28		23 41			00 04
Kings Langley d				21 31		22 00							22 33			23 10	23 33					00 09
Apsley d				21 34		22 04							22 37			23 14	23 36					00 12
Hemel Hempstead d	21 28			21 37	21 48	22 07					22 22		22 39	22 48		23 17	23 39		23 48			00 15
Berkhamsted d	21 32			21 42	21 53	22 12					22 29		22 44	22 53		23 22	23 44		23 53			00 20
Tring d	21 39			21 48		22 18					22 35		22 49			23 26	23 49					00 25
Cheddington d				21 53							22 40		22 54				23 54					
Leighton Buzzard d	21 50			21 58	22 06	22 25		22 18			22 47		23 00	23 07		23 35	00 01		00 07			00 35
Bletchley d	21 58			22a06	22 14	22a35					22 54		23 07	23 14		23 42	00 08		00 14			00 42
Milton Keynes Central a	22 05				22 19		22 17	22 32	22 39		23 02		23 15	23 22	23 28	23 50	00 16		00 22	00 27	00 27	00 50
d							22 17	22 32	22 40		23 02			23 23	23 29		00 17		00 22	00 28	00 28	
Wolverton d								22 36		←	23 06			23 27			00 21		00 26			
Northampton 68 a								22 50		22 50	23 20			23 40			00 34		00 40			
d								22 55		22 55												
Long Buckby 68 a			←					→		23 06												
Rugby 68 a		22 03	22 17						23 02	23 17					23 58					01 00	01 05	
Coventry 68 a			22 29				22 46			23 29					00 10					01 13	01 18	
Nuneaton 65 a									23 13													
Birmingham International 68 ✈ a			22 45				23 00			23 47					00 21					01 24	01 29	
Birmingham New Street 68 a			23 02				23 16			00 04					00 33					01 36	01 41	
Sandwell & Dudley 68 a			23 20				23 33															
Wolverhampton 68 a			23 35				23 46								01 02					02 05	02 10	

A To Chester
B To Liverpool Lime Street
C To Crewe
D To Manchester Piccadilly
E To Preston
F From London Euston to Crewe
G To Birmingham New Street
H From London Euston
I From Selhurst

Table T066-F

Saturdays

26 May to 8 December

London - Watford Junction, Milton Keynes, Northampton and West Midlands

	LM A	LM A	VT A	LM A	LM	LM	LM	SN	LM		LM	VT B	SN C	VT	VT	LM D	SN	VT E	VT E		SN	VT E	LM F	VT
London Euston ⊖60 d					00 05	00 34	01 34				05 34	06 05		06 23	07 03	06 24		06 55	07 20			07 35	07 05	07 23
East Croydon 176 d																					06 10			
Clapham Junction 176 d								05 07					05 39				06 09				06 40			
Imperial Wharf 176 d								05 12					05 43				06 14				06 45			
West Brompton ⊖176 d								05 15					05 46				06 17				06 48			
Kensington (Olympia) ⊖176 d								05 18					05 50				06 20				06 51			
Shepherd's Bush ⊖176 d								05 21					05 53				06 23				06 54			
Wembley Central ⊖60,176 d						00 44	01 45						06 07				06 38				07 09			
Harrow & Wealdstone ⊖60 d					00 17	00 49	01 50	05 40			05 46		06 12								07 14		07 18	
Bushey 60 d					00 22	00 54																	07 24	
Watford Junction 60 a					00 25	00 56	01 56	05 47			05 52		06 19			06 39	06 49				07 21		07 26	
d				00 04	00 25	00 57	01 57				05 53	06u20	06 20	06u37		06 41					07 21		07 27	07u37
Kings Langley d				00 09		01 02					05 57												07 31	
Apsley d				00 12		01 05					06 01												07 35	
Hemel Hempstead d				00 15	00 32	01 08	02 04				06 04		06 27			06 48					07 29		07 38	
Berkhamsted d				00 20	00 37	01 13	02 09				06 09		06 32			06 53					07 33		07 43	
Tring d				00 25	00 42	01 18	02 13				06 15		06 38			06 59					07 39		07 49	
Cheddington d					00 47	01 24					06 20					07 04							07 54	
Leighton Buzzard d	00 01	00 07		00 35	00 54	01 30	02 22				06 25		06 47			07 09					07 48		07 59	
Bletchley d	00 08	00 14		00 42	01 01	01 37	02 29		05 22		06 32		06 55			07 19					07 55		08 06	
Milton Keynes Central 10 a	00 16	00 22		00 50	01 09	01 45	02 37		05 28		06 37	06 39	07 00			07 24		07 25	07 50		08 00	08 05	08 11	
d	00 17	00 22	00 28		01 09	01 46			05 37		06 37	06 41				07 24							08 11	
Wolverton d	00 21	00 26			01 13	01 49			05 40		06 41					07 28							08 15	
Northampton 68 a	00 34	00 40			01 26	02 03			05 53		06 53					07 41							08 28	
d									05 55		06 55					07 45							08 37	
Long Buckby 68 a									06 06		07 06												→	
Rugby 68 a			01 05						06 17		07 17	07 02			07 51	08 04								
Coventry 68 a			01 18						06 29		07 29			07 22	08 02									08 22
Nuneaton 65 a																08 16								
Birmingham International 68 a			01 29						06 45		07 45			07 33	08 13									08 33
Birmingham New Street 12 68 a			01 41						07 01		08 01			07 45	08 26									08 45
Sandwell & Dudley 68 a																								
Wolverhampton 7 68 a			02 10																					

	VT B	LM D	LM	LM	VT		LM A	LM	VT G	LM	VT E	SN	LM	VT	VT H		LM D	LM	LM	VT I	VT	LM	VT J	LM
London Euston ⊖60 d	07 43	07 46	07 24	07 35	08 03			07 49	08 10	07 54	08 20		08 05	08 23	08 43		08 46	08 24	08 34	08 53	09 03	08 49	09 10	08 54
East Croydon 176 d												07 10												
Clapham Junction 176 d												07 40												
Imperial Wharf 176 d												07 45												
West Brompton ⊖176 d												07 48												
Kensington (Olympia) ⊖176 d												07 51												
Shepherd's Bush ⊖176 d												07 54												
Wembley Central ⊖60,176 d												08 09												
Harrow & Wealdstone ⊖60 d				07 46								08 14	08 18						08 46					
Bushey 60 d													08 24						08 52					
Watford Junction 60 a			07 39	07 53				08 03		08 09		08 21	08 26					08 39	08 54			09 03		09 09
d			07 41	07 55				08 03		08 11		08 21	08 27	08u37				08 41	08 55			09 03		09 11
Kings Langley d				07 59									08 31						08 59					
Apsley d				08 03									08 35						09 03					
Hemel Hempstead d			07 48	08 06						08 18		08 29	08 38					08 48	09 06					09 18
Berkhamsted d			07 53	08 10						08 23		08 33	08 43					08 53	09 10					09 23
Tring d			07 59	08a17								08 39	08a49					08 59	09a17					
Cheddington d			08 04															09 04						
Leighton Buzzard d			08 09							08 36		08 48						09 09						09 36
Bletchley d			08 19							08 43		08 55						09 16				09 24		09 43
Milton Keynes Central 10 a	08 13	08 18	08 24					08 24	08 40	08 48	08 50	09 00			09 13		09 18	09 21				09 29	09 40	09 48
d	08 13	08 19						08 25		08 49					09 13		09 19					09 29		09 49
Wolverton d							←			08 53														09 53
Northampton 68 a							08 28	08 40		09 05												09 44		10 06
d							08 37	08 55		09 16												09 55		
Long Buckby 68 a							08 48	09 06		09 27												10 06		
Rugby 68 a		08 41			08 51		08 59	09 17		09 37							09 41			09 44	09 51	10 17		
Coventry 68 a	08 42				09 02		09 10	09 29		09 49				09 22	09 42						10 02	10 29		
Nuneaton 65 a		08 54															09 53							
Birmingham International 68 a	08 53				09 13		09 28	09 45		10 04				09 33	09 53						10 13	10 45		
Birmingham New Street 12 68 a	09 05				09 25		09 42	10 01		10 17				09 45	10 04						10 25	11 01		
Sandwell & Dudley 68 a	09 24														10 24									
Wolverhampton 7 68 a	09 37														10 37									

A From London Euston
B To Glasgow Central
C From Balham
D To Crewe
E To Manchester Piccadilly
F To Birmingham New Street
G To Chester
H To Edinburgh
I To Blackpool North
J To Holyhead

Table T066-F

Saturdays

26 May to 8 December

London - Watford Junction, Milton Keynes, Northampton and West Midlands

	VT A		LM	SN	LM	VT	VT B	LM C	LM	LM	VT		LM	VT D	LM	VT A	VT E	LM	SN	LM	VT		VT F	LM C
London Euston ⊖60 d	09 20		09 13		09 05	09 23	09 43	09 46	09 24	09 34	10 03		09 49	10 10	09 54	10 20	10 36	10 13		10 04	10 23		10 43	10 46
East Croydon 176 d				08 10															09 10					
Clapham Junction 176 d				08 40															09 40					
Imperial Wharf 176 d				08 45															09 45					
West Brompton ⊖176 d				08 48															09 48					
Kensington (Olympia) ⊖176 d				08 51															09 51					
Shepherd's Bush ⊖176 d				08 54															09 54					
Wembley Central ⊖60,176 d				09 09															10 09	10 14				
Harrow & Wealdstone ⊖60 d				09 14	09 18					09 46									10 14	10 19				
Bushey 60 d					09 24					09 52										10 24				
Watford Junction 60 a				09 21	09 26				09 39	09 54			10 03		10 09				10 21	10 26				
d				09 21	09 27	09u37			09 41	09 55			10 03		10 11				10 21	10 27	10u37			
Kings Langley d					09 31					09 59										10 31				
Apsley d					09 35					10 03										10 35				
Hemel Hempstead d				09 29	09 38				09 48	10 06					10 18				10 29	10 38				
Berkhamsted d				09 33	09 43				09 53	10 10					10 23				10 33	10 43				
Tring d				09 39	09a49				09 59	10a17									10 39	10a49				
Cheddington d									10 04															
Leighton Buzzard d			09 42	09 50					10 09						10 36			10 42	10 48					
Bletchley d			09 50	09 57					10 16				10 24		10 43			10 50	10 55					
Milton Keynes Central 10 a	09 50		09 54	10 02			10 13	10 18	10 21				10 29	10 40	10 48	10 50		10 53	11 00				11 13	11 18
d			09 54				10 13	10 19					10 29		10 49			10 54					11 13	11 19
Wolverton d			09 58												10 53			10 58						
Northampton 68 a			10 13										10 45		11 06			11 12						
d			10 16										10 55					11 16						
Long Buckby 68 a			10 27										11 06					11 27						
Rugby 68 a			10 37					10 41			10 51		11 17				11 24	11 37						11 41
Coventry 68 a			10 49			10 22	10 42				11 02		11 29					11 49			11 22		11 42	
Nuneaton 65 a								10 53																11 53
Birmingham International 68 a			11 04			10 33	10 53				11 13		11 45					12 04			11 33		11 53	
Birmingham New Street 12 68 a			11 17			10 45	11 04				11 26		12 01					12 17			11 45		12 05	
Sandwell & Dudley 68 a							11 24																12 24	
Wolverhampton 7 68 a							11 37																12 37	

	LM	LM	VT	LM	VT D	LM	VT A		LM	SN	LM	VT G	VT	VT B	LM C	LM	LM		VT	LM	VT D	LM	VT A	LM
London Euston ⊖60 d	10 24	10 34	11 03	10 49	11 10	10 54	11 20		11 13		11 04	11 23	11 23	11 43	11 46	11 24	11 34		12 03	11 49	12 10	11 54	12 20	12 13
East Croydon 176 d										10 10														
Clapham Junction 176 d										10 40														
Imperial Wharf 176 d										10 45														
West Brompton ⊖176 d										10 48														
Kensington (Olympia) ⊖176 d										10 51														
Shepherd's Bush ⊖176 d										10 54														
Wembley Central ⊖60,176 d										11 09	11 14													
Harrow & Wealdstone ⊖60 d		10 46								11 14	11 19						11 46							
Bushey 60 d		10 52									11 24						11 52							
Watford Junction 60 a	10 39	10 54		11 03		11 09				11 21	11 26					11 40	11 54			12 03		12 09		
d	10 41	10 55		11 03		11 11				11 21	11 27	11u37	11u38			11 41	11 55			12 03		12 11		
Kings Langley d		10 59									11 31						11 59							
Apsley d		11 03									11 35						12 03							
Hemel Hempstead d	10 48	11 06				11 18				11 29	11 38					11 48	12 06					12 18		
Berkhamsted d	10 53	11 10				11 23				11 33	11 43					11 53	12 10					12 23		
Tring d	10 59	11a17								11 39	11a49					12 02	12a17							
Cheddington d	11 04															12 07								
Leighton Buzzard d	11 09					11 36			11 42	11 48						12 12						12 36		12 42
Bletchley d	11 16					11 43			11 50	11 55						12 19						12 43		12 50
Milton Keynes Central 10 a	11 21			11 24	11 40	11 48	11 50		11 54	12 00				12 13	12 18	12 24				12 24	12 40	12 48	12 50	12 53
d				11 25		11 49			11 54					12 13	12 19					12 25	12 41	12 49		12 54
Wolverton d						11 53			11 58													12 53		12 58
Northampton 68 a				11 40		12 06			12 11											12 40		13 06		13 12
d				11 55					12 16											12 55				13 16
Long Buckby 68 a				12 06					12 27											13 06				13 27
Rugby 68 a			11 51	12 17					12 37						12 41				12 51	13 17	13 03			13 37
Coventry 68 a			12 02	12 29					12 49			12 22	12 21	12 42					13 02	13 30				13 49
Nuneaton 65 a															12 53									
Birmingham International 68 a			12 13	12 45					13 04			12 33	12 32	12 53					13 13	13 45				14 04
Birmingham New Street 12 68 a			12 25	13 02					13 17			12 45	12 45	13 05					13 26	14 02				14 17
Sandwell & Dudley 68 a														13 24										
Wolverhampton 7 68 a												13 10		13 37										

A To Manchester Piccadilly
B To Glasgow Central
C To Crewe
D To Chester
E To Blackpool North
F To Edinburgh
G To Shrewsbury

London - Watford Junction, Milton Keynes, Northampton and West Midlands

		SN	LM	VT ◇	VT ◇ A	LM B	LM	LM	VT ◇	LM	VT ◇ C	LM	VT ◇ D	LM	SN	LM	VT ◇	VT ◇ E	LM B	LM	LM	VT ◇
London Euston ⊖60	d		12 04	12 23	12 43	12 46	12 24	12 34	13 03	12 49	13 10	12 54	13 20	13 13		13 04	13 23	13 43	13 46	13 24	13 34	14 03
East Croydon 176	d	11 10													12 10							
Clapham Junction 176	d	11 40													12 40							
Imperial Wharf 176	d	11 45													12 45							
West Brompton ⊖176	d	11 48													12 48							
Kensington (Olympia) ⊖176	d	11 51													12 51							
Shepherd's Bush ⊖176	d	11 54													12 54							
Wembley Central ⊖60,176	d	12 09	12 14												13 09	13 14						
Harrow & Wealdstone ⊖60	d	12 14	12 19					12 46							13 14	13 19					13 46	
Bushey 60	d		12 24					12 52								13 24					13 52	
Watford Junction 60	a	12 21	12 26				12 39	12 54		13 03		13 11			13 21	13 26				13 40	13 54	
	d	12 21	12 27	12u37			12 41	12 55		13 03		13 11			13 21	13 27	13u37			13 41	13 55	
Kings Langley	d		12 31					12 59								13 31					13 59	
Apsley	d		12 35					13 03								13 35					14 03	
Hemel Hempstead	d	12 29	12 38				12 48	13 06				13 18			13 29	13 38				13 48	14 06	
Berkhamsted	d	12 33	12 43				12 53	13 10				13 23			13 34	13 43				13 53	14 10	
Tring	d	12 39	12a49				12 59	13a17							13 40	13a49				13 59	14a17	
Cheddington	d						13 04													14 04		
Leighton Buzzard	d	12 48					13 09					13 36		13 42	13 48					14 09		
Bletchley	d	12 55					13 16					13 43		13 50	13 55					14 16		
Milton Keynes Central	a	13 00			13 13	13 18	13 21			13 24	13 40	13 48	13 50	13 53	14 00			14 13	14 18	14 23		
	d				13 13	13 19				13 25		13 49		13 54				14 13	14 19			
Wolverton	d											13 53		13 58								
Northampton 68	a									13 40		14 06		14 12								
	d									13 55				14 16								
Long Buckby 68	a									14 06				14 27								
Rugby 68	a					13 41			13 51	14 17				14 37					14 41			14 51
Coventry 68	a			13 22	13 42				14 02	14 29				14 49			14 22	14 42				15 02
Nuneaton 65	a					13 53													14 53			
Birmingham International 68 ✈	a			13 33	13 53				14 13	14 45				15 04			14 33	14 53				15 13
Birmingham New Street 68	a			13 45	14 05				14 25	15 01				15 17			14 45	15 05				15 26
Sandwell & Dudley 68	a				14 24													15 24				
Wolverhampton 68	a				14 37													15 37				

		LM	VT ◇ F	LM	VT ◇ D	LM	SN	LM	VT ◇	VT A	LM B	LM	LM	VT ◇	LM	VT ◇ C	LM	VT ◇ D	LM	SN	LM	VT ◇	VT E
London Euston ⊖60	d	13 49	14 10	13 54	14 20	14 13		14 04	14 23	14 43	14 46	14 24	14 34	15 03	14 49	15 10	14 54	15 20	15 13		15 04	15 23	15 43
East Croydon 176	d						13 10													14 10			
Clapham Junction 176	d						13 40													14 40			
Imperial Wharf 176	d						13 45													14 45			
West Brompton ⊖176	d						13 48													14 48			
Kensington (Olympia) ⊖176	d						13 51													14 51			
Shepherd's Bush ⊖176	d						13 54													14 54			
Wembley Central ⊖60,176	d						14 09	14 14												15 09	15 14		
Harrow & Wealdstone ⊖60	d						14 14	14 19					14 46							15 14	15 19		
Bushey 60	d							14 24					14 52								15 24		
Watford Junction 60	a	14 03		14 09			14 21	14 26				14 39	14 54		15 03		15 11			15 21	15 26		
	d	14 03		14 11			14 21	14 27	14u37			14 41	14 55		15 03		15 11			15 21	15 27	15u37	
Kings Langley	d							14 31					14 59								15 31		
Apsley	d							14 35					15 03								15 35		
Hemel Hempstead	d			14 18			14 29	14 38				14 48	15 06				15 18			15 29	15 38		
Berkhamsted	d			14 23			14 33	14 43				14 53	15 10				15 23			15 33	15 43		
Tring	d						14 39	14a49				14 59	15a17							15 39	15a49		
Cheddington	d											15 04											
Leighton Buzzard	d			14 36		14 42	14 48					15 09					15 36		15 42	15 48			
Bletchley	d			14 43		14 50	14 55					15 16					15 43		15 50	15 55			
Milton Keynes Central	a	14 24	14 40	14 48	14 50	14 53	15 00			15 13	15 18	15 21			15 24	15 40	15 48	15 50	15 53	16 00			16 13
	d	14 25		14 49		14 54				15 13	15 19				15 25		15 49		15 54				16 13
Wolverton	d			14 53		14 58											15 53		15 58				
Northampton 68	a	14 40		15 06		15 12									15 40		16 06		16 12				
	d	14 55				15 16									15 55				16 16				
Long Buckby 68	a	15 06				15 27									16 06				16 27				
Rugby 68	a	15 17				15 37					15 41			15 51	16 17				16 37				
Coventry 68	a	15 29				15 49			15 22	15 42				16 02	16 29				16 49			16 22	16 42
Nuneaton 65	a										15 53												
Birmingham International 68 ✈	a	15 45				16 04			15 33	15 53				16 13	16 45				17 04			16 33	16 53
Birmingham New Street 68	a	16 02				16 17			15 45	16 05				16 26	17 01				17 17			16 45	17 05
Sandwell & Dudley 68	a									16 24													17 24
Wolverhampton 68	a									16 37													17 37

A To Edinburgh
B To Crewe
C To Chester
D To Manchester Piccadilly
E To Glasgow Central
F To Holyhead

Table T066-F

Saturdays
26 May to 8 December

London - Watford Junction, Milton Keynes, Northampton and West Midlands

		LM A	LM	LM	VT ◇	LM	VT ◇ B	LM	VT ◇ C	LM	SN	LM	VT ◇	VT ◇ D	LM A	LM	LM	VT ◇	LM	VT ◇ E	LM	VT ◇ C	LM
London Euston ⊖60	d	15 46	15 24	15 34	16 03	15 49	16 10	15 54	16 20	16 13		16 05	16 23	16 43	16 46	16 24	16 34	17 03	16 49	17 10	16 54	17 20	17 13
East Croydon 176	d										15 10												
Clapham Junction 176	d										15 40												
Imperial Wharf 176	d										15 45												
West Brompton ⊖176	d										15 48												
Kensington (Olympia) ⊖176	d										15 51												
Shepherd's Bush ⊖176	d										15 54												
Wembley Central ⊖60,176	d										16 09												
Harrow & Wealdstone ⊖60	d			15 46							16 14	16 18					16 46						
Bushey 60	d			15 52								16 24					16 52						
Watford Junction 60	a		15 39	15 54		16 03		16 09			16 21	16 26				16 39	16 54		17 03		17 09		
	d		15 41	15 55		16 03		16 11			16 21	16 27	16u37			16 41	16 55		17 03		17 11		
Kings Langley	d			15 59								16 31					16 59						
Apsley	d			16 03								16 35					17 03						
Hemel Hempstead	d		15 48	16 06				16 18			16 29	16 38				16 48	17 06				17 18		
Berkhamsted	d		15 53	16 10				16 23			16 33	16 43				16 53	17 10				17 23		
Tring	d		15 59	16a17							16 39	16a49				16 59	17a17						
Cheddington	d		16 04													17 04							
Leighton Buzzard	d		16 09					16 36		16 42	16 48					17 09					17 36		17 42
Bletchley	d		16 16					16 43		16 50	16 56					17 16					17 43		17 50
Milton Keynes Central	a	16 18	16 21			16 24	16 40	16 48	16 50	16 54	17 01			17 13	17 18	17 21			17 24	17 40	17 48	17 50	17 53
	d	16 19				16 25		16 49		16 54				17 13	17 19				17 25		17 49		17 54
Wolverton	d							16 53		16 58											17 53		17 58
Northampton 68	a					16 41		17 06		17 12									17 41		18 06		18 12
	d					16 55				17 16									17 55				18 16
Long Buckby 68	a					17 06				17 27									18 06				18 27
Rugby 68	a	16 41			16 51	17 17				17 37					17 41			17 51	18 17				18 37
Coventry 68	a				17 02	17 29				17 49			17 22	17 42				18 02	18 29				18 49
Nuneaton 65	a	16 53													17 53								
Birmingham International 68 ✈	a				17 13	17 45				18 04			17 33	17 53				18 13	18 45				19 04
Birmingham New Street 68	a				17 26	18 01				18 17			17 45	18 05				18 26	19 01				19 17
Sandwell & Dudley 68	a													18 24									
Wolverhampton 68	a													18 37									

		SN	LM	VT ◇ F	VT ◇	VT ◇ D	LM A	LM	LM	VT ◇	LM	VT ◇ E	LM	VT ◇ C	LM	SN	LM	VT ◇ G	VT ◇	VT ◇ A	LM A	LM
London Euston ⊖60	d		17 05	17 07	17 23	17 43	17 46	17 24	17 34	18 03	17 49	18 10	17 54	18 20	18 13		18 05	18 23	18 23	18 43	18 46	18 24
East Croydon 176	d	16 10														17 10						
Clapham Junction 176	d	16 40														17 40						
Imperial Wharf 176	d	16 45														17 45						
West Brompton ⊖176	d	16 48														17 48						
Kensington (Olympia) ⊖176	d	16 51														17 51						
Shepherd's Bush ⊖176	d	16 54														17 54						
Wembley Central ⊖60,176	d	17 09														18 09						
Harrow & Wealdstone ⊖60	d	17 14	17 18						17 46							18 14	18 18					
Bushey 60	d		17 24						17 52								18 24					
Watford Junction 60	a	17 21	17 26					17 39	17 54		18 03		18 09			18 21	18 26					18 39
	d	17 21	17 27		17u37			17 41	17 55		18 03		18 11			18 21	18 27	18u37	18u37			18 41
Kings Langley	d		17 31						17 59								18 31					
Apsley	d		17 35						18 03								18 35					
Hemel Hempstead	d	17 29	17 38					17 48	18 06				18 18			18 29	18 38					18 48
Berkhamsted	d	17 33	17 43					17 53	18 10				18 23			18 33	18 43					18 53
Tring	d	17 39	17a49					17 59	18a17							18 39	18a49					18 59
Cheddington	d							18 04														19 04
Leighton Buzzard	d	17 48						18 09					18 36		18 44	18 48						19 09
Bletchley	d	17 55						18 16					18 43		18 52	18 57						19 16
Milton Keynes Central	a	18 00				18 13	18 18	18 21			18 24	18 40	18 48	18 50	18 56	19 02				19 13	19 18	19 21
	d					18 13	18 19				18 25		18 49		18 56					19 13	19 19	
Wolverton	d												18 53		19 00							
Northampton 68	a										18 41		19 06		19 13							
	d										18 55				19 16							
Long Buckby 68	a										19 06				19 27							
Rugby 68	a						18 41			18 52	19 17				19 37						19 41	
Coventry 68	a				18 22	18 42				19 03	19 29				19 49			19 22	19 24	19 42		
Nuneaton 65	a			18 02			18 53														19 53	
Birmingham International 68 ✈	a				18 33	18 53				19 13	19 45				20 04			19 33	19 34	19 53		
Birmingham New Street 68	a				18 45	19 05				19 26	20 02				20 17			19 45	19 45	20 06		
Sandwell & Dudley 68	a				18 58	19 24				19 43								19 58	19 58	20 24		
Wolverhampton 68	a				19 10	19 37				19 55								20 11	20 10	20 37		

A To Crewe
B To Holyhead
C To Manchester Piccadilly
D To Preston
E To Chester
F To Liverpool Lime Street
G To Shrewsbury

Table T066-F

Saturdays
26 May to 8 December

London - Watford Junction, Milton Keynes, Northampton and West Midlands

	LM	VT ◇	LM	LM	SN	LM	VT ◇ A	VT ◇ B	LM	LM	VT ◇	VT ◇	LM	VT ◇ A	LM	SN	LM	VT ◇ B	VT ◇	VT ◇ C	LM D	LM D
London Euston ⊖60 d	18 34	19 03	18 49	18 54		19 05	19 07	19 20	19 13	19 14	19 23	19 43	19 30	20 11	19 46		20 02	20 20	20 25	20 31	20 34	20 40
East Croydon 176 d					18 10											19 10						
Clapham Junction 176 d					18 40											19 36						
Imperial Wharf 176 d					18 45											19 41						
West Brompton ⊖176 d					18 48											19 44						
Kensington (Olympia) ⊖176 d					18 51											19 47						
Shepherd's Bush ⊖176 d					18 54											19 50						
Wembley Central ⊖60,176 d					19 08																	
Harrow & Wealdstone ⊖60 d	18 46				19 13	19 18							19 42			20 07						20 52
Bushey 60 d	18 52					19 24							19 48									20s57
Watford Junction 60 a	18 54		19 03	19 09	19 20	19 26				19 31			19 50		20 01	20 14	20 18				20 50	21 00
d	18 55		19 03	19 11		19 27				19 33	19u37		19 53		20 02		20 19		20u40	20u46	20 50	21 01
Kings Langley d	18 59					19 31							19 57		20 06							21 05
Apsley d	19 03					19 35							20 01		20 10							21 09
Hemel Hempstead d	19 06			19 18						19 41			20 04		20 13		20 26				20 57	
Berkhamsted d	19 10			19 23		19 41				19 46			20 09		20 18		20 31				21 02	
Tring d	19a17					19a47				19 51			20 13		20 23							21 19
Cheddington d										19 56					20 28						21 11	
Leighton Buzzard d				19 36					19 42	20 01			20 22		20 34		20 42				21 18	
Bletchley d				19 43					19 50	20 07			20 29		20 41		20 49				21 25	21 31
Milton Keynes Central a			19 24	19 48				19 50	19 53	20 13		20 20	20 34		20 49		20 54	21 03			21 33	21 39
d			19 25	19 49					19 54			20 20			20 49			21 05			21 33	21 40
Wolverton d				19 53					19 58						20 53						21 37	
Northampton 68 a			19 44	20 06					20 11						21 06						21 50	21 56
d			19 55						20 22						21 16						21 59	22 16
Long Buckby 68 a			20 06						20 33						21 27						→	→
Rugby 68 a		19 51	20 17						20 44					21 15	21 38					21 34		
Coventry 68 a		20 02	20 29						20 55		20 22	20 50			21 49				21 36			
Nuneaton 65 a							20 02											21 32				
Birmingham International 68 ✈ a		20 13	20 45						21 13		20 33	21 01			22 04				21 50			
Birmingham New Street 68 a		20 24	21 02						21 25		20 45	21 13			22 17				22 04			
Sandwell & Dudley 68 a		20 53									20 58								22 24			
Wolverhampton 68 a		21 08									21 12	21 37							22 37			

	VT ◇ B	VT ◇	LM E	LM E	LM	SN	LM D	VT ◇	LM E	LM	SN	LM	SN	LM	LM
London Euston ⊖60 d	21 00	21 03			21 07		21 28	21 43		21 54		22 34		23 04	23 40
East Croydon 176 d						20 10					21 10		22 10		
Clapham Junction 176 d						20 51					21 39		22 39		
Imperial Wharf 176 d						20 56					21 44		22 44		
West Brompton ⊖176 d						20 59					21 47		22 47		
Kensington (Olympia) ⊖176 d						21 03					21 50		22 50		
Shepherd's Bush ⊖176 d						21 06					21 53		22 53		
Wembley Central ⊖60,176 d						21 20					22 08		23 07		
Harrow & Wealdstone ⊖60 d						21 25				22 06	22 13		23 12	23 16	23 52
Bushey 60 d															
Watford Junction 60 a					21 24	21 33	21 43			22 12	22 26	22 49	23 19	23 23	23 58
d		21u18			21 24		21 44	21u58		22 14		22 50		23 24	23 59
Kings Langley d										22 18				23 28	00 03
Apsley d										22 22				23 32	00 07
Hemel Hempstead d					21 32		21 52			22 25		22 57		23 35	00 10
Berkhamsted d					21 37		21 57			22 30		23 02		23 40	00 15
Tring d										22 34				23 44	00 20
Cheddington d										22 39				23 49	00 25
Leighton Buzzard d					21 50		22 08			22 47		23 16		23 56	00 32
Bletchley d					21 57		22 15			22 54		23 23		00 03	00 39
Milton Keynes Central a	21 43	21 50			22 05		22 23	22 29		23 02		23 31		00 11	00 47
d		21 50			22 06		22 24	22 30		23 03		23 31		00 11	00 47
Wolverton d			←	←	22 10		22 28		←	23 07		23 35		00 15	00 51
Northampton 68 a			21 50	21 56	22 23		22 43		22 43	23 20		23 48		00 28	01 04
d			21 59	22 16			22 55		22 55						
Long Buckby 68 a			22 10	22 27			→		23 06						
Rugby 68 a		22 11	22 21	22 38				22 52	23 17						
Coventry 68 a		22 22	22 32	22 49				23 02	23 28						
Nuneaton 65 a															
Birmingham International 68 ✈ a		22 33	22 48	23 04				23 13	23 47						
Birmingham New Street 68 a		22 45	23 04	23 17				23 25	00 04						
Sandwell & Dudley 68 a		22 56						23 36							
Wolverhampton 68 a		23 08						23 48							

A To Liverpool Lime Street
B To Manchester Piccadilly
C To Preston
D To Birmingham New Street
E From London Euston

Table T066-F

Sundays
20 May to 2 December

London - Watford Junction, Milton Keynes, Northampton and West Midlands

	LM A	LM A	LM	LM 🚌	LM 🚌	LM 🚌	LM 🚌	LM 🚌	LM	LM	LM	VT ◇ B	VT ◇ C	VT ◇ B	LM D	SN	VT ◇ E	VT ◇	LM F	LM	VT ◇ C	VT ◇ B
London Euston ⊖60 d			00 15	02 00	02 00	02 00	02 00	02 00	06 54	07 24	07 52	08 10	08 15	08 20	08 24		08 45	08 50		08 55	09 14	09 20
East Croydon 176 d																						
Clapham Junction 176 d																08 15						
Imperial Wharf 176 d																08 19						
West Brompton ⊖176 d																08 22						
Kensington (Olympia) ⊖176 d																08 26						
Shepherd's Bush ⊖176 d																08 29						
Wembley Central ⊖60,176 d			00 24					02 30														
Harrow & Wealdstone ⊖60 d			00 29				02 35	02 45	07 06	07 36	08 04				08 36	08 47				09 07		
Bushey 60 d										07s41					08s41							
Watford Junction 60 a			00 35	02 50		02 50	02 55	03 05	07 12	07 44	08 10				08 44	08 55				09 13		
d			00 35	02 50		02 50	02 55	03 05	07 13	07 45	08 10				08 45			09u07		09 14		
Kings Langley d		00 03	00 40					03 20		07 49					08 49							
Apsley d		00 07	00 44					03 30		07 53					08 53							
Hemel Hempstead d		00 10	00 46		03 00	03 15		03 35	07 20	07 56	08 17				08 56					09 21		
Berkhamsted d		00 15	00 51				03 20	03 45	07 25	08 01	08 22				09 01					09 26		
Tring d		00 20	00 56					04 00	07 29		08 27									09 29		
Cheddington d		00 25	01 01					04 20	07 35		08 32									09 35		
Leighton Buzzard d		00 32	01 06			03 51		04 40	07 41	08 14	08 39				09 14					09 41		
Bletchley d	00 03	00 39	01 13			04 16		05 05	07 48	08 21	08 45				09 21					09 48		
Milton Keynes Central a	00 11	00 47	01 19	04 00	04 00	04 31	04 10	05 20	07 57	08 29	08 50	08 55		09 05	09 26		09 32	09 37		09 57		10 06
d	00 11	00 47	01 19						07 58	08 30	08 51				09 27		09 33	09 39		09 57		
Wolverton d	00 15	00 51	01 23						08 02	08 34	08 55				09 31				←	10 01		
Northampton 68 a	00 28	01 04	01 36						08 15	08 47	09 09				09 44				09 44	10 14		
d											09 26				10 00				10 00			
Long Buckby 68 a											09 37				→				10 11			
Rugby 68 a											09 48						10 07	10 13	10 22			
Coventry 68 a											09 59							10 24	10 33			
Nuneaton 65 a													09 43								10 44	
Birmingham International 68 ✈ a											10 09							10 35	10 51			
Birmingham New Street 68 a											10 26							10 47	11 03			
Sandwell & Dudley 68 a																		10 58				
Wolverhampton 68 a																		11 11				

	LM D	SN	VT ◇ G	VT ◇	LM F	LM H	LM	VT ◇ C	VT ◇ B	LM H	LM D	SN	VT ◇ E	VT ◇	LM F	LM	VT ◇ C	VT ◇ B	LM D	SN	VT ◇	VT ◇ B
London Euston ⊖60 d	09 24		09 45	09 50		09 54	10 01	10 15	10 20	10 24	10 28		10 45	10 50		10 54	11 15	11 20	11 24		11 50	12 17
East Croydon 176 d																						
Clapham Junction 176 d		09 13										10 17								11 16		
Imperial Wharf 176 d		09 17										10 21								11 20		
West Brompton ⊖176 d		09 20										10 24								11 23		
Kensington (Olympia) ⊖176 d		09 24										10 28								11 27		
Shepherd's Bush ⊖176 d		09 27										10 31								11 30		
Wembley Central ⊖60,176 d																						
Harrow & Wealdstone ⊖60 d	09 36	09 47					10 13				10 40	10 47				11 06			11 36	11 48		
Bushey 60 d	09s41															11s11						
Watford Junction 60 a	09 44	09 55				10 09	10 19			10 39	10 46	10 55				11 14			11 42	11 56		
d	09 45			10u05		10 10	10 19			10 40	10 46			11u05		11 14			11 42		12u05	
Kings Langley d	09 49										10 51								11 47			
Apsley d	09 53										10 55								11 51			
Hemel Hempstead d	09 56					10 17	10 26			10 47	10 57					11 21			11 53			
Berkhamsted d	10 01					10 22	10 31			10 52	11 02					11 26			11 58			
Tring d							10 36									11 31						
Cheddington d							10 41									11 36						
Leighton Buzzard d	10 14					10 35	10 47			11 05	11 15					11 43			12 12			
Bletchley d	10 21					10 42				11 12						11 50			12 19			
Milton Keynes Central a	10 26		10 32	10 37		10 50	10 58		11 06	11 20	11 27		11 32	11 37		11 58	12 02	12 08	12 27		12 28	12 50
d	10 27		10 33	10 38		10 50	10 58			11 20	11 28		11 33	11 38		11 58			12 28		12 30	
Wolverton d	10 31				←		11 02				11 32				←	12 02			12 32			
Northampton 68 a	10 44				10 44	11 06	11 16			11 38	11 45				11 45	12 15			12 44			
d	11 00				11 00	11 08				11 40	11 58				11 58				12 55			
Long Buckby 68 a	→				11 11	11 19				11 51	→				12 09				→			
Rugby 68 a			11 07	11 13	11 22	11 30				12 02			12 07	12 13	12 20						12 49	
Coventry 68 a				11 23	11 33									12 23	12 31						12 59	
Nuneaton 65 a						11 42		11 46		12 15												
Birmingham International 68 ✈ a				11 34	11 51									12 34	12 49						13 10	
Birmingham New Street 68 a				11 47	12 03									12 46	13 01						13 22	
Sandwell & Dudley 68 a				11 58										12 58								
Wolverhampton 68 a				12 11										13 10								

A not 20 May. From London Euston
B To Manchester Piccadilly
C To Liverpool Lime Street
D To Birmingham New Street
E To Glasgow Central
F From London Euston
G To Carlisle
H To Crewe

London - Watford Junction, Milton Keynes, Northampton and West Midlands

	LM ■	VT ◇■ 🍴	LM ■ A	LM ■	SN	VT ◇■ B 🍴	VT ◇■ 🍴	LM ■	LM ■ C	VT ◇■ D 🍴	LM ■	VT ◇■ 🍴	LM ■	SN	VT ◇■ E 🍴	VT ◇■ 🍴	LM ■	LM ■ C	VT ◇■ D 🍴	LM ■	VT ◇■ 🍴
London Euston ⊖60 d	11 54	12 20		12 14		12 40	13 00	12 34	12 50	13 17	12 54	13 20	13 14		13 40	14 00	13 34	13 50	14 17	13 54	14 20
East Croydon 176 d																					
Clapham Junction 176 d					12 05									13 05							
Imperial Wharf 176 d					12 09									13 09							
West Brompton ⊖176 d					12 12									13 12							
Kensington (Olympia) ⊖176 d					12 16									13 16							
Shepherd's Bush ⊖176 d					12 19									13 19							
Wembley Central ⊖60,176 d																					
Harrow & Wealdstone ⊖60 d	12 06			12 26	12 35						13 06		13 26	13 35						14 06	
Bushey 60 d	12s11			12 32									13 32								
Watford Junction 60 a	12 14			12 34	12 43			12 49	13 06		13 12		13 34	13 43			13 49	14 06		14 12	
d	12 14	12u34		12 35				12 50	13 06		13 13	13u34	13 35				13 50	14 06		14 13	14u34
Kings Langley d				12 39									13 39								
Apsley d				12 43									13 43								
Hemel Hempstead d	12 21			12 46				12 57			13 20		13 46				13 57			14 20	
Berkhamsted d	12 26			12 51				13 02			13 25		13 51				14 02			14 25	
Tring d	12 31			12a57							13 32		13a57							14 32	
Cheddington d	12 36										13 37									14 37	
Leighton Buzzard d	12 43							13 15	13 27		13 42						14 15	14 27		14 42	
Bletchley d	12 50							13 22			13 49						14 22			14 49	
Milton Keynes Central ■ a	12 58					13 13		13 27	13 36	13 50	13 54				14 13		14 27	14 37	14 50	14 54	
d	12 58					13 13		13 28	13 37						14 13		14 28	14 37			
Wolverton d	13 02		←					13 32									14 32				
Northampton 68 a	13 15		12 44					13 44	13 51								14 44	14 52			
d			12 55					13 55	14 02								14 55	15 02			
Long Buckby 68 a			13 06					14 06	14 13								15 06	15 13			
Rugby 68 a			13 17				13 51	14 17	14 24							14 51	15 17	15 24			
Coventry 68 a		13 22	13 29			13 42	14 02	14 29				14 22			14 42	15 02	15 29				15 22
Nuneaton 65 a									14 39									15 39			
Birmingham International 68 ✈ a		13 33	13 47			13 53	14 13	14 47				14 33			14 53	15 13	15 47				15 33
Birmingham New Street ■ 68 a		13 45	13 59			14 04	14 24	14 59				14 45			15 04	15 24	15 59				15 45
Sandwell & Dudley 68 a		13 56				14 25									15 26						
Wolverhampton ■ 68 a		14 08				14 37									15 37						

	LM ■	SN	VT ◇■ B 🍴	VT ◇■ 🍴	LM ■	LM ■ C	VT ◇■ F 🍴	VT ◇■ D 🍴	LM ■	VT ◇■ 🍴	LM ■	SN	VT ◇■ E 🍴	VT ◇■ 🍴	LM ■	LM ■ C	VT ◇■ F 🍴	VT ◇■ D 🍴	LM ■	VT ◇■ 🍴	LM ■	SN
London Euston ⊖60 d	14 14		14 40	15 00	14 34	14 50	15 08	15 17	14 54	15 20	15 14		15 40	16 00	15 34	15 50	16 08	16 17	15 54	16 20	16 14	
East Croydon 176 d																						
Clapham Junction 176 d		14 05										15 05										16 05
Imperial Wharf 176 d		14 09										15 09										16 09
West Brompton ⊖176 d		14 12										15 12										16 12
Kensington (Olympia) ⊖176 d		14 16										15 16										16 16
Shepherd's Bush ⊖176 d		14 19										15 19										16 19
Wembley Central ⊖60,176 d																						
Harrow & Wealdstone ⊖60 d	14 26	14 35							15 06		15 26	15 35							16 06		16 26	16 35
Bushey 60 d	14 32										15 32										16 32	
Watford Junction 60 a	14 34	14 43			14 49	15 06			15 12		15 34	15 43			15 49	16 06			16 12		16 34	16 43
d	14 35				14 50	15 06			15 13	15u34	15 35				15 50	16 06			16 13	16u34	16 35	
Kings Langley d	14 39										15 39										16 39	
Apsley d	14 43										15 43										16 43	
Hemel Hempstead d	14 46				14 57				15 20		15 46				15 57				16 20		16 46	
Berkhamsted d	14 51				15 02				15 25		15 51				16 02				16 25		16 51	
Tring d	14a57								15 32		15a57								16 32		16a57	
Cheddington d									15 37										16 37			
Leighton Buzzard d					15 15	15 27			15 42						16 15	16 27			16 42			
Bletchley d					15 22				15 49						16 22				16 49			
Milton Keynes Central ■ a			15 13		15 27	15 37	15 41	15 50	15 54				16 13		16 27	16 37	16 41	16 50	16 54			
d			15 13		15 28	15 37							16 13		16 28	16 37						
Wolverton d					15 32										16 32							
Northampton 68 a					15 44	15 52									16 44	16 53						
d					15 55	16 02									16 55	17 02						
Long Buckby 68 a					16 06	16 13									17 06	17 13						
Rugby 68 a				15 51	16 17	16 24								16 51	17 17	17 24						
Coventry 68 a			15 42	16 02	16 29					16 22			16 42	17 02	17 29					17 22		
Nuneaton 65 a						16 39										17 39						
Birmingham International 68 ✈ a			15 53	16 13	16 47					16 33			16 53	17 13	17 47					17 33		
Birmingham New Street ■ 68 a			16 05	16 23	16 59					16 45			17 04	17 24	17 59					17 45		
Sandwell & Dudley 68 a			16 25										17 25									
Wolverhampton ■ 68 a			16 37										17 37									

A From London Euston
B To Edinburgh
C To Crewe
D To Manchester Piccadilly
E To Glasgow Central
F To Chester

Table T066-F

Sundays
20 May to 2 December

London - Watford Junction, Milton Keynes, Northampton and West Midlands

	VT ◇■ A 🍴	VT ◇■ 🍴	LM ■	LM ■ B	VT ◇■ C 🍴	VT ◇■ D 🍴	LM ■	VT ◇■ E 🍴	VT ◇■ 🍴	LM ■	SN	VT ■ ■ F 🍴	VT ◇■ 🍴	LM ■	LM ■ B	VT ◇■ C 🍴	VT ◇■ D 🍴	LM ■	VT ◇■ G 🍴	VT ◇■ H 🍴	LM ■
London Euston ⊖60 d	16 40	17 00	16 34	16 50	17 08	17 17	16 54	17 05	17 20	17 14		17 40	18 00	17 34	17 50	18 08	18 17	17 54	18 20	18 20	18 14
East Croydon 176 d																					
Clapham Junction 176 d											17 05										
Imperial Wharf 176 d											17 09										
West Brompton ⊖176 d											17 12										
Kensington (Olympia) ⊖176 d											17 16										
Shepherd's Bush ⊖176 d											17 19										
Wembley Central ⊖60,176 d																					
Harrow & Wealdstone ⊖60 d							17 06			17 26	17 35							18 06			18 26
Bushey 60 d										17 32											18 32
Watford Junction 60 a			16 49	17 06			17 12			17 34	17 43			17 49	18 06			18 12			18 34
d			16 50	17 06			17 13		17u34	17 35				17 50	18 06			18 13	18u34	18u34	18 35
Kings Langley d										17 39											18 39
Apsley d										17 43											18 43
Hemel Hempstead d			16 57				17 20			17 46				17 57				18 20			18 46
Berkhamsted d			17 02				17 25			17 51				18 02				18 25			18 51
Tring d							17 32			17a57								18 32			18a57
Cheddington d							17 37											18 37			
Leighton Buzzard d			17 15	17 27			17 42							18 15	18 27			18 42			
Bletchley d			17 22				17 49							18 22				18 49			
Milton Keynes Central ■ a	17 13		17 27	17 37	17 41	17 50	17 54					18 13		18 27	18 37	18 41	18 50	18 54			
d	17 13		17 28	17 37								18 13		18 28	18 37						
Wolverton d			17 32											18 32							
Northampton 68 a			17 44	17 53										18 44	18 52						
d			17 55	18 02										18 55	19 02						
Long Buckby 68 a			18 06	18 13										19 06	19 13						
Rugby 68 a		17 51	18 17	18 24									18 51	19 17	19 24						
Coventry 68 a	17 44	18 02	18 29						18 22			18 44	19 02	19 29					19 22	19 24	
Nuneaton 65 a				18 39				18 03							19 39						
Birmingham International 68 ✈ a	17 54	18 13	18 47						18 33			18 54	19 13	19 47					19 33	19 34	
Birmingham New Street ■ 68 a	18 05	18 24	18 59						18 45			19 05	19 24	19 59					19 45	19 45	
Sandwell & Dudley 68 a	18 25											19 25	19 48								
Wolverhampton ■ 68 a	18 37											19 37	20 00								

	SN	VT ◇■ B 🍴	VT ◇■ 🍴	VT ◇■ I 🍴	LM ■	LM ■ B	VT ◇■ J 🍴	VT ◇■ D 🍴	LM ■	VT ◇■ E 🍴	VT ◇■ 🍴	LM ■	SN	VT ◇■ K 🍴	VT ◇■ H 🍴	VT ◇■ G 🍴	LM ■	LM ■ B	VT ◇■ E 🍴	VT ◇■ D 🍴	LM ■	VT ◇■ E 🍴
London Euston ⊖60 d		18 40	19 00	19 00	18 34	18 50	19 08	19 17	18 54	19 05	19 20	19 14		19 40	20 00	20 00	19 34	19 50	20 08	20 15	19 54	20 05
East Croydon 176 d																						
Clapham Junction 176 d	18 05												19 05									
Imperial Wharf 176 d	18 09												19 09									
West Brompton ⊖176 d	18 12												19 12									
Kensington (Olympia) ⊖176 d	18 16												19 16									
Shepherd's Bush ⊖176 d	18 19												19 19									
Wembley Central ⊖60,176 d																						
Harrow & Wealdstone ⊖60 d	18 35								19 06			19 26	19 35								20 06	
Bushey 60 d												19 32										
Watford Junction 60 a	18 43				18 49	19 06			19 12			19 34	19 43				19 49	20 06			20 12	
d					18 50	19 06			19 13		19u34	19 35					19 50	20 06			20 13	
Kings Langley d												19 39										
Apsley d												19 43										
Hemel Hempstead d					18 57				19 20			19 46					19 57				20 20	
Berkhamsted d					19 02				19 25			19 51					20 02				20 25	
Tring d									19 32			19a57									20 32	
Cheddington d									19 37												20 37	
Leighton Buzzard d					19 15	19 27			19 42								20 15	20 27			20 42	
Bletchley d					19 22				19 49								20 22				20 49	
Milton Keynes Central ■ a		19 13			19 27	19 37	19 41	19 50	19 54					20 13			20 27	20 37	20 41	20 48	20 54	
d		19 13			19 28	19 37								20 13			20 28	20 37				
Wolverton d					19 32												20 32					
Northampton 68 a					19 44	19 53											20 44	20 54				
d					19 55	20 02											20 55	21 06				
Long Buckby 68 a					20 06	20 13											21 06	21 17				
Rugby 68 a			19 50	19 52	20 17	20 24									20 51	20 51	21 17	21 28				
Coventry 68 a		19 42	20 01	20 03	20 29						20 22			20 42	21 02	21 03	21 29					
Nuneaton 65 a						20 39				20 03								21 43				21 03
Birmingham International 68 ✈ a		19 53	20 13	20 13	20 47						20 33			20 53	21 13	21 13	21 47					
Birmingham New Street ■ 68 a		20 04	20 24	20 24	20 59						20 45			21 05	21 24	21 24	21 59					
Sandwell & Dudley 68 a		20 24	20 35	20 35							20 56			21 24								
Wolverhampton ■ 68 a		20 37	20 47	20 47							21 11			21 37								

A To Edinburgh
B To Crewe
C To Chester
D To Manchester Piccadilly
E To Liverpool Lime Street
F To Glasgow Central
G from 16 September
H until 9 September
I To Shrewsbury
J To Holyhead
K To Preston

Table T066-F

Sundays
20 May to 2 December

London - Watford Junction, Milton Keynes, Northampton and West Midlands

	VT	LM	SN	VT	LM	VT	VT	LM	LM	VT	VT	LM	SN	VT	VT	LM	VT	LM	LM	SN	LM	VT
	◇■	■		◇■	■	◇■	◇■	■	■	◇■	◇■	■		◇■	◇■	■	◇■	■	■		■	◇■
					A	B		C		D	E			E		F		C				
	☕			☕		☕	☕			☕	☕			☕	☕		☕					☕
London Euston ■ ⊖60 d	20 18	20 14		20 38	20 34	20 50	20 54		21 06	21 21	21 25	21 30		21 51	21 55	22 00	22 25		22 28		22 58	23 25
East Croydon 176 🚊 d																						
Clapham Junction 176 d			20 05										21 19							22 19		
Imperial Wharf 176 d			20 09										21 23							22 23		
West Brompton ⊖176 d			20 12										21 26							22 26		
Kensington (Olympia) ⊖176 d			20 16										21 30							22 30		
Shepherd's Bush ⊖176 d			20 19										21 33							22 33		
Wembley Central ⊖60,176 d																						
Harrow & Wealdstone ⊖60 d		20 26	20 35									21 42	21 50			22 12			22 40	22 49	23 11	
Bushey 60 d		20 32										21s47							22s45			
Watford Junction 60 a		20 34	20 43		20 49				21 25			21 49	21 59			22 18			22 48	22 57	23 17	
d	20u32	20 35			20 50		21u10		21 25			21 50			22u09	22 19	22u39		22 49		23 18	23u39
Kings Langley d		20 39										21 54							22 53		23 22	
Apsley d		20 43										21 58							22 57		23 26	
Hemel Hempstead d		20 46			20 57				21 32			22 01				22 26			23 00		23 29	
Berkhamsted d		20 51			21 02				21 37			22 06				22 31			23 05		23 34	
Tring d		20a57							21 41							22 35					23 39	
Cheddington d									21 46							22 41					23 44	
Leighton Buzzard d					21 15				21 53			22 19				22 47			23 18		23 51	
Bletchley d					21 22				22 00			22 26				22 54			23 25		23 58	
Milton Keynes Central ■ a				21 16	21 28	21 35	21 41		22 08		22 17	22 34		22 37	22 43	23 02	23 11		23 33		00 06	00 11
d				21 16	21 29	21 37	21 43		22 08			22 34		22 39	22 45	23 03	23 12		23 33		00 06	00 12
Wolverton d					21 33			←	22 12			22 38				23 07		←	23 37		00 10	
Northampton 68 a					21 46			21 46	22 25			22 50				23 19		23 19	23 50		00 24	
d					21 55			21 55				22 52				23 32		23 32				
Long Buckby 68 a					→			22 06				23 03				→		23 43				
Rugby 68 a						21 59	22 05	22 17				23 14		23 18	23 22		23 46	23 54				00s46
Coventry 68 a	21 20			21 46			22 16	22 29				23 25			23 33		23 57	00 07				00s58
Nuneaton 65 a										22 56				23 29								
Birmingham International 68 ✈ a	21 31			21 57			22 27	22 47				23 55			23 44		00 08					01s09
Birmingham New Street ■ 68 🚊 a	21 45			22 09			22 39	22 59				00 07			23 56		00 21					01s22
Sandwell & Dudley 68 a	21 56			22 24			22 51															
Wolverhampton ■ 68 🚊 a	22 08			22 36			23 03								00 15		00 41					01 42

	LM
	■
London Euston ■ ⊖60 d	23 34
East Croydon 176 🚊 d	
Clapham Junction 176 d	
Imperial Wharf 176 d	
West Brompton ⊖176 d	
Kensington (Olympia) ⊖176 d	
Shepherd's Bush ⊖176 d	
Wembley Central ⊖60,176 d	
Harrow & Wealdstone ⊖60 d	23 46
Bushey 60 d	23s51
Watford Junction 60 a	23 54
d	23 55
Kings Langley d	23 59
Apsley d	00 03
Hemel Hempstead d	00 06
Berkhamsted d	00 11
Tring d	00 16
Cheddington d	00 21
Leighton Buzzard d	00 28
Bletchley d	00 35
Milton Keynes Central ■ a	00 43
d	00 43
Wolverton d	00 47
Northampton 68 a	01 00
d	
Long Buckby 68 a	
Rugby 68 a	
Coventry 68 a	
Nuneaton 65 a	
Birmingham International 68 ✈ a	
Birmingham New Street ■ 68 🚊 a	
Sandwell & Dudley 68 a	
Wolverhampton ■ 68 🚊 a	

A To Birmingham New Street
B To Preston
C From London Euston
D To Liverpool Lime Street
E To Manchester Piccadilly
F To Coventry

Table T066-R

Mondays to Fridays
21 May to 7 December

West Midlands, Northampton, Milton Keynes and Watford Junction - London

Miles	Miles	Miles		LM	LM	LM	VT	LM	LM	LM	SN	LM	LM	LM	LM	LM	LM	VT	SN	LM	LM	VT
				MX	MO	MX	MX															
				■	■	■	◇■	■	■	■	■	■	■	■	■	■	■	◇■	■	■	■	◇■
				A	B	B	C										D					
							☕											⊠				⊠
0	—	—	Wolverhampton ■ 68 🚊 d															05 00				
7½	—	—	Sandwell & Dudley 68 d																			
12¾	—	—	**Birmingham New Street** ■ 68 🚊 d															05 29				05 45
21¼	—	—	Birmingham International 68 ✈ d															05 40				05 55
—	—	—	Nuneaton 65 d																			
32	—	—	Coventry 68 d															05 51				06 06
43½	0	—	**Rugby** 68 d												05 16			06 03				06 20
53	—	—	Long Buckby 68 d												05 25							
62¼	—	—	**Northampton** 68 a												05 37							06 40
—	—	—	d						04 15	04 48		05 05			05 46						06 18	06 41
75¼	30	—	Wolverton d						04 27	05 00		05 17			05 58					←	06 30	
78¾	32¾	—	**Milton Keynes Central** ■ a						04 30	05 03		05 21			06 02			06 24			06 34	
—	—	—	d				00 24	03 30	04 30	05 04		05 21		05 54	06 02		06 19	06 26		06 19	06 35	
81¼	—	—	Bletchley d					03 35	04 35	05 09		05 26	05 38	05 59	06 07		→			06 24	06 40	
87¾	—	—	Leighton Buzzard d			00 03		03 42	04 42	05 15		05 33	05 45	06 06	06 15					06 31	06 47	
92	—	—	Cheddington d			00 12				05 24			05 50							06 37		
96¼	—	—	Tring d			00 18		03 54	04 55	05 30			05 57			06 23				06 42		
100	—	—	Berkhamsted d			00 23		03 59	05 01	05 35		05 50	06 02	06 18		06 28				06 46		
103½	—	—	Hemel Hempstead d			00 28		04 03	05 05	05 39		05 54	06 06	06 22		06 33				06 52		
105	—	—	Apsley d							05 42			06 09			06 36						
107	—	—	Kings Langley d							05 45			06 12			06 40						
110½	65	—	**Watford Junction** 60 a			00 35	00s52	04 10	05 13	05 49		06 01	06 17	06 29	06 33	06 44		06s47		06 59	07 04	
—	—	—	d			00 35		04 11	05 13	05 50	05 54	06 02	06 17	06 30	06 35	06 45			06 53	07 00	07 05	
112	—	—	Bushey 60 d	00 01	00 02								06 20			06 48						
116½	—	—	Harrow & Wealdstone ⊖60 d	00 07	00 08	00 42		04 17	05 20	05 56	06 00		06 26			06 53			07 00	07 06		
119¾	—	0	Wembley Central ⊖60,176 d			00 46		04 21	05 24		06 05								07 05			
—	—	4¼	Shepherd's Bush ⊖176 a								06 21								07 22			
—	—	5½	Kensington (Olympia) ⊖176 a								06 23								07 24			
—	—	7½	West Brompton ⊖176 a								06 26								07 27			
—	—	8	Imperial Wharf 176 a								06 29								07 30			
—	—	9	Clapham Junction 176 a								06 34								07 35			
—	—	16¾	East Croydon 176 🚊 a								06 59								08 01			
128	82½	—	**London Euston** ■ ⊖60 a	00 21	00 22	00 58	01 13	04 34	05 37	06 11		06 20	06 40	06 54	06 51	07 07		07 05		07 20	07 22	07 29

	VT	LM	LM	SN	LM	VT	LM	LM	VT	SN	VT	LM	LM	LM	LM	VT	SN	VT	LM	LM	VT	LM
	◇■	■	■	■	■	◇■	■	■	◇■	■	◇■	■	■	■	■	◇■	■	◇■	■	■	◇■	■
						E		D		F	G		D	A	D		H	I	J		E	
	⊠					⊠			⊠		⊠					⊠		⊠			⊠	
Wolverhampton ■ 68 🚊 d	05 24								05 45							06 04						
Sandwell & Dudley 68 d	05 34								05 55							06 15						
Birmingham New Street ■ 68 🚊 d	05 50							05 53	06 10						06 14	06 30						06 33
Birmingham International 68 ✈ d	06 00							06 05	06 20						06 30	06 40						06 45
Nuneaton 65 d						06 18													06 31		07 08	
Coventry 68 d	06 11						06 00	06 21	06 31						06 48	06 51						07 00
Rugby 68 d						06 32	06 11	06 32			06 54				06 59			07 08	06 47			07 12
Long Buckby 68 d							06 21	06 41							07 10				06 56			07 21
Northampton 68 a							06 33	06 54							07 24				07 09			07 35
d							06 38	07 09				07 00			07 38				07 16			07 42
Wolverton d							06 50	07 22				07 12		←	07 50							
Milton Keynes Central ■ a	06 38					06 51	06 54	07 25	06 59		07 13	07 16		07 25	07 54							
d	06 38				06 47	06 53	06 55	07 31	06 59	07 01	07 14	07 18	07 22	07 31	07 55							
Bletchley d		06 34			06 52		07 00	→		07 06			07 27		→					07 13		
Leighton Buzzard d		06 41			06 59		07 07			07 13		07 27	07 33	07 40								
Cheddington d					07 04								07 38				←					
Tring d		06 50	07 00		07 10					07 22			→				07 22			07 28		
Berkhamsted d		06 56	07 05		07 15					→							07 26			07 34		
Hemel Hempstead d		07 01	07 10		07 19												07 30			07 39		
Apsley d		07 04			07 23																	
Kings Langley d		07 08			07 26																	
Watford Junction 60 a		07 12	07 16		07 31											07s37	07 38			07 46		
d		07 13	07 19	07 24	07 32												07 38			07 46		
Bushey 60 d		07 15	07 22		07 35																	
Harrow & Wealdstone ⊖60 d		07 21		07 31	07 40												07 45					
Wembley Central ⊖60,176 d				07 36													07 50					
Shepherd's Bush ⊖176 a				07 49													08 11					
Kensington (Olympia) ⊖176 a				07 52													08 13					
West Brompton ⊖176 a				07 55													08 16					
Imperial Wharf 176 a				07 57													08 19					
Clapham Junction 176 a				08 02													08 24					
East Croydon 176 🚊 a				08 31													09 01					
London Euston ■ ⊖60 a	07 13	07 35	07 42		07 54	07 26	07 39		07 34		07 50	08 02		08 12		07 53		07 58	08 05	08 05	08 08	08 28

A From Birmingham New Street
B From Northampton
C From Wolverhampton
D To London Euston
E From Manchester Piccadilly
F To East Croydon
G From Liverpool Lime Street
H From Milton Keynes Central
I From Lancaster
J From Crewe

Table T066-R

Mondays to Fridays

21 May to 7 December

West Midlands, Northampton, Milton Keynes and Watford Junction - London

	VT ◇1 ⊠	LM 1	VT ◇1 A ⊠	LM 1 B	LM 1	LM 1	LM 1	LM 1	LM 1 C	LM 1	LM 1	SN 1	LM 1	VT ◇1 ⊠	VT ◇1 D ⊠	LM 1	VT ◇1 ⊠	VT ◇1 A ⊠	VT ◇1 ⊠	VT ◇1 A ⊠	LM 1	SN 1
Wolverhampton 7 68 ⛴ d	06 27													06 45			07 05					
Sandwell & Dudley 68 d	06 38													06 56			07 15					
Birmingham New Street 12 68 ⛴ d	06 50												06 54	07 10		07 14	07 30					
Birmingham International 68 ✈ d	07 00												07 05	07 20		07 30			07 41			
Nuneaton 65 d															07 35							
Coventry 68 d	07 11												07 21	07 31		07 43			07 52			
Rugby 68 d			07 30										07 32			07 54		07 54				
Long Buckby 68 d													07 41			08 04						
Northampton 68 a													07 54			08 16						
d								07 32					08 05			08 25						
Wolverton d									←				08 17			08 37						
Milton Keynes Central 10 a	07s40							07 46	07 54				08 21			08 40						
d								07 47	07 55	07 59		08 12	08 22			08 41				08 47		
Bletchley d					07 38			07 52	08 00	08 05		08 17	08 27			08 46						
Leighton Buzzard d				←	07 46			07 59	08 07	08 12		08 24	08 33			08 53						
Cheddington d				07 38				08 04														
Tring d				07 45			08 05	08 10			08 26	08 34									08 48	
Berkhamsted d				07 50	07 58			08 15			08 31	08 39									08 53	
Hemel Hempstead d				07 54	08 03			08 19		08 28	08 35	08 43									08 57	
Apsley d				07 58			08 14				08 38											
Kings Langley d				08 01			08 18				08 41											
Watford Junction 60 a				08 06	08 10		08 22	08 25		08 35	08 46	08 51									09 04	
d		07 55		08 06	08 11	08 15	08 23	08 27		08 36	08 46	08 52									09 05	09 16
Bushey 60 d		07 59				08 19					08 49										09 08	
Harrow & Wealdstone ⊖60 d		08 04			08 17	08 24	08 29	08 34			08 54	08 59									09 13	09 23
Wembley Central ⊖60,176 d												09 04										09 28
Shepherd's Bush ⊖176 a												09 22										09 46
Kensington (Olympia) ⊖176 a												09 24										09 48
West Brompton ⊖176 a												09 27										09 51
Imperial Wharf 176 a												09 30										09 54
Clapham Junction 176 a												09 35										09 59
East Croydon 176 ⛴ a												10 00										
London Euston 15 ⊖60 a	08 15	08 18	08 20	08 26	08 33	08 40	08 43	08 48	08 39	08 55	09 08		09 10	08 31	08 34	09 27	08 43	08 46	08 50	09 21	09 27	

	LM 1 E	LM 1 F	LM 1 E	SN 1 G	VT ◇1 ⊠	VT ◇1 H ⊠	LM 1 I	VT ◇1 A ⊠	VT ◇1 D ⊠	LM 1	LM 1	LM 1 C	VT ◇1 A ⊠	VT ◇1 ⊠	LM 1	SN 1	LM 1 F	LM 1	LM 1	LM 1	VT ◇1 A ⊠
Wolverhampton 7 68 ⛴ d					07 24	07 24	07 28	07 45													
Sandwell & Dudley 68 d							07 40	07 57													
Birmingham New Street 12 68 ⛴ d			07 33		07 50	07 50	07 54	08 10						08 30							
Birmingham International 68 ✈ d			07 45		08 00	08 00	08 05	08 21						08 40							
Nuneaton 65 d		08 19											08 46								
Coventry 68 d			08 04		08 10	08 11	08 21	08 31						08 51							
Rugby 68 d		08 34	08 15		08 23	08 23	08 39		08 47												
Long Buckby 68 d			08 25				08 48														
Northampton 68 a			08 37				09 00														
d			08 47				09 05											09 25			
Wolverton d			08 59				09 17				←	←				←	←	09 37			
Milton Keynes Central 10 a		08 55	09 03				09 21					09 03		09 18			09 21	09 41			
d	08 47	09 00	09 05	09 12			09 22				08 47	09 05		09 20		09 12	09 22	09 41		09 47	09 49
Bletchley d	→		→	→			→				08 52					09 17	09 27	09 46		09 52	
Leighton Buzzard d											08 59					09 24	09 34	09 53		09 59	
Cheddington d											09 04									10 04	
Tring d										09 01	09 10				09 26	09 34			09 56	10 10	
Berkhamsted d										09 06	09 15				09 31	09 39	09 46		10 01	10 15	
Hemel Hempstead d										09 10	09 19				09 36	09 43	09 51		10 05	10 19	
Apsley d										09 13					09 39				10 08		
Kings Langley d										09 16					09 42				10 11		
Watford Junction 60 a								09s16		09 21	09 26	09 28	09s32		09 46	09 51	09 58		10 15	10 26	
d										09 21	09 27	09 28			09 47	09 52	09 59		10 16	10 27	
Bushey 60 d										09 24					09 50				10 19		
Harrow & Wealdstone ⊖60 d										09 29	09 34				09 55	09 59			10 24		
Wembley Central ⊖60,176 d																10 04					
Shepherd's Bush ⊖176 a																10 22					
Kensington (Olympia) ⊖176 a																10 24					
West Brompton ⊖176 a																10 27					
Imperial Wharf 176 a																10 30					
Clapham Junction 176 a																10 35					
East Croydon 176 ⛴ a																10 59					
London Euston 15 ⊖60 a		09 37			09 13	09 13		09 33	09 41	09 43	09 48	09 46	09 49	09 53	10 11		10 19	10 23	10 39	10 45	10 26

A From Manchester Piccadilly
B From Milton Keynes Central
C From Birmingham New Street
D From Holyhead
E To London Euston
F From Crewe
G To East Croydon
H From Shrewsbury
I From Crewe to London Euston

Table T066-R

Mondays to Fridays

21 May to 7 December

West Midlands, Northampton, Milton Keynes and Watford Junction - London

	LM 1 A	LM 1 B	VT ◇1 ⊠	LM 1 B	VT ◇1 C ⊠	VT ◇1 D ⊠	LM 1 E	VT ◇1 F ⊠	SN 1 G	LM 1 H	LM 1	VT ◇1 ⊠	LM 1	SN 1 I	LM 1 E	VT ◇1 F ⊠	LM 1	LM 1	LM 1 B	VT ◇1 ⊠	LM 1 B	VT ◇1 ⊠
Wolverhampton 7 68 ⛴ d					08 45																	09 45
Sandwell & Dudley 68 d					08 55																	09 56
Birmingham New Street 12 68 ⛴ d		08 33	08 50	08 54	09 10						09 14	09 30							09 33	09 50	09 54	10 10
Birmingham International 68 ✈ d		08 45	09 00	09 05	09 20						09 30	09 40							09 45	10 00	10 05	10 20
Nuneaton 65 d	09 16							09 45														
Coventry 68 d		09 00	09 11	09 25	09 31						09 48	09 51							10 00	10 11	10 21	10 30
Rugby 68 d	09 32	09 12	09 23	09 38							09 59								10 12	10 23	10 32	
Long Buckby 68 d		09 21		09 47							10 08								10 21		10 41	
Northampton 68 a		09 33		09 59							10 20								10 33		10 54	
d		09 50		10 05							10 25								10 50		11 05	
Wolverton d				10 17			←			←	10 37										11 17	
Milton Keynes Central 10 a	09 53	10 04		10 21	09 58		10 04			10 21	10 41								11 04		11 21	10 58
d	09 54	10 07		10 22	10 00	10 03	10 07		10 12	10 22	10 41					10 47		10 47	11 07		11 22	11 00
Bletchley d		→		→					10 17	10 27	10 46							10 52	→		→	
Leighton Buzzard d									10 24	10 34	10 53							10 59				
Cheddington d																		11 04				
Tring d									10 34				10 26		←		10 56	11 10				
Berkhamsted d									10 39	10 46			10 31	←	10 46		11 01	11 15				
Hemel Hempstead d									10 43	→			10 35	10 43	10 51		11 05	11 19				
Apsley d									→				10 38				11 08					
Kings Langley d													10 41				11 11					
Watford Junction 60 a							10 30					10s39	10 46	10 51	10 58		11 16	11 26				
d							10 31						10 46	10 52	10 59		11 16	11 27				
Bushey 60 d													10 49				11 19					
Harrow & Wealdstone ⊖60 d													10 54	10 59			11 24					
Wembley Central ⊖60,176 d														11 04			11 29					
Shepherd's Bush ⊖176 a														11 22								
Kensington (Olympia) ⊖176 a														11 24								
West Brompton ⊖176 a														11 27								
Imperial Wharf 176 a														11 30								
Clapham Junction 176 a														11 35								
East Croydon 176 ⛴ a														11 59								
London Euston 15 ⊖60 a	10 29		10 13		10 32	10 37	10 46	10 51			11 27	10 56	11 08		11 19	11 20	11 41	11 45		11 15		11 34

	VT ◇1 J ⊠	VT ◇1 K ⊠	LM 1 E	SN TThO 1 L	SN MWFO 1 G	LM 1 A	LM 1 H	LM 1	VT ◇1 ⊠	LM 1	SN TThO 1 I	SN MWFO 1 I	LM 1 E	VT ◇1 F ⊠	LM 1	LM 1	LM 1 B	VT ◇1 ⊠	LM 1 B	VT ◇1 M ⊠	VT ◇1 D ⊠
Wolverhampton 7 68 ⛴ d	09 45																			10 45	
Sandwell & Dudley 68 d	09 56																			10 55	
Birmingham New Street 12 68 ⛴ d	10 10							10 14	10 30								10 33	10 50	10 54	11 10	
Birmingham International 68 ✈ d	10 20							10 30	10 40								10 45	11 00	11 05	11 20	
Nuneaton 65 d						10 36															
Coventry 68 d	10 31							10 48	10 51								11 00	11 11	11 21	11 31	
Rugby 68 d						10 53		10 59									11 12	11 23	11 32		
Long Buckby 68 d								11 08									11 21		11 41		
Northampton 68 a								11 20									11 33		11 54		
d								11 25									11 50		12 05		
Wolverton d			←				←	11 37											12 17		
Milton Keynes Central 10 a	10 58		11 04			11 14	11 21	11 41									12 04		12 21	11 58	
d	11 00	11 03	11 07	11 12	11 12	11 15	11 22	11 41						11 47		11 47	12 07		12 22	12 00	12 03
Bletchley d				11 17	11 17		11 27	11 46								11 52	→		→		
Leighton Buzzard d				11 24	11 24		11 34	11 53								11 59					
Cheddington d																12 04					
Tring d				11 34	11 34					11 26			←		11 56	12 10					
Berkhamsted d				11 39	11 39		11 46			11 31	←	←	11 46		12 01	12 15					
Hemel Hempstead d				11 43	11 43		→			11 35	11 43	11 43	11 51		12 05	12 19					
Apsley d				→	→					11 38					12 08						
Kings Langley d										11 41					12 11						
Watford Junction 60 a			11 30						11s39	11 46	11 51	11 51	11 58		12 16	12 26					
d			11 31							11 46	11 52	11 52	11 59		12 16	12 27					
Bushey 60 d										11 49					12 19						
Harrow & Wealdstone ⊖60 d										11 54	11 59	11 59			12 24						
Wembley Central ⊖60,176 d											12 03	12 03			12 29						
Shepherd's Bush ⊖176 a											12 22	12 22									
Kensington (Olympia) ⊖176 a											12 24	12 24									
West Brompton ⊖176 a											12 27	12 27									
Imperial Wharf 176 a											12 30	12 30									
Clapham Junction 176 a											12 35	12 35									
East Croydon 176 ⛴ a												12 59									
London Euston 15 ⊖60 a	11 34	11 37	11 46			11 50		12 27	11 55	12 08			12 18	12 20	12 41	12 45		12 14		12 33	12 37

A From Crewe
B To London Euston
C From Lancaster
D From Holyhead
E From Birmingham New Street
F From Manchester Piccadilly
G To East Croydon
H From Birmingham New Street to London Euston
I From Milton Keynes Central
J From Glasgow Central
K From Chester
L To Clapham Junction
M From Edinburgh

West Midlands, Northampton, Milton Keynes and Watford Junction - London

	LM	SN	LM	LM	LM	VT	LM	SN	LM	VT	LM	LM	LM	VT	LM	VT	VT	LM	SN	LM	LM	VT
	A	B	C	D				E	A	F			G		G	H	I	A	B	C	D	J
Wolverhampton 68 d																11 45						
Sandwell & Dudley 68 d																11 55						
Birmingham New Street 68 d					11 14	11 30							11 33	11 50	11 54	12 10						
Birmingham International 68 d					11 30	11 40							11 45	12 00	12 05	12 20						
Nuneaton 65 d			11 36																	12 36		
Coventry 68 d					11 48	11 51							12 00	12 11	12 21	12 31						
Rugby 68 d			11 53		11 59								12 18	12 23	12 32					12 53		13 00
Long Buckby 68 d					12 08								12 27		12 41							
Northampton 68 a					12 20								12 41		12 54							
d					12 25								12 50		13 05							
Wolverton d	←			←	12 37										13 17			←			←	
Milton Keynes Central a	12 04		12 14	12 21	12 41								13 04		13 21	12 58		13 04		13 14	13 21	
d	12 07	12 12	12 15	12 22	12 41					12 47		12 47	13 07		13 22	13 00	13 03	13 07	13 12	13 15	13 22	
Bletchley d		12 17		12 27	12 46							12 52	→		→				13 17		13 27	
Leighton Buzzard d		12 24		12 34	12 53							12 59							13 24		13 34	
Cheddington d												13 04										
Tring d		12 34					12 26		←		12 56	13 10							13 34			
Berkhamsted d		12 39		12 46			12 31	←	12 46		13 01	13 15							13 39		13 46	
Hemel Hempstead d		12 43		→			12 35	12 43	12 51		13 05	13 19							13 43		→	
Apsley d		→					12 38				13 08								→			
Kings Langley d							12 41				13 11											
Watford Junction 60 a	12 30					12s39	12 46	12 51	12 58		13 16	13 26						13 30				
d	12 31						12 46	12 52	12 59		13 16	13 27						13 31				
Bushey 60 d							12 49				13 19											
Harrow & Wealdstone ⊖60 d							12 54	12 59			13 24											
Wembley Central ⊖60,176 d								13 04			13 29											
Shepherd's Bush ⊖176 a								13 22														
Kensington (Olympia) ⊖176 a								13 24														
West Brompton ⊖176 a								13 27														
Imperial Wharf 176 a								13 30														
Clapham Junction 176 a								13 35														
East Croydon 176 a								13 59														
London Euston ⊖60 a	12 46		12 50		13 27	12 55	13 08		13 19	13 20	13 41	13 45		13 14		13 33	13 37	13 46		13 50		13 53

	LM	VT	LM	SN	LM	VT	LM	LM	LM	VT	LM	VT	VT	LM	SN	LM	LM	LM	VT	LM	SN	VT
				E	A	F			G		G	K	I	A	B	C	D				E	H
Wolverhampton 68 d												12 45										
Sandwell & Dudley 68 d												12 55										
Birmingham New Street 68 d	12 14	12 30							12 33	12 50	12 54	13 10						13 14	13 30			
Birmingham International 68 d	12 30	12 40							12 45	13 00	13 05	13 20						13 30	13 40			
Nuneaton 65 d																13 36						
Coventry 68 d	12 48	12 51							13 00	13 11	13 21	13 31						13 48	13 51			
Rugby 68 d	12 59								13 12	13 23	13 32					13 53		13 59				14 24
Long Buckby 68 d	13 08								13 21		13 41							14 08				
Northampton 68 a	13 21								13 34		13 53							14 20				
d	13 25								13 50		14 05							14 25				
Wolverton d	13 37										14 17			←			←	14 37				
Milton Keynes Central a	13 41								14 04		14 21	13 58		14 04		14 14	14 21	14 41				
d	13 41					13 47		13 47	14 07		14 22	14 00	14 03	14 07	14 12	14 15	14 22	14 41				
Bletchley d	13 46							13 52	→		→				14 17		14 27	14 46				
Leighton Buzzard d	13 53							13 59							14 24		14 34	14 53				
Cheddington d								14 04														
Tring d			13 26		←		13 56	14 10							14 34					14 26		
Berkhamsted d			13 31	←	13 46		14 01	14 15							14 39		14 46			14 31	←	
Hemel Hempstead d			13 35	13 43	13 51		14 05	14 19							14 43		→			14 35	14 43	
Apsley d			13 38				14 08								→					14 38		
Kings Langley d			13 41				14 11													14 42		
Watford Junction 60 a		13s42	13 46	13 51	13 58		14 16	14 26						14 30					14s39	14 46	14 51	
d			13 46	13 52	13 59		14 16	14 27						14 31						14 47	14 52	
Bushey 60 d			13 49				14 19													14 50		
Harrow & Wealdstone ⊖60 d			13 54	13 59			14 24													14 55	14 59	
Wembley Central ⊖60,176 d				14 04			14 29														15 04	
Shepherd's Bush ⊖176 a				14 22																	15 22	
Kensington (Olympia) ⊖176 a				14 24																	15 24	
West Brompton ⊖176 a				14 27																	15 27	
Imperial Wharf 176 a				14 30																	15 30	
Clapham Junction 176 a				14 35																	15 35	
East Croydon 176 a				14 59																	16 00	
London Euston ⊖60 a	14 27	13 59	14 08		14 18	14 20	14 41	14 45		14 14		14 33	14 38	14 47		14 50		15 27	14 55	15 11		15 13

A From Birmingham New Street
B To East Croydon
C From Crewe
D From Birmingham New Street to London Euston
E From Milton Keynes Central
F From Manchester Piccadilly
G To London Euston
H From Glasgow Central
I From Chester
J From Blackpool North
K From Edinburgh

West Midlands, Northampton, Milton Keynes and Watford Junction - London

	LM	LM	LM	VT	LM	VT	LM	VT	VT	LM	SN	LM	LM	LM	VT	VT MX	VT MO	LM	SN	LM	VT FO
	A			B	C		C	D	E	A	F	G	H			I	I		J	A	B
Wolverhampton 68 d								13 45													
Sandwell & Dudley 68 d								13 55													
Birmingham New Street 68 d					13 33	13 50	13 54	14 10						14 14	14 30						
Birmingham International 68 d					13 45	14 00	14 05	14 20						14 30	14 40						
Nuneaton 65 d												14 36									
Coventry 68 d					14 00	14 11	14 21	14 30						14 48	14 50						
Rugby 68 d					14 12	14 26	14 32					14 53		14 59		15 08	15 10				
Long Buckby 68 d					14 21		14 41							15 08							
Northampton 68 a					14 33		14 54							15 20							
d					14 50		15 05							15 25							
Wolverton d							15 17			←			←	15 37							
Milton Keynes Central a					15 04		15 21	14 58		15 04		15 14	15 21	15 41							
d			14 47	14 50	15 07		15 22	14 59	15 03	15 07	15 12	15 15	15 22	15 41							15 47
Bletchley d			14 52		→		→				15 17		15 27	15 46							
Leighton Buzzard d			14 59								15 24		15 34	15 53							
Cheddington d			15 04																		
Tring d	←	14 56	15 10								15 34							15 26		←	
Berkhamsted d	14 46	15 01	15 15								15 39		15 46					15 31	←	15 46	
Hemel Hempstead d	14 51	15 05	15 19								15 43		→					15 35	15 43	15 51	
Apsley d		15 08									→							15 38			
Kings Langley d		15 11																15 41			
Watford Junction 60 a	14 58	15 16	15 26							15 30					15s39			15 46	15 51	15 58	
d	14 59	15 16	15 27							15 31								15 46	15 52	15 59	
Bushey 60 d		15 19																15 49			
Harrow & Wealdstone ⊖60 d		15 24																15 54	15 59		
Wembley Central ⊖60,176 d		15 29																	16 04		
Shepherd's Bush ⊖176 a																			16 22		
Kensington (Olympia) ⊖176 a																			16 24		
West Brompton ⊖176 a																			16 27		
Imperial Wharf 176 a																			16 30		
Clapham Junction 176 a																			16 35		
East Croydon 176 a																			17 00		
London Euston ⊖60 a	15 19	15 41	15 45	15 28		15 16		15 33	15 36	15 48		15 50		16 27	15 56	15 59	15 59	16 08		16 19	16 22

	VT FX	SN	LM	LM	LM	VT	LM	VT	VT	LM	SN	LM	LM	LM	VT	LM	SN	LM	VT	LM	LM	LM
	B				C		C	K	L	A	F	G	H				J	A	B			C
Wolverhampton 68 d								14 45														
Sandwell & Dudley 68 d								14 55														
Birmingham New Street 68 d					14 33	14 50	14 54	15 10						15 14	15 30							15 33
Birmingham International 68 d					14 45	15 00	15 05	15 20						15 30	15 40							15 45
Nuneaton 65 d												15 36										
Coventry 68 d					15 00	15 11	15 21	15 31						15 48	15 51							16 00
Rugby 68 d					15 12	15 23	15 32					15 53		15 59								16 12
Long Buckby 68 d					15 21		15 41							16 08								16 21
Northampton 68 a					15 33		15 56							16 22								16 34
d					15 50		16 05							16 25								16 50
Wolverton d							16 17			←			←	16 37								
Milton Keynes Central a					16 04		16 21	15 58		16 04		16 14	16 21	16 41								17 04
d	15 47			15 47	16 07		16 22	16 00	16 03	16 07	16 12	16 15	16 22	16 41					16 47		16 47	17 07
Bletchley d				15 52	→		→				16 17		16 27	16 46							16 52	→
Leighton Buzzard d				15 59							16 24		16 34	16 53							16 59	
Cheddington d				16 04																	17 04	
Tring d			15 56	16 10							16 34					16 26		←		16 57	17 10	
Berkhamsted d			16 01	16 15							16 39		16 46			16 31	←	16 46		17 02	17 15	
Hemel Hempstead d			16 05	16 19							16 43		→			16 36	16 43	16 51		17 07	17 19	
Apsley d			16 08								→					16 39				17 10		
Kings Langley d			16 11													16 42				17 13		
Watford Junction 60 a			16 16	16 26						16 30					16s39	16 46	16 51	16 58		17 17	17 26	
d		16 12	16 16	16 27						16 31						16 47	16 52	16 59		17 18	17 27	
Bushey 60 d			16 19													16 50				17 21		
Harrow & Wealdstone ⊖60 d		16 20	16 24													16 55	16 59			17 26		
Wembley Central ⊖60,176 d		16 25	16 29														17 04					
Shepherd's Bush ⊖176 a		16 46															17 22					
Kensington (Olympia) ⊖176 a		16 48															17 24					
West Brompton ⊖176 a		16 51															17 27					
Imperial Wharf 176 a		16 54															17 30					
Clapham Junction 176 a		16 59															17 35					
East Croydon 176 a		17 30															18 00					
London Euston ⊖60 a	16 24		16 41	16 45		16 14		16 32	16 37	16 46		16 50		17 27	16 56	17 12		17 19	17 21	17 40	17 47	

A From Birmingham New Street
B From Manchester Piccadilly
C To London Euston
D From Glasgow Central
E From Chester
F To East Croydon
G From Crewe
H From Birmingham New Street to London Euston
I From Blackpool North
J From Milton Keynes Central
K From Edinburgh
L From Holyhead

West Midlands, Northampton, Milton Keynes and Watford Junction - London

		VT	LM	VT	VT	LM	VT	VT	LM	SN	LM	VT	LM	LM	VT	LM	LM	LM	VT	LM	VT	VT
		◇1	1	◇1	◇1	1	◇1	◇1	1	1	1	◇1	1	1	◇1	1	1	1	◇1	1	◇1	◇1
			A	B	C	D	E				F	G	D		H			A		A	I	J
		🛒		🛒	🛒		🛒	🛒				🛒			🛒				🛒		🛒	🛒
Wolverhampton 7 68	d			15 45			16 04														16 45	
Sandwell & Dudley 68	d			15 55																	16 55	
Birmingham New Street 12 68	d	15 50	15 54	16 10			16 30	16 30										16 33	16 50	16 54	17 10	
Birmingham International 68	d	16 00	16 05	16 20			16 40	16 40										16 45	17 00	17 05	17 20	
Nuneaton 65	d										16 36											
Coventry 68	d	16 11	16 21	16 31			16 51	16 51										17 00	17 11	17 21	17 31	
Rugby 68	d	16 23	16 32								16 53	17 07						17 16	17 23	17 32		
Long Buckby 68	d		16 41															17 26		17 41		
Northampton 68	a		16 57															17 38		17 56		
	d		17 05											17 25				17 50		18 05		
Wolverton	d		17 17			←							←	17 37						18 17		
Milton Keynes Central 10	a		17 21	16 58		17 04					17 14		17 21	17 41				18 04		18 21	17 58	
	d		17 22	16 59	17 03	17 07				17 12	17 15		17 22	17 41	17 47		17 47	18 07		18 22	17 59	18 03
Bletchley	d		→							17 17			17 27	17 46			17 52	→		→		
Leighton Buzzard	d									17 24			17 33	17 53			17 59					
Cheddington	d																18 04					
Tring	d								17 26	17 34						17 58	18 10					
Berkhamsted	d								17 31	17 39			17 46			18 03	18 15					
Hemel Hempstead	d								17 35	17 43			17 51			18 08	18 19					
Apsley	d								17 38							18 11						
Kings Langley	d								17 42							18 14						
Watford Junction 60	a					17 30	17s39	17s39	17 46	17 51			17 58			18 18	18 26					
	d					17 31			17 47	17 52			17 59			18 19	18 27					
Bushey 60	d								17 50							18 22						
Harrow & Wealdstone ⊖60	d								17 55	17 59						18 27						
Wembley Central ⊖60,176	d									18 04												
Shepherd's Bush ⊖176	a									18 22												
Kensington (Olympia) ⊖176	a									18 24												
West Brompton ⊖176	a									18 27												
Imperial Wharf 176	a									18 30												
Clapham Junction 176	a									18 35												
East Croydon 176	a									19 00												
London Euston 15 ⊖60	a	17 14		17 33	17 37	17 46	17 56	17 56	18 11		17 50	17 59	18 17	18 27	18 20	18 41	18 45		18 14		18 34	18 37

		LM	SN	LM	LM	VT	LM	VT	LM	SN	LM	LM	LM	VT	LM	VT	LM	VT	VT	LM	LM	SN	VT
		1	1	1	1	◇1	1	◇1	1	1	1	1	1	◇1	1	◇1	1	◇1	◇1	1	1	1	◇1
		D	K	F	L	M				N	D			H	A			B	J	D	F	K	H
						🛒		⊠						⊠		⊠		🛒	⊠				⊠
Wolverhampton 7 68	d																	17 45					
Sandwell & Dudley 68	d																	17 55					
Birmingham New Street 12 68	d						17 14	17 30							17 33	17 50	17 54	18 10					
Birmingham International 68	d						17 27	17 40							17 45	18 00	18 05	18 20					
Nuneaton 65	d			17 36																	18 36		
Coventry 68	d						17 42	17 51							18 00	18 10		18 31					
Rugby 68	d			17 55			17 56								18 12	18 23					18 53		
Long Buckby 68	d						18 05								18 21								
Northampton 68	a						18 17								18 37								
	d						18 25								18 50								
Wolverton	d	←			←		18 37													←			
Milton Keynes Central 10	a	18 04		18 15	18 21		18 41								19 04			18 58		19 04	19 14		
	d	18 07	18 12	18 15	18 22	18 24	18 41						18 47	18 49	19 07			18 59	19 02	19 07	19 15	19 15	19 34
Bletchley	d		18 17		18 27		18 46						18 52		→							19 20	
Leighton Buzzard	d		18 24		18 33		18 53						18 59									19 27	
Cheddington	d												19 04										
Tring	d		18 34						18 25		←	19 00	19 10									19 36	
Berkhamsted	d		18 39		18 46				18 30	←	18 46	19 05	19 15									→	
Hemel Hempstead	d		18 43		→				18 35	18 43	18 51	19 09	19 19										
Apsley	d		→						18 38			19 12											
Kings Langley	d								18 41			19 15											
Watford Junction 60	a	18 30						18s39	18 45	18 51	18 58	19 20	19 26							19 30			
	d	18 31							18 46	18 51	18 59	19 20	19 27							19 31			
Bushey 60	d								18 49			19 23											
Harrow & Wealdstone ⊖60	d								18 54	18 59		19 28											
Wembley Central ⊖60,176	d									19 05													
Shepherd's Bush ⊖176	a									19 22													
Kensington (Olympia) ⊖176	a									19 24													
West Brompton ⊖176	a									19 27													
Imperial Wharf 176	a									19 30													
Clapham Junction 176	a									19 35													
East Croydon 176	a									19 59													
London Euston 15 ⊖60	a	18 46		18 52		19 03	19 28	18 56	19 08		19 20	19 42	19 45	19 24		19 14	20 20	19 33	19 38	19 47	19 50		20 08

A To London Euston
B From Glasgow Central
C From Holyhead
D From Birmingham New Street
E From Shrewsbury
F From Crewe
G From Blackpool North
H From Manchester Piccadilly
I From Edinburgh
J From Chester
K To East Croydon
L From Birmingham New Street to London Euston
M From Liverpool Lime Street
N From Milton Keynes Central

West Midlands, Northampton, Milton Keynes and Watford Junction - London

		LM	VT	LM	SN	VT	LM	LM	LM	VT	LM	VT	LM	SN	LM	LM	VT	LM	VT	LM	SN	LM	VT
		1	◇1	1	1	◇1	1	1	1	◇1	1	1	1	1	1	1	◇1	1	◇1	1	1	1	◇1
					A	B			C		C	D	E	F	G	H	B				A	E	I
			⊠			⊠				⊠		🛒					⊠		🛒				⊠
Wolverhampton 7 68	d											18 45											
Sandwell & Dudley 68	d											18 55											
Birmingham New Street 12 68	d	18 14	18 30						18 33	18 50	18 54	19 10						19 14	19 30				
Birmingham International 68	d	18 30	18 40						18 45	19 00	19 05	19 20						19 30	19 40				
Nuneaton 65	d														19 36								
Coventry 68	d	18 48	18 51						19 00	19 11	19 21	19 31						19 48	19 51				
Rugby 68	d	18 59							19 18	19 23	19 32				19 53			19 59	20 03				
Long Buckby 68	d	19 08							19 27		19 41							20 10					
Northampton 68	a	19 21							19 41		19 54							20 23					
	d	19 25							19 50		20 05							20 25					
Wolverton	d	19 37									20 17		←			←		20 37					
Milton Keynes Central 10	a	19 40							20 04		20 24	19 58	20 04		20 14	20 24		20 41					
	d	19 41				19 47		19 47	20 07		20 25	20 00	20 07	20 12	20 15	20 25	20 33	20 41					20 47
Bletchley	d	19 46						19 52	→		→			20 19		20 30		20 46					
Leighton Buzzard	d	19 53						19 59						20 26		20 37		20 53					
Cheddington	d				←			20 04															
Tring	d			19 30	19 36		19 56	20 10						20 36						20 26		←	
Berkhamsted	d			19 35	19 41		20 01	20 15						20 40		20 49				20 31	←	20 49	
Hemel Hempstead	d			19 39	19 45		20 06	20 19						20 44		→				20 36	20 44	20 54	
Apsley	d			19 42			20 09							→						20 39			
Kings Langley	d			19 45			20 12													20 42			
Watford Junction 60	a		19s39	19 50	19 53		20 16	20 26					20 29						20s41	20 46	20 52	21 01	
	d			19 50	19 54		20 17	20 27					20 31							20 47	20 52	21 01	
Bushey 60	d			19 53			20 20													20 50			
Harrow & Wealdstone ⊖60	d			19 58	20 02		20 24													20 55	20 59		
Wembley Central ⊖60,176	d				20 06																21 04		
Shepherd's Bush ⊖176	a				20 22																21 18		
Kensington (Olympia) ⊖176	a				20 24																21 21		
West Brompton ⊖176	a				20 27																21 24		
Imperial Wharf 176	a				20 30																21 27		
Clapham Junction 176	a				20 35																21 32		
East Croydon 176	a				21 00																		
London Euston 15 ⊖60	a	20 27	19 56	20 13		20 21	20 39	20 45		20 15		20 32	20 48		20 51		21 06	21 28	20 57	21 11		21 20	21 20

		LM	LM	VT	LM	VT	VT	LM	LM	VT	SN	LM	VT	VT	VT	LM	VT	LM	VT	SN	LM	LM
		1	1	◇1	1	◇1	◇1	1	1	◇1	1	1	◇1	◇1	◇1	1	◇1	1	1	1	1	1
			C	B	C	I	J			K		E	B	I	B	C		C	D		E	
				🛒		⊠	🛒			🛒			🛒	🛒	🛒		🛒		⊠			
Wolverhampton 7 68	d					19 45													20 47			
Sandwell & Dudley 68	d					19 55													20 57			
Birmingham New Street 12 68	d				19 54	20 10										20 33	20 50	20 54	21 10			
Birmingham International 68	d				20 05	20 20										20 45	21 00	21 05	21 20			
Nuneaton 65	d									21 03												
Coventry 68	d				20 21	20 31										21 00	21 11	21 21	21 31			
Rugby 68	d				20 32									21 30		21 14	21 23	21 32				
Long Buckby 68	d				20 41											21 23		21 41				
Northampton 68	a				20 53											21 35		21 54				
	d				21 05											21 37		22 05				
Wolverton	d				21 17			←				←				21 49		22 17			←	
Milton Keynes Central 10	a				21 22	20 58						21 22		21 49		21 52		22 21	21 58		21 52	
	d		20 47	20 50	21 22	21 00	21 05	20 47			21 12	21 22	21 36	21 50	21 53	21 53		22 22	21 59		21 53	22 05
Bletchley	d		→		→			20 52			21 17	21 27				→		→			21 58	22 10
Leighton Buzzard	d							20 59			21 24	21 34									22 04	22 17
Cheddington	d							21 04													22 10	22 22
Tring	d	20 58						21 10	21 26		21 34										22 16	22 28
Berkhamsted	d	21 03						21 15	21 31		21 39	21 47									22 20	22 33
Hemel Hempstead	d	21 08						21 19	21 36		21 43	21 51									22 25	22 37
Apsley	d	21 11							21 39													22 40
Kings Langley	d	21 14							21 42													22 43
Watford Junction 60	a	21 18				21s19		21 27	21 46	21s49	21 51	21 58			22s13				22s20		22 32	22 48
	d	21 19						21 27	21 47		21 51	21 59								22 27	22 33	22 48
Bushey 60	d	21 22							21 50													22 51
Harrow & Wealdstone ⊖60	d	21 27							21 55		21 59									22 33		22 57
Wembley Central ⊖60,176	d																					
Shepherd's Bush ⊖176	a										22 18									22 57		
Kensington (Olympia) ⊖176	a										22 21									22 59		
West Brompton ⊖176	a										22 24									23 02		
Imperial Wharf 176	a										22 27									23 05		
Clapham Junction 176	a										22 31									23 10		
East Croydon 176	a										22 59											
London Euston 15 ⊖60	a	21 41		21 23		21 37	21 40	21 47	22 11	22 06		22 23	22 10	22 26	22 29		22 13		22 41		22 52	23 11

A From Milton Keynes Central
B From Manchester Piccadilly
C To London Euston
D From Edinburgh
E From Birmingham New Street
F To Clapham Junction
G From Crewe
H From Birmingham New Street to London Euston
I From Glasgow Central
J From Chester
K From Liverpool Lime Street

West Midlands, Northampton, Milton Keynes and Watford Junction - London

Station		SN	LM A	VT B	VT C	VT D	SN	LM E	VT	LM A	LM	VT
Wolverhampton 68	d								21 45			22 45
Sandwell & Dudley 68	d								21 55			22 55
Birmingham New Street 68	d							21 54	22 10			23 10
Birmingham International 68	d							22 05	22 20			23 20
Nuneaton 65	d				22 18							
Coventry 68	d							22 21	22 31			23 31
Rugby 68	d				22 32			22 32	22 45			23 44
Long Buckby 68	d							22 41				
Northampton 68	a							22 53				00s05
	d							22 55			23 35	
Wolverton	d		←					23 08		←	23 46	
Milton Keynes Central	a		22 21		22 54			23 12	23 06	23 12	23 51	00 23
	d	22 10	22 22	22 41	22 55	23 01		23 13	23 08	23 13	23 51	00 24
Bletchley	d	22 15	22 27					→		23 18	23 56	
Leighton Buzzard	d	22 22	22 33							23 24	00 03	
Cheddington	d									23 29	00 12	
Tring	d	22 34								23 38	00 18	
Berkhamsted	d	22 39	22 46							23 43	00 23	
Hemel Hempstead	d	22 43	22 51							23 47	00 28	
Apsley	d									23 50		
Kings Langley	d									23 53		
Watford Junction 60	a	22 52	23 01	23s15	23s25	23s30			23s39	23 58	00 35	00s52
	d	22 53	23 03				23 36			23 59	00 35	
Bushey 60	d									00 01		
Harrow & Wealdstone ⊖60	d	23 00					23 42			00 07	00 42	
Wembley Central ⊖60,176	d										00 46	
Shepherd's Bush ⊖176	a	23 21					00 05					
Kensington (Olympia) ⊖176	a	23 24					00 07					
West Brompton ⊖176	a	23 27					00 10					
Imperial Wharf 176	a	23 29					00 12					
Clapham Junction 176	a	23 34					00 17					
East Croydon 176	a											
London Euston ⊖60	a		23 21	23 34	23 43	23 48			00 03	00 21	00 58	01 13

Saturdays
26 May to 8 December

Station		LM A	LM F	VT G	LM	LM	SN	LM	LM	VT	SN	LM	LM	LM E	VT	LM	VT D	SN H	LM E	VT D	VT I	LM E	LM E
Wolverhampton 68	d														05 45								
Sandwell & Dudley 68	d														05 55								
Birmingham New Street 68	d									05 50					06 10								06 14
Birmingham International 68	d									06 00					06 20								06 30
Nuneaton 65	d																						
Coventry 68	d									06 11					06 31								06 48
Rugby 68	d									06 24							06 51						06 59
Long Buckby 68	d																						07 08
Northampton 68	a																						07 20
	d							05 15				06 05							07 05				07 35
Wolverton	d							05 27				06 17				←			07 17				07 47
Milton Keynes Central	a							05 31				06 21			06 59		07 11		07 21				07 51
	d			00 24	03 40	04 35		05 32				06 22		06 47	06 59	06 47	07 12	07 13	07 22	07 33	07 39	07 44	07 52
Bletchley	d				03 45	04 40		05 37	06 10			06 27	06 40	→		06 52		→	→			→	→
Leighton Buzzard	d		00 03		03 52	04 47		05 44	06 16			06 33	06 46			06 59							
Cheddington	d		00 12					05 51								07 04							
Tring	d		00 18		04 04	04 59		05 56	06 26			06 44	06 56			07 10							
Berkhamsted	d		00 23		04 09	05 04		06 01	06 31			06 49	07 01			07 15							
Hemel Hempstead	d		00 28		04 13	05 08		06 06	06 36			06 53	07 06			07 19							
Apsley	d							06 09	06 39				07 09										
Kings Langley	d							06 12	06 42				07 12										
Watford Junction 60	a		00 35	00s52	04 20	05 15		06 16	06 46			07 00	07 16		07s19	07 26	07s33						
	d		00 35		04 21	05 16	05 52	06 17	06 47		06 55	07 01	07 17			07 27							
Bushey 60	d	00 01						06 20	06 50				07 20										
Harrow & Wealdstone ⊖60	d	00 07	00 42		04 27	05 22	05 58	06 25	06 55		07 01		07 25										
Wembley Central ⊖60,176	d		00 46		04 32	05 27	06 03				07 06												
Shepherd's Bush ⊖176	a						06 19				07 21												
Kensington (Olympia) ⊖176	a						06 21				07 23												
West Brompton ⊖176	a						06 24				07 26												
Imperial Wharf 176	a						06 27				07 29												
Clapham Junction 176	a						06 32				07 34												
East Croydon 176	a						06 59				07 59												
London Euston ⊖60	a	00 21	00 58	01 13	04 45	05 39		06 39	07 09	07 15		07 20	07 39		07 36	07 45	07 50			08 07	08 14		

A From Birmingham New Street
B From Glasgow Central
C From Liverpool Lime Street
D From Manchester Piccadilly
E To London Euston
F From Northampton
G From Wolverhampton
H To East Croydon
I From Lancaster

West Midlands, Northampton, Milton Keynes and Watford Junction - London

Station		VT	VT A	LM	SN	VT	LM B	LM C	VT	LM	LM D	LM	VT E	LM F	SN G	LM H	LM	VT	LM	SN I	LM F	VT E	LM
Wolverhampton 68	d	06 06				06 27			06 45									07 05					
Sandwell & Dudley 68	d	06 17				06 37			06 56									07 15					
Birmingham New Street 68	d	06 30				06 50		06 54	07 10								07 14	07 30					
Birmingham International 68	d	06 40				07 00		07 05	07 20								07 30	07 40					
Nuneaton 65	d		06 59								07 27												
Coventry 68	d	06 51				07 11		07 21	07 31								07 48	07 51					
Rugby 68	d					07 23		07 32			07 43		07 54				07 59						
Long Buckby 68	d							07 41									08 08						
Northampton 68	a							07 54									08 20						
	d							08 05									08 25						
Wolverton	d				←		←	08 17				←		←		←	08 37						
Milton Keynes Central	a						07 21	08 21	07 58		08 04			07 51		08 21	08 41						
	d				07 13		07 22	08 22	07 59		08 05	07 44		07 52	08 13	08 22	08 41					08 47	
Bletchley	d			07 10	07 18		07 27	→				07 49		07 57	08 18	08 27	08 46						
Leighton Buzzard	d			07 16	07 25		07 33					07 56		08 03	08 25	08 33	08 53						
Cheddington	d											08 00											
Tring	d			07 26	07 34					07 56		08 07			08 34				08 26		←		08 56
Berkhamsted	d			07 31	07 39		07 46			08 01		08 12			08 39	08 46			08 31	←	08 46		09 01
Hemel Hempstead	d			07 36	07 43		07 51			08 06		08 16			08 43	→			08 35	08 43	08 51		09 06
Apsley	d			07 39						08 09					→				08 38				09 09
Kings Langley	d			07 42						08 12									08 41				09 12
Watford Junction 60	a	07s37	07s45	07 46	07 51		07 58			08 16		08 23		08 27				08s37	08 46	08 51	08 58		09 16
	d			07 47	07 52		07 59			08 17		08 24		08 28					08 46	08 52	08 59		09 17
Bushey 60	d			07 50						08 20									08 49				09 20
Harrow & Wealdstone ⊖60	d			07 55	07 59					08 25									08 54	08 59			09 25
Wembley Central ⊖60,176	d				08 04															09 04			
Shepherd's Bush ⊖176	a				08 19															09 19			
Kensington (Olympia) ⊖176	a				08 21															09 21			
West Brompton ⊖176	a				08 24															09 24			
Imperial Wharf 176	a				08 27															09 27			
Clapham Junction 176	a				08 32															09 32			
East Croydon 176	a				08 59															09 59			
London Euston ⊖60	a	07 53	08 02	08 09		08 17	08 18		08 33	08 39	08 40	08 42	08 45	08 46			09 27	08 54	09 08		09 19	09 21	09 39

Station		LM	VT J	LM C	VT	LM C	VT K	LM F	SN G	LM D	LM H	LM D	LM	VT	VT A	LM	SN I	LM F	VT E	LM	LM	LM C
Wolverhampton 68	d				07 25		07 45															
Sandwell & Dudley 68	d						07 55															
Birmingham New Street 68	d			07 33	07 50	07 54	08 10						08 14	08 30								08 33
Birmingham International 68	d			07 45	08 00	08 05	08 20						08 30	08 40								08 45
Nuneaton 65	d									08 27		08 47			09 05							
Coventry 68	d			08 00	08 11	08 21	08 31						08 48	08 51								09 00
Rugby 68	d			08 12	08 23	08 32				08 43		09 03	08 59									09 12
Long Buckby 68	d			08 21		08 41							09 08									09 21
Northampton 68	a			08 36		08 57							09 20									09 34
	d			08 50		09 05							09 25									09 50
Wolverton	d					09 17		←			←		09 37									
Milton Keynes Central	a			09 04		09 22	08 58	09 04		09 05	09 22	09 24	09 41									10 04
	d	08 47	08 53	09 07		09 22	08 59	09 07	09 12	09 15	09 22	09 25	09 41						09 47		09 47	10 07
Bletchley	d	08 52		→		→			09 17		09 27		09 46								09 52	→
Leighton Buzzard	d	08 59							09 24		09 34		09 53								09 59	
Cheddington	d	09 04																			10 04	
Tring	d	09 10							09 34							09 26		←		09 56	10 10	
Berkhamsted	d	09 15							09 39		09 46					09 31	←	09 46		10 01	10 15	
Hemel Hempstead	d	09 19							09 43		→					09 35	09 43	09 51		10 06	10 19	
Apsley	d								→							09 38				10 09		
Kings Langley	d															09 41				10 12		
Watford Junction 60	a	09 26						09 33						09s39		09 46	09 51	09 58		10 16	10 26	
	d	09 27						09 34								09 46	09 52	09 59		10 17	10 27	
Bushey 60	d															09 49				10 20		
Harrow & Wealdstone ⊖60	d															09 54	09 59			10 25		
Wembley Central ⊖60,176	d																10 04					
Shepherd's Bush ⊖176	a																10 19					
Kensington (Olympia) ⊖176	a																10 21					
West Brompton ⊖176	a																10 24					
Imperial Wharf 176	a																10 27					
Clapham Junction 176	a																10 32					
East Croydon 176	a																10 59					
London Euston ⊖60	a	09 45	09 30		09 13		09 34	09 49		09 52		10 00	10 27	09 57	10 04	10 08		10 19	10 21	10 39	10 45	

A From Liverpool Lime Street
B From Northampton
C To London Euston
D From Crewe
E From Manchester Piccadilly
F From Birmingham New Street
G To East Croydon
H From Birmingham New Street to London Euston
I From Milton Keynes Central
J From Chester
K From Preston

West Midlands, Northampton, Milton Keynes and Watford Junction - London

	VT	LM	VT	VT	LM	SN	LM	LM	LM	VT	VT	LM	SN	LM	VT	LM	LM	LM	VT	LM	VT	VT
	◇		◇	◇						◇	◇				◇				◇		◇	◇
		A		B	C	D	E	F		G			H	C	I			A		A	J	B
Wolverhampton 68 d										09 05											09 45	
Sandwell & Dudley 68 d																					09 55	
Birmingham New Street 68 d	08 50	08 54	09 10						09 14	09 30	09 30							09 33	09 50	09 54	10 10	
Birmingham International 68 d	09 00	09 05	09 20						09 30	09 40	09 40							09 45	10 00	10 05	10 20	
Nuneaton 65 d							09 36															
Coventry 68 d	09 11	09 21	09 31						09 48	09 51	09 51							10 00	10 11	10 21	10 31	
Rugby 68 d	09 23	09 32					09 53		09 59									10 12	10 23	10 32		
Long Buckby 68 d		09 41							10 08									10 21		10 41		
Northampton 68 a		09 54							10 20									10 34		10 54		
d		10 05							10 25									10 50		11 05		
Wolverton d		10 17			←			←	10 37											11 17		
Milton Keynes Central a		10 21	09 58		10 04		10 14	10 21	10 41									11 04		11 20	10 58	
d		10 22	09 59	10 03	10 07	10 12	10 15	10 22	10 41						10 47		10 47	11 07		11 22	10 59	11 03
Bletchley d		→				10 17		10 27	10 46								10 52	→		→		
Leighton Buzzard d						10 24		10 34	10 53								10 59					
Cheddington d																	11 04					
Tring d						10 34						10 26		←		10 56	11 10					
Berkhamsted d						10 39		10 46				10 31	←	10 46		11 01	11 15					
Hemel Hempstead d						10 43		→				10 35	10 43	10 51		11 05	11 19					
Apsley d						→						10 38				11 08						
Kings Langley d												10 41				11 11						
Watford Junction 60 a					10 30					10s39	10s39	10 46	10 51	10 58		11 16	11 26					
d					10 31							10 46	10 52	10 59		11 16	11 27					
Bushey 60 d												10 49				11 19						
Harrow & Wealdstone ⊖60 d												10 54	10 59			11 24						
Wembley Central ⊖60,176 d													11 04			11 29						
Shepherd's Bush ⊖176 a													11 19									
Kensington (Olympia) ⊖176 a													11 21									
West Brompton ⊖176 a													11 24									
Imperial Wharf 176 a													11 27									
Clapham Junction 176 a													11 32									
East Croydon 176 a													11 59									
London Euston ⊖60 a	10 15		10 33	10 36	10 46		10 50		11 27	10 56	10 56	11 08		11 19	11 21	11 41	11 45		11 14		11 33	11 36

	LM	SN	LM	LM	LM	VT	LM	SN	LM	VT	LM	LM	LM	VT	LM	VT	VT	LM	SN	LM	LM
						◇				◇				◇		◇	◇				
	C	D	E	F				H	C	I			A		A	K	B	C	D	E	F
Wolverhampton 68 d																10 45					
Sandwell & Dudley 68 d																10 55					
Birmingham New Street 68 d					10 14	10 30							10 33	10 50	10 54	11 10					
Birmingham International 68 d					10 30	10 40							10 45	11 00	11 05	11 20					
Nuneaton 65 d			10 36																	11 36	
Coventry 68 d					10 48	10 51							11 00	11 09	11 21	11 31					
Rugby 68 d			10 53		10 59								11 12	11 23	11 32					11 53	
Long Buckby 68 d					11 08								11 21		11 41						
Northampton 68 a					11 20								11 33		11 55						
d					11 25								11 50		12 05						
Wolverton d	←			←	11 37										12 17			←			←
Milton Keynes Central a	11 04		11 14	11 20	11 41								12 05		12 21	11 58		12 05		12 14	12 21
d	11 07	11 12	11 15	11 22	11 41					11 47		11 47	12 07		12 22	11 59	12 03	12 07	12 12	12 15	12 22
Bletchley d		11 17		11 27	11 46							11 52	→		→				12 17		12 27
Leighton Buzzard d		11 24		11 33	11 53							11 59							12 24		12 34
Cheddington d												12 04									
Tring d		11 34					11 26		←		11 56	12 10							12 34		
Berkhamsted d		11 39		11 46			11 31	←	11 46		12 01	12 15							12 39		12 46
Hemel Hempstead d		11 43		→			11 35	11 43	11 51		12 05	12 19							12 43		→
Apsley d		→					11 38				12 08								→		
Kings Langley d							11 41				12 11										
Watford Junction 60 a	11 30					11s39	11 46	11 51	11 58		12 16	12 26						12 30			
d	11 31						11 46	11 52	11 59		12 16	12 27						12 31			
Bushey 60 d							11 49				12 19										
Harrow & Wealdstone ⊖60 d							11 54	11 59			12 24										
Wembley Central ⊖60,176 d								12 04			12 29										
Shepherd's Bush ⊖176 a								12 19													
Kensington (Olympia) ⊖176 a								12 21													
West Brompton ⊖176 a								12 24													
Imperial Wharf 176 a								12 27													
Clapham Junction 176 a								12 32													
East Croydon 176 a								12 59													
London Euston ⊖60 a	11 46		11 50		12 27	11 55	12 08		12 19	12 21	12 41	12 45		12 13		12 33	12 36	12 46		12 50	

A To London Euston
B From Holyhead
C From Birmingham New Street
D To East Croydon
E From Crewe
F From Birmingham New Street to London Euston
G From Shrewsbury
H From Milton Keynes Central
I From Manchester Piccadilly
J From Glasgow Central
K From Edinburgh

West Midlands, Northampton, Milton Keynes and Watford Junction - London

	LM	VT	LM	SN	LM	VT	LM	LM	LM	VT	LM	VT	VT	LM	SN	LM	LM	VT	LM	VT	LM	SN
		◇				◇				◇		◇	◇					◇		◇		
				A	B	C			D		D	E	F	B	G	H	I	J				A
Wolverhampton 68 d												11 45										
Sandwell & Dudley 68 d												11 55										
Birmingham New Street 68 d	11 14	11 30							11 33	11 50	11 54	12 10							12 14	12 30		
Birmingham International 68 d	11 30	11 40							11 45	12 00	12 05	12 20							12 30	12 40		
Nuneaton 65 d																12 36						
Coventry 68 d	11 48	11 51							12 00	12 11	12 21	12 31							12 48	12 51		
Rugby 68 d	11 59								12 12	12 23	12 32					12 53		12 57	12 59			
Long Buckby 68 d	12 08								12 21		12 41								13 08			
Northampton 68 a	12 20								12 34		12 54								13 20			
d	12 25								12 50		13 05								13 25			
Wolverton d	12 37										13 17			←			←		13 37			
Milton Keynes Central a	12 41								13 05		13 21	12 58		13 05		13 14	13 21		13 41			
d	12 41					12 47		12 47	13 07		13 22	12 59	13 03	13 07	13 12	13 15	13 22		13 41			
Bletchley d	12 46							12 52	→		→				13 17		13 27		13 46			
Leighton Buzzard d	12 53							12 59							13 24		13 34		13 53			
Cheddington d								13 04														
Tring d			12 26		←		12 56	13 10							13 34						13 26	
Berkhamsted d			12 31	←	12 46		13 01	13 15							13 39		13 46				13 31	←
Hemel Hempstead d			12 35	12 43	12 51		13 05	13 19							13 43		→				13 35	13 43
Apsley d			12 38				13 08								→						13 38	
Kings Langley d			12 41				13 11														13 41	
Watford Junction 60 a		12s39	12 46	12 51	12 58		13 16	13 26						13 30						13s42	13 46	13 51
d			12 46	12 52	12 59		13 16	13 27						13 31							13 46	13 52
Bushey 60 d			12 49				13 19														13 49	
Harrow & Wealdstone ⊖60 d			12 54	12 59			13 24														13 54	13 59
Wembley Central ⊖60,176 d				13 04			13 29															14 04
Shepherd's Bush ⊖176 a				13 19																		14 19
Kensington (Olympia) ⊖176 a				13 21																		14 21
West Brompton ⊖176 a				13 24																		14 24
Imperial Wharf 176 a				13 27																		14 27
Clapham Junction 176 a				13 32																		14 32
East Croydon 176 a				13 59																		14 59
London Euston ⊖60 a	13 27	12 55	13 08		13 19	13 21	13 41	13 46		13 14		13 33	13 36	13 46		13 50		13 53	14 27	13 58	14 08	

	LM	VT	LM	LM	LM	VT	LM	VT	VT	LM	SN	LM	LM	LM	VT	LM	SN	VT	LM	LM	LM	VT
		◇				◇		◇	◇						◇			◇				◇
	B	C			D		D	K	F	B	G	H	I				A	E	B			C
Wolverhampton 68 d								12 45														
Sandwell & Dudley 68 d								12 55														
Birmingham New Street 68 d					12 33	12 50	12 54	13 10						13 14	13 30							
Birmingham International 68 d					12 45	13 00	13 05	13 20						13 30	13 40							
Nuneaton 65 d												13 36										
Coventry 68 d					13 00	13 09	13 21	13 31						13 48	13 51							
Rugby 68 d					13 12	13 23	13 32					13 53		13 59				14 24				
Long Buckby 68 d					13 21		13 41							14 08								
Northampton 68 a					13 34		13 54							14 20								
d					13 50		14 05							14 25								
Wolverton d							14 17			←			←	14 37								
Milton Keynes Central a					14 04		14 21	13 58		14 04		14 14	14 21	14 41								
d		13 47		13 47	14 07		14 22	14 00	14 03	14 07	14 12	14 15	14 22	14 41							14 47	14 50
Bletchley d				13 52	→		→				14 17		14 27	14 46							14 52	
Leighton Buzzard d				13 59							14 24		14 34	14 53							14 59	
Cheddington d				14 04																	15 04	
Tring d	←		13 56	14 10							14 34					14 26			←	14 56	15 10	
Berkhamsted d	13 46		14 01	14 15							14 39		14 46			14 31	←		14 46	15 01	15 15	
Hemel Hempstead d	13 51		14 05	14 19							14 43		→			14 35	14 43		14 51	15 05	15 19	
Apsley d			14 08								→					14 38				15 08		
Kings Langley d			14 11													14 41				15 11		
Watford Junction 60 a	13 58		14 16	14 26						14 30					14s39	14 46	14 51		14 58	15 16	15 26	
d	13 59		14 16	14 27						14 31						14 46	14 52		14 59	15 16	15 27	
Bushey 60 d			14 19													14 49				15 19		
Harrow & Wealdstone ⊖60 d			14 24													14 54	14 59			15 24		
Wembley Central ⊖60,176 d			14 29														15 04			15 29		
Shepherd's Bush ⊖176 a																	15 19					
Kensington (Olympia) ⊖176 a																	15 21					
West Brompton ⊖176 a																	15 24					
Imperial Wharf 176 a																	15 27					
Clapham Junction 176 a																	15 32					
East Croydon 176 a																	15 59					
London Euston ⊖60 a	14 19	14 20	14 41	14 45		14 13		14 33	14 36	14 46		14 50		15 27	14 56	15 08		15 13	15 19	15 41	15 45	15 28

A From Milton Keynes Central
B From Birmingham New Street
C From Manchester Piccadilly
D To London Euston
E From Glasgow Central
F From Chester
G To East Croydon
H From Crewe
I From Birmingham New Street to London Euston
J From Blackpool North
K From Edinburgh

Table T066-R

Saturdays

26 May to 8 December

West Midlands, Northampton, Milton Keynes and Watford Junction - London

	LM A	VT	LM A	VT B	VT C	LM D	SN E	LM F	LM G	LM	VT	VT H	LM	SN I	LM D	VT J	LM	LM	LM A	VT	LM A
Wolverhampton 68 d				13 45																	
Sandwell & Dudley 68 d				13 55																	
Birmingham New Street 68 d	13 33	13 50	13 54	14 10						14 14	14 30								14 33	14 50	14 54
Birmingham International 68 d	13 45	14 00	14 05	14 20						14 30	14 40								14 45	15 00	15 05
Nuneaton 65 d								14 36													
Coventry 68 d	14 00	14 11	14 21	14 30						14 48	14 51								15 00	15 09	15 21
Rugby 68 d	14 12	14 26	14 32					14 53		14 59		15 05							15 12	15 23	15 32
Long Buckby 68 d	14 21		14 41							15 08									15 21		15 41
Northampton 68 a	14 34		14 54							15 20									15 34		15 54
d	14 50		15 05							15 25									15 50		16 05
Wolverton d			15 17			←			←	15 37											16 17
Milton Keynes Central a	15 04		15 21	14 58		15 04		15 14	15 21	15 41									16 04		16 21
d	15 07		15 22	15 00	15 03	15 07	15 12	15 15	15 22	15 41						15 47		15 47	16 07		16 22
Bletchley d	→		→				15 17		15 27	15 46								15 52	→		→
Leighton Buzzard d							15 24		15 34	15 53								15 59			
Cheddington d																		16 04			
Tring d							15 34						15 26		←		15 56	16 10			
Berkhamsted d							15 39		15 46				15 31	←	15 46		16 01	16 15			
Hemel Hempstead d							15 43		→				15 35	15 43	15 51		16 05	16 19			
Apsley d							→						15 38				16 08				
Kings Langley d													15 41				16 11				
Watford Junction 60 a						15 30					15s39		15 46	15 51	15 58		16 16	16 26			
d						15 31							15 46	15 52	15 59		16 16	16 27			
Bushey 60 d													15 49				16 19				
Harrow & Wealdstone ⊖60 d													15 54	15 59			16 24				
Wembley Central ⊖60,176 d														16 04			16 29				
Shepherd's Bush ⊖176 a														16 19							
Kensington (Olympia) ⊖176 a														16 21							
West Brompton ⊖176 a														16 24							
Imperial Wharf 176 a														16 27							
Clapham Junction 176 a														16 32							
East Croydon 176 a														16 59							
London Euston ⊖60 a		15 16		15 32	15 36	15 46		15 50		16 27	15 55	15 58	16 08		16 19	16 21	16 41	16 46		16 14	

	VT K	VT C	LM D	SN E	LM F	LM G	LM	VT	LM	SN I	LM D	VT J	LM	LM	LM A	VT	LM A	VT B	VT L	LM D	SN E	LM F
Wolverhampton 68 d	14 45																	15 45				
Sandwell & Dudley 68 d	14 55																	15 54				
Birmingham New Street 68 d	15 10						15 14	15 30							15 33	15 50	15 54	16 10				
Birmingham International 68 d	15 20						15 30	15 40							15 45	16 00	16 05	16 20				
Nuneaton 65 d					15 36																	16 36
Coventry 68 d	15 31						15 48	15 51							16 00	16 11	16 21	16 30				
Rugby 68 d					15 53		15 59								16 12	16 23	16 32					16 53
Long Buckby 68 d							16 08								16 21		16 41					
Northampton 68 a							16 20								16 34		16 54					
d							16 25								16 50		17 05					
Wolverton d			←			←	16 37										17 17			←		
Milton Keynes Central a	15 58		16 04		16 14	16 21	16 41								17 04		17 21	16 58		17 04		17 14
d	15 59	16 03	16 07	16 12	16 15	16 22	16 41					16 47		16 47	17 07		17 22	16 59	17 03	17 07	17 12	17 15
Bletchley d				16 17		16 27	16 46							16 52	→		→				17 17	
Leighton Buzzard d				16 24		16 34	16 53							16 59							17 24	
Cheddington d														17 04								
Tring d				16 34					16 26		←		16 57	17 10							17 34	
Berkhamsted d				16 39		16 46			16 31	←	16 46		17 02	17 15							17 39	
Hemel Hempstead d				16 43		→			16 35	16 43	16 51		17 07	17 19							17 43	
Apsley d				→					16 38				17 10								→	
Kings Langley d									16 41				17 13									
Watford Junction 60 a			16 30					16s39	16 46	16 51	16 58		17 17	17 26						17 30		
d			16 31						16 46	16 52	16 59		17 18	17 27						17 31		
Bushey 60 d									16 49				17 21									
Harrow & Wealdstone ⊖60 d									16 54	16 59			17 26									
Wembley Central ⊖60,176 d										17 04												
Shepherd's Bush ⊖176 a										17 19												
Kensington (Olympia) ⊖176 a										17 21												
West Brompton ⊖176 a										17 24												
Imperial Wharf 176 a										17 27												
Clapham Junction 176 a										17 32												
East Croydon 176 a										17 59												
London Euston ⊖60 a	16 32	16 36	16 47		16 50		17 27	16 55	17 08		17 19	17 21	17 40	17 45		17 14		17 33	17 36	17 46		17 50

A To London Euston
B From Glasgow Central
C From Chester
D From Birmingham New Street
E To East Croydon
F From Crewe
G From Birmingham New Street to London Euston
H From Blackpool North
I From Milton Keynes Central
J From Manchester Piccadilly
K From Edinburgh
L From Holyhead

Table T066-R

Saturdays

26 May to 8 December

West Midlands, Northampton, Milton Keynes and Watford Junction - London

	LM A	VT B	LM	VT	LM	SN C	LM D	VT E	LM	LM	LM F	VT	LM F	VT G	VT H	LM D	SN I	LM J	VT K	LM F	VT
Wolverhampton 68 d		16 04												16 45							
Sandwell & Dudley 68 d														16 55							
Birmingham New Street 68 d			16 14	16 30							16 33	16 50	16 54	17 10						17 14	17 30
Birmingham International 68 d		16 40	16 30	16 40							16 45	17 00	17 05	17 20						17 31	17 40
Nuneaton 65 d																		17 36			
Coventry 68 d		16 51	16 48	16 50							17 00	17 11	17 21	17 31						17 49	17 51
Rugby 68 d			16 59								17 12	17 23	17 32					17 53	17 58	17 59	
Long Buckby 68 d			17 08								17 21		17 41							18 08	
Northampton 68 a			17 20								17 34		17 53							18 21	
d			17 25								17 50		18 05							18 31	
Wolverton d	←		17 37										18 17			←				18 43	
Milton Keynes Central a	17 21		17 41								18 04		18 21	17 58		18 04		18 14		18 47	
d	17 22		17 41					17 47		17 47	18 07		18 22	18 00	18 03	18 07	18 12	18 15		18 47	
Bletchley d	17 27		17 46							17 52	→		→				→			→	
Leighton Buzzard d	17 34		17 53							17 59											
Cheddington d										18 04											
Tring d					17 26		←		17 56	18 10											
Berkhamsted d	17 46				17 31	←	17 46		18 01	18 15											
Hemel Hempstead d	→				17 35	17 43	17 51		18 05	18 19											
Apsley d					17 38				18 08												
Kings Langley d					17 41				18 12												
Watford Junction 60 a		17s39		17s39	17 46	17 51	17 58		18 16	18 26						18 30					18s42
d					17 46	17 52	17 59		18 17	18 27						18 31					
Bushey 60 d					17 49				18 20												
Harrow & Wealdstone ⊖60 d					17 54	17 59			18 25												
Wembley Central ⊖60,176 d						18 04															
Shepherd's Bush ⊖176 a						18 19															
Kensington (Olympia) ⊖176 a						18 21															
West Brompton ⊖176 a						18 24															
Imperial Wharf 176 a						18 27															
Clapham Junction 176 a						18 32															
East Croydon 176 a						18 59															
London Euston ⊖60 a		17 56	18 27	17 56	18 08		18 19	18 21	18 39	18 45		18 14		18 33	18 37	18 46		18 50	18 53		18 58

	LM	SN	VT E	LM F	VT	LM D	LM F	VT L	LM	LM D	LM D	SN	SN I	LM J	VT E	LM F	VT	LM	SN	LM D	VT	LM
Wolverhampton 68 d								17 45														
Sandwell & Dudley 68 d								17 55														
Birmingham New Street 68 d				17 33	17 50		17 54	18 10								18 14	18 30				18 50	
Birmingham International 68 d				17 45	18 00		18 05	18 20								18 30	18 40				19 00	
Nuneaton 65 d														18 36								
Coventry 68 d				18 00	18 10		18 21	18 31								18 48	18 51				19 11	
Rugby 68 d				18 12	18 26		18 32							18 53		18 59					19 23	
Long Buckby 68 d				18 21			18 41									19 08						
Northampton 68 a				18 34			18 54									19 20						
d				18 50			19 05									19 31						
Wolverton d		←				←	19 17			←	←					19 43			←	←		
Milton Keynes Central a				19 04		18 21	19 21	18 58		18 47	19 04			19 14		19 46				19 21		
d		18 12	18 49	19 07		18 22	19 22	18 59		18 47	19 07		19 13	19 15	19 46	19 47			19 13	19 22		
Bletchley d		18 17		→		18 27	→			18 52			→			→			19 18	19 27		
Leighton Buzzard d		18 24				18 34				18 59									19 25	19 34		
Cheddington d										19 04												
Tring d	18 26	18 34							18 56	19 10								19 26	19 34			19 56
Berkhamsted d	18 31	18 39				18 46			19 01	19 15								19 31	19 39	19 46		20 01
Hemel Hempstead d	18 35	18 43				18 51			19 06	19 19								19 35	19 43	19 51		20 06
Apsley d	18 38								19 09									19 38				20 09
Kings Langley d	18 41								19 12									19 41				20 12
Watford Junction 60 a	18 46	18 51				18 58			19 16	19 27	19 30						19s39	19 46	19 50	19 58		20 16
d	18 46	18 51				18 59			19 17	19 27	19 31	19 31						19 46	19 51	19 59		20 17
Bushey 60 d	18 49								19 20									19 49				
Harrow & Wealdstone ⊖60 d	18 54	18 59							19 25			19 37						19 54	19 59			20 23
Wembley Central ⊖60,176 d		19 03										19 42							20 04			
Shepherd's Bush ⊖176 a		19 19										20 00							20 19			
Kensington (Olympia) ⊖176 a		19 21										20 03							20 22			
West Brompton ⊖176 a		19 24										20 06							20 25			
Imperial Wharf 176 a		19 27										20 09							20 28			
Clapham Junction 176 a		19 32										20 13							20 33			
East Croydon 176 a		19 59																	20 59			
London Euston ⊖60 a	19 08		19 22		19 15	19 18		19 32	19 39	19 46	19 46			19 50	20 34		19 55	20 08		20 19	20 23	20 37

A From Birmingham New Street to London Euston
B From Shrewsbury
C From Milton Keynes Central
D From Birmingham New Street
E From Manchester Piccadilly
F To London Euston
G From Edinburgh
H From Chester
I To East Croydon
J From Crewe
K From Blackpool North
L From Glasgow Central

Table T066-R

Saturdays
26 May to 8 December

West Midlands, Northampton, Milton Keynes and Watford Junction - London

	LM A	LM B	VT ◇ C	SN	LM A	VT ◇ D	LM	LM	LM B	VT ◇ D	SN	VT ◇ E	LM A	LM F	VT ◇ D	LM B	VT ◇ C	VT ◇ E	SN	LM A	VT ◇	SN
Wolverhampton 68 d			18 45							19 45							20 45				21 09	
Sandwell & Dudley 68 d			18 55							19 55							20 55				21 19	
Birmingham New Street 68 d		18 54	19 10				19 14		19 54	20 10						20 54	21 10				21 30	
Birmingham International 68 d		19 05	19 20				19 30		20 05	20 20						21 05	21 20				21 40	
Nuneaton 65 d														20 31								
Coventry 68 d		19 21	19 31				19 48		20 21	20 31						21 21	21 31				21 51	
Rugby 68 d		19 32	19 43				19 59		20 32	20 43				20 47		21 32	21 43				22 03	
Long Buckby 68 d		19 41					20 08		20 41							21 41						
Northampton 68 a		19 53					20 20		20 53					21 06		21 53						
Northampton d		20 02					20 32		21 02					21 21		22 05						
Wolverton d	←	20 14			←				21 14				←			22 17				←		
Milton Keynes Central a	19 46	20 18	20 05		20 18		20 47		21 17	21 04			21 17	21 35		22 20	22 04			22 20	22 24	
Milton Keynes Central d	19 47	20 18	20 07		20 18	20 44	20 47	20 50	21 18	21 05		21 11	21 18	21 35	21 52	22 21	22 05	22 11		22 21	22 26	
Bletchley d	19 52	→			20 23			20 55	→					21 40		→				22 26		
Leighton Buzzard d	19 59				20 30		20 56							21 47						22 32		
Cheddington d	20 04						21 03							21 52						22 37		
Tring d	20 10						21 08	21 12						21 59						22 44		
Berkhamsted d	20 15							21 17					21 40	22 04						22 49		
Hemel Hempstead d	20 19						21 15	21 21					21 44	22 09						22 53		
Apsley d							21 18							22 12						22 56		
Kings Langley d							21 21							22 15						23 00		
Watford Junction 60 a	20 26		20s34		20 51	21s15	21 26	21 30		21s35			21 51	22 19			22s34	22s40		23 06	23s12	
Watford Junction d	20 27			20 43	20 52		21 26	21 30			21 44		21 52	22 20					22 53	23 07		23 26
Bushey 60 d								21 33														
Harrow & Wealdstone ⊖60 d				20 49				21 39			21 50								22 59	23 13		23 32
Wembley Central ⊖60,176 d				20 54							21 55								23 04			23 37
Shepherd's Bush ⊖176 a				21 15							22 15								23 22			23 52
Kensington (Olympia) ⊖176 a				21 18							22 17								23 24			23 54
West Brompton ⊖176 a				21 21							22 26								23 27			23 57
Imperial Wharf 176 a				21 24							22 29								23 29			00 01
Clapham Junction 176 a				21 28							22 33								23 34			00 06
East Croydon 176 a				21 59							22 59											
London Euston ⊖60 a	20 46		20 53		21 12	21 33	21 46	21 52		21 56		21 59	22 12	22 38	22 42		22 53	22 59		23 27	23 33	

	LM	LM
Wolverhampton 68 d		
Sandwell & Dudley 68 d		
Birmingham New Street 68 d	21 34	22 14
Birmingham International 68 d	21 45	22 30
Nuneaton 65 d		
Coventry 68 d	22 00	22 48
Rugby 68 d	22 12	22 59
Long Buckby 68 d	22 21	23 08
Northampton 68 a	22 33	23 21
Northampton d	22 43	23 30
Wolverton d	22 55	23 42
Milton Keynes Central a	22 59	23 46
Milton Keynes Central d	22 59	23 46
Bletchley d	23 04	23 51
Leighton Buzzard d	23 11	23 58
Cheddington d	23 16	
Tring d	23 25	
Berkhamsted d	23 30	
Hemel Hempstead d	23 35	
Apsley d	23 38	
Kings Langley d	23 41	
Watford Junction 60 a	23 45	00 19
Watford Junction d	23 46	00 20
Bushey 60 d		
Harrow & Wealdstone ⊖60 d	23 52	
Wembley Central ⊖60,176 d		
Shepherd's Bush ⊖176 a		
Kensington (Olympia) ⊖176 a		
West Brompton ⊖176 a		
Imperial Wharf 176 a		
Clapham Junction 176 a		
East Croydon 176 a		
London Euston ⊖60 a	00 06	00 40

A From Birmingham New Street
B To London Euston
C From Edinburgh
D From Glasgow Central
E From Manchester Piccadilly
F From Crewe

Table T066-R

Sundays
20 May to 2 December

West Midlands, Northampton, Milton Keynes and Watford Junction - London

	LM A	LM (bus)	LM	LM (bus)	LM	LM	LM	SN	LM	LM	VT ◇	SN	LM	VT ◇ B	LM	LM C	VT ◇	VT ◇ B	SN	LM D	VT ◇ E	VT ◇ F
Wolverhampton 68 d											08 05						09 05					
Sandwell & Dudley 68 d											08 15						09 15					
Birmingham New Street 68 d											08 30					09 14	09 30					
Birmingham International 68 d											08 40					09 25	09 40					
Nuneaton 65 d																		09 56				
Coventry 68 d											08 51					09 44	09 51					
Rugby 68 d											09 04					09 55	10 04				10 33	
Long Buckby 68 d																10 05						
Northampton 68 a																10 17						
Northampton d				06 15			07 53		08 23	08 53			09 30		10 08	10 37						
Wolverton d				06 47			08 05		08 35	09 05			09 42		10 20	10 51				←		
Milton Keynes Central a				07 00			08 09		08 39	09 09	09 37		09 46		10 24	10 54	10 37			10 54	11 07	
Milton Keynes Central d			06 42		07 11	07 39	08 09		08 39	09 09	09 39		09 46	10 21	10 25	10 55	10 39			10 55	11 08	11 17
Bletchley d			06 47		07 16	07 44	08 14		08 44	09 14			09 51		10 30	→				11 00		
Leighton Buzzard d			06 53		07 23	07 51	08 21		08 51	09 21			09 58		10 37					11 06		
Cheddington d					07 27		08 26			09 26					10 41							
Tring d					07 37		08 35			09 35					10 49							
Berkhamsted d			07 09		07 42	08 06	08 40		09 06	09 39			10 14		10 53					11 21		
Hemel Hempstead d			07 14		07 46	08 11	08 45		09 11	09 43			10 18		10 58					11 26		
Apsley d			07 17			08 14			09 14				10 21							11 29		
Kings Langley d			07 20			08 17			09 17				10 24							11 32		
Watford Junction 60 a			07 24		07 53	08 21	08 52		09 22	09 51	10s07		10 29		11 05		11s11	11s16		11 37	11s43	
Watford Junction d	00 20	00 40	07 25		07 54	08 22	08 53	09 17	09 22	09 52		10 17	10 29		11 05				11 22	11 37		
Bushey 60 d						08 25			09 25				10 32							11 40		
Harrow & Wealdstone ⊖60 d		01 00	07 31		08 00	08 30	08 59	09 23	09 30	09 58		10 23	10 37		11 11				11 28	11 45		
Wembley Central ⊖60,176 d		01 15																				
Shepherd's Bush ⊖176 a								09 44				10 44							11 47			
Kensington (Olympia) ⊖176 a								09 46				10 46							11 49			
West Brompton ⊖176 a								09 49				10 49							11 52			
Imperial Wharf 176 a								09 52				10 52							11 55			
Clapham Junction 176 a								09 57				10 57							12 00			
East Croydon 176 a																						
London Euston ⊖60 a	00 40	01 45	07 45		08 14	08 44	09 13		09 45	10 13	10 25		10 51	11 05	11 26		11 31	11 34		11 59	12 03	12 06

	LM	LM C	VT ◇	LM D	VT ◇ B	SN	LM	LM G	VT ◇ E	LM	VT ◇ F	LM C	VT ◇	VT ◇ B	VT ◇	LM D	VT ◇ F	VT ◇	VT ◇ H	SN	LM G	LM
Wolverhampton 68 d			10 05										11 05					11 45				
Sandwell & Dudley 68 d			10 15										11 15					11 55				
Birmingham New Street 68 d		10 14	10 30									11 14	11 30		11 50			12 10				
Birmingham International 68 d		10 25	10 40									11 25	11 40		12 00			12 20				
Nuneaton 65 d					10 57			10 58						11 59					12 32		11 58	
Coventry 68 d		10 44	10 51									11 44	11 51		12 11			12 31				
Rugby 68 d		10 55	11 04					11 20	11 32			11 55	12 05		12 25						12 20	
Long Buckby 68 d		11 05						11 29				12 05									12 29	
Northampton 68 a		11 17						11 41				12 17									12 41	
Northampton d	11 06	11 26						11 50				12 26									12 50	
Wolverton d	11 18	11 38		←								12 38				←						
Milton Keynes Central a	11 22	11 42	11 37	11 42	11 45			12 04	12 07			12 41	12 26			12 41		13 00	13 04		13 04	
Milton Keynes Central d	11 23	11 42	11 39	11 42	11 47			12 07	12 09	12 11	12 22	12 42	12 27			12 42	12 52	13 01	13 05		13 07	
Bletchley d	11 28	→		11 47			11 57			12 16		→				12 47						
Leighton Buzzard d	11 35			11 54			12 03	12 15		12 23						12 53					13 15	
Cheddington d	11 39						12 09			12 28												
Tring d	11 47						12 15			12 35												13 14
Berkhamsted d	11 52			12 06			12 20			12 40						13 06						13 19
Hemel Hempstead d	11 57			12 11			12 24			12 44						13 11						13 24
Apsley d							12 27															13 27
Kings Langley d							12 30															13 30
Watford Junction 60 a	12 05		12s08	12 18			12 35	12 40		12 51				12s52		13 18					13 34	13 34
Watford Junction d	12 06			12 18		12 23	12 35	12 40		12 52						13 18				13 23	13 35	13 35
Bushey 60 d							12 38															13 38
Harrow & Wealdstone ⊖60 d	12 12			12 24		12 29	12 43			12 58						13 24				13 29		13 43
Wembley Central ⊖60,176 d																						
Shepherd's Bush ⊖176 a						12 47														13 47		
Kensington (Olympia) ⊖176 a						12 50														13 50		
West Brompton ⊖176 a						12 53														13 53		
Imperial Wharf 176 a						12 56														13 56		
Clapham Junction 176 a						13 00														14 00		
East Croydon 176 a																						
London Euston ⊖60 a	12 26		12 25	12 38	12 29		12 57	13 01	12 44	13 12	12 57		13 04	13 10	13 18	13 38	13 28	13 38	13 43		13 53	13 57

A not 20 May. From Birmingham New Street
B From Liverpool Lime Street
C To London Euston
D From Birmingham New Street
E From Preston
F From Manchester Piccadilly
G From Crewe
H From Chester

Table T066-R

Sundays

20 May to 2 December

West Midlands, Northampton, Milton Keynes and Watford Junction - London

	LM 1 A		LM 1 A	VT ◇1 ☕	LM 1	VT ◇1 ☕	VT ◇1 B ☕	VT ◇1 ☕	LM 1 C	VT ◇1 D ☕	SN		LM 1 E	LM 1	LM 1 A	LM 1 A	VT ◇1 ☕	LM 1	VT ◇1 ☕	VT ◇1 B ☕	VT ◇1 F ☕		LM 1 C	VT ◇1 D ☕
Wolverhampton 7 68 d								12 45													13 45			
Sandwell & Dudley 68 d								12 55													13 55			
Birmingham New Street 12 68 d			12 14	12 30		12 50		13 10								13 14	13 30		13 50		14 10			
Birmingham International 68 d			12 25	12 40		13 00		13 20								13 25	13 40		14 00		14 20			
Nuneaton 65 d													12 58											14 33
Coventry 68 d			12 44	12 51		13 11		13 31								13 44	13 51		14 11		14 31			
Rugby 68 d			12 55			13 27							13 20			13 55			14 22					
Long Buckby 68 d			13 05										13 29			14 05								
Northampton 68 a			13 17										13 41			14 17								
d			13 26										13 50			14 26								
Wolverton d			13 38		←				←							14 38		←					←	
Milton Keynes Central 10 a			13 41					13 58	13 41				14 04			14 41					14 58		14 41	15 03
d	13 11		13 42		13 11		13 49	13 59	13 42	14 04			14 07		14 11	14 42		14 11		14 51	14 59		14 42	15 04
Bletchley d	→		→		13 16				13 47						→	→		14 16					14 47	
Leighton Buzzard d					13 23				13 53				14 15					14 23					14 53	
Cheddington d					13 28													14 28						
Tring d					13 35									14 14				14 35						
Berkhamsted d					13 40				14 06					14 19				14 40					15 06	
Hemel Hempstead d					13 44				14 11					14 24				14 44					15 11	
Apsley d														14 27										
Kings Langley d														14 30										
Watford Junction 60 a				13s38	13 51				14 18				14 34	14 34			14s38	14 51					15 18	
d					13 52				14 18		14 23		14 35	14 35				14 52					15 18	
Bushey 60 d														14 38										
Harrow & Wealdstone ⊖60 d					13 58				14 24		14 29			14 43				14 58					15 24	
Wembley Central ⊖60,176 d																								
Shepherd's Bush ⊖176 a											14 47													
Kensington (Olympia) ⊖176 a											14 50													
West Brompton ⊖176 a											14 53													
Imperial Wharf 176 a											14 56													
Clapham Junction 176 a											15 00													
East Croydon 176 a																								
London Euston 15 ⊖60 a				13 57	14 12	14 19	14 28	14 36	14 38	14 41			14 53	14 57			14 57	15 12	15 15	15 26	15 37		15 38	15 42

	SN	LM 1 E	LM 1	LM 1 A	LM 1 A	VT ◇1 ☕	LM 1		VT ◇1 ☕	VT ◇1 B ☕	VT ◇1 G ☕	LM 1 C	VT ◇1 D ☕	SN	LM 1 E	LM 1	LM 1 A		LM 1 A	VT ◇1 ☕	LM 1	VT ◇1 ☕	VT ◇1 B ☕	VT ◇1 H ☕
Wolverhampton 7 68 d											14 45													15 45
Sandwell & Dudley 68 d											14 55													15 55
Birmingham New Street 12 68 d					14 14	14 30			14 50		15 10								15 14	15 30		15 50		16 10
Birmingham International 68 d					14 25	14 40			15 00		15 20								15 25	15 40		16 00		16 19
Nuneaton 65 d		13 58													14 58									
Coventry 68 d					14 44	14 51			15 11		15 31								15 44	15 51		16 11		16 30
Rugby 68 d		14 20			14 55				15 25						15 20				15 55			16 24		
Long Buckby 68 d		14 29			15 05										15 29				16 05					
Northampton 68 a		14 41			15 17										15 41				16 17					
d		14 50			15 26										15 50				16 26					
Wolverton d					15 38		←					←							16 38		←			
Milton Keynes Central 10 a		15 04			15 41						15 58	15 41			16 04				16 41					16 58
d		15 07		15 11	15 42		15 11			15 50	15 59	15 42	16 04		16 07		16 11		16 42		16 11		16 51	16 59
Bletchley d				→	→		15 16					15 47					→		→		16 16			
Leighton Buzzard d		15 15					15 23					15 53			16 15						16 23			
Cheddington d							15 28														16 28			
Tring d			15 14				15 35									16 14					16 35			
Berkhamsted d			15 19				15 40					16 06				16 19					16 40			
Hemel Hempstead d			15 24				15 44					16 11				16 24					16 44			
Apsley d			15 27													16 27								
Kings Langley d			15 30													16 30								
Watford Junction 60 a		15 34	15 34			15s38	15 51					16 18			16 34	16 34				16s38	16 51			
d	15 23	15 35	15 35				15 52					16 18		16 23	16 35	16 35					16 52			
Bushey 60 d			15 38													16 38								
Harrow & Wealdstone ⊖60 d	15 29		15 43				15 58					16 24		16 29		16 43					16 58			
Wembley Central ⊖60,176 d																								
Shepherd's Bush ⊖176 a	15 47													16 47										
Kensington (Olympia) ⊖176 a	15 50													16 50										
West Brompton ⊖176 a	15 53													16 53										
Imperial Wharf 176 a	15 56													16 56										
Clapham Junction 176 a	16 00													17 00										
East Croydon 176 a																								
London Euston 15 ⊖60 a		15 53	15 57			15 57	16 12		16 18	16 26	16 37	16 38	16 41		16 53	16 57				16 57	17 12	17 17	17 27	17 36

A To London Euston
B From Manchester Piccadilly
C From Birmingham New Street
D From Holyhead
E From Crewe
F From Lancaster
G From Edinburgh
H until 9 September. From Carlisle

Table T066-R

Sundays

20 May to 2 December

West Midlands, Northampton, Milton Keynes and Watford Junction - London

	VT ◇1 A ☕	LM 1 B	VT ◇1 C ☕		SN	LM 1 D	LM 1	LM 1 E	LM 1 E	VT ◇1 F ☕	VT ◇1 ☕	LM 1	VT ◇1 ☕		VT ◇1 G ☕	VT ◇1 H ☕	LM 1 B	VT ◇1 I ☕	SN	LM 1 D	LM 1	LM 1 E	LM 1 E	
Wolverhampton 7 68 d	15 45									16 04						16 45								
Sandwell & Dudley 68 d	15 55															16 55								
Birmingham New Street 12 68 d	16 10								16 14	16 30	16 30		16 50			17 10							17 14	
Birmingham International 68 d	16 19								16 25	16 40	16 40		17 00			17 20							17 25	
Nuneaton 65 d						15 58														16 58				
Coventry 68 d	16 31								16 44	16 51	16 51		17 11			17 30							17 44	
Rugby 68 d						16 20			16 55				17 25							17 20			17 55	
Long Buckby 68 d						16 29			17 05											17 29			18 05	
Northampton 68 a						16 41			17 17											17 41			18 17	
d						16 50			17 26											17 50			18 26	
Wolverton d		←							17 38			←					←						18 38	
Milton Keynes Central 10 a	16 58	16 41				17 04			17 41							17 58	17 41			18 04			18 41	
d	16 59	16 42	17 04			17 07		17 11	17 42			17 11			17 50	17 59	17 42	18 05		18 07		18 11	18 42	
Bletchley d		16 47						→	→			17 16					17 47					→	→	
Leighton Buzzard d		16 53				17 15						17 23					17 53			18 15				
Cheddington d												17 28												
Tring d							17 14					17 35									18 14			
Berkhamsted d		17 06					17 19					17 40					18 06				18 19			
Hemel Hempstead d		17 11					17 24					17 44					18 11				18 24			
Apsley d							17 27														18 27			
Kings Langley d							17 30														18 30			
Watford Junction 60 a		17 18				17 34	17 34			17s38	17s38	17 51					18 18			18 34	18 34			
d		17 18			17 23	17 35	17 35					17 52					18 18		18 23	18 35	18 35			
Bushey 60 d							17 38														18 38			
Harrow & Wealdstone ⊖60 d		17 24			17 29		17 43					17 58					18 24		18 29		18 43			
Wembley Central ⊖60,176 d																								
Shepherd's Bush ⊖176 a					17 47														18 47					
Kensington (Olympia) ⊖176 a					17 50														18 50					
West Brompton ⊖176 a					17 53														18 53					
Imperial Wharf 176 a					17 56														18 56					
Clapham Junction 176 a					18 00														19 00					
East Croydon 176 a																								
London Euston 15 ⊖60 a	17 36	17 38	17 41			17 53	17 57			17 57	17 57	18 12	18 18		18 27	18 36	18 38	18 41		18 53	18 57			

	VT ◇1 ☕	LM 1	VT ◇1 ☕	VT ◇1 G ☕	VT ◇1 A ☕	VT ◇1 J ☕	LM 1 B	VT ◇1 K ☕	SN		LM 1 D	LM 1	LM 1 E	LM 1 E	VT ◇1 ☕	LM 1	VT ◇1 ☕	VT ◇1 G ☕	VT ◇1 H ☕		LM 1 B	VT ◇1 K ☕	SN	LM 1
Wolverhampton 7 68 d					17 45	17 45													18 45					
Sandwell & Dudley 68 d					17 55	17 56													18 55					
Birmingham New Street 12 68 d	17 30		17 50		18 10	18 10								18 14	18 30		18 50		19 10					
Birmingham International 68 d	17 40		18 00		18 20	18 20								18 25	18 40		19 00		19 20					
Nuneaton 65 d											17 58													
Coventry 68 d	17 51		18 11		18 31	18 32								18 44	18 51		19 11		19 31					
Rugby 68 d			18 25								18 20			18 55			19 26							
Long Buckby 68 d											18 29			19 05										
Northampton 68 a											18 41			19 17										
d											18 50			19 26										
Wolverton d		←					←							19 38		←					←			
Milton Keynes Central 10 a					18 58	18 58	18 41				19 04			19 41					19 58		19 41			
d		18 11		18 50	18 59	19 00	18 42	19 05			19 07		19 11	19 42		19 11		19 50	20 00		19 42	20 04		
Bletchley d		18 16					18 47						→	→		19 16					19 47			
Leighton Buzzard d		18 23					18 53				19 15					19 23					19 53			
Cheddington d		18 28														19 28								
Tring d		18 35										19 14				19 35								20 14
Berkhamsted d		18 40					19 06					19 19				19 40					20 06			20 19
Hemel Hempstead d		18 44					19 11					19 24				19 44					20 11			20 24
Apsley d												19 27												20 27
Kings Langley d												19 30												20 30
Watford Junction 60 a	18s38	18 51					19 18				19 34	19 34			19s38	19 51					20 18			20 34
d		18 52					19 18		19 23		19 35	19 35				19 52					20 18		20 23	20 35
Bushey 60 d												19 38												20 38
Harrow & Wealdstone ⊖60 d		18 58					19 24		19 29			19 43				19 58					20 24		20 29	20 43
Wembley Central ⊖60,176 d																								
Shepherd's Bush ⊖176 a									19 47														20 47	
Kensington (Olympia) ⊖176 a									19 50														20 50	
West Brompton ⊖176 a									19 53														20 53	
Imperial Wharf 176 a									19 56														20 56	
Clapham Junction 176 a									20 00														21 00	
East Croydon 176 a																								
London Euston 15 ⊖60 a	18 57	19 12	19 17	19 27	19 37	19 37	19 38	19 42			19 53	19 57			19 57	20 12	20 18	20 27	20 37		20 38	20 41		20 57

A from 16 September. From Glasgow Central
B From Birmingham New Street
C From Holyhead
D From Crewe
E To London Euston
F From Shrewsbury
G From Manchester Piccadilly
H From Edinburgh
I From Liverpool Lime Street
J until 9 September. From Carlisle
K From Chester

Table T066-R

Sundays

20 May to 2 December

West Midlands, Northampton, Milton Keynes and Watford Junction - London

	LM	LM	LM	VT	LM	VT	SN	LM	VT	LM	LM	LM	VT	SN	VT	LM	VT	VT	LM	LM	VT	SN
	1	1	1	◇1	1	◇1		1	◇1	1	1	1	◇1		◇1	1	◇1	◇1	1	1	◇1	
	A	B	B			C		D	E	A		B			F	D	E	C	A	B		
				☕		☕			☕				☕		☕		☕	☕			☕	
Wolverhampton 7 68 ⇌ d									19 45												21 05	
Sandwell & Dudley 68 d									19 55												21 17	
Birmingham New Street 12 68 ⇌ d			19 14	19 30					20 10			20 14	20 30							21 14	21 30	
Birmingham International 68 ✈ d			19 25	19 40					20 20			20 25	20 40							21 25	21 40	
Nuneaton 65 d	18 58									20 01									20 58			
Coventry 68 d			19 44	19 51					20 31			20 44	20 51							21 44	21 51	
Rugby 68 d	19 20		19 55							20 17		20 55	21 05						21 20	21 55	22 04	
Long Buckby 68 d	19 29		20 05							20 26		21 05							21 29	22 05		
Northampton 68 a	19 41		20 17							20 38		21 17							21 41	22 17		
d	19 50		20 25							20 51		21 29							21 55	22 26		
Wolverton d	20 02		20 37		←			←		21 03		21 41				←			22 07	22 38		
Milton Keynes Central 10 a	20 06		20 40					20 40	20 59	21 07		21 44	21 26			21 44			22 11	22 41	22 35	
d	20 07	20 11	20 41		20 11	20 48		20 41	21 01	21 07	21 15	21 45	21 28		21 37	21 45	21 53	22 04	22 11	22 42	22 37	
Bletchley d		→	→		20 16			20 46			21 20	→				21 50			22 16	→		
Leighton Buzzard d	20 16				20 23			20 52		21 15	21 26					21 56			22 23			
Cheddington d					20 28						21 35								22 31			
Tring d					20 35						21 40								22 37			
Berkhamsted d					20 40			21 06			21 44					22 11			22 42			
Hemel Hempstead d					20 44			21 11			21 49					22 15			22 47			
Apsley d								21 14								22 18						
Kings Langley d								21 17								22 21						
Watford Junction 60 a	20 35			20s39	20 51			21 22		21 39	21 56		22s02			22 26	22s30		22 54		23s05	
d	20 35				20 52		21 17	21 22		21 40	21 56			22 18		22 26			22 54			23 17
Bushey 60 d											21 59								22 57			
Harrow & Wealdstone ⊖60 d					20 58		21 24	21 28			22 04			22 24		22 32			23 03			23 23
Wembley Central ⊖60,176 d																						
Shepherd's Bush ⊖176 a							21 43							22 44								23 44
Kensington (Olympia) ⊖176 a							21 45							22 47								23 47
West Brompton ⊖176 a							21 47							22 50								23 50
Imperial Wharf 176 a							21 50							22 53								23 53
Clapham Junction 176 a							21 54							22 57								23 57
East Croydon 176 ⇌ a																						
London Euston 15 ⊖60 a	20 54			20 57	21 14	21 31		21 43	21 46	21 58	22 19		22 22		22 25	22 48	22 53	22 56	23 17		23 23	

	LM	VT	VT	LM	VT	VT
	1	◇1	◇1	1	◇1	◇1
	D	C	F			
		☕	☕		☕	☕
Wolverhampton 7 68 ⇌ d					22 05	22 37
Sandwell & Dudley 68 d					22 16	22 48
Birmingham New Street 12 68 ⇌ d					22 30	23 00
Birmingham International 68 ✈ d					22 40	23 10
Nuneaton 65 d			22 19			
Coventry 68 d					22 51	23 21
Rugby 68 d			22 33		23 04	23 35
Long Buckby 68 d						
Northampton 68 a						23s54
d				23 00		
Wolverton d	←			23 12		
Milton Keynes Central 10 a	22 41		23 04	23 16	23 36	00s13
d	22 42	22 48	23 06	23 16	23 37	
Bletchley d	22 46			23 21		
Leighton Buzzard d	22 53			23 28		
Cheddington d				23 36		
Tring d				23 42		
Berkhamsted d	23 08			23 47		
Hemel Hempstead d	23 12			23 52		
Apsley d	23 15					
Kings Langley d	23 18					
Watford Junction 60 a	23 23	23s28	23s34	23 59	00s06	00s43
d	23 23			23 59		
Bushey 60 d				00 02		
Harrow & Wealdstone ⊖60 d	23 29			00 08		
Wembley Central ⊖60,176 d						
Shepherd's Bush ⊖176 a						
Kensington (Olympia) ⊖176 a						
West Brompton ⊖176 a						
Imperial Wharf 176 a						
Clapham Junction 176 a						
East Croydon 176 ⇌ a						
London Euston 15 ⊖60 a	23 43	23 46	23 52	00 22	00 25	01 03

A From Crewe
B To London Euston
C From Manchester Piccadilly
D From Birmingham New Street
E From Glasgow Central
F From Liverpool Lime Street

Table T067-F

Mondays to Fridays

21 May to 7 December

London - Stoke-on-Trent and Crewe

Miles	Miles		VT	XC	LM	LM	XC	VT	VT	LM	LM	XC	LM	LM	XC	LM	VT	LM	VT	VT	XC	VT
			◇1	◇1	1	1	◇1	◇1	◇1	1		◇1	1	1	◇1	1	◇1	1	◇1	◇1	◇1	◇1
											🚌											
			⊠				🛒	⊠	⊠			🛒			🛒		⊠		⊠	⊠	🛒	⊠
0	—	**London Euston** 15 ⊖66 d						05 27	05 31							06 24	06 36		06 43	07 07		07 10
17½	—	Watford Junction 66 d						05u45	05u50							06 41	06u51					
49¾	—	Milton Keynes Central 66 d						06 15	06 23							07 24			07 13			07 41
65¾	—	Northampton 68 d				05 45								06 35		07 45						
84½	—	Rugby d				06 06			06 45					06 59		08 04						
99	—	Nuneaton a				06 18		06 44						07 11		08 16						
—	—	d				06 20		06 45						07 12		08 16						
104	—	Atherstone d				06 26								07 18		08 22						
108	—	Polesworth d												07 23								
111½	—	Tamworth d				06 35								07 29		08 29						
117¾	—	Lichfield Trent Valley d				06 41								07 35		08 35						
125¾	—	Rugeley Trent Valley d				06 49								07 43		08 43						
135½	0	**Stafford** d	06 01	06 28	06 37	06 59	07 02	07 08		07 10		07 22	07 36	07 55	08 03	08 55		08 10		08 24	08 28	
—	—	Norton Bridge Station Drv d														→						
144½	—	Stone d				07 08								08 04								
—	—	Stone Crown Street d									07 14											
—	—	Stone Granville Square a																				
—	—	Barlaston Orchard Place d									07 23											
—	—	Wedgwood Old Road Bridge d																				
151¾	—	**Stoke-on-Trent** 50 d		06a44		07 16	07a19				07 47			08 12	08a18						08a43	
—	—	Hanley Bus Station a									07 57											
159	—	Kidsgrove 50 d				07 24								08 21								
161¼	—	Alsager 50 d				07 28								08 25								
167¾	24½	**Crewe** 65,50 a	06 20		06 57	07 38		07 27	07 30	07 32		07 42	07 56	08 34			08 10	08 30	09 07	08 41		08 47

	LM	LM	LM	VT	LM	XC	LM	VT	LM	VT	XC	VT	LM	VT	LM	XC	LM	LM	VT	LM	VT	XC
			1	◇1	1	◇1	1	◇1	1	◇1	◇1	◇1	1	◇1	1	◇1		1	◇1	1	◇1	◇1
	🚌	🚌															🚌					
				⊠		🛒		⊠		⊠	🛒	⊠		⊠		🛒			⊠		⊠	🛒
London Euston 15 ⊖66 d				07 35				07 43	07 46	08 07		08 10		08 40					08 43	08 46	09 07	
Watford Junction 66 d																						
Milton Keynes Central 66 d				08 06				08 13	08 19	08 38		08 43							09 13	09 19		
Northampton 68 d																						
Rugby d									08 42											09 42		
Nuneaton a									08 53											09 53		
d									08 54											09 54		
Atherstone d									09 00											10 00		
Polesworth d																						
Tamworth d									09 09											10 09		
Lichfield Trent Valley d									09 17											10 17		
Rugeley Trent Valley d					←				09 25						←					10 25		
Stafford d		08 35	08 36		08 55	09 03	09 10		09 42	09a27	09 28		09 35		09 42	10 02		10 10		10 42	10 24	10 28
Norton Bridge Station Drv d		08 53							→											→		
Stone d					09 04										09 51							
Stone Crown Street d	08 39	09a03															09 49					
Stone Granville Square a																						
Barlaston Orchard Place d	08 48																09 58					
Wedgwood Old Road Bridge d																						
Stoke-on-Trent 50 d	09 12				09 12	09a18					09a43				10 02	10a17	10 22					10a43
Hanley Bus Station a	09 19																10 29					
Kidsgrove 50 d					09 21										10 11							
Alsager 50 d					09 25										10 15							
Crewe 65,50 a			08 56	09 10	09 34		09 30	10 08				09 51	09 55	10 11	10 24			10 31	11 08		10 41	

	VT	LM	VT	LM	LM	XC	LM	LM	VT	LM	VT	XC	VT	LM	VT	LM	XC	LM	LM	VT	LM
	◇1	1	◇1		1	◇1		1	◇1	1	◇1	◇1	◇1	1	◇1	1	◇1		1	◇1	1
				🚌			🚌											🚌			
	⊠		⊠			🛒			⊠		⊠	🛒	⊠		⊠		🛒			☕	
London Euston 15 ⊖66 d	09 10		09 40						09 43	09 46	10 07		10 10		10 40					10 43	10 46
Watford Junction 66 d																					
Milton Keynes Central 66 d	09 41								10 13	10 19			10 41							11 13	11 19
Northampton 68 d																					
Rugby d										10 42											11 42
Nuneaton a										10 53											11 53
d										10 54											11 54
Atherstone d										11 00											12 00
Polesworth d																					
Tamworth d										11 09											12 09
Lichfield Trent Valley d										11 17											12 17
Rugeley Trent Valley d					←					11 25						←					12 25
Stafford d		10 35		10 35	10 42	11 03		11 10		11 42	11 24	11 28		11 35		11 42	12 03		12 10		12 42
Norton Bridge Station Drv d				10 53						→											→
Stone d					10 51											11 51					
Stone Crown Street d				11a03			10 49											11 49			
Stone Granville Square a																					
Barlaston Orchard Place d							10 58											11 58			
Wedgwood Old Road Bridge d																					
Stoke-on-Trent 50 d					11 02	11a18	11 22					11a43				12 02	12a18	12 22			
Hanley Bus Station a							11 29											12 29			
Kidsgrove 50 d					11 11											12 11					
Alsager 50 d					11 15											12 15					
Crewe 65,50 a	10 47	10 56	11 11		11 24			11 31	12 07		11 41		11 47	11 55	12 11	12 24			12 31	13 08	

Table T067-F

Mondays to Fridays

21 May to 7 December

London - Stoke-on-Trent and Crewe

	VT	XC	VT	LM	VT	LM	LM	XC	LM		LM	VT	LM	VT	XC	VT	LM	VT	LM		XC	LM	LM	VT
	◇■ ⊠	■ ⊤	◇■ ⊠	■	◇■ ⊠	bus	■	◇■ ⊤	bus		■	◇■ ⊠	■	◇■ ⊠	◇■ ⊤	◇■ ⊠	■	◇■ ⊠	■		◇■ ⊤	bus	■	◇■ ⊠
London Euston ⊖66 d	11 07		11 10		11 40							11 43	11 46	12 07		12 10		12 40						12 43
Watford Junction 66 d																								
Milton Keynes Central 66 d			11 41									12 13	12 19			12 41								13 13
Northampton 68 d																								
Rugby d													12 42			13 04								
Nuneaton a													12 53											
d													12 54											
Atherstone d													13 00											
Polesworth d																								
Tamworth d													13 09											
Lichfield Trent Valley d													13 17											
Rugeley Trent Valley d							←						13 25						←					
Stafford d	12 24	12 28		12 35		12 35	12 42	13 03			13 10		13 42	13 24	13 28		13 35		13 42		14 03		14 10	
Norton Bridge Station Drv d						12 53							→											
Stone d							12 51												13 51					
Stone Crown Street d						13a03			12 49													13 49		
Stone Granville Square a																								
Barlaston Orchard Place d									12 58													13 58		
Wedgwood Old Road Bridge d																								
Stoke-on-Trent 50 d		12a43					13 02	13a18	13 22						13a43				14 02		14a18	14 22		
Hanley Bus Station a									13 29													14 29		
Kidsgrove 50 d							13 11												14 11					
Alsager 50 d							13 15												14 15					
Crewe 65,50 a	12 41		12 47	12 55	13 11		13 24				13 31	14 07		13 41		13 50	13 56	14 11	14 24				14 31	15 07

	LM	VT	XC	VT	LM		VT	LM	XC	LM	LM	LM	VT	LM	VT		XC	VT	LM	VT	LM	XC	LM	LM
	■	◇■ ⊓	◇■ ⊤	◇■ ⊓	■		◇■ ⊓	■	◇■ ⊤	bus	bus	■	◇■ ⊓	■	◇■ ⊓		◇■ ⊤	◇■ ⊓	■	◇■ ⊓	■	◇■ ⊤	bus	■
London Euston ⊖66 d	12 46	13 07		13 10			13 40						13 43	13 46	14 07			14 10		14 40				
Watford Junction 66 d																								
Milton Keynes Central 66 d	13 19			13 41									14 13	14 19				14 41						
Northampton 68 d																								
Rugby d	13 42													14 42										
Nuneaton a	13 53													14 53										
d	13 54													14 54										
Atherstone d	14 00													15 00										
Polesworth d																								
Tamworth d	14 09													15 09										
Lichfield Trent Valley d	14 17													15 17										
Rugeley Trent Valley d	14 25							←						15 25							←			
Stafford d	14 42	14 24	14 28		14 35			14 42	15 03		15 05	15 10		15 42	15 24		15 28		15 35		15 42	16 03		16 10
Norton Bridge Station Drv d	→										15 23			→										
Stone d								14 51													15 51			
Stone Crown Street d										14 59	15a33												15 53	
Stone Granville Square a																								
Barlaston Orchard Place d										15 08													16 03	
Wedgwood Old Road Bridge d																							16 11	
Stoke-on-Trent 50 d			14a43					15 02	15a18	15 32							15a43				16 02	16a18	16 36	
Hanley Bus Station a										15 39													16 46	
Kidsgrove 50 d								15 11													16 11			
Alsager 50 d								15 15													16 15			
Crewe 65,50 a		14 41		14 47	14 54		15 10	15 24				15 30	16 07		15 41			15 47	15 55	16 11	16 24			16 31

	VT		LM	LM	VT	XC	VT	LM	VT	LM	XC		LM	VT	LM	LM	VT	XC	VT	LM	LM		VT	XC
	■ ⊓		bus	■	◇■ ⊓	◇■ ⊤	◇■ ⊓	■	◇■ ⊓	■	◇■ ⊤		■	■ ⊓	bus	■	◇■ ⊓	◇■ ⊤	◇■ ⊓	■	■		◇■ ⊓	◇■ ⊤
London Euston ⊖66 d	14 43			14 46	15 07		15 10		15 40					15 43		15 46	16 07		16 10				16 33	
Watford Junction 66 d																								
Milton Keynes Central 66 d	15 13			15 19			15 41							16 13		16 19			16u41					
Northampton 68 d																								
Rugby d				15 42												16 42							17 23	
Nuneaton a				15 53												16 53								
d				15 54												16 54								
Atherstone d				16 00												17 00								
Polesworth d																								
Tamworth d				16 09												17 09								
Lichfield Trent Valley d				16 17												17 17								
Rugeley Trent Valley d				16 25						←						17 25					←			
Stafford d			16 15	16 42	16 24	16 28		16 36		16 42	17 03		17 10		17 15	17 42	17 24	17 28		17 36	17 42		17 58	18 03
Norton Bridge Station Drv d			16a33	→											17 33	→								
Stone d										16 51											17 51			
Stone Crown Street d															17a43									
Stone Granville Square a																								
Barlaston Orchard Place d																								
Wedgwood Old Road Bridge d																								
Stoke-on-Trent 50 d						16a43				17 02	17a18							17a43			18 02			18a18
Hanley Bus Station a																								
Kidsgrove 50 d										17 11											18 11			
Alsager 50 d										17 15											18 15			
Crewe 65,50 a	17 08				16 41		16 47	16 56	17 11	17 24			17 30	18 08			17 41		17 47	17 56	18 24		18 17	

Table T067-F

Mondays to Fridays

21 May to 7 December

London - Stoke-on-Trent and Crewe

	VT	LM	LM	VT	LM	LM	VT		XC	VT	LM	LM	VT	XC	VT	LM	VT		LM	VT	XC	VT	LM	LM
	◇■ ⊓	bus	■	◇■ ⊓	bus	■	◇■ ⊠		◇■ ⊤	◇■ ⊠	■	■	◇■ ⊠	◇■ ⊤	◇■ ⊠	■	◇■ ⊓		■	◇■ ⊠	◇■ ⊤	◇■ ⊠	■	■
London Euston ⊖66 d	16 40			16 43		16 46	17 07			17 10			17 33		17 40		17 43		17 46	18 07		18 10		
Watford Junction 66 d																								
Milton Keynes Central 66 d				17 13		17 19				17u41							18u13		18 19			18u41		
Northampton 68 d																								
Rugby d						17 47							18 23						18 47					
Nuneaton a						17 59				18 11									18 59			19 12		
d						18 00				18 12									19 00			19 13		
Atherstone d						18 06													19 06					
Polesworth d																								
Tamworth d						18 15													19 15					
Lichfield Trent Valley d						18 22													19 22					
Rugeley Trent Valley d						18 30						←							19 30				←	
Stafford d			18 10			18 42	18 24		18 28		18 36	18 42	18 56	19 03		19 10			19 42	19 24	19 28		19 42	19 45
Norton Bridge Station Drv d						→													→					
Stone d																								19 54
Stone Crown Street d		17 54			18 49																			
Stone Granville Square a																								
Barlaston Orchard Place d		18 03			18a58																			
Wedgwood Old Road Bridge d																								
Stoke-on-Trent 50 d		18 27							18a43			19 07		19a18							19a43		20 02	20 07
Hanley Bus Station a		18 34																						
Kidsgrove 50 d																								20 15
Alsager 50 d																								20 20
Crewe 65,50 a	18 10		18 30	19 07			18 42			18 55	18 57	19 26	19 14		19 11	19 31	20 07			19 41		19 53	20 25	20 32

	VT	XC	VT		LM	VT	VT FO	XC	LM	VT ThFO	VT	VT	LM		XC	VT	LM	VT	LM	VT	XC	VT	LM	
	◇■ ⊠	◇■ ⊤	◇■ ⊠		■	◇■ ⊠	◇■ ⊓	◇■ ⊤	■	◇ ⊓	■ ⊓	◇■ ⊠	■		◇■ ⊤	◇■ ⊓	■	◇■ ⊓	■	◇■ ⊓	◇■	◇■ ⊓	■	
London Euston ⊖66 d	18 33		18 40			18 43	18 46		18 49	18 57	19 10					19 40		19 43	19 46	20 07		20 10		
Watford Junction 66 d																								
Milton Keynes Central 66 d						19 13	19 19		19 23		19u41		←					20 13	20 19			20 41		
Northampton 68 d									19 47				19 47											
Rugby d	19 23						19 41		→				20 06						20 42					
Nuneaton a											20 11		20 18						20 53	21 02				
d											20 12		20 19						21 00	21 03				
Atherstone d													20 24						21 06					
Polesworth d																								
Tamworth d			19 44										20 32			20 43			21 15					
Lichfield Trent Valley d			19 51										20 38			20 50			21 22					
Rugeley Trent Valley d												←	20 45						21 30				←	
Stafford d	19 54	20 03			20 10	20 51	20 24	20 28			20 37	20 51	20 55		21 03	21 04	21 10	21 55	21 42	21 27	21 29		21 42	
Norton Bridge Station Drv d						→												→	→					
Stone d													21 04										21 51	
Stone Crown Street d																								
Stone Granville Square a																								
Barlaston Orchard Place d																								
Wedgwood Old Road Bridge d																								
Stoke-on-Trent 50 d		20a19						20a43					21 12		21a18						21a45		22 02	
Hanley Bus Station a																								
Kidsgrove 50 d													21 21										22 11	
Alsager 50 d													21 25										22 15	
Crewe 65,50 a	20 13		20 17		20 30		20 42			20s33	20 53	21 15	21 34			21 21	21 32			21 46		21 47	22 24	

	VT	VT	VT	LM	XC	LM	LM	VT	VT		XC	LM	AW	VT	LM									
	◇■ ⊓	◇■ ⊓	◇■ ⊓	■	◇■	■	■	◇■ ⊓	◇■ ⊓		◇■	■	◇	◇■ ⊓	■									
London Euston ⊖66 d		20 30	20 40			20 46	20 49	21 07	21 10					22 00										
Watford Junction 66 d									21u25															
Milton Keynes Central 66 d						21 19	21 29	21 39						22 40										
Northampton 68 d							21 55																	
Rugby d						21 45	22 17		22 05					23 03										
Nuneaton a						21 57		22 07						23 13										
d						22 00		22 08						23 14										
Atherstone d						22 06																		
Polesworth d																								
Tamworth d		21 35				22 15								23s26										
Lichfield Trent Valley d		21 42				22 22								23s33										
Rugeley Trent Valley d	←					22 30									←									
Stafford d	21 55	22 00		22 10	22 28		23 53		22 37		23 01	23 21	23 43	23s48	23 53									
Norton Bridge Station Drv d							→																	
Stone d																								
Stone Crown Street d																								
Stone Granville Square a																								
Barlaston Orchard Place d																								
Wedgwood Old Road Bridge d																								
Stoke-on-Trent 50 d	22 11				22a43	22 51					23a17													
Hanley Bus Station a																								
Kidsgrove 50 d																								
Alsager 50 d																								
Crewe 65,50 a	22 30	22 17	22 10	22 34		23 10		22 53	22 58			23 49	00 10	00 17	00 22									

26 May to 8 December

London - Stoke-on-Trent and Crewe

	VT	XC	LM	LM	XC	LM	LM	XC	VT		LM	LM	LM	VT	VT	XC	LM	VT	XC		LM	LM	LM	VT
London Euston ⊖66 d									06 05				06 24	06 36				07 07						07 35
Watford Junction 66 d									06u20				06 41	06u51										
Milton Keynes Central 66 d									06 41				07 24											08 06
Northampton 68 d				05 41								06 38	07 45											
Rugby d				06 02					07 03			06 58	08 04											
Nuneaton a				06 14								07 10	08 16											
d				06 16								07 12	08 16											
Atherstone d				06 22								07 18	08 22											
Polesworth d												07 23												
Tamworth d				06 29								07 29	08 29											
Lichfield Trent Valley d				06 35								07 35	08 35											
Rugeley Trent Valley d				06 43								07 43	08 43											
Stafford d	06 01	06 28	06 36	06 58	07 03	07 10		07 31	07 34		07 36	07 55	08 55		07 59	08 03	08 10	08 24	08 28			08 35	08 36	
Norton Bridge Station Drv d													→									08 53		
Stone d				07 07								08 04												
Stone Crown Street d							07 14														08 39	09a03		
Stone Granville Square a																								
Barlaston Orchard Place d							07 23														08 48			
Wedgwood Old Road Bridge d																								
Stoke-on-Trent 50 d		06a44		07 15	07a18		07 47					08 15				08a18			08a43		09 12			
Hanley Bus Station a							07 57														09 19			
Kidsgrove 50 d				07 23								08 23												
Alsager 50 d				07 27								08 27												
Crewe 65,50 a	06 20		06 56	07 37		07 29		07 50	07 53		07 58	08 37		08 10	08 18		08 30	08 41					08 56	09 11

	LM	XC	LM	VT	LM		VT	XC	VT	LM	VT	LM	XC	LM	LM		VT	LM	VT	XC	VT	LM	VT	LM
London Euston ⊖66 d				07 43	07 46		08 07		08 10		08 40						08 43	08 46	09 07		09 10		09 40	
Watford Junction 66 d																								
Milton Keynes Central 66 d				08 13	08 19				08 41								09 13	09 19			09 41			
Northampton 68 d																								
Rugby d					08 42													09 42						
Nuneaton a					08 54													09 53						
d					08 54													09 54						
Atherstone d					09 00													10 00						
Polesworth d																								
Tamworth d					09 09													10 09						
Lichfield Trent Valley d					09 17													10 17						
Rugeley Trent Valley d	←				09 25							←						10 25						
Stafford d	08 55	09 03	09 10		09 42		09 24	09 28		09 35		09 42	10 03		10 10			10 42	10 26	10 28		10 35		10 35
Norton Bridge Station Drv d					→													→						10 53
Stone d	09 04											09 51												
Stone Crown Street d														09 49										11a03
Stone Granville Square a																								
Barlaston Orchard Place d														09 58										
Wedgwood Old Road Bridge d																								
Stoke-on-Trent 50 d	09 15	09a18						09a43				10 02	10a18	10 22						10a43				
Hanley Bus Station a														10 29										
Kidsgrove 50 d	09 23											10 11												
Alsager 50 d	09 28											10 15												
Crewe 65,50 a	09 37		09 30	10 08			09 41		09 47	09 55	10 11	10 24			10 30		11 08		10 44		10 47	10 55	11 11	

	LM		XC	LM	LM	VT	LM	VT	XC	VT	LM		VT	LM	XC	LM	LM	VT	LM	VT	XC		VT	LM
London Euston ⊖66 d						09 43	09 46	10 07		10 10			10 40					10 43	10 46	11 07			11 10	
Watford Junction 66 d																								
Milton Keynes Central 66 d						10 13	10 19			10 41								11 13	11 19				11 41	
Northampton 68 d																								
Rugby d							10 42												11 42					
Nuneaton a							10 53												11 53					
d							10 54												11 54					
Atherstone d							11 00												12 00					
Polesworth d																								
Tamworth d							11 09												12 09					
Lichfield Trent Valley d							11 17			11 24									12 17					
Rugeley Trent Valley d	←						11 25							←					12 25					
Stafford d	10 42		11 03		11 10		11 42	11 24	11 28		11 35			11 42	12 03		12 10		12 42	12 24	12 28			12 35
Norton Bridge Station Drv d							→												→					
Stone d	10 51													11 51										
Stone Crown Street d				10 49												11 49								
Stone Granville Square a																								
Barlaston Orchard Place d				10 58												11 58								
Wedgwood Old Road Bridge d																								
Stoke-on-Trent 50 d	11 02		11a18	11 22					11a43					12 02	12a18	12 22					12a43			
Hanley Bus Station a				11 29												12 29								
Kidsgrove 50 d	11 11													12 11										
Alsager 50 d	11 15													12 15										
Crewe 65,50 a	11 24				11 30	12 07		11 41		11 53	11 54		12 11	12 24			12 30	13 08		12 42			12 47	12 54

Table T067-F

Saturdays

26 May to 8 December

London - Stoke-on-Trent and Crewe

	VT	LM	LM	XC	LM	LM	VT		LM	VT	XC	VT	LM	VT	LM	XC	LM		LM	VT	LM	VT	XC	VT
London Euston ⊖66 d	11 40						11 43		11 46	12 07		12 10		12 40						12 43	12 46	13 07		13 10
Watford Junction 66 d																								
Milton Keynes Central 66 d							12 13		12 19			12 41								13 13	13 19			13 41
Northampton 68 d																								
Rugby d									12 42			13 04									13 42			
Nuneaton a									12 53												13 53			
d									12 54												13 54			
Atherstone d									13 00												14 00			
Polesworth d																								
Tamworth d									13 09												14 09			
Lichfield Trent Valley d									13 17												14 17			
Rugeley Trent Valley d			←						13 25						←						14 25			
Stafford d		12 35	12 42	13 03		13 10			13 42	13 24	13 28		13 35		13 42	14 03			14 10		14 42	14 24	14 28	
Norton Bridge Station Drv d		12 53							→												→			
Stone d			12 51												13 51									
Stone Crown Street d		13a03			12 49												13 49							
Stone Granville Square a																								
Barlaston Orchard Place d					12 58												13 58							
Wedgwood Old Road Bridge d																								
Stoke-on-Trent 50 d			13 02	13a18	13 22						13a43				14 02	14a18	14 22						14a43	
Hanley Bus Station a					13 29												14 29							
Kidsgrove 50 d			13 11												14 11									
Alsager 50 d			13 15												14 15									
Crewe 65,50 a	13 11		13 24			13 30	14 08			13 41		13 50	13 56	14 11	14 24				14 30	15 07		14 41		14 47

	LM	VT	LM		XC	LM	LM	LM	VT	LM	VT	XC	VT		LM	VT	LM	XC	LM	LM	VT	LM	LM	
London Euston ⊖66 d		13 40							13 43	13 46	14 07		14 10			14 40					14 43		14 46	
Watford Junction 66 d																								
Milton Keynes Central 66 d									14 13	14 19			14 41								15 13		15 19	
Northampton 68 d																								
Rugby d										14 42													15 42	
Nuneaton a										14 53													15 53	
d										14 54													15 54	
Atherstone d										15 00													16 00	
Polesworth d																								
Tamworth d										15 09													16 09	
Lichfield Trent Valley d										15 17													16 17	
Rugeley Trent Valley d			←							15 25							←						16 25	
Stafford d	14 35		14 42		15 03		15 05	15 10		15 42	15 24	15 28			15 35		15 42	16 03		16 10		16 15	16 42	
Norton Bridge Station Drv d							15 23			→												16a33	→	
Stone d			14 51														15 51							
Stone Crown Street d						14 59	15a33												15 53					
Stone Granville Square a																								
Barlaston Orchard Place d						15 08													16 03					
Wedgwood Old Road Bridge d																								
Stoke-on-Trent 50 d			15 02		15a18	15 32						15a43					16 02	16a18	16 36					
Hanley Bus Station a						15 39													16 46					
Kidsgrove 50 d			15 11														16 11							
Alsager 50 d			15 15														16 15							
Crewe 65,50 a	14 55	15 10	15 24					15 30	16 08		15 41		15 47		15 55	16 10	16 24			16 30	17 08			

	VT	XC	VT	LM	VT	LM	XC	LM	VT		LM	LM	VT	XC	VT	LM	LM	VT	XC		VT	LM	LM	VT
London Euston ⊖66 d	15 07		15 10		15 40				15 43			15 46	16 07		16 10			16 33			16 40			16 43
Watford Junction 66 d																								
Milton Keynes Central 66 d			15 41						16 13			16 19			16 41									17 13
Northampton 68 d																								
Rugby d												16 42												
Nuneaton a												16 53												
d												16 54												
Atherstone d												17 00												
Polesworth d																								
Tamworth d												17 09						17 38						
Lichfield Trent Valley d												17 17						17 45						
Rugeley Trent Valley d						←						17 25					←							
Stafford d	16 24	16 28		16 36		16 42	17 03	17 10			17 15	17 42	17 24	17 28		17 36	17 42	17a58	18 03				18 10	
Norton Bridge Station Drv d											17 33	→												
Stone d						16 51											17 51							
Stone Crown Street d											17a43											17 54		
Stone Granville Square a																								
Barlaston Orchard Place d																						18 03		
Wedgwood Old Road Bridge d																								
Stoke-on-Trent 50 d		16a43				17 02	17a18							17a43			18 02		18a18			18 27		
Hanley Bus Station a																						18 34		
Kidsgrove 50 d						17 11											18 11							
Alsager 50 d						17 15											18 15							
Crewe 65,50 a	16 41		16 47	16 55	17 11	17 24		17 30	18 07				17 41		17 47	17 55	18 24				18 10		18 30	19 08

Table T067-F

London - Stoke-on-Trent and Crewe

Saturdays
26 May to 8 December

		LM	LM	VT	XC	VT		VT	LM	VT	LM	XC	LM	VT	LM	VT		XC	VT	LM	LM	VT	XC	VT	VT
			■	◇■	◇■	◇■		◇■	■	◇■	■	◇■	■	◇■	■	◇■		◇■	◇■	■	■	◇■	◇■	◇■	◇■
		🚌		☕	🛒	☕		☕		☕		🛒		☕		☕		🛒	☕			☕	🛒	☕	☕
London Euston 15	⊖66 d		16 46	17 07		17 10		17 10		17 40				17 43	17 46	18 07			18 10			18 33		18 40	18 43
Watford Junction	66 d																								
Milton Keynes Central	66 d		17 19			17 40		17 41						18 13	18 19				18 41						19 13
Northampton	68 d																								
Rugby	d		17 42												18 42										
Nuneaton	a		17 53	18 02											18 53										
	d		17 54	18 03											18 54										
Atherstone	d		18 00												19 00										
Polesworth	d																								
Tamworth	d		18 09												19 09										
Lichfield Trent Valley	d		18 17												19 17							19 38			
Rugeley Trent Valley	d		18 25								←				19 25						←	19 45			
Stafford	d		18 44	18 27	18 28				18 36		18 44	19 03	19 10		19 42	19 24		19 28		19 36	19 42	19a58	20 03		20 51
Norton Bridge Station Drv	d		→												→										→
Stone	d										18 53										19 51				
Stone Crown Street	d	18 49																							
Stone Granville Square	a																								
Barlaston Orchard Place	d	18a58																							
Wedgwood Old Road Bridge	d																								
Stoke-on-Trent	50 d				18a43						19 02	19a18						19a43			20 02		20a18		
Hanley Bus Station	a																								
Kidsgrove	50 d										19 11										20 11				
Alsager	50 d										19 15										20 15				
Crewe	65,50 a			18 45		18 49		18 49	18 55	19 11	19 27		19 30	20 09		19 41			19 47	19 56	20 24			20 12	

		LM		VT	XC	LM	VT	LM	VT	VT	XC	LM		XC	VT	VT	VT	LM	XC	VT	XC	LM			
		■		◇■	◇■	■	◇■	■	◇■	◇■	◇■	■		◇■	◇■	◇■	◇■	■	◇■	◇■	◇■	■			
				☕			☕		☕	☕					☕	☕	☕			☕					
London Euston 15	⊖66 d	18 46		19 07			19 30			19 40					20 11	20 20	20 31			21 00					
Watford Junction	66 d																20u46								
Milton Keynes Central	66 d	19 19														21 05				21 45					
Northampton	68 d																								
Rugby	d	19 42													21 15		21 36								
Nuneaton	a	19 53		20 02												21 32									
	d	19 58		20 03												21 33									
Atherstone	d	20 04																							
Polesworth	d																								
Tamworth	d	20 14																							
Lichfield Trent Valley	d	20 21															21 53								
Rugeley Trent Valley	d	20 29						←	←								22 00								
Stafford	d	20 44		20 27	20 28	20 38		20 44	20 51		21 03	21 10		21 30	21 46			22 16	22 28	22 34	23 02	23 22			
Norton Bridge Station Drv	d	→																							
Stone	d											21 19													
Stone Crown Street	d																								
Stone Granville Square	a																								
Barlaston Orchard Place	d																								
Wedgwood Old Road Bridge	d																								
Stoke-on-Trent	50 d				20a43			21 02			21a18	21 27		21a46		22a05			22a43		23a19				
Hanley Bus Station	a																								
Kidsgrove	50 d											21 35													
Alsager	50 d											21 40													
Crewe	65,50 a			20 45		20 57	21 02	21 22	21 10	21 18		21 49			22 05		22 29	22 36		22 58		23 42			

Sundays
20 May to 2 December

		VT	VT	XC	VT	LM	XC	VT	LM	VT		LM	VT	XC	LM	VT	LM	LM	VT	LM		XC	VT	LM	LM
		◇■	◇■	◇■	◇■	■	◇■	◇■	■	◇■		■	◇■	◇■	■	◇■	■	■	◇■	■		◇■	◇■	■	■
		☕	☕	🛒	☕		🛒	☕		☕			☕	🛒		☕			☕			🛒	☕		
London Euston 15	⊖66 d		08 10		08 15			08 45		09 14			09 45		09 54	10 15		10 24	10 45				11 15		
Watford Junction	66 d														10 10			10 40							
Milton Keynes Central	66 d		08 56					09 33					10 33		10 50			11 20	11 33				12 04		
Northampton	68 d								09 40						11 08			11 40							
Rugby	d					08 52		10 09	10 03				11 09		11 30			12 03	12 09						
Nuneaton	a				09 43				10 15	10 44					11 42	11 46		12 15							
	d				09 44				10 16	10 45					11 43	11 47		12 16							
Atherstone	d								10 22						11 49			12 22							
Polesworth	d																								
Tamworth	d								10 30						11 57			12 30							
Lichfield Trent Valley	d								10 37	11 02					12 04			12 37							
Rugeley Trent Valley	d								10 44						12 09			12 44		←				←	
Stafford	d	09 17		09 33	10 08	10 17	10 33		11 00	11 15		11 17		11 32	12 21	12 14	12 17	13 00		12 21		12 29	12 53	13 00	13 09
Norton Bridge Station Drv	d														→			→							
Stone	d								11 09											12 30				13 09	
Stone Crown Street	d																								
Stone Granville Square	a																								
Barlaston Orchard Place	d																								
Wedgwood Old Road Bridge	d																								
Stoke-on-Trent	50 d			09a51			10a48		11 17					11a48						12 41		12a45		13 17	
Hanley Bus Station	a																								
Kidsgrove	50 d								11 25											12 49				13 25	
Alsager	50 d								11 30											12 53				13 30	
Crewe	65,50 a	09 35	10 17		10 28	10 37		10 55	11 41	11 34		11 37	11 55			12 32	12 37		12 56	13 03			13 12	13 41	13 30

Table T067-F

London - Stoke-on-Trent and Crewe

Sundays
20 May to 2 December

		VT	XC	VT	XC	LM		LM	VT	LM	VT	XC	VT	XC	LM	LM		VT	LM	VT	XC	VT	XC	LM	LM
		◇■	◇■	◇■	◇■	■		■	◇■	■	◇■	◇■	◇■	◇■	■	■		◇■	■	◇■	◇■	◇■	◇■	■	■
		☕	🛒	☕	🛒				☕		☕	🛒	☕	🛒				☕		☕	🛒	☕	🛒		
London Euston 15	⊖66 d	12 05		12 37					12 40	12 50	13 05		13 37					13 40	13 50	14 05		14 37			
Watford Junction	66 d									13 06									14 06						
Milton Keynes Central	66 d								13 13	13 37								14 13	14 37						
Northampton	68 d							13 02		14 02									15 02						
Rugby	d							13 26		14 26									15 26						
Nuneaton	a							13 40		14 39									15 39						
	d							13 40		14 40									15 40						
Atherstone	d							13 46		14 46									15 46						
Polesworth	d																								
Tamworth	d							13 55		14 55									15 55						
Lichfield Trent Valley	d							14 01		15 01									16 01						
Rugeley Trent Valley	d							14 09		15 09						←			16 09						←
Stafford	d	13 25	13 29		14 03	14 09		14 21		15 21	14 25	14 28		15 03	15 09	15 21			16 21	15 25	15 28		16 03	16 09	16 21
Norton Bridge Station Drv	d									→									→						
Stone	d							14 30								15 30									16 30
Stone Crown Street	d																								
Stone Granville Square	a																								
Barlaston Orchard Place	d																								
Wedgwood Old Road Bridge	d																								
Stoke-on-Trent	50 d		13a44		14a18			14 41				14a44		15a18		15 41					15a44		16a18		16 41
Hanley Bus Station	a																								
Kidsgrove	50 d							14 49								15 51									16 51
Alsager	50 d							14 54								15 55									16 55
Crewe	65,50 a	13 43		14 12		14 30		15 03	15 07		14 43		15 12		15 30	16 05		16 08		15 43		16 11		16 30	17 05

		VT		LM	VT	XC	VT	VT	XC	LM	LM	VT		LM	VT	XC	VT	VT	XC	LM	VT	LM		VT	LM
		◇■		■	◇■	◇■	◇■	◇■	◇■	■	■	◇■		■	◇■	◇■	◇■	◇■	◇■	■	◇■	■		◇■	■
		☕			☕	🛒	☕	☕	🛒			☕			☕	🛒	☕	☕	🛒		☕			☕	
London Euston 15	⊖66 d	14 40		14 50	15 05		15 08	15 37				15 40		15 50	16 05		16 08	16 37			16 40	16 50		17 05	
Watford Junction	66 d			15 06										16 06								17 06			
Milton Keynes Central	66 d	15 13		15 37			15 42					16 13		16 37			16 42				17 13	17 37			
Northampton	68 d			16 02										17 02								18 02			
Rugby	d			16 26										17 26								→			
Nuneaton	a			16 39										17 39										18 03	
	d			16 40										17 40										18 04	
Atherstone	d			16 46										17 46											
Polesworth	d																								
Tamworth	d			16 55										17 55											
Lichfield Trent Valley	d			17 01										18 01											
Rugeley Trent Valley	d			17 09							←			18 09											←
Stafford	d			17 21	16 25	16 28			17 03	17 09	17 21			18 21	17 26	17 29			18 03	18 09					18 21
Norton Bridge Station Drv	d			→										→											
Stone	d										17 30														18 30
Stone Crown Street	d																								
Stone Granville Square	a																								
Barlaston Orchard Place	d																								
Wedgwood Old Road Bridge	d																								
Stoke-on-Trent	50 d					16a44			17a18		17 41					17a45			18a18						18 41
Hanley Bus Station	a																								
Kidsgrove	50 d										17 51														18 52
Alsager	50 d										17 55														18 56
Crewe	65,50 a	17 07			16 43		16 50	17 12		17 30	18 05	18 07			17 44		17 50	18 12		18 30	19 07			18 44	19 06

		XC	VT	XC	VT	LM	LM	VT		LM	VT	XC	VT	VT	XC	LM	LM	XC		VT	LM	VT	VT	VT	VT
		◇■	◇■	◇■	◇■	■	■	■ ■		■	◇■	◇■	◇■	◇■	◇■	■	■	◇■		◇■	■	◇■	◇■	◇■	◇■
		🛒	☕	🛒	☕			☕			☕	🛒	☕	☕	🛒					☕		☕	☕	☕	☕
London Euston 15	⊖66 d		17 08		17 37			17 40		17 50	18 05		18 08	18 37						18 40	18 50	19 05	19 08		19 37
Watford Junction	66 d									18 06											19 06				
Milton Keynes Central	66 d		17 42				←	18 13		18 37			18 42							19 13	19 37		19 42		
Northampton	68 d						18 02			19 02											20 02				
Rugby	d						18 26			19 26											→				
Nuneaton	a						18 39			19 39												20 03			
	d						18 40			19 40												20 04			
Atherstone	d						18 46			19 46															
Polesworth	d																								
Tamworth	d						18 55			19 55															
Lichfield Trent Valley	d		18 24				19 01			20 01															
Rugeley Trent Valley	d						19 09			20 09							←							←	
Stafford	d	18 28	18 41	19 03		19 09	19 21			20 21	19 25	19 28			20 03	20 09	20 21	20 28		20 52		20 29		20 52	
Norton Bridge Station Drv	d									→										→					
Stone	d						19 30										20 30								
Stone Crown Street	d																								
Stone Granville Square	a																								
Barlaston Orchard Place	d																								
Wedgwood Old Road Bridge	d																								
Stoke-on-Trent	50 d	18a44		19a18			19 41					19a44			20a18		20 41	20a44							
Hanley Bus Station	a																								
Kidsgrove	50 d						19 52										20 52								
Alsager	50 d						19 56										20 56								
Crewe	65,50 a		18 59		19 12	19 30	20 06	20 07			19 43		19 50	20 12		20 31	21 06					20 47	20 50	21 10	21 12

Table T067-F

Sundays

20 May to 2 December

London - Stoke-on-Trent and Crewe

		XC	LM	XC		VT	LM	VT	VT	VT	VT	VT	LM	VT		LM	XC	VT	AW	VT
		◇■	■	◇■		◇■	■	◇■	◇■	◇■	◇■	◇■	■	◇■		■	◇■	◇■	◇	◇■
		✕				☕		☕	☕	☕	☕	☕		☕				☕		☕
London Euston ■	⊖66 d					19 40	19 50	20 05	20 08	20 25		20 35		20 50				21 21		21 51
Watford Junction	66 d						20 06													
Milton Keynes Central	66 d		←			20 13	20 37		20 41					21 37						22 39
Northampton	68 d		20 02				21 06													
Rugby	d		20 26				21 30							22 01		←				23 19
Nuneaton	a		20 39				21 43	21 03								21 43		22 56		23 29
	d		20 40				21 43	21 04								21 43		22 57		23 30
Atherstone	d		20 46				→									21 49				
Polesworth	d																			
Tamworth	d		20 55							21 32						21 58				
Lichfield Trent Valley	d		21 01							21 39						22 04				
Rugeley Trent Valley	d		21 09								←					22 10				
Stafford	d	21 06	21 21	21 30		21 56			21 33		21 56	22 00	22 17			22 23	22 28	23 23	23 31	23s54
Norton Bridge Station Drv	d					→														
Stone	d		21 30													22 32				
Stone Crown Street	d																			
Stone Granville Square	a																			
Barlaston Orchard Place	d																			
Wedgwood Old Road Bridge	d																			
Stoke-on-Trent	50 d	21a21	21 41	21a45												22 41	22a44			
Hanley Bus Station	a																			
Kidsgrove	50 d		21 52													22 49				
Alsager	50 d		21 56													22 53				
Crewe	65,50 a		22 06					21 44	21 53	22 10	22 16	22 20	22 36	22 49		23 03		23 44	23 57	00s16

Table T067-R

Mondays to Fridays

21 May to 7 December

Crewe and Stoke-on-Trent - London

Miles	Miles			AW	LM	LM	VT	XC	VT	LM		LM	VT	VT	LM	XC	LM	VT	LM	VT		VT	LM	LM	LM
					🚌	■	◇■	◇■	◇■	■		■	◇■	◇■	■	◇■	■	◇■	■	◇■		◇■	■	■	🚌
							⊠	✕	⊠				⊠	⊠		✕		⊠		⊠		⊠			
0	0	**Crewe**	65,50 d	04 59		05 21	05 36	05 47	06 02			06 19	06 28		06 35	06 39	06 49		06 52	06 53		07 17		07 17	
6¼	—	Alsager	50 d												06 44										
8½	—	Kidsgrove	50 d												06 48										
—	—	Hanley Bus Station	d		05 55																				07 30
15	—	**Stoke-on-Trent**	50 d		06 02			06 07							06 56			07 06	07 17						07 37
—	—	Wedgwood Old Road Bridge	d																						07 56
—	—	Barlaston Orchard Place	d		06 23																				08 04
—	—	Stone Granville Square	d		06a33																				08a19
—	—	Stone Crown Street	d																						
23¼	—	Stone	d												07 04										
—	—	Norton Bridge Station Drv	d																				←		
32¼	24½	**Stafford**	d	05a23			05 55	06a24	06 22			06a40		06 54	07a14	06a59	07 10	07 24	07 39			07 36	07 39	07a39	
42	—	Rugeley Trent Valley	d			06 00													→				07 49		
50	—	Lichfield Trent Valley	d			06 08				←				07 08									07 57		
56¼	—	Tamworth	d			06 15				06 15				07 15									08 03		
59¾	—	Polesworth	d			→																			
63¾	—	Atherstone	d							06 23													08 12		
68¾	—	Nuneaton	a				06 17			06 30			07 06							07 33			08 18		
—	—		d				06 18			06 31			07 08							07 35			08 19		
83¼	—	Rugby	a				06 31		06 52	06 46							08 36						08 34		
102	—	Northampton	68 a							07 09							09 00								
118	—	Milton Keynes Central	66 a				06 51		07 13								09 21						08 55		
150¼	—	Watford Junction	66 a														→	09s16							
167¾	—	**London Euston** ■	⊖66 a				07 26		07 50	08 05			08 08	08 23				09 33		08 34		08 54	09 37		

		XC	LM	XC	LM	VT		LM	LM	VT	VT	LM	VT	VT	LM	XC		LM	VT	XC	LM	VT	VT	LM	LM
		◇■	■	■	🚌	◇■		■	■	◇■	◇■	■	◇■	◇■	🚌	◇■		■	◇■	◇■	🚌	◇■	◇■	■	■
		✕		✕		⊠				⊠	⊠		⊠	⊠		✕			⊠	✕		⊠	⊠		
Crewe	65,50 d		07 49						07 55	07 57	08 01	08 18	08 23	08 29				08 49	08 56				09 01	09 02	09 19
Alsager	50 d								08 04															09 11	
Kidsgrove	50 d								08 08															09 15	
Hanley Bus Station	d														08 35										
Stoke-on-Trent	50 d	07 44		08 07		08 12			08 17						08 42	08 44				09 07		09 12		09 28	
Wedgwood Old Road Bridge	d																								
Barlaston Orchard Place	d														09 03										
Stone Granville Square	d														09a13						09 03				
Stone Crown Street	d																								
Stone	d								08 25															09 36	
Norton Bridge Station Drv	d				08 01																09 14				
Stafford	d	08a00	08a10	08a23	08a28				08 37			08a39	08 43			09a00		09a09		09a23	09a33			09 55	09a39
Rugeley Trent Valley	d								08 46															→	
Lichfield Trent Valley	d								08 54					09 01											
Tamworth	d								09 01					09 07											
Polesworth	d																								
Atherstone	d								09 09																
Nuneaton	a					08 44			09 16													09 44			
	d					08 46			09 16													09 45			
Rugby	a								09 32	08 45															
Northampton	68 a							←																	
Milton Keynes Central	66 a							09 21	09 53		09 58								10 02				10 58		
Watford Junction	66 a					09s32		09 58																	
London Euston ■	⊖66 a					09 49		10 19	10 29	09 41	10 32		10 00	10 16					10 37			10 51	11 34		

		VT		LM	VT	LM	XC	LM	VT	LM	VT	XC		LM	LM	VT	LM	VT	LM	VT FO	XC	LM		VT	LM
		◇■		■	◇■	🚌	◇■	■	◇■	■	◇■	◇■		■	■	◇■	■	◇■	🚌	◇■	◇■	■		◇■	■
		⊠			⊠		✕		⊠		⊠	✕				⊠		⊠		☕	✕			⊠	
Crewe	65,50 d	09 24			09 30			09 49	09 56		10 01			10 02	10 19	10 22		10 29		10 41		10 49		10 56	
Alsager	50 d													10 11											
Kidsgrove	50 d													10 15											
Hanley Bus Station	d					09 35													10 35						
Stoke-on-Trent	50 d					09 42	09 44					10 07		10 28					10 42		10 44				
Wedgwood Old Road Bridge	d																								
Barlaston Orchard Place	d					10 03													11 03						
Stone Granville Square	d					10a13													11a13						
Stone Crown Street	d																								
Stone	d													10 36											
Norton Bridge Station Drv	d			←													←								
Stafford	d	09 43		09 55			10a00	10a09				10a23		10 55	10a38	10 42	10 55				11a00	11a10			
Rugeley Trent Valley	d			10 05										→			11 05								
Lichfield Trent Valley	d			10 13													11 13								
Tamworth	d			10 20													11 20								
Polesworth	d																								
Atherstone	d			10 28													11 28								
Nuneaton	a			10 35													11 35								
	d			10 36													11 36								
Rugby	a			10 51													11 52								
Northampton	68 a									←															←
Milton Keynes Central	66 a			11 14					11 02	11 14	11 58						12 14							12 02	12 14
Watford Junction	66 a			→													→								
London Euston ■	⊖66 a	11 02			11 08				11 37	11 50	12 33					11 59		12 02		12 30				12 37	12 50

Table T067-R

Mondays to Fridays

21 May to 7 December

Crewe and Stoke-on-Trent - London

	VT	XC	LM	LM	LM	VT	LM	VT	LM	XC	LM	VT	LM	VT	XC	LM	LM	VT	LM	LM	VT	XC
	◇1 ⊠	◇1	bus	1	1	◇1 ⊠	1	◇1 ⊠	bus	◇1	1	◇1	1	◇1 ⊠	◇1	1	1	◇1	1	bus	◇1	◇1
Crewe 65,50 d	11 01			11 02	11 19	11 22		11 29			11 49	11 56		12 01		12 02	12 19	12 22			12 29	
Alsager 50 d				11 11												12 11						
Kidsgrove 50 d				11 15												12 15						
Hanley Bus Station d									11 35											12 25		
Stoke-on-Trent 50 d		11 07		11 28					11 42	11 44					12 07	12 28				12 42		12 44
Wedgwood Old Road Bridge d																						
Barlaston Orchard Place d									12 03											13 03		
Stone Granville Square d			11 03						12a13											13a13		
Stone Crown Street d																						
Stone d				11 36												12 36						
Norton Bridge Station Drv d			11 14				←												←			
Stafford d		11a24	11a33	11 55	11a39	11 42	11 55			12a00	12a10				12a23	12 55	12a39	12 42	12 55			13a00
Rugeley Trent Valley d				→			12 05									→			13 05			
Lichfield Trent Valley d							12 13												13 13			
Tamworth d							12 20												13 20			
Polesworth d																						
Atherstone d							12 28												13 28			
Nuneaton a							12 35												13 35			
d							12 36												13 36			
Rugby a							12 52												13 51			
Northampton 68 a													←									
Milton Keynes Central 66 a	12 58						13 14					13 02	13 14	13 58					14 14			
Watford Junction 66 a							→												→			
London Euston ⊖66 a	13 33					12 59		13 02				13 37	13 50	14 33				14 02			14 05	

	LM	VT	LM	VT	XC	LM	LM	LM	VT	LM	VT	LM	XC	LM	VT	LM	VT	XC	LM	LM	VT FX
	1	◇1	1	◇1 ⊠	◇1	bus	1	1	◇1	1	◇1	bus	◇1	1	◇1	1	◇1	◇1	1	1	◇1
Crewe 65,50 d	12 49	12 56		13 01			13 02	13 19	13 25		13 30			13 49	13 56		14 01		14 02	14 19	14 25
Alsager 50 d							13 11												14 11		
Kidsgrove 50 d							13 15												14 15		
Hanley Bus Station d												13 35									
Stoke-on-Trent 50 d					13 07		13 28					13 42	13 44					14 07	14 28		
Wedgwood Old Road Bridge d																					
Barlaston Orchard Place d												14 03									
Stone Granville Square d						13 03						14a13									
Stone Crown Street d																					
Stone d							13 36												14 36		
Norton Bridge Station Drv d						13 14				←											
Stafford d	13a09				13a25	13a33	13 55	13a39	13 44	13 55			14a00	14a09				14a23	14 55	14a38	14 45
Rugeley Trent Valley d							→			14 05									→		
Lichfield Trent Valley d										14 13											
Tamworth d										14 20											
Polesworth d																					
Atherstone d										14 28											
Nuneaton a										14 35											
d										14 36											
Rugby a										14 51											
Northampton 68 a			←													←					
Milton Keynes Central 66 a		14 02	14 14	14 58						15 14					15 02	15 14	15 58				
Watford Junction 66 a										→											
London Euston ⊖66 a		14 38	14 50	15 33					15 04		15 09				15 36	15 50	16 32				16 02

	VT FO	LM	VT FX	VT FO	XC	LM	LM	VT	LM	VT	XC	LM	LM	VT	LM	VT	XC	LM	LM	LM	VT	LM
	◇1	1	◇1	◇1	◇1	1	bus	◇1	1	◇1	◇1	1	1	◇1	1	◇1	◇1	bus	1	bus	◇1	1
Crewe 65,50 d	14 25		14 31	14 31		14 49		14 56		15 01		15 02	15 19	15 22		15 29			15 49		15 56	
Alsager 50 d												15 11										
Kidsgrove 50 d												15 15										
Hanley Bus Station d							14 50													15 50		
Stoke-on-Trent 50 d					14 44		14 57				15 07	15 28					15 44			15 57		
Wedgwood Old Road Bridge d																						
Barlaston Orchard Place d							15 18													16 18		
Stone Granville Square d							15a28											15 33		16a28		
Stone Crown Street d																						
Stone d												15 36										
Norton Bridge Station Drv d		←													←			15 44				
Stafford d	14 45	14 55			15a00	15a09					15a24	15 55	15a39	15 42	15 55		16a00	16a03	16a09			
Rugeley Trent Valley d		15 05										→			16 05							
Lichfield Trent Valley d		15 13													16 13							
Tamworth d		15 20													16 20							
Polesworth d																						
Atherstone d		15 28													16 28							
Nuneaton a		15 35													16 35							
d		15 36													16 36							
Rugby a		15 51													16 51							
Northampton 68 a									←													←
Milton Keynes Central 66 a		16 14						16 02	16 14	16 58					17 14						17 02	17 14
Watford Junction 66 a		→													→							
London Euston ⊖66 a	16 05		16 05	16 08				16 37	16 50	17 33				16 59		17 02					17 37	17 50

Table T067-R

Mondays to Fridays

21 May to 7 December

Crewe and Stoke-on-Trent - London

	VT	XC	LM	LM	VT	LM	VT	XC	LM	LM	VT	LM	XC	VT	VT	LM	LM	VT	LM	XC	LM	VT
	◇1	◇1	1	1	◇1	1	◇1	◇1	1	bus	◇1	1	◇1	◇1	◇1	1	1	◇1	bus	◇1	1	◇1 ⊠
Crewe 65,50 d	16 01		16 02	16 19	16 25		16 31		16 49		16 56				17 01	17 02	17 19	17 29			17 49	17 56
Alsager 50 d			16 11													17 11						
Kidsgrove 50 d			16 15													17 15						
Hanley Bus Station d																			17 30			
Stoke-on-Trent 50 d		16 07	16 28					16 44					17 07			17 28			17 37	17 44		
Wedgwood Old Road Bridge d																						
Barlaston Orchard Place d																			17 58			
Stone Granville Square d																			18a08			
Stone Crown Street d																						
Stone d			16 36													17 36						
Norton Bridge Station Drv d						←				16 54												
Stafford d		16a24	16 55	16a40	16 45	16 55		17a00	17a09	17a13			17a24	17 36		17 55	17a39			18a00	18a09	
Rugeley Trent Valley d			→			17 05										18 05						
Lichfield Trent Valley d						17 13										18 13						
Tamworth d						17 20										18 20						
Polesworth d																						
Atherstone d						17 28										18 28						
Nuneaton a						17 35										18 35						
d						17 36										18 36						
Rugby a						17 51										18 51						
Northampton 68 a												←										
Milton Keynes Central 66 a	17 58					18 15					18 02	18 15		18 23	18 58	19 14						19 01
Watford Junction 66 a						→										→		18s49				
London Euston ⊖66 a	18 34				18 02		18 05				18 37	18 52		19 03	19 33			19 06				19 38

	LM	VT	LM	XC	LM	VT	VT	VT	LM	XC	LM	XC	VT	LM	LM	VT	LM	VT	VT	XC	LM
	1	1	1	◇1	1	◇1 ⊠	◇1 ⊠	1	1	◇1	1	◇1	◇1 ⊠	1	1	◇1 ⊠	1	◇1 ⊠	◇1 ⊠	◇1	1
Crewe 65,50 d		18 01	18 02	18 07	18 19	18 24	18 29				18 49		19 01	19 02	19 19	19 22		19 29			19 55
Alsager 50 d			18 11											19 11							
Kidsgrove 50 d			18 15											19 15							
Hanley Bus Station d																					
Stoke-on-Trent 50 d			18 28							18 44		19 07		19 28						19 44	
Wedgwood Old Road Bridge d																					
Barlaston Orchard Place d																					
Stone Granville Square d																					
Stone Crown Street d																					
Stone d			18 36											19 36							
Norton Bridge Station Drv d									←								←				
Stafford d			18 55	18a25	18a40	18 43			18 55	19a00	19a10	19a24		19 50	19a39	19 42	19 50			20a00	20a15
Rugeley Trent Valley d			→						19 05					→			19 59				
Lichfield Trent Valley d									19 13								20 08				
Tamworth d									19 20								20 15				
Polesworth d																					
Atherstone d									19 28								20 23				
Nuneaton a									19 35								20 30				
d									19 36								20 30				
Rugby a									19 50								20 46				
Northampton 68 a	←							←									21 07		←		
Milton Keynes Central 66 a	19 14	19 58					19 33	19 58	20 14				20 58					20 31	20 58		
Watford Junction 66 a		→				19s47							→			20s45			21s19		
London Euston ⊖66 a	19 50					20 04	20 08	20 32	20 51							21 02		21 06	21 37		

	VT	XC	VT	LM	LM	VT	VT	VT	VT	LM	XC	LM	VT	XC	LM	VT	XC	LM	XC
	◇1	◇1	1 ⊠	1	1	◇1	◇1	◇1	1 ⊠	1	◇1	1	◇1 ⊠	◇1	1	◇1	◇1	1	◇1
Crewe 65,50 d	19 56		20 03	20 10	20 19	20 24	20 29	20 42				20 47	20 53		21 19	21 24		22 19	
Alsager 50 d				20 19															
Kidsgrove 50 d				20 23															
Hanley Bus Station d																			
Stoke-on-Trent 50 d		20 07		20 33							20 44			21 07			22 08		22 47
Wedgwood Old Road Bridge d																			
Barlaston Orchard Place d																			
Stone Granville Square d																			
Stone Crown Street d																			
Stone d				20 41															
Norton Bridge Station Drv d										←									
Stafford d		20a24		21 00	20a38		20 48			21 00	21a00	21a09	21a13	21a23	21a39	21 44	22a24	22a39	23a03
Rugeley Trent Valley d				→						21 09									
Lichfield Trent Valley d										21 18						21 58			
Tamworth d										21 25						22 05			
Polesworth d																			
Atherstone d										21 33									
Nuneaton a						21 02				21 40						22 17			
d						21 03				21 40						22 18			
Rugby a								21 28		21 55						22 31			
Northampton 68 a									←	22 17									
Milton Keynes Central 66 a	21 04		21 58				21 35	21 49	21 58							22 54			
Watford Junction 66 a			→			21s49			22s20							23s25			
London Euston ⊖66 a	21 40					22 06	22 10	22 26	22 41							23 43			

Crewe and Stoke-on-Trent - London

		AW	XC	VT	LM	LM	VT	VT	LM	XC	LM	LM	VT	LM	LM	VT	VT	VT	VT	LM	XC	LM	LM
			◇1	◇1	1	1	◇1	◇1	1	◇1	1	1	◇1	1	1	◇1	◇1	◇1	◇1	1	◇1	1	🚌
Crewe	65,50 d	04 59	05 47	06 00	06 01	06 11		06 29			06 49	07 00	07 01	07 18	07 19	07 20	07 29	07 41					
Alsager	50 d											07 08											
Kidsgrove	50 d											07 14											
Hanley Bus Station	d																						07 45
Stoke-on-Trent	50 d		06 08		06 24					06 39		07 22		07 38							07 44		07 52
Wedgwood Old Road Bridge	d																						08 11
Barlaston Orchard Place	d																						08 13
Stone Granville Square	d																						08a23
Stone Crown Street	d																						
Stone	d											07 31											
Norton Bridge Station Drv	d								←											←		←	
Stafford	d	05a24	06a25	06 19	06 48	06a30	06 36		06 48	06a55	07a08	07 48		08 08	07a38	07 39				07 48	08a00	08 08	
Rugeley Trent Valley	d				→				06 57			→		→						07 57		08 17	
Lichfield Trent Valley	d								07 05											08 05		08 25	
Tamworth	d								07 11											08 11		08 31	
Polesworth	d																						
Atherstone	d								07 20											08 20		08 40	
Nuneaton	a						06 58		07 26											08 26		08 46	
	d						06 59		07 27											08 27		08 47	
Rugby	a			06 50					07 42											08 42		09 02	
Northampton	68 a																		←				
Milton Keynes Central	66 a			07 11				07 31	08 04				08 58					08 52	08 58	09 05		09 24	
Watford Junction	66 a			07s33			07s45						→										
London Euston 15	⊖66 a			07 50			08 02	08 07	08 40							08 57	09 02	09 30	09 34	09 52		10 00	

		LM	VT	XC	LM	LM	LM	VT	LM	VT	LM	XC	LM	VT	LM	VT	XC	LM	LM	LM	VT	LM	VT
		1	◇1	◇1	🚌	1	1	◇1	1	◇1	🚌	◇1	1	◇1	1	◇1	◇1	🚌	1	1	◇1	1	◇1
Crewe	65,50 d	07 49	07 56			08 02	08 19	08 22		08 29			08 49	08 56		09 01			09 02	09 19	09 24		09 30
Alsager	50 d					08 11													09 11				
Kidsgrove	50 d					08 15													09 15				
Hanley Bus Station	d										08 35												
Stoke-on-Trent	50 d			08 07		08 28					08 42	08 44					09 07		09 28				
Wedgwood Old Road Bridge	d																						
Barlaston Orchard Place	d										09 03												
Stone Granville Square	d										09a13							09 03					
Stone Crown Street	d																						
Stone	d					08 36													09 36				
Norton Bridge Station Drv	d				08 11				←									09 14				←	
Stafford	d	08a09	08 15	08a24	08a28	08 55	08a39	08 42	08 55			09a00	09a10				09a23	09a33	09 55	09a39	09 43	09 55	
Rugeley Trent Valley	d					→			09 05										→			10 05	
Lichfield Trent Valley	d		08 30						09 13													10 13	
Tamworth	d		08 37						09 20													10 20	
Polesworth	d																						
Atherstone	d								09 28													10 28	
Nuneaton	a							09 04	09 35													10 35	
	d							09 05	09 36													10 36	
Rugby	a								09 51													10 51	
Northampton	68 a														←								
Milton Keynes Central	66 a								10 14					10 02	10 14	10 58						11 14	
Watford Junction	66 a								→													→	
London Euston 15	⊖66 a		09 43					10 04		10 08				10 36	10 50	11 33					11 02		11 07

		LM	XC	LM	VT	LM	VT	XC	LM	LM	VT	LM	VT	LM	XC	LM	VT	LM	VT	XC	LM	LM
		🚌	◇1	1	◇1	1	◇1	◇1	1	1	◇1	1	◇1	🚌	◇1	1	◇1	1	◇1	◇1	🚌	1
Crewe	65,50 d			09 49	09 56		10 01		10 02	10 19	10 22		10 29			10 49	10 56		11 02			11 02
Alsager	50 d								10 11													11 11
Kidsgrove	50 d								10 15													11 15
Hanley Bus Station	d	09 35												10 35								
Stoke-on-Trent	50 d	09 42	09 44					10 08	10 28					10 42	10 44					11 07		11 28
Wedgwood Old Road Bridge	d																					
Barlaston Orchard Place	d	10 03												11 03								
Stone Granville Square	d	10a13												11a13							11 03	
Stone Crown Street	d																					
Stone	d								10 36													11 36
Norton Bridge Station Drv	d											←									11 14	
Stafford	d		10a00	10a09				10a24	10 55	10a38	10 42	10 55			11a00	11a09				11a24	11a33	11 55
Rugeley Trent Valley	d								→			11 05										→
Lichfield Trent Valley	d											11 13										
Tamworth	d											11 20										
Polesworth	d																					
Atherstone	d											11 28										
Nuneaton	a											11 35										
	d											11 36										
Rugby	a											11 51										
Northampton	68 a					←												←				
Milton Keynes Central	66 a				11 02	11 14	11 58					12 14					12 02	12 14	12 58			
Watford Junction	66 a											→										
London Euston 15	⊖66 a				11 36	11 50	12 33				11 59		12 02				12 36	12 50	13 33			

		LM	VT	LM	VT	LM	XC	LM	VT	LM	VT	XC	LM	LM	VT	LM	VT	LM	XC	LM	VT	LM	VT
		1	◇1	1	◇1	🚌	◇1	1	◇1	1	◇1	◇1	1	1	◇1	1	◇1	🚌	◇1	1	◇1	1	◇1
Crewe	65,50 d	11 19	11 22		11 29			11 49	11 56		12 00		12 02	12 19	12 23		12 29			12 49	12 56		13 01
Alsager	50 d												12 11										
Kidsgrove	50 d												12 15										
Hanley Bus Station	d					11 35												12 35					
Stoke-on-Trent	50 d					11 42	11 44					12 07	12 28					12 42	12 44				
Wedgwood Old Road Bridge	d																						
Barlaston Orchard Place	d					12 03												13 03					
Stone Granville Square	d					12a13												13a13					
Stone Crown Street	d																						
Stone	d												12 36										
Norton Bridge Station Drv	d			←												←							
Stafford	d	11a38	11 42	11 55			12a00	12a09				12a23	12 55	12a39	12 43	12 55			13a00	13a09			
Rugeley Trent Valley	d			12 05									→			13 05							
Lichfield Trent Valley	d			12 13												13 13							
Tamworth	d			12 20												13 20							
Polesworth	d																						
Atherstone	d			12 28												13 28							
Nuneaton	a			12 35												13 35							
	d			12 36												13 36							
Rugby	a			12 51												13 51							
Northampton	68 a									←												←	
Milton Keynes Central	66 a			13 14					13 02	13 14	13 58					14 14					14 02	14 14	14 58
Watford Junction	66 a			→												→							
London Euston 15	⊖66 a		12 59		13 02				13 36	13 50	14 33				14 01		14 04				14 36	14 50	15 32

		XC	LM	LM	LM	VT	LM	VT	LM	XC	LM	VT	LM	VT	XC	LM	LM	VT	LM	VT	XC	LM
		◇1	🚌	1	1	◇1	1	◇1	🚌	◇1	1	◇1	1	◇1	◇1	1	1	◇1	1	◇1	◇1	1
Crewe	65,50 d			13 02	13 19	13 24		13 30			13 49	13 56		14 01		14 02	14 19	14 24		14 30		14 49
Alsager	50 d			13 11												14 11						
Kidsgrove	50 d			13 15												14 15						
Hanley Bus Station	d								13 35													
Stoke-on-Trent	50 d	13 07		13 28					13 42	13 44					14 07	14 28					14 44	
Wedgwood Old Road Bridge	d																					
Barlaston Orchard Place	d								14 03													
Stone Granville Square	d		13 03						14a13													
Stone Crown Street	d																					
Stone	d			13 36												14 36						
Norton Bridge Station Drv	d		13 14				←												←			
Stafford	d	13a24	13a33	13 55	13a38	13 43	13 55			14a00	14a09				14a24	14 55	14a39	14 44	14 55		15a00	15a09
Rugeley Trent Valley	d			→			14 05									→			15 05			
Lichfield Trent Valley	d						14 13												15 13			
Tamworth	d						14 20												15 20			
Polesworth	d																					
Atherstone	d						14 28												15 28			
Nuneaton	a						14 35												15 35			
	d						14 36												15 36			
Rugby	a						14 51												15 51			
Northampton	68 a												←									
Milton Keynes Central	66 a						15 14					15 02	15 14	15 58					16 14			
Watford Junction	66 a						→												→			
London Euston 15	⊖66 a					15 00		15 07				15 36	15 50	16 32				16 01		16 04		

		VT	LM	LM	XC	LM	VT	LM	VT	LM	VT	XC	LM	LM	LM	VT	LM	VT	XC	LM	LM	VT	LM
		◇1	1	🚌	◇1	1	◇1	1	◇1	1	◇1	◇1	🚌	1	🚌	◇1	1	◇1	◇1	1	1	◇1	1
Crewe	65,50 d	14 56				15 02	15 03	15 19	15 22		15 29			15 49		15 56		16 01		16 02	16 19	16 22	
Alsager	50 d					15 11														16 11			
Kidsgrove	50 d					15 15														16 15			
Hanley Bus Station	d			15 00											15 50								
Stoke-on-Trent	50 d			15 07	15 07	15 28						15 44			15 57				16 07	16 28			
Wedgwood Old Road Bridge	d																						
Barlaston Orchard Place	d			15 28											16 18								
Stone Granville Square	d			15a38									15 33		16a28								
Stone Crown Street	d																						
Stone	d					15 36														16 36			
Norton Bridge Station Drv	d									←			15 44										←
Stafford	d				15a25	15 55		15a39	15 42	15 55		16a00	16a03	16a09					16a23	16 55	16a38	16 42	16 55
Rugeley Trent Valley	d					→				16 05										→			17 05
Lichfield Trent Valley	d									16 13													17 13
Tamworth	d									16 20													17 20
Polesworth	d																						
Atherstone	d									16 28													17 28
Nuneaton	a									16 35													17 35
	d									16 36													17 36
Rugby	a									16 51													17 51
Northampton	68 a		←														←						
Milton Keynes Central	66 a	16 02	16 14				16 58			17 14						17 02	17 14	17 58					18 14
Watford Junction	66 a									→													→
London Euston 15	⊖66 a	16 36	16 50				17 33		16 59		17 03					17 36	17 50	18 33				17 59	

Table T067-R

Crewe and Stoke-on-Trent - London

Saturdays

26 May to 8 December

		VT	XC	LM	LM	VT		LM	VT	XC	LM	LM	VT	VT	LM	LM		XC	LM	XC	VT	VT	LM	LM	VT
		◇1	◇1	1	Bus	◇1		1	◇1	◇1	1	1	◇1	◇1	1	Bus		◇1	1	◇1	◇1	◇1	1	1	◇1
Crewe	65,50 d	16 29		16 49		16 56			17 01		17 02	17 19	17 23	17 29					17 49			18 01	18 02	18 19	18 29
Alsager	50 d										17 11												18 11		
Kidsgrove	50 d										17 15												18 15		
Hanley Bus Station	d															17 30									
Stoke-on-Trent	50 d		16 44							17 07	17 28					17 37		17 44		18 07			18 28		
Wedgwood Old Road Bridge	d																								
Barlaston Orchard Place	d																								
Stone Granville Square	d															17 58									
Stone Crown Street	d															18a08									
Stone	d										17 36												18 36		
Norton Bridge Station Drv	d				16 54										←										
Stafford	d		17a00	17a09	17a13					17a23	17 55	17a38	17 43		17 55			18a00	18a09	18a24	18 36		18 55	18a39	
Rugeley Trent Valley	d										→				18 05								19 05		
Lichfield Trent Valley	d												17 58		18 13								19 13		
Tamworth	d														18 20								19 20		
Polesworth	d																								
Atherstone	d														18 28								19 28		
Nuneaton	a														18 35								19 35		
	d														18 36								19 36		
Rugby	a														18 51							19 42	19 51		
Northampton	68 a							←															20 12		
Milton Keynes Central	66 a					18 02		18 14	18 58						19 14							20 05			
Watford Junction	66 a																					20s34			
London Euston	⊖66 a	18 02				18 37		18 50	19 32				19 07	19 03	19 50						19 59	20 53			20 02

		XC		LM	XC	LM	VT	LM	VT	VT	LM	XC		LM	XC	VT	LM	VT	XC	VT	VT	XC		LM	XC
		◇1		1	◇1	1	◇1	1	◇1	◇1	1	◇1		1	◇1	◇1	1	◇1	◇1	◇1	◇1	◇1		1	◇1
Crewe	65,50 d			18 49		19 02	19 03	19 19	19 23	19 29				19 49		20 01	20 19	20 23		20 47				21 19	
Alsager	50 d					19 11																			
Kidsgrove	50 d					19 15																			
Hanley Bus Station	d																								
Stoke-on-Trent	50 d	18 44			19 07	19 28						19 44			20 07				20 44			21 08			21 44
Wedgwood Old Road Bridge	d																								
Barlaston Orchard Place	d																								
Stone Granville Square	d																								
Stone Crown Street	d																								
Stone	d					19 36																			
Norton Bridge Station Drv	d										←														
Stafford	d	19a00		19a09	19a24	19 51		19a39	19 42		19 51	20a00		20a10	20a23		20a40	20 43	21a00			21a24		21a39	22a00
Rugeley Trent Valley	d					→					20 00														
Lichfield Trent Valley	d										20 08														
Tamworth	d										20 15														
Polesworth	d																								
Atherstone	d										20 23														
Nuneaton	a										20 30														
	d										20 31														
Rugby	a						20 42				20 46					21 42									
Northampton	68 a										21 06										←				
Milton Keynes Central	66 a						21 04				21 35					22 04				21 51	22 04				
Watford Junction	66 a						21s35				22 19					→					22s34				
London Euston	⊖66 a						21 56		21 17	21 20	22 38							22 15		22 42	22 53				

		VT	XC	VT	LM
		◇1	◇1	◇1	1
Crewe	65,50 d	21 44		22 06	22 19
Alsager	50 d				
Kidsgrove	50 d				
Hanley Bus Station	d				
Stoke-on-Trent	50 d		22 07		
Wedgwood Old Road Bridge	d				
Barlaston Orchard Place	d				
Stone Granville Square	d				
Stone Crown Street	d				
Stone	d				
Norton Bridge Station Drv	d				
Stafford	d	22a07	22a23	22a24	22a40
Rugeley Trent Valley	d				
Lichfield Trent Valley	d				
Tamworth	d				
Polesworth	d				
Atherstone	d				
Nuneaton	a				
	d				
Rugby	a				
Northampton	68 a				
Milton Keynes Central	66 a				
Watford Junction	66 a				
London Euston	⊖66 a				

Table T067-R

Crewe and Stoke-on-Trent - London

Sundays

20 May to 2 December

		VT	VT	XC	VT	LM	VT	XC	VT	LM		LM	LM	VT	VT	XC	VT	LM	VT	LM		LM	XC	LM	VT
		◇1	◇1	◇1	◇1	1	◇1	◇1	◇1	1		1	1	◇1	◇1	◇1	◇1	1	◇1	1		1	◇1	1	◇1
Crewe	65,50 d	08 43	08 53	09 05	09 13	09 32	09 43		10 14			10 21	10 37	10 43	10 55		11 14	11 37	11 49					12 19	12 23
Alsager	50 d					09 41							10 46					11 46							
Kidsgrove	50 d					09 45							10 50					11 50							
Hanley Bus Station	d																								
Stoke-on-Trent	50 d					09 53		10 07					10 59			11 07		11 59					12 07		
Wedgwood Old Road Bridge	d																								
Barlaston Orchard Place	d																								
Stone Granville Square	d																								
Stone Crown Street	d																								
Stone	d					10 01							11 07					12 07							
Norton Bridge Station Drv	d																								
Stafford	d	09 03		09a25	09 33	10 19		10a25	10 34			10a41	11 19			11a26	11 36	12 19					12a24	12a39	12 44
Rugeley Trent Valley	d					10 28							11 28					12 28							
Lichfield Trent Valley	d		09 25			10 36				←			11 36					12 36				←			
Tamworth	d					10 43				10 43			11 43					12 43				12 43			
Polesworth	d					→												→							
Atherstone	d									10 51			11 51									12 51			
Nuneaton	a				09 55				10 56	10 58			11 58				11 58		12 31			12 58			
	d				09 56				10 57	10 58			11 58				11 59		12 32			12 58			
Rugby	a						10 32			11 17			12 13	11 31								13 13			
Northampton	68 a									11 41			12 41							←		13 41			
Milton Keynes Central	66 a		10 19				11 07		11 45	12 04			13 04	12 07					13 04	13 04		14 04			
Watford Junction	66 a	10s34			11s16		11s43			12 40			→		12s37		12s52			13 34		→			
London Euston	⊖66 a	10 55	11 05		11 34		12 03		12 29	13 01				12 44	12 54		13 10		13 43	13 53					14 03

		VT	LM	VT	LM	VT		XC	LM	VT	VT	XC	LM	VT	VT	LM		LM	VT	XC	LM	VT	VT	XC	LM
		◇1	1	◇1	1	◇1		◇1	1	◇1	◇1	◇1	1	◇1	◇1	1		1	◇1	◇1	1	◇1	◇1	◇1	1
Crewe	65,50 d	12 30	12 37	12 55		13 01			13 19	13 23	13 30		13 37	13 52	13 53				14 01		14 19	14 23	14 30		14 32
Alsager	50 d		12 46										13 46												14 41
Kidsgrove	50 d		12 50										13 50												14 45
Hanley Bus Station	d																								
Stoke-on-Trent	50 d		12 59					13 07				13 45	13 59							14 07				14 44	14 53
Wedgwood Old Road Bridge	d																								
Barlaston Orchard Place	d																								
Stone Granville Square	d																								
Stone Crown Street	d																								
Stone	d		13 07										14 07												15 01
Norton Bridge Station Drv	d																								
Stafford	d		13 19					13a24	13a39	13 44		14a01	14 19							14a24	14a39	14 44		15a00	15 19
Rugeley Trent Valley	d		13 28										14 28												15 28
Lichfield Trent Valley	d		13 36										14 36					←							15 36
Tamworth	d		13 43										14 43					14 43							15 43
Polesworth	d												→												
Atherstone	d		13 51															14 51							15 51
Nuneaton	a		13 58											14 32	14 32			14 58							15 58
	d		13 58											14 33	14 33			14 58							15 58
Rugby	a		14 13															15 13							16 13
Northampton	68 a		14 41		←											←		15 41							16 41
Milton Keynes Central	66 a		15 04	14 03	14 04	14 58								15 03	15 03	15 04		16 04	15 58						17 04
Watford Junction	66 a		→		14 34											15 34		→							→
London Euston	⊖66 a	14 10		14 41	14 53	15 37				15 03	15 07			15 42	15 42	15 53			16 37			16 03	16 06		

		VT		VT	LM	VT	XC	LM	VT	VT	XC	LM		VT	LM	VT	XC	LM	VT	VT	XC	LM		VT	LM
		◇1		◇1	1	◇1	◇1	1	◇1	◇1	◇1	1		◇1	1	◇1	◇1	1	◇1	◇1	◇1	1		◇1	1
Crewe	65,50 d	14 55		14 56		15 01		15 19	15 23	15 30		15 37		15 54		16 01		16 19	16 23	16 30		16 37		16 54	
Alsager	50 d											15 46										16 46			
Kidsgrove	50 d											15 50										16 50			
Hanley Bus Station	d																								
Stoke-on-Trent	50 d						15 07				15 44	15 59					16 07				16 44	16 59			
Wedgwood Old Road Bridge	d																								
Barlaston Orchard Place	d																								
Stone Granville Square	d																								
Stone Crown Street	d																								
Stone	d											16 07										17 07			
Norton Bridge Station Drv	d																								
Stafford	d						15a23	15a40	15 44		16a00	16 19					16a24	16a39	16 44		17a00	17 19			
Rugeley Trent Valley	d											16 28										17 28			
Lichfield Trent Valley	d											16 36										17 36		17 27	
Tamworth	d											16 43										17 43			
Polesworth	d																								
Atherstone	d											16 51										17 51			
Nuneaton	a											16 58										17 58			
	d											16 58										17 58			
Rugby	a											17 13										18 13			
Northampton	68 a				←							17 41			←							18 41			←
Milton Keynes Central	66 a	16 03		16 03	16 04	16 58						18 04		17 03	17 04	17 58						19 04		18 04	18 04
Watford Junction	66 a				16 34							→			17 34							→			18 34
London Euston	⊖66 a	16 41		16 41	16 53	17 36			17 04	17 08				17 41	17 53	18 36			18 03	18 08				18 41	18 53

Table T067-R

Sundays

20 May to 2 December

Crewe and Stoke-on-Trent - London

		VT ◇■ 🍴	XC ◇■ 🛒	LM ■	VT ◇■ 🍴	VT ◇■ 🍴	XC ◇■ 🛒	LM ■		VT ◇■ 🍴	LM ■	VT ◇■ 🍴	XC ◇■ 🛒	LM ■	VT ◇■ 🍴	VT ◇■ 🍴	XC ◇■ 🛒	LM ■		VT ◇■ 🍴	LM ■	VT ◇■ 🍴	XC ◇■ 🛒	LM ■	VT ◇■ 🍴
Crewe	65,50 d	17 01		17 19	17 23	17 30		17 37		17 55		18 01		18 19	18 23	18 29		18 37		18 55		19 01		19 19	19 23
Alsager	50 d							17 46										18 46							
Kidsgrove	50 d							17 50										18 50							
Hanley Bus Station	d																								
Stoke-on-Trent	50 d		17 07				17 45	17 59					18 07				18 45	18 59					19 07		
Wedgwood Old Road Bridge	d																								
Barlaston Orchard Place	d																								
Stone Granville Square	d																								
Stone Crown Street	d																								
Stone	d							18 07										19 07							
Norton Bridge Station Drv.	d																								
Stafford	d		17a24	17a39	17 44		18a01	18 19					18a24	18a39	18 44		19a01	19 22					19a24	19a39	19 44
Rugeley Trent Valley	d							18 28										19 31							
Lichfield Trent Valley	d							18 36										19 39							
Tamworth	d							18 43										19 46							
Polesworth	d																								
Atherstone	d							18 51										19 54							
Nuneaton	a							18 58										20 01							
	d							18 58										20 01							
Rugby	a							19 13										20 16							
Northampton	68 a							19 41			←							20 38			←				
Milton Keynes Central	66 a	18 58						20 06		19 04	19 04	19 58						21 07		20 03	20 06	20 59			
Watford Junction	66 a							→			19 34							→			20 35				
London Euston ■	⊖66 a	19 37			19 03	19 06				19 42	19 53	20 37			20 04	20 07				20 41	20 54	21 46			21 03

		VT ◇■ 🍴	LM ■	XC ◇■ 🛒		LM ■	XC ◇■ 🛒	LM ■	VT ◇■ 🍴	XC ◇■	LM ■	VT ◇■ 🍴	LM ■	AW ◇		LM ■	VT ◇■ 🍴	VT ◇■ 🍴	XC ◇■	LM ■	XC ◇■				
Crewe	65,50 d	19 29				19 37		20 19	20 24		20 42	20 47		20 52		21 19	21 24	21 41		22 19					
Alsager	50 d					19 46					20 51														
Kidsgrove	50 d					19 50					20 55														
Hanley Bus Station	d																								
Stoke-on-Trent	50 d			19 45		19 59	20 06			20 45	21 07								21 45		22 45				
Wedgwood Old Road Bridge	d																								
Barlaston Orchard Place	d																								
Stone Granville Square	d																								
Stone Crown Street	d																								
Stone	d					20 07					21 15														
Norton Bridge Station Drv.	d																								
Stafford	d			20a01		20 19	20a24	20a38	20 43	21a01	21 27			21a13		21a39	21 44	22a00	22a04	22a39	23a01				
Rugeley Trent Valley	d					20 28					21 36														
Lichfield Trent Valley	d					20 36					21 44						22 01								
Tamworth	d					20 43					21 51						22 07								
Polesworth	d																								
Atherstone	d					20 51					21 59														
Nuneaton	a					20 58					22 06						22 18								
	d					20 58					22 06						22 19								
Rugby	a					21 13					22 21						22 31								
Northampton	68 a		←			21 41					22 44		←												
Milton Keynes Central	66 a		21 07			22 11			21 36			21 52	22 11				23 04								
Watford Junction	66 a		21 39			→						22s30	22 54				23s34								
London Euston ■	⊖66 a	21 08	21 58						22 25			22 53	23 17				23 52								

Table T068-F

Mondays to Fridays

21 May to 7 December

Northampton - Coventry - Birmingham - Wolverhampton - Stafford

Miles			VT MO ◇■ A 🍴	VT MX ◇■ A 🍴	VT MX ◇■ A 🍴	VT ◇■ B ☒	XC ◇■ C	LM ■ D	LM	VT ◇■ E ☒	LM ■		AW ◇ F 🛒	LM ■ G	XC ◇■ C 🛒	LM ■ D	LM	LM ■	XC ◇■ C 🛒	LM ■ H	LM ■ D		LM	VT ◇■ I ☒	LM ■
—	London Euston ■	⊖66 d																							
0	**Northampton**	66 d									05 16			05 45						05 55					06 16
9½	Long Buckby	d									05 27									06 06					06 27
18¾	Rugby	d		00 01	01 00						05 38			06 06						06 17					06 38
32¼	**Coventry**	a		00 10	01 13						05 49									06 29					06 49
—		d		00 10	01 13						05 50							06 11		06 30					06 50
34	Canley	d																06 14		06 33					
36	Tile Hill	d									05 55							06 18		06 37					06 55
38	Berkswell	d																06 21		06 40					
41¼	Hampton-in-Arden	d									06 01							06 25							07 01
43	**Birmingham International** ✈	a		00 21	01 24						06 04							06 28		06 45					07 04
—		d	00 09	00 21	01 24						06 05					06 18		06 29		06 46					07 05
45	Marston Green	d									06 08							06 32		06 49					07 08
46½	Lea Hall	d														06 23				06 52					
47¾	Stechford	d														06 26				06 55					
49½	Adderley Park	d														06 29									
51½	**BirminghamNewStreet** ■	a	00 21	00 33	01 36						06 18					06 33		06 42		07 01					07 17
—		d	00 24	00 35	01 37	05 30	05 57	06 01	06 04	06 15			06 25		06 30	06 36	06 39		06 51		07 01		07 08	07 15	
54¾	Smethwick Rolfe Street	d							06 10								06 45						07 14		
55½	Smethwick Galton Bridge ■	d						06 07	06 12				06 31				06 47				07 07		07 16		
56¾	Sandwell & Dudley	d							06 15	06 24							06 50						07 19	07 24	
57¾	Dudley Port	d							06 19								06 54						07 23		
58½	Tipton	d							06 21								06 56						07 25		
60	Coseley	d						06 14								06 47	06 59						07 28		
64¼	**Wolverhampton** ■	a	00 41	01 02	02 05	05 47	06 14	06 20	06 30	06 37			06 43		06 47	06 53	07 05		07 09		07 18		07 34	07 37	
—		d				05 48	06 15	06 21							06 48	06 54			07 10		07 20				
74¼	Penkridge	d						06 31								07 04					07 29				
79½	**Stafford**	a				06 00	06 27	06 37						06 58	06 59	07 10			07 21		07 36				

		LM ■ G	AW ◇ J 🛒	LM K	XC ◇■ C 🛒	LM	LM ■ L		LM ■ M	VT ◇■ ☒	XC ◇■ N 🛒	LM ■ L	LM ■	LM K	LM ■	VT ◇■ E ☒	LM ■		AW ■ F 🛒	VT ◇■ ☒	XC ◇■ O 🛒	LM	LM ■ D	LM P	LM ■
London Euston ■	⊖66 d									06 20			05 34			06 43				07 03					
Northampton	66 d	06 35											06 58				07 15								07 37
Long Buckby	d												07 09				07 26								07 48
Rugby	d	06 59								07 13			07 20				07 37			07 51					07 59
Coventry	a									07 22			07 31			07 42	07 48			08 02					08 10
	d								07 07	07 22	07 27		07 32			07 42	07 49			08 02					08 11
Canley	d								07 10				07 35												08 14
Tile Hill	d								07 14				07 39				07 54								08 18
Berkswell	d								07 17				07 42				07 57								08 21
Hampton-in-Arden	d								07 22								08 01								08 25
Birmingham International ✈	a								07 25	07 33	07 37		07 47			07 53	08 04			08 13					08 29
	d		07 09			07 18			07 25	07 33	07 38		07 48			07 53	08 05		08 09	08 13		08 17			08 29
Marston Green	d								07 29				07 51				08 08					08 20			08 32
Lea Hall	d					07 23							07 55									08 23			
Stechford	d					07 26							07 58									08 26			
Adderley Park	d					07 29							08 01									08 29			
BirminghamNewStreet ■	a		07 20			07 34			07 36	07 45	07 48		08 05			08 09	08 17		08 20	08 26		08 34			08 42
	d		07 23	07 27	07 31		07 36		07 39		07 57	08 01		08 05	08 09	08 15			08 24		08 31		08 36	08 39	
Smethwick Rolfe Street	d								07 45						08 15									08 45	
Smethwick Galton Bridge ■	d		07 29						07 47			08 07			08 17				08 31					08 47	
Sandwell & Dudley	d								07 50					08 13	08 20	08 24								08 50	
Dudley Port	d								07 54						08 24									08 54	
Tipton	d								07 56						08 26									08 56	
Coseley	d						07 47		07 59						08 29								08 47	08 59	
Wolverhampton ■	a		07 40	07 44	07 48		07 53		08 05		08 14	08 18		08 24	08 35	08 37			08 43		08 48		08 53	09 05	
	d				07 49		07 54				08 15	08 20									08 49		08 54		
Penkridge	d						08 04					08 29											09 04		
Stafford	a	07 53			08 02		08 10				08 27	08 35									09 02		09 10		

A From London Euston
B To Holyhead
C To Manchester Piccadilly
D To Liverpool Lime Street
E To Edinburgh
F To Aberystwyth
G To Crewe
H From Milton Keynes Central
I To Glasgow Central
J To Llandudno
K To Shrewsbury
L From Walsall to Liverpool Lime Street
M ■ to BirminghamNewStreet
N From Southampton Central to Manchester Piccadilly
O From Bristol Temple Meads to Manchester Piccadilly
P From Walsall

Table T068-F

Mondays to Fridays
21 May to 7 December

Northampton - Coventry - Birmingham - Wolverhampton - Stafford

		LM	VT	XC	LM	LM	LM	LM	VT	LM	AW	VT	XC	LM	LM	LM	LM	VT	XC	LM	LM	LM	LM
		■	◇■	◇■	■	■			◇■	■	◇	◇■	◇■		■	■	■	◇■	◇■	■	■		■
		A		B	C		D		E		F		G		C	H			I	C		D	H
			⊠	🛒					⊠		🛒	⊠	🛒					⊠	🛒				
London Euston ⊖66	d	06 24	07 23			06 34			07 43	07 13		08 03						08 23			07 49		
Northampton 66	d	07 45				07 55				08 13											08 55		
Long Buckby	d					08 06				08 24											09 06		
Rugby	d	08 04				08 17				08 35		08 51									09 17		
Coventry	a		08 22			08 29			08 42	08 46		09 02						09 22			09 29		
	d		08 22	08 27		08 30			08 42	08 50		09 02					09 11	09 22	09 27		09 30		
Canley	d					08 33											09 14				09 33		
Tile Hill	d					08 37				08 55							09 18				09 37		
Berkswell	d					08 40											09 21				09 40		
Hampton-in-Arden	d									09 01							09 25						
Birmingham International ✈	a		08 33	08 37		08 45			08 53	09 04		09 13					09 28	09 33	09 37		09 45		
	d		08 33	08 38		08 46			08 53	09 05	09 10	09 13		09 19			09 29	09 33	09 38		09 46		
Marston Green	d					08 49				09 08							09 32				09 49		
Lea Hall	d					08 52								09 23							09 52		
Stechford	d					08 55								09 26							09 55		
Adderley Park	d													09 29									
BirminghamNewStreet ⇌	a		08 45	08 48		09 02			09 05	09 18	09 21	09 26		09 34			09 42	09 45	09 49		10 01		
	d			08 57	09 01		09 05	09 08	09 15		09 25		09 31		09 36	09 39			09 57	10 01		10 05	10 08
Smethwick Rolfe Street	d							09 14								09 45							10 14
Smethwick Galton Bridge	d				09 07			09 16			09 31					09 47				10 07			10 16
Sandwell & Dudley	d						09 13	09 19	09 24							09 50						10 13	10 19
Dudley Port	d							09 23								09 54							10 23
Tipton	d							09 25								09 56							10 25
Coseley	d							09 28							09 47	09 59							10 28
Wolverhampton ⇌	a			09 14	09 18		09 24	09 34	09 37		09 43		09 48		09 53	10 05			10 14	10 18		10 24	10 34
	d			09 15	09 20								09 49		09 54				10 15	10 20			
Penkridge	d														10 04								
Stafford	a	08 54		09 27	09 33								10 01		10 10				10 27	10 33			

		VT	LM	AW	LM	VT	XC	LM	LM	LM	LM	VT	XC	LM	LM	LM	LM	VT	LM	AW	LM	VT	XC
		◇■	■	◇	■	◇■	◇■		■		■	◇■	◇■	■	■			◇■	■	◇	■	◇■	◇■
		J		K	L		M		C	H	N		I	C		D	H	E		F	L		O
		⊠		🛒		⊠	🛒					⊠	🛒					⊠		🛒		⊠	🛒
London Euston ⊖66	d	08 43	07 54			09 03						09 23			08 49			09 43	09 13			10 03	
Northampton 66	d		09 16		09 25										09 55				10 16		10 25		
Long Buckby	d		09 27		09 36										10 06				10 27		10 36		
Rugby	d		09 38		09 47	09 51					←				10 17				10 38		10 47	10 51	
Coventry	a	09 42	09 49		09 58	10 02					09 58	10 22			10 29			10 42	10 49		10 58	11 02	
	d	09 42	09 50		10 11	10 02					10 11	10 22	10 27		10 30			10 42	10 50		11 11	11 02	
Canley	d				→						10 14				10 33						→		
Tile Hill	d		09 55								10 18				10 37				10 55				
Berkswell	d										10 21				10 40								
Hampton-in-Arden	d		10 01								10 25								11 01				
Birmingham International ✈	a	09 53	10 04			10 13					10 28	10 33	10 37		10 45			10 53	11 04			11 13	
	d	09 53	10 05	10 09		10 13		10 19			10 29	10 33	10 38		10 46			10 53	11 05	11 10		11 13	
Marston Green	d		10 08								10 32				10 49				11 08				
Lea Hall	d							10 23							10 52								
Stechford	d							10 26							10 55								
Adderley Park	d							10 29															
BirminghamNewStreet ⇌	a	10 04	10 17	10 20		10 27		10 34			10 42	10 45	10 48		11 01			11 04	11 17	11 20		11 25	
	d	10 15		10 25			10 31		10 36	10 39			10 57	11 01		11 05	11 08	11 15		11 25			11 31
Smethwick Rolfe Street	d									10 45							11 14						
Smethwick Galton Bridge	d			10 31						10 47				11 07			11 16			11 31			
Sandwell & Dudley	d	10 24								10 50						11 13	11 19	11 24					
Dudley Port	d									10 54							11 23						
Tipton	d									10 56							11 25						
Coseley	d								10 47	10 59							11 28						
Wolverhampton ⇌	a	10 37		10 42			10 48		10 53	11 05			11 14	11 18		11 24	11 34	11 37		11 42			11 48
	d						10 49		10 54				11 15	11 20									11 49
Penkridge	d								11 04														
Stafford	a						11 02		11 10				11 27	11 33									12 02

A To Crewe
B From Southampton Central to Manchester Piccadilly
C To Liverpool Lime Street
D To Shrewsbury
E To Glasgow Central
F To Holyhead
G From Cardiff Central to Manchester Piccadilly
H From Walsall
I From Bournemouth to Manchester Piccadilly
J To Edinburgh
K To Aberystwyth
L To Birmingham New Street
M From Paignton to Manchester Piccadilly
N From Northampton
O From Bristol Temple Meads to Manchester Piccadilly

Table T068-F

Mondays to Fridays
21 May to 7 December

Northampton - Coventry - Birmingham - Wolverhampton - Stafford

		LM	LM	LM	LM	VT	XC	LM	LM	LM	LM	VT	LM	AW	LM	VT	XC	LM	LM	LM	LM	VT
			■		■	◇■	■	■	■		■	◇■	■		■	◇■	◇■		■	■	■	◇■
			A	B	C	D	E	A		D	B	F		G	H		I		A	B	C	
						⊠	🛒					🍽		🛒		⊠	🛒					⊠
London Euston ⊖66	d					10 23			09 49			10 43	10 13			11 03						11 23
Northampton 66	d								10 55				11 16		11 25							
Long Buckby	d								11 06				11 27		11 36							
Rugby	d				←				11 17				11 38		11 47	11 51					←	
Coventry	a				10 58	11 22			11 29			11 42	11 49		11 58	12 02					11 58	12 22
	d				11 11	11 22	11 27		11 30			11 42	11 50		12 11	12 02					12 11	12 22
Canley	d				11 14				11 33						→						12 14	
Tile Hill	d				11 18				11 37				11 55								12 18	
Berkswell	d				11 21				11 40												12 21	
Hampton-in-Arden	d				11 25								12 01								12 25	
Birmingham International ✈	a				11 28	11 33	11 37		11 45			11 53	12 04			12 13					12 28	12 33
	d	11 19			11 29	11 33	11 38		11 46			11 53	12 05	12 09		12 13		12 19			12 29	12 33
Marston Green	d				11 32				11 49				12 08								12 32	
Lea Hall	d	11 23							11 52									12 23				
Stechford	d	11 26							11 55									12 26				
Adderley Park	d	11 29																12 29				
BirminghamNewStreet ⇌	a	11 34			11 42	11 45	11 48		12 02			12 05	12 17	12 20		12 26		12 34			12 42	12 45
	d		11 36	11 39		11 53	11 57	12 01		12 05	12 08	12 15		12 25			12 31		12 36	12 39		
Smethwick Rolfe Street	d			11 45							12 14									12 45		
Smethwick Galton Bridge	d			11 47				12 07			12 16			12 31						12 47		
Sandwell & Dudley	d			11 50						12 13	12 19	12 24								12 50		
Dudley Port	d			11 54							12 23									12 54		
Tipton	d			11 56							12 25									12 56		
Coseley	d		11 47	11 59							12 28								12 47	12 59		
Wolverhampton ⇌	a		11 53	12 05		12 10	12 14	12 18		12 24	12 34	12 37		12 42			12 48		12 53	13 05		
	d		11 54				12 15	12 20									12 49		12 54			
Penkridge	d		12 04																13 04			
Stafford	a		12 10				12 27	12 33									13 02		13 10			

		XC	LM	LM	LM	LM	VT	LM	AW	LM	VT	XC	LM	LM	LM	LM	VT	XC	LM	LM	LM	LM
		◇■	■	■		■	◇■	■	◇	■	◇■	◇■		■	■	■	◇■	◇■	■	■		
		E	A		D	B	J		K	H		L		A	B	C		E	A		D	B
		🛒					⊠		🛒		⊠	🛒					⊠	🛒				
London Euston ⊖66	d			10 49			11 43	11 13			12 03						12 23			11 49		
Northampton 66	d			11 55				12 16		12 25										12 55		
Long Buckby	d			12 06				12 27		12 36										13 06		
Rugby	d			12 17				12 38		12 47	12 51					←				13 17		
Coventry	a			12 29			12 42	12 49		12 58	13 02					12 58	13 22			13 29		
	d	12 27		12 30			12 42	12 50		13 11	13 02					13 11	13 22	13 27		13 30		
Canley	d			12 33						→						13 14				13 33		
Tile Hill	d			12 37				12 55								13 18				13 37		
Berkswell	d			12 40												13 21				13 40		
Hampton-in-Arden	d							13 01								13 25						
Birmingham International ✈	a	12 37		12 45			12 53	13 04			13 13					13 28	13 33	13 37		13 45		
	d	12 38		12 46			12 53	13 05	13 08		13 13		13 19			13 29	13 33	13 38		13 46		
Marston Green	d			12 49				13 08								13 32				13 49		
Lea Hall	d			12 52									13 23							13 52		
Stechford	d			12 55									13 26							13 55		
Adderley Park	d												13 29									
BirminghamNewStreet ⇌	a	12 48		13 01			13 05	13 17	13 22		13 26		13 34			13 42	13 45	13 48		14 02		
	d	12 57	13 01		13 05	13 08	13 15		13 25			13 31		13 36	13 39			13 57	14 01		14 05	14 08
Smethwick Rolfe Street	d					13 14									13 45							14 14
Smethwick Galton Bridge	d		13 07			13 16			13 31						13 47				14 07			14 16
Sandwell & Dudley	d				13 13	13 19	13 24								13 50						14 13	14 19
Dudley Port	d					13 23									13 54							14 23
Tipton	d					13 25									13 56							14 25
Coseley	d					13 28								13 47	13 59							14 28
Wolverhampton ⇌	a	13 14	13 18		13 24	13 34	13 37		13 43			13 48		13 53	14 05			14 14	14 18		14 24	14 34
	d	13 15	13 20									13 49		13 54				14 15	14 20			
Penkridge	d													14 04								
Stafford	a	13 27	13 34									14 02		14 10				14 27	14 33			

A To Liverpool Lime Street
B From Walsall
C From Northampton
D To Shrewsbury
E From Bournemouth to Manchester Piccadilly
F To Edinburgh
G To Aberystwyth
H To Birmingham New Street
I From Bristol Temple Meads to Manchester Piccadilly
J To Glasgow Central
K To Holyhead
L From Paignton to Manchester Piccadilly

Table T068-F

Mondays to Fridays

21 May to 7 December

Northampton - Coventry - Birmingham - Wolverhampton - Stafford

Station		VT ◇■ A ⊠	LM ■	AW ◇ B	LM ■ C	VT ◇■	XC ◇■ D	LM	LM ■ E	LM ■ F	LM ■ G	VT ◇■	XC ◇■ H	LM ■ I	LM ■	LM J	LM	VT ◇■ K	LM ■	AW ◇ L	LM ■ C	VT ◇■	XC ◇■ M
London Euston ■ ⊖66	d	12 43	12 13			13 03						13 23			12 49			13 43	13 13			14 03	
Northampton 66	d		13 16		13 25										13 55				14 16		14 25		
Long Buckby	d		13 27		13 36										14 06				14 27		14 36		
Rugby	d		13 38		13 47	13 51					←				14 17				14 38		14 47	14 51	
Coventry	a	13 42	13 49		13 58	14 02					13 58	14 22			14 29			14 42	14 49		14 58	15 02	
	d	13 42	13 50		14 11	14 02					14 11	14 22	14 27		14 30			14 42	14 50		15 11	15 02	
Canley	d				→						14 14				14 33						→		
Tile Hill	d		13 55								14 18				14 37				14 55				
Berkswell	d										14 21				14 40								
Hampton-in-Arden	d		14 01								14 25								15 01				
Birmingham International ✈	a	13 53	14 04			14 13					14 28	14 33	14 37		14 45			14 53	15 04			15 13	
	d	13 53	14 05	14 09		14 13		14 19			14 29	14 33	14 38		14 46			14 53	15 05	15 09		15 13	
Marston Green	d		14 08								14 32				14 49				15 08				
Lea Hall	d							14 23							14 52								
Stechford	d							14 26							14 55								
Adderley Park	d							14 29															
BirminghamNewStreet ■	a	14 05	14 17	14 20		14 26		14 34			14 42	14 45	14 48		15 01			15 05	15 17	15 20		15 26	
	d	14 15		14 25			14 31		14 36	14 39			14 57	15 01		15 05	15 08	15 15		15 25			15 31
Smethwick Rolfe Street	d									14 45							15 14						
Smethwick Galton Bridge ■	d			14 31						14 47				15 07			15 16			15 29			
Sandwell & Dudley	d	14 24								14 50						15 13	15 19	15 24					
Dudley Port	d									14 54							15 23						
Tipton	d									14 56							15 25						
Coseley	d								14 47	14 59							15 28						
Wolverhampton ■	a	14 37		14 42			14 48		14 53	15 05			15 14	15 18		15 24	15 34	15 37		15 41			15 48
	d						14 49		14 54				15 15	15 20									15 49
Penkridge	d								15 04														
Stafford	a						15 02		15 10				15 27	15 33									16 02

Station		LM	LM ■ E	LM ■ F	LM ■ G	VT ◇■	XC ◇■ H	LM ■ E	LM ■	LM J	LM F	VT ■ A	LM ■	AW B	VT ◇■	XC ◇■ D	LM	LM ■ E	LM F	LM ■	VT ◇■	XC ◇■ H
London Euston ■ ⊖66	d					14 23			13 49			14 43	14 13		15 03						15 23	
Northampton 66	d								14 55				15 16							15 37		
Long Buckby	d								15 06				15 27							15 48		
Rugby	d				←				15 17				15 38		15 51					15 59		
Coventry	a				14 58	15 22			15 29			15 42	15 49		16 02					16 10	16 22	
	d				15 11	15 22	15 27		15 30			15 42	15 50		16 02					16 11	16 22	16 27
Canley	d				15 14				15 33											16 14		
Tile Hill	d				15 18				15 37				15 55							16 18		
Berkswell	d				15 21				15 40											16 21		
Hampton-in-Arden	d				15 25								16 01							16 25		
Birmingham International ✈	a				15 28	15 33	15 37		15 45			15 53	16 04		16 13					16 28	16 33	16 37
	d	15 19			15 29	15 33	15 38		15 46			15 53	16 05	16 09	16 13		16 19			16 29	16 33	16 38
Marston Green	d				15 32				15 49				16 08							16 32		
Lea Hall	d	15 23							15 52								16 23					
Stechford	d	15 26							15 55								16 26					
Adderley Park	d	15 29															16 29					
BirminghamNewStreet ■	a	15 34			15 42	15 45	15 48		16 01			16 05	16 17	16 20	16 27		16 34			16 42	16 45	16 48
	d		15 36	15 39			15 57	16 01		16 05	16 08	16 15		16 25		16 31		16 36	16 39			16 57
Smethwick Rolfe Street	d			15 45							16 14								16 45			
Smethwick Galton Bridge ■	d			15 47				16 07			16 16			16 31					16 47			
Sandwell & Dudley	d			15 50						16 13	16 19	16 24							16 50			
Dudley Port	d			15 54							16 23								16 54			
Tipton	d			15 56							16 25								16 56			
Coseley	d		15 47	15 59							16 28							16 47	16 59			
Wolverhampton ■	a		15 53	16 05			16 14	16 18		16 24	16 34	16 37		16 42		16 48		16 53	17 05			17 14
	d		15 54				16 15	16 20								16 49		16 54				17 15
Penkridge	d		16 04					16 29										17 04				
Stafford	a		16 10				16 27	16 35								17 02		17 10				17 27

A To Edinburgh
B To Aberystwyth
C To Birmingham New Street
D From Bristol Temple Meads to Manchester Piccadilly
E To Liverpool Lime Street
F From Walsall
G From Northampton
H From Bournemouth to Manchester Piccadilly
I From Walsall to Liverpool Lime Street
J To Shrewsbury
K To Glasgow Central
L To Holyhead
M From Penzance to Manchester Piccadilly

Table T068-F

Mondays to Fridays

21 May to 7 December

Northampton - Coventry - Birmingham - Wolverhampton - Stafford

Station		LM ■ A	LM ■	LM B	LM ■ C	VT ■ D	LM ■	AW ◇ E	VT ◇■	XC ◇■ F	LM	LM ■ A	LM C	LM ■	VT ◇■	LM B	XC ◇■ G	LM ■ A	LM ■	LM B	VT ◇■	LM ■ C
London Euston ■ ⊖66	d		14 49			15 43	15 13		16 03						16 23				15 49		16 43	
Northampton 66	d		15 55				16 16												16 55			
Long Buckby	d		16 06				16 27												17 06			
Rugby	d		16 17				16 38		16 51										17 17			
Coventry	a		16 29			16 42	16 49		17 02						17 22				17 29		17 42	
	d		16 30			16 42	16 50		17 02					17 11	17 22		17 27		17 30		17 42	
Canley	d		16 33											17 14					17 33			
Tile Hill	d		16 37				16 55							17 18					17 37			
Berkswell	d		16 40											17 21					17 40			
Hampton-in-Arden	d						17 01							17 25								
Birmingham International ✈	a		16 45			16 53	17 04		17 13					17 28	17 33		17 37		17 45		17 53	
	d		16 46			16 53	17 05	17 09	17 13		17 19			17 29	17 33		17 38		17 46		17 53	
Marston Green	d		16 49				17 08							17 32					17 49			
Lea Hall	d		16 52								17 23								17 52			
Stechford	d		16 55								17 26								17 55			
Adderley Park	d										17 29											
BirminghamNewStreet ■	a		17 02			17 05	17 17	17 20	17 26		17 34			17 42	17 45		17 48		18 01		18 05	
	d	17 01		17 05	17 08	17 15		17 25		17 31		17 36	17 39			17 49	17 57	18 01		18 05		18 08
Smethwick Rolfe Street	d				17 14								17 45									18 14
Smethwick Galton Bridge ■	d	17 07			17 16			17 31					17 47					18 07				18 16
Sandwell & Dudley	d			17 13	17 19	17 24							17 50							18 13		18 19
Dudley Port	d				17 23								17 54			17 59						18 23
Tipton	d				17 25								17 56			18 02						18 25
Coseley	d				17 28							17 47	17 59									18 28
Wolverhampton ■	a	17 18		17 24	17 34	17 37		17 42		17 48		17 53	18 05			18 10	18 14	18 18		18 24		18 34
	d	17 20								17 49		17 54					18 15	18 20				
Penkridge	d	17 29										18 04						18 29				
Stafford	a	17 35								18 02		18 10					18 27	18 35				

Station		VT ◇■ H	LM ■	AW ◇ I	VT ◇■ ⊠	XC ◇■ J	LM	LM ■ A	LM C	LM ■	VT ◇■ ⊠	XC ◇■ G	LM ■ K	LM ■	LM B	LM C	VT ◇■ D	AW ◇ L	LM ■	VT ◇■ ⊠	XC ◇■ M	LM	LM ■ A
London Euston ■ ⊖66	d	16 43	15 54		17 03						17 23			16 50			17 43		17 13	18 03			
Northampton 66	d		17 16											17 55					18 19				
Long Buckby	d		17 27											18 06					18 30				
Rugby	d		17 38		17 51									18 17					18 41	18 51			
Coventry	a	17 42	17 49		18 02						18 22			18 30			18 42		18 52	19 02			
	d	17 42	17 50		18 02					18 11	18 22	18 27		18 30			18 42		18 53	19 02			
Canley	d									18 14				18 33									
Tile Hill	d		17 55							18 18				18 37					18 58				
Berkswell	d									18 21				18 40									
Hampton-in-Arden	d		18 01							18 25									19 04				
Birmingham International ✈	a	17 53	18 04		18 13					18 28	18 33	18 37		18 46			18 53		19 07	19 13			
	d	17 53	18 05	18 09	18 13		18 19			18 29	18 33	18 38		18 46			18 53	19 04	19 08	19 13		19 19	
Marston Green	d		18 08							18 32				18 49					19 11				
Lea Hall	d						18 23							18 52								19 23	
Stechford	d						18 26							18 55								19 26	
Adderley Park	d						18 29															19 29	
BirminghamNewStreet ■	a	18 05	18 17	18 20	18 27		18 34			18 42	18 45	18 48		19 01			19 05	19 17	19 20	19 26		19 34	
	d	18 15		18 25		18 31		18 36	18 39			18 57	19 01		19 05	19 08	19 15	19 25		19 28	19 31		19 36
Smethwick Rolfe Street	d								18 45							19 14							
Smethwick Galton Bridge ■	d			18 31					18 47				19 07			19 16		19 31					
Sandwell & Dudley	d	18 24							18 50						19 13	19 19	19 24						
Dudley Port	d								18 54							19 23							
Tipton	d								18 56							19 25							
Coseley	d							18 47	18 59							19 28							19 47
Wolverhampton ■	a	18 37		18 42		18 48		18 53	19 05			19 14	19 18		19 24	19 34	19 37	19 43		19 59	19 48		19 53
	d					18 49		18 54				19 15	19 20								19 49		19 54
Penkridge	d							19 04					19 29										20 04
Stafford	a					19 02		19 10				19 27	19 36								20 02		20 10

A To Liverpool Lime Street
B To Shrewsbury
C From Walsall
D To Glasgow Central
E To Llandudno
F From Paignton to Manchester Piccadilly
G From Bournemouth to Manchester Piccadilly
H To Edinburgh
I To Aberystwyth
J From Bristol Temple Meads to Manchester Piccadilly
K To Crewe
L To Chester
M From Exeter St Davids to Manchester Piccadilly

Table T068-F

Mondays to Fridays
21 May to 7 December

Northampton - Coventry - Birmingham - Wolverhampton - Stafford

		LM	LM	VT	XC	LM	LM	LM	VT	AW	LM	VT	XC	LM	LM	LM	LM	LM	VT	XC	LM	LM
		1 A	1	◇1 ⊠	◇1 B 🍴	1	C	A	◇1 D ⊠	◇ E	1	1 🍽	◇1 F 🍴		1 G		1	1 D	1 🍽	◇1 H 🍴	1	C
London Euston 15 ⊖66	d		17 24	18 23		17 49			18 43		18 13	19 03					18 16	18 49	19 23		18 52	
Northampton 66	d		18 39			18 57					19 20						19 31	19 47			19 55	
Long Buckby	d		18 50			19 08					19 31						19 42				20 06	
Rugby	d		19 01			19 19					19 42	19 51					19 56	20 06			20 17	
Coventry	a		19 11	19 22		19 30			19 42		19 53	20 02					20 08		20 22		20 29	
	d		19 11	19 22	19 27	19 32			19 42		19 54	20 02					20 11		20 22	20 27	20 30	
Canley	d		19 14			19 35											20 14				20 33	
Tile Hill	d		19 18			19 39					19 59						20 18				20 37	
Berkswell	d		19 21			19 42											20 21				20 40	
Hampton-in-Arden	d		19 25								20 05						20 25					
Birmingham International ✈	a		19 29	19 33	19 37	19 47			19 53		20 08	20 13					20 28		20 33	20 37	20 45	
	d		19 29	19 33	19 38	19 48			19 53	20 04	20 09	20 13		20 19			20 29		20 33	20 38	20 46	
Marston Green	d		19 32			19 51					20 12						20 32				20 49	
Lea Hall	d					19 54								20 23							20 52	
Stechford	d					19 57								20 26							20 55	
Adderley Park	d													20 29								
BirminghamNewStreet 12	a		19 42	19 45	19 48	20 03			20 06	20 16	20 20	20 27		20 34			20 42		20 45	20 48	21 02	
	d	19 39		19 50	19 57		20 05	20 08	20 15	20 25			20 31		20 36	20 39			20 50	20 57		21 05
Smethwick Rolfe Street	d	19 45						20 14								20 45						
Smethwick Galton Bridge 7	d	19 47						20 16		20 31						20 47						
Sandwell & Dudley	d	19 50		19 59			20 13	20 19	20 24							20 50			20 59			21 13
Dudley Port	d	19 54						20 23								20 54						
Tipton	d	19 56						20 25								20 56						
Coseley	d	19 59						20 28							20 47	20 59						
Wolverhampton 7	a	20 05		20 11	20 14		20 24	20 34	20 37	20 42			20 48		20 53	21 05			21 10	21 14		21 24
	d				20 15				20 37				20 49		20 54					21 15		
Penkridge	d														21 04							
Stafford	a				20 27				20 50				21 02		21 10			20 55		21 28		

		LM	VT	AW	LM	VT	LM	LM	LM	LM	VT	XC	LM	VT	LM	LM	XC	VT	LM	LM	LM	XC	AW
			◇1 D 🍽	◇ I	1	◇1 🍽		1 G		1	◇1 🍽	◇1 B	1	◇1 🍽	C	1	◇1 I	◇1 🍽	1 D		1	◇1 J	◇ K
London Euston 15 ⊖66	d		19 43		19 13	20 03					20 23		19 49	20 43		20 13		21 03					
Northampton 66	d				20 19								20 55			21 16							
Long Buckby	d				20 30								21 06			21 27							
Rugby	d				20 41	20 51							21 17			21 38		21 58					
Coventry	a		20 42		20 52	21 02					21 24		21 29	21 42		21 49		22 07					
	d		20 42		20 53	21 02				21 11	21 25	21 27	21 30	21 42		21 50		22 08			22 11	22 25	
Canley	d									21 14			21 33								22 14		
Tile Hill	d				20 58					21 18			21 37			21 55					22 18		
Berkswell	d									21 21			21 40								22 21		
Hampton-in-Arden	d				21 04					21 25						22 01					22 25		
Birmingham International ✈	a		20 53		21 07	21 13				21 28	21 34	21 37	21 45	21 53		22 04		22 18			22 28	22 34	
	d		20 53	21 04	21 08	21 13	21 19			21 29	21 35	21 38	21 46	21 53		22 05		22 19		22 24	22 29	22 35	
Marston Green	d				21 11					21 32			21 49			22 08					22 32		
Lea Hall	d						21 23						21 52							22 28			
Stechford	d						21 26						21 55							22 31			
Adderley Park	d						21 29													22 34			
BirminghamNewStreet 12	a		21 04	21 16	21 20	21 26	21 34			21 42	21 46	21 48	22 02	22 05		22 18		22 30		22 39	22 42	22 45	
	d	21 08	21 15	21 25		21 28		21 36	21 39		21 49	21 57		22 08	22 14		22 30	22 32	22 39				22 52
Smethwick Rolfe Street	d	21 14							21 45						22 20				22 45				
Smethwick Galton Bridge 7	d	21 16		21 31					21 47						22 23				22 47				
Sandwell & Dudley	d	21 19	21 24						21 50		22 00			22 17	22 26			22 42	22 50				
Dudley Port	d	21 23							21 54						22 30				22 54				
Tipton	d	21 25							21 56						22 33				22 56				
Coseley	d	21 28						21 47	21 59						22 36				22 59				
Wolverhampton 7	a	21 34	21 37	21 42		21 57		21 53	22 05		22 10	22 14		22 28	22 42		22 47	22 53	23 04				23 26
	d		21 37					21 54				22 15					22 48		23 05				23 27
Penkridge	d							22 04											23 15				
Stafford	a		21 52					22 10				22 27					23 00		23 21				23 42

A From Walsall
B From Bournemouth to Manchester Piccadilly
C To Shrewsbury
D To Crewe
E To Aberystwyth
F From Bristol Temple Meads to Manchester Piccadilly
G To Liverpool Lime Street
H From Bournemouth to Manchester Piccadilly. 🍴 to BirminghamNewStreet
I To Manchester Piccadilly
J From Bournemouth
K To Holyhead

Table T068-F

Mondays to Fridays
21 May to 7 December

Northampton - Coventry - Birmingham - Wolverhampton - Stafford

		LM	VT	LM	AW TThO	AW MWFO	XC	LM	VT	VT FX	VT FO
		1 A	◇1 🍽	1	B	B	◇1 C	1	◇1 🍽	◇1 🍽	◇1 🍽
London Euston 15 ⊖66	d	20 49	21 43	21 13				21 49	22 30	23 30	23 30
Northampton 66	d	21 55		22 19				22 55			
Long Buckby	d	22 06		22 30				23 06			
Rugby	d	22 17		22 41				23 17	00 01	01 00	01 05
Coventry	a	22 29	22 46	22 52				23 29	00 10	01 13	01 18
	d	22 30	22 47	22 53			23 17	23 30	00 10	01 13	01 18
Canley	d	22 33		22 56				23 33			
Tile Hill	d	22 37		23 00				23 37			
Berkswell	d	22 40		23 03				23 40			
Hampton-in-Arden	d			23 07				23 44			
Birmingham International ✈	a	22 45	23 00	23 10			23 26	23 47	00 21	01 24	01 29
	d	22 46	23 01	23 11			23 27	23 48	00 21	01 24	01 29
Marston Green	d	22 49		23 14				23 51			
Lea Hall	d	22 52						23 54			
Stechford	d	22 55						23 57			
Adderley Park	d										
BirminghamNewStreet 12	a	23 02	23 16	23 22			23 56	00 04	00 33	01 36	01 41
	d	23 09	23 19		23 32	23 35			00 35	01 37	01 42
Smethwick Rolfe Street	d	23 15									
Smethwick Galton Bridge 7	d	23 17									
Sandwell & Dudley	d	23 20	23 34								
Dudley Port	d	23 24									
Tipton	d	23 26									
Coseley	d	23 29									
Wolverhampton 7	a	23 35	23 46		00 02	00 02			01 02	02 05	02 10
	d	23 36									
Penkridge	d	23 46									
Stafford	a	23 53									

Saturdays
26 May to 8 December

		VT	VT	VT	XC	LM	LM	LM	VT	AW	XC	LM	LM	LM	XC	LM	LM	LM	VT	LM	LM	VT	AW
		◇1 D 🍽	◇1 D 🍽	◇1 E 🍽	◇1 F	1 G	1 A		◇1 H 🍽	◇ I 🍴	◇1 F 🍴	1 G	J	1	◇1 F 🍴	1 K	1 G	J	◇1 L 🍽	1	1 A	◇1 M 🍽	E 🍴
London Euston 15 ⊖66	d																						
Northampton 66	d						05 41									05 55				06 16	06 38		
Long Buckby	d															06 06				06 27			
Rugby	d	00 01	01 05				06 02									06 17				06 38	06 58		
Coventry	a	00 10	01 18													06 29				06 49			
	d	00 10	01 18											06 11		06 30				06 50			
Canley	d													06 14		06 33							
Tile Hill	d													06 18		06 37				06 55			
Berkswell	d													06 21		06 40							
Hampton-in-Arden	d													06 25						07 01			
Birmingham International ✈	a	00 21	01 29											06 28		06 45				07 04			
	d	00 21	01 29									06 18		06 29		06 46				07 05			07 09
Marston Green	d													06 32		06 49				07 08			
Lea Hall	d											06 23				06 52							
Stechford	d											06 26				06 55							
Adderley Park	d											06 29											
BirminghamNewStreet 12	a	00 33	01 41									06 33		06 42		07 01				07 17			07 19
	d	00 35	01 42	05 30	05 57	06 01		06 08	06 15	06 25	06 31	06 36	06 39		06 57		07 01	07 08	07 15			07 21	07 24
Smethwick Rolfe Street	d							06 14					06 45					07 14					
Smethwick Galton Bridge 7	d					06 07		06 16		06 31			06 47				07 07	07 16					07 30
Sandwell & Dudley	d							06 19	06 24				06 50					07 19	07 24				
Dudley Port	d							06 23					06 54					07 23					
Tipton	d							06 25					06 56					07 25					
Coseley	d							06 28				06 47	06 59					07 28					
Wolverhampton 7	a	01 02	02 10	05 47	06 14	06 18		06 34	06 37	06 42	06 48	06 53	07 05		07 14		07 18	07 34	07 37			07 40	07 41
	d			05 48	06 15	06 20					06 49	06 54			07 15		07 20					07 41	
Penkridge	d					06 29						07 04					07 29						
Stafford	a			06 00	06 27	06 36	06 53				07 02	07 10			07 29		07 36				07 53	07 58	

A To Crewe
B To Shrewsbury
C From Reading
D From London Euston
E To Holyhead
F To Manchester Piccadilly
G To Liverpool Lime Street
H To Edinburgh
I To Aberystwyth
J From Walsall
K From Bletchley
L To Glasgow Central
M To Blackpool North

Northampton - Coventry - Birmingham - Wolverhampton - Stafford

		XC	LM	LM	LM	LM	VT	XC	LM	LM	LM	LM	VT	LM	AW	VT	XC	LM	LM	LM	LM	LM
		◇■ A ✕		■ B		■	◇■ 🛒	◇■ C ✕	■ B	■	D	E	◇■ F 🛒	■	■ G ✕	◇■ 🛒	◇■ H ✕		■ B	E	■	■ I
London Euston ⊖66	d						06 23			05 34						07 03						06 24
Northampton 66	d									06 55				07 16							07 37	07 45
Long Buckby	d									07 06				07 27							07 48	
Rugby	d									07 17				07 38		07 51					07 59	08 04
Coventry	a						07 22			07 29				07 49		08 02					08 10	
	d					07 11	07 22	07 27		07 30				07 50		08 02					08 11	
Canley	d					07 14				07 33											08 14	
Tile Hill	d					07 18				07 37				07 55							08 18	
Berkswell	d					07 21				07 40											08 21	
Hampton-in-Arden	d					07 25								08 01							08 25	
Birmingham International ✈	a					07 28	07 33	07 37		07 45				08 04		08 13					08 28	
	d		07 19			07 29	07 33	07 38		07 46				08 05	08 09	08 13		08 19			08 29	
Marston Green	d					07 32				07 49				08 08							08 32	
Lea Hall	d		07 23							07 52								08 23				
Stechford	d		07 26							07 55								08 26				
Adderley Park	d		07 29															08 29				
Birmingham New Street ■	a		07 34			07 42	07 45	07 48		08 01				08 17	08 20	08 26		08 34			08 42	
	d	07 31		07 36	07 39			07 57	08 01		08 05	08 08	08 15		08 25		08 31		08 36	08 39		
Smethwick Rolfe Street	d				07 45							08 14								08 45		
Smethwick Galton Bridge ■	d				07 47				08 07			08 16			08 31					08 47		
Sandwell & Dudley	d				07 50						08 13	08 19	08 24							08 50		
Dudley Port	d				07 54							08 23								08 54		
Tipton	d				07 56							08 25								08 56		
Coseley	d			07 47	07 59							08 28							08 47	08 59		
Wolverhampton ■	a	07 48		07 53	08 05			08 14	08 18		08 24	08 34	08 37		08 42		08 48		08 53	09 05		
	d	07 49		07 54				08 15	08 20								08 49		08 54			
Penkridge	d			08 04					08 29										09 04			
Stafford	a	08 02		08 10				08 27	08 35								09 02		09 10			08 52

		VT	XC	LM	LM	LM	LM	VT	LM	AW	VT	XC	LM	LM	LM	LM	VT	XC	LM	LM	LM	LM	VT
		◇■ 🛒	◇■ C ✕	■ B	■	D	E	◇■ J 🛒	■	■ K ✕	◇■ 🛒	◇■ L ✕		■ B	E	■	◇■ 🛒	◇■ M ✕	■ B	■	D	E	◇■ F 🛒
London Euston ⊖66	d	07 23						07 43			08 03					07 05	08 23			07 49			08 43
Northampton 66	d				07 55				08 16							08 37				08 55			
Long Buckby	d				08 06				08 27							08 48				09 06			
Rugby	d				08 17				08 38		08 51					08 59				09 17			
Coventry	a	08 22			08 29			08 42	08 49		09 02					09 10	09 22			09 29			09 42
	d	08 22	08 27		08 30			08 42	08 50		09 02					09 11	09 22	09 27		09 30			09 42
Canley	d				08 33											09 14				09 33			
Tile Hill	d				08 37				08 55							09 18				09 37			
Berkswell	d				08 40											09 21				09 40			
Hampton-in-Arden	d								09 01							09 25							
Birmingham International ✈	a	08 33	08 37		08 45			08 53	09 04		09 13					09 28	09 33	09 37		09 45			09 53
	d	08 33	08 38		08 46			08 53	09 05	09 10	09 13		09 19			09 29	09 33	09 38		09 46			09 53
Marston Green	d				08 49				09 08							09 32				09 49			
Lea Hall	d				08 52								09 23							09 52			
Stechford	d				08 55								09 26							09 55			
Adderley Park	d												09 29										
Birmingham New Street ■	a	08 45	08 48		09 01			09 05	09 17	09 20	09 25		09 34			09 42	09 45	09 48		10 01			10 04
	d		08 57	09 01		09 05	09 08	09 15		09 25		09 31		09 36	09 39			09 57	10 01		10 05	10 08	10 15
Smethwick Rolfe Street	d						09 14								09 45							10 14	
Smethwick Galton Bridge ■	d			09 07			09 16			09 31					09 47				10 07			10 16	
Sandwell & Dudley	d					09 13	09 19	09 24							09 50						10 13	10 19	10 24
Dudley Port	d						09 23								09 54							10 23	
Tipton	d						09 25								09 56							10 25	
Coseley	d						09 28							09 47	09 59							10 28	
Wolverhampton ■	a		09 14	09 18		09 24	09 34	09 37		09 43		09 48		09 53	10 05			10 14	10 18		10 24	10 34	10 37
	d		09 15	09 20								09 49		09 54				10 15	10 20				
Penkridge	d													10 04									
Stafford	a		09 27	09 33								10 02		10 10				10 27	10 33				

A To Manchester Piccadilly
B To Liverpool Lime Street
C From Southampton Central to Manchester Piccadilly
D To Shrewsbury
E From Walsall
F To Edinburgh
G To Aberystwyth
H From Bristol Temple Meads to Manchester Piccadilly
I To Crewe
J To Glasgow Central
K To Holyhead
L From Cardiff Central to Manchester Piccadilly
M From Bournemouth to Manchester Piccadilly

Northampton - Coventry - Birmingham - Wolverhampton - Stafford

		LM	AW	VT	XC	LM	LM	LM	LM	VT	XC	LM	LM	LM	LM	VT	LM	AW	LM	VT	XC	LM	LM
		■	■ A ✕	◇■ 🛒	◇■ B ✕		■ C	D	■	◇■ 🛒	◇■ E ✕	■ C	■	F	D	◇■ G 🛒	■	◇ H ✕	■ I	◇■ 🛒	◇■ J ✕		■ C
London Euston ⊖66	d	07 54		09 03						09 23			08 49			09 43	09 13			10 03			
Northampton 66	d	09 16							09 37				09 55				10 16		10 25				
Long Buckby	d	09 27							09 48				10 06				10 27		10 36				
Rugby	d	09 38		09 51					09 59				10 17				10 38		10 47	10 51			
Coventry	a	09 49		10 02					10 10	10 22			10 29			10 42	10 49		10 58	11 02			
	d	09 50		10 02					10 11	10 22	10 27		10 30			10 42	10 50		11 11	11 02			
Canley	d								10 14				10 33						→				
Tile Hill	d	09 55							10 18				10 37				10 55						
Berkswell	d								10 21				10 40										
Hampton-in-Arden	d	10 01							10 25								11 01						
Birmingham International ✈	a	10 04		10 13					10 28	10 33	10 37		10 45			10 53	11 04			11 13			
	d	10 05	10 09	10 13		10 19			10 29	10 33	10 38		10 46			10 53	11 05	11 10		11 13		11 19	
Marston Green	d	10 08							10 32				10 49				11 08						
Lea Hall	d					10 23							10 52									11 23	
Stechford	d					10 26							10 55									11 26	
Adderley Park	d					10 29																11 29	
Birmingham New Street ■	a	10 17	10 20	10 25		10 34			10 42	10 45	10 48		11 01			11 04	11 17	11 20		11 26		11 34	
	d		10 25		10 31		10 36	10 39			10 57	11 01		11 05	11 08	11 15		11 25			11 31		11 36
Smethwick Rolfe Street	d							10 45							11 14								
Smethwick Galton Bridge ■	d		10 31					10 47				11 07			11 16			11 31					
Sandwell & Dudley	d							10 50						11 13	11 19	11 24							
Dudley Port	d							10 54							11 23								
Tipton	d							10 56							11 25								
Coseley	d						10 47	10 59							11 28								11 47
Wolverhampton ■	a		10 42		10 48		10 53	11 05			11 14	11 18		11 24	11 34	11 37		11 43			11 48		11 53
	d				10 49		10 54				11 15	11 20									11 49		11 54
Penkridge	d						11 04																12 04
Stafford	a				11 02		11 10				11 27	11 33									12 02		12 10

		LM	LM	VT	XC	LM	LM	LM	LM	VT	LM	AW	LM	VT	XC	LM	LM	LM	LM	VT	XC	LM
		D	■ K	◇■ 🛒	◇■ E ✕	■ C	■	F	D	◇■ L 🛒	■	■ A ✕	■ I	◇■ 🛒	◇■ M ✕		■ C	D	■ K	◇■ F 🛒	◇■ E ✕	■ C
London Euston ⊖66	d			10 23			09 49			10 43	10 13			11 03						11 23		
Northampton 66	d						10 55				11 16		11 25									
Long Buckby	d						11 06				11 27		11 36									
Rugby	d		←				11 17				11 38		11 47	11 51					←			
Coventry	a		10 58	11 22			11 29			11 42	11 49		11 58	12 02					11 58	12 22		
	d		11 11	11 22	11 27		11 30			11 42	11 50		12 11	12 02					12 11	12 22	12 27	
Canley	d		11 14				11 33						→						12 14			
Tile Hill	d		11 18				11 37				11 55								12 18			
Berkswell	d		11 21				11 40												12 21			
Hampton-in-Arden	d		11 25								12 01								12 25			
Birmingham International ✈	a		11 28	11 33	11 37		11 45			11 53	12 04			12 13					12 28	12 33	12 37	
	d		11 29	11 33	11 38		11 46			11 53	12 05	12 09		12 13		12 19			12 29	12 33	12 38	
Marston Green	d		11 32				11 49				12 08								12 32			
Lea Hall	d						11 52									12 23						
Stechford	d						11 55									12 26						
Adderley Park	d															12 29						
Birmingham New Street ■	a		11 42	11 45	11 48		12 01			12 05	12 17	12 20		12 25		12 34			12 42	12 45	12 48	
	d	11 39			11 57	12 01		12 05	12 08	12 15		12 25			12 31		12 36	12 39		12 53	12 57	13 01
Smethwick Rolfe Street	d	11 45							12 14									12 45				
Smethwick Galton Bridge ■	d	11 47				12 07			12 16			12 31						12 47				13 07
Sandwell & Dudley	d	11 50						12 13	12 19	12 24								12 50				
Dudley Port	d	11 54							12 23									12 54				
Tipton	d	11 56							12 25									12 56				
Coseley	d	11 59							12 28								12 47	12 59				
Wolverhampton ■	a	12 05			12 14	12 18		12 24	12 34	12 37		12 42			12 48		12 53	13 05		13 10	13 14	13 18
	d				12 15	12 20									12 49		12 54				13 15	13 20
Penkridge	d																13 04					
Stafford	a				12 27	12 33									13 02		13 10				13 27	13 33

A To Aberystwyth
B From Paignton to Manchester Piccadilly
C To Liverpool Lime Street
D From Walsall
E From Bournemouth to Manchester Piccadilly
F To Shrewsbury
G To Glasgow Central
H To Holyhead
I To Birmingham New Street
J From Bristol Temple Meads to Manchester Piccadilly
K From Northampton
L To Edinburgh
M From Plymouth to Manchester Piccadilly

Table T068-F

Saturdays

26 May to 8 December

Northampton - Coventry - Birmingham - Wolverhampton - Stafford

	LM	LM	LM	VT	LM	AW	LM	VT	XC	LM	LM	LM	LM	VT	XC	LM	LM	LM	LM	VT	LM	AW
	■	A	B	◇■ C	■	◇ D	■ E	◇■	◇■ F		■ G	B	■ H	◇■	◇■ I	■ G	■	A	B	◇■ J	■	◇ K
London Euston ⊖66 d	10 49			11 43	11 13			12 03						12 23			11 49			12 43	12 13	
Northampton 66 d	11 55				12 16		12 25										12 55				13 16	
Long Buckby d	12 06				12 27		12 36										13 06				13 27	
Rugby d	12 17				12 38		12 47	12 51					←				13 17				13 38	
Coventry a	12 29			12 42	12 49		12 58	13 02					12 58	13 22			13 30			13 42	13 49	
d	12 30			12 42	12 50		13 11	13 02					13 11	13 22	13 27		13 30			13 42	13 50	
Canley d	12 33						→						13 14				13 33					
Tile Hill d	12 37				12 55								13 18				13 37				13 55	
Berkswell d	12 40												13 21				13 40					
Hampton-in-Arden d					13 01								13 25								14 01	
Birmingham International a	12 45			12 53	13 04			13 13					13 28	13 33	13 37		13 45			13 53	14 04	
d	12 46			12 53	13 05	13 10		13 13		13 19			13 29	13 33	13 38		13 46			13 53	14 05	14 09
Marston Green d	12 49				13 08								13 32				13 49				14 08	
Lea Hall d	12 52									13 23							13 52					
Stechford d	12 55									13 26							13 55					
Adderley Park d										13 29												
BirminghamNewStreet a	13 02			13 05	13 17	13 21		13 26		13 34			13 42	13 45	13 48		14 02			14 05	14 17	14 20
d		13 05	13 08	13 15		13 25			13 31		13 36	13 39			13 57	14 01		14 05	14 08	14 15		14 25
Smethwick Rolfe Street d			13 14									13 45							14 14			
Smethwick Galton Bridge d			13 16			13 31						13 47				14 07			14 16			14 31
Sandwell & Dudley d		13 13	13 19	13 24								13 50						14 13	14 19	14 24		
Dudley Port d			13 23									13 54							14 23			
Tipton d			13 25									13 56							14 25			
Coseley d			13 28								13 47	13 59							14 28			
Wolverhampton a		13 24	13 34	13 37		13 42			13 48		13 53	14 05			14 14	14 18		14 24	14 34	14 37		14 42
d									13 49		13 54				14 15	14 20						
Penkridge d											14 04											
Stafford a									14 02		14 10				14 27	14 33						

	LM	VT	XC	LM	LM	LM	LM	VT	XC	LM	LM	LM	LM	VT	LM	AW	LM	VT	XC	LM	LM
	■ E	◇■	◇■ L		■ G	B	■ H	◇■	◇■ I	■ G	■	A	B	◇■ C	■	■ D	■ E	◇■	◇■ M		■ G
London Euston ⊖66 d		13 03						13 23			12 49			13 43	13 13			14 03			
Northampton 66 d	13 25										13 55				14 16		14 25				
Long Buckby d	13 36										14 06				14 27		14 36				
Rugby d	13 47	13 51					←				14 17				14 38		14 47	14 51			
Coventry a	13 58	14 02					13 58	14 22			14 29			14 42	14 49		14 58	15 02			
d	14 11	14 02					14 11	14 22	14 27		14 30			14 42	14 50		15 11	15 02			
Canley d	→						14 14				14 33						→				
Tile Hill d							14 18				14 37				14 55						
Berkswell d							14 21				14 40										
Hampton-in-Arden d							14 25								15 01						
Birmingham International a		14 13					14 28	14 33	14 37		14 45			14 53	15 04			15 13			
d		14 13		14 19			14 29	14 33	14 38		14 46			14 53	15 05	15 09		15 13		15 19	
Marston Green d							14 32				14 49				15 08						
Lea Hall d				14 23							14 52									15 23	
Stechford d				14 26							14 55									15 26	
Adderley Park d				14 29																15 29	
BirminghamNewStreet a		14 25		14 34			14 42	14 45	14 48		15 01			15 05	15 17	15 20		15 26		15 34	
d			14 31		14 36	14 39			14 57	15 01		15 05	15 08	15 15		15 25			15 31		15 36
Smethwick Rolfe Street d						14 45							15 14								
Smethwick Galton Bridge d						14 47				15 07			15 16			15 31					
Sandwell & Dudley d						14 50						15 13	15 19	15 24							
Dudley Port d						14 54							15 23								
Tipton d						14 56							15 25								
Coseley d					14 47	14 59							15 28								15 47
Wolverhampton a			14 48		14 53	15 05			15 14	15 18		15 24	15 34	15 37		15 43			15 48		15 53
d			14 49		14 54				15 15	15 20									15 49		15 54
Penkridge d					15 04																16 04
Stafford a			15 02		15 10				15 27	15 34									16 02		16 10

A To Shrewsbury
B From Walsall
C To Glasgow Central
D To Holyhead
E To Birmingham New Street
F From Paignton to Manchester Piccadilly
G To Liverpool Lime Street
H From Northampton
I From Bournemouth to Manchester Piccadilly
J To Edinburgh
K To Aberystwyth
L From Bristol Temple Meads to Manchester Piccadilly
M From Penzance to Manchester Piccadilly

Table T068-F

Saturdays

26 May to 8 December

Northampton - Coventry - Birmingham - Wolverhampton - Stafford

	LM	LM	VT	XC	LM	LM	LM	LM	VT	LM	AW	LM	VT	XC	LM	LM	LM	LM	VT	XC	LM	LM
	A	■ B	◇■	◇■ C	■ D	■	E	A	■ F	■	◇ G	■ H	◇■	◇■ I		■ D	A	■ B	◇■	◇■ C	■ D	■
London Euston ⊖66 d			14 23			13 49			14 43	14 13			15 03						15 23			14 49
Northampton 66 d						14 55				15 16		15 25										15 55
Long Buckby d						15 06				15 27		15 36										16 06
Rugby d		←				15 17				15 38		15 47	15 51					←				16 17
Coventry a		14 58	15 22			15 29			15 42	15 49		15 58	16 02					15 58	16 22			16 29
d		15 11	15 22	15 27		15 30			15 42	15 50		16 11	16 02					16 11	16 22	16 27		16 30
Canley d		15 14				15 33						→						16 14				16 33
Tile Hill d		15 18				15 37				15 55								16 18				16 37
Berkswell d		15 21				15 40												16 21				16 40
Hampton-in-Arden d		15 25								16 01								16 25				
Birmingham International a		15 28	15 33	15 37		15 45			15 53	16 04			16 13					16 28	16 33	16 37		16 45
d		15 29	15 33	15 38		15 46			15 53	16 05	16 09		16 13		16 19			16 29	16 33	16 38		16 46
Marston Green d		15 32				15 49				16 08								16 32				16 49
Lea Hall d						15 52									16 23							16 52
Stechford d						15 55									16 26							16 55
Adderley Park d															16 29							
BirminghamNewStreet a		15 42	15 45	15 48		16 02			16 05	16 17	16 20		16 26		16 34			16 42	16 45	16 48		17 01
d	15 39			15 57	16 01		16 05	16 08	16 15		16 25			16 31		16 36	16 39			16 57	17 01	
Smethwick Rolfe Street d	15 45							16 14									16 45					
Smethwick Galton Bridge d	15 47				16 07			16 16			16 31						16 47				17 07	
Sandwell & Dudley d	15 50						16 13	16 19	16 24								16 50					
Dudley Port d	15 54							16 23									16 54					
Tipton d	15 56							16 25									16 56					
Coseley d	15 59							16 28								16 47	16 59					
Wolverhampton a	16 05			16 14	16 18		16 24	16 34	16 37		16 42			16 48		16 53	17 05			17 14	17 18	
d				16 15	16 20									16 49		16 54				17 15	17 20	
Penkridge d					16 29											17 04					17 29	
Stafford a				16 27	16 36									17 02		17 10				17 27	17 36	

	LM	LM	VT	LM	AW	LM	VT	XC	LM	LM	LM	LM	VT	XC	LM	LM	LM	LM	VT	LM	AW
	E	A	■ J	■	◇ K	■ H	◇■	◇■ L		■ D	A	■ B	◇■	◇■ C	■ D	■	E	A	◇■ M	■	◇ G
London Euston ⊖66 d			15 43	15 13			16 03						16 23			15 49			16 43	16 13	
Northampton 66 d				16 16		16 25										16 55				17 16	
Long Buckby d				16 27		16 36										17 06				17 27	
Rugby d				16 38		16 47	16 51					←				17 17				17 38	
Coventry a			16 42	16 49		16 58	17 02					16 58	17 22			17 29			17 42	17 49	
d			16 42	16 50		17 11	17 02					17 11	17 22	17 27		17 30			17 42	17 50	
Canley d						→						17 14				17 33					
Tile Hill d				16 55								17 18				17 37				17 55	
Berkswell d												17 21				17 40					
Hampton-in-Arden d				17 01								17 25								18 01	
Birmingham International a			16 53	17 04			17 13					17 28	17 33	17 37		17 45			17 53	18 04	
d			16 53	17 05	17 09		17 13		17 19			17 29	17 33	17 38		17 46			17 53	18 05	18 09
Marston Green d				17 08								17 32				17 49				18 08	
Lea Hall d									17 23							17 52					
Stechford d									17 26							17 55					
Adderley Park d									17 29												
BirminghamNewStreet a			17 05	17 17	17 21		17 26		17 34			17 42	17 45	17 48		18 01			18 05	18 17	18 21
d	17 05	17 08	17 15		17 25			17 31		17 36	17 39			17 57	18 01		18 05	18 08	18 15		18 25
Smethwick Rolfe Street d		17 14									17 45							18 14			
Smethwick Galton Bridge d		17 16			17 31						17 47				18 07			18 16			18 31
Sandwell & Dudley d	17 13	17 19	17 24								17 50						18 13	18 19	18 24		
Dudley Port d		17 23									17 54							18 23			
Tipton d		17 25									17 56							18 25			
Coseley d		17 28								17 47	17 59							18 28			
Wolverhampton a	17 24	17 34	17 37		17 43			17 48		17 53	18 05			18 14	18 18		18 24	18 34	18 37		18 42
d								17 49		17 54				18 15	18 20						
Penkridge d										18 04					18 29						
Stafford a								18 02		18 10				18 27	18 36						

A From Walsall
B From Northampton
C From Bournemouth to Manchester Piccadilly
D To Liverpool Lime Street
E To Shrewsbury
F To Edinburgh
G To Aberystwyth
H To Birmingham New Street
I From Bristol Temple Meads to Manchester Piccadilly
J To Glasgow Central
K To Holyhead
L From Paignton to Manchester Piccadilly
M To Preston

Northampton - Coventry - Birmingham - Wolverhampton - Stafford

		LM A	VT ◇	XC ◇ B	LM	LM C	LM D	LM E	VT ◇	XC ◇ F	LM G	LM	LM H	LM D	VT ◇ I	LM	AW ◇ J	XC ◇ K	LM A	VT ◇	LM	LM D
London Euston ⊖66	d		17 03						17 23			16 49			17 43	17 13				18 03		
Northampton 66	d	17 25										17 55				18 16			18 25			
Long Buckby	d	17 36										18 06				18 27			18 36			
Rugby	d	17 47	17 51					←				18 17				18 38			18 47	18 52		
Coventry	a	17 58	18 02					17 58	18 22			18 29			18 42	18 49			18 58	19 03		
	d	18 11	18 02					18 11	18 22	18 27		18 30			18 42	18 50			19 11	19 03		
Canley	d	→						18 14				18 33							→			
Tile Hill	d							18 18				18 37				18 55						
Berkswell	d							18 21				18 40										
Hampton-in-Arden	d							18 25								19 01						
Birmingham International ✈	a		18 13					18 28	18 33	18 37		18 45			18 53	19 04				19 13		
	d		18 13		18 19			18 29	18 33	18 38		18 46			18 53	19 05	19 09			19 13	19 19	
Marston Green	d							18 32				18 49				19 08						
Lea Hall	d				18 23							18 52									19 23	
Stechford	d				18 26							18 55									19 26	
Adderley Park	d				18 29																19 29	
BirminghamNewStreet	a		18 26		18 34			18 42	18 45	18 48		19 01			19 05	19 17	19 20			19 26	19 34	
	d			18 31		18 36	18 39		18 50	18 57	19 01		19 05	19 08	19 15		19 25	19 31		19 35		19 39
Smethwick Rolfe Street	d						18 45							19 14								19 45
Smethwick Galton Bridge	d						18 47				19 07			19 16			19 31					19 47
Sandwell & Dudley	d						18 50		18 59				19 13	19 19	19 24					19 44		19 50
Dudley Port	d						18 54							19 23								19 54
Tipton	d						18 56							19 25								19 56
Coseley	d					18 47	18 59							19 28								19 59
Wolverhampton	a			18 48		18 53	19 05		19 10	19 14	19 18		19 24	19 34	19 37		19 43	19 48		19 55		20 05
	d			18 49		18 54				19 15	19 20							19 49				
Penkridge	d					19 04					19 30											
Stafford	a			19 02		19 10				19 27	19 36							20 02				

		LM E	VT ◇	XC ◇ L	LM G	LM	LM H	LM	VT ◇ C	LM	AW ◇ M	XC ◇ B	VT ◇ N	LM	LM C	LM	VT ◇ O	LM	VT ◇	XC ◇ P	XC ◇ Q	XC ◇ R
London Euston ⊖66	d		18 23			17 49			18 43	18 13			19 03						19 23			
Northampton 66	d					18 55				19 16								19 37				
Long Buckby	d					19 06				19 27								19 48				
Rugby	d	←				19 17				19 38			19 51					19 59				
Coventry	a	18 58	19 24			19 29			19 42	19 49			20 02					20 10	20 22			
	d	19 11	19 25	19 27		19 30			19 42	19 50			20 02					20 11	20 22	20 27	20 27	
Canley	d	19 14				19 33												20 14				
Tile Hill	d	19 18				19 37				19 55								20 18				
Berkswell	d	19 21				19 40												20 21				
Hampton-in-Arden	d	19 25								20 01								20 25				
Birmingham International ✈	a	19 28	19 34	19 37		19 45			19 53	20 04			20 13					20 28	20 33	20 37	20 37	
	d	19 29	19 35	19 38		19 46			19 53	20 05	20 09		20 13	20 19				20 29	20 33	20 38	20 38	
Marston Green	d	19 32				19 49				20 08								20 32				
Lea Hall	d					19 52								20 23								
Stechford	d					19 55								20 26								
Adderley Park	d													20 29			←					
BirminghamNewStreet	a	19 42	19 45	19 48		20 02			20 06	20 17	20 20		20 24	20 34			20 24	20 42	20 45	20 48	20 48	
	d		19 50	19 57	20 01		20 05	20 08	20 15		20 25	20 31	20 42		20 36	20 39	20 42		20 50	20 57		20 57
Smethwick Rolfe Street	d							20 14					→			20 45						
Smethwick Galton Bridge	d				20 07			20 16			20 31					20 47						
Sandwell & Dudley	d		19 59				20 13	20 19	20 24							20 50	20 54		20 59			
Dudley Port	d							20 23								20 54						
Tipton	d							20 25								20 56						
Coseley	d							20 28							20 47	20 59						
Wolverhampton	a		20 10	20 14	20 19		20 24	20 34	20 37		20 42	20 48			20 53	21 05	21 08		21 12	21 16		21 16
	d			20 15	20 22				20 37			20 49			20 54					21 17		21 17
Penkridge	d				20 31										21 04							
Stafford	a			20 27	20 38				20 50			21 02			21 10					21 29		21 29

A To Birmingham New Street
B From Bristol Temple Meads to Manchester Piccadilly
C To Crewe
D From Walsall
E From Northampton
F From Bournemouth to Manchester Piccadilly
G To Liverpool Lime Street
H To Shrewsbury
I To Preston
J To Chester
K From Exeter St Davids to Manchester Piccadilly
L From Bournemouth to Manchester Piccadilly. ⚲ to BirminghamNewStreet
M To Aberystwyth
N To Wolverhampton
O From London Euston
P From 15 September. From Bournemouth to Manchester Piccadilly. ⚲ to BirminghamNewStreet
Q Until 8 September. From Bournemouth to Leeds
R Until 8 September. From Newquay to Manchester Piccadilly

Northampton - Coventry - Birmingham - Wolverhampton - Stafford

		LM	LM A	LM B	VT ◇	AW ◇ C	LM	LM	LM D	LM	LM	XC ◇ E	LM	LM A	LM B	VT ◇	LM	XC ◇ F	XC ◇ G	LM	AW ◇ D	LM D
London Euston ⊖66	d	18 49			19 43		19 13									20 25	19 46					
Northampton 66	d	19 55					20 22						20 55				21 16					
Long Buckby	d	20 06					20 33						21 06				21 27					
Rugby	d	20 17					20 44						21 17				21 38					
Coventry	a	20 29			20 50		20 55						21 29			21 36	21 49					
	d	20 30			20 50		20 56				21 11	21 27	21 30			21 36	21 50	22 01				
Canley	d	20 33					20 59				21 14		21 33									
Tile Hill	d	20 37					21 03				21 18		21 37				21 55					
Berkswell	d	20 40					21 06				21 21		21 40									
Hampton-in-Arden	d						21 10				21 25						22 01					
Birmingham International ✈	a	20 45			21 01		21 13				21 28	21 37	21 45			21 50	22 04	22 10				
	d	20 46			21 01	21 09	21 14	21 19			21 29	21 38	21 46			21 50	22 05	22 11		22 19		
Marston Green	d	20 49					21 17				21 32		21 49				22 08					
Lea Hall	d	20 52						21 23					21 52							22 23		
Stechford	d	20 55						21 26					21 55							22 26		
Adderley Park	d							21 29												22 29		
BirminghamNewStreet	a	21 02			21 13	21 20	21 25	21 34			21 42	21 48	22 01			22 04	22 17	22 21		22 34		
	d		21 05	21 08	21 17	21 25			21 36	21 39		21 57		22 05	22 08	22 16			22 31		22 35	22 39
Smethwick Rolfe Street	d			21 14						21 45					22 14							22 45
Smethwick Galton Bridge	d			21 16		21 31				21 47					22 16							22 47
Sandwell & Dudley	d		21 13	21 19						21 50				22 13	22 19	22 25						22 50
Dudley Port	d			21 23						21 54					22 23							22 54
Tipton	d			21 25						21 56					22 25							22 56
Coseley	d			21 28					21 47	21 59					22 28							22 59
Wolverhampton	a		21 24	21 34	21 37	21 43			21 53	22 05		22 14		22 24	22 34	22 37			22 48		22 52	23 04
	d								21 59			22 15							22 49			23 06
Penkridge	d								22 09													23 16
Stafford	a								22 15			22 27							23 01			23 22

		LM	VT ◇	XC ◇ H	LM	LM A	LM	VT ◇	AW A	LM
London Euston ⊖66	d		21 03		20 34		20 40	21 43		21 28
Northampton 66	d				21 59		22 16			22 55
Long Buckby	d				22 10		22 27			23 06
Rugby	d		22 12		22 21		22 38	22 53		23 17
Coventry	a		22 22		22 32		22 49	23 02		23 28
	d	22 11	22 23	22 26	22 33		22 50	23 03		23 30
Canley	d	22 14			22 36					23 33
Tile Hill	d	22 18			22 40		22 55			23 37
Berkswell	d	22 21			22 43					23 40
Hampton-in-Arden	d	22 25					23 01			23 44
Birmingham International ✈	a	22 28	22 33	22 36	22 48		23 04	23 13		23 47
	d	22 29	22 34	22 37	22 49		23 05	23 14		23 48
Marston Green	d	22 32			22 52		23 08			23 51
Lea Hall	d				22 55					23 54
Stechford	d				22 58					23 57
Adderley Park	d									
BirminghamNewStreet	a	22 42	22 45	22 47	23 04		23 17	23 25		00 04
	d		22 48			23 08		23 28	23 35	
Smethwick Rolfe Street	d					23 14				
Smethwick Galton Bridge	d					23 16				
Sandwell & Dudley	d		22 57			23 19		23 37		
Dudley Port	d					23 23				
Tipton	d					23 25				
Coseley	d					23 28				
Wolverhampton	a		23 08			23 34		23 48	23 53	
	d									
Penkridge	d									
Stafford	a									

A To Shrewsbury
B From Walsall
C To Chester
D To Crewe
E From Bournemouth to Manchester Piccadilly
F From Reading
G To Manchester Piccadilly
H From Bournemouth

Table T068-F

Sundays

20 May to 2 December

Northampton - Coventry - Birmingham - Wolverhampton - Stafford

Station		VT ◇■ A	XC ◇■ B	LM ■	LM	LM ■		VT ◇■ C	LM ■ D	LM ■	XC ◇■ B	AW ◇ E	AW ◇ F	LM G	VT ◇■ H	LM ■		LM ■	LM ■ I	LM ■ D	VT ◇■	XC ◇■ J	AW ◇ K	LM ■	LM G
London Euston ⊖66	d															07 52					08 50			08 24	
Northampton 66	d															09 26			09 40					10 00	
Long Buckby	d															09 37			09 51					10 11	
Rugby	d								08 52							09 48			10 03		10 14			10 22	
Coventry	a								09 04							09 59					10 24			10 33	
	d			08 37					09 07	09 11						10 00		10 11			10 24	10 29		10 34	
Canley	d			08 40						09 14								10 14						10 37	
Tile Hill	d			08 44					09 12	09 18								10 18						10 41	
Berkswell	d			08 47						09 21								10 21						10 44	
Hampton-in-Arden	d			08 51						09 25								10 25						10 48	
Birmingham International ✈	a			08 54					09 19	09 28						10 09		10 28			10 35	10 38		10 51	
	d			08 55		09 03			09 20	09 29		09 51	09 51			10 09		10 29			10 35	10 40	10 48	10 52	
Marston Green	d			08 58		09 06			09 23	09 32						10 12		10 32						10 55	
Lea Hall	d					09 09										10 16									
Stechford	d					09 12										10 18									
Adderley Park	d					09 15										10 22									
BirminghamNewStreet ■	a			09 06		09 20			09 31	09 40		10 01	10 01			10 26		10 40			10 47	10 50	10 58	11 03	
	d	08 45	09 01		09 08			09 20	09 42		10 01	10 04	10 04	10 08	10 20					10 42	10 50	11 01	11 05		11 08
Smethwick Rolfe Street	d				09 14									10 14											11 14
Smethwick Galton Bridge ■	d				09 16				09 49					10 16						10 49					11 16
Sandwell & Dudley	d				09 19									10 19							10 59				11 19
Dudley Port	d				09 23									10 23											11 23
Tipton	d				09 25									10 25											11 25
Coseley	d				09 28									10 28											11 28
Wolverhampton ■	a	09 03	09 18		09 34			09 37	10 00		10 18	10 22	10 22	10 33	10 37					11 00	11 11	11 18	11 26		11 33
	d	09 04	09 19						10 00		10 19									11 00		11 19			
Penkridge	d								10 10											11 10					
Stafford	a	09 17	09 32						10 16		10 32								10 58	11 16		11 31			

Station		VT ◇■ L		LM ■	LM ■ D	VT ◇■	XC ◇■ M	LM ■	LM G	LM ■ I	LM ■ I	VT ◇■ H		AW ◇ N	LM ■ D	LM ■	VT ◇■	XC ◇■ O	LM ■	LM G	VT ◇■ L	AW ◇ K		VT ◇■	XC ◇■ B
London Euston ⊖66	d					09 50		09 24		09 54	10 24						10 50		10 28					11 50	
Northampton 66	d							11 00		11 08	11 40								11 58						
Long Buckby	d							11 11		11 19	11 51								12 09						
Rugby	d					11 14		11 22		11 30	12 03						12 14		12 20					12 50	
Coventry	a					11 23		11 33									12 23		12 31					12 59	
	d			11 11		11 24	11 29	11 34								12 11	12 24	12 28	12 32					13 00	
Canley	d							11 37											12 35						
Tile Hill	d							11 41											12 39						
Berkswell	d							11 44											12 42						
Hampton-in-Arden	d							11 48											12 46						
Birmingham International ✈	a			11 20		11 34	11 39	11 51								12 20	12 34	12 38	12 49					13 10	
	d			11 20		11 35	11 41	11 52						12 07		12 20	12 35	12 40	12 50			13 07		13 10	
Marston Green	d			11 23				11 55								12 23			12 53						
Lea Hall	d			11 27												12 27									
Stechford	d			11 29												12 29									
Adderley Park	d			11 32												12 32									
BirminghamNewStreet ■	a			11 40		11 47	11 51	12 03						12 18		12 40	12 46	12 50	13 01			13 17		13 22	
	d	11 20			11 42	11 50	11 57		12 08			12 20		12 24	12 35		12 50	12 57		13 08	13 20	13 24			13 30
Smethwick Rolfe Street	d								12 14											13 14					
Smethwick Galton Bridge ■	d				11 49				12 16						12 42					13 16					
Sandwell & Dudley	d					11 59			12 19								12 59			13 19					
Dudley Port	d								12 23											13 23					
Tipton	d								12 25											13 25					
Coseley	d								12 28											13 28					
Wolverhampton ■	a	11 37			12 00	12 11	12 15		12 33			12 37		12 42	12 53		13 10	13 14		13 33	13 37	13 41			13 47
	d				12 00		12 16								12 53			13 16							13 49
Penkridge	d				12 10										13 03										
Stafford	a				12 16		12 28			12 20	12 59				13 09			13 28							14 02

A To Preston
B To Manchester Piccadilly
C To Carlisle
D To Liverpool Lime Street
E from 16 September. To Aberystwyth
F until 9 September. To Aberystwyth
G From Walsall
H To Edinburgh
I To Crewe
J From Reading to Manchester Piccadilly
K To Chester
L To Glasgow Central
M From Southampton Central to Manchester Piccadilly
N To Aberystwyth
O From Bournemouth to Manchester Piccadilly

Table T068-F

Sundays

20 May to 2 December

Northampton - Coventry - Birmingham - Wolverhampton - Stafford

Station		LM ■ A	LM ■	VT ◇■		XC ◇■ B	LM ■	LM C	VT ◇■ D	LM ■ E	AW ■ F	VT ◇■	XC ◇■ G	LM ■ A		LM ■	VT ◇■	XC ◇■ B	LM ■	LM C	LM ■ E	VT ◇■ H	XC ◇■ I	AW ◇ J
London Euston ⊖66	d			12 20			11 24		12 40			13 00					13 20		12 34		12 50	13 40		
Northampton 66	d						12 55			13 02									13 55		14 02			
Long Buckby	d						13 06			13 13									14 06		14 13			
Rugby	d						13 17			13 26		13 51							14 17		14 26			
Coventry	a			13 22			13 29		13 42			14 02					14 22		14 29			14 42		
	d		13 11	13 22		13 27	13 30		13 42			14 02				14 11	14 22	14 27	14 30			14 42	14 54	
Canley	d						13 33												14 33					
Tile Hill	d		13 16				13 37									14 16			14 37					
Berkswell	d						13 40												14 40					
Hampton-in-Arden	d						13 44												14 44					
Birmingham International ✈	a		13 23	13 33		13 36	13 47		13 53			14 13				14 23	14 33	14 36	14 47			14 53	15 03	
	d		13 23	13 33		13 38	13 48		13 53		14 07	14 13				14 23	14 33	14 38	14 48			14 53	15 04	15 07
Marston Green	d		13 26				13 51									14 26			14 51					
Lea Hall	d		13 30													14 30								
Stechford	d		13 32													14 32								
Adderley Park	d		13 35													14 35								
BirminghamNewStreet ■	a		13 42	13 45		13 48	13 59		14 04		14 18	14 24				14 42	14 45	14 48	14 59			15 04	15 14	15 18
	d	13 35		13 48		13 57		14 08	14 15		14 24		14 31	14 35				14 57		15 08		15 15		15 24
Smethwick Rolfe Street	d							14 14												15 14				
Smethwick Galton Bridge ■	d	13 42						14 16						14 42						15 16				
Sandwell & Dudley	d			13 57				14 19	14 26											15 19		15 27		
Dudley Port	d							14 23												15 23				
Tipton	d							14 25												15 25				
Coseley	d							14 28												15 28				
Wolverhampton ■	a	13 53		14 08		14 14		14 33	14 37		14 42		14 48	14 53				15 14		15 33		15 37		15 42
	d	13 53				14 15							14 49	14 53				15 15						
Penkridge	d	14 03												15 03										
Stafford	a	14 09				14 27				14 19			15 02	15 09				15 27			15 19			

Station		VT ◇■	XC ◇■ K	LM ■ A	LM ■	VT ◇■	XC ◇■ B	LM ■	LM C	LM ■ E		VT ◇■ D	XC ◇■ I	AW ■ F	VT ◇■	XC ◇■ K	LM ■ A	LM ■	VT ◇■	XC ◇■ B		LM ■	LM C	LM ■ E	VT ◇■ H
London Euston ⊖66	d	14 00				14 20		13 34		13 50		14 40			15 00				15 20			14 34		14 50	15 40
Northampton 66	d							14 55		15 02												15 55		16 02	
Long Buckby	d							15 06		15 13												16 06		16 13	
Rugby	d	14 51						15 17		15 26					15 51							16 17		16 26	
Coventry	a	15 02				15 22		15 29				15 42			16 02				16 22			16 29			16 42
	d	15 02			15 11	15 22	15 27	15 30				15 42	15 54		16 02			16 11	16 22	16 27		16 30			16 42
Canley	d							15 33														16 33			
Tile Hill	d				15 16			15 37										16 16				16 37			
Berkswell	d							15 40														16 40			
Hampton-in-Arden	d							15 44														16 44			
Birmingham International ✈	a	15 13			15 23	15 33	15 37	15 47				15 53	16 03		16 13			16 23	16 33	16 36		16 47			16 53
	d	15 13			15 23	15 33	15 38	15 48				15 53	16 04	16 07	16 13			16 23	16 33	16 38		16 48			16 53
Marston Green	d				15 26			15 51										16 26				16 51			
Lea Hall	d				15 30													16 30							
Stechford	d				15 32													16 32							
Adderley Park	d				15 35													16 35							
BirminghamNewStreet ■	a	15 24			15 42	15 45	15 48	15 59				16 05	16 14	16 18	16 23			16 42	16 45	16 48		16 59			17 04
	d		15 31	15 35			15 57		16 08			16 15		16 24		16 31	16 35			16 57			17 08		17 15
Smethwick Rolfe Street	d								16 14														17 14		
Smethwick Galton Bridge ■	d			15 42					16 16								16 42						17 16		
Sandwell & Dudley	d								16 19			16 26											17 19		17 26
Dudley Port	d								16 23														17 23		
Tipton	d								16 25														17 25		
Coseley	d								16 28														17 28		
Wolverhampton ■	a		15 48	15 53			16 14		16 33			16 37		16 42		16 48	16 53			17 14			17 33		17 37
	d		15 49	15 53			16 15									16 49	16 53			17 15					
Penkridge	d			16 03													17 03								
Stafford	a		16 02	16 09			16 27			16 19						17 02	17 09			17 28				17 19	

A To Liverpool Lime Street
B From Bournemouth to Manchester Piccadilly
C From Walsall
D To Edinburgh
E To Crewe
F To Aberystwyth
G From Paignton to Manchester Piccadilly
H To Glasgow Central
I From Reading
J To Chester
K From Plymouth to Manchester Piccadilly

Table T068-F

Sundays
20 May to 2 December

Northampton - Coventry - Birmingham - Wolverhampton - Stafford

		XC ◇■ A 🛒	AW ◇ B 🛒	VT ◇■ ☕	XC ◇■ C 🛒	LM ■ D	LM ■	VT ◇■ ☕	XC ◇■ E 🛒	LM ■	LM F	LM ■ G	VT ◇■ H ☕	XC ◇■ A 🛒	AW ◇ I	VT ◇■ ☕	XC ◇■ J 🛒	LM ■ D	LM ■	VT ◇■ ☕	XC ◇■ E 🛒	LM ■
London Euston ■ ⊖66	d			16 00				16 20		15 34		15 50	16 40			17 00				17 20		16 34
Northampton 66	d									16 55		17 02										17 55
Long Buckby	d									17 06		17 13										18 06
Rugby	d			16 51						17 17		17 26				17 51						18 17
Coventry	a			17 02				17 22		17 29			17 44			18 02				18 22		18 29
	d	16 54		17 02			17 11	17 22	17 27	17 30			17 45	17 54		18 02			18 11	18 22	18 27	18 30
Canley	d									17 33												18 33
Tile Hill	d						17 16			17 37									18 16			18 37
Berkswell	d									17 40												18 40
Hampton-in-Arden	d									17 44												18 44
Birmingham International ✈	a	17 03		17 13			17 23	17 33	17 36	17 47			17 54	18 03		18 13			18 23	18 33	18 36	18 47
	d	17 04	17 07	17 13			17 23	17 33	17 38	17 48			17 55	18 04	18 08	18 13			18 23	18 33	18 38	18 48
Marston Green	d						17 26			17 51									18 26			18 51
Lea Hall	d						17 30												18 30			
Stechford	d						17 32												18 32			
Adderley Park	d						17 35												18 35			
BirminghamNewStreet ■ ⛴	a	17 14	17 19	17 24			17 42	17 45	17 48	17 59			18 05	18 14	18 18	18 24			18 42	18 45	18 48	18 59
	d		17 24		17 31	17 35			17 57		18 08		18 15		18 24		18 31	18 35			18 57	
Smethwick Rolfe Street	d										18 14											
Smethwick Galton Bridge ■	d					17 42					18 16							18 42				
Sandwell & Dudley	d										18 19		18 26									
Dudley Port	d										18 23											
Tipton	d										18 25											
Coseley	d										18 28											
Wolverhampton ■ ⛴	a		17 42		17 48	17 53			18 14		18 33		18 37		18 42		18 48	18 53			19 14	
	d				17 49	17 53			18 15								18 49	18 53			19 15	
Penkridge	d					18 03												19 03				
Stafford	a				18 02	18 09			18 27			18 19					19 02	19 09			19 27	

		LM F	LM ■ G	VT ■ ■ K ☕	XC ◇■ A 🛒	AW ◇ L	XC ◇■ C 🛒	LM ■ D	VT ◇■ ☕	LM ■	VT ◇■ M ☕	VT ◇■ N ☕	XC ◇■ O 🛒	LM ■	LM F	LM ■ G	VT ◇■ G ☕	XC ◇■ A 🛒	AW ◇ I	VT ◇■ P ☕	XC ◇■ C 🛒	LM ■
London Euston ■ ⊖66	d		16 50	17 40					18 00		18 20	18 20		17 34		17 50	18 40			19 00		
Northampton 66	d		18 02											18 55		19 02						
Long Buckby	d		18 13											19 06		19 13						
Rugby	d		18 26						18 51					19 17		19 26				19 53		
Coventry	a			18 44					19 02		19 22	19 24		19 29			19 42			20 03		
	d			18 45	18 54				19 02	19 11	19 22	19 24	19 27	19 30			19 42	19 54		20 04		20 11
Canley	d													19 33								
Tile Hill	d									19 16				19 37								20 16
Berkswell	d													19 40								
Hampton-in-Arden	d													19 44								
Birmingham International ✈	a			18 54	19 03				19 13	19 23	19 33	19 34	19 36	19 47			19 53	20 03		20 13		20 23
	d			18 55	19 04	19 07			19 13	19 23	19 33	19 34	19 38	19 48			19 53	20 04	20 08	20 13		20 23
Marston Green	d									19 26				19 51								20 26
Lea Hall	d									19 30												20 30
Stechford	d									19 32												20 32
Adderley Park	d									19 35												20 35
BirminghamNewStreet ■ ⛴	a			19 05	19 14	19 20			19 24	19 42	19 45	19 45	19 48	19 59			20 04	20 14	20 18	20 24		20 42
	d	19 08		19 15		19 24	19 31	19 35	19 39				19 57		20 08		20 15		20 24	20 27	20 31	
Smethwick Rolfe Street	d	19 14													20 14							
Smethwick Galton Bridge ■	d	19 16						19 42							20 16							
Sandwell & Dudley	d	19 19		19 26					19 49						20 19		20 24			20 35		
Dudley Port	d	19 23													20 23							
Tipton	d	19 25													20 25							
Coseley	d	19 28													20 28							
Wolverhampton ■ ⛴	a	19 33		19 37		19 42	19 48	19 53	20 00				20 14		20 33		20 37		20 42	20 47	20 51	
	d						19 49	19 53					20 15				20 37				20 52	
Penkridge	d							20 03														
Stafford	a		19 19				20 02	20 09					20 27			20 19	20 51				21 05	

A From Reading
B To Holyhead
C From Bristol Temple Meads to Manchester Piccadilly
D To Liverpool Lime Street
E From Bournemouth to Manchester Piccadilly
F From Walsall
G To Crewe
H To Edinburgh
I To Aberystwyth
J From Penzance to Manchester Piccadilly
K To Glasgow Central
L To Chester
M From 16 September
N Until 9 September
O From Bournemouth to Manchester Piccadilly. 🛒 to BirminghamNewStreet
P To Shrewsbury

Table T068-F

Sundays
20 May to 2 December

Northampton - Coventry - Birmingham - Wolverhampton - Stafford

		VT ◇■ ☕	XC ◇■ A 🛒	LM ■	LM B	LM ■ C	VT ◇■ D ☕	XC ◇■ E	AW ◇ F	VT ◇■ G ☕	VT ◇■ H ☕	LM ■ I	LM ■	VT ◇■ ☕	XC ◇■ J	LM ■	LM B	LM ■ C	VT ◇■ ☕	XC ◇■ E	AW K	LM ■	VT ◇■ ☕
London Euston ■ ⊖66	d	19 20		18 34		18 50	19 40			20 00	20 00			20 18		19 34		19 50	20 38				20 54
Northampton 66	d			19 55		20 02										20 55		21 06					
Long Buckby	d			20 06		20 13										21 06		21 17					
Rugby	d			20 17		20 26				20 51	20 51					21 17		21 30					22 07
Coventry	a	20 22		20 29			20 42			21 02	21 03			21 20		21 29			21 46				22 16
	d	20 22	20 27	20 30			20 42	20 54		21 03	21 04		21 11	21 20	21 27	21 30			21 46	21 53		22 09	22 16
Canley	d			20 33												21 33							
Tile Hill	d			20 37									21 16			21 37							
Berkswell	d			20 40												21 40							
Hampton-in-Arden	d			20 44												21 44							
Birmingham International ✈	a	20 33	20 36	20 47			20 53	21 03		21 13	21 13		21 23	21 31	21 36	21 47			21 57	22 02		22 18	22 27
	d	20 33	20 38	20 48			20 53	21 04	21 08	21 13	21 13		21 23	21 31	21 38	21 48			21 57	22 03	22 11	22 18	22 27
Marston Green	d			20 51									21 26			21 51						22 21	
Lea Hall	d												21 30									22 25	
Stechford	d												21 32									22 27	
Adderley Park	d												21 35									22 31	
BirminghamNewStreet ■ ⛴	a	20 45	20 48	20 59			21 05	21 15	21 18	21 24	21 24		21 42	21 45	21 48	21 59			22 09	22 14	22 21	22 36	22 39
	d	20 48	20 57		21 08		21 15		21 24			21 42		21 48	21 57		22 08		22 16		22 24		22 43
Smethwick Rolfe Street	d				21 14												22 14						
Smethwick Galton Bridge ■	d				21 16							21 49					22 16						
Sandwell & Dudley	d	20 57			21 19		21 24							21 57			22 19		22 25				22 52
Dudley Port	d				21 23												22 23						
Tipton	d				21 25												22 25						
Coseley	d				21 28												22 28						
Wolverhampton ■ ⛴	a	21 11	21 15		21 33		21 37		21 42			22 00		22 08	22 14		22 33		22 36		22 41		23 03
	d		21 17				21 37					22 00			22 15								
Penkridge	d											22 10											
Stafford	a		21 29			21 18	21 55					22 16			22 27			22 23					

		XC ◇■ L	AW ◇ M	LM ■	LM B	XC ◇■ E	AW K	LM ■	LM ■ N	VT ◇■ ☕	LM ■ O	VT ◇■ ☕	LM ■	VT ◇■ ☕
London Euston ■ ⊖66	d			20 34					21 30	21 55		22 25	22 00	23 25
Northampton 66	d			21 55					22 52				23 32	
Long Buckby	d			22 06					23 03				23 43	
Rugby	d			22 17					23 14	23 23	←	23 48	23 54	00s46
Coventry	a			22 29					23 25	23 33	23 25	23 57	00 07	00s58
	d	22 24		22 30		22 54		23 09	23 38	23 33	23 38	23 58		
Canley	d			22 33					→		23 41			
Tile Hill	d			22 37							23 45			
Berkswell	d			22 40							23 48			
Hampton-in-Arden	d			22 44							23 52			
Birmingham International ✈	a	22 33		22 47		23 03		23 18		23 44	23 55	00 08		01s09
	d	22 34	22 40	22 48		23 04	23 08	23 18		23 44	23 56	00 09		
Marston Green	d			22 51				23 21			23 59			
Lea Hall	d							23 25						
Stechford	d							23 27						
Adderley Park	d							23 31						
BirminghamNewStreet ■ ⛴	a	22 43	22 50	22 59		23 14	23 18	23 36		23 56	00 07	00 21		01s22
	d		22 55		23 08		23 24			23 59		00 24		
Smethwick Rolfe Street	d				23 14									
Smethwick Galton Bridge ■	d				23 16									
Sandwell & Dudley	d				23 19									
Dudley Port	d				23 23									
Tipton	d				23 25									
Coseley	d				23 28									
Wolverhampton ■ ⛴	a		23 13		23 33		23 40			00 15		00 41		01 42
	d		23 15											
Penkridge	d													
Stafford	a		23 30											

A From Bournemouth to Manchester Piccadilly. 🛒 to BirminghamNewStreet
B From Walsall
C To Crewe
D To Preston
E From Reading
F To Chester
G Until 9 September
H From 16 September
I To Liverpool Lime Street
J From Bournemouth to Manchester Piccadilly
K To Shrewsbury
L From Bournemouth
M To Holyhead
N To Birmingham New Street
O From London Euston

Table T068-R

Mondays to Fridays
21 May to 7 December

Stafford - Wolverhampton - Birmingham - Coventry - Northampton

Miles			LM MX A	LM 1	VT ◇1 ⊠	VT ◇1 ⊠	VT ◇1 ⊠	LM 1	XC ◇1 B ⚒	AW C	VT ◇1 ⊠	LM 1	LM 1	AW D	VT ◇1 ⊠	LM 1 E	LM 1	AW F	LM	LM G	VT ◇1 ⊠	LM 1	XC ◇1 H ⚒
0	**Stafford**	d								05 24													06 25
5¾	Penkridge	d																					
10¾	**Wolverhampton 7**	a								05 39													06 38
—		d			05 00		05 24			05 40	05 45			05 59	06 04					06 14	06 27		06 41
18½	Coseley	d																		06 19			
20	Tipton	d																		06 22			
20¾	Dudley Port	d																		06 25			
22¾	Sandwell & Dudley	d					05 34				05 55				06 15					06 28	06 38		
24	Smethwick Galton Bridge 7	d												06 10						06 31			
24¾	Smethwick Rolfe Street	d																←		06 34			
28	**BirminghamNewStreet 12**	a			05 26		05 43			06 09	06 05			06 15	06 24			06 15		06 40	06 47		06 57
—		d			05 29	05 45	05 50	05 53	06 04		06 10		06 14	06 36	06 30		06 33	06 36	06 39		06 50	06 54	07 04
30	Adderley Park	d												→					06 44				
32	Stechford	d											06 20						06 47				
33	Lea Hall	d											06 23						06 50				
34¾	Marston Green	d	00 02					06 01					06 26				06 42					07 02	
36¾	**Birmingham International**	a	00 05		05 38	05 54	05 59	06 04	06 13		06 19		06 29		06 39		06 45	06 49	06 55		06 59	07 05	07 13
—		d	00 06		05 40	05 55	06 00	06 05	06 14		06 20		06 30		06 40		06 45				07 00	07 05	07 14
38¾	Hampton-in-Arden	d											06 33				06 48					07 08	
41½	Berkswell	d						06 11					06 38									07 13	
43½	Tile Hill	d						06 14					06 41				06 55						
45½	Canley	d						06 17					06 44									07 17	
47¼	**Coventry**	a	00 16		05 50	06 05	06 10	06 21	06 24		06 30		06 47		06 50		06 59				07 10	07 21	07 24
—		d			05 51	06 06	06 11	06 21			06 31	06 00	06 48		06 51		07 00				07 11	07 21	
60¾	Rugby	d		05 16	06 03	06 20		06 32				06 11	06 59			06 47	07 12					07 32	
70	Long Buckby	d		05 25				06 41				06 21	07 10			06 56	07 21					07 41	
79½	**Northampton** 66	a		05 37		06 40		06 54				06 33	07 24			07 09	07 35					07 54	
—	London Euston 15 ⊖66	a		06 51	07 05	07 29	07 13	08 12			07 34	07 39	08 39		07 53	08 05	08 28				08 15	09 10	

		VT ◇1 ⊠	LM 1	LM F	LM 1 I	VT ◇1 ⊠	VT ◇1 ⊠	LM 1	AW ◇ C	XC ◇1 J ⚒	LM	LM K	VT ◇1 F ⊠	LM 1 E	LM F	VT ◇1 L ⊠	XC ◇1 M ⚒	LM 1 E	VT ◇1 N ⊠	LM 1	LM 1 O
Stafford	d				06 40					07 01				07 10				07 15	07 24		
Penkridge	d				06 46									07 15							
Wolverhampton 7	a				06 57					07 12				07 26				07 29	07 40		
	d	06 45		06 49	07 00	07 05			07 12	07 16		07 19	07 24	07 28	07 33	07 37		07 40	07 45		07 50
Coseley	d			06 55	07 05							07 24						07 45			07 55
Tipton	d			06 58								07 27						07 48			07 58
Dudley Port	d			07 01								07 29						07 51			08 00
Sandwell & Dudley	d	06 56		07 05		07 15						07 33		07 40	07 45				07 57		08 04
Smethwick Galton Bridge 7	d			07 08					07 23			07 36		07 44				07 55			08 07
Smethwick Rolfe Street	d			07 11								07 38						07 57			08 09
BirminghamNewStreet 12	a	07 07		07 17	07 20	07 25			07 30	07 33		07 44	07 47	07 50	07 55	07 56		08 05	08 07		08 15
	d	07 10	07 14			07 30		07 33	07 36		07 39		07 50	07 54			08 04		08 10	08 14	
Adderley Park	d										07 44										
Stechford	d		07 20								07 47									08 20	
Lea Hall	d		07 23								07 50									08 23	
Marston Green	d		07 26					07 42						08 02						08 26	
Birmingham International	a	07 19	07 29					07 45	07 49		07 55		07 59	08 05			08 13		08 20	08 29	
	d	07 20	07 30				07 41	07 45					08 00	08 05			08 14		08 21	08 30	
Hampton-in-Arden	d							07 48												08 33	
Berkswell	d							07 53						08 11						08 38	
Tile Hill	d		07 38					07 56						08 14						08 41	
Canley	d							08 00						08 17						08 44	
Coventry	a	07 30	07 42				07 51	08 04					08 10	08 21			08 24		08 31	08 47	
	d	07 31	07 43				07 52	08 04					08 11	08 21					08 31	08 48	
Rugby	d		07 54					08 15					08 23	08 39						08 59	
Long Buckby	d		08 04					08 25						08 48							
Northampton 66	a		08 16					08 37						09 00						09 20	
London Euston 15 ⊖66	a	08 31	09 27			08 43	08 50	09 46					09 13	10 19					09 33		

A From Birmingham New Street
B To Bournemouth
C From Chester
D From Shrewsbury to Birmingham International
E From Crewe
F From Shrewsbury
G From Shrewsbury to Rugeley Trent Valley
H From Manchester Piccadilly to Bournemouth
I From Crewe to Walsall
J From Manchester Piccadilly to Bristol Temple Meads
K To Four Oaks
L From Preston
M From Nottingham to Bournemouth
N From Manchester Piccadilly
O To Walsall

Table T068-R

Mondays to Fridays
21 May to 7 December

Stafford - Wolverhampton - Birmingham - Coventry - Northampton

		LM 1 A	LM B	VT ◇1 ⊠	LM 1	AW ◇ C ⚒	XC ◇1 D ⚒	LM	LM E	LM 1 A	VT ◇1 ⊠	LM 1	LM B	XC 1 F ⚒	VT ◇1 G ⊠	LM 1	LM 1 E	LM 1 A	VT ◇1 ⊠	LM 1	AW ◇ H ⚒	XC ◇1 I ⚒	LM
Stafford	d	07 40					08 01			08 10				08 25				08 40				09 01	
Penkridge	d	07 46								08 16								08 46					
Wolverhampton 7	a	07 58					08 13			08 28				08 39				08 58				09 13	
	d	08 00	08 07			08 11	08 17		08 20	08 31			08 37	08 41	08 45		08 50	09 00			09 11	09 17	
Coseley	d	08 05							08 25								08 55	09 05					
Tipton	d								08 28								08 58						
Dudley Port	d								08 30								09 00						
Sandwell & Dudley	d								08 34				08 46		08 55		09 04						
Smethwick Galton Bridge 7	d					08 23			08 37	08 41							09 07				09 22		
Smethwick Rolfe Street	d								08 39								09 09						
BirminghamNewStreet 12	a	08 18	08 25			08 29	08 33		08 45	08 48			08 55	08 58	09 05		09 15	09 18			09 29	09 33	
	d			08 30	08 33	08 36		08 39			08 50	08 54		09 04	09 10	09 14			09 30	09 33	09 36		09 39
Adderley Park	d							08 44															09 44
Stechford	d							08 47								09 20							09 47
Lea Hall	d							08 50								09 23							09 50
Marston Green	d				08 42							09 02				09 26				09 42			
Birmingham International	a			08 39	08 45	08 49		08 55			08 59	09 05		09 13	09 19	09 29			09 39	09 45	09 49		09 55
	d			08 40	08 45						09 00	09 05		09 14	09 20	09 30			09 40	09 45			
Hampton-in-Arden	d				08 48											09 33				09 48			
Berkswell	d											09 11				09 38							
Tile Hill	d				08 55							09 14				09 41				09 55			
Canley	d											09 17				09 44							
Coventry	a			08 50	09 00						09 10	09 20		09 24	09 30	09 47			09 50	10 00			
	d			08 51	09 00						09 11	09 25			09 31	09 48			09 51	10 00			
Rugby	d				09 12						09 23	09 38				09 59				10 12			
Long Buckby	d				09 21							09 47				10 08				10 21			
Northampton 66	a				09 33							09 59				10 20				10 33			
London Euston 15 ⊖66	a			09 53	10 46						10 13	11 19			10 32	11 27			10 56	11 46			

		LM 1 E	LM 1 A	VT ◇1 ⊠	LM 1	LM B	XC ◇1 F ⚒	VT ◇1 ⊠	VT ◇1 J ⊠	LM 1	LM E	LM 1 A	VT ◇1 ⊠	LM 1	AW C ⚒	XC ◇1 D ⚒	LM	LM 1 E	LM 1 A	VT ◇1 ⊠	LM 1	LM B
Stafford	d		09 10				09 25					09 40				10 01			10 10			
Penkridge	d		09 16									09 46							10 16			
Wolverhampton 7	a		09 27				09 41					09 57				10 13			10 27			
	d	09 20	09 31			09 37	09 42	09 45	09 45		09 50	10 00			10 10	10 17		10 20	10 31			10 37
Coseley	d	09 25									09 55	10 05						10 25				
Tipton	d	09 28									09 58							10 28				
Dudley Port	d	09 30									10 00							10 30				
Sandwell & Dudley	d	09 34				09 46		09 56	09 56		10 04							10 34				10 46
Smethwick Galton Bridge 7	d	09 37	09 41								10 07				10 21			10 37	10 41			
Smethwick Rolfe Street	d	09 39									10 09							10 39				
BirminghamNewStreet 12	a	09 45	09 48			09 55	09 58	10 05	10 05		10 15	10 18			10 30	10 33		10 45	10 48			10 55
	d			09 50	09 54		10 04	10 10	10 10	10 14			10 30	10 33	10 36		10 39			10 50	10 54	
Adderley Park	d																10 44					
Stechford	d									10 20							10 47					
Lea Hall	d									10 23							10 50					
Marston Green	d				10 02					10 26				10 42							11 02	
Birmingham International	a			09 59	10 05		10 13	10 19	10 19	10 29			10 39	10 45	10 49		10 55			10 59	11 05	
	d			10 00	10 05		10 14	10 20	10 20	10 30			10 40	10 45						11 00	11 05	
Hampton-in-Arden	d									10 33				10 48								
Berkswell	d				10 11					10 38											11 11	
Tile Hill	d				10 14					10 41				10 55							11 14	
Canley	d				10 17					10 44											11 17	
Coventry	a			10 10	10 20		10 24	10 30	10 30	10 47			10 50	11 00						11 10	11 20	
	d			10 11	10 21			10 30	10 31	10 48			10 51	11 00						11 11	11 21	
Rugby	d			10 23	10 32					10 59				11 12						11 23	11 32	
Long Buckby	d				10 41					11 08				11 21							11 41	
Northampton 66	a				10 54					11 20				11 33							11 54	
London Euston 15 ⊖66	a			11 15	12 18			11 34	11 34	12 27			11 55	12 46						12 14	13 19	

A From Liverpool Lime Street
B From Shrewsbury
C From Aberystwyth
D From Manchester Piccadilly to Bristol Temple Meads
E To Walsall
F From Manchester Piccadilly to Bournemouth
G From Lancaster
H From Crewe
I From Manchester Piccadilly to Paignton
J From Glasgow Central

Table T068-R

Mondays to Fridays

21 May to 7 December

Stafford - Wolverhampton - Birmingham - Coventry - Northampton

		XC	VT	LM	LM	LM	VT	LM	AW	XC	LM	LM	LM	VT	LM	LM	XC	VT	LM	LM	LM	VT
		◇■ A	◇■ B	■	■ C	■ D	◇■	■	◇ E	◇■ F		■ C	■ D	◇■	■	E	◇■ A	◇■ G	■	■ C	■ D	◇■
Stafford	d	10 25				10 40				11 01			11 10				11 25				11 40	
Penkridge	d					10 46							11 16								11 46	
Wolverhampton	a	10 39				10 57				11 13			11 27				11 39				11 57	
	d	10 41	10 45		10 50	11 00			11 09	11 17		11 20	11 31			11 37	11 41	11 45		11 50	12 00	
Coseley	d				10 55	11 05						11 25								11 55	12 05	
Tipton	d				10 58							11 28								11 58		
Dudley Port	d				11 00							11 30								12 00		
Sandwell & Dudley	d		10 55		11 04							11 34				11 46		11 55		12 04		
Smethwick Galton Bridge	d				11 07				11 20			11 37	11 41							12 07		
Smethwick Rolfe Street	d				11 09							11 39								12 09		
Birmingham New Street	a	10 58	11 05		11 15	11 18			11 30	11 33		11 45	11 48			11 55	11 58	12 05		12 15	12 18	
	d	11 04	11 10	11 14			11 30	11 33	11 36		11 39			11 50	11 54		12 04	12 10	12 14			12 30
Adderley Park	d										11 44											
Stechford	d			11 20							11 47								12 20			
Lea Hall	d			11 23							11 50								12 23			
Marston Green	d			11 26				11 42							12 02				12 26			
Birmingham International	a	11 13	11 19	11 29			11 39	11 45	11 49		11 55			11 59	12 05		12 13	12 19	12 29			12 39
	d	11 14	11 20	11 30			11 40	11 45						12 00	12 05		12 14	12 20	12 30			12 40
Hampton-in-Arden	d			11 33				11 48											12 33			
Berkswell	d			11 38											12 11				12 38			
Tile Hill	d			11 41				11 55							12 14				12 41			
Canley	d			11 44											12 17				12 44			
Coventry	a	11 24	11 30	11 47			11 50	11 59						12 10	12 20		12 24	12 30	12 47			12 50
	d		11 31	11 48			11 51	12 00						12 11	12 21			12 31	12 48			12 51
Rugby	d			11 59				12 18						12 23	12 32				12 59			
Long Buckby	d			12 08				12 27							12 41				13 08			
Northampton 66	a			12 20				12 41							12 54				13 21			
London Euston ⊖66	a		12 33	13 27			12 55	13 46						13 14	14 18			13 33	14 27			13 59

		LM	AW	XC	LM	LM	LM	VT	LM	LM	XC	VT	LM	LM	LM	VT	LM	AW	XC	LM	LM	LM	VT
		■	◇ H	◇■ F		C	■ D	◇■	■	E	◇■ A	◇■ B	■	■ C	■ D	◇■	■	◇ I	◇■ J		■ C	■ D	◇■
Stafford	d			12 01			12 10				12 25				12 40				13 01			13 10	
Penkridge	d						12 16								12 46							13 16	
Wolverhampton	a			12 13			12 27				12 39				12 57				13 13			13 27	
	d		12 11	12 17		12 20	12 31			12 37	12 41	12 45		12 50	13 00			13 10	13 17		13 20	13 31	
Coseley	d					12 25								12 55	13 05						13 25		
Tipton	d					12 28								12 58							13 28		
Dudley Port	d					12 30								13 00							13 30		
Sandwell & Dudley	d					12 34				12 46		12 55		13 04							13 34		
Smethwick Galton Bridge	d		12 22			12 37	12 41							13 07				13 22			13 37	13 41	
Smethwick Rolfe Street	d					12 39								13 09							13 39		
Birmingham New Street	a		12 30	12 33		12 45	12 48			12 55	12 58	13 05		13 15	13 18			13 29	13 33		13 45	13 48	
	d	12 33	12 36		12 39			12 50	12 54		13 04	13 10	13 14			13 30	13 33	13 36		13 39			13 50
Adderley Park	d				12 44															13 44			
Stechford	d				12 47								13 20							13 47			
Lea Hall	d				12 50								13 23							13 50			
Marston Green	d	12 42							13 02				13 26				13 42						
Birmingham International	a	12 45	12 49		12 55			12 59	13 05		13 13	13 19	13 29			13 39	13 45	13 49		13 55			13 59
	d	12 45						13 00	13 05		13 14	13 20	13 30			13 40	13 45						14 00
Hampton-in-Arden	d	12 48											13 33				13 48						
Berkswell	d								13 11				13 38										
Tile Hill	d	12 55							13 14				13 41				13 55						
Canley	d								13 17				13 44										
Coventry	a	13 00						13 10	13 20		13 24	13 30	13 47			13 50	14 00						14 10
	d	13 00						13 11	13 21			13 31	13 48			13 51	14 00						14 11
Rugby	d	13 12						13 23	13 32				13 59				14 12						14 26
Long Buckby	d	13 21							13 41				14 08				14 21						
Northampton 66	a	13 34							13 53				14 20				14 33						
London Euston ⊖66	a	14 47						14 14	15 19			14 33	15 27			14 55	15 48						15 16

A From Manchester Piccadilly to Bournemouth
B From Edinburgh
C To Walsall
D From Liverpool Lime Street
E From Shrewsbury
F From Manchester Piccadilly to Bristol Temple Meads
G From Glasgow Central
H From Pwllheli
I From Holyhead
J From Manchester Piccadilly to Exeter St Davids

Table T068-R

Mondays to Fridays

21 May to 7 December

Stafford - Wolverhampton - Birmingham - Coventry - Northampton

		LM	LM	XC	VT	LM	LM	LM	VT	LM	AW	XC	LM	LM	LM	VT	LM	LM	XC	VT	LM	LM
		■	A	◇■ B	◇■ C	■	■ D	■ E	◇■	■	◇ F	◇■ G		■ D	■ E	◇■	■	A	◇■ B	◇■ H	■	D
Stafford	d			13 26				13 40				14 01			14 10				14 25			
Penkridge	d							13 46							14 16							
Wolverhampton	a			13 39				13 57				14 13			14 27				14 39			
	d		13 37	13 41	13 45		13 50	14 00			14 11	14 17		14 20	14 31			14 37	14 41	14 45		14 50
Coseley	d						13 55	14 05						14 25								14 55
Tipton	d						13 58							14 28								14 58
Dudley Port	d						14 00							14 30								15 00
Sandwell & Dudley	d		13 46		13 55		14 04							14 34				14 46		14 55		15 04
Smethwick Galton Bridge	d						14 07				14 23			14 37	14 41							15 07
Smethwick Rolfe Street	d						14 09							14 39								15 09
Birmingham New Street	a		13 55	13 58	14 05		14 15	14 18			14 30	14 34		14 45	14 48			14 55	14 58	15 05		15 15
	d	13 54		14 04	14 10	14 14			14 30	14 33	14 36		14 39			14 50	14 54		15 04	15 10	15 14	
Adderley Park	d												14 44									
Stechford	d					14 20							14 47								15 20	
Lea Hall	d					14 23							14 50								15 23	
Marston Green	d	14 02				14 26				14 42							15 02				15 26	
Birmingham International	a	14 05		14 13	14 19	14 29			14 39	14 45	14 49		14 55			14 59	15 05		15 13	15 19	15 29	
	d	14 05		14 14	14 20	14 30			14 40	14 45						15 00	15 05		15 14	15 20	15 30	
Hampton-in-Arden	d					14 33				14 48											15 33	
Berkswell	d	14 11				14 38											15 11				15 38	
Tile Hill	d	14 14				14 41				14 55							15 14				15 41	
Canley	d	14 17				14 44											15 17				15 44	
Coventry	a	14 20		14 24	14 29	14 47			14 50	15 00						15 10	15 20		15 24	15 30	15 47	
	d	14 21			14 30	14 48			14 50	15 00						15 11	15 21			15 31	15 48	
Rugby	d	14 32				14 59				15 12						15 23	15 32				15 59	
Long Buckby	d	14 41				15 08				15 21							15 41				16 08	
Northampton 66	a	14 54				15 20				15 33							15 56				16 22	
London Euston ⊖66	a	16 19			15 33	16 27			15 56	16 46						16 14	17 19			16 32	17 27	

		LM	VT	LM	AW	XC	LM	LM	LM	VT	LM	LM	XC	VT	LM	LM	LM	VT	VT	LM	AW	XC	LM
		■ E	◇■	■	◇ I	◇■ J		■ D	■ E	◇■	■	A	◇■ B	◇■ C	■	D	■ E	◇■	◇■ A	■	◇ F	◇■ G	
Stafford	d	14 40				15 01			15 10				15 25				15 40					16 01	
Penkridge	d	14 46							15 16								15 46						
Wolverhampton	a	14 57				15 13			15 27				15 39				15 57					16 13	
	d	15 00			15 11	15 17		15 20	15 31			15 37	15 41	15 45		15 50	16 00		16 04		16 10	16 17	
Coseley	d	15 05						15 25								15 55	16 05						
Tipton	d							15 28								15 58							
Dudley Port	d							15 30								16 00							
Sandwell & Dudley	d							15 34				15 46		15 55		16 04							
Smethwick Galton Bridge	d				15 22			15 37	15 41							16 07					16 22		
Smethwick Rolfe Street	d							15 39								16 09							
Birmingham New Street	a	15 18			15 30	15 33		15 45	15 48			15 55	15 58	16 05		16 15	16 18		16 22		16 30	16 33	
	d		15 30	15 33	15 36		15 39			15 50	15 54		16 04	16 10	16 14			16 30	16 30	16 33	16 36		16 39
Adderley Park	d						15 44																16 44
Stechford	d						15 47								16 20								16 47
Lea Hall	d						15 50								16 23								16 50
Marston Green	d			15 42							16 02				16 26					16 42			
Birmingham International	a		15 39	15 45	15 49		15 55			15 59	16 05		16 13	16 19	16 29			16 39	16 39	16 45	16 49		16 55
	d		15 40	15 45						16 00	16 05		16 14	16 20	16 30			16 40	16 40	16 45			
Hampton-in-Arden	d			15 48											16 33					16 48			
Berkswell	d										16 11				16 38								
Tile Hill	d			15 55							16 14				16 41					16 55			
Canley	d										16 17				16 44								
Coventry	a		15 50	16 00						16 10	16 20		16 24	16 30	16 49			16 50	16 50	17 00			
	d		15 51	16 00						16 11	16 21			16 31				16 51	16 51	17 00			
Rugby	d			16 12						16 23	16 32									17 16			
Long Buckby	d			16 21							16 41									17 26			
Northampton 66	a			16 34							16 57									17 38			
London Euston ⊖66	a		16 56	17 46						17 14	18 17			17 33				17 56	17 56	18 46			

A From Shrewsbury
B From Manchester Piccadilly to Bournemouth
C From Glasgow Central
D To Walsall
E From Liverpool Lime Street
F From Pwllheli
G From Manchester Piccadilly to Bristol Temple Meads
H From Edinburgh
I From Holyhead
J From Manchester Piccadilly to Paignton

Table T068-R

Mondays to Fridays
21 May to 7 December

Stafford - Wolverhampton - Birmingham - Coventry - Northampton

		LM	LM	VT	LM	LM	XC	VT	LM	LM	LM	VT	LM	AW	XC	LM	LM	LM	VT	LM	LM	XC	VT
		■ A	■ B	◇■ ⊏	■	C	◇■ D ⊼	◇■ E ⊏	■	■	■ B	◇■ ⊠	■	■ F ⊼	◇■ G ⊼		A	■ B	◇■ ⊠	■	C	◇■ D ⊼	◇■ H ⊏
Stafford	d		16 10				16 25				16 40				17 01			17 10				17 25	
Penkridge	d		16 16								16 46							17 16					
Wolverhampton ■	a		16 27				16 39				16 58				17 13			17 27				17 39	
	d	16 20	16 31			16 37	16 41	16 45		16 50	17 00			17 09	17 17		17 20	17 31			17 37	17 41	17 45
Coseley	d	16 25								16 55	17 05						17 25						
Tipton	d	16 28								16 58							17 28						
Dudley Port	d	16 30								17 00							17 30						
Sandwell & Dudley	d	16 34				16 46		16 55		17 04							17 34				17 46		17 55
Smethwick Galton Bridge ■	d	16 37	16 41							17 07				17 22			17 37	17 41					
Smethwick Rolfe Street	d	16 39								17 09							17 39						
BirminghamNewStreet ■	a	16 45	16 48			16 55	16 58	17 05		17 15	17 18			17 30	17 33		17 45	17 48			17 55	17 58	18 05
	d			16 50	16 54		17 04	17 10	17 14	17 17		17 30	17 33	17 36		17 39			17 50	17 54		18 04	18 10
Adderley Park	d									17 22						17 44							
Stechford	d								17 20							17 47							
Lea Hall	d									17 26						17 50							
Marston Green	d				17 02					17 29			17 42							18 02			
Birmingham International	a			16 59	17 05		17 13	17 19	17 26	17 32		17 39	17 45	17 49		17 55			17 59	18 05		18 13	18 19
	d			17 00	17 05		17 14	17 20	17 27	17 33		17 40	17 45						18 00	18 05		18 14	18 20
Hampton-in-Arden	d									17 36			17 48										
Berkswell	d				17 11					17 40										18 11			
Tile Hill	d				17 14				17 35				17 55							18 14			
Canley	d				17 17				17 38											18 17			
Coventry	a			17 10	17 20		17 24	17 30	17 41	17 49		17 50	18 00						18 10			18 24	18 30
	d			17 11	17 21			17 31	17 42			17 51	18 00						18 10				18 31
Rugby	d			17 23	17 32				17 56				18 12						18 23				
Long Buckby	d				17 41				18 05				18 21										
Northampton 66	a				17 56				18 17				18 37										
London Euston ■ ⊖66	a			18 14	19 20			18 34	19 28			18 56	19 47						19 14	20 20			19 33

		LM	LM	LM	VT	LM	AW	XC	LM	LM	LM	VT	LM	LM	XC	VT	LM	LM	LM	VT	LM	AW	XC
		■	■ A	■ B	◇■ ⊠	■	◇ I ⊼	◇■ J ⊼		A	■ B	◇■ ⊠	■	C	◇■ D ⊼	■ ■ E ⊏	■		■ B	◇■ ⊏	■	◇ F ⊼	◇■ K ⊼
Stafford	d			17 40				18 01			18 10				18 25				18 40				19 01
Penkridge	d			17 46							18 16								18 46				
Wolverhampton ■	a			17 58				18 13			18 27				18 39				18 59				19 13
	d		17 50	18 00			18 11	18 17		18 20	18 31			18 37	18 41	18 45		18 50	19 00			19 11	19 17
Coseley	d		17 55	18 05						18 25								18 55	19 05				
Tipton	d		17 58							18 28								18 58					
Dudley Port	d		18 00							18 30								19 00					
Sandwell & Dudley	d		18 04							18 34				18 46		18 55		19 04					
Smethwick Galton Bridge ■	d		18 07				18 22			18 37	18 41							19 07				19 22	
Smethwick Rolfe Street	d		18 09							18 39								19 09					
BirminghamNewStreet ■	a		18 15	18 18			18 30	18 33		18 45	18 48			18 55	18 58	19 05		19 16	19 18			19 30	19 33
	d	18 14			18 30	18 33	18 36		18 39			18 50	18 54		19 04	19 10	19 14			19 30	19 33	19 36	
Adderley Park	d								18 44														
Stechford	d	18 20							18 47								19 20						
Lea Hall	d	18 23							18 50								19 23						
Marston Green	d	18 26				18 42							19 02				19 26				19 42		
Birmingham International	a	18 29			18 39	18 45	18 49		18 55			18 59	19 05		19 13	19 19	19 29			19 39	19 45	19 49	
	d	18 30			18 40	18 45						19 00	19 05		19 14	19 20	19 30			19 40	19 45		
Hampton-in-Arden	d	18 33				18 48											19 33				19 48		
Berkswell	d	18 38											19 11				19 38						
Tile Hill	d	18 41				18 55							19 14				19 41				19 55		
Canley	d	18 44											19 17				19 44						
Coventry	a	18 47			18 50	19 00						19 10	19 20		19 24	19 30	19 47			19 49	20 00		
	d	18 48			18 51	19 00						19 11	19 21			19 31	19 48			19 51	20 00		
Rugby	d	18 59				19 18						19 23	19 32				19 59			20 03	20 15		
Long Buckby	d	19 08				19 27							19 41				20 10				20 24		
Northampton 66	a	19 21				19 41							19 54				20 23				20 38		
London Euston ■ ⊖66	a	20 27			19 56	20 48						20 15	21 20			20 32	21 28			20 57			

A To Walsall
B From Liverpool Lime Street
C From Shrewsbury
D From Manchester Piccadilly to Bournemouth
E From Edinburgh
F From Holyhead
G From Manchester Piccadilly to Bristol Temple Meads
H From Glasgow Central
I From Pwllheli
J From Manchester Piccadilly to Cardiff Central
K From Manchester Piccadilly to Plymouth

Table T068-R

Mondays to Fridays
21 May to 7 December

Stafford - Wolverhampton - Birmingham - Coventry - Northampton

		LM	LM	LM	LM	LM	XC	VT	LM	LM	LM	LM	LM	AW	XC	LM	LM	VT	LM	LM	LM	XC	VT
			A	■ B	■	C	◇■ D ⊼	◇■ E ⊠	■		■ B	■ F	■	◇ G ⊼	◇■ H ⊼			◇■ ⊏	■ B	■	C	◇■ I ⊼	■ ■ J ⊠
Stafford	d			19 10			19 25				19 40	19 50			20 01				20 16			20 25	
Penkridge	d			19 16							19 46								20 21				
Wolverhampton ■	a			19 28			19 39				19 57				20 13				20 32			20 42	
	d		19 20	19 31		19 37	19 41	19 45		19 50	20 00			20 11	20 17		20 20		20 33		20 37	20 44	20 47
Coseley	d		19 25							19 55	20 05						20 25						
Tipton	d		19 28							19 58							20 28						
Dudley Port	d		19 30							20 00							20 30						
Sandwell & Dudley	d		19 34			19 46		19 55		20 04							20 34				20 46		20 57
Smethwick Galton Bridge ■	d		19 37	19 41						20 07				20 22			20 37		20 43				
Smethwick Rolfe Street	d		19 39							20 09							20 39						
BirminghamNewStreet ■	a		19 45	19 48		19 55	19 58	20 05		20 16	20 18			20 29	20 33		20 46		20 50		20 55	21 00	21 05
	d	19 39			19 54		20 04	20 10	20 14				20 33	20 36		20 39		20 50		20 54		21 04	21 10
Adderley Park	d	19 44														20 44							
Stechford	d	19 47							20 20							20 47							
Lea Hall	d	19 50							20 23							20 50							
Marston Green	d				20 02				20 26				20 42							21 02			
Birmingham International	a	19 55			20 05		20 13	20 19	20 29				20 45	20 49		20 55		20 59		21 05		21 13	21 19
	d				20 05		20 14	20 20	20 30				20 45					21 00		21 05		21 14	21 20
Hampton-in-Arden	d								20 33				20 48										
Berkswell	d				20 11				20 38											21 11			
Tile Hill	d				20 14				20 41				20 55							21 14			
Canley	d				20 17				20 44											21 17			
Coventry	a				20 20		20 24	20 30	20 49				21 00					21 10		21 20		21 24	21 30
	d				20 21			20 31					21 00					21 11		21 21			21 31
Rugby	d				20 32							20 47	21 14					21 23		21 32			
Long Buckby	d				20 41								21 23							21 41			
Northampton 66	a				20 53							21 07	21 35							21 54			
London Euston ■ ⊖66	a				22 23			21 37					22 52					22 13		23 21			22 41

		LM	LM	LM	LM	XC	LM	LM	LM	LM	LM	VT	LM	XC	XC	VT	LM	LM	LM	AW	LM	LM
		■		■ B	■ F	◇■ K	■		A	■ B	■	◇■ E ⊠	C	◇■ K	◇■ L	◇■ ⊏	■		■ B	◇ G	■	A
Stafford	d			20 40	21 00	21 01				21 10		21 14		21 25					21 40			
Penkridge	d			20 46						21 16									21 46			
Wolverhampton ■	a			20 57		21 13				21 27		21 30		21 39					21 57			
	d		20 50	21 00		21 17			21 20	21 29		21 32	21 37	21 41		21 45		21 50	22 00	22 11		22 20
Coseley	d		20 55	21 05					21 25									21 55	22 05			22 25
Tipton	d		20 58						21 28									21 58				22 28
Dudley Port	d		21 00						21 30									22 00				22 30
Sandwell & Dudley	d		21 04						21 34				21 46			21 55		22 04				22 34
Smethwick Galton Bridge ■	d		21 07						21 37	21 41								22 07		22 22		22 37
Smethwick Rolfe Street	d		21 09						21 39									22 09				22 39
BirminghamNewStreet ■	a		21 16	21 18		21 33			21 45	21 48		21 54	21 57	22 00		22 06		22 15	22 18	22 31		22 45
	d	21 14					21 34	21 39			21 54				22 04	22 10	22 14				22 34	
Adderley Park	d							21 44														
Stechford	d	21 20						21 47									22 20					
Lea Hall	d	21 23						21 50									22 23					
Marston Green	d	21 26					21 42				22 02						22 26				22 42	
Birmingham International	a	21 29					21 45	21 55			22 05				22 13	22 19	22 29				22 45	
	d	21 30					21 45				22 05				22 14	22 20	22 30				22 45	
Hampton-in-Arden	d	21 33					21 48										22 33				22 48	
Berkswell	d	21 38									22 11						22 38					
Tile Hill	d	21 41					21 55				22 14						22 41				22 55	
Canley	d	21 44									22 17						22 44					
Coventry	a	21 49					22 00				22 20				22 24	22 30	22 49				23 00	
	d						22 00				22 21					22 31						
Rugby	d				21 58		22 12				22 32					22 45						
Long Buckby	d						22 21				22 41											
Northampton 66	a				22 17		22 35				22 53											
London Euston ■ ⊖66	a										00 21					00 03						

A To Walsall
B From Liverpool Lime Street
C From Shrewsbury
D From Manchester Piccadilly to Bournemouth. ⊼ to BirminghamNewStreet
E From Glasgow Central
F From Crewe
G From Aberystwyth
H From Manchester Piccadilly to Bristol Temple Meads
I From Manchester Piccadilly to Southampton Central. ⊼ to BirminghamNewStreet
J From Edinburgh
K From Manchester Piccadilly
L To Reading

Table T068-R

Mondays to Fridays
21 May to 7 December

Stafford - Wolverhampton - Birmingham - Coventry - Northampton

		VT	VT	LM	XC	VT	LM	AW	LM		XC	LM
		◇■	◇■	■	◇■	◇■		◇	■		◇■	
		A	B ☒		C			D	E		C	
Stafford	d				22 26				22 40		23 04	
Penkridge	d								22 46			
Wolverhampton ■	a				22 41				22 59		23 17	
	d	22 29	22 33		22 42	22 45		22 55	23 00		23 18	
Coseley	d								23 05			
Tipton	d								23 08			
Dudley Port	d								23 10			
Sandwell & Dudley	d					22 55			23 14			
Smethwick Galton Bridge ■	d								23 17			
Smethwick Rolfe Street	d								23 19			
BirminghamNewStreet ■	a	22 48	22 52		22 59	23 06		23 28	23 26		23 35	
	d			22 54		23 10	23 14					23 54
Adderley Park	d						23 19					
Stechford	d						23 22					
Lea Hall	d						23 25					
Marston Green	d			23 02			23 27					00 02
Birmingham International	a			23 05		23 19	23 30					00 05
	d			23 05		23 20	23 31					00 06
Hampton-in-Arden	d						23 34					
Berkswell	d			23 11			23 39					
Tile Hill	d			23 14			23 42					
Canley	d			23 17			23 45					
Coventry	a			23 20		23 30	23 50					00 16
	d			23 21		23 31						
Rugby	d			23 32		23 44						
Long Buckby	d			23 41								
Northampton 66	a			23 55		00s05						
London Euston ■ ⊖66	a					01 13						

Saturdays
26 May to 8 December

		LM	VT	AW	XC	VT	LM	AW	VT	LM		AW	LM	LM	VT	LM	XC	VT	LM	LM		VT	LM	AW	XC
			◇■		◇■	◇■	■		◇■	■					◇■	■	◇■	◇■	■	■		◇■	■		◇■
		F		G	H			I				J		J			K			L				J	M
Stafford	d			05 25													06 26			06 31					07 01
Penkridge	d																			06 36					
Wolverhampton ■	a			05 39													06 38			06 47					07 12
	d			05 40		05 45		06 02	06 06					06 19	06 27		06 41	06 45		06 50		07 05		07 12	07 17
Coseley	d													06 24						06 55					
Tipton	d													06 27						06 58					
Dudley Port	d													06 29						07 00					
Sandwell & Dudley	d					05 55			06 17					06 32	06 37			06 56		07 04		07 15			
Smethwick Galton Bridge ■	d							06 13						06 36						07 07				07 23	
Smethwick Rolfe Street	d											←		06 38						07 09					
BirminghamNewStreet ■	a			05 58		06 05		06 19	06 26			06 19		06 44	06 47		06 57	07 06		07 15		07 25		07 30	07 33
	d		05 50		06 04	06 10	06 14	06 36	06 30	06 33		06 36	06 39		06 50	06 54	07 04	07 10	07 14			07 30	07 33	07 36	
Adderley Park	d							→					06 44												
Stechford	d						06 20						06 47						07 20						
Lea Hall	d						06 23						06 50						07 23						
Marston Green	d	00 02					06 26			06 42						07 02			07 26				07 42		
Birmingham International	a	00 05	06 00		06 13	06 19	06 29		06 39	06 45		06 49	06 55		06 59	07 05	07 13	07 19	07 29			07 39	07 45	07 49	
	d	00 06	06 00		06 14	06 20	06 30		06 40	06 45					07 00	07 05	07 14	07 20	07 30			07 40	07 45		
Hampton-in-Arden	d						06 33			06 48									07 33				07 48		
Berkswell	d						06 38									07 11			07 38						
Tile Hill	d						06 41			06 55						07 14			07 41				07 55		
Canley	d						06 44									07 17			07 44						
Coventry	a	00 16	06 10		06 24	06 30	06 47		06 49	07 00					07 10	07 20	07 24	07 30	07 47			07 50	08 00		
	d		06 11			06 31	06 48		06 51	07 00					07 11	07 21		07 31	07 48			07 51	08 00		
Rugby	d		06 24				06 59			07 12					07 23	07 32			07 59				08 12		
Long Buckby	d						07 08			07 21						07 41			08 08				08 21		
Northampton 66	a						07 20			07 36						07 54			08 20				08 36		
London Euston ■ ⊖66	a		07 15			07 36	08 46		07 53						08 17	09 19		08 33	09 27			08 54	09 49		

A From Bangor (Gwynedd)
B From Edinburgh
C From Manchester Piccadilly
D From Holyhead
E From Liverpool Lime Street
F From Birmingham New Street
G From Chester
H To Bournemouth
I From Shrewsbury to Birmingham International
J From Shrewsbury
K From Manchester Piccadilly to Bournemouth
L From Crewe
M From Manchester Piccadilly to Bristol Temple Meads

Table T068-R

Saturdays
26 May to 8 December

Stafford - Wolverhampton - Birmingham - Coventry - Northampton

		LM		LM	VT	LM	LM	LM		XC	VT	LM		LM	LM	VT	LM	AW	XC	LM	LM	LM		VT	LM
					◇■	■	■			◇■	◇■	■			■	◇■	■	◇	◇■			■		◇■	■
Stafford	d					07 10									07 40				08 01			08 10			
Penkridge	d					07 16									07 46							08 16			
Wolverhampton ■	a					07 27									07 57				08 13			08 27			
	d			07 20	07 25	07 31		07 37			07 45			07 50	08 00			08 11	08 17		08 20	08 31			
Coseley	d			07 25										07 55	08 05						08 25				
Tipton	d			07 28										07 58							08 28				
Dudley Port	d			07 30										08 00							08 30				
Sandwell & Dudley	d			07 34				07 46			07 55			08 04							08 34				
Smethwick Galton Bridge ■	d			07 36		07 41								08 07				08 23			08 37	08 41			
Smethwick Rolfe Street	d			07 38										08 09							08 39				
BirminghamNewStreet ■	a			07 44	07 47	07 50		07 55			08 05			08 15	08 18			08 29	08 33		08 45	08 48			
	d	07 39			07 50		07 54			08 04	08 10	08 14				08 30	08 33	08 36		08 39				08 50	08 54
Adderley Park	d	07 44																		08 44					
Stechford	d	07 47										08 20								08 47					
Lea Hall	d	07 50										08 23								08 50					
Marston Green	d						08 02					08 26					08 42								09 02
Birmingham International	a	07 55			07 59		08 05			08 13	08 20	08 29				08 39	08 45	08 49		08 55				08 59	09 05
	d				08 00		08 05			08 14	08 20	08 30				08 40	08 45							09 00	09 05
Hampton-in-Arden	d											08 33					08 48								
Berkswell	d						08 11					08 38													09 11
Tile Hill	d						08 14					08 41					08 55								09 14
Canley	d						08 17					08 44													09 17
Coventry	a				08 10		08 20			08 24	08 30	08 47				08 50	09 00							09 10	09 20
	d				08 11		08 21				08 31	08 48				08 51	09 00							09 11	09 21
Rugby	d				08 23		08 32					08 59					09 12							09 23	09 32
Long Buckby	d						08 41					09 08					09 21								09 41
Northampton 66	a						08 57					09 20					09 34								09 54
London Euston ■ ⊖66	a				09 13		10 19				09 34	10 27				09 57	10 46							10 15	11 19

		LM	XC	VT	VT	LM	LM	LM		VT	VT	LM	AW	XC	LM	LM	LM	VT		LM	LM	XC	VT	LM	LM
			◇■	◇■	◇■	■		■		◇■	◇■	■	◇	◇■			■	◇■		■		◇■	◇■	■	
Stafford	d		08 25					08 40						09 01			09 10					09 25			
Penkridge	d							08 46									09 16								
Wolverhampton ■	a		08 39					08 58						09 15			09 27					09 38			
	d	08 37	08 41	08 45			08 50	09 00			09 05		09 12	09 17		09 20	09 31				09 37	09 41	09 45		09 50
Coseley	d						08 55	09 05								09 25									09 55
Tipton	d						08 58									09 28									09 58
Dudley Port	d						09 00									09 30									10 00
Sandwell & Dudley	d	08 46		08 56			09 04									09 34					09 46		09 55		10 04
Smethwick Galton Bridge ■	d						09 07						09 23			09 37	09 41								10 07
Smethwick Rolfe Street	d						09 09									09 39									10 09
BirminghamNewStreet ■	a	08 55	08 58	09 05			09 15	09 18			09 21		09 27	09 33		09 45	09 48				09 55	09 58	10 05		10 15
	d		09 04		09 10	09 14				09 30	09 30	09 33	09 36		09 39			09 50		09 54		10 04	10 10	10 14	
Adderley Park	d														09 44										
Stechford	d					09 20									09 47									10 20	
Lea Hall	d					09 23									09 50									10 23	
Marston Green	d					09 26						09 42								10 02				10 26	
Birmingham International	a		09 13		09 19	09 29				09 39	09 39	09 45	09 50		09 55			09 59		10 05		10 13	10 19	10 29	
	d		09 14		09 20	09 30				09 40	09 40	09 45						10 00		10 05		10 14	10 20	10 30	
Hampton-in-Arden	d					09 33						09 48												10 33	
Berkswell	d					09 38														10 11				10 38	
Tile Hill	d					09 41						09 55								10 14				10 41	
Canley	d					09 44														10 17				10 44	
Coventry	a		09 24		09 30	09 47				09 50	09 50	10 00						10 10		10 20		10 24	10 30	10 47	
	d				09 31	09 48				09 51	09 51	10 00						10 11		10 21			10 31	10 48	
Rugby	d					09 59						10 12						10 23		10 32				10 59	
Long Buckby	d					10 08						10 21								10 41				11 08	
Northampton 66	a					10 20						10 34								10 54				11 20	
London Euston ■ ⊖66	a				10 33	11 27				10 56	10 56	11 46						11 14		12 19			11 33	12 27	

Stafford - Wolverhampton - Birmingham - Coventry - Northampton

	LM	VT	LM	AW	XC	LM	LM	LM	VT	LM	LM	XC	VT	LM	LM	LM	VT	LM	AW	XC	LM	LM
	■ A	◇■	■	B	◇■ C		D	■ A	◇■	■	E	◇■ F	◇■ G	■	D	■ A	◇■	■	H	◇■ C		D
Stafford d	09 40				10 01			10 10				10 25				10 40				11 01		
Penkridge d	09 46							10 16								10 46						
Wolverhampton a	09 58				10 13			10 27				10 39				10 57				11 13		
Wolverhampton d	10 00			10 10	10 17		10 20	10 31			10 37	10 41	10 45		10 50	11 00			11 11	11 17		11 20
Coseley d	10 05						10 25								10 55	11 05						11 25
Tipton d							10 28								10 58							11 28
Dudley Port d							10 30								11 00							11 30
Sandwell & Dudley d							10 34				10 46		10 55		11 04							11 34
Smethwick Galton Bridge d				10 21			10 37	10 41							11 07				11 22			11 37
Smethwick Rolfe Street d							10 39								11 09							11 39
Birmingham New Street a	10 18			10 30	10 33		10 45	10 48			10 55	10 58	11 05		11 15	11 18			11 28	11 33		11 45
Birmingham New Street d		10 30	10 33	10 36		10 39			10 50	10 54		11 04	11 10	11 14			11 30	11 33	11 36		11 39	
Adderley Park d						10 44															11 44	
Stechford d						10 47								11 20							11 47	
Lea Hall d						10 50								11 23							11 50	
Marston Green d			10 42							11 02				11 26				11 42				
Birmingham International a		10 39	10 45	10 50		10 55			10 59	11 05		11 13	11 19	11 29			11 39	11 45	11 50		11 55	
Birmingham International d		10 40	10 45						11 00	11 05		11 14	11 20	11 30			11 40	11 45				
Hampton-in-Arden d			10 48											11 33				11 48				
Berkswell d										11 11				11 38								
Tile Hill d			10 55							11 14				11 41				11 55				
Canley d										11 17				11 44								
Coventry a		10 50	11 00						11 09	11 20		11 24	11 30	11 47			11 50	12 00				
Coventry d		10 51	11 00						11 09	11 21			11 31	11 48			11 51	12 00				
Rugby d			11 12						11 23	11 32				11 59				12 12				
Long Buckby d			11 21							11 41				12 08				12 21				
Northampton 66 a			11 33							11 55				12 20				12 34				
London Euston ⊖66 a		11 55	12 46						12 13	13 19			12 33	13 27			12 55	13 46				

	LM	VT	LM	LM	XC	VT	LM	LM	LM	VT	LM	AW	XC	LM	LM	LM	VT	LM	LM	XC	VT	LM
	■ A	◇■	■	E	◇■ F	◇■ I	■	D	■ A	◇■	■	J	◇■ C		D	■ A	◇■	■	E	◇■ F	◇■ G	■
Stafford d	11 10				11 25				11 40				12 01			12 10				12 25		
Penkridge d	11 16								11 46							12 16						
Wolverhampton a	11 27				11 39				11 57				12 13			12 27				12 39		
Wolverhampton d	11 31			11 37	11 41	11 45		11 50	12 00			12 13	12 17		12 20	12 31			12 37	12 41	12 45	
Coseley d								11 55	12 05						12 25							
Tipton d								11 58							12 28							
Dudley Port d								12 00							12 30							
Sandwell & Dudley d				11 46		11 55		12 04							12 34				12 46		12 55	
Smethwick Galton Bridge d	11 41							12 07				12 24			12 37	12 41						
Smethwick Rolfe Street d								12 09							12 39							
Birmingham New Street a	11 48			11 55	11 59	12 05		12 15	12 18			12 32	12 34		12 45	12 48			12 55	12 58	13 05	
Birmingham New Street d		11 50	11 54		12 04	12 10	12 14			12 30	12 33	12 36		12 39			12 50	12 54		13 04	13 10	13 14
Adderley Park d														12 44								
Stechford d							12 20							12 47								13 20
Lea Hall d							12 23							12 50								13 23
Marston Green d			12 02				12 26				12 42							13 02				13 26
Birmingham International a		11 59	12 05		12 13	12 19	12 29			12 39	12 45	12 50		12 55			12 59	13 05		13 13	13 19	13 29
Birmingham International d		12 00	12 05		12 14	12 20	12 30			12 40	12 45						13 00	13 05		13 14	13 20	13 30
Hampton-in-Arden d							12 33				12 48											13 33
Berkswell d			12 11				12 38											13 11				13 38
Tile Hill d			12 14				12 41				12 55							13 14				13 41
Canley d			12 17				12 44											13 17				13 44
Coventry a		12 10	12 20		12 24	12 30	12 47			12 50	13 00						13 09	13 20		13 24	13 30	13 47
Coventry d		12 11	12 21			12 31	12 48			12 51	13 00						13 09	13 21			13 31	13 48
Rugby d		12 23	12 32				12 59				13 12						13 23	13 32				13 59
Long Buckby d			12 41				13 08				13 21							13 41				14 08
Northampton 66 a			12 54				13 20				13 34							13 54				14 20
London Euston ⊖66 a		13 14	14 19			13 33	14 27			13 58	14 46						14 13	15 19			14 33	15 27

A From Liverpool Lime Street
B From Barmouth
C From Manchester Piccadilly to Bristol Temple Meads
D To Walsall
E From Shrewsbury
F From Manchester Piccadilly to Bournemouth
G From Edinburgh
H From Holyhead
I From Glasgow Central
J From Pwllheli

Stafford - Wolverhampton - Birmingham - Coventry - Northampton

	LM	LM	VT	LM	AW	XC	LM	LM	LM	VT	LM	LM	XC	VT	LM	LM	LM	VT	LM	AW	XC	LM
	A	■ B	◇■	■	C	◇■ D		A	■ B	◇■	■	E	◇■ F	◇■ G	■	A	■ B	◇■	■	H	◇■ I	
Stafford d		12 40				13 01			13 10				13 25				13 40				14 01	
Penkridge d		12 46							13 16								13 46					
Wolverhampton a		12 58				13 14			13 27				13 39				13 58				14 15	
Wolverhampton d	12 50	13 00			13 10	13 17		13 20	13 31			13 37	13 41	13 45		13 50	14 00			14 12	14 17	
Coseley d	12 55	13 05						13 25								13 55	14 05					
Tipton d	12 58							13 28								13 58						
Dudley Port d	13 00							13 30								14 00						
Sandwell & Dudley d	13 04							13 34				13 46		13 55		14 04						
Smethwick Galton Bridge d	13 07				13 21			13 37	13 41							14 07				14 24		
Smethwick Rolfe Street d	13 09							13 39								14 09						
Birmingham New Street a	13 15	13 18			13 28	13 34		13 45	13 48			13 55	13 58	14 05		14 15	14 18			14 30	14 35	
Birmingham New Street d			13 30	13 33	13 35		13 39			13 50	13 54		14 04	14 10	14 14			14 30	14 33	14 36		14 39
Adderley Park d							13 44															14 44
Stechford d							13 47								14 20							14 47
Lea Hall d							13 50								14 23							14 50
Marston Green d				13 42							14 02				14 26				14 42			
Birmingham International a			13 39	13 45	13 50		13 55			13 59	14 05		14 13	14 19	14 29			14 39	14 45	14 49		14 55
Birmingham International d			13 40	13 45						14 00	14 05		14 14	14 20	14 30			14 40	14 45			
Hampton-in-Arden d				13 48											14 33				14 48			
Berkswell d											14 11				14 38							
Tile Hill d				13 55							14 14				14 41				14 55			
Canley d											14 17				14 44							
Coventry a			13 50	14 00						14 10	14 20		14 24	14 29	14 47			14 50	15 00			
Coventry d			13 51	14 00						14 11	14 21			14 30	14 48			14 51	15 00			
Rugby d				14 12						14 26	14 32				14 59				15 12			
Long Buckby d				14 21							14 41				15 08				15 21			
Northampton 66 a				14 34							14 54				15 20				15 34			
London Euston ⊖66 a			14 56	15 46						15 16	16 19			15 32	16 27			15 55	16 47			

	LM	LM	VT	LM	LM	XC	VT	LM	LM	LM	VT	LM	AW	XC	LM	LM	LM	VT	LM	LM	XC
	A	■ B	◇■	■	E	◇■ F	◇■ J	■	A	■ B	◇■	■	C	◇■ I		A	■ B	◇■	■	E	◇■ F
Stafford d		14 10				14 25				14 40				15 01			15 10				15 26
Penkridge d		14 16								14 46							15 16				
Wolverhampton a		14 27				14 39				14 57				15 13			15 27				15 39
Wolverhampton d	14 20	14 31			14 37	14 41	14 45		14 50	15 00			15 11	15 17		15 20	15 31			15 37	15 41
Coseley d	14 25								14 55	15 05						15 25					
Tipton d	14 28								14 58							15 28					
Dudley Port d	14 30								15 00							15 30					
Sandwell & Dudley d	14 34				14 46		14 55		15 04							15 34				15 46	
Smethwick Galton Bridge d	14 37	14 41							15 07				15 22			15 37	15 41				
Smethwick Rolfe Street d	14 39								15 09							15 39					
Birmingham New Street a	14 45	14 48			14 55	14 58	15 05		15 15	15 18			15 28	15 33		15 45	15 48			15 55	15 58
Birmingham New Street d			14 50	14 54		15 04	15 10	15 14			15 30	15 33	15 36		15 39			15 50	15 54		16 04
Adderley Park d															15 44						
Stechford d								15 20							15 47						
Lea Hall d								15 23							15 50						
Marston Green d				15 02				15 26				15 42							16 02		
Birmingham International a			14 59	15 05		15 13	15 19	15 29			15 39	15 45	15 50		15 55			15 59	16 05		16 13
Birmingham International d			15 00	15 05		15 14	15 20	15 30			15 40	15 45						16 00	16 05		16 14
Hampton-in-Arden d								15 33				15 48									
Berkswell d				15 11				15 38											16 11		
Tile Hill d				15 14				15 41				15 55							16 14		
Canley d				15 17				15 44											16 17		
Coventry a			15 09	15 20		15 24	15 30	15 47			15 50	16 00						16 10	16 20		16 24
Coventry d			15 09	15 21			15 31	15 48			15 51	16 00						16 11	16 21		
Rugby d			15 23	15 32				15 59				16 12						16 23	16 32		
Long Buckby d				15 41				16 08				16 21							16 41		
Northampton 66 a				15 54				16 20				16 34							16 54		
London Euston ⊖66 a			16 14	17 19			16 32	17 27			16 55	17 46						17 14	18 19		

A To Walsall
B From Liverpool Lime Street
C From Holyhead
D From Manchester Piccadilly to Exeter St Davids
E From Shrewsbury
F From Manchester Piccadilly to Bournemouth
G From Glasgow Central
H From Pwllheli
I From Manchester Piccadilly to Bristol Temple Meads
J From Edinburgh

Table T068-R

Saturdays

26 May to 8 December

Stafford - Wolverhampton - Birmingham - Coventry - Northampton

		VT	LM	LM	LM	VT	VT	LM	AW	XC	LM	LM	LM	VT	LM	LM	XC	VT	LM	LM	LM	VT	LM
		A		B	C		D		E	F		B	C			D	G	H		B	C		
Stafford	d				15 40					16 01			16 10				16 25				16 40		
Penkridge	d				15 46								16 16								16 46		
Wolverhampton	a				15 58					16 13			16 27				16 39				16 57		
	d	15 45		15 50	16 00		16 04		16 10	16 17		16 20	16 31			16 37	16 41	16 45		16 50	17 00		
Coseley	d			15 55	16 05							16 25								16 55	17 05		
Tipton	d			15 58								16 28								16 58			
Dudley Port	d			16 00								16 30								17 00			
Sandwell & Dudley	d	15 54		16 04								16 34				16 46		16 55		17 04			
Smethwick Galton Bridge	d			16 07					16 22			16 37	16 41							17 07			
Smethwick Rolfe Street	d			16 09								16 39								17 09			
BirminghamNewStreet	a	16 05		16 15	16 18				16 30	16 33		16 45	16 48			16 55	16 58	17 05		17 15	17 18		
	d	16 10	16 14			16 30		16 33	16 36		16 39			16 50	16 54		17 04	17 10	17 14			17 30	17 33
Adderley Park	d										16 44								17 18				
Stechford	d		16 20								16 47								17 22				
Lea Hall	d		16 23								16 50								17 24				
Marston Green	d		16 26					16 42							17 02				17 27				17 42
Birmingham International	a	16 19	16 29			16 39	16 39	16 45	16 48		16 55			16 59	17 05		17 13	17 19	17 30			17 39	17 45
	d	16 20	16 30			16 40	16 40	16 45						17 00	17 05		17 14	17 20	17 31			17 40	17 45
Hampton-in-Arden	d		16 33					16 48											17 34				17 48
Berkswell	d		16 38												17 11				17 39				
Tile Hill	d		16 41					16 55							17 14				17 42				17 55
Canley	d		16 44												17 17				17 45				
Coventry	a	16 30	16 47			16 49	16 50	17 00						17 10	17 20		17 24	17 30	17 48			17 50	18 00
	d	16 30	16 48			16 50	16 51	17 00						17 11	17 21			17 31	17 49			17 51	18 00
Rugby	d		16 59					17 12						17 23	17 32				17 59				18 12
Long Buckby	d		17 08					17 21							17 41				18 08				18 21
Northampton 66	a		17 20					17 34							17 53				18 21				18 34
London Euston 66	a	17 33	18 27			17 56	17 56	18 46						18 14	19 18			18 33	19 46			18 58	19 46

		AW	XC	LM	LM	LM	VT	LM	LM	XC	VT	LM	LM	LM	VT	LM	AW	XC	LM	LM	LM	VT
		I	F		B	C			D	G	A		B	C			E	J		B	C	
Stafford	d		17 01			17 10				17 25				17 40				18 01			18 10	
Penkridge	d					17 16								17 46							18 16	
Wolverhampton	a		17 13			17 27				17 39				17 57				18 14			18 28	
	d	17 09	17 17		17 20	17 31			17 37	17 41	17 45		17 50	18 00			18 11	18 17		18 20	18 31	
Coseley	d				17 25								17 55	18 05						18 25		
Tipton	d				17 28								17 58							18 28		
Dudley Port	d				17 30								18 00							18 30		
Sandwell & Dudley	d				17 34				17 46		17 55		18 04							18 34		
Smethwick Galton Bridge	d	17 22			17 37	17 41							18 07				18 22			18 37	18 41	
Smethwick Rolfe Street	d				17 39								18 09							18 39		
BirminghamNewStreet	a	17 28	17 33		17 45	17 48			17 55	17 58	18 05		18 15	18 18			18 30	18 33		18 45	18 48	
	d	17 36		17 39			17 50	17 54		18 04	18 10	18 14			18 30	18 33	18 36		18 39			18 50
Adderley Park	d			17 44															18 44			
Stechford	d			17 47								18 20							18 47			
Lea Hall	d			17 50								18 23							18 50			
Marston Green	d							18 02				18 26				18 42						
Birmingham International	a	17 50		17 55			17 59	18 05		18 13	18 19	18 29			18 39	18 45	18 49		18 55			18 59
	d						18 00	18 05		18 14	18 20	18 30			18 40	18 45						19 00
Hampton-in-Arden	d											18 33				18 48						
Berkswell	d							18 11				18 38										
Tile Hill	d							18 14				18 41				18 55						
Canley	d							18 17				18 44										
Coventry	a						18 09	18 20		18 24	18 30	18 47			18 50	19 00						19 10
	d						18 10	18 21			18 31	18 48			18 51	19 00						19 11
Rugby	d						18 26	18 32				18 59				19 12						19 23
Long Buckby	d							18 41				19 08				19 21						
Northampton 66	a							18 54				19 20				19 34						
London Euston 66	a						19 15	20 19			19 32	20 46			19 55							20 23

A From Glasgow Central
B To Walsall
C From Liverpool Lime Street
D From Shrewsbury
E From Pwllheli
F From Manchester Piccadilly to Bristol Temple Meads
G From Manchester Piccadilly to Bournemouth
H From Edinburgh
I From Holyhead
J From Manchester Piccadilly to Cardiff Central

Table T068-R

Saturdays

26 May to 8 December

Stafford - Wolverhampton - Birmingham - Coventry - Northampton

		LM	LM	XC	VT	LM	LM	LM	LM	LM	AW	XC	LM	LM	LM	LM	LM	XC	VT	LM	LM	LM
			A	B	C			D	E		F	G		H	D		A	I	J			D
Stafford	d			18 25				18 40	18 55			19 01			19 10			19 25				19 40
Penkridge	d							18 46							19 16							19 46
Wolverhampton	a			18 39				18 57				19 13			19 28			19 40				19 58
	d		18 37	18 41	18 45		18 50	19 00			19 11	19 17		19 20	19 31		19 37	19 41	19 45		19 50	20 00
Coseley	d						18 55	19 05						19 25							19 55	20 05
Tipton	d						18 58							19 28							19 58	
Dudley Port	d						19 00							19 30							20 00	
Sandwell & Dudley	d		18 46		18 55		19 04							19 34			19 46		19 55		20 04	
Smethwick Galton Bridge	d						19 07				19 22			19 37	19 41						20 07	
Smethwick Rolfe Street	d						19 09							19 39							20 09	
BirminghamNewStreet	a		18 55	18 58	19 05		19 16	19 18			19 28	19 33		19 45	19 48		19 55	19 59	20 05		20 16	20 18
	d	18 54		19 04	19 10	19 14				19 33	19 36		19 39			19 54		20 04	20 10	20 14		
Adderley Park	d												19 44									
Stechford	d					19 20							19 47							20 20		
Lea Hall	d					19 23							19 50							20 23		
Marston Green	d	19 02				19 26				19 42						20 02				20 26		
Birmingham International	a	19 05		19 13	19 19	19 29				19 45	19 49		19 55			20 05		20 13	20 19	20 29		
	d	19 05		19 14	19 20	19 30				19 45						20 05		20 14	20 20	20 30		
Hampton-in-Arden	d					19 33				19 48										20 33		
Berkswell	d	19 11				19 38										20 11				20 38		
Tile Hill	d	19 14				19 41				19 55						20 14				20 41		
Canley	d	19 17				19 44										20 17				20 44		
Coventry	a	19 20		19 24	19 30	19 47				20 00						20 20		20 24	20 30	20 49		
	d	19 21			19 31	19 48				20 00						20 21			20 31			
Rugby	d	19 32			19 43	19 59			19 52	20 12						20 32			20 43			
Long Buckby	d	19 41				20 08				20 21						20 41						
Northampton 66	a	19 53				20 20			20 12	20 35						20 53						
London Euston 66	a	21 12			20 53	21 46										22 12			21 56			

		LM	LM	AW	XC	LM	LM	LM	LM	LM	XC	VT	LM	LM	LM	VT	XC	LM	LM	LM	VT	LM	LM
		E		K	G		H	D		A	L	C			D		M			H	J		A
Stafford	d	19 51			20 01			20 10			20 25				20 40		21 01						
Penkridge	d							20 16							20 46								
Wolverhampton	a				20 13			20 29			20 39				20 57		21 13						
	d			20 11	20 17		20 20	20 31		20 37	20 41	20 45		20 50	21 00	21 09	21 17			21 20	21 34		21 37
Coseley	d						20 25							20 55	21 05					21 25			
Tipton	d						20 28							20 58						21 28			
Dudley Port	d						20 30							21 00						21 30			
Sandwell & Dudley	d						20 34			20 46		20 55		21 04		21 19				21 34			21 46
Smethwick Galton Bridge	d			20 22			20 37	20 41						21 07						21 37			
Smethwick Rolfe Street	d						20 39							21 09						21 39			
BirminghamNewStreet	a			20 29	20 33		20 45	20 48		20 55	20 58	21 05		21 16	21 18	21 28	21 33			21 45	21 51		21 56
	d		20 33	20 35		20 39			20 54		21 04	21 10	21 14			21 30		21 34	21 39			21 54	
Adderley Park	d					20 44													21 44				
Stechford	d					20 47							21 20						21 47				
Lea Hall	d					20 50							21 23						21 50				
Marston Green	d		20 42						21 02				21 26					21 42				22 02	
Birmingham International	a		20 45	20 49		20 55			21 05		21 13	21 19	21 29			21 39		21 45	21 55			22 05	
	d		20 45						21 05		21 14	21 20	21 30			21 40		21 45				22 05	
Hampton-in-Arden	d		20 48										21 33					21 48					
Berkswell	d								21 11				21 38									22 11	
Tile Hill	d		20 55						21 14				21 41					21 55				22 14	
Canley	d								21 17				21 44									22 17	
Coventry	a		21 00						21 20		21 24	21 30	21 49			21 50		22 00				22 20	
	d		21 00						21 21			21 31				21 51		22 00				22 21	
Rugby	d	20 47	21 12						21 32			21 43				22 03		22 12				22 32	
Long Buckby	d		21 21						21 41									22 21				22 41	
Northampton 66	a	21 06	21 35						21 53									22 33				22 53	
London Euston 66	a	22 38							23 27			22 53				23 33		00 06					

A From Shrewsbury
B From Manchester Piccadilly to Bournemouth
C From Edinburgh
D From Liverpool Lime Street
E From Crewe
F From Holyhead
G From Manchester Piccadilly to Bristol Temple Meads
H To Walsall
I From Manchester Piccadilly to Bournemouth. ⚲ to BirminghamNewStreet
J From Glasgow Central
K From Aberystwyth
L From Manchester Piccadilly to Southampton Central. ⚲ to BirminghamNewStreet
M From Manchester Piccadilly

Table T068-R

Stafford - Wolverhampton - Birmingham - Coventry - Northampton

Saturdays

26 May to 8 December

		XC ◇1 A	LM 1	LM	LM 1 B	AW ◇ C	XC ◇1 A	LM 1	LM D	VT ◇1 E	LM 1	LM F	VT ◇1 G	XC ◇1 A	LM	LM	LM 1 B	AW ◇ H
Stafford	d	21 25			21 40		22 01			22 08			22 25	22 30			22 40	
Penkridge	d				21 46												22 46	
Wolverhampton 7	a	21 40			21 58		22 13			22 22			22 39	22 42			22 58	
	d	21 42		21 50	22 00	22 09	22 17		22 20	22 23		22 37	22 40	22 45		22 50	23 00	23 09
Coseley	d			21 55	22 05				22 25							22 55	23 05	
Tipton	d			21 58					22 28							22 58		
Dudley Port	d			22 00					22 30							23 00		
Sandwell & Dudley	d			22 04					22 34			22 46				23 04		
Smethwick Galton Bridge 7	d			22 07		22 20			22 37							23 07		
Smethwick Rolfe Street	d			22 09					22 39							23 09		
BirminghamNewStreet 12	a	21 59		22 16	22 18	22 31	22 33		22 45	22 48		22 55	22 58	23 01		23 16	23 18	23 30
	d		22 14					22 34			22 54				23 14			
Adderley Park	d														23 18			
Stechford	d		22 20												23 22			
Lea Hall	d		22 23												23 24			
Marston Green	d		22 26					22 42			23 02				23 27			
Birmingham International ✈	a		22 29					22 45			23 05				23 30			
	d		22 30					22 45			23 05				23 31			
Hampton-in-Arden	d		22 33					22 48							23 34			
Berkswell	d		22 38								23 11				23 39			
Tile Hill	d		22 41					22 55			23 14				23 42			
Canley	d		22 44								23 17				23 45			
Coventry	a		22 47					23 00			23 20				23 49			
	d		22 48								23 21							
Rugby	d		22 59								23 32							
Long Buckby	d		23 08								23 41							
Northampton 66	a		23 21								23 55							
London Euston 15 ⊖66	a		00 40															

Sundays

20 May to 2 December

		VT ◇1	LM 1	LM 1	LM	XC ◇1 I	LM 1	AW F	VT ◇1	LM 1	LM D	XC ◇1 J	LM 1	AW F	VT ◇1	LM 1	LM 1 K	LM D	XC ◇1 J	LM 1	AW ◇ L	LM 1 K	VT ◇1
Stafford	d											09 26					10 19		10 25			10 42	
Penkridge	d																					10 48	
Wolverhampton 7	a											09 40							10 38			11 01	
	d	08 05			08 22			09 00	09 05		09 22	09 41		09 59	10 05			10 22	10 41		10 57	11 02	11 05
Coseley	d				08 28						09 27							10 27					
Tipton	d				08 31						09 30							10 30					
Dudley Port	d				08 33						09 32							10 32					
Sandwell & Dudley	d	08 15			08 36				09 15		09 36				10 15			10 36					11 15
Smethwick Galton Bridge 7	d				08 40						09 38							10 38				11 12	
Smethwick Rolfe Street	d				08 42						09 40							10 40					
BirminghamNewStreet 12	a	08 24			08 49			09 15	09 24		09 46	09 57		10 14	10 24			10 46	10 57		11 13	11 19	11 26
	d	08 30	08 34	08 38		09 04	09 14	09 20	09 30	09 36		10 04	10 14	10 20	10 30	10 36			11 04	11 14	11 19		11 30
Adderley Park	d			08 42						09 41						10 41							
Stechford	d			08 46						09 44						10 44							
Lea Hall	d			08 48						09 47						10 47							
Marston Green	d		08 42	08 52			09 22			09 50			10 22			10 50				11 22			
Birmingham International ✈	a	08 39	08 45	08 55		09 13	09 25	09 32	09 39	09 53		10 13	10 25	10 32	10 39	10 53			11 13	11 25	11 31		11 39
	d	08 40	08 45			09 14	09 25		09 40	09 53		10 14	10 25		10 40	10 53			11 14	11 25			11 40
Hampton-in-Arden	d						09 28						10 28							11 28			
Berkswell	d		08 51				09 33						10 33							11 33			
Tile Hill	d		08 54				09 36						10 36							11 36			
Canley	d		08 57				09 40						10 40							11 40			
Coventry	a	08 50	09 00			09 24	09 44		09 50	10 04		10 24	10 44		10 50	11 04			11 24	11 44			11 50
	d	08 51					09 44		09 51				10 44		10 51					11 44			11 51
Rugby	d	09 04					09 55		10 04				10 55		11 04		11 20			11 55			12 05
Long Buckby	d						10 05						11 05				11 29			12 05			
Northampton 66	a						10 17						11 17				11 41			12 17			
London Euston 15 ⊖66	a	10 25					11 59		11 31				12 38		12 25		13 01			13 38			13 04

A From Manchester Piccadilly
B From Liverpool Lime Street
C From Aberystwyth
D To Walsall
E From Glasgow Central
F From Shrewsbury
G From Edinburgh
H From Holyhead
I To Bournemouth
J From Manchester Piccadilly to Bournemouth
K From Crewe
L From Chester

Table T068-R

Stafford - Wolverhampton - Birmingham - Coventry - Northampton

Sundays

20 May to 2 December

		LM 1	LM A	VT ◇1	VT ◇1 B	XC ◇1 C	VT ◇1	LM 1 D	LM 1	VT ◇1	XC ◇1 E	LM 1	AW F	LM A	VT ◇1	VT ◇1 B	XC ◇1 C	VT ◇1	LM 1 D	LM 1	LM 1 G	VT ◇1
Stafford	d					11 27		11 19									12 25		12 19		12 40	
Penkridge	d																				12 46	
Wolverhampton 7	a					11 41											12 38				12 56	
	d		11 22		11 32	11 42	11 45						12 17	12 22		12 32	12 41	12 45			12 58	
Coseley	d		11 27											12 27								
Tipton	d		11 30											12 30								
Dudley Port	d		11 32											12 32								
Sandwell & Dudley	d		11 36				11 55							12 36				12 55				
Smethwick Galton Bridge 7	d		11 38											12 38							13 08	
Smethwick Rolfe Street	d		11 40											12 40								
BirminghamNewStreet 12	a		11 46		11 50	11 58	12 06						12 33	12 46		12 50	12 57	13 06			13 15	
	d	11 36		11 50		12 04	12 10		12 14	12 30	12 33	12 36	12 41		12 50		13 04	13 10		13 14		13 30
Adderley Park	d	11 41										12 41										
Stechford	d	11 44										12 44										
Lea Hall	d	11 47										12 47										
Marston Green	d	11 50							12 22			12 50								13 22		
Birmingham International ✈	a	11 53		11 59		12 13	12 19		12 25	12 39	12 43	12 53	13 02		12 59		13 13	13 19		13 25		13 39
	d	11 53		12 00		12 14	12 20		12 25	12 40	12 44	12 53			13 00		13 14	13 20		13 25		13 40
Hampton-in-Arden	d								12 28											13 28		
Berkswell	d								12 33											13 33		
Tile Hill	d								12 36			13 01								13 36		
Canley	d								12 40											13 40		
Coventry	a	12 04		12 10		12 24	12 30		12 44	12 50	12 54	13 06			13 10		13 24	13 30		13 44		13 50
	d			12 11			12 31		12 44	12 51					13 11			13 31		13 44		13 51
Rugby	d			12 25				12 20	12 55						13 27				13 20	13 55		
Long Buckby	d							12 29	13 05										13 29	14 05		
Northampton 66	a							12 41	13 17										13 41	14 17		
London Euston 15 ⊖66	a			13 18			13 38	13 53	14 38	13 57					14 19			14 36	14 53	15 38		14 57

		LM 1	AW ◇ H	LM A	VT ◇1	XC ◇1 C	VT ◇1 I	LM 1 D	LM 1	LM 1 G	VT ◇1	XC ◇1 J	AW K	XC ◇1 L	LM 1	AW F	LM A	VT ◇1	XC ◇1 C	VT ◇1 M	LM 1 D	LM 1	LM 1 G
Stafford	d					13 25		13 19		13 40				14 02					14 25		14 19		14 40
Penkridge	d									13 46													14 46
Wolverhampton 7	a					13 37				13 57				14 15					14 39				14 57
	d		13 08	13 22		13 41	13 45			13 58			14 08	14 17			14 22		14 41	14 45			14 58
Coseley	d			13 27													14 27						
Tipton	d			13 30													14 30						
Dudley Port	d			13 32													14 32						
Sandwell & Dudley	d			13 36			13 55										14 36			14 55			
Smethwick Galton Bridge 7	d			13 38						14 08							14 38						15 08
Smethwick Rolfe Street	d			13 40												←	14 40						
BirminghamNewStreet 12	a		13 23	13 46		13 57	14 06			14 15			14 23	14 33		14 23	14 46		14 57	15 06			15 15
	d	13 36	13 39		13 50	14 04	14 10		14 14		14 30	14 33	14 39		14 36	14 39		14 50	15 04	15 10		15 14	
Adderley Park	d	13 41											→		14 41								
Stechford	d	13 44													14 44								
Lea Hall	d	13 47													14 47								
Marston Green	d	13 50							14 22						14 50							15 22	
Birmingham International ✈	a	13 53	13 57		14 00	14 13	14 19		14 25		14 39	14 43			14 53	15 00		15 00	15 13	15 19		15 25	
	d	13 53			14 00	14 14	14 20		14 25		14 40	14 44			14 53			15 00	15 14	15 20		15 25	
Hampton-in-Arden	d								14 28													15 28	
Berkswell	d								14 33													15 33	
Tile Hill	d	14 01							14 36						15 01							15 36	
Canley	d								14 40													15 40	
Coventry	a	14 06			14 10	14 24	14 30		14 44		14 50	14 54			15 06			15 11	15 24	15 30		15 44	
	d				14 11		14 31		14 44		14 51							15 11		15 31		15 44	
Rugby	d				14 22			14 20	14 55									15 25			15 20	15 55	
Long Buckby	d							14 29	15 05												15 29	16 05	
Northampton 66	a							14 41	15 17												15 41	16 17	
London Euston 15 ⊖66	a				15 15		15 37	15 53	16 38		15 57							16 18		16 37	16 53	17 38	

A To Walsall
B From Preston
C From Manchester Piccadilly to Bournemouth
D From Crewe
E To Reading
F From Aberystwyth
G From Liverpool Lime Street
H From Chester
I From Lancaster
J From Derby to Reading
K From Aberystwyth to Birmingham International
L From Manchester Piccadilly to Paignton
M From Edinburgh

Stafford - Wolverhampton - Birmingham - Coventry - Northampton

		VT	AW	XC	LM	AW	LM	VT	XC	VT	VT	LM	LM	LM	VT	VT	XC	AW	XC	LM	AW	LM	VT
		◇	◇ A	◇ B		◇ C	D	◇	◇ E	◇ F	◇ G	H		I	◇	◇ J	◇ K	L	◇ B		M	D	◇
Stafford	d			15 01					15 25			15 19		15 40					16 01				
Penkridge	d													15 46									
Wolverhampton	a			15 14					15 38					15 57					16 14				
	d		15 08	15 17			15 22		15 41	15 45	15 45			15 58		16 04		16 09	16 17			16 22	
Coseley	d						15 27															16 27	
Tipton	d						15 30															16 30	
Dudley Port	d						15 32															16 32	
Sandwell & Dudley	d						15 36			15 55	15 55											16 36	
Smethwick Galton Bridge	d						15 38							16 08								16 38	
Smethwick Rolfe Street	d					←	15 40														←	16 40	
BirminghamNewStreet	a		15 24	15 33		15 24	15 46		15 57	16 06	16 06			16 15		16 20		16 25	16 33		16 25	16 46	
	d	15 30	15 39		15 36	15 39		15 50	16 04	16 10	16 10		16 14		16 30	16 30	16 33	16 39		16 36	16 39		16 50
Adderley Park	d		→		15 41													→		16 41			
Stechford	d				15 44															16 44			
Lea Hall	d				15 47															16 47			
Marston Green	d				15 50								16 22							16 50			
Birmingham International	a	15 39			15 53	15 57		16 00	16 13	16 19	16 19		16 25		16 39	16 39	16 43			16 53	17 00		16 59
	d	15 40			15 53			16 00	16 14	16 19	16 19		16 25		16 40	16 40	16 44			16 53			17 00
Hampton-in-Arden	d												16 28										
Berkswell	d												16 33										
Tile Hill	d				16 01								16 36							17 01			
Canley	d												16 40										
Coventry	a	15 50			16 06			16 11	16 24	16 30	16 30		16 44		16 50	16 50	16 54			17 06			17 11
	d	15 51						16 11		16 30	16 31		16 44		16 51	16 51							17 11
Rugby	d							16 24				16 20	16 55										17 25
Long Buckby	d											16 29	17 05										
Northampton 66	a											16 41	17 17										
London Euston ⊖66	a	16 57						17 17		17 36	17 36	17 53	18 38		17 57	17 57							18 18

		XC	VT	LM	LM	LM	VT	XC	LM	AW	LM	VT	XC	VT	VT	LM	LM	LM	VT	XC	AW	XC	LM
		◇ E	◇ N	H		I	◇	◇ B		◇ C	D	◇	◇ E	◇ G	◇ F	H		I	◇	◇ O	P	◇ Q	
Stafford	d	16 25		16 19		16 40		17 01					17 25			17 19		17 40				18 02	
Penkridge	d					16 46												17 46					
Wolverhampton	a	16 39				16 57		17 14					17 39					17 57				18 15	
	d	16 41	16 45			16 58		17 15		17 19	17 22		17 41	17 45	17 45			17 58			18 09	18 17	
Coseley	d										17 27												
Tipton	d										17 30												
Dudley Port	d										17 32												
Sandwell & Dudley	d		16 55								17 36			17 55	17 56								
Smethwick Galton Bridge	d					17 08					17 38							18 08					
Smethwick Rolfe Street	d										17 40												
BirminghamNewStreet	a	16 57	17 06			17 15		17 32		17 37	17 46		17 57	18 05	18 05			18 15			18 27	18 33	
	d	17 04	17 10		17 14		17 30		17 36	17 39		17 50	18 04	18 10	18 10		18 14		18 30	18 33	18 39		18 36
Adderley Park	d								17 41												→		18 41
Stechford	d								17 44														18 44
Lea Hall	d								17 47														18 47
Marston Green	d				17 22				17 50								18 22						18 50
Birmingham International	a	17 13	17 19		17 25		17 39		17 53	17 57		17 59	18 13	18 19	18 19		18 25		18 39	18 43			18 53
	d	17 14	17 20		17 25		17 40		17 53			18 00	18 14	18 20	18 20		18 25		18 40	18 44			18 53
Hampton-in-Arden	d				17 28												18 28						
Berkswell	d				17 33												18 33						
Tile Hill	d				17 36				18 01								18 36						19 01
Canley	d				17 40												18 40						
Coventry	a	17 24	17 29		17 44		17 50		18 06			18 10	18 24	18 30	18 30		18 44		18 50	18 54			19 06
	d		17 30		17 44		17 51					18 11		18 31	18 32		18 44		18 51				
Rugby	d			17 20	17 55							18 25				18 20	18 55						
Long Buckby	d			17 29	18 05											18 29	19 05						
Northampton 66	a			17 41	18 17											18 41	19 17						
London Euston ⊖66	a		18 36	18 53	19 38		18 57					19 17		19 37	19 37	19 53	20 38		19 57				

A From Chester to Birmingham International
B From Manchester Piccadilly to Bristol Temple Meads
C From Chester
D To Walsall
E From Manchester Piccadilly to Bournemouth
F Until 9 September. From Carlisle
G From 16 September. From Glasgow Central
H From Crewe
I From Liverpool Lime Street
J From Shrewsbury
K From Newcastle to Reading
L From Aberystwyth to Birmingham International
M From Aberystwyth
N From Edinburgh
O From Edinburgh to Reading
P From Pwllheli to Birmingham International
Q From Manchester Piccadilly to Paignton

Table T068-R

Sundays
20 May to 2 December

Stafford - Wolverhampton - Birmingham - Coventry - Northampton

		AW	LM	VT	XC	VT	LM	LM	LM	VT	XC	AW	XC	LM	AW	LM	XC	VT	LM	LM	LM	VT	AW
		A	B	◇	◇ C	◇ D	E		F	◇	◇ G	◇ H	◇ I		◇ J	B	◇ K	◇ L	E		F	◇	◇ M
Stafford	d				18 25		18 19		18 40				19 02				19 25		19 22		19 40		
Penkridge	d								18 46												19 46		
Wolverhampton	a				18 37				18 57				19 15				19 38				19 57		
	d		18 22		18 41	18 45			18 58			19 08	19 17			19 22	19 41	19 45			19 58		20 07
Coseley	d		18 27													19 27							
Tipton	d		18 30													19 30							
Dudley Port	d		18 32													19 32							
Sandwell & Dudley	d		18 36			18 55										19 36		19 55					
Smethwick Galton Bridge	d		18 38						19 08							19 38					20 08		
Smethwick Rolfe Street	d	←	18 40												←	19 40							
BirminghamNewStreet	a	18 27	18 46		18 57	19 06			19 15			19 26	19 33		19 26	19 46	19 57	20 06			20 15		20 25
	d	18 39		18 50	19 04	19 10		19 14		19 30	19 33	19 39		19 36	19 39		20 04	20 10		20 14		20 30	20 39
Adderley Park	d											→		19 41									→
Stechford	d													19 44									
Lea Hall	d													19 47									
Marston Green	d							19 22						19 50						20 22			
Birmingham International	a	19 00		18 59	19 13	19 19		19 25		19 39	19 43			19 53	19 57		20 13	20 19		20 25		20 39	
	d			19 00	19 14	19 20		19 25		19 40	19 44			19 53			20 14	20 20		20 25		20 40	
Hampton-in-Arden	d							19 28												20 28			
Berkswell	d							19 33												20 33			
Tile Hill	d							19 36						20 01						20 36			
Canley	d							19 40												20 40			
Coventry	a			19 10	19 24	19 30		19 44		19 50	19 54			20 06			20 24	20 30		20 44		20 51	
	d			19 11		19 31		19 44		19 51								20 31		20 44		20 51	
Rugby	d			19 26			19 20	19 55											20 17	20 55		21 05	
Long Buckby	d						19 29	20 05											20 26	21 05			
Northampton 66	a						19 41	20 17											20 38	21 17			
London Euston ⊖66	a			20 18		20 37	20 54	21 43		20 57								21 46	21 58	22 48		22 22	

		XC	LM	AW	LM	LM	VT	XC	LM	LM	VT	AW	XC	LM	AW	LM	AW	LM	LM	LM	VT	AW
		◇ I		◇ N	E	B	◇ D	◇ O		F	◇	◇ H	◇ I		◇ J	B	◇ P	E		F	◇	◇ M
Stafford	d	20 02			20 19			20 26		20 40			21 02				21 13	21 27		21 40		
Penkridge	d									20 46										21 46		
Wolverhampton	a	20 15						20 38		20 57			21 15				21 29			21 57		
	d	20 17				20 22	20 33	20 41		20 58	21 05	21 12	21 17			21 22	21 35			21 58	22 05	22 09
Coseley	d					20 27										21 27						
Tipton	d					20 30										21 30						
Dudley Port	d					20 32										21 32						
Sandwell & Dudley	d					20 36					21 17					21 36					22 16	
Smethwick Galton Bridge	d					20 38				21 08						21 38				22 08		
Smethwick Rolfe Street	d			←		20 40									←	21 40						
BirminghamNewStreet	a	20 33		20 25		20 46	20 51	20 57		21 15	21 26	21 29	21 33		21 29	21 46	21 53			22 15	22 24	22 27
	d		20 36	20 39				21 04	21 14		21 30	21 39		21 36	21 39		21 56		22 14		22 30	22 39
Adderley Park	d		20 41									→		21 41								→
Stechford	d		20 44											21 44								
Lea Hall	d		20 47											21 47								
Marston Green	d		20 50						21 22					21 50					22 22			
Birmingham International	a		20 53	21 01				21 13	21 25		21 39			21 53	21 57		22 08		22 25		22 39	
	d		20 53					21 14	21 25		21 40			21 53					22 25		22 40	
Hampton-in-Arden	d								21 28										22 28			
Berkswell	d								21 33										22 33			
Tile Hill	d		21 01						21 36										22 36			
Canley	d								21 40										22 40			
Coventry	a		21 06					21 23	21 44		21 50			22 04					22 44		22 50	
	d								21 44		21 51								22 44		22 51	
Rugby	d				21 20				21 55		22 04							22 22	22 55		23 04	
Long Buckby	d				21 29				22 05									22 31	23 05			
Northampton 66	a				21 41				22 17									22 44	23 19			
London Euston ⊖66	a				23 17				23 43		23 23										00 25	

A From Pwllheli
B To Walsall
C From Manchester Piccadilly to Bournemouth
D From Edinburgh
E From Crewe
F From Liverpool Lime Street
G From Newcastle to Reading
H From Chester to Birmingham International
I From Manchester Piccadilly to Bristol Temple Meads
J From Chester
K From Manchester Piccadilly to Southampton Central
L From Glasgow Central
M From Aberystwyth to Birmingham International
N From Aberystwyth
O From Manchester Piccadilly to Reading. ⚲ to BirminghamNewStreet
P From Holyhead

Table T068-R

Sundays
20 May to 2 December

Stafford - Wolverhampton - Birmingham - Coventry - Northampton

Station		VT	LM	AW	XC	LM	VT	VT	LM	LM	XC
		◇■	■	◇	◇■		◇■	◇■	■	■	◇■
		A		B	C	D	E			F	C
		🍴					🍴	🍴			
Stafford	d	22 01			22 05					22 40	23 02
Penkridge	d									22 46	
Wolverhampton ■ ⇌	a	22 14			22 18					22 57	23 15
	d	22 16			22 19	22 25	22 32	22 37		22 58	23 17
Coseley	d					22 30					
Tipton	d					22 33					
Dudley Port	d					22 35					
Sandwell & Dudley	d					22 39		22 48			
Smethwick Galton Bridge ■	d					22 41				23 08	
Smethwick Rolfe Street	d			←		22 43					
BirminghamNewStreet ■ ⇌	a	22 33		22 27	22 36	22 49	22 53	22 56		23 16	23 33
	d		22 36	22 39				23 00	23 14		
Adderley Park	d		22 41						23 18		
Stechford	d		22 44						23 22		
Lea Hall	d		22 47						23 24		
Marston Green	d		22 50						23 27		
Birmingham International ✈	a		22 53	23 01				23 10	23 30		
	d		22 53					23 10	23 31		
Hampton-in-Arden	d								23 34		
Berkswell	d								23 39		
Tile Hill	d								23 42		
Canley	d								23 45		
Coventry	a		23 04					23 21	23 49		
	d							23 21			
Rugby	d							23 35			
Long Buckby	d										
Northampton 66	a							23s54			
London Euston ■ ⊖66	a							01 03			

A From Glasgow Central
B From Aberystwyth
C From Manchester Piccadilly
D To Walsall
E From Edinburgh
F From Liverpool Lime Street

Table T069-F

Mondays to Fridays
21 May to 27 July

Lichfield - Birmingham - Longbridge and Redditch

Miles	Miles	Station		LM	LM	LM	LM	LM	LM	LM	LM	LM	LM	LM	LM	XC	LM	LM	LM	LM	LM	LM	LM
																◇■ ✠							
0	—	**Lichfield Trent Valley**	d							06 08		06 20					06 50		07 10		07 20		07 40
1¼	—	**Lichfield City**	d							06 12		06 24			06 44		06 54		07 14		07 24		07 44
4¼	—	Shenstone	d							06 17					06 49				07 19				07 49
6¾	—	Blake Street	d					06 02		06 20		06 32			06 52		07 02		07 22		07 32		07 52
7½	—	Butlers Lane	d					06 04		06 23		06 34			06 54		07 04		07 24		07 34		07 54
8½	—	Four Oaks	d					06 06	06 16	06 25		06 36	06 46		06 56		07 06	07 16	07 26		07 36	07 46	07 56
9¾	—	Sutton Coldfield	d					06 10	06 20	06 29		06 40	06 50		07 00		07 10	07 20	07 30		07 40	07 50	08 00
11¼	—	Wylde Green	d					06 12	06 22	06 31		06 42	06 52		07 02		07 12	07 22	07 32		07 42	07 52	08 02
11¾	—	Chester Road	d					06 14	06 24	06 33		06 44	06 54		07 04		07 14	07 24	07 34		07 44	07 54	08 04
12¾	—	Erdington	d					06 17	06 27	06 36		06 47	06 57		07 07		07 17	07 27	07 37		07 47	07 57	08 07
13½	—	Gravelly Hill	d					06 19	06 29	06 38		06 49	06 59		07 09		07 19	07 29	07 39		07 49	07 59	08 09
14¾	—	Aston	d					06 23	06 33	06 42		06 53	07 03		07 13		07 23	07 33	07 43		07 53	08 03	08 13
16	—	Duddeston	d					06 26	06 36	06 45			07 06					07 36	07 46			08 06	08 16
17½	—	**Birmingham New Street** ■	a					06 30	06 41	06 49		07 00	07 11		07 20		07 31	07 40	07 51		08 01	08 12	08 21
—	—		d	05 53	06 03	06 13	06 23	06 33	06 45	06 53	07 00	07 03	07 15	07 20	07 23	07 30	07 33	07 43	07 53	08 00	08 03	08 15	08 23
18½	—	Five Ways	d	05 57	06 07	06 17	06 27	06 37	06 49	06 57		07 07	07 19		07 27		07 37	07 47	07 57		08 07	08 19	08 27
19¾	—	University	d	06 01	06 11	06 21	06 31	06 41	06 53	07 01	07 06	07 11	07 23	07 26	07 31	07a36	07 41	07 51	08 01	08 06	08 11	08 23	08 31
20¾	—	Selly Oak	d	06 03	06 13	06 23	06 33	06 43	06 55	07 03		07 13	07 25		07 33		07 43	07 53	08 03		08 13	08 25	08 33
21¾	—	Bournville	d	06 06	06 16	06 26	06 36	06 46	06 58	07 06		07 16	07 28		07 36		07 46	07 56	08 06		08 16	08 28	08 36
22¾	—	Kings Norton	d	06 09	06 19	06 29	06 39	06 49	07 01	07 09		07 19	07 31		07 39		07 49	07 59	08 09		08 19	08 31	08 39
24¼	—	Northfield	d	06 12	06 22	06 32	06 42	06 52	07 04	07 12		07 22	07 34		07 42		07 52	08 02	08 12		08 22	08 34	08 42
25¼	—	Longbridge	d	06a14	06 26	06a34	06 46	06a54	07 07	07a14		07 26	07a36		07 46		07a54	08 06	08a14		08 26	08a36	08 46
27¾	0	Barnt Green	d		06 31		06 51		07 11			07 31		07 39	07 51			08 11		08 17	08 31		08 51
29¾	—	Alvechurch	d		06 35		06 55		07 15			07 35			07 55			08 15			08 35		08 55
33	—	**Redditch**	a		06 41		07 03		07 21			07 41			08 03			08 21			08 41		09 03
—	3½	Bromsgrove	a								07 21			07 43						08 21			

Station		XC	LM	LM	LM	LM	LM	LM	LM	LM	XC	LM	LM	LM	LM	LM	LM	LM	XC	LM	LM	LM	LM
		◇■									◇■ ✠								◇■ ✠				
Lichfield Trent Valley	d		07 50				08 10			08 40		08 50				09 20				09 50			
Lichfield City	d		07 54		08 09		08 14	08 22		08 44		08 54			09 16	09 24		09 46		09 54			10 16
Shenstone	d						08 19	08 27		08 49		08 59				09 29				09 59			
Blake Street	d		08 02				08 22	08 31		08 52		09 02			09 22	09 32		09 52		10 02			10 22
Butlers Lane	d		08 04				08 24	08 33		08 54		09 04			09 24	09 34		09 54		10 04			10 24
Four Oaks	d		08 07	08 15	08 18		08 26	08 36	08 46	08 56		09 06	09 16		09 26	09 36	09 46	09 56		10 06	10 16		10 26
Sutton Coldfield	d		08 10	08 18	08 22		08 30	08 40	08 50	09 00		09 10	09 20		09 30	09 40	09 50	10 00		10 10	10 20		10 30
Wylde Green	d		08 12	08 21	08 24		08 32	08 42	08 52	09 02		09 12	09 22		09 32	09 42	09 52	10 02		10 12	10 22		10 32
Chester Road	d		08 14	08 23	08 26		08 34	08 44	08 54	09 04		09 14	09 24		09 34	09 44	09 54	10 04		10 14	10 24		10 34
Erdington	d		08 17	08 25	08 28		08 37	08 47	08 57	09 07		09 17	09 27		09 37	09 47	09 57	10 07		10 17	10 27		10 37
Gravelly Hill	d		08 19		08 30		08 39	08 49	08 59	09 09		09 19	09 29		09 39	09 49	09 59	10 09		10 19	10 29		10 39
Aston	d		08 23		08 33		08 43	08 53	09 03	09 13		09 23	09 33		09 43	09 53	10 03	10 13		10 23	10 33		10 43
Duddeston	d				08 36		08 46	08 56	09 06				09 36				10 06				10 36		
Birmingham New Street ■	a		08 31	08 37	08 41		08 51	09 00	09 13	09 21		09 31	09 41		09 50	10 01	10 11	10 21		10 31	10 41		10 50
	d	08 30	08 33		08 43	08 50	08 53	09 03	09 15	09 23	09 30	09 33	09 43	09 50	09 53	10 03	10 13	10 23	10 30	10 33	10 43	10 50	10 53
Five Ways	d		08 37		08 47		08 57	09 07	09 19	09 27		09 37	09 47		09 57	10 07	10 17	10 27		10 37	10 47		10 57
University	d	08a36	08 41		08 51	08 56	09 01	09 11	09 23	09 31	09a36	09 41	09 51	09 56	10 01	10 11	10 21	10 31	10a36	10 41	10 51	10 56	11 01
Selly Oak	d		08 43		08 53		09 03	09 13	09 25	09 33		09 43	09 53		10 03	10 13	10 23	10 33		10 43	10 53		11 03
Bournville	d		08 46		08 56		09 06	09 16	09 28	09 36		09 46	09 56		10 06	10 16	10 26	10 36		10 46	10 56		11 06
Kings Norton	d		08 49		08 59		09 09	09 19	09 31	09 39		09 49	09 59		10 09	10 19	10 29	10 39		10 49	10 59		11 09
Northfield	d		08 52		09 02		09 12	09 22	09 34	09 42		09 52	10 02		10 12	10 22	10 32	10 42		10 52	11 02		11 12
Longbridge	d		08a54		09 06		09a14	09 26	09a36	09 46		09a54	10 06		10a14	10 26	10a34	10 46		10a54	11 06		11a14
Barnt Green	d				09 11			09 31		09 51			10 11			10 31		10 51			11 11		
Alvechurch	d				09 16			09 35		09 55			10 15			10 35		10 55			11 15		
Redditch	a				09 21			09 41		10 03			10 21			10 41		11 03			11 21		
Bromsgrove	a					09 11								10 11								11 11	

Station		LM	LM	LM	XC	LM	LM	LM	LM	LM	LM	LM	XC	LM	LM	LM	LM	LM	LM	LM	XC	LM
					◇■ ✠								◇■ ✠								◇■ ✠	
Lichfield Trent Valley	d	10 20				10 50				11 20				11 50				12 20				12 50
Lichfield City	d	10 24		10 46		10 54			11 16	11 24		11 46		11 54			12 16	12 24		12 46		12 54
Shenstone	d	10 29				10 59				11 29				11 59				12 29				12 59
Blake Street	d	10 32		10 52		11 02			11 22	11 32		11 52		12 02			12 22	12 32		12 52		13 02
Butlers Lane	d	10 34		10 54		11 04			11 25	11 34		11 54		12 04			12 24	12 34		12 54		13 04
Four Oaks	d	10 36	10 46	10 56		11 06	11 16		11 26	11 36	11 46	11 56		12 06	12 16		12 26	12 36	12 46	12 56		13 06
Sutton Coldfield	d	10 40	10 50	11 00		11 10	11 20		11 30	11 40	11 50	12 00		12 10	12 20		12 30	12 40	12 50	13 00		13 10
Wylde Green	d	10 42	10 52	11 02		11 12	11 22		11 32	11 42	11 52	12 02		12 12	12 22		12 32	12 42	12 52	13 02		13 12
Chester Road	d	10 44	10 54	11 04		11 14	11 24		11 34	11 44	11 54	12 04		12 14	12 24		12 34	12 44	12 54	13 04		13 14
Erdington	d	10 47	10 57	11 07		11 17	11 27		11 37	11 47	11 57	12 07		12 17	12 27		12 37	12 47	12 57	13 07		13 17
Gravelly Hill	d	10 49	10 59	11 09		11 19	11 29		11 39	11 49	11 59	12 09		12 19	12 29		12 39	12 49	12 59	13 09		13 19
Aston	d	10 53	11 03	11 13		11 23	11 33		11 43	11 53	12 03	12 13		12 23	12 33		12 43	12 53	13 03	13 13		13 23
Duddeston	d		11 06				11 36				12 06				12 36				13 06			
Birmingham New Street ■	a	10 59	11 11	11 21		11 31	11 41		11 50	12 01	12 11	12 21		12 31	12 41		12 50	13 01	13 11	13 21		13 31
	d	11 03	11 13	11 23	11 30	11 33	11 43	11 50	11 53	12 03	12 13	12 23	12 30	12 33	12 43	12 50	12 53	13 03	13 13	13 23	13 30	13 33
Five Ways	d	11 07	11 17	11 27		11 37	11 47		11 57	12 07	12 17	12 27		12 37	12 47		12 57	13 07	13 17	13 27		13 37
University	d	11 11	11 21	11 31	11a36	11 41	11 51	11 56	12 01	12 11	12 21	12 31	12a36	12 41	12 51	12 56	13 01	13 11	13 21	13 31	13a36	13 41
Selly Oak	d	11 13	11 23	11 33		11 43	11 53		12 03	12 13	12 23	12 33		12 43	12 53		13 03	13 13	13 23	13 33		13 43
Bournville	d	11 16	11 26	11 36		11 46	11 56		12 06	12 16	12 26	12 36		12 46	12 56		13 06	13 16	13 26	13 36		13 46
Kings Norton	d	11 19	11 29	11 39		11 49	11 59		12 09	12 19	12 29	12 39		12 49	12 59		13 09	13 19	13 29	13 39		13 49
Northfield	d	11 22	11 32	11 42		11 52	12 02		12 12	12 22	12 32	12 42		12 52	13 02		13 12	13 22	13 32	13 42		13 52
Longbridge	d	11 26	11a34	11 46		11a54	12 06		12a14	12 26	12a34	12 46		12a54	13 06		13a14	13 26	13a34	13 46		13a54
Barnt Green	d	11 31		11 51			12 11			12 31		12 51			13 11			13 31		13 51		
Alvechurch	d	11 35		11 55			12 15			12 35		12 55			13 15			13 35		13 55		
Redditch	a	11 41		12 03			12 21			12 41		13 03			13 21			13 41		14 03		
Bromsgrove	a							12 11								13 11						

Lichfield - Birmingham - Longbridge and Redditch

		LM	LM	LM	LM	LM	LM	XC ◇1	LM	LM		LM	LM	LM	LM	LM	XC ◇1	LM	LM	LM		LM	LM	LM	LM
Lichfield Trent Valley	d				13 20				13 50					14 20				14 50					15 20		
Lichfield City	d			13 16	13 24		13 46		13 54				14 16	14 24		14 46		14 54				15 16	15 24		
Shenstone	d				13 29				13 59					14 29				14 59					15 29		
Blake Street	d			13 22	13 32		13 52		14 02				14 22	14 32		14 52		15 02				15 22	15 32		
Butlers Lane	d			13 24	13 34		13 54		14 04				14 24	14 34		14 54		15 04				15 24	15 34		
Four Oaks	d	13 16		13 26	13 36	13 46	13 56		14 06	14 16			14 26	14 36	14 46	14 56		15 06	15 16			15 26	15 36	15 46	
Sutton Coldfield	d	13 20		13 30	13 40	13 50	14 00		14 10	14 20			14 30	14 40	14 50	15 00		15 10	15 20			15 30	15 40	15 50	
Wylde Green	d	13 22		13 32	13 42	13 52	14 02		14 12	14 22			14 32	14 42	14 52	15 02		15 12	15 22			15 32	15 42	15 52	
Chester Road	d	13 24		13 34	13 44	13 54	14 04		14 14	14 24			14 34	14 44	14 54	15 04		15 14	15 24			15 34	15 44	15 54	
Erdington	d	13 27		13 37	13 47	13 57	14 07		14 17	14 27			14 38	14 47	14 57	15 07		15 17	15 27			15 37	15 47	15 57	
Gravelly Hill	d	13 29		13 39	13 49	13 59	14 09		14 19	14 29			14 39	14 49	14 59	15 09		15 19	15 29			15 39	15 49	15 59	
Aston	d	13 33		13 43	13 53	14 03	14 13		14 23	14 33			14 43	14 53	15 03	15 13		15 23	15 33			15 43	15 53	16 03	
Duddeston	d	13 36				14 06				14 36					15 06				15 36					16 06	
Birmingham New Street 12	a	13 41		13 50	14 01	14 11	14 21		14 31	14 41			14 50	15 01	15 11	15 21		15 31	15 41			15 50	16 00	16 10	
	d	13 43	13 50	13 53	14 03	14 13	14 23	14 30	14 33	14 43		14 50	14 53	15 03	15 13	15 23	15 30	15 33	15 43	15 50		15 53	16 03	16 15	16 20
Five Ways	d	13 47		13 57	14 07	14 17	14 27		14 37	14 47			14 57	15 07	15 17	15 27		15 37	15 47			15 57	16 07	16 19	
University	d	13 51	13 56	14 01	14 11	14 21	14 31	14a36	14 41	14 51		14 56	15 01	15 11	15 21	15 31	15a36	15 41	15 51	15 56		16 01	16 11	16 23	16 26
Selly Oak	d	13 53		14 03	14 13	14 23	14 33		14 43	14 53			15 03	15 13	15 23	15 33		15 43	15 53			16 03	16 13	16 25	
Bournville	d	13 56		14 06	14 16	14 26	14 36		14 46	14 56			15 06	15 16	15 26	15 36		15 46	15 56			16 06	16 16	16 28	
Kings Norton	d	13 59		14 09	14 19	14 29	14 39		14 49	14 59			15 09	15 19	15 29	15 39		15 49	15 59			16 09	16 19	16 31	
Northfield	d	14 02		14 12	14 22	14 32	14 42		14 52	15 02			15 12	15 22	15 32	15 42		15 52	16 02			16 12	16 22	16 34	
Longbridge	d	14 06		14a14	14 26	14a34	14 46		14a54	15 06			15a14	15 26	15a34	15 46		15a54	16 06			16a14	16 26	16a36	
Barnt Green	d	14 11			14 31		14 51			15 11				15 31		15 51			16 11				16 31		
Alvechurch	d	14 15			14 35		14 55			15 15				15 35		15 55			16 15				16 35		
Redditch	a	14 21			14 41		15 03			15 21				15 41		16 03			16 21				16 41		
Bromsgrove	a		14 11									15 11								16 11					16 41

		LM	XC ◇1	LM	LM	LM		LM	LM	LM	LM	LM	XC ◇1	LM	LM	LM		LM	LM	LM	LM	LM	LM	XC ◇1	LM
Lichfield Trent Valley	d			15 50					16 20					16 50						17 20			17 40		17 50
Lichfield City	d	15 46		15 54				16 16	16 24			16 46		16 54				17 16		17 24			17 45		17 54
Shenstone	d			15 59					16 29					16 59						17 29					17 59
Blake Street	d	15 52		16 02				16 22	16 32			16 52		17 02				17 22		17 32			17 52		18 02
Butlers Lane	d	15 54		16 04				16 25	16 34			16 54		17 04				17 25		17 34			17 54		18 04
Four Oaks	d	15 56		16 06	16 16			16 26	16 36	16 46		16 56		17 06	17 16			17 26		17 36	17 46		17 56		18 06
Sutton Coldfield	d	16 00		16 10	16 20			16 30	16 40	16 50		17 00		17 10	17 20			17 30		17 40	17 50		18 00		18 10
Wylde Green	d	16 02		16 12	16 22			16 32	16 42	16 52		17 02		17 12	17 22			17 32		17 42	17 52		18 02		18 12
Chester Road	d	16 04		16 14	16 24			16 34	16 44	16 54		17 04		17 14	17 24			17 34		17 44	17 54		18 04		18 14
Erdington	d	16 07		16 17	16 27			16 37	16 47	16 57		17 07		17 17	17 27			17 37		17 47	17 57		18 07		18 17
Gravelly Hill	d	16 09		16 19	16 29			16 39	16 49	16 59		17 09		17 19	17 29			17 39		17 49	17 59		18 09		18 19
Aston	d	16 13		16 23	16 33			16 43	16 53	17 03		17 13		17 23	17 33			17 43		17 53	18 03		18 13		18 23
Duddeston	d				16 36					17 06					17 36						18 06				
Birmingham New Street 12	a	16 21		16 31	16 41			16 50	17 00	17 11		17 21		17 31	17 41			17 50		18 00	18 11		18 21		18 31
	d	16 23	16 30	16 33	16 43	16 50		16 53	17 03	17 15	17 20	17 23	17 30	17 33	17 43	17 50		17 53	18 00	18 03	18 15	18 20	18 23	18 30	18 33
Five Ways	d	16 27		16 37	16 47			16 57	17 07	17 19		17 27		17 37	17 47			17 57		18 07	18 19		18 27		18 37
University	d	16 31	16a36	16 41	16 51	16 56		17 01	17 11	17 23	17 26	17 31	17 36	17 41	17 51	17 56		18 01	18 06	18 11	18 23	18 27	18 31	18 36	18 41
Selly Oak	d	16 33		16 43	16 53			17 03	17 13	17 25		17 33		17 43	17 53			18 03		18 13	18 25		18 33		18 43
Bournville	d	16 36		16 46	16 56			17 06	17 16	17 28		17 36		17 46	17 56			18 06		18 16	18 28		18 36		18 46
Kings Norton	d	16 39		16 49	16 59			17 09	17 19	17 31		17 39		17 49	17 59			18 09		18 19	18 31		18 39		18 49
Northfield	d	16 42		16 52	17 02			17 12	17 22	17 34		17 42		17 52	18 02			18 12		18 22	18 34		18 42		18 52
Longbridge	d	16 46		16a54	17 06			17a14	17 26	17a36		17 46		17a54	18 06			18a14		18 26	18a36		18 46		18a54
Barnt Green	d	16 51			17 11				17 31			17 51			18 11					18 31			18 51		
Alvechurch	d	16 55			17 15				17 35			17 55			18 15					18 35			18 55		
Redditch	a	17 03			17 21				17 41			18 03			18 21					18 41			19 03		
Bromsgrove	a					17 11					17 41		17 50			18 11			18 20			18 42		18 50	

		LM		LM	LM	LM	LM	LM	XC ◇1	LM	LM	LM		LM	LM	LM	LM	XC ◇1	LM	LM	LM	LM		LM	LM
Lichfield Trent Valley	d			18 10	18 20					18 50				19 20			19 40		19 58			20 28			20 58
Lichfield City	d			18 15	18 24			18 46		18 54		19 16		19 24			19 45		20 02			20 32			21 02
Shenstone	d				18 29					18 59				19 29					20 07			20 37			21 07
Blake Street	d			18 22	18 32			18 52		19 02		19 22		19 32			19 52		20 10			20 40			21 10
Butlers Lane	d			18 24	18 34			18 54		19 04		19 25		19 34			19 54		20 13			20 43			21 13
Four Oaks	d	18 16		18 26	18 36	18 46		18 56		19 06	19 16	19 27		19 36		19 46	19 56		20 15			20 45			21 15
Sutton Coldfield	d	18 20		18 30	18 40	18 50		19 00		19 10	19 20	19 30		19 40		19 50	20 00		20 19			20 49			21 19
Wylde Green	d	18 22		18 32	18 42	18 52		19 02		19 12	19 22	19 32		19 42		19 52	20 02		20 21			20 51			21 21
Chester Road	d	18 24		18 34	18 44	18 54		19 04		19 14	19 24	19 34		19 44		19 54	20 04		20 23			20 53			21 23
Erdington	d	18 27		18 37	18 47	18 57		19 07		19 17	19 27	19 37		19 47		19 57	20 07		20 26			20 56			21 26
Gravelly Hill	d	18 29		18 39	18 49	18 59		19 09		19 19	19 29	19 39		19 49		19 59	20 09		20 28			20 58			21 28
Aston	d	18 33		18 43	18 53	19 03		19 13		19 23	19 33	19 43		19 53		20 03	20 13		20 33			21 03			21 33
Duddeston	d	18 36				19 06					19 36					20 06			20 36			21 06			21 36
Birmingham New Street 12	a	18 41		18 49	19 00	19 11		19 21		19 31	19 41	19 50		19 59		20 11	20 21		20 41			21 10			21 40
	d	18 43		18 53	19 03	19 15	19 20	19 23	19 30	19 33	19 43	19 53			20 00	20 15	20 23	20 30	20 43	20 53	21 00	21 15		21 23	21 43
Five Ways	d	18 47		18 57	19 07	19 19		19 27		19 37	19 47	19 57				20 19	20 27		20 47	20 57		21 19		21 27	21 47
University	d	18 51		19 01	19 11	19 23	19 26	19 31	19a36	19 41	19 51	20 01			20 06	20 23	20 31	20a36	20 51	21 01	21 06	21 23		21 31	21 51
Selly Oak	d	18 53		19 03	19 13	19 25		19 33		19 43	19 53	20 03				20 25	20 33		20 53	21 03		21 25		21 33	21 53
Bournville	d	18 56		19 06	19 16	19 28		19 36		19 46	19 56	20 06				20 28	20 36		20 56	21 06		21 28		21 36	21 56
Kings Norton	d	18 59		19 09	19 19	19 31		19 39		19 49	19 59	20 09				20 31	20 39		20 59	21 09		21 31		21 39	21 59
Northfield	d	19 02		19 12	19 22	19 34		19 42		19 52	20 02	20 12				20 34	20 42		21 02	21 12		21 34		21 42	22 02
Longbridge	d	19 06		19a14	19 26	19a36		19 46		19a54	20 06	20a14				20 36	20a44		21 06	21a14		21 36		21a44	22 06
Barnt Green	d	19 11			19 31			19 51			20 11					20 41			21 11			21 41			22 11
Alvechurch	d	19 15			19 35			19 55			20 15					20 46			21 15			21 46			22 15
Redditch	a	19 21			19 41			20 03			20 21					20 51			21 21			21 51			22 21
Bromsgrove	a						19 42								20 20						21 21				

Lichfield - Birmingham - Longbridge and Redditch

		LM	LM	LM	LM	LM	LM	LM FO		LM FX	LM	LM	LM
Lichfield Trent Valley	d			21 28		21 58					22 28	22 55	23 23
Lichfield City	d			21 32		22 02					22 32	22 59	23 27
Shenstone	d			21 37		22 07					22 37	23 04	23 32
Blake Street	d			21 40		22 10					22 40	23 07	23 36
Butlers Lane	d			21 43		22 13					22 43	23 10	23 38
Four Oaks	d			21 45		22 15					22 45	23 12	23 41
Sutton Coldfield	d			21 49		22 19					22 49	23 16	23 44
Wylde Green	d			21 51		22 21					22 51	23 18	
Chester Road	d			21 53		22 23					22 53		
Erdington	d			21 56		22 26					22 56		
Gravelly Hill	d			21 58		22 28					22 58		
Aston	d			22 03		22 33					23 03		
Duddeston	d			22 06		22 36					23 06		
Birmingham New Street 12	a			22 12		22 41					23 10	23 29	23 57
	d	21 53	22 00	22 15	22 23	22 43	22 53	23 00		23 00	23 13	23 33	
Five Ways	d	21 57		22 19	22 27	22 47	22 57				23 17	23 37	
University	d	22 01	22 06	22 23	22 31	22 51	23 01	23 06		23 06	23 21	23 41	
Selly Oak	d	22 03		22 25	22 33	22 53	23 03				23 23	23 43	
Bournville	d	22 06		22 28	22 36	22 56	23 06				23 26	23 46	
Kings Norton	d	22 09		22 31	22 39	22 59	23 09				23 29	23 49	
Northfield	d	22 12		22 34	22 42	23 02	23 12				23 32	23 52	
Longbridge	d	22a14		22 36	22a44	23 06	23a14				23 36	23a54	
Barnt Green	d			22 41		23 11					23 41		
Alvechurch	d			22 46		23 15					23 45		
Redditch	a			22 51		23 21					23 51		
Bromsgrove	a		22 20					23 20		23 21			

Mondays to Fridays

30 July to 31 August

		LM	LM	LM	LM	LM	LM	LM	LM	LM		LM	LM	LM	XC ◇1	LM	LM	LM	LM	LM		LM	LM	XC ◇1	LM
Lichfield Trent Valley	d							06 08		06 20						06 50		07 10		07 20			07 40		07 50
Lichfield City	d							06 12		06 24				06 44		06 54		07 14		07 24			07 44		07 54
Shenstone	d							06 17						06 49				07 19					07 49		
Blake Street	d					06 02		06 20		06 32				06 52		07 02		07 22		07 32			07 52		08 02
Butlers Lane	d					06 04		06 23		06 34				06 54		07 04		07 24		07 34			07 54		08 04
Four Oaks	d					06 06	06 16	06 25		06 36		06 46		06 56		07 06	07 16	07 26		07 36		07 46	07 56		08 07
Sutton Coldfield	d					06 10	06 20	06 29		06 40		06 50		07 00		07 10	07 20	07 30		07 40		07 50	08 00		08 10
Wylde Green	d					06 12	06 22	06 31		06 42		06 52		07 02		07 12	07 22	07 32		07 42		07 52	08 02		08 12
Chester Road	d					06 14	06 24	06 33		06 44		06 54		07 04		07 14	07 24	07 34		07 44		07 54	08 04		08 14
Erdington	d					06 17	06 27	06 36		06 47		06 57		07 07		07 17	07 27	07 37		07 47		07 57	08 07		08 17
Gravelly Hill	d					06 19	06 29	06 38		06 49		06 59		07 09		07 19	07 29	07 39		07 49		07 59	08 09		08 19
Aston	d					06 23	06 33	06 42		06 53		07 03		07 13		07 23	07 33	07 43		07 53		08 03	08 13		08 23
Duddeston	d					06 26	06 36	06 45				07 06					07 36	07 46				08 06	08 16		
Birmingham New Street 12	a					06 30	06 41	06 49		07 00		07 11		07 20		07 31	07 40	07 51		08 01		08 12	08 21		08 31
	d	05 53	06 03	06 13	06 23	06 33	06 45	06 53	07 00	07 03		07 15	07 20	07 23	07 30	07 33	07 43	07 53	08 00	08 03		08 15	08 23	08 30	08 33
Five Ways	d	05 57	06 07	06 17	06 27	06 37	06 49	06 57		07 07		07 19		07 27		07 37	07 47	07 57		08 07		08 19	08 27		08 37
University	d	06 01	06 11	06 21	06 31	06 41	06 53	07 01	07 06	07 11		07 23	07 26	07 31	07a36	07 41	07 51	08 01	08 06	08 11		08 23	08 31	08a36	08 41
Selly Oak	d	06 03	06 13	06 23	06 33	06 43	06 55	07 03		07 13		07 25		07 33		07 43	07 53	08 03		08 13		08 25	08 33		08 43
Bournville	d	06 06	06 16	06 26	06 36	06 46	06 58	07 06		07 16		07 28		07 36		07 46	07 56	08 06		08 16		08 28	08 36		08 46
Kings Norton	d	06 09	06 19	06 29	06 39	06 49	07 01	07 09		07 19		07 31		07 39		07 49	07 59	08 09		08 19		08 31	08 39		08 49
Northfield	d	06 12	06 22	06 32	06 42	06 52	07 04	07 12		07 22		07 34		07 42		07 52	08 02	08 12		08 22		08 34	08 42		08 52
Longbridge	d	06 15	06 26	06 35	06 46	06 56	07 07	07 15		07 26		07 37		07 46		07 58	08 06	08 15		08 26		08 37	08 46		08 58
Barnt Green	d	06 19	06 31		06 51		07 11	07 19		07 31			07 39	07 51			08 11	08 19	08 17	08 31			08 51		
Alvechurch	d		06 35		06 55		07 15			07 35				07 55			08 15			08 35			08 55		
Redditch	a		06 41		07 03		07 21			07 41				08 03			08 21			08 41			09 03		
Bromsgrove	a	06 25		06 44		07 05		07 26	07 21			07 47	07 43			08 07		08 26	08 21			08 46			09 07

		LM	LM	LM	LM	LM		LM	LM	XC ◇1	LM	LM	LM	LM	LM	LM		LM	XC ◇1	LM	LM	LM	LM	LM	LM
Lichfield Trent Valley	d				08 10				08 40		08 50				09 20					09 50				10 20	
Lichfield City	d		08 09		08 14	08 22			08 44		08 54			09 16	09 24			09 46		09 54			10 16	10 24	
Shenstone	d				08 19	08 27			08 49		08 59				09 29					09 59				10 29	
Blake Street	d				08 22	08 31			08 52		09 02			09 22	09 32			09 52		10 02			10 22	10 32	
Butlers Lane	d				08 24	08 33			08 54		09 04			09 24	09 34			09 54		10 04			10 24	10 34	
Four Oaks	d	08 15	08 18		08 26	08 36		08 46	08 56		09 06	09 16		09 26	09 36	09 46		09 56		10 06	10 16		10 26	10 36	10 46
Sutton Coldfield	d	08 18	08 22		08 30	08 40		08 50	09 00		09 10	09 20		09 30	09 40	09 50		10 00		10 10	10 20		10 30	10 40	10 50
Wylde Green	d	08 21	08 24		08 32	08 42		08 52	09 02		09 12	09 22		09 32	09 42	09 52		10 02		10 12	10 22		10 32	10 42	10 52
Chester Road	d	08 23	08 26		08 34	08 44		08 54	09 04		09 14	09 24		09 34	09 44	09 54		10 04		10 14	10 24		10 34	10 44	10 54
Erdington	d	08 25	08 28		08 37	08 47		08 57	09 07		09 17	09 27		09 37	09 47	09 57		10 07		10 17	10 27		10 37	10 47	10 57
Gravelly Hill	d		08 30		08 39	08 49		08 59	09 09		09 19	09 29		09 39	09 49	09 59		10 09		10 19	10 29		10 39	10 49	10 59
Aston	d		08 33		08 43	08 53		09 03	09 13		09 23	09 33		09 43	09 53	10 03		10 13		10 23	10 33		10 43	10 53	11 03
Duddeston	d		08 36		08 46	08 56		09 06				09 36				10 06					10 36				11 06
Birmingham New Street 12	a	08 37	08 41		08 51	09 00		09 13	09 21		09 31	09 41		09 50	10 01	10 11		10 21		10 31	10 41		10 50	10 59	11 11
	d		08 43	08 50	08 53	09 03		09 15	09 23	09 30	09 33	09 43	09 50	09 53	10 03	10 13		10 23	10 30	10 33	10 43	10 50	10 53	11 03	11 13
Five Ways	d		08 47		08 57	09 07		09 19	09 27		09 37	09 47		09 57	10 07	10 17		10 27		10 37	10 47		10 57	11 07	11 17
University	d		08 51	08 56	09 01	09 11		09 23	09 31	09a36	09 41	09 51	09 56	10 01	10 11	10 21		10 31	10a36	10 41	10 51	10 56	11 01	11 11	11 21
Selly Oak	d		08 53		09 03	09 13		09 25	09 33		09 43	09 53		10 03	10 13	10 23		10 33		10 43	10 53		11 03	11 13	11 23
Bournville	d		08 56		09 06	09 16		09 28	09 36		09 46	09 56		10 06	10 16	10 26		10 36		10 46	10 56		11 06	11 16	11 26
Kings Norton	d		08 59		09 09	09 19		09 31	09 39		09 49	09 59		10 09	10 19	10 29		10 39		10 49	10 59		11 09	11 19	11 29
Northfield	d		09 02		09 12	09 22		09 34	09 42		09 52	10 02		10 12	10 22	10 32		10 42		10 52	11 02		11 12	11 22	11 32
Longbridge	d		09 06		09 15	09 26		09a36	09 46		09 58	10 06		10 15	10 26	10 36		10 46		10a54	11 06		11 15	11 26	11 36
Barnt Green	d		09 11		09 19	09 31			09 51			10 11		10 19	10 31			10 51			11 11		11 19	11 31	
Alvechurch	d		09 16			09 35			09 55			10 15			10 35			10 55			11 15			11 35	
Redditch	a		09 21			09 41			10 03			10 21			10 41			11 03			11 21			11 41	
Bromsgrove	a			09 11	09 25						10 07		10 11	10 25		10 45						11 11	11 25		11 45

Lichfield - Birmingham - Longbridge and Redditch

Mondays to Fridays

30 July to 31 August

Station		LM	XC ◇1	LM	LM	LM	LM	LM	LM	LM	XC ◇1	LM	LM	LM	LM	LM	LM	LM	XC ◇1	LM	LM	LM
Lichfield Trent Valley	d			10 50				11 20				11 50				12 20				12 50		
Lichfield City	d	10 46		10 54			11 16	11 24		11 46		11 54			12 16	12 24		12 46		12 54		
Shenstone	d			10 59				11 29				11 59				12 29				12 59		
Blake Street	d	10 52		11 02			11 22	11 32		11 52		12 02			12 22	12 32		12 52		13 02		
Butlers Lane	d	10 54		11 04			11 25	11 34		11 54		12 04			12 24	12 34		12 54		13 04		
Four Oaks	d	10 56		11 06	11 16		11 26	11 36	11 46	11 56		12 06	12 16		12 26	12 36	12 46	12 56		13 06	13 16	
Sutton Coldfield	d	11 00		11 10	11 20		11 30	11 40	11 50	12 00		12 10	12 20		12 30	12 40	12 50	13 00		13 10	13 20	
Wylde Green	d	11 02		11 12	11 22		11 32	11 42	11 52	12 02		12 12	12 22		12 32	12 42	12 52	13 02		13 12	13 22	
Chester Road	d	11 04		11 14	11 24		11 34	11 44	11 54	12 04		12 14	12 24		12 34	12 44	12 54	13 04		13 14	13 24	
Erdington	d	11 07		11 17	11 27		11 37	11 47	11 57	12 07		12 17	12 27		12 37	12 47	12 57	13 07		13 17	13 27	
Gravelly Hill	d	11 09		11 19	11 29		11 39	11 49	11 59	12 09		12 19	12 29		12 39	12 49	12 59	13 09		13 19	13 29	
Aston	d	11 13		11 23	11 33		11 43	11 53	12 03	12 13		12 23	12 33		12 43	12 53	13 03	13 13		13 23	13 33	
Duddeston	d				11 36				12 06				12 36				13 06				13 36	
Birmingham New Street 12	a	11 21		11 31	11 41		11 50	12 01	12 11	12 21		12 31	12 41		12 50	13 01	13 11	13 21		13 31	13 41	
	d	11 23	11 30	11 33	11 43	11 50	11 53	12 03	12 13	12 23	12 30	12 33	12 43	12 50	12 53	13 03	13 13	13 23	13 30	13 33	13 43	13 50
Five Ways	d	11 27		11 37	11 47		11 57	12 07	12 17	12 27		12 37	12 47		12 57	13 07	13 17	13 27		13 37	13 47	
University	d	11 31	11a36	11 41	11 51	11 56	12 01	12 11	12 21	12 31	12a36	12 41	12 51	12 56	13 01	13 11	13 21	13 31	13a36	13 41	13 51	13 56
Selly Oak	d	11 33		11 43	11 53		12 03	12 13	12 23	12 33		12 43	12 53		13 03	13 13	13 23	13 33		13 43	13 53	
Bournville	d	11 36		11 46	11 56		12 06	12 16	12 26	12 36		12 46	12 56		13 06	13 16	13 26	13 36		13 46	13 56	
Kings Norton	d	11 39		11 49	11 59		12 09	12 19	12 29	12 39		12 49	12 59		13 09	13 19	13 29	13 39		13 49	13 59	
Northfield	d	11 42		11 52	12 02		12 12	12 22	12 32	12 42		12 52	13 02		13 12	13 22	13 32	13 42		13 52	14 02	
Longbridge	d	11 46		11 58	12 06		12 17	12 26	12 36	12 46		12a54	13 06		13 15	13 26	13 36	13 46		13 58	14 06	
Barnt Green	d	11 51			12 11		12 22	12 31		12 51			13 11		13 19	13 31		13 51			14 11	
Alvechurch	d	11 55			12 15			12 35		12 55			13 15			13 35		13 55			14 15	
Redditch	a	12 03			12 21			12 41		13 03			13 21			13 41		14 03			14 21	
Bromsgrove	a			12 07		12 11	12 28		12 45					13 11	13 25		13 45			14 07		14 11

Station		LM	LM	LM	LM	XC ◇1	LM	LM	LM	LM	LM	LM	LM	XC ◇1	LM	LM	LM	LM	LM	LM	LM	LM	XC ◇1
Lichfield Trent Valley	d		13 20				13 50				14 20				14 50				15 20				
Lichfield City	d	13 16	13 24		13 46		13 54			14 16	14 24		14 46		14 54			15 16	15 24			15 46	
Shenstone	d		13 29				13 59				14 29				14 59				15 29				
Blake Street	d	13 22	13 32		13 52		14 02			14 22	14 32		14 52		15 02			15 22	15 32			15 52	
Butlers Lane	d	13 24	13 34		13 54		14 04			14 24	14 34		14 54		15 04			15 24	15 34			15 54	
Four Oaks	d	13 26	13 36	13 46	13 56		14 06	14 16		14 26	14 36	14 46	14 56		15 06	15 16		15 26	15 36	15 46		15 56	
Sutton Coldfield	d	13 30	13 40	13 50	14 00		14 10	14 20		14 30	14 40	14 50	15 00		15 10	15 20		15 30	15 40	15 50		16 00	
Wylde Green	d	13 32	13 42	13 52	14 02		14 12	14 22		14 32	14 42	14 52	15 02		15 12	15 22		15 32	15 42	15 52		16 02	
Chester Road	d	13 34	13 44	13 54	14 04		14 14	14 24		14 34	14 44	14 54	15 04		15 14	15 24		15 34	15 44	15 54		16 04	
Erdington	d	13 37	13 47	13 57	14 07		14 17	14 27		14 38	14 47	14 57	15 07		15 17	15 27		15 37	15 47	15 57		16 07	
Gravelly Hill	d	13 39	13 49	13 59	14 09		14 19	14 29		14 39	14 49	14 59	15 09		15 19	15 29		15 39	15 49	15 59		16 09	
Aston	d	13 43	13 53	14 03	14 13		14 23	14 33		14 43	14 53	15 03	15 13		15 23	15 33		15 43	15 53	16 03		16 13	
Duddeston	d			14 06				14 36				15 06				15 36				16 06			
Birmingham New Street 12	a	13 50	14 01	14 11	14 21		14 31	14 41		14 50	15 01	15 11	15 21		15 31	15 41		15 50	16 00	16 10		16 21	
	d	13 53	14 03	14 13	14 23	14 30	14 33	14 43	14 50	14 53	15 03	15 13	15 23	15 30	15 33	15 43	15 50	15 53	16 03	16 15	16 20	16 23	16 30
Five Ways	d	13 57	14 07	14 17	14 27		14 37	14 47		14 57	15 07	15 17	15 27		15 37	15 47		15 57	16 07	16 19		16 27	
University	d	14 01	14 11	14 21	14 31	14a36	14 41	14 51	14 56	15 01	15 11	15 21	15 31	15a36	15 41	15 51	15 56	16 01	16 11	16 23	16 26	16 31	16a36
Selly Oak	d	14 03	14 13	14 23	14 33		14 43	14 53		15 03	15 13	15 23	15 33		15 43	15 53		16 03	16 13	16 25		16 33	
Bournville	d	14 06	14 16	14 26	14 36		14 46	14 56		15 06	15 16	15 26	15 36		15 46	15 56		16 06	16 16	16 28		16 36	
Kings Norton	d	14 09	14 19	14 29	14 39		14 49	14 59		15 09	15 19	15 29	15 39		15 49	15 59		16 09	16 19	16 31		16 39	
Northfield	d	14 12	14 22	14 32	14 42		14 52	15 02		15 12	15 22	15 32	15 42		15 52	16 02		16 12	16 22	16 34		16 42	
Longbridge	d	14 15	14 26	14 36	14 46		14 58	15 06		15 15	15 26	15 36	15 46		15 58	16 06		16 15	16 26	16 36		16 46	
Barnt Green	d	14 19	14 31		14 51			15 11		15 19	15 31		15 51			16 11		16 19	16 31			16 51	
Alvechurch	d		14 35		14 55			15 15			15 35		15 55			16 15			16 35			16 55	
Redditch	a		14 41		15 03			15 21			15 41		16 03			16 21			16 41			17 03	
Bromsgrove	a	14 25		14 45			15 07		15 11	15 25		15 45			16 07		16 11	16 25		16 46	16 41		

Station		LM	LM	LM	LM	LM	LM	LM	LM	XC ◇1	LM	LM	LM	LM	LM	LM	LM	LM	LM	XC ◇1	LM	LM
Lichfield Trent Valley	d	15 50				16 20					16 50					17 20			17 40		17 50	
Lichfield City	d	15 54			16 16	16 24			16 46		16 54			17 16		17 24			17 45		17 54	
Shenstone	d	15 59				16 29					16 59					17 29					17 59	
Blake Street	d	16 02			16 22	16 32			16 52		17 02			17 22		17 32			17 52		18 02	
Butlers Lane	d	16 04			16 25	16 34			16 54		17 04			17 25		17 34			17 54		18 04	
Four Oaks	d	16 06	16 16		16 26	16 36	16 46		16 56		17 06	17 16		17 26		17 36	17 46		17 56		18 06	18 16
Sutton Coldfield	d	16 10	16 20		16 30	16 40	16 50		17 00		17 10	17 20		17 30		17 40	17 50		18 00		18 10	18 20
Wylde Green	d	16 12	16 22		16 32	16 42	16 52		17 02		17 12	17 22		17 32		17 42	17 52		18 02		18 12	18 22
Chester Road	d	16 14	16 24		16 34	16 44	16 54		17 04		17 14	17 24		17 34		17 44	17 54		18 04		18 14	18 24
Erdington	d	16 17	16 27		16 37	16 47	16 57		17 07		17 17	17 27		17 37		17 47	17 57		18 07		18 17	18 27
Gravelly Hill	d	16 19	16 29		16 39	16 49	16 59		17 09		17 19	17 29		17 39		17 49	17 59		18 09		18 19	18 29
Aston	d	16 23	16 33		16 43	16 53	17 03		17 13		17 23	17 33		17 43		17 53	18 03		18 13		18 23	18 33
Duddeston	d		16 36				17 06					17 36					18 06					18 36
Birmingham New Street 12	a	16 31	16 41		16 50	17 00	17 11		17 21		17 31	17 41		17 50		18 00	18 11		18 21		18 31	18 41
	d	16 33	16 43	16 50	16 53	17 03	17 15	17 20	17 23	17 30	17 33	17 43	17 50	17 53	18 00	18 03	18 15	18 20	18 23	18 30	18 33	18 43
Five Ways	d	16 37	16 47		16 57	17 07	17 19		17 27		17 37	17 47		17 57		18 07	18 19		18 27		18 37	18 47
University	d	16 41	16 51	16 56	17 01	17 11	17 23	17 26	17 31	17 36	17 41	17 51	17 56	18 01	18 06	18 11	18 23	18 27	18 31	18 36	18 41	18 51
Selly Oak	d	16 43	16 53		17 03	17 13	17 25		17 33		17 43	17 53		18 03		18 13	18 25		18 33		18 43	18 53
Bournville	d	16 46	16 56		17 06	17 16	17 28		17 36		17 46	17 56		18 06		18 16	18 28		18 36		18 46	18 56
Kings Norton	d	16 49	16 59		17 09	17 19	17 31		17 39		17 49	17 59		18 09		18 19	18 31		18 39		18 49	18 59
Northfield	d	16 52	17 02		17 12	17 22	17 34		17 42		17 52	18 02		18 12		18 22	18 34		18 42		18 52	19 02
Longbridge	d	16 58	17 06		17 15	17 26	17 36		17 46		17 58	18 06		18 15		18 26	18 36		18 46		18 58	19 06
Barnt Green	d		17 11		17 19	17 31			17 51			18 11		18 19		18 31			18 51			19 11
Alvechurch	d		17 15			17 35			17 55			18 15				18 35			18 55			19 15
Redditch	a		17 21			17 41			18 03			18 21				18 41			19 03			19 21
Bromsgrove	a	17 07		17 11	17 25		17 46	17 41		17 50	18 07		18 11	18 26	18 20		18 47	18 42		18 50	19 07	

Table T069-F

Lichfield - Birmingham - Longbridge and Redditch

Mondays to Fridays

30 July to 31 August

Station		LM	LM	LM	LM	LM	XC ◇1	LM	LM	LM	LM	LM	LM	LM	XC ◇1	LM	LM	LM	LM	LM	LM	LM	LM
Lichfield Trent Valley	d	18 10	18 20					18 50			19 20			19 40		19 58			20 28		20 58		
Lichfield City	d	18 15	18 24			18 46		18 54		19 16	19 24			19 45		20 02			20 32		21 02		
Shenstone	d		18 29					18 59			19 29					20 07			20 37		21 07		
Blake Street	d	18 22	18 32			18 52		19 02		19 22	19 32			19 52		20 10			20 40		21 10		
Butlers Lane	d	18 24	18 34			18 54		19 04		19 25	19 34			19 54		20 13			20 43		21 13		
Four Oaks	d	18 26	18 36	18 46		18 56		19 06	19 16	19 27	19 36		19 46	19 56		20 15			20 45		21 15		
Sutton Coldfield	d	18 30	18 40	18 50		19 00		19 10	19 20	19 30	19 40		19 50	20 00		20 19			20 49		21 19		
Wylde Green	d	18 32	18 42	18 52		19 02		19 12	19 22	19 32	19 42		19 52	20 02		20 21			20 51		21 21		
Chester Road	d	18 34	18 44	18 54		19 04		19 14	19 24	19 34	19 44		19 54	20 04		20 23			20 53		21 23		
Erdington	d	18 37	18 47	18 57		19 07		19 17	19 27	19 37	19 47		19 57	20 07		20 26			20 56		21 26		
Gravelly Hill	d	18 39	18 49	18 59		19 09		19 19	19 29	19 39	19 49		19 59	20 09		20 28			20 58		21 28		
Aston	d	18 43	18 53	19 03		19 13		19 23	19 33	19 43	19 53		20 03	20 13		20 33			21 03		21 33		
Duddeston	d			19 06					19 36				20 06			20 36			21 06		21 36		
Birmingham New Street 12	a	18 49	19 00	19 11		19 21		19 31	19 41	19 50	19 59		20 11	20 21		20 41			21 10		21 40		
	d	18 53	19 03	19 15	19 20	19 23	19 30	19 33	19 43	19 53		20 00	20 15	20 23	20 30	20 43	20 53	21 00	21 15	21 23	21 43	21 53	22 00
Five Ways	d	18 57	19 07	19 19		19 27		19 37	19 47	19 57			20 19	20 27		20 47	20 57		21 19	21 27	21 47	21 57	
University	d	19 01	19 11	19 23	19 26	19 31	19a36	19 41	19 51	20 01		20 06	20 23	20 31	20a36	20 51	21 01	21 06	21 23	21 31	21 51	22 01	22 06
Selly Oak	d	19 03	19 13	19 25		19 33		19 43	19 53	20 03			20 25	20 33		20 53	21 03		21 25	21 33	21 53	22 03	
Bournville	d	19 06	19 16	19 28		19 36		19 46	19 56	20 06			20 28	20 36		20 56	21 06		21 28	21 36	21 56	22 06	
Kings Norton	d	19 09	19 19	19 31		19 39		19 49	19 59	20 09			20 31	20 39		20 59	21 09		21 31	21 39	21 59	22 09	
Northfield	d	19 12	19 22	19 34		19 42		19 52	20 02	20 12			20 34	20 42		21 02	21 12		21 34	21 42	22 02	22 12	
Longbridge	d	19 15	19 26	19 36		19 46		19 58	20 06	20 15			20 36	20 46		21 06	21 15		21 36	21 46	22 06	22 15	
Barnt Green	d	19 19	19 31			19 51			20 11	20 19			20 41			21 11	21 19		21 41		22 11	22 19	
Alvechurch	d		19 35			19 55			20 15				20 46			21 15			21 46		22 15		
Redditch	a		19 41			20 03			20 21				20 51			21 21			21 51		22 21		
Bromsgrove	a	19 25		19 47	19 42			20 07		20 26		20 20		20 55			21 26	21 21		21 55		22 26	22 20

Station		LM	LM	LM	LM	LM FO	LM FX	LM	LM	LM
Lichfield Trent Valley	d	21 28		21 58				22 28	22 55	23 23
Lichfield City	d	21 32		22 02				22 32	22 59	23 27
Shenstone	d	21 37		22 07				22 37	23 04	23 32
Blake Street	d	21 40		22 10				22 40	23 07	23 36
Butlers Lane	d	21 43		22 13				22 43	23 10	23 38
Four Oaks	d	21 45		22 15				22 45	23 12	23 41
Sutton Coldfield	d	21 49		22 19				22 49	23 16	23 44
Wylde Green	d	21 51		22 21				22 51	23 18	
Chester Road	d	21 53		22 23				22 53		
Erdington	d	21 56		22 26				22 56		
Gravelly Hill	d	21 58		22 28				22 58		
Aston	d	22 03		22 33				23 03		
Duddeston	d	22 06		22 36				23 06		
Birmingham New Street 12	a	22 12		22 41				23 10	23 29	23 57
	d	22 15	22 23	22 43	22 53	23 00	23 00	23 13	23 33	
Five Ways	d	22 19	22 27	22 47	22 57			23 17	23 37	
University	d	22 23	22 31	22 51	23 01	23 06	23 06	23 21	23 41	
Selly Oak	d	22 25	22 33	22 53	23 03			23 23	23 43	
Bournville	d	22 28	22 36	22 56	23 06			23 26	23 46	
Kings Norton	d	22 31	22 39	22 59	23 09			23 29	23 49	
Northfield	d	22 34	22 42	23 02	23 12			23 32	23 52	
Longbridge	d	22 36	22 46	23 06	23 15			23 36	23a54	
Barnt Green	d	22 41		23 11	23 19			23 41		
Alvechurch	d	22 46		23 15				23 45		
Redditch	a	22 51		23 21				23 51		
Bromsgrove	a		22 55		23 26	23 20	23 21			

Mondays to Fridays

3 September to 5 October

Station		LM	LM	LM	LM	LM	LM	LM	LM	LM	LM	LM	LM	XC ◇1	LM	LM	LM	LM	LM	LM	LM	XC ◇1	LM
Lichfield Trent Valley	d							06 08		06 20					06 50		07 10		07 20		07 40		07 50
Lichfield City	d							06 12		06 24			06 44		06 54		07 14		07 24		07 44		07 54
Shenstone	d							06 17					06 49				07 19				07 49		
Blake Street	d					06 02		06 20		06 32			06 52		07 02		07 22		07 32		07 52		08 02
Butlers Lane	d					06 04		06 23		06 34			06 54		07 04		07 24		07 34		07 54		08 04
Four Oaks	d					06 06	06 16	06 25		06 36	06 46		06 56		07 06	07 16	07 26		07 36	07 46	07 56		08 07
Sutton Coldfield	d					06 10	06 20	06 29		06 40	06 50		07 00		07 10	07 20	07 30		07 40	07 50	08 00		08 10
Wylde Green	d					06 12	06 22	06 31		06 42	06 52		07 02		07 12	07 22	07 32		07 42	07 52	08 02		08 12
Chester Road	d					06 14	06 24	06 33		06 44	06 54		07 04		07 14	07 24	07 34		07 44	07 54	08 04		08 14
Erdington	d					06 17	06 27	06 36		06 47	06 57		07 07		07 17	07 27	07 37		07 47	07 57	08 07		08 17
Gravelly Hill	d					06 19	06 29	06 38		06 49	06 59		07 09		07 19	07 29	07 39		07 49	07 59	08 09		08 19
Aston	d					06 23	06 33	06 42		06 53	07 03		07 13		07 23	07 33	07 43		07 53	08 03	08 13		08 23
Duddeston	d					06 26	06 36	06 45			07 06					07 36	07 46			08 06	08 16		
Birmingham New Street 12	a					06 30	06 41	06 49		07 00	07 11		07 20		07 31	07 40	07 51		08 01	08 12	08 21		08 31
	d	05 53	06 03	06 13	06 23	06 33	06 45	06 53	07 00	07 03	07 15	07 20	07 23	07 30	07 33	07 43	07 53	08 00	08 03	08 15	08 23	08 30	08 33
Five Ways	d	05 57	06 07	06 17	06 27	06 37	06 49	06 57		07 07	07 19		07 27		07 37	07 47	07 57		08 07	08 19	08 27		08 37
University	d	06 01	06 11	06 21	06 31	06 41	06 53	07 01	07 06	07 11	07 23	07 26	07 31	07a36	07 41	07 51	08 01	08 06	08 11	08 23	08 31	08a36	08 41
Selly Oak	d	06 03	06 13	06 23	06 33	06 43	06 55	07 03		07 13	07 25		07 33		07 43	07 53	08 03		08 13	08 25	08 33		08 43
Bournville	d	06 06	06 16	06 26	06 36	06 46	06 58	07 06		07 16	07 28		07 36		07 46	07 56	08 06		08 16	08 28	08 36		08 46
Kings Norton	d	06 09	06 19	06 29	06 39	06 49	07 01	07 09		07 19	07 31		07 39		07 49	07 59	08 09		08 19	08 31	08 39		08 49
Northfield	d	06 12	06 22	06 32	06 42	06 52	07 04	07 12		07 22	07 34		07 42		07 52	08 02	08 12		08 22	08 34	08 42		08 52
Longbridge	d	06 15	06 26	06 35	06 46	06 56	07 07	07 15		07 26	07 37		07 46		07 58	08 06	08 15		08 26	08 37	08 46		08 58
Barnt Green	d	06 19	06 31		06 51		07 11	07 19		07 31		07 39	07 51			08 11	08 19	08 17	08 31		08 51		
Alvechurch	d		06 35		06 55		07 15			07 35			07 55			08 15			08 35		08 55		
Redditch	a		06 41		07 03		07 21			07 41			08 03			08 21			08 41		09 03		
Bromsgrove	a	06 25		06 44		07 05		07 26	07 21		07 47	07 43			08 07		08 26	08 21		08 46			09 07

Table T069-F

Mondays to Fridays

3 September to 5 October

Lichfield - Birmingham - Longbridge and Redditch

		LM	LM	LM	LM	LM		LM	LM	XC ◇1	LM	LM	LM	LM	LM	LM		LM	XC ◇1	LM	LM	LM	LM	LM	LM
Lichfield Trent Valley	d				08 10				08 40		08 50				09 20					09 50				10 20	
Lichfield City	d		08 09		08 14	08 22			08 44		08 54			09 16	09 24			09 46		09 54			10 16	10 24	
Shenstone	d				08 19	08 27			08 49		08 59				09 29					09 59				10 29	
Blake Street	d				08 22	08 31			08 52		09 02			09 22	09 32			09 52		10 02			10 22	10 32	
Butlers Lane	d				08 24	08 33			08 54		09 04			09 24	09 34			09 54		10 04			10 24	10 34	
Four Oaks	d	08 15	08 18		08 26	08 36		08 46	08 56		09 06	09 16		09 26	09 36	09 46		09 56		10 06	10 16		10 26	10 36	10 46
Sutton Coldfield	d	08 18	08 22		08 30	08 40		08 50	09 00		09 10	09 20		09 30	09 40	09 50		10 00		10 10	10 20		10 30	10 40	10 50
Wylde Green	d	08 21	08 24		08 32	08 42		08 52	09 02		09 12	09 22		09 32	09 42	09 52		10 02		10 12	10 22		10 32	10 42	10 52
Chester Road	d	08 23	08 26		08 34	08 44		08 54	09 04		09 14	09 24		09 34	09 44	09 54		10 04		10 14	10 24		10 34	10 44	10 54
Erdington	d	08 25	08 28		08 37	08 47		08 57	09 07		09 17	09 27		09 37	09 47	09 57		10 07		10 17	10 27		10 37	10 47	10 57
Gravelly Hill	d		08 30		08 39	08 49		08 59	09 09		09 19	09 29		09 39	09 49	09 59		10 09		10 19	10 29		10 39	10 49	10 59
Aston	d		08 33		08 43	08 53		09 03	09 13		09 23	09 33		09 43	09 53	10 03		10 13		10 23	10 33		10 43	10 53	11 03
Duddeston	d		08 36		08 46	08 56		09 06				09 36				10 06					10 36				11 06
Birmingham New Street	a	08 37	08 41		08 51	09 00		09 13	09 21		09 31	09 41		09 50	10 01	10 11		10 21		10 31	10 41		10 50	10 59	11 11
	d		08 43	08 50	08 53	09 03		09 15	09 23	09 30	09 33	09 43	09 50	09 53	10 03	10 13		10 23	10 30	10 33	10 43	10 50	10 53	11 03	11 13
Five Ways	d		08 47		08 57	09 07		09 19	09 27		09 37	09 47		09 57	10 07	10 17		10 27		10 37	10 47		10 57	11 07	11 17
University	d		08 51	08 56	09 01	09 11		09 23	09 31	09a36	09 41	09 51	09 56	10 01	10 11	10 21		10 31	10a36	10 41	10 51	10 56	11 01	11 11	11 21
Selly Oak	d		08 53		09 03	09 13		09 25	09 33		09 43	09 53		10 03	10 13	10 23		10 33		10 43	10 53		11 03	11 13	11 23
Bournville	d		08 56		09 06	09 16		09 28	09 36		09 46	09 56		10 06	10 16	10 26		10 36		10 46	10 56		11 06	11 16	11 26
Kings Norton	d		08 59		09 09	09 19		09 31	09 39		09 49	09 59		10 09	10 19	10 29		10 39		10 49	10 59		11 09	11 19	11 29
Northfield	d		09 02		09 12	09 22		09 34	09 42		09 52	10 02		10 12	10 22	10 32		10 42		10 52	11 02		11 12	11 22	11 32
Longbridge	d		09 06		09 15	09 26		09a36	09 46		09 58	10 06		10 15	10 26	10 36		10 46		10a54	11 06		11 15	11 26	11 36
Barnt Green	d		09 11		09 19	09 31			09 51			10 11		10 19	10 31			10 51			11 11		11 19	11 31	
Alvechurch	d		09 16			09 35			09 55			10 15			10 35			10 55			11 15			11 35	
Redditch	a		09 21			09 41			10 03			10 21			10 41			11 03			11 21			11 41	
Bromsgrove	a			09 11	09 25						10 07		10 11	10 25		10 45						11 11	11 25		11 45

		LM		XC ◇1	LM	LM	LM	LM	LM	LM	LM	XC ◇1		LM	LM	LM	LM	LM	LM	LM	XC ◇1	LM		LM	LM
Lichfield Trent Valley	d				10 50				11 20					11 50				12 20				12 50			
Lichfield City	d	10 46			10 54			11 16	11 24		11 46			11 54			12 16	12 24		12 46		12 54			
Shenstone	d				10 59				11 29					11 59				12 29				12 59			
Blake Street	d	10 52			11 02			11 22	11 32		11 52			12 02			12 22	12 32		12 52		13 02			
Butlers Lane	d	10 54			11 04			11 25	11 34		11 54			12 04			12 24	12 34		12 54		13 04			
Four Oaks	d	10 56			11 06	11 16		11 26	11 36	11 46	11 56			12 06	12 16		12 26	12 36	12 46	12 56		13 06		13 16	
Sutton Coldfield	d	11 00			11 10	11 20		11 30	11 40	11 50	12 00			12 10	12 20		12 30	12 40	12 50	13 00		13 10		13 20	
Wylde Green	d	11 02			11 12	11 22		11 32	11 42	11 52	12 02			12 12	12 22		12 32	12 42	12 52	13 02		13 12		13 22	
Chester Road	d	11 04			11 14	11 24		11 34	11 44	11 54	12 04			12 14	12 24		12 34	12 44	12 54	13 04		13 14		13 24	
Erdington	d	11 07			11 17	11 27		11 37	11 47	11 57	12 07			12 17	12 27		12 37	12 47	12 57	13 07		13 17		13 27	
Gravelly Hill	d	11 09			11 19	11 29		11 39	11 49	11 59	12 09			12 19	12 29		12 39	12 49	12 59	13 09		13 19		13 29	
Aston	d	11 13			11 23	11 33		11 43	11 53	12 03	12 13			12 23	12 33		12 43	12 53	13 03	13 13		13 23		13 33	
Duddeston	d					11 36				12 06					12 36				13 06					13 36	
Birmingham New Street	a	11 21			11 31	11 41		11 50	12 01	12 11	12 21			12 31	12 41		12 50	13 01	13 11	13 21		13 31		13 41	
	d	11 23		11 30	11 33	11 43	11 50	11 53	12 03	12 13	12 23	12 30		12 33	12 43	12 50	12 53	13 03	13 13	13 23	13 30	13 33		13 43	13 50
Five Ways	d	11 27			11 37	11 47		11 57	12 07	12 17	12 27			12 37	12 47		12 57	13 07	13 17	13 27		13 37		13 47	
University	d	11 31		11a36	11 41	11 51	11 56	12 01	12 11	12 21	12 31	12a36		12 41	12 51	12 56	13 01	13 11	13 21	13 31	13a36	13 41		13 51	13 56
Selly Oak	d	11 33			11 43	11 53		12 03	12 13	12 23	12 33			12 43	12 53		13 03	13 13	13 23	13 33		13 43		13 53	
Bournville	d	11 36			11 46	11 56		12 06	12 16	12 26	12 36			12 46	12 56		13 06	13 16	13 26	13 36		13 46		13 56	
Kings Norton	d	11 39			11 49	11 59		12 09	12 19	12 29	12 39			12 49	12 59		13 09	13 19	13 29	13 39		13 49		13 59	
Northfield	d	11 42			11 52	12 02		12 12	12 22	12 32	12 42			12 52	13 02		13 12	13 22	13 32	13 42		13 52		14 02	
Longbridge	d	11 46			11 58	12 06		12 17	12 26	12 36	12 46			12a54	13 06		13 15	13 26	13 36	13 46		13 58		14 06	
Barnt Green	d	11 51				12 11		12 22	12 31		12 51				13 11		13 19	13 31		13 51				14 11	
Alvechurch	d	11 55				12 15			12 35		12 55				13 15			13 35		13 55				14 15	
Redditch	a	12 03				12 21			12 41		13 03				13 21			13 41		14 03				14 21	
Bromsgrove	a				12 07		12 11	12 28		12 45						13 11	13 25		13 45			14 07			14 11

		LM	LM	LM	LM	XC ◇1	LM	LM		LM	LM	LM	LM	LM	XC ◇1	LM	LM	LM		LM	LM	LM	LM	LM	XC ◇1
Lichfield Trent Valley	d		13 20				13 50					14 20				14 50					15 20				
Lichfield City	d	13 16	13 24		13 46		13 54				14 16	14 24		14 46		14 54				15 16	15 24			15 46	
Shenstone	d		13 29				13 59					14 29				14 59					15 29				
Blake Street	d	13 22	13 32		13 52		14 02				14 22	14 32		14 52		15 02				15 22	15 32			15 52	
Butlers Lane	d	13 24	13 34		13 54		14 04				14 24	14 34		14 54		15 04				15 24	15 34			15 54	
Four Oaks	d	13 26	13 36	13 46	13 56		14 06	14 16			14 26	14 36	14 46	14 56		15 06	15 16			15 26	15 36	15 46		15 56	
Sutton Coldfield	d	13 30	13 40	13 50	14 00		14 10	14 20			14 30	14 40	14 50	15 00		15 10	15 20			15 30	15 40	15 50		16 00	
Wylde Green	d	13 32	13 42	13 52	14 02		14 12	14 22			14 32	14 42	14 52	15 02		15 12	15 22			15 32	15 42	15 52		16 02	
Chester Road	d	13 34	13 44	13 54	14 04		14 14	14 24			14 34	14 44	14 54	15 04		15 14	15 24			15 34	15 44	15 54		16 04	
Erdington	d	13 37	13 47	13 57	14 07		14 17	14 27			14 38	14 47	14 57	15 07		15 17	15 27			15 37	15 47	15 57		16 07	
Gravelly Hill	d	13 39	13 49	13 59	14 09		14 19	14 29			14 39	14 49	14 59	15 09		15 19	15 29			15 39	15 49	15 59		16 09	
Aston	d	13 43	13 53	14 03	14 13		14 23	14 33			14 43	14 53	15 03	15 13		15 23	15 33			15 43	15 53	16 03		16 13	
Duddeston	d			14 06				14 36					15 06				15 36					16 06			
Birmingham New Street	a	13 50	14 01	14 11	14 21		14 31	14 41			14 50	15 01	15 11	15 21		15 31	15 41			15 50	16 00	16 10		16 21	
	d	13 53	14 03	14 13	14 23	14 30	14 33	14 43		14 50	14 53	15 03	15 13	15 23	15 30	15 33	15 43	15 50		15 53	16 03	16 15	16 20	16 23	16 30
Five Ways	d	13 57	14 07	14 17	14 27		14 37	14 47			14 57	15 07	15 17	15 27		15 37	15 47			15 57	16 07	16 19		16 27	
University	d	14 01	14 11	14 21	14 31	14a36	14 41	14 51		14 56	15 01	15 11	15 21	15 31	15a36	15 41	15 51	15 56		16 01	16 11	16 23	16 26	16 31	16a36
Selly Oak	d	14 03	14 13	14 23	14 33		14 43	14 53			15 03	15 13	15 23	15 33		15 43	15 53			16 03	16 13	16 25		16 33	
Bournville	d	14 06	14 16	14 26	14 36		14 46	14 56			15 06	15 16	15 26	15 36		15 46	15 56			16 06	16 16	16 28		16 36	
Kings Norton	d	14 09	14 19	14 29	14 39		14 49	14 59			15 09	15 19	15 29	15 39		15 49	15 59			16 09	16 19	16 31		16 39	
Northfield	d	14 12	14 22	14 32	14 42		14 52	15 02			15 12	15 22	15 32	15 42		15 52	16 02			16 12	16 22	16 34		16 42	
Longbridge	d	14 15	14 26	14 36	14 46		14 58	15 06			15 15	15 26	15 36	15 46		15 58	16 06			16 15	16 26	16 36		16 46	
Barnt Green	d	14 19	14 31		14 51			15 11			15 19	15 31		15 51			16 11			16 19	16 31			16 51	
Alvechurch	d		14 35		14 55			15 15				15 35		15 55			16 15				16 35			16 55	
Redditch	a		14 41		15 03			15 21				15 41		16 03			16 21				16 41			17 03	
Bromsgrove	a	14 25		14 45			15 07			15 11	15 25		15 45			16 07		16 11		16 25		16 46	16 41		

Table T069-F

Mondays to Fridays

3 September to 5 October

Lichfield - Birmingham - Longbridge and Redditch

		LM	LM	LM		LM	LM	LM	LM	LM	XC ◇1	LM	LM	LM		LM	LM	LM	LM	LM	LM	XC ◇1	LM	LM
Lichfield Trent Valley	d	15 50					16 20					16 50						17 20			17 40		17 50	
Lichfield City	d	15 54				16 16	16 24			16 46		16 54				17 16		17 24			17 45		17 54	
Shenstone	d	15 59					16 29					16 59						17 29					17 59	
Blake Street	d	16 02				16 22	16 32			16 52		17 02				17 22		17 32			17 52		18 02	
Butlers Lane	d	16 04				16 25	16 34			16 54		17 04				17 25		17 34			17 54		18 04	
Four Oaks	d	16 06	16 16			16 26	16 36	16 46		16 56		17 06	17 16			17 26		17 36	17 46		17 56		18 06	18 16
Sutton Coldfield	d	16 10	16 20			16 30	16 40	16 50		17 00		17 10	17 20			17 30		17 40	17 50		18 00		18 10	18 20
Wylde Green	d	16 12	16 22			16 32	16 42	16 52		17 02		17 12	17 22			17 32		17 42	17 52		18 02		18 12	18 22
Chester Road	d	16 14	16 24			16 34	16 44	16 54		17 04		17 14	17 24			17 34		17 44	17 54		18 04		18 14	18 24
Erdington	d	16 17	16 27			16 37	16 47	16 57		17 07		17 17	17 27			17 37		17 47	17 57		18 07		18 17	18 27
Gravelly Hill	d	16 19	16 29			16 39	16 49	16 59		17 09		17 19	17 29			17 39		17 49	17 59		18 09		18 19	18 29
Aston	d	16 23	16 33			16 43	16 53	17 03		17 13		17 23	17 33			17 43		17 53	18 03		18 13		18 23	18 33
Duddeston	d		16 36					17 06					17 36						18 06					18 36
Birmingham New Street	a	16 31	16 41			16 50	17 00	17 11		17 21		17 31	17 41			17 50		18 00	18 11		18 21		18 31	18 41
	d	16 33	16 43	16 50		16 53	17 03	17 15	17 20	17 23	17 30	17 33	17 43	17 50		17 53	18 00	18 03	18 15	18 20	18 23	18 30	18 33	18 43
Five Ways	d	16 37	16 47			16 57	17 07	17 19		17 27		17 37	17 47			17 57		18 07	18 19		18 27		18 37	18 47
University	d	16 41	16 51	16 56		17 01	17 11	17 23	17 26	17 31	17 36	17 41	17 51	17 56		18 01	18 06	18 11	18 23	18 27	18 31	18 36	18 41	18 51
Selly Oak	d	16 43	16 53			17 03	17 13	17 25		17 33		17 43	17 53			18 03		18 13	18 25		18 33		18 43	18 53
Bournville	d	16 46	16 56			17 06	17 16	17 28		17 36		17 46	17 56			18 06		18 16	18 28		18 36		18 46	18 56
Kings Norton	d	16 49	16 59			17 09	17 19	17 31		17 39		17 49	17 59			18 09		18 19	18 31		18 39		18 49	18 59
Northfield	d	16 52	17 02			17 12	17 22	17 34		17 42		17 52	18 02			18 12		18 22	18 34		18 42		18 52	19 02
Longbridge	d	16 58	17 06			17 15	17 26	17 36		17 46		17 58	18 06			18 15		18 26	18 36		18 46		18 58	19 06
Barnt Green	d		17 11			17 19	17 31			17 51			18 11			18 19		18 31			18 51			19 11
Alvechurch	d		17 15				17 35			17 55			18 15					18 35			18 55			19 15
Redditch	a		17 21				17 41			18 03			18 21					18 41			19 03			19 21
Bromsgrove	a	17 07		17 11		17 25		17 46	17 41		17 50	18 07		18 11		18 26	18 20		18 47	18 42		18 50	19 07	

		LM	LM	LM	LM	LM	XC ◇1	LM	LM	LM		LM	LM	LM	LM	XC ◇1	LM	LM	LM	LM		LM	LM	LM	LM
Lichfield Trent Valley	d	18 10	18 20					18 50				19 20			19 40		19 58			20 28			20 58		
Lichfield City	d	18 15	18 24			18 46		18 54		19 16		19 24			19 45		20 02			20 32			21 02		
Shenstone	d		18 29					18 59				19 29					20 07			20 37			21 07		
Blake Street	d	18 22	18 32			18 52		19 02		19 22		19 32			19 52		20 10			20 40			21 10		
Butlers Lane	d	18 24	18 34			18 54		19 04		19 25		19 34			19 54		20 13			20 43			21 13		
Four Oaks	d	18 26	18 36	18 46		18 56		19 06	19 16	19 27		19 36		19 46	19 56		20 15			20 45			21 15		
Sutton Coldfield	d	18 30	18 40	18 50		19 00		19 10	19 20	19 30		19 40		19 50	20 00		20 19			20 49			21 19		
Wylde Green	d	18 32	18 42	18 52		19 02		19 12	19 22	19 32		19 42		19 52	20 02		20 21			20 51			21 21		
Chester Road	d	18 34	18 44	18 54		19 04		19 14	19 24	19 34		19 44		19 54	20 04		20 23			20 53			21 23		
Erdington	d	18 37	18 47	18 57		19 07		19 17	19 27	19 37		19 47		19 57	20 07		20 26			20 56			21 26		
Gravelly Hill	d	18 39	18 49	18 59		19 09		19 19	19 29	19 39		19 49		19 59	20 09		20 28			20 58			21 28		
Aston	d	18 43	18 53	19 03		19 13		19 23	19 33	19 43		19 53		20 03	20 13		20 33			21 03			21 33		
Duddeston	d			19 06					19 36					20 06			20 36			21 06			21 36		
Birmingham New Street	a	18 49	19 00	19 11		19 21		19 31	19 41	19 50		19 59		20 11	20 21		20 41			21 10			21 40		
	d	18 53	19 03	19 15	19 20	19 23	19 30	19 33	19 43	19 53			20 00	20 15	20 23	20 30	20 43	20 53	21 00	21 15		21 23	21 43	21 53	22 00
Five Ways	d	18 57	19 07	19 19		19 27		19 37	19 47	19 57				20 19	20 27		20 47	20 57		21 19		21 27	21 47	21 57	
University	d	19 01	19 11	19 23	19 26	19 31	19a36	19 41	19 51	20 01			20 06	20 23	20 31	20a36	20 51	21 01	21 06	21 23		21 31	21 51	22 01	22 06
Selly Oak	d	19 03	19 13	19 25		19 33		19 43	19 53	20 03				20 25	20 33		20 53	21 03		21 25		21 33	21 53	22 03	
Bournville	d	19 06	19 16	19 28		19 36		19 46	19 56	20 06				20 28	20 36		20 56	21 06		21 28		21 36	21 56	22 06	
Kings Norton	d	19 09	19 19	19 31		19 39		19 49	19 59	20 09				20 31	20 39		20 59	21 09		21 31		21 39	21 59	22 09	
Northfield	d	19 12	19 22	19 34		19 42		19 52	20 02	20 12				20 34	20 42		21 02	21 12		21 34		21 42	22 02	22 12	
Longbridge	d	19 15	19 26	19 36		19 46		19 58	20 06	20 15				20 36	20 46		21 06	21 15		21 36		21 46	22 06	22 15	
Barnt Green	d	19 19	19 31			19 51			20 11	20 19				20 41			21 11	21 19		21 41			22 11	22 19	
Alvechurch	d		19 35			19 55			20 15					20 46			21 15			21 46			22 15		
Redditch	a		19 41			20 03			20 21					20 51			21 21			21 51			22 21		
Bromsgrove	a	19 25		19 47	19 42			20 07		20 26			20 20		20 55			21 26	21 21			21 55		22 26	22 20

		LM	LM	LM	LM	LM FO		LM FX	LM	LM	LM
Lichfield Trent Valley	d	21 28		21 58					22 28	22 55	23 23
Lichfield City	d	21 32		22 02					22 32	22 59	23 27
Shenstone	d	21 37		22 07					22 37	23 04	23 32
Blake Street	d	21 40		22 10					22 40	23 07	23 36
Butlers Lane	d	21 43		22 13					22 43	23 10	23 38
Four Oaks	d	21 45		22 15					22 45	23 12	23 41
Sutton Coldfield	d	21 49		22 19					22 49	23 16	23 44
Wylde Green	d	21 51		22 21					22 51	23 18	
Chester Road	d	21 53		22 23					22 53		
Erdington	d	21 56		22 26					22 56		
Gravelly Hill	d	21 58		22 28					22 58		
Aston	d	22 03		22 33					23 03		
Duddeston	d	22 06		22 36					23 06		
Birmingham New Street	a	22 12		22 41					23 10	23 29	23 57
	d	22 15	22 23	22 43	22 53	23 00		23 00	23 13	23 33	
Five Ways	d	22 19	22 27	22 47	22 57				23 17	23 37	
University	d	22 23	22 31	22 51	23 01	23 06		23 06	23 21	23 41	
Selly Oak	d	22 25	22 33	22 53	23 03				23 23	23 43	
Bournville	d	22 28	22 36	22 56	23 06				23 26	23 46	
Kings Norton	d	22 31	22 39	22 59	23 09				23 29	23 49	
Northfield	d	22 34	22 42	23 02	23 12				23 32	23 52	
Longbridge	d	22 36	22 46	23 06	23 15				23 36	23a54	
Barnt Green	d	22 41		23 11	23 19				23 41		
Alvechurch	d	22 46		23 15					23 45		
Redditch	a	22 51		23 21					23 51		
Bromsgrove	a		22 55		23 26	23 20		23 21			

Table T069-F

Mondays to Fridays

8 October to 7 December

Lichfield - Birmingham - Longbridge and Redditch

		LM	LM	LM	LM	LM	LM	LM	LM	LM		LM	LM	LM	XC ◇1	LM	LM	LM	LM	LM		LM	LM	XC ◇1	LM
Lichfield Trent Valley	d							06 08		06 20						06 50		07 10		07 20			07 40		07 50
Lichfield City	d							06 12		06 24				06 44		06 54		07 14		07 24			07 44		07 54
Shenstone	d							06 17						06 49				07 19					07 49		
Blake Street	d					06 02		06 20		06 32				06 52		07 02		07 22		07 32			07 52		08 02
Butlers Lane	d					06 04		06 23		06 34				06 54		07 04		07 24		07 34			07 54		08 04
Four Oaks	d					06 06	06 16	06 25		06 36		06 46		06 56		07 06	07 16	07 26		07 36		07 46	07 56		08 07
Sutton Coldfield	d					06 10	06 20	06 29		06 40		06 50		07 00		07 10	07 20	07 30		07 40		07 50	08 00		08 10
Wylde Green	d					06 12	06 22	06 31		06 42		06 52		07 02		07 12	07 22	07 32		07 42		07 52	08 02		08 12
Chester Road	d					06 14	06 24	06 33		06 44		06 54		07 04		07 14	07 24	07 34		07 44		07 54	08 04		08 14
Erdington	d					06 17	06 27	06 36		06 47		06 57		07 07		07 17	07 27	07 37		07 47		07 57	08 07		08 17
Gravelly Hill	d					06 19	06 29	06 38		06 49		06 59		07 09		07 19	07 29	07 39		07 49		07 59	08 09		08 19
Aston	d					06 23	06 33	06 42		06 53		07 03		07 13		07 23	07 33	07 43		07 53		08 03	08 13		08 23
Duddeston	d					06 26	06 36	06 45				07 06					07 36	07 46				08 06	08 16		
Birmingham New Street 12	a					06 30	06 41	06 49		07 00		07 11		07 20		07 31	07 40	07 51		08 01		08 12	08 21		08 31
	d	05 53	06 03	06 13	06 23	06 33	06 45	06 53	07 00	07 03		07 15	07 20	07 23	07 30	07 33	07 43	07 53	08 00	08 03		08 15	08 23	08 30	08 33
Five Ways	d	05 57	06 07	06 17	06 27	06 37	06 49	06 57		07 07		07 19		07 27		07 37	07 47	07 57		08 07		08 19	08 27		08 37
University	d	06 01	06 11	06 21	06 31	06 41	06 53	07 01	07 06	07 11		07 23	07 26	07 31	07a36	07 41	07 51	08 01	08 06	08 11		08 23	08 31	08a36	08 41
Selly Oak	d	06 03	06 13	06 23	06 33	06 43	06 55	07 03		07 13		07 25		07 33		07 43	07 53	08 03		08 13		08 25	08 33		08 43
Bournville	d	06 06	06 16	06 26	06 36	06 46	06 58	07 06		07 16		07 28		07 36		07 46	07 56	08 06		08 16		08 28	08 36		08 46
Kings Norton	d	06 09	06 19	06 29	06 39	06 49	07 01	07 09		07 19		07 31		07 39		07 49	07 59	08 09		08 19		08 31	08 39		08 49
Northfield	d	06 12	06 22	06 32	06 42	06 52	07 04	07 12		07 22		07 34		07 42		07 52	08 02	08 12		08 22		08 34	08 42		08 52
Longbridge	d	06 15	06 26	06 35	06 46	06 56	07 07	07 15		07 26		07 37		07 46		07 58	08 06	08 15		08 26		08 37	08 46		08 58
Barnt Green	d	06 19	06 31		06 51		07 11	07 19		07 31			07 39	07 51			08 11	08 19	08 17	08 31			08 51		
Alvechurch	d		06 35		06 55		07 15			07 35				07 55			08 15			08 35			08 55		
Redditch	a		06 41		07 03		07 21			07 41				08 03			08 21			08 41			09 03		
Bromsgrove	a	06 25		06 44		07 05		07 26	07 21			07 47	07 43			08 07		08 26	08 21			08 46			09 07

		LM	LM	LM	LM	LM		LM	LM	XC ◇1	LM	LM	LM	LM	LM	LM		LM	XC ◇1	LM	LM	LM	LM	LM	LM
Lichfield Trent Valley	d				08 10				08 40		08 50				09 20					09 50				10 20	
Lichfield City	d		08 09		08 14	08 22			08 44		08 54			09 16	09 24			09 46		09 54			10 16	10 24	
Shenstone	d				08 19	08 27			08 49		08 59				09 29					09 59				10 29	
Blake Street	d				08 22	08 31			08 52		09 02			09 22	09 32			09 52		10 02			10 22	10 32	
Butlers Lane	d				08 24	08 33			08 54		09 04			09 24	09 34			09 54		10 04			10 24	10 34	
Four Oaks	d	08 15	08 18		08 26	08 36		08 46	08 56		09 06	09 16		09 26	09 36	09 46		09 56		10 06	10 16		10 26	10 36	10 46
Sutton Coldfield	d	08 18	08 22		08 30	08 40		08 50	09 00		09 10	09 20		09 30	09 40	09 50		10 00		10 10	10 20		10 30	10 40	10 50
Wylde Green	d	08 21	08 24		08 32	08 42		08 52	09 02		09 12	09 22		09 32	09 42	09 52		10 02		10 12	10 22		10 32	10 42	10 52
Chester Road	d	08 23	08 26		08 34	08 44		08 54	09 04		09 14	09 24		09 34	09 44	09 54		10 04		10 14	10 24		10 34	10 44	10 54
Erdington	d	08 25	08 28		08 37	08 47		08 57	09 07		09 17	09 27		09 37	09 47	09 57		10 07		10 17	10 27		10 37	10 47	10 57
Gravelly Hill	d		08 30		08 39	08 49		08 59	09 09		09 19	09 29		09 39	09 49	09 59		10 09		10 19	10 29		10 39	10 49	10 59
Aston	d		08 33		08 43	08 53		09 03	09 13		09 23	09 33		09 43	09 53	10 03		10 13		10 23	10 33		10 43	10 53	11 03
Duddeston	d		08 36		08 46	08 56		09 06				09 36				10 06					10 36				11 06
Birmingham New Street 12	a	08 37	08 41		08 51	09 00		09 13	09 21		09 31	09 41		09 50	10 01	10 11		10 21		10 31	10 41		10 50	10 59	11 11
	d		08 43	08 50	08 53	09 03		09 15	09 23	09 30	09 33	09 43	09 50	09 53	10 03	10 13		10 23	10 30	10 33	10 43	10 50	10 53	11 03	11 13
Five Ways	d		08 47		08 57	09 07		09 19	09 27		09 37	09 47		09 57	10 07	10 17		10 27		10 37	10 47		10 57	11 07	11 17
University	d		08 51	08 56	09 01	09 11		09 23	09 31	09a36	09 41	09 51	09 56	10 01	10 11	10 21		10 31	10a36	10 41	10 51	10 56	11 01	11 11	11 21
Selly Oak	d		08 53		09 03	09 13		09 25	09 33		09 43	09 53		10 03	10 13	10 23		10 33		10 43	10 53		11 03	11 13	11 23
Bournville	d		08 56		09 06	09 16		09 28	09 36		09 46	09 56		10 06	10 16	10 26		10 36		10 46	10 56		11 06	11 16	11 26
Kings Norton	d		08 59		09 09	09 19		09 31	09 39		09 49	09 59		10 09	10 19	10 29		10 39		10 49	10 59		11 09	11 19	11 29
Northfield	d		09 02		09 12	09 22		09 34	09 42		09 52	10 02		10 12	10 22	10 32		10 42		10 52	11 02		11 12	11 22	11 32
Longbridge	d		09 06		09 15	09 26		09a36	09 46		09 58	10 06		10 15	10 26	10 36		10 46		10a54	11 06		11 15	11 26	11 36
Barnt Green	d		09 11		09 19	09 31			09 51			10 11		10 19	10 31			10 51			11 11		11 19	11 31	
Alvechurch	d		09 16			09 35			09 55			10 15			10 35			10 55			11 15			11 35	
Redditch	a		09 21			09 41			10 03			10 21			10 41			11 03			11 21			11 41	
Bromsgrove	a			09 11	09 25						10 07		10 11	10 25		10 45						11 11	11 25		11 45

		LM		XC ◇1	LM	LM	LM	LM	LM	LM	LM	XC ◇1		LM	LM	LM	LM	LM	LM	LM	XC ◇1	LM		LM	LM
Lichfield Trent Valley	d				10 50				11 20					11 50				12 20				12 50			
Lichfield City	d	10 46			10 54			11 16	11 24		11 46			11 54			12 16	12 24		12 46		12 54			
Shenstone	d				10 59				11 29					11 59				12 29				12 59			
Blake Street	d	10 52			11 02			11 22	11 32		11 52			12 02			12 22	12 32		12 52		13 02			
Butlers Lane	d	10 54			11 04			11 25	11 34		11 54			12 04			12 24	12 34		12 54		13 04			
Four Oaks	d	10 56			11 06	11 16		11 26	11 36	11 46	11 56			12 06	12 16		12 26	12 36	12 46	12 56		13 06		13 16	
Sutton Coldfield	d	11 00			11 10	11 20		11 30	11 40	11 50	12 00			12 10	12 20		12 30	12 40	12 50	13 00		13 10		13 20	
Wylde Green	d	11 02			11 12	11 22		11 32	11 42	11 52	12 02			12 12	12 22		12 32	12 42	12 52	13 02		13 12		13 22	
Chester Road	d	11 04			11 14	11 24		11 34	11 44	11 54	12 04			12 14	12 24		12 34	12 44	12 54	13 04		13 14		13 24	
Erdington	d	11 07			11 17	11 27		11 37	11 47	11 57	12 07			12 17	12 27		12 37	12 47	12 57	13 07		13 17		13 27	
Gravelly Hill	d	11 09			11 19	11 29		11 39	11 49	11 59	12 09			12 19	12 29		12 39	12 49	12 59	13 09		13 19		13 29	
Aston	d	11 13			11 23	11 33		11 43	11 53	12 03	12 13			12 23	12 33		12 43	12 53	13 03	13 13		13 23		13 33	
Duddeston	d					11 36				12 06					12 36				13 06					13 36	
Birmingham New Street 12	a	11 21			11 31	11 41		11 50	12 01	12 11	12 21			12 31	12 41		12 50	13 01	13 11	13 21		13 31		13 41	
	d	11 23		11 30	11 33	11 43	11 50	11 53	12 03	12 13	12 23	12 30		12 33	12 43	12 50	12 53	13 03	13 13	13 23	13 30	13 33		13 43	13 50
Five Ways	d	11 27			11 37	11 47		11 57	12 07	12 17	12 27			12 37	12 47		12 57	13 07	13 17	13 27		13 37		13 47	
University	d	11 31		11a36	11 41	11 51	11 56	12 01	12 11	12 21	12 31	12a36		12 41	12 51	12 56	13 01	13 11	13 21	13 31	13a36	13 41		13 51	13 56
Selly Oak	d	11 33			11 43	11 53		12 03	12 13	12 23	12 33			12 43	12 53		13 03	13 13	13 23	13 33		13 43		13 53	
Bournville	d	11 36			11 46	11 56		12 06	12 16	12 26	12 36			12 46	12 56		13 06	13 16	13 26	13 36		13 46		13 56	
Kings Norton	d	11 39			11 49	11 59		12 09	12 19	12 29	12 39			12 49	12 59		13 09	13 19	13 29	13 39		13 49		13 59	
Northfield	d	11 42			11 52	12 02		12 12	12 22	12 32	12 42			12 52	13 02		13 12	13 22	13 32	13 42		13 52		14 02	
Longbridge	d	11 46			11 58	12 06		12 17	12 26	12 36	12 46			12a54	13 06		13 15	13 26	13 36	13 46		13 58		14 06	
Barnt Green	d	11 51				12 11		12 22	12 31		12 51				13 11		13 19	13 31		13 51				14 11	
Alvechurch	d	11 55				12 15			12 35		12 55				13 15			13 35		13 55				14 15	
Redditch	a	12 03				12 21			12 41		13 03				13 21			13 41		14 03				14 21	
Bromsgrove	a				12 07		12 11	12 28		12 45						13 11	13 25		13 45			14 07			14 11

Table T069-F

Mondays to Fridays

8 October to 7 December

Lichfield - Birmingham - Longbridge and Redditch

		LM	LM	LM	LM	XC ◇1	LM	LM		LM	LM	LM	LM	LM	XC ◇1	LM	LM	LM		LM	LM	LM	LM	LM	XC ◇1
Lichfield Trent Valley	d		13 20				13 50					14 20				14 50					15 20				
Lichfield City	d	13 16	13 24		13 46		13 54				14 16	14 24		14 46		14 54				15 16	15 24			15 46	
Shenstone	d		13 29				13 59					14 29				14 59					15 29				
Blake Street	d	13 22	13 32		13 52		14 02				14 22	14 32		14 52		15 02				15 22	15 32			15 52	
Butlers Lane	d	13 24	13 34		13 54		14 04				14 24	14 34		14 54		15 04				15 24	15 34			15 54	
Four Oaks	d	13 26	13 36	13 46	13 56		14 06	14 16			14 26	14 36	14 46	14 56		15 06	15 16			15 26	15 36	15 46		15 56	
Sutton Coldfield	d	13 30	13 40	13 50	14 00		14 10	14 20			14 30	14 40	14 50	15 00		15 10	15 20			15 30	15 40	15 50		16 00	
Wylde Green	d	13 32	13 42	13 52	14 02		14 12	14 22			14 32	14 42	14 52	15 02		15 12	15 22			15 32	15 42	15 52		16 02	
Chester Road	d	13 34	13 44	13 54	14 04		14 14	14 24			14 34	14 44	14 54	15 04		15 14	15 24			15 34	15 44	15 54		16 04	
Erdington	d	13 37	13 47	13 57	14 07		14 17	14 27			14 38	14 47	14 57	15 07		15 17	15 27			15 37	15 47	15 57		16 07	
Gravelly Hill	d	13 39	13 49	13 59	14 09		14 19	14 29			14 39	14 49	14 59	15 09		15 19	15 29			15 39	15 49	15 59		16 09	
Aston	d	13 43	13 53	14 03	14 13		14 23	14 33			14 43	14 53	15 03	15 13		15 23	15 33			15 43	15 53	16 03		16 13	
Duddeston	d			14 06				14 36					15 06				15 36					16 06			
Birmingham New Street 12	a	13 50	14 01	14 11	14 21		14 31	14 41			14 50	15 01	15 11	15 21		15 31	15 41			15 50	16 00	16 10		16 21	
	d	13 53	14 03	14 13	14 23	14 30	14 33	14 43		14 50	14 53	15 03	15 13	15 23	15 30	15 33	15 43	15 50		15 53	16 03	16 15	16 20	16 23	16 30
Five Ways	d	13 57	14 07	14 17	14 27		14 37	14 47			14 57	15 07	15 17	15 27		15 37	15 47			15 57	16 07	16 19		16 27	
University	d	14 01	14 11	14 21	14 31	14a36	14 41	14 51		14 56	15 01	15 11	15 21	15 31	15a36	15 41	15 51	15 56		16 01	16 11	16 23	16 26	16 31	16a36
Selly Oak	d	14 03	14 13	14 23	14 33		14 43	14 53			15 03	15 13	15 23	15 33		15 43	15 53			16 03	16 13	16 25		16 33	
Bournville	d	14 06	14 16	14 26	14 36		14 46	14 56			15 06	15 16	15 26	15 36		15 46	15 56			16 06	16 16	16 28		16 36	
Kings Norton	d	14 09	14 19	14 29	14 39		14 49	14 59			15 09	15 19	15 29	15 39		15 49	15 59			16 09	16 19	16 31		16 39	
Northfield	d	14 12	14 22	14 32	14 42		14 52	15 02			15 12	15 22	15 32	15 42		15 52	16 02			16 12	16 22	16 34		16 42	
Longbridge	d	14 15	14 26	14 36	14 46		14 58	15 06			15 15	15 26	15 36	15 46		15 58	16 06			16 15	16 26	16 36		16 46	
Barnt Green	d	14 19	14 31		14 51			15 11			15 19	15 31		15 51			16 11			16 19	16 31			16 51	
Alvechurch	d		14 35		14 55			15 15				15 35		15 55			16 15				16 35			16 55	
Redditch	a		14 41		15 03			15 21				15 41		16 03			16 21				16 41			17 03	
Bromsgrove	a	14 25		14 45			15 07			15 11	15 25		15 45			16 07		16 11		16 25		16 46	16 41		

		LM	LM	LM		LM	LM	LM	LM	LM	XC ◇1	LM	LM	LM		LM	LM	LM	LM	LM	LM	XC ◇1	LM	LM	
Lichfield Trent Valley	d	15 50					16 20					16 50						17 20			17 40		17 50		
Lichfield City	d	15 54				16 16	16 24			16 46		16 54				17 16		17 24			17 45		17 54		
Shenstone	d	15 59					16 29					16 59						17 29					17 59		
Blake Street	d	16 02				16 22	16 32			16 52		17 02				17 22		17 32			17 52		18 02		
Butlers Lane	d	16 04				16 25	16 34			16 54		17 04				17 25		17 34			17 54		18 04		
Four Oaks	d	16 06	16 16			16 26	16 36	16 46		16 56		17 06	17 16			17 26		17 36	17 46		17 56		18 06	18 16	
Sutton Coldfield	d	16 10	16 20			16 30	16 40	16 50		17 00		17 10	17 20			17 30		17 40	17 50		18 00		18 10	18 20	
Wylde Green	d	16 12	16 22			16 32	16 42	16 52		17 02		17 12	17 22			17 32		17 42	17 52		18 02		18 12	18 22	
Chester Road	d	16 14	16 24			16 34	16 44	16 54		17 04		17 14	17 24			17 34		17 44	17 54		18 04		18 14	18 24	
Erdington	d	16 17	16 27			16 37	16 47	16 57		17 07		17 17	17 27			17 37		17 47	17 57		18 07		18 17	18 27	
Gravelly Hill	d	16 19	16 29			16 39	16 49	16 59		17 09		17 19	17 29			17 39		17 49	17 59		18 09		18 19	18 29	
Aston	d	16 23	16 33			16 43	16 53	17 03		17 13		17 23	17 33			17 43		17 53	18 03		18 13		18 23	18 33	
Duddeston	d		16 36					17 06					17 36						18 06					18 36	
Birmingham New Street 12	a	16 31	16 41			16 50	17 00	17 11		17 21		17 31	17 41			17 50		18 00	18 11		18 21		18 31	18 41	
	d	16 33	16 43	16 50		16 53	17 03	17 15	17 20	17 23	17 30	17 33	17 43	17 50		17 53	18 00	18 03	18 15	18 20	18 23	18 30	18 33	18 43	
Five Ways	d	16 37	16 47			16 57	17 07	17 19		17 27		17 37	17 47			17 57		18 07	18 19		18 27		18 37	18 47	
University	d	16 41	16 51	16 56		17 01	17 11	17 23	17 26	17 31	17 36	17 41	17 51	17 56		18 01	18 06	18 11	18 23	18 27	18 31	18 36	18 41	18 51	
Selly Oak	d	16 43	16 53			17 03	17 13	17 25		17 33		17 43	17 53			18 03		18 13	18 25		18 33		18 43	18 53	
Bournville	d	16 46	16 56			17 06	17 16	17 28		17 36		17 46	17 56			18 06		18 16	18 28		18 36		18 46	18 56	
Kings Norton	d	16 49	16 59			17 09	17 19	17 31		17 39		17 49	17 59			18 09		18 19	18 31		18 39		18 49	18 59	
Northfield	d	16 52	17 02			17 12	17 22	17 34		17 42		17 52	18 02			18 12		18 22	18 34		18 42		18 52	19 02	
Longbridge	d	16 58	17 06			17 15	17 26	17 36		17 46		17 58	18 06			18 15		18 26	18 36		18 46		18 58	19 06	
Barnt Green	d		17 11			17 19	17 31			17 51			18 11			18 19		18 31			18 51			19 11	
Alvechurch	d		17 15				17 35			17 55			18 15					18 35			18 55			19 15	
Redditch	a		17 21				17 41			18 03			18 21					18 41			19 03			19 21	
Bromsgrove	a	17 07		17 11		17 25		17 46	17 41		17 50	18 07		18 11		18 26	18 20		18 47	18 42		18 50	19 07		

		LM	LM	LM	LM	LM	XC ◇1	LM	LM	LM		LM	LM	LM	LM	XC ◇1	LM	LM	LM	LM		LM	LM	LM	LM
Lichfield Trent Valley	d	18 10	18 20					18 50				19 20			19 40		19 58			20 28			20 58		
Lichfield City	d	18 15	18 24			18 46		18 54		19 16		19 24			19 45		20 02			20 32			21 02		
Shenstone	d		18 29					18 59				19 29					20 07			20 37			21 07		
Blake Street	d	18 22	18 32			18 52		19 02		19 22		19 32			19 52		20 10			20 40			21 10		
Butlers Lane	d	18 24	18 34			18 54		19 04		19 25		19 34			19 54		20 13			20 43			21 13		
Four Oaks	d	18 26	18 36	18 46		18 56		19 06	19 16	19 27		19 36		19 46	19 56		20 15			20 45			21 15		
Sutton Coldfield	d	18 30	18 40	18 50		19 00		19 10	19 20	19 30		19 40		19 50	20 00		20 19			20 49			21 19		
Wylde Green	d	18 32	18 42	18 52		19 02		19 12	19 22	19 32		19 42		19 52	20 02		20 21			20 51			21 21		
Chester Road	d	18 34	18 44	18 54		19 04		19 14	19 24	19 34		19 44		19 54	20 04		20 23			20 53			21 23		
Erdington	d	18 37	18 47	18 57		19 07		19 17	19 27	19 37		19 47		19 57	20 07		20 26			20 56			21 26		
Gravelly Hill	d	18 39	18 49	18 59		19 09		19 19	19 29	19 39		19 49		19 59	20 09		20 28			20 58			21 28		
Aston	d	18 43	18 53	19 03		19 13		19 23	19 33	19 43		19 53		20 03	20 13		20 33			21 03			21 33		
Duddeston	d			19 06					19 36					20 06			20 36			21 06			21 36		
Birmingham New Street 12	a	18 49	19 00	19 11		19 21		19 31	19 41	19 50		19 59		20 11	20 21		20 41			21 10			21 40		
	d	18 53	19 03	19 15	19 20	19 23	19 30	19 33	19 43	19 53			20 00	20 15	20 23	20 30	20 43	20 53	21 00	21 15		21 23	21 43	21 53	22 00
Five Ways	d	18 57	19 07	19 19		19 27		19 37	19 47	19 57				20 19	20 27		20 47	20 57		21 19		21 27	21 47	21 57	
University	d	19 01	19 11	19 23	19 26	19 31	19a36	19 41	19 51	20 01			20 06	20 23	20 31	20a36	20 51	21 01	21 06	21 23		21 31	21 51	22 01	22 06
Selly Oak	d	19 03	19 13	19 25		19 33		19 43	19 53	20 03				20 25	20 33		20 53	21 03		21 25		21 33	21 53	22 03	
Bournville	d	19 06	19 16	19 28		19 36		19 46	19 56	20 06				20 28	20 36		20 56	21 06		21 28		21 36	21 56	22 06	
Kings Norton	d	19 09	19 19	19 31		19 39		19 49	19 59	20 09				20 31	20 39		20 59	21 09		21 31		21 39	21 59	22 09	
Northfield	d	19 12	19 22	19 34		19 42		19 52	20 02	20 12				20 34	20 42		21 02	21 12		21 34		21 42	22 02	22 12	
Longbridge	d	19 15	19 26	19 36		19 46		19 58	20 06	20 15				20 36	20 46		21 06	21 15		21 36		21 46	22 06	22 15	
Barnt Green	d	19 19	19 31			19 51			20 11	20 19				20 41			21 11	21 19		21 41			22 11	22 19	
Alvechurch	d		19 35			19 55			20 15					20 46			21 15			21 46			22 15		
Redditch	a		19 41			20 03			20 21					20 51			21 21			21 51			22 21		
Bromsgrove	a	19 25		19 47	19 42			20 07		20 26			20 20		20 55			21 26	21 21			21 55		22 26	22 20

Table T069-F

Lichfield - Birmingham - Longbridge and Redditch

Mondays to Fridays

8 October to 7 December

		LM	LM	LM	LM	LM FO	LM FX	LM	LM	LM
Lichfield Trent Valley	d	21 28		21 58				22 28	22 55	23 23
Lichfield City	d	21 32		22 02				22 32	22 59	23 27
Shenstone	d	21 37		22 07				22 37	23 04	23 32
Blake Street	d	21 40		22 10				22 40	23 07	23 36
Butlers Lane	d	21 43		22 13				22 43	23 10	23 38
Four Oaks	d	21 45		22 15				22 45	23 12	23 41
Sutton Coldfield	d	21 49		22 19				22 49	23 16	23 44
Wylde Green	d	21 51		22 21				22 51	23 18	
Chester Road	d	21 53		22 23				22 53		
Erdington	d	21 56		22 26				22 56		
Gravelly Hill	d	21 58		22 28				22 58		
Aston	d	22 03		22 33				23 03		
Duddeston	d	22 06		22 36				23 06		
Birmingham New Street 12	a	22 12		22 41				23 10	23 29	23 57
	d	22 15	22 23	22 43	22 53	23 00	23 00	23 13	23 33	
Five Ways	d	22 19	22 27	22 47	22 57			23 17	23 37	
University	d	22 23	22 31	22 51	23 01	23 06	23 06	23 21	23 41	
Selly Oak	d	22 25	22 33	22 53	23 03			23 23	23 43	
Bournville	d	22 28	22 36	22 56	23 06			23 26	23 46	
Kings Norton	d	22 31	22 39	22 59	23 09			23 29	23 49	
Northfield	d	22 34	22 42	23 02	23 12			23 32	23 52	
Longbridge	d	22 36	22 46	23 06	23 15			23 36	23a54	
Barnt Green	d	22 41		23 11	23 19			23 41		
Alvechurch	d	22 46		23 15				23 45		
Redditch	a	22 51		23 21				23 51		
Bromsgrove	a		22 55		23 26	23 20	23 21			

Saturdays

26 May to 16 June

		XC ◇1	LM	LM	LM	LM	LM	LM	LM	LM	LM	LM	LM	XC ◇1	LM	LM	LM	LM	LM	LM	LM	XC ◇1	LM
Lichfield Trent Valley	d										06 20				06 50				07 20				07 50
Lichfield City	d										06 24	06 38			06 54	07 08			07 24		07 46		07 54
Shenstone	d										06 29				06 59				07 29				07 59
Blake Street	d						06 02				06 32				07 02				07 32		07 52		08 02
Butlers Lane	d						06 04				06 34				07 04				07 34		07 55		08 05
Four Oaks	d						06 07				06 36	06 48			07 06	07 18			07 36	07 46	07 56		08 06
Sutton Coldfield	d						06 10				06 40	06 51			07 10	07 21			07 40	07 50	08 00		08 10
Wylde Green	d						06 12				06 42	06 54			07 12	07 24			07 42	07 52	08 02		08 12
Chester Road	d						06 14				06 44	06 56			07 14	07 26			07 44	07 54	08 04		08 14
Erdington	d						06 17				06 47	06 58			07 17	07 28			07 47	07 57	08 07		08 17
Gravelly Hill	d						06 19				06 49	07 01			07 19	07 31			07 49	07 59	08 09		08 19
Aston	d						06 23				06 53	07 03			07 23	07 33			07 53	08 03	08 14		08 23
Duddeston	d						06 26				06 56	07 06			07 26	07 36				08 06			
Birmingham New Street 12	a						06 30				07 01	07 12			07 31	07 41			08 00	08 10	08 21		08 31
	d	05 42	05 53	06 03	06 13	06 23	06 33	06 43	06 50	06 53	07 03	07 14	07 23	07 30	07 33	07 43	07 50	07 53	08 03	08 14	08 23	08 30	08 33
Five Ways	d		05 57	06 07	06 17	06 27	06 37	06 47		06 57	07 07	07 18	07 27		07 37	07 47		07 57	08 07	08 18	08 27		08 37
University	d		06 01	06 11	06 21	06 31	06 41	06 51	06 56	07 01	07 11	07 22	07 31	07a36	07 41	07 51	07 56	08 01	08 11	08 22	08 31	08a36	08 41
Selly Oak	d		06 03	06 13	06 23	06 33	06 43	06 53		07 03	07 13	07 24	07 33		07 43	07 53		08 03	08 13	08 24	08 33		08 43
Bournville	d		06 06	06 16	06 26	06 36	06 46	06 56		07 06	07 16	07 27	07 36		07 46	07 56		08 06	08 16	08 27	08 36		08 46
Kings Norton	d		06 09	06 19	06 29	06 39	06 49	06 59		07 09	07 19	07 30	07 39		07 49	07 59		08 09	08 19	08 30	08 39		08 49
Northfield	d		06 12	06 22	06 32	06 42	06 52	07 02		07 12	07 22	07 33	07 42		07 52	08 02		08 12	08 22	08 33	08 42		08 52
Longbridge	d		06a14	06 25	06a34	06 45	06a55	07 05		07a14	07 25	07a35	07 45		07a54	08 05		08a14	08 25	08a35	08 45		08a54
Barnt Green	d			06 30		06 50		07 10			07 30		07 50			08 10			08 30		08 50		
Alvechurch	d			06 34		06 54		07 15			07 34		07 54			08 14			08 34		08 54		
Redditch	a			06 41		07 03		07 21			07 41		08 03			08 21			08 41		09 03		
Bromsgrove	a	06 03							07 11								08 11						

		LM	LM	LM	LM	LM	LM	XC ◇1	LM	LM	LM	LM	LM	LM	LM	XC ◇1	LM	LM	LM	LM	LM	LM	LM
Lichfield Trent Valley	d				08 20				08 50				09 20				09 50				10 20		
Lichfield City	d			08 16	08 24		08 46		08 54			09 16	09 24		09 46		09 54			10 16	10 24		10 46
Shenstone	d				08 29				08 59				09 29				09 59				10 29		
Blake Street	d			08 22	08 32		08 52		09 02			09 22	09 32		09 52		10 02			10 22	10 32		10 52
Butlers Lane	d			08 25	08 34		08 55		09 04			09 24	09 34		09 55		10 04			10 25	10 34		10 55
Four Oaks	d	08 16		08 26	08 36	08 46	08 56		09 06	09 16		09 26	09 36	09 46	09 56		10 06	10 16		10 26	10 36	10 46	10 56
Sutton Coldfield	d	08 20		08 30	08 40	08 50	09 00		09 10	09 20		09 30	09 40	09 50	10 00		10 10	10 20		10 30	10 40	10 50	11 00
Wylde Green	d	08 22		08 32	08 42	08 52	09 02		09 12	09 22		09 32	09 42	09 52	10 02		10 12	10 22		10 32	10 42	10 52	11 02
Chester Road	d	08 24		08 34	08 44	08 54	09 04		09 14	09 24		09 34	09 44	09 54	10 04		10 14	10 24		10 34	10 44	10 54	11 04
Erdington	d	08 27		08 37	08 47	08 57	09 07		09 17	09 27		09 37	09 47	09 57	10 07		10 17	10 27		10 37	10 47	10 57	11 07
Gravelly Hill	d	08 29		08 39	08 49	08 59	09 09		09 19	09 29		09 39	09 49	09 59	10 09		10 19	10 29		10 39	10 49	10 59	11 09
Aston	d	08 33		08 43	08 53	09 03	09 14		09 23	09 33		09 43	09 53	10 03	10 14		10 23	10 33		10 43	10 53	11 03	11 14
Duddeston	d	08 36				09 06				09 36				10 06				10 36				11 06	
Birmingham New Street 12	a	08 41		08 50	09 00	09 10	09 21		09 31	09 41		09 50	10 00	10 10	10 21		10 31	10 41		10 50	11 00	11 10	11 21
	d	08 43	08 50	08 53	09 03	09 14	09 23	09 30	09 33	09 43	09 50	09 53	10 03	10 14	10 23	10 30	10 33	10 43	10 50	10 53	11 03	11 14	11 23
Five Ways	d	08 47		08 57	09 07	09 18	09 27		09 37	09 47		09 57	10 07	10 18	10 27		10 37	10 47		10 57	11 07	11 18	11 27
University	d	08 51	08 56	09 01	09 11	09 22	09 31	09a36	09 41	09 51	09 56	10 01	10 11	10 22	10 31	10a36	10 41	10 51	10 56	11 01	11 11	11 22	11 31
Selly Oak	d	08 53		09 03	09 13	09 24	09 33		09 43	09 53		10 03	10 13	10 24	10 33		10 43	10 53		11 03	11 13	11 24	11 33
Bournville	d	08 56		09 06	09 16	09 27	09 36		09 46	09 56		10 06	10 16	10 27	10 36		10 46	10 56		11 06	11 16	11 27	11 36
Kings Norton	d	08 59		09 09	09 19	09 30	09 39		09 49	09 59		10 09	10 19	10 30	10 39		10 49	10 59		11 09	11 19	11 30	11 39
Northfield	d	09 02		09 12	09 22	09 33	09 42		09 52	10 02		10 12	10 22	10 33	10 42		10 52	11 02		11 12	11 22	11 33	11 42
Longbridge	d	09 06		09a14	09 25	09a35	09 45		09a54	10 06		10a14	10 25	10a35	10 45		10a54	11 06		11a14	11 25	11a35	11 45
Barnt Green	d	09 11			09 30		09 50			10 11			10 30		10 50			11 11			11 30		11 50
Alvechurch	d	09 15			09 34		09 54			10 15			10 34		10 54			11 15			11 34		11 54
Redditch	a	09 22			09 41		10 03			10 21			10 41		11 03			11 21			11 41		12 03
Bromsgrove	a		09 11								10 11								11 11				

Table T069-F

Lichfield - Birmingham - Longbridge and Redditch

Saturdays

26 May to 16 June

		XC ◇1	LM	LM	LM	LM	LM	LM	LM	XC ◇1	LM	LM	LM	LM	LM	LM	LM	XC ◇1	LM	LM	LM	LM
Lichfield Trent Valley	d		10 50				11 20				11 50				12 20				12 50			
Lichfield City	d		10 54			11 16	11 24		11 46		11 54			12 16	12 24		12 46		12 54			13 16
Shenstone	d		10 59				11 29				11 59				12 29				12 59			
Blake Street	d		11 02			11 22	11 32		11 52		12 02			12 22	12 32		12 52		13 02			13 22
Butlers Lane	d		11 04			11 25	11 34		11 54		12 04			12 25	12 34		12 55		13 04			13 25
Four Oaks	d		11 06	11 16		11 26	11 36	11 46	11 56		12 06	12 16		12 26	12 36	12 46	12 56		13 06	13 16		13 26
Sutton Coldfield	d		11 10	11 20		11 30	11 40	11 50	12 00		12 10	12 20		12 30	12 40	12 50	13 00		13 10	13 20		13 30
Wylde Green	d		11 12	11 22		11 32	11 42	11 52	12 02		12 12	12 22		12 32	12 42	12 52	13 02		13 12	13 22		13 32
Chester Road	d		11 14	11 24		11 34	11 44	11 54	12 04		12 14	12 24		12 34	12 44	12 54	13 04		13 14	13 24		13 34
Erdington	d		11 17	11 27		11 37	11 47	11 57	12 07		12 17	12 27		12 37	12 47	12 57	13 07		13 17	13 27		13 37
Gravelly Hill	d		11 19	11 29		11 39	11 49	11 59	12 09		12 19	12 29		12 39	12 49	12 59	13 09		13 19	13 29		13 39
Aston	d		11 23	11 33		11 43	11 53	12 03	12 14		12 23	12 33		12 43	12 53	13 03	13 14		13 23	13 33		13 43
Duddeston	d			11 36				12 06				12 36				13 06				13 36		
Birmingham New Street 12	a		11 31	11 41		11 50	12 00	12 10	12 21		12 31	12 41		12 50	13 00	13 10	13 21		13 31	13 41		13 50
	d	11 30	11 33	11 43	11 50	11 53	12 03	12 14	12 23	12 30	12 33	12 43	12 50	12 53	13 03	13 14	13 23	13 30	13 33	13 43	13 50	13 53
Five Ways	d		11 37	11 47		11 57	12 07	12 18	12 27		12 37	12 47		12 57	13 07	13 18	13 27		13 37	13 47		13 57
University	d	11a36	11 41	11 51	11 56	12 01	12 11	12 22	12 31	12a36	12 41	12 51	12 56	13 01	13 11	13 22	13 31	13a36	13 41	13 51	13 56	14 01
Selly Oak	d		11 43	11 53		12 03	12 13	12 24	12 33		12 43	12 53		13 03	13 13	13 24	13 33		13 43	13 53		14 03
Bournville	d		11 46	11 56		12 06	12 16	12 27	12 36		12 46	12 56		13 06	13 16	13 27	13 36		13 46	13 56		14 06
Kings Norton	d		11 49	11 59		12 09	12 19	12 30	12 39		12 49	12 59		13 09	13 19	13 30	13 39		13 49	13 59		14 09
Northfield	d		11 52	12 02		12 12	12 22	12 33	12 42		12 52	13 02		13 12	13 22	13 33	13 42		13 52	14 02		14 12
Longbridge	d		11a54	12 06		12a14	12 25	12a35	12 45		12a54	13 06		13a14	13 25	13a35	13 45		13a54	14 06		14a14
Barnt Green	d			12 11			12 30		12 50			13 11			13 30		13 50			14 11		
Alvechurch	d			12 15			12 34		12 54			13 15			13 34		13 54			14 15		
Redditch	a			12 21			12 41		13 03			13 21			13 41		14 03			14 21		
Bromsgrove	a				12 11								13 11								14 11	

		LM	LM	LM	XC ◇1	LM	LM	LM	LM	LM	LM	LM	XC ◇1	LM	LM	LM	LM	LM	LM	LM	LM	XC ◇1	LM
Lichfield Trent Valley	d	13 20				13 50				14 20				14 50				15 20					15 50
Lichfield City	d	13 24		13 46		13 54			14 16	14 24		14 46		14 54			15 16	15 24			15 46		15 54
Shenstone	d	13 29				13 59				14 29				14 59				15 29					15 59
Blake Street	d	13 32		13 52		14 02			14 22	14 32		14 52		15 02			15 22	15 32			15 52		16 02
Butlers Lane	d	13 34		13 55		14 04			14 25	14 34		14 55		15 04			15 25	15 34			15 55		16 04
Four Oaks	d	13 36	13 46	13 56		14 06	14 16		14 26	14 36	14 46	14 56		15 06	15 16		15 26	15 36	15 46		15 56		16 06
Sutton Coldfield	d	13 40	13 50	14 00		14 10	14 20		14 30	14 40	14 50	15 00		15 10	15 20		15 30	15 40	15 50		16 00		16 10
Wylde Green	d	13 42	13 52	14 02		14 12	14 22		14 32	14 42	14 52	15 02		15 12	15 22		15 32	15 42	15 52		16 02		16 12
Chester Road	d	13 44	13 54	14 04		14 14	14 24		14 34	14 44	14 54	15 04		15 14	15 24		15 34	15 44	15 54		16 04		16 14
Erdington	d	13 47	13 57	14 07		14 17	14 27		14 37	14 47	14 57	15 07		15 17	15 27		15 37	15 47	15 57		16 07		16 17
Gravelly Hill	d	13 49	13 59	14 09		14 19	14 29		14 39	14 49	14 59	15 09		15 19	15 29		15 39	15 49	15 59		16 09		16 19
Aston	d	13 53	14 03	14 14		14 23	14 33		14 43	14 53	15 03	15 14		15 23	15 33		15 43	15 53	16 03		16 14		16 23
Duddeston	d		14 06				14 36				15 06				15 36				16 06				
Birmingham New Street 12	a	14 00	14 10	14 21		14 31	14 41		14 50	15 00	15 10	15 21		15 31	15 41		15 50	16 00	16 11		16 21		16 31
	d	14 03	14 14	14 23	14 30	14 33	14 43	14 50	14 53	15 03	15 14	15 23	15 30	15 33	15 43	15 50	15 53	16 03	16 15	16 20	16 23	16 30	16 33
Five Ways	d	14 07	14 18	14 27		14 37	14 47		14 57	15 07	15 18	15 27		15 37	15 47		15 57	16 07	16 19		16 27		16 37
University	d	14 11	14 22	14 31	14a36	14 41	14 51	14 56	15 01	15 11	15 22	15 31	15a36	15 41	15 51	15 56	16 01	16 11	16 23		16 31	16a36	16 41
Selly Oak	d	14 13	14 24	14 33		14 43	14 53		15 03	15 13	15 24	15 33		15 43	15 53		16 03	16 13	16 25		16 33		16 43
Bournville	d	14 16	14 27	14 36		14 46	14 56		15 06	15 16	15 27	15 36		15 46	15 56		16 06	16 16	16 28		16 36		16 46
Kings Norton	d	14 19	14 30	14 39		14 49	14 59		15 09	15 19	15 30	15 39		15 49	15 59		16 09	16 19	16 31		16 39		16 49
Northfield	d	14 22	14 33	14 42		14 52	15 02		15 12	15 22	15 33	15 42		15 52	16 02		16 12	16 22	16 34		16 42		16 52
Longbridge	d	14 25	14a35	14 45		14a54	15 06		15a14	15 25	15a35	15 45		15a54	16 06		16a14	16 25	16a36		16 45		16a54
Barnt Green	d	14 30		14 50			15 11			15 30		15 50			16 11			16 30			16 50		
Alvechurch	d	14 34		14 54			15 15			15 34		15 54			16 15			16 34			16 54		
Redditch	a	14 41		15 03			15 21			15 41		16 03			16 21			16 41			17 03		
Bromsgrove	a							15 11								16 11				16 41			

		LM	LM	LM	LM	LM	LM	LM	XC ◇1	LM	LM	LM	LM	LM	LM	LM	XC ◇1	LM	LM	LM	LM	LM
Lichfield Trent Valley	d				16 20					16 50				17 20				17 50				18 20
Lichfield City	d			16 16	16 24			16 46		16 54			17 16	17 24		17 46		17 54			18 16	18 24
Shenstone	d				16 29					16 59				17 29				17 59				18 29
Blake Street	d			16 22	16 32			16 52		17 02			17 22	17 32		17 52		18 02			18 22	18 32
Butlers Lane	d			16 25	16 34			16 54		17 04			17 25	17 34		17 54		18 04			18 25	18 34
Four Oaks	d	16 16		16 26	16 36	16 46		16 56		17 06	17 16		17 26	17 36	17 46	17 56		18 06	18 16		18 26	18 36
Sutton Coldfield	d	16 20		16 30	16 40	16 50		17 00		17 10	17 20		17 30	17 40	17 50	18 00		18 10	18 20		18 30	18 40
Wylde Green	d	16 22		16 32	16 42	16 52		17 02		17 12	17 22		17 32	17 42	17 52	18 02		18 12	18 22		18 32	18 42
Chester Road	d	16 24		16 34	16 44	16 54		17 04		17 14	17 24		17 34	17 44	17 54	18 04		18 14	18 24		18 34	18 44
Erdington	d	16 27		16 37	16 47	16 57		17 07		17 17	17 27		17 37	17 47	17 57	18 07		18 17	18 27		18 37	18 47
Gravelly Hill	d	16 29		16 40	16 49	16 59		17 09		17 19	17 29		17 39	17 49	17 59	18 09		18 19	18 29		18 39	18 49
Aston	d	16 33		16 43	16 53	17 03		17 14		17 23	17 33		17 43	17 53	18 03	18 14		18 23	18 33		18 43	18 53
Duddeston	d	16 36				17 06					17 36				18 06				18 36			
Birmingham New Street 12	a	16 41		16 50	17 00	17 10		17 21		17 31	17 41		17 50	18 00	18 10	18 21		18 31	18 41		18 50	19 00
	d	16 43	16 50	16 53	17 03	17 14	17 20	17 23	17 30	17 33	17 43	17 50	17 53	18 03	18 14	18 23	18 30	18 33	18 43	18 50	18 53	19 03
Five Ways	d	16 47		16 57	17 07	17 18		17 27		17 37	17 47		17 57	18 07	18 18	18 27		18 37	18 47		18 57	19 07
University	d	16 51	16 56	17 01	17 11	17 22		17 31	17 36	17 41	17 51	17 56	18 01	18 11	18 22	18 31	18a36	18 41	18 51	18 56	19 01	19 11
Selly Oak	d	16 53		17 03	17 13	17 24		17 33		17 43	17 53		18 03	18 13	18 24	18 33		18 43	18 53		19 03	19 13
Bournville	d	16 56		17 06	17 16	17 27		17 36		17 46	17 56		18 06	18 16	18 27	18 36		18 46	18 56		19 06	19 16
Kings Norton	d	16 59		17 09	17 19	17 30		17 39		17 49	17 59		18 09	18 19	18 30	18 39		18 49	18 59		19 09	19 19
Northfield	d	17 02		17 12	17 22	17 33		17 42		17 52	18 02		18 12	18 22	18 33	18 42		18 52	19 02		19 12	19 22
Longbridge	d	17 06		17a14	17 25	17a35		17 45		17a54	18 06		18a14	18 25	18a35	18 45		18a54	19 06		19a14	19 25
Barnt Green	d	17 11			17 30			17 50			18 11			18 30		18 50			19 11			19 30
Alvechurch	d	17 15			17 34			17 54			18 15			18 34		18 54			19 15			19 34
Redditch	a	17 21			17 41			18 03			18 21			18 41		19 03			19 21			19 41
Bromsgrove	a		17 11				17 41		17 50			18 11								19 11		

Table T069-F

Saturdays
26 May to 16 June

Lichfield - Birmingham - Longbridge and Redditch

		LM	LM	LM	XC ◇1	LM	LM	LM	LM	LM	LM	XC ◇1	LM	LM	LM	LM	LM	LM	LM	LM	LM	LM	LM
Lichfield Trent Valley	d					18 50			19 20				19 58			20 28		20 58			21 28		21 58
Lichfield City	d			18 46		18 54		19 16	19 24		19 46		20 02			20 32		21 02			21 32		22 02
Shenstone	d					18 59			19 29				20 07			20 37		21 07			21 37		22 07
Blake Street	d			18 52		19 02		19 22	19 32		19 52		20 10			20 40		21 10			21 40		22 10
Butlers Lane	d			18 55		19 04		19 25	19 34		19 55		20 13			20 43		21 13			21 43		22 13
Four Oaks	d	18 46		18 56		19 06	19 16	19 26	19 36	19 46	19 56		20 15			20 45		21 15			21 45		22 15
Sutton Coldfield	d	18 50		19 00		19 10	19 20	19 30	19 40	19 50	20 00		20 19			20 49		21 19			21 49		22 19
Wylde Green	d	18 52		19 02		19 12	19 22	19 32	19 42	19 52	20 02		20 21			20 51		21 21			21 51		22 21
Chester Road	d	18 54		19 04		19 14	19 24	19 34	19 44	19 54	20 04		20 23			20 53		21 23			21 53		22 23
Erdington	d	18 57		19 07		19 17	19 27	19 37	19 47	19 57	20 07		20 26			20 56		21 26			21 56		22 26
Gravelly Hill	d	18 59		19 09		19 19	19 29	19 39	19 49	19 59	20 09		20 28			20 58		21 28			21 58		22 28
Aston	d	19 03		19 14		19 23	19 33	19 43	19 53	20 03	20 13		20 32			21 02		21 32			22 02		22 32
Duddeston	d	19 06					19 36		19 56	20 06			20 35			21 05		21 35			22 05		22 35
Birmingham New Street 12	a	19 10		19 21		19 31	19 41	19 50	20 01	20 10	20 21		20 40			21 11		21 40			22 09		22 40
	d	19 14	19 20	19 23	19 30	19 33	19 43	19 53		20 15	20 23	20 30	20 44	20 53	21 00	21 15	21 23	21 43	21 53	22 09	22 13	22 23	22 43
Five Ways	d	19 18		19 27		19 37	19 47	19 57		20 19	20 27		20 48	20 57		21 19	21 27	21 47	21 57		22 17	22 27	22 47
University	d	19 22	19 26	19 31	19a36	19 41	19 51	20 01		20 23	20 31	20a36	20 52	21 01	21 06	21 23	21 31	21 51	22 01	22 15	22 21	22 31	22 51
Selly Oak	d	19 24		19 33		19 43	19 53	20 03		20 25	20 33		20 54	21 03		21 25	21 33	21 53	22 03		22 23	22 33	22 53
Bournville	d	19 27		19 36		19 46	19 56	20 06		20 28	20 36		20 57	21 06		21 28	21 36	21 56	22 06		22 26	22 36	22 56
Kings Norton	d	19 30		19 39		19 49	19 59	20 09		20 31	20 39		21 00	21 09		21 31	21 39	21 59	22 09		22 29	22 39	22 59
Northfield	d	19 33		19 42		19 52	20 02	20 12		20 34	20 42		21 03	21 12		21 34	21 42	22 02	22 12		22 32	22 42	23 02
Longbridge	d	19a35		19 45		19a54	20 06	20a14		20 37	20a44		21 06	21a14		21 36	21a44	22 06	22a14		22 36	22a44	23 06
Barnt Green	d			19 50			20 11			20 41			21 11			21 40		22 11			22 41		23 11
Alvechurch	d			19 54			20 15			20 46			21 15			21 45		22 15			22 45		23 15
Redditch	a			20 03			20 21			20 51			21 21			21 51		22 22			22 51		23 22
Bromsgrove	a		19 41												21 20					22 29			

		LM	LM	LM	LM
Lichfield Trent Valley	d		22 28	22 55	23 23
Lichfield City	d		22 32	22 59	23 27
Shenstone	d		22 37	23 04	23 32
Blake Street	d		22 40	23 07	23 36
Butlers Lane	d		22 43	23 10	23 38
Four Oaks	d		22 45	23 12	23 41
Sutton Coldfield	d		22 49	23 16	23 44
Wylde Green	d		22 51	23 18	
Chester Road	d		22 53		
Erdington	d		22 56		
Gravelly Hill	d		22 58		
Aston	d		23 02		
Duddeston	d		23 05		
Birmingham New Street 12	a		23 09	23 29	23 59
	d	22 53	23 13	23 33	
Five Ways	d	22 57	23 17	23 37	
University	d	23 01	23 21	23 41	
Selly Oak	d	23 03	23 23	23 43	
Bournville	d	23 06	23 26	23 46	
Kings Norton	d	23 09	23 29	23 49	
Northfield	d	23 12	23 32	23 52	
Longbridge	d	23a14	23 35	23a54	
Barnt Green	d		23 40		
Alvechurch	d		23 44		
Redditch	a		23 51		
Bromsgrove	a				

Saturdays
23 June to 28 July

		XC ◇1	LM	LM	LM	LM	LM	LM	LM	LM	LM	LM	LM	XC ◇1	LM	LM	LM	LM	LM	LM	LM	XC ◇1	LM
Lichfield Trent Valley	d										06 20				06 50				07 20				07 50
Lichfield City	d										06 24	06 38			06 54	07 08			07 24		07 46		07 54
Shenstone	d										06 29				06 59				07 29				07 59
Blake Street	d						06 02				06 32				07 02				07 32		07 52		08 02
Butlers Lane	d						06 04				06 34				07 04				07 34		07 55		08 05
Four Oaks	d						06 07				06 36	06 48			07 06	07 18			07 36	07 46	07 56		08 06
Sutton Coldfield	d						06 10				06 40	06 51			07 10	07 21			07 40	07 50	08 00		08 10
Wylde Green	d						06 12				06 42	06 54			07 12	07 24			07 42	07 52	08 02		08 12
Chester Road	d						06 14				06 44	06 56			07 14	07 26			07 44	07 54	08 04		08 14
Erdington	d						06 17				06 47	06 58			07 17	07 28			07 47	07 57	08 07		08 17
Gravelly Hill	d						06 19				06 49	07 01			07 19	07 31			07 49	07 59	08 09		08 19
Aston	d						06 23				06 53	07 03			07 23	07 33			07 53	08 03	08 14		08 23
Duddeston	d						06 26				06 56	07 06			07 26	07 36				08 06			
Birmingham New Street 12	a						06 30				07 01	07 12			07 31	07 41			08 00	08 10	08 21		08 31
	d	05 42	05 53	06 03	06 13	06 23	06 33	06 43	06 50	06 53	07 03	07 14	07 23	07 30	07 33	07 43	07 50	07 53	08 03	08 14	08 23	08 30	08 33
Five Ways	d		05 57	06 07	06 17	06 27	06 37	06 47		06 57	07 07	07 18	07 27		07 37	07 47		07 57	08 07	08 18	08 27		08 37
University	d		06 01	06 11	06 21	06 31	06 41	06 51	06 56	07 01	07 11	07 22	07 31	07a36	07 41	07 51	07 56	08 01	08 11	08 22	08 31	08a36	08 41
Selly Oak	d		06 03	06 13	06 23	06 33	06 43	06 53		07 03	07 13	07 24	07 33		07 43	07 53		08 03	08 13	08 24	08 33		08 43
Bournville	d		06 06	06 16	06 26	06 36	06 46	06 56		07 06	07 16	07 27	07 36		07 46	07 56		08 06	08 16	08 27	08 36		08 46
Kings Norton	d		06 09	06 19	06 29	06 39	06 49	06 59		07 09	07 19	07 30	07 39		07 49	07 59		08 09	08 19	08 30	08 39		08 49
Northfield	d		06 12	06 22	06 32	06 42	06 52	07 02		07 12	07 22	07 33	07 42		07 52	08 02		08 12	08 22	08 33	08 42		08 52
Longbridge	d		06a14	06 25	06a34	06 45	06a55	07 05		07a14	07 25	07a35	07 45		07a54	08 05		08a14	08 25	08a35	08 45		08a54
Barnt Green	d			06 30		06 50		07 10			07 30		07 50			08 10			08 30		08 50		
Alvechurch	d			06 34		06 54		07 15			07 34		07 54			08 14			08 34		08 54		
Redditch	a			06 41		07 03		07 21			07 41		08 03			08 21			08 41		09 03		
Bromsgrove	a	06 03							07 11								08 11						

Table T069-F

Saturdays
23 June to 28 July

Lichfield - Birmingham - Longbridge and Redditch

		LM	LM	LM	LM	LM	LM	XC ◇1	LM	LM	LM	LM	LM	LM	LM	XC ◇1	LM	LM	LM	LM	LM	LM	LM
Lichfield Trent Valley	d				08 20				08 50				09 20				09 50				10 20		
Lichfield City	d			08 16	08 24		08 46		08 54			09 16	09 24		09 46		09 54			10 16	10 24		10 46
Shenstone	d				08 29				08 59				09 29				09 59				10 29		
Blake Street	d			08 22	08 32		08 52		09 02			09 22	09 32		09 52		10 02			10 22	10 32		10 52
Butlers Lane	d			08 25	08 34		08 55		09 04			09 24	09 34		09 55		10 04			10 25	10 34		10 55
Four Oaks	d	08 16		08 26	08 36	08 46	08 56		09 06	09 16		09 26	09 36	09 46	09 56		10 06	10 16		10 26	10 36	10 46	10 56
Sutton Coldfield	d	08 20		08 30	08 40	08 50	09 00		09 10	09 20		09 30	09 40	09 50	10 00		10 10	10 20		10 30	10 40	10 50	11 00
Wylde Green	d	08 22		08 32	08 42	08 52	09 02		09 12	09 22		09 32	09 42	09 52	10 02		10 12	10 22		10 32	10 42	10 52	11 02
Chester Road	d	08 24		08 34	08 44	08 54	09 04		09 14	09 24		09 34	09 44	09 54	10 04		10 14	10 24		10 34	10 44	10 54	11 04
Erdington	d	08 27		08 37	08 47	08 57	09 07		09 17	09 27		09 37	09 47	09 57	10 07		10 17	10 27		10 37	10 47	10 57	11 07
Gravelly Hill	d	08 29		08 39	08 49	08 59	09 09		09 19	09 29		09 39	09 49	09 59	10 09		10 19	10 29		10 39	10 49	10 59	11 09
Aston	d	08 33		08 43	08 53	09 03	09 14		09 23	09 33		09 43	09 53	10 03	10 14		10 23	10 33		10 43	10 53	11 03	11 14
Duddeston	d	08 36				09 06				09 36				10 06				10 36				11 06	
Birmingham New Street 12	a	08 41		08 50	09 00	09 10	09 21		09 31	09 41		09 50	10 00	10 10	10 21		10 31	10 41		10 50	11 00	11 10	11 21
	d	08 43	08 50	08 53	09 03	09 14	09 23	09 30	09 33	09 43	09 50	09 53	10 03	10 14	10 23	10 30	10 33	10 43	10 50	10 53	11 03	11 14	11 23
Five Ways	d	08 47		08 57	09 07	09 18	09 27		09 37	09 47		09 57	10 07	10 18	10 27		10 37	10 47		10 57	11 07	11 18	11 27
University	d	08 51	08 56	09 01	09 11	09 22	09 31	09a36	09 41	09 51	09 56	10 01	10 11	10 22	10 31	10a36	10 41	10 51	10 56	11 01	11 11	11 22	11 31
Selly Oak	d	08 53		09 03	09 13	09 24	09 33		09 43	09 53		10 03	10 13	10 24	10 33		10 43	10 53		11 03	11 13	11 24	11 33
Bournville	d	08 56		09 06	09 16	09 27	09 36		09 46	09 56		10 06	10 16	10 27	10 36		10 46	10 56		11 06	11 16	11 27	11 36
Kings Norton	d	08 59		09 09	09 19	09 30	09 39		09 49	09 59		10 09	10 19	10 30	10 39		10 49	10 59		11 09	11 19	11 30	11 39
Northfield	d	09 02		09 12	09 22	09 33	09 42		09 52	10 02		10 12	10 22	10 33	10 42		10 52	11 02		11 12	11 22	11 33	11 42
Longbridge	d	09 06		09a14	09 25	09a35	09 45		09a54	10 06		10a14	10 25	10a35	10 45		10a54	11 06		11a14	11 25	11a35	11 45
Barnt Green	d	09 11			09 30		09 50			10 11			10 30		10 50			11 11			11 30		11 50
Alvechurch	d	09 15			09 34		09 54			10 15			10 34		10 54			11 15			11 34		11 54
Redditch	a	09 22			09 41		10 03			10 21			10 41		11 03			11 21			11 41		12 03
Bromsgrove	a		09 11								10 11								11 11				

		XC ◇1	LM	LM	LM	LM	LM	LM	LM	XC ◇1	LM	LM	LM	LM	LM	LM	LM	XC ◇1	LM	LM	LM	LM
Lichfield Trent Valley	d		10 50				11 20				11 50				12 20				12 50			
Lichfield City	d		10 54			11 16	11 24		11 46		11 54			12 16	12 24		12 46		12 54			13 16
Shenstone	d		10 59				11 29				11 59				12 29				12 59			
Blake Street	d		11 02			11 22	11 32		11 52		12 02			12 22	12 32		12 52		13 02			13 22
Butlers Lane	d		11 04			11 25	11 34		11 54		12 04			12 25	12 34		12 55		13 04			13 25
Four Oaks	d		11 06	11 16		11 26	11 36	11 46	11 56		12 06	12 16		12 26	12 36	12 46	12 56		13 06	13 16		13 26
Sutton Coldfield	d		11 10	11 20		11 30	11 40	11 50	12 00		12 10	12 20		12 30	12 40	12 50	13 00		13 10	13 20		13 30
Wylde Green	d		11 12	11 22		11 32	11 42	11 52	12 02		12 12	12 22		12 32	12 42	12 52	13 02		13 12	13 22		13 32
Chester Road	d		11 14	11 24		11 34	11 44	11 54	12 04		12 14	12 24		12 34	12 44	12 54	13 04		13 14	13 24		13 34
Erdington	d		11 17	11 27		11 37	11 47	11 57	12 07		12 17	12 27		12 37	12 47	12 57	13 07		13 17	13 27		13 37
Gravelly Hill	d		11 19	11 29		11 39	11 49	11 59	12 09		12 19	12 29		12 39	12 49	12 59	13 09		13 19	13 29		13 39
Aston	d		11 23	11 33		11 43	11 53	12 03	12 14		12 23	12 33		12 43	12 53	13 03	13 14		13 23	13 33		13 43
Duddeston	d			11 36				12 06				12 36				13 06				13 36		
Birmingham New Street 12	a		11 31	11 41		11 50	12 00	12 10	12 21		12 31	12 41		12 50	13 00	13 10	13 21		13 31	13 41		13 50
	d	11 30	11 33	11 43	11 50	11 53	12 03	12 14	12 23	12 30	12 33	12 43	12 50	12 53	13 03	13 14	13 23	13 30	13 33	13 43	13 50	13 53
Five Ways	d		11 37	11 47		11 57	12 07	12 18	12 27		12 37	12 47		12 57	13 07	13 18	13 27		13 37	13 47		13 57
University	d	11a36	11 41	11 51	11 56	12 01	12 11	12 22	12 31	12a36	12 41	12 51	12 56	13 01	13 11	13 22	13 31	13a36	13 41	13 51	13 56	14 01
Selly Oak	d		11 43	11 53		12 03	12 13	12 24	12 33		12 43	12 53		13 03	13 13	13 24	13 33		13 43	13 53		14 03
Bournville	d		11 46	11 56		12 06	12 16	12 27	12 36		12 46	12 56		13 06	13 16	13 27	13 36		13 46	13 56		14 06
Kings Norton	d		11 49	11 59		12 09	12 19	12 30	12 39		12 49	12 59		13 09	13 19	13 30	13 39		13 49	13 59		14 09
Northfield	d		11 52	12 02		12 12	12 22	12 33	12 42		12 52	13 02		13 12	13 22	13 33	13 42		13 52	14 02		14 12
Longbridge	d		11a54	12 06		12a14	12 25	12a35	12 45		12a54	13 06		13a14	13 25	13a35	13 45		13a54	14 06		14a14
Barnt Green	d			12 11			12 30		12 50			13 11			13 30		13 50			14 11		
Alvechurch	d			12 15			12 34		12 54			13 15			13 34		13 54			14 15		
Redditch	a			12 21			12 41		13 03			13 21			13 41		14 03			14 21		
Bromsgrove	a				12 11								13 11								14 11	

		LM	LM	LM	XC ◇1	LM	LM	LM	LM	LM	LM	LM	XC ◇1	LM	LM	LM	LM	LM	LM	LM	LM	XC ◇1	LM
Lichfield Trent Valley	d	13 20				13 50				14 20				14 50				15 20					15 50
Lichfield City	d	13 24		13 46		13 54			14 16	14 24		14 46		14 54			15 16	15 24			15 46		15 54
Shenstone	d	13 29				13 59				14 29				14 59				15 29					15 59
Blake Street	d	13 32		13 52		14 02			14 22	14 32		14 52		15 02			15 22	15 32			15 52		16 02
Butlers Lane	d	13 34		13 55		14 04			14 25	14 34		14 55		15 04			15 25	15 34			15 55		16 04
Four Oaks	d	13 36	13 46	13 56		14 06	14 16		14 26	14 36	14 46	14 56		15 06	15 16		15 26	15 36	15 46		15 56		16 06
Sutton Coldfield	d	13 40	13 50	14 00		14 10	14 20		14 30	14 40	14 50	15 00		15 10	15 20		15 30	15 40	15 50		16 00		16 10
Wylde Green	d	13 42	13 52	14 02		14 12	14 22		14 32	14 42	14 52	15 02		15 12	15 22		15 32	15 42	15 52		16 02		16 12
Chester Road	d	13 44	13 54	14 04		14 14	14 24		14 34	14 44	14 54	15 04		15 14	15 24		15 34	15 44	15 54		16 04		16 14
Erdington	d	13 47	13 57	14 07		14 17	14 27		14 37	14 47	14 57	15 07		15 17	15 27		15 37	15 47	15 57		16 07		16 17
Gravelly Hill	d	13 49	13 59	14 09		14 19	14 29		14 39	14 49	14 59	15 09		15 19	15 29		15 39	15 49	15 59		16 09		16 19
Aston	d	13 53	14 03	14 14		14 23	14 33		14 43	14 53	15 03	15 14		15 23	15 33		15 43	15 53	16 03		16 14		16 23
Duddeston	d		14 06				14 36				15 06				15 36				16 06				
Birmingham New Street 12	a	14 00	14 10	14 21		14 31	14 41		14 50	15 00	15 10	15 21		15 31	15 41		15 50	16 00	16 11		16 21		16 31
	d	14 03	14 14	14 23	14 30	14 33	14 43	14 50	14 53	15 03	15 14	15 23	15 30	15 33	15 43	15 50	15 53	16 03	16 15	16 20	16 23	16 30	16 33
Five Ways	d	14 07	14 18	14 27		14 37	14 47		14 57	15 07	15 18	15 27		15 37	15 47		15 57	16 07	16 19		16 27		16 37
University	d	14 11	14 22	14 31	14a36	14 41	14 51	14 56	15 01	15 11	15 22	15 31	15a36	15 41	15 51	15 56	16 01	16 11	16 23		16 31	16a36	16 41
Selly Oak	d	14 13	14 24	14 33		14 43	14 53		15 03	15 13	15 24	15 33		15 43	15 53		16 03	16 13	16 25		16 33		16 43
Bournville	d	14 16	14 27	14 36		14 46	14 56		15 06	15 16	15 27	15 36		15 46	15 56		16 06	16 16	16 28		16 36		16 46
Kings Norton	d	14 19	14 30	14 39		14 49	14 59		15 09	15 19	15 30	15 39		15 49	15 59		16 09	16 19	16 31		16 39		16 49
Northfield	d	14 22	14 33	14 42		14 52	15 02		15 12	15 22	15 33	15 42		15 52	16 02		16 12	16 22	16 34		16 42		16 52
Longbridge	d	14 25	14a35	14 45		14a54	15 06		15a14	15 25	15a35	15 45		15a54	16 06		16a14	16 25	16a36		16 45		16a54
Barnt Green	d	14 30		14 50			15 11			15 30		15 50			16 11			16 30			16 50		
Alvechurch	d	14 34		14 54			15 15			15 34		15 54			16 15			16 34			16 54		
Redditch	a	14 41		15 03			15 21			15 41		16 03			16 21			16 41			17 03		
Bromsgrove	a							15 11								16 11				16 41			

Table T069-F

Saturdays

23 June to 28 July

Lichfield - Birmingham - Longbridge and Redditch

		LM	LM	LM	LM	LM	LM	LM	XC	LM	LM	LM	LM	LM	LM	LM	XC	LM	LM	LM	LM	LM
									◇1								◇1					
Lichfield Trent Valley	d				16 20					16 50				17 20				17 50				18 20
Lichfield City	d			16 16	16 24			16 46		16 54			17 16	17 24		17 46		17 54			18 16	18 24
Shenstone	d				16 29					16 59				17 29				17 59				18 29
Blake Street	d			16 22	16 32			16 52		17 02			17 22	17 32		17 52		18 02			18 22	18 32
Butlers Lane	d			16 25	16 34			16 54		17 04			17 25	17 34		17 54		18 04			18 25	18 34
Four Oaks	d	16 16		16 26	16 36	16 46		16 56		17 06	17 16		17 26	17 36	17 46	17 56		18 06	18 16		18 26	18 36
Sutton Coldfield	d	16 20		16 30	16 40	16 50		17 00		17 10	17 20		17 30	17 40	17 50	18 00		18 10	18 20		18 30	18 40
Wylde Green	d	16 22		16 32	16 42	16 52		17 02		17 12	17 22		17 32	17 42	17 52	18 02		18 12	18 22		18 32	18 42
Chester Road	d	16 24		16 34	16 44	16 54		17 04		17 14	17 24		17 34	17 44	17 54	18 04		18 14	18 24		18 34	18 44
Erdington	d	16 27		16 37	16 47	16 57		17 07		17 17	17 27		17 37	17 47	17 57	18 07		18 17	18 27		18 37	18 47
Gravelly Hill	d	16 29		16 40	16 49	16 59		17 09		17 19	17 29		17 39	17 49	17 59	18 09		18 19	18 29		18 39	18 49
Aston	d	16 33		16 43	16 53	17 03		17 14		17 23	17 33		17 43	17 53	18 03	18 14		18 23	18 33		18 43	18 53
Duddeston	d	16 36				17 06					17 36				18 06				18 36			
Birmingham New Street 12	a	16 41		16 50	17 00	17 10		17 21		17 31	17 41		17 50	18 00	18 10	18 21		18 31	18 41		18 50	19 00
	d	16 43	16 50	16 53	17 03	17 14	17 20	17 23	17 30	17 33	17 43	17 50	17 53	18 03	18 14	18 23	18 30	18 33	18 43	18 50	18 53	19 03
Five Ways	d	16 47		16 57	17 07	17 18		17 27		17 37	17 47		17 57	18 07	18 18	18 27		18 37	18 47		18 57	19 07
University	d	16 51	16 56	17 01	17 11	17 22		17 31	17 36	17 41	17 51	17 56	18 01	18 11	18 22	18 31	18a36	18 41	18 51	18 56	19 01	19 11
Selly Oak	d	16 53		17 03	17 13	17 24		17 33		17 43	17 53		18 03	18 13	18 24	18 33		18 43	18 53		19 03	19 13
Bournville	d	16 56		17 06	17 16	17 27		17 36		17 46	17 56		18 06	18 16	18 27	18 36		18 46	18 56		19 06	19 16
Kings Norton	d	16 59		17 09	17 19	17 30		17 39		17 49	17 59		18 09	18 19	18 30	18 39		18 49	18 59		19 09	19 19
Northfield	d	17 02		17 12	17 22	17 33		17 42		17 52	18 02		18 12	18 22	18 33	18 42		18 52	19 02		19 12	19 22
Longbridge	d	17 06		17a14	17 25	17a35		17 45		17a54	18 06		18a14	18 25	18a35	18 45		18a54	19 06		19a14	19 25
Barnt Green	d	17 11			17 30			17 50			18 11			18 30		18 50			19 11			19 30
Alvechurch	d	17 15			17 34			17 54			18 15			18 34		18 54			19 15			19 34
Redditch	a	17 21			17 41			18 03			18 21			18 41		19 03			19 21			19 41
Bromsgrove	a		17 11				17 41		17 50			18 11								19 11		

		LM	LM	LM	XC	LM	LM	LM	LM	LM	LM	XC	LM	LM	LM	LM	LM	LM	LM	LM	LM	LM	LM
					◇1							◇1											
Lichfield Trent Valley	d					18 50			19 20				19 58			20 28		20 58			21 28		21 58
Lichfield City	d			18 46		18 54		19 16	19 24		19 46		20 02			20 32		21 02			21 32		22 02
Shenstone	d					18 59			19 29				20 07			20 37		21 07			21 37		22 07
Blake Street	d			18 52		19 02		19 22	19 32		19 52		20 10			20 40		21 10			21 40		22 10
Butlers Lane	d			18 55		19 04		19 25	19 34		19 55		20 13			20 43		21 13			21 43		22 13
Four Oaks	d	18 46		18 56		19 06	19 16	19 26	19 36	19 46	19 56		20 15			20 45		21 15			21 45		22 15
Sutton Coldfield	d	18 50		19 00		19 10	19 20	19 30	19 40	19 50	20 00		20 19			20 49		21 19			21 49		22 19
Wylde Green	d	18 52		19 02		19 12	19 22	19 32	19 42	19 52	20 02		20 21			20 51		21 21			21 51		22 21
Chester Road	d	18 54		19 04		19 14	19 24	19 34	19 44	19 54	20 04		20 23			20 53		21 23			21 53		22 23
Erdington	d	18 57		19 07		19 17	19 27	19 37	19 47	19 57	20 07		20 26			20 56		21 26			21 56		22 26
Gravelly Hill	d	18 59		19 09		19 19	19 29	19 39	19 49	19 59	20 09		20 28			20 58		21 28			21 58		22 28
Aston	d	19 03		19 14		19 23	19 33	19 43	19 53	20 03	20 13		20 32			21 02		21 32			22 02		22 32
Duddeston	d	19 06					19 36		19 56	20 06			20 35			21 05		21 35			22 05		22 35
Birmingham New Street 12	a	19 10		19 21		19 31	19 41	19 50	20 01	20 10	20 21		20 40			21 11		21 40			22 09		22 40
	d	19 14	19 20	19 23	19 30	19 33	19 43	19 53		20 15	20 23	20 30	20 44	20 53	21 00	21 15	21 23	21 43	21 53	22 09	22 13	22 23	22 43
Five Ways	d	19 18		19 27		19 37	19 47	19 57		20 19	20 27		20 48	20 57		21 19	21 27	21 47	21 57		22 17	22 27	22 47
University	d	19 22	19 26	19 31	19a36	19 41	19 51	20 01		20 23	20 31	20a36	20 52	21 01	21 06	21 23	21 31	21 51	22 01	22 15	22 21	22 31	22 51
Selly Oak	d	19 24		19 33		19 43	19 53	20 03		20 25	20 33		20 54	21 03		21 25	21 33	21 53	22 03		22 23	22 33	22 53
Bournville	d	19 27		19 36		19 46	19 56	20 06		20 28	20 36		20 57	21 06		21 28	21 36	21 56	22 06		22 26	22 36	22 56
Kings Norton	d	19 30		19 39		19 49	19 59	20 09		20 31	20 39		21 00	21 09		21 31	21 39	21 59	22 09		22 29	22 39	22 59
Northfield	d	19 33		19 42		19 52	20 02	20 12		20 34	20 42		21 03	21 12		21 34	21 42	22 02	22 12		22 32	22 42	23 02
Longbridge	d	19a35		19 45		19a54	20 06	20a14		20 37	20a44		21 06	21a14		21 36	21a44	22 06	22a14		22 36	22a44	23 06
Barnt Green	d			19 50			20 11			20 41			21 11			21 40		22 11			22 41		23 11
Alvechurch	d			19 54			20 15			20 46			21 15			21 45		22 15			22 45		23 15
Redditch	a			20 03			20 21			20 51			21 21			21 51		22 22			22 51		23 22
Bromsgrove	a		19 41												21 20					22 29			

		LM	LM	LM	LM
Lichfield Trent Valley	d		22 28	22 55	23 23
Lichfield City	d		22 32	22 59	23 27
Shenstone	d		22 37	23 04	23 32
Blake Street	d		22 40	23 07	23 36
Butlers Lane	d		22 43	23 10	23 38
Four Oaks	d		22 45	23 12	23 41
Sutton Coldfield	d		22 49	23 16	23 44
Wylde Green	d		22 51	23 18	
Chester Road	d		22 53		
Erdington	d		22 56		
Gravelly Hill	d		22 58		
Aston	d		23 02		
Duddeston	d		23 05		
Birmingham New Street 12	a		23 09	23 29	23 59
	d	22 53	23 13	23 33	
Five Ways	d	22 57	23 17	23 37	
University	d	23 01	23 21	23 41	
Selly Oak	d	23 03	23 23	23 43	
Bournville	d	23 06	23 26	23 46	
Kings Norton	d	23 09	23 29	23 49	
Northfield	d	23 12	23 32	23 52	
Longbridge	d	23a14	23 35	23a54	
Barnt Green	d		23 40		
Alvechurch	d		23 44		
Redditch	a		23 51		
Bromsgrove	a				

Table T069-F

Saturdays

4 August to 1 September

Lichfield - Birmingham - Longbridge and Redditch

		XC	LM	LM	LM	LM	LM	LM	LM	LM	LM	LM	LM	XC	LM	LM	LM	LM	LM	LM	LM	XC	LM
		◇1												◇1								◇1	
Lichfield Trent Valley	d										06 20				06 50				07 20				07 50
Lichfield City	d										06 24	06 38			06 54	07 08			07 24		07 46		07 54
Shenstone	d										06 29				06 59				07 29				07 59
Blake Street	d						06 02				06 32				07 02				07 32		07 52		08 02
Butlers Lane	d						06 04				06 34				07 04				07 34		07 55		08 05
Four Oaks	d						06 07				06 36	06 48			07 06	07 18			07 36	07 46	07 56		08 06
Sutton Coldfield	d						06 10				06 40	06 51			07 10	07 21			07 40	07 50	08 00		08 10
Wylde Green	d						06 12				06 42	06 54			07 12	07 24			07 42	07 52	08 02		08 12
Chester Road	d						06 14				06 44	06 56			07 14	07 26			07 44	07 54	08 04		08 14
Erdington	d						06 17				06 47	06 58			07 17	07 28			07 47	07 57	08 07		08 17
Gravelly Hill	d						06 19				06 49	07 01			07 19	07 31			07 49	07 59	08 09		08 19
Aston	d						06 23				06 53	07 03			07 23	07 33			07 53	08 03	08 14		08 23
Duddeston	d						06 26				06 56	07 06			07 26	07 36				08 06			
Birmingham New Street 12	a						06 30				07 01	07 12			07 31	07 41			08 00	08 10	08 21		08 31
	d	05 42	05 53	06 03	06 13	06 23	06 33	06 43	06 50	06 53	07 03	07 14	07 23	07 30	07 33	07 43	07 50	07 53	08 03	08 14	08 23	08 30	08 33
Five Ways	d		05 57	06 07	06 17	06 27	06 37	06 47		06 57	07 07	07 18	07 27		07 37	07 47		07 57	08 07	08 18	08 27		08 37
University	d		06 01	06 11	06 21	06 31	06 41	06 51	06 56	07 01	07 11	07 22	07 31	07a36	07 41	07 51	07 56	08 01	08 11	08 22	08 31	08a36	08 41
Selly Oak	d		06 03	06 13	06 23	06 33	06 43	06 53		07 03	07 13	07 24	07 33		07 43	07 53		08 03	08 13	08 24	08 33		08 43
Bournville	d		06 06	06 16	06 26	06 36	06 46	06 56		07 06	07 16	07 27	07 36		07 46	07 56		08 06	08 16	08 27	08 36		08 46
Kings Norton	d		06 09	06 19	06 29	06 39	06 49	06 59		07 09	07 19	07 30	07 39		07 49	07 59		08 09	08 19	08 30	08 39		08 49
Northfield	d		06 12	06 22	06 32	06 42	06 52	07 02		07 12	07 22	07 33	07 42		07 52	08 02		08 12	08 22	08 33	08 42		08 52
Longbridge	d		06 15	06 25	06 35	06 45	06 59	07 05		07 15	07 25	07 36	07 45		07 58	08 05		08 15	08 25	08 36	08 45		08 58
Barnt Green	d		06 19	06 30		06 50		07 10		07 19	07 30		07 50			08 10		08 19	08 30		08 50		
Alvechurch	d			06 34		06 54		07 15			07 34		07 54			08 14			08 34		08 54		
Redditch	a			06 41		07 03		07 21			07 41		08 03			08 21			08 41		09 03		
Bromsgrove	a	06 03	06 25		06 44		07 08		07 11	07 25		07 46			08 07		08 11	08 25		08 46			09 07

		LM	LM	LM	LM	LM	LM	XC	LM	LM	LM	LM	LM	LM	LM	XC	LM	LM	LM	LM	LM	LM	LM
								◇1								◇1							
Lichfield Trent Valley	d				08 20				08 50				09 20				09 50				10 20		
Lichfield City	d			08 16	08 24		08 46		08 54			09 16	09 24		09 46		09 54			10 16	10 24		10 46
Shenstone	d				08 29				08 59				09 29				09 59				10 29		
Blake Street	d			08 22	08 32		08 52		09 02			09 22	09 32		09 52		10 02			10 22	10 32		10 52
Butlers Lane	d			08 25	08 34		08 55		09 04			09 24	09 34		09 55		10 04			10 25	10 34		10 55
Four Oaks	d	08 16		08 26	08 36	08 46	08 56		09 06	09 16		09 26	09 36	09 46	09 56		10 06	10 16		10 26	10 36	10 46	10 56
Sutton Coldfield	d	08 20		08 30	08 40	08 50	09 00		09 10	09 20		09 30	09 40	09 50	10 00		10 10	10 20		10 30	10 40	10 50	11 00
Wylde Green	d	08 22		08 32	08 42	08 52	09 02		09 12	09 22		09 32	09 42	09 52	10 02		10 12	10 22		10 32	10 42	10 52	11 02
Chester Road	d	08 24		08 34	08 44	08 54	09 04		09 14	09 24		09 34	09 44	09 54	10 04		10 14	10 24		10 34	10 44	10 54	11 04
Erdington	d	08 27		08 37	08 47	08 57	09 07		09 17	09 27		09 37	09 47	09 57	10 07		10 17	10 27		10 37	10 47	10 57	11 07
Gravelly Hill	d	08 29		08 39	08 49	08 59	09 09		09 19	09 29		09 39	09 49	09 59	10 09		10 19	10 29		10 39	10 49	10 59	11 09
Aston	d	08 33		08 43	08 53	09 03	09 14		09 23	09 33		09 43	09 53	10 03	10 14		10 23	10 33		10 43	10 53	11 03	11 14
Duddeston	d	08 36				09 06				09 36				10 06				10 36				11 06	
Birmingham New Street 12	a	08 41		08 50	09 00	09 10	09 21		09 31	09 41		09 50	10 00	10 10	10 21		10 31	10 41		10 50	11 00	11 10	11 21
	d	08 43	08 50	08 53	09 03	09 14	09 23	09 30	09 33	09 43	09 50	09 53	10 03	10 14	10 23	10 30	10 33	10 43	10 50	10 53	11 03	11 14	11 23
Five Ways	d	08 47		08 57	09 07	09 18	09 27		09 37	09 47		09 57	10 07	10 18	10 27		10 37	10 47		10 57	11 07	11 18	11 27
University	d	08 51	08 56	09 01	09 11	09 22	09 31	09a36	09 41	09 51	09 56	10 01	10 11	10 22	10 31	10a36	10 41	10 51	10 56	11 01	11 11	11 22	11 31
Selly Oak	d	08 53		09 03	09 13	09 24	09 33		09 43	09 53		10 03	10 13	10 24	10 33		10 43	10 53		11 03	11 13	11 24	11 33
Bournville	d	08 56		09 06	09 16	09 27	09 36		09 46	09 56		10 06	10 16	10 27	10 36		10 46	10 56		11 06	11 16	11 27	11 36
Kings Norton	d	08 59		09 09	09 19	09 30	09 39		09 49	09 59		10 09	10 19	10 30	10 39		10 49	10 59		11 09	11 19	11 30	11 39
Northfield	d	09 02		09 12	09 22	09 33	09 42		09 52	10 02		10 12	10 22	10 33	10 42		10 52	11 02		11 12	11 22	11 33	11 42
Longbridge	d	09 06		09 15	09 25	09 36	09 45		09 58	10 06		10 15	10 25	10 36	10 45		10 58	11 06		11 15	11 25	11 36	11 45
Barnt Green	d	09 11		09 19	09 30		09 50			10 11		10 19	10 30		10 50			11 11		11 19	11 30		11 50
Alvechurch	d	09 15			09 34		09 54			10 15			10 34		10 54			11 15			11 34		11 54
Redditch	a	09 22			09 41		10 03			10 21			10 41		11 03			11 21			11 41		12 03
Bromsgrove	a		09 11	09 25		09 46			10 07		10 11	10 25		10 46			11 07		11 11	11 25		11 46	

		XC	LM	LM	LM	LM	LM	LM	LM	XC	LM	LM	LM	LM	LM	LM	LM	XC	LM	LM	LM	LM
		◇1								◇1								◇1				
Lichfield Trent Valley	d		10 50				11 20				11 50				12 20				12 50			
Lichfield City	d		10 54			11 16	11 24		11 46		11 54			12 16	12 24		12 46		12 54			13 16
Shenstone	d		10 59				11 29				11 59				12 29				12 59			
Blake Street	d		11 02			11 22	11 32		11 52		12 02			12 22	12 32		12 52		13 02			13 22
Butlers Lane	d		11 04			11 25	11 34		11 54		12 04			12 25	12 34		12 55		13 04			13 25
Four Oaks	d		11 06	11 16		11 26	11 36	11 46	11 56		12 06	12 16		12 26	12 36	12 46	12 56		13 06	13 16		13 26
Sutton Coldfield	d		11 10	11 20		11 30	11 40	11 50	12 00		12 10	12 20		12 30	12 40	12 50	13 00		13 10	13 20		13 30
Wylde Green	d		11 12	11 22		11 32	11 42	11 52	12 02		12 12	12 22		12 32	12 42	12 52	13 02		13 12	13 22		13 32
Chester Road	d		11 14	11 24		11 34	11 44	11 54	12 04		12 14	12 24		12 34	12 44	12 54	13 04		13 14	13 24		13 34
Erdington	d		11 17	11 27		11 37	11 47	11 57	12 07		12 17	12 27		12 37	12 47	12 57	13 07		13 17	13 27		13 37
Gravelly Hill	d		11 19	11 29		11 39	11 49	11 59	12 09		12 19	12 29		12 39	12 49	12 59	13 09		13 19	13 29		13 39
Aston	d		11 23	11 33		11 43	11 53	12 03	12 14		12 23	12 33		12 43	12 53	13 03	13 14		13 23	13 33		13 43
Duddeston	d			11 36				12 06				12 36				13 06				13 36		
Birmingham New Street 12	a		11 31	11 41		11 50	12 00	12 10	12 21		12 31	12 41		12 50	13 00	13 10	13 21		13 31	13 41		13 50
	d	11 30	11 33	11 43	11 50	11 53	12 03	12 14	12 23	12 30	12 33	12 43	12 50	12 53	13 03	13 14	13 23	13 30	13 33	13 43	13 50	13 53
Five Ways	d		11 37	11 47		11 57	12 07	12 18	12 27		12 37	12 47		12 57	13 07	13 18	13 27		13 37	13 47		13 57
University	d	11a36	11 41	11 51	11 56	12 01	12 11	12 22	12 31	12a36	12 41	12 51	12 56	13 01	13 11	13 22	13 31	13a36	13 41	13 51	13 56	14 01
Selly Oak	d		11 43	11 53		12 03	12 13	12 24	12 33		12 43	12 53		13 03	13 13	13 24	13 33		13 43	13 53		14 03
Bournville	d		11 46	11 56		12 06	12 16	12 27	12 36		12 46	12 56		13 06	13 16	13 27	13 36		13 46	13 56		14 06
Kings Norton	d		11 49	11 59		12 09	12 19	12 30	12 39		12 49	12 59		13 09	13 19	13 30	13 39		13 49	13 59		14 09
Northfield	d		11 52	12 02		12 12	12 22	12 33	12 42		12 52	13 02		13 12	13 22	13 33	13 42		13 52	14 02		14 12
Longbridge	d		11 58	12 06		12 15	12 25	12 36	12 45		12 58	13 06		13 15	13 25	13 36	13 45		13 58	14 06		14 15
Barnt Green	d			12 11		12 19	12 30		12 50			13 11		13 19	13 30		13 50			14 11		14 19
Alvechurch	d			12 15			12 34		12 54			13 15			13 34		13 54			14 15		
Redditch	a			12 21			12 41		13 03			13 21			13 41		14 03			14 21		
Bromsgrove	a		12 07		12 11	12 25		12 46			13 07		13 11	13 25		13 46			14 07		14 11	14 25

Table T069-F

Saturdays
4 August to 1 September

Lichfield - Birmingham - Longbridge and Redditch

		LM	LM	LM	XC ◇1	LM	LM	LM	LM	LM	LM	LM	XC ◇1
Lichfield Trent Valley	d	13 20				13 50				14 20			
Lichfield City	d	13 24		13 46		13 54			14 16	14 24		14 46	
Shenstone	d	13 29				13 59				14 29			
Blake Street	d	13 32		13 52		14 02			14 22	14 32		14 52	
Butlers Lane	d	13 34		13 55		14 04			14 25	14 34		14 55	
Four Oaks	d	13 36	13 46	13 56		14 06	14 16		14 26	14 36	14 46	14 56	
Sutton Coldfield	d	13 40	13 50	14 00		14 10	14 20		14 30	14 40	14 50	15 00	
Wylde Green	d	13 42	13 52	14 02		14 12	14 22		14 32	14 42	14 52	15 02	
Chester Road	d	13 44	13 54	14 04		14 14	14 24		14 34	14 44	14 54	15 04	
Erdington	d	13 47	13 57	14 07		14 17	14 27		14 37	14 47	14 57	15 07	
Gravelly Hill	d	13 49	13 59	14 09		14 19	14 29		14 39	14 49	14 59	15 09	
Aston	d	13 53	14 03	14 14		14 23	14 33		14 43	14 53	15 03	15 14	
Duddeston	d		14 06				14 36				15 06		
Birmingham New Street	a	14 00	14 10	14 21		14 31	14 41		14 50	15 00	15 10	15 21	
	d	14 03	14 14	14 23	14 30	14 33	14 43	14 50	14 53	15 03	15 14	15 23	15 30
Five Ways	d	14 07	14 18	14 27		14 37	14 47		14 57	15 07	15 18	15 27	
University	d	14 11	14 22	14 31	14a36	14 41	14 51	14 56	15 01	15 11	15 22	15 31	15a36
Selly Oak	d	14 13	14 24	14 33		14 43	14 53		15 03	15 13	15 24	15 33	
Bournville	d	14 16	14 27	14 36		14 46	14 56		15 06	15 16	15 27	15 36	
Kings Norton	d	14 19	14 30	14 39		14 49	14 59		15 09	15 19	15 30	15 39	
Northfield	d	14 22	14 33	14 42		14 52	15 02		15 12	15 22	15 33	15 42	
Longbridge	d	14 25	14 36	14 45		14 58	15 06		15 15	15 25	15 36	15 45	
Barnt Green	d	14 30		14 50			15 11		15 19	15 30		15 50	
Alvechurch	d	14 34		14 54			15 15			15 34		15 54	
Redditch	a	14 41		15 03			15 21			15 41		16 03	
Bromsgrove	a		14 46			15 07		15 11	15 25		15 46		

		LM	LM	LM	LM	LM	LM	LM	LM	XC ◇1	LM
Lichfield Trent Valley	d	14 50				15 20					15 50
Lichfield City	d	14 54			15 16	15 24			15 46		15 54
Shenstone	d	14 59				15 29					15 59
Blake Street	d	15 02			15 22	15 32			15 52		16 02
Butlers Lane	d	15 04			15 25	15 34			15 55		16 04
Four Oaks	d	15 06	15 16		15 26	15 36	15 46		15 56		16 06
Sutton Coldfield	d	15 10	15 20		15 30	15 40	15 50		16 00		16 10
Wylde Green	d	15 12	15 22		15 32	15 42	15 52		16 02		16 12
Chester Road	d	15 14	15 24		15 34	15 44	15 54		16 04		16 14
Erdington	d	15 17	15 27		15 37	15 47	15 57		16 07		16 17
Gravelly Hill	d	15 19	15 29		15 39	15 49	15 59		16 09		16 19
Aston	d	15 23	15 33		15 43	15 53	16 03		16 14		16 23
Duddeston	d		15 36				16 06				
Birmingham New Street	a	15 31	15 41		15 50	16 00	16 11		16 21		16 31
	d	15 33	15 43	15 50	15 53	16 03	16 15	16 20	16 23	16 30	16 33
Five Ways	d	15 37	15 47		15 57	16 07	16 19		16 27		16 37
University	d	15 41	15 51	15 56	16 01	16 11	16 23		16 31	16a36	16 41
Selly Oak	d	15 43	15 53		16 03	16 13	16 25		16 33		16 43
Bournville	d	15 46	15 56		16 06	16 16	16 28		16 36		16 46
Kings Norton	d	15 49	15 59		16 09	16 19	16 31		16 39		16 49
Northfield	d	15 52	16 02		16 12	16 22	16 34		16 42		16 52
Longbridge	d	15 58	16 06		16 15	16 25	16 37		16 45		16 58
Barnt Green	d		16 11		16 19	16 30			16 50		
Alvechurch	d		16 15			16 34			16 54		
Redditch	a		16 21			16 41			17 03		
Bromsgrove	a	16 07		16 11	16 25		16 46	16 41			17 07

		LM	LM	LM	LM	LM	LM	LM	XC ◇1	LM	LM	LM	LM
Lichfield Trent Valley	d				16 20					16 50			
Lichfield City	d			16 16	16 24			16 46		16 54			17 16
Shenstone	d				16 29					16 59			
Blake Street	d			16 22	16 32			16 52		17 02			17 22
Butlers Lane	d			16 25	16 34			16 54		17 04			17 25
Four Oaks	d	16 16		16 26	16 36	16 46		16 56		17 06	17 16		17 26
Sutton Coldfield	d	16 20		16 30	16 40	16 50		17 00		17 10	17 20		17 30
Wylde Green	d	16 22		16 32	16 42	16 52		17 02		17 12	17 22		17 32
Chester Road	d	16 24		16 34	16 44	16 54		17 04		17 14	17 24		17 34
Erdington	d	16 27		16 37	16 47	16 57		17 07		17 17	17 27		17 37
Gravelly Hill	d	16 29		16 40	16 49	16 59		17 09		17 19	17 29		17 39
Aston	d	16 33		16 43	16 53	17 03		17 14		17 23	17 33		17 43
Duddeston	d	16 36				17 06					17 36		
Birmingham New Street	a	16 41		16 50	17 00	17 10		17 21		17 31	17 41		17 50
	d	16 43	16 50	16 53	17 03	17 14	17 20	17 23	17 30	17 33	17 43	17 50	17 53
Five Ways	d	16 47		16 57	17 07	17 18		17 27		17 37	17 47		17 57
University	d	16 51	16 56	17 01	17 11	17 22		17 31	17 36	17 41	17 51	17 56	18 01
Selly Oak	d	16 53		17 03	17 13	17 24		17 33		17 43	17 53		18 03
Bournville	d	16 56		17 06	17 16	17 27		17 36		17 46	17 56		18 06
Kings Norton	d	16 59		17 09	17 19	17 30		17 39		17 49	17 59		18 09
Northfield	d	17 02		17 12	17 22	17 33		17 42		17 52	18 02		18 12
Longbridge	d	17 06		17 15	17 25	17 36		17 45		17 58	18 06		18 15
Barnt Green	d	17 11		17 19	17 30			17 50			18 11		18 19
Alvechurch	d	17 15			17 34			17 54			18 15		
Redditch	a	17 21			17 41			18 03			18 21		
Bromsgrove	a		17 11	17 25		17 46	17 41		17 50	18 07		18 11	18 25

		LM	LM	LM	XC ◇1	LM	LM	LM	LM	LM
Lichfield Trent Valley	d	17 20				17 50				18 20
Lichfield City	d	17 24		17 46		17 54			18 16	18 24
Shenstone	d	17 29				17 59				18 29
Blake Street	d	17 32		17 52		18 02			18 22	18 32
Butlers Lane	d	17 34		17 54		18 04			18 25	18 34
Four Oaks	d	17 36	17 46	17 56		18 06	18 16		18 26	18 36
Sutton Coldfield	d	17 40	17 50	18 00		18 10	18 20		18 30	18 40
Wylde Green	d	17 42	17 52	18 02		18 12	18 22		18 32	18 42
Chester Road	d	17 44	17 54	18 04		18 14	18 24		18 34	18 44
Erdington	d	17 47	17 57	18 07		18 17	18 27		18 37	18 47
Gravelly Hill	d	17 49	17 59	18 09		18 19	18 29		18 39	18 49
Aston	d	17 53	18 03	18 14		18 23	18 33		18 43	18 53
Duddeston	d		18 06				18 36			
Birmingham New Street	a	18 00	18 10	18 21		18 31	18 41		18 50	19 00
	d	18 03	18 14	18 23	18 30	18 33	18 43	18 50	18 53	19 03
Five Ways	d	18 07	18 18	18 27		18 37	18 47		18 57	19 07
University	d	18 11	18 22	18 31	18a36	18 41	18 51	18 56	19 01	19 11
Selly Oak	d	18 13	18 24	18 33		18 43	18 53		19 03	19 13
Bournville	d	18 16	18 27	18 36		18 46	18 56		19 06	19 16
Kings Norton	d	18 19	18 30	18 39		18 49	18 59		19 09	19 19
Northfield	d	18 22	18 33	18 42		18 52	19 02		19 12	19 22
Longbridge	d	18 25	18 36	18 45		18 58	19 06		19 15	19 25
Barnt Green	d	18 30		18 50			19 11		19 19	19 30
Alvechurch	d	18 34		18 54			19 15			19 34
Redditch	a	18 41		19 03			19 21			19 41
Bromsgrove	a		18 46			19 07		19 11	19 25	

		LM	LM	LM	XC ◇1	LM	LM	LM	LM	LM	LM	XC ◇1	LM
Lichfield Trent Valley	d					18 50			19 20				19 58
Lichfield City	d			18 46		18 54		19 16	19 24		19 46		20 02
Shenstone	d					18 59			19 29				20 07
Blake Street	d			18 52		19 02		19 22	19 32		19 52		20 10
Butlers Lane	d			18 55		19 04		19 25	19 34		19 55		20 13
Four Oaks	d	18 46		18 56		19 06	19 16	19 26	19 36	19 46	19 56		20 15
Sutton Coldfield	d	18 50		19 00		19 10	19 20	19 30	19 40	19 50	20 00		20 19
Wylde Green	d	18 52		19 02		19 12	19 22	19 32	19 42	19 52	20 02		20 21
Chester Road	d	18 54		19 04		19 14	19 24	19 34	19 44	19 54	20 04		20 23
Erdington	d	18 57		19 07		19 17	19 27	19 37	19 47	19 57	20 07		20 26
Gravelly Hill	d	18 59		19 09		19 19	19 29	19 39	19 49	19 59	20 09		20 28
Aston	d	19 03		19 14		19 23	19 33	19 43	19 53	20 03	20 13		20 32
Duddeston	d	19 06					19 36		19 56	20 06			20 35
Birmingham New Street	a	19 10		19 21		19 31	19 41	19 50	20 01	20 10	20 21		20 40
	d	19 14	19 20	19 23	19 30	19 33	19 43	19 53		20 15	20 23	20 30	20 44
Five Ways	d	19 18		19 27		19 37	19 47	19 57		20 19	20 27		20 48
University	d	19 22	19 26	19 31	19a36	19 41	19 51	20 01		20 23	20 31	20a36	20 52
Selly Oak	d	19 24		19 33		19 43	19 53	20 03		20 25	20 33		20 54
Bournville	d	19 27		19 36		19 46	19 56	20 06		20 28	20 36		20 57
Kings Norton	d	19 30		19 39		19 49	19 59	20 09		20 31	20 39		21 00
Northfield	d	19 33		19 42		19 52	20 02	20 12		20 34	20 42		21 03
Longbridge	d	19 36		19 45		20 00	20 06	20 15		20 37	20 46		21 06
Barnt Green	d			19 50			20 11	20 19		20 41			21 11
Alvechurch	d			19 54			20 15			20 46			21 15
Redditch	a			20 03			20 21			20 51			21 21
Bromsgrove	a	19 46	19 41			20 09		20 25			20 55		

		LM	LM	LM	LM	LM	LM	LM	LM	LM	LM
Lichfield Trent Valley	d			20 28		20 58			21 28		21 58
Lichfield City	d			20 32		21 02			21 32		22 02
Shenstone	d			20 37		21 07			21 37		22 07
Blake Street	d			20 40		21 10			21 40		22 10
Butlers Lane	d			20 43		21 13			21 43		22 13
Four Oaks	d			20 45		21 15			21 45		22 15
Sutton Coldfield	d			20 49		21 19			21 49		22 19
Wylde Green	d			20 51		21 21			21 51		22 21
Chester Road	d			20 53		21 23			21 53		22 23
Erdington	d			20 56		21 26			21 56		22 26
Gravelly Hill	d			20 58		21 28			21 58		22 28
Aston	d			21 02		21 32			22 02		22 32
Duddeston	d			21 05		21 35			22 05		22 35
Birmingham New Street	a			21 11		21 40			22 09		22 40
	d	20 53	21 00	21 15	21 23	21 43	21 53	22 09	22 13	22 23	22 43
Five Ways	d	20 57		21 19	21 27	21 47	21 57		22 17	22 27	22 47
University	d	21 01	21 06	21 23	21 31	21 51	22 01	22 15	22 21	22 31	22 51
Selly Oak	d	21 03		21 25	21 33	21 53	22 03		22 23	22 33	22 53
Bournville	d	21 06		21 28	21 36	21 56	22 06		22 26	22 36	22 56
Kings Norton	d	21 09		21 31	21 39	21 59	22 09		22 29	22 39	22 59
Northfield	d	21 12		21 34	21 42	22 02	22 12		22 32	22 42	23 02
Longbridge	d	21 15		21 36	21 46	22 06	22 15		22 36	22a44	23 06
Barnt Green	d	21 20		21 40		22 11	22 19		22 41		23 11
Alvechurch	d			21 45		22 15			22 45		23 15
Redditch	a			21 51		22 22			22 51		23 22
Bromsgrove	a	21 26	21 20		21 55		22 25	22 29			

Table T069-F

Saturdays
4 August to 1 September

Lichfield - Birmingham - Longbridge and Redditch

		LM	LM	LM	LM
Lichfield Trent Valley	d		22 28	22 55	23 23
Lichfield City	d		22 32	22 59	23 27
Shenstone	d		22 37	23 04	23 32
Blake Street	d		22 40	23 07	23 36
Butlers Lane	d		22 43	23 10	23 38
Four Oaks	d		22 45	23 12	23 41
Sutton Coldfield	d		22 49	23 16	23 44
Wylde Green	d		22 51	23 18	
Chester Road	d		22 53		
Erdington	d		22 56		
Gravelly Hill	d		22 58		
Aston	d		23 02		
Duddeston	d		23 05		
Birmingham New Street	a		23 09	23 29	23 59
	d	22 53	23 13	23 33	
Five Ways	d	22 57	23 17	23 37	
University	d	23 01	23 21	23 41	
Selly Oak	d	23 03	23 23	23 43	
Bournville	d	23 06	23 26	23 46	
Kings Norton	d	23 09	23 29	23 49	
Northfield	d	23 12	23 32	23 52	
Longbridge	d	23a14	23 35	23a54	
Barnt Green	d		23 40		
Alvechurch	d		23 44		
Redditch	a		23 51		
Bromsgrove	a				

Saturdays
8 September to 8 December

		XC ◇1	LM	LM	LM	LM	LM	LM	LM	LM	LM	LM	LM
Lichfield Trent Valley	d										06 20		
Lichfield City	d										06 24	06 38	
Shenstone	d										06 29		
Blake Street	d						06 02				06 32		
Butlers Lane	d						06 04				06 34		
Four Oaks	d						06 07				06 36	06 48	
Sutton Coldfield	d						06 10				06 40	06 51	
Wylde Green	d						06 12				06 42	06 54	
Chester Road	d						06 14				06 44	06 56	
Erdington	d						06 17				06 47	06 58	
Gravelly Hill	d						06 19				06 49	07 01	
Aston	d						06 23				06 53	07 03	
Duddeston	d						06 26				06 56	07 06	
Birmingham New Street	a						06 30				07 01	07 12	
	d	05 42	05 53	06 03	06 13	06 23	06 33	06 43	06 50	06 53	07 03	07 14	07 23
Five Ways	d		05 57	06 07	06 17	06 27	06 37	06 47		06 57	07 07	07 18	07 27
University	d		06 01	06 11	06 21	06 31	06 41	06 51	06 56	07 01	07 11	07 22	07 31
Selly Oak	d		06 03	06 13	06 23	06 33	06 43	06 53		07 03	07 13	07 24	07 33
Bournville	d		06 06	06 16	06 26	06 36	06 46	06 56		07 06	07 16	07 27	07 36
Kings Norton	d		06 09	06 19	06 29	06 39	06 49	06 59		07 09	07 19	07 30	07 39
Northfield	d		06 12	06 22	06 32	06 42	06 52	07 02		07 12	07 22	07 33	07 42
Longbridge	d		06 15	06 25	06 35	06 45	06 59	07 05		07 15	07 25	07 36	07 45
Barnt Green	d		06 19	06 30		06 50		07 10		07 19	07 30		07 50
Alvechurch	d			06 34		06 54		07 15			07 34		07 54
Redditch	a			06 41		07 03		07 21			07 41		08 03
Bromsgrove	a	06 03	06 25		06 44		07 08		07 11	07 25		07 46	

		XC ◇1	LM	LM	LM	LM	LM	LM	LM	XC ◇1	LM
Lichfield Trent Valley	d		06 50				07 20				07 50
Lichfield City	d		06 54	07 08			07 24		07 46		07 54
Shenstone	d		06 59				07 29				07 59
Blake Street	d		07 02				07 32		07 52		08 02
Butlers Lane	d		07 04				07 34		07 55		08 05
Four Oaks	d		07 06	07 18			07 36	07 46	07 56		08 06
Sutton Coldfield	d		07 10	07 21			07 40	07 50	08 00		08 10
Wylde Green	d		07 12	07 24			07 42	07 52	08 02		08 12
Chester Road	d		07 14	07 26			07 44	07 54	08 04		08 14
Erdington	d		07 17	07 28			07 47	07 57	08 07		08 17
Gravelly Hill	d		07 19	07 31			07 49	07 59	08 09		08 19
Aston	d		07 23	07 33			07 53	08 03	08 14		08 23
Duddeston	d		07 26	07 36				08 06			
Birmingham New Street	a		07 31	07 41			08 00	08 10	08 21		08 31
	d	07 30	07 33	07 43	07 50	07 53	08 03	08 14	08 23	08 30	08 33
Five Ways	d		07 37	07 47		07 57	08 07	08 18	08 27		08 37
University	d	07a36	07 41	07 51	07 56	08 01	08 11	08 22	08 31	08a36	08 41
Selly Oak	d		07 43	07 53		08 03	08 13	08 24	08 33		08 43
Bournville	d		07 46	07 56		08 06	08 16	08 27	08 36		08 46
Kings Norton	d		07 49	07 59		08 09	08 19	08 30	08 39		08 49
Northfield	d		07 52	08 02		08 12	08 22	08 33	08 42		08 52
Longbridge	d		07 58	08 05		08 15	08 25	08 36	08 45		08 58
Barnt Green	d			08 10		08 19	08 30		08 50		
Alvechurch	d			08 14			08 34		08 54		
Redditch	a			08 21			08 41		09 03		
Bromsgrove	a		08 07		08 11	08 25		08 46			09 07

		LM	LM	LM	LM	LM	LM	XC ◇1	LM	LM	LM	LM	LM
Lichfield Trent Valley	d				08 20				08 50				09 20
Lichfield City	d			08 16	08 24		08 46		08 54			09 16	09 24
Shenstone	d				08 29				08 59				09 29
Blake Street	d			08 22	08 32		08 52		09 02			09 22	09 32
Butlers Lane	d			08 25	08 34		08 55		09 04			09 24	09 34
Four Oaks	d	08 16		08 26	08 36	08 46	08 56		09 06	09 16		09 26	09 36
Sutton Coldfield	d	08 20		08 30	08 40	08 50	09 00		09 10	09 20		09 30	09 40
Wylde Green	d	08 22		08 32	08 42	08 52	09 02		09 12	09 22		09 32	09 42
Chester Road	d	08 24		08 34	08 44	08 54	09 04		09 14	09 24		09 34	09 44
Erdington	d	08 27		08 37	08 47	08 57	09 07		09 17	09 27		09 37	09 47
Gravelly Hill	d	08 29		08 39	08 49	08 59	09 09		09 19	09 29		09 39	09 49
Aston	d	08 33		08 43	08 53	09 03	09 14		09 23	09 33		09 43	09 53
Duddeston	d	08 36				09 06				09 36			
Birmingham New Street	a	08 41		08 50	09 00	09 10	09 21		09 31	09 41		09 50	10 00
	d	08 43	08 50	08 53	09 03	09 14	09 23	09 30	09 33	09 43	09 50	09 53	10 03
Five Ways	d	08 47		08 57	09 07	09 18	09 27		09 37	09 47		09 57	10 07
University	d	08 51	08 56	09 01	09 11	09 22	09 31	09a36	09 41	09 51	09 56	10 01	10 11
Selly Oak	d	08 53		09 03	09 13	09 24	09 33		09 43	09 53		10 03	10 13
Bournville	d	08 56		09 06	09 16	09 27	09 36		09 46	09 56		10 06	10 16
Kings Norton	d	08 59		09 09	09 19	09 30	09 39		09 49	09 59		10 09	10 19
Northfield	d	09 02		09 12	09 22	09 33	09 42		09 52	10 02		10 12	10 22
Longbridge	d	09 06		09 15	09 25	09 36	09 45		09 58	10 06		10 15	10 25
Barnt Green	d	09 11		09 19	09 30		09 50			10 11		10 19	10 30
Alvechurch	d	09 15			09 34		09 54			10 15			10 34
Redditch	a	09 22			09 41		10 03			10 21			10 41
Bromsgrove	a		09 11	09 25		09 46			10 07		10 11	10 25	

		LM	LM	XC ◇1	LM	LM	LM	LM	LM	LM	LM
Lichfield Trent Valley	d				09 50				10 20		
Lichfield City	d		09 46		09 54			10 16	10 24		10 46
Shenstone	d				09 59				10 29		
Blake Street	d		09 52		10 02			10 22	10 32		10 52
Butlers Lane	d		09 55		10 04			10 25	10 34		10 55
Four Oaks	d	09 46	09 56		10 06	10 16		10 26	10 36	10 46	10 56
Sutton Coldfield	d	09 50	10 00		10 10	10 20		10 30	10 40	10 50	11 00
Wylde Green	d	09 52	10 02		10 12	10 22		10 32	10 42	10 52	11 02
Chester Road	d	09 54	10 04		10 14	10 24		10 34	10 44	10 54	11 04
Erdington	d	09 57	10 07		10 17	10 27		10 37	10 47	10 57	11 07
Gravelly Hill	d	09 59	10 09		10 19	10 29		10 39	10 49	10 59	11 09
Aston	d	10 03	10 14		10 23	10 33		10 43	10 53	11 03	11 14
Duddeston	d	10 06				10 36				11 06	
Birmingham New Street	a	10 10	10 21		10 31	10 41		10 50	11 00	11 10	11 21
	d	10 14	10 23	10 30	10 33	10 43	10 50	10 53	11 03	11 14	11 23
Five Ways	d	10 18	10 27		10 37	10 47		10 57	11 07	11 18	11 27
University	d	10 22	10 31	10a36	10 41	10 51	10 56	11 01	11 11	11 22	11 31
Selly Oak	d	10 24	10 33		10 43	10 53		11 03	11 13	11 24	11 33
Bournville	d	10 27	10 36		10 46	10 56		11 06	11 16	11 27	11 36
Kings Norton	d	10 30	10 39		10 49	10 59		11 09	11 19	11 30	11 39
Northfield	d	10 33	10 42		10 52	11 02		11 12	11 22	11 33	11 42
Longbridge	d	10 36	10 45		10 58	11 06		11 15	11 25	11 36	11 45
Barnt Green	d		10 50			11 11		11 19	11 30		11 50
Alvechurch	d		10 54			11 15			11 34		11 54
Redditch	a		11 03			11 21			11 41		12 03
Bromsgrove	a	10 46			11 07		11 11	11 25		11 46	

Table T069-F

Saturdays
8 September to 8 December

Lichfield - Birmingham - Longbridge and Redditch

		XC		LM	LM	LM	LM	LM	LM	LM	XC	LM		LM	LM	LM	LM	LM	LM	XC	LM	LM		LM	LM
		◇1 ⊤									◇1 ⊤									◇1 ⊤					
Lichfield Trent Valley	d			10 50				11 20				11 50					12 20				12 50				
Lichfield City	d			10 54			11 16	11 24		11 46		11 54				12 16	12 24		12 46		12 54				13 16
Shenstone	d			10 59				11 29				11 59					12 29				12 59				
Blake Street	d			11 02			11 22	11 32		11 52		12 02				12 22	12 32		12 52		13 02				13 22
Butlers Lane	d			11 04			11 25	11 34		11 54		12 04				12 25	12 34		12 55		13 04				13 25
Four Oaks	d			11 06	11 16		11 26	11 36	11 46	11 56		12 06		12 16		12 26	12 36	12 46	12 56		13 06	13 16			13 26
Sutton Coldfield	d			11 10	11 20		11 30	11 40	11 50	12 00		12 10		12 20		12 30	12 40	12 50	13 00		13 10	13 20			13 30
Wylde Green	d			11 12	11 22		11 32	11 42	11 52	12 02		12 12		12 22		12 32	12 42	12 52	13 02		13 12	13 22			13 32
Chester Road	d			11 14	11 24		11 34	11 44	11 54	12 04		12 14		12 24		12 34	12 44	12 54	13 04		13 14	13 24			13 34
Erdington	d			11 17	11 27		11 37	11 47	11 57	12 07		12 17		12 27		12 37	12 47	12 57	13 07		13 17	13 27			13 37
Gravelly Hill	d			11 19	11 29		11 39	11 49	11 59	12 09		12 19		12 29		12 39	12 49	12 59	13 09		13 19	13 29			13 39
Aston	d			11 23	11 33		11 43	11 53	12 03	12 14		12 23		12 33		12 43	12 53	13 03	13 14		13 23	13 33			13 43
Duddeston	d				11 36				12 06					12 36				13 06				13 36			
Birmingham New Street 12	a			11 31	11 41		11 50	12 00	12 10	12 21		12 31		12 41		12 50	13 00	13 10	13 21		13 31	13 41			13 50
	d	11 30		11 33	11 43	11 50	11 53	12 03	12 14	12 23	12 30	12 33		12 43	12 50	12 53	13 03	13 14	13 23	13 30	13 33	13 43		13 50	13 53
Five Ways	d			11 37	11 47		11 57	12 07	12 18	12 27		12 37		12 47		12 57	13 07	13 18	13 27		13 37	13 47			13 57
University	d	11a36		11 41	11 51	11 56	12 01	12 11	12 22	12 31	12a36	12 41		12 51	12 56	13 01	13 11	13 22	13 31	13a36	13 41	13 51		13 56	14 01
Selly Oak	d			11 43	11 53		12 03	12 13	12 24	12 33		12 43		12 53		13 03	13 13	13 24	13 33		13 43	13 53			14 03
Bournville	d			11 46	11 56		12 06	12 16	12 27	12 36		12 46		12 56		13 06	13 16	13 27	13 36		13 46	13 56			14 06
Kings Norton	d			11 49	11 59		12 09	12 19	12 30	12 39		12 49		12 59		13 09	13 19	13 30	13 39		13 49	13 59			14 09
Northfield	d			11 52	12 02		12 12	12 22	12 33	12 42		12 52		13 02		13 12	13 22	13 33	13 42		13 52	14 02			14 12
Longbridge	d			11 58	12 06		12 15	12 25	12 36	12 45		12 58		13 06		13 15	13 25	13 36	13 45		13 58	14 06			14 15
Barnt Green	d				12 11		12 19	12 30		12 50				13 11		13 19	13 30		13 50			14 11			14 19
Alvechurch	d				12 15			12 34		12 54				13 15			13 34		13 54			14 15			
Redditch	a				12 21			12 41		13 03				13 21			13 41		14 03			14 21			
Bromsgrove	a			12 07		12 11	12 25		12 46			13 07			13 11	13 25		13 46			14 07			14 11	14 25

		LM	LM	LM	XC	LM	LM	LM		LM	LM	LM	LM	XC	LM	LM	LM	LM		LM	LM	LM	LM	XC	LM
					◇1 ⊤									◇1 ⊤										◇1 ⊤	
Lichfield Trent Valley	d	13 20				13 50					14 20				14 50					15 20					15 50
Lichfield City	d	13 24		13 46		13 54				14 16	14 24		14 46		14 54			15 16		15 24			15 46		15 54
Shenstone	d	13 29				13 59					14 29				14 59					15 29					15 59
Blake Street	d	13 32		13 52		14 02				14 22	14 32		14 52		15 02			15 22		15 32			15 52		16 02
Butlers Lane	d	13 34		13 55		14 04				14 25	14 34		14 55		15 04			15 25		15 34			15 55		16 04
Four Oaks	d	13 36	13 46	13 56		14 06	14 16			14 26	14 36	14 46	14 56		15 06	15 16		15 26		15 36	15 46		15 56		16 06
Sutton Coldfield	d	13 40	13 50	14 00		14 10	14 20			14 30	14 40	14 50	15 00		15 10	15 20		15 30		15 40	15 50		16 00		16 10
Wylde Green	d	13 42	13 52	14 02		14 12	14 22			14 32	14 42	14 52	15 02		15 12	15 22		15 32		15 42	15 52		16 02		16 12
Chester Road	d	13 44	13 54	14 04		14 14	14 24			14 34	14 44	14 54	15 04		15 14	15 24		15 34		15 44	15 54		16 04		16 14
Erdington	d	13 47	13 57	14 07		14 17	14 27			14 37	14 47	14 57	15 07		15 17	15 27		15 37		15 47	15 57		16 07		16 17
Gravelly Hill	d	13 49	13 59	14 09		14 19	14 29			14 39	14 49	14 59	15 09		15 19	15 29		15 39		15 49	15 59		16 09		16 19
Aston	d	13 53	14 03	14 14		14 23	14 33			14 43	14 53	15 03	15 14		15 23	15 33		15 43		15 53	16 03		16 14		16 23
Duddeston	d		14 06				14 36					15 06				15 36					16 06				
Birmingham New Street 12	a	14 00	14 10	14 21		14 31	14 41			14 50	15 00	15 10	15 21		15 31	15 41		15 50		16 00	16 11		16 21		16 31
	d	14 03	14 14	14 23	14 30	14 33	14 43	14 50		14 53	15 03	15 14	15 23	15 30	15 33	15 43	15 50	15 53		16 03	16 15	16 20	16 23	16 30	16 33
Five Ways	d	14 07	14 18	14 27		14 37	14 47			14 57	15 07	15 18	15 27		15 37	15 47		15 57		16 07	16 19		16 27		16 37
University	d	14 11	14 22	14 31	14a36	14 41	14 51	14 56		15 01	15 11	15 22	15 31	15a36	15 41	15 51	15 56	16 01		16 11	16 23		16 31	16a36	16 41
Selly Oak	d	14 13	14 24	14 33		14 43	14 53			15 03	15 13	15 24	15 33		15 43	15 53		16 03		16 13	16 25		16 33		16 43
Bournville	d	14 16	14 27	14 36		14 46	14 56			15 06	15 16	15 27	15 36		15 46	15 56		16 06		16 16	16 28		16 36		16 46
Kings Norton	d	14 19	14 30	14 39		14 49	14 59			15 09	15 19	15 30	15 39		15 49	15 59		16 09		16 19	16 31		16 39		16 49
Northfield	d	14 22	14 33	14 42		14 52	15 02			15 12	15 22	15 33	15 42		15 52	16 02		16 12		16 22	16 34		16 42		16 52
Longbridge	d	14 25	14 36	14 45		14 58	15 06			15 15	15 25	15 36	15 45		15 58	16 06		16 15		16 25	16 37		16 45		16 58
Barnt Green	d	14 30		14 50			15 11			15 19	15 30		15 50			16 11		16 19		16 30			16 50		
Alvechurch	d	14 34		14 54			15 15				15 34		15 54			16 15				16 34			16 54		
Redditch	a	14 41		15 03			15 21				15 41		16 03			16 21				16 41			17 03		
Bromsgrove	a		14 46			15 07		15 11		15 25		15 46			16 07		16 11	16 25			16 46	16 41			17 07

		LM	LM	LM		LM	LM	LM	LM	XC	LM	LM	LM	LM		LM	LM	LM	XC	LM	LM	LM	LM	LM	
										◇1									◇1						
Lichfield Trent Valley	d					16 20					16 50					17 20				17 50				18 20	
Lichfield City	d			16 16		16 24			16 46		16 54			17 16		17 24		17 46		17 54			18 16	18 24	
Shenstone	d					16 29					16 59					17 29				17 59				18 29	
Blake Street	d			16 22		16 32			16 52		17 02			17 22		17 32		17 52		18 02			18 22	18 32	
Butlers Lane	d			16 25		16 34			16 54		17 04			17 25		17 34		17 54		18 04			18 25	18 34	
Four Oaks	d	16 16		16 26		16 36	16 46		16 56		17 06	17 16		17 26		17 36	17 46	17 56		18 06	18 16		18 26	18 36	
Sutton Coldfield	d	16 20		16 30		16 40	16 50		17 00		17 10	17 20		17 30		17 40	17 50	18 00		18 10	18 20		18 30	18 40	
Wylde Green	d	16 22		16 32		16 42	16 52		17 02		17 12	17 22		17 32		17 42	17 52	18 02		18 12	18 22		18 32	18 42	
Chester Road	d	16 24		16 34		16 44	16 54		17 04		17 14	17 24		17 34		17 44	17 54	18 04		18 14	18 24		18 34	18 44	
Erdington	d	16 27		16 37		16 47	16 57		17 07		17 17	17 27		17 37		17 47	17 57	18 07		18 17	18 27		18 37	18 47	
Gravelly Hill	d	16 29		16 40		16 49	16 59		17 09		17 19	17 29		17 39		17 49	17 59	18 09		18 19	18 29		18 39	18 49	
Aston	d	16 33		16 43		16 53	17 03		17 14		17 23	17 33		17 43		17 53	18 03	18 14		18 23	18 33		18 43	18 53	
Duddeston	d	16 36					17 06					17 36					18 06				18 36				
Birmingham New Street 12	a	16 41		16 50		17 00	17 10		17 21		17 31	17 41		17 50		18 00	18 10	18 21		18 31	18 41		18 50	19 00	
	d	16 43	16 50	16 53		17 03	17 14	17 20	17 23	17 30	17 33	17 43	17 50	17 53		18 03	18 14	18 23	18 30	18 33	18 43	18 50	18 53	19 03	
Five Ways	d	16 47		16 57		17 07	17 18		17 27		17 37	17 47		17 57		18 07	18 18	18 27		18 37	18 47		18 57	19 07	
University	d	16 51	16 56	17 01		17 11	17 22		17 31	17 36	17 41	17 51	17 56	18 01		18 11	18 22	18 31	18a36	18 41	18 51	18 56	19 01	19 11	
Selly Oak	d	16 53		17 03		17 13	17 24		17 33		17 43	17 53		18 03		18 13	18 24	18 33		18 43	18 53		19 03	19 13	
Bournville	d	16 56		17 06		17 16	17 27		17 36		17 46	17 56		18 06		18 16	18 27	18 36		18 46	18 56		19 06	19 16	
Kings Norton	d	16 59		17 09		17 19	17 30		17 39		17 49	17 59		18 09		18 19	18 30	18 39		18 49	18 59		19 09	19 19	
Northfield	d	17 02		17 12		17 22	17 33		17 42		17 52	18 02		18 12		18 22	18 33	18 42		18 52	19 02		19 12	19 22	
Longbridge	d	17 06		17 15		17 25	17 36		17 45		17 58	18 06		18 15		18 25	18 36	18 45		18 58	19 06		19 15	19 25	
Barnt Green	d	17 11		17 19		17 30			17 50			18 11		18 19		18 30		18 50			19 11		19 19	19 30	
Alvechurch	d	17 15				17 34			17 54			18 15				18 34		18 54			19 15			19 34	
Redditch	a	17 21				17 41			18 03			18 21				18 41		19 03			19 21			19 41	
Bromsgrove	a		17 11	17 25			17 46	17 41		17 50	18 07		18 11	18 25			18 46			19 07		19 11	19 25		

Table T069-F

Saturdays
8 September to 8 December

Lichfield - Birmingham - Longbridge and Redditch

		LM	LM	LM	XC	LM	LM	LM	LM	LM		LM	XC	LM	LM	LM	LM	LM	LM	LM		LM	LM	LM	LM
					◇1								◇1												
Lichfield Trent Valley	d					18 50			19 20					19 58			20 28		20 58				21 28		21 58
Lichfield City	d			18 46		18 54		19 16	19 24			19 46		20 02			20 32		21 02				21 32		22 02
Shenstone	d					18 59			19 29					20 07			20 37		21 07				21 37		22 07
Blake Street	d			18 52		19 02		19 22	19 32			19 52		20 10			20 40		21 10				21 40		22 10
Butlers Lane	d			18 55		19 04		19 25	19 34			19 55		20 13			20 43		21 13				21 43		22 13
Four Oaks	d	18 46		18 56		19 06	19 16	19 26	19 36	19 46		19 56		20 15			20 45		21 15				21 45		22 15
Sutton Coldfield	d	18 50		19 00		19 10	19 20	19 30	19 40	19 50		20 00		20 19			20 49		21 19				21 49		22 19
Wylde Green	d	18 52		19 02		19 12	19 22	19 32	19 42	19 52		20 02		20 21			20 51		21 21				21 51		22 21
Chester Road	d	18 54		19 04		19 14	19 24	19 34	19 44	19 54		20 04		20 23			20 53		21 23				21 53		22 23
Erdington	d	18 57		19 07		19 17	19 27	19 37	19 47	19 57		20 07		20 26			20 56		21 26				21 56		22 26
Gravelly Hill	d	18 59		19 09		19 19	19 29	19 39	19 49	19 59		20 09		20 28			20 58		21 28				21 58		22 28
Aston	d	19 03		19 14		19 23	19 33	19 43	19 53	20 03		20 13		20 32			21 02		21 32				22 02		22 32
Duddeston	d	19 06					19 36		19 56	20 06				20 35			21 05		21 35				22 05		22 35
Birmingham New Street 12	a	19 10		19 21		19 31	19 41	19 50	20 01	20 10		20 21		20 40			21 11		21 40				22 09		22 40
	d	19 14	19 20	19 23	19 30	19 33	19 43	19 53		20 15		20 23	20 30	20 44	20 53	21 00	21 15	21 23	21 43	21 53		22 09	22 13	22 23	22 43
Five Ways	d	19 18		19 27		19 37	19 47	19 57		20 19		20 27		20 48	20 57		21 19	21 27	21 47	21 57			22 17	22 27	22 47
University	d	19 22	19 26	19 31	19a36	19 41	19 51	20 01		20 23		20 31	20a36	20 52	21 01	21 06	21 23	21 31	21 51	22 01		22 15	22 21	22 31	22 51
Selly Oak	d	19 24		19 33		19 43	19 53	20 03		20 25		20 33		20 54	21 03		21 25	21 33	21 53	22 03			22 23	22 33	22 53
Bournville	d	19 27		19 36		19 46	19 56	20 06		20 28		20 36		20 57	21 06		21 28	21 36	21 56	22 06			22 26	22 36	22 56
Kings Norton	d	19 30		19 39		19 49	19 59	20 09		20 31		20 39		21 00	21 09		21 31	21 39	21 59	22 09			22 29	22 39	22 59
Northfield	d	19 33		19 42		19 52	20 02	20 12		20 34		20 42		21 03	21 12		21 34	21 42	22 02	22 12			22 32	22 42	23 02
Longbridge	d	19 36		19 45		20 00	20 06	20 15		20 37		20 46		21 06	21 15		21 36	21 46	22 06	22 15			22 36	22a44	23 06
Barnt Green	d			19 50			20 11	20 19		20 41				21 11	21 20		21 40		22 11	22 19			22 41		23 11
Alvechurch	d			19 54			20 15			20 46				21 15			21 45		22 15				22 45		23 15
Redditch	a			20 03			20 21			20 51				21 21			21 51		22 22				22 51		23 22
Bromsgrove	a	19 46	19 41			20 09		20 25				20 55			21 26	21 20		21 55		22 25		22 29			

		LM	LM	LM	LM
Lichfield Trent Valley	d		22 28	22 55	23 23
Lichfield City	d		22 32	22 59	23 27
Shenstone	d		22 37	23 04	23 32
Blake Street	d		22 40	23 07	23 36
Butlers Lane	d		22 43	23 10	23 38
Four Oaks	d		22 45	23 12	23 41
Sutton Coldfield	d		22 49	23 16	23 44
Wylde Green	d		22 51	23 18	
Chester Road	d		22 53		
Erdington	d		22 56		
Gravelly Hill	d		22 58		
Aston	d		23 02		
Duddeston	d		23 05		
Birmingham New Street 12	a		23 09	23 29	23 59
	d	22 53	23 13	23 33	
Five Ways	d	22 57	23 17	23 37	
University	d	23 01	23 21	23 41	
Selly Oak	d	23 03	23 23	23 43	
Bournville	d	23 06	23 26	23 46	
Kings Norton	d	23 09	23 29	23 49	
Northfield	d	23 12	23 32	23 52	
Longbridge	d	23a14	23 35	23a54	
Barnt Green	d		23 40		
Alvechurch	d		23 44		
Redditch	a		23 51		
Bromsgrove	a				

Sundays
20 May to 15 July

		LM	LM	LM	LM	LM	LM	LM	XC	LM		LM	LM	LM	XC	LM	LM	LM	LM	LM		LM	XC	LM	LM
									◇1 ⊤						◇1 ⊤								◇1 ⊤		
Lichfield Trent Valley	d					09 01				09 31			10 01			10 31		11 01				11 31			12 01
Lichfield City	d					09 05				09 35			10 05			10 35		11 05				11 35			12 05
Shenstone	d					09 10				09 40			10 10			10 40		11 10				11 40			12 10
Blake Street	d					09 13				09 43			10 13			10 43		11 13				11 43			12 13
Butlers Lane	d					09 16				09 46			10 16			10 46		11 16				11 46			12 16
Four Oaks	d					09 18		09 33		09 48			10 18			10 48		11 18				11 48			12 18
Sutton Coldfield	d					09 22		09 37		09 52			10 22			10 52		11 22				11 52			12 22
Wylde Green	d					09 24		09 39		09 54			10 24			10 54		11 24				11 54			12 24
Chester Road	d					09 26		09 41		09 56			10 26			10 56		11 26				11 56			12 26
Erdington	d					09 29		09 44		09 59			10 29			10 59		11 29				11 59			12 29
Gravelly Hill	d					09 31		09 46		10 01			10 31			11 01		11 31				12 01			12 31
Aston	d					09 35		09 50		10 05			10 35			11 05		11 35				12 05			12 35
Duddeston	d					09 38				10 08			10 38			11 08		11 38				12 08			12 38
Birmingham New Street 12	a					09 42		09 56		10 12			10 42			11 12		11 42				12 12			12 42
	d	08 55	09 03	09 15	09 34	09 45	10 00	10 03	10 12	10 15		10 34	10 45	11 03	11 12	11 15	11 34	11 45	12 00	12 03		12 15	12 30	12 34	12 45
Five Ways	d		09 07	09 19	09 38	09 49		10 07		10 19		10 38	10 49	11 07		11 19	11 38	11 49		12 07		12 19		12 38	12 49
University	d	09 01	09 11	09 23	09 42	09 53	10 06	10 11	10a18	10 23		10 42	10 53	11 11	11a18	11 23	11 42	11 53	12 06	12 11		12 23	12a36	12 42	12 53
Selly Oak	d		09 13	09 25	09 44	09 55		10 13		10 25		10 44	10 55	11 13		11 25	11 44	11 55		12 13		12 25		12 44	12 55
Bournville	d		09 16	09 28	09 47	09 58		10 16		10 28		10 47	10 58	11 16		11 28	11 47	11 58		12 16		12 28		12 47	12 58
Kings Norton	d		09 19	09 31	09 50	10 01		10 19		10 31		10 50	11 01	11 19		11 31	11 50	12 01		12 19		12 31		12 50	13 01
Northfield	d		09 22	09 34	09 53	10 04		10 22		10 34		10 53	11 04	11 22		11 34	11 53	12 04		12 22		12 34		12 53	13 04
Longbridge	d	09 09	09a24	09 37	09a55	10 07		10a24		10 37		10a55	11 07	11a24		11 37	11a55	12 07		12a24		12 37		12a55	13 07
Barnt Green	d			09 42		10 12				10 42			11 12			11 42		12 12				12 42			13 12
Alvechurch	d			09 46		10 16				10 46			11 16			11 46		12 16				12 46			13 16
Redditch	a	09 22		09 52		10 22				10 52			11 22			11 52		12 22				12 52			13 22
Bromsgrove	a						10 20												12 20						

Table T069-F

Sundays

20 May to 15 July

Lichfield - Birmingham - Longbridge and Redditch

		LM	LM	XC	LM	LM		LM	LM	LM	XC	LM	LM	LM	LM	XC		LM	LM	LM	LM	LM	XC	LM	LM
				◇1							◇1					◇1							◇1		
Lichfield Trent Valley	d		12 31			13 01				13 31			14 01		14 31				15 01			15 31			16 01
Lichfield City	d		12 35			13 05				13 35			14 05		14 35				15 05			15 35			16 05
Shenstone	d		12 40			13 10				13 40			14 10		14 40				15 10			15 40			16 10
Blake Street	d		12 43			13 13				13 43			14 13		14 43				15 13			15 43			16 13
Butlers Lane	d		12 46			13 16				13 46			14 16		14 46				15 16			15 46			16 16
Four Oaks	d		12 48			13 18				13 48			14 18		14 48				15 18			15 48			16 18
Sutton Coldfield	d		12 52			13 22				13 52			14 22		14 52				15 22			15 52			16 22
Wylde Green	d		12 54			13 24				13 54			14 24		14 54				15 24			15 54			16 24
Chester Road	d		12 56			13 26				13 56			14 26		14 56				15 26			15 56			16 26
Erdington	d		12 59			13 29				13 59			14 29		14 59				15 29			15 59			16 29
Gravelly Hill	d		13 01			13 31				14 01			14 31		15 01				15 31			16 01			16 31
Aston	d		13 05			13 35				14 05			14 35		15 05				15 35			16 05			16 35
Duddeston	d		13 08			13 38				14 08			14 38		15 08				15 38			16 08			16 38
Birmingham New Street	a		13 12			13 42				14 12			14 42		15 12				15 42			16 12			16 42
	d	13 03	13 15	13 30	13 34	13 45		14 00	14 03	14 15	14 30	14 34	14 45	15 03	15 15	15 30		15 34	15 45	16 00	16 03	16 15	16 30	16 34	16 45
Five Ways	d	13 07	13 19		13 38	13 49			14 07	14 19		14 38	14 49	15 07	15 19			15 38	15 49		16 07	16 19		16 38	16 49
University	d	13 11	13 23	13a36	13 42	13 53		14 06	14 11	14 23	14a36	14 42	14 53	15 11	15 23	15a36		15 42	15 53	16 06	16 11	16 23	16a36	16 42	16 53
Selly Oak	d	13 13	13 25		13 44	13 55			14 13	14 25		14 44	14 55	15 13	15 25			15 44	15 55		16 13	16 25		16 44	16 55
Bournville	d	13 16	13 28		13 47	13 58			14 16	14 28		14 47	14 58	15 16	15 28			15 47	15 58		16 16	16 28		16 47	16 58
Kings Norton	d	13 19	13 31		13 50	14 01			14 19	14 31		14 50	15 01	15 19	15 31			15 50	16 01		16 19	16 31		16 50	17 01
Northfield	d	13 22	13 34		13 53	14 04			14 22	14 34		14 53	15 04	15 22	15 34			15 53	16 04		16 22	16 34		16 53	17 04
Longbridge	d	13a24	13 37		13a55	14 07			14a24	14 37		14a55	15 07	15a24	15 37			15a55	16 07		16a24	16 37		16a55	17 07
Barnt Green	d		13 42			14 12				14 42			15 12		15 42				16 12			16 42			17 12
Alvechurch	d		13 46			14 16				14 46			15 16		15 46				16 16			16 46			17 16
Redditch	a		13 52			14 22				14 52			15 22		15 52				16 22			16 52			17 22
Bromsgrove	a							14 20												16 20					

		LM		LM	XC	LM	LM	LM	LM	LM	XC	LM		LM	LM	LM	LM	XC	LM	LM	LM	LM		LM	LM
					◇1						◇1							◇1							
Lichfield Trent Valley	d			16 31			17 01			17 31				18 01			18 31			19 01				19 31	
Lichfield City	d			16 35			17 05			17 35				18 05			18 35			19 05				19 35	
Shenstone	d			16 40			17 10			17 40				18 10			18 40			19 10				19 40	
Blake Street	d			16 43			17 13			17 43				18 13			18 43			19 13				19 43	
Butlers Lane	d			16 46			17 16			17 46				18 16			18 46			19 16				19 46	
Four Oaks	d			16 48			17 18			17 48				18 18			18 48			19 18				19 48	
Sutton Coldfield	d			16 52			17 22			17 52				18 22			18 52			19 22				19 52	
Wylde Green	d			16 54			17 24			17 54				18 24			18 54			19 24				19 54	
Chester Road	d			16 56			17 26			17 56				18 26			18 56			19 26				19 56	
Erdington	d			16 59			17 29			17 59				18 29			18 59			19 29				19 59	
Gravelly Hill	d			17 01			17 31			18 01				18 31			19 01			19 31				20 01	
Aston	d			17 05			17 35			18 05				18 35			19 05			19 35				20 05	
Duddeston	d			17 08			17 38			18 08				18 38			19 08			19 38				20 08	
Birmingham New Street	a			17 12			17 42			18 12				18 42			19 12			19 42				20 12	
	d	17 03		17 15	17 30	17 34	17 45	18 00	18 03	18 15	18 30	18 34		18 45	19 00	19 03	19 15	19 30	19 34	19 45	20 00	20 03		20 15	20 34
Five Ways	d	17 07		17 19		17 38	17 49		18 07	18 19		18 38		18 49		19 07	19 19		19 38	19 49		20 07		20 19	20 38
University	d	17 11		17 23	17a36	17 42	17 53	18 06	18 11	18 23	18a36	18 42		18 53	19 06	19 11	19 23	19a36	19 42	19 53	20 06	20 11		20 23	20 42
Selly Oak	d	17 13		17 25		17 44	17 55		18 13	18 25		18 44		18 55		19 13	19 25		19 44	19 55		20 13		20 25	20 44
Bournville	d	17 16		17 28		17 47	17 58		18 16	18 28		18 47		18 58		19 16	19 28		19 47	19 58		20 16		20 28	20 47
Kings Norton	d	17 19		17 31		17 50	18 01		18 19	18 31		18 50		19 01		19 19	19 31		19 50	20 01		20 19		20 31	20 50
Northfield	d	17 22		17 34		17 53	18 04		18 22	18 34		18 53		19 04		19 22	19 34		19 53	20 04		20 22		20 34	20 53
Longbridge	d	17a24		17 37		17a55	18 07		18a24	18 37		18a55		19 07		19a24	19 37		19a55	20 07		20a24		20 37	20a55
Barnt Green	d			17 42			18 12			18 42				19 12			19 42			20 12				20 42	
Alvechurch	d			17 46			18 16			18 46				19 16			19 46			20 16				20 46	
Redditch	a			17 52			18 22			18 52				19 22			19 52			20 22				20 52	
Bromsgrove	a							18 20							19 20						20 20				

		LM	LM	LM	LM	LM	LM	LM		LM	LM	LM	LM	LM	LM	LM
Lichfield Trent Valley	d	20 01			20 31		21 01				21 31		22 01		22 31	23 01
Lichfield City	d	20 05			20 35		21 05				21 35		22 05		22 35	23 05
Shenstone	d	20 10			20 40		21 10				21 40		22 10		22 40	23 10
Blake Street	d	20 13			20 43		21 13				21 43		22 13		22 43	23 13
Butlers Lane	d	20 16			20 46		21 16				21 46		22 16		22 46	23 16
Four Oaks	d	20 18			20 48		21 18				21 48		22 18		22 48	23 18
Sutton Coldfield	d	20 22			20 52		21 22				21 52		22 22		22 52	23 22
Wylde Green	d	20 24			20 54		21 24				21 54		22 24		22 54	23 24
Chester Road	d	20 26			20 56		21 26				21 56		22 26		22 56	
Erdington	d	20 29			20 59		21 29				21 59		22 29		22 59	
Gravelly Hill	d	20 31			21 01		21 31				22 01		22 31		23 01	
Aston	d	20 35			21 05		21 35				22 05		22 35		23 05	
Duddeston	d	20 38			21 08		21 38				22 08		22 38		23 08	
Birmingham New Street	a	20 42			21 12		21 42				22 12		22 42		23 12	23 39
	d	20 45	21 00	21 03	21 15	21 34	21 45	22 00		22 03	22 15	22 34	22 45	23 03	23 15	
Five Ways	d	20 49		21 07	21 19	21 38	21 49			22 07	22 19	22 38	22 49	23 07	23 19	
University	d	20 53	21 06	21 11	21 23	21 42	21 53	22 06		22 11	22 23	22 42	22 53	23 11	23 23	
Selly Oak	d	20 55		21 13	21 25	21 44	21 55			22 13	22 25	22 44	22 55	23 13	23 25	
Bournville	d	20 58		21 16	21 28	21 47	21 58			22 16	22 28	22 47	22 58	23 16	23 28	
Kings Norton	d	21 01		21 19	21 31	21 50	22 01			22 19	22 31	22 50	23 01	23 19	23 31	
Northfield	d	21 04		21 22	21 34	21 53	22 04			22 22	22 34	22 53	23 04	23 22	23 34	
Longbridge	d	21 07		21a24	21 37	21a55	22 07			22a24	22 37	22a55	23 07	23a24	23 37	
Barnt Green	d	21 12			21 42		22 12				22 42		23 12		23 42	
Alvechurch	d	21 16			21 46		22 16				22 46		23 16		23 46	
Redditch	a	21 22			21 52		22 22				22 52		23 22		23 52	
Bromsgrove	a		21 20					22 20								

Table T069-F

Sundays

22 July to 2 September

Lichfield - Birmingham - Longbridge and Redditch

		LM	LM	LM	LM	LM	LM	LM	LM	LM		LM	XC	LM	LM	LM	LM	LM	LM	XC		LM	LM	LM	LM
			A	B		A	B			A		B	◇1		A	B		A	B	◇1			A	B	
Lichfield Trent Valley	d							09 01						09 31			10 01					10 31			11 01
Lichfield City	d							09 05						09 35			10 05					10 35			11 05
Shenstone	d							09 10						09 40			10 10					10 40			11 10
Blake Street	d							09 13						09 43			10 13					10 43			11 13
Butlers Lane	d							09 16						09 46			10 16					10 46			11 16
Four Oaks	d							09 18		09 33		09 33		09 48			10 18					10 48			11 18
Sutton Coldfield	d							09 22		09 37		09 37		09 52			10 22					10 52			11 22
Wylde Green	d							09 24		09 39		09 39		09 54			10 24					10 54			11 24
Chester Road	d							09 26		09 41		09 41		09 56			10 26					10 56			11 26
Erdington	d							09 29		09 44		09 44		09 59			10 29					10 59			11 29
Gravelly Hill	d							09 31		09 46		09 46		10 01			10 31					11 01			11 31
Aston	d							09 35		09 50		09 50		10 05			10 35					11 05			11 35
Duddeston	d							09 38						10 08			10 38					11 08			11 38
Birmingham New Street	a							09 42		09 56		09 56		10 12			10 42					11 12			11 42
	d	08 55	09 03	09 03	09 15	09 34	09 34	09 45	10 00	10 03		10 03	10 12	10 15	10 37	10 37	10 45	11 03	11 03	11 12		11 15	11 34	11 34	11 45
Five Ways	d		09 07	09 07	09 19	09 38	09 38	09 49		10 07		10 07		10 19	10 41	10 41	10 49	11 07	11 07			11 19	11 38	11 38	11 49
University	d	09 01	09 11	09 11	09 23	09 42	09 42	09 53	10 06	10 11		10 11	10a18	10 23	10 45	10 45	10 53	11 11	11 11	11a18		11 23	11 42	11 42	11 53
Selly Oak	d		09 13	09 13	09 25	09 44	09 44	09 55		10 13		10 13		10 25	10 47	10 47	10 55	11 13	11 13			11 25	11 44	11 44	11 55
Bournville	d		09 16	09 16	09 28	09 47	09 47	09 58		10 16		10 16		10 28	10 50	10 50	10 58	11 16	11 16			11 28	11 47	11 47	11 58
Kings Norton	d		09 19	09 19	09 31	09 50	09 50	10 01		10 19		10 19		10 31	10 53	10 53	11 01	11 19	11 19			11 31	11 50	11 50	12 01
Northfield	d		09 22	09 22	09 34	09 53	09 53	10 04		10 22		10 22		10 34	10 56	10 56	11 04	11 22	11 22			11 34	11 53	11 53	12 04
Longbridge	d	09 09	09a24	09 25	09 37	09a55	09 56	10 07		10a24		10 27		10 37	10a58	10 59	11 07	11a24	11 27			11 37	11a55	11 58	12 07
Barnt Green	d			09 29	09 42			10 12				10 31		10 42			11 12		11 31			11 42			12 12
Alvechurch	d				09 46			10 16						10 46			11 16					11 46			12 16
Redditch	a	09 22			09 52			10 22						10 52			11 22					11 52			12 22
Bromsgrove	a			09 35			10 05		10 20			10 37				11 08			11 37					12 07	

		LM	LM	LM	LM	XC		LM	LM	LM	LM	LM	LM	XC	LM	LM		LM	LM	LM	LM	LM	XC	LM	LM
			A	B		◇1		A	B		A	B		◇1	A	B				A	B		◇1	A	B
Lichfield Trent Valley	d				11 31					12 01			12 31					13 01				13 31			
Lichfield City	d				11 35					12 05			12 35					13 05				13 35			
Shenstone	d				11 40					12 10			12 40					13 10				13 40			
Blake Street	d				11 43					12 13			12 43					13 13				13 43			
Butlers Lane	d				11 46					12 16			12 46					13 16				13 46			
Four Oaks	d				11 48					12 18			12 48					13 18				13 48			
Sutton Coldfield	d				11 52					12 22			12 52					13 22				13 52			
Wylde Green	d				11 54					12 24			12 54					13 24				13 54			
Chester Road	d				11 56					12 26			12 56					13 26				13 56			
Erdington	d				11 59					12 29			12 59					13 29				13 59			
Gravelly Hill	d				12 01					12 31			13 01					13 31				14 01			
Aston	d				12 05					12 35			13 05					13 35				14 05			
Duddeston	d				12 08					12 38			13 08					13 38				14 08			
Birmingham New Street	a				12 12					12 42			13 12					13 42				14 12			
	d	12 00	12 03	12 03	12 15	12 30		12 34	12 34	12 45	13 03	13 03	13 15	13 30	13 34	13 34		13 45	14 00	14 03	14 03	14 15	14 30	14 34	14 34
Five Ways	d		12 07	12 07	12 19			12 38	12 38	12 49	13 07	13 07	13 19		13 38	13 38		13 49		14 07	14 07	14 19		14 38	14 38
University	d	12 06	12 11	12 11	12 23	12a36		12 42	12 42	12 53	13 11	13 11	13 23	13a36	13 42	13 42		13 53	14 06	14 11	14 11	14 23	14a36	14 42	14 42
Selly Oak	d		12 13	12 13	12 25			12 44	12 44	12 55	13 13	13 13	13 25		13 44	13 44		13 55		14 13	14 13	14 25		14 44	14 44
Bournville	d		12 16	12 16	12 28			12 47	12 47	12 58	13 16	13 16	13 28		13 47	13 47		13 58		14 16	14 16	14 28		14 47	14 47
Kings Norton	d		12 19	12 19	12 31			12 50	12 50	13 01	13 19	13 19	13 31		13 50	13 50		14 01		14 19	14 19	14 31		14 50	14 50
Northfield	d		12 22	12 22	12 34			12 53	12 53	13 04	13 22	13 22	13 34		13 53	13 53		14 04		14 22	14 22	14 34		14 53	14 53
Longbridge	d		12a24	12 26	12 37			12a55	12 58	13 07	13a24	13 26	13 37		13a55	13 58		14 07		14a24	14 26	14 37		14a55	14 58
Barnt Green	d			12 31	12 42					13 12		13 31	13 42					14 12			14 31	14 42			
Alvechurch	d				12 46					13 16			13 46					14 16				14 46			
Redditch	a				12 52					13 22			13 52					14 22				14 52			
Bromsgrove	a	12 20		12 37					13 07			13 37				14 07			14 20		14 37				15 07

		LM		LM	LM	LM	XC	LM	LM	LM	LM	LM		LM	LM	XC	LM	LM	LM	LM	LM	LM		XC	LM
				A	B		◇1	A	B			A		B		◇1	A	B		A	B			◇1	A
Lichfield Trent Valley	d	14 01				14 31				15 01					15 31				16 01			16 31			
Lichfield City	d	14 05				14 35				15 05					15 35				16 05			16 35			
Shenstone	d	14 10				14 40				15 10					15 40				16 10			16 40			
Blake Street	d	14 13				14 43				15 13					15 43				16 13			16 43			
Butlers Lane	d	14 16				14 46				15 16					15 46				16 16			16 46			
Four Oaks	d	14 18				14 48				15 18					15 48				16 18			16 48			
Sutton Coldfield	d	14 22				14 52				15 22					15 52				16 22			16 52			
Wylde Green	d	14 24				14 54				15 24					15 54				16 24			16 54			
Chester Road	d	14 26				14 56				15 26					15 56				16 26			16 56			
Erdington	d	14 29				14 59				15 29					15 59				16 29			16 59			
Gravelly Hill	d	14 31				15 01				15 31					16 01				16 31			17 01			
Aston	d	14 35				15 05				15 35					16 05				16 35			17 05			
Duddeston	d	14 38				15 08				15 38					16 08				16 38			17 08			
Birmingham New Street	a	14 42				15 12				15 42					16 12				16 42			17 12			
	d	14 45		15 03	15 03	15 15	15 30	15 34	15 34	15 45	16 00	16 03		16 03	16 15	16 30	16 34	16 34	16 45	17 03	17 03	17 15		17 30	17 34
Five Ways	d	14 49		15 07	15 07	15 19		15 38	15 38	15 49		16 07		16 07	16 19		16 38	16 38	16 49	17 07	17 07	17 19			17 38
University	d	14 53		15 11	15 11	15 23	15a36	15 42	15 42	15 53	16 06	16 11		16 11	16 23	16a36	16 42	16 42	16 53	17 11	17 11	17 23		17a36	17 42
Selly Oak	d	14 55		15 13	15 13	15 25		15 44	15 44	15 55		16 13		16 13	16 25		16 44	16 44	16 55	17 13	17 13	17 25			17 44
Bournville	d	14 58		15 16	15 16	15 28		15 47	15 47	15 58		16 16		16 16	16 28		16 47	16 47	16 58	17 16	17 16	17 28			17 47
Kings Norton	d	15 01		15 19	15 19	15 31		15 50	15 50	16 01		16 19		16 19	16 31		16 50	16 50	17 01	17 19	17 19	17 31			17 50
Northfield	d	15 04		15 22	15 22	15 34		15 53	15 53	16 04		16 22		16 22	16 34		16 53	16 53	17 04	17 22	17 22	17 34			17 53
Longbridge	d	15 07		15a24	15 26	15 37		15a55	15 58	16 07		16a24		16 26	16 37		16a55	16 58	17 07	17a24	17 26	17 37			17a55
Barnt Green	d	15 12			15 31	15 42				16 12				16 31	16 42				17 12		17 31	17 42			
Alvechurch	d	15 16				15 46				16 16					16 46				17 16			17 46			
Redditch	a	15 22				15 52				16 22					16 52				17 22			17 52			
Bromsgrove	a				15 37				16 07		16 20			16 37				17 07			17 37				

A 22 July, 29 July

B not until 29 July

Table T069-F

Sundays

22 July to 2 September

Lichfield - Birmingham - Longbridge and Redditch

		LM A	LM	LM	LM B	LM A	LM	XC ◇1	LM B	LM A	LM	LM	LM B	LM A	LM	XC ◇1	LM B	LM A	LM	LM	LM B	LM A	LM
Lichfield Trent Valley	d		17 01				17 31				18 01				18 31				19 01				19 31
Lichfield City	d		17 05				17 35				18 05				18 35				19 05				19 35
Shenstone	d		17 10				17 40				18 10				18 40				19 10				19 40
Blake Street	d		17 13				17 43				18 13				18 43				19 13				19 43
Butlers Lane	d		17 16				17 46				18 16				18 46				19 16				19 46
Four Oaks	d		17 18				17 48				18 18				18 48				19 18				19 48
Sutton Coldfield	d		17 22				17 52				18 22				18 52				19 22				19 52
Wylde Green	d		17 24				17 54				18 24				18 54				19 24				19 54
Chester Road	d		17 26				17 56				18 26				18 56				19 26				19 56
Erdington	d		17 29				17 59				18 29				18 59				19 29				19 59
Gravelly Hill	d		17 31				18 01				18 31				19 01				19 31				20 01
Aston	d		17 35				18 05				18 35				19 05				19 35				20 05
Duddeston	d		17 38				18 08				18 38				19 08				19 38				20 08
Birmingham New Street 12	a		17 42				18 12				18 42				19 12				19 42				20 12
	d	17 34	17 45	18 00	18 03	18 03	18 15	18 30	18 34	18 34	18 45	19 00	19 03	19 03	19 15	19 30	19 34	19 34	19 45	20 00	20 03	20 03	20 15
Five Ways	d	17 38	17 49		18 07	18 07	18 19		18 38	18 38	18 49		19 07	19 07	19 19		19 38	19 38	19 49		20 07	20 07	20 19
University	d	17 42	17 53	18 06	18 11	18 11	18 23	18a36	18 42	18 42	18 53	19 06	19 11	19 11	19 23	19a36	19 42	19 42	19 53	20 06	20 11	20 11	20 23
Selly Oak	d	17 44	17 55		18 13	18 13	18 25		18 44	18 44	18 55		19 13	19 13	19 25		19 44	19 44	19 55		20 13	20 13	20 25
Bournville	d	17 47	17 58		18 16	18 16	18 28		18 47	18 47	18 58		19 16	19 16	19 28		19 47	19 47	19 58		20 16	20 16	20 28
Kings Norton	d	17 50	18 01		18 19	18 19	18 31		18 50	18 50	19 01		19 19	19 19	19 31		19 50	19 50	20 01		20 19	20 19	20 31
Northfield	d	17 53	18 04		18 22	18 22	18 34		18 53	18 53	19 04		19 22	19 22	19 34		19 53	19 53	20 04		20 22	20 22	20 34
Longbridge	d	17 58	18 07		18a24	18 26	18 37		18a55	18 58	19 07		19a24	19 26	19 37		19a55	19 58	20 07		20a24	20 26	20 37
Barnt Green	d		18 12			18 31	18 42				19 12			19 31	19 42				20 12			20 31	20 42
Alvechurch	d		18 16				18 46				19 16				19 46				20 16				20 46
Redditch	a		18 22				18 52				19 22				19 52				20 22				20 52
Bromsgrove	a	18 07		18 20		18 37				19 07		19 20		19 37				20 07		20 20		20 37	

		LM B	LM A	LM	LM	LM B	LM A	LM	LM B	LM A	LM	LM	LM B	LM A	LM	LM B	LM A	LM	LM B	LM A	LM	LM
Lichfield Trent Valley	d			20 01				20 31			21 01				21 31			22 01			22 31	23 01
Lichfield City	d			20 05				20 35			21 05				21 35			22 05			22 35	23 05
Shenstone	d			20 10				20 40			21 10				21 40			22 10			22 40	23 10
Blake Street	d			20 13				20 43			21 13				21 43			22 13			22 43	23 13
Butlers Lane	d			20 16				20 46			21 16				21 46			22 16			22 46	23 16
Four Oaks	d			20 18				20 48			21 18				21 48			22 18			22 48	23 18
Sutton Coldfield	d			20 22				20 52			21 22				21 52			22 22			22 52	23 22
Wylde Green	d			20 24				20 54			21 24				21 54			22 24			22 54	23 24
Chester Road	d			20 26				20 56			21 26				21 56			22 26			22 56	
Erdington	d			20 29				20 59			21 29				21 59			22 29			22 59	
Gravelly Hill	d			20 31				21 01			21 31				22 01			22 31			23 01	
Aston	d			20 35				21 05			21 35				22 05			22 35			23 05	
Duddeston	d			20 38				21 08			21 38				22 08			22 38			23 08	
Birmingham New Street 12	a			20 42				21 12			21 42				22 12			22 42			23 12	23 39
	d	20 34	20 34	20 45	21 00	21 03	21 03	21 15	21 34	21 34	21 45	22 00	22 03	22 03	22 15	22 34	22 34	22 45	23 03	23 03	23 15	
Five Ways	d	20 38	20 38	20 49		21 07	21 07	21 19	21 38	21 38	21 49		22 07	22 07	22 19	22 38	22 38	22 49	23 07	23 07	23 19	
University	d	20 42	20 42	20 53	21 06	21 11	21 11	21 23	21 42	21 42	21 53	22 06	22 11	22 11	22 23	22 42	22 42	22 53	23 11	23 11	23 23	
Selly Oak	d	20 44	20 44	20 55		21 13	21 13	21 25	21 44	21 44	21 55		22 13	22 13	22 25	22 44	22 44	22 55	23 13	23 13	23 25	
Bournville	d	20 47	20 47	20 58		21 16	21 16	21 28	21 47	21 47	21 58		22 16	22 16	22 28	22 47	22 47	22 58	23 16	23 16	23 28	
Kings Norton	d	20 50	20 50	21 01		21 19	21 19	21 31	21 50	21 50	22 01		22 19	22 19	22 31	22 50	22 50	23 01	23 19	23 19	23 31	
Northfield	d	20 53	20 53	21 04		21 22	21 22	21 34	21 53	21 53	22 04		22 22	22 22	22 34	22 53	22 53	23 04	23 22	23 22	23 34	
Longbridge	d	20a55	20 58	21 07		21a24	21 26	21 37	21a55	21 58	22 07		22 27	22 27	22 37	22a55	22 58	23 07	23a24	23 26	23 37	
Barnt Green	d			21 12			21 31	21 42			22 12		22a31	22 31	22 42			23 12		23 31	23 42	
Alvechurch	d			21 16				21 46			22 16				22 46			23 16			23 46	
Redditch	a			21 22				21 52			22 22				22 52			23 22			23 52	
Bromsgrove	a		21 07		21 20		21 37			22 07		22 20		22 37			23 07			23 37		

Sundays

9 September to 2 December

		LM	LM	LM	LM	LM	LM	LM	XC ◇1 ⊥	LM	LM	LM	LM	XC ◇1 ⊥	LM	LM	LM	LM	LM	LM	XC ◇1 ⊥	LM	LM
Lichfield Trent Valley	d					09 01				09 31		10 01			10 31		11 01			11 31			12 01
Lichfield City	d					09 05				09 35		10 05			10 35		11 05			11 35			12 05
Shenstone	d					09 10				09 40		10 10			10 40		11 10			11 40			12 10
Blake Street	d					09 13				09 43		10 13			10 43		11 13			11 43			12 13
Butlers Lane	d					09 16				09 46		10 16			10 46		11 16			11 46			12 16
Four Oaks	d					09 18		09 33		09 48		10 18			10 48		11 18			11 48			12 18
Sutton Coldfield	d					09 22		09 37		09 52		10 22			10 52		11 22			11 52			12 22
Wylde Green	d					09 24		09 39		09 54		10 24			10 54		11 24			11 54			12 24
Chester Road	d					09 26		09 41		09 56		10 26			10 56		11 26			11 56			12 26
Erdington	d					09 29		09 44		09 59		10 29			10 59		11 29			11 59			12 29
Gravelly Hill	d					09 31		09 46		10 01		10 31			11 01		11 31			12 01			12 31
Aston	d					09 35		09 50		10 05		10 35			11 05		11 35			12 05			12 35
Duddeston	d					09 38				10 08		10 38			11 08		11 38			12 08			12 38
Birmingham New Street 12	a					09 42		09 56		10 12		10 42			11 12		11 42			12 12			12 42
	d	08 55	09 03	09 15	09 34	09 45	10 00	10 03	10 12	10 15	10 34	10 45	11 03	11 12	11 15	11 34	11 45	12 00	12 03	12 15	12 30	12 34	12 45
Five Ways	d		09 07	09 19	09 38	09 49		10 07		10 19	10 38	10 49	11 07		11 19	11 38	11 49		12 07	12 19		12 38	12 49
University	d	09 01	09 11	09 23	09 42	09 53	10 06	10 11	10a18	10 23	10 42	10 53	11 11	11a18	11 23	11 42	11 53	12 06	12 11	12 23	12a36	12 42	12 53
Selly Oak	d		09 13	09 25	09 44	09 55		10 13		10 25	10 44	10 55	11 13		11 25	11 44	11 55		12 13	12 25		12 44	12 55
Bournville	d		09 16	09 28	09 47	09 58		10 16		10 28	10 47	10 58	11 16		11 28	11 47	11 58		12 16	12 28		12 47	12 58
Kings Norton	d		09 19	09 31	09 50	10 01		10 19		10 31	10 50	11 01	11 19		11 31	11 50	12 01		12 19	12 31		12 50	13 01
Northfield	d		09 22	09 34	09 53	10 04		10 22		10 34	10 53	11 04	11 22		11 34	11 53	12 04		12 22	12 34		12 53	13 04
Longbridge	d	09 09	09 25	09 37	09 56	10 07		10 27		10 37	10 56	11 07	11 27		11 37	11 58	12 07		12 26	12 37		12 58	13 07
Barnt Green	d		09 29	09 42		10 12		10 31		10 42		11 12	11 31		11 42		12 12		12 31	12 42			13 12
Alvechurch	d			09 46		10 16				10 46		11 16			11 46		12 16			12 46			13 16
Redditch	a	09 22		09 52		10 22				10 52		11 22			11 52		12 22			12 52			13 22
Bromsgrove	a		09 35		10 05		10 20	10 37			11 05		11 37			12 07		12 20	12 37			13 07	

A not until 29 July

B 22 July, 29 July

Table T069-F

Sundays

9 September to 2 December

Lichfield - Birmingham - Longbridge and Redditch

		LM	LM	XC ◇1 ⊥	LM	LM	LM	LM	LM	XC ◇1 ⊥	LM	LM	LM	LM	XC ◇1 ⊥	LM	LM	LM	LM	LM	XC ◇1	LM	LM
Lichfield Trent Valley	d		12 31			13 01			13 31			14 01		14 31			15 01			15 31			16 01
Lichfield City	d		12 35			13 05			13 35			14 05		14 35			15 05			15 35			16 05
Shenstone	d		12 40			13 10			13 40			14 10		14 40			15 10			15 40			16 10
Blake Street	d		12 43			13 13			13 43			14 13		14 43			15 13			15 43			16 13
Butlers Lane	d		12 46			13 16			13 46			14 16		14 46			15 16			15 46			16 16
Four Oaks	d		12 48			13 18			13 48			14 18		14 48			15 18			15 48			16 18
Sutton Coldfield	d		12 52			13 22			13 52			14 22		14 52			15 22			15 52			16 22
Wylde Green	d		12 54			13 24			13 54			14 24		14 54			15 24			15 54			16 24
Chester Road	d		12 56			13 26			13 56			14 26		14 56			15 26			15 56			16 26
Erdington	d		12 59			13 29			13 59			14 29		14 59			15 29			15 59			16 29
Gravelly Hill	d		13 01			13 31			14 01			14 31		15 01			15 31			16 01			16 31
Aston	d		13 05			13 35			14 05			14 35		15 05			15 35			16 05			16 35
Duddeston	d		13 08			13 38			14 08			14 38		15 08			15 38			16 08			16 38
Birmingham New Street 12	a		13 12			13 42			14 12			14 42		15 12			15 42			16 12			16 42
	d	13 03	13 15	13 30	13 34	13 45	14 00	14 03	14 15	14 30	14 34	14 45	15 03	15 15	15 30	15 34	15 45	16 00	16 03	16 15	16 30	16 34	16 45
Five Ways	d	13 07	13 19		13 38	13 49		14 07	14 19		14 38	14 49	15 07	15 19		15 38	15 49		16 07	16 19		16 38	16 49
University	d	13 11	13 23	13a36	13 42	13 53	14 06	14 11	14 23	14a36	14 42	14 53	15 11	15 23	15a36	15 42	15 53	16 06	16 11	16 23	16a36	16 42	16 53
Selly Oak	d	13 13	13 25		13 44	13 55		14 13	14 25		14 44	14 55	15 13	15 25		15 44	15 55		16 13	16 25		16 44	16 55
Bournville	d	13 16	13 28		13 47	13 58		14 16	14 28		14 47	14 58	15 16	15 28		15 47	15 58		16 16	16 28		16 47	16 58
Kings Norton	d	13 19	13 31		13 50	14 01		14 19	14 31		14 50	15 01	15 19	15 31		15 50	16 01		16 19	16 31		16 50	17 01
Northfield	d	13 22	13 34		13 53	14 04		14 22	14 34		14 53	15 04	15 22	15 34		15 53	16 04		16 22	16 34		16 53	17 04
Longbridge	d	13 26	13 37		13 58	14 07		14 26	14 37		14 58	15 07	15 26	15 37		15 58	16 07		16 26	16 37		16 58	17 07
Barnt Green	d	13 31	13 42			14 12		14 31	14 42			15 12	15 31	15 42			16 12		16 31	16 42			17 12
Alvechurch	d		13 46			14 16			14 46			15 16		15 46			16 16			16 46			17 16
Redditch	a		13 52			14 22			14 52			15 22		15 52			16 22			16 52			17 22
Bromsgrove	a	13 37			14 07		14 20	14 37			15 07		15 37			16 07		16 20	16 37			17 07	

		LM	LM	XC ◇1	LM	LM	LM	LM	LM	XC ◇1	LM	LM	LM	LM	LM	XC ◇1	LM	LM	LM	LM	LM	LM
Lichfield Trent Valley	d		16 31			17 01			17 31			18 01			18 31			19 01			19 31	
Lichfield City	d		16 35			17 05			17 35			18 05			18 35			19 05			19 35	
Shenstone	d		16 40			17 10			17 40			18 10			18 40			19 10			19 40	
Blake Street	d		16 43			17 13			17 43			18 13			18 43			19 13			19 43	
Butlers Lane	d		16 46			17 16			17 46			18 16			18 46			19 16			19 46	
Four Oaks	d		16 48			17 18			17 48			18 18			18 48			19 18			19 48	
Sutton Coldfield	d		16 52			17 22			17 52			18 22			18 52			19 22			19 52	
Wylde Green	d		16 54			17 24			17 54			18 24			18 54			19 24			19 54	
Chester Road	d		16 56			17 26			17 56			18 26			18 56			19 26			19 56	
Erdington	d		16 59			17 29			17 59			18 29			18 59			19 29			19 59	
Gravelly Hill	d		17 01			17 31			18 01			18 31			19 01			19 31			20 01	
Aston	d		17 05			17 35			18 05			18 35			19 05			19 35			20 05	
Duddeston	d		17 08			17 38			18 08			18 38			19 08			19 38			20 08	
Birmingham New Street 12	a		17 12			17 42			18 12			18 42			19 12			19 42			20 12	
	d	17 03	17 15	17 30	17 34	17 45	18 00	18 03	18 15	18 30	18 34	18 45	19 00	19 03	19 15	19 30	19 34	19 45	20 00	20 03	20 15	20 34
Five Ways	d	17 07	17 19		17 38	17 49		18 07	18 19		18 38	18 49		19 07	19 19		19 38	19 49		20 07	20 19	20 38
University	d	17 11	17 23	17a36	17 42	17 53	18 06	18 11	18 23	18a36	18 42	18 53	19 06	19 11	19 23	19a36	19 42	19 53	20 06	20 11	20 23	20 42
Selly Oak	d	17 13	17 25		17 44	17 55		18 13	18 25		18 44	18 55		19 13	19 25		19 44	19 55		20 13	20 25	20 44
Bournville	d	17 16	17 28		17 47	17 58		18 16	18 28		18 47	18 58		19 16	19 28		19 47	19 58		20 16	20 28	20 47
Kings Norton	d	17 19	17 31		17 50	18 01		18 19	18 31		18 50	19 01		19 19	19 31		19 50	20 01		20 19	20 31	20 50
Northfield	d	17 22	17 34		17 53	18 04		18 22	18 34		18 53	19 04		19 22	19 34		19 53	20 04		20 22	20 34	20 53
Longbridge	d	17 26	17 37		17 58	18 07		18 26	18 37		18 58	19 07		19 26	19 37		19 58	20 07		20 26	20 37	20 58
Barnt Green	d	17 31	17 42			18 12		18 31	18 42			19 12		19 31	19 42			20 12		20 31	20 42	
Alvechurch	d		17 46			18 16			18 46			19 16			19 46			20 16			20 46	
Redditch	a		17 52			18 22			18 52			19 22			19 52			20 22			20 52	
Bromsgrove	a	17 37			18 07		18 20	18 37			19 07		19 20	19 37			20 07		20 20	20 37		21 07

		LM	LM	LM	LM	LM	LM	LM	LM	LM	LM	LM	LM	LM	LM
Lichfield Trent Valley	d	20 01			20 31		21 01			21 31		22 01		22 31	23 01
Lichfield City	d	20 05			20 35		21 05			21 35		22 05		22 35	23 05
Shenstone	d	20 10			20 40		21 10			21 40		22 10		22 40	23 10
Blake Street	d	20 13			20 43		21 13			21 43		22 13		22 43	23 13
Butlers Lane	d	20 16			20 46		21 16			21 46		22 16		22 46	23 16
Four Oaks	d	20 18			20 48		21 18			21 48		22 18		22 48	23 18
Sutton Coldfield	d	20 22			20 52		21 22			21 52		22 22		22 52	23 22
Wylde Green	d	20 24			20 54		21 24			21 54		22 24		22 54	23 24
Chester Road	d	20 26			20 56		21 26			21 56		22 26		22 56	
Erdington	d	20 29			20 59		21 29			21 59		22 29		22 59	
Gravelly Hill	d	20 31			21 01		21 31			22 01		22 31		23 01	
Aston	d	20 35			21 05		21 35			22 05		22 35		23 05	
Duddeston	d	20 38			21 08		21 38			22 08		22 38		23 08	
Birmingham New Street 12	a	20 42			21 12		21 42			22 12		22 42		23 12	23 39
	d	20 45	21 00	21 03	21 15	21 34	21 45	22 00	22 03	22 15	22 34	22 45	23 03	23 15	
Five Ways	d	20 49		21 07	21 19	21 38	21 49		22 07	22 19	22 38	22 49	23 07	23 19	
University	d	20 53	21 06	21 11	21 23	21 42	21 53	22 06	22 11	22 23	22 42	22 53	23 11	23 23	
Selly Oak	d	20 55		21 13	21 25	21 44	21 55		22 13	22 25	22 44	22 55	23 13	23 25	
Bournville	d	20 58		21 16	21 28	21 47	21 58		22 16	22 28	22 47	22 58	23 16	23 28	
Kings Norton	d	21 01		21 19	21 31	21 50	22 01		22 19	22 31	22 50	23 01	23 19	23 31	
Northfield	d	21 04		21 22	21 34	21 53	22 04		22 22	22 34	22 53	23 04	23 22	23 34	
Longbridge	d	21 07		21 26	21 37	21 58	22 07		22 27	22 37	22 58	23 07	23 26	23 37	
Barnt Green	d	21 12		21 31	21 42		22 12		22 31	22 42		23 12	23 31	23 42	
Alvechurch	d	21 16			21 46		22 16			22 46		23 16		23 46	
Redditch	a	21 22			21 52		22 22			22 52		23 22		23 52	
Bromsgrove	a		21 20	21 37		22 07		22 20	22 37		23 07		23 37		

Redditch and Longbridge - Birmingham - Lichfield

Miles	Miles			LM	LM	LM	LM A	LM B	LM	LM	LM A	LM B	LM	LM	LM A	LM B	LM	LM A	LM B	LM	LM	LM	LM A
—	0	Bromsgrove	d				06 12		06 21		06 33		06 43		06 51			07 12			07 23		07 31
0	—	**Redditch**	d							06 12				06 32			06 55					07 12	
3¼	—	Alvechurch	d							06 17				06 37			07 00					07 17	
5¼	3½	Barnt Green	d							06 23				06 43	06 57		07 07					07 23	
7¾	—	Longbridge	d			06 12	06 22	06 22		06 32	06 42	06 42		06 52	07 02	07 02	07 12	07 22	07 22			07 32	07 42
8¾	—	Northfield	d			06 14	06 24	06 24		06 34	06 44	06 44		06 54	07 04	07 04	07 14	07 24	07 24			07 34	07 44
10¼	—	Kings Norton	d			06 17	06 27	06 27		06 37	06 47	06 47		06 57	07 07	07 07	07 17	07 27	07 27			07 37	07 47
11¼	—	Bournville	d			06 19	06 29	06 29		06 39	06 49	06 49		06 59	07 09	07 09	07 19	07 29	07 29			07 39	07 49
12¼	—	Selly Oak	d			06 22	06 32	06 32		06 42	06 52	06 52		07 02	07 12	07 12	07 22	07 32	07 32			07 42	07 52
13¼	—	University	d			06 25	06 35	06 35	06 40	06 45	06 55	06 55	07 00	07 05	07 15	07 15	07 25	07 35	07 35		07 40	07 45	07 55
14½	—	Five Ways	d			06 28	06 38	06 38		06 48	06 58	06 58		07 08	07 18	07 18	07 28	07 38	07 38			07 48	07 58
15¼	—	**Birmingham New Street**	a			06 32	06 42	06 42	06 49	06 52	07 03	07 03	07 09	07 12	07 22	07 22	07 33	07 42	07 42		07 49	07 52	08 03
—	—		d	06 01	06 25	06 35	06 45	06 45		06 55	07 05	07 05		07 15	07 25	07 25	07 35	07 45	07 45	07 47		07 55	08 05
16¾	—	Duddeston	d	06 06	06 29		06 49	06 49						07 19						07 52			
18¼	—	Aston	d	06 08	06 32	06 41	06 52	06 52		07 01	07 11	07 11		07 22	07 31	07 31	07 41			07 54		08 01	08 11
19¼	—	Gravelly Hill	d	06 12	06 34	06 44	06 56	06 56		07 04	07 14	07 14		07 26	07 34	07 34	07 44			07 57		08 04	08 14
20¼	—	Erdington	d	06 15	06 37	06 47	06 59	06 59		07 07	07 17	07 17		07 29	07 37	07 37	07 47			07 59		08 07	08 17
21¼	—	Chester Road	d	06 17	06 39	06 49	07 01	07 01		07 09	07 19	07 19		07 31	07 39	07 39	07 49			08 01		08 09	08 19
21¾	—	Wylde Green	d	06 19	06 42	06 52	07 03	07 03		07 12	07 22	07 22		07 33	07 42	07 42	07 52			08 03		08 12	08 22
23½	—	Sutton Coldfield	d	06 22	06 45	06 55	07 06	07 06		07 15	07 25	07 25		07 36	07 45	07 45	07 54	07 59	07 59	08 06		08 15	08 25
24½	—	Four Oaks	d	06 25	06 48	06 58	07a11	07a11		07 17	07 28	07 28		07a41	07 48	07 48		08 03	08 03	08a11		08 18	08 28
25½	—	Butlers Lane	d	06 28	06 51	07 01				07 21	07 31	07 31			07 51	07 51		08 05	08 05			08 21	08 31
26¼	—	Blake Street	d	06 30	06 53	07 03				07 23	07 33	07 33			07 53	07 53		08 08	08 08			08 23	08 33
28¾	—	Shenstone	d	06 34	06 56					07 26					07 56	07 56		08 12	08 12			08 26	08 36
31¾	—	**Lichfield City**	d	06a39	07 02	07 12				07 32	07 42	07 42			08 02	08 02	08a05	08a18	08a18			08 32	08 42
33	—	**Lichfield Trent Valley**	a		07 05	07 15				07 35	07 45	07 45			08 05	08 05						08 35	08 45

		LM B	LM	LM	XC ◇1	LM A	LM B	LM	LM	LM A	LM B	XC ◇1	LM	LM A	LM B	LM	LM	LM A	LM B	LM	LM	LM A	LM B
Bromsgrove	d				07 49	07 51				08 12		08 24		08 31		08 42		08 51			09 08	09 12	
Redditch	d			07 32				07 55					08 12				08 32			08 55			
Alvechurch	d			07 37				08 00					08 17				08 37			09 00			
Barnt Green	d			07 43		07 57		08 07					08 23				08 43	08 57		09 07			
Longbridge	d	07 43		07 52		08 02	08 02	08 12		08 22	08 22		08 32	08 42	08 43		08 52	09 02	09 02	09 12		09 22	09 22
Northfield	d	07 45		07 54		08 04	08 04	08 14		08 24	08 24		08 34	08 44	08 45		08 54	09 04	09 04	09 14		09 24	09 24
Kings Norton	d	07 48		07 57		08 07	08 07	08 17		08 27	08 27		08 37	08 47	08 48		08 57	09 07	09 07	09 17		09 27	09 27
Bournville	d	07 50		07 59		08 09	08 09	08 19		08 29	08 29		08 39	08 49	08 50		08 59	09 09	09 09	09 19		09 29	09 29
Selly Oak	d	07 53		08 02		08 12	08 12	08 22		08 32	08 32		08 42	08 52	08 53		09 02	09 12	09 12	09 22		09 32	09 32
University	d	07 56	08 00	08 05	08 10	08 15	08 15	08 25	08 30	08 35	08 35	08 39	08 45	08 55	08 56	09 00	09 05	09 15	09 15	09 25	09 30	09 35	09 35
Five Ways	d	07 59		08 08		08 18	08 18	08 29		08 38	08 38		08 48	08 58	08 59		09 08	09 18	09 18	09 28		09 38	09 38
Birmingham New Street	a	08 04	08 09	08 12	08 17	08 23	08 23	08 33	08 39	08 42	08 42	08 45	08 52	09 03	09 04	09 09	09 12	09 22	09 22	09 33	09 39	09 42	09 42
	d	08 06		08 15		08 25	08 25	08 35		08 45	08 45		08 55	09 05	09 06		09 15	09 25	09 25	09 35		09 45	09 45
Duddeston	d			08 19						08 49	08 49						09 19					09 49	09 49
Aston	d	08 12		08 22		08 31	08 31	08 41		08 52	08 52		09 01	09 11	09 12		09 22	09 31	09 31	09 41		09 52	09 52
Gravelly Hill	d	08 15		08 26		08 34	08 34	08 44		08 56	08 56		09 04	09 14	09 15		09 26	09 34	09 34	09 44		09 56	09 56
Erdington	d	08 18		08 29		08 37	08 37	08 47		08 59	08 59		09 07	09 17	09 18		09 29	09 37	09 37	09 47		09 59	09 59
Chester Road	d	08 20		08 31		08 39	08 39	08 49		09 01	09 01		09 09	09 19	09 20		09 31	09 39	09 39	09 49		10 01	10 01
Wylde Green	d	08 23		08 33		08 42	08 42	08 52		09 03	09 03		09 12	09 22	09 23		09 33	09 42	09 42	09 52		10 03	10 03
Sutton Coldfield	d	08 26		08 36		08 45	08 45	08 55		09 06	09 06		09 15	09 25	09 26		09 36	09 45	09 45	09 55		10 06	10 06
Four Oaks	d	08 29		08a41		08 48	08 48	08 58		09a11	09a11		09 18	09 28	09 29		09a41	09 48	09 48	09 58		10a11	10a11
Butlers Lane	d	08 32				08 51	08 51	09 01					09 21	09 31	09 32			09 51	09 51	10 01			
Blake Street	d	08 34				08 53	08 53	09 03					09 23	09 33	09 34			09 53	09 53	10 03			
Shenstone	d	08 37				08 56	08 56						09 26					09 56	09 56				
Lichfield City	d	08 43				09 02	09 02	09a11					09 32	09a41	09a42			10 02	10 02	10a11			
Lichfield Trent Valley	a	08 46				09 06	09 06						09 35					10 05	10 05				

		XC ◇1	LM	LM A	LM B	LM	LM	LM	LM	LM A	LM B	XC ◇1	LM	LM A	LM B	LM	LM	LM A	LM B	LM	LM	XC ◇1
Bromsgrove	d			09 30			09 53			10 12				10 30		10 43		10 51				
Redditch	d		09 12			09 32			09 55				10 12				10 32			10 55		
Alvechurch	d		09 17			09 37			10 00				10 17				10 37			11 00		
Barnt Green	d		09 23			09 43			10 07				10 23				10 43	10 57		11 07		
Longbridge	d		09 32	09 42	09 42	09 52		10 02	10 12	10 22	10 22		10 32	10 42	10 43		10 52	11 02	11 02	11 12	11 22	
Northfield	d		09 34	09 44	09 44	09 54		10 04	10 14	10 24	10 24		10 34	10 44	10 45		10 54	11 04	11 04	11 14	11 24	
Kings Norton	d		09 37	09 47	09 47	09 57		10 07	10 17	10 27	10 27		10 37	10 47	10 48		10 57	11 07	11 07	11 17	11 27	
Bournville	d		09 39	09 49	09 49	09 59		10 09	10 19	10 29	10 29		10 39	10 49	10 50		10 59	11 09	11 09	11 19	11 29	
Selly Oak	d		09 42	09 52	09 52	10 02		10 12	10 22	10 32	10 32		10 42	10 52	10 53		11 02	11 12	11 12	11 22	11 32	
University	d	09 39	09 45	09 55	09 55	10 05	10 10	10 15	10 25	10 35	10 35	10 39	10 45	10 55	10 56	11 00	11 05	11 15	11 15	11 25	11 35	11 39
Five Ways	d		09 48	09 58	09 58	10 08		10 18	10 28	10 38	10 38		10 48	10 58	10 59		11 08	11 18	11 18	11 28	11 38	
Birmingham New Street	a	09 45	09 52	10 02	10 02	10 12	10 19	10 22	10 33	10 42	10 42	10 45	10 52	11 03	11 04	11 09	11 12	11 22	11 22	11 33	11 42	11 45
	d		09 55	10 05	10 05	10 15		10 25	10 35	10 45	10 45		10 55	11 05	11 06		11 15	11 25	11 25	11 35	11 45	
Duddeston	d					10 19				10 49	10 49						11 19				11 49	
Aston	d		10 01	10 11	10 11	10 22		10 31	10 41	10 52	10 52		11 01	11 11	11 12		11 22	11 31	11 31	11 41	11 52	
Gravelly Hill	d		10 04	10 14	10 14	10 26		10 34	10 44	10 56	10 56		11 04	11 14	11 15		11 26	11 34	11 34	11 44	11 56	
Erdington	d		10 07	10 17	10 17	10 29		10 37	10 47	10 59	10 59		11 07	11 17	11 18		11 29	11 37	11 37	11 47	11 59	
Chester Road	d		10 09	10 19	10 19	10 31		10 39	10 49	11 01	11 01		11 09	11 19	11 20		11 31	11 39	11 39	11 49	12 01	
Wylde Green	d		10 12	10 22	10 22	10 33		10 42	10 52	11 03	11 03		11 12	11 22	11 23		11 33	11 42	11 42	11 52	12 03	
Sutton Coldfield	d		10 15	10 25	10 25	10 36		10 45	10 55	11 06	11 06		11 15	11 25	11 26		11 36	11 45	11 45	11 55	12 06	
Four Oaks	d		10 18	10 28	10 28	10a41		10 48	10 58	11a11	11a11		11 18	11 28	11 29		11a41	11 48	11 48	11 58	12a11	
Butlers Lane	d		10 21	10 31	10 31			10 51	11 01				11 21	11 31	11 32			11 51	11 51	12 01		
Blake Street	d		10 23	10 33	10 33			10 53	11 03				11 23	11 33	11 34			11 53	11 53	12 03		
Shenstone	d		10 26					10 56					11 26					11 56	11 56			
Lichfield City	d		10 32	10a41	10a41			11 02	11a11				11 32	11a41	11a42			12 02	12 02	12a11		
Lichfield Trent Valley	a		10 35					11 05					11 35					12 05	12 05			

A from 30 July

B until 27 July

Table T069-R

Mondays to Fridays

21 May to 31 August

Redditch and Longbridge - Birmingham - Lichfield

		LM	LM A	LM B	LM	LM	LM A	LM B	LM	LM A	LM B	XC ◇1	LM	LM A	LM B	LM	LM	LM A	LM B	LM	LM	XC ◇1	LM
Bromsgrove	d		11 33		11 43		11 51			12 12				12 33		12 43		12 51					
Redditch	d	11 12				11 32			11 55				12 12				12 32			12 55			13 12
Alvechurch	d	11 17				11 37			12 00				12 17				12 37			13 00			13 17
Barnt Green	d	11 23				11 43	11 57		12 07				12 23				12 43	12 57		13 07			13 23
Longbridge	d	11 32	11 42	11 43		11 52	12 02	12 02	12 12	12 22	12 22		12 32	12 42	12 43		12 52	13 02	13 02	13 12	13 22		13 32
Northfield	d	11 34	11 44	11 45		11 54	12 04	12 04	12 14	12 24	12 24		12 34	12 44	12 45		12 54	13 04	13 04	13 14	13 24		13 34
Kings Norton	d	11 37	11 47	11 48		11 57	12 07	12 07	12 17	12 27	12 27		12 37	12 47	12 48		12 57	13 07	13 07	13 17	13 27		13 37
Bournville	d	11 39	11 49	11 50		11 59	12 09	12 09	12 19	12 29	12 29		12 39	12 49	12 50		12 59	13 09	13 09	13 19	13 29		13 39
Selly Oak	d	11 42	11 52	11 53		12 02	12 12	12 12	12 22	12 32	12 32		12 42	12 52	12 53		13 02	13 12	13 12	13 22	13 32		13 42
University	d	11 45	11 55	11 56	12 00	12 05	12 15	12 15	12 25	12 35	12 35	12 39	12 45	12 55	12 56	13 00	13 05	13 15	13 15	13 25	13 35	13 39	13 45
Five Ways	d	11 48	11 58	11 59		12 08	12 18	12 18	12 28	12 38	12 38		12 48	12 58	12 59		13 08	13 18	13 18	13 28	13 38		13 48
Birmingham New Street	a	11 52	12 03	12 04	12 09	12 12	12 22	12 22	12 33	12 42	12 42	12 45	12 52	13 03	13 04	13 09	13 12	13 22	13 22	13 32	13 42	13 45	13 52
	d	11 55	12 05	12 06		12 15	12 25	12 25	12 35	12 45	12 45		12 55	13 05	13 06		13 15	13 25	13 25	13 35	13 45		13 55
Duddeston	d					12 19				12 49	12 49						13 19				13 49		
Aston	d	12 01	12 11	12 12		12 22	12 31	12 31	12 41	12 52	12 52		13 01	13 11	13 12		13 22	13 31	13 31	13 41	13 52		14 01
Gravelly Hill	d	12 04	12 14	12 15		12 26	12 34	12 34	12 44	12 56	12 56		13 04	13 14	13 15		13 26	13 34	13 34	13 44	13 56		14 04
Erdington	d	12 07	12 17	12 18		12 29	12 37	12 37	12 47	12 59	12 59		13 07	13 17	13 18		13 29	13 37	13 37	13 47	13 59		14 07
Chester Road	d	12 09	12 19	12 20		12 31	12 39	12 39	12 49	13 01	13 01		13 09	13 19	13 20		13 31	13 39	13 39	13 49	14 01		14 09
Wylde Green	d	12 12	12 22	12 23		12 33	12 42	12 42	12 52	13 03	13 03		13 12	13 22	13 23		13 33	13 42	13 42	13 52	14 03		14 12
Sutton Coldfield	d	12 15	12 25	12 26		12 36	12 45	12 45	12 55	13 06	13 06		13 15	13 25	13 26		13 36	13 45	13 45	13 55	14 06		14 15
Four Oaks	d	12 18	12 28	12 29		12a41	12 48	12 48	12 58	13a11	13a11		13 18	13 28	13 29		13a41	13 48	13 48	13 58	14a11		14 18
Butlers Lane	d	12 21	12 31	12 32			12 51	12 51	13 01				13 21	13 31	13 32			13 51	13 51	14 01			14 21
Blake Street	d	12 23	12 33	12 34			12 53	12 53	13 03				13 23	13 33	13 34			13 53	13 53	14 03			14 23
Shenstone	d	12 26					12 56	12 56					13 26					13 56	13 56				14 26
Lichfield City	d	12 32	12a41	12a42			13 02	13 02	13a11				13 32	13a41	13a42			14 02	14 02	14a11			14 32
Lichfield Trent Valley	a	12 35					13 04	13 04					13 35					14 05	14 05				14 35

		LM A	LM B	LM	LM	LM A	LM B	LM	LM A	LM B	XC ◇1	LM	LM A	LM B	LM	LM	LM A	LM B	LM	LM A	LM B	XC ◇1	LM
Bromsgrove	d	13 30		13 42		13 51			14 12				14 30		14 43		14 51			15 12			
Redditch	d				13 32			13 55				14 12				14 32			14 55				15 12
Alvechurch	d				13 37			14 00				14 17				14 37			15 00				15 17
Barnt Green	d				13 43	13 57		14 07				14 23				14 43	14 57		15 07				15 23
Longbridge	d	13 42	13 42		13 52	14 02	14 02	14 12	14 22	14 22		14 32	14 42	14 42		14 52	15 02	15 02	15 12	15 22	15 22		15 32
Northfield	d	13 44	13 44		13 54	14 04	14 04	14 14	14 24	14 24		14 34	14 44	14 44		14 54	15 04	15 04	15 14	15 24	15 24		15 34
Kings Norton	d	13 47	13 47		13 57	14 07	14 07	14 17	14 27	14 27		14 37	14 47	14 47		14 57	15 07	15 07	15 17	15 27	15 27		15 37
Bournville	d	13 49	13 49		13 59	14 09	14 09	14 19	14 29	14 29		14 39	14 49	14 49		14 59	15 09	15 09	15 19	15 29	15 29		15 39
Selly Oak	d	13 52	13 52		14 02	14 12	14 12	14 22	14 32	14 32		14 42	14 52	14 52		15 02	15 12	15 12	15 22	15 32	15 32		15 42
University	d	13 55	13 55	14 00	14 05	14 15	14 15	14 25	14 35	14 35	14 39	14 45	14 55	14 55	15 00	15 05	15 15	15 15	15 25	15 35	15 35	15 39	15 45
Five Ways	d	13 58	13 58		14 08	14 18	14 18	14 28	14 38	14 38		14 48	14 58	14 58		15 08	15 18	15 18	15 28	15 38	15 38		15 48
Birmingham New Street	a	14 03	14 03	14 09	14 12	14 22	14 22	14 33	14 42	14 42	14 45	14 52	15 03	15 03	15 09	15 12	15 22	15 22	15 33	15 42	15 42	15 45	15 52
	d	14 05	14 05		14 15	14 25	14 25	14 35	14 45	14 45		14 55	15 05	15 05		15 15	15 25	15 25	15 35	15 45	15 45		15 55
Duddeston	d				14 19				14 49	14 49						15 19				15 49	15 49		
Aston	d	14 11	14 11		14 22	14 31	14 31	14 41	14 52	14 52		15 01	15 11	15 11		15 22	15 31	15 31	15 41	15 52	15 52		16 01
Gravelly Hill	d	14 14	14 14		14 26	14 34	14 34	14 44	14 56	14 56		15 04	15 14	15 14		15 26	15 34	15 34	15 44	15 56	15 56		16 04
Erdington	d	14 17	14 17		14 29	14 37	14 37	14 47	14 59	14 59		15 07	15 17	15 17		15 29	15 37	15 37	15 47	15 59	15 59		16 07
Chester Road	d	14 19	14 19		14 31	14 39	14 39	14 49	15 01	15 01		15 09	15 19	15 19		15 31	15 39	15 39	15 49	16 01	16 01		16 09
Wylde Green	d	14 22	14 22		14 33	14 42	14 42	14 52	15 03	15 03		15 12	15 22	15 22		15 33	15 42	15 42	15 52	16 03	16 03		16 12
Sutton Coldfield	d	14 25	14 25		14 36	14 45	14 45	14 55	15 06	15 06		15 15	15 25	15 25		15 36	15 45	15 45	15 55	16 06	16 06		16 15
Four Oaks	d	14 28	14 28		14a41	14 48	14 48	14 58	15a11	15a11		15 18	15 28	15 28		15a41	15 48	15 48	15 58	16a11	16a11		16 18
Butlers Lane	d	14 31	14 31			14 51	14 51	15 01				15 21	15 31	15 31			15 51	15 51	16 01				16 21
Blake Street	d	14 33	14 33			14 53	14 53	15 03				15 23	15 33	15 33			15 53	15 53	16 03				16 23
Shenstone	d					14 56	14 56					15 26					15 56	15 56					16 26
Lichfield City	d	14a41	14a41			15 02	15 02	15a11				15 32	15a41	15a41			16 02	16 02	16a11				16 32
Lichfield Trent Valley	a					15 05	15 05					15 35					16 05	16 05					16 35

		LM A	LM B	LM	LM	LM A	LM B	LM	LM A	LM B	XC ◇1	LM	LM A	LM B	LM	LM	LM A	LM B	LM	LM A	LM B	XC ◇1
Bromsgrove	d	15 30		15 43		15 51			16 12				16 30		16 43		16 51			17 12		
Redditch	d				15 32			15 55				16 12				16 32			16 55			
Alvechurch	d				15 37			16 00				16 17				16 37			17 00			
Barnt Green	d				15 43	15 57		16 07				16 23				16 43	16 57		17 07			
Longbridge	d	15 42	15 42		15 52	16 02	16 02	16 12	16 22	16 22		16 32	16 42	16 42		16 52	17 02	17 02	17 12	17 22	17 22	
Northfield	d	15 44	15 44		15 54	16 04	16 04	16 14	16 24	16 24		16 34	16 44	16 44		16 54	17 04	17 04	17 14	17 24	17 24	
Kings Norton	d	15 47	15 47		15 57	16 07	16 07	16 17	16 27	16 27		16 37	16 47	16 47		16 57	17 07	17 07	17 17	17 27	17 27	
Bournville	d	15 49	15 49		15 59	16 09	16 09	16 19	16 29	16 29		16 39	16 49	16 49		16 59	17 09	17 09	17 19	17 29	17 29	
Selly Oak	d	15 52	15 52		16 02	16 12	16 12	16 22	16 32	16 32		16 42	16 52	16 52		17 02	17 12	17 12	17 22	17 32	17 32	
University	d	15 55	15 55	16 00	16 05	16 15	16 15	16 25	16 35	16 35	16 39	16 45	16 55	16 55	17 00	17 05	17 15	17 15	17 25	17 35	17 35	17 39
Five Ways	d	15 58	15 58		16 08	16 18	16 18	16 28	16 38	16 38		16 48	16 58	16 58		17 08	17 18	17 18	17 28	17 38	17 38	
Birmingham New Street	a	16 03	16 03	16 09	16 12	16 22	16 22	16 33	16 42	16 42	16 45	16 52	17 03	17 03	17 09	17 12	17 22	17 22	17 32	17 42	17 42	17 45
	d	16 05	16 05		16 15	16 25	16 25	16 35	16 45	16 45		16 55	17 05	17 05		17 15	17 25	17 25	17 35	17 45	17 45	
Duddeston	d				16 19				16 49	16 49						17 19				17 49	17 49	
Aston	d	16 11	16 11		16 22	16 31	16 31	16 41	16 52	16 52		17 01	17 11	17 11		17 22	17 31	17 31	17 41	17 52	17 52	
Gravelly Hill	d	16 14	16 14		16 26	16 34	16 34	16 44	16 56	16 56		17 04	17 14	17 14		17 26	17 34	17 34	17 44	17 56	17 56	
Erdington	d	16 17	16 17		16 29	16 37	16 37	16 47	16 59	16 59		17 07	17 17	17 17		17 29	17 37	17 37	17 47	17 59	17 59	
Chester Road	d	16 19	16 19		16 31	16 39	16 39	16 49	17 01	17 01		17 09	17 19	17 19		17 31	17 39	17 39	17 49	18 01	18 01	
Wylde Green	d	16 22	16 22		16 33	16 42	16 42	16 52	17 03	17 03		17 12	17 22	17 22		17 33	17 42	17 42	17 52	18 03	18 03	
Sutton Coldfield	d	16 25	16 25		16 36	16 45	16 45	16 55	17 06	17 06		17 15	17 25	17 25		17 36	17 45	17 45	17 55	18 06	18 06	
Four Oaks	d	16 28	16 28		16a41	16 48	16 48	16 58	17a11	17a11		17 18	17 28	17 28		17a41	17 48	17 48	17 58	18a11	18a11	
Butlers Lane	d	16 31	16 31			16 51	16 51	17 01				17 21	17 31	17 31			17 51	17 51	18 01			
Blake Street	d	16 33	16 33			16 53	16 53	17 03				17 23	17 33	17 33			17 53	17 53	18 03			
Shenstone	d					16 56	16 56					17 26	17 36	17 36			17 56	17 56	18 06			
Lichfield City	d	16a41	16a41			17 02	17 02	17a11				17 32	17 42	17 42			18 02	18 02	18 12			
Lichfield Trent Valley	a					17 05	17 05					17 35	17 45	17 45			18 05	18 05	18 15			

A from 30 July

B until 27 July

Table T069-R

Mondays to Fridays

21 May to 31 August

Redditch and Longbridge - Birmingham - Lichfield

		LM	LM	LM	LM	LM	LM	LM		LM	LM	LM	XC	LM	LM	LM	LM	LM		LM	LM	LM	LM	LM	XC
			A	B			A	B			A	B	◇■		A	B				A	B		A	B	◇■
Bromsgrove	d		17 30		17 42		17 51				18 12				18 31		18 42			18 51			19 12		
Redditch	d	17 12				17 32				17 55				18 12				18 32				18 55			
Alvechurch	d	17 17				17 37				18 00				18 17				18 37				19 00			
Barnt Green	d	17 23				17 43	17 57			18 07				18 23				18 43		18 57		19 07			
Longbridge	d	17 32	17 42	17 43		17 52	18 02	18 02		18 12	18 22	18 22		18 32	18 42	18 42		18 52		19 02	19 02	19 12	19 22	19 22	
Northfield	d	17 34	17 44	17 45		17 54	18 04	18 04		18 14	18 24	18 24		18 34	18 44	18 44		18 54		19 04	19 04	19 14	19 24	19 24	
Kings Norton	d	17 37	17 47	17 48		17 57	18 07	18 07		18 17	18 27	18 27		18 37	18 47	18 47		18 57		19 07	19 07	19 17	19 27	19 27	
Bournville	d	17 39	17 49	17 50		17 59	18 09	18 09		18 19	18 29	18 29		18 39	18 49	18 49		18 59		19 09	19 09	19 19	19 29	19 29	
Selly Oak	d	17 42	17 52	17 53		18 02	18 12	18 12		18 22	18 32	18 32		18 42	18 52	18 52		19 02		19 12	19 12	19 22	19 32	19 32	
University	d	17 45	17 55	17 56	18 00	18 05	18 15	18 15		18 25	18 35	18 35	18 39	18 45	18 55	18 55	19 00	19 05		19 15	19 15	19 25	19 35	19 35	19 39
Five Ways	d	17 48	17 58	17 59		18 08	18 18	18 18		18 28	18 38	18 38		18 48	18 58	18 58		19 08		19 18	19 18	19 28	19 38	19 38	
Birmingham New Street ■	a	17 52	18 03	18 04	18 09	18 12	18 22	18 22		18 33	18 42	18 42	18 45	18 52	19 03	19 03	19 09	19 12		19 23	19 23	19 33	19 42	19 42	19 45
	d	17 55	18 05	18 06		18 15	18 25	18 25		18 35	18 45	18 45		18 55	19 05	19 05		19 15				19 35			
Duddeston	d					18 19					18 49	18 49						19 19				19 39			
Aston	d	18 01	18 11	18 12		18 22	18 31	18 31		18 41	18 52	18 52		19 01	19 11	19 11		19 22				19 42			
Gravelly Hill	d	18 04	18 14	18 15		18 26	18 34	18 34		18 44	18 56	18 56		19 04	19 14	19 14		19 26				19 46			
Erdington	d	18 07	18 17	18 18		18 29	18 37	18 37		18 47	18 59	18 59		19 07	19 17	19 17		19 29				19 49			
Chester Road	d	18 09	18 19	18 20		18 31	18 39	18 39		18 49	19 01	19 01		19 09	19 19	19 19		19 31				19 51			
Wylde Green	d	18 12	18 22	18 23		18 33	18 42	18 42		18 52	19 03	19 03		19 12	19 22	19 22		19 33				19 53			
Sutton Coldfield	d	18 15	18 25	18 26		18 36	18 45	18 45		18 55	19 06	19 06		19 15	19 25	19 25		19 36				19 56			
Four Oaks	d	18 18	18 28	18 29		18a41	18 48	18 48		18 58	19a11	19a11		19 18	19 28	19 28		19a41				20 00			
Butlers Lane	d	18 21	18 31	18 32			18 51	18 51		19 01				19 21	19 31	19 31						20 03			
Blake Street	d	18 23	18 33	18 34			18 53	18 53		19 03				19 23	19 33	19 33						20 05			
Shenstone	d	18 26					18 56	18 56						19 26	19 36	19 36						20 09			
Lichfield City	d	18 32	18a41	18a42			19 02	19 02		19a11				19 32	19 42	19 42						20 14			
Lichfield Trent Valley	a	18 35					19 05	19 05						19 35	19 45	19 45						20 17			

		LM	LM	LM		LM	LM	LM	LM	LM	XC	LM	LM	LM		LM	LM	LM	LM	LM	LM	XC	LM	LM	
			A	B				A	B		◇■	A	B			A	B			A	B	◇■		A	
Bromsgrove	d		19 30				19 47	19 51				20 12				20 46		20 55		21 17				21 46	
Redditch	d	19 12				19 32				19 55				20 27					20 57				21 27		
Alvechurch	d	19 17				19 37				20 00				20 32					21 02				21 32		
Barnt Green	d	19 23				19 43		19 57		20 07				20 38		20 52			21 08				21 38	21 52	
Longbridge	d	19 32	19 42	19 42		19 52		20 02	20 02	20 12		20 27	20 27	20 42		20 57	20 57		21 12	21 27	21 27		21 42	21 57	
Northfield	d	19 34	19 44	19 44		19 54		20 04	20 04	20 14		20 29	20 29	20 44		20 59	20 59		21 14	21 29	21 29		21 44	21 59	
Kings Norton	d	19 37	19 47	19 47		19 57		20 07	20 07	20 17		20 32	20 32	20 47		21 02	21 02		21 17	21 32	21 32		21 47	22 02	
Bournville	d	19 39	19 49	19 49		19 59		20 09	20 09	20 19		20 34	20 34	20 49		21 04	21 04		21 19	21 34	21 34		21 49	22 04	
Selly Oak	d	19 42	19 52	19 52		20 02		20 12	20 12	20 22		20 37	20 37	20 52		21 07	21 07		21 22	21 37	21 37		21 52	22 07	
University	d	19 45	19 55	19 55		20 05	20 09	20 15	20 15	20 25	20 34	20 40	20 40	20 55		21 10	21 10	21 14	21 25	21 40	21 40	21 45	21 55	22 10	
Five Ways	d	19 48	19 58	19 58		20 08		20 18	20 18	20 28		20 43	20 43	20 58		21 13	21 13		21 28	21 43	21 43		21 58	22 13	
Birmingham New Street ■	a	19 52	20 03	20 03		20 12	20 17	20 23	20 23	20 33	20 40	20 47	20 47	21 03		21 17	21 17	21 20	21 33	21 48	21 48	21 51	22 02	22 17	
	d		20 05	20 05						20 35				21 05					21 35				22 05		
Duddeston	d		20 09	20 09						20 39				21 09					21 39				22 09		
Aston	d		20 12	20 12						20 42				21 12					21 42				22 12		
Gravelly Hill	d		20 16	20 16						20 46				21 16					21 46				22 16		
Erdington	d		20 19	20 19						20 49				21 19					21 49				22 19		
Chester Road	d		20 21	20 21						20 51				21 21					21 51				22 21		
Wylde Green	d		20 23	20 23						20 53				21 23					21 53				22 23		
Sutton Coldfield	d		20 26	20 26						20 56				21 26					21 56				22 26		
Four Oaks	d		20 30	20 30						21 00				21 30					22 00				22 30		
Butlers Lane	d		20 33	20 33						21 03				21 33					22 03				22 33		
Blake Street	d		20 35	20 35						21 05				21 35					22 05				22 35		
Shenstone	d		20 39	20 39						21 09				21 39					22 09				22 39		
Lichfield City	d		20 44	20 44						21 14				21 44					22 14				22 44		
Lichfield Trent Valley	a		20 47	20 47						21 17				21 47					22 17				22 47		

		LM	LM	LM	LM	LM	LM	LM	LM	LM		LM	LM	XC
		B		A	B			A	B			A	B	◇■
Bromsgrove	d			22 17		22 28		22 36				23 20		
Redditch	d		21 57				22 27			22 57				
Alvechurch	d		22 02				22 32			23 02				
Barnt Green	d		22 08				22 38	22 42		23 08				
Longbridge	d	21 57	22 12	22 27	22 27		22 42	22 52	22 52	23 12		23 30	23 30	
Northfield	d	21 59	22 14	22 29	22 29		22 44	22 54	22 54	23 14		23 32	23 32	
Kings Norton	d	22 02	22 17	22 32	22 32		22 47	22 57	22 57	23 17		23 35	23 35	
Bournville	d	22 04	22 19	22 34	22 34		22 49	22 59	22 59	23 19		23 37	23 37	
Selly Oak	d	22 07	22 22	22 37	22 37		22 52	23 02	23 02	23 22		23 40	23 40	
University	d	22 10	22 25	22 40	22 40	22 46	22 55	23 05	23 05	23 25		23 43	23 43	19 36
Five Ways	d	22 13	22 28	22 43	22 43		22 58	23 08	23 08	23 28		23 47	23 47	
Birmingham New Street ■	a	22 17	22 33	22 47	22 47	22 54	23 03	23 12	23 12	23 35		23 50	23 50	23 59
	d		22 35	22 55	22 55			23 15	23 15					
Duddeston	d		22 39	22 59	22 59			23 19	23 19					
Aston	d		22 42	23 02	23 02			23 22	23 22					
Gravelly Hill	d		22 46	23 06	23 06			23 26	23 26					
Erdington	d		22 49	23 09	23 09			23 29	23 29					
Chester Road	d		22 51	23 11	23 11			23 31	23 31					
Wylde Green	d		22 53	23 13	23 13			23 33	23 33					
Sutton Coldfield	d		22 56	23 16	23 16			23 36	23 36					
Four Oaks	d		23 00	23 19	23 19			23 39	23 39					
Butlers Lane	d		23 03	23 22	23 22			23 42	23 42					
Blake Street	d		23 05	23a25	23a25			23 44	23 44					
Shenstone	d		23 09					23 48	23 48					
Lichfield City	d		23 14					23a53	23a53					
Lichfield Trent Valley	a		23 17											

A from 30 July

B until 27 July

Table T069-R

Mondays to Fridays

3 September to 7 December

Redditch and Longbridge - Birmingham - Lichfield

		LM	LM	LM	LM	LM	LM	LM	LM	LM		LM	LM	LM	LM	LM	LM	LM	LM	LM		XC	LM	LM	LM
																						◇■			
Bromsgrove	d				06 12	06 21		06 33	06 43			06 51		07 12		07 23		07 31				07 49	07 51		
Redditch	d						06 12			06 32			06 55				07 12			07 32				07 55	
Alvechurch	d						06 17			06 37			07 00				07 17			07 37				08 00	
Barnt Green	d						06 23			06 43		06 57	07 07				07 23			07 43			07 57	08 07	
Longbridge	d			06 12	06 22		06 32	06 42		06 52		07 02	07 12	07 22			07 32	07 42		07 52			08 02	08 12	
Northfield	d			06 14	06 24		06 34	06 44		06 54		07 04	07 14	07 24			07 34	07 44		07 54			08 04	08 14	
Kings Norton	d			06 17	06 27		06 37	06 47		06 57		07 07	07 17	07 27			07 37	07 47		07 57			08 07	08 17	
Bournville	d			06 19	06 29		06 39	06 49		06 59		07 09	07 19	07 29			07 39	07 49		07 59			08 09	08 19	
Selly Oak	d			06 22	06 32		06 42	06 52		07 02		07 12	07 22	07 32			07 42	07 52		08 02			08 12	08 22	
University	d			06 25	06 35	06 40	06 45	06 55	07 00	07 05		07 15	07 25	07 35		07 40	07 45	07 55	08 00	08 05		08 10	08 15	08 25	08 30
Five Ways	d			06 28	06 38		06 48	06 58		07 08		07 18	07 28	07 38			07 48	07 58		08 08			08 18	08 29	
Birmingham New Street ■	a			06 32	06 42	06 49	06 52	07 03	07 09	07 12		07 22	07 33	07 42		07 49	07 52	08 03	08 09	08 12		08 17	08 23	08 33	08 39
	d	06 01	06 25	06 35	06 45		06 55	07 05		07 15		07 25	07 35	07 45	07 47		07 55	08 05		08 15			08 25	08 35	
Duddeston	d	06 06	06 29		06 49					07 19					07 52					08 19					
Aston	d	06 08	06 32	06 41	06 52		07 01	07 11		07 22		07 31	07 41		07 54		08 01	08 11		08 22			08 31	08 41	
Gravelly Hill	d	06 12	06 34	06 44	06 56		07 04	07 14		07 26		07 34	07 44		07 57		08 04	08 14		08 26			08 34	08 44	
Erdington	d	06 15	06 37	06 47	06 59		07 07	07 17		07 29		07 37	07 47		07 59		08 07	08 17		08 29			08 37	08 47	
Chester Road	d	06 17	06 39	06 49	07 01		07 09	07 19		07 31		07 39	07 49		08 01		08 09	08 19		08 31			08 39	08 49	
Wylde Green	d	06 19	06 42	06 52	07 03		07 12	07 22		07 33		07 42	07 52		08 03		08 12	08 22		08 33			08 42	08 52	
Sutton Coldfield	d	06 22	06 45	06 55	07 06		07 15	07 25		07 36		07 45	07 54	07 59	08 06		08 15	08 25		08 36			08 45	08 55	
Four Oaks	d	06 25	06 48	06 58	07a11		07 17	07 28		07a41		07 48		08 03	08a11		08 18	08 28		08a41			08 48	08 58	
Butlers Lane	d	06 28	06 51	07 01			07 21	07 31				07 51		08 05			08 21	08 31					08 51	09 01	
Blake Street	d	06 30	06 53	07 03			07 23	07 33				07 53		08 08			08 23	08 33					08 53	09 03	
Shenstone	d	06 34	06 56				07 26					07 56		08 12			08 26	08 36					08 56		
Lichfield City	d	06a39	07 02	07 12			07 32	07 42				08 02	08a05	08a18			08 32	08 42					09 02	09a11	
Lichfield Trent Valley	a		07 05	07 15			07 35	07 45				08 05					08 35	08 45					09 06		

		LM	XC	LM	LM	LM		LM	LM	LM	LM	LM	XC	LM	LM	LM		LM	LM	LM	LM	XC	LM	LM	LM
			◇■										◇■									◇■			
Bromsgrove	d	08 12	08 24		08 31	08 42			08 51		09 08	09 12			09 30			09 53			10 12			10 30	10 43
Redditch	d			08 12				08 32		08 55				09 12		09 32				09 55			10 12		
Alvechurch	d			08 17				08 37		09 00				09 17		09 37				10 00			10 17		
Barnt Green	d			08 23				08 43	08 57	09 07				09 23		09 43				10 07			10 23		
Longbridge	d	08 22		08 32	08 42			08 52	09 02	09 12		09 22		09 32	09 42	09 52			10 02	10 12	10 22		10 32	10 42	
Northfield	d	08 24		08 34	08 44			08 54	09 04	09 14		09 24		09 34	09 44	09 54			10 04	10 14	10 24		10 34	10 44	
Kings Norton	d	08 27		08 37	08 47			08 57	09 07	09 17		09 27		09 37	09 47	09 57			10 07	10 17	10 27		10 37	10 47	
Bournville	d	08 29		08 39	08 49			08 59	09 09	09 19		09 29		09 39	09 49	09 59			10 09	10 19	10 29		10 39	10 49	
Selly Oak	d	08 32		08 42	08 52			09 02	09 12	09 22		09 32		09 42	09 52	10 02			10 12	10 22	10 32		10 42	10 52	
University	d	08 35	08 39	08 45	08 55	09 00		09 05	09 15	09 25	09 30	09 35	09 39	09 45	09 55	10 05		10 10	10 15	10 25	10 35	10 39	10 45	10 55	11 00
Five Ways	d	08 38		08 48	08 58			09 08	09 18	09 28		09 38		09 48	09 58	10 08			10 18	10 28	10 38		10 48	10 58	
Birmingham New Street ■	a	08 42	08 45	08 52	09 03	09 09		09 12	09 22	09 33	09 39	09 42	09 45	09 52	10 02	10 12		10 19	10 22	10 33	10 42	10 45	10 52	11 03	11 09
	d	08 45		08 55	09 05			09 15	09 25	09 35		09 45		09 55	10 05	10 15			10 25	10 35	10 45		10 55	11 05	
Duddeston	d	08 49						09 19				09 49				10 19					10 49				
Aston	d	08 52		09 01	09 11			09 22	09 31	09 41		09 52		10 01	10 11	10 22			10 31	10 41	10 52		11 01	11 11	
Gravelly Hill	d	08 56		09 04	09 14			09 26	09 34	09 44		09 56		10 04	10 14	10 26			10 34	10 44	10 56		11 04	11 14	
Erdington	d	08 59		09 07	09 17			09 29	09 37	09 47		09 59		10 07	10 17	10 29			10 37	10 47	10 59		11 07	11 17	
Chester Road	d	09 01		09 09	09 19			09 31	09 39	09 49		10 01		10 09	10 19	10 31			10 39	10 49	11 01		11 09	11 19	
Wylde Green	d	09 03		09 12	09 22			09 33	09 42	09 52		10 03		10 12	10 22	10 33			10 42	10 52	11 03		11 12	11 22	
Sutton Coldfield	d	09 06		09 15	09 25			09 36	09 45	09 55		10 06		10 15	10 25	10 36			10 45	10 55	11 06		11 15	11 25	
Four Oaks	d	09a11		09 18	09 28			09a41	09 48	09 58		10a11		10 18	10 28	10a41			10 48	10 58	11a11		11 18	11 28	
Butlers Lane	d			09 21	09 31				09 51	10 01				10 21	10 31				10 51	11 01			11 21	11 31	
Blake Street	d			09 23	09 33				09 53	10 03				10 23	10 33				10 53	11 03			11 23	11 33	
Shenstone	d			09 26					09 56					10 26					10 56				11 26		
Lichfield City	d			09 32	09a41				10 02	10a11				10 32	10a41				11 02	11a11			11 32	11a41	
Lichfield Trent Valley	a			09 35					10 05					10 35					11 05				11 35		

		LM		LM	LM	LM	XC	LM	LM	LM	LM	LM		LM	LM	XC	LM	LM	LM	LM	LM	LM		LM	XC
							◇■									◇■									◇■
Bromsgrove	d			10 51					11 33	11 43		11 51			12 12			12 33	12 43		12 51				
Redditch	d	10 32			10 55			11 12			11 32			11 55			12 12			12 32		12 55			
Alvechurch	d	10 37			11 00			11 17			11 37			12 00			12 17			12 37		13 00			
Barnt Green	d	10 43		10 57	11 07			11 23			11 43	11 57		12 07			12 23			12 43	12 57	13 07			
Longbridge	d	10 52		11 02	11 12	11 22		11 32	11 42		11 52	12 02		12 12	12 22		12 32	12 42		12 52	13 02	13 12		13 22	
Northfield	d	10 54		11 04	11 14	11 24		11 34	11 44		11 54	12 04		12 14	12 24		12 34	12 44		12 54	13 04	13 14		13 24	
Kings Norton	d	10 57		11 07	11 17	11 27		11 37	11 47		11 57	12 07		12 17	12 27		12 37	12 47		12 57	13 07	13 17		13 27	
Bournville	d	10 59		11 09	11 19	11 29		11 39	11 49		11 59	12 09		12 19	12 29		12 39	12 49		12 59	13 09	13 19		13 29	
Selly Oak	d	11 02		11 12	11 22	11 32		11 42	11 52		12 02	12 12		12 22	12 32		12 42	12 52		13 02	13 12	13 22		13 32	
University	d	11 05		11 15	11 25	11 35	11 39	11 45	11 55	12 00	12 05	12 15		12 25	12 35	12 39	12 45	12 55	13 00	13 05	13 15	13 25		13 35	13 39
Five Ways	d	11 08		11 18	11 28	11 38		11 48	11 58		12 08	12 18		12 28	12 38		12 48	12 58		13 08	13 18	13 28		13 38	
Birmingham New Street ■	a	11 12		11 22	11 33	11 42	11 45	11 52	12 03	12 09	12 12	12 22		12 33	12 42	12 45	12 52	13 03	13 09	13 12	13 22	13 32		13 42	13 45
	d	11 15		11 25	11 35	11 45		11 55	12 05		12 15	12 25		12 35	12 45		12 55	13 05		13 15	13 25	13 35		13 45	
Duddeston	d	11 19				11 49					12 19				12 49					13 19				13 49	
Aston	d	11 22		11 31	11 41	11 52		12 01	12 11		12 22	12 31		12 41	12 52		13 01	13 11		13 22	13 31	13 41		13 52	
Gravelly Hill	d	11 26		11 34	11 44	11 56		12 04	12 14		12 26	12 34		12 44	12 56		13 04	13 14		13 26	13 34	13 44		13 56	
Erdington	d	11 29		11 37	11 47	11 59		12 07	12 17		12 29	12 37		12 47	12 59		13 07	13 17		13 29	13 37	13 47		13 59	
Chester Road	d	11 31		11 39	11 49	12 01		12 09	12 19		12 31	12 39		12 49	13 01		13 09	13 19		13 31	13 39	13 49		14 01	
Wylde Green	d	11 33		11 42	11 52	12 03		12 12	12 22		12 33	12 42		12 52	13 03		13 12	13 22		13 33	13 42	13 52		14 03	
Sutton Coldfield	d	11 36		11 45	11 55	12 06		12 15	12 25		12 36	12 45		12 55	13 06		13 15	13 25		13 36	13 45	13 55		14 06	
Four Oaks	d	11a41		11 48	11 58	12a11		12 18	12 28		12a41	12 48		12 58	13a11		13 18	13 28		13a41	13 48	13 58		14a11	
Butlers Lane	d			11 51	12 01			12 21	12 31			12 51		13 01			13 21	13 31			13 51	14 01			
Blake Street	d			11 53	12 03			12 23	12 33			12 53		13 03			13 23	13 33			13 53	14 03			
Shenstone	d			11 56				12 26				12 56					13 26				13 56				
Lichfield City	d			12 02	12a11			12 32	12a41			13 02		13a11			13 32	13a41			14 02	14a11			
Lichfield Trent Valley	a			12 05				12 35				13 04					13 35				14 05				

Table T069-R

Mondays to Fridays

3 September to 7 December

Redditch and Longbridge - Birmingham - Lichfield

		LM	LM	LM	LM	LM	LM	LM		XC	LM	LM	LM	LM	LM	LM	LM	XC		LM	LM	LM	LM	LM	LM
										◇1								◇1							
Bromsgrove	d		13 30	13 42		13 51		14 12				14 30	14 43		14 51		15 12				15 30	15 43		15 51	
Redditch	d	13 12			13 32		13 55				14 12			14 32		14 55				15 12			15 32		15 55
Alvechurch	d	13 17			13 37		14 00				14 17			14 37		15 00				15 17			15 37		16 00
Barnt Green	d	13 23			13 43	13 57	14 07				14 23			14 43	14 57	15 07				15 23			15 43	15 57	16 07
Longbridge	d	13 32	13 42		13 52	14 02	14 12	14 22			14 32	14 42		14 52	15 02	15 12	15 22			15 32	15 42		15 52	16 02	16 12
Northfield	d	13 34	13 44		13 54	14 04	14 14	14 24			14 34	14 44		14 54	15 04	15 14	15 24			15 34	15 44		15 54	16 04	16 14
Kings Norton	d	13 37	13 47		13 57	14 07	14 17	14 27			14 37	14 47		14 57	15 07	15 17	15 27			15 37	15 47		15 57	16 07	16 17
Bournville	d	13 39	13 49		13 59	14 09	14 19	14 29			14 39	14 49		14 59	15 09	15 19	15 29			15 39	15 49		15 59	16 09	16 19
Selly Oak	d	13 42	13 52		14 02	14 12	14 22	14 32			14 42	14 52		15 02	15 12	15 22	15 32			15 42	15 52		16 02	16 12	16 22
University	d	13 45	13 55	14 00	14 05	14 15	14 25	14 35		14 39	14 45	14 55	15 00	15 05	15 15	15 25	15 35	15 39		15 45	15 55	16 00	16 05	16 15	16 25
Five Ways	d	13 48	13 58		14 08	14 18	14 28	14 38			14 48	14 58		15 08	15 18	15 28	15 38			15 48	15 58		16 08	16 18	16 28
Birmingham New Street 12	a	13 52	14 03	14 09	14 12	14 22	14 33	14 42		14 45	14 52	15 03	15 09	15 12	15 22	15 33	15 42	15 45		15 52	16 03	16 09	16 12	16 22	16 33
	d	13 55	14 05		14 15	14 25	14 35	14 45			14 55	15 05		15 15	15 25	15 35	15 45			15 55	16 05		16 15	16 25	16 35
Duddeston	d				14 19			14 49						15 19			15 49						16 19		
Aston	d	14 01	14 11		14 22	14 31	14 41	14 52			15 01	15 11		15 22	15 31	15 41	15 52			16 01	16 11		16 22	16 31	16 41
Gravelly Hill	d	14 04	14 14		14 26	14 34	14 44	14 56			15 04	15 14		15 26	15 34	15 44	15 56			16 04	16 14		16 26	16 34	16 44
Erdington	d	14 07	14 17		14 29	14 37	14 47	14 59			15 07	15 17		15 29	15 37	15 47	15 59			16 07	16 17		16 29	16 37	16 47
Chester Road	d	14 09	14 19		14 31	14 39	14 49	15 01			15 09	15 19		15 31	15 39	15 49	16 01			16 09	16 19		16 31	16 39	16 49
Wylde Green	d	14 12	14 22		14 33	14 42	14 52	15 03			15 12	15 22		15 33	15 42	15 52	16 03			16 12	16 22		16 33	16 42	16 52
Sutton Coldfield	d	14 15	14 25		14 36	14 45	14 55	15 06			15 15	15 25		15 36	15 45	15 55	16 06			16 15	16 25		16 36	16 45	16 55
Four Oaks	d	14 18	14 28		14a41	14 48	14 58	15a11			15 18	15 28		15a41	15 48	15 58	16a11			16 18	16 28		16a41	16 48	16 58
Butlers Lane	d	14 21	14 31			14 51	15 01				15 21	15 31			15 51	16 01				16 21	16 31			16 51	17 01
Blake Street	d	14 23	14 33			14 53	15 03				15 23	15 33			15 53	16 03				16 23	16 33			16 53	17 03
Shenstone	d	14 26				14 56					15 26				15 56					16 26				16 56	
Lichfield City	d	14 32	14a41			15 02	15a11				15 32	15a41			16 02	16a11				16 32	16a41			17 02	17a11
Lichfield Trent Valley	a	14 35				15 05					15 35				16 05					16 35				17 05	

		LM	XC	LM		LM	LM	LM	LM	LM	LM	XC	LM	LM		LM	LM	LM	LM	LM	XC	LM	LM	LM
			◇1									◇1									◇1			
Bromsgrove	d	16 12				16 30	16 43		16 51		17 12			17 30		17 42		17 51		18 12			18 31	18 42
Redditch	d			16 12				16 32		16 55			17 12				17 32		17 55			18 12		
Alvechurch	d			16 17				16 37		17 00			17 17				17 37		18 00			18 17		
Barnt Green	d			16 23				16 43	16 57	17 07			17 23				17 43	17 57	18 07			18 23		
Longbridge	d	16 22		16 32		16 42		16 52	17 02	17 12	17 22		17 32	17 42			17 52	18 02	18 12	18 22		18 32	18 42	
Northfield	d	16 24		16 34		16 44		16 54	17 04	17 14	17 24		17 34	17 44			17 54	18 04	18 14	18 24		18 34	18 44	
Kings Norton	d	16 27		16 37		16 47		16 57	17 07	17 17	17 27		17 37	17 47			17 57	18 07	18 17	18 27		18 37	18 47	
Bournville	d	16 29		16 39		16 49		16 59	17 09	17 19	17 29		17 39	17 49			17 59	18 09	18 19	18 29		18 39	18 49	
Selly Oak	d	16 32		16 42		16 52		17 02	17 12	17 22	17 32		17 42	17 52			18 02	18 12	18 22	18 32		18 42	18 52	
University	d	16 35	16 39	16 45		16 55	17 00	17 05	17 15	17 25	17 35	17 39	17 45	17 55		18 00	18 05	18 15	18 25	18 35	18 39	18 45	18 55	19 00
Five Ways	d	16 38		16 48		16 58		17 08	17 18	17 28	17 38		17 48	17 58			18 08	18 18	18 28	18 38		18 48	18 58	
Birmingham New Street 12	a	16 42	16 45	16 52		17 03	17 09	17 12	17 22	17 32	17 42	17 45	17 52	18 03		18 09	18 12	18 22	18 33	18 42	18 45	18 52	19 03	19 09
	d	16 45		16 55		17 05		17 15	17 25	17 35	17 45		17 55	18 05			18 15	18 25	18 35	18 45		18 55	19 05	
Duddeston	d	16 49						17 19			17 49						18 19			18 49				
Aston	d	16 52		17 01		17 11		17 22	17 31	17 41	17 52		18 01	18 11			18 22	18 31	18 41	18 52		19 01	19 11	
Gravelly Hill	d	16 56		17 04		17 14		17 26	17 34	17 44	17 56		18 04	18 14			18 26	18 34	18 44	18 56		19 04	19 14	
Erdington	d	16 59		17 07		17 17		17 29	17 37	17 47	17 59		18 07	18 17			18 29	18 37	18 47	18 59		19 07	19 17	
Chester Road	d	17 01		17 09		17 19		17 31	17 39	17 49	18 01		18 09	18 19			18 31	18 39	18 49	19 01		19 09	19 19	
Wylde Green	d	17 03		17 12		17 22		17 33	17 42	17 52	18 03		18 12	18 22			18 33	18 42	18 52	19 03		19 12	19 22	
Sutton Coldfield	d	17 06		17 15		17 25		17 36	17 45	17 55	18 06		18 15	18 25			18 36	18 45	18 55	19 06		19 15	19 25	
Four Oaks	d	17a11		17 18		17 28		17a41	17 48	17 58	18a11		18 18	18 28			18a41	18 48	18 58	19a11		19 18	19 28	
Butlers Lane	d			17 21		17 31			17 51	18 01			18 21	18 31				18 51	19 01			19 21	19 31	
Blake Street	d			17 23		17 33			17 53	18 03			18 23	18 33				18 53	19 03			19 23	19 33	
Shenstone	d			17 26		17 36			17 56	18 06			18 26					18 56				19 26	19 36	
Lichfield City	d			17 32		17 42			18 02	18 12			18 32	18a41				19 02	19a11			19 32	19 42	
Lichfield Trent Valley	a			17 35		17 45			18 05	18 15			18 35					19 05				19 35	19 45	

		LM	LM	LM	LM	XC	LM	LM	LM	LM		LM	LM	XC	LM	LM	LM	LM	LM	LM		XC	LM	LM	LM
						◇1								◇1								◇1			
Bromsgrove	d		18 51		19 12			19 30		19 47		19 51			20 12		20 46	20 55		21 17				21 46	
Redditch	d	18 32		18 55			19 12		19 32				19 55			20 27			20 57				21 27		21 57
Alvechurch	d	18 37		19 00			19 17		19 37				20 00			20 32			21 02				21 32		22 02
Barnt Green	d	18 43	18 57	19 07			19 23		19 43			19 57	20 07			20 38	20 52		21 08				21 38	21 52	22 08
Longbridge	d	18 52	19 02	19 12	19 22		19 32	19 42	19 52			20 02	20 12		20 27	20 42	20 57		21 12	21 27			21 42	21 57	22 12
Northfield	d	18 54	19 04	19 14	19 24		19 34	19 44	19 54			20 04	20 14		20 29	20 44	20 59		21 14	21 29			21 44	21 59	22 14
Kings Norton	d	18 57	19 07	19 17	19 27		19 37	19 47	19 57			20 07	20 17		20 32	20 47	21 02		21 17	21 32			21 47	22 02	22 17
Bournville	d	18 59	19 09	19 19	19 29		19 39	19 49	19 59			20 09	20 19		20 34	20 49	21 04		21 19	21 34			21 49	22 04	22 19
Selly Oak	d	19 02	19 12	19 22	19 32		19 42	19 52	20 02			20 12	20 22		20 37	20 52	21 07		21 22	21 37			21 52	22 07	22 22
University	d	19 05	19 15	19 25	19 35	19 39	19 45	19 55	20 05	20 09		20 15	20 25	20 34	20 40	20 55	21 10	21 14	21 25	21 40		21 45	21 55	22 10	22 25
Five Ways	d	19 08	19 18	19 28	19 38		19 48	19 58	20 08			20 18	20 28		20 43	20 58	21 13		21 28	21 43			21 58	22 13	22 28
Birmingham New Street 12	a	19 12	19 23	19 33	19 42	19 45	19 52	20 03	20 12	20 17		20 23	20 33	20 40	20 47	21 03	21 17	21 20	21 33	21 48		21 51	22 02	22 17	22 33
	d	19 15		19 35				20 05					20 35			21 05			21 35				22 05		22 35
Duddeston	d	19 19		19 39				20 09					20 39			21 09			21 39				22 09		22 39
Aston	d	19 22		19 42				20 12					20 42			21 12			21 42				22 12		22 42
Gravelly Hill	d	19 26		19 46				20 16					20 46			21 16			21 46				22 16		22 46
Erdington	d	19 29		19 49				20 19					20 49			21 19			21 49				22 19		22 49
Chester Road	d	19 31		19 51				20 21					20 51			21 21			21 51				22 21		22 51
Wylde Green	d	19 33		19 53				20 23					20 53			21 23			21 53				22 23		22 53
Sutton Coldfield	d	19 36		19 56				20 26					20 56			21 26			21 56				22 26		22 56
Four Oaks	d	19a41		20 00				20 30					21 00			21 30			22 00				22 30		23 00
Butlers Lane	d			20 03				20 33					21 03			21 33			22 03				22 33		23 03
Blake Street	d			20 05				20 35					21 05			21 35			22 05				22 35		23 05
Shenstone	d			20 09				20 39					21 09			21 39			22 09				22 39		23 09
Lichfield City	d			20 14				20 44					21 14			21 44			22 14				22 44		23 14
Lichfield Trent Valley	a			20 17				20 47					21 17			21 47			22 17				22 47		23 17

Table T069-R

Mondays to Fridays

3 September to 7 December

Redditch and Longbridge - Birmingham - Lichfield

		LM	LM	LM	LM	LM		LM	XC
									◇1
Bromsgrove	d	22 17	22 28		22 36			23 20	
Redditch	d			22 27		22 57			
Alvechurch	d			22 32		23 02			
Barnt Green	d			22 38	22 42	23 08			
Longbridge	d	22 27		22 42	22 52	23 12		23 30	
Northfield	d	22 29		22 44	22 54	23 14		23 32	
Kings Norton	d	22 32		22 47	22 57	23 17		23 35	
Bournville	d	22 34		22 49	22 59	23 19		23 37	
Selly Oak	d	22 37		22 52	23 02	23 22		23 40	
University	d	22 40	22 46	22 55	23 05	23 25		23 43	19 36
Five Ways	d	22 43		22 58	23 08	23 28		23 47	
Birmingham New Street 12	a	22 47	22 54	23 03	23 12	23 35		23 50	23 59
	d	22 55			23 15				
Duddeston	d	22 59			23 19				
Aston	d	23 02			23 22				
Gravelly Hill	d	23 06			23 26				
Erdington	d	23 09			23 29				
Chester Road	d	23 11			23 31				
Wylde Green	d	23 13			23 33				
Sutton Coldfield	d	23 16			23 36				
Four Oaks	d	23 19			23 39				
Butlers Lane	d	23 22			23 42				
Blake Street	d	23a25			23 44				
Shenstone	d				23 48				
Lichfield City	d				23a53				
Lichfield Trent Valley	a								

Saturdays

26 May to 1 September

		LM	LM	LM	LM	LM	LM	LM	LM	LM		LM	LM	LM	LM	LM	LM	LM	LM	LM		XC	LM	LM	LM
					A	B		A	B				A	B		A	B		A	B		◇1			A
Bromsgrove	d				06 12			06 33				06 47	06 51			07 12			07 30			07 43		07 47	07 51
Redditch	d						06 12			06 32					06 55			07 12					07 32		
Alvechurch	d						06 17			06 37					07 00			07 17					07 37		
Barnt Green	d						06 23			06 43			06 57		07 07			07 23					07 43		07 57
Longbridge	d			06 12	06 22	06 22	06 32	06 42	06 42	06 52			07 02	07 02	07 12	07 22	07 22	07 32	07 42	07 43			07 52		08 02
Northfield	d			06 14	06 24	06 24	06 34	06 44	06 44	06 54			07 04	07 04	07 14	07 24	07 24	07 34	07 44	07 45			07 54		08 04
Kings Norton	d			06 17	06 27	06 27	06 37	06 47	06 47	06 57			07 07	07 07	07 17	07 27	07 27	07 37	07 47	07 48			07 57		08 07
Bournville	d			06 19	06 29	06 29	06 39	06 49	06 49	06 59			07 09	07 09	07 19	07 29	07 29	07 39	07 49	07 50			07 59		08 09
Selly Oak	d			06 22	06 32	06 32	06 42	06 52	06 52	07 02			07 12	07 12	07 22	07 32	07 32	07 42	07 52	07 53			08 02		08 12
University	d			06 25	06 35	06 35	06 45	06 55	06 55	07 05		07 10	07 15	07 15	07 25	07 35	07 35	07 45	07 55	07 56		08 00	08 05	08 10	08 15
Five Ways	d			06 29	06 38	06 38	06 49	06 58	06 58	07 09			07 19	07 19	07 29	07 38	07 38	07 49	07 59	08 00			08 09		08 19
Birmingham New Street 12	a			06 32	06 42	06 42	06 52	07 03	07 03	07 12		07 17	07 22	07 22	07 33	07 42	07 42	07 52	08 03	08 04		08 07	08 12	08 17	08 22
	d	05 55	06 25	06 36			06 55	07 06	07 06	07 15			07 25	07 25	07 35	07 45	07 45	07 55	08 06	08 07			08 15		08 25
Duddeston	d	05 59	06 29				06 59			07 19						07 49	07 49						08 19		
Aston	d	06 02	06 32	06 41			07 02	07 11	07 11	07 22			07 30	07 30	07 40	07 52	07 52	08 00	08 10	08 11			08 22		08 30
Gravelly Hill	d	06 06	06 36	06 45			07 06	07 15	07 15	07 26			07 34	07 34	07 44	07 56	07 56	08 04	08 14	08 15			08 26		08 34
Erdington	d	06 09	06 39	06 48			07 09	07 18	07 18	07 29			07 37	07 37	07 47	07 59	07 59	08 07	08 17	08 18			08 29		08 37
Chester Road	d	06 11	06 41	06 50			07 11	07 20	07 20	07 31			07 39	07 39	07 49	08 01	08 01	08 09	08 19	08 20			08 31		08 39
Wylde Green	d	06 13	06 43	06 52			07 13	07 22	07 22	07 33			07 41	07 41	07 51	08 03	08 03	08 11	08 21	08 22			08 33		08 41
Sutton Coldfield	d	06 16	06 46	06 55			07 16	07 25	07 25	07 36			07 44	07 44	07 54	08 06	08 06	08 14	08 24	08 25			08 36		08 44
Four Oaks	d	06 19	06 49	06 59			07 19	07 28	07 28	07a41			07 47	07 47	07 57	08a11	08a11	08 17	08 27	08 28			08a41		08 47
Butlers Lane	d	06 22	06 52	07 01			07 22	07 31	07 31				07 50	07 50	08 00			08 20	08 30	08 31					08 50
Blake Street	d	06 24	06 54	07 04			07 24	07 33	07 33				07 52	07 52	08 02			08 22	08 32	08 33					08 52
Shenstone	d	06 26	06 56				07 26						07 56	07 56				08 26							08 56
Lichfield City	d	06a34	07a04	07 12			07a34	07 42	07 42				08 02	08 02	08a11			08 32	08a41	08a42					09 02
Lichfield Trent Valley	a			07 15				07 45	07 45				08 05	08 05				08 35							09 05

		LM	LM	LM	LM	XC		LM	LM	LM	LM	LM	LM	LM	LM	LM		LM	XC	LM	LM	LM	LM	LM	LM
		B		A	B	◇1			A	B			A	B		A		B	◇1		A	B			A
Bromsgrove	d			08 12					08 30		08 43		08 51			09 12					09 30		09 43		09 51
Redditch	d		07 55					08 12				08 32			08 55					09 12				09 32	
Alvechurch	d		08 00					08 17				08 37			09 00					09 17				09 37	
Barnt Green	d		08 07					08 23				08 43	08 57		09 07					09 23				09 43	09 57
Longbridge	d	08 02	08 12	08 22	08 22			08 32	08 42	08 42		08 52	09 02	09 02	09 12	09 22		09 22		09 32	09 42	09 43		09 52	10 02
Northfield	d	08 04	08 14	08 24	08 24			08 34	08 44	08 44		08 54	09 04	09 04	09 14	09 24		09 24		09 34	09 44	09 45		09 54	10 04
Kings Norton	d	08 07	08 17	08 27	08 27			08 37	08 47	08 47		08 57	09 07	09 07	09 17	09 27		09 27		09 37	09 47	09 48		09 57	10 07
Bournville	d	08 09	08 19	08 29	08 29			08 39	08 49	08 49		08 59	09 09	09 09	09 19	09 29		09 29		09 39	09 49	09 50		09 59	10 09
Selly Oak	d	08 12	08 22	08 32	08 32			08 42	08 52	08 52		09 02	09 12	09 12	09 22	09 32		09 32		09 42	09 52	09 53		10 02	10 12
University	d	08 15	08 25	08 35	08 35	08 39		08 45	08 55	08 55	09 00	09 05	09 15	09 15	09 25	09 35		09 35	09 39	09 45	09 55	09 56	10 00	10 05	10 15
Five Ways	d	08 19	08 29	08 38	08 38			08 49	08 59	08 59		09 09	09 19	09 19	09 29	09 39		09 39		09 49	09 59	10 00		10 09	10 19
Birmingham New Street 12	a	08 22	08 33	08 42	08 42	08 45		08 52	09 03	09 03	09 09	09 12	09 22	09 22	09 33	09 42		09 42	09 45	09 52	10 03	10 04	10 09	10 12	10 22
	d	08 25	08 36	08 45	08 45			08 55	09 06	09 06		09 15	09 25	09 25	09 36	09 45		09 45		09 55	10 06	10 07		10 15	10 25
Duddeston	d			08 49	08 49							09 19				09 49		09 49						10 19	
Aston	d	08 30	08 41	08 52	08 52			09 00	09 11	09 11		09 22	09 30	09 30	09 41	09 52		09 52		10 00	10 11	10 12		10 22	10 30
Gravelly Hill	d	08 34	08 45	08 56	08 56			09 04	09 15	09 15		09 26	09 34	09 34	09 45	09 56		09 56		10 04	10 15	10 16		10 26	10 34
Erdington	d	08 37	08 48	08 59	08 59			09 07	09 18	09 18		09 29	09 37	09 37	09 48	09 59		09 59		10 07	10 18	10 19		10 29	10 37
Chester Road	d	08 39	08 50	09 01	09 01			09 09	09 20	09 20		09 31	09 39	09 39	09 50	10 01		10 01		10 09	10 20	10 21		10 31	10 39
Wylde Green	d	08 41	08 52	09 03	09 03			09 11	09 22	09 22		09 33	09 41	09 41	09 52	10 03		10 03		10 11	10 22	10 23		10 33	10 41
Sutton Coldfield	d	08 44	08 55	09 06	09 06			09 14	09 25	09 25		09 36	09 44	09 44	09 55	10 06		10 06		10 14	10 25	10 26		10 36	10 44
Four Oaks	d	08 47	08 58	09a11	09a11			09 17	09 28	09 28		09a41	09 47	09 47	09 58	10a11		10a11		10 17	10 28	10 29		10a41	10 47
Butlers Lane	d	08 50	09 01					09 20	09 31	09 31			09 50	09 50	10 01					10 20	10 31	10 32			10 50
Blake Street	d	08 52	09 03					09 22	09 33	09 33			09 52	09 52	10 03					10 22	10 33	10 34			10 52
Shenstone	d	08 56						09 26					09 56	09 56						10 26					10 56
Lichfield City	d	09 02	09a11					09 32	09a42	09a42			10 02	10 02	10a11					10 32	10a42	10a43			11 02
Lichfield Trent Valley	a	09 05						09 35					10 05	10 05						10 35					11 05

A from 4 August

B until 28 July

Table T069-R

Saturdays

26 May to 1 September

Redditch and Longbridge - Birmingham - Lichfield

		LM	LM	LM	LM	LM	XC	LM	LM	LM	LM	LM	LM	LM	LM	LM	LM	XC	LM	LM	LM	LM
		A		B	A		◇1		B	A			B	A		B	A	◇1		B	A	
Bromsgrove	d			10 12		10 08			10 30		10 43		10 51			11 12				11 30		11 43
Redditch	d		09 55					10 12				10 32			10 55				11 12			
Alvechurch	d		10 00					10 17				10 37			11 00				11 17			
Barnt Green	d		10 07					10 23				10 43	10 57		11 07				11 23			
Longbridge	d	10 02	10 12	10 22	10 22			10 32	10 42	10 43		10 52	11 02	11 02	11 12	11 22	11 22		11 32	11 42	11 42	
Northfield	d	10 04	10 14	10 24	10 24			10 34	10 44	10 45		10 54	11 04	11 04	11 14	11 24	11 24		11 34	11 44	11 44	
Kings Norton	d	10 07	10 17	10 27	10 27			10 37	10 47	10 48		10 57	11 07	11 07	11 17	11 27	11 27		11 37	11 47	11 47	
Bournville	d	10 09	10 19	10 29	10 29			10 39	10 49	10 50		10 59	11 09	11 09	11 19	11 29	11 29		11 39	11 49	11 49	
Selly Oak	d	10 12	10 22	10 32	10 32			10 42	10 52	10 53		11 02	11 12	11 12	11 22	11 32	11 32		11 42	11 52	11 52	
University	d	10 15	10 25	10 35	10 35		10 39	10 45	10 55	10 56	11 00	11 05	11 15	11 15	11 25	11 35	11 35	11 39	11 45	11 55	11 55	12 00
Five Ways	d	10 19	10 29	10 39	10 39			10 49	10 59	11 00		11 09	11 19	11 19	11 29	11 39	11 39		11 49	11 59	11 59	
Birmingham New Street 12	a	10 22	10 33	10 42	10 42	10 44	10 45	10 52	11 03	11 04	11 09	11 12	11 22	11 22	11 33	11 42	11 42	11 45	11 52	12 03	12 03	12 09
	d	10 25	10 36	10 45	10 45			10 55	11 06	11 07		11 15	11 25	11 25	11 36	11 45	11 45		11 55	12 06	12 06	
Duddeston	d			10 49	10 49							11 19				11 49	11 49					
Aston	d	10 30	10 41	10 52	10 52			11 00	11 11	11 12		11 22	11 30	11 30	11 41	11 52	11 52		12 00	12 11	12 11	
Gravelly Hill	d	10 34	10 45	10 56	10 56			11 04	11 15	11 16		11 26	11 34	11 34	11 45	11 56	11 56		12 04	12 15	12 15	
Erdington	d	10 37	10 48	10 59	10 59			11 07	11 18	11 19		11 29	11 37	11 37	11 48	11 59	11 59		12 07	12 18	12 18	
Chester Road	d	10 39	10 50	11 01	11 01			11 09	11 20	11 21		11 31	11 39	11 39	11 50	12 01	12 01		12 09	12 20	12 20	
Wylde Green	d	10 41	10 52	11 03	11 03			11 11	11 22	11 23		11 33	11 41	11 41	11 52	12 03	12 03		12 11	12 22	12 22	
Sutton Coldfield	d	10 44	10 55	11 06	11 06			11 14	11 25	11 26		11 36	11 44	11 44	11 55	12 06	12 06		12 14	12 25	12 25	
Four Oaks	d	10 47	10 58	11a11	11a11			11 17	11 28	11 29		11a41	11 47	11 47	11 58	12a11	12a11		12 17	12 28	12 28	
Butlers Lane	d	10 50	11 01					11 20	11 31	11 32			11 50	11 50	12 01				12 20	12 31	12 31	
Blake Street	d	10 52	11 03					11 22	11 33	11 34			11 52	11 52	12 03				12 22	12 33	12 33	
Shenstone	d	10 56						11 26					11 56	11 56					12 26			
Lichfield City	d	11 02	11a11					11 32	11a41	11a42			12 02	12 02	12a11				12 32	12a42	12a42	
Lichfield Trent Valley	a	11 05						11 35					12 05	12 05					12 35			

		LM	LM	LM	LM	LM	LM	XC	LM	LM	LM	LM	LM	LM	LM	LM	LM	LM	XC	LM	LM	LM	LM
			B	A		B	A	◇1		B	A			B	A		B	A	◇1		B	A	
Bromsgrove	d		11 51			12 12				12 30		12 43		12 51			13 12				13 30		13 43
Redditch	d	11 32			11 55				12 12				12 32			12 55				13 12			
Alvechurch	d	11 37			12 00				12 17				12 37			13 00				13 17			
Barnt Green	d	11 43	11 57		12 07				12 23				12 43	12 57		13 07				13 23			
Longbridge	d	11 52	12 02	12 02	12 12	12 22	12 22		12 32	12 42	12 42		12 52	13 02	13 02	13 12	13 22	13 22		13 32	13 42	13 43	
Northfield	d	11 54	12 04	12 04	12 14	12 24	12 24		12 34	12 44	12 44		12 54	13 04	13 04	13 14	13 24	13 24		13 34	13 44	13 45	
Kings Norton	d	11 57	12 07	12 07	12 17	12 27	12 27		12 37	12 47	12 47		12 57	13 07	13 07	13 17	13 27	13 27		13 37	13 47	13 48	
Bournville	d	11 59	12 09	12 09	12 19	12 29	12 29		12 39	12 49	12 49		12 59	13 09	13 09	13 19	13 29	13 29		13 39	13 49	13 50	
Selly Oak	d	12 02	12 12	12 12	12 22	12 32	12 32		12 42	12 52	12 52		13 02	13 12	13 12	13 22	13 32	13 32		13 42	13 52	13 53	
University	d	12 05	12 15	12 15	12 25	12 35	12 35	12 39	12 45	12 55	12 55	13 00	13 05	13 15	13 15	13 25	13 35	13 35	13 39	13 45	13 55	13 56	14 00
Five Ways	d	12 09	12 19	12 19	12 29	12 39	12 39		12 49	12 59	12 59		13 09	13 19	13 19	13 29	13 39	13 39		13 49	13 59	14 00	
Birmingham New Street 12	a	12 12	12 22	12 22	12 33	12 42	12 42	12 45	12 52	13 03	13 03	13 09	13 12	13 22	13 22	13 33	13 42	13 42	13 45	13 52	14 03	14 04	14 09
	d	12 15	12 25	12 25	12 36	12 45	12 45		12 55	13 06	13 06		13 15	13 25	13 25	13 36	13 45	13 45		13 55	14 06	14 07	
Duddeston	d	12 19				12 49	12 49						13 19				13 49	13 49					
Aston	d	12 22	12 30	12 30	12 41	12 52	12 52		13 00	13 11	13 11		13 22	13 30	13 30	13 41	13 52	13 52		14 00	14 11	14 12	
Gravelly Hill	d	12 26	12 34	12 34	12 45	12 56	12 56		13 04	13 15	13 15		13 26	13 34	13 34	13 45	13 56	13 56		14 04	14 15	14 16	
Erdington	d	12 29	12 37	12 37	12 48	12 59	12 59		13 07	13 18	13 18		13 29	13 37	13 37	13 48	13 59	13 59		14 07	14 18	14 19	
Chester Road	d	12 31	12 39	12 39	12 50	13 01	13 01		13 09	13 20	13 20		13 31	13 39	13 39	13 50	14 01	14 01		14 09	14 20	14 21	
Wylde Green	d	12 33	12 41	12 41	12 52	13 03	13 03		13 11	13 22	13 22		13 33	13 41	13 41	13 52	14 03	14 03		14 11	14 22	14 23	
Sutton Coldfield	d	12 36	12 44	12 44	12 55	13 06	13 06		13 14	13 25	13 25		13 36	13 44	13 44	13 55	14 06	14 06		14 14	14 25	14 26	
Four Oaks	d	12a41	12 47	12 47	12 58	13a11	13a11		13 17	13 28	13 28		13a41	13 47	13 47	13 58	14a11	14a11		14 17	14 28	14 29	
Butlers Lane	d		12 50	12 50	13 01				13 20	13 31	13 31			13 50	13 50	14 01				14 20	14 31	14 32	
Blake Street	d		12 52	12 52	13 03				13 22	13 33	13 33			13 52	13 52	14 03				14 22	14 33	14 34	
Shenstone	d		12 56	12 56					13 26					13 56	13 56					14 26			
Lichfield City	d		13 02	13 02	13a11				13 32	13a42	13a42			14 02	14 02	14a11				14 32	14a42	14a42	
Lichfield Trent Valley	a		13 05	13 05					13 35					14 05	14 05					14 35			

		LM	LM	LM	LM	LM	LM	XC	LM	LM	LM	LM	LM	LM	LM	LM	LM	LM	XC	LM	LM	LM
			B	A		B	A	◇1		B	A			B	A		B	A	◇1		B	A
Bromsgrove	d		13 51			14 12				14 30		14 43		14 51			15 12				15 30	
Redditch	d	13 32			13 55				14 12				14 32			14 55				15 12		
Alvechurch	d	13 37			14 00				14 17				14 37			15 00				15 17		
Barnt Green	d	13 43	13 57		14 07				14 23				14 43	14 57		15 07				15 23		
Longbridge	d	13 52	14 02	14 02	14 12	14 22	14 23		14 32	14 42	14 43		14 52	15 02	15 02	15 12	15 22	15 22		15 32	15 42	15 43
Northfield	d	13 54	14 04	14 04	14 14	14 24	14 25		14 34	14 44	14 45		14 54	15 04	15 04	15 14	15 24	15 24		15 34	15 44	15 45
Kings Norton	d	13 57	14 07	14 07	14 17	14 27	14 28		14 37	14 47	14 48		14 57	15 07	15 07	15 17	15 27	15 27		15 37	15 47	15 48
Bournville	d	13 59	14 09	14 09	14 19	14 29	14 30		14 39	14 49	14 50		14 59	15 09	15 09	15 19	15 29	15 29		15 39	15 49	15 50
Selly Oak	d	14 02	14 12	14 12	14 22	14 32	14 33		14 42	14 52	14 53		15 02	15 12	15 12	15 22	15 32	15 32		15 42	15 52	15 53
University	d	14 05	14 15	14 15	14 25	14 35	14 36	14 39	14 45	14 55	14 56	15 00	15 05	15 15	15 15	15 25	15 35	15 35	15 39	15 45	15 55	15 56
Five Ways	d	14 09	14 19	14 19	14 29	14 39	14 40		14 49	14 59	15 00		15 09	15 19	15 19	15 29	15 39	15 39		15 49	15 59	16 00
Birmingham New Street 12	a	14 12	14 22	14 22	14 33	14 42	14 43	14 45	14 52	15 03	15 04	15 09	15 12	15 22	15 22	15 33	15 42	15 42	15 45	15 52	16 03	16 04
	d	14 15	14 25	14 25	14 36	14 45	14 46		14 55	15 06	15 07		15 15	15 25	15 25	15 36	15 45	15 45		15 55	16 06	16 07
Duddeston	d	14 19				14 49	14 50						15 19				15 49	15 49				
Aston	d	14 22	14 30	14 30	14 41	14 52	14 53		15 00	15 11	15 12		15 22	15 30	15 30	15 41	15 52	15 52		16 00	16 11	16 12
Gravelly Hill	d	14 26	14 34	14 34	14 45	14 56	14 57		15 04	15 15	15 16		15 26	15 34	15 34	15 45	15 56	15 56		16 04	16 15	16 16
Erdington	d	14 29	14 37	14 37	14 48	14 59	15 00		15 07	15 18	15 19		15 29	15 37	15 37	15 48	15 59	15 59		16 07	16 18	16 19
Chester Road	d	14 31	14 39	14 39	14 50	15 01	15 02		15 09	15 20	15 21		15 31	15 39	15 39	15 50	16 01	16 01		16 09	16 20	16 21
Wylde Green	d	14 33	14 41	14 41	14 52	15 03	15 04		15 11	15 22	15 23		15 33	15 41	15 41	15 52	16 03	16 03		16 11	16 22	16 23
Sutton Coldfield	d	14 36	14 44	14 44	14 55	15 06	15 07		15 14	15 25	15 26		15 36	15 44	15 44	15 55	16 06	16 06		16 14	16 25	16 26
Four Oaks	d	14a41	14 47	14 47	14 58	15a11	15a12		15 17	15 28	15 29		15a41	15 47	15 47	15 58	16a11	16a11		16 17	16 28	16 29
Butlers Lane	d		14 50	14 50	15 01				15 20	15 31	15 32			15 50	15 50	16 01				16 20	16 31	16 32
Blake Street	d		14 52	14 52	15 03				15 22	15 33	15 34			15 52	15 52	16 03				16 22	16 33	16 34
Shenstone	d		14 56	14 56					15 26					15 56	15 56					16 26		
Lichfield City	d		15 02	15 02	15a11				15 32	15a42	15a43			16 02	16 02	16a11				16 32	16a41	16a42
Lichfield Trent Valley	a		15 05	15 05					15 35					16 05	16 05					16 35		

A until 28 July

B from 4 August

NRT MAY 2018 EDITION

Table T069-R

Saturdays

26 May to 1 September

Redditch and Longbridge - Birmingham - Lichfield

		LM	LM	LM	LM	LM	LM	LM	LM	XC	LM	LM	LM	LM	LM	LM	LM	LM	LM	LM	XC	LM	LM
				A	B		A	B		◇1		A	B			A	B		A	B	◇1		A
Bromsgrove	d	15 43		15 51			16 12		16 08			16 30		16 43		16 51			17 12				17 30
Redditch	d		15 32			15 55					16 12				16 32			16 55				17 12	
Alvechurch	d		15 37			16 00					16 17				16 37			17 00				17 17	
Barnt Green	d		15 43	15 57		16 07					16 23				16 43	16 57		17 07				17 23	
Longbridge	d		15 52	16 02	16 02	16 12	16 22	16 22			16 32	16 42	16 43		16 52	17 02	17 02	17 12	17 22	17 22		17 32	17 42
Northfield	d		15 54	16 04	16 04	16 14	16 24	16 24			16 34	16 44	16 45		16 54	17 04	17 04	17 14	17 24	17 24		17 34	17 44
Kings Norton	d		15 57	16 07	16 07	16 17	16 27	16 27			16 37	16 47	16 48		16 57	17 07	17 07	17 17	17 27	17 27		17 37	17 47
Bournville	d		15 59	16 09	16 09	16 19	16 29	16 29			16 39	16 49	16 50		16 59	17 09	17 09	17 19	17 29	17 29		17 39	17 49
Selly Oak	d		16 02	16 12	16 12	16 22	16 32	16 32			16 42	16 52	16 53		17 02	17 12	17 12	17 22	17 32	17 32		17 42	17 52
University	d	16 00	16 05	16 15	16 15	16 25	16 35	16 35		16 39	16 45	16 55	16 56	17 00	17 05	17 15	17 15	17 25	17 35	17 35	17 39	17 45	17 55
Five Ways	d		16 09	16 19	16 19	16 29	16 39	16 39			16 49	16 59	17 00		17 09	17 19	17 19	17 29	17 39	17 39		17 49	17 59
Birmingham New Street 12	a	16 09	16 12	16 22	16 22	16 33	16 42	16 42	16 44	16 45	16 52	17 03	17 04	17 09	17 12	17 22	17 22	17 33	17 42	17 42	17 45	17 52	18 03
	d		16 15	16 25	16 25	16 36	16 45	16 45			16 55	17 06	17 07		17 15	17 25	17 25	17 36	17 45	17 45		17 55	18 06
Duddeston	d		16 19				16 49	16 49							17 19				17 49	17 49			
Aston	d		16 22	16 30	16 30	16 41	16 52	16 52			17 00	17 11	17 12		17 22	17 30	17 30	17 41	17 52	17 52		18 00	18 11
Gravelly Hill	d		16 26	16 34	16 34	16 45	16 56	16 56			17 04	17 15	17 16		17 26	17 34	17 34	17 45	17 56	17 56		18 04	18 15
Erdington	d		16 29	16 37	16 37	16 48	16 59	16 59			17 07	17 18	17 19		17 29	17 37	17 37	17 48	17 59	17 59		18 07	18 18
Chester Road	d		16 31	16 39	16 39	16 50	17 01	17 01			17 09	17 20	17 21		17 31	17 39	17 39	17 50	18 01	18 01		18 09	18 20
Wylde Green	d		16 33	16 41	16 41	16 52	17 03	17 03			17 11	17 22	17 23		17 33	17 41	17 41	17 52	18 03	18 03		18 11	18 22
Sutton Coldfield	d		16 36	16 44	16 44	16 55	17 06	17 06			17 14	17 25	17 26		17 36	17 44	17 44	17 55	18 06	18 06		18 14	18 25
Four Oaks	d		16a41	16 47	16 47	16 58	17a11	17a11			17 17	17 28	17 29		17a41	17 47	17 47	17 58	18a11	18a11		18 17	18 28
Butlers Lane	d			16 50	16 50	17 01					17 20	17 31	17 32			17 50	17 50	18 01				18 20	18 31
Blake Street	d			16 52	16 52	17 03					17 22	17 33	17 34			17 52	17 52	18 03				18 22	18 33
Shenstone	d			16 56	16 56						17 26					17 56	17 56					18 26	
Lichfield City	d			17 02	17 02	17a11					17 32	17a42	17a43			18 02	18 02	18a11				18 32	18a42
Lichfield Trent Valley	a			17 05	17 05						17 35					18 05	18 05					18 35	

		LM	LM	LM	LM	LM	LM	LM	LM	XC	LM	LM	LM	LM	LM	LM	LM	LM	LM	LM	XC	LM	LM
		B			A	B		A	B	◇1		A	B			A	B		A	B	◇1		A
Bromsgrove	d		17 43		17 51			18 12				18 30		18 43		18 51			19 12				19 30
Redditch	d			17 32			17 55				18 12				18 32			18 55				19 12	
Alvechurch	d			17 37			18 00				18 17				18 37			19 00				19 17	
Barnt Green	d			17 43	17 57		18 07				18 23				18 43	18 57		19 07				19 23	
Longbridge	d	17 43		17 52	18 02	18 02	18 12	18 22	18 22		18 32	18 42	18 42		18 52	19 02	19 02	19 12	19 22	19 22		19 32	19 42
Northfield	d	17 45		17 54	18 04	18 04	18 14	18 24	18 24		18 34	18 44	18 44		18 54	19 04	19 04	19 14	19 24	19 24		19 34	19 44
Kings Norton	d	17 48		17 57	18 07	18 07	18 17	18 27	18 27		18 37	18 47	18 47		18 57	19 07	19 07	19 17	19 27	19 27		19 37	19 47
Bournville	d	17 50		17 59	18 09	18 09	18 19	18 29	18 29		18 39	18 49	18 49		18 59	19 09	19 09	19 19	19 29	19 29		19 39	19 49
Selly Oak	d	17 53		18 02	18 12	18 12	18 22	18 32	18 32		18 42	18 52	18 52		19 02	19 12	19 12	19 22	19 32	19 32		19 42	19 52
University	d	17 56	18 00	18 05	18 15	18 15	18 25	18 35	18 35	18 39	18 45	18 55	18 55	19 00	19 05	19 15	19 15	19 25	19 35	19 35	19 39	19 45	19 55
Five Ways	d	18 00		18 09	18 19	18 19	18 29	18 39	18 39		18 49	18 59	18 59		19 09	19 18	19 18	19 29	19 38	19 38		19 49	19 59
Birmingham New Street 12	a	18 04	18 09	18 12	18 22	18 22	18 33	18 42	18 42	18 45	18 52	19 03	19 03	19 09	19 12	19 23	19 23	19 32	19 43	19 43	19 45	19 52	20 03
	d	18 07		18 15	18 25	18 25	18 36	18 45	18 45		18 55	19 06	19 06		19 15			19 36					20 06
Duddeston	d			18 19				18 49	18 49						19 19			19 40					20 10
Aston	d	18 12		18 22	18 30	18 30	18 41	18 52	18 52		19 00	19 11	19 11		19 22			19 43					20 13
Gravelly Hill	d	18 16		18 26	18 34	18 34	18 45	18 56	18 56		19 04	19 15	19 15		19 26			19 47					20 17
Erdington	d	18 19		18 29	18 37	18 37	18 48	18 59	18 59		19 07	19 18	19 18		19 29			19 50					20 20
Chester Road	d	18 21		18 31	18 39	18 39	18 50	19 01	19 01		19 09	19 20	19 20		19 31			19 52					20 22
Wylde Green	d	18 23		18 33	18 41	18 41	18 52	19 03	19 03		19 11	19 22	19 22		19 33			19 54					20 24
Sutton Coldfield	d	18 26		18 36	18 44	18 44	18 55	19 06	19 06		19 14	19 25	19 25		19 36			19 57					20 27
Four Oaks	d	18 29		18a41	18 47	18 47	18 58	19a11	19a11		19 17	19 28	19 28		19a41			20 00					20 30
Butlers Lane	d	18 32			18 50	18 50	19 01				19 20	19 31	19 31					20 03					20 33
Blake Street	d	18 34			18 52	18 52	19 03				19 22	19 33	19 33					20 05					20 35
Shenstone	d				18 56	18 56					19 26							20 09					20 39
Lichfield City	d	18a43			19 02	19 02	19a11				19 32	19a42	19a42					20 14					20 44
Lichfield Trent Valley	a				19 05	19 05					19 35							20 17					20 47

		LM	LM	LM	LM	LM	XC	LM	LM	LM	LM	LM	LM	LM	LM	LM	LM	XC	LM	LM	LM	XC
		B		A	B		◇1	A	B		A	B			A	B		◇1	A	B		◇1
Bromsgrove	d			19 51				20 15			20 46		20 59		21 17			21 44	21 47			
Redditch	d		19 32			19 55				20 27				20 57			21 27				21 57	
Alvechurch	d		19 37			20 00				20 32				21 02			21 32				22 02	
Barnt Green	d		19 43	19 57		20 07				20 39	20 52			21 08			21 38		21 53		22 08	
Longbridge	d	19 43	19 52	20 02	20 02	20 12		20 27	20 27	20 43	20 57	20 57		21 12	21 27	21 28	21 42		21 58	21 58	22 12	
Northfield	d	19 45	19 54	20 04	20 04	20 14		20 29	20 29	20 45	20 59	20 59		21 14	21 29	21 30	21 44		22 00	22 00	22 14	
Kings Norton	d	19 48	19 57	20 07	20 07	20 17		20 32	20 32	20 49	21 02	21 02		21 17	21 32	21 33	21 47		22 03	22 03	22 17	
Bournville	d	19 50	19 59	20 09	20 09	20 19		20 33	20 33	20 50	21 04	21 04		21 19	21 34	21 35	21 49		22 05	22 05	22 19	
Selly Oak	d	19 53	20 02	20 12	20 12	20 22		20 37	20 37	20 53	21 07	21 07		21 22	21 37	21 38	21 52		22 08	22 08	22 22	
University	d	19 56	20 05	20 15	20 15	20 25	20 35	20 40	20 40	20 57	21 10	21 10	21 15	21 25	21 40	21 41	21 55	22 01	22 11	22 11	22 25	22 35
Five Ways	d	20 00	20 09	20 18	20 18	20 29		20 43	20 43	21 01	21 13	21 13		21 29	21 43	21 44	21 59		22 15	22 15	22 28	
Birmingham New Street 12	a	20 04	20 12	20 23	20 23	20 32	20 42	20 49	20 49	21 04	21 18	21 18	21 22	21 33	21 48	21 49	22 03	22 07	22 19	22 19	22 33	22 42
	d	20 07				20 36				21 06				21 36			22 06				22 35	
Duddeston	d	20 11				20 40				21 10				21 40			22 10				22 39	
Aston	d	20 14				20 43				21 13				21 43			22 13				22 42	
Gravelly Hill	d	20 18				20 47				21 17				21 47			22 17				22 46	
Erdington	d	20 21				20 50				21 20				21 50			22 20				22 49	
Chester Road	d	20 23				20 52				21 22				21 52			22 22				22 51	
Wylde Green	d	20 25				20 54				21 24				21 54			22 24				22 53	
Sutton Coldfield	d	20 28				20 57				21 27				21 57			22 27				22 56	
Four Oaks	d	20 31				21 00				21 30				22 00			22 30				22 59	
Butlers Lane	d	20 34				21 03				21 33				22 03			22 33				23 02	
Blake Street	d	20 36				21 05				21 35				22 05			22 35				23 04	
Shenstone	d	20 40				21 09				21 39				22 09			22 39				23 08	
Lichfield City	d	20 45				21 14				21 44				22 14			22 44				23 13	
Lichfield Trent Valley	a	20 48				21 17				21 48				22 17			22 47				23 17	

A from 4 August

B until 28 July

Table T069-R

Saturdays
26 May to 1 September

Redditch and Longbridge - Birmingham - Lichfield

		LM A	LM B	LM	LM A	LM B	LM	LM
Bromsgrove	d	22 17			22 41			
Redditch	d			22 27			22 57	
Alvechurch	d			22 32			23 02	
Barnt Green	d			22 38	22 47		23 08	
Longbridge	d	22 29	22 29	22 42	22 52	22 52	23 12	23 30
Northfield	d	22 31	22 31	22 44	22 54	22 54	23 14	23 32
Kings Norton	d	22 34	22 34	22 47	22 57	22 57	23 17	23 35
Bournville	d	22 36	22 36	22 49	22 59	22 59	23 19	23 37
Selly Oak	d	22 39	22 39	22 52	23 02	23 02	23 22	23 40
University	d	22 42	22 42	22 55	23 05	23 05	23 25	23 43
Five Ways	d	22 45	22 45	23 00	23 08	23 08	23 29	23 47
Birmingham New Street	a	22 49	22 49	23 03	23 13	23 13	23 33	23 50
	d	22 55	22 55		23 15	23 15		
Duddeston	d	22 59	22 59		23 19	23 19		
Aston	d	23 02	23 02		23 22	23 22		
Gravelly Hill	d	23 06	23 06		23 26	23 26		
Erdington	d	23 09	23 09		23 29	23 29		
Chester Road	d	23 11	23 11		23 31	23 31		
Wylde Green	d	23 13	23 13		23 33	23 33		
Sutton Coldfield	d	23 16	23 16		23 36	23 36		
Four Oaks	d	23 19	23 19		23 39	23 39		
Butlers Lane	d	23 22	23 22		23 42	23 42		
Blake Street	d	23a25	23a25		23 44	23 44		
Shenstone	d				23 48	23 48		
Lichfield City	d				23a54	23a54		
Lichfield Trent Valley	a							

Saturdays
8 September to 8 December

		LM	LM	LM	LM	LM	LM	LM	LM	LM	LM	LM	LM
Bromsgrove	d				06 12		06 33		06 47	06 51		07 12	
Redditch	d					06 12		06 32			06 55		07 12
Alvechurch	d					06 17		06 37			07 00		07 17
Barnt Green	d					06 23		06 43		06 57	07 07		07 23
Longbridge	d			06 12	06 22	06 32	06 42	06 52		07 02	07 12	07 22	07 32
Northfield	d			06 14	06 24	06 34	06 44	06 54		07 04	07 14	07 24	07 34
Kings Norton	d			06 17	06 27	06 37	06 47	06 57		07 07	07 17	07 27	07 37
Bournville	d			06 19	06 29	06 39	06 49	06 59		07 09	07 19	07 29	07 39
Selly Oak	d			06 22	06 32	06 42	06 52	07 02		07 12	07 22	07 32	07 42
University	d			06 25	06 35	06 45	06 55	07 05	07 10	07 15	07 25	07 35	07 45
Five Ways	d			06 29	06 38	06 49	06 58	07 09		07 19	07 29	07 38	07 49
Birmingham New Street	a			06 32	06 42	06 52	07 03	07 12	07 17	07 22	07 33	07 42	07 52
	d	05 55	06 25	06 36		06 55	07 06	07 15		07 25	07 35	07 45	07 55
Duddeston	d	05 59	06 29			06 59		07 19				07 49	
Aston	d	06 02	06 32	06 41		07 02	07 11	07 22		07 30	07 40	07 52	08 00
Gravelly Hill	d	06 06	06 36	06 45		07 06	07 15	07 26		07 34	07 44	07 56	08 04
Erdington	d	06 09	06 39	06 48		07 09	07 18	07 29		07 37	07 47	07 59	08 07
Chester Road	d	06 11	06 41	06 50		07 11	07 20	07 31		07 39	07 49	08 01	08 09
Wylde Green	d	06 13	06 43	06 52		07 13	07 22	07 33		07 41	07 51	08 03	08 11
Sutton Coldfield	d	06 16	06 46	06 55		07 16	07 25	07 36		07 44	07 54	08 06	08 14
Four Oaks	d	06 19	06 49	06 59		07 19	07 28	07a41		07 47	07 57	08a11	08 17
Butlers Lane	d	06 22	06 52	07 01		07 22	07 31			07 50	08 00		08 20
Blake Street	d	06 24	06 54	07 04		07 24	07 33			07 52	08 02		08 22
Shenstone	d	06 26	06 56			07 26				07 56			08 26
Lichfield City	d	06a34	07a04	07 12		07a34	07 42			08 02	08a11		08 32
Lichfield Trent Valley	a			07 15			07 45			08 05			08 35

		LM	XC ◇1	LM	LM	LM	LM	LM	XC ◇1	LM	LM
Bromsgrove	d	07 30	07 43		07 47	07 51		08 12			08 30
Redditch	d			07 32			07 55			08 12	
Alvechurch	d			07 37			08 00			08 17	
Barnt Green	d			07 43		07 57	08 07			08 23	
Longbridge	d	07 42		07 52		08 02	08 12	08 22		08 32	08 42
Northfield	d	07 44		07 54		08 04	08 14	08 24		08 34	08 44
Kings Norton	d	07 47		07 57		08 07	08 17	08 27		08 37	08 47
Bournville	d	07 49		07 59		08 09	08 19	08 29		08 39	08 49
Selly Oak	d	07 52		08 02		08 12	08 22	08 32		08 42	08 52
University	d	07 55	08 00	08 05	08 10	08 15	08 25	08 35	08 39	08 45	08 55
Five Ways	d	07 59		08 09		08 19	08 29	08 38		08 49	08 59
Birmingham New Street	a	08 03	08 07	08 12	08 17	08 22	08 33	08 42	08 45	08 52	09 03
	d	08 06		08 15		08 25	08 36	08 45		08 55	09 06
Duddeston	d			08 19				08 49			
Aston	d	08 10		08 22		08 30	08 41	08 52		09 00	09 11
Gravelly Hill	d	08 14		08 26		08 34	08 45	08 56		09 04	09 15
Erdington	d	08 17		08 29		08 37	08 48	08 59		09 07	09 18
Chester Road	d	08 19		08 31		08 39	08 50	09 01		09 09	09 20
Wylde Green	d	08 21		08 33		08 41	08 52	09 03		09 11	09 22
Sutton Coldfield	d	08 24		08 36		08 44	08 55	09 06		09 14	09 25
Four Oaks	d	08 27		08a41		08 47	08 58	09a11		09 17	09 28
Butlers Lane	d	08 30				08 50	09 01			09 20	09 31
Blake Street	d	08 32				08 52	09 03			09 22	09 33
Shenstone	d					08 56				09 26	
Lichfield City	d	08a41				09 02	09a11			09 32	09a42
Lichfield Trent Valley	a					09 05				09 35	

		LM	LM	LM	LM	LM	XC ◇1	LM	LM	LM	LM	LM	LM
Bromsgrove	d	08 43		08 51		09 12			09 30	09 43		09 51	
Redditch	d		08 32		08 55			09 12			09 32		09 55
Alvechurch	d		08 37		09 00			09 17			09 37		10 00
Barnt Green	d		08 43	08 57	09 07			09 23			09 43	09 57	10 07
Longbridge	d		08 52	09 02	09 12	09 22		09 32	09 42		09 52	10 02	10 12
Northfield	d		08 54	09 04	09 14	09 24		09 34	09 44		09 54	10 04	10 14
Kings Norton	d		08 57	09 07	09 17	09 27		09 37	09 47		09 57	10 07	10 17
Bournville	d		08 59	09 09	09 19	09 29		09 39	09 49		09 59	10 09	10 19
Selly Oak	d		09 02	09 12	09 22	09 32		09 42	09 52		10 02	10 12	10 22
University	d	09 00	09 05	09 15	09 25	09 35	09 39	09 45	09 55	10 00	10 05	10 15	10 25
Five Ways	d		09 09	09 19	09 29	09 39		09 49	09 59		10 09	10 19	10 29
Birmingham New Street	a	09 09	09 12	09 22	09 33	09 42	09 45	09 52	10 03	10 09	10 12	10 22	10 33
	d		09 15	09 25	09 36	09 45		09 55	10 06		10 15	10 25	10 36
Duddeston	d		09 19			09 49					10 19		
Aston	d		09 22	09 30	09 41	09 52		10 00	10 11		10 22	10 30	10 41
Gravelly Hill	d		09 26	09 34	09 45	09 56		10 04	10 15		10 26	10 34	10 45
Erdington	d		09 29	09 37	09 48	09 59		10 07	10 18		10 29	10 37	10 48
Chester Road	d		09 31	09 39	09 50	10 01		10 09	10 20		10 31	10 39	10 50
Wylde Green	d		09 33	09 41	09 52	10 03		10 11	10 22		10 33	10 41	10 52
Sutton Coldfield	d		09 36	09 44	09 55	10 06		10 14	10 25		10 36	10 44	10 55
Four Oaks	d		09a41	09 47	09 58	10a11		10 17	10 28		10a41	10 47	10 58
Butlers Lane	d			09 50	10 01			10 20	10 31			10 50	11 01
Blake Street	d			09 52	10 03			10 22	10 33			10 52	11 03
Shenstone	d			09 56				10 26				10 56	
Lichfield City	d			10 02	10a11			10 32	10a42			11 02	11a11
Lichfield Trent Valley	a			10 05				10 35				11 05	

		LM	LM	XC ◇1	LM	LM	LM	LM	LM	LM	LM
Bromsgrove	d	10 12	10 08			10 30	10 43		10 51		11 12
Redditch	d				10 12			10 32		10 55	
Alvechurch	d				10 17			10 37		11 00	
Barnt Green	d				10 23			10 43	10 57	11 07	
Longbridge	d	10 22			10 32	10 42		10 52	11 02	11 12	11 22
Northfield	d	10 24			10 34	10 44		10 54	11 04	11 14	11 24
Kings Norton	d	10 27			10 37	10 47		10 57	11 07	11 17	11 27
Bournville	d	10 29			10 39	10 49		10 59	11 09	11 19	11 29
Selly Oak	d	10 32			10 42	10 52		11 02	11 12	11 22	11 32
University	d	10 35		10 39	10 45	10 55	11 00	11 05	11 15	11 25	11 35
Five Ways	d	10 39			10 49	10 59		11 09	11 19	11 29	11 39
Birmingham New Street	a	10 42	10 44	10 45	10 52	11 03	11 09	11 12	11 22	11 33	11 42
	d	10 45			10 55	11 06		11 15	11 25	11 36	11 45
Duddeston	d	10 49						11 19			11 49
Aston	d	10 52			11 00	11 11		11 22	11 30	11 41	11 52
Gravelly Hill	d	10 56			11 04	11 15		11 26	11 34	11 45	11 56
Erdington	d	10 59			11 07	11 18		11 29	11 37	11 48	11 59
Chester Road	d	11 01			11 09	11 20		11 31	11 39	11 50	12 01
Wylde Green	d	11 03			11 11	11 22		11 33	11 41	11 52	12 03
Sutton Coldfield	d	11 06			11 14	11 25		11 36	11 44	11 55	12 06
Four Oaks	d	11a11			11 17	11 28		11a41	11 47	11 58	12a11
Butlers Lane	d				11 20	11 31			11 50	12 01	
Blake Street	d				11 22	11 33			11 52	12 03	
Shenstone	d				11 26				11 56		
Lichfield City	d				11 32	11a41			12 02	12a11	
Lichfield Trent Valley	a				11 35				12 05		

A from 4 August
B until 28 July

Table T069-R

Saturdays
8 September to 8 December

Redditch and Longbridge - Birmingham - Lichfield

		XC ◇1	LM	LM	and at the same minutes past each hour until	LM	LM	LM	LM	LM	XC ◇1	LM	LM
Bromsgrove	d			11 30		13 43		13 51		14 12			14 30
Redditch	d		11 12				13 32		13 55			14 12	
Alvechurch	d		11 17				13 37		14 00			14 17	
Barnt Green	d		11 23				13 43	13 57	14 07			14 23	
Longbridge	d		11 32	11 42			13 52	14 02	14 12	14 22		14 32	14 42
Northfield	d		11 34	11 44			13 54	14 04	14 14	14 24		14 34	14 44
Kings Norton	d		11 37	11 47			13 57	14 07	14 17	14 27		14 37	14 47
Bournville	d		11 39	11 49			13 59	14 09	14 19	14 29		14 39	14 49
Selly Oak	d		11 42	11 52			14 02	14 12	14 22	14 32		14 42	14 52
University	d	11 39	11 45	11 55		14 00	14 05	14 15	14 25	14 35	14 39	14 45	14 55
Five Ways	d		11 49	11 59			14 09	14 19	14 29	14 39		14 49	14 59
Birmingham New Street	a	11 45	11 52	12 03		14 09	14 12	14 22	14 33	14 42	14 45	14 52	15 03
	d		11 55	12 06			14 15	14 25	14 36	14 45		14 55	15 06
Duddeston	d						14 19			14 49			
Aston	d		12 00	12 11			14 22	14 30	14 41	14 52		15 00	15 11
Gravelly Hill	d		12 04	12 15			14 26	14 34	14 45	14 56		15 04	15 15
Erdington	d		12 07	12 18			14 29	14 37	14 48	14 59		15 07	15 18
Chester Road	d		12 09	12 20			14 31	14 39	14 50	15 01		15 09	15 20
Wylde Green	d		12 11	12 22			14 33	14 41	14 52	15 03		15 11	15 22
Sutton Coldfield	d		12 14	12 25			14 36	14 44	14 55	15 06		15 14	15 25
Four Oaks	d		12 17	12 28			14a41	14 47	14 58	15a11		15 17	15 28
Butlers Lane	d		12 20	12 31				14 50	15 01			15 20	15 31
Blake Street	d		12 22	12 33				14 52	15 03			15 22	15 33
Shenstone	d		12 26					14 56				15 26	
Lichfield City	d		12 32	12a42				15 02	15a11			15 32	15a42
Lichfield Trent Valley	a		12 35					15 05				15 35	

		LM	LM	LM	LM	LM	XC ◇1	LM	LM	LM
Bromsgrove	d	14 43		14 51		15 12			15 30	15 43
Redditch	d		14 32		14 55			15 12		
Alvechurch	d		14 37		15 00			15 17		
Barnt Green	d		14 43	14 57	15 07			15 23		
Longbridge	d		14 52	15 02	15 12	15 22		15 32	15 42	
Northfield	d		14 54	15 04	15 14	15 24		15 34	15 44	
Kings Norton	d		14 57	15 07	15 17	15 27		15 37	15 47	
Bournville	d		14 59	15 09	15 19	15 29		15 39	15 49	
Selly Oak	d		15 02	15 12	15 22	15 32		15 42	15 52	
University	d	15 00	15 05	15 15	15 25	15 35	15 39	15 45	15 55	16 00
Five Ways	d		15 09	15 19	15 29	15 39		15 49	15 59	
Birmingham New Street	a	15 09	15 12	15 22	15 33	15 42	15 45	15 52	16 03	16 09
	d		15 15	15 25	15 36	15 45		15 55	16 06	
Duddeston	d		15 19			15 49				
Aston	d		15 22	15 30	15 41	15 52		16 00	16 11	
Gravelly Hill	d		15 26	15 34	15 45	15 56		16 04	16 15	
Erdington	d		15 29	15 37	15 48	15 59		16 07	16 18	
Chester Road	d		15 31	15 39	15 50	16 01		16 09	16 20	
Wylde Green	d		15 33	15 41	15 52	16 03		16 11	16 22	
Sutton Coldfield	d		15 36	15 44	15 55	16 06		16 14	16 25	
Four Oaks	d		15a41	15 47	15 58	16a11		16 17	16 28	
Butlers Lane	d			15 50	16 01			16 20	16 31	
Blake Street	d			15 52	16 03			16 22	16 33	
Shenstone	d			15 56				16 26		
Lichfield City	d			16 02	16a11			16 32	16a41	
Lichfield Trent Valley	a			16 05				16 35		

		LM	LM	LM	LM	LM	XC ◇1	LM	LM	LM	LM	LM	LM
Bromsgrove	d		15 51		16 12	16 08			16 30	16 43		16 51	
Redditch	d	15 32		15 55				16 12			16 32		16 55
Alvechurch	d	15 37		16 00				16 17			16 37		17 00
Barnt Green	d	15 43	15 57	16 07				16 23			16 43	16 57	17 07
Longbridge	d	15 52	16 02	16 12	16 22			16 32	16 42		16 52	17 02	17 12
Northfield	d	15 54	16 04	16 14	16 24			16 34	16 44		16 54	17 04	17 14
Kings Norton	d	15 57	16 07	16 17	16 27			16 37	16 47		16 57	17 07	17 17
Bournville	d	15 59	16 09	16 19	16 29			16 39	16 49		16 59	17 09	17 19
Selly Oak	d	16 02	16 12	16 22	16 32			16 42	16 52		17 02	17 12	17 22
University	d	16 05	16 15	16 25	16 35		16 39	16 45	16 55	17 00	17 05	17 15	17 25
Five Ways	d	16 09	16 19	16 29	16 39			16 49	16 59		17 09	17 19	17 29
Birmingham New Street	a	16 12	16 22	16 33	16 42	16 44	16 45	16 52	17 03	17 09	17 12	17 22	17 33
	d	16 15	16 25	16 36	16 45			16 55	17 06		17 15	17 25	17 36
Duddeston	d	16 19			16 49						17 19		
Aston	d	16 22	16 30	16 41	16 52			17 00	17 11		17 22	17 30	17 41
Gravelly Hill	d	16 26	16 34	16 45	16 56			17 04	17 15		17 26	17 34	17 45
Erdington	d	16 29	16 37	16 48	16 59			17 07	17 18		17 29	17 37	17 48
Chester Road	d	16 31	16 39	16 50	17 01			17 09	17 20		17 31	17 39	17 50
Wylde Green	d	16 33	16 41	16 52	17 03			17 11	17 22		17 33	17 41	17 52
Sutton Coldfield	d	16 36	16 44	16 55	17 06			17 14	17 25		17 36	17 44	17 55
Four Oaks	d	16a41	16 47	16 58	17a11			17 17	17 28		17a41	17 47	17 58
Butlers Lane	d		16 50	17 01				17 20	17 31			17 50	18 01
Blake Street	d		16 52	17 03				17 22	17 33			17 52	18 03
Shenstone	d		16 56					17 26				17 56	
Lichfield City	d		17 02	17a11				17 32	17a42			18 02	18a11
Lichfield Trent Valley	a		17 05					17 35				18 05	

		LM	XC ◇1	LM	LM	LM	LM	LM	LM	LM	XC ◇1
Bromsgrove	d	17 12			17 30	17 43		17 51		18 12	
Redditch	d			17 12			17 32		17 55		
Alvechurch	d			17 17			17 37		18 00		
Barnt Green	d			17 23			17 43	17 57	18 07		
Longbridge	d	17 22		17 32	17 42		17 52	18 02	18 12	18 22	
Northfield	d	17 24		17 34	17 44		17 54	18 04	18 14	18 24	
Kings Norton	d	17 27		17 37	17 47		17 57	18 07	18 17	18 27	
Bournville	d	17 29		17 39	17 49		17 59	18 09	18 19	18 29	
Selly Oak	d	17 32		17 42	17 52		18 02	18 12	18 22	18 32	
University	d	17 35	17 39	17 45	17 55	18 00	18 05	18 15	18 25	18 35	18 39
Five Ways	d	17 39		17 49	17 59		18 09	18 19	18 29	18 39	
Birmingham New Street	a	17 42	17 45	17 52	18 03	18 09	18 12	18 22	18 33	18 42	18 45
	d	17 45		17 55	18 06		18 15	18 25	18 36	18 45	
Duddeston	d	17 49					18 19			18 49	
Aston	d	17 52		18 00	18 11		18 22	18 30	18 41	18 52	
Gravelly Hill	d	17 56		18 04	18 15		18 26	18 34	18 45	18 56	
Erdington	d	17 59		18 07	18 18		18 29	18 37	18 48	18 59	
Chester Road	d	18 01		18 09	18 20		18 31	18 39	18 50	19 01	
Wylde Green	d	18 03		18 11	18 22		18 33	18 41	18 52	19 03	
Sutton Coldfield	d	18 06		18 14	18 25		18 36	18 44	18 55	19 06	
Four Oaks	d	18a11		18 17	18 28		18a41	18 47	18 58	19a11	
Butlers Lane	d			18 20	18 31			18 50	19 01		
Blake Street	d			18 22	18 33			18 52	19 03		
Shenstone	d			18 26				18 56			
Lichfield City	d			18 32	18a42			19 02	19a11		
Lichfield Trent Valley	a			18 35				19 05			

		LM	LM	LM	LM	LM	LM	LM	XC ◇1	LM	LM	LM	LM
Bromsgrove	d		18 30	18 43		18 51		19 12			19 30		19 51
Redditch	d	18 12			18 32		18 55			19 12		19 32	
Alvechurch	d	18 17			18 37		19 00			19 17		19 37	
Barnt Green	d	18 23			18 43	18 57	19 07			19 23		19 43	19 57
Longbridge	d	18 32	18 42		18 52	19 02	19 12	19 22		19 32	19 42	19 52	20 02
Northfield	d	18 34	18 44		18 54	19 04	19 14	19 24		19 34	19 44	19 54	20 04
Kings Norton	d	18 37	18 47		18 57	19 07	19 17	19 27		19 37	19 47	19 57	20 07
Bournville	d	18 39	18 49		18 59	19 09	19 19	19 29		19 39	19 49	19 59	20 09
Selly Oak	d	18 42	18 52		19 02	19 12	19 22	19 32		19 42	19 52	20 02	20 12
University	d	18 45	18 55	19 00	19 05	19 15	19 25	19 35	19 39	19 45	19 55	20 05	20 15
Five Ways	d	18 49	18 59		19 09	19 18	19 29	19 38		19 49	19 59	20 09	20 18
Birmingham New Street	a	18 52	19 03	19 09	19 12	19 23	19 32	19 43	19 45	19 52	20 03	20 12	20 23
	d	18 55	19 06		19 15		19 36				20 06		
Duddeston	d				19 19		19 40				20 10		
Aston	d	19 00	19 11		19 22		19 43				20 13		
Gravelly Hill	d	19 04	19 15		19 26		19 47				20 17		
Erdington	d	19 07	19 18		19 29		19 50				20 20		
Chester Road	d	19 09	19 20		19 31		19 52				20 22		
Wylde Green	d	19 11	19 22		19 33		19 54				20 24		
Sutton Coldfield	d	19 14	19 25		19 36		19 57				20 27		
Four Oaks	d	19 17	19 28		19a41		20 00				20 30		
Butlers Lane	d	19 20	19 31				20 03				20 33		
Blake Street	d	19 22	19 33				20 05				20 35		
Shenstone	d	19 26					20 09				20 39		
Lichfield City	d	19 32	19a42				20 14				20 44		
Lichfield Trent Valley	a	19 35					20 17				20 47		

		LM	XC ◇1	LM	LM	LM	LM	LM	LM	LM	XC ◇1
Bromsgrove	d			20 15		20 46	20 59		21 17		21 44
Redditch	d	19 55			20 27			20 57		21 27	
Alvechurch	d	20 00			20 32			21 02		21 32	
Barnt Green	d	20 07			20 39	20 52		21 08		21 38	
Longbridge	d	20 12		20 27	20 43	20 57		21 12	21 27	21 42	
Northfield	d	20 14		20 29	20 45	20 59		21 14	21 29	21 44	
Kings Norton	d	20 17		20 32	20 49	21 02		21 17	21 32	21 47	
Bournville	d	20 19		20 33	20 50	21 04		21 19	21 34	21 49	
Selly Oak	d	20 22		20 37	20 53	21 07		21 22	21 37	21 52	
University	d	20 25	20 35	20 40	20 57	21 10	21 15	21 25	21 40	21 55	22 01
Five Ways	d	20 29		20 43	21 01	21 13		21 29	21 43	21 59	
Birmingham New Street	a	20 32	20 42	20 49	21 04	21 18	21 22	21 33	21 48	22 03	22 07
	d	20 36			21 06			21 36		22 06	
Duddeston	d	20 40			21 10			21 40		22 10	
Aston	d	20 43			21 13			21 43		22 13	
Gravelly Hill	d	20 47			21 17			21 47		22 17	
Erdington	d	20 50			21 20			21 50		22 20	
Chester Road	d	20 52			21 22			21 52		22 22	
Wylde Green	d	20 54			21 24			21 54		22 24	
Sutton Coldfield	d	20 57			21 27			21 57		22 27	
Four Oaks	d	21 00			21 30			22 00		22 30	
Butlers Lane	d	21 03			21 33			22 03		22 33	
Blake Street	d	21 05			21 35			22 05		22 35	
Shenstone	d	21 09			21 39			22 09		22 39	
Lichfield City	d	21 14			21 44			22 14		22 44	
Lichfield Trent Valley	a	21 17			21 48			22 17		22 47	

Saturdays

8 September to 8 December

Redditch and Longbridge - Birmingham - Lichfield

		LM	LM	XC ◇1	LM	LM	LM	LM	LM
Bromsgrove	d	21 47			22 17		22 41		
Redditch	d		21 57			22 27		22 57	
Alvechurch	d		22 02			22 32		23 02	
Barnt Green	d	21 53	22 08			22 38	22 47	23 08	
Longbridge	d	21 58	22 12		22 29	22 42	22 52	23 12	23 30
Northfield	d	22 00	22 14		22 31	22 44	22 54	23 14	23 32
Kings Norton	d	22 03	22 17		22 34	22 47	22 57	23 17	23 35
Bournville	d	22 05	22 19		22 36	22 49	22 59	23 19	23 37
Selly Oak	d	22 08	22 22		22 39	22 52	23 02	23 22	23 40
University	d	22 11	22 25	22 35	22 42	22 55	23 05	23 25	23 43
Five Ways	d	22 15	22 28		22 45	23 00	23 08	23 29	23 47
Birmingham New Street 12	a	22 19	22 33	22 42	22 49	23 03	23 13	23 33	23 50
	d		22 35		22 55		23 15		
Duddeston	d		22 39		22 59		23 19		
Aston	d		22 42		23 02		23 22		
Gravelly Hill	d		22 46		23 06		23 26		
Erdington	d		22 49		23 09		23 29		
Chester Road	d		22 51		23 11		23 31		
Wylde Green	d		22 53		23 13		23 33		
Sutton Coldfield	d		22 56		23 16		23 36		
Four Oaks	d		22 59		23 19		23 39		
Butlers Lane	d		23 02		23 22		23 42		
Blake Street	d		23 04		23a25		23 44		
Shenstone	d		23 08				23 48		
Lichfield City	d		23 13				23a54		
Lichfield Trent Valley	a		23 17						

Sundays

20 May to 7 October

		LM	LM	LM	LM	LM A	LM B	LM	LM A	LM B	LM	LM A	LM B	LM	LM A	LM C	LM D	LM	LM	LM A	LM B	LM	LM A
Bromsgrove	d			09 24		09 42			10 12			10 42			11 12			11 16		11 42			12 12
Redditch	d				09 27			09 57			10 27			10 57					11 27			11 57	
Alvechurch	d				09 32			10 02			10 32			11 02					11 32			12 02	
Barnt Green	d				09 38	09 48		10 08			10 38	10 48		11 08					11 38	11 48		12 08	
Longbridge	d		09 12		09 42	09 52	09 52	10 12	10 22	10 22	10 42	10 52	10 52	11 12	11 22	11 22	11 23		11 42	11 52	11 52	12 12	12 22
Northfield	d		09 14		09 44	09 54	09 54	10 14	10 24	10 24	10 44	10 54	10 54	11 14	11 24	11 24	11 25		11 44	11 54	11 54	12 14	12 24
Kings Norton	d		09 17		09 47	09 57	09 57	10 17	10 27	10 27	10 47	10 57	10 57	11 17	11 27	11 27	11 28		11 47	11 57	11 57	12 17	12 27
Bournville	d		09 19		09 49	09 59	09 59	10 19	10 29	10 29	10 49	10 59	10 59	11 19	11 29	11 29	11 30		11 49	11 59	11 59	12 19	12 29
Selly Oak	d		09 22		09 52	10 02	10 02	10 22	10 32	10 32	10 52	11 02	11 02	11 22	11 32	11 32	11 33		11 52	12 02	12 02	12 22	12 32
University	d		09 25	09 40	09 55	10 05	10 05	10 25	10 35	10 35	10 55	11 05	11 05	11 25	11 35	11 35	11 36	11 40	11 55	12 05	12 05	12 25	12 35
Five Ways	d		09 28		09 58	10 08	10 08	10 28	10 38	10 38	10 58	11 08	11 08	11 28	11 38	11 38	11 39		11 58	12 08	12 08	12 28	12 38
Birmingham New Street 12	a		09 32	09 47	10 03	10 13	10 13	10 33	10 42	10 42	11 03	11 13	11 13	11 33	11 43	11 43	11 44	11 46	12 03	12 13	12 13	12 33	12 42
	d	09 06	09 36		10 06			10 36			11 06			11 36					12 06			12 36	
Duddeston	d	09 10	09 40		10 10			10 40			11 10			11 40					12 10			12 40	
Aston	d	09 13	09 43		10 13			10 43			11 13			11 43					12 13			12 43	
Gravelly Hill	d	09 17	09 47		10 17			10 47			11 17			11 47					12 17			12 47	
Erdington	d	09 20	09 50		10 20			10 50			11 20			11 50					12 20			12 50	
Chester Road	d	09 22	09 52		10 22			10 52			11 22			11 52					12 22			12 52	
Wylde Green	d	09 24	09 54		10 24			10 54			11 24			11 54					12 24			12 54	
Sutton Coldfield	d	09 27	09 57		10 27			10 57			11 27			11 57					12 27			12 57	
Four Oaks	d	09 30	10 00		10 30			11 00			11 30			12 00					12 30			13 00	
Butlers Lane	d	09 33	10 03		10 33			11 03			11 33			12 03					12 33			13 03	
Blake Street	d	09 35	10 05		10 35			11 05			11 35			12 05					12 35			13 05	
Shenstone	d	09 39	10 09		10 39			11 09			11 39			12 09					12 39			13 09	
Lichfield City	d	09 44	10 14		10 44			11 14			11 44			12 14					12 44			13 14	
Lichfield Trent Valley	a	09 47	10 17		10 47			11 17			11 47			12 17					12 47			13 17	

		LM B	XC ◇1	LM	LM A	LM B	LM	LM	LM A	LM B	XC ◇1	LM	LM A	LM B	LM	LM A	LM B	XC ◇1	LM	LM A	LM B	LM	LM
Bromsgrove	d				12 42			13 08	13 12				13 42			14 12				14 42			15 08
Redditch	d			12 27			12 57					13 27			13 57				14 27			14 57	
Alvechurch	d			12 32			13 02					13 32			14 02				14 32			15 02	
Barnt Green	d			12 38	12 48		13 08					13 38	13 48		14 08				14 38	14 48		15 08	
Longbridge	d	12 23		12 42	12 52	12 52	13 12		13 22	13 23		13 42	13 52	13 52	14 12	14 22	14 23		14 42	14 52	14 52	15 12	
Northfield	d	12 25		12 44	12 54	12 54	13 14		13 24	13 25		13 44	13 54	13 54	14 14	14 24	14 25		14 44	14 54	14 54	15 14	
Kings Norton	d	12 28		12 47	12 57	12 57	13 17		13 27	13 28		13 47	13 57	13 57	14 17	14 27	14 28		14 47	14 57	14 57	15 17	
Bournville	d	12 30		12 49	12 59	12 59	13 19		13 29	13 30		13 49	13 59	13 59	14 19	14 29	14 30		14 49	14 59	14 59	15 19	
Selly Oak	d	12 33		12 52	13 02	13 02	13 22		13 32	13 33		13 52	14 02	14 02	14 22	14 32	14 33		14 52	15 02	15 02	15 22	
University	d	12 36	12 39	12 55	13 05	13 05	13 25	13 30	13 35	13 36	13 39	13 55	14 05	14 05	14 25	14 35	14 36	14 39	14 55	15 05	15 05	15 25	15 30
Five Ways	d	12 39		12 58	13 08	13 08	13 28		13 38	13 39		13 58	14 08	14 08	14 28	14 38	14 39		14 58	15 08	15 08	15 28	
Birmingham New Street 12	a	12 43	12 45	13 03	13 13	13 13	13 33	13 37	13 42	13 43	13 45	14 03	14 13	14 13	14 33	14 42	14 43	14 45	15 03	15 13	15 13	15 33	15 37
	d			13 06			13 36					14 06			14 36				15 06			15 36	
Duddeston	d			13 10			13 40					14 10			14 40				15 10			15 40	
Aston	d			13 13			13 43					14 13			14 43				15 13			15 43	
Gravelly Hill	d			13 17			13 47					14 17			14 47				15 17			15 47	
Erdington	d			13 20			13 50					14 20			14 50				15 20			15 50	
Chester Road	d			13 22			13 52					14 22			14 52				15 22			15 52	
Wylde Green	d			13 24			13 54					14 24			14 54				15 24			15 54	
Sutton Coldfield	d			13 27			13 57					14 27			14 57				15 27			15 57	
Four Oaks	d			13 30			14 00					14 30			15 00				15 30			16 00	
Butlers Lane	d			13 33			14 03					14 33			15 03				15 33			16 03	
Blake Street	d			13 35			14 05					14 35			15 05				15 35			16 05	
Shenstone	d			13 39			14 09					14 39			15 09				15 39			16 09	
Lichfield City	d			13 44			14 14					14 44			15 14				15 44			16 14	
Lichfield Trent Valley	a			13 47			14 17					14 47			15 17				15 47			16 17	

A from 5 August
B until 29 July
C 22 July, 29 July
D until 15 July

Sundays

20 May to 7 October

Redditch and Longbridge - Birmingham - Lichfield

		LM A	LM B	XC ◇1	LM	LM A	LM B	LM	LM A	LM B	XC ◇1	LM	LM A	LM B	LM	LM	LM A	LM B	XC ◇1	LM	LM A	LM B
Bromsgrove	d	15 12				15 42			16 12				16 42			17 08	17 12				17 42	
Redditch	d				15 27			15 57				16 27			16 57					17 27		
Alvechurch	d				15 32			16 02				16 32			17 02					17 32		
Barnt Green	d				15 38	15 48		16 08				16 38	16 48		17 08					17 38	17 48	
Longbridge	d	15 22	15 23		15 42	15 52	15 52	16 12	16 22	16 23		16 42	16 52	16 52	17 12		17 22	17 23		17 42	17 52	17 52
Northfield	d	15 24	15 25		15 44	15 54	15 54	16 14	16 24	16 25		16 44	16 54	16 54	17 14		17 24	17 25		17 44	17 54	17 54
Kings Norton	d	15 27	15 28		15 47	15 57	15 57	16 17	16 27	16 28		16 47	16 57	16 57	17 17		17 27	17 28		17 47	17 57	17 57
Bournville	d	15 29	15 30		15 49	15 59	15 59	16 19	16 29	16 30		16 49	16 59	16 59	17 19		17 29	17 30		17 49	17 59	17 59
Selly Oak	d	15 32	15 33		15 52	16 02	16 02	16 22	16 32	16 33		16 52	17 02	17 02	17 22		17 32	17 33		17 52	18 02	18 02
University	d	15 35	15 36	15 39	15 55	16 05	16 05	16 25	16 35	16 36	16 39	16 55	17 05	17 05	17 25	17 30	17 35	17 36	17 39	17 55	18 05	18 05
Five Ways	d	15 38	15 39		15 58	16 08	16 08	16 28	16 38	16 39		16 58	17 08	17 08	17 28		17 38	17 39		17 58	18 08	18 08
Birmingham New Street 12	a	15 42	15 43	15 45	16 03	16 13	16 13	16 33	16 42	16 43	16 45	17 03	17 13	17 13	17 33	17 37	17 42	17 43	17 45	18 03	18 13	18 13
	d				16 06			16 36				17 06			17 36					18 06		
Duddeston	d				16 10			16 40				17 10			17 40					18 10		
Aston	d				16 13			16 43				17 13			17 43					18 13		
Gravelly Hill	d				16 17			16 47				17 17			17 47					18 17		
Erdington	d				16 20			16 50				17 20			17 50					18 20		
Chester Road	d				16 22			16 52				17 22			17 52					18 22		
Wylde Green	d				16 24			16 54				17 24			17 54					18 24		
Sutton Coldfield	d				16 27			16 57				17 27			17 57					18 27		
Four Oaks	d				16 30			17 00				17 30			18 00					18 30		
Butlers Lane	d				16 33			17 03				17 33			18 03					18 33		
Blake Street	d				16 35			17 05				17 35			18 05					18 35		
Shenstone	d				16 39			17 09				17 39			18 09					18 39		
Lichfield City	d				16 44			17 14				17 44			18 14					18 44		
Lichfield Trent Valley	a				16 47			17 17				17 47			18 17					18 47		

		LM	LM A	LM B	XC ◇1	LM	LM	LM A	LM B	LM	LM	LM A	LM B	XC ◇1	LM	LM A	LM B	LM	LM A	LM B	XC ◇1	LM	LM
Bromsgrove	d		18 12			18 25		18 42			19 08	19 12				19 42			20 12			20 25	
Redditch	d	17 57					18 27			18 57					19 27			19 57					20 27
Alvechurch	d	18 02					18 32			19 02					19 32			20 02					20 32
Barnt Green	d	18 08					18 38	18 48		19 08					19 38	19 48		20 08					20 38
Longbridge	d	18 12	18 22	18 23			18 42	18 52	18 52	19 12		19 22	19 23		19 42	19 52	19 52	20 12	20 22	20 23			20 42
Northfield	d	18 14	18 24	18 25			18 44	18 54	18 54	19 14		19 24	19 25		19 44	19 54	19 54	20 14	20 24	20 25			20 44
Kings Norton	d	18 17	18 27	18 28			18 47	18 57	18 57	19 17		19 27	19 28		19 47	19 57	19 57	20 17	20 27	20 28			20 47
Bournville	d	18 19	18 29	18 30			18 49	18 59	18 59	19 19		19 29	19 30		19 49	19 59	19 59	20 19	20 29	20 30			20 49
Selly Oak	d	18 22	18 32	18 33			18 52	19 02	19 02	19 22		19 32	19 33		19 52	20 02	20 02	20 22	20 32	20 33			20 52
University	d	18 25	18 35	18 36	18 39	18 43	18 55	19 05	19 05	19 25	19 30	19 35	19 36	19 39	19 55	20 05	20 05	20 25	20 35	20 36	20 39	20 43	20 55
Five Ways	d	18 28	18 38	18 39			18 58	19 08	19 08	19 28		19 38	19 39		19 58	20 08	20 08	20 28	20 38	20 39			20 58
Birmingham New Street 12	a	18 33	18 42	18 43	18 45	18 49	19 03	19 13	19 13	19 33	19 37	19 42	19 43	19 45	20 03	20 13	20 13	20 33	20 42	20 43	20 45	20 49	21 03
	d	18 36					19 06			19 36					20 06			20 36					21 06
Duddeston	d	18 40					19 10			19 40					20 10			20 40					21 10
Aston	d	18 43					19 13			19 43					20 13			20 43					21 13
Gravelly Hill	d	18 47					19 17			19 47					20 17			20 47					21 17
Erdington	d	18 50					19 20			19 50					20 20			20 50					21 20
Chester Road	d	18 52					19 22			19 52					20 22			20 52					21 22
Wylde Green	d	18 54					19 24			19 54					20 24			20 54					21 24
Sutton Coldfield	d	18 57					19 27			19 57					20 27			20 57					21 27
Four Oaks	d	19 00					19 30			20 00					20 30			21 00					21 30
Butlers Lane	d	19 03					19 33			20 03					20 33			21 03					21 33
Blake Street	d	19 05					19 35			20 05					20 35			21 05					21 35
Shenstone	d	19 09					19 39			20 09					20 39			21 09					21 39
Lichfield City	d	19 14					19 44			20 14					20 44			21 14					21 44
Lichfield Trent Valley	a	19 17					19 47			20 17					20 47			21 17					21 47

		LM A	LM B	LM	LM	LM A	LM C	LM D	XC ◇1	LM	LM A	LM B	LM	LM A	LM B	XC ◇1	LM	LM A	LM B	LM	LM A	LM B
Bromsgrove	d	20 42			21 08	21 12					21 42			22 12				22 42			23 15	
Redditch	d			20 57						21 27			21 57				22 27			22 57		
Alvechurch	d			21 02						21 32			22 02				22 32			23 02		
Barnt Green	d	20 48		21 08						21 38	21 48		22 08				22 38	22 48		23 08		
Longbridge	d	20 52	20 52	21 12		21 22	21 22	21 23		21 42	21 52	21 52	22 12	22 22	22 23		22 42	22 52	22 52	23 12	23 25	23 25
Northfield	d	20 54	20 54	21 14		21 24	21 24	21 25		21 44	21 54	21 54	22 14	22 24	22 25		22 44	22 54	22 54	23 14	23 27	23 27
Kings Norton	d	20 57	20 57	21 17		21 27	21 27	21 28		21 47	21 57	21 57	22 17	22 27	22 28		22 47	22 57	22 57	23 17	23 30	23 30
Bournville	d	20 59	20 59	21 19		21 29	21 29	21 30		21 49	21 59	21 59	22 19	22 29	22 30		22 49	22 59	22 59	23 19	23 32	23 32
Selly Oak	d	21 02	21 02	21 22		21 32	21 32	21 33		21 52	22 02	22 02	22 22	22 32	22 33		22 52	23 02	23 02	23 22	23 35	23 35
University	d	21 05	21 05	21 25	21 30	21 35	21 35	21 36	21 39	21 55	22 05	22 05	22 25	22 35	22 36	22 39	22 55	23 05	23 05	23 25	23 38	23 38
Five Ways	d	21 08	21 08	21 28		21 38	21 38	21 39		21 58	22 08	22 08	22 28	22 38	22 39		22 58	23 08	23 08	23 28	23 42	23 42
Birmingham New Street 12	a	21 13	21 13	21 33	21 37	21 42	21 42	21 43	21 45	22 03	22 13	22 13	22 33	22 42	22 43	22 45	23 03	23 13	23 13	23 33	23 45	23 45
	d			21 36						22 06			22 36				23 06					
Duddeston	d			21 40						22 10			22 40				23 10					
Aston	d			21 43						22 13			22 43				23 13					
Gravelly Hill	d			21 47						22 17			22 47				23 17					
Erdington	d			21 50						22 20			22 50				23 20					
Chester Road	d			21 52						22 22			22 52				23 22					
Wylde Green	d			21 54						22 24			22 54				23 24					
Sutton Coldfield	d			21 57						22 27			22 57				23 27					
Four Oaks	d			22 00						22 30			23 00				23 30					
Butlers Lane	d			22 03						22 33			23 03				23 33					
Blake Street	d			22 05						22 35			23 05				23 35					
Shenstone	d			22 09						22 39			23 09				23 39					
Lichfield City	d			22 14						22 44			23 14				23 44					
Lichfield Trent Valley	a			22 17						22 47			23 17				23 47					

A from 5 August
B until 29 July
C 22 July, 29 July
D until 15 July

Table T069-R

Sundays

14 October to 2 December

Redditch and Longbridge - Birmingham - Lichfield

		LM	LM	LM	LM	LM	LM	LM	LM	LM	LM	LM	LM	LM	LM	LM	LM	XC	LM	LM	LM	LM	LM
																		◇■					
Bromsgrove	d			09 24		09 42		10 12		10 42		11 12	11 16		11 42		12 12			12 42		13 08	13 12
Redditch	d				09 27		09 57		10 27		10 57			11 27		11 57			12 27		12 57		
Alvechurch	d				09 32		10 02		10 32		11 02			11 32		12 02			12 32		13 02		
Barnt Green	d				09 38	09 48	10 08		10 38	10 48	11 08			11 38	11 48	12 08			12 38	12 48	13 08		
Longbridge	d		09 12		09 42	09 52	10 12	10 22	10 42	10 52	11 12	11 22		11 42	11 52	12 12	12 22		12 42	12 52	13 12		13 22
Northfield	d		09 14		09 44	09 54	10 14	10 24	10 44	10 54	11 14	11 24		11 44	11 54	12 14	12 24		12 44	12 54	13 14		13 24
Kings Norton	d		09 17		09 47	09 57	10 17	10 27	10 47	10 57	11 17	11 27		11 47	11 57	12 17	12 27		12 47	12 57	13 17		13 27
Bournville	d		09 19		09 49	09 59	10 19	10 29	10 49	10 59	11 19	11 29		11 49	11 59	12 19	12 29		12 49	12 59	13 19		13 29
Selly Oak	d		09 22		09 52	10 02	10 22	10 32	10 52	11 02	11 22	11 32		11 52	12 02	12 22	12 32		12 52	13 02	13 22		13 32
University	d		09 25	09 40	09 55	10 05	10 25	10 35	10 55	11 05	11 25	11 35	11 40	11 55	12 05	12 25	12 35	12 39	12 55	13 05	13 25	13 30	13 35
Five Ways	d		09 28		09 58	10 08	10 28	10 38	10 58	11 08	11 28	11 38		11 58	12 08	12 28	12 38		12 58	13 08	13 28		13 38
Birmingham New Street ■	a		09 32	09 47	10 03	10 13	10 33	10 42	11 03	11 13	11 33	11 43	11 46	12 03	12 13	12 33	12 42	12 45	13 03	13 13	13 33	13 37	13 42
	d	09 06	09 36		10 06		10 36		11 06		11 36			12 06		12 36			13 06		13 36		
Duddeston	d	09 10	09 40		10 10		10 40		11 10		11 40			12 10		12 40			13 10		13 40		
Aston	d	09 13	09 43		10 13		10 43		11 13		11 43			12 13		12 43			13 13		13 43		
Gravelly Hill	d	09 17	09 47		10 17		10 47		11 17		11 47			12 17		12 47			13 17		13 47		
Erdington	d	09 20	09 50		10 20		10 50		11 20		11 50			12 20		12 50			13 20		13 50		
Chester Road	d	09 22	09 52		10 22		10 52		11 22		11 52			12 22		12 52			13 22		13 52		
Wylde Green	d	09 24	09 54		10 24		10 54		11 24		11 54			12 24		12 54			13 24		13 54		
Sutton Coldfield	d	09 27	09 57		10 27		10 57		11 27		11 57			12 27		12 57			13 27		13 57		
Four Oaks	d	09 30	10 00		10 30		11 00		11 30		12 00			12 30		13 00			13 30		14 00		
Butlers Lane	d	09 33	10 03		10 33		11 03		11 33		12 03			12 33		13 03			13 33		14 03		
Blake Street	d	09 35	10 05		10 35		11 05		11 35		12 05			12 35		13 05			13 35		14 05		
Shenstone	d	09 39	10 09		10 39		11 09		11 39		12 09			12 39		13 09			13 39		14 09		
Lichfield City	d	09 44	10 14		10 44		11 14		11 44		12 14			12 44		13 14			13 44		14 14		
Lichfield Trent Valley	a	09 47	10 17		10 47		11 17		11 47		12 17			12 47		13 17			13 47		14 17		

		XC	LM	LM	LM	LM	XC	LM	LM	LM	LM	LM	XC	LM	LM	LM	LM	XC	LM	LM	LM	LM	LM
		◇■					◇■						◇■					◇■ 🛒					
Bromsgrove	d			13 42		14 12			14 42		15 08	15 12			15 42		16 12			16 42		17 08	17 12
Redditch	d		13 27		13 57			14 27		14 57				15 27		15 57			16 27		16 57		
Alvechurch	d		13 32		14 02			14 32		15 02				15 32		16 02			16 32		17 02		
Barnt Green	d		13 38	13 48	14 08			14 38	14 48	15 08				15 38	15 48	16 08			16 38	16 48	17 08		
Longbridge	d		13 42	13 52	14 12	14 22		14 42	14 52	15 12		15 22		15 42	15 52	16 12	16 22		16 42	16 52	17 12		17 22
Northfield	d		13 44	13 54	14 14	14 24		14 44	14 54	15 14		15 24		15 44	15 54	16 14	16 24		16 44	16 54	17 14		17 24
Kings Norton	d		13 47	13 57	14 17	14 27		14 47	14 57	15 17		15 27		15 47	15 57	16 17	16 27		16 47	16 57	17 17		17 27
Bournville	d		13 49	13 59	14 19	14 29		14 49	14 59	15 19		15 29		15 49	15 59	16 19	16 29		16 49	16 59	17 19		17 29
Selly Oak	d		13 52	14 02	14 22	14 32		14 52	15 02	15 22		15 32		15 52	16 02	16 22	16 32		16 52	17 02	17 22		17 32
University	d	13 39	13 55	14 05	14 25	14 35	14 39	14 55	15 05	15 25	15 30	15 35	15 39	15 55	16 05	16 25	16 35	16 39	16 55	17 05	17 25	17 30	17 35
Five Ways	d		13 58	14 08	14 28	14 38		14 58	15 08	15 28		15 38		15 58	16 08	16 28	16 38		16 58	17 08	17 28		17 38
Birmingham New Street ■	a	13 45	14 03	14 13	14 33	14 42	14 45	15 03	15 13	15 33	15 37	15 42	15 45	16 03	16 13	16 33	16 42	16 45	17 03	17 13	17 33	17 37	17 42
	d		14 06		14 36			15 06		15 36				16 06		16 36			17 06		17 36		
Duddeston	d		14 10		14 40			15 10		15 40				16 10		16 40			17 10		17 40		
Aston	d		14 13		14 43			15 13		15 43				16 13		16 43			17 13		17 43		
Gravelly Hill	d		14 17		14 47			15 17		15 47				16 17		16 47			17 17		17 47		
Erdington	d		14 20		14 50			15 20		15 50				16 20		16 50			17 20		17 50		
Chester Road	d		14 22		14 52			15 22		15 52				16 22		16 52			17 22		17 52		
Wylde Green	d		14 24		14 54			15 24		15 54				16 24		16 54			17 24		17 54		
Sutton Coldfield	d		14 27		14 57			15 27		15 57				16 27		16 57			17 27		17 57		
Four Oaks	d		14 30		15 00			15 30		16 00				16 30		17 00			17 30		18 00		
Butlers Lane	d		14 33		15 03			15 33		16 03				16 33		17 03			17 33		18 03		
Blake Street	d		14 35		15 05			15 35		16 05				16 35		17 05			17 35		18 05		
Shenstone	d		14 39		15 09			15 39		16 09				16 39		17 09			17 39		18 09		
Lichfield City	d		14 44		15 14			15 44		16 14				16 44		17 14			17 44		18 14		
Lichfield Trent Valley	a		14 47		15 17			15 47		16 17				16 47		17 17			17 47		18 17		

		XC	LM	LM	LM	LM	XC	LM	LM	LM	LM	LM	LM	XC	LM	LM	LM	LM	XC	LM	LM	LM
		◇■ 🛒					◇■ 🛒							◇■ 🛒					◇■ 🛒			
Bromsgrove	d			17 42		18 12		18 25		18 42		19 08	19 12			19 42		20 12		20 25		20 42
Redditch	d		17 27		17 57				18 27		18 57				19 27		19 57				20 27	
Alvechurch	d		17 32		18 02				18 32		19 02				19 32		20 02				20 32	
Barnt Green	d		17 38	17 48	18 08				18 38	18 48	19 08				19 38	19 48	20 08				20 38	20 48
Longbridge	d		17 42	17 52	18 12	18 22			18 42	18 52	19 12		19 22		19 42	19 52	20 12	20 22			20 42	20 52
Northfield	d		17 44	17 54	18 14	18 24			18 44	18 54	19 14		19 24		19 44	19 54	20 14	20 24			20 44	20 54
Kings Norton	d		17 47	17 57	18 17	18 27			18 47	18 57	19 17		19 27		19 47	19 57	20 17	20 27			20 47	20 57
Bournville	d		17 49	17 59	18 19	18 29			18 49	18 59	19 19		19 29		19 49	19 59	20 19	20 29			20 49	20 59
Selly Oak	d		17 52	18 02	18 22	18 32			18 52	19 02	19 22		19 32		19 52	20 02	20 22	20 32			20 52	21 02
University	d	17 39	17 55	18 05	18 25	18 35	18 39	18 43	18 55	19 05	19 25	19 30	19 35	19 39	19 55	20 05	20 25	20 35	20 39	20 43	20 55	21 05
Five Ways	d		17 58	18 08	18 28	18 38			18 58	19 08	19 28		19 38		19 58	20 08	20 28	20 38			20 58	21 08
Birmingham New Street ■	a	17 45	18 03	18 13	18 33	18 42	18 45	18 49	19 03	19 13	19 33	19 37	19 42	19 45	20 03	20 13	20 33	20 42	20 45	20 49	21 03	21 13
	d		18 06		18 36				19 06		19 36				20 06		20 36				21 06	
Duddeston	d		18 10		18 40				19 10		19 40				20 10		20 40				21 10	
Aston	d		18 13		18 43				19 13		19 43				20 13		20 43				21 13	
Gravelly Hill	d		18 17		18 47				19 17		19 47				20 17		20 47				21 17	
Erdington	d		18 20		18 50				19 20		19 50				20 20		20 50				21 20	
Chester Road	d		18 22		18 52				19 22		19 52				20 22		20 52				21 22	
Wylde Green	d		18 24		18 54				19 24		19 54				20 24		20 54				21 24	
Sutton Coldfield	d		18 27		18 57				19 27		19 57				20 27		20 57				21 27	
Four Oaks	d		18 30		19 00				19 30		20 00				20 30		21 00				21 30	
Butlers Lane	d		18 33		19 03				19 33		20 03				20 33		21 03				21 33	
Blake Street	d		18 35		19 05				19 35		20 05				20 35		21 05				21 35	
Shenstone	d		18 39		19 09				19 39		20 09				20 39		21 09				21 39	
Lichfield City	d		18 44		19 14				19 44		20 14				20 44		21 14				21 44	
Lichfield Trent Valley	a		18 47		19 17				19 47		20 17				20 47		21 17				21 47	

Table T069-R

Sundays

14 October to 2 December

Redditch and Longbridge - Birmingham - Lichfield

		LM	LM	LM	XC	LM	LM	LM	LM	XC	LM	LM	LM	LM
					◇■					◇■				
Bromsgrove	d		21 08	21 12			21 42		22 12			22 42		23 15
Redditch	d	20 57				21 27		21 57			22 27		22 57	
Alvechurch	d	21 02				21 32		22 02			22 32		23 02	
Barnt Green	d	21 08				21 38	21 48	22 08			22 38	22 48	23 08	
Longbridge	d	21 12		21 22		21 42	21 52	22 12	22 22		22 42	22 52	23 12	23 25
Northfield	d	21 14		21 24		21 44	21 54	22 14	22 24		22 44	22 54	23 14	23 27
Kings Norton	d	21 17		21 27		21 47	21 57	22 17	22 27		22 47	22 57	23 17	23 30
Bournville	d	21 19		21 29		21 49	21 59	22 19	22 29		22 49	22 59	23 19	23 32
Selly Oak	d	21 22		21 32		21 52	22 02	22 22	22 32		22 52	23 02	23 22	23 35
University	d	21 25	21 30	21 35	21 39	21 55	22 05	22 25	22 35	22 39	22 55	23 05	23 25	23 38
Five Ways	d	21 28		21 38		21 58	22 08	22 28	22 38		22 58	23 08	23 28	23 42
Birmingham New Street ■	a	21 33	21 37	21 42	21 45	22 03	22 13	22 33	22 42	22 45	23 03	23 13	23 33	23 45
	d	21 36				22 06		22 36			23 06			
Duddeston	d	21 40				22 10		22 40			23 10			
Aston	d	21 43				22 13		22 43			23 13			
Gravelly Hill	d	21 47				22 17		22 47			23 17			
Erdington	d	21 50				22 20		22 50			23 20			
Chester Road	d	21 52				22 22		22 52			23 22			
Wylde Green	d	21 54				22 24		22 54			23 24			
Sutton Coldfield	d	21 57				22 27		22 57			23 27			
Four Oaks	d	22 00				22 30		23 00			23 30			
Butlers Lane	d	22 03				22 33		23 03			23 33			
Blake Street	d	22 05				22 35		23 05			23 35			
Shenstone	d	22 09				22 39		23 09			23 39			
Lichfield City	d	22 14				22 44		23 14			23 44			
Lichfield Trent Valley	a	22 17				22 47		23 17			23 47			

Table T070-F

Birmingham - Walsall and Rugeley

Mondays to Fridays

21 May to 7 December

Miles	Station		LM MX A bus	LM	LM	LM ■	LM B	LM ■	LM	LM ■ C	LM	LM	LM	LM ■	LM	LM	LM	LM ■	LM	LM ■	LM	LM	LM
—	Wolverhampton ■ 68 bus	d					06 14			07 00				07 50		08 20		08 50		09 20		09 50	
0	**Birmingham New Street** ■	d		05 33	05 57	06 21	06 42	06 57	07 08	07 27	07 42	07 57	08 07	08 27	08 42	08 57	09 12	09 27	09 42	09 57	10 12	10 27	10 43
1½	Duddeston	d			06 02	06 26		07 02		07 32		08 02		08 32		09 02		09 32		10 02		10 32	
2¾	Aston	d			06 05	06 29		07 05		07 35		08 05		08 35		09 05		09 35		10 05		10 35	
3½	Witton	d			06 07	06 31		07 07		07 37		08 07		08 37		09 07		09 37		10 07		10 37	
4¼	Perry Barr	d			06 10	06 34		07 10		07 40		08 10		08 40		09 10		09 40		10 10		10 40	
5¾	Hamstead	d		05 43	06 13	06 37		07 13		07 43		08 13		08 43		09 13		09 43		10 13		10 43	
8½	Tame Bridge Parkway	d		05 47	06 17	06 41	06 54	07 17	07 22	07 47	07 54	08 18	08 23	08 47	08 57	09 17	09 27	09 47	09 57	10 17	10 27	10 47	10 57
9½	Bescot Stadium	d		05 50	06 20	06 44		07 20		07 50		08 20		08 50		09 20		09 50	10 00	10 20		10 50	11 00
10¾	**Walsall**	a		05 54	06 26	06 48	07 02	07 24	07 29	07 54	08 01	08 25	08 30	08 55	09 04	09 24	09 34	09 54	10 05	10 25	10 34	10 54	11 05
—		d			06 27		07 03		07 32		08 03		08 32		09 05		09 35		10 06		10 35		11 06
14	Bloxwich	d	00 06		06 32		07 08		07 37		08 10		08 37		09 10		09 40		10 11		10 40		11 11
14½	Bloxwich North	d	00 08		06 34		07 10		07 39		08 12		08 39		09 12		09 42		10 13		10 42		11 14
15¾	Landywood	d	00 18		06 38		07 14		07 43		08 16		08 43		09 16		09 46		10 17		10 46		11 18
18¾	Cannock	d	00 29		06 42		07 18		07 47		08 21		08 47		09 20		09 50		10 21		10 50		11 22
20¾	Hednesford	d	00a38		06 46		07 22		07 51		08 26		08 51		09 24		09 54		10 25		10 54		11 26
24¾	Rugeley Town	d			06 52		07 28		07 57		08 34		08 57		09 30		10 00		10 31		11 00		11 32
26¼	**Rugeley Trent Valley**	a			06 57		07 33		08 02		08 37		09 02		09 35		10 05		10 36		11 05		11 37

Station		LM ■	LM	LM ■	LM	LM ■	LM	LM ■	LM	LM	LM	LM ■	LM	LM ■	LM	LM ■	LM	LM ■	LM	LM	LM	LM ■	LM
Wolverhampton ■ 68 bus	d	10 20		10 50		11 20		11 50		12 20		12 50		13 20		13 50		14 20		14 50		15 20	
Birmingham New Street ■	d	10 57	11 12	11 27	11 42	11 57	12 12	12 27	12 42	12 57	13 12	13 27	13 42	13 57	14 12	14 27	14 42	14 57	15 12	15 27	15 42	15 57	16 12
Duddeston	d	11 02		11 32		12 02		12 32		13 02		13 32		14 02		14 32		15 02		15 32		16 02	
Aston	d	11 05		11 35		12 05		12 35		13 05		13 35		14 05		14 35		15 05		15 35		16 05	
Witton	d	11 07		11 37		12 07		12 37		13 07		13 37		14 07		14 37		15 07		15 37		16 07	
Perry Barr	d	11 10		11 40		12 10		12 40		13 10		13 40		14 10		14 40		15 10		15 40		16 10	
Hamstead	d	11 13		11 43		12 13		12 43		13 13		13 43		14 13		14 43		15 13		15 43		16 13	
Tame Bridge Parkway	d	11 17	11 27	11 47	11 57	12 17	12 27	12 47	12 57	13 17	13 27	13 47	13 57	14 17	14 27	14 47	14 57	15 17	15 27	15 47	15 54	16 17	16 24
Bescot Stadium	d	11 20		11 50	12 00	12 20		12 50	13 00	13 20		13 50	14 00	14 20		14 50	15 00	15 20		15 50		16 20	
Walsall	a	11 25	11 34	11 54	12 05	12 25	12 34	12 54	13 05	13 25	13 34	13 54	14 05	14 25	14 34	14 54	15 05	15 25	15 34	15 54	16 01	16 24	16 31
	d		11 35		12 06		12 35		13 06		13 35		14 06		14 35		15 06		15 35		16 02		16 32
Bloxwich	d		11 40		12 11		12 40		13 11		13 40		14 11		14 40		15 11		15 40		16 07		16 37
Bloxwich North	d		11 43		12 13		12 42		13 14		13 43		14 13		14 42		15 14		15 43		16 09		16 39
Landywood	d		11 47		12 17		12 46		13 18		13 47		14 17		14 46		15 18		15 47		16 13		16 43
Cannock	d		11 51		12 21		12 50		13 22		13 51		14 21		14 50		15 22		15 51		16 17		16 47
Hednesford	d		11 55		12 25		12 54		13 26		13 55		14 25		14 54		15 26		15 55		16 21		16 51
Rugeley Town	d		12 01		12 31		13 00		13 32		14 01		14 31		15 00		15 32		16 01		16 27		16 57
Rugeley Trent Valley	a		12 06		12 36		13 05		13 37		14 06		14 36		15 05		15 37		16 06		16 32		17 02

Station		LM	LM	LM ■	LM	LM	LM	LM	LM	LM ■	LM	LM	LM	LM	LM	LM	LM	LM	LM	LM	LM FX	LM FO
Wolverhampton ■ 68 bus	d	15 50		16 20				17 20		17 50		18 20		19 20				21 20		22 20		
Birmingham New Street ■	d	16 27	16 42	16 57	17 12	17 27	17 42	17 57	18 12	18 27	18 42	18 57	19 22	19 57	20 22	20 57	21 17	21 47	22 15	22 47	23 18	23 18
Duddeston	d	16 32		17 02		17 32		18 02		18 32		19 02	19 27	20 02		21 02		21 52		22 52	23 23	23 23
Aston	d	16 35		17 05		17 35		18 05		18 35		19 05	19 30	20 05		21 05		21 55		22 55	23 26	23 26
Witton	d	16 37		17 07		17 37		18 07		18 37		19 07	19 32	20 07		21 07		21 57		22 57	23 28	23 28
Perry Barr	d	16 40		17 10		17 40		18 10		18 40		19 10	19 35	20 10		21 10		22 00		23 00	23 31	23 31
Hamstead	d	16 43		17 13		17 43		18 13		18 43		19 13	19 38	20 13		21 13		22 03		23 03	23 34	23 34
Tame Bridge Parkway	d	16 47	16 57	17 17	17 27	17 47	17 57	18 17	18 27	18 47	18 54	19 17	19 42	20 17	20 34	21 17	21 30	22 07	22 26	23 07	23 39	23 39
Bescot Stadium	d	16 50		17 20		17 50		18 20		18 50		19 20	19 45	20 20		21 20		22 10		23 10	23 41	23 42
Walsall	a	16 54	17 04	17 24	17 34	17 54	18 04	18 24	18 34	18 54	19 01	19 24	19 50	20 24	20 41	21 24	21 38	22 15	22 34	23 14	23 46	23 46
	d		17 05		17 35		18 05		18 35		19 03		19 52		20 43		21 39		22 35			23 48
Bloxwich	d		17 10		17 40		18 10		18 40		19 09		19 59		20 48		21 44		22 41			23 53
Bloxwich North	d		17 13		17 43		18 12		18 42		19 12		20 01		20 50		21 46		22 44			23 55
Landywood	d		17 17		17 47		18 16		18 46		19 16		20 05		20 54		21 50		22 48			23 59
Cannock	d		17 21		17 51		18 20		18 50		19 21		20 10		20 58		21 54		22 53			00 03
Hednesford	d		17 25		17 55		18 24		18 54		19 26		20 15		21 02		21 58		22 58			00a07
Rugeley Town	d		17 31		18 01		18 30		19 00		19 34		20 23		21 08		22 04		23 06			
Rugeley Trent Valley	a		17 36		18 06		18 35		19 05		19 37		20 28		21 13		22 09		23 09			

Station		LM FX bus
Wolverhampton ■ 68 bus	d	
Birmingham New Street ■	d	
Duddeston	d	
Aston	d	
Witton	d	
Perry Barr	d	
Hamstead	d	
Tame Bridge Parkway	d	
Bescot Stadium	d	
Walsall	a	
	d	23 56
Bloxwich	d	00 06
Bloxwich North	d	00 08
Landywood	d	00 18
Cannock	d	00 29
Hednesford	d	00a38
Rugeley Town	d	
Rugeley Trent Valley	a	

A From Walsall
B From Shrewsbury
C From Crewe

For connections to Stafford refer to Table T67

Table T070-F

Birmingham - Walsall and Rugeley

Saturdays

26 May to 8 December

Station		LM A	LM	LM	LM	LM	LM	LM	LM	LM	LM	LM	LM	LM	LM	LM	LM	LM	
Wolverhampton ■ 68 bus	d			06 38					07 20		07 50		08 20		08 50		09 20		and at the same minutes past each hour until
Birmingham New Street ■	d		06 00		06 27	07 00	07 27	07 42	07 57	08 12	08 27	08 42	08 57	09 12	09 27	09 42	09 57	10 12	
Duddeston	d		06 04		06 32		07 32		08 02		08 32		09 02		09 32		10 02		
Aston	d		06 07		06 36	07 06	07 35		08 05		08 35		09 05		09 35		10 05		
Witton	d		06 09		06 38		07 37		08 07		08 37		09 07		09 37		10 07		
Perry Barr	d		06 12		06 41	07 10	07 40		08 10		08 40		09 10		09 40		10 10		
Hamstead	d		06 15		06 44	07 13	07 43		08 13		08 43		09 13		09 43		10 13		
Tame Bridge Parkway	d		06 20		06 48	07 18	07 47	07 57	08 17	08 27	08 47	08 57	09 17	09 24	09 47	09 57	10 17	10 27	
Bescot Stadium	d		06 22		06 51		07 50	08 00	08 20		08 50	09 00	09 20		09 50	10 00	10 20		
Walsall	a		06 28	06 51	06 56	07 25	07 54	08 05	08 24	08 34	08 54	09 05	09 24	09 31	09 54	10 05	10 24	10 34	
	d		06 29		06 58	07 26		08 06		08 35		09 06		09 33		10 06		10 35	
Bloxwich	d		06 34		07 03	07 31		08 11		08 40		09 11		09 38		10 11		10 40	
Bloxwich North	d		06 36		07 05	07 33		08 13		08 42		09 13		09 40		10 13		10 42	
Landywood	d		06 40		07 09	07 37		08 17		08 46		09 17		09 44		10 17		10 46	
Cannock	d	00 03	06 44		07 13	07 41		08 21		08 50		09 21		09 48		10 21		10 50	
Hednesford	d	00a07	06a48		07 17	07 45		08 25		08 54		09 25		09 52		10 25		10 54	
Rugeley Town	d				07 23	07 51		08 31		09 00		09 31		09 58		10 31		11 00	
Rugeley Trent Valley	a				07 28	07 56		08 37		09 05		09 36		10 03		10 36		11 05	

Station		LM	LM	LM	LM	LM	LM	LM	LM	LM	LM	LM	LM	LM	LM	LM	LM	LM	LM	LM	LM	LM	LM
Wolverhampton ■ 68 bus	d	14 50		15 20		15 50		16 20		16 50		17 20		17 50		18 20		19 20		20 20		21 20	
Birmingham New Street ■	d	15 27	15 42	15 57	16 12	16 27	16 42	16 57	17 12	17 27	17 42	17 57	18 12	18 27	18 42	18 57	19 19	19 57	20 19	20 47	21 19	21 57	22 19
Duddeston	d	15 32		16 02		16 32		17 02		17 32		18 02		18 32		19 02	19 23	20 02		20 52		22 02	
Aston	d	15 35		16 05		16 35		17 05		17 35		18 05		18 35		19 05	19 26	20 05		20 55		22 05	
Witton	d	15 37		16 07		16 37		17 07		17 37		18 07		18 37		19 07	19 28	20 07		20 57		22 07	
Perry Barr	d	15 40		16 10		16 40		17 09		17 40		18 10		18 40		19 10	19 31	20 10		21 00		22 10	
Hamstead	d	15 43		16 13		16 43		17 13		17 43		18 13		18 43		19 13	19 34	20 13		21 03		22 13	
Tame Bridge Parkway	d	15 47	15 57	16 17	16 27	16 47	16 57	17 17	17 27	17 47	17 57	18 17	18 27	18 47	18 57	19 17	19 39	20 17	20 31	21 07	21 31	22 17	22 31
Bescot Stadium	d	15 50	16 00	16 20		16 50	17 00	17 20		17 50	18 00	18 20		18 50	19 00	19 20	19 42	20 20		21 10		22 20	
Walsall	a	15 54	16 05	16 24	16 34	16 54	17 05	17 24	17 34	17 54	18 05	18 24	18 34	18 54	19 05	19 24	19 47	20 24	20 38	21 14	21 38	22 24	22 38
	d		16 06		16 35		17 06		17 35		18 06		18 35		19 06		19 48		20 39		21 39		22 39
Bloxwich	d		16 11		16 40		17 11		17 40		18 11		18 40		19 11		19 53		20 44		21 44		22 44
Bloxwich North	d		16 13		16 42		17 13		17 42		18 13		18 42		19 13		19 55		20 46		21 46		22 46
Landywood	d		16 17		16 46		17 17		17 46		18 17		18 46		19 17		19 59		20 50		21 50		22 50
Cannock	d		16 21		16 50		17 21		17 50		18 21		18 50		19 21		20 03		20 54		21 54		22 54
Hednesford	d		16 25		16 54		17 25		17 54		18 25		18 54		19 25		20 07		20 58		21 58		22 58
Rugeley Town	d		16 31		17 00		17 31		18 00		18 31		19 00		19 31		20 13		21 04		22 04		23 04
Rugeley Trent Valley	a		16 36		17 05		17 36		18 05		18 36		19 05		19 36		20 18		21 09		22 09		23 09

Station		LM	LM
Wolverhampton ■ 68 bus	d	22 20	
Birmingham New Street ■	d	22 47	23 19
Duddeston	d	22 52	23 23
Aston	d	22 55	23 26
Witton	d	22 57	23 28
Perry Barr	d	23 00	23 31
Hamstead	d	23 03	23 34
Tame Bridge Parkway	d	23 07	23 39
Bescot Stadium	d	23 10	23 42
Walsall	a	23 14	23 47
	d		23 48
Bloxwich	d		23 53
Bloxwich North	d		23 55
Landywood	d		23 59
Cannock	d		00 03
Hednesford	d		00a07
Rugeley Town	d		
Rugeley Trent Valley	a		

Sundays

20 May to 2 December

Station		LM B	LM	LM	LM bus	LM	LM	LM bus	LM	LM		LM	LM	LM	LM	LM	LM
Wolverhampton ■ 68 bus	d					09 22			10 22		and at the same minutes past each hour until	20 22		21 22		22 25	
Birmingham New Street ■	d		08 57	09 42		09 57	10 42		10 57	11 42		20 57	21 42	21 57	22 42	22 57	23 17
Duddeston	d		09 02			10 02			11 02			21 02		22 02		23 02	23 21
Aston	d		09 05			10 05			11 05			21 05		22 05		23 05	23 24
Witton	d		09 07			10 07			11 07			21 07		22 07		23 07	23 26
Perry Barr	d		09 09			10 09			11 09			21 09		22 09		23 09	23 29
Hamstead	d		09 12			10 12			11 12			21 12		22 12		23 12	23 31
Tame Bridge Parkway	d		09 16	09 54		10 16	10 54		11 16	11 54		21 16	21 54	22 16	22 54	23 16	23 35
Bescot Stadium	d		09 18			10 18			11 18			21 18		22 18		23 18	23 38
Walsall	a		09 23	10 04		10 23	11 04		11 23	12 01		21 23	22 01	22 23	23 01	23 23	23 42
	d				10 14			11 14		12 02			22 02		23 02		
Bloxwich	d				10 24			11 24		12 07			22 07		23 07		
Bloxwich North	d				10 26			11 26		12 09			22 09		23 09		
Landywood	d				10 36			11 36		12 13			22 13		23 13		
Cannock	d	00 03			10 47			11 47		12 17			22 17		23 17		
Hednesford	d	00a07			10 56			11 56		12 21			22 21		23a21		
Rugeley Town	d				11 07			12 07		12 27			22 27				
Rugeley Trent Valley	a				11 17			12 17		12 32			22 32				

A From Birmingham New Street
B not 20 May. From Birmingham New Street

For connections to Stafford refer to Table T67

Table T070-R

Rugeley and Walsall - Birmingham

Mondays to Fridays
21 May to 7 December

Miles	Station		LM MX A	LM	LM	LM [1] B	LM	LM [1] B	LM	LM [1] C	LM	LM	LM	LM [1]	LM	LM [1]	LM	LM [1] C	LM	LM [1] C	LM	LM	LM
0	**Rugeley Trent Valley**	d			05 56		06 39		07 05		07 42		08 12		08 42		09 12		09 42		10 12		10 42
1½	Rugeley Town	d			05 59		06 43		07 08		07 45		08 15		08 46		09 16		09 45		10 15		10 45
5½	Hednesford	d			06 06		06 51		07 16		07 53		08 23		08 54		09 24		09 53		10 23		10 53
7½	Cannock	d			06 10		06 55		07 19		07 56		08 26		08 58		09 28		09 56		10 26		10 56
9½	Landywood	d			06 14		06 58		07 23		08 00		08 30		09 01		09 31		10 00		10 30		11 00
11¾	Bloxwich North	d			06 18		07 03		07 27		08 04		08 34		09 06		09 36		10 04		10 34		11 04
12¾	Bloxwich	d			06 21		07 05		07 29		08 06		08 36		09 08		09 38		10 06		10 36		11 06
15½	**Walsall**	a			06 28		07 12		07 37		08 14		08 44		09 14		09 44		10 14		10 44		11 14
—		d		06 01	06 30	07 01	07 13	07 30	07 38	08 01	08 15	08 30	08 45	09 01	09 15	09 31	09 45	10 01	10 15	10 31	10 45	11 01	11 15
16¾	Bescot Stadium	d		06 04	06 34	07 04		07 34		08 04		08 34	08 49	09 04		09 34	09 49	10 04		10 34	10 49	11 04	
17¾	Tame Bridge Parkway	d		06 07	06 37	07 07	07 19	07 37	07 44	08 07	08 21	08 37	08 51	09 07	09 21	09 37	09 51	10 07	10 21	10 37	10 51	11 07	11 21
20½	Hamstead	d		06 11	06 41	07 11		07 41		08 11		08 41		09 11		09 41		10 11		10 41		11 11	
22	Perry Barr	d		06 14	06 44	07 14		07 44		08 14		08 44		09 14		09 44		10 14		10 44		11 14	
22¾	Witton	d		06 17	06 47	07 17		07 47		08 17		08 47		09 17		09 47		10 17		10 47		11 17	
23½	Aston	d		06 19	06 49	07 19		07 49		08 19		08 49		09 19		09 49		10 19		10 49		11 19	
24¾	Duddeston	d	00 01	06 22	06 52	07 22		07 52		08 22		08 51		09 22		09 52		10 22		10 52		11 22	
26¾	**Birmingham New Street** [12]	a	00 09	06 27	06 58	07 27	07 36	07 56	08 01	08 29	08 37	08 58	09 08	09 29	09 37	09 58	10 08	10 29	10 37	10 58	11 08	11 29	11 37
—	Wolverhampton [7] 68	a				07 53		08 18		09 05				10 05		10 34		11 05		11 34		12 05	

Station		LM [1]	LM	LM [1]	LM	LM [1]	LM	LM [1]	LM	LM	LM	LM [1]	LM	LM [1] B	LM	LM [1]	LM	LM [1] C	LM	LM	LM	LM [1]
Rugeley Trent Valley	d		11 12		11 42		12 12		12 42		13 12		13 42		14 12		14 42		15 12		15 42	
Rugeley Town	d		11 15		11 46		12 16		12 45		13 15		13 46		14 16		14 45		15 15		15 46	
Hednesford	d		11 23		11 54		12 24		12 53		13 23		13 54		14 24		14 53		15 23		15 54	
Cannock	d		11 26		11 58		12 28		12 56		13 26		13 58		14 28		14 56		15 26		15 58	
Landywood	d		11 30		12 01		12 31		13 00		13 30		14 01		14 31		15 00		15 30		16 01	
Bloxwich North	d		11 34		12 06		12 36		13 04		13 34		14 06		14 36		15 04		15 34		16 06	
Bloxwich	d		11 36		12 08		12 38		13 06		13 36		14 08		14 38		15 06		15 36		16 08	
Walsall	a		11 44		12 14		12 44		13 14		13 44		14 14		14 44		15 14		15 44		16 14	
	d	11 31	11 45	12 01	12 15	12 31	12 45	13 01	13 15	13 31	13 45	14 01	14 15	14 31	14 45	15 01	15 15	15 31	15 45	16 01	16 15	16 31
Bescot Stadium	d	11 34	11 49	12 04		12 34	12 49	13 04		13 34	13 49	14 04		14 34	14 49	15 04		15 34	15 49	16 04		16 34
Tame Bridge Parkway	d	11 37	11 51	12 07	12 21	12 37	12 51	13 07	13 21	13 37	13 51	14 07	14 21	14 37	14 51	15 07	15 21	15 37	15 51	16 07	16 21	16 37
Hamstead	d	11 41		12 11		12 41		13 11		13 41		14 11		14 41		15 11		15 41		16 11		16 41
Perry Barr	d	11 44		12 14		12 44		13 14		13 44		14 14		14 44		15 14		15 44		16 14		16 44
Witton	d	11 47		12 17		12 47		13 17		13 47		14 17		14 47		15 17		15 47		16 17		16 47
Aston	d	11 49		12 19		12 49		13 19		13 49		14 19		14 49		15 19		15 49		16 19		16 49
Duddeston	d	11 52		12 22		12 52		13 22		13 52		14 22		14 52		15 22		15 52		16 22		16 52
Birmingham New Street [12]	a	11 57	12 08	12 29	12 37	12 58	13 08	13 29	13 37	13 58	14 08	14 29	14 37	14 58	15 08	15 29	15 37	15 57	16 08	16 29	16 37	16 57
Wolverhampton [7] 68	a	12 34		13 05		13 34		14 05		14 34		15 05		15 18		16 05		16 34		17 05		17 34

Station		LM	LM	LM	LM [1]	LM	LM	LM	LM	LM	LM [1]	LM	LM	LM	LM	LM	LM	LM	LM	LM	LM	LM
Rugeley Trent Valley	d	16 12		16 42		17 12		17 42		18 12		18 42		19 22	19 42		20 42		21 45		22 42	
Rugeley Town	d	16 16		16 45		17 15		17 46		18 16		18 45		19 25	19 46		20 46		21 48		22 45	
Hednesford	d	16 24		16 53		17 23		17 54		18 24		18 53		19 33	19 54		20 54		21 55		22 53	
Cannock	d	16 28		16 56		17 26		17 58		18 28		18 56		19 36	19 58		20 58		21 59		22 56	
Landywood	d	16 31		17 00		17 30		18 01		18 31		19 00		19 40	20 01		21 01		22 02		23 00	
Bloxwich North	d	16 36		17 04		17 34		18 06		18 36		19 04		19 44	20 06		21 06		22 07		23 04	
Bloxwich	d	16 38		17 06		17 36		18 08		18 38		19 06		19 46	20 08		21 08		22 09		23 06	
Walsall	a	16 44		17 14		17 44		18 14		18 44		19 14		19 54	20 14		21 14		22 16		23 14	
	d	16 45	17 01	17 15	17 31	17 45	18 01	18 15	18 31	18 45	19 01	19 15	19 31	19 55	20 15	20 40	21 15	21 40	22 18	22 40	23 15	23 40
Bescot Stadium	d	16 49	17 04		17 34		18 04		18 34		19 04		19 34	20 00		20 43		21 43	22 22	22 43		23 43
Tame Bridge Parkway	d	16 52	17 07	17 21	17 37	17 51	18 07	18 20	18 37	18 51	19 07	19 21	19 37	20 03	20 21	20 46	21 21	21 46	22 25	22 46	23 21	23 46
Hamstead	d		17 11		17 41		18 11		18 41		19 11		19 41	20 07		20 50		21 50		22 50		23 50
Perry Barr	d		17 14		17 44		18 14		18 44		19 14		19 44	20 11		20 53		21 53		22 53		23 53
Witton	d		17 17		17 47		18 17		18 47		19 17		19 47	20 14		20 56		21 56		22 56		23 56
Aston	d		17 19		17 49		18 19		18 49		19 19		19 49	20 17		20 58		21 58		22 58		23 58
Duddeston	d		17 22		17 52		18 22		18 52		19 22		19 52	20 20		21 01		22 01		23 01		00 01
Birmingham New Street [12]	a	17 08	17 29	17 37	17 58	18 08	18 30	18 37	18 57	19 08	19 29	19 39	19 57	20 26	20 37	21 09	21 37	22 10	22 44	23 07	23 39	00 09
Wolverhampton [7] 68	a		18 05		18 34		19 05		19 34		20 05		20 34									

Saturdays
26 May to 8 December

Station		LM A	LM	LM	LM	LM	LM	LM	LM	LM	LM	LM	LM		LM	LM	LM	LM	LM	LM
Rugeley Trent Valley	d				06 28				07 42		08 12		08 42	and at the same minutes past each hour until		12 12		12 42		13 12
Rugeley Town	d				06 31				07 45		08 15		08 45			12 15		12 45		13 15
Hednesford	d				06 39	07 00			07 53		08 23		08 53			12 23		12 53		13 23
Cannock	d				06 42	07 04			07 56		08 26		08 56			12 26		12 56		13 26
Landywood	d				06 46	07 07			08 00		08 30		09 00			12 30		13 00		13 30
Bloxwich North	d				06 50	07 12			08 04		08 34		09 04			12 34		13 04		13 34
Bloxwich	d				06 52	07 14			08 06		08 36		09 06			12 36		13 06		13 36
Walsall	a				07 00	07 21			08 14		08 44		09 14			12 44		13 14		13 44
	d		06 01	06 31	07 01	07 22	07 31	08 01	08 15	08 31	08 45	09 01	09 15		12 31	12 45	13 01	13 15	13 31	13 45
Bescot Stadium	d		06 04	06 34	07 04		07 34	08 04		08 34	08 49	09 04			12 34	12 49	13 04		13 34	13 49
Tame Bridge Parkway	d		06 07	06 37	07 07	07 28	07 37	08 07	08 21	08 37	08 51	09 07	09 21		12 37	12 51	13 07	13 21	13 37	13 51
Hamstead	d		06 11	06 41	07 11		07 41	08 11		08 41		09 11			12 41		13 11		13 41	
Perry Barr	d		06 14	06 44	07 14		07 44	08 14		08 44		09 14			12 44		13 14		13 44	
Witton	d		06 17	06 47	07 18		07 47	08 17		08 47		09 17			12 47		13 17		13 47	
Aston	d		06 19	06 49	07 20		07 49	08 19		08 49		09 19			12 49		13 19		13 49	
Duddeston	d	00 01	06 22	06 52	07 23		07 52	08 22		08 52		09 22			12 52		13 22		13 52	
Birmingham New Street [12]	a	00 09	06 27	06 58	07 28	07 44	07 57	08 29	08 38	08 57	09 08	09 29	09 37		12 57	13 08	13 29	13 37	13 57	14 09
Wolverhampton [7] 68	a		07 05	07 34			08 34	09 05		09 34		10 05			13 34		14 05		14 34	

A From Walsall
B To Liverpool Lime Street
C [1] to Birmingham New Street

For connections from Stafford refer to Table T67

Table T070-R

Rugeley and Walsall - Birmingham

Saturdays
26 May to 8 December

Station		LM	LM	LM	LM		LM	LM	LM	LM	LM	LM	LM	LM	LM	LM	LM	LM	LM	LM	LM
Rugeley Trent Valley	d		13 42		14 12	and at the same minutes past each hour until		17 42		18 12		18 42	19 12	19 47		20 42		21 42		22 42	
Rugeley Town	d		13 45		14 15			17 45		18 15		18 45	19 15	19 50		20 45		21 45		22 45	
Hednesford	d		13 53		14 23			17 53		18 23		18 53	19 23	19 58		20 53		21 53		22 53	
Cannock	d		13 56		14 26			17 56		18 26		18 56	19 26	20 01		20 56		21 56		22 56	
Landywood	d		14 00		14 30			18 00		18 30		19 00	19 30	20 05		21 00		22 00		23 00	
Bloxwich North	d		14 04		14 34			18 04		18 34		19 04	19 34	20 09		21 04		22 04		23 04	
Bloxwich	d		14 06		14 36			18 06		18 36		19 06	19 36	20 11		21 06		22 06		23 06	
Walsall	a		14 14		14 44			18 14		18 44		19 14	19 44	20 19		21 14		22 14		23 14	
	d	14 01	14 15	14 31	14 45		18 01	18 15	18 31	18 45	19 01	19 15	19 45	20 20	20 40	21 15	21 40	22 15	22 40	23 15	23 40
Bescot Stadium	d	14 04		14 34	14 49		18 04		18 34	18 49	19 04	19 19	19 49		20 43		21 43		22 43		23 43
Tame Bridge Parkway	d	14 07	14 21	14 37	14 51		18 07	18 21	18 37	18 51	19 07	19 22	19 51	20 26	20 46	21 21	21 46	22 21	22 46	23 21	23 46
Hamstead	d	14 11		14 41			18 11		18 41		19 11	19 26	19 57		20 50		21 50		22 50		23 50
Perry Barr	d	14 14		14 44			18 14		18 44		19 14	19 30	20 00		20 53		21 53		22 53		23 53
Witton	d	14 17		14 47			18 17		18 47		19 17	19 33	20 03		20 56		21 56		22 56		23 56
Aston	d	14 19		14 49			18 19		18 49		19 19	19 37	20 07		20 58		21 58		22 58		23 58
Duddeston	d	14 22		14 52			18 22		18 52		19 22	19 40	20 10		21 01		22 01		23 01		00 01
Birmingham New Street [12]	a	14 29	14 37	14 57	15 08		18 29	18 37	18 57	19 08	19 29	19 44	20 14	20 44	21 06	21 37	22 07	22 37	23 07	23 37	00 08
Wolverhampton [7] 68	a	15 05		15 34			19 05		19 34		20 05				21 34		22 34				

Sundays
20 May to 2 December

Station		LM A	LM	LM (bus)	LM	LM	LM (bus)	LM	LM	LM (bus)	LM	LM	LM	LM	LM	LM	LM		LM	LM	LM
Rugeley Trent Valley	d			08 58			09 58			10 58			12 38		13 38		14 38	and at the same minutes past each hour until		22 38	
Rugeley Town	d			09 03			10 03			11 03			12 41		13 41		14 41			22 41	
Hednesford	d			09 14			10 14			11 14			12 49		13 49		14 49			22 49	
Cannock	d			09 21			10 21			11 21			12 52		13 52		14 52			22 52	
Landywood	d			09 32			10 32			11 32			12 56		13 56		14 56			22 56	
Bloxwich North	d			09 42			10 42			11 42			13 00		14 00		15 00			23 00	
Bloxwich	d			09 44			10 44			11 44			13 02		14 02		15 02			23 02	
Walsall	a			10 01			11 01			12 01			13 10		14 10		15 10			23 10	
	d		09 31		10 11	10 31		11 11	11 31		12 11	12 31	13 11	13 31	14 11	14 31	15 11		22 31	23 11	23 31
Bescot Stadium	d		09 35			10 35			11 35			12 35		13 35		14 35			22 35		23 35
Tame Bridge Parkway	d		09 38		10 17	10 38		11 17	11 38		12 17	12 38	13 17	13 38	14 17	14 38	15 17		22 38	23 17	23 38
Hamstead	d		09 41			10 41			11 41			12 41		13 41		14 41			22 41		23 41
Perry Barr	d		09 44			10 44			11 44			12 44		13 44		14 44			22 44		23 44
Witton	d		09 46			10 46			11 46			12 46		13 46		14 46			22 46		23 46
Aston	d		09 49			10 49			11 49			12 49		13 49		14 49			22 49		23 49
Duddeston	d	00 01	09 52			10 52			11 52			12 52		13 52		14 52			22 52		23 52
Birmingham New Street [12]	a	00 08	09 56		10 34	10 56		11 34	11 56		12 32	12 56	13 32	13 56	14 33	14 56	15 32		22 56	23 32	23 56
Wolverhampton [7] 68	a		10 33			11 33			12 33			13 33		14 33		15 33			23 33		

A not 20 May. From Walsall

For connections from Stafford refer to Table T67

Table T071-F

Mondays to Fridays

21 May to 7 December

Stratford-upon-Avon, Marylebone and Leamington Spa - Birmingham - Stourbridge, Worcester and Hereford

Miles	Miles	Miles	Station		LM	CH	CH	LM	GW	LM	LM	LM	GW		LM	CH	LM	LM	GW	LM	CH	CH	CH		LM
					MX	MX ◇	MX ◇												◇■ 🍴		A	B			
—	0	—	**Stratford-upon-Avon**	d																	06 06	06 06			06 26
—	1	—	Stratford-upon-Avon Parkway	d																	06 10	06 10			06 30
—	2¾	—	Wilmcote	d																	06 14	06 14			06 33
—	6½	—	Wootton Wawen	d																					06x37
—	8¼	—	Henley-in-Arden	d																					06 41
—	11¼	—	Danzey	d																					06x45
—	13	—	Wood End	d																					06x49
—	14¼	—	The Lakes	d																					06x51
—	15	—	Earlswood (West Midlands)	d																					06 54
—	16	—	Wythall	d																					06 57
—	17	—	Whitlocks End	d											06 28		06 46								07 00
—	18	—	Shirley	d											06 30		06 51								07 03
—	19¼	—	Yardley Wood	d											06 33		06 53								07 07
—	20½	—	Hall Green	d											06 36		06 57								07 10
—	21	—	Spring Road	d											06 39		06 59								07 13
—	—	—	**London Marylebone** 🅱 ⊖115	d																					
—	—	—	Banbury	d			00 03									06 04									
—	—	0	**Leamington Spa** ■	a			00 20									06 24					06 45	06 48			
—	—	—		d			00 21				05 47					06 25				06 31			06 51		
—	—	2	Warwick	d		00 03	00 25				05 52					06 30				06 36			06 56		
—	—	3¼	Warwick Parkway	d		00 07	00 29				05 55					06 33				06 39					
—	—	6	Hatton	d							05 59									06 43			07a03		
—	—	10¼	Lapworth	d							06 04									06 48					
—	—	12¾	Dorridge	d		00 18				05 40	06 09					06 44				06 54					
—	—	14¾	Widney Manor	d						05 45	06 13									06 58					
—	—	16¼	Solihull	d		00 24	00 41			05 48	06 17					06 50				07 02					
—	—	18	Olton	d						05 51	06 20									07 05					
—	—	19	Acocks Green	d						05 54	06 22									07 08					
—	22	20	Tyseley	d						05 57	06 25				06 42		07 02			07 10					07 16
—	23	21	Small Heath	d						05 59	06 27				06 44		07 05			07 13					07 18
—	24	—	Bordesley	d																					
—	24¾	—	**Birmingham Moor Street**	d	00 06	00a36	00a52			06 04	06 33				06 49	07 00	07 09			07 19					07 24
—	25¼	—	**Birmingham Snow Hill** ⇌	a	00 08					06 06	06 37				06 51	07 07	07 12			07 21					07 26
—	—	—		d						06 07					06 53		07 13			07 23					
—	26	—	Jewellery Quarter ⇌	d						06 10					06 55		07 15			07 25					
—	28½	—	The Hawthorns ⇌	d						06 14					06 59		07 19			07 29					
—	29	—	Smethwick Galton Bridge ■	d						06 17					07 02		07 22			07 32					
—	—	—	**Coventry**	a																					
—	—	—	**Birmingham Intl.** 68 ✈	a																					
0	—	24	**Birmingham New Street** ■ 68	a																					
—	—	—		d								07 00						07 20							
—	30¼	30¼	Langley Green	d						06 20					07 05					07 35					
—	32¼	—	Rowley Regis	d						06 23					07 09		07 28			07 39					
—	33½	—	Old Hill	d						06 26					07 12					07 42					
—	34¾	—	Cradley Heath	d						06 29					07 15		07 33			07 45					
—	36¼	—	Lye	d						06 32					07 18					07 48					
—	37¼	—	**Stourbridge Junction** ■	d						06 36					07 22		07a40			07 52					
—	39¼	—	Hagley	d						06 40					07 26					07 56					
—	41	—	Blakedown	d						06 43					07 29					07 59					
—	44¼	—	**Kidderminster**	d						06 48					07 34					08 04					
—	47¾	—	Hartlebury	d											07 39					08 09					
2½	—	—	University	d								07 06						07 26							
10½	—	—	Barnt Green	d														07 39							
13	—	—	Bromsgrove 69	d								07 22						07 44							
19¼	53½	—	Droitwich Spa	d						06 58		07 31			07 47			07 54		08 17					
25	—	—	**Worcester Shrub Hill** ■	a														08 01		08 24					
—	—	—		d				05 56	06 19				07 54					08 07	08 13	08 31					
25¾	58¾	—	**Worcester Foregate Street** ■	a				05 58	06 22	07 09		07 41	07 56		07 57			08 09	08 15	08 33					
—	—	—		d				05 59				07 42	07 57					08 11							
32½	—	—	Malvern Link	d				06 08				07 52	08 06					08 20							
33¾	—	—	**Great Malvern**	a				06 10				07 55	08 09					08 22							
—	—	—		d				06 11				08 00													
36½	—	—	Colwall	d				06 16				08 06													
40¾	—	—	Ledbury	a				06 23				08 13													
—	—	—		d				06 25				08 13													
54½	—	—	**Hereford** ■	a				06 49				08 29													

A until 5 October

B from 8 October

Table T071-F

Mondays to Fridays

21 May to 7 December

Stratford-upon-Avon, Marylebone and Leamington Spa - Birmingham - Stourbridge, Worcester and Hereford

Station		LM	LM	LM	LM	XC	CH	LM	XC		LM	LM	GW	LM	LM	LM	LM	CH	CH		XC	LM	LM	CH	GW
						◇■ 🍴	◇		◇■ 🍴				◇■ 🍴					◇	◇		◇■ 🍴			◇	◇
Stratford-upon-Avon	d			06 52				07 19			07 26				07 43			07 33							
Stratford-upon-Avon Parkway	d			06 56				07 23			07 30				07 47			07 37							
Wilmcote	d			06 59											07 50			07 41							
Wootton Wawen	d			07x03											07x54										
Henley-in-Arden	d			07 07				07 35							07 58										
Danzey	d			07x11											08x01										
Wood End	d			07x15											08x04										
The Lakes	d			07x17											08x07										
Earlswood (West Midlands)	d			07 20				07 43							08 10										
Wythall	d			07 23				07 46							08 13										
Whitlocks End	d			07 26				07 49				08 07			08 17								08 37		
Shirley	d			07 29				07 52				08 10			08 20								08 40		
Yardley Wood	d			07 32				07 55				08 12			08 23								08 42		
Hall Green	d			07 35				07 58				08 15			08 26								08 45		
Spring Road	d			07 37				08 01				08 17			08 29								08 47		
London Marylebone 🅱 ⊖115	d						06 05												06 17					07 11	
Banbury	d					06 57	07 03		07 26										07 49		07 57			08 07	
Leamington Spa ■	a					07 13	07 20		07 42									08 07	08 08		08 13			08 24	
	d				07 08	07 14	07 21		07 43					07 47			08 02		08 08		08 14			08 25	
Warwick	d				07 13		07 26							07 52			08 06		08 13					08 29	
Warwick Parkway	d				07 16		07 29							07 55			08 09							08 33	
Hatton	d				07 20		07 35							08 00			08 13		08a20						
Lapworth	d				07 25									08 05			08 18								
Dorridge	d	07 09			07 34		07 43				07 56			08 09		08 20	08 25								
Widney Manor	d	07 14			07 38		07 47				08 01			08 14		08 25	08 29								
Solihull	d	07 17			07 42		07 51				08 04			08 17		08 28	08 33							08 45	
Olton	d	07 20			07 45		07 55				08 08			08 20		08 32	08 36								
Acocks Green	d	07 23			07 48						08 11			08 23		08 35	08 39								
Tyseley	d	07 26		07 41	07 50						08 14	08 21		08 26	08 32	08 38	08 42						08 51		
Small Heath	d	07 28		07 43	07 53							08 23		08 29	08 34		08 45						08 52		
Bordesley	d																								
Birmingham Moor Street	d	07 33		07 49	07 58		08 03	08 08			08 19	08 28		08 34	08 39	08 42	08 49						08 58	08 54	
Birmingham Snow Hill ⇌	a	07 35		07 51	08 00		08 10	08 10			08 22	08 30		08 36	08 41	08 47	08 51						09 00	09 01	
	d	07 37		07 53	08 02			08 13			08 23	08 33		08 43			08 53						09 01		
Jewellery Quarter ⇌	d	07 39		07 55	08 04			08 15			08 25	08 35		08 45			08 55						09 04		
The Hawthorns ⇌	d	07 43		07 59	08 08			08 19			08 29	08 39		08 49			08 59						09 08		
Smethwick Galton Bridge ■	d	07 46		08 02	08 11			08 22			08 32	08 42		08 52			09 02						09 11		
Coventry	a					07 25															08 25				
Birmingham Intl. 68 ✈	a					07 37															08 37				
Birmingham New Street ■ 68	a					07 48			08 12												08 48				
	d		08 00																			08 50			
Langley Green	d			08 05	08 14							08 45					09 05								
Rowley Regis	d	07 52		08 08	08 18			08 28			08 38	08 48		08 58			09 08						09 17		
Old Hill	d			08 12	08 21							08 52					09 12								
Cradley Heath	d	07 57		08 15	08 24			08 33			08 43	08 55		09 03			09 15						09 22		
Lye	d			08 18	08 27							08 58					09 18								
Stourbridge Junction ■	d	08a03		08 22	08 31			08a40			08a48	09 02		09 09			09a22						09 29		
Hagley	d			08 26	08 35									09 12									09 33		
Blakedown	d			08 29	08 38									09 15									09 36		
Kidderminster	d			08 34	08a43							09a10		09 20									09a40		
Hartlebury	d			08 39																					
University	d		08 06																			08 56			
Barnt Green	d		08 17																						
Bromsgrove 69	d		08 22																			09 12			
Droitwich Spa	d		08 32		08 47									09 30								09 22			
Worcester Shrub Hill ■	a													09 40											
	d												09 21												10 00
Worcester Foregate Street ■	a		08 40		08 58								09 24									09 30			10 03
	d		08 41										09 25									09 32			10 03
Malvern Link	d		08 51										09 34									09 42			10 12
Great Malvern	a		08 53										09 37									09 44			10 15
	d		08 54																			09 45			
Colwall	d		08 59																			09 50			
Ledbury	a		09 06																			09 57			
	d		09 07																			09 59			
Hereford ■	a		09 22																			10 14			

Please note, Network Rail have stated that further updates to this timetable are possible during the validity period.

Table T071-F

Mondays to Fridays
21 May to 7 December

Stratford-upon-Avon, Marylebone and Leamington Spa - Birmingham - Stourbridge, Worcester and Hereford

		LM	CH	LM	XC	LM	LM	GW	LM	LM	CH	LM	XC	LM	CH	CH	CH	XC	GW	LM	LM	LM	CH
					◇1						◇		◇1		◇			◇1	◇1				◇
Stratford-upon-Avon	d			08 26												09 00					09 26		
Stratford-upon-Avon Parkway	d			08 30												09 04					09 30		
Wilmcote	d			08 33												09 07					09 33		
Wootton Wawen	d			08x37																	09x37		
Henley-in-Arden	d			08 41																	09 41		
Danzey	d			08x45																	09x45		
Wood End	d			08x49																	09x49		
The Lakes	d			08x51																	09x51		
Earlswood (West Midlands)	d			08 54																	09 54		
Wythall	d			08 57																	09 57		
Whitlocks End	d			09 00						09 19				09 40							10 00		
Shirley	d			09 03						09 22				09 42							10 03		
Yardley Wood	d			09 05						09 24				09 45							10 05		
Hall Green	d			09 09						09 27				09 48							10 09		
Spring Road	d			09 11						09 29				09 51							10 11		
London Marylebone 10 ⊖115	d										07 48				08 14								08 37
Banbury	d				08 30						08 50		08 57		09 08			09 34					09 40
Leamington Spa 8	a				08 46						09 07		09 13		09 25	09 37		09 50					09 57
	d		08 32		08 47						09 08		09 14		09 26		09 40	09 51					09 58
Warwick	d		08 38								09 12				09 30		09 45						10 03
Warwick Parkway	d										09 16				09 34								10 07
Hatton	d		08 44														09a52						
Lapworth	d		08 50																				
Dorridge	d	08 46	08 55				09 10				09 26	09 29								09 46		10 09	10 18
Widney Manor	d	08 51					09 14					09 33								09 51		10 14	
Solihull	d	08 54	09 01				09 18				09 31	09 37			09 46					09 54		10 17	10 24
Olton	d	08 57					09 21					09 40								09 57		10 20	
Acocks Green	d	09 00					09 24					09 42								10 00		10 23	
Tyseley	d	09 02								09 32										10 02			
Small Heath	d	09 05								09 35										10 05			
Bordesley	d																						
Birmingham Moor Street	d	09 09	09a17	09 18			09 31			09 39	09a42	09 49		09 59	09 55					10 09	10 18	10 29	10a35
Birmingham Snow Hill ⇌	a	09 12		09 20			09 35			09 42		09 52		10 01	10 02					10 12	10 20	10 32	
	d	09 13		09 23		09 33				09 43		09 53		10 03						10 13	10 23	10 33	
Jewellery Quarter ⇌	d	09 15		09 25		09 35				09 45		09 55		10 05						10 15	10 25	10 35	
The Hawthorns ⇌	d	09 19		09 29		09 39				09 49		09 59		10 09						10 19	10 29	10 39	
Smethwick Galton Bridge 7	d	09 22		09 32		09 42				09 52		10 02		10 12						10 22	10 32	10 42	
Coventry	a												09 25										
Birmingham Intl. 68 ✈	a												09 37										
Birmingham New Street 12 68	a				09 18								09 49					10 18					
	d								09 50														
Langley Green	d			09 35								10 05									10 35		
Rowley Regis	d	09 28		09 38		09 48				09 58		10 08		10 18						10 28	10 38	10 48	
Old Hill	d			09 42								10 12									10 42		
Cradley Heath	d	09 33		09 45		09 53				10 03		10 15		10 23						10 33	10 45	10 53	
Lye	d			09 48								10 18									10 48		
Stourbridge Junction 2	d	09 39		09a52		09 59				10 09		10a22		10 29						10 39	10a52	10 59	
Hagley	d					10 03				10 12				10 33								11 03	
Blakedown	d					10 06								10 36								11 06	
Kidderminster	d	09 47				10a10				10 18				10a40						10 47		11a10	
Hartlebury	d	09 52																		10 52			
University	d								09 56														
Barnt Green	d																						
Bromsgrove 69	d								10 12														
Droitwich Spa	d	10 00							10 22	10 30										11 00			
Worcester Shrub Hill 7	a																						
	d							10 16											10 49				
Worcester Foregate Street 7	a	10 09						10 19	10 30	10 39									10 52	11 09			
	d							10 19	10 32	10 42									10 53				
Malvern Link	d							10 28	10 42	10 52									11 02				
Great Malvern	a							10 31	10 44	10 57									11 05				
	d								10 45										11 07				
Colwall	d								10 50										11 13				
Ledbury	a								10 57										11 19				
	d								10 59										11 22				
Hereford 7	a								11 14										11 40				

Table T071-F

Mondays to Fridays
21 May to 7 December

Stratford-upon-Avon, Marylebone and Leamington Spa - Birmingham - Stourbridge, Worcester and Hereford

		XC	LM	GW	LM	LM	CH	LM	LM	CH	LM	XC	XC	LM	CH	XC	CH	GW	LM	LM	GW	LM
		◇1		◇1			◇					◇1 A	◇1 B		◇	1		◇			◇1	
Stratford-upon-Avon	d					10 03					10 26						10 37					11 03
Stratford-upon-Avon Parkway	d					10 07					10 30						10 41					11 07
Wilmcote	d										10 33						10 44					
Wootton Wawen	d										10x37											
Henley-in-Arden	d										10 41											
Danzey	d										10x45											
Wood End	d										10x49											
The Lakes	d										10x51											
Earlswood (West Midlands)	d										10 54											
Wythall	d										10 57											
Whitlocks End	d				10 19			10 40			11 00									11 19		
Shirley	d				10 22			10 42			11 03									11 22		
Yardley Wood	d				10 24			10 45			11 05									11 24		
Hall Green	d				10 27			10 48			11 09									11 27		
Spring Road	d				10 29			10 51			11 11									11 29		
London Marylebone 10 ⊖115	d						09 10								09 40							
Banbury	d	09 57					10 08					10 32	10 32		10 43	10 57						
Leamington Spa 8	a	10 12					10 24					10 49	10 49		11 00	11 13	11 14					
	d	10 14					10 25			10 32		10 50	10 50		11 01	11 14						
Warwick	d									10 38					11 05							
Warwick Parkway	d						10 32								11 09							
Hatton	d									10 44												
Lapworth	d									10 50												
Dorridge	d					10 29			10 46	10 55				11 09	11 19							11 29
Widney Manor	d					10 33			10 51					11 14								11 33
Solihull	d					10 37	10 45		10 54	11 01				11 17	11 25							11 37
Olton	d					10 40			10 57					11 20								11 40
Acocks Green	d					10 43			11 00					11 23								11 43
Tyseley	d				10 32				11 02											11 32		
Small Heath	d				10 35				11 05											11 35		
Bordesley	d																					
Birmingham Moor Street	d				10 39	10 49	10 54	10 59	11 09	11a17	11 18			11 29	11 35					11 39		11 49
Birmingham Snow Hill ⇌	a				10 42	10 52	11 01	11 01	11 12		11 20			11 32	11 42					11 42		11 52
	d				10 43	10 53		11 03	11 13		11 23			11 33						11 43		11 53
Jewellery Quarter ⇌	d				10 45	10 55		11 05	11 15		11 25			11 35						11 45		11 55
The Hawthorns ⇌	d				10 49	10 59		11 09	11 19		11 29			11 39						11 49		11 59
Smethwick Galton Bridge 7	d				10 52	11 02		11 12	11 22		11 32			11 42						11 52		12 02
Coventry	a	10 24														11 25						
Birmingham Intl. 68 ✈	a	10 37														11 37						
Birmingham New Street 12 68	a	10 48										11 18	11 18			11 48						
	d		10 50																11 50			
Langley Green	d					11 05					11 35											12 05
Rowley Regis	d				10 58	11 08		11 18	11 28		11 38			11 48						11 58		12 08
Old Hill	d					11 12					11 42											12 12
Cradley Heath	d				11 03	11 15		11 23	11 33		11 45			11 53						12 03		12 15
Lye	d					11 18					11 48											12 18
Stourbridge Junction 2	d				11 09	11a22		11 29	11 39		11a52			11 59						12 09		12a22
Hagley	d				11 12			11 33						12 03						12 12		
Blakedown	d							11 36						12 06								
Kidderminster	d				11 18			11a40	11 47					12a10						12 18		
Hartlebury	d								11 52													
University	d		10 56																11 56			
Barnt Green	d																					
Bromsgrove 69	d		11 12																12 12			
Droitwich Spa	d		11 22		11 30				12 00										12 22	12 30		
Worcester Shrub Hill 7	a				11 38															12 38		
	d			11 29														12 14			12 43	
Worcester Foregate Street 7	a		11 30	11 31					12 09									12 16	12 30		12 46	
	d		11 32															12 17	12 32		12 47	
Malvern Link	d		11 42															12 26	12 42		12 56	
Great Malvern	a		11 45															12 30	12 44		12 59	
	d		11 45																12 45		13 08	
Colwall	d		11 50																12 50		13 14	
Ledbury	a		11 57																12 57		13 20	
	d		11 58																12 59		13 31	
Hereford 7	a		12 14																13 15		13 47	

A until 20 July, from 8 October

B from 23 July until 5 October

Please note, Network Rail have stated that further updates to this timetable are possible during the validity period.

Table T071-F

Mondays to Fridays

21 May to 7 December

Stratford-upon-Avon, Marylebone and Leamington Spa - Birmingham - Stourbridge, Worcester and Hereford

		CH	CH	XC	LM	LM	LM		LM	LM	LM	CH	XC	LM	CH	LM	GW		LM	GW	CH	LM	XC	XC	LM
		◇		◇1 ✠								◇	◇1 ✠		◇		◇1 ✠			◇			◇1 A ✠	1 B	
Stratford-upon-Avon	d						11 26							12 03								12 26			
Stratford-upon-Avon Parkway	d						11 30							12 07								12 30			
Wilmcote	d						11 33															12 33			
Wootton Wawen	d						11x37															12x37			
Henley-in-Arden	d						11 41															12 41			
Danzey	d						11x45															12x45			
Wood End	d						11x49															12x49			
The Lakes	d						11x51															12x51			
Earlswood (West Midlands)	d						11 54															12 54			
Wythall	d						11 57															12 57			
Whitlocks End	d				11 40		12 00				12 19					12 40						13 00			
Shirley	d				11 42		12 03				12 22					12 42						13 03			
Yardley Wood	d				11 45		12 05				12 24					12 45						13 05			
Hall Green	d				11 48		12 09				12 27					12 48						13 09			
Spring Road	d				11 51		12 11				12 29					12 51						13 11			
London Marylebone ⊖115	d	10 10										10 40			11 10										
Banbury	d	11 07		11 30								11 46	11 57		12 07								12 32	12 32	
Leamington Spa	a	11 24		11 46								12 03	12 13		12 25								12 48	12 48	
	d	11 25	11 32	11 48								12 04	12 14		12 26						12 32		12 50	12 50	
Warwick	d		11 37									12 09									12 38				
Warwick Parkway	d	11 32										12 13			12 32										
Hatton	d		11a44																		12 44				
Lapworth	d																				12 50				
Dorridge	d					11 46			12 09			12 24		12 29					12 46		12 55				13 09
Widney Manor	d					11 51			12 14					12 33					12 51						13 14
Solihull	d	11 45				11 54			12 17			12 31		12 37	12 45				12 54		13 01				13 17
Olton	d					11 57			12 20					12 40					12 57						13 20
Acocks Green	d					12 00			12 23					12 43					13 00						13 23
Tyseley	d					12 02					12 32								13 02						
Small Heath	d					12 05					12 35								13 05						
Bordesley	d																								
Birmingham Moor Street	d	11a56			11 59	12 09	12 18		12 29		12 39	12 44		12 49	12a56	12 59			13 09		13a17	13 18			13 29
Birmingham Snow Hill	a				12 01	12 12	12 20		12 32		12 42	12 51		12 52		13 01			13 12			13 20			13 32
	d				12 03	12 13	12 23		12 33		12 43			12 53		13 03			13 13			13 23			13 33
Jewellery Quarter	d				12 05	12 15	12 25		12 35		12 45			12 55		13 05			13 15			13 25			13 35
The Hawthorns	d				12 09	12 19	12 29		12 39		12 49			12 59		13 09			13 19			13 29			13 39
Smethwick Galton Bridge	d				12 12	12 22	12 32		12 42		12 52			13 02		13 12			13 22			13 32			13 42
Coventry	a												12 25												
Birmingham Intl. 68	a												12 37												
Birmingham New Street 68	a			12 18									12 48										13 18	13 18	
	d									12 50															
Langley Green	d						12 35							13 05								13 35			
Rowley Regis	d				12 18	12 28	12 38		12 48		12 58			13 08		13 18			13 28			13 38			13 48
Old Hill	d						12 42							13 12								13 42			
Cradley Heath	d				12 23	12 33	12 45		12 53		13 03			13 15		13 23			13 33			13 45			13 53
Lye	d						12 48							13 18								13 48			
Stourbridge Junction	d				12 29	12 39	12a52		12 59		13 09			13a22		13a31			13 39			13a52			13 59
Hagley	d				12 33				13 03		13 12														14 03
Blakedown	d				12 36				13 06																14 06
Kidderminster	d				12a40	12 47			13a10		13 18								13 47						14a10
Hartlebury	d					12 52													13 52						
University	d									12 56															
Barnt Green	d																								
Bromsgrove 69	d									13 12															
Droitwich Spa	d					13 00				13 22	13 30								14 00						
Worcester Shrub Hill	a																		14 08						
	d																13 42			14 15					
Worcester Foregate Street	a					13 09				13 30	13 40						13 44			14 18					
	d					13 12				13 32										14 18					
Malvern Link	d					13 22				13 42										14 27					
Great Malvern	a					13 27				13 44										14 30					
	d									13 45															
Colwall	d									13 50															
Ledbury	a									13 57															
	d									13 59															
Hereford	a									14 16															

A until 20 July, from 8 October

B from 23 July until 5 October

Table T071-F

Mondays to Fridays

21 May to 7 December

Stratford-upon-Avon, Marylebone and Leamington Spa - Birmingham - Stourbridge, Worcester and Hereford

		CH	XC		LM	CH	LM	LM	CH	CH	XC	XC	LM		LM	LM	LM	CH	XC	LM	LM	LM	CH		LM
		◇	◇1 ✠						◇		1 A ✠	◇1 B ✠						◇	◇1 ✠				◇		
Stratford-upon-Avon	d					12 40		13 03								13 26						14 03			
Stratford-upon-Avon Parkway	d					12 44		13 07								13 30						14 07			
Wilmcote	d					12 47										13 33									
Wootton Wawen	d															13x37									
Henley-in-Arden	d															13 41									
Danzey	d															13x45									
Wood End	d															13x49									
The Lakes	d															13x51									
Earlswood (West Midlands)	d															13 54									
Wythall	d															13 57									
Whitlocks End	d						13 19						13 40			14 00					14 19				14 40
Shirley	d						13 22						13 42			14 03					14 22				14 42
Yardley Wood	d						13 24						13 45			14 05					14 24				14 45
Hall Green	d						13 27						13 48			14 09					14 27				14 48
Spring Road	d						13 29						13 51			14 11					14 29				14 51
London Marylebone ⊖115	d	11 40							12 10									12 40					13 10		
Banbury	d	12 40	12 57						13 08		13 31	13 31						13 40	13 57				14 10		
Leamington Spa	a	12 57	13 13			13 14			13 25		13 47	13 47						13 57	14 13				14 26		
	d	12 58	13 14						13 26	13 32	13 48	13 48						13 58	14 14				14 27		
Warwick	d	13 02								13 37								14 02							
Warwick Parkway	d	13 06							13 32									14 06					14 33		
Hatton	d									13a44															
Lapworth	d																								
Dorridge	d	13 16						13 29							13 46		14 09	14 16				14 29			
Widney Manor	d							13 33							13 51		14 14					14 33			
Solihull	d	13 22						13 37	13 45						13 54		14 17	14 22				14 37	14 45		
Olton	d							13 40							13 57		14 20					14 40			
Acocks Green	d							13 43							14 00		14 23					14 43			
Tyseley	d						13 32								14 02						14 32				
Small Heath	d						13 35								14 05						14 35				
Bordesley	d																								
Birmingham Moor Street	d	13 33					13 39	13 49	13a56				13 59		14 09	14 18	14 29	14 33			14 39	14 49	14a56		14 59
Birmingham Snow Hill	a	13 41					13 42	13 52					14 01		14 12	14 20	14 32	14 41			14 42	14 52			15 01
	d						13 43	13 53					14 03		14 13	14 23	14 33				14 43	14 53			15 03
Jewellery Quarter	d						13 45	13 55					14 05		14 15	14 25	14 35				14 45	14 55			15 05
The Hawthorns	d						13 49	13 59					14 09		14 19	14 29	14 39				14 50	14 59			15 09
Smethwick Galton Bridge	d						13 52	14 02					14 12		14 22	14 32	14 42				14 52	15 02			15 12
Coventry	a		13 25																14 25						
Birmingham Intl. 68	a		13 37																14 37						
Birmingham New Street 68	a		13 48								14 18	14 18							14 48						
	d				13 50															14 50					
Langley Green	d							14 05								14 35						15 05			
Rowley Regis	d						13 58	14 08					14 18		14 28	14 38	14 48				14 58	15 08			15 18
Old Hill	d							14 12								14 42						15 12			
Cradley Heath	d						14 03	14 15					14 23		14 33	14 45	14 53				15 03	15 15			15 23
Lye	d							14 18								14 48						15 18			
Stourbridge Junction	d						14 09	14a22					14 29		14 39	14a52	14 59				15 09	15a22			15 29
Hagley	d						14 12						14 33				15 03				15 12				15 33
Blakedown	d												14 36				15 06								15 36
Kidderminster	d						14 18						14a40		14 47		15a10				15 18				15a40
Hartlebury	d														14 52										
University	d				13 56															14 56					
Barnt Green	d																								
Bromsgrove 69	d				14 12															15 12					
Droitwich Spa	d				14 22		14 30								15 00					15 22	15 30				
Worcester Shrub Hill	a						14 40								15 10										
	d						14 45																		
Worcester Foregate Street	a				14 30		14 47													15 30	15 39				
	d				14 32		14 47													15 32					
Malvern Link	d				14 42		14 56													15 42					
Great Malvern	a				14 44		14 59													15 45					
	d				14 45															15 45					
Colwall	d				14 50															15 50					
Ledbury	a				14 57															15 57					
	d				14 59															15 59					
Hereford	a				15 14															16 14					

A until 20 July, from 8 October

B from 23 July until 5 October

Table T071-F

Stratford-upon-Avon, Marylebone and Leamington Spa - Birmingham - Stourbridge, Worcester and Hereford

Station		GW ◇1 🍴	GW ◇	LM	CH	LM	XC ◇1 🍴	LM	CH ◇		XC ◇1 🍴	LM	CH	LM	LM	CH ◇	CH	XC ◇1 🍴	LM		GW ◇1	LM	LM	LM	LM
Stratford-upon-Avon	d					14 26							14 37		15 03									15 26	
Stratford-upon-Avon Parkway	d					14 30							14 41		15 07									15 30	
Wilmcote	d					14 33							14 44											15 33	
Wootton Wawen	d					14x37																		15x37	
Henley-in-Arden	d					14 41																		15 41	
Danzey	d					14x45																		15x45	
Wood End	d					14x49																		15x49	
The Lakes	d					14x51																		15x51	
Earlswood (West Midlands)	d					14 54																		15 54	
Wythall	d					14 57																		15 57	
Whitlocks End	d					15 00								15 19					15 40					16 00	
Shirley	d					15 03								15 22					15 42					16 03	
Yardley Wood	d					15 05								15 24					15 45					16 05	
Hall Green	d					15 09								15 27					15 48					16 09	
Spring Road	d					15 11								15 29					15 51					16 11	
London Marylebone ■ ⊖115	d								13 40							14 10									
Banbury	d						14 31		14 40		14 57					15 07		15 32							
Leamington Spa ■	a						14 49		14 57		15 13		15 16			15 24		15 48							
	d				14 32		14 50		14 58		15 14					15 25	15 32	15 50							
Warwick	d				14 38				15 02								15 37								
Warwick Parkway	d								15 06							15 30									
Hatton	d				14 44												15a44								
Lapworth	d				14 50																				
Dorridge	d			14 46	14 55			15 09	15 16						15 29								15 46		16 09
Widney Manor	d			14 51				15 14							15 33								15 51		16 14
Solihull	d			14 54	15 01			15 17	15 22						15 37	15 45							15 54		16 17
Olton	d			14 57				15 20							15 40								15 57		16 20
Acocks Green	d			15 00				15 23							15 43								16 00		16 23
Tyseley	d			15 02										15 32									16 02		
Small Heath	d			15 05										15 35									16 05		
Bordesley	d																								
Birmingham Moor Street	d			15 09	15a17	15 18		15 29	15 33					15 39	15 49	15a56			15 59				16 09	16 18	16 29
Birmingham Snow Hill ⇌	a			15 12		15 20		15 32	15 41					15 42	15 52				16 01				16 12	16 20	16 32
	d			15 13		15 23		15 33						15 43	15 53				16 03				16 13	16 23	16 33
Jewellery Quarter ⇌	d			15 15		15 25		15 35						15 45	15 55				16 05				16 15	16 25	16 35
The Hawthorns ⇌	d			15 19		15 29		15 39						15 49	15 59				16 09				16 19	16 29	16 39
Smethwick Galton Bridge ■	d			15 22		15 32		15 42						15 52	16 02				16 12				16 22	16 32	16 42
Coventry	a										15 25														
Birmingham Intl. 68 ✈	a										15 37														
Birmingham New Street ■ 68	a						15 18				15 48							16 18							
	d											15 50										16 20			
Langley Green	d					15 35									16 05									16 35	
Rowley Regis	d			15 28		15 38		15 48						15 58	16 08				16 18				16 28	16 38	16 48
Old Hill	d					15 42									16 12									16 42	
Cradley Heath	d			15 33		15 45		15 53						16 03	16 15				16 23				16 33	16 45	16 53
Lye	d					15 48									16 18									16 48	
Stourbridge Junction ■	d			15 39		15a52		15 59						16 08	16a22				16 29				16 39	16a52	16 59
Hagley	d			15 43				16 03						16 12					16 33						17 03
Blakedown	d			15 47				16 06						16 15					16 36						17 06
Kidderminster	d			15 52				16a10						16 20					16a40				16 47		17a10
Hartlebury	d			15 57																			16 52		
University	d											15 56										16 26			
Barnt Green	d																								
Bromsgrove 69	d											16 12										16 42			
Droitwich Spa	d			16 06								16 21		16 31								16 52	17 00		
Worcester Shrub Hill ■	a			16 14																		16 58			
	d	15 39	16 14	16 21																	16 42	17 06			
Worcester Foregate Street ■	a	15 41	16 17	16 25								16 30		16 42							16 44	17 08	17 09		
	d		16 17									16 30										17 09			
Malvern Link	d		16 26									16 40										17 18			
Great Malvern	a		16 29									16 43										17 20			
	d											16 44													
Colwall	d											16 49													
Ledbury	a											16 57													
	d											16 59													
Hereford ■	a											17 15													

Table T071-F

Stratford-upon-Avon, Marylebone and Leamington Spa - Birmingham - Stourbridge, Worcester and Hereford

Station		CH ◇	XC ◇1 🍴	LM	GW ◇1 🍴		LM	LM	LM	CH ◇	LM	LM	GW	CH	LM		XC ◇1 🍴	LM	LM	LM	CH ◇	LM	XC ◇1 🍴	LM	CH ◇
Stratford-upon-Avon	d							16 03							16 26										
Stratford-upon-Avon Parkway	d							16 07							16 30										
Wilmcote	d														16 33										
Wootton Wawen	d														16x37										
Henley-in-Arden	d														16 41										
Danzey	d														16x45										
Wood End	d														16x49										
The Lakes	d														16x51										
Earlswood (West Midlands)	d														16 54										
Wythall	d														16 57										
Whitlocks End	d						16 19		16 40						17 00					17 19					
Shirley	d						16 22		16 42						17 03					17 22					
Yardley Wood	d						16 24		16 45						17 05					17 24					
Hall Green	d						16 27		16 48						17 09					17 27					
Spring Road	d						16 29		16 51						17 11					17 29					
London Marylebone ■ ⊖115	d	14 40								15 10											15 40				16 15
Banbury	d	15 42	15 57							16 09							16 31				16 40		16 57		17 08
Leamington Spa ■	a	15 59	16 13							16 26							16 47				16 57		17 13		17 25
	d	15 59	16 14							16 26				16 32			16 48				16 58		17 14		17 26
Warwick	d	16 03												16 38							17 02				
Warwick Parkway	d	16 07								16 32											17 06				17 32
Hatton	d													16 44											
Lapworth	d													16 50											
Dorridge	d	16 17						16 29				16 46		16 55					17 09		17 16	17 28			
Widney Manor	d							16 33				16 51							17 14			17 33			
Solihull	d	16 23						16 37		16 45		16 54		17 01					17 17		17 22	17 36			17 45
Olton	d							16 40				16 57							17 20			17 39			
Acocks Green	d							16 43				17 00							17 23			17 42			
Tyseley	d						16 32					17 02							17 25	17 34					
Small Heath	d						16 35					17 05							17 28	17 36					
Bordesley	d																								
Birmingham Moor Street	d	16 33					16 39	16 49	16 59	16 55		17 09		17a17	17 19				17 32	17 41	17 37	17 49			17 55
Birmingham Snow Hill ⇌	a	16 41					16 42	16 52	17 01	17 02		17 12			17 21				17 35	17 43	17 44	17 51			17 57
	d						16 43	16 54	17 03			17 13			17 23				17 36	17 43		17 53			17 59
Jewellery Quarter ⇌	d						16 45	16 56	17 05			17 15			17 25				17 39	17 47		17 56			
The Hawthorns ⇌	d						16 49	17 00	17 09			17 19			17 29				17 43	17 51		18 00			
Smethwick Galton Bridge ■	d						16 52	17 03	17 12			17 22			17 32				17 46	17 54		18 03			
Coventry	a		16 25																				17 25		
Birmingham Intl. 68 ✈	a		16 37																				17 37		
Birmingham New Street ■ 68	a		16 48														17 18						17 48		
	d			16 50							17 20							17 50						18 00	
Langley Green	d							17 06							17 35					17 57					
Rowley Regis	d						16 58	17 09	17 18			17 28			17 38				17 51	18 00		18 09			18 15
Old Hill	d							17 13							17 42					18 03					
Cradley Heath	d						17 03	17 16	17 23			17 33			17 45				17 57	18 07		18 14			
Lye	d							17 19							17 48					18 10					
Stourbridge Junction ■	d						17 10	17a22	17 29			17 39			17a52				18 02	18 14		18 20			18 27
Hagley	d						17 13		17 33			17 43							18 06	18 17		18 24			
Blakedown	d						17 17		17 36			17 47							18 09	18 21		18 27			
Kidderminster	d						17 23		17a40			17 52							18 14	18a27		18 32			18a44
Hartlebury	d						17 28												18 19			18 37			
University	d			16 56							17 26							17 56						18 06	
Barnt Green	d																								
Bromsgrove 69	d			17 12							17 42							18 12						18 22	
Droitwich Spa	d			17 22			17 37				17 52	18 04						18 22	18 28			18 45		18 35	
Worcester Shrub Hill ■	a			17 29							17 59	18 12						18 31						18 41	
	d			17 32	17 42						18 04		18 19					18 34						18 54	
Worcester Foregate Street ■	a			17 34	17 45		17 46				18 06		18 21					18 36	18 39			18 54		18 56	
	d			17 35	17 46						18 07		18 22					18 37						18 57	
Malvern Link	d			17 44	17 55						18 16		18 31					18 46						19 06	
Great Malvern	a			17 46	17 58						18 18		18 35					18 48						19 08	
	d			17 47							18 19							18 49							
Colwall	d			17 52							18 24							18 54							
Ledbury	a			17 59							18 31							19 02							
	d			18 00							18 31							19 04							
Hereford ■	a			18 17							18 46							19 19							

Please note, Network Rail have stated that further updates to this timetable are possible during the validity period.

Table T071-F

Mondays to Fridays

21 May to 7 December

Stratford-upon-Avon, Marylebone and Leamington Spa - Birmingham - Stourbridge, Worcester and Hereford

		LM	LM	CH	LM	XC	CH	CH	CH	GW	LM	GW	GW	LM	XC	LM	CH	CH	XC	LM	LM	LM
				◇		◇■	◇	◇		◇■		◇■	◇■		◇■			◇	◇■			
												A	B									
Stratford-upon-Avon	d		17 27					17 36						17 55								18 27
Stratford-upon-Avon Parkway	d		17 31					17 40						17 59								18 31
Wilmcote	d		17 34					17 43														18 34
Wootton Wawen	d		17x39																			18x39
Henley-in-Arden	d		17 43											18 07								18 43
Danzey	d		17x47																			18x47
Wood End	d		17x50																			18x50
The Lakes	d		17x53																			18x53
Earlswood (West Midlands)	d		17 56																			18 56
Wythall	d		17 58																			18 58
Whitlocks End	d	17 42	18 01											18 18							18 45	19 01
Shirley	d	17 44	18 04											18 21							18 47	19 04
Yardley Wood	d	17 47	18 07											18 24							18 50	19 07
Hall Green	d	17 50	18 10											18 27							18 53	19 10
Spring Road	d	17 52	18 12											18 29							18 56	19 12
London Marylebone ■ ⊖115	d			16 21			16 47										16 24	17 15				
Banbury	d			17 24		17 33	17 47								17 57		18 02	18 09	18 27			
Leamington Spa ■	a			17 41		17 50	18 04	18 09							18 13		18 21	18 26	18 44			
	d			17 41		17 51	18 04		18 11						18 14		18 22	18 27	18 45			
Warwick	d						18 08		18 16								18 26					
Warwick Parkway	d			17 47			18 12											18 34				
Hatton	d								18a23								18 39					
Lapworth	d																18 46					
Dorridge	d			17 57	18 04		18 22									18 24	18 51	18 45				
Widney Manor	d				18 08											18 29						
Solihull	d			18 03	18 12		18 27									18 32	18 57	18 50				
Olton	d				18 15											18 35						
Acocks Green	d				18 18											18 38						
Tyseley	d	17 56			18 21									18 32		18 40					18 59	
Small Heath	d	17 58			18 24									18 34		18 43						
Bordesley	d																					
Birmingham Moor Street	d	18 03	18 18	18 13	18 28		18a38							18 39		18 47	19 08	19 00			19 04	19 19
Birmingham Snow Hill	a	18 05	18 21	18 22	18 30									18 41		18 50	19 15	19 02			19 06	19 22
	d	18 08	18 23		18 31									18 43				19 04			19 10	
Jewellery Quarter	d	18 10	18 25		18 33									18 45							19 12	
The Hawthorns	d	18 14	18 29		18 38									18 49							19 16	
Smethwick Galton Bridge ■	d	18 17	18 32		18 41									18 52							19 19	
Coventry	a														18 25							
Birmingham Intl. 68 ✈	a														18 37							
Birmingham New Street ■ 68	a					18 18									18 48				19 18			
	d										18 20									19 20		
Langley Green	d	18 20	18 35		18 44																19 22	
Rowley Regis	d	18 24	18 39		18 47									18 58				19 17			19 25	
Old Hill	d	18 27	18 42		18 50																19 28	
Cradley Heath	d	18 30	18 45		18 54									19 03							19 32	
Lye	d	18 33	18 48		18 57																19 35	
Stourbridge Junction ■	d	18 37	18 52		19a02									19 09				19 28			19a39	
Hagley	d	18 41	18 56											19 12								
Blakedown	d	18 44	18 59											19 15								
Kidderminster	d	18a50	19a05											19 20				19a41				
Hartlebury	d																					
University	d										18 27									19 26		
Barnt Green	d																					
Bromsgrove 69	d										18 42									19 42		
Droitwich Spa	d										18 57			19 32						19 53		
Worcester Shrub Hill ■	a										19 10									20 05		
	d									19 07		19 35	19 35							20 13		
Worcester Foregate Street ■	a									19 10		19 38	19 38	19 43						20 15		
	d									19 11		19 39	19 39							20 16		
Malvern Link	d									19 20		19 48	19 48							20 25		
Great Malvern	a									19 24		19 51	19 51							20 28		
	d											19 52	19 52							20 28		
Colwall	d											19 58	19 58							20 34		
Ledbury	a											20 05	20 06							20 41		
	d											20 08	20 08							20 42		
Hereford ■	a											20 26	20 28							20 58		

A until 5 October B from 8 October

Table T071-F

Mondays to Fridays

21 May to 7 December

Stratford-upon-Avon, Marylebone and Leamington Spa - Birmingham - Stourbridge, Worcester and Hereford

		GW	LM	LM	CH	XC	LM	GW	GW	LM	LM	CH	LM	XC	CH	XC	LM	CH	GW	GW	LM	CH	LM
					◇	◇■		◇■	◇■			◇		◇■	◇	◇■		◇	◇■	◇■		◇	
								A	B										C	D			
Stratford-upon-Avon	d			18 51							19 03		19 26										20 26
Stratford-upon-Avon Parkway	d			18 55							19 07		19 30										20 30
Wilmcote	d			18 58									19 33										20 33
Wootton Wawen	d			19x03									19x37										20x37
Henley-in-Arden	d			19 07									19 41										20 41
Danzey	d												19x45										20x45
Wood End	d												19x49										20x49
The Lakes	d												19x51										20x51
Earlswood (West Midlands)	d												19 54										20 54
Wythall	d												19 57										20 57
Whitlocks End	d			19 17						19 25			20 00										21 00
Shirley	d			19 19						19 27			20 03										21 03
Yardley Wood	d			19 22						19 30			20 05										21 05
Hall Green	d			19 25						19 33			20 09										21 09
Spring Road	d			19 28						19 35			20 11										21 11
London Marylebone ■ ⊖115	d				17 46							18 15			18 47			18 24				19 15	
Banbury	d				18 48	18 57						19 09		19 30	19 51	19 57		20 06				20 16	
Leamington Spa ■	a				19 05	19 13						19 26		19 47	20 08	20 13		20 25				20 35	
	d				19 05	19 14						19 27		19 48	20 09	20 14		20 26				20 35	
Warwick	d				19 09										20 13								
Warwick Parkway	d				19 13							19 34			20 17			20 31				20 43	
Hatton	d																	20a38					
Lapworth	d										19 25												
Dorridge	d		19 00		19 23						19 30	19 45			20 27						20 29	20 53	
Widney Manor	d		19 05								19 35										20 33		
Solihull	d		19 08		19 29						19 38	19 51			20 33						20 37	20 58	
Olton	d		19 11								19 41										20 40		
Acocks Green	d		19 14								19 44										20 43		
Tyseley	d		19 17							19 38	19 47										20 45		
Small Heath	d		19 19							19 39	19 49										20 48		
Bordesley	d																						
Birmingham Moor Street	d		19 24	19 35	19 39					19 44	19 54	20 02	20 18		20 42						20 53	21a10	21 18
Birmingham Snow Hill	a		19 26	19 37	19 46					19 49	19 56	20 04	20 20		20 49						20 55		21 20
	d		19 28	19 40							19 58	20 06	20 23								20 58		21 23
Jewellery Quarter	d		19 30	19 42							20 00		20 25								21 00		21 25
The Hawthorns	d		19 34	19 46							20 04	20 13	20 29								21 04		21 29
Smethwick Galton Bridge ■	d		19 37	19 49							20 07	20 17	20 32								21 07		21 32
Coventry	a					19 26										20 26							
Birmingham Intl. 68 ✈	a					19 37										20 37							
Birmingham New Street ■ 68	a					19 48								20 18		20 48							
	d						20 00										21 00						
Langley Green	d		19 40								20 10		20 35								21 10		21 35
Rowley Regis	d		19 44	19 55							20 14	20 23	20 38								21 14		21 38
Old Hill	d		19 47								20 17		20 42								21 17		21 42
Cradley Heath	d		19 50	20 00							20 20		20 45								21 20		21 45
Lye	d		19 53								20 23		20 48								21 23		21 48
Stourbridge Junction ■	d		19 57	20a05							20 27	20 34	20a52								21 27		21a52
Hagley	d		20 01								20 31										21 31		
Blakedown	d		20 04								20 34										21 34		
Kidderminster	d		20 09								20 39	20a48									21 39		
Hartlebury	d		20 14																		21 44		
University	d						20 06										21 06						
Barnt Green	d																						
Bromsgrove 69	d						20 21										21 21						
Droitwich Spa	d		20 22				20 31				20 50						21 31				21 52		
Worcester Shrub Hill ■	a						20 38				20 59										21 59		
	d	20 19						20 42	20 42										21 58	21 58	22 06		
Worcester Foregate Street ■	a	20 22	20 31					20 44	20 44								21 39		22 01	22 01	22 08		
	d	20 23						20 46	20 46								21 41		22 02	22 02			
Malvern Link	d	20 32						20 55	20 55								21 51		22 12	22 12			
Great Malvern	a	20 35						20 58	20 58								21 54		22 15	22 15			
	d							20 59	20 59								21 54		22 20	22 20			
Colwall	d							21 06	21 06								21 59		22 26	22 26			
Ledbury	a							21 13	21 13								22 06		22 32	22 32			
	d							21 16	21 16								22 09		22 34	22 34			
Hereford ■	a							21 32	21 34								22 24		22 52	22 54			

A until 5 October. The Cathedrals Express
B from 8 October. The Cathedrals Express
C until 5 October
D from 8 October

Table T071-F

Stratford-upon-Avon, Marylebone and Leamington Spa - Birmingham - Stourbridge, Worcester and Hereford

Mondays to Fridays
21 May to 7 December

		XC ◇1	CH ◇		XC ◇1	GW ◇1 A	GW ◇1 B	LM	LM	CH ◇	LM	XC ◇1	CH ◇		CH ◇	XC ◇1	LM	CH ◇	LM	CH ◇	LM	CH ◇	XC ◇1		CH ◇
Stratford-upon-Avon	d										21 26				21 39						22 33				
Stratford-upon-Avon Parkway	d										21 30				21 43						22 37				
Wilmcote	d										21 33				21 47						22 40				
Wootton Wawen	d																								
Henley-in-Arden	d										21 39										22 46				
Danzey	d																								
Wood End	d										21x46														
The Lakes	d										21x48														
Earlswood (West Midlands)	d										21 51														
Wythall	d										21 54										22 56				
Whitlocks End	d										21 57										22 58				
Shirley	d										22 00										23 01				
Yardley Wood	d										22 02										23 03				
Hall Green	d										22 06										23 06				
Spring Road	d										22 08										23 08				
London Marylebone 10 ⊖115	d		19 47							20 10			20 37					20 43		21 10		21 40			22 10
Banbury	d	20 32	20 48		20 57					21 12		21 33	21 39			21 54		22 01		22 14		22 41	22 48		23 13
Leamington Spa 8	a	20 48	21 05		21 13					21 29		21 52	21 56		22 10	22 10		22 19		22 31		22 58	23 04		23 31
	d	20 50	21 05		21 14					21 30		21 53	21 57			22 12		22 20		22 31		22 59	23 05		23 31
Warwick	d		21 09										22 01					22 24				23 03			
Warwick Parkway	d		21 13							21 36			22 05							22 38		23 07			23 37
Hatton	d		21 18															22a31				23 12			
Lapworth	d		21 23																			23 18			
Dorridge	d		21 28						21 30				22 15						22 33			23 23			
Widney Manor	d								21 35										22 38			23 27			
Solihull	d		21 34						21 38	21 49			22 21						22 41	22 51		23 31			23 49
Olton	d								21 41										22 44						
Acocks Green	d								21 44										22 47						
Tyseley	d								21 47		22 11								22 50		23 12				
Small Heath	d								21 49		22 13								22 52		23 14				
Bordesley	d																								
Birmingham Moor Street	d		21 44						21 54	22 02	22 18		22 31						22 57	23 03	23 19	23 40			00a01
Birmingham Snow Hill ⇌	a		21 51						21 56	22 06	22 20		22 38						22 59	23 05	23 21	23 47			
	d								21 58	22 10	22 23								23 01	23 15					
Jewellery Quarter ⇌	d								22 00		22 25								23 03	23 18					
The Hawthorns ⇌	d								22 04	22 17	22 29								23 07	23 22					
Smethwick Galton Bridge 7	d								22 07	22 20	22 32								23 10	23 25					
Coventry	a				21 26											22 23							23 16		
Birmingham Intl. 68 ✈	a				21 37											22 34							23 26		
Birmingham New Street 12 68	a	21 23			21 48							22 18				22 45							23 56		
	d							22 00									23 00								
Langley Green	d								22 10		22 35								23 13	23 29					
Rowley Regis	d								22 14	22 25	22 38								23 17	23 33					
Old Hill	d								22 17		22 42								23 20	23 36					
Cradley Heath	d								22 20	22 31	22 45								23 23	23 40					
Lye	d								22 23		22 48								23 26	23 43					
Stourbridge Junction 2	d								22 27	22 37	22a52								23 30	23a49					
Hagley	d								22 31										23 34						
Blakedown	d								22 34										23 37						
Kidderminster	d								22 39	22a50									23 42						
Hartlebury	d								22 44										23 47						
University	d							22 06									23 06								
Barnt Green	d																								
Bromsgrove 69	d							22 21									23 21								
Droitwich Spa	d							22 34	22 52								23 31		23 54						
Worcester Shrub Hill 7	a							22 47	22 59								23 39		00 05						
	d					22 41	22 41		23 08																
Worcester Foregate Street 7	a					22 43	22 43		23 10																
	d					22 45	22 45		23 10																
Malvern Link	d					22 54	22 54		23 19																
Great Malvern	a					22 57	22 59		23 23																
	d																								
Colwall	d																								
Ledbury	a																								
	d																								
Hereford 7	a																								

A until 5 October

B from 8 October

Table T071-F

Stratford-upon-Avon, Marylebone and Leamington Spa - Birmingham - Stourbridge, Worcester and Hereford

Mondays to Fridays
21 May to 7 December

		CH	LM	CH ◇	CH ◇
Stratford-upon-Avon	d	23 15	23 30		
Stratford-upon-Avon Parkway	d		23 34		
Wilmcote	d				
Wootton Wawen	d				
Henley-in-Arden	d				
Danzey	d				
Wood End	d				
The Lakes	d				
Earlswood (West Midlands)	d				
Wythall	d				
Whitlocks End	d				
Shirley	d				
Yardley Wood	d				
Hall Green	d				
Spring Road	d				
London Marylebone 10 ⊖115	d			22 37	23 07
Banbury	d			23 41	00 03
Leamington Spa 8	a	23 38		23 58	00 20
	d			23 59	00 21
Warwick	d			00 03	00 25
Warwick Parkway	d			00 07	00 29
Hatton	d				
Lapworth	d				
Dorridge	d			00 18	
Widney Manor	d				
Solihull	d			00 24	00 41
Olton	d				
Acocks Green	d				
Tyseley	d				
Small Heath	d				
Bordesley	d				
Birmingham Moor Street	d		00 06	00a36	00a52
Birmingham Snow Hill ⇌	a		00 08		
	d				
Jewellery Quarter ⇌	d				
The Hawthorns ⇌	d				
Smethwick Galton Bridge 7	d				
Coventry	a				
Birmingham Intl. 68 ✈	a				
Birmingham New Street 12 68	a				
	d				
Langley Green	d				
Rowley Regis	d				
Old Hill	d				
Cradley Heath	d				
Lye	d				
Stourbridge Junction 2	d				
Hagley	d				
Blakedown	d				
Kidderminster	d				
Hartlebury	d				
University	d				
Barnt Green	d				
Bromsgrove 69	d				
Droitwich Spa	d				
Worcester Shrub Hill 7	a				
	d				
Worcester Foregate Street 7	a				
	d				
Malvern Link	d				
Great Malvern	a				
	d				
Colwall	d				
Ledbury	a				
	d				
Hereford 7	a				

Please note, Network Rail have stated that further updates to this timetable are possible during the validity period.

Table T071-F

Saturdays
26 May to 8 December

Stratford-upon-Avon, Marylebone and Leamington Spa - Birmingham - Stourbridge, Worcester and Hereford

	LM	CH ◇	CH ◇	CH A	CH B	LM	LM	LM	LM	GW ◇1	CH	LM	LM	XC ◇1	LM	LM	GW ◇1	LM	LM	CH	LM	XC ◇1
Stratford-upon-Avon d																			07 00			
Stratford-upon-Avon Parkway d																			07 04			
Wilmcote d																			07 07			
Wootton Wawen d																			07x11			
Henley-in-Arden d																			07 15			
Danzey d																			07x19			
Wood End d																			07x23			
The Lakes d																			07x25			
Earlswood (West Midlands) d																			07 28			
Wythall d																			07 31			
Whitlocks End d																07 03			07 33			
Shirley d																07 05			07 36			
Yardley Wood d																07 08			07 39			
Hall Green d																07 11			07 42			
Spring Road d																07 14			07 44			
London Marylebone ⊖115 d				00 20	00 20																	
Banbury d			00 03	01 35	01 35						06 00			06 57						07 03		07 29
Leamington Spa a			00 20	01 56	01 59						06 20			07 13						07 20		07 47
Leamington Spa d			00 21								06 21		06 29	07 14						07 21		07 47
Warwick d		00 03	00 25								06 25		06 33							07 25		
Warwick Parkway d		00 07	00 29								06 28		06 36							07 29		
Hatton d											06 34		06 40							07 34		
Lapworth d											06 39		06 46									
Dorridge d		00 18									06 44		06 50					07 26		07 42	08 07	
Widney Manor d													06 54					07 31			08 12	
Solihull d		00 24	00 41								06 49		06 58					07 34		07 48	08 15	
Olton d													07 01					07 37			08 18	
Acocks Green d													07 04					07 40			08 21	
Tyseley d													07 06			07 17		07 42	07 48		08 24	
Small Heath d													07 09			07 19		07 45	07 50			
Bordesley d																						
Birmingham Moor Street d	00 06	00a36	00a52						06 33		07a00	07 01	07 14			07 24		07 49	07 55	08a00	08 29	
Birmingham Snow Hill a	00 08								06 35			07 03	07 17			07 26		07 52	07 57		08 31	
Birmingham Snow Hill d									06 37			07 05				07 28		07 53	08 03		08 33	
Jewellery Quarter d									06 39			07 07				07 30		07 55	08 05		08 35	
The Hawthorns d									06 43			07 11				07 34		07 59	08 09		08 39	
Smethwick Galton Bridge d									06 46			07 14				07 37		08 02	08 12		08 42	
Coventry a														07 25								
Birmingham Intl. 68 a														07 37								
Birmingham New Street 68 a														07 48								08 18
Birmingham New Street d								06 50							07 50							
Langley Green d									06 49			07 17				07 40			08 15		08 45	
Rowley Regis d									06 52			07 20				07 43		08 08	08 19		08 48	
Old Hill d									06 56			07 24				07 47			08 22		08 52	
Cradley Heath d									06 59			07 27				07 50		08 13	08 25		08 55	
Lye d									07 02			07 30				07 53			08 28		08 58	
Stourbridge Junction d									07 06			07 34				07a57		08 19	08a32		09a02	
Hagley d									07 09			07 37						08 23				
Blakedown d									07 12			07 40						08 26				
Kidderminster d									07 17			07 45						08 31				
Hartlebury d									07 22													
University d								06 56							07 56							
Barnt Green d																						
Bromsgrove 69 d								07 12							08 12							
Droitwich Spa d								07 22	07 31			07 56			08 22			08 42				
Worcester Shrub Hill a									07 39			08 05										
Worcester Shrub Hill d						06 30	06 44			07 45		08 11					08 41					
Worcester Foregate Street a						06 32	06 47	07 30		07 48		08 13			08 30		08 44	08 51				
Worcester Foregate Street d						06 32	06 47	07 32		07 49		08 13			08 32		08 45					
Malvern Link d						06 42	06 56	07 42		07 58		08 22			08 42		08 54					
Great Malvern a						06 44	06 59	07 44		08 02		08 27			08 44		09 00					
Great Malvern d						06 45		07 45							08 45							
Colwall d						06 50		07 50							08 50							
Ledbury a						06 57		07 57							08 57							
Ledbury d						06 59		07 59							08 59							
Hereford a						07 19		08 15							09 14							

A until 6 October
B from 13 October

Table T071-F

Saturdays
26 May to 8 December

Stratford-upon-Avon, Marylebone and Leamington Spa - Birmingham - Stourbridge, Worcester and Hereford

	LM	LM	GW ◇1	LM	XC ◇1	LM	CH ◇	LM	CH ◇	CH	CH	LM	XC ◇1	XC ◇1	LM	GW	LM	LM	GW ◇1	LM	LM	CH ◇
Stratford-upon-Avon d		07 43							07 56			08 26								09 03		
Stratford-upon-Avon Parkway d		07 47							08 00			08 30								09 07		
Wilmcote d		07 50							08 03			08 33										
Wootton Wawen d		07x54										08x37										
Henley-in-Arden d		07 58										08 41										
Danzey d		08x02										08x45										
Wood End d		08x05										08x49										
The Lakes d		08x08										08x51										
Earlswood (West Midlands) d		08 11										08 54										
Wythall d		08 14										08 57										
Whitlocks End d		08 16				08 35						09 00						09 19			09 40	
Shirley d		08 19				08 38						09 03						09 22			09 42	
Yardley Wood d		08 22				08 40						09 05						09 24			09 45	
Hall Green d		08 25				08 43						09 09						09 27			09 48	
Spring Road d		08 27				08 45						09 11						09 29			09 51	
London Marylebone ⊖115 d							07 00															08 10
Banbury d					07 57		08 04				08 14		08 29	08 57								09 10
Leamington Spa a					08 13		08 22		08 28		08 33		08 47	09 13								09 27
Leamington Spa d				07 56	08 14		08 23			08 30	08 34		08 47	09 14								09 28
Warwick d				08 00						08 34	08 38											09 32
Warwick Parkway d				08 03			08 29				08 41											09 35
Hatton d				08 07						08a42	08 46											
Lapworth d				08 12							08 52											
Dorridge d				08 21			08 40	08 46			08 57				09 09					09 29		09 45
Widney Manor d				08 25				08 51							09 14					09 33		
Solihull d				08 29			08 47	08 54			09 03				09 17					09 37		09 51
Olton d				08 32				08 57							09 20					09 40		
Acocks Green d				08 35				09 00							09 23					09 43		
Tyseley d		08 31		08 37		08 48		09 02										09 32				
Small Heath d		08 33		08 40		08 51		09 05										09 35				
Bordesley d																						
Birmingham Moor Street d		08 38		08 45		08 55	09 00	09 09			09a15	09 18			09 29			09 39		09 49	09 58	10 02
Birmingham Snow Hill a		08 40		08 47		08 58	09 07	09 12				09 20			09 32			09 42		09 52	10 00	10 09
Birmingham Snow Hill d		08 43		08 53		09 03		09 13				09 23			09 33			09 43		09 53	10 03	
Jewellery Quarter d		08 45		08 55		09 05		09 15				09 25			09 35			09 45		09 55	10 05	
The Hawthorns d		08 49		08 59		09 09		09 19				09 29			09 39			09 49		09 59	10 09	
Smethwick Galton Bridge d		08 52		09 02		09 12		09 22				09 32			09 42			09 52		10 02	10 12	
Coventry a					08 25									09 25								
Birmingham Intl. 68 a					08 37									09 37								
Birmingham New Street 68 a					08 48								09 18	09 48								
Birmingham New Street d	08 50																09 50					
Langley Green d				09 05								09 35								10 05		
Rowley Regis d		08 58		09 08		09 18		09 28				09 38			09 48			09 58		10 08	10 18	
Old Hill d				09 12								09 42								10 12		
Cradley Heath d		09 03		09 15		09 23		09 33				09 45			09 53			10 03		10 15	10 23	
Lye d				09 18								09 48								10 18		
Stourbridge Junction d		09a09		09 22		09 29		09 39				09a52			09 59			10 09		10a22	10 29	
Hagley d				09 25		09 33									10 03			10 12			10 33	
Blakedown d				09 28		09 36									10 06						10 36	
Kidderminster d				09 33		09a40		09 47							10a10			10 18			10a40	
Hartlebury d								09 52														
University d	08 56																09 56					
Barnt Green d																						
Bromsgrove 69 d	09 12																10 12					
Droitwich Spa d	09 22			09 44				10 00									10 22	10 30				
Worcester Shrub Hill a				09 52														10 38				
Worcester Shrub Hill d			09 41													10 16			10 43			
Worcester Foregate Street a	09 30		09 44					10 09								10 18	10 30		10 45			
Worcester Foregate Street d	09 32		09 45													10 19	10 32		10 47			
Malvern Link d	09 42		09 54													10 28	10 42		10 56			
Great Malvern a	09 44		10 00													10 33	10 44		10 59			
Great Malvern d	09 45																10 45		11 08			
Colwall d	09 50																10 50		11 14			
Ledbury a	09 57																10 57		11 21			
Ledbury d	09 59																10 59		11 24			
Hereford a	10 14																11 14		11 41			

Table T071-F

Saturdays
26 May to 8 December

Stratford-upon-Avon, Marylebone and Leamington Spa - Birmingham - Stourbridge, Worcester and Hereford

		LM	LM	XC	LM	CH	XC	LM	LM	GW	LM	CH	LM	LM	CH	LM	XC	XC	LM	CH	XC	CH
				◇1		◇	◇1			◇1		◇					◇1 A	◇1 B		◇	◇1	
Stratford-upon-Avon	d		09 26								10 03					10 26						10 40
Stratford-upon-Avon Parkway	d		09 30								10 07					10 30						10 44
Wilmcote	d		09 33													10 33						10 47
Wootton Wawen	d		09x37													10x37						
Henley-in-Arden	d		09 41													10 41						
Danzey	d		09x45													10x45						
Wood End	d		09x49													10x49						
The Lakes	d		09x51													10x51						
Earlswood (West Midlands)	d		09 54													10 54						
Wythall	d		09 57													10 57						
Whitlocks End	d		10 00						10 19				10 40			11 00						
Shirley	d		10 03						10 22				10 42			11 03						
Yardley Wood	d		10 05						10 24				10 45			11 05						
Hall Green	d		10 09						10 27				10 48			11 09						
Spring Road	d		10 11						10 29				10 51			11 11						
London Marylebone 10 ⊖115	d					08 40						09 10								09 40		
Banbury	d			09 29		09 40	09 57					10 07					10 29	10 29		10 37	10 57	
Leamington Spa 5	a			09 46		09 57	10 13					10 24					10 46	10 46		10 54	11 13	11 16
	d			09 47		09 58	10 14					10 25			10 33		10 47	10 47		10 55	11 14	
Warwick	d					10 02									10 38					10 59		
Warwick Parkway	d					10 06						10 31								11 03		
Hatton	d														10 44							
Lapworth	d														10 50							
Dorridge	d	09 46			10 09	10 16					10 29			10 46	10 55				11 09	11 14		
Widney Manor	d	09 51			10 14						10 33			10 51					11 14			
Solihull	d	09 54			10 17	10 22					10 37	10 44		10 54	11 01				11 17	11 21		
Olton	d	09 57			10 20						10 40			10 57					11 20			
Acocks Green	d	10 00			10 23						10 43			11 00					11 23			
Tyseley	d	10 02							10 32					11 02								
Small Heath	d	10 05							10 35					11 05								
Bordesley	d																					
Birmingham Moor Street	d	10 09	10 18		10 29	10 34			10 39		10 49	10a58	10 59	11 09	11a15	11 18			11 29	11 34		
Birmingham Snow Hill ⇌	a	10 12	10 20		10 32	10 41			10 42		10 52		11 01	11 12		11 20			11 32	11 41		
	d	10 13	10 23		10 33				10 43		10 53		11 03	11 13		11 23			11 33			
Jewellery Quarter ⇌	d	10 15	10 25		10 35				10 45		10 55		11 05	11 15		11 25			11 35			
The Hawthorns ⇌	d	10 19	10 29		10 39				10 49		10 59		11 09	11 19		11 29			11 39			
Smethwick Galton Bridge 7	d	10 22	10 32		10 42				10 52		11 02		11 12	11 22		11 32			11 42			
Coventry	a						10 26														11 25	
Birmingham Intl. 68 ✈	a						10 37														11 37	
Birmingham New Street 12 68	a			10 18			10 48										11 18	11 18			11 48	
	d							10 50														
Langley Green	d		10 35								11 05					11 35						
Rowley Regis	d	10 28	10 38		10 48				10 58		11 08		11 18	11 28		11 38			11 48			
Old Hill	d		10 42								11 12					11 42						
Cradley Heath	d	10 33	10 45		10 53				11 03		11 15		11 23	11 33		11 45			11 53			
Lye	d		10 48								11 18					11 48						
Stourbridge Junction 2	d	10 39	10a52		10 59				11 09		11a22		11 29	11 39		11a52			11 59			
Hagley	d				11 03				11 12				11 33						12 03			
Blakedown	d				11 06								11 36						12 06			
Kidderminster	d	10 47			11a10				11 18				11a40	11 47					12a10			
Hartlebury	d	10 52												11 52								
University	d							10 56														
Barnt Green	d																					
Bromsgrove 69	d							11 12														
Droitwich Spa	d	11 00						11 22	11 30					12 00								
Worcester Shrub Hill 7	a								11 38													
	d									11 41												
Worcester Foregate Street 7	a	11 09						11 30		11 47				12 09								
	d	11 10						11 32														
Malvern Link	d	11 19						11 42														
Great Malvern	a	11 23						11 44														
	d							11 45														
Colwall	d							11 50														
Ledbury	a							11 57														
	d							11 59														
Hereford 7	a							12 14														

A until 21 July, from 13 October
B from 28 July until 6 October

Table T071-F

Saturdays
26 May to 8 December

Stratford-upon-Avon, Marylebone and Leamington Spa - Birmingham - Stourbridge, Worcester and Hereford

		GW	LM	LM	LM	CH	CH	XC	LM	GW	LM	LM	LM	CH	XC	LM	LM	GW	LM	CH	LM	LM	CH
		◇				◇		◇1		◇1				◇	◇1			◇1		◇			
Stratford-upon-Avon	d				11 03							11 26							12 03				
Stratford-upon-Avon Parkway	d				11 07							11 30							12 07				
Wilmcote	d											11 33											
Wootton Wawen	d											11x37											
Henley-in-Arden	d											11 41											
Danzey	d											11x45											
Wood End	d											11x49											
The Lakes	d											11x51											
Earlswood (West Midlands)	d											11 54											
Wythall	d											11 57											
Whitlocks End	d			11 19					11 40			12 00					12 19				12 40		
Shirley	d			11 22					11 42			12 03					12 22				12 42		
Yardley Wood	d			11 24					11 45			12 05					12 24				12 45		
Hall Green	d			11 27					11 48			12 09					12 27				12 48		
Spring Road	d			11 29					11 51			12 11					12 29				12 51		
London Marylebone 10 ⊖115	d					10 10								10 40						11 10			
Banbury	d					11 07		11 29						11 43	11 57					12 10			
Leamington Spa 5	a					11 24		11 46						12 00	12 13					12 26			
	d					11 25	11 32	11 47						12 01	12 14					12 27			12 33
Warwick	d						11 37							12 05									12 38
Warwick Parkway	d					11 32								12 09						12 34			
Hatton	d						11a44																12 44
Lapworth	d																						12 50
Dorridge	d				11 29						11 46		12 09	12 19					12 29			12 46	12 55
Widney Manor	d				11 33						11 51		12 14						12 33			12 51	
Solihull	d				11 37	11 45					11 54		12 17	12 25					12 37	12 46		12 54	13 01
Olton	d				11 40						11 57		12 20						12 40			12 57	
Acocks Green	d				11 43						12 00		12 23						12 43			13 00	
Tyseley	d			11 32							12 02						12 32					13 02	
Small Heath	d			11 35							12 05						12 35					13 05	
Bordesley	d																						
Birmingham Moor Street	d			11 39	11 49	11a59			11 59		12 09	12 18	12 29	12 34			12 39		12 49	12a59	12 59	13 09	13a14
Birmingham Snow Hill ⇌	a			11 42	11 52				12 01		12 12	12 20	12 32	12 41			12 42		12 52		13 01	13 12	
	d			11 43	11 53				12 03		12 13	12 23	12 33				12 43		12 53		13 03	13 13	
Jewellery Quarter ⇌	d			11 45	11 55				12 05		12 15	12 25	12 35				12 45		12 55		13 05	13 15	
The Hawthorns ⇌	d			11 49	11 59				12 09		12 19	12 29	12 39				12 49		12 59		13 09	13 19	
Smethwick Galton Bridge 7	d			11 52	12 02				12 12		12 22	12 32	12 42				12 52		13 02		13 12	13 22	
Coventry	a														12 26								
Birmingham Intl. 68 ✈	a														12 37								
Birmingham New Street 12 68	a							12 18							12 48								
	d		11 50													12 50							
Langley Green	d				12 05							12 35							13 05				
Rowley Regis	d			11 58	12 08				12 18		12 28	12 38	12 48				12 58		13 08		13 18	13 28	
Old Hill	d				12 12							12 42							13 12				
Cradley Heath	d			12 03	12 15				12 23		12 33	12 45	12 53				13 03		13 15		13 23	13 33	
Lye	d				12 18							12 48							13 18				
Stourbridge Junction 2	d			12 09	12a22				12 29		12 39	12a52	12 59				13 09		13a22		13 29	13 39	
Hagley	d			12 12					12 33				13 03				13 12				13 33		
Blakedown	d								12 36				13 06								13 36		
Kidderminster	d			12 18					12a40		12 47		13a10				13 18				13a40	13 47	
Hartlebury	d										12 52											13 52	
University	d		11 56													12 56							
Barnt Green	d																						
Bromsgrove 69	d		12 12													13 12							
Droitwich Spa	d		12 22	12 30							13 00					13 22	13 30					14 00	
Worcester Shrub Hill 7	a																13 38						
	d	12 14								12 48								13 44					
Worcester Foregate Street 7	a	12 17	12 30	12 39						12 50	13 09					13 30		13 46				14 09	
	d		12 32							12 52	13 10					13 32		13 48					
Malvern Link	d		12 42							13 01	13 19					13 42		13 57					
Great Malvern	a		12 44							13 04	13 23					13 44		14 03					
	d		12 45							13 08						13 45							
Colwall	d		12 50							13 14						13 50							
Ledbury	a		12 57							13 21						13 57							
	d		12 59							13 24						13 59							
Hereford 7	a		13 14							13 40						14 14							

Please note, Network Rail have stated that further updates to this timetable are possible during the validity period.

Table T071-F

Saturdays
26 May to 8 December

Stratford-upon-Avon, Marylebone and Leamington Spa - Birmingham - Stourbridge, Worcester and Hereford

		LM	XC ◇1 A	XC ◇1 B		LM	CH ◇	XC ◇1	CH	GW ◇	LM	LM	LM	CH ◇		CH	XC ◇1	LM	LM	LM	LM	CH ◇	XC ◇1	LM
Stratford-upon-Avon	d	12 26							12 42				13 03							13 26				
Stratford-upon-Avon Parkway	d	12 30							12 46				13 07							13 30				
Wilmcote	d	12 33							12 49											13 33				
Wootton Wawen	d	12x37																		13x37				
Henley-in-Arden	d	12 41																		13 41				
Danzey	d	12x45																		13x45				
Wood End	d	12x49																		13x49				
The Lakes	d	12x51																		13x51				
Earlswood (West Midlands)	d	12 54																		13 54				
Wythall	d	12 57																		13 57				
Whitlocks End	d	13 00										13 18						13 40		14 00				
Shirley	d	13 03										13 21						13 42		14 03				
Yardley Wood	d	13 05										13 23						13 45		14 05				
Hall Green	d	13 09										13 26						13 48		14 09				
Spring Road	d	13 11										13 28						13 51		14 11				
London Marylebone 10 ⊖115	d						11 40							12 10								12 40		
Banbury	d		12 29	12 29			12 37	12 57						13 07			13 29					13 37	13 57	
Leamington Spa 8	a		12 46	12 46			12 54	13 13	13 17					13 24			13 46					13 54	14 13	
	d		12 47	12 47			12 55	13 14						13 25		13 32	13 47					13 55	14 14	
Warwick	d						12 59									13 37						13 59		
Warwick Parkway	d						13 03							13 32								14 03		
Hatton	d															13a44								
Lapworth	d																							
Dorridge	d					13 09	13 15						13 29						13 46		14 09	14 13		
Widney Manor	d					13 14							13 33						13 51		14 14			
Solihull	d					13 17	13 21						13 37	13 45					13 54		14 17	14 21		
Olton	d					13 20							13 40						13 57		14 20			
Acocks Green	d					13 23							13 43						14 00		14 23			
Tyseley	d											13 31							14 02					
Small Heath	d											13 34							14 05					
Bordesley	d											13 36												
Birmingham Moor Street	d	13 18				13 29	13 34					13 39	13 49	13a59				13 59	14 09	14 18	14 29	14 34		
Birmingham Snow Hill ⇌	a	13 20				13 32	13 41					13 42	13 52					14 01	14 12	14 20	14 32	14 41		
	d	13 23				13 33						13 43	13 53					14 03	14 13	14 23	14 33			
Jewellery Quarter ⇌	d	13 25				13 35						13 45	13 55					14 05	14 15	14 25	14 35			
The Hawthorns ⇌	d	13 29				13 39						13 49	13 59					14 09	14 19	14 29	14 39			
Smethwick Galton Bridge 7	d	13 32				13 42						13 52	14 02					14 12	14 22	14 32	14 42			
Coventry	a							13 25															14 25	
Birmingham Intl. 68 ✈	a							13 37															14 37	
Birmingham New Street 12 68	a		13 18	13 18				13 48									14 18						14 48	
	d										13 50													14 50
Langley Green	d	13 35											14 05							14 35				
Rowley Regis	d	13 38				13 48						13 58	14 08					14 18	14 28	14 38	14 48			
Old Hill	d	13 42											14 12							14 42				
Cradley Heath	d	13 45				13 53						14 03	14 15					14 23	14 33	14 45	14 53			
Lye	d	13 48											14 18							14 48				
Stourbridge Junction 4	d	13a52				13 59						14 09	14a22					14 29	14 39	14a52	14 59			
Hagley	d					14 03						14 12						14 33			15 03			
Blakedown	d					14 06												14 36			15 06			
Kidderminster	d					14a10						14 18						14a40	14 47		15a10			
Hartlebury	d																		14 52					
University	d										13 56													14 56
Barnt Green	d																							
Bromsgrove 69	d										14 12													15 12
Droitwich Spa	d										14 22	14 30							15 00					15 22
Worcester Shrub Hill 7	a											14 39												
	d									14 15		14 44												
Worcester Foregate Street 7	a									14 17	14 30	14 46							15 09					15 30
	d									14 18	14 32	14 46												15 32
Malvern Link	d									14 27	14 42	14 55												15 42
Great Malvern	a									14 32	14 44	14 59												15 44
	d										14 45													15 45
Colwall	d										14 50													15 50
Ledbury	a										14 57													15 57
	d										14 59													15 59
Hereford 7	a										15 14													16 14

A until 21 July, from 13 October
B from 28 July until 6 October

Table T071-F

Saturdays
26 May to 8 December

Stratford-upon-Avon, Marylebone and Leamington Spa - Birmingham - Stourbridge, Worcester and Hereford

		LM	GW ◇1	LM	CH ◇	LM	LM	CH	LM	XC ◇1		LM	CH ◇	XC ◇1	CH	GW ◇	LM	LM	LM	CH ◇		CH	XC ◇1	LM	GW ◇1
Stratford-upon-Avon	d			14 03					14 26						14 42				15 03						
Stratford-upon-Avon Parkway	d			14 07					14 30						14 46				15 07						
Wilmcote	d								14 33						14 49										
Wootton Wawen	d								14x37																
Henley-in-Arden	d								14 41																
Danzey	d								14x45																
Wood End	d								14x49																
The Lakes	d								14x51																
Earlswood (West Midlands)	d								14 54																
Wythall	d								14 57																
Whitlocks End	d	14 19				14 40			15 00									15 19						15 40	
Shirley	d	14 22				14 42			15 03									15 22						15 42	
Yardley Wood	d	14 24				14 45			15 05									15 24						15 45	
Hall Green	d	14 27				14 48			15 09									15 27						15 48	
Spring Road	d	14 29				14 51			15 11									15 29						15 51	
London Marylebone 10 ⊖115	d				13 10								13 40							14 10					
Banbury	d				14 09					14 29			14 37	14 57						15 07			15 29		
Leamington Spa 8	a				14 25					14 46			14 54	15 13	15 17					15 24			15 46		
	d				14 27			14 33		14 47			14 55	15 14						15 25		15 32	15 47		
Warwick	d							14 38					14 59									15 37			
Warwick Parkway	d				14 33								15 03							15 32					
Hatton	d							14 44														15a44			
Lapworth	d							14 50																	
Dorridge	d			14 29			14 46	14 55				15 09	15 13						15 29						
Widney Manor	d			14 33			14 51					15 14							15 33						
Solihull	d			14 37	14 45		14 54	15 01				15 17	15 21						15 37	15 45					
Olton	d			14 40			14 57					15 20							15 40						
Acocks Green	d			14 43			15 00					15 23							15 43						
Tyseley	d	14 32					15 02											15 32							
Small Heath	d	14 35					15 05											15 35							
Bordesley	d																								
Birmingham Moor Street	d	14 39		14 49	14a59	14 59	15 09	15a14	15 18			15 29	15 34					15 39	15 49	15a59				15 59	
Birmingham Snow Hill ⇌	a	14 42		14 52		15 01	15 12		15 20			15 32	15 41					15 42	15 52					16 01	
	d	14 43		14 53		15 03	15 13		15 23			15 33						15 43	15 53					16 03	
Jewellery Quarter ⇌	d	14 45		14 55		15 05	15 15		15 25			15 35						15 45	15 55					16 05	
The Hawthorns ⇌	d	14 49		14 59		15 09	15 19		15 29			15 39						15 49	15 59					16 09	
Smethwick Galton Bridge 7	d	14 52		15 02		15 12	15 22		15 32			15 42						15 52	16 02					16 12	
Coventry	a													15 25											
Birmingham Intl. 68 ✈	a													15 37											
Birmingham New Street 12 68	a									15 18				15 48									16 18		
	d																15 50								
Langley Green	d			15 05					15 35										16 05						
Rowley Regis	d	14 58		15 08		15 18	15 28		15 38			15 48						15 58	16 08					16 18	
Old Hill	d			15 12					15 42										16 12						
Cradley Heath	d	15 03		15 15		15 23	15 33		15 45			15 53						16 03	16 15					16 23	
Lye	d			15 18					15 48										16 18						
Stourbridge Junction 4	d	15 09		15a22		15 29	15 39		15a52			15 59						16 09	16a22					16 29	
Hagley	d	15 12				15 33						16 03						16 12						16 33	
Blakedown	d					15 36						16 06												16 36	
Kidderminster	d	15 18				15a40	15 47					16a10						16 18						16a40	
Hartlebury	d						15 52																		
University	d																15 56								
Barnt Green	d																								
Bromsgrove 69	d																16 12								
Droitwich Spa	d	15 30					16 00										16 22	16 30							
Worcester Shrub Hill 7	a	15 38																							
	d		15 45													16 14									16 42
Worcester Foregate Street 7	a		15 48				16 09									16 17	16 30	16 39							16 44
	d		15 49													16 17	16 32								16 46
Malvern Link	d		15 58													16 26	16 42								16 55
Great Malvern	a		16 04													16 32	16 44								17 00
	d																16 45								
Colwall	d																16 50								
Ledbury	a																16 57								
	d																16 59								
Hereford 7	a																17 14								

Table T071-F

Saturdays

26 May to 8 December

Stratford-upon-Avon, Marylebone and Leamington Spa - Birmingham - Stourbridge, Worcester and Hereford

Station		LM	LM	LM	LM	CH ◇		XC ◇1	LM	LM	LM	CH ◇	LM	GW ◇1	LM	LM		GW	CH	LM	XC ◇1	LM	LM	CH ◇	XC ◇1
Stratford-upon-Avon	d			15 26							16 03									16 26					
Stratford-upon-Avon Parkway	d			15 30							16 07									16 30					
Wilmcote	d			15 33																16 33					
Wootton Wawen	d			15x37																16x37					
Henley-in-Arden	d			15 41																16 41					
Danzey	d			15x45																16x45					
Wood End	d			15x49																16x49					
The Lakes	d			15x51																16x51					
Earlswood (West Midlands)	d			15 54																16 54					
Wythall	d			15 57																16 57					
Whitlocks End	d			16 00						16 19			16 40							17 00					
Shirley	d			16 03						16 22			16 42							17 03					
Yardley Wood	d			16 05						16 24			16 45							17 05					
Hall Green	d			16 09						16 27			16 48							17 09					
Spring Road	d			16 11						16 29			16 51							17 11					
London Marylebone 10 ⊖115	d					14 40						15 10												15 40	
Banbury	d					15 37		15 57				16 09									16 29			16 37	16 57
Leamington Spa 8	a					15 54		16 13				16 25									16 46			16 54	17 13
	d					15 55		16 14				16 26							16 33		16 47			16 55	17 14
Warwick	d					15 59													16 38					16 59	
Warwick Parkway	d					16 03						16 33												17 03	
Hatton	d																		16 44						
Lapworth	d																		16 50						
Dorridge	d		15 46		16 09	16 13					16 29					16 46			16 55				17 09	17 13	
Widney Manor	d		15 51		16 14						16 33					16 51							17 14		
Solihull	d		15 54		16 17	16 21					16 37	16 45				16 54			17 01				17 17	17 21	
Olton	d		15 57		16 20						16 40					16 57							17 20		
Acocks Green	d		16 00		16 23						16 43					17 00							17 23		
Tyseley	d		16 02							16 32						17 02									
Small Heath	d		16 05							16 35						17 05									
Bordesley	d																								
Birmingham Moor Street	d		16 09	16 18	16 29	16 34				16 39	16 49	16a59	16 59			17 09			17a15	17 18			17 29	17 34	
Birmingham Snow Hill	a		16 12	16 20	16 32	16 41				16 42	16 52		17 01			17 12				17 20			17 32	17 41	
	d		16 13	16 23	16 33					16 43	16 53		17 03			17 13				17 23			17 33		
Jewellery Quarter	d		16 15	16 25	16 35					16 45	16 55		17 05			17 15				17 25			17 35		
The Hawthorns	d		16 19	16 29	16 39					16 49	16 59		17 09			17 19				17 29			17 39		
Smethwick Galton Bridge 7	d		16 22	16 32	16 42					16 52	17 02		17 12			17 22				17 32			17 42		
Coventry	a							16 25																	17 25
Birmingham Intl. 68 ✈	a							16 37																	17 37
Birmingham New Street 12 68	a							16 48													17 18				17 48
	d	16 20							16 50						17 20							17 50			
Langley Green	d			16 35							17 05									17 35					
Rowley Regis	d		16 28	16 38	16 48					16 58	17 08		17 18			17 28				17 38			17 48		
Old Hill	d			16 42							17 12									17 42					
Cradley Heath	d		16 33	16 45	16 53					17 03	17 15		17 23			17 33				17 45			17 53		
Lye	d			16 48							17 18									17 48					
Stourbridge Junction 2	d		16 39	16a52	16 59					17 09	17a22		17 29			17 41				17a52			17 59		
Hagley	d				17 03					17 12			17 33										18 03		
Blakedown	d				17 06								17 36										18 06		
Kidderminster	d		16 47		17a10					17 18			17a40			17 51							18 12		
Hartlebury	d		16 52													17 56							18 17		
University	d								16 56													17 56			
Barnt Green	d																								
Bromsgrove 69	d	16 42							17 12						17 42							18 12			
Droitwich Spa	d	16 52	17 00						17 22	17 30					17 52	18 04						18 22	18 26		
Worcester Shrub Hill 7	a	16 59													17 59	18 12						18 29	18 35		
	d													17 42				18 20				18 32			
Worcester Foregate Street 7	a		17 09						17 31	17 39				17 44				18 22				18 34			
	d		17 10						17 32					17 47				18 23				18 35			
Malvern Link	d		17 19						17 42					17 56				18 32				18 45			
Great Malvern	a		17 23						17 45					18 01				18 36				18 47			
	d								17 45													18 48			
Colwall	d								17 50													18 53			
Ledbury	a								17 57													19 00			
	d								17 59													19 01			
Hereford 7	a								18 14													19 16			

Table T071-F

Saturdays

26 May to 8 December

Stratford-upon-Avon, Marylebone and Leamington Spa - Birmingham - Stourbridge, Worcester and Hereford

Station		CH		LM	LM	CH ◇	CH	XC ◇1	LM	GW ◇1	LM	LM		CH ◇	LM	XC ◇1	LM	GW ◇1	LM	CH ◇	LM	CH		XC ◇1	LM
Stratford-upon-Avon	d	16 41			17 03						17 26				17 54						18 13				
Stratford-upon-Avon Parkway	d	16 45			17 07						17 30				17 58						18 17				
Wilmcote	d	16 48									17 33				18 01						18 20				
Wootton Wawen	d										17x37										18x24				
Henley-in-Arden	d										17 41				18 08						18 28				
Danzey	d										17x45										18x32				
Wood End	d										17x49										18x36				
The Lakes	d										17x51										18x38				
Earlswood (West Midlands)	d										17 54										18 42				
Wythall	d										17 57										18 44				
Whitlocks End	d			17 19							18 00				18 19						18 47				
Shirley	d			17 22							18 03				18 22						18 50				
Yardley Wood	d			17 24							18 05				18 24						18 53				
Hall Green	d			17 27							18 09				18 27						18 56				
Spring Road	d			17 29							18 11				18 29						18 58				
London Marylebone 10 ⊖115	d					16 10								16 40						17 10					
Banbury	d					17 07		17 29						17 37		17 57				18 09				18 29	
Leamington Spa 8	a	17 17				17 24		17 46						17 54		18 13				18 25				18 46	
	d					17 25	17 32	17 47						17 55		18 14				18 26		18 33		18 47	
Warwick	d						17 37							17 59								18 38			
Warwick Parkway	d					17 32								18 03						18 33					
Hatton	d						17a44															18 44			
Lapworth	d																					18 50			
Dorridge	d				17 29				17 46			18 09		18 13					18 29			18 55			
Widney Manor	d				17 33				17 51			18 14							18 33						
Solihull	d				17 37	17 45			17 54			18 17		18 21					18 37	18 48		19 02			
Olton	d				17 40				17 57			18 20							18 40						
Acocks Green	d				17 43				18 00			18 23							18 43						
Tyseley	d			17 32					18 02						18 32						19 02				
Small Heath	d			17 35					18 05						18 35						19 04				
Bordesley	d																								
Birmingham Moor Street	d			17 39	17 49	17a59			18 09		18 19	18 29		18 34	18 39				18 49	19 00	19 09	19a13			
Birmingham Snow Hill	a			17 42	17 52				18 12		18 21	18 32		18 41	18 43				18 52	19 02	19 11				
	d			17 43	17 53				18 13		18 23	18 33							18 53	19 05					
Jewellery Quarter	d			17 45	17 55				18 15		18 25	18 36							18 56						
The Hawthorns	d			17 49	17 59				18 19		18 29	18 40							19 00						
Smethwick Galton Bridge 7	d			17 52	18 02				18 22		18 32	18 43							19 03						
Coventry	a															18 25									
Birmingham Intl. 68 ✈	a															18 37									
Birmingham New Street 12 68	a							18 18								18 48								19 18	
	d																18 50								19 20
Langley Green	d				18 05				18 25			18 46							19 06						
Rowley Regis	d			17 58	18 08				18 28		18 38	18 49							19 09	19 18					
Old Hill	d				18 12				18 32			18 52							19 12						
Cradley Heath	d			18 03	18 15				18 35		18 43	18 56							19 16						
Lye	d				18 18				18 38			18 59							19 19						
Stourbridge Junction 2	d			18 09	18a22				18a42		18 49	19 03							19 23	19 30					
Hagley	d			18 13							18 52	19 06							19 26						
Blakedown	d			18 16							18 55	19 09							19 29						
Kidderminster	d			18 22							19 00	19a14							19 34	19a44					
Hartlebury	d			18 27							19 05														
University	d																18 56								19 26
Barnt Green	d																								
Bromsgrove 69	d																19 12								19 42
Droitwich Spa	d			18 37							19 14						19 22		19 46						19 52
Worcester Shrub Hill 7	a																19 29		19 54						
	d									18 54							19 35	19 42							
Worcester Foregate Street 7	a			18 46						18 56	19 23						19 37	19 44							20 00
	d									18 58	19 23						19 38								20 01
Malvern Link	d									19 07	19 33						19 48								20 11
Great Malvern	a									19 10	19 37						19 50								20 13
	d									19 11															20 25
Colwall	d									19 17															20 31
Ledbury	a									19 24															20 38
	d									19 29															20 39
Hereford 7	a									19 45															20 59

Please note, Network Rail have stated that further updates to this timetable are possible during the validity period.

Saturdays
26 May to 8 December

Stratford-upon-Avon, Marylebone and Leamington Spa - Birmingham - Stourbridge, Worcester and Hereford

		GW	LM	GW	CH	XC	CH	LM	LM	CH	CH	LM	XC	CH	XC	LM	LM	GW	CH	CH	LM	XC	CH
				◇1	◇	◇1				◇			◇1	◇	◇1			◇1	◇			◇1	◇
Stratford-upon-Avon	d						18 41	18 48				19 26									20 26		
Stratford-upon-Avon Parkway	d						18 45	18 52				19 30									20 30		
Wilmcote	d						18 48	18 55				19 33									20 33		
Wootton Wawen	d							18x59				19x37									20x37		
Henley-in-Arden	d							19 03				19 41									20 41		
Danzey	d							19x07				19x45									20x45		
Wood End	d							19x11				19x49									20x49		
The Lakes	d							19x13				19x51									20x51		
Earlswood (West Midlands)	d							19 17				19 54									20 54		
Wythall	d							19 19				19 57									20 57		
Whitlocks End	d							19 22				20 00									21 00		
Shirley	d							19 25				20 03									21 03		
Yardley Wood	d							19 28				20 05									21 05		
Hall Green	d							19 31				20 09									21 09		
Spring Road	d							19 33				20 11									21 11		
London Marylebone 10 ⊖115	d				17 40					18 10				18 40					19 10				19 40
Banbury	d				18 37	18 57				19 07			19 29	19 37	19 57				20 09			20 30	20 37
Leamington Spa 8	a				18 54	19 13	19 17			19 24			19 46	19 54	20 13				20 26			20 47	20 54
	d				18 55	19 14				19 26	19 32		19 47	19 55	20 14				20 27	20 33		20 48	20 55
Warwick	d				18 59						19 37			19 59						20 38			20 59
Warwick Parkway	d				19 03					19 33				20 03					20 33				21 03
Hatton	d										19a44									20 44			
Lapworth	d																			20 50			
Dorridge	d		19 00		19 13				19 29					20 13			20 29			20 55			21 13
Widney Manor	d		19 05						19 33								20 33						
Solihull	d		19 08		19 19				19 37	19 47				20 19			20 37		20 46	21 00			21 19
Olton	d		19 11						19 40								20 40						
Acocks Green	d		19 14						19 43								20 43						
Tyseley	d		19 17					19 37	19 45								20 45						
Small Heath	d		19 19					19 39	19 48								20 48						
Bordesley	d																						
Birmingham Moor Street	d		19 24		19 28			19 44	19 53	20 00		20 18		20 28			20 52		21a00	21a10	21 18		21 28
Birmingham Snow Hill ⇌	a		19 26		19 35			19 46	19 55	20 07		20 20		20 35			20 55				21 20		21 30
	d		19 28						19 56			20 23					20 56				21 23		21 33
Jewellery Quarter ⇌	d		19 30						19 58			20 25					20 58				21 25		
The Hawthorns ⇌	d		19 34						20 02			20 29					21 02				21 29		
Smethwick Galton Bridge 7	d		19 37						20 05			20 32					21 05				21 32		
Coventry	a					19 25									20 26								
Birmingham Intl. 68 ✈	a					19 37									20 37								
Birmingham New Street 12 68	a					19 48							20 18		20 48							21 16	
	d															21 00							
Langley Green	d		19 40						20 08			20 35					21 08				21 35		
Rowley Regis	d		19 43						20 11			20 38					21 11				21 38		21 45
Old Hill	d		19 47						20 15			20 42					21 15				21 42		
Cradley Heath	d		19 50						20 18			20 45					21 18				21 45		21 51
Lye	d		19 53						20 21			20 48					21 21				21 48		
Stourbridge Junction 2	d		19 57						20 25			20a52					21 25				21a52		21 59
Hagley	d		20 01						20 28								21 28						
Blakedown	d		20 04						20 31								21 31						
Kidderminster	d		20 09						20 36								21 36						22a12
Hartlebury	d		20 14																				
University	d															21 06							
Barnt Green	d																						
Bromsgrove 69	d															21 20							
Droitwich Spa	d		20 22						20 48							21 30	21 48						
Worcester Shrub Hill 7	a		20 31						20 56							21 38	21 56						
	d	20 20		20 46					20 59							21 47		22 06					
Worcester Foregate Street 7	a	20 22		20 49					21 01							21 49		22 08					
	d	20 23		20 50					21 02							21 50		22 09					
Malvern Link	d	20 32		20 59					21 11							21 59		22 18					
Great Malvern	a	20 35		21 02					21 15							22 01		22 24					
	d			21 03												22 02							
Colwall	d			21 09												22 07							
Ledbury	a			21 16												22 14							
	d			21 19												22 15							
Hereford 7	a			21 35												22 30							

Saturdays
26 May to 8 December

Stratford-upon-Avon, Marylebone and Leamington Spa - Birmingham - Stourbridge, Worcester and Hereford

		XC	LM	CH	LM	CH	CH	LM	XC	CH	LM	XC	CH	CH	XC	LM	CH	LM
		◇1				◇			◇1	◇		◇1	◇		◇1		◇	
Stratford-upon-Avon	d			20 42				21 26						22 15		22 33		23 30
Stratford-upon-Avon Parkway	d			20 46				21 30								22 37		23 34
Wilmcote	d			20 49				21 33								22 40		
Wootton Wawen	d																	
Henley-in-Arden	d							21 40								22 47		
Danzey	d																	
Wood End	d							21x46										
The Lakes	d							21x48										
Earlswood (West Midlands)	d							21 51										
Wythall	d							21 54								22 56		
Whitlocks End	d							21 57								22 59		
Shirley	d							22 00								23 02		
Yardley Wood	d							22 02								23 04		
Hall Green	d							22 06								23 07		
Spring Road	d							22 08								23 09		
London Marylebone 10 ⊖115	d					20 10				20 40			21 10				22 10	
Banbury	d	20 57				21 07			21 29	21 37		21 57	22 10		22 29		23 10	
Leamington Spa 8	a	21 13		21 17		21 24			21 46	21 54		22 13	22 27	22 40	22 46		23 27	
	d	21 14				21 25	21 32		21 49	21 55		22 14	22 28		22 47		23 28	
Warwick	d						21 37			21 59			22 32				23 32	
Warwick Parkway	d					21 32				22 03			22 36				23 37	
Hatton	d						21a44						22 41					
Lapworth	d												22 46					
Dorridge	d				21 29					22 13	22 33		22 51				23 47	
Widney Manor	d				21 33						22 38		22 55					
Solihull	d				21 37	21 45				22 19	22 41		22 58				23 53	
Olton	d				21 40						22 44							
Acocks Green	d				21 43						22 47							
Tyseley	d				21 45			22 11			22 50					23 12		
Small Heath	d				21 48			22 13			22 52					23 15		
Bordesley	d																	
Birmingham Moor Street	d				21 52	22a00		22 18		22 28	22 57		23 07			23 19	00a07	00 08
Birmingham Snow Hill ⇌	a				21 55			22 20		22 35	22 59		23 14			23 22		00 10
	d				21 56			22 23			23 01					23 23		
Jewellery Quarter ⇌	d				21 58			22 25			23 03					23 25		
The Hawthorns ⇌	d				22 02			22 29			23 07					23 29		
Smethwick Galton Bridge 7	d				22 05			22 32			23 10					23 32		
Coventry	a	21 26							22 00			22 25						
Birmingham Intl. 68 ✈	a	21 37							22 10			22 36						
Birmingham New Street 12 68	a	21 48							22 21			22 47			23 17			
	d		22 09															
Langley Green	d				22 08			22 35			23 13					23 35		
Rowley Regis	d				22 11			22 38			23 17					23 38		
Old Hill	d				22 15			22 42			23 20					23 42		
Cradley Heath	d				22 18			22 45			23 23					23 45		
Lye	d				22 21			22 48			23 26					23 48		
Stourbridge Junction 2	d				22 25			22a52			23 30					23a52		
Hagley	d				22 28						23 34							
Blakedown	d				22 31						23 37							
Kidderminster	d				22 36						23 42							
Hartlebury	d				22 41						23 47							
University	d		22 15															
Barnt Green	d																	
Bromsgrove 69	d		22 30															
Droitwich Spa	d		22 40		22 50						23 54							
Worcester Shrub Hill 7	a		22 47		22 57						00 05							
	d				23 02													
Worcester Foregate Street 7	a				23 04													
	d				23 05													
Malvern Link	d				23 14													
Great Malvern	a				23 16													
	d																	
Colwall	d																	
Ledbury	a																	
	d																	
Hereford 7	a																	

Table T071-F

Sundays
20 May to 2 December

Stratford-upon-Avon, Marylebone and Leamington Spa - Birmingham - Stourbridge, Worcester and Hereford

		LM	LM	LM	LM	LM	GW	LM	GW	LM	CH	LM	CH	XC	CH	CH	GW	GW	LM	CH	LM	XC	LM
		A					◇■		◇■		◇		◇	◇■	◇		◇■ B	◇■ C		◇		◇■	
Stratford-upon-Avon	d									09 29			09 38						10 29				
Stratford-upon-Avon Parkway	d									09 33			09 41						10 33				
Wilmcote	d									09 36			09 44						10 36				
Wootton Wawen	d																						
Henley-in-Arden	d									09 43									10 43				
Danzey	d																						
Wood End	d																						
The Lakes	d									09x49									10x49				
Earlswood (West Midlands)	d																						
Wythall	d									09 53									10 53				
Whitlocks End	d					09 06				09 56									10 56				
Shirley	d					09 09				09 59									10 59				
Yardley Wood	d					09 11				10 01									11 01				
Hall Green	d					09 15				10 05									11 05				
Spring Road	d					09 17				10 07									11 07				
London Marylebone ⊖115	d										08 15				09 10					09 40			
Banbury	d										09 29			09 55	10 07					10 37		10 55	
Leamington Spa	a										09 46		10 05	10 11	10 24					10 54		11 11	
	d										09 47			10 12	10 25	10 32				10 55		11 12	
Warwick	d										09 51					10 38				10 59			
Warwick Parkway	d										09 55				10 32					11 03			
Hatton	d										10 00					10 44							
Lapworth	d										10 06					10 50							
Dorridge	d		08 57								10 11	10 27				10 55				11 13	11 27		
Widney Manor	d		09 02									10 32									11 32		
Solihull	d		09 05								10 16	10 35			10 45	11 01				11 19	11 35		
Olton	d		09 08									10 38									11 38		
Acocks Green	d		09 11									10 41									11 41		
Tyseley	d									10 10									11 10				
Small Heath	d																						
Bordesley	d																						
Birmingham Moor Street	d	00 08	09 18			09 24				10 15	10 25	10 48			10 54	11a13			11 15	11 28	11 48		
Birmingham Snow Hill ⇌	a	00 10	09 20			09 26				10 17	10 32	10 50			11 01				11 17	11 35	11 50		
	d					09 28				10 22		10 52							11 22		11 52		
Jewellery Quarter ⇌	d					09 30				10 24		10 54							11 24		11 54		
The Hawthorns ⇌	d					09 34				10 28		10 58							11 28		11 58		
Smethwick Galton Bridge	d					09 37				10 31		11 01							11 31		12 01		
Coventry	a													10 25								11 25	
Birmingham Intl. 68 ✈	a													10 38								11 39	
Birmingham New Street 68	a													10 50								11 51	
	d							10 00															12 00
Langley Green	d											11 04									12 04		
Rowley Regis	d					09 43				10 37		11 07							11 37		12 07		
Old Hill	d											11 10									12 10		
Cradley Heath	d					09 48				10 42		11 14							11 42		12 14		
Lye	d											11 17									12 17		
Stourbridge Junction	d					09 54				10 47		11a21							11 47		12a21		
Hagley	d					09 57				10 51									11 51				
Blakedown	d									10 54									11 54				
Kidderminster	d					10 03				10 59									11 59				
Hartlebury	d																						
University	d							10 06															12 06
Barnt Green	d																						
Bromsgrove 69	d							10 20															12 20
Droitwich Spa	d					10 15		10 30		11 11									12 11				12 32
Worcester Shrub Hill	a					10 22		10 38		11 19									12 19				12 40
	d			09 06	09 43	10 30	10 34	10 51	11 01	11 33							12 07	12 09					12 47
Worcester Foregate Street	a			09 08	09 46	10 32	10 37	10 53	11 03	11 35							12 10	12 12					12 49
	d			09 09	09 46	10 32	10 39	10 54	11 05	11 35							12 10	12 13					12 50
Malvern Link	d			09 18		10 41	10 51	11 03	11 14	11 44							12 19	12 22					12 59
Great Malvern	a			09 20	09 58	10 45	10 54	11 05	11 17	11 48							12 25	12 25					13 01
	d			09 21				11 06	11 19														13 02
Colwall	d			09 26				11 11	11 25														13 07
Ledbury	a			09 32				11 18	11 32														13 14
	d			09 33				11 18	11 34														13 15
Hereford	a			09 51				11 34	11 51														13 32

A not 20 May
B until 9 September
C from 16 September

Table T071-F

Sundays
20 May to 2 December

Stratford-upon-Avon, Marylebone and Leamington Spa - Birmingham - Stourbridge, Worcester and Hereford

		CH	CH	GW	GW	LM	CH	LM	XC	CH	CH	CH	LM	CH	LM	CH	XC	CH	CH	LM	LM	XC	XC
		◇	◇	◇■ A	◇■ B		◇		◇■	◇		C		◇		D	◇■	◇				◇■ E	◇■ F
Stratford-upon-Avon	d					11 29						12 19	12 29			12 19							
Stratford-upon-Avon Parkway	d					11 33						12 23	12 33			12 23							
Wilmcote	d					11 36						12 26	12 36			12 26							
Wootton Wawen	d																						
Henley-in-Arden	d					11 43							12 43										
Danzey	d																						
Wood End	d																						
The Lakes	d					11x49							12x49										
Earlswood (West Midlands)	d																						
Wythall	d					11 53							12 53										
Whitlocks End	d					11 56							12 56										
Shirley	d					11 59							12 59										
Yardley Wood	d					12 01							13 01										
Hall Green	d					12 05							13 05										
Spring Road	d					12 07							13 07										
London Marylebone ⊖115	d	10 10	09 43				10 40			11 10				11 40				12 10					
Banbury	d	11 07	11 11				11 37		11 55	12 07				12 37			12 55	13 07				13 35	13 35
Leamington Spa	a	11 24	11 30				11 54		12 11	12 24		12 54		12 54		12 57	13 11	13 24				13 51	13 51
	d	11 25	11 32				11 55		12 12	12 25	12 32			12 55			13 12	13 25	13 32			13 52	13 52
Warwick	d		11 38				11 59				12 38			12 59					13 37				
Warwick Parkway	d	11 32					12 03			12 32				13 03				13 32					
Hatton	d		11a45								12 44								13a44				
Lapworth	d										12 50												
Dorridge	d						12 13	12 27			12 55			13 14	13 27								
Widney Manor	d							12 32							13 32								
Solihull	d	11 45					12 19	12 35		12 45	13 01			13 20	13 35			13 45					
Olton	d							12 38							13 38								
Acocks Green	d							12 41							13 41								
Tyseley	d					12 10							13 10										
Small Heath	d																						
Bordesley	d																						
Birmingham Moor Street	d	11a59				12 15	12 28	12 48		12a59	13a13		13 15	13 30	13 48			13a59					
Birmingham Snow Hill ⇌	a					12 17	12 35	12 50					13 17	13 37	13 50								
	d					12 22		12 52					13 22		13 52								
Jewellery Quarter ⇌	d					12 24		12 54					13 24		13 54								
The Hawthorns ⇌	d					12 28		12 58					13 28		13 58								
Smethwick Galton Bridge	d					12 31		13 01					13 31		14 01								
Coventry	a								12 25								13 23						
Birmingham Intl. 68 ✈	a								12 38								13 36						
Birmingham New Street 68	a								12 50								13 48					14 18	14 19
	d																				14 00		
Langley Green	d							13 04							14 04								
Rowley Regis	d					12 37		13 07					13 37		14 07								
Old Hill	d							13 10							14 10								
Cradley Heath	d					12 42		13 14					13 42		14 14								
Lye	d							13 17							14 17								
Stourbridge Junction	d					12 47		13a21					13 47		14a21								
Hagley	d					12 51							13 51										
Blakedown	d					12 54																	
Kidderminster	d					12 59							13 57										
Hartlebury	d																						
University	d																				14 06		
Barnt Green	d																						
Bromsgrove 69	d																				14 20		
Droitwich Spa	d					13 11							14 08								14 30		
Worcester Shrub Hill	a																				14 37		
	d			13 05	13 11															14 31	14 52		
Worcester Foregate Street	a			13 08	13 14	13 20							14 17							14 33	14 54		
	d			13 09	13 15															14 34	14 55		
Malvern Link	d			13 18	13 24															14 43	15 04		
Great Malvern	a			13 21	13 27															14 45	15 06		
	d			13 26	13 29																15 07		
Colwall	d			13 33	13 35																15 12		
Ledbury	a			13 41	13 42																15 19		
	d			13 51	13 51																15 19		
Hereford	a			14 07	14 07																15 35		

A until 9 September
B from 16 September
C until 30 September
D from 7 October
E from 22 July until 7 October
F until 15 July, from 14 October

Please note, Network Rail have stated that further updates to this timetable are possible during the validity period.

Table T071-F

Sundays
20 May to 2 December

Stratford-upon-Avon, Marylebone and Leamington Spa - Birmingham - Stourbridge, Worcester and Hereford

		GW ◇1 A	GW ◇1 B	LM	CH ◇	LM	XC ◇1	CH ◇	CH	XC ◇1	GW ◇1	LM	CH ◇	LM	XC ◇1	LM	CH	CH ◇	CH	XC ◇1	GW ◇1 A	GW ◇1 B
Stratford-upon-Avon	d			13 29								14 29					14 46					
Stratford-upon-Avon Parkway	d			13 33								14 33					14 50					
Wilmcote	d			13 36								14 36					14 53					
Wootton Wawen	d																					
Henley-in-Arden	d			13 43								14 43										
Danzey	d																					
Wood End	d																					
The Lakes	d			13x49								14x49										
Earlswood (West Midlands)	d																					
Wythall	d			13 53								14 53										
Whitlocks End	d			13 56								14 56										
Shirley	d			13 59								14 59										
Yardley Wood	d			14 01								15 01										
Hall Green	d			14 05								15 05										
Spring Road	d			14 07								15 07										
London Marylebone 10 ⊖115	d				12 40			13 10					13 40					14 10				
Banbury	d				13 39		13 55	14 07		14 24			14 39		14 55			15 07		15 24		
Leamington Spa 8	a				13 56		14 11	14 24		14 40			14 56		15 11		15 17	15 24		15 40		
	d				13 57		14 12	14 25	14 32	14 41			14 57		15 12			15 25	15 32	15 41		
Warwick	d				14 01				14 38				15 01						15 37			
Warwick Parkway	d				14 05			14 32					15 05					15 32				
Hatton	d								14 44										15a44			
Lapworth	d								14 50													
Dorridge	d				14 15	14 27			14 55				15 15	15 27								
Widney Manor	d					14 32								15 32								
Solihull	d				14 21	14 35		14 45	15 01				15 21	15 35				15 45				
Olton	d					14 38								15 38								
Acocks Green	d					14 41								15 41								
Tyseley	d			14 10								15 10										
Small Heath	d																					
Bordesley	d																					
Birmingham Moor Street	d			14 15	14 30	14 48		14a59	15a13			15 15	15 30	15 48				15a59				
Birmingham Snow Hill ⇌	a			14 17	14 37	14 50						15 17	15 37	15 50								
	d			14 22		14 52						15 22		15 52								
Jewellery Quarter ⇌	d			14 24		14 54						15 24		15 54								
The Hawthorns ⇌	d			14 28		14 58						15 28		15 58								
Smethwick Galton Bridge 7	d			14 31		15 01						15 31		16 01								
Coventry	a						14 23			14 52					15 23					15 52		
Birmingham Intl. 68 ✈	a						14 36			15 03					15 37					16 03		
Birmingham New Street 12 68	a						14 48			15 14					15 48					16 14		
	d															16 00						
Langley Green	d					15 04								16 04								
Rowley Regis	d			14 37		15 07						15 37		16 07								
Old Hill	d					15 10								16 10								
Cradley Heath	d			14 42		15 14						15 42		16 14								
Lye	d					15 17								16 17								
Stourbridge Junction 8	d			14 47		15a21						15 47		16a21								
Hagley	d			14 51								15 51										
Blakedown	d			14 54																		
Kidderminster	d			14 59								15 57										
Hartlebury	d																					
University	d															16 06						
Barnt Green	d																					
Bromsgrove 69	d															16 20						
Droitwich Spa	d			15 11								16 08				16 30						
Worcester Shrub Hill 7	a															16 38						
	d	15 05	15 06								16 04					16 43					17 08	17 09
Worcester Foregate Street 7	a	15 08	15 08	15 20							16 07	16 17				16 45					17 10	17 11
	d	15 09	15 10													16 46					17 12	17 13
Malvern Link	d	15 18	15 19													16 55					17 21	17 22
Great Malvern	a	15 21	15 22													16 57					17 24	17 25
	d	15 23	15 24													17 03					17 25	17 26
Colwall	d	15 29	15 30													17 09					17 31	17 32
Ledbury	a	15 36	15 37													17 16					17 38	17 39
	d	15 38	15 39													17 16					17 39	17 40
Hereford 7	a	15 55	15 56													17 34					17 56	17 57

A until 9 September
B from 16 September

Table T071-F

Sundays
20 May to 2 December

Stratford-upon-Avon, Marylebone and Leamington Spa - Birmingham - Stourbridge, Worcester and Hereford

		LM	CH ◇	LM	XC ◇1	CH ◇	LM	GW ◇	CH	XC ◇1	LM	CH ◇	LM	XC ◇1	LM	CH	CH ◇	CH	XC ◇1	GW ◇1 A	GW ◇1 B	LM	CH ◇
Stratford-upon-Avon	d	15 29									16 29					16 46						17 29	
Stratford-upon-Avon Parkway	d	15 33									16 33					16 50						17 33	
Wilmcote	d	15 36									16 36					16 53						17 36	
Wootton Wawen	d																						
Henley-in-Arden	d	15 43									16 43											17 43	
Danzey	d																						
Wood End	d																						
The Lakes	d	15x49									16x49											17x49	
Earlswood (West Midlands)	d																						
Wythall	d	15 53									16 53											17 53	
Whitlocks End	d	15 56									16 56											17 56	
Shirley	d	15 59									16 59											17 59	
Yardley Wood	d	16 01									17 01											18 01	
Hall Green	d	16 05									17 05											18 05	
Spring Road	d	16 07									17 07											18 07	
London Marylebone 10 ⊖115	d		14 40			15 10						15 40					16 10						16 40
Banbury	d		15 39		15 55	16 07				16 24		16 39		16 55			17 07		17 24				17 39
Leamington Spa 8	a		15 56		16 11	16 24				16 40		16 56		17 11		17 17	17 24		17 40				17 56
	d		15 57		16 12	16 25			16 32	16 41		16 57		17 12			17 25	17 32	17 41				17 57
Warwick	d		16 01						16 38			17 01						17 37					18 01
Warwick Parkway	d		16 05			16 32						17 05					17 32						18 05
Hatton	d								16 44									17a44					
Lapworth	d								16 50														
Dorridge	d		16 15	16 27					16 55			17 15	17 27										18 15
Widney Manor	d			16 32									17 32										
Solihull	d		16 21	16 35		16 45			17 01			17 21	17 35				17 45						18 21
Olton	d			16 38									17 38										
Acocks Green	d			16 41									17 41										
Tyseley	d	16 10									17 10											18 10	
Small Heath	d																						
Bordesley	d																						
Birmingham Moor Street	d	16 15	16 30	16 48		16a59	17 02		17a13		17 15	17 30	17 48				17a59					18 15	18 30
Birmingham Snow Hill ⇌	a	16 17	16 37	16 50			17 04				17 17	17 37	17 50									18 17	18 37
	d	16 22		16 51			17 06				17 22		17 52									18 22	
Jewellery Quarter ⇌	d	16 24		16 53							17 24		17 54									18 24	
The Hawthorns ⇌	d	16 28		16 57							17 28		17 58									18 28	
Smethwick Galton Bridge 7	d	16 31		17 00							17 31		18 01									18 31	
Coventry	a				16 23					16 52				17 23					17 52				
Birmingham Intl. 68 ✈	a				16 36					17 03				17 36					18 03				
Birmingham New Street 12 68	a				16 48					17 14				17 48					18 14				
	d														18 00								
Langley Green	d			17 03									18 04										
Rowley Regis	d	16 37		17 06							17 37		18 07									18 37	
Old Hill	d			17 09									18 10										
Cradley Heath	d	16 42		17 13							17 42		18 14									18 42	
Lye	d			17 16									18 17										
Stourbridge Junction 8	d	16 47		17a20			17 24				17 47		18a21									18 47	
Hagley	d	16 51					17 27				17 51											18 51	
Blakedown	d																					18 54	
Kidderminster	d	16 57					17 33				17 59											18 59	
Hartlebury	d																						
University	d														18 06								
Barnt Green	d																						
Bromsgrove 69	d														18 20								
Droitwich Spa	d	17 08					17 45				18 11				18 32							19 11	
Worcester Shrub Hill 7	a						17 52								18 41							19 19	
	d							18 04							18 52					19 07	19 08		
Worcester Foregate Street 7	a	17 17						18 06			18 21				18 54					19 10	19 11		
	d														18 55					19 11	19 12		
Malvern Link	d														19 04					19 20	19 21		
Great Malvern	a														19 06					19 22	19 23		
	d														19 07								
Colwall	d														19 12								
Ledbury	a														19 19								
	d														19 19								
Hereford 7	a														19 40								

A until 9 September
B from 16 September

Table T071-F

Sundays
20 May to 2 December

Stratford-upon-Avon, Marylebone and Leamington Spa - Birmingham - Stourbridge, Worcester and Hereford

		XC	LM	CH	CH	XC	GW	GW	LM	CH	XC	LM	CH	CH	CH	XC	LM	CH	XC	LM	CH	XC
		◇■		◇		◇■	◇■	◇■		◇	◇■			◇		◇■		◇	◇■		◇	◇■
							A	B														
		🍴				🍴	☕	☕			🍴					🍴			🍴			
Stratford-upon-Avon	d								18 29				18 46				19 29					
Stratford-upon-Avon Parkway	d								18 33				18 50				19 33					
Wilmcote	d								18 36				18 53				19 36					
Wootton Wawen	d																					
Henley-in-Arden	d								18 43								19 43					
Danzey	d																					
Wood End	d																					
The Lakes	d								18x49								19x49					
Earlswood (West Midlands)	d																					
Wythall	d								18 53								19 53					
Whitlocks End	d								18 56								19 56					
Shirley	d								18 59								19 59					
Yardley Wood	d								19 01								20 01					
Hall Green	d								19 05								20 05					
Spring Road	d								19 07								20 07					
London Marylebone ■ ⊖115	d			17 10						17 40				18 10				18 40			19 10	
Banbury	d	17 55		18 07		18 24				18 39	18 55			19 07		19 24		19 39	19 55		20 07	20 24
Leamington Spa ■	a	18 11		18 24		18 40				18 56	19 11		19 17	19 24		19 40		19 56	20 11		20 24	20 39
	d	18 12		18 25	18 32	18 41				18 57	19 12			19 25	19 32	19 41		19 57	20 12		20 25	20 41
Warwick	d				18 38					19 01					19 37			20 01				
Warwick Parkway	d			18 32						19 05				19 32				20 05			20 32	
Hatton	d				18 44										19a44							
Lapworth	d				18 50																	
Dorridge	d				18 55					19 15								20 15				
Widney Manor	d				18 59																	
Solihull	d			18 45	19 02					19 21				19 45				20 21			20 45	
Olton	d																					
Acocks Green	d																					
Tyseley	d								19 10								20 10					
Small Heath	d																					
Bordesley	d																					
Birmingham Moor Street	d			18a59	19a13				19 15	19 30				19 55			20 15	20 30			20a59	
Birmingham Snow Hill ⇌	a								19 17	19 37				19 57			20 17	20 37				
	d								19 22					19 59			20 22					
Jewellery Quarter ⇌	d								19 24								20 24					
The Hawthorns ⇌	d								19 28								20 28					
Smethwick Galton Bridge ■	d								19 31								20 31					
Coventry	a	18 23				18 52					19 23					19 52			20 23			20 52
Birmingham Intl. 68 ✈	a	18 36				19 03					19 36					20 03			20 36			21 03
Birmingham New Street ■ 68	a	18 48				19 14					19 48					20 14			20 48			21 15
	d		19 00									20 00								21 00		
Langley Green	d																					
Rowley Regis	d								19 37					20 12			20 37					
Old Hill	d																					
Cradley Heath	d								19 42								20 42					
Lye	d																					
Stourbridge Junction ■	d								19 47					20 23			20 47					
Hagley	d								19 51								20 51					
Blakedown	d																					
Kidderminster	d								19 57					20a36			20 57					
Hartlebury	d																					
University	d		19 06									20 06								21 06		
Barnt Green	d																					
Bromsgrove 69	d		19 20									20 20								21 20		
Droitwich Spa	d		19 30						20 09			20 30					21 09			21 30		
Worcester Shrub Hill ■	a		19 38						20 17			20 44					21 17			21 38		
	d		19 42				20 12	20 13				20 58					21 22			21 41		
Worcester Foregate Street ■	a		19 44				20 14	20 15				21 00					21 24			21 43		
	d						20 16	20 17									21 25			21 44		
Malvern Link	d						20 25	20 26									21 34			21 53		
Great Malvern	a						20 28	20 29									21 39			21 55		
	d						20 29	20 30												21 56		
Colwall	d						20 35	20 36												22 01		
Ledbury	a						20 42	20 43												22 08		
	d						20 44	20 45												22 09		
Hereford ■	a						21 00	21 01												22 27		

A until 9 September
B from 16 September

Table T071-F

Sundays
20 May to 2 December

Stratford-upon-Avon, Marylebone and Leamington Spa - Birmingham - Stourbridge, Worcester and Hereford

		CH	CH	XC	GW	GW	LM	CH	LM	XC	CH	XC	LM	CH	XC	CH
		◇	◇	◇■	◇■	◇■		◇		◇■	◇	◇■		◇	◇■	◇
					A	B										
					☕	☕										
Stratford-upon-Avon	d		20 38													
Stratford-upon-Avon Parkway	d		20 42													
Wilmcote	d		20 45													
Wootton Wawen	d															
Henley-in-Arden	d															
Danzey	d															
Wood End	d															
The Lakes	d															
Earlswood (West Midlands)	d															
Wythall	d															
Whitlocks End	d															
Shirley	d															
Yardley Wood	d															
Hall Green	d															
Spring Road	d															
London Marylebone ■ ⊖115	d	19 40						20 10			20 40			21 10		22 08
Banbury	d	20 39		20 55				21 07		21 24	21 39	21 55		22 07	22 24	23 09
Leamington Spa ■	a	20 56	21 07	21 11				21 24		21 40	21 56	22 11		22 24	22 40	23 26
	d	20 57		21 12				21 25		21 41	21 57	22 12		22 25	22 41	23 27
Warwick	d	21 01									22 01			22 29		23 31
Warwick Parkway	d	21 05						21 32			22 05			22 34		23 34
Hatton	d	21 10												22 40		
Lapworth	d	21 16												22 46		
Dorridge	d	21 21									22 15			22 51		23 44
Widney Manor	d	21 25												22 54		
Solihull	d	21 29						21 45			22 21			22 58		23 50
Olton	d															
Acocks Green	d															
Tyseley	d															
Small Heath	d															
Bordesley	d															
Birmingham Moor Street	d	21 38					21 43	21a56			22 30		22 52	23 07		23 59
Birmingham Snow Hill ⇌	a	21 40					21 45				22 32		22 54	23 14		00 07
	d	21 42					21 46				22 34		22 56			
Jewellery Quarter ⇌	d						21 48						22 58			
The Hawthorns ⇌	d						21 52						23 02			
Smethwick Galton Bridge ■	d						21 55						23 05			
Coventry	a			21 23						21 52		22 23			22 52	
Birmingham Intl. 68 ✈	a			21 36						22 02		22 33			23 03	
Birmingham New Street ■ 68	a			21 48						22 14		22 43			23 14	
	d								22 00							
Langley Green	d															
Rowley Regis	d	21 54					22 00				22 46		23 11			
Old Hill	d															
Cradley Heath	d	21 59					22 05				22 51		23 16			
Lye	d															
Stourbridge Junction ■	d	22 05					22 10				22 57		23 22			
Hagley	d						22 14						23 25			
Blakedown	d															
Kidderminster	d	22a18					22 20				23a10		23 31			
Hartlebury	d															
University	d								22 06							
Barnt Green	d															
Bromsgrove 69	d								22 20							
Droitwich Spa	d						22 31		22 36				23 43			
Worcester Shrub Hill ■	a						22 39		22 45				23 51			
	d				22 07	22 09			22 51							
Worcester Foregate Street ■	a				22 09	22 12			22 53							
	d				22 11	22 13			22 54							
Malvern Link	d				22 20	22 22			23 03							
Great Malvern	a				22 23	22 25			23 05							
	d															
Colwall	d															
Ledbury	a															
	d															
Hereford ■	a															

A from 16 September
B until 9 September

Please note, Network Rail have stated that further updates to this timetable are possible during the validity period.

Hereford, Worcester and Stourbridge - Birmingham - Leamington Spa, Marylebone and Stratford-upon-Avon

Miles	Miles	Miles			CH	CH	CH	CH	CH	LM	XC	CH	CH		CH	CH	CH	XC	CH	LM	LM	GW	LM		LM
					MX	◇	◇	◇	◇		◇■1	◇	◇					◇■1	◇			◇■1			
						A	B	A	B			A	B		A	B									
0	—	—	**Hereford** [7]	d																		04 47			
13¾	—	—	Ledbury	a																		05 03			
—	—	—		d																		05 04			
18	—	—	Colwall	d																		05 12			
20¾	—	—	**Great Malvern**	a																		05 16			
—	—	—		d																		05 17	05 48		
22	—	—	Malvern Link	d																		05 21	05 51		
28¾	0	—	**Worcester Foregate Street** [7]	a																		05 30	06 00		
—	—	—		d																		05 32	06 02		
29½	—	—	**Worcester Shrub Hill** [7]	a																		05 35			
—	—	—		d																	05 30				
34¼	5½	—	Droitwich Spa	d																	05 38		06 11		
40½	—	—	Bromsgrove 69	d																			06 21		
44	—	—	Barnt Green	d																					
52	—	—	University	d																			06 40		
—	11	—	Hartlebury	d																					
—	14¾	—	**Kidderminster**	d																	05 48				
—	17¾	—	Blakedown	d																					
—	19½	—	Hagley	d																					
—	21½	—	**Stourbridge Junction** [2]	d																	05 56				
—	22¾	—	Lye	d																	06 00				
—	24	—	Cradley Heath	d																	06 03				
—	25½	—	Old Hill	d																	06 07				
—	26¾	—	Rowley Regis	d																	06 10				
—	28½	0	Langley Green	d																	06 13				
54½	—	6¼	**Birmingham New Street** [12] 68	a																			06 49		
—	—	—		d							06 04							06 33							
—	—	—	**Birmingham Intl.** 68 ✈	d							06 14														
—	—	—	**Coventry**	d							06 25														
—	29½	—	Smethwick Galton Bridge [7]	d																	06 17				
—	30¼	—	The Hawthorns	d																	06 19				
—	32¾	—	Jewellery Quarter	d																	06 23				
—	33½	—	**Birmingham Snow Hill**	a																	06 27				
—	—	—		d						05 53										06 30	06 35				06 40
—	34	—	**Birmingham Moor Street**	d		05 15	05 15	05 42	05 42	05 56		06 10	06 10						06 28	06 33	06 38				06 43
—	34¾	—	Bordesley	d																					
—	35¾	9¼	Small Heath	d						05 59											06 41				06 46
—	36¾	10¼	Tyseley	d						06 02										06 38	06 45				06 49
—	—	11¼	Acocks Green	d						06 05											06 47				
—	—	12¼	Olton	d						06 07											06 50				
—	—	14	Solihull	d		05 24	05 24	05 51	05 51	06 11		06 19	06 19						06 38		06 54				
—	—	15½	Widney Manor	d						06 14											06 57				
—	—	17½	Dorridge	d				05 56	05 56	06 18		06 24	06 24						06 50		07a02				
—	—	20	Lapworth	d						06 22															
—	—	24¼	Hatton	d	00 05										06 32	06 32									
—	—	27	Warwick Parkway	d	00 10	05 36	05 36	06 05	06 05			06 34	06 34						06 59						
—	—	28¾	Warwick	d	00 13			06 08	06 08						06 40	06 40			07 02						
—	—	30¼	**Leamington Spa** [8]	a	00 17	05 41	05 41	06 12	06 12		06 36	06 40	06 40		06 45	06 48		06 58	07 06						
—	—	—		d	00 18	05 41	05 41	06 13	06 13		06 37	06 41	06 41				06 51	07 00	07 06						
—	—	—	Banbury	d	00a42	05 59	05 59	06 31	06 31		06a53	06 59	06 59					07a18	07 24						
—	—	—	**London Marylebone** [10] ⊖115	a		07 03	07 06	07 35	07 38			08 02	08 05						08 33						
—	37¼	—	Spring Road	d																06 41					06 52
—	38¼	—	Hall Green	d																06 43					06 54
—	39½	—	Yardley Wood	d																06 46					06 57
—	40¾	—	Shirley	d																06 49					07 00
—	41¾	—	Whitlocks End	d																06 52					07 03
—	42¾	—	Wythall	d																06 55					07 05
—	43¾	—	Earlswood (West Midlands)	d																					07 08
—	44½	—	The Lakes	d																					07x10
—	45¾	—	Wood End	d																					07x12
—	47½	—	Danzey	d																					07x15
—	50¼	—	Henley-in-Arden	d																07 05					07 20
—	52¼	—	Wootton Wawen	d																					07x23
—	56	—	Wilmcote	d						06 40							07 20								07 28
—	57¾	—	Stratford-upon-Avon Parkway	a						06 43							07 22			07 15					07 31
—	58¾	—	**Stratford-upon-Avon**	a						06 48							07 31			07 20					07 36

A until 5 October B from 8 October

Hereford, Worcester and Stourbridge - Birmingham - Leamington Spa, Marylebone and Stratford-upon-Avon

		CH	XC	LM	CH	CH	XC	CH	CH		CH	CH	LM	GW	LM	LM	LM	CH	CH		LM	GW	LM	XC	CH
		◇	◇■1		◇	◇	◇■1	◇	◇		◇			◇■1				◇	◇					◇■1	◇
					A	B		A	B									A	B						
Hereford [7]	d												05 28												
Ledbury	a												05 44												
	d												05 45												
Colwall	d												05 53												
Great Malvern	a												05 58												
	d												05 59									06 47			
Malvern Link	d												06 03									06 50			
Worcester Foregate Street [7]	a												06 12									06 58			
	d												06 14								06 53	06 59			
Worcester Shrub Hill [7]	a												06 17								06 55	07 01			
	d											06 12		06 25		06 35				06 50		07 06			
Droitwich Spa	d											06 20		06 33		06 43				07 03		07 13			
Bromsgrove 69	d													06 43								07 23			
Barnt Green	d																								
University	d													07 00								07 40			
Hartlebury	d											06 27				06 50				07 10					
Kidderminster	d	06 09										06 33				06 56	07 05	07 05		07 16				07 30
Blakedown	d											06 37				07 00				07 20					
Hagley	d											06 41				07 04				07 24					
Stourbridge Junction [2]	d	06 18		06 24	06 38	06 38						06 49				07 08	07 14	07 14		07 28				07 38
Lye	d			06 28								06 53				07 12				07 32					
Cradley Heath	d			06 31								06 56				07 15	07 22	07 22		07 35				07 44
Old Hill	d			06 34								07 00				07 18				07 38					
Rowley Regis	d	06 30		06 38	06 50	06 50						07 03				07 22	07 29	07 29		07 42				07 51
Langley Green	d			06 41								07 06				07 25				07 45					
Birmingham New Street [12] 68	a													07 09								07 49			
	d		07 04				07 33																	08 04	
Birmingham Intl. 68 ✈	d		07 14																					08 14	
Coventry	d		07 25																					08 25	
Smethwick Galton Bridge [7]	d	06 38		06 44	06 58	06 58						07 10				07 28	07 36	07 36		07 48				07 57
The Hawthorns	d	06 42		06 46								07 12				07 30	07 39	07 39		07 50				08 00
Jewellery Quarter	d			06 50								07 16				07 35	07 45	07 45		07 55					
Birmingham Snow Hill	a	06 48		06 54	07 05	07 05						07 22				07 38	07 48	07 48		07 59				08 06
	d	06 50		06 57	07 07	07 07					07 19	07 25			07 35	07 40	07 50	07 50		08 03				08 07
Birmingham Moor Street	d	06 55		07 00	07 11	07 11					07 22	07 28			07 38	07 43	07 54	07 54		08 06				08 10
Bordesley	d																								
Small Heath	d			07 03								07 31			07 41					08 09					
Tyseley	d			07 07								07 34			07 45	07 48				08 13					
Acocks Green	d			07 09							07 29					07 51									
Olton	d			07 12							07 32					07 54									
Solihull	d	07 04		07 16	07 20	07 20					07 36					07 57	08 03	08 03						08 19
Widney Manor	d			07 19							07 40					08 01									
Dorridge	d			07 30	07 27	07 27					07 52					08a06								08 24
Lapworth	d			07 35							07 56														
Hatton	d			07 40				07 55	07 55			08 02													
Warwick Parkway	d	07 18		07 44	07 39	07 39		08 00	08 00								08 15	08 15						08 34
Warwick	d			07 47				08 03	08 03			08 07												08 37
Leamington Spa [8]	a	07 23	07 37	07 53	07 44	07 44	07 59	08 07	08 07			08 16					08 20	08 20					08 37	08 42
	d	07 24	07 38		07 46	07 46	08 00	08 08	08 08		08 08						08 21	08 21					08 38	08 43
Banbury	d		07a54		08 06	08 06	08a16	08 27	08 27								08 41	08 41					08a55	09 02
London Marylebone [10] ⊖115	a	08 34			09 07	09 10		09 35	09 38								09 38	09 41						09 59
Spring Road	d											07 37			07 47					08 15					
Hall Green	d											07 39			07 50					08 18					
Yardley Wood	d											07 42			07 52					08 20					
Shirley	d											07 45			07 56					08 24					
Whitlocks End	d											07 48			07a58					08a27					
Wythall	d											07 51													
Earlswood (West Midlands)	d											07 53													
The Lakes	d											07x56													
Wood End	d											07x58													
Danzey	d											08x01													
Henley-in-Arden	d											08 06													
Wootton Wawen	d											08x09													
Wilmcote	d									08 35		08 15													
Stratford-upon-Avon Parkway	a									08 37		08 18													
Stratford-upon-Avon	a									08 46		08 23													

A until 5 October B from 8 October

Table T071-R

Mondays to Fridays
21 May to 7 December

Hereford, Worcester and Stourbridge - Birmingham - Leamington Spa, Marylebone and Stratford-upon-Avon

Station		LM	LM	XC	GW	CH	CH	LM	LM	LM	LM	CH	CH	LM	LM	CH	XC	LM	GW	CH	CH	CH	LM
				◇■ ✠	◇■ A	◇ B	◇ C					◇ B	◇ C				■ ✠		◇■ ✠		◇ B	◇ C	
Hereford ■	d				06 42						07 09							07 32					
Ledbury	a				06 58						07 24							07 49					
	d				07 02						07 25							07 50					
Colwall	d				07 09						07 31							07 57					
Great Malvern	a				07 14						07 36							08 01					
	d		07 02		07 15						07 36							08 07					
Malvern Link	d		07 05		07 20						07 39							08 10					
Worcester Foregate Street ■	a		07 14		07 28						07 48							08 18					
	d	07 14	07 16		07 31						07 48				08 02			08 24	08 25				
Worcester Shrub Hill ■	a		07 18		07 34						07 51								08 28				
	d		07 23						07 35		07 54												
Droitwich Spa	d	07 23	07 33						07 43		08 02				08 11			08 33					
Bromsgrove 69	d																	08 42					
Barnt Green	d																						
University	d		08 00								08 30							09 00					
Hartlebury	d	07 30													08 18								
Kidderminster	d	07 36							07 54			08 09	08 09		08 24								
Blakedown	d	07 40							07 59			08 14	08 14		08 28								
Hagley	d	07 44							08 03			08 19	08 19		08 31								
Stourbridge Junction ■	d	07 48						07 57	08 07	08 15		08 23	08 23		08 35								08 44
Lye	d							08 01		08 19					08 39								
Cradley Heath	d	07 54						08 04	08 13	08 22		08 29	08 29		08 42								08 50
Old Hill	d							08 07		08 25					08 46								
Rowley Regis	d	07 59						08 11	08 19	08 29		08 35	08 35		08 49								08 55
Langley Green	d							08 14		08 32					08 52								
Birmingham New Street ■ 68	a		08 09								08 39							09 09					
	d			08 33													09 04						
Birmingham Intl. 68 ✈	d																09 14						
Coventry	d																09 25						
Smethwick Galton Bridge ■	d	08 05						08 17	08 25	08 35		08 41	08 41		08 56								09 01
The Hawthorns	d	08 07						08 19	08 28	08 37		08 44	08 44		08 58								09 03
Jewellery Quarter	d	08 11						08 23	08 32	08 41		08 49	08 49		09 02								09 07
Birmingham Snow Hill	a	08 15						08 26	08 35	08 45		08 51	08 51		09 07								09 12
	d	08 17				08 22	08 22	08 28	08 37	08 47		08 52	08 52	08 58	09 08						09 12	09 12	09 17
Birmingham Moor Street	d	08 20				08 25	08 25	08 31	08 40	08 50		08 55	08 55	09 01	09 11						09 15	09 15	09 20
Bordesley	d																						
Small Heath	d								08 43						09 14								
Tyseley	d								08 46						09 18								
Acocks Green	d	08 26							08 49					09 07									09 26
Olton	d	08 29							08 52					09 10									09 29
Solihull	d	08 32				08 37	08 37		08 56			09 07	09 07	09 13							09 24	09 24	09 32
Widney Manor	d	08 36							08 59					09 17									09 36
Dorridge	d	08a41				08 52	08 52		09a05					09 21							09 29	09 29	09a41
Lapworth	d																						
Hatton	d															09 21							
Warwick Parkway	d					09 02	09 02					09 19	09 19								09 39	09 39	
Warwick	d					09 06	09 06									09 28					09 42	09 42	
Leamington Spa ■	a			08 58		09 11	09 11					09 24	09 24			09 37	09 38				09 46	09 46	
	d			09 00		09 12	09 12					09 25	09 25				09 39			09 40	09 46	09 46	
Banbury	d			09a18		09 31	09 31					09 44	09 44				09a55				10 04	10 04	
London Marylebone ■ ⊖115	a					10 36	10 39					10 40	10 43								11 08	11 11	
Spring Road	d							08 37		08 56					09 20								
Hall Green	d							08 39		08 59					09 23								
Yardley Wood	d							08 42		09 01					09 25								
Shirley	d							08 45		09 05					09 29								
Whitlocks End	d							08 48		09a07					09a31								
Wythall	d							08 51															
Earlswood (West Midlands)	d							08 53															
The Lakes	d							08x56															
Wood End	d							08x58															
Danzey	d							09x01															
Henley-in-Arden	d							09 06															
Wootton Wawen	d							09x09															
Wilmcote	d							09 15												10 06			
Stratford-upon-Avon Parkway	a							09 18						09 45						10 08			
Stratford-upon-Avon	a							09 23						09 49						10 17			

A The Cathedrals Express
B until 5 October
C from 8 October

Table T071-R

Mondays to Fridays
21 May to 7 December

Hereford, Worcester and Stourbridge - Birmingham - Leamington Spa, Marylebone and Stratford-upon-Avon

Station		LM	XC	CH	LM	LM	CH	LM	GW	CH	LM	LM	XC	LM	CH	CH	LM	LM	LM	LM	GW	XC
			◇■ ✠				◇ A		◇	◇ B			◇■ ✠		◇ A	◇ B					◇■ ✠	◇■ ✠
Hereford ■	d													08 45								
Ledbury	a													09 03								
	d													09 06								
Colwall	d													09 13								
Great Malvern	a													09 17								
	d							08 38	08 50					09 18							09 54	
Malvern Link	d							08 41	08 53					09 21							09 58	
Worcester Foregate Street ■	a							08 49	09 02					09 30							10 08	
	d					08 38		08 50	09 03			09 03		09 31							10 09	
Worcester Shrub Hill ■	a					08 40			09 06					09 33							10 12	
	d					08 43								09 36						09 52		
Droitwich Spa	d					08 53		08 59				09 12		09 43						10 00		
Bromsgrove 69	d							09 08						09 53								
Barnt Green	d																					
University	d							09 30						10 10								
Hartlebury	d											09 19										
Kidderminster	d				08 57	09 06						09 25					09 36		09 55	10 10		
Blakedown	d				09 01	09 10						09 29					09 40		09 59			
Hagley	d				09 05	09 14						09 33					09 44		10 03			
Stourbridge Junction ■	d	08 53			09 09	09 18					09 27	09 37					09 48	09 57	10 07	10 18		
Lye	d	08 57									09 31							10 01				
Cradley Heath	d	08 59			09 15	09 24					09 34	09 43					09 54	10 04	10 13	10 24		
Old Hill	d	09 03									09 37							10 07				
Rowley Regis	d	09 06			09 20	09 29					09 41	09 48					09 59	10 11	10 18	10 29		
Langley Green	d	09 09									09 44							10 14				
Birmingham New Street ■ 68	a							09 39						10 19								
	d		09 33										10 04									10 33
Birmingham Intl. 68 ✈	d												10 14									
Coventry	d												10 25									
Smethwick Galton Bridge ■	d	09 12			09 26	09 35					09 47	09 54					10 05	10 17	10 24	10 35		
The Hawthorns	d	09 14			09 28	09 37					09 49	09 56					10 07	10 19	10 26	10 37		
Jewellery Quarter	d	09 18			09 32	09 41					09 53	10 00					10 11	10 23	10 30	10 41		
Birmingham Snow Hill	a	09 21			09 36	09 45					09 56	10 04					10 15	10 26	10 34	10 45		
	d	09 28			09 37	09 47					09 58	10 07			10 12	10 12	10 17	10 28	10 37	10 47		
Birmingham Moor Street	d	09 31		09 34	09 40	09 50	09 55			09 55	10 01	10 10			10 15	10 15	10 20	10 31	10 40	10 50		
Bordesley	d																					
Small Heath	d				09 43							10 13							10 43			
Tyseley	d				09 47							10 17							10 47			
Acocks Green	d				09 49						10 07						10 26		10 49			
Olton	d				09 52						10 10						10 28		10 52			
Solihull	d			09 43	09 56		10 04			10 04	10 13				10 24	10 24	10 32		10 56			
Widney Manor	d				09 59						10 17						10 36		10 59			
Dorridge	d			09 52	10a04						10 21				10 29	10 29	10a41		11a04			
Lapworth	d			09 56																		
Hatton	d			10 02																		
Warwick Parkway	d						10 16			10 16					10 39	10 39						
Warwick	d			10 08											10 42	10 42						
Leamington Spa ■	a		09 59	10 17			10 21			10 21			10 37		10 46	10 46						10 58
	d		10 00				10 22			10 22			10 38		10 46	10 46						11 00
Banbury	d		10a17				10 40			10 40			10a54		11 04	11 04						11a17
London Marylebone ■ ⊖115	a						11 40			11 43					12 08	12 11						
Spring Road	d	09 37				09 56						10 19						10 37		10 56		
Hall Green	d	09 39				09 59						10 22						10 39		10 59		
Yardley Wood	d	09 42				10 01						10 24						10 42		11 01		
Shirley	d	09 45				10 05						10 28						10 45		11 05		
Whitlocks End	d	09 48				10a07						10a30						10 48		11a07		
Wythall	d	09 51																10 51				
Earlswood (West Midlands)	d	09 53																10 53				
The Lakes	d	09x56																10x56				
Wood End	d	09x58																10x58				
Danzey	d	10x01																11x01				
Henley-in-Arden	d	10 06																11 06				
Wootton Wawen	d	10x09																11x09				
Wilmcote	d	10 15																11 15				
Stratford-upon-Avon Parkway	a	10 18									10 37							11 18				
Stratford-upon-Avon	a	10 23									10 41							11 23				

A until 5 October
B from 8 October

Please note, Network Rail have stated that further updates to this timetable are possible during the validity period.

Hereford, Worcester and Stourbridge - Birmingham - Leamington Spa, Marylebone and Stratford-upon-Avon

		CH	CH	CH	LM	LM	CH		XC	CH	CH	LM	LM	LM	XC	CH	LM		LM	CH	GW	GW	CH	LM	LM
			◇ A	◇ B					◇■ ⚲	◇ A	◇ B				◇■ ⚲					◇ A	■	◇ ⚲	◇ B		
Hereford 7	d													09 39											
Ledbury	a													09 56											
	d													09 58											
Colwall	d													10 05											
Great Malvern	a													10 10											
	d													10 10							10 48	10 59			
Malvern Link	d													10 13							10 51	11 02			
Worcester Foregate Street 7	a													10 22							11 00	11 10			
	d											10 16		10 24							11 03	11 15			
Worcester Shrub Hill 7	a																				11 06	11 17			
	d																		10 52						
Droitwich Spa	d											10 25		10 33					11 00						
Bromsgrove 69	d													10 43											
Barnt Green	d																								
University	d													11 00											
Hartlebury	d											10 32													
Kidderminster	d					10 25						10 38					10 55		11 10						11 25
Blakedown	d					10 29											10 59								11 29
Hagley	d					10 33						10 44					11 03								11 33
Stourbridge Junction 2	d				10 28	10 37						10 48	10 57				11 07		11 18					11 27	11 37
Lye	d				10 31								11 01											11 31	
Cradley Heath	d				10 34	10 43						10 54	11 04				11 13		11 24					11 34	11 43
Old Hill	d				10 37								11 07											11 37	
Rowley Regis	d				10 41	10 48						10 59	11 11				11 18		11 29					11 41	11 48
Langley Green	d				10 44								11 14											11 44	
Birmingham New Street 12 68	a													11 09											
	d								11 04						11 33										
Birmingham Intl. 68 ✈	d								11 14																
Coventry	d								11 25																
Smethwick Galton Bridge 7	d				10 47	10 54						11 05	11 17				11 24		11 35					11 47	11 54
The Hawthorns	d				10 49	10 56						11 07	11 19				11 26		11 37					11 49	11 56
Jewellery Quarter	d				10 53	11 00						11 11	11 23				11 30		11 41					11 53	12 00
Birmingham Snow Hill	a				10 56	11 04						11 15	11 26				11 34		11 45					11 56	12 04
	d				10 58	11 07				11 12	11 12	11 17	11 28				11 37		11 47					11 58	12 07
Birmingham Moor Street	d		10 55	10 55	11 01	11 10				11 15	11 15	11 20	11 31			11 34	11 40		11 50	11 55			11 55	12 01	12 10
Bordesley	d																								
Small Heath	d					11 13											11 43								12 13
Tyseley	d					11 17											11 47								12 17
Acocks Green	d				11 07							11 26					11 49							12 07	
Olton	d				11 10							11 29					11 52							12 10	
Solihull	d		11 04	11 04	11 13					11 24	11 24	11 32				11 43	11 56			12 04			12 04	12 13	
Widney Manor	d				11 17							11 36					11 59							12 17	
Dorridge	d				11 21					11 29	11 29	11a41				11 52	12a04							12 21	
Lapworth	d															11 56									
Hatton	d	10 58														12 02									
Warwick Parkway	d		11 17	11 17						11 39	11 39									12 16			12 16		
Warwick	d	11 04								11 42	11 42					12 08									
Leamington Spa 5	a	11 14	11 22	11 22					11 37	11 46	11 46				12 00	12 17				12 21			12 21		
	d		11 23	11 23			11 32		11 38	11 46	11 46				12 01					12 22			12 22		
Banbury	d		11 40	11 40					11a54	12 04	12 04				12a18					12 40			12 40		
London Marylebone 10 ⊖115	a		12 43	12 46						13 09	13 12									13 43			13 46		
Spring Road	d					11 19							11 37						11 56						12 19
Hall Green	d					11 22							11 39						11 59						12 22
Yardley Wood	d					11 24							11 42						12 01						12 24
Shirley	d					11 28							11 45						12 05						12 28
Whitlocks End	d					11a30							11 48						12a07						12a30
Wythall	d												11 51												
Earlswood (West Midlands)	d												11 53												
The Lakes	d												11x56												
Wood End	d												11x58												
Danzey	d												12x01												
Henley-in-Arden	d												12 06												
Wootton Wawen	d												12x09												
Wilmcote	d						11 55						12 15												
Stratford-upon-Avon Parkway	a				11 37		11 57						12 18											12 37	
Stratford-upon-Avon	a				11 41		12 06						12 23											12 41	

A until 5 October
B from 8 October

Hereford, Worcester and Stourbridge - Birmingham - Leamington Spa, Marylebone and Stratford-upon-Avon

		XC	CH		CH	LM	LM	LM	XC	LM	LM	GW	CH		CH	CH	LM	LM	CH	XC	CH	CH	LM		LM
		◇■ ⚲	◇ A		◇ B				◇■ ⚲			◇■ ⚲			◇ A	◇ B				◇■ ⚲	◇ A	◇ B			
Hereford 7	d							10 39																	
Ledbury	a							10 56																	
	d							10 58																	
Colwall	d							11 05																	
Great Malvern	a							11 10																	
	d							11 10			11 35														
Malvern Link	d							11 13			11 38														
Worcester Foregate Street 7	a							11 22			11 48														
	d					11 16		11 24			11 51	12 00											12 16		
Worcester Shrub Hill 7	a											12 03													
	d																								
Droitwich Spa	d					11 25		11 33			12 00												12 25		
Bromsgrove 69	d							11 43																	
Barnt Green	d																								
University	d							12 00																	
Hartlebury	d					11 32																	12 32		
Kidderminster	d					11 38				11 55	12 10							12 25					12 38		
Blakedown	d									11 59								12 29							
Hagley	d					11 44				12 03								12 33					12 44		
Stourbridge Junction 2	d					11 48	11 57			12 07	12 18						12 27	12 37					12 48		12 57
Lye	d						12 01										12 31								13 01
Cradley Heath	d					11 54	12 04			12 13	12 24						12 34	12 43					12 54		13 04
Old Hill	d						12 07										12 37								13 07
Rowley Regis	d					11 59	12 11			12 18	12 29						12 41	12 48					12 59		13 11
Langley Green	d						12 14										12 44								13 14
Birmingham New Street 12 68	a							12 09																	
	d	12 04							12 33											13 04					
Birmingham Intl. 68 ✈	d	12 14																		13 14					
Coventry	d	12 25																		13 25					
Smethwick Galton Bridge 7	d					12 05	12 17			12 24	12 35						12 47	12 54					13 05		13 17
The Hawthorns	d					12 07	12 19			12 26	12 37						12 49	12 56					13 07		13 19
Jewellery Quarter	d					12 11	12 23			12 30	12 41						12 53	13 00					13 11		13 23
Birmingham Snow Hill	a					12 15	12 26			12 34	12 45						12 56	13 04					13 15		13 26
	d		12 12		12 12	12 17	12 28			12 37	12 47						12 58	13 07			13 12	13 12	13 17		13 28
Birmingham Moor Street	d		12 15		12 15	12 20	12 31			12 40	12 50				12 55	12 55	13 01	13 10			13 15	13 15	13 20		13 31
Bordesley	d																								
Small Heath	d									12 43								13 13							
Tyseley	d									12 47								13 17							
Acocks Green	d					12 26				12 49							13 07						13 26		
Olton	d					12 29				12 52							13 10						13 29		
Solihull	d		12 24		12 24	12 32				12 56					13 04	13 04	13 13				13 24	13 24	13 32		
Widney Manor	d					12 36				12 59							13 17						13 36		
Dorridge	d		12 29		12 29	12a41				13a04							13 21				13 30	13 30	13a41		
Lapworth	d																								
Hatton	d												12 58												
Warwick Parkway	d		12 39		12 39										13 17	13 17					13 40	13 40			
Warwick	d		12 42		12 42								13 04								13 44	13 44			
Leamington Spa 5	a	12 37	12 46		12 46				12 59				13 14		13 22	13 22				13 37	13 48	13 48			
	d	12 38	12 46		12 46				13 00						13 23	13 23			13 32	13 38	13 49	13 49			
Banbury	d	12a54	13 04		13 04				13a18						13 41	13 41				13a54	14 07	14 07			
London Marylebone 10 ⊖115	a		14 09		14 12										14 43	14 46					15 08	15 11			
Spring Road	d						12 37				12 56							13 19							13 37
Hall Green	d						12 39				12 59							13 22							13 39
Yardley Wood	d						12 42				13 01							13 24							13 42
Shirley	d						12 45				13 05							13 28							13 45
Whitlocks End	d						12 48				13a07							13a30							13 48
Wythall	d						12 51																		13 51
Earlswood (West Midlands)	d						12 53																		13 53
The Lakes	d						12x56																		13x56
Wood End	d						12x58																		13x58
Danzey	d						13x01																		14x01
Henley-in-Arden	d						13 06																		14 06
Wootton Wawen	d						13x09																		14x09
Wilmcote	d						13 15												13 59						14 15
Stratford-upon-Avon Parkway	a						13 18										13 37		14 01						14 18
Stratford-upon-Avon	a						13 23										13 41		14 12						14 23

A until 5 October
B from 8 October

Table T071-R

Mondays to Fridays
21 May to 7 December

Hereford, Worcester and Stourbridge - Birmingham - Leamington Spa, Marylebone and Stratford-upon-Avon

		LM	XC	CH	LM	LM	CH	GW	GW	CH	LM	LM	XC	CH	CH	LM	LM	LM	XC	LM	LM	GW	CH
			◇1				◇	◇1	◇	◇			◇1	◇	◇				◇1			◇1	
							A			B				A	B								
			✕					✕					✕						✕			✕	
Hereford 7	d	11 39						12 09										12 39					
Ledbury	a	11 55						12 25										12 57					
	d	11 58						12 27										12 58					
Colwall	d	12 05						12 34										13 05					
Great Malvern	a	12 10						12 39										13 10					
	d	12 10						12 40	12 51									13 10					
Malvern Link	d	12 13						12 44	12 54									13 13					
Worcester Foregate Street 7	a	12 22						12 53	13 03									13 22					
	d	12 24						12 55	13 03									13 24			13 51	13 55	
Worcester Shrub Hill 7	a							12 58	13 06													13 58	
	d					12 52										13 17							
Droitwich Spa	d	12 33				13 00										13 25		13 33			14 00		
Bromsgrove 69	d	12 43																13 42					
Barnt Green	d																						
University	d	13 00																14 00					
Hartlebury	d															13 32							
Kidderminster	d				12 55	13 10										13 38				13 55	14 10		
Blakedown	d				12 59															13 59			
Hagley	d				13 03											13 44				14 03			
Stourbridge Junction 2	d				13 07	13 18					13 27	13 37				13 48	13 57			14 07	14 18		
Lye	d										13 31						14 01						
Cradley Heath	d				13 13	13 24					13 34	13 43				13 54	14 04			14 13	14 24		
Old Hill	d										13 37						14 07						
Rowley Regis	d				13 18	13 29					13 41	13 48				13 59	14 11			14 18	14 29		
Langley Green	d										13 44						14 14						
Birmingham New Street 12 68	a	13 09																14 09					
	d		13 33										14 04						14 33				
Birmingham Intl. 68 ✈	d												14 14										
Coventry	d												14 25										
Smethwick Galton Bridge 7	d				13 24	13 35					13 47	13 54				14 05	14 17			14 24	14 35		
The Hawthorns ⇌	d				13 26	13 37					13 49	13 56				14 07	14 19			14 26	14 37		
Jewellery Quarter ⇌	d				13 30	13 41					13 53	14 00				14 11	14 23			14 30	14 41		
Birmingham Snow Hill ⇌	a				13 34	13 45					13 56	14 04				14 15	14 26			14 34	14 45		
	d				13 37	13 47					13 58	14 07		14 12	14 12	14 17	14 28			14 37	14 47		
Birmingham Moor Street	d			13 34	13 40	13 50	13 55			13 55	14 01	14 10		14 15	14 15	14 20	14 31			14 40	14 50		
Bordesley	d																						
Small Heath	d				13 43							14 13								14 43			
Tyseley	d				13 47							14 17								14 47			
Acocks Green	d				13 49						14 07					14 26				14 49			
Olton	d				13 52						14 10					14 29				14 52			
Solihull	d			13 43	13 56		14 04			14 04	14 13			14 24	14 24	14 32				14 56			
Widney Manor	d				13 59						14 17					14 36				14 59			
Dorridge	d			13 51	14a04						14 21			14 29	14 29	14a41				15a04			
Lapworth	d			13 54																			
Hatton	d			14 00																			14 58
Warwick Parkway	d						14 16			14 16				14 39	14 39								
Warwick	d			14 05										14 42	14 42								15 05
Leamington Spa 8	a		13 59	14 17			14 21			14 21			14 37	14 46	14 46				14 58				15 16
	d		14 00				14 22			14 22			14 38	14 46	14 46				15 00				
Banbury	d		14a17				14 40			14 40			14a54	15 04	15 04				15a17				
London Marylebone 10 ⊖115	a						15 40			15 43				16 08	16 11								
Spring Road	d					13 56						14 19					14 37				14 56		
Hall Green	d					13 59						14 22					14 39				14 59		
Yardley Wood	d					14 01						14 24					14 42				15 01		
Shirley	d					14 05						14 28					14 45				15 05		
Whitlocks End	d					14a07						14a30					14 48				15a07		
Wythall	d																14 51						
Earlswood (West Midlands)	d																14 53						
The Lakes	d																14x56						
Wood End	d																14x58						
Danzey	d																15x01						
Henley-in-Arden	d																15 06						
Wootton Wawen	d																15x09						
Wilmcote	d																15 15						
Stratford-upon-Avon Parkway	a										14 37						15 18						
Stratford-upon-Avon	a										14 41						15 23						

A until 5 October
B from 8 October

Table T071-R

Mondays to Fridays
21 May to 7 December

Hereford, Worcester and Stourbridge - Birmingham - Leamington Spa, Marylebone and Stratford-upon-Avon

		CH	CH	LM	LM	CH	XC	CH	CH	LM	LM	LM	XC	CH	LM	LM	CH	GW	CH	LM	LM	XC	CH
		◇	◇				◇1	◇	◇				◇1				◇	◇	◇			◇1	◇
		A	B					A	B								A		B				A
							✕						✕									✕	
Hereford 7	d											13 41											
Ledbury	a											13 58											
	d											14 00											
Colwall	d											14 05											
Great Malvern	a											14 10											
	d									14 00		14 10						14 50					
Malvern Link	d									14 03		14 13						14 53					
Worcester Foregate Street 7	a									14 12		14 23						15 02					
	d									14 16		14 24						15 03					
Worcester Shrub Hill 7	a																	15 06					
	d															14 52							
Droitwich Spa	d									14 25		14 33				15 00							
Bromsgrove 69	d											14 43											
Barnt Green	d																						
University	d											15 00											
Hartlebury	d									14 32													
Kidderminster	d				14 25					14 38					14 55	15 10					15 25		
Blakedown	d				14 29										14 59						15 29		
Hagley	d				14 33					14 44					15 03						15 33		
Stourbridge Junction 2	d			14 27	14 37					14 48	14 57				15 07	15 18				15 27	15 37		
Lye	d			14 31							15 01									15 31			
Cradley Heath	d			14 34	14 43					14 54	15 04				15 13	15 24				15 34	15 43		
Old Hill	d			14 37							15 07									15 37			
Rowley Regis	d			14 41	14 48					14 59	15 11				15 18	15 29				15 41	15 48		
Langley Green	d			14 44							15 14									15 44			
Birmingham New Street 12 68	a											15 09											
	d						15 04						15 33									16 04	
Birmingham Intl. 68 ✈	d						15 14															16 14	
Coventry	d						15 25															16 25	
Smethwick Galton Bridge 7	d			14 47	14 54					15 05	15 17				15 24	15 35				15 47	15 54		
The Hawthorns ⇌	d			14 49	14 56					15 07	15 19				15 26	15 37				15 49	15 56		
Jewellery Quarter ⇌	d			14 53	15 00					15 11	15 23				15 30	15 41				15 53	16 00		
Birmingham Snow Hill ⇌	a			14 56	15 04					15 15	15 26				15 34	15 45				15 56	16 04		
	d			14 58	15 07			15 12	15 12	15 17	15 28				15 37	15 47				15 58	16 07		16 12
Birmingham Moor Street	d	14 55	14 55	15 01	15 10			15 15	15 15	15 20	15 31			15 34	15 40	15 50	15 55		15 55	16 01	16 10		16 15
Bordesley	d																						
Small Heath	d				15 13										15 43						16 13		
Tyseley	d				15 17										15 47						16 17		
Acocks Green	d			15 07						15 26					15 49					16 07			
Olton	d			15 10						15 29					15 52					16 10			
Solihull	d	15 04	15 04	15 13				15 24	15 24	15 32				15 43	15 56		16 04		16 04	16 13			16 24
Widney Manor	d			15 17						15 36					15 59					16 17			
Dorridge	d			15 21				15 30	15 30	15a41				15 52	16a04					16a22			16 29
Lapworth	d													15 56									
Hatton	d													16 02									
Warwick Parkway	d	15 16	15 16					15 40	15 40								16 17		16 17				16 39
Warwick	d							15 43	15 43					16 08									16 42
Leamington Spa 8	a	15 21	15 21				15 37	15 47	15 47				16 00	16 18			16 22		16 22			16 37	16 46
	d	15 21	15 21			15 32	15 38	15 47	15 47				16 01				16 23		16 23			16 38	16 46
Banbury	d	15 39	15 39				15a54	16 05	16 05				16a17				16 41		16 41			16a54	17 04
London Marylebone 10 ⊖115	a	16 42	16 45					17 12	17 15								17 45		17 48				18 13
Spring Road	d				15 19						15 37					15 56					16 19		
Hall Green	d				15 22						15 39					15 59					16 22		
Yardley Wood	d				15 24						15 42					16 01					16 24		
Shirley	d				15 28						15 45					16 05					16 28		
Whitlocks End	d				15a30						15 48					16a07					16a30		
Wythall	d										15 51												
Earlswood (West Midlands)	d										15 53												
The Lakes	d										15x56												
Wood End	d										15x58												
Danzey	d										16x01												
Henley-in-Arden	d										16 06												
Wootton Wawen	d										16x09												
Wilmcote	d					15 59					16 15												
Stratford-upon-Avon Parkway	a			15 37		16 01					16 18												
Stratford-upon-Avon	a			15 41		16 12					16 23												

A until 5 October
B from 8 October

Table T071-R

Mondays to Fridays
21 May to 7 December

Hereford, Worcester and Stourbridge - Birmingham - Leamington Spa, Marylebone and Stratford-upon-Avon

		CH ◇ A	LM	LM	LM	XC ◇■ ✕	LM	LM	GW ◇■	GW ◇■	CH ◇ B	CH ◇ A	LM	LM	XC ◇■ ✕	CH ◇ B	CH ◇ A	LM	XC ◇■ ✕	CH	LM	LM
Hereford ■	d				14 39					15 14												
Ledbury	a				14 57					15 30												
	d				14 58					15 31												
Colwall	d				15 05					15 39												
Great Malvern	a				15 10					15 44												
	d				15 10			15 21		15 45												
Malvern Link	d				15 13			15 24		15 50												
Worcester Foregate Street ■	a				15 22			15 33		15 59												
	d				15 24			15 33	15 51	16 01											16 13	
Worcester Shrub Hill ■	a							15 36	15 54	16 04												
	d		15 17					15 47														
Droitwich Spa	d		15 25		15 33			15 55													16 22	
Bromsgrove 69	d				15 43																	
Barnt Green	d																					
University	d				16 00																	
Hartlebury	d		15 32																		16 29	
Kidderminster	d		15 38				15 55	16 06						16 23							16 35	
Blakedown	d		15 42				15 59	16 10						16 27							16 40	
Hagley	d		15 46				16 03	16 14						16 31							16 44	
Stourbridge Junction ■	d		15 50	15 57			16 07	16 18					16 27	16 35							16 48	16 57
Lye	d			16 01									16 31									17 01
Cradley Heath	d		15 55	16 04			16 13	16 24					16 34	16 41							16 54	17 04
Old Hill	d			16 07									16 37									17 07
Rowley Regis	d		16 00	16 11			16 18	16 29					16 41	16 46							16 59	17 11
Langley Green	d			16 14									16 44									17 14
Birmingham New Street ■ 68	a				16 09																	
	d					16 33									17 04				17 33			
Birmingham Intl. 68 ✈	d														17 14							
Coventry	d														17 25							
Smethwick Galton Bridge ■	d		16 06	16 17			16 24	16 35					16 47	16 52							17 05	17 17
The Hawthorns ⇌	d		16 08	16 19			16 26	16 37					16 49	16 54							17 09	17 19
Jewellery Quarter ⇌	d		16 12	16 23			16 30	16 41					16 53	16 58							17 13	17 23
Birmingham Snow Hill ⇌	a		16 16	16 26			16 34	16 45					16 56	17 01							17 18	17 26
	d	16 12	16 17	16 28			16 37	16 47			16 52	16 52	16 58	17 03		17 07	17 07	17 14			17 22	17 28
Birmingham Moor Street	d	16 15	16 20	16 31			16 40	16 50			16 55	16 55	17 01	17 06		17 10	17 10	17 17		17 21	17 25	17 31
Bordesley	d																					
Small Heath	d						16 43	16 53										17 20				
Tyseley	d			16 36			16 47	16 57					17 06					17 24				17 36
Acocks Green	d		16 26				16 49						17 09								17 31	
Olton	d		16 29				16 52						17 11								17 34	
Solihull	d	16 24	16 32				16 56				17 04	17 04	17 15			17 19	17 19			17 30	17 37	
Widney Manor	d		16 36				16 59						17 18			17 22	17 22				17 41	
Dorridge	d	16 29	16a41				17a04						17a23			17 26	17 26			17 35	17a48	
Lapworth	d																			17 39		
Hatton	d																			17 45		
Warwick Parkway	d	16 39									17 16	17 16				17 36	17 36					
Warwick	d	16 42									17 19	17 19				17 39	17 39			17 51		
Leamington Spa ■	a	16 46				16 58					17 23	17 23			17 37	17 43	17 43		17 59	18 01		
	d	16 46				17 00					17 23	17 23			17 38	17 43	17 43		18 01			
Banbury	d	17 04				17a17					17 41	17 41			17a54	18 01	18 01		18a18			
London Marylebone ■ ⊖115	a	18 16									18 39	18 42				19 11	19 14					
Spring Road	d			16 38				16 59						17 12				17 26				17 38
Hall Green	d			16 41				17 02						17 15				17 29				17 41
Yardley Wood	d			16 43				17 04						17 17				17 31				17 43
Shirley	d			16 46				17 08						17 21				17 35				17 46
Whitlocks End	d			16 49				17a10						17 23				17a38				17 49
Wythall	d			16 52										17 26								17 52
Earlswood (West Midlands)	d			16 54																		17 54
The Lakes	d			16x57																		17x57
Wood End	d			16x59																		17x59
Danzey	d			17x02																		18x02
Henley-in-Arden	d			17 07										17 36								18 07
Wootton Wawen	d			17x10																		18x10
Wilmcote	d			17 16																		18 16
Stratford-upon-Avon Parkway	a			17 19										17 46								18 19
Stratford-upon-Avon	a			17 24										17 49								18 24

A from 8 October
B until 5 October

Table T071-R

Mondays to Fridays
21 May to 7 December

Hereford, Worcester and Stourbridge - Birmingham - Leamington Spa, Marylebone and Stratford-upon-Avon

		LM	CH ◇ A	CH ◇ B	CH A	CH B	LM	LM	LM	GW	CH ◇ A	CH ◇ B	LM	LM	XC ◇■ ✕	CH ◇ A	CH ◇ B	LM	LM	LM	XC ◇■ ✕	GW ◇■ ✕	LM
Hereford ■	d	15 39																		16 39			
Ledbury	a	15 56																		16 56			
	d	15 58																		16 57			
Colwall	d	16 05																		17 04			
Great Malvern	a	16 10																		17 08			
	d	16 10								16 48										17 09			17 41
Malvern Link	d	16 13								16 51										17 12			17 44
Worcester Foregate Street ■	a	16 22								17 00										17 21			17 52
	d	16 22						16 34	16 47	17 02								17 15		17 24		17 26	17 53
Worcester Shrub Hill ■	a							16 36		17 04												17 29	18 00
	d							16 40															
Droitwich Spa	d	16 33						16 48	16 55									17 25		17 33			
Bromsgrove 69	d	16 43																		17 42			
Barnt Green	d																						
University	d	17 00																		18 00			
Hartlebury	d							16 55										17 32					
Kidderminster	d						16 53	17 01	17 06					17 25				17 38					
Blakedown	d						16 57		17 10					17 29				17 42					
Hagley	d						17 01		17 14					17 33				17 46					
Stourbridge Junction ■	d						17 05	17 12	17 18				17 27	17 37				17 50	17 57				
Lye	d												17 31						18 01				
Cradley Heath	d						17 11	17 18	17 24				17 34	17 43				17 56	18 04				
Old Hill	d												17 37						18 07				
Rowley Regis	d						17 16	17 23	17 29				17 41	17 48				18 01	18 11				
Langley Green	d												17 44						18 14				
Birmingham New Street ■ 68	a	17 09																		18 09			
	d														18 04						18 33		
Birmingham Intl. 68 ✈	d														18 14								
Coventry	d														18 25								
Smethwick Galton Bridge ■	d						17 22	17 29	17 35				17 47	17 54				18 07	18 17				
The Hawthorns ⇌	d						17 24	17 31	17 37				17 49	17 56				18 09	18 19				
Jewellery Quarter ⇌	d						17 28	17 35	17 41				17 53	18 00				18 13	18 23				
Birmingham Snow Hill ⇌	a						17 32	17 39	17 45				17 56	18 04				18 17	18 26				
	d						17 36	17 42	17 47		17 52	17 52	17 58	18 07		18 12	18 12	18 22	18 28				
Birmingham Moor Street	d						17 39	17 45	17 50		17 55	17 55	18 01	18 10		18 15	18 15	18 25	18 31				
Bordesley	d																						
Small Heath	d						17 42	17 49	17 53				18 04	18 13					18 34				
Tyseley	d						17 47	17 52	17 57				18 08	18 17					18 37				
Acocks Green	d						17 49	17 55					18 10					18 31					
Olton	d						17 52	17 57					18 13					18 34					
Solihull	d						17 56	18 01			18 06	18 06	18 17			18 24	18 24	18 37					
Widney Manor	d						17 59	18 04					18 20					18 41					
Dorridge	d						18 03	18a09			18 12	18 12	18 24			18 29	18 29	18a48					
Lapworth	d						18 07						18 28			18 34	18 34						
Hatton	d		17 58	17 58			18 12									18 40	18 40						
Warwick Parkway	d						18 16				18 22	18 22				18 45	18 45						
Warwick	d		18 05	18 05			18 19									18 48	18 48						
Leamington Spa ■	a		18 09	18 09			18 26				18 27	18 27			18 37	18 52	18 52				19 00		
	d		18 09	18 09	18 11	18 11					18 28	18 28			18 38	18 53	18 53				19 01		
Banbury	d		18 28	18 28							18 46	18 46			18a55	19 12	19 12				19a17		
London Marylebone ■ ⊖115	a		19 41	19 44							19 44	19 47				20 23	20 26						
Spring Road	d								17 59					18 19					18 40				
Hall Green	d								18 02					18 22					18 42				
Yardley Wood	d								18 04					18 24					18 45				
Shirley	d								18 08					18 28					18 48				
Whitlocks End	d								18 10					18a30					18 51				
Wythall	d								18 13										18 53				
Earlswood (West Midlands)	d								18 15										18 56				
The Lakes	d								18x18										18x58				
Wood End	d								18x20										19x00				
Danzey	d								18x23										19x02				
Henley-in-Arden	d								18 28										19 07				
Wootton Wawen	d								18x31										19x10				
Wilmcote	d				18 44	18 44			18 37										19 16				
Stratford-upon-Avon Parkway	a				18 46	18 46			18 40				18 55						19 19				
Stratford-upon-Avon	a				18 51	18 54			18 43				18 59						19 23				

A until 5 October
B from 8 October

Please note, Network Rail have stated that further updates to this timetable are possible during the validity period.

Table T071-R

Mondays to Fridays

21 May to 7 December

Hereford, Worcester and Stourbridge - Birmingham - Leamington Spa, Marylebone and Stratford-upon-Avon

		CH ◇ A	CH ◇ B	LM	LM	XC ◇1 ♈	LM	CH ◇ A	CH ◇ B	LM	LM	LM	GW ◇1 ♈	LM	GW	XC ◇1 ♈	CH ◇ A	CH ◇ B	XC ◇1	LM	CH ◇ A	CH ◇ B
Hereford 7	d						17 39													18 48		
Ledbury	a						17 56													19 03		
	d						17 58													19 04		
Colwall	d						18 05													19 10		
Great Malvern	a						18 09													19 14		
	d						18 10						18 29		18 50					19 15		
Malvern Link	d						18 13						18 33		18 53					19 18		
Worcester Foregate Street 7	a						18 23						18 41		19 02					19 26		
	d				17 56		18 24						18 43	18 46	19 03					19 28		
Worcester Shrub Hill 7	a												18 46		19 06							
	d											18 37										
Droitwich Spa	d				18 05		18 33					18 45		18 55						19 37		
Bromsgrove 69	d						18 42													19 47		
Barnt Green	d																					
University	d						19 00													20 09		
Hartlebury	d													19 02								
Kidderminster	d			18 00	18 15					18 38		18 55		19 10								
Blakedown	d			18 05						18 42		18 59		19 15								
Hagley	d			18 08	18 21					18 46		19 03		19 18								
Stourbridge Junction 2	d			18 12	18 25					18 50		19 06		19 25								
Lye	d				18 29					18 54				19 29								
Cradley Heath	d			18 18	18 32					18 57		19 13		19 32								
Old Hill	d				18 36					19 00				19 35								
Rowley Regis	d			18 24	18 39					19 04		19 18		19 39								
Langley Green	d				18 42					19 07				19 42								
Birmingham New Street 12 68	a						19 09													20 17		
	d					19 04										19 33			20 04			
Birmingham Intl. 68 ✈	d					19 14													20 14			
Coventry	d					19 25													20 25			
Smethwick Galton Bridge 7	d			18 29	18 46					19 10		19 24		19 45								
The Hawthorns 🚊	d			18 31	18 48					19 12		19 26		19 47								
Jewellery Quarter 🚊	d			18 36	18 52					19 16		19 30		19 51								
Birmingham Snow Hill 🚊	a			18 43	18 55					19 20		19 34		19 55								
	d	18 40	18 40	18 45	18 57			19 17	19 17	19 22	19 28			19 57							20 15	20 15
Birmingham Moor Street	d	18 43	18 43	18 48	19 00			19 20	19 20	19 25	19 31			20 00							20 18	20 18
Bordesley	d																					
Small Heath	d			18 51	19 03						19 34			20 03								
Tyseley	d			18 55	19 07						19 37			20 07								
Acocks Green	d			18 57						19 31				20 09								
Olton	d			19 00						19 34				20 12								
Solihull	d	18 52	18 52	19 04				19 29	19 29	19 37				20 16							20 27	20 27
Widney Manor	d			19 07						19 41				20 19								
Dorridge	d	18 57	18 57	19 11				19 34	19 34	19a48				20a24							20 32	20 32
Lapworth	d			19 15				19 38	19 38													
Hatton	d			19 20				19 44	19 44													
Warwick Parkway	d	19 07	19 07	19 24				19 49	19 49												20 42	20 42
Warwick	d			19 27				19 52	19 52												20 45	20 45
Leamington Spa 8	a	19 12	19 12	19 34		19 37		19 56	19 56							20 00			20 37		20 49	20 49
	d	19 12	19 12			19 38		19 57	19 57							20 02	20 26	20 26	20 38		20 50	20 50
Banbury	d	19 30	19 30			19a54		20 16	20 16							20a19			20a55		21 13	21 13
London Marylebone 15 ⊖115	a	20 37	20 40					21 35	21 38												22 12	22 15
Spring Road	d				19 09						19 40											
Hall Green	d				19 12						19 42											
Yardley Wood	d				19 14						19 45											
Shirley	d				19 18						19 48											
Whitlocks End	d				19a20						19 51											
Wythall	d										19 53											
Earlswood (West Midlands)	d										19 56											
The Lakes	d										19x58											
Wood End	d										20x00											
Danzey	d										20x02											
Henley-in-Arden	d										20 07											
Wootton Wawen	d										20x10											
Wilmcote	d										20 15						20 48	20 48				
Stratford-upon-Avon Parkway	a										20 18						20 50	20 50				
Stratford-upon-Avon	a										20 23						20 54	20 57				

A until 5 October

B from 8 October

Table T071-R

Mondays to Fridays

21 May to 7 December

Hereford, Worcester and Stourbridge - Birmingham - Leamington Spa, Marylebone and Stratford-upon-Avon

		LM	LM	GW ◇1 ♈	XC ◇1	XC ◇1	LM	CH ◇ A	CH ◇ B	LM	LM	GW ◇1	LM	GW	CH ◇ A	CH ◇ B	CH ◇	XC ◇1	CH	LM	CH	LM	LM
Hereford 7	d						19 50						20 56										21 29
Ledbury	a						20 06						21 12										21 45
	d						20 09						21 14										21 45
Colwall	d						20 15						21 20										21 52
Great Malvern	a						20 19						21 25										21 56
	d			19 42			20 20						21 25	21 36									21 57
Malvern Link	d			19 46			20 22						21 28	21 39									22 00
Worcester Foregate Street 7	a			19 55			20 31						21 36	21 47									22 09
	d		19 46	19 57			20 31				20 51	20 59	21 37	21 49									22 10
Worcester Shrub Hill 7	a			20 00			20 34					21 02	21 39	21 51									
	d						20 37															21 54	
Droitwich Spa	d		19 55				20 45				21 00											22 02	22 19
Bromsgrove 69	d						20 55																22 28
Barnt Green	d																						
University	d						21 14																22 46
Hartlebury	d		20 02								21 07												
Kidderminster	d		20 10								21 13											22 13	
Blakedown	d		20 15								21 17											22 17	
Hagley	d		20 18								21 21											22 21	
Stourbridge Junction 2	d	19 57	20 25							20 57	21 25									21 57		22 25	
Lye	d	20 01	20 29							21 01	21 29									22 01		22 29	
Cradley Heath	d	20 04	20 32							21 04	21 32									22 04		22 32	
Old Hill	d	20 07	20 35							21 07	21 35									22 07		22 35	
Rowley Regis	d	20 11	20 39							21 11	21 39									22 11		22 39	
Langley Green	d	20 14	20 42							21 14	21 42									22 14		22 42	
Birmingham New Street 12 68	a						21 20																22 54
	d				20 34	21 04												22 04					
Birmingham Intl. 68 ✈	d					21 14												22 14					
Coventry	d					21 25												22 25					
Smethwick Galton Bridge 7	d	20 17	20 45							21 17	21 45									22 17		22 45	
The Hawthorns 🚊	d	20 19	20 47							21 19	21 47									22 19		22 47	
Jewellery Quarter 🚊	d	20 23	20 51							21 23	21 51									22 23		22 51	
Birmingham Snow Hill 🚊	a	20 26	20 55							21 26	21 55									22 26		22 55	
	d	20 28	20 57					21 15	21 15	21 28	21 57								22 12	22 28		22 57	
Birmingham Moor Street	d	20 31	21 00					21 18	21 18	21 31	22 00								22 15	22 31		23 00	
Bordesley	d																						
Small Heath	d	20 34	21 03							21 34	22 03									22 34		23 03	
Tyseley	d	20 37	21 07							21 37	22 07								22 20	22 37		23 07	
Acocks Green	d		21 09								22 09								22 23			23 09	
Olton	d		21 12								22 12								22 26			23 12	
Solihull	d		21 16					21 27	21 27		22 16								22 30			23 16	
Widney Manor	d		21 19								22 19								22 33			23 19	
Dorridge	d		21a24					21 32	21 32		22a24								22 37			23 23	
Lapworth	d							21 36	21 36										22 41			23 27	
Hatton	d							21 42	21 42						21 59	21 59			22 47			23 32	
Warwick Parkway	d							21 47	21 47										22 52			23 36	
Warwick	d							21 50	21 50						22 06	22 06			22 55		23 34	23 39	
Leamington Spa 8	a				20 59	21 37		21 54	21 54						22 10	22 10		22 37	22 59		23 38	23 44	
	d				21 00	21 38		21 55	21 55						22 10	22 10	22 20	22 38	23 00		23 39		
Banbury	d				21a17	21a54		22 13	22 13						22 30	22 30		22a54	23a26		23a57		
London Marylebone 15 ⊖115	a							23 12	23 15						23 58	00 01							
Spring Road	d	20 40								21 40										22 40			
Hall Green	d	20 42								21 42										22 42			
Yardley Wood	d	20 45								21 45										22 45			
Shirley	d	20 48								21 48										22 48			
Whitlocks End	d	20 51								21 51										22 51			
Wythall	d	20 53								21 53										22 53			
Earlswood (West Midlands)	d	20 56								21 56										22 56			
The Lakes	d	20x58								21x58										22x58			
Wood End	d	21x00								22x00										23x00			
Danzey	d	21x02								22x02										23x02			
Henley-in-Arden	d	21 07								22 07										23 07			
Wootton Wawen	d	21x10								22x10										23x10			
Wilmcote	d	21 15								22 15							22 43			23 15			
Stratford-upon-Avon Parkway	a	21 18								22 18							22 45			23 18			
Stratford-upon-Avon	a	21 23								22 23							22 56			23 23			

A until 5 October

B from 8 October

Please note, Network Rail have stated that further updates to this timetable are possible during the validity period.

Table T071-R

Mondays to Fridays
21 May to 7 December

Hereford, Worcester and Stourbridge - Birmingham - Leamington Spa, Marylebone and Stratford-upon-Avon

		CH	LM	GW ◇■	LM
Hereford ■	d			21 51	22 59
Ledbury	a			22 08	23 15
	d			22 11	23 15
Colwall	d			22 18	23 22
Great Malvern	a			22 23	23 26
	d			22 24	23 27
Malvern Link	d				23 30
Worcester Foregate Street ■	a			22 34	23 39
	d		22 17	22 36	23 40
Worcester Shrub Hill ■	a		22 19	22 39	23 47
	d		22 27		
Droitwich Spa	d		22 35		
Bromsgrove 69	d				
Barnt Green	d				
University	d				
Hartlebury	d		22 42		
Kidderminster	d		22 51		
Blakedown	d				
Hagley	d				
Stourbridge Junction ■	d		23 00		
Lye	d		23 04		
Cradley Heath	d		23 07		
Old Hill	d		23 10		
Rowley Regis	d		23 14		
Langley Green	d		23 17		
Birmingham New Street ■ 68	a				
	d				
Birmingham Intl. 68 ✈	d				
Coventry	d				
Smethwick Galton Bridge ■	d		23 20		
The Hawthorns ⇌	d		23 22		
Jewellery Quarter ⇌	d		23 26		
Birmingham Snow Hill ⇌	a		23 29		
	d	23 30	23 34		
Birmingham Moor Street	d	23 33	23 37		
Bordesley	d				
Small Heath	d		23 40		
Tyseley	d	23 38	23 44		
Acocks Green	d	23 41			
Olton	d	23 44			
Solihull	d	23 48			
Widney Manor	d	23 51			
Dorridge	d	23 55			
Lapworth	d	23 59			
Hatton	d	00 05			
Warwick Parkway	d	00 10			
Warwick	d	00 13			
Leamington Spa ■	a	00 17			
	d	00 18			
Banbury	d	00a42			
London Marylebone ■ ⊖115	a				
Spring Road	d		23 46		
Hall Green	d		23 49		
Yardley Wood	d		23 51		
Shirley	d		23 55		
Whitlocks End	d		23a57		
Wythall	d				
Earlswood (West Midlands)	d				
The Lakes	d				
Wood End	d				
Danzey	d				
Henley-in-Arden	d				
Wootton Wawen	d				
Wilmcote	d				
Stratford-upon-Avon Parkway	a				
Stratford-upon-Avon	a				

Table T071-R

Saturdays
26 May to 8 December

Hereford, Worcester and Stourbridge - Birmingham - Leamington Spa, Marylebone and Stratford-upon-Avon

		CH	XC ◇■ ✕	CH ◇ A	CH ◇ B	XC ◇■	CH ◇ A	CH ◇ B	LM	LM		XC ◇■ ✕	GW ◇■	CH ◇ A	CH ◇ B	LM	XC ◇■ ✕	CH	LM	LM		CH ◇ A	CH ◇ B	LM	GW ◇■
Hereford ■	d																								06 17
Ledbury	a																								06 33
	d																								06 34
Colwall	d																								06 42
Great Malvern	a																								06 46
	d												05 54							06 17					06 48
Malvern Link	d												05 58							06 20					06 52
Worcester Foregate Street ■	a												06 07							06 27					07 01
	d												06 09							06 28					07 03
Worcester Shrub Hill ■	a												06 12												07 06
	d								05 43	06 07									06 21					07 01	
Droitwich Spa	d								05 51	06 15									06 29	06 37				07 09	
Bromsgrove 69	d																			06 47					
Barnt Green	d																								
University	d																			07 10					
Hartlebury	d								05 59										06 36					07 16	
Kidderminster	d								06 05					06 37	06 37				06 43			07 12	07 12	07 22	
Blakedown	d								06 09										06 47					07 26	
Hagley	d								06 13										06 51					07 30	
Stourbridge Junction ■	d								06 17					06 45	06 45				06 57			07 22	07 22	07 35	
Lye	d								06 21										07 01					07 39	
Cradley Heath	d								06 24					06 51	06 51				07 04					07 42	
Old Hill	d								06 27										07 08					07 45	
Rowley Regis	d								06 31					06 57	06 57				07 11			07 33	07 33	07 49	
Langley Green	d								06 34										07 14					07 52	
Birmingham New Street ■ 68	a									06 47										07 17					
	d		06 04			06 33						07 04					07 33								
Birmingham Intl. 68 ✈	d		06 14									07 14													
Coventry	d		06 25									07 25													
Smethwick Galton Bridge ■	d								06 37					07 02	07 02				07 18			07 41	07 41	07 55	
The Hawthorns ⇌	d								06 39					07 05	07 05				07 20			07 44	07 44	07 57	
Jewellery Quarter ⇌	d								06 43										07 24					08 01	
Birmingham Snow Hill ⇌	a								06 47					07 11	07 11				07 28			07 49	07 49	08 05	
	d			06 12	06 12		06 46	06 46	06 50					07 12	07 12	07 25			07 33			07 51	07 51	08 07	
Birmingham Moor Street	d			06 15	06 15		06 49	06 49	06 53					07 15	07 15	07 28		07 34	07 36			07 55	07 55	08 10	
Bordesley	d																								
Small Heath	d								06 56							07 31								08 13	
Tyseley	d								06 59							07 34								08 17	
Acocks Green	d								07 02										07 43						
Olton	d								07 05										07 46						
Solihull	d			06 24	06 24		07 02	07 02	07 09					07 24	07 24			07 42	07 49			08 05	08 05		
Widney Manor	d								07 12										07 53						
Dorridge	d			06 29	06 29				07a17					07 29	07 29			07 53	07a58						
Lapworth	d			06 33	06 33													07 57							
Hatton	d	00 05		06 39	06 39													08 03							
Warwick Parkway	d	00 10		06 44	06 44		07 14	07 14						07 39	07 39							08 18	08 18		
Warwick	d	00 13		06 47	06 47									07 42	07 42			08 09							
Leamington Spa ■	a	00 17	06 37	06 51	06 51	06 58	07 19	07 19				07 37		07 46	07 46		08 00	08 19				08 23	08 23		
	d	00 18	06 38	06 52	06 52	07 00	07 20	07 20				07 38		07 46	07 46		08 01					08 24	08 24		
Banbury	d	00a42	06a54	07 10	07 10	07a17	07 39	07 39				07a54		08 04	08 04		08a17					08 44	08 44		
London Marylebone ■ ⊖115	a			08 14	08 17		08 42	08 45						09 11	09 14							09 41	09 44		
Spring Road	d															07 37								08 19	
Hall Green	d															07 39								08 22	
Yardley Wood	d															07 42								08 24	
Shirley	d															07 45								08 28	
Whitlocks End	d															07 48								08a30	
Wythall	d															07 51									
Earlswood (West Midlands)	d															07 53									
The Lakes	d															07x56									
Wood End	d															07x58									
Danzey	d															08x01									
Henley-in-Arden	d															08 06									
Wootton Wawen	d															08x09									
Wilmcote	d															08 15									
Stratford-upon-Avon Parkway	a															08 18									
Stratford-upon-Avon	a															08 21									

A until 6 October
B from 13 October

Table T071-R

Saturdays

26 May to 8 December

Hereford, Worcester and Stourbridge - Birmingham - Leamington Spa, Marylebone and Stratford-upon-Avon

		CH	CH	CH	XC	XC	LM	CH	CH	LM	LM	LM	LM	GW	XC	CH	CH	LM	LM	XC	CH	CH	LM
		◇ A	◇ B		◇■ C	◇■ D		◇ A	◇ B					◇■	◇■	◇ A	◇ B			◇■	◇ A	◇ B	
Hereford ■	d													07 13									
Ledbury	a													07 29									
	d													07 30									
Colwall	d													07 38									
Great Malvern	a													07 42									
	d						07 12							07 44									
Malvern Link	d						07 15							07 48									
Worcester Foregate Street ■	a						07 23							07 57									
	d						07 24						07 47	07 59									
Worcester Shrub Hill ■	a						07 26							08 02									
	d						07 29																08 15
Droitwich Spa	d						07 37						07 56										08 23
Bromsgrove 69	d						07 47																
Barnt Green	d																						
University	d						08 10																
Hartlebury	d																						08 31
Kidderminster	d										07 47		08 06			08 13	08 13						08 36
Blakedown	d										07 51		08 11										08 41
Hagley	d										07 55		08 14										08 44
Stourbridge Junction ■	d										07 59	08 05	08 19			08 24	08 24		08 35				08 48
Lye	d											08 09							08 39				
Cradley Heath	d										08 04	08 12	08 25			08 30	08 30		08 42				08 54
Old Hill	d											08 15							08 45				
Rowley Regis	d										08 10	08 19	08 30			08 36	08 36		08 49				08 59
Langley Green	d											08 22							08 52				
Birmingham New Street ■ 68	a						08 17																
	d				08 04	08 04									08 33					09 04			
Birmingham Intl. 68 ✈	d				08 14	08 14														09 14			
Coventry	d				08 25	08 25														09 25			
Smethwick Galton Bridge ■	d										08 16	08 25	08 36			08 42	08 42		08 55				09 05
The Hawthorns	d										08 18	08 27	08 38			08 45	08 45		08 57				09 07
Jewellery Quarter	d										08 22	08 31	08 42						09 01				09 11
Birmingham Snow Hill	a										08 26	08 35	08 45			08 51	08 51		09 05				09 15
	d									08 17	08 28	08 37	08 47			08 53	08 53	08 58	09 07		09 12	09 12	09 17
Birmingham Moor Street	d							08 15	08 15	08 20	08 31	08 40	08 50			08 56	08 56	09 01	09 10		09 15	09 15	09 20
Bordesley	d																						
Small Heath	d											08 43							09 13				
Tyseley	d											08 47							09 17				
Acocks Green	d									08 26		08 49						09 07					09 26
Olton	d									08 29		08 52						09 10					09 29
Solihull	d							08 24	08 24	08 32		08 56				09 05	09 05	09 13			09 24	09 24	09 32
Widney Manor	d									08 36		08 59						09 17					09 36
Dorridge	d							08 29	08 29	08a41		09a04						09 21			09 29	09 29	09a41
Lapworth	d																						
Hatton	d	08 17	08 17																				
Warwick Parkway	d							08 39	08 39							09 16	09 16				09 39	09 39	
Warwick	d	08 24	08 24					08 42	08 42												09 42	09 42	
Leamington Spa ■	a	08 28	08 28		08 37	08 37		08 46	08 46						08 58	09 21	09 21			09 37	09 46	09 46	
	d	08 29	08 29	08 30	08 38	08 38		08 46	08 46						09 00	09 22	09 22			09 38	09 46	09 46	
Banbury	d	08 48	08 48		08a54	08a54		09 04	09 04						09a17	09 40	09 40			09a55	10 05	10 05	
London Marylebone ■ ⊖115	a	10 05	10 08					10 11	10 14							10 41	10 44				11 11	11 14	
Spring Road	d										08 37		08 56						09 19				
Hall Green	d										08 39		08 59						09 22				
Yardley Wood	d										08 42		09 01						09 24				
Shirley	d										08 45		09 05						09 28				
Whitlocks End	d										08 48		09a07						09a30				
Wythall	d										08 51												
Earlswood (West Midlands)	d										08 53												
The Lakes	d										08x56												
Wood End	d										08x58												
Danzey	d										09x01												
Henley-in-Arden	d										09 06												
Wootton Wawen	d										09x09												
Wilmcote	d			08 58							09 15												
Stratford-upon-Avon Parkway	a			09 01							09 18							09 45					
Stratford-upon-Avon	a			09 12							09 23							09 49					

A until 6 October
B from 13 October
C until 21 July, from 8 September
D from 28 July until 1 September

Table T071-R

Saturdays

26 May to 8 December

Hereford, Worcester and Stourbridge - Birmingham - Leamington Spa, Marylebone and Stratford-upon-Avon

		LM	LM	XC	CH	LM	LM	CH	CH	LM	LM	GW	XC	CH	CH	LM	LM	LM	XC	LM	LM	LM
				◇■				◇ A	◇ B			◇■	◇■	◇ A	◇ B				◇■			
Hereford ■	d		07 37															08 39				
Ledbury	a		07 53															08 56				
	d		07 58															08 58				
Colwall	d		08 05															09 05				
Great Malvern	a		08 09															09 10				
	d		08 10									08 43				09 00		09 10				
Malvern Link	d		08 13									08 47				09 02		09 13				
Worcester Foregate Street ■	a		08 21									08 56				09 12		09 22				
	d		08 24							08 56		08 58				09 16		09 24				09 51
Worcester Shrub Hill ■	a											09 01										
	d																			09 44		
Droitwich Spa	d		08 33							09 05						09 25		09 33		09 52		10 00
Bromsgrove 69	d		08 43															09 43		10 08		
Barnt Green	d																					
University	d		09 00															10 00				
Hartlebury	d															09 32						
Kidderminster	d							09 10	09 10	09 16	09 25					09 38					09 55	10 10
Blakedown	d										09 29										09 59	
Hagley	d										09 33					09 44					10 03	
Stourbridge Junction ■	d	08 57				09 07		09 20	09 20	09 27	09 37					09 48	09 57				10 07	10 18
Lye	d	09 01								09 31							10 01					
Cradley Heath	d	09 04				09 13				09 34	09 43					09 54	10 04				10 13	10 24
Old Hill	d	09 07								09 37							10 07					
Rowley Regis	d	09 11				09 18		09 31	09 31	09 41	09 48					09 59	10 11				10 18	10 30
Langley Green	d	09 14								09 44							10 14					
Birmingham New Street ■ 68	a		09 09															10 09		10 44		
	d			09 33									10 04						10 33			
Birmingham Intl. 68 ✈	d												10 14									
Coventry	d												10 25									
Smethwick Galton Bridge ■	d	09 17				09 24		09 39	09 39	09 47	09 54					10 05	10 17				10 24	10 35
The Hawthorns	d	09 19				09 26		09 42	09 42	09 49	09 56					10 07	10 19				10 26	10 37
Jewellery Quarter	d	09 23				09 30				09 53	10 00					10 11	10 23				10 30	10 41
Birmingham Snow Hill	a	09 26				09 34		09 50	09 50	09 56	10 04					10 15	10 26				10 34	10 45
	d	09 28				09 37	09 47	09 51	09 51	09 58	10 07			10 12	10 12	10 17	10 28				10 37	10 47
Birmingham Moor Street	d	09 31			09 34	09 40	09 50	09 55	09 55	10 01	10 10			10 15	10 15	10 20	10 31				10 40	10 50
Bordesley	d																					
Small Heath	d					09 43					10 13										10 43	
Tyseley	d					09 47					10 17										10 47	
Acocks Green	d					09 49				10 07						10 26					10 49	
Olton	d					09 52				10 10						10 29					10 52	
Solihull	d				09 43	09 56		10 04	10 04	10 13				10 24	10 24	10 32					10 56	
Widney Manor	d					09 59				10 17						10 36					10 59	
Dorridge	d				09 54	10a04				10 21				10 29	10 29	10a41					11a04	
Lapworth	d				09 58																	
Hatton	d				10 04																	
Warwick Parkway	d							10 19	10 19					10 39	10 39							
Warwick	d				10 10									10 42	10 42							
Leamington Spa ■	a			09 59	10 19			10 24	10 24				10 37	10 46	10 46				10 58			
	d			10 00				10 25	10 25				10 38	10 46	10 46				11 00			
Banbury	d			10a17				10 44	10 44				10a54	11 05	11 05				11a17			
London Marylebone ■ ⊖115	a							11 46	11 49					12 11	12 14							
Spring Road	d	09 37					09 56				10 19						10 37					10 56
Hall Green	d	09 39					09 59				10 22						10 39					10 59
Yardley Wood	d	09 42					10 01				10 24						10 42					11 01
Shirley	d	09 45					10 05				10 28						10 45					11 05
Whitlocks End	d	09 48					10a07				10a30						10 48					11a07
Wythall	d	09 51															10 51					
Earlswood (West Midlands)	d	09 53															10 53					
The Lakes	d	09x56															10x56					
Wood End	d	09x58															10x58					
Danzey	d	10x01															11x01					
Henley-in-Arden	d	10 06															11 06					
Wootton Wawen	d	10x09															11x09					
Wilmcote	d	10 15															11 15					
Stratford-upon-Avon Parkway	a	10 18								10 37							11 18					
Stratford-upon-Avon	a	10 23								10 41							11 23					

A until 6 October
B from 13 October

Please note, Network Rail have stated that further updates to this timetable are possible during the validity period.

Table T071-R

Saturdays
26 May to 8 December

Hereford, Worcester and Stourbridge - Birmingham - Leamington Spa, Marylebone and Stratford-upon-Avon

		GW	CH	CH	CH	LM	LM	CH		XC	CH	CH	LM	LM	LM	XC	CH	LM		LM	CH	GW	GW	CH	LM
		◇1		◇	◇					◇1	◇	◇				◇1					◇	◇1	1	◇	
				A	B						A	B									A			B	
		☕								🍴						🍴						☕			
Hereford 7	d														09 39										
Ledbury	a														09 56										
	d														09 58										
Colwall	d														10 05										
Great Malvern	a														10 10										
	d	09 45													10 10							10 45	10 57		
Malvern Link	d	09 49													10 13							10 49	11 00		
Worcester Foregate Street 7	a	09 58													10 22							10 58	11 09		
	d	10 00											10 16		10 24							11 00	11 10		
Worcester Shrub Hill 7	a	10 03																				11 03	11 12		
	d																			10 52					
Droitwich Spa	d												10 25		10 33					11 00					
Bromsgrove 69	d														10 43										
Barnt Green	d																								
University	d														11 00										
Hartlebury	d												10 32												
Kidderminster	d						10 25						10 38					10 55		11 10					
Blakedown	d						10 29											10 59							
Hagley	d						10 33						10 44					11 03							
Stourbridge Junction 2	d					10 27	10 37						10 48	10 57				11 07		11 18					11 27
Lye	d					10 31								11 01											11 31
Cradley Heath	d					10 34	10 43						10 54	11 04				11 13		11 24					11 34
Old Hill	d					10 37								11 07											11 37
Rowley Regis	d					10 41	10 48						10 59	11 11				11 18		11 30					11 41
Langley Green	d					10 44								11 14											11 44
Birmingham New Street 12 68	a														11 09										
	d									11 04						11 33									
Birmingham Intl. 68 ✈	d									11 14															
Coventry	d									11 25															
Smethwick Galton Bridge 2	d					10 47	10 54						11 05	11 17				11 24		11 35					11 47
The Hawthorns 🚊	d					10 49	10 56						11 07	11 19				11 26		11 37					11 49
Jewellery Quarter 🚊	d					10 53	11 00						11 11	11 23				11 30		11 41					11 53
Birmingham Snow Hill 🚊	a					10 56	11 04						11 15	11 26				11 34		11 45					11 56
	d					10 58	11 07				11 12	11 12	11 17	11 28				11 37		11 47					11 58
Birmingham Moor Street	d			10 55	10 55	11 01	11 10				11 15	11 15	11 20	11 31			11 34	11 40		11 50	11 55			11 55	12 01
Bordesley	d																								
Small Heath	d						11 13											11 43							
Tyseley	d						11 17											11 47							
Acocks Green	d					11 07							11 26					11 49							12 07
Olton	d					11 10							11 29					11 52							12 10
Solihull	d			11 04	11 04	11 13					11 24	11 24	11 32				11 43	11 56			12 04			12 04	12 13
Widney Manor	d					11 17							11 36					11 59							12 17
Dorridge	d					11 21					11 29	11 29	11a41				11 54	12a04							12 21
Lapworth	d																11 58								
Hatton	d		11 02														12 04								
Warwick Parkway	d			11 16	11 16						11 39	11 39									12 19			12 19	
Warwick	d		11 08								11 42	11 42					12 09								
Leamington Spa 8	a		11 16	11 21	11 21					11 37	11 46	11 46				11 58	12 19				12 25			12 25	
	d			11 21	11 21			11 32		11 38	11 46	11 46				12 00					12 25			12 25	
Banbury	d			11 39	11 39					11a54	12 05	12 05				12a17					12 44			12 44	
London Marylebone 10 ⊖115	a			12 41	12 44						13 11	13 14									13 41			13 44	
Spring Road	d						11 19							11 37						11 56					
Hall Green	d						11 22							11 39						11 59					
Yardley Wood	d						11 24							11 42						12 01					
Shirley	d						11 28							11 45						12 05					
Whitlocks End	d						11a30							11 48						12a07					
Wythall	d													11 51											
Earlswood (West Midlands)	d													11 53											
The Lakes	d													11x56											
Wood End	d													11x58											
Danzey	d													12x01											
Henley-in-Arden	d													12 06											
Wootton Wawen	d													12x09											
Wilmcote	d													12 15											
Stratford-upon-Avon Parkway	a					11 37		11 55						12 18											12 37
Stratford-upon-Avon	a					11 41		12 05						12 23											12 41

A until 6 October
B from 13 October

Table T071-R

Saturdays
26 May to 8 December

Hereford, Worcester and Stourbridge - Birmingham - Leamington Spa, Marylebone and Stratford-upon-Avon

		LM	XC	CH		CH	LM	LM	LM	XC	LM	LM	GW	CH		CH	CH	LM	LM	CH	XC	CH	CH	LM
			◇1	◇		◇				◇1			◇1			◇	◇				◇1	◇	◇	
				A		B										A	B					A	B	
			🍴							🍴			☕								🍴			
Hereford 7	d								10 39															
Ledbury	a								10 56															
	d								10 58															
Colwall	d								11 05															
Great Malvern	a								11 10															
	d								11 10			11 37												
Malvern Link	d								11 13			11 39												
Worcester Foregate Street 7	a								11 22			11 48												
	d								11 24			11 51	12 06											12 16
Worcester Shrub Hill 7	a												12 09											
	d						11 17																	
Droitwich Spa	d						11 25		11 33			12 00												12 25
Bromsgrove 69	d								11 43															
Barnt Green	d																							
University	d								12 00															
Hartlebury	d						11 32																	12 32
Kidderminster	d	11 25					11 38				11 55	12 10							12 25					12 38
Blakedown	d	11 29									11 59								12 29					
Hagley	d	11 33					11 44				12 03								12 33					12 44
Stourbridge Junction 2	d	11 37					11 48	11 57			12 07	12 18						12 27	12 37					12 48
Lye	d							12 01										12 31						
Cradley Heath	d	11 43					11 54	12 04			12 13	12 24						12 34	12 43					12 54
Old Hill	d							12 07										12 37						
Rowley Regis	d	11 48					11 59	12 11			12 18	12 30						12 41	12 48					12 59
Langley Green	d							12 14										12 44						
Birmingham New Street 12 68	a								12 09															
	d		12 04							12 33											13 04			
Birmingham Intl. 68 ✈	d		12 14																		13 14			
Coventry	d		12 25																		13 25			
Smethwick Galton Bridge 2	d	11 54					12 05	12 17			12 24	12 35						12 47	12 54					13 05
The Hawthorns 🚊	d	11 56					12 07	12 19			12 26	12 37						12 49	12 56					13 07
Jewellery Quarter 🚊	d	12 00					12 11	12 23			12 30	12 41						12 53	13 00					13 11
Birmingham Snow Hill 🚊	a	12 04					12 15	12 26			12 34	12 45						12 56	13 04					13 15
	d	12 07		12 12		12 12	12 17	12 28			12 37	12 47						12 58	13 07			13 12	13 12	13 17
Birmingham Moor Street	d	12 10		12 15		12 15	12 20	12 31			12 40	12 50				12 55	12 55	13 01	13 10			13 15	13 15	13 20
Bordesley	d																							
Small Heath	d	12 13									12 43								13 13					
Tyseley	d	12 17									12 47								13 17					
Acocks Green	d						12 26				12 49							13 07						13 26
Olton	d						12 29				12 52							13 10						13 29
Solihull	d			12 24		12 24	12 32				12 56					13 04	13 04	13 13				13 24	13 24	13 32
Widney Manor	d						12 36				12 59							13 17						13 36
Dorridge	d			12 29		12 29	12a41				13a04							13 21				13 29	13 29	13a41
Lapworth	d																							
Hatton	d													13 03										
Warwick Parkway	d			12 39		12 39										13 16	13 16					13 38	13 38	
Warwick	d			12 42		12 42								13 09								13 41	13 41	
Leamington Spa 8	a		12 37	12 46		12 46				12 58				13 17		13 21	13 21				13 37	13 45	13 45	
	d		12 38	12 46		12 46				13 00						13 22	13 22			13 32	13 38	13 46	13 46	
Banbury	d		12a54	13 05		13 05				13a17						13 40	13 40				13a54	14 07	14 07	
London Marylebone 10 ⊖115	a			14 11		14 14										14 41	14 44					15 11	15 14	
Spring Road	d	12 19						12 37				12 56							13 19					
Hall Green	d	12 22						12 39				12 59							13 22					
Yardley Wood	d	12 24						12 42				13 01							13 24					
Shirley	d	12 28						12 45				13 05							13 28					
Whitlocks End	d	12a30						12 48				13a07							13a30					
Wythall	d							12 51																
Earlswood (West Midlands)	d							12 53																
The Lakes	d							12x56																
Wood End	d							12x58																
Danzey	d							13x01																
Henley-in-Arden	d							13 06																
Wootton Wawen	d							13x09																
Wilmcote	d							13 15												13 57				
Stratford-upon-Avon Parkway	a							13 18										13 37		14 00				
Stratford-upon-Avon	a							13 23										13 41		14 09				

A until 6 October
B from 13 October

Table T071-R

Hereford, Worcester and Stourbridge - Birmingham - Leamington Spa, Marylebone and Stratford-upon-Avon

Saturdays
26 May to 8 December

		LM	LM	XC	GW	CH	LM	LM	CH	GW	CH	LM	LM	XC	CH	CH	LM	LM	LM	XC	LM	LM	CH
				◇■	◇				◇ A	◇■	◇ B			◇■	◇ A	◇ B				◇■			
Hereford ■	d		11 39							12 13									12 39				
Ledbury	a		11 56							12 29									12 56				
	d		11 58							12 30									12 58				
Colwall	d		12 05							12 38									13 05				
Great Malvern	a		12 10							12 42									13 10				
	d		12 10							12 46									13 10			13 37	
Malvern Link	d		12 13							12 50									13 13			13 39	
Worcester Foregate Street ■	a		12 22							12 59									13 22			13 48	
	d		12 24		12 41			12 51		13 01									13 24			13 51	
Worcester Shrub Hill ■	a				12 43					13 04													
	d																13 17						
Droitwich Spa	d		12 33					13 00									13 25		13 33			14 00	
Bromsgrove 69	d		12 43																13 43				
Barnt Green	d																						
University	d		13 00																14 00				
Hartlebury	d																13 32						
Kidderminster	d						12 55	13 10					13 25				13 38				13 55	14 10	
Blakedown	d						12 59						13 29								13 59		
Hagley	d						13 03						13 33				13 44				14 03		
Stourbridge Junction ■	d	12 57					13 07	13 18				13 27	13 37				13 48	13 57			14 07	14 18	
Lye	d	13 01										13 31						14 01					
Cradley Heath	d	13 04					13 13	13 24				13 34	13 43				13 54	14 04			14 13	14 24	
Old Hill	d	13 07										13 37						14 07					
Rowley Regis	d	13 11					13 18	13 30				13 41	13 48				13 59	14 11			14 18	14 30	
Langley Green	d	13 14										13 44						14 14					
Birmingham New Street ■ 68	a		13 09																14 09				
	d			13 33										14 04						14 33			
Birmingham Intl. 68 ✈	d													14 14									
Coventry	d													14 25									
Smethwick Galton Bridge ■	d	13 17					13 24	13 35				13 47	13 54				14 05	14 17			14 24	14 35	
The Hawthorns	d	13 19					13 26	13 37				13 49	13 56				14 07	14 19			14 26	14 37	
Jewellery Quarter	d	13 23					13 30	13 41				13 53	14 00				14 11	14 23			14 30	14 41	
Birmingham Snow Hill	a	13 26					13 34	13 45				13 56	14 04				14 15	14 26			14 34	14 45	
	d	13 28					13 37	13 47				13 58	14 07		14 12	14 12	14 17	14 28			14 37	14 47	
Birmingham Moor Street	d	13 31				13 34	13 40	13 50	13 55		13 55	14 01	14 10		14 15	14 15	14 20	14 31			14 40	14 50	
Bordesley	d																						
Small Heath	d						13 43						14 13								14 43		
Tyseley	d						13 47						14 17								14 47		
Acocks Green	d						13 49					14 07					14 26				14 49		
Olton	d						13 52					14 10					14 29				14 52		
Solihull	d					13 43	13 56		14 04		14 04	14 13			14 24	14 24	14 32				14 56		
Widney Manor	d						13 59					14 17					14 36				14 59		
Dorridge	d					13 54	14a04					14 21			14 29	14 29	14a41				15a04		
Lapworth	d					13 59																	
Hatton	d					14 05																	15 03
Warwick Parkway	d								14 16		14 16				14 39	14 39							
Warwick	d					14 11									14 42	14 42							15 09
Leamington Spa ■	a			13 58		14 17			14 22		14 22			14 37	14 46	14 46				14 58			15 17
	d			14 00					14 22		14 22			14 38	14 46	14 46				15 00			
Banbury	d			14a18					14 41		14 41			14a55	15 05	15 05				15a21			
London Marylebone ■ ⊖115	a								15 41		15 44				16 11	16 14							
Spring Road	d	13 37						13 56					14 19					14 37				14 56	
Hall Green	d	13 39						13 59					14 22					14 39				14 59	
Yardley Wood	d	13 42						14 01					14 24					14 42				15 01	
Shirley	d	13 45						14 05					14 28					14 45				15 05	
Whitlocks End	d	13 48						14a07					14a30					14 48				15a07	
Wythall	d	13 51																14 51					
Earlswood (West Midlands)	d	13 53																14 53					
The Lakes	d	13x56																14x56					
Wood End	d	13x58																14x58					
Danzey	d	14x01																15x01					
Henley-in-Arden	d	14 06																15 06					
Wootton Wawen	d	14x09																15x09					
Wilmcote	d	14 15																15 15					
Stratford-upon-Avon Parkway	a	14 18										14 37						15 18					
Stratford-upon-Avon	a	14 23										14 41						15 23					

A until 6 October

B from 13 October

Table T071-R

Hereford, Worcester and Stourbridge - Birmingham - Leamington Spa, Marylebone and Stratford-upon-Avon

Saturdays
26 May to 8 December

		CH	CH	LM	LM	CH	XC	CH	CH	LM	LM	LM	XC	CH	LM	LM	CH	GW	GW	CH	LM	LM	XC
		◇ A	◇ B				◇■	◇ A	◇ B				◇■				◇ A	◇■	◇	◇ B			◇■
Hereford ■	d											13 39											
Ledbury	a											13 55											
	d											13 58											
Colwall	d											14 05											
Great Malvern	a											14 10											
	d											14 10						14 35	14 50				
Malvern Link	d											14 13						14 39	14 53				
Worcester Foregate Street ■	a											14 22						14 53	15 03				
	d									14 16		14 24						14 57	15 03				
Worcester Shrub Hill ■	a																	15 00	15 06				
	d															14 52							
Droitwich Spa	d									14 25		14 33				15 00							
Bromsgrove 69	d											14 43											
Barnt Green	d																						
University	d											15 00											
Hartlebury	d									14 32													
Kidderminster	d				14 25					14 38					14 55	15 10						15 25	
Blakedown	d				14 29										14 59							15 29	
Hagley	d				14 33					14 44					15 03							15 33	
Stourbridge Junction ■	d			14 27	14 37					14 48	14 57				15 07	15 18					15 27	15 37	
Lye	d			14 31							15 01										15 31		
Cradley Heath	d			14 34	14 43					14 54	15 04				15 13	15 24					15 34	15 43	
Old Hill	d			14 37							15 07										15 37		
Rowley Regis	d			14 41	14 48					14 59	15 11				15 18	15 30					15 41	15 48	
Langley Green	d			14 44							15 14										15 44		
Birmingham New Street ■ 68	a											15 09											
	d						15 04						15 33										16 04
Birmingham Intl. 68 ✈	d						15 14																16 14
Coventry	d						15 25																16 25
Smethwick Galton Bridge ■	d			14 47	14 54					15 05	15 17				15 24	15 35					15 47	15 54	
The Hawthorns	d			14 49	14 56					15 07	15 19				15 26	15 37					15 49	15 56	
Jewellery Quarter	d			14 53	15 00					15 11	15 23				15 30	15 41					15 53	16 00	
Birmingham Snow Hill	a			14 56	15 04					15 15	15 26				15 34	15 45					15 56	16 04	
	d			14 58	15 07			15 12	15 12	15 17	15 28				15 37	15 47					15 58	16 07	
Birmingham Moor Street	d	14 55	14 55	15 01	15 10			15 15	15 15	15 20	15 31			15 34	15 40	15 50	15 55			15 55	16 01	16 10	
Bordesley	d																						
Small Heath	d				15 13										15 43							16 13	
Tyseley	d				15 17										15 47							16 17	
Acocks Green	d			15 07						15 26					15 49						16 07		
Olton	d			15 10						15 29					15 52						16 10		
Solihull	d	15 04	15 04	15 13				15 24	15 24	15 32				15 43	15 56		16 04			16 04	16 13		
Widney Manor	d			15 17						15 36					15 59						16 17		
Dorridge	d			15 21				15 29	15 29	15a41				15 54	16a04						16 21		
Lapworth	d													15 59									
Hatton	d													16 05									
Warwick Parkway	d	15 16	15 16					15 39	15 39								16 16			16 16			
Warwick	d							15 42	15 42					16 11									
Leamington Spa ■	a	15 21	15 21				15 37	15 46	15 46				16 00	16 17			16 21			16 21			16 37
	d	15 22	15 22			15 32	15 38	15 46	15 46				16 02				16 22			16 22			16 38
Banbury	d	15 41	15 41				15a54	16 05	16 05				16a18				16 41			16 41			16a54
London Marylebone ■ ⊖115	a	16 46	16 49					17 11	17 14								17 41			17 44			
Spring Road	d				15 19						15 37					15 56						16 19	
Hall Green	d				15 22						15 39					15 59						16 22	
Yardley Wood	d				15 24						15 42					16 01						16 24	
Shirley	d				15 28						15 45					16 05						16 28	
Whitlocks End	d				15a30						15 48					16a07						16a30	
Wythall	d										15 51												
Earlswood (West Midlands)	d										15 53												
The Lakes	d										15x56												
Wood End	d										15x58												
Danzey	d										16x01												
Henley-in-Arden	d										16 06												
Wootton Wawen	d										16x09												
Wilmcote	d					15 56					16 15												
Stratford-upon-Avon Parkway	a			15 37		15 58					16 18										16 37		
Stratford-upon-Avon	a			15 41		16 08					16 23										16 41		

A until 6 October

B from 13 October

Please note, Network Rail have stated that further updates to this timetable are possible during the validity period.

Table T071-R

Saturdays
26 May to 8 December

Hereford, Worcester and Stourbridge - Birmingham - Leamington Spa, Marylebone and Stratford-upon-Avon

		CH ◇ A	CH ◇ B	LM	LM	LM	XC ◇1	LM	LM	LM	GW ◇1	CH	CH ◇ A	CH ◇ B	LM	LM	CH	XC ◇1	CH ◇ A	CH ◇ B	LM	LM
Hereford	d					14 39					15 13											
Ledbury	a					14 55					15 29											
	d					14 58					15 30											
Colwall	d					15 05					15 38											
Great Malvern	a					15 10					15 42											
	d					15 10				15 33	15 44											
Malvern Link	d					15 13				15 35	15 48											
Worcester Foregate Street	a					15 22				15 45	15 57											
	d			15 16		15 24				15 51	15 59										16 14	
Worcester Shrub Hill	a										16 02											
	d							15 44														
Droitwich Spa	d			15 25		15 33		15 52		16 00											16 23	
Bromsgrove 69	d					15 43		16 08														
Barnt Green	d																					
University	d					16 00																
Hartlebury	d			15 32																	16 31	
Kidderminster	d			15 38					15 55	16 10						16 25					16 36	
Blakedown	d								15 59							16 29					16 41	
Hagley	d			15 44					16 03							16 32					16 44	
Stourbridge Junction	d			15 48	15 57				16 07	16 18					16 27	16 37					16 48	16 57
Lye	d				16 01										16 31							17 01
Cradley Heath	d			15 54	16 04				16 13	16 24					16 34	16 43					16 54	17 04
Old Hill	d				16 07										16 37							17 07
Rowley Regis	d			15 59	16 11				16 18	16 30					16 41	16 48					16 59	17 11
Langley Green	d				16 14										16 44							17 14
Birmingham New Street 68	a					16 09		16 44														
	d						16 33											17 04				
Birmingham Intl. 68 ✈	d																	17 14				
Coventry	d																	17 25				
Smethwick Galton Bridge	d			16 05	16 17				16 24	16 35					16 47	16 54					17 05	17 17
The Hawthorns	d			16 07	16 19				16 26	16 37					16 49	16 56					17 07	17 19
Jewellery Quarter	d			16 11	16 23				16 30	16 41					16 53	17 00					17 11	17 23
Birmingham Snow Hill	a			16 15	16 26				16 34	16 45					16 56	17 03					17 15	17 26
	d	16 12	16 12	16 17	16 28				16 37	16 47					16 58	17 07			17 12	17 12	17 17	17 28
Birmingham Moor Street	d	16 15	16 15	16 20	16 31				16 40	16 50			16 55	16 55	17 01	17 10			17 15	17 15	17 20	17 31
Bordesley	d																					
Small Heath	d								16 43	16 53						17 13						
Tyseley	d				16 36				16 47	16 57						17 17						17 36
Acocks Green	d			16 26					16 49						17 07						17 26	
Olton	d			16 29					16 52						17 10						17 29	
Solihull	d	16 24	16 24	16 32					16 56				17 04	17 04	17 13				17 24	17 24	17 32	
Widney Manor	d			16 36					16 59						17 17						17 36	
Dorridge	d	16 29	16 29	16a41					17a04						17 21				17 29	17 29	17a41	
Lapworth	d																					
Hatton	d											17 03										
Warwick Parkway	d	16 39	16 39										17 16	17 16					17 39	17 39		
Warwick	d	16 42	16 42									17 09							17 42	17 42		
Leamington Spa	a	16 46	16 46				16 59					17 17	17 21	17 21				17 37	17 46	17 46		
	d	16 46	16 46				17 00						17 22	17 22			17 32	17 38	17 46	17 46		
Banbury	d	17 05	17 05				17a17						17 41	17 41				17a54	18 05	18 05		
London Marylebone ⊖115	a	18 11	18 14										18 41	18 44					19 11	19 14		
Spring Road	d				16 38					16 59						17 19						17 38
Hall Green	d				16 41					17 02						17 22						17 41
Yardley Wood	d				16 43					17 04						17 24						17 43
Shirley	d				16 46					17 08						17 28						17 47
Whitlocks End	d				16 49					17a10						17 30						17a49
Wythall	d				16 52											17 33						
Earlswood (West Midlands)	d				16 54											17 35						
The Lakes	d				16x56											17x37						
Wood End	d				16x58											17x40						
Danzey	d				17x01											17x43						
Henley-in-Arden	d				17 06											17 48						
Wootton Wawen	d				17x09											17x51						
Wilmcote	d				17 15											17 56	18 02					
Stratford-upon-Avon Parkway	a				17 18										17 37	17 59	18 05					
Stratford-upon-Avon	a				17 23										17 41	18 03	18 15					

A until 6 October
B from 13 October

Table T071-R

Saturdays
26 May to 8 December

Hereford, Worcester and Stourbridge - Birmingham - Leamington Spa, Marylebone and Stratford-upon-Avon

		LM	XC ◇1	CH	LM	LM	GW ◇1	GW	CH ◇ A	CH ◇ B	LM	LM	XC ◇1	CH ◇ A	CH ◇ B	LM	LM	LM	XC ◇1	CH	CH ◇ A	CH ◇ B	LM
Hereford	d	15 39																16 39					
Ledbury	a	15 55																16 56					
	d	15 58																16 58					
Colwall	d	16 05																17 05					
Great Malvern	a	16 10																17 10					
	d	16 10					16 35	16 50										17 10					
Malvern Link	d	16 13					16 39	16 53										17 13					
Worcester Foregate Street	a	16 22					16 53	17 03										17 22					
	d	16 24				16 47	16 57	17 04										17 24					17 47
Worcester Shrub Hill	a						17 00	17 06															
	d															17 15							
Droitwich Spa	d	16 33				16 56										17 24		17 33					17 56
Bromsgrove 69	d	16 43																17 43					
Barnt Green	d																						
University	d	17 00																18 00					
Hartlebury	d															17 31							
Kidderminster	d				16 55	17 06						17 25				17 36							18 06
Blakedown	d				16 59	17 11						17 29				17 41							18 11
Hagley	d				17 03	17 14						17 33				17 44							18 14
Stourbridge Junction	d				17 07	17 18					17 27	17 37				17 48	17 57						18 18
Lye	d										17 31						18 01						
Cradley Heath	d				17 13	17 24					17 34	17 43				17 54	18 04						18 24
Old Hill	d										17 37						18 07						
Rowley Regis	d				17 18	17 29					17 41	17 48				18 00	18 11						18 30
Langley Green	d										17 44						18 14						
Birmingham New Street 68	a	17 09																18 09					
	d		17 33										18 04						18 33				
Birmingham Intl. 68 ✈	d												18 14										
Coventry	d												18 25										
Smethwick Galton Bridge	d				17 24	17 35					17 47	17 54				18 05	18 17						18 35
The Hawthorns	d				17 26	17 37					17 49	17 56				18 07	18 19						18 37
Jewellery Quarter	d				17 30	17 41					17 53	18 00				18 11	18 23						18 41
Birmingham Snow Hill	a				17 34	17 45					17 56	18 04				18 15	18 26						18 45
	d				17 37	17 47					17 58	18 07		18 12	18 12	18 17	18 28						18 55
Birmingham Moor Street	d			17 34	17 40	17 50			17 55	17 55	18 01	18 10		18 15	18 15	18 20	18 31				18 55	18 55	18 58
Bordesley	d																						
Small Heath	d				17 43	17 53						18 13				18 23							19 01
Tyseley	d				17 47	17 57						18 17				18 26							19 05
Acocks Green	d				17 49						18 07					18 29							19 07
Olton	d				17 52						18 10					18 31							19 10
Solihull	d			17 43	17 56				18 04	18 04	18 13			18 24	18 24	18 35					19 04	19 04	19 14
Widney Manor	d				17 59						18 17					18 38							19 17
Dorridge	d			17 54	18a04						18a23			18 29	18 29	18a43							19a22
Lapworth	d			17 59																			
Hatton	d			18 05																19 03			
Warwick Parkway	d								18 16	18 16				18 39	18 39						19 16	19 16	
Warwick	d			18 11										18 42	18 42					19 09			
Leamington Spa	a		18 00	18 17					18 22	18 22			18 37	18 46	18 46				18 58	19 17	19 21	19 21	
	d		18 02						18 22	18 22			18 38	18 46	18 46				19 00		19 22	19 22	
Banbury	d		18a18						18 41	18 41			18a54	19 05	19 05				19a17		19 41	19 41	
London Marylebone ⊖115	a								19 41	19 44				20 11	20 14						20 41	20 44	
Spring Road	d					17 59						18 19					18 37						
Hall Green	d					18 02						18 22					18 39						
Yardley Wood	d					18 04						18 24					18 42						
Shirley	d					18 08						18 28					18 45						
Whitlocks End	d					18 10						18a30					18 48						
Wythall	d					18 13											18 51						
Earlswood (West Midlands)	d					18 15											18 53						
The Lakes	d					18x18											18x56						
Wood End	d					18x20											18x58						
Danzey	d					18x23											19x01						
Henley-in-Arden	d					18 28											19 06						
Wootton Wawen	d					18x31											19x09						
Wilmcote	d					18 37											19 15						
Stratford-upon-Avon Parkway	a					18 40											19 18						
Stratford-upon-Avon	a					18 43											19 23						

A until 6 October
B from 13 October

Table T071-R

Saturdays
26 May to 8 December

Hereford, Worcester and Stourbridge - Birmingham - Leamington Spa, Marylebone and Stratford-upon-Avon

Station		LM	GW ◇1	CH	XC ◇1	CH ◇ A	CH ◇ B	LM	LM	LM	XC ◇1	GW ◇	CH	CH ◇ A	CH ◇ B	LM	GW	XC ◇1	CH ◇ A	CH ◇ B	LM	XC ◇1
Hereford 7	d									17 39												
Ledbury	a									17 55												
	d									17 58												
Colwall	d									18 05												
Great Malvern	a									18 10												
	d		17 45					17 59		18 10		18 35					18 50					
Malvern Link	d		17 49					18 01		18 13		18 38					18 53					
Worcester Foregate Street 7	a		17 58					18 11		18 22		18 47					19 04					
	d		18 00					18 12		18 24		18 48				18 51	19 05					
Worcester Shrub Hill 7	a		18 03					18 14				18 50					19 07					
	d							18 17														
Droitwich Spa	d							18 25		18 33						19 00						
Bromsgrove 69	d									18 43												
Barnt Green	d																					
University	d									19 00												
Hartlebury	d															19 07						
Kidderminster	d							18 37								19 13					19 43	
Blakedown	d							18 41								19 17					19 47	
Hagley	d							18 45								19 21					19 51	
Stourbridge Junction 2	d	18 27						18 50	18 57							19 25					19 57	
Lye	d	18 31							19 01							19 29					20 01	
Cradley Heath	d	18 34						18 56	19 04							19 32					20 04	
Old Hill	d	18 37							19 07							19 35					20 07	
Rowley Regis	d	18 41						19 01	19 11							19 39					20 11	
Langley Green	d	18 44							19 14							19 42					20 14	
Birmingham New Street 12 68	a									19 09												
	d				19 04						19 33							20 04				20 33
Birmingham Intl. 68 ✈	d				19 14													20 14				
Coventry	d				19 25													20 25				
Smethwick Galton Bridge 7	d	18 47						19 07	19 17							19 45					20 17	
The Hawthorns	d	18 49						19 09	19 19							19 47					20 19	
Jewellery Quarter	d	18 53						19 13	19 23							19 51					20 23	
Birmingham Snow Hill	a	18 58						19 16	19 26							19 55					20 26	
	d	19 02				19 12	19 12	19 17	19 28							19 57			20 12	20 12	20 28	
Birmingham Moor Street	d	19 05				19 15	19 15	19 20	19 31				19 34	19 55	19 55	20 00			20 15	20 15	20 31	
Bordesley	d																					
Small Heath	d	19 08						19 23	19 34							20 03					20 34	
Tyseley	d	19 12						19 27	19 37							20 07					20 37	
Acocks Green	d							19 29								20 09						
Olton	d							19 32								20 12						
Solihull	d					19 24	19 24	19 36					19 43	20 04	20 04	20 16			20 24	20 24		
Widney Manor	d							19 39								20 19						
Dorridge	d					19 29	19 29	19a44					19 55			20a24			20 29	20 29		
Lapworth	d												20 00									
Hatton	d												20 06									
Warwick Parkway	d					19 39	19 39							20 16	20 16				20 39	20 39		
Warwick	d					19 42	19 42						20 12						20 42	20 42		
Leamington Spa 5	a				19 37	19 46	19 46				20 01		20 18	20 22	20 22			20 37	20 46	20 46		20 59
	d			19 32	19 38	19 46	19 46				20 03			20 23	20 23			20 38	20 46	20 46		21 00
Banbury	d				19a54	20 05	20 05				20a19			20 41	20 41			20a54	21 05	21 05		21a19
London Marylebone 10 ⊖115	a					21 11	21 14							21 41	21 44				22 11	22 14		
Spring Road	d	19 14							19 40												20 40	
Hall Green	d	19 17							19 42												20 42	
Yardley Wood	d	19 19							19 45												20 45	
Shirley	d	19 23							19 48												20 48	
Whitlocks End	d	19a25							19 51												20 51	
Wythall	d								19 53												20 53	
Earlswood (West Midlands)	d								19 56												20 56	
The Lakes	d								19x58												20x58	
Wood End	d								20x00												21x00	
Danzey	d								20x02												21x02	
Henley-in-Arden	d								20 07												21 07	
Wootton Wawen	d								20x10												21x10	
Wilmcote	d			19 58					20 15												21 15	
Stratford-upon-Avon Parkway	a			20 00					20 18												21 18	
Stratford-upon-Avon	a			20 10					20 23												21 23	

A until 6 October
B from 13 October

Table T071-R

Saturdays
26 May to 8 December

Hereford, Worcester and Stourbridge - Birmingham - Leamington Spa, Marylebone and Stratford-upon-Avon

Station		CH	CH A	CH B	LM	GW ◇1	CH	XC ◇1	LM	CH ◇ A	CH ◇ B	LM	LM	GW ◇1	GW	CH	CH	LM	LM	LM	LM	LM	GW 1
Hereford 7	d				19 11				19 59					20 20						21 35			
Ledbury	a				19 28				20 15					20 36						21 50			
	d				19 28				20 15					20 41						21 51			
Colwall	d				19 34				20 22					20 48						21 57			
Great Malvern	a				19 39				20 26					20 53						22 02			
	d				19 39				20 27					20 54	21 15				21 30	22 03			22 41
Malvern Link	d				19 42				20 30					20 58	21 18				21 32	22 06			22 45
Worcester Foregate Street 7	a				19 51				20 38					21 09	21 27				21 42	22 14			22 54
	d				19 51	20 04			20 40					21 11	21 28				21 42	22 15			22 56
Worcester Shrub Hill 7	a					20 07								21 14	21 30				21 45	22 18			22 59
	d												20 52						21 54			22 47	
Droitwich Spa	d				20 00				20 49				21 00						22 02			22 55	
Bromsgrove 69	d								20 59														
Barnt Green	d																						
University	d								21 15														
Hartlebury	d				20 07								21 07										
Kidderminster	d				20 13								21 13						22 13			23 05	
Blakedown	d				20 17								21 17						22 17			23 10	
Hagley	d				20 21								21 21						22 21			23 14	
Stourbridge Junction 2	d				20 25							20 57	21 25					21 57	22 25		22 57	23 18	
Lye	d				20 29							21 01	21 29					22 01	22 29		23 01		
Cradley Heath	d				20 32							21 04	21 32					22 04	22 32		23 04		
Old Hill	d				20 35							21 07	21 35					22 07	22 35		23 07		
Rowley Regis	d				20 39							21 11	21 39					22 11	22 39		23 11		
Langley Green	d				20 42							21 14	21 42					22 14	22 42		23 14		
Birmingham New Street 12 68	a								21 22														
	d							21 04															
Birmingham Intl. 68 ✈	d							21 14															
Coventry	d							21 25															
Smethwick Galton Bridge 7	d				20 45							21 17	21 45					22 17	22 45		23 17		
The Hawthorns	d				20 47							21 19	21 47					22 19	22 47		23 19		
Jewellery Quarter	d				20 51							21 23	21 51					22 23	22 51		23 23		
Birmingham Snow Hill	a				20 55							21 26	21 54					22 26	22 55		23 26	23 36	
	d				20 57					21 15	21 15	21 28	21 57				22 15	22 28	22 57		23 28	23 37	
Birmingham Moor Street	d		20 45	20 45	21 00					21 18	21 18	21 31	22 00				22 18	22 31	23 00		23 31	23 40	
Bordesley	d																						
Small Heath	d				21 03							21 34	22 03					22 34	23 03		23 34	23 43	
Tyseley	d				21 07							21 37	22 07				22 23	22 37	23 07		23 37	23 47	
Acocks Green	d				21 09								22 09				22 26		23 09			23 49	
Olton	d				21 12								22 12				22 29		23 12			23 52	
Solihull	d		20 55	20 55	21 16					21 27	21 27		22 16				22 33		23 16			23 56	
Widney Manor	d				21 19					21 30	21 30		22 19				22 36		23 19			23 59	
Dorridge	d		21 01	21 01	21a24					21 34	21 34		22a24				22 40		23 23			00 03	
Lapworth	d									21 38	21 38						22 44		23 26			00 06	
Hatton	d	21 02								21 44	21 44						22 50		23 32			00 12	
Warwick Parkway	d		21 13	21 13						21 49	21 49						22 55		23 35			00 15	
Warwick	d	21 09	21 17	21 17						21 52	21 52					22 35	22 58		23 38			00 18	
Leamington Spa 5	a	21 17	21 21	21 21				21 37		21 56	21 56					22 40	23 03		23 44			00 25	
	d		21 22	21 22			21 32	21 38		21 57	21 57					22 41	23 04						
Banbury	d		21 40	21 40				21a54		22 16	22 16					23a02	23a24						
London Marylebone 10 ⊖115	a		22 41	22 44						23 48	23 51												
Spring Road	d											21 40						22 40			23 40		
Hall Green	d											21 42						22 42			23 42		
Yardley Wood	d											21 45						22 45			23 45		
Shirley	d											21 48						22 48			23 48		
Whitlocks End	d											21 51						22 51			23a52		
Wythall	d											21 53						22 53					
Earlswood (West Midlands)	d											21 56						22 56					
The Lakes	d											21x58						22x58					
Wood End	d											22x00						23x00					
Danzey	d											22x02						23x02					
Henley-in-Arden	d											22 07						23 07					
Wootton Wawen	d											22x10						23x10					
Wilmcote	d						21 58					22 15						23 15					
Stratford-upon-Avon Parkway	a						22 00					22 18						23 18					
Stratford-upon-Avon	a						22 10					22 23						23 23					

A until 6 October
B from 13 October

Table T071-R

Saturdays
26 May to 8 December

Hereford, Worcester and Stourbridge - Birmingham - Leamington Spa, Marylebone and Stratford-upon-Avon

Station		LM
Hereford 7	d	22 49
Ledbury	a	23 04
	d	23 05
Colwall	d	23 11
Great Malvern	a	23 16
	d	23 17
Malvern Link	d	23 20
Worcester Foregate Street 7	a	23 28
	d	23 29
Worcester Shrub Hill 7	a	23 36
	d	
Droitwich Spa	d	
Bromsgrove 69	d	
Barnt Green	d	
University	d	
Hartlebury	d	
Kidderminster	d	
Blakedown	d	
Hagley	d	
Stourbridge Junction 2	d	
Lye	d	
Cradley Heath	d	
Old Hill	d	
Rowley Regis	d	
Langley Green	d	
Birmingham New Street 12 68	a	
	d	
Birmingham Intl. 68 ✈	d	
Coventry	d	
Smethwick Galton Bridge 7	d	
The Hawthorns 🚊	d	
Jewellery Quarter 🚊	d	
Birmingham Snow Hill 🚊	a	
	d	
Birmingham Moor Street	d	
Bordesley	d	
Small Heath	d	
Tyseley	d	
Acocks Green	d	
Olton	d	
Solihull	d	
Widney Manor	d	
Dorridge	d	
Lapworth	d	
Hatton	d	
Warwick Parkway	d	
Warwick	d	
Leamington Spa 8	a	
	d	
Banbury	d	
London Marylebone 10 ⊖115	a	
Spring Road	d	
Hall Green	d	
Yardley Wood	d	
Shirley	d	
Whitlocks End	d	
Wythall	d	
Earlswood (West Midlands)	d	
The Lakes	d	
Wood End	d	
Danzey	d	
Henley-in-Arden	d	
Wootton Wawen	d	
Wilmcote	d	
Stratford-upon-Avon Parkway	a	
Stratford-upon-Avon	a	

Table T071-R

Sundays
20 May to 2 December

Hereford, Worcester and Stourbridge - Birmingham - Leamington Spa, Marylebone and Stratford-upon-Avon

Station		LM A	CH ◇ B	CH ◇ C	GW ◇	CH ◇ B	CH ◇ C	XC ◇1 ✠	LM	CH ◇ B		CH ◇ C	LM	CH ◇ B	CH ◇ C	CH	CH ◇ B	CH ◇ C	XC ◇1 ✠	CH ◇ B		CH ◇ C	LM	GW ◇1 D	GW ◇1 E
Hereford 7	d																								
Ledbury	a																								
	d																								
Colwall	d																								
Great Malvern	a																								
	d																						09 07	09 20	09 24
Malvern Link	d																						09 09	09 24	09 28
Worcester Foregate Street 7	a																						09 19	09 32	09 36
	d				08 30				09 01														09 20	09 34	09 38
Worcester Shrub Hill 7	a				08 32				09 03														09 22	09 37	09 41
	d								09 06														09 26		
Droitwich Spa	d								09 14														09 35		
Bromsgrove 69	d								09 24																
Barnt Green	d																								
University	d								09 40																
Hartlebury	d																								
Kidderminster	d																			09 40		09 40	09 45		
Blakedown	d																						09 49		
Hagley	d																						09 53		
Stourbridge Junction 2	d																			09 48		09 48	09 57		
Lye	d																								
Cradley Heath	d																			09 54		09 54	10 03		
Old Hill	d																								
Rowley Regis	d																			10 00		10 00	10 08		
Langley Green	d																								
Birmingham New Street 12 68	a								09 47																
	d							09 04											10 04						
Birmingham Intl. 68 ✈	d							09 14											10 14						
Coventry	d							09 25											10 25						
Smethwick Galton Bridge 7	d																						10 13		
The Hawthorns 🚊	d																						10 15		
Jewellery Quarter 🚊	d																						10 19		
Birmingham Snow Hill 🚊	a																			10 11		10 11	10 22		
	d									09 12		09 12	09 27							10 12		10 12	10 27		
Birmingham Moor Street	d		08 25	08 25		08 55	08 55			09 15		09 15	09 30			09 41	09 55	09 55		10 15		10 15	10 30		
Bordesley	d																								
Small Heath	d																								
Tyseley	d												09 35										10 35		
Acocks Green	d																								
Olton	d																								
Solihull	d		08 34	08 34		09 04	09 04			09 24		09 24				09 50	10 04	10 04		10 24		10 24			
Widney Manor	d																								
Dorridge	d	00 03	08 39	08 39						09 29		09 29				09 55				10 29		10 29			
Lapworth	d	00 06														09 59									
Hatton	d	00 12												09 55	09 55	10 05									
Warwick Parkway	d	00 15	08 49	08 49		09 16	09 16			09 39		09 39					10 16	10 16		10 39		10 39			
Warwick	d	00 18	08 52	08 52						09 42		09 42		10 01	10 01	10 11				10 42		10 42			
Leamington Spa 8	a	00 25	08 57	08 57		09 21	09 21	09 37		09 46		09 46		10 05	10 05	10 17	10 21	10 21	10 37	10 46		10 46			
	d		08 58	08 58		09 22	09 22	09 38		09 46		09 46		10 06	10 06		10 22	10 22	10 38	10 46		10 46			
Banbury	d		09 16	09 16		09 40	09 40	09a54		10 07		10 07		10 24	10 24		10 40	10 40	10a54	11 07		11 07			
London Marylebone 10 ⊖115	a		10 18	10 21		10 41	10 44			11 09		11 12		11 39	11 42		11 42	11 45		12 10		12 13			
Spring Road	d												09 37										10 37		
Hall Green	d												09 40										10 40		
Yardley Wood	d												09 42										10 42		
Shirley	d												09 45										10 45		
Whitlocks End	d												09 48										10 48		
Wythall	d												09 51										10 51		
Earlswood (West Midlands)	d																								
The Lakes	d												09x53										10x53		
Wood End	d																								
Danzey	d																								
Henley-in-Arden	d												10 01										11 01		
Wootton Wawen	d																								
Wilmcote	d												10 09										11 09		
Stratford-upon-Avon Parkway	a												10 12										11 12		
Stratford-upon-Avon	a												10 15										11 15		

A not 20 May
B until 30 September
C from 7 October
D from 16 September
E until 9 September

Table T071-R

Sundays
20 May to 2 December

Hereford, Worcester and Stourbridge - Birmingham - Leamington Spa, Marylebone and Stratford-upon-Avon

	CH ◇ A	CH ◇ B	LM	CH ◇	XC ◇1	CH ◇ A	CH ◇ B	LM	LM	CH	CH ◇ A	CH ◇ B	LM	XC ◇1	CH ◇ A	CH ◇ B	LM	GW ◇ C	GW ◇1 D	CH A	CH B	XC ◇1
Hereford d									10 05													
Ledbury a									10 22													
d									10 22													
Colwall d									10 29													
Great Malvern a									10 33													
d								10 07	10 34								10 57	11 13	11 13			
Malvern Link d								10 09	10 37								10 59	11 17	11 17			
Worcester Foregate Street a								10 18	10 45								11 17	11 26	11 26			
d								10 26	10 46								11 18	11 28	11 28			
Worcester Shrub Hill a									10 48								11 20	11 31	11 31			
d									10 58								11 26					
Droitwich Spa d								10 35	11 06								11 35					
Bromsgrove 69 d									11 16													
Barnt Green d																						
University d									11 40													
Hartlebury d																						
Kidderminster d			10 14					10 45			11 13	11 13					11 45					
Blakedown d			10 18																			
Hagley d			10 22					10 51									11 51					
Stourbridge Junction d			10 26					10 57			11 22	11 22	11 26				11 57					
Lye d			10 30										11 30									
Cradley Heath d			10 33					11 03					11 33				12 03					
Old Hill d			10 36										11 36									
Rowley Regis d			10 40					11 08			11 33	11 33	11 40				12 08					
Langley Green d			10 43										11 43									
Birmingham New Street 68 a									11 46													
d					11 04									12 04								12 33
Birmingham Intl. 68 ✈ d					11 14									12 14								12 44
Coventry d					11 25									12 25								12 55
Smethwick Galton Bridge d			10 46					11 13					11 46				12 13					
The Hawthorns d			10 48					11 15					11 48				12 15					
Jewellery Quarter d			10 52					11 19					11 52				12 19					
Birmingham Snow Hill a			10 55					11 22			11 44	11 44	11 55				12 22					
d			10 57			11 12	11 12	11 27			11 49	11 49	11 57		12 12	12 12	12 27					
Birmingham Moor Street d	10 55	10 55	11 00			11 15	11 15	11 30		11 41	11 55	11 55	12 00		12 15	12 15	12 30					
Bordesley d																						
Small Heath d																						
Tyseley d								11 35									12 35					
Acocks Green d			11 06										12 06									
Olton d			11 09										12 09									
Solihull d	11 04	11 04	11 12			11 24	11 24			11 50	12 04	12 04	12 12		12 24	12 24						
Widney Manor d			11 16										12 16									
Dorridge d			11a21			11 29	11 29			11 55			12a21		12 29	12 29						
Lapworth d										11 59												
Hatton d										12 05										12 38	12 38	
Warwick Parkway d	11 16	11 16				11 39	11 39				12 16	12 16			12 39	12 39						
Warwick d						11 42	11 42			12 11					12 42	12 42				12 47	12 47	
Leamington Spa a	11 21	11 21			11 37	11 46	11 46			12 17	12 21	12 21		12 37	12 46	12 46				12 54	12 57	13 07
d	11 22	11 22		11 32	11 38	11 46	11 46				12 22	12 22		12 38	12 46	12 46						13 08
Banbury d	11 40	11 40			11a54	12 07	12 07				12 40	12 40		12a54	13 07	13 07						13a24
London Marylebone ⊖115 a	12 40	12 43				13 10	13 13				13 40	13 43			14 10	14 13						
Spring Road d								11 37									12 37					
Hall Green d								11 40									12 40					
Yardley Wood d								11 42									12 42					
Shirley d								11 45									12 45					
Whitlocks End d								11 48									12 48					
Wythall d								11 51									12 51					
Earlswood (West Midlands) d																						
The Lakes d								11x53									12x53					
Wood End d																						
Danzey d																						
Henley-in-Arden d								12 01									13 01					
Wootton Wawen d																						
Wilmcote d				11 55				12 09									13 09					
Stratford-upon-Avon Parkway a				11 57				12 12									13 12					
Stratford-upon-Avon a				12 07				12 15									13 15					

A until 30 September
B from 7 October
C until 9 September
D from 16 September

Table T071-R

Sundays
20 May to 2 December

Hereford, Worcester and Stourbridge - Birmingham - Leamington Spa, Marylebone and Stratford-upon-Avon

	CH ◇ A	CH ◇ B	LM	CH	XC ◇1	CH ◇ A	CH ◇ B	LM	XC ◇1	LM	CH	CH ◇ A	CH ◇ B	LM	XC ◇1	CH ◇ A	CH ◇ B	LM	GW ◇1 C	GW ◇1 D	GW ◇1
Hereford d										12 02											13 32
Ledbury a										12 18											13 50
d										12 18											13 51
Colwall d										12 25											13 58
Great Malvern a										12 29											14 03
d								12 07		12 30									13 20	13 20	14 07
Malvern Link d								12 09		12 33									13 23	13 24	14 11
Worcester Foregate Street a								12 20		12 41									13 32	13 32	14 19
d								12 21		12 42								13 26	13 32	13 33	14 22
Worcester Shrub Hill a								12 23		12 44									13 35	13 36	14 25
d								12 26		12 50											
Droitwich Spa d								12 35		12 58								13 35			
Bromsgrove 69 d										13 08											
Barnt Green d																					
University d										13 30											
Hartlebury d																					
Kidderminster d								12 45										13 45			
Blakedown d								12 49													
Hagley d								12 53										13 51			
Stourbridge Junction d			12 26					12 57						13 26				13 57			
Lye d			12 30											13 30							
Cradley Heath d			12 33					13 03						13 33				14 03			
Old Hill d			12 36											13 36							
Rowley Regis d			12 40					13 08						13 40				14 08			
Langley Green d			12 43											13 43							
Birmingham New Street 68 a										13 37											
d					13 04				13 33						14 04						
Birmingham Intl. 68 ✈ d					13 14										14 14						
Coventry d					13 25										14 25						
Smethwick Galton Bridge d			12 46					13 13						13 46				14 13			
The Hawthorns d			12 48					13 15						13 48				14 15			
Jewellery Quarter d			12 52					13 19						13 52				14 19			
Birmingham Snow Hill a			12 55					13 22						13 56				14 22			
d			12 57			13 12	13 12	13 27						13 57		14 12	14 12	14 27			
Birmingham Moor Street d	12 55	12 55	13 00			13 15	13 15	13 30			13 41	13 55	13 55	14 00		14 15	14 15	14 30			
Bordesley d																					
Small Heath d																					
Tyseley d								13 35										14 35			
Acocks Green d			13 06											14 06							
Olton d			13 09											14 09							
Solihull d	13 04	13 04	13 12			13 24	13 24				13 50	14 04	14 04	14 12		14 24	14 24				
Widney Manor d			13 16											14 16							
Dorridge d			13a22			13 29	13 29				13 55			14a21		14 29	14 29				
Lapworth d											13 59										
Hatton d											14 05										
Warwick Parkway d	13 16	13 16				13 39	13 39					14 16	14 16			14 39	14 39				
Warwick d						13 42	13 42				14 11					14 42	14 42				
Leamington Spa a	13 21	13 21			13 37	13 46	13 46		13 58		14 17	14 21	14 21		14 37	14 46	14 46				
d	13 22	13 22		13 32	13 38	13 46	13 46		13 59			14 22	14 22		14 38	14 46	14 46				
Banbury d	13 40	13 40			13a54	14 07	14 07		14a15			14 40	14 40		14a54	15 07	15 07				
London Marylebone ⊖115 a	14 40	14 43				15 10	15 13					15 40	15 43			16 10	16 13				
Spring Road d								13 37										14 37			
Hall Green d								13 40										14 40			
Yardley Wood d								13 42										14 42			
Shirley d								13 45										14 45			
Whitlocks End d								13 48										14 48			
Wythall d								13 51										14 51			
Earlswood (West Midlands) d																					
The Lakes d								13x53										14x53			
Wood End d																					
Danzey d																					
Henley-in-Arden d								14 01										15 01			
Wootton Wawen d																					
Wilmcote d				13 54				14 09										15 09			
Stratford-upon-Avon Parkway a				13 56				14 12										15 12			
Stratford-upon-Avon a				14 06				14 15										15 15			

A until 30 September
B from 7 October
C from 16 September
D until 9 September

Please note, Network Rail have stated that further updates to this timetable are possible during the validity period.

Sundays

20 May to 2 December

Hereford, Worcester and Stourbridge - Birmingham - Leamington Spa, Marylebone and Stratford-upon-Avon

		XC ◇■	CH	CH ◇ A	CH ◇ B	LM	CH	XC ◇■		CH ◇ A	CH ◇ B	LM	XC ◇■	LM	GW ◇■ C	GW ◇■ D	CH	CH ◇ A		CH ◇ B	LM	XC ◇■	CH ◇ A	CH ◇ B	LM
Hereford ■	d													14 02	14 32	14 32									
Ledbury	a													14 18	14 50	14 50									
	d													14 19	14 51	14 52									
Colwall	d													14 26	14 58	14 59									
Great Malvern	a													14 30	15 04	15 04									
	d													14 31	15 09	15 09									
Malvern Link	d													14 34	15 13	15 13									
Worcester Foregate Street ■	a													14 42	15 21	15 21									
	d											14 26		14 43	15 24	15 24									15 28
Worcester Shrub Hill ■	a													14 45	15 27	15 27									
	d													14 50											
Droitwich Spa	d											14 35		14 58											15 37
Bromsgrove 69	d													15 08											
Barnt Green	d																								
University	d													15 30											
Hartlebury	d																								
Kidderminster	d											14 45													15 47
Blakedown	d											14 49													
Hagley	d											14 53													15 53
Stourbridge Junction ■	d					14 26						14 57									15 26				15 57
Lye	d					14 30															15 30				
Cradley Heath	d					14 33						15 03									15 33				16 03
Old Hill	d					14 36															15 36				
Rowley Regis	d					14 40						15 08									15 40				16 08
Langley Green	d					14 43															15 43				
Birmingham New Street ■ 68	a													15 37											
	d	14 33						15 04					15 33									16 04			
Birmingham Intl. 68 ✈	d	14 44						15 14														16 14			
Coventry	d	14 55						15 25														16 25			
Smethwick Galton Bridge ■	d					14 46						15 13									15 46				16 13
The Hawthorns	d					14 48						15 15									15 48				16 15
Jewellery Quarter	d					14 52						15 19									15 52				16 19
Birmingham Snow Hill	a					14 55						15 22									15 55				16 23
	d					14 57				15 12	15 12	15 27									15 57		16 12	16 12	16 27
Birmingham Moor Street	d			14 55	14 55	15 00				15 15	15 15	15 30					15 41	15 55		15 55	16 00		16 15	16 15	16 30
Bordesley	d																								
Small Heath	d																								
Tyseley	d											15 35													16 35
Acocks Green	d					15 06															16 06				
Olton	d					15 09															16 09				
Solihull	d			15 04	15 04	15 12				15 24	15 24						15 50	16 04		16 04	16 12		16 24	16 24	
Widney Manor	d					15 16															16 16				
Dorridge	d					15a22				15 29	15 29						15 55				16a21		16 29	16 29	
Lapworth	d																15 59								
Hatton	d		15 04														16 05								
Warwick Parkway	d			15 16	15 16					15 39	15 39							16 16		16 16			16 39	16 39	
Warwick	d		15 11							15 42	15 42						16 11						16 42	16 42	
Leamington Spa ■	a	15 08	15 17	15 21	15 21			15 37		15 46	15 46		15 58				16 17	16 21		16 21		16 37	16 46	16 46	
	d	15 09		15 22	15 22		15 32	15 38		15 46	15 46		15 59					16 22		16 22		16 38	16 46	16 46	
Banbury	d	15a26		15 40	15 40			15a54		16 07	16 07		16a15					16 40		16 40		16a54	17 07	17 07	
London Marylebone ■ ⊖115	a			16 40	16 43					17 10	17 13							17 40		17 43			18 10	18 13	
Spring Road	d											15 37													16 37
Hall Green	d											15 40													16 40
Yardley Wood	d											15 42													16 42
Shirley	d											15 45													16 45
Whitlocks End	d											15 48													16 48
Wythall	d											15 51													16 51
Earlswood (West Midlands)	d																								
The Lakes	d											15x53													16x53
Wood End	d																								
Danzey	d																								
Henley-in-Arden	d											16 01													17 01
Wootton Wawen	d																								
Wilmcote	d						15 54					16 09													17 09
Stratford-upon-Avon Parkway	a						15 56					16 12													17 12
Stratford-upon-Avon	a						16 06					16 15													17 15

A until 30 September
B from 7 October
C from 16 September
D until 9 September

Sundays

20 May to 2 December

Hereford, Worcester and Stourbridge - Birmingham - Leamington Spa, Marylebone and Stratford-upon-Avon

		LM	XC ◇■	CH		CH ◇ A	CH ◇ B	LM	CH	XC ◇■	CH ◇ A	CH ◇ B	LM	GW ◇■		XC ◇■	LM	GW ◇■ C	GW ◇■ D	CH	CH ◇ A	CH ◇ B	LM	XC ◇■	
Hereford ■	d																15 57	16 34	16 34						
Ledbury	a																16 14	16 51	16 51						
	d																16 14	16 51	16 52						
Colwall	d																16 21	17 00	17 00						
Great Malvern	a																16 25	17 04	17 04						
	d	15 32															16 26	17 05	17 05						
Malvern Link	d	15 35															16 29	17 09	17 09						
Worcester Foregate Street ■	a	15 43															16 37	17 19	17 19						
	d	15 45											16 26	16 28			16 38	17 24	17 24						
Worcester Shrub Hill ■	a													16 31			16 40	17 27	17 27						
	d																16 50								
Droitwich Spa	d	15 54											16 35				16 58								
Bromsgrove 69	d																17 08								
Barnt Green	d																								
University	d																17 30								
Hartlebury	d																								
Kidderminster	d	16 04											16 45												
Blakedown	d	16 09																							
Hagley	d	16 13											16 51												
Stourbridge Junction ■	d	16 17						16 26					16 57										17 26		
Lye	d							16 30															17 30		
Cradley Heath	d							16 33					17 03										17 33		
Old Hill	d							16 36															17 36		
Rowley Regis	d							16 40					17 08										17 40		
Langley Green	d							16 43															17 43		
Birmingham New Street ■ 68	a																17 37								
	d		16 33							17 04						17 33								18 04	
Birmingham Intl. 68 ✈	d		16 44							17 14														18 14	
Coventry	d		16 55							17 25														18 25	
Smethwick Galton Bridge ■	d	16 30						16 46					17 13										17 46		
The Hawthorns	d							16 48					17 15										17 48		
Jewellery Quarter	d							16 52					17 19										17 52		
Birmingham Snow Hill	a	16 36						16 55					17 22										17 55		
	d	16 43						16 57			17 12	17 12	17 27										17 57		
Birmingham Moor Street	d	16a45				16 55	16 55	17 00			17 15	17 15	17 30							17 41	17 55	17 55	18 00		
Bordesley	d																								
Small Heath	d																								
Tyseley	d												17 35												
Acocks Green	d							17 06															18 06		
Olton	d							17 09															18 09		
Solihull	d					17 04	17 04	17 12			17 24	17 24								17 50	18 04	18 04	18 12		
Widney Manor	d							17 16															18 16		
Dorridge	d							17a22			17 29	17 29								17 55			18a21		
Lapworth	d																			17 59					
Hatton	d			17 04																18 05					
Warwick Parkway	d					17 16	17 16				17 39	17 39									18 16	18 16			
Warwick	d			17 11							17 42	17 42								18 11					
Leamington Spa ■	a		17 08	17 17		17 21	17 21			17 37	17 46	17 46				17 58				18 17	18 21	18 21		18 37	
	d		17 09			17 22	17 22		17 32	17 38	17 46	17 46				17 59					18 22	18 22		18 38	
Banbury	d		17a25			17 40	17 40			17a54	18 07	18 07				18a16					18 40	18 40		18a54	
London Marylebone ■ ⊖115	a					18 40	18 43				19 10	19 13									19 40	19 43			
Spring Road	d												17 37												
Hall Green	d												17 40												
Yardley Wood	d												17 42												
Shirley	d												17 45												
Whitlocks End	d												17 48												
Wythall	d												17 51												
Earlswood (West Midlands)	d																								
The Lakes	d												17x53												
Wood End	d																								
Danzey	d																								
Henley-in-Arden	d												18 01												
Wootton Wawen	d																								
Wilmcote	d								17 54				18 09												
Stratford-upon-Avon Parkway	a								17 56				18 12												
Stratford-upon-Avon	a								18 06				18 15												

A until 30 September
B from 7 October
C from 16 September
D until 9 September

Table T071-R

Sundays
20 May to 2 December

Hereford, Worcester and Stourbridge - Birmingham - Leamington Spa, Marylebone and Stratford-upon-Avon

		CH	CH	LM	XC	LM	GW	GW	CH	CH	CH	CH	XC	CH	CH	LM	XC	LM	GW	GW	CH	CH	XC
		◇	◇		◇■		◇	◇■		◇	◇		◇■	◇	◇		◇■		◇■	◇■	◇	◇	◇■
		A	B				C	D		A	B			A	B				C	D	A	B	
					🛒								🛒				🛒		🍴	🍴			🛒
Hereford ■	d																	18 03	18 38	18 38			
Ledbury	a																	18 19	18 55	18 55			
	d																	18 19	18 57	18 57			
Colwall	d																	18 26	19 04	19 04			
Great Malvern	a																	18 30	19 09	19 09			
	d																	18 31	19 11	19 12			
Malvern Link	d																	18 34	19 15	19 16			
Worcester Foregate Street ■	a																	18 42	19 24	19 25			
	d			17 27			18 26	18 26								18 26		18 43	19 30	19 30			
Worcester Shrub Hill ■	a						18 29	18 29										18 45	19 33	19 33			
	d					17 59												18 50					
Droitwich Spa	d			17 36		18 07										18 35		18 58					
Bromsgrove	69 d					18 25												19 08					
Barnt Green	d																						
University	d					18 43												19 30					
Hartlebury	d																						
Kidderminster	d			17 46												18 45							
Blakedown	d			17 51																			
Hagley	d			17 55												18 51							
Stourbridge Junction ■	d			17 59												18 55							
Lye	d																						
Cradley Heath	d			18 05												19 01							
Old Hill	d																						
Rowley Regis	d			18 10												19 06							
Langley Green	d																						
Birmingham New Street ■■	68 a					18 49												19 37					
	d				18 33								19 04				19 33						20 04
Birmingham Intl.	68 ✈ d				18 44								19 14				19 44						20 14
Coventry	d				18 55								19 25				19 55						20 25
Smethwick Galton Bridge ■	d			18 15												19 12							
The Hawthorns 🚊	d			18 17												19 14							
Jewellery Quarter 🚊	d			18 21												19 18							
Birmingham Snow Hill 🚊	a			18 24												19 21							
	d	18 12	18 12	18 27										19 12	19 12	19 23							
Birmingham Moor Street	d	18 15	18 15	18 30						18 55	18 55			19 15	19 15	19a25					19 39	19 39	
Bordesley	d																						
Small Heath	d																						
Tyseley	d			18 35																			
Acocks Green	d																						
Olton	d																						
Solihull	d	18 24	18 24							19 04	19 04			19 24	19 24						19 48	19 48	
Widney Manor	d																				19 51	19 51	
Dorridge	d	18 29	18 29											19 29	19 29						19 56	19 56	
Lapworth	d																				20 00	20 00	
Hatton	d								19 04												20 06	20 06	
Warwick Parkway	d	18 39	18 39							19 16	19 16			19 39	19 39								
Warwick	d	18 42	18 42						19 11					19 42	19 42						20 11	20 11	
Leamington Spa ■	a	18 46	18 46		19 08				19 17	19 21	19 21		19 37	19 46	19 46		20 08				20 16	20 16	20 37
	d	18 46	18 46		19 09					19 22	19 22	19 32	19 38	19 46	19 46		20 09				20 17	20 17	20 38
Banbury	d	19 07	19 07		19a25					19 41	19 41		19a54	20 07	20 07		20a25				20 36	20 36	20a54
London Marylebone ■ ⊖115	a	20 10	20 13							20 45	20 48			21 10	21 13						21 53	21 56	
Spring Road	d			18 37																			
Hall Green	d			18 40																			
Yardley Wood	d			18 42																			
Shirley	d			18 45																			
Whitlocks End	d			18 48																			
Wythall	d			18 51																			
Earlswood (West Midlands)	d																						
The Lakes	d			18x53																			
Wood End	d																						
Danzey	d																						
Henley-in-Arden	d			19 01																			
Wootton Wawen	d																						
Wilmcote	d			19 09								19 54											
Stratford-upon-Avon Parkway	a			19 12								19 56											
Stratford-upon-Avon	a			19 15								20 06											

A until 30 September
B from 7 October
C until 9 September
D from 16 September

Table T071-R

Sundays
20 May to 2 December

Hereford, Worcester and Stourbridge - Birmingham - Leamington Spa, Marylebone and Stratford-upon-Avon

		CH	CH	LM	XC	XC	LM	GW	GW	CH	CH	XC	CH	CH	LM	LM	LM	LM	LM
		◇	◇		◇■	◇		◇	◇	◇	◇	◇■	◇	◇					
		A	B		C	D		E	F	A	B		A	B					
Hereford ■	d															20 03			22 39
Ledbury	a															20 19			22 56
	d															20 19			22 58
Colwall	d															20 26			23 05
Great Malvern	a															20 30			23 09
	d							20 15	20 15							20 31		22 10	23 10
Malvern Link	d							20 18	20 18							20 34		22 12	23 12
Worcester Foregate Street ■	a							20 27	20 27							20 42		22 22	23 22
	d						19 55	20 28	20 28							20 43	21 18	22 23	23 23
Worcester Shrub Hill ■	a						19 57	20 30	20 31							20 46	21 20	22 25	23 27
	d			19 38			20 02								20 38	20 50	21 25	22 29	
Droitwich Spa	d			19 46			20 10								20 46	20 58	21 33	22 37	
Bromsgrove	69 d						20 25									21 08			
Barnt Green	d																		
University	d						20 43									21 30			
Hartlebury	d																		
Kidderminster	d			19 56											20 56		21 43	22 47	
Blakedown	d																		
Hagley	d			20 03											21 03		21 49	22 53	
Stourbridge Junction ■	d			20 07											21 07		21 53	22 57	
Lye	d																		
Cradley Heath	d			20 13											21 13		21 59	23 03	
Old Hill	d																		
Rowley Regis	d			20 18											21 18		22 04	23 08	
Langley Green	d																		
Birmingham New Street ■■	68 a						20 49									21 37			
	d				20 33	20 33						21 04							
Birmingham Intl.	68 ✈ d											21 14							
Coventry	d											21 24							
Smethwick Galton Bridge ■	d			20 23											21 23		22 09	23 14	
The Hawthorns 🚊	d			20 25											21 25		22 11	23 16	
Jewellery Quarter 🚊	d			20 29											21 29		22 15	23 20	
Birmingham Snow Hill 🚊	a			20 33											21 33		22 19	23 25	
	d	20 12	20 12	20 34									21 15	21 15	21 34		22 21		
Birmingham Moor Street	d	20 15	20 15	20a37									21 18	21 18	21a37		22a23		
Bordesley	d																		
Small Heath	d																		
Tyseley	d																		
Acocks Green	d																		
Olton	d																		
Solihull	d	20 24	20 24										21 27	21 27					
Widney Manor	d												21 30	21 30					
Dorridge	d	20 29	20 29										21 34	21 34					
Lapworth	d																		
Hatton	d									20 56	20 56								
Warwick Parkway	d	20 39	20 39										21 44	21 44					
Warwick	d	20 42	20 42							21 03	21 03		21 47	21 47					
Leamington Spa ■	a	20 46	20 46		20 58	20 59				21 07	21 07	21 35	21 51	21 51					
	d	20 46	20 46		21 00	21 00				21 08	21 08	21 36	21 52	21 52					
Banbury	d	21 07	21 07		21a17	21a17				21 28	21 28	21a52	22 15	22 15					
London Marylebone ■ ⊖115	a	22 13	22 16							22 53	22 56		23 42	23 45					
Spring Road	d																		
Hall Green	d																		
Yardley Wood	d																		
Shirley	d																		
Whitlocks End	d																		
Wythall	d																		
Earlswood (West Midlands)	d																		
The Lakes	d																		
Wood End	d																		
Danzey	d																		
Henley-in-Arden	d																		
Wootton Wawen	d																		
Wilmcote	d																		
Stratford-upon-Avon Parkway	a																		
Stratford-upon-Avon	a																		

A until 30 September
B from 7 October
C until 15 July, from 9 September
D from 22 July until 2 September
E from 16 September
F until 9 September

Table T072-F

Mondays to Fridays
21 May to 7 December

Stourbridge Junction - Stourbridge Town

Miles			LM	LM	LM	LM	LM	LM	and at the same minutes past each hour until	LM	LM	LM	LM	LM	LM		LM	LM	LM	LM	LM
0	Stourbridge Junction ■	d	05 45	05 55	06 05	06 15	06 25	06 35		21 45	21 55	22 05	22 15	22 25	22 35		22 45	23 00	23 15	23 35	23 54
0¾	Stourbridge Town	a	05 48	05 58	06 08	06 18	06 28	06 38		21 48	21 58	22 08	22 18	22 28	22 38		22 48	23 03	23 18	23 38	23 57

Saturdays
26 May to 8 December

		LM	LM	LM	LM	LM	LM	LM	LM	LM	and at the same minutes past each hour until	LM	LM	LM	LM	LM	LM		LM	LM	LM	LM	LM	LM
Stourbridge Junction ■	d	05 59	06 20	06 50	07 05	07 15	07 25	07 35	07 45	07 55		21 05	21 15	21 25	21 35	21 45	21 55		22 05	22 15	22 25	22 35	22 55	23 05
Stourbridge Town	a	06 02	06 23	06 53	07 08	07 18	07 28	07 38	07 48	07 58		21 08	21 18	21 28	21 38	21 48	21 58		22 08	22 18	22 28	22 38	22 58	23 08

			LM	LM	LM
Stourbridge Junction ■	d		23 15	23 35	23 54
Stourbridge Town	a		23 18	23 38	23 57

Sundays
20 May to 2 December

		LM	LM	and every 15 minutes until	LM	LM
Stourbridge Junction ■	d	09 43	10 00		19 30	19 53
Stourbridge Town	a	09 46	10 03		19 33	19 56

Table T072-R

Mondays to Fridays
21 May to 7 December

Stourbridge Town - Stourbridge Junction

Miles			LM	LM	LM	LM	LM	LM	and at the same minutes past each hour until	LM	LM	LM	LM	LM	LM		LM	LM	LM	LM	LM
0	Stourbridge Town	d	05 50	06 00	06 10	06 20	06 30	06 40		21 50	22 00	22 10	22 20	22 30	22 40		22 50	23 05	23 20	23 40	23 59
0¾	Stourbridge Junction ■	a	05 53	06 03	06 13	06 23	06 33	06 43		21 53	22 03	22 13	22 23	22 33	22 43		22 53	23 08	23 23	23 43	00 02

Saturdays
26 May to 8 December

		LM	LM	LM	LM	LM	LM	LM	LM	LM	and at the same minutes past each hour until	LM	LM	LM	LM	LM	LM		LM	LM	LM	LM	LM	LM
Stourbridge Town	d	06 05	06 38	06 55	07 10	07 20	07 30	07 40	07 50	08 00		21 10	21 20	21 30	21 40	21 50	22 00		22 10	22 20	22 30	22 40	23 00	23 10
Stourbridge Junction ■	a	06 08	06 41	06 58	07 13	07 23	07 33	07 43	07 53	08 03		21 13	21 23	21 33	21 43	21 53	22 03		22 13	22 23	22 33	22 43	23 03	23 13

			LM	LM	LM
Stourbridge Town	d		23 20	23 40	23 59
Stourbridge Junction ■	a		23 23	23 43	00 02

Sundays
20 May to 2 December

		LM	LM	and every 15 minutes until	LM	LM
Stourbridge Town	d	09 48	10 05		19 35	19 58
Stourbridge Junction ■	a	09 51	10 08		19 38	20 01

Table T074-F

Mondays to Fridays
21 May to 7 December

Birmingham - Wolverhampton - Telford - Shrewsbury

Miles			AW MO	AW MX	AW MX	LM	AW	LM	AW	LM	LM		AW	LM	AW	LM	AW	LM	AW	VT	LM		AW	LM	AW
			A	B			◇ C ✠		◇ D ✠				■ C ✠		◇ E ✠		◇ C ✠		◇ E ✠	◇■ F ⊠			■ C ✠		◇ E ✠
—	Birmingham International 68	d							07 09				08 09		09 10		10 09		11 10	11 33			12 09		13 08
0	**Birmingham New Street** ■ 68	d					06 25		07 23	07 27	08 05		08 24	09 05	09 25	10 05	10 25	11 05	11 25	11 53	12 05		12 25	13 05	13 25
4	Smethwick Galton Bridge ■ 68	d					06 31		07 29				08 31		09 31		10 31		11 31				12 31		13 31
5¼	Sandwell & Dudley 68	d									08 13			09 13		10 13		11 13			12 13			13 13	
13	**Wolverhampton** ■ 68 ⇌	d		00 03	00 20	06 10	06 43	06 51	07 42	07 46	08 25		08 44	09 25	09 43	10 25	10 43	11 25	11 42	12 11	12 25		12 43	13 25	13 43
17	Bilbrook	d		00 09		06 16		06 57		07 52	08 31			09 31		10 31		11 31			12 31			13 31	
17½	Codsall	d		00 12		06 19		07 00		07 55	08 34			09 34		10 34		11 34			12 34			13 34	
20¾	Albrighton	d		00 16		06 24		07 05		07 59	08 38			09 38		10 38		11 38			12 38			13 38	
22¼	Cosford	d	00 02	00 20		06 27		07 08		08 02	08 41			09 41		10 41		11 41			12 41			13 41	
25½	Shifnal	d	00 07	00 25		06 32		07 13		08 07	08 46			09 46		10 46		11 46			12 46			13 46	
28½	**Telford Central**	d	00 13	00 30	00 36	06 38	07 01	07 19	07 59	08 13	08 52		09 00	09 52	09 59	10 52	10 59	11 52	11 59	12 28	12 52		12 59	13 52	14 00
29½	Oakengates	d	00 15	00 32		06 40		07 21		08 15	08 54			09 54		10 54		11 54			12 54			13 54	
32½	Wellington (Shropshire)	d	00 20	00 37	00 43	06 46	07 07	07 27	08 05	08 21	09 00		09 07	10 00	10 05	11 00	11 06	12 00	12 05	12 35	13 00		13 06	14 00	14 06
43	**Shrewsbury**	a	00 36	00 53	01 00	07 00	07 22	07 41	08 19	08 34	09 14		09 20	10 14	10 21	11 14	11 19	12 14	12 19	12 51	13 14		13 19	14 14	14 20

		LM	AW	LM	AW	LM	AW		LM	AW	LM	LM	AW	LM	AW	VT	LM		AW	LM	AW	LM	AW TThO	AW MWFO
			◇ C ✠		◇ E ✠		■ C ✠			◇ D			◇ C		◇ G	◇■ F ⊠			◇ C		◇ H			
Birmingham International 68	d		14 09		15 09		16 09			17 09			18 09		19 04	19 33			20 04		21 04			
Birmingham New Street ■ 68	d	14 05	14 25	15 05	15 25	16 05	16 25		17 05	17 25	17 49	18 05	18 25	19 05	19 25	19 50	20 05		20 25	21 05	21 25	22 14	23 32	23 35
Smethwick Galton Bridge ■ 68	d		14 31		15 29		16 31			17 31			18 31		19 31				20 31		21 31	22 23		
Sandwell & Dudley 68	d	14 13		15 13		16 13			17 13			18 13		19 13		19 59	20 13			21 13		22 26		
Wolverhampton ■ 68 ⇌	d	14 25	14 43	15 25	15 42	16 25	16 43		17 25	17 42	18 10	18 25	18 43	19 25	19 43	20 19	20 25		20 43	21 25	21 42	22 44	00 03	00 03
Bilbrook	d	14 31		15 31		16 31			17 31		18 16	18 31		19 31			20 31			21 31		22 50	00 09	00 09
Codsall	d	14 34		15 34		16 34			17 34		18 19	18 34		19 34			20 34			21 34		22 52	00 12	00 12
Albrighton	d	14 38		15 38		16 38			17 38		18 24	18 38		19 38			20 38			21 38		22 57	00 16	00 16
Cosford	d	14 41		15 41		16 41			17 41		18 27	18 41		19 41			20 41			21 41		23 00	00 20	00 20
Shifnal	d	14 46		15 46		16 46			17 46		18 32	18 46		19 46			20 46			21 46		23 04	00 25	00 25
Telford Central	d	14 52	14 59	15 52	15 58	16 52	16 59		17 52	18 01	18 37	18 52	18 59	19 52	20 00	20 36	20 52		20 59	21 52	21 58	23 10	00 30	00 30
Oakengates	d	14 54		15 54		16 54			17 54		18 39	18 54		19 54			20 54			21 54		23 12	00 32	00 32
Wellington (Shropshire)	d	15 00	15 06	16 00	16 05	17 00	17 06		18 00	18 06	18 45	19 00	19 06	20 00	20 06	20 43	21 00		21 05	22 00	22 06	23 18	00 37	00 37
Shrewsbury	a	15 14	15 19	16 14	16 19	17 14	17 19		18 14	18 20	19 00	19 14	19 19	20 14	20 19	20 55	21 14		21 18	22 14	22 18	23 30	00 53	00 53

Saturdays
26 May to 8 December

		AW	AW	AW	LM	AW	LM	AW	LM	AW		LM	AW	LM	AW	LM	AW	VT	LM	AW		LM	AW	LM	AW
		B		◇ C ✠		■ E ✠		■ C ✠		■ E ✠			■ C ✠		◇ E ✠		■ C ✠	◇■ F ☕		◇ E ✠			◇ C ✠		■ E ✠
Birmingham International 68	d					07 09		08 09		09 10			10 09		11 10		12 09	12 33		13 10			14 09		15 09
Birmingham New Street ■ 68	d			06 25		07 24	08 05	08 25	09 05	09 25		10 05	10 25	11 05	11 25	12 05	12 25	12 53	13 05	13 25		14 05	14 25	15 05	15 25
Smethwick Galton Bridge ■ 68	d			06 31		07 30		08 31		09 31			10 31		11 31		12 31			13 31			14 31		15 31
Sandwell & Dudley 68	d						08 13		09 13			10 13		11 13		12 13			13 13			14 13		15 13	
Wolverhampton ■ 68 ⇌	d	00 03	00 20	06 43	07 25	07 43	08 25	08 43	09 25	09 43		10 25	10 43	11 25	11 44	12 25	12 43	13 11	13 25	13 42		14 25	14 43	15 25	15 43
Bilbrook	d	00 09			07 31		08 31		09 31			10 31		11 31		12 31			13 31			14 31		15 31	
Codsall	d	00 12			07 34		08 34		09 34			10 34		11 34		12 34			13 34			14 34		15 34	
Albrighton	d	00 16			07 38		08 38		09 38			10 38		11 38		12 38			13 38			14 38		15 38	
Cosford	d	00 20			07 41		08 41		09 41			10 41		11 41		12 41			13 41			14 41		15 41	
Shifnal	d	00 25			07 46		08 46		09 46			10 46		11 46		12 46			13 46			14 46		15 46	
Telford Central	d	00 30	00 36	06 59	07 52	07 59	08 52	09 00	09 52	10 00		10 52	10 59	11 52	12 00	12 52	12 59	13 28	13 52	13 59		14 52	15 00	15 52	16 00
Oakengates	d	00 32			07 54		08 54		09 54			10 54		11 54		12 54			13 54			14 54		15 54	
Wellington (Shropshire)	d	00 37	00 43	07 06	08 00	08 05	09 00	09 07	10 00	10 06		11 00	11 06	12 00	12 08	13 00	13 07	13 35	14 00	14 06		15 00	15 07	16 00	16 07
Shrewsbury	a	00 53	01 00	07 19	08 14	08 20	09 14	09 20	10 14	10 18		11 14	11 19	12 14	12 21	13 14	13 20	13 54	14 14	14 19		15 14	15 20	16 14	16 20

		LM	AW	LM	AW	LM		AW	LM	AW	VT	LM	AW	LM	AW	LM		AW	LM	AW
			◇ C ✠		◇ E			◇ C ✠		◇ G	◇■ F ☕		◇ C		◇ G			◇ I		
Birmingham International 68	d		16 09		17 09			18 09		19 09	19 33		20 09		21 09					
Birmingham New Street ■ 68	d	16 05	16 25	17 05	17 25	18 05		18 25	19 05	19 25	19 50	20 05	20 25	21 05	21 25	22 05		22 35	23 08	23 35
Smethwick Galton Bridge ■ 68	d		16 31		17 31			18 31		19 31			20 31		21 31				23 16	
Sandwell & Dudley 68	d	16 13		17 13		18 13			19 13		19 59	20 13		21 13		22 13			23 19	
Wolverhampton ■ 68 ⇌	d	16 25	16 43	17 25	17 43	18 25		18 43	19 25	19 43	20 19	20 25	20 43	21 25	21 43	22 25		22 53	23 35	23 54
Bilbrook	d	16 31		17 31		18 31			19 31			20 31		21 31		22 31				00 01
Codsall	d	16 34		17 34		18 34			19 34			20 34		21 34		22 34				00 04
Albrighton	d	16 38		17 38		18 38			19 38			20 38		21 38		22 38				00 08
Cosford	d	16 41		17 41		18 41			19 41			20 41		21 41		22 41				00 12
Shifnal	d	16 46		17 46		18 46			19 46			20 46		21 46		22 46				00 17
Telford Central	d	16 52	16 59	17 52	18 00	18 52		18 59	19 52	20 00	20 36	20 52	20 59	21 52	22 00	22 52		23 09	23 51	00 22
Oakengates	d	16 54		17 54		18 54			19 54			20 54		21 54		22 54				00 25
Wellington (Shropshire)	d	17 00	17 07	18 00	18 07	19 00		19 06	20 00	20 06	20 43	21 00	21 06	22 00	22 06	23 00		23 16	23 58	00 30
Shrewsbury	a	17 14	17 20	18 14	18 20	19 14		19 19	20 14	20 20	20 55	21 14	21 20	22 14	22 23	23 14		23 28	00 11	00 45

A From Birmingham International
B From Birmingham New Street
C To Aberystwyth
D To Llandudno
E To Holyhead
F From London Euston
G To Chester
H To Manchester Piccadilly
I To Crewe

Table T074-F

Birmingham - Wolverhampton - Telford - Shrewsbury

Sundays
20 May to 2 December

		AW	AW	AW	AW	AW	AW	AW	AW	AW	AW	AW	AW	AW	AW	AW	AW	AW	AW	AW	VT	AW	AW
		A		◇ B	◇ C 🍴		◇ D	◇ E 🍴		◇ D 🍴	■ E 🍴		◇ D 🍴	■ E 🍴		◇ F 🍴	◇ E		◇ D	◇ E	◇1 G ⓡ	◇ D	
Birmingham International	68 d			09 51	09 51		10 48	12 07		13 07	14 07		15 07	16 07		17 07	18 08		19 07	20 08	20 13	21 08	22 11
Birmingham New Street ■12	68 d			10 04	10 04		11 05	12 24		13 24	14 24		15 24	16 24		17 24	18 24		19 24	20 24	20 27	21 24	22 24
Smethwick Galton Bridge ■5	68 d																						
Sandwell & Dudley	68 d																				20 35		
Wolverhampton ■7	68 ⇌ d		00 18	10 22	10 22	11 06	11 27	12 42	13 06	13 42	14 43	15 06	15 43	16 43	17 06	17 43	18 43	19 06	19 43	20 43	20 56	21 43	22 42
Bilbrook	d	00 01		10 28	10 28	11 12	11 33		13 12			15 12			17 12			19 12				21 49	22 48
Codsall	d	00 04		10 31	10 31	11 15	11 35		13 15			15 15			17 15			19 15				21 51	22 50
Albrighton	d	00 08		10 35	10 35	11 19	11 40		13 19			15 19			17 19			19 19				21 56	22 55
Cosford	d	00 12		10 39	10 39	11 23	11 43		13 23			15 23			17 23			19 23				21 59	22 58
Shifnal	d	00 17		10 44	10 44	11 28	11 48		13 28			15 28			17 28			19 28				22 04	23 03
Telford Central	d	00 22	00 36	10 49	10 49	11 34	11 54	12 59	13 34	13 58	14 59	15 34	15 59	16 59	17 34	17 59	18 59	19 34	19 59	20 59	21 13	22 10	23 09
Oakengates	d	00 25		10 51	10 51	11 37	11 56		13 37			15 37			17 37			19 37				22 12	23 11
Wellington (Shropshire)	d	00 30	00 43	10 57	10 57	11 43	12 01	13 05	13 43	14 04	15 06	15 43	16 06	17 06	17 43	18 05	19 06	19 43	20 06	21 06	21 20	22 17	23 16
Shrewsbury	a	00 45	00 59	11 10	11 10	11 58	12 14	13 19	13 58	14 18	15 19	15 58	16 22	17 19	17 59	18 19	19 19	19 58	20 19	21 19	21 35	22 30	23 32

		AW
Birmingham International	68 d	23 08
Birmingham New Street ■12	68 d	23 24
Smethwick Galton Bridge ■5	68 d	
Sandwell & Dudley	68 d	
Wolverhampton ■7	68 ⇌ d	23 46
Bilbrook	d	23 52
Codsall	d	23 54
Albrighton	d	23 59
Cosford	d	00 02
Shifnal	d	00 07
Telford Central	d	00 13
Oakengates	d	00 15
Wellington (Shropshire)	d	00 20
Shrewsbury	a	00 36

A not 20 May. From Birmingham New Street
B until 9 September. To Aberystwyth
C from 16 September. To Aberystwyth
D To Chester
E To Aberystwyth
F To Holyhead
G From London Euston

Table T074-R

Shrewsbury - Telford - Wolverhampton - Birmingham

Mondays to Fridays
21 May to 7 December

Miles			AW MX	AW	LM	LM	AW	VT	LM	LM	AW	LM	AW	LM	AW	LM	AW	LM	AW	LM	AW	LM	AW
			◇ A		B		◇ A	◇1 C ⊠			◇ D 🍴		◇ E 🍴		■ D 🍴		◇ 🍴		◇ F 🍴		◇ G 🍴		◇ F 🍴
0	**Shrewsbury**	d		05 18	05 24	05 58	06 33	06 39	06 53	07 15	07 33	07 47	08 32	08 47	09 33	09 47	10 32	10 47	11 33	11 47	12 33	12 47	13 34
10½	Wellington (Shropshire)	d		05 31	05 38	06 11	06 46	06 53	07 06	07 28	07 46	08 00	08 45	09 00	09 46	10 00	10 46	11 00	11 46	12 00	12 46	13 00	13 48
13½	Oakengates	d			05 42	06 16				07 33		08 05		09 05		10 05		11 05		12 05		13 05	
14½	**Telford Central**	d		05 38	05 45	06 19	06 53	07 00	07 13	07 37	07 53	08 08	08 52	09 08	09 53	10 08	10 52	11 08	11 53	12 08	12 53	13 08	13 54
17½	Shifnal	d			05 50	06 24			07 18	07 42		08 13		09 13		10 13		11 13		12 13		13 13	
20¾	Cosford	d			05 55	06 29				07 47		08 18		09 18		10 18		11 18		12 18		13 18	
22¼	Albrighton	d			05 58	06 32				07 50		08 21		09 21		10 21		11 21		12 21		13 21	
25½	Codsall	d	00 05		06 04	06 38				07 56		08 27		09 27		10 27		11 27		12 27		13 27	
26	Bilbrook	d	00 06		06 06	06 40				07 59		08 29		09 29		10 29		11 29		12 29		13 29	
30	**Wolverhampton ■7** 68 ⇌	a	00 17	05 58	06 13	06 47	07 11	07 17	07 32	08 06	08 11	08 36	09 10	09 36	10 10	10 36	11 09	11 36	12 11	12 36	13 10	13 36	14 10
37¾	Sandwell & Dudley 68	a			06 27	07 04			07 45			08 46		09 46		10 46		11 46		12 46		13 46	
39	Smethwick Galton Bridge ■5 68	a		06 10	06 31	07 08	07 23				08 22		09 22		10 21		11 20		12 22		13 22		14 23
43	**Birmingham New Street ■12** 68	a		06 15	06 40	07 17	07 30	07 47	07 55	08 25	08 29	08 55	09 29	09 55	10 30	10 55	11 30	11 55	12 30	12 55	13 29	13 55	14 30
—	Birmingham International 68	a		06 49			07 49	07 59			08 49		09 49		10 49		11 49		12 49		13 49		14 49

		LM	AW	LM	VT	AW	LM	AW	LM	AW	LM	AW	LM	AW	LM	LM	AW	LM	AW	AW
			◇ G 🍴		◇1 C ⓡ	◇ F 🍴		■ G 🍴		◇ F 🍴		◇ G 🍴		◇ D 🍴			◇ D		◇ G	◇ A
Shrewsbury	d	13 47	14 33	14 47	15 24	15 33	15 47	16 33	16 47	17 33	17 47	18 33	18 47	19 33	19 47	20 47	21 33	21 47	22 18	23 24
Wellington (Shropshire)	d	14 00	14 46	15 00	15 38	15 46	16 00	16 47	17 00	17 46	18 00	18 46	19 00	19 46	20 00	21 00	21 47	22 00	22 32	23 38
Oakengates	d	14 05		15 05			16 05		17 05		18 05		19 05		20 05	21 05		22 05		23 42
Telford Central	d	14 08	14 53	15 08	15 44	15 53	16 08	16 54	17 08	17 53	18 08	18 53	19 08	19 53	20 08	21 08	21 53	22 08	22 38	23 45
Shifnal	d	14 13		15 13			16 13		17 13		18 13		19 13		20 13	21 13		22 13		23 50
Cosford	d	14 18		15 18			16 18		17 18		18 18		19 18		20 18	21 18		22 18		23 55
Albrighton	d	14 21		15 21			16 21		17 21		18 21		19 21		20 21	21 21		22 21		23 59
Codsall	d	14 27		15 27			16 27		17 27		18 27		19 27		20 27	21 27		22 27		00 05
Bilbrook	d	14 29		15 29			16 29		17 29		18 29		19 29		20 29	21 29		22 29		00 06
Wolverhampton ■7 68 ⇌	a	14 36	15 11	15 36	16 01	16 10	16 36	17 09	17 36	18 11	18 36	19 11	19 36	20 11	20 36	21 36	22 11	22 38	22 55	00 17
Sandwell & Dudley 68	a	14 46		15 46			16 46		17 46		18 46		19 46		20 46	21 46				
Smethwick Galton Bridge ■5 68	a		15 22			16 22		17 22		18 22		19 22		20 22			22 22			
Birmingham New Street ■12 68	a	14 55	15 30	15 55	16 22	16 30	16 55	17 30	17 55	18 30	18 55	19 30	19 55	20 29	20 55	21 57	22 31		23 28	
Birmingham International 68	a		15 49		16 39	16 49		17 49		18 49		19 49		20 49						

Saturdays
26 May to 8 December

		AW	AW	LM	AW	LM	AW	LM	VT	AW	LM	AW	LM	AW	LM	AW	LM	AW	LM	AW	LM	AW	LM
		◇ A					◇ D 🍴		◇1 C ⓡ	◇ G		■ H 🍴		■ G 🍴		■ F 🍴		■ G 🍴		■ F 🍴		■ G 🍴	
Shrewsbury	d		05 22	05 29	06 33	06 47	07 33	07 47	08 18	08 33	08 47	09 33	09 47	10 33	10 47	11 34	11 47	12 33	12 47	13 35	13 47	14 33	14 47
Wellington (Shropshire)	d		05 35	05 42	06 46	07 00	07 46	08 00	08 32	08 46	09 00	09 47	10 00	10 46	11 00	11 48	12 00	12 46	13 00	13 48	14 00	14 46	15 00
Oakengates	d			05 47		07 05		08 05			09 05		10 05		11 05		12 05		13 05		14 05		15 05
Telford Central	d		05 42	05 50	06 53	07 08	07 53	08 08	08 39	08 53	09 08	09 53	10 08	10 53	11 08	11 55	12 08	12 53	13 08	13 55	14 08	14 53	15 08
Shifnal	d			05 55		07 13		08 13			09 13		10 13		11 13		12 13		13 13		14 13		15 13
Cosford	d			06 00		07 18		08 18			09 18		10 18		11 18		12 18		13 18		14 18		15 18
Albrighton	d			06 03		07 21		08 21			09 21		10 21		11 21		12 21		13 21		14 21		15 21
Codsall	d	00 05		06 09		07 27		08 27			09 27		10 27		11 27		12 27		13 27		14 27		15 27
Bilbrook	d	00 06		06 11		07 29		08 29			09 29		10 29		11 29		12 29		13 29		14 29		15 29
Wolverhampton ■7 68 ⇌	a	00 17	06 01	06 18	07 11	07 36	08 11	08 36	09 00	09 11	09 36	10 10	10 36	11 11	11 36	12 12	12 36	13 10	13 36	14 12	14 36	15 11	15 36
Sandwell & Dudley 68	a			06 32		07 46		08 46			09 46		10 46		11 46		12 46		13 46		14 46		15 46
Smethwick Galton Bridge ■5 68	a		06 13	06 35	07 23		08 22			09 23		10 21		11 22		12 24		13 21		14 24		15 22	
Birmingham New Street ■12 68	a		06 19	06 44	07 30	07 55	08 29	08 55	09 21	09 27	09 55	10 30	10 55	11 28	11 55	12 32	12 55	13 28	13 55	14 30	14 55	15 28	15 55
Birmingham International 68	a		06 49		07 49		08 49		09 39	09 50		10 50		11 50		12 50		13 50		14 49		15 50	

		VT	AW	LM	AW	LM	AW	LM	AW	LM	AW	LM	LM	AW	LM	AW	AW
		◇1 C ⓡ	◇ F 🍴		■ G 🍴		◇ F 🍴		■ G 🍴		◇ D 🍴			◇ D		◇ G	◇ A
Shrewsbury	d	15 24	15 33	15 47	16 34	16 47	17 33	17 47	18 33	18 47	19 32	19 47	20 47	21 33	21 47	22 31	23 26
Wellington (Shropshire)	d	15 38	15 46	16 00	16 48	17 00	17 46	18 00	18 46	19 00	19 46	20 00	21 00	21 46	22 00	22 45	23 40
Oakengates	d			16 05		17 05		18 05		19 05		20 05	21 05		22 05		23 44
Telford Central	d	15 44	15 53	16 08	16 54	17 08	17 53	18 08	18 53	19 08	19 53	20 08	21 08	21 53	22 08	22 51	23 47
Shifnal	d			16 13		17 13		18 13		19 13		20 13	21 13		22 13		23 52
Cosford	d			16 18		17 18		18 18		19 18		20 18	21 18		22 18		23 57
Albrighton	d			16 21		17 21		18 21		19 21		20 21	21 21		22 21		00 02
Codsall	d			16 27		17 27		18 27		19 27		20 27	21 27		22 27		00 07
Bilbrook	d			16 29		17 29		18 29		19 29		20 29	21 29		22 29		00 09
Wolverhampton ■7 68 ⇌	a	16 01	16 10	16 36	17 09	17 36	18 11	18 36	19 11	19 37	20 10	20 36	21 36	22 09	22 36	23 08	00 16
Sandwell & Dudley 68	a			16 46		17 46		18 46		19 46		20 46	21 46		22 46		
Smethwick Galton Bridge ■5 68	a		16 22		17 22		18 22		19 22		20 22			22 20			
Birmingham New Street ■12 68	a		16 30	16 55	17 28	17 55	18 30	18 55	19 28	19 55	20 29	20 55	21 56	22 31	22 55	23 30	
Birmingham International 68	a	16 39	16 48		17 50		18 49		19 49		20 49						

A From Chester
B To Rugeley Trent Valley
C To London Euston
D From Aberystwyth
E From Crewe
F From Pwllheli
G From Holyhead
H From Barmouth

Table T074-R

Sundays

20 May to 2 December

Shrewsbury - Telford - Wolverhampton - Birmingham

		AW	AW	AW	AW	AW	AW	AW	AW	AW	AW	AW	VT	AW	AW	AW	AW	AW	AW	AW	AW	AW	AW
		◇ A				◇ B 🍴	■ C 🍴		◇ B 🍴	■ C 🍴		◇ B	◇■ D ⊡	■ C 🍴		◇ B	■ E 🍴		◇ B	◇ C 🍴	◇ B	◇ C	◇ F
Shrewsbury	d		08 10	09 09	09 55	10 20	11 40	12 10	12 31	13 31	14 10	14 31	15 24	15 33	16 10	16 40	17 33	18 10	18 31	19 31	20 23	21 31	22 23
Wellington (Shropshire)	d		08 24	09 23	10 09	10 34	11 54	12 24	12 45	13 45	14 23	14 45	15 38	15 47	16 23	16 54	17 47	18 23	18 45	19 45	20 37	21 45	22 37
Oakengates	d		08 28	09 27	10 14			12 29			14 29				16 29			18 29			20 41		22 43
Telford Central	d		08 31	09 30	10 17	10 40	12 00	12 32	12 51	13 51	14 32	14 51	15 44	15 53	16 32	17 00	17 53	18 32	18 51	19 51	20 44	21 51	22 45
Shifnal	d		08 36	09 35	10 22			12 37			14 37				16 37			18 37			20 49		22 51
Cosford	d		08 41	09 40	10 28			12 43			14 43				16 43			18 43			20 54		22 56
Albrighton	d	00 02	08 44	09 43	10 31			12 46			14 46				16 46			18 46			20 57		22 59
Codsall	d	00 07	08 50	09 49	10 37			12 52			14 52				16 52			18 52			21 02		23 05
Bilbrook	d	00 09	08 52	09 51	10 39			12 55			14 54				16 54			18 54			21 04		23 07
Wolverhampton [7] 68	a	00 16	08 59	09 58	10 50	10 56	12 16	13 03	13 07	14 07	15 03	15 07	16 01	16 09	17 03	17 15	18 09	19 03	19 07	20 07	21 11	22 07	23 14
Sandwell & Dudley 68	a																						
Smethwick Galton Bridge [3] 68	a																						
Birmingham New Street [12] 68	a		09 15	10 14		11 13	12 33		13 23	14 23		15 24	16 20	16 25		17 37	18 27		19 26	20 25	21 29	22 27	
Birmingham International 68	a		09 32	10 32		11 31	13 02		13 57	15 00		15 57	16 39	17 00		17 57	19 00		19 57	21 01	21 57	23 01	

		AW
		◇ G
Shrewsbury	d	22 24
Wellington (Shropshire)	d	22 38
Oakengates	d	22 43
Telford Central	d	22 46
Shifnal	d	22 51
Cosford	d	22 56
Albrighton	d	22 59
Codsall	d	23 05
Bilbrook	d	23 07
Wolverhampton [7] 68	a	23 14
Sandwell & Dudley 68	a	
Smethwick Galton Bridge [3] 68	a	
Birmingham New Street [12] 68	a	
Birmingham International 68	a	

A not 20 May. From Chester
B From Chester
C From Aberystwyth
D To London Euston
E From Pwllheli
F from 16 September. From Chester
G until 9 September. From Holyhead

Table T075-F

Mondays to Fridays

21 May to 7 December

Birmingham - Shrewsbury - Chester - Holyhead

Network Diagram - see first page of Table 74

Miles	Miles			AW MX	AW	AW	VT	AW	AW	AW	AW	AW	AW	AW	AW	AW	AW	AW	AW	AW	AW	AW FO	AW FX
				A			◇■ B		◇ 🍴	◇ 🍴	◇ 🍴	◇ 🍴	◇ C 🍴	◇ 🍴	■ 🍴	◇ 🍴	◇ 🍴	◇ 🍴	■ 🍴	◇	BHX ■ ⊠		
0	—	Birmingham International 68	d							07 09		09 10		11 10		13 08		15 09		17 09			
8¼	—	**Birmingham New Street** [12] 74,68	d							07 23		09 25		11 25		13 25		15 25		17 25			
12¼	—	Smethwick Galton Bridge [3] 74,68	d							07 29		09 31		11 31		13 31		15 29		17 31			
20¼	—	**Wolverhampton** [7] 68,74	d							07 42		09 43		11 42		13 43		15 42		17 42			
35¾	—	Telford Central 74	d							07 59		09 59		11 59		14 00		15 58		18 01			
39¾	—	Wellington (Shropshire) 74	d							08 05		10 05		12 05		14 06		16 05		18 06			
—	0	**Cardiff Central** [7] 131	d						05 08		07 21		09 21		11 21		13 21		15 21		17 16		
—	11¾	Newport (South Wales) 131	d						05 27		07 36		09 35		11 36		13 35		15 36		17 31		
—	55¾	Hereford 131	d						06 25		08 27		10 27		12 27		14 25		16 28		18 25		
50	106	**Shrewsbury** 74	a						07 22	08 19	09 19	10 21	11 21	12 19	13 21	14 20	15 23	16 19	17 24	18 20	19 08		
—	—		d		05 20	06 10		07 00	07 25	08 25	09 25	10 23	11 25	12 25	13 26	14 25	15 29	16 24	17 25	18 25	19 09	19 27	19 27
68	124	Gobowen	d		05 38	06 29		07 19	07 43	08 43	09 43	10 43	11 42	12 42	13 43	14 43	15 46	16 43	17 43	18 43		19 45	19 45
71	127	Chirk	d	00 03	05 43	06 34		07 24	07 48	08 48	09 48	10 48	11 48	12 48	13 49	14 48	15 52	16 48	17 48	18 48		19 50	19 50
75½	131½	Ruabon	d	00 09	05 50	06 41		07 31	07 55	08 55	09 55	10 55	11 54	12 54	13 55	14 55	15 58	16 55	17 55	18 55		19 57	19 57
80¼	136¼	Wrexham General	a	00 15	05 56	06 49		07 40	08 01	09 01	10 01	11 00	12 00	13 00	14 01	15 01	16 04	17 01	18 01	19 01	19 37	20 03	20 03
—	—		d	00 15	06 06		07 00		08 01	09 02	10 01	11 00	12 01	13 01	14 02	15 01	16 05	17 02	18 01	19 03	19 38	20 03	20 03
92¼	148¼	**Chester** 81	a	00 35	06 25		07 17		08 20	09 19	10 20	11 20	12 19	13 19	14 19	15 18	16 23	17 21	18 19	19 23	19 57	20 24	20 25
104¾	160¾	Flint 81	a						08 38	09 37	10 40	11 37	12 36	13 35	14 36	15 37	16 39	17 40	18 38	19 46	20 14		
118¾	174¾	Prestatyn 81	a						08 51	09 51	10 53	11 51	12 49	13 49	14 50	15 50	16 53	17 54	18 51	20 00			
122¼	178¼	Rhyl 81	a						08 57	09 57	10 59	11 57	12 55	13 55	14 56	15 56	16 59	18 00	18 57	20 06	20 30		
132¾	188¾	Colwyn Bay 81	a						09 11	10 11	11 10	12 11	13 06	14 05	15 06	16 07	17 09	18 14	19 11	20 20	20 42		
136¾	192¾	Llandudno Junction 81	a						09 17	10 16	11 15	12 16	13 11	14 11	15 12	16 12	17 15	18 19	19 17	20 25	20 49		
139¾	195¾	Llandudno 81	a						09 27	10 31										20 42			
158	214	Bangor (Gwynedd) 81	a								11 39	12 33	13 29	14 34	15 30	16 42	17 37	18 46	19 34		21 06		
182¾	238¾	**Holyhead** 81	a								12 23	13 17	14 14	15 07	16 14	17 16	18 21	19 17	20 20		21 41		

		AW	AW	AW	AW
		◇	◇	◇ D	
Birmingham International 68	d	19 04		21 04	
Birmingham New Street [12] 74,68	d	19 25		21 25	
Smethwick Galton Bridge [3] 74,68	d	19 31		21 31	
Wolverhampton [7] 68,74	d	19 43		21 42	
Telford Central 74	d	20 00		21 58	
Wellington (Shropshire) 74	d	20 06		22 06	
Cardiff Central [7] 131	d		19 34		
Newport (South Wales) 131	d		19 48		
Hereford 131	d		20 39		
Shrewsbury 74	a	20 19	21 37	22 18	
	d	20 28	21 39	22 24	23 40
Gobowen	d	20 46	21 56	22 42	23 57
Chirk	d	20 51	22 02	22 47	00 03
Ruabon	d	20 58	22 08	22 53	00 09
Wrexham General	a	21 04	22 12	22 59	00 15
	d	21 04	22 13	23 00	00 15
Chester 81	a	21 23	22 36	23 17	00 35
Flint 81	a		23 10		
Prestatyn 81	a		23 24		
Rhyl 81	a		23 30		
Colwyn Bay 81	a		23 44		
Llandudno Junction 81	a		23 49		
Llandudno 81	a				
Bangor (Gwynedd) 81	a		00 13		
Holyhead 81	a		00 48		

A From Shrewsbury
B To London Euston
C From Maesteg
D To Manchester Piccadilly

Table T075-F

Saturdays
26 May to 8 December

Birmingham - Shrewsbury - Chester - Holyhead

Network Diagram - see first page of Table 74

	AW	AW	AW	AW	AW	AW	AW	AW	AW	AW	AW	AW	AW	AW	AW	AW	AW	AW	AW	AW	AW
	A		B 🍴	◇ 🍴	■ 🍴	◇ 🍴	■ 🍴	◇ 🍴	◇ 🍴	■ C 🍴	◇ 🍴	◇ C 🍴	■ 🍴	■ 🍴	◇		■	◇	◇	◇	
Birmingham International 68 ✈ d					07 09		09 10		11 10		13 10		15 09		17 09			19 09		21 09	
Birmingham New Street 12 74,68 d					07 24		09 25		11 25		13 25		15 25		17 25			19 25		21 25	
Smethwick Galton Bridge 3 74,68 d					07 30		09 31		11 31		13 31		15 31		17 31			19 31		21 31	
Wolverhampton 7 68,74 ⛴ d					07 43		09 43		11 44		13 42		15 43		17 43			19 43		21 43	
Telford Central 74 d					07 59		10 00		12 00		13 59		16 00		18 00			20 00		22 00	
Wellington (Shropshire) 74 d					08 05		10 06		12 08		14 06		16 07		18 07			20 06		22 06	
Cardiff Central 7 131 d				05 21		07 21		09 21		11 21		13 21		15 21			17 21		19 34		
Newport (South Wales) 131 d				05 35		07 36		09 35		11 35		13 36		15 36			17 35		19 48		
Hereford 131 d				06 25		08 27		10 26		12 28		14 27		16 29			18 27		20 39		
Shrewsbury 74 a				07 22	08 20	09 23	10 18	11 23	12 21	13 20	14 19	15 24	16 20	17 22	18 20		19 19	20 20	21 35	22 23	
d		05 20	06 10	07 25	08 22	09 25	10 22	11 25	12 25	13 25	14 22	15 30	16 25	17 24	18 25		19 28	20 25	21 39	22 25	23 33
Gobowen d		05 38	06 29	07 43	08 40	09 43	10 41	11 42	12 43	13 42	14 40	15 47	16 43	17 41	18 43		19 45	20 43	21 56	22 43	23 52
Chirk d	00 03	05 43	06 34	07 48	08 45	09 48	10 46	11 48	12 49	13 48	14 46	15 53	16 49	17 47	18 48		19 51	20 48	22 02	22 48	23 58
Ruabon d	00 09	05 50	06 41	07 55	08 52	09 55	10 53	11 54	12 55	13 54	14 52	15 59	16 55	17 53	18 55		19 57	20 55	22 08	22 55	00 04
Wrexham General a	00 15	05 56	06 48	08 01	08 59	10 01	10 59	12 00	13 01	14 00	14 58	16 05	17 01	17 59	19 01		20 03	21 01	22 14	23 01	00 10
d	00 15	05 56	06 50	08 01	08 59	10 01	11 02	12 01	13 03	14 01	14 59	16 06	17 03	18 00	19 02	19 48	20 04	21 01	22 15	23 01	00 14
Chester 81 a	00 35	06 17	07 09	08 19	09 17	10 19	11 21	12 18	13 20	14 19	15 20	16 23	17 19	18 17	19 21	20 06	20 23	21 20	22 33	23 22	00 33
Flint 81 a				08 36	09 36	10 36	11 38	12 35	13 37	14 35	15 35	16 40	17 38	18 38	19 41		20 46		22 52		
Prestatyn 81 a				08 50	09 50	10 49	11 52	12 49	13 51	14 49	15 49	16 54	17 52	18 52	19 55		21 00		23 06		
Rhyl 81 a				08 56	09 56	10 55	11 58	12 56	13 57	14 56	15 55	17 00	17 58	18 58	20 01		21 06		23 12		
Colwyn Bay 81 a				09 06	10 06	11 06	12 08	13 07	14 07	15 07	16 05	17 10	18 12	19 08	20 15		21 19		23 26		
Llandudno Junction 81 a				09 12	10 12	11 11	12 14	13 14	14 13	15 14	16 11	17 16	18 17	19 14	20 20		21 24		23 38		
Llandudno 81 a																					
Bangor (Gwynedd) 81 a				09 35	10 30	11 35	12 32	13 32	14 37	15 32	16 34	17 39	18 41	19 32	20 47		21 42				
Holyhead 81 a				10 15	11 05	12 09	13 12	14 13	15 09	16 13	17 12	18 19	19 13	20 18	21 31		22 25				

Sundays
20 May to 2 December

	AW	AW	AW	AW	AW	AW	AW	AW	AW	AW
	D	🍴	◇	◇ 🍴	■ 🍴	◇ 🍴	■ 🍴	◇ 🍴	◇	
Birmingham International 68 ✈ d			10 48	13 07		15 07		17 07	19 07	
Birmingham New Street 12 74,68 d			11 05	13 24		15 24		17 24	19 24	
Smethwick Galton Bridge 3 74,68 d										
Wolverhampton 7 68,74 ⛴ d			11 27	13 42		15 43		17 43	19 43	
Telford Central 74 d			11 54	13 58		15 59		17 59	19 59	
Wellington (Shropshire) 74 d			12 01	14 04		16 06		18 05	20 06	
Cardiff Central 7 131 d					13 14		15 15			
Newport (South Wales) 131 d					13 35		15 34			
Hereford 131 d					14 26		16 28			
Shrewsbury 74 a			12 14	14 18	15 21	16 22	17 23	18 19	20 19	
d		10 16	12 18	14 20	15 24	16 24	17 30	18 20	20 23	
Gobowen d		10 34	12 36	14 38	15 42	16 42	17 48	18 38	20 41	
Chirk d		10 39	12 41	14 43	15 48	16 47	17 53	18 43	20 47	
Ruabon d	00 04	10 46	12 48	14 50	15 54	16 54	18 00	18 50	20 53	
Wrexham General a	00 10	10 52	12 54	14 56	16 00	17 00	18 06	18 56	20 59	
d	00 14	10 52	12 54	14 56	16 01	17 05	18 06	18 56	21 00	22 35
Chester 81 a	00 33	11 12	13 17	15 18	16 20	17 26	18 25	19 15	21 20	22 55
Flint 81 a					16 50		18 44	19 53		
Prestatyn 81 a					17 04		18 58	20 10		
Rhyl 81 a					17 10		19 04	20 16		
Colwyn Bay 81 a					17 24		19 18	20 30		
Llandudno Junction 81 a					17 29		19 23	20 36		
Llandudno 81 a										
Bangor (Gwynedd) 81 a					17 52		19 48	20 57		
Holyhead 81 a					18 37		20 18	21 34		

A From Shrewsbury
B To Manchester Piccadilly
C From Maesteg
D not 20 May. From Shrewsbury

Table T075-R

Mondays to Fridays
21 May to 7 December

Holyhead - Chester - Shrewsbury - Birmingham

Network Diagram - see first page of Table 74

Miles	Miles		AW	AW	AW	AW BHX	AW	AW	AW	AW	AW	AW	AW	AW	AW	AW	AW	AW	AW	VT	AW	AW
			◇		◇ 🍴	■ ⊠		◇ 🍴	■ 🍴	◇ 🍴	◇ 🍴	■ A 🍴	◇ 🍴	■ B 🍴	■ 🍴	◇ 🍴	◇ 🍴	■ 🍴	◇ 🍴	◇1 C ⊠		◇
0	0	**Holyhead** 81 d			04 25	05 34		06 28		08 05	09 23	10 41	11 27	12 32	13 24	14 36	15 47	16 51	17 31			19 21
24¾	24¾	Bangor (Gwynedd) 81 d			04 57	06 02		07 06		09 02	10 02	11 07	12 00	13 07	14 04	15 04	16 26	17 19	18 10			20 00
43	43	Llandudno 81 d							08 30													
46	46	Llandudno Junction 81 d			05 15	06 20		07 25	08 39	09 25	10 25	11 25	12 23	13 25	14 29	15 27	16 49	17 37	18 33			20 23
50	50	Colwyn Bay 81 d			05 21	06 28		07 31	08 45	09 31	10 31	11 31	12 29	13 31	14 35	15 33		17 43				20 29
60½	60½	Rhyl 81 d			05 31	06 39		07 41	08 56	09 41	10 41	11 41	12 40	13 41	14 45	15 43		17 53				20 39
64	64	Prestatyn 81 d			05 37			07 47		09 47	10 47	11 47	12 45	13 47	14 51	15 49		17 59				20 45
78	78	Flint 81 d			05 50	06 56		08 00		10 00	11 00	12 00	12 59	14 00	15 04	16 00		18 12				20 58
90½	90½	**Chester** 81 d	05 35	05 45	06 18	07 16		08 19	09 27	10 21	11 36	12 19	13 30	14 20	15 36	16 22	17 34	18 30	19 18	20 22		21 21
102½	102½	Wrexham General a	05 49	06 03	06 34	07 30		08 33	09 42	10 35	11 49	12 33	13 44	14 34	15 50	16 37	17 48	18 45	19 32	20 38		21 35
—	—	d	05 50		06 34	07 34	07 50	08 35	09 42	10 36	11 50	12 34	13 45	14 34	15 51	16 37	17 50	18 46	19 33		20 49	21 38
107¼	107¼	Ruabon a	05 56		06 41		07 57	08 42	09 49	10 42	11 58	12 40	13 51	14 41	15 57	16 44	17 56	18 52	19 40		20 56	21 44
111¾	111¾	Chirk a	06 03		06 47		08 04	08 48	09 55	10 49	12 04	12 47	13 58	14 47	16 04	16 50	18 03	18 59	19 46		21 02	21 50
114¾	114¾	Gobowen a	06 08		06 53		08 09	08 54	10 01	10 54	12 10	12 52	14 03	14 53	16 09	16 56	18 08	19 04	19 52		21 08	21 56
132¾	132¾	**Shrewsbury** 74 a	06 27		07 12	08 03	08 28	09 12	10 20	11 13	12 29	13 11	14 23	15 11	16 29	17 14	18 27	19 23	20 14		21 28	22 14
—	183½	Hereford 131 a			08 09	08 55		10 09		12 06		14 09		16 09		18 12		20 19				
—	227	Newport (South Wales) 131 a			08 59	09 40		11 01	11 53	12 56		14 54		16 59		19 00		21 15				
—	238¾	**Cardiff Central** 7 131 a			09 19	09 58		11 15	12 10	13 20		15 10		17 16		19 20		21 35				
143	—	Wellington (Shropshire) 74 a	06 46								12 45		14 45		16 47		18 46					22 31
147	—	Telford Central 74 a	06 53								12 53		14 53		16 53		18 53					22 37
162½	—	**Wolverhampton** 7 68,74 ⛴ a	07 11								13 10		15 11		17 09		19 11					22 55
170½	—	Smethwick Galton Bridge 3 74,68 ✈ a	07 23								13 22		15 22		17 22		19 22					
174½	—	**Birmingham New Street** 12 74,68 a	07 30								13 29		15 30		17 30		19 30					23 28
182¾	—	Birmingham International 68 a	07 49								13 49		15 49		17 49		19 49					

	AW
	◇
Holyhead 81 d	
Bangor (Gwynedd) 81 d	
Llandudno 81 d	
Llandudno Junction 81 d	
Colwyn Bay 81 d	
Rhyl 81 d	
Prestatyn 81 d	
Flint 81 d	
Chester 81 d	22 32
Wrexham General a	22 44
d	22 45
Ruabon a	22 51
Chirk a	22 57
Gobowen a	23 03
Shrewsbury 74 a	23 21
Hereford 131 a	
Newport (South Wales) 131 a	
Cardiff Central 7 131 a	
Wellington (Shropshire) 74 a	23 37
Telford Central 74 a	23 45
Wolverhampton 7 68,74 ⛴ a	00 17
Smethwick Galton Bridge 3 74,68 ✈ a	
Birmingham New Street 12 74,68 a	
Birmingham International 68 a	

Saturdays
26 May to 8 December

	AW	AW	AW	AW	AW	AW	AW	AW	AW	AW	AW	AW	AW	AW	AW	AW	AW	AW	AW
		◇ D 🍴	◇ E	◇	◇ B 🍴	■ 🍴	◇ 🍴	■ 🍴	■ 🍴	■ 🍴	◇ B 🍴	■ 🍴	◇ 🍴	■ 🍴	◇ 🍴	◇ 🍴		◇	◇
Holyhead 81 d		04 25		05 23	06 35	07 15	08 20	09 23	10 33	11 23	12 38	13 28	14 27	15 23	16 52	17 32		19 22	
Bangor (Gwynedd) 81 d		04 57		06 02	07 07	08 02	09 02	10 02	11 05	12 02	13 07	14 07	14 55	16 02	17 20	18 11		20 01	
Llandudno 81 d																			
Llandudno Junction 81 d		05 15		06 25	07 25	08 25	09 25	10 25	11 23	12 25	13 25	14 25	15 18	16 25	17 38	18 34		20 24	
Colwyn Bay 81 d		05 21		06 31	07 31	08 31	09 31	10 31	11 29	12 31	13 31	14 31	15 24	16 31	17 44	18 40		20 30	
Rhyl 81 d		05 31		06 41	07 41	08 41	09 41	10 41	11 39	12 41	13 41	14 41	15 35	16 41	17 54	18 50		20 40	
Prestatyn 81 d		05 37		06 47	07 47	08 47	09 47	10 47	11 45	12 47	13 47	14 47	15 40	16 47	18 00	18 56		20 46	
Flint 81 d		05 50		07 00	08 00	09 00	10 00	11 00	11 58	13 00	14 00	15 00	15 54	17 00	18 13	19 09		20 59	
Chester 81 d	05 37	06 20	06 20	07 30	08 20	09 30	10 19	11 36	12 19	13 35	14 19	15 36	16 21	17 30	18 32	19 31	20 26	21 22	22 30
Wrexham General a	05 55	06 34	06 34	07 44	08 34	09 44	10 33	11 50	12 33	13 49	14 33	15 50	16 36	17 44	18 47	19 45	20 40	21 36	22 46
d		06 35	06 35	07 45	08 34	09 45	10 34	11 51	12 33	13 50	14 33	15 51	16 36	17 45	18 47	19 46	20 41	21 37	22 46
Ruabon a		06 41	06 41	07 51	08 41	09 51	10 41	11 57	12 40	13 56	14 40	15 58	16 43	17 51	18 54	19 52	20 48	21 44	22 53
Chirk a		06 48	06 48	07 58	08 47	09 57	10 47	12 04	12 46	14 03	14 46	16 04	16 49	17 58	19 00	19 59	20 54	21 50	22 59
Gobowen a		06 53	06 53	08 03	08 53	10 03	10 52	12 09	12 51	14 08	14 52	16 10	16 55	18 03	19 06	20 04	21 00	21 56	23 05
Shrewsbury 74 a		07 12	07 12	08 22	09 11	10 29	11 11	12 27	13 10	14 28	15 10	16 29	17 13	18 22	19 24	20 26	21 21	22 14	23 23
Hereford 131 a		08 10	08 10		10 07		12 04		14 09		16 01		18 05		20 20				
Newport (South Wales) 131 a		09 00	09 00		10 57		12 54		15 04		16 51		18 55		21 14				
Cardiff Central 7 131 a		09 18	09 18		11 13		13 17		15 24		17 08		19 15		21 35				
Wellington (Shropshire) 74 a				08 46		10 46		12 45		14 45		16 47		18 46				22 44	23 39
Telford Central 74 a				08 53		10 53		12 53		14 53		16 53		18 53				22 50	23 47
Wolverhampton 7 68,74 ⛴ a				09 11		11 11		13 10		15 11		17 09		19 11				23 08	00 16
Smethwick Galton Bridge 3 74,68 ✈ a				09 23		11 22		13 21		15 22		17 22		19 22					
Birmingham New Street 12 74,68 a				09 27		11 28		13 28		15 28		17 28		19 28				23 30	
Birmingham International 68 a				09 50		11 50		13 50		15 50		17 50		19 49					

A To Llanelli
B To Maesteg
C From London Euston
D from 15 September. To Maesteg
E until 8 September. To Maesteg

Table T075-R

Sundays

20 May to 2 December

Holyhead - Chester - Shrewsbury - Birmingham

Network Diagram - see first page of Table 74

	AW	AW	AW	AW	AW	AW	AW	AW	AW	AW	AW	AW	AW
		◇	◇	■	◇	◇	◇	■	◇	◇ A	◇ B		
		⊼	⊼	⊼				⊼					
Holyhead 81 d				10 20				16 25			19 17		
Bangor (Gwynedd) 81 d				10 59				17 04			19 56		
Llandudno 81 d													
Llandudno Junction 81 d				11 22				17 25			20 24		
Colwyn Bay 81 d				11 28				17 31			20 30		
Rhyl 81 d				11 41				17 44			20 44		
Prestatyn 81 d				11 46				17 49			20 49		
Flint 81 d				12 00				18 03			21 03		
Chester 81 d	08 15	09 26	11 35	12 28	13 35	15 32	17 31	18 25	19 26	21 28	21 28	22 04	23 00
Wrexham General a	08 33	09 40	11 50	12 43	13 50	15 47	17 46	18 40	19 40	21 44	21 44	22 22	
d		09 41	11 50	12 44	13 50	15 47	17 46	18 40	19 41	21 44	21 45		
Ruabon a		09 47	11 57	12 50	13 57	15 54	17 53	18 47	19 47	21 51	21 51		
Chirk a		09 54	12 03	12 56	14 03	16 00	17 59	18 52	19 53	21 57	21 58		
Gobowen a		09 59	12 09	13 02	14 09	16 06	18 05	18 59	19 59	22 03	22 03		
Shrewsbury 74 a		10 18	12 27	13 21	14 27	16 24	18 23	19 17	20 17	22 20	22 22		00 14
Hereford 131 a				14 20				20 18					
Newport (South Wales) 131 a				15 10				21 10					
Cardiff Central 7 131 a				15 34				21 37					
Wellington (Shropshire) 74 a		10 33	12 44		14 44	16 53	18 45		20 36	22 36	22 37		
Telford Central 74 a		10 39	12 50		14 50	16 59	18 51		20 44	22 45	22 46		
Wolverhampton 7 68,74 ⇌ a		10 56	13 07		15 07	17 15	19 07		21 11	23 14	23 14		
Smethwick Galton Bridge 5 74,68 ✈ a													
Birmingham New Street 12 74,68 a		11 13	13 23		15 24	17 37	19 26		21 29				
Birmingham International 68 a		11 31	13 57		15 57	17 57	19 57		21 57				

A from 16 September

B until 9 September

Table T076-F

Mondays to Fridays

21 May to 7 December

Birmingham - Shrewsbury - Aberystwyth, Barmouth - Pwllheli

Miles	Miles		AW	AW	AW	AW	AW	AW	AW	AW	AW		AW	AW	AW	AW		AW		AW	AW	
											■					■					■	
						◇		◇	◇	◇			◇	◇	◇			◇				
								⊼	⊼		⊼			⊼		⊼		⊼			⊼	
—	—	Birmingham International 68 ✈ d									08 09			10 09		12 09		14 09			16 09	
0	—	**Birmingham New Street** 12 74,68 d							06 25		08 24			10 25		12 25		14 25			16 25	
4	—	Smethwick Galton Bridge 5 74,68 d							06 31		08 31			10 31		12 31		14 31			16 31	
12¾	—	**Wolverhampton** 7 68,74 ⇌ d							06 43		08 44			10 43		12 43		14 43			16 43	
28¼	—	Telford Central 74 d							07 01		09 00			10 59		12 59		14 59			16 59	
32¾	—	Wellington (Shropshire) 74 d							07 07		09 07			11 06		13 06		15 06			17 06	
42¾	—	**Shrewsbury** 74 a							07 22		09 20			11 19		13 19		15 19			17 19	
—	—	d						06 25	07 27		09 30		10 29	11 27		13 29		15 30			17 29	
62½	—	Welshpool d						06 48	07 49		09 52		10 51	11 49		13 51		15 52			17 51	
76½	—	Newtown (Powys) d						07 03	08 03		10 06		11 06	12 03		14 05		16 06			18 05	
82	—	Caersws d						07 10	08 10		10 13		11 13	12 10		14 12		16 13			18 12	
103¾	0	**Machynlleth** 4 a						07 40	08 41		10 44		11 40	12 41		14 43		16 44			18 41	
—	—																					
—	—	d	04 53	05 07	05 45	06 43	06 47	07 46	08 48	08 52	10 50	10 55	11 41	12 47	12 51	14 49	14 56	16 50	16 55	18 01	18 49	19 04
107¾	4	Dovey Junction 5 d	04 59	05 13	05 54	06 49	06 55	07 56	08 55	08 58	10 56	11 01	11 54	12 54	12 57	14 56	15 02	16 56	17 01		18 58	19 10
116	—	Borth d	05 09		06 04		07 05	08 06	09 05		11 06		12 04	13 04		15 06		17 06			19 08	
124¼	—	**Aberystwyth** a	05 22		06 17		07 17	08 20	09 20		11 20		12 20	13 20		15 20		17 20		18 27	19 20	
—	9	Penhelig d		05x22		06x58				09x07		11x10			13x06		15x11		17x10			19x20
—	10	Aberdovey d		05 26		07 02				09 11		11 14			13 10		15 15		17 14			19 23
—	13½	Tywyn a		05 33		07 11				09 20		11 23			13 19		15 24		17 24			19 32
—	—	d		05 33		07 14				09 24		11 30			13 25		15 26		17 29			19 33
—	16	Tonfanau d		05x37		07x17				09x27		11x33			13x29		15x30		17x32			19x37
—	20	Llwyngwril d		05x43		07x24				09x34		11x40			13x35		15x36		17x39			19x44
—	22¾	Fairbourne d		05 52		07 32				09 42		11 49			13 44		15 45		17 47			19 51
—	23¾	Morfa Mawddach d		05x53		07x34				09x44		11x50			13x45		15x46		17x49			19x54
—	25½	**Barmouth** a		06 04		07 45				09 53		11 59			13 55		15 56		17 58			20 03
—	—	d				07 47				09 58		12 01			13 57		15 58		18 00			20 04
—	26¾	Llanaber d				07x50				10x02		12x03			14x00		16x01		18x03			20x08
—	29¾	Talybont d				07x54				10x05		12x08			14x04		16x05		18x07			20x13
—	30¼	Dyffryn Ardudwy d				07x57				10x08		12x11			14x07		16x08		18x10			20x16
—	32½	Llanbedr d				08x01				10x12		12x15			14x11		16x12		18x14			20x20
—	33¼	Pensarn d				08x03				10x15		12x17			14x13		16x14		18x16			20x22
—	34	Llandanwg d				08x05				10x17		12x19			14x15		16x16		18x18			20x24
—	35¾	Harlech a				08 11				10 25		12 25			14 21		16 22		18 24			20 30
—	—	d				08 25				10 28		12 27			14 31		16 29		18 33			20 30
—	38½	Tygwyn d				08x29				10x31		12x31			14x35		16x32		18x36			20x35
—	39¼	Talsarnau d				08x31				10x34		12x33			14x37		16x35		18x39			20x37
—	40½	Llandecwyn d				08x34				10x37		12x36			14x40		16x38		18x42			20x40
—	41¼	Penrhyndeudraeth d				08 38				10 41		12 40			14 44		16 42		18 46			20 43
—	42½	Minffordd d				08 42				10 44		12 44			14 48		16 45		18 49			20 47
—	44½	Porthmadog a				08 49				10 52		12 51			14 55		16 53		18 57			20 55
—	—	d				08 50				10 52		12 52			14 56		16 53		18 57			20 55
—	49½	Criccieth d				08 57				11 00		12 59			15 03		17 00		19 04			21 03
—	54	Penychain d				09x02				11x05		13x04			15x08		17x05		19x11			21x09
—	55½	Abererch d				09x06				11x08		13x08			15x12		17x08		19x14			21x12
—	57½	**Pwllheli** a				09 12				11 14		13 15			15 20		17 18		19 20			21 18

For connections from London Euston refer to Table T66

For connections from Manchester Piccadilly and Crewe refer to Table T131

Table T076-F

Mondays to Fridays

21 May to 7 December

Birmingham - Shrewsbury - Aberystwyth, Barmouth - Pwllheli

		AW ◇ ⊥	AW ◇	AW ◇	AW ◇	AW ◇
Birmingham International 68 ✈	d		18 09			20 04
Birmingham New Street 74,68	d		18 25			20 25
Smethwick Galton Bridge 74,68	d		18 31			20 31
Wolverhampton 68,74	d		18 43			20 43
Telford Central 74	d		18 59			20 59
Wellington (Shropshire) 74	d		19 06			21 05
Shrewsbury 74	a		19 19			21 18
	d	18 31	19 30		20 32	21 50
Welshpool	d	18 53	19 52		20 53	22 12
Newtown (Powys)	d	19 07	20 06		21 08	22 27
Caersws	d	19 14	20 13		21 16	22 34
Machynlleth	a	19 45	20 47		21 43	23 02
	d	19 48	20 49	21 47	21 49	23 07
Dovey Junction	d	19 57	20 57	21 53	21 57	23 13
Borth	d	20 07	21 07		22 07	23 23
Aberystwyth	a	20 20	21 20		22 20	23 37
Penhelig	d			22x02		
Aberdovey	d			22 06		
Tywyn	a			22 15		
	d			22 16		
Tonfanau	d			22x20		
Llwyngwril	d			22x26		
Fairbourne	d			22 35		
Morfa Mawddach	d			22x36		
Barmouth	a			22 46		
	d			22 47		
Llanaber	d			22x51		
Talybont	d			22x54		
Dyffryn Ardudwy	d			22x57		
Llanbedr	d			23x01		
Pensarn	d			23x04		
Llandanwg	d			23x06		
Harlech	a			23 12		
	d			23 13		
Tygwyn	d			23x17		
Talsarnau	d			23x20		
Llandecwyn	d			23x23		
Penrhyndeudraeth	d			23 26		
Minffordd	d			23 30		
Porthmadog	a			23 37		
	d			23 38		
Criccieth	d			23 46		
Penychain	d			23x51		
Abererch	d			23x54		
Pwllheli	a			00 01		

For connections from London Euston refer to Table T66

For connections from Manchester Piccadilly and Crewe refer to Table T131

Table T076-F

Saturdays

26 May to 8 December

Birmingham - Shrewsbury - Aberystwyth, Barmouth - Pwllheli

		AW	AW	AW	AW ◇	AW	AW ◇ ⊥	AW ◇ ⊥	AW ◇
Birmingham International 68 ✈	d								
Birmingham New Street 74,68	d							06 25	
Smethwick Galton Bridge 74,68	d							06 31	
Wolverhampton 68,74	d							06 43	
Telford Central 74	d							06 59	
Wellington (Shropshire) 74	d							07 06	
Shrewsbury 74	a							07 19	
	d						06 25	07 29	
Welshpool	d						06 48	07 52	
Newtown (Powys)	d						07 03	08 06	
Caersws	d						07 10	08 13	
Machynlleth	a						07 42	08 44	
	d	04 53	05 07	05 47	06 43	06 47	07 48	08 49	08 53
Dovey Junction	d	04 59	05 13	05 56	06 49	06 56	07 55	08 56	08 59
Borth	d	05 09		06 06		07 06	08 05	09 06	
Aberystwyth	a	05 26		06 20		07 20	08 20	09 20	
Penhelig	d		05x22		06x58				09x08
Aberdovey	d		05 26		07 02				09 12
Tywyn	a		05 33		07 11				09 21
	d		05 33		07 14				09 22
Tonfanau	d		05x37		07x17				09x26
Llwyngwril	d		05x43		07x24				09x32
Fairbourne	d		05 52		07 32				09 41
Morfa Mawddach	d		05x53		07x34				09x42
Barmouth	a		06 04		07 45				09 52
	d				07 47				09 58
Llanaber	d				07x50				10x01
Talybont	d				07x54				10x05
Dyffryn Ardudwy	d				07x57				10x08
Llanbedr	d				08x01				10x12
Pensarn	d				08x03				10x14
Llandanwg	d				08x05				10x16
Harlech	a				08 11				10 25
	d				08 25				10 27
Tygwyn	d				08x29				10x31
Talsarnau	d				08x31				10x33
Llandecwyn	d				08x34				10x36
Penrhyndeudraeth	d				08 38				10 40
Minffordd	d				08 42				10 44
Porthmadog	a				08 49				10 51
	d				08 50				10 52
Criccieth	d				08 57				10 59
Penychain	d				09x02				11x04
Abererch	d				09x06				11x08
Pwllheli	a				09 13				11 14

		AW ■ ⊥		AW ◇	AW ■ ⊥		AW ■ ⊥		AW ◇ ⊥		AW	AW ◇ ⊥	AW ◇	AW ◇ ⊥	AW ◇ ⊥
Birmingham International 68 ✈	d	08 09			10 09		12 09		14 09			16 09			18 09
Birmingham New Street 74,68	d	08 25			10 25		12 25		14 25			16 25			18 25
Smethwick Galton Bridge 74,68	d	08 31			10 31		12 31		14 31			16 31			18 31
Wolverhampton 68,74	d	08 43			10 43		12 43		14 43			16 43			18 43
Telford Central 74	d	09 00			10 59		12 59		15 00			16 59			18 59
Wellington (Shropshire) 74	d	09 07			11 06		13 07		15 07			17 07			19 06
Shrewsbury 74	a	09 20			11 19		13 20		15 20			17 20			19 19
	d	09 31		10 29	11 29		13 29		15 30			17 27		18 27	19 30
Welshpool	d	09 53		10 51	11 51		13 51		15 52			17 49		18 49	19 52
Newtown (Powys)	d	10 07		11 06	12 05		14 05		16 06			18 03		19 03	20 06
Caersws	d	10 14		11 13	12 12		14 12		16 13			18 10		19 10	20 13
Machynlleth	a	10 45		11 41	12 43		14 43		16 44			18 41		19 42	20 47
	d	10 51	10 55	11 45	12 49	12 52	14 49	14 56	16 50	16 55	18 01	18 51	19 04	19 46	20 52
Dovey Junction	d	10 57	11 01	11 54	12 57	12 58	14 55	15 02	16 56	17 01		18 59	19 10	19 55	21 00
Borth	d	11 07		12 04	13 07		15 05		17 06			19 09		20 05	21 10
Aberystwyth	a	11 20		12 20	13 20		15 20		17 20		18 30	19 22		20 20	21 23
Penhelig	d		11x10			13x07		15x11		17x10			19x19		
Aberdovey	d		11 14			13 11		15 15		17 14			19 23		
Tywyn	a		11 23			13 19		15 24		17 24			19 32		
	d		11 30			13 24		15 25		17 29			19 33		
Tonfanau	d		11x33			13x28		15x29		17x32			19x36		
Llwyngwril	d		11x40			13x34		15x35		17x39			19x43		
Fairbourne	d		11 48			13 43		15 44		17 47			19 51		
Morfa Mawddach	d		11x50			13x44		15x45		17x49			19x53		
Barmouth	a		11 59			13 54		15 55		17 58			20 02		
	d		12 00			13 56		15 57		18 00			20 04		
Llanaber	d		12x03			13x59		16x00		18x03			20x08		
Talybont	d		12x07			14x03		16x04		18x07			20x13		
Dyffryn Ardudwy	d		12x10			14x06		16x07		18x10			20x16		
Llanbedr	d		12x14			14x10		16x11		18x14			20x20		
Pensarn	d		12x17			14x12		16x13		18x16			20x22		
Llandanwg	d		12x19			14x14		16x15		18x18			20x24		
Harlech	a		12 25			14 20		16 21		18 24			20 30		
	d		12 28			14 31		16 29		18 33			20 30		
Tygwyn	d		12x31			14x35		16x32		18x36			20x35		
Talsarnau	d		12x34			14x37		16x35		18x39			20x37		
Llandecwyn	d		12x37			14x40		16x38		18x42			20x40		
Penrhyndeudraeth	d		12 41			14 44		16 42		18 46			20 43		
Minffordd	d		12 44			14 48		16 45		18 49			20 47		
Porthmadog	a		12 52			14 55		16 53		18 57			20 55		
	d		12 52			14 56		16 53		18 57			20 55		
Criccieth	d		13 00			15 03		17 00		19 04			21 03		
Penychain	d		13x05			15x08		17x05		19x09			21x09		
Abererch	d		13x08			15x12		17x08		19x12			21x12		
Pwllheli	a		13 15			15 20		17 16		19 19			21 18		

For connections from London Euston refer to Table T66

For connections from Manchester Piccadilly and Crewe refer to Table T131

Table T076-F

Saturdays
26 May to 8 December

Birmingham - Shrewsbury - Aberystwyth, Barmouth - Pwllheli

		AW ◇	AW ◇	AW ◇
Birmingham International 68 ✈	d			20 09
Birmingham New Street 74,68	d			20 25
Smethwick Galton Bridge 74,68	d			20 31
Wolverhampton 68,74	d			20 43
Telford Central 74	d			20 59
Wellington (Shropshire) 74	d			21 06
Shrewsbury 74	a			21 20
	d		20 32	21 43
Welshpool	d		20 53	22 05
Newtown (Powys)	d		21 08	22 20
Caersws	d		21 15	22 27
Machynlleth	a		21 42	22 55
	d	21 47	21 49	23 02
Dovey Junction	d	21 53	21 57	23 08
Borth	d		22 07	23 18
Aberystwyth	a		22 20	23 31
Penhelig	d	22x02		
Aberdovey	d	22 06		
Tywyn	a	22 15		
	d	22 17		
Tonfanau	d	22x20		
Llwyngwril	d	22x27		
Fairbourne	d	22 35		
Morfa Mawddach	d	22x37		
Barmouth	a	22 46		
	d	22 48		
Llanaber	d	22x51		
Talybont	d	22x54		
Dyffryn Ardudwy	d	22x58		
Llanbedr	d	23x02		
Pensarn	d	23x05		
Llandanwg	d	23x07		
Harlech	a	23 12		
	d	23 14		
Tygwyn	d	23x17		
Talsarnau	d	23x20		
Llandecwyn	d	23x23		
Penrhyndeudraeth	d	23 27		
Minffordd	d	23 30		
Porthmadog	a	23 38		
	d	23 38		
Criccieth	d	23 46		
Penychain	d	23x51		
Abererch	d	23x53		
Pwllheli	a	00 01		

For connections from London Euston refer to Table T66

For connections from Manchester Piccadilly and Crewe refer to Table T131

Table T076-F

Sundays
20 May to 9 September

Birmingham - Shrewsbury - Aberystwyth, Barmouth - Pwllheli

		AW	AW ◇	AW ◇	AW	AW ◇	AW	AW ◇ 🚲		AW ■ 🚲	AW ◇ 🚲	AW ■ 🚲		AW ◇	AW ◇	AW ◇
Birmingham International 68 ✈	d					09 51		12 07		14 07		16 07			18 08	20 08
Birmingham New Street 74,68	d					10 04		12 24		14 24		16 24			18 24	20 24
Smethwick Galton Bridge 74,68	d															
Wolverhampton 68,74	d					10 22		12 42		14 43		16 43			18 43	20 43
Telford Central 74	d					10 49		12 59		14 59		16 59			18 59	20 59
Wellington (Shropshire) 74	d					10 57		13 05		15 06		17 06			19 06	21 06
Shrewsbury 74	a					11 10		13 19		15 19		17 19			19 19	21 19
	d		08 30			11 28		13 28		15 27	16 29	17 27		18 28	19 27	21 27
Welshpool	d		08 52			11 50		13 50		15 51	16 51	17 49		18 50	19 49	21 49
Newtown (Powys)	d		09 06			12 04		14 04		16 05	17 05	18 03		19 04	20 03	22 03
Caersws	d		09 13			12 11		14 12		16 12	17 12	18 11		19 11	20 10	22 10
Machynlleth	a		09 45			12 45		14 43		16 43	17 42	18 42		19 40	20 41	22 39
	d	08 50	09 47	10 10	10 49	12 50	13 51	14 48	14 52	16 48	17 45	18 48	18 55	19 42	20 47	22 45
Dovey Junction	d	08 56	09 55	10 16	10 58	12 58	13 59	14 58	14 58	16 55	17 55	18 56	19 01	19 56	20 55	22 52
Borth	d	09 06	10 05		11 08	13 08	14 09	15 08		17 05	18 05	19 06		20 06	21 05	23 02
Aberystwyth	a	09 20	10 20		11 20	13 21	14 21	15 20		17 20	18 20	19 20		20 20	21 20	23 15
Penhelig	d			10x25					15x07				19x10			
Aberdovey	d			10 29					15 11				19 14			
Tywyn	a			10 35					15 17				19 20			
	d			10 36					15 31				19 25			
Tonfanau	d			10x39					15x34				19x29			
Llwyngwril	d			10x47					15x41				19x36			
Fairbourne	d			10 54					15 49				19 44			
Morfa Mawddach	d			10x56					15x51				19x45			
Barmouth	a			11 03					15 57				19 52			
	d			11 04					15 59				19 54			
Llanaber	d			11x08					16x02				19x56			
Talybont	d			11x11					16x06				20x01			
Dyffryn Ardudwy	d			11x15					16x10				20x04			
Llanbedr	d			11x19					16x14				20x08			
Pensarn	d			11x21					16x16				20x11			
Llandanwg	d			11x23					16x18				20x13			
Harlech	a			11 30					16 25				20 20			
	d			11 32					16 25				20 22			
Tygwyn	d			11x36					16x29				20x26			
Talsarnau	d			11x39					16x32				20x29			
Llandecwyn	d			11x42					16x36				20x32			
Penrhyndeudraeth	d			11 46					16 39				20 36			
Minffordd	d			11 49					16 42				20 39			
Porthmadog	a			11 54					16 47				20 44			
	d			11 57					16 48				20 45			
Criccieth	d			12 05					16 55				20 53			
Penychain	d			12x11					17x01				20x58			
Abererch	d			12x13					17x04				21x01			
Pwllheli	a			12 21					17 14				21 12			

For connections from London Euston refer to Table T66

For connections from Manchester Piccadilly and Crewe refer to Table T131

Table T076-F

Sundays

16 September to 2 December

Birmingham - Shrewsbury - Aberystwyth, Barmouth - Pwllheli

		AW	AW	AW	AW	AW	AW	AW	AW	AW	AW		AW	AW	AW
				🚌		◇ 🛒		◇ 🛒	■ 🛒	◇ 🛒	■ 🛒		◇	◇	◇
Birmingham International 68 ✈	d					09 51		12 07	14 07		16 07			18 08	20 08
Birmingham New Street 12 74,68	d					10 04		12 24	14 24		16 24			18 24	20 24
Smethwick Galton Bridge 5 74,68	d														
Wolverhampton 7 68,74 🚉	d					10 22		12 42	14 43		16 43			18 43	20 43
Telford Central 74	d					10 49		12 59	14 59		16 59			18 59	20 59
Wellington (Shropshire) 74	d					10 57		13 05	15 06		17 06			19 06	21 06
Shrewsbury 74	a					11 10		13 19	15 19		17 19			19 19	21 19
	d			08 30		11 28		13 28	15 27	16 29	17 27		18 28	19 27	21 27
Welshpool	d			09 05		11 50		13 50	15 51	16 51	17 49		18 50	19 49	21 49
Newtown (Powys)	d			09 30		12 04		14 04	16 05	17 05	18 03		19 04	20 03	22 03
Caersws	d			09 45		12 11		14 12	16 12	17 12	18 11		19 11	20 10	22 10
Machynlleth 4	a			10 25		12 45		14 43	16 43	17 42	18 42		19 40	20 41	22 39
	d	08 50	09 47	10 25	10 49	12 50	13 51	14 48	16 48	17 45	18 48	18 55	19 42	20 47	22 45
Dovey Junction 5	d	08 56	09 55		10 58	12 58	13 59	14 58	16 55	17 55	18 56	19 01	19 56	20 55	22 52
Borth	d	09 06	10 05	10 50	11 08	13 08	14 09	15 08	17 05	18 05	19 06		20 06	21 05	23 02
Aberystwyth	a	09 20	10 20	11 10	11 20	13 21	14 21	15 20	17 20	18 20	19 20		20 20	21 20	23 15
Penhelig	d											19x10			
Aberdovey	d											19 14			
Tywyn	a											19 20			
	d											19 25			
Tonfanau	d											19x29			
Llwyngwril	d											19x36			
Fairbourne	d											19 44			
Morfa Mawddach	d											19x45			
Barmouth	a											19 52			
	d											19 54			
Llanaber	d											19x56			
Talybont	d											20x01			
Dyffryn Ardudwy	d											20x04			
Llanbedr	d											20x08			
Pensarn	d											20x11			
Llandanwg	d											20x13			
Harlech	a											20 20			
	d											20 22			
Tygwyn	d											20x26			
Talsarnau	d											20x29			
Llandecwyn	d											20x32			
Penrhyndeudraeth	d											20 36			
Minffordd	d											20 39			
Porthmadog	a											20 44			
	d											20 45			
Criccieth	d											20 53			
Penychain	d											20x58			
Abererch	d											21x01			
Pwllheli	a											21 12			

For connections from London Euston refer to Table T66

For connections from Manchester Piccadilly and Crewe refer to Table T131

Table T076-R

Mondays to Fridays

21 May to 7 December

Pwllheli - Barmouth, Aberystwyth - Shrewsbury - Birmingham

Miles	Miles			AW MX	AW	AW	AW	AW	AW	AW	AW	AW	AW	AW	AW	AW	AW	AW	AW	AW	AW	AW	AW
				A	◇ 🛒		◇	■ 🛒	◇	◇ 🛒	◇ B 🛒	◇ 🛒	◇ B 🛒	◇ 🛒	◇	◇ B 🛒	◇ 🛒	◇ B 🛒	◇ 🛒	◇	◇ 🛒	◇	◇
—	0	**Pwllheli**	d						06 29		07 24		09 34			11 37		13 38		15 37			17 42
—	1¾	Abererch	d						06x32		07x27		09x37			11x40		13x41		15x40			17x45
—	3¼	Penychain	d						06x35		07x30		09x40			11x43		13x44		15x43			17x48
—	7¾	Criccieth	d						06 43		07 38		09 48			11 51		13 52		15 51			17 56
—	12¾	Porthmadog	a						06 51		07 46		09 56			11 59		14 00		15 59			18 04
—	—		d						06 53		07 47		09 57			12 01		14 02		16 01			18 06
—	15	Minffordd	d						06 57		07 52		10 01			12 05		14 06		16 05			18 10
—	16¼	Penrhyndeudraeth	d						07 01		07 56		10 05			12 09		14 10		16 09			18 14
—	17	Llandecwyn	d						07x03		07x58		10x07			12x11		14x12		16x11			18x16
—	18¾	Talsarnau	d						07x05		08x00		10x09			12x13		14x14		16x13			18x18
—	19	Tygwyn	d						07x08		08x03		10x12			12x16		14x17		16x16			18x21
—	21½	Harlech	a						07 15		08 09		10 20			12 24		14 25		16 24			18 27
—	—		d						07 17		08 21		10 29			12 28		14 28		16 29			18 30
—	23½	Llandanwg	d						07x22		08x25		10x34			12x33		14x33		16x34			18x36
—	24¼	Pensarn	d						07x23		08x27		10x35			12x34		14x34		16x35			18x37
—	30½	Llanbedr	d						07x26		08x29		10x38			12x37		14x37		16x38			18x39
—	27	Dyffryn Ardudwy	d						07x30		08x33		10x42			12x41		14x41		16x42			18x43
—	28¾	Talybont	d						07x33		08x36		10x45			12x44		14x44		16x45			18x46
—	25	Llanaber	d						07x37		08x41		10x49			12x48		14x48		16x49			18x50
—	32	**Barmouth**	a						07 42		08 45		10 54			12 53		14 53		16 54			18 55
—	—		d				06 45		07 46		08 50		10 59			12 55		14 55		16 56			18 57
—	33¾	Morfa Mawddach	d				06x49		07x50		08x54		11x03			12x59		14x59		17x00			19x01
—	34¾	Fairbourne	d				06 53		07 54		08 58		11 07			13 03		15 03		17 04			19 05
—	37¼	Llwyngwril	d				06x59		08x01		09x04		11x14			13x09		15x09		17x10			19x12
—	41½	Tonfanau	d				07x06		08x09		09x11		11x21			13x16		15x16		17x17			19x19
—	44¼	Tywyn	a				07 13		08 12		09 21		11 27			13 23		15 24		17 24			19 25
—	—		d				07 14		08 16		09 27		11 30			13 25		15 26		17 27			19 34
—	47½	Aberdovey	d				07 20		08 22		09 33		11 36			13 31		15 32		17 33			19 40
—	48½	Penhelig	d				07x23		08x24		09x35		11x38			13x33		15x35		17x35			19x43
0	—	**Aberystwyth**	d		05 30	06 30		07 30		08 30		09 30		11 30	12 30		13 30		15 30		17 30	18 32	
8¼	—	Borth	d		05 43	06 43		07 43		08 43		09 43		11 43	12 43		13 43		15 43		17 43	18 45	
16½	53½	Dovey Junction 5	d	00 03	05 53	06 53	07 35	07 53	08 38	08 58	09 47	09 53	11 49	11 53	12 57	13 45	13 53	15 46	15 53	17 47	17 53	18 56	19 56
20½	57½	**Machynlleth** 4	a	00 12	06 00	07 00	07 43	08 00	08 45	09 05	09 54	10 00	11 57	12 01	13 04	13 52	14 00	15 54	16 00	17 55	18 00	19 03	20 04
—	—																						
—	—		d		06 01	07 04		08 05		09 06	10 08		12 04		13 06	14 07		16 08			18 05	19 09	
42¼	—	Caersws	d		06 28	07 31		08 28		09 33	10 35		12 32		13 33	14 34		16 31			18 30	19 32	
47¾	—	Newtown (Powys)	d		06 35	07 38		08 39		09 40	10 42		12 39		13 40	14 41		16 42			18 41	19 43	
61¾	—	Welshpool	d		06 50	07 52		08 54		09 55	10 56		12 54		13 54	14 55		16 56			18 56	19 57	
81½	—	**Shrewsbury** 74	a		07 12	08 14		09 16		10 17	11 18		13 16		14 18	15 19		17 20			19 18	20 22	
—	—		d		07 33			09 33			11 33		13 34			15 33		17 33			19 33		
92	—	Wellington (Shropshire) 74	d		07 46			09 46			11 46		13 48			15 46		17 46			19 46		
96	—	Telford Central 74	d		07 53			09 53			11 53		13 54			15 53		17 53			19 53		
112	—	**Wolverhampton** 7 68,74 🚉	a		08 11			10 10			12 11		14 10			16 10		18 11			20 11		
120¾	—	Smethwick Galton Bridge 5 68,74	a		08 22			10 21			12 22		14 23			16 22		18 22			20 22		
124¾	—	**Birmingham New Street** 12 74,68	a		08 29			10 30			12 30		14 30			16 30		18 30			20 29		
—	—	Birmingham International 68 ✈	a		08 49			10 49			12 49		14 49			16 49		18 49			20 49		

A From Aberystwyth

B 🛒 from Machynlleth

For connections to London Euston refer to Table T66

For connections to Crewe and Manchester Piccadilly refer to Table T131

Table T076-R

Mondays to Fridays

21 May to 7 December

Pwllheli - Barmouth, Aberystwyth - Shrewsbury - Birmingham

	AW	AW	AW	AW	AW	AW
	◇			◇		
Pwllheli d				20 26		
Abererch d				20x29		
Penychain d				20x32		
Criccieth d				20 40		
Porthmadog a				20 48		
d				20 55		
Minffordd d				20 59		
Penrhyndeudraeth d				21 03		
Llandecwyn d				21x05		
Talsarnau d				21x07		
Tygwyn d				21x10		
Harlech a				21 17		
d				21 19		
Llandanwg d				21x24		
Pensarn d				21x25		
Llanbedr d				21x28		
Dyffryn Ardudwy d				21x32		
Talybont d				21x35		
Llanaber d				21x40		
Barmouth a				21 44		
d				21 46		
Morfa Mawddach d				21x50		
Fairbourne d				21 54		
Llwyngwril d				22x01		
Tonfanau d				22x08		
Tywyn a				22 14		
d				22 17		
Aberdovey d				22 23		
Penhelig d				22x25		
Aberystwyth d	19 30	20 30	21 30		22 30	23 40
Borth d	19 43	20 43	21 43		22 43	23 53
Dovey Junction ■ d	19 59	20 55	21 56	22 38	22 53	00 03
Machynlleth ■ a	20 06	21 04	22 05	22 45	23 02	00 12
d	20 11					
Caersws d	20 34					
Newtown (Powys) d	20 44					
Welshpool d	20 59					
Shrewsbury 74 a	21 21					
d	21 33					
Wellington (Shropshire) 74 d	21 47					
Telford Central 74 d	21 53					
Wolverhampton ■ 68,74 ⇌ a	22 11					
Smethwick Galton Bridge ■ 68,74 a	22 22					
Birmingham New Street ■ 74,68 a	22 31					
Birmingham International 68 ✈ a						

For connections to London Euston refer to Table T66

For connections to Crewe and Manchester Piccadilly refer to Table T131

Table T076-R

Saturdays

26 May to 8 December

Pwllheli - Barmouth, Aberystwyth - Shrewsbury - Birmingham

	AW	AW	AW	AW	AW	AW	AW	AW	AW	AW	AW	AW	AW	AW	AW	AW	AW	AW	AW	AW	AW	AW
				■	■			■	■	■	■											
		◇		◇		◇	◇	◇		◇		◇	◇	◇	◇	◇	◇	◇	◇	◇	◇	
	A			B				B		B			C		C							
		🍴		🍴	🍴		🍴	🍴	🍴	🍴	🍴		🍴	🍴	🍴	🍴		🍴				
Pwllheli d						06 29		07 24		09 34			11 37		13 38		15 37			17 42		
Abererch d						06x32		07x27		09x37			11x40		13x41		15x40			17x45		
Penychain d						06x35		07x30		09x40			11x43		13x44		15x43			17x48		
Criccieth d						06 43		07 38		09 48			11 51		13 52		15 51			17 56		
Porthmadog a						06 51		07 46		09 56			11 59		14 00		15 59			18 04		
d						06 53		07 47		09 58			12 01		14 02		16 01			18 06		
Minffordd d						06 57		07 52		10 02			12 05		14 06		16 05			18 10		
Penrhyndeudraeth d						07 01		07 56		10 06			12 09		14 10		16 09			18 14		
Llandecwyn d						07x03		07x58		10x08			12x11		14x12		16x11			18x16		
Talsarnau d						07x05		08x00		10x10			12x13		14x14		16x13			18x18		
Tygwyn d						07x08		08x03		10x13			12x16		14x17		16x16			18x21		
Harlech a						07 15		08 09		10 21			12 24		14 25		16 24			18 27		
d						07 17		08 16		10 28			12 28		14 26		16 29			18 30		
Llandanwg d						07x22		08x20		10x33			12x33		14x31		16x34			18x36		
Pensarn d						07x23		08x22		10x34			12x34		14x32		16x35			18x37		
Llanbedr d						07x26		08x24		10x37			12x37		14x35		16x38			18x39		
Dyffryn Ardudwy d						07x30		08x28		10x41			12x41		14x39		16x42			18x43		
Talybont d						07x33		08x31		10x44			12x44		14x42		16x45			18x46		
Llanaber d						07x37		08x36		10x48			12x48		14x46		16x49			18x50		
Barmouth a						07 42		08 40		10 53			12 53		14 51		16 54			18 55		
d				06 45		07 46		08 47		10 58			12 55		14 55		16 56			18 57		
Morfa Mawddach d				06x49		07x50		08x51		11x02			12x59		14x59		17x00			19x01		
Fairbourne d				06 53		07 54		08 55		11 06			13 03		15 03		17 04			19 05		
Llwyngwril d				06x59		08x01		09x01		11x13			13x10		15x09		17x10			19x12		
Tonfanau d				07x06		08x09		09x08		11x20			13x17		15x16		17x17			19x19		
Tywyn a				07 13		08 12		09 15		11 26			13 23		15 24		17 24			19 25		
d				07 14		08 16		09 24		11 30			13 25		15 26		17 27			19 35		
Aberdovey d				07 20		08 22		09 30		11 36			13 31		15 32		17 33			19 41		
Penhelig d				07x23		08x24		09x32		11x39			13x33		15x35		17x35			19x43		
Aberystwyth d		05 30	06 30		07 30		08 30		09 30		11 30	12 30		13 30		15 30		17 30	18 33		19 30	20 36
Borth d		05 43	06 43		07 43		08 43		09 43		11 43	12 43		13 43		15 43		17 43	18 45		19 43	20 49
Dovey Junction ■ d	00 03	05 54	06 54	07 35	07 54	08 38	08 59	09 44	09 53	11 51	11 55	12 58	13 45	13 53	15 46	15 53	17 47	17 53	18 56	19 56	19 59	21 01
Machynlleth ■ a	00 12	06 01	07 01	07 43	08 01	08 47	09 06	09 52	09 58	11 58	12 00	13 05	13 53	13 58	15 55	15 58	17 55	18 00	19 03	20 03	20 04	21 08
d		06 02	07 03	08 08			09 08	10 08		12 07		13 06	14 07		16 08			18 05	19 05		20 11	
Caersws d		06 29	07 30	08 31			09 35	10 35		12 34		13 33	14 34		16 31			18 28	19 28		20 34	
Newtown (Powys) d		06 36	07 37	08 42			09 42	10 42		12 41		13 40	14 41		16 42			18 39	19 39		20 44	
Welshpool d		06 51	07 52	08 56			09 56	10 56		12 55		13 55	14 55		16 56			18 53	20 00		21 02	
Shrewsbury 74 a		07 13	08 13	09 18			10 18	11 18		13 17		14 16	15 17		17 19			19 15	20 22		21 24	
d		07 33		09 33				11 34		13 35			15 33		17 33			19 32			21 33	
Wellington (Shropshire) 74 d		07 46		09 47				11 48		13 48			15 46		17 46			19 46			21 46	
Telford Central 74 d		07 53		09 53				11 55		13 55			15 53		17 53			19 53			21 53	
Wolverhampton ■ 68,74 ⇌ a		08 11		10 10				12 12		14 12			16 10		18 11			20 10			22 09	
Smethwick Galton Bridge ■ 68,74 a		08 22		10 21				12 24		14 24			16 22		18 22			20 22			22 20	
Birmingham New Street ■ 74,68 a		08 29		10 30				12 32		14 30			16 30		18 30			20 29			22 31	
Birmingham International 68 ✈ a		08 49		10 50				12 50		14 49			16 48		18 49			20 49				

A From Aberystwyth

B 🍴 ■ from Machynlleth ◇ to Machynlleth

C 🍴 from Machynlleth

For connections to London Euston refer to Table T66

For connections to Crewe and Manchester Piccadilly refer to Table T131

Table T076-R

Saturdays
26 May to 8 December

Pwllheli - Barmouth, Aberystwyth - Shrewsbury - Birmingham

		AW	AW	AW	AW
			◇		
Pwllheli	d		20 26		
Abererch	d		20x29		
Penychain	d		20x32		
Criccieth	d		20 40		
Porthmadog	a		20 48		
	d		20 56		
Minffordd	d		21 01		
Penrhyndeudraeth	d		21 04		
Llandecwyn	d		21x06		
Talsarnau	d		21x09		
Tygwyn	d		21x11		
Harlech	a		21 18		
	d		21 20		
Llandanwg	d		21x24		
Pensarn	d		21x26		
Llanbedr	d		21x28		
Dyffryn Ardudwy	d		21x32		
Talybont	d		21x35		
Llanaber	d		21x40		
Barmouth	a		21 45		
	d		21 47		
Morfa Mawddach	d		21x51		
Fairbourne	d		21 55		
Llwyngwril	d		22x02		
Tonfanau	d		22x09		
Tywyn	a		22 15		
	d		22 17		
Aberdovey	d		22 23		
Penhelig	d		22x25		
Aberystwyth	d	21 35		22 30	23 35
Borth	d	21 48		22 43	23 48
Dovey Junction ■	d	21 58	22 38	22 53	23 58
Machynlleth ■	a	22 05	22 45	23 00	00 07
	d				
Caersws	d				
Newtown (Powys)	d				
Welshpool	d				
Shrewsbury 74	a				
	d				
Wellington (Shropshire) 74	d				
Telford Central 74	d				
Wolverhampton ■ 68,74 ⇌	a				
Smethwick Galton Bridge ■ 68,74	a				
Birmingham New Street ■ 74,68	a				
Birmingham International 68 ✈	a				

For connections to London Euston refer to Table T66

For connections to Crewe and Manchester Piccadilly refer to Table T131

Table T076-R

Sundays
20 May to 9 September

Pwllheli - Barmouth, Aberystwyth - Shrewsbury - Birmingham

		AW	AW	AW	AW	AW	AW	AW	AW	AW	AW	AW	AW	AW	AW	AW
		■		■		■		■	■							
			◇		◇		◇	◇		◇		◇	◇			
								A								
		⚭	⚭	⚭		⚭		⚭	⚭	⚭						
Pwllheli	d				11 28			13 48				17 36				
Abererch	d				11x32			13x51				17x40				
Penychain	d				11x35			13x54				17x44				
Criccieth	d				11 41			14 02				17 50				
Porthmadog	a				11 48			14 10				17 59				
	d				11 57			14 12				18 00				
Minffordd	d				12 02			14 16				18 05				
Penrhyndeudraeth	d				12 06			14 20				18 09				
Llandecwyn	d				12x09			14x22				18x12				
Talsarnau	d				12x11			14x24				18x14				
Tygwyn	d				12x13			14x27				18x16				
Harlech	a				12 18			14 32				18 21				
	d				12 19			14 34				18 22				
Llandanwg	d				12x25			14x38				18x28				
Pensarn	d				12x28			14x40				18x30				
Llanbedr	d				12x30			14x42				18x32				
Dyffryn Ardudwy	d				12x34			14x46				18x36				
Talybont	d				12x37			14x49				18x39				
Llanaber	d				12x42			14x54				18x45				
Barmouth	a				12 45			14 59				18 48				
	d				12 48			15 01				18 50				
Morfa Mawddach	d				12x53			15x05				18x55				
Fairbourne	d				12 56			15 09				18 57				
Llwyngwril	d				13x04			15x15				19x05				
Tonfanau	d				13x11			15x22				19x12				
Tywyn	a				13 16			15 27				19 19				
	d				13 16			15 28				19 24				
Aberdovey	d				13 22			15 35				19 30				
Penhelig	d				13x26			15x37				19x34				
Aberystwyth	d	09 30	10 30	11 30		13 30	14 34		15 30	17 30	18 30		19 30	20 30	21 30	23 20
Borth	d	09 43	10 43	11 43		13 43	14 47		15 43	17 43	18 43		19 43	20 43	21 43	23 33
Dovey Junction ■	d	09 53	10 56	11 53	13 36	13 57	14 57	15 49	15 53	17 53	19 02	19 46	19 53	20 53	21 53	23 43
Machynlleth ■	a	10 00	11 03	12 00	13 46	14 04	15 04	15 59	16 00	18 00	19 10	19 54	20 00	21 03	22 02	23 54
	d	10 08	11 05	12 06		14 06	15 08	16 05		18 05			20 05			
Caersws	d	10 31	11 28	12 29		14 29	15 31	16 30		18 28			20 28			
Newtown (Powys)	d	10 41	11 38	12 40		14 40	15 41	16 41		18 39			20 39			
Welshpool	d	10 57	11 54	12 54		14 55	15 56	16 55		18 54			20 53			
Shrewsbury 74	a	11 19	12 17	13 16		15 17	16 20	17 17		19 16			21 16			
	d	11 40		13 31		15 33		17 33		19 31			21 31			
Wellington (Shropshire) 74	d	11 54		13 45		15 47		17 47		19 45			21 45			
Telford Central 74	d	12 00		13 51		15 53		17 53		19 51			21 51			
Wolverhampton ■ 68,74 ⇌	a	12 16		14 07		16 09		18 09		20 07			22 07			
Smethwick Galton Bridge ■ 68,74	a															
Birmingham New Street ■ 74,68	a	12 33		14 23		16 25		18 27		20 25			22 27			
Birmingham International 68 ✈	a	13 02		15 00		17 00		19 00		21 01			23 01			

A ⚭ ■ from Machynlleth ◇ to Machynlleth

For connections to London Euston refer to Table T66

For connections to Crewe and Manchester Piccadilly refer to Table T131

Table T076-R

Sundays

16 September to 2 December

Pwllheli - Barmouth, Aberystwyth - Shrewsbury - Birmingham

		AW	AW	AW	AW	AW		AW	AW	AW	AW	AW	AW	AW	AW
		■		■	■			■	■						
			◇			◇		◇		◇		◇			
								A							
		⌶	⌶	⌶	⌶			⌶	⌶	⌶					
Pwllheli	d							13 48							
Abererch	d							13x51							
Penychain	d							13x54							
Criccieth	d							14 02							
Porthmadog	a							14 10							
	d							14 12							
Minffordd	d							14 16							
Penrhyndeudraeth	d							14 20							
Llandecwyn	d							14x22							
Talsarnau	d							14x24							
Tygwyn	d							14x27							
Harlech	a							14 32							
	d							14 34							
Llandanwg	d							14x38							
Pensarn	d							14x40							
Llanbedr	d							14x42							
Dyffryn Ardudwy	d							14x46							
Talybont	d							14x49							
Llanaber	d							14x54							
Barmouth	a							14 59							
	d							15 01							
Morfa Mawddach	d							15x05							
Fairbourne	d							15 09							
Llwyngwril	d							15x15							
Tonfanau	d							15x22							
Tywyn	a							15 27							
	d							15 28							
Aberdovey	d							15 35							
Penhelig	d							15x37							
Aberystwyth	d	09 30	10 30	11 30	13 30	14 34			15 30	17 30	18 30	19 30	20 30	21 30	23 20
Borth	d	09 43	10 43	11 43	13 43	14 47			15 43	17 43	18 43	19 43	20 43	21 43	23 33
Dovey Junction ■	d	09 53	10 56	11 53	13 57	14 57		15 49	15 53	17 53	19 02	19 53	20 53	21 53	23 43
Machynlleth ■	a	10 00	11 03	12 00	14 04	15 04		15 59	16 00	18 00	19 10	20 00	21 03	22 02	23 54
	d	10 08	11 05	12 06	14 06	15 08		16 05		18 05		20 05			
Caersws	d	10 31	11 28	12 29	14 29	15 31		16 30		18 28		20 28			
Newtown (Powys)	d	10 41	11 38	12 40	14 40	15 41		16 41		18 39		20 39			
Welshpool	d	10 57	11 54	12 54	14 55	15 56		16 55		18 54		20 53			
Shrewsbury 74	a	11 19	12 17	13 16	15 17	16 20		17 17		19 16		21 16			
	d	11 40		13 31	15 33			17 33		19 31		21 31			
Wellington (Shropshire) 74	d	11 54		13 45	15 47			17 47		19 45		21 45			
Telford Central 74	d	12 00		13 51	15 53			17 53		19 51		21 51			
Wolverhampton ■ 68,74	a	12 16		14 07	16 09			18 09		20 07		22 07			
Smethwick Galton Bridge ■ 68,74	a														
Birmingham New Street ■ 74,68	a	12 33		14 23	16 25			18 27		20 25		22 27			
Birmingham International 68	a	13 02		15 00	17 00			19 00		21 01		23 01			

A ⌶ ■ from Machynlleth ◇ to Machynlleth

For connections to London Euston refer to Table T66

For connections to Crewe and Manchester Piccadilly refer to Table T131

Table T078-F

Mondays to Fridays

21 May to 7 December

Sheffield, Chinley, Marple and Romiley Manchester and Manchester Airport

Miles	Miles	Miles			NT MX	NT MX	TP MX	TP MO	TP MX	TP	NT	NT	NT		NT	NT	TP	NT	NT	NT	NT	EM	NT		NT
							◇■	◇■	◇■	◇■						◇	◇■					◇			
					A	A	B		A		C		C			D	E			C		F			C
0	—	—	**Sheffield ■**	d			03 24	03 45		05 11							06 09					06 18			
4¾	—	—	Dore & Totley	d													06 15					06 25			
9¾	—	—	Grindleford	d																		06 33			
11¼	—	—	Hathersage	d																		06 38			
13	—	—	Bamford	d																		06 42			
14¾	—	—	Hope (Derbyshire)	d																		06 46			
20	—	—	Edale	d		00 01																06 53			
25½	—	0	**Chinley**	d		00 09															06 48	07 01			
—	—	8½	Hazel Grove 86	a																					
—	—	—	Stockport 86	a		00 26											06 53					07 24			
29¼	—	—	New Mills Central	d								06 05						06 32			06 55				
30¾	—	—	Strines	d								06 08						06 35			06 58				
33	—	—	**Marple**	d								06 11						06 38			07 02				
—	0	—	**Rose Hill Marple**	d											06 20				06 44				07 13		
34¼	2	—	**Romiley**	d								06 15			06 25			06 42	06 49		07 09		07 18		
—	3¼	—	Woodley	d											06 29				06 52				07 22		
—	4¾	—	Hyde Central	d											06 32				06 56				07 25		
—	6	—	Hyde North	d											06 35				06 58				07 28		
—	7¾	—	Guide Bridge	d							06 13		06 36		06 40	06 44			07 03	07 07			07 32		07 38
—	9	—	Fairfield	d											06 43				07 06				07 35		
—	10	—	Gorton	d							06 16				06 46				07 08				07 38		
35½	—	—	Bredbury	d								06 19						06 45			07 12				
36½	—	—	Brinnington	d								06 22						06 48			07 14				
38¼	—	—	Reddish North	d	00 02							06 25						06 51			07 18				
39¼	—	—	Ryder Brow	d	00 03							06 28						06 54							
39½	—	—	Belle Vue	d	00 05							06 29						06 55							
40½	11	—	Ashburys	d	00 08						06 19	06 33	06 41		06 49			06 58		07 13	07 24		07 41		07 44
41½	12	—	Ardwick	d					←											07 15					
42	12½	8¾	**Manchester Piccadilly ■**	a	00 15	00 35	04 52	04 35	04 52	06 03	06 25	06 38	06 47		06 54	06 56	07 02	07 04	07 16	07 19	07 32	07 38	07 46		07 51
—	—	—	**Manchester Airport** 85	a			→	05 11	05 12	06 25							07 26								

		NT	TP	NT	NT	NT	NT	NT	NT		EM	EM	NT	NT	NT	NT	TP	NT	NT		NT	NT	NT	NT	EM
			◇■								◇	◇			◇		◇■							◇	◇
			G	H			H				I	J	H		D		G	H				H			F
			⌶														⌶								
Sheffield ■	d		07 08						07 12		07 32	07 33					08 08							08 33	08 41
Dore & Totley	d		07 14						07 20		07 39	07 40					08 14								
Grindleford	d								07 28																
Hathersage	d								07 32																
Bamford	d								07 36																
Hope (Derbyshire)	d								07 40																
Edale	d								07 47															08 57	
Chinley	d								07 56		08 03	08 03												09 05	
Hazel Grove 86	a										08 16	08 16													
Stockport 86	a		07 53								08 25	08 25					08 53								09 25
New Mills Central	d	07 26				07 44			08 04							08 26								09 12	
Strines	d					07 47										08 29									
Marple	d	07 31				07 50		07 58	08 09							08 32					08 54			09 18	
Rose Hill Marple	d				07 45									08 20					08 45				09 13		
Romiley	d	07 35			07 50	07 54		08 02	08 13					08 25		08 36			08 50		08 58		09 18	09 22	
Woodley	d				07 53									08 29					08 53				09 22		
Hyde Central	d				07 57									08 32					08 57				09 26		
Hyde North	d				07 59									08 35					08 59						
Guide Bridge	d			07 51	08 04		08 11						08 34	08 39	08 45			08 50	09 04			09 13	09 32		
Fairfield	d													08 42									09 35		
Gorton	d			07 55	08 08		08 14							08 45				08 54	09 08				09 38		
Bredbury	d	07 38				07 57		08 05								08 39					09 01			09 25	
Brinnington	d	07 41				08 00		08 08								08 42					09 03			09 27	
Reddish North	d	07 44				08 03		08 11								08 45					09 07			09 30	
Ryder Brow	d	07 47						08 14								08 48					09 09				
Belle Vue	d							08 16								08 49									
Ashburys	d	07 52		07 58			08 17	08 20					08 40	08 48		08 53		08 57			09 13	09 19	09 41		
Ardwick	d	07 54																							
Manchester Piccadilly ■	a	07 58	08 03	08 04	08 16	08 13	08 23	08 26	08 28		08 37	08 37	08 46	08 53	08 55	08 58	09 02	09 03	09 16		09 19	09 24	09 46	09 41	09 37
Manchester Airport 85	a		08 26														09 26								

A From Sheffield
B To Manchester Airport
C From Hadfield
D From Huddersfield
E From Doncaster
F From Nottingham to Liverpool Lime Street
G From Cleethorpes
H From Manchester Piccadilly
I until 27 July, from 8 October. From Nottingham to Liverpool Lime Street
J from 30 July until 5 October. From Nottingham to Liverpool Lime Street

Sheffield, Chinley, Marple and Romiley Manchester and Manchester Airport

	NT A	TP ◇1 B	NT	NT	NT A	NT ◇	EM ◇ C	NT	NT A		TP ◇1 B	NT	NT	NT A	NT ◇	EM ◇ D	EM ◇ E	NT	NT A		TP ◇1 B	NT	NT
Sheffield 7 d		09 11				09 14	09 40				10 10				10 14	10 40	10 41				11 11		
Dore & Totley d						09 21									10 21								
Grindleford d						09 29									10 29								
Hathersage d						09 32									10 32								
Bamford d						09 36									10 36								
Hope (Derbyshire) d						09 40									10 40								
Edale d						09 47									10 47								
Chinley d						09 55									10 55								
Hazel Grove 86 a																							
Stockport 86 a		09 52					10 25				10 52					11 25	11 25				11 52		
New Mills Central d			09 32			10 03						10 26			11 03							11 32	
Strines d												10 29											
Marple d			09 37			10 08						10 32			11 08							11 37	
Rose Hill Marple d				09 45				10 14					10 45					11 14					11 45
Romiley d			09 41	09 50		10 12		10 19				10 36	10 50		11 12			11 19				11 41	11 50
Woodley d				09 53				10 22					10 53					11 22					11 53
Hyde Central d				09 57				10 26					10 57					11 26					11 57
Hyde North d				09 59									10 59										11 59
Guide Bridge d	09 37			10 05	10 09			10 32	10 39				11 07	11 11				11 32	11 39				12 04
Fairfield d								10 35										11 35					
Gorton d				10 09				10 38					11 11					11 38					12 08
Bredbury d			09 44			10 15						10 39			11 15							11 44	
Brinnington d			09 47			10 17						10 42			11 17							11 47	
Reddish North d			09 50			10 20						10 45			11 20							11 50	
Ryder Brow d			09 53									10 48										11 53	
Belle Vue d			09 54																			11 54	
Ashburys d	09 47		09 58		10 14			10 41	10 44			10 55		11 16				11 41	11 44			11 58	
Ardwick d																							
Manchester Piccadilly 10 a	09 54	10 02	10 03	10 16	10 25	10 33	10 37	10 46	10 53		11 02	11 03	11 18	11 23	11 33	11 37	11 37	11 46	11 53		12 02	12 03	12 16
Manchester Airport 85 a		10 26									11 26										12 26		

	NT A	NT ◇	EM ◇ C	NT	NT A	TP ◇1 B		NT	NT	NT A	NT ◇	EM ◇ D	NT	NT A	TP ◇1 B	NT		NT	NT A	NT ◇	EM ◇ C	NT	NT A	TP ◇1 B
Sheffield 7 d		11 14	11 41			12 11					12 14	12 41			13 11					13 14	13 40			14 11
Dore & Totley d		11 21									12 21													
Grindleford d		11 29									12 29									13 26				
Hathersage d		11 32									12 32													
Bamford d		11 36									12 36									13 32				
Hope (Derbyshire) d		11 39									12 39									13 35				
Edale d		11 47									12 47													
Chinley d		11 55									12 55									13 48				
Hazel Grove 86 a																								
Stockport 86 a			12 25			12 52						13 25			13 52						14 25			14 52
New Mills Central d		12 02						12 31			13 03					13 32				14 01				
Strines d								12 34																
Marple d		12 07						12 37			13 08					13 37				14 06				
Rose Hill Marple d				12 14					12 45				13 14					13 45				14 14		
Romiley d		12 11		12 19				12 41	12 50		13 12		13 19			13 41		13 50		14 10		14 19		
Woodley d				12 22					12 53				13 22					13 53				14 22		
Hyde Central d				12 26					12 57				13 26					13 57				14 26		
Hyde North d									12 59									13 59						
Guide Bridge d	12 09			12 32	12 39				13 04	13 09			13 32	13 39				14 04	14 09			14 32	14 39	
Fairfield d				12 35									13 35									14 35		
Gorton d				12 38					13 08				13 38					14 08				14 38		
Bredbury d		12 14						12 44			13 15					13 44				14 14				
Brinnington d		12 17						12 47			13 17					13 47				14 17				
Reddish North d		12 20						12 50			13 20					13 50				14 20				
Ryder Brow d								12 53								13 53								
Belle Vue d																13 54								
Ashburys d	12 14			12 41	12 44			12 57		13 14			13 41	13 44		13 58			14 14			14 41	14 44	
Ardwick d																								
Manchester Piccadilly 10 a	12 23	12 33	12 37	12 46	12 53	13 02		13 03	13 16	13 23	13 33	13 37	13 46	13 53	14 02	14 03		14 16	14 23	14 33	14 37	14 46	14 53	15 02
Manchester Airport 85 a						13 26									14 26									15 26

A From Hadfield
B From Cleethorpes
C From Norwich to Liverpool Lime Street
D until 31 August, from 8 October. From Norwich to Liverpool Lime Street
E from 3 September until 5 October. From Norwich to Liverpool Lime Street

Table T078-F

Mondays to Fridays

21 May to 7 December

Sheffield, Chinley, Marple and Romiley Manchester and Manchester Airport

	NT	NT	NT A	NT ◇	EM ◇ B	NT	NT A	TP ◇1 C		NT	NT A	NT	NT	EM ◇ B	NT	NT A	NT ◇	TP ◇1 C		NT	NT A	NT	EM ◇ B	NT D
Sheffield 7 d				14 14	14 41			15 11						15 40			15 45	16 11				16 14	16 40	
Dore & Totley d				14 21																		16 21		
Grindleford d				14 29																		16 29		
Hathersage d				14 32																		16 32		
Bamford d				14 36																		16 36		
Hope (Derbyshire) d				14 40													16 06					16 40		
Edale d				14 47																		16 47		
Chinley d				14 55													16 19					16 55		
Hazel Grove 86 a																								
Stockport 86 a					15 25			15 52						16 25				16 52					17 25	
New Mills Central d	14 27			15 03						15 32			16 03				16 32					17 03		
Strines d	14 30																16 35							
Marple d	14 33			15 08						15 37			16 08				16 38					17 08		
Rose Hill Marple d		14 45				15 14						15 56			16 14					16 45				
Romiley d	14 37	14 51		15 12		15 19				15 41		16 01	16 12		16 19		16 42			16 50		17 12		
Woodley d		14 54				15 22						16 04			16 22					16 53				
Hyde Central d		14 59				15 26						16 08			16 26					16 57				
Hyde North d		15 01										16 10								16 59				
Guide Bridge d		15 06	15 09			15 32	15 39				16 09	16 15			16 32	16 39				17 04	17 09			17 34
Fairfield d						15 35									16 35									
Gorton d		15 10				15 38						16 19			16 38					17 08				
Bredbury d	14 40			15 15						15 44			16 15				16 45					17 15		
Brinnington d	14 43			15 17						15 47			16 17				16 48					17 17		
Reddish North d	14 46			15 20						15 50			16 21				16 51					17 20		
Ryder Brow d	14 49									15 53							16 53							
Belle Vue d										15 54														
Ashburys d	14 56		15 15			15 41	15 44			15 58	16 14				16 41	16 44	16 58				17 14			17 39
Ardwick d																								
Manchester Piccadilly 10 a	15 03	15 17	15 23	15 33	15 37	15 46	15 53	16 02		16 03	16 21	16 27	16 31	16 37	16 46	16 53	17 03	17 02		17 16	17 21	17 31	17 37	17 46
Manchester Airport 85 a								16 26										17 26						

	NT	NT	NT D	TP ◇1 C		NT	NT D	NT	EM ◇ B	NT D	NT E	NT F	NT ◇ G	NT		NT D	TP ◇1 C	NT	NT D	NT	EM ◇ B	NT	NT A	NT
Sheffield 7 d				17 11				17 14	17 40								18 11			18 14	18 40			
Dore & Totley d								17 21												18 21				
Grindleford d								17 29												18 29				
Hathersage d								17 32												18 32				
Bamford d								17 36												18 36				
Hope (Derbyshire) d								17 40												18 40				
Edale d								17 47												18 47				
Chinley d								17 55												18 55				
Hazel Grove 86 a																								
Stockport 86 a				17 52					18 25								18 52				19 25			
New Mills Central d		17 27						18 03						18 30						19 03				19 26
Strines d														18 33										19 29
Marple d		17 32						18 08				18 26		18 37						19 08				19 33
Rose Hill Marple d	17 20					17 45					18 24							18 45				19 14		
Romiley d	17 25	17 36				17 50		18 12			18 30	18 30		18 40				18 50		19 12		19 19		19 37
Woodley d	17 28					17 55												18 53				19 22		
Hyde Central d	17 32					17 59												18 57				19 26		
Hyde North d						18 01												18 59						
Guide Bridge d	17 38		17 50			18 06	18 15			18 34			18 44			18 48		19 04	19 10			19 32	19 39	
Fairfield d	17 41					18 09																19 35		
Gorton d	17 44					18 15												19 08				19 38		
Bredbury d		17 39						18 15			18 33	18 33		18 43						19 15				19 40
Brinnington d		17 42						18 17			18 36	18 36		18 46						19 17				19 42
Reddish North d		17 45						18 20			18 39	18 39		18 49						19 20				19 46
Ryder Brow d		17 48									18 42	18 42												19 48
Belle Vue d		17 49									18 43	18 43												
Ashburys d	17 47	17 53	17 56				18 20			18 39	18 47	18 47				18 55			19 15			19 41	19 44	19 53
Ardwick d																								
Manchester Piccadilly 10 a	17 52	17 58	18 01	18 02		18 23	18 28	18 31	18 37	18 46	18 52	18 52	18 54	18 58		19 01	19 02	19 16	19 21	19 33	19 37	19 46	19 51	19 58
Manchester Airport 85 a				18 26													19 26							

A From Hadfield
B From Norwich to Liverpool Lime Street
C From Cleethorpes
D From Manchester Piccadilly
E until 31 August
F from 3 September
G From Huddersfield

Table T078-F

Mondays to Fridays

21 May to 7 December

Sheffield, Chinley, Marple and Romiley Manchester and Manchester Airport

		TP ◇1 A	NT B	NT ◇	EM ◇ C	NT	NT B	TP ◇1 A	NT	NT B	NT ◇	EM ◇ D	NT	NT B	NT	TP ◇1 A	NT B	NT ◇	NT B	NT	TP ◇1 A	NT B	NT
Sheffield 7 ⇌	d	19 11		19 14	19 40			20 11			20 14	20 31				21 11		21 14			22 11		
Dore & Totley	d			19 21							20 21												
Grindleford	d			19 29														21 27					
Hathersage	d			19 32							20 32							21 31					
Bamford	d			19 36														21 34					
Hope (Derbyshire)	d			19 40							20 38							21 38					
Edale	d			19 47														21 45					
Chinley	d			19 55							20 51							21 53					
Hazel Grove 86	a																						
Stockport 86	a	19 52			20 25			20 52				21 25				21 52					22 52		
New Mills Central	d			20 03					20 32		20 59				21 31			22 01		22 26			23 15
Strines	d								20 35											22 29			23 18
Marple	d			20 08					20 38		21 04				21 36			22 06		22 32			23 21
Rose Hill Marple	d					20 13							21 13										
Romiley	d			20 12		20 18			20 42		21 08		21 18		21 40			22 10		22 36			23 25
Woodley	d					20 22							21 22										
Hyde Central	d					20 25							21 25										
Hyde North	d					20 28							21 28										
Guide Bridge	d		20 09			20 32	20 39			21 09			21 32	21 39			22 09		22 38			23 09	
Fairfield	d					20 35							21 35										
Gorton	d					20 38				21 12			21 38				22 12					23 12	
Bredbury	d			20 15					20 45		21 11				21 43			22 13		22 39			23 28
Brinnington	d			20 17					20 47		21 13				21 46			22 15		22 42			23 31
Reddish North	d			20 20					20 50		21 16				21 49			22 18		22 45			23 34
Ryder Brow	d								20 53						21 52					22 48			23 37
Belle Vue	d								20 54						21 53					22 49			23 38
Ashburys	d		20 14			20 41	20 44		20 58	21 15			21 41	21 47	21 57		22 15		22 43	22 53		23 15	23 42
Ardwick	d																						
Manchester Piccadilly 10 ⇌	a	20 02	20 21	20 33	20 37	20 46	20 51	21 01	21 03	21 23	21 27	21 36	21 46	21 54	22 02	22 09	22 21	22 33	22 51	22 58	23 01	23 22	23 47
Manchester Airport 85 ⇌✈	a	20 26						21 26													23 26		

		NT	NT
Sheffield 7 ⇌	d	22 47	23 27
Dore & Totley	d	22 54	23 34
Grindleford	d	23 02	23 42
Hathersage	d	23 06	23 46
Bamford	d	23 10	23 50
Hope (Derbyshire)	d	23 13	23 54
Edale	d	23 21	00 01
Chinley	d	23 29	00 09
Hazel Grove 86	a		
Stockport 86	a		00 26
New Mills Central	d	23 39	
Strines	d	23 44	
Marple	d	23 48	
Rose Hill Marple	d		
Romiley	d	23 52	
Woodley	d		
Hyde Central	d		
Hyde North	d		
Guide Bridge	d		
Fairfield	d		
Gorton	d		
Bredbury	d	23 55	
Brinnington	d	23 57	
Reddish North	d	00 02	
Ryder Brow	d	00 03	
Belle Vue	d	00 05	
Ashburys	d	00 08	
Ardwick	d		
Manchester Piccadilly 10 ⇌	a	00 15	00 35
Manchester Airport 85 ⇌✈	a		

A From Cleethorpes
B From Hadfield
C From Norwich to Liverpool Lime Street
D From Norwich

Table T078-F

Saturdays

26 May to 8 December

Sheffield, Chinley, Marple and Romiley Manchester and Manchester Airport

		NT A	NT A	TP ◇1	TP ◇1	NT B	NT	NT B	TP ◇1 C	NT	NT B	NT	EM ◇ D	NT	NT B	NT	TP ◇1 E 🍴	NT	NT B	NT	EM ◇ F	EM ◇ G	NT
Sheffield 7 ⇌	d			03 24	05 11				06 09				06 20				07 08			07 14	07 32	07 33	
Dore & Totley	d								06 15				06 27				07 14			07 21	07 39	07 40	
Grindleford	d												06 35							07 29			
Hathersage	d												06 39							07 32			
Bamford	d												06 43							07 36			
Hope (Derbyshire)	d												06 47							07 40			
Edale	d		00 01										06 54							07 47			
Chinley	d		00 09									06 48	07 02							07 55	08 04	08 04	
Hazel Grove 86	a																				08 16	08 16	
Stockport 86	a		00 26						06 52				07 26				07 52				08 25	08 25	
New Mills Central	d						06 00			06 32		06 55				07 26				08 03			
Strines	d						06 03			06 35		06 58											
Marple	d						06 06			06 38		07 02				07 31				08 08			
Rose Hill Marple	d													07 13				07 45					08 14
Romiley	d						06 10			06 42		07 09		07 18		07 35		07 50		08 12			08 19
Woodley	d													07 22				07 53					08 22
Hyde Central	d													07 25				07 57					08 26
Hyde North	d													07 28				07 59					
Guide Bridge	d					06 13		06 39			07 09			07 32	07 39			08 04	08 09				08 32
Fairfield	d													07 35									08 35
Gorton	d					06 16		06 42			07 12			07 38				08 08					08 38
Bredbury	d						06 14			06 45		07 12				07 38				08 15			
Brinnington	d						06 17			06 48		07 14				07 41				08 17			
Reddish North	d	00 02					06 20			06 51		07 18				07 45				08 20			
Ryder Brow	d	00 03					06 23			06 54						07 47							
Belle Vue	d	00 05					06 24			06 55													
Ashburys	d	00 08				06 19	06 28	06 45		06 59	07 15	07 24		07 41	07 44	07 52			08 14				08 41
Ardwick	d															07 54							
Manchester Piccadilly 10 ⇌	a	00 15	00 35	04 52	06 03	06 25	06 33	06 51	07 02	07 04	07 21	07 32	07 39	07 46	07 51	07 58	08 02	08 16	08 21	08 33	08 37	08 37	08 46
Manchester Airport 85 ⇌✈	a			05 12	06 25				07 26								08 26						

		NT B	NT	TP ◇1 E 🍴	NT	NT B	NT ◇	EM ◇ D	NT	NT B	TP ◇1 E 🍴	NT	NT	NT B	NT ◇	EM ◇ H	NT	NT B	TP ◇1 E 🍴	NT	NT	NT B
Sheffield 7 ⇌	d			08 08			08 13	08 40			09 11				09 14	09 40			10 10			
Dore & Totley	d			08 14			08 20								09 21							
Grindleford	d						08 27								09 29							
Hathersage	d						08 31								09 32							
Bamford	d						08 35								09 36							
Hope (Derbyshire)	d						08 38								09 40							
Edale	d						08 46								09 47							
Chinley	d						08 54								09 55							
Hazel Grove 86	a																					
Stockport 86	a			08 53				09 25			09 52					10 26			10 52			
New Mills Central	d		08 26				09 01					09 32			10 03					10 26		
Strines	d		08 29																	10 29		
Marple	d		08 32				09 06					09 37			10 08					10 32		
Rose Hill Marple	d				08 45				09 13				09 45				10 14				10 45	
Romiley	d		08 36		08 50		09 10		09 18			09 41	09 50		10 12		10 19			10 36	10 50	
Woodley	d				08 53				09 22				09 53				10 22				10 53	
Hyde Central	d				08 57				09 26				09 57				10 26				10 57	
Hyde North	d				08 59								09 59								10 59	
Guide Bridge	d	08 39			09 04	09 09			09 32	09 37			10 05	10 10			10 32	10 39			11 07	11 11
Fairfield	d								09 35								10 35					
Gorton	d				09 08				09 38				10 09				10 38				11 11	
Bredbury	d		08 39				09 13					09 44			10 15					10 39		
Brinnington	d		08 42				09 16					09 47			10 17					10 42		
Reddish North	d		08 45				09 19					09 50			10 20					10 45		
Ryder Brow	d		08 48									09 53								10 48		
Belle Vue	d		08 49									09 54										
Ashburys	d	08 44	08 53			09 14			09 41	09 47		09 58		10 15			10 41	10 44		10 55		11 16
Ardwick	d																					
Manchester Piccadilly 10 ⇌	a	08 51	08 58	09 02	09 16	09 21	09 31	09 37	09 46	09 54	10 02	10 03	10 16	10 23	10 33	10 37	10 46	10 53	11 02	11 03	11 18	11 23
Manchester Airport 85 ⇌✈	a			09 26							10 26								11 26			

A From Sheffield
B From Hadfield
C From Doncaster
D From Nottingham to Liverpool Lime Street
E From Cleethorpes
F from 23 June. From Nottingham to Liverpool Lime Street
G until 16 June. From Nottingham to Liverpool Lime Street
H From Norwich to Liverpool Lime Street

Table T078-F

Saturdays
26 May to 8 December

Sheffield, Chinley, Marple and Romiley Manchester and Manchester Airport

		NT ◇	EM ◇ A	NT	NT B	TP ◇1 C	NT	NT	NT B	NT ◇	EM ◇ A	NT	NT B	TP ◇1 C	NT	NT	NT B	NT ◇	EM ◇ A	NT	NT B	TP ◇1 C
Sheffield [7]	d	10 14	10 40			11 11				11 14	11 40			12 11				12 14	12 40			13 11
Dore & Totley	d	10 21								11 21								12 21				
Grindleford	d	10 29								11 29								12 29				
Hathersage	d	10 32								11 32								12 32				
Bamford	d	10 36								11 36								12 36				
Hope (Derbyshire)	d	10 40								11 40								12 40				
Edale	d	10 47								11 47								12 47				
Chinley	d	10 55								11 55								12 55				
Hazel Grove 86	a																					
Stockport 86	a		11 25			11 52					12 25			12 52					13 25			13 52
New Mills Central	d	11 03					11 32			12 03					12 31			13 03				
Strines	d														12 34							
Marple	d	11 08					11 37			12 08					12 37			13 08				
Rose Hill Marple	d			11 14				11 45				12 14				12 45				13 14		
Romiley	d	11 12		11 19			11 41	11 50		12 12		12 19			12 41	12 50		13 12		13 19		
Woodley	d			11 22				11 53				12 22				12 53				13 22		
Hyde Central	d			11 26				11 57				12 26				12 57				13 26		
Hyde North	d							11 59								12 59						
Guide Bridge	d			11 32	11 39			12 04	12 09			12 32	12 39			13 04	13 09			13 32	13 39	
Fairfield	d			11 35								12 35								13 35		
Gorton	d			11 38				12 08				12 38				13 08				13 38		
Bredbury	d	11 15					11 44			12 15					12 44			13 15				
Brinnington	d	11 17					11 47			12 17					12 47			13 17				
Reddish North	d	11 20					11 50			12 20					12 50			13 20				
Ryder Brow	d						11 53								12 53							
Belle Vue	d						11 54															
Ashburys	d			11 41	11 44		11 58		12 14			12 41	12 44		12 57		13 14			13 41	13 44	
Ardwick	d																					
Manchester Piccadilly [10]	a	11 33	11 37	11 46	11 53	12 02	12 03	12 16	12 23	12 33	12 37	12 46	12 53	13 02	13 03	13 16	13 23	13 31	13 37	13 46	13 53	14 02
Manchester Airport 85	a					12 26								13 26								14 26

		NT	NT	NT B	NT ◇	EM ◇ A	NT	NT B	TP ◇1 C	NT	NT	NT B	NT ◇	EM ◇ A	NT	NT B	TP ◇1 C	NT	NT B	NT	NT ◇	EM ◇ A	NT
Sheffield [7]	d				13 14	13 40			14 11				14 14	14 40			15 11				15 14	15 40	
Dore & Totley	d				13 21								14 21								15 21		
Grindleford	d				13 29								14 29								15 29		
Hathersage	d				13 32								14 32								15 32		
Bamford	d				13 36								14 36								15 36		
Hope (Derbyshire)	d				13 40								14 40								15 40		
Edale	d				13 47								14 47								15 47		
Chinley	d				13 55								14 55								15 55		
Hazel Grove 86	a																						
Stockport 86	a					14 25			14 52					15 25			15 52					16 25	
New Mills Central	d	13 32			14 03					14 27			15 03					15 32			16 03		
Strines	d									14 30													
Marple	d	13 37			14 08					14 33			15 08					15 37			16 08		
Rose Hill Marple	d		13 45				14 14				14 45				15 14					15 56			16 14
Romiley	d	13 41	13 50		14 12		14 19			14 37	14 51		15 12		15 19			15 41		16 01	16 12		16 19
Woodley	d		13 53				14 22				14 54				15 22					16 04			16 22
Hyde Central	d		13 57				14 26				14 59				15 26					16 08			16 26
Hyde North	d		13 59								15 01									16 10			
Guide Bridge	d		14 04	14 09			14 32	14 39			15 06	15 09			15 32	15 39			16 09	16 15			16 32
Fairfield	d						14 35								15 35								16 35
Gorton	d		14 08				14 38				15 10				15 38					16 19			16 38
Bredbury	d	13 44			14 15					14 40			15 15					15 44			16 15		
Brinnington	d	13 47			14 17					14 43			15 17					15 47			16 17		
Reddish North	d	13 50			14 20					14 46			15 20					15 50			16 20		
Ryder Brow	d	13 53								14 49								15 53					
Belle Vue	d	13 54																15 54					
Ashburys	d	13 58		14 14			14 41	14 44		14 56		15 15			15 41	15 44		15 58	16 14				16 41
Ardwick	d																						
Manchester Piccadilly [10]	a	14 03	14 16	14 23	14 31	14 37	14 46	14 53	15 03	15 03	15 17	15 23	15 33	15 37	15 46	15 53	16 02	16 03	16 21	16 27	16 31	16 37	16 46
Manchester Airport 85	a								15 26								16 26						

A From Norwich to Liverpool Lime Street
B From Hadfield
C From Cleethorpes

Table T078-F

Saturdays
26 May to 8 December

Sheffield, Chinley, Marple and Romiley Manchester and Manchester Airport

		NT A	TP ◇1 B	NT	NT	NT A	NT	EM ◇ C	NT	NT A	NT	TP ◇1 B	NT	NT A	NT	EM ◇ C	NT	NT A	NT	TP ◇1 B	NT	NT A
Sheffield [7]	d		16 11				16 14	16 40				17 11			17 14	17 38				18 11		
Dore & Totley	d						16 21								17 21							
Grindleford	d						16 29								17 29							
Hathersage	d						16 32								17 32							
Bamford	d						16 36								17 36							
Hope (Derbyshire)	d						16 40								17 40							
Edale	d						16 47								17 47							
Chinley	d						16 55								17 55							
Hazel Grove 86	a																					
Stockport 86	a		16 52					17 25				17 52				18 25				18 52		
New Mills Central	d			16 32			17 03				17 27				18 03				18 26			
Strines	d			16 35															18 29			
Marple	d			16 38			17 08				17 32				18 08				18 32			
Rose Hill Marple	d				16 45				17 14				17 45				18 14				18 45	
Romiley	d			16 42	16 50		17 12		17 19		17 36		17 50		18 12		18 19		18 36		18 50	
Woodley	d				16 53				17 22				17 53				18 22				18 53	
Hyde Central	d				16 57				17 26				17 57				18 26				18 57	
Hyde North	d				16 59								17 59								18 59	
Guide Bridge	d	16 39			17 04	17 09			17 32	17 39			18 04	18 09			18 32	18 39			19 04	19 09
Fairfield	d								17 35				18 07				18 35					
Gorton	d				17 08				17 38				18 09				18 38				19 08	
Bredbury	d			16 45			17 15				17 39				18 15				18 39			
Brinnington	d			16 48			17 17				17 42				18 17				18 42			
Reddish North	d			16 51			17 20				17 45				18 20				18 45			
Ryder Brow	d			16 54							17 48								18 48			
Belle Vue	d										17 49								18 49			
Ashburys	d	16 44		16 58		17 14			17 41	17 44	17 53			18 15			18 41	18 44	18 53			19 14
Ardwick	d																					
Manchester Piccadilly [10]	a	16 53	17 02	17 04	17 16	17 21	17 31	17 37	17 46	17 51	17 58	18 02	18 16	18 21	18 31	18 37	18 46	18 51	18 58	19 02	19 16	19 21
Manchester Airport 85	a		17 26									18 26								19 26		

		NT	EM ◇ C	NT	NT A	NT	TP ◇1 B	NT A	NT ◇	EM ◇ C	NT	NT A	NT	TP ◇1 B	NT A	NT ◇	EM ◇ D	NT	NT A	NT	TP ◇1 B	NT A	NT ◇
Sheffield [7]	d	18 14	18 37				19 11		19 14	19 40				20 11		20 14	20 34				21 11		21 14
Dore & Totley	d	18 21							19 21							20 21							
Grindleford	d	18 29							19 29														21 27
Hathersage	d	18 32							19 32							20 32							21 31
Bamford	d	18 36							19 36														21 34
Hope (Derbyshire)	d	18 40							19 40							20 38							21 38
Edale	d	18 47							19 47														21 45
Chinley	d	18 55							19 55							20 51							21 53
Hazel Grove 86	a																						
Stockport 86	a		19 25				19 52			20 25				20 52			21 19				21 52		
New Mills Central	d	19 03				19 26			20 03				20 26			20 59				21 27			22 01
Strines	d					19 29							20 29										
Marple	d	19 08				19 33			20 08				20 32			21 04				21 32			22 06
Rose Hill Marple	d			19 14							20 13							21 13					
Romiley	d	19 12		19 19		19 37			20 12		20 18		20 36			21 08		21 18		21 36			22 10
Woodley	d			19 22							20 22							21 22					
Hyde Central	d			19 26							20 25							21 25					
Hyde North	d										20 28							21 28					
Guide Bridge	d			19 32	19 39			20 09			20 32	20 39			21 09			21 32	21 39			22 09	
Fairfield	d			19 35							20 35							21 35					
Gorton	d			19 38							20 38				21 12			21 38				22 12	
Bredbury	d	19 15				19 40			20 15				20 39			21 11				21 39			22 13
Brinnington	d	19 17				19 42			20 17				20 42			21 13				21 42			22 15
Reddish North	d	19 20				19 46			20 20				20 45			21 16				21 45			22 18
Ryder Brow	d					19 48							20 48							21 48			
Belle Vue	d												20 49							21 49			
Ashburys	d			19 41	19 44	19 53		20 14			20 41	20 44	20 53		21 15			21 41	21 47	21 53		22 15	
Ardwick	d																						
Manchester Piccadilly [10]	a	19 33	19 37	19 46	19 51	19 58	20 03	20 21	20 33	20 37	20 46	20 51	20 58	21 04	21 23	21 27	21 29	21 46	21 54	21 58	22 04	22 21	22 33
Manchester Airport 85	a						20 26							21 26									

A From Hadfield
B From Cleethorpes
C From Norwich to Liverpool Lime Street
D From Norwich

Table T078-F

Saturdays
26 May to 8 December

Sheffield, Chinley, Marple and Romiley Manchester and Manchester Airport

		NT	NT	TP	NT	NT	NT
				◇1			
		A		B	A		
Sheffield 7 ⇌	d			22 11		22 24	
Dore & Totley	d					22 31	
Grindleford	d					22 38	
Hathersage	d					22 42	
Bamford	d					22 46	
Hope (Derbyshire)	d					22 49	
Edale	d					22 56	
Chinley	d					23 04	
Hazel Grove 86	a						
Stockport 86	a			22 54			
New Mills Central	d		22 26			23 12	23 36
Strines	d		22 29				23 39
Marple	d		22 32			23 17	23 42
Rose Hill Marple	d						
Romiley	d		22 36			23 21	23 46
Woodley	d						
Hyde Central	d						
Hyde North	d						
Guide Bridge	d	22 38			23 09		
Fairfield	d						
Gorton	d				23 12		
Bredbury	d		22 39			23 24	23 49
Brinnington	d		22 42			23 26	23 52
Reddish North	d		22 45			23 30	23 55
Ryder Brow	d		22 48				23 58
Belle Vue	d		22 49				23 59
Ashburys	d	22 43	22 53		23 15		00 03
Ardwick	d						
Manchester Piccadilly 10 ⇌	a	22 51	22 59	23 03	23 22	23 41	00 08
Manchester Airport 85 ⇌✈	a			23 26			

Sundays
20 May to 9 September

		NT	TP	NT	TP	NT	NT	NT	TP	NT	NT	EM	NT	TP	NT	NT	EM	NT	TP	NT	NT	EM	NT
			◇1		◇1				◇1			◇		◇1			◇		◇1			◇	
		C	⊼		⊼	A		D	E ⊼	A		F	A	B ⊼	A		F	A	B ⊼	A		F	A
Sheffield 7 ⇌	d		07 51	08 14	09 11		09 14		10 14		10 17	10 41		11 11		11 14	11 39		12 11		12 14	12 39	
Dore & Totley	d			08 20			09 21				10 23	10 48				11 21					12 23		
Grindleford	d			08 27			09 28				10 30					11 28					12 30		
Hathersage	d			08 31			09 32				10 34					11 31					12 33		
Bamford	d			08 35			09 36				10 38					11 35					12 37		
Hope (Derbyshire)	d			08 38			09 39				10 41					11 39					12 41		
Edale	d			08 46			09 47				10 48					11 46					12 48		
Chinley	d			08 54			09 55				10 56					11 54					12 56		
Hazel Grove 86	a																						
Stockport 86	a		08 32		09 52							11 26		11 56			12 25		12 52			13 25	
New Mills Central	d			09 02			10 03				11 05					12 03					13 05		
Strines	d			09 05			10 06				11 08					12 06					13 08		
Marple	d			09 09			10 10				11 11					12 09					13 11		
Rose Hill Marple	d																						
Romiley	d			09 12			10 13				11 15					12 13					13 15		
Woodley	d																						
Hyde Central	d																						
Hyde North	d																						
Guide Bridge	d					10 14		10 38		11 08			11 38		12 08			12 38		13 08			13 38
Fairfield	d																						
Gorton	d					10 17		10 41		11 11			11 41		12 11			12 41		13 11			13 41
Bredbury	d			09 15			10 16				11 18					12 16					13 18		
Brinnington	d			09 18			10 19				11 20					12 18					13 20		
Reddish North	d			09 21			10 22				11 23					12 21					13 23		
Ryder Brow	d																						
Belle Vue	d																						
Ashburys	d	00 03				10 22		10 44		11 14			11 44		12 14			12 44		13 14			13 44
Ardwick	d																						
Manchester Piccadilly 10 ⇌	a	00 08	08 42	09 33	10 02	10 28	10 33	10 51	11 03	11 20	11 34	11 37	11 52	12 10	12 21	12 33	12 37	12 50	13 02	13 21	13 34	13 37	13 50
Manchester Airport 85 ⇌✈	a		09 04		10 27				11 26					12 27					13 26				

A From Hadfield
B From Cleethorpes
C not 20 May. From New Mills Central
D From Manchester Piccadilly
E From Doncaster
F From Nottingham to Liverpool Lime Street

Table T078-F

Sundays
20 May to 9 September

Sheffield, Chinley, Marple and Romiley Manchester and Manchester Airport

		TP	NT	NT	EM	NT	TP	NT	NT	EM	NT	TP	NT	NT	EM	NT	TP	NT	NT	EM	NT	TP
		◇1			◇		◇1			◇		◇1			◇		◇1			◇		◇1
		A ⊼	B		C	B	A ⊼	B		C	B	A ⊼	B		D	B	A ⊼	B		E	B	A ⊼
Sheffield 7 ⇌	d	13 11		13 14	13 38		14 11		14 14	14 37		15 11		15 14	15 43		16 11		16 14	16 39		17 11
Dore & Totley	d			13 20					14 20					15 20					16 20			
Grindleford	d			13 27					14 27					15 27					16 27			
Hathersage	d			13 31					14 31					15 31					16 31			
Bamford	d			13 35					14 35					15 35					16 35			
Hope (Derbyshire)	d			13 38					14 38					15 38					16 38			
Edale	d			13 46					14 46					15 46					16 46			
Chinley	d			13 54					14 54					15 54					16 54			
Hazel Grove 86	a																					
Stockport 86	a	13 52			14 26		14 53			15 25		15 53			16 25		16 53			17 28		17 53
New Mills Central	d			14 02					15 02					16 02					17 02			
Strines	d			14 05					15 05					16 05					17 05			
Marple	d			14 09					15 09					16 09					17 09			
Rose Hill Marple	d																					
Romiley	d			14 12					15 12					16 12					17 12			
Woodley	d																					
Hyde Central	d																					
Hyde North	d																					
Guide Bridge	d		14 09			14 38		15 08			15 38		16 08			16 38		17 08			17 38	
Fairfield	d																					
Gorton	d		14 12			14 41		15 11			15 41		16 11			16 41		17 11			17 41	
Bredbury	d			14 15					15 15					16 15					17 15			
Brinnington	d			14 18					15 18					16 18					17 18			
Reddish North	d			14 21					15 21					16 21					17 21			
Ryder Brow	d																					
Belle Vue	d																					
Ashburys	d		14 15			14 44		15 14			15 44		16 14			16 44		17 14			17 44	
Ardwick	d																					
Manchester Piccadilly 10 ⇌	a	14 02	14 21	14 33	14 37	14 50	15 03	15 20	15 33	15 37	15 50	16 02	16 20	16 33	16 37	16 51	17 02	17 21	17 34	17 38	17 51	18 03
Manchester Airport 85 ⇌✈	a	14 26					15 26					16 26					17 26					18 26

		NT	NT	EM	NT	TP	NT	NT	EM	NT	TP	NT	NT	EM	NT	TP	NT	NT	EM	TP	NT	TP	NT
				◇		◇1			◇		◇1			◇		◇1			◇	◇1		◇1	
		B		C	B	A ⊼	B		C	B	A	B		F	B	A	B		F	A	B	A	
Sheffield 7 ⇌	d		17 14	17 44		18 11		18 14	18 37		19 11		19 14	19 35		20 11		20 14	20 35	21 11		22 13	22 16
Dore & Totley	d		17 20					18 20					19 20					20 20					22 22
Grindleford	d		17 27					18 27					19 27					20 27					22 29
Hathersage	d		17 31					18 31					19 31					20 31					22 33
Bamford	d		17 35					18 35					19 35					20 35					22 37
Hope (Derbyshire)	d		17 38					18 38					19 38					20 38					22 40
Edale	d		17 46					18 46					19 46					20 46					22 48
Chinley	d		17 54					18 54					19 54					20 54					22 56
Hazel Grove 86	a																						
Stockport 86	a			18 25		18 53			19 25		19 53			20 26		20 53			21 25	21 56		23 03	
New Mills Central	d		18 02					19 02					20 02					21 02					23 04
Strines	d		18 05					19 05					20 05					21 05					23 07
Marple	d		18 09					19 09					20 09					21 09					23 11
Rose Hill Marple	d																						
Romiley	d		18 12					19 12					20 12					21 12					23 14
Woodley	d																						
Hyde Central	d																						
Hyde North	d																						
Guide Bridge	d	18 08			18 38		19 08			19 38		20 08			20 38		21 08				22 08		
Fairfield	d																						
Gorton	d	18 11			18 41		19 11			19 41		20 11			20 41		21 11				22 11		
Bredbury	d		18 15					19 15					20 15					21 15					23 17
Brinnington	d		18 18					19 18					20 18					21 18					23 20
Reddish North	d		18 21					19 21					20 21					21 21					23 23
Ryder Brow	d																						
Belle Vue	d																						
Ashburys	d	18 14			18 44		19 14			19 44		20 14			20 44		21 14				22 14		23 30
Ardwick	d																						
Manchester Piccadilly 10 ⇌	a	18 21	18 33	18 37	18 50	19 03	19 20	19 33	19 37	19 50	20 04	20 20	20 32	20 38	20 51	21 04	21 20	21 32	21 37	22 05	22 20	23 16	23 36
Manchester Airport 85 ⇌✈	a					19 26					20 26					21 26				22 26			

A From Cleethorpes
B From Hadfield
C From Norwich to Liverpool Lime Street
D From Nottingham to Liverpool Lime Street
E From Peterborough to Liverpool Lime Street
F From Norwich

Table T078-F

Sundays

16 September to 2 December

Sheffield, Chinley, Marple and Romiley Manchester and Manchester Airport

		NT A	TP ◇1 🛒	NT	TP ◇1 🛒	NT B	NT	NT C	TP ◇1 D 🛒	NT B	NT	EM ◇ E	NT B	TP ◇1 F 🛒	NT B	NT	EM ◇ E	NT B	TP ◇1 F 🛒	NT B	NT	EM ◇ E	NT B
Sheffield 7	d		07 51	08 14	09 11		09 14		10 14		10 17	10 41		11 11		11 14	11 39		12 11		12 14	12 39	
Dore & Totley	d			08 20			09 21				10 23	10 48				11 21					12 23		
Grindleford	d			08 27			09 28				10 30					11 28					12 30		
Hathersage	d			08 31			09 32				10 34					11 31					12 33		
Bamford	d			08 35			09 36				10 38					11 35					12 37		
Hope (Derbyshire)	d			08 38			09 39				10 41					11 39					12 41		
Edale	d			08 46			09 47				10 48					11 46					12 48		
Chinley	d			08 54			09 55				10 56					11 54					12 56		
Hazel Grove 86	a																						
Stockport 86	a		08 32		09 52							11 26		11 56			12 25		12 52			13 25	
New Mills Central	d			09 02			10 03				11 05					12 08					13 05		
Strines	d			09 05			10 06				11 08					12 11					13 08		
Marple	d			09 09			10 10				11 11					12 15					13 11		
Rose Hill Marple	d																						
Romiley	d			09 12			10 13				11 15					12 19					13 15		
Woodley	d																						
Hyde Central	d																						
Hyde North	d																						
Guide Bridge	d					10 14		10 38		11 08			11 38		12 08			12 38		13 08			13 38
Fairfield	d																						
Gorton	d					10 17		10 41		11 11			11 41		12 11			12 41		13 11			13 41
Bredbury	d			09 15			10 16				11 18					12 22					13 18		
Brinnington	d			09 18			10 19				11 20					12 25					13 20		
Reddish North	d			09 21			10 22				11 23					12 29					13 23		
Ryder Brow	d																						
Belle Vue	d																						
Ashburys	d	00 03				10 22		10 44		11 14			11 44		12 14			12 44		13 14			13 44
Ardwick	d																						
Manchester Piccadilly 10	a	00 08	08 42	09 33	10 03	10 28	10 33	10 51	11 03	11 21	11 34	11 37	11 51	12 10	12 25	12 43	12 37	12 51	13 04	13 21	13 34	13 37	13 50
Manchester Airport 85	a		09 04		10 25				11 26					12 27					13 26				

		TP ◇1 F 🛒	NT B	NT	EM ◇ E	NT B	TP ◇1 F 🛒	NT B	NT	EM ◇ G	NT B	TP ◇1 F 🛒	NT B	NT	EM ◇ E	NT B	TP ◇1 F 🛒	NT B	NT	EM ◇ H	NT B	TP ◇1 F 🛒
Sheffield 7	d	13 11		13 14	13 38		14 11		14 14	14 37		15 11		15 14	15 43		16 11		16 14	16 39		17 11
Dore & Totley	d			13 20					14 20					15 20					16 20			
Grindleford	d			13 27					14 27					15 27					16 27			
Hathersage	d			13 31					14 31					15 31					16 31			
Bamford	d			13 35					14 35					15 35					16 35			
Hope (Derbyshire)	d			13 38					14 38					15 38					16 38			
Edale	d			13 46					14 46					15 46					16 46			
Chinley	d			13 54					14 54					15 54					16 54			
Hazel Grove 86	a																					
Stockport 86	a	13 52			14 26		14 53			15 25		15 53			16 25		16 53			17 28		17 53
New Mills Central	d			14 02					15 02					16 02					17 02			
Strines	d			14 05					15 05					16 05					17 05			
Marple	d			14 09					15 09					16 09					17 09			
Rose Hill Marple	d																					
Romiley	d			14 12					15 12					16 12					17 12			
Woodley	d																					
Hyde Central	d																					
Hyde North	d																					
Guide Bridge	d		14 09			14 38		15 08			15 38		16 08			16 38		17 08			17 38	
Fairfield	d																					
Gorton	d		14 12			14 41		15 11			15 41		16 11			16 41		17 11			17 41	
Bredbury	d			14 15					15 15					16 15					17 15			
Brinnington	d			14 18					15 18					16 18					17 18			
Reddish North	d			14 21					15 21					16 21					17 21			
Ryder Brow	d																					
Belle Vue	d																					
Ashburys	d		14 15			14 44		15 14			15 44		16 14			16 44		17 14			17 44	
Ardwick	d																					
Manchester Piccadilly 10	a	14 02	14 21	14 33	14 37	14 50	15 03	15 20	15 33	15 37	15 50	16 02	16 20	16 33	16 37	16 51	17 02	17 21	17 34	17 38	17 51	18 03
Manchester Airport 85	a	14 26					15 26					16 26					17 26					18 26

A From New Mills Central
B From Hadfield
C From Manchester Piccadilly
D From Doncaster
E From Nottingham to Liverpool Lime Street
F From Cleethorpes
G From Norwich to Liverpool Lime Street
H From Peterborough to Liverpool Lime Street

Table T078-F

Sundays

16 September to 2 December

Sheffield, Chinley, Marple and Romiley Manchester and Manchester Airport

		NT A	NT	EM ◇ B	NT A	TP ◇1 C 🛒	NT A	NT	EM ◇ B	NT A	TP ◇1 C	NT A	NT	EM ◇ D	NT A	TP ◇1 C	NT A	NT	EM ◇ D	TP ◇1 C	NT A	TP ◇1 C
Sheffield 7	d		17 14	17 44		18 11		18 14	18 37		19 11		19 14	19 35		20 11		20 14	20 35	21 11		22 13
Dore & Totley	d		17 20					18 20					19 20					20 20				
Grindleford	d		17 27					18 27					19 27					20 27				
Hathersage	d		17 31					18 31					19 31					20 31				
Bamford	d		17 35					18 35					19 35					20 35				
Hope (Derbyshire)	d		17 38					18 38					19 38					20 38				
Edale	d		17 46					18 46					19 46					20 46				
Chinley	d		17 54					18 54					19 54					20 54				
Hazel Grove 86	a																					
Stockport 86	a			18 25		18 53			19 25		19 53			20 26		20 53			21 25	21 56		23 03
New Mills Central	d		18 02					19 02					20 02					21 02				
Strines	d		18 05					19 05					20 05					21 05				
Marple	d		18 09					19 09					20 09					21 09				
Rose Hill Marple	d																					
Romiley	d		18 12					19 12					20 12					21 12				
Woodley	d																					
Hyde Central	d																					
Hyde North	d																					
Guide Bridge	d	18 08			18 38		19 08			19 38		20 08			20 38		21 08				22 08	
Fairfield	d																					
Gorton	d	18 11			18 41		19 11			19 41		20 11			20 41		21 11				22 11	
Bredbury	d		18 15					19 15					20 15					21 15				
Brinnington	d		18 18					19 18					20 18					21 18				
Reddish North	d		18 21					19 21					20 21					21 21				
Ryder Brow	d																					
Belle Vue	d																					
Ashburys	d	18 14			18 44		19 14			19 44		20 14			20 44		21 14				22 14	
Ardwick	d																					
Manchester Piccadilly 10	a	18 21	18 33	18 37	18 50	19 03	19 20	19 33	19 37	19 50	20 04	20 20	20 32	20 38	20 51	21 04	21 20	21 32	21 37	22 05	22 20	23 16
Manchester Airport 85	a					19 26					20 26					21 26				22 26		

		NT
Sheffield 7	d	22 16
Dore & Totley	d	22 22
Grindleford	d	22 29
Hathersage	d	22 33
Bamford	d	22 37
Hope (Derbyshire)	d	22 40
Edale	d	22 48
Chinley	d	22 56
Hazel Grove 86	a	
Stockport 86	a	
New Mills Central	d	23 04
Strines	d	23 07
Marple	d	23 11
Rose Hill Marple	d	
Romiley	d	23 14
Woodley	d	
Hyde Central	d	
Hyde North	d	
Guide Bridge	d	
Fairfield	d	
Gorton	d	
Bredbury	d	23 17
Brinnington	d	23 20
Reddish North	d	23 23
Ryder Brow	d	
Belle Vue	d	
Ashburys	d	23 30
Ardwick	d	
Manchester Piccadilly 10	a	23 36
Manchester Airport 85	a	

A From Hadfield
B From Norwich to Liverpool Lime Street
C From Cleethorpes
D From Norwich

Manchester Airport and Manchester Romiley, Marple, Chinley and Sheffield

Miles	Miles	Miles			NT A	NT	NT A	NT ◇ B	NT	TP ◇1 C	NT A	NT D		NT	NT E	NT F	NT	NT ◇ B	NT F	NT D	NT G	NT E		TP ◇1 C ✠	NT E
—	—	—	**Manchester Airport** 85	d						05 54														06 53	
0	0	—	**Manchester Piccadilly** 10	a						06 11														07 12	
—	—	—		d	05 32	05 46	05 52	05 56	06 11	06 17	06 24	06 34		06 38		06 47	06 54	07 01	07 07	07 09	07 11			07 18	
0½	0½	—	Ardwick	d																					
1½	1½	—	Ashburys	d	05 36		05 56		06 15		06 28	06 38				06 51			07 11		07 15				
2½	—	—	Belle Vue	d					06 17																
2¾	—	—	Ryder Brow	d					06 19								07 00								
3¾	—	—	Reddish North	d					06 22					06 47			07 03				07 21				
5½	—	—	Brinnington	d					06 25					06 51			07 07				07 24				
6½	—	—	Bredbury	d					06 28					06 54			07 10				07 28				
—	2½	—	Gorton	d								06 41								07 16					
—	3½	—	Fairfield	d								06 43							07 15						
—	4¾	—	Guide Bridge	a	05 41		06 01	06 04			06 33	06 46				06 56		07 09	07 18	07 21					
—	—	—		d								06 46								07 21					
—	6½	—	Hyde North	d								06 50								07 25					
—	7¾	—	Hyde Central	d								06 53								07 28					
—	9¼	—	Woodley	d								06 56			←					07 31		←			
7½	10½	—	**Romiley**	d					06 31			07 00		06 57	07 00		07 13			07 35	07 31	07 35			
—	12½	—	Rose Hill Marple	a								→			07 05					→		07 40			
9	—	—	**Marple**	d					06 35					07 00			07 17				07 35				
11¼	—	—	Strines	d																					
12¾	—	—	New Mills Central	a					06 40					07 06			07 22				07 40				
—	—	—		d										07 06							07 41				
—	—	—	Stockport 86	d		05 56				06 24														07 28	
—	—	0	Hazel Grove 86	d		06 04																			
16½	—	8½	**Chinley**	d		06 15								07 13							07 48				
22	—	—	Edale	d		06 23								07 22							07 57				
27¼	—	—	Hope (Derbyshire)	d		06 30								07 29							08 04				
29	—	—	Bamford	d		06 33								07 32							08 07				
30¾	—	—	Hathersage	d		06 37								07 36							08 10				
32¼	—	—	Grindleford	d		06 41								07 40							08 14				←
37¾	—	—	Dore & Totley	d		06 50								07 57							08 24			08 03	08 24
42	—	—	**Sheffield** 7	a		06 56				07 06				08 04							→			08 09	08 32

		NT F	NT	NT	EM ◇ H	NT F	NT F	NT		TP ◇1 C ✠	NT	NT A	NT	EM ◇ H	NT	NT A	NT	TP ◇1 C ✠		NT	NT A	NT D	NT ◇	NT E	EM ◇ I
Manchester Airport 85	d									07 53								08 53							
Manchester Piccadilly 10	a									08 11								09 11							
	d	07 26	07 29	07 40	07 42	07 42	08 02	08 09		08 19	08 19	08 29	08 39	08 43	08 49	08 59	09 08	09 19		09 19	09 29	09 34	09 40		09 42
Ardwick	d																								
Ashburys	d	07 30		07 44		07 46	08 06				08 23	08 33	08 43			09 03				09 23	09 33	09 38			
Belle Vue	d			07 46																09 25					
Ryder Brow	d			07 48							08 26									09 27					
Reddish North	d			07 51							08 29				08 57					09 30			09 48		
Brinnington	d			07 55							08 32				09 00					09 33			09 51		
Bredbury	d			07 58							08 35				09 03					09 36			09 54		
Gorton	d		07 35					08 15					08 46				09 14					09 42			
Fairfield	d		07 37										08 48									09 44			
Guide Bridge	a	07 35	07 40			07 51	08 11	08 19				08 38	08 51			09 08	09 18				09 38	09 47			
	d		07 40					08 19					08 51				09 18					09 47			
Hyde North	d							08 23									09 22								
Hyde Central	d		07 47					08 26					08 56				09 25					09 53			
Woodley	d		07 51					08 29					09 00				09 28					09 56		←	
Romiley	d		07 54	08 03				08 33			08 38		09 04		09 07		09 32			09 39		10 01	09 57	10 01	
Rose Hill Marple	a		07 59					08 40					09 09				09 38					→		10 06	
Marple	d			08 07							08 42				09 11					09 43			10 01		
Strines	d										08 46									09 47					
New Mills Central	a			08 12							08 49				09 16					09 50			10 06		
	d														09 17								10 07		
Stockport 86	d				07 54					08 28				08 54				09 28							09 54
Hazel Grove 86	d																								
Chinley	d														09 23								10 14		
Edale	d														09 32								10 23		
Hope (Derbyshire)	d														09 38								10 30		
Bamford	d														09 42								10 34		
Hathersage	d														09 45								10 37		
Grindleford	d														09 49								10 41		
Dore & Totley	d				08 28										09 58								10 58		
Sheffield 7	a				08 34					09 08				09 35	10 05			10 08					11 04		10 32

A To Hadfield
B To Huddersfield
C To Cleethorpes
D To Rose Hill Marple
E From Manchester Piccadilly
F To Manchester Piccadilly
G To Sheffield
H From Liverpool Lime Street to Norwich
I from 3 September until 5 October. From Liverpool Lime Street to Norwich

Table T078-R

Mondays to Fridays

21 May to 7 December

Manchester Airport and Manchester Romiley, Marple, Chinley and Sheffield

		EM ◇ A	NT B	NT		TP ◇1 C ✠	NT	NT B	NT	EM ◇ D	NT ◇	NT B	NT	TP ◇1 C ✠		NT	NT B	NT	EM ◇ D	NT ◇	NT B	NT	TP ◇1 C ✠	NT
Manchester Airport 85	d					09 53								10 53									11 53	
Manchester Piccadilly 10	a					10 11								11 11									12 11	
	d	09 42	09 59	10 09		10 19	10 19	10 29	10 39	10 42	10 49	10 59	11 09	11 19		11 19	11 29	11 34	11 42	11 49	11 59	12 06	12 19	12 19
Ardwick	d																							
Ashburys	d		10 03				10 23	10 33	10 43			11 03				11 23	11 33	11 38			12 03			12 23
Belle Vue	d						10 25																	12 25
Ryder Brow	d						10 27									11 26								12 27
Reddish North	d						10 30				10 57					11 29				11 57				12 30
Brinnington	d						10 33				11 00					11 32				12 00				12 33
Bredbury	d						10 36				11 03					11 35				12 03				12 36
Gorton	d			10 15					10 46				11 15					11 42				12 12		
Fairfield	d								10 48									11 44						
Guide Bridge	a		10 08	10 19				10 38	10 51			11 08	11 19				11 38	11 47			12 08	12 16		
	d			10 19					10 51				11 19					11 47				12 16		
Hyde North	d			10 23									11 23									12 20		
Hyde Central	d			10 26					10 56				11 26					11 53				12 23		
Woodley	d			10 29					10 59				11 29					11 56				12 26		
Romiley	d			10 33			10 39		11 03		11 06		11 33			11 38		12 00		12 06		12 30		12 39
Rose Hill Marple	a			10 40					11 08				11 38					12 05				12 35		
Marple	d						10 43				11 10					11 42				12 10				12 43
Strines	d															11 46								
New Mills Central	a						10 48				11 15					11 49				12 15				12 48
	d										11 16									12 16				
Stockport 86	d	09 54				10 28				10 54				11 28					11 54				12 28	
Hazel Grove 86	d																							
Chinley	d										11 22									12 24				
Edale	d										11 31									12 32				
Hope (Derbyshire)	d										11 37									12 39				
Bamford	d										11 41									12 42				
Hathersage	d										11 44									12 45				
Grindleford	d										11 48									12 49				
Dore & Totley	d										11 58									12 58				
Sheffield 7	a	10 34				11 08				11 35	12 04			12 08					12 35	13 04			13 08	

		NT B	NT	EM ◇ D	NT ◇	NT B	NT	TP ◇1 C ✠	NT	NT B		NT	EM ◇ D	NT ◇	NT B	NT	TP ◇1 C ✠	NT	NT B	NT		EM ◇ D	NT ◇	NT B	NT
Manchester Airport 85	d							12 53									13 53								
Manchester Piccadilly 10	a							13 11									14 11								
	d	12 29	12 39	12 42	12 49	12 59	13 09	13 19	13 19	13 29		13 39	13 42	13 49	13 59	14 09	14 19	14 19	14 29	14 39		14 42	14 49	14 59	15 09
Ardwick	d																								
Ashburys	d	12 33	12 43			13 03			13 23	13 33		13 43			14 03			14 23	14 33	14 43				15 03	
Belle Vue	d																	14 25							
Ryder Brow	d								13 26									14 27							
Reddish North	d				12 57				13 29					13 57				14 30					14 57		
Brinnington	d				13 00				13 32					14 00				14 33					15 00		
Bredbury	d				13 03				13 35					14 03				14 36					15 03		
Gorton	d		12 46				13 15					13 46				14 15				14 46					15 15
Fairfield	d		12 48									13 48								14 48					
Guide Bridge	a	12 38	12 51			13 08	13 19			13 38		13 51			14 08	14 19			14 38	14 51				15 08	15 19
	d		12 51				13 19					13 51				14 19				14 51					15 19
Hyde North	d						13 23									14 23									15 23
Hyde Central	d		12 56				13 26					13 56				14 26				14 56					15 26
Woodley	d		12 59				13 29					13 59				14 29				14 59					15 29
Romiley	d		13 03		13 06		13 33		13 38			14 03		14 06		14 33		14 39		15 03			15 06		15 33
Rose Hill Marple	a		13 08				13 38					14 08				14 40				15 08					15 38
Marple	d				13 10				13 42					14 10				14 43					15 10		
Strines	d								13 46																
New Mills Central	a				13 15				13 49					14 15				14 48					15 15		
	d				13 16									14 16									15 16		
Stockport 86	d			12 54				13 28					13 54				14 28					14 54			
Hazel Grove 86	d																								
Chinley	d				13 23									14 23									15 23		
Edale	d				13 32									14 32									15 32		
Hope (Derbyshire)	d				13 38									14 38									15 38		
Bamford	d				13 42									14 42									15 42		
Hathersage	d				13 45									14 45									15 45		
Grindleford	d				13 49									14 49									15 49		
Dore & Totley	d				13 58									14 58									15 58		
Sheffield 7	a			13 34	14 04			14 08					14 35	15 04			15 08					15 34	16 04		

A until 31 August, from 8 October. From Liverpool Lime Street to Norwich
B To Hadfield
C To Cleethorpes
D From Liverpool Lime Street to Norwich

Table T078-R

Mondays to Fridays

21 May to 7 December

Manchester Airport and Manchester Romiley, Marple, Chinley and Sheffield

		TP ◇■ A	NT	NT B	NT	EM ◇ C	NT	NT B	NT	TP ◇■ A	NT	NT D
Manchester Airport 85	d	14 53								15 53		
Manchester Piccadilly	a	15 11								16 11		
	d	15 19	15 19	15 29	15 39	15 42	15 49	15 57	16 08	16 19	16 19	16 29
Ardwick	d											
Ashburys	d		15 23	15 33	15 43			16 01			16 23	16 33
Belle Vue	d										16 25	
Ryder Brow	d		15 26								16 27	
Reddish North	d		15 29				15 57				16 30	
Brinnington	d		15 32				16 00				16 33	
Bredbury	d		15 35				16 03				16 36	
Gorton	d				15 46				16 15			
Fairfield	d				15 48							
Guide Bridge	a			15 38	15 51			16 06	16 19			16 38
	d				15 51				16 19			
Hyde North	d								16 23			
Hyde Central	d				15 56				16 26			
Woodley	d				15 59				16 29			
Romiley	d		15 38		16 03		16 06		16 33		16 39	
Rose Hill Marple	a				16 08				16 38			
Marple	d		15 42				16 10				16 43	
Strines	d		15 46								16 47	
New Mills Central	a		15 49				16 15				16 50	
	d						16 16					
Stockport 86	d	15 28				15 54				16 28		
Hazel Grove 86	d											
Chinley	d						16 23					
Edale	d						16 32					
Hope (Derbyshire)	d						16 38					
Bamford	d						16 42					
Hathersage	d						16 45					
Grindleford	d						16 49					
Dore & Totley	d						16 58					
Sheffield 7	a	16 08				16 34	17 04			17 08		

		NT	NT	NT D	EM ◇ C	NT	NT D	NT	TP ◇■ A	NT	NT D	NT
Manchester Airport 85	d								16 53			
Manchester Piccadilly	a								17 11			
	d	16 32	16 35	16 41	16 42	16 49	17 04	17 10	17 19	17 19	17 25	17 32
Ardwick	d		16 38									
Ashburys	d		16 40	16 45			17 11			17 23	17 29	
Belle Vue	d									17 25		
Ryder Brow	d	16 38								17 27		
Reddish North	d	16 41				16 57				17 30		17 40
Brinnington	d	16 45				17 01				17 33		17 43
Bredbury	d	16 48				17 04				17 36		17 46
Gorton	d			16 47				17 16				
Fairfield	d		16 44					17 18				
Guide Bridge	a		16 47	16 51			17 16	17 21			17 34	
	d		16 47					17 21				
Hyde North	d		16 51					17 25				
Hyde Central	d		16 54					17 28				
Woodley	d		16 58					17 31				
Romiley	d	16 53	17 03			17 07		17 35		17 39		17 50
Rose Hill Marple	a		17 08					17 40				
Marple	d	16 57				17 11				17 43		17 54
Strines	d									17 47		17 58
New Mills Central	a	17 02				17 16				17 50		18 01
	d					17 16						
Stockport 86	d				16 54				17 28			
Hazel Grove 86	d											
Chinley	d				17 09	17 24						
Edale	d					17 34						
Hope (Derbyshire)	d					17 41						
Bamford	d					17 44						
Hathersage	d					17 47						
Grindleford	d					17 51						
Dore & Totley	d				17 31	18 00			18 04			
Sheffield 7	a				17 39	18 06			18 10			

		NT E	NT F	NT D	EM ◇ G	EM ◇ H	NT	NT I	NT ◇ J	NT D	NT	TP ◇■ A
Manchester Airport 85	d											17 53
Manchester Piccadilly	a											18 11
	d	17 34	17 34	17 40	17 42	17 42	17 49		17 59	18 05	18 09	18 19
Ardwick	d								18 02			
Ashburys	d	17 38	17 38	17 44						18 09		
Belle Vue	d											
Ryder Brow	d											
Reddish North	d						17 58					
Brinnington	d						18 01					
Bredbury	d						18 04					
Gorton	d	17 41	17 41	17 46							18 15	
Fairfield	d	17 43	17 43									
Guide Bridge	a	17 46	17 46	17 50					18 09	18 14	18 19	
	d	17 46	17 46								18 19	
Hyde North	d	17 51	17 51								18 23	
Hyde Central	d	17 54	17 54								18 26	
Woodley	d	17 57	18 07					←			18 29	
Romiley	d	18 01	18 11				18 07	18 11			18 33	
Rose Hill Marple	a	18 06	→								18 38	
Marple	d						18 11	18a14				
Strines	d											
New Mills Central	a						18 16					
	d						18 16					
Stockport 86	d				17 54	17 54						18 28
Hazel Grove 86	d											
Chinley	d				18 09	18 09	18 24					
Edale	d						18 32					
Hope (Derbyshire)	d						18 39					
Bamford	d						18 42					
Hathersage	d						18 46					
Grindleford	d						18 50					
Dore & Totley	d				18 40	18 41	18 58					19 03
Sheffield 7	a				18 48	18 49	19 06					19 09

		NT	NT B	NT	NT	EM ◇ C	NT ◇	NT B	NT	TP ◇■ A	NT
Manchester Airport 85	d									18 53	
Manchester Piccadilly	a									19 11	
	d	18 19	18 27	18 32	18 34	18 42	18 49	18 59	19 09	19 19	19 19
Ardwick	d										
Ashburys	d	18 23	18 31		18 38			19 03			19 23
Belle Vue	d	18 25									19 25
Ryder Brow	d	18 27		18 38							19 27
Reddish North	d	18 30		18 41			18 57				19 30
Brinnington	d	18 33		18 45			19 00				19 33
Bredbury	d	18 36		18 48			19 04				19 36
Gorton	d		18 33		18 41				19 15		
Fairfield	d				18 43						
Guide Bridge	a		18 37		18 46			19 08	19 19		
	d				18 46				19 19		
Hyde North	d				18 50				19 23		
Hyde Central	d				18 53				19 26		
Woodley	d				18 56				19 29		
Romiley	d	18 39		18 52	19 00		19 07		19 33		19 39
Rose Hill Marple	a				19 05				19 40		
Marple	d	18 43		18 56			19 10				19 43
Strines	d	18 47									
New Mills Central	a	18 50		19 01			19 16				19 48
	d	18 51					19 16				
Stockport 86	d					18 54				19 28	
Hazel Grove 86	d										
Chinley	d	18a58					19 24				
Edale	d						19 32				
Hope (Derbyshire)	d						19 39				
Bamford	d						19 42				
Hathersage	d						19 46				
Grindleford	d						19 50				
Dore & Totley	d						19 58			20 03	
Sheffield 7	a					19 35	20 05			20 09	

A To Cleethorpes
B To Hadfield
C From Liverpool Lime Street to Norwich
D To Manchester Piccadilly
E until 31 August
F from 3 September. To Marple
G from 8 October. From Liverpool Lime Street to Nottingham
H until 5 October. From Liverpool Lime Street to Nottingham
I from 3 September. From Manchester Piccadilly
J To Huddersfield

Table T078-R

Mondays to Fridays

21 May to 7 December

Manchester Airport and Manchester Romiley, Marple, Chinley and Sheffield

		NT A	NT	EM ◇ B	NT ◇	NT A	NT	TP ◇■ C	NT	NT A	EM ◇ B	NT ◇
Manchester Airport 85	d							19 53				
Manchester Piccadilly	a							20 11				
	d	19 29	19 39	19 42	19 49	19 59	20 09	20 19	20 19	20 29	20 42	20 49
Ardwick	d											
Ashburys	d	19 33	19 43			20 03			20 23	20 33		
Belle Vue	d											
Ryder Brow	d								20 26			
Reddish North	d				19 57				20 29			20 57
Brinnington	d				20 00				20 32			21 00
Bredbury	d				20 04				20 35			21 03
Gorton	d		19 46				20 15					
Fairfield	d		19 48									
Guide Bridge	a	19 38	19 51			20 08	20 19			20 38		
	d		19 51				20 19					
Hyde North	d						20 23					
Hyde Central	d		19 56				20 26					
Woodley	d		19 59				20 29					
Romiley	d		20 03		20 07		20 33		20 38			21 06
Rose Hill Marple	a		20 08				20 40					
Marple	d				20 10				20 42			21 10
Strines	d								20 46			
New Mills Central	a				20 16				20 49			21 15
	d				20 16							21 16
Stockport 86	d			19 54				20 28			20 54	
Hazel Grove 86	d											
Chinley	d				20 24							21 22
Edale	d											21 30
Hope (Derbyshire)	d											21 37
Bamford	d											21 40
Hathersage	d											21 43
Grindleford	d											21 47
Dore & Totley	d				20 48			21 03				21 55
Sheffield 7	a			20 35	20 55			21 09			21 35	22 05

		NT A	NT	TP ◇■ C	NT ◇	NT A	NT	NT A	TP ◇■ D	EM ◇ B	NT A	NT
Manchester Airport 85	d			20 53					21 53			
Manchester Piccadilly	a			21 11					22 11			
	d	20 59	21 09	21 19	21 19	21 28	21 49	21 58	22 19	22 28	22 29	22 40
Ardwick	d											
Ashburys	d	21 03				21 33	21 54	22 02			22 33	22 44
Belle Vue	d				21 25							22 46
Ryder Brow	d				21 27							22 48
Reddish North	d				21 30		21 59					22 51
Brinnington	d				21 33		22 03					22 54
Bredbury	d				21 37		22 06					22 57
Gorton	d		21 15					22 04			22 35	
Fairfield	d		21 17									
Guide Bridge	a	21 08	21 20			21 38		22 08			22 39	
	d		21 20									
Hyde North	d		21 24									
Hyde Central	d		21 27									
Woodley	d		21 30									
Romiley	d		21 34		21 40		22 09					23 00
Rose Hill Marple	a		21 40									
Marple	d				21 44		22 13					23 04
Strines	d				21 48							23 08
New Mills Central	a				21 51		22 21					23 11
	d				21 52							
Stockport 86	d			21 28						22 38		
Hazel Grove 86	d											
Chinley	d				22 12					22 53		
Edale	d									23 01		
Hope (Derbyshire)	d				22 25					23 07		
Bamford	d				22 28					23 11		
Hathersage	d				22 32					23 15		
Grindleford	d									23 19		
Dore & Totley	d			22 03	22 46					23 28		
Sheffield 7	a			22 10	22 52				23 09	23 35		

		NT	NT E	TP ◇■
Manchester Airport 85	d			23 30
Manchester Piccadilly	a			23 45
	d	23 24	23 27	23 50
Ardwick	d			
Ashburys	d	23 28	23 31	
Belle Vue	d	23 30		
Ryder Brow	d	23 32		
Reddish North	d	23 35		
Brinnington	d	23 38		
Bredbury	d	23 41		
Gorton	d		23 33	
Fairfield	d			
Guide Bridge	a		23 37	
	d			
Hyde North	d			
Hyde Central	d			
Woodley	d			
Romiley	d	23 44		
Rose Hill Marple	a			
Marple	d	23 48		
Strines	d	23 52		
New Mills Central	a	23 55		
	d			
Stockport 86	d			
Hazel Grove 86	d			
Chinley	d			
Edale	d			
Hope (Derbyshire)	d			
Bamford	d			
Hathersage	d			
Grindleford	d			
Dore & Totley	d			
Sheffield 7	a			01 21

A To Hadfield
B From Liverpool Lime Street to Nottingham
C To Cleethorpes
D To Doncaster
E To Glossop

Table T078-R

Saturdays

26 May to 8 December

Manchester Airport and Manchester Romiley, Marple, Chinley and Sheffield

	NT	NT A	NT	TP ◇■ B	NT A	NT C	NT	NT D	NT A		NT	TP ◇■ B ✠	NT	NT A	NT	EM ◇ E	NT	NT A	NT		TP ◇■ B ✠	NT	NT A	NT
Manchester Airport 85 ✈ d				05 56								06 53									07 53			
Manchester Piccadilly 10 a				06 13								07 12									08 11			
d	05 46	05 59	06 11	06 17	06 29	06 34	06 38		06 59		07 09	07 19	07 19	07 29	07 33	07 42	07 49	07 59	08 09		08 19	08 19	08 29	08 39
Ardwick d																								
Ashburys d		06 03	06 15		06 33	06 38			07 03				07 23	07 33				08 03				08 23	08 33	08 43
Belle Vue d			06 17										07 25											
Ryder Brow d			06 19										07 27									08 26		
Reddish North d			06 22				06 47						07 30				07 57					08 29		
Brinnington d			06 25				06 51						07 33				08 00					08 32		
Bredbury d			06 28				06 54						07 36				08 03					08 35		
Gorton d						06 41					07 16				07 39				08 15					08 46
Fairfield d						06 43									07 41									08 48
Guide Bridge a		06 08			06 38	06 46			07 08		07 21			07 38	07 44			08 08	08 19				08 38	08 51
d						06 46					07 21				07 44				08 19					08 51
Hyde North d						06 50					07 25								08 23					
Hyde Central d						06 53					07 28				07 50				08 26					08 56
Woodley d						06 56		←			07 31				07 53				08 29					09 00
Romiley d			06 31			07 00	06 57	07 00			07 35		07 39		07 56		08 06		08 33			08 38		09 04
Rose Hill Marple a						→		07 05			07 40				08 01				08 40					09 09
Marple d			06 35				07 00						07 43				08 10					08 42		
Strines d																						08 46		
New Mills Central a			06 40				07 06						07 48				08 15					08 49		
d							07 06										08 16							
Stockport 86 d	05 56			06 26								07 28				07 55					08 28			
Hazel Grove 86 d	06 04																							
Chinley d	06 15						07 13										08 23							
Edale d	06 23						07 22										08 32							
Hope (Derbyshire) d	06 30						07 29										08 38							
Bamford d	06 33						07 32										08 42							
Hathersage d	06 37						07 36										08 45							
Grindleford d	06 41						07 40										08 49							
Dore & Totley d	06 50						07 57					08 03				08 28	08 58							
Sheffield 7 a	06 56			07 08			08 04					08 09				08 35	09 05				09 08			

	EM ◇ E	NT	NT A	NT	TP ◇■ B ✠		NT	NT A	NT	EM ◇ E	NT ◇	NT A	NT	TP ◇■ B ✠	NT		NT A	NT	EM ◇ E	NT ◇	NT A	NT	TP ◇■ B ✠	NT
Manchester Airport 85 ✈ d					08 53									09 53									10 53	
Manchester Piccadilly 10 a					09 11									10 11									11 11	
d	08 43	08 49	08 59	09 08	09 19		09 19	09 29	09 34	09 42	09 49	09 59	10 09	10 19	10 19		10 29	10 39	10 43	10 49	10 59	11 09	11 19	11 19
Ardwick d																								
Ashburys d			09 03				09 23	09 33	09 38			10 03			10 23		10 33	10 43			11 03			11 23
Belle Vue d							09 25								10 25									
Ryder Brow d							09 27								10 27									11 26
Reddish North d		08 57					09 30				09 57				10 30					10 57				11 29
Brinnington d		09 00					09 33				10 00				10 33					11 00				11 32
Bredbury d		09 03					09 36				10 03				10 36					11 03				11 35
Gorton d				09 14					09 42				10 15					10 46				11 15		
Fairfield d									09 44									10 48						
Guide Bridge a			09 08	09 18				09 38	09 47			10 08	10 19				10 38	10 51			11 08	11 19		
d				09 18					09 47				10 19					10 51				11 19		
Hyde North d				09 22									10 23									11 23		
Hyde Central d				09 25					09 53				10 26					10 56				11 26		
Woodley d				09 28					09 56				10 29					10 59				11 29		
Romiley d		09 07		09 32			09 39		10 01		10 06		10 33		10 39			11 03		11 06		11 33		11 38
Rose Hill Marple a				09 38					10 06				10 40					11 08				11 38		
Marple d		09 11					09 43				10 10				10 43					11 10				11 42
Strines d							09 47																	11 46
New Mills Central a		09 16					09 50				10 15				10 48					11 15				11 49
d		09 17									10 16									11 16				
Stockport 86 d	08 54				09 28					09 54				10 28					10 54				11 28	
Hazel Grove 86 d																								
Chinley d		09 23									10 23									11 22				
Edale d		09 32									10 32									11 31				
Hope (Derbyshire) d		09 38									10 38									11 37				
Bamford d		09 42									10 42									11 41				
Hathersage d		09 45									10 45									11 44				
Grindleford d		09 49									10 49									11 48				
Dore & Totley d		09 58									10 58									11 58				
Sheffield 7 a	09 34	10 05			10 08					10 34	11 05			11 08					11 35	12 04			12 08	

A To Hadfield
B To Cleethorpes
C To Rose Hill Marple
D From Manchester Piccadilly
E From Liverpool Lime Street to Norwich

Table T078-R

Saturdays

26 May to 8 December

Manchester Airport and Manchester Romiley, Marple, Chinley and Sheffield

	NT A		NT	EM ◇ B	NT ◇	NT A	NT	TP ◇■ C ✠	NT	NT A	NT		EM ◇ B	NT ◇	NT A	NT	TP ◇■ C ✠	NT	NT A	NT	EM ◇ B		NT ◇	NT A
Manchester Airport 85 ✈ d								11 53									12 53							
Manchester Piccadilly 10 a								12 11									13 11							
d	11 29		11 34	11 42	11 49	11 59	12 06	12 19	12 19	12 29	12 39		12 42	12 49	12 59	13 09	13 19	13 19	13 29	13 39	13 42		13 49	13 59
Ardwick d																								
Ashburys d	11 33		11 38			12 03			12 23	12 33	12 43				13 03			13 23	13 33	13 43				14 03
Belle Vue d									12 25															
Ryder Brow d									12 27									13 26						
Reddish North d					11 57				12 30					12 57				13 29					13 57	
Brinnington d					12 00				12 33					13 00				13 32					14 00	
Bredbury d					12 03				12 36					13 03				13 35					14 03	
Gorton d			11 42				12 12				12 46					13 15				13 46				
Fairfield d			11 44								12 48									13 48				
Guide Bridge a	11 38		11 47			12 08	12 16			12 38	12 51				13 08	13 19			13 38	13 51				14 08
d			11 47				12 16				12 51					13 19				13 51				
Hyde North d							12 20									13 23								
Hyde Central d			11 53				12 23				12 56					13 26				13 56				
Woodley d			11 56				12 26				12 59					13 29				13 59				
Romiley d			12 00		12 06		12 30		12 39		13 03			13 06		13 33		13 38		14 03			14 06	
Rose Hill Marple a			12 05				12 35				13 08					13 38				14 08				
Marple d					12 10				12 43					13 10				13 42					14 10	
Strines d																		13 46						
New Mills Central a					12 15				12 48					13 15				13 49					14 15	
d					12 16									13 16									14 16	
Stockport 86 d				11 54				12 28					12 54				13 28				13 54			
Hazel Grove 86 d																								
Chinley d					12 23									13 23									14 23	
Edale d					12 32									13 32									14 32	
Hope (Derbyshire) d					12 38									13 38									14 38	
Bamford d					12 42									13 42									14 42	
Hathersage d					12 45									13 45									14 45	
Grindleford d					12 49									13 49									14 49	
Dore & Totley d					12 58									13 58									14 58	
Sheffield 7 a				12 35	13 05			13 08					13 34	14 04			14 08				14 33		15 05	

	NT	TP ◇■ C ✠	NT	NT A	NT	EM ◇ B	NT ◇		NT A	NT	TP ◇■ C ✠	NT	NT A	NT	EM ◇ B	NT	NT A		NT	TP ◇■ C ✠	NT	NT A	NT	EM ◇ B
Manchester Airport 85 ✈ d		13 53									14 53									15 53				
Manchester Piccadilly 10 a		14 11									15 13									16 11				
d	14 09	14 19	14 19	14 29	14 39	14 42	14 49		14 59	15 09	15 19	15 19	15 29	15 39	15 42	15 49	15 57		16 08	16 19	16 19	16 27	16 35	16 42
Ardwick d																							16 38	
Ashburys d			14 23	14 33	14 43				15 03			15 23	15 33	15 43			16 01				16 23	16 33	16 40	
Belle Vue d			14 25																		16 25			
Ryder Brow d			14 27									15 26									16 27			
Reddish North d			14 30				14 57					15 29				15 57					16 30			
Brinnington d			14 33				15 00					15 32				16 00					16 33			
Bredbury d			14 36				15 03					15 35				16 03					16 36			
Gorton d	14 15				14 46					15 15				15 46					16 15					
Fairfield d					14 48									15 48									16 44	
Guide Bridge a	14 19			14 38	14 51				15 08	15 19			15 38	15 51			16 06		16 19			16 38	16 47	
d	14 19				14 51					15 19				15 51					16 19				16 47	
Hyde North d	14 23									15 23									16 23				16 51	
Hyde Central d	14 26				14 56					15 26				15 56					16 26				16 54	
Woodley d	14 29				14 59					15 29				15 59					16 29				16 58	
Romiley d	14 33		14 39		15 03		15 06			15 33		15 38		16 03		16 06			16 33		16 39		17 03	
Rose Hill Marple a	14 40				15 08					15 38				16 08					16 38				17 08	
Marple d			14 43				15 10					15 42				16 10					16 43			
Strines d												15 46									16 47			
New Mills Central a			14 48				15 15					15 49				16 15					16 50			
d							15 16									16 16								
Stockport 86 d		14 28				14 54					15 28				15 54					16 28				16 54
Hazel Grove 86 d																								
Chinley d							15 23									16 23								17 09
Edale d							15 32									16 32								
Hope (Derbyshire) d							15 38									16 38								
Bamford d							15 42									16 42								
Hathersage d							15 45									16 45								
Grindleford d							15 49									16 49								
Dore & Totley d							15 58									16 58								17 31
Sheffield 7 a		15 08				15 34	16 04				16 08				16 34	17 04				17 08				17 37

A To Hadfield
B From Liverpool Lime Street to Norwich
C To Cleethorpes

Saturdays
26 May to 8 December

Manchester Airport and Manchester Romiley, Marple, Chinley and Sheffield

	NT	NT A	NT	TP ◇1 B	NT	NT A	NT	EM ◇ C	NT	NT A	NT	TP ◇1 B	NT	NT A	NT	EM ◇ D	NT ◇	NT A	NT	TP ◇1 B	NT
Manchester Airport 85 d				16 53								17 53								18 53	
Manchester Piccadilly 10 a				17 13								18 11								19 13	
d	16 49	16 59	17 10	17 19	17 19	17 29	17 34	17 42	17 49	17 59	18 09	18 19	18 19	18 27	18 34	18 42	18 49	18 59	19 09	19 19	19 19
Ardwick d																					
Ashburys d		17 03			17 23	17 33	17 38			18 03			18 23	18 31	18 38			19 03			19 23
Belle Vue d					17 25								18 25								19 25
Ryder Brow d					17 27								18 27								19 27
Reddish North d	16 57				17 30				17 57				18 30				18 57				19 30
Brinnington d	17 01				17 33				18 00				18 33				19 00				19 33
Bredbury d	17 04				17 36				18 04				18 36				19 04				19 36
Gorton d			17 16				17 41				18 15			18 33	18 41				19 15		
Fairfield d			17 18				17 43								18 43						
Guide Bridge a		17 08	17 21			17 38	17 46			18 08	18 19			18 37	18 46			19 08	19 19		
d			17 21				17 47				18 19				18 46				19 19		
Hyde North d			17 25				17 51				18 23				18 50				19 23		
Hyde Central d			17 28				17 54				18 26				18 53				19 26		
Woodley d			17 31				17 57				18 29				18 56				19 29		
Romiley d	17 07		17 35		17 39		18 01		18 07		18 33		18 39		19 00		19 07		19 33		19 39
Rose Hill Marple a			17 40				18 06				18 40				19 05				19 40		
Marple d	17 11				17 43				18 10				18 43				19 10				19 43
Strines d					17 47								18 47								
New Mills Central a	17 16				17 50				18 16				18 50				19 16				19 48
d	17 16								18 16								19 16				
Stockport 86 d				17 28				17 54				18 28				18 54				19 28	
Hazel Grove 86 d																					
Chinley d	17 24							18 09	18 24								19 24				
Edale d	17 34								18 32								19 32				
Hope (Derbyshire) d	17 41								18 39								19 39				
Bamford d	17 44								18 42								19 42				
Hathersage d	17 47								18 46								19 46				
Grindleford d	17 51								18 50								19 50				
Dore & Totley d	18 00			18 04					18 58			19 03					19 58			20 03	
Sheffield 7 a	18 06			18 10				18 37	19 04			19 09				19 34	20 05			20 09	

	NT A	NT	EM ◇ C	NT ◇	NT A	NT	TP ◇1 B	NT	NT A	EM ◇ C	NT ◇	NT A	NT	TP ◇1 B	NT ◇	NT A	EM ◇ C	NT	NT A	TP ◇1 E	EM ◇ C	NT A
Manchester Airport 85 d							19 56							20 53						21 53		
Manchester Piccadilly 10 a							20 13							21 13						22 12		
d	19 29	19 39	19 42	19 49	19 59	20 09	20 19	20 19	20 29	20 43	20 49	20 59	21 09	21 19	21 19	21 28	21 41	21 49	21 58	22 19	22 28	22 29
Ardwick d																						
Ashburys d	19 33	19 43			20 03			20 23	20 33			21 03				21 33			22 02			22 33
Belle Vue d																		21 55				
Ryder Brow d								20 26										21 57				
Reddish North d				19 57				20 29			20 57				21 27			22 00				
Brinnington d				20 00				20 32			21 00				21 30			22 03				
Bredbury d				20 03				20 35			21 03				21 34			22 07				
Gorton d		19 46				20 15							21 15						22 04			22 35
Fairfield d		19 48											21 17									
Guide Bridge a	19 38	19 51			20 08	20 19			20 38			21 08	21 20			21 38			22 08			22 39
d		19 51				20 19							21 20									
Hyde North d						20 23							21 24									
Hyde Central d		19 56				20 26							21 27									
Woodley d		19 59				20 29							21 30									
Romiley d		20 03		20 06		20 33		20 38			21 06		21 34		21 38			22 10				
Rose Hill Marple a		20 08				20 40							21 40									
Marple d				20 10				20 42			21 10				21 42			22 14				
Strines d								20 46							21 46							
New Mills Central a				20 15				20 49			21 15				21 49			22 21				
d				20 16							21 16				21 50							
Stockport 86 d			19 55				20 28			20 55				21 28			21 52				22 38	
Hazel Grove 86 d																						
Chinley d				20 23							21 22				21 56						22 53	
Edale d				20 32							21 30										23 01	
Hope (Derbyshire) d				20 38							21 37										23 07	
Bamford d				20 42							21 40										23 11	
Hathersage d				20 45							21 43										23 15	
Grindleford d				20 49							21 47										23 19	
Dore & Totley d				20 58			21 03				21 55			22 03	22 20						23 28	
Sheffield 7 a			20 34	21 05			21 09			21 35	22 05			22 10	22 27		22 31			23 10	23 35	

A To Hadfield
B To Cleethorpes
C From Liverpool Lime Street to Nottingham
D From Liverpool Lime Street to Norwich
E To Doncaster

Saturdays
26 May to 8 December

Manchester Airport and Manchester Romiley, Marple, Chinley and Sheffield

	NT	NT	NT A
Manchester Airport 85 d			
Manchester Piccadilly 10 a			
d	22 40	23 24	23 27
Ardwick d			
Ashburys d	22 44	23 28	23 31
Belle Vue d	22 46	23 30	
Ryder Brow d	22 48	23 32	
Reddish North d	22 51	23 35	
Brinnington d	22 54	23 38	
Bredbury d	22 57	23 41	
Gorton d			23 33
Fairfield d			
Guide Bridge a			23 37
d			
Hyde North d			
Hyde Central d			
Woodley d			
Romiley d	23 00	23 44	
Rose Hill Marple a			
Marple d	23 04	23 48	
Strines d	23 08	23 52	
New Mills Central a	23 11	23 55	
d			
Stockport 86 d			
Hazel Grove 86 d			
Chinley d			
Edale d			
Hope (Derbyshire) d			
Bamford d			
Hathersage d			
Grindleford d			
Dore & Totley d			
Sheffield 7 a			

Sundays
20 May to 9 September

	NT	TP ◇1 B	NT	TP ◇1 B	NT C	NT	NT D	TP ◇1 B	NT D	NT	NT D	TP ◇1 B	NT D	NT	NT D	TP ◇1 B	NT D	EM ◇ E	NT	NT D	TP ◇1 B	NT D
Manchester Airport 85 d		07 49		08 46				09 56				10 55				11 56					12 56	
Manchester Piccadilly 10 a		08 09		09 02				10 10				11 15				12 13					13 13	
d	07 42	08 13	08 31	09 10	09 29	09 45	09 59	10 14	10 29	10 45	10 56	11 19	11 26	11 42	11 59	12 19	12 29	12 43	12 45	12 59	13 19	13 29
Ardwick d																						
Ashburys d	07 46				09 33		10 03		10 33		11 00		11 30		12 03		12 33			13 03		13 33
Belle Vue d																						
Ryder Brow d																						
Reddish North d	07 51		08 38			09 52				10 52				11 51					12 52			
Brinnington d	07 54		08 42			09 56				10 56				11 54					12 56			
Bredbury d	07 57		08 45			09 59				10 59				11 57					12 59			
Gorton d					09 36		10 05		10 35		11 03		11 33		12 05		12 35			13 05		13 35
Fairfield d																						
Guide Bridge a					09 39		10 09		10 39		11 07		11 37		12 09		12 39			13 09		13 39
d																						
Hyde North d																						
Hyde Central d																						
Woodley d																						
Romiley d	08 01		08 48			10 02				11 02				12 00					13 02			
Rose Hill Marple a																						
Marple d	08 04		08 51			10 05				11 05				12 04					13 05			
Strines d	08 08		08 55			10 09				11 09				12 08					13 09			
New Mills Central a	08 12		08 59			10 13				11 13				12 11					13 13			
d	08 12		08 59			10 13				11 13				12 11					13 13			
Stockport 86 d		08 23		09 18				10 23				11 29				12 28		12 55			13 28	
Hazel Grove 86 d																						
Chinley d	08 21		09 06			10 20				11 20				12 19					13 20			
Edale d	08 30		09 15			10 29				11 29				12 28					13 29			
Hope (Derbyshire) d	08 37		09 22			10 36				11 36				12 35					13 36			
Bamford d	08 41		09 25			10 39				11 39				12 38					13 39			
Hathersage d	08 45		09 29			10 43				11 43				12 42					13 43			
Grindleford d	08 49		09 33			10 47				11 47				12 46					13 47			
Dore & Totley d	08 58		09 41			10 55				11 55				12 55					13 55			
Sheffield 7 a	09 04	09 08	09 48	10 08		11 02		11 05		12 02		12 09		13 02		13 08		13 37	14 02		14 08	

A To Glossop
B To Cleethorpes
C To Manchester Piccadilly
D To Hadfield
E To Norwich

Table T078-R

Sundays
20 May to 9 September

Manchester Airport and Manchester Romiley, Marple, Chinley and Sheffield

	NT	EM	NT	TP	NT	EM	NT	NT	TP	NT	EM	NT	NT	TP	NT	EM	NT	NT	TP	NT	EM	NT
		◇ A	B	◇1 C 🍴	B	◇ A		B	◇1 C 🍴	B	◇ A		B	◇1 C 🍴	B	◇ A		B	◇1 C 🍴	B	◇ D	
Manchester Airport 85 d				13 56					14 56					15 56					16 56			
Manchester Piccadilly 10 a				14 13					15 13					16 13					17 13			
d	13 42	13 43	13 59	14 19	14 29	14 43	14 45	14 59	15 19	15 29	15 42	15 45	15 59	16 19	16 29	16 42	16 45	16 59	17 19	17 29	17 42	17 45
Ardwick d																						
Ashburys d			14 03		14 33			15 03		15 33			16 03		16 33			17 03		17 33		
Belle Vue d																						
Ryder Brow d																						
Reddish North d	13 49						14 52					15 52					16 52					17 52
Brinnington d	13 53						14 56					15 56					16 56					17 56
Bredbury d	13 56						14 59					15 59					16 59					17 59
Gorton d			14 05		14 35			15 05		15 35			16 05		16 35			17 05		17 35		
Fairfield d																						
Guide Bridge a			14 09		14 39			15 09		15 39			16 09		16 39			17 09		17 39		
d																						
Hyde North d																						
Hyde Central d																						
Woodley d																						
Romiley d	13 59						15 02					16 02					17 02					18 02
Rose Hill Marple a																						
Marple d	14 02						15 05					16 05					17 05					18 05
Strines d	14 06						15 09					16 09					17 09					18 09
New Mills Central a	14 10						15 13					16 13					17 13					18 13
d	14 10						15 13					16 13					17 13					18 13
Stockport 86 d		13 51		14 28		14 54			15 28		15 53			16 28		16 54			17 28		17 54	
Hazel Grove 86 d																						
Chinley d	14 17						15 20					16 20					17 20					18 20
Edale d	14 26						15 29					16 29					17 29					18 29
Hope (Derbyshire) d	14 32						15 36					16 36					17 36					18 36
Bamford d	14 35						15 39					16 39					17 39					18 39
Hathersage d	14 39						15 43					16 43					17 43					18 43
Grindleford d	14 42						15 47					16 47					17 47					18 47
Dore & Totley d	14 50						15 55					16 55					17 55		18 03			18 55
Sheffield 7 a	14 59	14 37		15 08		15 35	16 02		16 08		16 37	17 02		17 08		17 35	18 01		18 09		18 36	19 02

	NT	TP	NT	EM	NT	NT	TP	NT	EM	NT	NT	TP	NT	EM	NT	TP	NT	EM	TP	TP
	B	◇1 C 🍴	B	◇ A		B	◇1 C	B	◇ D		B	◇1 C		◇ D	B	◇1 C		◇ D	◇1 E	◇1
Manchester Airport 85 d		17 56					18 56					19 56				20 55			21 56	22 56
Manchester Piccadilly 10 a		18 13					19 13					20 13				21 13			22 15	23 11
d	17 59	18 19	18 29	18 42	18 45	18 59	19 19	19 29	19 42	19 45	19 59	20 18	20 42	20 43	20 59	21 19	21 45	22 11	22 19	23 20
Ardwick d																				
Ashburys d	18 03		18 33			19 03		19 33			20 03				21 03					
Belle Vue d																				
Ryder Brow d																				
Reddish North d					18 52					19 52			20 49				21 52			
Brinnington d					18 56					19 56			20 53				21 56			
Bredbury d					18 59					19 59			20 56				21 59			
Gorton d	18 05		18 35			19 05		19 35			20 05				21 05					
Fairfield d																				
Guide Bridge a	18 09		18 39			19 09		19 39			20 09				21 09					
d																				
Hyde North d																				
Hyde Central d																				
Woodley d																				
Romiley d					19 02					20 02			20 59				22 02			
Rose Hill Marple a																				
Marple d					19 05					20 05			21 02				22 05			
Strines d					19 09					20 09			21 06				22 09			
New Mills Central a					19 13					20 13			21 10				22 13			
d					19 13					20 13			21 10				22 13			
Stockport 86 d		18 28		18 53			19 28		19 54			20 28		20 53		21 28		22 30	22 27	23 28
Hazel Grove 86 d																				
Chinley d					19 20					20 20			21 17				22 20	22 46		
Edale d					19 29					20 29			21 26				22 29	22 54		
Hope (Derbyshire) d					19 36					20 36			21 32				22 36	22 59		
Bamford d					19 39					20 39			21 35				22 39	23 02		
Hathersage d					19 43					20 43			21 39				22 43	23 05		
Grindleford d					19 47					20 47			21 42				22 47	23 12		
Dore & Totley d		19 03			19 55		20 03			20 55		21 03				22 05	22 55	23 18		
Sheffield 7 a		19 09		19 35	20 02		20 09		20 35	21 02		21 09	21 58	21 34		22 11	23 02	23 26	23 09	00 10

A From Liverpool Lime Street to Norwich
B To Hadfield
C To Cleethorpes
D From Liverpool Lime Street to Nottingham
E To Doncaster

Table T078-R

Sundays
16 September to 21 October

Manchester Airport and Manchester Romiley, Marple, Chinley and Sheffield

	NT	TP	NT	TP	NT	NT	NT	TP	NT	NT	NT	TP	NT	NT	NT	TP	NT	EM	NT	NT	TP	NT
		◇1 A 🍴		◇1 A 🍴	B		C	◇1 A 🍴	C		C	◇1 A 🍴	C		C	◇1 A 🍴	C	◇ D		C	◇1 A 🍴	C
Manchester Airport 85 d		07 49		08 46				09 56				10 55				11 56					12 56	
Manchester Piccadilly 10 a		08 06		09 02				10 10				11 15				12 13					13 13	
d	07 42	08 12	08 45	09 10	09 29	09 31	10 01	10 14	10 29	10 45	10 59	11 19	11 29	11 45	11 58	12 19	12 30	12 43	12 52	13 00	13 19	13 29
Ardwick d																						
Ashburys d	07 46				09 33				10 33		11 03		11 33		12 03		12 34			13 04		13 33
Belle Vue d																						
Ryder Brow d																						
Reddish North d	07 51		08 52			09 39				10 52				11 52								
Brinnington d	07 54		08 56			09 42				10 56				11 56								
Bredbury d	07 57		08 59			09 45				10 59				11 59					13 03			
Gorton d					09 36				10 35		11 05		11 35		12 05					13 06		13 35
Fairfield d																						
Guide Bridge a					09 39		10 09		10 39		11 09		11 39		12 09		12 39			13 10		13 39
d																						
Hyde North d																						
Hyde Central d																						
Woodley d																						
Romiley d	08 01		09 02			09 48				11 02				12 02					13 06			
Rose Hill Marple a																						
Marple d	08 04		09 05			09 52				11 05				12 05					13 09			
Strines d	08 08		09 09			09 56				11 09				12 09								
New Mills Central a	08 12		09 13			09 59				11 13				12 13					13 15			
d	08 12		09 13			09 59				11 13				12 13					13 15			
Stockport 86 d		08 22		09 18				10 23				11 29				12 28		12 55			13 28	
Hazel Grove 86 d																						
Chinley d	08 21		09 20			10 07				11 20				12 20					13 22			
Edale d	08 30		09 29			10 16				11 29				12 29					13 31			
Hope (Derbyshire) d	08 37		09 36			10 23				11 36				12 36					13 37			
Bamford d	08 41		09 39			10 26				11 39				12 39					13 40			
Hathersage d	08 45		09 43			10 30				11 43				12 43					13 44			
Grindleford d	08 49		09 47			10 33				11 47				12 47					13 47			
Dore & Totley d	08 58		09 55			10 42				11 55				12 55					13 55			
Sheffield 7 a	09 04	09 08	10 02	10 08		10 48		11 05		12 02		12 09		13 02		13 08		13 37	14 02		14 08	

	NT	EM	NT	TP	NT	EM	NT	NT	TP	NT	EM	NT	NT	TP	NT	EM	NT	NT	TP	NT	EM	NT
		◇ E	C	◇1 A 🍴	C	◇ E		C	◇1 A 🍴	C	◇ E		C	◇1 A 🍴	C	◇ E		C	◇1 A 🍴	C	◇ F	
Manchester Airport 85 d				13 56					14 56					15 56					16 56			
Manchester Piccadilly 10 a				14 13					15 13					16 13					17 13			
d	13 42	13 43	13 59	14 19	14 29	14 43	14 45	14 59	15 19	15 29	15 42	15 45	15 59	16 19	16 29	16 42	16 45	16 59	17 19	17 29	17 42	17 45
Ardwick d																						
Ashburys d			14 03		14 33			15 03		15 33			16 03		16 33			17 03		17 33		
Belle Vue d																						
Ryder Brow d																						
Reddish North d	13 49						14 52					15 52					16 52					17 52
Brinnington d	13 53						14 56					15 56					16 56					17 56
Bredbury d	13 56						14 59					15 59					16 59					17 59
Gorton d			14 05		14 35			15 05		15 35			16 05		16 35			17 05		17 35		
Fairfield d																						
Guide Bridge a			14 09		14 39			15 09		15 39			16 09		16 39			17 09		17 39		
d																						
Hyde North d																						
Hyde Central d																						
Woodley d																						
Romiley d	13 59						15 02					16 02					17 02					18 02
Rose Hill Marple a																						
Marple d	14 02						15 05					16 05					17 05					18 05
Strines d	14 06						15 09					16 09					17 09					18 09
New Mills Central a	14 10						15 13					16 13					17 13					18 13
d	14 10						15 13					16 13					17 13					18 13
Stockport 86 d		13 51		14 28		14 54			15 28		15 53			16 28		16 54			17 28		17 54	
Hazel Grove 86 d																						
Chinley d	14 17						15 20					16 20					17 20					18 20
Edale d	14 26						15 29					16 29					17 29					18 29
Hope (Derbyshire) d	14 32						15 36					16 36					17 36					18 36
Bamford d	14 35						15 39					16 39					17 39					18 39
Hathersage d	14 39						15 43					16 43					17 43					18 43
Grindleford d	14 42						15 47					16 47					17 47					18 47
Dore & Totley d	14 50						15 55					16 55					17 55		18 03			18 55
Sheffield 7 a	14 59	14 37		15 08		15 35	16 02		16 08		16 37	17 02		17 08		17 35	18 01		18 09		18 36	19 02

A To Cleethorpes
B To Manchester Piccadilly
C To Hadfield
D To Norwich
E From Liverpool Lime Street to Norwich
F From Liverpool Lime Street to Nottingham

Table T078-R

Sundays 16 September to 21 October

Manchester Airport and Manchester Romiley, Marple, Chinley and Sheffield

Station		NT A	TP ◇1 B 🚲	NT A	EM ◇ C	NT	NT A	TP ◇1 B	NT A	EM ◇ D	NT	NT A	TP ◇1 B	NT	EM ◇ D	NT A	TP ◇1 B	NT	EM ◇ D	TP ◇1 E	TP ◇1
Manchester Airport 85	d		17 56					18 56					19 56				20 55			21 56	22 56
Manchester Piccadilly 10	a		18 13					19 13					20 13				21 13			22 15	23 11
	d	17 59	18 19	18 29	18 42	18 45	18 59	19 19	19 29	19 42	19 45	19 59	20 18	20 42	20 43	20 59	21 19	21 45	22 11	22 19	23 20
Ardwick	d																				
Ashburys	d	18 03		18 33			19 03		19 33			20 03				21 03					
Belle Vue	d																				
Ryder Brow	d																				
Reddish North	d					18 52					19 52			20 49				21 52			
Brinnington	d					18 56					19 56			20 53				21 56			
Bredbury	d					18 59					19 59			20 56				21 59			
Gorton	d	18 05		18 35			19 05		19 35			20 05				21 05					
Fairfield	d																				
Guide Bridge	a	18 09		18 39			19 09		19 39			20 09				21 09					
	d																				
Hyde North	d																				
Hyde Central	d																				
Woodley	d																				
Romiley	d					19 02					20 02			20 59				22 02			
Rose Hill Marple	a																				
Marple	d					19 05					20 05			21 02				22 05			
Strines	d					19 09					20 09			21 06				22 09			
New Mills Central	a					19 13					20 13			21 10				22 13			
	d					19 13					20 13			21 10				22 13			
Stockport 86	d		18 28		18 53			19 28		19 54			20 28		20 53		21 28		22 30	22 27	23 28
Hazel Grove 86	d																				
Chinley	d					19 20					20 20			21 17				22 20	22 46		
Edale	d					19 29					20 29			21 26				22 29	22 54		
Hope (Derbyshire)	d					19 36					20 36			21 32				22 36	22 59		
Bamford	d					19 39					20 39			21 35				22 39	23 02		
Hathersage	d					19 43					20 43			21 39				22 43	23 05		
Grindleford	d					19 47					20 47			21 42				22 47	23 12		
Dore & Totley	d		19 03			19 55		20 03			20 55		21 03				22 05	22 55	23 18		
Sheffield 7	a		19 09		19 35	20 02		20 09		20 35	21 02		21 09	21 58	21 34		22 11	23 02	23 26	23 09	00 10

Sundays 28 October to 2 December

Station		NT	TP ◇1 B 🚲	NT	TP ◇1 B 🚲	NT F	NT	NT A	TP ◇1 B 🚲	NT A	NT	NT A	TP ◇1 B 🚲	NT A	NT	NT A	TP ◇1 B 🚲	NT A	EM ◇ G	NT	NT A	TP ◇1 B 🚲	NT A
Manchester Airport 85	d								09 56				10 55				11 56					12 56	
Manchester Piccadilly 10	a								10 10				11 15				12 13					13 13	
	d	07 42	08 12	08 45	09 10	09 29	09 31	10 01	10 14	10 29	10 45	10 59	11 19	11 29	11 45	11 58	12 19	12 30	12 43	12 52	13 00	13 19	13 29
Ardwick	d																						
Ashburys	d	07 46				09 33				10 33		11 03		11 33		12 03		12 34			13 04		13 33
Belle Vue	d																						
Ryder Brow	d																						
Reddish North	d	07 51		08 52			09 39				10 52				11 52								
Brinnington	d	07 54		08 56			09 42				10 56				11 56								
Bredbury	d	07 57		08 59			09 45				10 59				11 59					13 03			
Gorton	d					09 36				10 35		11 05		11 35		12 05					13 06		13 35
Fairfield	d																						
Guide Bridge	a					09 39		10 09		10 39		11 09		11 39		12 09		12 39			13 10		13 39
	d																						
Hyde North	d																						
Hyde Central	d																						
Woodley	d																						
Romiley	d	08 01		09 02			09 48				11 02				12 02					13 06			
Rose Hill Marple	a																						
Marple	d	08 04		09 05			09 52				11 05				12 05					13 09			
Strines	d	08 08		09 09			09 56				11 09				12 09								
New Mills Central	a	08 12		09 13			09 59				11 13				12 13					13 15			
	d	08 12		09 13			09 59				11 13				12 13					13 15			
Stockport 86	d		08 22		09 18				10 23				11 29				12 28		12 55			13 28	
Hazel Grove 86	d																						
Chinley	d	08 21		09 20			10 07				11 20				12 20					13 22			
Edale	d	08 30		09 29			10 16				11 29				12 29					13 31			
Hope (Derbyshire)	d	08 37		09 36			10 23				11 36				12 36					13 37			
Bamford	d	08 41		09 39			10 26				11 39				12 39					13 40			
Hathersage	d	08 45		09 43			10 30				11 43				12 43					13 44			
Grindleford	d	08 49		09 47			10 33				11 47				12 47					13 47			
Dore & Totley	d	08 58		09 55			10 42				11 55				12 55					13 55			
Sheffield 7	a	09 04	09 08	10 02	10 08		10 48		11 05		12 02		12 09		13 02		13 08		13 37	14 02		14 08	

A To Hadfield
B To Cleethorpes
C From Liverpool Lime Street to Norwich
D From Liverpool Lime Street to Nottingham
E To Doncaster
F To Manchester Piccadilly
G To Norwich

Table T078-R

Sundays 28 October to 2 December

Manchester Airport and Manchester Romiley, Marple, Chinley and Sheffield

Station		NT	EM ◇ A	NT B	TP ◇1 C 🚲	NT B	EM ◇ A	NT	NT B	TP ◇1 C 🚲	NT B	EM ◇ A	NT	NT B	TP ◇1 C 🚲	NT B	EM ◇ A	NT	NT B	TP ◇1 C 🚲	NT B	EM ◇ D	NT
Manchester Airport 85	d				13 56					14 56					15 56					16 56			
Manchester Piccadilly 10	a				14 13					15 13					16 13					17 13			
	d	13 42	13 43	13 59	14 19	14 29	14 43	14 45	14 59	15 19	15 29	15 42	15 45	15 59	16 19	16 29	16 42	16 45	16 59	17 19	17 29	17 42	17 45
Ardwick	d																						
Ashburys	d			14 03		14 33			15 03		15 33			16 03		16 33			17 03		17 33		
Belle Vue	d																						
Ryder Brow	d																						
Reddish North	d	13 49						14 52					15 52					16 52					17 52
Brinnington	d	13 53						14 56					15 56					16 56					17 56
Bredbury	d	13 56						14 59					15 59					16 59					17 59
Gorton	d			14 05		14 35			15 05		15 35			16 05		16 35			17 05		17 35		
Fairfield	d																						
Guide Bridge	a			14 09		14 39			15 09		15 39			16 09		16 39			17 09		17 39		
	d																						
Hyde North	d																						
Hyde Central	d																						
Woodley	d																						
Romiley	d	13 59						15 02					16 02					17 02					18 02
Rose Hill Marple	a																						
Marple	d	14 02						15 05					16 05					17 05					18 05
Strines	d	14 06						15 09					16 09					17 09					18 09
New Mills Central	a	14 10						15 13					16 13					17 13					18 13
	d	14 10						15 13					16 13					17 13					18 13
Stockport 86	d		13 51		14 28		14 54			15 28		15 53			16 28		16 54			17 28		17 54	
Hazel Grove 86	d																						
Chinley	d	14 17						15 20					16 20					17 20					18 20
Edale	d	14 26						15 29					16 29					17 29					18 29
Hope (Derbyshire)	d	14 32						15 36					16 36					17 36					18 36
Bamford	d	14 35						15 39					16 39					17 39					18 39
Hathersage	d	14 39						15 43					16 43					17 43					18 43
Grindleford	d	14 42						15 47					16 47					17 47					18 47
Dore & Totley	d	14 50						15 55					16 55					17 55		18 03			18 55
Sheffield 7	a	14 59	14 37		15 08		15 35	16 02		16 08		16 37	17 02		17 08		17 35	18 01		18 09		18 36	19 02

Station		NT B	TP ◇1 C 🚲	NT B	EM ◇ A	NT	NT B	TP ◇1 C	NT B	EM ◇ D	NT	NT B	TP ◇1 C	NT	EM ◇ D	NT B	TP ◇1 C	NT	EM ◇ D	TP ◇1 E	TP ◇1
Manchester Airport 85	d		17 56					18 56					19 56				20 55			21 56	22 56
Manchester Piccadilly 10	a		18 13					19 13					20 13				21 13			22 15	23 11
	d	17 59	18 19	18 29	18 42	18 45	18 59	19 19	19 29	19 42	19 45	19 59	20 18	20 42	20 43	20 59	21 19	21 45	22 11	22 19	23 20
Ardwick	d																				
Ashburys	d	18 03		18 33			19 03		19 33			20 03				21 03					
Belle Vue	d																				
Ryder Brow	d																				
Reddish North	d					18 52					19 52			20 49				21 52			
Brinnington	d					18 56					19 56			20 53				21 56			
Bredbury	d					18 59					19 59			20 56				21 59			
Gorton	d	18 05		18 35			19 05		19 35			20 05				21 05					
Fairfield	d																				
Guide Bridge	a	18 09		18 39			19 09		19 39			20 09				21 09					
	d																				
Hyde North	d																				
Hyde Central	d																				
Woodley	d																				
Romiley	d					19 02					20 02			20 59				22 02			
Rose Hill Marple	a																				
Marple	d					19 05					20 05			21 02				22 05			
Strines	d					19 09					20 09			21 06				22 09			
New Mills Central	a					19 13					20 13			21 10				22 13			
	d					19 13					20 13			21 10				22 13			
Stockport 86	d		18 28		18 53			19 28		19 54			20 28		20 53		21 28		22 30	22 27	23 28
Hazel Grove 86	d																				
Chinley	d					19 20					20 20			21 17				22 20	22 46		
Edale	d					19 29					20 29			21 26				22 29	22 54		
Hope (Derbyshire)	d					19 36					20 36			21 32				22 36	22 59		
Bamford	d					19 39					20 39			21 35				22 39	23 02		
Hathersage	d					19 43					20 43			21 39				22 43	23 05		
Grindleford	d					19 47					20 47			21 42				22 47	23 12		
Dore & Totley	d		19 03			19 55		20 03			20 55		21 03				22 05	22 55	23 18		
Sheffield 7	a		19 09		19 35	20 02		20 09		20 35	21 02		21 09	21 58	21 34		22 11	23 02	23 26	23 09	00 10

A From Liverpool Lime Street to Norwich
B To Hadfield
C To Cleethorpes
D From Liverpool Lime Street to Nottingham
E To Doncaster

Table T078A-F

Mondays to Fridays
21 May to 7 December

Stockport - Reddish South - Denton and Stalybridge

Miles				NT ◇	NT ◇	NT ◇
0	Stockport	84,86	d			
1½	Reddish South		d			
3½	Denton		d			
5	Guide Bridge	78,79	d			
7½	Stalybridge	39	a			
—	Stalybridge		d	06 37	08 39	18 38
—	Guide Bridge		d	06a44	08a44	18a44
—	Denton		d			
—	Reddish South		d			
—	Stockport		a			

No Saturday or Sunday Service

No Southbound Service from Stalybridge - Denton - Stockport

Table T079-F

Mondays to Fridays
21 May to 7 December

Manchester - Glossop and Hadfield

Miles	Miles				NT	NT	NT	NT	NT	NT	NT	NT	NT		NT	NT	NT	NT	NT	NT	NT	NT	NT
0	—	Manchester Picc. 10	78 ⇌	d	05 32	05 52	06 24	06 47	07 07	07 26	07 42	08 02	08 29	and every 30 minutes until	15 29	15 57	16 29	16 41	17 04	17 25	17 40	18 05	18 27
0½	—	Ardwick	78	d																			
1½	—	Ashburys	78	d	05 36	05 56	06 28	06 51	07 11	07 30	07 46	08 06	08 33		15 33	16 01	16 33	16 45	17 11	17 29	17 44	18 09	18 31
2½	—	Gorton	78	d														16 47			17 46		18 33
4¾	—	Guide Bridge	78	d	05 41	06 01	06 33	06 56	07 18	07 35	07 51	08 12	08 38		15 38	16 06	16 38	16 51	17 16	17 34	17 50	18 14	18 37
6¾	—	Flowery Field		d		06 04	06 36	06 59	07 21	07 38	07 55	08 15	08 41		15 41	16 09	16 41	16 54	17 19	17 37	17 54	18 17	18 40
7½	—	Newton for Hyde		d		06 07	06 39	07 02	07 23	07 41	07 57	08 18	08 43		15 43	16 11	16 44	16 56	17 22	17 40	17 57	18 20	18 42
8½	—	Godley		d		06 10	06 41	07 04	07 25	07 43	08 00	08 20	08 45		15 45	16 13	16 46	16 58	17 25	17 42	17 59	18 22	18 44
9	—	Hattersley		d		06 12	06 44	07 07	07 28	07 46	08 02	08 23	08 47		15 47	16 15	16 49	17 00	17 28	17 45	18 02	18 25	18 46
10	—	Broadbottom		d		06 16	06 47	07 10	07 31	07 49	08 05	08 26	08 50		15 50	16 18	16 52	17 02	17 31	17 48	18 05	18 28	18 49
12¼	0	Dinting 3		d		06 22	06 53	07 16	07 37	07 59	08 11	08 34	08 55		15 55	16 25	16 58	17 08	17 37	17 58	18 11	18 34	18 55
13¼	—	Glossop		a		06 25	06 56						08 59		15 59	16 29	17 01	17 12	17 41	18 01	18 15	18 37	18 59
—	—			d		06 28	06 59						09 01		16 01	16 31	17 04	17 18	17 43	18 04	18 18	18 40	19 01
15	0¾	Hadfield		a	05 55	06 34	07 05	07 19	07 40	08 02	08 14	08 37	09 07		16 07	16 37	17 10	17 24	17 49	18 10	18 25	18 46	19 07

			NT		NT	NT	NT	NT	NT
Manchester Picc. 10	78 ⇌	d	18 59	and every 30 minutes until	20 59	21 28	21 58	22 29	23 27
Ardwick	78	d							
Ashburys	78	d	19 03		21 03	21 33	22 02	22 33	23 31
Gorton	78	d					22 04	22 35	23 33
Guide Bridge	78	d	19 08		21 08	21 38	22 08	22 39	23 37
Flowery Field		d	19 11		21 11	21 41	22 11	22 42	23 40
Newton for Hyde		d	19 13		21 13	21 43	22 13	22 44	23 42
Godley		d	19 15		21 15	21 45	22 15	22 46	23 44
Hattersley		d	19 17		21 17	21 47	22 17	22 48	23 46
Broadbottom		d	19 20		21 20	21 50	22 20	22 51	23 48
Dinting 3		d	19 25		21 25	21 55	22 25	22 56	23 54
Glossop		a	19 29		21 29	21 59	22 29	23 00	
		d	19 31		21 31	22 01	22 31	23 02	
Hadfield		a	19 37		21 37	22 07	22 37	23 08	23 56

Saturdays
26 May to 8 December

			NT		NT	NT	NT	NT	NT	NT	NT	NT		NT	NT	NT	NT	NT
Manchester Picc. 10	78 ⇌	d	05 59	and every 30 minutes until	15 29	15 57	16 27	16 59	17 29	17 59	18 27	18 59	and every 30 minutes until	20 59	21 28	21 58	22 29	23 27
Ardwick	78	d																
Ashburys	78	d	06 03		15 33	16 01	16 33	17 03	17 33	18 03	18 31	19 03		21 03	21 33	22 02	22 33	23 31
Gorton	78	d									18 33					22 04	22 35	23 33
Guide Bridge	78	d	06 08		15 38	16 06	16 38	17 08	17 38	18 08	18 37	19 08		21 08	21 38	22 08	22 39	23 37
Flowery Field		d	06 11		15 41	16 09	16 41	17 11	17 41	18 11	18 40	19 11		21 11	21 41	22 11	22 42	23 40
Newton for Hyde		d	06 13		15 43	16 11	16 43	17 13	17 43	18 13	18 42	19 13		21 13	21 43	22 13	22 44	23 42
Godley		d	06 15		15 45	16 13	16 45	17 15	17 45	18 15	18 44	19 15		21 15	21 45	22 15	22 46	23 44
Hattersley		d	06 17		15 47	16 15	16 47	17 17	17 47	18 17	18 46	19 17		21 17	21 47	22 17	22 48	23 46
Broadbottom		d	06 20		15 50	16 18	16 50	17 20	17 50	18 20	18 49	19 20		21 20	21 50	22 20	22 51	23 48
Dinting 3		d	06 25		15 55	16 25	16 55	17 25	17 55	18 25	18 55	19 25		21 25	21 55	22 25	22 56	23 54
Glossop		a	06 29		15 59	16 29	16 59	17 29	17 59	18 29	18 59	19 29		21 29	21 59	22 29	23 00	
		d	06 31		16 01	16 31	17 01	17 31	18 01	18 31	19 01	19 31		21 31	22 01	22 31	23 02	
Hadfield		a	06 37		16 07	16 37	17 07	17 37	18 07	18 37	19 07	19 37		21 37	22 07	22 37	23 08	23 56

Sundays
20 May to 9 September

			NT	NT	NT	NT	NT	NT		NT	NT
Manchester Picc. 10	78 ⇌	d	09 29	09 59	10 29	10 56	11 26	11 59	and every 30 minutes until	19 59	20 59
Ardwick	78	d									
Ashburys	78	d	09 33	10 03	10 33	11 00	11 30	12 03		20 03	21 03
Gorton	78	d	09 36	10 05	10 35	11 03	11 33	12 05		20 05	21 05
Guide Bridge	78	d	09 44	10 09	10 39	11 07	11 39	12 09		20 09	21 09
Flowery Field		d	09 47	10 12	10 42	11 11	11 42	12 12		20 12	21 12
Newton for Hyde		d	09 50	10 14	10 44	11 13	11 44	12 14		20 14	21 14
Godley		d	09 52	10 16	10 46	11 16	11 46	12 16		20 16	21 16
Hattersley		d	09 55	10 18	10 48	11 18	11 48	12 18		20 18	21 18
Broadbottom		d	09 58	10 20	10 50	11 20	11 50	12 20		20 20	21 20
Dinting 3		d	10 04	10 26	10 56	11 26	11 56	12 26		20 26	21 26
Glossop		a		10 29	10 59	11 29	11 59	12 29		20 29	21 29
		d		10 32	11 02	11 32	12 02	12 32		20 32	21 32
Hadfield		a	10 06	10 38	11 08	11 38	12 08	12 38		20 38	21 38

Sundays
16 September to 2 December

			NT	NT	NT	NT	NT	NT	NT	NT	NT		NT	NT
Manchester Picc. 10	78 ⇌	d	09 29	10 01	10 29	10 59	11 29	11 58	12 30	13 00	13 29	and every 30 minutes until	19 59	20 59
Ardwick	78	d												
Ashburys	78	d	09 33		10 33	11 03	11 33	12 03	12 34	13 04	13 33		20 03	21 03
Gorton	78	d	09 36		10 35	11 05	11 35	12 05		13 06	13 35		20 05	21 05
Guide Bridge	78	d	09 44	10 09	10 39	11 09	11 39	12 09	12 39	13 10	13 39		20 09	21 09
Flowery Field		d	09 47		10 42	11 12	11 42	12 12	12 42	13 13	13 42		20 12	21 12
Newton for Hyde		d	09 50	10 13	10 44	11 14	11 44	12 14	12 44	13 15	13 44		20 14	21 14
Godley		d	09 52		10 46	11 16	11 46	12 16	12 46	13 17	13 46		20 16	21 16
Hattersley		d	09 55	10 18	10 48	11 18	11 48	12 18	12 48	13 19	13 48		20 18	21 18
Broadbottom		d	09 58	10 20	10 50	11 20	11 50	12 20	12 50	13 21	13 50		20 20	21 20
Dinting 3		d	10 04	10 26	10 56	11 26	11 56	12 26	12 56	13 27	13 56		20 26	21 26
Glossop		a		10 29	10 59	11 29	11 59	12 29	12 59	13 30	13 59		20 29	21 29
		d		10 32	11 02	11 32	12 02	12 32	13 02	13 33	14 02		20 32	21 32
Hadfield		a	10 06	10 38	11 08	11 38	12 08	12 38	13 08	13 39	14 08		20 38	21 38

Table T079-R

Hadfield and Glossop - Manchester

Mondays to Fridays

21 May to 7 December

Miles	Miles				NT	NT	NT	NT	NT	NT	NT	NT	NT	NT	NT	NT	NT	NT		NT	NT	NT	NT
0	0	**Hadfield**		d	05 45	06 05	06 37	07 08	07 21	07 42	08 04	08 17	08 39	09 10	09 40	10 10	10 40	11 10	and	14 10	14 40	15 10	15 40
1¾	—	**Glossop**		a	05 50	06 11	06 43	07 14	07 27	07 48	08 10	08 23	08 45	09 15	09 45	10 15	10 45	11 15	every 30	14 15	14 45	15 15	15 45
—	—			d	05 53	06 13	06 45	07 16	07 30	07 51	08 13	08 25	08 49	09 18	09 48	10 18	10 48	11 18	minutes	14 18	14 48	15 18	15 48
2¾	0¾	Dinting 3		d	05 56	06 17	06 49	07 20	07 34	07 55	08 17	08 29	08 53	09 21	09 51	10 21	10 51	11 21	until	14 21	14 51	15 21	15 51
5	—	Broadbottom		d	06 00	06 22	06 54	07 25	07 38	07 59	08 21	08 34	08 58	09 25	09 57	10 27	10 57	11 27		14 27	14 57	15 27	15 57
6	—	Hattersley		d	06 03	06 24	06 56	07 27	07 41	08 01	08 24	08 37	09 00	09 28	09 59	10 29	10 59	11 29		14 29	14 59	15 29	15 59
6½	—	Godley		d	06 05	06 27	06 59	07 30	07 43	08 03	08 26	08 39	09 03	09 30	10 01	10 31	11 01	11 31		14 31	15 01	15 31	16 01
7½	—	Newton for Hyde		d	06 07	06 29	07 01	07 32	07 45	08 05	08 28	08 42	09 06	09 32	10 03	10 33	11 03	11 33		14 33	15 03	15 33	16 03
8¾	—	Flowery Field		d	06 09	06 32	07 03	07 34	07 48	08 07	08 31	08 45	09 09	09 34	10 05	10 35	11 05	11 35		14 35	15 05	15 35	16 05
10¼	—	Guide Bridge	78	a	06 12	06 35	07 07	07 38	07 51	08 10	08 34	08 50	09 12	09 37	10 09	10 39	11 11	11 39		14 39	15 09	15 39	16 09
12½	—	Gorton	78	a	06 16				07 55	08 14		08 54											
13½	—	Ashburys	78	a	06 19	06 41	07 13	07 43	07 58	08 17	08 39	08 57	09 19	09 47	10 14	10 44	11 16	11 44		14 44	15 15	15 44	16 14
14½	—	Ardwick	78	a			07 15																
15	—	**Manchester Picc.** 10	78 ⇌	a	06 25	06 47	07 19	07 51	08 04	08 23	08 46	09 03	09 24	09 54	10 25	10 53	11 23	11 53		14 53	15 23	15 53	16 21

			NT	NT	NT	NT	NT	NT	NT	NT	NT	NT	NT	NT	NT	NT	NT	NT	NT
Hadfield		d	16 10	16 40	17 13	17 28	17 52	18 13	18 27	18 49	19 10	19 40	20 10	20 40	21 10	21 40	22 10	22 40	23 59
Glossop		a	16 15	16 45							19 15	19 45	20 15	20 45	21 15	21 45	22 15	22 45	00 04
		d	16 18	16 48							19 18	19 48	20 18	20 48	21 18	21 48	22 18	22 48	
Dinting 3		d	16 21	16 51	17 16	17 30	17 55	18 16	18 30	18 52	19 21	19 51	20 21	20 51	21 21	21 51	22 21	22 51	
Broadbottom		d	16 27	16 57	17 20	17 35	17 59	18 20	18 35	18 56	19 27	19 57	20 27	20 57	21 27	21 57	22 27	22 57	
Hattersley		d	16 29	16 59	17 23	17 37	18 02	18 23	18 37	18 59	19 29	19 59	20 29	20 59	21 29	21 59	22 29	22 59	
Godley		d	16 31	17 01	17 25	17 40	18 05	18 25	18 40	19 01	19 31	20 01	20 31	21 01	21 31	22 01	22 31	23 01	
Newton for Hyde		d	16 33	17 03	17 28	17 42	18 07	18 28	18 42	19 04	19 33	20 03	20 33	21 03	21 33	22 03	22 33	23 03	
Flowery Field		d	16 35	17 05	17 30	17 44	18 10	18 30	18 45	19 06	19 35	20 05	20 35	21 05	21 35	22 05	22 35	23 05	
Guide Bridge	78	a	16 39	17 09	17 34	17 50	18 15	18 34	18 48	19 10	19 39	20 09	20 39	21 09	21 39	22 09	22 38	23 09	
Gorton	78	a												21 12		22 12		23 12	
Ashburys	78	a	16 44	17 14	17 39	17 56	18 20	18 39	18 55	19 15	19 44	20 14	20 44	21 15	21 47	22 15	22 43	23 15	
Ardwick	78	a																	
Manchester Picc. 10	78 ⇌	a	16 53	17 21	17 46	18 01	18 28	18 46	19 01	19 21	19 51	20 21	20 51	21 23	21 54	22 21	22 51	23 22	

Saturdays

26 May to 8 December

			NT	NT	NT	NT		NT	NT	NT	NT	NT	NT		NT	NT	NT	NT	NT	NT	NT	NT
Hadfield		d	05 45	06 10	06 40	07 10	and	08 40	09 10	09 40	10 10	10 40	11 10	and	14 10	14 40	15 10	15 40	16 10	16 40	17 10	17 40
Glossop		a	05 50	06 15	06 45	07 15	every 30	08 45	09 15	09 45	10 15	10 45	11 15	every 30	14 15	14 45	15 15	15 45	16 15	16 45	17 15	17 45
		d	05 53	06 18	06 48	07 18	minutes	08 48	09 18	09 48	10 18	10 48	11 18	minutes	14 18	14 48	15 18	15 48	16 18	16 48	17 18	17 48
Dinting 3		d	05 56	06 21	06 51	07 21	until	08 51	09 21	09 51	10 21	10 51	11 21	until	14 21	14 51	15 21	15 51	16 21	16 51	17 21	17 51
Broadbottom		d	06 00	06 27	06 57	07 27		08 57	09 25	09 57	10 27	10 57	11 27		14 27	14 57	15 27	15 57	16 27	16 57	17 27	17 57
Hattersley		d	06 03	06 29	06 59	07 29		08 59	09 28	09 59	10 29	10 59	11 29		14 29	14 59	15 29	15 59	16 29	16 59	17 29	17 59
Godley		d	06 05	06 31	07 01	07 31		09 01	09 30	10 01	10 31	11 01	11 31		14 31	15 01	15 31	16 01	16 31	17 01	17 31	18 01
Newton for Hyde		d	06 07	06 33	07 03	07 33		09 03	09 32	10 03	10 33	11 03	11 33		14 33	15 03	15 33	16 03	16 33	17 03	17 33	18 03
Flowery Field		d	06 09	06 35	07 05	07 35		09 05	09 34	10 05	10 35	11 05	11 35		14 35	15 05	15 35	16 05	16 35	17 05	17 35	18 05
Guide Bridge	78	a	06 12	06 39	07 09	07 39		09 09	09 37	10 10	10 39	11 11	11 39		14 39	15 09	15 39	16 09	16 39	17 09	17 39	18 09
Gorton	78	a	06 16	06 42	07 12																	
Ashburys	78	a	06 19	06 45	07 15	07 44		09 14	09 47	10 15	10 44	11 16	11 44		14 44	15 15	15 44	16 14	16 44	17 14	17 44	18 15
Ardwick	78	a																				
Manchester Picc. 10	78 ⇌	a	06 25	06 51	07 21	07 51		09 21	09 54	10 23	10 53	11 23	11 53		14 53	15 23	15 53	16 21	16 53	17 21	17 51	18 21

			NT		NT	NT	NT	NT	NT	NT	NT
Hadfield		d	18 10	and	20 10	20 40	21 10	21 40	22 10	22 40	23 59
Glossop		a	18 15	every 30	20 15	20 45	21 15	21 45	22 15	22 45	00 04
		d	18 18	minutes	20 18	20 48	21 18	21 48	22 18	22 48	
Dinting 3		d	18 21	until	20 21	20 51	21 21	21 51	22 21	22 51	
Broadbottom		d	18 27		20 27	20 57	21 27	21 57	22 27	22 57	
Hattersley		d	18 29		20 29	20 59	21 29	21 59	22 29	22 59	
Godley		d	18 31		20 31	21 01	21 31	22 01	22 31	23 01	
Newton for Hyde		d	18 33		20 33	21 03	21 33	22 03	22 33	23 03	
Flowery Field		d	18 35		20 35	21 05	21 35	22 05	22 35	23 05	
Guide Bridge	78	a	18 39		20 39	21 09	21 39	22 09	22 38	23 09	
Gorton	78	a				21 12		22 12		23 12	
Ashburys	78	a	18 44		20 44	21 15	21 47	22 15	22 43	23 15	
Ardwick	78	a									
Manchester Picc. 10	78 ⇌	a	18 51		20 51	21 23	21 54	22 21	22 51	23 22	

Sundays

20 May to 9 September

			NT	NT	NT	NT	NT	NT	NT	NT	NT	NT		NT	NT		NT	NT		NT
Hadfield		d	09 47	10 11	10 41	11 11	11 41	12 11	12 41	13 11	13 42	14 11	and	15 41	16 11	and	17 41	18 11	and	19 41
Glossop		a	09 52	10 16	10 46	11 16	11 46	12 16	12 46	13 16	13 47	14 16	every 30	15 46	16 16	every 30	17 46	18 16	every 30	19 46
		d	09 55	10 19	10 49	11 19	11 49	12 19	12 49	13 19	13 50	14 19	minutes	15 49	16 19	minutes	17 49	18 19	minutes	19 49
Dinting 3		d	09 58	10 22	10 52	11 22	11 52	12 22	12 52	13 22	13 53	14 22	until	15 52	16 22	until	17 52	18 22	until	19 52
Broadbottom		d	10 02	10 26	10 56	11 26	11 56	12 26	12 56	13 26	13 57	14 26		15 56	16 26		17 56	18 26		19 56
Hattersley		d	10 05	10 29	10 59	11 29	11 59	12 29	12 59	13 29	14 00	14 29		15 59	16 29		17 59	18 29		19 59
Godley		d	10 07	10 31	11 01	11 31	12 01	12 31	13 01	13 31	14 02	14 31		16 01	16 31		18 01	18 31		20 01
Newton for Hyde		d	10 09	10 33	11 03	11 33	12 03	12 33	13 03	13 33	14 04	14 33		16 03	16 33		18 03	18 33		20 03
Flowery Field		d	10 11	10 35	11 05	11 35	12 05	12 35	13 05	13 35	14 06	14 35		16 05	16 35		18 05	18 35		20 05
Guide Bridge	78	a	10 14	10 38	11 08	11 38	12 08	12 38	13 08	13 38	14 09	14 38		16 08	16 38		18 08	18 38		20 08
Gorton	78	a	10 17	10 41	11 11	11 41	12 11	12 41	13 11	13 41	14 12	14 41		16 11	16 41		18 11	18 41		20 11
Ashburys	78	a	10 22	10 44	11 14	11 44	12 14	12 44	13 14	13 44	14 15	14 44		16 14	16 44		18 14	18 44		20 14
Ardwick	78	a																		
Manchester Picc. 10	78 ⇌	a	10 28	10 51	11 20	11 52	12 21	12 50	13 21	13 50	14 21	14 50		16 20	16 51		18 21	18 50		20 20

Table T079-R

Hadfield and Glossop - Manchester

Sundays

20 May to 9 September

			NT	NT	NT
Hadfield		d	20 11	20 41	21 41
Glossop		a	20 16	20 46	21 46
		d	20 19	20 49	21 49
Dinting 3		d	20 22	20 52	21 52
Broadbottom		d	20 26	20 56	21 56
Hattersley		d	20 29	20 59	21 59
Godley		d	20 31	21 01	22 01
Newton for Hyde		d	20 33	21 03	22 03
Flowery Field		d	20 35	21 05	22 05
Guide Bridge	78	a	20 38	21 08	22 08
Gorton	78	a	20 41	21 11	22 11
Ashburys	78	a	20 44	21 14	22 14
Ardwick	78	a			
Manchester Picc. 10	78 ⇌	a	20 51	21 20	22 20

Sundays

16 September to 2 December

			NT	NT	NT	NT	NT	NT	NT	NT	NT	NT		NT	NT		NT	NT		NT
Hadfield		d	09 47	10 11	10 41	11 11	11 41	12 11	12 41	13 11	13 42	14 11	and	15 41	16 11	and	17 41	18 11	and	19 41
Glossop		a	09 52	10 16	10 46	11 16	11 46	12 16	12 46	13 16	13 47	14 16	every 30	15 46	16 16	every 30	17 46	18 16	every 30	19 46
		d	09 55	10 19	10 49	11 19	11 49	12 19	12 49	13 19	13 50	14 19	minutes	15 49	16 19	minutes	17 49	18 19	minutes	19 49
Dinting 3		d	09 58	10 22	10 52	11 22	11 52	12 22	12 52	13 22	13 53	14 22	until	15 52	16 22	until	17 52	18 22	until	19 52
Broadbottom		d	10 02	10 26	10 56	11 26	11 56	12 26	12 56	13 26	13 57	14 26		15 56	16 26		17 56	18 26		19 56
Hattersley		d	10 05	10 29	10 59	11 29	11 59	12 29	12 59	13 29	14 00	14 29		15 59	16 29		17 59	18 29		19 59
Godley		d	10 07	10 31	11 01	11 31	12 01	12 31	13 01	13 31	14 02	14 31		16 01	16 31		18 01	18 31		20 01
Newton for Hyde		d	10 09	10 33	11 03	11 33	12 03	12 33	13 03	13 33	14 04	14 33		16 03	16 33		18 03	18 33		20 03
Flowery Field		d	10 11	10 35	11 05	11 35	12 05	12 35	13 05	13 35	14 06	14 35		16 05	16 35		18 05	18 35		20 05
Guide Bridge	78	a	10 14	10 38	11 08	11 38	12 08	12 38	13 08	13 38	14 09	14 38		16 08	16 38		18 08	18 38		20 08
Gorton	78	a	10 17	10 41	11 11	11 41	12 11	12 41	13 11	13 41	14 12	14 41		16 11	16 41		18 11	18 41		20 11
Ashburys	78	a	10 22	10 44	11 14	11 44	12 14	12 44	13 14	13 44	14 15	14 44		16 14	16 44		18 14	18 44		20 14
Ardwick	78	a																		
Manchester Picc. 10	78 ⇌	a	10 28	10 51	11 21	11 51	12 25	12 51	13 21	13 50	14 21	14 50		16 20	16 51		18 21	18 50		20 20

			NT	NT	NT
Hadfield		d	20 11	20 41	21 41
Glossop		a	20 16	20 46	21 46
		d	20 19	20 49	21 49
Dinting 3		d	20 22	20 52	21 52
Broadbottom		d	20 26	20 56	21 56
Hattersley		d	20 29	20 59	21 59
Godley		d	20 31	21 01	22 01
Newton for Hyde		d	20 33	21 03	22 03
Flowery Field		d	20 35	21 05	22 05
Guide Bridge	78	a	20 38	21 08	22 08
Gorton	78	a	20 41	21 11	22 11
Ashburys	78	a	20 44	21 14	22 14
Ardwick	78	a			
Manchester Picc. 10	78 ⇌	a	20 51	21 20	22 20

London and Birmingham - Crewe and Manchester - Chester and North Wales

Miles	Miles		AW MX A	AW MX ◇ B	AW MO ◇ C	AW MO ◇ D	AW MO A	AW MX ◇ B	AW MO ◇ A	AW MX ◇ E	AW		AW MX	NT F	AW	AW	AW	VT ◇■ ⊠	AW ◇ 🛒	AW ◇ 🛒	AW		AW	NT
—	—	London Euston ■ ⊖65 d																						
—	—	Birmingham New Street ■ 65 d																05 30						
—	—	Manchester Airport 84,85 ✈ d																	05 33					
—	—	Cardiff Central ■ 131 d																						
0	—	**Crewe** ■ d				00 01		00 07	00 10	00 15								06 23		06 56			07 11	
—	0	**Manchester Pic'dilly** ■ 90 ⇌ d											00 32						05 47					06 13
—	0½	**Manchester Oxford Road** 90 d																	05 50					
—	16¼	Newton-le-Willows 90 d																	06 08					
—	18	Earlestown ■ 90 d												05 32					06 11					
—	22	Warrington Bank Quay 90 d												05 42					06 21					
—	27	Runcorn East d					00 01							05 50					06 28					
—	30¼	Frodsham d					00 06							05 55					06 33					
—	32¾	Helsby d	00 03				00 10							05a59					06 37					
21	40¼	**Chester** a	00 15			00 22	00 24	00 31	00 34	00 37			01 36					06 43	06 49	07 19			07 35	07 40
—	—	d				00 38				00 40								06 44	06 55	07 21				
29	—	Shotton d																		07 30				
33½	—	Flint d				00 51				00 53								06 57	07 08	07 36				
47½	—	Prestatyn d				01 04				01 06								07 10	07 21	07 49				
51	—	Rhyl d				01 10				01 12								07 16	07 27	07 55				
55¼	—	Abergele & Pensarn d																		08 01				
61½	—	Colwyn Bay d				01 21				01 23								07 27	07 38	08 09				
65½	0	**Llandudno Junction** a				01 27				01 28								07 32	07 43	08 14				
—	—	d				01 28				01 29	05 40				06 13	06 51	07 31	07 33	07 44	08 16	08 19			
—	1¼	Deganwy d									05x43				06x16	06x54	07x34		07x48		08x22			
—	3	**Llandudno** a									05 49				06 23	07 01	07 41		07 56		08 27			
66½	—	Conwy d																		08x18				
70¾	—	Penmaenmawr d			00x02															08x24				
73¼	—	Llanfairfechan d		00x04	00x05															08x28				
80¼	—	**Bangor (Gwynedd)** a		00 13	00 13	01 44				01 46								07 49		08 37				
—	—	d		00 14	00 16	01 44				01 46								07 50		08 38				
84½	—	Llanfairpwll d																		08x45				
93½	—	Bodorgan d																		08x55				
96¼	—	Ty Croes d																		09x00				
98	—	Rhosneigr d																		09x03				
102	—	Valley d																		09x09				
105½	—	**Holyhead** ■ a		00 48	00 51	02 20				02 15								08 20		09 22				

	AW ◇ 🛒	AW ◇ 🛒	NT	AW	AW ■ 🛒	AW ◇ G	VT ◇■ ⊠		NT	AW ◇ D 🛒	AW	AW ◇ 🛒	AW	AW 🛒	NT ◇	VT ◇■ ⊠	AW ◇ 🛒		AW	AW	AW ◇ 🛒	NT ◇	VT ◇■ ⊠	AW ◇ D 🛒
London Euston ■ ⊖65 d							07 10									08 10							09 10	
Birmingham New Street ■ 65 d										07 23														09 25
Manchester Airport 84,85 ✈ d																								
Cardiff Central ■ 131 d		05 08															07 21							
Crewe ■ d				08 23			08 49				09 23		09 40			09 53				10 23			10 49	
Manchester Pic'dilly ■ 90 ⇌ d	06 50		07 09		07 50				07 40			08 52			08 41						09 53	09 41		
Manchester Oxford Road 90 d	06 53				07 54							08 55									09u57			
Newton-le-Willows 90 d	07 09				08 16							09 15									10 16			
Earlestown ■ 90 d	07 13				08 19							09 19									10 21			
Warrington Bank Quay 90 d	07 24				08 26							09 26									10 31			
Runcorn East d	07 31				08 34							09 33									10 39			
Frodsham d	07 36				08 39							09 38									10 44			
Helsby d	07 40				08 43							09 42									10 50			
Chester a	07 52	08 20	08 38	08 46	08 55		09 11		09 11	09 19	09 46	09 54	10 01		10 10	10 13	10 20			10 46	11 02	11 10	11 13	11 20
d	07 55	08 22			08 57					09 23		09 58		10 03		10 16	10 25				11 03		11 16	11 25
Shotton d	08 04	08 32								09 32				10 12			10 34							
Flint d	08 10	08 38			09 10					09 38				10 18		10 29	10 40							11 38
Prestatyn d	08 23	08 52			09 23					09 51				10 31		10 42	10 54				11 28			11 51
Rhyl d	08 29	08 58			09 29					09 57				10 37		10 48	11 00				11 34		11 43	11 57
Abergele & Pensarn d	08 35	09 04								10 03				10 43										12 03
Colwyn Bay d	08 43	09 12			09 40					10 11				10 51		10 59	11 10						11 54	12 11
Llandudno Junction a	08 51	09 17			09 45					10 16		10 35		10 56		11 04	11 15				11 47		12 00	12 16
d		09 18			09 46	09 50				10 18		10 36		10 58		11 06	11 17		11 28		11 49		12 01	12 18
Deganwy d		09x22				09x53				10x21				11x02					11x31					
Llandudno a		09 27				09 58				10 31				11 09					11 38					
Conwy d					09x48												11x19							
Penmaenmawr d					09x55												11x25							
Llanfairfechan d					09x59												11x30							
Bangor (Gwynedd) a					10 09							10 52				11 24	11 39				12 05		12 17	12 33
d					10 09							10 53				11 25	11 40				12 06		12 18	12 36
Llanfairpwll d																	11x47							12x41
Bodorgan d																	11x57							12x51
Ty Croes d																	12x02							12x56
Rhosneigr d																	12x05							12x59
Valley d																	12x11							13x05
Holyhead ■ a					10 37							11 19				11 55	12 23				12 36		12 50	13 17

A From Manchester Piccadilly
B From Cardiff Central
C From Crewe
D From Birmingham International
E From Birmingham New Street
F From Liverpool Lime Street to Ellesmere Port
G From Blaenau Ffestiniog

London and Birmingham - Crewe and Manchester - Chester and North Wales

	AW ◇ A	AW	AW ◇ 🛒		AW	VT ◇■ ⊠	AW ◇ B 🛒	NT ◇	AW	AW ◇ 🛒	NT ◇	VT ◇■ ⊠	AW ◇ C 🛒		AW	AW	AW ◇ 🛒	NT ◇	VT ◇■ ⊠	AW ■ 🛒	AW	AW ◇ 🛒	VT ◇■ ◫	
London Euston ■ ⊖65 d						10 10						11 10							12 10				13 10	
Birmingham New Street ■ 65 d													11 25											
Manchester Airport 84,85 ✈ d			10 37							11 37							12 35					13 37		
Cardiff Central ■ 131 d							09 21													11 21				
Crewe ■ d		11 23				11 49			12 23			12 49				13 23			13 52		14 23		14 49	
Manchester Pic'dilly ■ 90 ⇌ d			10 52					10 41		11 52	11 41						12 52	12 41				13 52		
Manchester Oxford Road 90 d			10 56							11 56							12 55					13 56		
Newton-le-Willows 90 d			11 16							12 16							13 16					14 16		
Earlestown ■ 90 d			11 19							12 20							13 19					14 19		
Warrington Bank Quay 90 d			11 26							12 27							13 27					14 27		
Runcorn East d			11 33							12 34							13 34					14 34		
Frodsham d			11 38							12 39							13 38					14 38		
Helsby d			11 42							12 43							13 42					14 42		
Chester a		11 46	11 54			12 11	12 19	12 19	12 46	12 55	13 10	13 11	13 19			13 46	13 54	14 10	14 13	14 19	14 46	14 54	15 10	
d			11 55				12 23			12 56			13 23				13 56			14 24		14 56		
Shotton d			12 04							13 05							14 05					15 05		
Flint d			12 10				12 36			13 11			13 36				14 11			14 37		15 11		
Prestatyn d			12 24				12 50			13 25			13 49				14 24			14 50		15 24		
Rhyl d			12 30				12 56			13 31			13 55				14 30			14 56		15 30		
Abergele & Pensarn d			12 36							13 37							14 36					15 36		
Colwyn Bay d			12 44				13 06			13 45			14 06				14 44			15 07		15 44		
Llandudno Junction a			12 51				13 11			13 50			14 11				14 49			15 12		15 49		
d	12 35				12 57		13 13			13 52			14 12		14 28		14 51			15 13		15 51		
Deganwy d	12x38				13x00					13x56					14x31		14x54					15x54		
Llandudno a	12 45				13 07					14 04					14 38		15 03					16 03		
Conwy d													14x17											
Penmaenmawr d													14x21											
Llanfairfechan d													14x25											
Bangor (Gwynedd) a							13 29						14 34							15 30				
d							13 31						14 36							15 31				
Llanfairpwll d							13x37													15x37				
Bodorgan d							13x47													15x47				
Ty Croes d							13x51													15x52				
Rhosneigr d							13x54													15x55				
Valley d							14x00													16x01				
Holyhead ■ a							14 14						15 07							16 14				

	NT	AW ◇ A	AW ◇ C 🛒	AW	AW ◇ 🛒	VT ◇■ ◫	NT ◇	AW ◇ 🛒	AW		AW ◇ 🛒	NT	VT ◇■ ◫	AW ◇ C 🛒	AW	AW	AW ◇ A	AW ■ 🛒	VT ◇■ ◫		NT	AW ■ 🛒	AW	AW
London Euston ■ ⊖65 d						14 10							15 10						16 10					
Birmingham New Street ■ 65 d			13 25											15 25										
Manchester Airport 84,85 ✈ d					14 37						15 37													
Cardiff Central ■ 131 d								13 21														15 21		
Crewe ■ d				15 23		15 49			16 23				16 49			17 23			17 49					18 23
Manchester Pic'dilly ■ 90 ⇌ d	13 41				14 52		14 41				15 52	15 41						16 50			16 41		17 15	
Manchester Oxford Road 90 d					14 56						15 56							16u54					17 18	
Newton-le-Willows 90 d					15 16						16 16							17 13					17 35	
Earlestown ■ 90 d					15 19						16 19							17 17					17 39	
Warrington Bank Quay 90 d					15 27						16 26							17 28					17 46	
Runcorn East d					15 34						16 33							17 36					17 54	
Frodsham d					15 38						16 37							17 43					17 59	
Helsby d					15 42						16 41							17 48					18 03	
Chester a	15 10		15 18	15 46	15 54	16 10	16 10	16 23	16 46		16 54	17 10	17 11	17 21		17 46		18 01	18 08		18 10	18 19	18 19	18 46
d			15 24		15 56			16 27			16 55			17 26				18 03	18 10			18 23		
Shotton d					16 05						17 04			17 35								18 32		
Flint d			15 37		16 11			16 40			17 10			17 41					18 23			18 38		
Prestatyn d			15 51		16 24			16 53			17 23			17 54				18 26	18 36			18 52		
Rhyl d			15 57		16 30			16 59			17 29			18 00				18 33	18 42			18 58		
Abergele & Pensarn d					16 36						17 35			18 06								19 04		
Colwyn Bay d			16 07		16 44			17 10			17 43			18 14				18 45	18 53			19 12		
Llandudno Junction a			16 12		16 49			17 15			17 49			18 19				18 50	18 58			19 17		
d		16 05	16 20		16 51			17 15			17 50			18 25	18 26		18 41	18 52	19 00			19 18		
Deganwy d		16x08			16x55						17x54				18x29		18x44	18x57						
Llandudno a		16 17			17 03						18 02				18 36		18 53	19 04						
Conwy d			16x23					17x18						18x28										
Penmaenmawr d			16x30					17x24						18x33										
Llanfairfechan d			16x32					17x28						18x37										
Bangor (Gwynedd) a			16 42					17 37						18 46					19 18			19 34		
d			16 44					17 39						18 47								19 34		
Llanfairpwll d								17x46														19x41		
Bodorgan d								17x56														19x51		
Ty Croes d								18x00														19x56		
Rhosneigr d								18x03														19x59		
Valley d								18x09														20x05		
Holyhead ■ a			17 16					18 21						19 17								20 20		

A From Blaenau Ffestiniog
B From Maesteg
C From Birmingham International

Table T081-F

London and Birmingham - Crewe and Manchester - Chester and North Wales

Mondays to Fridays
21 May to 7 December

	AW	AW	AW	NT	VT	VT	AW	AW	AW	AW BHX	AW	NT	VT	AW	AW	AW	AW	AW	NT	VT	VT	AW
	■		■ A ⊥		◇■ ⊠	◇■ ⊠	◇ B			■ ⊠		◇	◇■ C ⊠	◇	◇ D			■ E ⊥	◇	■ 1 ⊏	■ 1 ⊏	◇ B
London Euston [15] ⊖65 d					17 10	17 10							18 10							19 10	19 10	
Birmingham New Street [12] 65 d							17 25															19 25
Manchester Airport 84,85 ✈ d																						
Cardiff Central [7] 131 d			16 21							17 16								18 21				
Crewe [10] d			18 45		18 57	18 57		19 23					19 56			20 23		20 48		20 55	20 55	
Manchester Pic'dilly [10] 90 ⇌ d	17 52			17 41					18 43			18 41					19 52		19 40			
Manchester Oxford Road 90 d	17 55								18 48								19 55					
Newton-le-Willows 90 d	18 16								19 06								20 16					
Earlestown [8] 90 d	18 19								19 11								20 19					
Warrington Bank Quay 90 d	18 27								19 22								20 26					
Runcorn East d	18 34								19 29								20 33					
Frodsham d	18 39								19 34								20 37					
Helsby d	18 44								19 38								20 41					
Chester a	18 56		19 05	19 09	19 16	19 16	19 23	19 46	19 50	19 57		20 09	20 15			20 46	20 53	21 08	21 10	21 17	21 20	21 23
d	18 57					19 23	19 32			20 02			20 26	20 34							21 25	
Shotton d	19 06						19 41							20 43								
Flint d	19 12					19 36	19 47			20 14				20 49							21 38	
Prestatyn d	19 26					19 49	20 00							21 02							21 51	
Rhyl d	19 32					19 55	20 06			20 31			20 53	21 08							21 58	
Abergele & Pensarn d							20 12							21 14								
Colwyn Bay d	19 42					20 06	20 20			20 44			21 04	21 22							22 09	
Llandudno Junction a	19 47					20 11	20 25			20 49			21 09	21 27							22 14	
d	19 52	19 55				20 13	20 30			20 51	20 58		21 10	21 29	21 32						22 15	
Deganwy d		19x58					20x33				21x01				21x35							
Llandudno a		20 05					20 42				21 08				21 44							
Conwy d	19x54													21x31								
Penmaenmawr d	20x00													21x37								
Llanfairfechan d	20x05													21x41								
Bangor (Gwynedd) a	20 15					20 28				21 06			21 25	21 51							22 30	
d	20 16					20 29				21 07			21 27	21 52							22 32	
Llanfairpwll d														21x58								
Bodorgan d														22x08								
Ty Croes d														22x13								
Rhosneigr d														22x16								
Valley d														22x21								
Holyhead [30] a	20 45					21 00				21 41			21 56	22 35							23 01	

	AW	AW	VT	NT	AW	AW	AW	NT	AW	AW	AW	NT	AW	AW	AW	NT
		◇	◇■ ⊏	◇	◇			◇	◇ F			◇		◇	◇	
London Euston [15] ⊖65 d			20 10													
Birmingham New Street [12] 65 d									21 25						22 52	
Manchester Airport 84,85 ✈ d	20 35						21 32									
Cardiff Central [7] 131 d					19 34									21 17		
Crewe [10] d		21 36	21 49			22 23					23 30			00 07	00 15	
Manchester Pic'dilly [10] 90 ⇌ d	20 50			20 41			21 50	21 40		22 12		22 40	23 14			23 41
Manchester Oxford Road 90 d	20 54						21 53			22 15			23 17			
Newton-le-Willows 90 d	21 11						22 10			22 37			23 35			
Earlestown [8] 90 d	21 14						22 14			22 40			23 38			
Warrington Bank Quay 90 d	21 26						22 23			22 48			23 48			
Runcorn East d	21 33						22 30			22 55			23 55			
Frodsham d	21 37						22 34			23 00			23 59			
Helsby d	21 41						22 38			23 04			00 03			
Chester a	21 55	21 59	22 13	22 13	22 36	22 48	22 50	23 14	23 17	23 17	23 52	00 11	00 15	00 31	00 37	01 07
d		22 04			22 56										00 40	
Shotton d		22 13			23 05											
Flint d		22 19			23 11										00 53	
Prestatyn d		22 32			23 24										01 06	
Rhyl d		22 38			23 30										01 12	
Abergele & Pensarn d		22 44			23 36											
Colwyn Bay d		22 52			23 44										01 23	
Llandudno Junction a		22 57			23 49										01 28	
d		22 59			23 52										01 29	
Deganwy d																
Llandudno a																
Conwy d		23x01			23x54											
Penmaenmawr d		23x07			23x59											
Llanfairfechan d		23x12			00x04											
Bangor (Gwynedd) a		23 21			00 13										01 46	
d		23 22			00 14										01 46	
Llanfairpwll d		23x29														
Bodorgan d		23x39														
Ty Croes d		23x44														
Rhosneigr d		23x47														
Valley d		23x53														
Holyhead [30] a		00 05			00 48										02 15	

A From Swansea
B From Birmingham International
C ⊠ to Chester
D From Blaenau Ffestiniog
E From Llanelli
F From Birmingham International to Manchester Piccadilly

Table T081-F

London and Birmingham - Crewe and Manchester - Chester and North Wales

Saturdays
26 May to 8 December

	AW	AW	AW	AW	AW	AW	NT	AW	AW	VT	AW	AW	AW	NT	AW	AW	AW	AW	NT	AW	AW	NT
	A	◇ B	◇ B	◇ C			D			◇■ ⊏	◇ ⊥	◇ ⊥				◇ ⊥	◇ ⊥				◇ ⊥	
London Euston [15] ⊖65 d																						
Birmingham New Street [12] 65 d										05 30												
Manchester Airport 84,85 ✈ d											05 33											
Cardiff Central [7] 131 d																	05 21					
Crewe [10] d			00 07	00 15						06 23		07 03			07 23					08 23		
Manchester Pic'dilly [10] 90 ⇌ d						00 27					05 48			06 13		06 50			07 08		07 52	07 40
Manchester Oxford Road 90 d											05 52					06 53					07 55	
Newton-le-Willows 90 d											06 08					07 09					08 16	
Earlestown [8] 90 d							05 32				06 11					07 14					08 19	
Warrington Bank Quay 90 d							05 42				06 21					07 23					08 28	
Runcorn East d							05 50				06 28					07 30					08 36	
Frodsham d							05 55				06 33					07 34					08 41	
Helsby d	00 03						05a59				06 37					07 38					08 45	
Chester a	00 15		00 31	00 37		01 31				06 43	06 49	07 23		07 40	07 46	07 50	08 19		08 39	08 46	08 57	09 11
d				00 40						06 44	06 55	07 25				07 55	08 23				08 59	
Shotton d											07 04					08 04					09 08	
Flint d				00 53						06 57	07 10	07 39				08 10	08 37				09 14	
Prestatyn d				01 06						07 10	07 23	07 52				08 23	08 50				09 27	
Rhyl d				01 12						07 16	07 29	07 58				08 29	08 56				09 33	
Abergele & Pensarn d											07 35					08 35					09 39	
Colwyn Bay d				01 23						07 27	07 43	08 09				08 43	09 07				09 47	
Llandudno Junction a				01 28						07 32	07 48	08 14				08 48	09 12				09 52	
d				01 29	06 13			06 51	07 31	07 33	07 50	08 15	08 28			08 50	09 13	09 28			09 54	
Deganwy d					06x16			06x54	07x34		07x54		08x31			08x54		09x31			09x58	
Llandudno a					06 23			07 01	07 41		08 02		08 38			09 02		09 38			10 05	
Conwy d												08x17					09x16					
Penmaenmawr d												08x23					09x22					
Llanfairfechan d		00x04										08x27					09x26					
Bangor (Gwynedd) a		00 13		01 46						07 49		08 36					09 35					
d		00 14		01 46						07 50		08 38					09 37					
Llanfairpwll d												08x44										
Bodorgan d												08x54					09x52					
Ty Croes d												08x59					09x56					
Rhosneigr d												09x02					09x59					
Valley d												09x08										
Holyhead [30] a		00 48		02 15						08 20		09 21					10 15					

	AW	AW	AW	AW	AW	VT	NT	AW	AW	AW	AW	NT	VT	AW	AW	AW	AW	AW	AW	VT	AW	NT
	◇ E	■ F ⊥			◇ ⊥	◇■ ⊏	◇	◇ ⊥			■ ⊥	◇	◇■ ⊏	■ F ⊥			◇ E	■ ⊥		◇■ ⊏	◇ ⊥	◇
London Euston [15] ⊖65 d						08 10							09 10							10 10		
Birmingham New Street [12] 65 d		07 24												09 25								
Manchester Airport 84,85 ✈ d											09 37							10 37				
Cardiff Central [7] 131 d								07 21													09 21	
Crewe [10] d				09 23		09 49				10 23			10 49			11 23				11 56		
Manchester Pic'dilly [10] 90 ⇌ d					08 52		08 41				09 53	09 41						10 53				10 41
Manchester Oxford Road 90 d					08 55						09 56							10 56				
Newton-le-Willows 90 d					09 16						10 16							11 16				
Earlestown [8] 90 d					09 19						10 19							11 19				
Warrington Bank Quay 90 d					09 27						10 27							11 27				
Runcorn East d					09 34						10 34							11 34				
Frodsham d					09 38						10 38							11 38				
Helsby d					09 42						10 42							11 42				
Chester a		09 17		09 46	09 54	10 10	10 10	10 19		10 46	10 54	11 10	11 13	11 21		11 46		11 54		12 17	12 18	12 19
d		09 24			09 56			10 23			10 56		11 16	11 24				11 56			12 23	
Shotton d					10 05						11 05							12 05				
Flint d		09 37			10 11			10 36			11 11			11 39				12 11			12 36	
Prestatyn d		09 50			10 24			10 50			11 24			11 52				12 24			12 50	
Rhyl d		09 56			10 30			10 56			11 30		11 43	11 58				12 30			12 57	
Abergele & Pensarn d					10 36						11 36							12 36				
Colwyn Bay d		10 07			10 44			11 06			11 44		11 54	12 09				12 44			13 09	
Llandudno Junction a		10 12			10 49			11 11			11 49		12 00	12 14				12 49			13 14	
d	10 07	10 13	10 28		10 51			11 13	11 26		11 51		12 01	12 15	12 25		12 35	12 50	12 57		13 15	
Deganwy d	10x10		10x31		10x55				11x29		11x55				12x28		12x38		13x00			
Llandudno a	10 17		10 38		11 02				11 36		12 02				12 35		12 45		13 07			
Conwy d								11x15										12x52				
Penmaenmawr d								11x21										12x58				
Llanfairfechan d								11x26										13x02				
Bangor (Gwynedd) a		10 30						11 35					12 16	12 32				13 15			13 32	
d		10 31						11 36					12 17	12 33							13 33	
Llanfairpwll d		10x38												12x40							13x40	
Bodorgan d														12x50							13x50	
Ty Croes d														12x55							13x55	
Rhosneigr d														12x58							13x58	
Valley d		10x56												13x04							14x04	
Holyhead [30] a		11 05						12 09					12 47	13 12							14 13	

A From Manchester Piccadilly
B From Cardiff Central
C From Birmingham New Street
D From Liverpool Lime Street to Ellesmere Port
E From Blaenau Ffestiniog
F From Birmingham International

London and Birmingham - Crewe and Manchester - Chester and North Wales

		AW		AW ■ ✠	NT ◇	VT ◇■ ☕	AW ◇ A ✠	AW	AW	AW ◇ ✠	NT ◇	VT ◇■ ☕		AW ■ B ✠	AW	AW	AW ◇ ✠	VT ◇■ ☕	NT ◇	AW ◇ C	AW ◇ A ✠	AW		AW	AW ◇ ✠
London Euston 15 ⊖65	d					11 10						12 10						13 10							
Birmingham New Street 12 65	d						11 25														13 25				
Manchester Airport 84,85 ✈	d			11 37						12 37							13 37								14 37
Cardiff Central 7 131	d													11 21											
Crewe 10	d	12 23				12 49			13 23			13 52				14 23		14 49						15 23	
Manchester Pic'dilly 10 90 ⛴	d			11 53	11 41					12 53	12 41						13 53		13 41						14 53
Manchester Oxford Road 90	d			11 56						12 56							13 56								14 56
Newton-le-Willows 90	d			12 16						13 16							14 16								15 16
Earlestown 8 90	d			12 19						13 19							14 19								15 19
Warrington Bank Quay 90	d			12 27						13 27							14 27								15 27
Runcorn East	d			12 34						13 34							14 34								15 34
Frodsham	d			12 38						13 38							14 39								15 38
Helsby	d			12 42						13 42							14 43								15 42
Chester	a	12 46		12 54	13 10	13 11	13 20		13 46	13 54	14 10	14 15		14 19		14 46	14 55	15 09	15 14		15 20			15 46	15 54
	d			12 56			13 25			13 56				14 23			14 56				15 21				15 56
Shotton	d			13 05						14 05							15 05								16 05
Flint	d			13 11			13 38			14 11				14 36			15 11				15 36				16 11
Prestatyn	d			13 24			13 51			14 24				14 50			15 25				15 49				16 24
Rhyl	d			13 30			13 57			14 30				14 57			15 31				15 55				16 30
Abergele & Pensarn	d			13 36						14 36							15 37								16 36
Colwyn Bay	d			13 44			14 08			14 44				15 09			15 45				16 06				16 44
Llandudno Junction	a			13 49			14 13			14 49				15 14			15 50				16 11				16 49
	d			13 51			14 14	14 28		14 51				15 15	15 30		15 51			16 05	16 12	16 26			16 51
Deganwy	d			13x55				14x31		14x55					15x33		15x55			16x08		16x29			16x55
Llandudno	a			14 02				14 38		15 02					15 40		16 03			16 15		16 36			17 02
Conwy	d						14x18														16x18				
Penmaenmawr	d						14x24														16x20				
Llanfairfechan	d						14x28														16x25				
Bangor (Gwynedd)	a						14 37							15 32							16 34				
	d						14 39							15 32							16 35				
Llanfairpwll	d													15x39											
Bodorgan	d													15x49											
Ty Croes	d													15x54											
Rhosneigr	d													15x57											
Valley	d													16x03											
Holyhead 30	a						15 09							16 13							17 12				

		VT ◇■ ☕	NT ◇	AW ◇ B ✠	AW	AW	AW ◇ ✠	VT ◇■ ☕		AW ■ A ✠	AW	NT ◇	AW	AW ◇ C	AW ◇ ✠	VT ◇■ ☕	NT	AW ■ ✠		AW	AW	AW ◇ D	AW ◇ E ✠	VT ◇■ ☕	VT ◇■ ☕
London Euston 15 ⊖65	d	14 10						15 10								16 10								17 10	17 10
Birmingham New Street 12 65	d									15 25															
Manchester Airport 84,85 ✈	d						15 37								16 37							17 37			
Cardiff Central 7 131	d			13 21														15 21							
Crewe 10	d	15 49				16 23		16 49					17 23			17 49					18 23			18 52	18 52
Manchester Pic'dilly 10 90 ⛴	d		14 41				15 53					15 41			16 53		16 41					17 53			
Manchester Oxford Road 90	d						15 56								16 56							17 56			
Newton-le-Willows 90	d						16 16								17 16							18 14			
Earlestown 8 90	d						16 19								17 19							18 17			
Warrington Bank Quay 90	d						16 27								17 27							18 27	18 27		
Runcorn East	d						16 34								17 34							18 34	18 34		
Frodsham	d						16 38								17 38							18 38	18 38		
Helsby	d						16 42								17 42							18 42	18 42		
Chester	a	16 10	16 10	16 23		16 46	16 54	17 11		17 19		17 25	17 46		17 54	18 10	18 10	18 17			18 46	18 54	18 54	19 11	19 11
	d	16 12		16 28			16 56			17 24					17 56	18 16		18 24				18 56	18 56		19 18
Shotton	d						17 05			17 33					18 05			18 33				19 05	19 05		
Flint	d	16 25		16 41			17 11			17 39					18 11	18 29		18 39				19 11	19 11		19 31
Prestatyn	d	16 38		16 54			17 24			17 52					18 24	18 42		18 52				19 24	19 24		19 44
Rhyl	d	16 45		17 00			17 30			17 58					18 30	18 49		18 58				19 30	19 30		19 51
Abergele & Pensarn	d						17 36			18 04					18 36							19 36	19 36		
Colwyn Bay	d	16 56		17 11			17 44			18 12					18 44	19 00		19 09				19 44	19 44		20 02
Llandudno Junction	a	17 01		17 16			17 49			18 17					18 49	19 05		19 14				19 49	19 49		20 07
	d	17 02		17 17	17 28		17 51			18 19	18 26			18 41	18 51	19 06		19 16		19 28		19 51	19 51		20 08
Deganwy	d				17x31		17x55				18x29			18x44	18x56					19x31		19x55	19x55		
Llandudno	a				17 38		18 03				18 36			18 53	19 03					19 38		20 02	20 02		
Conwy	d			17x20						18x22															
Penmaenmawr	d			17x26						18x27															
Llanfairfechan	d			17x30						18x32															
Bangor (Gwynedd)	a	17 17		17 39						18 41						19 21		19 32							20 23
	d	17 19		17 41						18 43						19 23		19 33							20 25
Llanfairpwll	d			17x47														19x40							
Bodorgan	d			17x57														19x50							
Ty Croes	d			18x01														19x55							
Rhosneigr	d			18x04														19x58							
Valley	d			18x10														20x04							
Holyhead 30	a	17 48		18 19						19 13						19 52		20 18							20 54

A From Birmingham International
B From Maesteg
C From Blaenau Ffestiniog
D not 2 June
E 2 June

London and Birmingham - Crewe and Manchester - Chester and North Wales

		NT	AW ◇ A	AW		AW	AW	VT ◇■ ☕	NT ◇	AW ■	AW ◇ B	AW	AW	NT ◇		AW ◇ A	AW ◇	AW	AW	NT	AW ◇	AW 🚌	AW	AW
London Euston 15 ⊖65	d							18 10																
Birmingham New Street 12 65	d		17 25													19 25								
Manchester Airport 84,85 ✈	d						18 37											20 35						
Cardiff Central 7 131	d									17 21											19 34			
Crewe 10	d					19 23		19 49				20 23					21 00		21 36				22 23	
Manchester Pic'dilly 10 90 ⛴	d	17 41					18 53		18 41				19 52	19 40				20 50		20 41				21 51
Manchester Oxford Road 90	d						18 56						19 55					20 53						21 54
Newton-le-Willows 90	d						19 16						20 16					21 11						22 11
Earlestown 8 90	d						19 19						20 20					21 16						22 14
Warrington Bank Quay 90	d						19 27						20 30					21 30						22 24
Runcorn East	d						19 34						20 37					21 37						22 31
Frodsham	d						19 39						20 42					21 41						22 35
Helsby	d						19 43						20 46					21 45						22 39
Chester	a	19 12	19 21			19 46	19 55	20 09	20 09	20 23		20 46	20 58	21 10		21 20	21 21	21 58	22 00	22 09	22 33		22 45	22 54
	d		19 27							20 32							21 26				22 38			
Shotton	d		19 36							20 41							21 35				22 47			
Flint	d		19 42							20 47							21 41				22 53			
Prestatyn	d		19 55							21 00							21 54				23 06			
Rhyl	d		20 01							21 06							22 00				23 12			
Abergele & Pensarn	d		20 07														22 06				23 18			
Colwyn Bay	d		20 15							21 19							22 14				23 26			
Llandudno Junction	a		20 20							21 24							22 19				23 38			
	d		20 27	20 30						21 26	21 32						22 21					23 48		
Deganwy	d			20x33							21x35													
Llandudno	a			20 40							21 44													
Conwy	d		20x30														22x23							
Penmaenmawr	d		20x35														22x30							
Llanfairfechan	d		20x39														22x34							
Bangor (Gwynedd)	a		20 47							21 42							22 43					00 13		
	d		20 48							21 43							22 45					00 13		
Llanfairpwll	d		20x55							21x50														
Bodorgan	d		21x05							22x00														
Ty Croes	d		21x10							22x04														
Rhosneigr	d		21x13							22x07														
Valley	d		21x19							22x13														
Holyhead 30	a		21 31							22 25							23 18					00 48		

		NT	AW	AW ◇ A	AW	NT ◇	AW	AW ◇	NT
London Euston 15 ⊖65	d								
Birmingham New Street 12 65	d			21 25					
Manchester Airport 84,85 ✈	d								
Cardiff Central 7 131	d							20 55	
Crewe 10	d				23 21			23 57	
Manchester Pic'dilly 10 90 ⛴	d	21 37	22 12			22 40	23 14		23 41
Manchester Oxford Road 90	d		22 15				23 17		
Newton-le-Willows 90	d		22 37				23 35		
Earlestown 8 90	d		22 40				23 38		
Warrington Bank Quay 90	d		22 48				23 48		
Runcorn East	d		22 55				23 55		
Frodsham	d		23 00				23 59		
Helsby	d		23 04				00 03		
Chester	a	23 09	23 19	23 22	23 42	00 09	00 15	00 22	01 07
	d								
Shotton	d								
Flint	d								
Prestatyn	d								
Rhyl	d								
Abergele & Pensarn	d								
Colwyn Bay	d								
Llandudno Junction	a								
	d								
Deganwy	d								
Llandudno	a								
Conwy	d								
Penmaenmawr	d								
Llanfairfechan	d								
Bangor (Gwynedd)	a								
	d								
Llanfairpwll	d								
Bodorgan	d								
Ty Croes	d								
Rhosneigr	d								
Valley	d								
Holyhead 30	a								

A From Birmingham International
B From Blaenau Ffestiniog

London and Birmingham - Crewe and Manchester - Chester and North Wales

		AW A	AW B 🚌	AW ◇	AW ◇	AW	AW 🚌	AW ◇ ⊼	AW	AW		NT ◇	AW	AW	VT ◇1 ☕	AW	AW	AW ◇ C	AW ◇ ⊼	AW		AW ⊼	AW	NT ◇	AW
London Euston ■ ⊖65	d																								
Birmingham New Street ■ 65	d																								
Manchester Airport 84,85 ✈	d																								
Cardiff Central ■ 131	d																								
Crewe ■	d				08 27			09 25		09 57					10 42		10 57		11 27				11 55		
Manchester Pic'dilly ■ 90	d						07 18					09 04	09 48									10 52		10 58	
Manchester Oxford Road 90	d						07 33						09 51									10 57			
Newton-le-Willows 90	d						08 03						10 06									11 13			
Earlestown ■ 90	d						08 13						10 09									11 16			
Warrington Bank Quay 90	d						08 38						10 20									11 26			
Runcorn East	d						08 58						10 27									11 33			
Frodsham	d						09 13						10 32									11 38			
Helsby	d	00 03					09 18						10 36									11 42			
Chester	a	00 15			08 49		09 38	09 47		10 20		10 39	10 50		11 02		11 20		11 46			11 54	12 18	12 26	
	d			06 20	09 00			09 48							11 07				12 03						
Shotton	d							09 57											12 12						
Flint	d			06 33	09 13			10 03											12 18						
Prestatyn	d			06 47	09 26			10 17							11 30				12 31						
Rhyl	d			06 53	09 32			10 23							11 37				12 37						
Abergele & Pensarn	d							10 29																	
Colwyn Bay	d			07 03	09 43			10 37							11 48				12 48						
Llandudno Junction	a			07 08	09 47			10 42							11 53				12 53						
	d			07 10	09 54	10 00		10 43	10 50					11 25	11 54	12 00		12 42	12 54	12 58					13 39
Deganwy	d					10x03			10x53					11x28		12x03		12x45		13x01					13x43
Llandudno	a					10 10			11 00					11 35		12 10		12 54		13 08					13 49
Conwy	d							10x45																	
Penmaenmawr	d							10x51																	
Llanfairfechan	d							10x55																	
Bangor (Gwynedd)	a			07 25	10 11			11 03							12 09				13 10						
	d		00 13	07 26	10 12			11 06							12 11				13 11						
Llanfairpwll	d							11x12																	
Bodorgan	d							11x22																	
Ty Croes	d							11x26																	
Rhosneigr	d							11x29																	
Valley	d							11x35																	
Holyhead ■	a		00 48	08 00	10 48			11 49							12 40				13 40						

		AW ◇ ⊼	AW	AW ⊼	AW ◇ D	AW		AW ■ ⊼	AW	AW ⊼	AW	NT ◇	AW	AW ■ ⊼	AW	AW ⊼		AW ◇ D ⊼	AW	AW	AW ■	AW	AW	AW ■ ⊼	AW
London Euston ■ ⊖65	d																								
Birmingham New Street ■ 65	d				11 05													13 24							
Manchester Airport 84,85 ✈	d																								
Cardiff Central ■ 131	d																							13 14	
Crewe ■	d	12 27				12 57		13 27			13 57			14 27					14 57		15 27				
Manchester Pic'dilly ■ 90	d			11 56						12 56		13 06				13 56							14 56		
Manchester Oxford Road 90	d			11 59						12 59						13 59							14 59		
Newton-le-Willows 90	d			12 17						13 17						14 17							15 17		
Earlestown ■ 90	d			12 20						13 23						14 20							15 20		
Warrington Bank Quay 90	d			12 29						13 31						14 27							15 28		
Runcorn East	d			12 36						13 38						14 34							15 35		
Frodsham	d			12 41						13 43						14 39							15 40		
Helsby	d			12 45						13 47						14 43							15 44		
Chester	a	12 52		12 57	13 17	13 20		13 51		13 59	14 20	14 40		14 51		14 55		15 18	15 20		15 49		15 56	16 20	
	d	13 02						14 04						15 02							16 02			16 36	
Shotton	d	13 11						14 13						15 11							16 11			16 45	
Flint	d	13 17						14 19						15 17							16 17			16 51	
Prestatyn	d	13 30						14 32						15 30							16 30			17 04	
Rhyl	d	13 36						14 38						15 36							16 36			17 10	
Abergele & Pensarn	d	13 42						14 44						15 42							16 42			17 16	
Colwyn Bay	d	13 50						14 52						15 50							16 50			17 24	
Llandudno Junction	a	13 55						14 57						15 55							16 55			17 29	
	d	13 57	14 02					14 59	15 02				15 30	15 57	16 04					16 39	16 57	17 05		17 31	17 40
Deganwy	d		14x05						15x05				15x33		16x07					16x42		17x08			17x43
Llandudno	a		14 12						15 12				15 40		16 14					16 49		17 15			17 50
Conwy	d	13x59												15x59										17x33	
Penmaenmawr	d	14x05												16x05										17x39	
Llanfairfechan	d	14x09												16x09										17x43	
Bangor (Gwynedd)	a	14 17						15 14						16 17							17 12			17 52	
	d	14 19						15 16						16 19							17 14			17 54	
Llanfairpwll	d							15x22													17x20			18x00	
Bodorgan	d							15x32													17x30			18x10	
Ty Croes	d							15x36													17x34			18x15	
Rhosneigr	d							15x39													17x37			18x19	
Valley	d							15x45													17x43			18x25	
Holyhead ■	a	14 53						15 55						16 53							17 57			18 37	

A not 20 May. From Manchester Piccadilly
B not 20 May. From Llandudno Junction
C From Blaenau Ffestiniog
D From Birmingham International

Table T081-F

Sundays
20 May to 9 September

London and Birmingham - Crewe and Manchester - Chester and North Wales

		AW		NT ◇	AW ■	AW ◇ A	AW	VT ◇1 ☕	AW ◇ B ⊼	AW	AW ⊼	VT ◇1 ☕		AW ■ ⊼	NT ◇	AW ◇	AW ⊼	AW ◇ C ⊼	VT ◇1 ☕	AW ◇ B ⊼	VT ◇1 ☕	AW		AW	VT ◇1 ☕
London Euston ■ ⊖65	d							15 08				16 08							17 08		17 08				18 08
Birmingham New Street ■ 65	d								15 24									17 24							
Manchester Airport 84,85 ✈	d																								
Cardiff Central ■ 131	d													15 15											
Crewe ■	d	15 57			16 27			16 52		17 27		17 52				18 27			19 01		19 01	19 24			19 52
Manchester Pic'dilly ■ 90	d			15 06			15 56				16 56				17 06		17 56							18 56	
Manchester Oxford Road 90	d						15 59				16 59						17 59							18 59	
Newton-le-Willows 90	d						16 17				17 17						18 17							19 17	
Earlestown ■ 90	d						16 20				17 20						18 20							19 20	
Warrington Bank Quay 90	d						16 27				17 27						18 27							19 30	
Runcorn East	d						16 34				17 34						18 34							19 37	
Frodsham	d						16 39				17 38						18 39							19 41	
Helsby	d						16 43				17 42						18 43			←				19 45	
Chester	a	16 20		16 40	16 49		16 55	17 11	17 26	17 50	17 55	18 12		18 25	18 34	18 49	18 55	19 15	19 19	19 15	19 20	19 47		19 58	20 11
	d				17 02									18 30		18 52		19 38	19 29	19 38					
Shotton	d				17 11									18 39		19 01		→		19 48					
Flint	d				17 17									18 45		19 07			19 42	19 55					
Prestatyn	d				17 30									18 58		19 21			19 55	20 11					
Rhyl	d				17 36									19 04		19 27			20 02	20 17					
Abergele & Pensarn	d				17 42									19 10		19 33				20 23					
Colwyn Bay	d				17 50									19 18		19 41			20 13	20 31					
Llandudno Junction	a				17 55									19 23		19 46			20 18	20 36					
	d				17 57	18 31								19 25		19 47			20 19	20 37					
Deganwy	d					18x34																			
Llandudno	a					18 43																			
Conwy	d				17x59									19x27		19x49				20x40					
Penmaenmawr	d				18x05									19x33		19x55				20x45					
Llanfairfechan	d				18x09									19x38		19x59				20x49					
Bangor (Gwynedd)	a				18 17									19 48		20 07			20 34	20 57					
	d				18 19									19 49		20 09			20 36	20 59					
Llanfairpwll	d																								
Bodorgan	d																								
Ty Croes	d																								
Rhosneigr	d																								
Valley	d																								
Holyhead ■	a				18 54									20 18		20 44			21 03	21 34					

		VT ◇1 ☕	NT ◇	AW	AW	VT ◇1 ☕	AW ◇ B	AW ◇		AW	AW	NT ◇	AW ◇	AW	AW ◇ B	AW	AW	AW ◇ B		AW	AW ◇ D				
London Euston ■ ⊖65	d	18 08				19 08																			
Birmingham New Street ■ 65	d						19 24								21 24			22 55							
Manchester Airport 84,85 ✈	d																								
Cardiff Central ■ 131	d																				21 12				
Crewe ■	d	19 52		20 27		20 55		21 28			21 57		22 29		23 06		23 38	00 01			00 10				
Manchester Pic'dilly ■ 90	d		19 06		19 56					20 56		21 06		21 56		22 56				23 25					
Manchester Oxford Road 90	d				19 59					20 59				21 59		22 59				23 28					
Newton-le-Willows 90	d				20 16					21 17				22 17		23 20				23 45					
Earlestown ■ 90	d				20 19					21 19				22 20		23 23				23 47					
Warrington Bank Quay 90	d				20 31					21 28				22 26		23 30				23 54					
Runcorn East	d				20 38					21 35				22 33		23 37				00 01					
Frodsham	d				20 43					21 39				22 38		23 41				00 06					
Helsby	d				20 47					21 43				22 42		23 45				00 10					
Chester	a	20 13	20 34	20 50	20 59	21 13	21 20	21 51		21 56	22 20	22 36	22 52	22 54	23 31	23 57	00 01	00 22		00 24	00 34				
	d	20 18				21 17		22 01					23 02					00 38							
Shotton	d							22 10					23 11												
Flint	d	20 31				21 30		22 16					23 17					00 51							
Prestatyn	d	20 44				21 43		22 29					23 30					01 04							
Rhyl	d	20 51				21 50		22 35					23 36					01 10							
Abergele & Pensarn	d							22 41																	
Colwyn Bay	d	21 02				22 01		22 49					23 47					01 21							
Llandudno Junction	a	21 07				22 06		22 54					23 52					01 27							
	d	21 08				22 07		22 56					23 53					01 28							
Deganwy	d																								
Llandudno	a																								
Conwy	d												23x55												
Penmaenmawr	d												00x02												
Llanfairfechan	d												00x05												
Bangor (Gwynedd)	a	21 23				22 22		23 11					00 13					01 44							
	d	21 25				22 24		23 13					00 16					01 44							
Llanfairpwll	d							23x19																	
Bodorgan	d							23x29																	
Ty Croes	d							23x33																	
Rhosneigr	d							23x36																	
Valley	d							23x42																	
Holyhead ■	a	21 54				22 53		23 55					00 51					02 20							

A From Blaenau Ffestiniog
B From Birmingham International
C From Birmingham International to Holyhead
D From Manchester Piccadilly

Table T081-F

Sundays

16 September to 2 December

London and Birmingham - Crewe and Manchester - Chester and North Wales

		AW	AW	AW	AW	AW	NT	AW	VT	AW	AW	AW
		A	B 🚌	🚌	◇ 🚲		◇		◇1 🛒		◇ 🚲	🚲
London Euston ⊖65	d											
Birmingham New Street 65	d											
Manchester Airport 84,85 ✈	d											
Cardiff Central 131	d											
Crewe	d				09 25	10 07			10 42	11 05	11 27	
Manchester Pic'dilly 90 ⇌	d			07 18			09 04	09 48				10 52
Manchester Oxford Road 90	d			07 33				09 51				10 57
Newton-le-Willows 90	d			08 03				10 06				11 13
Earlestown 90	d			08 13				10 09				11 16
Warrington Bank Quay 90	d			08 38				10 20				11 26
Runcorn East	d			08 58				10 27				11 33
Frodsham	d			09 13				10 32				11 38
Helsby	d	00 03		09 18				10 36				11 42
Chester	a	00 15		09 38	09 47	10 30	10 39	10 50	11 02	11 30	11 46	11 54
	d				09 48				11 07		12 03	
Shotton	d				09 57						12 12	
Flint	d				10 03						12 18	
Prestatyn	d				10 17				11 30		12 31	
Rhyl	d				10 23				11 37		12 37	
Abergele & Pensarn	d				10 29							
Colwyn Bay	d				10 37				11 48		12 48	
Llandudno Junction	a				10 42				11 53		12 53	
	d				10 43				11 54		12 54	
Deganwy	d											
Llandudno	a											
Conwy	d				10x45							
Penmaenmawr	d				10x51							
Llanfairfechan	d				10x55							
Bangor (Gwynedd)	a				11 03				12 09		13 10	
	d		00 13		11 06				12 11		13 11	
Llanfairpwll	d				11x12							
Bodorgan	d				11x22							
Ty Croes	d				11x26							
Rhosneigr	d				11x29							
Valley	d				11x35							
Holyhead	a		00 48		11 49				12 40		13 40	

		AW	NT	AW	AW	AW	AW	AW	AW	AW	NT	AW
			◇	◇ 🚲	🚲	◇ C		▪ 🚲	🚲		◇	▪ 🚲
London Euston ⊖65	d											
Birmingham New Street 65	d					11 05						
Manchester Airport 84,85 ✈	d											
Cardiff Central 131	d											
Crewe	d	11 55		12 27			12 54	13 27		13 57		14 27
Manchester Pic'dilly 90 ⇌	d		10 58		11 56				12 56		13 06	
Manchester Oxford Road 90	d				11 59				12 59			
Newton-le-Willows 90	d				12 17				13 17			
Earlestown 90	d				12 20				13 23			
Warrington Bank Quay 90	d				12 29				13 31			
Runcorn East	d				12 36				13 38			
Frodsham	d				12 41				13 43			
Helsby	d				12 45				13 47			
Chester	a	12 18	12 26	12 52	12 57	13 17	13 17	13 51	13 59	14 20	14 40	14 51
	d			13 02				14 04				15 02
Shotton	d			13 11				14 13				15 11
Flint	d			13 17				14 19				15 17
Prestatyn	d			13 30				14 32				15 30
Rhyl	d			13 36				14 38				15 36
Abergele & Pensarn	d			13 42				14 44				15 42
Colwyn Bay	d			13 50				14 52				15 50
Llandudno Junction	a			13 55				14 57				15 55
	d			13 57				14 59				15 57
Deganwy	d											
Llandudno	a											
Conwy	d			13x59								15x59
Penmaenmawr	d			14x05								16x05
Llanfairfechan	d			14x09								16x09
Bangor (Gwynedd)	a			14 17				15 14				16 17
	d			14 19				15 16				16 19
Llanfairpwll	d							15x22				
Bodorgan	d							15x32				
Ty Croes	d							15x36				
Rhosneigr	d							15x39				
Valley	d							15x45				
Holyhead	a			14 53				15 55				16 53

		AW	AW	AW	AW	AW	AW	NT	AW	AW	VT	AW
		🚲	◇ C 🚲		▪		▪ 🚲	◇	▪		◇1 🛒	◇ C 🚲
London Euston ⊖65	d										15 08	
Birmingham New Street 65	d		13 24									15 24
Manchester Airport 84,85 ✈	d											
Cardiff Central 131	d						13 14					
Crewe	d			14 57	15 27				16 27		16 52	
Manchester Pic'dilly 90 ⇌	d	13 56				14 56		15 06		15 56		
Manchester Oxford Road 90	d	13 59				14 59				15 59		
Newton-le-Willows 90	d	14 17				15 17				16 17		
Earlestown 90	d	14 20				15 20				16 20		
Warrington Bank Quay 90	d	14 27				15 28				16 27		
Runcorn East	d	14 34				15 35				16 34		
Frodsham	d	14 39				15 40				16 39		
Helsby	d	14 43				15 44				16 43		
Chester	a	14 55	15 18	15 20	15 49	15 56	16 20	16 40	16 49	16 55	17 11	17 26
	d				16 02		16 36		17 02			
Shotton	d				16 11		16 45		17 11			
Flint	d				16 17		16 51		17 17			
Prestatyn	d				16 30		17 04		17 30			
Rhyl	d				16 36		17 10		17 36			
Abergele & Pensarn	d				16 42		17 16		17 42			
Colwyn Bay	d				16 50		17 24		17 50			
Llandudno Junction	a				16 55		17 29		17 55			
	d				16 57		17 31		17 57			
Deganwy	d											
Llandudno	a											
Conwy	d						17x33		17x59			
Penmaenmawr	d						17x39		18x05			
Llanfairfechan	d						17x43		18x09			
Bangor (Gwynedd)	a				17 12		17 52		18 17			
	d				17 14		17 54		18 19			
Llanfairpwll	d				17x20		18x00					
Bodorgan	d				17x30		18x10					
Ty Croes	d				17x34		18x15					
Rhosneigr	d				17x37		18x19					
Valley	d				17x43		18x25					
Holyhead	a				17 57		18 37		18 54			

		AW	AW	VT	AW	NT	AW	AW	AW	VT	AW	VT
		▪	🚲	◇1 🛒	▪ 🚲	◇	◇	🚲	◇ D 🚲	◇1 🛒	◇ C 🚲	◇1 🛒
London Euston ⊖65	d			16 08						17 08		17 08
Birmingham New Street 65	d								17 24			
Manchester Airport 84,85 ✈	d											
Cardiff Central 131	d				15 15							
Crewe	d	17 27		17 52			18 27			19 01		19 01
Manchester Pic'dilly 90 ⇌	d		16 56			17 06		17 56				
Manchester Oxford Road 90	d		16 59					17 59				
Newton-le-Willows 90	d		17 17					18 17				
Earlestown 90	d		17 20					18 20				
Warrington Bank Quay 90	d		17 27					18 27				
Runcorn East	d		17 34					18 34				
Frodsham	d		17 38					18 39				
Helsby	d		17 42					18 43			←	
Chester	a	17 49	17 55	18 12	18 25	18 34	18 49	18 55	19 15	19 19	19 15	19 20
	d	18 02			18 30		18 52		19 38	19 29	19 38	
Shotton	d	18 11			18 39		19 01		→		19 48	
Flint	d	18 17			18 45		19 07			19 42	19 55	
Prestatyn	d	18 30			18 58		19 21			19 55	20 11	
Rhyl	d	18 36			19 04		19 27			20 02	20 17	
Abergele & Pensarn	d	18 42			19 10		19 33				20 23	
Colwyn Bay	d	18 50			19 18		19 41			20 13	20 31	
Llandudno Junction	a	18 55			19 23		19 46			20 18	20 36	
	d	18 57			19 25		19 47			20 19	20 37	
Deganwy	d											
Llandudno	a											
Conwy	d				19x27		19x49				20x40	
Penmaenmawr	d				19x33		19x55				20x45	
Llanfairfechan	d				19x38		19x59				20x49	
Bangor (Gwynedd)	a	19 12			19 48		20 07			20 34	20 57	
	d	19 14			19 49		20 09			20 36	20 59	
Llanfairpwll	d	19x20										
Bodorgan	d	19x30										
Ty Croes	d	19x34										
Rhosneigr	d	19x37										
Valley	d	19x43										
Holyhead	a	19 54			20 18		20 44			21 03	21 34	

A From Manchester Piccadilly
B From Llandudno Junction
C From Birmingham International
D From Birmingham International to Holyhead

Table T081-F

Sundays

16 September to 2 December

London and Birmingham - Crewe and Manchester - Chester and North Wales

		AW	AW	VT	VT	NT	AW	AW	VT	AW	AW
				◇1 🛒	◇1 🛒	◇			◇1 🛒	◇ A	◇
London Euston ⊖65	d			18 08	18 08				19 08		
Birmingham New Street 65	d									19 24	
Manchester Airport 84,85 ✈	d										
Cardiff Central 131	d										
Crewe	d	19 26		19 52	19 52		20 27		20 55		21 28
Manchester Pic'dilly 90 ⇌	d		18 56			19 06		19 56			
Manchester Oxford Road 90	d		18 59					19 59			
Newton-le-Willows 90	d		19 17					20 16			
Earlestown 90	d		19 20					20 19			
Warrington Bank Quay 90	d		19 30					20 31			
Runcorn East	d		19 37					20 38			
Frodsham	d		19 41					20 43			
Helsby	d		19 45					20 47			
Chester	a	19 47	19 58	20 11	20 13	20 34	20 50	20 59	21 13	21 20	21 51
	d				20 18				21 17		22 01
Shotton	d										22 10
Flint	d				20 31				21 30		22 16
Prestatyn	d				20 44				21 43		22 29
Rhyl	d				20 51				21 50		22 35
Abergele & Pensarn	d										22 41
Colwyn Bay	d				21 02				22 01		22 49
Llandudno Junction	a				21 07				22 06		22 54
	d				21 08				22 07		22 56
Deganwy	d										
Llandudno	a										
Conwy	d										
Penmaenmawr	d										
Llanfairfechan	d										
Bangor (Gwynedd)	a				21 23				22 22		23 11
	d				21 25				22 24		23 13
Llanfairpwll	d										23x19
Bodorgan	d										23x29
Ty Croes	d										23x33
Rhosneigr	d										23x36
Valley	d										23x42
Holyhead	a				21 54				22 53		23 55

		AW	AW	NT	AW	AW	AW	AW	AW	AW	AW	AW
				◇	◇		◇ A			◇ A		◇ B
London Euston ⊖65	d											
Birmingham New Street 65	d						21 24			22 55		
Manchester Airport 84,85 ✈	d											
Cardiff Central 131	d											21 12
Crewe	d		22 03		22 29		23 06		23 38	00 01		00 10
Manchester Pic'dilly 90 ⇌	d	20 56		21 06		21 56		22 56			23 25	
Manchester Oxford Road 90	d	20 59				21 59		22 59			23 28	
Newton-le-Willows 90	d	21 17				22 17		23 20			23 45	
Earlestown 90	d	21 19				22 20		23 23			23 47	
Warrington Bank Quay 90	d	21 28				22 26		23 30			23 54	
Runcorn East	d	21 35				22 33		23 37			00 01	
Frodsham	d	21 39				22 38		23 41			00 06	
Helsby	d	21 43				22 42		23 45			00 10	
Chester	a	21 56	22 26	22 36	22 52	22 54	23 31	23 57	00 01	00 22	00 24	00 34
	d				23 02					00 38		
Shotton	d				23 11							
Flint	d				23 17					00 51		
Prestatyn	d				23 30					01 04		
Rhyl	d				23 36					01 10		
Abergele & Pensarn	d											
Colwyn Bay	d				23 47					01 21		
Llandudno Junction	a				23 52					01 27		
	d				23 53					01 28		
Deganwy	d											
Llandudno	a											
Conwy	d				23x55							
Penmaenmawr	d				00x02							
Llanfairfechan	d				00x05							
Bangor (Gwynedd)	a				00 13					01 44		
	d				00 16					01 44		
Llanfairpwll	d											
Bodorgan	d											
Ty Croes	d											
Rhosneigr	d											
Valley	d											
Holyhead	a				00 51					02 20		

A From Birmingham International
B From Manchester Piccadilly

North Wales and Chester - Manchester and Crewe - Birmingham and London

Miles	Miles		AW	AW	AW	AW	AW	AW	AW	NT	AW	VT	AW	AW	AW	NT	NT	AW	AW BHX	VT	VT	AW
						◇ A					◇ 🛒	◇1 ⊠	◇				B	◇ 🛒	■ ⊠	◇1 C ⊠	◇1 ⊠	◇ 🛒
0	—	**Holyhead** d									04 25	04 48						05 14	05 34		05 51	
3½	—	Valley d									04x31											
7½	—	Rhosneigr d																				
9¾	—	Ty Croes d																				
12	—	Bodorgan d																				
21	—	Llanfairpwll d									04x48							05x35				
24¾	—	**Bangor (Gwynedd)** a									04 55	05 14						05 43	06 01		06 17	
—	—	d									04 57	05 14						05 44	06 02		06 18	
32¼	—	Llanfairfechan d																05x51				
34¾	—	Penmaenmawr d																05x55				
39	—	Conwy d																06x01				
—	0	**Llandudno** d												05 54								
—	1¾	Deganwy d												05x58								
40	3	**Llandudno Junction** a									05 13	05 32		06 02				06 05	06 19		06 35	
—	—	d					04 38				05 15	05 32	05 46					06 07	06 20		06 36	
44	—	Colwyn Bay d					04 44				05 21	05 38	05 52					06 13	06 28		06 42	
50¼	—	Abergele & Pensarn d					04 51											06 20				
54½	—	Rhyl d					04 57				05 31	05 49	06 02					06 26	06 39		06 53	
58	—	Prestatyn d					05 02				05 37		06 08					06 31			06 58	
72	—	Flint d					05 16				05 50		06 21					06 45	06 56		07 12	
76¼	—	Shotton d					05 22						06 27					06 51				
84¼	0	**Chester** a					05 34				06 06	06 17	06 39					07 03	07 11		07 26	
—	—	d	03 34	04 22	04 55	05 35	05 37	05 38	05 51	05 58	06 18	06 26	06 41		06 45	06 51		07 12	07 16	07 35	07 35	07 38
—	7½	Helsby d						05 47					06 50				07 04	07 21				07 49
—	10	Frodsham d						05 51					06 55				07 09	07 25				07 54
—	13¾	Runcorn East d						05 56					07 00				07 14	07 31				08 00
—	18¾	Warrington Bank Quay 90 a						06 05					07 10				07 21	07 39				08 08
—	22¾	Earlestown 90 a						06 13					07 18					07 47				08 21
—	24	Newton-le-Willows 90 a						06 15					07 20					07 49				08 25
—	39¾	**Manchester Oxford Road** 90 a						06 34					07 42					08 07				08s48
—	40¾	**Manchester Pic'dilly** 90 ⇌ a	04 42					06 43		07 32			07 50			08 18		08 12				08 53
105½	—	**Crewe** a		04 44	05 20		05 58		06 15			06 47			07 06					07 54	07 54	
—	—	Cardiff Central 131 a									09 19								09 58			
—	—	Manchester Airport 84,85 ✈ a	05 04																			
—	—	Birmingham New Street 65 a		06 09		07 30																
—	—	London Euston ⊖65 a										08 34								09 41	09 41	

	AW	NT	AW	AW	VT	AW	AW	AW	NT	AW	AW	VT	AW	AW	NT	AW	VT	AW	AW	AW	NT	VT
	◇			◇ 🛒	◇1 ⊠	◇ 🛒			◇	◇	■ 🛒	◇1 ⊠	◇ 🛒		◇	◇ 🛒	◇1 ⊠	◇ 🛒	◇ D		◇	◇1 ⊒
Holyhead d				06 28	06 55					07 15						08 05	08 55					
Valley d				06x34						07x21						08x11						
Rhosneigr d				06x40						07x26						08x17						
Ty Croes d				06x43						07x30						08x20						
Bodorgan d				06x48						07x34						08x25						
Llanfairpwll d				06x57						07x44						08x34						
Bangor (Gwynedd) a				07 05	07 21					07 52						08 42	09 21					
d				07 06	07 22					08 02						09 02	09 22					
Llanfairfechan d										08x09						09x09						
Penmaenmawr d										08x13						09x13						
Conwy d										08x19						09x19						
Llandudno d	06 46		07 08			07 45	08 02				08 30							09 45	10 08			
Deganwy d	06x50		07x12			07x49	08x06				08x34							09x49	10x12			
Llandudno Junction a	06 55		07 18	07 22	07 39	07 53	08 12			08 23	08 38					09 23	09 39	09 53	10 18			
d	06 57			07 25	07 40	07 54				08 25	08 39		08 54			09 25	09 40	09 54				
Colwyn Bay d	07 03			07 31	07 47	08 00				08 31	08 45		09 00			09 31	09 47	10 00				
Abergele & Pensarn d	07 10					08 07							09 07					10 07				
Rhyl d	07 16			07 41	07 58	08 13				08 41	08 56		09 13			09 41	09 58	10 13				
Prestatyn d	07 22			07 47	08 04	08 19				08 47			09 19			09 47	10 04	10 19				
Flint d	07 36			08 00	08 17	08 32				09 00			09 32			10 00	10 17	10 32				
Shotton d	07 42					08 38							09 38					10 38				
Chester a	07 54			08 16	08 31	08 50				09 15	09 24		09 50			10 16	10 31	10 50				
d	07 55	07 58		08 19	08 35	08 52		08 55	09 00	09 17	09 27	09 35	09 52	09 55	10 02	10 21	10 35	10 52		10 55	11 02	11 35
Helsby d						09 01							10 01					11 01				
Frodsham d						09 05							10 05					11 05				
Runcorn East d						09 11							10 11					11 11				
Warrington Bank Quay 90 a						09 18							10 18					11 18				
Earlestown 90 a						09 28							10 28					11 28				
Newton-le-Willows 90 a						09 30							10 30					11 30				
Manchester Oxford Road 90 a						09 48							10 48					11 48				
Manchester Pic'dilly 90 ⇌ a		09 31				09 53			10 30				10 53		11 30			11 53			12 30	
Crewe a	08 19				08 54			09 18		09 37		09 54		10 18			10 54			11 18		11 54
Cardiff Central 131 a				11 15							12 10					13 20						
Manchester Airport 84,85 ✈ a						10 19							11 19					12 20				
Birmingham New Street 65 a																						
London Euston ⊖65 a					10 37							11 37					12 37					13 37

A To Birmingham International
B From Ellesmere Port
C From Wrexham General
D To Blaenau Ffestiniog

Table T081-R

Mondays to Fridays

21 May to 7 December

North Wales and Chester - Manchester and Crewe - Birmingham and London

	AW	AW	AW	AW	NT	AW	VT	AW	AW	NT	AW	VT	AW	AW	AW	AW	NT	AW	VT	VT	AW
	◇ A 🛒	◇ 🛒			◇	■ B 🛒	◇1 ⊒	◇ 🛒	🛒	◇	◇ A 🛒	◇1 ⊒	◇ 🛒		◇ C		◇	■ D 🛒	◇1 ⊒	◇1 ⊒	◇ 🛒
Holyhead d	09 23					10 41					11 27							12 32		12 53	13 05
Valley d	09x29										11x33										
Rhosneigr d	09x34																	12x42			
Ty Croes d	09x38																	12x46			
Bodorgan d	09x42																	12x50			
Llanfairpwll d	09x52										11x51										
Bangor (Gwynedd) a	10 00					11 06					11 59							13 05		13 19	13 31
d	10 02					11 07					12 00							13 07		13 21	13 32
Llanfairfechan d	10x09										12x07										
Penmaenmawr d	10x13										12x11										
Conwy d	10x19										12x17										
Llandudno d		10 44	11 12					11 44						12 46	13 08						
Deganwy d		10x48	11x16					11x48						12x50	13x12						
Llandudno Junction a	10 23	10 52	11 20			11 23		11 52			12 22			12 56	13 18			13 23		13 37	13 49
d	10 25	10 53				11 25		11 53			12 23		12 53					13 25		13 39	13 50
Colwyn Bay d	10 31	10 59				11 31		11 59			12 29		12 59					13 31		13 45	13 58
Abergele & Pensarn d		11 06						12 06					13 06								14 05
Rhyl d	10 41	11 12				11 41		12 12			12 40		13 12					13 41		13 56	14 12
Prestatyn d	10 47	11 18				11 47		12 18			12 45		13 18					13 47		14 01	14 18
Flint d	11 00	11 31				12 00		12 31			12 59		13 31					14 00		14 15	14 31
Shotton d		11 37						12 37					13 37								
Chester a	11 16	11 49				12 15		12 49			13 14		13 49					14 16		14 28	14 46
d	11 36	11 52		11 55	11 55	12 19	12 35	12 52	12 55	13 02	13 30	13 35	13 51			13 55	14 02	14 20	14 35	14 35	14 48
Helsby d		12 01						13 01					14 00								14 58
Frodsham d		12 06						13 05					14 04								15 03
Runcorn East d		12 11						13 11					14 10								15 08
Warrington Bank Quay 90 a		12 20						13 18					14 19								15 18
Earlestown 90 a		12 28						13 28					14 28								15 29
Newton-le-Willows 90 a		12 30						13 30					14 31								
Manchester Oxford Road 90 a		12 48						13 48					14 48								
Manchester Pic'dilly 90 ⇌ a		12 53			13 30			13 53		14 30			14 53				15 30				15 54
Crewe a				12 18			12 54		13 18			13 54				14 18			14 54	14 54	
Cardiff Central 131 a						15 10												17 16			
Manchester Airport 84,85 ✈ a		13 20						14 19					15 19								
Birmingham New Street 65 a	13 29										15 30										
London Euston ⊖65 a							14 38					15 36							16 37	16 37	

	AW	AW	NT	AW	VT	AW	AW	AW	NT	AW	AW	VT	AW	NT	AW	AW	AW	AW	VT	AW	NT	AW
			◇	■ A 🛒	◇1 ⊒	■ E 🛒	◇ 🛒		◇	◇ 🛒	◇ 🛒	◇1 ⊒			■	🛒	◇ C	◇ A 🛒	◇1 ⊠			◇ 🛒
Holyhead d				13 24	13 58						14 36							15 47				
Valley d				13x30														15x53				
Rhosneigr d				13x36														15x58				
Ty Croes d				13x40														16x02				
Bodorgan d				13x44														16x06				
Llanfairpwll d				13x55														16x16				
Bangor (Gwynedd) a				14 03	14 24						15 02							16 24				
d				14 04	14 25						15 04							16 26				
Llanfairfechan d				14x12							15x11							16x33				
Penmaenmawr d				14x16							15x15							16x37				
Conwy d				14x23							15x21							16x43				
Llandudno d	14 08						14 40			15 08					16 07		16 20					17 07
Deganwy d	14x12						14x44			15x12					16x11		16x24					17x11
Llandudno Junction a	14 18			14 27	14 42		14 48			15 16	15 25				16 15		16 28	16 47				17 15
d				14 29	14 43		14 49			15 17	15 27				16 16	16 25		16 49				17 17
Colwyn Bay d				14 35	14 50		14 55			15 23	15 33				16 22	16 31						17 23
Abergele & Pensarn d							15 02			15 30					16 29							17 29
Rhyl d				14 45	15 00		15 08			15 36	15 43				16 35	16 43						17 35
Prestatyn d				14 51			15 14			15 42	15 49				16 40	16 48						17 41
Flint d				15 04			15 27			15 55	16 00				16 54	17 02						17 54
Shotton d				15 10		←	15 33			16 01					17 00							18 00
Chester a				15 24	15 28	15 24	15 45			16 14	16 18				17 15	17 17		17 29				18 14
d		14 55	15 02	15 36	15 35	15 36	15 49	15 55	16 02	16 20	16 22	16 35	16 55	17 02	17 20			17 34	17 35	17 55	18 01	18 16
Helsby d				→			15 58			16 30					17 29							18 25
Frodsham d							16 03			16 34					17 34							18 30
Runcorn East d							16 08			16 40					17 39							18 35
Warrington Bank Quay 90 a							16 18			16 49					17 47							18 44
Earlestown 90 a							16 28			16 57					17 56							18 56
Newton-le-Willows 90 a							16 30			16 59					17 59							18 58
Manchester Oxford Road 90 a							16 48			17 20					18 19							19 19
Manchester Pic'dilly 90 ⇌ a			16 30				16 54		17 30	17 25				18 30	18 27						19 30	19 23
Crewe a		15 18			15 54			16 18				16 54	17 18						17 54	18 18		
Cardiff Central 131 a											19 20											
Manchester Airport 84,85 ✈ a																						
Birmingham New Street 65 a						17 30												19 30				
London Euston ⊖65 a					17 37							18 37							19 38			

A To Birmingham International
B To Llanelli
C To Blaenau Ffestiniog
D To Maesteg
E From Holyhead to Birmingham International

Table T081-R

Mondays to Fridays
21 May to 7 December

North Wales and Chester - Manchester and Crewe - Birmingham and London

	AW	AW	AW	AW	NT	AW	AW	VT	NT	AW	AW	AW	NT	AW	AW	AW	AW	AW	NT	AW	VT
		◇				◇ A		◇	B	◇	◇ C		◇	◇	◇					◇	◇
Holyhead d	16 51					17 31								18 23						19 21	
Valley d						17x37								18x29						19x27	
Rhosneigr d						17x42								18x34						19x32	
Ty Croes d						17x46								18x38						19x36	
Bodorgan d						17x50								18x42						19x40	
Llanfairpwll d						18x00								18x52						19x50	
Bangor (Gwynedd) a	17 17					18 08								19 00						19 58	
d	17 19					18 10								19 02						20 00	20 20
Llanfairfechan d						18x17								19x09						20x07	
Penmaenmawr d						18x21								19x13						20x11	
Conwy d						18x27								19x19						20x17	
Llandudno d			18 08							18 44	19 05				19 34		20 08				
Deganwy d			18x12							18x48	19x09				19x40		20x12				
Llandudno Junction a	17 35		18 18			18 31				18 52	19 13			19 24	19 44		20 17			20 21	20 36
d	17 37					18 33	18 39			18 53				19 26	19 46					20 23	20 38
Colwyn Bay d	17 43						18 45			18 59				19 32	19 54					20 29	20 44
Abergele & Pensarn d										19 06					20 02						
Rhyl d	17 53						18 55			19 12				19 42	20 09					20 39	20 55
Prestatyn d	17 59						19 01			19 18				19 48	20 16					20 45	21 01
Flint d	18 12						19 14			19 31				20 01	20 30					20 58	21 14
Shotton d										19 37										21 04	
Chester a	18 27					19 13	19 31			19 49				20 17	20 45					21 16	21 28
d	18 30	18 50		18 55	19 01			19 35		19 52		19 55	20 01	20 19	20 47	20 52		20 55	21 02	21 21	21 35
Helsby d		19 00							19 21	20 01						21 01					
Frodsham d		19 05							19 25	20 05						21 06					
Runcorn East d		19 10							19 32	20 11						21 11					
Warrington Bank Quay 90 a		19 18							19 42	20 18						21 19					
Earlestown 90 a		19 28							19 52	20 28						21 27					
Newton-le-Willows 90 a		19 31							19 57	20 30						21 30					
Manchester Oxford Road 90 a		19 49								20 49						21 49					
Manchester Pic'dilly 90 a		19 53			20 30					20 53			21 31			21 53			22 32		
Crewe a				19 18				19 54				20 18		20 41	21 07			21 18			21 54
Cardiff Central 131 a	21 35																				
Manchester Airport 84,85 a		20 19								21 20											
Birmingham New Street 65 a																				23 28	22 48
London Euston ⊖65 a								21 40													

	AW	AW	NT	AW	NT	AW	AW
	◇		◇	◇			◇ D
Holyhead d				20 32			
Valley d							
Rhosneigr d							
Ty Croes d							
Bodorgan d							
Llanfairpwll d							
Bangor (Gwynedd) a				20 59			
d				21 01			
Llanfairfechan d				21x08			
Penmaenmawr d				21x12			
Conwy d				21x18			
Llandudno d	20 43	21 11				21 45	
Deganwy d	20x47	21x14				21x49	
Llandudno Junction a	20 51	21 22		21 22		21 53	
d	20 52			21 28		21 55	
Colwyn Bay d	20 58			21 34		22 01	
Abergele & Pensarn d	21 05			21 41		22 09	
Rhyl d	21 11			21 47		22 16	
Prestatyn d	21 17			21 52		22 22	
Flint d	21 30			22 06		22 37	
Shotton d	21 36			22 12		22 44	
Chester a	21 48			22 23		22 55	
d	21 51		22 01	22 25	22 46	23 01	23 22
Helsby d	22 00						23 31
Frodsham d	22 04						23 35
Runcorn East d	22 10						23 41
Warrington Bank Quay 90 a	22 17						23 51
Earlestown 90 a	22 25						23 58
Newton-le-Willows 90 a	22 28						00 02
Manchester Oxford Road 90 a	22 49						
Manchester Pic'dilly 90 a	22 55		23 31		00 26		00 25
Crewe a				22 52		23 26	
Cardiff Central 131 a							
Manchester Airport 84,85 a							
Birmingham New Street 65 a							
London Euston ⊖65 a							

A To Shrewsbury
B From Ellesmere Port to Manchester Victoria
C To Blaenau Ffestiniog
D From Birmingham International

Table T081-R

Saturdays
26 May to 8 December

North Wales and Chester - Manchester and Crewe - Birmingham and London

	AW	AW	AW	AW	AW	AW	NT	AW	AW	AW	AW	AW	NT	NT	AW	VT	AW	AW	AW	AW	NT	AW
								◇ A	◇ B	◇ C	◇ D			E	F	◇	◇ G	◇			◇	◇ H
Holyhead d								04 25		04 25							05 23					06 35
Valley d								04 32		04x32							05x29					06x41
Rhosneigr d																	05x34					
Ty Croes d																	05x38					
Bodorgan d																	05x42					
Llanfairpwll d								04 49		04x49							05x52					06x58
Bangor (Gwynedd) a								04 56		04 56							06 00					07 05
d								04 57		04 57							06 02					07 07
Llanfairfechan d																	06x09					
Penmaenmawr d																	06x13					
Conwy d																	06x19					
Llandudno d																		06 34	07 08			
Deganwy d																		06x38	07x12			
Llandudno Junction a								05 13		05 13							06 23	06 42	07 18			07 23
d				04 38				05 15		05 15		05 37					06 25	06 44				07 25
Colwyn Bay d				04 44				05 21		05 21		05 43					06 31	06 50				07 31
Abergele & Pensarn d				04 51								05 50						06 57				
Rhyl d				04 57				05 31		05 31		05 56					06 41	07 03				07 41
Prestatyn d				05 02				05 37		05 37		06 01					06 47	07 08				07 47
Flint d				05 16				05 50		05 50		06 15					07 00	07 21				08 00
Shotton d				05 22								06 21						07 27				
Chester a				05 34				06 05		06 05		06 33					07 16	07 39				08 15
d	03 36	04 22	04 55	05 37	05 38	05 51	05 58	06 13	06 13	06 20	06 20	06 35	06 51		07 12	07 17	07 30	07 41		07 55	07 58	08 20
Helsby d					05 47			06 22	06 22					07 04	07 21			07 50				
Frodsham d					05 52			06 26	06 26					07 09	07 25			07 54				
Runcorn East d					05 57			06 32	06 32					07 14	07 31			08 00				
Warrington Bank Quay 90 a					06 05			06 39	06 39					07 21	07 38			08 07				
Earlestown 90 a					06 15			06 47	06 47						07 46			08 29				
Newton-le-Willows 90 a					06 18			06 50	06 50						07 49			08 32				
Manchester Oxford Road 90 a					06 40			07 11	07 11						08 07			08 49				
Manchester Pic'dilly 90 a	04 39				06 44		07 32	07 19	07 19				08 18		08 16			08 53			09 31	
Crewe a		04 43	05 20	05 58		06 15						07 00				07 36				08 18		
Cardiff Central 131 a										09 18	09 18											11 13
Manchester Airport 84,85 a	05 04																	09 19				
Birmingham New Street 65 a		05 58															09 27					
London Euston ⊖65 a																09 30						

	VT	AW	AW	AW	NT	AW	VT	AW	AW	AW	NT	AW	VT	AW	AW	AW	NT	VT	AW	AW	AW	AW
	◇	◇			◇	G	◇	◇			◇	◇	◇				◇	◇	G	◇ I	◇	
Holyhead d	06 52					07 15	07 55					08 20	08 55						09 23			
Valley d						07x21						08x26							09x29			
Rhosneigr d						07x26						08x32							09x34			
Ty Croes d						07x30						08x35							09x38			
Bodorgan d						07x34						08x40							09x42			
Llanfairpwll d						07x44						08x49							09x52			
Bangor (Gwynedd) a	07 18					07 52	08 21					08 57	09 21						10 00			
d	07 20					08 02	08 22					09 02	09 22						10 02			
Llanfairfechan d						08x09						09x09							10x09			
Penmaenmawr d						08x13						09x13							10x13			
Conwy d						08x19						09x19							10x19			
Llandudno d		07 45	08 08					08 45	09 08					09 45	10 10					10 22	10 44	11 08
Deganwy d		07x49	08x12					08x49	09x12					09x49	10x14					10x26	10x48	11x12
Llandudno Junction a	07 36	07 53	08 18			08 23	08 39	08 53	09 18			09 23	09 39	09 53	10 20				10 23	10 32	10 52	11 18
d	07 38	07 54				08 25	08 40	08 54				09 25	09 40	09 54					10 25		10 53	
Colwyn Bay d	07 44	08 00				08 31	08 47	09 00				09 31	09 47	10 00					10 31		10 59	
Abergele & Pensarn d		08 07						09 07						10 07							11 06	
Rhyl d	07 55	08 13				08 41	08 58	09 13				09 41	09 58	10 13					10 41		11 12	
Prestatyn d	08 01	08 19				08 47	09 04	09 19				09 47	10 03	10 19					10 47		11 18	
Flint d	08 15	08 32				09 00	09 17	09 32				10 00		10 32					11 00		11 31	
Shotton d		08 38						09 38						10 38							11 37	
Chester a	08 28	08 50				09 16	09 31	09 50				10 15	10 28	10 50					11 17		11 49	
d	08 35	08 52		08 55	09 00	09 30	09 35	09 52		09 55	10 02	10 19	10 35	10 52		10 55	11 02	11 35	11 36		11 52	
Helsby d		09 01						10 01						11 01							12 01	
Frodsham d		09 05						10 05						11 05							12 06	
Runcorn East d		09 11						10 11						11 11							12 11	
Warrington Bank Quay 90 a		09 18						10 18						11 18							12 20	
Earlestown 90 a		09 28						10 28						11 28							12 28	
Newton-le-Willows 90 a		09 30						10 30						11 30							12 30	
Manchester Oxford Road 90 a		09 48						10 48						11 49							12 48	
Manchester Pic'dilly 90 a		09 53			10 30			10 53			11 30			11 54			12 30				12 53	
Crewe a	08 54			09 18			09 54			10 18			10 54			11 18		11 54				
Cardiff Central 131 a												13 17										
Manchester Airport 84,85 a		10 19						11 19						12 19							13 19	
Birmingham New Street 65 a						11 28													13 28			
London Euston ⊖65 a	10 36						11 36						12 36					13 36				

A until 8 September
B from 15 September
C from 15 September. To Maesteg
D until 8 September. To Maesteg
E From Ellesmere Port
F From Shrewsbury
G To Birmingham International
H To Maesteg
I To Blaenau Ffestiniog

Table T081-R

Saturdays

26 May to 8 December

North Wales and Chester - Manchester and Crewe - Birmingham and London

		AW		NT	AW	VT	AW	AW	AW	NT	AW	VT	
				◇	■ ⊥	◇■ ⊏	◇ ⊥			◇	■ A ⊥	◇■ ⊏	
Holyhead ■	d				10 33						11 23		
Valley	d				10x39						11x29		
Rhosneigr	d										11x34		
Ty Croes	d										11x38		
Bodorgan	d										11x42		
Llanfairpwll	d				10x56						11x52		
Bangor (Gwynedd)	a				11 03						12 00		
	d				11 05						12 02		
Llanfairfechan	d										12x09		
Penmaenmawr	d										12x13		
Conwy	d										12x19		
Llandudno	d						11 44	12 08					
Deganwy	d						11x48	12x12					
Llandudno Junction	a				11 21		11 52	12 18			12 23		
	d				11 23		11 53				12 25		
Colwyn Bay	d				11 29		11 59				12 31		
Abergele & Pensarn	d						12 06						
Rhyl	d				11 39		12 12				12 41		
Prestatyn	d				11 45		12 18				12 47		
Flint	d				11 58		12 31				13 00		
Shotton	d						12 37						
Chester	a				12 13		12 49				13 16		
	d	11 55		11 55	12 19	12 35	12 51		12 55	13 02	13 35	13 35	
Helsby	d						13 00						
Frodsham	d						13 05						
Runcorn East	d						13 11						
Warrington Bank Quay 90	a						13 18						
Earlestown ■ 90	a						13 28						
Newton-le-Willows 90	a						13 30						
Manchester Oxford Road 90	a						13 48						
Manchester Pic'dilly ■ 90 ⛴	a			13 30			13 53			14 30			
Crewe ■	a	12 18				12 54			13 18			13 54	
Cardiff Central ■ 131	a				15 24								
Manchester Airport 84,85 ✈	a						14 19						
Birmingham New Street ■ 65	a										15 28		
London Euston ■ ⊖65	a					14 36						15 36	

		AW	AW	AW	AW	NT	AW	VT	AW	AW		AW	NT
		◇ ⊥		◇ B		◇	◇ C ⊥	◇■ ⊏	◇ ⊥				◇
Holyhead ■	d						12 38						
Valley	d												
Rhosneigr	d												
Ty Croes	d												
Bodorgan	d												
Llanfairpwll	d												
Bangor (Gwynedd)	a						13 05						
	d						13 07		13 33				
Llanfairfechan	d								13x40				
Penmaenmawr	d								13x44				
Conwy	d								13x50				
Llandudno	d	12 40	12 46	13 08						14 08			
Deganwy	d	12x44	12x50	13x12						14x12			
Llandudno Junction	a	12 48	12 56	13 18			13 23		13 55	14 18			
	d	12 53					13 25		13 56				
Colwyn Bay	d	12 59					13 31		14 02				
Abergele & Pensarn	d	13 06							14 09				
Rhyl	d	13 12					13 41		14 15				
Prestatyn	d	13 18					13 47		14 21				
Flint	d	13 31					14 00		14 34				
Shotton	d	13 37							14 40				
Chester	a	13 49					14 15		14 52				
	d	13 52			13 55	14 02	14 19	14 35	14 54			14 55	15 02
Helsby	d	14 02							15 03				
Frodsham	d	14 06							15 07				
Runcorn East	d	14 12							15 13				
Warrington Bank Quay 90	a	14 20							15 20				
Earlestown ■ 90	a	14 28							15 28				
Newton-le-Willows 90	a	14 31							15 31				
Manchester Oxford Road 90	a	14 49							15 48				
Manchester Pic'dilly ■ 90 ⛴	a	14 53				15 30			15 53				16 30
Crewe ■	a				14 18			14 54				15 18	
Cardiff Central ■ 131	a						17 08						
Manchester Airport 84,85 ✈	a	15 19							16 19				
Birmingham New Street ■ 65	a												
London Euston ■ ⊖65	a							16 36					

		AW	VT	AW	AW	AW	NT	AW		VT	AW	AW	AW
		■ A ⊥	◇■ ⊏	■ D ⊥	◇ ⊥		◇	◇ ⊥		◇■ ⊏		◇ ⊥	
Holyhead ■	d	13 28	13 58					14 27					
Valley	d	13x34											
Rhosneigr	d	13x39											
Ty Croes	d	13x43											
Bodorgan	d	13x47											
Llanfairpwll	d	13x57											
Bangor (Gwynedd)	a	14 05	14 24					14 53					
	d	14 07	14 25					14 55					
Llanfairfechan	d							15x02					
Penmaenmawr	d							15x06					
Conwy	d							15x12					
Llandudno	d				14 42						15 08	15 44	16 07
Deganwy	d				14x46						15x12	15x48	16x11
Llandudno Junction	a	14 23	14 42		14 50			15 16			15 18	15 52	16 17
	d	14 25	14 43		14 51			15 18				15 53	
Colwyn Bay	d	14 31	14 50		14 57			15 24				15 59	
Abergele & Pensarn	d				15 04							16 06	
Rhyl	d	14 41	15 00		15 10			15 35				16 12	
Prestatyn	d	14 47			15 16			15 40				16 18	
Flint	d	15 00			15 29			15 54				16 31	
Shotton	d			←	15 35							16 37	
Chester	a	15 18	15 27	15 18	15 47			16 08				16 49	
	d	15 36	15 35	15 36	15 49	15 55	16 02	16 21		16 35		16 52	
Helsby	d	→			15 58							17 01	
Frodsham	d				16 03							17 06	
Runcorn East	d				16 08							17 11	
Warrington Bank Quay 90	a				16 18							17 19	
Earlestown ■ 90	a				16 29							17 28	
Newton-le-Willows 90	a				16 31							17 30	
Manchester Oxford Road 90	a				16 49							17 48	
Manchester Pic'dilly ■ 90 ⛴	a				16 53		17 30					17 53	
Crewe ■	a		15 54			16 18				16 54			
Cardiff Central ■ 131	a							19 15					
Manchester Airport 84,85 ✈	a				17 19							18 19	
Birmingham New Street ■ 65	a			17 28									
London Euston ■ ⊖65	a		17 36							18 37			

		AW	NT	AW	VT	AW		AW	AW	AW	NT	AW	NT
				■ A ⊥	◇■ ⊏	◇ B		◇ ⊥				◇ ⊥	
Holyhead ■	d			15 23								16 52	
Valley	d			15x29									
Rhosneigr	d			15x34									
Ty Croes	d			15x38									
Bodorgan	d			15x42									
Llanfairpwll	d			15x52									
Bangor (Gwynedd)	a			16 00								17 18	
	d			16 02								17 20	
Llanfairfechan	d			16x09									
Penmaenmawr	d			16x13									
Conwy	d			16x19									
Llandudno	d					16 20		16 44	17 08				
Deganwy	d					16x24		16x48	17x12				
Llandudno Junction	a			16 23		16 30		16 52	17 18			17 36	
	d			16 25				16 53				17 38	
Colwyn Bay	d			16 31				16 59				17 44	
Abergele & Pensarn	d							17 06					
Rhyl	d			16 41				17 12				17 54	
Prestatyn	d			16 47				17 18				18 00	
Flint	d			17 00				17 31				18 13	
Shotton	d							17 37					
Chester	a			17 16				17 49				18 28	
	d	16 55	17 02	17 30	17 35			17 51		17 55	18 01	18 32	18 48
Helsby	d							18 00					
Frodsham	d							18 05					
Runcorn East	d							18 10					
Warrington Bank Quay 90	a							18 18					
Earlestown ■ 90	a							18 26					
Newton-le-Willows 90	a							18 29					
Manchester Oxford Road 90	a							18 49					
Manchester Pic'dilly ■ 90 ⛴	a		18 30					18 53			19 30		20 18
Crewe ■	a	17 18			17 54					18 18			
Cardiff Central ■ 131	a											21 35	
Manchester Airport 84,85 ✈	a												
Birmingham New Street ■ 65	a			19 28									
London Euston ■ ⊖65	a												

A To Birmingham International
B To Blaenau Ffestiniog
C To Maesteg
D From Holyhead to Birmingham International

Table T081-R

Saturdays

26 May to 8 December

North Wales and Chester - Manchester and Crewe - Birmingham and London

		AW	AW	AW		AW	AW	NT	AW	AW	AW	AW	NT
		◇				◇ A ⊥	B ⊥	C	◇	◇ D			◇
Holyhead ■	d					17 32							
Valley	d					17x38							
Rhosneigr	d					17x43							
Ty Croes	d					17x47							
Bodorgan	d					17x51							
Llanfairpwll	d					18x01							
Bangor (Gwynedd)	a					18 09							
	d					18 11							
Llanfairfechan	d					18x18							
Penmaenmawr	d					18x22							
Conwy	d					18x28							
Llandudno	d	17 44	18 08						18 44	19 03	19 13		
Deganwy	d	17x48	18x12						18x48	19x07	19x17		
Llandudno Junction	a	17 52	18 18			18 32			18 52	19 11	19 21		
	d	17 53				18 34			18 53				
Colwyn Bay	d	17 59				18 40			18 59				
Abergele & Pensarn	d	18 06							19 06				
Rhyl	d	18 12				18 50			19 12				
Prestatyn	d	18 18				18 56			19 18				
Flint	d	18 31				19 09			19 31				
Shotton	d	18 37							19 37				
Chester	a	18 49				19 25			19 49				
	d	18 52		18 55			19 35		19 51			19 55	20 01
Helsby	d	19 01						19 21	20 00				
Frodsham	d	19 06						19 25	20 05				
Runcorn East	d	19 11						19 32	20 10				
Warrington Bank Quay 90	a	19 20						19 42	20 18				
Earlestown ■ 90	a	19 28						19 52	20 26				
Newton-le-Willows 90	a	19 30						19 57	20 29				
Manchester Oxford Road 90	a	19 48							20 49				
Manchester Pic'dilly ■ 90 ⛴	a	19 53							20 56				21 26
Crewe ■	a			19 18			20 00					20 18	
Cardiff Central ■ 131	a												
Manchester Airport 84,85 ✈	a	20 19											
Birmingham New Street ■ 65	a												
London Euston ■ ⊖65	a												

		AW		VT	AW	AW	AW	NT	AW	AW	AW	NT	
		◇		◇ ⊏	◇				◇			◇	
Holyhead ■	d	18 23							19 22				
Valley	d	18x29							19x28				
Rhosneigr	d	18x34							19x33				
Ty Croes	d	18x38							19x37				
Bodorgan	d	18x42							19x41				
Llanfairpwll	d	18x52							19x51				
Bangor (Gwynedd)	a	19 00							19 59				
	d	19 03							20 01				
Llanfairfechan	d	19x10							20x08				
Penmaenmawr	d	19x14							20x12				
Conwy	d	19x20							20x18				
Llandudno	d				19 42	20 08				20 43			
Deganwy	d				19x46	20x12				20x47			
Llandudno Junction	a	19 22			19 50	20 18			20 22	20 51			
	d	19 26			19 51				20 24	20 52			
Colwyn Bay	d	19 32			19 57				20 30	20 58			
Abergele & Pensarn	d				20 04					21 05			
Rhyl	d	19 42			20 10				20 40	21 11			
Prestatyn	d	19 48			20 16				20 46	21 17			
Flint	d	20 01			20 29				20 59	21 30			
Shotton	d				20 35					21 36			
Chester	a	20 17			20 47				21 15	21 48			
	d	20 19		20 35	20 50		20 55	21 01	21 22		21 53	22 01	
Helsby	d				20 59						22 02		
Frodsham	d				21 04						22 06		
Runcorn East	d				21 09						22 12		
Warrington Bank Quay 90	a				21 19						22 20		
Earlestown ■ 90	a				21 27						22 27		
Newton-le-Willows 90	a				21 30						22 31		
Manchester Oxford Road 90	a				21 49						22 50		
Manchester Pic'dilly ■ 90 ⛴	a				21 56			22 28			22 55	23 31	
Crewe ■	a	20 41		20 54			21 18						
Cardiff Central ■ 131	a												
Manchester Airport 84,85 ✈	a												
Birmingham New Street ■ 65	a								23 30				
London Euston ■ ⊖65	a												

		AW	NT	AW	AW
		◇		◇	
Holyhead ■	d	20 37			
Valley	d				
Rhosneigr	d				
Ty Croes	d				
Bodorgan	d				
Llanfairpwll	d				
Bangor (Gwynedd)	a	21 05			
	d	21 06			
Llanfairfechan	d	21x13			
Penmaenmawr	d	21x17			
Conwy	d	21x23			
Llandudno	d			21 45	
Deganwy	d			21x49	
Llandudno Junction	a	21 28		21 53	
	d	21 29		21 55	
Colwyn Bay	d	21 35		22 01	
Abergele & Pensarn	d	21 42		22 09	
Rhyl	d	21 48		22 16	
Prestatyn	d	21 54		22 22	
Flint	d	22 07		22 37	
Shotton	d	22 13		22 44	
Chester	a	22 24		22 55	
	d	22 27	22 46	23 01	23 22
Helsby	d				23 31
Frodsham	d				23 35
Runcorn East	d				23 41
Warrington Bank Quay 90	a				23 50
Earlestown ■ 90	a				23 58
Newton-le-Willows 90	a				00 01
Manchester Oxford Road 90	a				
Manchester Pic'dilly ■ 90 ⛴	a		00 26		00 22
Crewe ■	a	22 50		23 26	
Cardiff Central ■ 131	a				
Manchester Airport 84,85 ✈	a				
Birmingham New Street ■ 65	a				
London Euston ■ ⊖65	a				

A To Shrewsbury
B until 8 September
C From Ellesmere Port to Manchester Victoria
D To Blaenau Ffestiniog

North Wales and Chester - Manchester and Crewe - Birmingham and London

	AW	AW	AW	AW	NT	AW	AW	AW	AW	AW	AW	AW	AW	NT	AW	VT	AW	AW	AW	AW	AW	VT
				◇	◇	◇ A 🛒		◇ 🛒		🛒	◇	◇ B				◇1 ☕	◇ A 🛒	🛒			■ 🛒	◇1 ☕
Holyhead 30 d				07 16				07 50			08 45										10 20	10 55
Valley d								07 56													10x26	
Rhosneigr d								08 02													10x31	
Ty Croes d								08 05													10x35	
Bodorgan d								08 10													10x39	
Llanfairpwll d								08 19													10x49	
Bangor (Gwynedd) a				07 42				08 27			09 12										10 57	11 21
d				07 43				08 28			09 13										10 59	11 22
Llanfairfechan d								08x36													11x06	
Penmaenmawr d								08x40													11x10	
Conwy d								08x46													11x16	
Llandudno d												10 22			11 07							
Deganwy d												10x26			11x11							
Llandudno Junction a				07 58				08 50			09 29	10 30			11 17						11 20	11 38
d				08 00				08 51			09 35										11 22	11 40
Colwyn Bay d				08 07				08 57			09 41										11 28	11 46
Abergele & Pensarn d				08 14							09 48										11 35	
Rhyl d				08 20				09 08			09 54										11 41	11 57
Prestatyn d				08 25							09 59										11 46	12 03
Flint d				08 39							10 13										12 00	12 16
Shotton d				08 45				09 28			10 19										12 06	
Chester a				08 57				09 40			10 31										12 19	12 30
d	07 56	08 27	08 39	08 58	08 59	09 26	09 27	09 42	09 57	10 36	10 39		10 57	10 59		11 28	11 35	11 36	11 57	12 23	12 28	12 33
Helsby d			08 50					09 51		10 45								11 45				
Frodsham d			08 54					09 55		10 49								11 49				
Runcorn East d			08 59					10 00		10 54								11 54				
Warrington Bank Quay 90 a			09 07					10 09		11 03								12 03				
Earlestown 8 90 a			09 16					10 17		11 12								12 10				
Newton-le-Willows 90 a			09 18					10 20		11 15								12 13				
Manchester Oxford Road 90 a			09 36					10 38		11 34								12 33				
Manchester Pic'dilly 10 90 a			09 45		10 31			10 47		11 41				12 33				12 41				
Crewe 10 a	08 20	08 51		09 21			09 50		10 20		11 03		11 20			11 47			12 20	12 44		12 53
Cardiff Central 7 131 a																					15 34	
Manchester Airport 84,85 ✈ a																						
Birmingham New Street 12 65 a						11 13											13 23					
London Euston 15 ⊖65 a																13 43						14 41

	AW	AW	AW	AW	NT	VT	VT	AW	AW	AW	AW	AW	VT	VT	AW	AW	AW	AW	AW	NT	AW	VT
	🛒				◇	◇1 ☕	◇1 ☕		◇ A				◇1 ☕	◇1 ☕	◇ B					◇	◇ A	◇1 ☕
Holyhead 30 d						11 50							12 50									13 55
Valley d																						
Rhosneigr d																						
Ty Croes d																						
Bodorgan d																						
Llanfairpwll d																						
Bangor (Gwynedd) a						12 16							13 16									14 21
d						12 17							13 18									14 22
Llanfairfechan d																						
Penmaenmawr d																						
Conwy d																						
Llandudno d		11 40	12 18					13 19							13 30	13 50	14 20					
Deganwy d		11x44	12x22					13x23							13x34	13x54	14x24					
Llandudno Junction a		11 50	12 28			12 34		13 29					13 34		13 38	14 00	14 30					14 39
d						12 35							13 36									14 40
Colwyn Bay d						12 42							13 42									14 46
Abergele & Pensarn d																						
Rhyl d						12 53							13 53									14 57
Prestatyn d						12 59							13 59									15 03
Flint d													14 13									
Shotton d																						
Chester a						13 24							14 26									15 31
d	12 36			12 57	12 59	13 30	13 30		13 35	13 36	13 57	14 24	14 33	14 33				14 36	14 57	15 04	15 32	15 33
Helsby d	12 45									13 45								14 45				
Frodsham d	12 49									13 49								14 49				
Runcorn East d	12 54									13 54								14 54				
Warrington Bank Quay 90 a	13 03									14 03								15 03				
Earlestown 8 90 a	13 11									14 11								15 11				
Newton-le-Willows 90 a	13 13									14 13								15 13				
Manchester Oxford Road 90 a	13 31									14 33								15 31				
Manchester Pic'dilly 10 90 a	13 40				14 35					14 41								15 40		16 40		
Crewe 10 a				13 20		13 50	13 50				14 20	14 48	14 54	14 54					15 20			15 52
Cardiff Central 7 131 a																						
Manchester Airport 84,85 ✈ a																						
Birmingham New Street 12 65 a									15 24												17 37	
London Euston 15 ⊖65 a						15 42	15 42						16 41	16 41								17 41

A To Birmingham International

B To Blaenau Ffestiniog

North Wales and Chester - Manchester and Crewe - Birmingham and London

	AW	AW	AW	AW	AW	AW	AW	AW	NT	AW	VT	AW	AW	AW	AW	VT	AW	AW	AW	AW	NT
	🛒				■ 🛒				◇	◇ A	◇1 ☕	◇ 🛒			■ 🛒	◇1 ☕					
Holyhead 30 d					14 30							15 44			16 25						
Valley d					14x36										16x31						
Rhosneigr d					14x42										16x36						
Ty Croes d					14x45										16x40						
Bodorgan d					14x50										16x44						
Llanfairpwll d					14x59										16x54						
Bangor (Gwynedd) a					15 07							16 10			17 02						
d					15 08							16 12			17 04						
Llanfairfechan d												16x20									
Penmaenmawr d												16x24									
Conwy d												16x30									
Llandudno d		15 13				15 44	16 16						16 52				17 20	18 05			
Deganwy d		15x17				15x48	16x20						16x56				17x24	18x09			
Llandudno Junction a		15 23			15 25	15 54	16 26					16 33	17 02		17 20		17 30	18 15			
d					15 28							16 35			17 25						
Colwyn Bay d					15 34							16 41			17 31						
Abergele & Pensarn d					15 41							16 48			17 38						
Rhyl d					15 47							16 54			17 44						
Prestatyn d					15 52							16 59			17 49						
Flint d					16 06							17 13			18 03						
Shotton d					16 12							17 19			18 11						
Chester a					16 21							17 35			18 22						
d	15 36		15 57	16 27	16 36			16 57	17 07	17 31	17 35	17 36		17 59	18 25	18 35			18 36	18 59	19 04
Helsby d	15 45				16 45							17 45							18 45		
Frodsham d	15 49				16 49							17 49							18 49		
Runcorn East d	15 54				16 54							17 54							18 54		
Warrington Bank Quay 90 a	16 03				17 03							18 03							19 03		
Earlestown 8 90 a	16 11				17 11							18 11							19 11		
Newton-le-Willows 90 a	16 13				17 13							18 13							19 13		
Manchester Oxford Road 90 a	16 31				17 31							18 31							19 31		
Manchester Pic'dilly 10 90 a	16 40				17 40				18 39			18 40							19 40		20 38
Crewe 10 a			16 20	16 51				17 20			17 53			18 22		18 53				19 20	
Cardiff Central 7 131 a															21 37						
Manchester Airport 84,85 ✈ a																					
Birmingham New Street 12 65 a										19 26											
London Euston 15 ⊖65 a											19 42					20 41					

	AW	AW	AW	VT	AW	AW	AW	AW	VT	AW	NT	AW	AW	AW	AW	AW	AW	AW	AW
	■ 🛒		◇ A	◇ ☕			◇ A		◇ ☕			◇ B					◇	C	◇
Holyhead 30 d	17 30						18 25					19 17					20 35		21 40
Valley d							18x31					19x23					20x41		
Rhosneigr d							18x36					19x28					20x46		
Ty Croes d							18x40					19x32					20x50		
Bodorgan d							18x44					19x36					20x54		
Llanfairpwll d							18x54					19x46					21x04		
Bangor (Gwynedd) a	17 57						19 02					19 54					21 12		22 07
d	17 59						19 04					19 56					21 14		22 09
Llanfairfechan d	18x06											20x04					21x21		
Penmaenmawr d	18x10											20x09					21x25		
Conwy d	18x16											20x15					21x31		
Llandudno d		18 55																	
Deganwy d		18x59																	
Llandudno Junction a	18 20	19 05					19 20					20 18					21 35		22 25
d	18 24						19 24					20 24					21 37		22 27
Colwyn Bay d	18 30						19 30					20 30					21 43		22 33
Abergele & Pensarn d	18 37						19 37					20 38					21 50		
Rhyl d	18 43						19 43					20 44					21 56		22 43
Prestatyn d	18 48						19 48					20 49					22 01		22 49
Flint d	19 02						20 02					21 03					22 15		23 02
Shotton d	19 10						20 10					21 10					22 21		
Chester a	19 22						20 20					21 22					22 33		23 17
d	19 25		19 26	19 35	19 36	19 57	20 27	20 36	20 37	20 57	20 59		21 27	21 43	21 57	22 06	22 35	23 00	
Helsby d					19 45			20 45						21 52		22 15			
Frodsham d					19 49			20 49						21 56		22 19			
Runcorn East d					19 54			20 54						22 01		22 24			
Warrington Bank Quay 90 a					20 03			21 03						22 10		22 33			
Earlestown 8 90 a					20 11			21 10						22 18		22 41			
Newton-le-Willows 90 a					20 13			21 13						22 21		22 43			
Manchester Oxford Road 90 a					20 31			21 32						22 39		23 01			
Manchester Pic'dilly 10 90 a					20 40			21 40			22 28			22 48		23 10			
Crewe 10 a	19 49			19 56		20 20	20 48		20 56	21 20			21 50		22 21		23 01	23 21	
Cardiff Central 7 131 a																			
Manchester Airport 84,85 ✈ a																			
Birmingham New Street 12 65 a			21 29				21 53												
London Euston 15 ⊖65 a																			

A To Birmingham International

B To Wolverhampton

C To Shrewsbury

North Wales and Chester - Manchester and Crewe - Birmingham and London

Sundays

16 September to 2 December

		AW	AW	NT	AW	AW	AW	AW	AW	NT		VT	AW	AW	AW	AW	VT	AW	NT	AW		VT	VT	AW	AW
				◇	◇ A ✠			✠	◇	◇		◇■ 🍴	◇ A ✠	✠		■ ✠	◇■ 🍴	✠	◇			◇■ 🍴	◇■ 🍴	◇ A	
Holyhead	d								08 45							10 20	10 55					11 50			
Valley	d															10x26									
Rhosneigr	d															10x31									
Ty Croes	d															10x35									
Bodorgan	d															10x39									
Llanfairpwll	d															10x49									
Bangor (Gwynedd)	a								09 12							10 57	11 21					12 16			
	d								09 13							10 59	11 22					12 17			
Llanfairfechan	d															11x06									
Penmaenmawr	d															11x10									
Conwy	d															11x16									
Llandudno	d																								
Deganwy	d																								
Llandudno Junction	a								09 29							11 20	11 38					12 34			
	d								09 35							11 22	11 40					12 35			
Colwyn Bay	d								09 41							11 28	11 46					12 42			
Abergele & Pensarn	d								09 48							11 35									
Rhyl	d								09 54							11 41	11 57					12 53			
Prestatyn	d								09 59							11 46	12 03					12 59			
Flint	d								10 13							12 00	12 16								
Shotton	d								10 19							12 06									
Chester	a								10 31							12 19	12 30					13 24			
	d	08 27	08 39	08 59	09 26	09 39	09 42	10 36	10 39	10 59		11 28	11 35	11 36	12 23	12 28	12 33	12 36	12 59	13 20		13 30	13 30	13 35	13 36
Helsby	d		08 50				09 51	10 45						11 45				12 45							13 45
Frodsham	d		08 54				09 55	10 49						11 49				12 49							13 49
Runcorn East	d		08 59				10 00	10 54						11 54				12 54							13 54
Warrington Bank Quay 90	a		09 07				10 09	11 03						12 03				13 03							14 03
Earlestown ■ 90	a		09 16				10 17	11 12						12 10				13 11							14 11
Newton-le-Willows 90	a		09 18				10 20	11 15						12 13				13 13							14 13
Manchester Oxford Road 90	a		09 36				10 38	11 34						12 33				13 31							14 33
Manchester Pic'dilly ■ 90	a		09 45	10 31			10 46	11 41		12 29				12 41				13 40	14 35						14 41
Crewe ■	a	08 51				10 02			11 03			11 47			12 44		12 53			13 43		13 50	13 50		
Cardiff Central ■ 131	a															15 34									
Manchester Airport 84,85 ✈	a																								
Birmingham New Street ■ 65	a				11 13								13 23											15 24	
London Euston ■ ⊖65	a											13 43					14 41					15 42	15 42		

		AW	VT	VT	AW	NT		AW	VT	AW	AW	AW	AW	NT	AW	AW		VT	AW	AW	VT	AW	AW	NT	AW
			◇■ 🍴	◇■ 🍴		◇		◇ A	◇■ 🍴	✠			■ ✠	◇	◇	◇ A		◇■ 🍴		■ ✠	◇■ 🍴				■ ✠
Holyhead	d		12 50						13 55				14 30		15 30					16 25					17 30
Valley	d												14x36							16x31					
Rhosneigr	d												14x42							16x36					
Ty Croes	d												14x45							16x40					
Bodorgan	d												14x50							16x44					
Llanfairpwll	d												14x59							16x54					
Bangor (Gwynedd)	a		13 16						14 21				15 07		15 56					17 02					17 57
	d		13 18						14 22				15 08		15 58					17 04					17 59
Llanfairfechan	d														16x05										18x06
Penmaenmawr	d														16x09										18x10
Conwy	d														16x15										18x16
Llandudno	d																								
Deganwy	d																								
Llandudno Junction	a		13 34						14 39				15 25		16 19					17 20					18 20
	d		13 36						14 40				15 28		16 25					17 25					18 24
Colwyn Bay	d		13 42						14 46				15 34		16 31					17 31					18 30
Abergele & Pensarn	d												15 41		16 38					17 38					18 37
Rhyl	d		13 53						14 57				15 47		16 44					17 44					18 43
Prestatyn	d		13 59						15 03				15 52		16 49					17 49					18 48
Flint	d		14 13										16 06		17 03					18 03					19 02
Shotton	d												16 12		17 09					18 11					19 10
Chester	a		14 26						15 31				16 21		17 21					18 22					19 22
	d	14 23	14 33	14 33	14 36	15 04		15 32	15 33	15 36	16 00	16 27	16 36	17 07	17 22	17 31		17 35	17 36	18 25	18 35	18 36	19 00	19 04	19 25
Helsby	d				14 45					15 45			16 45						17 45			18 45			
Frodsham	d				14 49					15 49			16 49						17 49			18 49			
Runcorn East	d				14 54					15 54			16 54						17 54			18 54			
Warrington Bank Quay 90	a				15 03					16 03			17 03						18 03			19 03			
Earlestown ■ 90	a				15 11					16 11			17 11						18 11			19 11			
Newton-le-Willows 90	a				15 13					16 13			17 13						18 13			19 13			
Manchester Oxford Road 90	a				15 31					16 31			17 31						18 31			19 31			
Manchester Pic'dilly ■ 90	a				15 40	16 40				16 40			17 40	18 39					18 40			19 40		20 38	
Crewe ■	a	14 46	14 54	14 54					15 52		16 25	16 51			17 42			17 53			18 53		19 21		19 49
Cardiff Central ■ 131	a																			21 37					
Manchester Airport 84,85 ✈	a																								
Birmingham New Street ■ 65	a							17 37								19 26									
London Euston ■ ⊖65	a		16 41	16 41					17 41									19 42			20 41				

A To Birmingham International

North Wales and Chester - Manchester and Crewe - Birmingham and London

Sundays

16 September to 2 December

		AW		VT	AW	AW	AW	AW	VT	AW	NT	AW		AW	AW	AW	AW	AW	AW
		◇ A		◇ 🍴			◇ A		◇ 🍴			◇					◇	B	◇
Holyhead	d						18 25					19 40					20 35		21 40
Valley	d						18x31										20x41		
Rhosneigr	d						18x36										20x46		
Ty Croes	d						18x40										20x50		
Bodorgan	d						18x44										20x54		
Llanfairpwll	d						18x54										21x04		
Bangor (Gwynedd)	a						19 02					20 07					21 12		22 07
	d						19 04					20 09					21 14		22 09
Llanfairfechan	d											20x16					21x21		
Penmaenmawr	d											20x20					21x25		
Conwy	d											20x26					21x31		
Llandudno	d																		
Deganwy	d																		
Llandudno Junction	a						19 20					20 30					21 35		22 25
	d						19 24					20 37					21 37		22 27
Colwyn Bay	d						19 30					20 43					21 43		22 33
Abergele & Pensarn	d						19 37					20 50					21 50		
Rhyl	d						19 43					20 56					21 56		22 43
Prestatyn	d						19 48					21 02					22 01		22 49
Flint	d						20 02					21 16					22 15		23 02
Shotton	d						20 10					21 22					22 21		
Chester	a						20 20					21 34					22 33		23 17
	d	19 26		19 35	19 36	19 52	20 27	20 36	20 37	20 50	20 59	21 36		21 43	21 50	22 06	22 35	23 00	
Helsby	d				19 45			20 45						21 52		22 15			
Frodsham	d				19 49			20 49						21 56		22 19			
Runcorn East	d				19 54			20 54						22 01		22 24			
Warrington Bank Quay 90	a				20 03			21 03						22 10		22 33			
Earlestown ■ 90	a				20 11			21 10						22 18		22 41			
Newton-le-Willows 90	a				20 13			21 13						22 21		22 43			
Manchester Oxford Road 90	a				20 31			21 32						22 39		23 01			
Manchester Pic'dilly ■ 90	a				20 40			21 40			22 28			22 48		23 10			
Crewe ■	a			19 56		20 13	20 48		20 56	21 13		22 00			22 13		23 01	23 21	
Cardiff Central ■ 131	a																		
Manchester Airport 84,85 ✈	a																		
Birmingham New Street ■ 65	a	21 29					21 53												
London Euston ■ ⊖65	a																		

A To Birmingham International

B To Shrewsbury

Table T082-F

Mondays to Fridays

21 May to 7 December

Manchester - Bolton - Wigan, Kirkby, Southport, Preston, Blackpool North and Barrow-in-Furness

Miles	Miles	Miles	Miles	Miles			NT	NT	NT	NT	NT	NT	NT	NT	NT		NT	TP	NT	TP	NT	NT	NT	NT	NT
							MX	MX	MX	MX	MX	MX	MX												
												◇					◇	◇1		◇1		◇			◇
							A	B	C	C	C	A	C	D				E		F			G		H
										🚌	🚌		🚌					🛒	🚌						
0	0	0	—	—	**Manchester Airport** 85 ✈	d											04 34			05 03		05 20			
1½	1½	1½	—	—	Heald Green 85	d											04 38					05 24			
—	—	—	—	—	Buxton 86	d																			
—	—	—	—	—	Hazel Grove 86	d																			
—	—	—	—	—	Stockport 84	d																			
9¾	9¾	9¾	—	—	**Manchester Piccadilly** 10	d						00 09					04 51	05 00	05 00	05 17		05 42			
10¼	10¼	10¼	—	—	**Manchester Oxford Road**	d											04 54			05 20		05 45			
10½	10½	10½	—	—	Deansgate	d																			
—	—	—	—	—	Rochdale 41	d																			
—	—	—	0	—	**Manchester Victoria**	d														05a26	05 33		05 44		
—	—	—	0¾	—	Salford Central	d															05 36		05 47		
12	12	12	1¾	—	**Salford Crescent**	a															05 39		05 50		
—	—	—	—	—		d															05 40		05 51		
—	—	—	5¾	—	Swinton	d																			
—	—	—	6½	—	Moorside	d																			
—	—	—	8¼	—	Walkden	d																			
—	—	—	11¾	—	Atherton	d		00 04																	
—	—	—	13	—	Hag Fold	d		00 06																	
—	—	—	13¼	—	Daisy Hill	d		00 10																	
15	15	15	—	—	Clifton	d																			
18	18	18	—	—	Kearsley	d																			
18¾	18	18¾	—	—	Farnworth	d																			
19¾	19¾	19¾	—	—	Moses Gate	d																			
21	21	21	—	—	**Bolton**	a													05 25				06 02		
—	—	—	—	—		d							00 05						05 25						
—	—	25½	—	—	Westhoughton	d																			
—	—	28	15¾	—	Hindley	d		00 15																	
—	—	29½	17¼	0	Ince	d		00 18																	
—	—	—	—	0¾	Wigan North Western	a																06 16			
—	—	30½	18¼	—	**Wigan Wallgate**	a		00 23													06 02				
—	—	—	—	—		d															06 04			06 37	
—	—	—	20	—	Pemberton	d															06 08				
—	—	—	22	—	Orrell	d															06 12				
—	—	—	23¼	—	Upholland	d															06 15				
—	—	—	25¼	—	Rainford	d															06 19				
—	—	—	30½	—	**Kirkby**	a															06 29				
—	—	33¼	—	—	Gathurst	d																		06 41	
—	—	35	—	—	Appley Bridge	d																		06 45	
—	—	37¼	—	—	Parbold	d																		06 49	
—	—	38¾	—	—	Hoscar	d																		06 52	
—	—	40¼	—	—	Burscough Bridge	d																		06 56	
—	—	41½	—	—	New Lane	d																		06 58	
—	—	43½	—	—	Bescar Lane	d																		07 02	
—	—	46¾	—	—	Meols Cop	d																		07 07	
—	—	48	—	—	**Southport**	a																		07 14	
24	24	—	—	—	Lostock	d							00 23												
26	26	—	—	—	Horwich Parkway	d							00 31						05 44						
27½	27½	—	—	—	Blackrod	d							00 37												
29½	29½	—	—	—	Adlington (Lancashire)	d							00 44												
33½	33½	—	—	—	Chorley	d					00 06		00 54						06 01						
36	36	—	—	—	Buckshaw Parkway	d				00 09	00 21		01 09						06 16						
37	37	—	—	—	Leyland	d			00 17	00 23			01 23									06 29			
41	41	—	—	—	**Preston** 8 65,97	a			00 23	00 43	00 46	00 59	01s43				05 46	05 35	06 41			06 36			
—	—	—	—	—		d			00 25			01 01		05 16				05 40				06 38			
48¾	—	—	—	—	Kirkham & Wesham 97	a						01 10	02s08									06 47			
55¼	—	—	—	—	Poulton-le-Fylde 97	a			00 41			01 18	02s28									06 55			
57¼	—	—	—	—	Layton 97	a						01 22	02s38									06 59			
58½	—	—	—	—	**Blackpool North** 97	a			00 48			01 29	02 48									07 04			
—	62	—	—	—	**Lancaster** 6 65	a								05 36				05 55							
—	—	—	—	—		d								05 36	05 40			05 56							06 48
—	81	—	—	—	Oxenholme Lake District 65	a									06 18			06 10							
—	91	—	—	—	Windermere 83	a									06 39										
—	68	—	—	—	Carnforth	d								05 46											06a58
—	71¾	—	—	—	Silverdale	d								05 51											
—	74	—	—	—	Arnside	d								05 56											
—	77¼	—	—	—	Grange-over-Sands	d								06 02											
—	79½	—	—	—	Kents Bank	d	00 04							06 06											
—	81½	—	—	—	Cark	d	00 08							06 10											
—	87½	—	—	—	Ulverston	d	00 16							06 18											
—	90¾	—	—	—	Dalton	d	00 24							06 27											
—	95	—	—	—	Roose	d	00 30							06 33											
—	96¾	—	—	—	**Barrow-in-Furness**	a	00 37							06 40											

A From Manchester Airport
B From Blackburn
C From Manchester Piccadilly
D To Carlisle
E To Glasgow Central
F To Newcastle
G To Clitheroe
H To Leeds

Table T082-F

Mondays to Fridays

21 May to 7 December

Manchester - Bolton - Wigan, Kirkby, Southport, Preston, Blackpool North and Barrow-in-Furness

		NT	NT	NT	NT	NT	TP	NT	TP	NT		NT	TP	NT	NT	NT	NT	NT	NT	NT		TP	NT	NT
		◇		◇			◇1		◇1				◇1	◇		◇		◇				◇1		
			A		B		C		D				E		F	G				H		I	J	K
									🛒													🛒		
Manchester Airport 85 ✈	d		05 36	05 42			05 48		06 10				06 19	06 35				06 39				06 47		
Heald Green 85	d			05 46										06 39										
Buxton 86	d																							
Hazel Grove 86	d																							
Stockport 84	d									06 13													07 06	
Manchester Piccadilly 10	d		05 51	06 01			06 05		06 26	06 30			06 34	06 55				07 01				07 05	07 17	
Manchester Oxford Road	d		05 55	06 05			06 09			06 33			06 38	06 58				07 04				07 08	07 20	
Deansgate	d			06 07						06 36								07 07					07 22	
Rochdale 41	d				←			05 53								06 39				06 42				07 09
Manchester Victoria	d		06 05		06 05	06 08	06a14	06 15				06 36	06a45		06 50	06 55	07 00		07 05	07 08		07a14		07 25
Salford Central	d		→		06 08	06 12		06 18				06 39			06 53	06 58	07 03		07 08	07 12				07 28
Salford Crescent	a			06 10	06 13	06 17		06 21		06 40		06 44			06 57	07 01	07 06	07 11	07 12	07 18			07 27	07 31
	d			06 11	06 14	06 18		06 22		06 40		06 45			06 57	07 02	07 07	07 11	07 14	07 18			07 28	07 32
Swinton	d							06 28				06 52					07 13							
Moorside	d											06 54					07 16							
Walkden	d							06 33				06 58				07 10	07 19							07 42
Atherton	d							06 39				07 04				07 16	07 25							07 49
Hag Fold	d							06 41				07 06					07 28							
Daisy Hill	d							06 44				07 10				07 19	07 31							07 53
Clifton	d																							
Kearsley	d					06 25									07 05									
Farnworth	d					06 27									07 07									
Moses Gate	d					06 30									07 09									
Bolton	a			06 21	06 26	06 33				06 51					07 13			07 22	07 26	07 30			07 39	
	d			06 22	06 26	06 34				06 51					07 13			07 22	07 26				07 39	
Westhoughton	d					06 41									07 21								07 47	
Hindley	d					06 45		06 49				07 14			07 28		07 35						07 53	08 00
Ince	d							06 52									07 38							
Wigan North Western	a					06 53								07 28	07 33								07 59	
Wigan Wallgate	a							06 55				07 19				07 29	07 41							08 05
	d							06 57				07 21					07 43							08 06
Pemberton	d							07 01									07 47							
Orrell	d							07 05									07 51							
Upholland	d							07 08									07 54							
Rainford	d							07 12									07 58							
Kirkby	a							07 22									08 08							
Gathurst	d											07 25												08 11
Appley Bridge	d											07 29												08 15
Parbold	d											07 34												08 19
Hoscar	d																							08 22
Burscough Bridge	d											07 39												08 25
New Lane	d																							08 28
Bescar Lane	d																							08 31
Meols Cop	d											07 47												08 37
Southport	a											07 54												08 44
Lostock	d				06 32					06 56									07 33					
Horwich Parkway	d			06 29	06 36					07 00								07 31	07 37					
Blackrod	d				06 40					07 03									07 40					
Adlington (Lancashire)	d				06 44					07 07									07 44					
Chorley	d			06 37	06 49					07 12								07 38	07 49					
Buckshaw Parkway	d			06 40	06a54					07 16								07 42	07a56					
Leyland	d			06 46										07 39										
Preston 8 65,97	a			06 54					07 01	07 25				07 47				07 53						
	d	06 44							07 03	07 28				07 48										
Kirkham & Wesham 97	a													07 57										
Poulton-le-Fylde 97	a									07 44				08 06										
Layton 97	a													08 10										
Blackpool North 97	a									07 53				08 14										
Lancaster 6 65	a	07 01							07 18															
	d	07 02							07 18															
Oxenholme Lake District 65	a								07 31															
Windermere 83	a																							
Carnforth	d	07 11																						
Silverdale	d	07 17																						
Arnside	d	07 21																						
Grange-over-Sands	d	07 27																						
Kents Bank	d																							
Cark	d	07 33																						
Ulverston	d	07 41																						
Dalton	d	07 49																						
Roose	d	07 56																						
Barrow-in-Furness	a	08 03																						

A To Buckshaw Parkway
B From Manchester Airport
C To Hull
D To Edinburgh
E To Newcastle
F From Stalybridge
G From Leeds
H To Blackburn
I To Middlesbrough
J From Alderley Edge
K From Blackburn

Table T082-F

Mondays to Fridays
21 May to 7 December

Manchester - Bolton - Wigan, Kirkby, Southport, Preston, Blackpool North and Barrow-in-Furness

		NT	TP ◇1 A	NT	NT	NT	NT B	TP ◇1 C	NT ◇	NT D	NT ◇ E	NT ◇	NT ◇	NT	NT F	TP ◇1 G	NT H	NT I	TP ◇1 J	NT ◇ K		NT	NT B
Manchester Airport 85	d		07 10					07 19	07 24				07 40			07 47			08 10				
Heald Green 85	d								07 28				07 44										
Buxton 86	d																						
Hazel Grove 86	d																						
Stockport 84	d																08 06						
Manchester Piccadilly	d		07 26		07 31			07 35	07 43				08 01			08 05	08 18		08 26	08 30			
Manchester Oxford Road	d				07 34			07 38	07 50				08 04			08 08	08 22			08 34			
Deansgate	d				07 36								08 07							08 37			
Rochdale 41	d						07 14				07 38				07 42			08 06					08 14
Manchester Victoria	d					07 37	07 41	07a45		07 50	07 55			08 05	08 08	08a14		08 26				08 37	08 41
Salford Central	d					07 40	07 44			07 53	07 58			08 08	08 12			08 29				08 40	08 44
Salford Crescent	a				07 40	07 44	07 48			07 56	08 01		08 11	08 11	08 18		08 28	08 32		08 41		08 44	08 48
	d				07 41	07 45	07 48			07 57	08 07		08 11	08 14	08 18		08 28	08 33		08 41		08 45	08 48
Swinton	d					07 52												08 39				08 52	
Moorside	d					07 54																08 54	
Walkden	d					07 58					08 15							08 44				08 58	
Atherton	d					08 04					08 21							08 50				09 04	
Hag Fold	d					08 07																09 07	
Daisy Hill	d					08 10					08 25							08 54				09 10	
Clifton	d																						
Kearsley	d									08 04													
Farnworth	d									08 07													
Moses Gate	d									08 09													
Bolton	a				07 51		08 00			08 13			08 22	08 26	08 30		08 39			08 52			09 00
	d				07 55					08 13			08 22	08 26			08 40			08 52			
Westhoughton	d									08 21							08 47						
Hindley	d					08 15				08 28							08 53	08 59				09 15	
Ince	d					08 18				08 31												09 18	
Wigan North Western	a								08 18	08 35							09 00						
Wigan Wallgate	a					08 21					08 38							09 04				09 21	
	d					08 23					08 39							09 06				09 23	
Pemberton	d					08 27																09 27	
Orrell	d					08 31																09 31	
Upholland	d					08 34																09 34	
Rainford	d					08 38																09 38	
Kirkby	a					08 48																09 48	
Gathurst	d										08 44							09 10					
Appley Bridge	d										08 48							09 14					
Parbold	d										08 52							09 18					
Hoscar	d																						
Burscough Bridge	d										08 57							09 23					
New Lane	d																						
Bescar Lane	d																						
Meols Cop	d										09 05							09 31					
Southport	a										09 13							09 38					
Lostock	d				08 00									08 32						08 57			
Horwich Parkway	d				08 05								08 29	08 36						09 01			
Blackrod	d				08 08									08 40									
Adlington (Lancashire)	d				08 12									08 44									
Chorley	d				08 17								08 37	08 49						09 09			
Buckshaw Parkway	d				08 21								08 41	08a56						09 13			
Leyland	d				08 28				08 32											09 16			
Preston 65,97	a		08 02		08 36				08 39				08 52						09 02	09 24			
	d		08 03		08 38				08 41			08 42							09 04	09 29	09 32		
Kirkham & Wesham 97	a								08 50												09 41		
Poulton-le-Fylde 97	a				08 54				08 58												09 50		
Layton 97	a								09 02														
Blackpool North 97	a				09 01				09 07												09 59		
Lancaster 65	a		08 18									08 59							09 19	09 50			
	d	07 36		08 23								09 00							09 19	09 59			
Oxenholme Lake District 65	a																		09 32	10 18			
Windermere 83	a																			10 41			
Carnforth	d	07 45		08 32								09 10											
Silverdale	d	07 51		08 38								09 16											
Arnside	d	07 55		08 42								09 20											
Grange-over-Sands	d	08 01		08 48								09 26											
Kents Bank	d	08 05		08 52								09 30											
Cark	d	08 09		08 56								09 34											
Ulverston	d	08 17		09 04								09 42											
Dalton	d	08 26		09 13								09 50											
Roose	d	08 32		09 19								09 56											
Barrow-in-Furness	a	08 39		09 26								10 03											

A To Glasgow Central
B To Clitheroe
C To Newcastle
D From Stalybridge
E From Leeds
F To Blackburn
G To Middlesbrough
H From Alderley Edge
I From Blackburn
J To Edinburgh
K ◇ from Preston

Table T082-F

Mondays to Fridays
21 May to 7 December

Manchester - Bolton - Wigan, Kirkby, Southport, Preston, Blackpool North and Barrow-in-Furness

		TP ◇1 A	NT ◇	NT B	NT ◇ C	NT	NT ◇	NT	NT D	TP ◇1 E	NT F	NT G	TP ◇1 H	NT	NT	NT I	TP ◇1 A	NT ◇ J	NT ◇	NT ◇	NT B	NT ◇ C
Manchester Airport 85	d	08 17	08 28				08 41			08 47			09 10				09 19			09 29		
Heald Green 85	d						08 45													09 33		
Buxton 86	d					08 00																
Hazel Grove 86	d					08 35																
Stockport 84	d					08 45					09 06											
Manchester Piccadilly	d	08 35	08 47			08 57	09 01			09 05	09 18		09 26	09 31			09 35			09 47		
Manchester Oxford Road	d	08 38	08 51			09 00	09 04			09 08	09 22			09 34			09 38			09 51		
Deansgate	d					09 03	09 07							09 37								
Rochdale 41	d				08 39				08 42			09 09				09 14						09 39
Manchester Victoria	d	08a45		08 50	08 55	09a07		09 05	09 08	09a14		09 26			09 37	09 41	09a45				09 50	09 55
Salford Central	d			08 53	08 58			09 08	09 12			09 29			09 40	09 44					09 53	09 58
Salford Crescent	a			08 56	09 01		09 11	09 11	09 18		09 27	09 32		09 40	09 44	09 48					09 56	10 01
	d			08 57	09 02		09 11	09 14	09 18		09 29	09 33		09 41	09 45	09 48					09 57	10 02
Swinton	d											09 39			09 51							
Moorside	d														09 54							
Walkden	d				09 10							09 44			09 57							10 10
Atherton	d				09 16							09 50			10 03							10 16
Hag Fold	d														10 05							
Daisy Hill	d				09 20							09 54			10 09							10 20
Clifton	d																					
Kearsley	d			09 04																	10 04	
Farnworth	d			09 07																	10 07	
Moses Gate	d			09 09																	10 09	
Bolton	a			09 13			09 21	09 26	09 30		09 39			09 51		10 00					10 13	
	d			09 13			09 22	09 26			09 40			09 52							10 13	
Westhoughton	d			09 21							09 47										10 21	
Hindley	d			09 31							09 53	09 59			10 13						10 29	
Ince	d											10 02										
Wigan North Western	a		09 19	09 36							09 59									10 18	10 34	
Wigan Wallgate	a				09 28							10 05			10 18							10 28
	d				09 30							10 07			10 20							10 30
Pemberton	d														10 24							
Orrell	d														10 28							
Upholland	d														10 31							
Rainford	d														10 35							
Kirkby	a														10 45							
Gathurst	d				09 34							10 11										10 34
Appley Bridge	d				09 38							10 15										10 38
Parbold	d				09 43							10 19										10 43
Hoscar	d											10 22										
Burscough Bridge	d				09 48							10 25										10 48
New Lane	d											10 28										
Bescar Lane	d											10 31										
Meols Cop	d				09 56							10 37										10 56
Southport	a				10 03							10 44										11 03
Lostock	d							09 32						09 57								
Horwich Parkway	d						09 28	09 36						10 01								
Blackrod	d							09 40														
Adlington (Lancashire)	d							09 44														
Chorley	d						09 36	09 49						10 09								
Buckshaw Parkway	d						09 39	09a56						10 12								
Leyland	d		09 31											10 18						10 30		
Preston 65,97	a		09 40				09 49						10 02	10 24						10 41		
	d		09 45				09 57						10 04	10 26					10 44	10 46		
Kirkham & Wesham 97	a		09 54																	10 55		
Poulton-le-Fylde 97	a		10 03											10 42						11 03		
Layton 97	a		10 07																	11 07		
Blackpool North 97	a		10 13											10 51						11 12		
Lancaster 65	a						10 13						10 19						11 01			
	d						10 14						10 20					10 45	11 02			
Oxenholme Lake District 65	a												10 33									
Windermere 83	a																					
Carnforth	d						10 22											10a55	11 11			
Silverdale	d						10 28															
Arnside	d						10 32												11 20			
Grange-over-Sands	d						10 37												11 26			
Kents Bank	d						10 41															
Cark	d						10 45															
Ulverston	d						10 53												11 39			
Dalton	d						11 01															
Roose	d						11 06															
Barrow-in-Furness	a						11 15												11 58			

A To Newcastle
B From Stalybridge
C From Leeds
D To Blackburn
E To Middlesbrough
F From Alderley Edge
G From Blackburn
H To Glasgow Central
I To Clitheroe
J To Leeds

Table T082-F

Mondays to Fridays

21 May to 7 December

Manchester - Bolton - Wigan, Kirkby, Southport, Preston, Blackpool North and Barrow-in-Furness

	NT ◇	NT	NT A	TP ◇■ B	NT C	NT D	TP ◇■ E	NT	NT	NT F	TP ◇■ G	NT ◇	NT H	NT ◇ I	NT ◇	NT	NT A	TP ◇■ B	NT C	NT D	NT J	TP ◇■ K
Manchester Airport 85 ✈ d	09 40			09 47			10 10				10 19	10 29			10 40			10 47				10 59
Heald Green 85 d	09 44											10 33			10 44							
Buxton 86 d																						
Hazel Grove 86 d																						
Stockport 84 d					10 06														11 06			
Manchester Piccadilly ■ d	10 01			10 05	10 18		10 26	10 31			10 35	10 47			11 01			11 05	11 18			11 22
Manchester Oxford Road d	10 04			10 08	10 21			10 34			10 38	10 51			11 04			11 08	11 21			
Deansgate d	10 07							10 37							11 07							
Rochdale 41 d			09 42			10 09				10 14				10 38			10 42			11 09		
Manchester Victoria d		10 05	10 08	10a14		10 26			10 37	10 41	10a45		10 50	10 54		11 05	11 08	11a14		11 26		
Salford Central d		10 08	10 12			10 29			10 40	10 44			10 53	10 57		11 08	11 12			11 29		
Salford Crescent a	10 11	10 11	10 18		10 26	10 32		10 40	10 44	10 48			10 56	11 00	11 11	11 11	11 18		11 26	11 32		
d	10 11	10 14	10 18		10 28	10 33		10 41	10 45	10 48			10 57	11 01	11 11	11 14	11 18		11 28	11 33		
Swinton d						10 39			10 52											11 39		
Moorside d									10 54													
Walkden d						10 44			10 58					11 09						11 44		
Atherton d						10 50			11 04					11 15						11 50		
Hag Fold d									11 07													
Daisy Hill d						10 54			11 10					11 19						11 54		
Clifton d																						
Kearsley d													11 04									
Farnworth d													11 07									
Moses Gate d													11 09									
Bolton a	10 22	10 26	10 31		10 39			10 51		11 00			11 13		11 22	11 26	11 31		11 39			
d	10 22	10 26			10 39			10 52					11 13		11 22	11 26			11 39			
Westhoughton d					10 47								11 21						11 47			
Hindley d					10 53	10 59			11 15				11 29						11 53	11 59		
Ince d									11 18													
Wigan North Western a					10 59							11 20	11 34						11 59			
Wigan Wallgate a						11 04			11 21					11 28						12 04		
d						11 05			11 23					11 30						12 05		
Pemberton d									11 27													
Orrell d									11 31													
Upholland d									11 34													
Rainford d									11 38													
Kirkby a									11 48													
Gathurst d						11 10								11 34						12 10		
Appley Bridge d						11 14								11 38						12 14		
Parbold d						11 18								11 43						12 18		
Hoscar d																				12 21		
Burscough Bridge d						11 23								11 48						12 24		
New Lane d																				12 27		
Bescar Lane d																				12 30		
Meols Cop d						11 31								11 56						12 36		
Southport a						11 38								12 03						12 43		
Lostock d		10 32						10 57								11 32						
Horwich Parkway d	10 29	10 36						11 01							11 29	11 36						
Blackrod d		10 40														11 40						
Adlington (Lancashire) d		10 44														11 44						
Chorley d	10 37	10 49						11 09							11 37	11 49						
Buckshaw Parkway d	10 41	10a56						11 12							11 41	11a56						
Leyland d								11 16				11 33										
Preston ■ 65,97 a	10 52						11 02	11 24				11 42			11 53							11 59
d								11 25				11 45										12 04
Kirkham & Wesham 97 a												11 54										
Poulton-le-Fylde 97 a								11 41				12 03										
Layton 97 a												12 07										
Blackpool North 97 a								11 50				12 11										
Lancaster ■ 65 a																						12 19
d																					12 02	12 20
Oxenholme Lake District 65 a																						12 33
Windermere 83 a																						
Carnforth d																					12 11	
Silverdale d																					12 17	
Arnside d																					12 21	
Grange-over-Sands d																					12 27	
Kents Bank d																					12 31	
Cark d																					12 35	
Ulverston d																					12 43	
Dalton d																					12 58	
Roose d																					13 04	
Barrow-in-Furness a																					13 11	

A To Blackburn
B To Middlesbrough
C From Alderley Edge
D From Blackburn
E To Edinburgh
F To Clitheroe
G To Newcastle
H From Stalybridge
I From Leeds
J To Carlisle
K To Glasgow Central

Table T082-F

Mondays to Fridays

21 May to 7 December

Manchester - Bolton - Wigan, Kirkby, Southport, Preston, Blackpool North and Barrow-in-Furness

	NT ◇	NT	NT	NT A	TP ◇■ B	NT ◇	NT C	NT ◇ D	NT E	NT ◇	NT	NT F	TP ◇■ G	NT H	NT I	TP ◇■ J	NT	NT	NT A	TP ◇■ B	NT ◇	NT C
Manchester Airport 85 ✈ d					11 19	11 29				11 41			11 47			12 10				12 19	12 29	
Heald Green 85 d						11 33				11 45											12 33	
Buxton 86 d																						
Hazel Grove 86 d																						
Stockport 84 d														12 06								
Manchester Piccadilly ■ d		11 31			11 35	11 47				12 01			12 05	12 18		12 26	12 31			12 35	12 47	
Manchester Oxford Road d		11 34			11 38	11 51				12 04			12 08	12 21			12 34			12 38	12 51	
Deansgate d		11 37								12 07							12 37					
Rochdale 41 d				11 16				11 39				11 42			12 09				12 17			
Manchester Victoria d			11 36	11 41	11a45		11 50	11 55			12 05	12 08	12a14		12 26			12 36	12 41	12a45		12 50
Salford Central d			11 39	11 44			11 53	11 58			12 08	12 12			12 29			12 40	12 44			12 53
Salford Crescent a		11 41	11 44	11 48			11 56	12 01		12 11	12 11	12 18		12 26	12 32		12 41	12 44	12 48			12 56
d		11 41	11 45	11 48			11 57	12 02		12 11	12 14	12 18		12 29	12 33		12 41	12 45	12 48			12 57
Swinton d			11 52												12 39			12 52				
Moorside d			11 54															12 54				
Walkden d			11 58					12 10							12 44			12 58				
Atherton d			12 04					12 16							12 50			13 04				
Hag Fold d			12 07															13 07				
Daisy Hill d			12 10					12 20							12 54			13 10				
Clifton d																						
Kearsley d							12 04															13 04
Farnworth d							12 07															13 07
Moses Gate d							12 09															13 09
Bolton a		11 52		12 00			12 13			12 21	12 26	12 30		12 39			12 52		13 00			13 13
d		11 52					12 13			12 22	12 26			12 40			12 52					13 13
Westhoughton d							12 21							12 47								13 21
Hindley d			12 15				12 29							12 53	12 59			13 15				13 29
Ince d			12 18															13 18				
Wigan North Western a						12 19	12 34							12 59							13 19	13 34
Wigan Wallgate a			12 21					12 28							13 04			13 21				
d			12 23					12 30							13 05			13 23				
Pemberton d			12 27															13 27				
Orrell d			12 31															13 31				
Upholland d			12 34															13 34				
Rainford d			12 38															13 38				
Kirkby a			12 48															13 48				
Gathurst d								12 34							13 10							
Appley Bridge d								12 38							13 14							
Parbold d								12 43							13 18							
Hoscar d																						
Burscough Bridge d								12 48							13 23							
New Lane d																						
Bescar Lane d																						
Meols Cop d								12 56							13 31							
Southport a								13 03							13 38							
Lostock d		11 57									12 32						12 57					
Horwich Parkway d		12 01								12 28	12 36						13 01					
Blackrod d											12 40											
Adlington (Lancashire) d											12 44											
Chorley d		12 09								12 36	12 49						13 09					
Buckshaw Parkway d		12 13								12 39	12a56						13 13					
Leyland d		12 16				12 30											13 17				13 31	
Preston ■ 65,97 a		12 23				12 35				12 48						13 02	13 23				13 42	
d	12 17	12 25				12 38				12 57						13 03	13 25				13 45	
Kirkham & Wesham 97 a						12 47															13 54	
Poulton-le-Fylde 97 a		12 42				12 56											13 42				14 03	
Layton 97 a						13 00															14 07	
Blackpool North 97 a		12 49				13 10											13 49				14 13	
Lancaster ■ 65 a	12 37									13 13						13 18						
d	12 37								12 45	13 14						13 19						
Oxenholme Lake District 65 a	13 00															13 32						
Windermere 83 a	13 24																					
Carnforth d									12a54	13 22												
Silverdale d										13 28												
Arnside d										13 32												
Grange-over-Sands d										13 37												
Kents Bank d										13 41												
Cark d										13 45												
Ulverston d										13 53												
Dalton d										14 01												
Roose d										14 06												
Barrow-in-Furness a										14 14												

A To Clitheroe
B To Newcastle
C From Stalybridge
D From Leeds
E From Morecambe to Leeds
F To Blackburn
G To Middlesbrough
H From Alderley Edge
I From Blackburn
J To Edinburgh

Table T082-F

Mondays to Fridays
21 May to 7 December

Manchester - Bolton - Wigan, Kirkby, Southport, Preston, Blackpool North and Barrow-in-Furness

		NT	NT	NT	NT	TP	NT	NT	NT	TP	NT	NT	NT	NT	TP	NT	NT	NT	NT	NT	NT	NT
		◇	◇			◇1				◇1	◇				◇1	◇		◇		◇		
		A			B	C	D	E		F				G	H		I	A				B
Manchester Airport 85	d		12 40			12 47				13 10					13 19	13 29				13 40		
Heald Green 85	d		12 44													13 33				13 44		
Buxton 86	d																					
Hazel Grove 86	d																					
Stockport 84	d						13 06															
Manchester Piccadilly	d		13 01			13 05	13 18			13 26		13 31			13 35	13 47				14 01		
Manchester Oxford Road	d		13 04			13 08	13 21					13 34			13 38	13 51				14 04		
Deansgate	d		13 07									13 37								14 07		
Rochdale 41	d	12 39			12 42			13 09						13 16				13 39				13 42
Manchester Victoria	d	12 55		13 05	13 08	13a14		13 26					13 36	13 41	13a45		13 50	13 55			14 05	14 08
Salford Central	d	12 58		13 08	13 12			13 29					13 39	13 44			13 53	13 58			14 08	14 12
Salford Crescent	a	13 01	13 11	13 11	13 18		13 26	13 32				13 41	13 44	13 48			13 56	14 01		14 11	14 11	14 18
	d	13 02	13 11	13 14	13 18		13 29	13 33				13 41	13 45	13 48			13 57	14 02		14 11	14 14	14 18
Swinton	d							13 39					13 52									
Moorside	d												13 54									
Walkden	d	13 10						13 44					13 58					14 10				
Atherton	d	13 16						13 50					14 04					14 16				
Hag Fold	d												14 07									
Daisy Hill	d	13 20						13 54					14 10					14 20				
Clifton	d																					
Kearsley	d																14 04					
Farnworth	d																14 07					
Moses Gate	d																14 09					
Bolton	a		13 22	13 26	13 31		13 39					13 52		14 00			14 13			14 22	14 26	14 30
	d		13 22	13 26			13 40					13 52					14 13			14 22	14 26	
Westhoughton	d						13 47										14 21					
Hindley	d						13 53	13 59					14 15				14 29					
Ince	d												14 18									
Wigan North Western	a						13 59									14 19	14 34					
Wigan Wallgate	a	13 28						14 04					14 23					14 28				
	d	13 30						14 05										14 30	14 40			
Pemberton	d																		14 44			
Orrell	d																		14 48			
Upholland	d																		14 51			
Rainford	d																		14 55			
Kirkby	a																		15 07			
Gathurst	d	13 34						14 10										14 34				
Appley Bridge	d	13 38						14 14										14 38				
Parbold	d	13 43						14 18										14 43				
Hoscar	d																					
Burscough Bridge	d	13 48						14 23										14 48				
New Lane	d																					
Bescar Lane	d																					
Meols Cop	d	13 56						14 31										14 56				
Southport	a	14 03						14 38										15 03				
Lostock	d			13 32								13 57									14 32	
Horwich Parkway	d		13 29	13 36								14 01								14 29	14 36	
Blackrod	d			13 40																	14 40	
Adlington (Lancashire)	d			13 44																	14 44	
Chorley	d		13 37	13 49								14 09								14 37	14 49	
Buckshaw Parkway	d		13 41	13a56								14 13								14 41	14a56	
Leyland	d											14 18				14 31						
Preston 65,97	a		13 57							14 02		14 24				14 41				14 57		
	d									14 04	14 10	14 26				14 45						
Kirkham & Wesham 97	a															14 54						
Poulton-le-Fylde 97	a											14 42				15 03						
Layton 97	a															15 07						
Blackpool North 97	a											14 51				15 13						
Lancaster 65	a									14 19	14 30											
	d								14 02	14 19	14 30											
Oxenholme Lake District 65	a									14 32	14 51											
Windermere 83	a										15 09											
Carnforth	d								14 11													
Silverdale	d								14 17													
Arnside	d								14 22													
Grange-over-Sands	d								14 28													
Kents Bank	d								14 31													
Cark	d								14 35													
Ulverston	d								14 43													
Dalton	d								14 52													
Roose	d								14 58													
Barrow-in-Furness	a								15 05													

A From Leeds
B To Blackburn
C To Middlesbrough
D From Alderley Edge
E From Blackburn
F To Glasgow Central
G To Clitheroe
H To Newcastle
I From Stalybridge

Table T082-F

Mondays to Fridays
21 May to 7 December

Manchester - Bolton - Wigan, Kirkby, Southport, Preston, Blackpool North and Barrow-in-Furness

		TP	NT	NT	NT	NT	TP	NT	NT	NT	NT	TP	NT	NT	NT	NT	NT	NT	TP	NT	NT	TP	NT
		◇1			◇		◇1					◇1	◇		◇	◇			◇1			◇1	
		A	B	C	D	E	F	G			H	I		J	K			L	A	B	C	M	
Manchester Airport 85	d	13 47					14 10					14 19	14 29			14 40			14 47			15 10	
Heald Green 85	d												14 33			14 44							
Buxton 86	d																						
Hazel Grove 86	d																						
Stockport 84	d		14 06																	15 06			
Manchester Piccadilly	d	14 05	14 18				14 26		14 31			14 35	14 47			15 01			15 05	15 18		15 26	15 31
Manchester Oxford Road	d	14 08	14 21						14 34			14 38	14 51			15 04			15 08	15 21			15 34
Deansgate	d								14 37							15 07							15 37
Rochdale 41	d			14 09							14 13				14 39			14 42			15 09		
Manchester Victoria	d	14a14		14 26						14 37	14 41	14a45		14 50	14 55		15 05	15 08	15a14		15 26		
Salford Central	d			14 29						14 40	14 44			14 53	14 58		15 08	15 12			15 29		
Salford Crescent	a		14 26	14 32					14 40	14 44	14 48			14 56	15 01	15 11	15 11	15 18		15 26	15 32		15 40
	d		14 29	14 33					14 41	14 45	14 49			14 57	15 02	15 11	15 14	15 18		15 29	15 33		15 41
Swinton	d			14 39						14 52											15 39		
Moorside	d									14 54													
Walkden	d			14 44						14 58					15 10						15 44		
Atherton	d			14 50						15 04					15 16						15 50		
Hag Fold	d									15 07													
Daisy Hill	d			14 54						15 10					15 20						15 54		
Clifton	d																						
Kearsley	d													15 04									
Farnworth	d													15 07									
Moses Gate	d													15 09									
Bolton	a		14 39						14 51		15 00			15 13		15 22	15 26	15 31		15 40			15 51
	d		14 40						14 52					15 13		15 22	15 26			15 40			15 52
Westhoughton	d		14 47											15 21						15 48			
Hindley	d		14 53	14 59						15 15				15 29						15 54	15 59		
Ince	d									15 18													
Wigan North Western	a		14 59										15 19	15 34						16 00			
Wigan Wallgate	a			15 04						15 21					15 28						16 04		
	d			15 05						15 23					15 30						16 05		
Pemberton	d									15 27													
Orrell	d									15 31													
Upholland	d									15 34													
Rainford	d									15 38													
Kirkby	a									15 48													
Gathurst	d			15 10											15 34						16 10		
Appley Bridge	d			15 14											15 38						16 14		
Parbold	d			15 18											15 43						16 18		
Hoscar	d			15 21																			
Burscough Bridge	d			15 24											15 48						16 23		
New Lane	d			15 27																			
Bescar Lane	d			15 30																			
Meols Cop	d			15 36											15 56						16 31		
Southport	a			15 43											16 03						16 38		
Lostock	d								14 57								15 32						15 57
Horwich Parkway	d								15 01							15 29	15 36						16 01
Blackrod	d																15 40						
Adlington (Lancashire)	d																15 44						
Chorley	d								15 09							15 37	15 49						16 09
Buckshaw Parkway	d								15 12							15 40	15a56						16 12
Leyland	d								15 18				15 31										16 18
Preston 65,97	a						15 03		15 24				15 41			15 52						16 02	16 24
	d						15 04		15 25				15 43									16 04	16 25
Kirkham & Wesham 97	a												15 52										
Poulton-le-Fylde 97	a								15 41				16 00										16 41
Layton 97	a												16 04										16 46
Blackpool North 97	a								15 50				16 11										16 52
Lancaster 65	a						15 19															16 19	
	d				14 51	15 03		16 13														16 19	
Oxenholme Lake District 65	a																					16 32	
Windermere 83	a																						
Carnforth	d				15a23	15 12		16 22															
Silverdale	d					15 18		16 28															
Arnside	d					15 23		16 32															
Grange-over-Sands	d					15 29		16 38															
Kents Bank	d					15 32		16 42															
Cark	d					15 36		16 46															
Ulverston	d					15 45		16 54															
Dalton	d					15 53		17 02															
Roose	d					16 00		17 08															
Barrow-in-Furness	a					16 07		17 16															

A To Middlesbrough
B From Alderley Edge
C From Blackburn
D To Leeds
E To Sellafield
F To Edinburgh
G To Carlisle
H To Clitheroe
I To Newcastle
J From Stalybridge
K From Leeds
L To Blackburn
M To Glasgow Central

Table T082-F

Mondays to Fridays
21 May to 7 December

Manchester - Bolton - Wigan, Kirkby, Southport, Preston, Blackpool North and Barrow-in-Furness

		NT	NT	TP	NT	NT	NT	NT	NT	NT	TP	NT	NT	NT	TP	NT	NT	NT	NT	TP	NT	NT
				◇1	◇		◇	◇			◇1				◇1					◇1	◇	
			A	B		C	D			A	E	F	G	H	I				A	B		C
				🍴							🍴				🍴					🍴		
Manchester Airport	85 d			15 19	15 29			15 40			15 47				16 10					16 19	16 24	
Heald Green	85 d				15 33			15 44													16 28	
Buxton	86 d																					
Hazel Grove	86 d																					
Stockport	84 d											16 06										
Manchester Piccadilly [10]	d			15 35	15 47			16 01			16 05	16 18			16 26		16 31			16 35	16 45	
Manchester Oxford Road	d			15 38	15 51			16 04			16 08	16 21					16 34			16 38	16 49	
Deansgate	d							16 07									16 37					
Rochdale	41 d		15 16				15 39			15 42			16 09						16 14			
Manchester Victoria	d	15 37	15 41	15a45		15 50	15 55		16 05	16 08	16a15		16 26					16 37	16 41	16a45		16 49
Salford Central	d	15 40	15 44			15 53	15 58		16 08	16 12			16 29					16 40	16 44			16 52
Salford Crescent	a	15 44	15 48			15 56	16 01	16 11	16 11	16 18		16 28	16 32				16 40	16 44	16 48			16 55
	d	15 45	15 48			15 57	16 02	16 11	16 14	16 18		16 29	16 33				16 41	16 45	16 48			16 57
Swinton	d	15 52											16 39					16 52				
Moorside	d	15 54																16 54				
Walkden	d	15 58					16 10						16 44					16 58				
Atherton	d	16 04					16 16						16 50					17 04				
Hag Fold	d	16 07																17 07				
Daisy Hill	d	16 10					16 20						16 54					17 10				
Clifton	d																					
Kearsley	d					16 04																17 04
Farnworth	d					16 07																17 07
Moses Gate	d					16 09																17 09
Bolton	a		16 00			16 13		16 22	16 26	16 30		16 39					16 51		17 00			17 13
	d					16 13		16 22	16 26			16 40					16 52					17 13
Westhoughton	d					16 21						16 47										17 21
Hindley	d	16 15				16 30						16 53	16 59					17 15				17 29
Ince	d	16 18																17 18				
Wigan North Western	a				16 19	16 35						17 02									17 19	17 34
Wigan Wallgate	a	16 21					16 28						17 04					17 21				
	d	16 23					16 30						17 05					17 23				
Pemberton	d	16 27																17 27				
Orrell	d	16 31																17 31				
Upholland	d	16 34																17 34				
Rainford	d	16 38																17 38				
Kirkby	a	16 48																17 48				
Gathurst	d						16 34						17 10									
Appley Bridge	d						16 38						17 14									
Parbold	d						16 43						17 18									
Hoscar	d												17 21									
Burscough Bridge	d						16 48						17 24									
New Lane	d												17 27									
Bescar Lane	d												17 30									
Meols Cop	d						16 56						17 36									
Southport	a						17 03						17 43									
Lostock	d							16 27	16 32								16 57					
Horwich Parkway	d							16 31	16 36								17 01					
Blackrod	d								16 40								17 04					
Adlington (Lancashire)	d								16 44								17 08					
Chorley	d							16 39	16 49								17 13					
Buckshaw Parkway	d							16 43	16a56								17 16					
Leyland	d				16 31												17 22					
Preston [8]	65,97 a				16 41			16 58							17 02		17 30				17 38	
	d				16 43										17 03	17 20	17 32				17 40	
Kirkham & Wesham	97 a				16 52												17 41				17 50	
Poulton-le-Fylde	97 a				17 00												17 49				17 59	
Layton	97 a				17 04												17 54				18 03	
Blackpool North	97 a				17 09												18 00				18 07	
Lancaster [6]	65 a														17 18	17 37						
	d													17 01	17 19	17 38						
Oxenholme Lake District	65 a														17 32							
Windermere	83 a																					
Carnforth	d													17 10		17 47						
Silverdale	d															17 53						
Arnside	d													17 19		17 57						
Grange-over-Sands	d													17 25		18 03						
Kents Bank	d															18 07						
Cark	d															18 11						
Ulverston	d													17 38		18 19						
Dalton	d													17 46		18 27						
Roose	d													17 52		18 33						
Barrow-in-Furness	a													17 59		18 40						

A To Clitheroe
B To Newcastle
C From Stalybridge
D From Leeds
E To Middlesbrough
F From Alderley Edge
G From Blackburn
H To Carlisle
I To Edinburgh

Table T082-F

Mondays to Fridays
21 May to 7 December

Manchester - Bolton - Wigan, Kirkby, Southport, Preston, Blackpool North and Barrow-in-Furness

		NT	NT	NT	NT	NT	NT	TP	NT	NT	NT	TP	NT	NT	NT	NT	NT	TP	NT	NT	NT	NT	NT
		◇	◇	◇	◇			◇1				◇1		◇				◇1	◇		◇	◇	
		A	B	A			C	D		E	F	G	H				I	J		K	A		
								🍴				🍴						🍴					
Manchester Airport	85 d				16 40			16 47				17 10						17 19	17 26			17 42	
Heald Green	85 d				16 44														17 30			17 46	
Buxton	86 d																						
Hazel Grove	86 d																						
Stockport	84 d									17 06													
Manchester Piccadilly [10]	d				17 01			17 05		17 19		17 27			17 31			17 35	17 47			18 01	
Manchester Oxford Road	d				17 04			17 08							17 34			17 38	17 51			18 04	
Deansgate	d				17 07					17 22					17 37							18 07	
Rochdale	41 d	16 39					16 34				17 09						17 14				17 40		
Manchester Victoria	d	16 55				17 05	17 08	17a14	17 14		17 25					17 37	17 41	17a45		17 50	17 56		18 05
Salford Central	d	16 58				17 08	17 12		17 18		17 29					17 40	17 44			17 53	17 59		18 08
Salford Crescent	a	17 01			17 11	17 11	17 18		17 21	17 26	17 32				17 41	17 44	17 48			17 56	18 02	18 10	18 11
	d	17 02			17 11	17 14	17 18		17 22	17 29	17 33				17 41	17 45	17 48			17 57	18 02	18 11	18 14
Swinton	d								17 28							17 52							
Moorside	d										17 39					17 54							
Walkden	d	17 10							17 33		17 43					17 58					18 11		
Atherton	d	17 16							17 39		17 49					18 04					18 17		
Hag Fold	d								17 41							18 07							
Daisy Hill	d	17 20							17 44		17 53					18 10					18 21		
Clifton	d																			18 01			
Kearsley	d																			18 06			
Farnworth	d						17 27													18 09			
Moses Gate	d																			18 11			
Bolton	a				17 22	17 26	17 32			17 40					17 52		18 00			18 15		18 21	18 26
	d				17 22	17 26				17 40					17 52					18 15		18 21	18 26
Westhoughton	d									17 49										18 23			
Hindley	d								17 49	17 55	17 59					18 15				18 29			
Ince	d									17 58						18 18				18 32			
Wigan North Western	a								17 57		18 04								18 19	18 36			
Wigan Wallgate	a	17 28								18 01						18 21					18 29		
	d	17 30								18 03						18 23					18 30		
Pemberton	d															18 27							
Orrell	d															18 31							
Upholland	d															18 34							
Rainford	d															18 38							
Kirkby	a															18 48							
Gathurst	d	17 34								18 07											18 35		
Appley Bridge	d	17 38								18 11											18 39		
Parbold	d	17 43								18 15											18 43		
Hoscar	d									18 18													
Burscough Bridge	d	17 48								18 22											18 48		
New Lane	d									18 24													
Bescar Lane	d									18 28													
Meols Cop	d	17 56								18 33											18 56		
Southport	a	18 03								18 40											19 04		
Lostock	d				17 27	17 32									17 57							18 26	18 32
Horwich Parkway	d				17 31	17 36									18 01							18 30	18 36
Blackrod	d					17 40									18 04								18 40
Adlington (Lancashire)	d					17 44									18 08								18 44
Chorley	d				17 39	17 49									18 13							18 37	18 49
Buckshaw Parkway	d				17 43	17a56									18 16							18 41	18a56
Leyland	d														18 21				18 32				
Preston [8]	65,97 a				17 57							18 02			18 27				18 41			18 50	
	d			17 45								18 03		18 20	18 29				18 44			18 58	
Kirkham & Wesham	97 a														18 38				18 53				
Poulton-le-Fylde	97 a														18 46				19 01				
Layton	97 a														18 51				19 05				
Blackpool North	97 a														18 57				19 10				
Lancaster [6]	65 a			18 02								18 18		18 40								19 13	
	d		17 45	18 03								18 19	18 35	18 40								19 14	
Oxenholme Lake District	65 a											18 32		18 59									
Windermere	83 a													19 22									
Carnforth	d		17a55	18 12									18 44									19 22	
Silverdale	d			18 18									18 50									19 28	
Arnside	d			18 22									18 54									19 32	
Grange-over-Sands	d			18 28									19 00									19 37	
Kents Bank	d			18 32									19 04									19 41	
Cark	d			18 36									19 08									19 45	
Ulverston	d			18 44									19 16									19 53	
Dalton	d			18 52									19 24									20 01	
Roose	d			18 58									19 31									20 07	
Barrow-in-Furness	a			19 05									19 38									20 14	

A From Leeds
B From Morecambe to Leeds
C To Blackburn
D To Middlesbrough
E From Alderley Edge
F From Blackburn
G To Glasgow Central
H To Millom
I To Clitheroe
J To Newcastle
K From Stalybridge

Table T082-F

Mondays to Fridays
21 May to 7 December

Manchester - Bolton - Wigan, Kirkby, Southport, Preston, Blackpool North and Barrow-in-Furness

	TP	NT	NT	NT	TP	NT	NT	NT	TP	NT	NT	NT	NT	NT	NT	TP	NT	NT	NT	TP	NT	NT
	◇■				◇■				◇■	◇		◇	◇			◇■				◇■		
	A	B	C	D	E			F	G		H	I			F	A	C	D	J	K		
Manchester Airport 85 d	17 47				18 10				18 19	18 29			18 40			18 47				19 10		
Heald Green 85 d										18 33			18 44									
Buxton 86 d																						
Hazel Grove 86 d																						
Stockport 84 d			18 06														19 06					
Manchester Piccadilly d	18 05		18 18		18 26	18 31			18 35	18 48			19 01			19 05	19 18			19 26	19 31	
Manchester Oxford Road d	18 08		18 22			18 34			18 38	18 52			19 04			19 08	19 21				19 34	
Deansgate d						18 37							19 06								19 37	
Rochdale 41 d		17 53		18 09				18 18				18 39						19 09				
Manchester Victoria d	18a15	18 16		18 26			18 37	18 41	18a45		18 49	18 55		19 05	19 09	19a14		19 26				19 37
Salford Central d		18 19		18 29			18 40	18 44			18 52	18 58		19 08	19 13			19 29				19 40
Salford Crescent a		18 22	18 28	18 32		18 40	18 44	18 48			18 55	19 01	19 10	19 11	19 18		19 26	19 32			19 41	19 44
d		18 23	18 29	18 33		18 41	18 45	18 48			18 57	19 02	19 10	19 14	19 18		19 28	19 33			19 41	19 45
Swinton d				18 39			18 52											19 39				19 52
Moorside d							18 54															19 54
Walkden d				18 44			18 58					19 10						19 44				19 58
Atherton d				18 50			19 04					19 16						19 50				20 04
Hag Fold d							19 07															20 06
Daisy Hill d				18 54			19 10					19 20						19 54				20 10
Clifton d																						
Kearsley d											19 04											
Farnworth d											19 07											
Moses Gate d											19 09											
Bolton a		18 34	18 39			18 51		19 00			19 13		19 21	19 26	19 31		19 39				19 52	
d			18 40			18 52					19 13		19 21	19 26			19 39				19 52	
Westhoughton d			18 48								19 21						19 47					
Hindley d			18 54	18 59							19 29						19 53	19 59				20 14
Ince d				19 02														20 02				
Wigan North Western a										19 20	19 34						19 59					
Wigan Wallgate a			18 59	19 05			19 20					19 28						20 05				20 21
d			19 01	19 07								19 30						20 07				
Pemberton d				19 11																		
Orrell d				19 16																		
Upholland d				19 20																		
Rainford d				19 24																		
Kirkby a				19 34																		
Gathurst d			19 05									19 34						20 11				
Appley Bridge d			19 09									19 38						20 15				
Parbold d			19 13									19 43						20 19				
Hoscar d																						
Burscough Bridge d			19 18									19 48						20 24				
New Lane d																						
Bescar Lane d																						
Meols Cop d			19 26									19 56						20 32				
Southport a			19 33									20 03						20 39				
Lostock d						18 57								19 32							19 57	
Horwich Parkway d						19 01							19 28	19 36							20 01	
Blackrod d														19 40								
Adlington (Lancashire) d														19 44								
Chorley d						19 08							19 36	19 49							20 09	
Buckshaw Parkway d						19 12							19 40	19 53							20 13	
Leyland d						19 18				19 32				20 02							20 18	
Preston 65,97 a					19 02	19 24				19 43			19 51	20 10						20 02	20 24	
d					19 04	19 26				19 45										20 04	20 26	
Kirkham & Wesham 97 a										19 54												
Poulton-le-Fylde 97 a						19 42				20 02											20 42	
Layton 97 a										20 06												
Blackpool North 97 a						19 51				20 13											20 51	
Lancaster 65 a					19 19															20 19		
d					19 21														20 02	20 20		
Oxenholme Lake District 65 a					19 34															20 33		
Windermere 83 a																						
Carnforth d																			20 12			
Silverdale d																			20 17			
Arnside d																			20 22			
Grange-over-Sands d																			20 28			
Kents Bank d																			20 32			
Cark d																			20 36			
Ulverston d																			20 44			
Dalton d																			20 52			
Roose d																			21 02			
Barrow-in-Furness a																			21 09			

A To Middlesbrough
B To Blackburn
C From Alderley Edge
D From Blackburn
E To Edinburgh
F To Clitheroe
G To York
H From Stalybridge
I From Leeds
J To Millom
K To Glasgow Central

Table T082-F

Mondays to Fridays
21 May to 7 December

Manchester - Bolton - Wigan, Kirkby, Southport, Preston, Blackpool North and Barrow-in-Furness

	NT	TP	NT	NT	NT	NT	NT	NT	NT	NT	NT	TP	NT	NT	TP	NT	NT	NT	TP	NT	NT
		◇■		◇	◇		◇	◇	◇			◇■			◇■				◇■		◇
	A	B	C		D	E	F				G	H	I	J	K			A	B	E	
Manchester Airport 85 d		19 19		19 29					19 40			19 47			20 10				20 19		20 29
Heald Green 85 d				19 33					19 44												
Buxton 86 d																					
Hazel Grove 86 d																					
Stockport 84 d													20 05								
Manchester Piccadilly d		19 35		19 47					20 01			20 05	20 18		20 26	20 31			20 35		20 43
Manchester Oxford Road d		19 38		19 51					20 04			20 08	20 21			20 34			20 38		20 49
Deansgate d									20 07							20 37					
Rochdale 41 d	19 14				19 40						19 42			20 09				20 14			
Manchester Victoria d	19 41	19a45	19 49		19 56					20 05	20 09	20a14		20 26			20 37	20 41	20a45	20 49	
Salford Central d	19 44		19 52		19 59					20 08	20 13			20 29			20 40	20 44		20 53	
Salford Crescent a	19 48		19 55		20 02				20 10	20 11	20 18		20 26	20 32		20 41	20 44	20 48		20 56	
d	19 48		19 57		20 02				20 11	20 14	20 18		20 28	20 33		20 41	20 45	20 48		20 57	
Swinton d														20 39			20 52				
Moorside d																	20 54				
Walkden d					20 11									20 44			20 58				
Atherton d					20 17									20 50			21 04				
Hag Fold d																	21 07				
Daisy Hill d					20 20									20 54			21 10				
Clifton d																					
Kearsley d			20 04																	21 04	
Farnworth d			20 07																	21 07	
Moses Gate d			20 09																	21 09	
Bolton a	20 00		20 13						20 21	20 26	20 30		20 39			20 52		21 00		21 13	
d			20 13						20 22	20 26			20 39			20 52				21 13	
Westhoughton d			20 21			←							20 47							21 21	
Hindley d			20 29		20 25	20 29							20 53	20 59						21 26	
Ince d			→											21 02							
Wigan North Western a				20 19	20 33	20 36							20 59							21 33	
Wigan Wallgate a														21 05			21 20				
d														21 07							
Pemberton d																					
Orrell d																					
Upholland d																					
Rainford d																					
Kirkby a																					
Gathurst d														21 11							
Appley Bridge d														21 15							
Parbold d														21 19							
Hoscar d														21 22							
Burscough Bridge d														21 26							
New Lane d														21 28							
Bescar Lane d														21 32							
Meols Cop d														21 37							
Southport a														21 44							
Lostock d										20 32						20 57					
Horwich Parkway d									20 29	20 36						21 01					
Blackrod d										20 40											
Adlington (Lancashire) d										20 44											
Chorley d									20 36	20 49						21 09					
Buckshaw Parkway d									20 40	20 53						21 13					
Leyland d				20 31						21 02						21 18					21 34
Preston 65,97 a				20 41					20 50	21 13					21 02	21 24					21 42
d				20 45				20 45							21 04	21 26					21 47
Kirkham & Wesham 97 a				20 54																	21 56
Poulton-le-Fylde 97 a				21 02												21 42					22 04
Layton 97 a				21 06																	22 08
Blackpool North 97 a				21 13												21 49					22 12
Lancaster 65 a								21 02							21 19						
d							20 30	21 03							21 20						
Oxenholme Lake District 65 a															21 33						
Windermere 83 a																					
Carnforth d							20a40	21 12													
Silverdale d								21 18													
Arnside d								21 22													
Grange-over-Sands d								21 28													
Kents Bank d								21 32													
Cark d								21 36													
Ulverston d								21 44													
Dalton d								21 52													
Roose d								21 58													
Barrow-in-Furness a								22 05													

A To Clitheroe
B To York
C From Stalybridge to Wigan North Western
D From Leeds
E From Stalybridge
F From Morecambe to Leeds
G To Blackburn
H To Middlesbrough
I From Alderley Edge
J From Blackburn
K To Edinburgh

Manchester - Bolton - Wigan, Kirkby, Southport, Preston, Blackpool North and Barrow-in-Furness

		NT	NT	NT	TP	NT	NT	NT	TP	NT	NT	NT	NT	NT	NT	NT FO	NT FX	NT FX	NT FO	NT FX	NT FX	NT FO	TP
		◇	◇		◇1				◇1				◇		◇	◇	◇	bus		bus			◇1
		A		B	C	D	E		F	G		H		I	A				H	H	I	I	J
Manchester Airport 85	d		20 39		20 45				21 05				21 29			21 37	21 37						22 07
Heald Green 85	d		20 43																				
Buxton 86	d																						
Hazel Grove 86	d																						
Stockport 84	d									21 09													
Manchester Piccadilly 10	d		20 57		21 05				21 22	21 27	21 31		21 43			22 01	22 01						22 22
Manchester Oxford Road	d		21 00		21 08					21 30	21 34		21 49			22 04	22 04						22 25
Deansgate	d		21 03								21 37					22 06	22 07						
Rochdale 41	d	20 39		20 42		21 09						21 15			21 39				21 42				
Manchester Victoria	d	20 55		21 08	21a14	21 26						21 40		21 49	21 55				22 15	22 15	22 20	22 20	22a31
Salford Central	d	20 58		21 12		21 29						21 43		21 52	21 59				22 18		22 23	22 23	
Salford Crescent	a	21 01	21 08	21 18		21 32				21 36	21 40	21 47		21 55	22 02	22 10	22 10		22 22	22 25	22 28	22 28	
	d	21 02	21 09	21 18		21 33				21 36	21 41	21 47		21 56	22 03	22 10	22 11		22 23	22 25	22 29	22 29	
Swinton	d	21 09				21 39									22 09								
Moorside	d					21 42																	
Walkden	d	21 14				21 46									22 14								
Atherton	d	21 20				21 51									22 20								
Hag Fold	d					21 54																	
Daisy Hill	d	21 24				21 57									22 24						22 45		
Clifton	d																						
Kearsley	d													22 03									
Farnworth	d													22 06									
Moses Gate	d													22 08									
Bolton	a		21 20	21 32						21 47	21 51	21 59		22 12		22 22	22 22		22 34	22 50		22 39	
	d		21 20							21 47	21 52			22 12		22 22	22 22	22 30				22 40	
Westhoughton	d									21 56				22 20								22 47	
Hindley	d	21 28				22 01				22 06				22 27							22 49	22 51	
Ince	d									22 09													
Wigan North Western	a												22 17	22 32									
Wigan Wallgate	a	21 35				22 08				22 14					22 35						22 56	22 58	
	d									22 15					22 37								
Pemberton	d																						
Orrell	d																						
Upholland	d																						
Rainford	d																						
Kirkby	a																						
Gathurst	d									22 20					22 41								
Appley Bridge	d									22 24					22 45								
Parbold	d									22 28					22 50								
Hoscar	d																						
Burscough Bridge	d									22 33					22 55								
New Lane	d																						
Bescar Lane	d																						
Meols Cop	d									22 43					23 03								
Southport	a									22 48					23 10								
Lostock	d										21 57												
Horwich Parkway	d		21 27								22 02					22 29		22 49					
Blackrod	d		21 30								22 05												
Adlington (Lancashire)	d		21 34								22 09												
Chorley	d		21 39								22 14					22 37		23 06					
Buckshaw Parkway	d		21 43								22 18					22 41		23 21					
Leyland	d										22 26												
Preston 8 65,97	a		21 54						22 02		22 33		22 39			22 56	22 58	23 46					
	d								22 03		22 35		22 42			22 58	23 00						
Kirkham & Wesham 97	a												22 51										
Poulton-le-Fylde 97	a										22 51		22 59			23 14	23 16						
Layton 97	a												23 03										
Blackpool North 97	a										22 58		23 08			23 21	23 23						
Lancaster 6 65	a								22 18														
	d						21 34	22 06	22 19														
Oxenholme Lake District 65	a								22 32														
Windermere 83	a																						
Carnforth	d						21a43	22 15															
Silverdale	d							22 21															
Arnside	d							22 25															
Grange-over-Sands	d							22 31															
Kents Bank	d							22 35															
Cark	d							22 39															
Ulverston	d							22 47															
Dalton	d							22 55															
Roose	d							23 01															
Barrow-in-Furness	a							23 09															

A From Leeds
B To Blackburn
C To Scarborough
D From Blackburn
E To Skipton
F To Glasgow Central
G From Alderley Edge
H To Clitheroe
I From Stalybridge
J To York

Manchester - Bolton - Wigan, Kirkby, Southport, Preston, Blackpool North and Barrow-in-Furness

		NT	NT FX	NT FX	NT FO	NT	TP	NT FO	NT FO	NT FX	NT FX	NT FX	NT FO	NT FX	TP	NT FX	NT FO	NT FX	NT FO	NT FX	NT	TP
			bus				◇1		◇	◇	bus	bus		bus	◇1					bus		◇1
						A	B	C				D	D	E	F	C	C				A	F
Manchester Airport 85	d	22 10							22 34	22 34					22 47							23 19
Heald Green 85	d								22 38	22 38												
Buxton 86	d																					
Hazel Grove 86	d																					
Stockport 84	d																					
Manchester Piccadilly 10	d	22 26	22 30	22 31	22 31		22 35		22 56	22 56	23 05				23 05			23 29	23 29	23 30		23 35
Manchester Oxford Road	d			22 34	22 34		22 38		23 00	23 00					23 08			23 32	23 32			23 38
Deansgate	d			22 37	22 37				23 02	23 02								23 35	23 35			
Rochdale 41	d					22 14							22 43								23 11	
Manchester Victoria	d					22 40	22a43	22 51				23 10	23 12		23a14	23 19	23 19				23 37	23a45
Salford Central	d					22 43		22 54					23 15	←		23 22	23 22				23 40	
Salford Crescent	a		22 40	22 40	22 41	22 46		22 57	23 06			23 20	23 19	23 20		23 27	23 27	23 38	23 38	23 40	23 43	
	d		22 40	22 41	22 41	22 47		22 58	23 06			23 20	23 19	23 20		23 28	23 28	23 39	23 39	23 40	23 44	
Swinton	d					22 54						→									23 51	
Moorside	d					22 56															23 53	
Walkden	d					23 00															23 57	
Atherton	d					23 06															00 04	
Hag Fold	d					23 09															00 06	
Daisy Hill	d					23 12										23 44					00 10	
Clifton	d																					
Kearsley	d																23 35					
Farnworth	d							23 06									23 37					
Moses Gate	d																23 40					
Bolton	a		23 05		22 52			23 11	23 17		23 30		23 31	23 45			23 43		23 49	00 05		
	d		23 05		22 52			23 11	23 17		23 30						23 44		23 50	00 05		
Westhoughton	d							23 19									23 51					
Hindley	d					23 17		23 24								23 50	23 57				00 15	
Ince	d					23 20															00 18	
Wigan North Western	a	22 56		23 04				23 31								23 56	00 03	00 03				
Wigan Wallgate	a					23 23															00 23	
	d					23 25																
Pemberton	d																					
Orrell	d																					
Upholland	d																					
Rainford	d																					
Kirkby	a																					
Gathurst	d					23 29																
Appley Bridge	d					23 33																
Parbold	d					23 37																
Hoscar	d																					
Burscough Bridge	d					23 42																
New Lane	d																					
Bescar Lane	d																					
Meols Cop	d					23 50																
Southport	a					23 57																
Lostock	d		23 23		22 57														23 55	00 23		
Horwich Parkway	d		23 31		23 01				23 24		23 49								23 59	00 31		
Blackrod	d		23 37		23 04														00 02	00 37		
Adlington (Lancashire)	d		23 44		23 08														00 06	00 44		
Chorley	d		23 54		23 13				23 32		00 06								00 11	00 54		
Buckshaw Parkway	d		00 09		23 17				23 36		00 21								00 14	01 09		
Leyland	d		00 23	23 21	23 22				23 43	23 44								00 17	00 20	01 23		
Preston 8 65,97	a	23 14	00 43	23 27	23 28				23 51	23 51	00 46							00 23	00 26	01s43		
	d	23 15		23 30	23 30				23 53	23 53								00 25	00 28			
Kirkham & Wesham 97	a								00 02	00 02										02s08		
Poulton-le-Fylde 97	a			23 46	23 46				00 10	00 10								00 41	00 44	02s28		
Layton 97	a								00 14	00 14										02s38		
Blackpool North 97	a			23 53	23 53				00 21	00 21								00 48	00 51	02 48		
Lancaster 6 65	a	23 33																				
	d	23 33																				
Oxenholme Lake District 65	a																					
Windermere 83	a																					
Carnforth	d	23 43																				
Silverdale	d	23 48																				
Arnside	d	23 53																				
Grange-over-Sands	d	23 59																				
Kents Bank	d	00 04																				
Cark	d	00 08																				
Ulverston	d	00 16																				
Dalton	d	00 24																				
Roose	d	00 30																				
Barrow-in-Furness	a	00 37																				

A From Blackburn
B To Leeds
C From Stalybridge
D To Blackburn
E From Manchester Victoria to Blackburn
F To York

Table T082-F

Manchester - Bolton - Wigan, Kirkby, Southport, Preston, Blackpool North and Barrow-in-Furness

Mondays to Fridays

21 May to 7 December

		NT	NT
			◇
		A	
Manchester Airport 85 ✈	d	23 25	23 46
Heald Green 85	d		23 50
Buxton 86	d		
Hazel Grove 86	d		
Stockport 84	d		
Manchester Piccadilly 10	d	23 43	00 09
Manchester Oxford Road	d	23 46	
Deansgate	d		
Rochdale 41	d		
Manchester Victoria	d	23a55	
Salford Central	d		
Salford Crescent	a		
	d		
Swinton	d		
Moorside	d		
Walkden	d		
Atherton	d		
Hag Fold	d		
Daisy Hill	d		
Clifton	d		
Kearsley	d		
Farnworth	d		
Moses Gate	d		
Bolton	a		
	d		
Westhoughton	d		
Hindley	d		
Ince	d		
Wigan North Western	a		
Wigan Wallgate	a		
	d		
Pemberton	d		
Orrell	d		
Upholland	d		
Rainford	d		
Kirkby	a		
Gathurst	d		
Appley Bridge	d		
Parbold	d		
Hoscar	d		
Burscough Bridge	d		
New Lane	d		
Bescar Lane	d		
Meols Cop	d		
Southport	a		
Lostock	d		
Horwich Parkway	d		
Blackrod	d		
Adlington (Lancashire)	d		
Chorley	d		
Buckshaw Parkway	d		
Leyland	d		
Preston 8 65,97	a		00 59
	d		01 01
Kirkham & Wesham 97	a		01 10
Poulton-le-Fylde 97	a		01 18
Layton 97	a		01 22
Blackpool North 97	a		01 29
Lancaster 6 65	a		
	d		
Oxenholme Lake District 65	a		
Windermere 83	a		
Carnforth	d		
Silverdale	d		
Arnside	d		
Grange-over-Sands	d		
Kents Bank	d		
Cark	d		
Ulverston	d		
Dalton	d		
Roose	d		
Barrow-in-Furness	a		

A From Wilmslow

Table T082-F

Manchester - Bolton - Wigan, Kirkby, Southport, Preston, Blackpool North and Barrow-in-Furness

Saturdays

26 May to 8 December

		NT	NT	NT	NT	NT	NT	NT	TP	NT		TP	NT	NT	NT	NT	NT	NT	NT	NT		NT	NT	NT	TP
					◇	◇			◇1	◇		◇1		◇			◇	◇		◇					◇1
		A	B	C	B		D		E 🍴			F			G		H		I			B			J
Manchester Airport 85 ✈	d									04 46		04 54		05 20					05 36	05 42					05 48
Heald Green 85	d									04 50				05 24						05 46					
Buxton 86	d																								
Hazel Grove 86	d																								
Stockport 84	d																								
Manchester Piccadilly 10	d				00 09				04 54	05 04		05 10		05 42					05 52	06 01					06 05
Manchester Oxford Road	d									05 07		05 13		05 45					05 56	06 05					06 09
Deansgate	d									05 09										06 07					
Rochdale 41	d																					←		05 53	
Manchester Victoria	d					00 25						05a19	05 33		05 44				06 05			06 05	06 08	06 15	06a16
Salford Central	d												05 36		05 47				→			06 08	06 12	06 18	
Salford Crescent	a					00 29				05 13			05 39		05 50					06 10		06 13	06 17	06 21	
	d					00 30				05 13			05 40		05 51					06 11		06 14	06 18	06 22	
Swinton	d																							06 28	
Moorside	d																								
Walkden	d																							06 33	
Atherton	d			00 04																				06 39	
Hag Fold	d			00 06																				06 41	
Daisy Hill	d			00 10																				06 44	
Clifton	d																								
Kearsley	d																						06 25		
Farnworth	d																						06 27		
Moses Gate	d																						06 30		
Bolton	a					00 40				05 24					06 02					06 21		06 26	06 33		
	d					00 41				05 24										06 22		06 26	06 34		
Westhoughton	d																						06 41		
Hindley	d			00 15																			06 45	06 49	
Ince	d			00 18																				06 52	
Wigan North Western	a													06 16									06 53		
Wigan Wallgate	a			00 23									06 02											06 55	
	d												06 04			06 37								06 57	
Pemberton	d												06 08											07 01	
Orrell	d												06 12											07 05	
Upholland	d												06 15											07 08	
Rainford	d												06 19											07 12	
Kirkby	a												06 29											07 22	
Gathurst	d															06 41									
Appley Bridge	d															06 45									
Parbold	d															06 49									
Hoscar	d															06 52									
Burscough Bridge	d															06 56									
New Lane	d															06 58									
Bescar Lane	d															07 02									
Meols Cop	d															07 07									
Southport	a															07 14									
Lostock	d																					06 32			
Horwich Parkway	d									05 31										06 29		06 36			
Blackrod	d	00 02																				06 40			
Adlington (Lancashire)	d	00 06																				06 44			
Chorley	d	00 11								05 39										06 37		06 49			
Buckshaw Parkway	d	00 14								05 43										06 40		06a54			
Leyland	d	00 20												06 29						06 46					
Preston 8 65,97	a	00 26			00 59	01 06			05 30	05 55				06 36						06 54					
	d	00 28			01 01		05 16		05 40					06 38				06 44							
Kirkham & Wesham 97	a				01 10									06 47											
Poulton-le-Fylde 97	a	00 44			01 18									06 55											
Layton 97	a				01 22									06 59											
Blackpool North 97	a	00 51			01 29									07 04											
Lancaster 6 65	a						05 36		05 55									07 01							
	d						05 36	05 40	05 56								06 48	07 02							
Oxenholme Lake District 65	a							06 18	06 10																
Windermere 83	a							06 39																	
Carnforth	d						05 46										06a58	07 11							
Silverdale	d						05 51											07 17							
Arnside	d						05 56											07 21							
Grange-over-Sands	d						06 02											07 27							
Kents Bank	d		00 04				06 06																		
Cark	d		00 08				06 10											07 33							
Ulverston	d		00 16				06 18											07 41							
Dalton	d		00 24				06 27											07 49							
Roose	d		00 30				06 33											07 56							
Barrow-in-Furness	a		00 37				06 40											08 03							

A From Manchester Piccadilly
B From Manchester Airport
C From Blackburn
D To Carlisle
E To Glasgow Central
F To Newcastle
G To Clitheroe
H To Leeds
I To Buckshaw Parkway
J To Middlesbrough

Table T082-F

Saturdays
26 May to 8 December

Manchester - Bolton - Wigan, Kirkby, Southport, Preston, Blackpool North and Barrow-in-Furness

		TP ◇1 A 🍴	NT	NT	TP ◇1 B	NT ◇	NT C	NT ◇ D	NT	NT ◇	NT	NT E	TP ◇1 F 🍴	NT G	NT H	NT	TP ◇1 I 🍴	NT	NT	NT J	TP ◇1 B 🍴	NT ◇	NT C
Manchester Airport 85	d	06 10			06 19	06 35				06 39			06 47				07 10				07 19	07 28	
Heald Green 85	d					06 39																07 32	
Buxton 86	d																						
Hazel Grove 86	d																						
Stockport 84	d		06 13											07 06									
Manchester Piccadilly 10	d	06 26	06 30		06 35	06 55				07 01			07 05	07 17			07 26	07 31			07 35	07 46	
Manchester Oxford Road	d		06 33		06 38	06 58				07 04			07 08	07 20				07 34			07 38	07 51	
Deansgate	d		06 36							07 07				07 22				07 36					
Rochdale 41	d							06 39				06 42			07 09					07 14			
Manchester Victoria	d			06 36	06a45		06 50	06 55	07 00		07 05	07 08	07a14		07 25				07 37	07 41	07a44		07 50
Salford Central	d			06 39			06 53	06 58	07 03		07 08	07 12			07 28				07 40	07 44			07 53
Salford Crescent	a		06 40	06 44			06 57	07 01	07 06	07 11	07 12	07 18		07 27	07 31			07 40	07 44	07 48			07 56
	d		06 40	06 45			06 57	07 02	07 07	07 11	07 14	07 18		07 28	07 32			07 41	07 45	07 48			07 57
Swinton	d			06 52					07 13										07 52				
Moorside	d			06 54					07 16										07 54				
Walkden	d			06 58				07 10	07 19						07 42				07 58				
Atherton	d			07 04				07 16	07 25						07 49				08 04				
Hag Fold	d			07 06					07 28										08 07				
Daisy Hill	d			07 10				07 19	07 31						07 53				08 10				
Clifton	d																						
Kearsley	d						07 05																08 04
Farnworth	d						07 07																08 07
Moses Gate	d						07 09																08 09
Bolton	a		06 51				07 13			07 22	07 26	07 30		07 39				07 51		08 00			08 13
	d		06 51				07 13			07 22	07 26			07 39				07 55					08 13
Westhoughton	d						07 21							07 47									08 21
Hindley	d			07 14			07 28		07 35					07 53	08 00				08 15				08 28
Ince	d								07 38										08 18				08 31
Wigan North Western	a					07 28	07 33							07 59								08 18	08 35
Wigan Wallgate	a			07 19				07 29	07 41						08 05				08 21				
	d			07 21					07 43						08 06				08 23				
Pemberton	d								07 47										08 27				
Orrell	d								07 51										08 31				
Upholland	d								07 54										08 34				
Rainford	d								07 58										08 38				
Kirkby	a								08 08										08 48				
Gathurst	d			07 25											08 11								
Appley Bridge	d			07 29											08 15								
Parbold	d			07 34											08 19								
Hoscar	d														08 22								
Burscough Bridge	d			07 39											08 25								
New Lane	d														08 28								
Bescar Lane	d														08 31								
Meols Cop	d			07 47											08 37								
Southport	a			07 54											08 44								
Lostock	d		06 56									07 33						08 00					
Horwich Parkway	d		07 00								07 31	07 37						08 05					
Blackrod	d		07 03									07 40						08 08					
Adlington (Lancashire)	d		07 07									07 44						08 12					
Chorley	d		07 12								07 38	07 49						08 17					
Buckshaw Parkway	d		07 16								07 42	07a56						08 21					
Leyland	d					07 39												08 28				08 32	
Preston 8 65,97	a	07 01	07 25			07 47					07 53						08 01	08 36				08 39	
	d	07 03	07 28			07 48											08 03	08 38				08 41	
Kirkham & Wesham 97	a					07 57																08 50	
Poulton-le-Fylde 97	a		07 44			08 06												08 54				08 58	
Layton 97	a					08 10																09 02	
Blackpool North 97	a		07 53			08 14												09 01				09 07	
Lancaster 6 65	a	07 18															08 18						
	d	07 18														07 36	08 18						
Oxenholme Lake District 65	a	07 31															08 31						
Windermere 83	a																						
Carnforth	d															07 45							
Silverdale	d															07 51							
Arnside	d															07 55							
Grange-over-Sands	d															08 01							
Kents Bank	d															08 05							
Cark	d															08 09							
Ulverston	d															08 17							
Dalton	d															08 26							
Roose	d															08 32							
Barrow-in-Furness	a															08 39							

A To Edinburgh
B To Newcastle
C From Stalybridge
D From Leeds
E To Blackburn
F To Middlesbrough
G From Alderley Edge
H From Blackburn
I To Glasgow Central
J To Clitheroe

Table T082-F

Saturdays
26 May to 8 December

Manchester - Bolton - Wigan, Kirkby, Southport, Preston, Blackpool North and Barrow-in-Furness

		NT ◇ A	NT	NT ◇	NT ◇	NT	NT B	TP ◇1 C 🍴	NT D	NT E	TP ◇1 F 🍴	NT ◇ G		NT	NT H	TP ◇1 I 🍴	NT ◇	NT J	NT ◇ A	NT ◇	NT K	NT B
Manchester Airport 85	d				07 40			07 47			08 10					08 17	08 28			08 41		
Heald Green 85	d				07 44															08 45		
Buxton 86	d																					
Hazel Grove 86	d																					
Stockport 84	d								08 06													
Manchester Piccadilly 10	d				08 01			08 05	08 18		08 26	08 30				08 35	08 47			09 01		
Manchester Oxford Road	d				08 04			08 08	08 22			08 34				08 38	08 51			09 04		
Deansgate	d				08 07							08 37								09 07		
Rochdale 41	d	07 38					07 42			08 06					08 14				08 39			08 42
Manchester Victoria	d	07 55				08 05	08 08	08a15		08 26				08 37	08 41	08a45		08 50	08 55		09 05	09 08
Salford Central	d	07 58				08 08	08 12			08 29				08 40	08 44			08 53	08 58		09 08	09 12
Salford Crescent	a	08 01			08 11	08 11	08 18		08 28	08 32		08 41		08 44	08 48			08 56	09 01	09 11	09 11	09 18
	d	08 07			08 11	08 14	08 18		08 28	08 33		08 41		08 45	08 48			08 57	09 02	09 11	09 14	09 18
Swinton	d									08 39				08 52								
Moorside	d													08 54								
Walkden	d	08 15								08 44				08 58					09 10			
Atherton	d	08 21								08 50				09 04					09 16			
Hag Fold	d													09 07								
Daisy Hill	d	08 25								08 54				09 10					09 20			
Clifton	d																					
Kearsley	d																	09 04				
Farnworth	d																	09 07				
Moses Gate	d																	09 09				
Bolton	a				08 22	08 26	08 30		08 39			08 52			09 00			09 13		09 21	09 26	09 30
	d				08 22	08 26			08 40			08 52						09 13		09 22	09 26	
Westhoughton	d								08 47									09 21				
Hindley	d								08 53	08 59				09 15				09 31				
Ince	d													09 18								
Wigan North Western	a								09 00								09 19	09 36				
Wigan Wallgate	a	08 38								09 04				09 21					09 28			
	d	08 39								09 06				09 23					09 30			
Pemberton	d													09 27								
Orrell	d													09 31								
Upholland	d													09 34								
Rainford	d													09 38								
Kirkby	a													09 48								
Gathurst	d	08 44								09 10									09 34			
Appley Bridge	d	08 48								09 14									09 38			
Parbold	d	08 52								09 18									09 43			
Hoscar	d																					
Burscough Bridge	d	08 57								09 23									09 48			
New Lane	d																					
Bescar Lane	d																					
Meols Cop	d	09 05								09 31									09 56			
Southport	a	09 13								09 38									10 03			
Lostock	d					08 32						08 57									09 32	
Horwich Parkway	d				08 29	08 36						09 01								09 28	09 36	
Blackrod	d					08 40																
Adlington (Lancashire)	d					08 44																
Chorley	d				08 37	08 49						09 09								09 36	09 44	
Buckshaw Parkway	d				08 41	08a56						09 13								09 39	09 48	
Leyland	d											09 16					09 31				→	
Preston 8 65,97	a				08 52						09 02	09 24					09 40			09 49		
	d			08 42							09 04	09 29	09 32				09 45			09 57		
Kirkham & Wesham 97	a												09 41				09 54					
Poulton-le-Fylde 97	a												09 50				10 03					
Layton 97	a																10 07					
Blackpool North 97	a												09 59				10 13					
Lancaster 6 65	a			08 59							09 19	09 50								10 13		
	d		08 23	09 00								09 59								10 14		
Oxenholme Lake District 65	a											10 18										
Windermere 83	a											10 41										
Carnforth	d		08 32	09 10																10 22		
Silverdale	d		08 38	09 16																10 28		
Arnside	d		08 42	09 20																10 32		
Grange-over-Sands	d		08 48	09 26																10 37		
Kents Bank	d		08 52	09 30																10 41		
Cark	d		08 56	09 34																10 45		
Ulverston	d		09 04	09 42																10 53		
Dalton	d		09 13	09 50																11 01		
Roose	d		09 19	09 56																11 06		
Barrow-in-Furness	a		09 26	10 03																11 15		

A From Leeds
B To Blackburn
C To Middlesbrough
D From Alderley Edge
E From Blackburn
F To Edinburgh
G ◇ from Preston
H To Clitheroe
I To Newcastle
J From Stalybridge
K To Blackpool North

Table T082-F

Saturdays
26 May to 8 December

Manchester - Bolton - Wigan, Kirkby, Southport, Preston, Blackpool North and Barrow-in-Furness

	TP	NT	NT	NT	TP	NT	NT	NT	TP	NT	NT	NT	NT	NT	NT	NT	NT	TP	NT	NT	TP	NT
	◇1				◇1				◇1	◇	◇	◇		◇	◇			◇1			◇1	
	A		B	C	D	E		F	G	H			I	J			K	A	B	C	L	
Manchester Airport 85 d	08 47				09 10				09 19			09 29			09 40			09 47			10 10	
Heald Green 85 d												09 33			09 44							
Buxton 86 d																						
Hazel Grove 86 d																						
Stockport 84 d			09 06																10 06			
Manchester Piccadilly d	09 05	09 14	09 18		09 26				09 35			09 47			10 01			10 05	10 18		10 26	10 31
Manchester Oxford Road d	09 08	09 18	09 22						09 38			09 51			10 04			10 08	10 21			10 34
Deansgate d		09 20													10 07							10 37
Rochdale 41 d				09 09				09 14						09 39			09 42			10 09		
Manchester Victoria d	09a15			09 26			09 37	09 41	09a45				09 50	09 55		10 05	10 08	10a14		10 26		
Salford Central d				09 29			09 40	09 44					09 53	09 58		10 08	10 12			10 29		
Salford Crescent a			09 27	09 32			09 44	09 48					09 56	10 01	10 11	10 11	10 18		10 26	10 32		10 40
d			09 29	09 33			09 45	09 48					09 57	10 02	10 11	10 14	10 18		10 28	10 33		10 41
Swinton d				09 39			09 52													10 39		
Moorside d							09 54															
Walkden d				09 44			09 58							10 10						10 44		
Atherton d				09 50			10 04							10 16						10 50		
Hag Fold d							10 07															
Daisy Hill d				09 54			10 10							10 20						10 54		
Clifton d																						
Kearsley d													10 04									
Farnworth d													10 07									
Moses Gate d													10 09									
Bolton a		09 33	09 39					10 00					10 13		10 22	10 26	10 31		10 39			10 51
d		09 34	09 40										10 13		10 22	10 26			10 39			10 52
Westhoughton d			09 47										10 21						10 47			
Hindley d			09 53	09 59			10 15						10 29						10 53	10 59		
Ince d							10 18													11 02		
Wigan North Western a			09 59									10 18	10 34						10 59			
Wigan Wallgate a				10 04			10 21							10 28						11 05		
d				10 05			10 23							10 30						11 07		
Pemberton d							10 27															
Orrell d							10 31															
Upholland d							10 34															
Rainford d							10 38															
Kirkby a							10 48															
Gathurst d				10 10										10 34						11 11		
Appley Bridge d				10 14										10 38						11 15		
Parbold d				10 18										10 43						11 19		
Hoscar d				10 21																		
Burscough Bridge d				10 24										10 48						11 24		
New Lane d				10 27																		
Bescar Lane d				10 30																		
Meols Cop d				10 36										10 56						11 32		
Southport a				10 43										11 03						11 39		
Lostock d		09 39														10 32						10 57
Horwich Parkway d		09 44													10 29	10 36						11 01
Blackrod d		09 47														10 40						
Adlington (Lancashire) d		09 51														10 44						
Chorley d		09 56				←									10 37	10 49						11 09
Buckshaw Parkway d		10a03				09 48									10 41	10a56						11 12
Leyland d						09 52						10 30										11 16
Preston 65,97 a					10 03	10 03						10 41			10 52						11 02	11 24
d					10 04	10 08					10 44	10 46										11 25
Kirkham & Wesham 97 a												10 55										
Poulton-le-Fylde 97 a						10 24						11 03										11 41
Layton 97 a												11 07										
Blackpool North 97 a						10 33						11 12										11 50
Lancaster 65 a					10 20						11 01											
d					10 20					10 45	11 02											
Oxenholme Lake District 65 a					10 34																	
Windermere 83 a																						
Carnforth d										10a55	11 11											
Silverdale d																						
Arnside d											11 20											
Grange-over-Sands d											11 26											
Kents Bank d																						
Cark d																						
Ulverston d											11 39											
Dalton d																						
Roose d																						
Barrow-in-Furness a											11 58											

A To Middlesbrough
B From Alderley Edge
C From Blackburn
D To Glasgow Central
E From Manchester Victoria
F To Clitheroe
G To Newcastle
H To Leeds
I From Stalybridge
J From Leeds
K To Blackburn
L To Edinburgh

Table T082-F

Saturdays
26 May to 8 December

Manchester - Bolton - Wigan, Kirkby, Southport, Preston, Blackpool North and Barrow-in-Furness

	NT	NT	TP	NT	NT	NT	NT	NT	NT	TP	NT	TP	NT	NT	NT	NT	NT	NT	TP	NT	NT
			◇1	◇		◇	◇			◇1		◇1			◇				◇1	◇	
		A	B		C	D			E	F		G	H	I				A	B		C
Manchester Airport 85 d			10 19	10 29			10 40			10 47		10 59							11 19	11 29	
Heald Green 85 d				10 33			10 44													11 33	
Buxton 86 d																					
Hazel Grove 86 d																					
Stockport 84 d													11 06								
Manchester Piccadilly d			10 35	10 47			11 01			11 05		11 14	11 18			11 22			11 35	11 47	
Manchester Oxford Road d			10 38	10 51			11 04			11 08			11 21			11 25			11 38	11 51	
Deansgate d							11 07									11 28					
Rochdale 41 d		10 14				10 38			10 42					11 09				11 13			
Manchester Victoria d	10 37	10 41	10a45		10 50	10 54		11 05	11 08	11a14				11 26			11 36	11 41	11a45		11 50
Salford Central d	10 40	10 44			10 53	10 57		11 08	11 12					11 29			11 39	11 44			11 53
Salford Crescent a	10 44	10 48			10 56	11 00	11 11	11 11	11 18				11 26	11 32		11 36	11 44	11 48			11 56
d	10 45	10 48			10 57	11 01	11 11	11 14	11 18				11 28	11 33		11 36	11 45	11 48			11 57
Swinton d	10 51													11 39			11 52				
Moorside d	10 54																11 54				
Walkden d	10 57					11 09								11 44			11 58				
Atherton d	11 03					11 15								11 50			12 04				
Hag Fold d	11 05																12 07				
Daisy Hill d	11 08					11 19								11 54			12 10				
Clifton d																					
Kearsley d					11 04																12 04
Farnworth d					11 07																12 07
Moses Gate d					11 09																12 09
Bolton a		11 00			11 13		11 22	11 26	11 31				11 39			11 47		12 00			12 13
d					11 13		11 22	11 26					11 39			11 47					12 13
Westhoughton d					11 21								11 47								12 21
Hindley d	11 13				11 29								11 53	11 59			12 15				12 29
Ince d																	12 18				
Wigan North Western a				11 20	11 34								11 59							12 19	12 34
Wigan Wallgate a	11 18					11 28								12 04			12 21				
d	11 19					11 30								12 05			12 23				
Pemberton d	11 23																12 27				
Orrell d	11 27																12 31				
Upholland d	11 31																12 34				
Rainford d	11 34																12 38				
Kirkby a	11 44																12 48				
Gathurst d						11 34								12 10							
Appley Bridge d						11 38								12 14							
Parbold d						11 43								12 18							
Hoscar d														12 21							
Burscough Bridge d						11 48								12 24							
New Lane d														12 27							
Bescar Lane d														12 30							
Meols Cop d						11 56								12 36							
Southport a						12 03								12 43							
Lostock d								11 32								11 53					
Horwich Parkway d							11 29	11 36								11 57					
Blackrod d								11 40													
Adlington (Lancashire) d								11 44													
Chorley d							11 37	11 49								12 09					
Buckshaw Parkway d							11 41	11a56								12 13					
Leyland d				11 33												12 18				12 30	
Preston 65,97 a				11 42			11 52					11 58				12 24				12 35	
d				11 45								12 04			12 17	12 26				12 38	
Kirkham & Wesham 97 a				11 54																12 47	
Poulton-le-Fylde 97 a				12 03												12 42				12 56	
Layton 97 a				12 07																13 00	
Blackpool North 97 a				12 11												12 51				13 10	
Lancaster 65 a												12 19			12 37						
d											12 02	12 20			12 37						
Oxenholme Lake District 65 a												12 33			13 00						
Windermere 83 a															13 24						
Carnforth d											12 11										
Silverdale d											12 17										
Arnside d											12 21										
Grange-over-Sands d											12 27										
Kents Bank d											12 31										
Cark d											12 35										
Ulverston d											12 43										
Dalton d											12 53										
Roose d											12 59										
Barrow-in-Furness a											13 06										

A To Clitheroe
B To Newcastle
C From Stalybridge
D From Leeds
E To Blackburn
F To Middlesbrough
G To Glasgow Central
H From Alderley Edge
I From Blackburn

Table T082-F

Saturdays
26 May to 8 December

Manchester - Bolton - Wigan, Kirkby, Southport, Preston, Blackpool North and Barrow-in-Furness

	NT ◇ A	NT B	NT ◇	NT	NT C	TP ◇■ D ✠	NT E	NT F	TP ◇■ G ✠		NT	NT	NT H	TP ◇■ I ✠	NT ◇	NT J	NT ◇ A	NT ◇	NT		NT C	TP ◇■ D ✠	NT E	NT F
Manchester Airport 85 d			11 41			11 47			12 10					12 19	12 29			12 40				12 47		
Heald Green 85 d			11 45												12 33			12 44						
Buxton 86 d																								
Hazel Grove 86 d																								
Stockport 84 d							12 06																13 06	
Manchester Piccadilly 10 d			12 01			12 05	12 18		12 26		12 31			12 35	12 47			13 01				13 05	13 18	
Manchester Oxford Road d			12 04			12 08	12 21				12 34			12 38	12 51			13 04				13 08	13 21	
Deansgate d			12 07								12 37							13 07						
Rochdale 41 d	11 39				11 42			12 09					12 17				12 39				12 42			13 09
Manchester Victoria d	11 55			12 05	12 08	12a14		12 26				12 36	12 41	12a45		12 50	12 55		13 05		13 08	13a14		13 26
Salford Central d	11 58			12 08	12 12			12 29				12 40	12 44			12 53	12 58		13 08		13 12			13 29
Salford Crescent a	12 01		12 11	12 11	12 18		12 26	12 32			12 41	12 44	12 48			12 56	13 01	13 11	13 11		13 18		13 26	13 32
d	12 02		12 11	12 14	12 18		12 29	12 33			12 41	12 45	12 48			12 57	13 02	13 11	13 14		13 18		13 29	13 33
Swinton d								12 39				12 52												13 39
Moorside d												12 54												
Walkden d	12 10							12 44				12 58					13 10							13 44
Atherton d	12 16							12 50				13 04					13 16							13 50
Hag Fold d												13 07												
Daisy Hill d	12 20							12 54				13 10					13 20							13 54
Clifton d																								
Kearsley d																13 04								
Farnworth d																13 07								
Moses Gate d																13 09								
Bolton a			12 21	12 26	12 30		12 39				12 52		13 00			13 13		13 22	13 26		13 31		13 39	
d			12 22	12 26			12 40				12 52					13 13		13 22	13 26				13 40	
Westhoughton d							12 47									13 21							13 47	
Hindley d							12 53	12 59				13 15				13 29							13 53	13 59
Ince d												13 18												
Wigan North Western a							12 59								13 19	13 34							13 59	
Wigan Wallgate a	12 28							13 04				13 21					13 28							14 04
d	12 30							13 05				13 23					13 30							14 05
Pemberton d												13 27												
Orrell d												13 31												
Upholland d												13 34												
Rainford d												13 38												
Kirkby a												13 48												
Gathurst d	12 34							13 10									13 34							14 10
Appley Bridge d	12 38							13 14									13 38							14 14
Parbold d	12 43							13 18									13 43							14 18
Hoscar d																								
Burscough Bridge d	12 48							13 23									13 48							14 23
New Lane d																								
Bescar Lane d																								
Meols Cop d	12 56							13 31									13 56							14 31
Southport a	13 03							13 38									14 03							14 38
Lostock d				12 32							12 57								13 32					
Horwich Parkway d			12 28	12 36							13 01							13 29	13 36					
Blackrod d				12 40															13 40					
Adlington (Lancashire) d				12 44															13 44					
Chorley d			12 36	12 49							13 09							13 37	13 49					
Buckshaw Parkway d			12 39	12a56							13 13							13 41	13a56					
Leyland d											13 17				13 31									
Preston 8 65,97 a			12 48						13 02		13 23				13 42			13 57						
d			12 57						13 03		13 25				13 45									
Kirkham & Wesham 97 a															13 54									
Poulton-le-Fylde 97 a											13 42				14 03									
Layton 97 a															14 07									
Blackpool North 97 a											13 49				14 13									
Lancaster 6 65 a			13 13						13 19															
d		12 45	13 14						13 20															
Oxenholme Lake District 65 a									13 33															
Windermere 83 a																								
Carnforth d		12a54	13 22																					
Silverdale d			13 28																					
Arnside d			13 32																					
Grange-over-Sands d			13 37																					
Kents Bank d			13 41																					
Cark d			13 45																					
Ulverston d			13 53																					
Dalton d			14 01																					
Roose d			14 06																					
Barrow-in-Furness a			14 14																					

A From Leeds
B From Morecambe to Leeds
C To Blackburn
D To Middlesbrough
E From Alderley Edge
F From Blackburn
G To Edinburgh
H To Clitheroe
I To Newcastle
J From Stalybridge

Table T082-F

Saturdays
26 May to 8 December

Manchester - Bolton - Wigan, Kirkby, Southport, Preston, Blackpool North and Barrow-in-Furness

	NT	TP ◇■ A ✠	NT ◇	NT	NT		NT B	TP ◇■ C ✠	NT ◇	NT D	NT ◇ E	NT ◇	NT	NT F	TP ◇■ G ✠		NT H	NT I	NT ◇ J	NT K	TP ◇■ L ✠	NT K	NT	NT
Manchester Airport 85 d		13 10						13 19	13 29			13 40			13 47						14 10			
Heald Green 85 d									13 33			13 44												
Buxton 86 d																								
Hazel Grove 86 d																								
Stockport 84 d																	14 06							
Manchester Piccadilly 10 d		13 26		13 31				13 35	13 47			14 01			14 05		14 18				14 26		14 31	
Manchester Oxford Road d								13 38	13 51			14 04			14 08		14 21						14 34	
Deansgate d												14 07											14 37	
Rochdale 41 d							13 16				13 39			13 42				14 09						
Manchester Victoria d					13 37		13 41	13a45		13 50	13 55		14 05	14 08	14a14			14 26						14 37
Salford Central d					13 40		13 44			13 53	13 58		14 08	14 12				14 29						14 40
Salford Crescent a				13 36	13 44		13 48			13 56	14 01	14 11	14 11	14 18			14 26	14 32					14 40	14 44
d				13 37	13 45		13 48			13 57	14 02	14 11	14 14	14 18			14 29	14 33					14 41	14 45
Swinton d					13 52													14 39						14 52
Moorside d					13 54																			14 54
Walkden d					13 58						14 10							14 44						14 58
Atherton d					14 04						14 16							14 50						15 04
Hag Fold d					14 07																			15 07
Daisy Hill d					14 10						14 20							14 54						15 10
Clifton d																								
Kearsley d										14 04														
Farnworth d										14 07														
Moses Gate d										14 09														
Bolton a				13 47			14 00			14 13		14 22	14 26	14 30			14 39						14 51	
d				13 48						14 13		14 22	14 26				14 40						14 52	
Westhoughton d										14 21							14 47							
Hindley d					14 15					14 29							14 53	14 59						15 15
Ince d					14 18																			15 18
Wigan North Western a									14 19	14 34							14 59							
Wigan Wallgate a					14 21						14 28							15 04						15 21
d					14 23						14 30							15 05						15 23
Pemberton d					14 27																			15 27
Orrell d					14 31																			15 31
Upholland d					14 34																			15 34
Rainford d					14 38																			15 38
Kirkby a					14 48																			15 48
Gathurst d											14 34							15 10						
Appley Bridge d											14 38							15 14						
Parbold d											14 43							15 18						
Hoscar d																		15 21						
Burscough Bridge d											14 48							15 24						
New Lane d																		15 27						
Bescar Lane d																		15 30						
Meols Cop d											14 56							15 36						
Southport a											15 03							15 43						
Lostock d				13 53									14 32										14 57	
Horwich Parkway d				13 57								14 29	14 36										15 01	
Blackrod d													14 40											
Adlington (Lancashire) d													14 44											
Chorley d				14 05								14 37	14 49										15 09	
Buckshaw Parkway d				14 08								14 41	14a56										15 12	
Leyland d				14 14					14 31														15 18	
Preston 8 65,97 a		14 02		14 23					14 41			14 57									15 03		15 24	
d		14 04	14 10	14 25					14 45												15 04		15 25	
Kirkham & Wesham 97 a									14 54															
Poulton-le-Fylde 97 a				14 41					15 03														15 41	
Layton 97 a									15 07															
Blackpool North 97 a				14 50					15 13														15 50	
Lancaster 6 65 a		14 19	14 30																		15 19			
d	14 02	14 19	14 30																14 46	15 03		16 13		
Oxenholme Lake District 65 a		14 32	14 51																					
Windermere 83 a			15 09																					
Carnforth d	14 11																		15a23	15 12		16 22		
Silverdale d	14 17																			15 18		16 28		
Arnside d	14 22																			15 23		16 32		
Grange-over-Sands d	14 28																			15 29		16 38		
Kents Bank d	14 31																			15 32		16 42		
Cark d	14 35																			15 36		16 46		
Ulverston d	14 43																			15 45		16 54		
Dalton d	14 52																			15 53		17 02		
Roose d	14 58																			16 00		17 08		
Barrow-in-Furness a	15 05																			16 07		17 16		

A To Glasgow Central
B To Clitheroe
C To Newcastle
D From Stalybridge
E From Leeds
F To Blackburn
G To Middlesbrough
H From Alderley Edge
I From Blackburn
J To Leeds
K To Carlisle
L To Edinburgh

Table T082-F

Saturdays
26 May to 8 December

Manchester - Bolton - Wigan, Kirkby, Southport, Preston, Blackpool North and Barrow-in-Furness

		NT A	TP ◇■ B	NT ◇	NT C	NT ◇ D	NT ◇	NT	NT E	TP ◇■ F	NT G	NT H	TP ◇■ I	NT	NT	NT A	TP ◇■ B	NT ◇	NT C	NT ◇ D	NT ◇	NT
Manchester Airport 85	d		14 19	14 29			14 40			14 47			15 10				15 19	15 29			15 40	
Heald Green 85	d			14 33			14 44											15 33			15 44	
Buxton 86	d																					
Hazel Grove 86	d																					
Stockport 84	d										15 06											
Manchester Piccadilly	d		14 35	14 47			15 01			15 05	15 18		15 26	15 31			15 35	15 47			16 01	
Manchester Oxford Road	d		14 38	14 51			15 04			15 08	15 21			15 34			15 38	15 51			16 04	
Deansgate	d						15 07							15 37							16 07	
Rochdale 41	d	14 13				14 39			14 42			15 09				15 14				15 39		
Manchester Victoria	d	14 41	14a45		14 50	14 55		15 05	15 08	15a14		15 26			15 37	15 41	15a45		15 50	15 55		16 05
Salford Central	d	14 44			14 53	14 58		15 08	15 12			15 29			15 40	15 44			15 53	15 58		16 08
Salford Crescent	a	14 48			14 56	15 01	15 11	15 11	15 18		15 26	15 32		15 40	15 44	15 48			15 56	16 01	16 11	16 11
	d	14 49			14 57	15 02	15 11	15 14	15 18		15 29	15 33		15 41	15 45	15 48			15 57	16 02	16 11	16 14
Swinton	d											15 39			15 52							
Moorside	d														15 54							
Walkden	d					15 10						15 44			15 58					16 10		
Atherton	d					15 16						15 50			16 04					16 16		
Hag Fold	d														16 07							
Daisy Hill	d					15 20						15 54			16 10					16 20		
Clifton	d																					
Kearsley	d				15 04														16 04			
Farnworth	d				15 07														16 07			
Moses Gate	d				15 09														16 09			
Bolton	a	15 00			15 13		15 22	15 26	15 31		15 40			15 51		16 00			16 13		16 22	16 26
	d				15 13		15 22	15 26			15 40			15 52					16 13		16 22	16 26
Westhoughton	d				15 21						15 48								16 21			
Hindley	d				15 29						15 54	15 59			16 15				16 30			
Ince	d														16 18							
Wigan North Western	a			15 19	15 34						16 00							16 19	16 35			
Wigan Wallgate	a					15 28						16 04			16 21					16 28		
	d					15 30						16 05			16 23					16 30		
Pemberton	d														16 27							
Orrell	d														16 31							
Upholland	d														16 34							
Rainford	d														16 38							
Kirkby	a														16 48							
Gathurst	d					15 34						16 10								16 34		
Appley Bridge	d					15 38						16 14								16 38		
Parbold	d					15 43						16 18								16 43		
Hoscar	d																					
Burscough Bridge	d					15 48						16 23								16 48		
New Lane	d																					
Bescar Lane	d																					
Meols Cop	d					15 56						16 31								16 56		
Southport	a					16 03						16 38								17 03		
Lostock	d							15 32						15 57							16 27	16 32
Horwich Parkway	d						15 29	15 36						16 01							16 31	16 36
Blackrod	d							15 40														16 40
Adlington (Lancashire)	d							15 44														16 44
Chorley	d						15 37	15 49						16 09							16 39	16 49
Buckshaw Parkway	d						15 40	15a56						16 12							16 43	16a56
Leyland	d			15 31										16 18				16 31				
Preston 65,97	a			15 41			15 53						16 02	16 24				16 41			16 58	
	d			15 43									16 03	16 25				16 43				
Kirkham & Wesham 97	a			15 52														16 52				
Poulton-le-Fylde 97	a			16 00										16 41				17 00				
Layton 97	a			16 04										16 46				17 04				
Blackpool North 97	a			16 11										16 52				17 09				
Lancaster 65	a												16 18									
	d												16 19									
Oxenholme Lake District 65	a												16 32									
Windermere 83	a																					
Carnforth	d																					
Silverdale	d																					
Arnside	d																					
Grange-over-Sands	d																					
Kents Bank	d																					
Cark	d																					
Ulverston	d																					
Dalton	d																					
Roose	d																					
Barrow-in-Furness	a																					

A To Clitheroe
B To Newcastle
C From Stalybridge
D From Leeds
E To Blackburn
F To Middlesbrough
G From Alderley Edge
H From Blackburn
I To Glasgow Central

Table T082-F

Saturdays
26 May to 8 December

Manchester - Bolton - Wigan, Kirkby, Southport, Preston, Blackpool North and Barrow-in-Furness

		NT A	TP ◇■ B	NT C	NT D	NT E	TP ◇■ F	NT	NT	NT	NT A	TP ◇■ G	NT ◇	NT H	NT ◇ I	NT ◇ J	NT ◇ I	NT ◇	NT	NT K	TP ◇■ B	NT	NT C
Manchester Airport 85	d		15 47				16 10					16 19	16 29					16 40			16 47		
Heald Green 85	d												16 33					16 44					
Buxton 86	d																						
Hazel Grove 86	d																						
Stockport 84	d			16 06																			17 06
Manchester Piccadilly	d		16 05	16 18			16 26		16 31			16 35	16 47					17 01			17 05		17 19
Manchester Oxford Road	d		16 08	16 21					16 34			16 38	16 51					17 04			17 08		
Deansgate	d								16 37									17 07					17 22
Rochdale 41	d	15 42			16 09						16 14				16 39					16 42			
Manchester Victoria	d	16 08	16a14		16 26					16 37	16 41	16a45		16 49	16 55				17 05	17 08	17a14	17 14	
Salford Central	d	16 12			16 29					16 40	16 44			16 52	16 58				17 08	17 12		17 18	
Salford Crescent	a	16 18		16 28	16 32				16 40	16 44	16 48			16 55	17 01			17 11	17 11	17 18		17 21	17 26
	d	16 18		16 29	16 33				16 41	16 45	16 48			16 57	17 02			17 11	17 14	17 18		17 22	17 29
Swinton	d				16 39					16 52												17 28	
Moorside	d									16 54													
Walkden	d				16 44					16 58					17 10							17 33	
Atherton	d				16 50					17 04					17 16							17 39	
Hag Fold	d									17 07												17 41	
Daisy Hill	d				16 54					17 10					17 20							17 44	
Clifton	d																						
Kearsley	d													17 04									
Farnworth	d													17 07						17 27			
Moses Gate	d													17 09									
Bolton	a	16 30		16 39					16 51		17 00			17 13				17 22	17 26	17 32			17 40
	d			16 40					16 52					17 13				17 22	17 26				17 40
Westhoughton	d			16 47										17 21									17 49
Hindley	d			16 53	16 59					17 15				17 29								17 49	17 55
Ince	d									17 18													17 58
Wigan North Western	a			17 02									17 19	17 34								17 57	
Wigan Wallgate	a				17 04					17 21					17 28								18 01
	d				17 05					17 23					17 30								18 03
Pemberton	d									17 27													
Orrell	d									17 31													
Upholland	d									17 34													
Rainford	d									17 38													
Kirkby	a									17 48													
Gathurst	d				17 10										17 34								18 07
Appley Bridge	d				17 14										17 38								18 11
Parbold	d				17 18										17 43								18 15
Hoscar	d				17 21																		18 18
Burscough Bridge	d				17 24										17 48								18 22
New Lane	d				17 27																		18 24
Bescar Lane	d				17 30																		18 28
Meols Cop	d				17 36										17 56								18 33
Southport	a				17 43										18 03								18 40
Lostock	d								16 57									17 27	17 32				
Horwich Parkway	d								17 01									17 31	17 36				
Blackrod	d								17 04										17 40				
Adlington (Lancashire)	d								17 08										17 44				
Chorley	d								17 13									17 39	17 49				
Buckshaw Parkway	d								17 16									17 43	17a56				
Leyland	d								17 22														
Preston 65,97	a						17 02		17 30				17 38					17 57					
	d						17 03	17 20	17 32				17 40				17 45						
Kirkham & Wesham 97	a								17 41				17 50										
Poulton-le-Fylde 97	a								17 49				17 59										
Layton 97	a								17 54				18 03										
Blackpool North 97	a								18 00				18 07										
Lancaster 65	a						17 18	17 37									18 02						
	d					17 01	17 19	17 38								17 45	18 03						
Oxenholme Lake District 65	a						17 32																
Windermere 83	a																						
Carnforth	d					17 10		17 47								17a55	18 12						
Silverdale	d							17 53									18 18						
Arnside	d					17 19		17 57									18 22						
Grange-over-Sands	d					17 25		18 03									18 28						
Kents Bank	d							18 07									18 32						
Cark	d							18 11									18 36						
Ulverston	d					17 38		18 19									18 44						
Dalton	d					17 46		18 27									18 52						
Roose	d					17 52		18 33									18 58						
Barrow-in-Furness	a					17 59		18 40									19 05						

A To Clitheroe
B To Middlesbrough
C From Alderley Edge
D From Blackburn
E To Carlisle
F To Edinburgh
G To Newcastle
H From Stalybridge
I From Leeds
J From Morecambe to Leeds
K To Blackburn

Manchester - Bolton - Wigan, Kirkby, Southport, Preston, Blackpool North and Barrow-in-Furness

Station		NT A	TP ◇1 B ✠	NT	NT ◇	NT	NT	NT C	TP ◇1 D ✠	NT ◇	NT E	NT ◇ F	NT ◇	NT	TP ◇1 G ✠	NT H	NT I	NT A	TP ◇1 J ✠	NT	NT	NT C
Manchester Airport 85	d		17 10						17 19	17 26			17 42		17 47				18 10			
Heald Green 85	d									17 30			17 46									
Buxton 86	d																					
Hazel Grove 86	d																					
Stockport 84	d																18 06					
Manchester Piccadilly	d		17 27			17 31			17 35	17 47			18 01		18 05		18 18		18 26	18 31		
Manchester Oxford Road	d					17 34			17 38	17 51			18 04		18 08		18 22			18 34		
Deansgate	d					17 37							18 07							18 37		
Rochdale 41	d	17 09						17 14				17 40				17 53		18 09				18 18
Manchester Victoria	d	17 25					17 37	17 41	17a45		17 50	17 56		18 05	18a15	18 16		18 26			18 37	18 41
Salford Central	d	17 29					17 40	17 44			17 53	17 59		18 08		18 19		18 29			18 40	18 44
Salford Crescent	a	17 32				17 41	17 44	17 48			17 56	18 02	18 10	18 11		18 22	18 28	18 32		18 40	18 44	18 48
	d	17 33				17 41	17 45	17 48			17 57	18 02	18 11	18 14		18 23	18 29	18 33		18 41	18 45	18 48
Swinton	d						17 52											18 39			18 52	
Moorside	d	17 39					17 54														18 54	
Walkden	d	17 43					17 58					18 11						18 44			18 58	
Atherton	d	17 49					18 04					18 17						18 50			19 04	
Hag Fold	d						18 07														19 07	
Daisy Hill	d	17 53					18 10					18 21						18 54			19 10	
Clifton	d										18 01											
Kearsley	d										18 06											
Farnworth	d										18 09											
Moses Gate	d										18 11											
Bolton	a					17 52		18 00			18 15		18 21	18 26		18 34	18 39			18 51		19 00
	d					17 52					18 15		18 21	18 26			18 40			18 52		
Westhoughton	d										18 23						18 48					
Hindley	d	17 59					18 15				18 29						18 54	18 59				
Ince	d						18 18				18 32							19 02				
Wigan North Western	a	18 04								18 19	18 36											
Wigan Wallgate	a						18 21					18 29					18 59	19 05			19 20	
	d						18 23					18 30					19 01	19 07				
Pemberton	d						18 27											19 11				
Orrell	d						18 31											19 16				
Upholland	d						18 34											19 20				
Rainford	d						18 38											19 24				
Kirkby	a						18 48											19 34				
Gathurst	d											18 35					19 05					
Appley Bridge	d											18 39					19 09					
Parbold	d											18 43					19 13					
Hoscar	d																					
Burscough Bridge	d											18 48					19 18					
New Lane	d																					
Bescar Lane	d																					
Meols Cop	d											18 56					19 26					
Southport	a											19 04					19 33					
Lostock	d					17 57							18 26	18 32						18 57		
Horwich Parkway	d					18 01							18 30	18 36						19 01		
Blackrod	d					18 04								18 40								
Adlington (Lancashire)	d					18 08								18 44								
Chorley	d					18 13							18 37	18 49						19 08		
Buckshaw Parkway	d					18 16							18 41	18a56						19 12		
Leyland	d					18 21				18 32										19 18		
Preston 65,97	a		18 02			18 27				18 41			18 50						19 03	19 24		
	d		18 03		18 20	18 29				18 44			18 58						19 05	19 26		
Kirkham & Wesham 97	a					18 38				18 53												
Poulton-le-Fylde 97	a					18 46				19 01										19 42		
Layton 97	a					18 51				19 05												
Blackpool North 97	a					18 57				19 10										19 51		
Lancaster 65	a		18 18		18 40								19 13						19 20			
	d		18 19	18 35	18 40								19 14						19 21			
Oxenholme Lake District 65	a		18 32		18 59														19 34			
Windermere 83	a				19 22																	
Carnforth	d			18 44									19 22									
Silverdale	d			18 50									19 28									
Arnside	d			18 54									19 32									
Grange-over-Sands	d			19 00									19 37									
Kents Bank	d			19 04									19 41									
Cark	d			19 08									19 45									
Ulverston	d			19 16									19 53									
Dalton	d			19 24									20 01									
Roose	d			19 30									20 07									
Barrow-in-Furness	a			19 38									20 14									

A From Blackburn
B To Glasgow Central
C To Clitheroe
D To Newcastle
E From Stalybridge
F From Leeds
G To Middlesbrough
H To Blackburn
I From Alderley Edge
J To Edinburgh

Table T082-F

Saturdays
26 May to 8 December

Manchester - Bolton - Wigan, Kirkby, Southport, Preston, Blackpool North and Barrow-in-Furness

Station		TP ◇1 A ✠	NT ◇	NT B	NT ◇ C	NT ◇	NT	NT D	TP ◇1 E	NT F	NT G	NT H	TP ◇1 I ✠	NT	NT	NT D	TP ◇1 A	NT J	NT ◇	NT ◇ C	NT B	NT ◇ K	NT ◇
Manchester Airport 85	d	18 19	18 29			18 40			18 47				19 10				19 19		19 29				
Heald Green 85	d		18 33			18 44													19 33				
Buxton 86	d																						
Hazel Grove 86	d																						
Stockport 84	d									19 06													
Manchester Piccadilly	d	18 35	18 48			19 01			19 05	19 18			19 26	19 31			19 35		19 47				
Manchester Oxford Road	d	18 38	18 52			19 04			19 08	19 21				19 34			19 38		19 51				
Deansgate	d					19 06								19 37									
Rochdale 41	d				18 39						19 09					19 14				19 40			
Manchester Victoria	d	18a45		18 49	18 55		19 05	19 09	19a14		19 26				19 37	19 41	19a45	19 49		19 56			
Salford Central	d			18 52	18 58		19 08	19 13			19 29				19 40	19 44		19 52		19 59			
Salford Crescent	a			18 55	19 01	19 10	19 11	19 18		19 26	19 32			19 41	19 44	19 48		19 55		20 02			
	d			18 57	19 02	19 10	19 14	19 18		19 28	19 33			19 41	19 45	19 48		19 57		20 02			
Swinton	d										19 39				19 52								
Moorside	d														19 54								
Walkden	d				19 10						19 44				19 58					20 11			
Atherton	d				19 16						19 50				20 04					20 17			
Hag Fold	d														20 06								
Daisy Hill	d				19 20						19 54				20 10					20 20			
Clifton	d																						
Kearsley	d			19 04														20 04					
Farnworth	d			19 07														20 07					
Moses Gate	d			19 09														20 09					
Bolton	a			19 13		19 21	19 26	19 31		19 39				19 52		20 00		20 13					
	d			19 13		19 21	19 26			19 39				19 52				20 13					
Westhoughton	d			19 21						19 47								20 21			←		
Hindley	d			19 29						19 53	19 59				20 14			20 29		20 25	20 29		
Ince	d										20 02							→					
Wigan North Western	a		19 20	19 34						19 59									20 19	20 33	20 36		
Wigan Wallgate	a				19 28						20 05				20 21								
	d				19 30						20 07												
Pemberton	d																						
Orrell	d																						
Upholland	d																						
Rainford	d																						
Kirkby	a																						
Gathurst	d				19 34						20 11												
Appley Bridge	d				19 38						20 15												
Parbold	d				19 43						20 19												
Hoscar	d																						
Burscough Bridge	d				19 48						20 24												
New Lane	d																						
Bescar Lane	d																						
Meols Cop	d				19 56						20 32												
Southport	a				20 03						20 39												
Lostock	d						19 32							19 57									
Horwich Parkway	d					19 28	19 36							20 01									
Blackrod	d						19 40																
Adlington (Lancashire)	d						19 44																
Chorley	d					19 36	19 49							20 09									
Buckshaw Parkway	d					19 40	19 53							20 13									
Leyland	d		19 32				20 02							20 18					20 31				
Preston 65,97	a		19 43			19 51	20 10						20 02	20 24					20 41				
	d		19 45										20 04	20 26					20 45				20 45
Kirkham & Wesham 97	a		19 54																20 54				
Poulton-le-Fylde 97	a		20 02											20 42					21 02				
Layton 97	a		20 06																21 06				
Blackpool North 97	a		20 13											20 51					21 13				
Lancaster 65	a												20 19										21 02
	d											20 05	20 19									20 30	21 03
Oxenholme Lake District 65	a												20 32										
Windermere 83	a																						
Carnforth	d											20 15										20a40	21 12
Silverdale	d											20 20											21 18
Arnside	d											20 25											21 22
Grange-over-Sands	d											20 31											21 28
Kents Bank	d											20 35											21 32
Cark	d											20 39											21 36
Ulverston	d											20 47											21 44
Dalton	d											20 55											21 52
Roose	d											21 02											21 58
Barrow-in-Furness	a											21 09											22 05

A To York
B From Stalybridge
C From Leeds
D To Clitheroe
E To Middlesbrough
F From Alderley Edge
G From Blackburn
H To Millom
I To Edinburgh
J From Stalybridge to Wigan North Western
K From Morecambe to Leeds

Table T082-F	Saturdays 26 May to 8 December

Manchester - Bolton - Wigan, Kirkby, Southport, Preston, Blackpool North and Barrow-in-Furness

		NT	NT	NT	TP	NT	NT	NT	NT	NT	TP	NT	NT	NT	NT	NT	NT	TP	NT	NT	NT	NT	NT
		◇			◇1						◇1	◇		◇	◇			◇1					
				A	B	C	D			E	F		G	H		A	D	I	C	J	K	L	
Manchester Airport 85	d	19 40			19 47						20 19	20 29			20 39			21 06					
Heald Green 85	d	19 44													20 43								
Buxton 86	d																						
Hazel Grove 86	d																						
Stockport 84	d					20 05													21 09				
Manchester Piccadilly 10	d	20 01			20 07	20 18		20 31			20 35	20 43			20 57			21 22	21 27				21 31
Manchester Oxford Road	d	20 04			20 10	20 21		20 34			20 38	20 49			21 00			21 25	21 30				21 34
Deansgate	d	20 07						20 37							21 03								21 37
Rochdale 41	d			19 42			20 09			20 14				20 39		20 42	21 09						
Manchester Victoria	d		20 05	20 09	20a16		20 26		20 37	20 41	20a45		20 49	20 55		21 08	21 26	21a30					
Salford Central	d		20 08	20 13			20 29		20 40	20 44			20 53	20 58		21 12	21 29						
Salford Crescent	a	20 10	20 11	20 18		20 26	20 32	20 41	20 44	20 48			20 56	21 01	21 08	21 18	21 32		21 36				21 40
	d	20 11	20 14	20 18		20 28	20 33	20 41	20 45	20 48			20 57	21 02	21 09	21 18	21 33		21 36				21 41
Swinton	d						20 39		20 52					21 09			21 39						
Moorside	d								20 54								21 42						
Walkden	d						20 44		20 58					21 14			21 46						
Atherton	d						20 50		21 04					21 20			21 51						
Hag Fold	d								21 07								21 54						
Daisy Hill	d						20 54		21 10					21 24			21 57						
Clifton	d																						
Kearsley	d												21 04										
Farnworth	d												21 07										
Moses Gate	d												21 09										
Bolton	a	20 21	20 26	20 30		20 39		20 52		21 00			21 13		21 20	21 32			21 47				21 51
	d	20 22	20 26			20 39		20 52					21 13		21 20				21 47				21 52
Westhoughton	d					20 47							21 21						21 56				
Hindley	d					20 53	20 59						21 26	21 28			22 01		22 06				
Ince	d						21 02												22 09				
Wigan North Western	a					20 59						21 22	21 33										
Wigan Wallgate	a						21 05		21 20					21 35			22 08		22 14				
	d						21 07												22 15				
Pemberton	d																						
Orrell	d																						
Upholland	d																						
Rainford	d																						
Kirkby	a																						
Gathurst	d						21 11												22 20				
Appley Bridge	d						21 15												22 24				
Parbold	d						21 19												22 28				
Hoscar	d						21 22																
Burscough Bridge	d						21 26												22 33				
New Lane	d						21 28																
Bescar Lane	d						21 32																
Meols Cop	d						21 37												22 43				
Southport	a						21 44												22 48				
Lostock	d		20 32					20 57															21 57
Horwich Parkway	d	20 29	20 36					21 01							21 27								22 02
Blackrod	d		20 40												21 30								22 05
Adlington (Lancashire)	d		20 44												21 34								22 09
Chorley	d	20 37	20 49					21 09							21 39								22 14
Buckshaw Parkway	d	20 43	20 53					21 13							21 43								22 18
Leyland	d		20 59					21 18				21 35											22 26
Preston 8 65,97	a	20 57	21 10					21 24				21 43			21 54								22 33
	d							21 26				21 44									22 05		22 35
Kirkham & Wesham 97	a											21 53											
Poulton-le-Fylde 97	a							21 42				22 01											22 51
Layton 97	a											22 05											
Blackpool North 97	a							21 49				22 10											22 58
Lancaster 6 65	a																				22 25		
	d																			21 34	22 26	22 26	
Oxenholme Lake District 65	a																						
Windermere 83	a																						
Carnforth	d																			21a43	22 35	22 35	
Silverdale	d																				22 41	22 41	
Arnside	d																				22 45	22 45	
Grange-over-Sands	d																				22 51	22 51	
Kents Bank	d																				22 55	22 55	
Cark	d																				22 59	22 59	
Ulverston	d																				23 07	23 07	
Dalton	d																				23 15	23 15	
Roose	d																				23 21	23 21	
Barrow-in-Furness	a																				23 29	23 29	

A To Blackburn
B To Middlesbrough
C From Alderley Edge
D From Blackburn
E To Clitheroe
F To York
G From Stalybridge
H From Leeds
I To Scarborough
J To Skipton
K from 23 June until 8 September
L until 16 June, from 15 September

Table T082-F	Saturdays 26 May to 8 December

Manchester - Bolton - Wigan, Kirkby, Southport, Preston, Blackpool North and Barrow-in-Furness

		NT	NT	NT	NT	NT	NT	NT	TP	NT	NT	NT	NT	NT	NT	NT	NT	NT	NT	TP	NT	TP
			◇		◇	◇			◇1	◇		◇				◇				◇1		◇1
		A		B	C		A	B	D	E	F	F		G	B		H	B		D		I
Manchester Airport 85	d		21 29			21 37			22 07	22 10		22 10				22 34				23 07		23 19
Heald Green 85	d															22 38						
Buxton 86	d																					
Hazel Grove 86	d																					
Stockport 84	d																					
Manchester Piccadilly 10	d		21 43			22 01			22 22	22 26		22 26	22 31			22 56				23 26	23 30	23 35
Manchester Oxford Road	d		21 49			22 04			22 25	22 29		22 29	22 34			23 00				23 29	23 33	23 38
Deansgate	d					22 06							22 37			23 02					23 36	
Rochdale 41	d	21 19			21 39		21 42							22 14			22 43					
Manchester Victoria	d	21 40		21 49	21 55		22 15	22 20	22a31					22 40	22 51		23 08	23 16	23 20	23a35		23a45
Salford Central	d	21 43		21 52	21 59		22 18	22 23						22 43	22 54		23 12	23 19	23 23			
Salford Crescent	a	21 47		21 55	22 02	22 10	22 22	22 28					22 41	22 46	22 57	23 06	23 16	23 22	23 26		23 39	
	d	21 47		21 56	22 03	22 10	22 23	22 29					22 41	22 47	22 58	23 06	23 16	23 23	23 27		23 40	
Swinton	d				22 09									22 54					23 33			
Moorside	d													22 56					23 36			
Walkden	d				22 14									23 00					23 40			
Atherton	d				22 20									23 06					23 45			
Hag Fold	d													23 09					23 48			
Daisy Hill	d				22 24									23 12					23 51			
Clifton	d																					
Kearsley	d			22 03														23 30				
Farnworth	d			22 06											23 06			23 32				
Moses Gate	d			22 08														23 35				
Bolton	a	21 59		22 12		22 22	22 34	22 39					22 52		23 11	23 17	23 28	23 38			23 50	
	d			22 12		22 22		22 40					22 52		23 11	23 17		23 39			23 51	
Westhoughton	d			22 20				22 47							23 19			23 46				
Hindley	d			22 27				22 51						23 17	23 24			23 51	23 56			
Ince	d													23 20					23 59			
Wigan North Western	a		22 17	22 32											23 31			23 58				
Wigan Wallgate	a				22 35			22 58						23 23					00 04			
	d				22 37									23 25								
Pemberton	d																					
Orrell	d																					
Upholland	d																					
Rainford	d																					
Kirkby	a																					
Gathurst	d				22 41									23 29								
Appley Bridge	d				22 45									23 33								
Parbold	d				22 50									23 37								
Hoscar	d																					
Burscough Bridge	d				22 55									23 42								
New Lane	d																					
Bescar Lane	d																					
Meols Cop	d				23 03									23 50								
Southport	a				23 10									23 57								
Lostock	d												22 57			23 22						
Horwich Parkway	d					22 29							23 01			23 27					23 58	
Blackrod	d												23 04			23 30						
Adlington (Lancashire)	d												23 08			23 34						
Chorley	d					22 37							23 13			23 39					00 06	
Buckshaw Parkway	d					22 41							23 17			23 42					00 09	
Leyland	d												23 22			23 48					00 13	
Preston 8 65,97	a		22 39			22 56				23 09		23 09	23 28			23 54					00 21	
	d		22 42			22 58				23 10			23 30			23 56					00 23	
Kirkham & Wesham 97	a		22 51													00 05						
Poulton-le-Fylde 97	a		22 59			23 14							23 46			00 13					00 39	
Layton 97	a		23 03													00 17						
Blackpool North 97	a		23 08			23 21							23 53			00 24					00 46	
Lancaster 6 65	a									23 28												
	d									23 28	23 28											
Oxenholme Lake District 65	a																					
Windermere 83	a																					
Carnforth	d									23 38	23 38											
Silverdale	d									23 43	23 43											
Arnside	d									23 48	23 48											
Grange-over-Sands	d									23 54	23 54											
Kents Bank	d									23 58	23 58											
Cark	d									00 02	00 02											
Ulverston	d									00 10	00 10											
Dalton	d									00 19	00 19											
Roose	d									00 25	00 25											
Barrow-in-Furness	a									00 32	00 32											

A To Clitheroe
B From Stalybridge
C From Leeds
D To York
E from 23 June until 8 September
F until 16 June, from 15 September
G From Blackburn
H To Blackburn
I until 20 October. To York

Table T082-F

Saturdays

26 May to 8 December

Manchester - Bolton - Wigan, Kirkby, Southport, Preston, Blackpool North and Barrow-in-Furness

		NT	NT
		A	
Manchester Airport 85	d		23 28
Heald Green 85	d		23 32
Buxton 86	d		
Hazel Grove 86	d		
Stockport 84	d		
Manchester Piccadilly	d	23 43	23 51
Manchester Oxford Road	d	23 46	23 54
Deansgate	d		23 56
Rochdale 41	d		
Manchester Victoria	d	23a55	
Salford Central	d		
Salford Crescent	a		00 01
	d		00 02
Swinton	d		
Moorside	d		
Walkden	d		
Atherton	d		
Hag Fold	d		
Daisy Hill	d		
Clifton	d		
Kearsley	d		
Farnworth	d		
Moses Gate	d		
Bolton	a		00 12
	d		
Westhoughton	d		
Hindley	d		
Ince	d		
Wigan North Western	a		
Wigan Wallgate	a		
	d		
Pemberton	d		
Orrell	d		
Upholland	d		
Rainford	d		
Kirkby	a		
Gathurst	d		
Appley Bridge	d		
Parbold	d		
Hoscar	d		
Burscough Bridge	d		
New Lane	d		
Bescar Lane	d		
Meols Cop	d		
Southport	a		
Lostock	d		
Horwich Parkway	d		
Blackrod	d		
Adlington (Lancashire)	d		
Chorley	d		
Buckshaw Parkway	d		
Leyland	d		
Preston 65,97	a		
	d		
Kirkham & Wesham 97	a		
Poulton-le-Fylde 97	a		
Layton 97	a		
Blackpool North 97	a		
Lancaster 65	a		
	d		
Oxenholme Lake District 65	a		
Windermere 83	a		
Carnforth	d		
Silverdale	d		
Arnside	d		
Grange-over-Sands	d		
Kents Bank	d		
Cark	d		
Ulverston	d		
Dalton	d		
Roose	d		
Barrow-in-Furness	a		

A From Wilmslow

Table T082-F

Sundays

20 May to 2 December

Manchester - Bolton - Wigan, Kirkby, Southport, Preston, Blackpool North and Barrow-in-Furness

		NT	NT	NT	NT	NT	NT	NT	NT	TP		TP	NT	NT	TP	TP	TP	NT	NT	NT		NT	NT	NT	NT
		◇					◇	◇	◇	◇■		◇■			◇■	◇■	◇■		■					◇	◇
		A	B	C	D	E	F	G	H	I		J			K	L	M	N	O			E		P	
Manchester Airport 85	d						07 42	07 42		07 46		07 46			08 22	08 25									08 33
Heald Green 85	d						07 46	07 46																	
Buxton 86	d																								
Hazel Grove 86	d																								
Stockport 84	d																								
Manchester Piccadilly	d						07 59	08 00		08 04		08 06			08 36	08 38	08 43								08 52
Manchester Oxford Road	d						08 03	08 03	08 03	08 07		08 09			08 39	08 41									08 55
Deansgate	d						08 05	08 06	08 06																
Rochdale 41	d																								
Manchester Victoria	d					07 55				08a13		08a15	08 20	08 25	08a47	08a50				08 31		08 41	08 55		
Salford Central	d												08 23	08 28						08 34		08 44	08 58		
Salford Crescent	a					08 00	08 09	08 09	08 09				08 26	08 31						08 37		08 47	09 02		
	d			00 02		08 00	08 10	08 10	08 10				08 27	08 32						08 37		08 48	09 03		
Swinton	d													08 39									09 10		
Moorside	d																						09 12		
Walkden	d													08 44									09 16		
Atherton	d													08 49									09 22		
Hag Fold	d																						09 25		
Daisy Hill	d													08 53									09 28		
Clifton	d																								
Kearsley	d																								
Farnworth	d																								
Moses Gate	d																								
Bolton	a			00 12		08 14	08 20	08 20	08 20				08 37							08 48		09 00			
	d						08 21	08 21	08 21				08 38							08 48					
Westhoughton	d												08 45												
Hindley	d												08 51	08 58									09 33		
Ince	d																						09 36		
Wigan North Western	a												08 57												09 22
Wigan Wallgate	a													09 03									09 41		
	d													09 04											
Pemberton	d																								
Orrell	d																								
Upholland	d																								
Rainford	d																								
Kirkby	a																								
Gathurst	d													09 09											
Appley Bridge	d													09 13											
Parbold	d													09 17											
Hoscar	d																								
Burscough Bridge	d													09 22											
New Lane	d																								
Bescar Lane	d																								
Meols Cop	d													09 30											
Southport	a													09 37											
Lostock	d						08 26	08 26	08 26											08 53					
Horwich Parkway	d						08 31	08 31	08 31											08 57					
Blackrod	d						08 34	08 34	08 34											09 00					
Adlington (Lancashire)	d						08 38	08 38	08 38											09 04					
Chorley	d				00 06		08 43	08 43	08 43											09 09					
Buckshaw Parkway	d				00 09		08 47	08 47	08 47											09 12					
Leyland	d				00 13		08 51	08 51	08 51											09 19					
Preston 65,97	a				00 21		09 01	09 01	09 01								09 22			09 25					09 40
	d				00 23												09 23			09 27				09 38	09 41
Kirkham & Wesham 97	a																			09 36					09 50
Poulton-le-Fylde 97	a				00 39															09 44					09 59
Layton 97	a																								
Blackpool North 97	a				00 46															09 52					10 05
Lancaster 65	a																09 38							09 58	
	d																	09 45						09 59	
Oxenholme Lake District 65	a																							10 18	
Windermere 83	a																							10 52	
Carnforth	d																	10a10	10 20						
Silverdale	d																		10 26						
Arnside	d																		10 30						
Grange-over-Sands	d																		10 36						
Kents Bank	d																		10 40						
Cark	d	00 02	00 02																10 44						
Ulverston	d	00 10	00 10																10 52						
Dalton	d	00 19	00 19																11 00						
Roose	d	00 25	00 25																11 06						
Barrow-in-Furness	a	00 32	00 32																11 14						

A from 24 June until 9 September. From Manchester Airport
B from 27 May until 17 June, from 16 September. From Lancaster
C not 20 May. From Manchester Airport
D not 20 May. From Manchester Piccadilly
E To Clitheroe
F from 16 September until 21 October
G until 9 September
H from 28 October
I from 16 September until 21 October. To Scarborough
J until 9 September. To Scarborough
K until 9 September, from 28 October. To Middlesbrough
L from 16 September until 21 October. To Middlesbrough
M from 24 June. To Edinburgh
N until 17 June
O until 17 June. To Carlisle
P from 24 June

Table T082-F

Sundays

20 May to 2 December

Manchester - Bolton - Wigan, Kirkby, Southport, Preston, Blackpool North and Barrow-in-Furness

	NT	NT	NT	NT	TP	TP	NT	TP	NT	NT	NT	NT	NT	NT	NT	NT	NT	NT	TP	NT	NT	NT
	◇	A	B	C	◇1 D	◇1 E		◇1 F	G		◇ H	I	◇ J	◇ K	◇ I	◇	◇ J	◇ L	◇1 M	A	B	
Manchester Airport 85 d	08 42				09 05	09 05		09 19								09 33	09 43	09 43	10 10			
Heald Green 85 d	08 46																09 47	09 47				
Buxton 86 d																						
Hazel Grove 86 d																						
Stockport 84 d																						
Manchester Piccadilly d	09 01				09 22	09 22		09 33								09 53	09 59	10 01	10 26			
Manchester Oxford Road d	09 04							09 37								09 58	10 02	10 04				
Deansgate d	09 07																10 06	10 06				
Rochdale 41 d			09 03																		10 03	
Manchester Victoria d		09 20	09 25				09 31	09a43	09 45	09 55										10 19	10 25	10 31
Salford Central d		09 23	09 29				09 34		09 48	09 58										10 22	10 29	10 34
Salford Crescent a	09 13	09 26	09 32				09 37		09 51	10 01							10 10	10 10		10 25	10 32	10 37
d	09 13	09 27	09 32				09 37		09 52	10 02							10 10	10 10		10 26	10 32	10 37
Swinton d			09 39							10 09											10 39	
Moorside d										10 11												
Walkden d			09 44							10 15											10 44	
Atherton d			09 49							10 21											10 49	
Hag Fold d										10 24												
Daisy Hill d			09 53							10 27											10 53	
Clifton d																						
Kearsley d																						
Farnworth d																						
Moses Gate d																						
Bolton a	09 24	09 37					09 48		10 04								10 21	10 21		10 36		10 48
d	09 24	09 38					09 48										10 21	10 21		10 37		10 48
Westhoughton d		09 45																		10 44		
Hindley d		09 51	09 58							10 32										10 50	10 58	
Ince d										10 35												
Wigan North Western a		09 57														10 29				10 56		
Wigan Wallgate a			10 03							10 40											11 03	
d			10 04																		11 04	
Pemberton d																						
Orrell d																						
Upholland d																						
Rainford d																						
Kirkby a																						
Gathurst d			10 09																		11 09	
Appley Bridge d			10 13																		11 13	
Parbold d			10 17																		11 17	
Hoscar d																						
Burscough Bridge d			10 22																		11 22	
New Lane d																						
Bescar Lane d																						
Meols Cop d			10 30																		11 30	
Southport a			10 37																		11 37	
Lostock d							09 53															10 53
Horwich Parkway d	09 31						09 57										10 28	10 28				10 57
Blackrod d							10 00															11 00
Adlington (Lancashire) d							10 04															11 04
Chorley d	09 39						10 09										10 36	10 36				11 09
Buckshaw Parkway d	09 42						10 12										10 40	10 40				11 12
Leyland d							10 19															11 19
Preston 65,97 a	09 55				10 02	10 01	10 25									10 47	10 54	10 54	11 04			11 25
d					10 03	10 24	10 27					10 36	10 45	10 45		10 48			11 09			11 27
Kirkham & Wesham 97 a							10 36									10 57						11 36
Poulton-le-Fylde 97 a							10 44									11 06						11 44
Layton 97 a																						
Blackpool North 97 a							10 52									11 12						11 52
Lancaster 65 a					10 18	10 39						10 56	11 05	11 05					11 24			
d				10 11	10 19	10 40					10 41	10 57	11 05	11 06	11 06				11 25			
Oxenholme Lake District 65 a					10 32	10 53						11 16							11 38			
Windermere 83 a												11 36										
Carnforth d				10 20							10a51		11 15	11 16	11 16							
Silverdale d				10 26									11 21	11 21	11 21							
Arnside d				10 30									11 25	11 26	11 26							
Grange-over-Sands d				10 36									11 31	11 32	11 32							
Kents Bank d				10 40									11 35	11 35	11 35							
Cark d				10 44									11 39	11 39	11 39							
Ulverston d				10 52									11 47	11 48	11 48							
Dalton d				11 00									11 55	11 56	11 56							
Roose d				11 06									12 01	12 02	12 02							
Barrow-in-Furness a				11 14									12 09	12 09	12 09							

A From Stalybridge
B From Blackburn
C from 24 June. To Carlisle
D from 24 June. To Glasgow Central
E until 17 June. To Glasgow Central
F To Newcastle
G To Clitheroe
H To Leeds
I until 17 June
J from 16 September
K from 24 June until 9 September
L until 9 September
M To Edinburgh

Table T082-F

Sundays

20 May to 2 December

Manchester - Bolton - Wigan, Kirkby, Southport, Preston, Blackpool North and Barrow-in-Furness

	TP	NT	TP	NT	NT	NT	NT	NT	NT	NT	TP	NT	NT	NT	NT	NT	NT	NT	TP	NT	NT
	◇1 A	B	◇1 C		◇	◇	◇	D	E	◇ F	◇1 G		◇ H	B		◇	D	I	◇1 J	E	
Manchester Airport 85 d	10 19		10 20			10 43					11 10		11 43								
Heald Green 85 d						10 47															
Buxton 86 d																					
Hazel Grove 86 d																					
Stockport 84 d																					
Manchester Piccadilly d	10 36		10 37			11 01					11 26		12 01								
Manchester Oxford Road d	10 39		10 40			11 05	11 07						12 05			12 07					
Deansgate d							11 09									12 09					
Rochdale 41 d									11 03											12 03	
Manchester Victoria d	10a45	10 45	10a46	10 55				11 19	11 25			11 31		11 45	11 55		12 19		12 23	12 25	12 31
Salford Central d		10 48		10 58				11 22	11 29			11 34		11 48	11 58		12 22			12 29	12 34
Salford Crescent a		10 51		11 01			11 12	11 25	11 32			11 37		11 51	12 01	12 12	12 25			12 32	12 37
d		10 52		11 02			11 13	11 26	11 32			11 37		11 52	12 02	12 13	12 26			12 32	12 37
Swinton d				11 09					11 39						12 09					12 39	
Moorside d				11 11											12 11						
Walkden d				11 15					11 44						12 15					12 44	
Atherton d				11 21					11 49						12 21					12 49	
Hag Fold d				11 24											12 24						
Daisy Hill d				11 27					11 53						12 27					12 53	
Clifton d																					
Kearsley d																					
Farnworth d																					
Moses Gate d																					
Bolton a		11 04					11 23	11 36				11 48		12 04		12 23	12 36				12 48
d							11 24	11 37				11 48				12 24	12 37				12 48
Westhoughton d								11 44									12 44				
Hindley d				11 32				11 50	11 58						12 32		12 50			12 58	
Ince d				11 35											12 35						
Wigan North Western a						11 32		11 56					12 33				12 56				
Wigan Wallgate a				11 40					12 03						12 40					13 03	
d									12 04											13 04	
Pemberton d																					
Orrell d																					
Upholland d																					
Rainford d																					
Kirkby a																					
Gathurst d									12 09											13 09	
Appley Bridge d									12 13											13 13	
Parbold d									12 17											13 17	
Hoscar d																					
Burscough Bridge d									12 22											13 22	
New Lane d																					
Bescar Lane d																					
Meols Cop d									12 30											13 30	
Southport a									12 37											13 37	
Lostock d												11 53									12 53
Horwich Parkway d							11 31					11 57				12 31					12 57
Blackrod d												12 00									13 00
Adlington (Lancashire) d												12 04									13 04
Chorley d							11 39					12 09				12 39					13 09
Buckshaw Parkway d							11 42					12 12				12 42					13 12
Leyland d												12 19									13 19
Preston 65,97 a						11 50	12 01				12 02	12 25	12 51			12 58			13 02		13 25
d					11 27	11 52					12 04	12 27	12 52						13 04		13 27
Kirkham & Wesham 97 a						12 01						12 36	13 01								13 36
Poulton-le-Fylde 97 a						12 09						12 44	13 10								13 44
Layton 97 a																					
Blackpool North 97 a						12 16						12 52	13 16								13 52
Lancaster 65 a					11 47						12 19								13 19		
d					11 47					12 15	12 20							13 13	13 19		
Oxenholme Lake District 65 a											12 33								13 32		
Windermere 83 a																					
Carnforth d					11 57					12a50								13 22			
Silverdale d					12 03													13 28			
Arnside d					12 07													13 32			
Grange-over-Sands d					12 13													13 38			
Kents Bank d					12 17													13 42			
Cark d					12 21													13 46			
Ulverston d					12 29													13 54			
Dalton d					12 37													14 02			
Roose d					12 43													14 08			
Barrow-in-Furness a					12 51													14 16			

A from 16 September. To Newcastle
B To Clitheroe
C until 9 September. To Newcastle
D From Stalybridge
E From Blackburn
F To Leeds
G To Glasgow Central
H until 9 September
I To Carlisle
J To Edinburgh

Table T082-F

Sundays
20 May to 2 December

Manchester - Bolton - Wigan, Kirkby, Southport, Preston, Blackpool North and Barrow-in-Furness

	TP ◇1 A ✠	NT B	NT	NT ◇	NT ◇	NT ◇	TP ◇1 C ✠	NT D	NT E	TP ◇1 F ✠	TP ◇1 G ✠	NT	TP ◇1 A ✠	NT B	NT	NT ◇	NT ◇	NT ◇	TP ◇1 H ✠	NT D	NT E	NT ◇ I
Manchester Airport 85 d	12 19				12 41		12 47			13 10	13 10		13 19				13 33	13 41	13 47			
Heald Green 85 d																	13 37	13 45				
Buxton 86 d																						
Hazel Grove 86 d																						
Stockport 84 d																						
Manchester Piccadilly 10 d	12 35				13 00		13 05			13 26	13 26		13 35				13 51	14 00	14 05			
Manchester Oxford Road d	12 38				13 05	13 07	13 09						13 38				14 07	14 05	14 09			
Deansgate d						13 09											14 09					
Rochdale 41 d									13 03												14 03	
Manchester Victoria d	12a45	12 45	12 55				13a15	13 19	13 25			13 31	13a45	13 45	13 55				14a15	14 19	14 25	
Salford Central d		12 48	12 58					13 22	13 29			13 34		13 48	13 58					14 22	14 29	
Salford Crescent a		12 51	13 01			13 13		13 25	13 32			13 37		13 51	14 01		14 12			14 25	14 32	
d		12 52	13 02			13 13		13 26	13 32			13 37		13 52	14 02		14 13			14 26	14 32	
Swinton d			13 09						13 39						14 09						14 39	
Moorside d			13 11												14 11							
Walkden d			13 15						13 44						14 15						14 44	
Atherton d			13 21						13 49						14 21						14 49	
Hag Fold d			13 24												14 24							
Daisy Hill d			13 27						13 53						14 27						14 53	
Clifton d																						
Kearsley d																						
Farnworth d																						
Moses Gate d																						
Bolton a		13 04				13 24		13 36				13 48		14 04			14 23			14 36		
d						13 24		13 37				13 48					14 24			14 37		
Westhoughton d								13 44												14 44		
Hindley d			13 32					13 50	13 58						14 32					14 50	14 58	
Ince d			13 35												14 35							
Wigan North Western a					13 33			13 56										14 33		14 56		
Wigan Wallgate a			13 40						14 03						14 40						15 03	
d									14 04												15 04	
Pemberton d																						
Orrell d																						
Upholland d																						
Rainford d																						
Kirkby a																						
Gathurst d									14 09												15 09	
Appley Bridge d									14 13												15 13	
Parbold d									14 17												15 17	
Hoscar d																						
Burscough Bridge d									14 22												15 22	
New Lane d																						
Bescar Lane d																						
Meols Cop d									14 30												15 30	
Southport a									14 37												15 37	
Lostock d												13 53										
Horwich Parkway d						13 31						13 57					14 31					
Blackrod d												14 00										
Adlington (Lancashire) d												14 04										
Chorley d						13 39						14 09					14 39					
Buckshaw Parkway d						13 43						14 12					14 42					
Leyland d												14 19										
Preston 8 65,97 a					13 51	13 58				14 03	14 03	14 25					14 59	14 51				
d				13 29	13 52					14 04	14 04	14 27				14 29		14 52				
Kirkham & Wesham 97 a					14 01							14 36						15 01				
Poulton-le-Fylde 97 a					14 10							14 44						15 10				
Layton 97 a																						
Blackpool North 97 a					14 16							14 52						15 16				
Lancaster 6 65 a				13 49						14 19	14 20					14 49						
d				13 49						14 20	14 20					14 49						15 15
Oxenholme Lake District 65 a										14 33	14 34											
Windermere 83 a																						
Carnforth d				13 59												14 59						15a50
Silverdale d																15 04						
Arnside d				14 08												15 09						
Grange-over-Sands d				14 14												15 15						
Kents Bank d																15 18						
Cark d																15 22						
Ulverston d				14 27												15 31						
Dalton d																15 39						
Roose d																15 45						
Barrow-in-Furness a				14 45												15 52						

A To Newcastle
B To Clitheroe
C until 9 September. To Middlesbrough
D From Stalybridge
E From Blackburn
F from 16 September. To Glasgow Central
G until 9 September. To Glasgow Central
H To Middlesbrough
I To Leeds

Table T082-F

Sundays
20 May to 2 December

Manchester - Bolton - Wigan, Kirkby, Southport, Preston, Blackpool North and Barrow-in-Furness

	TP ◇1 A ✠	NT B	NT	TP ◇1 C ✠	NT D	NT	NT ◇	NT ◇	TP ◇1 E ✠	NT F	NT G	TP ◇1 H ✠	NT	TP ◇1 C ✠	NT D	NT	NT ◇	NT ◇	NT ◇	TP ◇1 E ✠	NT F
Manchester Airport 85 d	14 10			14 19			14 33	14 41	14 47			15 10		15 19				15 33	15 41	15 47	
Heald Green 85 d							14 37	14 45										15 37	15 45		
Buxton 86 d																					
Hazel Grove 86 d																					
Stockport 84 d																					
Manchester Piccadilly 10 d	14 26			14 35			14 51	15 00	15 05			15 26		15 35				15 51	16 00	16 05	
Manchester Oxford Road d				14 38			15 07	15 05	15 09					15 38				16 07	16 05	16 09	
Deansgate d							15 09											16 09			
Rochdale 41 d											15 03										
Manchester Victoria d			14 31	14a45	14 45	14 55			15a14	15 19	15 25		15 31	15a45	15 45	15 55				16a14	16 19
Salford Central d			14 34		14 48	14 58				15 22	15 29		15 34		15 48	15 58					16 22
Salford Crescent a			14 37		14 51	15 01	15 12			15 25	15 32		15 37		15 51	16 01		16 12			16 25
d			14 37		14 52	15 02	15 13			15 26	15 32		15 37		15 52	16 02		16 13			16 26
Swinton d						15 09					15 39					16 09					
Moorside d						15 11										16 11					
Walkden d						15 15					15 44					16 15					
Atherton d						15 21					15 49					16 21					
Hag Fold d						15 24										16 24					
Daisy Hill d						15 27					15 53					16 27					
Clifton d																					
Kearsley d																					
Farnworth d																					
Moses Gate d																					
Bolton a			14 48		15 04		15 23			15 36			15 48		16 04			16 23			16 36
d			14 48				15 24			15 37			15 48					16 24			16 37
Westhoughton d										15 44											16 44
Hindley d						15 32				15 50	15 58					16 32					16 50
Ince d						15 35										16 35					
Wigan North Western a								15 33		15 56									16 33		16 56
Wigan Wallgate a						15 40					16 03					16 40					
d											16 04										
Pemberton d																					
Orrell d																					
Upholland d																					
Rainford d																					
Kirkby a																					
Gathurst d											16 09										
Appley Bridge d											16 13										
Parbold d											16 17										
Hoscar d																					
Burscough Bridge d											16 22										
New Lane d																					
Bescar Lane d																					
Meols Cop d											16 30										
Southport a											16 37										
Lostock d			14 53										15 53								
Horwich Parkway d			14 57				15 31						15 57					16 31			
Blackrod d			15 00										16 00								
Adlington (Lancashire) d			15 04										16 04								
Chorley d			15 09				15 39						16 09					16 39			
Buckshaw Parkway d			15 12				15 42						16 12					16 42			
Leyland d			15 19										16 19								
Preston 8 65,97 a	15 03		15 25				15 58	15 51				16 03	16 25					16 57	16 50		
d	15 04		15 27					15 52				16 04	16 27				16 29		16 51		
Kirkham & Wesham 97 a			15 36					16 01					16 36						17 01		
Poulton-le-Fylde 97 a			15 44					16 10					16 44						17 10		
Layton 97 a																					
Blackpool North 97 a			15 52					16 16					16 52						17 16		
Lancaster 6 65 a	15 19											16 20					16 49				
d		16 13										16 20					16 49				
Oxenholme Lake District 65 a												16 34									
Windermere 83 a																					
Carnforth d		16 22															16 59				
Silverdale d		16 28															17 05				
Arnside d		16 32															17 09				
Grange-over-Sands d		16 38															17 15				
Kents Bank d		16 42															17 19				
Cark d		16 46															17 23				
Ulverston d		16 54															17 31				
Dalton d		17 02															17 39				
Roose d		17 08															17 45				
Barrow-in-Furness a		17 16															17 53				

A To Edinburgh
B To Carlisle
C To Newcastle
D To Clitheroe
E To Middlesbrough
F From Stalybridge
G From Blackburn
H To Glasgow Central

Table T082-F

Sundays

20 May to 2 December

Manchester - Bolton - Wigan, Kirkby, Southport, Preston, Blackpool North and Barrow-in-Furness

		NT A	NT ◇ B	TP ◇■ C ✠	NT	TP ◇■ D ✠	NT E	NT	NT ◇	NT ◇	NT ◇	TP ◇■ F ✠	NT G	NT A	TP ◇■ H ✠	TP ◇■ I ✠	TP ◇■ J ✠	NT	TP ◇■ D ✠	NT E	NT	NT ◇	NT ◇
Manchester Airport 85 ✈	d			16 10		16 19				16 33	16 41	16 47			17 10	17 10			17 19			17 33	17 41
Heald Green 85	d									16 37	16 45											17 37	17 45
Buxton 86	d																						
Hazel Grove 86	d																						
Stockport 84	d																						
Manchester Piccadilly ■	d			16 26		16 35				16 51	17 00	17 05			17 26	17 27			17 35			17 51	18 00
Manchester Oxford Road	d					16 38				17 07	17 05	17 09							17 38			18 07	18 05
Deansgate	d									17 09												18 09	
Rochdale 41	d	16 03												17 03									
Manchester Victoria	d	16 25			16 31	16a45	16 45	16 55				17a14	17 19	17 25				17 31	17a45	17 45	17 55		
Salford Central	d	16 29			16 34		16 48	16 58					17 22	17 29				17 34		17 48	17 58		
Salford Crescent	a	16 32			16 37		16 51	17 01		17 12			17 25	17 32				17 37		17 51	18 01	18 12	
	d	16 32			16 37		16 52	17 02		17 13			17 26	17 32				17 37		17 52	18 02	18 13	
Swinton	d	16 39						17 09						17 39							18 09		
Moorside	d							17 11													18 11		
Walkden	d	16 44						17 15						17 44							18 15		
Atherton	d	16 49						17 21						17 49							18 21		
Hag Fold	d							17 24													18 24		
Daisy Hill	d	16 53						17 27						17 53							18 27		
Clifton	d																						
Kearsley	d																						
Farnworth	d																						
Moses Gate	d																						
Bolton	a				16 48		17 04			17 23			17 36					17 48		18 13		18 23	
	d				16 48					17 24			17 37					17 48				18 24	
Westhoughton	d												17 44										
Hindley	d	16 58						17 32					17 50	17 58							18 32		
Ince	d							17 35													18 35		
Wigan North Western	a										17 33		17 56										18 33
Wigan Wallgate	a	17 03						17 40						18 03							18 40		
	d	17 04												18 04									
Pemberton	d																						
Orrell	d																						
Upholland	d																						
Rainford	d																						
Kirkby	a																						
Gathurst	d	17 09												18 09									
Appley Bridge	d	17 13												18 13									
Parbold	d	17 17												18 17									
Hoscar	d																						
Burscough Bridge	d	17 22												18 22									
New Lane	d																						
Bescar Lane	d																						
Meols Cop	d	17 30												18 30									
Southport	a	17 37												18 37									
Lostock	d				16 53													17 53					
Horwich Parkway	d				16 57					17 31								17 57				18 31	
Blackrod	d				17 00													18 00					
Adlington (Lancashire)	d				17 04													18 04					
Chorley	d				17 09					17 39								18 09				18 39	
Buckshaw Parkway	d				17 12					17 42								18 12				18 42	
Leyland	d				17 19												←	18 19					
Preston ■ 65,97	a			17 02	17 25					18 05	17 51				18 04	18 03	18 04	18 25				18 59	18 51
	d			17 03	17 27				17 29		17 52				18 06	18 04	18 06	18 27					18 52
Kirkham & Wesham 97	a				17 36						18 01				→			18 36					19 01
Poulton-le-Fylde 97	a				17 44						18 10							18 44					19 10
Layton 97	a																						
Blackpool North 97	a				17 52						18 16							18 52					19 16
Lancaster ■ 65	a			17 18					17 49							18 20	18 21						
	d		17 15	17 19					17 49							18 20	18 21						
Oxenholme Lake District 65	a			17 32												18 34	18 34						
Windermere 83	a																						
Carnforth	d		17a50						17 59														
Silverdale	d								18 05														
Arnside	d								18 09														
Grange-over-Sands	d								18 15														
Kents Bank	d								18 19														
Cark	d								18 23														
Ulverston	d								18 31														
Dalton	d								18 39														
Roose	d								18 45														
Barrow-in-Furness	a								18 53														

A From Blackburn
B To Leeds
C To Edinburgh
D To Newcastle
E To Clitheroe
F To Middlesbrough
G From Stalybridge
H from 16 September. To Glasgow Central
I until 9 September. To Glasgow Central
J from 16 September. From Manchester Airport to Glasgow Central

Table T082-F

Sundays

20 May to 2 December

Manchester - Bolton - Wigan, Kirkby, Southport, Preston, Blackpool North and Barrow-in-Furness

		TP ◇■ A ✠	NT B	NT C	NT	TP ◇■ D ✠	NT ◇	NT	TP ◇■ E ✠	NT F	NT	NT ◇	NT ◇	TP ◇■ A	NT B	NT C	NT ◇ G	TP ◇■ H ✠	NT	TP ◇■ I	NT F	NT	NT ◇
Manchester Airport 85 ✈	d	17 47				18 10			18 19			18 33	18 41	18 47				19 10		19 19			
Heald Green 85	d											18 37	18 45										
Buxton 86	d																						
Hazel Grove 86	d																						
Stockport 84	d																						
Manchester Piccadilly ■	d	18 07				18 26			18 35			18 51	19 00	19 05				19 26		19 35			
Manchester Oxford Road	d	18 10							18 38			19 07	19 05	19 09						19 38			
Deansgate	d											19 09											
Rochdale 41	d			18 03												19 03							
Manchester Victoria	d	18a16	18 19	18 25				18 31	18a45	18 45	18 55			19a14	19 19	19 25			19 31	19a45	19 45	19 55	
Salford Central	d		18 22	18 29				18 34		18 48	18 58				19 22	19 29			19 34		19 48	19 58	
Salford Crescent	a		18 25	18 32				18 37		18 51	19 01	19 12			19 25	19 32			19 37		19 51	20 01	
	d		18 26	18 32				18 37		18 52	19 02	19 13			19 26	19 32			19 37		19 52	20 02	
Swinton	d			18 39							19 09					19 39						20 09	
Moorside	d										19 11											20 11	
Walkden	d			18 44							19 15					19 44						20 15	
Atherton	d			18 49							19 21					19 49						20 21	
Hag Fold	d										19 24											20 24	
Daisy Hill	d			18 53							19 27					19 53						20 27	
Clifton	d																						
Kearsley	d																						
Farnworth	d																						
Moses Gate	d																						
Bolton	a		18 36					18 48		19 04		19 23			19 36				19 48		20 04		
	d		18 37					18 48				19 24			19 37				19 48				
Westhoughton	d		18 44												19 44								
Hindley	d		18 50	18 58							19 32				19 50	19 58						20 32	
Ince	d										19 35											20 35	
Wigan North Western	a		18 56										19 33		19 56								
Wigan Wallgate	a			19 03							19 40					20 03						20 40	
	d			19 04												20 04							
Pemberton	d																						
Orrell	d																						
Upholland	d																						
Rainford	d																						
Kirkby	a																						
Gathurst	d			19 09												20 09							
Appley Bridge	d			19 13												20 13							
Parbold	d			19 17												20 17							
Hoscar	d																						
Burscough Bridge	d			19 22												20 22							
New Lane	d																						
Bescar Lane	d																						
Meols Cop	d			19 30												20 30							
Southport	a			19 37												20 37							
Lostock	d							18 53											19 53				
Horwich Parkway	d							18 57				19 31							19 57				
Blackrod	d							19 00											20 00				
Adlington (Lancashire)	d							19 04											20 04				
Chorley	d							19 09				19 39							20 09				
Buckshaw Parkway	d							19 12				19 42							20 12				
Leyland	d							19 19											20 19				
Preston ■ 65,97	a					19 02		19 25				19 58	19 51					20 02	20 25				
	d					19 04	19 26	19 27					19 52					20 04	20 27				20 29
Kirkham & Wesham 97	a							19 36					20 02						20 36				
Poulton-le-Fylde 97	a							19 44					20 10						20 44				
Layton 97	a																						
Blackpool North 97	a							19 52					20 17						20 52				
Lancaster ■ 65	a					19 19	19 46											20 19					20 49
	d				19 13	19 19	19 47										19 51	20 20					20 49
Oxenholme Lake District 65	a					19 32												20 33					
Windermere 83	a																						
Carnforth	d				19 22		19 57										20a01						20 59
Silverdale	d				19 28		20 02																21 05
Arnside	d				19 32		20 07																21 09
Grange-over-Sands	d				19 38		20 13																21 15
Kents Bank	d				19 42		20 16																21 19
Cark	d				19 46		20 20																21 23
Ulverston	d				19 54		20 29																21 31
Dalton	d				20 02		20 37																21 39
Roose	d				20 08		20 43																21 45
Barrow-in-Furness	a				20 16		20 50																21 53

A To Middlesbrough
B From Stalybridge
C From Blackburn
D To Edinburgh
E To Newcastle
F To Clitheroe
G To Leeds
H To Glasgow Central
I To York

Manchester - Bolton - Wigan, Kirkby, Southport, Preston, Blackpool North and Barrow-in-Furness

		NT		NT	TP	NT	NT	NT	TP	NT	NT	NT		NT	NT	NT	TP	NT	NT	NT	NT	NT		NT	NT
		◇		◇	◇■				◇■		◇	◇					◇■			◇	◇				
					A	B	C		D					E	B		D	C				E			B
Manchester Airport 85 ✈	d	19 33		19 41	20 10				20 19		20 33	20 41					21 04			21 33	21 41				
Heald Green 85	d	19 37		19 45							20 37	20 45								21 37	21 45				
Buxton 86	d																								
Hazel Grove 86	d																								
Stockport 84	d																								
Manchester Piccadilly ■	d	19 51		20 00	20 26				20 35		20 51	21 00					21 22			21 52	22 01				
Manchester Oxford Road	d	20 07		20 05					20 38		21 07	21 05					21 25			22 06	22 04				
Deansgate	d	20 09									21 09									22 08					
Rochdale 41	d						20 03											21 09							
Manchester Victoria	d					20 19	20 25	20 31	20a45	20 55				21 12	21 19	21 25	21a31	21 32	21 51			22 07			22 19
Salford Central	d					20 22	20 29	20 34		20 58				21 15	21 22	21 28		21 35	21 54			22 10			22 22
Salford Crescent	a	20 12				20 25	20 32	20 37		21 01	21 12			21 18	21 25	21 31		21 38	22 01	22 11		22 15			22 25
	d	20 13				20 26	20 32	20 37		21 02	21 13			21 19	21 26	21 31		21 39	22 02	22 12		22 16			22 26
Swinton	d						20 39			21 09								21 45	22 09						
Moorside	d									21 11									22 11						
Walkden	d						20 44			21 15								21 50	22 15						
Atherton	d						20 49			21 21								21 56	22 21						
Hag Fold	d									21 24									22 24						
Daisy Hill	d						20 53			21 27								22 00	22 27						
Clifton	d																								
Kearsley	d																								
Farnworth	d																								
Moses Gate	d																								
Bolton	a	20 23				20 36		20 48			21 23			21 31	21 36	21 42				22 22		22 27			22 36
	d	20 24				20 37		20 48			21 24				21 37	21 42				22 23					22 37
Westhoughton	d					20 44									21 44										22 44
Hindley	d					20 50	20 58			21 32					21 50			22 05	22 32						22 50
Ince	d									21 35									22 35						
Wigan North Western	a			20 33		20 56						21 35			21 56						22 31				22 56
Wigan Wallgate	a						21 03			21 40								22 10	22 40						
	d						21 04											22 12							
Pemberton	d																								
Orrell	d																								
Upholland	d																								
Rainford	d																								
Kirkby	a																								
Gathurst	d						21 09											22 16							
Appley Bridge	d						21 13											22 20							
Parbold	d						21 17											22 24							
Hoscar	d																								
Burscough Bridge	d						21 22											22 29							
New Lane	d																								
Bescar Lane	d																								
Meols Cop	d						21 30											22 37							
Southport	a						21 37											22 45							
Lostock	d							20 53								21 47									
Horwich Parkway	d	20 31						20 57			21 31					21 51				22 30					
Blackrod	d							21 00								21 54									
Adlington (Lancashire)	d							21 04								21 58									
Chorley	d	20 39						21 09			21 39					22 03				22 38					
Buckshaw Parkway	d	20 42						21 12			21 42					22 06				22 41					
Leyland	d							21 19								22 13									
Preston ■ 65,97	a	21 03		20 51	21 02			21 25			21 57	21 54				22 21				22 55	22 49				
	d			20 52	21 04			21 27				21 54				22 22					22 50				
Kirkham & Wesham 97	a			21 01				21 36				22 04				22 31					22 59				
Poulton-le-Fylde 97	a			21 10				21 44				22 13				22 40					23 08				
Layton 97	a																								
Blackpool North 97	a			21 16				21 52				22 19				22 47					23 14				
Lancaster ■ 65	a				21 19																				
	d				21 20																			22 15	
Oxenholme Lake District 65	a				21 33																				
Windermere 83	a																								
Carnforth	d																							22 24	
Silverdale	d																							22 29	
Arnside	d																							22 34	
Grange-over-Sands	d																							22 40	
Kents Bank	d																							22 43	
Cark	d																							22 47	
Ulverston	d																							22 55	
Dalton	d																							23 03	
Roose	d																							23 09	
Barrow-in-Furness	a																							23 17	

A To Edinburgh
B From Stalybridge
C From Blackburn
D To Scarborough
E To Clitheroe

Manchester - Bolton - Wigan, Kirkby, Southport, Preston, Blackpool North and Barrow-in-Furness

		TP	TP	NT	NT	NT	NT	TP
		◇■	◇■		◇			◇■
		A	A			B	C	A
Manchester Airport 85 ✈	d	22 06	22 19		22 43			23 27
Heald Green 85	d				22 47			
Buxton 86	d							
Hazel Grove 86	d							
Stockport 84	d							
Manchester Piccadilly ■	d	22 23	22 35		23 01			23 41
Manchester Oxford Road	d	22 26	22 38		23 05			23 44
Deansgate	d				23 07			
Rochdale 41	d							
Manchester Victoria	d	22a32	22a44	22 55		23 14	23 19	23a49
Salford Central	d			22 58		23 17	23 22	
Salford Crescent	a			23 01		23 20	23 25	
	d			23 02		23 21	23 26	
Swinton	d			23 09				
Moorside	d			23 11				
Walkden	d			23 15				
Atherton	d			23 21				
Hag Fold	d			23 24				
Daisy Hill	d			23 27				
Clifton	d							
Kearsley	d							
Farnworth	d							
Moses Gate	d							
Bolton	a					23 33	23 36	
	d						23 37	
Westhoughton	d						23 44	
Hindley	d			23 32			23 50	
Ince	d			23 35				
Wigan North Western	a				23 33		23 56	
Wigan Wallgate	a			23 40				
	d							
Pemberton	d							
Orrell	d							
Upholland	d							
Rainford	d							
Kirkby	a							
Gathurst	d							
Appley Bridge	d							
Parbold	d							
Hoscar	d							
Burscough Bridge	d							
New Lane	d							
Bescar Lane	d							
Meols Cop	d							
Southport	a							
Lostock	d							
Horwich Parkway	d							
Blackrod	d							
Adlington (Lancashire)	d							
Chorley	d							
Buckshaw Parkway	d							
Leyland	d							
Preston ■ 65,97	a				23 51			
	d				23 52			
Kirkham & Wesham 97	a				00 01			
Poulton-le-Fylde 97	a				00 10			
Layton 97	a							
Blackpool North 97	a				00 16			
Lancaster ■ 65	a							
	d							
Oxenholme Lake District 65	a							
Windermere 83	a							
Carnforth	d							
Silverdale	d							
Arnside	d							
Grange-over-Sands	d							
Kents Bank	d							
Cark	d							
Ulverston	d							
Dalton	d							
Roose	d							
Barrow-in-Furness	a							

A To York
B To Blackburn
C From Stalybridge

Table T082-R

Mondays to Fridays

21 May to 7 December

Barrow-in-Furness, Blackpool North, Preston, Southport, Kirkby and Wigan - Bolton - Manchester

Miles	Miles	Miles	Miles	Miles			NT MO A	NT MX B 🚌	NT MX C 🚌	TP ThO ◇1 D ⌶	TP TW FO ◇1 D ⌶	NT MX C 🚌	NT ◇	NT 🚌	NT ◇	NT 🚌	NT E	NT 🚌	NT	NT	NT F	NT	NT ◇	NT ◇
—	0	—	—	—	**Barrow-in-Furness**	d																		04 53
—	1¾	—	—	—	Roose	d																		
—	6	—	—	—	Dalton	d																		
—	9¾	—	—	—	Ulverston	d																		05 09
—	15¼	—	—	—	Cark	d																		
—	17¼	—	—	—	Kents Bank	d																		
—	19½	—	—	—	Grange-over-Sands	d																		05 21
—	22¼	—	—	—	Arnside	d																		05 27
—	25	—	—	—	Silverdale	d																		
—	28¾	—	—	—	Carnforth	d																		05 37
—	—	—	—	—	Windermere 83	d																		
—	—	—	—	—	Oxenholme Lake District 65	d																		
—	34¾	—	—	—	**Lancaster** 6 65	a																		05 45
—	—	—	—	—		d																		05 46
0	—	—	—	—	**Blackpool North** 97	d							03 33		04 46				05 23				05 39	
1¼	—	—	—	—	Layton 97	d																	05 42	
3¾	—	—	—	—	Poulton-le-Fylde 97	d									04 52				05 29				05 46	
9¾	—	—	—	—	Kirkham & Wesham 97	d																	05 55	
—	55¾	—	—	—	**Preston** 8 65,97	a							03 55		05 08				05 46				06 05	06 06
—	—	—	—	—		d				00 57	00 57		03 57	04 05	05 09			05 16	05 48			06 01	06 07	
21½	59¾	—	—	—	Leyland	d						00 11							05 55			06 07	06 12	
23¾	62	—	—	—	Buckshaw Parkway	d						00 25							06 00			06 13		
26	64¼	—	—	—	Chorley	d						00 40						05 41	06 05			06 18		
29	67¼	—	—	—	Adlington (Lancashire)	d						00 50										06 23		
31	69¼	—	—	—	Blackrod	d			00 05			00 57										06 27		
32½	70¾	—	—	—	Horwich Parkway	d			00 11			01 03						05 56	06 13			06 31		
34½	72¾	—	—	—	Lostock	d			00 19			01 11							06 17			06 35		
—	—	0	—	—	**Southport**	d																		
—	—	1¾	—	—	Meols Cop	d																		
—	—	4½	—	—	Bescar Lane	d																		
—	—	6½	—	—	New Lane	d																		
—	—	7¾	—	—	Burscough Bridge	d																		
—	—	9¼	—	—	Hoscar	d																		
—	—	10¾	—	—	Parbold	d																		
—	—	13	—	—	Appley Bridge	d																		
—	—	14¾	—	—	Gathurst	d																		
—	—	—	0	—	**Kirkby**	d																		
—	—	—	5¼	—	Rainford	d																		
—	—	—	7¼	—	Upholland	d																		
—	—	—	8½	—	Orrell	d																		
—	—	—	10½	—	Pemberton	d																		
—	—	17½	12¼	—	**Wigan Wallgate**	a																		
—	—	—	—	—		d														06 01	06 08			
—	—	—	—	0	Wigan North Western	d							04 16				05 48						06 23	
—	—	18½	13¼	0¾	Ince	d														06 04				
—	—	20	14¾	—	Hindley	d											05 54			06 08	06 13			
—	—	22½	—	—	Westhoughton	d											06 01				06 18			
37½	75¾	27	—	—	**Bolton**	a			00 37			01 29		04 40			06 09	06 15	06 22		06 26	06 40		
—	—	—	—	—		d		00 15	00 37			01 29		04 40		05 30	06 09	06 15	06 22		06 26	06 40		
38¼	76½	27¾	—	—	Moses Gate	d															06 29			
39¾	78	29¼	—	—	Farnworth	d															06 31			
40½	78¾	30	—	—	Kearsley	d															06 33			
43½	81¾	33	—	—	Clifton	d																		
—	—	—	17¼	—	Daisy Hill	d														06 12				
—	—	—	17½	—	Hag Fold	d														06 15				
—	—	—	18¾	—	Atherton	d														06 18				
—	—	—	22¼	—	Walkden	d														06 24				
—	—	—	24	—	Moorside	d														06 28				
—	—	—	24¾	—	Swinton	d														06 31				
46½	84¾	36	28¾	—	**Salford Crescent**	a		00 40	01s02			01s54				05 55	06 21		06 34	06 39	06 44	06 52		
—	—	—	—	—		d		00 40								05 55	06 22		06 35	06 40	06 45	06 53		
—	—	—	29¾	—	Salford Central	d	00 03													06 43	06 48	06 56		
—	—	—	30½	—	**Manchester Victoria** ⇌	a	00 06	00 50												06 46	06 51	06 59		
—	—	—	—	—	Rochdale 41	a																		
48	86¼	37½	—	—	Deansgate ⇌	a											06 29							
48¼	86½	37¾	—	—	**Manchester Oxford Road**	a									05 52		06 32		06 41				06 52	
48¾	87	38¼	—	—	**Manchester Piccadilly** 10 ⇌	a			01 12	01 43	01 43	02 04	04 46	05 05	05 56	06 02	06 36	06 40	06 46				06 57	
—	—	—	—	—	Stockport 84	a											06 52							
—	—	—	—	—	Hazel Grove 86	a																		
—	—	—	—	—	Buxton 86	a																		
57	95¼	46½	—	—	Heald Green 85	a									06 13									
58½	96¾	48	—	—	**Manchester Airport** 85 ⇌✈	a					01 58		05 04		06 20								07 18	

A From Southport
B From Blackburn
C From Preston
D From Edinburgh
E To Alderley Edge
F To Stalybridge

Table T082-R

Mondays to Fridays

21 May to 7 December

Barrow-in-Furness, Blackpool North, Preston, Southport, Kirkby and Wigan - Bolton - Manchester

		NT A	NT ◇	TP ◇1	NT B	NT	NT	NT C	NT ◇ D	NT E	NT	NT F	NT	NT	NT ◇	NT ◇ G	NT H	NT E	NT ◇	NT	NT C	NT ◇ D
Barrow-in-Furness	d					05 49										06 11			06 11			
Roose	d					05 53																
Dalton	d					05 59																
Ulverston	d					06 08										06 26			06 26			
Cark	d					06 15																
Kents Bank	d					06 19																
Grange-over-Sands	d					06 23										06 39			06 39			
Arnside	d					06 29										06 45			06 45			
Silverdale	d					06 34																
Carnforth	d				06 24	06 41										06 55			06 55			
Windermere 83	d																					
Oxenholme Lake District 65	d																					
Lancaster 6 65	a				06 32	06 51										07 02			07 02			
	d			06 20												07 03			07 03			
Blackpool North 97	d													06 34	06 38							
Layton 97	d														06 41							
Poulton-le-Fylde 97	d													06 40	06 45							
Kirkham & Wesham 97	d													06 49	06 54							
Preston 8 65,97	a			06 38										07 00	07 05	07 22			07 22			
	d		06 21	06 47										07 02	07 07				07 28			
Leyland	d													07 08	07 12							
Buckshaw Parkway	d		06 30										07 08	07 15					07 36			
Chorley	d		06 35										07 13	07 20					07 40			
Adlington (Lancashire)	d												07 18									
Blackrod	d												07 22	07 27								
Horwich Parkway	d		06 44										07 26	07 31					07 48			
Lostock	d												07 30	07 35								
Southport	d							06 17				06 34					06 48				07 17	
Meols Cop	d							06 22				06 40					06 53				07 22	
Bescar Lane	d																06 58					
New Lane	d																07 02					
Burscough Bridge	d							06 31				06 48					07 05				07 31	
Hoscar	d																07 08					
Parbold	d							06 36				06 53					07 11				07 36	
Appley Bridge	d							06 40				06 57					07 16				07 40	
Gathurst	d							06 44				07 01					07 19				07 44	
Kirkby	d										06 36											
Rainford	d										06 44											
Upholland	d										06 48											
Orrell	d										06 52											
Pemberton	d										06 55											
Wigan Wallgate	a							06 49			07 00	07 06					07 24				07 49	
	d							06 50			07 01	07 07					07 25			07 40	07 50	
Wigan North Western	d						06 42		06 56						07 23							07 56
Ince	d										07 04									07 43		
Hindley	d							06 56			07 08	07 12					07 31			07 46	07 56	
Westhoughton	d							07 01				07 17									08 01	
Bolton	a		06 51					07 09				07 25	07 35	07 40					07 54		08 09	
	d	06 49	06 52					07 09		07 19		07 25	07 35	07 40				07 49	07 55		08 09	
Moses Gate	d											07 28										
Farnworth	d											07 30										
Kearsley	d											07 32										
Clifton	d											07 37										
Daisy Hill	d						06 50		07 05		07 13						07 35			07 51		08 05
Hag Fold	d						06 53				07 16									07 54		
Atherton	d						06 56		07 09		07 19						07 39			07 57		08 09
Walkden	d						07 02		07 15		07 25						07 45			08 03		08 15
Moorside	d						07 06				07 29									08 06		
Swinton	d						07 09				07 32									08 09		
Salford Crescent	a	07 01	07 04				07 17	07 21	07 28	07 32	07 39	07 44	07 47	07 52			07 56	08 02	08 06	08 17	08 21	08 28
	d	07 01	07 06				07 18	07 22	07 28	07 33	07 40	07 44	07 47	07 53			07 57	08 02	08 07	08 18	08 22	08 28
Salford Central	d	07 04					07 21		07 32	07 36	07 43	07 48		07 56			08 00	08 06		08 21		08 32
Manchester Victoria ⇌	a	07 07					07 24		07 35	07 41	07 46	07 51		07 59			08 03	08 08		08 24		08 36
Rochdale 41	a	07 31							07 49	08 06							08 17	08 31				08 51
Deansgate ⇌	a							07 28					07 51								08 29	
Manchester Oxford Road	a		07 11					07 30					07 53		07 57				08 11		08 31	
Manchester Piccadilly 10 ⇌	a		07 15	07 27				07 35					07 57		08 01				08 15		08 37	
Stockport 84	a							07 50													08 51	
Hazel Grove 86	a																					
Buxton 86	a																					
Heald Green 85	a		07 29																08 27			
Manchester Airport 85 ⇌✈	a		07 35	07 47											08 23				08 34			

A From Blackburn
B From Skipton
C To Alderley Edge
D To Leeds
E From Clitheroe
F To Stalybridge
G 28 May
H To Blackburn

Table T082-R

Mondays to Fridays
21 May to 7 December

Barrow-in-Furness, Blackpool North, Preston, Southport, Kirkby and Wigan - Bolton - Manchester

		NT	NT	TP	NT	NT	NT	NT	NT	NT	NT	NT	NT	NT	NT	NT	NT	NT	TP	NT	NT	NT	NT
		A		◇■ B		C	◇	◇			D	E	◇		F	◇ G	A		◇■ H	C	◇	◇	
Barrow-in-Furness	d							06 47	07 08													07 46	
Roose	d							06 51	07 12													07 50	
Dalton	d							06 57	07 18													07 56	
Ulverston	d							07 05	07 27													08 05	
Cark	d							07 13	07 34													08 12	
Kents Bank	d								07 38														
Grange-over-Sands	d							07 20	07 42													08 19	
Arnside	d							07 25	07 49													08 25	
Silverdale	d							07 30	07 54													08 30	
Carnforth	d							07 37	08 01													08 37	
Windermere 83	d																						
Oxenholme Lake District 65	d			07 09															08 14				
Lancaster ■ 65	a			07 23				07 45	08 10										08 28			08 45	
	d			07 25				07 46											08 28			08 46	
Blackpool North 97	d		07 16				07 38											08 21			08 38		
Layton 97	d						07 41														08 41		
Poulton-le-Fylde 97	d		07 22				07 45											08 27			08 45		
Kirkham & Wesham 97	d		07 31				07 54														08 54		
Preston ■ 65,97	a		07 42	07 45			08 04	08 06										08 44	08 46		09 04	09 08	
	d		07 45	07 47			08 06						08 24					08 45	08 47		09 06		
Leyland	d		07 52				08 12											08 52			09 12		
Buckshaw Parkway	d		07 57							08 09			08 33					08 58					09 09
Chorley	d		08 02							08 18			08 38					09 04					09 18
Adlington (Lancashire)	d		08 06							08 23													09 23
Blackrod	d		08 10							08 27													09 27
Horwich Parkway	d		08 14							08 31			08 46					09 13					09 31
Lostock	d		08 17							08 35								09 17					09 35
Southport	d										07 47					08 24							
Meols Cop	d										07 52					08 29							
Bescar Lane	d										07 57												
New Lane	d										08 01												
Burscough Bridge	d										08 04					08 38							
Hoscar	d										08 07												
Parbold	d										08 11					08 43							
Appley Bridge	d										08 15					08 47							
Gathurst	d										08 19					08 51							
Kirkby	d				07 36									08 15									
Rainford	d				07 44									08 23									
Upholland	d				07 48									08 27									
Orrell	d				07 52									08 31									
Pemberton	d				07 55									08 34									
Wigan Wallgate	a				08 00						08 24			08 39		08 55							
	d				08 01						08 25			08 41		08 57							
Wigan North Western	d					08 08	08 23								08 50					09 08	09 23		
Ince	d				08 04									08 44									
Hindley	d				08 08	08 13					08 31			08 47	08 56					09 13			
Westhoughton	d					08 18									09 01					09 18			
Bolton	a		08 22			08 26				08 40			08 54		09 09			09 22		09 26			09 40
	d	08 17	08 23			08 27				08 40		08 49	08 54		09 09		09 17	09 22		09 26			09 40
Moses Gate	d					08 30														09 29			
Farnworth	d	08 21				08 32														09 31			
Kearsley	d					08 34											09 21			09 33			
Clifton	d																						
Daisy Hill	d				08 13						08 35			08 51		09 05							
Hag Fold	d				08 16									08 54									
Atherton	d				08 19						08 39			08 57		09 09							
Walkden	d				08 25						08 45			09 03		09 15							
Moorside	d													09 07									
Swinton	d				08 30									09 09									
Salford Crescent	a	08 32	08 36		08 39	08 44				08 52	08 56	09 01	09 06	09 17	09 21	09 28	09 32	09 36		09 44			09 52
	d	08 33	08 36		08 40	08 45				08 53	08 57	09 01	09 07	09 18	09 22	09 28	09 33	09 36		09 45			09 53
Salford Central	d	08 36			08 42	08 48				08 56	09 00	09 04		09 21		09 32	09 36			09 48			09 56
Manchester Victoria ⇌	a	08 41			08 46	08 51				09 00	09 03	09 07		09 26		09 36	09 41			09 51			09 59
Rochdale 41	a	09 06									09 17	09 31				09 50	10 06						
Deansgate ⇌	a		08 40												09 29			09 40					
Manchester Oxford Road	a		08 42				08 55						09 11		09 32			09 42			09 52		
Manchester Piccadilly ■ ⇌	a		08 45	08 27			08 59						09 15		09 36			09 45	09 27		09 57		
Stockport 84	a														09 51								
Hazel Grove 86	a																						
Buxton 86	a																						
Heald Green 85	a						09 15						09 29								10 14		
Manchester Airport 85 ⇌✈	a			08 47			09 19						09 35						09 47		10 19		

A From Clitheroe
B From Glasgow Central
C To Stalybridge
D To Blackburn
E From Blackburn
F To Alderley Edge
G To Leeds
H From Edinburgh

Table T082-R

Mondays to Fridays
21 May to 7 December

Barrow-in-Furness, Blackpool North, Preston, Southport, Kirkby and Wigan - Bolton - Manchester

		NT	NT	NT	NT	NT	NT	NT	NT	TP	NT	NT	NT	NT	NT	NT	NT	NT	NT	NT	NT	NT
		A	B	◇		C	◇ D	E		◇■ F	G	◇	◇	◇ H		A	B	◇		C	◇ D	E
Barrow-in-Furness	d												08 46									
Roose	d												08 50									
Dalton	d												08 56									
Ulverston	d												09 04									
Cark	d												09 12									
Kents Bank	d												09 16									
Grange-over-Sands	d												09 20									
Arnside	d												09 25									
Silverdale	d												09 30									
Carnforth	d												09 37	09 57								
Windermere 83	d																					
Oxenholme Lake District 65	d									09 13												
Lancaster ■ 65	a									09 27			09 45	10 05								
	d									09 28			09 46									
Blackpool North 97	d								09 21			09 38										
Layton 97	d											09 41										
Poulton-le-Fylde 97	d								09 26			09 45										
Kirkham & Wesham 97	d											09 54										
Preston ■ 65,97	a								09 43	09 45		10 04	10 06									
	d			09 24					09 45	09 47		10 06						10 24				
Leyland	d								09 54			10 12										
Buckshaw Parkway	d			09 33					10 02						10 09			10 33				
Chorley	d			09 38					10 06						10 18			10 38				
Adlington (Lancashire)	d														10 23							
Blackrod	d														10 27							
Horwich Parkway	d			09 46					10 14						10 31			10 46				
Lostock	d								10 18						10 35							
Southport	d	08 52					09 24									09 47					10 24	
Meols Cop	d	08 57					09 29									09 52					10 29	
Bescar Lane	d															09 57						
New Lane	d															10 01						
Burscough Bridge	d	09 06					09 38									10 04					10 38	
Hoscar	d															10 07						
Parbold	d	09 10					09 43									10 10					10 43	
Appley Bridge	d	09 15					09 47									10 15					10 47	
Gathurst	d	09 18					09 51									10 18					10 51	
Kirkby	d				09 15														10 15			
Rainford	d				09 23														10 23			
Upholland	d				09 27														10 27			
Orrell	d				09 31														10 31			
Pemberton	d				09 34														10 34			
Wigan Wallgate	a	09 23			09 39		09 55									10 23			10 39		10 55	
	d	09 24			09 41		09 57									10 24			10 41		10 57	
Wigan North Western	d					09 50					10 08	10 23								10 50		
Ince	d				09 44														10 44			
Hindley	d	09 30			09 47	09 56					10 13					10 30			10 47	10 56		
Westhoughton	d					10 01					10 18									11 01		
Bolton	a			09 54		10 09			10 23		10 27				10 40			10 54		11 09		
	d		09 49	09 54		10 09		10 19	10 23		10 27				10 40		10 49	10 54		11 09		11 19
Moses Gate	d										10 30											
Farnworth	d										10 32											
Kearsley	d										10 34											
Clifton	d																					
Daisy Hill	d	09 34			09 51		10 05									10 34			10 51		11 05	
Hag Fold	d				09 54														10 54			
Atherton	d	09 38			09 57		10 09									10 38			10 57		11 09	
Walkden	d	09 44			10 03		10 15									10 44			11 03		11 15	
Moorside	d				10 07														11 07			
Swinton	d	09 49			10 09											10 49			11 09			
Salford Crescent	a	09 56	10 01	10 06	10 17	10 21	10 28	10 32	10 36		10 45				10 52	10 56	11 01	11 06	11 17	11 21	11 28	11 32
	d	09 57	10 01	10 07	10 18	10 22	10 28	10 33	10 36		10 46				10 53	10 57	11 01	11 07	11 18	11 22	11 28	11 33
Salford Central	d	10 00	10 04		10 21		10 32	10 36			10 49				10 56	11 00	11 04		11 21		11 32	11 36
Manchester Victoria ⇌	a	10 03	10 07		10 26		10 36	10 41			10 52				10 59	11 03	11 07		11 26		11 36	11 41
Rochdale 41	a	10 17	10 31				10 50	11 06								11 17	11 31				11 50	12 03
Deansgate ⇌	a					10 29			10 40											11 29		
Manchester Oxford Road	a			10 11		10 32			10 42			10 52						11 11		11 32		
Manchester Piccadilly ■ ⇌	a			10 15		10 36			10 45	10 27		10 57						11 15		11 36		
Stockport 84	a					10 51														11 51		
Hazel Grove 86	a																					
Buxton 86	a																					
Heald Green 85	a			10 29								11 14						11 29				
Manchester Airport 85 ⇌✈	a			10 35						10 47		11 18						11 35				

A To Blackburn
B From Blackburn
C To Alderley Edge
D To Leeds
E From Clitheroe
F From Glasgow Central
G To Stalybridge
H From Leeds

Table T082-R

Mondays to Fridays

21 May to 7 December

Barrow-in-Furness, Blackpool North, Preston, Southport, Kirkby and Wigan - Bolton - Manchester

		NT	NT ◇ A	TP ◇1 B	NT C	NT D	NT ◇	NT	NT E	NT F	NT ◇	NT	NT G	NT ◇ H	NT I	NT	TP ◇1 J	NT D	NT ◇	NT ◇	NT ◇ K	NT	NT E
Barrow-in-Furness	d				09 58															10 48			
Roose	d				10 02																		
Dalton	d				10 08															10 57			
Ulverston	d				10 17															11 05			
Cark	d				10 24															11 13			
Kents Bank	d				10 28																		
Grange-over-Sands	d				10 32															11 20			
Arnside	d				10 39															11 25			
Silverdale	d				10 43															11 30			
Carnforth	d				10 56															11 37	12 01		
Windermere 83	d		09 34																				
Oxenholme Lake District 65	d		09 55	10 13													11 13						
Lancaster 8 65	a		10 13	10 29	11 07												11 29			11 45	12 10		
	d		10 14	10 30													11 30			11 46			
Blackpool North 97	d	10 12					10 32									11 20			11 38				
Layton 97	d						10 35												11 41				
Poulton-le-Fylde 97	d	10 17					10 39									11 25			11 45				
Kirkham & Wesham 97	d						10 48												11 54				
Preston 8 65,97	a	10 34	10 37	10 47			10 58									11 42	11 47		12 04	12 08			
	d	10 44		10 49			11 00				11 24					11 44	11 49		12 06				
Leyland	d	10 54					11 06									11 53			12 12				
Buckshaw Parkway	d	11 02						11 09			11 33					11 59						12 09	
Chorley	d	11 06						11 18			11 38					12 04						12 18	
Adlington (Lancashire)	d							11 23														12 23	
Blackrod	d							11 27														12 27	
Horwich Parkway	d	11 14						11 31			11 46					12 13						12 31	
Lostock	d	11 18						11 35								12 17						12 35	
Southport	d								10 52					11 24									11 47
Meols Cop	d								10 57					11 29									11 52
Bescar Lane	d																						11 57
New Lane	d																						12 01
Burscough Bridge	d								11 06					11 38									12 04
Hoscar	d																						12 07
Parbold	d								11 10					11 43									12 10
Appley Bridge	d								11 15					11 47									12 15
Gathurst	d								11 18					11 51									12 18
Kirkby	d																						
Rainford	d																						
Upholland	d																						
Orrell	d																						
Pemberton	d																						
Wigan Wallgate	a								11 23					11 55									12 23
	d								11 24			11 41		11 57									12 24
Wigan North Western	d					11 08	11 23						11 50					12 08	12 23				
Ince	d											11 44											
Hindley	d					11 13			11 30			11 47	11 56					12 13					12 30
Westhoughton	d					11 18							12 01					12 18					
Bolton	a	11 23				11 27		11 40			11 54		12 09			12 22		12 26				12 40	
	d	11 23				11 27		11 40		11 49	11 54		12 09		12 19	12 22		12 26				12 40	
Moses Gate	d					11 30												12 29					
Farnworth	d					11 32												12 31					
Kearsley	d					11 34												12 33					
Clifton	d																						
Daisy Hill	d								11 34			11 51		12 05									12 34
Hag Fold	d											11 54											
Atherton	d								11 38			11 57		12 09									12 38
Walkden	d								11 44			12 03		12 15									12 44
Moorside	d											12 07											
Swinton	d								11 49			12 09											12 49
Salford Crescent	a	11 36				11 45		11 52	11 56	12 01	12 06	12 17	12 21	12 28	12 32	12 36		12 44				12 52	12 56
	d	11 36				11 46		11 53	11 57	12 02	12 07	12 18	12 22	12 28	12 33	12 36		12 45				12 53	12 57
Salford Central	d					11 48		11 56	12 00	12 05		12 21		12 32	12 36			12 48				12 56	13 00
Manchester Victoria ⇌	a					11 51		11 59	12 03	12 08		12 26		12 36	12 41			12 51				12 59	13 03
Rochdale 41	a								12 17	12 32				12 50	13 06								13 17
Deansgate ⇌	a	11 40											12 29			12 40							
Manchester Oxford Road	a	11 42					11 55				12 11		12 32			12 42			12 52				
Manchester Piccadilly 10 ⇌	a	11 45		11 27			11 59				12 15		12 36			12 45	12 27		12 57				
Stockport 84	a												12 51										
Hazel Grove 86	a																						
Buxton 86	a																						
Heald Green 85	a						12 15				12 29								13 14				
Manchester Airport 85 ⇌✈	a			11 47			12 20				12 35						12 48		13 19				

A ◇ to Preston
B From Edinburgh
C From Carlisle
D To Stalybridge
E To Blackburn
F From Blackburn
G To Alderley Edge
H To Leeds
I From Clitheroe
J From Glasgow Central
K From Leeds to Morecambe

Table T082-R

Mondays to Fridays

21 May to 7 December

Barrow-in-Furness, Blackpool North, Preston, Southport, Kirkby and Wigan - Bolton - Manchester

		NT A	NT ◇	NT	NT B	NT ◇ C	NT D	NT	TP ◇1 E	NT F	NT ◇	NT	NT G	NT A	NT ◇	NT	TP ◇1 H	NT	NT	NT B	NT ◇ C	NT ◇ I	NT D
Barrow-in-Furness	d														11 53			12 51					
Roose	d														11 57								
Dalton	d														12 03			13 00					
Ulverston	d														12 11			13 09					
Cark	d														12 18			13 16					
Kents Bank	d														12 22			13 20					
Grange-over-Sands	d														12 26			13 24					
Arnside	d														12 33			13 30					
Silverdale	d														12 37			13 35					
Carnforth	d														12 44			13 42				14 01	
Windermere 83	d															12 32							
Oxenholme Lake District 65	d								12 13							12 53	13 13						
Lancaster 8 65	a								12 27						12 51	13 14	13 27	13 52				14 13	
	d								12 28						12 52		13 28						
Blackpool North 97	d							12 20			12 38												
Layton 97	d										12 41												
Poulton-le-Fylde 97	d							12 25			12 45												
Kirkham & Wesham 97	d										12 54												
Preston 8 65,97	a							12 42	12 45		13 04				13 11		13 45						
	d		12 24					12 44	12 47		13 06				13 25		13 47						
Leyland	d							12 55			13 12												
Buckshaw Parkway	d		12 33					13 02				13 09			13 33								
Chorley	d		12 38					13 06				13 18			13 37								
Adlington (Lancashire)	d											13 23											
Blackrod	d											13 27											
Horwich Parkway	d		12 46					13 14				13 31			13 46								
Lostock	d							13 18				13 35											
Southport	d					12 24							12 52								13 24		
Meols Cop	d					12 29							12 57								13 29		
Bescar Lane	d																						
New Lane	d																						
Burscough Bridge	d					12 38							13 06								13 38		
Hoscar	d																						
Parbold	d					12 43							13 10								13 43		
Appley Bridge	d					12 47							13 15								13 47		
Gathurst	d					12 51							13 18								13 51		
Kirkby	d			12 15															13 15				
Rainford	d			12 23															13 23				
Upholland	d			12 27															13 27				
Orrell	d			12 31															13 31				
Pemberton	d			12 34															13 34				
Wigan Wallgate	a			12 39		12 55							13 23						13 39		13 55		
	d			12 41		12 57							13 24						13 41		13 57		
Wigan North Western	d				12 50					13 08	13 24									13 50			
Ince	d			12 44															13 44				
Hindley	d			12 47	12 56					13 13			13 30						13 47	13 56			
Westhoughton	d				13 01					13 18										14 01			
Bolton	a		12 54		13 09			13 23		13 27		13 40			13 52					14 09			
	d	12 49	12 54		13 09		13 19	13 23		13 27		13 40		13 49	13 55					14 09			14 18
Moses Gate	d									13 30													
Farnworth	d									13 32													
Kearsley	d									13 34													
Clifton	d																						
Daisy Hill	d			12 51		13 05							13 34						13 51		14 05		
Hag Fold	d			12 54															13 54				
Atherton	d			12 57		13 09							13 38						13 57		14 09		
Walkden	d			13 03		13 15							13 44						14 03		14 15		
Moorside	d			13 07															14 07				
Swinton	d			13 09									13 49						14 09				
Salford Crescent	a	13 01	13 06	13 17	13 21	13 28	13 32			13 45		13 52	13 56	14 01	14 06				14 17	14 21	14 28		14 32
	d	13 01	13 07	13 18	13 22	13 28	13 33			13 46		13 53	13 57	14 01	14 07				14 18	14 22	14 28		14 32
Salford Central	d	13 04		13 21		13 32	13 36			13 48		13 56	14 00	14 04					14 21		14 32		14 37
Manchester Victoria ⇌	a	13 07		13 26		13 36	13 41			13 51		13 59	14 03	14 07					14 26		14 35		14 41
Rochdale 41	a	13 31				13 50	14 06						14 17	14 31							14 49		15 08
Deansgate ⇌	a				13 29			13 39												14 29			
Manchester Oxford Road	a		13 11		13 32			13 41			13 53				14 11					14 32			
Manchester Piccadilly 10 ⇌	a		13 15		13 36			13 44	13 27		13 58				14 15		14 27			14 36			
Stockport 84	a				13 51															14 51			
Hazel Grove 86	a																						
Buxton 86	a																						
Heald Green 85	a		13 29								14 14				14 28								
Manchester Airport 85 ⇌✈	a		13 35						13 47		14 18				14 35		14 47						

A From Blackburn
B To Alderley Edge
C To Leeds
D From Clitheroe
E From Edinburgh
F To Stalybridge
G To Blackburn
H From Glasgow Central
I From Leeds

Table T082-R

21 May to 7 December

Barrow-in-Furness, Blackpool North, Preston, Southport, Kirkby and Wigan - Bolton - Manchester

		NT	NT A	NT ◇	NT	NT B	NT C	NT ◇	TP ◇1 D	NT E	NT	NT F	NT ◇ G	NT H	NT	NT A	NT ◇	NT	NT B	NT C	NT ◇	NT ◇
Barrow-in-Furness	d									13 47												
Roose	d									13 51												
Dalton	d									13 57												
Ulverston	d									14 06												
Cark	d									14 13												
Kents Bank	d									14 17												
Grange-over-Sands	d									14 21												
Arnside	d									14 28												
Silverdale	d									14 33												
Carnforth	d									14 40												
Windermere 83	d																					14 25
Oxenholme Lake District 65	d								14 13													14 47
Lancaster 8 65	a								14 27	14 50												15 08
	d								14 28													15 09
Blackpool North 97	d	13 23		13 38											14 23		14 38					
Layton 97	d			13 41													14 41					
Poulton-le-Fylde 97	d	13 28		13 45											14 29		14 45					
Kirkham & Wesham 97	d			13 54													14 54					
Preston 8 65,97	a	13 48		14 04					14 45						14 48		15 04					15 33
	d	13 50		14 06				14 24	14 47						14 50		15 06				15 23	
Leyland	d	13 56		14 12											14 57		15 12					
Buckshaw Parkway	d	14 01			14 09			14 33							15 02			15 09			15 32	
Chorley	d	14 06			14 18			14 38							15 06			15 18			15 37	
Adlington (Lancashire)	d				14 23													15 23				
Blackrod	d				14 27													15 27				
Horwich Parkway	d	14 14			14 31			14 46							15 14			15 31			15 45	
Lostock	d	14 17			14 35										15 18			15 35				
Southport	d					13 52							14 24						14 47			
Meols Cop	d					13 57							14 29						14 52			
Bescar Lane	d																		14 57			
New Lane	d																		15 01			
Burscough Bridge	d					14 06							14 38						15 04			
Hoscar	d																		15 07			
Parbold	d					14 10							14 43						15 10			
Appley Bridge	d					14 15							14 47						15 15			
Gathurst	d					14 18							14 51						15 18			
Kirkby	d										14 15											
Rainford	d										14 23											
Upholland	d										14 27											
Orrell	d										14 31											
Pemberton	d										14 34											
Wigan Wallgate	a					14 23					14 39		14 55						15 23			
	d					14 24					14 41		14 57						15 24			
Wigan North Western	d		14 08	14 23								14 50				15 08	15 23					
Ince	d										14 44											
Hindley	d		14 13			14 30					14 47	14 56				15 13			15 30			
Westhoughton	d		14 18									15 01				15 18						
Bolton	a	14 22	14 26		14 40			14 54				15 09			15 23	15 27		15 40			15 52	
	d	14 23	14 27		14 40		14 49	14 54				15 09		15 19	15 23	15 27		15 40		15 49	15 53	
Moses Gate	d		14 30													15 30						
Farnworth	d		14 32													15 32						
Kearsley	d		14 34													15 34						
Clifton	d																					
Daisy Hill	d					14 34					14 51		15 05						15 34			
Hag Fold	d										14 54											
Atherton	d					14 38					14 57		15 09						15 38			
Walkden	d					14 44					15 03		15 15						15 44			
Moorside	d										15 07											
Swinton	d					14 49					15 09								15 49			
Salford Crescent	a	14 35	14 45		14 52	14 56	15 01	15 06			15 17	15 21	15 28	15 32	15 36	15 45		15 52	15 56	16 01	16 05	
	d	14 36	14 45		14 53	14 57	15 01	15 07			15 18	15 22	15 28	15 33	15 36	15 46		15 53	15 57	16 01	16 07	
Salford Central	d		14 48		14 56	15 00	15 04				15 21		15 31	15 37		15 48		15 56	16 00	16 04		
Manchester Victoria ⇌	a		14 51		14 59	15 03	15 07				15 26		15 34	15 40		15 51		15 59	16 03	16 07		
Rochdale 41	a					15 17	15 31						15 49	16 03					16 17	16 31		
Deansgate ⇌	a	14 39										15 29			15 40							
Manchester Oxford Road	a	14 41		14 53				15 11				15 32			15 42		15 53				16 11	
Manchester Piccadilly 10 ⇌	a	14 45		14 57				15 15	15 27			15 36			15 45		15 58				16 15	
Stockport 84	a											15 51										
Hazel Grove 86	a																					
Buxton 86	a																					
Heald Green 85	a			15 13				15 29									16 15				16 29	
Manchester Airport 85 ⇌✈	a			15 18				15 35	15 47								16 19				16 35	

A To Stalybridge
B To Blackburn
C From Blackburn
D From Edinburgh
E From Carlisle
F To Alderley Edge
G To Leeds
H From Clitheroe

Table T082-R

21 May to 7 December

Barrow-in-Furness, Blackpool North, Preston, Southport, Kirkby and Wigan - Bolton - Manchester

		NT	NT A	NT ◇ B	NT C	NT	TP ◇1 D	NT E	NT ◇	NT	NT F	NT G	NT ◇	NT ◇ H	NT	NT A	NT ◇ B	NT C	NT	TP ◇1 I	NT J	NT E	NT ◇
Barrow-in-Furness	d												14 48								15 50		
Roose	d												14 52								15 54		
Dalton	d												14 58								16 00		
Ulverston	d												15 06								16 08		
Cark	d												15 13								16 16		
Kents Bank	d												15 17								16 20		
Grange-over-Sands	d												15 21								16 24		
Arnside	d												15 28								16 30		
Silverdale	d												15 32								16 35		
Carnforth	d												15 39	15 59							16 42		
Windermere 83	d																						
Oxenholme Lake District 65	d						15 13													16 13			
Lancaster 8 65	a						15 27						15 46	16 08						16 27	16 52		
	d						15 28						15 47							16 28			
Blackpool North 97	d					15 20			15 38										16 15				16 38
Layton 97	d								15 41														16 41
Poulton-le-Fylde 97	d					15 25			15 45										16 21				16 45
Kirkham & Wesham 97	d								15 54														16 54
Preston 8 65,97	a					15 42	15 46		16 04				16 06						16 38	16 46			17 04
	d					15 44	15 47		16 06				16 24						16 39	16 47			17 06
Leyland	d					15 51			16 12										16 46				17 12
Buckshaw Parkway	d					15 57				16 09			16 32						16 52				
Chorley	d					16 02				16 18			16 36						16 57				
Adlington (Lancashire)	d									16 23									17 02				
Blackrod	d									16 27									17 06				
Horwich Parkway	d					16 11				16 31			16 44						17 10				
Lostock	d					16 14				16 35									17 14				
Southport	d			15 24							15 47						16 19						
Meols Cop	d			15 29							15 52						16 24						
Bescar Lane	d										15 57												
New Lane	d										16 01												
Burscough Bridge	d			15 38							16 04						16 33						
Hoscar	d										16 07												
Parbold	d			15 43							16 10						16 38						
Appley Bridge	d			15 47							16 15						16 42						
Gathurst	d			15 51							16 18						16 46						
Kirkby	d	15 15													16 15								
Rainford	d	15 23													16 23								
Upholland	d	15 27													16 27								
Orrell	d	15 31													16 31								
Pemberton	d	15 34													16 34								
Wigan Wallgate	a	15 39		15 55							16 23				16 39		16 50						
	d	15 41		15 57							16 24				16 41		16 52						
Wigan North Western	d		15 50					16 08	16 23							16 46						17 07	17 23
Ince	d	15 44													16 44								
Hindley	d	15 47	15 56					16 13			16 30				16 47		16 57					17 12	
Westhoughton	d		16 01					16 18								16 56	17 02					17 17	
Bolton	a		16 09			16 19		16 26		16 40			16 51			17 04	17 10		17 19			17 25	
	d		16 09		16 19	16 22		16 26		16 40		16 49	16 52			17 07	17 13	17 19	17 22			17 26	
Moses Gate	d							16 29														17 29	
Farnworth	d							16 31														17 31	
Kearsley	d							16 33														17 33	
Clifton	d																						
Daisy Hill	d	15 51		16 05							16 34				16 51								
Hag Fold	d	15 54													16 54								
Atherton	d	15 57		16 09							16 38				16 57								
Walkden	d	16 03		16 15							16 44				17 03								
Moorside	d	16 07													17 07								
Swinton	d	16 09									16 49				17 09								
Salford Crescent	a	16 17	16 21	16 28	16 32	16 36		16 44		16 52	16 56	17 01	17 04		17 17	17 21	17 25	17 32	17 35			17 44	
	d	16 18	16 22	16 28	16 33	16 36		16 45		16 53	16 57	17 01	17 07		17 18	17 22	17 25	17 32	17 36			17 45	
Salford Central	d	16 21		16 32	16 36			16 48		16 56	17 00	17 04			17 21		17 29	17 36				17 48	
Manchester Victoria ⇌	a	16 26		16 36	16 41			16 51		16 59	17 03	17 07			17 26		17 33	17 41				17 51	
Rochdale 41	a			16 50	17 10						17 17	17 31					17 50	18 06					
Deansgate ⇌	a		16 29			16 40										17 29			17 39				
Manchester Oxford Road	a		16 32			16 42			16 53				17 11			17 32			17 41				17 52
Manchester Piccadilly 10 ⇌	a		16 36			16 45	16 27		16 58				17 15			17 37			17 45	17 29			17 57
Stockport 84	a		16 51													17 51							
Hazel Grove 86	a																						
Buxton 86	a																						
Heald Green 85	a								17 14				17 29										18 13
Manchester Airport 85 ⇌✈	a						16 47		17 18				17 35							17 48			18 18

A To Alderley Edge
B To Leeds
C From Clitheroe
D From Glasgow Central
E To Stalybridge
F To Blackburn
G From Blackburn
H From Leeds to Morecambe
I From Edinburgh
J From Carlisle

Table T082-R

Mondays to Fridays

21 May to 7 December

Barrow-in-Furness, Blackpool North, Preston, Southport, Kirkby and Wigan - Bolton - Manchester

	NT	NT	NT	NT	NT	NT	NT	NT	TP	NT	NT	NT	NT	NT	NT	NT	NT	TP	NT	NT	NT
			◇			◇			◇1		◇						◇	◇1			
		A			B	C	D		E	F			G		A	D		H			B
Barrow-in-Furness d												16 49	17 19						18 02		
Roose d													17 23						18 06		
Dalton d												16 58	17 29						18 12		
Ulverston d												17 06	17 37						18 21		
Cark d												17 14	17 45						18 28		
Kents Bank d												17 18							18 32		
Grange-over-Sands d												17 22	17 52						18 36		
Arnside d												17 27	17 58						18 42		
Silverdale d												17 32	18 03						18 47		
Carnforth d												17 39	18 10						18 54		
Windermere 83 d																					
Oxenholme Lake District 65 d									17 10									18 13			
Lancaster 65 a									17 27			17 47	18 23					18 27	19 05		
d									17 28			17 48						18 28			
Blackpool North 97 d								17 11			17 38										
Layton 97 d								17 14			17 41										
Poulton-le-Fylde 97 d								17 18			17 45										
Kirkham & Wesham 97 d								17 27			17 54										
Preston 65,97 a								17 38	17 46		18 04	18 08						18 46			
d			17 24					17 40	17 47		18 06						18 23	18 47			
Leyland d								17 46			18 12										
Buckshaw Parkway d	17 09		17 33					17 52						18 09			18 33				
Chorley d	17 18		17 38					17 57						18 18			18 38				
Adlington (Lancashire) d	17 23							18 02						18 23							
Blackrod d	17 27							18 06						18 27							
Horwich Parkway d	17 31		17 46					18 10						18 31			18 46				
Lostock d	17 35							18 14						18 35							
Southport d		16 52				17 24									17 52						
Meols Cop d		16 57				17 29									17 57						
Bescar Lane d																					
New Lane d																					
Burscough Bridge d		17 06				17 38									18 06						
Hoscar d																					
Parbold d		17 10				17 43									18 10						
Appley Bridge d		17 15				17 47									18 15						
Gathurst d		17 18				17 51									18 18						
Kirkby d				17 15																18 15	
Rainford d				17 23																18 23	
Upholland d				17 27																18 27	
Orrell d				17 31																18 31	
Pemberton d				17 34																18 34	
Wigan Wallgate a		17 23		17 39		17 55									18 23					18 39	
d		17 24		17 41		17 57									18 24					18 41	
Wigan North Western d					17 49					18 08	18 23										18 50
Ince d				17 44	17 52															18 44	
Hindley d		17 30		17 47	17 56					18 13					18 30					18 47	18 56
Westhoughton d					18 01					18 18											19 01
Bolton a	17 40		17 54		18 09			18 19		18 26				18 40			18 54				19 09
d	17 40		17 54		18 09		18 18	18 22		18 26				18 40		18 49	18 54				19 10
Moses Gate d										18 29											
Farnworth d										18 31											
Kearsley d										18 33											
Clifton d																					
Daisy Hill d		17 34		17 51		18 05									18 34					18 51	
Hag Fold d				17 54																18 54	
Atherton d		17 38		17 57		18 09									18 38					18 57	
Walkden d		17 44		18 03		18 15									18 44					19 03	
Moorside d				18 07																19 07	
Swinton d		17 49		18 09											18 49					19 09	
Salford Crescent a	17 52	17 56	18 06	18 18	18 21	18 28	18 32	18 35		18 44				18 52	18 56	19 01	19 06			19 17	19 21
d	17 53	17 57	18 07	18 18	18 22	18 28	18 32	18 36		18 45				18 53	18 57	19 01	19 07			19 18	19 22
Salford Central d	17 56	18 00		18 21		18 32	18 36			18 48				18 56	19 00	19 04				19 21	
Manchester Victoria a	18 00	18 03		18 26		18 36	18 41			18 51				18 59	19 03	19 07				19 26	
Rochdale 41 a		18 17				18 50	19 06								19 17	19 32					
Deansgate a					18 29			18 39													19 29
Manchester Oxford Road a			18 11		18 32			18 41			18 52						19 11				19 32
Manchester Piccadilly 10 a			18 15		18 36			18 45	18 23		18 57						19 15	19 27			19 36
Stockport 84 a					18 49																19 51
Hazel Grove 86 a																					
Buxton 86 a																					
Heald Green 85 a			18 29								19 13						19 29				
Manchester Airport 85 a			18 35						18 43		19 18						19 35	19 46			

A To Blackburn
B To Alderley Edge
C To Leeds
D From Clitheroe
E From Glasgow Central
F To Stalybridge
G From Carlisle
H From Edinburgh

Table T082-R

Mondays to Fridays

21 May to 7 December

Barrow-in-Furness, Blackpool North, Preston, Southport, Kirkby and Wigan - Bolton - Manchester

	NT	NT	NT	NT	NT	NT	NT	NT	NT	NT	NT	NT	NT	NT	NT	NT	TP	NT	NT	NT	NT	NT
	◇				◇				◇	◇	◇			◇			◇1		◇	◇		◇
	A	B		C			D	E			F		G	A	B		H	C			D	
Barrow-in-Furness d																				19 00		
Roose d																						
Dalton d																						
Ulverston d																				19 16		
Cark d																						
Kents Bank d																						
Grange-over-Sands d																				19 28		
Arnside d																				19 35		
Silverdale d																						
Carnforth d											19 14									19 46		
Windermere 83 d										18 30												
Oxenholme Lake District 65 d										18 49							19 13					
Lancaster 65 a										19 08	19 23						19 27			19 54		
d										19 09							19 28			19 55		
Blackpool North 97 d			18 24		18 37											19 16			19 39			
Layton 97 d					18 40														19 42			
Poulton-le-Fylde 97 d			18 30		18 44											19 21			19 46			
Kirkham & Wesham 97 d					18 53														19 55			
Preston 65,97 a			18 48		19 03					19 32						19 38	19 46		20 05	20 18		
d			18 50		19 05				19 23							19 44	19 47		20 07			20 22
Leyland d			18 56		19 11											19 51			20 13			
Buckshaw Parkway d			19 01			19 09			19 33							19 57						20 33
Chorley d			19 06			19 18			19 38							20 01						20 38
Adlington (Lancashire) d						19 23										20 06						
Blackrod d						19 27										20 10						
Horwich Parkway d			19 14			19 31			19 46							20 13						20 46
Lostock d			19 17			19 35										20 17						
Southport d	18 24						18 47							19 24								
Meols Cop d	18 29						18 52							19 29								
Bescar Lane d							18 57															
New Lane d							19 01															
Burscough Bridge d	18 38						19 04							19 38								
Hoscar d							19 07															
Parbold d	18 43						19 10							19 43								
Appley Bridge d	18 47						19 15							19 47								
Gathurst d	18 51						19 18							19 51								
Kirkby d																					19 43	
Rainford d																					19 51	
Upholland d																					19 55	
Orrell d																					19 59	
Pemberton d																					20 03	
Wigan Wallgate a	18 55						19 23							19 55							20 07	
d	18 57						19 24					19 38		19 57							20 17	
Wigan North Western d				19 08	19 23								19 50					20 08	20 25			
Ince d												19 41									20 20	
Hindley d				19 13			19 30					19 45	19 56					20 13			20 24	
Westhoughton d				19 18									20 01					20 18				
Bolton a			19 22	19 26		19 40			19 54				20 09			20 22		20 26				20 54
d		19 18	19 23	19 26		19 40		19 49	19 54				20 09		20 18	20 22		20 26				20 54
Moses Gate d				19 29														20 29				
Farnworth d				19 31														20 31				
Kearsley d				19 33														20 33				
Clifton d																						
Daisy Hill d	19 05						19 34					19 50		20 05							20 28	
Hag Fold d												19 53									20 31	
Atherton d	19 09						19 38					19 56		20 09							20 34	
Walkden d	19 15						19 44					20 02		20 15							20 40	
Moorside d												20 06									20 44	
Swinton d							19 49					20 09									20 46	
Salford Crescent a	19 28	19 31	19 35	19 44		19 52	19 56	20 01	20 06			20 17	20 21	20 28	20 31	20 35		20 44			20 56	21 06
d	19 28	19 32	19 36	19 45		19 53	19 57	20 01	20 07			20 18	20 22	20 28	20 32	20 35		20 45			20 57	21 07
Salford Central d	19 32	19 35		19 48		19 56	20 00	20 04				20 21		20 32	20 36			20 48			21 00	
Manchester Victoria a	19 36	19 40		19 51		19 59	20 03	20 07				20 27		20 36	20 41			20 51			21 03	
Rochdale 41 a	19 50	20 05					20 17	20 31						20 50	21 05						21 17	
Deansgate a			19 39										20 29			20 39						
Manchester Oxford Road a			19 41		19 53				20 11				20 31			20 41			20 53			21 11
Manchester Piccadilly 10 a					19 57				20 15				20 36			20 45	20 27		20 57			21 15
Stockport 84 a													20 50									
Hazel Grove 86 a																						
Buxton 86 a																						
Heald Green 85 a					20 12				20 27										21 13			21 29
Manchester Airport 85 a					20 17				20 33								20 47		21 18			21 35

A To Leeds
B From Clitheroe
C To Stalybridge
D To Blackburn
E From Blackburn
F From Leeds to Morecambe
G To Alderley Edge
H From Glasgow Central

Table T082-R

Mondays to Fridays

21 May to 7 December

Barrow-in-Furness, Blackpool North, Preston, Southport, Kirkby and Wigan - Bolton - Manchester

		NT	NT	NT	NT	TP	NT	NT	NT	NT	NT	NT	TP	NT	NT	NT FO	NT	NT FX	NT FX	NT FO	NT FX	NT FX	NT FO
				A		◇■ B 🍴	◇	◇ C	D	◇	◇		◇■ E 🍴			A		F 🚌	G 🚌	◇	H 🚌	◇	D
Barrow-in-Furness	d						19 43							20 42									
Roose	d						19 47							20 46									
Dalton	d						19 53							20 52									
Ulverston	d						20 02							21 01									
Cark	d						20 09							21 08									
Kents Bank	d						20 13							21 12									
Grange-over-Sands	d						20 17							21 16									
Arnside	d						20 23							21 22									
Silverdale	d						20 28							21 27									
Carnforth	d						20 35	21 05						21 36									
Windermere	83 d																						
Oxenholme Lake District	65 d					20 14							21 09										
Lancaster ■	65 a					20 28	20 43	21 13					21 23	21 48									
	d					20 28	20 43						21 24										
Blackpool North	97 d				20 14					20 38							21 17						
Layton	97 d									20 41													
Poulton-le-Fylde	97 d				20 20					20 45							21 22						
Kirkham & Wesham	97 d									20 54													
Preston ■	65,97 a				20 37	20 46	21 03			21 04			21 41				21 39						
	d				20 39	20 47	21 05			21 06	21 08		21 43				21 48		21 50	22 22		22 22	
Leyland	d				20 46					21 12							21 54		22 10				
Buckshaw Parkway	d				20 53						21 18						21 59		22 24	22 31			
Chorley	d				20 59						21 23						22 04		22 39	22 36			
Adlington (Lancashire)	d				21 04						21 28						22 09		→				
Blackrod	d				21 08						21 31						22 12						
Horwich Parkway	d				21 12						21 35						22 16			22 45			
Lostock	d				21 16						21 38						22 20						
Southport	d		20 18									21 08											
Meols Cop	d		20 23									21 13											
Bescar Lane	d																						
New Lane	d																						
Burscough Bridge	d		20 32									21 22											
Hoscar	d																						
Parbold	d		20 37									21 26											
Appley Bridge	d		20 41									21 31											
Gathurst	d		20 45									21 34											
Kirkby	d																						
Rainford	d																						
Upholland	d																						
Orrell	d																						
Pemberton	d																						
Wigan Wallgate	a		20 49									21 39											
	d		20 51									21 40											
Wigan North Western	d	20 41							21 15	21 23					21 46								22 50
Ince	d	20 44										21 43											
Hindley	d	20 48	20 56						21 20			21 47			21 52								22 56
Westhoughton	d		21 01						21 25						21 56								23 00
Bolton	a		21 09		21 21				21 33		21 43				22 04		22 25			22 52			23 08
	d		21 09	21 18	21 21				21 34		21 44				22 05	22 19	22 25	22 45		22 53			23 09
Moses Gate	d								21 37						22 08								
Farnworth	d								21 39						22 10								
Kearsley	d								21 41						22 12								
Clifton	d																						
Daisy Hill	d	20 52										21 51											
Hag Fold	d	20 55										21 54											
Atherton	d	20 58										21 57											
Walkden	d	21 04										22 03											
Moorside	d	21 07										22 07											
Swinton	d	21 10										22 10									←		
Salford Crescent	a	21 18	21 21	21 30	21 33				21 51		21 56	22 17			22 22	22 32	22 37	23 10		23 06	23 10		23 21
	d	21 18	21 22	21 30	21 34				21 53		21 59	22 18			22 23	22 33	22 37	23 10		23 06	23 10		23 21
Salford Central	d	21 21	21 25	21 33					22 01			22 21			22 25	22 36		→					23 24
Manchester Victoria	a	21 24	21 28	21 36					22 06			22 24			22 28	22 42					23 20		23 27
Rochdale	41 a			22 01																			
Deansgate	a				21 37																		
Manchester Oxford Road	a				21 39		21 43			21 53	22 07						22 42			23 11		23 11	
Manchester Piccadilly ■	a				21 43	21 27	21 47			21 57			22 22				22 46			23 15		23 15	
Stockport	84 a																						
Hazel Grove	86 a																						
Buxton	86 a																						
Heald Green	85 a									22 11										23 29		23 29	
Manchester Airport	85 a					21 44	22 05			22 17			22 40							23 35		23 35	

A From Clitheroe
B From Edinburgh
C From Leeds
D To Stalybridge
E From Glasgow Central
F From Blackburn to Manchester Victoria
G To Manchester Piccadilly
H From Blackburn

Table T082-R

Mondays to Fridays

21 May to 7 December

Barrow-in-Furness, Blackpool North, Preston, Southport, Kirkby and Wigan - Bolton - Manchester

		NT FX	NT FX	NT FX	TP	NT FX	NT FX	NT	NT FO	NT FX	NT FX	NT	NT FO	NT FX	NT FX	NT	NT	NT FX	NT FO	NT FX	NT	NT FX
		A 🚌	B	C 🚌	◇■ D 🍴	◇	C 🚌		◇	E 🚌	F 🚌		G	E 🚌	C 🚌	H	I	◇	◇	E 🚌		🚌
Barrow-in-Furness	d															21 45						
Roose	d															21 49						
Dalton	d															21 55						
Ulverston	d															22 04						
Cark	d															22 11						
Kents Bank	d															22 15						
Grange-over-Sands	d															22 19						
Arnside	d															22 26						
Silverdale	d															22 30						
Carnforth	d															22 38						
Windermere	83 d																				22 45	
Oxenholme Lake District	65 d				22 11																23 06	
Lancaster ■	65 a				22 25											22 46					23 23	
	d				22 26											22 46	23 03				23 24	
Blackpool North	97 d					22 25			22 25									23 13	23 13			
Layton	97 d					22 28			22 28									23 16	23 16			
Poulton-le-Fylde	97 d					22 32			22 32									23 20	23 20			
Kirkham & Wesham	97 d					22 41			22 41									23 30	23 30			
Preston ■	65,97 a				22 44	22 51			22 51							23 09	23 24	23 41	23 41		23 45	
	d			22 22	22 45	22 54			22 54						22 59			23 42	23 45			23 51
Leyland	d					22 59			22 59						23 19			23 49	23 51			00 11
Buckshaw Parkway	d	←		22 47					23 05						23 33				23 57			00 25
Chorley	d	22 39		23 02					23 10						23 48				00 01			00 40
Adlington (Lancashire)	d	22 49							23 15						23 58				00 06			00 50
Blackrod	d	22 56							23 18						00 05				00 10			00 57
Horwich Parkway	d	23 02		23 17					23 22						00 11				00 13	←		01 03
Lostock	d	23 10							23 26						00 19				00 17	00 19		01 11
Southport	d							22 18				23 10			→							
Meols Cop	d							22 23				23 15										
Bescar Lane	d							22 28														
New Lane	d							22 32														
Burscough Bridge	d							22 35				23 24										
Hoscar	d							22 38														
Parbold	d							22 41				23 28										
Appley Bridge	d							22 46				23 33										
Gathurst	d							22 49				23 36										
Kirkby	d																					
Rainford	d																					
Upholland	d																					
Orrell	d																					
Pemberton	d																					
Wigan Wallgate	a							22 54				23 43										
	d						22 50	22 55														
Wigan North Western	d		22 50																			
Ince	d							22 58														
Hindley	d		22 56				23 00	23 02														
Westhoughton	d						23 10							←								
Bolton	a	23 28		23s36			23 30		23 32					23s36					00 22	00 37		01 29
	d	23 28					23 30		23 32				23 46						00 22	00 37		01 29
Moses Gate	d			→																		
Farnworth	d																					
Kearsley	d																					
Clifton	d																					
Daisy Hill	d							23 06														
Hag Fold	d							23 09														
Atherton	d							23 11														
Walkden	d							23 17														
Moorside	d							23 20														
Swinton	d							23 23		←	←											
Salford Crescent	a	23s53	23 21				23s55	23 32	23 44	23s53	23s55		23 57	00s01					00 34	01s02		01s54
	d		23 21					23 33	23 44				23 59						00 35			
Salford Central	d	→	23 24				→	23 36					00 02									
Manchester Victoria	a		23 27					23 39					00 06									
Rochdale	41 a																					
Deansgate	a																					
Manchester Oxford Road	a					23 41			23 49													
Manchester Piccadilly ■	a				23 24	23 53			23 53	00 03	00 05			00 11				00 40	00 41	01 12		02 04
Stockport	84 a																					
Hazel Grove	86 a																					
Buxton	86 a																					
Heald Green	85 a																	00 55	00 54			
Manchester Airport	85 a				23 41	00 11			00 11									01 01	01 01			

A From Preston to Manchester Piccadilly
B To Stalybridge
C To Manchester Piccadilly
D From Edinburgh
E From Preston
F From Wigan Wallgate
G From Clitheroe
H From Carlisle
I From Morecambe

Table T082-R

Saturdays
26 May to 8 December

Barrow-in-Furness, Blackpool North, Preston, Southport, Kirkby and Wigan - Bolton - Manchester

		NT	NT	TP	NT	NT	NT	NT	NT	NT	NT	NT	NT	NT	NT	NT	NT	NT	NT	NT	NT	TP	NT
		◇		◇1	◇		◇						◇	◇		◇			◇			◇1	
		A	B	C		bus		D			E				F			D	G	B			H
				bike																			
Barrow-in-Furness	d													04 53									
Roose	d																						
Dalton	d																						
Ulverston	d													05 09									
Cark	d																						
Kents Bank	d																						
Grange-over-Sands	d													05 21									
Arnside	d													05 27									
Silverdale	d																						
Carnforth	d													05 37									06 22
Windermere 83	d																						
Oxenholme Lake District 65	d																						
Lancaster 8 65	a													05 45									06 32
	d													05 46								06 29	
Blackpool North 97	d				03 33		04 28		05 23				05 39								06 16		
Layton 97	d												05 42										
Poulton-le-Fylde 97	d						04 34		05 29				05 46								06 21		
Kirkham & Wesham 97	d												05 55										
Preston 8 65,97	a				03 54		04 51		05 46				06 05	06 06							06 38	06 47	
	d			00 57	03 55	04 05	04 54		05 48			06 01	06 07			06 21					06 40	06 48	
Leyland	d								05 55			06 07	06 12								06 47		
Buckshaw Parkway	d				04 05		05 05		06 00			06 13				06 30					06 53		
Chorley	d	00 01			04 10		05 10		06 05			06 18				06 35					06 58		
Adlington (Lancashire)	d	00 06										06 23											
Blackrod	d	00 10										06 27											
Horwich Parkway	d	00 13			04 18		05 19		06 13			06 31				06 43					07 06		
Lostock	d	00 17							06 17			06 35									07 10		
Southport	d																	06 17					
Meols Cop	d																	06 22					
Bescar Lane	d																						
New Lane	d																						
Burscough Bridge	d																	06 31					
Hoscar	d																						
Parbold	d																	06 36					
Appley Bridge	d																	06 40					
Gathurst	d																	06 44					
Kirkby	d																						
Rainford	d																						
Upholland	d																						
Orrell	d																						
Pemberton	d																						
Wigan Wallgate	a																	06 49					
	d									06 01	06 08							06 50					
Wigan North Western	d							05 48					06 23				06 42		06 56				
Ince	d									06 04													
Hindley	d							05 54		06 08	06 13							06 56					
Westhoughton	d							06 01			06 18							07 01					
Bolton	a	00 22			04 25	04 40	05 26	06 09	06 22		06 26	06 40				06 50		07 09			07 15		
	d	00 22			04 26	04 40	05 27	06 09	06 22		06 26	06 40			06 47	06 51		07 09		07 19	07 22		
Moses Gate	d										06 29												
Farnworth	d										06 31												
Kearsley	d										06 33												
Clifton	d																						
Daisy Hill	d									06 12							06 50		07 05				
Hag Fold	d									06 15							06 53						
Atherton	d									06 18							06 56		07 09				
Walkden	d									06 24							07 02		07 15				
Moorside	d									06 28							07 06						
Swinton	d									06 31							07 09						
Salford Crescent	a	00 34			04 38		05 39	06 21	06 34	06 39	06 44	06 52			06 58	07 02	07 17	07 21	07 28	07 32	07 36		
	d	00 35			04 38		05 39	06 22	06 35	06 40	06 45	06 53			06 59	07 03	07 18	07 22	07 28	07 33	07 36		
Salford Central	d		00 02							06 43	06 48	06 56			07 04		07 21		07 32	07 36			
Manchester Victoria	a		00 06							06 46	06 51	06 59			07 07		07 24		07 35	07 41			
Rochdale 41	a														07 31				07 49	08 06			
Deansgate	a							06 29										07 28			07 40		
Manchester Oxford Road	a						05 44	06 32					06 52			07 07		07 30			07 42		
Manchester Piccadilly 10	a	00 41		01 43	04 44	05 05	05 48	06 36	06 46				06 57			07 11		07 35			07 45	07 27	
Stockport 84	a							06 52										07 50					
Hazel Grove 86	a																						
Buxton 86	a																						
Heald Green 85	a	00 54					06 03									07 28							
Manchester Airport 85	a	01 01		01 58	05 04		06 10						07 18			07 35						07 47	

A From Blackpool North
B From Clitheroe
C From Edinburgh
D To Alderley Edge
E To Stalybridge
F From Blackburn
G To Leeds
H From Skipton

Table T082-R

Saturdays
26 May to 8 December

Barrow-in-Furness, Blackpool North, Preston, Southport, Kirkby and Wigan - Bolton - Manchester

		NT	NT	NT	NT	NT	NT	NT	NT	NT	NT	NT	NT	NT	TP	NT	NT	NT	NT	NT	NT	NT	NT
					◇				◇			◇			◇1			◇	◇				
				A			B	C			D	E	C		F		A					B	G
															bike								
Barrow-in-Furness	d	05 49							06 11										06 47	07 08			
Roose	d	05 53																	06 51	07 12			
Dalton	d	05 59																	06 57	07 18			
Ulverston	d	06 08							06 26										07 05	07 27			
Cark	d	06 15																	07 13	07 34			
Kents Bank	d	06 19																		07 38			
Grange-over-Sands	d	06 23							06 39										07 20	07 42			
Arnside	d	06 29							06 45										07 25	07 49			
Silverdale	d	06 34																	07 30	07 54			
Carnforth	d	06 41							06 55										07 37	08 01			
Windermere 83	d																						
Oxenholme Lake District 65	d														07 09								
Lancaster 8 65	a	06 51							07 02						07 23				07 45	08 10			
	d								07 03						07 24				07 46				
Blackpool North 97	d				06 38									07 16				07 38					
Layton 97	d				06 41													07 41					
Poulton-le-Fylde 97	d				06 45									07 22				07 45					
Kirkham & Wesham 97	d				06 54									07 31				07 54					
Preston 8 65,97	a				07 05				07 22					07 42	07 44			08 04	08 06				
	d				07 07				07 28					07 45	07 45			08 06					
Leyland	d				07 12									07 51				08 12					
Buckshaw Parkway	d					07 09			07 36					07 57							08 09		
Chorley	d					07 18			07 40					08 02							08 18		
Adlington (Lancashire)	d					07 23								08 06							08 23		
Blackrod	d					07 27								08 10							08 27		
Horwich Parkway	d					07 31			07 48					08 14							08 31		
Lostock	d					07 35								08 17							08 35		
Southport	d			06 34			06 48				07 17											07 47	
Meols Cop	d			06 40			06 53				07 22											07 52	
Bescar Lane	d						06 58															07 57	
New Lane	d						07 02															08 01	
Burscough Bridge	d			06 48			07 05				07 31											08 04	
Hoscar	d						07 08															08 07	
Parbold	d			06 53			07 11				07 36											08 11	
Appley Bridge	d			06 57			07 16				07 40											08 15	
Gathurst	d			07 01			07 19				07 44											08 19	
Kirkby	d		06 36													07 36							
Rainford	d		06 44													07 44							
Upholland	d		06 48													07 48							
Orrell	d		06 52													07 52							
Pemberton	d		06 55													07 55							
Wigan Wallgate	a		07 00	07 06			07 24				07 49					08 00						08 24	
	d		07 01	07 07			07 25			07 40	07 50					08 01						08 25	
Wigan North Western	d				07 23							07 56					08 08	08 23					
Ince	d		07 04							07 43						08 04							
Hindley	d		07 08	07 12			07 31			07 46	07 56					08 08	08 13					08 31	
Westhoughton	d			07 17							08 01						08 18						
Bolton	a			07 25		07 40			07 54		08 09			08 22			08 26				08 40		
	d			07 25		07 40		07 49	07 55		08 09		08 17	08 23			08 27				08 40		08 49
Moses Gate	d			07 28													08 30						
Farnworth	d			07 30									08 21				08 32						
Kearsley	d			07 32													08 34						
Clifton	d			07 37																			
Daisy Hill	d		07 13				07 35			07 51		08 05				08 13						08 35	
Hag Fold	d		07 16							07 54						08 16							
Atherton	d		07 19				07 39			07 57		08 09				08 19						08 39	
Walkden	d		07 25				07 45			08 03		08 15				08 25						08 45	
Moorside	d		07 29							08 06													
Swinton	d		07 32							08 09						08 30							
Salford Crescent	a		07 39	07 44		07 52	07 56	08 02	08 05	08 17	08 21	08 28	08 32	08 36		08 39	08 44				08 52	08 56	09 01
	d		07 40	07 44		07 53	07 57	08 02	08 06	08 18	08 22	08 28	08 33	08 36		08 40	08 45				08 53	08 57	09 01
Salford Central	d		07 43	07 48		07 56	08 00	08 06		08 21		08 32	08 36			08 42	08 48				08 56	09 00	09 04
Manchester Victoria	a		07 46	07 51		07 59	08 03	08 08		08 24		08 36	08 41			08 46	08 51				09 00	09 03	09 07
Rochdale 41	a						08 17	08 31				08 51	09 06									09 17	09 31
Deansgate	a										08 29			08 40									
Manchester Oxford Road	a				07 57				08 12		08 31			08 42				08 55					
Manchester Piccadilly 10	a				08 01				08 15		08 37			08 45	08 27			08 59					
Stockport 84	a										08 51												
Hazel Grove 86	a																						
Buxton 86	a																						
Heald Green 85	a								08 27									09 15					
Manchester Airport 85	a				08 23				08 35						08 47			09 19					

A To Stalybridge
B To Blackburn
C From Clitheroe
D To Alderley Edge
E To Leeds
F From Glasgow Central
G From Blackburn

Table T082-R

Saturdays
26 May to 8 December

Barrow-in-Furness, Blackpool North, Preston, Southport, Kirkby and Wigan - Bolton - Manchester

	NT ◇	NT	NT A	NT ◇ B	NT C	NT	TP ◇1 D	NT E	NT ◇	NT ◇	NT	NT F	NT G	NT ◇	NT	NT A	NT ◇ B	NT C	NT	TP ◇1 H	NT E
Barrow-in-Furness d										07 46											
Roose d										07 50											
Dalton d										07 56											
Ulverston d										08 05											
Cark d										08 12											
Kents Bank d																					
Grange-over-Sands d										08 19											
Arnside d										08 25											
Silverdale d										08 30											
Carnforth d										08 37											
Windermere 83 d																					
Oxenholme Lake District 65 d							08 13													09 14	
Lancaster 6 65 a							08 27			08 45										09 28	
d							08 28			08 46										09 29	
Blackpool North 97 d						08 21			08 38										09 21		
Layton 97 d									08 41												
Poulton-le-Fylde 97 d						08 27			08 45										09 26		
Kirkham & Wesham 97 d									08 54												
Preston 8 65,97 a						08 44	08 45		09 04	09 08									09 43	09 46	
d	08 24					08 45	08 47		09 06					09 24					09 45	09 48	
Leyland d						08 52			09 12										09 54		
Buckshaw Parkway d	08 33					08 58					09 09			09 33					10 02		
Chorley d	08 38					09 04					09 18			09 38					10 06		
Adlington (Lancashire) d											09 23										
Blackrod d											09 27										
Horwich Parkway d	08 46					09 13					09 31			09 46					10 14		
Lostock d						09 17					09 35								10 18		
Southport d				08 24								08 52					09 24				
Meols Cop d				08 29								08 57					09 29				
Bescar Lane d																					
New Lane d																					
Burscough Bridge d				08 38								09 06					09 38				
Hoscar d																					
Parbold d				08 43								09 10					09 43				
Appley Bridge d				08 47								09 15					09 47				
Gathurst d				08 51								09 18					09 51				
Kirkby d		08 15													09 15						
Rainford d		08 23													09 23						
Upholland d		08 27													09 27						
Orrell d		08 31													09 31						
Pemberton d		08 34													09 34						
Wigan Wallgate a		08 39		08 55								09 23			09 39		09 55				
d		08 41		08 57								09 24			09 41		09 57				
Wigan North Western d			08 50					09 08	09 23							09 50					10 08
Ince d		08 44													09 44						
Hindley d		08 47	08 56					09 13				09 30			09 47	09 56					10 13
Westhoughton d			09 01					09 18								10 01					10 18
Bolton a	08 54		09 09			09 22		09 26			09 40			09 54		10 09			10 23		10 27
d	08 54		09 09		09 17	09 22		09 26			09 40		09 49	09 54		10 09		10 19	10 23		10 27
Moses Gate d								09 29													10 30
Farnworth d								09 31													10 32
Kearsley d					09 21			09 33													10 34
Clifton d																					
Daisy Hill d		08 51		09 05								09 34			09 51		10 05				
Hag Fold d		08 54													09 54						
Atherton d		08 57		09 09								09 38			09 57		10 09				
Walkden d		09 03		09 15								09 44			10 03		10 15				
Moorside d		09 07													10 07						
Swinton d		09 09										09 49			10 09						
Salford Crescent a	09 06	09 17	09 21	09 28	09 32	09 36		09 44			09 52	09 56	10 01	10 06	10 17	10 21	10 28	10 32	10 36		10 45
d	09 07	09 18	09 22	09 28	09 33	09 36		09 45			09 53	09 57	10 01	10 07	10 18	10 22	10 28	10 33	10 36		10 46
Salford Central d		09 21		09 32	09 36			09 48			09 56	10 00	10 04		10 21		10 32	10 36			10 49
Manchester Victoria a		09 26		09 36	09 41			09 51			09 59	10 03	10 07		10 26		10 36	10 41			10 52
Rochdale 41 a				09 50	10 06							10 17	10 31				10 50	11 06			
Deansgate a			09 29			09 40										10 29			10 40		
Manchester Oxford Road a	09 11		09 32			09 42			09 52					10 11		10 32			10 42		
Manchester Piccadilly 10 a	09 15		09 36			09 45	09 27		09 57					10 15		10 36			10 45	10 27	
Stockport 84 a			09 51													10 51					
Hazel Grove 86 a																					
Buxton 86 a																					
Heald Green 85 a	09 29								10 14					10 29							
Manchester Airport 85 a	09 35						09 47		10 19					10 35						10 47	

A To Alderley Edge
B To Leeds
C From Clitheroe
D From Edinburgh
E To Stalybridge
F To Blackburn
G From Blackburn
H From Glasgow Central

Table T082-R

Saturdays
26 May to 8 December

Barrow-in-Furness, Blackpool North, Preston, Southport, Kirkby and Wigan - Bolton - Manchester

	NT ◇	NT ◇	NT ◇ A	NT	NT B	NT C	NT ◇	NT	NT D	NT ◇ E	NT F	NT	NT ◇ G	TP ◇1 H	NT I	NT J	NT ◇	NT	NT B	NT C	NT ◇	NT
Barrow-in-Furness d		08 46													09 58							
Roose d		08 50													10 02							
Dalton d		08 56													10 08							
Ulverston d		09 04													10 17							
Cark d		09 12													10 24							
Kents Bank d		09 16													10 28							
Grange-over-Sands d		09 20													10 32							
Arnside d		09 25													10 39							
Silverdale d		09 30													10 43							
Carnforth d		09 37	09 57												10 56							
Windermere 83 d													09 34									
Oxenholme Lake District 65 d													09 55	10 14								
Lancaster 6 65 a		09 45	10 05										10 13	10 28	11 07							
d		09 46											10 14	10 29								
Blackpool North 97 d	09 38											10 12					10 36					
Layton 97 d	09 41																10 39					
Poulton-le-Fylde 97 d	09 45											10 17					10 43					
Kirkham & Wesham 97 d	09 54																10 52					
Preston 8 65,97 a	10 04	10 06										10 34	10 37	10 46			11 03					
d	10 06						10 24					10 44		10 48			11 04				11 24	
Leyland d	10 12											10 54					11 10					
Buckshaw Parkway d				10 09			10 33					11 02						11 09			11 33	
Chorley d				10 18			10 38					11 06						11 18			11 38	
Adlington (Lancashire) d				10 23														11 23				
Blackrod d				10 27														11 27				
Horwich Parkway d				10 31			10 46					11 14						11 31			11 46	
Lostock d				10 35								11 18						11 35				
Southport d					09 47					10 24									10 52			
Meols Cop d					09 52					10 29									10 57			
Bescar Lane d					09 57																	
New Lane d					10 01																	
Burscough Bridge d					10 04					10 38									11 06			
Hoscar d					10 07																	
Parbold d					10 10					10 43									11 10			
Appley Bridge d					10 15					10 47									11 15			
Gathurst d					10 18					10 51									11 18			
Kirkby d								10 15														11 15
Rainford d								10 23														11 23
Upholland d								10 27														11 27
Orrell d								10 31														11 31
Pemberton d								10 34														11 34
Wigan Wallgate a					10 23			10 39		10 55									11 23			11 39
d					10 24			10 41		10 57									11 24			11 41
Wigan North Western d	10 23								10 50							11 08	11 22					
Ince d								10 44														11 44
Hindley d					10 30			10 47	10 56							11 13			11 30			11 47
Westhoughton d									11 01							11 18						
Bolton a				10 40			10 54		11 09			11 23				11 27		11 40			11 54	
d				10 40		10 49	10 54		11 09		11 19	11 23				11 27		11 40		11 49	11 54	
Moses Gate d																11 30						
Farnworth d																11 32						
Kearsley d																11 34						
Clifton d																						
Daisy Hill d					10 34			10 51		11 05									11 34			11 51
Hag Fold d								10 54														11 54
Atherton d					10 38			10 57		11 09									11 38			11 57
Walkden d					10 44			11 03		11 15									11 44			12 03
Moorside d								11 07														12 07
Swinton d					10 49			11 09											11 49			12 09
Salford Crescent a				10 52	10 56	11 01	11 06	11 17	11 21	11 28	11 32	11 36				11 45		11 52	11 56	12 01	12 06	12 17
d				10 53	10 57	11 01	11 07	11 18	11 22	11 28	11 33	11 36				11 46		11 53	11 57	12 02	12 07	12 18
Salford Central d				10 56	11 00	11 04		11 21		11 32	11 36					11 48		11 56	12 00	12 05		12 21
Manchester Victoria a				10 59	11 03	11 07		11 26		11 36	11 41					11 51		11 59	12 03	12 08		12 26
Rochdale 41 a					11 17	11 31				11 50	12 03								12 17	12 32		
Deansgate a									11 29			11 40										
Manchester Oxford Road a	10 52						11 11		11 32			11 42					11 55				12 11	
Manchester Piccadilly 10 a	10 57						11 15		11 36			11 45		11 27			11 59				12 15	
Stockport 84 a									11 51													
Hazel Grove 86 a																						
Buxton 86 a																						
Heald Green 85 a	11 14						11 29										12 15				12 29	
Manchester Airport 85 a	11 18						11 35							11 47			12 19				12 35	

A From Leeds
B To Blackburn
C From Blackburn
D To Alderley Edge
E To Leeds
F From Clitheroe
G ◇ to Preston
H From Edinburgh
I From Carlisle
J To Stalybridge

Table T082-R

Saturdays
26 May to 8 December

Barrow-in-Furness, Blackpool North, Preston, Southport, Kirkby and Wigan - Bolton - Manchester

		NT	NT	NT	NT	TP	NT	NT	NT	NT	NT	NT	NT	NT	NT	NT	NT	NT	NT	TP	NT	NT
		A	◇ B	C		◇1 D	E	◇	◇	◇ F		G	H	◇		A	◇ B	C		◇1 I	E	◇
Barrow-in-Furness	d								10 48													
Roose	d																					
Dalton	d								10 57													
Ulverston	d								11 05													
Cark	d								11 13													
Kents Bank	d																					
Grange-over-Sands	d								11 20													
Arnside	d								11 25													
Silverdale	d								11 30													
Carnforth	d								11 37	12 01												
Windermere	83 d																					
Oxenholme Lake District	65 d					11 12														12 14		
Lancaster 6	65 a					11 26			11 45	12 10										12 28		
	d					11 27			11 46											12 29		
Blackpool North	97 d				11 20			11 35											12 20			12 38
Layton	97 d							11 38														12 41
Poulton-le-Fylde	97 d				11 25			11 42											12 25			12 45
Kirkham & Wesham	97 d							11 51														12 54
Preston 8	65,97 a				11 42	11 45		12 01	12 08										12 42	12 46		13 04
	d				11 44	11 47		12 03						12 24					12 44	12 48		13 06
Leyland	d				11 53														12 55			13 12
Buckshaw Parkway	d				11 59						12 09			12 33					13 02			
Chorley	d				12 04						12 18			12 38					13 06			
Adlington (Lancashire)	d										12 23											
Blackrod	d										12 27											
Horwich Parkway	d				12 13						12 31			12 46					13 14			
Lostock	d				12 17						12 35								13 18			
Southport	d		11 24									11 47					12 24					
Meols Cop	d		11 29									11 52					12 29					
Bescar Lane	d											11 57										
New Lane	d											12 01										
Burscough Bridge	d		11 38									12 04					12 38					
Hoscar	d											12 07										
Parbold	d		11 43									12 10					12 43					
Appley Bridge	d		11 47									12 15					12 47					
Gathurst	d		11 51									12 18					12 51					
Kirkby	d																					
Rainford	d																					
Upholland	d																					
Orrell	d																					
Pemberton	d																					
Wigan Wallgate	a		11 55									12 23					12 55					
	d		11 57									12 24			12 41		12 57					
Wigan North Western	d	11 50					12 08	12 19								12 50					13 08	13 24
Ince	d														12 44							
Hindley	d	11 56					12 13					12 30			12 47	12 56					13 13	
Westhoughton	d	12 01					12 18									13 01					13 18	
Bolton	a	12 09			12 22		12 26				12 40			12 54		13 09			13 23		13 27	
	d	12 09		12 19	12 22		12 26				12 40		12 49	12 54		13 09		13 19	13 23		13 27	
Moses Gate	d						12 29														13 30	
Farnworth	d						12 31														13 32	
Kearsley	d						12 33														13 34	
Clifton	d																					
Daisy Hill	d		12 05									12 34			12 51		13 05					
Hag Fold	d														12 54							
Atherton	d		12 09									12 38			12 57		13 09					
Walkden	d		12 15									12 44			13 03		13 15					
Moorside	d														13 07							
Swinton	d											12 49			13 09							
Salford Crescent	a	12 21	12 28	12 32	12 36		12 44				12 52	12 56	13 01	13 06	13 17	13 21	13 28	13 32	13 36		13 45	
	d	12 22	12 28	12 33	12 36		12 45				12 53	12 57	13 01	13 07	13 18	13 22	13 28	13 33	13 36		13 46	
Salford Central	d		12 32	12 36			12 48				12 56	13 00	13 04		13 21		13 32	13 36			13 48	
Manchester Victoria	⇌ a		12 36	12 41			12 51				12 59	13 03	13 07		13 26		13 36	13 41			13 51	
Rochdale	41 a		12 50	13 06								13 17	13 31				13 50	14 06				
Deansgate	⇌ a	12 29			12 40											13 29						
Manchester Oxford Road	a	12 32			12 42			12 52						13 11		13 32			13 41			13 53
Manchester Piccadilly 10	⇌ a	12 36			12 45	12 27		12 57						13 15		13 36			13 45	13 27		13 58
Stockport	84 a	12 51														13 51						
Hazel Grove	86 a																					
Buxton	86 a																					
Heald Green	85 a							13 14						13 29								14 15
Manchester Airport	85 ⇌✈ a					12 47		13 19						13 35						13 47		14 19

A To Alderley Edge
B To Leeds
C From Clitheroe
D From Glasgow Central
E To Stalybridge
F From Leeds to Morecambe
G To Blackburn
H From Blackburn
I From Edinburgh

Table T082-R

Saturdays
26 May to 8 December

Barrow-in-Furness, Blackpool North, Preston, Southport, Kirkby and Wigan - Bolton - Manchester

		NT	NT	NT	NT	NT	NT	NT	NT	NT	NT	TP	NT	NT	NT	NT	NT	NT	NT	NT	NT	NT	NT
			A	B	◇			C	◇ D	E		◇1 F		◇ G	H	◇		A	B	◇		C	◇ D
Barrow-in-Furness	d				11 53								12 51										
Roose	d				11 57																		
Dalton	d				12 03								13 00										
Ulverston	d				12 11								13 09										
Cark	d				12 18								13 16										
Kents Bank	d				12 22								13 20										
Grange-over-Sands	d				12 26								13 24										
Arnside	d				12 33								13 30										
Silverdale	d				12 37								13 35										
Carnforth	d				12 44								13 42	14 02									
Windermere	83 d					12 31																	
Oxenholme Lake District	65 d					12 52						13 14											
Lancaster 6	65 a				12 51	13 12						13 28	13 52	14 13									
	d				12 52							13 29											
Blackpool North	97 d										13 20					13 38							
Layton	97 d															13 41							
Poulton-le-Fylde	97 d										13 25					13 45							
Kirkham & Wesham	97 d															13 54							
Preston 8	65,97 a				13 11						13 42	13 47				14 04							
	d				13 25						13 44	13 48				14 06				14 24			
Leyland	d										13 54					14 12							
Buckshaw Parkway	d	13 09			13 33						14 01						14 05			14 33			
Chorley	d	13 18			13 37						14 05						14 18			14 38			
Adlington (Lancashire)	d	13 23															14 23						
Blackrod	d	13 27															14 27						
Horwich Parkway	d	13 31			13 46						14 13						14 31			14 46			
Lostock	d	13 35									14 17						14 35						
Southport	d		12 52						13 24									13 52					14 24
Meols Cop	d		12 57						13 29									13 57					14 29
Bescar Lane	d																						
New Lane	d																						
Burscough Bridge	d		13 06						13 38									14 06					14 38
Hoscar	d																						
Parbold	d		13 10						13 43									14 10					14 43
Appley Bridge	d		13 15						13 47									14 15					14 47
Gathurst	d		13 18						13 51									14 18					14 51
Kirkby	d						13 15														14 15		
Rainford	d						13 23														14 23		
Upholland	d						13 27														14 27		
Orrell	d						13 31														14 31		
Pemberton	d						13 34														14 34		
Wigan Wallgate	a		13 23				13 39		13 55									14 23			14 39		14 55
	d		13 24				13 41		13 57									14 24			14 41		14 57
Wigan North Western	d							13 50							14 08	14 24						14 50	
Ince	d						13 44														14 44		
Hindley	d		13 30				13 47	13 56							14 13			14 30			14 47	14 56	
Westhoughton	d							14 01							14 18							15 01	
Bolton	a	13 40			13 52			14 09			14 22				14 26		14 40			14 54		15 09	
	d	13 40		13 49	13 55			14 09		14 18	14 22				14 27		14 40		14 49	14 54		15 09	
Moses Gate	d														14 30								
Farnworth	d														14 32								
Kearsley	d														14 34								
Clifton	d																						
Daisy Hill	d		13 34				13 51		14 05									14 34			14 51		15 05
Hag Fold	d						13 54														14 54		
Atherton	d		13 38				13 57		14 09									14 38			14 57		15 09
Walkden	d		13 44				14 03		14 15									14 44			15 03		15 15
Moorside	d						14 07														15 07		
Swinton	d		13 49				14 09											14 49			15 09		
Salford Crescent	a	13 52	13 56	14 01	14 06		14 17	14 21	14 28	14 32	14 35				14 45		14 52	14 56	15 01	15 06	15 17	15 21	15 28
	d	13 53	13 57	14 01	14 07		14 18	14 22	14 28	14 32	14 36				14 45		14 53	14 57	15 01	15 07	15 18	15 22	15 28
Salford Central	d	13 56	14 00	14 04			14 21		14 32	14 37					14 48		14 56	15 00	15 04		15 21		15 31
Manchester Victoria	⇌ a	13 59	14 03	14 07			14 26		14 35	14 41					14 51		14 59	15 03	15 07		15 26		15 34
Rochdale	41 a		14 17	14 31					14 49	15 08								15 17	15 31				15 49
Deansgate	⇌ a							14 29			14 39											15 29	
Manchester Oxford Road	a				14 11			14 32			14 41					14 53				15 11		15 32	
Manchester Piccadilly 10	⇌ a				14 15			14 36			14 45	14 27				14 57				15 15		15 36	
Stockport	84 a							14 51														15 51	
Hazel Grove	86 a																						
Buxton	86 a																						
Heald Green	85 a				14 28											15 14				15 29			
Manchester Airport	85 ⇌✈ a				14 35							14 47				15 19				15 35			

A To Blackburn
B From Blackburn
C To Alderley Edge
D To Leeds
E From Clitheroe
F From Glasgow Central
G From Leeds
H To Stalybridge

Table T082-R

Saturdays
26 May to 8 December

Barrow-in-Furness, Blackpool North, Preston, Southport, Kirkby and Wigan - Bolton - Manchester

		NT A	NT	TP ◇1 B	NT C	NT D	NT ◇	NT	NT E	NT F	NT ◇	NT ◇	NT	NT G	NT ◇ H	NT A	NT	TP ◇1 I	NT D	NT ◇	NT	NT E	NT F
Barrow-in-Furness	d				13 47																		
Roose	d				13 51																		
Dalton	d				13 57																		
Ulverston	d				14 06																		
Cark	d				14 13																		
Kents Bank	d				14 17																		
Grange-over-Sands	d				14 21																		
Arnside	d				14 28																		
Silverdale	d				14 33																		
Carnforth	d				14 40																		
Windermere 83	d											14 25											
Oxenholme Lake District 65	d			14 14								14 47						15 12					
Lancaster 65	a			14 28	14 50							15 08						15 26					
	d			14 29								15 09						15 27					
Blackpool North 97	d		14 20				14 38										15 20			15 38			
Layton 97	d						14 41													15 41			
Poulton-le-Fylde 97	d		14 25				14 45										15 25			15 45			
Kirkham & Wesham 97	d						14 54													15 54			
Preston 65,97	a		14 42	14 46			15 04					15 32					15 42	15 46		16 04			
	d		14 44	14 48			15 06				15 23						15 44	15 47		16 06			
Leyland	d		14 54				15 12										15 51			16 12			
Buckshaw Parkway	d		15 02					15 09			15 32						15 57				16 09		
Chorley	d		15 06					15 18			15 37						16 02				16 18		
Adlington (Lancashire)	d							15 23													16 23		
Blackrod	d							15 27													16 27		
Horwich Parkway	d		15 14					15 31			15 45						16 11				16 31		
Lostock	d		15 18					15 35									16 14				16 35		
Southport	d								14 47						15 24							15 47	
Meols Cop	d								14 52						15 29							15 52	
Bescar Lane	d								14 57													15 57	
New Lane	d								15 01													16 01	
Burscough Bridge	d								15 04						15 38							16 04	
Hoscar	d								15 07													16 07	
Parbold	d								15 10						15 43							16 10	
Appley Bridge	d								15 15						15 47							16 15	
Gathurst	d								15 18						15 51							16 18	
Kirkby	d												15 15										
Rainford	d												15 23										
Upholland	d												15 27										
Orrell	d												15 31										
Pemberton	d												15 34										
Wigan Wallgate	a								15 23				15 39		15 55							16 23	
	d								15 24				15 41		15 57							16 24	
Wigan North Western	d					15 08	15 23							15 50					16 08	16 23			
Ince	d												15 44										
Hindley	d					15 13			15 30				15 47	15 56					16 13			16 30	
Westhoughton	d					15 18								16 01					16 18				
Bolton	a		15 23			15 27		15 40			15 52			16 09			16 19		16 26		16 40		
	d	15 19	15 23			15 27		15 40		15 49	15 53			16 09		16 19	16 22		16 26		16 40		16 49
Moses Gate	d					15 30													16 29				
Farnworth	d					15 32													16 31				
Kearsley	d					15 34													16 33				
Clifton	d																						
Daisy Hill	d								15 34				15 51		16 05							16 34	
Hag Fold	d												15 54										
Atherton	d								15 38				15 57		16 09							16 38	
Walkden	d								15 44				16 03		16 15							16 44	
Moorside	d												16 07										
Swinton	d								15 49				16 09									16 49	
Salford Crescent	a	15 32	15 36			15 45		15 52	15 56	16 01	16 05		16 17	16 21	16 28	16 32	16 36		16 44		16 52	16 56	17 01
	d	15 33	15 36			15 46		15 53	15 57	16 01	16 07		16 18	16 22	16 28	16 33	16 36		16 45		16 53	16 57	17 01
Salford Central	d	15 37				15 48		15 56	16 00	16 04			16 21		16 32	16 36			16 48		16 56	17 00	17 04
Manchester Victoria	a	15 40				15 51		15 59	16 03	16 07			16 26		16 36	16 41			16 51		16 59	17 03	17 07
Rochdale 41	a	16 03							16 17	16 31					16 50	17 10						17 17	17 31
Deansgate	a		15 40											16 29			16 40						
Manchester Oxford Road	a		15 42				15 53				16 11			16 32			16 42			16 53			
Manchester Piccadilly	a		15 45	15 27			15 58				16 15			16 36			16 45	16 27		16 58			
Stockport 84	a													16 51									
Hazel Grove 86	a																						
Buxton 86	a																						
Heald Green 85	a						16 15				16 29									17 14			
Manchester Airport 85	a			15 47			16 19				16 35							16 47		17 18			

A From Clitheroe
B From Edinburgh
C From Carlisle
D To Stalybridge
E To Blackburn
F From Blackburn
G To Alderley Edge
H To Leeds
I From Glasgow Central

Table T082-R

Saturdays
26 May to 8 December

Barrow-in-Furness, Blackpool North, Preston, Southport, Kirkby and Wigan - Bolton - Manchester

		NT ◇	NT ◇ A	NT	NT B	NT ◇ C	NT D	NT	TP ◇1 E	NT F	NT G	NT ◇	NT	NT H	NT ◇	NT	NT B	NT ◇ C	NT D	NT	TP ◇1 I	NT G
Barrow-in-Furness	d	14 57								15 50												
Roose	d	15 01								15 54												
Dalton	d	15 07								16 00												
Ulverston	d	15 15								16 08												
Cark	d	15 22								16 16												
Kents Bank	d	15 26								16 20												
Grange-over-Sands	d	15 30								16 24												
Arnside	d	15 37								16 30												
Silverdale	d	15 41								16 35												
Carnforth	d	15 48	15 59							16 42												
Windermere 83	d																					
Oxenholme Lake District 65	d								16 15												17 14	
Lancaster 65	a	15 55	16 08						16 29	16 52											17 28	
	d	16 03							16 30												17 29	
Blackpool North 97	d							16 15				16 38								17 11		
Layton 97	d											16 41								17 14		
Poulton-le-Fylde 97	d							16 21				16 45								17 18		
Kirkham & Wesham 97	d											16 54								17 27		
Preston 65,97	a	16 22						16 38	16 47			17 04								17 38	17 47	
	d	16 28						16 39	16 49			17 06			17 22					17 40	17 48	
Leyland	d							16 46				17 12								17 46		
Buckshaw Parkway	d	16 36						16 52					17 09		17 33					17 52		
Chorley	d	16 40						16 57					17 18		17 38					17 57		
Adlington (Lancashire)	d							17 02					17 23							18 02		
Blackrod	d							17 06					17 27							18 06		
Horwich Parkway	d	16 48						17 10					17 31		17 46					18 10		
Lostock	d							17 14					17 35							18 14		
Southport	d					16 24								16 52				17 24				
Meols Cop	d					16 30								16 57				17 29				
Bescar Lane	d																					
New Lane	d																					
Burscough Bridge	d					16 38								17 06				17 38				
Hoscar	d																					
Parbold	d					16 43								17 10				17 43				
Appley Bridge	d					16 47								17 15				17 47				
Gathurst	d					16 51								17 18				17 51				
Kirkby	d			16 15												17 15						
Rainford	d			16 23												17 23						
Upholland	d			16 27												17 27						
Orrell	d			16 31												17 31						
Pemberton	d			16 34												17 34						
Wigan Wallgate	a			16 39		16 56								17 23		17 39		17 55				
	d			16 41		16 57								17 24		17 41		17 57				
Wigan North Western	d				16 50						17 07	17 23					17 49					18 08
Ince	d			16 44												17 44	17 52					
Hindley	d			16 47	16 56						17 12			17 30		17 47	17 56					18 13
Westhoughton	d				17 01						17 17						18 01					18 18
Bolton	a	16 54			17 09			17 19			17 25		17 40		17 54		18 09			18 19		18 26
	d	16 55			17 10		17 19	17 22			17 26		17 40		17 54		18 09		18 18	18 22		18 26
Moses Gate	d										17 29											18 29
Farnworth	d										17 31											18 31
Kearsley	d										17 33											18 33
Clifton	d																					
Daisy Hill	d			16 51		17 05								17 34		17 51		18 05				
Hag Fold	d			16 54												17 54						
Atherton	d			16 57		17 10								17 38		17 57		18 09				
Walkden	d			17 03		17 16								17 44		18 03		18 15				
Moorside	d			17 07												18 07						
Swinton	d			17 09										17 49		18 09						
Salford Crescent	a	17 06		17 17	17 21	17 28	17 32	17 35			17 44		17 52	17 56	18 06	18 18	18 21	18 28	18 32	18 35		18 44
	d	17 07		17 18	17 22	17 28	17 32	17 36			17 45		17 53	17 57	18 07	18 18	18 22	18 28	18 32	18 36		18 45
Salford Central	d			17 21		17 32	17 36				17 48		17 56	18 00		18 21		18 32	18 36			18 48
Manchester Victoria	a			17 26		17 36	17 41				17 51		18 00	18 03		18 26		18 36	18 41			18 51
Rochdale 41	a					17 50	18 06							18 17				18 50	19 06			
Deansgate	a				17 29			17 39									18 29			18 39		
Manchester Oxford Road	a	17 11			17 32			17 41				17 52			18 11		18 32			18 41		
Manchester Piccadilly	a	17 15			17 37			17 45	17 29			17 57			18 15		18 36			18 45	18 27	
Stockport 84	a				17 51												18 51					
Hazel Grove 86	a																					
Buxton 86	a																					
Heald Green 85	a	17 29										18 13			18 29							
Manchester Airport 85	a	17 35							17 47			18 18			18 35						18 47	

A From Leeds to Morecambe
B To Alderley Edge
C To Leeds
D From Clitheroe
E From Edinburgh
F From Carlisle
G To Stalybridge
H To Blackburn
I From Glasgow Central

Table T082-R

Saturdays

26 May to 8 December

Barrow-in-Furness, Blackpool North, Preston, Southport, Kirkby and Wigan - Bolton - Manchester

		NT ◇	NT	NT A	NT	NT B	NT C	NT ◇	NT	NT D	NT ◇ E	NT C	NT	TP ◇1 F	NT	NT G	NT ◇	NT	NT B	NT H	NT ◇	NT ◇	NT ◇ I
Barrow-in-Furness	d		16 49	17 19											18 02								
Roose	d			17 23											18 06								
Dalton	d		16 58	17 29											18 12								
Ulverston	d		17 06	17 37											18 21								
Cark	d		17 14	17 45											18 28								
Kents Bank	d		17 18												18 32								
Grange-over-Sands	d		17 22	17 52											18 36								
Arnside	d		17 27	17 58											18 42								
Silverdale	d		17 32	18 03											18 47								
Carnforth	d		17 39	18 10											18 54								19 10
Windermere 83	d																					18 30	
Oxenholme Lake District 65	d													18 14								18 49	
Lancaster 65	a		17 47	18 24										18 28	19 05							19 08	19 19
	d		17 48											18 29								19 09	
Blackpool North 97	d	17 38											18 20				18 37						
Layton 97	d	17 41															18 40						
Poulton-le-Fylde 97	d	17 45											18 25				18 44						
Kirkham & Wesham 97	d	17 54															18 53						
Preston 65,97	a	18 04	18 08										18 42	18 47			19 03					19 32	
	d	18 06						18 24					18 44	18 48			19 05				19 24		
Leyland	d	18 12											18 51				19 11						
Buckshaw Parkway	d				18 09			18 33					18 59					19 09			19 33		
Chorley	d				18 18			18 38					19 04					19 18			19 38		
Adlington (Lancashire)	d				18 23													19 23					
Blackrod	d				18 27													19 27					
Horwich Parkway	d				18 31			18 46					19 12					19 31			19 46		
Lostock	d				18 35								19 16					19 35					
Southport	d					17 52					18 24								18 47				
Meols Cop	d					17 57					18 29								18 52				
Bescar Lane	d																		18 57				
New Lane	d																		19 01				
Burscough Bridge	d					18 06					18 38								19 04				
Hoscar	d																		19 07				
Parbold	d					18 10					18 43								19 10				
Appley Bridge	d					18 15					18 47								19 15				
Gathurst	d					18 18					18 51								19 18				
Kirkby	d								18 15														
Rainford	d								18 23														
Upholland	d								18 27														
Orrell	d								18 31														
Pemberton	d								18 34														
Wigan Wallgate	a					18 23			18 39		18 55								19 23				
	d					18 24			18 41		18 57								19 24				
Wigan North Western	d	18 23								18 50						19 08	19 23						
Ince	d								18 44														
Hindley	d					18 30			18 47	18 56						19 13			19 30				
Westhoughton	d									19 01						19 18							
Bolton	a				18 40			18 54		19 09			19 21			19 26		19 40			19 54		
	d				18 40		18 49	18 54		19 10		19 18	19 23			19 26		19 40		19 49	19 54		
Moses Gate	d															19 29							
Farnworth	d															19 31							
Kearsley	d															19 33							
Clifton	d																						
Daisy Hill	d					18 34			18 51		19 05								19 34				
Hag Fold	d								18 54														
Atherton	d					18 38			18 57		19 09								19 38				
Walkden	d					18 44			19 03		19 15								19 44				
Moorside	d								19 07														
Swinton	d					18 49			19 09										19 49				
Salford Crescent	a				18 52	18 56	19 01	19 06	19 17	19 21	19 28	19 31	19 35			19 44		19 52	19 56	20 01	20 06		
	d				18 53	18 57	19 01	19 07	19 18	19 22	19 28	19 32	19 35			19 45		19 53	19 57	20 01	20 07		
Salford Central	d				18 56	19 00	19 04		19 21		19 32	19 35				19 48		19 56	20 00	20 04			
Manchester Victoria	a				18 59	19 03	19 07		19 26		19 36	19 40				19 51		19 59	20 03	20 07			
Rochdale 41	a					19 17	19 32				19 50	20 05							20 17	20 31			
Deansgate	a									19 29			19 39										
Manchester Oxford Road	a	18 52						19 11		19 32			19 41				19 53				20 11		
Manchester Piccadilly	a	18 57						19 15		19 36			19 45	19 27			19 57				20 15		
Stockport 84	a									19 51													
Hazel Grove 86	a																						
Buxton 86	a																						
Heald Green 85	a	19 13						19 29									20 12				20 27		
Manchester Airport 85	a	19 18						19 35						19 47			20 17				20 33		

A From Carlisle
B To Blackburn
C From Clitheroe
D To Alderley Edge
E To Leeds
F From Edinburgh
G To Stalybridge
H From Blackburn
I From Leeds to Morecambe

Table T082-R

Saturdays

26 May to 8 December

Barrow-in-Furness, Blackpool North, Preston, Southport, Kirkby and Wigan - Bolton - Manchester

		NT	NT A	NT ◇ B	NT C	NT	TP ◇1 D	NT E	NT ◇	NT F	NT ◇	NT ◇	NT	NT	NT C	NT	TP ◇1 G	NT ◇	NT E	NT ◇	NT ◇	TP ◇1 D
Barrow-in-Furness	d											19 10						19 34				
Roose	d																	19 38				
Dalton	d																	19 44				
Ulverston	d											19 26						19 53				
Cark	d																	20 00				
Kents Bank	d																	20 04				
Grange-over-Sands	d											19 38						20 08				
Arnside	d											19 44						20 14				
Silverdale	d																	20 19				
Carnforth	d											19 55						20 26				
Windermere 83	d																					
Oxenholme Lake District 65	d						19 14										20 14					20 55
Lancaster 65	a						19 28					20 03					20 28	20 34				21 09
	d						19 29					20 03					20 29	20 34				21 09
Blackpool North 97	d					19 12			19 36							20 16				20 38		
Layton 97	d								19 39											20 41		
Poulton-le-Fylde 97	d					19 18			19 43							20 21				20 45		
Kirkham & Wesham 97	d								19 52											20 54		
Preston 65,97	a					19 35	19 47		20 02			20 26				20 38	20 46	20 54		21 04		21 27
	d					19 40	19 48		20 04		20 22					20 40	20 48	21 05		21 06	21 22	21 28
Leyland	d					19 47			20 10							20 47				21 12		
Buckshaw Parkway	d					19 54					20 33					20 52					21 32	
Chorley	d					20 00					20 38					20 58					21 37	
Adlington (Lancashire)	d					20 05										21 03						
Blackrod	d					20 09										21 07						
Horwich Parkway	d					20 13					20 46					21 11					21 45	
Lostock	d					20 17										21 15						
Southport	d			19 24										20 18								
Meols Cop	d			19 29										20 23								
Bescar Lane	d																					
New Lane	d																					
Burscough Bridge	d			19 38										20 32								
Hoscar	d																					
Parbold	d			19 43										20 37								
Appley Bridge	d			19 47										20 41								
Gathurst	d			19 51										20 45								
Kirkby	d	19 15								19 43												
Rainford	d	19 23								19 51												
Upholland	d	19 27								19 55												
Orrell	d	19 31								19 59												
Pemberton	d	19 34								20 03												
Wigan Wallgate	a	19 39		19 55						20 07				20 49								
	d	19 41		19 57						20 17				20 51								
Wigan North Western	d		19 50					20 08	20 22				20 41						21 15	21 23		
Ince	d	19 44								20 20			20 44									
Hindley	d	19 47	19 56					20 13		20 24			20 48	20 56					21 21			
Westhoughton	d		20 01					20 18						21 01					21 26			
Bolton	a		20 09			20 22		20 26			20 54			21 09		21 20			21 34		21 53	
	d		20 09		20 18	20 22		20 26			20 54			21 09	21 18	21 21			21 34		21 53	
Moses Gate	d							20 29											21 37			
Farnworth	d							20 31											21 39			
Kearsley	d							20 33											21 41			
Clifton	d																					
Daisy Hill	d	19 51		20 05						20 28			20 52									
Hag Fold	d	19 54								20 31			20 55									
Atherton	d	19 57		20 09						20 34			20 58									
Walkden	d	20 03		20 15						20 40			21 04									
Moorside	d	20 07								20 44			21 07									
Swinton	d	20 09								20 46			21 10									
Salford Crescent	a	20 17	20 21	20 28	20 31	20 35		20 44		20 56	21 06		21 18	21 21	21 30	21 33			21 52		22 05	
	d	20 18	20 22	20 28	20 32	20 35		20 45		20 57	21 07		21 18	21 22	21 30	21 34			21 54		22 06	
Salford Central	d	20 21		20 32	20 36			20 48		21 00			21 21	21 25	21 33				21 59			
Manchester Victoria	a	20 26		20 36	20 41			20 51		21 03			21 24	21 28	21 36				22 04			
Rochdale 41	a			20 50	21 05					21 17					22 01							
Deansgate	a		20 29			20 39										21 37						
Manchester Oxford Road	a		20 31			20 41			20 53		21 11					21 39		21 42		21 53	22 10	
Manchester Piccadilly	a		20 36			20 45	20 27		20 57		21 15					21 44	21 27	21 49		21 57	22 14	22 09
Stockport 84	a		20 51																			
Hazel Grove 86	a																					
Buxton 86	a																					
Heald Green 85	a								21 13		21 29									22 11		
Manchester Airport 85	a						20 47		21 18		21 35						21 47	22 05		22 17	22 32	22 26

A To Alderley Edge
B To Leeds
C From Clitheroe
D From Glasgow Central
E To Stalybridge
F To Blackburn
G From Edinburgh

Table T082-R

Barrow-in-Furness, Blackpool North, Preston, Southport, Kirkby and Wigan - Bolton - Manchester

Saturdays
26 May to 8 December

		NT ◇ A	NT B	NT	NT	NT C	NT D	NT	NT ◇	NT C	NT	NT ◇	NT ◇ E	NT ◇ B	NT	NT D	NT ◇	NT B 🚌	NT E	NT B 🚌
Barrow-in-Furness	d			20 42									21 46	21 46						
Roose	d			20 46									21 50	21 50						
Dalton	d			20 52									21 56	21 56						
Ulverston	d			21 01									22 04	22 04						
Cark	d			21 08									22 12	22 12						
Kents Bank	d			21 12									22 16	22 16						
Grange-over-Sands	d			21 16									22 20	22 20						
Arnside	d			21 22									22 26	22 26						
Silverdale	d			21 27									22 30	22 30						
Carnforth	d	21 05		21 36									22 38	22 38						
Windermere	83 d		20 43																22 26	22 25
Oxenholme Lake District	65 d		21 02																22 47	23 10
Lancaster	65 a	21 13	21 21	21 48									22 46	22 47					23 05	23 55
	d												22 46					22 55	23 06	23 55
Blackpool North	97 d							21 17				22 25					23 02			
Layton	97 d											22 28					23 05			
Poulton-le-Fylde	97 d							21 22				22 32					23 09			
Kirkham & Wesham	97 d											22 41					23 18			
Preston	65,97 a							21 39				22 51	23 09				23 29	23 35	23 29	00 35
	d							21 48	22 22			22 54					23 31			
Leyland	d							21 54				22 59					23 37			
Buckshaw Parkway	d							21 59	22 31			23 05					23 43			
Chorley	d							22 04	22 36			23 10					23 48			
Adlington (Lancashire)	d							22 09				23 15					23 53			
Blackrod	d							22 12				23 18					23 56			
Horwich Parkway	d							22 16	22 45			23 22					23 59			
Lostock	d							22 20				23 26					00 04			
Southport	d				21 08						22 18				23 10					
Meols Cop	d				21 13						22 23				23 15					
Bescar Lane	d										22 28									
New Lane	d										22 32									
Burscough Bridge	d				21 22						22 35				23 24					
Hoscar	d										22 38									
Parbold	d				21 26						22 41				23 28					
Appley Bridge	d				21 31						22 46				23 33					
Gathurst	d				21 34						22 49				23 36					
Kirkby	d																			
Rainford	d																			
Upholland	d																			
Orrell	d																			
Pemberton	d																			
Wigan Wallgate	a				21 39						22 54				23 43					
	d				21 40						22 55									
Wigan North Western	d					21 46				22 50										
Ince	d				21 43						22 58									
Hindley	d				21 47	21 52				22 56	23 02									
Westhoughton	d					21 56				23 00										
Bolton	a					22 04		22 25	22 52	23 08		23 31					00 09			
	d					22 05	22 19	22 25	22 53	23 09		23 32				23 48	00 09			
Moses Gate	d					22 08														
Farnworth	d					22 10														
Kearsley	d					22 12														
Clifton	d																			
Daisy Hill	d				21 51						23 06									
Hag Fold	d				21 54						23 09									
Atherton	d				21 57						23 11									
Walkden	d				22 03						23 17									
Moorside	d				22 07						23 20									
Swinton	d				22 10						23 23									
Salford Crescent	a				22 17	22 22	22 32	22 37	23 06	23 21	23 32	23 44				23 59	00 21			
	d				22 18	22 23	22 33	22 37	23 06	23 21	23 33	23 44				00 01	00 22			
Salford Central	d				22 21	22 26	22 36			23 24	23 36									
Manchester Victoria	a				22 24	22 29	22 42			23 27	23 39					00 08				
Rochdale	41 a																			
Deansgate	a																			
Manchester Oxford Road	a							22 42	23 11			23 49								
Manchester Piccadilly	a							22 46	23 15			23 53					00 27			
Stockport	84 a																			
Hazel Grove	86 a																			
Buxton	86 a																			
Heald Green	85 a								23 29								00 41			
Manchester Airport	85 ✈ a								23 35			00 10					00 47			

A From Leeds
B until 16 June, from 15 September
C To Stalybridge
D From Clitheroe
E from 23 June until 8 September

Table T082-R

Barrow-in-Furness, Blackpool North, Preston, Southport, Kirkby and Wigan - Bolton - Manchester

Sundays
20 May to 2 December

		NT A	NT ◇ B	NT	NT C	NT D	NT ◇	NT	NT E	NT ◇	NT ◇	NT C	NT D	NT ◇	NT	NT F	NT ◇	NT ◇ G	NT G	NT H	NT ◇ I	NT ◇ J	NT ◇ K
Barrow-in-Furness	d																	08 39	09 05	09 05			
Roose	d																	08 43		09 09			
Dalton	d																	08 49		09 15			
Ulverston	d																	08 57	09 21	09 24			
Cark	d																	09 05		09 31			
Kents Bank	d																	09 09		09 35			
Grange-over-Sands	d																	09 13	09 34	09 39			
Arnside	d																	09 19	09 40	09 45			
Silverdale	d																	09 24		09 50			
Carnforth	d																	09 31	09 50	09a57	10 15		
Windermere	83 d																						
Oxenholme Lake District	65 d																						
Lancaster	65 a																	09 40	10 00		10 25		
	d																	09 40					
Blackpool North	97 d						07 48			08 21	08 43						09 21					09 41	09 41
Layton	97 d									08 24							09 24						
Poulton-le-Fylde	97 d									08 27	08 49						09 27					09 47	09 47
Kirkham & Wesham	97 d									08 37	08 58						09 37					09 56	09 56
Preston	65,97 a						08 09			08 48	09 08						09 48	10 04				10 06	10 06
	d						08 11			08 49	09 10			09 22			09 49					10 08	10 08
Leyland	d									08 56							09 56						
Buckshaw Parkway	d						08 21			09 01				09 32			10 01						
Chorley	d						08 27			09 06				09 36			10 06						
Adlington (Lancashire)	d									09 11							10 11						
Blackrod	d									09 15							10 15						
Horwich Parkway	d						08 36			09 19				09 45			10 19						
Lostock	d		00 04							09 22							10 22						
Southport	d											08 47											
Meols Cop	d											08 53											
Bescar Lane	d																						
New Lane	d																						
Burscough Bridge	d											09 01											
Hoscar	d																						
Parbold	d											09 06											
Appley Bridge	d											09 10											
Gathurst	d											09 14											
Kirkby	d																						
Rainford	d																						
Upholland	d																						
Orrell	d																						
Pemberton	d																						
Wigan Wallgate	a											09 18											
	d			08 05	08 18			08 50				09 20			09 52								
Wigan North Western	d					08 21					09 24		09 27									10 24	10 24
Ince	d			08 08				08 53							09 55								
Hindley	d			08 11		08 26		08 56				09 25	09 32		09 58								
Westhoughton	d					08 31							09 37										
Bolton	a		00 09			08 39	08 45			09 27			09 45	09 52			10 27						
	d		00 09			08 39	08 46		09 19	09 28			09 45	09 53		10 19	10 28						
Moses Gate	d																						
Farnworth	d																						
Kearsley	d																						
Clifton	d																						
Daisy Hill	d			08 15	08 26			09 00				09 29			10 02								
Hag Fold	d			08 18				09 03							10 05								
Atherton	d			08 21	08 30			09 06				09 33			10 08								
Walkden	d			08 27	08 36			09 12				09 39			10 14								
Moorside	d			08 31				09 16							10 18								
Swinton	d			08 34	08 41			09 19				09 44			10 21								
Salford Crescent	a		00 21	08 44	08 51	08 55		09 26	09 32	09 39		09 51	09 57	10 05	10 29	10 33	10 39						
	d	00 01	00 22	08 45	08 52	08 55		09 27	09 32	09 40		09 52	09 58	10 05	10 30	10 33	10 40						
Salford Central	d			08 47	08 54	08 58		09 29	09 35	09 42		09 55	10 01		10 32	10 36	10 42						
Manchester Victoria	a	00 08		08 50	08 57	09 01		09 34	09 39	09 45		09 58	10 05		10 37	10 40	10 45						
Rochdale	41 a				09 19							10 20											
Deansgate	a						09 01							10 09									
Manchester Oxford Road	a						09 05				09 57			10 13								10 58	11 00
Manchester Piccadilly	a		00 27								10 00											11 01	
Stockport	84 a																						
Hazel Grove	86 a																						
Buxton	86 a																						
Heald Green	85 a		00 41																				
Manchester Airport	85 ✈ a		00 47								10 19											11 20	

A not 20 May. From Clitheroe
B not 20 May. From Blackpool North
C To Blackburn
D To Stalybridge
E From Blackburn
F From Clitheroe
G from 24 June
H until 17 June
I From Leeds
J until 9 September
K from 16 September

Table T082-R

Sundays
20 May to 2 December

Barrow-in-Furness, Blackpool North, Preston, Southport, Kirkby and Wigan - Bolton - Manchester

		NT	NT	NT	NT	NT	NT	TP	NT	NT	NT	NT	NT	NT	NT	NT	TP	TP	NT	NT	NT	TP	NT
				◇			◇	◇1	◇	◇	◇	◇			◇	◇					◇	◇1	◇
		A	B			C		D	E	F	G	H	A	B			I	J		C		K	
Barrow-in-Furness	d										09 47	09 47				10 21							
Roose	d										09 51	09 51											
Dalton	d										09 57	09 57											
Ulverston	d										10 05	10 05				10 37							
Cark	d										10 13	10 13											
Kents Bank	d										10 17	10 17											
Grange-over-Sands	d										10 21	10 21				10 49							
Arnside	d										10 27	10 27				10 56							
Silverdale	d										10 32	10 32											
Carnforth	d										10 39	10 39				11 06							
Windermere 83	d																						
Oxenholme Lake District 65	d							10 26									11 11	11 11				11 23	
Lancaster 6 65	a							10 40			10 48	10 48				11 15	11 25	11 25				11 37	
	d							10 41			10 48	10 52				11 15	11 26	11 26				11 38	
Blackpool North 97	d						10 21		10 41	10 41											11 21		11 41
Layton 97	d						10 24														11 24		
Poulton-le-Fylde 97	d						10 27		10 47	10 47											11 27		11 47
Kirkham & Wesham 97	d						10 37		10 56	10 56											11 37		11 56
Preston 8 65,97	a						10 48	10 57	11 06	11 06	11 12	11 16				11 39	11 41	11 41			11 48	11 56	12 06
	d			10 22			10 49	11 02	11 08	11 08					11 22		11 43	11 43			11 49	11 58	12 08
Leyland	d						10 56														11 56		
Buckshaw Parkway	d			10 32			11 01								11 32						12 01		
Chorley	d			10 36			11 06								11 36						12 06		
Adlington (Lancashire)	d						11 11														12 11		
Blackrod	d						11 15														12 15		
Horwich Parkway	d			10 45			11 19								11 45						12 19		
Lostock	d						11 22														12 22		
Southport	d	09 47											10 47										
Meols Cop	d	09 53											10 53										
Bescar Lane	d																						
New Lane	d																						
Burscough Bridge	d	10 01											11 01										
Hoscar	d																						
Parbold	d	10 06											11 06										
Appley Bridge	d	10 10											11 10										
Gathurst	d	10 14											11 14										
Kirkby	d																						
Rainford	d																						
Upholland	d																						
Orrell	d																						
Pemberton	d																						
Wigan Wallgate	a	10 18											11 18										
	d	10 20			10 51								11 20						11 51				
Wigan North Western	d		10 27						11 24	11 24				11 27									12 24
Ince	d				10 54														11 54				
Hindley	d	10 25	10 32		10 57								11 25	11 32					11 57				
Westhoughton	d		10 37											11 37									
Bolton	a		10 45	10 52			11 27							11 45	11 52						12 27		
	d		10 45	10 53		11 19	11 28							11 45	11 53					12 19	12 28		
Moses Gate	d																						
Farnworth	d																						
Kearsley	d																						
Clifton	d																						
Daisy Hill	d	10 29			11 01								11 29						12 01				
Hag Fold	d				11 04														12 04				
Atherton	d	10 33			11 07								11 33						12 07				
Walkden	d	10 39			11 13								11 39						12 13				
Moorside	d				11 17														12 17				
Swinton	d	10 44			11 20								11 44						12 20				
Salford Crescent	a	10 51	10 57	11 05	11 29	11 33	11 39						11 51	11 57	12 05				12 29	12 33	12 39		
	d	10 52	10 58	11 05	11 30	11 33	11 40						11 52	11 58	12 05				12 30	12 33	12 40		
Salford Central	d	10 55	11 01		11 32	11 36	11 42						11 55	12 01					12 32	12 36	12 42		
Manchester Victoria ⇌	a	10 59	11 05		11 37	11 40	11 45	11 49					12 00	12 05					12 37	12 40	12 45		
Rochdale 41	a	11 21											12 21										
Deansgate ⇌	a			11 09											12 09								
Manchester Oxford Road	a			11 13					11 58	11 58					12 13								12 58
Manchester Piccadilly 10 ⇌	a								12 01	12 01							12 21	12 23				12 41	13 01
Stockport 84	a																						
Hazel Grove 86	a																						
Buxton 86	a																						
Heald Green 85	a																						
Manchester Airport 85 ⇌✈	a								12 18	12 19							12 40	12 40				13 00	13 17

A To Blackburn
B To Stalybridge
C From Clitheroe
D from 24 June. From Glasgow Central
E from 16 September
F until 9 September
G from 24 June
H until 17 June
I from 16 September. From Edinburgh
J from 24 June until 9 September. From Edinburgh
K until 17 June. From Edinburgh

Table T082-R

Sundays
20 May to 2 December

Barrow-in-Furness, Blackpool North, Preston, Southport, Kirkby and Wigan - Bolton - Manchester

		NT	NT	NT	NT	NT	NT	NT	TP	NT	NT	NT	NT	NT	TP	NT	NT	NT	NT	NT	NT	NT
			◇		◇			◇	◇1	◇	◇			◇	◇1					◇	◇	
		A	B	C			D		E			A	C		F	G	H		D			A
Barrow-in-Furness	d									11 33						12 53	13 17					
Roose	d									11 37						12 57	13 21					
Dalton	d									11 43						13 03	13 27					
Ulverston	d									11 51						13 11	13 35					
Cark	d									11 59												
Kents Bank	d									12 03												
Grange-over-Sands	d									12 07						13 24	13 48					
Arnside	d									12 13						13 30	13 54					
Silverdale	d									12 18						13 35	13 59					
Carnforth	d		12 02							12 26						13 42	14 06					
Windermere 83	d																					
Oxenholme Lake District 65	d								12 13						13 13							
Lancaster 6 65	a		12 13						12 27	12 34					13 27	13 52	14 16					
	d								12 28	12 35					13 28							
Blackpool North 97	d							12 17			12 40									13 21	13 41	
Layton 97	d							12 20												13 24		
Poulton-le-Fylde 97	d							12 23			12 46									13 27	13 47	
Kirkham & Wesham 97	d							12 33			12 55									13 37	13 56	
Preston 8 65,97	a							12 44	12 45	12 59	13 05				13 47					13 48	14 06	
	d				12 22			12 45	12 47		13 07			13 22	13 48					13 49	14 08	
Leyland	d							12 52												13 56		
Buckshaw Parkway	d				12 32			12 57						13 32						14 01		
Chorley	d				12 36			13 02						13 36						14 06		
Adlington (Lancashire)	d							13 07												14 11		
Blackrod	d							13 11												14 15		
Horwich Parkway	d				12 45			13 15						13 45						14 19		
Lostock	d							13 18												14 22		
Southport	d	11 47										12 47										13 47
Meols Cop	d	11 53										12 53										13 53
Bescar Lane	d																					
New Lane	d																					
Burscough Bridge	d	12 01										13 01										14 01
Hoscar	d																					
Parbold	d	12 06										13 06										14 06
Appley Bridge	d	12 10										13 10										14 10
Gathurst	d	12 14										13 14										14 14
Kirkby	d																					
Rainford	d																					
Upholland	d																					
Orrell	d																					
Pemberton	d																					
Wigan Wallgate	a	12 18										13 18										14 18
	d	12 20				12 51						13 20						13 51				14 20
Wigan North Western	d			12 27							13 23		13 26								14 24	
Ince	d					12 54												13 54				
Hindley	d	12 25		12 32		12 57						13 25	13 31					13 57				14 25
Westhoughton	d			12 37									13 36									
Bolton	a			12 45	12 52			13 23					13 44	13 52						14 27		
	d			12 45	12 53		13 19	13 28					13 44	13 53					14 19	14 28		
Moses Gate	d																					
Farnworth	d																					
Kearsley	d																					
Clifton	d																					
Daisy Hill	d	12 29				13 01						13 29						14 01				14 29
Hag Fold	d					13 04												14 04				
Atherton	d	12 33				13 07						13 33						14 07				14 33
Walkden	d	12 39				13 13						13 39						14 13				14 39
Moorside	d					13 17												14 17				
Swinton	d	12 44				13 20						13 44						14 20				14 44
Salford Crescent	a	12 51		12 57	13 05	13 29	13 33	13 39				13 51	13 56	14 05				14 29	14 33	14 39		14 51
	d	12 52		12 58	13 05	13 30	13 33	13 40				13 52	13 57	14 05				14 30	14 33	14 40		14 52
Salford Central	d	12 55		13 01		13 32	13 36	13 42				13 55	14 02					14 32	14 36	14 42		14 55
Manchester Victoria ⇌	a	13 00		13 04		13 37	13 40	13 45				14 00	14 05					14 37	14 40	14 45		15 00
Rochdale 41	a	13 22										14 22										15 22
Deansgate ⇌	a				13 09									14 09								
Manchester Oxford Road	a				13 11						13 58			14 11							14 56	
Manchester Piccadilly 10 ⇌	a				13 15				13 27		14 01			14 15	14 27						15 00	
Stockport 84	a																					
Hazel Grove 86	a																					
Buxton 86	a																					
Heald Green 85	a				13 28									14 28								
Manchester Airport 85 ⇌✈	a				13 35				13 47		14 17			14 35	14 47						15 17	

A To Blackburn
B From Leeds
C To Stalybridge
D From Clitheroe
E From Edinburgh
F From Glasgow Central
G from 24 June. From Carlisle
H until 17 June. From Carlisle

Table T082-R

Sundays
20 May to 2 December

Barrow-in-Furness, Blackpool North, Preston, Southport, Kirkby and Wigan - Bolton - Manchester

		NT	NT	TP	NT	NT	NT	NT	NT	NT	NT	NT	NT	TP	NT	NT	NT	NT	NT	NT	NT	NT	TP
		A	◇	◇■ B 🍴		C	◇	◇	◇	D	◇ E	A	◇	◇■ F 🍴		C	◇	◇	◇	D	A	◇	◇■ B 🍴
Barrow-in-Furness	d								13 45										14 45				
Roose	d								13 49										14 49				
Dalton	d								13 55										14 55				
Ulverston	d								14 03										15 03				
Cark	d								14 11										15 11				
Kents Bank	d								14 15										15 15				
Grange-over-Sands	d								14 19										15 19				
Arnside	d								14 25										15 25				
Silverdale	d								14 30										15 30				
Carnforth	d								14 37		15 02								15 37				
Windermere 83	d																						
Oxenholme Lake District 65	d			14 12										15 15									16 12
Lancaster 65	a			14 26					14 46		15 13			15 29					15 46				16 26
	d			14 27					14 46					15 29					15 46				16 27
Blackpool North 97	d						14 21	14 41									15 21	15 41					
Layton 97	d						14 24										15 24						
Poulton-le-Fylde 97	d						14 27	14 47									15 27	15 47					
Kirkham & Wesham 97	d						14 37	14 56									15 37	15 56					
Preston 65,97	a			14 45			14 48	15 06	15 10					15 47			15 48	16 06	16 10				16 44
	d		14 22	14 46			14 49	15 08					15 22	15 48			15 49	16 08				16 22	16 46
Leyland	d						14 56										15 56						
Buckshaw Parkway	d		14 32				15 02						15 32				16 01					16 32	
Chorley	d		14 36				15 07						15 36				16 06					16 36	
Adlington (Lancashire)	d						15 12										16 11						
Blackrod	d						15 16										16 15						
Horwich Parkway	d		14 45				15 20						15 45				16 19					16 45	
Lostock	d						15 23										16 22						
Southport	d									14 47										15 47			
Meols Cop	d									14 53										15 53			
Bescar Lane	d																						
New Lane	d																						
Burscough Bridge	d									15 01										16 01			
Hoscar	d																						
Parbold	d									15 06										16 06			
Appley Bridge	d									15 10										16 10			
Gathurst	d									15 14										16 14			
Kirkby	d																						
Rainford	d																						
Upholland	d																						
Orrell	d																						
Pemberton	d																						
Wigan Wallgate	a									15 18										16 18			
	d				14 51					15 20					15 51					16 20			
Wigan North Western	d	14 27						15 25				15 27						16 24			16 27		
Ince	d				14 54										15 54								
Hindley	d	14 32			14 57					15 25		15 32			15 57					16 25	16 32		
Westhoughton	d	14 37										15 37									16 37		
Bolton	a	14 45	14 52				15 28					15 45	15 52				16 27				16 45	16 52	
	d	14 45	14 53			15 19	15 29					15 45	15 53			16 19	16 28				16 45	16 53	
Moses Gate	d																						
Farnworth	d																						
Kearsley	d																						
Clifton	d																						
Daisy Hill	d				15 01					15 29					16 01					16 29			
Hag Fold	d				15 04										16 04								
Atherton	d				15 07					15 33					16 07					16 33			
Walkden	d				15 13					15 39					16 13					16 39			
Moorside	d				15 17										16 17								
Swinton	d				15 20					15 44					16 20					16 44			
Salford Crescent	a	14 57	15 05		15 29	15 33	15 40			15 51		15 57	16 05		16 29	16 33	16 39			16 51	16 57	17 05	
	d	14 58	15 05		15 30	15 33	15 41			15 52		15 58	16 05		16 30	16 33	16 40			16 52	16 58	17 06	
Salford Central	d	15 01			15 32	15 36	15 43			15 55		16 01			16 32	16 36	16 42			16 55	17 01		
Manchester Victoria	a	15 05			15 37	15 40	15 46			16 00		16 05			16 37	16 40	16 45			17 00	17 05		
Rochdale 41	a									16 22										17 22			
Deansgate	a		15 09										16 09									17 09	
Manchester Oxford Road	a		15 11					15 58					16 11					16 57				17 11	
Manchester Piccadilly	a		15 15	15 26				16 01					16 15	16 26				17 01				17 15	17 26
Stockport 84	a																						
Hazel Grove 86	a																						
Buxton 86	a																						
Heald Green 85	a		15 28										16 28									17 28	
Manchester Airport 85	a		15 35	15 47				16 17					16 35	16 47				17 17				17 35	17 43

A To Stalybridge
B From Edinburgh
C From Clitheroe
D To Blackburn
E From Leeds
F From Glasgow Central

Table T082-R

Sundays
20 May to 2 December

Barrow-in-Furness, Blackpool North, Preston, Southport, Kirkby and Wigan - Bolton - Manchester

		NT	NT	NT	NT	NT	NT	NT	NT	NT	TP	NT	NT	NT	NT	NT	NT	NT	NT	TP	NT	NT
		A		◇ B	C	◇	◇	D	E	◇	◇■ F 🍴		C	◇	◇	◇	D	E	◇	◇■ G 🍴		C
Barrow-in-Furness	d	15 50														16 44						
Roose	d	15 54														16 48						
Dalton	d	16 00														16 54						
Ulverston	d	16 08														17 02						
Cark	d	16 16														17 10						
Kents Bank	d	16 20														17 14						
Grange-over-Sands	d	16 24														17 18						
Arnside	d	16 30														17 24						
Silverdale	d	16 35														17 29						
Carnforth	d	16 42		17 02												17 36						
Windermere 83	d																					
Oxenholme Lake District 65	d										17 14									18 14		
Lancaster 65	a	16 52		17 13							17 28					17 45				18 28		
	d										17 29					17 45				18 29		
Blackpool North 97	d					16 21	16 41							17 21	17 41							
Layton 97	d					16 24								17 24								
Poulton-le-Fylde 97	d					16 27	16 47							17 27	17 47							
Kirkham & Wesham 97	d					16 37	16 56							17 37	17 56							
Preston 65,97	a					16 48	17 06				17 47			17 48	18 06	18 09				18 46		
	d					16 49	17 08			17 22	17 48			17 49	18 08				18 22	18 48		
Leyland	d					16 56								17 56								
Buckshaw Parkway	d					17 01				17 32				18 01					18 32			
Chorley	d					17 06				17 36				18 06					18 36			
Adlington (Lancashire)	d					17 11								18 11								
Blackrod	d					17 15								18 15								
Horwich Parkway	d					17 19				17 45				18 19					18 45			
Lostock	d					17 22								18 22								
Southport	d							16 47									17 47					
Meols Cop	d							16 53									17 53					
Bescar Lane	d																					
New Lane	d																					
Burscough Bridge	d							17 01									18 01					
Hoscar	d																					
Parbold	d							17 06									18 06					
Appley Bridge	d							17 10									18 10					
Gathurst	d							17 14									18 14					
Kirkby	d																					
Rainford	d																					
Upholland	d																					
Orrell	d																					
Pemberton	d																					
Wigan Wallgate	a							17 18									18 18					
	d		16 51					17 20				17 51					18 20				18 51	
Wigan North Western	d						17 24		17 27						18 24			18 27				
Ince	d		16 54									17 54									18 54	
Hindley	d		16 57					17 25	17 32			17 57					18 25	18 32			18 57	
Westhoughton	d								17 37									18 37				
Bolton	a					17 27			17 45	17 52				18 27				18 45	18 52			
	d				17 19	17 28			17 45	17 53			18 19	18 28				18 45	18 53			19 21
Moses Gate	d																					
Farnworth	d																					
Kearsley	d																					
Clifton	d																					
Daisy Hill	d		17 01					17 29				18 01					18 29				19 01	
Hag Fold	d		17 04									18 04									19 04	
Atherton	d		17 07					17 33				18 07					18 33				19 07	
Walkden	d		17 13					17 39				18 13					18 39				19 13	
Moorside	d		17 17									18 17									19 17	
Swinton	d		17 20					17 44				18 20					18 44				19 20	
Salford Crescent	a		17 29		17 33	17 39		17 51	17 57	18 05		18 29	18 33	18 39			18 51	18 57	19 05		19 29	19 33
	d		17 30		17 33	17 40		17 52	17 58	18 05		18 30	18 33	18 40			18 52	18 58	19 05		19 30	19 33
Salford Central	d		17 32		17 36	17 42		17 55	18 01			18 32	18 36	18 42			18 55	19 01			19 32	19 36
Manchester Victoria	a		17 37		17 40	17 45		18 00	18 05			18 37	18 40	18 45			19 00	19 04			19 37	19 40
Rochdale 41	a							18 22									19 22					
Deansgate	a									18 09									19 09			
Manchester Oxford Road	a						17 58			18 11					18 58				19 11			
Manchester Piccadilly	a						18 01			18 15	18 27				19 01				19 15	19 26		
Stockport 84	a																					
Hazel Grove 86	a																					
Buxton 86	a																					
Heald Green 85	a									18 28									19 28			
Manchester Airport 85	a						18 17			18 35	18 47				19 17				19 35	19 47		

A From Carlisle
B From Leeds
C From Clitheroe
D To Blackburn
E To Stalybridge
F From Glasgow Central
G From Edinburgh

Table T082-R

Sundays
20 May to 2 December

Barrow-in-Furness, Blackpool North, Preston, Southport, Kirkby and Wigan - Bolton - Manchester

	NT ◇	NT ◇	NT A	NT B	NT ◇	NT C	NT ◇ D	TP ◇ E	TP ◇ F	NT	NT ◇	NT ◇	NT ◇	NT A	NT B	NT G	NT ◇	TP ◇ H	NT	NT G	NT ◇	NT ◇
Barrow-in-Furness d						17 46							18 58									
Roose d						17 50																
Dalton d						17 56																
Ulverston d						18 05							19 14									
Cark d						18 12																
Kents Bank d						18 16																
Grange-over-Sands d						18 20							19 26									
Arnside d						18 27							19 32									
Silverdale d						18 32																
Carnforth d						18 41	19 02						19 43									
Windermere 83 d																						
Oxenholme Lake District 65 d								19 14	19 14									20 13				
Lancaster 6 65 a						18 49	19 13	19 28	19 29				19 51					20 27				
d						19 02		19 29	19 29				19 51					20 28				
Blackpool North 97 d	18 21	18 41									19 21	19 41									20 21	20 41
Layton 97 d	18 24										19 24										20 24	
Poulton-le-Fylde 97 d	18 27	18 47									19 27	19 47									20 27	20 47
Kirkham & Wesham 97 d	18 37	18 56									19 37	19 56									20 37	20 56
Preston 8 65,97 a	18 48	19 06				19 25		19 47	19 48		19 48	20 06	20 15					20 45			20 48	21 06
d	18 49	19 08			19 22			19 48	19 49		19 49	20 08					20 22	20 47			20 49	21 08
Leyland d	18 56										19 56										20 56	
Buckshaw Parkway d	19 01				19 32						20 01						20 32				21 01	
Chorley d	19 06				19 36						20 06						20 36				21 06	
Adlington (Lancashire) d	19 11										20 11										21 11	
Blackrod d	19 15										20 15										21 15	
Horwich Parkway d	19 19				19 45						20 19						20 45				21 19	
Lostock d	19 22										20 22										21 22	
Southport d			18 47											19 47								
Meols Cop d			18 53											19 53								
Bescar Lane d																						
New Lane d																						
Burscough Bridge d			19 01											20 01								
Hoscar d																						
Parbold d			19 06											20 06								
Appley Bridge d			19 10											20 10								
Gathurst d			19 14											20 14								
Kirkby d																						
Rainford d																						
Upholland d																						
Orrell d																						
Pemberton d																						
Wigan Wallgate a			19 18											20 18								
d			19 20							19 51				20 20					20 51			
Wigan North Western d		19 24		19 27								20 26			20 27							21 24
Ince d										19 54									20 54			
Hindley d			19 25	19 32						19 57				20 25	20 32				20 57			
Westhoughton d				19 37											20 37							
Bolton a	19 27			19 45	19 52						20 27				20 45		20 52				21 27	
d	19 28			19 45	19 53						20 28				20 45	20 49	20 53			21 19	21 28	
Moses Gate d																						
Farnworth d																						
Kearsley d																						
Clifton d																						
Daisy Hill d			19 29							20 01				20 29					21 01			
Hag Fold d										20 04									21 04			
Atherton d			19 33							20 07				20 33					21 07			
Walkden d			19 39							20 13				20 39					21 13			
Moorside d										20 17									21 17			
Swinton d			19 44							20 20				20 44					21 20			
Salford Crescent a	19 39		19 51	19 57	20 05					20 29	20 39			20 51	20 57	21 01	21 05		21 29	21 33	21 39	
d	19 40		19 52	19 58	20 05					20 30	20 40			20 52	20 58	21 01	21 05		21 30	21 33	21 40	
Salford Central d	19 42		19 55	20 01						20 32	20 42			20 55	21 01	21 05			21 32	21 36	21 42	
Manchester Victoria ⇌ a	19 45		20 00	20 05						20 37	20 45			21 00	21 05	21 09			21 37	21 40	21 45	
Rochdale 41 a			20 22											21 22								
Deansgate ⇌ a					20 09												21 09					
Manchester Oxford Road a		19 58			20 11							20 58					21 11					21 58
Manchester Piccadilly 10 ⇌ a		20 01			20 15			20 26	20 26			21 01					21 15	21 25				22 01
Stockport 84 a																						
Hazel Grove 86 a																						
Buxton 86 a																						
Heald Green 85 a					20 28												21 27					
Manchester Airport 85 ⇌✈ a		20 17			20 36			20 47	20 47			21 17					21 34	21 42				22 16

A To Blackburn
B To Stalybridge
C From Carlisle
D From Leeds
E from 16 September. From Glasgow Central
F until 9 September. From Glasgow Central
G From Clitheroe
H From Edinburgh

Table T082-R

Sundays
20 May to 2 December

Barrow-in-Furness, Blackpool North, Preston, Southport, Kirkby and Wigan - Bolton - Manchester

	NT ◇	NT A	NT B	NT ◇	NT	NT ◇ C	TP ◇ D	TP ◇ E	NT F	NT ◇ G	NT	NT ◇	NT	NT B	NT ◇	TP ◇ H	NT	NT	NT I	NT F	NT	NT
Barrow-in-Furness d	19 45										20 46											
Roose d	19 49										20 50											
Dalton d	19 55										20 56											
Ulverston d	20 03										21 05											
Cark d	20 11										21 12											
Kents Bank d	20 15										21 16											
Grange-over-Sands d	20 19										21 20											
Arnside d	20 25										21 26											
Silverdale d	20 30										21 31											
Carnforth d	20 37										21 38											
Windermere 83 d																			21 44			
Oxenholme Lake District 65 d							21 15	21 16								22 12			22 16			
Lancaster 6 65 a	20 46						21 30	21 30			21 48					22 26			22 34			
d	20 46						21 31	21 31								22 27			22 35			
Blackpool North 97 d						21 21						21 41						22 21				
Layton 97 d						21 24												22 24				
Poulton-le-Fylde 97 d						21 27						21 47						22 27				
Kirkham & Wesham 97 d						21 37						21 56						22 37				
Preston 8 65,97 a	21 10					21 48	21 49	21 50		←		22 06				22 44		22 48	22 57			
d				21 22		21 49	21 51	21 51				22 08			22 22	22 46		22 49				
Leyland d						21 56				21 56								22 56				
Buckshaw Parkway d				21 32		→				22 01					22 32			23 01				
Chorley d				21 36						22 06					22 36			23 06				
Adlington (Lancashire) d										22 11								23 11				
Blackrod d										22 15								23 15				
Horwich Parkway d				21 45						22 19					22 44			23 19				
Lostock d										22 22								23 22				
Southport d		20 47											21 47									22 54
Meols Cop d		20 53											21 53									22 59
Bescar Lane d																						
New Lane d																						
Burscough Bridge d		21 01											22 01									23 08
Hoscar d																						
Parbold d		21 06											22 06									23 12
Appley Bridge d		21 10											22 10									23 17
Gathurst d		21 14											22 14									23 20
Kirkby d																						
Rainford d																						
Upholland d																						
Orrell d																						
Pemberton d																						
Wigan Wallgate a		21 18											22 18									23 25
d		21 20			21 51								22 20				22 51					23 26
Wigan North Western d			21 27									22 24		22 27							23 21	
Ince d					21 54												22 54					
Hindley d		21 25	21 32		21 57								22 25	22 32			22 57				23 26	
Westhoughton d			21 37											22 37							23 31	
Bolton a			21 45	21 52				22s10		22 27				22 45	22 52			23 27			23 40	
d			21 45	21 53					22 19	22 28				22 45	22 52			23 28		23 36	23 40	
Moses Gate d																						
Farnworth d																						
Kearsley d																						
Clifton d																						
Daisy Hill d		21 29			22 01								22 29				23 01					23 34
Hag Fold d					22 04												23 04					23 37
Atherton d		21 33			22 07								22 33				23 07					23 40
Walkden d		21 39			22 13								22 39				23 13					23 45
Moorside d					22 17												23 17					23 49
Swinton d		21 44			22 20								22 44				23 20					23 52
Salford Crescent a		21 51	21 57	22 05	22 29				22 33	22 39			22 51	22 57	23 04		23 29	23 39		23 48	23 52	23 58
d		21 52	21 58	22 05	22 30				22 33	22 40			22 52	22 58	23 04		23 30	23 40		23 48	23 53	23 59
Salford Central d		21 55	22 01		22 32				22 36	22 42			22 55	23 01			23 32	23 42		23 51	23 56	00 03
Manchester Victoria ⇌ a		22 00	22 05		22 37				22 40	22 45			23 00	23 04			23 37	23 45		23 55	23 59	00 06
Rochdale 41 a		22 22											23 23									
Deansgate ⇌ a				22 11											23 08							
Manchester Oxford Road a				22 13								22 58			23 10							
Manchester Piccadilly 10 ⇌ a				22 17			22 27	22 26				23 01			23 17	23 27						
Stockport 84 a																						
Hazel Grove 86 a																						
Buxton 86 a																						
Heald Green 85 a				22 31											23 30							
Manchester Airport 85 ⇌✈ a				22 38			22 44	22 44				23 17			23 37	23 44						

A To Blackburn
B To Stalybridge
C To Manchester Victoria
D until 9 September. From Glasgow Central
E from 16 September. From Glasgow Central
F From Clitheroe
G From Blackpool North
H From Edinburgh
I from 24 June

Table T083-F

Mondays to Fridays

21 May to 7 December

Oxenholme - Lake District - Windermere

Miles			NT A	NT	NT	NT	NT ◇ B	NT	NT	NT ◇ C	NT	NT ◇ C	NT	NT	NT	NT	NT ◇ C	NT	NT	NT
0	**Oxenholme Lake District**	d	06 19	07 28	08 27	09 12	10 19	11 18	12 06	13 02	14 00	14 51	15 37	16 27	17 15	18 05	19 00	20 18	21 17	22 19
2¼	Kendal	d	06 23	07 32	08 31	09 16	10 23	11 22	12 10	13 06	14 04	14 55	15 41	16 31	17 19	18 09	19 05	20 22	21 21	22 23
4	Burneside	d	06 27	07 36	08 35		10 27	11 26	12 14	13 10	14 08		15 45		17 23	18 13	19 09	20 26	21 25	22 27
6½	Staveley	d	06 33	07 43	08 41		10 34	11 33	12 21	13 16	14 15		15 52		17 30	18 19	19 15	20 33	21 32	22 34
10	**Windermere**	a	06 39	07 49	08 47	09 29	10 41	11 39	12 27	13 24	14 21	15 09	15 58	16 44	17 36	18 25	19 22	20 39	21 38	22 40

Saturdays

26 May to 8 December

		NT A	NT	NT	NT	NT ◇ B	NT	NT	NT ◇ C	NT	NT ◇ C	NT	NT	NT	NT	NT ◇ C	NT	NT D (bus)	NT E	NT D (bus)	NT E
Oxenholme Lake District	d	06 19	07 28	08 27	09 12	10 19	11 18	12 06	13 02	14 00	14 51	15 37	16 27	17 15	18 05	19 00	20 18	21 15	21 16	22 00	22 01
Kendal	d	06 23	07 32	08 31	09 16	10 23	11 22	12 10	13 06	14 04	14 55	15 41	16 31	17 19	18 09	19 05	20 22	21 25	21 20	22 10	22 05
Burneside	d	06 27	07 36	08 35		10 27	11 26	12 14	13 10	14 08		15 45		17 23	18 13	19 09	20 26	21 35	21 24	22 20	22 09
Staveley	d	06 33	07 43	08 41		10 34	11 33	12 21	13 16	14 15		15 52		17 30	18 19	19 15	20 33	21 45	21 30	22 30	22 15
Windermere	a	06 39	07 49	08 47	09 29	10 41	11 39	12 27	13 24	14 21	15 09	15 58	16 44	17 36	18 25	19 22	20 39	21 55	21 36	22 40	22 21

Sundays

20 May to 2 December

		NT F (bus)	NT ◇ G	NT C	NT	NT	NT ◇	NT	NT	NT ◇	NT	NT	NT ◇	NT	NT F	NT H
Oxenholme Lake District	d	09 45	10 30	11 19	12 01	12 47	13 31	14 29	15 38	16 40	17 37	18 26	19 26	20 18	21 14	21 18
Kendal	d	09 55	10 34	11 23	12 05	12 51	13 35	14 33	15 42	16 44	17 41	18 30	19 30	20 22	21 18	21 22
Burneside	d	10 05	10 38				13 39	14 37	15 46	16 48	17 45	18 34	19 34	20 26	21 22	21 26
Staveley	d	10 15	10 44				13 46	14 44	15 53	16 55	17 52	18 41	19 41	20 33	21 28	21 33
Windermere	a	10 25	10 52	11 36	12 19	13 04	13 53	14 50	15 59	17 02	17 58	18 47	19 48	20 39	21 34	21 39

A From Lancaster
B From Manchester Piccadilly
C From Preston
D until 16 June, from 15 September
E from 23 June until 8 September
F until 17 June
G from 24 June. From Preston
H from 24 June

Table T083-R

Mondays to Fridays

21 May to 7 December

Windermere - Oxenholme - Lake District

Miles			NT	NT	NT	NT ◇ A	NT	NT	NT B	NT	NT ◇ C	NT	NT	NT	NT	NT ◇ C	NT	NT	NT	NT C
0	**Windermere**	d	06 43	07 55	08 51	09 34	10 47	11 43	12 32	13 35	14 25	15 13	16 02	16 48	17 40	18 30	19 45	20 44	21 45	22 45
3½	Staveley	d	06 49	08 01		09 40	10 53		12 38	13 41	14 31	15 19		16 54	17 46		19 51	20 50	21 51	22 51
6	Burneside	d	06 54	08 06		09 45	10 58		12 43	13 46	14 36	15 24		16 59	17 51		19 56	20 55	21 56	22 56
7¾	Kendal	d	06 58	08 10	09 03	09 48	11 02	11 56	12 47	13 50	14 40	15 28	16 14	17 03	17 55	18 42	20 00	20 59	22 00	22 59
10	**Oxenholme Lake District**	a	07 03	08 15	09 08	09 53	11 07	12 01	12 52	13 55	14 45	15 33	16 19	17 08	18 00	18 47	20 05	21 04	22 05	23 04

Saturdays

26 May to 8 December

		NT	NT	NT	NT ◇ A	NT	NT	NT B	NT	NT ◇ C	NT	NT	NT	NT	NT ◇ C	NT	NT D	NT E	NT E	NT F (bus)	NT G (bus)	NT H
Windermere	d	06 43	07 55	08 51	09 34	10 47	11 43	12 31	13 35	14 25	15 13	16 02	16 48	17 40	18 30	19 45	20 43	20 44	21 40	21 40	22 25	22 26
Staveley	d	06 49	08 01		09 40	10 53		12 37	13 41	14 31	15 19		16 54	17 46		19 51		20 50		21 50	22 35	22 32
Burneside	d	06 54	08 06		09 45	10 58		12 42	13 46	14 36	15 24		16 59	17 51		19 56		20 55		22 00	22 45	22 37
Kendal	d	06 58	08 10	09 03	09 48	11 02	11 56	12 46	13 50	14 40	15 28	16 14	17 03	17 55	18 42	20 00	20 55	20 59	21 52	22 10	22 55	22 40
Oxenholme Lake District	a	07 03	08 15	09 08	09 53	11 07	12 01	12 51	13 55	14 45	15 33	16 19	17 08	18 00	18 47	20 05	21 00	21 04	21 57	22 25	23 10	22 45

Sundays

20 May to 2 December

		NT I (bus)	NT	NT	NT	NT ◇	NT	NT	NT ◇	NT	NT	NT ◇	NT	NT	NT J	NT K
Windermere	d	10 30	10 56	11 40	12 23	13 08	13 58	14 55	16 03	17 06	18 02	18 51	19 52	20 44	21 38	21 44
Staveley	d	10 40	11 02		12 29		14 04	15 01		17 12	18 08	18 57	19 58	20 50		21 50
Burneside	d	10 50	11 07		12 34		14 09	15 06		17 17	18 13	19 02	20 03	20 55		21 55
Kendal	d	11 00	11 10	11 52	12 38	13 20	14 13	15 10	16 15	17 21	18 17	19 06	20 07	20 59	21 50	21 59
Oxenholme Lake District	a	11 15	11 15	11 57	12 43	13 25	14 18	15 15	16 20	17 26	18 22	19 11	20 12	21 04	21 55	22 04

A To Manchester Piccadilly
B To Lancaster
C To Preston
D until 16 June, from 15 September. To Lancaster
E from 23 June until 8 September
F until 16 June, from 15 September
G until 16 June, from 15 September. To Preston
H from 23 June until 8 September. To Preston
I until 17 June
J until 17 June. To Preston
K from 24 June. To Preston

Stoke-on-Trent and Crewe - Manchester Airport, Stockport and Manchester

Miles	Miles	Miles			VT MO ◇■ A	NT MX B	NT MX C	NT	NT D	NT E	NT	VT ◇■	NT	NT F	TP ◇■ G	AW	NT E	NT H	NT D	XC ◇■	NT ◇	NT B	NT F
—	—	—	London Euston ■ ⊖65	d																			
—	—	—	Birmingham New Street ■ 68	d																05 57			
—	—	—	Wolverhampton ■ 68 ⇌	d																06 15			
—	—	—	Stafford 65,67	d																06 28			
0	—	—	**Stoke-on-Trent** 50	d																06 45	06 29		
3	—	—	Longport 50	d																	06 33		
6¼	—	—	Kidsgrove 50	d																	06 37		
—	0	—	**Crewe** ■	d				00 44			05 44	06 11				06 27			06 16				
—	4¾	—	Sandbach	d							05 51								06 23				
—	8½	—	Holmes Chapel	d							05 56								06 28				
—	10½	—	Goostrey	d							06 00												
—	14¼	—	Chelford	d							06 05												
—	17¼	—	Alderley Edge	d							06 09							06 49	06 38				
—	19	0	**Wilmslow**	d					05 42		06 13	06 27				06 45		06 52	06 42				
—	—	2	Styal	d					05 45										06 46				
—	—	4¼	**Manchester Airport** ✈	a				01 09	05 53										06 54				
—	20½	—	Handforth	d							06 16							06 55					
11¾	—	—	Congleton	d																06 57	06 44		
19¾	—	—	**Macclesfield**	a																07 05	06 51		
—	—	—		d									06 17							07 06	06 52		
22½	—	—	Prestbury	d									06 21								06 56		
24½	—	—	Adlington (Cheshire)	d									06 24								06 59		
26½	—	—	Poynton	d									06 27								07 03		
28	—	—	Bramhall	d									06 30								07 05		
29½	22¾	—	Cheadle Hulme	d							06 20		06 34					06 59			07 08		
31¾	25	—	**Stockport**	a							06 25	06 36	06 38			06 54		07 06		07 19	07 13		
—	—	—		d	00 04	00 13	00 26			06 20	06 27	06 37	06 39	06 45	06 53	06 55	06 57	07 06		07 20	07 13	07 17	07 21
31¾	26½	—	Heaton Chapel	d							06 31		06 42				07 01				07 17		07 25
34¾	28	—	Levenshulme	d							06 34		06 45				07 04				07 20		07 28
37¾	31	—	**Manchester Picc.** ■ 85,89 ⇌	a	00 13	00 26	00 35	01 28	06 20	06 29	06 44	06 48	06 54	06 56	07 02	07 09	07 14	07 16	07 21	07 28	07 30	07 32	07 36
38¼	31½	—	**Manchester Oxford Road** 85,89	a					06 24									07 19	07 24				
38¾	32	—	Deansgate 85,89 ⇌	a					06 31									07 22	07 32				

		EM ◇ I	NT E	NT ◇	VT ◇■	NT ◇	NT F	NT	XC ◇■ ⊥	TP ◇■ J ⊥	AW ◇ K	NT H	NT B	NT ◇ D	XC ◇■ ⊥	VT ◇■ ⊠	NT	NT F	EM ◇ I	NT E	NT	VT ◇■ ⊠	NT ◇
London Euston ■ ⊖65	d															06 16						06 36	
Birmingham New Street ■ 68	d								06 30						06 51								
Wolverhampton ■ 68 ⇌	d								06 48						07 10								
Stafford 65,67	d								07 02						07 22								
Stoke-on-Trent 50	d					06 58			07 20							07 45							07 56
Longport 50	d																						08 00
Kidsgrove 50	d					07 05																	08 05
Crewe ■	d			06 48	07 10						07 26			07 13	07 44						07 48	08 11	
Sandbach	d			06 55										07 20							07 55		
Holmes Chapel	d			07 00										07 25							08 00		
Goostrey	d			07 03										07 29							08 03		
Chelford	d			07 08										07 34							08 08		
Alderley Edge	d			07 13				07 29				07 49		07 39							08 13		
Wilmslow	d			07 16	07 26			07 32			07 49	07 52		07 42	08 01						08 16	08 27	
Styal	d													07 46									
Manchester Airport ✈	a													07 53									
Handforth	d			07 19				07 35				07 55									08 19		
Congleton	d					07 12																	08 12
Macclesfield	a					07 19			07 37							08 01							08 19
	d					07 20			07 38							08 02	07 49						08 19
Prestbury	d					07 24											07 53						08 23
Adlington (Cheshire)	d					07 27																	08 26
Poynton	d					07 30											07 57						08 30
Bramhall	d					07 33											08 00						08 33
Cheadle Hulme	d			07 24		07 37		07 40				07 59					08 03				08 24		08 37
Stockport	a			07 29	07 36	07 41			07 49		07 58	08 05			08 13	08 17	08 11				08 28	08 35	08 41
	d	07 25	07 30	07 29	07 37	07 42	07 46		07 50	07 53	07 59	08 06	08 09		08 14	08 18	08 13	08 20	08 25	08 30	08 29	08 36	08 42
Heaton Chapel	d			07 33				07 47									08 17	08 24			08 32		
Levenshulme	d			07 36				07 50									08 20	08 27			08 35		
Manchester Picc. ■ 85,89 ⇌	a	07 38	07 40	07 43	07 47	07 53	07 56	07 57	07 59	08 03	08 10	08 16	08 18	08 21	08 24	08 27	08 32	08 36	08 37	08 40	08 43	08 46	08 53
Manchester Oxford Road 85,89	a	07 42										08 20		08 24					08 41				
Deansgate 85,89 ⇌	a													08 32									

A From London Euston
B From Chester
C From Sheffield
D To Liverpool Lime Street
E From Hazel Grove
F From Buxton
G From Doncaster to Manchester Airport
H To Wigan North Western
I From Nottingham to Liverpool Lime Street
J From Cleethorpes to Manchester Airport
K From Cardiff Central

Stoke-on-Trent and Crewe - Manchester Airport, Stockport and Manchester

		NT A	XC ◇■ ⊥	TP ◇■ B ⊥	VT ◇■ ⊠	AW ◇ C ⊥	NT D	NT ◇ E	XC ◇■ F ⊥	VT ◇■ ⊠	NT G	NT H	EM ◇ I	NT H	NT	VT ◇■ ⊠	NT	NT J	XC ◇■ K ⊥	TP ◇■ B ⊥	VT ◇■ ⊠	AW ◇ L ⊥	NT D
London Euston ■ ⊖65	d				06 55					07 20						07 35					08 00		
Birmingham New Street ■ 68	d		07 31						07 57										08 31				
Wolverhampton ■ 68 ⇌	d		07 49						08 15										08 49				
Stafford 65,67	d		08 03						08 28										09 03				
Stoke-on-Trent 50	d		08 20		08 25				08 44	08 48							08 56		09 20		09 25		
Longport 50	d																						
Kidsgrove 50	d																09 03						
Crewe ■	d					08 28		08 16							08 48	09 11						09 30	
Sandbach	d							08 23							08 55								
Holmes Chapel	d							08 28							09 00								
Goostrey	d														09 03								
Chelford	d														09 08								
Alderley Edge	d						08 49	08 38							09 13								09 49
Wilmslow	d					08 48	08 52	08 42							09 16	09 27						09 49	09 52
Styal	d							08 46															
Manchester Airport ✈	a							08 53															
Handforth	d						08 55								09 19								09 56
Congleton	d																09 10						
Macclesfield	a		08 36		08 41				09 01								09 17		09 36		09 41		
	d		08 37		08 41				09 02								09 18		09 37		09 41		
Prestbury	d																09 22						
Adlington (Cheshire)	d																09 25						
Poynton	d																09 29						
Bramhall	d																09 31						
Cheadle Hulme	d						09 00								09 24		09 35						10 00
Stockport	a		08 49		08 54	08 59	09 06		09 13	09 16					09 28	09 36	09 39		09 49		09 54	09 58	10 06
	d	08 45	08 50	08 53	08 56	08 59	09 06		09 14	09 17	09 17	09 20	09 25	09 30	09 29	09 37	09 40	09 46	09 50	09 53	09 55	09 58	10 06
Heaton Chapel	d											09 24			09 32		09 43						
Levenshulme	d										09 24				09 35			09 50					
Manchester Picc. ■ 85,89 ⇌	a	08 55	08 59	09 02	09 04	09 13	09 17	09 21	09 25	09 27	09 31	09 34	09 37	09 40	09 43	09 45	09 53	09 56	09 59	10 02	10 05	10 13	10 17
Manchester Oxford Road 85,89	a	08 59					09 21	09 25					09 41										10 20
Deansgate 85,89 ⇌	a	09 02						09 32															

		NT ◇ E	XC ◇■ F ⊥	VT ◇■ ⊠	NT ◇ G	NT J	EM ◇ M	NT H	NT	VT ◇■ ⊠	NT	NT J	XC ◇■ C ⊥	TP ◇■ B ⊥	VT ◇■ ⊠	AW ■ L ⊥	NT D	XC ◇■ N ⊥	NT ◇ E	VT ◇■ ⊠	NT ◇ G	NT J
London Euston ■ ⊖65	d			08 20						08 40					09 00					09 20		
Birmingham New Street ■ 68	d		08 57										09 31					09 57				
Wolverhampton ■ 68 ⇌	d		09 15										09 49					10 15				
Stafford 65,67	d		09 28										10 02					10 28				
Stoke-on-Trent 50	d		09 44	09 48							09 56		10 20		10 25			10 44		10 48		
Longport 50	d																					
Kidsgrove 50	d										10 03											
Crewe ■	d	09 16							09 48	10 12						10 30			10 16			
Sandbach	d	09 23							09 55										10 23			
Holmes Chapel	d	09 28							10 00										10 28			
Goostrey	d								10 03													
Chelford	d								10 08													
Alderley Edge	d	09 38							10 13								10 49		10 38			
Wilmslow	d	09 42							10 16	10 27						10 48	10 52		10 42			
Styal	d	09 46																	10 45			
Manchester Airport ✈	a	09 53																	10 53			
Handforth	d								10 19								10 55					
Congleton	d										10 10											
Macclesfield	a		10 01								10 17		10 36		10 41			11 01				
	d		10 02								10 18		10 37		10 41			11 02				
Prestbury	d										10 22											
Adlington (Cheshire)	d										10 25											
Poynton	d										10 29											
Bramhall	d										10 31											
Cheadle Hulme	d								10 24		10 35						10 59					
Stockport	a		10 13	10 16					10 28	10 36	10 39		10 49		10 54	10 58	11 05	11 13		11 16		
	d		10 14	10 17	10 18	10 21	10 25	10 30	10 29	10 37	10 40	10 45	10 50	10 53	10 56	10 58	11 06	11 14		11 17	11 17	11 20
Heaton Chapel	d					10 25			10 32		10 43											11 24
Levenshulme	d					10 28			10 35			10 50										11 27
Manchester Picc. ■ 85,89 ⇌	a	10 21	10 25	10 28	10 30	10 36	10 37	10 40	10 43	10 46	10 52	10 56	11 00	11 02	11 05	11 13	11 17	11 24	11 25	11 28	11 30	11 36
Manchester Oxford Road 85,89	a	10 24					10 41										11 20		11 28			
Deansgate 85,89 ⇌	a	10 32																	11 32			

A From Buxton to Manchester Victoria
B From Cleethorpes to Manchester Airport
C From Cardiff Central
D To Wigan North Western
E To Liverpool Lime Street
F From Southampton Central
G From Chester
H From Hazel Grove
I From Nottingham to Liverpool Lime Street
J From Buxton
K From Bristol Temple Meads
L From Carmarthen
M From Norwich to Liverpool Lime Street
N From Bournemouth

Table T084-F

Mondays to Fridays

21 May to 7 December

Stoke-on-Trent and Crewe - Manchester Airport, Stockport and Manchester

	EM	NT	NT	VT	NT	NT	XC	TP	VT	AW	NT	NT	XC	VT	NT	NT	EM	NT	NT	VT	NT	NT
	◇			◇■			◇■	◇■	◇■	◇		◇	◇■	◇■	◇		◇			◇■		
	A	B				C	D	E		F	G	H	I		J	C	A	B				C
London Euston ⊖65 d				09 40					10 00					10 20						10 40		
Birmingham New Street 68 d							10 31						10 57									
Wolverhampton 68 d							10 49						11 15									
Stafford 65,67 d							11 03						11 28									
Stoke-on-Trent 50 d					10 56		11 20		11 25				11 44	11 48							11 56	
Longport 50 d																						
Kidsgrove 50 d					11 03																12 03	
Crewe d			10 48	11 12						11 30		11 17							11 48	12 12		
Sandbach d			10 55									11 24							11 55			
Holmes Chapel d			11 00									11 29							12 00			
Goostrey d			11 03																12 03			
Chelford d			11 08																12 08			
Alderley Edge d			11 13								11 49	11 38							12 13			
Wilmslow d			11 16	11 27						11 49	11 52	11 42							12 16	12 27		
Styal d												11 45										
Manchester Airport ✈ a												11 53										
Handforth d			11 19								11 56								12 19			
Congleton d					11 10																12 10	
Macclesfield a					11 17		11 36		11 41				12 01								12 17	
d					11 18		11 37		11 41				12 02								12 18	
Prestbury d					11 22																12 22	
Adlington (Cheshire) d					11 25																12 25	
Poynton d					11 29																12 28	
Bramhall d					11 31																12 31	
Cheadle Hulme d			11 24		11 35						12 00								12 24		12 35	
Stockport a			11 28	11 35	11 39		11 49		11 54	11 58	12 06		12 13	12 16					12 28	12 35	12 39	
d	11 25	11 30	11 29	11 36	11 40	11 45	11 50	11 53	11 56	11 58	12 06		12 14	12 17	12 17	12 20	12 25	12 30	12 29	12 36	12 40	12 45
Heaton Chapel d			11 32		11 43											12 24			12 32		12 43	
Levenshulme d			11 35			11 50										12 27			12 35			12 50
Manchester Picc. 85,89 a	11 37	11 40	11 43	11 46	11 52	11 56	11 59	12 02	12 05	12 13	12 17	12 21	12 25	12 28	12 30	12 36	12 37	12 40	12 43	12 46	12 52	12 56
Manchester Oxford Road 85,89 a	11 41										12 20	12 24					12 41					
Deansgate 85,89 a												12 32										

	XC	TP	VT	AW	NT	NT	XC	VT	NT	NT	EM	NT	NT	VT	NT	NT	XC	TP	VT	AW	NT
	◇■	◇■	◇■	■		◇	■	◇■	◇		◇			◇■			◇■	◇■	◇■	■	
	K	E		F	G	H	I		J	C	L	B				C	K	E		M	G
London Euston ⊖65 d			11 00					11 20						11 40					12 00		
Birmingham New Street 68 d	11 31						11 57										12 31				
Wolverhampton 68 d	11 49						12 15										12 49				
Stafford 65,67 d	12 03						12 28										13 03				
Stoke-on-Trent 50 d	12 20		12 25				12 44	12 48							12 58		13 20		13 25		
Longport 50 d																					
Kidsgrove 50 d															13 05						
Crewe d				12 30		12 17							12 48	13 12						13 30	
Sandbach d						12 24							12 55								
Holmes Chapel d						12 29							13 00								
Goostrey d													13 03								
Chelford d													13 08								
Alderley Edge d					12 49	12 38							13 13								13 49
Wilmslow d				12 49	12 52	12 42							13 16	13 27						13 49	13 52
Styal d						12 46															
Manchester Airport ✈ a						12 53															
Handforth d					12 56								13 19								13 56
Congleton d															13 12						
Macclesfield a	12 36		12 41				13 01								13 19		13 36		13 41		
d	12 37		12 41				13 02								13 20		13 37		13 41		
Prestbury d															13 24						
Adlington (Cheshire) d															13 27						
Poynton d															13 30						
Bramhall d															13 33						
Cheadle Hulme d					13 00								13 24		13 37						14 00
Stockport a	12 49		12 55	12 58	13 06		13 12	13 16					13 28	13 35			13 49		13 54	13 58	14 06
d	12 50	12 53	12 56	12 58	13 06		13 13	13 17	13 17	13 20	13 25	13 30	13 29	13 36		13 46	13 50	13 53	13 56	13 58	14 06
Heaton Chapel d										13 24			13 32								
Levenshulme d										13 27			13 35								
Manchester Picc. 85,89 a	12 59	13 02	13 05	13 13	13 17	13 21	13 25	13 28	13 30	13 36	13 37	13 40	13 43	13 46	13 54	13 56	13 59	14 02	14 05	14 13	14 17
Manchester Oxford Road 85,89 a					13 20	13 24					13 41										14 20
Deansgate 85,89 a						13 32															

A From Norwich to Liverpool Lime Street
B From Hazel Grove
C From Buxton
D From Paignton
E From Cleethorpes to Manchester Airport
F From Milford Haven
G To Wigan North Western
H To Liverpool Lime Street
I From Bournemouth
J From Chester
K From Bristol Temple Meads
L until 31 August, from 8 October. From Norwich to Liverpool Lime Street
M From Fishguard Harbour

Table T084-F

Mondays to Fridays

21 May to 7 December

Stoke-on-Trent and Crewe - Manchester Airport, Stockport and Manchester

	NT	XC	VT	NT	NT	EM	NT	NT	VT	NT	NT	XC	TP	VT	AW	NT	NT	XC	VT	NT	NT	EM
	◇	◇■	◇■	◇		◇			◇■			◇■	◇■	◇■	■		◇	◇■	◇■	◇		◇
	A	B		C	D	E	F				D	G	H		I	J	A	B		C	D	E
London Euston ⊖65 d			12 20						12 40					13 00					13 20			
Birmingham New Street 68 d		12 57										13 31						13 57				
Wolverhampton 68 d		13 15										13 49						14 15				
Stafford 65,67 d		13 28										14 03						14 28				
Stoke-on-Trent 50 d		13 44	13 48							13 56		14 20		14 25				14 44	14 48			
Longport 50 d																						
Kidsgrove 50 d										14 03												
Crewe d	13 18							13 48	14 12						14 30		14 16					
Sandbach d	13 25							13 55									14 23					
Holmes Chapel d	13 30							14 00									14 28					
Goostrey d								14 03														
Chelford d								14 08														
Alderley Edge d	13 39							14 13								14 49	14 38					
Wilmslow d	13 43							14 16	14 27						14 49	14 52	14 42					
Styal d	13 46																14 46					
Manchester Airport ✈ a	13 54																14 53					
Handforth d								14 19								14 56						
Congleton d										14 10												
Macclesfield a		14 01								14 17		14 36		14 41				15 01				
d		14 02								14 18		14 37		14 41				15 02				
Prestbury d										14 22												
Adlington (Cheshire) d										14 25												
Poynton d										14 29												
Bramhall d										14 31												
Cheadle Hulme d								14 24		14 35						15 00						
Stockport a		14 13	14 16					14 28	14 35	14 39		14 49		14 54	14 58	15 06		15 13	15 16			
d		14 14	14 17	14 17	14 20	14 25	14 30	14 29	14 36	14 40	14 45	14 50	14 53	14 56	14 58	15 06		15 14	15 17	15 17	15 20	15 25
Heaton Chapel d					14 24			14 32		14 43											15 24	
Levenshulme d					14 27			14 35			14 50										15 27	
Manchester Picc. 85,89 a	14 21	14 25	14 28	14 30	14 36	14 37	14 40	14 43	14 46	14 52	14 56	14 59	15 02	15 05	15 13	15 17	15 21	15 25	15 28	15 30	15 36	15 37
Manchester Oxford Road 85,89 a	14 24					14 41										15 20	15 24					15 41
Deansgate 85,89 a	14 32																15 32					

	NT	NT	VT	NT	NT	XC	TP	VT	AW	NT	NT	XC	VT	NT	NT	EM	NT	NT	VT	NT	NT	XC
			◇■			◇■	◇■	◇■	◇		◇	◇■	◇■	◇		◇			◇■			◇■
	F				D	K	H		L	J	A	B		C	D	E	F				D	M
London Euston ⊖65 d			13 40					14 00					14 20						14 40			
Birmingham New Street 68 d						14 31						14 57										15 31
Wolverhampton 68 d						14 49						15 15										15 49
Stafford 65,67 d						15 03						15 28										16 03
Stoke-on-Trent 50 d				14 56		15 20		15 25				15 44	15 48							15 56		16 20
Longport 50 d																						
Kidsgrove 50 d				15 03																16 03		
Crewe d		14 48	15 11						15 30		15 07							15 48	16 12			
Sandbach d		14 55									15 23							15 55				
Holmes Chapel d		15 00									15 28							16 00				
Goostrey d		15 03																16 03				
Chelford d		15 08																16 08				
Alderley Edge d		15 13								15 49	15 38							16 13				
Wilmslow d		15 16	15 27						15 49	15 52	15 42							16 16	16 27			
Styal d											15 46											
Manchester Airport ✈ a											15 53											
Handforth d		15 19								15 56								16 19				
Congleton d				15 10																16 10		
Macclesfield a				15 17		15 36		15 41				16 01								16 17		16 36
d				15 18		15 37		15 41				16 02								16 18		16 37
Prestbury d				15 22																16 22		
Adlington (Cheshire) d				15 25																16 25		
Poynton d				15 29																16 29		
Bramhall d				15 31																16 31		
Cheadle Hulme d		15 24		15 35						16 00								16 24		16 35		
Stockport a		15 28	15 35	15 39		15 49		15 54	15 58	16 06		16 13	16 16					16 28	16 35	16 39		16 49
d	15 30	15 29	15 36	15 40	15 45	15 50	15 53	15 56	15 58	16 06		16 14	16 17	16 17	16 20	16 25	16 30	16 29	16 36	16 40	16 45	16 50
Heaton Chapel d		15 32		15 43											16 24			16 32		16 43		
Levenshulme d		15 35			15 50										16 27			16 35			16 50	
Manchester Picc. 85,89 a	15 40	15 43	15 46	15 52	15 56	15 59	16 02	16 05	16 13	16 17	16 21	16 25	16 28	16 30	16 36	16 37	16 40	16 43	16 46	16 52	16 56	16 59
Manchester Oxford Road 85,89 a										16 20	16 24					16 41						
Deansgate 85,89 a											16 32											

A To Liverpool Lime Street
B From Bournemouth
C From Chester
D From Buxton
E From Norwich to Liverpool Lime Street
F From Hazel Grove
G From Paignton
H From Cleethorpes to Manchester Airport
I From Milford Haven
J To Wigan North Western
K From Bristol Temple Meads
L From Carmarthen
M From Penzance

Stoke-on-Trent and Crewe - Manchester Airport, Stockport and Manchester

	TP	VT	AW	NT	NT	XC	VT	NT	NT	EM	NT	NT	VT	NT	NT	XC	TP	VT	AW	NT	NT
	◇ A	◇	B	C	◇ D	◇ E	◇	◇ F	G	◇ H	I		◇		G	◇ J	◇ A	◇	K	C	◇
London Euston ⊖65 d		15 00					15 20						15 40					16 00			
Birmingham New Street 68 d						15 57										16 31					
Wolverhampton 68 d						16 15										16 49					
Stafford 65,67 d						16 28										17 03					
Stoke-on-Trent 50 d		16 25				16 44	16 48							16 56		17 20		17 25			
Longport 50 d																					
Kidsgrove 50 d														17 03							
Crewe d			16 30		16 16							16 48	17 12						17 30		17 16
Sandbach d					16 23							16 55									17 23
Holmes Chapel d					16 28							17 00									17 28
Goostrey d												17 03									
Chelford d												17 08									
Alderley Edge d				16 49	16 38							17 13								17 49	17 38
Wilmslow d			16 49	16 52	16 42							17 16	17 27						17 49	17 52	17 42
Styal d					16 46																17 46
Manchester Airport a					16 53																17 53
Handforth d				16 56								17 19								17 56	
Congleton d														17 10							
Macclesfield a		16 41				17 01	17 05							17 17		17 36		17 41			
d		16 41				17 02	17 06							17 18		17 37		17 41			
Prestbury d														17 22							
Adlington (Cheshire) d														17 25							
Poynton d														17 29							
Bramhall d														17 31							
Cheadle Hulme d				17 00								17 24		17 35						18 00	
Stockport a		16 54	16 59	17 06		17 13	17 17					17 28	17 36	17 39		17 49		17 54	17 58	18 06	
d	16 53	16 56	16 59	17 06		17 14	17 18	17 16	17 20	17 25	17 30	17 29	17 37	17 40	17 45	17 50	17 53	17 56	17 58	18 06	
Heaton Chapel d									17 24			17 32		17 43							
Levenshulme d									17 27			17 35			17 50						
Manchester Picc. 85,89 a	17 02	17 05	17 13	17 17	17 21	17 25	17 28	17 30	17 36	17 37	17 40	17 43	17 46	17 52	17 56	17 59	18 02	18 05	18 13	18 17	18 22
Manchester Oxford Road 85,89 a					17 25					17 41										18 21	
Deansgate 85,89 a				17 22	17 32																

	XC	VT	NT	NT	EM	NT	NT	VT	NT	NT	XC	TP	VT	AW	NT	NT	XC	VT	NT	NT	EM	NT
	◇ E	◇	F	G	◇ H	I		◇		G	◇ L	◇ A	◇	B	M	◇	◇ E	◇	F	I	◇ H	
London Euston ⊖65 d		16 20						16 40					17 00					17 20				
Birmingham New Street 68 d	16 57										17 31						17 57					
Wolverhampton 68 d	17 15										17 49						18 15					
Stafford 65,67 d	17 28										18 03						18 28					
Stoke-on-Trent 50 d	17 44	17 48							17 56		18 20		18 25				18 44	18 48				
Longport 50 d																						
Kidsgrove 50 d									18 03													
Crewe d							17 48	18 11						18 30		18 17						18 48
Sandbach d							17 55									18 24						18 55
Holmes Chapel d							18 00									18 29						19 00
Goostrey d							18 03															19 03
Chelford d							18 08															19 08
Alderley Edge d							18 13								18 49	18 39						19 13
Wilmslow d							18 16	18 27						18 49	18 52	18 42						19 16
Styal d																18 46						
Manchester Airport a																18 53						
Handforth d							18 19								18 56							19 19
Congleton d									18 10													
Macclesfield a	18 01								18 17		18 36		18 41				19 01					
d	18 02								18 18		18 37		18 41				19 02					
Prestbury d									18 22													
Adlington (Cheshire) d									18 25													
Poynton d									18 29													
Bramhall d									18 31													
Cheadle Hulme d							18 24		18 35						19 00							19 24
Stockport a	18 13	18 16					18 28	18 36	18 39		18 49		18 54	18 58	19 06		19 13	19 16				19 28
d	18 14	18 17	18 17	18 20	18 25	18 30	18 29	18 37	18 40	18 45	18 50	18 53	18 56	18 58	19 06		19 14	19 17	19 17	19 20	19 25	19 29
Heaton Chapel d				18 24			18 32		18 43											19 24		
Levenshulme d				18 27			18 35			18 50										19 27		
Manchester Picc. 85,89 a	18 25	18 27	18 30	18 36	18 37	18 40	18 43	18 48	18 54	18 56	18 59	19 02	19 05	19 13	19 17	19 21	19 24	19 28	19 30	19 36	19 37	19 39
Manchester Oxford Road 85,89 a					18 41										19 20						19 41	
Deansgate 85,89 a																						

A From Cleethorpes to Manchester Airport
B From Milford Haven
C To Southport
D To Liverpool Lime Street
E From Bournemouth
F From Chester
G From Buxton
H From Norwich to Liverpool Lime Street
I From Hazel Grove
J From Bristol Temple Meads
K From Carmarthen
L From Paignton
M To Wigan North Western

Table T084-F

Mondays to Fridays
21 May to 7 December

Stoke-on-Trent and Crewe - Manchester Airport, Stockport and Manchester

	VT	NT	NT	XC	TP	VT	NT	AW	NT	XC	VT	NT	NT	EM	NT	VT	NT	XC	TP	VT	AW
	◇	◇	A	◇ B	◇ C	◇	D	E	F	◇ G	◇	H	I	◇ J	◇	◇	◇	◇ K	◇ C		L
London Euston ⊖65 d	17 40					18 00					18 20					18 40				19 00	
Birmingham New Street 68 d				18 31						18 57								19 31			
Wolverhampton 68 d				18 49						19 15								19 49			
Stafford 65,67 d				19 03						19 28								20 03			
Stoke-on-Trent 50 d		18 58		19 20		19 25				19 44	19 48						19 58	20 20		20 25	
Longport 50 d																					
Kidsgrove 50 d		19 05															20 05				
Crewe d	19 12							19 37							19 48	20 18					20 24
Sandbach d															19 55						
Holmes Chapel d															20 00						
Goostrey d															20 03						
Chelford d															20 08						
Alderley Edge d							19 48								20 13						
Wilmslow d	19 27						19 51	19 57	19 43						20 16	20 33					20 41
Styal d									19 46												
Manchester Airport a									19 54												
Handforth d							19 54								20 19						
Congleton d		19 12															20 12				
Macclesfield a		19 19		19 36		19 41				20 01							20 19	20 36			
d		19 20		19 37		19 41				20 02							20 20	20 37			
Prestbury d		19 24															20 24				
Adlington (Cheshire) d		19 27															20 27				
Poynton d		19 30															20 30				
Bramhall d		19 33															20 33				
Cheadle Hulme d		19 37					19 58								20 24		20 37				
Stockport a	19 36	19 41		19 49		19 54	20 05	20 04		20 13	20 16				20 28	20 42	20 41	20 48		20 53	20 52
d	19 37	19 42	19 46	19 50	19 53	19 56	20 05	20 05		20 14	20 17	20 17	20 20	20 25	20 29	20 43	20 42	20 49	20 52	20 54	20 52
Heaton Chapel d													20 24		20 32						
Levenshulme d															20 35						
Manchester Picc. 85,89 a	19 45	19 54	19 56	19 59	20 02	20 05	20 17	20 19	20 21	20 25	20 28	20 30	20 35	20 37	20 43	20 52	20 57	20 59	21 01	21 05	21 09
Manchester Oxford Road 85,89 a							20 20		20 24					20 41							
Deansgate 85,89 a									20 32												

	VT ThFO	NT	NT	NT	XC	VT	NT	EM	NT	NT	VT	NT	XC	VT	TP	AW	NT	NT	XC	NT	NT	NT
	◇	A	F	M	◇ G		◇ H	◇ N	◇	I	◇	◇	◇ B	◇	◇ O	◇ E	F	A	◇ G	H	I	◇
London Euston ⊖65 d	18 57					19 20					19 40			20 00								
Birmingham New Street 68 d					19 57								20 31						20 57			
Wolverhampton 68 d					20 15								20 49						21 15			
Stafford 65,67 d					20 28						21 04		21 03						21 29			
Stoke-on-Trent 50 d					20 44	20 50						20 58	21 20	21 26					21 46			
Longport 50 d																						
Kidsgrove 50 d												21 05										
Crewe d	20s33								20 48		21 23					21 35						21 48
Sandbach d									20 55													21 56
Holmes Chapel d									21 00													22 01
Goostrey d									21 03													22 04
Chelford d									21 08													22 09
Alderley Edge d				20 52					21 13													22 14
Wilmslow d			20 43	20 55					21 16		21 38					21 52	21 34					22 17
Styal d			20 46														21 37					
Manchester Airport a			20 54														21 45					
Handforth d				20 58					21 19													22 20
Congleton d												21 12										
Macclesfield a					21 01	21 06						21 19	21 36	21 41					22 02			
d					21 02	21 07						21 20	21 37	21 42					22 03			
Prestbury d												21 24										
Adlington (Cheshire) d												21 27										
Poynton d												21 30										
Bramhall d												21 33										
Cheadle Hulme d				21 02					21 24			21 37										22 25
Stockport a				21 08	21 13	21 19			21 28			21 41	21 49	21 54		22 01			22 15			22 29
d		21 05		21 09	21 14	21 20	21 17	21 25	21 29	21 34		21 42	21 50	21 55	21 58	22 02		22 06	22 16	22 18	22 22	22 30
Heaton Chapel d							21 20		21 32			21 45									22 25	22 33
Levenshulme d							21 24		21 35			21 49									22 28	22 36
Manchester Picc. 85,89 a	21 09	21 15	21 17	21 25	21 25	21 28	21 31	21 36	21 43	21 46	21 54	21 58	21 59	22 04	22 09	22 15	22 17	22 17	22 25	22 32	22 35	22 43
Manchester Oxford Road 85,89 a			21 20	21 29													22 20					
Deansgate 85,89 a			21 31														22 33					

A From Buxton
B From Bristol Temple Meads
C From Cleethorpes to Manchester Airport
D To Wigan North Western
E From Carmarthen
F To Liverpool Lime Street
G From Bournemouth
H From Chester
I From Hazel Grove
J From Norwich to Liverpool Lime Street
K From Exeter St Davids
L From Milford Haven
M To Southport
N From Norwich
O From Cleethorpes

Table T084-F

Stoke-on-Trent and Crewe - Manchester Airport, Stockport and Manchester

Mondays to Fridays
21 May to 7 December

	VT	TP	NT	VT	NT	XC	NT	NT	NT	NT	VT	AW	NT	NT	XC	AW	VT
	◇■	◇■ A	B	◇■	C	◇■ D	◇	◇ E	F	G	◇■	◇ H	B		◇■	◇ I	◇■
London Euston ⊖65 d	20 40			21 00							21 40						23 00
Birmingham New Street 68 d						21 57									22 30	21 25	
Wolverhampton 68 d						22 15									22 48	21 42	
Stafford 65,67 d						22 28									23 01		
Stoke-on-Trent 50 d				22 28		22 44	22 20				23 08				23 20		01s18
Longport 50 d																	
Kidsgrove 50 d							22 27										
Crewe d	22 11											23 06		23 12			
Sandbach d														23 19			
Holmes Chapel d														23 24			
Goostrey d														23 27			
Chelford d														23 32			
Alderley Edge d														23 37			
Wilmslow d	22 27				22 35					23 10		23 23		23 40			
Styal d					22 38												
Manchester Airport a					22 46					23 18							
Handforth d														23 43			
Congleton d							22 34										
Macclesfield a				22 44		23 01	22 41				23 24						01s34
d				22 44		23 02	22 49				23 24						
Prestbury d							22 53										
Adlington (Cheshire) d							22 56										
Poynton d							22 59										
Bramhall d							23 02										
Cheadle Hulme d							23 05							23 48			
Stockport a	22 36			22 58		23 13	23 09				23 38	23 32		23 52			01s48
d	22 37	22 52	22 56	22 59		23 14	23 13	23 17	23 20		23 39	23 32	23 45	23 53			
Heaton Chapel d							23 16		23 23					23 56			
Levenshulme d							23 19		23 26					23 59			
Manchester Picc. 85,89 a	22 46	23 01	23 05	23 08	23 20	23 25	23 30	23 31	23 35	23 41	23 49	23 50	23 56	00 06	00 11	00 25	01 59
Manchester Oxford Road 85,89 a					23 24					23 45							
Deansgate 85,89 a					23 27												

Saturdays
26 May to 8 December

	NT	NT	NT	NT	NT	NT	NT	NT	TP	AW	NT	NT	XC	NT	NT	EM	NT	NT	NT	NT	XC	TP
	E	J		C	F			B	◇■ K		L	C	◇■	E	B	◇ M	F	◇	◇	B	◇■	◇■ A
London Euston ⊖65 d																						
Birmingham New Street 68 d													05 57								06 31	
Wolverhampton 68 d													06 15								06 49	
Stafford 65,67 d													06 28								07 03	
Stoke-on-Trent 50 d													06 45						06 58		07 20	
Longport 50 d																						
Kidsgrove 50 d																			07 05			
Crewe d			00 44			05 44				06 27		06 16						06 48				
Sandbach d						05 51						06 23						06 55				
Holmes Chapel d						05 56						06 28						07 00				
Goostrey d						06 00												07 03				
Chelford d						06 05												07 08				
Alderley Edge d						06 09					06 49	06 38						07 13				
Wilmslow d				05 42		06 13				06 45	06 52	06 42						07 16				
Styal d				05 45								06 46										
Manchester Airport a			01 09	05 53								06 54										
Handforth d						06 16					06 55							07 19				
Congleton d													06 58						07 12			
Macclesfield a													07 05						07 19		07 36	
d							06 16						07 06						07 20		07 37	
Prestbury d							06 20												07 24			
Adlington (Cheshire) d							06 23												07 27			
Poynton d							06 27												07 30			
Bramhall d							06 30												07 33			
Cheadle Hulme d						06 20	06 34				06 59							07 24	07 37			
Stockport a						06 25	06 38			06 55	07 06		07 18					07 29	07 41		07 49	
d	00 13	00 26			06 20	06 27	06 39	06 45	06 53	06 55	07 06		07 19	07 17	07 21	07 26	07 30	07 29	07 42	07 46	07 50	07 53
Heaton Chapel d						06 31	06 42								07 25			07 33				
Levenshulme d						06 34	06 45								07 28			07 36				
Manchester Picc. 85,89 a	00 26	00 35	01 28	06 20	06 29	06 44	06 55	06 56	07 02	07 07	07 16	07 21	07 28	07 32	07 36	07 39	07 40	07 43	07 53	07 56	07 59	08 02
Manchester Oxford Road 85,89 a				06 24							07 19	07 24				07 42						
Deansgate 85,89 a				06 31							07 22	07 32										

A From Cleethorpes to Manchester Airport
B From Buxton
C To Liverpool Lime Street
D From Bournemouth
E From Chester
F From Hazel Grove
G To Manchester Victoria
H From Cardiff Central
I From Birmingham International
J From Sheffield
K From Doncaster to Manchester Airport
L To Wigan North Western
M From Nottingham to Liverpool Lime Street

Table T084-F

Stoke-on-Trent and Crewe - Manchester Airport, Stockport and Manchester

Saturdays
26 May to 8 December

	AW	NT	NT	NT	XC	NT	EM	NT	NT	VT	NT	NT	XC	TP	VT	AW	NT	NT	XC	VT	NT	NT
	◇ A	B	C	◇ D	◇■	E	◇ F	G		◇■	◇	E	◇■	◇■ H	◇■	◇ A	B	◇ D	◇■ I	◇■	◇ C	G
London Euston ⊖65 d										06 36					06 55					07 20		
Birmingham New Street 68 d					06 57								07 31						07 57			
Wolverhampton 68 d					07 15								07 49						08 15			
Stafford 65,67 d					07 31								08 03						08 28			
Stoke-on-Trent 50 d											07 56		08 20		08 25				08 44	08 48		
Longport 50 d											08 00											
Kidsgrove 50 d											08 05											
Crewe d	07 27			07 13	07 52				07 55	08 11						08 28		08 16				
Sandbach d				07 20					08 02									08 23				
Holmes Chapel d				07 25					08 07									08 28				
Goostrey d				07 29																		
Chelford d				07 34																		
Alderley Edge d		07 49		07 39					08 16								08 49	08 38				
Wilmslow d	07 44	07 52		07 42	08 08				08 20	08 27						08 45	08 52	08 42				
Styal d				07 46														08 46				
Manchester Airport a				07 53														08 53				
Handforth d		07 55							08 23								08 55					
Congleton d											08 12											
Macclesfield a											08 19		08 36		08 41				09 01			
d											08 19		08 37		08 41				09 02			
Prestbury d											08 23											
Adlington (Cheshire) d											08 26											
Poynton d											08 30											
Bramhall d											08 33											
Cheadle Hulme d		07 59							08 27		08 37						09 00					
Stockport a	07 58	08 05			08 16				08 32	08 35	08 41		08 50		08 54	08 59	09 06		09 13	09 16		
d	07 58	08 06	08 09		08 16	08 20	08 25	08 30	08 32	08 36	08 42	08 45	08 51	08 53	08 56	08 59	09 06		09 14	09 17	09 17	09 20
Heaton Chapel d						08 24																09 24
Levenshulme d						08 27																09 27
Manchester Picc. 85,89 a	08 10	08 16	08 18	08 21	08 29	08 36	08 37	08 40	08 43	08 46	08 54	08 56	08 59	09 02	09 04	09 13	09 17	09 21	09 25	09 28	09 31	09 34
Manchester Oxford Road 85,89 a		08 20		08 24			08 41										09 21	09 25				
Deansgate 85,89 a				08 32														09 32				

	EM	NT	NT	VT	NT	NT	XC	TP	VT	AW	NT	NT	XC	VT	NT	NT	EM	NT	NT	VT	NT
	◇ F	G		◇■		E	◇■ J	◇■ H	◇■	◇ K	B	◇ D	◇■ I	◇■	◇ C	E	◇ L	G		◇■	
London Euston ⊖65 d				07 35					08 00					08 20						08 40	
Birmingham New Street 68 d							08 31						08 57								
Wolverhampton 68 d							08 49						09 15								
Stafford 65,67 d							09 03						09 28								
Stoke-on-Trent 50 d					08 56		09 20		09 25				09 44	09 48							09 56
Longport 50 d																					
Kidsgrove 50 d					09 03																10 03
Crewe d			08 48	09 12						09 30		09 16							09 48	10 12	
Sandbach d			08 55									09 23							09 55		
Holmes Chapel d			09 00									09 28							10 00		
Goostrey d			09 03																10 03		
Chelford d			09 08																10 08		
Alderley Edge d			09 13								09 49	09 38							10 13		
Wilmslow d			09 16	09 28						09 47	09 52	09 42							10 16	10 27	
Styal d												09 46									
Manchester Airport a												09 53									
Handforth d			09 19								09 56								10 19		
Congleton d					09 10																10 10
Macclesfield a					09 17		09 36		09 41				10 01								10 17
d					09 18		09 37		09 41				10 02								10 18
Prestbury d					09 22																10 22
Adlington (Cheshire) d					09 25																10 25
Poynton d					09 29																10 29
Bramhall d					09 31																10 31
Cheadle Hulme d			09 24		09 35						10 00								10 24		10 35
Stockport a			09 28	09 36	09 39		09 49		09 54	09 58	10 06		10 13	10 16					10 28	10 36	10 40
d	09 25	09 30	09 29	09 37	09 40	09 46	09 50	09 53	09 55	09 58	10 06		10 14	10 17	10 18	10 21	10 27	10 30	10 29	10 37	10 40
Heaton Chapel d			09 32		09 43											10 25			10 32		10 44
Levenshulme d			09 35			09 50										10 28			10 35		
Manchester Picc. 85,89 a	09 37	09 40	09 43	09 45	09 53	09 56	09 59	10 02	10 04	10 13	10 17	10 21	10 24	10 28	10 30	10 36	10 37	10 40	10 43	10 46	10 52
Manchester Oxford Road 85,89 a	09 41										10 20	10 24					10 41				
Deansgate 85,89 a												10 32									

A From Cardiff Central
B To Wigan North Western
C From Chester
D To Liverpool Lime Street
E From Buxton
F From Nottingham to Liverpool Lime Street
G From Hazel Grove
H From Cleethorpes to Manchester Airport
I From Southampton Central
J From Bristol Temple Meads
K From Carmarthen
L From Norwich to Liverpool Lime Street

Table T084-F

Saturdays

26 May to 8 December

Stoke-on-Trent and Crewe - Manchester Airport, Stockport and Manchester

	NT	XC	TP	VT	AW	NT	NT	XC	VT	NT	NT	EM	NT	NT	VT	NT	NT	XC	TP	VT	AW	NT
	A	◇■ B ✠	◇■ C ✠	◇■ ⎍	■ D ✠	E	◇ F	◇■ G ✠	◇■ ⎍	◇ H	A	◇ I	J		◇■ ⎍		A	◇■ K ✠	◇■ C ✠	◇■ ⎍	■ L ✠	E
London Euston ⊖65 d				09 00					09 20						09 40					10 00		
Birmingham New Street 68 d		09 31						09 57										10 31				
Wolverhampton 68 d		09 49						10 15										10 49				
Stafford 65,67 d		10 03						10 28										11 03				
Stoke-on-Trent 50 d		10 20		10 25				10 44	10 48							10 56		11 20		11 25		
Longport 50 d																						
Kidsgrove 50 d																11 03						
Crewe d					10 30		10 16							10 48	11 12						11 30	
Sandbach d							10 23							10 55								
Holmes Chapel d							10 28							11 00								
Goostrey d														11 03								
Chelford d														11 08								
Alderley Edge d						10 49	10 38							11 13								11 49
Wilmslow d					10 48	10 52	10 42							11 16	11 27						11 49	11 52
Styal d							10 45															
Manchester Airport ✈ a							10 53															
Handforth d						10 55								11 19								11 56
Congleton d																11 10						
Macclesfield a		10 36		10 41				11 01								11 17		11 36		11 41		
d		10 37		10 41				11 02								11 18		11 37		11 41		
Prestbury d																11 22						
Adlington (Cheshire) d																11 25						
Poynton d																11 29						
Bramhall d																11 31						
Cheadle Hulme d						10 59								11 24		11 35						12 00
Stockport a		10 49		10 54	10 58	11 05		11 13	11 16					11 28	11 35	11 39		11 49		11 54	11 58	12 06
d	10 45	10 50	10 53	10 56	10 58	11 06		11 14	11 17	11 17	11 20	11 26	11 30	11 29	11 36	11 40	11 45	11 50	11 53	11 56	11 58	12 06
Heaton Chapel d											11 24			11 32		11 43						
Levenshulme d	10 50										11 27			11 35			11 50					
Manchester Picc. 85,89 a	10 56	11 00	11 02	11 04	11 13	11 17	11 24	11 25	11 28	11 30	11 36	11 37	11 40	11 43	11 46	11 52	11 56	11 59	12 02	12 04	12 13	12 17
Manchester Oxford Road 85,89 a						11 20	11 28					11 41										12 20
Deansgate 85,89 a							11 31															

	NT	XC	VT	NT	NT	EM	NT	NT	VT	NT	NT	XC	TP	VT	AW	NT	NT	XC	VT	NT	NT
	◇ F	◇■ G ✠	◇■ ⎍	◇ H	A	◇ I	J		◇■ ⎍		A	◇■ M ✠	◇■ C ✠	◇■ ⎍	◇ L ✠	E	◇ F	◇■ G ✠	◇■ ⎍	◇ H	A
London Euston ⊖65 d			10 20						10 40					11 00					11 20		
Birmingham New Street 68 d		10 57										11 31						11 57			
Wolverhampton 68 d		11 15										11 49						12 15			
Stafford 65,67 d		11 28										12 03						12 28			
Stoke-on-Trent 50 d		11 44	11 48							11 56		12 20		12 25				12 44	12 48		
Longport 50 d																					
Kidsgrove 50 d										12 03											
Crewe d	11 17							11 48	12 12						12 30		12 17				
Sandbach d	11 24							11 55									12 24				
Holmes Chapel d	11 29							12 00									12 29				
Goostrey d								12 03													
Chelford d								12 08													
Alderley Edge d	11 38							12 13								12 49	12 38				
Wilmslow d	11 42							12 16	12 27						12 49	12 52	12 42				
Styal d	11 45																12 46				
Manchester Airport ✈ a	11 53																12 53				
Handforth d								12 19								12 56					
Congleton d										12 10											
Macclesfield a		12 01								12 17		12 36		12 41				13 01			
d		12 02								12 18		12 37		12 41				13 02			
Prestbury d										12 22											
Adlington (Cheshire) d										12 25											
Poynton d										12 28											
Bramhall d										12 31											
Cheadle Hulme d								12 24		12 35						13 00					
Stockport a		12 13	12 16					12 28	12 35	12 39		12 49		12 55	12 58	13 06		13 13	13 16		
d		12 14	12 17	12 17	12 20	12 26	12 30	12 29	12 36	12 40	12 45	12 50	12 53	12 56	12 58	13 06		13 14	13 17	13 17	13 20
Heaton Chapel d					12 24			12 32		12 43											13 24
Levenshulme d					12 27			12 35			12 50										13 27
Manchester Picc. 85,89 a	12 21	12 25	12 28	12 30	12 36	12 37	12 40	12 43	12 46	12 52	12 56	12 59	13 02	13 04	13 13	13 17	13 21	13 25	13 28	13 30	13 36
Manchester Oxford Road 85,89 a	12 24					12 41										13 20	13 24				
Deansgate 85,89 a	12 32																13 36				

A From Buxton
B From Cardiff Central
C From Cleethorpes to Manchester Airport
D From Carmarthen
E To Wigan North Western
F To Liverpool Lime Street
G From Bournemouth
H From Chester
I From Norwich to Liverpool Lime Street
J From Hazel Grove
K From Paignton
L From Milford Haven
M From Bristol Temple Meads

Table T084-F

Saturdays

26 May to 8 December

Stoke-on-Trent and Crewe - Manchester Airport, Stockport and Manchester

	EM	NT	NT	VT	NT	NT	XC	TP	VT	AW	NT	NT	XC	VT	NT	NT	EM	NT	NT	VT	NT	NT
	◇ A	B		◇■ ⎍	◇	C	◇■ D ✠	◇■ E ✠	◇■ ⎍	◇ F ✠	G	◇ H	◇■ I ✠	◇■ ⎍	◇ J	C	◇ A	B		◇■ ⎍	◇	C
London Euston ⊖65 d				11 40					12 00					12 20						12 40		
Birmingham New Street 68 d							12 31						12 57									
Wolverhampton 68 d							12 49						13 15									
Stafford 65,67 d							13 03						13 28									
Stoke-on-Trent 50 d					12 56		13 20		13 25				13 44	13 48							13 58	
Longport 50 d																						
Kidsgrove 50 d					13 03																14 05	
Crewe d			12 48	13 12						13 30		13 18							13 48	14 12		
Sandbach d			12 55									13 25							13 55			
Holmes Chapel d			13 00									13 30							14 00			
Goostrey d			13 03																14 03			
Chelford d			13 08																14 08			
Alderley Edge d			13 13								13 49	13 39							14 13			
Wilmslow d			13 16	13 27						13 47	13 52	13 43							14 16	14 27		
Styal d												13 46										
Manchester Airport ✈ a												13 54										
Handforth d			13 19								13 56								14 19			
Congleton d					13 10																14 12	
Macclesfield a					13 17		13 36		13 41				14 01								14 19	
d					13 18		13 37		13 41				14 02								14 20	
Prestbury d					13 22																14 24	
Adlington (Cheshire) d					13 25																14 27	
Poynton d					13 29																14 30	
Bramhall d					13 31																14 33	
Cheadle Hulme d			13 24		13 35						14 00								14 24			
Stockport a			13 28	13 35	13 39		13 49		13 54	13 58	14 06		14 13	14 16					14 28	14 35		
d	13 26	13 30	13 29	13 36	13 40	13 45	13 50	13 53	13 56	13 58	14 06		14 14	14 17	14 17	14 20	14 26	14 30	14 29	14 36		14 45
Heaton Chapel d			13 32		13 43											14 24			14 32		14 43	
Levenshulme d			13 35			13 50										14 27			14 35		14 46	
Manchester Picc. 85,89 a	13 37	13 40	13 43	13 46	13 52	13 56	13 59	14 02	14 05	14 14	14 17	14 21	14 25	14 28	14 30	14 36	14 37	14 40	14 43	14 46	14 52	14 56
Manchester Oxford Road 85,89 a	13 41										14 20	14 24					14 41					
Deansgate 85,89 a												14 32										

	XC	TP	VT	AW	NT	NT	XC	VT	NT	NT	EM	NT	NT	VT	NT	NT	XC	TP	VT	AW	NT	NT
	◇■ K ✠	◇■ E ✠	◇■ ⎍	■ L ✠	G	◇ H	◇■ I ✠	◇■ ⎍	◇ J	C	◇ A	B		◇■ ⎍		C	◇■ M ✠	◇■ E ✠	◇■ ⎍	■ N ✠	G	◇ H
London Euston ⊖65 d			13 00					13 20						13 40					14 00			
Birmingham New Street 68 d	13 31						13 57										14 31					
Wolverhampton 68 d	13 49						14 15										14 49					
Stafford 65,67 d	14 03						14 28										15 03					
Stoke-on-Trent 50 d	14 20		14 25				14 44	14 48							14 56		15 20		15 25			
Longport 50 d																						
Kidsgrove 50 d															15 03							
Crewe d				14 30		14 16							14 48	15 11						15 30		15 07
Sandbach d						14 23							14 55									15 23
Holmes Chapel d						14 28							15 00									15 28
Goostrey d													15 03									
Chelford d													15 08									
Alderley Edge d					14 49	14 38							15 13								15 49	15 38
Wilmslow d				14 47	14 52	14 42							15 16	15 27						15 47	15 52	15 42
Styal d						14 46																15 46
Manchester Airport ✈ a						14 53																15 53
Handforth d					14 56								15 19								15 56	
Congleton d															15 10							
Macclesfield a	14 36		14 41				15 01								15 17		15 36		15 41			
d	14 37		14 41				15 02								15 18		15 37		15 41			
Prestbury d															15 22							
Adlington (Cheshire) d															15 25							
Poynton d															15 29							
Bramhall d															15 31							
Cheadle Hulme d					15 00								15 24		15 35						16 00	
Stockport a	14 49		14 54	14 58	15 06		15 13	15 16					15 28	15 35	15 39		15 49		15 54	15 58	16 06	
d	14 50	14 53	14 56	14 59	15 06		15 14	15 17	15 17	15 20	15 26	15 30	15 29	15 36	15 40	15 45	15 50	15 53	15 56	15 59	16 06	
Heaton Chapel d										15 24			15 32		15 43							
Levenshulme d										15 27			15 35			15 50						
Manchester Picc. 85,89 a	14 59	15 03	15 05	15 15	15 17	15 21	15 25	15 28	15 30	15 36	15 37	15 40	15 43	15 46	15 52	15 56	15 59	16 02	16 05	16 15	16 17	16 21
Manchester Oxford Road 85,89 a					15 20	15 24					15 41										16 20	16 24
Deansgate 85,89 a						15 32																16 32

A From Norwich to Liverpool Lime Street
B From Hazel Grove
C From Buxton
D From Plymouth
E From Cleethorpes to Manchester Airport
F From Fishguard Harbour
G To Wigan North Western
H To Liverpool Lime Street
I From Bournemouth
J From Chester
K From Paignton
L From Milford Haven
M From Bristol Temple Meads
N From Carmarthen

Stoke-on-Trent and Crewe - Manchester Airport, Stockport and Manchester

	XC	VT	NT	NT	EM	NT	NT	VT	NT	NT	XC	TP	VT	AW	NT	NT	XC	VT	NT	NT	EM
	◇1	◇1	◇		◇			◇1	◇		◇1	◇1	◇1	■		◇	◇1	◇1	◇		◇
	A		B	C	D	E				C	F	G		H	I	J	A		B	C	D
	🛒	☕						☕			🛒	🛒	☕	🛒			🛒	☕			
London Euston 15 ⊖65 d		14 20						14 40					15 00					15 20			
Birmingham New Street 12 68 d	14 57										15 31						15 57				
Wolverhampton 7 68 d	15 15										15 49						16 15				
Stafford 65,67 d	15 28										16 03						16 28				
Stoke-on-Trent 50 d	15 44	15 48							15 58		16 20		16 25				16 44	16 48			
Longport 50 d																					
Kidsgrove 50 d									16 05												
Crewe 10 d							15 48	16 11						16 30		16 16					
Sandbach d							15 55									16 23					
Holmes Chapel d							16 00									16 28					
Goostrey d							16 03														
Chelford d							16 08														
Alderley Edge d							16 13								16 49	16 38					
Wilmslow d							16 16	16 27						16 47	16 52	16 42					
Styal d																16 46					
Manchester Airport ✈ a																16 53					
Handforth d							16 19								16 56						
Congleton d									16 12												
Macclesfield a	16 01								16 19		16 36		16 41				17 01				
d	16 02								16 20		16 37		16 41				17 02				
Prestbury d									16 24												
Adlington (Cheshire) d									16 27												
Poynton d									16 30												
Bramhall d									16 33												
Cheadle Hulme d							16 24		16 37						17 00						
Stockport a	16 13	16 16					16 28	16 36			16 49		16 54	16 59	17 06		17 13	17 16			
d	16 14	16 17	16 17	16 20	16 26	16 30	16 29	16 37		16 46	16 50	16 53	16 56	16 59	17 06		17 14	17 17	17 16	17 20	17 26
Heaton Chapel d				16 24			16 32													17 24	
Levenshulme d				16 27			16 35													17 27	
Manchester Picc. 10 85,89 a	16 25	16 28	16 30	16 36	16 37	16 40	16 43	16 46	16 54	16 56	16 59	17 02	17 04	17 14	17 17	17 21	17 25	17 28	17 30	17 36	17 37
Manchester Oxford Road 85,89 a					16 41											17 25					17 41
Deansgate 85,89 a															17 22	17 32					

	NT	NT	VT	NT	NT	XC	TP	VT	AW	NT	NT	XC	VT	NT	NT	EM	NT	NT	VT	NT	NT	XC
			◇1			◇1	◇1	◇1	◇		◇	◇1	◇1			◇			◇1			◇1
	E				C	K	G		L	I		A		B	C	D	E				C	M
			☕			🛒	🛒	☕	🛒			🛒	☕						☕			🛒
London Euston 15 ⊖65 d			15 40					16 00					16 20						16 40			
Birmingham New Street 12 68 d						16 31						16 57										17 31
Wolverhampton 7 68 d						16 49						17 15										17 49
Stafford 65,67 d						17 03						17 28										18 03
Stoke-on-Trent 50 d				16 56		17 20		17 25				17 44	17 48							17 56		18 20
Longport 50 d																						
Kidsgrove 50 d				17 03																18 03		
Crewe 10 d		16 48	17 12						17 30		17 16							17 48	18 11			
Sandbach d		16 55									17 23							17 55				
Holmes Chapel d		17 00									17 28							18 00				
Goostrey d		17 03																18 03				
Chelford d		17 08																18 08				
Alderley Edge d		17 13								17 49	17 38							18 13				
Wilmslow d		17 16	17 27						17 47	17 52	17 42							18 16	18 27			
Styal d											17 46											
Manchester Airport ✈ a											17 53											
Handforth d		17 19								17 56								18 19				
Congleton d				17 10																18 10		
Macclesfield a				17 17		17 36		17 41				18 01								18 17		18 36
d				17 18		17 37		17 41				18 02								18 18		18 37
Prestbury d				17 22																18 22		
Adlington (Cheshire) d				17 25																18 25		
Poynton d				17 29																18 29		
Bramhall d				17 31																18 31		
Cheadle Hulme d		17 24		17 35						18 00								18 24		18 35		
Stockport a		17 28	17 36	17 39		17 49		17 54	17 58	18 06		18 13	18 16					18 28	18 36	18 39		18 49
d	17 30	17 29	17 37	17 40	17 45	17 50	17 53	17 56	17 59	18 06		18 14	18 17	18 17	18 21	18 26	18 30	18 29	18 37	18 40	18 45	18 50
Heaton Chapel d		17 32		17 43											18 24			18 32		18 43		
Levenshulme d		17 35			17 50										18 27			18 35			18 50	
Manchester Picc. 10 85,89 a	17 40	17 43	17 46	17 51	17 56	17 59	18 02	18 04	18 15	18 17	18 22	18 25	18 27	18 30	18 36	18 37	18 40	18 43	18 45	18 54	18 56	18 59
Manchester Oxford Road 85,89 a										18 21						18 41						
Deansgate 85,89 a																						

A From Bournemouth
B From Chester
C From Buxton
D From Norwich to Liverpool Lime Street
E From Hazel Grove
F From Penzance
G From Cleethorpes to Manchester Airport
H From Milford Haven
I To Southport
J To Liverpool Lime Street
K From Bristol Temple Meads
L From Carmarthen
M From Paignton

Table T084-F

Saturdays

26 May to 8 December

Stoke-on-Trent and Crewe - Manchester Airport, Stockport and Manchester

	TP	VT	AW	NT	NT	XC	VT	NT	NT	EM	NT	VT	NT	NT	XC	TP	VT	AW	NT	NT	NT
	◇1	◇1	■		◇	◇1	◇1			◇		◇1	◇		◇1	◇1	◇1	■			
	A		B	C		D		E	F	G				H	I	A		J	C	E	K
	🛒	☕	🛒			🛒	☕					☕			🛒		☕	🛒			
London Euston 15 ⊖65 d		17 00					17 20					17 40					18 00				
Birmingham New Street 12 68 d						17 57									18 31						
Wolverhampton 7 68 d						18 15									18 49						
Stafford 65,67 d						18 28									19 03						
Stoke-on-Trent 50 d		18 25				18 44	18 48						18 58		19 20		19 25				
Longport 50 d																					
Kidsgrove 50 d													19 05								
Crewe 10 d			18 30		18 07						18 48	19 12						19 30			
Sandbach d					18 23						18 55										
Holmes Chapel d					18 28						19 00										
Goostrey d											19 03										
Chelford d											19 08										
Alderley Edge d				18 49	18 38						19 13								19 48		
Wilmslow d			18 47	18 52	18 42						19 16	19 27						19 47	19 51		19 43
Styal d					18 46																19 46
Manchester Airport ✈ a					18 54																19 54
Handforth d				18 56							19 19								19 54		
Congleton d													19 12								
Macclesfield a		18 41				19 01							19 19		19 36		19 41				
d		18 41				19 02							19 20		19 37		19 41				
Prestbury d													19 24								
Adlington (Cheshire) d													19 27								
Poynton d													19 30								
Bramhall d													19 33								
Cheadle Hulme d				19 00							19 24		19 37						19 58		
Stockport a		18 54	18 58	19 06		19 13	19 16				19 28	19 36	19 41		19 49		19 54	19 58	20 05		
d	18 53	18 56	18 58	19 06		19 14	19 17	19 17	19 20	19 26	19 29	19 37	19 42	19 46	19 50	19 52	19 56	19 58	20 05	20 09	
Heaton Chapel d									19 24		19 32										
Levenshulme d									19 27		19 35										
Manchester Picc. 10 85,89 a	19 02	19 05	19 15	19 17	19 21	19 24	19 28	19 30	19 36	19 37	19 43	19 45	19 54	19 56	19 59	20 03	20 04	20 15	20 17	20 18	20 21
Manchester Oxford Road 85,89 a				19 20						19 41									20 20		20 24
Deansgate 85,89 a																					20 32

	XC	VT	EM	NT	VT	NT	NT	XC	TP	VT	AW	NT	NT	XC	NT	NT	EM	VT	NT	NT	VT	NT
	◇1	◇1	◇	◇	◇1		◇	◇1	◇1	◇1	■			◇1		◇	◇	◇1		◇	◇1	◇
	D		G			F		L	A		B	H	K	D	M	E	N		F			
	🛒	☕			☕			🛒		☕	🛒							☕			☕	
London Euston 15 ⊖65 d		18 20			18 40					19 00								19 20			19 40	
Birmingham New Street 12 68 d	18 57							19 31						19 57								
Wolverhampton 7 68 d	19 15							19 49						20 15								
Stafford 65,67 d	19 28							20 03						20 28								
Stoke-on-Trent 50 d	19 44	19 48					19 58	20 20		20 25				20 44				20 48				20 58
Longport 50 d																						
Kidsgrove 50 d							20 05															21 05
Crewe 10 d				19 48	20 12						20 30									20 48	21 19	
Sandbach d				19 55																20 55		
Holmes Chapel d				20 00																21 00		
Goostrey d				20 03																21 03		
Chelford d				20 08																21 08		
Alderley Edge d				20 13											20 52					21 13		
Wilmslow d				20 16	20 28						20 47		20 43		20 55					21 16	21 34	
Styal d													20 46									
Manchester Airport ✈ a													20 54									
Handforth d				20 19											20 58					21 19		
Congleton d							20 12															21 12
Macclesfield a	20 01						20 19	20 36		20 41				21 01								21 19
d	20 02						20 20	20 37		20 41				21 02								21 20
Prestbury d							20 24															21 24
Adlington (Cheshire) d							20 27															21 27
Poynton d							20 30															21 30
Bramhall d							20 33															21 33
Cheadle Hulme d				20 24			20 37								21 02					21 24		21 37
Stockport a	20 13	20 16		20 28	20 36		20 41	20 49		20 54	20 59			21 13	21 08			21 20		21 28	21 44	21 41
d	20 14	20 17	20 26	20 29	20 37	20 32	20 42	20 50	20 52	20 56	20 59	21 05		21 14	21 09	21 16	21 20	21 21	21 32	21 29	21 45	21 42
Heaton Chapel d						20 36														21 32		21 45
Levenshulme d				20 33																21 35		21 49
Manchester Picc. 10 85,89 a	20 25	20 28	20 37	20 40	20 45	20 46	20 57	20 59	21 04	21 04	21 15	21 15	21 16	21 24	21 25	21 26	21 29	21 32	21 42	21 43	21 53	21 58
Manchester Oxford Road 85,89 a			20 41										21 19		21 29							
Deansgate 85,89 a													21 29									

A From Cleethorpes to Manchester Airport
B From Milford Haven
C To Wigan North Western
D From Bournemouth
E From Chester
F From Hazel Grove
G From Norwich to Liverpool Lime Street
H From Buxton
I From Bristol Temple Meads
J From Carmarthen
K To Liverpool Lime Street
L From Exeter St Davids
M To Southport
N From Norwich

Table T084-F

Saturdays
26 May to 8 December

Stoke-on-Trent and Crewe - Manchester Airport, Stockport and Manchester

	XC	TP	AW	NT	NT	NT	XC	NT	NT	VT	NT	TP	NT	XC	NT	VT	NT	AW	NT	NT	NT	XC
	◇■ A	◇■ B	◇ C	D	E	F	◇■ G	H	◇	◇■	E	◇■ I	D	◇■ J	◇ F	◇■	K	◇ L	◇	E		◇■
London Euston ⊖65 d										20 20						21 00						
Birmingham New Street 68 d	20 31						20 57							21 57								22 31
Wolverhampton 68 d	20 49						21 17							22 15								22 49
Stafford 65,67 d	21 03						21 30							22 28		22 34						23 02
Stoke-on-Trent 50 d	21 20						21 47			22 05				22 44					22 55			23 20
Longport 50 d																						
Kidsgrove 50 d																			23 02			
Crewe d			21 30						21 48							22 59		23 06			23 12	
Sandbach d									21 56												23 19	
Holmes Chapel d									22 01												23 24	
Goostrey d									22 04												23 27	
Chelford d									22 09												23 32	
Alderley Edge d									22 14												23 37	
Wilmslow d			21 47	21 37					22 17				22 39			23 15	23 20	23 24			23 40	
Styal d				21 40									22 42									
Manchester Airport ✈ a				21 48									22 50									
Handforth d									22 20												23 43	
Congleton d																			23 09			
Macclesfield a	21 36						22 04			22 21				23 01					23 16			23 38
d	21 37						22 05			22 21				23 02					23 17			23 39
Prestbury d																			23 21			
Adlington (Cheshire) d																			23 24			
Poynton d																			23 27			
Bramhall d																			23 30			
Cheadle Hulme d									22 25										23 33		23 48	
Stockport a	21 49		21 59				22 16		22 29	22 35				23 13		23 26		23 32	23 38		23 52	23 53
d	21 50	21 53	22 00		22 06	22 17	22 21	22 26	22 30	22 36	22 44	22 54		23 14	23 18	23 27		23 33	23 38	23 42	23 53	23 54
Heaton Chapel d								22 29	22 33		22 48										23 56	
Levenshulme d								22 32	22 36		22 51										23 59	
Manchester Picc. 85,89 a	21 59	22 04	22 14	22 17	22 17	22 28	22 33	22 39	22 43	22 50	23 00	23 03	23 20	23 29	23 31	23 39	23 41	23 49	23 49	23 57	00 06	00 10
Manchester Oxford Road 85,89 a				22 20									23 24				23 45					
Deansgate 85,89 a				22 33									23 27									

Sundays
20 May to 9 September

	NT	TP	NT	AW	NT	NT	NT	TP	AW	NT	NT	NT	XC	NT	VT	NT	VT	AW	NT	NT	XC	EM
	M	◇■ N	E		D	◇	E	◇■ N		H	D	◇ F	◇■	◇	◇■	E	◇■	◇ O	D	◇	◇■	◇ P
London Euston ⊖65 d															08 10		08 20					
Birmingham New Street 68 d													09 01								10 01	
Wolverhampton 68 d													09 19								10 19	
Stafford 65,67 d													09 33								10 33	
Stoke-on-Trent 50 d													09 52				10 21			10 30	10 52	
Longport 50 d																						
Kidsgrove 50 d																				10 37		
Crewe d				08 28		08 56			09 28					09 56	10 19			10 28				
Sandbach d						09 03								10 03								
Holmes Chapel d						09 07								10 07								
Goostrey d						09 10								10 10								
Chelford d						09 15								10 15								
Alderley Edge d						09 19			09 46					10 19								
Wilmslow d				08 47	08 38	09 22			09 49		09 42			10 22	10 34			10 47	10 43			
Styal d					08 41						09 45								10 46			
Manchester Airport ✈ a					08 49						09 53								10 54			
Handforth d						09 25								10 25								
Congleton d																				10 44		
Macclesfield a													10 09				10 36			10 51	11 08	
d													10 10				10 38			10 52	11 09	
Prestbury d																				10 56		
Adlington (Cheshire) d																				10 59		
Poynton d																				11 02		
Bramhall d																				11 05		
Cheadle Hulme d						09 30								10 30						11 09		
Stockport a						09 34							10 22	10 34	10 43		10 50	10 58		11 13	11 22	
d	00 13	08 33	09 00			09 35	09 43	09 53		09 59		10 18	10 27	10 35	10 44	10 46	10 52	10 58		11 14	11 23	11 26
Heaton Chapel d			09 04							10 03		10 21								11 18		
Levenshulme d			09 07							10 06		10 25								11 21		
Manchester Picc. 85,89 a	00 26	08 42	09 13	09 14	09 16	09 48	09 56	10 02	10 12	10 14	10 20	10 31	10 38	10 47	10 53	10 56	11 02	11 17	11 19	11 31	11 33	11 37
Manchester Oxford Road 85,89 a					09 20						10 24								11 23			11 41
Deansgate 85,89 a					09 27						10 31								11 32			

A From Bristol Temple Meads
B From Cleethorpes
C From Carmarthen
D To Liverpool Lime Street
E From Buxton
F From Chester
G From Newquay
H From Hazel Grove
I From Cleethorpes to Manchester Airport
J From Bournemouth
K To Manchester Victoria
L From Maesteg
M not 20 May. From Chester
N From Sheffield to Manchester Airport
O From Shrewsbury
P From Nottingham to Liverpool Lime Street

Table T084-F

Sundays
20 May to 9 September

Stoke-on-Trent and Crewe - Manchester Airport, Stockport and Manchester

	NT	NT	AW	VT	TP	NT	NT	NT	EM	XC	NT	NT	TP	VT	AW	NT	NT	XC	EM	NT	VT	NT
	◇	A	◇ B	◇■	◇■ C	D	E	F	◇ G	◇■ H	◇	A	◇■ C	◇■	■ B	D	E	◇■ I	◇ G	◇	◇■	A
London Euston ⊖65 d				09 20										10 20							11 20	
Birmingham New Street 68 d										11 01								11 57				
Wolverhampton 68 d										11 19								12 16				
Stafford 65,67 d										11 32								12 29				
Stoke-on-Trent 50 d				11 23						11 52				12 25				12 46			13 11	
Longport 50 d																						
Kidsgrove 50 d																						
Crewe d	10 54		11 23								11 58				12 28					12 57		
Sandbach d	11 01										12 05									13 04		
Holmes Chapel d	11 05										12 09									13 08		
Goostrey d	11 08										12 12									13 11		
Chelford d	11 13										12 17									13 16		
Alderley Edge d	11 17										12 21									13 20		
Wilmslow d	11 20		11 42				11 38				12 24				12 48		12 43			13 23		
Styal d							11 41										12 46					
Manchester Airport ✈ a							11 49										12 55					
Handforth d	11 23										12 27									13 26		
Congleton d																						
Macclesfield a				11 38						12 09				12 40				13 04			13 26	
d				11 39						12 10				12 42				13 05			13 28	
Prestbury d																						
Adlington (Cheshire) d																						
Poynton d																						
Bramhall d																						
Cheadle Hulme d	11 28										12 32									13 31		
Stockport a	11 32			11 52						12 24	12 36			12 55	12 58			13 16		13 35	13 41	
d	11 33	11 44		11 53	11 57	12 03		12 20	12 26	12 30	12 37	12 43	12 52	12 56	12 58	13 03		13 17	13 26	13 36	13 42	13 49
Heaton Chapel d						12 07		12 23								13 07						
Levenshulme d						12 10		12 26								13 10						
Manchester Picc. 85,89 a	11 46	11 56	12 03	12 04	12 10	12 17	12 21	12 33	12 37	12 41	12 47	12 56	13 02	13 05	13 13	13 17	13 21	13 29	13 37	13 46	13 50	13 58
Manchester Oxford Road 85,89 a							12 24		12 41								13 24		13 41			
Deansgate 85,89 a							12 32										13 32					

	TP	AW	NT	NT	XC	NT	VT	NT	EM	NT	VT	NT	XC	TP	VT	AW	NT	NT	XC	VT	EM
	◇■ C	■ J	D	E	◇■ K	◇	◇■	◇ F	◇ L	◇	◇■	A	◇■	◇■ C	◇■	◇ B	D	E	◇■ K	◇■	◇ L
London Euston ⊖65 d							12 17				12 37				12 57					13 17	
Birmingham New Street 68 d					12 57								13 30						13 57		
Wolverhampton 68 d					13 16								13 49						14 15		
Stafford 65,67 d					13 29								14 03						14 28		
Stoke-on-Trent 50 d					13 45	13 25	13 50						14 20		14 26				14 45	14 50	
Longport 50 d																					
Kidsgrove 50 d						13 32															
Crewe d		13 29									14 13					14 28					
Sandbach d																					
Holmes Chapel d																					
Goostrey d																					
Chelford d																					
Alderley Edge d										14 19											
Wilmslow d		13 49		13 39						14 22	14 28					14 48		14 39			
Styal d				13 42														14 42			
Manchester Airport ✈ a				13 50														14 50			
Handforth d										14 25											
Congleton d						13 39															
Macclesfield a					14 04	13 46							14 36		14 42				15 01		
d					14 05	13 47							14 37		14 42				15 02		
Prestbury d						13 51															
Adlington (Cheshire) d						13 54															
Poynton d						13 57															
Bramhall d						14 00															
Cheadle Hulme d						14 04				14 30											
Stockport a		13 59			14 16	14 08	14 22			14 34	14 38		14 50		14 55	14 58			15 14	15 20	
d	13 53	13 59	14 04		14 17	14 13	14 23	14 21	14 27	14 35	14 39	14 45	14 51	14 54	14 56	15 00	15 04		15 15	15 21	15 26
Heaton Chapel d			14 07			14 17		14 25									15 07				
Levenshulme d			14 10			14 20		14 28									15 10				
Manchester Picc. 85,89 a	14 02	14 17	14 17	14 21	14 29	14 30	14 32	14 35	14 37	14 44	14 48	14 55	14 59	15 03	15 06	15 15	15 17	15 21	15 24	15 31	15 37
Manchester Oxford Road 85,89 a				14 24					14 41									15 24			15 41
Deansgate 85,89 a				14 32														15 32			

A From Buxton
B From Cardiff Central
C From Cleethorpes to Manchester Airport
D From Hazel Grove
E To Liverpool Lime Street
F From Chester
G From Nottingham to Liverpool Lime Street
H From Reading
I From Southampton Central
J From Carmarthen
K From Bournemouth
L From Norwich to Liverpool Lime Street

Table T084-F

Sundays

20 May to 9 September

Stoke-on-Trent and Crewe - Manchester Airport, Stockport and Manchester

	NT	VT	NT	XC	TP	VT	AW		NT	NT	XC	VT	EM	NT	NT	VT	NT		XC	TP	VT	AW	NT	NT
	◇	◇■	A	◇■ B	◇■ C	◇■	■ D		E	F	◇■ G	◇■	◇ H	◇ I	◇	◇■	A		◇■ J	◇■ C	◇■	■ K	E	F
London Euston ■ ⊖65 d		13 37				13 57						14 17				14 37					14 57			
Birmingham New Street ■ 68 d				14 31							14 57								15 31					
Wolverhampton ■ 68 d				14 49							15 15								15 49					
Stafford 65,67 d				15 03							15 28								16 03					
Stoke-on-Trent 50 d				15 20		15 26					15 45	15 50							16 20		16 27			
Longport 50 d																								
Kidsgrove 50 d																								
Crewe ■ d	14 56	15 13					15 28								15 56	16 12						16 28		
Sandbach d	15 03														16 03									
Holmes Chapel d	15 07														16 07									
Goostrey d	15 10														16 10									
Chelford d	15 15														16 15									
Alderley Edge d	15 19														16 19									
Wilmslow d	15 22	15 29					15 47			15 39					16 22	16 29						16 47		16 39
Styal d										15 42														16 42
Manchester Airport ✈ a										15 50														16 50
Handforth d	15 25														16 25									
Congleton d																								
Macclesfield a				15 36		15 42					16 04								16 36		16 42			
d				15 37		15 42					16 05								16 37		16 42			
Prestbury d																								
Adlington (Cheshire) d																								
Poynton d																								
Bramhall d																								
Cheadle Hulme d	15 30														16 30									
Stockport a	15 34	15 38		15 50		15 55	15 57				16 16	16 23			16 34	16 35			16 50		16 56	16 57		
d	15 35	15 39	15 43	15 51	15 54	15 56	15 57		16 04		16 17	16 24	16 26	16 24	16 35	16 36	16 43		16 51	16 54	16 57	16 57	17 04	
Heaton Chapel d									16 07					16 28									17 07	
Levenshulme d									16 10					16 31									17 10	
Manchester Picc. ■ 85,89 a	15 45	15 48	15 54	15 59	16 02	16 05	16 14		16 17	16 21	16 29	16 32	16 37	16 40	16 45	16 48	16 54		16 59	17 02	17 06	17 14	17 17	17 21
Manchester Oxford Road 85,89 a										16 24			16 41											17 24
Deansgate 85,89 a										16 32														17 32

	XC	NT	VT		EM	NT	VT	NT	XC	TP	VT	AW	NT		NT	XC	VT	EM	NT	NT	VT	NT	XC	
	◇■ G	◇	◇■		◇ L	◇	◇■	A	◇■ J	◇■ C	◇■	■ D	E		F	◇■ G	◇■	◇ M	◇ I	◇	◇■	A	◇■ N	
London Euston ■ ⊖65 d			15 17				15 37				15 57						16 17				16 37			
Birmingham New Street ■ 68 d	15 57								16 31							16 57							17 31	
Wolverhampton ■ 68 d	16 15								16 49							17 15							17 49	
Stafford 65,67 d	16 28								17 03							17 29							18 03	
Stoke-on-Trent 50 d	16 45	16 30	16 53						17 20		17 26					17 46	17 50						18 20	
Longport 50 d																								
Kidsgrove 50 d		16 37																						
Crewe ■ d						16 56	17 13					17 28								17 56	18 13			
Sandbach d						17 03														18 03				
Holmes Chapel d						17 07														18 07				
Goostrey d						17 10														18 10				
Chelford d						17 15														18 15				
Alderley Edge d						17 19														18 19				
Wilmslow d						17 22	17 29					17 45			17 39					18 22	18 29			
Styal d															17 42									
Manchester Airport ✈ a															17 50									
Handforth d						17 25														18 25				
Congleton d		16 44																						
Macclesfield a	17 04	16 51							17 36		17 42					18 04							18 36	
d	17 05	16 52							17 37		17 42					18 05							18 37	
Prestbury d		16 56																						
Adlington (Cheshire) d		16 59																						
Poynton d		17 02																						
Bramhall d		17 05																						
Cheadle Hulme d		17 09				17 30														18 30				
Stockport a	17 16	17 14	17 23			17 34	17 38		17 50		17 55	17 57				18 16	18 23			18 34	18 38		18 50	
d	17 17	17 14	17 24		17 29	17 35	17 39	17 43	17 51	17 54	17 56	17 57	18 09			18 17	18 24	18 26	18 25	18 35	18 39	18 43	18 51	
Heaton Chapel d		17 18																	18 29					
Levenshulme d		17 21																	18 32					
Manchester Picc. ■ 85,89 a	17 29	17 31	17 32		17 38	17 45	17 48	17 54	17 59	18 03	18 05	18 18	18 18		18 21	18 29	18 32	18 37	18 39	18 45	18 48	18 54	18 59	
Manchester Oxford Road 85,89 a					17 41										18 24			18 41						
Deansgate 85,89 a															18 32									

A From Buxton
B From Paignton
C From Cleethorpes to Manchester Airport
D From Milford Haven
E From Hazel Grove
F To Liverpool Lime Street
G From Bournemouth
H From Nottingham to Liverpool Lime Street
I From Chester
J From Plymouth
K From Cardiff Central
L From Peterborough to Liverpool Lime Street
M From Norwich to Liverpool Lime Street
N From Bristol Temple Meads

Table T084-F

Sundays

20 May to 9 September

Stoke-on-Trent and Crewe - Manchester Airport, Stockport and Manchester

	TP	VT	AW	NT	NT	XC	VT	EM	NT		VT	NT	XC	TP	VT	AW	NT	NT	XC		VT	NT	EM	NT
	◇■ A	◇■	■ B	C	D	◇■ E	◇■	◇ F	◇		◇■	G	◇■ H	◇■ A	◇■	■ I	C	D	◇■ E		◇■	J	◇ K	◇
London Euston ■ ⊖65 d		16 57					17 17				17 37				17 57						18 17			
Birmingham New Street ■ 68 d						17 57							18 31						18 57					
Wolverhampton ■ 68 d						18 15							18 49						19 15					
Stafford 65,67 d						18 28							19 03						19 28					
Stoke-on-Trent 50 d		18 26				18 47	18 50						19 20		19 26				19 47		19 50			
Longport 50 d																								
Kidsgrove 50 d																								
Crewe ■ d			18 28						18 56		19 13					19 28								19 56
Sandbach d									19 03															20 03
Holmes Chapel d									19 07															20 07
Goostrey d									19 10															20 10
Chelford d									19 15															20 15
Alderley Edge d									19 19															20 19
Wilmslow d			18 47		18 39				19 22		19 29					19 47		19 39						20 22
Styal d					18 42													19 42						
Manchester Airport ✈ a					18 50													19 50						
Handforth d									19 25															20 25
Congleton d																								
Macclesfield a		18 42				19 04							19 36		19 42				20 04					
d		18 42				19 05							19 37		19 42				20 05					
Prestbury d																								
Adlington (Cheshire) d																								
Poynton d																								
Bramhall d																								
Cheadle Hulme d									19 30															20 30
Stockport a		18 56	18 57			19 17	19 23		19 34		19 38		19 50		19 56	19 57			20 16		20 23			20 34
d	18 54	18 57	18 57	19 04		19 18	19 24	19 26	19 35		19 39	19 43	19 51	19 54	19 57	19 57	20 04		20 17		20 24	20 22	20 27	20 35
Heaton Chapel d				19 07													20 07					20 26		
Levenshulme d				19 10													20 10					20 29		
Manchester Picc. ■ 85,89 a	19 03	19 06	19 15	19 17	19 21	19 28	19 32	19 37	19 44		19 48	19 54	19 59	20 04	20 06	20 16	20 17	20 21	20 28		20 32	20 38	20 38	20 44
Manchester Oxford Road 85,89 a					19 24			19 42										20 24						
Deansgate 85,89 a					19 32													20 32						

	VT	NT	XC	TP	VT		AW	NT	NT	XC	VT	NT	EM	NT	VT		NT	XC	TP	VT	NT	AW	XC	NT
	◇■	G	◇■ L	◇■ A	◇■		■ B	D	C	◇■ E	◇■	◇	◇ K	◇	◇■		G	◇■ L	◇■ A	◇■	D	■ I	◇■ E	J
London Euston ■ ⊖65 d	18 37				18 57						19 17				19 37					19 57				
Birmingham New Street ■ 68 d			19 31							19 57								20 31					20 57	
Wolverhampton ■ 68 d			19 49							20 15								20 52					21 17	
Stafford 65,67 d			20 03							20 28								21 06					21 30	
Stoke-on-Trent 50 d			20 20		20 26					20 45	20 50	20 30						21 22		21 26			21 46	
Longport 50 d																								
Kidsgrove 50 d												20 37												
Crewe ■ d	20 13						20 29							20 55	21 13							21 28		
Sandbach d														21 02										
Holmes Chapel d														21 06										
Goostrey d														21 09										
Chelford d														21 14										
Alderley Edge d														21 18								21 46		
Wilmslow d	20 29						20 47	20 37						21 21	21 29						21 37	21 48		
Styal d								20 40													21 40			
Manchester Airport ✈ a								20 48													21 50			
Handforth d														21 24										
Congleton d												20 44												
Macclesfield a			20 36		20 42					21 02		20 51						21 39		21 43			22 03	
d			20 37		20 42					21 03		20 52						21 40		21 43			22 04	
Prestbury d												20 56												
Adlington (Cheshire) d												20 59												
Poynton d												21 02												
Bramhall d												21 05												
Cheadle Hulme d												21 09		21 29										
Stockport a	20 38		20 50		20 56		20 57			21 15	21 19	21 13		21 33	21 38			21 52		21 59		22 01	22 15	
d	20 39	20 43	20 51	20 54	20 57		20 57		21 05	21 16	21 20	21 14	21 25	21 34	21 39		21 45	21 53	21 56	22 00		22 01	22 16	22 19
Heaton Chapel d									21 09			21 17												
Levenshulme d									21 12			21 21												
Manchester Picc. ■ 85,89 a	20 48	20 54	20 59	21 04	21 06		21 15	21 17	21 18	21 29	21 31	21 33	21 37	21 43	21 49		21 55	22 02	22 05	22 09	22 18	22 19	22 26	22 28
Manchester Oxford Road 85,89 a								21 20													22 21			
Deansgate 85,89 a								21 29													22 31			

A From Cleethorpes to Manchester Airport
B From Cardiff Central
C From Hazel Grove
D To Liverpool Lime Street
E From Bournemouth
F From Norwich to Liverpool Lime Street
G From Buxton
H From Penzance
I From Milford Haven
J From Chester
K From Norwich
L From Bristol Temple Meads

Sundays
20 May to 9 September

Stoke-on-Trent and Crewe - Manchester Airport, Stockport and Manchester

		VT	NT	VT	NT	TP	XC	NT	NT	NT	NT	VT	VT
		◇■	◇	◇■	A	◇■ B	◇■ C	D		A	◇	◇■	◇■
London Euston ⊖65	d	20 15		20 35								21 25	21 51
Birmingham New Street 68	d						21 57						
Wolverhampton 68	d						22 15						
Stafford 65,67	d			22 00			22 28						23s54
Stoke-on-Trent 50	d	21 50					22 45				23 00	23 33	
Longport 50	d												
Kidsgrove 50	d										23 07		
Crewe	d		21 55	22 21					22 56				00s16
Sandbach	d		22 02						23 03				
Holmes Chapel	d		22 06						23 07				
Goostrey	d		22 09						23 10				
Chelford	d		22 14						23 15				
Alderley Edge	d		22 18						23 19				
Wilmslow	d		22 21	22 36				22 52	23 22				
Styal	d							22 55					
Manchester Airport ✈	a							23 03					
Handforth	d		22 24						23 25				
Congleton	d										23 14		
Macclesfield	a						23 01				23 21	23 49	
	d						23 02				23 27	23 50	
Prestbury	d										23 31		
Adlington (Cheshire)	d										23 34		
Poynton	d										23 37		
Bramhall	d										23 40		
Cheadle Hulme	d		22 29						23 30		23 44		
Stockport	a	22 21	22 33	22 45			23 14		23 34		23 48	00 03	00s38
	d	22 22	22 34	22 46	22 49	23 03	23 15		23 35	23 45	23 50	00 04	
Heaton Chapel	d		22 37						23 38				
Levenshulme	d		22 40						23 41				
Manchester Picc. 85,89	a	22 31	22 47	22 54	23 00	23 16	23 24	23 31	23 49	23 55	00 01	00 13	00 48
Manchester Oxford Road 85,89	a							23 35					
Deansgate 85,89	a							23 38					

Sundays
16 September to 2 December

		NT	TP	NT	AW	NT	NT	NT	TP	AW	NT	NT	NT	XC	NT	VT	NT	VT	AW	NT	NT	XC	EM
		E	◇■ F	A		D	◇	A	◇■ F		G	D	◇ E	◇■	◇	◇■	A	◇■	◇ H	D	◇	◇■	◇ I
London Euston ⊖65	d															08 10		08 20					
Birmingham New Street 68	d													09 01								10 01	
Wolverhampton 68	d													09 19								10 19	
Stafford 65,67	d													09 33								10 33	
Stoke-on-Trent 50	d													09 52				10 21			10 30	10 52	
Longport 50	d																						
Kidsgrove 50	d																				10 37		
Crewe	d				08 28		08 56			09 28					09 56	10 19			10 28				
Sandbach	d						09 03								10 03								
Holmes Chapel	d						09 07								10 07								
Goostrey	d						09 10								10 10								
Chelford	d						09 15								10 15								
Alderley Edge	d						09 19			09 46					10 19								
Wilmslow	d				08 47	08 38	09 22			09 49		09 43			10 22	10 34			10 47	10 43			
Styal	d					08 41						09 46								10 46			
Manchester Airport ✈	a					08 49						09 54								10 54			
Handforth	d						09 25								10 25								
Congleton	d																				10 44		
Macclesfield	a													10 09				10 36			10 51	11 08	
	d													10 10				10 38			10 52	11 09	
Prestbury	d																				10 56		
Adlington (Cheshire)	d																				10 59		
Poynton	d																				11 02		
Bramhall	d																				11 05		
Cheadle Hulme	d						09 30								10 30						11 09		
Stockport	a						09 34							10 22	10 34	10 43		10 50	10 58		11 13	11 22	
	d	00 13	08 33	09 00			09 35	09 43	09 53		09 59		10 18	10 27	10 35	10 44	10 46	10 52	10 58		11 14	11 23	11 26
Heaton Chapel	d			09 04							10 03		10 22								11 18		
Levenshulme	d			09 07							10 06		10 25								11 21		
Manchester Picc. 85,89	a	00 26	08 42	09 13	09 14	09 16	09 48	09 54	10 03	10 12	10 13	10 20	10 31	10 38	10 47	10 53	10 56	11 02	11 17	11 19	11 31	11 33	11 37
Manchester Oxford Road 85,89	a					09 20						10 24								11 23			11 41
Deansgate 85,89	a					09 27						10 31								11 32			

A From Buxton
B From Cleethorpes
C From Bournemouth
D To Liverpool Lime Street
E From Chester
F From Sheffield to Manchester Airport
G From Hazel Grove
H From Shrewsbury
I From Nottingham to Liverpool Lime Street

Sundays
16 September to 2 December

Stoke-on-Trent and Crewe - Manchester Airport, Stockport and Manchester

		NT	NT	AW	VT	TP	NT	NT	NT	EM	XC	NT	NT	TP	VT	AW	NT	XC	EM	NT	VT	NT	TP
		◇	A	◇ B	◇■	◇■ C	D	E	◇ F	◇ G	◇■ H	◇	A	◇■ C	◇■	■ B	E	◇■ I	◇ G	◇	◇■	A	◇■ C
London Euston ⊖65	d				09 20										10 20						11 20		
Birmingham New Street 68	d										11 01							11 57					
Wolverhampton 68	d										11 19							12 16					
Stafford 65,67	d										11 32							12 29					
Stoke-on-Trent 50	d				11 23						11 52				12 25			12 46			13 11		
Longport 50	d																						
Kidsgrove 50	d																						
Crewe	d	10 54		11 23								11 58				12 28				12 57			
Sandbach	d	11 01										12 05								13 04			
Holmes Chapel	d	11 05										12 09								13 08			
Goostrey	d	11 08										12 12								13 11			
Chelford	d	11 13										12 17								13 16			
Alderley Edge	d	11 17										12 21								13 20			
Wilmslow	d	11 20		11 42				11 38				12 24				12 48	12 43			13 23			
Styal	d							11 41									12 46						
Manchester Airport ✈	a							11 49									12 55						
Handforth	d	11 23										12 27								13 26			
Congleton	d																						
Macclesfield	a				11 38						12 09				12 40			13 04			13 26		
	d				11 39						12 10				12 42			13 05			13 28		
Prestbury	d																						
Adlington (Cheshire)	d																						
Poynton	d																						
Bramhall	d																						
Cheadle Hulme	d	11 28										12 32								13 31			
Stockport	a	11 32			11 52						12 24	12 36			12 55	12 58		13 16		13 35	13 41		
	d	11 33	11 44		11 53	11 57	12 03		12 17	12 26	12 30	12 37	12 43	12 52	12 56	12 58		13 17	13 26	13 36	13 42	13 49	13 53
Heaton Chapel	d						12 07																
Levenshulme	d						12 10																
Manchester Picc. 85,89	a	11 46	11 56	12 03	12 04	12 10	12 17	12 21	12 29	12 37	12 41	12 47	12 56	13 04	13 05	13 13	13 21	13 29	13 37	13 46	13 50	13 58	14 02
Manchester Oxford Road 85,89	a							12 24		12 41							13 24		13 41				
Deansgate 85,89	a							12 32									13 32						

		AW	NT	NT	XC	NT	VT	NT	EM	NT	VT	NT	XC	TP	VT	AW	NT	NT	XC	VT	EM	NT
		◇ B	D	E	◇■ J	◇	◇■	◇ F	◇ G	◇	◇■	A	◇■	◇■ C	◇■	◇ B	D	E	◇■ J	◇■	◇ K	◇
London Euston ⊖65	d						12 17				12 37				12 57					13 17		
Birmingham New Street 68	d				12 57								13 30						13 57			
Wolverhampton 68	d				13 16								13 49						14 15			
Stafford 65,67	d				13 29								14 03						14 28			
Stoke-on-Trent 50	d				13 45	13 25	13 50						14 20		14 26				14 45	14 50		
Longport 50	d																					
Kidsgrove 50	d					13 32																
Crewe	d	13 29									14 13					14 28						14 56
Sandbach	d																					15 03
Holmes Chapel	d																					15 07
Goostrey	d																					15 10
Chelford	d																					15 15
Alderley Edge	d									14 19												15 19
Wilmslow	d	13 49		13 39						14 22	14 28					14 48		14 39				15 22
Styal	d			13 42														14 42				
Manchester Airport ✈	a			13 50														14 50				
Handforth	d									14 25												15 25
Congleton	d					13 39																
Macclesfield	a				14 04	13 46							14 36		14 42				15 01			
	d				14 05	13 47							14 37		14 42				15 02			
Prestbury	d					13 51																
Adlington (Cheshire)	d					13 54																
Poynton	d					13 57																
Bramhall	d					14 00																
Cheadle Hulme	d					14 04				14 30												15 30
Stockport	a	13 59			14 16	14 08	14 22			14 34	14 38		14 50		14 55	14 58			15 14	15 20		15 34
	d	13 59	14 04		14 17	14 13	14 23	14 21	14 27	14 35	14 39	14 45	14 51	14 54	14 56	15 00	15 04		15 15	15 21	15 26	15 35
Heaton Chapel	d		14 07			14 17		14 25									15 07					
Levenshulme	d		14 10			14 20		14 28									15 10					
Manchester Picc. 85,89	a	14 17	14 17	14 21	14 29	14 30	14 32	14 35	14 37	14 44	14 48	14 55	14 59	15 03	15 06	15 15	15 17	15 21	15 24	15 31	15 37	15 45
Manchester Oxford Road 85,89	a			14 24					14 41									15 24			15 41	
Deansgate 85,89	a			14 32														15 32				

A From Buxton
B From Cardiff Central
C From Cleethorpes to Manchester Airport
D From Hazel Grove
E To Liverpool Lime Street
F From Chester
G From Nottingham to Liverpool Lime Street
H From Reading
I From Southampton Central
J From Bournemouth
K From Norwich to Liverpool Lime Street

Table T084-F

Sundays

16 September to 2 December

Stoke-on-Trent and Crewe - Manchester Airport, Stockport and Manchester

	VT	NT	XC	TP	VT	AW	NT	NT	XC	VT	EM	NT	NT	VT	NT	XC	TP	VT	AW	NT	NT	XC
		A	B	C		D	E	F	G		H	I			A	J	C		K	E	F	G
London Euston ⊖65 d	13 37				13 57					14 17				14 37				14 57				
Birmingham New Street 68 d			14 31						14 57							15 31						15 57
Wolverhampton 68 d			14 49						15 15							15 49						16 15
Stafford 65,67 d			15 03						15 28							16 03						16 28
Stoke-on-Trent 50 d			15 20		15 26				15 45	15 50						16 20		16 27				16 45
Longport 50 d																						
Kidsgrove 50 d																						
Crewe d	15 13					15 28							15 56	16 12					16 28			
Sandbach d													16 03									
Holmes Chapel d													16 07									
Goostrey d													16 10									
Chelford d													16 15									
Alderley Edge d													16 19									
Wilmslow d	15 29					15 47		15 39					16 22	16 29					16 47		16 39	
Styal d								15 42													16 42	
Manchester Airport ✈ a								15 50													16 50	
Handforth d													16 25									
Congleton d																						
Macclesfield a			15 36		15 42				16 04							16 36		16 42				17 04
d			15 37		15 42				16 05							16 37		16 42				17 05
Prestbury d																						
Adlington (Cheshire) d																						
Poynton d																						
Bramhall d																						
Cheadle Hulme d													16 30									
Stockport a	15 38		15 50		15 55	15 57			16 16	16 23			16 34	16 35		16 50		16 56	16 57			17 16
d	15 39	15 43	15 51	15 54	15 56	15 57	16 04		16 17	16 24	16 26	16 24	16 35	16 36	16 43	16 51	16 54	16 57	16 57	17 04		17 17
Heaton Chapel d							16 07					16 28								17 07		
Levenshulme d							16 10					16 31								17 10		
Manchester Picc. 85,89 a	15 48	15 54	15 59	16 02	16 05	16 14	16 17	16 21	16 29	16 32	16 37	16 40	16 45	16 48	16 54	16 59	17 02	17 06	17 14	17 17	17 21	17 29
Manchester Oxford Road 85,89 a								16 24			16 41										17 24	
Deansgate 85,89 a								16 32													17 32	

	NT	VT	EM	NT	VT	NT	XC	TP	VT	AW	NT	NT	XC	VT	EM	NT	NT	VT	NT	XC	TP
			L			A	J	C		M	E	F	G		N	I			A	O	C
London Euston ⊖65 d		15 17			15 37				15 57					16 17				16 37			
Birmingham New Street 68 d							16 31						16 57							17 31	
Wolverhampton 68 d							16 49						17 15							17 49	
Stafford 65,67 d							17 03						17 29							18 03	
Stoke-on-Trent 50 d	16 30	16 53					17 20		17 26				17 46	17 50						18 20	
Longport 50 d																					
Kidsgrove 50 d	16 37																				
Crewe d				16 56	17 13					17 28							17 56	18 13			
Sandbach d				17 03													18 03				
Holmes Chapel d				17 07													18 07				
Goostrey d				17 10													18 10				
Chelford d				17 15													18 15				
Alderley Edge d				17 19													18 19				
Wilmslow d				17 22	17 29					17 45		17 39					18 22	18 29			
Styal d												17 42									
Manchester Airport ✈ a												17 50									
Handforth d				17 25													18 25				
Congleton d	16 44																				
Macclesfield a	16 51						17 36		17 42				18 04							18 36	
d	16 52						17 37		17 42				18 05							18 37	
Prestbury d	16 56																				
Adlington (Cheshire) d	16 59																				
Poynton d	17 02																				
Bramhall d	17 05																				
Cheadle Hulme d	17 09			17 30													18 30				
Stockport a	17 14	17 23		17 34	17 38		17 50		17 55	17 57			18 16	18 23			18 34	18 38		18 50	
d	17 14	17 24	17 29	17 35	17 39	17 43	17 51	17 54	17 56	17 57	18 09		18 17	18 24	18 26	18 25	18 35	18 39	18 43	18 51	18 54
Heaton Chapel d	17 18															18 29					
Levenshulme d	17 21															18 32					
Manchester Picc. 85,89 a	17 31	17 32	17 38	17 45	17 48	17 54	17 59	18 03	18 05	18 18	18 18	18 21	18 29	18 32	18 37	18 39	18 45	18 48	18 54	18 59	19 03
Manchester Oxford Road 85,89 a			17 41									18 24			18 41						
Deansgate 85,89 a												18 32									

A From Buxton
B From Paignton
C From Cleethorpes to Manchester Airport
D From Carmarthen
E From Hazel Grove
F To Liverpool Lime Street
G From Bournemouth
H From Nottingham to Liverpool Lime Street
I From Chester
J From Plymouth
K From Cardiff Central
L From Peterborough to Liverpool Lime Street
M From Milford Haven
N From Norwich to Liverpool Lime Street
O From Bristol Temple Meads

Table T084-F

Sundays

16 September to 2 December

Stoke-on-Trent and Crewe - Manchester Airport, Stockport and Manchester

	VT	AW	NT	NT	XC	VT	EM	NT	VT	NT	XC	TP	VT	AW	NT	NT	XC	VT	NT	EM	NT	VT
		A	B	C	D		E			F	G	H		I	B	C	D		J	K		
London Euston ⊖65 d	16 57					17 17			17 37				17 57					18 17				18 37
Birmingham New Street 68 d					17 57						18 31						18 57					
Wolverhampton 68 d					18 15						18 49						19 15					
Stafford 65,67 d					18 28						19 03						19 28					
Stoke-on-Trent 50 d	18 26				18 47	18 50					19 20		19 26				19 47	19 50				
Longport 50 d																						
Kidsgrove 50 d																						
Crewe d		18 28						18 56	19 13					19 28							19 56	20 13
Sandbach d								19 03													20 03	
Holmes Chapel d								19 07													20 07	
Goostrey d								19 10													20 10	
Chelford d								19 15													20 15	
Alderley Edge d								19 19													20 19	
Wilmslow d		18 47		18 39				19 22	19 29					19 47		19 39					20 22	20 29
Styal d				18 42												19 42						
Manchester Airport ✈ a				18 50												19 50						
Handforth d								19 25													20 25	
Congleton d																						
Macclesfield a	18 42				19 04						19 36		19 42				20 04					
d	18 42				19 05						19 37		19 42				20 05					
Prestbury d																						
Adlington (Cheshire) d																						
Poynton d																						
Bramhall d																						
Cheadle Hulme d								19 30													20 30	
Stockport a	18 56	18 57			19 17	19 23		19 34	19 38		19 50		19 56	19 57			20 16	20 23			20 34	20 38
d	18 57	18 57	19 04		19 18	19 24	19 26	19 35	19 39	19 43	19 51	19 54	19 57	19 57	20 04		20 17	20 24	20 22	20 27	20 35	20 39
Heaton Chapel d			19 07												20 07				20 26			
Levenshulme d			19 10												20 10				20 29			
Manchester Picc. 85,89 a	19 06	19 15	19 17	19 21	19 28	19 32	19 37	19 44	19 48	19 54	19 59	20 04	20 06	20 16	20 17	20 21	20 28	20 32	20 38	20 38	20 44	20 48
Manchester Oxford Road 85,89 a				19 24			19 42									20 24						
Deansgate 85,89 a				19 32												20 32						

	NT	XC	TP	VT	AW	NT	NT	XC	VT	NT	EM	NT	VT	NT	XC	TP	VT	NT	AW	XC	NT	VT
	F	L	H		A	C	B	D			K			F	L	H		C	I	D	J	
London Euston ⊖65 d				18 57					19 17				19 37				19 57					20 15
Birmingham New Street 68 d		19 31						19 57							20 31					20 57		
Wolverhampton 68 d		19 49						20 15							20 52					21 17		
Stafford 65,67 d		20 03						20 28							21 06					21 30		
Stoke-on-Trent 50 d		20 20		20 26				20 45	20 50	20 30					21 22		21 26			21 46		21 50
Longport 50 d																						
Kidsgrove 50 d										20 37												
Crewe d					20 29							20 55	21 13						21 28			
Sandbach d												21 02										
Holmes Chapel d												21 06										
Goostrey d												21 09										
Chelford d												21 14										
Alderley Edge d												21 18							21 46			
Wilmslow d					20 47	20 37						21 21	21 29					21 37	21 48			
Styal d						20 40												21 40				
Manchester Airport ✈ a						20 48												21 50				
Handforth d												21 24										
Congleton d										20 44												
Macclesfield a		20 36		20 42				21 02		20 51					21 39		21 43			22 03		
d		20 37		20 42				21 03		20 52					21 40		21 43			22 04		
Prestbury d										20 56												
Adlington (Cheshire) d										20 59												
Poynton d										21 02												
Bramhall d										21 05												
Cheadle Hulme d										21 09		21 29										
Stockport a		20 50		20 56	20 57			21 15	21 19	21 13		21 33	21 38		21 52		21 59		22 01	22 15		22 21
d	20 43	20 51	20 54	20 57	20 57		21 05	21 16	21 20	21 14	21 25	21 34	21 39	21 45	21 53	21 56	22 00		22 01	22 16	22 19	22 22
Heaton Chapel d							21 09			21 17												
Levenshulme d							21 12			21 21												
Manchester Picc. 85,89 a	20 54	20 59	21 04	21 06	21 15	21 17	21 18	21 29	21 31	21 33	21 37	21 43	21 49	21 55	22 02	22 05	22 09	22 18	22 19	22 26	22 28	22 31
Manchester Oxford Road 85,89 a						21 20												22 21				
Deansgate 85,89 a						21 29												22 31				

A From Cardiff Central
B From Hazel Grove
C To Liverpool Lime Street
D From Bournemouth
E From Norwich to Liverpool Lime Street
F From Buxton
G From Penzance
H From Cleethorpes to Manchester Airport
I From Milford Haven
J From Chester
K From Norwich
L From Bristol Temple Meads

Table T084-F

Sundays
16 September to 2 December

Stoke-on-Trent and Crewe - Manchester Airport, Stockport and Manchester

		NT		VT	NT	TP	XC	NT	NT	NT	NT	VT		VT
		◇		◇■		◇■	◇■				◇	◇■		◇■
					A	B	C	D		A				
				☕								☕		☕
London Euston ■ ⊖65	d			20 35								21 25		21 51
Birmingham New Street ■ 68	d						21 57							
Wolverhampton ■ 68	d						22 15							
Stafford 65,67	d			22 00			22 28							23s54
Stoke-on-Trent 50	d						22 45				23 00	23 33		
Longport 50	d													
Kidsgrove 50	d										23 07			
Crewe ■	d	21 55		22 21					22 56					00s16
Sandbach	d	22 02							23 03					
Holmes Chapel	d	22 06							23 07					
Goostrey	d	22 09							23 10					
Chelford	d	22 14							23 15					
Alderley Edge	d	22 18							23 19					
Wilmslow	d	22 21		22 36				22 52	23 22					
Styal	d							22 55						
Manchester Airport ✈	a							23 03						
Handforth	d	22 24							23 25					
Congleton	d										23 14			
Macclesfield	a						23 01				23 21	23 49		
	d						23 02				23 27	23 50		
Prestbury	d										23 31			
Adlington (Cheshire)	d										23 34			
Poynton	d										23 37			
Bramhall	d										23 40			
Cheadle Hulme	d	22 29							23 30		23 44			
Stockport	a	22 33		22 45			23 14		23 34		23 48	00 03		00s38
	d	22 34		22 46	22 49	23 03	23 15		23 35	23 45	23 50	00 04		
Heaton Chapel	d	22 37							23 38					
Levenshulme	d	22 40							23 41					
Manchester Picc. ■ 85,89	a	22 47		22 54	23 00	23 16	23 24	23 31	23 49	23 55	00 01	00 13		00 48
Manchester Oxford Road 85,89	a							23 35						
Deansgate 85,89	a							23 38						

A From Buxton
B From Cleethorpes
C From Bournemouth
D To Liverpool Lime Street

Table T084-R

Mondays to Fridays
21 May to 7 December

Manchester, Stockport and Manchester Airport - Crewe and Stoke-on-Trent

Miles	Miles	Miles			NT MX	VT	XC	NT	NT	NT	NT	VT		XC	NT	VT	NT	NT	TP	NT	VT	AW		NT	VT
						◇■	◇■			◇		◇■		◇■		◇■	◇		◇■		◇■	◇		◇	◇■
					A		B				C			D			E	F	G	H		I			
						⊠	⌶					⊠		⌶		⊠					⊠	⌶			⊠
0	0	—	Deansgate 85,89	d																					
0½	0½	—	**Manchester Oxford Road** 85,89	d													06 09								
1	1	—	**Manchester Picc.** ■ 85,89	d		05 05	05 11	05 19		05 38	05 46	05 55		06 00	06 03	06 10	06 13	06 13	06 17	06 24	06 27	06 29		06 32	06 35
4	4	—	Levenshulme	d																06 30				06 37	
5½	5½	—	Heaton Chapel	d											06 10					06 33				06 40	
7	7	—	**Stockport**	a		05 11				05 47	05 55	06 02		06 07	06 14	06 17		06 22	06 24	06 36	06 34	06 38		06 44	06 42
—	—	—		d		05 13				05 47		06 03		06 08	06 14	06 18					06 35	06 39		06 44	06 43
9¼	9¼	—	Cheadle Hulme	d						05 52					06 20									06 51	
9¾	—	—	Bramhall	d						05 55														06 54	
12¼	—	—	Poynton	d						05 58														06 57	
14¼	—	—	Adlington (Cheshire)	d						06 02														07 01	
16¼	—	—	Prestbury	d						06 05														07 04	
19	—	—	**Macclesfield**	a						06 08						06 30					06 47			07 07	06 55
—	—	—		d					06 00	06 09						06 31					06 48			07 08	06 56
27	—	—	Congleton	d					06 07	06 20														07 15	
—	11½	—	Handforth	d											06 24										
—	—	0	**Manchester Airport** ✈	d				05 45									06a27								
—	—	2¼	Styal	d				05 49																	
—	13	4	**Wilmslow**	d	00 02			05 53				06 11		06 16	06 27							06 47			
—	14¾	—	Alderley Edge	d	00 06			05 56							06 32										
—	17¾	—	Chelford	d	00 10			06 01							06 37										
—	21½	—	Goostrey	d	00 15			06 06							06 42										
—	23½	—	Holmes Chapel	d	00 19			06 09							06 45										
—	27¼	—	Sandbach	d	00 24			06 14							06 51										
—	32	—	**Crewe** ■	a	00 34	05 33	05 43	06 25				06 27		06 37	07 01							07 07			
32½	—	—	Kidsgrove 50	a					06 13	06 26														07 21	
35¾	—	—	Longport 50	a																					
38¾	—	—	**Stoke-on-Trent** 50	a			06 06		06 23	06 37						06 46					07 04			07 31	07 11
—	—	—	Stafford 65,67	a		05 54	06 24							06 59							07 22				
—	—	—	Wolverhampton ■ 68	a			06 38							07 12							07 40				
—	—	—	Birmingham New Street ■ 68	a			06 57							07 33							08 07				
—	—	—	London Euston ■ ⊖65	a		07 26						08 08				08 20					09 33				08 46

		NT	VT	NT	NT	VT	NT	XC		NT	VT	TP	NT	XC	AW	VT	NT	NT		NT	VT	NT	XC	NT	VT
			◇■			◇■		◇■			◇■	◇■		■ ■	◇	◇■		◇			◇■	◇	◇■		◇■
		J		K	H			D		F		G	H	B	L		F			K			M	K	
			⊠			⊠		⌶			⊠	⌶		⌶	⌶	⊠					⊠		⌶		⊠
Deansgate 85,89	d	06 30																							
Manchester Oxford Road 85,89	d	06 33																							
Manchester Picc. ■ 85,89	d	06 37	06 43	06 48	06 51	06 58	07 01	07 05		07 09	07 15	07 18	07 22	07 27	07 30	07 36	07 40	07 44		07 52	07 55	08 01	08 05	08 08	08 15
Levenshulme	d	06 45			06 58		07 07						07 30									08 07			
Heaton Chapel	d	06 49			07 01		07 10						07 33									08 10			
Stockport	a	06 52	06 50	06 59	07 05		07 13	07 12		07 17	07 22	07 28	07 36	07 35	07 39	07 42	07 50	07 55		08 01	08 03	08 15	08 12	08 20	08 22
	d	06 56	06 51			07u05	07 20	07 13			07 23			07 36	07 39	07 43		07 56			08 04	08 19	08 13		08 23
Cheadle Hulme	d	07 00					07 24											08 00				08 23			
Bramhall	d																	08 03							
Poynton	d																	08 06							
Adlington (Cheshire)	d																	08 09							
Prestbury	d																	08 12							
Macclesfield	a							07 25						07 48		07 55		08 16					08 25		
	d							07 26						07 49		07 56		08 16					08 26		
Congleton	d																	08 23							
Handforth	d	07 05					07 28															08 27			
Manchester Airport ✈	d																								
Styal	d																								
Wilmslow	d	07 08	06 59				07 32								07 47						08 11	08 30			
Alderley Edge	d	07a13					07 35															08 33			
Chelford	d						07 39															08 38			
Goostrey	d						07 44															08 43			
Holmes Chapel	d						07 48															08 46			
Sandbach	d						07 53															08 52			
Crewe ■	a		07 15				08 03								08 05						08 27	09 02			
Kidsgrove 50	a																	08 29							
Longport 50	a																								
Stoke-on-Trent 50	a							07 43			07 48			08 06		08 11		08 40					08 43		08 49
Stafford 65,67	a		07 35					08 00						08 23									09 00		
Wolverhampton ■ 68	a							08 13						08 39									09 13		
Birmingham New Street ■ 68	a							08 33						08 58									09 33		
London Euston ■ ⊖65	a		08 54			09 00					09 21					09 49					10 16				10 26

A From Manchester Piccadilly
B To Bournemouth
C To Sheffield
D To Bristol Temple Meads
E From Manchester Victoria
F To Chester
G From Manchester Airport to Cleethorpes
H To Hazel Grove
I not from 26 June until 29 June. To Milford Haven
J From Wigan North Western
K To Buxton
L To Carmarthen
M To Paignton

Manchester, Stockport and Manchester Airport - Crewe and Stoke-on-Trent

		TP	NT	XC	AW	VT	NT	NT	NT	VT	NT	XC	NT	VT	TP	NT	XC	AW	VT	NT	NT	NT
		◇1 A 🛒	B	◇1 C 🛒	◇ D 🛒	◇1 ⊠	◇ E	◇	F	◇1 ⊠	◇	◇1 G 🛒	F	◇1 ⊠	◇1 A 🛒	B	◇1 C 🛒	◇ H 🛒	◇1 ⊠	I	◇ E	◇
Deansgate 85,89 ⇌	d																			09 30		
Manchester Oxford Road 85,89	d																			09 33		
Manchester Picc. 10 85,89 ⇌	d	08 19	08 24	08 27	08 31	08 35	08 41	08 44	08 47	08 55	09 01	09 05	09 11	09 15	09 19	09 24	09 27	09 31	09 35	09 37	09 41	09 44
Levenshulme	d		08 30						08 55		09 07					09 30				09 44		
Heaton Chapel	d		08 33						08 58		09 10					09 33				09 47		
Stockport	a	08 27	08 36	08 35	08 39	08 42	08 50	08 56	09 02	09 03	09 13	09 12	09 20	09 22	09 27	09 36	09 35	09 39	09 43	09 51	09 51	09 57
	d			08 36	08 39	08 43		08 57		09 04	09 14	09 13		09 23			09 36	09 39	09 44	09 51		09 57
Cheadle Hulme	d							09 01			09 20									09 56		10 01
Bramhall	d							09 04														10 04
Poynton	d							09 07														10 07
Adlington (Cheshire)	d							09 11														10 11
Prestbury	d							09 14														10 14
Macclesfield	a			08 48		08 55		09 17				09 25					09 48		09 55			10 17
	d			08 49		08 56		09 18				09 26					09 49		09 56			10 18
Congleton	d							09 25														10 25
Handforth	d										09 24									10 00		
Manchester Airport ✈	d																					
Styal	d																					
Wilmslow	d				08 47					09 11	09 27							09 47		10 03		
Alderley Edge	d										09 30									10a08		
Chelford	d										09 35											
Goostrey	d										09 40											
Holmes Chapel	d										09 43											
Sandbach	d										09 49											
Crewe 10	a				09 07					09 29	09 59							10 06				
Kidsgrove 50	a							09 31														10 31
Longport 50	a																					
Stoke-on-Trent 50	a			09 06		09 11		09 41				09 43		09 49			10 06		10 11			10 41
Stafford 65,67	a			09 23								10 00					10 23					
Wolverhampton 7 68 ⇌	a			09 41								10 13					10 39					
Birmingham New Street 12 68	a			09 58								10 33					10 58					
London Euston 15 ⊖65	a					10 51				11 08				11 20					11 40			

		NT	VT	NT	XC	NT	VT	TP	NT	XC	AW	VT	NT	NT	NT	NT	VT	NT	XC	NT	VT	TP	NT
		F	◇1 ⊠		◇1 G 🛒	F	◇1 ⊠	◇1 A 🛒	B	◇1 C 🛒	◇ D 🛒	◇1 ⊠	I	◇ E	◇	F	◇1 ⊠		◇1 G 🛒	F	◇1 🍽	◇1 A 🛒	B
Deansgate 85,89 ⇌	d												10 30										
Manchester Oxford Road 85,89	d												10 33										
Manchester Picc. 10 85,89 ⇌	d	09 48	09 55	10 01	10 05	10 11	10 15	10 19	10 24	10 27	10 31	10 35	10 37	10 41	10 44	10 47	10 55	11 01	11 05	11 11	11 15	11 19	11 24
Levenshulme	d	09 55		10 07					10 30				10 44			10 55		11 07					11 30
Heaton Chapel	d	09 58		10 10					10 33				10 47			10 58		11 10					11 33
Stockport	a	10 02	10 03	10 13	10 12	10 20	10 22	10 27	10 36	10 35	10 39	10 42	10 51	10 50	10 57	11 02	11 03	11 13	11 12	11 20	11 22	11 27	11 36
	d		10 04	10 14	10 13		10 23			10 36	10 39	10 43	10 51		10 57		11 04	11 14	11 13		11 23		
Cheadle Hulme	d			10 21									10 56		11 01			11 21					
Bramhall	d														11 04								
Poynton	d														11 07								
Adlington (Cheshire)	d														11 11								
Prestbury	d														11 14								
Macclesfield	a				10 25					10 48		10 55			11 17				11 25				
	d				10 26					10 49		10 56			11 18				11 26				
Congleton	d														11 25								
Handforth	d			10 25									11 00					11 25					
Manchester Airport ✈	d																						
Styal	d																						
Wilmslow	d		10 11	10 28							10 47		11 03				11 11	11 28					
Alderley Edge	d			10 31									11a08					11 31					
Chelford	d			10 36														11 36					
Goostrey	d			10 41														11 41					
Holmes Chapel	d			10 44														11 44					
Sandbach	d			10 50														11 50					
Crewe 10	a		10 27	11 00							11 06						11 27	12 00					
Kidsgrove 50	a														11 31								
Longport 50	a																						
Stoke-on-Trent 50	a				10 43		10 49			11 06		11 11			11 41				11 43		11 49		
Stafford 65,67	a				11 00					11 24									12 00				
Wolverhampton 7 68 ⇌	a				11 13					11 39									12 13				
Birmingham New Street 12 68	a				11 33					11 58									12 33				
London Euston 15 ⊖65	a		12 02				12 20					12 40					13 02				13 20		

A From Manchester Airport to Cleethorpes
B To Hazel Grove
C To Bournemouth
D To Milford Haven
E To Chester
F To Buxton
G To Bristol Temple Meads
H To Carmarthen
I From Wigan North Western

Manchester, Stockport and Manchester Airport - Crewe and Stoke-on-Trent

		XC	AW	VT	NT	NT	NT	NT	VT	NT	XC	NT	VT	TP	NT	XC	AW	VT	NT	NT	NT	NT	VT
		◇1 A 🛒	◇ B 🛒	◇1 🍽	C	◇ D	◇	E	◇1 🍽		◇1 F 🛒	E	◇1 🍽	◇1 G 🛒	H	◇1 A 🛒	■ I 🛒	◇1 🍽	C	◇ D	◇	E	◇1 🍽
Deansgate 85,89 ⇌	d				11 30														12 30				
Manchester Oxford Road 85,89	d				11 33														12 33				
Manchester Picc. 10 85,89 ⇌	d	11 27	11 31	11 35	11 37	11 41	11 44	11 47	11 55	12 01	12 05	12 11	12 15	12 19	12 24	12 27	12 31	12 35	12 37	12 41	12 44	12 47	12 55
Levenshulme	d				11 44			11 55		12 07					12 30				12 44			12 55	
Heaton Chapel	d				11 47			11 58		12 10					12 33				12 47			12 58	
Stockport	a	11 35	11 39	11 42	11 51	11 50	11 57	12 02	12 03	12 13	12 12	12 20	12 22	12 27	12 36	12 35	12 39	12 42	12 51	12 50	12 57	13 02	13 03
	d	11 36	11 39	11 43	11 51		11 57		12 04	12 14	12 13		12 23			12 36	12 39	12 43	12 51		12 57		13 04
Cheadle Hulme	d				11 56		12 01			12 21									12 56		13 01		
Bramhall	d						12 04														13 04		
Poynton	d						12 07														13 07		
Adlington (Cheshire)	d						12 11														13 11		
Prestbury	d						12 14														13 14		
Macclesfield	a	11 48		11 55			12 17				12 25					12 48		12 55			13 17		
	d	11 49		11 56			12 18				12 26					12 49		12 56			13 18		
Congleton	d						12 25														13 25		
Handforth	d				12 00					12 25									13 00				
Manchester Airport ✈	d																						
Styal	d																						
Wilmslow	d		11 47		12 03				12 11	12 28							12 47		13 03				13 11
Alderley Edge	d				12a08					12 31									13a08				
Chelford	d									12 36													
Goostrey	d									12 41													
Holmes Chapel	d									12 44													
Sandbach	d									12 50													
Crewe 10	a		12 06						12 27	13 00							13 06						13 29
Kidsgrove 50	a						12 31														13 31		
Longport 50	a																						
Stoke-on-Trent 50	a	12 06		12 11			12 41				12 43		12 49			13 06		13 11			13 41		
Stafford 65,67	a	12 23									13 00					13 25							
Wolverhampton 7 68 ⇌	a	12 39									13 13					13 39							
Birmingham New Street 12 68	a	12 58									13 33					13 58							
London Euston 15 ⊖65	a			13 40					14 05				14 20					14 41					15 09

		NT	XC	NT	VT	TP	NT	XC	AW	VT	NT	NT	NT	NT	VT FX	VT FO	NT	XC	NT	VT FO	VT FX	TP
			◇1 J 🛒	E	◇1 🍽	◇1 G 🛒	H	◇1 A 🛒	■ K 🛒	◇1 🍽	C	D	◇	E	◇1 🍽	◇1 🍽		◇1 L 🛒	E	◇1 🍽	◇1 🍽	◇1 G 🛒
Deansgate 85,89 ⇌	d										13 30											
Manchester Oxford Road 85,89	d										13 33											
Manchester Picc. 10 85,89 ⇌	d	13 01	13 05	13 11	13 15	13 19	13 24	13 27	13 31	13 35	13 37	13 41	13 44	13 47	13 55	13 55	14 01	14 05	14 11	14 15	14 15	14 19
Levenshulme	d	13 07					13 30				13 44			13 55			14 07					
Heaton Chapel	d	13 10					13 33				13 47			13 58			14 10					
Stockport	a	13 13	13 12	13 20	13 22	13 27	13 36	13 35	13 39	13 42	13 51	13 50	13 57	14 02	14 03	14 03	14 13	14 12	14 20	14 22	14 22	14 27
	d	13 14	13 13		13 23			13 36	13 39	13 43	13 51		13 57		14 04	14 04	14 14	14 13		14 23	14 23	
Cheadle Hulme	d	13 21									13 56		14 01				14 20					
Bramhall	d												14 04									
Poynton	d												14 07									
Adlington (Cheshire)	d												14 11									
Prestbury	d												14 14									
Macclesfield	a		13 25					13 48		13 55			14 17					14 25				
	d		13 26					13 49		13 56			14 18					14 26				
Congleton	d												14 25									
Handforth	d	13 25									14 00						14 24					
Manchester Airport ✈	d																					
Styal	d																					
Wilmslow	d	13 28							13 47		14 03				14 11	14 11	14 27					
Alderley Edge	d	13 31									14a08						14 30					
Chelford	d	13 36															14 35					
Goostrey	d	13 41															14 40					
Holmes Chapel	d	13 44															14 43					
Sandbach	d	13 50															14 49					
Crewe 10	a	14 00							14 06						14 29	14 29	14 59					
Kidsgrove 50	a												14 31									
Longport 50	a																					
Stoke-on-Trent 50	a		13 43		13 49			14 06		14 11			14 41					14 43		14 48	14 48	
Stafford 65,67	a		14 00					14 23										15 00				
Wolverhampton 7 68 ⇌	a		14 13					14 39										15 13				
Birmingham New Street 12 68	a		14 34					14 58										15 33				
London Euston 15 ⊖65	a				15 28					15 39					16 05	16 08				16 22	16 24	

A To Bournemouth
B To Carmarthen
C From Wigan North Western
D To Chester
E To Buxton
F To Exeter St Davids
G From Manchester Airport to Cleethorpes
H To Hazel Grove
I To Milford Haven
J To Bristol Temple Meads
K To Tenby
L To Paignton

Table T084-R

Mondays to Fridays
21 May to 7 December

Manchester, Stockport and Manchester Airport - Crewe and Stoke-on-Trent

	NT	XC	AW	VT	NT	NT	NT	NT	VT	NT	XC	NT	VT	TP	NT	XC	AW	VT	NT	NT	NT	NT
	A	◇■ B ✠	■ C ✠	◇■ ☕	D	◇ E	◇	F	◇■ ☕		◇■ G ✠	F	◇■ ☕	◇■ H ✠	A	◇■ B ✠	■ I ✠	◇■ ☕	D	E	◇	F
Deansgate 85,89 d					14 30														15 30			
Manchester Oxford Road 85,89 d					14 33														15 33			
Manchester Picc. 85,89 d	14 24	14 27	14 31	14 35	14 37	14 41	14 44	14 47	14 55	15 01	15 05	15 11	15 15	15 19	15 24	15 27	15 31	15 35	15 37	15 41	15 44	15 47
Levenshulme d	14 30				14 44			14 55		15 07					15 30				15 44			15 55
Heaton Chapel d	14 33				14 47			14 58		15 10					15 33				15 47			15 58
Stockport a	14 36	14 35	14 39	14 42	14 51	14 50	14 57	15 02	15 03	15 13	15 12	15 20	15 22	15 27	15 36	15 35	15 39	15 42	15 51	15 50	15 57	16 02
d		14 36	14 39	14 43	14 51		14 57		15 04	15 14	15 13		15 23			15 36	15 39	15 43	15 51		15 57	
Cheadle Hulme d					14 56		15 01			15 20									15 56		16 01	
Bramhall d							15 04														16 04	
Poynton d							15 07														16 07	
Adlington (Cheshire) d							15 11														16 11	
Prestbury d							15 14														16 14	
Macclesfield a		14 48		14 55			15 17				15 25					15 48		15 55			16 17	
d		14 49		14 56			15 18				15 26					15 49		15 56			16 18	
Congleton d							15 25														16 25	
Handforth d					15 00					15 24									16 00			
Manchester Airport d																						
Styal d																						
Wilmslow d			14 47		15 03				15 11	15 27							15 47		16 03			
Alderley Edge d					15a08					15 30									16a08			
Chelford d										15 35												
Goostrey d										15 40												
Holmes Chapel d										15 43												
Sandbach d										15 49												
Crewe a			15 06						15 27	15 59							16 06					
Kidsgrove 50 a							15 31														16 31	
Longport 50 a																						
Stoke-on-Trent 50 a		15 06		15 11			15 41				15 43		15 48			16 06		16 11			16 41	
Stafford 65,67 a		15 24									16 00					16 24						
Wolverhampton 68 a		15 39									16 13					16 39						
Birmingham New Street 68 a		15 58									16 33					16 58						
London Euston ⊖65 a				16 40					17 02				17 21					17 40				

	VT	NT	XC	NT	VT	TP	NT	XC	AW	VT	NT	NT	NT	NT	VT	NT	XC	NT	VT	TP	NT
	◇■ ☕		◇■ G ✠	F	◇■ ☕	◇■ H ✠	A	◇■ B ✠	■ C ✠	◇■ ☕	D	E	◇	F	◇■ ☕		◇■ J ✠	F	◇■ ☒	◇■ H ✠	
Deansgate 85,89 d											16 30										
Manchester Oxford Road 85,89 d											16 33										
Manchester Picc. 85,89 d	15 55	16 01	16 05	16 11	16 15	16 19	16 24	16 27	16 31	16 35	16 37	16 41	16 44	16 47	16 55	17 01	17 05	17 11	17 15	17 19	17 21
Levenshulme d		16 07					16 30				16 44			16 55		17 07					
Heaton Chapel d		16 10					16 33				16 47			16 58		17 10					
Stockport a	16 03	16 13	16 12	16 20	16 22	16 27	16 36	16 35	16 39	16 42	16 51	16 50	16 57	17 02	17 03	17 13	17 12	17 20	17 22	17 27	17 30
d	16 04	16 14	16 13		16 23			16 36	16 39	16 43	16 51		16 57		17 04	17 14	17 13		17 23		17 30
Cheadle Hulme d		16 21									16 56		17 01			17 22					17 34
Bramhall d													17 04								17 37
Poynton d													17 07								17 40
Adlington (Cheshire) d													17 11								17 44
Prestbury d													17 14								17 47
Macclesfield a			16 25					16 48		16 55			17 17				17 25				17 53
d			16 26					16 49		16 56			17 18				17 26				
Congleton d													17 25								
Handforth d		16 25									17 00					17 26					
Manchester Airport d																					
Styal d																					
Wilmslow d	16 11	16 28							16 47		17 04				17 11	17 29					
Alderley Edge d		16 31									17a08					17 32					
Chelford d		16 36														17 37					
Goostrey d		16 41														17 42					
Holmes Chapel d		16 44														17 45					
Sandbach d		16 50														17 51					
Crewe a	16 29	17 00							17 06						17 27	18 01					
Kidsgrove 50 a													17 31								
Longport 50 a																					
Stoke-on-Trent 50 a			16 43		16 48			17 07		17 11			17 41				17 43		17 48		
Stafford 65,67 a			17 00					17 24									18 00				
Wolverhampton 68 a			17 13					17 39									18 13				
Birmingham New Street 68 a			17 33					17 58									18 33				
London Euston ⊖65 a	18 05				18 20					18 40					19 06				19 24		

A To Hazel Grove
B To Bournemouth
C To Milford Haven
D From Wigan North Western
E To Chester
F To Buxton
G To Bristol Temple Meads
H From Manchester Airport to Cleethorpes
I To Carmarthen
J To Cardiff Central

Table T084-R

Mondays to Fridays
21 May to 7 December

Manchester, Stockport and Manchester Airport - Crewe and Stoke-on-Trent

	NT	XC	AW	VT	NT	NT	NT	NT	VT	NT	XC	NT	VT	TP	NT	XC	AW	AW	NT	VT	NT	NT
	A	◇■ B ✠	■ C ✠	◇■ ☒	D	E	◇	F	◇■ ☒		◇■ G ✠	F	◇■ ☒	◇■ H ✠	A	◇■ B ✠	FX ◇ I	FO ◇ I	◇	◇■ ☒	D	◇ E
Deansgate 85,89 d					17 29																18 30	
Manchester Oxford Road 85,89 d					17 33																18 33	
Manchester Picc. 85,89 d	17 24	17 27	17 31	17 35	17 38	17 41	17 44	17 47	17 55	18 01	18 05	18 11	18 15	18 19	18 24	18 27	18 29	18 31	18 34	18 35	18 37	18 41
Levenshulme d	17 30				17 44			17 55		18 07					18 30						18 43	
Heaton Chapel d	17 33				17 47			17 58		18 10					18 33						18 46	
Stockport a	17 36	17 35	17 39	17 42	17 51	17 50	17 57	18 02	18 03	18 13	18 12	18 20	18 22	18 27	18 36	18 35	18 37	18 39		18 42	18 49	18 49
d		17 35	17 39	17 43	17 51		17 57		18 04	18 14	18 13		18 23			18 36	18 37	18 39		18 43	18 50	
Cheadle Hulme d					17 56		18 01			18 21											18 54	
Bramhall d							18 04															
Poynton d							18 07															
Adlington (Cheshire) d							18 11															
Prestbury d							18 14															
Macclesfield a				17 55			18 17				18 25									18 54		
d				17 56			18 18				18 26									18 55		
Congleton d							18 25									18 55						
Handforth d					18 00					18 25											18 59	
Manchester Airport d																			19 02			
Styal d																			19 12			
Wilmslow d		17 45	17 48		18 03				18 10	18 28							18 45	18 47	19 18		19 02	
Alderley Edge d					18a08					18 31									19 21		19a06	
Chelford d										18 36												
Goostrey d										18 41												
Holmes Chapel d										18 44									19 30			
Sandbach d										18 50									19 35			
Crewe a		18 04	18 08						18 27	19 00							19 06	19 06	19 43			
Kidsgrove 50 a							18 31															
Longport 50 a																						
Stoke-on-Trent 50 a				18 11			18 41				18 43		18 49			19 07				19 10		
Stafford 65,67 a		18 25									19 00					19 24						
Wolverhampton 68 a		18 39									19 13					19 39						
Birmingham New Street 68 a		18 58									19 33					19 58						
London Euston ⊖65 a				19 41					20 08				20 21							20 39		

	NT	NT	VT	NT	XC	NT	VT	TP	NT	XC	AW	NT	NT	NT	NT	NT	VT	NT	XC	VT	TP	NT
	◇	F	◇■ ☒		◇■ J ✠	F	◇■ ☕	◇■ H	A	◇■ K ✠	◇ I	◇	D	◇ E	◇	F	◇■ ☕	◇	◇■	◇■ ☕	◇■ H	A
Deansgate 85,89 d													19 30									
Manchester Oxford Road 85,89 d													19 33									
Manchester Picc. 85,89 d	18 44	18 49	18 55	19 01	19 05	19 11	19 15	19 19	19 24	19 27	19 31	19 31	19 38	19 40	19 44	19 47	19 55	20 01	20 05	20 15	20 19	20 24
Levenshulme d		18 55		19 07					19 30				19 44			19 55		20 07				20 30
Heaton Chapel d		18 58		19 10					19 33				19 47			19 58		20 10				20 33
Stockport a	18 57	19 02	19 03	19 13	19 12	19 20	19 22	19 27	19 36	19 35	19 39		19 51	19 50	19 57	20 02	20 03	20 13	20 12	20 22	20 27	20 36
d	18 57		19 04	19 14	19 13		19 23			19 36	19 40		19 51		19 57		20 04	20 14	20 13	20 23		
Cheadle Hulme d	19 01			19 21									19 56		20 01			20 21				
Bramhall d	19 04														20 04							
Poynton d	19 07														20 07							
Adlington (Cheshire) d	19 11														20 11							
Prestbury d	19 14														20 14							
Macclesfield a	19 17				19 25		19 35			19 48					20 17				20 25	20 35		
d	19 18				19 26		19 36			19 49					20 18				20 26	20 36		
Congleton d	19 25														20 25							
Handforth d				19 25									20 00					20 25				
Manchester Airport d												20 03										
Styal d												20 10										
Wilmslow d			19 11	19 28							19 47	20a14	20 03				20 11	20 28				
Alderley Edge d				19 31									20a08					20 31				
Chelford d				19 36														20 36				
Goostrey d				19 41														20 41				
Holmes Chapel d				19 44														20 44				
Sandbach d				19 50														20 50				
Crewe a			19 27	20 00							20 07						20 27	21 00				
Kidsgrove 50 a	19 31														20 31							
Longport 50 a																						
Stoke-on-Trent 50 a	19 41				19 43		19 51			20 06					20 41				20 43	20 51		
Stafford 65,67 a					20 00					20 24							20 47		21 00			
Wolverhampton 68 a					20 13					20 42									21 13			
Birmingham New Street 68 a					20 33					21 00									21 33			
London Euston ⊖65 a			21 06				21 23										22 10			22 29		

A To Hazel Grove
B To Bournemouth
C To Cardiff Central
D From Wigan North Western
E To Chester
F To Buxton
G To Plymouth
H From Manchester Airport to Cleethorpes
I To Carmarthen
J To Bristol Temple Meads
K To Southampton Central

Table T084-R

Mondays to Fridays
21 May to 7 December

Manchester, Stockport and Manchester Airport - Crewe and Stoke-on-Trent

	XC	AW	NT	NT	NT	NT	NT	VT	TP	NT	XC	AW	NT	NT	NT	NT	XC	NT	NT	AW	NT
	◇■	◇ A	B	◇ C	◇	D	◇	◇■	◇■ E	F	◇■	◇ G	◇ C	◇	D	◇	◇■		F	◇ G	◇ C
Deansgate 85,89 ⇌ d			20 29																		
Manchester Oxford Road 85,89 d			20 33																		
Manchester Picc. ■ 85,89 ⇌ d	20 27	20 31	20 37	20 41	20 44	20 47	21 01	21 15	21 19	21 23	21 27	21 36	21 40	21 43	21 49	22 01	22 07	22 18	22 22	22 36	22 40
Levenshulme d			20 44			20 55	21 07			21 29					21 56	22 07			22 30		
Heaton Chapel d			20 47			20 58	21 10			21 32					21 59	22 10			22 33		
Stockport a	20 35	20 39	20 50	20 49	20 57	21 02	21 13	21 22	21 27	21 35	21 35	21 44	21 49	21 57	22 02	22 13	22 14	22 27	22 36	22 43	22 52
d	20 36	20 40	20 51		20 57		21 14	21 23			21 36	21 45		21 57		22 14	22 16	22 28		22 44	
Cheadle Hulme d			20 55		21 01		21 21							22 01		22 18		22 32			
Bramhall d					21 04									22 04				22 36			
Poynton d					21 07									22 07				22 39			
Adlington (Cheshire) d					21 11									22 11				22 43			
Prestbury d					21 14									22 14				22 47			
Macclesfield a	20 48				21 17			21 35			21 48			22 17			22 28	22 54			
d	20 49				21 18			21 36			21 49			22 18			22 29				
Congleton d					21 25									22 25							
Handforth d			21 00				21 25									22 22					
Manchester Airport ✈ d																					
Styal d																					
Wilmslow d		20 47	21 03				21 28					21 52				22 25				22 52	
Alderley Edge d			21a07				21 31									22 28					
Chelford d							21 36									22 33					
Goostrey d							21 41									22 38					
Holmes Chapel d							21 44									22 41					
Sandbach d							21 50									22 47					
Crewe ■ a		21 10					22 00					22 11				22 57				23 10	
Kidsgrove 50 a					21 31									22 31							
Longport 50 a																					
Stoke-on-Trent 50 a	21 06				21 41			21 51			22 06			22 41			22 46				
Stafford 65,67 a	21 23										22 24						23 03				
Wolverhampton ■ 68 ⇌ a	21 39										22 41						23 17				
Birmingham New Street ■ 68 a	22 00										22 59						23 35				
London Euston ■ ⊖65 a								23 48													

	TP	NT	NT	NT	NT	NT	NT
	◇■ H		D		F		C
Deansgate 85,89 ⇌ d							
Manchester Oxford Road 85,89 d							
Manchester Picc. ■ 85,89 ⇌ d	22 43	23 01	23 11	23 14	23 24	23 38	23 41
Levenshulme d		23 07			23 30	23 44	
Heaton Chapel d		23 10			23 33	23 47	
Stockport a		23 13	23 20	23 23	23 36	23 50	23 50
d		23 16		23 23		23 51	
Cheadle Hulme d		23 20		23 27		23 55	
Bramhall d				23 31			
Poynton d				23 34			
Adlington (Cheshire) d				23 38			
Prestbury d				23 41			
Macclesfield a				23 45			
d							
Congleton d							
Handforth d		23 24				23 59	
Manchester Airport ✈ d	23a00						
Styal d							
Wilmslow d		23 27				00 02	
Alderley Edge d		23a34				00 06	
Chelford d						00 10	
Goostrey d						00 15	
Holmes Chapel d						00 19	
Sandbach d						00 24	
Crewe ■ a						00 34	
Kidsgrove 50 a							
Longport 50 a							
Stoke-on-Trent 50 a							
Stafford 65,67 a							
Wolverhampton ■ 68 ⇌ a							
Birmingham New Street ■ 68 a							
London Euston ■ ⊖65 a							

A To Cardiff Central
B From Wigan North Western
C To Chester
D To Buxton
E From Manchester Airport to Cleethorpes
F To Hazel Grove
G To Shrewsbury
H From Hull

Table T084-R

Saturdays
26 May to 8 December

Manchester, Stockport and Manchester Airport - Crewe and Stoke-on-Trent

	NT	XC	NT	VT	NT	NT	NT	VT	XC	NT	VT	NT	NT	TP	NT	AW	VT	NT	NT	NT	VT	NT
	A	◇■ B		◇■		◇	C	◇■	◇■ D		◇■	◇ E	F	◇■ G	H	◇ I	◇■	J	◇	K	◇■	
Deansgate 85,89 ⇌ d																		06 30				
Manchester Oxford Road 85,89 d												06 09						06 33				
Manchester Picc. ■ 85,89 ⇌ d		05 11	05 19	05 25		05 38	05 46	05 55	06 00	06 03	06 10	06 13	06 13	06 17	06 24	06 30	06 35	06 37	06 45	06 48	06 55	07 01
Levenshulme d															06 30			06 45		06 55		07 07
Heaton Chapel d										06 10					06 33			06 49		06 58		07 10
Stockport a				05 33		05 47	05 55	06 02	06 07	06 14	06 18		06 22	06 26	06 36	06 38	06 42	06 52	06 55	07 01	07 03	07 13
d				05 34		05 47		06 03	06 08	06 14	06 19					06 39	06 43	06 54	06 57		07 04	07 20
Cheadle Hulme d						05 52				06 18								06 58	07 01			07 24
Bramhall d						05 55													07 04			
Poynton d						05 58													07 07			
Adlington (Cheshire) d						06 02													07 11			
Prestbury d						06 05													07 14			
Macclesfield a						06 08			06 20		06 30						06 55		07 17			
d					05 55	06 09			06 21		06 31						06 56		07 18			
Congleton d					06 02	06 20													07 25			
Handforth d										06 22								07 03				07 28
Manchester Airport ✈ d			05 45									06a27										
Styal d			05 49																			
Wilmslow d	00 02		05 53	05 41				06 11		06 26						06 47		07 06			07 11	07 32
Alderley Edge d	00 06		05 56							06 29								07a11				07 35
Chelford d	00 10		06 01							06 33												07 39
Goostrey d	00 15		06 06							06 38												07 44
Holmes Chapel d	00 19		06 09							06 42												07 48
Sandbach d	00 24		06 14							06 47												07 53
Crewe ■ a	00 34	05 42	06 25	05 57				06 27		06 57						07 05					07 27	08 03
Kidsgrove 50 a					06 08	06 26													07 32			
Longport 50 a																						
Stoke-on-Trent 50 a		06 07			06 18	06 37			06 38		06 46						07 11		07 42			
Stafford 65,67 a		06 25		06 18					06 55													
Wolverhampton ■ 68 ⇌ a		06 38							07 12													
Birmingham New Street ■ 68 a		06 57							07 33													
London Euston ■ ⊖65 a				07 50				08 07			08 25						08 45				09 02	

	XC	NT	VT	TP	NT	XC	AW	VT	NT	NT	NT	VT	NT	XC	NT	VT	TP	NT	XC	AW	VT	NT
	◇■ D	F	◇■	◇■ G	H	◇■ B	◇ L	◇■	F	◇	K	◇■	◇	◇■ M	K	◇■	◇■ G	H	◇■ B	■ I	◇■	◇ F
Deansgate 85,89 ⇌ d																						
Manchester Oxford Road 85,89 d																						
Manchester Picc. ■ 85,89 ⇌ d	07 05	07 08	07 15	07 19	07 22	07 27	07 30	07 35	07 40	07 44	07 52	07 55	08 01	08 05	08 08	08 15	08 19	08 24	08 27	08 30	08 35	08 41
Levenshulme d					07 30								08 07					08 30				
Heaton Chapel d					07 33								08 10					08 33				
Stockport a	07 12	07 18	07 22	07 27	07 36	07 35	07 39	07 42	07 50	07 55	08 01	08 03	08 13	08 12	08 20	08 22	08 27	08 36	08 35	08 39	08 42	08 50
d	07 13		07 23			07 36	07 40	07 43		07 56		08 04	08 14	08 13		08 23			08 36	08 39	08 43	
Cheadle Hulme d										08 00			08 21									
Bramhall d										08 03												
Poynton d										08 06												
Adlington (Cheshire) d										08 09												
Prestbury d										08 12												
Macclesfield a	07 25					07 48		07 55		08 16				08 25					08 48		08 55	
d	07 26					07 49		07 56		08 16				08 26					08 49		08 56	
Congleton d										08 23												
Handforth d													08 25									
Manchester Airport ✈ d																						
Styal d																						
Wilmslow d							07 47					08 11	08 28							08 47		
Alderley Edge d													08 31									
Chelford d													08 36									
Goostrey d													08 41									
Holmes Chapel d													08 44									
Sandbach d													08 50									
Crewe ■ a							08 06					08 27	09 00							09 06		
Kidsgrove 50 a										08 29												
Longport 50 a																						
Stoke-on-Trent 50 a	07 43		07 49			08 06		08 11		08 40				08 43		08 48			09 06		09 11	
Stafford 65,67 a	08 00					08 24								09 00					09 23			
Wolverhampton ■ 68 ⇌ a	08 13					08 39								09 15					09 38			
Birmingham New Street ■ 68 a	08 33					08 58								09 33					09 58			
London Euston ■ ⊖65 a			09 21					09 40				10 08				10 21					10 41	

A From Manchester Piccadilly
B To Bournemouth
C To Sheffield
D To Bristol Temple Meads
E From Manchester Victoria
F To Chester
G From Manchester Airport to Cleethorpes
H To Hazel Grove
I To Milford Haven
J From Wigan North Western
K To Buxton
L To Carmarthen
M To Paignton

Manchester, Stockport and Manchester Airport - Crewe and Stoke-on-Trent

		NT ◇	NT A	VT ◇■	NT ◇	XC ◇■ B	NT A	VT ◇■	TP ◇■ C	NT D	XC ◇■ E	AW ◇ F	VT ◇■	NT G	NT ◇ H	NT ◇	NT A	VT ◇■	NT	XC ◇■ B	NT A	VT ◇■
Deansgate 85,89	d													09 30								
Manchester Oxford Road 85,89	d													09 33								
Manchester Picc. 85,89	d	08 44	08 47	08 55	09 01	09 05	09 11	09 15	09 19	09 24	09 27	09 30	09 35	09 37	09 41	09 44	09 48	09 55	10 01	10 05	10 11	10 15
Levenshulme	d		08 55		09 07					09 30				09 44			09 55		10 07			
Heaton Chapel	d		08 58		09 10					09 33				09 47			09 58		10 10			
Stockport	a	08 56	09 02	09 03	09 13	09 12	09 20	09 22	09 28	09 36	09 36	09 39	09 42	09 51	09 51	09 57	10 02	10 03	10 13	10 12	10 20	10 22
	d	08 57		09 04	09 14	09 13		09 23			09 37	09 40	09 43	09 51		09 57		10 04	10 14	10 13		10 23
Cheadle Hulme	d	09 01			09 20									09 56		10 01			10 21			
Bramhall	d	09 04														10 04						
Poynton	d	09 07														10 07						
Adlington (Cheshire)	d	09 11														10 11						
Prestbury	d	09 14														10 14						
Macclesfield	a	09 17				09 25					09 49		09 55			10 17				10 25		
	d	09 18				09 26					09 50		09 56			10 18				10 26		
Congleton	d	09 25														10 25						
Handforth	d				09 24									10 00					10 25			
Manchester Airport	d																					
Styal	d																					
Wilmslow	d			09 11	09 27							09 48		10 03				10 11	10 28			
Alderley Edge	d				09 30									10a08					10 31			
Chelford	d				09 35														10 36			
Goostrey	d				09 40														10 41			
Holmes Chapel	d				09 43														10 44			
Sandbach	d				09 49														10 50			
Crewe	a			09 29	09 59							10 07						10 27	11 00			
Kidsgrove 50	a	09 31														10 31						
Longport 50	a																					
Stoke-on-Trent 50	a	09 41				09 43		09 49			10 07		10 11			10 41				10 43		10 48
Stafford 65,67	a					10 00					10 24									11 00		
Wolverhampton 68	a					10 13					10 39									11 13		
Birmingham New Street 68	a					10 33					10 58									11 33		
London Euston ⊖65	a			11 07				11 21					11 41					12 02				12 21

		TP ◇■ C	NT D	XC ◇■ E	AW I	VT ◇■	NT G	NT ◇ H	NT ◇	NT A	VT ◇■	NT	XC ◇■ B	NT A	VT ◇■	TP ◇■ C	NT D	XC ◇■ E	AW ◇ F	VT ◇■	NT G	NT ◇ H	NT ◇
Deansgate 85,89	d						10 30														11 30		
Manchester Oxford Road 85,89	d						10 33														11 33		
Manchester Picc. 85,89	d	10 19	10 24	10 27	10 31	10 35	10 37	10 41	10 44	10 47	10 55	11 01	11 05	11 11	11 15	11 19	11 24	11 27	11 31	11 35	11 37	11 41	11 44
Levenshulme	d		10 30				10 44			10 55		11 07					11 30				11 44		
Heaton Chapel	d		10 33				10 47			10 58		11 10					11 33				11 47		
Stockport	a	10 27	10 36	10 35	10 39	10 42	10 51	10 51	10 57	11 02	11 03	11 13	11 12	11 20	11 22	11 27	11 36	11 35	11 39	11 42	11 51	11 50	11 57
	d			10 36	10 40	10 43	10 51		10 57		11 04	11 14	11 13		11 23			11 36	11 39	11 43	11 51		11 57
Cheadle Hulme	d						10 56		11 01			11 21									11 56		12 01
Bramhall	d								11 04														12 04
Poynton	d								11 07														12 07
Adlington (Cheshire)	d								11 11														12 11
Prestbury	d								11 14														12 14
Macclesfield	a			10 48		10 56			11 17				11 25					11 48		11 55			12 17
	d			10 49		10 57			11 18				11 26					11 49		11 56			12 18
Congleton	d								11 25														12 25
Handforth	d						11 00					11 25									12 00		
Manchester Airport	d																						
Styal	d																						
Wilmslow	d				10 47		11 03				11 11	11 28							11 47		12 03		
Alderley Edge	d						11a08					11 31									12a08		
Chelford	d											11 36											
Goostrey	d											11 41											
Holmes Chapel	d											11 44											
Sandbach	d											11 50											
Crewe	a				11 06						11 27	12 00							12 06				
Kidsgrove 50	a								11 31														12 31
Longport 50	a																						
Stoke-on-Trent 50	a			11 06		11 11			11 41				11 43		11 48			12 06		12 11			12 41
Stafford 65,67	a			11 24									12 00					12 23					
Wolverhampton 68	a			11 39									12 13					12 39					
Birmingham New Street 68	a			11 59									12 34					12 58					
London Euston ⊖65	a					12 42					13 02				13 21					13 39			

A To Buxton
B To Bristol Temple Meads
C From Manchester Airport to Cleethorpes
D To Hazel Grove
E To Bournemouth
F To Carmarthen
G From Wigan North Western
H To Chester
I To Milford Haven

Table T084-R

Saturdays
26 May to 8 December

Manchester, Stockport and Manchester Airport - Crewe and Stoke-on-Trent

		NT A	VT ◇■	NT	XC ◇■ B	NT A	VT ◇■	TP ◇■ C	NT D	XC ◇■ E	AW ◇■ F	VT ◇■	NT G	NT ◇ H	NT ◇	NT A	VT ◇■	NT	XC ◇■ I	NT A	VT ◇■	TP ◇■ C
Deansgate 85,89	d												12 30									
Manchester Oxford Road 85,89	d												12 33									
Manchester Picc. 85,89	d	11 47	11 55	12 01	12 05	12 11	12 15	12 19	12 24	12 27	12 31	12 35	12 37	12 41	12 44	12 47	12 55	13 01	13 05	13 11	13 15	13 19
Levenshulme	d	11 55		12 07					12 30				12 44			12 55		13 07				
Heaton Chapel	d	11 58		12 10					12 33				12 47			12 58		13 10				
Stockport	a	12 02	12 03	12 13	12 12	12 20	12 22	12 27	12 36	12 35	12 39	12 42	12 51	12 50	12 57	13 02	13 03	13 13	13 12	13 20	13 22	13 27
	d		12 04	12 14	12 13		12 23			12 36	12 39	12 43	12 51		12 57		13 04	13 14	13 13		13 23	
Cheadle Hulme	d			12 22									12 56		13 01			13 21				
Bramhall	d														13 04							
Poynton	d														13 07							
Adlington (Cheshire)	d														13 11							
Prestbury	d														13 14							
Macclesfield	a				12 25					12 48		12 55			13 17				13 25			
	d				12 26					12 49		12 56			13 18				13 26			
Congleton	d														13 25							
Handforth	d			12 26									13 00					13 25				
Manchester Airport	d																					
Styal	d																					
Wilmslow	d		12 11	12 29							12 47		13 03				13 11	13 28				
Alderley Edge	d			12 32									13a08					13 31				
Chelford	d			12 37														13 36				
Goostrey	d			12 42														13 41				
Holmes Chapel	d			12 45														13 44				
Sandbach	d			12 51														13 50				
Crewe	a		12 27	13 01							13 06						13 29	14 00				
Kidsgrove 50	a														13 31							
Longport 50	a																					
Stoke-on-Trent 50	a				12 43		12 48			13 06		13 11			13 41				13 43		13 48	
Stafford 65,67	a				13 00					13 24									14 00			
Wolverhampton 68	a				13 14					13 39									14 15			
Birmingham New Street 68	a				13 34					13 58									14 35			
London Euston ⊖65	a		14 04				14 20					14 41					15 07				15 28	

		NT D	XC ◇■ E	AW J	VT ◇■	NT G	NT ◇ H	NT ◇	NT A	VT ◇■	NT	XC ◇■ I	NT A	VT ◇■	TP ◇■ C	NT D	XC ◇■ E	AW K	VT ◇■	NT G	NT ◇ H	NT ◇	NT A
Deansgate 85,89	d					13 30														14 30			
Manchester Oxford Road 85,89	d					13 33														14 33			
Manchester Picc. 85,89	d	13 24	13 27	13 31	13 35	13 37	13 41	13 44	13 47	13 55	14 01	14 05	14 11	14 15	14 19	14 24	14 27	14 31	14 35	14 37	14 41	14 44	14 47
Levenshulme	d	13 30				13 44			13 55		14 07					14 30				14 44			14 55
Heaton Chapel	d	13 33				13 47			13 58		14 10					14 33				14 47			14 58
Stockport	a	13 36	13 35	13 39	13 42	13 51	13 50	13 55	14 02	14 03	14 13	14 12	14 20	14 22	14 27	14 36	14 35	14 39	14 42	14 51	14 50	14 57	15 02
	d		13 36	13 39	13 43	13 51		13 57		14 04	14 14	14 13		14 23			14 36	14 40	14 43	14 51		14 57	
Cheadle Hulme	d					13 56		14 01			14 20									14 56		15 01	
Bramhall	d							14 04														15 04	
Poynton	d							14 07														15 07	
Adlington (Cheshire)	d							14 11														15 11	
Prestbury	d							14 14														15 14	
Macclesfield	a		13 48		13 55			14 17				14 25					14 48		14 55			15 17	
	d		13 49		13 56			14 18				14 26					14 49		14 56			15 18	
Congleton	d							14 25														15 25	
Handforth	d					14 00					14 24									15 00			
Manchester Airport	d																						
Styal	d																						
Wilmslow	d			13 47		14 03				14 11	14 27							14 47		15 03			
Alderley Edge	d					14a08					14 30									15a08			
Chelford	d										14 35												
Goostrey	d										14 40												
Holmes Chapel	d										14 43												
Sandbach	d										14 49												
Crewe	a			14 06						14 28	14 59							15 06					
Kidsgrove 50	a							14 31														15 31	
Longport 50	a																						
Stoke-on-Trent 50	a		14 06		14 11			14 41				14 43		14 48			15 06		15 11			15 41	
Stafford 65,67	a		14 24									15 00					15 25						
Wolverhampton 68	a		14 39									15 13					15 39						
Birmingham New Street 68	a		14 58									15 33					15 58						
London Euston ⊖65	a				15 41					16 04				16 21					16 40				

A To Buxton
B To Exeter St Davids
C From Manchester Airport to Cleethorpes
D To Hazel Grove
E To Bournemouth
F To Milford Haven
G From Wigan North Western
H To Chester
I To Bristol Temple Meads
J To Pembroke Dock
K not 23 June. To Milford Haven

Table T084-R

Saturdays
26 May to 8 December

Manchester, Stockport and Manchester Airport - Crewe and Stoke-on-Trent

	VT ◇■	NT	XC ◇■ A	NT B	VT ◇■	TP ◇■ C	NT D	XC ◇■ E	AW F	VT ◇■	NT G	NT ◇ H	NT ◇	NT B	VT ◇■	NT	XC ◇■ A	NT B	VT ◇■	TP ◇■ C	NT D	XC ◇■ E
Deansgate 85,89 d											15 30											
Manchester Oxford Road 85,89 d											15 33											
Manchester Picc. 85,89 d	14 55	15 01	15 05	15 11	15 15	15 19	15 24	15 27	15 31	15 35	15 37	15 41	15 44	15 47	15 55	16 01	16 05	16 11	16 15	16 19	16 24	16 27
Levenshulme d		15 07					15 30				15 44			15 55		16 07					16 30	
Heaton Chapel d		15 10					15 33				15 47			15 58		16 10					16 33	
Stockport a	15 03	15 13	15 12	15 20	15 22	15 27	15 36	15 35	15 39	15 42	15 51	15 50	15 57	16 02	16 03	16 13	16 12	16 20	16 22	16 27	16 36	16 35
Stockport d	15 04	15 14	15 13		15 23			15 36	15 39	15 43	15 51		15 57		16 04	16 14	16 13		16 23			16 36
Cheadle Hulme d		15 20									15 56		16 01			16 21						
Bramhall d													16 04									
Poynton d													16 07									
Adlington (Cheshire) d													16 11									
Prestbury d													16 14									
Macclesfield a			15 25					15 48		15 55			16 17				16 25					16 48
Macclesfield d			15 26					15 49		15 56			16 18				16 26					16 49
Congleton d													16 25									
Handforth d		15 24									16 00					16 25						
Manchester Airport d																						
Styal d																						
Wilmslow d	15 11	15 27							15 47		16 03				16 11	16 28						
Alderley Edge d		15 30									16a08					16 31						
Chelford d		15 35														16 36						
Goostrey d		15 40														16 41						
Holmes Chapel d		15 43														16 44						
Sandbach d		15 49														16 50						
Crewe a	15 27	15 59							16 06						16 27	17 00						
Kidsgrove 50 a													16 31									
Longport 50 a																						
Stoke-on-Trent 50 a			15 43		15 48			16 06		16 11			16 41				16 43		16 48			17 06
Stafford 65,67 a			16 00					16 23									17 00					17 23
Wolverhampton 68 a			16 13					16 39									17 13					17 39
Birmingham New Street 68 a			16 33					16 58									17 33					17 58
London Euston 65 a	17 03				17 21					17 41					18 02				18 21			

	AW I	VT ◇■	NT G	NT H	NT ◇	NT B	VT ◇■	NT	XC ◇■ J	NT B	VT ◇■	TP ◇■ C	NT D	XC ◇■ E	AW J	VT ◇■	NT G	NT H	NT ◇	NT B	VT ◇■
Deansgate 85,89 d			16 30														17 29				
Manchester Oxford Road 85,89 d			16 33														17 33				
Manchester Picc. 85,89 d	16 31	16 35	16 37	16 41	16 44	16 47	16 55	17 01	17 05	17 11	17 15	17 19	17 24	17 27	17 31	17 35	17 38	17 41	17 44	17 47	17 55
Levenshulme d			16 44			16 55		17 07					17 30				17 44			17 55	
Heaton Chapel d			16 47			16 58		17 10					17 33				17 47			17 58	
Stockport a	16 39	16 42	16 51	16 50	16 57	17 02	17 03	17 13	17 12	17 20	17 22	17 27	17 36	17 34	17 39	17 42	17 51	17 50	17 57	18 02	18 03
Stockport d	16 39	16 43	16 51		16 57		17 04	17 14	17 13		17 23			17 36	17 39	17 43	17 51		17 57		18 04
Cheadle Hulme d			16 56		17 01			17 22									17 56		18 01		
Bramhall d					17 04														18 04		
Poynton d					17 07														18 07		
Adlington (Cheshire) d					17 11														18 11		
Prestbury d					17 14														18 14		
Macclesfield a		16 55			17 17				17 25							17 55			18 17		
Macclesfield d		16 56			17 18				17 26							17 56			18 18		
Congleton d					17 25									17 55					18 25		
Handforth d			17 00					17 26									18 00				
Manchester Airport d																					
Styal d																					
Wilmslow d	16 47		17 03				17 11	17 29							17 47		18 03				18 11
Alderley Edge d			17a08					17 32									18a08				
Chelford d								17 37													
Goostrey d								17 42													
Holmes Chapel d								17 45													
Sandbach d								17 51													
Crewe a	17 06						17 27	18 01							18 06						18 27
Kidsgrove 50 a					17 31														18 31		
Longport 50 a																					
Stoke-on-Trent 50 a		17 11			17 41				17 43		17 48			18 06		18 11			18 41		
Stafford 65,67 a									18 00					18 24							
Wolverhampton 68 a									18 14					18 39							
Birmingham New Street 68 a									18 33					18 58							
London Euston 65 a		18 41					19 03				19 22					19 39					20 02

A To Bristol Temple Meads
B To Buxton
C From Manchester Airport to Cleethorpes
D To Hazel Grove
E To Bournemouth
F To Pembroke Dock
G From Wigan North Western
H To Chester
I To Milford Haven
J To Cardiff Central

Table T084-R

Saturdays
26 May to 8 December

Manchester, Stockport and Manchester Airport - Crewe and Stoke-on-Trent

	NT	XC ◇■ A	NT B	VT ◇■	TP ◇■ C	NT D	XC ◇■ E	AW ◇ F	NT ◇	VT ◇■	NT G	NT ◇ H	NT ◇	NT B	VT ◇■	NT	XC ◇■ A	NT B	TP ◇■ C	NT D	XC ◇■ I	AW ◇ J
Deansgate 85,89 d											18 30											
Manchester Oxford Road 85,89 d											18 33											
Manchester Picc. 85,89 d	18 01	18 05	18 11	18 15	18 19	18 24	18 27	18 31	18 33	18 35	18 37	18 41	18 44	18 49	18 55	19 01	19 05	19 11	19 19	19 24	19 27	19 31
Levenshulme d	18 07					18 30					18 44			18 55		19 07				19 30		
Heaton Chapel d	18 10					18 33					18 47			18 58		19 10				19 33		
Stockport a	18 13	18 12	18 20	18 22	18 27	18 36	18 34	18 39		18 42	18 51	18 50	18 57	19 02	19 03	19 13	19 12	19 20	19 27	19 36	19 35	19 39
Stockport d	18 14	18 13		18 23			18 36	18 39		18 43	18 51		18 57		19 04	19 14	19 13				19 36	19 40
Cheadle Hulme d	18 21										18 56		19 01			19 21						
Bramhall d													19 04									
Poynton d													19 07									
Adlington (Cheshire) d													19 11									
Prestbury d													19 14									
Macclesfield a		18 25								18 55			19 17				19 25				19 48	
Macclesfield d		18 26								18 56			19 18				19 26				19 49	
Congleton d							18 55						19 25									
Handforth d	18 25										19 00					19 25						
Manchester Airport d									19 05													
Styal d									19 12													
Wilmslow d	18 28							18 47	19 18		19 03				19 11	19 28						19 47
Alderley Edge d	18 31								19 21		19a08					19 31						
Chelford d	18 36															19 36						
Goostrey d	18 41															19 41						
Holmes Chapel d	18 44								19 30							19 44						
Sandbach d	18 50								19 35							19 50						
Crewe a	19 00							19 08	19 43						19 27	20 00						20 06
Kidsgrove 50 a													19 31									
Longport 50 a																						
Stoke-on-Trent 50 a		18 43		18 48			19 07			19 11			19 41				19 43				20 06	
Stafford 65,67 a		19 00					19 24										20 00				20 23	
Wolverhampton 68 a		19 13					19 40										20 13				20 39	
Birmingham New Street 68 a		19 33					19 59										20 33				20 58	
London Euston 65 a				20 34						20 57					21 20							

	NT ◇	VT ◇■	NT G	NT ◇ H	NT ◇	NT B	NT ◇	XC ◇■	TP ◇■ C	NT D	XC ◇■	AW ◇ J	VT ◇■	NT G	NT H	NT	NT B	NT ◇	XC ◇■	TP ◇■ C	NT D
Deansgate 85,89 d			19 30											20 29							
Manchester Oxford Road 85,89 d			19 33											20 33							
Manchester Picc. 85,89 d	19 31	19 35	19 37	19 40	19 44	19 47	20 00	20 05	20 19	20 24	20 27	20 30	20 35	20 37	20 41	20 44	20 47	21 01	21 05	21 19	21 23
Levenshulme d			19 45			19 55	20 07			20 30				20 45			20 55	21 07			21 29
Heaton Chapel d			19 48			19 58	20 10			20 33				20 48			20 58	21 10			21 32
Stockport a		19 42	19 51	19 50	19 57	20 02	20 13	20 12	20 27	20 36	20 35	20 39	20 42	20 51	20 50	20 57	21 02	21 13	21 12	21 27	21 35
Stockport d		19 43	19 52		19 57		20 14	20 13			20 36	20 39	20 43	20 52		20 57		21 17	21 13		
Cheadle Hulme d			19 56		20 01		20 21							20 56		21 01		21 22			
Bramhall d					20 04											21 04					
Poynton d					20 07											21 07					
Adlington (Cheshire) d					20 11											21 11					
Prestbury d					20 14											21 14					
Macclesfield a		19 56			20 17			20 25			20 48		20 55			21 17			21 25		
Macclesfield d		19 57			20 18			20 26			20 49		20 56			21 18			21 26		
Congleton d					20 25											21 25					
Handforth d			20 01				20 25							21 01				21 26			
Manchester Airport d	20 07																				
Styal d	20 11																				
Wilmslow d	20a15		20 04				20 28					20 47		21 04				21 29			
Alderley Edge d			20a08				20 31							21a08				21 32			
Chelford d							20 36											21 37			
Goostrey d							20 41											21 42			
Holmes Chapel d							20 44											21 45			
Sandbach d							20 50											21 51			
Crewe a							21 00					21 05						22 01			
Kidsgrove 50 a					20 31											21 31					
Longport 50 a																					
Stoke-on-Trent 50 a		20 11			20 41			20 43			21 06		21 11			21 41			21 43		
Stafford 65,67 a								21 00			21 24								22 00		
Wolverhampton 68 a								21 13			21 40								22 13		
Birmingham New Street 68 a								21 33			21 59								22 33		
London Euston 65 a		21 59											22 59								

A To Bristol Temple Meads
B To Buxton
C From Manchester Airport to Cleethorpes
D To Hazel Grove
E To Bournemouth
F To Carmarthen
G From Wigan North Western
H To Chester
I To Southampton Central
J To Cardiff Central

Table T084-R

Manchester, Stockport and Manchester Airport - Crewe and Stoke-on-Trent

Saturdays

26 May to 8 December

		XC	AW	NT	NT	NT	NT	NT	NT	AW	NT	TP	NT	NT	NT	NT	NT	NT
		◇1	◇ A	B	◇	C	◇		D	◇ A	◇ B	◇1 E		C		D		B
Deansgate 85,89	d																	
Manchester Oxford Road 85,89	d																	
Manchester Picc. 10 85,89	d	21 27	21 33	21 37	21 43	21 47	22 01	22 18	22 22	22 35	22 40	22 42	23 04	23 07	23 14	23 14	23 38	23 41
Levenshulme	d					21 55	22 07		22 30				23 10			23 20	23 44	
Heaton Chapel	d					21 58	22 10		22 33				23 13			23 23	23 47	
Stockport	a	21 34	21 42	21 46	21 57	22 02	22 13	22 27	22 36	22 43	22 48		23 16	23 16	23 23	23 26	23 50	23 50
	d	21 35	21 43		21 57		22 14	22 27		22 44			23 20		23 23		23 51	
Cheadle Hulme	d				22 01		22 18	22 32					23 24		23 27		23 55	
Bramhall	d				22 04			22 35							23 31			
Poynton	d				22 07			22 39							23 34			
Adlington (Cheshire)	d				22 11			22 43							23 38			
Prestbury	d				22 14			22 46							23 41			
Macclesfield	a	21 47			22 17			22 54							23 45			
	d	21 49			22 18													
Congleton	d				22 25													
Handforth	d						22 22						23 28				23 59	
Manchester Airport ✈	d											23a00						
Styal	d																	
Wilmslow	d		21 50				22 25			22 52			23 31				00 02	
Alderley Edge	d						22 28						23 34				00a07	
Chelford	d						22 33						23 38					
Goostrey	d						22 38						23 43					
Holmes Chapel	d						22 41						23 46					
Sandbach	d						22 47						23 50					
Crewe 10	a		22 11				22 57			23 10			23 59					
Kidsgrove 50	a				22 31													
Longport 50	a																	
Stoke-on-Trent 50	a	22 06			22 41													
Stafford 65,67	a	22 23																
Wolverhampton 7 68	a	22 42																
Birmingham New Street 12 68	a	23 01																
London Euston 15 ⊖65	a																	

Sundays

20 May to 9 September

		NT	VT	NT	TP	VT	NT	XC	NT	NT	NT	NT	TP	VT	NT	XC	AW	NT	NT	TP	VT	XC	AW
		F	◇1		◇1 G	◇1		◇1 H	C	◇	◇	◇ B	◇1 G	◇1	D	◇1 H	I	C	◇	◇1 G	◇1	◇1 H	J
Deansgate 85,89	d																						
Manchester Oxford Road 85,89	d																						
Manchester Picc. 10 85,89	d		08 05	08 09	08 13	08 20	08 23	08 27	08 50	08 53	08 59	09 04	09 10	09 20	09 23	09 27	09 30	09 45	09 55	10 14	10 20	10 26	10 31
Levenshulme	d								08 56						09 29								
Heaton Chapel	d								08 59						09 32								
Stockport	a		08 13	08 17	08 21	08 28		08 34	09 02	09 02	09 08	09 12	09 18	09 28	09 35	09 35	09 40	09 54	10 04	10 23	10 28	10 34	10 40
	d		08 14	08 18		08 28		08 36		09 02	09 08			09 28		09 36	09 40		10 06		10 29	10 36	10 40
Cheadle Hulme	d			08 23						09 06	09 13								10 12				
Bramhall	d									09 09													
Poynton	d									09 12													
Adlington (Cheshire)	d									09 16													
Prestbury	d									09 19													
Macclesfield	a					08 41				09 22				09 40		09 48						10 48	
	d					08 41				09 23				09 40		09 49						10 49	
Congleton	d									09 30													
Handforth	d			08 27							09 17								10 16				
Manchester Airport ✈	d						08 50																
Styal	d						08 56																
Wilmslow	d	00 02	08 22	08 30			08a59	08 43			09 20						09 48		10 19		10 37		10 48
Alderley Edge	d	00a07		08 33							09 23						09 53		10 22				
Chelford	d										09 27								10 26				
Goostrey	d										09 31								10 31				
Holmes Chapel	d										09 34								10 34				
Sandbach	d			08 43							09 39								10 39				
Crewe 10	a		08 39	08 53				09 01			09 49						10 08		10 49		10 53		11 07
Kidsgrove 50	a									09 36													
Longport 50	a																						
Stoke-on-Trent 50	a					08 57				09 44				09 59		10 05						11 06	
Stafford 65,67	a		09 01					09 25								10 25						11 26	
Wolverhampton 7 68	a							09 40								10 38						11 41	
Birmingham New Street 12 68	a							09 57								10 57						11 58	
London Euston 15 ⊖65	a		10 55			10 59								12 06							12 54		

A To Shrewsbury
B To Chester
C To Buxton
D To Hazel Grove
E From Hull
F not 20 May. From Manchester Piccadilly
G From Manchester Airport to Cleethorpes
H To Bournemouth
I To Cardiff Central
J To Milford Haven

Table T084-R

Manchester, Stockport and Manchester Airport - Crewe and Stoke-on-Trent

Sundays

20 May to 9 September

		NT	VT	NT	NT	NT	VT	TP	XC	AW	VT	NT	NT	VT	NT	VT	TP	NT	XC	AW	VT	EM	NT
		A	◇1	B	◇ C		◇1	◇1 D	◇1 E	F	◇1	◇	B	◇1	◇	◇1	◇1 D	A	◇1 E	G	◇1	◇ H	B
Deansgate 85,89	d																						
Manchester Oxford Road 85,89	d																						
Manchester Picc. 10 85,89	d	10 34	10 35	10 43	10 58	11 06	11 15	11 19	11 27	11 30	11 35	11 41	11 49	11 55	12 02	12 15	12 19	12 23	12 26	12 32	12 35	12 43	12 48
Levenshulme	d			10 49									11 55					12 29					12 54
Heaton Chapel	d			10 52									11 58					12 32					12 57
Stockport	a	10 43	10 45	10 56	11 07	11 15	11 23	11 28	11 34	11 41	11 44	11 50	12 02	12 04	12 10	12 22	12 27	12 35	12 34	12 41	12 42	12 52	13 00
	d		10 46			11 16	11 24		11 36	11 43	11 44	11 52		12 05	12 11	12 23			12 35	12 42	12 43		
Cheadle Hulme	d					11 22						11 56			12 15								
Bramhall	d											11 59											
Poynton	d											12 02											
Adlington (Cheshire)	d											12 06											
Prestbury	d											12 09											
Macclesfield	a		10 57						11 49		11 57	12 12							12 48		12 57		
	d		10 57						11 49		11 57	12 13							12 49		12 57		
Congleton	d											12 20											
Handforth	d					11 26									12 19								
Manchester Airport ✈	d																						
Styal	d																						
Wilmslow	d					11 29				11 50				12 12	12 22					12 50			
Alderley Edge	d					11 32									12 25								
Chelford	d														12 29								
Goostrey	d														12 33								
Holmes Chapel	d					11 40									12 36								
Sandbach	d					11 45									12 41								
Crewe 10	a					11 55				12 10				12 28	12 51					13 09			
Kidsgrove 50	a											12 26											
Longport 50	a																						
Stoke-on-Trent 50	a		11 14				11 51		12 06		12 14	12 37				12 49			13 06		13 14		
Stafford 65,67	a								12 24										13 24				
Wolverhampton 7 68	a								12 38										13 37				
Birmingham New Street 12 68	a								12 57										13 57				
London Euston 15 ⊖65	a		12 57				13 28				13 47			14 10		14 28					14 48		

		VT	XC	NT	NT	VT	TP	NT	XC	AW	VT	NT	VT	XC	NT	VT	TP	NT	XC	AW	VT	NT
		◇1	◇1 I	◇ C	◇	◇1	◇1 D	A	◇1 E	F	◇1	B	◇1	◇1 J	◇	◇1	◇1 D	A	◇1 E	G	◇1	◇
Deansgate 85,89	d																					
Manchester Oxford Road 85,89	d																					
Manchester Picc. 10 85,89	d	12 55	13 05	13 06	13 08	13 15	13 19	13 23	13 27	13 30	13 35	13 51	13 55	14 05	14 08	14 15	14 19	14 23	14 27	14 30	14 35	14 45
Levenshulme	d							13 29				13 57						14 29				
Heaton Chapel	d							13 32				14 00						14 32				
Stockport	a	13 03	13 12	13 16	13 17	13 22	13 28	13 35	13 35	13 39	13 42	14 03	14 03	14 12	14 17	14 22	14 27	14 35	14 34	14 38	14 42	14 54
	d	13 05	13 13		13 18	13 23			13 36	13 40	13 42		14 05	14 13	14 18	14 22			14 36	14 40	14 42	14 56
Cheadle Hulme	d				13 22										14 22							15 01
Bramhall	d																					15 04
Poynton	d																					15 07
Adlington (Cheshire)	d																					15 10
Prestbury	d																					15 13
Macclesfield	a		13 25						13 48		13 55			14 25					14 48		14 55	15 17
	d		13 26						13 49		13 55			14 26					14 49		14 55	15 17
Congleton	d																					15 24
Handforth	d				13 26										14 26							
Manchester Airport ✈	d																					
Styal	d																					
Wilmslow	d	13 13			13 29					13 47			14 12		14 29					14 48		
Alderley Edge	d				13 32										14 32							
Chelford	d				13 36										14 36							
Goostrey	d				13 40										14 40							
Holmes Chapel	d				13 43										14 43							
Sandbach	d				13 48										14 48							
Crewe 10	a	13 29			14 02					14 07			14 28		15 02					15 08		
Kidsgrove 50	a																					15 30
Longport 50	a																					
Stoke-on-Trent 50	a		13 44			13 50			14 06		14 12			14 43		14 49			15 06		15 12	15 40
Stafford 65,67	a		14 01						14 24					15 00					15 23			
Wolverhampton 7 68	a		14 15						14 39					15 14					15 38			
Birmingham New Street 12 68	a		14 33						14 57					15 33					15 57			
London Euston 15 ⊖65	a	15 07				15 26					15 46		16 06			16 26					16 46	

A To Hazel Grove
B To Buxton
C To Chester
D From Manchester Airport to Cleethorpes
E To Bournemouth
F To Cardiff Central
G To Milford Haven
H To Norwich
I To Paignton
J To Bristol Temple Meads

Table T084-R

Manchester, Stockport and Manchester Airport - Crewe and Stoke-on-Trent

		NT	VT	XC	NT	NT	VT	TP	NT	XC	AW	VT	NT	VT	XC	NT	VT	TP	NT	XC	AW	VT	NT
			◇■	◇■	◇	◇	◇■	◇■		◇■	■	◇■		◇■	◇■	◇	◇■	◇■		◇■	■	◇■	
		A		B	C			D	E	F	G		A		B			D	E	F	G		A
			☕	🛒			☕	🛒		🛒	🛒	☕		☕	🛒		☕	🛒		🛒	🛒	☕	
Deansgate 85,89 ⇌	d																						
Manchester Oxford Road 85,89	d																						
Manchester Picc. [10] 85,89 ⇌	d	14 49	14 55	15 05	15 06	15 08	15 15	15 19	15 24	15 27	15 30	15 35	15 49	15 55	16 05	16 08	16 15	16 19	16 23	16 27	16 30	16 35	16 49
Levenshulme	d	14 55							15 30				15 55						16 29				16 55
Heaton Chapel	d	14 58							15 33				15 58						16 32				16 58
Stockport	a	15 01	15 03	15 12	15 16	15 17	15 22	15 27	15 36	15 35	15 40	15 42	16 01	16 02	16 12	16 17	16 22	16 27	16 35	16 34	16 39	16 42	17 01
	d		15 04	15 13		15 18	15 22			15 36	15 40	15 42		16 03	16 13	16 18	16 23			16 36	16 39	16 42	
Cheadle Hulme	d					15 22										16 22							
Bramhall	d																						
Poynton	d																						
Adlington (Cheshire)	d																						
Prestbury	d																						
Macclesfield	a			15 25						15 48		15 55			16 25					16 48		16 55	
	d			15 26						15 49		15 55			16 26					16 49		16 55	
Congleton	d																						
Handforth	d					15 26										16 26							
Manchester Airport ✈	d																						
Styal	d																						
Wilmslow	d		15 12			15 29					15 48			16 11		16 29					16 48		
Alderley Edge	d					15 32										16 32							
Chelford	d					15 36										16 36							
Goostrey	d					15 40										16 40							
Holmes Chapel	d					15 43										16 43							
Sandbach	d					15 48										16 48							
Crewe [10]	a		15 28			16 02					16 07			16 27		17 02					17 07		
Kidsgrove 50	a																						
Longport 50	a																						
Stoke-on-Trent 50	a			15 43			15 49			16 06		16 12			16 43		16 48			17 06		17 12	
Stafford 65,67	a			16 00						16 24					17 00					17 24			
Wolverhampton [7] 68 ⇌	a			16 14						16 39					17 14					17 39			
Birmingham New Street [12] 68	a			16 33						16 57					17 32					17 57			
London Euston [15] ⊖65	a		17 08				17 27					17 44		18 08			18 27					18 46	

		VT	XC	NT	NT	VT	TP	NT	XC	AW	VT	NT	VT	XC	NT	VT	TP	NT	XC	AW	VT	NT
		◇■	◇■	◇	◇	◇■	◇■		◇■	■	◇■		◇■	◇■	◇	◇■	◇■		◇■	■	◇■	◇
			H	C			D	E	F	C		A		B			D	E	I	G		
		☕	🛒			☕	🛒		🛒	🛒	☕		☕	🛒		☕	🛒		🛒		☕	
Deansgate 85,89 ⇌	d																					
Manchester Oxford Road 85,89	d																					
Manchester Picc. [10] 85,89 ⇌	d	16 55	17 05	17 06	17 08	17 15	17 19	17 23	17 27	17 30	17 35	17 49	17 55	18 05	18 09	18 15	18 19	18 23	18 27	18 30	18 35	18 46
Levenshulme	d							17 29				17 55						18 29				
Heaton Chapel	d							17 32				17 58						18 32				
Stockport	a	17 02	17 12	17 16	17 17	17 22	17 27	17 35	17 34	17 39	17 42	18 01	18 02	18 12	18 18	18 22	18 27	18 35	18 34	18 39	18 42	18 54
	d	17 03	17 13		17 18	17 22			17 36	17 40	17 42		18 03	18 13	18 19	18 22			18 36	18 40	18 42	18 56
Cheadle Hulme	d				17 23										18 23							19 00
Bramhall	d																					19 03
Poynton	d																					19 06
Adlington (Cheshire)	d																					19 10
Prestbury	d																					19 13
Macclesfield	a		17 25						17 48		17 55			18 25					18 48		18 55	19 16
	d		17 26						17 49		17 55			18 26					18 49		18 55	19 17
Congleton	d																					19 24
Handforth	d				17 27										18 27							
Manchester Airport ✈	d																					
Styal	d																					
Wilmslow	d	17 11			17 30					17 47			18 11		18 30					18 48		
Alderley Edge	d				17 33										18 33							
Chelford	d				17 37										18 37							
Goostrey	d				17 42										18 42							
Holmes Chapel	d				17 45										18 45							
Sandbach	d				17 50										18 50							
Crewe [10]	a	17 27			18 02					18 07			18 27		19 02					19 07		
Kidsgrove 50	a																					19 30
Longport 50	a																					
Stoke-on-Trent 50	a		17 44			17 49			18 06		18 12			18 44		18 50			19 06		19 12	19 42
Stafford 65,67	a		18 01						18 24					19 01					19 24			
Wolverhampton [7] 68 ⇌	a		18 15						18 37					19 15					19 38			
Birmingham New Street [12] 68	a		18 33						18 57					19 33					19 57			
London Euston [15] ⊖65	a	19 06				19 27					19 46		20 07			20 27					20 45	

A To Buxton
B To Bristol Temple Meads
C To Chester
D From Manchester Airport to Cleethorpes
E To Hazel Grove
F To Bournemouth
G To Cardiff Central
H To Paignton
I To Southampton Central

Table T084-R

Manchester, Stockport and Manchester Airport - Crewe and Stoke-on-Trent

		NT	VT	XC	NT	NT	VT	TP	NT	XC	AW	VT	NT	XC	NT	TP	VT	AW	NT	NT	VT	XC	NT
			◇■	◇■	◇	◇	◇■	◇■		◇■	◇	◇■		◇■	◇	◇■	◇■	◇			◇■	◇■	◇
		A		B	C			D	E	F	G		A	B		D		G	E	A			C
			☕	🛒			☕			🛒		☕					☕				☕		
Deansgate 85,89 ⇌	d																						
Manchester Oxford Road 85,89	d																						
Manchester Picc. [10] 85,89 ⇌	d	18 49	18 55	19 05	19 06	19 08	19 15	19 19	19 23	19 27	19 30	19 35	19 49	20 05	20 08	20 18	20 21	20 30	20 33	20 49	20 55	21 05	21 06
Levenshulme	d	18 55							19 29				19 55						20 39	20 55			
Heaton Chapel	d	18 58							19 32				19 58						20 42	20 58			
Stockport	a	19 01	19 02	19 12	19 16	19 17	19 22	19 27	19 35	19 34	19 39	19 41	20 01	20 13	20 17	20 26	20 27	20 38	20 45	21 01	21 03	21 12	21 16
	d		19 03	19 13		19 18	19 22			19 36	19 40	19 41		20 14	20 18		20 27	20 40			21 03	21 13	
Cheadle Hulme	d					19 22									20 23								
Bramhall	d																						
Poynton	d																						
Adlington (Cheshire)	d																						
Prestbury	d																						
Macclesfield	a			19 25						19 48		19 54		20 26			20 40				21 16	21 25	
	d			19 26						19 49		19 54		20 27			20 40				21 16	21 26	
Congleton	d																						
Handforth	d					19 26									20 27								
Manchester Airport ✈	d																						
Styal	d																						
Wilmslow	d		19 11			19 29					19 48				20 30			20 48					
Alderley Edge	d					19 32									20 33								
Chelford	d					19 36									20 37								
Goostrey	d					19 40									20 41								
Holmes Chapel	d					19 43									20 44								
Sandbach	d					19 48									20 49								
Crewe [10]	a		19 27			20 02					20 08				21 02			21 07					
Kidsgrove 50	a																						
Longport 50	a																						
Stoke-on-Trent 50	a			19 44			19 49			20 06		20 11		20 44			20 57				21 33	21 44	
Stafford 65,67	a			20 01						20 24				21 01								22 04	
Wolverhampton [7] 68 ⇌	a			20 15						20 38				21 15								22 18	
Birmingham New Street [12] 68	a			20 33						20 57				21 33								22 36	
London Euston [15] ⊖65	a		21 08				21 31					22 01					22 56				23 46		

		NT	TP	NT	AW	NT	NT	XC	NT	TP	NT	AW	NT	NT	TP	NT
			◇■			◇		◇■	◇	◇■					◇■	
			D	E			A			H	E		A		I	E
Deansgate 85,89 ⇌	d															
Manchester Oxford Road 85,89	d															
Manchester Picc. [10] 85,89 ⇌	d	21 12	21 19	21 23	21 34	21 49	21 50	22 05	22 15	22 19	22 25	22 35	22 48	23 00	23 20	23 26
Levenshulme	d			21 29			21 56				22 32		22 54			23 33
Heaton Chapel	d			21 32			21 59				22 35		22 57			23 36
Stockport	a	21 20	21 27	21 35	21 43	21 58	22 02	22 12	22 24	22 27	22 38		23 00	23 08	23 28	23 39
	d	21 23			21 47	21 59		22 13	22 24					23 10		
Cheadle Hulme	d	21 27				22 03			22 28					23 14		
Bramhall	d					22 06										
Poynton	d					22 09										
Adlington (Cheshire)	d					22 12										
Prestbury	d					22 15										
Macclesfield	a					22 19		22 25								
	d					22 29		22 26								
Congleton	d					22 36										
Handforth	d	21 31							22 32					23 18		
Manchester Airport ✈	d															
Styal	d															
Wilmslow	d	21 34			21 57				22 35			22 50		23 21		
Alderley Edge	d	21 37							22 38			22 54		23a28		
Chelford	d	21 41							22 42							
Goostrey	d	21 45							22 47							
Holmes Chapel	d	21 48							22 50							
Sandbach	d	21 53							22 55							
Crewe [10]	a	22 03			22 16				23 05			23 13				
Kidsgrove 50	a					22 42										
Longport 50	a															
Stoke-on-Trent 50	a					22 53		22 44								
Stafford 65,67	a							23 01								
Wolverhampton [7] 68 ⇌	a							23 15								
Birmingham New Street [12] 68	a							23 33								
London Euston [15] ⊖65	a															

A To Buxton
B To Bristol Temple Meads
C To Chester
D From Manchester Airport to Cleethorpes
E To Hazel Grove
F To Reading
G To Cardiff Central
H From Manchester Airport to Doncaster
I From Manchester Airport to Sheffield

Table T084-R

Sundays

16 September to 2 December

Manchester, Stockport and Manchester Airport - Crewe and Stoke-on-Trent

	NT	TP	VT	NT	TP	VT	NT	XC	NT	NT	NT	TP	NT	NT	TP	VT	NT	XC	AW	NT	TP	NT
	A	B	◇		◇ C	◇	B	◇ D	E	F	◇	G	◇	◇ H	◇ C	◇	I	◇ D	J	F	◇ K	◇
Deansgate 85,89 d																						
Manchester Oxford Road 85,89 d												08 46										
Manchester Picc. 85,89 d		00 40	08 05	08 09	08 12	08 20	08 23	08 27	08 30	08 50	08 53	08 56	08 59	09 04	09 10	09 20	09 23	09 27	09 30	09 45	09 52	09 55
Levenshulme d										08 56							09 29					
Heaton Chapel d										08 59							09 32					
Stockport a			08 13	08 17	08 21	08 28		08 34		09 02	09 02		09 08	09 12	09 18	09 28	09 35	09 35	09 40	09 54		10 03
Stockport d			08 14	08 18		08 28		08 36			09 02		09 08			09 28		09 36	09 40			10 06
Cheadle Hulme d				08 23							09 06		09 13									10 12
Bramhall d											09 09											
Poynton d											09 12											
Adlington (Cheshire) d											09 16											
Prestbury d											09 19											
Macclesfield a						08 41					09 22					09 40		09 48				
Macclesfield d						08 41					09 23					09 40		09 49				
Congleton d											09 30											
Handforth d				08 27									09 17									10 16
Manchester Airport d		01a05					08 50		09 11			09a10									10a07	
Styal d							08 56		09 16													
Wilmslow d	00 02		08 22	08 30			08a59	08 43	09a19				09 20						09 48			10 19
Alderley Edge d	00a07			08 33									09 23						09 53			10 22
Chelford d													09 27									10 26
Goostrey d													09 31									10 31
Holmes Chapel d													09 34									10 34
Sandbach d				08 43									09 39									10 39
Crewe a			08 39	08 53				09 01					09 49						10 08			10 49
Kidsgrove 50 a											09 36											
Longport 50 a																						
Stoke-on-Trent 50 a						08 57					09 44					09 59		10 05				
Stafford 65,67 a			09 01					09 25										10 25				
Wolverhampton 68 a								09 40										10 38				
Birmingham New Street 68 a								09 57										10 57				
London Euston ⊖65 a			10 55			10 59										12 06						

	TP	VT	NT	XC	AW	VT	NT	NT	NT	VT	TP	XC	AW	VT	NT	NT	VT	NT	VT	TP	XC	AW
	◇ C	◇	I	◇ D	L	◇	F	◇ H		◇	◇ C	◇ D	J	◇	◇	F	◇	◇	◇	◇ C	◇ D	L
Deansgate 85,89 d																						
Manchester Oxford Road 85,89 d																						
Manchester Picc. 85,89 d	10 14	10 20	10 23	10 26	10 31	10 35	10 45	10 58	11 06	11 15	11 19	11 27	11 30	11 35	11 41	11 49	11 55	12 01	12 15	12 19	12 26	12 32
Levenshulme d			10 29				10 51									11 55						
Heaton Chapel d			10 32				10 54									11 58						
Stockport a	10 23	10 28	10 35	10 34	10 39	10 45	10 58	11 07	11 15	11 23	11 27	11 34	11 41	11 44	11 50	12 02	12 04	12 10	12 22	12 28	12 34	12 41
Stockport d		10 29		10 36	10 40	10 46			11 16	11 24		11 36	11 43	11 44	11 52		12 05	12 11	12 23		12 35	12 42
Cheadle Hulme d									11 22						11 56			12 15				
Bramhall d															11 59							
Poynton d															12 02							
Adlington (Cheshire) d															12 06							
Prestbury d															12 09							
Macclesfield a				10 48		10 57						11 49		11 57	12 12						12 48	
Macclesfield d				10 49		10 57						11 49		11 57	12 13						12 49	
Congleton d															12 20							
Handforth d									11 26									12 19				
Manchester Airport d																						
Styal d																						
Wilmslow d		10 37			10 48				11 29				11 50				12 12	12 22				12 50
Alderley Edge d									11 32									12 25				
Chelford d																		12 29				
Goostrey d																		12 33				
Holmes Chapel d									11 40									12 36				
Sandbach d									11 45									12 41				
Crewe a		10 53			11 07				11 55				12 10				12 28	12 51				13 09
Kidsgrove 50 a															12 26							
Longport 50 a																						
Stoke-on-Trent 50 a				11 06		11 14				11 51		12 06		12 14	12 37				12 49		13 06	
Stafford 65,67 a				11 26								12 24									13 24	
Wolverhampton 68 a				11 41								12 38									13 37	
Birmingham New Street 68 a				11 58								12 57									13 57	
London Euston ⊖65 a		12 54				12 57				13 28				13 47			14 10		14 28			

- A From Manchester Piccadilly
- B from 28 October
- C From Manchester Airport to Cleethorpes
- D To Bournemouth
- E until 21 October
- F To Buxton
- G from 28 October. From Manchester Victoria
- H To Chester
- I To Hazel Grove
- J To Cardiff Central
- K from 28 October. From Greenfield
- L To Milford Haven

Table T084-R

Sundays

16 September to 2 December

Manchester, Stockport and Manchester Airport - Crewe and Stoke-on-Trent

	VT	EM	NT	VT	XC	NT	NT	VT	TP	NT	XC	AW	VT	NT	VT	XC	NT	VT	TP	NT	XC
	◇	◇ A	B	◇	◇ C	◇ D	◇	◇	◇ E	F	◇ G	H	◇	B	◇	◇ I	◇	◇	◇ E	F	◇ G
Deansgate 85,89 d																					
Manchester Oxford Road 85,89 d																					
Manchester Picc. 85,89 d	12 35	12 43	12 49	12 55	13 05	13 06	13 08	13 15	13 19	13 23	13 27	13 30	13 35	13 51	13 55	14 05	14 08	14 15	14 19	14 23	14 27
Levenshulme d			12 55							13 29				13 57						14 29	
Heaton Chapel d			12 58							13 32				14 00						14 32	
Stockport a	12 42	12 52	13 02	13 04	13 12	13 16	13 17	13 22	13 28	13 35	13 35	13 39	13 42	14 03	14 03	14 12	14 17	14 22	14 27	14 35	14 34
Stockport d	12 43			13 05	13 13		13 18	13 23			13 36	13 40	13 42		14 05	14 13	14 18	14 22			14 36
Cheadle Hulme d							13 22										14 22				
Bramhall d																					
Poynton d																					
Adlington (Cheshire) d																					
Prestbury d																					
Macclesfield a	12 57				13 25						13 48		13 55			14 25					14 48
Macclesfield d	12 57				13 26						13 49		13 55			14 26					14 49
Congleton d																					
Handforth d							13 26										14 26				
Manchester Airport d																					
Styal d																					
Wilmslow d				13 13			13 29					13 47			14 12		14 29				
Alderley Edge d							13 32										14 32				
Chelford d							13 36										14 36				
Goostrey d							13 40										14 40				
Holmes Chapel d							13 43										14 43				
Sandbach d							13 48										14 48				
Crewe a				13 29			14 02					14 07			14 28		15 02				
Kidsgrove 50 a																					
Longport 50 a																					
Stoke-on-Trent 50 a	13 14				13 44			13 50			14 06		14 12			14 43		14 49			15 06
Stafford 65,67 a					14 01						14 24					15 00					15 23
Wolverhampton 68 a					14 15						14 39					15 14					15 38
Birmingham New Street 68 a					14 33						14 57					15 33					15 57
London Euston ⊖65 a	14 48			15 07				15 26					15 46		16 06			16 26			

	AW	VT	NT	NT	VT	XC	NT	NT	VT	TP	NT	XC	AW	VT	NT	VT	XC	NT	VT	TP	NT	XC
	J	◇	◇	B	◇	◇ I	◇ D	◇	◇	◇ E	F	◇ G	H	◇	B	◇	◇ I	◇	◇	◇ E	F	◇ G
Deansgate 85,89 d																						
Manchester Oxford Road 85,89 d																						
Manchester Picc. 85,89 d	14 30	14 35	14 45	14 49	14 55	15 05	15 06	15 08	15 15	15 19	15 24	15 27	15 30	15 35	15 49	15 55	16 05	16 08	16 15	16 19	16 23	16 27
Levenshulme d				14 55							15 30				15 55						16 29	
Heaton Chapel d				14 58							15 33				15 58						16 32	
Stockport a	14 38	14 42	14 54	15 01	15 03	15 12	15 16	15 17	15 22	15 27	15 36	15 35	15 40	15 42	16 01	16 02	16 12	16 17	16 22	16 27	16 35	16 34
Stockport d	14 40	14 42	14 56		15 04	15 13		15 18	15 22			15 36	15 40	15 42		16 03	16 13	16 18	16 23			16 36
Cheadle Hulme d			15 01					15 22										16 22				
Bramhall d			15 04																			
Poynton d			15 07																			
Adlington (Cheshire) d			15 10																			
Prestbury d			15 13																			
Macclesfield a		14 55	15 17			15 25						15 48		15 55			16 25					16 48
Macclesfield d		14 55	15 17			15 26						15 49		15 55			16 26					16 49
Congleton d			15 24																			
Handforth d								15 26										16 26				
Manchester Airport d																						
Styal d																						
Wilmslow d	14 48				15 12			15 29					15 48			16 11		16 29				
Alderley Edge d								15 32										16 32				
Chelford d								15 36										16 36				
Goostrey d								15 40										16 40				
Holmes Chapel d								15 43										16 43				
Sandbach d								15 48										16 48				
Crewe a	15 08				15 28			16 02					16 07			16 27		17 02				
Kidsgrove 50 a			15 30																			
Longport 50 a																						
Stoke-on-Trent 50 a		15 12	15 40			15 43			15 49			16 06		16 12			16 43		16 48			17 06
Stafford 65,67 a						16 00						16 24					17 00					17 24
Wolverhampton 68 a						16 14						16 39					17 14					17 39
Birmingham New Street 68 a						16 33						16 57					17 32					17 57
London Euston ⊖65 a		16 46			17 08				17 27					17 44		18 08			18 27			

- A To Norwich
- B To Buxton
- C To Paignton
- D To Chester
- E From Manchester Airport to Cleethorpes
- F To Hazel Grove
- G To Bournemouth
- H To Cardiff Central
- I To Bristol Temple Meads
- J To Milford Haven

Manchester, Stockport and Manchester Airport - Crewe and Stoke-on-Trent

	AW	VT	NT	VT	XC	NT	NT	VT	TP	NT	XC	AW	VT	NT	VT	XC	NT	VT	TP	NT	XC
	■	◇■		◇■	◇■	◇	◇	◇■	◇■		◇■	■	◇■		◇■	◇■	◇	◇■	◇■		◇■
	A		B		C	D			E	F	G	D		B		H			E	F	I
Deansgate 85,89 d																					
Manchester Oxford Road 85,89 d																					
Manchester Picc. 85,89 d	16 30	16 35	16 49	16 55	17 05	17 06	17 08	17 15	17 19	17 23	17 27	17 30	17 35	17 49	17 55	18 05	18 09	18 15	18 19	18 23	18 27
Levenshulme d			16 55							17 29				17 55						18 29	
Heaton Chapel d			16 58							17 32				17 58						18 32	
Stockport a	16 39	16 42	17 01	17 02	17 12	17 16	17 17	17 22	17 27	17 35	17 34	17 39	17 42	18 01	18 02	18 12	18 18	18 22	18 27	18 35	18 34
d	16 39	16 42		17 03	17 13		17 18	17 22			17 36	17 40	17 42		18 03	18 13	18 19	18 22			18 36
Cheadle Hulme d							17 23										18 23				
Bramhall d																					
Poynton d																					
Adlington (Cheshire) d																					
Prestbury d																					
Macclesfield a		16 55			17 25						17 48		17 55			18 25					18 48
d		16 55			17 26						17 49		17 55			18 26					18 49
Congleton d																					
Handforth d							17 27										18 27				
Manchester Airport d																					
Styal d																					
Wilmslow d	16 48			17 11			17 30					17 47			18 11		18 30				
Alderley Edge d							17 33										18 33				
Chelford d							17 37										18 37				
Goostrey d							17 42										18 42				
Holmes Chapel d							17 45										18 45				
Sandbach d							17 50										18 50				
Crewe a	17 07			17 27			18 02					18 07			18 27		19 02				
Kidsgrove 50 a																					
Longport 50 a																					
Stoke-on-Trent 50 a		17 12			17 44			17 49			18 06		18 12			18 44		18 50			19 06
Stafford 65,67 a					18 01						18 24					19 01					19 24
Wolverhampton 68 a					18 15						18 37					19 15					19 38
Birmingham New Street 68 a					18 33						18 57					19 33					19 57
London Euston ⊖65 a		18 46		19 06				19 27					19 46		20 07			20 27			

	AW	VT	NT	NT	VT	XC	NT	NT	VT	TP	NT	XC	AW	VT	NT	XC	NT	TP	VT	AW	NT	NT
	■	◇■	◇		◇■	◇■	◇	◇	◇■	◇■		◇■	◇	◇■		◇■	◇	◇■	◇■	◇		
	A			B		H	D			E	F	J	A		B	H		E		A	F	B
Deansgate 85,89 d																						
Manchester Oxford Road 85,89 d																						
Manchester Picc. 85,89 d	18 30	18 35	18 46	18 49	18 55	19 05	19 06	19 08	19 15	19 19	19 23	19 27	19 30	19 35	19 49	20 05	20 08	20 18	20 21	20 30	20 33	20 49
Levenshulme d				18 55							19 29				19 55						20 39	20 55
Heaton Chapel d				18 58							19 32				19 58						20 42	20 58
Stockport a	18 39	18 42	18 54	19 01	19 02	19 12	19 16	19 17	19 22	19 27	19 35	19 34	19 39	19 41	20 01	20 13	20 17	20 26	20 27	20 38	20 45	21 01
d	18 40	18 42	18 56		19 03	19 13		19 18	19 22			19 36	19 40	19 41		20 14	20 18		20 27	20 40		
Cheadle Hulme d			19 00					19 22									20 23					
Bramhall d			19 03																			
Poynton d			19 06																			
Adlington (Cheshire) d			19 10																			
Prestbury d			19 13																			
Macclesfield a		18 55	19 16			19 25						19 48		19 54		20 26			20 40			
d		18 55	19 17			19 26						19 49		19 54		20 27			20 40			
Congleton d			19 24																			
Handforth d								19 26									20 27					
Manchester Airport d																						
Styal d																						
Wilmslow d	18 48				19 11			19 29					19 48				20 30			20 48		
Alderley Edge d								19 32									20 33					
Chelford d								19 36									20 37					
Goostrey d								19 40									20 41					
Holmes Chapel d								19 43									20 44					
Sandbach d								19 48									20 49					
Crewe a	19 07				19 27			20 02					20 08				21 02			21 07		
Kidsgrove 50 a			19 30																			
Longport 50 a																						
Stoke-on-Trent 50 a		19 12	19 42			19 44			19 49			20 06		20 11		20 44			20 57			
Stafford 65,67 a						20 01						20 24				21 01						
Wolverhampton 68 a						20 15						20 38				21 15						
Birmingham New Street 68 a						20 33						20 57				21 33						
London Euston ⊖65 a		20 45			21 08				21 31					22 01					22 56			

A To Cardiff Central
B To Buxton
C To Plymouth
D To Chester
E From Manchester Airport to Cleethorpes
F To Hazel Grove
G To Bournemouth
H To Bristol Temple Meads
I To Southampton Central
J To Reading

Table T084-R

Sundays

16 September to 2 December

Manchester, Stockport and Manchester Airport - Crewe and Stoke-on-Trent

	VT	XC	NT	NT	TP	NT	AW	NT	NT	XC	NT	TP	NT	AW	NT	NT	TP	NT
	◇■	◇■	◇		◇■			◇		◇■	◇	◇■					◇■	
			A		B	C			D			E	C		D		F	C
Deansgate 85,89 d																		
Manchester Oxford Road 85,89 d																		
Manchester Picc. 85,89 d	20 55	21 05	21 06	21 12	21 19	21 23	21 34	21 49	21 50	22 05	22 15	22 19	22 25	22 35	22 48	23 00	23 20	23 26
Levenshulme d						21 29			21 56				22 32		22 54			23 33
Heaton Chapel d						21 32			21 59				22 35		22 57			23 36
Stockport a	21 03	21 12	21 16	21 20	21 27	21 35	21 43	21 58	22 02	22 12	22 24	22 27	22 38		23 00	23 08	23 28	23 39
d	21 03	21 13		21 23			21 47	21 59		22 13	22 24					23 10		
Cheadle Hulme d				21 27				22 03			22 28					23 14		
Bramhall d								22 06										
Poynton d								22 09										
Adlington (Cheshire) d								22 12										
Prestbury d								22 15										
Macclesfield a	21 16	21 25						22 19		22 25								
d	21 16	21 26						22 29		22 26								
Congleton d								22 36										
Handforth d				21 31							22 32					23 18		
Manchester Airport d																		
Styal d																		
Wilmslow d				21 34			21 57				22 35			22 50		23 21		
Alderley Edge d				21 37							22 38			22 54		23a28		
Chelford d				21 41							22 42							
Goostrey d				21 45							22 47							
Holmes Chapel d				21 48							22 50							
Sandbach d				21 53							22 55							
Crewe a				22 03			22 16				23 05			23 13				
Kidsgrove 50 a								22 42										
Longport 50 a																		
Stoke-on-Trent 50 a	21 33	21 44						22 53		22 44								
Stafford 65,67 a		22 04								23 01								
Wolverhampton 68 a		22 18								23 15								
Birmingham New Street 68 a		22 36								23 33								
London Euston ⊖65 a	23 46																	

A To Chester
B From Manchester Airport to Cleethorpes
C To Hazel Grove
D To Buxton
E From Manchester Airport to Doncaster
F From Manchester Airport to Sheffield

Table T085-F

Manchester Airport - Manchester

Mondays to Fridays

21 May to 7 December

Miles	Station	NT MX	NT MO	TP MX	TP MO	NT	TP	NT	TP	NT		AW	NT	TP	TP	NT	TP	TP	NT	NT		TP	TP	NT
		◇		◇1	◇1		◇1	◇	◇1	◇		◇ 🍴	◇	◇1	◇1		◇1 🍴	◇1	◇	◇		◇1 🍴	◇1 🍴	
—	Crewe 10 84 d					00 44																		06 16
—	Wilmslow 84 d															05 42								06 42
0	**Manchester Airport** d		00 05	00 38	00 45	01 13	04 22	04 34	05 03	05 20		05 33	05 42	05 48	05 54	05 59	06 10	06 19	06 35	06 39		06 47	06 53	06 58
1½	Heald Green d							04 38		05 24			05 46			06 03			06 39					07 02
4	Gatley d												05 49			06 06				06 45				07 05
5¼	East Didsbury d									05 28						06 08			06 44					07 07
6¼	Burnage d									05 31						06 11				06 49				07 10
7¼	Mauldeth Road d	00 01								05 33						06 13				06 51				07 12
—	**Manchester Piccadilly 10** a	00 08	00 20	00 51	00 58	01 28	04 35	04 50	05 16	05 41		05 46	06 00	06 04	06 11	06 20	06 24	06 32	06 53	06 59		07 03	07 12	07 21
—	d							04 51	05 17	05 42		05 47	06 01	06 05		06 22		06 34	06 55	07 01		07 05		07 22
—	**Manchester Oxford Rd.** a							04 53	05 19	05 44		05 49	06 03	06 07		06 24		06 36	06 57	07 03		07 07		07 24
—	Deansgate a												06 07			06 31				07 07				07 32

Station	TP	TP	NT	NT	TP	TP		NT	TP	TP	NT	NT	TP	TP	NT	TP		TP	NT	NT	TP	TP	NT	TP
	◇1 🍴	◇1 🍴	◇	◇	◇1 🍴	◇1 🍴		◇	◇1 🍴	◇1 🍴	◇	◇	◇1 🍴	◇1 🍴	◇	◇1 🍴		◇1 🍴	◇	◇	◇1 🍴	◇1 🍴	◇	◇1 🍴
Crewe 10 84 d								07 13							08 16								09 16	
Wilmslow 84 d								07 42							08 42								09 42	
Manchester Airport d	07 10	07 19	07 24	07 40	07 47	07 53		07 59	08 10	08 17	08 28	08 41	08 47	08 53	08 59	09 10		09 19	09 29	09 40	09 47	09 53	09 58	10 10
Heald Green d			07 28	07 44				08 03				08 45			09 03				09 33	09 44			10 03	
Gatley d				07 47				08 06		08 22					09 06					09 47			10 06	
East Didsbury d			07 32					08 08			08 34				09 08				09 37				10 08	
Burnage d				07 51				08 11			08 37				09 11					09 51			10 11	
Mauldeth Road d								08 13			08 39				09 13								10 13	
Manchester Piccadilly 10 a	07 25	07 33	07 41	07 59	08 03	08 11		08 21	08 25	08 33	08 46	08 59	09 03	09 11	09 21	09 25		09 33	09 46	09 59	10 03	10 11	10 21	10 25
d		07 35	07 43	08 01	08 05			08 22		08 35	08 47	09 01	09 05		09 22			09 35	09 47	10 01	10 05		10 22	
Manchester Oxford Rd. a		07 37	07 45	08 03	08 07			08 24		08 37	08 49	09 03	09 07		09 25			09 37	09 49	10 03	10 07		10 24	
Deansgate a				08 07				08 32				09 07			09 32					10 07			10 32	

Station	TP	NT		AW	NT	TP	TP	TP	NT	TP	NT	AW		NT	TP	TP	NT	TP	TP	NT	AW	NT		TP
	◇1 🍴	◇		◇ 🍴	◇	◇1 🍴	◇1 🍴	◇1 🍴	◇	◇1 🍴	◇	◇ 🍴		◇	◇1 🍴	◇1 🍴	◇	◇1 🍴	◇1 🍴	◇	◇ 🍴	◇		◇1 🍴
Crewe 10 84 d									10 16								11 17							
Wilmslow 84 d									10 42								11 42							
Manchester Airport d	10 19	10 29		10 37	10 40	10 47	10 53	10 59	11 02	11 19	11 29	11 37		11 41	11 47	11 53	11 57	12 10	12 19	12 29	12 35	12 40		12 47
Heald Green d		10 33			10 44				11 06		11 33			11 45			12 02			12 33		12 44		
Gatley d					10 47				11 09					11 48			12 05					12 47		
East Didsbury d		10 37		10 43					11 11		11 37	11 43					12 08			12 37	12 41			
Burnage d					10 51				11 14					11 52			12 10					12 51		
Mauldeth Road d									11 16								12 13							
Manchester Piccadilly 10 a	10 33	10 46		10 51	10 59	11 03	11 11	11 21	11 25	11 33	11 46	11 51		11 59	12 03	12 11	12 21	12 25	12 33	12 46	12 50	12 59		13 03
d	10 35	10 47		10 52	11 01	11 05			11 26	11 35	11 47	11 52		12 01	12 05		12 22		12 35	12 47	12 52	13 01		13 05
Manchester Oxford Rd. a	10 37	10 49		10 54	11 03	11 07			11 28	11 37	11 50	11 54		12 03	12 07		12 24		12 37	12 50	12 54	13 03		13 07
Deansgate a					11 07				11 32					12 07			12 32					13 07		

Station	TP	NT	TP	TP	NT	AW	NT	TP		TP	NT	TP	TP	NT	AW	NT	TP	TP		NT	TP	TP	NT	AW
	◇1 🍴	◇	◇1 🍴	◇1 🍴	◇	◇ 🍴	◇	◇1 🍴		◇1 🍴	◇	◇1 🍴	◇1 🍴	◇	◇ 🍴	◇	◇1 🍴	◇1 🍴		◇	◇1 🍴	◇1 🍴	◇	◇ 🍴
Crewe 10 84 d		12 17									13 18									14 16				
Wilmslow 84 d		12 42									13 43									14 42				
Manchester Airport d	12 53	12 59	13 10	13 19	13 29	13 37	13 40	13 47		13 53	13 58	14 10	14 19	14 29	14 37	14 40	14 47	14 53		14 58	15 10	15 19	15 29	15 37
Heald Green d		13 03			13 33		13 44				14 03			14 33		14 44				15 03			15 33	
Gatley d		13 06					13 47				14 06					14 47				15 06				
East Didsbury d		13 08			13 37	13 43					14 08			14 37	14 43					15 08			15 37	15 43
Burnage d		13 11					13 51				14 11					14 51				15 11				
Mauldeth Road d		13 13									14 13									15 13				
Manchester Piccadilly 10 a	13 11	13 21	13 25	13 33	13 46	13 51	13 59	14 03		14 11	14 21	14 25	14 33	14 46	14 51	14 59	15 03	15 11		15 21	15 25	15 33	15 46	15 51
d		13 22		13 35	13 47	13 52	14 01	14 05			14 22		14 35	14 47	14 52	15 01	15 05			15 22		15 35	15 47	15 52
Manchester Oxford Rd. a		13 24		13 37	13 50	13 54	14 03	14 07			14 24		14 37	14 50	14 54	15 03	15 07			15 24		15 37	15 50	15 54
Deansgate a		13 32					14 07				14 32					15 07				15 32				

Station	TP	TP	NT	TP		TP	NT	TP	TP	NT	TP	TP	NT	TP		TP	NT	TP	TP	NT	NT	TP	TP	NT
	◇1 🍴	◇1 🍴	◇	◇1 🍴		◇1 🍴	◇	◇1 🍴	◇1 🍴	◇	◇1 🍴	◇1 🍴	◇	◇1 🍴		◇1 🍴	◇	◇1 🍴	◇1 🍴	◇	◇	◇1	◇1	◇
Crewe 10 84 d			15 07							16 16							17 16							18 17
Wilmslow 84 d			15 42							16 42							17 42							18 42
Manchester Airport d	15 47	15 53	15 59	16 10		16 19	16 24	16 47	16 53	16 59	17 10	17 19	17 26	17 47		17 53	17 59	18 10	18 19	18 29	18 40	18 47	18 53	18 59
Heald Green d			16 03				16 28			17 03			17 30				18 03			18 33	18 44			19 03
Gatley d			16 06							17 06			17 33				18 06				18 47			19 06
East Didsbury d			16 08				16 32			17 08			17 36				18 08			18 37				19 08
Burnage d			16 11							17 11			17 38				18 11				18 51			19 11
Mauldeth Road d			16 13							17 13							18 13							19 13
Manchester Piccadilly 10 a	16 03	16 11	16 21	16 25		16 33	16 41	17 03	17 11	17 21	17 25	17 33	17 46	18 03		18 11	18 22	18 25	18 33	18 46	18 59	19 03	19 11	19 21
d	16 05		16 22			16 35	16 45	17 05		17 23		17 35	17 47	18 05					18 35	18 48	19 01	19 05		
Manchester Oxford Rd. a	16 07		16 24			16 37	16 47	17 07		17 25		17 37	17 50	18 07					18 37	18 50	19 03	19 07		
Deansgate a			16 32							17 32											19 06			

Table T085-F

Manchester Airport - Manchester

Mondays to Fridays

21 May to 7 December

Station	TP	TP	NT	NT	TP	TP		NT	TP	TP	NT	AW	NT	TP	TP	NT		TP	TP	NT	AW	NT	TP	NT
	◇1 🍴	◇1	◇	◇	◇1	◇1			◇1 🍴	◇1	◇		◇	◇1	◇1			◇1 🍴	◇1	◇		◇	◇1	
Crewe 10 84 d																								
Wilmslow 84 d								19 43								20 43								21 34
Manchester Airport d	19 10	19 19	19 29	19 40	19 47	19 53		19 59	20 10	20 19	20 29	20 35	20 39	20 45	20 53	20 58		21 05	21 22	21 29	21 32	21 37	21 53	21 58
Heald Green d			19 33	19 44				20 03					20 43			21 02								22 02
Gatley d				19 47				20 06					20 46			21 05								22 05
East Didsbury d			19 37					20 08								21 07								22 07
Burnage d				19 51				20 11							21 00								22 00	
Mauldeth Road d								20 13							21 03								22 03	
Manchester Piccadilly 10 a	19 25	19 33	19 46	19 59	20 05	20 11		20 21	20 25	20 33	20 41	20 48	20 56	21 00	21 11	21 17		21 21	21 36	21 42	21 48	21 53	22 11	22 17
d		19 35	19 47	20 01	20 05			20 22		20 35	20 43	20 50	20 57	21 05		21 18				21 43	21 50	22 01		22 18
Manchester Oxford Rd. a		19 37	19 50	20 03	20 08			20 24		20 37	20 45	20 52	20 59	21 07		21 20				21 45	21 52	22 03		22 20
Deansgate a				20 07				20 32					21 02			21 31						22 06		22 33

Station	TP	NT		NT	TP	NT	TP	NT	TP	NT
	◇1			◇	◇1		◇1		◇1	◇
Crewe 10 84 d										
Wilmslow 84 d						22 35		23 10		
Manchester Airport d	22 07	22 10		22 34	22 47	23 01	23 19	23 25	23 30	23 46
Heald Green d				22 38		23 05				23 50
Gatley d				22 41		23 08				23 53
East Didsbury d										23 55
Burnage d				22 45		23 11		23 32		23 58
Mauldeth Road d						23 14				00 01
Manchester Piccadilly 10 a	22 21	22 25		22 54	23 03	23 20	23 33	23 41	23 45	00 08
d	22 22			22 56	23 05	23 22	23 35	23 43		
Manchester Oxford Rd. a	22 24			22 58	23 07	23 24	23 37	23 45		
Deansgate a				23 02		23 27				

Saturdays

26 May to 8 December

Station	NT	TP	NT	TP	NT	TP	NT	AW	NT		TP	TP	NT	TP	TP	NT	NT	TP	TP		NT	TP	TP	NT
	◇	◇1		◇1	◇	◇1	◇	◇ 🍴	◇		◇1	◇1		◇1 🍴	◇1	◇	◇	◇1 🍴	◇1 🍴			◇1 🍴	◇1 🍴	◇
Crewe 10 84 d			00 44																		06 16			
Wilmslow 84 d													05 42								06 42			
Manchester Airport d		00 38	01 13	04 12	04 46	04 54	05 20	05 33	05 42		05 48	05 56	05 59	06 10	06 19	06 35	06 39	06 47	06 53		06 58	07 10	07 19	07 28
Heald Green d					04 50		05 24		05 46				06 03			06 39					07 02			07 32
Gatley d									05 49				06 06				06 45				07 05			
East Didsbury d							05 28						06 08			06 44					07 07			07 36
Burnage d							05 31						06 11				06 49				07 10			
Mauldeth Road d	00 01						05 33						06 13				06 51				07 12			
Manchester Piccadilly 10 a	00 08	00 52	01 28	04 25	05 02	05 09	05 41	05 47	06 00		06 04	06 13	06 20	06 24	06 33	06 53	06 59	07 03	07 12		07 21	07 25	07 33	07 45
d					05 04	05 10	05 42	05 48	06 01		06 05		06 22		06 35	06 55	07 01	07 05			07 22		07 35	07 46
Manchester Oxford Rd. a					05 06	05 12	05 44	05 50	06 03		06 07		06 24		06 37	06 57	07 03	07 07			07 24		07 37	07 48
Deansgate a					05 09				06 07				06 31				07 07				07 32			

Station	NT	TP	TP	NT	TP		TP	NT	NT	TP	TP	NT	TP	TP	NT		AW	NT	TP	TP	NT	TP	TP	NT
	◇	◇1 🍴	◇1 🍴	◇	◇1 🍴		◇1 🍴	◇	◇	◇1 🍴	◇1 🍴	◇	◇1 🍴	◇1 🍴	◇		■ 🍴	◇	◇1 🍴	◇1 🍴	◇	◇1 🍴	◇1 🍴	◇
Crewe 10 84 d				07 13								08 16									09 16			
Wilmslow 84 d				07 42								08 42									09 42			
Manchester Airport d	07 40	07 47	07 53	07 59	08 10		08 17	08 28	08 41	08 47	08 53	08 59	09 10	09 19	09 29		09 37	09 40	09 47	09 53	09 58	10 10	10 19	10 29
Heald Green d	07 44			08 03					08 45			09 03			09 33			09 44			10 03			10 33
Gatley d	07 47			08 06			08 22					09 06						09 47			10 06			
East Didsbury d				08 08				08 34				09 08			09 37		09 43				10 08			10 37
Burnage d	07 51			08 11				08 37				09 11						09 51			10 11			
Mauldeth Road d				08 13				08 39				09 13									10 13			
Manchester Piccadilly 10 a	07 59	08 03	08 11	08 21	08 25		08 33	08 46	08 59	09 03	09 11	09 21	09 25	09 33	09 46		09 52	09 59	10 03	10 11	10 21	10 25	10 33	10 46
d	08 01	08 05		08 22			08 35	08 47	09 01	09 05		09 22		09 35	09 47		09 53	10 01	10 05		10 22		10 35	10 47
Manchester Oxford Rd. a	08 03	08 07		08 24			08 37	08 49	09 03	09 07		09 25		09 37	09 49		09 55	10 03	10 07		10 24		10 37	10 49
Deansgate a	08 07			08 32					09 07			09 32						10 07			10 32			

Station	AW		NT	TP	TP	TP	NT	TP	NT	AW	NT		TP	TP	NT	TP	TP	NT	AW	NT	TP		TP	NT
	■ 🍴		◇	◇1 🍴	◇1 🍴	◇1 🍴	◇	◇1 🍴	◇	■ 🍴	◇		◇1 🍴	◇1 🍴	◇	◇1 🍴	◇1 🍴	◇	◇ 🍴	◇	◇1 🍴		◇1 🍴	◇
Crewe 10 84 d							10 16								11 17									12 17
Wilmslow 84 d							10 42								11 42									12 42
Manchester Airport d	10 37		10 40	10 47	10 53	10 59	11 02	11 19	11 29	11 37	11 41		11 47	11 53	11 57	12 10	12 19	12 29	12 37	12 40	12 47		12 53	12 59
Heald Green d			10 44				11 06		11 33		11 45				12 02			12 33		12 44				13 03
Gatley d			10 47				11 09				11 48				12 05					12 47				13 06
East Didsbury d	10 43						11 11		11 37	11 43					12 08			12 37	12 43					13 08
Burnage d			10 51				11 14				11 52				12 10					12 51				13 11
Mauldeth Road d							11 16								12 13									13 13
Manchester Piccadilly 10 a	10 52		10 59	11 03	11 11	11 13	11 24	11 33	11 46	11 52	11 59		12 03	12 11	12 21	12 25	12 33	12 46	12 52	12 59	13 03		13 11	13 21
d	10 53		11 01	11 05			11 26	11 35	11 47	11 53	12 01		12 05		12 22		12 35	12 47	12 53	13 01	13 05			13 22
Manchester Oxford Rd. a	10 55		11 03	11 07			11 28	11 37	11 50	11 55	12 03		12 07		12 24		12 37	12 50	12 55	13 03	13 07			13 24
Deansgate a			11 07				11 31				12 07				12 32					13 07				13 36

Table T085-F

Manchester Airport - Manchester

Saturdays

26 May to 8 December

	TP ◇■ 🍴	TP ◇■ 🍴	NT ◇	AW ◇ 🍴	NT ◇	TP ◇■ 🍴	TP ◇■ 🍴	NT ◇	TP ◇■ 🍴	TP ◇■ 🍴	NT ◇	AW ◇ 🍴	NT ◇	TP ◇■ 🍴	TP ◇■ 🍴	NT ◇	TP ◇■ 🍴	TP ◇■ 🍴	NT ◇	AW ◇ 🍴	TP ◇■ 🍴
Crewe ■ 84 d								13 18								14 16					
Wilmslow 84 d								13 43								14 42					
Manchester Airport d	13 10	13 19	13 29	13 37	13 40	13 47	13 53	13 58	14 10	14 19	14 29	14 37	14 40	14 47	14 53	14 59	15 10	15 19	15 29	15 37	15 47
Heald Green d			13 33		13 44			14 03			14 33		14 44			15 03			15 33		
Gatley d					13 47			14 06					14 47			15 06					
East Didsbury d			13 37	13 43				14 08			14 37	14 43				15 08			15 37	15 43	
Burnage d					13 51			14 11					14 51			15 11					
Mauldeth Road d								14 13								15 13					
Manchester Piccadilly ■ a	13 25	13 33	13 46	13 52	13 59	14 03	14 11	14 21	14 25	14 33	14 46	14 52	14 59	15 03	15 13	15 21	15 25	15 33	15 46	15 52	16 03
d		13 35	13 47	13 53	14 01	14 05		14 22		14 35	14 47	14 53	15 01	15 05		15 22		15 35	15 47	15 53	16 05
Manchester Oxford Rd. a		13 37	13 50	13 55	14 03	14 07		14 24		14 37	14 50	14 55	15 03	15 07		15 24		15 37	15 50	15 55	16 07
Deansgate a					14 07			14 32					15 07			15 32					

	TP ◇■ 🍴	NT ◇	TP ◇■ 🍴	TP ◇■ 🍴	NT ◇	AW ◇ 🍴	TP ◇■ 🍴	TP ◇■ 🍴	NT ◇	TP ◇■ 🍴	TP ◇■ 🍴	NT ◇	AW ◇ A	TP ◇■ 🍴	TP ◇■ 🍴	NT ◇	TP ◇■ 🍴	TP ◇■ 🍴	NT ◇	AW	NT ◇	TP ◇■
Crewe ■ 84 d		15 07							16 16							17 16						
Wilmslow 84 d		15 42							16 42							17 42						
Manchester Airport d	15 53	15 59	16 10	16 19	16 29	16 37	16 47	16 53	16 59	17 10	17 19	17 26	17 37	17 47	17 53	17 59	18 10	18 19	18 29	18 37	18 40	18 47
Heald Green d		16 03			16 33				17 03			17 30				18 03			18 33		18 44	
Gatley d		16 06							17 06			17 33				18 06					18 47	
East Didsbury d		16 08			16 37	16 43			17 08			17 36	17 43			18 08			18 37	18 43		
Burnage d		16 11							17 11			17 38				18 11					18 51	
Mauldeth Road d		16 13							17 13							18 13						
Manchester Piccadilly ■ a	16 11	16 21	16 25	16 33	16 46	16 52	17 03	17 13	17 21	17 25	17 33	17 46	17 52	18 03	18 11	18 22	18 25	18 33	18 46	18 52	18 59	19 03
d		16 22		16 35	16 47	16 53	17 05		17 23		17 35	17 47	17 53	18 05				18 35	18 48	18 53	19 01	19 05
Manchester Oxford Rd. a		16 24		16 37	16 50	16 55	17 07		17 25		17 37	17 50	17 55	18 07				18 37	18 50	18 55	19 03	19 07
Deansgate a		16 32							17 32												19 06	

	TP ◇■	NT ◇	TP ◇■ 🍴	TP ◇■	NT ◇	NT ◇	TP ◇■	TP ◇■	NT	TP ◇■	NT ◇	AW	NT ◇	TP ◇■	NT	TP ◇■	TP ◇■	NT ◇	NT ◇	TP ◇■	NT	TP ◇■
Crewe ■ 84 d		18 07																				
Wilmslow 84 d		18 42							19 43						20 43						21 37	
Manchester Airport d	18 53	18 59	19 10	19 19	19 29	19 40	19 47	19 56	19 59	20 19	20 29	20 35	20 39	20 53	20 58	21 06	21 19	21 29	21 37	21 53	21 58	22 07
Heald Green d		19 03			19 33	19 44			20 03				20 43		21 02						22 02	
Gatley d		19 06				19 47			20 06				20 46		21 05						22 05	
East Didsbury d		19 08			19 37				20 08						21 07						22 07	
Burnage d		19 11				19 51			20 11					21 02						22 00		
Mauldeth Road d		19 13							20 13					21 05						22 03		
Manchester Piccadilly ■ a	19 13	19 21	19 25	19 33	19 46	19 59	20 06	20 13	20 21	20 33	20 41	20 48	20 56	21 13	21 16	21 20	21 36	21 42	21 53	22 12	22 17	22 21
d				19 35	19 47	20 01	20 07		20 22	20 35	20 43	20 50	20 57		21 17	21 22		21 43	22 01		22 18	22 22
Manchester Oxford Rd. a				19 37	19 50	20 03	20 09		20 24	20 37	20 45	20 52	20 59		21 19	21 24		21 45	22 03		22 20	22 24
Deansgate a						20 07			20 32				21 02		21 29				22 06		22 33	

	NT ◇	NT	TP ◇■	TP ◇■ B	TP ◇■ C	TP C 🚌	NT
Crewe ■ 84 d							
Wilmslow 84 d		22 39					
Manchester Airport d	22 10	22 59	23 07	23 19	23 19	23 20	23 28
Heald Green d		23 03					23 32
Gatley d		23 06					23 35
East Didsbury d		23 08					23 37
Burnage d		23 11					23 40
Mauldeth Road d		23 13					23 42
Manchester Piccadilly ■ a	22 25	23 20	23 24	23 33	23 35	23 45	23 49
d	22 26	23 22	23 26	23 35			23 51
Manchester Oxford Rd. a	22 28	23 24	23 28	23 37			23 53
Deansgate a		23 27					23 56

Sundays

20 May to 2 December

	TP ◇■ D	TP E 🚌	TP E 🚌	TP ◇■ D	TP E 🚌	NT E 🚌	NT D	TP E 🚌	TP ◇■ D	NT F 🚌	NT G	NT H	TP E 🚌	TP ◇■ D 🍴	TP E 🚌	TP ◇■ H 🍴	TP ◇■ G 🍴	TP ◇■ H 🍴	TP ◇■ G 🍴	NT G	NT I 🚌	TP ◇■ F 🍴
Crewe ■ 84 d																						
Wilmslow 84 d																						
Manchester Airport d	01 00	01 00	03 30	04 22	04 55	05 50	05 52	06 05	06 27	06 50	06 51	06 51	07 00	07 27	07 35	07 46	07 46	07 49	07 49	08 00	08 00	08 22
Heald Green d						05 55	05 56			06 55		06 55								08 04	08 05	
Gatley d						06 03	05 59			07 03		06 58								08 07	08 13	
East Didsbury d						06 11	06 02			07 11		07 01								08 10	08 21	
Burnage d						06 16	06 04			07 16		07 03								08 12	08 26	
Mauldeth Road d						06 21	06 07			07 21		07 06								08 15	08 31	
Manchester Piccadilly ■ a	01 14	01 25	03 55	04 36	05 20	06 32	06 15	06 30	06 41	07 32	07 05	07 14	07 25	07 41	08 00	08 02	08 04	08 06	08 09	08 22	08 42	08 35
d																08 04	08 06			08 23		08 36
Manchester Oxford Rd. a																08 06	08 08			08 25		08 38
Deansgate a																				08 29		

A not 2 June
B until 20 October
C from 27 October
D until 21 October
E from 28 October
F until 9 September, from 28 October
G until 9 September
H from 16 September until 21 October
I from 16 September

Table T085-F

Manchester Airport - Manchester

Sundays

20 May to 2 December

	TP ◇■ A 🍴	NT ◇	TP B 🚌	NT ◇	TP ◇■ C 🍴	NT	TP ◇■ 🍴	TP ◇■ 🍴	NT ◇ D	NT ◇ E	NT ◇ E	NT ◇ D	TP ◇■ 🍴	NT D	NT E	TP ◇■ 🍴	TP ◇■ E 🍴	TP ◇■ D 🍴	NT ◇	TP ◇■ 🍴	NT
Crewe ■ 84 d																					
Wilmslow 84 d						08 38								09 42	09 43						10 43
Manchester Airport d	08 25	08 33	08 35	08 42	08 46	08 53	09 05	09 19	09 33	09 33	09 43	09 43	09 56	09 59	09 59	10 10	10 19	10 20	10 43	10 55	10 58
Heald Green d				08 46		08 58					09 47	09 47		10 03	10 03				10 47		11 02
Gatley d						09 01								10 06	10 06						11 05
East Didsbury d						09 03								10 08	10 08						11 08
Burnage d						09 06								10 11	10 11						11 10
Mauldeth Road d						09 08								10 13	10 13						11 13
Manchester Piccadilly ■ a	08 38	08 50	09 00	08 59	09 02	09 16	09 20	09 32	09 50	09 51	09 57	10 00	10 10	10 20	10 20	10 24	10 34	10 35	10 59	11 15	11 19
d	08 38	08 52		09 01		09 18		09 33	09 53	09 53	09 59	10 01		10 22	10 22		10 36	10 37	11 01		11 21
Manchester Oxford Rd. a	08 40	08 54		09 03		09 20		09 35	09 55	09 55	10 01	10 03		10 24	10 24		10 38	10 39	11 03		11 23
Deansgate a				09 06		09 27					10 04	10 06		10 31	10 31						11 32

	TP ◇■ 🍴	NT ◇ D	TP ◇■ 🍴	NT	TP ◇■ 🍴	NT ◇	TP ◇■ D 🍴	TP ◇■ 🍴	NT	TP ◇■ 🍴	TP ◇■ 🍴	NT ◇	NT ◇	TP ◇■ 🍴	TP ◇■ 🍴	NT		TP ◇■ 🍴	TP ◇■ 🍴	NT ◇	NT ◇	TP ◇■ 🍴
Crewe ■ 84 d																	and at the same minutes past each hour until					
Wilmslow 84 d				11 38					12 43							13 39						
Manchester Airport d	11 10	11 43	11 56	11 59	12 19	12 41	12 47	12 56	12 59	13 10	13 19	13 33	13 41	13 47	13 56	13 59		16 10	16 19	16 33	16 41	16 47
Heald Green d				12 03					13 03			13 37	13 45			14 03				16 37	16 45	
Gatley d				12 06					13 06							14 06						
East Didsbury d				12 09					13 08							14 09						
Burnage d				12 11					13 11							14 11						
Mauldeth Road d				12 14					13 13							14 14						
Manchester Piccadilly ■ a	11 23	12 00	12 13	12 21	12 33	12 59	13 04	13 13	13 21	13 25	13 33	13 49	13 59	14 04	14 13	14 21		16 25	16 33	16 49	16 59	17 04
d		12 01		12 22	12 35	13 00	13 05		13 22		13 35	13 51	14 00	14 05		14 22			16 35	16 51	17 00	17 05
Manchester Oxford Rd. a		12 03		12 24	12 37	13 02	13 07		13 24		13 37	13 53	14 02	14 07		14 24			16 37	16 53	17 02	17 07
Deansgate a				12 32					13 32			14 09				14 32				17 09		

	TP ◇■ 🍴	NT	TP ◇■ 🍴	TP ◇■ 🍴	NT ◇	NT ◇	TP ◇■ 🍴	TP ◇■ 🍴	NT	TP ◇■ 🍴	TP ◇■ 🍴	NT ◇	NT ◇	TP ◇■	TP ◇■	NT	TP ◇■ 🍴	TP ◇■	NT ◇	NT ◇	TP ◇■
Crewe ■ 84 d																					
Wilmslow 84 d		16 39							17 39							18 39					
Manchester Airport d	16 56	16 59	17 10	17 19	17 33	17 41	17 47	17 56	17 59	18 10	18 19	18 33	18 41	18 47	18 56	18 59	19 10	19 19	19 33	19 41	19 56
Heald Green d		17 03			17 37	17 45			18 03			18 37	18 45			19 03			19 37	19 45	
Gatley d		17 06							18 06							19 06					
East Didsbury d		17 09							18 09							19 09					
Burnage d		17 11							18 11							19 11					
Mauldeth Road d		17 14							18 14							19 14					
Manchester Piccadilly ■ a	17 13	17 21	17 25	17 33	17 49	17 59	18 06	18 13	18 21	18 25	18 33	18 49	18 59	19 04	19 13	19 21	19 25	19 33	19 49	19 59	20 13
d		17 22		17 35	17 51	18 00	18 07		18 22		18 35	18 51	19 00	19 05		19 22		19 35	19 51	20 00	
Manchester Oxford Rd. a		17 24		17 37	17 53	18 02	18 09		18 24		18 37	18 53	19 02	19 07		19 24		19 37	19 53	20 02	
Deansgate a		17 32			18 09				18 32			19 09				19 32			20 09		

	NT	TP ◇■ 🍴	TP ◇■	NT ◇	NT ◇	TP ◇■	NT	TP ◇■	NT ◇	NT ◇	TP ◇■	NT	TP ◇■	TP ◇■	NT ◇	TP ◇■	NT	TP ◇■
Crewe ■ 84 d																		
Wilmslow 84 d	19 39						20 37					21 37					22 52	
Manchester Airport d	19 59	20 10	20 19	20 33	20 41	20 55	20 58	21 04	21 33	21 41	21 56	21 59	22 06	22 19	22 43	22 56	23 09	23 27
Heald Green d	20 03			20 37	20 45		21 02		21 37	21 45		22 03			22 47		23 13	
Gatley d	20 06						21 05					22 06					23 16	
East Didsbury d	20 09						21 07					22 08					23 19	
Burnage d	20 11					21 02					22 03						23 21	
Mauldeth Road d	20 14					21 05					22 06						23 24	
Manchester Piccadilly ■ a	20 21	20 25	20 33	20 49	20 59	21 13	21 17	21 21	21 49	21 59	22 15	22 18	22 22	22 33	23 00	23 11	23 31	23 39
d	20 22		20 35	20 51	21 00		21 18	21 22	21 52	22 01		22 19	22 23	22 35	23 01		23 33	23 41
Manchester Oxford Rd. a	20 24		20 37	20 53	21 02		21 20	21 24	21 54	22 03		22 21	22 25	22 37	23 03		23 35	23 43
Deansgate a	20 32			21 09			21 29		22 08			22 31			23 07		23 38	

A from 16 September until 21 October
B from 28 October
C until 21 October
D until 9 September
E from 16 September

Table T085-R

Mondays to Fridays
21 May to 7 December

Manchester - Manchester Airport

Miles		TP	NT	TP	NT	TP	TP	TP	NT	NT	AW	NT	TP	TP	TP	NT	TP	TP	NT	TP	NT	NT
		MO	MO	MX	MX	MO	TW FO						MO	MX			MX	MO				
		◇1	◇	◇1	◇	◇1	◇1 🛒	◇1		◇		◇	◇1	◇1	◇1		◇1	◇1	◇	◇1	◇	◇
—	Deansgate 84,89 d		00 25																			06 18
—	Manchester Oxford Rd. 84,89 d		00 28														05 46	05 46	05 54		06 09	06 21
0	Manchester Piccadilly 10 a		00 30														05 49	05 49	05 56		06 12	06 23
—	d	00 06	00 32	00 37	00 42	00 44	01 44	03 43	03 46	04 12	04 46	04 49	04 55	04 56	04 59	05 19	05 50	05 50	05 58	06 07	06 13	06 25
3½	Mauldeth Road d		00 38													05 26						06 32
4½	Burnage d		00 40													05 29						06 35
5½	East Didsbury d		00 43		00 50											05 31			06 07			06 37
6¾	Gatley d		00 45													05 34			06 10			06 40
8¼	Heald Green d		00 48		00 55											05 37			06 13			06 43
9¾	**Manchester Airport** ✈ a	00 23	00 53	00 52	01 01	00 59	01 58	04 00	04 01	04 28	05 04	05 04	05 11	05 12	05 15	05 41	06 09	06 10	06 20	06 25	06 27	06 47
—	Wilmslow 84 a															05 53						07 15
—	Crewe 10 84 a															06 25						07 42

	TP	NT	TP	NT	TP	TP	NT	TP	NT	TP	NT	TP	TP	NT	TP	NT	TP	NT	TP	TP	NT
	◇1	◇	◇1	◇	◇1	◇1		◇1	◇	◇1 🛒	◇	◇1 🛒	◇1 🛒		◇1 🛒	◇	◇1 🛒	◇	◇1 🛒	◇1 🛒	◇
Deansgate 84,89 d							07 22							08 22							09 22
Manchester Oxford Rd. 84,89 d	06 49	06 54		07 13	07 16		07 27	07 47	07 59		08 13	08 16		08 27	08 47	08 56		09 13	09 16		09 27
Manchester Piccadilly 10 a	06 53	06 57		07 15	07 20		07 31	07 49	08 01		08 15	08 19		08 31	08 49	08 59		09 15	09 19		09 31
d	06 55	06 59	07 07	07 17	07 20	07 29	07 33	07 51	08 03	08 07	08 17	08 20	08 29	08 33	08 51	09 00	09 07	09 17	09 20	09 29	09 33
Mauldeth Road d		07 05					07 40		08 10					08 39							09 40
Burnage d		07 07					07 42		08 12					08 42		09 07					09 42
East Didsbury d				07 24			07 45					08 29		08 44				09 24			09 45
Gatley d		07 11					07 47		08 16					08 47		09 11					09 47
Heald Green d				07 29			07 50				08 27			08 50		09 15		09 29			09 50
Manchester Airport ✈ a	07 08	07 18	07 26	07 35	07 38	07 47	07 57	08 07	08 23	08 26	08 34	08 36	08 47	08 57	09 09	09 19	09 26	09 35	09 36	09 47	09 57
Wilmslow 84 a							08 15							09 15							10 15
Crewe 10 84 a							08 42							09 42							10 42

	TP	AW	NT	TP	NT	TP	TP	NT	TP	AW	NT	TP	NT	TP	TP	NT	TP	AW	NT	TP	NT	TP
	◇1 🛒	◇ 🛒	◇	◇1 🛒	◇	◇1 🛒	◇1 🛒	◇	◇1 🛒	◇ 🛒	◇	◇1 🛒	◇	◇1 🛒	◇1 🛒	◇	◇1 🛒	◇ 🛒	◇	◇1 🛒	◇	◇1 🛒
Deansgate 84,89 d								10 22								11 22						
Manchester Oxford Rd. 84,89 d	09 46	09 49	09 54		10 13	10 15		10 27	10 46	10 49	10 54		11 13	11 15		11 27	11 47	11 49	11 57		12 12	12 15
Manchester Piccadilly 10 a	09 49	09 53	09 57		10 15	10 20		10 31	10 49	10 53	10 57		11 15	11 20		11 31	11 50	11 53	11 59		12 15	12 20
d	09 51	09 55	09 59	10 07	10 17	10 20	10 29	10 33	10 50	10 55	10 59	11 07	11 17	11 20	11 29	11 33	11 51	11 55	12 01	12 07	12 17	12 20
Mauldeth Road d								10 39								11 40						
Burnage d			10 07					10 42			11 06					11 42			12 08			
East Didsbury d		10 04			10 24			10 44		11 04			11 24			11 45		12 04			12 24	
Gatley d			10 11					10 47			11 10					11 47			12 12			
Heald Green d			10 14		10 29			10 50			11 14		11 29			11 50			12 15		12 29	
Manchester Airport ✈ a	10 08	10 19	10 19	10 26	10 35	10 36	10 47	10 57	11 09	11 19	11 18	11 26	11 35	11 36	11 47	11 56	12 09	12 20	12 20	12 26	12 35	12 39
Wilmslow 84 a								11 16								12 15						
Crewe 10 84 a								11 43								12 42						

	TP	NT	TP	AW	NT	TP	NT	TP	TP	NT	TP	AW	NT	TP	NT	TP	TP	NT	TP	AW	NT	TP
	◇1 🛒	◇	◇1 🛒	◇ 🛒	◇	◇1 🛒	◇	◇1 🛒	◇1 🛒	◇	◇1 🛒	◇ 🛒	◇	◇1 🛒	◇	◇1 🛒	◇1 🛒	◇	◇1 🛒	◇ 🛒	◇	◇1 🛒
Deansgate 84,89 d		12 22								13 22								14 22				
Manchester Oxford Rd. 84,89 d		12 27	12 46	12 49	12 54		13 12	13 15		13 27	13 46	13 49	13 54		14 12	14 15		14 27	14 46	14 50	14 54	
Manchester Piccadilly 10 a		12 31	12 49	12 53	12 57		13 15	13 20		13 31	13 49	13 53	13 58		14 15	14 20		14 31	14 49	14 53	14 57	
d	12 29	12 33	12 50	12 55	12 59	13 07	13 17	13 20	13 29	13 33	13 50	13 55	13 59	14 07	14 17	14 20	14 29	14 33	14 50	14 55	14 59	15 07
Mauldeth Road d		12 40								13 40								14 39				
Burnage d		12 42			13 07					13 42			14 06					14 42			15 06	
East Didsbury d		12 45		13 04			13 24			13 45		14 04			14 24			14 44		15 04		
Gatley d		12 47			13 11					13 47			14 10					14 47			15 10	
Heald Green d		12 50			13 14		13 29			13 50			14 14		14 29			14 50			15 13	
Manchester Airport ✈ a	12 48	12 57	13 09	13 20	13 19	13 26	13 35	13 36	13 47	13 57	14 08	14 19	14 18	14 26	14 35	14 36	14 47	14 57	15 08	15 19	15 18	15 26
Wilmslow 84 a		13 16								14 15								15 15				
Crewe 10 84 a		13 43								14 42								15 42				

	NT	TP	TP	NT	TP	NT	TP	NT	TP	TP	NT	TP	NT	TP	NT	TP	TP	NT	TP	NT	TP
	◇	◇1 🛒	◇1 🛒	◇	◇1 🛒	◇	◇1 🛒	◇	◇1 🛒	◇1 🛒	◇	◇1 🛒	◇	◇1 🛒	◇	◇1 🛒	◇1 🛒	◇	◇1 🛒	◇	◇1 🛒
Deansgate 84,89 d				15 22							16 22							17 23			
Manchester Oxford Rd. 84,89 d	15 12	15 15		15 27	15 46	15 54		16 12	16 15		16 27	16 46	16 55		17 12	17 15		17 28	17 46	17 54	
Manchester Piccadilly 10 a	15 15	15 20		15 31	15 49	15 58		16 15	16 20		16 31	16 49	16 58		17 15	17 20		17 33	17 49	17 57	
d	15 17	15 20	15 29	15 33	15 50	15 59	16 07	16 17	16 20	16 29	16 33	16 50	17 00	17 07	17 17	17 20	17 30	17 34	17 50	17 59	18 07
Mauldeth Road d				15 39							16 39							17 40			
Burnage d				15 41		16 07					16 41		17 07					17 43		18 06	
East Didsbury d	15 24			15 44				16 24			16 44		17 09			17 29		17 45			
Gatley d				15 46		16 11					16 46			17 18				17 48		18 10	
Heald Green d	15 29			15 49		16 15		16 29			16 49		17 14		17 29			17 51		18 13	
Manchester Airport ✈ a	15 35	15 36	15 47	15 57	16 09	16 19	16 26	16 35	16 36	16 47	16 57	17 09	17 18	17 26	17 35	17 36	17 48	17 58	18 08	18 18	18 26
Wilmslow 84 a				16 15							17 16							18 15			
Crewe 10 84 a				16 42							17 43							18 43			

Table T085-R

Mondays to Fridays
21 May to 7 December

Manchester - Manchester Airport

	NT	TP	TP	NT	TP	NT	TP	NT	TP	TP	NT	TP	AW	NT	TP	NT	TP	TP	NT	TP	AW
	◇	◇1 🛒	◇1 🛒	◇	◇1 🛒	◇	◇1 🛒	◇	◇1 🛒	◇1 🛒	◇	◇1 🛒	◇	◇	◇1	◇	◇1	◇1 🛒		◇1	◇
Deansgate 84,89 d																			20 22		
Manchester Oxford Rd. 84,89 d	18 13	18 16			18 46	18 54		19 13	19 15			19 46	19 50	19 55		20 13	20 16		20 27	20 47	20 50
Manchester Piccadilly 10 a	18 15	18 19			18 49	18 57		19 15	19 19			19 49	19 53	19 57		20 15	20 19		20 31	20 49	20 53
d	18 17	18 20	18 25	18 34	18 51	18 59	19 07	19 17	19 21	19 29	19 31	19 50	19 55	19 59	20 06	20 17	20 20	20 29	20 33	20 51	20 55
Mauldeth Road d				18 41							19 39								20 39		
Burnage d				18 43		19 06					19 42								20 41		
East Didsbury d	18 24			18 46				19 24			19 44								20 44		
Gatley d				18 48		19 10					19 47			20 09					20 46		
Heald Green d	18 29			18 51		19 13		19 29			19 50			20 12		20 27			20 49		
Manchester Airport ✈ a	18 35	18 36	18 43	18 57	19 09	19 18	19 26	19 35	19 36	19 46	19 57	20 08	20 19	20 17	20 26	20 33	20 36	20 47	20 57	21 13	21 20
Wilmslow 84 a				19 16							20 14								21 10		
Crewe 10 84 a				19 43																	

	NT	TP	NT	TP	TP	NT	NT	NT	TP	TP	NT	TP	TP	NT	TP	TP	NT	NT
																		FX
	◇	◇1	◇	◇1	◇1 🛒		◇	◇	◇1	◇1 🛒		◇1	◇1	◇	◇1 🛒	◇1		◇
Deansgate 84,89 d						21 22					22 25						23 26	
Manchester Oxford Rd. 84,89 d	20 55		21 13	21 16		21 27	21 45	21 55	22 01		22 28			23 13		23 24	23 30	23 50
Manchester Piccadilly 10 a	20 57		21 15	21 20		21 31	21 47	21 57	22 05		22 31			23 15		23 28	23 32	23 53
d	20 59	21 07	21 17	21 20	21 29	21 33	21 49	21 59	22 05	22 24	22 32	22 43	23 08	23 17	23 25	23 28	23 34	23 55
Mauldeth Road d						21 39					22 38						23 40	
Burnage d	21 06					21 41					22 41						23 42	
East Didsbury d			21 24			21 44					22 43			23 24			23 45	
Gatley d	21 10					21 46		22 07			22 46						23 47	
Heald Green d	21 13		21 29			21 49		22 11			22 49			23 29			23 50	
Manchester Airport ✈ a	21 18	21 26	21 35	21 36	21 44	21 57	22 05	22 17	22 22	22 40	22 54	23 00	23 26	23 35	23 41	23 44	23 55	00 11
Wilmslow 84 a						22 12					23 06							
Crewe 10 84 a																		

Saturdays
26 May to 8 December

	TP	TP	TP	NT	NT	TP	AW	NT	TP	NT	NT	TP	TP	NT	NT	TP	NT	TP	NT	TP	TP	NT
	◇1	◇1 🛒	◇1		◇	◇1		◇	◇1		◇	◇1	◇1	◇	◇	◇1	◇	◇1	◇	◇1	◇1	
Deansgate 84,89 d															06 18							07 22
Manchester Oxford Rd. 84,89 d											05 45	05 51		06 09	06 21	06 49	06 54		07 09	07 16		07 27
Manchester Piccadilly 10 a											05 48	05 53		06 12	06 23	06 53	06 57		07 11	07 20		07 31
d	00 37	01 44	03 34	03 46	04 12	04 34	04 46	04 49	04 56	05 19	05 49	05 55	06 08	06 13	06 25	06 55	06 59	07 07	07 13	07 20	07 29	07 33
Mauldeth Road d										05 26					06 32		07 05					07 40
Burnage d										05 29					06 35		07 07					07 42
East Didsbury d										05 31	05 57				06 37				07 23			07 45
Gatley d										05 34	06 00				06 40		07 11					07 47
Heald Green d										05 37	06 03				06 43				07 28			07 50
Manchester Airport ✈ a	00 52	01 58	03 52	04 01	04 28	04 50	05 04	05 04	05 12	05 41	06 10	06 11	06 25	06 27	06 47	07 08	07 18	07 26	07 35	07 38	07 47	07 57
Wilmslow 84 a										05 53					07 15							08 15
Crewe 10 84 a										06 25					07 42							08 41

	TP	NT	TP	NT	TP	TP	NT	TP	AW	NT	TP	NT	TP	TP	NT	TP	AW	NT	TP	NT	TP	TP
	◇1	◇	◇1 🛒	◇	◇1 🛒	◇1 🛒		◇1 🛒	◇ 🛒	◇	◇1 🛒	◇	◇1 🛒	◇1 🛒	◇	◇1 🛒	◇ 🛒	◇	◇1 🛒	◇	◇1 🛒	◇1 🛒
Deansgate 84,89 d							08 22								09 22							
Manchester Oxford Rd. 84,89 d	07 47	07 59		08 13	08 16		08 29	08 46	08 51	08 56		09 13	09 16		09 27	09 46	09 49	09 54		10 13	10 15	
Manchester Piccadilly 10 a	07 49	08 01		08 15	08 19		08 33	08 49	08 53	08 59		09 15	09 19		09 31	09 49	09 53	09 57		10 15	10 20	
d	07 51	08 03	08 07	08 17	08 20	08 30	08 35	08 50	08 55	09 00	09 07	09 17	09 20	09 29	09 33	09 50	09 55	09 59	10 07	10 17	10 20	10 29
Mauldeth Road d		08 10					08 41								09 40							
Burnage d		08 12					08 43			09 07					09 42			10 07				
East Didsbury d					08 29		08 46		09 03			09 24			09 45		10 05			10 24		
Gatley d		08 16					08 48			09 11					09 47			10 11				
Heald Green d				08 27			08 52			09 15		09 29			09 50			10 14		10 29		
Manchester Airport ✈ a	08 09	08 23	08 26	08 35	08 36	08 47	08 58	09 09	09 19	09 19	09 26	09 35	09 36	09 47	09 57	10 08	10 19	10 19	10 26	10 35	10 36	10 47
Wilmslow 84 a							09 15								10 15							
Crewe 10 84 a							09 42								10 42							

	NT	TP	AW	NT	TP	NT	TP	TP	NT	TP	AW	NT	TP	NT	TP	TP	NT	TP	AW	NT	TP
		◇1 🛒	◇ 🛒	◇	◇1 🛒	◇	◇1 🛒	◇1 🛒	◇	◇1 🛒	■ 🛒	◇	◇1 🛒	◇	◇1 🛒	◇1 🛒	◇	◇1 🛒	◇ 🛒	◇	◇1 🛒
Deansgate 84,89 d	10 22								11 22								12 22				
Manchester Oxford Rd. 84,89 d	10 27	10 46	10 49	10 54		11 13	11 15		11 27	11 47	11 50	11 56		12 12	12 15		12 27	12 47	12 50	12 54	
Manchester Piccadilly 10 a	10 31	10 49	10 53	10 57		11 15	11 20		11 31	11 50	11 54	11 59		12 15	12 20		12 31	12 49	12 53	12 57	
d	10 33	10 50	10 55	10 59	11 06	11 17	11 20	11 29	11 33	11 51	11 55	12 00	12 07	12 17	12 20	12 29	12 33	12 51	12 55	12 59	13 07
Mauldeth Road d	10 40								11 40								12 40				
Burnage d	10 42			11 06					11 42			12 07					12 42			13 07	
East Didsbury d	10 45		11 04			11 24			11 45		12 05			12 24			12 45		13 05		
Gatley d	10 47			11 10					11 47			12 11					12 47			13 11	
Heald Green d	10 50			11 14		11 29			11 50			12 15		12 29			12 50			13 14	
Manchester Airport ✈ a	10 57	11 09	11 19	11 18	11 26	11 35	11 36	11 47	11 56	12 09	12 19	12 19	12 26	12 35	12 39	12 47	12 57	13 09	13 19	13 19	13 26
Wilmslow 84 a	11 17								12 15								13 16				
Crewe 10 84 a	11 43								12 42								13 43				

Manchester - Manchester Airport

Saturdays
26 May to 8 December

	NT	TP	TP	NT	TP	AW	NT	TP	NT	TP	TP	NT	TP	AW	NT	TP	NT	TP	TP	NT	TP
	◇	◇1 🛒	◇1 🛒		◇1 🛒	◇ 🛒	◇	◇1 🛒	◇	◇1 🛒	◇1 🛒	◇	◇1 🛒	◇ 🛒	◇	◇1 🛒	◇	◇1 🛒	◇1 🛒	◇	◇1 🛒
Deansgate 84,89 d				13 22								14 22								15 22	
Manchester Oxford Rd. 84,89 d	13 12	13 15		13 27	13 47	13 49	13 54		14 12	14 15		14 27	14 46	14 50	14 54		15 12	15 15		15 27	15 46
Manchester Piccadilly 10 a	13 15	13 20		13 31	13 49	13 53	13 58		14 15	14 20		14 31	14 49	14 53	14 57		15 15	15 20		15 31	15 49
d	13 17	13 20	13 29	13 33	13 51	13 55	13 59	14 07	14 17	14 20	14 29	14 33	14 50	14 54	14 59	15 09	15 17	15 20	15 29	15 33	15 50
Mauldeth Road d				13 39								14 39								15 39	
Burnage d				13 41			14 07					14 42			15 07					15 41	
East Didsbury d	13 24			13 44		14 05			14 24			14 44		15 04			15 24			15 44	
Gatley d				13 46			14 11					14 47			15 11					15 46	
Heald Green d	13 29			13 49			14 15		14 29			14 53			15 14		15 29			15 49	
Manchester Airport a	13 35	13 36	13 47	13 57	14 08	14 19	14 19	14 26	14 35	14 36	14 47	15 03	15 08	15 19	15 19	15 26	15 35	15 36	15 47	15 57	16 09
Wilmslow 84 a				14 15								15 15								16 15	
Crewe 10 84 a				14 42								15 42								16 42	

	AW	NT	TP	NT	TP	TP	NT	TP	AW	NT	TP	NT	TP	TP	NT	TP	AW	NT	TP	NT	TP	TP
	◇ 🛒	◇	◇1 🛒	◇	◇1 🛒	◇1 🛒	◇	◇1 🛒	◇ 🛒	◇	◇1 🛒	◇	◇1 🛒	◇1 🛒	◇	◇1 🛒	◇ 🛒	◇	◇1 🛒	◇	◇1 🛒	◇1 🛒
Deansgate 84,89 d							16 22								17 23							
Manchester Oxford Rd. 84,89 d	15 50	15 54		16 12	16 15		16 27	16 46	16 50	16 55		17 12	17 15		17 28	17 46	17 50	17 54		18 13	18 16	
Manchester Piccadilly 10 a	15 53	15 58		16 15	16 20		16 31	16 50	16 53	16 58		17 15	17 20		17 33	17 49	17 53	17 57		18 15	18 19	
d	15 54	15 59	16 09	16 17	16 20	16 29	16 33	16 51	16 55	17 00	17 07	17 17	17 20	17 30	17 34	17 50	17 54	17 59	18 07	18 17	18 20	18 29
Mauldeth Road d							16 39								17 40							
Burnage d		16 07					16 41			17 07					17 43			18 06				
East Didsbury d	16 05			16 24			16 44		17 05	17 09					17 45		18 04			18 24		
Gatley d		16 11					16 46				17 18				17 48			18 10				
Heald Green d		16 15		16 29			16 49			17 14		17 29			17 51			18 13		18 29		
Manchester Airport a	16 19	16 19	16 26	16 35	16 36	16 47	16 57	17 09	17 19	17 18	17 26	17 35	17 36	17 47	17 58	18 08	18 19	18 18	18 26	18 35	18 36	18 47
Wilmslow 84 a							17 16								18 15							
Crewe 10 84 a							17 43								18 43							

	NT	TP	NT	TP	NT	TP	TP	NT	TP	AW	NT	TP	NT	TP	TP	NT	TP	NT	TP	NT	TP	TP
	◇	◇1 🛒	◇	◇1 🛒	◇	◇1 🛒	◇1 🛒	◇	◇1 🛒	◇	◇	◇1	◇	◇1	◇1 🛒		◇1	◇	◇1	◇	◇1	◇1 🛒
Deansgate 84,89 d																20 22						
Manchester Oxford Rd. 84,89 d		18 46	18 54		19 13	19 16			19 46	19 49	19 55		20 13	20 16		20 27	20 46	20 55		21 13	21 16	
Manchester Piccadilly 10 a		18 49	18 57		19 15	19 20			19 49	19 53	19 57		20 15	20 19		20 31	20 49	20 57		21 15	21 20	
d	18 33	18 50	18 59	19 08	19 17	19 22	19 29	19 31	19 50	19 54	19 59	20 08	20 17	20 20	20 29	20 33	20 50	20 59	21 08	21 17	21 20	21 29
Mauldeth Road d	18 40							19 40								20 39						
Burnage d	18 42		19 06					19 42								20 41		21 06				
East Didsbury d	18 45				19 24			19 45								20 44				21 24		
Gatley d	18 47		19 10					19 47			20 09					20 46		21 10				
Heald Green d	18 50		19 13		19 29			19 50			20 12		20 27			20 49		21 13		21 29		
Manchester Airport a	19 00	19 09	19 18	19 26	19 35	19 36	19 47	19 57	20 07	20 19	20 17	20 26	20 33	20 36	20 47	20 57	21 12	21 18	21 26	21 35	21 36	21 47
Wilmslow 84 a	19 16							20 15								21 10						
Crewe 10 84 a	19 43																					

	NT	NT	NT	TP	TP	NT	NT	TP	TP	NT	TP	NT
		◇	◇	◇1	◇1 🛒	◇		◇1	◇1	◇	◇1	
Deansgate 84,89 d	21 22						22 25					23 26
Manchester Oxford Rd. 84,89 d	21 27	21 46	21 55	22 01		22 12	22 28			23 13	23 24	23 30
Manchester Piccadilly 10 a	21 31	21 49	21 57	22 05		22 14	22 31			23 15	23 27	23 32
d	21 33	21 50	21 59	22 05	22 11	22 16	22 32	22 42	23 09	23 17	23 27	23 34
Mauldeth Road d	21 39						22 38					23 40
Burnage d	21 41						22 41					23 42
East Didsbury d	21 44						22 43			23 24		23 45
Gatley d	21 46		22 07				22 46					23 47
Heald Green d	21 49		22 11				22 49			23 29		23 50
Manchester Airport a	21 57	22 05	22 17	22 22	22 26	22 32	22 53	23 00	23 26	23 35	23 44	23 55
Wilmslow 84 a	22 11						23 16					
Crewe 10 84 a												

Sundays
20 May to 2 December

	TP	TP	TP	TP	TP	NT	NT	TP	NT	NT	TP	NT	NT	NT	TP	TP	NT	NT	TP	TP	TP	NT
	◇1		◇1		◇1						◇1					◇1			◇1	◇1	1	
	A	B	C	B	C	C	B	B	B	C	C	D	E	C	B	C	E	D		C	B	
		🚌		🚌			🚌	🚌	🚌				🚌		🚌				🛒	🛒	🛒	
Deansgate 84,89 d																						
Manchester Oxford Rd. 84,89 d																				08 46	08 46	09 13
Manchester Piccadilly 10 a																				08 49	08 49	09 15
d	00 35	00 40	03 47	03 55	05 21	05 24	05 25	05 55	06 20	06 21	06 36	07 18	07 20	07 29	07 45	07 50	08 23	08 30	08 46	08 56	08 56	09 17
Mauldeth Road d						05 31	05 36		06 31	06 28		07 25	07 31				08 30					09 23
Burnage d						05 34	05 41		06 36	06 31		07 28	07 36				08 32					09 26
East Didsbury d						05 37	05 47		06 42	06 34		07 30	07 42				08 35	08 44				09 28
Gatley d						05 39	05 52		06 47	06 36		07 33	07 47				08 37	08 46				09 31
Heald Green d						05 42	06 00		06 55	06 39		07 36	07 55				08 40	08 49				09 34
Manchester Airport a	00 52	01 05	04 02	04 20	05 36	05 48	06 05	06 20	07 00	06 44	06 52	07 41	08 00	07 48	08 10	08 04	08 45	08 54	09 04	09 10	09 10	09 39
Wilmslow 84 a																	08 59	09 19				09 56
Crewe 10 84 a																						

A from 27 May until 21 October
B from 28 October
C until 21 October
D from 16 September until 21 October
E until 9 September, from 28 October

Manchester - Manchester Airport

Sundays
20 May to 2 December

	TP	TP	NT	TP	TP	NT	NT	TP	NT	TP	NT	NT	TP	TP	TP	TP	NT	TP	TP	NT	TP
	◇1	◇1	◇	◇1	◇1		◇	◇1		◇1	◇	◇	◇1	◇1				◇1	◇1	◇	◇1
	A	B		B	A		A				B	A		A	B	C		D			
	🛒	🛒		🛒	🛒			🛒		🛒			🛒	🛒				🛒	🛒		🛒
Deansgate 84,89 d						10 24			11 23								12 22				
Manchester Oxford Rd. 84,89 d	09 47		09 58			10 27	10 59		11 26	11 47	11 59	11 59		12 16			12 25		12 49	12 59	
Manchester Piccadilly 10 a	09 50		10 00			10 30	11 01		11 29	11 49	12 01	12 01		12 19			12 27		12 51	13 01	
d	09 52	09 52	10 05	10 10	10 11	10 40	11 06	11 09	11 33	11 52	12 04	12 04	12 13	12 20	12 23	12 25	12 29	12 43	12 53	13 03	13 09
Mauldeth Road d						10 47			11 40								12 36				
Burnage d						10 49			11 43								12 38				
East Didsbury d						10 52			11 47			12 12					12 41				
Gatley d						10 54			11 50								12 43				
Heald Green d						10 57			11 55								12 46				
Manchester Airport a	10 05	10 07	10 19	10 25	10 27	11 02	11 20	11 26	12 03	12 08	12 18	12 19	12 27	12 37	12 40	12 40	12 51	13 00	13 06	13 17	13 26
Wilmslow 84 a						11 14			12 19								13 12				
Crewe 10 84 a																					

	NT	TP	TP	NT	TP	NT	TP	NT	TP	TP	NT	TP	NT	TP	NT	TP	TP	NT	TP	NT	TP	NT
	◇	◇1 🛒	◇1 🛒		◇1 🛒	◇	◇1 🛒	◇	◇1 🛒	◇1 🛒		◇1 🛒	◇	◇1 🛒	◇	◇1 🛒	◇1 🛒		◇1 🛒	◇	◇1 🛒	◇
Deansgate 84,89 d	13 09			13 21				14 09			14 22				15 09			15 21				16 09
Manchester Oxford Rd. 84,89 d	13 12	13 16		13 26	13 47	13 59		14 12	14 16		14 27	14 47	14 57		15 12	15 16		15 26	15 47	15 59		16 12
Manchester Piccadilly 10 a	13 15	13 19		13 31	13 49	14 01		14 15	14 20		14 31	14 50	15 00		15 15	15 19		15 31	15 49	16 01		16 15
d	13 17	13 20	13 29	13 33	13 51	14 03	14 09	14 17	14 20	14 29	14 33	14 51	15 01	15 09	15 17	15 20	15 29	15 33	15 51	16 03	16 09	16 17
Mauldeth Road d				13 40							14 40							15 40				
Burnage d				13 42							14 42							15 42				
East Didsbury d				13 45							14 45							15 45				
Gatley d				13 47							14 47							15 47				
Heald Green d	13 28			13 50				14 28			14 50				15 28			15 50				16 28
Manchester Airport a	13 35	13 38	13 47	13 55	14 06	14 17	14 26	14 35	14 38	14 47	14 55	15 05	15 17	15 26	15 35	15 38	15 47	15 55	16 05	16 17	16 26	16 35
Wilmslow 84 a				14 12							15 12							16 12				
Crewe 10 84 a																						

	TP	TP	NT	TP	NT	TP	NT	TP	TP	NT	TP	NT	TP	NT	TP	TP	NT	TP	NT	TP	NT
	◇1 🛒	◇1 🛒		◇1 🛒	◇	◇1 🛒	◇	◇1 🛒	◇1 🛒		◇1 🛒	◇	◇1 🛒	◇	◇1 🛒	◇1 🛒		◇1 🛒	◇	◇1 🛒	◇
Deansgate 84,89 d			16 21				17 09			17 21				18 09			18 22				19 09
Manchester Oxford Rd. 84,89 d	16 16		16 26	16 47	16 58		17 13	17 16		17 26	17 47	17 59		18 12	18 16		18 27	18 47	18 59		19 12
Manchester Piccadilly 10 a	16 20		16 31	16 49	17 01		17 15	17 20		17 31	17 49	18 01		18 15	18 20		18 31	18 49	19 01		19 15
d	16 20	16 29	16 33	16 51	17 02	17 09	17 17	17 20	17 28	17 33	17 51	18 03	18 09	18 17	18 20	18 29	18 33	18 51	19 03	19 09	19 17
Mauldeth Road d			16 40							17 40							18 40				
Burnage d			16 42							17 42							18 42				
East Didsbury d			16 45							17 45							18 45				
Gatley d			16 47							17 47							18 47				
Heald Green d			16 50				17 28			17 50				18 28			18 50				19 28
Manchester Airport a	16 38	16 47	16 55	17 06	17 17	17 26	17 35	17 38	17 43	17 55	18 05	18 17	18 26	18 35	18 38	18 47	18 55	19 06	19 17	19 26	19 35
Wilmslow 84 a			17 12							18 12							19 12				
Crewe 10 84 a																					

	TP	TP	NT	TP	NT	TP	NT	TP	TP	NT	TP	NT	TP	NT	TP	TP	NT	AW	NT	TP	NT	TP
	◇1 🛒	◇1 🛒		◇1 🛒	◇	◇1	◇	◇1	◇1 🛒		◇1	◇	◇1	◇	◇1	◇1 🛒			◇	◇1	◇	◇1 B 🛒
Deansgate 84,89 d			19 21				20 09			20 21				21 09			21 21				22 11	
Manchester Oxford Rd. 84,89 d	19 16		19 26	19 47	19 59		20 12	20 16		20 26	20 47	20 59		21 12	21 16		21 26		21 59		22 15	
Manchester Piccadilly 10 a	19 20		19 31	19 49	20 01		20 15	20 19		20 31	20 49	21 01		21 15	21 20		21 31		22 01		22 17	
d	19 20	19 29	19 33	19 51	20 03	20 09	20 17	20 20	20 29	20 33	20 51	21 03	21 08	21 17	21 21	21 27	21 33	21 34	22 03	22 09	22 19	22 28
Mauldeth Road d			19 40							20 40							21 40					
Burnage d			19 42							20 43							21 42					
East Didsbury d			19 45							20 47							21 45					
Gatley d			19 47							20 50							21 47					
Heald Green d			19 50				20 28			20 54				21 27			21 50				22 31	
Manchester Airport a	19 38	19 47	19 55	20 05	20 17	20 26	20 36	20 39	20 47	21 01	21 11	21 17	21 26	21 34	21 37	21 42	21 55		22 16	22 26	22 38	22 44
Wilmslow 84 a			20 12							21 15							22 10	21 56				
Crewe 10 84 a																		22 16				

	TP	NT	AW	NT	TP	NT	TP	NT
	◇1 A 🛒			◇	◇1	◇	◇1 🛒	
Deansgate 84,89 d		22 21				23 08		23 21
Manchester Oxford Rd. 84,89 d		22 28		22 59	23 04	23 14		23 26
Manchester Piccadilly 10 a		22 32		23 01	23 09	23 17		23 31
d	22 29	22 33	22 35	23 03	23 10	23 19	23 29	23 33
Mauldeth Road d		22 39						23 39
Burnage d		22 42						23 41
East Didsbury d		22 44						23 44
Gatley d		22 47						23 46
Heald Green d		22 50				23 30		23 49
Manchester Airport a	22 44	22 55		23 17	23 25	23 37	23 44	23 54
Wilmslow 84 a		23 12	22 50					00 10
Crewe 10 84 a			23 13					

A until 9 September
B from 16 September
C from 24 June until 9 September
D until 17 June

Table T086-F

Buxton and Hazel Grove - Manchester

Mondays to Fridays
21 May to 7 December

Miles			NT	NT	NT	NT	NT	NT	NT	EM ◇ A	NT	NT B	NT	NT	NT	NT	NT	NT	NT	NT	NT	NT	NT
0	**Buxton**	d		06 00		06 32		07 01	07 36			08 00			08 58	09 34		10 02	10 34		11 02	11 34	
3	Dove Holes	d		06 06		06 38			07 42						09 05	09 40						11 40	
5¾	Chapel-en-le-Frith	d		06 12		06 44		07 11	07 48			08 10			09 10	09 46		10 12	10 44		11 12	11 46	
9½	Whaley Bridge	d		06 18		06 50		07 17	07 54			08 17			09 16	09 52		10 18	10 50		11 18	11 52	
10¾	Furness Vale	d		06 21		06 53		07 21	07 57			08 20			09 20	09 55			10 54			11 55	
11½	New Mills Newtown	d		06 25		06 57		07 24	08 01			08 24			09 23	09 59		10 23	10 57		11 23	11 59	
13¼	Disley	d		06 28		07 00		07 28	08 04			08 27			09 27	10 02		10 27	11 01		11 27	12 02	
14¾	Middlewood	d		06 32		07 04			08 08						09 30				11 05				
17	**Hazel Grove**	a		06 36		07 08		07 35	08 12			08 34			09 35	10 09		10 34	11 09		11 34	12 09	
—		d	06 11	06 37	06 49	07 09	07 21	07 35	08 13	08 17	08 21	08 35	09 10	09 21	09 35	10 10	10 21	10 35	11 10	11 21	11 35	12 10	12 21
18	Woodsmoor	d	06 13		06 51	07 12	07 23	07 38			08 23	08 38	09 13	09 23	09 38	10 13	10 23	10 38	11 13	11 23	11 38	12 13	12 23
18¾	Davenport	d	06 15		06 53	07 14	07 25	07 40			08 25	08 40	09 15	09 25	09 41	10 15	10 25	10 40	11 15	11 25	11 40	12 15	12 25
19¾	**Stockport** 84	a	06 20	06 45	06 57	07 20	07 29	07 45	08 20	08 25	08 29	08 45	09 20	09 29	09 45	10 21	10 29	10 45	11 20	11 29	11 45	12 20	12 29
21¼	Heaton Chapel 84	a			07 01	07 25			08 24				09 24			10 25			11 24			12 24	
22¾	Levenshulme 84	a			07 04	07 28			08 27						09 50	10 28		10 50	11 27		11 50	12 27	
25¾	**Manchester Picc.** 10 84 ⇌	a	06 29	06 56	07 14	07 36	07 40	07 56	08 36	08 37	08 40	08 55	09 34	09 40	09 56	10 36	10 40	10 56	11 36	11 40	11 56	12 36	12 40
—	Manchester Oxford Road	a								08 41		08 59											
—	Deansgate ⇌	a										09 02											

		NT	NT	NT	NT	NT	NT	NT	NT	NT	NT	NT	NT	NT	NT	NT	NT	NT	NT	NT	NT	NT	NT
Buxton	d	12 02	12 34		13 02	13 34		14 02	14 34		15 02	15 34		16 00	16 36		17 00	17 35		18 00		19 00	
Dove Holes	d					13 40						15 40					17 06			18 06			
Chapel-en-le-Frith	d	12 12	12 44		13 12	13 46		14 12	14 44		15 12	15 46		16 10	16 46		17 11	17 45		18 11		19 10	
Whaley Bridge	d	12 18	12 50		13 18	13 52		14 18	14 50		15 18	15 52		16 16	16 52		17 17	17 51		18 17		19 16	
Furness Vale	d		12 54			13 55			14 54			15 55		16 19	16 55		17 21	17 54		18 21		19 20	
New Mills Newtown	d	12 23	12 57		13 23	13 59		14 23	14 57		15 23	15 59		16 23	16 59		17 24	17 58		18 24		19 23	
Disley	d	12 27	13 01		13 27	14 02		14 27	15 01		15 27	16 02		16 26	17 02		17 27	18 01		18 27		19 26	
Middlewood	d		13 05						15 05					16 30				18 05				19 30	
Hazel Grove	a	12 34	13 09		13 34	14 09		14 34	15 09		15 34	16 09		16 34	17 09		17 34	18 09		18 34		19 34	
	d	12 35	13 10	13 21	13 35	14 10	14 22	14 35	15 10	15 21	15 35	16 10	16 21	16 35	17 10	17 21	17 35	18 10	18 21	18 35	19 08	19 35	20 09
Woodsmoor	d	12 38	13 13	13 23	13 38	14 13	14 24	14 38	15 13	15 23	15 38	16 13	16 23	16 38	17 13	17 23	17 38	18 13	18 23	18 38	19 11	19 38	20 11
Davenport	d	12 40	13 15	13 25	13 40	14 15	14 26	14 40	15 15	15 25	15 40	16 15	16 25	16 40	17 15	17 25	17 40	18 15	18 25	18 40	19 15	19 40	20 16
Stockport 84	a	12 45	13 20	13 29	13 45	14 20	14 29	14 45	15 20	15 29	15 45	16 20	16 29	16 45	17 20	17 29	17 45	18 20	18 29	18 45	19 20	19 45	20 20
Heaton Chapel 84	a		13 24			14 24			15 24			16 24			17 24			18 24			19 24		20 24
Levenshulme 84	a	12 50	13 27			14 27		14 50	15 27		15 50	16 27		16 50	17 27		17 50	18 27		18 50	19 27		
Manchester Picc. 10 84 ⇌	a	12 56	13 36	13 40	13 56	14 36	14 40	14 56	15 36	15 40	15 56	16 36	16 40	16 56	17 36	17 40	17 56	18 36	18 40	18 56	19 36	19 56	20 35
Manchester Oxford Road	a																						
Deansgate ⇌	a																						

		NT	NT	NT	NT	NT	NT	NT
Buxton	d	20 18		21 21		22 13		22 59
Dove Holes	d	20 24				22 19		23 05
Chapel-en-le-Frith	d	20 29		21 31		22 24		23 10
Whaley Bridge	d	20 36		21 37		22 30		23 16
Furness Vale	d	20 39		21 41		22 34		23 20
New Mills Newtown	d	20 43		21 44		22 37		23 23
Disley	d	20 46		21 48		22 40		23 27
Middlewood	d	20 50		21 51		22 44		23 30
Hazel Grove	a	20 54		21 56		22 48		23 35
	d	20 55	21 25	21 56	22 08	22 49	23 08	23 35
Woodsmoor	d	20 58	21 27	21 59	22 11		23 10	23 38
Davenport	d	21 00	21 30	22 02	22 15		23 13	23 40
Stockport 84	a	21 05	21 34	22 06	22 21	22 56	23 17	23 45
Heaton Chapel 84	a				22 25		23 23	
Levenshulme 84	a				22 28		23 26	
Manchester Picc. 10 84 ⇌	a	21 15	21 46	22 17	22 35	23 05	23 35	23 56
Manchester Oxford Road	a							
Deansgate ⇌	a							

Saturdays
26 May to 8 December

		NT	NT	NT	NT	NT	NT	EM ◇ A	NT	NT	NT	NT	NT	NT	NT	NT	NT	NT	NT	NT	NT	NT	NT
Buxton	d		06 00	06 33		07 01	07 36			08 00			08 58	09 34		10 02	10 34		11 02	11 34		12 02	12 34
Dove Holes	d		06 06	06 39			07 42						09 05	09 40						11 40			
Chapel-en-le-Frith	d		06 12	06 45		07 11	07 48			08 10			09 10	09 46		10 12	10 44		11 12	11 46		12 12	12 44
Whaley Bridge	d		06 18	06 51		07 17	07 54			08 17			09 16	09 52		10 18	10 50		11 18	11 52		12 18	12 50
Furness Vale	d		06 21	06 54		07 21	07 57			08 20			09 20	09 55			10 54			11 55			12 54
New Mills Newtown	d		06 25	06 58		07 24	08 01			08 24			09 23	09 59		10 23	10 57		11 23	11 59		12 23	12 57
Disley	d		06 28	07 01		07 28	08 04			08 27			09 27	10 02		10 27	11 01		11 27	12 02		12 27	13 01
Middlewood	d		06 32	07 05			08 08						09 30				11 05						13 05
Hazel Grove	a		06 36	07 09		07 35	08 12			08 34			09 35	10 09		10 34	11 09		11 34	12 09		12 34	13 09
	d	06 11	06 37	07 10	07 21	07 35	08 13	08 17	08 21	08 35	09 10	09 21	09 35	10 10	10 21	10 35	11 10	11 21	11 35	12 10	12 21	12 35	13 10
Woodsmoor	d	06 13		07 13	07 23	07 38			08 23	08 38	09 13	09 23	09 38	10 13	10 23	10 38	11 13	11 23	11 38	12 13	12 23	12 38	13 13
Davenport	d	06 15		07 15	07 25	07 40			08 25	08 40	09 15	09 25	09 41	10 15	10 25	10 40	11 15	11 25	11 40	12 15	12 25	12 40	13 15
Stockport 84	a	06 20	06 45	07 21	07 29	07 45	08 20	08 25	08 29	08 45	09 20	09 29	09 45	10 21	10 29	10 45	11 20	11 29	11 45	12 20	12 29	12 45	13 20
Heaton Chapel 84	a			07 25			08 24				09 24			10 25			11 24			12 24			13 24
Levenshulme 84	a			07 28			08 27				09 27		09 50	10 28		10 50	11 27		11 50	12 27		12 50	13 27
Manchester Picc. 10 84 ⇌	a	06 29	06 56	07 36	07 40	07 56	08 36	08 37	08 40	08 56	09 34	09 40	09 56	10 36	10 40	10 56	11 36	11 40	11 56	12 36	12 40	12 56	13 36
Manchester Oxford Road	a							08 41															
Deansgate ⇌	a																						

A From Nottingham to Liverpool Lime Street
B To Manchester Victoria

Table T086-F

Buxton and Hazel Grove - Manchester

Saturdays
26 May to 8 December

		NT	NT	NT	NT	NT	NT	NT	NT	NT	NT	NT	NT	NT	NT	NT	NT	NT	NT	NT	NT	NT
Buxton	d		13 02	13 34		14 02	14 34		15 02	15 34		16 00	16 36		17 00	17 35		18 00		19 00		20 18
Dove Holes	d			13 40						15 40					17 06			18 06				20 24
Chapel-en-le-Frith	d		13 12	13 46		14 12	14 44		15 12	15 46		16 10	16 46		17 11	17 45		18 11		19 10		20 29
Whaley Bridge	d		13 18	13 52		14 18	14 50		15 18	15 52		16 16	16 52		17 17	17 51		18 17		19 16		20 36
Furness Vale	d			13 55			14 54			15 55		16 19	16 55		17 21	17 54		18 21		19 20		20 39
New Mills Newtown	d		13 23	13 59		14 23	14 57		15 23	15 59		16 23	16 59		17 24	17 58		18 24		19 23		20 43
Disley	d		13 27	14 02		14 27	15 01		15 27	16 02		16 26	17 02		17 27	18 01		18 27		19 26		20 46
Middlewood	d						15 05					16 30				18 05				19 30		20 50
Hazel Grove	a		13 34	14 09		14 34	15 09		15 34	16 09		16 34	17 09		17 34	18 09		18 34		19 34		20 54
	d	13 21	13 35	14 10	14 22	14 35	15 10	15 21	15 35	16 10	16 21	16 35	17 10	17 21	17 35	18 10	18 21	18 35	19 08	19 35	20 23	20 55
Woodsmoor	d	13 23	13 38	14 13	14 24	14 38	15 13	15 23	15 38	16 13	16 23	16 38	17 13	17 23	17 38	18 13	18 23	18 38	19 11	19 38	20 25	20 58
Davenport	d	13 25	13 40	14 15	14 26	14 40	15 15	15 25	15 40	16 15	16 25	16 40	17 15	17 25	17 40	18 15	18 25	18 40	19 15	19 40	20 28	21 00
Stockport 84	a	13 29	13 45	14 20	14 29	14 45	15 20	15 29	15 45	16 20	16 29	16 45	17 20	17 29	17 45	18 20	18 29	18 45	19 20	19 45	20 32	21 05
Heaton Chapel 84	a			14 24			15 24			16 24			17 24			18 24			19 24		20 36	
Levenshulme 84	a		13 50	14 27			15 27		15 50	16 27			17 27		17 50	18 27		18 50	19 27			
Manchester Picc. 10 84 ⇌	a	13 40	13 56	14 36	14 40	14 56	15 36	15 40	15 56	16 36	16 40	16 56	17 36	17 40	17 56	18 36	18 40	18 56	19 36	19 56	20 46	21 15
Manchester Oxford Road	a																					
Deansgate ⇌	a																					

		NT	NT	NT	NT	NT
Buxton	d		21 21		21 59	22 56
Dove Holes	d				22 05	23 02
Chapel-en-le-Frith	d		21 31		22 10	23 07
Whaley Bridge	d		21 37		22 16	23 13
Furness Vale	d		21 41		22 20	23 17
New Mills Newtown	d		21 44		22 23	23 20
Disley	d		21 48		22 26	23 24
Middlewood	d		21 51		22 30	23 27
Hazel Grove	a		21 56		22 34	23 32
	d	21 23	21 56	22 12	22 35	23 32
Woodsmoor	d	21 25	21 59	22 15	22 37	23 35
Davenport	d	21 28	22 02	22 19	22 39	23 37
Stockport 84	a	21 32	22 06	22 25	22 44	23 42
Heaton Chapel 84	a			22 29	22 48	
Levenshulme 84	a			22 32	22 51	
Manchester Picc. 10 84 ⇌	a	21 42	22 17	22 39	23 00	23 57
Manchester Oxford Road	a					
Deansgate ⇌	a					

Sundays
20 May to 2 December

		NT	NT A	NT B	NT A	NT B	NT	NT	NT	NT	NT	NT B	NT	NT	NT	NT	NT	NT	NT	NT	NT	NT	NT
Buxton	d	08 14	08 56	08 56			10 03		10 59		11 59		13 00		13 58		14 58		15 58		16 58		17 58
Dove Holes	d	08 20	09 02	09 02					11 05				13 06				15 04				17 04		
Chapel-en-le-Frith	d	08 25	09 07	09 07			10 12		11 10		12 08		13 11		14 07		15 09		16 07		17 09		18 07
Whaley Bridge	d	08 32	09 14	09 14			10 19		11 17		12 15		13 18		14 14		15 15		16 14		17 15		18 14
Furness Vale	d	08 35	09 17	09 17			10 22		11 20		12 18		13 21		14 17		15 18		16 17		17 18		18 17
New Mills Newtown	d	08 38	09 20	09 20			10 25		11 23		12 21		13 24		14 20		15 21		16 20		17 21		18 20
Disley	d	08 42	09 24	09 24			10 29		11 27		12 25		13 28		14 24		15 25		16 24		17 25		18 24
Middlewood	d	08 45	09 27	09 27			10 32				12 28				14 27				16 27				18 27
Hazel Grove	a	08 49	09 32	09 32			10 37		11 34		12 33		13 35		14 32		15 32		16 32		17 32		18 32
	d	08 50	09 32	09 32	09 50	09 50	10 37	10 54	11 34	11 54	12 33	12 54	13 35	13 54	14 32	14 54	15 32	15 54	16 32	16 54	17 32	18 00	18 32
Woodsmoor	d	08 53	09 35	09 35	09 52	09 52	10 40	10 56	11 37	11 56	12 36	12 56	13 38	13 56	14 35	14 56	15 35	15 56	16 35	16 56	17 35	18 02	18 35
Davenport	d	08 55	09 37	09 37	09 55	09 55	10 42	10 59	11 39	11 59	12 38	12 59	13 43	13 59	14 37	14 59	15 37	15 59	16 37	16 59	17 37	18 05	18 37
Stockport 84	a	09 00	09 42	09 42	09 59	09 59	10 46	11 03	11 43	12 03	12 42	13 03	13 49	14 03	14 42	15 03	15 42	16 03	16 42	17 03	17 42	18 09	18 42
Heaton Chapel 84	a	09 04			10 03	10 03				12 07		13 07		14 07		15 07		16 07		17 07			
Levenshulme 84	a	09 07			10 06	10 06				12 10		13 10		14 10		15 10		16 10		17 10			
Manchester Picc. 10 84 ⇌	a	09 13	09 54	09 56	10 13	10 14	10 56		11 56	12 17	12 56	13 17	13 58	14 17	14 55	15 17	15 54	16 17	16 54	17 17	17 54	18 18	18 54
Manchester Oxford Road	a																						
Deansgate ⇌	a																						

		NT	NT	NT	NT	NT	NT	NT	NT
Buxton	d		18 58		19 58		21 00	22 05	22 59
Dove Holes	d		19 04				21 06		23 05
Chapel-en-le-Frith	d		19 09		20 07		21 11	22 14	23 10
Whaley Bridge	d		19 15		20 14		21 18	22 21	23 17
Furness Vale	d		19 18		20 17		21 21	22 24	23 20
New Mills Newtown	d		19 21		20 20		21 24	22 27	23 23
Disley	d		19 25		20 24		21 28	22 31	23 27
Middlewood	d				20 27			22 34	23 30
Hazel Grove	a		19 32		20 32		21 35	22 39	23 35
	d	18 54	19 32	19 54	20 32	20 57	21 35	22 39	23 35
Woodsmoor	d	18 56	19 35	19 56	20 35	20 59	21 38	22 42	23 38
Davenport	d	18 59	19 37	19 59	20 37	21 01	21 40	22 44	23 40
Stockport 84	a	19 03	19 42	20 03	20 42	21 05	21 44	22 49	23 44
Heaton Chapel 84	a	19 07		20 07		21 09			
Levenshulme 84	a	19 10		20 10		21 12			
Manchester Picc. 10 84 ⇌	a	19 17	19 54	20 17	20 54	21 18	21 55	23 00	23 55
Manchester Oxford Road	a								
Deansgate ⇌	a								

A from 16 September
B until 9 September

Table T086-R

Manchester - Hazel Grove and Buxton

Mondays to Fridays

21 May to 7 December

Miles	Station		NT A	NT	NT	NT	NT	NT	NT	NT	NT	NT	NT	NT	NT	NT	NT	NT	NT	NT	NT	NT	NT
—	Deansgate	d																					
—	Manchester Oxford Road	d																					
0	**Manchester Picc.** [10] 84	d	05 46	06 24	06 48	06 51	07 22	07 52	08 08	08 24	08 47	09 11	09 24	09 48	10 11	10 24	10 47	11 11	11 24	11 47	12 11	12 24	12 47
3	Levenshulme 84	d		06 30		06 58	07 30			08 30	08 55		09 30	09 55		10 30	10 55		11 30	11 55		12 30	12 55
4½	Heaton Chapel 84	d		06 33		07 01	07 33			08 33	08 58		09 33	09 58		10 33	10 58		11 33	11 58		12 33	12 58
6	**Stockport** 84	d	05 56	06 37	06 59	07 05	07 37	08 02	08 22	08 37	09 02	09 21	09 37	10 02	10 21	10 37	11 02	11 21	11 37	12 02	12 21	12 37	13 02
7	Davenport	d		06 40	07 04		07 40	08 06	08 26	08 40	09 07	09 25	09 40	10 07	10 25	10 40	11 07	11 25	11 40	12 07	12 25	12 40	13 07
7¼	Woodsmoor	d		06 43	07 06		07 43	08 08		08 43	09 09	09 27	09 43	10 09	10 27	10 43	11 09	11 27	11 43	12 09	12 27	12 43	13 09
8¾	**Hazel Grove**	a	06 03	06 45	07 09	07 13	07 45	08 11	08 29	08 45	09 12	09 30	09 45	10 12	10 30	10 45	11 12	11 30	11 45	12 12	12 30	12 45	13 12
—		d			07 09			08 12	08 30		09 13	09 30		10 12	10 30		11 12	11 30		12 12	12 30		13 12
11	Middlewood	d			07 14						09 17			10 17						12 17			
12½	Disley	d			07 18			08 19	08 38		09 21	09 38		10 21	10 37		11 19	11 37		12 21	12 37		13 19
14¼	New Mills Newtown	d			07 22			08 22	08 42		09 25	09 42		10 24	10 41		11 23	11 41		12 24	12 41		13 23
15¼	Furness Vale	d			07 25			08 25	08 45		09 28	09 45		10 27			11 26			12 27			13 26
16¼	Whaley Bridge	d			07 28			08 28	08 48		09 31	09 48		10 30	10 47		11 29	11 47		12 30	12 47		13 29
20½	Chapel-en-le-Frith	d			07 35			08 36	08 55		09 38	09 56		10 37	10 54		11 36	11 54		12 37	12 54		13 36
22¾	Dove Holes	d			07 40				09 00			10 01					11 41						13 41
25¾	**Buxton**	a			07 48			08 48	09 09		09 50	10 09		10 49	11 06		11 49	12 06		12 49	13 06		13 49

Station		NT	NT	NT	NT	NT	NT	NT	NT	NT	NT	NT	NT	NT	NT	NT	NT	NT	NT	NT	NT	NT
Deansgate	d																					
Manchester Oxford Road	d																					
Manchester Picc. [10] 84	d	13 11	13 24	13 47	14 11	14 24	14 47	15 11	15 24	15 47	16 11	16 24	16 47	17 11	17 24	17 47	18 11	18 24	18 49	19 11	19 24	19 47
Levenshulme 84	d		13 30	13 55		14 30	14 55		15 30	15 55		16 30	16 55		17 30	17 55		18 30	18 55		19 30	19 55
Heaton Chapel 84	d		13 33	13 58		14 33	14 58		15 33	15 58		16 33	16 58		17 33	17 58		18 33	18 58		19 33	19 58
Stockport 84	d	13 21	13 37	14 02	14 21	14 37	15 02	15 21	15 37	16 02	16 21	16 37	17 02	17 21	17 37	18 02	18 21	18 37	19 02	19 21	19 37	20 02
Davenport	d	13 25	13 40	14 07	14 25	14 40	15 07	15 25	15 40	16 07	16 25	16 40	17 07		17 40	18 07	18 25	18 40	19 07		19 40	20 07
Woodsmoor	d	13 27	13 43	14 09	14 27	14 43	15 09	15 27	15 43	16 09	16 27	16 43	17 09		17 43	18 09	18 27	18 43	19 09		19 43	20 09
Hazel Grove	a	13 30	13 45	14 12	14 30	14 45	15 12	15 30	15 45	16 12	16 30	16 45	17 12	17 28	17 45	18 12	18 30	18 45	19 12	19 28	19 45	20 12
	d	13 30		14 12	14 30		15 12	15 30		16 12	16 30		17 12	17 28		18 12	18 30		19 12	19 29		20 12
Middlewood	d			14 17						16 17			17 17			18 17			19 17			
Disley	d	13 37		14 21	14 37		15 19	15 37		16 21	16 37		17 21	17 35		18 21	18 37		19 21	19 36		20 19
New Mills Newtown	d	13 41		14 24	14 41		15 23	15 41		16 24	16 41		17 24	17 39		18 25	18 41		19 24	19 40		20 23
Furness Vale	d			14 27			15 26			16 27	16 44		17 27	17 42		18 28	18 44		19 27	19 43		20 26
Whaley Bridge	d	13 47		14 30	14 47		15 29	15 47		16 30	16 48		17 31	17 45		18 31	18 47		19 30	19 46		20 29
Chapel-en-le-Frith	d	13 54		14 37	14 54		15 36	15 54		16 37	16 55		17 38	17 52		18 38	18 55		19 38	19 53		20 36
Dove Holes	d						15 41						17 43				19 00		19 43			20 41
Buxton	a	14 06		14 49	15 06		15 49	16 06		16 49	17 07		17 51	18 04		18 50	19 08		19 51	20 05		20 49

Station		NT	NT	NT	NT	NT	NT	NT
Deansgate	d							
Manchester Oxford Road	d							
Manchester Picc. [10] 84	d	20 24	20 47	21 23	21 49	22 22	23 11	23 24
Levenshulme 84	d	20 30	20 55	21 29	21 56	22 30		23 30
Heaton Chapel 84	d	20 33	20 58	21 32	21 59	22 33		23 33
Stockport 84	d	20 37	21 02	21 36	22 03	22 46	23 21	23 37
Davenport	d	20 40	21 07	21 39	22 07	22 49		23 40
Woodsmoor	d	20 43	21 09	21 42	22 09	22 52		23 43
Hazel Grove	a	20 45	21 12	21 44	22 12	22 54	23 28	23 45
	d		21 12		22 12		23 28	
Middlewood	d		21 17				23 33	
Disley	d		21 21		22 19		23 37	
New Mills Newtown	d		21 24		22 23		23 41	
Furness Vale	d		21 27		22 26		23 44	
Whaley Bridge	d		21 30		22 29		23 47	
Chapel-en-le-Frith	d		21 37		22 36		23 54	
Dove Holes	d				22 41		23 59	
Buxton	a		21 49		22 49		00 07	

Saturdays

26 May to 8 December

Station		NT A	NT	NT	NT	NT	NT	NT	NT	NT	NT	NT	NT	NT	NT	NT	NT	NT	NT	NT	NT	NT	NT
Deansgate	d																						
Manchester Oxford Road	d																						
Manchester Picc. [10] 84	d	05 46	06 24	06 48	07 22	07 52	08 08	08 24	08 47	09 11	09 24	09 48	10 11	10 24	10 47	11 11	11 24	11 47	12 11	12 24	12 47	13 11	13 24
Levenshulme 84	d		06 30	06 55	07 30			08 30	08 55		09 30	09 55		10 30	10 55		11 30	11 55		12 30	12 55		13 30
Heaton Chapel 84	d		06 33	06 58	07 33			08 33	08 58		09 33	09 58		10 33	10 58		11 33	11 58		12 33	12 58		13 33
Stockport 84	d	05 56	06 37	07 02	07 37	08 02	08 22	08 37	09 02	09 21	09 37	10 02	10 21	10 37	11 02	11 21	11 37	12 02	12 21	12 37	13 02	13 21	13 37
Davenport	d		06 40	07 06	07 40	08 06	08 26	08 40	09 07	09 25	09 40	10 07	10 25	10 40	11 07	11 25	11 40	12 07	12 25	12 40	13 07	13 25	13 40
Woodsmoor	d		06 43	07 08	07 43	08 08		08 43	09 09	09 27	09 43	10 09	10 27	10 43	11 09	11 27	11 43	12 09	12 27	12 43	13 09	13 27	13 43
Hazel Grove	a	06 03	06 45	07 11	07 45	08 11	08 29	08 45	09 12	09 30	09 45	10 12	10 30	10 45	11 12	11 30	11 45	12 12	12 30	12 45	13 12	13 30	13 45
	d			07 12		08 12	08 30		09 13	09 30		10 12	10 30		11 12	11 30		12 12	12 30		13 12	13 30	
Middlewood	d			07 16					09 17			10 17						12 17					
Disley	d			07 20		08 19	08 38		09 21	09 38		10 21	10 37		11 19	11 37		12 21	12 37		13 19	13 37	
New Mills Newtown	d			07 24		08 22	08 42		09 25	09 42		10 24	10 41		11 23	11 41		12 24	12 41		13 23	13 41	
Furness Vale	d			07 27		08 25	08 45		09 28	09 45		10 27			11 26			12 27			13 26		
Whaley Bridge	d			07 30		08 28	08 48		09 31	09 48		10 30	10 47		11 29	11 47		12 30	12 47		13 29	13 47	
Chapel-en-le-Frith	d			07 37		08 36	08 55		09 38	09 56		10 37	10 54		11 36	11 54		12 37	12 54		13 36	13 54	
Dove Holes	d			07 42			09 00			10 01					11 41						13 41		
Buxton	a			07 50		08 48	09 09		09 50	10 09		10 49	11 06		11 49	12 06		12 49	13 06		13 49	14 06	

A To Sheffield

Table T086-R

Manchester - Hazel Grove and Buxton

Saturdays

26 May to 8 December

Station		NT	NT	NT	NT	NT	NT	NT	NT	NT	NT	NT	NT	NT	NT	NT	NT	NT	NT	NT	NT	NT
Deansgate	d																					
Manchester Oxford Road	d																					
Manchester Picc. [10] 84	d	13 47	14 11	14 24	14 47	15 11	15 24	15 47	16 11	16 24	16 47	17 11	17 24	17 47	18 11	18 24	18 49	19 11	19 24	19 47	20 24	20 47
Levenshulme 84	d	13 55		14 30	14 55		15 30	15 55		16 30	16 55		17 30	17 55		18 30	18 55		19 30	19 55	20 30	20 55
Heaton Chapel 84	d	13 58		14 33	14 58		15 33	15 58		16 33	16 58		17 33	17 58		18 33	18 58		19 33	19 58	20 33	20 58
Stockport 84	d	14 02	14 21	14 37	15 02	15 21	15 37	16 02	16 21	16 37	17 02	17 21	17 37	18 02	18 21	18 37	19 02	19 21	19 37	20 02	20 37	21 02
Davenport	d	14 07	14 25	14 40	15 07	15 25	15 40	16 07	16 25	16 40	17 07		17 40	18 07	18 25	18 40	19 07		19 40	20 07	20 40	21 07
Woodsmoor	d	14 09	14 27	14 43	15 09	15 27	15 43	16 09	16 27	16 43	17 09		17 43	18 09	18 27	18 43	19 09		19 43	20 09	20 43	21 09
Hazel Grove	a	14 12	14 30	14 45	15 12	15 30	15 45	16 12	16 30	16 45	17 12	17 28	17 45	18 12	18 30	18 45	19 12	19 28	19 45	20 12	20 45	21 12
	d	14 12	14 30		15 12	15 30		16 12	16 30		17 12	17 28		18 12	18 30		19 12	19 29		20 12		21 12
Middlewood	d	14 17						16 17			17 17			18 17			19 17					21 17
Disley	d	14 21	14 37		15 19	15 37		16 21	16 37		17 21	17 35		18 21	18 37		19 21	19 36		20 19		21 21
New Mills Newtown	d	14 24	14 41		15 23	15 41		16 24	16 41		17 24	17 39		18 25	18 41		19 24	19 40		20 23		21 24
Furness Vale	d	14 27			15 26			16 27	16 44		17 27	17 42		18 28	18 44		19 27	19 43		20 26		21 27
Whaley Bridge	d	14 30	14 47		15 29	15 47		16 30	16 48		17 31	17 45		18 31	18 47		19 30	19 46		20 29		21 30
Chapel-en-le-Frith	d	14 37	14 54		15 36	15 54		16 37	16 55		17 38	17 52		18 38	18 55		19 38	19 53		20 36		21 37
Dove Holes	d				15 41						17 43				19 00		19 43			20 41		
Buxton	a	14 49	15 06		15 49	16 06		16 49	17 07		17 51	18 04		18 50	19 08		19 51	20 05		20 49		21 49

Station		NT	NT	NT	NT	NT
Deansgate	d					
Manchester Oxford Road	d					
Manchester Picc. [10] 84	d	21 23	21 47	22 22	23 07	23 14
Levenshulme 84	d	21 29	21 55	22 30		23 20
Heaton Chapel 84	d	21 32	21 58	22 33		23 23
Stockport 84	d	21 36	22 05	22 42	23 17	23 27
Davenport	d	21 39	22 10	22 45	23 21	
Woodsmoor	d	21 42	22 12	22 48	23 23	
Hazel Grove	a	21 44	22 15	22 50	23 26	23 33
	d		22 15		23 26	
Middlewood	d				23 31	
Disley	d		22 22		23 35	
New Mills Newtown	d		22 26		23 39	
Furness Vale	d		22 29		23 42	
Whaley Bridge	d		22 32		23 45	
Chapel-en-le-Frith	d		22 39		23 52	
Dove Holes	d		22 44		23 57	
Buxton	a		22 52		00 05	

Sundays

20 May to 2 December

Station		NT	NT	NT	NT A	NT B	NT B	NT A	NT	NT	NT B	NT B	NT A	NT	NT	NT	NT	NT	NT	NT	NT	NT	NT
Deansgate	d																						
Manchester Oxford Road	d																						
Manchester Picc. [10] 84	d	08 50	09 23	09 45	10 23	10 34	10 43	10 45		11 49	12 23	12 48	12 49	13 23	13 51	14 23	14 49	15 24	15 49	16 23	16 49	17 23	17 49
Levenshulme 84	d	08 56	09 29		10 29		10 49	10 51		11 55	12 29	12 54	12 55	13 29	13 57	14 29	14 55	15 30	15 55	16 29	16 55	17 29	17 55
Heaton Chapel 84	d	08 59	09 32		10 32		10 52	10 54		11 58	12 32	12 57	12 58	13 32	14 00	14 32	14 58	15 33	15 58	16 32	16 58	17 32	17 58
Stockport 84	d	09 03	09 36	09 55	10 36	10 44	10 56	10 58	11 36	12 02	12 36	13 01	13 02	13 36	14 04	14 36	15 02	15 37	16 02	16 36	17 02	17 36	18 02
Davenport	d	09 07	09 39	09 59	10 39		11 00	11 02	11 39	12 06	12 39	13 05	13 06	13 39	14 08	14 39	15 06	15 40	16 06	16 39	17 06	17 39	18 06
Woodsmoor	d	09 09	09 41	10 01	10 41		11 02	11 04	11 41	12 08	12 41	13 07	13 08	13 41	14 10	14 41	15 08	15 42	16 08	16 41	17 08	17 41	18 08
Hazel Grove	a	09 12	09 43	10 04	10 43	10 50	11 05	11 07	11 43	12 11	12 43	13 10	13 11	13 43	14 13	14 43	15 11	15 44	16 11	16 43	17 11	17 43	18 11
	d	09 12		10 04			11 06	11 08		12 12		13 10	13 12		14 13		15 11		16 11		17 11		18 11
Middlewood	d	09 17		10 09						12 16					14 18				16 16				18 16
Disley	d	09 21		10 13			11 13	11 15		12 20		13 17	13 19		14 22		15 18		16 20		17 18		18 20
New Mills Newtown	d	09 25		10 17			11 17	11 19		12 24		13 21	13 23		14 26		15 22		16 24		17 22		18 24
Furness Vale	d	09 27		10 19			11 19	11 21		12 27		13 24	13 25		14 28		15 25		16 26		17 25		18 26
Whaley Bridge	d	09 31		10 23			11 23	11 25		12 30		13 27	13 29		14 32		15 28		16 30		17 28		18 30
Chapel-en-le-Frith	d	09 38		10 30			11 30	11 32		12 37		13 34	13 36		14 39		15 35		16 37		17 35		18 37
Dove Holes	d	09 43					11 35	11 37				13 39	13 41				15 40				17 40		
Buxton	a	09 51		10 41			11 43	11 45		12 49		13 47	13 49		14 50		15 48		16 48		17 48		18 48

Station		NT	NT	NT	NT	NT	NT	NT	NT	NT	NT	NT
Deansgate	d											
Manchester Oxford Road	d											
Manchester Picc. [10] 84	d	18 23	18 49	19 23	19 49	20 33	20 49	21 23	21 50	22 25	22 48	23 26
Levenshulme 84	d	18 29	18 55	19 29	19 55	20 39	20 55	21 29	21 56	22 32	22 54	23 33
Heaton Chapel 84	d	18 32	18 58	19 32	19 58	20 42	20 58	21 32	21 59	22 35	22 57	23 36
Stockport 84	d	18 36	19 02	19 36	20 02	20 46	21 02	21 36	22 03	22 39	23 01	23 40
Davenport	d	18 39	19 06	19 39	20 06	20 49	21 06	21 39	22 07	22 42	23 05	23 43
Woodsmoor	d	18 41	19 08	19 41	20 08	20 51	21 08	21 41	22 09	22 44	23 07	23 45
Hazel Grove	a	18 43	19 11	19 43	20 11	20 53	21 11	21 43	22 12	22 46	23 10	23 47
	d		19 11		20 11		21 11		22 12		23 10	
Middlewood	d				20 16				22 17		23 15	
Disley	d		19 18		20 20		21 18		22 21		23 19	
New Mills Newtown	d		19 22		20 24		21 22		22 25		23 23	
Furness Vale	d		19 25		20 26		21 25		22 27		23 25	
Whaley Bridge	d		19 28		20 30		21 28		22 31		23 29	
Chapel-en-le-Frith	d		19 35		20 37		21 35		22 38		23 36	
Dove Holes	d		19 40				21 40				23 41	
Buxton	a		19 48		20 48		21 48		22 49		23 49	

A from 16 September

B until 9 September

Table T088-F

Manchester - Northwich and Chester

Mondays to Fridays
21 May to 7 December

Miles	Station		NT MX	NT	NT	NT	NT	NT ◇	NT ◇	NT ◇	NT ◇		NT	NT	NT	NT	NT ◇	NT ◇	NT ◇	NT ◇	NT ◇	NT
0	Manchester Picc. 84	d		06 13	07 09	07 40		08 41	09 41	10 41	11 41	and hourly until	16 41		17 41		18 41	19 40	20 41	21 40	22 40	23 41
6½	Stockport 84	d		06 22	07 18	07 52	08 18	08 52	09 52	10 52	11 52		16 52	17 18	17 52	18 18	18 52	19 52	20 54	21 52	22 56	23 50
14¾	Navigation Road	d	00 06	06 37	07 34	08 07	08 33	09 07	10 07	11 10	12 07		17 07	17 33	18 07	18 33	19 07	20 08	21 09	22 07		00 06
15¼	Altrincham	a	00 08	06 39	07 36	08 09	08 35	09 09	10 09	11 12	12 09		17 09	17 35	18 09	18 35	19 09	20 10	21 11	22 09	23 13	00 08
—		d	00 08	06 40	07 36	08 10	08 36	09 10	10 10	11 13	12 10		17 10	17 36	18 10	18 36	19 10	20 10	21 11	22 10	23 13	00 08
16	Hale	d	00 11	06 43	07 39	08 12	08 39	09 13	10 13	11 15	12 13		17 13	17 39	18 12	18 39	19 12	20 13	21 14	22 12	23 16	00 11
17¾	Ashley	d	00 14	06 46	07 43	08 16	08 42	09 16	10 16	11 19	12 16		17 16	17 42	18 16	18 42	19 16	20 16	21 17	22 16	23 19	00 14
18½	Mobberley	d	00 18	06 50	07 47	08 19	08 46	09 20	10 20	11 22	12 20		17 20	17 46	18 19	18 46	19 19	20 20	21 21	22 19	23 22	00 18
22¼	Knutsford	d	00 23	06 55	07 52	08 24	08 51	09 25	10 25	11 27	12 25		17 25	17 51	18 24	18 51	19 24	20 24	21 26	22 24	23 27	00 23
24¾	Plumley	d	00 27	06 59	07 56	08 28	08 55	09 29	10 29	11 31	12 29		17 29	17 55	18 29	18 55	19 29	20 29	21 30	22 29	23 31	00 27
26¾	Lostock Gralam	d	00 31	07 03	08 00	08 32	08 59	09 33	10 33	11 35	12 33		17 33	17 59	18 32	18 59	19 32	20 32	21 34	22 32	23 35	00 31
28¼	Northwich	d	00 35	07 07	08 05	08 37	09 03	09 37	10 37	11 39	12 37		17 37	18 03	18 37	19 03	19 37	20 37	21 38	22 37	23 39	00 35
30	Greenbank	d	00 40	07 13	08 10	08 42	09 09	09 43	10 43	11 45	12 43		17 43	18 08	18 42	19 09	19 42	20 42	21 44	22 42	23 44	00 40
32¾	Cuddington	d	00 45	07 18	08 15	08 47	09 14	09 48	10 48	11 50	12 48		17 48	18 13	18 47	19 14	19 47	20 47	21 49	22 47	23 49	00 45
35¾	Delamere	d	00 50	07 23	08 20	08 52	09 19	09 53	10 53	11 55	12 53		17 53	18 18	18 52	19 19	19 52	20 52	21 53	22 52	23 54	00 50
38¾	Mouldsworth	d	00 55	07 28	08 26	08 57	09 24	09 58	10 58	12 07	12 58		17 58	18 23	18 57	19 24	19 57	20 57	21 59	23 00	23 59	00 55
45¼	Chester 81	a	01 07	07 40	08 38	09 11	09 36	10 10	11 10	12 19	13 10		18 10	18 35	19 09	19 36	20 09	21 10	22 13	23 14	00 11	01 07

Saturdays
26 May to 8 December

Station		NT	NT	NT	NT	NT ◇	NT ◇	NT ◇	NT ◇	NT ◇	NT ◇	NT ◇	NT ◇	NT	NT	NT ◇	NT ◇	NT	NT	NT ◇	NT
Manchester Picc. 84	d		06 13	07 08	07 40	08 41	09 41	10 41	11 41	12 41	13 41	14 41	15 41	16 41	17 41	18 41	19 40	20 41	21 37	22 40	23 41
Stockport 84	d		06 22	07 19	07 52	08 52	09 52	10 52	11 52	12 52	13 52	14 52	15 52	16 52	17 52	18 52	19 52	20 52	21 51	22 52	23 50
Navigation Road	d	00 06	06 37	07 35	08 07	09 07	10 07	11 12	12 07	13 07	14 12	15 07	16 12	17 07	18 07	19 07	20 08	21 07	22 06	23 07	00 06
Altrincham	a	00 08	06 39	07 37	08 09	09 09	10 09	11 14	12 09	13 09	14 14	15 09	16 14	17 09	18 09	19 09	20 10	21 09	22 08	23 09	00 08
	d	00 08	06 40	07 37	08 10	09 10	10 10	11 15	12 10	13 10	14 15	15 10	16 15	17 10	18 10	19 10	20 10	21 10	22 09	23 10	00 08
Hale	d	00 11	06 43	07 40	08 12	09 13	10 13	11 18	12 13	13 13	14 17	15 13	16 18	17 13	18 13	19 12	20 13	21 12	22 11	23 12	00 11
Ashley	d	00 14	06 46	07 44	08 16	09 16	10 16	11 21	12 16	13 16	14 21	15 16	16 22	17 16	18 16	19 16	20 16	21 16	22 15	23 16	00 14
Mobberley	d	00 18	06 50	07 48	08 19	09 20	10 20	11 25	12 20	13 20	14 24	15 20	16 26	17 20	18 20	19 19	20 20	21 19	22 18	23 19	00 18
Knutsford	d	00 23	06 55	07 53	08 24	09 25	10 25	11 30	12 25	13 25	14 29	15 25	16 31	17 25	18 25	19 24	20 24	21 24	22 23	23 24	00 23
Plumley	d	00 27	06 59	07 57	08 28	09 29	10 29	11 34	12 29	13 29	14 34	15 29	16 36	17 29	18 29	19 29	20 29	21 29	22 28	23 29	00 27
Lostock Gralam	d	00 31	07 03	08 01	08 32	09 33	10 33	11 38	12 33	13 33	14 37	15 33	16 40	17 33	18 33	19 32	20 32	21 32	22 31	23 32	00 31
Northwich	d	00 35	07 07	08 06	08 37	09 37	10 37	11 42	12 37	13 37	14 41	15 37	16 44	17 37	18 37	19 37	20 37	21 37	22 36	23 37	00 35
Greenbank	d	00 40	07 13	08 11	08 42	09 43	10 43	11 48	12 43	13 43	14 46	15 43	16 50	17 43	18 43	19 42	20 42	21 42	22 41	23 42	00 40
Cuddington	d	00 45	07 18	08 16	08 47	09 48	10 48	11 53	12 48	13 48	14 51	15 48	16 55	17 48	18 48	19 47	20 47	21 47	22 46	23 47	00 45
Delamere	d	00 50	07 23	08 21	08 52	09 53	10 53	11 58	12 53	13 53	14 56	15 53	17 00	17 53	18 53	19 52	20 52	21 52	22 51	23 52	00 50
Mouldsworth	d	00 55	07 28	08 27	08 57	09 58	10 58	12 07	12 58	13 58	15 01	15 58	17 14	17 58	19 00	19 57	20 57	21 57	22 58	23 57	00 55
Chester 81	a	01 07	07 40	08 39	09 11	10 10	11 10	12 19	13 10	14 10	15 14	16 10	17 25	18 10	19 12	20 09	21 10	22 09	23 09	00 09	01 07

Sundays
20 May to 2 December

Station		NT A	NT ◇	NT ◇	NT ◇	NT ◇	NT ◇	NT ◇	NT ◇
Manchester Picc. 84	d		09 04	10 58	13 06	15 06	17 06	19 06	21 06
Stockport 84	d		09 20	11 07	13 17	15 19	17 17	19 17	21 18
Navigation Road	d	00 06	09 34	11 22	13 32	15 34	17 31	19 31	21 33
Altrincham	a	00 08	09 36	11 24	13 34	15 36	17 33	19 33	21 35
	d	00 08	09 37	11 24	13 34	15 37	17 34	19 34	21 35
Hale	d	00 11	09 39	11 27	13 37	15 39	17 36	19 36	21 38
Ashley	d	00 14	09 43	11 31	13 41	15 43	17 40	19 40	21 42
Mobberley	d	00 18	09 47	11 34	13 44	15 47	17 44	19 44	21 45
Knutsford	d	00 23	09 52	11 39	13 49	15 52	17 49	19 49	21 50
Plumley	d	00 27	09 56	11 44	13 54	15 56	17 53	19 53	21 55
Lostock Gralam	d	00 31	10 00	11 48	13 58	16 00	17 57	19 57	21 59
Northwich	d	00 35	10 05	11 52	14 02	16 05	18 02	20 02	22 03
Greenbank	d	00 40	10 10	11 58	14 08	16 10	18 07	20 07	22 09
Cuddington	d	00 45	10 15	12 03	14 13	16 15	18 12	20 12	22 14
Delamere	d	00 50	10 20	12 08	14 18	16 20	18 17	20 17	22 19
Mouldsworth	d	00 55	10 26	12 14	14 24	16 26	18 23	20 23	22 25
Chester 81	a	01 07	10 39	12 26	14 40	16 40	18 34	20 34	22 36

A not 20 May

Table T088-R

Chester and Northwich - Manchester

Mondays to Fridays
21 May to 7 December

Miles	Station		NT	NT	NT	NT	NT	NT ◇	NT ◇	NT ◇	NT ◇	NT ◇	NT ◇	NT ◇	NT ◇	NT	NT	NT	NT ◇	NT	NT ◇	NT
0	Chester 81	d	05 58	06 21	06 51	07 15	07 58	09 00	10 02	11 02	11 55	13 02	14 02	15 02	16 02	17 02	18 01	19 01	20 01	21 02	22 01	22 46
6½	Mouldsworth	d	06 10	06 32	07 03	07 31	08 11	09 13	10 13	11 13	12 07	13 13	14 13	15 14	16 13	17 13	18 13	19 12	20 12	21 14	22 13	22 59
9½	Delamere	d	06 15	06 38	07 08	07 37	08 16	09 18	10 18	11 18	12 12	13 18	14 18	15 19	16 18	17 18	18 18	19 17	20 17	21 19	22 18	23 05
12½	Cuddington	d	06 20	06 42	07 13	07 42	08 21	09 23	10 23	11 23	12 17	13 23	14 23	15 24	16 23	17 23	18 23	19 22	20 22	21 23	22 23	23 09
15¼	Greenbank	d	06 25	06 47	07 18	07 47	08 26	09 27	10 27	11 27	12 23	13 27	14 27	15 28	16 27	17 27	18 27	19 26	20 26	21 28	22 27	23 14
17	Northwich	d	06 30	06 53	07 23	07 52	08 31	09 33	10 33	11 33	12 30	13 33	14 33	15 34	16 33	17 33	18 33	19 32	20 32	21 33	22 33	23 20
18½	Lostock Gralam	d	06 33	06 56	07 26	07 56	08 34	09 36	10 36	11 36	12 33	13 36	14 36	15 37	16 36	17 36	18 36	19 35	20 35	21 36	22 36	23 23
20½	Plumley	d	06 37	07 00	07 30	08 00	08 38	09 39	10 39	11 39	12 37	13 39	14 39	15 40	16 39	17 39	18 39	19 38	20 38	21 40	22 39	23 27
23	Knutsford	d	06 42	07 05	07 35	08 05	08 43	09 44	10 44	11 44	12 43	13 44	14 44	15 45	16 44	17 44	18 44	19 44	20 44	21 45	22 44	23 33
26¾	Mobberley	d	06 47	07 10	07 40	08 10	08 48	09 49	10 49	11 49	12 48	13 49	14 49	15 50	16 49	17 49	18 49	19 48	20 48	21 50	22 49	23 37
27½	Ashley	d	06 50	07 14	07 43	08 14	08 51	09 52	10 52	11 52	12 52	13 52	14 52	15 53	16 52	17 52	18 52	19 52	20 52	21 53	22 52	23 41
29¼	Hale	d	06 54	07 18	07 47	08 18	08 55	09 56	10 56	11 56	12 56	13 56	14 56	15 57	16 56	17 56	18 56	19 56	20 56	21 57	22 56	23 45
30	Altrincham	a	06 58	07 21	07 51	08 22	08 59	09 59	10 59	11 59	12 59	13 59	14 59	16 00	16 59	17 59	18 59	19 59	20 59	22 01	22 59	23 49
—		d	06 58	07 24	07 51	08 22	08 59	10 00	11 00	12 00	13 00	14 00	15 00	16 01	17 00	18 00	19 00	20 00	21 00	22 01	23 00	23 49
30½	Navigation Road	d	07 01	07 26	07 54	08 25	09 02	10 02	11 02	12 02	13 02	14 02	15 02	16 03	17 02	18 02	19 02	20 02	21 02	22 03	23 02	23 52
38¾	Stockport 84	a	07 16	07 46	08 08	08 39	09 16	10 16	11 16	12 16	13 16	14 16	15 16	16 16	17 16	18 16	19 16	20 16	21 16	22 18	23 16	00 12
44¾	Manchester Picc. 81	a	07 32		08 18		09 31	10 30	11 30	12 30	13 30	14 30	15 30	16 30	17 30	18 30	19 30	20 30	21 31	22 32	23 31	00 26

Saturdays
26 May to 8 December

Station		NT	NT	NT ◇	NT ◇	NT ◇	NT ◇	NT ◇	NT ◇	NT ◇	NT ◇	NT ◇	NT	NT	NT	NT ◇	NT	NT ◇	NT
Chester 81	d	05 58	06 51	07 58	09 00	10 02	11 02	11 55	13 02	14 02	15 02	16 02	17 02	18 01	18 48	20 01	21 01	22 01	22 46
Mouldsworth	d	06 10	07 03	08 11	09 13	10 13	11 13	12 07	13 13	14 13	15 14	16 13	17 13	18 13	19 04	20 12	21 12	22 12	22 59
Delamere	d	06 15	07 08	08 16	09 18	10 18	11 18	12 12	13 18	14 18	15 19	16 18	17 18	18 18	19 09	20 17	21 17	22 17	23 05
Cuddington	d	06 20	07 13	08 21	09 23	10 23	11 23	12 17	13 23	14 23	15 24	16 23	17 23	18 23	19 14	20 22	21 22	22 22	23 09
Greenbank	d	06 25	07 18	08 26	09 27	10 27	11 27	12 23	13 27	14 27	15 28	16 27	17 27	18 27	19 19	20 26	21 26	22 26	23 14
Northwich	d	06 30	07 23	08 31	09 33	10 33	11 33	12 30	13 33	14 33	15 34	16 33	17 33	18 33	19 24	20 32	21 32	22 32	23 20
Lostock Gralam	d	06 33	07 26	08 34	09 36	10 36	11 36	12 33	13 36	14 36	15 37	16 36	17 36	18 36	19 27	20 35	21 35	22 35	23 23
Plumley	d	06 37	07 30	08 38	09 39	10 39	11 39	12 37	13 39	14 39	15 40	16 39	17 39	18 39	19 31	20 38	21 38	22 39	23 27
Knutsford	d	06 42	07 35	08 43	09 44	10 44	11 44	12 43	13 44	14 44	15 45	16 44	17 44	18 44	19 36	20 44	21 44	22 44	23 33
Mobberley	d	06 47	07 40	08 48	09 49	10 49	11 49	12 48	13 49	14 49	15 50	16 49	17 49	18 49	19 41	20 48	21 48	22 48	23 37
Ashley	d	06 50	07 43	08 51	09 52	10 52	11 52	12 52	13 52	14 52	15 53	16 52	17 52	18 52	19 44	20 52	21 52	22 52	23 41
Hale	d	06 54	07 47	08 55	09 56	10 56	11 56	12 56	13 56	14 56	15 57	16 56	17 56	18 56	19 48	20 55	21 56	22 56	23 45
Altrincham	a	06 58	07 51	08 59	09 59	10 59	11 59	12 59	13 59	14 59	16 00	16 59	17 59	18 59	19 52	20 59	21 59	22 59	23 49
	d	06 58	07 51	08 59	10 00	11 00	12 00	13 00	14 00	15 00	16 01	17 00	18 00	19 00	19 52	20 59	22 00	23 00	23 49
Navigation Road	d	07 01	07 54	09 02	10 02	11 02	12 02	13 02	14 02	15 02	16 03	17 02	18 02	19 02	19 54	21 01	22 02	23 02	23 52
Stockport 84	a	07 16	08 08	09 16	10 16	11 16	12 16	13 16	14 16	15 16	16 16	17 16	18 16	19 16	20 09	21 16	22 16	23 17	00 12
Manchester Picc. 81	a	07 32	08 18	09 31	10 30	11 30	12 30	13 30	14 30	15 30	16 30	17 30	18 30	19 30	20 18	21 26	22 28	23 31	00 26

Sundays
20 May to 2 December

Station		NT ◇ A	NT ◇ B	NT ◇ B	NT A	NT ◇	NT ◇	NT ◇	NT	NT
Chester 81	d	08 59	08 59	10 59	10 59	12 59	15 04	17 07	19 04	20 59
Mouldsworth	d	09 10	09 10	11 10	11 10	13 10	15 15	17 18	19 15	21 10
Delamere	d	09 16	09 16	11 16	11 16	13 16	15 21	17 23	19 21	21 16
Cuddington	d	09 20	09 20	11 20	11 20	13 20	15 25	17 28	19 25	21 20
Greenbank	d	09 25	09 25	11 25	11 25	13 25	15 30	17 33	19 30	21 25
Northwich	d	09 31	09 31	11 31	11 31	13 31	15 36	17 38	19 36	21 31
Lostock Gralam	d	09 34	09 34	11 34	11 34	13 34	15 39	17 41	19 39	21 34
Plumley	d	09 38	09 38	11 38	11 38	13 38	15 43	17 45	19 43	21 38
Knutsford	d	09 43	09 43	11 43	11 43	13 43	15 48	17 50	19 48	21 43
Mobberley	d	09 48	09 48	11 48	11 48	13 48	15 53	17 54	19 53	21 48
Ashley	d	09 51	09 51	11 51	11 51	13 51	15 56	17 58	19 56	21 51
Hale	d	09 55	09 55	11 55	11 55	13 55	16 00	18 02	20 00	21 55
Altrincham	a	09 59	09 59	11 59	11 59	13 59	16 04	18 05	20 04	21 59
	d	09 59	09 59	11 59	11 59	13 59	16 04	18 06	20 04	21 59
Navigation Road	d	10 02	10 02	12 02	12 02	14 02	16 07	18 08	20 07	22 02
Stockport 84	a	10 16	10 17	12 16	12 16	14 17	16 24	18 25	20 21	22 17
Manchester Picc. 81	a	10 31	10 31	12 29	12 33	14 35	16 40	18 39	20 38	22 28

A until 9 September

B from 16 September

Manchester Airport and Manchester - Warrington Central - Liverpool

Miles		NT MX A	NT	NT ◇	NT	NT B	NT	NT	NT ◇	NT	NT C	EM ◇ D	NT	NT ◇	NT	NT ◇ C	EM ◇ E	EM ◇ F	NT	NT ◇	NT	NT ◇ C
0	**Manchester Airport** 85 d			05 51		05 59			06 50		06 58			07 50		07 59						08 59
—	Sheffield [7] 78 d											06 18					07 32	07 33				
—	Stockport 84 d											07 25					08 25	08 25				
9¾	**Manchester Picc** [10] 78,84,85 d			06 09		06 22			07 09		07 22	07 39		08 09		08 22	08 38	08 38				09 22
10½	**Manchester Oxford Road** 84,85 d			06 13	06 20	06 29		06 49	07 12		07 30	07 42	07 48	08 12	08 16	08 30	08 42	08 42	08 45	09 12	09 16	09 30
10¾	Deansgate 84,85 d				06 23	06 32		06 51			07 32		07 50			08 32			08 48			09 32
13¾	Trafford Park d				06 28										08 22						09 22	
14½	Humphrey Park d				06 30																09 24	
15½	Urmston d				06 33			06 59					07 58		08 25				08 56		09 27	
16	Chassen Road d				06 35										08 27							
16¾	Flixton d				06 37								08 01		08 30						09 30	
19	Irlam d				06 42			07 05					08 05		08 34				09 02		09 34	
20¼	Glazebrook d				06 45								08 08									
23	Birchwood d			06 27	06 50			07 12	07 27				08 13	08 27	08 40				09 07	09 27	09 40	
24½	Padgate d	00 02			06 53								08 16		08 43						09 43	
25¾	**Warrington Central** a	00 06		06 32	06 56			07 18	07 32			07 58	08 19	08 32	08 46		08 58	08 58	09 12	09 32	09 46	
—	d	00 06	05 57	06 33	06 57		07 11		07 32	07 40		07 58	08 20	08 32	08 47		08 58	08 58	09 13	09 32	09 47	
28¾	Sankey for Penketh d	00 10	06 01		07 01		07 15			07 44			08 24						09 17			
32¼	Widnes d	00 16	06 07		07 06		07 21			07 50		08 06	08 30		08 55		09 06	09 06	09 23		09 55	
34	Hough Green d	00 20	06 10		07 10		07 25			07 53		08 10	08 33		08 58				09 26		09 59	
35½	Halewood d	00 24	06 14		07 14		07 29			07 58			08 37						09 30			
37½	Hunts Cross 103 d	00 27	06 18		07 17		07 32			08 01		08s15	08 40						09 33			
39	L'pool Sth Parkway [7] 91,103 d	00 33	06 23	06 51	07 23		07 38		07 49	08 06		08 20	08 46	08 51	09 06		09 15	09 15	09 39	09 50	10 07	
40	West Allerton 91 a		06 26		07 26		07 41			08 10			08 49		09 10				09 42		10 11	
40¾	Mossley Hill 91 a		06 29		07 28		07 44			08 12			08 52		09 13				09 45		10 13	
43¾	Edge Hill 90,91 a		06 35		07 34	07 21	07 50			08 20	08 17		08 57			09 22			09 50			10 22
44½	**Liverpool Lime Street** [10] 90,91 a	00 46	06 39	07 04	07 38	07 30	07 54		08 01	08 24	08 26	08 34	09 02	09 09	09 24	09 30	09 28	09 28	09 55	10 02	10 23	10 30

	EM ◇ D	NT	NT ◇	NT	NT ◇ C	EM ◇ G	NT	NT ◇	NT	NT ◇ C	EM ◇ H	EM ◇ I	NT	NT ◇	NT	NT ◇ C	EM ◇ G	NT	NT ◇	NT	NT ◇ C	EM ◇ H
Manchester Airport 85 d			09 50		09 58			10 50		11 02				11 50		11 57			12 50		12 59	
Sheffield [7] 78 d	08 41					09 40					10 40	10 41					11 41					12 41
Stockport 84 d	09 25					10 25					11 25	11 25					12 25					13 25
Manchester Picc [10] 78,84,85 d	09 39		10 09		10 22	10 38		11 09		11 26	11 38	11 38		12 09		12 22	12 38		13 09		13 22	13 38
Manchester Oxford Road 84,85 d	09 42	09 45	10 13	10 15	10 30	10 42	10 46	11 12	11 15	11 30	11 42	11 42	11 46	12 12	12 15	12 30	12 42	12 46	13 12	13 15	13 30	13 42
Deansgate 84,85 d		09 48			10 32		10 48			11 32			11 48			12 32		12 48			13 32	
Trafford Park d									11 22											13 22		
Humphrey Park d									11 24											13 24		
Urmston d		09 56		10 24			10 56		11 27				11 56		12 24			12 56		13 27		
Chassen Road d				10 26											12 26							
Flixton d				10 29					11 30						12 28					13 30		
Irlam d		10 02		10 33			11 02		11 34				12 02		12 33			13 02		13 34		
Glazebrook d				10 36											12 36							
Birchwood d		10 07	10 27	10 41			11 07	11 27	11 40				12 07	12 27	12 40			13 07	13 27	13 40		
Padgate d				10 44					11 43						12 43					13 43		
Warrington Central a	09 58	10 12	10 32	10 47		10 58	11 12	11 32	11 46		11 58	11 58	12 12	12 32	12 47		12 58	13 12	13 32	13 46		13 58
d	09 58	10 13	10 33	10 48		10 58	11 13	11 32	11 47		11 58	11 58	12 13	12 32	12 47		12 58	13 13	13 33	13 47		13 58
Sankey for Penketh d		10 17					11 17						12 17					13 17				
Widnes d	10 06	10 23		10 56		11 06	11 23		11 55		12 06	12 06	12 23		12 55		13 06	13 23		13 55		14 06
Hough Green d		10 26		10 59			11 26		11 59				12 26		12 59			13 26		13 59		
Halewood d		10 30					11 30						12 30					13 30				
Hunts Cross 103 d		10 33					11 33						12 33					13 33				
L'pool Sth Parkway [7] 91,103 d	10 15	10 39	10 50	11 07		11 15	11 39	11 50	12 07		12 15	12 15	12 39	12 49	13 07		13 15	13 39	13 50	14 07		14 15
West Allerton 91 a		10 42		11 11			11 42		12 11				12 42		13 11			13 42		14 11		
Mossley Hill 91 a		10 45		11 14			11 45		12 13				12 45		13 13			13 45		14 13		
Edge Hill 90,91 a		10 50			11 23		11 50			12 21			12 50			13 22		13 50			14 22	
Liverpool Lime Street [10] 90,91 a	10 31	10 55	11 02	11 24	11 30	11 32	11 55	12 02	12 23	12 30	12 32	12 32	12 55	13 01	13 23	13 30	13 32	13 55	14 02	14 23	14 30	14 32

A From Manchester Oxford Road
B From Wilmslow
C From Crewe
D From Nottingham
E until 27 July, from 8 October. From Nottingham
F from 30 July until 5 October. From Nottingham
G From Norwich
H until 31 August, from 8 October. From Norwich
I from 3 September until 5 October. From Norwich

Manchester Airport and Manchester - Warrington Central - Liverpool

	NT	NT ◇	NT	NT ◇ A	EM ◇ B	NT	NT ◇	NT	NT ◇ A	EM ◇ B	NT	NT ◇	NT	NT ◇ A	EM ◇ B	NT	NT ◇	NT	NT ◇ A	EM ◇ B	NT	NT ◇
Manchester Airport 85 d		13 50		13 58			14 50		14 58			15 50		15 59			16 50		16 59			17 50
Sheffield [7] 78 d					13 40					14 41					15 40					16 40		
Stockport 84 d					14 25					15 25					16 25					17 25		
Manchester Picc [10] 78,84,85 d		14 09		14 22	14 38		15 09		15 22	15 38		16 09		16 22	16 38		17 10		17 23	17 38		18 09
Manchester Oxford Road 84,85 d	13 46	14 12	14 15	14 30	14 42	14 46	15 12	15 16	15 30	15 42	15 46	16 12	16 15	16 30	16 42	16 46	17 13	17 15	17 30	17 42	17 46	18 13
Deansgate 84,85 d	13 48			14 32		14 48			15 32		15 48			16 32		16 48			17 32		17 48	
Trafford Park d								15 22								16 54		17 23			17 54	
Humphrey Park d								15 24										17 25			17 56	
Urmston d	13 56		14 24			14 56		15 27			15 56		16 24			16 58		17 28			17 59	
Chassen Road d			14 26										16 26					17 30			18 01	
Flixton d			14 28					15 30					16 28			17 01		17 33			18 04	
Irlam d	14 02		14 33			15 02		15 34			16 02		16 33			17 05		17 38		17 53	18 09	
Glazebrook d			14 36										16 36					17 41			18 12	
Birchwood d	14 07	14 27	14 40			15 07	15 27	15 40			16 07	16 27	16 40			17 11	17 28	17 46		17 58	18 17	18 28
Padgate d			14 43					15 43					16 43			17 14		17 49			18 20	
Warrington Central a	14 12	14 32	14 47		14 58	15 12	15 32	15 46		15 58	16 12	16 32	16 47		16 58	17 17	17 33	17 52		18 03	18 23	18 33
d	14 13	14 33	14 47		14 58	15 13	15 33	15 47		15 58	16 13	16 32	16 47		16 58	17 18	17 33	17 53		18 04	18 24	18 33
Sankey for Penketh d	14 17					15 17					16 17					17 22		17 57				
Widnes d	14 23		14 55		15 06	15 23		15 55		16 06	16 23		16 55		17 06	17 28		18 03		18 12		
Hough Green d	14 26		14 59			15 26		15 58			16 26		16 59			17 31		18 06			18 33	
Halewood d	14 30					15 30					16 30					17 35		18 10				
Hunts Cross 103 d	14 33					15 33					16 33					17 38		18 13			18 38	
L'pool Sth Parkway [7] 91,103 d	14 39	14 50	15 07		15 15	15 39	15 50	16 06		16 15	16 39	16 50	17 08		17 15	17 46	17 51	18 19		18 23	18 46	18 50
West Allerton 91 a	14 42		15 11			15 42		16 10			16 42		17 11			17 49		18 22			18 49	
Mossley Hill 91 a	14 45		15 13			15 45		16 13			16 45		17 14			17 52		18 25			18 53	
Edge Hill 90,91 a	14 50			15 22		15 50			16 24		16 50			17 25		17 57		18 33	18 24		19 02	
Liverpool Lime Street [10] 90,91 a	14 55	15 02	15 23	15 29	15 32	15 55	16 02	16 22	16 30	16 32	16 55	17 04	17 23	17 31	17 32	18 02	18 09	18 37	18 30	18 36	19 06	19 04

	NT	EM ◇ B	NT	NT ◇	NT	EM ◇ B	NT	NT ThX ◇	NT ThO ◇	NT	NT C	EM ◇ B	NT	NT ◇	NT C	NT	NT ◇	NT C	NT	NT ◇	NT C	NT
Manchester Airport 85 d				18 50				19 50	19 50		19 59			20 48	20 58		21 50	21 58		22 50	23 01	
Sheffield [7] 78 d		17 40				18 40						19 40										
Stockport 84 d		18 25				19 25						20 25										
Manchester Picc [10] 78,84,85 d		18 38		19 09		19 38		20 09	20 09		20 22	20 38		21 11	21 18		22 07	22 18		23 09	23 22	
Manchester Oxford Road 84,85 d	18 16	18 42	18 46	19 12	19 15	19 42	19 46	20 12	20 12	20 15	20 30	20 42	20 46	21 14	21 29	21 46	22 11	22 31	22 43	23 12	23 25	23 29
Deansgate 84,85 d			18 48				19 48				20 32		20 48		21 31	21 48		22 34	22 45		23 28	23 31
Trafford Park d	18 22		18 54				19 54						20 54			21 54						23 37
Humphrey Park d	18 24		18 56				19 56						20 56			21 56						23 39
Urmston d	18 27		18 59		19 24		19 59			20 26			20 59			21 59			22 52			23 42
Chassen Road d	18 29		19 01		19 26					20 28						22 01						23 44
Flixton d	18 31		19 03		19 28					20 30						22 03						23 47
Irlam d	18 36		19 08		19 33		20 04			20 35			21 04			22 08			22 58			23 52
Glazebrook d			19 11				20 07						21 07			22 11						23 55
Birchwood d	18 42		19 15	19 27			20 12	20 27	20 27	20 41			21 12	21 29		22 15	22 26		23 04	23 29		23 59
Padgate d			19 18				20 15						21 15			22 18						00 02
Warrington Central a	18 47	18 58	19 22	19 32	19 41	19 58	20 18	20 32	20 32	20 46		20 58	21 18	21 34		22 22	22 31		23 09	23 34		00 06
d	18 47	18 58	19 22	19 32	19 42	19 58	20 19	20 32	20 32	20 46		20 58	21 19	21 34		22 22	22 31		23 09	23 35		00 06
Sankey for Penketh d	18 51						20 23						21 23				22 35		23 13			00 10
Widnes d	18 57	19 06		19 40		20 06	20 29			20 55		21 06	21 29				22 41		23 19			00 16
Hough Green d	19 01		19 32		19 51		20 32			20 58			21 32			22 32			23 23			00 20
Halewood d	19 05		19 36				20 36						21 36			22 36			23 27			00 24
Hunts Cross 103 d	19 08	19 13	19 39				20 39						21 39			22 39			23 30			00 27
L'pool Sth Parkway [7] 91,103 d	19 16	19 20	19 46	19 51	20 02	20 17	20 46	20 49	20 49	21 09		21 20	21 46	21 53		22 49	22 53		23 36	23 52		00 33
West Allerton 91 a	19 19		19 49		20 06					21 12			21 49			22 52			23 39			
Mossley Hill 91 a	19 23		19 52		20 10		20 50			21 14			21 52			22 54			23 42			
Edge Hill 90,91 a	19 30				20 19		20 56				21 24		21 57		22 20	23 03		23 26	23 49		00 20	
Liverpool Lime Street [10] 90,91 a	19 35	19 35	20 01	20 09	20 23	20 34	21 00	21 04	21 12	21 24	21 30	21 36	22 02	22 09	22 28	23 08	23 05	23 34	23 54	00 05	00 28	00 46

A From Crewe
B From Norwich
C From Wilmslow

Table T089-F

Saturdays

26 May to 8 December

Manchester Airport and Manchester - Warrington Central - Liverpool

	NT A	NT	NT ◇	NT	NT B	NT	NT	NT ◇	NT	NT C	EM ◇ D	NT	NT ◇	NT	NT ◇ C	EM ◇ E	EM ◇ F	NT	NT ◇	NT	NT ◇ C	EM ◇ D
Manchester Airport 85 d			05 51		05 59			06 50		06 58			07 50		07 59						08 59	
Sheffield 78 d											06 20					07 32	07 33					08 40
Stockport 84 d											07 26					08 25	08 25					09 25
ManchesterPicc 78,84,85 d			06 09		06 22			07 09		07 22	07 39		08 09		08 22	08 38	08 38				09 22	09 38
Manchester Oxford Road 84,85 d			06 13	06 20	06 29		06 49	07 12		07 30	07 42	07 48	08 12	08 16	08 30	08 42	08 42	08 45	09 12	09 16	09 30	09 42
Deansgate 84,85 d				06 23	06 32		06 51			07 32		07 50			08 32			08 48			09 32	
Trafford Park d				06 28										08 22						09 22		
Humphrey Park d				06 30																09 24		
Urmston d				06 33			06 59					07 58		08 25				08 56		09 27		
Chassen Road d				06 35										08 27								
Flixton d				06 37								08 01		08 30						09 30		
Irlam d				06 42			07 05					08 05		08 34				09 02		09 34		
Glazebrook d				06 45								08 08										
Birchwood d			06 27	06 50			07 12	07 27				08 13	08 27	08 40				09 07	09 27	09 40		
Padgate d	00 02			06 53								08 16		08 43						09 43		
Warrington Central a	00 06		06 32	06 56			07 18	07 32			07 58	08 19	08 32	08 46		08 58	08 58	09 12	09 32	09 46		09 58
d	00 06	05 57	06 33	06 57		07 11		07 32	07 40		07 58	08 20	08 32	08 47		08 58	08 58	09 13	09 32	09 47		09 58
Sankey for Penketh d	00 10	06 01		07 01		07 15			07 44			08 24						09 17				
Widnes d	00 16	06 07		07 06		07 21			07 50		08 06	08 30		08 55		09 06	09 06	09 23		09 55		10 06
Hough Green d	00 20	06 10		07 10		07 25			07 53		08 10	08 33		08 58				09 26		09 59		
Halewood d	00 24	06 14		07 14		07 29			07 58			08 37						09 30				
Hunts Cross 103 d	00 27	06 18		07 17		07 32			08 01		08s15	08 40						09 33				
L'pool Sth Parkway 91,103 d	00 33	06 23	06 51	07 23		07 38		07 49	08 06		08 20	08 46	08 51	09 06		09 15	09 15	09 39	09 50	10 07		10 15
West Allerton 91 a		06 26		07 26		07 41			08 10			08 49		09 10				09 42		10 11		
Mossley Hill 91 a		06 29		07 28		07 44			08 12			08 52		09 13				09 45		10 13		
Edge Hill 90,91 a		06 35		07 34	07 21	07 50			08 20	08 19		08 57			09 22			09 50			10 22	
Liverpool Lime Street 90,91 a	00 46	06 39	07 04	07 38	07 30	07 54		08 01	08 24	08 27	08 33	09 02	09 09	09 24	09 30	09 31	09 31	09 55	10 02	10 23	10 30	10 31

	NT	NT ◇	NT	NT ◇ C	EM ◇ G	NT	NT ◇	NT	NT ◇ C	EM ◇ G	NT	NT ◇	NT	NT ◇ C	EM ◇ G	NT	NT ◇	NT	NT ◇ C	EM ◇ G	NT
Manchester Airport 85 d		09 50		09 58			10 50		11 02			11 50		11 57			12 50		12 59		
Sheffield 78 d					09 40					10 40					11 40					12 40	
Stockport 84 d					10 27					11 26					12 26					13 26	
ManchesterPicc 78,84,85 d		10 10		10 22	10 38		11 09		11 26	11 38		12 09		12 22	12 38		13 09		13 22	13 38	
Manchester Oxford Road 84,85 d	09 45	10 13	10 16	10 30	10 42	10 46	11 13	11 15	11 29	11 42	11 46	12 12	12 15	12 30	12 42	12 46	13 12	13 15	13 34	13 42	13 46
Deansgate 84,85 d	09 48			10 32		10 48			11 31		11 48			12 32		12 48			13 37		13 48
Trafford Park d								11 22										13 22			
Humphrey Park d								11 24										13 24			
Urmston d	09 56		10 25			10 56		11 27			11 56		12 24			12 56		13 27			13 56
Chassen Road d			10 27										12 26								
Flixton d			10 29					11 30					12 28					13 30			
Irlam d	10 02		10 34			11 02		11 34			12 02		12 33			13 02		13 34			14 02
Glazebrook d			10 37										12 36								
Birchwood d	10 07	10 28	10 41			11 07	11 28	11 40			12 07	12 27	12 40			13 07	13 27	13 40			14 07
Padgate d			10 44					11 43					12 43					13 43			
Warrington Central a	10 12	10 33	10 48		10 58	11 12	11 33	11 46		11 58	12 12	12 32	12 47		12 58	13 12	13 32	13 46		13 58	14 12
d	10 13	10 33	10 48		10 58	11 13	11 34	11 47		11 58	12 13	12 32	12 47		12 58	13 13	13 33	13 47		13 58	14 13
Sankey for Penketh d	10 17					11 17					12 17					13 17					14 17
Widnes d	10 23		10 56		11 06	11 23		11 55		12 06	12 23		12 55		13 06	13 23		13 55		14 06	14 23
Hough Green d	10 26		11 00			11 26		11 59			12 26		12 59			13 26		13 59			14 26
Halewood d	10 30					11 30					12 30					13 30					14 30
Hunts Cross 103 d	10 33					11 33					12 33					13 33					14 33
L'pool Sth Parkway 91,103 d	10 39	10 50	11 08		11 15	11 39	11 51	12 07		12 15	12 39	12 51	13 07		13 15	13 39	13 50	14 07		14 15	14 39
West Allerton 91 a	10 42		11 12			11 42		12 11			12 42		13 11			13 42		14 11			14 42
Mossley Hill 91 a	10 45		11 14			11 45		12 13			12 45		13 13			13 45		14 13			14 45
Edge Hill 90,91 a	10 50			11 23		11 50			12 23		12 50			13 22		13 50			14 26		14 50
Liverpool Lime Street 90,91 a	10 55	11 02	11 24	11 30	11 32	11 55	12 03	12 23	12 30	12 32	12 55	13 03	13 23	13 30	13 32	13 55	14 02	14 23	14 34	14 32	14 55

	NT ◇	NT	NT ◇ C	EM ◇ G	NT	NT ◇	NT	NT ◇ C	EM ◇ G	NT	NT ◇	NT	NT ◇ C	EM ◇ G	NT	NT ◇	NT	NT ◇ C	EM ◇ G	NT	NT ◇	NT
Manchester Airport 85 d	13 50		13 58			14 50		14 59			15 50		15 59			16 50		16 59			17 50	
Sheffield 78 d				13 40					14 40					15 40					16 40			
Stockport 84 d				14 26					15 26					16 26					17 26			
ManchesterPicc 78,84,85 d	14 09		14 22	14 38		15 09		15 22	15 38		16 09		16 22	16 38		17 10		17 23	17 38		18 09	
Manchester Oxford Road 84,85 d	14 12	14 15	14 30	14 42	14 46	15 12	15 15	15 30	15 42	15 46	16 12	16 16	16 30	16 42	16 46	17 13	17 15	17 30	17 42	17 46	18 13	18 16
Deansgate 84,85 d			14 32		14 48			15 32		15 48			16 32		16 48			17 32		17 48		
Trafford Park d							15 22								16 54		17 23			17 54		18 22
Humphrey Park d							15 24										17 25			17 56		18 24
Urmston d		14 24			14 56		15 27			15 56		16 24			16 58		17 28			17 59		18 27
Chassen Road d		14 26										16 26					17 30			18 01		18 29
Flixton d		14 28					15 30					16 28			17 01		17 33			18 04		18 31
Irlam d		14 33			15 02		15 34			16 02		16 33			17 05		17 38		17 53	18 09		18 36
Glazebrook d		14 36										16 36					17 41			18 12		
Birchwood d	14 27	14 40			15 07	15 27	15 40			16 07	16 27	16 40			17 11	17 28	17 46		17 58	18 17	18 28	18 42
Padgate d		14 43					15 43					16 43			17 14		17 49			18 20		
Warrington Central a	14 32	14 47		14 58	15 12	15 32	15 46		15 58	16 12	16 32	16 47		16 58	17 17	17 33	17 52		18 03	18 23	18 33	18 47
d	14 33	14 47		14 58	15 13	15 33	15 47		15 58	16 13	16 32	16 47		16 58	17 18	17 33	17 53		18 04	18 24	18 33	18 47
Sankey for Penketh d					15 17					16 17					17 22		17 57					18 51
Widnes d		14 55		15 06	15 23		15 55		16 06	16 23		16 55		17 06	17 28		18 03		18 12			18 57
Hough Green d		14 59			15 26		15 58			16 26		16 59			17 31		18 06			18 33		19 01
Halewood d					15 30					16 30					17 35		18 10					19 05
Hunts Cross 103 d					15 33					16 33					17 38		18 13			18 38		19 08
L'pool Sth Parkway 91,103 d	14 50	15 07		15 15	15 39	15 50	16 08		16 15	16 39	16 50	17 08		17 15	17 46	17 50	18 19		18 23	18 46	18 50	19 16
West Allerton 91 a		15 11			15 42		16 12			16 42		17 11			17 49		18 22			18 49		19 19
Mossley Hill 91 a		15 13			15 45		16 15			16 45		17 14			17 52		18 25			18 53		19 23
Edge Hill 90,91 a			15 22		15 50			16 24		16 50			17 25		17 57		18 33	18 24		19 02		19 30
Liverpool Lime Street 90,91 a	15 02	15 23	15 29	15 31	15 55	16 02	16 24	16 30	16 32	16 55	17 04	17 23	17 31	17 32	18 02	18 07	18 37	18 30	18 36	19 06	19 04	19 35

A From Manchester Oxford Road
B From Wilmslow
C From Crewe
D From Nottingham
E from 23 June. From Nottingham
F until 16 June. From Nottingham
G From Norwich

Table T089-F

Saturdays

26 May to 8 December

Manchester Airport and Manchester - Warrington Central - Liverpool

	EM ◇ A	NT	NT ◇	NT	EM ◇ A	NT	NT ◇	NT	NT B	EM ◇ A	NT	NT ◇	NT B	NT	NT ◇	NT B	NT	NT ◇	NT	NT B
Manchester Airport 85 d			18 50				19 50		19 59			20 48	20 58		21 50	21 58		22 50		22 59
Sheffield 78 d	17 38				18 37					19 40										
Stockport 84 d	18 26				19 26					20 26										
ManchesterPicc 78,84,85 d	18 38		19 09		19 38		20 11		20 22	20 38		21 11	21 17		22 07	22 18		23 09		23 22
Manchester Oxford Road 84,85 d	18 42	18 46	19 12	19 15	19 42	19 46	20 14	20 17	20 30	20 42	20 46	21 14	21 27	21 46	22 11	22 31	22 43	23 12	23 20	23 25
Deansgate 84,85 d		18 48				19 48			20 32		20 48		21 29	21 48		22 34	22 45		23 22	23 28
Trafford Park d		18 54				19 54					20 54			21 54					23 28	
Humphrey Park d		18 56				19 56					20 56			21 56					23 30	
Urmston d		18 59		19 24		19 59		20 26			20 59			21 59			22 52		23 33	
Chassen Road d		19 01		19 26				20 28						22 01					23 35	
Flixton d		19 03		19 28				20 30						22 03					23 38	
Irlam d		19 08		19 33		20 04		20 35			21 04			22 08			22 58		23 43	
Glazebrook d		19 11				20 07					21 07			22 11					23 46	
Birchwood d		19 15	19 27			20 12	20 29	20 41			21 12	21 29		22 15	22 26		23 04	23 29	23 51	
Padgate d		19 18				20 15					21 15			22 18					23 54	
Warrington Central a	18 58	19 22	19 32	19 41	19 58	20 18	20 34	20 46		20 58	21 18	21 34		22 22	22 31		23 09	23 34	23 57	
d	18 58	19 22	19 32	19 42	19 58	20 19	20 34	20 46		20 58	21 19	21 34		22 22	22 31		23 09	23 35	23 58	
Sankey for Penketh d						20 23					21 23				22 35		23 13		00 02	
Widnes d	19 06		19 40		20 06	20 29		20 55		21 06	21 29				22 41		23 19		00 08	
Hough Green d		19 32		19 51		20 32		20 58			21 32			22 32			23 23		00 11	
Halewood d		19 36				20 36					21 36			22 36			23 27		00 15	
Hunts Cross 103 d	19 13	19 39				20 39					21 39			22 39			23 30		00 19	
L'pool Sth Parkway 91,103 d	19 20	19 46	19 51	20 02	20 18	20 46	20 51	21 09		21 20	21 46	21 53		22 49	22 53		23 36	23 52	00 24	
West Allerton 91 a		19 49		20 06				21 12			21 49			22 52			23 39			
Mossley Hill 91 a		19 52		20 10		20 50		21 14			21 52			22 54			23 42			
Edge Hill 90,91 a				20 19		20 56			21 24		21 57		22 19	23 03		23 24	23 50			00 19
Liverpool Lime Street 90,91 a	19 36	20 01	20 09	20 23	20 33	21 00	21 04	21 24	21 30	21 32	22 02	22 09	22 26	23 08	23 05	23 31	23 55	00 05	00 37	00 28

Sundays

20 May to 2 December

	NT C	NT	NT ◇ D	NT ◇ E	NT ◇ F	NT E	NT G	NT	NT B	NT	NT ◇	NT B	NT	NT ◇	NT B	EM ◇ H	NT	NT ◇	NT B	EM ◇ H	NT	NT ◇ G
Manchester Airport 85 d				07 52		08 00			08 53			09 59		10 50	10 58			11 51	11 59			
Sheffield 78 d																10 41				11 39		
Stockport 84 d																11 26				12 26		
ManchesterPicc 78,84,85 d				08 14		08 23	08 24		09 18			10 22		11 11	11 21	11 38		12 11	12 22	12 38		
Manchester Oxford Road 84,85 d		07 46	08 17	08 17	08 17	08 27	08 27	08 39	09 25	09 46	10 17	10 29	10 43	11 14	11 30	11 42	11 46	12 14	12 30	12 42	12 45	13 12
Deansgate 84,85 d		07 48				08 29	08 29	08 41	09 27	09 48		10 32	10 45		11 32		11 48		12 32		12 47	
Trafford Park d																						
Humphrey Park d																						
Urmston d		07 55						08 49		09 55			10 52				11 55				12 54	
Chassen Road d																						
Flixton d		07 58						08 52		09 58			10 55				11 58				12 57	
Irlam d		08 02						08 57		10 02			10 59				12 02				13 01	
Glazebrook d																						
Birchwood d		08 07	08 31	08 31	08 31			09 03		10 07	10 32		11 05	11 29			12 07	12 29			13 06	13 27
Padgate d																						
Warrington Central a		08 12	08 36	08 36	08 36			09 08		10 12	10 37		11 10	11 34		11 58	12 12	12 34		12 58	13 11	13 32
d		08 13	08 37	08 37	08 37			09 08		10 13	10 37		11 10	11 34		11 59	12 13	12 34		12 59	13 12	13 33
Sankey for Penketh d	00 02																					
Widnes d	00 08	08 21						09 17		10 21			11 19			12 06	12 21			13 06	13 20	
Hough Green d	00 11	08 25						09 21		10 25			11 23				12 25				13 23	
Halewood d	00 15	08 29						09 26		10 29			11 27				12 29				13 27	
Hunts Cross 103 d	00 19	08 32						09 32		10 32			11 30				12 32				13 30	
L'pool Sth Parkway 91,103 d	00 24	08 37	08 54	08 54	08 54			09 37		10 37	11 01		11 35	11 51		12 17	12 37	12 51		13 17	13 36	13 50
West Allerton 91 a		08 40						09 40		10 40			11 38				12 40				13 39	
Mossley Hill 91 a		08 43						09 43		10 43			11 41				12 43				13 41	
Edge Hill 90,91 a																						
Liverpool Lime Street 90,91 a	00 37	08 52	09 09	09 10	09 10	09 29	09 29	09 52	10 24	10 52	11 14	11 28	11 50	12 03	12 29	12 30	12 52	13 03	13 29	13 30	13 50	14 03

	NT ◇ E	NT B	EM ◇ H	NT	NT ◇	NT B	EM ◇ A	NT	NT ◇	NT B	EM ◇ A	NT	NT ◇	NT B	EM ◇ H	NT	NT ◇	NT B	EM ◇ I	NT	NT ◇	NT B
Manchester Airport 85 d	12 51	12 59			13 51	13 59			14 51	14 59			15 51	15 59			16 51	16 59			17 51	17 59
Sheffield 78 d			12 39				13 38				14 37				15 43				16 39			
Stockport 84 d			13 26				14 27				15 26				16 26				17 29			
ManchesterPicc 78,84,85 d	13 09	13 22	13 38		14 09	14 22	14 38		15 09	15 22	15 38		16 09	16 22	16 38		17 09	17 22	17 38		18 12	18 22
Manchester Oxford Road 84,85 d	13 13	13 30	13 42	13 46	14 13	14 30	14 42	14 46	15 13	15 30	15 42	15 46	16 13	16 30	16 42	16 46	17 13	17 30	17 42	17 46	18 16	18 30
Deansgate 84,85 d		13 32		13 48		14 32		14 48		15 32		15 48		16 32		16 48		17 32		17 48		18 32
Trafford Park d																						
Humphrey Park d																						
Urmston d				13 55				14 55				15 55				16 55				17 55		
Chassen Road d																						
Flixton d				13 58				14 58				15 58				16 58				17 58		
Irlam d				14 02				15 02				16 02				17 02				18 02		
Glazebrook d																						
Birchwood d	13 27			14 07	14 27			15 07	15 27			16 07	16 27			17 07	17 27			18 07	18 30	
Padgate d																						
Warrington Central a	13 32		13 58	14 12	14 32		14 58	15 12	15 32		15 58	16 12	16 32		16 58	17 12	17 32		17 58	18 12	18 35	
d	13 33		13 58	14 13	14 33		14 58	15 13	15 33		15 58	16 13	16 33		16 58	17 13	17 33		17 59	18 13	18 36	
Sankey for Penketh d																						
Widnes d			14 06	14 21			15 06	15 21			16 06	16 21			17 06	17 21			18 06	18 21		
Hough Green d				14 25				15 25				16 25				17 25				18 25		
Halewood d				14 29				15 29				16 29				17 29				18 29		
Hunts Cross 103 d				14 32				15 32				16 32				17 32				18 32		
L'pool Sth Parkway 91,103 d	13 50		14 16	14 37	14 50		15 16	15 37	15 50		16 16	16 37	16 50		17 16	17 37	17 50		18 17	18 37	18 53	
West Allerton 91 a				14 40				15 40				16 40				17 40				18 40		
Mossley Hill 91 a				14 43				15 43				16 43				17 43				18 43		
Edge Hill 90,91 a																						
Liverpool Lime Street 90,91 a	14 02	14 29	14 32	14 52	15 02	15 29	15 30	15 52	16 02	16 29	16 30	16 52	17 02	17 29	17 30	17 52	18 02	18 29	18 30	18 52	19 05	19 29

A From Norwich
B From Wilmslow
C not 20 May. From Manchester Oxford Road
D from 16 September until 21 October
E until 9 September
F from 28 October
G from 16 September
H From Nottingham
I From Peterborough

Table T089-F

Sundays

20 May to 2 December

Manchester Airport and Manchester - Warrington Central - Liverpool

	EM	NT	NT	NT	EM	NT	NT	NT	NT	NT	NT	NT	NT	NT	NT	NT	NT
	◇		◇		◇		◇			◇			◇			◇	
	A			B	A			B			B			B			B
Manchester Airport 85 d			18 51	18 59			19 51	19 59		20 49	20 58		21 51	21 59		22 51	23 09
Sheffield [7] 78 d	17 44				18 37												
Stockport 84 d	18 26				19 26												
ManchesterPicc [10] 78,84,85 d	18 38		19 09	19 22	19 39		20 09	20 22		21 09	21 18		22 09	22 19		23 09	23 33
Manchester Oxford Road 84,85 d	18 42	18 46	19 13	19 30	19 43	19 46	20 13	20 30	20 46	21 13	21 27	21 45	22 13	22 29	22 43	23 13	23 36
Deansgate 84,85 d		18 48		19 32		19 48		20 32	20 48		21 29	21 47		22 31	22 46		23 38
Trafford Park d																	
Humphrey Park d																	
Urmston d		18 55				19 55			20 55			21 54			22 53		
Chassen Road d																	
Flixton d		18 58				19 58			20 58			21 57			22 56		
Irlam d		19 02				20 02			21 02			22 01			23 00		
Glazebrook d																	
Birchwood d		19 07	19 27			20 07	20 27		21 07	21 27		22 06	22 27		23 06	23 27	
Padgate d																	
Warrington Central a	18 58	19 12	19 32		19 59	20 12	20 32		21 12	21 32		22 11	22 32		23 11	23 32	
d	18 58	19 13	19 33		19 59	20 13	20 33		21 13	21 33		22 12	22 33		23 11	23 33	
Sankey for Penketh d																	
Widnes d	19 06	19 21			20 07	20 21			21 21			22 21			23 21		
Hough Green d		19 25				20 25			21 25			22 25			23 25		
Halewood d		19 29				20 29			21 29			22 29			23 29		
Hunts Cross 103 d		19 32				20 32			21 32			22 32			23 32		
L'pool Sth Parkway [7] 91,103 d	19 17	19 37	19 50		20 17	20 37	20 50		21 37	21 50		22 37	22 50		23 37	23 50	
West Allerton 91 a		19 40				20 40			21 40			22 40			23 40		
Mossley Hill 91 a		19 43				20 43			21 43			22 43			23 43		
Edge Hill 90,91 a																	
Liverpool Lime Street [10] 90,91 a	19 30	19 52	20 02	20 29	20 31	20 52	21 02	21 29	21 52	22 02	22 26	22 52	23 02	23 31	23 52	00 05	00 34

A From Norwich

B From Wilmslow

Table T089-R

Mondays to Fridays

21 May to 7 December

Liverpool - Warrington Central - Manchester and Manchester Airport

Miles		NT	NT	NT	NT	NT	NT	NT	NT	EM	NT	NT	NT	NT	NT	EM	NT	NT	NT	NT	EM	EM
		MX																				
			◇	◇			◇			◇			◇			◇		◇		◇	◇	◇
		A		B					B	C					B	C				B	D	E
0	**Liverpool Lime Street** [10] 90,91 d		03 37	05 24		05 49	06 14	06 20	06 28	06 47		06 50	07 09	07 19	07 28	07 42	07 45	08 16	08 19	08 28	08 52	08 52
1¼	Edge Hill 90,91 d			05 28		05 53			06 32			06 54		07 23	07 32				08 23	08 32		
3¾	Mossley Hill 91 d					05 58		06 28				06 59		07 28			07 54		08 28			
4½	West Allerton 91 d					06 01		06 31				07 01		07 31			07 57		08 31			
5½	L'pool Sth Parkway [7] 91,103 d					06 04	06 25	06 34		06 58		07 04	07 19	07 34		07 53	08 01	08 30	08 34		09 03	09 03
7	Hunts Cross 103 d					06 07						07 08				07 59	08 04					
8	Halewood d					06 10						07 11					08 07					
10½	Hough Green d	00 03				06 14		06 40				07 15		07 43			08 12		08 42			
12¼	Widnes d	00 07				06 18		06 44		07 07		07 19	07 28			08 05	08 16		08 46		09 11	09 11
15¾	Sankey for Penketh d	00 12				06 23						07 24					08 21					
18¼	**Warrington Central** a	00 17				06 28	06 39	06 52		07 14		07 29	07 37	07 52		08 13	08 26	08 45	08 54		09 18	09 18
—	d	00 18			05 58		06 40	06 53		07 15	07 23		07 38	07 53		08 13	08 26	08 46	08 54		09 19	09 19
20	Padgate d				06 01			06 56			07 26			07 56					08 58			
21½	Birchwood d				06 05		06 45	06 59		07 19	07 30		07 43	08 00		08 18	08 31	08 50	09 01			
24¼	Glazebrook d				06 10			07 04			07 35			08 05					09 06			
25½	Irlam d				06 13		06 51	07 08			07 38		07 49	08 08			08 38		09 10			
27¾	Flixton d				06 17			07 12			07 42			08 13			08 42		09 14			
28½	Chassen Road d				06 19			07 14			07 44			08 15			08 44		09 16			
29	Urmston d				06 22		06 56	07 17			07 47			08 17			08 47		09 18			
30	Humphrey Park d				06 25			07 20			07 50			08 21			08 50		09 21			
30¾	Trafford Park d				06 28			07 23			07 53			08 24			08 53		09 24			
33¾	Deansgate 84,85 a			06 18	06 36			07 31	07 22		08 01			08 32	08 22		09 01		09 32	09 22		
34	**Manchester Oxford Road** 84,85 a			06 20	06 38		07 07	07 33	07 24	07 37	08 03		08 07	08 34	08 24	08 38	09 03	09 07	09 34	09 24	09 38	09 38
34¾	**ManchesterPicc** [10] 78,84,85 a	00 38	04 11	06 23			07 11		07 31	07 41					08 31	08 41		09 11		09 31	09 41	09 41
—	Stockport 84 a									07 54						08 54					09 54	09 54
—	Sheffield [7] 78 a									08 34						09 35					10 32	10 34
44½	**Manchester Airport** 85,84 a		04 28	06 47			07 31		07 57						08 57			09 30		09 57		

	NT	NT	NT	NT	EM	NT	NT	NT	NT	EM	NT	NT	NT	NT	EM	NT	NT	NT	NT	EM	NT
		◇		◇	◇		◇		◇	◇		◇		◇	◇		◇		◇	◇	
				B	C				B	C				B	C				B	C	
Liverpool Lime Street [10] 90,91 d	08 55	09 16	09 19	09 28	09 52	09 55	10 16	10 19	10 28	10 52	10 55	11 16	11 19	11 28	11 52	11 55	12 16	12 19	12 28	12 52	12 55
Edge Hill 90,91 d	08 59			09 32		09 59			10 32		10 59			11 32		11 59			12 32		12 59
Mossley Hill 91 d	09 04		09 28			10 04		10 28			11 04		11 28			12 04		12 28			13 04
West Allerton 91 d	09 07		09 31			10 07		10 31			11 07		11 31			12 07		12 31			13 07
L'pool Sth Parkway [7] 91,103 d	09 10	09 30	09 34		10 03	10 10	10 30	10 34		11 03	11 10	11 30	11 34		12 03	12 10	12 30	12 34		13 03	13 10
Hunts Cross 103 d	09 13					10 13					11 13					12 13					13 13
Halewood d	09 16					10 16					11 16					12 16					13 16
Hough Green d	09 20		09 41			10 20		10 41			11 20		11 41			12 20		12 41			13 20
Widnes d	09 24		09 45		10 11	10 24		10 45		11 11	11 24		11 45		12 11	12 24		12 45		13 11	13 24
Sankey for Penketh d	09 29					10 29					11 29					12 29					13 29
Warrington Central a	09 34	09 44	09 53		10 18	10 34	10 44	10 53		11 18	11 34	11 44	11 53		12 18	12 34	12 44	12 53		13 18	13 34
d	09 35	09 45	09 54		10 19	10 35	10 45	10 54		11 19	11 35	11 45	11 54		12 19	12 35	12 45	12 54		13 19	13 35
Padgate d			09 58					10 58					11 58					12 58			
Birchwood d	09 39	09 50	10 02			10 39	10 50	11 02			11 39	11 50	12 02			12 39	12 50	13 02			13 39
Glazebrook d								11 07										13 07			
Irlam d	09 46		10 08			10 46		11 10			11 46		12 08			12 46		13 10			13 46
Flixton d			10 12					11 14					12 12					13 14			
Chassen Road d								11 16										13 16			
Urmston d	09 51		10 16			10 51		11 19			11 51		12 16			12 51		13 19			13 51
Humphrey Park d			10 19										12 19								
Trafford Park d			10 21										12 21								
Deansgate 84,85 a	10 01		10 32	10 22		11 01		11 32	11 22		12 01		12 32	12 22		13 01		13 32	13 22		14 01
Manchester Oxford Road 84,85 a	10 03	10 07	10 35	10 24	10 38	11 03	11 07	11 35	11 24	11 38	12 03	12 07	12 35	12 24	12 38	13 03	13 07	13 35	13 24	13 38	14 03
ManchesterPicc [10] 78,84,85 a		10 11		10 31	10 41		11 11		11 31	11 41		12 11		12 31	12 41		13 11		13 31	13 41	
Stockport 84 a					10 54					11 54					12 53					13 54	
Sheffield [7] 78 a					11 35					12 35					13 34					14 35	
Manchester Airport 85,84 a		10 30		10 57			11 30		11 56			12 30		12 57			13 30		13 57		

A From Liverpool Lime Street

B To Crewe

C To Norwich

D from 3 September until 5 October. To Norwich

E until 31 August, from 8 October. To Norwich

Table T089-R

Mondays to Fridays

21 May to 7 December

Liverpool - Warrington Central - Manchester and Manchester Airport

	NT	NT	NT	EM	NT	NT	NT	NT	EM	NT	NT	NT	NT	EM	NT	NT	NT	NT	NT	EM	EM	NT
	◇		◇	◇		◇		◇	◇		◇		◇	◇			◇		◇	◇	◇	
			A	B				A	B				A	B		C			A	D	E	
Liverpool Lime Street 90,91 d	13 16	13 19	13 28	13 52	13 55	14 16	14 19	14 28	14 52	14 55	15 16	15 19	15 28	15 52	15 55	16 00	16 16	16 19	16 28	16 52	16 52	16 55
Edge Hill 90,91 d			13 32		13 59			14 32		14 59			15 32		15 59	16a04			16 32			16 59
Mossley Hill 91 d		13 28			14 04		14 28			15 04		15 28			16 04			16 28				17 04
West Allerton 91 d		13 31			14 07		14 31			15 07		15 31			16 07			16 31				17 07
L'pool Sth Parkway 91,103 d	13 30	13 34		14 03	14 10	14 30	14 34		15 03	15 10	15 30	15 34		16 03	16 10		16 30	16 34		17 03	17 03	17 10
Hunts Cross 103 d					14 13					15 13					16 14							17 13
Halewood d					14 16					15 16					16 17							17 16
Hough Green d		13 41			14 20		14 41			15 20		15 41			16 21			16 41				17 20
Widnes d		13 45		14 11	14 24		14 45		15 11	15 24		15 45		16 11	16 25			16 45		17 11	17 11	17 24
Sankey for Penketh d					14 29					15 29					16 30							17 29
Warrington Central a	13 44	13 53		14 18	14 34	14 44	14 53		15 18	15 34	15 44	15 53		16 18	16 35		16 45	16 53		17 18	17 18	17 34
d	13 45	13 54		14 19	14 35	14 45	14 54		15 19	15 35	15 45	15 54		16 19	16 35		16 45	16 54		17 19	17 19	17 35
Padgate d		13 58					14 58					15 58						16 58				
Birchwood d	13 50	14 02			14 39	14 50	15 02			15 39	15 50	16 02			16 40		16 50	17 02				17 39
Glazebrook d							15 07											17 07				
Irlam d		14 08			14 46		15 10			15 46		16 08			16 46			17 10				17 46
Flixton d		14 12					15 14					16 12						17 14				
Chassen Road d							15 16											17 16				
Urmston d		14 16			14 51		15 19			15 51		16 16			16 51			17 19				17 51
Humphrey Park d		14 19										16 19										
Trafford Park d		14 21										16 21										
Deansgate 84,85 a		14 32	14 22		15 01		15 32	15 22		16 01		16 32	16 22		17 01			17 32	17 23			18 01
Manchester Oxford Road 84,85 a	14 07	14 35	14 24	14 38	15 03	15 07	15 35	15 24	15 38	16 03	16 07	16 35	16 24	16 38	17 03		17 07	17 35	17 25	17 38	17 38	18 03
ManchesterPicc 78,84,85 a	14 11		14 31	14 41		15 11		15 31	15 41		16 11		16 31	16 41			17 11		17 33	17 41	17 41	
Stockport 84 a				14 54					15 54					16 54						17 54	17 54	
Sheffield 78 a				15 34					16 34					17 39						18 48	18 49	
Manchester Airport 85,84 a	14 30		14 57			15 30		15 57			16 30		16 57				17 32		17 58			

	NT	NT	EM	NT	NT	NT	EM	NT	NT	NT	NT	EM	NT	NT	NT	NT	NT	NT	EM	NT	NT
	◇		◇		◇		◇		◇			◇		◇					◇		◇
			B				F				G	F				G		G	F		
Liverpool Lime Street 90,91 d	17 15	17 19	17 52	17 55	18 16	18 19	18 52	18 55	19 15	19 19	19 28	19 52	19 55	20 19	20 26	20 28	20 54	21 29	21 37	21 55	22 29
Edge Hill 90,91 d				17 59				18 59			19 32		19 59			20 32	20 58	21 33		21 59	
Mossley Hill 91 d		17 27		18 04		18 28		19 04		19 28			20 04		20 34		21 03			22 04	
West Allerton 91 d		17 30		18 07		18 31		19 07		19 31			20 07		20 37		21 05			22 07	
L'pool Sth Parkway 91,103 d	17 26	17 33	18 03	18 10	18 29	18 34	19 03	19 10	19 29	19 34		20 03	20 10	20 31	20 40		21 08		21 48	22 10	22 40
Hunts Cross 103 d		17 36		18 13		18 38		19 13					20 13				21 13			22 13	
Halewood d		17 39		18 16		18 41		19 16					20 16				21 15			22 16	
Hough Green d		17 44		18 20		18 45		19 20		19 41			20 20		20 46		21 19			22 20	
Widnes d		17 47	18 11	18 24		18 48	19 11	19 24		19 45		20 11	20 24		20 50		21 23		21 56	22 24	
Sankey for Penketh d		17 52		18 29		18 53		19 29					20 29				21 28			22 29	
Warrington Central a	17 41	17 57	18 18	18 34	18 45	18 58	19 18	19 34	19 45	19 53		20 18	20 34	20 45	20 58		21 33		22 03	22 34	22 54
d	17 45	17 58	18 19	18 35	18 46	18 59	19 19	19 35	19 45	19 53		20 19	20 35	20 46	20 58		21 33		22 04	22 35	22 54
Padgate d		18 01				19 02				19 57			20 38		21 02		21 36			22 38	
Birchwood d	17 50	18 05		18 39	18 51	19 05		19 40	19 50	20 00			20 41	20 50	21 05		21 39			22 41	22 59
Glazebrook d						19 10				20 05					21 10		21 44			22 46	
Irlam d		18 11		18 46		19 14		19 46		20 09			20 47		21 14		21 47			22 50	
Flixton d		18 15				19 18				20 13					21 18		21 51			22 54	
Chassen Road d						19 20									21 20		21 53			22 56	
Urmston d		18 18		18 51		19 22		19 52		20 16			20 52		21 22		21 56			22 58	
Humphrey Park d		18 21								20 19							21 58			23 01	
Trafford Park d		18 24								20 22							22 01			23 04	
Deansgate 84,85 a		18 32				19 32		20 03		20 32	20 22		21 02		21 32	21 22	22 09	22 25		23 12	
Manchester Oxford Road 84,85 a	18 07	18 35	18 38	19 02	19 07	19 34	19 38	20 05	20 07	20 35	20 24	20 38	21 05	21 07	21 34	21 24	22 11	22 27	22 23	23 14	23 16
ManchesterPicc 78,84,85 a	18 11		18 41		19 11		19 41		20 11		20 31	20 41		21 11		21 31	22 15	22 31	22 26		23 20
Stockport 84 a			18 54				19 54					20 53							22 37		
Sheffield 78 a			19 35				20 35					21 35							23 35		
Manchester Airport 85,84 a	18 30				19 30				20 29		20 57			21 31		21 57	22 31	22 54			23 36

	NT	NT
Liverpool Lime Street 90,91 d	22 30	23 38
Edge Hill 90,91 d	22 34	23 42
Mossley Hill 91 d		23 47
West Allerton 91 d		23 50
L'pool Sth Parkway 91,103 d		23 53
Hunts Cross 103 d		23 56
Halewood d		23 59
Hough Green d		00 03
Widnes d		00 07
Sankey for Penketh d		00 12
Warrington Central a		00 17
d		00 18
Padgate d		
Birchwood d		
Glazebrook d		
Irlam d		
Flixton d		
Chassen Road d		
Urmston d		
Humphrey Park d		
Trafford Park d		
Deansgate 84,85 a	23 26	
Manchester Oxford Road 84,85 a	23 28	
ManchesterPicc 78,84,85 a	23 32	00 38
Stockport 84 a		
Sheffield 78 a		
Manchester Airport 85,84 a	23 55	

A To Crewe
B To Norwich
C To Earlestown
D from 8 October. To Nottingham
E until 5 October. To Nottingham
F To Nottingham
G To Wilmslow

Table T089-R

Saturdays

26 May to 8 December

Liverpool - Warrington Central - Manchester and Manchester Airport

	NT	NT	NT	NT	NT	NT	NT	NT	EM	NT	NT	NT	NT	NT	EM	NT	NT	NT	NT	EM	NT	NT
		◇	◇			◇			◇			◇			◇		◇		◇	◇		◇
	A		B					B	C					B	C				B	C		
Liverpool Lime Street 90,91 d		03 37	05 24		05 49	06 12	06 20	06 28	06 47		06 50	07 09	07 19	07 28	07 42	07 45	08 16	08 19	08 28	08 52	08 55	09 16
Edge Hill 90,91 d			05 28		05 53			06 32			06 54		07 23	07 32				08 23	08 32		08 59	
Mossley Hill 91 d					05 58		06 28				06 59		07 28			07 54		08 28			09 04	
West Allerton 91 d					06 01		06 31				07 01		07 31			07 57		08 31			09 07	
L'pool Sth Parkway 91,103 d					06 04	06 25	06 34		06 58		07 04	07 19	07 34		07 52	08 01	08 30	08 34		09 03	09 10	09 30
Hunts Cross 103 d					06 07						07 08				07 59	08 04					09 13	
Halewood d					06 10						07 11					08 07					09 16	
Hough Green d	00 03				06 14		06 40				07 15		07 43			08 12		08 42			09 20	
Widnes d	00 07				06 18		06 44		07 07		07 19	07 28			08 05	08 16		08 46		09 11	09 24	
Sankey for Penketh d	00 12				06 23						07 24					08 21					09 29	
Warrington Central a	00 17				06 28	06 39	06 52		07 15		07 29	07 37	07 52		08 13	08 26	08 45	08 54		09 18	09 34	09 44
d	00 18			05 58		06 39	06 53		07 15	07 23		07 38	07 53		08 13	08 26	08 46	08 54		09 19	09 35	09 45
Padgate d				06 01			06 56			07 26			07 56					08 58				
Birchwood d				06 05		06 44	06 59		07 20	07 30		07 43	08 00		08 18	08 31	08 50	09 01			09 39	09 50
Glazebrook d				06 10			07 04			07 35			08 05					09 06				
Irlam d				06 13		06 50	07 08			07 38		07 49	08 08			08 38		09 10			09 46	
Flixton d				06 17			07 12			07 42			08 13			08 42		09 14				
Chassen Road d				06 19			07 14			07 44			08 15			08 44		09 16				
Urmston d				06 22			07 17			07 47			08 17			08 47		09 18			09 51	
Humphrey Park d				06 25			07 20			07 50			08 21			08 50		09 21				
Trafford Park d				06 28			07 23			07 53			08 24			08 53		09 24				
Deansgate 84,85 a			06 18	06 36			07 31	07 22		08 01			08 32	08 22		09 01		09 32	09 22		10 01	
Manchester Oxford Road 84,85 a			06 20	06 38		07 03	07 33	07 24	07 38	08 03		08 07	08 34	08 24	08 38	09 03	09 07	09 34	09 24	09 38	10 03	10 07
ManchesterPicc 78,84,85 a	00 38	04 11	06 23			07 07		07 31	07 41					08 33	08 41		09 11		09 31	09 41		10 11
Stockport 84 a									07 54						08 54					09 54		
Sheffield 78 a									08 35						09 34					10 34		
Manchester Airport 85,84 a		04 28	06 47			07 31		07 57						08 58			09 30		09 57			10 30

	NT	NT	EM	NT	NT	NT	NT	EM	NT	NT	NT	NT	EM	NT	NT	NT	NT	EM	NT	NT	NT	NT
			◇		◇		◇	◇		◇		◇	◇		◇			◇		◇		◇
		B	C				B	C				B	C				B	C				B
Liverpool Lime Street 90,91 d	09 19	09 28	09 52	09 55	10 16	10 19	10 28	10 52	10 55	11 16	11 19	11 28	11 52	11 55	12 16	12 19	12 28	12 52	12 55	13 16	13 19	13 28
Edge Hill 90,91 d		09 32		09 59			10 32		10 59			11 32		11 59			12 32		12 59			13 32
Mossley Hill 91 d	09 28			10 04		10 28			11 04		11 28			12 04		12 28			13 04		13 28	
West Allerton 91 d	09 31			10 07		10 31			11 07		11 31			12 07		12 31			13 07		13 31	
L'pool Sth Parkway 91,103 d	09 34		10 03	10 10	10 30	10 34		11 03	11 10	11 30	11 34		12 03	12 10	12 30	12 34		13 03	13 10	13 30	13 34	
Hunts Cross 103 d				10 13					11 13					12 13					13 13			
Halewood d				10 16					11 16					12 16					13 16			
Hough Green d	09 41			10 20		10 41			11 20		11 41			12 20		12 41			13 20		13 41	
Widnes d	09 45		10 11	10 24		10 45		11 11	11 24		11 45		12 11	12 24		12 45		13 11	13 24		13 45	
Sankey for Penketh d				10 29					11 29					12 29					13 29			
Warrington Central a	09 53		10 18	10 34	10 44	10 53		11 18	11 34	11 44	11 53		12 18	12 34	12 44	12 53		13 18	13 34	13 44	13 53	
d	09 54		10 19	10 35	10 45	10 54		11 19	11 35	11 45	11 54		12 19	12 35	12 45	12 54		13 19	13 35	13 45	13 54	
Padgate d	09 58					10 58					11 58					12 58					13 58	
Birchwood d	10 02			10 39	10 50	11 02			11 39	11 50	12 02			12 39	12 50	13 02			13 39	13 50	14 02	
Glazebrook d						11 07										13 07						
Irlam d	10 08			10 46		11 10			11 46		12 08			12 46		13 10			13 46		14 08	
Flixton d	10 12					11 14					12 12					13 14					14 12	
Chassen Road d						11 16										13 16						
Urmston d	10 16			10 51		11 19			11 51		12 16			12 51		13 19			13 51		14 16	
Humphrey Park d	10 19										12 19										14 19	
Trafford Park d	10 21										12 21										14 21	
Deansgate 84,85 a	10 32	10 22		11 01		11 32	11 22		12 01		12 32	12 22		13 01		13 32	13 22		14 01		14 32	14 22
Manchester Oxford Road 84,85 a	10 35	10 24	10 38	11 03	11 07	11 35	11 24	11 38	12 03	12 07	12 35	12 24	12 38	13 03	13 07	13 35	13 24	13 38	14 03	14 07	14 35	14 24
ManchesterPicc 78,84,85 a		10 31	10 41		11 11		11 31	11 41		12 11		12 31	12 41		13 11		13 31	13 41		14 11		14 31
Stockport 84 a			10 54					11 54					12 54					13 54				
Sheffield 78 a			11 35					12 35					13 34					14 33				
Manchester Airport 85,84 a		10 57			11 30		11 56			12 30		12 57			13 30		13 57			14 30		15 03

	EM	NT	NT	NT	NT	EM	NT	NT	NT	NT	EM	NT	NT	NT	NT	EM	NT	NT	NT	EM	NT
	◇		◇		◇	◇		◇		◇	◇		◇		◇	◇		◇		◇	
	C				B	C				B	C				B	D				C	
Liverpool Lime Street 90,91 d	13 52	13 55	14 16	14 19	14 28	14 52	14 55	15 16	15 19	15 28	15 52	15 55	16 16	16 19	16 28	16 52	16 55	17 15	17 19	17 52	17 55
Edge Hill 90,91 d		13 59			14 32		14 59			15 32		15 59			16 32		16 59				17 59
Mossley Hill 91 d		14 04		14 28			15 04		15 28			16 04		16 28			17 04		17 27		18 04
West Allerton 91 d		14 07		14 31			15 07		15 31			16 07		16 31			17 07		17 30		18 07
L'pool Sth Parkway 91,103 d	14 03	14 10	14 30	14 34		15 03	15 10	15 30	15 34		16 03	16 10	16 30	16 34		17 03	17 10	17 26	17 33	18 03	18 10
Hunts Cross 103 d		14 13					15 13					16 14					17 13		17 36		18 13
Halewood d		14 16					15 16					16 17					17 16		17 39		18 16
Hough Green d		14 20		14 41			15 20		15 41			16 21		16 41			17 20		17 44		18 20
Widnes d	14 11	14 24		14 45		15 11	15 24		15 45		16 11	16 25		16 45		17 11	17 24		17 47	18 11	18 24
Sankey for Penketh d		14 29					15 29					16 30					17 29		17 52		18 29
Warrington Central a	14 18	14 34	14 44	14 53		15 18	15 34	15 44	15 53		16 18	16 35	16 45	16 53		17 18	17 34	17 41	17 57	18 18	18 34
d	14 19	14 35	14 45	14 54		15 19	15 35	15 45	15 54		16 19	16 35	16 45	16 54		17 19	17 35	17 45	17 58	18 19	18 35
Padgate d				14 58					15 58					16 58					18 01		
Birchwood d		14 39	14 50	15 02			15 39	15 50	16 02			16 40	16 50	17 02			17 39	17 50	18 05		18 39
Glazebrook d				15 07										17 07							
Irlam d		14 46		15 10			15 46		16 08			16 46		17 10			17 46		18 11		18 46
Flixton d				15 14					16 12					17 14					18 15		
Chassen Road d				15 16										17 16							
Urmston d		14 51		15 19			15 51		16 16			16 51		17 19			17 51		18 18		18 51
Humphrey Park d									16 19										18 21		
Trafford Park d									16 21										18 24		
Deansgate 84,85 a		15 01		15 32	15 22		16 01		16 32	16 22		17 01		17 32	17 23		18 01		18 32		
Manchester Oxford Road 84,85 a	14 38	15 03	15 07	15 35	15 24	15 38	16 03	16 07	16 35	16 24	16 38	17 03	17 07	17 35	17 25	17 38	18 03	18 07	18 35	18 38	19 02
ManchesterPicc 78,84,85 a	14 41		15 11		15 31	15 41		16 11		16 31	16 41		17 11		17 33	17 41		18 11		18 41	
Stockport 84 a	14 54					15 54					16 54					17 54				18 54	
Sheffield 78 a	15 34					16 34					17 37					18 37				19 34	
Manchester Airport 85,84 a			15 30		15 57			16 30		16 57			17 32		17 58			18 30			

A From Liverpool Lime Street
B To Crewe
C To Norwich
D To Nottingham

Liverpool - Warrington Central - Manchester and Manchester Airport

Saturdays
26 May to 8 December

	NT ◇	NT	EM ◇ A	NT	NT ◇	NT	NT B	EM ◇ A	NT	NT ◇	NT	NT B	EM ◇ A	NT	NT ◇	NT B	EM ◇ A	NT	NT ◇	NT	NT
Liverpool Lime Street 90,91 d	18 16	18 19	18 52	18 55	19 15	19 19	19 28	19 52	19 55	20 19	20 26	20 28	20 49	20 56	21 29	21 29	21 37	21 55	22 29	22 30	23 38
Edge Hill 90,91 d				18 59			19 32		19 59			20 32		21 00		21 33		21 59		22 34	23 42
Mossley Hill 91 d		18 28		19 04		19 28			20 04		20 34			21 05				22 04			23 47
West Allerton 91 d		18 31		19 07		19 31			20 07		20 37			21 07				22 07			23 50
L'pool Sth Parkway 91,103 d	18 29	18 34	19 03	19 10	19 29	19 34		20 03	20 10	20 31	20 40		21 00	21 10	21 40		21 48	22 10	22 40		23 53
Hunts Cross 103 d		18 38		19 13					20 13					21 15				22 13			23 56
Halewood d		18 41		19 16					20 16					21 17				22 16			23 59
Hough Green d		18 45		19 20		19 41			20 20		20 46			21 21				22 20			00 03
Widnes d		18 48	19 11	19 24		19 45		20 11	20 24		20 50		21 08	21 25			21 56	22 24			00 07
Sankey for Penketh d		18 53		19 29					20 29					21 30				22 29			00 12
Warrington Central a	18 45	18 58	19 18	19 34	19 45	19 53		20 19	20 34	20 45	20 58		21 15	21 35	21 54		22 03	22 34	22 54		00 17
d	18 46	18 59	19 19	19 35	19 45	19 53		20 19	20 35	20 46	20 58		21 16	21 35	21 54		22 04	22 35	22 54		00 18
Padgate d		19 02				19 57			20 38		21 02			21 38				22 38			
Birchwood d	18 51	19 05		19 40	19 50	20 00			20 41	20 50	21 05			21 41	21 59			22 41	22 59		
Glazebrook d		19 10				20 05					21 10			21 46				22 46			
Irlam d		19 14		19 46		20 09			20 47		21 14			21 50				22 50			
Flixton d		19 18				20 13					21 18			21 54				22 54			
Chassen Road d		19 20									21 20			21 56				22 56			
Urmston d		19 22		19 52		20 16			20 52		21 22			21 58				22 58			
Humphrey Park d						20 19								22 01				23 01			
Trafford Park d						20 22								22 04				23 04			
Deansgate 84,85 a		19 32		20 03		20 32	20 22		21 02		21 32	21 22		22 12		22 25		23 12		23 26	
Manchester Oxford Road 84,85 a	19 07	19 34	19 38	20 05	20 07	20 35	20 24	20 39	21 05	21 07	21 34	21 24	21 37	22 14	22 17	22 27	22 24	23 14	23 16	23 28	
ManchesterPicc 78,84,85 a	19 11		19 41		20 11		20 31	20 41		21 11		21 31	21 40		22 21	22 31	22 26		23 22	23 32	00 40
Stockport 84 a			19 54					20 54					21 51				22 37				
Sheffield 78 a			20 34					21 35					22 31				23 35				
Manchester Airport 85,84 a	19 30				20 29		20 57			21 31		21 57			22 39	22 53				23 55	

Sundays
20 May to 2 December

	NT C	NT B	NT ◇	NT	NT ◇ D	NT ◇ E	NT	NT B	NT ◇	NT	NT B	NT ◇ D	NT ◇ E	NT	NT B	NT ◇	NT	NT B	EM ◇ F	NT ◇	NT	NT B
Liverpool Lime Street 90,91 d		08 15	08 21	08 25	09 14	09 14	09 27	09 30	10 13	10 27	10 30	11 17	11 19	11 25	11 28	12 14	12 25	12 28	12 52	13 14	13 25	13 29
Edge Hill 90,91 d																						
Mossley Hill 91 d				08 33			09 35			10 35				11 33			12 33				13 33	
West Allerton 91 d				08 35			09 37			10 37				11 35			12 35				13 35	
L'pool Sth Parkway 91,103 d			08 31	08 39	09 25	09 25	09 41		10 25	10 41		11 29	11 31	11 40		12 25	12 40		13 03	13 25	13 40	
Hunts Cross 103 d				08 42			09 44			10 44				11 44			12 43				13 43	
Halewood d				08 45			09 47			10 47				11 47			12 46				13 46	
Hough Green d	00 03			08 49			09 51			10 51				11 51			12 50				13 50	
Widnes d	00 07			08 53			09 55			10 55				11 55			12 54		13 11		13 54	
Sankey for Penketh d	00 12																					
Warrington Central a	00 17		08 45	09 02	09 44	09 44	10 03		10 44	11 03		11 43	11 45	12 03		12 44	13 02		13 18	13 44	14 02	
d	00 18		08 46	09 04	09 44	09 44	10 03		10 44	11 04		11 44	11 45	12 04		12 44	13 03		13 19	13 44	14 03	
Padgate d																						
Birchwood d			08 50	09 08	09 49	09 49	10 08		10 49	11 09		11 49	11 50	12 09		12 49	13 08			13 49	14 08	
Glazebrook d																						
Irlam d				09 14			10 14			11 15				12 15			13 14				14 14	
Flixton d				09 18			10 18			11 19				12 19			13 18				14 18	
Chassen Road d																						
Urmston d				09 21			10 21			11 22				12 22			13 21				14 21	
Humphrey Park d																						
Trafford Park d																						
Deansgate 84,85 a				09 31			10 31	10 24		11 35	11 23			12 34	12 22		13 32	13 21			14 34	14 22
Manchester Oxford Road 84,85 a		09 12	09 07	09 34	10 06	10 06	10 33	10 26	11 06	11 37	11 25	12 06	12 08	12 36	12 24	13 06	13 35	13 23	13 38	14 06	14 36	14 24
ManchesterPicc 78,84,85 a	00 40	09 15	09 11		10 10	10 11		10 30	11 10		11 29	12 09			12 27	13 10		13 31	13 41	14 10		14 31
Stockport 84 a																			13 51			
Sheffield 78 a																			14 37			
Manchester Airport 85,84 a		09 39	09 31		10 32	10 35		11 02	11 31		12 03	12 26			12 51	13 30		13 55		14 30		14 55

	EM ◇ F	NT ◇	NT	NT B	EM ◇ F	NT ◇	NT	NT B	EM ◇ F	NT ◇	NT	NT B	EM ◇ A	NT ◇	NT	NT B	EM ◇ F	NT ◇	NT	NT B	EM ◇ A	NT ◇
Liverpool Lime Street 90,91 d	13 52	14 14	14 25	14 28	14 52	15 14	15 25	15 28	15 52	16 19	16 25	16 28	16 52	17 14	17 25	17 29	17 52	18 14	18 25	18 28	18 52	19 14
Edge Hill 90,91 d																						
Mossley Hill 91 d			14 33				15 33				16 33				17 33				18 33			
West Allerton 91 d			14 35				15 35				16 35				17 35				18 35			
L'pool Sth Parkway 91,103 d	14 03	14 25	14 40		15 03	15 25	15 40		16 03	16 30	16 40		17 03	17 25	17 40		18 03	18 25	18 40		19 03	19 25
Hunts Cross 103 d			14 43				15 43				16 43				17 43				18 43			
Halewood d			14 46				15 46				16 46				17 46				18 46			
Hough Green d			14 50				15 50				16 50				17 50				18 50			
Widnes d	14 11		14 54		15 11		15 54		16 11		16 54		17 11		17 54		18 11		18 54		19 11	
Sankey for Penketh d																						
Warrington Central a	14 18	14 44	15 02		15 18	15 44	16 02		16 18	16 44	17 02		17 18	17 44	18 02		18 18	18 44	19 02		19 18	19 44
d	14 19	14 44	15 03		15 19	15 44	16 03		16 19	16 44	17 03		17 19	17 44	18 03		18 19	18 44	19 03		19 19	19 44
Padgate d																						
Birchwood d		14 49	15 08			15 49	16 08			16 49	17 08			17 49	18 08			18 49	19 08			19 49
Glazebrook d																						
Irlam d			15 14				16 14				17 14				18 14				19 14			
Flixton d			15 18				16 18				17 18				18 18				19 18			
Chassen Road d																						
Urmston d			15 21				16 21				17 21				18 21				19 21			
Humphrey Park d																						
Trafford Park d																						
Deansgate 84,85 a			15 32	15 21			16 32	16 21			17 32	17 21			18 32	18 22			19 32	19 21		
Manchester Oxford Road 84,85 a	14 39	15 06	15 35	15 23	15 38	16 06	16 35	16 23	16 38	17 06	17 35	17 23	17 38	18 06	18 35	18 24	18 38	19 06	19 35	19 23	19 38	20 06
ManchesterPicc 78,84,85 a	14 42	15 11		15 31	15 41	16 10		16 31	16 41	17 10		17 31	17 41	18 10		18 31	18 41	19 10		19 31	19 41	20 10
Stockport 84 a	14 51				15 51				16 51				17 51				18 51				19 50	
Sheffield 78 a	15 35				16 37				17 35				18 36				19 35				20 35	
Manchester Airport 85,84 a		15 30		15 55		16 30		16 55		17 30		17 55		18 30		18 55		19 30		19 55		20 30

A To Nottingham
B To Wilmslow
C not 20 May. From Liverpool Lime Street
D until 9 September
E from 16 September
F To Norwich

Liverpool - Warrington Central - Manchester and Manchester Airport

Sundays
20 May to 2 December

	NT	NT A	EM ◇ B	NT ◇	NT	NT A	EM ◇ B	NT ◇	NT	NT A	NT ◇	NT	NT A	NT ◇
Liverpool Lime Street 90,91 d	19 25	19 28	19 52	20 09	20 25	20 28	21 16	21 19	21 25	21 28	22 14	22 25	22 28	23 30
Edge Hill 90,91 d														
Mossley Hill 91 d	19 33				20 33				21 33			22 33		
West Allerton 91 d	19 35				20 35				21 35			22 35		
L'pool Sth Parkway 91,103 d	19 40		20 03	20 23	20 40		21 26	21 33	21 40		22 25	22 40		
Hunts Cross 103 d	19 43				20 44				21 43			22 43		
Halewood d	19 46				20 47				21 46			22 46		
Hough Green d	19 50				20 51				21 50			22 50		
Widnes d	19 54		20 11		20 55		21 34		21 54			22 54		
Sankey for Penketh d														
Warrington Central a	20 02		20 18	20 44	21 03		21 42	21 47	22 02		22 44	23 02		
d	20 03		20 19	20 44	21 04		21 42	21 48	22 03		22 45	23 03		
Padgate d														
Birchwood d	20 08			20 49	21 09			21 53	22 08		22 50	23 08		
Glazebrook d														
Irlam d	20 14				21 15				22 14			23 14		
Flixton d	20 18				21 19				22 18			23 18		
Chassen Road d														
Urmston d	20 21				21 22				22 21			23 21		
Humphrey Park d														
Trafford Park d														
Deansgate 84,85 a	20 32	20 21			21 33	21 21			22 31	22 21		23 33	23 21	00 25
Manchester Oxford Road 84,85 a	20 35	20 23	20 38	21 06	21 36	21 23	22 06	22 10	22 33	22 23	23 07	23 35	23 23	00 27
ManchesterPicc 78,84,85 a		20 31	20 41	21 11		21 31	22 09	22 13		22 32	23 13		23 31	00 30
Stockport 84 a			20 51				22 22							
Sheffield 78 a			21 34				23 26							
Manchester Airport 85,84 a		21 01		21 30		21 55		22 34		22 55	23 32		23 54	00 53

A To Wilmslow
B To Nottingham

Table T090-F

Mondays to Fridays
21 May to 7 December

Manchester Airport, Manchester, Preston, Wigan and Newton-le-Willows - St Helens and Liverpool

Miles	Miles	Miles	Miles	Station		NT MX A	NT ◇ B	NT	NT ◇	NT C	NT	AW ◇ D	TP ◇1	NT	NT	NT	NT ◇ B	NT	AW ◇ E	TP ◇1 F	NT	NT	NT G
—	—	—	0	**Manchester Airport** 85	d				04 34			05 33											
—	—	—	9¾	**Manchester Piccadilly** 10	d				04 51			05 47							06 50				
—	—	—	10¼	**Manchester Oxford Road**	d				04 54			05 50							06 53				
0	—	—	—	**Manchester Victoria**	d						05 28		05 55		06 00					06 56			
4	—	—	14¼	Eccles	d						05 35												
5	—	—	15¼	Patricroft	d						05 37												
—	—	—	—	Blackpool North 97	d		03 33										05 39	06 03					
—	0	0	—	**Preston** 8 65,82	d		03 57		05a46								06 07	06 29					
—	4	4	—	Leyland 82	d												06 12	06 35					
—	6¾	6¾	—	Euxton Balshaw Lane	d													06 39					
—	15	15	—	**Wigan North Western** 65	a		04 16										06 23	06 47					
—	—	—	—		d			05 35								06 21		06 48			06 52	07 02	
15½	—	22	26	**Newton-le-Willows**	d						05 48	06 08			06 17				07 09			07 17	
—	—	—	—	Warrington Bank Quay	d																		
17	—	23½	27½	Earlestown 8	d					05 32	05 50	06 11			06 19				07 13			07 20	07 37
—	—	—	—	Warrington Bank Quay	a					05 39		06 19							07 23				07 47
19¾	—	26¼	30¼	**St Helens Junction**	d						05 55				06 24							07 24	
21	—	27½	31½	Lea Green	d						05 58		06 16		06 27					07 19		07 27	
22¾	—	29¼	33¼	Rainhill	d	00 02					06 02				06 31							07 30	
24¼	—	30¾	34¾	Whiston	d	00 05					06 05				06 34							07 33	
—	18¾	—	—	Bryn	d			05 41								06 27					06 58		
—	20	—	—	Garswood	d			05 44								06 31					07 01		
—	23¼	—	—	**St Helens Central**	a			05 51								06 37		07 00			07 08		
—	—	—	—		d			05 51						06 08		06 38		07 00			07 08		
—	25¼	—	—	Thatto Heath	d			05 55						06 12		06 42					07 12		
—	26¼	—	—	Eccleston Park	d			05 57						06 14		06 44					07 14		
—	27¼	—	—	Prescot	d			06 00						06 17		06 47					07 17		
26¼	29½	32¾	36¾	Huyton	d	00 09		06 04			06 09			06 21	06 38	06 51		07 08			07 23	07 37	
26¾	30	33¼	37¼	Roby	d	00 11		06 07			06 11			06 24	06 40	06 54					07 26	07 39	
28¼	31½	34¾	38¾	Broad Green	d	00 14		06 10			06 14			06 27	06 43	06 57					07 29	07 42	
29¼	32½	35¾	39¾	Wavertree Technology Park	d	00 17		06 13			06 17			06 30	06 46	07 00					07 32	07 45	
30	33¼	36½	40½	Edge Hill 91	d	00 20		06 16			06 20			06 33	06 49	07 03					07 35	07 48	
31¾	35	38¼	42¼	**Liverpool Lime Street** 10 91	a	00 28		06 23			06 28		06 32	06 39	06 54	07 09		07 19		07 35	07 39	07 54	

Station		NT ◇	TP ◇1 H	NT	NT ◇ B	NT	AW ■ ◇ I	TP ◇1 J	NT	NT	TP ◇1 H	NT	NT ◇ B	NT	NT	EM ◇ K	NT	NT	AW ◇ I	NT L	TP ◇1 H	NT ◇	NT
Manchester Airport 85	d	06 50																					
Manchester Piccadilly 10	d	07 09					07 50									08 38			08 52	08 57			
Manchester Oxford Road	d	07 12					07 54								08 16	08 42			08 55	09 00		09 12	
Manchester Victoria	d		07 24					07 55			08 24									09a07	09 23		
Eccles	d																						
Patricroft	d																						
Blackpool North 97	d				06 38	07 03							07 38				08 04						
Preston 8 65,82	d				07 07	07 29							08 06				08 30						
Leyland 82	d				07 12	07 35							08 12				08 36						
Euxton Balshaw Lane	d					07 39											08 40						
Wigan North Western 65	a				07 23	07 47							08 23				08 50						
	d			07 21		07 48			07 51	08 06		08 21		08 47			08 51						09 21
Newton-le-Willows	d		07 41				08 16			08 20	08 41								09 15		09 41		
Warrington Bank Quay	d																	09 09					
Earlestown 8	d						08 19			08 22								09 16	09 19				
Warrington Bank Quay	a						08 26												09 26				
St Helens Junction	d									08 27								09 21					
Lea Green	d							08 16		08 30								09 24					
Rainhill	d									08 33								09 28					
Whiston	d									08 36								09 31					
Bryn	d			07 27					07 58			08 27					08 59						09 27
Garswood	d			07 31		07 57			08 02			08 31					09 02						09 31
St Helens Central	a			07 37		08 03			08 08			08 37		08 59			09 09						09 37
	d			07 38		08 04			08 09			08 38		08 59			09 09						09 38
Thatto Heath	d			07 42					08 13			08 42					09 13						09 42
Eccleston Park	d			07 44					08 15			08 44					09 15						09 44
Prescot	d			07 47		08 09			08 18			08 47					09 17						09 47
Huyton	d			07 53		08 13			08 22	08 40		08 54		09 07			09 22	09 35					09 51
Roby	d			07 56		08 15			08 25	08 42		08 57					09 24	09 37					09 54
Broad Green	d			07 59		08 18			08 28	08 45		09 00					09 27	09 40					09 57
Wavertree Technology Park	d			08 04					08 31	08 48		09 03					09 30	09 43					10 00
Edge Hill 91	d			08 08					08 34	08 51		09 06					09 33	09 46					10 03
Liverpool Lime Street 10 91	a	08 01	08 02	08 12		08 28		08 32	08 40	08 57	09 02	09 12		09 19	09 24	09 28	09 40	09 52			10 02	10 02	10 09

A From Wilmslow
B To Manchester Airport
C From Liverpool Lime Street to Ellesmere Port
D To Llandudno
E To Llandudno Junction
F From York
G From Liverpool Lime Street
H From Newcastle
I To Holyhead
J From Middlesbrough
K From Nottingham
L From Buxton

Table T090-F

Mondays to Fridays
21 May to 7 December

Manchester Airport, Manchester, Preston, Wigan and Newton-le-Willows - St Helens and Liverpool

Station		NT ◇ A	NT	NT	NT B	EM ◇ C	NT ◇	AW ◇ D	NT	NT B	NT ◇	TP ◇1 E	NT	NT ◇ A	NT ◇	NT	EM ◇ F	NT	NT ◇ A	NT	NT B	NT ◇	TP ◇1 E
Manchester Airport 85	d										09 50											10 50	
Manchester Piccadilly 10	d					09 39		09 53			10 09						10 38					11 09	
Manchester Oxford Road	d			09 16		09 42		09u57			10 13					10 15	10 42					11 12	
Manchester Victoria	d											10 24											11 24
Eccles	d																						
Patricroft	d																						
Blackpool North 97	d	08 38					09 03							09 38	10 01				10 32				
Preston 8 65,82	d	09 06					09 29							10 06	10 29				11 00				
Leyland 82	d	09 12					09 35							10 12	10 35				11 06				
Euxton Balshaw Lane	d						09 39								10 39								
Wigan North Western 65	a	09 23					09 50							10 23	10 47				11 20				
	d		09 47				09 51						10 21		10 48			10 51					
Newton-le-Willows	d							10 16				10 42											11 43
Warrington Bank Quay	d								10 12											11 12			
Earlestown 8	d				09 38			10 21	10 22	10 37										11 19	11 33		
Warrington Bank Quay	a				09 48			10 30		10 45											11 44		
St Helens Junction	d								10 26											11 24			
Lea Green	d								10 29											11 27			
Rainhill	d								10 33											11 31			
Whiston	d								10 36											11 34			
Bryn	d						09 57						10 27					10 58					
Garswood	d						10 00						10 31					11 02					
St Helens Central	a		09 59				10 07						10 37		11 00			11 08					
	d		09 59				10 07						10 38		11 00			11 09					
Thatto Heath	d						10 11						10 42					11 13					
Eccleston Park	d						10 13						10 44					11 15					
Prescot	d						10 15						10 47					11 18					
Huyton	d		10 07				10 20		10 40				10 51		11 08			11 22		11 38			
Roby	d						10 22		10 42				10 54					11 25		11 40			
Broad Green	d						10 25		10 45				10 57					11 28		11 43			
Wavertree Technology Park	d						10 28		10 48				11 00					11 31		11 46			
Edge Hill 91	d						10 31		10 51				11 03					11 34		11 49			
Liverpool Lime Street 10 91	a		10 19	10 23		10 31	10 38		10 56		11 02	11 02	11 09		11 19	11 24	11 32	11 40		11 55		12 02	12 02

Station		NT	NT ◇	NT	EM ◇ F	NT	NT	NT B	NT ◇	TP ◇1 E	NT	NT ◇ A	NT ◇	NT	EM ◇ F	NT	NT	NT B	NT ◇	TP ◇1 E	NT	NT ◇ A
Manchester Airport 85	d								11 50										12 50			
Manchester Piccadilly 10	d				11 38				12 09						12 38				13 09			
Manchester Oxford Road	d			11 15	11 42				12 12					12 15	12 42				13 12			
Manchester Victoria	d									12 24										13 24		
Eccles	d																					
Patricroft	d																					
Blackpool North 97	d		11 01									11 38	12 01									12 38
Preston 8 65,82	d		11 29									12 06	12 29									13 06
Leyland 82	d		11 35									12 12	12 35									13 12
Euxton Balshaw Lane	d		11 39										12 39									
Wigan North Western 65	a		11 47									12 23	12 47									13 23
	d	11 21	11 48			11 51					12 21		12 48			12 52					13 21	
Newton-le-Willows	d									12 42										13 42		
Warrington Bank Quay	d						12 12										13 11					
Earlestown 8	d						12 19	12 33									13 18	13 37				
Warrington Bank Quay	a							12 45										13 48				
St Helens Junction	d						12 24										13 23					
Lea Green	d						12 27										13 26					
Rainhill	d						12 31										13 30					
Whiston	d						12 34										13 33					
Bryn	d	11 27				11 58					12 27					12 58					13 27	
Garswood	d	11 31				12 02					12 31					13 02					13 31	
St Helens Central	a	11 37	12 00			12 08					12 37		13 00			13 08					13 37	
	d	11 38	12 00			12 09					12 38		13 00			13 09					13 38	
Thatto Heath	d	11 42				12 13					12 42					13 13					13 42	
Eccleston Park	d	11 44				12 15					12 44					13 15					13 44	
Prescot	d	11 47				12 21					12 47					13 18					13 47	
Huyton	d	11 51	12 08			12 25	12 38				12 51		13 08			13 22	13 37				13 51	
Roby	d	11 54				12 28	12 40				12 54					13 25	13 39				13 54	
Broad Green	d	11 57				12 31	12 43				12 57					13 28	13 42				13 57	
Wavertree Technology Park	d	12 02				12 34	12 46				13 00					13 31	13 45				14 00	
Edge Hill 91	d	12 05				12 37	12 49				13 03					13 34	13 48				14 03	
Liverpool Lime Street 10 91	a	12 09	12 19	12 23	12 32	12 43	12 55		13 01	13 02	13 09		13 19	13 23	13 32	13 41	13 53		14 02	14 02	14 09	

A To Manchester Airport
B From Liverpool Lime Street
C From Nottingham
D To Holyhead
E From Newcastle
F From Norwich

Table T090-F

Mondays to Fridays
21 May to 7 December

Manchester Airport, Manchester, Preston, Wigan and Newton-le-Willows - St Helens and Liverpool

	NT	NT	EM	NT	NT	NT	NT		TP	NT	NT	NT	NT	EM	NT	NT	NT		NT	TP	NT	NT	NT	NT
	◇		◇ A			B	◇		◇1 C ✠		◇ D	◇		◇ E			B		◇	◇1 C ✠		◇ D	◇	
Manchester Airport 85 d							13 50												14 50					
Manchester Piccadilly d			13 38				14 09							14 38					15 09					
Manchester Oxford Road d		13 15	13 42				14 12						14 15	14 42					15 12					15 16
Manchester Victoria d									14 24											15 24				
Eccles d																								
Patricroft d																								
Blackpool North 97 d	13 05										13 38	14 01										14 38	15 05	
Preston 65,82 d	13 31										14 06	14 29										15 06	15 31	
Leyland 82 d	13 37										14 12	14 35										15 12	15 37	
Euxton Balshaw Lane d	13 41											14 39											15 41	
Wigan North Western 65 a	13 49										14 23	14 47										15 23	15 49	
Wigan North Western d	13 50			13 53						14 21		14 48			14 52						15 21		15 50	
Newton-le-Willows d									14 42											15 42				
Warrington Bank Quay d					14 11											15 12								
Earlestown d					14 18	14 36										15 19	15 38							
Warrington Bank Quay a						14 44											15 46							
St Helens Junction d					14 23											15 24								
Lea Green d					14 26											15 27								
Rainhill d					14 30											15 31								
Whiston d					14 33											15 34								
Bryn d				14 00						14 27					14 58						15 27			
Garswood d				14 03						14 31					15 02						15 31			
St Helens Central a	14 02			14 10						14 37		15 00			15 08						15 37		16 02	
St Helens Central d	14 02			14 10						14 38		15 00			15 09						15 38		16 02	
Thatto Heath d				14 14						14 42					15 13						15 42			
Eccleston Park d				14 16						14 44					15 15						15 44			
Prescot d				14 18						14 47					15 18						15 47			
Huyton d	14 10			14 23	14 37					14 51		15 08			15 22	15 38					15 51		16 10	
Roby d				14 25	14 39					14 54					15 25	15 40					15 54			
Broad Green d				14 28	14 42					14 57					15 29	15 43					15 57			
Wavertree Technology Park d				14 31	14 45					15 00					15 32	15 46					16 00			
Edge Hill 91 d				14 34	14 48					15 03					15 35	15 49					16 03			
Liverpool Lime Street 91 a	14 22	14 23	14 32	14 41	14 53		15 02		15 02	15 09		15 19	15 23	15 32	15 41	15 54			16 02	16 02	16 09		16 21	16 22

	EM	NT	NT		TP	NT	NT	NT	NT	NT	EM	AW	NT		NT	NT	AW	TP	NT	NT	NT	NT	NT	
	◇ E				◇1 C ✠	◇		◇ D		◇	◇ E	■ F ✠				B	G	◇1 C ✠	◇		◇ D		◇	
Manchester Airport 85 d						15 50													16 50					
Manchester Piccadilly d	15 38					16 09					16 38	16 50					17 15		17 10					
Manchester Oxford Road d	15 42					16 12			16 15		16 42	16u54					17 18		17 13					
Manchester Victoria d					16 24										17 01			17 24						
Eccles d															17 09									
Patricroft d															17 11									
Blackpool North 97 d								15 38		16 01											16 38		17 01	
Preston 65,82 d								16 06		16 31											17 06		17 30	
Leyland 82 d								16 12		16 37											17 12		17 36	
Euxton Balshaw Lane d										16 41													17 40	
Wigan North Western 65 a								16 23		16 51											17 23		17 50	
Wigan North Western d		15 51					16 21			16 52			16 56							17 21		17 38	17 51	
Newton-le-Willows d					16 42							17 13			17 22		17 35	17 40						
Warrington Bank Quay d			16 12																					
Earlestown d			16 19									17 17			17 24	17 34	17 39							
Warrington Bank Quay a												17 26				17 44	17 46							
St Helens Junction d			16 24												17 29									
Lea Green d			16 27												17 32									
Rainhill d			16 31												17 35									
Whiston d			16 34												17 38									
Bryn d		15 58					16 27						17 02							17 27		17 44		
Garswood d		16 02					16 31						17 06							17 31		17 47		
St Helens Central a		16 08					16 37			17 04			17 12							17 37		17 54	18 03	
St Helens Central d		16 09					16 38			17 04			17 13							17 38		17 54	18 03	
Thatto Heath d		16 13					16 42						17 17							17 42		17 58		
Eccleston Park d		16 15					16 44						17 19							17 44		18 00		
Prescot d		16 18					16 47						17 22							17 47		18 02		
Huyton d		16 22	16 38				16 51			17 12			17 28		17 42					17 53		18 07	18 11	
Roby d		16 25	16 40				16 54						17 31		17 44					17 56		18 09		
Broad Green d		16 29	16 43				16 57						17 34		17 47					17 59			18 14	
Wavertree Technology Park d		16 32	16 46				17 00						17 37		17 50					18 02		18 13		
Edge Hill 91 d		16 35	16 49				17 03						17 40		17 53					18 05				
Liverpool Lime Street 91 a	16 32	16 41	16 54		17 02	17 04	17 09		17 23	17 24	17 32		17 44		17 59			18 05	18 09	18 09		18 21	18 24	

A until 31 August, from 8 October. From Norwich
B From Liverpool Lime Street
C From Newcastle
D To Manchester Airport
E From Norwich
F To Llandudno
G To Chester

Table T090-F

Mondays to Fridays
21 May to 7 December

Manchester Airport, Manchester, Preston, Wigan and Newton-le-Willows - St Helens and Liverpool

	EM	AW	NT	TP	NT	NT	NT	NT	NT		AW	NT	NT	NT	TP	NT	NT	NT	NT		NT	NT	NT	EM
	◇ A	■ B		◇1 C ✠	◇		◇ D	◇	◇		E			F	◇1 C ✠	◇		◇ D	◇			G	◇	◇ A
Manchester Airport 85 d					17 50											18 50								
Manchester Piccadilly d	17 38	17 52			18 09						18 43					19 09								19 38
Manchester Oxford Road d	17 42	17 55			18 13						18 48					19 12					19 15			19 42
Manchester Victoria d				18 23					18 30						19 25								19 31	
Eccles d									18 38														19 38	
Patricroft d									18 40														19 40	
Blackpool North 97 d							17 38	18 03										18 37	19 05					
Preston 65,82 d							18 06	18 29										19 05	19 31					
Leyland 82 d							18 12	18 35										19 11	19 37					
Euxton Balshaw Lane d								18 39											19 41					
Wigan North Western 65 a							18 23	18 47										19 23	19 49					
Wigan North Western d						18 21		18 48				18 52					19 21		19 50					
Newton-le-Willows d		18 16		18 41					18 51		19 06				19 43								19 51	
Warrington Bank Quay d			18 12										19 11									19 44		
Earlestown d		18 19	18 19						18 54		19 11		19 19	19 34								19a52	19 53	
Warrington Bank Quay a		18 26									19 21			19 46										
St Helens Junction d			18 24						18 58				19 24										19 57	
Lea Green d			18 27						19 01				19 27										20 00	
Rainhill d			18 31						19 04				19 31										20 04	
Whiston d			18 34						19 07				19 34										20 07	
Bryn d						18 27						18 58					19 27							
Garswood d						18 31						19 02					19 31							
St Helens Central a						18 37		19 00				19 08					19 37		20 02					
St Helens Central d						18 38		19 00				19 09					19 38		20 02					
Thatto Heath d						18 42						19 13					19 42							
Eccleston Park d						18 44						19 15					19 44							
Prescot d						18 47						19 18					19 47							
Huyton d			18 38			18 53		19 08	19 11			19 23	19 38				19 51		20 10				20 11	
Roby d			18 40			18 56			19 13			19 26	19 40				19 54						20 13	
Broad Green d			18 43			18 59			19 16			19 29	19 43				19 57						20 16	
Wavertree Technology Park d			18 46			19 02			19 19			19 32	19 46				20 00						20 19	
Edge Hill 91 d			18 49			19 05			19 22			19 35	19 49				20 03				20 19		20 22	
Liverpool Lime Street 91 a	18 36		18 54	19 02	19 04	19 09		19 19	19 30			19 41	19 54		20 03	20 09	20 09		20 21		20 23		20 30	20 34

	AW	NT	NT	TP	NT ThX		NT	NT	NT ThO	NT	NT	EM	NT	AW	NT		TP	NT	NT	NT	NT	NT	AW	AW
	E			◇1 C	◇			◇ D	◇	◇		◇ A	◇ H	E			◇1 C		◇ D			◇ H	E	E
Manchester Airport 85 d					19 50				19 50				20 29	20 35								21 29	21 32	
Manchester Piccadilly d	19 52				20 09				20 09			20 38	20 43	20 50								21 43	21 50	22 12
Manchester Oxford Road d	19 55				20 12				20 12		20 15	20 42	20 49	20 54								21 49	21 53	22 15
Manchester Victoria d				20 24													21 24							
Eccles d																								
Patricroft d																								
Blackpool North 97 d								19 39		20 01									20 38	21 00				
Preston 65,82 d								20 07		20 29									21 06	21 30				
Leyland 82 d								20 13		20 35			21a33						21 12	21 36				
Euxton Balshaw Lane d										20 39										21 40				
Wigan North Western 65 a								20 24		20 47									21 23	21 49		22 17		
Wigan North Western d		19 54					20 21			20 48					20 52			21 21		21 50	22 02			
Newton-le-Willows d	20 16			20 40										21 11			21 40						22 10	22 37
Warrington Bank Quay d			20 12																					
Earlestown d	20 19		20 19											21 14									22 14	22 40
Warrington Bank Quay a	20 25													21 25									22 22	22 47
St Helens Junction d			20 24																					
Lea Green d			20 27	20 46													21 46							
Rainhill d			20 31																					
Whiston d			20 34																					
Bryn d		20 00					20 27								20 58			21 27			22 08			
Garswood d		20 04					20 31								21 02			21 31			22 12			
St Helens Central a		20 10					20 37			21 00					21 08			21 37		22 02	22 19			
St Helens Central d		20 11					20 38			21 00					21 09			21 38		22 02	22 19			
Thatto Heath d		20 15					20 42								21 13			21 42			22 23			
Eccleston Park d		20 17					20 44								21 15			21 44			22 25			
Prescot d		20 20					20 47								21 18			21 47			22 28			
Huyton d		20 24	20 38				20 51			21 08					21 22			21 53		22 11	22 32			
Roby d		20 27	20 40				20 54								21 25			21 56		22 14	22 35			
Broad Green d		20 30	20 43				20 57								21 28			21 59		22 17	22 38			
Wavertree Technology Park d		20 33	20 46				21 00								21 31			22 02		22 20	22 41			
Edge Hill 91 d		20 36	20 49				21 03								21 34			22 05		22 23	22 44			
Liverpool Lime Street 91 a		20 42	20 54	21 03	21 04		21 09		21 12	21 19	21 24	21 36			21 40		22 03	22 09		22 29	22 50			

A From Norwich
B To Holyhead
C From Newcastle
D To Manchester Airport
E To Chester
F From Liverpool Lime Street
G From Ellesmere Port to Manchester Victoria
H To Blackpool North

Manchester Airport, Manchester, Preston, Wigan and Newton-le-Willows - St Helens and Liverpool

Mondays to Fridays
21 May to 7 December

	TP ◇■ A	NT	NT FX ◇ B	TP ◇■ C	NT FX ◇ D	NT FX ◇ B	AW E	TP ◇■ A	NT F	NT FO	NT F
Manchester Airport 85 d					22 34				23 01		23 25
Manchester Piccadilly d				22 35	22 56		23 14		23 22		23 43
Manchester Oxford Road d				22 38	23 00		23 17		23 25		23 46
Manchester Victoria d	22 24			22a43				23 23		23 40	23a55
Eccles d									23 34	23 47	
Patricroft d									23 37	23 49	
Blackpool North 97 d		22 18	22 25			23 13					
Preston 65,82 d		22 43	22 54			23 42					
Leyland 82 d		22 49	22a59		23a43	23a49					
Euxton Balshaw Lane d		22 53									
Wigan North Western 65 a		23 01									
d		23 02									
Newton-le-Willows d	22 41						23 35	23 40	23 47	00 01	
Warrington Bank Quay d											
Earlestown d							23 38		23 50	00 04	
Warrington Bank Quay a							23 47				
St Helens Junction d									23 54	00 08	
Lea Green d	22 47							23 46	23 57	00 11	
Rainhill d									00 02	00 15	
Whiston d									00 05	00 18	
Bryn d		23 08									
Garswood d		23 12									
St Helens Central a		23 18									
d		23 19									
Thatto Heath d		23 23									
Eccleston Park d		23 25									
Prescot d		23 28									
Huyton d		23 32							00 09	00 24	
Roby d		23 35							00 11	00 26	
Broad Green d		23 38							00 14	00 29	
Wavertree Technology Park d		23 41							00 17	00 32	
Edge Hill 91 d		23 44							00 20	00 35	
Liverpool Lime Street 91 a	23 04	23 50						00 03	00 28	00 42	

Saturdays
26 May to 8 December

	NT F	NT G	NT H	NT	NT	AW ◇ I ✠	TP ◇■	NT	NT	TP ◇■	NT	NT ◇ B	NT	AW ◇ I ✠	TP ◇■ J	NT	NT	NT K	NT ◇	TP ◇■ A	NT	NT ◇ B
Manchester Airport 85 d						05 33													06 50			
Manchester Piccadilly d						05 48								06 50					07 09			
Manchester Oxford Road d						05 52								06 53					07 12			
Manchester Victoria d					05 28		05 55		06 00	06 24					06 56					07 23		
Eccles d					05 35																	
Patricroft d					05 37																	
Blackpool North 97 d												05 39	06 03									06 38
Preston 65,82 d												06 07	06 29									07 07
Leyland 82 d												06 12	06 35									07 12
Euxton Balshaw Lane d													06 39									
Wigan North Western 65 a												06 23	06 47									07 23
d				05 35							06 21		06 48			06 52	07 02				07 21	
Newton-le-Willows d		00 01			05 48	06 08			06 17	06 40				07 09			07 17			07 41		
Warrington Bank Quay d																						
Earlestown d		00 04	05 32		05 50	06 11			06 19					07 14			07 20	07 37				
Warrington Bank Quay a			05 39			06 21								07 22				07 47				
St Helens Junction d		00 08			05 55				06 24								07 24					
Lea Green d		00 11			05 58		06 16		06 27						07 19		07 27					
Rainhill d	00 02	00 15			06 02				06 31								07 30					
Whiston d	00 05	00 18			06 05				06 34								07 33					
Bryn d				05 41							06 27					06 58					07 27	
Garswood d				05 44							06 31					07 01					07 31	
St Helens Central a				05 51							06 37		07 00			07 08					07 37	
d				05 51				06 08			06 38		07 00			07 08					07 38	
Thatto Heath d				05 55				06 12			06 42					07 12					07 42	
Eccleston Park d				05 57				06 14			06 44					07 14					07 44	
Prescot d				06 00				06 17			06 47					07 17					07 47	
Huyton d	00 09	00 24		06 04	06 09			06 21	06 38		06 51		07 08			07 23	07 37				07 53	
Roby d	00 11	00 26		06 07	06 11			06 24	06 40		06 54					07 26	07 39				07 56	
Broad Green d	00 14	00 29		06 10	06 14			06 27	06 43		06 57					07 29	07 42				07 59	
Wavertree Technology Park d	00 17	00 32		06 13	06 17			06 30	06 46		07 00					07 32	07 45				08 04	
Edge Hill 91 d	00 20	00 35		06 16	06 20			06 33	06 49		07 03					07 35	07 48				08 08	
Liverpool Lime Street 91 a	00 28	00 42		06 23	06 28		06 32	06 39	06 54	07 02	07 09		07 19		07 35	07 39	07 54		08 01	08 02	08 12	

A From Newcastle
B To Manchester Airport
C To Leeds
D To Blackpool North
E To Chester
F From Wilmslow
G From Manchester Victoria
H From Liverpool Lime Street to Ellesmere Port
I To Llandudno
J From York
K From Liverpool Lime Street

Table T090-F

Manchester Airport, Manchester, Preston, Wigan and Newton-le-Willows - St Helens and Liverpool

Saturdays
26 May to 8 December

	NT	AW ◇ A ✠	TP ◇■ B ✠	NT	NT	NT C	TP ◇■ D ✠	NT	NT ◇ E	NT	NT	EM ◇ F	NT	NT	AW ◇ A ✠	NT ◇	TP ◇■ D ✠	NT	NT ◇ E	NT	NT	EM ◇ F
Manchester Airport 85 d																						
Manchester Piccadilly d		07 52										08 38			08 52							09 38
Manchester Oxford Road d		07 55									08 16	08 42			08 55	09 12					09 16	09 42
Manchester Victoria d			07 55				08 24										09 23					
Eccles d																						
Patricroft d																						
Blackpool North 97 d	07 03								07 38				08 04						08 38			
Preston 65,82 d	07 29								08 06				08 30						09 06			
Leyland 82 d	07 35								08 12				08 36						09 12			
Euxton Balshaw Lane d	07 39												08 40									
Wigan North Western 65 a	07 47								08 23				08 50						09 23			
d	07 48			07 51				08 21		08 47			08 51					09 21		09 47		
Newton-le-Willows d		08 16					08 41								09 16		09 41					
Warrington Bank Quay d					08 14									09 09								
Earlestown d		08 19			08 22	08 38								09 16	09 19							
Warrington Bank Quay a		08 27				08 47									09 26							
St Helens Junction d					08 27									09 21								
Lea Green d			08 16		08 30									09 24								
Rainhill d					08 33									09 28								
Whiston d					08 36									09 31								
Bryn d				07 58				08 27					08 59					09 27				
Garswood d	07 57			08 02				08 31					09 02					09 31				
St Helens Central a	08 03			08 08				08 37		08 59			09 09					09 37		09 59		
d	08 04			08 09				08 38		08 59			09 09					09 38		09 59		
Thatto Heath d				08 13				08 42					09 13					09 42				
Eccleston Park d				08 15				08 44					09 15					09 44				
Prescot d	08 09			08 18				08 47					09 17					09 47				
Huyton d	08 13			08 22	08 40			08 54		09 07			09 22	09 35				09 54		10 07		
Roby d	08 15			08 25	08 42			08 57					09 24	09 37				09 57				
Broad Green d	08 18			08 28	08 45			09 00					09 27	09 40				10 00				
Wavertree Technology Park d				08 31	08 48			09 03					09 30	09 43				10 03				
Edge Hill 91 d				08 34	08 51			09 06					09 33	09 46				10 06				
Liverpool Lime Street 91 a	08 28		08 32	08 40	08 57		09 02	09 12		09 19	09 24	09 31	09 40	09 52		10 02	10 09	10 10		10 19	10 23	10 31

	NT ◇	NT C	NT	NT C	NT ◇	TP ◇■ D ✠	NT	NT ◇ E	NT ◇	NT	EM ◇ G	NT	NT ◇ E	NT	NT C	TP ◇■ D ✠	NT ◇	NT	NT ◇	NT	EM ◇ G
Manchester Airport 85 d					09 50												10 50				
Manchester Piccadilly d					10 10						10 38						11 09				11 38
Manchester Oxford Road d					10 13					10 16	10 42						11 13			11 15	11 42
Manchester Victoria d						10 24										11 24					
Eccles d																					
Patricroft d																					
Blackpool North 97 d	09 03							09 38	10 01				10 36						11 03		
Preston 65,82 d	09 29							10 06	10 29				11 04						11 29		
Leyland 82 d	09 35							10 12	10 35				11 10						11 35		
Euxton Balshaw Lane d	09 39								10 39										11 39		
Wigan North Western 65 a	09 50							10 23	10 47				11 21						11 47		
d	09 51						10 21		10 48			10 51						11 21	11 48		
Newton-le-Willows d						10 42										11 42					
Warrington Bank Quay d			10 12											11 12							
Earlestown d		09 38	10 22	10 37										11 19	11 33						
Warrington Bank Quay a		09 48		10 45											11 44						
St Helens Junction d			10 26											11 24							
Lea Green d			10 29											11 27							
Rainhill d			10 33											11 31							
Whiston d			10 36											11 34							
Bryn d	09 57						10 27					10 58						11 27			
Garswood d	10 00						10 31					11 02						11 31			
St Helens Central a	10 07						10 37		11 00			11 08						11 37	12 00		
d	10 07						10 38		11 00			11 09						11 38	12 00		
Thatto Heath d	10 11						10 42					11 13						11 42			
Eccleston Park d	10 13						10 44					11 15						11 44			
Prescot d	10 15						10 47					11 18						11 47			
Huyton d	10 20		10 40				10 51		11 08			11 22		11 38				11 51	12 08		
Roby d	10 22		10 42				10 54					11 25		11 40				11 54			
Broad Green d	10 25		10 45				10 57					11 28		11 43				11 57			
Wavertree Technology Park d	10 28		10 48				11 00					11 31		11 46				12 02			
Edge Hill 91 d	10 31		10 51				11 03					11 34		11 49				12 05			
Liverpool Lime Street 91 a	10 40		10 56		11 02	11 02	11 09		11 19	11 24	11 32	11 40		11 55		12 02	12 03	12 09	12 19	12 23	12 32

A To Llandudno
B From Middlesbrough
C From Liverpool Lime Street
D From Newcastle
E To Manchester Airport
F From Nottingham
G From Norwich

Table T090-F

Saturdays
26 May to 8 December

Manchester Airport, Manchester, Preston, Wigan and Newton-le-Willows - St Helens and Liverpool

Station		NT	NT ◇ A	NT	NT B	TP ◇1 C	NT ◇	NT		NT ◇	NT	EM ◇ D	NT	NT	NT B	NT ◇	TP ◇1 C	NT		NT ◇ A	NT ◇	NT	EM ◇ D	NT	NT
Manchester Airport 85	d						11 50									12 50									
Manchester Piccadilly	d						12 09					12 38				13 09							13 38		
Manchester Oxford Road	d						12 12				12 15	12 42				13 12						13 15	13 42		
Manchester Victoria	d					12 24											13 24								
Eccles	d																								
Patricroft	d																								
Blackpool North 97	d		11 35							12 01										12 38	13 05				
Preston 65,82	d		12 03							12 29										13 06	13 31				
Leyland 82	d									12 35										13 12	13 37				
Euxton Balshaw Lane	d									12 39											13 41				
Wigan North Western 65	a		12 18							12 47										13 23	13 49				
	d	11 51						12 21		12 48			12 52					13 21			13 50			13 53	
Newton-le-Willows	d					12 42											13 42								
Warrington Bank Quay	d			12 12										13 11											14 11
Earlestown	d			12 19	12 33									13 18	13 37										14 18
Warrington Bank Quay	a				12 45										13 48										
St Helens Junction	d			12 24										13 23											14 23
Lea Green	d			12 27										13 26											14 26
Rainhill	d			12 31										13 30											14 30
Whiston	d			12 34										13 33											14 33
Bryn	d	11 58						12 27					12 58					13 27						14 00	
Garswood	d	12 02						12 31					13 02					13 31						14 03	
St Helens Central	a	12 08						12 37		13 00			13 08					13 37			14 02			14 10	
	d	12 09						12 38		13 00			13 09					13 38			14 02			14 10	
Thatto Heath	d	12 13						12 42					13 13					13 42						14 14	
Eccleston Park	d	12 15						12 44					13 15					13 44						14 16	
Prescot	d	12 21						12 47					13 18					13 47						14 18	
Huyton	d	12 25		12 38				12 51		13 08			13 22	13 37				13 51			14 10			14 23	14 37
Roby	d	12 28		12 40				12 54					13 25	13 39				13 54						14 25	14 39
Broad Green	d	12 31		12 43				12 57					13 28	13 42				13 57						14 28	14 42
Wavertree Technology Park	d	12 34		12 46				13 00					13 31	13 45				14 00						14 31	14 45
Edge Hill 91	d	12 37		12 49				13 03					13 34	13 48				14 03						14 34	14 48
Liverpool Lime Street 91	a	12 43		12 55		13 02	13 03	13 09		13 19	13 23	13 32	13 41	13 53		14 02	14 02	14 09			14 22	14 23	14 32	14 41	14 53

Station		NT B	NT ◇	TP ◇1 C		NT	NT ◇ A	NT ◇	NT	EM ◇ D	NT	NT	NT B	NT ◇		TP ◇1 C	NT	NT ◇ A	NT ◇	NT	EM ◇ D	NT	NT	NT B	
Manchester Airport 85	d		13 50											14 50											
Manchester Piccadilly	d		14 09							14 38				15 09							15 38				
Manchester Oxford Road	d		14 12						14 15	14 42				15 12						15 15	15 42				
Manchester Victoria	d			14 24												15 24									
Eccles	d																								
Patricroft	d																								
Blackpool North 97	d						13 38	14 01										14 38	15 05						
Preston 65,82	d						14 06	14 29										15 06	15 31						
Leyland 82	d						14 12	14 35										15 12	15 37						
Euxton Balshaw Lane	d							14 39											15 41						
Wigan North Western 65	a						14 24	14 47										15 23	15 49						
	d					14 21		14 48			14 52						15 21		15 50			15 51			
Newton-le-Willows	d			14 42												15 42									
Warrington Bank Quay	d											15 12											16 12		
Earlestown	d	14 40										15 19	15 36										16 19	16 38	
Warrington Bank Quay	a	14 48											15 44											16 50	
St Helens Junction	d											15 24											16 24		
Lea Green	d											15 27											16 27		
Rainhill	d											15 31											16 31		
Whiston	d											15 34											16 34		
Bryn	d					14 27					14 58						15 27					15 58			
Garswood	d					14 31					15 02						15 31					16 02			
St Helens Central	a					14 37		15 00			15 08						15 37		16 02			16 08			
	d					14 38		15 00			15 09						15 38		16 02			16 09			
Thatto Heath	d					14 42					15 13						15 42					16 13			
Eccleston Park	d					14 44					15 15						15 44					16 15			
Prescot	d					14 47					15 18						15 47					16 18			
Huyton	d					14 51		15 08			15 22	15 38					15 51		16 10			16 22	16 38		
Roby	d					14 54					15 25	15 40					15 54					16 25	16 40		
Broad Green	d					14 57					15 29	15 43					15 57					16 29	16 43		
Wavertree Technology Park	d					15 00					15 32	15 46					16 00					16 32	16 46		
Edge Hill 91	d					15 03					15 35	15 49					16 03					16 35	16 49		
Liverpool Lime Street 91	a		15 02	15 02		15 09		15 19	15 23	15 31	15 41	15 54		16 02		16 02	16 09		16 21	16 24	16 32	16 41	16 54		

A To Manchester Airport
B From Liverpool Lime Street
C From Newcastle
D From Norwich

Table T090-F

Saturdays
26 May to 8 December

Manchester Airport, Manchester, Preston, Wigan and Newton-le-Willows - St Helens and Liverpool

Station		TP ◇1 A	NT ◇	NT	NT ◇ B	NT	NT ◇	EM ◇ C	NT	NT		NT D	TP ◇1 A	NT ◇	NT	NT ◇ B	NT	NT ◇	EM ◇ C	NT		TP ◇1 A	NT ◇	NT	NT ◇ B
Manchester Airport 85	d		15 50											16 50									17 50		
Manchester Piccadilly	d		16 09					16 38						17 10					17 38				18 09		
Manchester Oxford Road	d		16 12			16 16		16 42						17 13					17 42				18 13		
Manchester Victoria	d	16 23											17 24									18 23			
Eccles	d																								
Patricroft	d																								
Blackpool North 97	d				15 38		16 01									16 38		17 01							17 38
Preston 65,82	d				16 06		16 31									17 06		17 30							18 06
Leyland 82	d				16 12		16 37									17 12		17 36							18 12
Euxton Balshaw Lane	d						16 41											17 40							
Wigan North Western 65	a				16 23		16 51									17 23		17 50							18 23
	d			16 21			16 52		16 56						17 21		17 38	17 51						18 21	
Newton-le-Willows	d	16 42											17 40									18 41			
Warrington Bank Quay	d									17 11										18 12					
Earlestown	d									17 19		17 34								18 19					
Warrington Bank Quay	a											17 44													
St Helens Junction	d									17 24										18 24					
Lea Green	d									17 27										18 27					
Rainhill	d									17 31										18 31					
Whiston	d									17 34										18 34					
Bryn	d			16 27					17 02						17 27		17 44							18 27	
Garswood	d			16 31					17 06						17 31		17 47							18 31	
St Helens Central	a			16 37			17 04		17 12						17 37		17 54	18 03						18 37	
	d			16 38			17 04		17 13						17 38		17 54	18 03						18 38	
Thatto Heath	d			16 42					17 17						17 42		17 58							18 42	
Eccleston Park	d			16 44					17 19						17 44		18 00							18 44	
Prescot	d			16 47					17 22						17 47		18 02							18 47	
Huyton	d			16 51			17 12		17 28	17 38					17 53		18 07	18 11		18 38				18 53	
Roby	d			16 54					17 31	17 40					17 56		18 09			18 40				18 56	
Broad Green	d			16 57					17 34	17 43					17 59			18 14		18 43				18 59	
Wavertree Technology Park	d			17 00					17 37	17 46					18 02		18 13			18 46				19 02	
Edge Hill 91	d			17 03					17 40	17 49					18 05					18 49				19 05	
Liverpool Lime Street 91	a	17 02	17 04	17 09		17 23	17 24	17 32	17 44	17 54			18 05	18 07	18 09		18 21	18 24	18 36	18 54		19 02	19 04	19 09	

Station		NT ◇	NT ◇	NT	NT	NT D		TP ◇1 A	NT ◇	NT	NT ◇ B	NT ◇	NT	NT E	NT ◇	EM ◇ C		NT	NT ◇ B	NT	AW F	TP ◇1 A	NT ◇	NT	NT ◇
Manchester Airport 85	d								18 50														19 50		
Manchester Piccadilly	d								19 09							19 38					19 52		20 11		
Manchester Oxford Road	d								19 12				19 15			19 42					19 55		20 14		
Manchester Victoria	d		18 30					19 25							19 31							20 24			
Eccles	d		18 38												19 38										
Patricroft	d		18 40												19 40										
Blackpool North 97	d	18 03									18 37	19 05							19 36						20 01
Preston 65,82	d	18 29									19 05	19 31							20 04						20 29
Leyland 82	d	18 35									19 11	19 37							20 10						20 35
Euxton Balshaw Lane	d	18 39										19 41													20 39
Wigan North Western 65	a	18 47									19 23	19 49							20 21						20 47
	d	18 48		18 52						19 21		19 50						19 54						20 21	20 48
Newton-le-Willows	d		18 51					19 43							19 51						20 16	20 40			
Warrington Bank Quay	d				19 10									19 44						20 11					
Earlestown	d		18 54		19 19	19 34								19a52	19 53					20 19	20 20				
Warrington Bank Quay	a					19 46															20 30				
St Helens Junction	d		18 58		19 24										19 57					20 24					
Lea Green	d		19 01		19 27										20 00					20 27		20 46			
Rainhill	d		19 04		19 31										20 04					20 31					
Whiston	d		19 07		19 34										20 07					20 34					
Bryn	d			18 58						19 27								20 00						20 27	
Garswood	d			19 02						19 31								20 04						20 31	
St Helens Central	a	19 00		19 08						19 37		20 02						20 10						20 37	21 00
	d	19 00		19 09						19 38		20 02						20 11						20 38	21 00
Thatto Heath	d			19 13						19 42								20 15						20 42	
Eccleston Park	d			19 15						19 44								20 17						20 44	
Prescot	d			19 18						19 47								20 20						20 47	
Huyton	d	19 08	19 11	19 23	19 38					19 51		20 10			20 11			20 24		20 38				20 51	21 08
Roby	d		19 13	19 26	19 40					19 54					20 13			20 27		20 40				20 54	
Broad Green	d		19 16	19 29	19 43					19 57					20 16			20 30		20 43				20 57	
Wavertree Technology Park	d		19 19	19 32	19 46					20 00					20 19			20 33		20 46				21 00	
Edge Hill 91	d		19 22	19 35	19 49					20 03			20 19		20 22			20 36		20 49				21 03	
Liverpool Lime Street 91	a	19 19	19 30	19 41	19 54			20 03	20 09	20 09		20 21	20 23		20 29	20 33		20 42		20 54		21 03	21 04	21 09	21 19

A From Newcastle
B To Manchester Airport
C From Norwich
D From Liverpool Lime Street
E From Ellesmere Port to Manchester Victoria
F To Chester

Table T090-F

Saturdays
26 May to 8 December

Manchester Airport, Manchester, Preston, Wigan and Newton-le-Willows - St Helens and Liverpool

		NT	EM	NT	NT	NT	AW	NT	TP	NT	NT	NT	AW	AW	TP	NT	NT	AW	TP	NT	NT
			◇ A			◇ B	C	◇ D	◇■ E			◇ B	C	C	◇■ E		◇ F	C	◇■ E		G
Manchester Airport 85	d					20 29	20 35					21 29					22 10				
Manchester Piccadilly	d		20 38			20 43	20 50					21 43	21 51	22 12			22 26	23 14			23 43
Manchester Oxford Road	d	20 17	20 42			20 49	20 53					21 49	21 54	22 15			22 29	23 17			23 46
Manchester Victoria	d								21 24						22 23				23 23	23 31	23a55
Eccles	d																			23 38	
Patricroft	d																			23 41	
Blackpool North 97	d							20 38		21 00						22 18					
Preston 65,82	d							21 06		21 30						22 43	23a09				
Leyland 82	d							21 12		21 36						22 49					
Euxton Balshaw Lane	d									21 40						22 53					
Wigan North Western 65	a					21 22		21 23		21 49		22 17				23 01					
	d			20 52	21 21					21 50	22 02					23 02					
Newton-le-Willows	d						21 11		21 40				22 11	22 37	22 40			23 35	23 40	23 52	
Warrington Bank Quay	d																				
Earlestown	d						21 16						22 14	22 40				23 38		23 54	
Warrington Bank Quay	a						21 29						22 23	22 47				23 47			
St Helens Junction	d																			23 59	
Lea Green	d								21 46						22 46				23 46	00 02	
Rainhill	d																			00 05	
Whiston	d																			00 08	
Bryn	d			20 58	21 27						22 08					23 08					
Garswood	d			21 02	21 31						22 12					23 12					
St Helens Central	a			21 08	21 37					22 02	22 19					23 18					
	d			21 09	21 38					22 02	22 19					23 19					
Thatto Heath	d			21 13	21 42						22 23					23 23					
Eccleston Park	d			21 15	21 44						22 25					23 25					
Prescot	d			21 18	21 47						22 28					23 28					
Huyton	d			21 22	21 53					22 11	22 32					23 32				00 12	
Roby	d			21 25	21 56					22 14	22 35					23 35				00 14	
Broad Green	d			21 28	21 59					22 17	22 38					23 38				00 18	
Wavertree Technology Park	d			21 31	22 02					22 20	22 41					23 43				00 21	
Edge Hill 91	d			21 34	22 05					22 23	22 44					23 47				00 24	
Liverpool Lime Street 91	a	21 24	21 32	21 40	22 09				22 03	22 29	22 50				23 03	23 51			00 03	00 32	

Sundays
20 May to 2 December

		NT	AW	TP	NT	NT	NT	NT	NT	TP	NT	NT	NT	AW	TP	NT	TP	NT	NT	NT	NT	NT	AW
		H	C	◇■ 🍴	◇ I	◇ J	◇	K		◇■ L 🍴	◇	◇ B	◇ D	C	◇■ L 🍴		◇■ E 🍴	◇	◇ M	◇ B	◇		C 🍴
Manchester Airport 85	d											08 33								09 33			
Manchester Piccadilly	d		07 18					08 24				08 52		09 48						09 53			10 52
Manchester Oxford Road	d		07 33		08 17	08 17		08 27				08 55		09 51						09 58	10 17		10 57
Manchester Victoria	d			08 25						09 10					09 56		10 24						
Eccles	d							08 35															
Patricroft	d							08 37															
Blackpool North 97	d						07 55				08 32		08 43					09 32	09 41				
Preston 65,82	d						08 22				08 59		09 10					09 58	10 08				
Leyland 82	d						08 28				09 05							10 05					
Euxton Balshaw Lane	d						08 32				09 10							10 09					
Wigan North Western 65	a						08 41				09 18	09 22	09 23					10 17	10 24	10 29			
	d						08 41		08 53		09 19					09 54		10 18				10 49	
Newton-le-Willows	d		08 03					08 48		09 27				10 06			10 42						11 13
Warrington Bank Quay	d																						
Earlestown	d		08 13					08 50						10 09									11 16
Warrington Bank Quay	a		08 38											10 17									11 26
St Helens Junction	d							08 54															
Lea Green	d	00 02		08 45				08 57							10 16								
Rainhill	d	00 05						09 01															
Whiston	d	00 08						09 04															
Bryn	d								08 59							10 00						10 55	
Garswood	d						08 50		09 02		09 28					10 03		10 27				10 58	
St Helens Central	a						08 57		09 09		09 34					10 10		10 33				11 05	
	d						08 57		09 09		09 35					10 10		10 34				11 05	
Thatto Heath	d						09 01		09 13		09 38					10 14		10 37				11 09	
Eccleston Park	d								09 15							10 16						11 11	
Prescot	d						09 05		09 17		09 42					10 18		10 41				11 13	
Huyton	d	00 12					09 09	09 11	09 21		09 47					10 22		10 50				11 17	
Roby	d	00 14						09 13	09 23		09 49					10 24		10 52				11 19	
Broad Green	d	00 18						09 16	09 26		09 52					10 27		10 56				11 22	
Wavertree Technology Park	d	00 21						09 19	09 29		09 55					10 30		10 59				11 25	
Edge Hill 91	d	00 24																					
Liverpool Lime Street 91	a	00 32		09 02	09 09	09 10	09 21	09 29	09 38	09 48	10 03				10 32	10 39	11 02	11 09			11 14	11 34	

A From Norwich
B To Blackpool North
C To Chester
D To Manchester Airport
E From Newcastle
F until 16 June, from 15 September
G From Wilmslow
H not 20 May. From Manchester Victoria
I from 16 September until 21 October
J from 28 October
K from 16 September
L From York
M To Manchester Oxford Road

Table T090-F

Sundays
20 May to 2 December

Manchester Airport, Manchester, Preston, Wigan and Newton-le-Willows - St Helens and Liverpool

		TP	NT	NT	NT	TP	EM	NT	AW	TP	NT	NT	NT	NT	TP	EM	NT	AW	TP	NT	NT	NT	TP
		◇■ A 🍴	◇	◇ B	◇ C	◇■ D 🍴	◇ E		F 🍴	◇■ A 🍴	◇	◇ B	◇ G	◇ H	◇■ D 🍴	◇ E		F 🍴	◇■ A 🍴	◇	◇ B	◇ C	◇■ I 🍴
Manchester Airport 85	d				10 43									11 43								12 41	
Manchester Piccadilly	d				11 01		11 38		11 56					12 01		12 38		12 56				13 00	
Manchester Oxford Road	d				11 05	11 10	11 42		11 59				12 03	12 05	12 09	12 42		12 59				13 05	13 09
Manchester Victoria	d	11 24				11a16				12 27					12a15				13 24				13a15
Eccles	d																						
Patricroft	d																						
Blackpool North 97	d		10 33	10 41							11 32	11 41								12 24	12 40		
Preston 65,82	d		11 00	11 08							11 59	12 08								12 51	13 07		
Leyland 82	d		11 06								12 05									12 57			
Euxton Balshaw Lane	d		11 10								12 10									13 02			
Wigan North Western 65	a		11 19	11 24	11 32						12 21	12 24	12 33	12 33						13 12	13 22	13 33	
	d		11 19					11 53			12 21						12 53			13 12			
Newton-le-Willows	d	11 40							12 17	12 43								13 17	13 40				
Warrington Bank Quay	d																						
Earlestown	d								12 20									13 23					
Warrington Bank Quay	a								12 29									13 31					
St Helens Junction	d																						
Lea Green	d																						
Rainhill	d																						
Whiston	d																						
Bryn	d							11 59									12 59						
Garswood	d		11 28					12 02			12 30						13 02			13 21			
St Helens Central	a		11 36					12 09			12 37						13 09			13 28			
	d		11 36					12 09			12 37						13 09			13 28			
Thatto Heath	d		11 40					12 13			12 41						13 13			13 32			
Eccleston Park	d							12 15									13 15						
Prescot	d		11 44					12 17			12 45						13 17			13 36			
Huyton	d		11 48					12 23			12 51						13 21			13 42			
Roby	d		11 50					12 25			12 54						13 23			13 51			
Broad Green	d		11 53					12 28			12 57						13 26			13 54			
Wavertree Technology Park	d		11 56					12 31			13 00						13 29			13 57			
Edge Hill 91	d																						
Liverpool Lime Street 91	a	12 01	12 05				12 30	12 38		13 04	13 09					13 30	13 38		14 01	14 03			

		NT	EM	NT	AW	TP	NT	NT	NT	EM	NT	AW	TP	NT	NT	NT	EM	NT	AW	TP	NT	NT
		◇ J	◇ E		F 🍴	◇■ A 🍴	◇	◇ B	◇ C	◇ K		F	◇■ A 🍴	◇	◇ B	◇ C	◇ K		F	◇■ A 🍴	◇	◇ B
Manchester Airport 85	d								13 41							14 41						
Manchester Piccadilly	d		13 38		13 56				14 00	14 38		14 56				15 00	15 38		15 56			
Manchester Oxford Road	d	13 12	13 42		13 59				14 05	14 42		14 59				15 05	15 42		15 59			
Manchester Victoria	d					14 24							15 24							16 24		
Eccles	d																					
Patricroft	d																					
Blackpool North 97	d						13 32	13 41						14 32	14 41						15 32	15 41
Preston 65,82	d						14 00	14 08						15 01	15 08						16 01	16 08
Leyland 82	d						14 06							15 07							16 07	
Euxton Balshaw Lane	d						14 10							15 11							16 11	
Wigan North Western 65	a						14 18	14 23	14 33					15 20	15 24	15 33					16 20	16 24
	d			13 53			14 19				14 53			15 20				15 53			16 20	
Newton-le-Willows	d				14 17	14 42						15 17	15 40						16 17	16 42		
Warrington Bank Quay	d																					
Earlestown	d				14 20							15 20							16 20			
Warrington Bank Quay	a				14 27							15 28							16 27			
St Helens Junction	d																					
Lea Green	d																					
Rainhill	d																					
Whiston	d																					
Bryn	d			13 59							14 59							15 59				
Garswood	d			14 02			14 28				15 02			15 29				16 02			16 29	
St Helens Central	a			14 09			14 34				15 09			15 36				16 09			16 36	
	d			14 09			14 35				15 09			15 36				16 09			16 36	
Thatto Heath	d			14 13			14 38				15 13			15 40				16 13			16 40	
Eccleston Park	d			14 15							15 15							16 15				
Prescot	d			14 17			14 42				15 17			15 44				16 17			16 44	
Huyton	d			14 21			14 50				15 21			15 48				16 21			16 51	
Roby	d			14 23			14 52				15 23			15 52				16 23			16 53	
Broad Green	d			14 26			14 55				15 26			15 55				16 26			16 56	
Wavertree Technology Park	d			14 29			14 58				15 29			15 58				16 29			16 59	
Edge Hill 91	d																					
Liverpool Lime Street 91	a	14 03	14 32	14 38		15 02	15 05			15 30	15 38		16 02	16 07			16 30	16 38		17 02	17 05	

A From Newcastle
B To Manchester Airport
C To Blackpool North
D To Middlesbrough
E From Nottingham
F To Chester
G from 16 September. To Blackpool North
H until 9 September. To Blackpool North
I from 16 September. To Middlesbrough
J from 16 September
K From Norwich

Manchester Airport, Manchester, Preston, Wigan and Newton-le-Willows - St Helens and Liverpool

	NT	EM	NT	AW	TP	NT	NT		NT	EM	NT	AW	TP	NT	NT	NT	EM		NT	AW	TP	NT	NT	NT
	◇	◇			◇1	◇	◇		◇	◇			◇1	◇	◇	◇	◇				◇1	◇	◇	◇
	A	B		C ✠	D ✠		E		A	F		C ✠	D ✠		E	A	G			C	D ✠		E	A
Manchester Airport 85 d	15 41								16 41							17 41								18 41
Manchester Piccadilly 10 d	16 00	16 38		16 56					17 00	17 38		17 56				18 00	18 38			18 56				19 00
Manchester Oxford Road d	16 05	16 42		16 59					17 05	17 42		17 59				18 05	18 42			18 59				19 05
Manchester Victoria d					17 24								18 24								19 24			
Eccles d																								
Patricroft d																								
Blackpool North 97 d						16 32	16 41							17 34	17 41							18 32	18 41	
Preston 8 65,82 d						16 59	17 08							18 01	18 08							18 59	19 08	
Leyland 82 d						17 05																19 05		
Euxton Balshaw Lane d						17 10								18 10								19 10		
Wigan North Western 65 a	16 33					17 19	17 23		17 33					18 18	18 23	18 33						19 19	19 23	19 33
d			16 53			17 19					17 53			18 19					18 53			19 19		
Newton-le-Willows d				17 17	17 41							18 17	18 41							19 17	19 41			
Warrington Bank Quay d																								
Earlestown 8 d				17 20								18 20								19 20				
Warrington Bank Quay a				17 26								18 27								19 29				
St Helens Junction d																								
Lea Green d																								
Rainhill d																								
Whiston d																								
Bryn d			16 59								17 59								18 59					
Garswood d			17 02			17 28					18 02			18 28					19 02			19 28		
St Helens Central a			17 09			17 35					18 09			18 35					19 09			19 35		
d			17 09			17 35					18 09			18 35					19 09			19 35		
Thatto Heath d			17 13			17 39					18 13			18 39					19 13			19 39		
Eccleston Park d			17 15								18 15								19 15					
Prescot d			17 17			17 43					18 17			18 43					19 17			19 43		
Huyton d			17 21			17 49					18 21			18 49					19 21			19 49		
Roby d			17 23			17 51					18 23			18 51					19 23			19 51		
Broad Green d			17 26			17 54					18 26			18 54					19 26			19 54		
Wavertree Technology Park d			17 29			17 57					18 29			18 57					19 29			19 57		
Edge Hill 91 d																								
Liverpool Lime Street 10 91 a		17 30	17 38		18 02	18 04				18 30	18 38		19 02	19 04			19 30		19 38		20 02	20 04		

	EM	NT	AW		TP	NT	NT	NT	NT	AW	TP	NT	NT		NT	NT	NT	AW	NT	TP	NT	NT	AW	
	◇				◇1	◇	◇	◇			◇1	◇	◇		◇		◇		◇	◇1		◇		
	G		C		D		E	A		C	D		E		A		E	C	A	D			C	
Manchester Airport 85 d								19 41							20 41				21 41					
Manchester Piccadilly 10 d	19 39		19 56					20 00		20 56					21 00			21 56	22 01				22 56	
Manchester Oxford Road d	19 43		19 59					20 05		20 59					21 05			21 59	22 04				22 59	
Manchester Victoria d					20 24						21 23									22 24				
Eccles d																								
Patricroft d																								
Blackpool North 97 d						19 32	19 41					20 32	20 41				21 41					22 05		
Preston 8 65,82 d						20 00	20 08					20 59	21 08				22 08					22 32		
Leyland 82 d						20 07						21 06										22 38		
Euxton Balshaw Lane d						20 11						21 10										22 46		
Wigan North Western 65 a						20 22	20 26	20 33				21 19	21 23		21 35		22 23		22 31			22 56		
d		19 53				20 22			20 53			21 19				21 53					22 36	22 57		
Newton-le-Willows d			20 16		20 40					21 17	21 40							22 17		22 40			23 20	
Warrington Bank Quay d																								
Earlestown 8 d			20 19							21 19								22 20					23 23	
Warrington Bank Quay a			20 30							21 27								22 26					23 29	
St Helens Junction d																								
Lea Green d					20 46						21 46									22 46				
Rainhill d																								
Whiston d																								
Bryn d		19 59							20 59							21 59						23 03		
Garswood d		20 02				20 31			21 02			21 28				22 02					22 45	23 07		
St Helens Central a		20 09				20 38			21 09			21 35				22 09					22 51	23 13		
d		20 09				20 38			21 09			21 35				22 09					22 52	23 14		
Thatto Heath d		20 13				20 42			21 13			21 39				22 13					22 55	23 17		
Eccleston Park d		20 15							21 15							22 15						23 20		
Prescot d		20 17				20 46			21 17			21 43				22 17					22 59	23 22		
Huyton d		20 21				20 52			21 21			21 50				22 21					23 03	23 26		
Roby d		20 23				20 55			21 23			21 54				22 23						23 28		
Broad Green d		20 26				20 58			21 26			21 57				22 26						23 31		
Wavertree Technology Park d		20 29				21 01			21 29			22 00				22 29						23 34		
Edge Hill 91 d																								
Liverpool Lime Street 10 91 a	20 31	20 38			21 03	21 07			21 38		22 03	22 08				22 38				23 04	23 15	23 46		

A To Blackpool North
B From Nottingham
C To Chester
D From Newcastle
E To Manchester Airport
F From Peterborough
G From Norwich

Table T090-F

Sundays

20 May to 2 December

Manchester Airport, Manchester, Preston, Wigan and Newton-le-Willows - St Helens and Liverpool

	NT	TP	AW
	◇	◇1	
	A	B	C
Manchester Airport 85 d	22 43		
Manchester Piccadilly 10 d	23 01		23 25
Manchester Oxford Road d	23 05		23 28
Manchester Victoria d		23 24	
Eccles d			
Patricroft d			
Blackpool North 97 d			
Preston 8 65,82 d			
Leyland 82 d			
Euxton Balshaw Lane d			
Wigan North Western 65 a	23 33		
d			
Newton-le-Willows d		23 40	23 45
Warrington Bank Quay d			
Earlestown 8 d			23 47
Warrington Bank Quay a			23 54
St Helens Junction d			
Lea Green d		23 46	
Rainhill d			
Whiston d			
Bryn d			
Garswood d			
St Helens Central a			
d			
Thatto Heath d			
Eccleston Park d			
Prescot d			
Huyton d			
Roby d			
Broad Green d			
Wavertree Technology Park d			
Edge Hill 91 d			
Liverpool Lime Street 10 91 a		00 03	

A To Blackpool North
B From Newcastle
C To Chester

Table T090-R

Mondays to Fridays
21 May to 7 December

Liverpool and St Helens - Newton-le-Willows, Wigan, Preston, Manchester and Manchester Airport

Miles	Miles	Miles	Miles			NT MO ◇ A	NT MO A	NT MX A	NT MX A	NT MX B	NT ◇ C	NT D	TP ◇1 E	NT ◇ F	NT G	AW H	NT ◇ I	NT ◇ C	NT	NT	NT ◇	NT ◇ J	NT
0	0	0	—	**Liverpool Lime Street**	91 d							05 10	05 20	05 24					05 46		06 14		06 15
1¾	1¾	1¾	—	Edge Hill	91 d							05 14		05 28					05 50				06 19
2½	2½	2½	—	Wavertree Technology Park	d									05 30					05 52				06 21
3½	3½	3½	—	Broad Green	d									05 33					05 55				06 24
5	5	5	—	Roby	d									05 36					05 58				06 27
5½	5½	5½	—	Huyton	d							05 20		05 38					06 01				06 30
—	7½	—	—	Prescot	d														06 05				06 34
—	8¾	—	—	Eccleston Park	d														06 07				06 36
—	9¾	—	—	Thatto Heath	d														06 10				06 39
—	11¼	—	—	**St Helens Central**	a														06 13				06 42
—	—	—	—		d														06 14				06 43
—	15	—	—	Garswood	d														06 20				06 49
—	16¼	—	—	Bryn	d														06 23				06 52
7½	—	7½	—	Whiston	d									05 42									
9	—	9	—	Rainhill	d									05 45									
10¾	—	10¾	—	Lea Green	d								05 32	05 48									
12	—	12	—	**St Helens Junction**	d							05 27		05 51									
—	—	—	—	Warrington Bank Quay	d											06 06							
14¾	—	14¾	—	Earlestown	d	00 02		00 05				05 32		05 55		06 13							
—	—	—	—	Warrington Bank Quay	a							05 39											
16¾	—	16¾	0	**Newton-le-Willows**	d	00 05		00 07					05 38	05 58		06 16							
—	20	23¼	—	**Wigan North Western**	65,82 a														06 32				07 01
—	—	—	—		d					00 04	04 16				05 48		06 17	06 23		06 42		06 56	
—	28¾	31½	—	Euxton Balshaw Lane	d		00 04		00 08														
—	31	34¾	—	Leyland	82 a		00 10		00 12	00 17							06 29						
—	35	38¾	—	**Preston**	65,82 a		00 16		00 21	00 23							06 36						
—	52½	—	—	Blackpool North	97 a		00 41			00 48							07 04						
26¾	—	—	10½	Patricroft	d	00 15		00 17						06 08									
27¾	—	—	11½	Eccles	d	00 17		00 20						06 10									
31¾	—	—	—	**Manchester Victoria**	a			00 29					05 57							07 24		07 35	
—	—	—	15¾	**Manchester Oxford Road**	a	00 27								06 20	06 32	06 34		06 52			07 07		
—	—	—	16¼	**Manchester Piccadilly**	a	00 30					04 46			06 23	06 36	06 43		06 57			07 11		
—	—	—	26	**Manchester Airport**	85 a	00 53					05 04			06 47				07 18			07 31		

		TP ◇1 E	NT F	NT	AW ◇ K	NT ◇ C	NT ◇ I	NT	NT ◇ J	NT	NT	TP ◇1 E	AW ◇ L	NT F	NT	NT M	AW ◇ H	NT ◇ I	NT ◇ C	NT	NT	NT ◇	NT G
Liverpool Lime Street	91 d	06 25	06 28	06 36				06 45		07 03	07 15	07 25		07 28	07 36					07 43	07 57	08 16	
Edge Hill	91 d		06 32					06 49		07 07	07 19			07 32						07 47	08 01		
Wavertree Technology Park	d		06 34					06 52		07 09	07 21			07 34						07 49	08 03		
Broad Green	d		06 37					06 55		07 12	07 24			07 37						07 52	08 06		
Roby	d		06 40					06 58		07 15	07 27			07 40						07 55	08 09		
Huyton	d		06 42	06 45				07 00		07 17	07 30			07 42	07 45					07 58	08 11		
Prescot	d							07 04			07 34									08 04			
Eccleston Park	d							07 06			07 36									08 06			
Thatto Heath	d							07 09			07 39									08 09			
St Helens Central	a			06 53				07 12			07 42				07 53					08 12			
	d			06 53				07 13			07 43				07 53					08 13			
Garswood	d							07 19			07 49									08 19			
Bryn	d							07 22			07 52									08 22			
Whiston	d		06 46							07 21				07 46							08 15		
Rainhill	d		06 49							07 24				07 49							08 18		
Lea Green	d		06 52							07 27				07 52							08 21		
St Helens Junction	d		06 55							07 30				07 55							08 24		
Warrington Bank Quay	d				07 10								07 39				08 09						
Earlestown	d		06 59		07 18					07 37			07 47	07 59			08 22				08 28		
Warrington Bank Quay	a									07 47													
Newton-le-Willows	d	06 43	07 02		07 21							07 42	07 50	08 02			08 27				08 31		
Wigan North Western	65,82 a			07 06				07 31			08 01				08 06					08 31			
	d			07 06		07 23	07 28		07 56						08 06	08 08		08 18	08 23				08 50
Euxton Balshaw Lane	d			07 15											08 15								
Leyland	82 a			07 19			07 39								08 19			08 32					
Preston	65,82 a			07 27			07 47								08 27			08 39					
Blackpool North	97 a			07 55			08 14								08 52			09 07					
Patricroft	d		07 12											08 12							08 41		
Eccles	d		07 14											08 14							08 43		
Manchester Victoria	a	07 00							08 36			08 01				08 51					08 55		
Manchester Oxford Road	a		07 24		07 42	07 57							08 07	08 24			08s48		08 55			09 07	09 32
Manchester Piccadilly	a		07 31		07 50	08 01							08 12	08 31			08 53		08 59			09 11	09 36
Manchester Airport	85 a		07 57			08 23								08 57					09 19			09 30	

A From Liverpool Lime Street
B From Manchester Piccadilly
C From Blackpool North
D To Ellesmere Port
E To Newcastle
F To Crewe
G To Alderley Edge
H From Chester
I From Manchester Airport
J To Leeds
K From Llandudno Junction
L From Holyhead
M To Stalybridge

Table T090-R

Mondays to Fridays
21 May to 7 December

Liverpool and St Helens - Newton-le-Willows, Wigan, Preston, Manchester and Manchester Airport

		NT	TP ◇1 A	NT ◇ B	NT ◇	NT C	NT D	AW ◇ E	NT ◇ F	NT ◇ G	NT	NT H	NT	NT	NT ◇	TP ◇1 A	NT ◇ B	NT ◇	NT C	NT D	NT ◇ F	NT ◇ G	NT
Liverpool Lime Street	91 d	08 16	08 25	08 28	08 36						08 45		09 00	09 15	09 16	09 25	09 28	09 36					09 45
Edge Hill	91 d	08 20		08 32							08 49		09 04	09 19			09 32						09 49
Wavertree Technology Park	d	08 22		08 34							08 51		09 06	09 21			09 34						09 51
Broad Green	d	08 25		08 37							08 54		09 09	09 24			09 37						09 54
Roby	d	08 28		08 40							08 57		09 12	09 27			09 40						09 57
Huyton	d	08 31		08 42	08 45						09 00		09 14	09 30			09 42	09 45					10 00
Prescot	d	08 35									09 04			09 34									10 04
Eccleston Park	d	08 37									09 06			09 36									10 06
Thatto Heath	d	08 40									09 09			09 39									10 09
St Helens Central	a	08 43			08 53						09 12			09 42				09 53					10 12
	d	08 44			08 53						09 13			09 43				09 53					10 13
Garswood	d	08 50									09 19			09 49									10 19
Bryn	d	08 53									09 22			09 52									10 22
Whiston	d			08 46									09 18				09 46						
Rainhill	d			08 49									09 21				09 49						
Lea Green	d			08 52									09 25				09 52						
St Helens Junction	d			08 55									09 28				09 55						
Warrington Bank Quay	d						09 09	09 19												10 12			
Earlestown	d			08 59			09a16	09 28					09 38				09 59			10a22			
Warrington Bank Quay	a												09 48										
Newton-le-Willows	d		08 42	09 02				09 30								09 43	10 02						
Wigan North Western	65,82 a	09 02			09 06						09 31			10 01				10 06					10 31
	d				09 06	09 08			09 20	09 23		09 50						10 06	10 08		10 18	10 23	
Euxton Balshaw Lane	d				09 15													10 15					
Leyland	82 a				09 19				09 31									10 19			10 30		
Preston	65,82 a				09 27				09 40									10 27			10 41		
Blackpool North	97 a				09 51				10 13									10 55			11 12		
Patricroft	d			09 12													10 12						
Eccles	d			09 14													10 14						
Manchester Victoria	a		09 01			09 51										10 01			10 52				
Manchester Oxford Road	a			09 24				09 48		09 52		10 32			10 07		10 24					10 52	
Manchester Piccadilly	a			09 31				09 53		09 57		10 36			10 11		10 31					10 57	
Manchester Airport	85 a			09 57				10 19		10 19					10 30		10 57					11 18	

		AW ◇ I	NT	NT H	NT	NT ◇	TP ◇1 A	NT ◇ B	NT ◇	NT C	NT D	AW ◇ E	NT ◇ F	NT ◇ G	NT	NT H	NT	NT	NT ◇	TP ◇1 A	NT ◇ B	NT ◇
Liverpool Lime Street	91 d		10 00		10 15	10 16	10 25	10 28	10 36						10 45		11 00	11 15	11 16	11 25	11 28	11 36
Edge Hill	91 d		10 04		10 19			10 32							10 49		11 04	11 19			11 32	
Wavertree Technology Park	d		10 06		10 21			10 34							10 51		11 06	11 21			11 34	
Broad Green	d		10 09		10 24			10 37							10 54		11 09	11 24			11 37	
Roby	d		10 12		10 27			10 40							10 57		11 12	11 27			11 40	
Huyton	d		10 14		10 30			10 42	10 45						11 00		11 14	11 30			11 42	11 45
Prescot	d				10 34										11 04			11 34				
Eccleston Park	d				10 36										11 06			11 36				
Thatto Heath	d				10 39										11 09			11 39				
St Helens Central	a				10 42				10 53						11 12			11 42				11 53
	d				10 43				10 53						11 13			11 43				11 53
Garswood	d				10 49										11 19			11 49				
Bryn	d				10 52										11 22			11 52				
Whiston	d		10 18					10 46									11 18				11 46	
Rainhill	d		10 21					10 49									11 21				11 49	
Lea Green	d		10 24					10 52									11 24				11 52	
St Helens Junction	d		10 27					10 55									11 27				11 55	
Warrington Bank Quay	d	10 19									11 12	11 19										
Earlestown	d	10 28	10 37					10 59			11a19	11 28					11 33				11 59	
Warrington Bank Quay	a		10 45														11 44					
Newton-le-Willows	d	10 30					10 43	11 02				11 30								11 42	12 02	
Wigan North Western	65,82 a				11 01				11 06						11 31			12 01				12 06
	d			10 50					11 06	11 08			11 21	11 23		11 50						12 06
Euxton Balshaw Lane	d								11 15													12 15
Leyland	82 a								11 19				11 32									12 19
Preston	65,82 a								11 28				11 42									12 27
Blackpool North	97 a								11 53				12 11									12 52
Patricroft	d							11 12													12 12	
Eccles	d							11 14													12 14	
Manchester Victoria	a						11 01			11 51										12 01		
Manchester Oxford Road	a	10 48		11 32		11 07		11 24				11 48		11 55		12 32			12 07		12 24	
Manchester Piccadilly	a	10 53		11 36		11 11		11 31				11 53		11 59		12 36			12 11		12 31	
Manchester Airport	85 a	11 19				11 30		11 56				12 20		12 20					12 30		12 57	

A To Newcastle
B To Crewe
C To Stalybridge
D To Liverpool Lime Street
E From Llandudno
F From Manchester Airport
G From Blackpool North
H To Alderley Edge
I From Llandudno Junction

Liverpool and St Helens - Newton-le-Willows, Wigan, Preston, Manchester and Manchester Airport

	NT A	NT B	NT ◇ C	NT ◇ D	NT	AW ◇ E	NT	NT F	NT	NT ◇	TP ◇■ G	NT ◇ H	NT ◇	NT A	NT B	NT ◇ C	NT ◇ D	NT	AW ◇ E	NT	NT F	NT
Liverpool Lime Street 91 d					11 45		12 00		12 14	12 16	12 25	12 28	12 37					12 45		13 00		13 15
Edge Hill 91 d					11 49		12 04		12 18			12 32						12 49		13 04		13 19
Wavertree Technology Park d					11 51		12 06		12 20			12 34						12 51		13 06		13 21
Broad Green d					11 54		12 09		12 24			12 37						12 54		13 09		13 24
Roby d					11 57		12 12		12 27			12 40						12 57		13 12		13 27
Huyton d					12 00		12 14		12 30			12 42	12 46					13 00		13 14		13 30
Prescot d					12 04				12 34									13 04				13 34
Eccleston Park d					12 06				12 36									13 06				13 36
Thatto Heath d					12 09				12 39									13 09				13 39
St Helens Central a					12 12				12 42				12 54					13 12				13 42
d					12 13				12 43				12 54					13 13				13 43
Garswood d					12 19				12 49									13 19				13 49
Bryn d					12 22				12 52									13 22				13 52
Whiston d							12 18					12 46								13 18		
Rainhill d							12 21					12 49								13 21		
Lea Green d							12 24					12 52								13 24		
St Helens Junction d							12 27					12 55								13 27		
Warrington Bank Quay d		12 12				12 20									13 11				13 19			
Earlestown d		12a19				12 28	12 33					12 59			13a18				13 28	13 37		
Warrington Bank Quay a							12 45													13 48		
Newton-le-Willows d						12 30					12 43	13 02							13 30			
Wigan North Western 65,82 a					12 31				13 01				13 07					13 31				14 01
d	12 08		12 19	12 23				12 50					13 07	13 08		13 19	13 24				13 50	
Euxton Balshaw Lane d													13 16									
Leyland 82 a			12 30										13 20			13 31						
Preston 65,82 a			12 35										13 28			13 42						
Blackpool North 97 a			13 10										13 53			14 13						
Patricroft d												13 12										
Eccles d												13 14										
Manchester Victoria a	12 51										13 01			13 51								
Manchester Oxford Road a				12 52		12 48		13 32		13 07		13 24					13 53		13 48		14 32	
Manchester Piccadilly a				12 57		12 53		13 36		13 11		13 31					13 58		13 53		14 36	
Manchester Airport 85 a				13 19		13 20				13 30		13 57					14 18		14 19			

	NT ◇	TP ◇■ G	NT ◇ H	NT ◇	NT A	NT B	NT ◇ C	NT ◇ D	NT	AW ◇ I	NT	NT F	NT	NT ◇	TP ◇■ G	NT ◇ H	NT ◇	NT A	NT B	AW ◇ J	NT ◇ C
Liverpool Lime Street 91 d	13 16	13 25	13 28	13 37					13 45		14 00		14 15	14 16	14 25	14 28	14 37				
Edge Hill 91 d			13 32						13 49		14 04		14 19			14 32					
Wavertree Technology Park d			13 34						13 51		14 06		14 21			14 34					
Broad Green d			13 37						13 54		14 09		14 24			14 37					
Roby d			13 40						13 57		14 12		14 27			14 40					
Huyton d			13 42	13 46					14 00		14 14		14 30			14 42	14 46				
Prescot d									14 04				14 34								
Eccleston Park d									14 06				14 36								
Thatto Heath d									14 09				14 39								
St Helens Central a				13 53					14 12				14 42				14 53				
d				13 54					14 13				14 43				14 54				
Garswood d									14 19				14 49								
Bryn d									14 22				14 52								
Whiston d			13 46								14 18					14 46					
Rainhill d			13 49								14 21					14 49					
Lea Green d			13 52								14 24					14 52					
St Helens Junction d			13 55								14 27					14 55					
Warrington Bank Quay d						14 11				14 19									15 12	15 19	
Earlestown d			13 59			14a18				14 28	14 36					14 59			15a19	15 30	
Warrington Bank Quay a											14 44										
Newton-le-Willows d		13 43	14 02							14 31					14 43	15 02					
Wigan North Western 65,82 a				14 06					14 31				15 01				15 06				
d				14 07	14 08		14 19	14 23				14 50					15 07	15 08			15 19
Euxton Balshaw Lane d				14 16													15 16				
Leyland 82 a				14 20			14 31										15 20				15 31
Preston 65,82 a				14 28			14 41										15 27				15 41
Blackpool North 97 a				14 53			15 13										15 53				16 11
Patricroft d			14 12													15 12					
Eccles d			14 14													15 14					
Manchester Victoria a		14 01			14 51										15 01			15 51			
Manchester Oxford Road a	14 07		14 24					14 53		14 48		15 32		15 07		15 24					
Manchester Piccadilly a	14 11		14 31					14 57		14 53		15 36		15 11		15 31				15 54	
Manchester Airport 85 a	14 30		14 57					15 18		15 19				15 30		15 57					

A To Stalybridge
B To Liverpool Lime Street
C From Manchester Airport
D From Blackpool North
E From Llandudno
F To Alderley Edge
G To Newcastle
H To Crewe
I From Llandudno Junction
J From Holyhead

Liverpool and St Helens - Newton-le-Willows, Wigan, Preston, Manchester and Manchester Airport

	NT ◇ A	NT	NT B	NT	NT	NT ◇	TP ◇■ C	NT ◇ D	NT	NT E	NT F	NT ◇ G	AW ◇ H	NT ◇ A	NT	NT B	NT	NT	NT ◇	TP ◇■ C	AW ◇ H	NT ◇ D
Liverpool Lime Street 91 d		14 45		15 00	15 15	15 16	15 25	15 28	15 37						15 45		16 00	16 15	16 16	16 25		16 28
Edge Hill 91 d		14 49		15 04	15 19			15 32							15 49		16 04	16 19				16 32
Wavertree Technology Park d		14 51		15 06	15 21			15 34							15 51		16 06	16 21				16 34
Broad Green d		14 54		15 09	15 24			15 37							15 54		16 09	16 24				16 37
Roby d		14 57		15 12	15 27			15 40							15 57		16 12	16 27				16 40
Huyton d		15 00		15 14	15 30			15 42	15 46						16 00		16 14	16 30				16 42
Prescot d		15 04			15 34										16 04			16 34				
Eccleston Park d		15 06			15 36										16 06			16 36				
Thatto Heath d		15 09			15 39										16 09			16 39				
St Helens Central a		15 12			15 42				15 54						16 12			16 42				
d		15 13			15 43				15 54						16 13			16 43				
Garswood d		15 19			15 49										16 19			16 49				
Bryn d		15 22			15 52										16 22			16 52				
Whiston d				15 18				15 46									16 18					16 46
Rainhill d				15 21				15 49									16 21					16 49
Lea Green d				15 24				15 52									16 25					16 52
St Helens Junction d				15 27				15 55									16 28					16 55
Warrington Bank Quay d											16 12		16 20								16 49	
Earlestown d				15 38				15 59			16a19		16 28				16a33				16 57	17 00
Warrington Bank Quay a				15 46																		
Newton-le-Willows d							15 43	16 02					16 30							16 43	17 00	17 03
Wigan North Western 65,82 a		15 31			16 01				16 07						16 31			17 01				
d	15 23		15 50						16 07	16 08		16 19		16 23		16 46						
Euxton Balshaw Lane d									16 16													
Leyland 82 a									16 20			16 31										
Preston 65,82 a									16 28			16 41										
Blackpool North 97 a									16 56			17 09										
Patricroft d								16 12														17 13
Eccles d								16 14														17 15
Manchester Victoria a							16 01			16 51										17 01		
Manchester Oxford Road a	15 53		16 32			16 07		16 24					16 48	16 53		17 32			17 07		17 20	17 25
Manchester Piccadilly a	15 58		16 36			16 11		16 31					16 54	16 58		17 37			17 11		17 25	17 33
Manchester Airport 85 a	16 19					16 30		16 57						17 18					17 32			17 58

	NT ◇	NT E	NT ◇ G	NT ◇ A	NT	NT B	NT	NT	NT	NT ◇	NT I	TP ◇■ C	NT J	NT ◇	AW ■ H	NT F	NT ◇ G	NT ◇ A	NT	NT	NT B	NT
Liverpool Lime Street 91 d	16 36				16 45		17 00	17 09	17 13	17 15	17 17	17 26	←	17 36					17 48	17 59		18 13
Edge Hill 91 d					16 49		17 04		17 17		17 21		17 21						17 52	18 03		18 17
Wavertree Technology Park d					16 51		17 06		17 19		→		17 24						17 54	18 05		18 19
Broad Green d					16 54		17 09		17 22				17 27						17 57	18 08		18 22
Roby d					16 57		17 12		17 25				17 30						18 00	18 11		18 25
Huyton d	16 45				17 00		17 14	17 18	17 27				17 35	17 45					18 03	18 13		18 28
Prescot d					17 04			17 23	17 31					17 49					18 07			18 32
Eccleston Park d					17 06			17 26	17 34					17 51					18 09			18 34
Thatto Heath d					17 09			17 29	17 36					17 54					18 12			18 37
St Helens Central a	16 53				17 12			17 32	17 40					17 57					18 15			18 40
d	16 53				17 13			17 33	17 40					17 58					18 16			18 41
Garswood d					17 19			17 40	17 47					18 04					18 22			18 47
Bryn d					17 22			17 44	17 50					18 07					18 25			18 50
Whiston d							17 18						17 38							18 17		
Rainhill d							17 21						17 41							18 20		
Lea Green d							17 24						17 45							18 23		
St Helens Junction d							17 27						17 48							18 26		
Warrington Bank Quay d															17 48	18 12						
Earlestown d							17 34						17 52		17 56	18a19				18 30		
Warrington Bank Quay a							17 44															
Newton-le-Willows d												17 42	17 54		17 59					18 33		
Wigan North Western 65,82 a	17 06				17 31			17 52	17 59					18 14					18 34	18 49		18 59
d	17 06	17 07	17 19	17 23		17 49		17 52						18 14			18 20	18 23			18 50	
Euxton Balshaw Lane d	17 15							18 02						18 23								
Leyland 82 a	17 19							18 06						18 27			18 32					
Preston 65,82 a	17 27		17 38					18 14						18 35			18 41					
Blackpool North 97 a	17 50		18 07											19 00			19 10					
Patricroft d													18 04									
Eccles d													18 07									
Manchester Victoria a		17 51										18 00	18 21									
Manchester Oxford Road a				17 52		18 32				18 07					18 19			18 52			19 32	
Manchester Piccadilly a				17 57		18 36				18 11					18 27			18 57			19 36	
Manchester Airport 85 a				18 18						18 30								19 18				

A From Blackpool North
B To Alderley Edge
C To Newcastle
D To Crewe
E To Stalybridge
F To Liverpool Lime Street
G From Manchester Airport
H From Llandudno
I To Manchester Victoria
J From Liverpool Lime Street

Table T090-R

Mondays to Fridays
21 May to 7 December

Liverpool and St Helens - Newton-le-Willows, Wigan, Preston, Manchester and Manchester Airport

	NT	NT	TP	NT	NT	AW	NT	NT	NT	NT	NT	AW	NT	NT	NT	NT	TP	NT	NT	NT	NT
	◇	◇ A	◇1 B	◇ C	◇	◇ D ✠	E	F	◇ G	◇ H		◇ I		◇	J		◇1 B	K	L	◇	E
Liverpool Lime Street 91 d	18 16	18 17	18 26	←	18 35						18 47		19 00	19 15		19 15	19 25		19 28	19 36	
Edge Hill 91 d		18 21		18 21							18 51		19 04			19 19			19 32		
Wavertree Technology Park d		→		18 23							18 53		19 06			19 21			19 34		
Broad Green d				18 26							18 56		19 09			19 24			19 37		
Roby d				18 29							18 59		19 12			19 27			19 40		
Huyton d				18 35	18 45						19 02		19 14			19 30			19 42	19 45	
Prescot d											19 06					19 34					
Eccleston Park d											19 08					19 36					
Thatto Heath d											19 11					19 39					
St Helens Central a					18 53						19 14					19 42				19 53	
d					18 53						19 15					19 43				19 53	
Garswood d											19 21					19 49					
Bryn d											19 24					19 52					
Whiston d				18 39									19 18						19 46		
Rainhill d				18 42									19 21						19 49		
Lea Green d				18 45									19 24						19 52		
St Helens Junction d				18 48									19 27						19 55		
Warrington Bank Quay d						18 45		19 11				19 19						19 44			
Earlestown d				18 52		18 56		19a18				19 28	19 34					19 54	19 59		
Warrington Bank Quay a													19 46								
Newton-le-Willows d			18 44	18 55		18 59						19 31					19 43	19 57	20 02		
Wigan North Western 65,82 a					19 06						19 33					20 01				20 06	
d					19 07		19 08		19 20	19 23					19 50					20 06	20 08
Euxton Balshaw Lane d					19 17															20 15	
Leyland 82 a					19 21				19 32											20 19	
Preston 65,82 a					19 29				19 43											20 28	
Blackpool North 97 a					19 54				20 13											20 53	
Patricroft d				19 05															20 12		
Eccles d				19 07															20 14		
Manchester Victoria a			19 01	19 21			19 51										20 01	20 17			20 51
Manchester Oxford Road a	19 07					19 19				19 53		19 49		20 07	20 31				20 24		
Manchester Piccadilly a	19 11					19 23				19 57		19 53		20 11	20 36				20 31		
Manchester Airport 85 a	19 30									20 17		20 19		20 29					20 57		

	NT	NT	NT	NT	NT	NT	AW	NT	TP	NT	NT	NT	AW	NT	NT	NT	NT	TP	NT	NT	AW	NT
	F	◇ G	◇ H				◇ D	◇	◇1 B	L	◇	E	I	◇ H			◇	◇1 B	L	◇ G	◇ D	E
Liverpool Lime Street 91 d				19 45		20 15		20 19	20 24	20 28	20 36				20 45		21 15	21 24	21 29			
Edge Hill 91 d				19 49		20 19				20 32					20 49		21 19		21 33			
Wavertree Technology Park d				19 51		20 21				20 34					20 51		21 21		21 35			
Broad Green d				19 54		20 24				20 37					20 54		21 24		21 38			
Roby d				19 57		20 27				20 40					20 57		21 27		21 41			
Huyton d				20 00		20 30				20 42	20 45				21 00		21 30		21 43			
Prescot d				20 04		20 34									21 04		21 34					
Eccleston Park d				20 06		20 36									21 06		21 36					
Thatto Heath d				20 09		20 39									21 09		21 39					
St Helens Central a				20 12		20 42					20 53				21 12		21 42					
d				20 13		20 43					20 53				21 13		21 43					
Garswood d				20 19		20 49									21 19		21 49					
Bryn d				20 22		20 52									21 22		21 52					
Whiston d										20 46									21 47			
Rainhill d										20 49									21 50			
Lea Green d									20 36	20 52								21 36	21 53			
St Helens Junction d										20 55									21 56			
Warrington Bank Quay d	20 12						20 19						21 20								22 18	
Earlestown d	20a19						20 28			20 59			21 27						22 00		22 26	
Warrington Bank Quay a																						
Newton-le-Willows d							20 31		20 43	21 02			21 30					21 44	22 03		22 29	
Wigan North Western 65,82 a				20 31		21 01					21 06				21 31		21 59					
d		20 19	20 25		20 41						21 06	21 15		21 23		21 46	21 59			22 17		22 50
Euxton Balshaw Lane d											21 15						22 08					
Leyland 82 a		20 31									21 20						22 12					
Preston 65,82 a		20 41									21 27						22 20			22 39		
Blackpool North 97 a		21 13									21 54						22 45			23 08		
Patricroft d										21 12									22 16			
Eccles d										21 14									22 19			
Manchester Victoria a					21 24				21 01			22 06				22 28		22 01				23 27
Manchester Oxford Road a			20 53				20 49	21 07		21 24			21 49	21 53					22 27		22 49	
Manchester Piccadilly a			20 57				20 53	21 11		21 31			21 53	21 57					22 31		22 55	
Manchester Airport 85 a			21 18				21 20	21 31		21 57				22 17					22 54			

A To Manchester Victoria
B To Newcastle
C From Liverpool Lime Street
D From Llandudno
E To Stalybridge
F To Liverpool Lime Street
G From Manchester Airport
H From Blackpool North
I From Chester
J To Alderley Edge
K From Ellesmere Port
L To Wilmslow

Table T090-R

Mondays to Fridays
21 May to 7 December

Liverpool and St Helens - Newton-le-Willows, Wigan, Preston, Manchester and Manchester Airport

	NT	NT	TP	NT	NT	NT FX	NT	NT
	A	◇	◇1 B	◇		C		
Liverpool Lime Street 91 d		22 15	22 24	22 29	22 30		23 15	23 31
Edge Hill 91 d		22 19			22 34		23 19	23 35
Wavertree Technology Park d		22 21			22 36		23 21	23 37
Broad Green d		22 24			22 39		23 24	23 40
Roby d		22 27			22 42		23 27	23 43
Huyton d		22 30			22 45		23 30	23 45
Prescot d		22 34					23 34	
Eccleston Park d		22 36					23 36	
Thatto Heath d		22 39					23 39	
St Helens Central a		22 42					23 42	
d		22 44					23 43	
Garswood d		22 51					23 49	
Bryn d		22 54					23 52	
Whiston d					22 48			23 49
Rainhill d					22 52			23 52
Lea Green d			22 36		22 55			23 55
St Helens Junction d					22 59			23 58
Warrington Bank Quay d								
Earlestown d					23 03			00 05
Warrington Bank Quay a								
Newton-le-Willows d			22 42		23 07			00 07
Wigan North Western 65,82 a		23 01					23 59	
d	22 57	23 01				23 05	23 59	
Euxton Balshaw Lane d		23 10					00 08	
Leyland 82 a		23 14				23 21	00 12	
Preston 65,82 a	23 14	23 22				23 27	00 21	
Blackpool North 97 a		23 47				23 53		
Patricroft d					23 17			00 17
Eccles d					23 20			00 20
Manchester Victoria a			23 00					00 29
Manchester Oxford Road a				23 16	23 28			
Manchester Piccadilly a				23 20	23 32			
Manchester Airport 85 a				23 36	23 55			

Saturdays
26 May to 8 December

	NT	NT	NT	TP	NT	NT	AW	NT	NT	NT	NT	NT	NT	NT	TP	AW	NT	NT	NT	NT	NT	NT
	D	D	E	◇1 F	◇ G	H	I	◇ J	◇ K			◇	◇ L		◇1 F ✠	◇ M	G		◇ K	◇ J		◇ L
Liverpool Lime Street 91 d			05 10	05 20	05 24					05 46		06 12		06 15	06 25		06 28	06 36			06 45	
Edge Hill 91 d			05 14		05 28					05 50				06 19			06 32				06 49	
Wavertree Technology Park d					05 30					05 52				06 21			06 34				06 52	
Broad Green d					05 33					05 55				06 24			06 37				06 55	
Roby d					05 36					05 58				06 27			06 40				06 58	
Huyton d			05 20		05 38					06 01				06 30			06 42	06 45			07 00	
Prescot d										06 05				06 34							07 04	
Eccleston Park d										06 07				06 36							07 06	
Thatto Heath d										06 10				06 39							07 09	
St Helens Central a										06 13				06 42				06 53			07 12	
d										06 14				06 43				06 53			07 13	
Garswood d										06 20				06 49							07 19	
Bryn d										06 23				06 52							07 22	
Whiston d					05 42												06 46					
Rainhill d					05 45												06 49					
Lea Green d				05 32	05 48												06 52					
St Helens Junction d			05 27		05 51												06 55					
Warrington Bank Quay d							06 06									06 40						
Earlestown d	00 05		05 32		05 55		06 15									06 47	06 59					
Warrington Bank Quay a			05 39																			
Newton-le-Willows d	00 07			05 38	05 58		06 18								06 43	06 50	07 02					
Wigan North Western 65,82 a										06 32				07 01				07 06			07 31	
d						05 48		06 17	06 23		06 42		06 56					07 06	07 23	07 28		07 56
Euxton Balshaw Lane d		00 08																07 15				
Leyland 82 a		00 12						06 29										07 19		07 39		
Preston 65,82 a		00 21						06 36										07 27		07 47		
Blackpool North 97 a								07 04										07 55		08 14		
Patricroft d	00 17				06 08												07 12					
Eccles d	00 20				06 10												07 14					
Manchester Victoria a	00 29			05 57							07 24		07 35		07 00							08 36
Manchester Oxford Road a					06 20	06 32	06 40		06 52			07 03				07 11	07 24		07 57			
Manchester Piccadilly a					06 23	06 36	06 44		06 57			07 07				07 19	07 31		08 01			
Manchester Airport 85 a					06 47				07 18			07 31					07 57		08 23			

A From Manchester Airport to Barrow-in-Furness
B To York
C From Manchester Piccadilly
D From Liverpool Lime Street
E To Ellesmere Port
F To Newcastle
G To Crewe
H To Alderley Edge
I From Chester
J From Manchester Airport
K From Blackpool North
L To Leeds
M From Holyhead

Liverpool and St Helens - Newton-le-Willows, Wigan, Preston, Manchester and Manchester Airport

	NT	NT	TP ◇1 A	AW B	NT C	NT	NT D	NT E	NT ◇ F	AW ◇ G	NT ◇ H	NT	NT	NT ◇	NT I	NT	TP ◇1 A	NT ◇ C	NT ◇	NT D	NT E	AW ◇ G
Liverpool Lime Street 91 d	07 03	07 15	07 25		07 28	07 36						07 43	08 01	08 16		08 16	08 25	08 28	08 36			
Edge Hill 91 d	07 07	07 19			07 32							07 47	08 05			08 20		08 32				
Wavertree Technology Park d	07 09	07 21			07 34							07 49	08 07			08 22		08 34				
Broad Green d	07 12	07 24			07 37							07 52	08 10			08 25		08 37				
Roby d	07 15	07 27			07 40							07 55	08 13			08 28		08 40				
Huyton d	07 17	07 30			07 42	07 45						07 58	08 16			08 31		08 42	08 45			
Prescot d		07 34										08 04				08 35						
Eccleston Park d		07 36										08 06				08 37						
Thatto Heath d		07 39										08 09				08 40						
St Helens Central a		07 42				07 53						08 12				08 43			08 53			
d		07 43				07 53						08 13				08 44			08 53			
Garswood d		07 49										08 19				08 50						
Bryn d		07 52										08 22				08 53						
Whiston d	07 21				07 46								08 19					08 46				
Rainhill d	07 24				07 49								08 22					08 49				
Lea Green d	07 27				07 52								08 26					08 52				
St Helens Junction d	07 30				07 55								08 29					08 55				
Warrington Bank Quay d				07 39				08 14		08 19											09 09	09 19
Earlestown d	07 37			07 46	07 59			08a22		08 29			08 38					08 59			09a16	09 28
Warrington Bank Quay a	07 47												08 47									
Newton-le-Willows d			07 42	07 49	08 02					08 32							08 42	09 02				09 30
Wigan North Western 65,82 a		08 01				08 06						08 31				09 02			09 06			
d						08 06	08 08		08 18		08 23				08 50				09 06	09 08		
Euxton Balshaw Lane d						08 15													09 15			
Leyland 82 a						08 19			08 32										09 19			
Preston 65,82 a						08 27			08 39										09 27			
Blackpool North 97 a						08 52			09 07										09 51			
Patricroft d					08 12													09 12				
Eccles d					08 14													09 14				
Manchester Victoria a			08 01				08 51										09 01			09 51		
Manchester Oxford Road a				08 07	08 24					08 49	08 55			09 07	09 32			09 24				09 48
Manchester Piccadilly a				08 16	08 33					08 53	08 59			09 11	09 36			09 31				09 53
Manchester Airport 85 a					08 58					09 19	09 19			09 30				09 57				10 19

	NT ◇ F	NT ◇ H	NT	NT I	NT	NT	NT ◇	TP ◇1 A	NT C	NT ◇	NT D	NT E	NT ◇ F	NT ◇ H	NT	AW ◇ G	NT	NT I	NT	NT ◇	TP ◇1 A
Liverpool Lime Street 91 d			08 45		09 00	09 15	09 16	09 25	09 28	09 36					09 45		10 00		10 15	10 16	10 25
Edge Hill 91 d			08 49		09 04	09 19			09 32						09 49		10 04		10 19		
Wavertree Technology Park d			08 51		09 06	09 21			09 34						09 51		10 06		10 21		
Broad Green d			08 54		09 09	09 24			09 37						09 54		10 09		10 24		
Roby d			08 57		09 12	09 27			09 40						09 57		10 12		10 27		
Huyton d			09 00		09 14	09 30			09 42	09 45					10 00		10 14		10 30		
Prescot d			09 04			09 34									10 04				10 34		
Eccleston Park d			09 06			09 36									10 06				10 36		
Thatto Heath d			09 09			09 39									10 09				10 39		
St Helens Central a			09 12			09 42				09 53					10 12				10 42		
d			09 13			09 43				09 53					10 13				10 43		
Garswood d			09 19			09 49									10 19				10 49		
Bryn d			09 22			09 52									10 22				10 52		
Whiston d					09 18				09 46								10 18				
Rainhill d					09 21				09 49								10 21				
Lea Green d					09 25				09 52								10 24				
St Helens Junction d					09 28				09 55								10 27				
Warrington Bank Quay d												10 12				10 19					
Earlestown d					09 38				09 59			10a22				10 28	10 37				
Warrington Bank Quay a					09 48												10 45				
Newton-le-Willows d								09 43	10 02							10 30					10 43
Wigan North Western 65,82 a			09 31			10 01				10 06					10 31				11 01		
d	09 20	09 23		09 50						10 06	10 08		10 18	10 23				10 50			
Euxton Balshaw Lane d										10 15											
Leyland 82 a	09 31									10 19			10 30								
Preston 65,82 a	09 40									10 27			10 41								
Blackpool North 97 a	10 13									10 55			11 12								
Patricroft d									10 12												
Eccles d									10 14												
Manchester Victoria a								10 01			10 52										11 01
Manchester Oxford Road a		09 52		10 32			10 07		10 24					10 52		10 48		11 32		11 07	
Manchester Piccadilly a		09 57		10 36			10 11		10 31					10 57		10 53		11 36		11 11	
Manchester Airport 85 a		10 19					10 30		10 57					11 18		11 19				11 30	

A To Newcastle
B From Shrewsbury
C To Crewe
D To Stalybridge
E To Liverpool Lime Street
F From Manchester Airport
G From Llandudno
H From Blackpool North
I To Alderley Edge

Table T090-R
Saturdays
26 May to 8 December

Liverpool and St Helens - Newton-le-Willows, Wigan, Preston, Manchester and Manchester Airport

	NT ◇ A	NT ◇	NT B	NT C	AW D	NT ◇ E	NT ◇ F	NT	NT G	NT	NT	NT ◇	TP ◇1 H	NT ◇ A	NT ◇	NT B	NT C	NT ◇ E	AW ◇ D	NT ◇ F	NT	NT G
Liverpool Lime Street 91 d	10 28	10 36						10 45		11 00	11 15	11 16	11 25	11 28	11 36						11 45	
Edge Hill 91 d	10 32							10 49		11 04	11 19			11 32							11 49	
Wavertree Technology Park d	10 34							10 51		11 06	11 21			11 34							11 51	
Broad Green d	10 37							10 54		11 09	11 24			11 37							11 54	
Roby d	10 40							10 57		11 12	11 27			11 40							11 57	
Huyton d	10 42	10 45						11 00		11 14	11 30			11 42	11 45						12 00	
Prescot d								11 04			11 34										12 04	
Eccleston Park d								11 06			11 36										12 06	
Thatto Heath d								11 09			11 39										12 09	
St Helens Central a		10 53						11 12			11 42				11 53						12 12	
d		10 53						11 13			11 43				11 53						12 13	
Garswood d								11 19			11 49										12 19	
Bryn d								11 22			11 52										12 22	
Whiston d	10 46									11 18				11 46								
Rainhill d	10 49									11 21				11 49								
Lea Green d	10 52									11 24				11 52								
St Helens Junction d	10 55									11 27				11 55								
Warrington Bank Quay d				11 12	11 19												12 12		12 20			
Earlestown d	10 59			11a19	11 28					11 33				11 59			12a19		12 28			
Warrington Bank Quay a										11 44												
Newton-le-Willows d	11 02				11 30								11 42	12 02					12 30			
Wigan North Western 65,82 a		11 06						11 31			12 01				12 06						12 31	
d		11 06	11 08			11 21	11 22		11 50						12 06	12 08		12 19		12 19		12 50
Euxton Balshaw Lane d		11 15													12 15							
Leyland 82 a		11 19				11 32									12 19			12 30				
Preston 65,82 a		11 28				11 42									12 27			12 35				
Blackpool North 97 a		11 53				12 11									12 52			13 10				
Patricroft d	11 12													12 12								
Eccles d	11 14													12 14								
Manchester Victoria a			11 51										12 00			12 51						
Manchester Oxford Road a	11 24				11 49		11 55		12 32			12 07		12 24					12 48	12 52		13 32
Manchester Piccadilly a	11 31				11 54		11 59		12 36			12 11		12 31					12 53	12 57		13 36
Manchester Airport 85 a	11 56				12 19		12 19					12 30		12 57					13 19	13 19		

	NT	NT	NT ◇	TP ◇1 H	NT A	NT ◇	NT B	NT C	AW ◇ D	NT ◇ E	NT ◇ F	NT	NT G	NT	NT	NT ◇	TP ◇1 H	NT ◇ A	NT B	NT ◇	NT C
Liverpool Lime Street 91 d	12 00	12 14	12 16	12 25	12 28	12 37						12 45		13 00	13 15	13 16	13 25	13 28		13 37	
Edge Hill 91 d	12 04	12 18			12 32							12 49		13 04	13 19			13 32			
Wavertree Technology Park d	12 06	12 20			12 34							12 51		13 06	13 21			13 34			
Broad Green d	12 09	12 24			12 37							12 54		13 09	13 24			13 37			
Roby d	12 12	12 27			12 40							12 57		13 12	13 27			13 40			
Huyton d	12 14	12 30			12 42	12 46						13 00		13 14	13 30			13 42		13 51	
Prescot d		12 34										13 04			13 34						
Eccleston Park d		12 36										13 06			13 36						
Thatto Heath d		12 39										13 09			13 39						
St Helens Central a		12 42				12 54						13 12			13 42					13 58	
d		12 43				12 54						13 13			13 43					13 59	
Garswood d		12 49										13 19			13 49						
Bryn d		12 52										13 22			13 52						
Whiston d	12 18				12 46									13 18				13 46			
Rainhill d	12 21				12 49									13 21				13 49			
Lea Green d	12 24				12 52									13 24				13 52			
St Helens Junction d	12 27				12 55									13 27				13 55			
Warrington Bank Quay d								13 11	13 19												14 11
Earlestown d	12 33				12 59			13a18	13 28					13 37				13 59			14a18
Warrington Bank Quay a	12 45													13 48							
Newton-le-Willows d				12 43	13 02				13 30								13 43	14 02			
Wigan North Western 65,82 a		13 01				13 07						13 31			14 01					14 11	
d						13 07	13 08			13 19	13 24		13 50						14 08	14 12	
Euxton Balshaw Lane d						13 16														14 21	
Leyland 82 a						13 20				13 31										14 27	
Preston 65,82 a						13 28				13 42										14 35	
Blackpool North 97 a						13 53				14 13										15 00	
Patricroft d					13 12													14 12			
Eccles d					13 14													14 14			
Manchester Victoria a				13 01			13 51										14 01		14 51		
Manchester Oxford Road a			13 07		13 24				13 48		13 53		14 32			14 07		14 24			
Manchester Piccadilly a			13 11		13 31				13 53		13 58		14 36			14 11		14 31			
Manchester Airport 85 a			13 30		13 57				14 19		14 19					14 30		15 03			

A To Crewe
B To Stalybridge
C To Liverpool Lime Street
D From Llandudno
E From Manchester Airport
F From Blackpool North
G To Alderley Edge
H To Newcastle

Table T090-R

Saturdays
26 May to 8 December

Liverpool and St Helens - Newton-le-Willows, Wigan, Preston, Manchester and Manchester Airport

		NT ◇ A	AW ◇ B	NT ◇ C	NT	NT D	NT	NT	NT ◇	TP ◇[1] E	NT ◇ F	NT	NT G	NT H	NT ◇ A	AW ◇ I	NT ◇ C	NT	NT D	NT	NT	NT ◇	TP ◇[1] E
Liverpool Lime Street [10] 91	d				13 45		14 00	14 15	14 16	14 25	14 28	14 37						14 45		15 00	15 15	15 16	15 25
Edge Hill 91	d				13 49		14 04	14 19			14 32							14 49		15 04	15 19		
Wavertree Technology Park	d				13 51		14 06	14 21			14 34							14 51		15 06	15 21		
Broad Green	d				13 54		14 09	14 24			14 37							14 54		15 09	15 24		
Roby	d				13 57		14 12	14 27			14 40							14 57		15 12	15 27		
Huyton	d				14 00		14 14	14 30			14 42	14 46						15 00		15 14	15 30		
Prescot	d				14 04			14 34										15 04			15 34		
Eccleston Park	d				14 06			14 36										15 06			15 36		
Thatto Heath	d				14 09			14 39										15 09			15 39		
St Helens Central	a				14 12			14 42				14 53						15 12			15 42		
	d				14 13			14 43				14 54						15 13			15 43		
Garswood	d				14 19			14 49										15 19			15 49		
Bryn	d				14 22			14 52										15 22			15 52		
Whiston	d						14 18				14 46									15 18			
Rainhill	d						14 21				14 49									15 21			
Lea Green	d						14 24				14 52									15 24			
St Helens Junction	d						14 27				14 55									15 27			
Warrington Bank Quay	d		14 20											15 12		15 21							
Earlestown [8]	d		14 28				14 40				14 59			15a19		15 28				15 36			
Warrington Bank Quay	a						14 48													15 44			
Newton-le-Willows	d		14 31							14 43	15 02					15 31							15 44
Wigan North Western 65,82	a				14 31			15 01				15 06						15 31			16 01		
	d	14 19		14 24		14 50						15 07	15 08		15 19		15 23		15 50				
Euxton Balshaw Lane	d											15 16											
Leyland 82	a	14 31										15 20			15 31								
Preston [8] 65,82	a	14 41										15 28			15 41								
Blackpool North 97	a	15 13										15 53			16 11								
Patricroft	d										15 12												
Eccles	d										15 14												
Manchester Victoria	a									15 01			15 51										16 01
Manchester Oxford Road	a		14 49	14 53		15 32			15 07		15 24					15 48	15 53		16 32			16 07	
Manchester Piccadilly [10]	a		14 53	14 57		15 36			15 11		15 31					15 53	15 58		16 36			16 11	
Manchester Airport 85	a		15 19	15 19					15 30		15 57					16 19	16 19					16 30	

		NT ◇ F	NT	NT G	NT H	NT ◇ A	NT ◇ C	NT	AW ◇ B	NT	NT D	NT	NT ◇	TP ◇[1] E	NT ◇ F	NT ◇	NT G	NT H	NT ◇ A	NT ◇ C	NT	AW ◇ B	NT
Liverpool Lime Street [10] 91	d	15 28	15 37					15 45		16 00		16 15	16 16	16 25	16 28	16 36					16 45		17 00
Edge Hill 91	d	15 32						15 49		16 04		16 19			16 32						16 49		17 04
Wavertree Technology Park	d	15 34						15 51		16 06		16 21			16 34						16 51		17 06
Broad Green	d	15 37						15 54		16 09		16 24			16 37						16 54		17 09
Roby	d	15 40						15 57		16 12		16 27			16 40						16 57		17 12
Huyton	d	15 42	15 46					16 00		16 14		16 30			16 42	16 45					17 00		17 14
Prescot	d							16 04				16 34									17 04		
Eccleston Park	d							16 06				16 36									17 06		
Thatto Heath	d							16 09				16 39									17 09		
St Helens Central	a		15 54					16 12				16 42				16 53					17 12		
	d		15 54					16 13				16 43				16 53					17 13		
Garswood	d							16 19				16 49									17 19		
Bryn	d							16 22				16 52									17 22		
Whiston	d	15 46								16 18					16 46								17 18
Rainhill	d	15 49								16 21					16 49								17 21
Lea Green	d	15 52								16 25					16 52								17 24
St Helens Junction	d	15 55								16 28					16 55								17 27
Warrington Bank Quay	d				16 12				16 20									17 11				17 19	
Earlestown [8]	d	15 59			16a19				16 29	16 38					17 00			17a19				17 28	17 34
Warrington Bank Quay	a									16 50													17 44
Newton-le-Willows	d	16 02							16 31					16 43	17 03							17 30	
Wigan North Western 65,82	a		16 07					16 31				17 01				17 06					17 31		
	d		16 07	16 08		16 19	16 23				16 50					17 06	17 07		17 19	17 23			
Euxton Balshaw Lane	d		16 16													17 15							
Leyland 82	a		16 20			16 31										17 19							
Preston [8] 65,82	a		16 28			16 41										17 27			17 38				
Blackpool North 97	a		16 56			17 09										17 50			18 07				
Patricroft	d	16 12													17 13								
Eccles	d	16 14													17 15								
Manchester Victoria	a			16 51										17 01			17 51						
Manchester Oxford Road	a	16 24					16 53		16 49		17 32		17 07		17 25					17 52		17 48	
Manchester Piccadilly [10]	a	16 31					16 58		16 53		17 37		17 11		17 33					17 57		17 53	
Manchester Airport 85	a	16 57					17 18		17 19				17 32		17 58					18 18		18 19	

A From Manchester Airport
B From Llandudno
C From Blackpool North
D To Alderley Edge
E To Newcastle
F To Crewe
G To Stalybridge
H To Liverpool Lime Street
I From Bangor (Gwynedd)

Table T090-R

Saturdays
26 May to 8 December

Liverpool and St Helens - Newton-le-Willows, Wigan, Preston, Manchester and Manchester Airport

		NT A	NT	NT	NT ◇	NT B	TP ◇[1] C	NT D	NT ◇	NT E	AW ◇ F	NT ◇ G	NT ◇ H	NT	NT	NT A	NT	NT ◇	NT ◇ B	TP ◇[1] C	NT ◇ D	NT ◇
Liverpool Lime Street [10] 91	d		17 09	17 13	17 15	17 17	17 26	←	17 36					17 48	17 59		18 13	18 16	18 17	18 26	←	18 35
Edge Hill 91	d			17 17		17 21		17 21						17 52	18 03		18 17		18 21		18 21	
Wavertree Technology Park	d			17 19		→		17 24						17 54	18 05		18 19		→		18 23	
Broad Green	d			17 22				17 27						17 57	18 08		18 22				18 26	
Roby	d			17 25				17 30						18 00	18 11		18 25				18 29	
Huyton	d		17 18	17 27				17 35	17 45					18 03	18 13		18 28				18 35	18 45
Prescot	d		17 23	17 31					17 49					18 07			18 32					
Eccleston Park	d		17 26	17 34					17 51					18 09			18 34					
Thatto Heath	d		17 29	17 36					17 54					18 12			18 37					
St Helens Central	a		17 32	17 40					17 57					18 15			18 40					18 53
	d		17 33	17 40					17 58					18 16			18 41					18 53
Garswood	d		17 40	17 47					18 04					18 22			18 47					
Bryn	d		17 44	17 50					18 07					18 25			18 50					
Whiston	d							17 38							18 17						18 39	
Rainhill	d							17 41							18 20						18 42	
Lea Green	d							17 45							18 23						18 45	
St Helens Junction	d							17 48							18 26						18 48	
Warrington Bank Quay	d									18 12	18 19											
Earlestown [8]	d							17 52		18a19	18 26				18 30						18 52	
Warrington Bank Quay	a																					
Newton-le-Willows	d						17 42	17 54			18 29				18 33					18 43	18 55	
Wigan North Western 65,82	a		17 52	17 59					18 14					18 34	18 49		18 59					19 06
	d	17 49	17 52						18 14			18 20	18 23			18 50						19 07
Euxton Balshaw Lane	d		18 02						18 23													19 17
Leyland 82	a		18 06						18 27			18 32										19 21
Preston [8] 65,82	a		18 14						18 35			18 41										19 29
Blackpool North 97	a								19 00			19 10										19 54
Patricroft	d							18 04													19 05	
Eccles	d							18 07													19 07	
Manchester Victoria	a						18 00	18 21												19 02	19 21	
Manchester Oxford Road	a	18 32			18 07						18 49		18 52			19 32		19 07				
Manchester Piccadilly [10]	a	18 36			18 11						18 53		18 57			19 36		19 11				
Manchester Airport 85	a				18 30								19 18					19 30				

		NT I	NT E	NT ◇ G	NT ◇ H	NT	AW ◇ F	NT	NT ◇	NT A	NT	TP ◇[1] C	NT J	NT K	NT ◇	NT I	NT E	AW ◇ F	NT ◇ G	NT ◇ H	NT	NT	NT
Liverpool Lime Street [10] 91	d					18 47		19 00	19 15		19 15	19 25		19 28	19 36						19 45		20 15
Edge Hill 91	d					18 51		19 04			19 19			19 32							19 49		20 19
Wavertree Technology Park	d					18 53		19 06			19 21			19 34							19 51		20 21
Broad Green	d					18 56		19 09			19 24			19 37							19 54		20 24
Roby	d					18 59		19 12			19 27			19 40							19 57		20 27
Huyton	d					19 02		19 14			19 30			19 42	19 45						20 00		20 30
Prescot	d					19 06					19 34										20 04		20 34
Eccleston Park	d					19 08					19 36										20 06		20 36
Thatto Heath	d					19 11					19 39										20 09		20 39
St Helens Central	a					19 14					19 42				19 53						20 12		20 42
	d					19 15					19 43				19 53						20 13		20 43
Garswood	d					19 21					19 49										20 19		20 49
Bryn	d					19 24					19 52										20 22		20 52
Whiston	d							19 18						19 46									
Rainhill	d							19 21						19 49									
Lea Green	d							19 24						19 52									
St Helens Junction	d							19 27						19 55									
Warrington Bank Quay	d		19 10				19 20						19 44				20 11	20 19					
Earlestown [8]	d		19a19				19 28	19 34					19 54	19 59			20a19	20 26					
Warrington Bank Quay	a							19 46															
Newton-le-Willows	d						19 30					19 43	19 57	20 02				20 29					
Wigan North Western 65,82	a					19 33					20 01				20 06						20 31		21 01
	d	19 08		19 20	19 23					19 50					20 06	20 08			20 19	20 22		20 41	
Euxton Balshaw Lane	d														20 15								
Leyland 82	a			19 32											20 19				20 31				
Preston [8] 65,82	a			19 43											20 28				20 41				
Blackpool North 97	a			20 13											20 53				21 13				
Patricroft	d													20 12									
Eccles	d													20 14									
Manchester Victoria	a	19 51										20 01	20 17			20 51						21 24	
Manchester Oxford Road	a				19 53		19 48		20 07	20 31				20 24				20 49		20 53			
Manchester Piccadilly [10]	a				19 57		19 53		20 11	20 36				20 31				20 56		20 57			
Manchester Airport 85	a				20 17		20 19		20 29					20 57						21 18			

A To Alderley Edge
B To Manchester Victoria
C To Newcastle
D From Liverpool Lime Street
E To Liverpool Lime Street
F From Llandudno
G From Manchester Airport
H From Blackpool North
I To Stalybridge
J From Ellesmere Port
K To Wilmslow

Table T090-R

Saturdays
26 May to 8 December

Liverpool and St Helens - Newton-le-Willows, Wigan, Preston, Manchester and Manchester Airport

		NT	TP	NT	NT	NT	AW	NT	NT	NT	NT	NT	TP	NT	NT	NT	AW	NT	NT	TP	NT	NT
		◇	◇1		◇		◇	◇	◇			◇	◇1	◇		◇			◇	◇1	◇	
			A	B		C	D	E	F		C		G		B	E	H	C		G		
Liverpool Lime Street	91 d	20 19	20 24	20 28	20 36					20 45		21 15	21 24	21 29	21 29				22 15	22 24	22 29	22 30
Edge Hill	91 d			20 32						20 49		21 19			21 33				22 19			22 34
Wavertree Technology Park	d			20 34						20 51		21 21			21 35				22 21			22 36
Broad Green	d			20 37						20 54		21 24			21 38				22 24			22 39
Roby	d			20 40						20 57		21 27			21 41				22 27			22 42
Huyton	d			20 42	20 45					21 00		21 30			21 43				22 30			22 45
Prescot	d									21 04		21 34							22 34			
Eccleston Park	d									21 06		21 36							22 36			
Thatto Heath	d									21 09		21 39							22 39			
St Helens Central	a				20 53					21 12		21 42							22 42			
	d				20 53					21 13		21 43							22 44			
Garswood	d									21 19		21 49							22 51			
Bryn	d									21 22		21 52							22 54			
Whiston	d			20 46											21 47							22 48
Rainhill	d			20 49											21 50							22 52
Lea Green	d		20 36	20 52									21 36		21 53					22 36		22 55
St Helens Junction	d			20 55											21 56							22 59
Warrington Bank Quay	d						21 20										22 20					
Earlestown 8	d			20 59			21 27								22 00		22 28					23 03
Warrington Bank Quay	a																					
Newton-le-Willows	d		20 43	21 02			21 30						21 42		22 03		22 31			22 42		23 07
Wigan North Western	65,82 a				21 06					21 31		21 59							23 01			
	d				21 06	21 15		21 23	21 23		21 46	21 59				22 17		22 50	23 01			
Euxton Balshaw Lane	d				21 15							22 08							23 10			
Leyland	82 a				21 20			21 34				22 12							23 14			
Preston 8	65,82 a				21 27			21 43				22 20				22 39			23 22			
Blackpool North	97 a				21 54			22 10				22 45				23 08			23 47			
Patricroft	d			21 12											22 16							23 17
Eccles	d			21 14											22 19							23 20
Manchester Victoria	a		21 01			22 04					22 29		22 00					23 27		23 00		
Manchester Oxford Road	a	21 07		21 24			21 49		21 53					22 17	22 27		22 50				23 16	23 28
Manchester Piccadilly 10	a	21 11		21 31			21 56		21 57					22 21	22 31		22 55				23 22	23 32
Manchester Airport	85 a	21 31		21 57					22 17					22 39	22 53							23 55

		NT	NT	NT	AW
					H
Liverpool Lime Street	91 d	23 00	23 15	23 21	
Edge Hill	91 d		23 19	23 25	
Wavertree Technology Park	d		23 22	23 28	
Broad Green	d		23 25	23 31	
Roby	d		23 28	23 34	
Huyton	d	23 09	23 30	23 36	
Prescot	d		23 34		
Eccleston Park	d		23 37		
Thatto Heath	d		23 39		
St Helens Central	a	23 17	23 43		
	d	23 17	23 43		
Garswood	d		23 50		
Bryn	d		23 53		
Whiston	d			23 39	
Rainhill	d			23 42	
Lea Green	d			23 46	
St Helens Junction	d			23 49	
Warrington Bank Quay	d				23 50
Earlestown 8	d			23 53	23 58
Warrington Bank Quay	a				
Newton-le-Willows	d			23 56	00 02
Wigan North Western	65,82 a	23 31	23 59		
	d		23 59		
Euxton Balshaw Lane	d		00 09		
Leyland	82 a		00 13		
Preston 8	65,82 a		00 21		
Blackpool North	97 a				
Patricroft	d			00 06	
Eccles	d			00 08	
Manchester Victoria	a			00 17	
Manchester Oxford Road	a				
Manchester Piccadilly 10	a				00 22
Manchester Airport	85 a				

A To Newcastle
B To Wilmslow
C To Stalybridge
D From Llandudno
E From Manchester Airport
F From Blackpool North
G To York
H From Chester

Table T090-R

Sundays
20 May to 2 December

Liverpool and St Helens - Newton-le-Willows, Wigan, Preston, Manchester and Manchester Airport

		AW	NT	NT	TP	NT	NT	NT	NT	AW	NT	NT	NT	NT	NT	NT	NT	TP	NT	AW	AW	NT	NT
					◇1			◇	◇		◇	◇			◇	◇	◇	◇1			◇	◇	◇
		A	B	B	C	D	E			F	G	H	E			I	J	C	D	K	L	M	N
Liverpool Lime Street	91 d				08 12	08 15		08 21	08 32					08 45	09 10	09 14	09 14	09 23	09 30				
Edge Hill	91 d																						
Wavertree Technology Park	d					08 22			08 38					08 51	09 18				09 37				
Broad Green	d					08 25			08 41					08 54	09 21				09 40				
Roby	d					08 28			08 44					08 57	09 24				09 43				
Huyton	d					08 30			08 46					08 59	09 26				09 45				
Prescot	d								08 50					09 03	09 30								
Eccleston Park	d													09 05									
Thatto Heath	d								08 53					09 08	09 33								
St Helens Central	a								08 57					09 11	09 37								
	d								08 57					09 12	09 37								
Garswood	d								09 04					09 18	09 44								
Bryn	d													09 21									
Whiston	d					08 34													09 48				
Rainhill	d					08 37													09 51				
Lea Green	d				08 28	08 40													09 55				
St Helens Junction	d					08 44													09 58				
Warrington Bank Quay	d									09 08										10 10	10 10		
Earlestown 8	d					08 48				09 16									10 02	10 17	10 17		
Warrington Bank Quay	a																						
Newton-le-Willows	d	00 02			08 34	08 51				09 19								09 39	10 04	10 20	10 20		
Wigan North Western	65,82 a								09 11					09 30	09 51								
	d						08 21		09 12		09 22	09 24	09 27		09 52							10 24	10 24
Euxton Balshaw Lane	d			00 09					09 21						10 01								
Leyland	82 a			00 13					09 27						10 07								
Preston 8	65,82 a			00 21					09 33		09 40				10 13								
Blackpool North	97 a								09 58		10 05				10 38								
Patricroft	d		00 06			09 01													10 14				
Eccles	d		00 08			09 03													10 17				
Manchester Victoria	a		00 17		08 55		09 01						10 05					09 57					
Manchester Oxford Road	a					09 12		09 07		09 36		09 57				10 06	10 06		10 26	10 38	10 38	10 58	11 00
Manchester Piccadilly 10	a	00 22				09 15		09 11		09 45		10 00				10 10	10 11		10 30	10 46	10 47	11 01	
Manchester Airport	85 a					09 39		09 31				10 19				10 32	10 35		11 02			11 20	

		NT	NT	NT	NT	NT	TP	NT	AW	NT	NT	NT	NT	NT	NT	NT	TP	NT	AW	NT	NT	NT	NT
			◇		◇	◇	◇1			◇	◇			◇	◇	◇	◇1			◇			◇
		E	G				C	D	F	N	M	E		G		I	C	D	F	H	E		G
Liverpool Lime Street	91 d			09 45	10 13	10 16	10 24	10 30					10 45		11 15	11 17	11 25	11 28				11 45	
Edge Hill	91 d																						
Wavertree Technology Park	d			09 51		10 22		10 36					10 51		11 20			11 33				11 50	
Broad Green	d			09 54		10 25		10 39					10 54		11 23			11 36				11 53	
Roby	d			09 57		10 28		10 42					10 57		11 26			11 39				11 56	
Huyton	d			09 59		10 30		10 44					10 59		11 29			11 41				11 59	
Prescot	d			10 03		10 35							11 03		11 33							12 03	
Eccleston Park	d			10 05									11 05									12 05	
Thatto Heath	d			10 08		10 38							11 08		11 36							12 08	
St Helens Central	a			10 11		10 42							11 11		11 40							12 11	
	d			10 12		10 42							11 12		11 40							12 12	
Garswood	d			10 18		10 49							11 18		11 47							12 18	
Bryn	d			10 21									11 21									12 21	
Whiston	d							10 47										11 45					
Rainhill	d							10 50										11 48					
Lea Green	d							10 54										11 51					
St Helens Junction	d							10 57										11 54					
Warrington Bank Quay	d								11 03										12 03				
Earlestown 8	d							11 01	11 12									11 58	12 10				
Warrington Bank Quay	a																						
Newton-le-Willows	d						10 43	11 03	11 15								11 43	12 01	12 13				
Wigan North Western	65,82 a			10 30		10 59							11 30		11 54							12 32	
	d	10 27	10 29			10 59				11 24	11 24	11 27		11 33	11 55					12 24	12 27		12 33
Euxton Balshaw Lane	d					11 08									12 04								
Leyland	82 a					11 14									12 10								
Preston 8	65,82 a		10 47			11 20								11 50	12 16								12 51
Blackpool North	97 a		11 12			11 46								12 16	12 41								13 16
Patricroft	d							11 13										12 12					
Eccles	d							11 16										12 14					
Manchester Victoria	a	11 05					11 00					12 05					12 00				13 04		
Manchester Oxford Road	a				11 06			11 25	11 34	11 58	11 58					12 06		12 24	12 33	12 58			
Manchester Piccadilly 10	a				11 10			11 29	11 41	12 01	12 01					12 09		12 27	12 41	13 01			
Manchester Airport	85 a				11 31			12 03		12 18	12 19					12 26		12 51		13 17			

A not 20 May. From Chester
B not 20 May. From Liverpool Lime Street
C To Newcastle
D To Wilmslow
E To Stalybridge
F From Chester
G From Manchester Airport
H From Blackpool North
I until 9 September
J from 16 September
K from 16 September. From Chester
L until 9 September. From Holyhead
M until 9 September. From Blackpool North
N from 16 September. From Blackpool North

Liverpool and St Helens - Newton-le-Willows, Wigan, Preston, Manchester and Manchester Airport

	NT ◇	NT ◇	TP ◇1 A ⌶	NT B	AW C ⌶	NT ◇ D	NT E	NT	NT ◇ F	NT ◇	NT ◇	TP ◇1 A ⌶	NT B	AW C	NT ◇ D	NT E	NT	NT ◇ F	NT ◇	NT	TP ◇1 A ⌶
Liverpool Lime Street 91 d	12 14	12 15	12 24	12 28				12 45		13 14	13 15	13 25	13 29				13 45		14 14	14 15	14 25
Edge Hill 91 d																					
Wavertree Technology Park d		12 20		12 33				12 50			13 20		13 34				13 50			14 20	
Broad Green d		12 23		12 36				12 53			13 23		13 37				13 53			14 23	
Roby d		12 26		12 39				12 56			13 26		13 40				13 56			14 26	
Huyton d		12 29		12 41				12 59			13 29		13 42				13 59			14 29	
Prescot d		12 33						13 03			13 33						14 03			14 33	
Eccleston Park d								13 05									14 05				
Thatto Heath d		12 36						13 08			13 36						14 08			14 36	
St Helens Central a		12 40						13 11			13 40						14 11			14 40	
d		12 40						13 12			13 40						14 12			14 40	
Garswood d		12 47						13 18			13 47						14 18			14 47	
Bryn d								13 21									14 21				
Whiston d				12 45									13 46								
Rainhill d				12 48									13 49								
Lea Green d				12 51									13 52								
St Helens Junction d				12 54									13 55								
Warrington Bank Quay d					13 03									14 03							
Earlestown d				12 58	13 11								13 59	14 11							
Warrington Bank Quay a																					
Newton-le-Willows d			12 43	13 01	13 14							13 43	14 02	14 14							14 43
Wigan North Western 65,82 a		12 54						13 30			13 54						14 30			14 54	
d		12 55				13 23	13 26		13 33		13 55				14 24	14 27		14 33		14 55	
Euxton Balshaw Lane d		13 04									14 04									15 04	
Leyland 82 a		13 10									14 10									15 10	
Preston 65,82 a		13 16							13 51		14 16							14 51		15 16	
Blackpool North 97 a		13 41							14 16		14 41							15 16		15 41	
Patricroft d				13 11									14 12								
Eccles d				13 13									14 14								
Manchester Victoria a			13 00				14 05					14 00				15 05					15 01
Manchester Oxford Road a	13 06			13 23	13 31	13 58				14 06			14 24	14 33	14 56				15 06		
Manchester Piccadilly a	13 10			13 31	13 40	14 01				14 10			14 31	14 41	15 00				15 11		
Manchester Airport 85 a	13 30			13 55		14 17				14 30			14 55		15 17				15 30		

	NT B	AW C	NT ◇ D	NT E	NT	NT ◇ F	NT ◇	NT ◇	TP ◇1 A ⌶	NT B	AW C ⌶	NT ◇ D	NT E	NT	NT ◇ F	NT ◇	NT ◇	TP ◇1 A ⌶	NT B	AW ■ G ⌶	NT ◇ D	NT
Liverpool Lime Street 91 d	14 28				14 45		15 14	15 15	15 25	15 28				15 45		16 15	16 19	16 25	16 28			16 45
Edge Hill 91 d																						
Wavertree Technology Park d	14 33				14 50			15 20		15 33				15 50		16 20			16 33			16 50
Broad Green d	14 36				14 53			15 23		15 36				15 53		16 23			16 36			16 53
Roby d	14 39				14 56			15 26		15 39				15 56		16 26			16 39			16 56
Huyton d	14 41				14 59			15 29		15 41				15 59		16 29			16 41			16 59
Prescot d					15 03			15 33						16 03		16 33						17 03
Eccleston Park d					15 05									16 05								17 05
Thatto Heath d					15 08			15 36						16 08		16 36						17 08
St Helens Central a					15 11			15 40						16 11		16 40						17 11
d					15 12			15 40						16 12		16 40						17 12
Garswood d					15 18			15 47						16 18		16 47						17 18
Bryn d					15 21									16 21								17 21
Whiston d	14 45									15 45									16 45			
Rainhill d	14 48									15 48									16 48			
Lea Green d	14 51									15 51									16 51			
St Helens Junction d	14 54									15 54									16 54			
Warrington Bank Quay d		15 03									16 03									17 03		
Earlestown d	14 58	15 11								15 58	16 11								16 58	17 11		
Warrington Bank Quay a																						
Newton-le-Willows d	15 01	15 14							15 43	16 01	16 14							16 43	17 01	17 14		
Wigan North Western 65,82 a					15 30			15 54						16 30		16 54						17 30
d			15 25	15 27		15 33		15 55				16 24	16 27		16 33	16 55					17 24	
Euxton Balshaw Lane d								16 04								17 04						
Leyland 82 a								16 10								17 10						
Preston 65,82 a						15 51		16 16							16 50	17 16						
Blackpool North 97 a						16 16		16 41							17 16	17 41						
Patricroft d	15 11									16 11									17 11			
Eccles d	15 13									16 13									17 13			
Manchester Victoria a				16 05					16 00				17 05					17 00				
Manchester Oxford Road a	15 23	15 31	15 58				16 06			16 23	16 31	16 57					17 06		17 23	17 31	17 58	
Manchester Piccadilly a	15 31	15 40	16 01				16 10			16 31	16 40	17 01					17 10		17 31	17 40	18 01	
Manchester Airport 85 a	15 55		16 17				16 30			16 55		17 17					17 30		17 55		18 17	

A To Newcastle
B To Wilmslow
C From Chester
D From Blackpool North
E To Stalybridge
F From Manchester Airport
G From Holyhead

Liverpool and St Helens - Newton-le-Willows, Wigan, Preston, Manchester and Manchester Airport

	NT ◇ A	NT ◇	NT ◇	TP ◇1 B ⌶	NT C	AW D	AW ◇ E ⌶	NT ◇ F	NT G	NT	NT ◇ A	NT ◇	NT ◇	TP ◇1 B	NT C	AW H	NT ◇ F	NT G	NT	NT ◇ A	NT ◇
Liverpool Lime Street 91 d		17 14	17 15	17 25	17 29					17 45		18 14	18 15	18 25	18 28				18 45		19 14
Edge Hill 91 d																					
Wavertree Technology Park d			17 20		17 34					17 50			18 20		18 33				18 50		
Broad Green d			17 23		17 37					17 53			18 23		18 36				18 53		
Roby d			17 26		17 40					17 56			18 26		18 39				18 56		
Huyton d			17 29		17 42					17 59			18 29		18 41				18 59		
Prescot d			17 33							18 03			18 33						19 03		
Eccleston Park d										18 05									19 05		
Thatto Heath d			17 36							18 08			18 36						19 08		
St Helens Central a			17 40							18 11			18 40						19 11		
d			17 40							18 12			18 40						19 12		
Garswood d			17 47							18 18			18 47						19 18		
Bryn d										18 21									19 21		
Whiston d					17 46										18 45						
Rainhill d					17 49										18 48						
Lea Green d					17 52										18 51						
St Helens Junction d					17 55										18 54						
Warrington Bank Quay d						18 03	18 04									19 03					
Earlestown d					17 59	18 11	18 11								18 58	19 11					
Warrington Bank Quay a																					
Newton-le-Willows d				17 43	18 02	18 14	18 14							18 43	19 01	19 14					
Wigan North Western 65,82 a			17 54							18 30			18 54						19 30		
d	17 33		17 55					18 24	18 27		18 33		18 55				19 24	19 27		19 33	
Euxton Balshaw Lane d			18 04										19 04								
Leyland 82 a			18 10										19 10								
Preston 65,82 a	17 51		18 16								18 51		19 16							19 51	
Blackpool North 97 a	18 16		18 41								19 16		19 41							20 17	
Patricroft d					18 12										19 11						
Eccles d					18 14										19 13						
Manchester Victoria a				18 00					19 04					19 00				20 05			
Manchester Oxford Road a		18 06			18 24	18 31	18 31	18 58				19 06			19 23	19 31	19 58				20 06
Manchester Piccadilly a		18 10			18 31	18 40	18 40	19 01				19 10			19 31	19 40	20 01				20 10
Manchester Airport 85 a		18 30			18 55			19 17				19 30			19 55		20 17				20 30

	NT ◇	TP ◇1 B	NT C	AW H	NT ◇ F	NT G	NT	NT ◇ A	NT ◇	NT ◇	TP ◇1 B	NT C	AW H	NT ◇ F	NT G	NT	NT ◇ A	TP ◇1	NT	NT ◇	TP ◇1 B	NT C
Liverpool Lime Street 91 d	19 15	19 25	19 28				19 45		20 09	20 15	20 24	20 28				20 45		20 52	21 15	21 19	21 24	21 28
Edge Hill 91 d																						
Wavertree Technology Park d	19 20		19 33				19 50			20 20		20 33				20 50			21 20			21 33
Broad Green d	19 23		19 36				19 53			20 23		20 36				20 53			21 23			21 36
Roby d	19 26		19 39				19 56			20 26		20 39				20 56			21 26			21 39
Huyton d	19 29		19 41				19 59			20 29		20 41				20 59			21 29			21 41
Prescot d	19 33						20 03			20 33						21 03			21 33			
Eccleston Park d							20 05									21 05						
Thatto Heath d	19 36						20 08			20 36						21 08			21 36			
St Helens Central a	19 40						20 11			20 40						21 11			21 40			
d	19 40						20 12			20 40						21 12			21 40			
Garswood d	19 47						20 18			20 47						21 18			21 47			
Bryn d							20 21									21 21						
Whiston d			19 45									20 45										21 45
Rainhill d			19 48									20 48										21 48
Lea Green d			19 51								20 36	20 51									21 36	21 51
St Helens Junction d			19 54									20 54										21 54
Warrington Bank Quay d				20 03									21 03									
Earlestown d			19 58	20 11								20 58	21 10									21 58
Warrington Bank Quay a																						
Newton-le-Willows d		19 43	20 01	20 14							20 43	21 01	21 13								21 42	22 01
Wigan North Western 65,82 a	19 54						20 32			20 54						21 30			21 54			
d	19 55				20 26	20 27		20 33		20 55				21 24	21 27		21 35		21 55			
Euxton Balshaw Lane d	20 04									21 04									22 04			
Leyland 82 a	20 10									21 10									22 10			
Preston 65,82 a	20 16							20 51		21 16							21 54		22 16			
Blackpool North 97 a	20 41							21 16		21 41							22 19		22 41			
Patricroft d			20 11									21 11										22 11
Eccles d			20 13									21 13										22 13
Manchester Victoria a		20 00				21 05					21 00				22 05			21 27			22 00	
Manchester Oxford Road a			20 23	20 31	20 58				21 06			21 23	21 32	21 58						22 10		22 23
Manchester Piccadilly a			20 31	20 40	21 01				21 11			21 31	21 40	22 01						22 13		22 32
Manchester Airport 85 a			21 01		21 17				21 30			21 55		22 16						22 34		22 55

A From Manchester Airport
B To Newcastle
C To Wilmslow
D from 16 September. From Chester
E until 9 September. From Holyhead
F From Blackpool North
G To Stalybridge
H From Chester

Table T090-R

Sundays
20 May to 2 December

Liverpool and St Helens - Newton-le-Willows, Wigan, Preston, Manchester and Manchester Airport

	AW	NT	NT	NT	NT	NT	NT	TP	AW	NT	NT	NT	NT	NT
		◇			◇	◇	◇	◇1				◇		◇
	A	B	C		D			E	A	F		D		
Liverpool Lime Street 10 91 d				21 45		22 14	22 15	22 20		22 28			23 15	23 30
Edge Hill 91 d														
Wavertree Technology Park d				21 50			22 20			22 33			23 20	23 35
Broad Green d				21 53			22 23			22 36			23 23	23 38
Roby d				21 56			22 26			22 39			23 26	23 41
Huyton d				21 59			22 29			22 41			23 29	23 43
Prescot d				22 03			22 33						23 33	
Eccleston Park d				22 05										
Thatto Heath d				22 08			22 36						23 36	
St Helens Central a				22 11			22 40						23 40	
d				22 12			22 40						23 40	
Garswood d				22 18			22 47						23 47	
Bryn d				22 21										
Whiston d										22 45				23 47
Rainhill d										22 48				23 50
Lea Green d								22 34		22 51				23 53
St Helens Junction d										22 54				23 56
Warrington Bank Quay d	22 11								22 33					
Earlestown 8 d	22 18								22 41	22 58				00 02
Warrington Bank Quay a														
Newton-le-Willows d	22 21							22 40	22 44	23 01				00 05
Wigan North Western 65,82 a				22 30			22 54						23 54	
d		22 24	22 27		22 31		22 55				23 21	23 33	23 55	
Euxton Balshaw Lane d							23 04						00 04	
Leyland 82 a							23 10						00 10	
Preston 8 65,82 a					22 49		23 16					23 51	00 16	
Blackpool North 97 a					23 14		23 41					00 16	00 41	
Patricroft d										23 11				00 15
Eccles d										23 13				00 17
Manchester Victoria a			23 04					22 58			23 59			
Manchester Oxford Road a	22 39	22 58				23 07			23 01	23 23				00 27
Manchester Piccadilly 10 a	22 48	23 01				23 13			23 10	23 31				00 30
Manchester Airport 85 a		23 17				23 32				23 54				00 53

A From Chester
B From Blackpool North
C To Stalybridge
D From Manchester Airport
E To York
F To Wilmslow

Table T091-F

Mondays to Fridays
21 May to 7 December

Crewe and Runcorn - Liverpool

Miles		VT	NT	LM	NT	LM	NT	LM	NT	LM		NT	NT	VT	NT	LM	EM	LM	NT	NT		LM	VT	NT
		MO	MX																					
		◇1		1		1	◇	1		1			◇	◇1		1	◇	1		◇		1	◇1	
				A																				
		☕												⊠									⊠	
—	London Euston ⊖65 d													05 27									07 07	
—	Birmingham New Street 12 65 d									06 01						06 36		07 01				07 36		
0	Crewe 10 65 d			05 40		06 03		06 33		06 59				07 28		07 33		07 59				08 32	08 43	
7½	Winsford d					06 12		06 42		07 06						07 42		08 07						
11¾	Hartford d					06 17		06 47		07 11						07 47		08 12				08 42		
14½	Acton Bridge d					06 21		06 51		07 15						07 51		08 16						
22½	Runcorn a			05 59		06 29		06 59		07 24				07 45		07 59		08 24				08 52	09 00	
—	d	00 04		06 01		06 30		07 00		07 25				07 45		08 00		08 25				08 52	09 00	
30	Liverpool South Parkway 7 a			06 08		06 38		07 08		07 33						08 09		08 32				09 01		
—	d		00 33	06 09	06 23	06 39	06 51	07 09	07 23	07 33		07 38	07 49		08 06	08 09	08 20	08 33	08 46	08 51		09 01		09 06
31	West Allerton d				06 26				07 26			07 41			08 10				08 49					09 10
31¾	Mossley Hill d				06 29				07 28			07 44			08 12				08 52					09 13
34¼	Edge Hill 90 d				06 35				07 34			07 50			08 20				08 57					
35½	Liverpool Lime Street 10 90 a	00 28	00 46	06 21	06 39	06 51	07 04	07 21	07 38	07 46		07 54	08 01	08 03	08 24	08 21	08 34	08 44	09 02	09 09		09 11	09 20	09 24

	EM	LM	NT	NT	LM	VT		NT	EM	LM	NT	NT	LM	VT	VT	NT		EM	LM	NT	NT	LM	VT	NT
														MO	MX									
	◇	1		◇	1	◇1			◇	1		◇	1	◇1	◇1			◇	1		◇	1	◇1	
						⊠								⊠	⊠								⊠	
London Euston ⊖65 d						08 07								09 07	09 07								10 07	
Birmingham New Street 12 65 d		08 01			08 36					09 01			09 36						10 01			10 36		
Crewe 10 65 d		08 57			09 32					09 57			10 33	10 43	10 43				10 57			11 33	11 43	
Winsford d		09 07								10 07									11 07					
Hartford d		09 12			09 42					10 12									11 12					
Acton Bridge d										10 16														
Runcorn a		09 21			09 52	10 01				10 24			10 51	11 01	11 03				11 21			11 51	12 00	
d		09 22			09 52	10 02				10 25			10 51	11 01	11 03				11 22			11 51	12 00	
Liverpool South Parkway 7 a		09 30			10 01					10 32			11 00						11 30			12 00		
d	09 15	09 31	09 39	09 50	10 01			10 07	10 15	10 33	10 39	10 50	11 00			11 07		11 15	11 31	11 39	11 50	12 00		12 07
West Allerton d			09 42					10 11			10 42					11 11				11 42				12 11
Mossley Hill d			09 45					10 13			10 45					11 14				11 45				12 13
Edge Hill 90 d			09 50								10 50									11 50				
Liverpool Lime Street 10 90 a	09 28	09 42	09 55	10 02	10 11	10 19		10 23	10 31	10 44	10 55	11 02	11 10	11 19	11 21	11 24		11 32	11 42	11 55	12 02	12 10	12 19	12 23

	EM	LM		NT	NT	LM	VT	NT	EM	LM	NT	NT		LM	VT	NT	EM	LM	NT	NT	LM	VT		NT
	◇	1			◇	1	◇1		◇	1		◇		1	◇1		◇	1		◇	1	◇1		
																	B							
							⊠								⊠							☕		
London Euston ⊖65 d							11 07								12 07							13 07		
Birmingham New Street 12 65 d		11 01				11 36				12 01				12 36				13 01			13 36			
Crewe 10 65 d		11 57				12 33	12 43			12 57				13 33	13 43			13 57			14 33	14 43		
Winsford d		12 07								13 07								14 07						
Hartford d		12 12								13 12								14 12						
Acton Bridge d		12 16																						
Runcorn a		12 25				12 51	13 00			13 21				13 51	14 00			14 21			14 53	15 00		
d		12 25				12 51	13 00			13 22				13 51	14 00			14 22			14 53	15 00		
Liverpool South Parkway 7 a		12 33				13 00				13 30				14 00				14 30			15 02			
d	12 15	12 33		12 39	12 49	13 00		13 07	13 15	13 31	13 39	13 50		14 00		14 07	14 15	14 31	14 39	14 50	15 02			15 07
West Allerton d				12 42				13 11			13 42					14 11			14 42					15 11
Mossley Hill d				12 45				13 13			13 45					14 13			14 45					15 13
Edge Hill 90 d				12 50							13 50								14 50					
Liverpool Lime Street 10 90 a	12 32	12 44		12 55	13 01	13 10	13 19	13 23	13 32	13 42	13 55	14 02		14 10	14 19	14 23	14 32	14 42	14 55	15 02	15 12	15 19		15 23

	EM	LM	NT	NT	LM	VT	NT	EM		LM	NT	NT	LM	VT	NT	EM	LM	NT		NT	LM	VT	NT	EM
	◇	1		◇	1	◇1		◇		1		◇	1	◇1		◇	1			◇	1	◇1		◇
						☕								☕								☕		
London Euston ⊖65 d						14 07								15 07								16 07		
Birmingham New Street 12 65 d		14 01			14 36					15 01			15 36				16 01				16 36			
Crewe 10 65 d		14 57			15 33	15 43				15 57			16 33	16 43			16 57				17 32	17 43		
Winsford d		15 07								16 07							17 07							
Hartford d		15 12								16 12							17 12				17 42			
Acton Bridge d										16 16							17 16							
Runcorn a		15 22			15 51	16 00				16 24			16 51	17 00			17 24				17 52	18 00		
d		15 22			15 51	16 00				16 25			16 51	17 00			17 25				17 52	18 00		
Liverpool South Parkway 7 a		15 31			16 00					16 32			17 00				17 33				18 01			
d	15 15	15 31	15 39	15 50	16 00		16 06	16 15		16 33	16 39	16 50	17 00		17 08	17 15	17 33	17 46		17 51	18 01		18 19	18 23
West Allerton d			15 42				16 10				16 42				17 11			17 49					18 22	
Mossley Hill d			15 45				16 13				16 45				17 14			17 52					18 25	
Edge Hill 90 d			15 50								16 50							17 57					18 33	
Liverpool Lime Street 10 90 a	15 32	15 42	15 55	16 02	16 10	16 20	16 22	16 32		16 44	16 55	17 04	17 11	17 20	17 23	17 32	17 44	18 02		18 09	18 11	18 19	18 37	18 36

A from 28 May
B until 31 August, from 8 October

Table T091-F

Crewe and Runcorn - Liverpool

Mondays to Fridays
21 May to 7 December

	LM	NT	NT	LM	VT	NT	EM	LM	VT	NT	NT	NT	LM	VT	EM	VT	NT	NT ThX	VT	NT ThO	LM
	■		◇	■	◇■ ⊠		◇	■	◇■ ⊠		◇		■	◇■ ⊠	◇	◇■ ⊠		◇	■ ■ ⊏	◇	■
London Euston ⊖65 d					17 07				17 33					18 07		18 33			19 07		
Birmingham New Street 65 d	17 01			17 36				18 01					18 36								19 36
Crewe 65 d	17 57			18 32	18 44			18 59	19 16				19 33	19 43		20 16					20 33
Winsford d	18 07							19 07					19 42								20 42
Hartford d	18 12			18 45				19 12					19 47								20 47
Acton Bridge d	18 16			18 48																	
Runcorn a	18 24			18 56	19 00			19 21	19 33				19 56	20 00		20 33			20 50		20 56
d	18 25			18 57	19 00			19 22	19 33				19 56	20 00		20 33			20 50		20 56
Liverpool South Parkway a	18 32			19 05				19 30					20 05								21 05
d	18 33	18 46	18 50	19 06		19 16	19 20	19 31		19 46	19 51	20 02	20 05		20 17		20 46	20 49		20 49	21 05
West Allerton d		18 49				19 20				19 49		20 06									
Mossley Hill d		18 53				19 24				19 52		20 10					20 50				
Edge Hill 90 d		19 02				19 30						20 19					20 56				
Liverpool Lime Street 90 a	18 44	19 06	19 04	19 17	19 20	19 35	19 35	19 42	19 52	20 01	20 09	20 23	20 17	20 20	20 34	20 53	21 00	21 04	21 08	21 12	21 18

	NT	EM	NT	NT	LM	VT	NT	NT	LM	VT	NT	NT
		◇		◇	■	◇■ ⊏		◇	■	◇■ ⊏		◇
London Euston ⊖65 d						20 07				21 07		
Birmingham New Street 65 d					20 36				21 36			
Crewe 65 d					21 33	21 48			22 36	22 53		
Winsford d					21 42				22 42			
Hartford d					21 47				22 48			
Acton Bridge d									22 52			
Runcorn a					21 55	22 05			22 59	23 11		
d					21 56	22 05			23 00	23 11		
Liverpool South Parkway a					22 04				23 08			
d	21 09	21 20	21 46	21 53	22 05		22 49	22 53	23 09		23 36	23 52
West Allerton d	21 12		21 49				22 52				23 39	
Mossley Hill d	21 14		21 52				22 54				23 42	
Edge Hill 90 d			21 57				23 03				23 49	
Liverpool Lime Street 90 a	21 24	21 36	22 02	22 09	22 16	22 22	23 08	23 05	23 20	23 34	23 54	00 05

Saturdays
26 May to 8 December

	NT	LM	NT	LM	NT	LM	NT	LM	NT	NT	NT	LM	EM	LM	NT	NT	LM	VT	NT	EM	LM	NT
		■		■	◇	■		■		◇		■	◇	■		◇	■	◇■ ⊏		◇	■	
London Euston ⊖65 d																		07 07				
Birmingham New Street 65 d								06 01				06 36		07 01			07 36				08 01	
Crewe 65 d		05 48		06 15		06 33		06 59				07 33		07 59			08 32	08 43			08 57	
Winsford d						06 42		07 07				07 42		08 07							09 07	
Hartford d						06 47		07 12				07 47		08 12			08 42				09 12	
Acton Bridge d						06 51		07 16				07 51		08 16								
Runcorn a		06 07		06 34		07 00		07 24				07 59		08 24			08 52	09 00			09 21	
d		06 07		06 34		07 00		07 25				08 00		08 25			08 52	09 00			09 22	
Liverpool South Parkway a		06 16		06 43		07 09		07 33				08 09		08 32			09 01				09 30	
d	00 33	06 16	06 23	06 43	06 51	07 09	07 23	07 33	07 38	07 49	08 06	08 09	08 20	08 33	08 46	08 51	09 01		09 06	09 15	09 31	09 39
West Allerton d			06 26				07 26		07 41		08 10				08 49				09 10			09 42
Mossley Hill d			06 29				07 28		07 44		08 12				08 52				09 13			09 45
Edge Hill 90 d			06 35				07 34		07 50		08 20				08 57							09 50
Liverpool Lime Street 90 a	00 46	06 26	06 39	06 54	07 04	07 21	07 38	07 44	07 54	08 01	08 24	08 21	08 33	08 44	09 02	09 09	09 11	09 20	09 24	09 31	09 42	09 55

	NT	LM	VT	NT	EM	LM	NT	NT	LM	VT	NT	EM	LM	NT	NT	LM	VT	NT	EM	LM	NT	NT
	◇	■	◇■ ⊏		◇	■		◇	■	◇■ ⊏		◇	■		◇	■	◇■ ⊏		◇	■		◇
London Euston ⊖65 d			08 07							09 07							10 07					
Birmingham New Street 65 d		08 36				09 01			09 36				10 01			10 36				11 01		
Crewe 65 d		09 32	09 43			09 57			10 32	10 46			10 57			11 32	11 43			11 57		
Winsford d						10 07							11 07							12 07		
Hartford d		09 42				10 12			10 42				11 12			11 42				12 12		
Acton Bridge d						10 16														12 16		
Runcorn a		09 52	10 00			10 24			10 52	11 03			11 21			11 52	12 00			12 24		
d		09 52	10 00			10 25			10 52	11 03			11 22			11 52	12 00			12 25		
Liverpool South Parkway a		10 01				10 32			11 01				11 30			12 01				12 32		
d	09 50	10 01		10 07	10 15	10 33	10 39	10 50	11 01		11 08	11 15	11 31	11 39	11 51	12 01		12 07	12 15	12 33	12 39	12 51
West Allerton d				10 11			10 42				11 12			11 42				12 11			12 42	
Mossley Hill d				10 13			10 45				11 14			11 45				12 13			12 45	
Edge Hill 90 d							10 50							11 50							12 50	
Liverpool Lime Street 90 a	10 02	10 11	10 19	10 23	10 31	10 44	10 55	11 02	11 11	11 20	11 24	11 32	11 42	11 55	12 03	12 11	12 19	12 23	12 32	12 44	12 55	13 03

	LM	VT	NT	EM	LM	NT	NT	LM	VT	NT	EM	LM	NT	NT	LM	VT	NT	EM	LM	NT	NT
	■	◇■ ⊏		◇	■		◇	■	◇■ ⊏		◇	■		◇	■	◇■ ⊏		◇	■		◇
London Euston ⊖65 d		11 07							12 07							13 07					
Birmingham New Street 65 d	11 36				12 01			12 36				13 01			13 36				14 01		
Crewe 65 d	12 32	12 43			12 57			13 32	13 43			13 57			14 32	14 43			14 57		
Winsford d					13 07							14 07							15 07		
Hartford d	12 42				13 12			13 42				14 12			14 42				15 12		
Acton Bridge d																					
Runcorn a	12 52	13 00			13 22			13 52	14 00			14 21			14 52	15 00			15 21		
d	12 52	13 00			13 22			13 52	14 00			14 22			14 52	15 00			15 22		
Liverpool South Parkway a	13 01				13 31			14 01				14 30			15 01				15 30		
d	13 01		13 07	13 15	13 31	13 39	13 50	14 01		14 07	14 15	14 31	14 39	14 50	15 01		15 07	15 15	15 31	15 39	15 50
West Allerton d			13 11			13 42				14 11			14 42				15 11			15 42	
Mossley Hill d			13 13			13 45				14 13			14 45				15 13			15 45	
Edge Hill 90 d						13 50							14 50							15 50	

Table T091-F

Crewe and Runcorn - Liverpool

Saturdays
26 May to 8 December

	LM	VT	NT	EM	LM	NT	NT	LM	VT	NT	EM	LM	NT	NT	LM	VT	NT	EM	LM	VT	NT
	■	◇■ ⊏		◇	■		◇	■	◇■ ⊏		◇	■		◇	■	◇■ ⊏		◇	■	◇■ ⊏	
London Euston ⊖65 d		14 07							15 07							16 07				16 33	
Birmingham New Street 65 d	14 36				15 01			15 36				16 01			16 36				17 01		
Crewe 65 d	15 32	15 43			15 57			16 32	16 43			16 57			17 32	17 43			17 57		
Winsford d					16 07							17 07							18 07		
Hartford d	15 42				16 12			16 42				17 12			17 42				18 12		
Acton Bridge d					16 16							17 16							18 16		
Runcorn a	15 52	16 00			16 25			16 52	17 00			17 24			17 52	18 00			18 24	18 32	
d	15 52	16 00			16 25			16 52	17 00			17 25			17 52	18 00			18 25	18 32	
Liverpool South Parkway a	16 01				16 33			17 01				17 33			18 01				18 32		
d	16 01		16 08	16 15	16 33	16 39	16 50	17 01		17 08	17 15	17 34	17 46	17 50	18 01		18 19	18 23	18 33		18 46
West Allerton d			16 12			16 42				17 11			17 49				18 22				18 49
Mossley Hill d			16 15			16 45				17 14			17 52				18 25				18 53
Edge Hill 90 d						16 50							17 57				18 33				19 02
Liverpool Lime Street 90 a	16 11	16 20	16 24	16 32	16 44	16 55	17 04	17 11	17 20	17 23	17 32	17 44	18 02	18 07	18 11	18 19	18 37	18 36	18 44	18 52	19 06

	NT	LM	VT	NT	EM	LM	NT	NT	VT	NT	EM	LM	VT	NT	NT	NT	VT	EM	LM	NT	NT	VT
	◇	■	◇■ ⊏		◇	■		◇	◇■ ⊏		◇	■	◇■ ⊏		◇		◇■ ⊏	◇	■		◇	◇■ ⊏
London Euston ⊖65 d			17 07						18 07				18 33				19 07					20 11
Birmingham New Street 65 d		17 36				18 01						19 01							20 01			
Crewe 65 d		18 32	18 47			18 57			19 43			19 57					20 47		20 59			22 06
Winsford d						19 07						20 07							21 06			
Hartford d		18 42				19 12						20 12							21 11			
Acton Bridge d												20 16										
Runcorn a		18 52	19 04			19 21			20 00			20 25	20 31				21 05		21 20			22 24
d		18 52	19 04			19 22			20 00			20 25	20 32				21 05		21 21			22 24
Liverpool South Parkway a		19 01				19 30						20 33							21 29			
d	18 50	19 01		19 16	19 20	19 31	19 46	19 51		20 02	20 18	20 33		20 46	20 51	21 09		21 20	21 30	21 46	21 53	
West Allerton d				19 20			19 49			20 06						21 12				21 49		
Mossley Hill d				19 24			19 52			20 10				20 50		21 14				21 52		
Edge Hill 90 d				19 30						20 19				20 56						21 57		
Liverpool Lime Street 90 a	19 04	19 11	19 22	19 35	19 36	19 42	20 01	20 09	20 18	20 23	20 33	20 44	20 51	21 00	21 04	21 24	21 27	21 32	21 40	22 02	22 09	22 42

	NT	NT	NT	NT
		◇		◇
London Euston ⊖65 d				
Birmingham New Street 65 d				
Crewe 65 d				
Winsford d				
Hartford d				
Acton Bridge d				
Runcorn a				
d				
Liverpool South Parkway a				
d	22 49	22 53	23 36	23 52
West Allerton d	22 52		23 39	
Mossley Hill d	22 54		23 42	
Edge Hill 90 d	23 03		23 50	
Liverpool Lime Street 90 a	23 08	23 05	23 55	00 05

Sundays
20 May to 2 December

	NT	NT	NT	NT	NT	NT	VT	NT	LM	NT	NT	VT	LM	EM	NT	NT	VT	LM	EM	NT	VT	NT
	A		◇ B	◇ C			◇■ ⊏	◇	■		◇	◇■ ⊏	■	◇		◇	◇■ ⊏	■	◇		◇■ ⊏	◇ D
London Euston ⊖65 d							08 15					09 14					10 15				11 15	
Birmingham New Street 65 d									09 42				10 42					11 42				
Crewe 65 d							10 30		10 38			11 36	11 38				12 34	12 38			13 15	
Winsford d									10 45				11 45					12 45				
Hartford d									10 50				11 50					12 50				
Acton Bridge d																						
Runcorn a							10 48		11 00			11 53	12 00				12 51	13 01			13 32	
d							10 48		11 01			11 53	12 01				12 51	13 01			13 32	
Liverpool South Parkway a									11 09				12 09					13 10				
d	00 24	08 37	08 54	08 54	09 37	10 37		11 01	11 10	11 35	11 51		12 10	12 17	12 37	12 51		13 10	13 17	13 36		13 50
West Allerton d		08 40			09 40	10 40				11 38					12 40					13 39		
Mossley Hill d		08 43			09 43	10 43				11 41					12 43					13 41		
Edge Hill 90 d																						
Liverpool Lime Street 90 a	00 37	08 52	09 09	09 10	09 52	10 52	11 06	11 14	11 21	11 50	12 03	12 11	12 21	12 30	12 52	13 03	13 08	13 21	13 30	13 50	13 54	14 02

	NT	LM	VT	EM	NT	NT	LM	VT	EM	NT	NT	LM	VT	EM	NT	NT	LM	VT	EM	NT	NT	LM
	◇ E	■	◇■ ⊏	◇		◇	■	◇■ ⊏	◇		◇	■	◇■ ⊏	◇		◇	■	◇■ ⊏	◇		◇	■
London Euston ⊖65 d			12 05					13 05					14 05					15 05				
Birmingham New Street 65 d		12 35					13 35					14 35					15 35					16 35
Crewe 65 d		13 31	13 45				14 31	14 45				15 31	15 45				16 31	16 45				17 31
Winsford d		13 38					14 38					15 38					16 38					17 38
Hartford d		13 43					14 43					15 43					16 43					17 43
Acton Bridge d																						
Runcorn a		13 54	14 02				14 53	15 02				15 53	16 02				16 54	17 02				17 54
d		13 54	14 02				14 54	15 02				15 54	16 02				16 54	17 02				17 54
Liverpool South Parkway a		14 03					15 02					16 02					17 03					18 03
d	13 50	14 03		14 16	14 37	14 50	15 03		15 16	15 37	15 50	16 03		16 16	16 37	16 50	17 03		17 16	17 37	17 50	18 03
West Allerton d					14 40					15 40					16 40					17 40		
Mossley Hill d					14 43					15 43					16 43					17 43		
Edge Hill 90 d																						
Liverpool Lime Street 90 a	14 03	14 14	14 20	14 32	14 52	[illegible]	[illegible]	[illegible]	[illegible]	[illegible]	[illegible]	[illegible]	[illegible]	[illegible]	[illegible]	[illegible]	[illegible]	[illegible]	[illegible]	[illegible]	[illegible]	[illegible]

Table T091-F

Sundays
20 May to 2 December

Crewe and Runcorn - Liverpool

	VT	EM	NT	NT	LM	VT	EM		NT	NT	LM	VT	EM	NT	NT	LM	VT		NT	NT	VT	VT	NT	NT
	◇1 ☕	◇		◇	1	◇1 ☕	◇			◇	1	◇1 ☕	◇		◇	1	◇1 ☕			◇	◇1 ☕	◇1 ☕		◇
London Euston ⊖65 d	16 05					17 05						18 05					19 05				20 05	20 08		
Birmingham New Street 12 65 d					17 35						18 35					19 35								
Crewe 10 65 d	17 46				18 31	18 46					19 31	19 45				20 31	20 49				21 46	21 55		
Winsford d					18 38						19 38					20 38								
Hartford d					18 43						19 43					20 43								
Acton Bridge d																								
Runcorn a	18 02				18 54	19 02					19 54	20 02				20 54	21 06				22 03	22 12		
d	18 02				18 54	19 02					19 54	20 02				20 54	21 06				22 03	22 12		
Liverpool South Parkway 7 ✈ a					19 03						20 03					21 03								
d		18 17	18 37	18 53	19 03		19 17		19 37	19 50	20 03		20 17	20 37	20 50	21 03			21 37	21 50			22 37	22 50
West Allerton d			18 40						19 40					20 40					21 40				22 40	
Mossley Hill d			18 43						19 43					20 43					21 43				22 43	
Edge Hill 90 d																								
Liverpool Lime Street 10 90 a	18 21	18 30	18 52	19 05	19 14	19 21	19 30		19 52	20 02	20 14	20 20	20 31	20 52	21 02	21 14	21 23		21 52	22 02	22 20	22 29	22 52	23 02

	LM	NT	NT		VT
	1		◇		◇1 ☕
London Euston ⊖65 d					21 21
Birmingham New Street 12 65 d	21 42				
Crewe 10 65 d	22 38				23 46
Winsford d	22 45				
Hartford d	22 50				
Acton Bridge d					
Runcorn a	22 59				00 04
d	23 00				00 04
Liverpool South Parkway 7 ✈ a	23 10				
d	23 10	23 37	23 50		
West Allerton d		23 40			
Mossley Hill d		23 43			
Edge Hill 90 d					
Liverpool Lime Street 10 90 a	23 24	23 52	00 05		00 28

Table T091-R

Mondays to Fridays
21 May to 7 December

Liverpool - Runcorn and Crewe

Miles		LM MO	LM MX	NT	VT	NT	VT		NT	NT	NT	LM	EM	NT	VT	LM	NT		NT	NT	LM	EM	NT	VT
		1	1	◇	◇1 ⊠		◇1 ⊠		◇			1	◇		◇1 ⊠	1	◇				1	◇		◇1 ⊠
0	**Liverpool Lime Street** 10 90 d			05 24	05 26	05 49	06 05		06 14	06 20	06 28	06 30	06 47	06 50	07 00	07 04	07 09		07 19	07 28	07 34	07 42	07 45	07 47
1¼	Edge Hill 90 d			05 28		05 53					06 32			06 54					07 23	07 32				
3¾	Mossley Hill d					05 58				06 28				06 59					07 28				07 54	
4½	West Allerton d					06 01				06 31				07 01					07 31				07 57	
5½	**Liverpool South Parkway** 7 ✈ a					06 04			06 24	06 34		06 39	06 58	07 04		07 14	07 19		07 34		07 44	07 52	08 00	
—	d											06 40				07 15					07 44			
13	**Runcorn** a				05 42		06 20					06 47				07 23					07 52			08 02
—	d				05 43		06 21					06 48			07u15	07 23					07 52			08 03
21	Acton Bridge d		00 04									06 57				07 32								
23¾	Hartford d	00 02	00 08									07 01				07 36					08 03			
28	Winsford d	00 07	00 13									07 06				07 40					08 08			
35½	**Crewe** 10 65 a	00 20	00 26	07 42	06 00						08 42	07 15				07 48				09 42	08 16			08 21
—	Birmingham New Street 12 65 a											08 18				08 48					09 18			
—	London Euston ⊖65 a				07 50		08 23								09 04									10 00

	LM	NT	NT		NT	LM	VT	EM	NT	LM	NT	NT	NT		LM	VT	EM	NT	LM	NT	NT	NT	LM	
	1	◇			◇	1	◇1 ⊠	◇		1	◇		◇		1	◇1 ⊠	◇		1	◇		◇	1	
Liverpool Lime Street 10 90 d	08 04	08 16	08 19		08 28	08 34	08 47	08 52	08 55	09 04	09 16	09 19	09 28		09 34	09 47	09 52	09 55	10 04	10 16	10 19	10 28	10 34	
Edge Hill 90 d			08 23		08 32				08 59				09 32					09 59				10 32		
Mossley Hill d			08 28						09 04			09 28						10 04			10 28			
West Allerton d			08 31						09 07			09 31						10 07			10 31			
Liverpool South Parkway 7 ✈ a	08 14	08 29	08 34			08 43		09 02	09 10	09 16	09 29	09 34			09 43		10 02	10 10	10 16	10 29	10 34		10 43	
d	08 15					08 44				09 16					09 44				10 16				10 44	
Runcorn a	08 23					08 51	09 02			09 25					09 51	10 02			10 25				10 51	
d	08 23					08 52	09 03			09 25					09 52	10 03			10 25				10 52	
Acton Bridge d	08 34					09 01																		
Hartford d						09 05				09 36					10 02				10 36				11 02	
Winsford d						09 10									10 07								11 07	
Crewe 10 65 a	08 46				10 42	09 18	09 22			09 46			11 43		10 17	10 21			10 46			12 42	11 16	
Birmingham New Street 12 65 a	09 48					10 18				10 48					11 18				11 48				12 18	
London Euston ⊖65 a							11 02									11 59								

	VT	EM	NT	LM	NT	NT	NT	LM	VT		EM	NT	LM	NT	NT	NT	LM	VT	EM		NT	LM	NT	NT
	◇1 ⊠	◇		1	◇		◇	1	◇1 ☕		◇		1	◇		◇	1	◇1 ☕	◇			1	◇	
Liverpool Lime Street 10 90 d	10 47	10 52	10 55	11 04	11 16	11 19	11 28	11 34	11 47		11 52	11 55	12 04	12 16	12 19	12 28	12 34	12 47	12 52		12 55	13 04	13 16	13 19
Edge Hill 90 d			10 59				11 32					11 59				12 32					12 59			
Mossley Hill d			11 04			11 28						12 04			12 28						13 04			13 28
West Allerton d			11 07			11 31						12 07			12 31						13 07			13 31
Liverpool South Parkway 7 ✈ a		11 02	11 10	11 16	11 29	11 34		11 43			12 02	12 10	12 16	12 29	12 34		12 43		13 02		13 10	13 16	13 29	13 34
d				11 16				11 44					12 16				12 44					13 16		
Runcorn a	11 02			11 25				11 51	12 02				12 25				12 51	13 02				13 25		
d	11 03			11 25				11 52	12 03				12 25				12 52	13 03				13 25		
Acton Bridge d																	13 01							
Hartford d				11 36				12 04					12 36				13 05					13 36		
Winsford d								12 08									13 10							
Crewe 10 65 a	11 21			11 46			13 43	12 17	12 21				12 46			14 42	13 18	13 23				13 46		
Birmingham New Street 12 65 a				12 48				13 18					13 48				14 18					14 48		
London Euston ⊖65 a	12 59								14 02									15 04						

	NT	LM	VT FX	VT FO	EM		NT	LM	NT	NT	NT	LM	VT	EM	NT		LM	NT	NT	NT	LM	VT	EM	NT
	◇	1	◇1 ☕	◇1 ☕	◇			1	◇		◇	1	◇1 ☕	◇			1	◇		◇	1	◇1 ☕	◇	
Liverpool Lime Street 10 90 d	13 28	13 34	13 47	13 47	13 52		13 55	14 04	14 16	14 19	14 28	14 34	14 47	14 52	14 55		15 04	15 16	15 19	15 28	15 34	15 47	15 52	15 55
Edge Hill 90 d	13 32						13 59				14 32				14 59					15 32				15 59
Mossley Hill d							14 04			14 28					15 04				15 28					16 04
West Allerton d							14 07			14 31					15 07				15 31					16 07
Liverpool South Parkway 7 ✈ a		13 43			14 02		14 10	14 16	14 29	14 34		14 43		15 02	15 10		15 16	15 29	15 34		15 43		16 02	16 10
d		13 44						14 16				14 44					15 16				15 44			
Runcorn a		13 51	14 02	14 02				14 25				14 51	15 02				15 25				15 51	16 02		
d		13 52	14 03	14 03				14 25				14 52	15 03				15 25				15 52	16 03		
Acton Bridge d																								
Hartford d		14 02						14 36				15 02					15 36				16 02			
Winsford d		14 07										15 07									16 07			
Crewe 10 65 a	15 42	14 17	14 24	14 24				14 46			16 42	15 17	15 21				15 46			17 43	16 17	16 24		
Birmingham New Street 12 65 a		15 18						15 48				16 18					16 48				17 18			
London Euston ⊖65 a			16 02	16 05									16 59									18 02		

	NT		LM	NT	NT	NT	LM	VT	EM	NT	LM		NT	NT	LM	VT	EM	NT	LM	NT	NT		LM	VT
			1	◇		◇	1	◇1 ☕	◇		1		◇		1	◇1 ⊠	◇		1	◇			1	◇1 ⊠
Liverpool Lime Street 10 90 d	16 00		16 04	16 16	16 19	16 28	16 34	16 47	16 52	16 55	17 04		17 15	17 19	17 34	17 47	17 52	17 55	18 04	18 16	18 19		18 34	18 47
Edge Hill 90 d	16a04					16 32				16 59								17 59						
Mossley Hill d					16 28					17 04				17 27				18 04			18 28			
West Allerton d					16 31					17 07				17 30				18 07			18 31			
Liverpool South Parkway 7 ✈ a			16 16	16 29	16 34		16 43		17 02	17 10	17 16		17 25	17 33	17 43		18 02	18 10	18 14	18 28	18 34		18 43	
d			16 16				16 44				17 16				17 44				18 15				18 44	
Runcorn a			16 25				16 51	17 02			17 25				17 51	18 02			18 23				18 51	19 02
d			16 25				16 52	17 03			17 25				17 52	18 03			18 25				18 52	19 03
Acton Bridge d							17 01								18 01									
Hartford d			16 36				17 05				17 36				18 05				18 36				19 02	
Winsford d											17 40				18 10				18 40				19 07	
Crewe 10 65 a			16 46			18 43	17 19				17 46				18 18	18 22			18 48				19 17	19 21
Birmingham New Street 12 65 a			17 48				18 18				18 48				19 18				19 48				20 18	
London Euston ⊖65 a								19 03								20 04								21 02

Table T091-R

Liverpool - Runcorn and Crewe

Mondays to Fridays
21 May to 7 December

	EM ◇	NT	LM ■	NT ◇	NT	NT	LM ■	VT ◇■ ☕	EM ◇	NT	LM ■	NT ◇	NT	NT	LM ■	VT ◇■ ☕	NT	NT	LM ■	EM ◇	NT
Liverpool Lime Street ■ 90 d	18 52	18 55	19 12	19 15	19 19	19 28	19 34	19 47	19 52	19 55	20 04	20 19	20 26	20 28	20 34	20 48	20 54	21 29	21 34	21 37	21 55
Edge Hill 90 d		18 59				19a32				19 59				20a32			20 58	21a33			21 59
Mossley Hill d		19 04			19 28					20 04			20 34				21 03				22 04
West Allerton d		19 07			19 31					20 07			20 37				21 05				22 07
Liverpool South Parkway ■ ✈ a	19 02	19 10	19 22	19 29	19 34		19 43		20 02	20 10	20 15	20 31	20 40		20 43		21 08		21 43	21 47	22 10
d			19 22				19 44				20 15				20 44				21 44		
Runcorn a			19 30				19 51	20 02			20 24				20 51	21 03			21 51		
d			19 30				19 52	20 03			20 25				20 52	21 04			21 52		
Acton Bridge d			19 40																		
Hartford d							20 04								21 04				22 04		
Winsford d							20 08								21 08				22 08		
Crewe ■ 65 a			19 53				20 16	20 22			20 44				21 16	21 22			22 16		
Birmingham New Street ■ 65 a			20 50				21 18				21 48				22 18				23 26		
London Euston ⊖65 a								22 06								23 43					

	NT ◇	NT	LM ■	LM ■	NT
Liverpool Lime Street ■ 90 d	22 29	22 30	22 34	23 34	23 38
Edge Hill 90 d		22a34			23 42
Mossley Hill d					23 47
West Allerton d					23 50
Liverpool South Parkway ■ ✈ a	22 39		22 45	23 46	23 53
d			22 46	23 46	
Runcorn a			22 55	23 55	
d			22 55	23 55	
Acton Bridge d			23 04	00 04	
Hartford d			23 08	00 08	
Winsford d			23 13	00 13	
Crewe ■ 65 a			23 24	00 26	
Birmingham New Street ■ 65 a					
London Euston ⊖65 a					

Saturdays
26 May to 8 December

	LM ■	NT ◇	VT ◇■ ☕	NT	NT ◇	NT	NT	LM ■	VT ◇■ ☕	EM ◇	NT	LM ■	NT ◇	VT ◇■ ☕	NT	NT	LM ■	EM ◇	NT	VT ◇■ ☕	LM ■	NT ◇
Liverpool Lime Street ■ 90 d		05 24	05 46	05 49	06 12	06 20	06 28	06 32	06 44	06 47	06 50	07 04	07 09	07 16	07 19	07 28	07 34	07 42	07 45	07 47	08 04	08 16
Edge Hill 90 d		05 28		05 53			06 32				06 54				07 23	07 32						
Mossley Hill d				05 58		06 28					06 59				07 28				07 54			
West Allerton d				06 01		06 31					07 01				07 31				07 57			
Liverpool South Parkway ■ ✈ a				06 04	06 24	06 34		06 41		06 58	07 04	07 14	07 19		07 34		07 43	07 52	08 00		08 15	08 29
d								06 42				07 15					07 44				08 15	
Runcorn a			06 02					06 49	07 00			07 23		07 32			07 51			08 02	08 24	
d			06 03					06 50	07 01			07 23		07 33			07 52			08 03	08 25	
Acton Bridge d	00 04											07 32									08 34	
Hartford d	00 08							07 00				07 36					08 02					
Winsford d	00 13							07 05									08 07					
Crewe ■ 65 a	00 26	07 42					08 41	07 15	07 19			07 47		07 54		09 42	08 17			08 21	08 47	
Birmingham New Street ■ 65 a								08 18				08 48					09 18				09 48	
London Euston ⊖65 a			08 02						08 57					09 43						10 04		

	NT	NT ◇	LM ■	VT ◇■ ☕	EM ◇	NT	LM ■	NT ◇	NT	NT	LM ■	VT ◇■ ☕	EM ◇	NT	LM ■	NT ◇	NT	NT ◇	LM ■	VT ◇■ ☕	EM ◇	NT
Liverpool Lime Street ■ 90 d	08 19	08 28	08 34	08 47	08 52	08 55	09 04	09 16	09 19	09 28	09 34	09 47	09 52	09 55	10 04	10 16	10 19	10 28	10 34	10 47	10 52	10 55
Edge Hill 90 d	08 23	08 32				08 59				09 32				09 59				10 32				10 59
Mossley Hill d	08 28					09 04			09 28					10 04			10 28					11 04
West Allerton d	08 31					09 07			09 31					10 07			10 31					11 07
Liverpool South Parkway ■ ✈ a	08 34		08 43		09 02	09 10	09 16	09 29	09 34		09 43		10 02	10 10	10 16	10 29	10 34		10 43		11 02	11 10
d			08 44				09 16				09 44				10 16				10 44			
Runcorn a			08 51	09 02			09 25				09 51	10 02			10 25				10 51	11 02		
d			08 52	09 03			09 25				09 52	10 03			10 25				10 52	11 03		
Acton Bridge d			09 01																			
Hartford d			09 05				09 36				10 02				10 36				11 02			
Winsford d			09 10								10 07								11 07			
Crewe ■ 65 a		10 42	09 18	09 22			09 46			11 43	10 17	10 21			10 46			12 42	11 17	11 21		
Birmingham New Street ■ 65 a			10 18				10 48				11 18				11 48				12 18			
London Euston ⊖65 a				11 02								11 59								12 59		

	LM ■	NT ◇	NT	NT ◇	LM ■	VT ◇■ ☕	EM ◇	NT	LM ■	NT ◇	NT	NT	LM ■	VT ◇■ ☕	EM ◇	NT	LM ■	NT ◇	NT	NT ◇	LM ■
Liverpool Lime Street ■ 90 d	11 04	11 16	11 19	11 28	11 34	11 47	11 52	11 55	12 04	12 16	12 19	12 28	12 34	12 47	12 52	12 55	13 04	13 16	13 19	13 28	13 34
Edge Hill 90 d				11 32				11 59				12 32				12 59				13 32	
Mossley Hill d			11 28					12 04			12 28					13 04			13 28		
West Allerton d			11 31					12 07			12 31					13 07			13 31		
Liverpool South Parkway ■ ✈ a	11 16	11 29	11 34		11 43		12 02	12 10	12 16	12 29	12 34		12 43		13 02	13 10	13 16	13 29	13 34		13 43
d	11 16				11 44				12 16				12 44				13 16				13 44
Runcorn a	11 25				11 51	12 02			12 25				12 51	13 02			13 25				13 51
d	11 25				11 52	12 03			12 25				12 52	13 03			13 25				13 52
Acton Bridge d													13 01								
Hartford d	11 36				12 02				12 36				13 05				13 36				14 02
Winsford d					12 07								13 10								14 07
Crewe ■ 65 a	11 46			13 43	12 18	12 22			12 46			14 42	13 18	13 22			13 46			15 42	14 17
Birmingham New Street ■ 65 a	12 48				13 18				13 48				14 18				14 48				15 18
London Euston ⊖65 a						14 01								15 00							

Table T091-R

Liverpool - Runcorn and Crewe

Saturdays
26 May to 8 December

	VT ◇■ ☕	EM ◇	NT	LM ■	NT ◇	NT	NT ◇	LM ■	VT ◇■ ☕	EM ◇	NT	LM ■	NT ◇	NT	NT ◇	LM ■	VT ◇■ ☕	EM ◇	NT	LM ■	NT ◇
Liverpool Lime Street ■ 90 d	13 47	13 52	13 55	14 04	14 16	14 19	14 28	14 34	14 47	14 52	14 55	15 04	15 16	15 19	15 28	15 34	15 47	15 52	15 55	16 04	16 16
Edge Hill 90 d			13 59				14 32				14 59				15 32				15 59		
Mossley Hill d			14 04			14 28					15 04			15 28					16 04		
West Allerton d			14 07			14 31					15 07			15 31					16 07		
Liverpool South Parkway ■ ✈ a		14 02	14 10	14 16	14 29	14 34		14 43		15 02	15 10	15 16	15 29	15 34		15 43		16 02	16 10	16 16	16 29
d				14 16				14 44				15 16				15 44				16 16	
Runcorn a	14 02			14 25				14 51	15 02			15 25				15 51	16 02			16 25	
d	14 03			14 25				14 52	15 03			15 25				15 52	16 03			16 25	
Acton Bridge d																					
Hartford d				14 36				15 02				15 36				16 02				16 36	
Winsford d								15 07								16 07					
Crewe ■ 65 a	14 23			14 46			16 42	15 17	15 21			15 46			17 43	16 17	16 21			16 46	
Birmingham New Street ■ 65 a				15 48				16 18				16 48				17 18				17 48	
London Euston ⊖65 a	16 01								16 59								17 59				

	NT	NT ◇	LM ■	VT ◇■ ☕	EM ◇	NT	LM ■	NT ◇	NT	LM ■	VT ◇■ ☕	EM ◇	NT	LM ■	NT ◇	NT	LM ■	VT ◇■ ☕	EM ◇	NT	LM ■	NT ◇
Liverpool Lime Street ■ 90 d	16 19	16 28	16 34	16 47	16 52	16 55	17 04	17 15	17 19	17 34	17 47	17 52	17 55	18 04	18 16	18 19	18 34	18 47	18 52	18 55	19 04	19 15
Edge Hill 90 d		16 32				16 59							17 59							18 59		
Mossley Hill d	16 28					17 04			17 27				18 04			18 28				19 04		
West Allerton d	16 31					17 07			17 30				18 07			18 31				19 07		
Liverpool South Parkway ■ ✈ a	16 34		16 43		17 02	17 10	17 16	17 25	17 33	17 43		18 02	18 10	18 14	18 28	18 34	18 43		19 02	19 10	19 13	19 29
d			16 44				17 16			17 44				18 15			18 44				19 14	
Runcorn a			16 51	17 02			17 25			17 51	18 02			18 23			18 51	19 02			19 21	
d			16 52	17 03			17 25			17 52	18 03			18 24			18 52	19 03			19 25	
Acton Bridge d			17 01							18 01											19 34	
Hartford d			17 05				17 36			18 05				18 36			19 02					
Winsford d							17 40							18 40			19 07					
Crewe ■ 65 a		18 43	17 17	17 22			17 49			18 19				18 48			19 18	19 21			19 49	
Birmingham New Street ■ 65 a			18 18				18 48			19 18				19 48			20 18				20 48	
London Euston ⊖65 a				19 07							19 59							21 17				

	NT	NT	LM ■	VT ◇■ ☕	EM ◇	NT	NT ◇	NT	NT	LM ■	EM ◇	NT	NT ◇	NT	LM ■	EM ◇	NT	LM ■	NT ◇	NT	NT
Liverpool Lime Street ■ 90 d	19 19	19 28	19 34	19 48	19 52	19 55	20 19	20 26	20 28	20 34	20 49	20 56	21 29	21 29	21 34	21 37	21 55	22 04	22 29	22 30	23 38
Edge Hill 90 d		19a32				19 59			20a32			21 00		21a33			21 59			22a34	23 42
Mossley Hill d	19 28					20 04		20 34				21 05					22 04				23 47
West Allerton d	19 31					20 07		20 37				21 07					22 07				23 50
Liverpool South Parkway ■ ✈ a	19 34		19 43		20 03	20 10	20 31	20 40		20 43	20 59	21 10	21 39		21 43	21 47	22 10	22 14	22 39		23 53
d			19 44							20 44					21 44			22 15			
Runcorn a			19 51	20 03						20 51					21 51			22 22			
d			19 52	20 04						20 52					21 52			22 23			
Acton Bridge d																					
Hartford d			20 02							21 02					22 04			22 33			
Winsford d			20 07							21 07					22 09			22 38			
Crewe ■ 65 a			20 17	20 22						21 16					22 17			22 47			
Birmingham New Street ■ 65 a			21 18							22 18					23 18						
London Euston ⊖65 a				22 15																	

Sundays
20 May to 2 December

	VT ◇■ ☕	NT ◇	NT	VT ◇■ ☕	NT ◇	NT	VT ◇■ ☕	NT ◇	NT	VT ◇■ ☕	NT ◇ A	NT ◇ B	NT	LM ■	VT ◇■ ☕	NT ◇	NT	LM ■	VT ◇■ ☕	EM ◇	NT ◇	NT
Liverpool Lime Street ■ 90 d	08 18	08 21	08 25	08 38	09 14	09 27	09 38	10 13	10 27	10 38	11 17	11 19	11 25	11 34	11 47	12 14	12 25	12 34	12 47	12 52	13 14	13 25
Edge Hill 90 d																						
Mossley Hill d			08 33			09 35			10 35				11 33				12 33					13 33
West Allerton d			08 35			09 37			10 37				11 35				12 35					13 35
Liverpool South Parkway ■ ✈ a		08 31	08 38		09 24	09 40		10 24	10 40		11 29	11 30	11 39	11 43		12 24	12 39	12 43		13 02	13 24	13 39
d														11 44				12 44				
Runcorn a	08 34			08 53			09 53			10 53				11 51	12 02			12 51	13 02			
d	08 35			08 54			09 54			10 54				11 52	12 03			12 52	13 03			
Acton Bridge d																						
Hartford d														12 03				13 03				
Winsford d														12 08				13 08				
Crewe ■ 65 a	08 52			09 11			10 12			11 12				12 18	12 21			13 18	13 21			
Birmingham New Street ■ 65 a														13 15				14 15				
London Euston ⊖65 a	11 05			11 34			12 29			13 10					14 03				15 03			

	LM ■	VT ◇■ ☕	EM ◇	NT ◇	NT	LM ■	VT ◇■ ☕	EM ◇	NT ◇	NT	LM ■	VT ◇■ ☕	EM ◇	VT ◇■ ☕	NT ◇	NT	LM ■	VT ◇■ ☕	EM ◇	NT ◇	NT	LM ■
Liverpool Lime Street ■ 90 d	13 34	13 47	13 52	14 14	14 25	14 34	14 47	14 52	15 14	15 25	15 34	15 47	15 52	16 16	16 19	16 25	16 34	16 47	16 52	17 14	17 25	17 34
Edge Hill 90 d																						
Mossley Hill d					14 33					15 33						16 33					17 33	
West Allerton d					14 35					15 35						16 35					17 35	
Liverpool South Parkway ■ ✈ a	13 43		14 02	14 24	14 39	14 43		15 02	15 24	15 39	15 43		16 02		16 29	16 39	16 43		17 02	17 24	17 39	17 43
d	13 44					14 44					15 44						16 44					17 44
Runcorn a	13 51	14 02				14 51	15 02				15 51	16 02		16 31			16 51	17 02				17 51
d	13 52	14 03				14 52	15 03				15 52	16 03		16 32			16 52	17 03				17 52
Acton Bridge d																						
Hartford d	14 03					15 03					16 03						17 03					18 03
Winsford d	14 08					15 08					16 08						17 08					18 08
Crewe ■ 65 a	14 17	14 21				15 18	15 21				16 18	16 21		16 51			17 18	17 21				18 18
Birmingham New Street ■ 65 a	15 15					16 15					17 15						18 15					19 15
London Euston ⊖65 a		16 03					17 04					18 03		18 41				19 03				

Table T091-R

Sundays

20 May to 2 December

Liverpool - Runcorn and Crewe

	VT ◇1	EM ◇	NT ◇	NT	LM 1	VT ◇1	EM ◇	NT ◇	NT	LM 1	VT ◇1	EM ◇	NT ◇	NT	LM 1	VT ◇1	EM ◇	NT ◇	NT	LM 1	NT ◇	NT
Liverpool Lime Street 10 . 90 d	17 47	17 52	18 14	18 25	18 34	18 47	18 52	19 14	19 25	19 34	19 47	19 52	20 09	20 25	20 34	20 47	21 16	21 19	21 25	21 34	22 14	22 25
Edge Hill 90 d																						
Mossley Hill d				18 33					19 33					20 33					21 33			22 33
West Allerton d				18 35					19 35					20 35					21 35			22 35
Liverpool South Parkway 7 a		18 02	18 24	18 39	18 43		19 02	19 24	19 39	19 43		20 02	20 22	20 39	20 43		21 26	21 32	21 39	21 43	22 25	22 39
d					18 44					19 44					20 44					21 44		
Runcorn a	18 02				18 51	19 02				19 51	20 02				20 51	21 02				21 51		
d	18 03				18 52	19 03				19 52	20 03				20 52	21 03				21 52		
Acton Bridge d																						
Hartford d					19 03					20 03					21 03					22 03		
Winsford d					19 08					20 08					21 08					22 08		
Crewe 10 65 a	18 21				19 17	19 21				20 17	20 22				21 17	21 22				22 17		
Birmingham New Street 12 65 a					20 15					21 15					22 15					23 16		
London Euston ⊖65 a	20 04					21 03					22 25					23 52						

	LM 1
Liverpool Lime Street 10 . 90 d	23 30
Edge Hill 90 d	
Mossley Hill d	
West Allerton d	
Liverpool South Parkway 7 a	23 41
d	23 42
Runcorn a	23 51
d	23 52
Acton Bridge d	
Hartford d	00 02
Winsford d	00 07
Crewe 10 65 a	00 20
Birmingham New Street 12 65 a	
London Euston ⊖65 a	

Table T094-F

Mondays to Fridays

21 May to 7 December

Manchester and Bolton - Blackburn - Clitheroe

Miles		NT MX	NT	NT	NT	NT	NT	NT	NT	NT	NT	NT	NT	NT	NT	NT	NT	NT	NT	NT	NT	NT
0	Manchester Victoria 82 d			05 44		07 08	07 41	08 08	08 41	09 08	09 41	10 08	10 41	11 08	11 41	12 08	12 41	13 08	13 41	14 08	14 41	15 08
0¾	Salford Central 82 d			05 47		07 12	07 44	08 12	08 44	09 12	09 44	10 12	10 44	11 12	11 44	12 12	12 44	13 12	13 44	14 12	14 44	15 12
—	Manchester Piccadilly 10 82 d																					
1¾	Salford Crescent 82 d			05 51		07 18	07 48	08 18	08 48	09 18	09 48	10 18	10 48	11 18	11 48	12 18	12 48	13 18	13 48	14 18	14 49	15 18
10¾	Bolton 82 d			06 03		07 31	08 00	08 31	09 00	09 31	10 00	10 32	11 00	11 32	12 00	12 31	13 00	13 32	14 00	14 31	15 01	15 32
12½	Hall I' Th' Wood d			06 08		07 36	08 06	08 36	09 06	09 36	10 06	10 37	11 06	11 37	12 06	12 36	13 06	13 37	14 06	14 36	15 06	15 37
13½	Bromley Cross d			06 11		07 41	08 10	08 41	09 10	09 41	10 10	10 41	11 10	11 41	12 10	12 41	13 10	13 41	14 10	14 41	15 11	15 41
16½	Entwistle d			06x18			08x17		09x17		10x17		11x17		12x17		13x17		14x17		15x17	
20¼	Darwen a			06 24		07 52	08 23	08 52	09 23	09 52	10 23	10 52	11 23	11 52	12 23	12 52	13 23	13 52	14 23	14 52	15 24	15 52
—	d	00 20		06 25		07 55	08 25	08 55	09 25	09 55	10 25	10 55	11 25	11 55	12 25	12 57	13 25	13 55	14 25	14 55	15 25	15 55
—	Blackpool North 97 d																					
—	Preston 8 97 d																					
24½	Blackburn a	00 35		06 32		08 07	08 32	09 07	09 32	10 08	10 32	11 06	11 32	12 06	12 32	13 07	13 32	14 05	14 32	15 07	15 33	16 05
—	d		06 11	06 33	07 32		08 33		09 33		10 33		11 33		12 33		13 34		14 33		15 33	
27¼	Ramsgreave & Wilpshire d		06 17	06 39	07 38		08 39		09 39		10 39		11 39		12 39		13 40		14 39		15 39	
29¾	Langho d		06 22	06 44	07 43		08 44		09 44		10 44		11 44		12 44		13 45		14 44		15 44	
31¾	Whalley d		06 26	06 48	07 47		08 48		09 48		10 48		11 48		12 48		13 49		14 48		15 48	
34¼	Clitheroe a		06 35	06 57	07 56		08 56		09 56		10 56		11 56		12 56		13 57		14 56		15 57	

	NT	NT	NT	NT	NT	NT	NT	NT	NT	NT	NT	NT	NT	NT FO	NT FX	NT FO	NT FX
Manchester Victoria 82 d	15 41	16 08	16 41	17 08	17 41	18 16	18 41	19 09	19 41	20 09	20 41	21 08	21 40	22 15	22 15	23 12	23 10
Salford Central 82 d	15 44	16 12	16 44	17 12	17 44	18 19	18 44	19 13	19 44	20 13	20 44	21 12	21 43	22 18		23 15	
Manchester Piccadilly 10 82 d																	
Salford Crescent 82 d	15 48	16 18	16 48	17 18	17 48	18 23	18 48	19 18	19 48	20 18	20 48	21 18	21 47	22 23	22 25	23 19	23 20
Bolton 82 d	16 00	16 31	17 00	17 33	18 00	18 35	19 00	19 31	20 00	20 31	21 00	21 32	21 59	22 35	22 50	23 32	23 45
Hall I' Th' Wood d	16 06	16 36	17 06	17 38	18 06	18 40	19 06	19 37	20 06	20 36	21 06	21 38	22 05	22 40	22 58	23 37	23 53
Bromley Cross d	16 10	16 41	17 10	17 42	18 10	18 43	19 10	19 41	20 10	20 41	21 10	21 41	22 10	22 43	23 04	23 43	23 59
Entwistle d	16x17		17x17	17x48	18x17		19x17		20x17		21x17		22x16	22x50		23x49	
Darwen a	16 23	16 52	17 23	17 55	18 23	18 55	19 23	19 52	20 23	20 52	21 23	21 53	22 23	22 56	23 25	23 56	00 20
d	16 25	16 55	17 25	17 55	18 25	18 55	19 25	19 55	20 25	20 55	21 25	21 55	22 24	22 57	23 25	23 56	00 20
Blackpool North 97 d																	
Preston 8 97 d																	
Blackburn a	16 32	17 07	17 32	18 05	18 32	19 06	19 32	20 07	20 32	21 05	21 32	22 05	22 31	23 04	23 40	00 05	00 35
d	16 33	17 09	17 33		18 33		19 33	20 08	20 33		21 33		22 32	23 05	23 40		
Ramsgreave & Wilpshire d	16 39	17 15	17 39		18 39		19 39	20 14	20 39		21 39		22 38	23 11	23 48		
Langho d	16 44	17 20	17 44		18 44		19 44	20 19	20 44		21 44		22 43	23 16	23 53		
Whalley d	16 48	17 24	17 48		18 48		19 48	20 23	20 48		21 48		22 47	23 20	23 59		
Clitheroe a	16 56	17 32	17 56		18 56		19 56	20 33	20 56		21 56		22 55	23 28	00 09		

Saturdays

26 May to 8 December

	NT	NT	NT	NT	NT	NT	NT	NT	NT	NT	NT	NT	NT	NT	NT	NT	NT	NT	NT	NT	NT	NT
Manchester Victoria 82 d		05 44		07 08	07 41	08 08	08 41	09 08	09 41	10 08	10 41	11 08	11 41	12 08	12 41	13 08	13 41	14 08	14 41	15 08	15 41	16 08
Salford Central 82 d		05 47		07 12	07 44	08 12	08 44	09 12	09 44	10 12	10 44	11 12	11 44	12 12	12 44	13 12	13 44	14 12	14 44	15 12	15 44	16 12
Manchester Piccadilly 10 82 d																						
Salford Crescent 82 d		05 51		07 18	07 48	08 18	08 48	09 18	09 48	10 18	10 48	11 18	11 48	12 18	12 48	13 18	13 48	14 18	14 49	15 18	15 48	16 18
Bolton 82 d		06 03		07 31	08 00	08 31	09 00	09 31	10 00	10 32	11 00	11 32	12 00	12 31	13 00	13 32	14 00	14 31	15 01	15 32	16 00	16 31
Hall I' Th' Wood d		06 08		07 36	08 06	08 36	09 06	09 36	10 06	10 37	11 06	11 37	12 06	12 36	13 06	13 37	14 06	14 36	15 06	15 37	16 06	16 36
Bromley Cross d		06 11		07 41	08 10	08 41	09 10	09 41	10 10	10 41	11 10	11 41	12 10	12 41	13 10	13 41	14 10	14 41	15 11	15 41	16 10	16 41
Entwistle d		06x18			08x17		09x17		10x17		11x17		12x17		13x17		14x17		15x17		16x17	
Darwen a		06 24		07 52	08 23	08 52	09 23	09 52	10 23	10 52	11 23	11 52	12 23	12 52	13 23	13 52	14 23	14 52	15 24	15 52	16 23	16 52
d		06 25		07 55	08 25	08 55	09 25	09 55	10 25	10 55	11 25	11 55	12 25	12 57	13 25	13 55	14 25	14 55	15 25	15 55	16 25	16 55
Blackpool North 97 d																						
Preston 8 97 d																						
Blackburn a		06 32		08 07	08 32	09 07	09 32	10 08	10 32	11 06	11 32	12 06	12 32	13 07	13 32	14 05	14 32	15 07	15 33	16 05	16 32	17 07
d	06 11	06 33	07 32		08 33		09 33		10 33		11 33		12 33		13 34		14 33		15 33		16 33	17 09
Ramsgreave & Wilpshire d	06 17	06 39	07 38		08 39		09 39		10 39		11 39		12 39		13 40		14 39		15 39		16 39	17 15
Langho d	06 22	06 44	07 43		08 44		09 44		10 44		11 44		12 44		13 45		14 44		15 44		16 44	17 20
Whalley d	06 26	06 48	07 47		08 48		09 48		10 48		11 48		12 48		13 49		14 48		15 48		16 48	17 24
Clitheroe a	06 35	06 57	07 56		08 56		09 56		10 56		11 56		12 56		13 57		14 56		15 57		16 56	17 32

	NT	NT	NT	NT	NT	NT	NT	NT	NT	NT	NT	NT	NT
Manchester Victoria 82 d	16 41	17 08	17 41	18 16	18 41	19 09	19 41	20 09	20 41	21 08	21 40	22 15	23 08
Salford Central 82 d	16 44	17 12	17 44	18 19	18 44	19 13	19 44	20 13	20 44	21 12	21 43	22 18	23 12
Manchester Piccadilly 10 82 d													
Salford Crescent 82 d	16 48	17 18	17 48	18 23	18 48	19 18	19 48	20 18	20 48	21 18	21 47	22 23	23 16
Bolton 82 d	17 00	17 33	18 00	18 35	19 00	19 31	20 00	20 31	21 00	21 32	21 59	22 35	23 29
Hall I' Th' Wood d	17 06	17 38	18 06	18 40	19 06	19 37	20 06	20 36	21 06	21 38	22 05	22 40	23 34
Bromley Cross d	17 10	17 42	18 10	18 43	19 10	19 41	20 10	20 41	21 10	21 41	22 10	22 43	23 39
Entwistle d	17x17	17x48	18x17		19x17		20x17		21x17		22x16	22x50	23x45
Darwen a	17 23	17 55	18 23	18 55	19 23	19 52	20 23	20 52	21 23	21 53	22 23	22 56	23 52
d	17 25	17 55	18 25	18 55	19 25	19 55	20 25	20 55	21 25	21 55	22 24	22 57	23 53
Blackpool North 97 d													
Preston 8 97 d													
Blackburn a	17 32	18 05	18 32	19 06	19 32	20 07	20 32	21 05	21 32	22 05	22 31	23 04	00 02
d	17 33		18 33		19 33	20 08	20 33		21 33		22 32	23 05	
Ramsgreave & Wilpshire d	17 39		18 39		19 39	20 14	20 39		21 39		22 38	23 11	
Langho d	17 44		18 44		19 44	20 19	20 44		21 44		22 43	23 16	
Whalley d	17 48		18 48		19 48	20 23	20 48		21 48		22 47	23 20	
Clitheroe a	17 56		18 56		19 56	20 33	20 56		21 56		22 55	23 28	

Table T094-F

Sundays
20 May to 2 December

Manchester and Bolton - Blackburn - Clitheroe

		NT	NT ◇	NT	NT		NT	NT	NT	NT	NT	NT	NT
Manchester Victoria 82 ⇌	d	07 55		08 41	09 45	and hourly until	16 45	17 45	18 45	19 45	21 12	22 07	23 14
Salford Central 82	d			08 44	09 48		16 48	17 48	18 48	19 48	21 15	22 10	23 17
Manchester Piccadilly 10 82 ⇌	d												
Salford Crescent 82	d	08 00		08 48	09 52		16 52	17 52	18 52	19 52	21 19	22 16	23 21
Bolton 82	d	08 15		09 00	10 04		17 04	18 18	19 04	20 04	21 32	22 28	23 33
Hall I' Th' Wood	d	08 20		09 05	10 09		17 09	18 23	19 09	20 09	21 37	22 33	23 38
Bromley Cross	d	08 23		09 09	10 12		17 12	18 26	19 12	20 12	21 41	22 36	23 41
Entwistle	d	08x29		09x16	10x19		17x19	18x33	19x19	20x19	21x48		23x48
Darwen	a	08 36		09 22	10 25		17 25	18 39	19 25	20 25	21 54	22 47	23 54
	d	08 36		09 23	10 26		17 26	18 40	19 26	20 26	21 55	22 47	23 55
Blackpool North 97	d		08 40										
Preston 8 97	d		09 07										
Blackburn	a	08 43	09 28	09 32	10 33		17 33	18 47	19 33	20 33	22 04	22 55	00 05
	d	08 44	09 28	09 38	10 34		17 34	18 48	19 34	20 34	22 05	22 55	
Ramsgreave & Wilpshire	d	08 50	09 35	09 47	10 40		17 40	18 54	19 40	20 40	22 11	23 01	
Langho	d	08 55	09 40	09 52	10 45		17 45	18 59	19 45	20 45	22 16	23 06	
Whalley	d	08 59	09 44	09 56	10 49		17 49	19 03	19 49	20 49	22 20	23 10	
Clitheroe	a	09 08	09 51	10 05	10 58		17 58	19 12	19 58	20 58	22 29	23 19	

Table T094-R

Mondays to Fridays
21 May to 7 December

Clitheroe - Blackburn - Bolton and Manchester

Miles			NT MX (bus)	NT	NT	NT	NT	NT	NT	NT	NT	NT	NT	NT	NT	NT	NT	NT	NT	NT	NT	NT	NT
0	**Clitheroe**	d					06 25		06 49	07 25			08 25			09 25			10 25			11 25	
2½	Whalley	d					06 31		06 55	07 31			08 31			09 31			10 31			11 31	
4½	Langho	d					06 36		07 00	07 36			08 36			09 36			10 36			11 36	
7	Ramsgreave & Wilpshire	d					06 40		07 04	07 40			08 40			09 40			10 40			11 40	
9¾	**Blackburn**	a					06 47		07 11	07 47			08 47			09 47			10 47			11 47	
—		d		06 13	06 16	06 19	06 48	07 14	07 18	07 48	08 18	08 19	08 48	09 18	09 19	09 48	10 18	10 19	10 48	11 17	11 19	11 48	12 18
—	Preston 8 97	a		06 39																			
—	Blackpool North 97	a																					
14	Darwen	a			06 23		06 55		07 25	07 55	08 25		08 55	09 25		09 55	10 25		10 55	11 24		11 55	12 25
—		d			06 27		06 56		07 27	07 56	08 27		08 56	09 27		09 56	10 27		10 56	11 27		11 56	12 27
17¾	Entwistle	d			06x34		07x03		07x34	08x03			09x03			10x03			11x03			12x03	
20¾	Bromley Cross	d			06 40		07 09		07 40	08 09	08 40		09 08	09 40		10 09	10 40		11 09	11 40		12 09	12 40
21¾	Hall I' Th' Wood	d	00 07		06 43		07 12		07 43	08 12	08 43		09 11	09 43		10 12	10 43		11 12	11 43		12 12	12 43
23½	**Bolton** 82	a	00 15		06 48		07 17		07 48	08 17	08 48		09 16	09 48		10 17	10 48		11 17	11 49		12 17	12 48
32½	Salford Crescent 82	a	00 40		07 01		07 32		08 02	08 32	09 01		09 32	10 01		10 32	11 01		11 32	12 01		12 32	13 01
—	Manchester Piccadilly 10 82 ⇌	a																					
33½	Salford Central 82	a			07 04		07 36		08 05	08 35	09 04		09 35	10 04		10 36	11 04		11 36	12 04		12 36	13 04
34¼	**Manchester Victoria** 82 ⇌	a	00 50		07 07	07 23	07 41	08 24	08 08	08 41	09 07	09 24	09 41	10 07	10 24	10 41	11 07	11 24	11 41	12 08	12 24	12 41	13 07

		NT	NT	NT	NT	NT	NT	NT	NT	NT	NT	NT	NT	NT	NT	NT	NT	NT	NT	NT	NT	NT
Clitheroe	d		12 25			13 23			14 25			15 25			16 25		17 25	17 53		18 25		
Whalley	d		12 31			13 29			14 31			15 31			16 31		17 31	17 59		18 31		
Langho	d		12 36			13 34			14 36			15 36			16 36		17 36	18 04		18 36		
Ramsgreave & Wilpshire	d		12 40			13 38			14 40			15 40			16 40		17 40	18 08		18 40		
Blackburn	a		12 47			13 45			14 47			15 47			16 47		17 47	18 16		18 47		
	d	12 19	12 48	13 16	13 19	13 47	14 16	14 19	14 48	15 18	15 19	15 48	16 17	16 18	16 48	17 19	17 48	18 18	18 19	18 48	19 18	19 19
Preston 8 97	a																					
Blackpool North 97	a																					
Darwen	a		12 55	13 23		13 54	14 23		14 55	15 25		15 55		16 25	16 55		17 56	18 25		18 55	19 25	
	d		12 56	13 27		13 56	14 27		14 56	15 27		15 56		16 27	16 56		17 56	18 28		18 56	19 27	
Entwistle	d		13x03			14x03			15x03			16x03			17x03		18x03			19x03		
Bromley Cross	d		13 09	13 40		14 09	14 40		15 09	15 40		16 09		16 40	17 09		18 09	18 40		19 09	19 40	
Hall I' Th' Wood	d		13 12	13 43		14 12	14 43		15 12	15 43		16 12		16 43	17 12		18 12	18 43		19 12	19 43	
Bolton 82	a		13 17	13 48		14 17	14 48		15 17	15 48		16 17		16 48	17 17		18 17	18 48		19 17	19 48	
Salford Crescent 82	a		13 32	14 01		14 32	15 01		15 32	16 01		16 32		17 01	17 32		18 32	19 01		19 31	20 01	
Manchester Piccadilly 10 82 ⇌	a																					
Salford Central 82	a		13 36	14 04		14 35	15 04		15 37	16 04		16 36		17 04	17 36		18 36	19 04		19 35	20 04	
Manchester Victoria 82 ⇌	a	13 24	13 41	14 07	14 24	14 41	15 07	15 24	15 40	16 07	16 24	16 41	17 24	17 07	17 41	18 24	18 41	19 07	19 24	19 40	20 07	20 24

		NT	NT	NT	NT	NT FO	NT FX	NT FX (bus)	NT	NT FO	NT FX	NT	NT FX (bus)	NT FO
Clitheroe	d	19 10		20 25		21 25	21 25			22 54	22 58			23 39
Whalley	d	19 16		20 31		21 31	21 31			23 00	23 04			23 45
Langho	d	19 21		20 36		21 36	21 36			23 05	23 09			23 50
Ramsgreave & Wilpshire	d	19 25		20 40		21 40	21 40			23 09	23 13			23 54
Blackburn	a	19 32		20 47		21 47	21 48			23 17	23 22			00 02
	d	19 46	20 17	20 48	21 20	21 48		21 55	22 19	23 17		23 25	23 25	
Preston 8 97	a													
Blackpool North 97	a													
Darwen	a	19 53		20 55		21 55		22 10		23 25			23 40	
	d	19 56		20 56		21 56		22 10		23 25			23 40	
Entwistle	d	20x03		21x03		22x03				23x32				
Bromley Cross	d	20 09		21 09		22 09		22 30		23 38			23 59	
Hall I' Th' Wood	d	20 12		21 12		22 12		22 37		23 40			00 07	
Bolton 82	a	20 17		21 17		22 17		22 45		23 45			00 15	
Salford Crescent 82	a	20 31		21 30		22 32		23 10		23 57			00 40	
Manchester Piccadilly 10 82 ⇌	a													
Salford Central 82	a	20 35		21 33		22 36				00 01				
Manchester Victoria 82 ⇌	a	20 41	21 24	21 36	22 29	22 42		23 20	23 33	00 06		00 33	00 50	

Saturdays
26 May to 8 December

		NT	NT	NT	NT	NT	NT	NT	NT	NT	NT	NT	NT	NT	NT	NT	NT	NT	NT	NT	NT	NT	NT
Clitheroe	d				06 25		06 49	07 25			08 25			09 25			10 25			11 25			12 25
Whalley	d				06 31		06 55	07 31			08 31			09 31			10 31			11 31			12 31
Langho	d				06 36		07 00	07 36			08 36			09 36			10 36			11 36			12 36
Ramsgreave & Wilpshire	d				06 40		07 04	07 40			08 40			09 40			10 40			11 40			12 40
Blackburn	a				06 47		07 11	07 47			08 47			09 47			10 47			11 47			12 47
	d	06 13	06 16	06 19	06 48	07 14	07 18	07 48	08 18	08 19	08 48	09 18	09 19	09 48	10 18	10 19	10 48	11 17	11 19	11 48	12 18	12 19	12 48
Preston 8 97	a	06 39																					
Blackpool North 97	a																						
Darwen	a		06 23		06 55		07 25	07 55	08 25		08 55	09 25		09 55	10 25		10 55	11 24		11 55	12 25		12 55
	d		06 25		06 56		07 27	07 56	08 27		08 56	09 27		09 56	10 27		10 56	11 27		11 56	12 27		12 56
Entwistle	d		06x32		07x03		07x34	08x03			09x03			10x03			11x03			12x03			13x03
Bromley Cross	d		06 38		07 09		07 40	08 09	08 40		09 08	09 40		10 09	10 40		11 09	11 40		12 09	12 40		13 09
Hall I' Th' Wood	d		06 41		07 12		07 43	08 12	08 43		09 11	09 43		10 12	10 43		11 12	11 43		12 12	12 43		13 12
Bolton 82	a		06 46		07 17		07 48	08 17	08 48		09 16	09 48		10 17	10 48		11 17	11 49		12 17	12 48		13 17
Salford Crescent 82	a		06 58		07 32		08 02	08 32	09 01		09 32	10 01		10 32	11 01		11 32	12 01		12 32	13 01		13 32
Manchester Piccadilly 10 82 ⇌	a																						
Salford Central 82	a		07 01		07 36		08 05	08 35	09 04		09 35	10 04		10 36	11 04		11 36	12 04		12 36	13 04		13 36
Manchester Victoria 82 ⇌	a		07 07	07 23	07 41	08 24	08 08	08 41	09 07	09 24	09 41	10 07	10 24	10 41	11 07	11 24	11 41	12 08	12 24	12 41	13 07	13 24	13 41

Table T094-R

Saturdays

26 May to 8 December

Clitheroe - Blackburn - Bolton and Manchester

Station		NT		NT	NT	NT	NT	NT	NT	NT	NT	NT		NT	NT	NT	NT	NT	NT	NT	NT	NT		NT	NT
Clitheroe	d				13 23			14 25			15 25				16 25		17 25	17 53		18 25				19 10	
Whalley	d				13 29			14 31			15 31				16 31		17 31	17 59		18 31				19 16	
Langho	d				13 34			14 36			15 36				16 36		17 36	18 04		18 36				19 21	
Ramsgreave & Wilpshire	d				13 38			14 40			15 40				16 40		17 40	18 08		18 40				19 25	
Blackburn	a				13 45			14 47			15 47				16 47		17 47	18 16		18 47				19 32	
	d	13 16		13 19	13 47	14 16	14 19	14 48	15 18	15 19	15 48	16 17		16 18	16 48	17 19	17 48	18 18	18 19	18 48	19 18	19 19		19 46	20 17
Preston 8 97	a																								
Blackpool North 97	a																								
Darwen	a	13 23			13 54	14 23		14 55	15 25		15 55			16 25	16 55		17 56	18 25		18 55	19 25			19 53	
	d	13 27			13 56	14 27		14 56	15 27		15 56			16 27	16 56		17 56	18 28		18 56	19 27			19 56	
Entwistle	d				14x03			15x03			16x03				17x03		18x03			19x03				20x03	
Bromley Cross	d	13 40			14 09	14 40		15 09	15 40		16 09			16 40	17 09		18 09	18 40		19 09	19 40			20 09	
Hall I' Th' Wood	d	13 43			14 12	14 43		15 12	15 43		16 12			16 43	17 12		18 12	18 43		19 12	19 43			20 12	
Bolton 82	a	13 48			14 17	14 48		15 17	15 48		16 17			16 48	17 17		18 17	18 48		19 17	19 48			20 17	
Salford Crescent 82	a	14 01			14 32	15 01		15 32	16 01		16 32			17 01	17 32		18 32	19 01		19 31	20 01			20 31	
Manchester Piccadilly 10 82	a																								
Salford Central 82	a	14 04			14 35	15 04		15 37	16 04		16 36			17 04	17 36		18 36	19 04		19 35	20 04			20 35	
Manchester Victoria 82	a	14 07		14 24	14 41	15 07	15 24	15 40	16 07	16 24	16 41	17 24		17 07	17 41	18 24	18 41	19 07	19 24	19 40	20 07	20 24		20 41	21 24

Station		NT	NT	NT	NT	NT	NT	NT
Clitheroe	d	20 25		21 25		22 54		23 39
Whalley	d	20 31		21 31		23 00		23 45
Langho	d	20 36		21 36		23 05		23 50
Ramsgreave & Wilpshire	d	20 40		21 40		23 09		23 54
Blackburn	a	20 47		21 47		23 17		00 02
	d	20 48	21 20	21 48	22 19	23 18	23 19	
Preston 8 97	a							
Blackpool North 97	a							
Darwen	a	20 55		21 55		23 25		
	d	20 56		21 56		23 26		
Entwistle	d	21x03		22x03		23x33		
Bromley Cross	d	21 09		22 09		23 39		
Hall I' Th' Wood	d	21 12		22 12		23 42		
Bolton 82	a	21 17		22 17		23 47		
Salford Crescent 82	a	21 30		22 32		23 59		
Manchester Piccadilly 10 82	a							
Salford Central 82	a	21 33		22 36				
Manchester Victoria 82	a	21 36	22 29	22 42	23 33	00 08	00 24	

Sundays

20 May to 2 December

Station		NT	NT	NT	NT	NT	and at the same minutes past each hour until	NT	NT	NT		NT	NT	NT	NT	NT ◇ H	NT	NT	NT	NT		NT	NT
Clitheroe	d					09 25			17 25			18 25			19 47	20 00	20 25		21 25				22 45
Whalley	d					09 31			17 31			18 31			19 53	20 06	20 31		21 31				22 51
Langho	d					09 36			17 36			18 36			19 58	20 11	20 36		21 36				22 55
Ramsgreave & Wilpshire	d					09 40			17 40			18 40			20 02	20 16	20 40		21 40				23 00
Blackburn	a					09 47			17 47			18 47			20 12	20 25	20 47		21 47				23 07
	d	07 48	08 12	08 48	09 12	09 48		17 12	17 48	18 12		18 50	19 12	20 16	20 17	20 25	20 48	21 13	21 48	22 13		23 00	23 07
Preston 8 97	a															20 46							
Blackpool North 97	a															21 14							
Darwen	a			08 55		09 55			17 55			18 57			20 26		20 55		21 55				23 15
	d			08 56		09 56			17 56			18 58			20 27		20 56		21 56				23 15
Entwistle	d			09x03		10x03			18x03			19x05			20x34		21x03		22x03				23x22
Bromley Cross	d			09 09		10 09			18 09			19 11			20 40		21 09		22 09				23 28
Hall I' Th' Wood	d			09 13		10 12			18 12			19 14			20 43		21 12		22 12				23 30
Bolton 82	a			09 18		10 17			18 17			19 19			20 48		21 17		22 17				23 35
Salford Crescent 82	a			09 32		10 33			18 33			19 33			21 01		21 33		22 33				23 48
Manchester Piccadilly 10 82	a																						
Salford Central 82	a			09 35		10 36			18 36			19 36			21 04		21 36		22 36				23 51
Manchester Victoria 82	a	08 59	09 24	09 39	10 24	10 40		18 24	18 40	19 24		19 40	20 24	21 30	21 09		21 40	22 25	22 40	23 25		00 11	23 55

Table T097-F

Mondays to Fridays

21 May to 7 December

Colne, Burnley, Accrington and Blackburn - Preston - Blackpool

Miles	Miles	Station		NT MX A	NT MX ◇ B	NT MO ◇ C	NT MX ◇ C	NT MO D	NT MX E	NT MX ◇ C	NT	NT		NT ◇ C	NT	NT	NT F	NT	NT D	NT	NT ◇	NT ◇ C		NT	NT
0	—	**Colne**	d								05 23					06 11									07 09
2	—	Nelson	d								05 27					06 16									07 14
3¼	—	Brierfield	d								05 30					06 19									07 17
5½	—	**Burnley Central**	d								05 35					06 24									07 22
6	—	Burnley Barracks	d								05x37					06x27									07x25
—	0	Manchester Victoria	d															06 00							
—	10½	Rochdale	d															06 14							
—	19¼	Todmorden	d															06 29							
—	—	Leeds 10 41	d																		05 55				
—	28	Burnley Manchester Road 41	d															06 45			07 04				
7	—	Rose Grove	d								05 40					06 30		06 48							07 29
8½	—	Hapton	d								05x43					06x33									07x32
10	—	Huncoat	d								05 46					06 37									07 35
11¼	34	Accrington	d								05 51					06 41		06 55			07 13				07 40
12½	—	Church & Oswaldtwistle	d								05 53					06 44									07 44
14¼	—	Rishton	d								05 56					06 48									07 48
18	39½	**Blackburn**	a								06 02					06 54		07 06			07 21				07 54
—	—	Clitheroe 94	d																						
—	—	**Blackburn**	d								06 02					06 54					07 22				07 54
19¼	—	Mill Hill (Lancashire)	d													06 57					07 25				07 57
20	—	Cherry Tree	d													06 59									07 59
21	—	Pleasington	d													07x02									08x02
26	—	Bamber Bridge	d													07 09					07 33				08 09
27¼	—	Lostock Hall	d	00 01												07 11					07 36				08 11
30	0	**Preston 8**	a	00 11							06 21					07 20					07 44				08 21
—	—		d					00 17	00 25	01 01		06 31		06 38	07 05		07 28		07 32	07 35		07 48		08 05	
35¼	5¼	Salwick	d																	07 42					
37¾	7¾	Kirkham & Wesham	d			00 02	00 02	00 27		01 10		06 40		06 47					07 41	07 47		07 58			
41	—	Moss Side	d									06 46								07 53					
43½	—	Lytham	d									06 50								07 57					
44¾	—	Ansdell & Fairhaven	d									06 53								08 00					
46¾	—	St Annes-on-the-Sea	d									06 57								08 04					
48¼	—	Squires Gate	d									07 01								08 07					
49½	—	Blackpool Pleasure Beach	d									07 03								08 10					
50	—	**Blackpool South**	a									07 06								08 12					
—	14¼	Poulton-le-Fylde	d		00 04	00 10	00 10	00 35	00 41	01 19				06 56	07 21		07 44		07 49			08 06		08 21	
—	16¼	Layton	d				00 14			01 23				06 59								08 10			
—	17½	**Blackpool North**	a		00 11	00 16	00 21	00 41	00 48	01 29				07 04	07 29		07 53		07 55			08 14		08 29	

Station		NT D	NT	NT	NT E	NT ◇ C	NT ◇	NT		VT ◇ 1 G	NT	NT ◇ D	NT H	NT E	NT	NT ◇	NT ◇ C	NT		NT	NT E	NT H	NT ◇ D	NT	NT ◇
Colne	d										08 11									09 11					
Nelson	d										08 16									09 16					
Brierfield	d										08 19									09 19					
Burnley Central	d										08 24									09 24					
Burnley Barracks	d										08x27									09x27					
Manchester Victoria	d		07 04										08 04									09 04			
Rochdale	d		07 18										08 18									09 18			
Todmorden	d		07 35										08 35									09 35			
Leeds 10 41	d						06 52									07 52									08 51
Burnley Manchester Road 41	d		07 51				08 04						08 51			09 03						09 51			10 03
Rose Grove	d		07 54								08 30		08 54							09 30		09 54			
Hapton	d										08x33									09x33					
Huncoat	d										08 37									09 37					
Accrington	d		08 01				08 13				08 41		09 01			09 12				09 41		10 01			10 12
Church & Oswaldtwistle	d										08 44									09 44					
Rishton	d										08 48									09 48					
Blackburn	a		08 12				08 22				08 54		09 12			09 21				09 54		10 12			10 20
Clitheroe 94	d																								
Blackburn	d						08 23				08 54					09 22				09 54					10 20
Mill Hill (Lancashire)	d						08 26				08 57									09 57					
Cherry Tree	d										08 59									09 59					
Pleasington	d										09x02									10x02					
Bamber Bridge	d						08 34				09 09									10 09					
Lostock Hall	d						08 37				09 11									10 11					
Preston 8	a						08 46				09 21					09 43				10 21					10 38
	d	08 29		08 34	08 38	08 41		09 05		09 17		09 29		09 32	09 35		09 45	10 12			10 26		10 29	10 34	
Salwick	d																								
Kirkham & Wesham	d	08 38		08 43		08 50								09 42	09 44		09 55						10 41	10 44	
Moss Side	d			08 49											09 50									10 50	
Lytham	d			08 53											09 54									10 54	
Ansdell & Fairhaven	d			08 56											09 57									10 57	
St Annes-on-the-Sea	d			09 00											10 01									11 01	
Squires Gate	d			09 04											10 05									11 04	
Blackpool Pleasure Beach	d			09 06											10 08									11 07	
Blackpool South	a			09 09											10 10									11 09	
Poulton-le-Fylde	d	08 46			08 54	08 59		09 21				09 45		09 50			10 03				10 42		10 49		
Layton	d					09 02											10 07								
Blackpool North	a	08 52			09 01	09 07		09 29		09 37		09 51		09 59			10 13	10 34			10 51		10 55		

A From Colne
B From Leeds
C From Manchester Airport
D From Liverpool Lime Street
E From Manchester Piccadilly
F From Stockport
G From London Euston
H From Southport

Colne, Burnley, Accrington and Blackburn - Preston - Blackpool

		NT ◇ A	NT	NT	NT B	NT C	NT ◇ D	VT ◇1 E ⊏	NT	NT ◇	NT ◇ A	NT	NT	NT B	NT C	NT ◇ D	NT	NT ◇ A	NT ◇	VT ◇1 E ⊏	NT	NT
Colne	d			10 11									11 11									12 11
Nelson	d			10 16									11 16									12 16
Brierfield	d			10 19									11 19									12 19
Burnley Central	d			10 24									11 24									12 24
Burnley Barracks	d			10x26									11x26									12x27
Manchester Victoria	d					10 04									11 04							
Rochdale	d					10 18									11 18							
Todmorden	d					10 33									11 33							
Leeds 10 41	d									09 51									10 51			
Burnley Manchester Road 41	d					10 49				11 03					11 49				12 03			
Rose Grove	d			10 30		10 52							11 30		11 52							12 30
Hapton	d			10x33									11x33									12x33
Huncoat	d			10 36									11 36									12 37
Accrington	d			10 41		10 59				11 12			11 41		11 59				12 12			12 41
Church & Oswaldtwistle	d			10 44									11 44									12 44
Rishton	d			10 47									11 47									12 48
Blackburn	a			10 53		11 10				11 20			11 53		12 10				12 20			12 54
Clitheroe 94	d																					
Blackburn	d			10 54						11 20			11 54						12 21			12 54
Mill Hill (Lancashire)	d			10 57									11 57									12 57
Cherry Tree	d			10 59									11 59									12 59
Pleasington	d			11x01									12x01									13x02
Bamber Bridge	d			11 08									12 08									13 09
Lostock Hall	d			11 11									12 11									13 11
Preston 8	a			11 20						11 39			12 20						12 39			13 20
	d	10 46	11 05		11 25		11 30	11 33	11 36		11 45	12 05		12 25		12 29	12 34	12 38		13 00	13 06	
Salwick	d																					
Kirkham & Wesham	d	10 55					11 39		11 46		11 55					12 38	12 43	12 48				
Moss Side	d								11 52								12 49					
Lytham	d								11 56								12 53					
Ansdell & Fairhaven	d								11 59								12 56					
St Annes-on-the-Sea	d								12 03								13 00					
Squires Gate	d								12 07								13 04					
Blackpool Pleasure Beach	d								12 09								13 06					
Blackpool South	a								12 12								13 09					
Poulton-le-Fylde	d	11 04	11 21		11 41		11 47				12 03	12 21		12 42		12 46		12 57			13 22	
Layton	d	11 07									12 07							13 00				
Blackpool North	a	11 12	11 29		11 50		11 53	11 56			12 11	12 29		12 49		12 52		13 10		13 20	13 30	

		NT B	NT C	NT ◇ D	NT	NT ◇	NT ◇ A	NT	NT	NT B	NT C	NT ◇ D	NT	NT ◇	NT ◇ A	NT	NT	NT B	NT C	NT ◇ D	NT	NT ◇	NT ◇ A
Colne	d								13 11								14 11						
Nelson	d								13 16								14 16						
Brierfield	d								13 19								14 19						
Burnley Central	d								13 24								14 24						
Burnley Barracks	d								13x26								14x26						
Manchester Victoria	d		12 04								13 04								14 04				
Rochdale	d		12 18								13 18								14 18				
Todmorden	d		12 33								13 33								14 33				
Leeds 10 41	d					11 51								12 51								13 51	
Burnley Manchester Road 41	d		12 49			13 03					13 49			14 03					14 49			15 03	
Rose Grove	d		12 52						13 30		13 52						14 30		14 52				
Hapton	d								13x33								14x33						
Huncoat	d								13 36								14 36						
Accrington	d		12 59			13 12			13 41		13 59			14 12			14 41		14 59			15 12	
Church & Oswaldtwistle	d								13 44								14 44						
Rishton	d								13 47								14 47						
Blackburn	a		13 10			13 20			13 53		14 10			14 20			14 53		15 10			15 20	
Clitheroe 94	d																						
Blackburn	d					13 20			13 54					14 20			14 54					15 20	
Mill Hill (Lancashire)	d								13 57								14 57						
Cherry Tree	d								13 59								14 59						
Pleasington	d								14x01								15x01						
Bamber Bridge	d								14 08								15 08						
Lostock Hall	d								14 11								15 11						
Preston 8	a					13 38			14 20					14 38			15 20					15 38	
	d	13 25		13 30	13 35		13 45	14 05		14 26		14 29	14 36		14 45	15 05		15 25		15 29	15 34		15 43
Salwick	d																				15 41		
Kirkham & Wesham	d			13 39	13 44		13 55					14 39	14 46		14 55					15 39	15 46		15 52
Moss Side	d				13 50								14 52								15 52		
Lytham	d				13 54								14 56								15 56		
Ansdell & Fairhaven	d				13 57								14 59								15 59		
St Annes-on-the-Sea	d				14 01								15 03								16 03		
Squires Gate	d				14 05								15 06								16 06		
Blackpool Pleasure Beach	d				14 07								15 09								16 09		
Blackpool South	a				14 10								15 11								16 11		
Poulton-le-Fylde	d	13 42		13 47			14 03	14 21		14 42		14 47			15 03	15 21		15 41		15 47			16 01
Layton	d						14 07								15 07								16 04
Blackpool North	a	13 49		13 53			14 13	14 29		14 51		14 53			15 13	15 29		15 50		15 53			16 11

A From Manchester Airport
B From Manchester Piccadilly
C From Southport
D From Liverpool Lime Street
E From London Euston

Table T097-F

Mondays to Fridays
21 May to 7 December

Colne, Burnley, Accrington and Blackburn - Preston - Blackpool

		NT	NT	NT A	NT B	NT C	NT	NT ◇	NT ◇ D	NT	NT	NT ◇ C	NT B	NT A	NT	NT ◇ D	NT ◇ E	NT	NT	NT A	NT B	NT	NT ◇ C
Colne	d		15 11								16 11								17 11				
Nelson	d		15 16								16 16								17 16				
Brierfield	d		15 19								16 19								17 19				
Burnley Central	d		15 24								16 24								17 24				
Burnley Barracks	d		15x27								16x27								17x27				
Manchester Victoria	d				15 04								16 04								17 04		
Rochdale	d				15 18								16 18								17 18		
Todmorden	d				15 33								16 35								17 35		
Leeds 10 41	d							14 51									15 51						
Burnley Manchester Road 41	d				15 49			16 03					16 51				17 03				17 51		
Rose Grove	d		15 30		15 52						16 30		16 54						17 30		17 54		
Hapton	d		15x33								16x33								17x33				
Huncoat	d		15 37								16 37								17 37				
Accrington	d		15 41		15 59			16 12			16 41		17 01				17 12		17 41		18 01		
Church & Oswaldtwistle	d		15 44								16 44								17 44				
Rishton	d		15 48								16 48								17 48				
Blackburn	a		15 54		16 10			16 20			16 54		17 11				17 20		17 54		18 12		
Clitheroe 94	d																						
Blackburn	d		15 54					16 21			16 54						17 20		17 54				
Mill Hill (Lancashire)	d		15 57								16 57								17 57				
Cherry Tree	d		15 59								16 59								17 59				
Pleasington	d		16x02								17x02								18x02				
Bamber Bridge	d		16 09								17 09								18 09				
Lostock Hall	d		16 11								17 11								18 11				
Preston 8	a		16 21					16 38			17 21						17 41		18 21				
	d	16 05		16 25		16 30	16 35		16 43	17 05		17 29		17 32	17 35	17 40		18 05		18 29		18 32	18 37
Salwick	d														17 42								
Kirkham & Wesham	d					16 42	16 45		16 52					17 41	17 47	17 51				18 38		18 41	18 46
Moss Side	d						16 51								17 53							18 47	
Lytham	d						16 55								17 57							18 52	
Ansdell & Fairhaven	d						16 58								18 00							18 55	
St Annes-on-the-Sea	d						17 02								18 04							18 59	
Squires Gate	d						17 05								18 07							19 02	
Blackpool Pleasure Beach	d						17 08								18 10							19 05	
Blackpool South	a						17 10								18 12							19 08	
Poulton-le-Fylde	d	16 21		16 42		16 50			17 01	17 21		17 44		17 50		17 59		18 21		18 47			18 54
Layton	d			16 46					17 04					17 54		18 03				18 51			
Blackpool North	a	16 29		16 52		16 56			17 09	17 29		17 50		18 00		18 07		18 30		18 57			19 00

		NT ◇	NT ◇ D	VT ◇1 F ⊏	NT	NT A	NT B	NT ◇ C	NT	NT ◇	NT ◇ D	NT	NT	NT A	NT B	NT ◇ C	NT	NT ◇	NT ◇ D	NT	NT	NT A
Colne	d				18 11								19 11								20 11	
Nelson	d				18 16								19 16								20 16	
Brierfield	d				18 19								19 19								20 19	
Burnley Central	d				18 24								19 24								20 24	
Burnley Barracks	d				18x27								19x27								20x27	
Manchester Victoria	d						18 04								19 04							
Rochdale	d						18 18								19 18							
Todmorden	d						18 35								19 33							
Leeds 10 41	d	16 51								17 51								18 51				
Burnley Manchester Road 41	d	18 03					18 51			19 04					19 49			20 03				
Rose Grove	d				18 30		18 54						19 30		19 52						20 30	
Hapton	d				18x33								19x33								20x33	
Huncoat	d				18 37								19 37								20 37	
Accrington	d	18 12			18 41		19 01			19 13			19 41		19 59			20 12			20 41	
Church & Oswaldtwistle	d				18 44								19 44								20 44	
Rishton	d				18 48								19 48								20 48	
Blackburn	a	18 20			18 54		19 12			19 21			19 54		20 09			20 20			20 54	
Clitheroe 94	d																					
Blackburn	d	18 21			18 54					19 22			19 54					20 20			20 54	
Mill Hill (Lancashire)	d				18 57								19 57								20 57	
Cherry Tree	d				18 59								19 59								20 59	
Pleasington	d				19x02								20x02								21x02	
Bamber Bridge	d				19 09								20 09								21 09	
Lostock Hall	d				19 11								20 11								21 11	
Preston 8	a	18 38			19 21					19 40			20 20					20 38			21 21	
	d		18 44	19 05		19 26		19 31	19 36		19 45	20 05		20 26		20 29	20 34		20 45	21 05		21 26
Salwick	d																					
Kirkham & Wesham	d		18 53	19 15				19 40	19 46		19 54					20 38	20 44		20 54			
Moss Side	d								19 52								20 50					
Lytham	d								19 56								20 54					
Ansdell & Fairhaven	d								19 59								20 57					
St Annes-on-the-Sea	d								20 03								21 01					
Squires Gate	d								20 06								21 04					
Blackpool Pleasure Beach	d								20 09								21 07					
Blackpool South	a								20 11								21 09					
Poulton-le-Fylde	d		19 02	19 24		19 42		19 48			20 03	20 21		20 42		20 46			21 03	21 21		21 42
Layton	d		19 05								20 06								21 06			
Blackpool North	a		19 10	19 30		19 51		19 54			20 13	20 29		20 51		20 53			21 13	21 29		21 49

A From Manchester Piccadilly
B From Southport
C From Liverpool Lime Street
D From Manchester Airport
E To Barrow-in-Furness
F From London Euston

Table T097-F

Mondays to Fridays

21 May to 7 December

Colne, Burnley, Accrington and Blackburn - Preston - Blackpool

Station		NT A	NT ◇ B	NT	NT ◇	NT ◇ C	NT	NT ◇ B	NT D	NT	NT ◇ C	NT E	NT ◇	NT	NT	NT	NT FO ◇ C	NT FX ◇ C	NT ◇ B	NT D	NT ◇	NT ◇ C	NT
Colne	d									21 26					22 24								23 11
Nelson	d									21 31					22 29								23 16
Brierfield	d									21 34					22 32								23 19
Burnley Central	d									21 39					22 37								23 24
Burnley Barracks	d									21x42					22x40								23x27
Manchester Victoria	d	20 04										21 04				22 04							
Rochdale	d	20 18										21 18				22 18							
Todmorden	d	20 33										21 35				22 35							
Leeds 10	41 d				19 51								20 49								22 00		
Burnley Manchester Road	41 d	20 49			21 03							21 51	22 03			22 51					23 11		
Rose Grove	d	20 52								21 45		21 54			22 43	22 54							23 30
Hapton	d									21x48					22x46								
Huncoat	d									21 52					22 50								
Accrington	d	20 59			21 12					21 56		22 01	22 12		22 54	23 01					23 20		23 37
Church & Oswaldtwistle	d									21 59					22 57								
Rishton	d									22 03					23 01								
Blackburn	a	21 10			21 20					22 09		22 12	22 20		23 09	23 13					23 28		23 46
Clitheroe	94 d																						
Blackburn	d				21 21					22 09			22 21								23 29		23 47
Mill Hill (Lancashire)	d									22 12													23 50
Cherry Tree	d									22 14													
Pleasington	d									22x17													
Bamber Bridge	d									22 24													23 58
Lostock Hall	d									22 26													00 01
Preston 8	a				21 39					22 36			22 42								23 46		00 11
	d		21 29	21 36		21 47	22 05	22 22	22 35		22 42			22 45			22 58	23 00	23 24	23 30	23 48	23 53	
Salwick	d																						
Kirkham & Wesham	d		21 40	21 45		21 56		22 31			22 51			22 55					23 33			00 02	
Moss Side	d			21 51										23 01									
Lytham	d			21 56										23 05									
Ansdell & Fairhaven	d			21 59										23 08									
St Annes-on-the-Sea	d			22 03										23 12									
Squires Gate	d			22 06										23 15									
Blackpool Pleasure Beach	d			22 09										23 18									
Blackpool South	a			22 11										23 20									
Poulton-le-Fylde	d		21 48			22 04	22 21	22 39	22 51		23 00						23 14	23 16	23 41	23 46	00 04	00 10	
Layton	d					22 08					23 03											00 14	
Blackpool North	a		21 54			22 12	22 31	22 45	22 58		23 08						23 21	23 23	23 47	23 53	00 11	00 21	

Station		NT
Colne	d	
Nelson	d	
Brierfield	d	
Burnley Central	d	
Burnley Barracks	d	
Manchester Victoria	d	23 04
Rochdale	d	23 18
Todmorden	d	23 33
Leeds 10	41 d	
Burnley Manchester Road	41 d	23 49
Rose Grove	d	23 52
Hapton	d	
Huncoat	d	
Accrington	d	23 59
Church & Oswaldtwistle	d	
Rishton	d	
Blackburn	a	00 10
Clitheroe	94 d	
Blackburn	d	
Mill Hill (Lancashire)	d	
Cherry Tree	d	
Pleasington	d	
Bamber Bridge	d	
Lostock Hall	d	
Preston 8	a	
	d	
Salwick	d	
Kirkham & Wesham	d	
Moss Side	d	
Lytham	d	
Ansdell & Fairhaven	d	
St Annes-on-the-Sea	d	
Squires Gate	d	
Blackpool Pleasure Beach	d	
Blackpool South	a	
Poulton-le-Fylde	d	
Layton	d	
Blackpool North	a	

A From Southport
B From Liverpool Lime Street
C From Manchester Airport
D From Manchester Piccadilly
E From Kirkby

Table T097-F

Saturdays

26 May to 8 December

Colne, Burnley, Accrington and Blackburn - Preston - Blackpool

Station		NT A	NT ◇ B	NT ◇ C	NT D	NT ◇ C	NT	NT ◇ C	NT	NT	NT	NT E	NT	NT F	NT	NT ◇	NT ◇ C	NT	NT	NT F	NT	NT D	NT ◇ C
Colne	d						05 23				06 11								07 09				
Nelson	d						05 27				06 16								07 14				
Brierfield	d						05 30				06 19								07 17				
Burnley Central	d						05 35				06 24								07 22				
Burnley Barracks	d						05x37				06x27								07x25				
Manchester Victoria	d												06 00								07 04		
Rochdale	d												06 14								07 18		
Todmorden	d												06 29								07 35		
Leeds 10	41 d															05 55							
Burnley Manchester Road	41 d												06 45			07 04					07 51		
Rose Grove	d						05 40				06 30		06 48						07 29		07 54		
Hapton	d						05x43				06x33								07x32				
Huncoat	d						05 46				06 37								07 35				
Accrington	d						05 51				06 41		06 55			07 13			07 40		08 01		
Church & Oswaldtwistle	d						05 53				06 44								07 44				
Rishton	d						05 56				06 48								07 48				
Blackburn	a						06 02				06 54		07 06			07 21			07 54		08 12		
Clitheroe	94 d																						
Blackburn	d						06 02				06 54					07 22			07 54				
Mill Hill (Lancashire)	d										06 57					07 25			07 57				
Cherry Tree	d										06 59								07 59				
Pleasington	d										07x02								08x02				
Bamber Bridge	d										07 09					07 33			08 09				
Lostock Hall	d	00 01									07 11					07 36			08 11				
Preston 8	a	00 11					06 21				07 20					07 44			08 21				
	d				00 28	01 01		06 38	06 56	07 05		07 28		07 32	07 43		07 48	08 05		08 29		08 38	08 41
Salwick	d														07 50								
Kirkham & Wesham	d			00 02		01 10		06 47	07 05					07 41	08 00		07 58			08 38			08 50
Moss Side	d								07 11						08 06								
Lytham	d								07 15						08 10								
Ansdell & Fairhaven	d								07 18						08 13								
St Annes-on-the-Sea	d								07 22						08 17								
Squires Gate	d								07 26						08 20								
Blackpool Pleasure Beach	d								07 28						08 23								
Blackpool South	a								07 31						08 25								
Poulton-le-Fylde	d		00 04	00 10	00 44	01 19		06 56		07 21		07 44		07 49			08 06	08 21		08 46		08 54	08 59
Layton	d			00 14		01 23		06 59									08 10						09 02
Blackpool North	a		00 11	00 21	00 51	01 29		07 04		07 29		07 53		07 55			08 14	08 29		08 52		09 01	09 07

Station		NT ◇	NT	NT	VT ◇1 G	NT	NT ◇ F	NT H	NT D	NT ◇	NT ◇ C	NT	NT	NT	NT ◇ F	NT H	NT ◇	NT ◇ C	NT	NT	NT D	NT H	NT ◇ F
Colne	d					08 11								09 11						10 11			
Nelson	d					08 16								09 16						10 16			
Brierfield	d					08 19								09 19						10 19			
Burnley Central	d					08 24								09 24						10 24			
Burnley Barracks	d					08x27								09x27						10x26			
Manchester Victoria	d							08 04					09 05			09 04						10 04	
Rochdale	d							08 18								09 18						10 18	
Todmorden	d							08 35								09 35						10 33	
Leeds 10	41 d	06 52								07 52							08 51						
Burnley Manchester Road	41 d	08 04						08 51		09 03						09 51	10 03					10 49	
Rose Grove	d					08 30		08 54						09 30		09 54				10 30		10 52	
Hapton	d					08x33								09x33						10x33			
Huncoat	d					08 37								09 37						10 36			
Accrington	d	08 13				08 41		09 01		09 12				09 41		10 01	10 12			10 41		10 59	
Church & Oswaldtwistle	d					08 44								09 44						10 44			
Rishton	d					08 48								09 48						10 47			
Blackburn	a	08 22				08 54		09 12		09 21				09 54		10 12	10 20			10 53		11 10	
Clitheroe	94 d																						
Blackburn	d	08 23				08 54				09 22				09 54			10 20			10 54			
Mill Hill (Lancashire)	d	08 26				08 57								09 57						10 57			
Cherry Tree	d					08 59								09 59						10 59			
Pleasington	d					09x02								10x02						11x01			
Bamber Bridge	d	08 34				09 09								10 09						11 08			
Lostock Hall	d	08 37				09 11								10 11						11 11			
Preston 8	a	08 46				09 21				09 43			10 03	10 21			10 38			11 20			
	d		08 56	09 05	09 11		09 29		09 32		09 45	09 54	10 08		10 29			10 46	11 05		11 25		11 30
Salwick	d																						
Kirkham & Wesham	d		09 05						09 42		09 55	10 03			10 41			10 55					11 39
Moss Side	d		09 11									10 09											
Lytham	d		09 15									10 13											
Ansdell & Fairhaven	d		09 18									10 16											
St Annes-on-the-Sea	d		09 22									10 20											
Squires Gate	d		09 26									10 24											
Blackpool Pleasure Beach	d		09 28									10 27											
Blackpool South	a		09 31									10 29											
Poulton-le-Fylde	d			09 21			09 45		09 50		10 03		10 24		10 49			11 04	11 21		11 41		11 47
Layton	d										10 07							11 07					
Blackpool North	a			09 29	09 32		09 51		09 59		10 13		10 33		10 55			11 12	11 29		11 50		11 53

A From Colne
B From Leeds
C From Manchester Airport
D From Manchester Piccadilly
E From Stockport
F From Liverpool Lime Street
G From Birmingham New Street
H From Southport

Table T097-F

Saturdays

26 May to 8 December

Colne, Burnley, Accrington and Blackburn - Preston - Blackpool

		VT ◇■ A		NT ◇	NT ◇ B	NT	NT	NT	NT C	NT D	NT ◇ E	NT ◇ B		NT ◇	NT	VT ◇■ A	NT	NT	NT C	NT D	NT ◇ E	NT ◇		NT ◇ B	NT
Colne	d							11 11										12 11							
Nelson	d							11 16										12 16							
Brierfield	d							11 19										12 19							
Burnley Central	d							11 24										12 24							
Burnley Barracks	d							11x26										12x27							
Manchester Victoria	d									11 04										12 04					
Rochdale	d									11 18										12 18					
Todmorden	d									11 33										12 33					
Leeds 10 41	d			09 51										10 51								11 51			
Burnley Manchester Road 41	d			11 03						11 49				12 03						12 49		13 03			
Rose Grove	d							11 30		11 52								12 30		12 52					
Hapton	d							11x33										12x33							
Huncoat	d							11 36										12 37							
Accrington	d			11 12				11 41		11 59				12 12				12 41		12 59		13 12			
Church & Oswaldtwistle	d							11 44										12 44							
Rishton	d							11 47										12 48							
Blackburn	a			11 20				11 53		12 10				12 20				12 54		13 10		13 20			
Clitheroe 94	d																								
Blackburn	d			11 20				11 54						12 21				12 54				13 20			
Mill Hill (Lancashire)	d							11 57										12 57							
Cherry Tree	d							11 59										12 59							
Pleasington	d							12x01										13x02							
Bamber Bridge	d							12 08										13 09							
Lostock Hall	d							12 11										13 11							
Preston 8	a			11 39				12 20						12 39				13 20				13 38			
	d	11 33			11 45	11 57	12 05		12 26		12 29	12 38			12 53	13 00	13 06		13 25		13 30			13 45	13 52
Salwick	d																								
Kirkham & Wesham	d				11 55	12 07					12 38	12 48			13 03						13 39			13 55	14 03
Moss Side	d					12 13									13 09										14 09
Lytham	d					12 17									13 13										14 13
Ansdell & Fairhaven	d					12 20									13 16										14 16
St Annes-on-the-Sea	d					12 24									13 20										14 20
Squires Gate	d					12 27									13 24										14 23
Blackpool Pleasure Beach	d					12 30									13 26										14 26
Blackpool South	a					12 32									13 29										14 28
Poulton-le-Fylde	d				12 03		12 21		12 42		12 46	12 57					13 22		13 42		13 47			14 03	
Layton	d				12 07							13 00												14 07	
Blackpool North	a	11 56			12 11		12 29		12 51		12 52	13 10				13 20	13 30		13 49		13 53			14 13	

		NT	NT	NT C	NT D	NT ◇ E	NT ◇	NT ◇ B		NT	NT	NT	NT C	NT D	NT E	NT ◇	NT ◇ B	NT		NT	NT	NT C	NT D	NT E	NT ◇
Colne	d		13 11									14 11									15 11				
Nelson	d		13 16									14 16									15 16				
Brierfield	d		13 19									14 19									15 19				
Burnley Central	d		13 24									14 24									15 24				
Burnley Barracks	d		13x26									14x26									15x27				
Manchester Victoria	d				13 04									14 04									15 04		
Rochdale	d				13 18									14 18									15 18		
Todmorden	d				13 33									14 33									15 33		
Leeds 10 41	d						12 51									13 51									14 51
Burnley Manchester Road 41	d				13 49		14 03							14 49		15 03							15 49		16 03
Rose Grove	d		13 30		13 52							14 30		14 52							15 30		15 52		
Hapton	d		13x33									14x33									15x33				
Huncoat	d		13 36									14 36									15 37				
Accrington	d		13 41		13 59		14 12					14 41		14 59		15 12					15 41		15 59		16 12
Church & Oswaldtwistle	d		13 44									14 44									15 44				
Rishton	d		13 47									14 47									15 48				
Blackburn	a		13 53		14 10		14 20					14 53		15 10		15 20					15 54		16 10		16 20
Clitheroe 94	d																								
Blackburn	d		13 54				14 20					14 54				15 20					15 54				16 21
Mill Hill (Lancashire)	d		13 57									14 57									15 57				
Cherry Tree	d		13 59									14 59									15 59				
Pleasington	d		14x01									15x01									16x02				
Bamber Bridge	d		14 08									15 08									16 09				
Lostock Hall	d		14 11									15 11									16 11				
Preston 8	a		14 20				14 38					15 20				15 38					16 21				16 38
	d	14 05		14 25		14 36		14 45		14 52	15 05		15 25		15 29		15 43	15 48		16 05		16 25		16 30	
Salwick	d																	15 55							
Kirkham & Wesham	d					14 46		14 55		15 02					15 39		15 52	16 00						16 42	
Moss Side	d									15 08								16 06							
Lytham	d									15 12								16 10							
Ansdell & Fairhaven	d									15 15								16 13							
St Annes-on-the-Sea	d									15 19								16 17							
Squires Gate	d									15 22								16 20							
Blackpool Pleasure Beach	d									15 25								16 23							
Blackpool South	a									15 27								16 25							
Poulton-le-Fylde	d	14 21		14 41		14 54		15 03			15 21		15 41		15 47		16 01			16 21		16 42		16 50	
Layton	d							15 07									16 04					16 46			
Blackpool North	a	14 29		14 50		15 00		15 13			15 29		15 50		15 53		16 11			16 29		16 52		16 56	

A From London Euston
B From Manchester Airport
C From Manchester Piccadilly
D From Southport
E From Liverpool Lime Street

Table T097-F

Saturdays

26 May to 8 December

Colne, Burnley, Accrington and Blackburn - Preston - Blackpool

		NT ◇ A	NT	NT		NT	NT ◇ B	NT C	NT D	NT ◇ A	NT ◇ E	NT	NT	NT		NT D	NT C	NT ◇ B	NT ◇	NT ◇ A	NT	NT	NT D	NT C
Colne	d					16 11								17 11								18 11		
Nelson	d					16 16								17 16								18 16		
Brierfield	d					16 19								17 19								18 19		
Burnley Central	d					16 24								17 24								18 24		
Burnley Barracks	d					16x27								17x27								18x27		
Manchester Victoria	d							16 04									17 04							18 04
Rochdale	d							16 18									17 18							18 18
Todmorden	d							16 35									17 35							18 35
Leeds 10 41	d										15 51								16 51					
Burnley Manchester Road 41	d							16 51			17 03						17 51		18 03					18 51
Rose Grove	d					16 30		16 54						17 30			17 54					18 30		18 54
Hapton	d					16x33								17x33								18x33		
Huncoat	d					16 37								17 37								18 37		
Accrington	d					16 41		17 01			17 12			17 41			18 01		18 12			18 41		19 01
Church & Oswaldtwistle	d					16 44								17 44								18 44		
Rishton	d					16 48								17 48								18 48		
Blackburn	a					16 54		17 11			17 20			17 54			18 12		18 20			18 54		19 12
Clitheroe 94	d																							
Blackburn	d					16 54					17 20			17 54					18 21			18 54		
Mill Hill (Lancashire)	d					16 57								17 57								18 57		
Cherry Tree	d					16 59								17 59								18 59		
Pleasington	d					17x02								18x02								19x02		
Bamber Bridge	d					17 09								18 09								19 09		
Lostock Hall	d					17 11								18 11								19 11		
Preston 8	a					17 21					17 41			18 21					18 38			19 21		
	d	16 43	16 53	17 05			17 29		17 32	17 40		17 52	18 05			18 29		18 37		18 44	18 55		19 26	
Salwick	d											17 59												
Kirkham & Wesham	d	16 52	17 03						17 41	17 51		18 04				18 38		18 46		18 53	19 04			
Moss Side	d		17 09									18 10									19 10			
Lytham	d		17 13									18 14									19 14			
Ansdell & Fairhaven	d		17 16									18 17									19 17			
St Annes-on-the-Sea	d		17 20									18 21									19 21			
Squires Gate	d		17 23									18 24									19 25			
Blackpool Pleasure Beach	d		17 26									18 27									19 27			
Blackpool South	a		17 28									18 29									19 30			
Poulton-le-Fylde	d	17 01		17 21			17 44		17 50	17 59			18 21			18 47		18 54		19 02			19 42	
Layton	d	17 04							17 54	18 03						18 51				19 05				
Blackpool North	a	17 09		17 29			17 50		18 00	18 07			18 30			18 57		19 00		19 10			19 51	

		NT ◇ B	NT ◇	NT ◇ A	NT	NT	NT	NT D	NT C	NT ◇ B		NT ◇	NT ◇ A	NT	NT	NT	NT D	NT C	NT ◇ B	NT ◇		NT ◇ A	NT	NT	NT ◇ B
Colne	d						19 11									20 11									
Nelson	d						19 16									20 16									
Brierfield	d						19 19									20 19									
Burnley Central	d						19 24									20 24									
Burnley Barracks	d						19x27									20x27									
Manchester Victoria	d								19 04									20 04							
Rochdale	d								19 18									20 18							
Todmorden	d								19 33									20 33							
Leeds 10 41	d		17 51									18 51								19 51					
Burnley Manchester Road 41	d		19 04						19 49			20 03						20 49		21 03					
Rose Grove	d						19 30		19 52							20 30		20 52							
Hapton	d						19x33									20x33									
Huncoat	d						19 37									20 37									
Accrington	d		19 13				19 41		19 59			20 12				20 41		20 59		21 12					
Church & Oswaldtwistle	d						19 44									20 44									
Rishton	d						19 48									20 48									
Blackburn	a		19 21				19 54		20 09			20 20				20 54		21 10		21 20					
Clitheroe 94	d																								
Blackburn	d		19 22				19 54					20 20				20 54				21 21					
Mill Hill (Lancashire)	d						19 57									20 57									
Cherry Tree	d						19 59									20 59									
Pleasington	d						20x02									21x02									
Bamber Bridge	d						20 09									21 09									
Lostock Hall	d						20 11									21 11									
Preston 8	a		19 40				20 20					20 38				21 21				21 39					
	d	19 31		19 45	19 57	20 05		20 26		20 29			20 45	20 52	21 05		21 26		21 29			21 44	21 59	22 05	22 22
Salwick	d																								
Kirkham & Wesham	d	19 40		19 54	20 07					20 38			20 54	21 03					21 40			21 53	22 08		22 31
Moss Side	d				20 13									21 09									22 14		
Lytham	d				20 17									21 13									22 19		
Ansdell & Fairhaven	d				20 20									21 16									22 22		
St Annes-on-the-Sea	d				20 24									21 20									22a25		
Squires Gate	d				20 27									21 23											
Blackpool Pleasure Beach	d				20 30									21 26											
Blackpool South	a				20 32									21 28											
Poulton-le-Fylde	d	19 48		20 03		20 21		20 42		20 46			21 03		21 21		21 42		21 48			22 02		22 21	22 39
Layton	d			20 06									21 06									22 05			
Blackpool North	a	19 54		20 13		20 29		20 51		20 53			21 13		21 29		21 49		21 54			22 10		22 31	22 45

A From Manchester Airport
B From Liverpool Lime Street
C From Southport
D From Manchester Piccadilly
E To Barrow-in-Furness

Table T097-F

Saturdays
26 May to 8 December

Colne, Burnley, Accrington and Blackburn - Preston - Blackpool

		NT A	NT	NT ◇ B	NT C	NT ◇	NT	NT	NT	NT ◇ B	NT ◇ D	NT A	NT ◇	NT ◇ B	NT	NT	NT
Colne	d		21 26					22 24							23 11		
Nelson	d		21 31					22 29							23 16		
Brierfield	d		21 34					22 32							23 19		
Burnley Central	d		21 39					22 37							23 24		
Burnley Barracks	d		21x42					22x40							23x27		
Manchester Victoria	d				21 04				22 04							22 42	23 04
Rochdale	d				21 18				22 18							23 03	23 18
Todmorden	d				21 35				22 35							23 15	23 33
Leeds 10 41	d					20 49							22 00				
Burnley Manchester Road 41	d				21 51	22 03			22 51				23 11			23 31	23 49
Rose Grove	d		21 45		21 54			22 43	22 54						23 30	23 34	23 52
Hapton	d		21x48					22x46									
Huncoat	d		21 52					22 50									
Accrington	d		21 56		22 01	22 12		22 54	23 01				23 20		23 37	23 41	23 59
Church & Oswaldtwistle	d		21 59					22 57									
Rishton	d		22 03					23 01									
Blackburn	a		22 09		22 12	22 20		23 09	23 13				23 28		23 46	23 52	00 10
Clitheroe 94	d																
Blackburn	d		22 09			22 21							23 29		23 47		
Mill Hill (Lancashire)	d		22 12												23 50		
Cherry Tree	d		22 14														
Pleasington	d		22x17														
Bamber Bridge	d		22 24												23 58		
Lostock Hall	d		22 26												00 01		
Preston 8	a		22 36			22 42							23 46		00 11		
	d	22 35		22 42			22 45			22 58	23 24	23 30	23 48	23 56			
Salwick	d																
Kirkham & Wesham	d			22 51			22 54				23 33			00 05			
Moss Side	d						23 00										
Lytham	d						23 05										
Ansdell & Fairhaven	d						23 08										
St Annes-on-the-Sea	d						23 12										
Squires Gate	d						23 15										
Blackpool Pleasure Beach	d						23 18										
Blackpool South	a						23 20										
Poulton-le-Fylde	d	22 51		23 00						23 14	23 41	23 46	00 04	00 13			
Layton	d			23 03										00 17			
Blackpool North	a	22 58		23 08						23 21	23 47	23 53	00 11	00 24			

Sundays
20 May to 2 December

		NT E	NT ◇ F	NT ◇ G	NT H	NT	NT	NT	NT ◇ D	NT	NT ◇ B	NT ◇ D	NT	NT	NT I	NT ◇ B	NT ◇ J	NT ◇ D	NT	NT	NT K	NT ◇ B	NT ◇ J
Colne	d													09 20						10 21			
Nelson	d													09 26						10 26			
Brierfield	d													09 29						10 29			
Burnley Central	d													09 34						10 34			
Burnley Barracks	d													09x36						10x37			
Manchester Victoria	d						08 31	08 33					09 31		08 59				10 31		10 00		
Rochdale	d							08 54							09 20						10 21		
Todmorden	d							09 09							09 35						10 36		
Leeds 10 41	d																09 02						10 02
Burnley Manchester Road 41	d							09 25							09 51		10 20				10 52		11 20
Rose Grove	d							09 28						09 40	09 54					10 40	10 55		
Hapton	d													09x43						10x43			
Huncoat	d													09 46						10 47			
Accrington	d							09 36						09 51	10 02		10 29			10 51	11 03		11 29
Church & Oswaldtwistle	d							09 40						09 54	10 04					10 54	11 05		
Rishton	d													09 57						10 58			
Blackburn	a							09 52						10 03	10 16		10 38			11 04	11 17		11 38
Clitheroe 94	d																						
Blackburn	d													10 04			10 39			11 04			11 39
Mill Hill (Lancashire)	d													10 07						11 07			
Cherry Tree	d													10 09						11 09			
Pleasington	d													10x11						11x12			
Bamber Bridge	d													10 18						11 19			
Lostock Hall	d	00 01												10 21						11 26			
Preston 8	a	00 11					09 25						10 25	10 30			10 57		11 25	11 34			11 57
	d				00 23	08 34	09 27		09 34	09 38	09 41	10 14	10 27	10 36		10 48	10 59	11 22	11 27	11 36		11 52	11 59
Salwick	d																						
Kirkham & Wesham	d			00 05		08 43	09 36		09 44	09 47	09 51	10 24	10 36	10 45		10 58		11 31	11 36	11 45		12 01	
Moss Side	d					08 49				09 53				10 51						11 51			
Lytham	d					08 53				09 57				10 55						11 55			
Ansdell & Fairhaven	d					08 56				10 00				10 58						11 58			
St Annes-on-the-Sea	d					09 00				10 04				11 02						12 02			
Squires Gate	d					09 04				10 08				11 06						12 06			
Blackpool Pleasure Beach	d					09 06				10 10				11 08						12 08			
Blackpool South	a					09 10				10 14				11 12						12 12			
Poulton-le-Fylde	d		00 04	00 13	00 39		09 45		09 52		09 59	10 32	10 45			11 06	11 15	11 40	11 45			12 10	12 15
Layton	d			00 17																			
Blackpool North	a		00 11	00 24	00 46		09 52		09 58		10 05	10 38	10 52			11 12	11 22	11 46	11 52			12 16	12 22

- **A** From Manchester Piccadilly
- **B** From Manchester Airport
- **C** From Kirkby
- **D** From Liverpool Lime Street
- **E** not 20 May. From Colne
- **F** not 20 May. From Leeds
- **G** not 20 May. From Manchester Airport
- **H** not 20 May. From Manchester Piccadilly
- **I** From Wigan Wallgate
- **J** From York
- **K** From Southport

Table T097-F

Sundays
20 May to 2 December

Colne, Burnley, Accrington and Blackburn - Preston - Blackpool

		NT ◇ A	NT	NT	NT B	NT ◇ C	NT ◇ D	NT ◇ A	NT	NT	NT B	NT ◇ C	NT ◇ D	NT ◇ A	NT	NT	NT B	NT ◇ C	NT ◇ D	NT A	NT	NT	NT B
Colne	d			11 21						12 21						13 21						14 21	
Nelson	d			11 26						12 26						13 26						14 26	
Brierfield	d			11 29						12 29						13 29						14 29	
Burnley Central	d			11 34						12 34						13 34						14 34	
Burnley Barracks	d			11x37						12x37						13x37						14x37	
Manchester Victoria	d		11 31		11 01				12 31		12 01				13 31		13 02				14 31		14 02
Rochdale	d				11 21						12 21						13 22						14 22
Todmorden	d				11 36						12 36						13 37						14 37
Leeds 10 41	d						11 02						12 02						13 08				
Burnley Manchester Road 41	d				11 52		12 20				12 52		13 20				13 53		14 21				14 53
Rose Grove	d			11 40	11 55					12 40	12 55					13 40	13 56					14 40	14 56
Hapton	d			11x43						12x43						13x43						14x43	
Huncoat	d			11 47						12 47						13 47						14 47	
Accrington	d			11 51	12 03		12 29			12 51	13 03		13 29			13 51	14 03		14 30			14 51	15 03
Church & Oswaldtwistle	d			11 54	12 05					12 54	13 05					13 54	14 05					14 54	15 05
Rishton	d			11 58						12 58						13 58						14 58	
Blackburn	a			12 04	12 17		12 38			13 04	13 17		13 38			14 04	14 17		14 39			15 04	15 17
Clitheroe 94	d																						
Blackburn	d			12 04			12 39			13 04			13 39			14 04			14 39			15 04	
Mill Hill (Lancashire)	d			12 07						13 07						14 07						15 07	
Cherry Tree	d			12 09						13 09						14 09						15 09	
Pleasington	d			12x12						13x12						14x12						15x12	
Bamber Bridge	d			12 19						13 19						14 19						15 19	
Lostock Hall	d			12 26						13 26						14 26						15 26	
Preston 8	a		12 25	12 34			12 57		13 25	13 34			13 57		14 25	14 34			14 57		15 25	15 34	
	d	12 17	12 27	12 36		12 52	12 59	13 17	13 27	13 36		13 52	13 59	14 17	14 27	14 36		14 52	14 59	15 17	15 27	15 36	
Salwick	d																						
Kirkham & Wesham	d	12 27	12 36	12 45		13 02		13 27	13 36	13 45		14 02		14 27	14 36	14 45		15 02		15 27	15 36	15 45	
Moss Side	d			12 51						13 51						14 51						15 51	
Lytham	d			12 55						13 55						14 55						15 55	
Ansdell & Fairhaven	d			12 58						13 58						14 58						15 58	
St Annes-on-the-Sea	d			13 02						14 02						15 02						16 02	
Squires Gate	d			13 06						14 06						15 06						16 06	
Blackpool Pleasure Beach	d			13 08						14 08						15 08						16 08	
Blackpool South	a			13 12						14 12						15 12						16 12	
Poulton-le-Fylde	d	12 35	12 45			13 10	13 15	13 35	13 45			14 10	14 15	14 35	14 45			15 10	15 15	15 35	15 45		
Layton	d																						
Blackpool North	a	12 41	12 52			13 16	13 22	13 41	13 52			14 16	14 22	14 41	14 52			15 16	15 22	15 41	15 52		

		NT ◇ C	NT ◇ D	NT ◇ A	NT	NT	NT B	NT ◇ C	NT ◇ D	NT ◇ A	NT	NT	NT B	NT ◇ C	NT ◇ D	NT ◇ A	NT	NT	NT B	NT ◇ C	NT ◇ D	NT ◇ A
Colne	d					15 21						16 21						17 21				
Nelson	d					15 26						16 26						17 26				
Brierfield	d					15 29						16 29						17 29				
Burnley Central	d					15 34						16 34						17 34				
Burnley Barracks	d					15x37						16x37						17x37				
Manchester Victoria	d				15 31		15 02				16 31		16 02				17 31		17 02			
Rochdale	d						15 22						16 22						17 22			
Todmorden	d						15 37						16 37						17 37			
Leeds 10 41	d		14 08						15 03						16 03						17 03	
Burnley Manchester Road 41	d		15 21				15 53		16 20				16 53		17 20				17 53		18 20	
Rose Grove	d					15 40	15 56					16 40	16 56					17 40	17 56			
Hapton	d					15x43						16x43						17x43				
Huncoat	d					15 47						16 47						17 47				
Accrington	d		15 30			15 51	16 03		16 29			16 51	17 03		17 29			17 51	18 03		18 29	
Church & Oswaldtwistle	d					15 54	16 05					16 54	17 05					17 54	18 05			
Rishton	d					15 58						16 58						17 58				
Blackburn	a		15 39			16 04	16 17		16 38			17 04	17 17		17 38			18 04	18 17		18 38	
Clitheroe 94	d																					
Blackburn	d		15 39			16 04			16 39			17 04			17 39			18 04			18 39	
Mill Hill (Lancashire)	d					16 07						17 07						18 07				
Cherry Tree	d					16 09						17 09						18 09				
Pleasington	d					16x12						17x12						18x12				
Bamber Bridge	d					16 19						17 19						18 19				
Lostock Hall	d					16 26						17 26						18 26				
Preston 8	a		15 57		16 25	16 34			16 57		17 25	17 34			17 57		18 25	18 34			18 57	
	d	15 52	15 59	16 17	16 27	16 36		16 51	16 59	17 17	17 27	17 36		17 52	17 59	18 17	18 27	18 36		18 52	18 59	19 17
Salwick	d																					
Kirkham & Wesham	d	16 02		16 27	16 36	16 45		17 02		17 27	17 36	17 45		18 02		18 27	18 36	18 45		19 02		19 27
Moss Side	d					16 51						17 51						18 51				
Lytham	d					16 55						17 55						18 55				
Ansdell & Fairhaven	d					16 58						17 58						18 58				
St Annes-on-the-Sea	d					17 02						18 02						19 02				
Squires Gate	d					17 06						18 06						19 06				
Blackpool Pleasure Beach	d					17 08						18 08						19 08				
Blackpool South	a					17 12						18 12						19 12				
Poulton-le-Fylde	d	16 10	16 15	16 35	16 45			17 10	17 15	17 35	17 45			18 10	18 15	18 35	18 45			19 10	19 15	19 35
Layton	d																					
Blackpool North	a	16 16	16 22	16 41	16 52			17 16	17 22	17 41	17 52			18 16	18 22	18 41	18 52			19 16	19 22	19 41

- **A** From Liverpool Lime Street
- **B** From Southport
- **C** From Manchester Airport
- **D** From York

Table T097-F

Sundays
20 May to 2 December

Colne, Burnley, Accrington and Blackburn - Preston - Blackpool

Station		NT	NT	NT A	NT ◇ B	NT ◇ C	NT ◇ D	NT	NT	NT A	NT ◇ E	NT ◇ B	NT ◇ C	NT ◇ D	NT	NT	NT A	NT ◇ B	NT ◇ C	NT D	NT	NT	NT ◇ B
Colne	d		18 21						19 21							20 21						21 25	
Nelson	d		18 26						19 26							20 26						21 30	
Brierfield	d		18 29						19 29							20 29						21 33	
Burnley Central	d		18 34						19 34							20 34						21 38	
Burnley Barracks	d		18x37						19x37							20x37						21x41	
Manchester Victoria	d	18 31		18 02				19 31		19 02					20 31		20 02				21 25		
Rochdale	d			18 22						19 22							20 22						
Todmorden	d			18 37						19 37							20 37						
Leeds 10	41 d					18 03							19 04						20 03				
Burnley Manchester Road	41 d			18 53		19 20				19 53			20 20				20 53		21 20				
Rose Grove	d		18 40	18 56					19 40	19 56						20 40	20 56					21 44	
Hapton	d		18x43						19x43							20x43						21x47	
Huncoat	d		18 47						19 47							20 47						21 51	
Accrington	d		18 51	19 03		19 29			19 51	20 03			20 29			20 51	21 03		21 29			21 55	
Church & Oswaldtwistle	d		18 54	19 05					19 54	20 05						20 54	21 05					21 58	
Rishton	d		18 58						19 58							20 58						22 02	
Blackburn	a		19 04	19 17		19 38			20 04	20 17			20 38			21 04	21 17		21 38			22 08	
Clitheroe	94 d										20 00												
Blackburn	d		19 04			19 39			20 04		20 25		20 39			21 04			21 39			22 08	
Mill Hill (Lancashire)	d		19 07						20 07							21 07						22 11	
Cherry Tree	d		19 09						20 09							21 09						22 13	
Pleasington	d		19x12						20x12							21x12						22x16	
Bamber Bridge	d		19 19						20 19		20 35					21 19						22 23	
Lostock Hall	d		19 26						20 26		20 37					21 26						22 25	
Preston 8	a	19 25	19 34			19 57		20 25	20 34		20 46		20 57		21 25	21 34			21 59		22 21	22 34	
	d	19 27	19 36		19 52	19 59	20 17	20 27	20 36		20 47	20 52	20 59	21 17	21 27	21 36		21 54	22 02	22 17	22 22		22 50
Salwick	d																						
Kirkham & Wesham	d	19 36	19 45		20 02		20 27	20 36	20 45		20 57	21 02		21 27	21 36	21 45		22 04		22 27	22 32		23 00
Moss Side	d		19 51						20 51							21 51							
Lytham	d		19 55						20 55							21 55							
Ansdell & Fairhaven	d		19 58						20 58							21 58							
St Annes-on-the-Sea	d		20 02						21 02							22 02							
Squires Gate	d		20 06						21 06							22 06							
Blackpool Pleasure Beach	d		20 08						21 08							22 08							
Blackpool South	a		20 12						21 12							22 12							
Poulton-le-Fylde	d	19 45			20 10	20 15	20 35	20 45			21 05	21 10	21 15	21 35	21 45			22 13	22 18	22 35	22 40		23 08
Layton	d																						
Blackpool North	a	19 52			20 17	20 22	20 41	20 52			21 14	21 16	21 22	21 41	21 52			22 19	22 24	22 41	22 47		23 14

Station		NT A	NT ◇ C	NT ◇ D	NT A	NT ◇ B
Colne	d					
Nelson	d					
Brierfield	d					
Burnley Central	d					
Burnley Barracks	d					
Manchester Victoria	d	21 02			22 02	
Rochdale	d	21 22			22 22	
Todmorden	d	21 37			22 37	
Leeds 10	41 d		21 08			
Burnley Manchester Road	41 d	21 53	22 25		22 53	
Rose Grove	d	21 56			22 56	
Hapton	d					
Huncoat	d					
Accrington	d	22 03	22 34		23 03	
Church & Oswaldtwistle	d	22 05			23 05	
Rishton	d					
Blackburn	a	22 17	22 42		23 17	
Clitheroe	94 d					
Blackburn	d		22 43			
Mill Hill (Lancashire)	d					
Cherry Tree	d					
Pleasington	d					
Bamber Bridge	d					
Lostock Hall	d					
Preston 8	a		23 01			
	d		23 04	23 17		23 52
Salwick	d					
Kirkham & Wesham	d			23 27		00 02
Moss Side	d					
Lytham	d					
Ansdell & Fairhaven	d					
St Annes-on-the-Sea	d					
Squires Gate	d					
Blackpool Pleasure Beach	d					
Blackpool South	a					
Poulton-le-Fylde	d		23 20	23 35		00 10
Layton	d					
Blackpool North	a		23 26	23 41		00 16

A From Southport
B From Manchester Airport
C From York
D From Liverpool Lime Street
E From Carlisle

Table T097-R

Mondays to Fridays
21 May to 7 December

Blackpool - Preston - Blackburn, Accrington, Burnley and Colne

Miles	Miles	Miles	Station		NT MX A	NT ◇ B	NT	NT ◇ B	NT ◇	NT C	NT	NT D	NT E	NT	NT ◇ B	NT F	NT	NT G	NT ◇	NT	NT E	NT G	NT
—	0	—	**Blackpool North**	d		03 33		04 46	05 19	05 23					05 39	06 03	06 21						
—	1¼	—	Layton	d											05 42								
—	3¼	—	Poulton-le-Fylde	d				04 52	05 25	05 29					05 46	06 08	06 27						
0	—	—	**Blackpool South**	d							05 14									06 12			
0½	—	—	Blackpool Pleasure Beach	d							05 16									06 14			
1¾	—	—	Squires Gate	d							05 18									06 16			
3¼	—	—	St Annes-on-the-Sea	d							05 22									06 20			
5¼	—	—	Ansdell & Fairhaven	d							05 26									06 24			
6½	—	—	Lytham	d							05 29									06 27			
9	—	—	Moss Side	d							05 34									06 32			
12¼	9¾	—	Kirkham & Wesham	d							05 41				05 55	06 17				06 39			
14¾	12¼	—	Salwick	d																06 43			
20	17½	—	**Preston** 8	a		03 55		05 08	05 43	05 46	05 52				06 05	06 27	06 46			06 52			
—	—	—		d			05 05		05 44					05 56					06 48				06 57
22¾	—	—	Lostock Hall	d										06 02									07 03
24	—	—	Bamber Bridge	d										06 06									07 07
29	—	—	Pleasington	d										06x13									07x14
30	—	—	Cherry Tree	d										06 17									07 18
30¾	—	—	Mill Hill (Lancashire)	d										06 19									07 20
32	—	—	**Blackburn**	a			05 23		06 03					06 23					07 04				07 24
—	—	—	Clitheroe	94 a																			
—	—	0	**Blackburn**	d			05 23		06 03			06 16	06 19	06 23				06 48	07 04		07 14	07 18	07 24
35¼	—	—	Rishton	d			05 28							06 28									07 29
37½	—	—	Church & Oswaldtwistle	d			05 31							06 31									07 32
38¼	—	5¼	**Accrington**	d			05 35		06 11				06 27	06 35					07 12		07 21		07 36
40	—	—	Huncoat	d			05 39							06 39									07 40
41½	—	—	Hapton	d			05x42							06x42									07x43
43	—	—	Rose Grove	d			05 46						06 34	06 46							07 28		07 47
—	—	11¼	Burnley Manchester Road	41 a					06 20				06 37						07 21		07 32		
—	—	—	Leeds 10	41 a					07 40										08 38				
—	—	20¼	Todmorden	d	00 04								06 55								07 49		
—	—	29	Rochdale	d	00 18								07 09								08 06		
—	—	39½	Manchester Victoria	a	00 33							07 07	07 23					07 41			08 24	08 08	
44	—	—	Burnley Barracks	d			05x49							06x49									07x50
44½	—	—	**Burnley Central**	d			05 52							06 51									07 53
46¾	—	—	Brierfield	d			05 56							06 56									07 57
48	—	—	Nelson	d			06 00							06 59									08 01
50	—	—	**Colne**	a			06 06							07 05									08 07

Station		NT	NT ◇ B	NT F	NT C	NT G	NT ◇	NT	NT D	NT E	NT	NT	NT ◇ B	NT F	NT C	NT G	NT ◇	NT	NT D	NT E	NT	NT	NT ◇ B
Blackpool North	d	06 34	06 38	07 03	07 16							07 32	07 38	08 04	08 21							08 32	08 38
Layton	d		06 41										07 41										08 41
Poulton-le-Fylde	d	06 40	06 45	07 08	07 22							07 38	07 45	08 09	08 27							08 38	08 45
Blackpool South	d							07 11										08 16					
Blackpool Pleasure Beach	d							07 13										08 18					
Squires Gate	d							07 15										08 20					
St Annes-on-the-Sea	d							07 19										08 24					
Ansdell & Fairhaven	d							07 23										08 28					
Lytham	d							07 26										08 31					
Moss Side	d							07 31										08 36					
Kirkham & Wesham	d	06 49	06 54	07 17	07 31			07 41					07 54	08 18				08 44					08 54
Salwick	d							07 45															
Preston 8	a	07 00	07 05	07 26	07 42			07 54				07 58	08 04	08 28	08 44			08 55				09 02	09 04
	d	07 02					07 50				07 57						08 50				08 57		
Lostock Hall	d										08 03										09 03		
Bamber Bridge	d										08 07										09 07		
Pleasington	d										08x14										09x14		
Cherry Tree	d										08 18										09 18		
Mill Hill (Lancashire)	d										08 20										09 20		
Blackburn	a						08 05				08 24						09 05				09 24		
Clitheroe	94 a																						
Blackburn	d					07 48	08 06		08 18	08 19	08 24					08 48	09 06		09 18	09 19	09 24		
Rishton	d										08 29										09 29		
Church & Oswaldtwistle	d										08 32										09 32		
Accrington	d						08 14			08 27	08 36						09 14			09 27	09 36		
Huncoat	d										08 40										09 40		
Hapton	d										08x43										09x43		
Rose Grove	d									08 34	08 47									09 34	09 47		
Burnley Manchester Road	41 a						08 22			08 37							09 22			09 37			
Leeds 10	41 a						09 42										10 43						
Todmorden	d									08 55										09 55			
Rochdale	d									09 09										10 09			
Manchester Victoria	a	07 59				08 41			09 07	09 24						09 41			10 07	10 24			
Burnley Barracks	d										08x50										09x50		
Burnley Central	d										08 53										09 53		
Brierfield	d										08 57										09 57		
Nelson	d										09 01										10 01		
Colne	a										09 07										10 07		

A From Blackburn
B To Manchester Airport
C To Manchester Piccadilly
D To Rochdale
E To Southport
F To Liverpool Lime Street
G From Clitheroe to Rochdale

Table T097-R

Mondays to Fridays

21 May to 7 December

Blackpool - Preston - Blackburn, Accrington, Burnley and Colne

		NT	NT	NT	NT		NT	NT	NT	NT	NT	NT	NT	NT	NT		NT	NT	NT	NT	NT	NT	NT	NT	NT
		◇			◇						◇		◇				◇					◇		◇	
		A	B	C				D	E		F		A	B	C				D	E		F		A	B
Blackpool North	d	09 03	09 21								09 38	09 45	10 01	10 12								10 32	10 37	11 01	11 20
Layton	d										09 41											10 35			
Poulton-le-Fylde	d	09 08	09 26								09 45		10 06	10 17								10 39	10 43	11 06	11 25
Blackpool South	d						09 13											10 14							
Blackpool Pleasure Beach	d						09 15											10 16							
Squires Gate	d						09 17											10 18							
St Annes-on-the-Sea	d						09 21											10 22							
Ansdell & Fairhaven	d						09 25											10 26							
Lytham	d						09 28											10 29							
Moss Side	d						09 33											10 34							
Kirkham & Wesham	d	09 17					09 41				09 54		10 15					10 41				10 48		11 15	
Salwick	d																								
Preston	a	09 27	09 43				09 52				10 04	10 08	10 25	10 34				10 52				10 58	11 02	11 25	11 42
	d				09 48					09 57							10 47				10 57				
Lostock Hall	d									10 03											11 03				
Bamber Bridge	d									10 07											11 07				
Pleasington	d									10x14											11x14				
Cherry Tree	d									10 18											11 18				
Mill Hill (Lancashire)	d									10 20											11 20				
Blackburn	a				10 04					10 24							11 03				11 24				
Clitheroe 94	a																								
Blackburn	d			09 48	10 05			10 18	10 19	10 24					10 48		11 03		11 17	11 19	11 24				
Rishton	d									10 29											11 29				
Church & Oswaldtwistle	d									10 32											11 32				
Accrington	d				10 13				10 27	10 36							11 11			11 27	11 36				
Huncoat	d									10 40											11 40				
Hapton	d									10x43											11x43				
Rose Grove	d								10 34	10 47										11 34	11 47				
Burnley Manchester Road 41	a				10 21				10 37								11 20			11 37					
Leeds 41	a				11 39												12 38								
Todmorden	d								10 55											11 55					
Rochdale	d								11 09											12 09					
Manchester Victoria	a			10 41				11 07	11 24						11 41				12 08	12 24					
Burnley Barracks	d									10x50											11x50				
Burnley Central	d									10 53											11 53				
Brierfield	d									10 57											11 57				
Nelson	d									11 01											12 01				
Colne	a									11 07											12 07				

			NT	NT	NT	NT	NT	NT	NT	NT	NT		NT	NT	NT	NT	NT	NT	NT	NT	NT		NT	NT	NT
				◇						◇	◇				◇						◇		◇		◇
			C			D	E			F	A		B	C			D	E			F		A	C	
Blackpool North	d								11 32	11 38	12 01		12 20							12 32	12 38		13 05		
Layton	d									11 41											12 41				
Poulton-le-Fylde	d								11 38	11 45	12 06		12 25							12 38	12 45		13 10		
Blackpool South	d				11 13											12 16									
Blackpool Pleasure Beach	d				11 15											12 18									
Squires Gate	d				11 17											12 20									
St Annes-on-the-Sea	d				11 21											12 24									
Ansdell & Fairhaven	d				11 24											12 28									
Lytham	d				11 27											12 31									
Moss Side	d				11 32											12 36									
Kirkham & Wesham	d				11 39					11 54	12 15					12 43					12 54		13 19		
Salwick	d																								
Preston	a				11 50				11 58	12 04	12 25		12 42			12 54				12 59	13 04		13 29		
	d			11 47				11 57							12 47				12 57						13 47
Lostock Hall	d							12 03											13 03						
Bamber Bridge	d							12 07											13 07						
Pleasington	d							12x14											13x14						
Cherry Tree	d							12 18											13 18						
Mill Hill (Lancashire)	d							12 20											13 20						
Blackburn	a			12 03				12 24							13 03				13 24						14 03
Clitheroe 94	a																								
Blackburn	d		11 48	12 03		12 18	12 19	12 24						12 48	13 03		13 16	13 19	13 24					13 47	14 03
Rishton	d							12 29											13 29						
Church & Oswaldtwistle	d							12 32											13 32						
Accrington	d			12 11			12 27	12 36							13 11			13 27	13 36						14 11
Huncoat	d							12 40											13 40						
Hapton	d							12x43											13x43						
Rose Grove	d						12 34	12 47										13 34	13 47						
Burnley Manchester Road 41	a			12 20			12 37								13 20			13 37							14 20
Leeds 41	a			13 38											14 38										15 37
Todmorden	d						12 55											13 55							
Rochdale	d						13 09											14 09							
Manchester Victoria	a		12 41			13 07	13 24							13 41			14 07	14 24						14 41	
Burnley Barracks	d							12x50											13x50						
Burnley Central	d							12 53											13 53						
Brierfield	d							12 57											13 57						
Nelson	d							13 01											14 01						
Colne	a							13 07											14 07						

A To Liverpool Lime Street
B To Manchester Piccadilly
C From Clitheroe to Rochdale
D To Rochdale
E To Southport
F To Manchester Airport

Table T097-R

Mondays to Fridays

21 May to 7 December

Blackpool - Preston - Blackburn, Accrington, Burnley and Colne

		NT	NT	NT	NT	NT	NT		NT	NT	NT	NT	NT	NT	NT	NT	NT		NT	NT	NT	NT	NT	NT	NT
									◇	◇		◇								◇	◇			◇	
		A		B	C				D	E	F		A		B	C				D	E	A	F		
Blackpool North	d	13 23					13 32		13 38	14 01			14 23						14 32	14 38	15 05	15 20			
Layton	d								13 41											14 41					
Poulton-le-Fylde	d	13 28					13 38		13 45	14 06			14 29						14 38	14 45	15 10	15 25			
Blackpool South	d		13 15											14 15											15 17
Blackpool Pleasure Beach	d		13 17											14 17											15 19
Squires Gate	d		13 19											14 19											15 21
St Annes-on-the-Sea	d		13 23											14 23											15 25
Ansdell & Fairhaven	d		13 27											14 27											15 29
Lytham	d		13 30											14 30											15 32
Moss Side	d		13 35											14 35											15 37
Kirkham & Wesham	d		13 44						13 54	14 15				14 45						14 54	15 19				15 43
Salwick	d																								
Preston	a	13 48	13 55				14 02		14 04	14 25			14 48	14 56					15 02	15 04	15 29	15 42			15 54
	d					13 57						14 47					14 58							15 47	
Lostock Hall	d					14 03											15 04								
Bamber Bridge	d					14 07											15 08								
Pleasington	d					14x14											15x15								
Cherry Tree	d					14 18											15 19								
Mill Hill (Lancashire)	d					14 20											15 21								
Blackburn	a					14 24						15 04					15 25							16 04	
Clitheroe 94	a																								
Blackburn	d			14 16	14 19	14 24					14 48	15 04			15 18	15 19	15 25						15 48	16 04	
Rishton	d					14 29											15 30								
Church & Oswaldtwistle	d					14 32											15 33								
Accrington	d				14 27	14 36						15 12				15 27	15 36							16 12	
Huncoat	d					14 40											15 41								
Hapton	d					14x43											15x44								
Rose Grove	d				14 34	14 47										15 34	15 47								
Burnley Manchester Road 41	a				14 37							15 21				15 37								16 21	
Leeds 41	a											16 39												17 39	
Todmorden	d				14 55											15 55									
Rochdale	d				15 09											16 09									
Manchester Victoria	a			15 07	15 24						15 40				16 07	16 24							16 41		
Burnley Barracks	d					14x50											15x50								
Burnley Central	d					14 53											15 53								
Brierfield	d					14 57											15 57								
Nelson	d					15 01											16 01								
Colne	a					15 07											16 07								

		NT	NT		NT	NT	NT	NT	NT	NT	NT	NT	NT		NT	NT	NT	NT	NT	NT	NT	NT	NT		NT
							◇	◇			◇						◇	◇		◇					
		G	B				D	E	A	F			H				D	E	F		A		F		C
Blackpool North	d					15 32	15 38	16 01	16 15							16 32	16 38	17 01			17 11				
Layton	d						15 41										16 41				17 14				
Poulton-le-Fylde	d					15 38	15 45	16 06	16 21							16 38	16 45	17 06			17 18				
Blackpool South	d											16 15										17 14			
Blackpool Pleasure Beach	d											16 17										17 16			
Squires Gate	d											16 19										17 18			
St Annes-on-the-Sea	d											16 23										17 22			
Ansdell & Fairhaven	d											16 27										17 26			
Lytham	d											16 30										17 29			
Moss Side	d											16 35										17 34			
Kirkham & Wesham	d						15 54	16 15				16 42					16 54	17 15			17 27	17 41			
Salwick	d																	17 19				17 45			
Preston	a					15 59	16 04	16 25	16 38			16 53				17 02	17 04	17 28			17 38	17 54			
	d				15 57						16 47				16 57					17 35					
Lostock Hall	d				16 03										17 03					17 42					
Bamber Bridge	d				16 07										17 07					17 45					
Pleasington	d				16x14										17x14					17 53					
Cherry Tree	d				16 18										17 18					17 56					
Mill Hill (Lancashire)	d				16 20										17 20					17 59					
Blackburn	a				16 24						17 04				17 24					18 02					
Clitheroe 94	a																								
Blackburn	d	16 17	16 18		16 24					16 48	17 04		17 19		17 24				17 48	18 03			18 18		18 19
Rishton	d				16 29										17 29										
Church & Oswaldtwistle	d				16 32										17 32										
Accrington	d	16 25			16 36						17 12		17 27		17 36					18 11					18 27
Huncoat	d				16 40										17 40										
Hapton	d				16x43										17x43										
Rose Grove	d	16 32			16 47								17 34		17 47										18 34
Burnley Manchester Road 41	a	16 35									17 21		17 37							18 20					18 37
Leeds 41	a										18 41									19 37					
Todmorden	d	16 53											17 55												18 55
Rochdale	d	17 09											18 09												19 09
Manchester Victoria	a	17 24	17 07							17 41			18 24						18 41				19 07		19 24
Burnley Barracks	d				16x50										17x50										
Burnley Central	d				16 53										17 53										
Brierfield	d				16 57										17 57										
Nelson	d				17 01										18 01										
Colne	a				17 07										18 07										

A To Manchester Piccadilly
B To Rochdale
C To Southport
D To Manchester Airport
E To Liverpool Lime Street
F From Clitheroe to Rochdale
G To Wigan North Western
H To Kirkby

Blackpool - Preston - Blackburn, Accrington, Burnley and Colne

		NT	NT	NT ◇ A	NT ◇ B	NT C	NT ◇	NT D	NT	NT E	NT F	NT	NT ◇ A	NT ◇ B	NT G	NT C	NT ◇	NT	NT	NT H	NT	NT ◇ A	NT ◇ B
Blackpool North	d		17 32	17 38	18 03			18 24					18 37	19 05	19 16				19 32			19 39	20 01
Layton	d			17 41									18 40									19 42	
Poulton-le-Fylde	d		17 38	17 45	18 08			18 30					18 44	19 10	19 21				19 38			19 46	20 06
Blackpool South	d								18 16									19 13					
Blackpool Pleasure Beach	d								18 18									19 15					
Squires Gate	d								18 20									19 17					
St Annes-on-the-Sea	d								18 24									19 21					
Ansdell & Fairhaven	d								18 28									19 25					
Lytham	d								18 31									19 28					
Moss Side	d								18 36									19 33					
Kirkham & Wesham	d			17 54	18 17				18 43				18 53	19 19				19 40				19 55	20 15
Salwick	d																						
Preston 8	a		18 02	18 04	18 27			18 48	18 54				19 03	19 29	19 38			19 51	19 57			20 05	20 25
	d	17 57					18 47					18 57					19 47				19 57		
Lostock Hall	d	18 03										19 03									20 03		
Bamber Bridge	d	18 07										19 07									20 07		
Pleasington	d	18x14										19x14									20x14		
Cherry Tree	d	18 18										19 18									20 18		
Mill Hill (Lancashire)	d	18 20										19 20									20 20		
Blackburn	a	18 24					19 03					19 24					20 02				20 24		
Clitheroe 94	a																						
Blackburn	d	18 24				18 48	19 03			19 18	19 19	19 24				19 46	20 03			20 17	20 24		
Rishton	d	18 29										19 29									20 29		
Church & Oswaldtwistle	d	18 32										19 32									20 32		
Accrington	d	18 36					19 11				19 27	19 36					20 10			20 25	20 36		
Huncoat	d	18 40										19 40									20 40		
Hapton	d	18x43										19x43									20x43		
Rose Grove	d	18 47									19 34	19 47								20 32	20 47		
Burnley Manchester Road 41	a						19 20				19 37						20 19			20 35			
Leeds 10 41	a						20 39										21 37						
Todmorden	d										19 55									20 53			
Rochdale	d										20 09									21 09			
Manchester Victoria	a					19 40				20 07	20 24					20 41				21 24			
Burnley Barracks	d	18x50										19x50									20x50		
Burnley Central	d	18 53										19 53									20 53		
Brierfield	d	18 57										19 57									20 57		
Nelson	d	19 01										20 01									21 01		
Colne	a	19 07										20 07									21 07		

		NT G	NT C	NT ◇	NT	NT F	NT	NT	NT ◇ A	NT B	NT G	NT FO I	NT FX 🚌	NT ◇	NT	NT H	NT	NT	NT B	NT	NT ◇ A	NT	NT
Blackpool North	d	20 14						20 32	20 38	21 00	21 17							21 32	22 18		22 25		
Layton	d								20 41									21 35			22 28		
Poulton-le-Fylde	d	20 20						20 38	20 45	21 06	21 22							21 39	22 23		22 32		
Blackpool South	d				20 15										21 13							22 15	
Blackpool Pleasure Beach	d				20 17										21 15							22 17	
Squires Gate	d				20 19										21 17							22 20	
St Annes-on-the-Sea	d				20 23										21 21							22 24	
Ansdell & Fairhaven	d				20 26										21 25							22 27	
Lytham	d				20 29										21 28							22 31	
Moss Side	d				20 34										21 33							22 36	
Kirkham & Wesham	d				20 43				20 54	21 15					21 40			21 47			22 41	22 48	
Salwick	d																						
Preston 8	a	20 37			20 54			21 02	21 04	21 25	21 39				21 51			21 59	22 41		22 51	22 58	
	d			20 47			20 57							21 47			21 57			22 47			23 23
Lostock Hall	d						21 03										22 03			22 53			
Bamber Bridge	d						21 07										22 07			22 57			
Pleasington	d						21x14										22x14			23x04			
Cherry Tree	d						21 18										22 18			23 08			
Mill Hill (Lancashire)	d						21 20										22 20			23 10			
Blackburn	a			21 03			21 24							22 03			22 24			23 13			23 40
Clitheroe 94	a																						
Blackburn	d		20 48	21 03		21 20	21 24					21 48	21 55	22 03		22 19	22 24			23 15			
Rishton	d						21 29										22 29			23 20			
Church & Oswaldtwistle	d						21 32										22 32			23 23			
Accrington	d			21 11		21 30	21 36							22 11		22 27	22 36			23 26			
Huncoat	d						21 40										22 40			23 31			
Hapton	d						21x43										22x43			23x34			
Rose Grove	d					21 37	21 47									22 34	22 47			23 37			
Burnley Manchester Road 41	a			21 20		21 40								22 20		22 37							
Leeds 10 41	a			22 38										23 37									
Todmorden	d					21 58										22 55							
Rochdale	d					22 14										23 11							
Manchester Victoria	a		21 36			22 29						22 42	23 20			23 33							
Burnley Barracks	d						21x50										22x50			23x40			
Burnley Central	d						21 53										22 53			23 42			
Brierfield	d						21 57										22 57			23 47			
Nelson	d						22 01										23 01			23 50			
Colne	a						22 07										23 07			23 55			

A To Manchester Airport
B To Liverpool Lime Street
C From Clitheroe to Rochdale
D To Manchester Oxford Road
E To Rochdale
F To Southport
G To Manchester Piccadilly
H To Wigan Wallgate
I From Clitheroe

Table T097-R

Blackpool - Preston - Blackburn, Accrington, Burnley and Colne

Mondays to Fridays

21 May to 7 December

		NT ◇ A	NT FO B	NT	NT	NT FX 🚌
Blackpool North	d	23 13				
Layton	d	23 16				
Poulton-le-Fylde	d	23 20				
Blackpool South	d			23 24		
Blackpool Pleasure Beach	d			23 26		
Squires Gate	d			23 28		
St Annes-on-the-Sea	d			23 32		
Ansdell & Fairhaven	d			23 35		
Lytham	d			23 38		
Moss Side	d			23 43		
Kirkham & Wesham	d	23 30		23 50		
Salwick	d					
Preston 8	a	23 41		00 02		
	d					
Lostock Hall	d					
Bamber Bridge	d					
Pleasington	d					
Cherry Tree	d					
Mill Hill (Lancashire)	d					
Blackburn	a					
Clitheroe 94	a					
Blackburn	d		23 17		23 25	23 25
Rishton	d					
Church & Oswaldtwistle	d					
Accrington	d				23 33	
Huncoat	d					
Hapton	d					
Rose Grove	d				23 41	
Burnley Manchester Road 41	a				23 44	
Leeds 10 41	a					
Todmorden	d				00 04	
Rochdale	d				00 18	
Manchester Victoria	a		00 06		00 33	00 50
Burnley Barracks	d					
Burnley Central	d					
Brierfield	d					
Nelson	d					
Colne	a					

Saturdays

26 May to 8 December

		NT C	NT ◇ A	NT ◇ A	NT	NT ◇	NT D	NT E	NT F	NT	NT ◇ A	NT	NT G	NT D	NT H	NT ◇	NT F	NT H	NT	NT	NT ◇ A	NT	NT G
Blackpool North	d		03 33	04 28		05 19	05 23				05 39		06 03	06 16						06 32	06 38		07 03
Layton	d										05 42										06 41		
Poulton-le-Fylde	d			04 34		05 25	05 29				05 46		06 08	06 21						06 38	06 45		07 08
Blackpool South	d											05 35										06 35	
Blackpool Pleasure Beach	d											05 37										06 37	
Squires Gate	d											05 39										06 39	
St Annes-on-the-Sea	d											05 43										06 43	
Ansdell & Fairhaven	d											05 47										06 47	
Lytham	d											05 50										06 50	
Moss Side	d											05 55										06 55	
Kirkham & Wesham	d										05 55	06 02	06 17								06 54	07 02	07 17
Salwick	d																					07 06	
Preston 8	a		03 54	04 51		05 43	05 46				06 05	06 13	06 27	06 38						07 02	07 05	07 15	07 26
	d				05 05	05 44				05 56						06 48			06 57				
Lostock Hall	d									06 02									07 03				
Bamber Bridge	d									06 06									07 07				
Pleasington	d									06x13									07x14				
Cherry Tree	d									06 17									07 18				
Mill Hill (Lancashire)	d									06 19									07 20				
Blackburn	a				05 23	06 03				06 23						07 04			07 24				
Clitheroe 94	a																						
Blackburn	d				05 23	06 03		06 16	06 19	06 23					06 48	07 04	07 14	07 18	07 24				
Rishton	d				05 28					06 28									07 29				
Church & Oswaldtwistle	d				05 31					06 31									07 32				
Accrington	d				05 35	06 11			06 27	06 35						07 12	07 21		07 36				
Huncoat	d				05 39					06 39									07 40				
Hapton	d				05x42					06x42									07x43				
Rose Grove	d				05 46				06 34	06 46							07 28		07 47				
Burnley Manchester Road 41	a					06 20			06 37							07 21	07 32						
Leeds 10 41	a					07 40										08 38							
Todmorden	d	00 04							06 55								07 49						
Rochdale	d	00 18							07 09								08 06						
Manchester Victoria	a	00 33						07 07	07 23						07 41		08 24	08 08					
Burnley Barracks	d				05x49					06x49									07x50				
Burnley Central	d				05 52					06 51									07 53				
Brierfield	d				05 56					06 56									07 57				
Nelson	d				06 00					06 59									08 01				
Colne	a				06 06					07 05									08 07				

A To Manchester Airport
B From Clitheroe
C From Blackburn
D To Manchester Piccadilly
E To Rochdale
F To Southport
G To Liverpool Lime Street
H From Clitheroe to Rochdale

Blackpool - Preston - Blackburn, Accrington, Burnley and Colne

		NT A	NT B	NT ◇	NT C	NT D	NT	NT	NT ◇ E	NT	NT F	NT A	NT B	NT ◇	NT C	NT D	NT	NT	NT ◇ E	NT	NT ◇ F	NT A	NT B
Blackpool North	d	07 16						07 32	07 38		08 04	08 21						08 32	08 38		09 03	09 21	
Layton	d								07 41										08 41				
Poulton-le-Fylde	d	07 22						07 38	07 45		08 09	08 27						08 38	08 45		09 08	09 26	
Blackpool South	d									07 35										08 35			
Blackpool Pleasure Beach	d									07 37										08 37			
Squires Gate	d									07 39										08 39			
St Annes-on-the-Sea	d									07 43										08 43			
Ansdell & Fairhaven	d									07 47										08 47			
Lytham	d									07 50										08 50			
Moss Side	d									07 55										08 55			
Kirkham & Wesham	d	07 31							07 54	08 02	08 18								08 54	09 02	09 17		
Salwick	d									08 07													
Preston	a	07 42						07 58	08 04	08 16	08 28	08 44						09 02	09 04	09 15	09 27	09 43	
	d			07 50			07 57							08 50			08 57						
Lostock Hall	d						08 03										09 03						
Bamber Bridge	d						08 07										09 07						
Pleasington	d						08x14										09x14						
Cherry Tree	d						08 18										09 18						
Mill Hill (Lancashire)	d						08 20										09 20						
Blackburn	a			08 05			08 24							09 05			09 24						
Clitheroe 94	a																						
Blackburn	d		07 48	08 06	08 18	08 19	08 24						08 48	09 06	09 18	09 19	09 24						09 48
Rishton	d						08 29										09 29						
Church & Oswaldtwistle	d						08 32										09 32						
Accrington	d			08 14		08 27	08 36							09 14		09 27	09 36						
Huncoat	d						08 40										09 40						
Hapton	d						08x43										09x43						
Rose Grove	d					08 34	08 47									09 34	09 47						
Burnley Manchester Road 41	a			08 22		08 37								09 22		09 37							
Leeds 41	a			09 42										10 43									
Todmorden	d					08 55										09 55							
Rochdale	d					09 09										10 09							
Manchester Victoria	a		08 41		09 07	09 24							09 41		10 07	10 24							10 41
Burnley Barracks	d						08x50										09x50						
Burnley Central	d						08 53										09 53						
Brierfield	d						08 57										09 57						
Nelson	d						09 01										10 01						
Colne	a						09 07										10 07						

		NT ◇	NT C	NT D	NT	NT ◇ E	NT	NT ◇ F	NT A	NT B	NT ◇	NT C	NT D	NT	NT	NT ◇ E	NT	NT ◇ F	NT A	NT B	NT ◇	NT
Blackpool North	d					09 38		10 01	10 12						10 33	10 36		11 03	11 20			11 32
Layton	d					09 41										10 39						
Poulton-le-Fylde	d					09 45		10 06	10 17						10 39	10 43		11 08	11 25			11 38
Blackpool South	d						09 35										10 35					
Blackpool Pleasure Beach	d						09 37										10 37					
Squires Gate	d						09 39										10 39					
St Annes-on-the-Sea	d						09 43										10 43					
Ansdell & Fairhaven	d						09 47										10 47					
Lytham	d						09 50										10 50					
Moss Side	d						09 55										10 55					
Kirkham & Wesham	d					09 54	10 02	10 15								10 52	11 02	11 17				
Salwick	d																					
Preston	a					10 04	10 13	10 25	10 34						11 01	11 03	11 13	11 27	11 42			11 57
	d	09 48			09 57						10 47			10 57							11 47	
Lostock Hall	d				10 03									11 03								
Bamber Bridge	d				10 07									11 07								
Pleasington	d				10x14									11x14								
Cherry Tree	d				10 18									11 18								
Mill Hill (Lancashire)	d				10 20									11 20								
Blackburn	a	10 04			10 24						11 03			11 24							12 03	
Clitheroe 94	a																					
Blackburn	d	10 05	10 18	10 19	10 24					10 48	11 03	11 17	11 19	11 24						11 48	12 03	
Rishton	d				10 29									11 29								
Church & Oswaldtwistle	d				10 32									11 32								
Accrington	d	10 13		10 27	10 36						11 11		11 27	11 36							12 11	
Huncoat	d				10 40									11 40								
Hapton	d				10x43									11x43								
Rose Grove	d			10 34	10 47								11 34	11 47								
Burnley Manchester Road 41	a	10 21		10 37							11 20		11 37								12 20	
Leeds 41	a	11 39									12 38										13 38	
Todmorden	d			10 55									11 55									
Rochdale	d			11 09									12 09									
Manchester Victoria	a		11 07	11 24						11 41		12 08	12 24							12 41		
Burnley Barracks	d				10x50									11x50								
Burnley Central	d				10 53									11 53								
Brierfield	d				10 57									11 57								
Nelson	d				11 01									12 01								
Colne	a				11 07									12 07								

A To Manchester Piccadilly
B From Clitheroe to Rochdale
C To Rochdale
D To Southport
E To Manchester Airport
F To Liverpool Lime Street

Table T097-R

Saturdays

26 May to 8 December

Blackpool - Preston - Blackburn, Accrington, Burnley and Colne

		NT A	NT B	NT	NT ◇ C	NT	NT ◇ D	NT E	NT F	NT ◇	NT A	NT B	NT	NT	NT ◇ C	NT	NT ◇ D	NT E	NT F	NT ◇	NT A	NT B	NT
Blackpool North	d				11 35		12 01	12 20						12 32	12 38		13 05	13 20					
Layton	d				11 38										12 41								
Poulton-le-Fylde	d				11 42		12 06	12 25						12 38	12 45		13 10	13 25					
Blackpool South	d					11 36										12 36							
Blackpool Pleasure Beach	d					11 38										12 38							
Squires Gate	d					11 40										12 40							
St Annes-on-the-Sea	d					11 44										12 44							
Ansdell & Fairhaven	d					11 47										12 48							
Lytham	d					11 50										12 51							
Moss Side	d					11 55										12 56							
Kirkham & Wesham	d				11 51	12 02	12 15								12 54	13 03	13 19						
Salwick	d																						
Preston	a				12 01	12 13	12 25	12 42						12 59	13 04	13 14	13 29	13 42					
	d			11 57						12 47			12 57							13 47			13 57
Lostock Hall	d			12 03									13 03										14 03
Bamber Bridge	d			12 07									13 07										14 07
Pleasington	d			12x14									13x14										14x14
Cherry Tree	d			12 18									13 18										14 18
Mill Hill (Lancashire)	d			12 20									13 20										14 20
Blackburn	a			12 24						13 03			13 24							14 03			14 24
Clitheroe 94	a																						
Blackburn	d	12 18	12 19	12 24					12 48	13 03	13 16	13 19	13 24						13 47	14 03	14 16	14 19	14 24
Rishton	d			12 29									13 29										14 29
Church & Oswaldtwistle	d			12 32									13 32										14 32
Accrington	d		12 27	12 36						13 11		13 27	13 36							14 11		14 27	14 36
Huncoat	d			12 40									13 40										14 40
Hapton	d			12x43									13x43										14x43
Rose Grove	d		12 34	12 47								13 34	13 47									14 34	14 47
Burnley Manchester Road 41	a		12 37							13 20		13 37								14 20		14 37	
Leeds 41	a									14 38										15 37			
Todmorden	d		12 55									13 55										14 55	
Rochdale	d		13 09									14 09										15 09	
Manchester Victoria	a	13 07	13 24						13 41		14 07	14 24							14 41		15 07	15 24	
Burnley Barracks	d			12x50									13x50										14x50
Burnley Central	d			12 53									13 53										14 53
Brierfield	d			12 57									13 57										14 57
Nelson	d			13 01									14 01										15 01
Colne	a			13 07									14 07										15 07

		NT	NT ◇ C	NT	NT ◇ D	NT E	NT F	NT ◇	NT A	NT B	NT	NT	NT ◇ C	NT	NT ◇ D	NT E	NT F	NT ◇	NT G	NT A	NT	NT
Blackpool North	d	13 32	13 38		14 01	14 20						14 32	14 38		15 05	15 20						15 32
Layton	d		13 41										14 41									
Poulton-le-Fylde	d	13 38	13 45		14 06	14 25						14 38	14 45		15 10	15 25						15 38
Blackpool South	d			13 35										14 35								
Blackpool Pleasure Beach	d			13 37										14 37								
Squires Gate	d			13 39										14 39								
St Annes-on-the-Sea	d			13 43										14 43								
Ansdell & Fairhaven	d			13 47										14 47								
Lytham	d			13 50										14 50								
Moss Side	d			13 55										14 55								
Kirkham & Wesham	d		13 54	14 02	14 15								14 54	15 02	15 19							
Salwick	d																					
Preston	a	14 02	14 04	14 13	14 25	14 42						15 02	15 04	15 13	15 29	15 42						15 58
	d							14 47			14 57							15 47			15 57	
Lostock Hall	d										15 03										16 03	
Bamber Bridge	d										15 07										16 07	
Pleasington	d										15x14										16x14	
Cherry Tree	d										15 18										16 18	
Mill Hill (Lancashire)	d										15 20										16 20	
Blackburn	a							15 04			15 24							16 04			16 24	
Clitheroe 94	a																					
Blackburn	d						14 48	15 04	15 18	15 19	15 24						15 48	16 04	16 17	16 18	16 24	
Rishton	d										15 29										16 29	
Church & Oswaldtwistle	d										15 32										16 32	
Accrington	d							15 12		15 27	15 35							16 12	16 25		16 36	
Huncoat	d										15 40										16 40	
Hapton	d										15x43										16x43	
Rose Grove	d									15 34	15 46								16 32		16 47	
Burnley Manchester Road 41	a							15 21		15 37								16 21	16 35			
Leeds 41	a							16 39										17 39				
Todmorden	d									15 55									16 53			
Rochdale	d									16 09									17 09			
Manchester Victoria	a						15 40		16 07	16 24							16 41		17 24	17 07		
Burnley Barracks	d										15x49										16x50	
Burnley Central	d										15 52										16 53	
Brierfield	d										15 56										16 57	
Nelson	d										16 00										17 01	
Colne	a										16 06										17 07	

A To Rochdale
B To Southport
C To Manchester Airport
D To Liverpool Lime Street
E To Manchester Piccadilly
F From Clitheroe to Rochdale
G To Wigan North Western

Table T097-R

Blackpool - Preston - Blackburn, Accrington, Burnley and Colne

Saturdays

26 May to 8 December

		NT ◇ A	NT	NT ◇ B	NT C	NT D	NT ◇	NT E	NT	NT	NT ◇ A	NT	NT ◇ B	NT D	NT ◇	NT C	NT D	NT F	NT	NT	NT ◇ A	NT	NT ◇ B
Blackpool North	d	15 38		16 01	16 15					16 32	16 38		17 01			17 11				17 32	17 38		18 03
Layton	d	15 41									16 41					17 14					17 41		
Poulton-le-Fylde	d	15 45		16 06	16 21					16 38	16 45		17 06			17 18				17 38	17 45		18 08
Blackpool South	d		15 35									16 35										17 35	
Blackpool Pleasure Beach	d		15 37									16 37										17 37	
Squires Gate	d		15 39									16 39										17 39	
St Annes-on-the-Sea	d		15 43									16 43										17 43	
Ansdell & Fairhaven	d		15 47									16 47										17 47	
Lytham	d		15 50									16 50										17 50	
Moss Side	d		15 55									16 55										17 55	
Kirkham & Wesham	d	15 54	16 01	16 15							16 54	17 02	17 15			17 27					17 54	18 02	18 17
Salwick	d												17 19										
Preston 8	a	16 04	16 12	16 25	16 38					17 02	17 04	17 13	17 28			17 38				18 02	18 04	18 13	18 27
	d						16 47		16 57						17 35				17 57				
Lostock Hall	d								17 03						17 42				18 03				
Bamber Bridge	d								17 07						17 45				18 07				
Pleasington	d								17x14						17 53				18x14				
Cherry Tree	d								17 18						17 56				18 18				
Mill Hill (Lancashire)	d								17 20						17 59				18 20				
Blackburn	a						17 04		17 24						18 02				18 24				
Clitheroe 94	a																						
Blackburn	d					16 48	17 04	17 19	17 24					17 48	18 03		18 18	18 19	18 24				
Rishton	d								17 29										18 29				
Church & Oswaldtwistle	d								17 32										18 32				
Accrington	d						17 12	17 27	17 36						18 11			18 27	18 36				
Huncoat	d								17 40										18 40				
Hapton	d								17x43										18x43				
Rose Grove	d							17 34	17 47									18 34	18 47				
Burnley Manchester Road 41	a						17 21	17 37							18 20			18 37					
Leeds 10 41	a						18 41								19 37								
Todmorden	d							17 55										18 55					
Rochdale	d							18 09										19 09					
Manchester Victoria	a					17 41		18 24						18 41			19 07	19 24					
Burnley Barracks	d								17x50										18x50				
Burnley Central	d								17 53										18 53				
Brierfield	d								17 57										18 57				
Nelson	d								18 01										19 01				
Colne	a								18 07										19 07				

		NT C	NT D	NT ◇	NT G	NT F	NT	NT ◇ A	NT	NT ◇ B	NT C	NT D	NT ◇	NT H	NT	NT	NT ◇ A	NT	NT ◇ B	NT C	NT D	NT ◇	NT F
Blackpool North	d	18 20						18 37		19 05	19 12					19 32	19 36		20 01	20 16			
Layton	d							18 40									19 39						
Poulton-le-Fylde	d	18 25						18 44		19 10	19 18					19 38	19 43		20 06	20 21			
Blackpool South	d								18 35									19 35					
Blackpool Pleasure Beach	d								18 37									19 37					
Squires Gate	d								18 39									19 39					
St Annes-on-the-Sea	d								18 43									19 43					
Ansdell & Fairhaven	d								18 47									19 47					
Lytham	d								18 50									19 50					
Moss Side	d								18 55									19 55					
Kirkham & Wesham	d							18 53	19 02	19 19							19 52	20 02	20 15				
Salwick	d																						
Preston 8	a	18 42						19 03	19 13	19 29	19 35					19 57	20 02	20 13	20 25	20 38			
	d			18 47			18 56						19 47		19 56							20 47	
Lostock Hall	d						19 03								20 03								
Bamber Bridge	d						19 07								20 07								
Pleasington	d						19x14								20x14								
Cherry Tree	d						19 18								20 18								
Mill Hill (Lancashire)	d						19 20								20 20								
Blackburn	a			19 03			19 24						20 02		20 24							21 03	
Clitheroe 94	a																						
Blackburn	d		18 48	19 03	19 18	19 19	19 24					19 46	20 03	20 17	20 24						20 48	21 03	21 20
Rishton	d						19 29								20 29								
Church & Oswaldtwistle	d						19 32								20 32								
Accrington	d			19 11		19 27	19 36						20 10	20 25	20 36							21 11	21 30
Huncoat	d						19 40								20 40								
Hapton	d						19x43								20x43								
Rose Grove	d					19 34	19 47							20 32	20 47								21 37
Burnley Manchester Road 41	a			19 20		19 37							20 19	20 35								21 20	21 40
Leeds 10 41	a			20 39									21 37									22 38	
Todmorden	d					19 55								20 53									21 58
Rochdale	d					20 09								21 09									22 14
Manchester Victoria	a		19 40		20 07	20 24						20 41		21 24							21 36		22 29
Burnley Barracks	d						19x50								20x50								
Burnley Central	d						19 53								20 53								
Brierfield	d						19 57								20 57								
Nelson	d						20 01								21 01								
Colne	a						20 07								21 07								

A To Manchester Airport
B To Liverpool Lime Street
C To Manchester Piccadilly
D From Clitheroe to Rochdale
E To Kirkby
F To Southport
G To Rochdale
H To Wigan Wallgate

Table T097-R

Blackpool - Preston - Blackburn, Accrington, Burnley and Colne

Saturdays

26 May to 8 December

		NT	NT	NT ◇ A	NT	NT B	NT C	NT D	NT ◇	NT	NT	NT	NT	NT B	NT ◇ A	NT D	NT	NT	NT	NT ◇ A	NT
Blackpool North	d		20 32	20 38		21 00	21 17					21 32		22 18	22 25					23 02	
Layton	d			20 41								21 35			22 28					23 05	
Poulton-le-Fylde	d		20 38	20 45		21 06	21 22					21 39		22 23	22 32					23 09	
Blackpool South	d				20 36								21 35								23 24
Blackpool Pleasure Beach	d				20 38								21 37								23 26
Squires Gate	d				20 40								21 39								23 28
St Annes-on-the-Sea	d				20 44								21 43						22 29		23 32
Ansdell & Fairhaven	d				20 47								21 47						22 32		23 35
Lytham	d				20 50								21 50						22 35		23 38
Moss Side	d				20 55								21 55						22 40		23 43
Kirkham & Wesham	d			20 54	21 02	21 15						21 47	22 02		22 41				22 48	23 18	23 50
Salwick	d																				
Preston 8	a		21 02	21 04	21 13	21 25	21 39					21 59	22 13	22 41	22 51				22 58	23 29	00 02
	d	20 57							21 47		21 57							22 57			
Lostock Hall	d	21 03									22 03							23 03			
Bamber Bridge	d	21 07									22 07							23 07			
Pleasington	d	21x14									22x14							23x14			
Cherry Tree	d	21 18									22 18							23 18			
Mill Hill (Lancashire)	d	21 20									22 20							23 20			
Blackburn	a	21 24							22 03		22 24							23 24			
Clitheroe 94	a																				
Blackburn	d	21 24						21 48	22 03	22 19	22 24					23 18	23 19	23 24			
Rishton	d	21 29									22 29							23 29			
Church & Oswaldtwistle	d	21 32									22 32							23 32			
Accrington	d	21 36							22 11	22 27	22 36						23 27	23 36			
Huncoat	d	21 40									22 40							23 40			
Hapton	d	21x43									22x43							23x43			
Rose Grove	d	21 47								22 34	22 47						23 34	23 47			
Burnley Manchester Road 41	a								22 20	22 37							23 37				
Leeds 10 41	a								23 37												
Todmorden	d									22 55							23 55				
Rochdale	d									23 11							00 09				
Manchester Victoria	a							22 42		23 33						00 08	00 24				
Burnley Barracks	d	21x50									22x50							23x50			
Burnley Central	d	21 53									22 53							23a52			
Brierfield	d	21 57									22 57										
Nelson	d	22 01									23 01										
Colne	a	22 07									23 07										

Sundays

20 May to 2 December

		NT E	NT	NT ◇ F	NT G	NT	NT ◇ B	NT	NT ◇	NT ◇ H	NT G	NT	NT ◇ B	NT ◇ I 🍴	NT ◇ A	NT ◇ H	NT D	NT ◇	NT G	NT	NT ◇ B	NT ◇ F	NT ◇ H
Blackpool North	d			07 48			07 55		08 21				08 32	08 40	08 43	09 05		09 21			09 32	09 41	10 05
Layton	d								08 24									09 24					
Poulton-le-Fylde	d						08 01		08 27				08 38	08 46	08 49	09 11		09 27			09 38	09 47	10 11
Blackpool South	d																			09 16			
Blackpool Pleasure Beach	d																			09 18			
Squires Gate	d																			09 20			
St Annes-on-the-Sea	d																			09 24			
Ansdell & Fairhaven	d																			09 28			
Lytham	d																			09 31			
Moss Side	d																			09 36			
Kirkham & Wesham	d						08 10		08 37				08 47	08 55	08 58			09 37		09 43	09 47	09 56	
Salwick	d																						
Preston 8	a			08 09			08 20		08 48				08 57	09 06	09 08	09 29		09 48		09 54	09 57	10 06	10 29
	d					08 15			08 49			08 56		09 07		09 30		09 49		09 55			10 30
Lostock Hall	d					08 21						09 02		09 14						10 02			
Bamber Bridge	d					08 25						09 06		09 17						10 06			
Pleasington	d											09x13								10x13			
Cherry Tree	d											09 17								10 17			
Mill Hill (Lancashire)	d											09 19								10 19			
Blackburn	a					08 36						09 23		09 28		09 47				10 23			10 47
Clitheroe 94	a													09 51									
Blackburn	d		07 48		08 12	08 37		08 48		08 48	09 12	09 23				09 47	09 48		10 12	10 23			10 47
Rishton	d											09 28								10 28			
Church & Oswaldtwistle	d		07 53		08 17						09 17	09 31							10 17	10 31			
Accrington	d		07 56		08 21	08 45				08 56	09 21	09 35				09 55			10 21	10 35			10 55
Huncoat	d											09 39								10 39			
Hapton	d											09x42								10x42			
Rose Grove	d		08 03		08 28	08 52					09 28	09 46							10 28	10 46			
Burnley Manchester Road 41	a		08 07		08 31					09 04	09 31					10 04			10 31				11 04
Leeds 10 41	a									10 19						11 19							12 19
Todmorden	d		08 24		08 49						09 49								10 49				
Rochdale	d	00 09	08 38		09 03						10 03								11 03				
Manchester Victoria	a	00 24	08 59		09 24			09 39	09 45		10 24						10 40	10 45	11 24				
Burnley Barracks	d											09x49								10x49			
Burnley Central	d					08 57						09 52								10 52			
Brierfield	d					09 01						09 56								10 56			
Nelson	d					09 05						10 00								11 00			
Colne	a					09 11						10 06								11 06			

A To Manchester Airport
B To Liverpool Lime Street
C To Manchester Piccadilly
D From Clitheroe
E not 20 May. From Blackburn
F To Manchester Oxford Road
G To Southport
H To York
I To Carlisle

Table T097-R

Blackpool - Preston - Blackburn, Accrington, Burnley and Colne

		NT A	NT ◇	NT B	NT	NT ◇ C	NT ◇ D	NT ◇ E	NT A	NT ◇	NT B	NT	NT ◇ C	NT ◇ D	NT ◇ E	NT A	NT ◇	NT ◇ C	NT B	NT	NT ◇ D	NT ◇ E	NT A
Blackpool North	d		10 21			10 33	10 41	11 05		11 21			11 32	11 41	12 05		12 17	12 24			12 40	13 05	
Layton	d		10 24							11 24							12 20						
Poulton-le-Fylde	d		10 27			10 39	10 47	11 11		11 27			11 38	11 47	12 11		12 23	12 30			12 46	13 11	
Blackpool South	d				10 18							11 16								12 16			
Blackpool Pleasure Beach	d				10 20							11 18								12 18			
Squires Gate	d				10 22							11 20								12 20			
St Annes-on-the-Sea	d				10 26							11 24								12 24			
Ansdell & Fairhaven	d				10 29							11 28								12 28			
Lytham	d				10 32							11 31								12 31			
Moss Side	d				10 37							11 36								12 36			
Kirkham & Wesham	d		10 37		10 44	10 48	10 56			11 37		11 43	11 47	11 56			12 33	12 39		12 43	12 55		
Salwick	d																						
Preston	a		10 48		10 55	10 59	11 06	11 29		11 48		11 54	11 57	12 06	12 29		12 44	12 49		12 54	13 05	13 29	
	d		10 49		10 56			11 30		11 49		11 56			12 30		12 45			12 56		13 30	
Lostock Hall	d				11 07							12 07								13 07			
Bamber Bridge	d				11 10							12 10								13 10			
Pleasington	d				11x18							12x17								13x17			
Cherry Tree	d				11 21							12 21								13 21			
Mill Hill (Lancashire)	d				11 24							12 23								13 23			
Blackburn	a				11 27			11 47				12 27			12 47					13 27		13 47	
Clitheroe 94	a																						
Blackburn	d	10 48		11 12	11 28			11 47	11 48		12 12	12 27			12 47	12 48			13 12	13 27		13 47	13 48
Rishton	d				11 33							12 32								13 32			
Church & Oswaldtwistle	d			11 17	11 36						12 17	12 35							13 17	13 35			
Accrington	d			11 21	11 39			11 55			12 21	12 39			12 55				13 21	13 39		13 55	
Huncoat	d				11 44							12 43								13 43			
Hapton	d				11x47							12x46								13x46			
Rose Grove	d			11 28	11 50						12 28	12 50							13 28	13 50			
Burnley Manchester Road 41	a			11 31				12 04			12 31				13 04				13 31			14 04	
Leeds 41	a							13 19							14 23							15 19	
Todmorden	d			11 49							12 49								13 49				
Rochdale	d			12 03							13 03								14 03				
Manchester Victoria	a	11 40	11 45	12 24					12 40	12 45	13 24					13 40	13 45		14 24				14 40
Burnley Barracks	d				11x53							12x53								13x53			
Burnley Central	d				11 56							12 56								13 56			
Brierfield	d				12 01							13 00								14 00			
Nelson	d				12 04							13 04								14 04			
Colne	a				12 11							13 10								14 10			

		NT ◇	NT B	NT	NT ◇ C	NT ◇ D	NT ◇ E	NT A	NT ◇	NT B	NT	NT ◇ C	NT ◇ D	NT ◇ E	NT A	NT ◇	NT B	NT	NT ◇ C	NT ◇ D	NT ◇ E	NT A
Blackpool North	d	13 21			13 32	13 41	13 52		14 21			14 32	14 41	15 05		15 21			15 32	15 41	16 05	
Layton	d	13 24							14 24							15 24						
Poulton-le-Fylde	d	13 27			13 38	13 47	13 58		14 27			14 38	14 47	15 11		15 27			15 38	15 47	16 11	
Blackpool South	d			13 16							14 16							15 16				
Blackpool Pleasure Beach	d			13 18							14 18							15 18				
Squires Gate	d			13 20							14 20							15 20				
St Annes-on-the-Sea	d			13 24							14 24							15 24				
Ansdell & Fairhaven	d			13 28							14 28							15 28				
Lytham	d			13 31							14 31							15 31				
Moss Side	d			13 36							14 36							15 36				
Kirkham & Wesham	d	13 37		13 43	13 47	13 56			14 37		14 43	14 47	14 56			15 37		15 43	15 47	15 56		
Salwick	d																					
Preston	a	13 48		13 53	13 58	14 06	14 16		14 48		14 54	14 59	15 06	15 29		15 48		15 54	15 59	16 06	16 29	
	d	13 49		13 55			14 18		14 49		14 56			15 30		15 49		15 56			16 30	
Lostock Hall	d			14 07							15 07							16 07				
Bamber Bridge	d			14 10							15 10							16 10				
Pleasington	d			14x17							15x17							16x17				
Cherry Tree	d			14 21							15 21							16 21				
Mill Hill (Lancashire)	d			14 23							15 23							16 23				
Blackburn	a			14 27			14 37				15 27			15 47				16 27			16 47	
Clitheroe 94	a																					
Blackburn	d		14 12	14 27			14 39	14 48		15 12	15 27			15 47	15 48		16 12	16 27			16 47	16 48
Rishton	d			14 32							15 32							16 32				
Church & Oswaldtwistle	d		14 17	14 35						15 17	15 35						16 17	16 35				
Accrington	d		14 21	14 39			14 47			15 21	15 39			15 55			16 21	16 39			16 55	
Huncoat	d			14 43							15 43							16 43				
Hapton	d			14x46							15x46							16x46				
Rose Grove	d		14 28	14 50						15 28	15 50						16 28	16 50				
Burnley Manchester Road 41	a		14 31				14 57			15 31				16 04			16 31				17 04	
Leeds 41	a						16 15							17 19							18 20	
Todmorden	d		14 49							15 49							16 49					
Rochdale	d		15 03							16 03							17 03					
Manchester Victoria	a	14 45	15 24					15 40	15 46	16 24					16 40	16 45	17 24					17 40
Burnley Barracks	d			14x53							15x53							16x53				
Burnley Central	d			14 56							15 56							16 56				
Brierfield	d			15 00							16 00							17 00				
Nelson	d			15 04							16 04							17 04				
Colne	a			15 10							16 10							17 10				

A From Clitheroe
B To Southport
C To Liverpool Lime Street
D To Manchester Airport
E To York

Table T097-R

Blackpool - Preston - Blackburn, Accrington, Burnley and Colne

		NT ◇	NT A	NT	NT ◇ B	NT ◇ C	NT ◇ D	NT E	NT ◇	NT A	NT	NT ◇ B	NT ◇ C	NT ◇ D	NT E	NT ◇	NT A	NT	NT ◇ B	NT ◇ C	NT ◇ D	NT ◇	NT A
Blackpool North	d	16 21			16 32	16 41	17 05		17 21			17 34	17 41	17 52		18 21			18 32	18 41	19 05	19 21	
Layton	d	16 24							17 24							18 24						19 24	
Poulton-le-Fylde	d	16 27			16 38	16 47	17 11		17 27			17 40	17 47	17 58		18 27			18 38	18 47	19 11	19 27	
Blackpool South	d			16 16							17 16							18 16					
Blackpool Pleasure Beach	d			16 18							17 18							18 18					
Squires Gate	d			16 20							17 20							18 20					
St Annes-on-the-Sea	d			16 24							17 24							18 24					
Ansdell & Fairhaven	d			16 28							17 28							18 28					
Lytham	d			16 31							17 31							18 31					
Moss Side	d			16 36							17 36							18 36					
Kirkham & Wesham	d	16 37		16 43	16 47	16 56			17 37		17 43	17 49	17 56			18 37		18 43	18 47	18 56		19 37	
Salwick	d																						
Preston	a	16 48		16 54	16 57	17 06	17 29		17 48		17 54	17 59	18 06	18 17		18 48		18 54	18 57	19 06	19 29	19 48	
	d	16 49		16 56			17 30		17 49		17 56			18 19		18 49		18 56			19 30	19 49	
Lostock Hall	d			17 07							18 02							19 07					
Bamber Bridge	d			17 10							18 06							19 10					
Pleasington	d			17x17							18x13							19x17					
Cherry Tree	d			17 21							18 17							19 21					
Mill Hill (Lancashire)	d			17 23							18 19							19 23					
Blackburn	a			17 27			17 47				18 23			18 35				19 27			19 47		
Clitheroe 94	a																						
Blackburn	d		17 12	17 27			17 47	17 48		18 12	18 23			18 36	18 50		19 12	19 27			19 47		20 16
Rishton	d			17 32							18 28							19 32					
Church & Oswaldtwistle	d		17 17	17 35						18 17	18 31						19 17	19 35					20 21
Accrington	d		17 21	17 39			17 55			18 21	18 35			18 45			19 21	19 39			19 55		20 25
Huncoat	d			17 43							18 39							19 43					
Hapton	d			17x46							18x42							19x46					
Rose Grove	d		17 28	17 50						18 28	18 46						19 28	19 50					20 32
Burnley Manchester Road 41	a		17 31				18 04			18 31				18 58			19 31				20 04		20 35
Leeds 41	a						19 18							20 17							21 19		
Todmorden	d		17 49							18 49							19 49						20 55
Rochdale	d		18 03							19 03							20 03						21 09
Manchester Victoria	a	17 45	18 24					18 40	18 45	19 24					19 40	19 45	20 24					20 45	21 30
Burnley Barracks	d			17x53							18x49							19x53					
Burnley Central	d			17 56							18 52							19 56					
Brierfield	d			18 00							18 56							20 00					
Nelson	d			18 04							19 00							20 04					
Colne	a			18 10							19 06							20 10					

		NT E	NT	NT ◇ B	NT ◇ C	NT ◇	NT E	NT ◇	NT	NT	NT ◇ B	NT ◇ C	NT ◇	NT E	NT ◇	NT	NT	NT ◇ C	NT ◇ B	NT	NT	NT
Blackpool North	d			19 32	19 41	20 00		20 21			20 32	20 41	21 05		21 21			21 41	22 05	22 21		
Layton	d							20 24							21 24					22 24		
Poulton-le-Fylde	d			19 38	19 47	20 06		20 27			20 38	20 47	21 11		21 27			21 47	22 11	22 27		
Blackpool South	d		19 16							20 16							21 18				22 18	
Blackpool Pleasure Beach	d		19 18							20 18							21 20				22 20	
Squires Gate	d		19 20							20 20							21 22				22 22	
St Annes-on-the-Sea	d		19 24							20 24							21 26				22 26	
Ansdell & Fairhaven	d		19 28							20 28							21 30				22 30	
Lytham	d		19 31							20 31							21 33				22 33	
Moss Side	d		19 36							20 36							21 38				22 38	
Kirkham & Wesham	d		19 43	19 47	19 56			20 37		20 43	20 47	20 56			21 37		21 45	21 56	22 20	22 37	22 45	
Salwick	d																					
Preston	a		19 54	19 59	20 06	20 24		20 48		20 53	20 58	21 06	21 29		21 48		21 56	22 06	22 31	22 48	22 56	
	d		19 55			20 29		20 49		20 54			21 30		21 49		22 01			22 49		
Lostock Hall	d		20 07							21 07							22 07					
Bamber Bridge	d		20 10							21 10							22 11					
Pleasington	d		20x17							21x17							22x18					
Cherry Tree	d		20 21							21 21							22 22					
Mill Hill (Lancashire)	d		20 23							21 23							22 24					
Blackburn	a		20 27			20 46				21 27			21 47				22 28					
Clitheroe 94	a																					
Blackburn	d	20 17	20 27			20 46	20 48		21 13	21 27			21 47	21 48		22 13	22 28					23 00
Rishton	d		20 32							21 32							22 33					
Church & Oswaldtwistle	d		20 35						21 18	21 35						22 18	22 36					23 05
Accrington	d		20 39			20 54			21 22	21 39			21 55			22 22	22 40					23 08
Huncoat	d		20 43							21 43							22 44					
Hapton	d		20x46							21x46							22x47					
Rose Grove	d		20 50						21 29	21 50						22 29	22 51					23 15
Burnley Manchester Road 41	a					21 03			21 32				22 04			22 32						23 19
Leeds 41	a					22 18							23 22									
Todmorden	d								21 50							22 50						23 35
Rochdale	d								22 04							23 04						23 49
Manchester Victoria	a	21 09					21 40	21 45	22 25					22 40	22 45	23 25				23 45		00 11
Burnley Barracks	d		20x53							21x53							22x54					
Burnley Central	d		20 56							21 56							22 57					
Brierfield	d		21 00							22 00							23 01					
Nelson	d		21 04							22 04							23 05					
Colne	a		21 10							22 10							23 12					

A To Southport
B To Liverpool Lime Street
C To Manchester Airport
D To York
E From Clitheroe

Table T097-R

Sundays
20 May to 2 December

Blackpool - Preston - Blackburn, Accrington, Burnley and Colne

			NT	NT
				A
Blackpool North		d	23 01	
Layton		d		
Poulton-le-Fylde		d	23 07	
Blackpool South		d		
Blackpool Pleasure Beach		d		
Squires Gate		d		
St Annes-on-the-Sea		d		
Ansdell & Fairhaven		d		
Lytham		d		
Moss Side		d		
Kirkham & Wesham		d	23 16	
Salwick		d		
Preston 8		a	23 26	
		d		
Lostock Hall		d		
Bamber Bridge		d		
Pleasington		d		
Cherry Tree		d		
Mill Hill (Lancashire)		d		
Blackburn		a		
Clitheroe	94	a		
Blackburn		d		23 07
Rishton		d		
Church & Oswaldtwistle		d		
Accrington		d		
Huncoat		d		
Hapton		d		
Rose Grove		d		
Burnley Manchester Road	41	a		
Leeds 10	41	a		
Todmorden		d		
Rochdale	⇌	d		
Manchester Victoria	⇌	a		23 55
Burnley Barracks		d		
Burnley Central		d		
Brierfield		d		
Nelson		d		
Colne		a		

A From Clitheroe

Table T098-F

Mondays to Fridays
21 May to 7 December

Lancaster - Morecambe and Heysham

Miles				NT	NT	NT	NT	NT	NT	NT	NT	NT	NT	NT	NT	NT	NT	NT	NT	NT	NT	NT	NT	NT
													◇				◇		◇					
0	**Lancaster** 8	82	d	05 31	05 40	06 18	07 23	07 56	08 41	09 50	10 50	11 28	12 14	12 49	13 52	14 39	14 51	15 23	16 22	16 49	17 13	17 49	18 30	19 01
2½	Bare Lane		d	05 36	05 45	06 23	07 28	08 01	08 46	09 55	10 55	11 33	12 20	12 54	13 57	14 44	14 56	15 28	16 28	16 54	17 18	17 54	18 35	19 06
4¼	**Morecambe**		a	05 40	05 49	06 27	07 32	08 05	08 50	09 59	10 59	11 37	12 24	12 58	14 01	14 48	15 00	15 32	16 32	16 58	17 22	17 58	18 39	19 10
—			d											13 02										
8¼	**Heysham Port**	⛴	a											13 17										

			NT	NT	NT	NT	NT
			◇				
Lancaster 8	82	d	19 39	20 36	21 30	22 02	22 39
Bare Lane		d	19 46	20 41	21 35	22 07	22 44
Morecambe		a	19 50	20 45	21 39	22 11	22 48
		d					
Heysham Port	⛴	a					

Saturdays
26 May to 8 December

			NT	NT	NT	NT	NT	NT	NT	NT	NT	NT	NT	NT	NT	NT	NT	NT	NT	NT	NT	NT	NT	NT
												◇			◇	◇		◇						◇
Lancaster 8	82	d	05 31	05 40	06 18	07 23	07 56	08 41	09 50	10 50	11 28	12 14	12 49	13 52	14 46	14 51	15 27	16 22	16 49	17 13	17 49	18 30	19 01	19 34
Bare Lane		d	05 36	05 45	06 23	07 28	08 01	08 46	09 55	10 55	11 33	12 20	12 54	13 57	14 51	14 56	15 32	16 28	16 54	17 18	17 54	18 35	19 06	19 41
Morecambe		a	05 40	05 49	06 27	07 32	08 05	08 50	09 59	10 59	11 37	12 24	12 58	14 01	14 55	15 01	15 36	16 32	16 58	17 22	17 58	18 39	19 10	19 45
		d											13 02											
Heysham Port	⛴	a											13 17											

			NT	NT	NT	NT
Lancaster 8	82	d	20 36	21 30	22 06	22 39
Bare Lane		d	20 41	21 35	22 11	22 44
Morecambe		a	20 45	21 39	22 15	22 48
		d				
Heysham Port	⛴	a				

Sundays
20 May to 2 December

			NT	NT	NT	NT	NT	NT	NT	NT	NT	NT	NT	NT		NT
						◇				◇			◇			
			A													
Lancaster 8	82	d	09 30	10 30	11 30	12 15	12 30	13 40	14 30	15 15	15 30	16 30	17 15	17 30	and hourly until	21 30
Bare Lane		d	09 35	10 35	11 35	12 20	12 35	13 45	14 35	15 20	15 35	16 35	17 20	17 35		21 35
Morecambe		a	09 39	10 39	11 39	12 24	12 39	13 49	14 39	15 24	15 39	16 39	17 24	17 39		21 39
		d					12 43									
Heysham Port	⛴	a					12 58									

A from 24 June

Table T098-R

Mondays to Fridays

21 May to 7 December

Heysham and Morecambe - Lancaster

Miles			NT	NT	NT	NT	NT	NT	NT	NT	NT	NT	NT	NT	NT	NT	NT	NT	NT	NT	NT	NT	NT
															◇					◇			
0	**Heysham Port** ⛴	d											13 20										
4¼	**Morecambe**	a											13 35										
—		d	05 53	05 57	07 08	07 41	08 23	08 54	10 32	11 15	11 41	12 32	13 38	14 22	15 04	15 09	15 42	16 36	17 02	17 31	18 08	18 45	19 23
6	Bare Lane	d	05a57	06 01	07 12	07 45	08 27	08 58	10 36	11 19	11 45	12 36	13 42	14 26	15a08	15 13	15 46	16 40	17 06	17 35	18 12	18 49	19 27
8½	**Lancaster** 🅱	82 a		06 07	07 19	07 51	08 33	09 04	10 42	11 24	11 50	12 42	13 48	14 31		15 18	15 51	16 45	17 12	17 41	18 17	18 54	19 33

		NT	NT	NT	NT	NT
		◇				
Heysham Port ⛴	d					
Morecambe	a					
	d	20 10	21 08	21 43	22 22	22 52
Bare Lane	d	20 14	21 12	21 47	22 26	22 56
Lancaster 🅱	82 a	20 20	21 18	21 52	22 32	23 02

Saturdays

26 May to 8 December

		NT	NT	NT	NT	NT	NT	NT	NT	NT	NT	NT	NT	NT	NT	NT	NT	NT	NT	NT	NT	NT	NT	NT
													◇	◇					◇				◇
Heysham Port ⛴	d											13 20											
Morecambe	a											13 35											
	d	05 53	05 57	07 08	07 41	08 23	08 54	10 32	11 15	11 41	12 32	13 38	14 33	15 04	15 09	15 42	16 36	17 02	17 31	18 08	18 45	19 23	20 10
Bare Lane	d	05a57	06 01	07 12	07 45	08 27	08 58	10 36	11 19	11 45	12 36	13 42	14 37	15a08	15 13	15 46	16 40	17 06	17 35	18 12	18 49	19 27	20 14
Lancaster 🅱	82 a		06 07	07 19	07 51	08 33	09 04	10 42	11 24	11 50	12 42	13 48	14 42		15 18	15 51	16 45	17 12	17 41	18 17	18 54	19 33	20 20

		NT	NT	NT	NT
Heysham Port ⛴	d				
Morecambe	a				
	d	21 08	21 43	22 24	22 52
Bare Lane	d	21 12	21 47	22 28	22 56
Lancaster 🅱	82 a	21 18	21 52	22 36	23 01

Sundays

20 May to 2 December

		NT	NT	NT	NT	NT	NT	NT	NT	NT	NT	NT	NT	NT	NT	NT	NT	NT
					◇					◇			◇					
		A				B	C											
Heysham Port ⛴	d					13 03	13 05											
Morecambe	a					13 19	13 21											
	d	10 00	11 00	11 50	12 36	13 23	13 25	13 57	14 57	15 36	15 57	16 57	17 36	17 57	18 57	20 00	20 57	22 00
Bare Lane	d	10 04	11 04	11 54	12a40	13 27	13 29	14 01	15 01	15a40	16 01	17 01	17a40	18 01	19 01	20 04	21 01	22 04
Lancaster 🅱	82 a	10 10	11 10	12 00		13 33	13 35	14 07	15 07		16 07	17 07		18 07	19 07	20 10	21 07	22 10

A from 24 June
B until 9 September
C from 16 September

Table T099-F

Mondays to Saturdays

21 May to 8 December

Ormskirk - Preston

Miles			NT SX	NT SO	NT	NT	NT	NT SX	NT SO	NT	NT	NT SO	NT SX	NT SX	NT SO	NT	NT	NT	NT	NT	NT SX	NT SO	NT
0	**Ormskirk**	d	07 01	07 01	08 01	09 01	10 01	11 01	11 01	12 01	13 01	14 01	14 01	15 01	15 01	16 01	17 01	18 01	19 01	20 01	21 01	21 01	22 01
2½	Burscough Junction	d	07 05	07 05	08 05	09 05	10 05	11 05	11 05	12 05	13 05	14 05	14 05	15 05	15 05	16 05	17 05	18 05	19 05	20 05	21 05	21 05	22 05
5½	Rufford	d	07 11	07 11	08 11	09 11	10 11	11 11	11 11	12 11	13 11	14 11	14 11	15 11	15 11	16 11	17 11	18 11	19 11	20 11	21 11	21 11	22 11
8	Croston	d	07 16	07 16	08 16	09 16	10 16	11 16	11 16	12 16	13 16	14 16	14 16	15 16	15 16	16 16	17 16	18 16	19 16	20 16	21 16	21 16	22 16
15	**Preston** 🅱	a	07 30	07 31	08 32	09 32	10 32	11 34	11 35	12 32	13 33	14 32	14 33	15 32	15 33	16 33	17 32	18 30	19 34	20 32	21 32	21 35	22 30

		NT
Ormskirk	d	23 11
Burscough Junction	d	23 15
Rufford	d	23 21
Croston	d	23 26
Preston 🅱	a	23 40

For connections from Liverpool Central refer to Table T105

No Sunday Service

Table T099-R

Mondays to Saturdays

21 May to 8 December

Preston - Ormskirk

Miles			NT	NT	NT	NT	NT	NT	NT	NT	NT	NT	NT	NT	NT	NT	NT	NT
0	**Preston** 🅱	d	06 25	07 26	08 26	09 26	10 26	11 26	12 26	13 26	14 26	15 26	16 26	17 26	18 26	19 26	20 26	21 26	22 37
7	Croston	d	06 39	07 39	08 39	09 39	10 39	11 39	12 39	13 39	14 39	15 39	16 39	17 39	18 39	19 40	20 39	21 39	22 50
9½	Rufford	d	06 44	07 44	08 44	09 44	10 44	11 44	12 44	13 44	14 44	15 44	16 44	17 44	18 44	19 45	20 44	21 44	22 55
12½	Burscough Junction	d	06 50	07 50	08 50	09 50	10 50	11 50	12 50	13 50	14 50	15 50	16 50	17 50	18 50	19 51	20 50	21 50	23 01
15	**Ormskirk**	a	06 56	07 56	08 56	09 56	10 56	11 56	12 56	13 56	14 56	15 56	16 56	17 56	18 56	19 57	20 56	21 56	23 07

For connections to Liverpool Central refer to Table T103

No Sunday Service

Table T100-F

Barrow-in-Furness - Whitehaven and Carlisle

Mondays to Fridays
21 May to 7 December

Miles		NT	NT	NT	NT	NT	NT	NT	NT	NT
—	Lancaster ■ 82 d				05 36					
0	**Barrow-in-Furness** d			05 50	06 50	07 50	09 18	10 22	11 20	12 06
6	Askam d			06 02	07 00	08 00	09 30	10 32	11 30	12 16
9¼	Kirkby-in-Furness d			06x08	07x04	08x04	09 34	10x36	11x34	12x20
11¼	Foxfield d			06 13	07 08	08 08	09 39	10 40	11 38	12 24
13½	Green Road d			06x18	07x12	08x11	09 43	10x43	11x41	12x27
16	Millom a			06 23	07 18	08 17	09 48	10 49	11 47	12 33
—	d			06 24	07 18	08 18	09 49	10 50	11 47	12 34
19	Silecroft d			06x30	07x23	08x23		10x54	11x52	12x38
24½	Bootle d			06x38	07x30	08x29		11x01	11x58	12x45
29¼	Ravenglass for Eskdale d			06 45	07 37	08 35	10 06	11 07	12 04	12 51
31	Drigg d			06x50	07x40	08x38		11x10	12x07	12x54
33¼	Seascale d			06 54	07 44	08 42	10 13	11 14	12 11	12 57
35	Sellafield d			06 59	07 53	08 49	10 17	11 22	12 17	13 03
37	Braystones d				07x57			11x26		13x07
38¼	Nethertown d				07x59			11x28		13x09
41¼	St Bees d			07 13	08 05	09 00	10 30	11 34	12 27	13 28
44¾	Corkickle d			07 20	08 11	09 05	10 37	11 40	12 32	13 34
45¾	**Whitehaven** a			07 23	08 14	09 08	10 40	11 43	12 35	13 36
—	d		06 57	07 25	08 16	09 09	10 43	11 45	12 36	13 38
47	Parton d		07x00	07x29	08x20	09x13	10x49	11x48		13x41
50½	Harrington d		07 09	07 40	08 28	09 21	11 00	11 57		13 50
52¼	**Workington** d	06 05	07 15	07 46	08 34	09 27	11 06	12 03	12 53	13 56
56	Flimby d	06x09	07x19	07x53	08x39	09x32		12x07		14x00
58	Maryport d	06 13	07 23	07 57	08 43	09 36	11 15	12 11	13 01	14 04
65½	Aspatria d	06 23	07 33	08 08	08 53	09 46	11 26	12 21		14 14
71¾	Wigton d	06 35	07 44	08 20	09 04	09 57	11 38	12 33	13 22	14 26
81¼	Dalston d	06 44	07 53	08 30	09 13	10 06		12 42		14 35
85¾	**Carlisle** ■ a	06 55	08 04	08 42	09 24	10 17	11 57	12 53	13 40	14 49

	NT	NT	NT	NT	NT	NT	NT	NT	NT	NT	NT	NT
Lancaster ■ 82 d	12 02					15 03	16 13	17 01		18 35		20 02
Barrow-in-Furness d	13 16	14 19	14 52	15 31		16 13	17 17	18 06	19 12	19 44	20 20	21 12
Askam d	13 26	14 29	15 04	15 43		16 23	17 28	18 16	19 22	19 54	20 30	21 22
Kirkby-in-Furness d	13x30	14x33		15x48		16x27	17x32	18x20	19x26	19x58	20x34	21x26
Foxfield d	13 34	14 37		15 53		16 32	17 36	18 24	19 30	20 02	20 38	21 30
Green Road d	13x37	14x40		15x58		16x35	17x39	18x27	19x33	20x05	20x41	21x34
Millom a	13 43	14 46	15 19	16 03		16 41	17 45	18 33	19 39	20 12	20 47	21 40
d	13 44	14 47	15 20	16 04		16 42	17 45	18 33	19 40		20 47	
Silecroft d	13x48	14x51		16x10		16x46	17x50		19x44		20x52	
Bootle d	13x55	14x58		16x18		16x53	17x56		19x51		20x58	
Ravenglass for Eskdale d	14 01	15 04	15 37	16 25		16 59	18 02	18 49	19 57		21 04	
Drigg d	14x04	15x07		16x29		17x02	18x05	18 52	20x00		21x07	
Seascale d	14 07	15 10	15 44	16 34		17 06	18 09	18 56	20 03		21 11	
Sellafield d	14 13	15 16	15 49	16 39		17a10	18 14	19 00	20 12		21 16	
Braystones d		15x19							20x15			
Nethertown d		15x22							20x18			
St Bees d	14 26	15 30	16 01	16 49			18 26	19 12	20 27		21 26	
Corkickle d	14 32	15 35	16 09	16 56			18 32	19 17	20 32		21 31	
Whitehaven a	14 34	15 39	16 12	16 59			18 34	19 20	20 36		21 34	
d	14 38	15 40	16 13	17 01	17 49		18 35	19 21	20 37		21 35	
Parton d	14x41	15x47	16x18		17x52		18x39	19x25	20x41		21x39	
Harrington d	14 50	15 55	16 29		18 01		18 47	19 33	20 49		21 47	
Workington d	14 56	16 01	16 35	17 19	18 07		18 53	19 39	20 55		21 53	
Flimby d	15x00	16x06	16x41		18x11		18x58	19x43	21x00		21x58	
Maryport d	15 05	16 10	16 45	17 28	18 16		19 02	19 47	21 04		22 02	
Aspatria d	15 15	16 20	16 57		18 26		19 12	19 57	21 14		22 12	
Wigton d	15 26	16 31	17 09	17 50	18 37		19 23	20 09	21 25		22 23	
Dalston d	15 35	16 40	17 19	18 00	18 46		19 32	20 18	21 34		22 32	
Carlisle ■ a	15 46	16 51	17 30	18 11	18 57		19 43	20 31	21 45		22 43	

	NT	NT
Lancaster ■ 82 d		
Barrow-in-Furness d		22 11
Askam d		22 21
Kirkby-in-Furness d		22x25
Foxfield d		22 29
Green Road d		22x33
Millom a		22 39
d		
Silecroft d		
Bootle d		
Ravenglass for Eskdale d		
Drigg d		
Seascale d		
Sellafield d		
Braystones d		
Nethertown d		
St Bees d		
Corkickle d		
Whitehaven a		
d	22 09	
Parton d	22x12	
Harrington d	22 21	
Workington d	22 27	
Flimby d	22x32	
Maryport d	22 36	
Aspatria d	22 46	
Wigton d	22 57	
Dalston d	23 06	
Carlisle ■ a	23 17	

Saturdays
26 May to 8 December

	NT	NT	NT	NT	NT	NT	NT	NT	NT
Lancaster ■ 82 d				05 36					
Barrow-in-Furness d			05 50	06 50	07 54	09 02	10 22	11 20	12 06
Askam d			06 02	07 00	08 04	09 14	10 32	11 30	12 16
Kirkby-in-Furness d			06x08	07x04	08x08	09x19	10x36	11x34	12x20
Foxfield d			06 13	07 08	08 12	09 24	10 40	11 38	12 24
Green Road d			06x18	07x12	08x15	09x29	10x43	11x41	12x27
Millom a			06 23	07 18	08 21	09 34	10 49	11 47	12 33
d			06 24	07 18	08 22	09 35	10 50	11 47	12 34
Silecroft d			06x30	07x23	08x27	09x40	10x54	11x52	12x38
Bootle d			06x38	07x30	08x33	09x49	11x01	11x58	12x45
Ravenglass for Eskdale d			06 45	07 37	08 39	09 56	11 07	12 04	12 51
Drigg d			06x50	07x40	08x42	10x00	11x10	12x07	12x54
Seascale d			06 54	07 44	08 46	10 05	11 14	12 11	12 57
Sellafield d			06 59	07 53	08 52	10 09	11 22	12 17	13 03
Braystones d				07x57	08x55		11x26		13x07
Nethertown d				07x59	08x58		11x28		13x09
St Bees d			07 13	08 05	09 03	10 20	11 34	12 27	13 28
Corkickle d			07 20	08 11	09 08	10 27	11 40	12 32	13 34
Whitehaven a			07 23	08 14	09 12	10 30	11 43	12 35	13 36
d		06 57	07 25	08 16	09 14	10 32	11 45	12 36	13 38
Parton d		07x00	07x29	08x20	09x18	10x39	11x48		13x41
Harrington d		07 09	07 40	08 28	09 26	10 50	11 57		13 50
Workington d	05 48	07 15	07 46	08 34	09 32	10 56	12 03	12 53	13 56
Flimby d	05x52	07x19	07x53	08x39	09x37	11x02	12x07		14x00
Maryport d	05 56	07 23	07 57	08 43	09 41	11 06	12 11	13 01	14 04
Aspatria d	06 06	07 33	08 08	08 53	09 51	11 18	12 21		14 14
Wigton d	06 18	07 44	08 20	09 04	10 02	11 30	12 33	13 22	14 26
Dalston d	06 27	07 53	08 30	09 13	10 11	11 40	12 42		14 35
Carlisle ■ a	06 38	08 04	08 42	09 24	10 22	11 51	12 53	13 40	14 49

	NT	NT	NT	NT	NT	NT	NT	NT	NT	NT	NT	NT	NT
Lancaster ■ 82 d					15 03	16 13	17 01					20 05	
Barrow-in-Furness d	13 16	14 19	14 52	15 31	16 09	17 17	18 06	18 57	19 44		20 19	21 12	22 11
Askam d	13 26	14 29	15 04	15 43	16 19	17 28	18 16	19 07	19 54		20 29	21 22	22 21
Kirkby-in-Furness d	13x30	14x33		15x48	16x23	17x32	18x20	19x11	19x58		20x33	21x26	22x25
Foxfield d	13 34	14 37		15 53	16 27	17 36	18 24	19 15	20 02		20 37	21 30	22 29
Green Road d	13x37	14x40		15x58	16x30	17x39	18x27	19x19	20x05		20x40	21x34	22x33
Millom a	13 43	14 46	15 19	16 03	16 36	17 45	18 33	19 25	20 11		20 47	21 40	22 39
d	13 44	14 47	15 20	16 04	16 37	17 45	18 33	19 25	20 11				
Silecroft d	13x48	14x51		16x10	16x41	17x50		19x29	20x16				
Bootle d	13x55	14x58		16x18	16x48	17x56		19x36	20x22				
Ravenglass for Eskdale d	14 01	15 04	15 37	16 25	16 54	18 02	18 49	19 42	20 28				
Drigg d	14x04	15x07		16x29	16x57	18x05	18 52	19x45	20x31				
Seascale d	14 07	15 10	15 44	16 34	17 00	18 09	18 56	19 48	20 35				
Sellafield d	14 13	15 17	15 49	16 42	17 07	18 14	19 00	19 53	20 41				
Braystones d		15x20			17x10				20x44				
Nethertown d		15x23			17x13				20x47				
St Bees d	14 26	15 32	16 01	16 52	17 19	18 26	19 12	20 03	20 52				
Corkickle d	14 32	15 37	16 09	16 59	17 24	18 32	19 17	20 08	20 57				
Whitehaven a	14 34	15 41	16 12	17 02	17 28	18 34	19 20	20 12	21 01				
d	14 38	15 45	16 13	17 04	17 29	18 35	19 21	20 13	21 02	22 09			
Parton d	14x41	15x50	16x18		17x33	18x39	19x25	20x17		22x12			
Harrington d	14 50	15 58	16 29		17 41	18 47	19 33	20 25		22 21			
Workington d	14 56	16 04	16 35	17 22	17 47	18 53	19 39	20 31	21 19	22 27			
Flimby d	15x00	16x09	16x41		17x52	18x58	19x43	20x36	21x24	22x32			
Maryport d	15 05	16 13	16 45	17 31	17 56	19 02	19 47	20 40	21a27	22a36			
Aspatria d	15 15	16 23	16 57		18 06	19 12	19 57	20 50					
Wigton d	15 26	16 34	17 09	17 53	18 17	19 23	20 09	21 01					
Dalston d	15 35	16 43	17 19	18 03	18 26	19 32	20 18	21 10					
Carlisle ■ a	15 46	16 54	17 30	18 14	18 41	19 43	20 31	21 21					

Table T100-F

Barrow-in-Furness - Whitehaven and Carlisle

Sundays
20 May to 17 June

	NT	NT	VT	NT	NT	VT	NT	NT	VT
			◇■		■	◇■			◇■
Lancaster ■ 82 d			11 18			12 55			14 58
Barrow-in-Furness d	09 05			09 50	11 15		12 18	12 58	
Askam d	09 15			10 00	11 25		12 28	13 08	
Kirkby-in-Furness d	09x19			10x04	11x29		12x32	13x12	
Foxfield d	09 23			10 08	11 33		12 36	13 16	
Green Road d	09x26			10x11	11x37		12x39	13x19	
Millom a	09 33			10 17	11 43		12 45	13 25	
d				10 18	11 43		12 45	13 25	
Silecroft d				10x22	11x47		12x50	13x30	
Bootle d				10x29	11x54		12x56	13x36	
Ravenglass for Eskdale d				10 35	12 00		13 02	13 42	
Drigg d				10x38	12x03		13x05	13x45	
Seascale d				10 41	12 06		13 09	13 49	
Sellafield d				10 47	12 12		13 15	13 54	
Braystones d								13x58	
Nethertown d								14x00	
St Bees d				11 00	12 25		13 28	14 05	
Corkickle d				11 06	12 30		13 33	14 10	
Whitehaven a				11 08	12 33		13 37	14 14	
d		10 16		11 10	12 34		13 38	14 16	
Parton d		10x20		11x13	12x38		13x42	14x20	
Harrington d		10 28		11 22	12 46		13 50	14 28	
Workington d		10 34		11 28	12 52		13 56	14 34	
Flimby d		10x39		11x32	12x57		14x01	14x39	
Maryport d		10 43		11 36	13 01		14 05	14 43	
Aspatria d		10 53		11 46	13 11		14 15	14 53	
Wigton d		11 04		11 58	13 22		14 26	15 04	
Dalston d		11 13		12 07	13 31		14 35	15 13	
Carlisle ■ a		11 24	12 11	12 18	13 42	13 49	14 46	15 24	15 47

	NT	NT	NT	NT	NT	NT	NT	NT	NT
Lancaster ■ 82 d	13 13				16 13				
Barrow-in-Furness d	14 17	14 51		15 58	17 17	18 12	19 07		
Askam d	14 27	15 01		16 08	17 28	18 22	19 17		
Kirkby-in-Furness d		15x05		16x12	17x32	18x26	19x21		
Foxfield d		15 09		16 16	17 36	18 30	19 25		
Green Road d		15x12		16x19	17x39	18x33	19x28		
Millom a	14 41	15 18		16 25	17 45	18 40	19 35		
d	14 43	15 19		16 25	17 46				
Silecroft d		15x24		16x30	17x50				
Bootle d		15x30		16x36	17x57				
Ravenglass for Eskdale d	14 58	15 36		16 42	18 03				
Drigg d		15x39		16x45	18x06				
Seascale d		15 43		16 49	18 09				
Sellafield d	15 06	15a50		16 54	18 15				
Braystones d				16x58	18x18				
Nethertown d				17x00	18x21				
St Bees d	15 15			17 05	18 29				
Corkickle d	15 21			17 10	18 34				
Whitehaven a	15 23			17 14	18 38				
d	15 25		16 11	17 16	18 39			19 38	20 30
Parton d	15x28		16x15	17x20	18x43			19x41	20x33
Harrington d	15 37		16 24	17 28	18 51			19 50	20 42
Workington d	15 44		16 29	17 34	18 57			19 56	20 48
Flimby d	15x48		16x34	17x39	19x02			20x01	20x53
Maryport d	15 53		16 38	17 43	19 06			20 05	20 57
Aspatria d	16 03		16 48	17 53	19 16			20 15	21 07
Wigton d	16 15		16 59	18 04	19 27			20 26	21 18
Dalston d	16 24		17 08	18 13	19 36			20 35	21 27
Carlisle ■ a	16 35		17 19	18 24	19 47			20 46	21 38

Sundays
24 June to 9 September

	NT	NT	NT	NT	VT	NT	NT	VT	NT
					◇■			◇■	
Lancaster ■ 82 d					11 18		10 11	12 55	
Barrow-in-Furness d		09 05				09 50	11 15		12 18
Askam d		09 15				10 00	11 25		12 28
Kirkby-in-Furness d		09x19				10x04	11x29		12x32
Foxfield d		09 23				10 08	11 33		12 36
Green Road d		09x26				10x11	11x37		12x39
Millom a		09 33				10 17	11 43		12 45
d						10 18	11 43		12 45
Silecroft d						10x22	11x47		12x50
Bootle d						10x29	11x54		12x56
Ravenglass for Eskdale d						10 35	12 00		13 02
Drigg d						10x38	12x03		13x05
Seascale d						10 41	12 06		13 09
Sellafield d						10 47	12 12		13 15
Braystones d									
Nethertown d									
St Bees d						11 00	12 25		13 28
Corkickle d						11 06	12 30		13 33
Whitehaven a						11 08	12 33		13 37
d				10 16		11 10	12 34		13 38
Parton d				10x20		11x13	12x38		13x42
Harrington d				10 28		11 22	12 46		13 50
Workington d	08 55		09 40	10 34		11 28	12 52		13 56
Flimby d	09x00		09x45	10x39		11x32	12x57		14x01
Maryport d	09 04		09 49	10 43		11 36	13 01		14 05
Aspatria d	09 14		09 59	10 53		11 46	13 11		14 15
Wigton d	09 25		10 10	11 04		11 58	13 22		14 26
Dalston d	09 34		10 19	11 13		12 07	13 31		14 35
Carlisle ■ a	09 45		10 30	11 24	12 11	12 18	13 42	13 49	14 46

	NT	VT	NT	NT	NT	NT	NT	NT	NT	NT	NT
		◇■									
Lancaster ■ 82 d		14 58	13 13				16 13				
Barrow-in-Furness d	12 58		14 17	14 51		15 58	17 17	18 12	19 07		
Askam d	13 08		14 27	15 01		16 08	17 28	18 22	19 17		
Kirkby-in-Furness d	13x12			15x05		16x12	17x32	18x26	19x21		
Foxfield d	13 16			15 09		16 16	17 36	18 30	19 25		
Green Road d	13x19			15x12		16x19	17x39	18x33	19x28		
Millom a	13 25		14 41	15 18		16 25	17 45	18 40	19 35		
d	13 25		14 43	15 19		16 25	17 46				
Silecroft d	13x30			15x24		16x30	17x50				
Bootle d	13x36			15x30		16x36	17x57				
Ravenglass for Eskdale d	13 42		14 58	15 36		16 42	18 03				
Drigg d	13x45			15x39		16x45	18x06				
Seascale d	13 49			15 43		16 49	18 09				
Sellafield d	13 54		15 06	15a50		16 54	18 15				
Braystones d	13x58					16x58	18x18				
Nethertown d	14x00					17x00	18x21				
St Bees d	14 05		15 15			17 05	18 29				
Corkickle d	14 10		15 21			17 10	18 34				
Whitehaven a	14 14		15 23			17 14	18 38				
d	14 16		15 25		16 11	17 16	18 39			19 38	20 30
Parton d	14x20		15x28		16x15	17x20	18x43			19x41	20x33
Harrington d	14 28		15 37		16 24	17 28	18 51			19 50	20 42
Workington d	14 34		15 44		16 29	17 34	18 57			19 56	20 48
Flimby d	14x39		15x48		16x34	17x39	19x02			20x01	20x53
Maryport d	14 43		15 53		16 38	17 43	19 06			20 05	20 57
Aspatria d	14 53		16 03		16 48	17 53	19 16			20 15	21 07
Wigton d	15 04		16 15		16 59	18 04	19 27			20 26	21 18
Dalston d	15 13		16 24		17 08	18 13	19 36			20 35	21 27
Carlisle ■ a	15 24	15 47	16 35		17 19	18 24	19 47			20 46	21 38

No Sunday Service Barrow-in-Furness to Whitehaven

Table T100-F

Sundays

16 September to 2 December

Barrow-in-Furness - Whitehaven and Carlisle

		NT	NT	NT	NT	NT	NT	NT	NT	NT	NT	NT	NT	NT	NT	NT	NT	NT
Lancaster 8 82	d						10 11			13 13				16 13				
Barrow-in-Furness	d		09 05			09 50	11 15	12 18	12 58	14 17	14 51		15 58	17 17	18 12	19 07		
Askam	d		09 15			10 00	11 25	12 28	13 08	14 27	15 01		16 08	17 28	18 22	19 17		
Kirkby-in-Furness	d		09x19			10x04	11x29	12x32	13x12		15x05		16x12	17x32	18x26	19x21		
Foxfield	d		09 23			10 08	11 33	12 36	13 16		15 09		16 16	17 36	18 30	19 25		
Green Road	d		09x26			10x11	11x37	12x39	13x19		15x12		16x19	17x39	18x33	19x28		
Millom	a		09 33			10 17	11 43	12 45	13 25	14 41	15 18		16 25	17 45	18 40	19 35		
	d					10 18	11 43	12 45	13 25	14 43	15 19		16 25	17 46				
Silecroft	d					10x22	11x47	12x50	13x30		15x24		16x30	17x50				
Bootle	d					10x29	11x54	12x56	13x36		15x30		16x36	17x57				
Ravenglass for Eskdale	d					10 35	12 00	13 02	13 42	14 58	15 36		16 42	18 03				
Drigg	d					10x38	12x03	13x05	13x45		15x39		16x45	18x06				
Seascale	d					10 41	12 06	13 09	13 49		15 43		16 49	18 09				
Sellafield	d					10 47	12 12	13 15	13 54	15 06	15a50		16 54	18 15				
Braystones	d								13x58				16x58	18x18				
Nethertown	d								14x00				17x00	18x21				
St Bees	d					11 00	12 25	13 28	14 05	15 15			17 05	18 29				
Corkickle	d					11 06	12 30	13 33	14 10	15 21			17 10	18 34				
Whitehaven	a					11 08	12 33	13 37	14 14	15 23			17 14	18 38				
	d				10 16	11 10	12 34	13 38	14 16	15 25		16 11	17 16	18 39			19 38	20 30
Parton	d				10x20	11x13	12x38	13x42	14x20	15x28		16x15	17x20	18x43			19x41	20x33
Harrington	d				10 28	11 22	12 46	13 50	14 28	15 37		16 24	17 28	18 51			19 50	20 42
Workington	d	08 55		09 40	10 34	11 28	12 52	13 56	14 34	15 44		16 29	17 34	18 57			19 56	20 48
Flimby	d	09x00		09x45	10x39	11x32	12x57	14x01	14x39	15x48		16x34	17x39	19x02			20x01	20x53
Maryport	d	09 04		09 49	10 43	11 36	13 01	14 05	14 43	15 53		16 38	17 43	19 06			20 05	20 57
Aspatria	d	09 14		09 59	10 53	11 46	13 11	14 15	14 53	16 03		16 48	17 53	19 16			20 15	21 07
Wigton	d	09 25		10 10	11 04	11 58	13 22	14 26	15 04	16 15		16 59	18 04	19 27			20 26	21 18
Dalston	d	09 34		10 19	11 13	12 07	13 31	14 35	15 13	16 24		17 08	18 13	19 36			20 35	21 27
Carlisle 8	a	09 45		10 30	11 24	12 18	13 42	14 46	15 24	16 35		17 19	18 24	19 47			20 46	21 38

No Sunday Service Barrow-in-Furness to Whitehaven

Table T100-R

Mondays to Fridays

21 May to 7 December

Carlisle and Whitehaven - Barrow-in-Furness

Miles			NT	NT	NT	NT	NT	NT	NT	NT	NT	NT	NT	NT	NT	NT	NT	NT	NT	NT	NT	NT	NT
0	**Carlisle 8**	d		05 53	06 16	07 10	08 10	09 03	10 13	11 07	12 08	13 07	14 11	14 41	15 12	15 59		17 06	17 45	18 46	19 09	20 55	22 01
4	Dalston	d		06 02	06 25	07 19		09 12	10 22	11 15		13 15	14 19	14 51	15 20	16 07		17 14	17 54	18 54	19 17	21 03	22 09
11½	Wigton	d		06 11	06 35	07 31	08 27	09 22	10 31	11 25	12 26	13 25	14 29	15 01	15 29	16 17		17 24	18 04	19 04	19 27	21 13	22 19
19¾	Aspatria	d		06 22	06 47	07 41		09 34	10 42	11 35		13 35	14 39	15 11	15 40	16 27		17 34	18 16	19 14	19 37	21 23	22 29
27¼	Maryport	d	05 48	06 33	06 59	07 52	08 48	09 46	10 53	11 46	12 48	13 46	14 50	15 22	15 50	16 38		17 45	18 28	19 25	19 48	21 34	22 40
29¼	Flimby	d	05x51	06x36	07x03	07x55		09x50	10x56	11x49		13x49	14x53	15x25	15x53	16x41		17x48	18x32	19x28	19x51	21x37	22x43
33	**Workington**	d	05 58	06 44	07 10	08 05	08 58	09 57	11 03	11 57	12 58	13 57	15 01	15 33	16 01	16 48		17 56	18 39	19 36	19 59	21 45	22 51
34¾	Harrington	d	06 02	06 48	07 15	08 09		10 02	11 07	12 01		14 01	15 05	15 37	16 05	16 52		18 00	18 44	19 40	20 03	21 49	22 55
38¼	Parton	d	06x11	06x57	07x26	08x18		10x13	11x16	12x09		14x09	15x13	15x45	16x13	17x01		18x08	18x55	19x49	20x11	21x57	23x03
39½	**Whitehaven**	a	06 16	07 02	07 30	08 23	09 14	10 17	11 21	12 15	13 15	14 15	15 19	15 51	16 19	17 08		18 16	19 00	19 56	20 16	22 04	23 10
—		d	06 18	07 04	07 32	08 25	09 16	10 19	11 23	12 16	13 17	14 16	15 20	15 52	16 20			18 18	19 01		20 18		
40½	Corkickle	d	06 20	07 06	07 35	08 27	09 18	10 22	11 25	12 19	13 20	14 19	15 23	15 55	16 23			18 20	19 05		20 20		
44	St Bees	d	06 26	07 12	07 42	08 33	09 29	10 32	11 33	12 28	13 27	14 30	15 29	16 02	16 28			18 27	19 13		20 28		
47	Nethertown	d	06x30						11x37					16x06				18x31			20x32		
48¼	Braystones	d	06x33						11x40					16x08				18x34			20x34		
50¼	Sellafield	d	06 39	07 24	07 53	08 44	09 39	10 43	11 45	12 38	13 38	14 45	15 40	16 14	16 39		17 18	18 40	19 24		20 40		
52	Seascale	d	06 43	07 28	07 58	08 47	09 43	10 48	11 49	12 42	13 43	14 48	15 44	16 18	16 43		17 22	18 43	19 28		20 44		
54¼	Drigg	d	06x46	07x31		08x50	09x46		11x52	12x45		14x52	15x48	16x21	16x46		17x26		19x33		20x47		
56	Ravenglass for Eskdale	d	06 50	07 34	08 05	08 54	09 49	10 55	11 55	12 48	13 50	14 56	15 52	16 25	16 50		17 30	18 49	19 37		20 50		
60¾	Bootle	d	06x55	07x40		08x59	09x55		12x01	12x54		15x01	15x58	16x31	16x56		17x36		19x44		20x56		
66¼	Silecroft	d	07x02	07x46		09x06	10x01		12x07	13x00		15x08	16x05	16x38	17x03		17x44		19x52		21x02		
69¼	Millom	a	07 08	07 53	08 21	09 12	10 08	11 11	12 14	13 07	14 06	15 15	16 11	16 44	17 10		17 49	19 05	19 58		21 09		
—		d	07 09	07 53	08 22	09 14	10 09	11 12	12 14	13 07	14 07	15 16	16 12	16 45	17 10		17 49	19 05	19 58		21 09		
71¾	Green Road	d	07x13	07x57		09x18	10x13		12x18	13x11		15x20	16x16	16x49	17x15		17x54	19x09	20x04		21x13		
73¾	Foxfield	d	07 17	08 01		09 22	10 17		12 22	13 15	14 16	15 24	16 20	16 53	17 19		17 59	19 13	20 09		21 17		
76	Kirkby-in-Furness	d	07x21	08x05		09x26	10x21		12x26	13x19	14x20	15x28	16x24	16x58	17x24		18x04	19x17	20x14		21x21		
79¼	Askam	d	07 26	08 11	08 39	09 31	10 26	11 29	12 31	13 24	14 26	15 33	16 29	17 03	17 29		18 09	19 22	20 20		21 26		
85¼	**Barrow-in-Furness**	a	07 41	08 26	08 54	09 46	10 41	11 45	12 46	13 39	14 41	15 48	16 44	17 17	17 44		18 24	19 37	20 37		21 41		
—	Lancaster 8 82	a				11 07				14 50		16 52		18 23							22 46		

Saturdays

26 May to 8 December

		NT	NT	NT	NT	NT	NT	NT	NT	NT	NT	NT	NT	NT	NT	NT	NT	NT	NT	NT	NT	NT
Carlisle 8	d		05 53	06 16	07 10	08 15	08 51	10 13	11 07	12 08	13 07	14 11	14 41	15 12	16 26	17 06	17 45	18 46	19 09	20 00	21 06	21 47
Dalston	d		06 02	06 25	07 19		09 00	10 22	11 15		13 15	14 19	14 51	15 20	16 34	17 14	17 54	18 54	19 17	20 08	21 14	21 55
Wigton	d		06 11	06 35	07 31	08 32	09 10	10 31	11 25	12 26	13 25	14 29	15 01	15 29	16 44	17 24	18 04	19 04	19 27	20 18	21 24	22 04
Aspatria	d		06 22	06 47	07 41		09 22	10 42	11 35		13 35	14 39	15 11	15 40	16 54	17 34	18 16	19 14	19 37	20 28	21 34	22 15
Maryport	d	05 48	06 33	06 59	07 52	08 53	09 34	10 53	11 46	12 48	13 46	14 50	15 22	15 50	17 05	17 45	18 28	19 25	19 48	20 39	21 45	22 25
Flimby	d	05x51	06x36	07x03	07x55		09x38	10x56	11x49		13x49	14x53	15x25	15x53	17x08	17x48	18x32	19x28	19x51	20x42	21x48	22x29
Workington	d	05 58	06 44	07 10	08 05	09 03	09 45	11 03	11 57	12 58	13 57	15 01	15 33	16 01	17 15	17 56	18 39	19 36	19 59	20 50	21 56	22 35
Harrington	d	06 02	06 48	07 15	08 09		09 50	11 07	12 01		14 01	15 05	15 37	16 05	17 19	18 00	18 44	19 40	20 03	20 54	22 00	22 39
Parton	d	06x11	06x57	07x26	08x18		10x01	11x16	12x09		14x09	15x13	15x45	16x13	17x28	18x08	18x55	19x49	20x11	21x02	22x08	22x49
Whitehaven	a	06 16	07 02	07 30	08 23	09 19	10 05	11 21	12 15	13 15	14 15	15 19	15 51	16 19	17 33	18 16	19 00	19 56	20 19	21 09	22 15	22 55
	d	06 18	07 04	07 32	08 25	09 21	10 07	11 23	12 16	13 17	14 16	15 20	15 52	16 20	17 35	18 18	19 01		20 20			
Corkickle	d	06 20	07 06	07 35	08 27	09 23	10 10	11 25	12 19	13 20	14 19	15 23	15 55	16 23	17 37	18 20	19 05		20 23			
St Bees	d	06 26	07 12	07 42	08 33	09 33	10 21	11 33	12 28	13 27	14 30	15 29	16 02	16 28	17 43	18 27	19 13		20 28			
Nethertown	d	06x30						11x37	12x32				16x06			18x31			20x32			
Braystones	d	06x33						11x40	12x34				16x08			18x34			20x35			
Sellafield	d	06 39	07 24	07 53	08 44	09 43	10 32	11 45	12 40	13 38	14 45	15 40	16 14	16 39	17 53	18 40	19 24		20 40			
Seascale	d	06 43	07 28	07 58	08 47	09 46	10 37	11 49	12 44	13 43	14 48	15 44	16 18	16 43	17 57	18 43	19 28		20 44			
Drigg	d	06x46	07x31		08x50	09x49	10x41	11x52	12x47		14x52	15x48	16x21	16x46	18x00		19x33		20x47			
Ravenglass for Eskdale	d	06 50	07 34	08 05	08 54	09 53	10 46	11 55	12 50	13 50	14 56	15 52	16 25	16 50	18 04	18 49	19 37		20 50			
Bootle	d	06x55	07x40		08x59	09x58	10x52	12x01	12x56		15x01	15x58	16x31	16x56	18x09		19x44		20x56			
Silecroft	d	07x02	07x46		09x06	10x05	11x00	12x07	13x02		15x08	16x05	16x38	17x03	18x16		19x52		21x02			
Millom	a	07 08	07 53	08 21	09 12	10 11	11 06	12 14	13 09	14 06	15 15	16 11	16 44	17 10	18 23	19 05	19 58		21 09			
	d	07 09	07 53	08 22	09 14	10 11	11 06	12 14	13 09	14 07	15 16	16 12	16 45	17 10	18 23	19 05	19 58		21 09			
Green Road	d	07x13	07x57		09x18	10x15		12x18	13x13		15x20	16x16	16x49	17x15	18x27	19x09	20x04		21x13			
Foxfield	d	07 17	08 01		09 22	10 19	11 15	12 22	13 17	14 16	15 24	16 20	16 53	17 19	18 31	19 13	20 09		21 17			
Kirkby-in-Furness	d	07x21	08x05		09x26	10x23	11x20	12x26	13x21	14x20	15x28	16x24	16x58	17x24	18x35	19x17	20x14		21x21			
Askam	d	07 26	08 11	08 39	09 31	10 28	11 26	12 31	13 26	14 26	15 33	16 29	17 03	17 29	18 40	19 22	20 20		21 26			
Barrow-in-Furness	a	07 41	08 26	08 54	09 46	10 43	11 41	12 46	13 41	14 41	15 48	16 44	17 17	17 44	18 55	19 37	20 37		21 41			
Lancaster 8 82	a				11 07				14 50		16 52		18 24									

Table T100-R

Sundays

20 May to 17 June

Carlisle and Whitehaven - Barrow-in-Furness

		NT	NT	NT		NT	NT	VT	NT	NT	NT	NT	NT	NT	NT		NT
								◇1									
Carlisle 8	d			10 41		11 06	12 07	13 07	13 16	14 12		15 10	16 16	17 10	18 10		21 10
Dalston	d			10 49		11 14	12 15		13 24	14 20		15 18	16 24	17 18	18 18		21 18
Wigton	d			10 58		11 24	12 25		13 34	14 30		15 28	16 34	17 28	18 28		21 28
Aspatria	d			11 09		11 34	12 35		13 44	14 40		15 38	16 44	17 38	18 38		21 38
Maryport	d	09 17	10 24	11 20		11 45	12 46		13 55	14 51		15 49	16 55	17 49	18 49		21 49
Flimby	d	09x20		11x23		11x48			13x58	14x54		15x52	16x58	17x52	18x52		21x52
Workington	d	09 27	10 33	11 30		11 56	12 58		14 06	15 02		16 00	17 06	18 00	19 00		22 00
Harrington	d	09 31		11 34		12 00	13 02		14 10	15 06		16 04	17 10	18 04	19 04		22 04
Parton	d	09x40	10x45	11x43		12x08	13x10		14x18	15x14		16x12	17x18	18x12	19x12		22x12
Whitehaven	a	09 45	10 50	11 48		12 14	13 16		14 24	15 21		16 17	17 24	18 18	19 19		22 19
	d	09 47	10 51	11 50		12 15	13 18		14 25			16 19	17 25	18 19			
Corkickle	d	09 49	10 54	11 52		12 18	13 21		14 28			16 22	17 28	18 22		and hourly until	
St Bees	d	09 55	10 59	11 58		12 24	13 27		14 33			16 29	17 33	18 28			
Nethertown	d	09x59		12x02								16x33		18x32			
Braystones	d	10x01		12x04								16x35		18x34			
Sellafield	d	10 07	11 09	12 10		12 34	13 37		14 44		16 04	16 42	17 44	18 40			
Seascale	d	10 11	11 13	12 14		12 38	13 40		14 48		16 08	16 46	17 48	18 43			
Drigg	d	10x14	11x16	12x17		12x41	13x43		14x51		16x11		17x51	18x46			
Ravenglass for Eskdale	d	10 17	11 19	12 21		12 44	13 47		14 54		16 14	16 52	17 54	18 50			
Bootle	d	10x23	11x25	12x27		12x50	13x52		15x00		16x20		18x00	18x55			
Silecroft	d	10x29	11x31	12x33		12x56	13x59		15x06		16x26		18x06	19x02			
Millom	a	10 36	11 38	12 40		13 03	14 05		15 13		16 33	17 07	18 13	19 08			
	d	10 36	11 38	12 40		13 03	14 06		15 14		16 34	17 09	18 14	19 08			
Green Road	d	10x40	11x42	12x44		13x07	14x10		15x18		16x38		18x18	19x12			
Foxfield	d	10 44	11 45	12 48		13 11	14 14		15 22		16 42	17 16	18 22	19 16			
Kirkby-in-Furness	d	10x48	11x49	12x52		13x15	14x18		15x26		16x46	17x20	18x26	19x20			
Askam	d	10 53	11 54	12 58		13 20	14 23		15 31		16 51	17 25	18 31	19 25			
Barrow-in-Furness	a	11 08	12 09	13 15		13 35	14 38		15 46		17 06	17 40	18 46	19 40			
Lancaster 6 82	a			14 16				13 54	16 52			18 49					

Sundays

24 June to 9 September

		NT	NT	NT	NT	NT	VT	NT	NT	NT		NT	NT	NT	NT		NT
							◇1										
Carlisle 8	d		09 45	10 23	11 06	12 07	13 07	13 16	14 12			15 10	16 16	17 10	18 10		21 10
Dalston	d		09 53	10 32	11 14	12 15		13 24	14 20			15 18	16 24	17 18	18 18		21 18
Wigton	d		10 02	10 41	11 24	12 25		13 34	14 30			15 28	16 34	17 28	18 28		21 28
Aspatria	d		10 13	10 52	11 34	12 35		13 44	14 40			15 38	16 44	17 38	18 38		21 38
Maryport	d	09 17	10 24	11 03	11 45	12 46		13 55	14 51			15 49	16 55	17 49	18 49		21 49
Flimby	d	09x20		11x06	11x48			13x58	14x54			15x52	16x58	17x52	18x52		21x52
Workington	d	09 27	10 33	11 13	11 56	12 58		14 06	15 02			16 00	17 06	18 00	19 00		22 00
Harrington	d	09 31		11 17	12 00	13 02		14 10	15 06			16 04	17 10	18 04	19 04		22 04
Parton	d	09x40	10x45	11x26	12x08	13x10		14x18	15x14			16x12	17x18	18x12	19x12		22x12
Whitehaven	a	09 45	10 50	11 31	12 14	13 16		14 24	15 21			16 17	17 24	18 18	19 19		22 19
	d	09 47	10 51	11 33	12 15	13 18		14 25				16 19	17 25	18 19			
Corkickle	d	09 49	10 54	11 35	12 18	13 21		14 28				16 22	17 28	18 22		and hourly until	
St Bees	d	09 55	10 59	11 41	12 24	13 27		14 33				16 29	17 33	18 28			
Nethertown	d	09x59										16x33		18x32			
Braystones	d	10x01										16x35		18x34			
Sellafield	d	10 07	11 09	11 51	12 34	13 37		14 44		16 04		16 42	17 44	18 40			
Seascale	d	10 11	11 13	11 54	12 38	13 40		14 48		16 08		16 46	17 48	18 43			
Drigg	d	10x14	11x16	11x57	12x41	13x43		14x51		16x11			17x51	18x46			
Ravenglass for Eskdale	d	10 17	11 19	12 01	12 44	13 47		14 54		16 14		16 52	17 54	18 50			
Bootle	d	10x23	11x25	12x06	12x50	13x52		15x00		16x20			18x00	18x55			
Silecroft	d	10x29	11x31	12x13	12x56	13x59		15x06		16x26			18x06	19x02			
Millom	a	10 36	11 38	12 19	13 03	14 05		15 13		16 33		17 07	18 13	19 08			
	d	10 36	11 38	12 19	13 03	14 06		15 14		16 34		17 09	18 14	19 08			
Green Road	d	10x40	11x42	12x23	13x07	14x10		15x18		16x38			18x18	19x12			
Foxfield	d	10 44	11 45	12 27	13 11	14 14		15 22		16 42		17 16	18 22	19 16			
Kirkby-in-Furness	d	10x48	11x49	12x31	13x15	14x18		15x26		16x46		17x20	18x26	19x20			
Askam	d	10 53	11 54	12 36	13 20	14 23		15 31		16 51		17 25	18 31	19 25			
Barrow-in-Furness	a	11 08	12 09	12 51	13 35	14 38		15 46		17 06		17 40	18 46	19 40			
Lancaster 6 82	a			13 52			13 54	16 52				18 49					

No Sunday Service Whitehaven to Barrow-in-Furness

Table T100-R

Sundays

16 September to 2 December

Carlisle and Whitehaven - Barrow-in-Furness

		NT	NT	NT	NT		NT	NT	NT	NT	NT	NT	NT	NT		NT
Carlisle 8	d		09 45	10 23	11 06		12 07	13 16	14 12		15 10	16 16	17 10	18 10		21 10
Dalston	d		09 53	10 32	11 14		12 15	13 24	14 20		15 18	16 24	17 18	18 18		21 18
Wigton	d		10 02	10 41	11 24		12 25	13 34	14 30		15 28	16 34	17 28	18 28		21 28
Aspatria	d		10 13	10 52	11 34		12 35	13 44	14 40		15 38	16 44	17 38	18 38		21 38
Maryport	d	09 17	10 24	11 03	11 45		12 46	13 55	14 51		15 49	16 55	17 49	18 49		21 49
Flimby	d	09x20		11x06	11x48			13x58	14x54		15x52	16x58	17x52	18x52		21x52
Workington	d	09 27	10 33	11 13	11 56		12 58	14 06	15 02		16 00	17 06	18 00	19 00		22 00
Harrington	d	09 31		11 17	12 00		13 02	14 10	15 06		16 04	17 10	18 04	19 04		22 04
Parton	d	09x40	10x45	11x26	12x08		13x10	14x18	15x14		16x12	17x18	18x12	19x12		22x12
Whitehaven	a	09 45	10 50	11 31	12 14		13 16	14 24	15 21		16 17	17 24	18 18	19 19		22 19
	d	09 47	10 51	11 33	12 15		13 18	14 25			16 19	17 25	18 19			
Corkickle	d	09 49	10 54	11 35	12 18		13 21	14 28			16 22	17 28	18 22		and hourly until	
St Bees	d	09 55	10 59	11 41	12 24		13 27	14 33			16 29	17 33	18 28			
Nethertown	d	09x59									16x33		18x32			
Braystones	d	10x01									16x35		18x34			
Sellafield	d	10 07	11 09	11 51	12 34		13 37	14 44		16 04	16 42	17 44	18 40			
Seascale	d	10 11	11 13	11 54	12 38		13 40	14 48		16 08	16 46	17 48	18 43			
Drigg	d	10x14	11x16	11x57	12x41		13x43	14x51		16x11		17x51	18x46			
Ravenglass for Eskdale	d	10 17	11 19	12 01	12 44		13 47	14 54		16 14	16 52	17 54	18 50			
Bootle	d	10x23	11x25	12x06	12x50		13x52	15x00		16x20		18x00	18x55			
Silecroft	d	10x29	11x31	12x13	12x56		13x59	15x06		16x26		18x06	19x02			
Millom	a	10 36	11 38	12 19	13 03		14 05	15 13		16 33	17 07	18 13	19 08			
	d	10 36	11 38	12 19	13 03		14 06	15 14		16 34	17 09	18 14	19 08			
Green Road	d	10x40	11x42	12x23	13x07		14x10	15x18		16x38		18x18	19x12			
Foxfield	d	10 44	11 45	12 27	13 11		14 14	15 22		16 42	17 16	18 22	19 16			
Kirkby-in-Furness	d	10x48	11x49	12x31	13x15		14x18	15x26		16x46	17x20	18x26	19x20			
Askam	d	10 53	11 54	12 36	13 20		14 23	15 31		16 51	17 25	18 31	19 25			
Barrow-in-Furness	a	11 08	12 09	12 51	13 35		14 38	15 46		17 06	17 40	18 46	19 40			
Lancaster 6 82	a			13 52				16 52			18 49					

No Sunday Service Whitehaven to Barrow-in-Furness

Table T101-F

Mondays to Fridays
21 May to 7 December

Wrexham - Bidston

Miles			AW	AW	AW	AW	AW	AW	AW	AW	AW	AW	AW	AW	AW	AW
0	**Wrexham Central**	d		07 28	08 30	09 30	10 30	11 30	12 30	13 30	14 30	15 30	16 30	17 43	19 44	21 55
0½	**Wrexham General**	a		07 30	08 32	09 32	10 32	11 32	12 32	13 32	14 32	15 32	16 32	17 45	19 48	21 57
—		d	06 31	07 30	08 32	09 32	10 32	11 32	12 32	13 32	14 32	15 32	16 32	17 45	19 48	21 57
2¼	Gwersyllt	d	06 35	07 34	08 36	09 36	10 36	11 36	12 36	13 36	14 36	15 36	16 36	17 49	19 50	22 01
4	Cefn-y-Bedd	d	06 40	07 39	08 41	09 41	10 41	11 41	12 41	13 41	14 41	15 41	16 41	17 54	19 55	22 06
4¾	Caergwrle	d	06 42	07 41	08 43	09 43	10 43	11 43	12 43	13 43	14 43	15 43	16 43	17 56	19 57	22 08
5¼	Hope (Flintshire)	d	06 44	07 43	08 45	09 45	10 45	11 45	12 45	13 45	14 45	15 45	16 45	17 58	19 59	22 10
7¼	Penyffordd	d	06 48	07 47	08 49	09 49	10 49	11 49	12 49	13 49	14 49	15 49	16 49	18 02	20 03	22 14
8½	Buckley	d	06 51	07 50	08 52	09 52	10 52	11 52	12 52	13 52	14 52	15 52	16 52	18 05	20 06	22 17
10½	Hawarden	d	06 55	07 54	08 56	09 56	10 56	11 56	12 56	13 56	14 56	15 56	16 56	18 09	20 10	22 21
12¾	Shotton High Level	d	06 59	07 59	09 00	10 00	11 00	12 00	13 00	14 00	15 00	16 00	17 00	18 13	20 14	22 25
13¼	Hawarden Bridge	d	07x01	08x01									17x02			
18¾	Neston	d	07 10	08 10	09 10	10 10	11 10	12 10	13 10	14 10	15 10	16 10	17 11	18 23	20 24	22 35
21¼	Heswall	d	07 15	08 15	09 15	10 15	11 15	12 15	13 15	14 15	15 15	16 15	17 16	18 28	20 29	22 40
25½	Upton	d	07 21	08 21	09 21	10 21	11 21	12 21	13 21	14 21	15 21	16 21	17 22	18 34	20 35	22 46
27½	**Bidston**	a	07 30	08 30	09 31	10 30	11 30	12 30	13 30	14 30	15 30	16 30	17 31	18 45	20 44	22 55

Saturdays
26 May to 8 December

		AW	AW	AW	AW	AW	AW	AW	AW	AW	AW	AW	AW	AW	AW
Wrexham Central	d		07 28	08 30	09 30	10 30	11 30	12 30	13 30	14 30	15 30	16 30	17 43	19 44	21 55
Wrexham General	a		07 30	08 32	09 32	10 32	11 32	12 32	13 32	14 32	15 32	16 32	17 45	19 48	21 57
	d	06 31	07 30	08 32	09 32	10 32	11 32	12 32	13 32	14 32	15 32	16 32	17 45	19 48	21 57
Gwersyllt	d	06 35	07 34	08 36	09 36	10 36	11 36	12 36	13 36	14 36	15 36	16 36	17 49	19 50	22 01
Cefn-y-Bedd	d	06 40	07 39	08 41	09 41	10 41	11 41	12 41	13 41	14 41	15 41	16 41	17 54	19 55	22 06
Caergwrle	d	06 42	07 41	08 43	09 43	10 43	11 43	12 43	13 43	14 43	15 43	16 43	17 56	19 57	22 08
Hope (Flintshire)	d	06 44	07 43	08 45	09 45	10 45	11 45	12 45	13 45	14 45	15 45	16 45	17 58	19 59	22 10
Penyffordd	d	06 48	07 47	08 49	09 49	10 49	11 49	12 49	13 49	14 49	15 49	16 49	18 02	20 03	22 14
Buckley	d	06 51	07 50	08 52	09 52	10 52	11 52	12 52	13 52	14 52	15 52	16 52	18 05	20 06	22 17
Hawarden	d	06 55	07 54	08 56	09 56	10 56	11 56	12 56	13 56	14 56	15 56	16 56	18 09	20 10	22 21
Shotton High Level	d	06 59	07 59	09 00	10 00	11 00	12 00	13 00	14 00	15 00	16 00	17 00	18 13	20 14	22 25
Hawarden Bridge	d	07x01	08x01									17x02			
Neston	d	07 10	08 10	09 10	10 10	11 10	12 10	13 10	14 10	15 10	16 10	17 11	18 23	20 24	22 35
Heswall	d	07 15	08 15	09 15	10 15	11 15	12 15	13 15	14 15	15 15	16 15	17 16	18 28	20 29	22 40
Upton	d	07 21	08 21	09 21	10 21	11 21	12 21	13 21	14 21	15 21	16 21	17 22	18 34	20 35	22 46
Bidston	a	07 30	08 30	09 31	10 30	11 30	12 30	13 30	14 30	15 30	16 30	17 31	18 45	20 44	22 55

Sundays
20 May to 2 December

		AW	AW	AW	AW	AW	AW
Wrexham Central	d		11 05	13 35	16 05	18 35	21 05
Wrexham General	a		11 07	13 37	16 07	18 37	21 07
	d	08 44	11 08	13 38	16 08	18 38	21 08
Gwersyllt	d	08 48	11 12	13 42	16 12	18 42	21 12
Cefn-y-Bedd	d	08 53	11 17	13 47	16 17	18 47	21 17
Caergwrle	d	08 55	11 19	13 49	16 19	18 49	21 19
Hope (Flintshire)	d	08 57	11 21	13 51	16 21	18 51	21 21
Penyffordd	d	09 01	11 25	13 55	16 25	18 55	21 25
Buckley	d	09 04	11 28	13 58	16 28	18 58	21 28
Hawarden	d	09 08	11 32	14 02	16 32	19 02	21 32
Shotton High Level	d	09 12	11 36	14 06	16 36	19 06	21 36
Hawarden Bridge	d	09x14	11x38	14x08	16x38	19x08	21x38
Neston	d	09 23	11 47	14 17	16 47	19 17	21 47
Heswall	d	09 28	11 52	14 22	16 52	19 22	21 52
Upton	d	09 34	11 58	14 28	16 58	19 28	21 58
Bidston	a	09 41	12 06	14 36	17 06	19 36	22 06

For connections to Liverpool Lime Street refer to Table T106

Table T101-R

Mondays to Fridays
21 May to 7 December

Bidston - Wrexham

Miles			AW	AW	AW	AW	AW	AW	AW	AW	AW	AW	AW	AW	AW	AW	AW
0	**Bidston**	d		07 31	08 31	09 32	10 32	11 32	12 32	13 32	14 32	15 32	16 35	17 45	18 46	20 56	22 56
2	Upton	d		07 32	08 32	09 33	10 33	11 33	12 33	13 33	14 33	15 33	16 36	17 46	18 47	20 57	22 57
6¼	Heswall	d		07 39	08 39	09 40	10 40	11 40	12 40	13 40	14 40	15 40	16 43	17 53	18 54	21 04	23 04
8¾	Neston	d		07 44	08 44	09 45	10 45	11 45	12 45	13 45	14 45	15 45	16 48	17 58	18 59	21 09	23 09
14¼	Hawarden Bridge	d		07x53	08x53								16x57	18x07			
14¾	Shotton High Level	d		07 55	08 55	09 55	10 55	11 55	12 55	13 55	14 55	15 55	16 59	18 09	19 09	21 19	23 20
17½	Hawarden	d		08 00	09 00	10 00	11 00	12 00	13 00	14 00	15 00	16 00	17 04	18 14	19 14	21 24	23 25
19	Buckley	d		08 05	09 05	10 05	11 05	12 05	13 05	14 05	15 05	16 05	17 09	18 19	19 19	21 29	23 30
20¼	Penyffordd	d		08 08	09 08	10 08	11 08	12 08	13 08	14 08	15 08	16 08	17 12	18 22	19 22	21 32	23 33
22¼	Hope (Flintshire)	d		08 12	09 12	10 12	11 12	12 12	13 12	14 12	15 12	16 12	17 16	18 26	19 26	21 36	23 37
22¾	Caergwrle	d		08 14	09 14	10 14	11 14	12 14	13 14	14 14	15 14	16 14	17 18	18 28	19 28	21 38	23 39
23½	Cefn-y-Bedd	d		08 16	09 16	10 16	11 16	12 16	13 16	14 16	15 16	16 16	17 20	18 30	19 30	21 40	23 40
25¼	Gwersyllt	d		08 20	09 20	10 20	11 20	12 20	13 20	14 20	15 20	16 20	17 24	18 34	19 34	21 44	23 46
27	**Wrexham General**	a		08 27	09 27	10 27	11 27	12 27	13 27	14 27	15 27	16 27	17 31	18 41	19 41	21 51	23 53
—		d	07 10	08 27	09 27	10 27	11 27	12 27	13 27	14 27	15 27	16 27	17 31	18 41	19 41	21 51	
27½	**Wrexham Central**	a	07 13	08 32	09 32	10 32	11 32	12 32	13 32	14 32	15 32	16 32	17 36	18 46	19 46	21 56	

Saturdays
26 May to 8 December

		AW	AW	AW	AW	AW	AW	AW	AW	AW	AW	AW	AW	AW	AW
Bidston	d		07 31	08 31	09 32	10 32	11 32	12 32	13 32	14 32	15 32	16 35	17 45	20 56	22 56
Upton	d		07 32	08 32	09 33	10 33	11 33	12 33	13 33	14 33	15 33	16 36	17 46	20 57	22 57
Heswall	d		07 39	08 39	09 40	10 40	11 40	12 40	13 40	14 40	15 40	16 43	17 53	21 04	23 04
Neston	d		07 44	08 44	09 45	10 45	11 45	12 45	13 45	14 45	15 45	16 48	17 58	21 09	23 09
Hawarden Bridge	d		07x53	08x53								16x57	18x07		
Shotton High Level	d		07 55	08 55	09 55	10 55	11 55	12 55	13 55	14 55	15 55	16 59	18 09	21 19	23 20
Hawarden	d		08 00	09 00	10 00	11 00	12 00	13 00	14 00	15 00	16 00	17 04	18 14	21 24	23 25
Buckley	d		08 05	09 05	10 05	11 05	12 05	13 05	14 05	15 05	16 05	17 09	18 19	21 29	23 30
Penyffordd	d		08 08	09 08	10 08	11 08	12 08	13 08	14 08	15 08	16 08	17 12	18 22	21 32	23 33
Hope (Flintshire)	d		08 12	09 12	10 12	11 12	12 12	13 12	14 12	15 12	16 12	17 16	18 26	21 36	23 37
Caergwrle	d		08 14	09 14	10 14	11 14	12 14	13 14	14 14	15 14	16 14	17 18	18 28	21 38	23 39
Cefn-y-Bedd	d		08 16	09 16	10 16	11 16	12 16	13 16	14 16	15 16	16 16	17 20	18 30	21 40	23 40
Gwersyllt	d		08 20	09 20	10 20	11 20	12 20	13 20	14 20	15 20	16 20	17 24	18 34	21 44	23 46
Wrexham General	a		08 27	09 27	10 27	11 27	12 27	13 27	14 27	15 27	16 27	17 31	18 41	21 51	23 53
	d	07 10	08 27	09 27	10 27	11 27	12 27	13 27	14 27	15 27	16 27	17 31	18 41	21 51	
Wrexham Central	a	07 13	08 32	09 32	10 32	11 32	12 32	13 32	14 32	15 32	16 32	17 36	18 46	21 56	

Sundays
20 May to 2 December

		AW	AW	AW	AW	AW	AW
Bidston	d	09 57	12 27	14 57	17 27	19 57	22 27
Upton	d	09 58	12 28	14 58	17 28	19 58	22 28
Heswall	d	10 05	12 35	15 05	17 35	20 05	22 35
Neston	d	10 10	12 40	15 10	17 40	20 10	22 40
Hawarden Bridge	d	10x19	12x49	15x19	17x49	20x19	22x49
Shotton High Level	d	10 21	12 51	15 21	17 51	20 21	22 51
Hawarden	d	10 26	12 56	15 26	17 56	20 26	22 56
Buckley	d	10 31	13 01	15 31	18 01	20 31	23 01
Penyffordd	d	10 34	13 04	15 34	18 04	20 34	23 04
Hope (Flintshire)	d	10 38	13 08	15 38	18 08	20 38	23 08
Caergwrle	d	10 40	13 10	15 40	18 10	20 40	23 10
Cefn-y-Bedd	d	10 42	13 12	15 42	18 12	20 42	23 12
Gwersyllt	d	10 46	13 16	15 46	18 16	20 46	23 16
Wrexham General	a	10 51	13 23	15 53	18 23	20 53	23 26
	d	10 52	13 24	15 54	18 24	20 54	
Wrexham Central	a	10 59	13 26	15 59	18 29	20 59	

For connections from Liverpool Lime Street refer to Table T106

Table T102-F

Mondays to Saturdays

21 May to 8 December

Llandudno - Blaenau Ffestiniog

Miles			AW SO ◇	AW SX ◇	AW SO ◇	AW SX ◇	AW SX ◇	AW SO ◇	AW ◇	AW ◇	AW SO ◇	AW SX ◇
0	**Llandudno**	81 d					10 08	10 22	13 08	16 20	19 03	19 05
1¾	Deganwy	81 d					10x12	10x26	13x12	16x24	19x07	19x09
3	**Llandudno Junction**	81 d	05 30	05 30	07 26	07 26	10 28	10 34	13 30	16 33	19 19	19 23
5	Glan Conwy	d			07x29	07x29	10x31	10x37	13x33	16x36	19x22	19x26
8½	Tal-y-Cafn	d	05 38	05 38	07 35	07 35	10 37	10 43	13 39	16 42	19 28	19 32
11½	Dolgarrog	d			07x40	07x40	10x42	10x48	13x44	16x47	19x33	19x37
14½	North Llanrwst	d			07x47	07x47	10x48	10x54	13x50	16x53	19x39	19x43
15	Llanrwst	d	05 48	05 48	07 49	07 49	10 50	10 56	13 52	16 55	19 41	19 45
18½	Betws-y-Coed	d	05 54	05 54	07 55	07 55	10 56	11 02	13 58	17 01	19 47	19 51
22¾	Pont-y-Pant	d			08x03	08x03	11x04	11x10	14x06	17x09	19x55	19x59
24¼	Dolwyddelan	d			08x06	08x06	11x07	11x13	14x09	17x12	19x58	20x02
26	Roman Bridge	d			08x10	08x10	11x11	11x17	14x13	17x16	20x02	20x06
31	**Blaenau Ffestiniog**	a	06 21	06 24	08 26	08 29	11 30	11 36	14 32	17 35	20 21	20 23

For connections from Crewe, Chester, Rhyl and Bangor (Gwynedd), refer to Table T81

No Sunday Service

Table T102-R

Mondays to Saturdays

21 May to 8 December

Blaenau Ffestiniog - Llandudno

Miles			AW ◇	AW SX ◇	AW SO ◇	AW ◇	AW SO ◇	AW SX ◇	AW SX ◇	AW SO ◇	AW ◇
0	**Blaenau Ffestiniog**	d	06 24	08 35	08 46	11 35	14 57	14 57	17 36	17 37	20 23
5	Roman Bridge	d	06x34	08x45	08x56	11x45	15x07	15x07	17x46	17x47	20x33
6¾	Dolwyddelan	d	06x37	08x49	09x00	11x49	15x11	15x11	17x50	17x51	20x37
8¼	Pont-y-Pant	d	06x40	08x52	09x03	11x52	15x14	15x14	17x53	17x54	20x40
12½	Betws-y-Coed	d	06 50	09 02	09 13	12 02	15 24	15 24	18 03	18 04	20 50
16	Llanrwst	d	06 56	09 08	09 19	12 08	15 30	15 30	18 09	18 10	20 56
16½	North Llanrwst	d	06x57	09x09	09x20	12x09	15x31	15x31	18x10	18x11	20x57
19½	Dolgarrog	d	07x03	09x16	09x27	12x16	15x38	15x38	18x17	18x18	21x04
22½	Tal-y-Cafn	d	07x09	09x22	09x33	12x22	15x44	15x44	18x23	18x24	21x10
26	Glan Conwy	d	07x15	09x28	09x39	12x28	15x50	15x50	18x29	18x30	21x16
28	**Llandudno Junction**	81 a	07 20	09 33	09 44	12 33	15 55	15 55	18 34	18 35	21 21
29¼	Deganwy	81 a		09x53	10x10	12x38	16x08	16x08	18x44	18x44	21x35
31	**Llandudno**	81 a		09 58	10 17	12 45	16 15	16 17	18 53	18 53	21 44

For connections to Bangor (Gwynedd), Rhyl, Chester and Crewe refer to Table T81

No Sunday Service

Table T103-F

Mondays to Fridays

21 May to 7 December

Hunts Cross - Southport

Miles			ME A	ME	ME	ME	ME	ME	ME	ME		ME	ME	ME	ME	ME	ME	ME		ME	ME
0	**Hunts Cross**	89 d					06 01	06 21	06 36	06 51	and every 15 minutes until	07 51	08 06	08 21	08 36	08 51	09 06	09 21	and every 15 minutes until	14 06	14 21
1½	**Liverpool Sth Parkway** 7 89 ✈	d					06 04	06 24	06 39	06 54		07 54	08 09	08 24	08 39	08 54	09 09	09 24		14 09	14 24
2½	Cressington	d					06 07	06 27	06 42	06 57		07 57	08 12	08 27	08 42	08 57	09 12	09 27		14 12	14 27
3¼	Aigburth	d					06 09	06 29	06 44	06 59		07 59	08 14	08 29	08 44	08 59	09 14	09 29		14 14	14 29
4½	St Michaels	d					06 11	06 31	06 46	07 01		08 01	08 16	08 31	08 46	09 01	09 16	09 31		14 16	14 31
5¾	Brunswick	d					06 14	06 34	06 49	07 04		08 04	08 19	08 34	08 49	09 04	09 19	09 34		14 19	14 34
7¼	**Liverpool Central** 10	a					06 23	06 38	06 53	07 08		08 08	08 23	08 38	08 53	09 08	09 23	09 38		14 23	14 38
—		d				06 08	06 23	06 38	06 53	07 08		08 08	08 23	08 38	08 53	09 08	09 23	09 38		14 23	14 38
7½	**Moorfields** 10	d				06 10	06 25	06 41	06 55	07 11		08 11	08 26	08 41	08 56	09 11	09 26	09 41		14 26	14 41
9¼	Sandhills	d			05 59	06 14	06 29	06 45	06 59	07 15		08 15	08 30	08 45	09 00	09 15	09 30	09 45		14 30	14 45
10	Bank Hall	d			06 02	06 17	06 32	06 47	07 02	07 17		08 17	08 32	08 47	09 02	09 17	09 32	09 47		14 32	14 47
10¾	Bootle Oriel Road	d			06 04	06 19	06 34	06 49	07 04	07 19		08 19	08 34	08 49	09 04	09 19	09 34	09 49		14 34	14 49
11	Bootle New Strand	d			06 06	06 21	06 36	06 51	07 06	07 21		08 21	08 36	08 51	09 06	09 21	09 36	09 51		14 36	14 51
12	Seaforth & Litherland	d			06 08	06 23	06 38	06 53	07 08	07 23		08 23	08 38	08 53	09 08	09 23	09 38	09 53		14 38	14 53
13¼	Waterloo	d			06 10	06 25	06 40	06 55	07 10	07 25		08 25	08 40	08 55	09 10	09 25	09 40	09 55		14 40	14 55
14¼	Blundellsands & Crosby	d			06 13	06 28	06 43	06 58	07 13	07 28		08 28	08 43	08 58	09 13	09 28	09 43	09 58		14 43	14 58
15	Hall Road	d			06 15	06 30	06 45	07 00	07 15	07 30		08 30	08 45	09 00	09 15	09 30	09 45	10 00		14 45	15 00
17	Hightown	d		00 03	06 18	06 33	06 48	07 03	07 18	07 33		08 33	08 48	09 03	09 18	09 33	09 48	10 03		14 48	15 03
19	Formby	d		00 07	06 22	06 37	06 52	07 07	07 22	07 37		08 37	08 52	09 07	09 22	09 37	09 52	10 07		14 52	15 07
20	Freshfield	d		00 09	06 24	06 39	06 54	07 09	07 24	07 39		08 39	08 54	09 09	09 24	09 39	09 54	10 09		14 54	15 09
22¾	Ainsdale	d		00 13	06 28	06 43	06 58	07 13	07 28	07 43		08 43	08 58	09 13	09 28	09 43	09 58	10 13		14 58	15 13
24½	Hillside	d	00 01	00 16	06 31	06 46	07 01	07 16	07 31	07 46		08 46	09 01	09 16	09 31	09 46	10 01	10 16		15 01	15 16
25¼	Birkdale	d	00 03	00 18	06 33	06 48	07 03	07 18	07 33	07 48		08 48	09 03	09 18	09 33	09 48	10 03	10 18		15 03	15 18
26¼	**Southport**	a	00 10	00 25	06 40	06 53	07 10	07 25	07 40	07 55		08 55	09 08	09 23	09 38	09 55	10 08	10 25		15 10	15 23

		ME	ME	ME	ME	ME	ME	ME	ME	ME	ME	ME	ME	ME	ME		ME	ME	ME	ME	ME	ME
Hunts Cross	89 d	14 36	14 51	15 06	15 21	15 36	15 51	16 06	16 21	16 36	16 51	17 06	17 21	17 36	17 51	and every 15 minutes until	19 21	19 36	19 51	20 06	20 21	20 36
Liverpool Sth Parkway 7 89 ✈	d	14 39	14 54	15 09	15 24	15 39	15 54	16 10	16 24	16 39	16 54	17 09	17 24	17 39	17 54		19 24	19 39	19 54	20 09	20 24	20 39
Cressington	d	14 42	14 57	15 12	15 27	15 42	15 57	16 12	16 27	16 42	16 57	17 12	17 27	17 42	17 57		19 27	19 42	19 57	20 12	20 27	20 42
Aigburth	d	14 44	14 59	15 14	15 29	15 44	15 59	16 14	16 29	16 44	16 59	17 14	17 29	17 44	17 59		19 29	19 44	19 59	20 14	20 29	20 44
St Michaels	d	14 46	15 01	15 16	15 31	15 46	16 01	16 17	16 31	16 46	17 01	17 16	17 31	17 46	18 01		19 31	19 46	20 01	20 16	20 31	20 46
Brunswick	d	14 49	15 04	15 19	15 34	15 49	16 04	16 19	16 34	16 49	17 04	17 19	17 34	17 49	18 04		19 34	19 49	20 04	20 19	20 34	20 49
Liverpool Central 10	a	14 53	15 08	15 23	15 38	15 53	16 08	16 23	16 38	16 53	17 08	17 23	17 38	17 53	18 08		19 38	19 53	20 08	20 23	20 38	20 53
	d	14 53	15 08	15 23	15 38	15 53	16 08	16 23	16 38	16 53	17 08	17 23	17 38	17 53	18 08		19 38	19 53	20 08	20 23	20 38	20 53
Moorfields 10	d	14 56	15 11	15 26	15 41	15 56	16 11	16 26	16 41	16 56	17 11	17 26	17 41	17 56	18 11		19 41	19 55	20 11	20 25	20 41	20 55
Sandhills	d	15 00	15 15	15 30	15 45	16 00	16 15	16 30	16 45	17 00	17 15	17 30	17 45	18 00	18 15		19 45	19 59	20 15	20 29	20 45	20 59
Bank Hall	d	15 02	15 17	15 32	15 47	16 02	16 17	16 32	16 47	17 02	17 17	17 32	17 47	18 02	18 17		19 47	20 02	20 17	20 32	20 47	21 02
Bootle Oriel Road	d	15 04	15 19	15 34	15 49	16 04	16 19	16 34	16 49	17 04	17 19	17 34	17 49	18 04	18 19		19 49	20 04	20 19	20 34	20 49	21 04
Bootle New Strand	d	15 06	15 21	15 36	15 51	16 06	16 21	16 36	16 51	17 06	17 21	17 36	17 51	18 06	18 21		19 51	20 06	20 21	20 36	20 51	21 06
Seaforth & Litherland	d	15 08	15 23	15 38	15 53	16 08	16 23	16 38	16 53	17 08	17 23	17 38	17 53	18 08	18 23		19 53	20 08	20 23	20 38	20 53	21 08
Waterloo	d	15 10	15 25	15 40	15 55	16 10	16 25	16 40	16 55	17 10	17 25	17 40	17 55	18 10	18 25		19 55	20 10	20 25	20 40	20 55	21 10
Blundellsands & Crosby	d	15 13	15 28	15 43	15 58	16 13	16 28	16 43	16 58	17 13	17 28	17 43	17 58	18 13	18 28		19 58	20 13	20 28	20 43	20 58	21 13
Hall Road	d	15 15	15 30	15 45	16 00	16 15	16 30	16 45	17 00	17 15	17 30	17 45	18 00	18 15	18 30		20 00	20 15	20 30	20 45	21 00	21 15
Hightown	d	15 18	15 33	15 48	16 03	16 18	16 33	16 48	17 03	17 18	17 33	17 48	18 03	18 18	18 33		20 03	20 18	20 33	20 48	21 03	21 18
Formby	d	15 22	15 37	15 52	16 07	16 22	16 37	16 52	17 07	17 22	17 37	17 52	18 07	18 22	18 37		20 07	20 22	20 37	20 52	21 07	21 22
Freshfield	d	15 24	15 39	15 54	16 09	16 24	16 39	16 54	17 09	17 24	17 39	17 54	18 09	18 24	18 39		20 09	20 24	20 39	20 54	21 09	21 24
Ainsdale	d	15 28	15 43	15 58	16 13	16 28	16 43	16 58	17 13	17 28	17 43	17 58	18 13	18 28	18 43		20 13	20 28	20 43	20 58	21 13	21 28
Hillside	d	15 31	15 46	16 01	16 16	16 31	16 46	17 01	17 16	17 31	17 46	18 01	18 16	18 31	18 46		20 16	20 31	20 46	21 01	21 16	21 31
Birkdale	d	15 33	15 48	16 03	16 18	16 33	16 48	17 03	17 18	17 33	17 48	18 03	18 18	18 33	18 48		20 18	20 33	20 48	21 03	21 18	21 33
Southport	a	15 40	15 53	16 10	16 23	16 38	16 55	17 10	17 25	17 38	17 55	18 08	18 25	18 38	18 55		20 25	20 40	20 55	21 10	21 25	21 40

		ME	ME	ME	ME	ME	ME	ME	ME	ME	ME	ME
Hunts Cross	89 d	20 51	21 06	21 21	21 36	21 51	22 06	22 21	22 36	22 51	23 06	23 21
Liverpool Sth Parkway 7 89 ✈	d	20 54	21 09	21 24	21 39	21 54	22 09	22 24	22 39	22 54	23 09	23 24
Cressington	d	20 57	21 12	21 27	21 42	21 57	22 12	22 27	22 42	22 57	23 12	23 27
Aigburth	d	20 59	21 14	21 29	21 44	21 59	22 14	22 29	22 44	22 59	23 14	23 29
St Michaels	d	21 01	21 16	21 31	21 46	22 01	22 16	22 31	22 46	23 01	23 16	23 31
Brunswick	d	21 04	21 19	21 34	21 49	22 04	22 19	22 34	22 49	23 04	23 19	23 34
Liverpool Central 10	a	21 08	21 23	21 38	21 53	22 08	22 23	22 38	22 53	23 08	23 23	23 38
	d	21 08	21 23	21 38	21 53	22 08	22 23	22 38	22 53	23 08	23 23	23 38
Moorfields 10	d	21 11	21 25	21 41	21 55	22 11	22 25	22 41	22 55	23 11	23 26	23 41
Sandhills	d	21 15	21 29	21 45	21 59	22 15	22 29	22 45	22 59	23 15	23 29	23 44
Bank Hall	d	21 17	21 32	21 47	22 02	22 17	22 32	22 47	23 02	23 17	23 32	23 47
Bootle Oriel Road	d	21 19	21 34	21 49	22 04	22 19	22 34	22 49	23 04	23 19	23 34	23 49
Bootle New Strand	d	21 21	21 36	21 51	22 06	22 21	22 36	22 51	23 06	23 21	23 36	23 51
Seaforth & Litherland	d	21 23	21 38	21 53	22 08	22 23	22 38	22 53	23 08	23 23	23 38	23 53
Waterloo	d	21 25	21 40	21 55	22 10	22 25	22 40	22 55	23 10	23 25	23 40	23 55
Blundellsands & Crosby	d	21 28	21 43	21 58	22 13	22 28	22 43	22 58	23 13	23 28	23 43	23 58
Hall Road	d	21 30	21 45	22 00	22 15	22 30	22 45	23 00	23 15	23 30	23 45	23 59
Hightown	d	21 33	21 48	22 03	22 18	22 33	22 48	23 03	23 18	23 33	23 48	00 03
Formby	d	21 37	21 52	22 07	22 22	22 37	22 52	23 07	23 22	23 37	23 52	00 07
Freshfield	d	21 39	21 54	22 09	22 24	22 39	22 54	23 09	23 24	23 39	23 54	00 09
Ainsdale	d	21 43	21 58	22 13	22 28	22 43	22 58	23 13	23 28	23 43	23 58	00 13
Hillside	d	21 46	22 01	22 16	22 31	22 46	23 01	23 16	23 31	23 46	00 01	00 16
Birkdale	d	21 48	22 03	22 18	22 33	22 48	23 03	23 18	23 33	23 48	00 03	00 18
Southport	a	21 55	22 10	22 25	22 40	22 55	23 10	23 25	23 40	23 55	00 10	00 25

A MX until 21 September, from 25 September

For alternative services between Liverpool and Sandhills refer to Tables T104 and T105

Table T103-F

Saturdays

26 May to 8 December

Hunts Cross - Southport

		ME	ME	ME	ME	ME	ME	ME	ME	ME		ME	ME	ME		ME	ME	ME		ME		ME	ME
Hunts Cross 89	d					06 01	06 21	06 36	06 51	07 06		07 21	07 36	07 51	and every 15 minutes until	15 51	16 06	16 21	and every 15 minutes until	19 21		19 36	19 51
Liverpool Sth Parkway 89	d					06 04	06 24	06 39	06 54	07 09		07 24	07 39	07 54		15 54	16 10	16 24		19 24		19 39	19 54
Cressington	d					06 07	06 27	06 42	06 57	07 12		07 27	07 42	07 57		15 57	16 12	16 27		19 27		19 42	19 57
Aigburth	d					06 09	06 29	06 44	06 59	07 14		07 29	07 44	07 59		15 59	16 14	16 29		19 29		19 44	19 59
St Michaels	d					06 11	06 31	06 46	07 01	07 16		07 31	07 46	08 01		16 01	16 17	16 31		19 31		19 46	20 01
Brunswick	d					06 14	06 34	06 49	07 04	07 19		07 34	07 49	08 04		16 04	16 19	16 34		19 34		19 49	20 04
Liverpool Central 10	a					06 23	06 38	06 53	07 08	07 23		07 38	07 53	08 08		16 08	16 23	16 38		19 38		19 53	20 08
	d				06 08	06 23	06 38	06 53	07 08	07 23		07 38	07 53	08 08		16 08	16 23	16 38		19 38		19 53	20 08
Moorfields 10	d				06 10	06 25	06 41	06 55	07 11	07 26		07 41	07 56	08 11		16 11	16 26	16 41		19 41		19 55	20 11
Sandhills	d			05 59	06 14	06 29	06 45	06 59	07 15	07 30		07 45	08 00	08 15		16 15	16 30	16 45		19 45		19 59	20 15
Bank Hall	d			06 02	06 17	06 32	06 47	07 02	07 17	07 32		07 47	08 02	08 17		16 17	16 32	16 47		19 47		20 02	20 17
Bootle Oriel Road	d			06 04	06 19	06 34	06 49	07 04	07 19	07 34		07 49	08 04	08 19		16 19	16 34	16 49		19 49		20 04	20 19
Bootle New Strand	d			06 06	06 21	06 36	06 51	07 06	07 21	07 36		07 51	08 06	08 21		16 21	16 36	16 51		19 51		20 06	20 21
Seaforth & Litherland	d			06 08	06 23	06 38	06 53	07 08	07 23	07 38		07 53	08 08	08 23		16 23	16 38	16 53		19 53		20 08	20 23
Waterloo	d			06 10	06 25	06 40	06 55	07 10	07 25	07 40		07 55	08 10	08 25		16 25	16 40	16 55		19 55		20 10	20 25
Blundellsands & Crosby	d			06 13	06 28	06 43	06 58	07 13	07 28	07 43		07 58	08 13	08 28		16 28	16 43	16 58		19 58		20 13	20 28
Hall Road	d			06 15	06 30	06 45	07 00	07 15	07 30	07 45		08 00	08 15	08 30		16 30	16 45	17 00		20 00		20 15	20 30
Hightown	d		00 03	06 18	06 33	06 48	07 03	07 18	07 33	07 48		08 03	08 18	08 33		16 33	16 48	17 03		20 03		20 18	20 33
Formby	d		00 07	06 22	06 37	06 52	07 07	07 22	07 37	07 52		08 07	08 22	08 37		16 37	16 52	17 07		20 07		20 22	20 37
Freshfield	d		00 09	06 24	06 39	06 54	07 09	07 24	07 39	07 54		08 09	08 24	08 39		16 39	16 54	17 09		20 09		20 24	20 39
Ainsdale	d		00 13	06 28	06 43	06 58	07 13	07 28	07 43	07 58		08 13	08 28	08 43		16 43	16 58	17 13		20 13		20 28	20 43
Hillside	d	00 01	00 16	06 31	06 46	07 01	07 16	07 31	07 46	08 01		08 16	08 31	08 46		16 46	17 01	17 16		20 16		20 31	20 46
Birkdale	d	00 03	00 18	06 33	06 48	07 03	07 18	07 33	07 48	08 03		08 18	08 33	08 48		16 48	17 03	17 18		20 18		20 33	20 48
Southport	a	00 10	00 25	06 40	06 55	07 10	07 25	07 40	07 55	08 10		08 25	08 39	08 55		16 55	17 10	17 25		20 25		20 40	20 55

		ME	ME	ME	ME	ME	ME	ME		ME	ME	ME	ME	ME	ME	ME
Hunts Cross 89	d	20 06	20 21	20 36	20 51	21 06	21 21	21 36		21 51	22 06	22 21	22 36	22 51	23 06	23 21
Liverpool Sth Parkway 89	d	20 09	20 24	20 39	20 54	21 09	21 24	21 39		21 54	22 09	22 24	22 39	22 54	23 09	23 23
Cressington	d	20 12	20 27	20 42	20 57	21 12	21 27	21 42		21 57	22 12	22 27	22 42	22 57	23 12	23 27
Aigburth	d	20 14	20 29	20 44	20 59	21 14	21 29	21 44		21 59	22 14	22 29	22 44	22 59	23 14	23 29
St Michaels	d	20 16	20 31	20 46	21 01	21 16	21 31	21 46		22 01	22 16	22 31	22 46	23 01	23 16	23 30
Brunswick	d	20 19	20 34	20 49	21 04	21 19	21 34	21 49		22 04	22 19	22 34	22 49	23 04	23 19	23 34
Liverpool Central 10	a	20 23	20 38	20 53	21 08	21 23	21 38	21 53		22 08	22 23	22 38	22 53	23 08	23 23	23 38
	d	20 23	20 38	20 53	21 08	21 23	21 38	21 53		22 08	22 23	22 38	22 53	23 08	23 23	23 38
Moorfields 10	d	20 25	20 41	20 55	21 11	21 25	21 41	21 55		22 11	22 25	22 41	22 55	23 11	23 26	23 41
Sandhills	d	20 29	20 45	20 59	21 15	21 29	21 45	21 59		22 15	22 29	22 45	22 59	23 15	23 30	23 44
Bank Hall	d	20 32	20 47	21 02	21 17	21 32	21 47	22 02		22 17	22 32	22 47	23 02	23 17	23 32	23 47
Bootle Oriel Road	d	20 34	20 49	21 04	21 19	21 34	21 49	22 04		22 19	22 34	22 49	23 04	23 19	23 34	23 49
Bootle New Strand	d	20 36	20 51	21 06	21 21	21 36	21 51	22 06		22 21	22 36	22 51	23 06	23 21	23 36	23 51
Seaforth & Litherland	d	20 38	20 53	21 08	21 23	21 38	21 53	22 08		22 23	22 38	22 53	23 08	23 23	23 38	23 53
Waterloo	d	20 40	20 55	21 10	21 25	21 40	21 55	22 10		22 25	22 40	22 55	23 10	23 25	23 40	23 55
Blundellsands & Crosby	d	20 43	20 58	21 13	21 28	21 43	21 58	22 13		22 28	22 43	22 58	23 13	23 28	23 43	23 58
Hall Road	d	20 45	21 00	21 15	21 30	21 45	22 00	22 15		22 30	22 45	23 00	23 15	23 30	23 45	23 59
Hightown	d	20 48	21 03	21 18	21 33	21 48	22 03	22 18		22 33	22 48	23 03	23 18	23 33	23 48	00 03
Formby	d	20 52	21 07	21 22	21 37	21 52	22 07	22 22		22 37	22 52	23 07	23 22	23 37	23 52	00 07
Freshfield	d	20 54	21 09	21 24	21 39	21 54	22 09	22 24		22 39	22 54	23 09	23 24	23 39	23 54	00 09
Ainsdale	d	20 58	21 13	21 28	21 43	21 58	22 13	22 28		22 43	22 58	23 13	23 28	23 43	23 58	00 13
Hillside	d	21 01	21 16	21 31	21 46	22 01	22 16	22 31		22 46	23 01	23 16	23 31	23 46	00 01	00 16
Birkdale	d	21 03	21 18	21 33	21 48	22 03	22 18	22 33		22 48	23 03	23 18	23 33	23 48	00 03	00 18
Southport	a	21 10	21 25	21 40	21 55	22 10	22 25	22 40		22 55	23 10	23 25	23 40	23 55	00 10	00 25

Sundays

20 May to 2 December

		ME A	ME A	ME	ME	ME	ME B	ME C	ME	ME D	ME	ME D		ME	ME D	ME	ME D		ME	ME D	ME	ME	ME D	ME
Hunts Cross 89	d				08 06	08 36	09 06	09 06	09 36		10 06		and at the same minutes past each hour until	18 36		19 06			19 36		20 06	20 36		21 06
Liverpool Sth Parkway 89	d				08 09	08 39	09 09	09 09	09 39		10 09			18 39		19 09			19 39		20 09	20 39		21 09
Cressington	d				08 12	08 42	09 12	09 12	09 42		10 12			18 42		19 12			19 42		20 12	20 42		21 12
Aigburth	d				08 14	08 44	09 14	09 14	09 44		10 14			18 44		19 14			19 44		20 14	20 44		21 14
St Michaels	d				08 16	08 46	09 16	09 16	09 46		10 16			18 46		19 16			19 46		20 16	20 46		21 16
Brunswick	d				08 19	08 49	09 19	09 19	09 49		10 19			18 49		19 19			19 49		20 19	20 49		21 19
Liverpool Central 10	a				08 23	08 53	09 23	09 23	09 53		10 23			18 53		19 23			19 53		20 23	20 53		21 23
	d			08 07	08 23	08 53	09 23	09 23	09 53	10 07	10 23	10 37		18 53	19 07	19 23	19 37		19 53	20 07	20 23	20 53	21 07	21 23
Moorfields 10	d			08 10	08 25	08 55	09 25	09 25	09 55	10 10	10 25	10 40		18 55	19 10	19 25	19 40		19 55	20 10	20 25	20 55	21 10	21 25
Sandhills	d			08 14	08 29	08 59	09 29	09 29	09 59	10 14	10 29	10 44		18 59	19 14	19 29	19 44		19 59	20 14	20 29	20 59	21 14	21 29
Bank Hall	d			08 17	08 32	09 02	09 32	09 32	10 02	10 16	10 32	10 46		19 02	19 16	19 32	19 46		20 02	20 16	20 32	21 02	21 16	21 32
Bootle Oriel Road	d			08 19	08 34	09 04	09 34	09 34	10 04	10 18	10 34	10 48		19 04	19 18	19 34	19 48		20 04	20 18	20 34	21 04	21 18	21 34
Bootle New Strand	d			08 21	08 36	09 06	09 36	09 36	10 06	10 20	10 36	10 50		19 06	19 20	19 36	19 50		20 06	20 20	20 36	21 06	21 20	21 36
Seaforth & Litherland	d			08 23	08 38	09 08	09 38	09 38	10 08	10 22	10 38	10 52		19 08	19 22	19 38	19 52		20 08	20 22	20 38	21 08	21 22	21 38
Waterloo	d			08 25	08 40	09 10	09 40	09 40	10 10	10 24	10 40	10 54		19 10	19 24	19 40	19 54		20 10	20 24	20 40	21 10	21 24	21 40
Blundellsands & Crosby	d			08 28	08 43	09 13	09 43	09 43	10 13	10 27	10 43	10 57		19 13	19 27	19 43	19 57		20 13	20 27	20 43	21 13	21 27	21 43
Hall Road	d			08 30	08 45	09 15	09 45	09 45	10 15	10 29	10 45	10 59		19 15	19 29	19 45	19 59		20 15	20 29	20 45	21 15	21 29	21 45
Hightown	d		00 03	08 33	08 48	09 18	09 48	09 48	10 18	10 32	10 48	11 02		19 18	19 32	19 48	20 02		20 18	20 32	20 48	21 18	21 32	21 48
Formby	d		00 07	08 37	08 52	09 22	09 52	09 52	10 22	10 36	10 52	11 06		19 22	19 36	19 52	20 06		20 22	20 36	20 52	21 22	21 36	21 52
Freshfield	d		00 09	08 39	08 54	09 24	09 54	09 54	10 24	10 38	10 54	11 08		19 24	19 38	19 54	20 08		20 24	20 38	20 54	21 24	21 38	21 54
Ainsdale	d		00 13	08 43	08 58	09 28	09 58	09 58	10 28	10 42	10 58	11 12		19 28	19 42	19 58	20 12		20 28	20 42	20 58	21 28	21 42	21 58
Hillside	d	00 01	00 16	08 46	09 01	09 31	10 01	10 01	10 31	10 45	11 01	11 15		19 31	19 45	20 01	20 15		20 31	20 45	21 01	21 31	21 45	22 01
Birkdale	d	00 03	00 18	08 48	09 03	09 33	10 03	10 03	10 33	10 47	11 03	11 17		19 33	19 47	20 03	20 17		20 33	20 47	21 03	21 33	21 47	22 03
Southport	a	00 10	00 25	08 55	09 10	09 40	10 10	10 11	10 40	10 54	11 10	11 24		19 40	19 54	20 10	20 24		20 40	20 54	21 10	21 40	21 54	22 10

A not 20 May
B until 1 July, from 30 September
C from 8 July until 23 September
D until 23 September

For alternative services between Liverpool and Sandhills refer to Tables T104 and T105

Table T103-F

Sundays

20 May to 2 December

Hunts Cross - Southport

		ME A	ME	ME A		ME	ME A	ME	ME A	ME B	ME A	ME
Hunts Cross 89	d		21 36			22 06		22 36		23 06	23 06	
Liverpool Sth Parkway 89	d		21 39			22 09		22 39		23 09	23 09	
Cressington	d		21 42			22 12		22 42		23 12	23 12	
Aigburth	d		21 44			22 14		22 44		23 14	23 14	
St Michaels	d		21 46			22 16		22 46		23 16	23 16	
Brunswick	d		21 49			22 19		22 49		23 19	23 19	
Liverpool Central 10	a		21 53			22 23		22 53		23 23	23 23	
	d	21 37	21 53	22 07		22 23	22 37	22 53	23 07	23 23	23 23	23 37
Moorfields 10	d	21 40	21 55	22 10		22 25	22 40	22 55	23 10	23 25	23 25	23 40
Sandhills	d	21 44	21 59	22 14		22 29	22 44	22 59	23 14	23 29	23a29	23 44
Bank Hall	d	21 46	22 02	22 16		22 32	22 46	23 02	23 16	23 32		23 47
Bootle Oriel Road	d	21 48	22 04	22 18		22 34	22 48	23 04	23 18	23 34		23 49
Bootle New Strand	d	21 50	22 06	22 20		22 36	22 50	23 06	23 20	23 36		23 51
Seaforth & Litherland	d	21 52	22 08	22 22		22 38	22 52	23 08	23 22	23 38		23 53
Waterloo	d	21 54	22 10	22 24		22 40	22 54	23 10	23 24	23 40		23 55
Blundellsands & Crosby	d	21 57	22 13	22 27		22 43	22 57	23 13	23 27	23 43		23 58
Hall Road	d	21 59	22 15	22 29		22 45	22 59	23 15	23 29	23 45		23 59
Hightown	d	22 02	22 18	22 32		22 48	23 02	23 18	23 32	23 48		00 03
Formby	d	22 06	22 22	22 36		22 52	23 06	23 22	23 36	23 52		00 07
Freshfield	d	22 08	22 24	22 38		22 54	23 08	23 24	23 38	23 54		00 09
Ainsdale	d	22 12	22 28	22 42		22 58	23 12	23 28	23 42	23 58		00 13
Hillside	d	22 15	22 31	22 45		23 01	23 15	23 31	23 45	00 01		00 16
Birkdale	d	22 17	22 33	22 47		23 03	23 17	23 33	23 47	00 03		00 18
Southport	a	22 24	22 40	22 54		23 10	23 24	23 40	23 54	00 10		00 25

A until 23 September
B from 30 September

For alternative services between Liverpool and Sandhills refer to Tables T104 and T105

Table T103-R

Southport - Hunts Cross

Mondays to Fridays
21 May to 7 December

Miles			ME	ME		ME	ME		ME	ME
0	**Southport**	d		05 38	and every 15 minutes until	06 23	06 43	and every 15 minutes until	22 58	23 18
1	Birkdale	d		05 42		06 27	06 47		23 02	23 22
2	Hillside	d		05 44		06 29	06 49		23 04	23 24
3½	Ainsdale	d		05 47		06 32	06 52		23 07	23 27
6¼	Freshfield	d		05 51		06 36	06 56		23 11	23 31
7¼	Formby	d		05 53		06 38	06 58		23 13	23 33
9¾	Hightown	d		05 57		06 42	07 02		23 17	23 37
11¼	Hall Road	d		06 00		06 45	07 05		23 20	23 40
12	Blundellsands & Crosby	d		06 02		06 47	07 07		23 22	23 42
13	Waterloo	d		06 05		06 50	07 10		23 25	23 45
14¾	Seaforth & Litherland	d		06 07		06 52	07 12		23 27	23 47
15¼	Bootle New Strand	d		06 10		06 55	07 15		23 30	23 50
15½	Bootle Oriel Road	d		06 11		06 56	07 16		23 31	23 51
16¼	Bank Hall	d		06 18		07 03	07 18		23 33	23 53
17	Sandhills	d	06 06	06 21		07 06	07 21		23 36	23 56
18½	**Moorfields [10]**	d	06 10	06 25		07 10	07 25		23 40	23 59
19	**Liverpool Central [10]**	a	06 13	06 28		07 13	07 28		23 43	00 03
—		d	06 13	06 28		07 13	07 28		23 43	
20½	Brunswick	d	06 17	06 32		07 17	07 32		23 47	
21¼	St Michaels	d	06 20	06 35		07 20	07 35		23 50	
23	Aigburth	d	06 22	06 37		07 22	07 37		23 52	
23¾	Cressington	d	06 24	06 39		07 24	07 39		23 54	
24¾	**Liverpool Sth Parkway [7] 89** ✈	d	06 27	06 42		07 27	07 42		23 57	
26¼	**Hunts Cross** 89	a	06 32	06 47		07 32	07 47		00 02	

Saturdays
26 May to 8 December

		ME	ME		ME	ME		ME	ME
Southport	d		05 38	and every 15 minutes until	06 23	06 43	and every 15 minutes until	22 58	23 18
Birkdale	d		05 42		06 27	06 47		23 02	23 22
Hillside	d		05 44		06 29	06 49		23 04	23 24
Ainsdale	d		05 47		06 32	06 52		23 07	23 27
Freshfield	d		05 51		06 36	06 56		23 11	23 31
Formby	d		05 53		06 38	06 58		23 13	23 33
Hightown	d		05 57		06 42	07 02		23 17	23 37
Hall Road	d		06 00		06 45	07 05		23 20	23 40
Blundellsands & Crosby	d		06 02		06 47	07 07		23 22	23 42
Waterloo	d		06 05		06 50	07 10		23 25	23 45
Seaforth & Litherland	d		06 07		06 52	07 12		23 27	23 47
Bootle New Strand	d		06 10		06 55	07 15		23 30	23 50
Bootle Oriel Road	d		06 11		06 56	07 16		23 31	23 51
Bank Hall	d		06 18		07 03	07 18		23 33	23 53
Sandhills	d	06 05	06 21		07 06	07 21		23 36	23 56
Moorfields [10]	d	06 10	06 25		07 10	07 25		23 40	23 59
Liverpool Central [10]	a	06 13	06 28		07 13	07 28		23 43	00 03
	d	06 13	06 28		07 13	07 28		23 43	
Brunswick	d	06 17	06 32		07 17	07 32		23 47	
St Michaels	d	06 20	06 35		07 20	07 35		23 50	
Aigburth	d	06 22	06 37		07 22	07 37		23 52	
Cressington	d	06 24	06 39		07 24	07 39		23 54	
Liverpool Sth Parkway [7] 89 ✈	d	06 27	06 42		07 27	07 42		23 57	
Hunts Cross 89	a	06 32	06 47		07 32	07 47		00 02	

Sundays
20 May to 2 December

		ME	ME		ME	ME A	ME	ME A	ME	ME A		ME	ME A	ME	ME A	ME	ME A	ME	ME
Southport	d		07 58	and every 30 minutes until	09 58	10 13	10 28	10 43	10 58	11 13	and at the same minutes past each hour until	21 28	21 43	21 58	22 13	22 28	22 43	22 58	23 18
Birkdale	d		08 02		10 02	10 17	10 32	10 47	11 02	11 17		21 32	21 47	22 02	22 17	22 32	22 47	23 02	23 22
Hillside	d		08 04		10 04	10 19	10 34	10 49	11 04	11 19		21 34	21 49	22 04	22 19	22 34	22 49	23 04	23 24
Ainsdale	d		08 07		10 07	10 22	10 37	10 52	11 07	11 22		21 37	21 52	22 07	22 22	22 37	22 52	23 07	23 27
Freshfield	d		08 11		10 11	10 26	10 41	10 56	11 11	11 26		21 41	21 56	22 11	22 26	22 41	22 56	23 11	23 31
Formby	d		08 13		10 13	10 28	10 43	10 58	11 13	11 28		21 43	21 58	22 13	22 28	22 43	22 58	23 13	23 33
Hightown	d		08 17		10 17	10 32	10 47	11 02	11 17	11 32		21 47	22 02	22 17	22 32	22 47	23 02	23 17	23 37
Hall Road	d		08 20		10 20	10 35	10 50	11 05	11 20	11 35		21 50	22 05	22 20	22 35	22 50	23 05	23 20	23 40
Blundellsands & Crosby	d		08 22		10 22	10 37	10 52	11 07	11 22	11 37		21 52	22 07	22 22	22 37	22 52	23 07	23 22	23 42
Waterloo	d		08 25		10 25	10 40	10 55	11 10	11 25	11 40		21 55	22 10	22 25	22 40	22 55	23 10	23 25	23 45
Seaforth & Litherland	d		08 27		10 27	10 42	10 57	11 12	11 27	11 42		21 57	22 12	22 27	22 42	22 57	23 12	23 27	23 47
Bootle New Strand	d		08 30		10 30	10 45	11 00	11 15	11 30	11 45		22 00	22 15	22 30	22 45	23 00	23 15	23 30	23 50
Bootle Oriel Road	d		08 31		10 31	10 46	11 01	11 16	11 31	11 46		22 01	22 16	22 31	22 46	23 01	23 16	23 31	23 51
Bank Hall	d		08 33		10 33	10 48	11 03	11 18	11 33	11 48		22 03	22 18	22 33	22 48	23 03	23 18	23 33	23 53
Sandhills	d		08 36		10 36	10 52	11 06	11 21	11 36	11 51		22 06	22 21	22 36	22 51	23 06	23 21	23 36	23 56
Moorfields [10]	d		08 40		10 40	10 55	11 10	11 25	11 40	11 55		22 10	22 25	22 40	22 55	23 10	23 25	23 40	23 59
Liverpool Central [10]	a		08 43		10 43	10 58	11 13	11 28	11 43	11 58		22 13	22 28	22 43	22 58	23 13	23 28	23 43	00 03
	d	08 13	08 43		10 43		11 13		11 43			22 13		22 43		23 13		23 43	
Brunswick	d	08 17	08 47		10 47		11 17		11 47			22 17		22 47		23 17		23 47	
St Michaels	d	08 20	08 50		10 50		11 20		11 50			22 20		22 50		23 20		23 50	
Aigburth	d	08 22	08 52		10 52		11 22		11 52			22 22		22 52		23 22		23 52	
Cressington	d	08 24	08 54		10 54		11 24		11 54			22 24		22 54		23 24		23 54	
Liverpool Sth Parkway [7] 89 ✈	d	08 27	08 57		10 57		11 27		11 57			22 27		22 57		23 27		23 57	
Hunts Cross 89	a	08 32	09 02		11 02		11 32		12 02			22 32		23 02		23 32		00 02	

A until 23 September

For alternative services between Sandhills and Liverpool refer to Tables T104 and T105

Table T104-F

Liverpool Central - Kirkby

Mondays to Saturdays
21 May to 8 December

Miles			ME	ME	ME	ME		ME	ME SX	ME SO	ME		ME	ME SX	ME SO	ME		ME
0	**Liverpool Central [10]**	d		06 05	06 35	07 05	and every 15 minutes until	09 05	09 20	09 20	09 35	and every 15 minutes until	16 35	16 50	16 50	17 05	and every 15 minutes until	19 35
0½	**Moorfields [10]**	d		06 06	06 38	07 08		09 08	09 23	09 23	09 38		16 38	16 53	16 53	17 08		19 38
2	Sandhills	d	00 01	06 10	06 41	07 11		09 11	09 25	09 26	09 41		16 41	16 55	16 56	17 11		19 41
3	Kirkdale	d	00 04	06 14	06 44	07 14		09 14	09 29	09 29	09 44		16 44	16 59	16 59	17 14		19 44
4¼	Rice Lane	d	00 07	06 17	06 47	07 17		09 17	09 32	09 32	09 47		16 47	17 02	17 02	17 17		19 47
5¾	Fazakerley	d	00 10	06 20	06 49	07 20		09 20	09 35	09 35	09 50		16 50	17 05	17 05	17 20		19 50
7½	**Kirkby**	a	00 14	06 23	06 54	07 24		09 24	09 39	09 39	09 54		16 54	17 09	17 09	17 24		19 54

		ME		ME	ME
Liverpool Central [10]	d	20 05	and every 30 minutes until	23 35	23 55
Moorfields [10]	d	20 08		23 38	23 58
Sandhills	d	20 11		23 41	00 01
Kirkdale	d	20 14		23 44	00 04
Rice Lane	d	20 17		23 47	00 07
Fazakerley	d	20 20		23 50	00 10
Kirkby	a	20 24		23 54	00 14

Sundays
20 May to 2 December

		ME A	ME	ME	ME	ME	ME	ME	ME	ME	ME	ME	ME		ME	ME	ME		ME	ME
Liverpool Central [10]	d		08 05	08 26	08 35	08 56	09 05	09 26	09 35	09 56	10 05	10 26	10 35	and every 30 minutes until	14 05	14 26	14 35	and every 30 minutes until	23 35	23 55
Moorfields [10]	d		08 08	08 28	08 38	08 58	09 08	09 28	09 38	09 58	10 08	10 28	10 38		14 08	14 28	14 38		23 38	23 58
Sandhills	d	00 01	08 11	08 32	08 41	09 02	09 11	09 32	09 41	10 02	10 11	10 32	10 41		14 11	14 32	14 41		23 41	00 01
Kirkdale	d	00 04	08 14	08 35	08 44	09 05	09 14	09 35	09 44	10 05	10 14	10 35	10 44		14 14	14 35	14 44		23 44	00 04
Rice Lane	d	00 07	08 17	08 38	08 47	09 08	09 17	09 38	09 47	10 08	10 17	10 38	10 47		14 17	14 38	14 47		23 47	00 07
Fazakerley	d	00 10	08 20	08 41	08 50	09 11	09 20	09 41	09 50	10 11	10 20	10 41	10 50		14 20	14 41	14 50		23 50	00 10
Kirkby	a	00 14	08 24	08 44	08 54	09 14	09 24	09 44	09 54	10 14	10 24	10 44	10 54		14 24	14 44	14 54		23 54	00 14

A not 20 May

For additional trains Liverpool-Kirkdale refer to Table T105

For additional trains between Liverpool and Sandhills refer to Tables T103 and T105

Table T104-R

Kirkby - Liverpool Central

Mondays to Saturdays
21 May to 8 December

Miles			ME		ME	ME		ME	ME SO	ME SX	ME		ME	ME SX	ME SO	ME		ME
0	**Kirkby**	d	05 43	and every 30 minutes until	07 13	07 28	and every 15 minutes until	14 43	14 58	14 58	15 13	and every 15 minutes until	16 43	16 58	16 58	17 13	and every 15 minutes until	19 43
1¾	Fazakerley	d	05 46		07 16	07 31		14 46	15 01	15 01	15 16		16 46	17 01	17 01	17 16		19 46
3¼	Rice Lane	d	05 49		07 19	07 34		14 49	15 04	15 04	15 19		16 49	17 04	17 04	17 19		19 49
4½	Kirkdale	d	05 52		07 22	07 37		14 52	15 07	15 07	15 22		16 52	17 07	17 07	17 22		19 52
5½	Sandhills	d	05 55		07 25	07 40		14 55	15 10	15 10	15 25		16 55	17 10	17 10	17 25		19 55
7	**Moorfields [10]**	d	05 58		07 28	07 43		14 58	15 13	15 13	15 28		16 58	17 13	17 14	17 28		19 58
7½	**Liverpool Central [10]**	a	06 01		07 31	07 46		15 01	15 16	15 17	15 31		17 01	17 16	17 16	17 31		20 01

		ME		ME
Kirkby	d	20 13	and every 30 minutes until	23 13
Fazakerley	d	20 16		23 16
Rice Lane	d	20 19		23 19
Kirkdale	d	20 22		23 22
Sandhills	d	20 25		23 25
Moorfields [10]	d	20 28		23 28
Liverpool Central [10]	a	20 31		23 31

Sundays
20 May to 2 December

		ME		ME
Kirkby	d	08 13	and every 30 minutes until	23 13
Fazakerley	d	08 16		23 16
Rice Lane	d	08 19		23 19
Kirkdale	d	08 22		23 22
Sandhills	d	08 25		23 25
Moorfields [10]	d	08 28		23 28
Liverpool Central [10]	a	08 31		23 31

For additional trains Liverpool-Kirkdale refer to Table T105

For additional trains between Liverpool and Sandhills refer to Tables T103 and T105

Table T105-F

Mondays to Saturdays

21 May to 8 December

Liverpool Central - Ormskirk

Miles	Station		ME MO A	ME MO B	ME MX C	ME MX D	ME	ME	ME	ME D	ME E	ME	ME D	ME E	ME	ME	ME D	ME E	ME	ME D	ME E	ME	ME
0	**Liverpool Central**	d						06 05	06 08	06 17	06 17	06 23	06 32	06 32	06 35	06 38	06 47	06 47	06 53	07 02	07 02	07 05	07 08
0½	**Moorfields**	d						06 06	06 10	06 20	06 20	06 25	06 35	06 35	06 38	06 41	06 50	06 50	06 55	07 05	07 05	07 08	07 11
2	Sandhills	d					00 01	06 10	06a14	06 23	06 23	06a29	06 38	06 38	06 41	06a44	06 53	06 53	06a59	07 08	07 08	07 11	07a14
3	Kirkdale	d					00a04	06a14		06 26	06 26		06 41	06 41	06a44		06 56	06 56		07 11	07 11	07a14	
4¼	Walton	d								06 29	06 29		06 44	06 44			06 59	06 59		07 14	07 14		
4½	Orrell Park	d	00 01	00 01	00 01	00 01				06 30	06 30		06 45	06 45			07 00	07 00		07 15	07 15		
5½	Aintree	d	00 04	00 04	00 04	00 04				06 33	06 33		06 48	06 48			07 03	07 03		07 18	07 18		
6¼	Old Roan	d	00 06	00 06	00 06	00 06				06 35	06 35		06 50	06 50			07 05	07 05		07 20	07 20		
8	Maghull	d	00 09	00 09	00 09	00 09				06 38	06 38		06 53	06 53			07 08	07 08		07 23	07 23		
—	Maghull North Station	d	⌇	00 11	00 11	⌇				⌇	06 40		⌇	06 55			⌇	07 10		⌇	07 25		
10½	Town Green	d	00 15	00 15	00 15	00 15				06 44	06 44		06 59	06 59			07 14	07 14		07 29	07 29		
11½	Aughton Park	d	00 17	00 17	00 17	00 17				06 46	06 46		07 01	07 01			07 16	07 16		07 31	07 31		
12¾	**Ormskirk**	a	00 22	00 22	00 23	00 23				06 52	06 52		07 07	07 07			07 22	07 22		07 37	07 37		

Station		ME D	ME E	ME	ME	ME D	ME E	ME	ME	ME D	ME E	ME	ME	ME D	ME E	ME	ME	ME D	ME E	ME	ME	ME D	ME E
Liverpool Central	d	07 17	07 17	07 20	07 23	07 32	07 32	07 35	07 38	07 47	07 47	07 50	07 53	08 02	08 02	08 05	08 08	08 17	08 17	08 20	08 23	08 32	08 32
Moorfields	d	07 20	07 20	07 23	07 26	07 35	07 35	07 38	07 41	07 50	07 50	07 53	07 56	08 05	08 05	08 08	08 11	08 20	08 20	08 23	08 26	08 35	08 35
Sandhills	d	07 23	07 23	07 26	07a29	07 38	07 38	07 41	07a44	07 53	07 53	07 56	07a59	08 08	08 08	08 11	08a14	08 23	08 23	08 26	08a29	08 38	08 38
Kirkdale	d	07 26	07 26	07a29		07 41	07 41	07a44		07 56	07 56	07a59		08 11	08 11	08a14		08 26	08 26	08a29		08 41	08 41
Walton	d	07 29	07 29			07 44	07 44			07 59	07 59			08 14	08 14			08 29	08 29			08 44	08 44
Orrell Park	d	07 30	07 30			07 45	07 45			08 00	08 00			08 15	08 15			08 30	08 30			08 45	08 45
Aintree	d	07 33	07 33			07 48	07 48			08 03	08 03			08 18	08 18			08 33	08 33			08 48	08 48
Old Roan	d	07 35	07 35			07 50	07 50			08 05	08 05			08 20	08 20			08 35	08 35			08 50	08 50
Maghull	d	07 38	07 38			07 53	07 53			08 08	08 08			08 23	08 23			08 38	08 38			08 53	08 53
Maghull North Station	d	⌇	07 40			⌇	07 55			⌇	08 10			⌇	08 25			⌇	08 40			⌇	08 55
Town Green	d	07 44	07 44			07 59	07 59			08 14	08 14			08 29	08 29			08 44	08 44			08 59	08 59
Aughton Park	d	07 46	07 46			08 01	08 01			08 16	08 16			08 31	08 31			08 46	08 46			09 01	09 01
Ormskirk	a	07 52	07 52			08 07	08 07			08 22	08 22			08 37	08 37			08 52	08 52			09 07	09 07

Station		ME	ME	ME D	ME E	ME	ME	ME D	ME E	ME	ME	ME D	ME E	ME SX	ME SO	ME	ME D	ME E	ME	ME	ME D	ME E
Liverpool Central	d	08 35	08 38	08 47	08 47	08 50	08 53	09 02	09 02	09 05	09 08	09 17	09 17	09 20	09 20	09 23	09 32	09 32	09 35	09 38	09 47	09 47
Moorfields	d	08 38	08 41	08 50	08 50	08 53	08 56	09 05	09 05	09 08	09 11	09 20	09 20	09 23	09 23	09 26	09 35	09 35	09 38	09 41	09 50	09 50
Sandhills	d	08 41	08a44	08 53	08 53	08 56	08a59	09 08	09 08	09 11	09a14	09 23	09 23	09 25	09 26	09a30	09 38	09 38	09 41	09a44	09 53	09 53
Kirkdale	d	08a44		08 56	08 56	08a59		09 11	09 11	09a14		09 26	09 26	09a28	09a29		09 41	09 41	09a44		09 56	09 56
Walton	d			08 59	08 59			09 14	09 14			09 29	09 29				09 44	09 44			09 59	09 59
Orrell Park	d			09 00	09 00			09 15	09 15			09 30	09 30				09 45	09 45			10 00	10 00
Aintree	d			09 03	09 03			09 18	09 18			09 33	09 33				09 48	09 48			10 03	10 03
Old Roan	d			09 05	09 05			09 20	09 20			09 35	09 35				09 50	09 50			10 05	10 05
Maghull	d			09 08	09 08			09 23	09 23			09 38	09 38				09 53	09 53			10 08	10 08
Maghull North Station	d			⌇	09 10			⌇	09 25			⌇	09 40				⌇	09 55			⌇	10 10
Town Green	d			09 14	09 14			09 29	09 29			09 44	09 44				09 59	09 59			10 14	10 14
Aughton Park	d			09 16	09 16			09 31	09 31			09 46	09 46				10 01	10 01			10 16	10 16
Ormskirk	a			09 22	09 22			09 37	09 37			09 52	09 52				10 07	10 07			10 22	10 22

Station		ME	ME	ME D	ME E	ME	ME	ME D	ME E	ME	ME	ME D	ME E	ME	ME	ME D	ME E	ME	ME	ME D	ME E	ME	ME
Liverpool Central	d	09 50	09 53	10 02	10 02	10 05	10 08	10 17	10 17	10 20	10 23	10 32	10 32	10 35	10 38	10 47	10 47	10 50	10 53	11 02	11 02	11 05	11 08
Moorfields	d	09 53	09 56	10 05	10 05	10 08	10 11	10 20	10 20	10 23	10 26	10 35	10 35	10 38	10 41	10 50	10 50	10 53	10 56	11 05	11 05	11 08	11 11
Sandhills	d	09 56	09a59	10 08	10 08	10 11	10a14	10 23	10 23	10 26	10a29	10 38	10 38	10 41	10a44	10 53	10 53	10 56	10a59	11 08	11 08	11 11	11a14
Kirkdale	d	09a59		10 11	10 11	10a14		10 26	10 26	10a29		10 41	10 41	10a44		10 56	10 56	10a59		11 11	11 11	11a14	
Walton	d			10 14	10 14			10 29	10 29			10 44	10 44			10 59	10 59			11 14	11 14		
Orrell Park	d			10 15	10 15			10 30	10 30			10 45	10 45			11 00	11 00			11 15	11 15		
Aintree	d			10 18	10 18			10 33	10 33			10 48	10 48			11 03	11 03			11 18	11 18		
Old Roan	d			10 20	10 20			10 35	10 35			10 50	10 50			11 05	11 05			11 20	11 20		
Maghull	d			10 23	10 23			10 38	10 38			10 53	10 53			11 08	11 08			11 23	11 23		
Maghull North Station	d			⌇	10 25			⌇	10 40			⌇	10 55			⌇	11 10			⌇	11 25		
Town Green	d			10 29	10 29			10 44	10 44			10 59	10 59			11 14	11 14			11 29	11 29		
Aughton Park	d			10 31	10 31			10 46	10 46			11 01	11 01			11 16	11 16			11 31	11 31		
Ormskirk	a			10 37	10 37			10 52	10 52			11 07	11 07			11 22	11 22			11 37	11 37		

Station		ME D	ME E	ME	ME	ME D	ME E	ME	ME	ME D	ME E	ME	ME	ME D	ME E	ME	ME	ME D	ME E	ME	ME	ME D	ME E
Liverpool Central	d	11 17	11 17	11 20	11 23	11 32	11 32	11 35	11 38	11 47	11 47	11 50	11 53	12 02	12 02	12 05	12 08	12 17	12 17	12 20	12 23	12 32	12 32
Moorfields	d	11 20	11 20	11 23	11 26	11 35	11 35	11 38	11 41	11 50	11 50	11 53	11 56	12 05	12 05	12 08	12 11	12 20	12 20	12 23	12 26	12 35	12 35
Sandhills	d	11 23	11 23	11 26	11a29	11 38	11 38	11 41	11a44	11 53	11 53	11 56	11a59	12 08	12 08	12 11	12a14	12 23	12 23	12 26	12a29	12 38	12 38
Kirkdale	d	11 26	11 26	11a29		11 41	11 41	11a44		11 56	11 56	11a59		12 11	12 11	12a14		12 26	12 26	12a29		12 41	12 41
Walton	d	11 29	11 29			11 44	11 44			11 59	11 59			12 14	12 14			12 29	12 29			12 44	12 44
Orrell Park	d	11 30	11 30			11 45	11 45			12 00	12 00			12 15	12 15			12 30	12 30			12 45	12 45
Aintree	d	11 33	11 33			11 48	11 48			12 03	12 03			12 18	12 18			12 33	12 33			12 48	12 48
Old Roan	d	11 35	11 35			11 50	11 50			12 05	12 05			12 20	12 20			12 35	12 35			12 50	12 50
Maghull	d	11 38	11 38			11 53	11 53			12 08	12 08			12 23	12 23			12 38	12 38			12 53	12 53
Maghull North Station	d	⌇	11 40			⌇	11 55			⌇	12 10			⌇	12 25			⌇	12 40			⌇	12 55
Town Green	d	11 44	11 44			11 59	11 59			12 14	12 14			12 29	12 29			12 44	12 44			12 59	12 59
Aughton Park	d	11 46	11 46			12 01	12 01			12 16	12 16			12 31	12 31			12 46	12 46			13 01	13 01
Ormskirk	a	11 52	11 52			12 07	12 07			12 22	12 22			12 37	12 37			12 52	12 52			13 07	13 07

A until 18 June
B from 25 June
C from 19 June
D until 16 June
E from 18 June

For additional trains between Liverpool and Kirkdale refer to Table T104

For additional trains between Liverpool and Sandhills refer to Tables T103 and T104

Table T105-F

Mondays to Saturdays

21 May to 8 December

Liverpool Central - Ormskirk

Station		ME	ME	ME A	ME B	ME	ME	ME A	ME B	ME	ME	ME A	ME B	ME	ME	ME A	ME B	ME	ME	ME A	ME B	ME	ME
Liverpool Central	d	12 35	12 38	12 47	12 47	12 50	12 53	13 02	13 02	13 05	13 08	13 17	13 17	13 20	13 23	13 32	13 32	13 35	13 38	13 47	13 47	13 50	13 53
Moorfields	d	12 38	12 41	12 50	12 50	12 53	12 56	13 05	13 05	13 08	13 11	13 20	13 20	13 23	13 26	13 35	13 35	13 38	13 41	13 50	13 50	13 53	13 56
Sandhills	d	12 41	12a44	12 53	12 53	12 56	12a59	13 08	13 08	13 11	13a14	13 23	13 23	13 26	13a29	13 38	13 38	13 41	13a44	13 53	13 53	13 56	13a59
Kirkdale	d	12a44		12 56	12 56	12a59		13 11	13 11	13a14		13 26	13 26	13a29		13 41	13 41	13a44		13 56	13 56	13a59	
Walton	d			12 59	12 59			13 14	13 14			13 29	13 29			13 44	13 44			13 59	13 59		
Orrell Park	d			13 00	13 00			13 15	13 15			13 30	13 30			13 45	13 45			14 00	14 00		
Aintree	d			13 03	13 03			13 18	13 18			13 33	13 33			13 48	13 48			14 03	14 03		
Old Roan	d			13 05	13 05			13 20	13 20			13 35	13 35			13 50	13 50			14 05	14 05		
Maghull	d			13 08	13 08			13 23	13 23			13 38	13 38			13 53	13 53			14 08	14 08		
Maghull North Station	d			⌇	13 10			⌇	13 25			⌇	13 40			⌇	13 55			⌇	14 10		
Town Green	d			13 14	13 14			13 29	13 29			13 44	13 44			13 59	13 59			14 14	14 14		
Aughton Park	d			13 16	13 16			13 31	13 31			13 46	13 46			14 01	14 01			14 16	14 16		
Ormskirk	a			13 22	13 22			13 37	13 37			13 52	13 52			14 07	14 07			14 22	14 22		

Station		ME A	ME B	ME	ME	ME A	ME B	ME	ME	ME A	ME B	ME	ME	ME A	ME B	ME	ME	ME A	ME B	ME	ME	ME A
Liverpool Central	d	14 02	14 02	14 05	14 08	14 17	14 17	14 20	14 23	14 32	14 32	14 35	14 38	14 47	14 47	14 50	14 53	15 02	15 02	15 05	15 08	15 17
Moorfields	d	14 05	14 05	14 08	14 11	14 20	14 20	14 23	14 26	14 35	14 35	14 38	14 41	14 50	14 50	14 53	14 56	15 05	15 05	15 08	15 11	15 20
Sandhills	d	14 08	14 08	14 11	14a14	14 23	14 23	14 26	14a29	14 38	14 38	14 41	14a44	14 53	14 53	14 56	14a59	15 08	15 08	15 11	15a14	15 23
Kirkdale	d	14 11	14 11	14a14		14 26	14 26	14a29		14 41	14 41	14a44		14 56	14 56	14a59		15 11	15 11	15a14		15 26
Walton	d	14 14	14 14			14 29	14 29			14 44	14 44			14 59	14 59			15 14	15 14			15 29
Orrell Park	d	14 15	14 15			14 30	14 30			14 45	14 45			15 00	15 00			15 15	15 15			15 30
Aintree	d	14 18	14 18			14 33	14 33			14 48	14 48			15 03	15 03			15 18	15 18			15 33
Old Roan	d	14 20	14 20			14 35	14 35			14 50	14 50			15 05	15 05			15 20	15 20			15 35
Maghull	d	14 23	14 23			14 38	14 38			14 53	14 53			15 08	15 08			15 23	15 23			15 38
Maghull North Station	d	⌇	14 25			⌇	14 40			⌇	14 55			⌇	15 10			⌇	15 25			⌇
Town Green	d	14 29	14 29			14 44	14 44			14 59	14 59			15 14	15 14			15 29	15 29			15 44
Aughton Park	d	14 31	14 31			14 46	14 46			15 01	15 01			15 16	15 16			15 31	15 31			15 46
Ormskirk	a	14 37	14 37			14 52	14 52			15 07	15 07			15 22	15 22			15 37	15 37			15 52

Station		ME B	ME	ME	ME A	ME B	ME	ME	ME A	ME B	ME	ME	ME A	ME B	ME	ME	ME A	ME B	ME	ME	ME A	ME B	ME
Liverpool Central	d	15 17	15 20	15 23	15 32	15 32	15 35	15 38	15 47	15 47	15 50	15 53	16 02	16 02	16 05	16 08	16 17	16 17	16 20	16 23	16 32	16 32	16 35
Moorfields	d	15 20	15 23	15 26	15 35	15 35	15 38	15 41	15 50	15 50	15 53	15 56	16 05	16 05	16 08	16 11	16 20	16 20	16 23	16 26	16 35	16 35	16 38
Sandhills	d	15 23	15 26	15a29	15 38	15 38	15 41	15a44	15 53	15 53	15 56	15a59	16 08	16 08	16 11	16a14	16 23	16 23	16 26	16a29	16 38	16 38	16 41
Kirkdale	d	15 26	15a29		15 41	15 41	15a44		15 56	15 56	15a59		16 11	16 11	16a14		16 26	16 26	16a29		16 41	16 41	16a44
Walton	d	15 29			15 44	15 44			15 59	15 59			16 14	16 14			16 29	16 29			16 44	16 44	
Orrell Park	d	15 30			15 45	15 45			16 00	16 00			16 15	16 15			16 30	16 30			16 45	16 45	
Aintree	d	15 33			15 48	15 48			16 03	16 03			16 18	16 18			16 33	16 33			16 48	16 48	
Old Roan	d	15 35			15 50	15 50			16 05	16 05			16 20	16 20			16 35	16 35			16 50	16 50	
Maghull	d	15 38			15 53	15 53			16 08	16 08			16 23	16 23			16 38	16 38			16 53	16 53	
Maghull North Station	d	15 40			⌇	15 55			⌇	16 10			⌇	16 25			⌇	16 40			⌇	16 55	
Town Green	d	15 44			15 59	15 59			16 14	16 14			16 29	16 29			16 44	16 44			16 59	16 59	
Aughton Park	d	15 46			16 01	16 01			16 16	16 16			16 31	16 31			16 46	16 46			17 01	17 01	
Ormskirk	a	15 52			16 07	16 07			16 22	16 22			16 37	16 37			16 52	16 52			17 07	17 07	

Station		ME	ME A	ME B	ME SX	ME SO	ME	ME A	ME B	ME	ME	ME A	ME B	ME	ME	ME A	ME B	ME	ME	ME A	ME B	ME	ME
Liverpool Central	d	16 38	16 47	16 47	16 50	16 50	16 53	17 02	17 02	17 05	17 08	17 17	17 17	17 20	17 23	17 32	17 32	17 35	17 38	17 47	17 47	17 50	17 53
Moorfields	d	16 41	16 50	16 50	16 53	16 53	16 56	17 05	17 05	17 08	17 11	17 20	17 20	17 23	17 26	17 35	17 35	17 38	17 41	17 50	17 50	17 53	17 56
Sandhills	d	16a44	16 53	16 53	16 55	16 56	16a59	17 08	17 08	17 11	17a14	17 23	17 23	17 26	17a29	17 38	17 38	17 41	17a44	17 53	17 53	17 56	17a59
Kirkdale	d		16 56	16 56	16a58	16a59		17 11	17 11	17a14		17 26	17 26	17a29		17 41	17 41	17a44		17 56	17 56	17a59	
Walton	d		16 59	16 59				17 14	17 14			17 29	17 29			17 44	17 44			17 59	17 59		
Orrell Park	d		17 00	17 00				17 15	17 15			17 30	17 30			17 45	17 45			18 00	18 00		
Aintree	d		17 03	17 03				17 18	17 18			17 33	17 33			17 48	17 48			18 03	18 03		
Old Roan	d		17 05	17 05				17 20	17 20			17 35	17 35			17 50	17 50			18 05	18 05		
Maghull	d		17 08	17 08				17 23	17 23			17 38	17 38			17 53	17 53			18 08	18 08		
Maghull North Station	d		⌇	17 10				⌇	17 25			⌇	17 40			⌇	17 55			⌇	18 10		
Town Green	d		17 14	17 14				17 29	17 29			17 44	17 44			17 59	17 59			18 14	18 14		
Aughton Park	d		17 16	17 16				17 31	17 31			17 46	17 46			18 01	18 01			18 16	18 16		
Ormskirk	a		17 22	17 22				17 37	17 37			17 52	17 52			18 07	18 07			18 22	18 22		

Station		ME A	ME B	ME	ME	ME A	ME B	ME	ME	ME A	ME B	ME	ME	ME A	ME B	ME	ME	ME A	ME B	ME	ME	ME A
Liverpool Central	d	18 02	18 02	18 05	18 08	18 17	18 17	18 20	18 23	18 32	18 32	18 35	18 38	18 47	18 47	18 50	18 53	19 02	19 02	19 05	19 08	19 17
Moorfields	d	18 05	18 05	18 08	18 11	18 20	18 20	18 23	18 26	18 35	18 35	18 38	18 41	18 50	18 50	18 53	18 56	19 05	19 05	19 08	19 11	19 20
Sandhills	d	18 08	18 08	18 11	18a14	18 23	18 23	18 26	18a29	18 38	18 38	18 41	18a44	18 53	18 53	18 56	18a59	19 08	19 08	19 11	19a14	19 23
Kirkdale	d	18 11	18 11	18a14		18 26	18 26	18a29		18 41	18 41	18a44		18 56	18 56	18a59		19 11	19 11	19a14		19 26
Walton	d	18 14	18 14			18 29	18 29			18 44	18 44			18 59	18 59			19 14	19 14			19 29
Orrell Park	d	18 15	18 15			18 30	18 30			18 45	18 45			19 00	19 00			19 15	19 15			19 30
Aintree	d	18 18	18 18			18 33	18 33			18 48	18 48			19 03	19 03			19 18	19 18			19 33
Old Roan	d	18 20	18 20			18 35	18 35			18 50	18 50			19 05	19 05			19 20	19 20			19 35
Maghull	d	18 23	18 23			18 38	18 38			18 53	18 53			19 08	19 08			19 23	19 23			19 38
Maghull North Station	d	⌇	18 25			⌇	18 40			⌇	18 55			⌇	19 10			⌇	19 25			⌇
Town Green	d	18 29	18 29			18 44	18 44			18 59	18 59			19 14	19 14			19 29	19 29			19 44
Aughton Park	d	18 31	18 31			18 46	18 46			19 01	19 01			19 16	19 16			19 31	19 31			19 46
Ormskirk	a	18 37	18 37			18 52	18 52			19 07	19 07			19 22	19 22			19 37	19 37			19 52

A until 16 June
B from 18 June

For additional trains between Liverpool and Kirkdale refer to Table T104

For additional trains between Liverpool and Sandhills refer to Tables T103 and T104

Table T105-F

Mondays to Saturdays

21 May to 8 December

Liverpool Central - Ormskirk

		ME A	ME	ME	ME	ME	ME B	ME A	ME	ME	ME	ME B	ME A	ME	ME	ME	ME B	ME A	ME	ME	ME	ME B
Liverpool Central	d	19 17	19 20	19 23	19 35	19 38	19 47	19 47	19 53	20 05	20 08	20 17	20 17	20 23	20 35	20 38	20 47	20 47	20 53	21 05	21 08	21 17
Moorfields	d	19 20	19 23	19 26	19 38	19 41	19 50	19 50	19 55	20 08	20 11	20 20	20 20	20 25	20 38	20 41	20 50	20 50	20 55	21 08	21 11	21 20
Sandhills	d	19 23	19 26	19a29	19 41	19a44	19 53	19 53	19a59	20 11	20a14	20 23	20 23	20a29	20 41	20a44	20 53	20 53	20a59	21 11	21a14	21 23
Kirkdale	d	19 26	19a29		19a44		19 56	19 56		20a14		20 26	20 26		20a44		20 56	20 56		21a14		21 26
Walton	d	19 29					19 59	19 59				20 29	20 29				20 59	20 59				21 29
Orrell Park	d	19 30					20 00	20 00				20 30	20 30				21 00	21 00				21 30
Aintree	d	19 33					20 03	20 03				20 33	20 33				21 03	21 03				21 33
Old Roan	d	19 35					20 05	20 05				20 35	20 35				21 05	21 05				21 35
Maghull	d	19 38					20 08	20 08				20 38	20 38				21 08	21 08				21 38
Maghull North Station	d	19 40						20 10					20 40					21 10				
Town Green	d	19 44					20 14	20 14				20 44	20 44				21 14	21 14				21 44
Aughton Park	d	19 46					20 16	20 16				20 46	20 46				21 16	21 16				21 46
Ormskirk	a	19 52					20 22	20 22				20 52	20 52				21 22	21 22				21 52

		ME A	ME	ME	ME	ME B	ME A	ME	ME	ME	ME B	ME A	ME	ME	ME	ME B	ME A	ME	ME	ME	ME B	ME A	ME
Liverpool Central	d	21 17	21 23	21 35	21 38	21 47	21 47	21 53	22 05	22 08	22 17	22 17	22 23	22 35	22 38	22 47	22 47	22 53	23 05	23 08	23 17	23 17	23 23
Moorfields	d	21 20	21 25	21 38	21 41	21 50	21 50	21 55	22 08	22 11	22 20	22 20	22 25	22 38	22 41	22 50	22 50	22 55	23 08	23 11	23 20	23 20	23 26
Sandhills	d	21 23	21a29	21 41	21a44	21 53	21 53	21a59	22 11	22a14	22 23	22 23	22a29	22 41	22a44	22 53	22 53	22a59	23 11	23a14	23 23	23 23	23a29
Kirkdale	d	21 26		21a44		21 56	21 56		22a14		22 26	22 26		22a44		22 56	22 56		23a14		23 26	23 26	
Walton	d	21 29				21 59	21 59				22 29	22 29				22 59	22 59				23 29	23 29	
Orrell Park	d	21 30				22 00	22 00				22 30	22 30				23 00	23 00				23 30	23 30	
Aintree	d	21 33				22 03	22 03				22 33	22 33				23 03	23 03				23 33	23 33	
Old Roan	d	21 35				22 05	22 05				22 35	22 35				23 05	23 05				23 35	23 35	
Maghull	d	21 38				22 08	22 08				22 38	22 38				23 08	23 08				23 38	23 38	
Maghull North Station	d	21 40					22 10					22 40					23 10					23 40	
Town Green	d	21 44				22 14	22 14				22 44	22 44				23 14	23 14				23 44	23 44	
Aughton Park	d	21 46				22 16	22 16				22 46	22 46				23 16	23 16				23 46	23 46	
Ormskirk	a	21 52				22 22	22 22				22 52	22 52				23 22	23 22				23 52	23 52	

		ME	ME	ME B	ME A	ME
Liverpool Central	d	23 35	23 38	23 47	23 47	23 55
Moorfields	d	23 38	23 41	23 50	23 50	23 58
Sandhills	d	23 41	23a44	23 53	23 53	00 01
Kirkdale	d	23a44		23 56	23 56	00a04
Walton	d			23 59	23 59	
Orrell Park	d			00 01	00 01	
Aintree	d			00 04	00 04	
Old Roan	d			00 06	00 06	
Maghull	d			00 09	00 09	
Maghull North Station	d				00 11	
Town Green	d			00 15	00 15	
Aughton Park	d			00 17	00 17	
Ormskirk	a			00 23	00 23	

Sundays

20 May to 2 December

		ME C	ME D	ME E	ME	ME	ME F	ME D	ME	ME	ME	ME F	ME D	ME	ME	ME	ME F	ME D	ME	ME	ME	ME F	ME D
Liverpool Central	d				08 05	08 07	08 17	08 17	08 23	08 26	08 35	08 47	08 47	08 53	08 56	09 05	09 17	09 17	09 23	09 26	09 35	09 47	09 47
Moorfields	d				08 08	08 10	08 20	08 20	08 25	08 28	08 38	08 50	08 50	08 55	08 58	09 08	09 20	09 20	09 25	09 28	09 38	09 50	09 50
Sandhills	d			00 01	08 11	08a14	08 23	08 23	08a29	08 32	08 41	08 53	08 53	08a59	09 02	09 11	09 23	09 23	09a29	09 32	09 41	09 53	09 53
Kirkdale	d			00a04	08a14		08 26	08 26		08a35	08a44	08 56	08 56		09a05	09a14	09 26	09 26		09a35	09a44	09 56	09 56
Walton	d						08 29	08 29				08 59	08 59				09 29	09 29				09 59	09 59
Orrell Park	d	00 01	00 01				08 30	08 30				09 00	09 00				09 30	09 30				10 00	10 00
Aintree	d	00 04	00 04				08 33	08 33				09 03	09 03				09 33	09 33				10 03	10 03
Old Roan	d	00 06	00 06				08 35	08 35				09 05	09 05				09 35	09 35				10 05	10 05
Maghull	d	00 09	00 09				08 38	08 38				09 08	09 08				09 38	09 38				10 08	10 08
Maghull North Station	d		00 11					08 40					09 10					09 40					10 10
Town Green	d	00 15	00 15				08 44	08 44				09 14	09 14				09 44	09 44				10 14	10 14
Aughton Park	d	00 17	00 17				08 46	08 46				09 16	09 16				09 46	09 46				10 16	10 16
Ormskirk	a	00 23	00 23				08 52	08 52				09 22	09 22				09 52	09 52				10 22	10 22

		ME	ME	ME	ME G	ME F	ME D	ME	ME	ME	ME G	ME F	ME D	ME	ME	ME G	ME F	ME D	ME
Liverpool Central	d	09 53	09 56	10 05	10 07	10 17	10 17	10 23	10 26	10 35	10 37	10 47	10 47	10 53	11 05	11 07	11 17	11 17	11 23
Moorfields	d	09 55	09 58	10 08	10 10	10 20	10 20	10 25	10 28	10 38	10 40	10 50	10 50	10 55	11 08	11 10	11 20	11 20	11 25
Sandhills	d	09a59	10 02	10 11	10a14	10 23	10 23	10a29	10 32	10 41	10a44	10 53	10 53	10a59	11 11	11a14	11 23	11 23	11a29
Kirkdale	d		10a05	10a14		10 26	10 26		10a35	10a44		10 56	10 56		11a14		11 26	11 26	
Walton	d					10 29	10 29					10 59	10 59				11 29	11 29	
Orrell Park	d					10 30	10 30					11 00	11 00				11 30	11 30	
Aintree	d					10 33	10 33					11 03	11 03				11 33	11 33	
Old Roan	d					10 35	10 35					11 05	11 05				11 35	11 35	
Maghull	d					10 38	10 38					11 08	11 08				11 38	11 38	
Maghull North Station	d						10 40						11 10					11 40	
Town Green	d					10 44	10 44					11 14	11 14				11 44	11 44	
Aughton Park	d					10 46	10 46					11 16	11 16				11 46	11 46	
Ormskirk	a					10 52	10 52					11 22	11 22				11 52	11 52	

and at the same minutes past each hour until

A from 18 June
B until 16 June
C from 27 May until 17 June
D from 24 June
E not 20 May
F until 17 June
G until 23 September

For additional trains between Liverpool and Kirkdale refer to Table T104

For additional trains between Liverpool and Sandhills refer to Tables T103 and T104

Table T105-F

Sundays

20 May to 2 December

Liverpool Central - Ormskirk

		ME	ME A	ME B	ME C	ME	ME	ME A	ME B	ME C	ME	ME	ME	ME A	ME B	ME C	ME	ME	ME A	ME B	ME C	ME
Liverpool Central	d	13 35	13 37	13 47	13 47	13 53	14 05	14 07	14 17	14 17	14 23	14 26	14 35	14 37	14 47	14 47	14 53	15 05	15 07	15 17	15 17	15 23
Moorfields	d	13 38	13 40	13 50	13 50	13 55	14 08	14 10	14 20	14 20	14 25	14 28	14 38	14 40	14 50	14 50	14 55	15 08	15 10	15 20	15 20	15 25
Sandhills	d	13 41	13a44	13 53	13 53	13a59	14 11	14a14	14 23	14 23	14a29	14 32	14 41	14a44	14 53	14 53	14a59	15 11	15a14	15 23	15 23	15a29
Kirkdale	d	13a44		13 56	13 56		14a14		14 26	14 26		14a35	14a44		14 56	14 56		15a14		15 26	15 26	
Walton	d			13 59	13 59				14 29	14 29					14 59	14 59				15 29	15 29	
Orrell Park	d			14 00	14 00				14 30	14 30					15 00	15 00				15 30	15 30	
Aintree	d			14 03	14 03				14 33	14 33					15 03	15 03				15 33	15 33	
Old Roan	d			14 05	14 05				14 35	14 35					15 05	15 05				15 35	15 35	
Maghull	d			14 08	14 08				14 38	14 38					15 08	15 08				15 38	15 38	
Maghull North Station	d				14 10					14 40						15 10					15 40	
Town Green	d			14 14	14 14				14 44	14 44					15 14	15 14				15 44	15 44	
Aughton Park	d			14 16	14 16				14 46	14 46					15 16	15 16				15 46	15 46	
Ormskirk	a			14 22	14 22				14 52	14 52					15 22	15 22				15 52	15 52	

and at the same minutes past each hour until

		ME	ME A	ME B	ME C	ME	ME	ME A	ME B	ME C	ME	ME	ME B	ME C	ME	ME	ME A	ME B	ME C	ME	ME	ME A	ME B
Liverpool Central	d	19 35	19 37	19 47	19 47	19 53	20 05	20 07	20 17	20 17	20 23	20 35	20 47	20 47	20 53	21 05	21 07	21 17	21 17	21 23	21 35	21 37	21 47
Moorfields	d	19 38	19 40	19 50	19 50	19 55	20 08	20 10	20 20	20 20	20 25	20 38	20 50	20 50	20 55	21 08	21 10	21 20	21 20	21 25	21 38	21 40	21 50
Sandhills	d	19 41	19a44	19 53	19 53	19a59	20 11	20a14	20 23	20 23	20a29	20 41	20 53	20 53	20a59	21 11	21a14	21 23	21 23	21a29	21 41	21a44	21 53
Kirkdale	d	19a44		19 56	19 56		20a14		20 26	20 26		20a44	20 56	20 56		21a14		21 26	21 26		21a44		21 56
Walton	d			19 59	19 59				20 29	20 29			20 59	20 59				21 29	21 29				21 59
Orrell Park	d			20 00	20 00				20 30	20 30			21 00	21 00				21 30	21 30				22 00
Aintree	d			20 03	20 03				20 33	20 33			21 03	21 03				21 33	21 33				22 03
Old Roan	d			20 05	20 05				20 35	20 35			21 05	21 05				21 35	21 35				22 05
Maghull	d			20 08	20 08				20 38	20 38			21 08	21 08				21 38	21 38				22 08
Maghull North Station	d				20 10					20 40				21 10					21 40				
Town Green	d			20 14	20 14				20 44	20 44			21 14	21 14				21 44	21 44				22 14
Aughton Park	d			20 16	20 16				20 46	20 46			21 16	21 16				21 46	21 46				22 16
Ormskirk	a			20 22	20 22				20 52	20 52			21 22	21 22				21 52	21 52				22 22

		ME C	ME	ME	ME A	ME B	ME C	ME	ME	ME A	ME B	ME C	ME	ME	ME A	ME B	ME C	ME	ME	ME	ME B	ME C	ME
Liverpool Central	d	21 47	21 53	22 05	22 07	22 17	22 17	22 23	22 35	22 37	22 47	22 47	22 53	23 05	23 07	23 17	23 17	23 23	23 35	23 37	23 47	23 47	23 55
Moorfields	d	21 50	21 55	22 08	22 10	22 20	22 20	22 25	22 38	22 40	22 50	22 50	22 55	23 08	23 10	23 20	23 20	23 25	23 38	23 40	23 50	23 50	23 58
Sandhills	d	21 53	21a59	22 11	22a14	22 23	22 23	22a29	22 41	22a44	22 53	22 53	22a59	23 11	23a14	23 23	23 23	23a29	23 41	23a44	23 53	23 53	00 01
Kirkdale	d	21 56		22a14		22 26	22 26		22a44		22 56	22 56		23a14		23 26	23 26		23a44		23 56	23 56	00a04
Walton	d	21 59				22 29	22 29				22 59	22 59				23 29	23 29				23 59	23 59	
Orrell Park	d	22 00				22 30	22 30				23 00	23 00				23 30	23 30				00 01	00 01	
Aintree	d	22 03				22 33	22 33				23 03	23 03				23 33	23 33				00 04	00 04	
Old Roan	d	22 05				22 35	22 35				23 05	23 05				23 35	23 35				00 06	00 06	
Maghull	d	22 08				22 38	22 38				23 08	23 08				23 38	23 38				00 09	00 09	
Maghull North Station	d	22 10					22 40					23 10					23 40					00 11	
Town Green	d	22 14				22 44	22 44				23 14	23 14				23 44	23 44				00 15	00 15	
Aughton Park	d	22 16				22 46	22 46				23 16	23 16				23 46	23 46				00 17	00 17	
Ormskirk	a	22 22				22 52	22 52				23 22	23 22				23 52	23 52				00 22	00 22	

A until 23 September
B until 17 June
C from 24 June

For additional trains between Liverpool and Kirkdale refer to Table T104

For additional trains between Liverpool and Sandhills refer to Tables T103 and T104

Table T105-R

Mondays to Saturdays

21 May to 8 December

Ormskirk - Liverpool Central

Miles			ME MX	ME MO	ME	ME SO	ME SX	ME A	ME B	ME	ME	ME	ME A	ME B	ME	ME	ME	ME A	ME B	ME	ME	ME B	ME A
0	**Ormskirk**	d						05 49	05 49				06 19	06 19				06 49	06 49			07 04	07 04
1¼	Aughton Park	d						05 52	05 52				06 22	06 22				06 52	06 52			07 07	07 07
2¼	Town Green	d						05 54	05 54				06 24	06 24				06 54	06 54			07 09	07 09
—	Maghull North Station	d						05 58					06 28					06 58					07 13
4¾	Maghull	d						06 01	06 01				06 31	06 31				07 01	07 01			07 16	07 16
6½	Old Roan	d						06 04	06 04				06 34	06 34				07 04	07 04			07 19	07 19
7¼	Aintree	d						06 06	06 06				06 36	06 36				07 06	07 06			07 21	07 21
8¼	Orrell Park	d						06 08	06 08				06 38	06 38				07 08	07 08			07 23	07 23
8½	Walton	d						06 11	06 11				06 41	06 41				07 11	07 11			07 26	07 26
9¾	Kirkdale	d	00 02	00 02	05 52			06 14	06 14		06 22		06 44	06 44		06 52		07 14	07 14		07 22	07 29	07 29
10½	Sandhills	d	00 04	00 04	05 55	06 05	06 06	06 16	06 16	06 21	06 25	06 36	06 46	06 46	06 51	06 55	07 06	07 16	07 16	07 21	07 25	07 31	07 31
12¼	**Moorfields**	d	00 08	00 08	05 58	06 10	06 10	06 20	06 20	06 25	06 28	06 40	06 50	06 50	06 55	06 58	07 10	07 20	07 20	07 25	07 28	07 35	07 35
12¾	**Liverpool Central**	a	00 11	00 12	06 01	06 13	06 13	06 23	06 23	06 28	06 31	06 43	06 53	06 53	06 58	07 01	07 13	07 23	07 23	07 28	07 31	07 38	07 38

		ME	ME	ME A	ME B	ME	ME	ME A	ME B	ME	ME	ME A	ME B	ME	ME	ME A	ME B	ME	ME	ME A	ME B	ME
Ormskirk	d			07 19	07 19			07 34	07 34			07 49	07 49			08 04	08 04			08 19	08 19	
Aughton Park	d			07 22	07 22			07 37	07 37			07 52	07 52			08 07	08 07			08 22	08 22	
Town Green	d			07 24	07 24			07 39	07 39			07 54	07 54			08 09	08 09			08 24	08 24	
Maghull North Station	d			07 28				07 43				07 58				08 13				08 28		
Maghull	d			07 31	07 31			07 46	07 46			08 01	08 01			08 16	08 16			08 31	08 31	
Old Roan	d			07 34	07 34			07 49	07 49			08 04	08 04			08 19	08 19			08 34	08 34	
Aintree	d			07 36	07 36			07 51	07 51			08 06	08 06			08 21	08 21			08 36	08 36	
Orrell Park	d			07 38	07 38			07 53	07 53			08 08	08 08			08 23	08 23			08 38	08 38	
Walton	d			07 41	07 41			07 56	07 56			08 11	08 11			08 26	08 26			08 41	08 41	
Kirkdale	d		07 37	07 44	07 44		07 52	07 59	07 59		08 07	08 14	08 14		08 22	08 29	08 29		08 37	08 44	08 44	
Sandhills	d	07 36	07 40	07 46	07 46	07 51	07 55	08 01	08 01	08 06	08 10	08 16	08 16	08 21	08 25	08 31	08 31	08 36	08 40	08 46	08 46	08 51
Moorfields	d	07 40	07 43	07 50	07 50	07 55	07 58	08 05	08 05	08 10	08 13	08 20	08 20	08 25	08 28	08 35	08 35	08 40	08 43	08 50	08 50	08 55
Liverpool Central	a	07 43	07 46	07 53	07 53	07 58	08 01	08 08	08 08	08 13	08 16	08 23	08 23	08 28	08 31	08 38	08 38	08 43	08 46	08 53	08 53	08 58

		ME	ME B	ME A	ME	ME	ME A	ME B	ME	ME	ME A	ME B	ME	ME	ME A	ME B	ME	ME	ME B	ME A	ME	ME	ME A
Ormskirk	d		08 34	08 34			08 49	08 49			09 04	09 04			09 19	09 19			09 34	09 34			09 49
Aughton Park	d		08 37	08 37			08 52	08 52			09 07	09 07			09 22	09 22			09 37	09 37			09 52
Town Green	d		08 39	08 39			08 54	08 54			09 09	09 09			09 24	09 24			09 39	09 39			09 54
Maghull North Station	d			08 43			08 58				09 13				09 28					09 43			09 58
Maghull	d		08 46	08 46			09 01	09 01			09 16	09 16			09 31	09 31			09 46	09 46			10 01
Old Roan	d		08 49	08 49			09 04	09 04			09 19	09 19			09 34	09 34			09 49	09 49			10 04
Aintree	d		08 51	08 51			09 06	09 06			09 21	09 21			09 36	09 36			09 51	09 51			10 06
Orrell Park	d		08 53	08 53			09 08	09 08			09 23	09 23			09 38	09 38			09 53	09 53			10 08
Walton	d		08 56	08 56			09 11	09 11			09 26	09 26			09 41	09 41			09 56	09 56			10 11
Kirkdale	d	08 52	08 59	08 59		09 07	09 14	09 14		09 22	09 29	09 29		09 37	09 44	09 44		09 52	09 59	09 59		10 07	10 14
Sandhills	d	08 55	09 01	09 01	09 06	09 10	09 16	09 16	09 21	09 25	09 31	09 31	09 36	09 40	09 46	09 46	09 51	09 55	10 01	10 01	10 06	10 10	10 16
Moorfields	d	08 58	09 05	09 05	09 10	09 13	09 20	09 20	09 25	09 28	09 35	09 35	09 40	09 43	09 50	09 50	09 55	09 58	10 05	10 05	10 10	10 13	10 20
Liverpool Central	a	09 01	09 08	09 08	09 13	09 16	09 23	09 23	09 28	09 31	09 38	09 38	09 43	09 46	09 53	09 53	09 58	10 01	10 08	10 08	10 13	10 16	10 23

		ME B	ME	ME	ME A	ME B	ME	ME	ME B	ME A	ME	ME	ME A	ME B	ME	ME	ME A	ME B	ME	ME	ME B	ME A	ME
Ormskirk	d	09 49			10 04	10 04			10 19	10 19			10 34	10 34			10 49	10 49			11 04	11 04	
Aughton Park	d	09 52			10 07	10 07			10 22	10 22			10 37	10 37			10 52	10 52			11 07	11 07	
Town Green	d	09 54			10 09	10 09			10 24	10 24			10 39	10 39			10 54	10 54			11 09	11 09	
Maghull North Station	d				10 13					10 28			10 43				10 58					11 13	
Maghull	d	10 01			10 16	10 16			10 31	10 31			10 46	10 46			11 01	11 01			11 16	11 16	
Old Roan	d	10 04			10 19	10 19			10 34	10 34			10 49	10 49			11 04	11 04			11 19	11 19	
Aintree	d	10 06			10 21	10 21			10 36	10 36			10 51	10 51			11 06	11 06			11 21	11 21	
Orrell Park	d	10 08			10 23	10 23			10 38	10 38			10 53	10 53			11 08	11 08			11 23	11 23	
Walton	d	10 11			10 26	10 26			10 41	10 41			10 56	10 56			11 11	11 11			11 26	11 26	
Kirkdale	d	10 14		10 22	10 29	10 29		10 37	10 44	10 44		10 52	10 59	10 59		11 07	11 14	11 14		11 22	11 29	11 29	
Sandhills	d	10 16	10 21	10 25	10 31	10 31	10 36	10 40	10 46	10 46	10 51	10 55	11 01	11 01	11 06	11 10	11 16	11 16	11 21	11 25	11 31	11 31	11 36
Moorfields	d	10 20	10 25	10 28	10 35	10 35	10 40	10 43	10 50	10 50	10 55	10 58	11 05	11 05	11 10	11 13	11 20	11 20	11 25	11 28	11 35	11 35	11 40
Liverpool Central	a	10 23	10 28	10 31	10 38	10 38	10 43	10 46	10 53	10 53	10 58	11 01	11 08	11 08	11 13	11 16	11 23	11 23	11 28	11 31	11 38	11 38	11 43

		ME	ME A	ME B	ME	ME	ME A	ME B	ME	ME	ME A	ME B	ME	ME	ME A	ME B	ME	ME	ME A	ME B	ME	ME
Ormskirk	d		11 19	11 19			11 34	11 34			11 49	11 49			12 04	12 04			12 19	12 19		
Aughton Park	d		11 22	11 22			11 37	11 37			11 52	11 52			12 07	12 07			12 22	12 22		
Town Green	d		11 24	11 24			11 39	11 39			11 54	11 54			12 09	12 09			12 24	12 24		
Maghull North Station	d		11 28				11 43				11 58				12 13				12 28			
Maghull	d		11 31	11 31			11 46	11 46			12 01	12 01			12 16	12 16			12 31	12 31		
Old Roan	d		11 34	11 34			11 49	11 49			12 04	12 04			12 19	12 19			12 34	12 34		
Aintree	d		11 36	11 36			11 51	11 51			12 06	12 06			12 21	12 21			12 36	12 36		
Orrell Park	d		11 38	11 38			11 53	11 53			12 08	12 08			12 23	12 23			12 38	12 38		
Walton	d		11 41	11 41			11 56	11 56			12 11	12 11			12 26	12 26			12 41	12 41		
Kirkdale	d	11 37	11 44	11 44		11 52	11 59	11 59		12 07	12 14	12 14		12 22	12 29	12 29		12 37	12 44	12 44		12 52
Sandhills	d	11 40	11 46	11 46	11 51	11 55	12 01	12 01	12 06	12 10	12 16	12 16	12 21	12 25	12 31	12 31	12 36	12 40	12 46	12 46	12 51	12 55
Moorfields	d	11 43	11 50	11 50	11 55	11 58	12 05	12 05	12 10	12 13	12 20	12 20	12 25	12 28	12 35	12 35	12 40	12 43	12 50	12 50	12 55	12 58
Liverpool Central	a	11 46	11 53	11 53	11 58	12 01	12 08	12 08	12 13	12 16	12 23	12 23	12 28	12 31	12 38	12 38	12 43	12 46	12 53	12 53	12 58	13 01

A from 18 June

B until 16 June

For additional trains between Liverpool and Kirkdale refer to Table T104

For additional trains between Liverpool and Sandhills refer to Tables T103 and T104

Table T105-R

Mondays to Saturdays

21 May to 8 December

Ormskirk - Liverpool Central

		ME A	ME B	ME	ME	ME A	ME B	ME	ME	ME A	ME B	ME	ME	ME A	ME B	ME	ME	ME A	ME B	ME	ME	ME A
Ormskirk	d	12 34	12 34			12 49	12 49			13 04	13 04			13 19	13 19			13 34	13 34			13 49
Aughton Park	d	12 37	12 37			12 52	12 52			13 07	13 07			13 22	13 22			13 37	13 37			13 52
Town Green	d	12 39	12 39			12 54	12 54			13 09	13 09			13 24	13 24			13 39	13 39			13 54
Maghull North Station	d	12 43				12 58				13 13				13 28				13 43				13 58
Maghull	d	12 46	12 46			13 01	13 01			13 16	13 16			13 31	13 31			13 46	13 46			14 01
Old Roan	d	12 49	12 49			13 04	13 04			13 19	13 19			13 34	13 34			13 49	13 49			14 04
Aintree	d	12 51	12 51			13 06	13 06			13 21	13 21			13 36	13 36			13 51	13 51			14 06
Orrell Park	d	12 53	12 53			13 08	13 08			13 23	13 23			13 38	13 38			13 53	13 53			14 08
Walton	d	12 56	12 56			13 11	13 11			13 26	13 26			13 41	13 41			13 56	13 56			14 11
Kirkdale	d	12 59	12 59		13 07	13 14	13 14		13 22	13 29	13 29		13 37	13 44	13 44		13 52	13 59	13 59		14 07	14 14
Sandhills	d	13 01	13 01	13 06	13 10	13 16	13 16	13 21	13 25	13 31	13 31	13 36	13 40	13 46	13 46	13 51	13 55	14 01	14 01	14 06	14 10	14 16
Moorfields	d	13 05	13 05	13 10	13 13	13 20	13 20	13 25	13 28	13 35	13 35	13 40	13 43	13 50	13 50	13 55	13 58	14 05	14 05	14 10	14 13	14 20
Liverpool Central	a	13 08	13 08	13 13	13 16	13 23	13 23	13 28	13 31	13 38	13 38	13 43	13 46	13 53	13 53	13 58	14 01	14 08	14 08	14 13	14 16	14 23

		ME B	ME	ME	ME A	ME B	ME	ME	ME A	ME B	ME	ME	ME A	ME B	ME	ME SO	ME SX	ME A	ME B	ME	ME	ME A	ME B
Ormskirk	d	13 49			14 04	14 04			14 19	14 19			14 34	14 34				14 49	14 49			15 04	15 04
Aughton Park	d	13 52			14 07	14 07			14 22	14 22			14 37	14 37				14 52	14 52			15 07	15 07
Town Green	d	13 54			14 09	14 09			14 24	14 24			14 39	14 39				14 54	14 54			15 09	15 09
Maghull North Station	d				14 13				14 28				14 43					14 58				15 13	
Maghull	d	14 01			14 16	14 16			14 31	14 31			14 46	14 46				15 01	15 01			15 16	15 16
Old Roan	d	14 04			14 19	14 19			14 34	14 34			14 49	14 49				15 04	15 04			15 19	15 19
Aintree	d	14 06			14 21	14 21			14 36	14 36			14 51	14 51				15 06	15 06			15 21	15 21
Orrell Park	d	14 08			14 23	14 23			14 38	14 38			14 53	14 53				15 08	15 08			15 23	15 23
Walton	d	14 11			14 26	14 26			14 41	14 41			14 56	14 56				15 11	15 11			15 26	15 26
Kirkdale	d	14 14		14 22	14 29	14 29		14 37	14 44	14 44		14 52	14 59	14 59		15 07	15 07	15 14	15 14		15 22	15 29	15 29
Sandhills	d	14 16	14 21	14 25	14 31	14 31	14 36	14 40	14 46	14 46	14 51	14 55	15 01	15 01	15 06	15 10	15 10	15 16	15 16	15 21	15 25	15 31	15 31
Moorfields	d	14 20	14 25	14 28	14 35	14 35	14 40	14 43	14 50	14 50	14 55	14 58	15 05	15 05	15 10	15 13	15 13	15 20	15 20	15 25	15 28	15 35	15 35
Liverpool Central	a	14 23	14 28	14 31	14 38	14 38	14 43	14 46	14 53	14 53	14 58	15 01	15 08	15 08	15 13	15 16	15 17	15 23	15 23	15 28	15 31	15 38	15 38

		ME	ME	ME A	ME B	ME	ME	ME A	ME B	ME	ME	ME A	ME B	ME	ME	ME A	ME B	ME	ME	ME A	ME B	ME	ME
Ormskirk	d			15 19	15 19			15 34	15 34			15 49	15 49			16 04	16 04			16 19	16 19		
Aughton Park	d			15 22	15 22			15 37	15 37			15 52	15 52			16 07	16 07			16 22	16 22		
Town Green	d			15 24	15 24			15 39	15 39			15 54	15 54			16 09	16 09			16 24	16 24		
Maghull North Station	d			15 28				15 43				15 58				16 13				16 28			
Maghull	d			15 31	15 31			15 46	15 46			16 01	16 01			16 16	16 16			16 31	16 31		
Old Roan	d			15 34	15 34			15 49	15 49			16 04	16 04			16 19	16 19			16 34	16 34		
Aintree	d			15 36	15 36			15 51	15 51			16 06	16 06			16 21	16 21			16 36	16 36		
Orrell Park	d			15 38	15 38			15 53	15 53			16 08	16 08			16 23	16 23			16 38	16 38		
Walton	d			15 41	15 41			15 56	15 56			16 11	16 11			16 26	16 26			16 41	16 41		
Kirkdale	d		15 37	15 44	15 44		15 52	15 59	15 59		16 07	16 14	16 14		16 22	16 29	16 29		16 37	16 44	16 44		16 52
Sandhills	d	15 36	15 40	15 46	15 46	15 51	15 55	16 01	16 01	16 06	16 10	16 16	16 16	16 21	16 25	16 31	16 31	16 36	16 40	16 46	16 46	16 51	16 55
Moorfields	d	15 40	15 43	15 50	15 50	15 55	15 58	16 05	16 05	16 10	16 13	16 20	16 20	16 25	16 28	16 35	16 35	16 40	16 43	16 50	16 50	16 55	16 58
Liverpool Central	a	15 43	15 46	15 53	15 53	15 58	16 01	16 08	16 08	16 13	16 16	16 23	16 23	16 28	16 31	16 38	16 38	16 43	16 46	16 53	16 53	16 58	17 01

		ME A	ME B	ME	ME SX	ME SO	ME A	ME B	ME	ME	ME B	ME A	ME	ME	ME A	ME B	ME	ME	ME A	ME B	ME	ME
Ormskirk	d	16 34	16 34				16 49	16 49			17 04	17 04			17 19	17 19			17 34	17 34		
Aughton Park	d	16 37	16 37				16 52	16 52			17 07	17 07			17 22	17 22			17 37	17 37		
Town Green	d	16 39	16 39				16 54	16 54			17 09	17 09			17 24	17 24			17 39	17 39		
Maghull North Station	d	16 43					16 58					17 13			17 28				17 43			
Maghull	d	16 46	16 46				17 01	17 01			17 16	17 16			17 31	17 31			17 46	17 46		
Old Roan	d	16 49	16 49				17 04	17 04			17 19	17 19			17 34	17 34			17 49	17 49		
Aintree	d	16 51	16 51				17 06	17 06			17 21	17 21			17 36	17 36			17 51	17 51		
Orrell Park	d	16 53	16 53				17 08	17 08			17 23	17 23			17 38	17 38			17 53	17 53		
Walton	d	16 56	16 56				17 11	17 11			17 26	17 26			17 41	17 41			17 56	17 56		
Kirkdale	d	16 59	16 59		17 07	17 07	17 14	17 14		17 22	17 29	17 29		17 37	17 44	17 44		17 52	17 59	17 59		18 07
Sandhills	d	17 01	17 01	17 06	17 10	17 10	17 16	17 16	17 21	17 25	17 31	17 31	17 36	17 40	17 46	17 46	17 51	17 55	18 01	18 01	18 06	18 10
Moorfields	d	17 05	17 05	17 10	17 13	17 14	17 20	17 20	17 25	17 28	17 35	17 35	17 40	17 43	17 50	17 50	17 55	17 58	18 05	18 05	18 10	18 13
Liverpool Central	a	17 08	17 08	17 13	17 16	17 16	17 23	17 23	17 28	17 31	17 38	17 38	17 43	17 46	17 53	17 53	17 58	18 01	18 08	18 08	18 13	18 16

		ME A	ME B	ME	ME	ME A	ME B	ME	ME	ME A	ME B	ME	ME	ME A	ME B	ME	ME	ME A	ME B	ME	ME	ME B	ME A
Ormskirk	d	17 49	17 49			18 04	18 04			18 19	18 19			18 34	18 34			18 49	18 49			19 04	19 04
Aughton Park	d	17 52	17 52			18 07	18 07			18 22	18 22			18 37	18 37			18 52	18 52			19 07	19 07
Town Green	d	17 54	17 54			18 09	18 09			18 24	18 24			18 39	18 39			18 54	18 54			19 09	19 09
Maghull North Station	d	17 58				18 13				18 28				18 43				18 58					19 13
Maghull	d	18 01	18 01			18 16	18 16			18 31	18 31			18 46	18 46			19 01	19 01			19 16	19 16
Old Roan	d	18 04	18 04			18 19	18 19			18 34	18 34			18 49	18 49			19 04	19 04			19 19	19 19
Aintree	d	18 06	18 06			18 21	18 21			18 36	18 36			18 51	18 51			19 06	19 06			19 21	19 21
Orrell Park	d	18 08	18 08			18 23	18 23			18 38	18 38			18 53	18 53			19 08	19 08			19 23	19 23
Walton	d	18 11	18 11			18 26	18 26			18 41	18 41			18 56	18 56			19 11	19 11			19 26	19 26
Kirkdale	d	18 14	18 14		18 22	18 29	18 29		18 37	18 44	18 44		18 52	18 59	18 59		19 07	19 14	19 14		19 22	19 29	19 29
Sandhills	d	18 16	18 16	18 21	18 25	18 31	18 31	18 36	18 40	18 46	18 46	18 51	18 55	19 01	19 01	19 06	19 10	19 16	19 16	19 21	19 25	19 31	19 31
Moorfields	d	18 20	18 20	18 25	18 28	18 35	18 35	18 40	18 43	18 50	18 50	18 55	18 58	19 05	19 05	19 10	19 13	19 20	19 20	19 25	19 28	19 35	19 35
Liverpool Central	a	18 23	18 23	18 28	18 31	18 38	18 38	18 43	18 46	18 53	18 53	18 58	19 01	19 08	19 08	19 13	19 16	19 23	19 23	19 28	19 31	19 38	19 38

A from 18 June

B until 16 June

For additional trains between Liverpool and Kirkdale refer to Table T104

For additional trains between Liverpool and Sandhills refer to Tables T103 and T104

Table T105-R

Mondays to Saturdays

21 May to 8 December

Ormskirk - Liverpool Central

		ME	ME	ME A	ME B	ME	ME	ME SO C	ME SO B	ME SX A		ME SX D	ME	ME	ME	ME A	ME B	ME	ME	ME		ME A	ME B	ME	ME
Ormskirk	d			19 19	19 19			19 34	19 34	19 34		19 34				20 07	20 07					20 37	20 37		
Aughton Park	d			19 22	19 22			19 37	19 37	19 37		19 37				20 10	20 10					20 40	20 40		
Town Green	d			19 24	19 24			19 39	19 39	19 39		19 39				20 12	20 12					20 42	20 42		
Maghull North Station	d			19 28				19 43		19 43						20 16						20 46			
Maghull	d			19 31	19 31			19 46	19 46	19 46		19 46				20 19	20 19					20 49	20 49		
Old Roan	d			19 34	19 34			19 49	19 49	19 49		19 49				20 22	20 22					20 52	20 52		
Aintree	d			19 36	19 36			19 51	19 51	19 51		19 51				20 24	20 24					20 54	20 54		
Orrell Park	d			19 38	19 38			19 53	19 53	19 53		19 53				20 26	20 26					20 56	20 56		
Walton	d			19 41	19 41			19 56	19 56	19 56		19 56				20 28	20 28					20 58	20 58		
Kirkdale	d		19 37	19 44	19 44		19 52	19 59	19 59	19 59		19 59			20 22	20 31	20 31			20 52		21 01	21 01		
Sandhills	d	19 36	19 40	19 46	19 46	19 51	19 55	20 01	20 01	20 01		20 01	20 06	20 21	20 25	20 33	20 33	20 36	20 51	20 55		21 03	21 03	21 06	21 21
Moorfields	d	19 40	19 43	19 50	19 50	19 55	19 58	20 05	20 05	20 05		20 05	20 10	20 25	20 28	20 37	20 37	20 40	20 55	20 58		21 07	21 07	21 10	21 25
Liverpool Central	a	19 43	19 46	19 53	19 53	19 58	20 01	20 08	20 08	20 11		20 11	20 13	20 28	20 31	20 40	20 40	20 43	20 58	21 01		21 11	21 11	21 13	21 28

		ME	ME A	ME B	ME	ME		ME	ME B	ME A	ME	ME	ME	ME A	ME B	ME		ME	ME	ME A	ME B	ME	ME	ME	ME A
Ormskirk	d		21 07	21 07					21 37	21 37				22 07	22 07					22 37	22 37				23 07
Aughton Park	d		21 10	21 10					21 40	21 40				22 10	22 10					22 40	22 40				23 10
Town Green	d		21 12	21 12					21 42	21 42				22 12	22 12					22 42	22 42				23 12
Maghull North Station	d		21 16							21 46				22 16						22 46					23 16
Maghull	d		21 19	21 19					21 49	21 49				22 19	22 19					22 49	22 49				23 19
Old Roan	d		21 22	21 22					21 52	21 52				22 22	22 22					22 52	22 52				23 22
Aintree	d		21 24	21 24					21 54	21 54				22 24	22 24					22 54	22 54				23 24
Orrell Park	d		21 26	21 26					21 56	21 56				22 26	22 26					22 56	22 56				23 26
Walton	d		21 28	21 28					21 58	21 58				22 28	22 28					22 58	22 58				23 28
Kirkdale	d	21 22	21 31	21 31				21 52	22 01	22 01			22 22	22 31	22 31				22 52	23 01	23 01			23 22	23 31
Sandhills	d	21 25	21 33	21 33	21 36	21 51		21 55	22 03	22 03	22 06	22 21	22 25	22 33	22 33	22 36		22 51	22 55	23 03	23 03	23 06	23 21	23 25	23 33
Moorfields	d	21 28	21 37	21 37	21 40	21 55		21 58	22 07	22 07	22 10	22 25	22 28	22 37	22 37	22 40		22 55	22 58	23 07	23 07	23 10	23 25	23 28	23 37
Liverpool Central	a	21 31	21 41	21 41	21 43	21 58		22 01	22 11	22 11	22 13	22 28	22 31	22 41	22 41	22 43		22 58	23 01	23 11	23 11	23 13	23 28	23 31	23 41

		ME B		ME	ME	ME A	ME B
Ormskirk	d	23 07				23 37	23 37
Aughton Park	d	23 10				23 40	23 40
Town Green	d	23 12				23 42	23 42
Maghull North Station	d					23 46	
Maghull	d	23 19				23 49	23 49
Old Roan	d	23 22				23 52	23 52
Aintree	d	23 24				23 54	23 54
Orrell Park	d	23 26				23 56	23 56
Walton	d	23 28				23 59	23 59
Kirkdale	d	23 31				00 02	00 02
Sandhills	d	23 33		23 36	23 56	00 04	00 04
Moorfields	d	23 37		23 40	23 59	00 08	00 08
Liverpool Central	a	23 41		23 43	00 03	00 11	00 11

Sundays

20 May to 2 December

		ME E	ME	ME F	ME G	ME	ME	ME F	ME G	ME		ME	ME F	ME G	ME	ME	ME F	ME G	ME	ME		ME F	ME G	ME	ME H
Ormskirk	d			08 07	08 07			08 37	08 37				09 07	09 07			09 37	09 37				10 07	10 07		
Aughton Park	d			08 10	08 10			08 40	08 40				09 10	09 10			09 40	09 40				10 10	10 10		
Town Green	d			08 12	08 12			08 42	08 42				09 12	09 12			09 42	09 42				10 12	10 12		
Maghull North Station	d			08 16				08 46					09 16				09 46					10 16			
Maghull	d			08 19	08 19			08 49	08 49				09 19	09 19			09 49	09 49				10 19	10 19		
Old Roan	d			08 22	08 22			08 52	08 52				09 22	09 22			09 52	09 52				10 22	10 22		
Aintree	d			08 24	08 24			08 54	08 54				09 24	09 24			09 54	09 54				10 24	10 24		
Orrell Park	d			08 26	08 26			08 56	08 56				09 26	09 26			09 56	09 56				10 26	10 26		
Walton	d			08 28	08 28			08 58	08 58				09 28	09 28			09 58	09 58				10 28	10 28		
Kirkdale	d	00 02	08 22	08 31	08 31		08 52	09 01	09 01			09 22	09 31	09 31		09 52	10 01	10 01		10 22		10 31	10 31		
Sandhills	d	00 04	08 25	08 33	08 33	08 36	08 55	09 03	09 03	09 06		09 25	09 33	09 33	09 36	09 55	10 03	10 03	10 06	10 25		10 33	10 33	10 36	10 51
Moorfields	d	00 08	08 28	08 37	08 37	08 40	08 58	09 07	09 07	09 10		09 28	09 37	09 37	09 40	09 58	10 07	10 07	10 10	10 28		10 37	10 37	10 40	10 55
Liverpool Central	a	00 11	08 31	08 41	08 41	08 43	09 01	09 11	09 11	09 13		09 31	09 41	09 41	09 43	10 01	10 11	10 11	10 13	10 31		10 41	10 41	10 43	10 58

		ME H	ME	ME F	ME G	ME	ME H	ME	ME F	ME G	ME	ME H		ME	ME F	ME G	ME	ME H	ME	ME F	ME G	ME	ME H
Ormskirk	d			10 37	10 37				11 07	11 07			and at the same minutes past each hour until		14 37	14 37				15 07	15 07		
Aughton Park	d			10 40	10 40				11 10	11 10					14 40	14 40				15 10	15 10		
Town Green	d			10 42	10 42				11 12	11 12					14 42	14 42				15 12	15 12		
Maghull North Station	d			10 46					11 16						14 46					15 16			
Maghull	d			10 49	10 49				11 19	11 19					14 49	14 49				15 19	15 19		
Old Roan	d			10 52	10 52				11 22	11 22					14 52	14 52				15 22	15 22		
Aintree	d			10 54	10 54				11 24	11 24					14 54	14 54				15 24	15 24		
Orrell Park	d			10 56	10 56				11 26	11 26					14 56	14 56				15 26	15 26		
Walton	d			10 58	10 58				11 28	11 28					14 58	14 58				15 28	15 28		
Kirkdale	d		10 52	11 01	11 01			11 22	11 31	11 31				14 52	15 01	15 01			15 22	15 31	15 31		
Sandhills	d	10 52	10 55	11 03	11 03	11 06	11 21	11 25	11 33	11 33	11 36	11 51		14 55	15 03	15 03	15 06	15 21	15 25	15 33	15 33	15 36	15 51
Moorfields	d	10 55	10 58	11 07	11 07	11 10	11 25	11 28	11 37	11 37	11 40	11 55		14 58	15 07	15 07	15 10	15 25	15 28	15 37	15 37	15 40	15 55
Liverpool Central	a	10 58	11 01	11 11	11 11	11 13	11 28	11 31	11 41	11 41	11 43	11 58		15 01	15 11	15 11	15 13	15 28	15 31	15 41	15 41	15 43	15 58

A from 18 June
B until 16 June
C from 23 June
D until 15 June
E not 20 May
F from 24 June
G until 17 June
H until 23 September

For additional trains between Liverpool and Kirkdale refer to Table T104

For additional trains between Liverpool and Sandhills refer to Tables T103 and T104

Table T105-R

Sundays

20 May to 2 December

Ormskirk - Liverpool Central

		ME	ME A	ME B	ME	ME C	ME	ME B	ME A	ME	ME C	ME	ME A	ME B	ME	ME C	ME	ME A	ME B	
Ormskirk	d		15 37	15 37				16 07	16 07				16 37	16 37				17 07	17 07	and at the same minutes past each hour until
Aughton Park	d		15 40	15 40				16 10	16 10				16 40	16 40				17 10	17 10	
Town Green	d		15 42	15 42				16 12	16 12				16 42	16 42				17 12	17 12	
Maghull North Station	d		15 46						16 16				16 46					17 16		
Maghull	d		15 49	15 49				16 19	16 19				16 49	16 49				17 19	17 19	
Old Roan	d		15 52	15 52				16 22	16 22				16 52	16 52				17 22	17 22	
Aintree	d		15 54	15 54				16 24	16 24				16 54	16 54				17 24	17 24	
Orrell Park	d		15 56	15 56				16 26	16 26				16 56	16 56				17 26	17 26	
Walton	d		15 58	15 58				16 28	16 28				16 58	16 58				17 28	17 28	
Kirkdale	d	15 52	16 01	16 01			16 22	16 31	16 31			16 52	17 01	17 01			17 22	17 31	17 31	
Sandhills	d	15 55	16 03	16 03	16 06	16 21	16 25	16 33	16 33	16 36	16 51	16 55	17 03	17 03	17 06	17 21	17 25	17 33	17 33	
Moorfields	d	15 58	16 07	16 07	16 10	16 25	16 28	16 37	16 37	16 40	16 55	16 58	17 07	17 07	17 10	17 25	17 28	17 37	17 37	
Liverpool Central	a	16 01	16 11	16 11	16 13	16 28	16 31	16 41	16 41	16 43	16 58	17 01	17 11	17 11	17 13	17 28	17 31	17 41	17 41	

		ME	ME C	ME	ME A	ME B	ME	ME C	ME	ME A	ME B		ME	ME	ME A	ME B
Ormskirk	d				22 37	22 37				23 07	23 07				23 37	23 37
Aughton Park	d				22 40	22 40				23 10	23 10				23 40	23 40
Town Green	d				22 42	22 42				23 12	23 12				23 42	23 42
Maghull North Station	d				22 46					23 16					23 46	
Maghull	d				22 49	22 49				23 19	23 19				23 49	23 49
Old Roan	d				22 52	22 52				23 22	23 22				23 52	23 52
Aintree	d				22 54	22 54				23 24	23 24				23 54	23 54
Orrell Park	d				22 56	22 56				23 26	23 26				23 56	23 56
Walton	d				22 58	22 58				23 28	23 28				23 59	23 59
Kirkdale	d			22 52	23 01	23 01			23 22	23 31	23 31				00 02	00 02
Sandhills	d	22 36	22 51	22 55	23 03	23 03	23 06	23 21	23 25	23 33	23 33		23 36	23 56	00 04	00 04
Moorfields	d	22 40	22 55	22 58	23 07	23 07	23 10	23 25	23 28	23 37	23 37		23 40	23 59	00 08	00 08
Liverpool Central	a	22 43	22 58	23 01	23 11	23 11	23 13	23 28	23 31	23 41	23 41		23 43	00 03	00 12	00 12

A from 24 June
B until 17 June
C until 23 September

For additional trains between Liverpool and Kirkdale refer to Table T104

For additional trains between Liverpool and Sandhills refer to Tables T103 and T104

Table T106-F

Mondays to Saturdays

21 May to 8 December

Liverpool and Birkenhead - New Brighton and West Kirby

Miles	Miles			ME	ME	ME	ME	ME	ME	ME	ME	ME	ME	ME	ME	ME	ME SO	ME SX	ME	ME	ME	ME	ME
0	0	Moorfields	d			06 16	06 21	06 46	06 51	07 16	07 21	07 31	07 36	07 46	07 51	08 01	08 06	08 06	08 16	08 21	08 31	08 36	08 46
0½	0½	Liverpool Lime Street	d			06 18	06 23	06 48	06 53	07 18	07 23	07 33	07 38	07 48	07 53	08 03	08 08	08 08	08 18	08 23	08 33	08 38	08 48
1	1	Liverpool Central	d			06 20	06 25	06 50	06 55	07 20	07 25	07 35	07 40	07 50	07 55	08 05	08 10	08 10	08 20	08 25	08 35	08 40	08 50
1½	1½	James Street	d			06 22	06 27	06 52	06 57	07 22	07 27	07 37	07 42	07 52	07 57	08 07	08 12	08 12	08 22	08 27	08 37	08 42	08 52
2¼	2¼	Hamilton Square	d			06 25	06 30	06 55	07 00	07 25	07 30	07 40	07 45	07 55	08 00	08 10	08 15	08 15	08 25	08 30	08 40	08 45	08 55
3¼	3¼	Conway Park	d			06 27	06 32	06 57	07 02	07 27	07 32	07 42	07 47	07 57	08 02	08 12	08 17	08 17	08 27	08 32	08 42	08 47	08 57
4	4	Birkenhead Park	d			06 29	06 34	06 59	07 04	07 29	07 34	07 44	07 49	07 59	08 04	08 14	08 19	08 20	08 29	08 34	08 44	08 49	08 59
4¾	4¾	Birkenhead North	d		00 02	06 32	06 37	07 02	07 07	07 32	07 37	07 47	07 52	08 02	08 07	08 17	08 22	08 22	08 32	08 37	08 47	08 52	09 02
—	6¼	Wallasey Village	d		00 07	06 37		07 07		07 37		07 52		08 07		08 22			08 37		08 52		09 07
—	6½	Wallasey Grove Road	d		00 08	06 38		07 08		07 38		07 53		08 08		08 23			08 38		08 53		09 08
—	7¾	**New Brighton**	a		00 13	06 43		07 13		07 43		07 58		08 13		08 28			08 43		08 58		09 13
5¼	—	Bidston	d				06 40		07 10		07 40		07 55		08 10		08 25	08 25		08 40		08 55	
6½	—	Leasowe	d				06 42		07 12		07 42		07 57		08 12		08 27	08 27		08 42		08 57	
7	—	Moreton	d				06 44		07 14		07 44		07 59		08 14		08 29	08 29		08 44		08 59	
8¼	—	Meols	d				06 48		07 18		07 48		08 03		08 18		08 33	08 33		08 48		09 03	
9½	—	Manor Road	d				06 50		07 20		07 50		08 05		08 20		08 35	08 35		08 50		09 05	
10	—	Hoylake	d	00 02			06 52		07 22		07 52		08 07		08 22		08 37	08 37		08 52		09 07	
11¼	—	**West Kirby**	a	00 07			06 57		07 27		07 57		08 12		08 27		08 42	08 42		08 57		09 12	

		ME SX	ME	ME	ME	ME	ME	ME	ME	ME		ME	ME	ME	ME	ME	ME	ME	ME	ME	ME	ME
Moorfields	d	08 48	08 51	09 01	09 06	09 16	09 21	09 31	09 36	09 46		17 51	18 01	18 06	18 16	18 21	18 31	18 36	18 46	18 51	19 01	19 06
Liverpool Lime Street	d	08 50	08 53	09 03	09 08	09 18	09 23	09 33	09 38	09 48		17 53	18 03	18 08	18 18	18 23	18 33	18 38	18 48	18 53	19 03	19 08
Liverpool Central	d	08 52	08 55	09 05	09 10	09 20	09 25	09 35	09 40	09 50		17 55	18 05	18 10	18 20	18 25	18 35	18 40	18 50	18 55	19 05	19 10
James Street	d	08 54	08 57	09 07	09 12	09 22	09 27	09 37	09 42	09 52		17 57	18 07	18 12	18 22	18 27	18 37	18 42	18 52	18 57	19 07	19 12
Hamilton Square	d	08 57	09 00	09 10	09 15	09 25	09 30	09 40	09 45	09 55	and at the same minutes past each hour until	18 00	18 10	18 15	18 25	18 30	18 40	18 45	18 55	19 00	19 10	19 15
Conway Park	d	09 00	09 02	09 12	09 17	09 27	09 32	09 42	09 47	09 57		18 02	18 12	18 17	18 27	18 32	18 42	18 47	18 57	19 02	19 12	19 17
Birkenhead Park	d	09 02	09 04	09 14	09 19	09 29	09 34	09 44	09 49	09 59		18 04	18 14	18 19	18 29	18 34	18 44	18 49	18 59	19 04	19 14	19 19
Birkenhead North	d	09a05	09 07	09 17	09 22	09 32	09 37	09 47	09 52	10 02		18 07	18 17	18 22	18 32	18 37	18 47	18 52	19 02	19 07	19 17	19 22
Wallasey Village	d			09 22		09 37		09 52		10 07			18 22		18 37		18 52		19 07		19 22	
Wallasey Grove Road	d			09 23		09 38		09 53		10 08			18 23		18 38		18 53		19 08		19 23	
New Brighton	a			09 28		09 43		09 58		10 13			18 28		18 43		18 58		19 13		19 28	
Bidston	d		09 10		09 25		09 40		09 55			18 10		18 25		18 40		18 55		19 10		19 25
Leasowe	d		09 12		09 27		09 42		09 57			18 12		18 27		18 42		18 57		19 12		19 27
Moreton	d		09 14		09 29		09 44		09 59			18 14		18 29		18 44		18 59		19 14		19 29
Meols	d		09 18		09 33		09 48		10 03			18 18		18 33		18 48		19 03		19 18		19 33
Manor Road	d		09 20		09 35		09 50		10 05			18 20		18 35		18 50		19 05		19 20		19 35
Hoylake	d		09 22		09 37		09 52		10 07			18 22		18 37		18 52		19 07		19 22		19 37
West Kirby	a		09 27		09 42		09 57		10 12			18 27		18 42		18 57		19 12		19 27		19 42

		ME	ME	ME	ME		ME	ME	ME	ME	ME	ME	ME
Moorfields	d	19 16	19 31	19 46	20 01		22 16	22 31	22 46	23 01	23 16	23 31	23 46
Liverpool Lime Street	d	19 18	19 33	19 48	20 03		22 18	22 33	22 48	23 03	23 18	23 33	23 48
Liverpool Central	d	19 20	19 35	19 50	20 05		22 20	22 35	22 50	23 05	23 20	23 35	23 50
James Street	d	19 22	19 37	19 52	20 07		22 22	22 37	22 52	23 07	23 22	23 37	23 52
Hamilton Square	d	19 25	19 40	19 55	20 10	and at the same minutes past each hour until	22 25	22 40	22 55	23 10	23 25	23 40	23 55
Conway Park	d	19 27	19 42	19 57	20 12		22 27	22 42	22 57	23 12	23 27	23 42	23 57
Birkenhead Park	d	19 29	19 44	19 59	20 14		22 29	22 44	22 59	23 14	23 29	23 44	23 59
Birkenhead North	d	19 32	19 47	20 02	20 17		22 32	22 47	23 02	23 17	23 32	23 47	00 02
Wallasey Village	d	19 37		20 07			22 37		23 07		23 37		00 07
Wallasey Grove Road	d	19 38		20 08			22 38		23 08		23 38		00 08
New Brighton	a	19 43		20 13			22 43		23 13		23 43		00 13
Bidston	d		19 50		20 20			22 50		23 20		23 50	
Leasowe	d		19 52		20 22			22 52		23 22		23 52	
Moreton	d		19 54		20 24			22 54		23 24		23 54	
Meols	d		19 58		20 28			22 58		23 28		23 58	
Manor Road	d		20 00		20 30			23 00		23 30		23 59	
Hoylake	d		20 02		20 32			23 02		23 32		00 02	
West Kirby	a		20 07		20 37			23 07		23 37		00 07	

Sundays

20 May to 2 December

		ME A	ME A	ME	ME	ME	ME		ME	ME	ME	ME	ME	ME	ME	ME
Moorfields	d			08 01	08 16	08 31	08 46		22 01	22 16	22 31	22 46	23 01	23 16	23 31	23 46
Liverpool Lime Street	d			08 03	08 18	08 33	08 48		22 03	22 18	22 33	22 48	23 03	23 18	23 33	23 48
Liverpool Central	d			08 05	08 20	08 35	08 50		22 05	22 20	22 35	22 50	23 05	23 20	23 35	23 50
James Street	d			08 07	08 22	08 37	08 52		22 07	22 22	22 37	22 52	23 07	23 22	23 37	23 52
Hamilton Square	d			08 10	08 25	08 40	08 55	and at the same minutes past each hour until	22 10	22 25	22 40	22 55	23 10	23 25	23 40	23 55
Conway Park	d			08 12	08 27	08 42	08 57		22 12	22 27	22 42	22 57	23 12	23 27	23 42	23 57
Birkenhead Park	d			08 14	08 29	08 44	08 59		22 14	22 29	22 44	22 59	23 14	23 29	23 44	23 59
Birkenhead North	d		00 02	08 17	08 32	08 47	09 02		22 17	22 32	22 47	23 02	23 17	23 32	23 47	00 02
Wallasey Village	d		00 07		08 37		09 07			22 37		23 07		23 37		00 07
Wallasey Grove Road	d		00 08		08 38		09 08			22 38		23 08		23 38		00 08
New Brighton	a		00 13		08 43		09 13			22 43		23 13		23 43		00 13
Bidston	d			08 20		08 50			22 20		22 50		23 20		23 50	
Leasowe	d			08 22		08 52			22 22		22 52		23 22		23 52	
Moreton	d			08 24		08 54			22 24		22 54		23 24		23 54	
Meols	d			08 28		08 58			22 28		22 58		23 28		23 58	
Manor Road	d			08 30		09 00			22 30		23 00		23 30		23 59	
Hoylake	d	00 02		08 32		09 02			22 32		23 02		23 32		00 02	
West Kirby	a	00 07		08 37		09 07			22 37		23 07		23 37		00 07	

A not 20 May

Table T106-R

Mondays to Saturdays

21 May to 8 December

West Kirby and New Brighton - Birkenhead and Liverpool

Miles	Miles			ME	ME	ME	ME	ME	ME	ME	ME	ME	ME	ME	ME		ME	ME	ME	ME	ME	ME	ME
0	—	**West Kirby**	d		05 51		06 21		06 51		07 06		07 21		07 36			17 51		18 06		18 21	
1	—	Hoylake	d		05 54		06 24		06 54		07 09		07 24		07 39			17 54		18 09		18 24	
1¾	—	Manor Road	d		05 56		06 26		06 56		07 11		07 26		07 41			17 56		18 11		18 26	
3	—	Meols	d		05 58		06 28		06 58		07 13		07 28		07 43			17 58		18 13		18 28	
4¼	—	Moreton	d		06 01		06 31		07 01		07 16		07 31		07 46			18 01		18 16		18 31	
4¾	—	Leasowe	d		06 03		06 33		07 03		07 18		07 33		07 48	and at the same minutes past each hour until		18 03		18 18		18 33	
5¾	—	Bidston	d		06 06		06 36		07 06		07 21		07 36		07 51			18 06		18 21		18 36	
—	0	**New Brighton**	d	05 53		06 23		06 53		07 08		07 23		07 38			17 53		18 08		18 23		18 38
—	1¼	Wallasey Grove Road	d	05 57		06 27		06 57		07 12		07 27		07 42			17 57		18 12		18 27		18 42
—	1½	Wallasey Village	d	05 59		06 29		06 59		07 14		07 29		07 44			17 59		18 14		18 29		18 44
6½	3	Birkenhead North	d	06 04	06 09	06 34	06 39	07 04	07 09	07 19	07 24	07 34	07 39	07 49	07 54		18 04	18 09	18 19	18 24	18 34	18 39	18 49
7½	3¾	Birkenhead Park	d	06 06	06 11	06 36	06 41	07 06	07 11	07 21	07 26	07 36	07 41	07 51	07 56		18 06	18 11	18 21	18 26	18 36	18 41	18 51
8¼	4½	Conway Park	d	06 09	06 14	06 39	06 44	07 09	07 14	07 24	07 29	07 39	07 44	07 54	07 59		18 09	18 14	18 24	18 29	18 39	18 44	18 54
8¾	5	Hamilton Square	d	06 11	06 16	06 41	06 46	07 11	07 16	07 26	07 31	07 41	07 46	07 56	08 01		18 11	18 16	18 26	18 31	18 41	18 46	18 56
8¾	6¼	James Street	d	06 14	06 19	06 44	06 49	07 14	07 19	07 29	07 34	07 44	07 49	07 59	08 04		18 14	18 19	18 29	18 34	18 44	18 49	18 59
10¼	7¾	Moorfields	a	06 16	06 21	06 46	06 51	07 16	07 21	07 31	07 36	07 46	07 51	08 01	08 06		18 16	18 21	18 31	18 36	18 46	18 51	19 01
9¾	7¼	Liverpool Lime Street	a	06 18	06 23	06 48	06 53	07 18	07 23	07 33	07 38	07 48	07 53	08 03	08 08		18 18	18 23	18 33	18 38	18 48	18 53	19 03
9¼	6¾	**Liverpool Central**	a	06 20	06 25	06 50	06 55	07 20	07 25	07 35	07 40	07 50	07 55	08 05	08 10		18 20	18 25	18 35	18 40	18 50	18 55	19 05

		ME	ME	ME	ME	ME		ME	ME	ME	ME	ME	ME	ME
West Kirby	d	18 36		19 01		19 31			22 01		22 31		23 01	
Hoylake	d	18 39		19 04		19 34			22 04		22 34		23 04	
Manor Road	d	18 41		19 06		19 36			22 06		22 36		23 06	
Meols	d	18 43		19 08		19 38			22 08		22 38		23 08	
Moreton	d	18 46		19 11		19 41			22 11		22 41		23 11	
Leasowe	d	18 48		19 13		19 43	and at the same minutes past each hour until		22 13		22 43		23 13	
Bidston	d	18 51		19 16		19 46			22 16		22 46		23 16	
New Brighton	d		18 53		19 23			21 53		22 23		22 53		23 23
Wallasey Grove Road	d		18 57		19 27			21 57		22 27		22 57		23 27
Wallasey Village	d		18 59		19 29			21 59		22 29		22 59		23 29
Birkenhead North	d	18 54	19 04	19 19	19 34	19 49		22 04	22 19	22 34	22 49	23 04	23 19	23 34
Birkenhead Park	d	18 56	19 06	19 21	19 36	19 51		22 06	22 21	22 36	22 51	23 06	23 21	23 36
Conway Park	d	18 59	19 09	19 24	19 39	19 54		22 09	22 24	22 39	22 54	23 09	23 24	23 39
Hamilton Square	d	19 01	19 11	19 26	19 41	19 56		22 11	22 26	22 41	22 56	23 11	23 26	23 41
James Street	d	19 04	19 14	19 29	19 44	19 59		22 14	22 29	22 44	22 59	23 14	23 29	23 44
Moorfields	a	19 06	19 16	19 31	19 46	20 01		22 16	22 31	22 46	23 01	23 16	23 31	23 46
Liverpool Lime Street	a	19 08	19 18	19 33	19 48	20 03		22 18	22 33	22 48	23 03	23 18	23 33	23 48
Liverpool Central	a	19 10	19 20	19 35	19 50	20 05		22 20	22 35	22 50	23 05	23 20	23 35	23 50

Sundays

20 May to 2 December

		ME	ME	ME	ME		ME	ME	ME	ME	ME	ME	ME
West Kirby	d		08 01		08 31			22 01		22 31		23 01	
Hoylake	d		08 04		08 34			22 04		22 34		23 04	
Manor Road	d		08 06		08 36			22 06		22 36		23 06	
Meols	d		08 08		08 38			22 08		22 38		23 08	
Moreton	d		08 11		08 41			22 11		22 41		23 11	
Leasowe	d		08 13		08 43	and at the same minutes past each hour until		22 13		22 43		23 13	
Bidston	d		08 16		08 46			22 16		22 46		23 16	
New Brighton	d	07 53		08 23			21 53		22 23		22 53		23 23
Wallasey Grove Road	d	07 57		08 27			21 57		22 27		22 57		23 27
Wallasey Village	d	07 59		08 29			21 59		22 29		22 59		23 29
Birkenhead North	d	08 04	08 19	08 34	08 49		22 04	22 19	22 34	22 49	23 04	23 19	23 34
Birkenhead Park	d	08 06	08 21	08 36	08 51		22 06	22 21	22 36	22 51	23 06	23 21	23 36
Conway Park	d	08 09	08 24	08 39	08 54		22 09	22 24	22 39	22 54	23 09	23 24	23 39
Hamilton Square	d	08 11	08 26	08 41	08 56		22 11	22 26	22 41	22 56	23 11	23 26	23 41
James Street	d	08 14	08 29	08 44	08 59		22 14	22 29	22 44	22 59	23 14	23 29	23 44
Moorfields	a	08 16	08 31	08 46	09 01		22 16	22 31	22 46	23 01	23 16	23 31	23 46
Liverpool Lime Street	a	08 18	08 33	08 48	09 03		22 18	22 33	22 48	23 03	23 18	23 33	23 48
Liverpool Central	a	08 20	08 35	08 50	09 05		22 20	22 35	22 50	23 05	23 20	23 35	23 50

Table T107-F

Liverpool - Chester & Ellesmere Port

Mondays to Saturdays

21 May to 8 December

Miles	Miles			ME	ME	ME	ME	ME	ME	ME	ME	ME		ME	ME	ME SX	ME SO	ME SX	ME	ME SX	ME	ME SX		ME SO	ME SX
0	—	Moorfields	d			05 36	05 56	06 06	06 26	06 41	06 56	07 11		07 26	07 41	07 53	07 56		08 11	08 19	08 26	08 33		08 41	08 41
0½	—	Liverpool Lime Street	d			05 38	05 58	06 08	06 28	06 43	06 58	07 13		07 28	07 43	07 55	07 58		08 13	08 21	08 28	08 35		08 43	08 43
1	—	Liverpool Central	d			05 40	06 00	06 10	06 30	06 45	07 00	07 15		07 30	07 45	07 57	08 00		08 15	08 23	08 30	08 37		08 45	08 45
1½	—	James Street	d			05 42	06 02	06 12	06 32	06 47	07 02	07 17		07 32	07 47	07 59	08 02		08 17	08 25	08 32	08 39		08 47	08 47
2¾	—	Hamilton Square	d			05 45	06 05	06 15	06 35	06 50	07 05	07 20		07 35	07 50	08 02	08 05		08 20	08 28	08 35	08 42		08 50	08 50
3	—	Birkenhead Central	d			05 47	06 07	06 17	06 37	06 52	07 07	07 22		07 37	07 52	08 05	08 07		08 22	08 30	08 37	08a44		08 52	08 53
3¾	—	Green Lane	d			05 49	06 09	06 19	06 39	06 54	07 09	07 24		07 39	07 54	08 07	08 09		08 24	08 32	08 39			08 54	08 55
4½	—	Rock Ferry	d			05 52	06 12	06 22	06 42	06 57	07 12	07 27		07 42	07 57	08 09	08 12		08 27	08 35	08 42			08 57	08 57
5½	—	Bebington	d			05 54	06 14	06 24	06 44	06 59	07 14	07 29		07 44	07 59	08 12	08 14		08 29	08 37	08 44			08 59	09 00
6½	—	Port Sunlight	d		00 01	05 56	06 16	06 26	06 46	07 01	07 16	07 31		07 46	08 01	08 14	08 16		08 31	08 39	08 46			09 01	09 02
7	—	Spital	d		00 03	05 58	06 18	06 28	06 48	07 03	07 18	07 33		07 48	08 03	08 16	08 18		08 33	08 41	08 48			09 03	09 04
7¾	—	Bromborough Rake	d		00 05	06 00	06 20	06 30	06 50	07 05	07 20	07 35		07 50	08 05	08 18	08 20		08 35	08 43	08 50			09 05	09 06
8½	—	Bromborough	d		00 07	06 02	06 22	06 32	06 52	07 07	07 22	07 37		07 52	08 07	08 20	08 22		08 37	08 45	08 52			09 07	09 08
9	—	Eastham Rake	d		00 10	06 05	06 25	06 35	06 55	07 10	07 25	07 40		07 55	08 10	08 22	08 25		08 40	08 48	08 55			09 10	09 10
10	0	Hooton	d		00 12	06 07	06 27	06 37	06 57	07 12	07 27	07 43		07 57	08 13	08 24	08 27	08 29	08 42	08 50	08 57			09 12	09 12
—	1½	Little Sutton	d	00 01			06 31		07 01		07 31			08 01			08 31	08 34			09 01				
—	2½	Overpool	d	00 03			06 33		07 03		07 33			08 03			08 33	08 36			09 03				
—	4	**Ellesmere Port**	a	00 07			06 38		07 08		07 38			08 08			08 38	08 39			09 08				
13	—	Capenhurst	d		00 17	06 12		06 42		07 17		07 48			08 18	08 29			08 47	08 55				09 17	09 17
16¾	—	Bache	d		00 22	06 17		06 47		07 22		07 54			08 24	08 35			08 52	09 00				09 22	09 23
18½	—	**Chester**	a		00 26	06 26		06 56		07 27		07 58			08 28	08 38			08 57	09 07				09 27	09 27

		ME SO	ME SO	ME SX	ME	ME SO	ME SX	ME		ME	ME	ME	ME	ME	ME	ME	ME	ME		ME	ME	ME	ME	ME	
Moorfields	d	08 48	08 56	08 56	09 11	09 18	09 19	09 26		09 41	09 48	09 56	10 11	10 18	10 26	10 41	10 48	10 56		11 11	11 18	11 26	11 41	11 48	
Liverpool Lime Street	d	08 50	08 58	08 58	09 13	09 20	09 21	09 28		09 43	09 50	09 58	10 13	10 20	10 28	10 43	10 50	10 58		11 13	11 20	11 28	11 43	11 50	
Liverpool Central	d	08 52	09 00	09 00	09 15	09 22	09 23	09 30		09 45	09 52	10 00	10 15	10 22	10 30	10 45	10 52	11 00		11 15	11 22	11 30	11 45	11 52	
James Street	d	08 54	09 02	09 02	09 17	09 24	09 25	09 32		09 47	09 54	10 02	10 17	10 24	10 32	10 47	10 54	11 02		11 17	11 24	11 32	11 47	11 54	
Hamilton Square	d	08 57	09 05	09 05	09 20	09 27	09 28	09 35		09 50	09 57	10 05	10 20	10 27	10 35	10 50	10 57	11 05		11 20	11 27	11 35	11 50	11 57	
Birkenhead Central	d	09 00	09 07	09 07	09 22	09 30	09 30	09 37		09 52	10 00	10 07	10 22	10 30	10 37	10 52	11 00	11 07		11 22	11 30	11 37	11 52	12 00	
Green Lane	d	09 02	09 09	09 09	09 24	09 32	09 32	09 39		09 54	10 02	10 09	10 24	10 32	10 39	10 54	11 02	11 09		11 24	11 32	11 39	11 54	12 02	
Rock Ferry	d	09 04	09 12	09 12	09 27	09 34	09 35	09 42		09 57	10 04	10 12	10 27	10 34	10 42	10 57	11 04	11 12		11 27	11 34	11 42	11 57	12 04	
Bebington	d	09 07	09 14	09 14	09 29	09 37	09 37	09 44		09 59	10 07	10 14	10 29	10 37	10 44	10 59	11 07	11 14		11 29	11 37	11 44	11 59	12 07	
Port Sunlight	d	09 09	09 16	09 16	09 31	09 39	09 39	09 46		10 01	10 09	10 16	10 31	10 39	10 46	11 01	11 09	11 16		11 31	11 39	11 46	12 01	12 09	
Spital	d	09 11	09 18	09 18	09 33	09 41	09 41	09 48		10 03	10 11	10 18	10 33	10 41	10 48	11 03	11 11	11 18		11 33	11 41	11 48	12 03	12 11	
Bromborough Rake	d	09 13	09 20	09 20	09 35	09 43	09 43	09 50		10 05	10 13	10 20	10 35	10 43	10 50	11 05	11 13	11 20		11 35	11 43	11 50	12 05	12 13	
Bromborough	d	09 15	09 22	09 22	09 37	09 45	09 45	09 52		10 07	10 15	10 22	10 37	10 45	10 52	11 07	11 15	11 22		11 37	11 45	11 52	12 07	12 15	
Eastham Rake	d	09 17	09 25	09 25	09 40	09 47	09 48	09 55		10 10	10 17	10 25	10 40	10 47	10 55	11 10	11 17	11 25		11 40	11 47	11 55	12 10	12 17	
Hooton	d	09 19	09 27	09 27	09 42	09 49	09 50	09 57		10 12	10 19	10 27	10 42	10 49	10 57	11 12	11 19	11 27		11 42	11 49	11 57	12 12	12 19	
Little Sutton	d	09 24		09 31		09 54	09 54				10 24			10 54			11 24				11 54			12 24	
Overpool	d	09 26		09 33		09 56	09 56				10 26			10 56			11 26				11 56			12 26	
Ellesmere Port	a	09 32		09 38		10 00	10 00				10 30			11 00			11 30				12 00			12 31	
Capenhurst	d				09 47					10 17			10 47			11 17				11 47			12 17		
Bache	d		09 36		09 52			10 06		10 22		10 36	10 52		11 06	11 22		11 36		11 52		12 06	12 22		
Chester	a		09 41		09 57			10 11		10 27		10 41	10 57		11 11	11 27		11 41		11 57		12 11	12 27		

		ME	ME	ME	ME	ME	ME		ME	ME	ME	ME	ME	ME		ME	ME	ME	ME	ME SX	ME	ME	ME SO	ME SX
Moorfields	d	11 56	12 11	12 18	12 26	12 41	12 48		14 56	15 11	15 18	15 26	15 41	15 48		15 56	16 11	16 18	16 26	16 33	16 41	16 48	16 56	16 56
Liverpool Lime Street	d	11 58	12 13	12 20	12 28	12 43	12 50		14 58	15 13	15 20	15 28	15 43	15 50		15 58	16 13	16 20	16 28	16 35	16 43	16 50	16 58	16 58
Liverpool Central	d	12 00	12 15	12 22	12 30	12 45	12 52		15 00	15 15	15 22	15 30	15 45	15 52		16 00	16 15	16 22	16 30	16 37	16 45	16 52	17 00	17 00
James Street	d	12 02	12 17	12 24	12 32	12 47	12 54		15 02	15 17	15 24	15 32	15 47	15 54		16 02	16 17	16 24	16 32	16 39	16 47	16 54	17 02	17 02
Hamilton Square	d	12 05	12 20	12 27	12 35	12 50	12 57		15 05	15 20	15 27	15 35	15 50	15 57		16 05	16 20	16 27	16 35	16 42	16 50	16 57	17 05	17 05
Birkenhead Central	d	12 07	12 22	12 30	12 37	12 52	13 00		15 07	15 22	15 30	15 37	15 52	16 00		16 07	16 22	16 30	16 37	16 45	16 52	17 00	17 07	17 07
Green Lane	d	12 09	12 24	12 32	12 39	12 54	13 02	and at	15 09	15 24	15 32	15 39	15 54	16 02		16 09	16 24	16 32	16 39	16 47	16 54	17 02	17 09	17 09
Rock Ferry	d	12 12	12 27	12 34	12 42	12 57	13 04	the same	15 12	15 27	15 34	15 42	15 57	16 04		16 12	16 27	16 34	16 42	16 49	16 57	17 04	17 12	17 12
Bebington	d	12 14	12 29	12 37	12 44	12 59	13 07	minutes	15 14	15 29	15 37	15 44	15 59	16 07		16 14	16 29	16 37	16 44	16 52	16 59	17 07	17 14	17 14
Port Sunlight	d	12 16	12 31	12 39	12 46	13 01	13 09	past	15 16	15 31	15 39	15 46	16 01	16 09		16 16	16 31	16 39	16 46	16 54	17 01	17 09	17 16	17 16
Spital	d	12 18	12 33	12 41	12 48	13 03	13 11	each	15 18	15 33	15 41	15 48	16 03	16 11		16 18	16 33	16 41	16 48	16 56	17 03	17 11	17 18	17 18
Bromborough Rake	d	12 20	12 35	12 43	12 50	13 05	13 13	hour until	15 20	15 35	15 43	15 50	16 05	16 13		16 20	16 35	16 43	16 50	16 58	17 05	17 13	17 20	17 20
Bromborough	d	12 22	12 37	12 45	12 52	13 07	13 15		15 22	15 37	15 45	15 52	16 07	16 15		16 22	16 37	16 45	16 52	17 00	17 07	17 15	17 22	17 22
Eastham Rake	d	12 25	12 40	12 47	12 55	13 10	13 17		15 25	15 40	15 47	15 55	16 10	16 17		16 25	16 40	16 47	16 55	17 02	17 10	17 17	17 25	17 25
Hooton	d	12 27	12 42	12 49	12 57	13 12	13 19		15 27	15 42	15 49	15 57	16 12	16 19		16 27	16 42	16 49	16 57	17 04	17 12	17 19	17 27	17 27
Little Sutton	d			12 54			13 24				15 54			16 24				16 54		17 09		17 24		
Overpool	d			12 56			13 26				15 56			16 26				16 56		17 11		17 26		
Ellesmere Port	a			13 00			13 30				16 00			16 30				17 00		17 16		17 30		
Capenhurst	d		12 47			13 17				15 47			16 17				16 47				17 17			17 32
Bache	d	12 36	12 52		13 06	13 22			15 36	15 52		16 06	16 22			16 36	16 52		17 06		17 22		17 36	17 37
Chester	a	12 41	12 57		13 11	13 27			15 41	15 57		16 11	16 27			16 41	16 57		17 11		17 27		17 41	17 41

			ME SX	ME	ME	ME SO	ME SX	ME SX	ME	ME	ME		ME	ME	ME	ME	ME	ME	ME	ME	ME		ME	ME	ME SO
Moorfields	d		17 03	17 11	17 18	17 26	17 26	17 33	17 41	17 48	17 56		18 11	18 18	18 26	18 41	18 48	18 56	19 11	19 26	19 41		19 56	20 11	20 26
Liverpool Lime Street	d		17 05	17 13	17 20	17 28	17 28	17 35	17 43	17 50	17 58		18 13	18 20	18 28	18 43	18 50	18 58	19 13	19 28	19 43		19 58	20 13	20 28
Liverpool Central	d		17 07	17 15	17 22	17 30	17 30	17 37	17 45	17 52	18 00		18 15	18 22	18 30	18 45	18 52	19 00	19 15	19 30	19 45		20 00	20 15	20 30
James Street	d		17 09	17 17	17 24	17 32	17 32	17 39	17 47	17 54	18 02		18 17	18 24	18 32	18 47	18 54	19 02	19 17	19 32	19 47		20 02	20 17	20 32
Hamilton Square	d		17 12	17 20	17 27	17 35	17 35	17 42	17 50	17 57	18 05		18 20	18 27	18 35	18 50	18 57	19 05	19 20	19 35	19 50		20 05	20 20	20 35
Birkenhead Central	d		17 15	17 22	17 30	17 37	17 37	17 45	17 52	18 00	18 07		18 22	18 30	18 37	18 52	19 00	19 07	19 22	19 37	19 52		20 07	20 22	20 37
Green Lane	d		17 17	17 24	17 32	17 39	17 39	17 47	17 54	18 02	18 09		18 24	18 32	18 39	18 54	19 02	19 09	19 24	19 39	19 54		20 09	20 24	20 39
Rock Ferry	d		17 19	17 27	17 34	17 42	17 42	17 49	17 57	18 04	18 12		18 27	18 34	18 42	18 57	19 04	19 12	19 27	19 42	19 57		20 12	20 27	20 42
Bebington	d		17 22	17 29	17 37	17 44	17 44	17 52	17 59	18 07	18 14		18 29	18 37	18 44	18 59	19 07	19 14	19 29	19 44	19 59		20 14	20 29	20 44
Port Sunlight	d		17 24	17 31	17 39	17 46	17 46	17 54	18 01	18 09	18 16		18 31	18 39	18 46	19 01	19 09	19 16	19 31	19 46	20 01		20 16	20 31	20 46
Spital	d		17 26	17 33	17 41	17 48	17 48	17 56	18 03	18 11	18 18		18 33	18 41	18 48	19 03	19 11	19 18	19 33	19 48	20 03		20 18	20 33	20 48
Bromborough Rake	d		17 28	17 35	17 43	17 50	17 50	17 58	18 05	18 13	18 20		18 35	18 43	18 50	19 05	19 13	19 20	19 35	19 50	20 05		20 20	20 35	20 50
Bromborough	d		17 30	17 37	17 45	17 52	17 52	18 00	18 07	18 15	18 22		18 37	18 45	18 52	19 07	19 15	19 22	19 37	19 52	20 07		20 22	20 37	20 52
Eastham Rake	d		17 32	17 40	17 47	17 55	17 55	18 02	18 10	18 17	18 25		18 40	18 47	18 55	19 10	19 17	19 25	19 40	19 55	20 10		20 25	20 40	20 55
Hooton	d		17 34	17 42	17 49	17 57	17 57	18 04	18 12	18 19	18 27		18 42	18 49	18 57	19 12	19 19	19 27	19 42	19 57	20 12		20 27	20 42	20 57
Little Sutton	d		17 39		17 54			18 09		18 24				18 54			19 24			20 01			20 31		21 01
Overpool	d		17 41		17 56			18 11		18 26				18 56			19 26			20 03			20 33		21 03
Ellesmere Port	a		17 46		18 00			18 16		18 30				19 00			19 30			20 08			20 38		21 08
Capenhurst	d			17 47			18 02		18 17				18 47			19 17			19 47		20 17			20 47	
Bache	d			17 52		18 06	18 07		18 22		18 36		18 52		19 06	19 22		19 36	19 52		20 22			20 52	
Chester	a			17 57		18 11	18 11		18 26		18 39		18 56		19 10	19 26		19 41	19 56		20 26			20 56	

Table T107-F

Liverpool - Chester & Ellesmere Port

Mondays to Saturdays

21 May to 8 December

		ME SX	ME	ME	ME	ME	ME		ME	ME	ME	ME	ME	ME	ME	ME
Moorfields	d	20 27	20 41	20 56	21 11	21 26	21 41		21 56	22 11	22 26	22 41	22 56	23 11	23 26	23 41
Liverpool Lime Street	d	20 29	20 43	20 58	21 13	21 28	21 43		21 58	22 13	22 28	22 43	22 58	23 13	23 28	23 43
Liverpool Central	d	20 31	20 45	21 00	21 15	21 30	21 45		22 00	22 15	22 30	22 45	23 00	23 15	23 30	23 45
James Street	d	20 33	20 47	21 02	21 17	21 32	21 47		22 02	22 17	22 32	22 47	23 02	23 17	23 32	23 47
Hamilton Square	d	20 36	20 50	21 05	21 20	21 35	21 50		22 05	22 20	22 35	22 50	23 05	23 20	23 35	23 50
Birkenhead Central	d	20 38	20 52	21 07	21 22	21 37	21 52		22 07	22 22	22 37	22 52	23 07	23 22	23 37	23 52
Green Lane	d	20 40	20 54	21 09	21 24	21 39	21 54		22 09	22 24	22 39	22 54	23 09	23 24	23 39	23 54
Rock Ferry	d	20 43	20 57	21 12	21 27	21 42	21 57		22 12	22 27	22 42	22 57	23 12	23 27	23 42	23 57
Bebington	d	20 45	20 59	21 14	21 29	21 44	21 59		22 14	22 29	22 44	22 59	23 14	23 29	23 44	23 59
Port Sunlight	d	20 47	21 01	21 16	21 31	21 46	22 01		22 16	22 31	22 46	23 01	23 16	23 31	23 46	00 01
Spital	d	20 49	21 03	21 18	21 33	21 48	22 03		22 18	22 33	22 48	23 03	23 18	23 33	23 48	00 03
Bromborough Rake	d	20 51	21 05	21 20	21 35	21 50	22 05		22 20	22 35	22 50	23 05	23 20	23 35	23 50	00 05
Bromborough	d	20 53	21 07	21 22	21 37	21 52	22 07		22 22	22 37	22 52	23 07	23 22	23 37	23 52	00 07
Eastham Rake	d	20 56	21 10	21 25	21 40	21 55	22 10		22 25	22 40	22 55	23 10	23 25	23 40	23 55	00 10
Hooton	d	20 58	21 12	21 27	21 42	21 57	22 12		22 27	22 42	22 57	23 12	23 27	23 42	23 57	00 12
Little Sutton	d	21 02		21 31		22 01			22 31		23 01		23 31		00 01	
Overpool	d	21 04		21 33		22 03			22 33		23 03		23 33		00 03	
Ellesmere Port	a	21 09		21 38		22 08			22 38		23 08		23 37		00 07	
Capenhurst	d		21 17		21 47		22 17			22 47		23 17		23 47		00 17
Bache	d		21 22		21 52		22 22			22 52		23 22		23 52		00 22
Chester	a		21 26		21 56		22 26			22 56		23 26		23 56		00 26

Sundays

20 May to 2 December

		ME A	ME A	ME	ME	ME	ME		ME	ME	ME	ME		ME	ME	ME	ME
Moorfields	d			07 56	08 11	08 26	08 41		21 56	22 11	22 26	22 41		22 56	23 11	23 26	23 41
Liverpool Lime Street	d			07 58	08 13	08 28	08 43		21 58	22 13	22 28	22 43		22 58	23 13	23 28	23 43
Liverpool Central	d			08 00	08 15	08 30	08 45		22 00	22 15	22 30	22 45		23 00	23 15	23 30	23 45
James Street	d			08 02	08 17	08 32	08 47		22 02	22 17	22 32	22 47		23 02	23 17	23 32	23 47
Hamilton Square	d			08 05	08 20	08 35	08 50		22 05	22 20	22 35	22 50		23 05	23 20	23 35	23 50
Birkenhead Central	d			08 07	08 22	08 37	08 52		22 07	22 22	22 37	22 52		23 07	23 22	23 37	23 52
Green Lane	d			08 09	08 24	08 39	08 54	and at	22 09	22 24	22 39	22 54		23 09	23 24	23 39	23 54
Rock Ferry	d			08 12	08 27	08 42	08 57	the same	22 12	22 27	22 42	22 57		23 12	23 27	23 42	23 57
Bebington	d			08 14	08 29	08 44	08 59	minutes	22 14	22 29	22 44	22 59		23 14	23 29	23 44	23 59
Port Sunlight	d		00 01	08 16	08 31	08 46	09 01	past	22 16	22 31	22 46	23 01		23 16	23 31	23 46	00 01
Spital	d		00 03	08 18	08 33	08 48	09 03	each	22 18	22 33	22 48	23 03		23 18	23 33	23 48	00 03
Bromborough Rake	d		00 05	08 20	08 35	08 50	09 05	hour until	22 20	22 35	22 50	23 05		23 20	23 35	23 50	00 05
Bromborough	d		00 07	08 22	08 37	08 52	09 07		22 22	22 37	22 52	23 07		23 22	23 37	23 52	00 07
Eastham Rake	d		00 10	08 25	08 40	08 55	09 10		22 25	22 40	22 55	23 10		23 25	23 40	23 55	00 10
Hooton	d		00 12	08 27	08 42	08 57	09 12		22 27	22 42	22 57	23 12		23 27	23 42	23 57	00 12
Little Sutton	d	00 01		08 31		09 01			22 31		23 01			23 31		00 01	
Overpool	d	00 03		08 33		09 03			22 33		23 03			23 33		00 03	
Ellesmere Port	a	00 07		08 38		09 08			22 38		23 08			23 37		00 07	
Capenhurst	d		00 17		08 47		09 17			22 47		23 17			23 47		00 17
Bache	d		00 22		08 52		09 22			22 52		23 22			23 52		00 22
Chester	a		00 26		08 56		09 26			22 56		23 26			23 56		00 26

A not 20 May

Table T107-R

Mondays to Saturdays

21 May to 8 December

Chester, Ellesmere Port - Liverpool

Miles	Miles			ME	ME	ME	ME	ME	ME	ME	ME SX	ME SO	ME SX	ME SO	ME SX	ME SX	ME	ME SX	ME SO	ME SX	ME SX	ME SO	ME SO
0	—	**Chester**	d			05 55		06 30		07 00			07 22	07 30		07 37		07 52	08 00		08 07		08 15
1½	—	Bache	d			05 58		06 33		07 03			07 26	07 33		07 41		07 56	08 03		08 11		08 18
5¼	—	Capenhurst	d			06 04		06 39		07 09			07 32	07 39		07 47		08 02	08 09		08 17		08 24
—	0	**Ellesmere Port**	d				06 17		06 47		07 17	07 19			07 31		07 49			08 01		08 12	
—	1½	Overpool	d				06 20		06 50		07 20	07 22			07 34		07 52			08 04		08 15	
—	2½	Little Sutton	d				06 22		06 52		07 22	07 24			07 36		07 54			08 06		08 17	
8¼	4	Hooton	d	05 39	05 59	06 09	06 26	06 44	06 56	07 14	07 26	07 29	07 36	07 44	07 44	07 52	07 59	08 06	08 14	08 14	08 21	08 21	08 29
9¼	—	Eastham Rake	d	05 41	06 01	06 11	06 28	06 46	06 58	07 16	07 28	07 31	07 38	07 46	07 46	07 54	08 01	08 08	08 16	08 16	08 23	08 23	08 31
9¾	—	Bromborough	d	05 43	06 03	06 13	06 31	06 48	07 01	07 18	07 31	07 33	07 41	07 48	07 48	07 56	08 03	08 11	08 18	08 18	08 26	08 26	08 33
10½	—	Bromborough Rake	d	05 45	06 05	06 15	06 33	06 50	07 03	07 20	07 33	07 35	07 43	07 50	07 50	07 58	08 05	08 13	08 20	08 20	08 28	08 28	08 35
11¼	—	Spital	d	05 47	06 07	06 17	06 35	06 52	07 05	07 22	07 35	07 37	07 45	07 52	07 52	08 00	08 07	08 15	08 22	08 22	08 30	08 30	08 37
11¾	—	Port Sunlight	d	05 49	06 09	06 19	06 37	06 54	07 07	07 24	07 37	07 39	07 47	07 54	07 54	08 02	08 09	08 17	08 24	08 24	08 32	08 32	08 39
12¾	—	Bebington	d	05 51	06 11	06 21	06 39	06 56	07 09	07 26	07 39	07 41	07 49	07 56	07 56	08 04	08 11	08 19	08 26	08 26	08 34	08 34	08 41
13¾	—	Rock Ferry	d	05 54	06 14	06 24	06 42	06 59	07 12	07 29	07 42	07 44	07 52	07 59	07 59	08 07	08 14	08 22	08 29	08 29	08 37	08 37	08 44
14½	—	Green Lane	d	05 57	06 17	06 27	06 44	07 02	07 14	07 32	07 44	07 47	07 54	08 02	08 02	08 10	08 17	08 24	08 32	08 32	08 39	08 39	08 47
15	—	Birkenhead Central	d	05 59	06 19	06 34	06 49	07 04	07 19	07 34	07 47	07 49	07 57	08 04	08 04	08 12	08 19	08 27	08 34	08 34	08 42	08 42	08 49
15½	—	Hamilton Square	d	06 01	06 21	06 36	06 51	07 06	07 21	07 36	07 49	07 51	07 59	08 06	08 06	08 14	08 21	08 29	08 36	08 36	08 44	08 44	08 51
16¾	—	James Street	d	06 04	06 24	06 39	06 54	07 09	07 24	07 39	07 52	07 54	08 02	08 09	08 09	08 17	08 24	08 32	08 39	08 39	08 47	08 47	08 54
17	—	Moorfields 10	a	06 06	06 26	06 41	06 56	07 11	07 26	07 41	07 53	07 56	08 03	08 11	08 11	08 19	08 26	08 33	08 41	08 41	08 48	08 48	08 56
17½	—	Liverpool Lime Street 10	a	06 08	06 28	06 43	06 58	07 13	07 28	07 43	07 55	07 58	08 05	08 13	08 13	08 21	08 28	08 35	08 43	08 43	08 50	08 50	08 58
18	—	**Liverpool Central** 10	a	06 10	06 30	06 45	07 00	07 15	07 30	07 45	07 57	08 00	08 07	08 15	08 15	08 23	08 30	08 37	08 45	08 45	08 52	08 52	09 00

		ME SX	ME	ME SO	ME SX	ME	ME	ME	ME	ME	ME		ME	ME	ME	ME	ME	ME	ME	ME	ME	ME	ME
Chester	d		08 31			08 45	09 01		09 15	09 31			16 45	17 01		17 15	17 31		17 45	18 01		18 15	18 30
Bache	d		08 35			08 48	09 05		09 18	09 35			16 48	17 05		17 18	17 35		17 48	18 05		18 18	18 33
Capenhurst	d					08 54			09 24				16 54			17 24			17 54			18 24	18 39
Ellesmere Port	d	08 17		08 42	08 42			09 12			09 42				17 12			17 42			18 12		
Overpool	d	08 20		08 45	08 45			09 15			09 45				17 15			17 45			18 15		
Little Sutton	d	08 22		08 47	08 47			09 17			09 47				17 17			17 47			18 17		
Hooton	d	08 29	08 44	08 51	08 52	08 59	09 14	09 21	09 29	09 44	09 51	and at the same minutes past each hour until	16 59	17 14	17 21	17 29	17 44	17 51	17 59	18 14	18 21	18 29	18 44
Eastham Rake	d	08 31	08 46	08 53	08 54	09 01	09 16	09 23	09 31	09 46	09 53		17 01	17 16	17 23	17 31	17 46	17 53	18 01	18 16	18 23	18 31	18 46
Bromborough	d	08 33	08 48	08 56	08 56	09 03	09 18	09 26	09 33	09 48	09 56		17 03	17 18	17 26	17 33	17 48	17 56	18 03	18 18	18 26	18 33	18 48
Bromborough Rake	d	08 35	08 50	08 58	08 58	09 05	09 20	09 28	09 35	09 50	09 58		17 05	17 20	17 28	17 35	17 50	17 58	18 05	18 20	18 28	18 35	18 50
Spital	d	08 37	08 52	09 00	09 00	09 07	09 22	09 30	09 37	09 52	10 00		17 07	17 22	17 30	17 37	17 52	18 00	18 07	18 22	18 30	18 37	18 52
Port Sunlight	d	08 39	08 54	09 02	09 02	09 09	09 24	09 32	09 39	09 54	10 02		17 09	17 24	17 32	17 39	17 54	18 02	18 09	18 24	18 32	18 39	18 54
Bebington	d	08 41	08 56	09 04	09 04	09 11	09 26	09 34	09 41	09 56	10 04		17 11	17 26	17 34	17 41	17 56	18 04	18 11	18 26	18 34	18 41	18 56
Rock Ferry	d	08 44	08 59	09 07	09 07	09 14	09 29	09 37	09 44	09 59	10 07		17 14	17 29	17 37	17 44	17 59	18 07	18 14	18 29	18 37	18 44	18 59
Green Lane	d	08 47	09 02	09 09	09 10	09 17	09 32	09 39	09 47	10 02	10 09		17 17	17 32	17 39	17 47	18 02	18 09	18 17	18 32	18 39	18 47	19 02
Birkenhead Central	d	08 49	09 04	09 12	09 12	09 19	09 34	09 42	09 49	10 04	10 12		17 19	17 34	17 42	17 49	18 04	18 12	18 19	18 34	18 42	18 49	19 04
Hamilton Square	d	08 51	09 06	09 14	09 14	09 21	09 36	09 44	09 51	10 06	10 14		17 21	17 36	17 44	17 51	18 06	18 14	18 21	18 36	18 44	18 51	19 06
James Street	d	08 54	09 09	09 17	09 17	09 24	09 39	09 47	09 54	10 09	10 17		17 24	17 39	17 47	17 54	18 09	18 17	18 24	18 39	18 47	18 54	19 09
Moorfields 10	a	08 56	09 11	09 18	09 19	09 26	09 41	09 48	09 56	10 11	10 18		17 26	17 41	17 48	17 56	18 11	18 18	18 26	18 41	18 48	18 56	19 11
Liverpool Lime Street 10	a	08 58	09 13	09 20	09 21	09 28	09 43	09 50	09 58	10 13	10 20		17 28	17 43	17 50	17 58	18 13	18 20	18 28	18 43	18 50	18 58	19 13
Liverpool Central 10	a	09 00	09 15	09 22	09 23	09 30	09 45	09 52	10 00	10 15	10 22		17 30	17 45	17 52	18 00	18 15	18 22	18 30	18 45	18 52	19 00	19 15

		ME	ME	ME	ME	ME SO	ME SX	ME	ME	ME	ME	ME	ME	ME	ME	ME	ME	ME	ME	ME	ME	ME
Chester	d		19 00		19 30			20 00		20 30		21 00		21 30		22 00		22 30		23 00		23 30
Bache	d		19 03		19 33			20 03		20 33		21 03		21 33		22 03		22 33		23 03		23 33
Capenhurst	d		19 09		19 39			20 09		20 39		21 09		21 39		22 09		22 39		23 09		23 39
Ellesmere Port	d	18 46		19 16		19 49	19 49		20 19		20 49		21 19		21 49		22 19		22 49		23 19	
Overpool	d	18 49		19 19		19 52	19 52		20 22		20 52		21 22		21 52		22 22		22 52		23 22	
Little Sutton	d	18 51		19 21		19 54	19 54		20 24		20 54		21 24		21 54		22 24		22 54		23 24	
Hooton	d	18 59	19 14	19 29	19 44	19 59	20 00	20 14	20 29	20 44	20 59	21 14	21 29	21 44	21 59	22 14	22 29	22 44	22 59	23 14	23 29	23a44
Eastham Rake	d	19 01	19 16	19 31	19 46	20 01	20 02	20 16	20 31	20 46	21 01	21 16	21 31	21 46	22 01	22 16	22 31	22 46	23 01	23 16	23 31	
Bromborough	d	19 03	19 18	19 33	19 48	20 03	20 04	20 18	20 33	20 48	21 03	21 18	21 33	21 48	22 03	22 18	22 33	22 48	23 03	23 18	23 33	
Bromborough Rake	d	19 05	19 20	19 35	19 50	20 05	20 06	20 20	20 35	20 50	21 05	21 20	21 35	21 50	22 05	22 20	22 35	22 50	23 05	23 20	23 35	
Spital	d	19 07	19 22	19 37	19 52	20 07	20 08	20 22	20 37	20 52	21 07	21 22	21 37	21 52	22 07	22 22	22 37	22 52	23 07	23 22	23 37	
Port Sunlight	d	19 09	19 24	19 39	19 54	20 09	20 10	20 24	20 39	20 54	21 09	21 24	21 39	21 54	22 09	22 24	22 39	22 54	23 09	23 24	23 39	
Bebington	d	19 11	19 26	19 41	19 56	20 11	20 12	20 26	20 41	20 56	21 11	21 26	21 41	21 56	22 11	22 26	22 41	22 56	23 11	23 26	23 41	
Rock Ferry	d	19 14	19 29	19 44	19 59	20 14	20 15	20 29	20 44	20 59	21 14	21 29	21 44	21 59	22 14	22 29	22 44	22 59	23 14	23 29	23 44	
Green Lane	d	19 17	19 32	19 47	20 02	20 17	20 18	20 32	20 47	21 02	21 17	21 32	21 47	22 02	22 17	22 32	22 47	23 02	23 17	23 32	23 47	
Birkenhead Central	d	19 19	19 34	19 49	20 04	20 19	20 20	20 34	20 49	21 04	21 19	21 34	21 49	22 04	22 19	22 34	22 49	23 04	23 19	23 34	23 49	
Hamilton Square	d	19 21	19 36	19 51	20 06	20 21	20 22	20 36	20 51	21 06	21 21	21 36	21 51	22 06	22 21	22 36	22 51	23 06	23 21	23 36	23 51	
James Street	d	19 24	19 39	19 54	20 09	20 24	20 25	20 39	20 54	21 09	21 24	21 39	21 54	22 09	22 24	22 39	22 54	23 09	23 24	23 39	23 54	
Moorfields 10	a	19 26	19 41	19 56	20 11	20 26	20 27	20 41	20 56	21 11	21 26	21 41	21 56	22 11	22 26	22 41	22 56	23 11	23 26	23 41	23 56	
Liverpool Lime Street 10	a	19 28	19 43	19 58	20 13	20 28	20 29	20 43	20 58	21 13	21 28	21 43	21 58	22 13	22 28	22 43	22 58	23 13	23 28	23 43	23 58	
Liverpool Central 10	a	19 30	19 45	20 00	20 15	20 30	20 31	20 45	21 00	21 15	21 30	21 45	22 00	22 15	22 30	22 45	23 00	23 15	23 30	23 45	23 59	

Sundays

20 May to 2 December

		ME	ME	ME	ME	ME		ME	ME	ME	ME	ME	ME	ME	ME
Chester	d			08 00		08 30			22 00		22 30		23 00		23 30
Bache	d			08 03		08 33			22 03		22 33		23 03		23 33
Capenhurst	d			08 09		08 39			22 09		22 39		23 09		23 39
Ellesmere Port	d		07 49		08 19			21 49		22 19		22 49		23 19	
Overpool	d		07 52		08 22			21 52		22 22		22 52		23 22	
Little Sutton	d		07 54		08 24			21 54		22 24		22 54		23 24	
Hooton	d	07 44	07 59	08 14	08 29	08 44	and at the same minutes past each hour until	21 59	22 14	22 29	22 44	22 59	23 14	23 29	23a44
Eastham Rake	d	07 46	08 01	08 16	08 31	08 46		22 01	22 16	22 31	22 46	23 01	23 16	23 31	
Bromborough	d	07 48	08 03	08 18	08 33	08 48		22 03	22 18	22 33	22 48	23 03	23 18	23 33	
Bromborough Rake	d	07 50	08 05	08 20	08 35	08 50		22 05	22 20	22 35	22 50	23 05	23 20	23 35	
Spital	d	07 52	08 07	08 22	08 37	08 52		22 07	22 22	22 37	22 52	23 07	23 22	23 37	
Port Sunlight	d	07 54	08 09	08 24	08 39	08 54		22 09	22 24	22 39	22 54	23 09	23 24	23 39	
Bebington	d	07 56	08 11	08 26	08 41	08 56		22 11	22 26	22 41	22 56	23 11	23 26	23 41	
Rock Ferry	d	07 59	08 14	08 29	08 44	08 59		22 14	22 29	22 44	22 59	23 14	23 29	23 44	
Green Lane	d	08 02	08 17	08 32	08 47	09 02		22 17	22 32	22 47	23 02	23 17	23 32	23 47	
Birkenhead Central	d	08 04	08 19	08 34	08 49	09 04		22 19	22 34	22 49	23 04	23 19	23 34	23 49	
Hamilton Square	d	08 06	08 21	08 36	08 51	09 06		22 21	22 36	22 51	23 06	23 21	23 36	23 51	
James Street	d	08 09	08 24	08 39	08 54	09 09		22 24	22 39	22 54	23 09	23 24	23 39	23 54	
Moorfields 10	a	08 11	08 26	08 41	08 56	09 11		22 26	22 41	22 56	23 11	23 26	23 41	23 56	
Liverpool Lime Street 10	a	08 13	08 28	08 43	08 58	09 13		22 28	22 43	22 58	23 13	23 28	23 43	23 58	
Liverpool Central 10	a	08 15	08 30	08 45	09 00	09 15		22 30	22 45	23 00	23 15	23 30	23 45	23 59	

Table T109-F

Mondays to Fridays

21 May to 7 December

Ellesmere Port - Helsby

Miles			NT	NT	NT A
0	**Ellesmere Port**	d	06 19	06 53	19 10
2½	Stanlow & Thornton	d	06 23	06 57	19 14
3¼	Ince & Elton	d	06 26	07 00	19 17
5¼	**Helsby**	d	06a30	07 04	19 21
—	Warrington Bank Quay 81	a		07 21	19 42

Saturdays

26 May to 8 December

		NT	NT	NT A
Ellesmere Port	d	06 19	06 53	19 10
Stanlow & Thornton	d	06 23	06 57	19 14
Ince & Elton	d	06 26	07 00	19 17
Helsby	d	06a30	07 04	19 21
Warrington Bank Quay 81	a		07 21	19 42

A To Manchester Victoria

No Sunday Service

Table T109-R

Mondays to Fridays

21 May to 7 December

Helsby - Ellesmere Port

Miles			NT A	NT	NT
—	Warrington Bank Quay 81	d	05 42		
0	**Helsby**	d	06 00	06 33	18 50
2	Ince & Elton	d	06 03	06 36	18 53
2¾	Stanlow & Thornton	d	06 06	06 38	18 55
5¼	**Ellesmere Port**	a	06 12	06 45	19 01

Saturdays

26 May to 8 December

		NT A	NT	NT
Warrington Bank Quay 81	d	05 42		
Helsby	d	06 00	06 33	18 50
Ince & Elton	d	06 03	06 36	18 53
Stanlow & Thornton	d	06 06	06 38	18 55
Ellesmere Port	a	06 12	06 45	19 01

A From Liverpool Lime Street

No Sunday Service

Table T114-F

London - Amersham and Aylesbury

Mondays to Fridays

21 May to 7 December

Miles			CH A	CH MX B	CH MX C	CH D	CH E	CH E	CH D	CH	CH D	CH E	CH	CH D	CH E	CH	CH D	CH E	CH	CH D	CH E	CH	CH D
0	**London Marylebone**	⊖ d				06 33	06 33	06 52	06 52	07 26	07 57	07 57	08 27	08 57	08 57	09 27	09 57	09 57	10 27	10 57	10 57	11 27	11 57
9	Harrow-on-the-Hill §	⊖ d		00 09	00 09	06 45	06 45	07 04	07 04	07 39	08 09	08 09	08 39	09 09	09 09	09 39	10 09	10 09	10 39	11 09	11 09	11 39	12 09
17	Rickmansworth §	⊖ d		00 19	00 19	06 55	06 55	07 14	07 14	07 49	08 19	08 19	08 49	09 19	09 19	09 49	10 19	10 19	10 49	11 19	11 19	11 49	12 19
19¼	Chorleywood §	⊖ d		00 24	00 24	07 00	07 00	07 19	07 19	07 54	08 24	08 24	08 54	09 24	09 24	09 54	10 24	10 24	10 54	11 24	11 24	11 54	12 24
21½	Chalfont & Latimer §	⊖ d		00 28	00 28	07 04	07 04	07 23	07 23	07 58	08 28	08 28	08 58	09 28	09 28	09 58	10 28	10 28	10 58	11 28	11 28	11 58	12 28
23½	**Amersham** §	⊖ d	00 02	00 32	00 32	07 08	07 08	07 27	07 27	08 02	08 32	08 32	09 02	09 32	09 32	10 02	10 32	10 32	11 02	11 32	11 32	12 02	12 32
28¾	Great Missenden	d	00 09	00 39	00 39	07 15	07 15	07 34	07 34	08 09	08 39	08 39	09 09	09 39	09 39	10 09	10 39	10 39	11 09	11 39	11 39	12 09	12 39
33¼	Wendover	d	00 15	00 45	00 45	07 21	07 21	07 40	07 40	08 15	08 45	08 45	09 15	09 45	09 45	10 15	10 45	10 45	11 15	11 45	11 45	12 15	12 45
35¼	Stoke Mandeville	d	00 19	00 49	00 49	07 25	07 25	07 44	07 44	08 19	08 49	08 49	09 19	09 49	09 49	10 19	10 49	10 49	11 19	11 49	11 49	12 19	12 49
37¾	**Aylesbury**	d	00a29	00 54	00 54	07 30	07 30	07 53	07 56	08a28	08 54	08 54	09a29	09 54	09 54	10a29	10 54	10 54	11a29	11 54	11 54	12a31	12 54
40½	**Aylesbury Vale Parkway**	a		01 03	01 06	07 39	07 42	08 04	08 04		09 03	09 06		10 03	10 06		11 03	11 06		12 03	12 06		13 03

		CH E	CH	CH D	CH E	CH	CH D	CH E	CH	CH D	CH E	CH D	CH E	CH	CH D	CH E	CH	CH D	CH E	CH	CH D	CH E	CH
London Marylebone	⊖ d	11 57	12 27	12 57	12 57	13 27	13 57	13 57	14 27	14 57	14 57	15 27	15 27	15 56	16 12	16 12	16 27	16 42	16 42	17 11	17 30	17 30	17 40
Harrow-on-the-Hill §	⊖ d	12 09	12 39	13 09	13 09	13 39	14 09	14 09	14 39	15 09	15 09	15 39	15 39	16 09	16 24	16 24		16 54	16 54	17 23			17 54
Rickmansworth §	⊖ d	12 19	12 49	13 19	13 19	13 49	14 19	14 19	14 49	15 19	15 19	15 49	15 49	16 19	16 34	16 34		17 04	17 04				18 04
Chorleywood §	⊖ d	12 24	12 54	13 24	13 24	13 54	14 24	14 24	14 54	15 24	15 24	15 54	15 54	16 24	16 39	16 39		17 09	17 09	17 37			18 09
Chalfont & Latimer §	⊖ d	12 28	12 58	13 28	13 28	13 58	14 28	14 28	14 58	15 28	15 28	15 58	15 58	16 28	16 43	16 43		17 13	17 13	17 41			18 13
Amersham §	⊖ d	12 32	13 02	13 32	13 32	14 02	14 32	14 32	15 02	15 32	15 32	16 02	16 02	16 32	16 47	16 47	16 57	17 17	17 17	17 45			18 17
Great Missenden	d	12 39	13 09	13 39	13 39	14 09	14 39	14 39	15 09	15 39	15 39	16 09	16 09	16 39	16 54	16 54	17 04	17 24	17 24	17 52	18 06	18 06	18 24
Wendover	d	12 45	13 15	13 45	13 45	14 15	14 45	14 45	15 15	15 45	15 45	16 15	16 15	16 45	17 00	17 00	17 10	17 30	17 30	17 58	18 12	18 12	18 30
Stoke Mandeville	d	12 49	13 19	13 49	13 49	14 19	14 49	14 49	15 19	15 49	15 49	16 19	16 19	16 49	17 04	17 04	17 14	17 34	17 34	18 02	18 17	18 17	18 34
Aylesbury	d	12 54	13a29	13 54	13 54	14a29	14 54	14 54	15a32	15 54	15 54	16 26	16 26	16a58	17 09	17 09	17a21	17 39	17 39	18a12	18 24	18 24	18a42
Aylesbury Vale Parkway	a	13 06		14 03	14 06		15 03	15 06		16 03	16 06	16 34	16 37		17 18	17 21		17 48	17 51		18 32	18 35	

		CH D	CH E	CH	CH D	CH E	CH	CH D	CH E	CH	CH D	CH E	CH D	CH E	CH	CH D	CH E	CH	CH D	CH E	CH	CH D
London Marylebone	⊖ d	17 58	17 58	18 12	18 32	18 32	18 43	18 59	18 59	19 18	19 32	19 32	19 56	19 56	20 23	20 57	20 57	21 27	21 57	21 57	22 27	22 57
Harrow-on-the-Hill §	⊖ d			18 24			18 55	19 11	19 11		19 45	19 45	20 08	20 08	20 35	21 09	21 09	21 39	22 09	22 09	22 39	23 09
Rickmansworth §	⊖ d			18 34				19 22	19 22		19 55	19 55	20 18	20 18	20 45	21 19	21 19	21 49	22 19	22 19	22 49	23 19
Chorleywood §	⊖ d			18 39			19 10	19 26	19 26		20 00	20 00	20 23	20 23	20 50	21 24	21 24	21 54	22 24	22 24	22 54	23 24
Chalfont & Latimer §	⊖ d			18 43			19 14	19 30	19 30		20 04	20 04	20 27	20 27	20 54	21 28	21 28	21 58	22 28	22 28	22 58	23 28
Amersham §	⊖ d	18 29	18 29	18 47			19 18	19 34	19 34	19 51	20 08	20 08	20 31	20 31	20 58	21 32	21 32	22 02	22 32	22 32	23 02	23 32
Great Missenden	d	18 37	18 37	18 54	19 08	19 08	19 25	19 42	19 42	19 58	20 15	20 15	20 38	20 38	21 05	21 39	21 39	22 09	22 39	22 39	23 09	23 39
Wendover	d	18 43	18 43	19 00	19 14	19 14	19 31	19 49	19 49	20 04	20 21	20 21	20 44	20 44	21 11	21 45	21 45	22 15	22 45	22 45	23 15	23 45
Stoke Mandeville	d	18 47	18 47	19 04	19 19	19 19	19 35	19 54	19 54	20 09	20 25	20 25	20 48	20 48	21 15	21 49	21 49	22 19	22 49	22 49	23 19	23 49
Aylesbury	d	18 52	18 52	19a14	19 25	19 25	19a45	20 03	20 03	20a16	20 31	20 31	20 53	20 53	21a25	21 54	21 54	22a29	22 54	22 54	23a29	23 54
Aylesbury Vale Parkway	a	19 01	19 04		19 33	19 36		20 11	20 14		20 39	20 42	21 02	21 05		22 03	22 06		23 03	23 06		00 03

		CH E	CH	CH D	CH E
London Marylebone	⊖ d	22 57	23 27	23 57	23 57
Harrow-on-the-Hill §	⊖ d	23 09	23 39	00 09	00 09
Rickmansworth §	⊖ d	23 19	23 49	00 19	00 19
Chorleywood §	⊖ d	23 24	23 54	00 24	00 24
Chalfont & Latimer §	⊖ d	23 28	23 58	00 28	00 28
Amersham §	⊖ d	23 32	00 02	00 32	00 32
Great Missenden	d	23 39	00 09	00 39	00 39
Wendover	d	23 45	00 15	00 45	00 45
Stoke Mandeville	d	23 49	00 19	00 49	00 49
Aylesbury	d	23 54	00a26	00 54	00 54
Aylesbury Vale Parkway	a	00 06		01 03	01 06

Saturdays

26 May to 8 December

		CH A	CH F	CH G	CH	CH H	CH I	CH H	CH I	CH	CH H	CH I	CH	CH H	CH I	CH	CH H	CH I	CH	CH H	CH I	CH	CH H
London Marylebone	⊖ d					07 27	07 27	07 57	07 57	08 27	08 57	08 57	09 27	09 57	09 57	10 27	10 57	10 57	11 27	11 57	11 57	12 27	12 57
Harrow-on-the-Hill §	⊖ d		00 09	00 09		07 39	07 39	08 09	08 09	08 39	09 09	09 09	09 39	10 09	10 09	10 39	11 09	11 09	11 39	12 09	12 09	12 39	13 09
Rickmansworth §	⊖ d		00 19	00 19		07 49	07 49	08 19	08 19	08 49	09 19	09 19	09 49	10 19	10 19	10 49	11 19	11 19	11 49	12 19	12 19	12 49	13 19
Chorleywood §	⊖ d		00 24	00 24		07 54	07 54	08 24	08 24	08 54	09 24	09 24	09 54	10 24	10 24	10 54	11 24	11 24	11 54	12 24	12 24	12 54	13 24
Chalfont & Latimer §	⊖ d		00 28	00 28		07 58	07 58	08 28	08 28	08 58	09 28	09 28	09 58	10 28	10 28	10 58	11 28	11 28	11 58	12 28	12 28	12 58	13 28
Amersham §	⊖ d	00 02	00 32	00 32	07 02	08 02	08 02	08 32	08 32	09 02	09 32	09 32	10 02	10 32	10 32	11 02	11 32	11 32	12 02	12 32	12 32	13 02	13 32
Great Missenden	d	00 09	00 39	00 39	07 09	08 09	08 09	08 39	08 39	09 09	09 39	09 39	10 09	10 39	10 39	11 09	11 39	11 39	12 09	12 39	12 39	13 09	13 39
Wendover	d	00 15	00 45	00 45	07 15	08 15	08 15	08 45	08 45	09 15	09 45	09 45	10 15	10 45	10 45	11 15	11 45	11 45	12 15	12 45	12 45	13 15	13 45
Stoke Mandeville	d	00 19	00 49	00 49	07 19	08 19	08 19	08 49	08 49	09 19	09 49	09 49	10 19	10 49	10 49	11 19	11 49	11 49	12 19	12 49	12 49	13 19	13 49
Aylesbury	d	00a26	00 54	00 54	07a26	08 24	08 24	08 54	08 54	09a26	09 54	09 54	10a26	10 54	10 54	11a26	11 54	11 54	12a26	12 54	12 54	13a26	13 54
Aylesbury Vale Parkway	a		01 03	01 06		08 33	08 36	09 03	09 06		10 03	10 06		11 03	11 06		12 03	12 06		13 03	13 06		14 03

§ London Underground Limited (Metropolitan Line) services operate between Harrow-on-the-Hill, Rickmansworth, Chorleywood, Chalfont & Latimer and Amersham
A From London Marylebone
B until 5 October. From London Marylebone
C from 9 October. From London Marylebone
D until 5 October
E from 8 October
F until 6 October. From London Marylebone
G from 13 October. From London Marylebone
H until 6 October
I from 13 October

For additional services between London and Aylesbury refer to Table T115

Table T114-F

London - Amersham and Aylesbury

Saturdays

26 May to 8 December

		CH A	CH	CH B	CH A	CH	CH B	CH A	CH	CH B	CH A	CH	CH B	CH A	CH	CH B	CH A	CH	CH B	CH A	CH	CH B
London Marylebone	⊖ d	12 57	13 27	13 57	13 57	14 27	14 57	14 57	15 27	15 57	15 57	16 27	16 57	16 57	17 27	17 57	17 57	18 27	18 57	18 57	19 27	19 57
Harrow-on-the-Hill §	⊖ d	13 09	13 39	14 09	14 09	14 39	15 09	15 09	15 39	16 09	16 09	16 39	17 09	17 09	17 39	18 09	18 09	18 39	19 09	19 09	19 39	20 09
Rickmansworth §	⊖ d	13 19	13 49	14 19	14 19	14 49	15 19	15 19	15 49	16 19	16 19	16 49	17 19	17 19	17 49	18 19	18 19	18 49	19 19	19 19	19 49	20 19
Chorleywood §	⊖ d	13 24	13 54	14 24	14 24	14 54	15 24	15 24	15 54	16 24	16 24	16 54	17 24	17 24	17 54	18 24	18 24	18 54	19 24	19 24	19 54	20 24
Chalfont & Latimer §	⊖ d	13 28	13 58	14 28	14 28	14 58	15 28	15 28	15 58	16 28	16 28	16 58	17 28	17 28	17 58	18 28	18 28	18 58	19 28	19 28	19 58	20 28
Amersham §	⊖ d	13 32	14 02	14 32	14 32	15 02	15 32	15 32	16 02	16 32	16 32	17 02	17 32	17 32	18 02	18 32	18 32	19 02	19 32	19 32	20 02	20 32
Great Missenden	d	13 39	14 09	14 39	14 39	15 09	15 39	15 39	16 09	16 39	16 39	17 09	17 39	17 39	18 09	18 39	18 39	19 09	19 39	19 39	20 09	20 39
Wendover	d	13 45	14 15	14 45	14 45	15 15	15 45	15 45	16 15	16 45	16 45	17 15	17 45	17 45	18 15	18 45	18 45	19 15	19 45	19 45	20 15	20 45
Stoke Mandeville	d	13 49	14 19	14 49	14 49	15 19	15 49	15 49	16 19	16 49	16 49	17 19	17 49	17 49	18 19	18 49	18 49	19 19	19 49	19 49	20 19	20 49
Aylesbury	d	13 54	14a26	14 54	14 54	15a26	15 54	15 54	16a26	16 54	16 54	17a29	17 54	17 54	18a26	18 54	18 54	19a29	19 54	19 54	20a26	20 54
Aylesbury Vale Parkway	a	14 06		15 03	15 06		16 03	16 06		17 03	17 06		18 03	18 06		19 03	19 06		20 03	20 06		21 03

		CH A	CH	CH B	CH A	CH	CH B	CH A	CH B	CH A	CH B	CH A	CH	CH
London Marylebone	⊖ d	19 57	20 27	20 57	20 57	21 27	21 57	21 57	22 27	22 27	22 57	22 57	23 27	23 57
Harrow-on-the-Hill §	⊖ d	20 09	20 39	21 09	21 09	21 39	22 09	22 09	22 39	22 39	23 09	23 09	23 39	00 09
Rickmansworth §	⊖ d	20 19	20 49	21 19	21 19	21 49	22 19	22 19	22 49	22 49	23 19	23 19	23 49	00 19
Chorleywood §	⊖ d	20 24	20 54	21 24	21 24	21 54	22 24	22 24	22 54	22 54	23 24	23 24	23 54	00 24
Chalfont & Latimer §	⊖ d	20 28	20 58	21 28	21 28	21 58	22 28	22 28	22 58	22 58	23 28	23 28	23 58	00 28
Amersham §	⊖ d	20 32	21 02	21 32	21 32	22 02	22 32	22 32	23 02	23 02	23 32	23 32	00 02	00 32
Great Missenden	d	20 39	21 09	21 39	21 39	22 09	22 39	22 39	23 09	23 09	23 39	23 39	00 09	00 39
Wendover	d	20 45	21 15	21 45	21 45	22 15	22 45	22 45	23 15	23 15	23 45	23 45	00 15	00 45
Stoke Mandeville	d	20 49	21 19	21 49	21 49	22 19	22 49	22 49	23 19	23 19	23 49	23 49	00 19	00 49
Aylesbury	d	20 54	21a29	21 54	21 54	22a26	22 54	22 54	23 24	23 24	23 54	23 54	00a26	00a56
Aylesbury Vale Parkway	a	21 06		22 03	22 06		23 03	23 06	23 33	23 36	00 03	00 06		

Sundays

20 May to 2 December

		CH C	CH C	CH D	CH E	CH D	CH E	CH D	CH E	CH D	CH E	CH D	CH E	CH D	CH E	CH D	CH E	CH D	CH E	CH	CH D	CH E	CH
London Marylebone	⊖ d			07 57	07 57	08 57	08 57	09 57	09 57	10 57	10 57	11 57	11 57	12 57	12 57	13 57	13 57	14 57	14 57	15 27	15 57	15 57	16 27
Harrow-on-the-Hill §	⊖ d		00 09	08 09	08 09	09 09	09 09	10 09	10 09	11 09	11 09	12 09	12 09	13 09	13 09	14 09	14 09	15 09	15 09	15 39	16 09	16 09	16 39
Rickmansworth §	⊖ d		00 19	08 19	08 19	09 19	09 19	10 19	10 19	11 19	11 19	12 19	12 19	13 19	13 19	14 19	14 19	15 19	15 19	15 49	16 19	16 19	16 49
Chorleywood §	⊖ d		00 24	08 24	08 24	09 24	09 24	10 24	10 24	11 24	11 24	12 24	12 24	13 24	13 24	14 24	14 24	15 24	15 24	15 54	16 24	16 24	16 54
Chalfont & Latimer §	⊖ d		00 28	08 28	08 28	09 28	09 28	10 28	10 28	11 28	11 28	12 28	12 28	13 28	13 28	14 28	14 28	15 28	15 28	15 58	16 28	16 28	16 58
Amersham §	⊖ d	00 02	00 32	08 32	08 32	09 32	09 32	10 32	10 32	11 32	11 32	12 32	12 32	13 32	13 32	14 32	14 32	15 32	15 32	16 02	16 32	16 32	17 02
Great Missenden	d	00 09	00 39	08 39	08 39	09 39	09 39	10 39	10 39	11 39	11 39	12 39	12 39	13 39	13 39	14 39	14 39	15 39	15 39	16 09	16 39	16 39	17 09
Wendover	d	00 15	00 45	08 45	08 45	09 45	09 45	10 45	10 45	11 45	11 45	12 45	12 45	13 45	13 45	14 45	14 45	15 45	15 45	16 15	16 45	16 45	17 15
Stoke Mandeville	d	00 19	00 49	08 49	08 49	09 49	09 49	10 49	10 49	11 49	11 49	12 49	12 49	13 49	13 49	14 49	14 49	15 49	15 49	16 19	16 49	16 49	17 19
Aylesbury	d	00a26	00a56	08 54	08 54	09 54	09 54	10 54	10 54	11 54	11 54	12 54	12 54	13 54	13 54	14 54	14 54	15 54	15 54	16a26	16 54	16 54	17a26
Aylesbury Vale Parkway	a			09 03	09 06	10 03	10 06	11 03	11 06	12 03	12 06	13 03	13 06	14 03	14 06	15 03	15 06	16 03	16 06		17 03	17 06	

		CH D	CH E	CH	CH D	CH E	CH	CH D	CH E	CH	CH D	CH E	CH	CH D	CH E	CH D	CH E	CH	CH D	CH E	CH	CH
London Marylebone	⊖ d	16 57	16 57	17 27	17 57	17 57	18 27	18 57	18 57	19 27	19 57	19 57	20 27	20 57	20 57	21 27	21 27	21 57	22 27	22 27	22 57	23 27
Harrow-on-the-Hill §	⊖ d	17 09	17 09	17 39	18 09	18 09	18 39	19 09	19 09	19 39	20 09	20 09	20 39	21 09	21 09	21 39	21 39	22 09	22 39	22 39	23 09	23 39
Rickmansworth §	⊖ d	17 19	17 19	17 49	18 19	18 19	18 49	19 19	19 19	19 49	20 19	20 19	20 49	21 19	21 19	21 49	21 49	22 19	22 49	22 49	23 19	23 49
Chorleywood §	⊖ d	17 24	17 24	17 54	18 24	18 24	18 54	19 24	19 24	19 54	20 24	20 24	20 54	21 24	21 24	21 54	21 54	22 24	22 54	22 54	23 24	23 54
Chalfont & Latimer §	⊖ d	17 28	17 28	17 58	18 28	18 28	18 58	19 28	19 28	19 58	20 28	20 28	20 58	21 28	21 28	21 58	21 58	22 28	22 58	22 58	23 28	23 58
Amersham §	⊖ d	17 32	17 32	18 02	18 32	18 32	19 02	19 32	19 32	20 02	20 32	20 32	21 02	21 32	21 32	22 02	22 02	22 32	23 02	23 02	23 32	00 02
Great Missenden	d	17 39	17 39	18 09	18 39	18 39	19 09	19 39	19 39	20 09	20 39	20 39	21 09	21 39	21 39	22 09	22 09	22 39	23 09	23 09	23 39	00 09
Wendover	d	17 45	17 45	18 15	18 45	18 45	19 15	19 45	19 45	20 15	20 45	20 45	21 15	21 45	21 45	22 15	22 15	22 45	23 15	23 15	23 45	00 15
Stoke Mandeville	d	17 49	17 49	18 19	18 49	18 49	19 19	19 49	19 49	20 19	20 49	20 49	21 19	21 49	21 49	22 19	22 19	22 49	23 19	23 19	23 49	00 19
Aylesbury	d	17 54	17 54	18a26	18 54	18 54	19a29	19 54	19 54	20a26	20 54	20 54	21a29	21 54	21 54	22 24	22 24	22a56	23 24	23 24	23a56	00a26
Aylesbury Vale Parkway	a	18 03	18 06		19 03	19 06		20 03	20 06		21 03	21 06		22 03	22 06	22 33	22 36		23 33	23 36		

§ London Underground Limited (Metropolitan Line) services operate between Harrow-on-the-Hill, Rickmansworth, Chorleywood, Chalfont & Latimer and Amersham
A from 13 October
B until 6 October
C not 20 May. From London Marylebone
D until 30 September
E from 7 October

For additional services between London and Aylesbury refer to Table T115

Table T114-R

Mondays to Fridays

21 May to 7 December

Aylesbury and Amersham - London

Miles			CH A	CH B	CH A	CH B	CH A	CH B	CH A	CH B	CH A	CH B	CH A	CH B	CH A	CH B	CH A	CH B	CH A	CH B	CH A	CH B	CH A
0	Aylesbury Vale Parkway	d	05 13	05 16	05 41	05 44			06 16	06 19			06 50	06 53			07 22	07 25			07 48	07 51	08 09
2¼	Aylesbury	d	05 18	05 21	05 46	05 49	06 04	06 07	06 21	06 24	06 35	06 38	06 55	06 58	07 04	07 10	07 27	07 30	07 38	07 41	07 59	08 02	08 14
5¼	Stoke Mandeville	d	05 23	05 26	05 51	05 54	06 08	06 11	06 26	06 29	06 40	06 43	07 00	07 03	07 09	07 15	07 32	07 35	07 43	07 46	08 04	08 07	08 19
7¼	Wendover	d	05 27	05 30	05 55	05 58	06 12	06 15	06 30	06 33	06 44	06 47	07 04	07 07	07 13	07 19	07 36	07 39	07 47	07 50	08 08	08 11	08 23
11¾	Great Missenden	d	05 33	05 36	06 01	06 04	06 18	06 21	06 37	06 40	06 50	06 53	07 11	07 14	07 19	07 25	07 43	07 46	07 53	07 56	08 15	08 18	08 29
17	Amersham §	⊖ d	05 40	05 43	06 08	06 11	06 25	06 28	06 44	06 47	06 57	07 00	07 18	07 21	07 26	07 32	07 50	07 53	08 00	08 03	08 22	08 25	08 36
19	Chalfont & Latimer §	⊖ d			06 12	06 15	06 29	06 32			07 01	07 04			07 30	07 36			08 04	08 07			08 40
21¼	Chorleywood §	⊖ d			06 17	06 18	06 34	06 35			07 06	07 07			07 35	07 39			08 09	08 10			08 45
23¼	Rickmansworth §	⊖ d			06 23	06 23	06 40	06 40			07 12	07 12							08 15	08 15			
31¼	Harrow-on-the-Hill §	⊖ d	06 01	06 01	06 34	06 34	06 51	06 51			07 23	07 23			07 50	07 53			08 26	08 26			09 01
40¼	London Marylebone	⊖ a	06 16	06 16	06 49	06 49	07 07	07 07	07 22	07 22	07 38	07 38	07 53	07 53	08 06	08 09	08 26	08 26	08 41	08 41	09 00	09 00	09 17

		CH B	CH A	CH B	CH A	CH B	CH A	CH B	CH A	CH B	CH A	CH B	CH A	CH B	CH A	CH B	CH A	CH B	CH A	CH B	CH A	CH B
Aylesbury Vale Parkway	d	08 12	08 36	08 39			09 15	09 18			10 10	10 13			11 10	11 13			12 10	12 13		
Aylesbury	d	08 17	08 41	08 44	08 59	09 02	09 20	09 23	09 42	09 48	10 15	10 18	10 45	10 48	11 15	11 18	11 45	11 48	12 15	12 18	12 45	12 48
Stoke Mandeville	d	08 22	08 45	08 48	09 03	09 06	09 24	09 27	09 46	09 52	10 19	10 22	10 49	10 52	11 19	11 22	11 49	11 52	12 19	12 22	12 49	12 52
Wendover	d	08 26	08 49	08 52	09 07	09 10	09 28	09 31	09 50	09 56	10 23	10 26	10 53	10 56	11 23	11 26	11 53	11 56	12 23	12 26	12 53	12 56
Great Missenden	d	08 32	08 55	08 58	09 13	09 16	09 34	09 37	09 56	10 02	10 29	10 32	10 59	11 02	11 29	11 32	11 59	12 02	12 29	12 32	12 59	13 02
Amersham §	⊖ d	08 39	09 02	09 05	09 20	09 23	09 41	09 44	10 03	10 09	10 36	10 39	11 06	11 09	11 36	11 39	12 06	12 09	12 36	12 39	13 06	13 09
Chalfont & Latimer §	⊖ d	08 43	09 06	09 09	09 24	09 27	09 46	09 48	10 07	10 13	10 40	10 43	11 10	11 13	11 40	11 43	12 10	12 13	12 40	12 43	13 10	13 13
Chorleywood §	⊖ d	08 46	09 11	09 12	09 29	09 30	09 50	09 52	10 12	10 16	10 45	10 46	11 15	11 16	11 45	11 46	12 15	12 16	12 45	12 46	13 15	13 16
Rickmansworth §	⊖ d		09 17	09 17	09 35	09 35	09 56	09 56	10 18	10 21	10 51	10 51	11 21	11 21	11 51	11 51	12 21	12 21	12 51	12 51	13 21	13 21
Harrow-on-the-Hill §	⊖ d	09 01	09 28	09 28	09 46	09 46	10 08	10 08	10 29	10 32	11 02	11 02	11 32	11 32	12 02	12 02	12 32	12 32	13 02	13 02	13 32	13 32
London Marylebone	⊖ a	09 17	09 44	09 44	10 04	10 04	10 23	10 23	10 46	10 49	11 20	11 20	11 50	11 50	12 20	12 20	12 50	12 50	13 20	13 20	13 50	13 50

		CH A	CH B	CH A	CH B	CH A	CH B	CH A	CH B	CH A	CH B	CH A	CH B	CH A	CH B	CH A	CH B	CH A	CH B	CH A	CH B	CH	CH A
Aylesbury Vale Parkway	d	13 10	13 13			14 10	14 13			15 10	15 13			16 10	16 13	16 40	16 43			17 34	17 34	18 06	
Aylesbury	d	13 15	13 18	13 45	13 48	14 15	14 18	14 45	14 48	15 15	15 18	15 45	15 48	16 15	16 18	16 45	16 48	17 12	17 15	17 47	17 50	18a11	18 17
Stoke Mandeville	d	13 19	13 22	13 49	13 52	14 19	14 22	14 49	14 52	15 19	15 22	15 49	15 52	16 19	16 22	16 49	16 52	17 16	17 19	17 51	17 54		18 22
Wendover	d	13 23	13 26	13 53	13 56	14 23	14 26	14 53	14 56	15 23	15 26	15 53	15 56	16 23	16 26	16 53	16 56	17 20	17 23	17 55	17 58		18 26
Great Missenden	d	13 29	13 32	13 59	14 02	14 29	14 32	14 59	15 02	15 29	15 32	15 59	16 02	16 29	16 32	16 59	17 02	17 26	17 29	18 01	18 04		18 32
Amersham §	⊖ d	13 36	13 39	14 06	14 09	14 36	14 39	15 06	15 09	15 36	15 39	16 06	16 09	16 36	16 39	17 06	17 09	17 33	17 36	18 08	18 11		18 39
Chalfont & Latimer §	⊖ d	13 40	13 43	14 10	14 13	14 40	14 43	15 10	15 13	15 40	15 43	16 10	16 13	16 40	16 43	17 10	17 13	17 37	17 40	18 12	18 15		18 43
Chorleywood §	⊖ d	13 45	13 46	14 15	14 16	14 45	14 46	15 15	15 16	15 45	15 46	16 15	16 16	16 45	16 46	17 15	17 16	17 42	17 43	18 17	18 18		18 48
Rickmansworth §	⊖ d	13 51	13 51	14 21	14 21	14 51	14 51	15 21	15 21	15 51	15 51	16 21	16 21	16 51	16 51	17 21	17 21	17 48	17 48	18 23	18 23		18 54
Harrow-on-the-Hill §	⊖ d	14 02	14 02	14 32	14 32	15 02	15 02	15 32	15 32	16 02	16 02	16 32	16 32	17 02	17 02	17 32	17 32	17 59	17 59	18 34	18 34		19 05
London Marylebone	⊖ a	14 20	14 20	14 50	14 50	15 20	15 20	15 50	15 50	16 20	16 20	16 50	16 50	17 20	17 20	17 48	17 48	18 15	18 15	18 50	18 50		19 20

		CH B	CH A	CH B	CH A	CH B	CH A	CH B	CH FO C	CH B	CH FX A	CH A	CH B	CH A	CH B	CH A	CH B	CH A	CH B
Aylesbury Vale Parkway	d		18 39	18 42			19 40	19 43				20 45	20 48	21 10	21 13				
Aylesbury	d	18 20	18 44	18 47	19 15	19 18	19 45	19 48	20 18	20 21	20 21	20 50	20 53	21 15	21 18	21 45	21 48	22 45	22 48
Stoke Mandeville	d	18 25	18 48	18 51	19 19	19 22	19 49	19 52	20 22	20 25	20 25	20 54	20 57	21 19	21 22	21 49	21 52	22 49	22 52
Wendover	d	18 29	18 52	18 55	19 23	19 26	19 53	19 56	20 26	20 29	20 29	20 58	21 01	21 23	21 26	21 53	21 56	22 53	22 56
Great Missenden	d	18 35	18 58	19 01	19 29	19 32	19 59	20 02	20 32	20 35	20 35	21 04	21 07	21 29	21 32	21 59	22 02	22 59	23 02
Amersham §	⊖ d	18 42	19 05	19 08	19 36	19 39	20 06	20 09	20 39	20 42	20 42	21 11	21 14	21 36	21 39	22 06	22 09	23 06	23 09
Chalfont & Latimer §	⊖ d	18 46	19 09	19 12	19 40	19 43	20 10	20 13	20 43	20 46	20 46	21 15	21 18	21 40	21 43	22 10	22 13	23 10	23 13
Chorleywood §	⊖ d	18 49	19 14	19 15	19 45	19 46	20 15	20 16	20 48	20 49	20 51	21 20	21 21	21 45	21 46	22 15	22 16	23 15	23 16
Rickmansworth §	⊖ d	18 54	19 20	19 20	19 51	19 51	20 21	20 21	20 54	20 54	20 57	21 26	21 26	21 51	21 51	22 21	22 21	23 21	23 21
Harrow-on-the-Hill §	⊖ d	19 05	19 31	19 31	20 02	20 02	20 32	20 32	21 05	21 05	21 08	21 37	21 37	22 02	22 02	22 32	22 32	23 32	23 32
London Marylebone	⊖ a	19 20	19 48	19 48	20 20	20 20	20 49	20 49	21 21	21 21	21 24	21 53	21 53	22 19	22 19	22 48	22 48	23 50	23 50

Saturdays

26 May to 8 December

		CH D	CH E	CH D	CH E	CH D	CH E	CH D	CH E	CH D	CH E	CH D	CH E	CH D	CH E	CH D	CH E	CH D	CH E	CH D	CH E	CH D	CH E
Aylesbury Vale Parkway	d	06 10	06 13			07 10	07 13			08 10	08 13			09 10	09 13			10 10	10 13			11 10	11 13
Aylesbury	d	06 15	06 18	06 45	06 48	07 15	07 18	07 45	07 48	08 15	08 18	08 45	08 48	09 15	09 18	09 45	09 48	10 15	10 18	10 45	10 48	11 15	11 18
Stoke Mandeville	d	06 19	06 22	06 49	06 52	07 19	07 22	07 49	07 52	08 19	08 22	08 49	08 52	09 19	09 22	09 49	09 52	10 19	10 22	10 49	10 52	11 19	11 22
Wendover	d	06 23	06 26	06 53	06 56	07 23	07 26	07 53	07 56	08 23	08 26	08 53	08 56	09 23	09 26	09 53	09 56	10 23	10 26	10 53	10 56	11 23	11 26
Great Missenden	d	06 29	06 32	06 59	07 02	07 29	07 32	07 59	08 02	08 29	08 32	08 59	09 02	09 29	09 32	09 59	10 02	10 29	10 32	10 59	11 02	11 29	11 32
Amersham §	⊖ d	06 36	06 39	07 06	07 09	07 36	07 39	08 06	08 09	08 36	08 39	09 06	09 09	09 36	09 39	10 06	10 09	10 36	10 39	11 06	11 09	11 36	11 39
Chalfont & Latimer §	⊖ d	06 40	06 43	07 10	07 13	07 40	07 43	08 10	08 13	08 40	08 43	09 10	09 13	09 40	09 43	10 10	10 13	10 40	10 43	11 10	11 13	11 40	11 43
Chorleywood §	⊖ d	06 45	06 46	07 15	07 16	07 45	07 46	08 15	08 16	08 45	08 46	09 15	09 16	09 45	09 46	10 15	10 16	10 45	10 46	11 15	11 16	11 45	11 46
Rickmansworth §	⊖ d	06 51	06 51	07 21	07 21	07 51	07 51	08 21	08 21	08 51	08 51	09 21	09 21	09 51	09 51	10 21	10 21	10 51	10 51	11 21	11 21	11 51	11 51
Harrow-on-the-Hill §	⊖ d	07 02	07 02	07 32	07 32	08 02	08 02	08 32	08 32	09 02	09 02	09 32	09 32	10 02	10 02	10 32	10 32	11 02	11 02	11 32	11 32	12 02	12 02
London Marylebone	⊖ a	07 18	07 18	07 50	07 50	08 18	08 18	08 50	08 50	09 20	09 20	09 50	09 50	10 20	10 20	10 50	10 50	11 20	11 20	11 50	11 50	12 20	12 20

		CH D	CH E	CH D	CH E	CH D	CH E	CH D	CH E	CH D	CH E	CH D	CH E	CH D	CH E	CH D	CH E	CH D	CH E	CH D	CH E	CH D	CH E
Aylesbury Vale Parkway	d			12 10	12 13			13 10	13 13			14 10	14 13			15 10	15 13			16 10	16 13		
Aylesbury	d	11 45	11 48	12 15	12 18	12 45	12 48	13 15	13 18	13 45	13 48	14 15	14 18	14 45	14 48	15 15	15 18	15 45	15 48	16 15	16 18	16 45	16 48
Stoke Mandeville	d	11 49	11 52	12 19	12 22	12 49	12 52	13 19	13 22	13 49	13 52	14 19	14 22	14 49	14 52	15 19	15 22	15 49	15 52	16 19	16 22	16 49	16 52
Wendover	d	11 53	11 56	12 23	12 26	12 53	12 56	13 23	13 26	13 53	13 56	14 23	14 26	14 53	14 56	15 23	15 26	15 53	15 56	16 23	16 26	16 53	16 56
Great Missenden	d	11 59	12 02	12 29	12 32	12 59	13 02	13 29	13 32	13 59	14 02	14 29	14 32	14 59	15 02	15 29	15 32	15 59	16 02	16 29	16 32	16 59	17 02
Amersham §	⊖ d	12 06	12 09	12 36	12 39	13 06	13 09	13 36	13 39	14 06	14 09	14 36	14 39	15 06	15 09	15 36	15 39	16 06	16 09	16 36	16 39	17 06	17 09
Chalfont & Latimer §	⊖ d	12 10	12 13	12 40	12 43	13 10	13 13	13 40	13 43	14 10	14 13	14 40	14 43	15 10	15 13	15 40	15 43	16 10	16 13	16 40	16 43	17 10	17 13
Chorleywood §	⊖ d	12 15	12 16	12 45	12 46	13 15	13 16	13 45	13 46	14 15	14 16	14 45	14 46	15 15	15 16	15 45	15 46	16 15	16 16	16 45	16 46	17 15	17 16
Rickmansworth §	⊖ d	12 21	12 21	12 51	12 51	13 21	13 21	13 51	13 51	14 21	14 21	14 51	14 51	15 21	15 21	15 51	15 51	16 21	16 21	16 51	16 51	17 21	17 21
Harrow-on-the-Hill §	⊖ d	12 32	12 32	13 02	13 02	13 32	13 32	14 02	14 02	14 32	14 32	15 02	15 02	15 32	15 32	16 02	16 02	16 32	16 32	17 02	17 02	17 32	17 32
London Marylebone	⊖ a	12 50	12 50	13 20	13 20	13 50	13 50	14 18	14 18	14 50	14 50	15 20	15 20	15 50	15 50	16 20	16 20	16 50	16 50	17 20	17 20	17 50	17 50

§ London Underground Limited (Metropolitan Line) services operate between Harrow-on-the-Hill, Rickmansworth, Chorleywood, Chalfont & Latimer and Amersham

A from 8 October
B until 5 October
C from 12 October
D from 13 October
E until 6 October

For additional services between London and Aylesbury refer to Table T115

Table T114-R

Saturdays

26 May to 8 December

Aylesbury and Amersham - London

		CH A	CH B	CH A	CH B	CH A	CH B	CH A	CH B	CH A	CH B	CH A	CH B	CH A	CH B	CH A	CH B	CH A	CH B	CH A	CH B	CH A	CH B
Aylesbury Vale Parkway	d	17 10	17 13			18 10	18 13			19 10	19 13			20 10	20 13			21 10	21 13			22 10	22 13
Aylesbury	d	17 15	17 18	17 45	17 48	18 15	18 18	18 45	18 48	19 15	19 18	19 45	19 48	20 15	20 18	20 45	20 48	21 15	21 18	21 45	21 48	22 15	22 18
Stoke Mandeville	d	17 19	17 22	17 49	17 52	18 19	18 22	18 49	18 52	19 19	19 22	19 49	19 52	20 19	20 22	20 49	20 52	21 19	21 22	21 49	21 52	22 19	22 22
Wendover	d	17 23	17 26	17 53	17 56	18 23	18 26	18 53	18 56	19 23	19 26	19 53	19 56	20 23	20 26	20 53	20 56	21 23	21 26	21 53	21 56	22 23	22 26
Great Missenden	d	17 29	17 32	17 59	18 02	18 29	18 32	18 59	19 02	19 29	19 32	19 59	20 02	20 29	20 32	20 59	21 02	21 29	21 32	21 59	22 02	22 29	22 32
Amersham §	⊖ d	17 36	17 39	18 06	18 09	18 36	18 39	19 06	19 09	19 36	19 39	20 06	20 09	20 36	20 39	21 06	21 09	21 36	21 39	22 06	22 09	22 36	22 39
Chalfont & Latimer §	⊖ d	17 40	17 43	18 10	18 13	18 40	18 43	19 10	19 13	19 40	19 43	20 10	20 13	20 40	20 43	21 10	21 13	21 40	21 43	22 10	22 13	22 40	22 43
Chorleywood §	⊖ d	17 45	17 46	18 15	18 16	18 45	18 46	19 15	19 16	19 45	19 46	20 15	20 16	20 45	20 46	21 15	21 16	21 45	21 46	22 15	22 16	22 45	22 46
Rickmansworth §	⊖ d	17 51	17 51	18 21	18 21	18 51	18 51	19 21	19 21	19 51	19 51	20 21	20 21	20 51	20 51	21 21	21 21	21 51	21 51	22 21	22 21	22 51	22 51
Harrow-on-the-Hill §	⊖ d	18 02	18 02	18 32	18 32	19 02	19 02	19 32	19 32	20 02	20 02	20 32	20 32	21 02	21 02	21 32	21 32	22 02	22 02	22 32	22 32	23 02	23 02
London Marylebone	⊖ a	18 20	18 20	18 50	18 50	19 20	19 20	19 50	19 50	20 20	20 20	20 50	20 50	21 20	21 20	21 50	21 50	22 20	22 20	22 50	22 50	23 20	23 20

		CH A	CH B
Aylesbury Vale Parkway	d		
Aylesbury	d	23 15	23 18
Stoke Mandeville	d	23 19	23 22
Wendover	d	23 23	23 26
Great Missenden	d	23 29	23 32
Amersham §	⊖ d	23a39	23a42
Chalfont & Latimer §	⊖ d		
Chorleywood §	⊖ d		
Rickmansworth §	⊖ d		
Harrow-on-the-Hill §	⊖ d		
London Marylebone	⊖ a		

Sundays

20 May to 2 December

		CH C	CH D	CH C	CH D	CH C	CH D	CH C	CH D	CH C	CH D	CH C	CH D	CH C	CH D	CH C	CH D	CH C	CH D	CH C	CH D	CH C	CH D
Aylesbury Vale Parkway	d	07 10	07 13	08 10	08 13			09 10	09 13			10 10	10 13	11 10	11 13	12 10	12 13	13 10	13 13	14 10	14 13	15 10	15 13
Aylesbury	d	07 15	07 18	08 15	08 18	08 45	08 48	09 15	09 18	09 45	09 48	10 15	10 18	11 15	11 18	12 15	12 18	13 15	13 18	14 15	14 18	15 15	15 18
Stoke Mandeville	d	07 19	07 22	08 19	08 22	08 49	08 52	09 19	09 22	09 49	09 52	10 19	10 22	11 19	11 22	12 19	12 22	13 19	13 22	14 19	14 22	15 19	15 22
Wendover	d	07 23	07 26	08 23	08 26	08 53	08 56	09 23	09 26	09 53	09 56	10 23	10 26	11 23	11 26	12 23	12 26	13 23	13 26	14 23	14 26	15 23	15 26
Great Missenden	d	07 29	07 32	08 29	08 32	08 59	09 02	09 29	09 32	09 59	10 02	10 29	10 32	11 29	11 32	12 29	12 32	13 29	13 32	14 29	14 32	15 29	15 32
Amersham §	⊖ d	07 36	07 39	08 36	08 39	09 06	09 09	09 36	09 39	10 06	10 09	10 36	10 39	11 36	11 39	12 36	12 39	13 36	13 39	14 36	14 39	15 36	15 39
Chalfont & Latimer §	⊖ d	07 40	07 43	08 40	08 43	09 10	09 13	09 40	09 43	10 10	10 13	10 40	10 43	11 40	11 43	12 40	12 43	13 40	13 43	14 40	14 43	15 40	15 43
Chorleywood §	⊖ d	07 45	07 46	08 45	08 46	09 15	09 16	09 45	09 46	10 15	10 16	10 45	10 46	11 45	11 46	12 45	12 46	13 45	13 46	14 45	14 46	15 45	15 46
Rickmansworth §	⊖ d	07 51	07 51	08 51	08 51	09 21	09 21	09 51	09 51	10 21	10 21	10 51	10 51	11 51	11 51	12 51	12 51	13 51	13 51	14 51	14 51	15 51	15 51
Harrow-on-the-Hill §	⊖ d	08 02	08 02	09 02	09 02	09 32	09 32	10 02	10 02	10 32	10 32	11 02	11 02	12 02	12 02	13 02	13 02	14 02	14 02	15 02	15 02	16 02	16 02
London Marylebone	⊖ a	08 20	08 20	09 18	09 18	09 50	09 50	10 20	10 20	10 50	10 50	11 20	11 20	12 20	12 20	13 20	13 20	14 20	14 20	15 20	15 20	16 20	16 20

		CH C	CH D	CH C	CH D	CH C	CH D	CH C	CH D	CH C	CH D	CH C	CH D	CH C	CH D	CH C	CH D	CH C	CH D	CH C	CH D	CH C	CH D
Aylesbury Vale Parkway	d			16 10	16 13			17 10	17 13			18 10	18 13			19 10	19 13			20 10	20 13		
Aylesbury	d	15 45	15 48	16 15	16 18	16 45	16 48	17 15	17 18	17 45	17 48	18 15	18 18	18 45	18 48	19 15	19 18	19 45	19 48	20 15	20 18	20 45	20 48
Stoke Mandeville	d	15 49	15 52	16 19	16 22	16 49	16 52	17 19	17 22	17 49	17 52	18 19	18 22	18 49	18 52	19 19	19 22	19 49	19 52	20 19	20 22	20 49	20 52
Wendover	d	15 53	15 56	16 23	16 26	16 53	16 56	17 23	17 26	17 53	17 56	18 23	18 26	18 53	18 56	19 23	19 26	19 53	19 56	20 23	20 26	20 53	20 56
Great Missenden	d	15 59	16 02	16 29	16 32	16 59	17 02	17 29	17 32	17 59	18 02	18 29	18 32	18 59	19 02	19 29	19 32	19 59	20 02	20 29	20 32	20 59	21 02
Amersham §	⊖ d	16 06	16 09	16 36	16 39	17 06	17 09	17 36	17 39	18 06	18 09	18 36	18 39	19 06	19 09	19 36	19 39	20 06	20 09	20 36	20 39	21 06	21 09
Chalfont & Latimer §	⊖ d	16 10	16 13	16 40	16 43	17 10	17 13	17 40	17 43	18 10	18 13	18 40	18 43	19 10	19 13	19 40	19 43	20 10	20 13	20 40	20 43	21 10	21 13
Chorleywood §	⊖ d	16 15	16 16	16 45	16 46	17 15	17 16	17 45	17 46	18 15	18 16	18 45	18 46	19 15	19 16	19 45	19 46	20 15	20 16	20 45	20 46	21 15	21 16
Rickmansworth §	⊖ d	16 21	16 21	16 51	16 51	17 21	17 21	17 51	17 51	18 21	18 21	18 51	18 51	19 21	19 21	19 51	19 51	20 21	20 21	20 51	20 51	21 21	21 21
Harrow-on-the-Hill §	⊖ d	16 32	16 32	17 02	17 02	17 32	17 32	18 02	18 02	18 32	18 32	19 02	19 02	19 32	19 32	20 02	20 02	20 32	20 32	21 02	21 02	21 32	21 32
London Marylebone	⊖ a	16 50	16 50	17 20	17 20	17 50	17 50	18 20	18 20	18 50	18 50	19 20	19 20	19 48	19 48	20 20	20 20	20 50	20 50	21 20	21 20	21 50	21 50

		CH C	CH D	CH C	CH D	CH C	CH D
Aylesbury Vale Parkway	d	21 10	21 13			22 40	22 43
Aylesbury	d	21 15	21 18	21 45	21 48	22 45	22 48
Stoke Mandeville	d	21 19	21 22	21 49	21 52	22 49	22 52
Wendover	d	21 23	21 26	21 53	21 56	22 53	22 56
Great Missenden	d	21 29	21 32	21 59	22 02	22 59	23 02
Amersham §	⊖ d	21 36	21 39	22 06	22 09	23 06	23 09
Chalfont & Latimer §	⊖ d	21 40	21 43	22 10	22 13	23 10	23 13
Chorleywood §	⊖ d	21 45	21 46	22 15	22 16	23 15	23 16
Rickmansworth §	⊖ d	21 51	21 51	22 21	22 21	23 21	23 21
Harrow-on-the-Hill §	⊖ d	22 02	22 02	22 32	22 32	23 32	23 32
London Marylebone	⊖ a	22 20	22 20	22 50	22 50	23 48	23 48

§ London Underground Limited (Metropolitan Line) services operate between Harrow-on-the-Hill, Rickmansworth, Chorleywood, Chalfont & Latimer and Amersham

A from 13 October
B until 6 October
C from 7 October
D until 30 September

For additional services between London and Aylesbury refer to Table T115

Table T115-F

Mondays to Fridays
21 May to 7 December

London - High Wycombe, Aylesbury, Oxford Parkway, Banbury, Stratford-upon-Avon, Birmingham Snow Hill and Kidderminster

Miles	Miles	Miles	Miles			CH MX ◇ A	CH MX ◇ B	CH MX ◇ A	CH MX ◇ B	CH MX ◇ A	CH MX ◇ B	CH MX ◇ A	CH MX ◇ B	CH MO ◇ C	CH MO ◇ D	CH MX E	CH MO E	CH MX A	CH MX B	CH MX ◇ F	CH MX ◇ G	CH MO C	CH MO D	CH MX
0	—	—	—	**London Marylebone** ⊖	d															00 01	00 01			00 05
—	—	—	—	**London Paddington** ⊖	d																			
6½	—	—	—	Wembley Stadium	d																			
8	—	—	—	Sudbury & Harrow Road	d																			
8¾	—	—	—	Sudbury Hill Harrow	d																			
9¾	—	—	—	Northolt Park	d																			
11½	—	—	—	South Ruislip § ⊖	d																	00 02	00 02	
13¼	—	—	—	West Ruislip § ⊖	d																	00 06	00 06	
16	—	—	—	Denham	d																	00 10	00 10	
17	—	—	—	Denham Golf Club	d																	00 13	00 13	
18¾	—	—	—	Gerrards Cross	d													00 02	00 02			00 17	00 17	00 24
21¼	—	—	—	Seer Green	d																	00 21	00 21	
23	—	—	—	Beaconsfield	d													00 09	00 09			00 25	00 25	00 30
27¾	—	—	—	**High Wycombe**	d												00 04	00 15	00 15	00 28	00 28	00 31	00 31	00 36
32¾	—	—	—	Saunderton	d											00 04						00 37	00 37	
36	0	—	—	**Princes Risborough**	d			00 03	00 03							00 10	00 14	00 26	00 26			00 45	00 45	00 45
—	1½	—	—	Monks Risborough	d			00 07	00 07									00 29	00 29			00 48	00 48	
—	3	—	—	Little Kimble	d			00 11	00 11									00 33	00 33			00 52	00 52	
—	7½	—	—	**Aylesbury**	a			00 21	00 24									00 44	00 47			01 06	01 09	
44¾	—	—	0	Haddenham & Thame Parkway	d									00 03	00 03	00 17	00 21							00 52
—	—	—	10	Bicester Village	d							00 10	00 10	00 18	00 18					00 55	00 55			
—	—	—	16	Islip	d																			
—	—	—	18¾	Oxford Parkway 116	a							00 18	00 18	00 26	00 26					01 03	01 03			
—	—	—	21¾	Oxford	a							00 28	00 31	00 35	00 38					01 13	01 16			
54¾	—	—	—	**Bicester North**	d											00 30	00 34							01 05
65¾	—	—	—	Kings Sutton	d											00 42								
68¾	—	—	—	**Banbury**	d					00 03	00 03					00a50	00a55							01a22
88¾	—	0	—	**Leamington Spa**	d					00 21	00 21													
90¾	—	2	—	Warwick	d	00 03	00 03			00 25	00 25													
92	—	3¼	—	Warwick Parkway	d	00 07	00 07			00 29	00 29													
94¾	—	6	—	Hatton	d																			
—	—	7¾	—	Claverdon	d																			
—	—	11	—	Bearley	d																			
—	—	12½	—	Wilmcote	d																			
—	—	14¼	—	Stratford-upon-Avon Parkway	a																			
—	—	15¼	—	**Stratford-upon-Avon**	a																			
99	—	—	—	Lapworth	a																			
101¼	—	—	—	Dorridge	a	00 17	00 17																	
104¾	—	—	—	Solihull	a	00 23	00 23			00 40	00 40													
111¼	—	—	—	**Birmingham Moor Street**	a	00 36	00 39			00 52	00 55													
112	—	—	—	**Birmingham Snow Hill**	a																			
—	—	—	—	Rowley Regis	a																			
—	—	—	—	Cradley Heath	a																			
—	—	—	—	**Stourbridge Junction**	a																			
—	—	—	—	**Kidderminster**	a																			

§ London Underground Limited (Central Line) also operate services between South Ruislip and West Ruislip at frequent intervals
A until 5 October. From London Marylebone
B from 9 October. From London Marylebone
C until 1 October. From London Marylebone
D from 8 October. From London Marylebone
E From London Marylebone
F until 5 October
G from 9 October

For complete services between Banbury and Birmingham, refer to Table T71

For principal services between London and Aylesbury refer to Table T114

Table T115-F

Mondays to Fridays
21 May to 7 December

London - High Wycombe, Aylesbury, Oxford Parkway, Banbury, Stratford-upon-Avon, Birmingham Snow Hill and Kidderminster

		CH MO	CH MX A	CH MX B	CH	CH	CH ◇ A	CH ◇ C	CH	LM D	CH	CH ◇	CH ◇	CH A	CH C	CH ◇ A	CH ◇ C	CH	CH ◇	CH ◇ A	CH ◇ C	CH	CH
London Marylebone ⊖	d	00 05	00 10	00 10			06 09	06 09	05 55			06 05	06 17			06 48	06 48	06 40	07 11	07 14	07 14	07 00	07 18
London Paddington ⊖	d																						
Wembley Stadium	d		00 19	00 19					06 05				06 27					06 50				07 09	07 27
Sudbury & Harrow Road	d																						
Sudbury Hill Harrow	d																					07 13	
Northolt Park	d		00 24	00 24					06 10				06 32									07 16	
South Ruislip § ⊖	d		00 28	00 28					06 23									07 02				07 28	
West Ruislip § ⊖	d		00 32	00 32					06 27				06 37									07 31	07a40
Denham	d		00 37	00 37					06 32				06 42					07 08				07 36	
Denham Golf Club	d								06 34									07 10					
Gerrards Cross	d	00 25	00 42	00 42			06 28	06 28	06 38				06 47			07 05	07 05	07 14				07 41	
Seer Green	d		00 46	00 46					06 42				06 52									07 46	
Beaconsfield	d	00 32	00 50	00 50			06 34	06 34	06 46				06 55			07 11	07 11	07 20				07 49	
High Wycombe	d	00 38	00 56	00 56		06 05	06 40	06 40	06a53				07 01			07 17	07 17	07 26		07 38	07 38	07 55	
Saunderton	d		01 02	01 02		06 11							07 07									08 02	
Princes Risborough	d	00 48	01 09	01 09		06 16	06 49	06 49					07 13	07 23	07 23	07 26	07 26	07a38				08 07	
Monks Risborough	d		01 12	01 12										07 27	07 27								
Little Kimble	d		01 16	01 16										07 31	07 31								
Aylesbury	a		01 27	01 30										07 41	07 44								
Haddenham & Thame Parkway	d	00 55				06 23	06 55	06 55					07 20			07 32	07 32					08 13	
Bicester Village	d						07 08	07 08								07 45	07 45			08 02	08 02		
Islip	d						07 15	07 15												08 09	08 09		
Oxford Parkway 116	a						07 18	07 18								07 52	07 52			08 12	08 12		
Oxford	a						07 33	07 36								08 02	08 05			08 22	08 25		
Bicester North	d	01 08			05 46	06 38						06 47	07 33						07 54			08 28	
Kings Sutton	d	01 19										06 57	07 44									08 39	
Banbury	d	01a27			06 04	06a52						07 03	07 49						08 07			08a45	
Leamington Spa	d				06 25						06 51	07 21	08 08						08 25				
Warwick	d				06 30						06 56	07 26	08 13						08 29				
Warwick Parkway	d				06 33							07 29							08 33				
Hatton	d										07 04	07 35	08 21										
Claverdon	d									06x31	07 10		08 26										
Bearley	d									06x35			08 31										
Wilmcote	d									06 40	07 20		08 35										
Stratford-upon-Avon Parkway	a									06 43	07 22		08 37										
Stratford-upon-Avon	a									06 48	07 31		08 46										
Lapworth	a																						
Dorridge	a				06 43							07 42											
Solihull	a				06 49							07 50							08 44				
Birmingham Moor Street	a				06 59							08 02							08 53				
Birmingham Snow Hill	a				07 07							08 10							09 01				
Rowley Regis	a																						
Cradley Heath	a																						
Stourbridge Junction	a																						
Kidderminster	a																						

§ London Underground Limited (Central Line) also operate services between South Ruislip and West Ruislip at frequent intervals
A until 5 October
B from 9 October
C from 8 October
D From Birmingham Snow Hill

For complete services between Banbury and Birmingham, refer to Table T71

For principal services between London and Aylesbury refer to Table T114

Please note, Network Rail have stated that further updates to this timetable are possible during the validity period.

Table T115-F

Mondays to Fridays

21 May to 7 December

London - High Wycombe, Aylesbury, Oxford Parkway, Banbury, Stratford-upon-Avon, Birmingham Snow Hill and Kidderminster

		CH	CH	CH	CH	CH	CH	CH	CH	CH	CH	CH	CH	CH	CH	CH	CH	CH	CH	CH	CH	CH	CH
			◇	◇		◇	◇			◇	◇	◇								◇	◇	◇	◇
			A	B	A	A	B			A	B		B	A	B	A		B		A	B	A	B
London Marylebone ⊖	d	07 29	07 40	07 40		07 48	07 48	07 44	07 51	08 11	08 11	08 14		08 17	08 17		08 21			08 37	08 37	08 41	08 41
London Paddington ⊖	d																						
Wembley Stadium	d								08 00								08 30						
Sudbury & Harrow Road	d																						
Sudbury Hill Harrow	d								08 04														
Northolt Park	d								08 07														
South Ruislip § ⊖	d							08 02															
West Ruislip § ⊖	d								08 13					08 32	08 32								
Denham	d							08 09									08 40						
Denham Golf Club	d							08 11															
Gerrards Cross	d	07 48						08 15	08a22					08 39	08 39		08 45						
Seer Green	d							08 20									08 50						
Beaconsfield	d	07 54						08 23						08 45	08 45		08 53						
High Wycombe	d	08a03	08 04	08 04		08 14	08 14	08a32						08 51	08 51		09a02					09 06	09 06
Saunderton	d													08 57	08 57								
Princes Risborough	d		08 13	08 13	08 23								08 23	09 06	09 06	09 15		09 15					
Monks Risborough	d				08 27								08 27			09 19		09 19					
Little Kimble	d				08 31								08 31			09 23		09 23					
Aylesbury	a				08 41								08 44	09 23	09 26	09 33		09 36					
Haddenham & Thame Parkway	d		08 19	08 19																09 14	09 14		
Bicester Village	d		08 31	08 31						08 54	08 54											09 31	09 31
Islip	d																						
Oxford Parkway 116	a		08 39	08 39						09 01	09 01											09 38	09 38
Oxford	a		08 48	08 51						09 11	09 14											09 47	09 50
Bicester North	d					08 36	08 36													09 26	09 26		
Kings Sutton	d																						
Banbury	d					08 50	08 50					09 08								09 40	09 40		
Leamington Spa	d					09 08	09 08					09 26							09 40	09 58	09 58		
Warwick	d					09 12	09 12					09 30							09 45	10 03	10 03		
Warwick Parkway	d					09 16	09 16					09 34								10 07	10 07		
Hatton	d																		09 52				
Claverdon	d																		09 57				
Bearley	d																		10 02				
Wilmcote	d																		10 06				
Stratford-upon-Avon Parkway	a																		10 08				
Stratford-upon-Avon	a																		10 17				
Lapworth	a																						
Dorridge	a					09 25	09 25													10 17	10 17		
Solihull	a					09 31	09 31					09 45								10 23	10 23		
Birmingham Moor Street	a					09 42	09 45					09 54								10 35	10 38		
Birmingham Snow Hill	a											10 02											
Rowley Regis	a																						
Cradley Heath	a																						
Stourbridge Junction	a																						
Kidderminster	a																						

§ London Underground Limited (Central Line) also operate services between South Ruislip and West Ruislip at frequent intervals

A until 5 October
B from 8 October

For complete services between Banbury and Birmingham, refer to Table T71

For principal services between London and Aylesbury refer to Table T114

Table T115-F

Mondays to Fridays

21 May to 7 December

London - High Wycombe, Aylesbury, Oxford Parkway, Banbury, Stratford-upon-Avon, Birmingham Snow Hill and Kidderminster

		CH	CH	CH	CH	CH	CH	CH	CH	CH	CH	CH	CH	CH	CH	CH	CH	CH	CH	CH	CH	CH	CH
					◇	◇	◇				◇	◇	◇				◇	◇	◇	◇			
					A	B			A		A	B		B			A	B	A	B		A	B
London Marylebone ⊖	d	08 44	08 33	08 50	09 00	09 00	09 10	09 13		09 17	09 35	09 35	09 40		09 43	09 46	10 06	10 06	10 10	10 10		10 13	10 13
London Paddington ⊖	d																						
Wembley Stadium	d			08 59						09 26						09 55							
Sudbury & Harrow Road	d																						
Sudbury Hill Harrow	d			09 03												09 59							
Northolt Park	d			09 06												10 02							
South Ruislip § ⊖	d		08 59	09 13																			
West Ruislip § ⊖	d									09 35					09 58								
Denham	d		09 05													10 09							
Denham Golf Club	d	09 01														10 11							
Gerrards Cross	d	09 05	09 10	09a24				09 33		09 42					10 05	10a18						10 32	10 32
Seer Green	d									09 46												10 36	10 36
Beaconsfield	d	09 11	09 17							09 50			10 02		10 12							10 40	10 40
High Wycombe	d	09 17	09a24				09 36	09 43		09a59	10 00	10 00			10 18				10 36	10 36		10 46	10 46
Saunderton	d							09 49														10 53	10 53
Princes Risborough	d	09 26						09a58	10 07					10 07	10 27							11 00	11 00
Monks Risborough	d								10 11					10 11								11 03	11 03
Little Kimble	d								10 15					10 15									
Aylesbury	a								10 25					10 28								11 16	11 19
Haddenham & Thame Parkway	d	09 32			09 39	09 39									10 34		10 40	10 40					
Bicester Village	d				09 52	09 52					10 23	10 23					10 53	10 53					
Islip	d				09 58	09 58																	
Oxford Parkway 116	a				10 01	10 01					10 30	10 30					11 01	11 01					
Oxford	a				10 11	10 14					10 38	10 41					11 09	11 12					
Bicester North	d	09 45											10 29		10 47								
Kings Sutton	d	09 56																					
Banbury	d	10a03					10 08						10 43		11a02				11 07	11 07			
Leamington Spa	d						10 25						11 01						11 25	11 25	11 32		
Warwick	d												11 05								11 37		
Warwick Parkway	d						10 32						11 09						11 32	11 32			
Hatton	d																				11 44		
Claverdon	d																						
Bearley	d																						
Wilmcote	d																				11 55		
Stratford-upon-Avon Parkway	a																				11 57		
Stratford-upon-Avon	a																				12 06		
Lapworth	a																						
Dorridge	a												11 18										
Solihull	a						10 44						11 24						11 44	11 44			
Birmingham Moor Street	a						10 53						11 33						11 56	11 59			
Birmingham Snow Hill	a						11 01						11 42										
Rowley Regis	a																						
Cradley Heath	a																						
Stourbridge Junction	a																						
Kidderminster	a																						

§ London Underground Limited (Central Line) also operate services between South Ruislip and West Ruislip at frequent intervals

A until 5 October
B from 8 October

For complete services between Banbury and Birmingham, refer to Table T71

For principal services between London and Aylesbury refer to Table T114

Please note, Network Rail have stated that further updates to this timetable are possible during the validity period.

Table T115-F

Mondays to Fridays
21 May to 7 December

London - High Wycombe, Aylesbury, Oxford Parkway, Banbury, Stratford-upon-Avon, Birmingham Snow Hill and Kidderminster

		CH ◇	CH ◇ A	CH ◇ B	CH ◇	CH	CH	CH ◇ A	CH ◇ B	CH ◇ A	CH ◇ B	CH A	CH B	CH ◇	CH ◇ A	CH ◇ B	CH ◇	CH	CH	CH	CH ◇ A	CH ◇ B	CH ◇ A
London Marylebone 10 ⊖	d	10 16	10 35	10 35	10 40	10 43	10 46	11 07	11 07	11 10	11 10	11 13	11 13	11 17	11 35	11 35	11 40	11 43		11 47	12 07	12 07	12 10
London Paddington 15 ⊖	d																		11 35				
Wembley Stadium	d	10 25					10 55							11 26						11 56			
Sudbury & Harrow Road	d																						
Sudbury Hill Harrow	d						10 59													12 00			
Northolt Park	d						11 01													12 02			
South Ruislip § ⊖	d	10 32												11 33									
West Ruislip 3 § ⊖	d						11 06													12 07			
Denham	d						11 11													12 12			
Denham Golf Club	d					11 00												12 00					
Gerrards Cross 1	d	10 42				11 04	11a19					11 32	11 32	11 42				12 04		12a19			
Seer Green	d											11 36	11 36										
Beaconsfield	d	10 48				11 10						11 40	11 40	11 48				12 10					
High Wycombe 1	d	10a58	11 00	11 00		11 16				11 35	11 35	11 46	11 46	11a58	12 00	12 00		12 16	12a27				12 34
Saunderton	d											11 53	11 53										
Princes Risborough 2	d					11 25						12 00	12 00					12 25					
Monks Risborough	d											12 03	12 03										
Little Kimble	d																						
Aylesbury	a											12 17	12 20										
Haddenham & Thame Parkway	d					11 32		11 41	11 41									12 32			12 41	12 41	
Bicester Village	d		11 24	11 24				11 54	11 54						12 23	12 23					12 54	12 54	
Islip	d																				13 00	13 00	
Oxford Parkway 116	a		11 32	11 32				12 02	12 02						12 30	12 30					13 04	13 04	
Oxford	a		11 39	11 42				12 10	12 13						12 38	12 41					13 12	13 15	
Bicester North 3	d				11 32	11 45											12 27	12 45					
Kings Sutton	d																	12 55					
Banbury	d				11 46	12a02				12 07	12 07						12 40	13a03					13 08
Leamington Spa 8	d				12 04					12 26	12 26						12 58						13 26
Warwick	d				12 09												13 02						
Warwick Parkway	d				12 13					12 32	12 32						13 06						13 32
Hatton	d																						
Claverdon	d																						
Bearley	d																						
Wilmcote	d																						
Stratford-upon-Avon Parkway	a																						
Stratford-upon-Avon	a																						
Lapworth	a																						
Dorridge	a				12 23												13 15						
Solihull	a				12 30					12 44	12 44						13 21						13 44
Birmingham Moor Street	a				12 43					12 56	12 59						13 33						13 56
Birmingham Snow Hill ⇌	a				12 51												13 41						
Rowley Regis	a																						
Cradley Heath	a																						
Stourbridge Junction 2	a																						
Kidderminster	a																						

§ London Underground Limited (Central Line) also operate services between South Ruislip and West Ruislip at frequent intervals

A until 5 October
B from 8 October

For complete services between Banbury and Birmingham, refer to Table T71

For principal services between London and Aylesbury refer to Table T114

Table T115-F

Mondays to Fridays
21 May to 7 December

London - High Wycombe, Aylesbury, Oxford Parkway, Banbury, Stratford-upon-Avon, Birmingham Snow Hill and Kidderminster

		CH ◇ A	CH	CH B	CH A	CH ◇	CH ◇ B	CH ◇ A	CH ◇	CH	CH	CH ◇ B	CH ◇ A	CH ◇ B	CH ◇ A	CH B	CH A	CH ◇	CH ◇ B	CH ◇ A	CH ◇	CH	CH
London Marylebone 10 ⊖	d	12 10		12 13	12 13	12 17	12 35	12 35	12 40	12 43	12 47	13 06	13 06	13 10	13 10	13 13	13 13	13 17	13 35	13 35	13 40	13 43	13 47
London Paddington 15 ⊖	d																						
Wembley Stadium	d					12 26					12 56							13 26					13 56
Sudbury & Harrow Road	d																						
Sudbury Hill Harrow	d										13 00												
Northolt Park	d										13 02												14 01
South Ruislip § ⊖	d					12 33												13 33					
West Ruislip 3 § ⊖	d										13 07												14 06
Denham	d										13 12												14 10
Denham Golf Club	d									13 00												14 00	
Gerrards Cross 1	d			12 32	12 32	12 42				13 04	13a19					13 32	13 32	13 42				14 04	14a18
Seer Green	d			12 36	12 36											13 36	13 36						
Beaconsfield	d			12 40	12 40	12 48				13 10						13 40	13 40	13 48				14 10	
High Wycombe 1	d	12 34		12 47	12 47	12a57	12 59	12 59		13 16				13 34	13 34	13 46	13 46	13a57	13 59	13 59		14 16	
Saunderton	d			12 53	12 53											13 53	13 53						
Princes Risborough 2	d			13 00	13 00					13 25						14 00	14 00					14 25	
Monks Risborough	d			13 03	13 03											14 03	14 03						
Little Kimble	d			13 07	13 07																		
Aylesbury	a			13 21	13 24											14 17	14 20						
Haddenham & Thame Parkway	d									13 32		13 41	13 41									14 32	
Bicester Village	d						13 21	13 21				13 54	13 54						14 21	14 21			
Islip	d																						
Oxford Parkway 116	a						13 30	13 30				14 02	14 02						14 30	14 30			
Oxford	a						13 38	13 41				14 10	14 13						14 38	14 41			
Bicester North 3	d								13 27	13 45											14 27	14 45	
Kings Sutton	d																						
Banbury	d	13 08							13 40	14a04				14 10	14 10						14 40	15a02	
Leamington Spa 8	d	13 26	13 32						13 58					14 27	14 27						14 58		
Warwick	d		13 37						14 02												15 02		
Warwick Parkway	d	13 32							14 06					14 33	14 33						15 06		
Hatton	d		13 44																				
Claverdon	d		13 49																				
Bearley	d		13 55																				
Wilmcote	d		13 59																				
Stratford-upon-Avon Parkway	a		14 01																				
Stratford-upon-Avon	a		14 12																				
Lapworth	a																						
Dorridge	a								14 15												15 15		
Solihull	a	13 44							14 21					14 44	14 44						15 21		
Birmingham Moor Street	a	13 59							14 33					14 56	14 59						15 33		
Birmingham Snow Hill ⇌	a								14 41												15 41		
Rowley Regis	a																						
Cradley Heath	a																						
Stourbridge Junction 2	a																						
Kidderminster	a																						

§ London Underground Limited (Central Line) also operate services between South Ruislip and West Ruislip at frequent intervals

A from 8 October
B until 5 October

For complete services between Banbury and Birmingham, refer to Table T71

For principal services between London and Aylesbury refer to Table T114

Please note, Network Rail have stated that further updates to this timetable are possible during the validity period.

London - High Wycombe, Aylesbury, Oxford Parkway, Banbury, Stratford-upon-Avon, Birmingham Snow Hill and Kidderminster

		CH ◇ A	CH ◇ B	CH ◇ A	CH ◇ B	CH	CH A	CH B	CH ◇	CH ◇ A	CH ◇ B	CH ◇	CH	CH	CH ◇ A	CH ◇ B	CH ◇	CH A	CH B	CH ◇	CH ◇ A	CH ◇ B	CH ◇
London Marylebone ⊖	d	14 06	14 06	14 10	14 10		14 13	14 13	14 17	14 35	14 35	14 40	14 43	14 47	15 05	15 05	15 10	15 13	15 13	15 17	15 35	15 35	15 40
London Paddington ⊖	d																						
Wembley Stadium	d								14 26					14 56						15 26			
Sudbury & Harrow Road	d																						
Sudbury Hill Harrow	d								14 30														
Northolt Park	d													15 01									
South Ruislip § ⊖	d								14 35											15 33			
West Ruislip § ⊖	d													15 06									
Denham	d													15 10				15 29	15 29				
Denham Golf Club	d													15 12									
Gerrards Cross	d						14 32	14 32	14 44				15 02	15a19				15 34	15 34	15 41			
Seer Green	d						14 36	14 36												15 45			
Beaconsfield	d						14 40	14 40	14 50				15 08					15 40	15 40	15 49			
High Wycombe	d			14 34	14 34		14 46	14 46	15a01	15 03	15 03		15 14				15 35	15 46	15 46	15a59	16 01	16 01	
Saunderton	d						14 53	14 53										15 53	15 53				
Princes Risborough	d						15 00	15 00					15 23					16 00	16 00				
Monks Risborough	d						15 03	15 03										16 03	16 03				
Little Kimble	d						15 07	15 07															
Aylesbury	a						15 18	15 21										16 17	16 20				
Haddenham & Thame Parkway	d	14 41	14 41										15 30				15 48						
Bicester Village	d	14 54	14 54							15 26	15 26				15 55	15 55					16 23	16 23	
Islip	d									15 32	15 32												
Oxford Parkway 116	a	15 02	15 02							15 35	15 35				16 03	16 03					16 30	16 30	
Oxford	a	15 10	15 13							15 46	15 49				16 12	16 15					16 38	16 41	
Bicester North	d											15 29	15 43										16 27
Kings Sutton	d												15 56										
Banbury	d			15 07	15 07							15 42	16a04				16 09						16 40
Leamington Spa	d			15 25	15 25	15 32						15 59					16 26						16 58
Warwick	d					15 37						16 03											17 02
Warwick Parkway	d			15 30	15 30							16 07					16 32						17 06
Hatton	d					15 44																	
Claverdon	d					15 49																	
Bearley	d					15 55																	
Wilmcote	d					15 59																	
Stratford-upon-Avon Parkway	a					16 01																	
Stratford-upon-Avon	a					16 12																	
Lapworth	a																						
Dorridge	a											16 16											17 15
Solihull	a			15 44	15 44							16 22					16 44						17 21
Birmingham Moor Street	a			15 56	15 59							16 33					16 54						17 36
Birmingham Snow Hill	a											16 41					17 02						17 44
Rowley Regis	a																						
Cradley Heath	a																						
Stourbridge Junction	a																						
Kidderminster	a																						

§ London Underground Limited (Central Line) also operate services between South Ruislip and West Ruislip at frequent intervals

A until 5 October
B from 8 October

For complete services between Banbury and Birmingham, refer to Table T71

For principal services between London and Aylesbury refer to Table T114

London - High Wycombe, Aylesbury, Oxford Parkway, Banbury, Stratford-upon-Avon, Birmingham Snow Hill and Kidderminster

		CH	CH A	CH B	CH	CH ◇	CH ◇ A	CH ◇ B	CH ◇	CH A	CH B	CH C	CH A	CH B	CH	CH	CH ◇ A	CH ◇ B	CH ◇ A	CH ◇ B	CH A	CH B	CH
London Marylebone ⊖	d	15 43	16 00	16 00	15 50	16 15	16 18	16 18	16 21			16 24	16 27	16 27	16 30	16 33	16 47	16 47	16 50	16 50	16 53	16 53	17 00
London Paddington ⊖	d																						
Wembley Stadium	d				15 59											16 42							17 10
Sudbury & Harrow Road	d															16 45							
Sudbury Hill Harrow	d				16 03																		
Northolt Park	d				16 06											16 49							
South Ruislip § ⊖	d				16 14											16 53							
West Ruislip § ⊖	d	15 57														16a59					17 08	17 08	
Denham	d				16 20										16 47						17 13	17 13	
Denham Golf Club	d				16 22										16 50								
Gerrards Cross	d	16 04	16 18	16 18	16a28							16 43			16 54						17 18	17 18	17 24
Seer Green	d											16 47									17 22	17 22	
Beaconsfield	d	16 10	16 24	16 24					16 42						17 01						17 26	17 26	17 30
High Wycombe	d	16 16	16 30	16 30					16 48			16 55			17a10				17 13	17 13	17 32	17 32	17a39
Saunderton	d	16 23										17 02											
Princes Risborough	d	16 28							16 56	17 02	17 02	17 07							17 22	17 22	17 46	17 46	
Monks Risborough	d									17 06	17 06										17 50	17 50	
Little Kimble	d									17 10	17 10										17 54	17 54	
Aylesbury	a									17 20	17 23		17 21	17 24							18 07	18 10	
Haddenham & Thame Parkway	d	16 35					16 53	16 53				17 13					17 22	17 22					
Bicester Village	d		16 52	16 52			17 06	17 06											17 39	17 39			
Islip	d																		17 45	17 45			
Oxford Parkway 116	a		16 59	16 59			17 13	17 13											17 48	17 48			
Oxford	a		17 10	17 13			17 22	17 25											17 56	17 59			
Bicester North	d	16 48							17 11			17 26					17 34	17 34					
Kings Sutton	d											17 37											
Banbury	d	17a03				17 08			17 24			→					17 47	17 47					
Leamington Spa	d					17 26			17 41								18 04	18 04					
Warwick	d																18 08	18 08					
Warwick Parkway	d					17 32			17 47								18 12	18 12					
Hatton	d																						
Claverdon	d																						
Bearley	d																						
Wilmcote	d																						
Stratford-upon-Avon Parkway	a																						
Stratford-upon-Avon	a																						
Lapworth	a																						
Dorridge	a								17 56								18 21	18 21					
Solihull	a					17 44			18 02								18 26	18 26					
Birmingham Moor Street	a					17 54			18 11								18 38	18 41					
Birmingham Snow Hill	a					17 57			18 22														
Rowley Regis	a					18 13																	
Cradley Heath	a																						
Stourbridge Junction	a					18 25																	
Kidderminster	a					18 44																	

§ London Underground Limited (Central Line) also operate services between South Ruislip and West Ruislip at frequent intervals

A until 5 October
B from 8 October
C To Birmingham Snow Hill

For complete services between Banbury and Birmingham, refer to Table T71

For principal services between London and Aylesbury refer to Table T114

Table T115-F

Mondays to Fridays

21 May to 7 December

London - High Wycombe, Aylesbury, Oxford Parkway, Banbury, Stratford-upon-Avon, Birmingham Snow Hill and Kidderminster

	CH	CH A	CH B		CH C	CH ◇	CH ◇ A	CH ◇ B	CH FO	CH FX	CH	CH	CH D	CH	CH ◇	CH ◇ A	CH ◇ B	CH A	CH B		CH D	CH	CH	CH ◇
London Marylebone ⊖ d	16 56					17 15	17 18	17 18	17 21	17 21	17 24	17 27	17 30	17 34	17 46	17 50	17 50	17 53	17 53		17 58	18 01	18 04	18 15
London Paddington ⊖ d																								
Wembley Stadium d														17 43									18 13	
Sudbury & Harrow Road d												17 38												
Sudbury Hill Harrow d	17 07																						18 18	
Northolt Park d	17 10											17 42											18 21	
South Ruislip § ⊖ d	17 18											17 50											18 35	
West Ruislip § ⊖ d												17a59										18 16		
Denham d											17 41							18 10	18 10					
Denham Golf Club d																		18 12	18 12					
Gerrards Cross d	17a29										17 46			17 56				18 16	18 16			18 23	18a45	
Seer Green d											17 50							18 21	18 21					
Beaconsfield d									17 45	17 45				18 02				18 24	18 24			18 29		
High Wycombe d									17 53	17 53	17 58			18a11		18 14	18 14	18 30	18 30			18a38		
Saunderton d											18 05													
Princes Risborough d									18 03	18 03	18 10					18 23	18 23	18 42	18 42					
Monks Risborough d																		18 45	18 45					
Little Kimble d																		18 49	18 49					
Aylesbury a													18 23					19 00	19 03		18 51			
Haddenham & Thame Parkway d									18 11	18 11	18 17				18 23									
Bicester Village d							18 05	18 05								18 40	18 40							
Islip d																								
Oxford Parkway 116 a							18 12	18 12								18 47	18 47							
Oxford a							18 22	18 25								18 55	18 58							
Bicester North d					←				18 23	18a25	18a33				18 35									
Kings Sutton d					17 37																			
Banbury d					18 02	18 09			18a41						18 48									19 09
Leamington Spa d		18 11	18 11		18 22	18 27									19 05									19 27
Warwick d		18 16	18 16		18 26										19 09									
Warwick Parkway d						18 34									19 13									19 34
Hatton d		18 27	18 27		18 39																			
Claverdon d		18 33	18 33																					
Bearley d		18 39	18 39																					
Wilmcote d		18 44	18 44																					
Stratford-upon-Avon Parkway a		18 46	18 46																					
Stratford-upon-Avon a		18 51	18 54																					
Lapworth a					18 46																			
Dorridge a					18 50	18 44									19 22									19 45
Solihull a					18 57	18 49									19 28									19 50
Birmingham Moor Street a					19 07	18 59									19 38									20 00
Birmingham Snow Hill a					19 15	19 02									19 46									20 04
Rowley Regis a						19 15																		20 22
Cradley Heath a																								
Stourbridge Junction a						19 26																		20 33
Kidderminster a						19 41																		20 48

§ London Underground Limited (Central Line) also operate services between South Ruislip and West Ruislip at frequent intervals

A until 5 October
B from 8 October
C From London Marylebone
D To Aylesbury Vale Parkway

For complete services between Banbury and Birmingham, refer to Table T71

For principal services between London and Aylesbury refer to Table T114

Table T115-F

Mondays to Fridays

21 May to 7 December

London - High Wycombe, Aylesbury, Oxford Parkway, Banbury, Stratford-upon-Avon, Birmingham Snow Hill and Kidderminster

	CH ◇ A	CH ◇ B	CH		CH ◇	CH ◇ C	CH ◇ D	CH	CH E	CH	CH ◇ C	CH ◇ D	CH C	CH D	CH C	CH D	CH	CH	CH ◇ C		CH ◇ D	CH C	CH D	CH ◇ C
London Marylebone ⊖ d	18 18	18 18	18 21		18 47	18 24	18 24	18 28	18 32	18 36	18 50	18 50			18 53	18 53	19 03	18 56	19 15		19 15	19 18	19 18	19 21
London Paddington ⊖ d																								
Wembley Stadium d								18 37										19 05						
Sudbury & Harrow Road d								18 40																
Sudbury Hill Harrow d								18 43																
Northolt Park d						18 36	18 36											19 10						
South Ruislip § ⊖ d								18 51										19 17						
West Ruislip § ⊖ d								18a57																
Denham d						18 44	18 44								19 08	19 08								
Denham Golf Club d															19 13	19 13		19 23						
Gerrards Cross d						18 49	18 49			18 56					19 18	19 18	19 23	19a29						
Seer Green d						18 54	18 54								19 22	19 22								
Beaconsfield d			18 44							19 03					19 26	19 26	19 30							
High Wycombe d			18 50			19 02	19 02			19a12	19 16	19 16			19 32	19 32	19a39							19 45
Saunderton d						19 08	19 08																	
Princes Risborough d			19 00			19 13	19 13				19 25	19 25	19 32	19 32	19 43	19 43								
Monks Risborough d													19 35	19 35										
Little Kimble d													19 39	19 39										
Aylesbury a									19 24				19 49	19 52	19 59	20 02						20 16	20 19	
Haddenham & Thame Parkway d	18 54	18 54	19 06		19 25																			19 58
Bicester Village d	19 08	19 08									19 42	19 42												20 11
Islip d																								
Oxford Parkway 116 a	19 15	19 15									19 49	19 49												20 18
Oxford a	19 25	19 28									19 57	20 00												20 27
Bicester North d			19 20		19 37	19 44	19 44												20 02		20 02			
Kings Sutton d						19 55	19 55																	
Banbury d			19a37		19 51	20 06	20 06												20 16		20 16			
Leamington Spa d					20 09	20 26	20 26												20 35		20 35			
Warwick d					20 13																			
Warwick Parkway d					20 17	20 31	20 31												20 43		20 43			
Hatton d						20 38	20 38																	
Claverdon d																								
Bearley d																								
Wilmcote d						20 48	20 48																	
Stratford-upon-Avon Parkway a						20 50	20 50																	
Stratford-upon-Avon a						20 54	20 57																	
Lapworth a																								
Dorridge a					20 26														20 52		20 52			
Solihull a					20 32														20 58		20 58			
Birmingham Moor Street a					20 41														21 10		21 13			
Birmingham Snow Hill a					20 49																			
Rowley Regis a																								
Cradley Heath a																								
Stourbridge Junction a																								
Kidderminster a																								

§ London Underground Limited (Central Line) also operate services between South Ruislip and West Ruislip at frequent intervals

A until 5 October. The Oxford Flyer
B from 8 October. The Oxford Flyer
C until 5 October
D from 8 October
E To Aylesbury Vale Parkway

For complete services between Banbury and Birmingham, refer to Table T71

For principal services between London and Aylesbury refer to Table T114

Please note, Network Rail have stated that further updates to this timetable are possible during the validity period.

Table T115-F

Mondays to Fridays

21 May to 7 December

London - High Wycombe, Aylesbury, Oxford Parkway, Banbury, Stratford-upon-Avon, Birmingham Snow Hill and Kidderminster

		CH ◇ A	CH	CH ◇		CH ◇	CH ◇ B	CH ◇ A	CH B	CH ◇	CH	CH ◇ B	CH ◇ A	CH ◇	CH A	CH B	CH A	CH ◇	CH ◇	CH ◇ B		CH ◇ A	CH ◇	CH	CH ◇ B
London Marylebone ⊖	d	19 21	19 24	19 28		19 47	19 50	19 50		19 53	19 36	20 07	20 07	20 10		20 13	20 13	20 16	20 37	20 40		20 40	20 43	20 46	21 02
London Paddington ⊖	d																								
Wembley Stadium	d										19 45							20 25						20 55	
Sudbury & Harrow Road	d										19 48														
Sudbury Hill Harrow	d										19 51													20 59	
Northolt Park	d										19 54							20 30						21 02	
South Ruislip § ⊖	d										20 07							20 34							
West Ruislip § ⊖	d			19 43												20 28	20 28							21 07	
Denham	d			19 48												20 33	20 33							21 12	
Denham Golf Club	d			19 50																				21 15	
Gerrards Cross	d		19 44	19 54						20 12	20a18					20 38	20 38	20 42					21 02	21a21	
Seer Green	d		19 48							20 17								20 47							
Beaconsfield	d		19 52	20 00						20 21						20 44	20 44	20 50					21 08		
High Wycombe	d	19 45	19 58	20a09			20 14	20 14		20a30				20 35		20 50	20 50	20a59		21 05		21 05	21 14		
Saunderton	d		20 04													20 56	20 56								
Princes Risborough	d		20a12			20 17	20 23	20 23	20 33						20 33	21 04	21 04						21 23		
Monks Risborough	d								20 37						20 37	21 08	21 08								
Little Kimble	d								20 41						20 41										
Aylesbury	a								20 51						20 54	21 23	21 26								
Haddenham & Thame Parkway	d	19 58				20 23								20 48					21 11				21 30		21 42
Bicester Village	d	20 11					20 39	20 39				20 52	20 52							21 28		21 28			21 55
Islip	d											20 58	20 58												
Oxford Parkway 116	a	20 18					20 46	20 46				21 02	21 02							21 35		21 35			22 02
Oxford	a	20 30					20 56	20 59				21 12	21 15							21 45		21 48			22 11
Bicester North	d					20 35								20 59					21 24				21 43		
Kings Sutton	d																						21 55		
Banbury	d					20 48								21 12					21 39				22 01		
Leamington Spa	d					21 05								21 30					21 57				22 20		
Warwick	d					21 09													22 01				22 24		
Warwick Parkway	d					21 13								21 36					22 05						
Hatton	d					21 18																	22 31		
Claverdon	d																						22 36		
Bearley	d																								
Wilmcote	d																						22 43		
Stratford-upon-Avon Parkway	a																						22 45		
Stratford-upon-Avon	a																						22 56		
Lapworth	a					21 23																			
Dorridge	a					21 28													22 14						
Solihull	a					21 33								21 48					22 20						
Birmingham Moor Street	a					21 43								21 58					22 30						
Birmingham Snow Hill	a					21 51								22 06					22 38						
Rowley Regis	a													22 25											
Cradley Heath	a													22 30											
Stourbridge Junction	a													22 36											
Kidderminster	a													22 50											

§ London Underground Limited (Central Line) also operate services between South Ruislip and West Ruislip at frequent intervals

A from 8 October
B until 5 October

For complete services between Banbury and Birmingham, refer to Table T71

For principal services between London and Aylesbury refer to Table T114

Table T115-F

Mondays to Fridays

21 May to 7 December

London - High Wycombe, Aylesbury, Oxford Parkway, Banbury, Stratford-upon-Avon, Birmingham Snow Hill and Kidderminster

		CH ◇ A	CH ◇	CH B		CH A	CH ◇	CH ◇ B	CH ◇ A	CH ◇	CH B	CH A	CH ◇	CH ◇ B	CH ◇ A	CH ◇ B	CH ◇ A	CH B	CH A	CH ◇		CH ◇ B	CH ◇ A	CH ◇ B	CH ◇ A
London Marylebone ⊖	d	21 02	21 10	21 13		21 13	21 16	21 32	21 32	21 40	21 43	21 43	21 46	22 07	22 07	22 10	22 10	22 13	22 13	22 16		22 37	22 37	22 40	22 40
London Paddington ⊖	d																								
Wembley Stadium	d						21 25						21 55							22 25					
Sudbury & Harrow Road	d																								
Sudbury Hill Harrow	d																								
Northolt Park	d												22 00												
South Ruislip § ⊖	d						21 32													22 32					
West Ruislip § ⊖	d												22 05												
Denham	d						21 38						22 10							22 38					
Denham Golf Club	d												22 12							22 40					
Gerrards Cross	d			21 32		21 32	21 43				22 02	22 02	22 16					22 32	22 32	22 44					
Seer Green	d			21 36		21 36												22 36	22 36						
Beaconsfield	d			21 40		21 40	21 49				22 08	22 08	22 22					22 40	22 40	22 50					
High Wycombe	d		21 36	21 46		21 46	21a58	21 59	21 59	22 04	22 14	22 14	22a31			22 35	22 35	22 46	22 46	23a00		23 02	23 02	23 07	23 07
Saunderton	d			21 52		21 52												22 52	22 52						
Princes Risborough	d			21 59		21 59					22 25	22 25						22 59	22 59						
Monks Risborough	d			22 02		22 02												23 02	23 02						
Little Kimble	d			22 06		22 06												23 06	23 06						
Aylesbury	a			22 17		22 20					22 41	22 44						23 17	23 20						
Haddenham & Thame Parkway	d	21 42								22 17						22 48	22 48					23 15	23 15		
Bicester Village	d	21 55						22 26	22 26					22 53	22 53									23 33	23 33
Islip	d													22 59	22 59										
Oxford Parkway 116	a	22 02						22 34	22 34					23 02	23 02									23 41	23 41
Oxford	a	22 14						22 41	22 44					23 12	23 15									23 50	23 53
Bicester North	d		21 59							22 28						22 59	22 59					23 27	23 27		
Kings Sutton	d																								
Banbury	d		22 14							22 41						23 13	23 13					23 41	23 41		
Leamington Spa	d		22 31							22 59						23 31	23 31					23 59	23 59		
Warwick	d									23 03												00 03	00 03		
Warwick Parkway	d		22 38							23 07						23 37	23 37					00 07	00 07		
Hatton	d									23 12															
Claverdon	d																								
Bearley	d																								
Wilmcote	d																								
Stratford-upon-Avon Parkway	a																								
Stratford-upon-Avon	a																								
Lapworth	a									23 17															
Dorridge	a									23 22												00 17	00 17		
Solihull	a		22 50							23 30						23 48	23 48					00 23	00 23		
Birmingham Moor Street	a		23 00							23 39						00 01	00 04					00 36	00 39		
Birmingham Snow Hill	a		23 05							23 47															
Rowley Regis	a		23 32																						
Cradley Heath	a		23 39																						
Stourbridge Junction	a		23 49																						
Kidderminster	a																								

§ London Underground Limited (Central Line) also operate services between South Ruislip and West Ruislip at frequent intervals

A from 8 October
B until 5 October

For complete services between Banbury and Birmingham, refer to Table T71

For principal services between London and Aylesbury refer to Table T114

Table T115-F

Mondays to Fridays
21 May to 7 December

London - High Wycombe, Aylesbury, Oxford Parkway, Banbury, Stratford-upon-Avon, Birmingham Snow Hill and Kidderminster

		CH	CH ◇ A	CH ◇ B	CH ◇ A	CH ◇ B	CH ◇ A	CH ◇ B	CH	CH FX C	CH FX B	CH FO A	CH FO D
London Marylebone ⊖	d	22 43	23 10	23 10	23 00	23 00	23 07	23 07	23 20	23 30	23 30	23 45	23 45
London Paddington ⊖	d												
Wembley Stadium	d	22 52	23 19	23 19	23 09	23 09			23 29	23 39	23 39	23 54	23 54
Sudbury & Harrow Road	d												
Sudbury Hill Harrow	d												
Northolt Park	d				23 14	23 14				23 44	23 44	23 59	23 59
South Ruislip § ⊖	d				23 27	23 27				23 47	23 47	00 02	00 02
West Ruislip § ⊖	d				23 31	23 31				23 51	23 51	00 06	00 06
Denham	d								23 39	23 56	23 56	00 11	00 11
Denham Golf Club	d				23 36	23 36				23 58	23 58	00 13	00 13
Gerrards Cross	d	23 05			23 40	23 40			23 44	00 02	00 02	00 17	00 17
Seer Green	d								23 48				
Beaconsfield	d	23 11			23 46	23 46			23 52	00 09	00 09	00 24	00 24
High Wycombe	d	23 17	23 39	23 39	23 52	23 52			23 58	00 15	00 15	00 30	00 30
Saunderton	d								00 04				
Princes Risborough	d	23 26	23 48	23 48	00 03	00 03			00 10	00 26	00 26	00 41	00 41
Monks Risborough	d				00 07	00 07				00 29	00 29	00 44	00 44
Little Kimble	d				00 11	00 11				00 33	00 33	00 48	00 48
Aylesbury	a				00 21	00 24				00 44	00 47	00 59	01 02
Haddenham & Thame Parkway	d	23 33	23 55	23 55					00 17				
Bicester Village	d		00 10	00 10									
Islip	d												
Oxford Parkway 116	a		00 18	00 18									
Oxford	a		00 28	00 31									
Bicester North	d	23a47					23 50	23 50	00 30				
Kings Sutton	d								00 42				
Banbury	d						00 03	00 03	00a50				
Leamington Spa	d						00 21	00 21					
Warwick	d						00 25	00 25					
Warwick Parkway	d						00 29	00 29					
Hatton	d												
Claverdon	d												
Bearley	d												
Wilmcote	d												
Stratford-upon-Avon Parkway	a												
Stratford-upon-Avon	a												
Lapworth	a												
Dorridge	a												
Solihull	a						00 40	00 40					
Birmingham Moor Street	a						00 52	00 55					
Birmingham Snow Hill	a												
Rowley Regis	a												
Cradley Heath	a												
Stourbridge Junction	a												
Kidderminster	a												

§ London Underground Limited (Central Line) also operate services between South Ruislip and West Ruislip at frequent intervals

A until 5 October
B from 8 October
C until 4 October
D from 12 October

For complete services between Banbury and Birmingham, refer to Table T71

For principal services between London and Aylesbury refer to Table T114

Table T115-F

Saturdays
26 May to 8 December

London - High Wycombe, Aylesbury, Oxford Parkway, Banbury, Stratford-upon-Avon, Birmingham Snow Hill and Kidderminster

		CH ◇ A	CH ◇ B	CH ◇ A	CH ◇ B	CH ◇ A	CH ◇ B	CH C	CH A	CH B	CH ◇ A	CH ◇ B	CH ◇ D	CH ◇ E	CH	CH D	CH E	CH ◇ D	CH ◇ E	CH D	CH E	CH ◇ D	CH ◇ E
London Marylebone ⊖	d												00 10	00 10	00 20	00 25	00 25	01 10	01 10			05 56	05 56
London Paddington ⊖	d																						
Wembley Stadium	d															00 34	00 34					06 05	06 05
Sudbury & Harrow Road	d																						
Sudbury Hill Harrow	d																						
Northolt Park	d															00 39	00 39						
South Ruislip § ⊖	d								00 02	00 02						00 43	00 43						
West Ruislip § ⊖	d								00 06	00 06						00 47	00 47						
Denham	d								00 11	00 11						00 52	00 52						
Denham Golf Club	d								00 13	00 13													
Gerrards Cross	d								00 17	00 17					00 39	00 57	00 57	01 29	01 29				
Seer Green	d															01 01	01 01						
Beaconsfield	d								00 24	00 24					00 45	01 05	01 05	01 35	01 35				
High Wycombe	d								00 30	00 30			00 38	00 38	00 51	01 11	01 11	01 41	01 41	06 12	06 12	06 26	06 26
Saunderton	d							00 04								01 17	01 17			06 18	06 18		
Princes Risborough	d			00 03	00 03			00 10	00 41	00 41					01 00	01 24	01 24	01 51	01 51	06 24	06 24		
Monks Risborough	d			00 07	00 07				00 44	00 44						01 27	01 27						
Little Kimble	d			00 11	00 11				00 48	00 48						01 31	01 31						
Aylesbury	a			00 21	00 24				00 59	01 02						01 42	01 45						
Haddenham & Thame Parkway	d							00 17							01 07			01 58	01 58	06 31	06 31	06 40	06 40
Bicester Village	d										00 10	00 10	01 05	01 05				02 12	02 12			06 55	06 55
Islip	d																						
Oxford Parkway 116	a										00 18	00 18	01 13	01 13				02 20	02 20			07 03	07 03
Oxford	a										00 28	00 31	01 25	01 28				02 29	02 32			07 11	07 14
Bicester North	d							00 30							01 20					06 45	06 45		
Kings Sutton	d							00 42												06 57	06 57		
Banbury	d					00 03	00 03	00a50							01 35					07 03	07 03		
Leamington Spa	d					00 21	00 21								01a59					07 21	07 21		
Warwick	d	00 03	00 03			00 25	00 25													07 25	07 25		
Warwick Parkway	d	00 07	00 07			00 29	00 29													07 29	07 29		
Hatton	d																			07 34	07 34		
Claverdon	d																						
Bearley	d																						
Wilmcote	d																						
Stratford-upon-Avon Parkway	a																						
Stratford-upon-Avon	a																						
Lapworth	a																						
Dorridge	a	00 17	00 17																	07 41	07 41		
Solihull	a	00 23	00 23			00 40	00 40													07 47	07 47		
Birmingham Moor Street	a	00 36	00 39			00 52	00 55													08 00	08 03		
Birmingham Snow Hill	a																						
Rowley Regis	a																						
Cradley Heath	a																						
Stourbridge Junction	a																						
Kidderminster	a																						

§ London Underground Limited (Central Line) also operate services between South Ruislip and West Ruislip at frequent intervals

A until 6 October. From London Marylebone
B from 13 October. From London Marylebone
C From London Marylebone
D until 6 October
E from 13 October

For complete services between Banbury and Birmingham, refer to Table T71

For principal services between London and Aylesbury refer to Table T114

Please note, Network Rail have stated that further updates to this timetable are possible during the validity period.

Table T115-F

Saturdays

26 May to 8 December

London - High Wycombe, Aylesbury, Oxford Parkway, Banbury, Stratford-upon-Avon, Birmingham Snow Hill and Kidderminster

		CH ◇ A	CH ◇ B	CH A	CH B	CH	CH ◇	CH	CH ◇ A	CH ◇ B	CH A	CH B	CH ◇ A	CH ◇ B	CH	CH	CH ◇ A	CH ◇ B	CH ◇	CH A	CH B	CH ◇ A	CH ◇ B
London Marylebone ⊖	d	06 25	06 25	06 20	06 20	06 29	07 00		07 06	07 06	07 09	07 09	07 40	07 40	07 43	07 46	08 06	08 06	08 10	08 13	08 13	08 35	08 35
London Paddington ⊖	d																						
Wembley Stadium	d			06 29	06 29	06 38					07 18	07 18				07 55				08 22	08 22		
Sudbury & Harrow Road	d																						
Sudbury Hill Harrow	d																						
Northolt Park	d					06 43					07 23	07 23				08 00							
South Ruislip § ⊖	d			06 41	06 41	06 46					07 26	07 26				08 03							
West Ruislip § ⊖	d					06 50					07 30	07 30				08 07							
Denham	d					06 54					07 34	07 34				08 11				08 32	08 32		
Denham Golf Club	d					06 57					07 37	07 37			08 00								
Gerrards Cross	d			06 49	06 49	07 00					07 41	07 41			08 04	08a22				08 36	08 36		
Seer Green	d					07 05					07 45	07 45			08 09					08 41	08 41		
Beaconsfield	d			06 55	06 55	07 08					07 48	07 48			08 12					08 44	08 44		
High Wycombe	d	06 52	06 52	07 01	07 01	07a15	07 23		07 30	07 30	07 54	07 54	08 03	08 03	08 18				08 34	08 50	08 50	08 58	08 58
Saunderton	d			07 07	07 07						08 01	08 01								08 56	08 56		
Princes Risborough	d	07 02	07 02	07 14	07 14		07 32				08 08	08 08			08 27					09 03	09 03		
Monks Risborough	d			07 17	07 17						08 11	08 11								09 06	09 06		
Little Kimble	d			07 21	07 21						08 15	08 15								09 10	09 10		
Aylesbury	a			07 32	07 35						08 26	08 29								09 21	09 24		
Haddenham & Thame Parkway	d	07 09	07 09				07 38		07 43	07 43					08 34		08 41	08 41					
Bicester Village	d	07 24	07 24						07 56	07 56			08 26	08 26			08 54	08 54				09 21	09 21
Islip	d	07 31	07 31										08 32	08 32								09 27	09 27
Oxford Parkway 116	a	07 35	07 35						08 03	08 03			08 35	08 35			09 01	09 01				09 31	09 31
Oxford	a	07 47	07 50						08 12	08 15			08 44	08 47			09 10	09 13				09 39	09 42
Bicester North	d						07 50								08 47				08 56				
Kings Sutton	d														08 58								
Banbury	d						08 04								09a05				09 10				
Leamington Spa	d						08 23	08 30											09 28				
Warwick	d							08 34											09 32				
Warwick Parkway	d						08 29												09 35				
Hatton	d							08 42															
Claverdon	d							08 48															
Bearley	d							08 53															
Wilmcote	d							08 58															
Stratford-upon-Avon Parkway	a							09 01															
Stratford-upon-Avon	a							09 12															
Lapworth	a																						
Dorridge	a						08 39												09 45				
Solihull	a						08 46												09 50				
Birmingham Moor Street	a						08 59												10 01				
Birmingham Snow Hill	a						09 07												10 09				
Rowley Regis	a																						
Cradley Heath	a																						
Stourbridge Junction	a																						
Kidderminster	a																						

§ London Underground Limited (Central Line) also operate services between South Ruislip and West Ruislip at frequent intervals

A until 6 October
B from 13 October

For complete services between Banbury and Birmingham, refer to Table T71

For principal services between London and Aylesbury refer to Table T114

Table T115-F

Saturdays

26 May to 8 December

London - High Wycombe, Aylesbury, Oxford Parkway, Banbury, Stratford-upon-Avon, Birmingham Snow Hill and Kidderminster

		CH ◇	CH	CH	CH ◇ A	CH ◇ B	CH ◇ A	CH ◇ B	CH A	CH B	CH ◇ A	CH ◇ B	CH ◇	CH	CH	CH ◇ A	CH ◇ B	CH ◇ A	CH ◇ B	CH	CH A	CH B	CH ◇ A
London Marylebone ⊖	d	08 40	08 43	08 46	09 06	09 06	09 10	09 10	09 13	09 13	09 35	09 35	09 40	09 43	09 46	10 06	10 06	10 10	10 10		10 13	10 13	10 35
London Paddington ⊖	d																						
Wembley Stadium	d			08 55					09 22	09 22					09 55						10 22	10 22	
Sudbury & Harrow Road	d																						
Sudbury Hill Harrow	d																						
Northolt Park	d			09 00											10 00								
South Ruislip § ⊖	d			09 03											10 03								
West Ruislip § ⊖	d			09 07											10 07								
Denham	d			09 11					09 32	09 32					10 11						10 32	10 32	
Denham Golf Club	d		09 00											10 00									
Gerrards Cross	d		09 04	09a22					09 37	09 37				10 04	10a22						10 37	10 37	
Seer Green	d		09 09											10 09									
Beaconsfield	d		09 12						09 43	09 43				10 12							10 43	10 43	
High Wycombe	d		09 18				09 34	09 34	09 49	09 49	09 58	09 58		10 18				10 34	10 34		10 49	10 49	10 59
Saunderton	d								09 56	09 56											10 55	10 55	
Princes Risborough	d		09 27						10 03	10 03				10 27							11 02	11 02	
Monks Risborough	d								10 06	10 06											11 05	11 05	
Little Kimble	d								10 10	10 10													
Aylesbury	a								10 21	10 24											11 19	11 22	
Haddenham & Thame Parkway	d		09 34		09 41	09 41								10 34		10 41	10 41						
Bicester Village	d				09 54	09 54					10 22	10 22				10 54	10 54						11 22
Islip	d																						
Oxford Parkway 116	a				10 01	10 01					10 29	10 29				11 01	11 01						11 29
Oxford	a				10 10	10 13					10 38	10 41				11 10	11 13						11 39
Bicester North	d	09 26	09 47										10 24	10 47									
Kings Sutton	d																						
Banbury	d	09 40	10a02				10 07	10 07					10 37	11a02				11 07	11 07				
Leamington Spa	d	09 58					10 25	10 25					10 55					11 25	11 25	11 32			
Warwick	d	10 02											10 59							11 37			
Warwick Parkway	d	10 06					10 31	10 31					11 03					11 32	11 32				
Hatton	d																			11 44			
Claverdon	d																						
Bearley	d																						
Wilmcote	d																						
Stratford-upon-Avon Parkway	a																			11 55			
Stratford-upon-Avon	a																			12 05			
Lapworth	a																						
Dorridge	a	10 15											11 13										
Solihull	a	10 21					10 43	10 43					11 20					11 44	11 44				
Birmingham Moor Street	a	10 33					10 55	10 58					11 33					11 56	11 59				
Birmingham Snow Hill	a	10 41											11 41										
Rowley Regis	a																						
Cradley Heath	a																						
Stourbridge Junction	a																						
Kidderminster	a																						

§ London Underground Limited (Central Line) also operate services between South Ruislip and West Ruislip at frequent intervals

A until 6 October
B from 13 October

For complete services between Banbury and Birmingham, refer to Table T71

For principal services between London and Aylesbury refer to Table T114

Table T115-F

Saturdays
26 May to 8 December

London - High Wycombe, Aylesbury, Oxford Parkway, Banbury, Stratford-upon-Avon, Birmingham Snow Hill and Kidderminster

		CH	CH	CH	CH	CH	CH	CH		CH	CH	CH	CH	CH	CH	CH	CH	CH	CH	CH	CH	CH	CH	CH
		◇	◇			◇	◇	◇		◇			◇	◇	◇			◇	◇	◇	◇			
		A				B	A	B		A	B	A	B	A				B	A	B	A		B	A
London Marylebone ⊖	d	10 35	10 40	10 43	10 46	11 06	11 06	11 10		11 10	11 13	11 13	11 35	11 35	11 40	11 43	11 46	12 06	12 06	12 10	12 10		12 13	12 13
London Paddington ⊖	d																							
Wembley Stadium	d				10 55						11 22	11 22					11 55						12 22	12 22
Sudbury & Harrow Road	d																							
Sudbury Hill Harrow	d																							
Northolt Park	d				11 00												12 00							
South Ruislip § ⊖	d				11 03												12 03							
West Ruislip § ⊖	d				11 07												12 07							
Denham	d				11 11						11 32	11 32					12 11						12 32	12 32
Denham Golf Club	d			11 00												12 00								
Gerrards Cross	d			11 04	11a22						11 37	11 37				12 04	12a22						12 37	12 37
Seer Green	d			11 09												12 09								
Beaconsfield	d			11 12							11 43	11 43				12 12							12 43	12 43
High Wycombe	d	10 59		11 18				11 34		11 34	11 49	11 49	11 58	11 58		12 18				12 34	12 34		12 49	12 49
Saunderton	d										11 56	11 56											12 56	12 56
Princes Risborough	d			11 27							12 03	12 03				12 27							13 03	13 03
Monks Risborough	d										12 06	12 06											13 06	13 06
Little Kimble	d										12 10	12 10											13 10	13 10
Aylesbury	a										12 21	12 24											13 21	13 24
Haddenham & Thame Parkway	d			11 34		11 40	11 40									12 34		12 41	12 41					
Bicester Village	d	11 22				11 53	11 53						12 22	12 22				12 54	12 54					
Islip	d												12 28	12 28										
Oxford Parkway 116	a	11 29				12 01	12 01						12 31	12 31				13 01	13 01					
Oxford	a	11 42				12 09	12 12						12 39	12 42				13 10	13 13					
Bicester North	d		11 28	11 47											12 24	12 47								
Kings Sutton	d			11 58																				
Banbury	d		11 43	12a05				12 10		12 10					12 37	13a02				13 07	13 07			
Leamington Spa	d		12 01					12 27		12 27					12 55					13 25	13 25	13 32		
Warwick	d		12 05												12 59							13 37		
Warwick Parkway	d		12 09					12 34		12 34					13 03					13 32	13 32			
Hatton	d																					13 44		
Claverdon	d																					13 49		
Bearley	d																					13 54		
Wilmcote	d																					13 57		
Stratford-upon-Avon Parkway	a																					14 00		
Stratford-upon-Avon	a																					14 09		
Lapworth	a																							
Dorridge	a		12 18												13 14									
Solihull	a		12 24					12 45		12 45					13 20					13 44	13 44			
Birmingham Moor Street	a		12 33					12 56		12 59					13 33					13 56	13 59			
Birmingham Snow Hill	a		12 41												13 41									
Rowley Regis	a																							
Cradley Heath	a																							
Stourbridge Junction	a																							
Kidderminster	a																							

§ London Underground Limited (Central Line) also operate services between South Ruislip and West Ruislip at frequent intervals

A from 13 October
B until 6 October

For complete services between Banbury and Birmingham, refer to Table T71

For principal services between London and Aylesbury refer to Table T114

Table T115-F

Saturdays
26 May to 8 December

London - High Wycombe, Aylesbury, Oxford Parkway, Banbury, Stratford-upon-Avon, Birmingham Snow Hill and Kidderminster

		CH	CH	CH	CH	CH	CH	CH		CH	CH	CH	CH	CH	CH	CH	CH	CH	CH	CH	CH	CH	CH	CH
		◇	◇	◇			◇	◇		◇	◇			◇	◇	◇			◇	◇	◇	◇		
		A	B				A	B		A	B	A	B	A	B				A	B	A	B		A
London Marylebone ⊖	d	12 35	12 35	12 40	12 43	12 46	13 06	13 06		13 10	13 10	13 13	13 13	13 35	13 35	13 40	13 43	13 46	14 06	14 06	14 10	14 10		14 13
London Paddington ⊖	d																							
Wembley Stadium	d					12 55						13 22	13 22					13 55						14 22
Sudbury & Harrow Road	d																							
Sudbury Hill Harrow	d																							
Northolt Park	d					13 00												14 00						
South Ruislip § ⊖	d					13 03												14 03						
West Ruislip § ⊖	d					13 07												14 07						
Denham	d					13 11						13 32	13 32					14 11						14 32
Denham Golf Club	d				13 00												14 00							
Gerrards Cross	d				13 04	13a19						13 37	13 37				14 04	14a19						14 37
Seer Green	d				13 09												14 09							
Beaconsfield	d				13 12							13 43	13 43				14 12							14 43
High Wycombe	d	12 58	12 58		13 18					13 35	13 35	13 49	13 49	13 58	13 58		14 18				14 34	14 34		14 49
Saunderton	d											13 55	13 55											14 55
Princes Risborough	d				13 27							14 02	14 02				14 27							15 02
Monks Risborough	d											14 05	14 05											15 05
Little Kimble	d											14 09	14 09											15 09
Aylesbury	a											14 20	14 23											15 20
Haddenham & Thame Parkway	d				13 34		13 41	13 41									14 34		14 41	14 41				
Bicester Village	d	13 22	13 22				13 54	13 54						14 22	14 22				14 54	14 54				
Islip	d																							
Oxford Parkway 116	a	13 29	13 29				14 01	14 01						14 29	14 29				15 01	15 01				
Oxford	a	13 40	13 43				14 10	14 13						14 38	14 41				15 10	15 13				
Bicester North	d			13 24	13 47											14 24	14 47							
Kings Sutton	d				13 58																			
Banbury	d			13 37	14a04					14 09	14 09					14 37	15a02				15 07	15 07		
Leamington Spa	d			13 55						14 27	14 27					14 55					15 25	15 25	15 32	
Warwick	d			13 59												14 59							15 37	
Warwick Parkway	d			14 03						14 33	14 33					15 03					15 32	15 32		
Hatton	d																						15 44	
Claverdon	d																						15 49	
Bearley	d																							
Wilmcote	d																						15 56	
Stratford-upon-Avon Parkway	a																						15 58	
Stratford-upon-Avon	a																						16 08	
Lapworth	a																							
Dorridge	a			14 12												15 12								
Solihull	a			14 20						14 44	14 44					15 20					15 44	15 44		
Birmingham Moor Street	a			14 33						14 56	14 59					15 33					15 56	15 59		
Birmingham Snow Hill	a			14 41												15 41								
Rowley Regis	a																							
Cradley Heath	a																							
Stourbridge Junction	a																							
Kidderminster	a																							

§ London Underground Limited (Central Line) also operate services between South Ruislip and West Ruislip at frequent intervals

A until 6 October
B from 13 October

For complete services between Banbury and Birmingham, refer to Table T71

For principal services between London and Aylesbury refer to Table T114

Please note, Network Rail have stated that further updates to this timetable are possible during the validity period.

Table T115-F

Saturdays

26 May to 8 December

London - High Wycombe, Aylesbury, Oxford Parkway, Banbury, Stratford-upon-Avon, Birmingham Snow Hill and Kidderminster

		CH A	CH ◇ B	CH ◇ A	CH ◇	CH	CH	CH ◇ B	CH ◇ A	CH ◇ B	CH ◇ A	CH B	CH A	CH ◇ B	CH ◇ A	CH ◇	CH	CH	CH ◇ B	CH ◇ A	CH ◇ B	CH ◇ A	CH
London Marylebone ⊖	d	14 13	14 35	14 35	14 40	14 43	14 46	15 06	15 06	15 10	15 10	15 13	15 13	15 35	15 35	15 40	15 43	15 46	16 06	16 06	16 10	16 10	
London Paddington ⊖	d																						
Wembley Stadium	d	14 22					14 55					15 22	15 22					15 55					
Sudbury & Harrow Road	d																						
Sudbury Hill Harrow	d																						
Northolt Park	d						15 00											16 00					
South Ruislip § ⊖	d						15 03											16 03					
West Ruislip § ⊖	d						15 07											16 07					
Denham	d	14 32					15 11					15 32	15 32					16 11					
Denham Golf Club	d					15 00											16 00						
Gerrards Cross	d	14 37				15 04	15a22					15 37	15 37				16 04	16a22					
Seer Green	d					15 09											16 09						
Beaconsfield	d	14 43				15 12						15 43	15 43				16 12						
High Wycombe	d	14 49	14 58	14 58		15 18				15 34	15 34	15 49	15 49	15 58	15 58		16 18				16 34	16 34	
Saunderton	d	14 55										15 55	15 55										
Princes Risborough	d	15 02				15 27						16 02	16 02				16 27						
Monks Risborough	d	15 05										16 05	16 05										
Little Kimble	d	15 09										16 09	16 09										
Aylesbury	a	15 23										16 20	16 23										
Haddenham & Thame Parkway	d					15 34		15 41	15 41								16 34		16 41	16 41			
Bicester Village	d		15 22	15 22				15 54	15 54					16 22	16 22				16 54	16 54			
Islip	d		15 28	15 28																			
Oxford Parkway 116	a		15 31	15 31				16 01	16 01					16 29	16 29				17 01	17 01			
Oxford	a		15 40	15 43				16 11	16 14					16 37	16 40				17 10	17 13			
Bicester North	d				15 24	15 47										16 24	16 47						
Kings Sutton	d					15 58																	
Banbury	d				15 37	16a04				16 09	16 09					16 37	17a02				17 07	17 07	
Leamington Spa	d				15 55					16 26	16 26					16 55					17 25	17 25	17 32
Warwick	d				15 59											16 59							17 37
Warwick Parkway	d				16 03					16 33	16 33					17 03					17 32	17 32	
Hatton	d																						17 47
Claverdon	d																						17 52
Bearley	d																						17 57
Wilmcote	d																						18 02
Stratford-upon-Avon Parkway	a																						18 05
Stratford-upon-Avon	a																						18 15
Lapworth	a																						
Dorridge	a				16 12											17 12							
Solihull	a				16 20					16 44	16 44					17 20					17 44	17 44	
Birmingham Moor Street	a				16 33					16 56	16 59					17 33					17 56	17 59	
Birmingham Snow Hill	a				16 41											17 41							
Rowley Regis	a																						
Cradley Heath	a																						
Stourbridge Junction	a																						
Kidderminster	a																						

§ London Underground Limited (Central Line) also operate services between South Ruislip and West Ruislip at frequent intervals

A from 13 October
B until 6 October

For complete services between Banbury and Birmingham, refer to Table T71

For principal services between London and Aylesbury refer to Table T114

Table T115-F

Saturdays

26 May to 8 December

London - High Wycombe, Aylesbury, Oxford Parkway, Banbury, Stratford-upon-Avon, Birmingham Snow Hill and Kidderminster

		CH A	CH B	CH ◇ A	CH ◇ B	CH ◇	CH	CH	CH ◇ A	CH ◇ B	CH ◇	CH A	CH B	CH ◇ A	CH ◇ B	CH ◇	CH	CH	CH ◇ A	CH ◇ B	CH ◇	CH	CH A
London Marylebone ⊖	d	16 13	16 13	16 35	16 35	16 40	16 43	16 46	17 06	17 06	17 10	17 13	17 13	17 35	17 35	17 40	17 43	17 46	18 06	18 06	18 10		18 13
London Paddington ⊖	d																						
Wembley Stadium	d	16 22	16 22					16 55				17 22	17 22					17 55					18 22
Sudbury & Harrow Road	d																						
Sudbury Hill Harrow	d																						
Northolt Park	d							17 00										18 00					
South Ruislip § ⊖	d							17 03										18 03					
West Ruislip § ⊖	d							17 07										18 07					
Denham	d	16 32	16 32					17 11				17 32	17 32					18 11					18 32
Denham Golf Club	d						17 00										18 00						
Gerrards Cross	d	16 37	16 37				17 04	17a22				17 37	17 37				18 04	18a22					18 37
Seer Green	d						17 09										18 09						
Beaconsfield	d	16 43	16 43				17 12					17 43	17 43				18 12						18 43
High Wycombe	d	16 49	16 49	16 58	16 58		17 18				17 34	17 49	17 49	17 58	17 58		18 18				18 34		18 49
Saunderton	d	16 55	16 55									17 55	17 55										18 55
Princes Risborough	d	17 02	17 02				17 27					18 02	18 02				18 27						19 02
Monks Risborough	d	17 05	17 05									18 05	18 05										19 05
Little Kimble	d	17 09	17 09									18 09	18 09										19 09
Aylesbury	a	17 20	17 23									18 20	18 23										19 20
Haddenham & Thame Parkway	d						17 34		17 41	17 41							18 34		18 41	18 41			
Bicester Village	d			17 22	17 22				17 54	17 54				18 22	18 22				18 54	18 54			
Islip	d													18 28	18 28								
Oxford Parkway 116	a			17 29	17 29				18 01	18 01				18 31	18 31				19 01	19 01			
Oxford	a			17 38	17 41				18 12	18 15				18 39	18 42				19 10	19 13			
Bicester North	d					17 24	17 47									18 24	18 47						
Kings Sutton	d						17 58																
Banbury	d					17 37	18a04				18 09					18 37	19a02				19 07		
Leamington Spa	d					17 55					18 26					18 55					19 26	19 32	
Warwick	d					17 59										18 59						19 37	
Warwick Parkway	d					18 03					18 33					19 03					19 33		
Hatton	d																					19 44	
Claverdon	d																					19 49	
Bearley	d																					19 54	
Wilmcote	d																					19 58	
Stratford-upon-Avon Parkway	a																					20 00	
Stratford-upon-Avon	a																					20 10	
Lapworth	a																						
Dorridge	a					18 12										19 12							
Solihull	a					18 20					18 47					19 18					19 46		
Birmingham Moor Street	a					18 33					18 58					19 27					19 58		
Birmingham Snow Hill	a					18 41					19 02					19 35					20 07		
Rowley Regis	a										19 16												
Cradley Heath	a																						
Stourbridge Junction	a										19 27												
Kidderminster	a										19 44												

§ London Underground Limited (Central Line) also operate services between South Ruislip and West Ruislip at frequent intervals

A until 6 October
B from 13 October

For complete services between Banbury and Birmingham, refer to Table T71

For principal services between London and Aylesbury refer to Table T114

Table T115-F

Saturdays
26 May to 8 December

London - High Wycombe, Aylesbury, Oxford Parkway, Banbury, Stratford-upon-Avon, Birmingham Snow Hill and Kidderminster

		CH	CH	CH	CH	CH	CH	CH	CH	CH	CH	CH	CH	CH	CH	CH	CH	CH	CH	CH	CH	CH	CH
			◇	◇	◇			◇	◇	◇	◇			◇	◇	◇			◇	◇	◇	◇	
		A	B	A				B	A	B	A	B	A	B	A				B	A	B	A	
London Marylebone ⊖	d	18 13	18 35	18 35	18 40	18 43	18 46	19 06	19 06	19 10	19 10	19 13	19 13	19 35	19 35	19 40	19 43	19 46	20 06	20 06	20 10	20 10	
London Paddington ⊖	d																						
Wembley Stadium	d	18 22					18 55					19 22	19 22					19 55					
Sudbury & Harrow Road	d																						
Sudbury Hill Harrow	d																						
Northolt Park	d						19 00											20 00					
South Ruislip § ⊖	d						19 03											20 03					
West Ruislip § ⊖	d						19 07											20 07					
Denham	d	18 32					19 11					19 32	19 32					20 11					
Denham Golf Club	d					19 00											20 00						
Gerrards Cross	d	18 37				19 04	19a19					19 37	19 37				20 04	20a22					
Seer Green	d					19 09											20 09						
Beaconsfield	d	18 43				19 12						19 43	19 43				20 12						
High Wycombe	d	18 49	18 58	18 58		19 18				19 34	19 34	19 49	19 49	19 58	19 58		20 18				20 34	20 34	
Saunderton	d	18 55										19 55	19 55										
Princes Risborough	d	19 02				19 27						20 02	20 02				20 27						
Monks Risborough	d	19 05										20 05	20 05										
Little Kimble	d	19 09										20 09	20 09										
Aylesbury	a	19 23										20 20	20 23										
Haddenham & Thame Parkway	d					19 34		19 41	19 41								20 34		20 41	20 41			
Bicester Village	d		19 22	19 22				19 54	19 54					20 22	20 22				20 54	20 54			
Islip	d																						
Oxford Parkway 116	a		19 29	19 29				20 01	20 01					20 29	20 29				21 01	21 01			
Oxford	a		19 38	19 41				20 10	20 13					20 37	20 40				21 10	21 13			
Bicester North	d				19 24	19 47										20 24	20 47						
Kings Sutton	d					19 58																	
Banbury	d				19 37	20a04				20 09	20 09					20 37	21a02				21 07	21 07	
Leamington Spa	d				19 55					20 27	20 27					20 55					21 25	21 25	21 32
Warwick	d				19 59											20 59							21 37
Warwick Parkway	d				20 03					20 33	20 33					21 03					21 32	21 32	
Hatton	d																						21 44
Claverdon	d																						21 49
Bearley	d																						21 54
Wilmcote	d																						21 58
Stratford-upon-Avon Parkway	a																						22 00
Stratford-upon-Avon	a																						22 10
Lapworth	a																						
Dorridge	a				20 12											21 12							
Solihull	a				20 18					20 45	20 45					21 18					21 44	21 44	
Birmingham Moor Street	a				20 27					20 57	21 00					21 27					21 57	22 00	
Birmingham Snow Hill	a				20 35											21 30							
Rowley Regis	a															21 44							
Cradley Heath	a															21 50							
Stourbridge Junction	a															21 56							
Kidderminster	a															22 12							

§ London Underground Limited (Central Line) also operate services between South Ruislip and West Ruislip at frequent intervals

A from 13 October
B until 6 October

For complete services between Banbury and Birmingham, refer to Table T71

For principal services between London and Aylesbury refer to Table T114

Table T115-F

Saturdays
26 May to 8 December

London - High Wycombe, Aylesbury, Oxford Parkway, Banbury, Stratford-upon-Avon, Birmingham Snow Hill and Kidderminster

		CH	CH	CH	CH	CH	CH	CH	CH	CH	CH	CH	CH	CH	CH	CH	CH	CH	CH	CH	CH	CH	CH
				◇	◇	◇			◇	◇	◇			◇	◇			◇	◇	◇	◇		
		A	B	A	B				A	B		A	B	A	B			A	B	A	B	A	B
London Marylebone ⊖	d	20 13	20 13	20 35	20 35	20 40	20 43	20 46	21 06	21 06	21 10	21 13	21 13	21 35	21 35	21 40	21 46	22 06	22 06	22 10	22 10	22 13	22 13
London Paddington ⊖	d																						
Wembley Stadium	d	20 22	20 22					20 55				21 22	21 22				21 55					22 22	22 22
Sudbury & Harrow Road	d																						
Sudbury Hill Harrow	d																						
Northolt Park	d							21 00									22 00					22 27	22 27
South Ruislip § ⊖	d							21 03									22 03					22 30	22 30
West Ruislip § ⊖	d							21 07									22 07					22 34	22 34
Denham	d	20 32	20 32					21 11				21 32	21 32				22 11					22 38	22 38
Denham Golf Club	d						21 00									21 57						22 41	22 41
Gerrards Cross	d	20 37	20 37				21 04	21a19				21 37	21 37			22 01	22a22					22 45	22 45
Seer Green	d						21 09									22 06						22 50	22 50
Beaconsfield	d	20 43	20 43				21 12					21 43	21 43			22 10						22 53	22 53
High Wycombe	d	20 49	20 49	20 58	20 58		21 18				21 34	21 49	21 49	21 59	21 59	22 16				22 34	22 34	22 59	22 59
Saunderton	d	20 56	20 56									21 56	21 56			22 23						23 06	23 06
Princes Risborough	d	21 03	21 03				21 27					22 03	22 03			22 28						23 13	23 13
Monks Risborough	d	21 06	21 06									22 06	22 06									23 16	23 16
Little Kimble	d	21 10	21 10									22 10	22 10									23 20	23 20
Aylesbury	a	21 21	21 24									22 21	22 24									23 31	23 34
Haddenham & Thame Parkway	d						21 34		21 41	21 41						22 35		22 40	22 40				
Bicester Village	d			21 22	21 22				21 54	21 54				22 22	22 22			22 53	22 53				
Islip	d			21 28	21 28																		
Oxford Parkway 116	a			21 31	21 31				22 01	22 01				22 29	22 29			23 01	23 01				
Oxford	a			21 39	21 42				22 10	22 13				22 39	22 42			23 09	23 12				
Bicester North	d					21 24	21 47				21 57					22 48				22 57	22 57		
Kings Sutton	d						21 58																
Banbury	d					21 37	22a05				22 10					23a10				23 10	23 10		
Leamington Spa	d					21 55					22 28									23 28	23 28		
Warwick	d					21 59					22 32									23 32	23 32		
Warwick Parkway	d					22 03					22 36									23 37	23 37		
Hatton	d										22 41												
Claverdon	d																						
Bearley	d																						
Wilmcote	d																						
Stratford-upon-Avon Parkway	a																						
Stratford-upon-Avon	a																						
Lapworth	a										22 46												
Dorridge	a					22 12					22 51									23 46	23 46		
Solihull	a					22 18					22 58									23 52	23 52		
Birmingham Moor Street	a					22 27					23 06									00 04	00 07		
Birmingham Snow Hill	a					22 35					23 14												
Rowley Regis	a																						
Cradley Heath	a																						
Stourbridge Junction	a																						
Kidderminster	a																						

§ London Underground Limited (Central Line) also operate services between South Ruislip and West Ruislip at frequent intervals

A until 6 October
B from 13 October

For complete services between Banbury and Birmingham, refer to Table T71

For principal services between London and Aylesbury refer to Table T114

Please note, Network Rail have stated that further updates to this timetable are possible during the validity period.

Table T115-F

Saturdays
26 May to 8 December

London - High Wycombe, Aylesbury, Oxford Parkway, Banbury, Stratford-upon-Avon, Birmingham Snow Hill and Kidderminster

		CH	CH	CH	CH	CH	CH	CH	CH	CH
		◇	◇		◇	◇				
		A	B		A	B		A	B	
London Marylebone ⊖	d	22 35	22 35	22 40	23 10	23 10	23 15	23 19	23 19	23 45
London Paddington ⊖	d									
Wembley Stadium	d	22 45	22 45	22 49	23 19	23 19	23 24	23 29	23 29	23 55
Sudbury & Harrow Road	d									
Sudbury Hill Harrow	d									
Northolt Park	d							23 34	23 34	
South Ruislip § ⊖	d							23 37	23 37	
West Ruislip § ⊖	d							23 41	23 41	
Denham	d							23 45	23 45	
Denham Golf Club	d							23 48	23 48	
Gerrards Cross	d			23 02			23 37	23 51	23 51	00 08
Seer Green	d							23 56	23 56	
Beaconsfield	d			23 08			23 43	23 59	23 59	00 15
High Wycombe	d	23 06	23 06	23 14	23 36	23 36	23 49	00 05	00 05	00 21
Saunderton	d							00 11	00 11	
Princes Risborough	d			23 23			23 59	00 18	00 18	00 31
Monks Risborough	d							00 21	00 21	
Little Kimble	d							00 25	00 25	
Aylesbury	a							00 36	00 39	
Haddenham & Thame Parkway	d			23 30			00 06			00 38
Bicester Village	d	23 33	23 33		23 59	23 59				
Islip	d				00 05	00 05				
Oxford Parkway 116	a	23 41	23 41		00 09	00 09				
Oxford	a	23 47	23 50		00 18	00 21				
Bicester North	d			23 43			00 19			00 51
Kings Sutton	d									01 03
Banbury	d			00a03			00a40			01a14
Leamington Spa	d									
Warwick	d									
Warwick Parkway	d									
Hatton	d									
Claverdon	d									
Bearley	d									
Wilmcote	d									
Stratford-upon-Avon Parkway	a									
Stratford-upon-Avon	a									
Lapworth	a									
Dorridge	a									
Solihull	a									
Birmingham Moor Street	a									
Birmingham Snow Hill	a									
Rowley Regis	a									
Cradley Heath	a									
Stourbridge Junction	a									
Kidderminster	a									

§ London Underground Limited (Central Line) also operate services between South Ruislip and West Ruislip at frequent intervals

A until 6 October
B from 13 October

For complete services between Banbury and Birmingham, refer to Table T71

For principal services between London and Aylesbury refer to Table T114

Table T115-F

Sundays
20 May to 2 December

London - High Wycombe, Aylesbury, Oxford Parkway, Banbury, Stratford-upon-Avon, Birmingham Snow Hill and Kidderminster

		CH	CH	CH	CH	CH	CH	CH	CH	CH	CH	CH	CH	CH	CH	CH	CH	CH	CH	CH	CH	CH	CH
		◇	◇						◇	◇			◇			◇	◇			◇	◇	◇	
		A	B	A	B	C	C		D	E	F	G		H	I	D	E			D	E		D
London Marylebone ⊖	d							00 10	07 35	07 35	07 50	07 50	08 15			08 35	08 35	08 40	08 46	09 05	09 05	09 10	09 13
London Paddington ⊖	d																						
Wembley Stadium	d							00 19			07 59	07 59							08 55				09 22
Sudbury & Harrow Road	d																						
Sudbury Hill Harrow	d																						
Northolt Park	d							00 24			08 04	08 04							09 00				
South Ruislip § ⊖	d							00 27			08 07	08 07							09 03				
West Ruislip § ⊖	d							00 31			08 11	08 11							09 07				
Denham	d							00 35			08 15	08 15							09 11				
Denham Golf Club	d							00 38			08 18	08 18											
Gerrards Cross	d						00 08	00 42	07 53	07 53	08 22	08 22	08 33					09 00	09a22				09 35
Seer Green	d							00 46			08 27	08 27						09 05					
Beaconsfield	d						00 15	00 50	07 59	07 59	08 30	08 30	08 39					09 08					09 41
High Wycombe	d			00 05	00 05		00 21	00 56	08 05	08 05	08 36	08 36	08 45	←	←	08 59	08 59	09 14				09 34	09 47
Saunderton	d			00 11	00 11			01 02			08 43	08 43		08 43	08 43			09 21					09 54
Princes Risborough	d			00 18	00 18		00 31	01 09	08 14	08 14	→	→	08 53	09 01	09 01			09 26					10 01
Monks Risborough	d			00 21	00 21			01 12						09 04	09 04								10 04
Little Kimble	d			00 25	00 25			01 16						09 08	09 08								10 08
Aylesbury	a			00 36	00 39			01 30						09 19	09 22								10 19
Haddenham & Thame Parkway	d					00 06	00 38		08 21	08 21			09 00					09 33		09 40	09 40		
Bicester Village	d								08 34	08 34						09 22	09 22			09 53	09 53		
Islip	d	00 05	00 05						08 40	08 40													
Oxford Parkway 116	a	00 09	00 09						08 43	08 43						09 29	09 29			10 00	10 00		
Oxford	a	00 18	00 21						08 51	08 54						09 37	09 40			10 09	10 12		
Bicester North	d					00 19	00 51						09 10					09 46					
Kings Sutton	d						01 03						09 20										
Banbury	d					00a40	01a14						09 29					10a02				10 07	
Leamington Spa	d												09 47									10 25	
Warwick	d												09 51										
Warwick Parkway	d												09 55									10 32	
Hatton	d												10 00										
Claverdon	d																						
Bearley	d																						
Wilmcote	d																						
Stratford-upon-Avon Parkway	a																						
Stratford-upon-Avon	a																						
Lapworth	a												10 06										
Dorridge	a												10 10										
Solihull	a												10 16									10 44	
Birmingham Moor Street	a												10 24									10 53	
Birmingham Snow Hill	a												10 32									11 01	
Rowley Regis	a																						
Cradley Heath	a																						
Stourbridge Junction	a																						
Kidderminster	a																						

§ London Underground Limited (Central Line) also operate services between South Ruislip and West Ruislip at frequent intervals

A from 27 May until 7 October. From London Marylebone
B from 14 October. From London Marylebone
C not 20 May. From London Marylebone
D until 30 September
E from 7 October
F from 7 October. To Aylesbury
G until 30 September. To Aylesbury
H until 30 September. From London Marylebone
I from 7 October. From London Marylebone

For complete services between Banbury and Birmingham, refer to Table T71

For principal services between London and Aylesbury refer to Table T114

Table T115-F

Sundays

20 May to 2 December

London - High Wycombe, Aylesbury, Oxford Parkway, Banbury, Stratford-upon-Avon, Birmingham Snow Hill and Kidderminster

		CH	CH	CH	CH	CH	CH	CH	CH	CH	CH	CH	CH	CH	CH	CH	CH	CH	CH	CH	CH	CH	CH
		A	◇ B	◇ A	◇	◇ C		◇ B	◇ A	◇ B	◇ A	◇ D	B	A	◇ B	◇ A	◇			◇ B	◇ A	◇ B	◇ A
London Marylebone ⊖	d	09 13	09 35	09 35	09 40	09 43	09 46	10 05	10 05	10 10	10 10		10 13	10 13	10 35	10 35	10 40	10 43	10 46	11 05	11 05	11 10	11 10
London Paddington ⊖	d																						
Wembley Stadium	d	09 22					09 55						10 22	10 22					10 55				
Sudbury & Harrow Road	d																						
Sudbury Hill Harrow	d																						
Northolt Park	d						10 00												11 00				
South Ruislip § ⊖	d						10 03												11 03				
West Ruislip § ⊖	d																		11 07				
Denham	d						10 09												11 11				
Denham Golf Club	d					10 00																	
Gerrards Cross	d	09 35				10 04	10a19						10 35	10 35				11 02	11a19				
Seer Green	d					10 09												11 07					
Beaconsfield	d	09 41				10 12							10 41	10 41				11 10					
High Wycombe	d	09 47	09 58	09 58		10 18				10 34	10 34		10 47	10 47	10 58	10 58		11 16				11 34	11 34
Saunderton	d	09 54											10 54	10 54									
Princes Risborough	d	10 01				10 27							11 01	11 01				11 25					
Monks Risborough	d	10 04											11 04	11 04									
Little Kimble	d	10 08											11 08	11 08									
Aylesbury	a	10 22											11 19	11 22									
Haddenham & Thame Parkway	d					10 34		10 40	10 40									11 32		11 40	11 40		
Bicester Village	d		10 21	10 21				10 53	10 53						11 21	11 21				11 53	11 53		
Islip	d		10 27	10 27																			
Oxford Parkway 116	a		10 30	10 30				11 00	11 00						11 28	11 28				12 00	12 00		
Oxford	a		10 39	10 42				11 09	11 12			←			11 37	11 40				12 09	12 12		
Bicester North	d				10 24	10 47						10 47					11 24	11 45					
Kings Sutton	d					→												11 56					
Banbury	d				10 37					11 07	11 07	11 11					11 37	12a02				12 07	12 07
Leamington Spa	d				10 55					11 25	11 25	11 32					11 55					12 25	12 25
Warwick	d				10 59							11 38					11 59						
Warwick Parkway	d				11 03					11 32	11 32						12 03					12 32	12 32
Hatton	d											11 45											
Claverdon	d																						
Bearley	d																						
Wilmcote	d											11 55											
Stratford-upon-Avon Parkway	a											11 57											
Stratford-upon-Avon	a											12 07											
Lapworth	a																						
Dorridge	a				11 12												12 12						
Solihull	a				11 18					11 44	11 44						12 18					12 44	12 44
Birmingham Moor Street	a				11 27					11 56	11 59						12 27					12 56	12 59
Birmingham Snow Hill	a				11 35												12 35						
Rowley Regis	a																						
Cradley Heath	a																						
Stourbridge Junction	a																						
Kidderminster	a																						

§ London Underground Limited (Central Line) also operate services between South Ruislip and West Ruislip at frequent intervals

A from 7 October
B until 30 September
C To Stratford-upon-Avon
D From London Marylebone

For complete services between Banbury and Birmingham, refer to Table T71

For principal services between London and Aylesbury refer to Table T114

Table T115-F

Sundays

20 May to 2 December

London - High Wycombe, Aylesbury, Oxford Parkway, Banbury, Stratford-upon-Avon, Birmingham Snow Hill and Kidderminster

		CH	CH	CH	CH	CH	CH	CH	CH	CH	CH	CH	CH	CH	CH	CH	CH	CH	CH	CH	CH	CH	CH
		A	B	◇ A	◇ B	◇			◇ A	◇ B	◇ A	◇ B		A	B	◇ A	◇ B	◇			◇ A	◇ B	◇ A
London Marylebone ⊖	d	11 13	11 13	11 35	11 35	11 40	11 43	11 46	12 05	12 05	12 10	12 10		12 13	12 13	12 35	12 35	12 40	12 43	12 46	13 05	13 05	13 10
London Paddington ⊖	d																						
Wembley Stadium	d	11 22	11 22					11 55						12 22	12 22					12 55			
Sudbury & Harrow Road	d																						
Sudbury Hill Harrow	d																						
Northolt Park	d							12 00												13 00			
South Ruislip § ⊖	d							12 03												13 03			
West Ruislip § ⊖	d																			13 07			
Denham	d							12 09												13 11			
Denham Golf Club	d						12 00																
Gerrards Cross	d	11 36	11 36				12 04	12a16						12 36	12 36				13 02	13a22			
Seer Green	d						12 09												13 07				
Beaconsfield	d	11 42	11 42				12 12							12 42	12 42			13 01	13 10				
High Wycombe	d	11 48	11 48	11 58	11 58		12 18				12 34	12 34		12 48	12 48	12 59	12 59		13 16				13 34
Saunderton	d	11 55	11 55											12 55	12 55								
Princes Risborough	d	12 02	12 02				12 27							13 02	13 02				13 25				
Monks Risborough	d	12 05	12 05											13 05	13 05								
Little Kimble	d	12 09	12 09											13 09	13 09								
Aylesbury	a	12 20	12 23											13 20	13 23								
Haddenham & Thame Parkway	d						12 34		12 40	12 40									13 32		13 40	13 40	
Bicester Village	d			12 21	12 21				12 53	12 53						13 22	13 22				13 53	13 53	
Islip	d			12 27	12 27																		
Oxford Parkway 116	a			12 30	12 30				13 00	13 00						13 29	13 29				14 00	14 00	
Oxford	a			12 39	12 42				13 09	13 12						13 37	13 40				14 09	14 12	
Bicester North	d					12 24	12 47											13 26	13 45				
Kings Sutton	d																		13 56				
Banbury	d					12 37	13a02				13 07	13 07						13 39	14a02				14 07
Leamington Spa	d					12 55					13 25	13 25	13 32					13 57					14 25
Warwick	d					12 59							13 37					14 01					
Warwick Parkway	d					13 03					13 32	13 32						14 05					14 32
Hatton	d												13 44										
Claverdon	d																						
Bearley	d																						
Wilmcote	d												13 54										
Stratford-upon-Avon Parkway	a												13 56										
Stratford-upon-Avon	a												14 06										
Lapworth	a																						
Dorridge	a					13 13												14 14					
Solihull	a					13 19					13 44	13 44						14 20					14 44
Birmingham Moor Street	a					13 29					13 56	13 59						14 29					14 56
Birmingham Snow Hill	a					13 37												14 37					
Rowley Regis	a																						
Cradley Heath	a																						
Stourbridge Junction	a																						
Kidderminster	a																						

§ London Underground Limited (Central Line) also operate services between South Ruislip and West Ruislip at frequent intervals

A until 30 September
B from 7 October

For complete services between Banbury and Birmingham, refer to Table T71

For principal services between London and Aylesbury refer to Table T114

Table T115-F

Sundays

20 May to 2 December

London - High Wycombe, Aylesbury, Oxford Parkway, Banbury, Stratford-upon-Avon, Birmingham Snow Hill and Kidderminster

	CH ◇ A	CH B	CH A	CH ◇ B	CH ◇ A	CH ◇	CH		CH	CH ◇ B	CH ◇ A	CH ◇ B	CH ◇ A	CH	CH B	CH A	CH ◇ B	CH ◇ A	CH ◇	CH	CH	CH ◇ B	CH ◇ A
London Marylebone ⊖ d	13 10	13 13	13 13	13 35	13 35	13 40	13 43		13 46	14 05	14 05	14 10	14 10		14 13	14 13	14 35	14 35	14 40	14 43	14 46	15 05	15 05
London Paddington ⊖ d																							
Wembley Stadium d		13 22	13 22						13 55						14 22	14 22					14 55		
Sudbury & Harrow Road d																							
Sudbury Hill Harrow d																							
Northolt Park d									14 00												15 00		
South Ruislip § ⊖ d									14 03												15 03		
West Ruislip § ⊖ d																					15 07		
Denham d									14 09												15 11		
Denham Golf Club d							14 00																
Gerrards Cross d		13 35	13 35				14 04		14a19						14 35	14 35				15 02	15a21		
Seer Green d							14 09													15 07			
Beaconsfield d		13 41	13 41			14 01	14 12								14 41	14 41			15 01	15 10			
High Wycombe d	13 34	13 47	13 47	13 59	13 59		14 18					14 34	14 34		14 47	14 47	14 59	14 59		15 16			
Saunderton d		13 54	13 54												14 54	14 54							
Princes Risborough d		14 01	14 01				14 27								15 01	15 01				15 25			
Monks Risborough d		14 04	14 04												15 04	15 04							
Little Kimble d		14 08	14 08												15 08	15 08							
Aylesbury a		14 19	14 22												15 19	15 22							
Haddenham & Thame Parkway d							14 34			14 40	14 40									15 32		15 40	15 40
Bicester Village d				14 22	14 22					14 53	14 53						15 22	15 22				15 53	15 53
Islip d				14 28	14 28																		
Oxford Parkway 116 a				14 31	14 31					15 00	15 00						15 29	15 29				16 00	16 00
Oxford a				14 39	14 42					15 09	15 12						15 37	15 40				16 09	16 12
Bicester North d						14 26	14 47												15 26	15 45			
Kings Sutton d																				15 56			
Banbury d	14 07					14 39	15a02					15 07	15 07						15 39	16a02			
Leamington Spa d	14 25					14 57						15 25	15 25	15 32					15 57				
Warwick d						15 01								15 37					16 01				
Warwick Parkway d	14 32					15 05						15 32	15 32						16 05				
Hatton d														15 44									
Claverdon d																							
Bearley d																							
Wilmcote d														15 54									
Stratford-upon-Avon Parkway a														15 56									
Stratford-upon-Avon a														16 06									
Lapworth a																							
Dorridge a						15 14													16 14				
Solihull a	14 44					15 20						15 44	15 44						16 20				
Birmingham Moor Street a	14 59					15 29						15 56	15 59						16 29				
Birmingham Snow Hill a						15 37													16 37				
Rowley Regis a																							
Cradley Heath a																							
Stourbridge Junction a																							
Kidderminster a																							

§ London Underground Limited (Central Line) also operate services between South Ruislip and West Ruislip at frequent intervals

A from 7 October
B until 30 September

For complete services between Banbury and Birmingham, refer to Table T71

For principal services between London and Aylesbury refer to Table T114

Table T115-F

Sundays

20 May to 2 December

London - High Wycombe, Aylesbury, Oxford Parkway, Banbury, Stratford-upon-Avon, Birmingham Snow Hill and Kidderminster

	CH ◇ A	CH ◇ B	CH A	CH B	CH ◇ A	CH ◇ B	CH ◇		CH	CH	CH ◇ A	CH ◇ B	CH ◇ A	CH ◇ B	CH	CH A	CH B	CH ◇ A	CH ◇ B	CH ◇	CH	CH	CH ◇ A
London Marylebone ⊖ d	15 10	15 10	15 13	15 13	15 35	15 35	15 40		15 43	15 46	16 05	16 05	16 10	16 10		16 13	16 13	16 35	16 35	16 40	16 43	16 46	17 05
London Paddington ⊖ d																							
Wembley Stadium d			15 22	15 22						15 55						16 22	16 22					16 55	
Sudbury & Harrow Road d																							
Sudbury Hill Harrow d																							
Northolt Park d										16 00												17 00	
South Ruislip § ⊖ d										16 03												17 03	
West Ruislip § ⊖ d																						17 07	
Denham d										16 09												17 11	
Denham Golf Club d									16 00														
Gerrards Cross d			15 35	15 35					16 04	16a19						16 35	16 35				17 02	17a21	
Seer Green d									16 09												17 07		
Beaconsfield d			15 41	15 41			16 01		16 12							16 41	16 41			17 01	17 10		
High Wycombe d	15 34	15 34	15 47	15 47	15 59	15 59			16 18				16 34	16 34		16 47	16 47	16 59	16 59		17 16		
Saunderton d			15 54	15 54												16 54	16 54						
Princes Risborough d			16 01	16 01					16 27							17 01	17 01				17 25		
Monks Risborough d			16 04	16 04												17 04	17 04						
Little Kimble d			16 08	16 08												17 08	17 08						
Aylesbury a			16 19	16 22												17 19	17 22						
Haddenham & Thame Parkway d									16 34		16 40	16 40									17 32		17 40
Bicester Village d					16 22	16 22					16 53	16 53						17 22	17 22				17 53
Islip d					16 28	16 28																	
Oxford Parkway 116 a					16 31	16 31					17 00	17 00						17 29	17 29				18 00
Oxford a					16 39	16 42					17 09	17 12						17 37	17 40				18 09
Bicester North d							16 26		16 47											17 26	17 45		
Kings Sutton d																					17 56		
Banbury d	16 07	16 07					16 39		17a02				17 07	17 07						17 39	18a02		
Leamington Spa d	16 25	16 25					16 57						17 25	17 25	17 32					17 57			
Warwick d							17 01								17 37					18 01			
Warwick Parkway d	16 32	16 32					17 05						17 32	17 32						18 05			
Hatton d															17 44								
Claverdon d																							
Bearley d																							
Wilmcote d															17 54								
Stratford-upon-Avon Parkway a															17 56								
Stratford-upon-Avon a															18 06								
Lapworth a																							
Dorridge a							17 14													18 14			
Solihull a	16 44	16 44					17 20						17 44	17 44						18 20			
Birmingham Moor Street a	16 56	16 59					17 29						17 56	17 59						18 29			
Birmingham Snow Hill a							17 37													18 37			
Rowley Regis a																							
Cradley Heath a																							
Stourbridge Junction a																							
Kidderminster a																							

§ London Underground Limited (Central Line) also operate services between South Ruislip and West Ruislip at frequent intervals

A until 30 September
B from 7 October

For complete services between Banbury and Birmingham, refer to Table T71

For principal services between London and Aylesbury refer to Table T114

Please note, Network Rail have stated that further updates to this timetable are possible during the validity period.

Table T115-F

Sundays
20 May to 2 December

London - High Wycombe, Aylesbury, Oxford Parkway, Banbury, Stratford-upon-Avon, Birmingham Snow Hill and Kidderminster

		CH ◇ A	CH ◇ B	CH ◇ A	CH B	CH A	CH ◇ B	CH ◇ A	CH ◇	CH	CH	CH ◇ B	CH ◇ A	CH ◇	CH	CH B	CH A	CH ◇ B	CH ◇ A	CH ◇	CH	CH	CH ◇ B
London Marylebone ⊖	d	17 05	17 10	17 10	17 13	17 13	17 35	17 35	17 40	17 43	17 46	18 05	18 05	18 10		18 13	18 13	18 35	18 35	18 40	18 43	18 46	19 05
London Paddington ⊖	d																						
Wembley Stadium	d				17 22	17 22					17 55					18 22	18 22					18 55	
Sudbury & Harrow Road	d																						
Sudbury Hill Harrow	d																						
Northolt Park	d										18 00											19 00	
South Ruislip § ⊖	d										18 03											19 03	
West Ruislip § ⊖	d																					19 07	
Denham	d										18 09											19 11	
Denham Golf Club	d									18 00													
Gerrards Cross	d				17 35	17 35				18 04	18a19					18 35	18 35				19 02	19a18	
Seer Green	d									18 09											19 07		
Beaconsfield	d				17 41	17 41			18 01	18 12						18 41	18 41			19 01	19 10		
High Wycombe	d		17 34	17 34	17 47	17 47	17 59	17 59		18 18				18 35		18 47	18 47	18 59	18 59		19 16		
Saunderton	d				17 54	17 54										18 54	18 54						
Princes Risborough	d				18 01	18 01				18 27						19 01	19 01				19 25		
Monks Risborough	d				18 04	18 04										19 04	19 04						
Little Kimble	d				18 08	18 08										19 08	19 08						
Aylesbury	a				18 19	18 22										19 19	19 22						
Haddenham & Thame Parkway	d	17 40								18 34		18 40	18 40								19 32		19 40
Bicester Village	d	17 53					18 22	18 22				18 53	18 53					19 22	19 22				19 53
Islip	d																						
Oxford Parkway 116	a	18 00					18 29	18 29				19 00	19 00					19 29	19 29				20 00
Oxford	a	18 12					18 39	18 42				19 09	19 12					19 37	19 40				20 09
Bicester North	d								18 26	18 47										19 26	19 45		
Kings Sutton	d																				19 56		
Banbury	d		18 07	18 07					18 39	19a02				19 07						19 39	20a02		
Leamington Spa	d		18 25	18 25					18 57					19 25	19 32					19 57			
Warwick	d								19 01						19 37					20 01			
Warwick Parkway	d		18 32	18 32					19 05					19 32						20 05			
Hatton	d														19 44								
Claverdon	d																						
Bearley	d																						
Wilmcote	d														19 54								
Stratford-upon-Avon Parkway	a														19 56								
Stratford-upon-Avon	a														20 06								
Lapworth	a																						
Dorridge	a								19 14											20 14			
Solihull	a		18 44	18 44					19 20					19 43						20 20			
Birmingham Moor Street	a		18 56	18 59					19 29					19 53						20 29			
Birmingham Snow Hill	a								19 37					19 57						20 37			
Rowley Regis	a													20 10									
Cradley Heath	a																						
Stourbridge Junction	a													20 21									
Kidderminster	a													20 36									

§ London Underground Limited (Central Line) also operate services between South Ruislip and West Ruislip at frequent intervals

A from 7 October
B until 30 September

For complete services between Banbury and Birmingham, refer to Table T71

For principal services between London and Aylesbury refer to Table T114

Table T115-F

Sundays
20 May to 2 December

London - High Wycombe, Aylesbury, Oxford Parkway, Banbury, Stratford-upon-Avon, Birmingham Snow Hill and Kidderminster

		CH ◇ A	CH ◇ B	CH ◇ A	CH B	CH A	CH ◇ B	CH ◇ A	CH ◇	CH	CH	CH ◇ B	CH ◇ A	CH ◇ B	CH ◇ A	CH B	CH A	CH ◇ B	CH ◇ A	CH ◇	CH	CH	CH ◇ B
London Marylebone ⊖	d	19 05	19 10	19 10	19 13	19 13	19 35	19 35	19 40	19 43	19 47	20 05	20 05	20 10	20 10	20 13	20 13	20 35	20 35	20 40	20 44	20 47	21 05
London Paddington ⊖	d																						
Wembley Stadium	d				19 22	19 22					19 56					20 22	20 22					20 56	
Sudbury & Harrow Road	d																						
Sudbury Hill Harrow	d																						
Northolt Park	d										20 01											21 01	
South Ruislip § ⊖	d										20 04											21 04	
West Ruislip § ⊖	d																					21 08	
Denham	d										20 10											21 12	
Denham Golf Club	d									20 00													
Gerrards Cross	d				19 35	19 35				20 04	20a20					20 35	20 35				21 03	21a22	
Seer Green	d									20 09											21 08		
Beaconsfield	d				19 41	19 41			20 01	20 12						20 41	20 41			21 01	21 11		
High Wycombe	d		19 34	19 34	19 47	19 47	19 59	19 59		20 18				20 34	20 34	20 47	20 47	20 58	20 58		21 17		
Saunderton	d				19 54	19 54										20 54	20 54						
Princes Risborough	d				20 01	20 01				20 27						21 01	21 01				21 26		
Monks Risborough	d				20 04	20 04										21 04	21 04						
Little Kimble	d				20 08	20 08										21 08	21 08						
Aylesbury	a				20 19	20 22										21 19	21 22						
Haddenham & Thame Parkway	d	19 40								20 34		20 40	20 40								21 33		21 39
Bicester Village	d	19 53					20 22	20 22				20 53	20 53					21 20	21 20				21 51
Islip	d						20 28	20 28															
Oxford Parkway 116	a	20 00					20 31	20 31				21 00	21 00					21 28	21 28				21 59
Oxford	a	20 12					20 39	20 42				21 09	21 12					21 36	21 39				22 08
Bicester North	d								20 26	20 47										21 26	21 46		
Kings Sutton	d																				21 57		
Banbury	d		20 07	20 07					20 39	21a02				21 07	21 07					21 39	22a02		
Leamington Spa	d		20 25	20 25					20 57					21 25	21 25					21 57			
Warwick	d								21 01											22 01			
Warwick Parkway	d		20 32	20 32					21 05					21 32	21 32					22 05			
Hatton	d								21 10														
Claverdon	d																						
Bearley	d																						
Wilmcote	d																						
Stratford-upon-Avon Parkway	a																						
Stratford-upon-Avon	a																						
Lapworth	a								21 15														
Dorridge	a								21 20											22 14			
Solihull	a		20 44	20 44					21 28					21 44	21 44					22 20			
Birmingham Moor Street	a		20 56	20 59					21 37					21 56	21 59					22 29			
Birmingham Snow Hill	a								21 40											22 32			
Rowley Regis	a								21 53											22 45			
Cradley Heath	a								21 59											22 51			
Stourbridge Junction	a								22 04											22 56			
Kidderminster	a								22 18											23 10			

§ London Underground Limited (Central Line) also operate services between South Ruislip and West Ruislip at frequent intervals

A from 7 October
B until 30 September

For complete services between Banbury and Birmingham, refer to Table T71

For principal services between London and Aylesbury refer to Table T114

Please note, Network Rail have stated that further updates to this timetable are possible during the validity period.

Table T115-F

Sundays
20 May to 2 December

London - High Wycombe, Aylesbury, Oxford Parkway, Banbury, Stratford-upon-Avon, Birmingham Snow Hill and Kidderminster

		CH ◇ A	CH ◇	CH B	CH A	CH ◇ B	CH ◇ A	CH	CH B	CH A	CH ◇	CH ◇ B	CH ◇ A	CH	CH B	CH A	CH ◇ B	CH ◇ A	CH	CH B	CH A
London Marylebone ⊖	d	21 05	21 10	21 13	21 13	21 35	21 35	21 40	21 45	21 45	22 08	22 15	22 15	22 40	22 45	22 45	23 15	23 15	23 30	23 45	23 45
London Paddington ⊖	d																				
Wembley Stadium	d			21 22	21 22				21 54	21 54					22 55	22 55			23 39	23 54	23 54
Sudbury & Harrow Road	d																				
Sudbury Hill Harrow	d																				
Northolt Park	d								21 59	21 59					23 00	23 00				23 59	23 59
South Ruislip § ⊖	d								22 02	22 02					23 03	23 03				00 02	00 02
West Ruislip § ⊖	d								22 06	22 06					23 07	23 07				00 06	00 06
Denham	d								22 10	22 10					23 11	23 11				00 10	00 10
Denham Golf Club	d							21 57							23 14	23 14				00 13	00 13
Gerrards Cross	d			21 35	21 35			22 01	22 15	22 15				22 57	23 18	23 18	23 35	23 35	23 52	00 17	00 17
Seer Green	d							22 06							23 22	23 22				00 21	00 21
Beaconsfield	d			21 41	21 41			22 09	22 21	22 21				23 03	23 26	23 26	23 41	23 41	23 58	00 25	00 25
High Wycombe	d		21 34	21 47	21 47	21 59	21 59	22 15	22 27	22 27	22 34			23 09	23 32	23 32	23 47	23 47	00 04	00 31	00 31
Saunderton	d			21 54	21 54				22 33	22 33					23 38	23 38				00 37	00 37
Princes Risborough	d			22 01	22 01			22 24	22 40	22 40				23 17	23 45	23 45	23 56	23 56	00 14	00 45	00 45
Monks Risborough	d			22 04	22 04				22 43	22 43					23 48	23 48				00 48	00 48
Little Kimble	d			22 08	22 08				22 47	22 47					23 52	23 52				00 52	00 52
Aylesbury	a			22 19	22 22				22 58	23 01					00 03	00 06				01 06	01 09
Haddenham & Thame Parkway	d	21 39						22 31				22 54	22 54	23 24			00 03	00 03	00 21		
Bicester Village	d	21 51				22 22	22 22					23 09	23 09				00 18	00 18			
Islip	d					22 28	22 28														
Oxford Parkway 116	a	21 59				22 31	22 31					23 17	23 17				00 26	00 26			
Oxford	a	22 11				22 39	22 42					23 26	23 29				00 35	00 38			
Bicester North	d							22a50			22 56			23 35					00 34		
Kings Sutton	d																				
Banbury	d		22 07								23 09			23a53					00a55		
Leamington Spa	d		22 25								23 27										
Warwick	d		22 29								23 31										
Warwick Parkway	d		22 34								23 34										
Hatton	d		22 40																		
Claverdon	d																				
Bearley	d																				
Wilmcote	d																				
Stratford-upon-Avon Parkway	a																				
Stratford-upon-Avon	a																				
Lapworth	a		22 45																		
Dorridge	a		22 50								23 44										
Solihull	a		22 57								23 49										
Birmingham Moor Street	a		23 06								23 58										
Birmingham Snow Hill	a		23 14								00 07										
Rowley Regis	a																				
Cradley Heath	a																				
Stourbridge Junction	a																				
Kidderminster	a																				

§ London Underground Limited (Central Line) also operate services between South Ruislip and West Ruislip at frequent intervals

A from 7 October
B until 30 September

For complete services between Banbury and Birmingham, refer to Table T71

For principal services between London and Aylesbury refer to Table T114

Table T115-R

Mondays to Fridays
21 May to 7 December

Kidderminster, Birmingham Snow Hill, Stratford-upon-Avon, Banbury, Oxford Parkway, Aylesbury, High Wycombe - London

Miles	Miles	Miles	Miles			CH MX A	CH MX B	CH C	CH D	CH C	CH D	CH C	CH D	CH C	CH D	CH ◇ C	CH ◇ D	CH ◇ C	CH ◇ D	CH	CH C	CH E	CH F	CH D
—	—	—	—	**Kidderminster**	d																			
—	—	—	—	**Stourbridge Junction**	d																			
—	—	—	—	Cradley Heath	d																			
—	—	—	—	Rowley Regis	d																			
0	—	—	—	**Birmingham Snow Hill**	d																			
0¾	—	—	—	**Birmingham Moor Street**	d													05 15	05 15					
7¼	—	—	—	Solihull	d													05 24	05 24					
10½	—	—	—	Dorridge	d																			
13	—	—	—	Lapworth	d																			
—	—	0	—	**Stratford-upon-Avon**	d																			
—	—	1	—	Stratford-upon-Avon Parkway	d																			
—	—	2¾	—	Wilmcote	d																			
—	—	4¼	—	Bearley	d																			
—	—	7¼	—	Claverdon	d																			
17¼	—	9¼	—	Hatton	d																			
20	—	12	—	Warwick Parkway	d													05 36	05 36					
21¼	—	13¼	—	Warwick	d																			
23¼	—	15¼	—	**Leamington Spa**	d													05 41	05 41					
43¾	—	—	—	**Banbury**	d					05 17	05 17							05 59	05 59					
46¾	—	—	—	Kings Sutton	d					05 22	05 22													
57¼	—	—	—	**Bicester North**	d					05 33	05 33							06 11	06 11					
—	—	—	0	Oxford	d											05 36	05 36							
—	—	—	3½	Oxford Parkway 116	d											05 42	05 42							
—	—	—	5¾	Islip	d																			
—	—	—	11¾	Bicester Village	d											05 52	05 52							
70¼	—	—	21¾	Haddenham & Thame Parkway	d					05 45	05 45					06 06	06 06	06 22	06 22					
—	0	—	—	**Aylesbury**	d			05 02	05 02			05 35	05 35							06 05		06 21	06 24	
—	4½	—	—	Little Kimble	d			05 11	05 11			05 44	05 44							06 14				
—	6	—	—	Monks Risborough	d			05 15	05 15			05 48	05 48							06 18				
76	7½	—	—	**Princes Risborough**	d			05 20	05 20			05 54	05 54			06 13	06 13			06a26				
79¼	—	—	—	Saunderton	d			05 25	05 25							06 18	06 18							
84¼	—	—	—	**High Wycombe**	d			05 31	05 31	05 59	05 59	06 04	06 04	06 19	06 19	06 25	06 25	06 35	06 35					
89	—	—	—	Beaconsfield	d			05 38	05 38	06 05	06 05	06 11	06 11	06 26	06 26	06 31	06 31				06 46			06 46
90¾	—	—	—	Seer Green	d			05 41	05 41			06 14	06 14											
93¼	—	—	—	Gerrards Cross	d			05 46	05 46	06 11	06 11	06 19	06 19	06 32	06 32	06 37	06 37				06 52			06 52
95	—	—	—	Denham Golf Club	d			05 49	05 49			06 22	06 22											
96	—	—	—	Denham	d			05 52	05 52			06 25	06 25								06 56			06 56
98¾	—	—	—	West Ruislip § ⊖	d			05 56	05 56					06 49	06 49									
100½	—	—	—	South Ruislip § ⊖	d			06 00	06 00			06 31	06 31								07 02			07 02
102¼	—	—	—	Northolt Park	d			06 04	06 04			06 35	06 35	06 55	06 55									
103¾	—	—	—	Sudbury Hill Harrow	d									06 58	06 58									
104	—	—	—	Sudbury & Harrow Road	d									07 01	07 01									
105½	—	—	—	Wembley Stadium	d	00 06	00 06	06 09	06 09			06 40	06 40	07 04	07 04									
—	—	—	—	**London Paddington** ⊖	a																			
112	—	—	—	**London Marylebone** ⊖	a	00 19	00 22	06 19	06 22	06 31	06 34	06 51	06 54	07 16	07 19	07 00	07 03	07 03	07 06		07 19	07 22	07 22	07 22

§ London Underground Limited (Central Line) also operate services between South Ruislip and West Ruislip at frequent intervals

A until 5 October. From Aylesbury
B from 9 October. From Aylesbury
C until 5 October
D from 8 October
E from 8 October. From Aylesbury Vale Parkway
F until 5 October. From Aylesbury Vale Parkway

For complete services between Banbury and Birmingham, refer to Table T71

For principal services between London and Aylesbury refer to Table T114

Table T115-R

Kidderminster, Birmingham Snow Hill, Stratford-upon-Avon, Banbury, Oxford Parkway, Aylesbury, High Wycombe - London

Mondays to Fridays
21 May to 7 December

		CH	CH	CH	CH	CH	CH	CH	CH	CH	CH	CH	CH	CH	CH	CH		CH	CH	CH	CH	CH	LM	CH	CH
		◇ A	◇ B		A	◇ A	B	◇ B	◇ A	◇ B	A	B	C	D	A	B		◇ A	◇ B	◇ A	◇ B		E	A	B
Kidderminster	d																								
Stourbridge Junction	d																								
Cradley Heath	d																								
Rowley Regis	d																								
Birmingham Snow Hill	d																								
Birmingham Moor Street	d								05 42	05 42										06 10	06 10				
Solihull	d								05 51	05 51										06 19	06 19				
Dorridge	d								05 56	05 56										06 24	06 24				
Lapworth	d																								
Stratford-upon-Avon	d																					06 06	07 26		
Stratford-upon-Avon Parkway	d																					06 10	07a29		
Wilmcote	d																					06 14			
Bearley	d																								
Claverdon	d																					06 21			
Hatton	d																					06 32			
Warwick Parkway	d								06 05	06 05										06 34	06 34				
Warwick	d								06 08	06 08												06 40			
Leamington Spa	d								06 13	06 13										06 41	06 41	06a48			
Banbury	d								06 31	06 31										06 59	06 59				
Kings Sutton	d								06 36	06 36															
Bicester North	d				06 23		06 23		06 46	06 46										07 11	07 11				
Oxford	d	06 01	06 01			06 25		06 25										06 43	06 43						
Oxford Parkway 116	d	06 07	06 07			06 31		06 31										06 50	06 50						
Islip	d																								
Bicester Village	d	06 17	06 17			06 40		06 40										06 59	06 59						
Haddenham & Thame Parkway	d				06 35		06 35											07 11	07 11						
Aylesbury	d			06 23									06 55	06 58	06 46	06 46									
Little Kimble	d														06 54	06 54									
Monks Risborough	d														06 58	06 58									
Princes Risborough	d	06 36	06 36	06a42	06 44		06 44								07 02	07 02		07 18	07 18						
Saunderton	d														07 07	07 07									
High Wycombe	d	06 46	06 46		06 54		06 54				07 10	07 10			07 14	07 14		07 27	07 27						
Beaconsfield	d				07 02		07 02								07 20	07 20		07 34	07 34						
Seer Green	d	06 53	06 53												07 24	07 24									
Gerrards Cross	d	06 58	06 58								07 21	07 21			07 29	07 29									
Denham Golf Club	d	07 01	07 01																						
Denham	d					07 13		07 13																	
West Ruislip § ⊖	d	07 06	07 06																					07 46	07 46
South Ruislip § ⊖	d										07 29	07 29			07 37	07 37									
Northolt Park	d										07 33	07 33													
Sudbury Hill Harrow	d																							07 52	07 52
Sudbury & Harrow Road	d																							07 55	07 55
Wembley Stadium	d														07 44	07 44								07 58	07 58
London Paddington ⊖	a																								
London Marylebone ⊖	a	07 23	07 26		07 28	07 30	07 31	07 33	07 35	07 38	07 49	07 52	07 53	07 53	07 56	07 59		07 57	08 00	08 02	08 05			08 12	08 15

§ London Underground Limited (Central Line) also operate services between South Ruislip and West Ruislip at frequent intervals

A until 5 October
B from 8 October
C from 8 October. From Aylesbury Vale Parkway
D until 5 October. From Aylesbury Vale Parkway
E To Stourbridge Junction

For complete services between Banbury and Birmingham, refer to Table T71

For principal services between London and Aylesbury refer to Table T114

Table T115-R

Kidderminster, Birmingham Snow Hill, Stratford-upon-Avon, Banbury, Oxford Parkway, Aylesbury, High Wycombe - London

Mondays to Fridays
21 May to 7 December

		CH	CH	CH	CH	CH	CH	CH	CH	CH	CH	CH	CH	CH	CH	CH		CH	CH	CH	CH	CH	CH	CH	CH
		A	B	A	◇ C	B	D	E	A	◇	B	◇		A	B	A		B	A	B	◇ A	◇ B	D	E	
Kidderminster	d											06 09													
Stourbridge Junction	d											06 18													
Cradley Heath	d																								
Rowley Regis	d											06 30													
Birmingham Snow Hill	d											06 50													
Birmingham Moor Street	d									06 28		06 55													
Solihull	d									06 38		07 04													
Dorridge	d									06 50															
Lapworth	d																								
Stratford-upon-Avon	d																								
Stratford-upon-Avon Parkway	d																								
Wilmcote	d																								
Bearley	d																								
Claverdon	d																								
Hatton	d																								
Warwick Parkway	d									06 59		07 18													
Warwick	d									07 02															
Leamington Spa	d									07 06		07 24													
Banbury	d									07 24															07 50
Kings Sutton	d																								07 55
Bicester North	d			07 17		07 17				07 40															08 07
Oxford	d				07 17																07 43	07 43			
Oxford Parkway 116	d				07 25																07 50	07 50			
Islip	d																								
Bicester Village	d				07 35																07 59	07 59			
Haddenham & Thame Parkway	d			07 30		07 30				07 52											08 11	08 11			
Aylesbury	d						07 27	07 30					07 47										07 59	08 02	
Little Kimble	d												07 56												
Monks Risborough	d												08 00												
Princes Risborough	d	07 26	07 26						07 51		07 51		08a05						08 08	08 08	08 18	08 18			
Saunderton	d																		08 13	08 13					
High Wycombe	d	07 36	07 36	07 44		07 44			08 00		08 00					08 11		08 11	08 19	08 19	08 27	08 27			08 31
Beaconsfield	d			07 51		07 51			08 07		08 07					08 18		08 18	08 26	08 26					
Seer Green	d	07 43	07 43													08 21		08 21							
Gerrards Cross	d	07 48	07 48	07 57		07 57								08 22	08 22	08 26		08 26	08 32	08 32					
Denham Golf Club	d	07 51	07 51																						
Denham	d	07 54	07 54													08 30		08 30							
West Ruislip § ⊖	d													08 29	08 29				08 50	08 50					
South Ruislip § ⊖	d															08 36		08 36							
Northolt Park	d													08 35	08 35										
Sudbury Hill Harrow	d																		08 57	08 57					
Sudbury & Harrow Road	d																								
Wembley Stadium	d	08 04	08 04													08 43		08 43							08 52
London Paddington ⊖	a																								
London Marylebone ⊖	a	08 16	08 19	08 19	08 20	08 22	08 26	08 26	08 30	08 33	08 33	08 34		08 51	08 54	08 55		08 58	09 12	09 15	08 57	09 00	09 00	09 00	09 05

§ London Underground Limited (Central Line) also operate services between South Ruislip and West Ruislip at frequent intervals

A until 5 October
B from 8 October
C The Oxford Flyer
D from 8 October. From Aylesbury Vale Parkway
E until 5 October. From Aylesbury Vale Parkway

For complete services between Banbury and Birmingham, refer to Table T71

For principal services between London and Aylesbury refer to Table T114

Please note, Network Rail have stated that further updates to this timetable are possible during the validity period.

Kidderminster, Birmingham Snow Hill, Stratford-upon-Avon, Banbury, Oxford Parkway, Aylesbury, High Wycombe - London

		CH ◇ A	CH ◇ B	CH A	CH B	CH A	CH B	CH ◇ A	CH ◇ B	CH ◇ A	CH ◇ B	CH ◇ A	CH ◇ B	CH ◇ A	CH ◇ B	CH	CH A	CH A	CH B	CH B	CH ◇ A	CH ◇	CH ◇ B	CH A
Kidderminster	d													07 05	07 05							07 30		
Stourbridge Junction	d	06 38	06 38											07 14	07 14							07 38		
Cradley Heath	d													07 22	07 22							07 44		
Rowley Regis	d	06 50	06 50											07 29	07 29							07 51		
Birmingham Snow Hill	d	07 07	07 07											07 50	07 50							08 07		
Birmingham Moor Street	d	07 11	07 11											07 54	07 54							08 10		
Solihull	d	07 20	07 20											08 03	08 03							08 19		
Dorridge	d	07 27	07 27																			08 24		
Lapworth	d																							
Stratford-upon-Avon	d											07 33	07 33											
Stratford-upon-Avon Parkway	d											07 37	07 37											
Wilmcote	d											07 41	07 41											
Bearley	d																							
Claverdon	d											07 49	07 49											
Hatton	d											07 55	07 55											
Warwick Parkway	d	07 39	07 39									08 00	08 00	08 15	08 15							08 34		
Warwick	d											08 03	08 03									08 37		
Leamington Spa	d	07 46	07 46									08 08	08 08	08 21	08 21							08 43		
Banbury	d	08 06	08 06									08 27	08 27	08 41	08 41							09 02		
Kings Sutton	d																							
Bicester North	d											08 41	08 41	08 55	08 55									
Oxford	d							08 01	08 01	08 21	08 21										08 40		08 40	
Oxford Parkway 116	d							08 08	08 08	08 27	08 27										08 50		08 50	
Islip	d							08 12	08 12															
Bicester Village	d							08 20	08 20	08 36	08 36										08 59		08 59	
Haddenham & Thame Parkway	d											08 52	08 52								09 11		09 11	
Aylesbury	d															08 47								
Little Kimble	d															08 56								
Monks Risborough	d															09 00								
Princes Risborough	d							08 39	08 39	08 52	08 52					09a09					09 18		09 18	
Saunderton	d							08 44	08 44															
High Wycombe	d					08 40	08 40	08 51	08 51	09 01	09 01	09 05	09 05					09 17		09 17	09 27		09 27	
Beaconsfield	d					08 47	08 47	08 58	08 58									09 24		09 24				
Seer Green	d					08 50	08 50					09 12	09 12											
Gerrards Cross	d			08 49	08 49	08 55	08 55			09 10	09 10							09 30		09 30				09 42
Denham Golf Club	d			08 53	08 53																			09 45
Denham	d					08 59	08 59														09 38		09 38	
West Ruislip § ⊖	d																09 26		09 26					
South Ruislip § ⊖	d					09 05	09 05											09 37		09 37				
Northolt Park	d			09 02	09 02												09 32		09 32					09 54
Sudbury Hill Harrow	d																09 35		09 35					
Sudbury & Harrow Road	d			09 06	09 06																			
Wembley Stadium	d					09 12	09 12										09 39		09 39					09 59
London Paddington ⊖	a																							
London Marylebone ⊖	a	09 07	09 10	09 21	09 24	09 25	09 28	09 27	09 30	09 30	09 33	09 35	09 38	09 38	09 41		09 52	09 55	09 55	09 57	09 56	09 59	09 59	10 12

§ London Underground Limited (Central Line) also operate services between South Ruislip and West Ruislip at frequent intervals

A until 5 October
B from 8 October

For complete services between Banbury and Birmingham, refer to Table T71

For principal services between London and Aylesbury refer to Table T114

Kidderminster, Birmingham Snow Hill, Stratford-upon-Avon, Banbury, Oxford Parkway, Aylesbury, High Wycombe - London

		CH A	CH B	CH A	CH ◇ B	CH ◇ A	CH B	CH A	CH ◇ B	CH ◇ A	CH ◇ B	CH ◇ A	CH ◇ B	CH ◇ B	CH ◇ A	CH	CH ◇ A	LM C	CH B	CH A	CH B	CH ◇ B	CH A	CH ◇ A
Kidderminster	d												08 09		08 09									
Stourbridge Junction	d												08 23		08 23									
Cradley Heath	d												08 29		08 29									
Rowley Regis	d												08 35		08 35									
Birmingham Snow Hill	d										08 22	08 22	08 52		08 52							09 12		09 12
Birmingham Moor Street	d										08 25	08 25	08 55		08 55							09 15		09 15
Solihull	d										08 37	08 37	09 07		09 07							09 24		09 24
Dorridge	d										08 52	08 52										09 29		09 29
Lapworth	d																							
Stratford-upon-Avon	d															09 00		10 03						
Stratford-upon-Avon Parkway	d															09 04		10a06						
Wilmcote	d															09 07								
Bearley	d															09 11								
Claverdon	d															09 16								
Hatton	d															09 21								
Warwick Parkway	d										09 02	09 02	09 19		09 19							09 39		09 39
Warwick	d										09 06	09 06				09 28						09 42		09 42
Leamington Spa	d										09 12	09 12	09 25		09 25	09a37						09 46		09 46
Banbury	d						09 07	09 07			09 31	09 31	09 44		09 44							10 04		10 04
Kings Sutton	d						09 12	09 12																
Bicester North	d						09 30	09 30			09 43	09 43										10 16		10 16
Oxford	d				09 10	09 10								09 36			09 36							
Oxford Parkway 116	d				09 16	09 16								09 45			09 45							
Islip	d													09 49			09 49							
Bicester Village	d				09 25	09 25								09 57			09 57							
Haddenham & Thame Parkway	d						09 42	09 42			09 54	09 54										10 27		10 27
Aylesbury	d								09 33	09 33														
Little Kimble	d								09 41	09 41														
Monks Risborough	d								09 45	09 45														
Princes Risborough	d				09 42	09 42			09 49	09 49											10 16		10 16	
Saunderton	d								09 54	09 54														
High Wycombe	d		09 36	09 36	09 52	09 52	09 57	09 57	10 02	10 02	10 07	10 07							10 20	10 20	10 26		10 26	
Beaconsfield	d		09 43	09 43			10 03	10 03											10 27	10 27	10 32		10 32	
Seer Green	d		09 46	09 46																	10 35		10 35	
Gerrards Cross	d	09 42	09 51	09 51							10 16	10 16							10 33	10 33	10 40		10 40	
Denham Golf Club	d	09 45																						
Denham	d		09 55	09 55																	10 44		10 44	
West Ruislip § ⊖	d								10 29	10 29														
South Ruislip § ⊖	d		10 00	10 00															10 41	10 41				
Northolt Park	d	09 54							10 35	10 35														
Sudbury Hill Harrow	d								10 38	10 38														
Sudbury & Harrow Road	d								10 41	10 41														
Wembley Stadium	d	09 59																	10 48	10 48				
London Paddington ⊖	a																							
London Marylebone ⊖	a	10 14	10 18	10 21	10 19	10 22	10 32	10 35	10 55	10 58	10 36	10 39	10 40	10 41	10 43		10 44		10 59	11 02	11 05	11 08	11 08	11 11

§ London Underground Limited (Central Line) also operate services between South Ruislip and West Ruislip at frequent intervals

A from 8 October
B until 5 October
C To Stourbridge Junction

For complete services between Banbury and Birmingham, refer to Table T71

For principal services between London and Aylesbury refer to Table T114

Table T115-R

Mondays to Fridays

21 May to 7 December

Kidderminster, Birmingham Snow Hill, Stratford-upon-Avon, Banbury, Oxford Parkway, Aylesbury, High Wycombe - London

	CH ◇ A	CH ◇ B	CH A	CH B	CH A	CH B	CH ◇ A	CH ◇ B	CH ◇ A	CH ◇ B	CH ◇ A	CH ◇ B	CH A	CH B	CH ◇ A		CH ◇ B	CH	LM C	CH ◇ A	CH ◇ B	CH A	CH B	CH A
Kidderminster d																								
Stourbridge Junction ■ d																								
Cradley Heath d																								
Rowley Regis d																								
Birmingham Snow Hill ⇌ d															10 12		10 12							
Birmingham Moor Street d							09 55	09 55							10 15		10 15							
Solihull d							10 04	10 04							10 24		10 24							
Dorridge d															10 29		10 29							
Lapworth d																								
Stratford-upon-Avon d																		10 37	11 03					
Stratford-upon-Avon Parkway d																		10 41	11a06					
Wilmcote d																		10 44						
Bearley d																		10 48						
Claverdon d																		10 53						
Hatton d																		10 58						
Warwick Parkway d							10 16	10 16							10 39		10 39							
Warwick d															10 42		10 42	11 04						
Leamington Spa ■ d							10 22	10 22							10 46		10 46	11a14						
Banbury d							10 40	10 40					10 45	10 45	11 04		11 04							
Kings Sutton d													10 50	10 50										
Bicester North ■ d													11 01	11 01	11 16		11 16							
Oxford d	10 10	10 10							10 41	10 41										11 08	11 08			
Oxford Parkway 116 d	10 17	10 17							10 47	10 47										11 15	11 15			
Islip d																								
Bicester Village d	10 26	10 26							10 56	10 56										11 24	11 24			
Haddenham & Thame Parkway d	10 38	10 38											11 13	11 13						11 37	11 37			
Aylesbury d					10 30	10 30																		11 29
Little Kimble d																								11 37
Monks Risborough d					10 41	10 41																		11 41
Princes Risborough ■ d					10 45	10 45							11 20	11 20										11 45
Saunderton d					10 50	10 50																		11 50
High Wycombe ■ d	10 51	10 51			10 57	10 57	11 10	11 10			11 20	11 20	11 30	11 30						11 51	11 51			11 56
Beaconsfield d					11 03	11 03					11 26	11 26	11 36	11 36										12 02
Seer Green d					11 06	11 06																		12 05
Gerrards Cross ■ d			10 49	10 49	11 11	11 11					11 32	11 32	11 42	11 42								11 49	11 49	12 10
Denham Golf Club d			10 52	10 52																		11 52	11 52	
Denham d			10 55	10 55							11 36	11 36										11 55	11 55	
West Ruislip ■ § ⊖ d			11 05	11 05																		12 05	12 05	
South Ruislip § ⊖ d											11 41	11 41												
Northolt Park d			11 11	11 11																		12 11	12 11	
Sudbury Hill Harrow d			11 14	11 14																		12 14	12 14	
Sudbury & Harrow Road d																								
Wembley Stadium d			11 18	11 18							11 48	11 48										12 18	12 18	
London Paddington ■ ⊖ a																								
London Marylebone ■ ⊖ a	11 18	11 21	11 32	11 35	11 36	11 39	11 40	11 43	11 46	11 49	11 59	12 02	12 05	12 08	12 08		12 11			12 18	12 21	12 32	12 35	12 36

§ London Underground Limited (Central Line) also operate services between South Ruislip and West Ruislip at frequent intervals

A until 5 October
B from 8 October
C To Stourbridge Junction

For complete services between Banbury and Birmingham, refer to Table T71

For principal services between London and Aylesbury refer to Table T114

Table T115-R

Mondays to Fridays

21 May to 7 December

Kidderminster, Birmingham Snow Hill, Stratford-upon-Avon, Banbury, Oxford Parkway, Aylesbury, High Wycombe - London

	CH A	CH ◇ B	CH ◇ A	CH ◇ B	CH ◇ A	LM C	CH ◇ B	CH ◇ A	CH B	CH A	CH ◇ B	CH ◇ A	CH ◇ B	CH ◇ A	CH B		CH A	CH B	CH A	CH ◇ B	CH ◇ A	CH ◇ B	CH ◇ A	CH ◇ B
Kidderminster d																								
Stourbridge Junction ■ d																								
Cradley Heath d																								
Rowley Regis d																								
Birmingham Snow Hill ⇌ d											11 12	11 12												
Birmingham Moor Street d		10 55	10 55								11 15	11 15								11 55	11 55			
Solihull d		11 04	11 04								11 24	11 24								12 04	12 04			
Dorridge d											11 29	11 29												
Lapworth d																								
Stratford-upon-Avon d						12 03																		
Stratford-upon-Avon Parkway d						12a06																		
Wilmcote d																								
Bearley d																								
Claverdon d																								
Hatton d																								
Warwick Parkway d		11 17	11 17								11 39	11 39								12 16	12 16			
Warwick d											11 42	11 42												
Leamington Spa ■ d		11 23	11 23								11 46	11 46								12 22	12 22			
Banbury d		11 40	11 40						11 48	11 48	12 04	12 04								12 40	12 40			
Kings Sutton d																								
Bicester North ■ d									12 03	12 03	12 16	12 16												
Oxford d				11 42	11 42								12 11	12 11								12 41	12 41	
Oxford Parkway 116 d				11 48	11 48								12 17	12 17								12 47	12 47	
Islip d																								
Bicester Village d				11 57	11 57								12 26	12 26								12 56	12 56	
Haddenham & Thame Parkway d											12 27	12 27	12 38	12 38										
Aylesbury d	11 29																	12 32	12 32					
Little Kimble d	11 37																							
Monks Risborough d	11 41																	12 43	12 43					
Princes Risborough ■ d	11 45								12 20	12 20								12 47	12 47					
Saunderton d	11 50																	12 52	12 52					
High Wycombe ■ d	11 56	12 13	12 13				12 20	12 20	12 30	12 30			12 51	12 51				12 58	12 58	13 13	13 13			13 20
Beaconsfield d	12 02						12 26	12 26	12 36	12 36								13 05	13 05					13 27
Seer Green d	12 05																	13 08	13 08					
Gerrards Cross ■ d	12 10						12 32	12 32	12 42	12 42					12 49		12 49	13 13	13 13					13 33
Denham Golf Club d															12 52		12 52							
Denham d															12 55		12 55							
West Ruislip ■ § ⊖ d															13 05		13 05							
South Ruislip § ⊖ d							12 39	12 39																13 40
Northolt Park d															13 11		13 11							
Sudbury Hill Harrow d															13 14		13 14							
Sudbury & Harrow Road d																								
Wembley Stadium d							12 46	12 46							13 18		13 18							13 47
London Paddington ■ ⊖ a																								
London Marylebone ■ ⊖ a	12 39	12 43	12 46	12 46	12 49		12 59	13 01	13 05	13 08	13 09	13 12	13 18	13 21	13 32		13 35	13 38	13 41	13 43	13 46	13 46	13 49	13 59

§ London Underground Limited (Central Line) also operate services between South Ruislip and West Ruislip at frequent intervals

A from 8 October
B until 5 October
C To Stourbridge Junction

For complete services between Banbury and Birmingham, refer to Table T71

For principal services between London and Aylesbury refer to Table T114

Please note, Network Rail have stated that further updates to this timetable are possible during the validity period.

Table T115-R

Mondays to Fridays

21 May to 7 December

Kidderminster, Birmingham Snow Hill, Stratford-upon-Avon, Banbury, Oxford Parkway, Aylesbury, High Wycombe - London

		CH ◇ A	CH B	CH A	CH ◇ B	CH ◇ A	CH	LM C	CH ◇ B	CH ◇ A	CH B	CH A	CH B	CH A	CH ◇ B	CH ◇ A		CH ◇ B	CH ◇ A	LM C	CH ◇ B	CH ◇ A	CH B	CH A	CH ◇ B
Kidderminster	d																								
Stourbridge Junction	d																								
Cradley Heath	d																								
Rowley Regis	d																								
Birmingham Snow Hill	d				12 12	12 12																			13 12
Birmingham Moor Street	d				12 15	12 15									12 55	12 55									13 15
Solihull	d				12 24	12 24									13 04	13 04									13 24
Dorridge	d				12 29	12 29																			13 30
Lapworth	d																								
Stratford-upon-Avon	d						12 40	13 03												14 03					
Stratford-upon-Avon Parkway	d						12 44	13a06												14a06					
Wilmcote	d						12 47																		
Bearley	d																								
Claverdon	d																								
Hatton	d						12 58																		
Warwick Parkway	d				12 39	12 39									13 17	13 17									13 40
Warwick	d				12 42	12 42	13 04																		13 44
Leamington Spa	d				12 46	12 46	13a14								13 23	13 23									13 49
Banbury	d		12 44	12 44	13 04	13 04									13 41	13 41							13 45	13 45	14 07
Kings Sutton	d																						13 50	13 50	
Bicester North	d		13 01	13 01	13 17	13 17																	14 01	14 01	14 20
Oxford	d								13 11	13 11								13 38	13 38						
Oxford Parkway 116	d								13 17	13 17								13 45	13 45						
Islip	d																	13 48	13 48						
Bicester Village	d								13 26	13 26								13 56	13 56						
Haddenham & Thame Parkway	d		13 13	13 13					13 38	13 38													14 13	14 13	
Aylesbury	d												13 31	13 31											
Little Kimble	d												13 39	13 39											
Monks Risborough	d												13 43	13 43											
Princes Risborough	d		13 20	13 20									13 47	13 47									14 20	14 20	
Saunderton	d												13 52	13 52											
High Wycombe	d	13 20	13 30	13 30					13 51	13 51			13 58	13 58	14 13	14 13					14 20	14 20	14 30	14 30	
Beaconsfield	d	13 27	13 36	13 36									14 05	14 05							14 27	14 27	14 36	14 36	
Seer Green	d												14 08	14 08											
Gerrards Cross	d	13 33	13 42	13 42							13 49	13 49	14 13	14 13							14 33	14 33	14 42	14 42	
Denham Golf Club	d										13 52	13 52													
Denham	d										13 55	13 55													
West Ruislip § ⊖	d										14 05	14 05													
South Ruislip § ⊖	d	13 40																			14 40	14 40			
Northolt Park	d										14 11	14 11													
Sudbury Hill Harrow	d										14 14	14 14													
Sudbury & Harrow Road	d																								
Wembley Stadium	d	13 47									14 18	14 18	14 26	14 26							14 47	14 47			
London Paddington ⊖	a																								
London Marylebone ⊖	a	14 02	14 05	14 08	14 09	14 12			14 18	14 21	14 32	14 35	14 40	14 43	14 43	14 46		14 46	14 49		14 59	15 02	15 05	15 08	15 08

§ London Underground Limited (Central Line) also operate services between South Ruislip and West Ruislip at frequent intervals

A from 8 October
B until 5 October
C To Stourbridge Junction

For complete services between Banbury and Birmingham, refer to Table T71

For principal services between London and Aylesbury refer to Table T114

Table T115-R

Mondays to Fridays

21 May to 7 December

Kidderminster, Birmingham Snow Hill, Stratford-upon-Avon, Banbury, Oxford Parkway, Aylesbury, High Wycombe - London

		CH ◇ A	CH ◇ B	CH ◇ A	CH B	CH A	CH B	CH A	CH ◇ B	CH ◇ A	CH ◇ B	CH ◇ A	CH ◇ B	CH ◇ A	CH B	CH A		CH ◇ B	CH ◇ A	CH	LM C	CH ◇ B	CH ◇ A	CH B	CH A
Kidderminster	d																								
Stourbridge Junction	d																								
Cradley Heath	d																								
Rowley Regis	d																								
Birmingham Snow Hill	d	13 12																14 12	14 12						
Birmingham Moor Street	d	13 15							13 55	13 55								14 15	14 15						
Solihull	d	13 24							14 04	14 04								14 24	14 24						
Dorridge	d	13 30																14 29	14 29						
Lapworth	d																								
Stratford-upon-Avon	d																			14 37	15 03				
Stratford-upon-Avon Parkway	d																			14 41	15a06				
Wilmcote	d																			14 44					
Bearley	d																			14 48					
Claverdon	d																			14 53					
Hatton	d																			14 58					
Warwick Parkway	d	13 40							14 16	14 16								14 39	14 39						
Warwick	d	13 44																14 42	14 42	15 05					
Leamington Spa	d	13 49							14 22	14 22								14 46	14 46	15a16					
Banbury	d	14 07							14 40	14 40					14 47	14 47		15 04	15 04						
Kings Sutton	d																								
Bicester North	d	14 20													15 01	15 01		15 16	15 16						
Oxford	d		14 10	14 10							14 41	14 41										15 11	15 11		
Oxford Parkway 116	d		14 17	14 17							14 47	14 47										15 19	15 19		
Islip	d																								
Bicester Village	d		14 26	14 26							14 56	14 56										15 28	15 28		
Haddenham & Thame Parkway	d		14 38	14 38											15 13	15 13						15 40	15 40		
Aylesbury	d						14 31	14 31																	
Little Kimble	d						14 39	14 39																	
Monks Risborough	d						14 43	14 43																	
Princes Risborough	d						14 47	14 47							15 20	15 20									
Saunderton	d						14 52	14 52																	
High Wycombe	d		14 51	14 51			14 58	14 58	15 10	15 10			15 20	15 20	15 30	15 30		15 37	15 37			15 53	15 53		
Beaconsfield	d						15 05	15 05					15 26	15 26	15 36	15 36						15 59	15 59		
Seer Green	d						15 08	15 08																	
Gerrards Cross	d				14 49	14 49	15 13	15 13					15 32	15 32	15 42	15 42		15 47	15 47					15 53	15 53
Denham Golf Club	d				14 52	14 52																		15 56	15 56
Denham	d				14 55	14 55																		15 59	15 59
West Ruislip § ⊖	d				15 05	15 05																		16 09	16 09
South Ruislip § ⊖	d												15 40	15 40											
Northolt Park	d				15 11	15 11																		16 15	16 15
Sudbury Hill Harrow	d				15 14	15 14																		16 18	16 18
Sudbury & Harrow Road	d																								
Wembley Stadium	d				15 18	15 18							15 47	15 47								16 12	16 12	16 22	16 22
London Paddington ⊖	a																								
London Marylebone ⊖	a	15 11	15 18	15 21	15 32	15 35	15 36	15 39	15 40	15 43	15 43	15 46	15 59	16 02	16 05	16 08		16 08	16 11			16 23	16 26	16 35	16 38

§ London Underground Limited (Central Line) also operate services between South Ruislip and West Ruislip at frequent intervals

A from 8 October
B until 5 October
C To Stourbridge Junction

For complete services between Banbury and Birmingham, refer to Table T71

For principal services between London and Aylesbury refer to Table T114

Table T115-R

Mondays to Fridays

21 May to 7 December

Kidderminster, Birmingham Snow Hill, Stratford-upon-Avon, Banbury, Oxford Parkway, Aylesbury, High Wycombe - London

	CH A	CH B	CH ◇ A	CH ◇ B	CH ◇ A	CH ◇ B	LM C	CH A	CH B	CH A	CH B	CH ◇ A	CH ◇ B	CH ◇ A	CH ◇ B	CH A	CH B	CH A	CH B	CH ◇ A	CH ◇ B	CH ◇ A	CH ◇ B
Kidderminster d																							
Stourbridge Junction 2 d																							
Cradley Heath d																							
Rowley Regis d																							
Birmingham Snow Hill ⇌ d												15 12	15 12										
Birmingham Moor Street d			14 55	14 55								15 15	15 15							15 55	15 55		
Solihull d			15 04	15 04								15 24	15 24							16 04	16 04		
Dorridge d												15 30	15 30										
Lapworth d																							
Stratford-upon-Avon d							16 03																
Stratford-upon-Avon Parkway d							16a06																
Wilmcote d																							
Bearley d																							
Claverdon d																							
Hatton d																							
Warwick Parkway d			15 16	15 16								15 40	15 40							16 17	16 17		
Warwick d												15 43	15 43										
Leamington Spa 8 d			15 21	15 21								15 47	15 47							16 23	16 23		
Banbury d			15 39	15 39						15 48	15 48	16 05	16 05							16 41	16 41		
Kings Sutton d																							
Bicester North 3 d										16 03	16 03	16 17	16 17										
Oxford d					15 41	15 41								16 11	16 11							16 38	16 38
Oxford Parkway 116 d					15 49	15 49								16 17	16 17							16 44	16 44
Islip d																						16 48	16 48
Bicester Village d					15 58	15 58								16 26	16 26							16 56	16 56
Haddenham & Thame Parkway d												16 28	16 28	16 38	16 38								
Aylesbury d	15 33	15 33														16 29	16 29						
Little Kimble d																16 37	16 37						
Monks Risborough d	15 44	15 44														16 41	16 41						
Princes Risborough 2 d	15 48	15 48								16 20	16 20					16 46	16 46						
Saunderton d	15 53	15 53														16 51	16 51						
High Wycombe 1 d	15 59	15 59	16 10	16 10				16 21	16 21	16 30	16 30			16 51	16 51	16 57	16 57	17 03	17 03	17 13	17 13		
Beaconsfield d	16 06	16 06						16 28	16 28	16 36	16 36					17 04	17 04	17 10	17 10				
Seer Green d	16 09	16 09																17 13	17 13				
Gerrards Cross 1 d	16 14	16 14						16 34	16 34	16 42	16 42					17 10	17 10	17 18	17 18				
Denham Golf Club d								16 37	16 37														
Denham d								16 40	16 40					17 02	17 02								
West Ruislip 3 § ⊖ d								16 53	16 53									17 34	17 34				
South Ruislip § ⊖ d	16 21	16 21														17 17	17 17						
Northolt Park d																17 21	17 21						
Sudbury Hill Harrow d																		17 41	17 41				
Sudbury & Harrow Road d																							
Wembley Stadium d								17 02	17 02							17 26	17 26						
London Paddington 15 ⊖ a																							
London Marylebone 10 ⊖ a	16 39	16 42	16 42	16 45	16 45	16 48		17 16	17 19	17 09	17 12	17 12	17 15	17 21	17 24	17 39	17 42	17 57	18 00	17 45	17 48	17 50	17 53

§ London Underground Limited (Central Line) also operate services between South Ruislip and West Ruislip at frequent intervals

A until 5 October
B from 8 October
C To Stourbridge Junction

For complete services between Banbury and Birmingham, refer to Table T71

For principal services between London and Aylesbury refer to Table T114

Table T115-R

Mondays to Fridays

21 May to 7 December

Kidderminster, Birmingham Snow Hill, Stratford-upon-Avon, Banbury, Oxford Parkway, Aylesbury, High Wycombe - London

	CH ◇ A	CH ◇ B	CH A	CH B	CH ◇ A	CH ◇ B	CH ◇ A	CH ◇ B	CH ◇ A	CH	CH ◇ B	CH ◇ A	CH ◇ B	CH ◇ A	CH ◇ B	CH FX ◇ C	CH FX ◇ B	CH FO ◇	CH A	CH B	CH ◇ A	CH ◇ B	CH A
Kidderminster d																							
Stourbridge Junction 2 d																							
Cradley Heath d																							
Rowley Regis d																							
Birmingham Snow Hill ⇌ d					16 12	16 12								16 52	16 52								
Birmingham Moor Street d					16 15	16 15								16 55	16 55								
Solihull d					16 24	16 24								17 04	17 04								
Dorridge d					16 29	16 29																	
Lapworth d																							
Stratford-upon-Avon d																							
Stratford-upon-Avon Parkway d																							
Wilmcote d																							
Bearley d																							
Claverdon d																							
Hatton d																							
Warwick Parkway d					16 39	16 39								17 16	17 16								
Warwick d					16 42	16 42								17 19	17 19								
Leamington Spa 8 d					16 46	16 46								17 23	17 23								
Banbury d			16 45	16 45	17 04	17 04								17 41	17 41								17 46
Kings Sutton d			16 50	16 50																			17 51
Bicester North 3 d			17 03	17 03	17 16	17 16																	18 03
Oxford d							16 54	16 54				17 23	17 23			17 37	17 37	17 37					
Oxford Parkway 116 d							17 03	17 03				17 29	17 29			17 46	17 46	17 46					
Islip d																17 50	17 50	17 50					
Bicester Village d							17 20	17 20				17 38	17 38			17 58	17 58	17 58					
Haddenham & Thame Parkway d					17 27	17 27						17 50	17 50										
Aylesbury d										17 29													
Little Kimble d										17 38													
Monks Risborough d										17 42													
Princes Risborough 2 d			17 20	17 20						17a48		17 57	17 57										18 21
Saunderton d			17 25	17 25																			18 26
High Wycombe 1 d	17 23	17 23	17 31	17 31			17 45	17 45	17 52		17 52	18 06	18 06	18 11	18 11						18 22	18 22	18 33
Beaconsfield d	17 30	17 30	17 38	17 38					17 59		17 59										18 29	18 29	
Seer Green d									18 02		18 02												
Gerrards Cross 1 d	17 36	17 36	17 44	17 44			17 54	17 54	18 07		18 07										18 35	18 35	18 43
Denham Golf Club d	17 39	17 39																			18 38	18 38	
Denham d	17 42	17 42					17 58	17 58													18 41	18 41	
West Ruislip 3 § ⊖ d																			18 32	18 32			
South Ruislip § ⊖ d			17 52	17 52			18 04	18 04	18 14		18 14								18 36	18 36			18 50
Northolt Park d									18 18		18 18												
Sudbury Hill Harrow d																			18 41	18 41			
Sudbury & Harrow Road d																							
Wembley Stadium d	17 54	17 54					18 11	18 11											18 45	18 45	18 51	18 51	
London Paddington 15 ⊖ a																							
London Marylebone 10 ⊖ a	18 07	18 10	18 10	18 13	18 13	18 16	18 26	18 29	18 33		18 36	18 35	18 38	18 39	18 42	18 48	18 51	18 53	18 59	19 02	19 04	19 07	19 08

§ London Underground Limited (Central Line) also operate services between South Ruislip and West Ruislip at frequent intervals

A until 5 October
B from 8 October
C until 4 October

For complete services between Banbury and Birmingham, refer to Table T71

For principal services between London and Aylesbury refer to Table T114

Please note, Network Rail have stated that further updates to this timetable are possible during the validity period.

Table T115-R

Mondays to Fridays

21 May to 7 December

Kidderminster, Birmingham Snow Hill, Stratford-upon-Avon, Banbury, Oxford Parkway, Aylesbury, High Wycombe - London

		CH A	CH ◇ B	CH ◇ A	CH ◇ B	CH ◇ A	CH	CH B	CH A	CH ◇ B	CH ◇ A	CH ◇ B	CH ◇ A	CH ◇ B	CH ◇ A	CH ◇ B	CH ◇ A	LM C	CH ◇ B	CH ◇ A	CH B	CH FX ◇ D	CH A	CH FX ◇ A
Kidderminster	d																							
Stourbridge Junction	d																							
Cradley Heath	d																							
Rowley Regis	d																							
Birmingham Snow Hill	d		17 07	17 07												17 52	17 52							
Birmingham Moor Street	d		17 10	17 10												17 55	17 55							
Solihull	d		17 19	17 19												18 06	18 06							
Dorridge	d		17 26	17 26												18 12	18 12							
Lapworth	d																							
Stratford-upon-Avon	d													17 36	17 36			19 03						
Stratford-upon-Avon Parkway	d													17 40	17 40			19a06						
Wilmcote	d													17 43	17 43									
Bearley	d													17 47	17 47									
Claverdon	d													17 52	17 52									
Hatton	d													17 58	17 58									
Warwick Parkway	d		17 36	17 36												18 22	18 22							
Warwick	d		17 39	17 39										18 05	18 05									
Leamington Spa	d		17 43	17 43										18 09	18 09	18 28	18 28							
Banbury	d	17 46	18 01	18 01										18 28	18 28	18 46	18 46							
Kings Sutton	d	17 51																						
Bicester North	d	18 03	18 14	18 14										18 45	18 45	18 58	18 58				19 03		19 03	
Oxford	d				18 01	18 01						18 23	18 23									19 01		19 01
Oxford Parkway 116	d				18 10	18 10						18 29	18 29									19 07		19 07
Islip	d				18 14	18 14																19 10		19 10
Bicester Village	d				18 23	18 23						18 38	18 38									19 18		19 18
Haddenham & Thame Parkway	d		18 25	18 25								18 50	18 50								19 15		19 15	
Aylesbury	d						18 22																	
Little Kimble	d						18 31																	
Monks Risborough	d						18 35																	
Princes Risborough	d	18 21					18a47					18 57	18 57								19 22		19 22	
Saunderton	d	18 26																			19 27		19 27	
High Wycombe	d	18 33	18 38	18 38	18 45	18 45				18 51	18 51	19 06	19 06						19 20	19 20	19 34		19 34	
Beaconsfield	d		18 45	18 45						18 58	18 58								19 27	19 27				
Seer Green	d									19 01	19 01								19 30	19 30				
Gerrards Cross	d	18 43						18 58	18 58	19 06	19 06								19 35	19 35				
Denham Golf Club	d																							
Denham	d							19 02	19 02										19 39	19 39				
West Ruislip § ⊖	d																							
South Ruislip § ⊖	d	18 50																	19 44	19 44				
Northolt Park	d							19 09	19 09															
Sudbury Hill Harrow	d																							
Sudbury & Harrow Road	d																							
Wembley Stadium	d							19 14	19 14										19 51	19 51				
London Paddington ⊖	a																							
London Marylebone ⊖	a	19 11	19 11	19 14	19 12	19 15		19 27	19 30	19 30	19 33	19 33	19 36	19 41	19 44	19 44	19 47		20 04	20 07	20 08	20 09	20 11	20 12

§ London Underground Limited (Central Line) also operate services between South Ruislip and West Ruislip at frequent intervals

A from 8 October
B until 5 October
C To Worcester Shrub Hill
D until 4 October

For complete services between Banbury and Birmingham, refer to Table T71

For principal services between London and Aylesbury refer to Table T114

Table T115-R

Mondays to Fridays

21 May to 7 December

Kidderminster, Birmingham Snow Hill, Stratford-upon-Avon, Banbury, Oxford Parkway, Aylesbury, High Wycombe - London

		CH FO ◇	CH ◇ A	CH ◇ B	CH	CH A	CH B	CH A	CH ◇ A	CH B	CH ◇ B	CH ◇ A	CH ◇ B	CH	CH ◇ A	CH ◇ B	CH ◇ A	CH ◇ B	CH A	CH B	CH ◇ A	CH ◇ B	CH ◇ A	CH ◇ B
Kidderminster	d																							
Stourbridge Junction	d																							
Cradley Heath	d																							
Rowley Regis	d																							
Birmingham Snow Hill	d		18 12	18 12					18 40		18 40										19 17	19 17		
Birmingham Moor Street	d		18 15	18 15					18 43		18 43										19 20	19 20		
Solihull	d		18 24	18 24					18 52		18 52										19 29	19 29		
Dorridge	d		18 29	18 29					18 57		18 57										19 34	19 34		
Lapworth	d		18 34	18 34																	19 38	19 38		
Stratford-upon-Avon	d				19 12																			
Stratford-upon-Avon Parkway	d				19 16																			
Wilmcote	d				19 20																			
Bearley	d				19 24																			
Claverdon	d				19 29																			
Hatton	d		18 40	18 40	19a39																19 44	19 44		
Warwick Parkway	d		18 45	18 45					19 07		19 07										19 49	19 49		
Warwick	d		18 48	18 48																	19 52	19 52		
Leamington Spa	d		18 53	18 53					19 12		19 12										19 57	19 57		
Banbury	d		19 12	19 12					19 30		19 30										20 16	20 16		
Kings Sutton	d		19 17	19 17																				
Bicester North	d		19 28	19 28					19 42		19 42										20 30	20 30		
Oxford	d	19 01										19 28	19 28				20 00	20 00					20 26	20 26
Oxford Parkway 116	d	19 07										19 37	19 37				20 09	20 09					20 32	20 32
Islip	d	19 10																						
Bicester Village	d	19 18										19 47	19 47				20 19	20 19					20 41	20 41
Haddenham & Thame Parkway	d		19 40	19 40					19 53		19 53	19 59	19 59								20 42	20 42	20 53	20 53
Aylesbury	d					19 13	19 13							20 09										
Little Kimble	d													20 18										
Monks Risborough	d					19 24	19 24							20 22										
Princes Risborough	d					19 34	19 34		20 00		20 00			20a31			20 36	20 36			20 49	20 49		
Saunderton	d																				20 54	20 54		
High Wycombe	d					19 44	19 44		20 09		20 09	20 13	20 13		20 17	20 17					21 01	21 01	21 09	21 09
Beaconsfield	d					19 50	19 50					20 19	20 19		20 24	20 24					21 07	21 07		
Seer Green	d														20 27	20 27								
Gerrards Cross	d					19 56	19 56	20 03		20 03					20 32	20 32			20 56	20 56	21 13	21 13		
Denham Golf Club	d							20 06		20 06									20 59	20 59				
Denham	d							20 09		20 09									21 02	21 02				
West Ruislip § ⊖	d					20 07	20 07								20 39	20 39			21 07	21 07				
South Ruislip § ⊖	d							20 15		20 15														
Northolt Park	d					20 13	20 13												21 13	21 13				
Sudbury Hill Harrow	d							20 19		20 19														
Sudbury & Harrow Road	d																							
Wembley Stadium	d					20 18	20 18								20 48	20 48			21 18	21 18				
London Paddington ⊖	a																							
London Marylebone ⊖	a	20 13	20 23	20 26		20 31	20 34	20 34	20 37	20 37	20 40	20 43	20 46		21 03	21 06	21 10	21 13	21 32	21 35	21 35	21 38	21 38	21 41

§ London Underground Limited (Central Line) also operate services between South Ruislip and West Ruislip at frequent intervals

A until 5 October
B from 8 October

For complete services between Banbury and Birmingham, refer to Table T71

For principal services between London and Aylesbury refer to Table T114

Table T115-R

Mondays to Fridays

21 May to 7 December

Kidderminster, Birmingham Snow Hill, Stratford-upon-Avon, Banbury, Oxford Parkway, Aylesbury, High Wycombe - London

		CH	CH	CH	CH	CH	CH	CH	CH	CH	CH	CH	CH	CH FO	CH FX	CH FX	CH FO	CH	CH	CH	CH	CH	CH	CH
		◇	◇	◇	◇	◇	◇	◇	◇						◇	◇		◇	◇			◇	◇	◇
		A	B	A	B	A	B	A	B	A	B	A	B	A	C	B	D	A	B	A	B	A	B	A
Kidderminster	d																							
Stourbridge Junction	d																							
Cradley Heath	d																							
Rowley Regis	d																							
Birmingham Snow Hill	d					20 15	20 15															21 15	21 15	
Birmingham Moor Street	d					20 18	20 18															21 18	21 18	
Solihull	d					20 27	20 27															21 27	21 27	
Dorridge	d					20 32	20 32															21 32	21 32	
Lapworth	d																					21 36	21 36	
Stratford-upon-Avon	d																							
Stratford-upon-Avon Parkway	d																							
Wilmcote	d																							
Bearley	d																							
Claverdon	d																							
Hatton	d																					21 42	21 42	
Warwick Parkway	d					20 42	20 42															21 47	21 47	
Warwick	d					20 45	20 45															21 50	21 50	
Leamington Spa	d					20 50	20 50															21 55	21 55	
Banbury	d					21 13	21 13													21 34	21 34	22 13	22 13	
Kings Sutton	d																							
Bicester North	d					21 25	21 25													21 48	21 48	22 25	22 25	
Oxford	d			20 55	20 55			21 15	21 15									21 37	21 37					22 15
Oxford Parkway 116	d			21 01	21 01			21 21	21 21									21 48	21 48					22 21
Islip	d																							
Bicester Village	d			21 10	21 10			21 30	21 30									21 57	21 57					22 30
Haddenham & Thame Parkway	d			21 22	21 22													22 09	22 09	22 01	22 01			22 42
Aylesbury	d											21 24	21 24											
Little Kimble	d											21 33	21 33											
Monks Risborough	d											21 37	21 37											
Princes Risborough	d			21 29	21 29							21 48	21 48							22 18	22 18			22 49
Saunderton	d											21 53	21 53											22 54
High Wycombe	d	21 19	21 19	21 38	21 38	21 45	21 45					21 59	21 59	22 08	22 08	22 08	22 08	22 22	22 22	22 28	22 28	22 45	22 45	23 00
Beaconsfield	d	21 26	21 26									22 06	22 06	22 15	22 15	22 15	22 15			22 34	22 34			23 07
Seer Green	d	21 29	21 29									22 09	22 09											23 10
Gerrards Cross	d	21 34	21 34							22 01	22 01	22 14	22 14	22 21	22 21	22 21	22 21			22 40	22 40			23 15
Denham Golf Club	d									22 04	22 04													23 18
Denham	d									22 07	22 07			22 25	22 25	22 25	22 25							23 21
West Ruislip § ⊖	d									22 12	22 12			22 35	22 35	22 35	22 35							23 26
South Ruislip § ⊖	d	21 42	21 42									22 22	22 22							22 48	22 48			23 30
Northolt Park	d									22 18	22 18													23 34
Sudbury Hill Harrow	d																							
Sudbury & Harrow Road	d																							
Wembley Stadium	d	21 49	21 49							22 23	22 23	22 29	22 29	22 44	22 44	22 44	22 44	22 39	22 39	22 55	22 55			23 39
London Paddington ⊖	a																							
London Marylebone ⊖	a	22 02	22 05	22 05	22 08	22 12	22 15	22 18	22 21	22 36	22 39	22 42	22 45	22 55	22 57	23 00	23 00	22 52	22 55	23 08	23 11	23 12	23 15	23 52

§ London Underground Limited (Central Line) also operate services between South Ruislip and West Ruislip at frequent intervals

A until 5 October
B from 8 October
C until 4 October
D from 12 October

For complete services between Banbury and Birmingham, refer to Table T71

For principal services between London and Aylesbury refer to Table T114

Table T115-R

Mondays to Fridays

21 May to 7 December

Kidderminster, Birmingham Snow Hill, Stratford-upon-Avon, Banbury, Oxford Parkway, Aylesbury, High Wycombe - London

		CH	CH	CH	CH	CH	CH	CH	CH	CH FO	CH FO	CH	LM
		◇	◇	◇	◇	◇				◇	◇		
		A	B	A	B	A	B	A		B	C		D
Kidderminster	d												
Stourbridge Junction	d												
Cradley Heath	d												
Rowley Regis	d												
Birmingham Snow Hill	d												
Birmingham Moor Street	d												
Solihull	d												
Dorridge	d												
Lapworth	d												
Stratford-upon-Avon	d		21 39	21 39								23 15	23 30
Stratford-upon-Avon Parkway	d		21 43	21 43									23a33
Wilmcote	d		21 47	21 47									
Bearley	d												
Claverdon	d		21 54	21 54									
Hatton	d		21 59	21 59									
Warwick Parkway	d												
Warwick	d		22 06	22 06								23 34	
Leamington Spa	d		22 10	22 10								23 39	
Banbury	d		22 30	22 30								23 58	
Kings Sutton	d		22 35	22 35									
Bicester North	d		22 46	22 46									
Oxford	d	22 15			22 41	22 41			23 15	23 35	23 35	00a22	
Oxford Parkway 116	d	22 21			22 47	22 47			23 21	23 42	23 42		
Islip	d				22 50	22 50							
Bicester Village	d	22 30			22 58	22 58			23 31	23 51	23 51		
Haddenham & Thame Parkway	d	22 42	22 59	22 59	23 10	23 10			23 44				
Aylesbury	d						23 16	23 16					
Little Kimble	d						23 24	23 24					
Monks Risborough	d						23 28	23 28					
Princes Risborough	d	22 49	23 07	23 07	23 17	23 17	23 32	23 32	23 51				
Saunderton	d	22 54											
High Wycombe	d	23 00	23 17	23 17	23 26	23 26	23 42	23 42	00a07	00 13	00 13		
Beaconsfield	d	23 07	23 24	23 24	23 32	23 32	23 48	23 48					
Seer Green	d	23 10			23 35	23 35							
Gerrards Cross	d	23 15	23 30	23 30	23 39	23 39	23 54	23 54					
Denham Golf Club	d	23 18											
Denham	d	23 21			23 43	23 43							
West Ruislip § ⊖	d	23 26			23 47	23 47							
South Ruislip § ⊖	d	23 30											
Northolt Park	d	23 34			23 53	23 53							
Sudbury Hill Harrow	d												
Sudbury & Harrow Road	d												
Wembley Stadium	d	23 39			23 58	23 58	00 06	00 06					
London Paddington ⊖	a												
London Marylebone ⊖	a	23 55	23 58	00 01	00 11	00 14	00 19	00 22		00 40	00 43		

§ London Underground Limited (Central Line) also operate services between South Ruislip and West Ruislip at frequent intervals

A from 8 October
B until 5 October
C from 12 October
D To Birmingham Snow Hill

For complete services between Banbury and Birmingham, refer to Table T71

For principal services between London and Aylesbury refer to Table T114

Please note, Network Rail have stated that further updates to this timetable are possible during the validity period.

Kidderminster, Birmingham Snow Hill, Stratford-upon-Avon, Banbury, Oxford Parkway, Aylesbury, High Wycombe - London

	CH	CH	CH	CH	CH	CH	CH	CH	CH	CH	CH	CH	CH	CH	CH	CH	CH	CH	CH	CH	CH	CH
			◇	◇							◇	◇			◇	◇					◇	◇
	A	B	C	D	E	F	E	F	E	F	E	F	E	F	E	F	E	F	E	F	E	F
Kidderminster d																						
Stourbridge Junction d																						
Cradley Heath d																						
Rowley Regis d																						
Birmingham Snow Hill d																					06.12	06.12
Birmingham Moor Street d																					06.15	06.15
Solihull d																					06.24	06.24
Dorridge d																					06.29	06.29
Lapworth d																					06.33	06.33
Stratford-upon-Avon d																						
Stratford-upon-Avon Parkway d																						
Wilmcote d																						
Bearley d																						
Claverdon d																						
Hatton d																					06.39	06.39
Warwick Parkway d																					06.44	06.44
Warwick d																					06.47	06.47
Leamington Spa d																					06.52	06.52
Banbury d									06.04	06.04			06.24	06.24							07.10	07.10
Kings Sutton d													06.29	06.29								
Bicester North d									06.18	06.18			06.39	06.39							07.22	07.22
Oxford d											06.12	06.12			06.37	06.37						
Oxford Parkway 116 d											06.18	06.18			06.43	06.43						
Islip d																						
Bicester Village d											06.28	06.28			06.52	06.52						
Haddenham & Thame Parkway d									06.30	06.30	06.42	06.42	06.50	06.50							07.33	07.33
Aylesbury d					05.15	05.15	05.55	05.55									06.52	06.52				
Little Kimble d					05.23	05.23	06.03	06.03									07.00	07.00				
Monks Risborough d					05.27	05.27	06.07	06.07									07.04	07.04				
Princes Risborough d					05.31	05.31	06.11	06.11	06.37	06.37							07.09	07.09				
Saunderton d					05.36	05.36	06.16	06.16									07.14	07.14				
High Wycombe d			00.13	00.13	05.43	05.43	06.23	06.23	06.47	06.47	06.56	06.56	07.03	07.03			07.21	07.21	07.31	07.31	07.46	07.46
Beaconsfield d					05.50	05.50	06.29	06.29	06.53	06.53			07.09	07.09			07.27	07.27	07.37	07.37		
Seer Green d					05.53	05.53	06.32	06.32									07.30	07.30				
Gerrards Cross d					05.58	05.58	06.37	06.37	06.59	06.59			07.15	07.15			07.35	07.35	07.43	07.43		
Denham Golf Club d					06.01	06.01	06.41	06.41											07.46	07.46		
Denham d					06.04	06.04	06.44	06.44											07.49	07.49		
West Ruislip § ⊖ d					06.09	06.09	06.49	06.49									07.42	07.42	07.59	07.59		
South Ruislip § ⊖ d					06.13	06.13	06.53	06.53									07.46	07.46	08.03	08.03		
Northolt Park d					06.17	06.17	06.57	06.57									07.50	07.50	08.07	08.07		
Sudbury Hill Harrow d																						
Sudbury & Harrow Road d																						
Wembley Stadium d	00.06	00.06			06.22	06.22	07.02	07.02	07.11	07.11							07.55	07.55	08.12	08.12		
London Paddington ⊖ a																						
London Marylebone ⊖ a	00.19	00.22	00.40	00.43	06.35	06.38	07.15	07.18	07.24	07.27	07.27	07.30	07.36	07.39	07.40	07.43	08.09	08.12	08.25	08.28	08.14	08.17

§ London Underground Limited (Central Line) also operate services between South Ruislip and West Ruislip at frequent intervals

A until 6 October. From Aylesbury
B from 13 October. From Aylesbury
C until 6 October. From Oxford
D from 13 October. From Oxford
E until 6 October
F from 13 October

For complete services between Banbury and Birmingham, refer to Table T71

For principal services between London and Aylesbury refer to Table T114

Table T115-R

Saturdays

26 May to 8 December

Kidderminster, Birmingham Snow Hill, Stratford-upon-Avon, Banbury, Oxford Parkway, Aylesbury, High Wycombe - London

	CH	CH	CH	CH	CH	CH	CH	CH	CH	CH	CH	CH	CH	CH	CH	CH	CH	CH	CH	CH	CH	CH
	◇	◇			◇	◇	◇	◇			◇	◇	◇	◇					◇	◇	◇	◇
	A	B	A	B	A	B	A	B	A	B	A	B	A	B	A	B	A	B	A	B	A	B
Kidderminster d											06.37	06.37							07.12	07.12		
Stourbridge Junction d											06.45	06.45							07.22	07.22		
Cradley Heath d											06.51	06.51										
Rowley Regis d											06.57	06.57							07.33	07.33		
Birmingham Snow Hill d					06.46	06.46					07.12	07.12							07.51	07.51		
Birmingham Moor Street d					06.49	06.49					07.15	07.15							07.55	07.55		
Solihull d					07.02	07.02					07.24	07.24							08.05	08.05		
Dorridge d											07.29	07.29										
Lapworth d																						
Stratford-upon-Avon d																						
Stratford-upon-Avon Parkway d																						
Wilmcote d																						
Bearley d																						
Claverdon d																						
Hatton d																						
Warwick Parkway d					07.14	07.14					07.39	07.39							08.18	08.18		
Warwick d											07.42	07.42										
Leamington Spa d					07.20	07.20					07.46	07.46							08.24	08.24		
Banbury d					07.39	07.39			07.44	07.44	08.04	08.04							08.44	08.44		
Kings Sutton d									07.49	07.49												
Bicester North d					07.51	07.51			08.00	08.00	08.16	08.16										
Oxford d	07.10	07.10					07.36	07.36					08.11	08.11							08.40	08.40
Oxford Parkway 116 d	07.16	07.16					07.44	07.44					08.17	08.17							08.47	08.47
Islip d	07.19	07.19																				
Bicester Village d	07.27	07.27					07.55	07.55					08.26	08.26							08.58	08.58
Haddenham & Thame Parkway d	07.41	07.41							08.13	08.13			08.38	08.38								
Aylesbury d			07.32	07.32													08.29	08.29				
Little Kimble d			07.40	07.40													08.37	08.37				
Monks Risborough d			07.44	07.44													08.41	08.41				
Princes Risborough d			07.49	07.49					08.20	08.20	08.31	08.31					08.45	08.45				
Saunderton d			07.54	07.54													08.50	08.50				
High Wycombe d	07.55	07.55	08.01	08.01	08.11	08.11			08.30	08.30			08.51	08.51			08.57	08.57	09.14	09.14		
Beaconsfield d			08.07	08.07					08.36	08.36							09.03	09.03				
Seer Green d			08.10	08.10													09.06	09.06				
Gerrards Cross d			08.14	08.14					08.42	08.42					08.49	08.49	09.11	09.11				
Denham Golf Club d															08.52	08.52						
Denham d			08.18	08.18											08.55	08.55	09.15	09.15				
West Ruislip § ⊖ d															09.05	09.05						
South Ruislip § ⊖ d															09.09	09.09						
Northolt Park d															09.13	09.13						
Sudbury Hill Harrow d																						
Sudbury & Harrow Road d																						
Wembley Stadium d									08.54	08.54					09.18	09.18						
London Paddington ⊖ a																						
London Marylebone ⊖ a	08.28	08.31	08.39	08.42	08.42	08.45	08.54	08.57	09.07	09.10	09.11	09.14	09.18	09.21	09.32	09.35	09.36	09.39	09.41	09.44	09.46	09.49

§ London Underground Limited (Central Line) also operate services between South Ruislip and West Ruislip at frequent intervals

A until 6 October
B from 13 October

For complete services between Banbury and Birmingham, refer to Table T71

For principal services between London and Aylesbury refer to Table T114

Table T115-R

Saturdays
26 May to 8 December

Kidderminster, Birmingham Snow Hill, Stratford-upon-Avon, Banbury, Oxford Parkway, Aylesbury, High Wycombe - London

		CH ◇ A	CH ◇ B	CH ◇ A	CH ◇ B	LM C	CH ◇ A	CH ◇ B	CH A	CH B	CH A	CH B	CH ◇ A	CH ◇ B	CH ◇ A	CH ◇ B	CH A	CH B	CH ◇ A	CH ◇ B	LM C	CH ◇ A	CH ◇ B
Kidderminster	d												08 13	08 13									
Stourbridge Junction 2	d												08 24	08 24									
Cradley Heath	d												08 30	08 30									
Rowley Regis	d												08 36	08 36									
Birmingham Snow Hill	d												08 53	08 53					09 12	09 12			
Birmingham Moor Street	d			08 15	08 15								08 56	08 56					09 15	09 15			
Solihull	d			08 24	08 24								09 05	09 05					09 24	09 24			
Dorridge	d			08 29	08 29														09 29	09 29			
Lapworth	d																						
Stratford-upon-Avon	d	07 56	07 56			09 03															10 03		
Stratford-upon-Avon Parkway	d	08 00	08 00			09a06															10a06		
Wilmcote	d	08 03	08 03																				
Bearley	d																						
Claverdon	d	08 11	08 11																				
Hatton	d	08 17	08 17																				
Warwick Parkway	d			08 39	08 39								09 16	09 16					09 39	09 39			
Warwick	d	08 24	08 24	08 42	08 42														09 42	09 42			
Leamington Spa 3	d	08 29	08 29	08 46	08 46								09 22	09 22					09 46	09 46			
Banbury	d	08 48	08 48	09 04	09 04								09 40	09 40			09 44	09 44	10 05	10 05			
Kings Sutton	d	08 53	08 53														09 49	09 49					
Bicester North 3	d	09 03	09 03	09 16	09 16												10 01	10 01	10 18	10 18			
Oxford	d						09 09	09 09							09 42	09 42						10 09	10 09
Oxford Parkway 116	d						09 15	09 15							09 48	09 48						10 15	10 15
Islip	d						09 18	09 18														10 18	10 18
Bicester Village	d						09 26	09 26							09 57	09 57						10 26	10 26
Haddenham & Thame Parkway	d	09 14	09 14				09 38	09 38									10 13	10 13				10 38	10 38
Aylesbury	d										09 29	09 29											
Little Kimble	d										09 37	09 37											
Monks Risborough	d										09 41	09 41											
Princes Risborough 2	d	09 21	09 21	09 31	09 31						09 45	09 45					10 20	10 20					
Saunderton	d										09 50	09 50											
High Wycombe 1	d	09 30	09 30				09 51	09 51			09 57	09 57	10 14	10 14			10 30	10 30				10 51	10 51
Beaconsfield	d	09 36	09 36								10 03	10 03					10 36	10 36					
Seer Green	d										10 06	10 06											
Gerrards Cross 1	d	09 41	09 41						09 49	09 49	10 11	10 11					10 42	10 42					
Denham Golf Club	d								09 52	09 52													
Denham	d								09 55	09 55	10 15	10 15											
West Ruislip 3 § ⊖	d								10 05	10 05													
South Ruislip § ⊖	d								10 09	10 09													
Northolt Park	d								10 13	10 13													
Sudbury Hill Harrow	d																						
Sudbury & Harrow Road	d																						
Wembley Stadium	d	09 52	09 52						10 18	10 18							10 54	10 54					
London Paddington 15 ⊖	a																						
London Marylebone 10 ⊖	a	10 05	10 08	10 11	10 14		10 18	10 21	10 32	10 35	10 36	10 39	10 41	10 44	10 48	10 51	11 07	11 10	11 11	11 14		11 18	11 21

§ London Underground Limited (Central Line) also operate services between South Ruislip and West Ruislip at frequent intervals

A until 6 October
B from 13 October
C To Stourbridge Junction

For complete services between Banbury and Birmingham, refer to Table T71

For principal services between London and Aylesbury refer to Table T114

Table T115-R

Saturdays
26 May to 8 December

Kidderminster, Birmingham Snow Hill, Stratford-upon-Avon, Banbury, Oxford Parkway, Aylesbury, High Wycombe - London

		CH A	CH B	CH A	CH B	CH A	CH B	CH ◇ A	CH ◇ B	CH ◇ A	CH ◇ B	CH A	CH B	CH ◇ A	CH ◇ B	CH	LM C	CH ◇ A	CH ◇ B	CH A	CH B	CH A	CH B
Kidderminster	d							09 10	09 10														
Stourbridge Junction 2	d							09 20	09 20														
Cradley Heath	d																						
Rowley Regis	d							09 31	09 31														
Birmingham Snow Hill	d							09 51	09 51					10 12	10 12								
Birmingham Moor Street	d							09 55	09 55					10 15	10 15								
Solihull	d							10 04	10 04					10 24	10 24								
Dorridge	d													10 29	10 29								
Lapworth	d																						
Stratford-upon-Avon	d															10 40	11 03						
Stratford-upon-Avon Parkway	d															10 44	11a06						
Wilmcote	d															10 47							
Bearley	d															10 51							
Claverdon	d															10 56							
Hatton	d															11 02							
Warwick Parkway	d							10 19	10 19					10 39	10 39								
Warwick	d													10 42	10 42	11 08							
Leamington Spa 3	d							10 25	10 25					10 46	10 46	11a16							
Banbury	d					10 24	10 24	10 44	10 44			10 48	10 48	11 05	11 05								
Kings Sutton	d					10 31	10 31																
Bicester North 3	d					10 42	10 42					11 03	11 03	11 18	11 18								
Oxford	d									10 44	10 44							11 11	11 11				
Oxford Parkway 116	d									10 50	10 50							11 17	11 17				
Islip	d																						
Bicester Village	d									10 59	10 59							11 26	11 26				
Haddenham & Thame Parkway	d											11 15	11 15					11 38	11 38				
Aylesbury	d			10 29	10 29																	11 30	11 30
Little Kimble	d			10 37	10 37																		
Monks Risborough	d			10 41	10 41																	11 41	11 41
Princes Risborough 2	d			10 45	10 45							11 22	11 22									11 45	11 45
Saunderton	d			10 50	10 50																	11 50	11 50
High Wycombe 1	d			10 57	10 57	11 10	11 10	11 18	11 18			11 32	11 32					11 51	11 51			11 57	11 57
Beaconsfield	d			11 03	11 03							11 38	11 38									12 03	12 03
Seer Green	d			11 06	11 06																	12 06	12 06
Gerrards Cross 1	d	10 49	10 49	11 11	11 11							11 44	11 44							11 51	11 51	12 11	12 11
Denham Golf Club	d	10 52	10 52																	11 54	11 54		
Denham	d	10 55	10 55	11 15	11 15															11 57	11 57	12 15	12 15
West Ruislip 3 § ⊖	d	11 05	11 05																	12 06	12 06		
South Ruislip § ⊖	d	11 09	11 09																	12 10	12 10		
Northolt Park	d	11 13	11 13																	12 14	12 14		
Sudbury Hill Harrow	d																						
Sudbury & Harrow Road	d																						
Wembley Stadium	d	11 18	11 18									11 56	11 56							12 19	12 19		
London Paddington 15 ⊖	a																						
London Marylebone 10 ⊖	a	11 32	11 35	11 36	11 39	11 41	11 44	11 46	11 49	11 49	11 52	12 08	12 11	12 11	12 14			12 19	12 22	12 32	12 35	12 36	12 39

§ London Underground Limited (Central Line) also operate services between South Ruislip and West Ruislip at frequent intervals

A until 6 October
B from 13 October
C To Stourbridge Junction

For complete services between Banbury and Birmingham, refer to Table T71

For principal services between London and Aylesbury refer to Table T114

Please note, Network Rail have stated that further updates to this timetable are possible during the validity period.

Table T115-R

Saturdays

26 May to 8 December

Kidderminster, Birmingham Snow Hill, Stratford-upon-Avon, Banbury, Oxford Parkway, Aylesbury, High Wycombe - London

Station		CH	CH	CH	CH	CH	CH	CH	CH	LM	CH	CH	CH	CH	CH	CH	CH	CH	CH	CH	CH	CH	CH
		◇	◇	◇	◇			◇	◇		◇	◇					◇	◇	◇	◇			◇
		A	B	A	B	A	B	A	B	C	A	B	A	B	A	B	A	B	A	B	A	B	A
Kidderminster	d																						
Stourbridge Junction	d																						
Cradley Heath	d																						
Rowley Regis	d																						
Birmingham Snow Hill	d							11 12	11 12														12 12
Birmingham Moor Street	d	10 55	10 55					11 15	11 15								11 55	11 55					12 15
Solihull	d	11 04	11 04					11 24	11 24								12 04	12 04					12 24
Dorridge	d							11 29	11 29														12 29
Lapworth	d																						
Stratford-upon-Avon	d									12 03													
Stratford-upon-Avon Parkway	d									12a06													
Wilmcote	d																						
Bearley	d																						
Claverdon	d																						
Hatton	d																						
Warwick Parkway	d	11 16	11 16					11 39	11 39								12 19	12 19					12 39
Warwick	d							11 42	11 42														12 42
Leamington Spa	d	11 21	11 21					11 46	11 46								12 25	12 25					12 46
Banbury	d	11 39	11 39			11 43	11 43	12 05	12 05								12 44	12 44			12 49	12 49	13 05
Kings Sutton	d																						
Bicester North	d					12 01	12 01	12 18	12 18												13 02	13 02	13 18
Oxford	d			11 42	11 42						12 09	12 09							12 42	12 42			
Oxford Parkway 116	d			11 48	11 48						12 15	12 15							12 48	12 48			
Islip	d										12 18	12 18											
Bicester Village	d			11 57	11 57						12 26	12 26							12 57	12 57			
Haddenham & Thame Parkway	d					12 13	12 13				12 38	12 38									13 14	13 14	
Aylesbury	d														12 29	12 29							
Little Kimble	d														12 37	12 37							
Monks Risborough	d														12 41	12 41							
Princes Risborough	d					12 20	12 20								12 45	12 45					13 21	13 21	
Saunderton	d														12 50	12 50							
High Wycombe	d	12 14	12 14			12 30	12 30				12 51	12 51			12 57	12 57	13 14	13 14			13 31	13 31	
Beaconsfield	d					12 36	12 36								13 03	13 03					13 37	13 37	
Seer Green	d														13 06	13 06							
Gerrards Cross	d					12 42	12 42						12 49	12 49	13 11	13 11					13 43	13 43	
Denham Golf Club	d												12 52	12 52									
Denham	d												12 55	12 55	13 15	13 15							
West Ruislip § ⊖	d												13 05	13 05									
South Ruislip § ⊖	d												13 09	13 09									
Northolt Park	d												13 13	13 13									
Sudbury Hill Harrow	d																						
Sudbury & Harrow Road	d																						
Wembley Stadium	d					12 54	12 54						13 18	13 18							13 55	13 55	
London Paddington ⊖	a																						
London Marylebone ⊖	a	12 41	12 44	12 46	12 49	13 07	13 10	13 11	13 14		13 18	13 21	13 32	13 35	13 36	13 39	13 41	13 44	13 46	13 49	14 08	14 11	14 11

§ London Underground Limited (Central Line) also operate services between South Ruislip and West Ruislip at frequent intervals

A until 6 October
B from 13 October
C To Stourbridge Junction

For complete services between Banbury and Birmingham, refer to Table T71

For principal services between London and Aylesbury refer to Table T114

Table T115-R

Saturdays

26 May to 8 December

Kidderminster, Birmingham Snow Hill, Stratford-upon-Avon, Banbury, Oxford Parkway, Aylesbury, High Wycombe - London

Station		CH	CH	LM	CH	CH	CH	CH	CH	CH	CH	CH	CH	CH	CH	CH	CH	CH	LM	CH	CH	CH	CH
		◇			◇	◇					◇	◇	◇	◇			◇	◇		◇	◇		
		A		B	C	A	C	A	C	A	C	A	C	A	C	A	C	A	B	C	A	C	A
Kidderminster	d																						
Stourbridge Junction	d																						
Cradley Heath	d																						
Rowley Regis	d																						
Birmingham Snow Hill	d	12 12															13 12	13 12					
Birmingham Moor Street	d	12 15									12 55	12 55					13 15	13 15					
Solihull	d	12 24									13 04	13 04					13 24	13 24					
Dorridge	d	12 29															13 29	13 29					
Lapworth	d																						
Stratford-upon-Avon	d		12 42	13 03															14 03				
Stratford-upon-Avon Parkway	d		12 46	13a06															14a06				
Wilmcote	d		12 49																				
Bearley	d																						
Claverdon	d		12 57																				
Hatton	d		13 03																				
Warwick Parkway	d	12 39									13 16	13 16					13 38	13 38					
Warwick	d	12 42	13 09														13 41	13 41					
Leamington Spa	d	12 46	13a17								13 22	13 22					13 46	13 46					
Banbury	d	13 05									13 40	13 40			13 47	13 47	14 07	14 07					
Kings Sutton	d																						
Bicester North	d	13 18													14 02	14 02	14 20	14 20					
Oxford	d				13 11	13 11							13 43	13 43						14 11	14 11		
Oxford Parkway 116	d				13 17	13 17							13 49	13 49						14 17	14 17		
Islip	d																						
Bicester Village	d				13 26	13 26							13 58	13 58						14 26	14 26		
Haddenham & Thame Parkway	d				13 38	13 38									14 14	14 14				14 38	14 38		
Aylesbury	d								13 29	13 29													
Little Kimble	d								13 37	13 37													
Monks Risborough	d								13 41	13 41													
Princes Risborough	d								13 45	13 45					14 21	14 21							
Saunderton	d								13 50	13 50													
High Wycombe	d				13 51	13 51			13 57	13 57	14 14	14 14			14 31	14 31				14 51	14 51		
Beaconsfield	d								14 03	14 03					14 37	14 37							
Seer Green	d								14 06	14 06													
Gerrards Cross	d						13 51	13 51	14 11	14 11					14 43	14 43						14 50	14 50
Denham Golf Club	d						13 54	13 54														14 53	14 53
Denham	d						13 57	13 57	14 15	14 15												14 56	14 56
West Ruislip § ⊖	d						14 07	14 07														15 05	15 05
South Ruislip § ⊖	d						14 11	14 11														15 09	15 09
Northolt Park	d						14 15	14 15														15 13	15 13
Sudbury Hill Harrow	d																						
Sudbury & Harrow Road	d																						
Wembley Stadium	d						14 20	14 20							14 55	14 55						15 18	15 18
London Paddington ⊖	a																						
London Marylebone ⊖	a	14 14			14 21	14 24	14 33	14 36	14 36	14 39	14 41	14 44	14 46	14 49	15 08	15 11	15 11	15 14		15 18	15 21	15 32	15 35

§ London Underground Limited (Central Line) also operate services between South Ruislip and West Ruislip at frequent intervals

A from 13 October
B To Stourbridge Junction
C until 6 October

For complete services between Banbury and Birmingham, refer to Table T71

For principal services between London and Aylesbury refer to Table T114

Table T115-R

Saturdays

26 May to 8 December

Kidderminster, Birmingham Snow Hill, Stratford-upon-Avon, Banbury, Oxford Parkway, Aylesbury, High Wycombe - London

		CH	CH	CH	CH	CH	CH	CH	CH	CH	CH	CH	LM	CH	CH	CH	CH	CH	CH	CH	CH	CH	CH
				◇	◇	◇	◇			◇	◇			◇	◇					◇	◇	◇	◇
		A	B	A	B	A	B	A	B	A	B		C	A	B	A	B	A	B	A	B	A	B
Kidderminster	d																						
Stourbridge Junction 2	d																						
Cradley Heath	d																						
Rowley Regis	d																						
Birmingham Snow Hill ⇌	d									14 12	14 12												
Birmingham Moor Street	d			13 55	13 55					14 15	14 15									14 55	14 55		
Solihull	d			14 04	14 04					14 24	14 24									15 04	15 04		
Dorridge	d									14 29	14 29												
Lapworth	d																						
Stratford-upon-Avon	d											14 42	15 03										
Stratford-upon-Avon Parkway	d											14 46	15a06										
Wilmcote	d											14 49											
Bearley	d																						
Claverdon	d											14 57											
Hatton	d											15 03											
Warwick Parkway	d			14 16	14 16					14 39	14 39									15 16	15 16		
Warwick	d									14 42	14 42	15 09											
Leamington Spa 8	d			14 22	14 22					14 46	14 46	15a17								15 22	15 22		
Banbury	d			14 41	14 41			14 44	14 44	15 05	15 05									15 41	15 41		
Kings Sutton	d							14 49	14 49														
Bicester North 8	d							15 01	15 01	15 18	15 18												
Oxford	d					14 42	14 42							15 09	15 09							15 43	15 43
Oxford Parkway 116	d					14 48	14 48							15 15	15 15							15 49	15 49
Islip	d													15 18	15 18								
Bicester Village	d					14 57	14 57							15 26	15 26							15 58	15 58
Haddenham & Thame Parkway	d							15 13	15 13					15 38	15 38								
Aylesbury	d	14 29	14 29															15 30	15 30				
Little Kimble	d	14 37	14 37																				
Monks Risborough	d	14 41	14 41															15 41	15 41				
Princes Risborough 2	d	14 45	14 45					15 20	15 20									15 45	15 45				
Saunderton	d	14 50	14 50															15 50	15 50				
High Wycombe 1	d	14 57	14 57	15 14	15 14			15 30	15 30					15 51	15 51			15 57	15 57	16 14	16 14		
Beaconsfield	d	15 03	15 03					15 36	15 36									16 03	16 03				
Seer Green	d	15 06	15 06															16 06	16 06				
Gerrards Cross 1	d	15 11	15 11					15 42	15 42							15 49	15 49	16 11	16 11				
Denham Golf Club	d															15 52	15 52						
Denham	d	15 15	15 15													15 55	15 55	16 15	16 15				
West Ruislip 8 § ⊖	d															16 05	16 05						
South Ruislip § ⊖	d															16 09	16 09						
Northolt Park	d															16 13	16 13						
Sudbury Hill Harrow	d																						
Sudbury & Harrow Road	d																						
Wembley Stadium	d							15 54	15 54							16 18	16 18						
London Paddington 15 ⊖	a																						
London Marylebone 15 ⊖	a	15 36	15 39	15 41	15 44	15 47	15 50	16 07	16 10	16 11	16 14			16 18	16 21	16 32	16 35	16 36	16 39	16 46	16 49	16 49	16 52

§ London Underground Limited (Central Line) also operate services between South Ruislip and West Ruislip at frequent intervals

A until 6 October
B from 13 October
C To Stourbridge Junction

For complete services between Banbury and Birmingham, refer to Table T71

For principal services between London and Aylesbury refer to Table T114

Table T115-R

Saturdays

26 May to 8 December

Kidderminster, Birmingham Snow Hill, Stratford-upon-Avon, Banbury, Oxford Parkway, Aylesbury, High Wycombe - London

		CH	CH	CH	CH	LM	CH	CH	CH	CH	CH	CH	CH	CH	CH	CH	CH	CH	CH	CH	CH	LM	CH
				◇	◇		◇	◇					◇	◇	◇	◇			◇	◇			◇
		A	B	A	B	C	A	B	A	B	A	B	A	B	A	B	A	B	A	B		C	A
Kidderminster	d																						
Stourbridge Junction 2	d																						
Cradley Heath	d																						
Rowley Regis	d																						
Birmingham Snow Hill ⇌	d			15 12	15 12														16 12	16 12			
Birmingham Moor Street	d			15 15	15 15								15 55	15 55					16 15	16 15			
Solihull	d			15 24	15 24								16 04	16 04					16 24	16 24			
Dorridge	d			15 29	15 29														16 29	16 29			
Lapworth	d																						
Stratford-upon-Avon	d					16 03															16 41	17 03	
Stratford-upon-Avon Parkway	d					16a06															16 45	17a06	
Wilmcote	d																				16 48		
Bearley	d																				16 52		
Claverdon	d																				16 57		
Hatton	d																				17 03		
Warwick Parkway	d			15 39	15 39								16 16	16 16					16 39	16 39			
Warwick	d			15 42	15 42														16 42	16 42	17 09		
Leamington Spa 8	d			15 46	15 46								16 22	16 22					16 46	16 46	17a17		
Banbury	d	15 47	15 47	16 05	16 05								16 41	16 41			16 44	16 44	17 05	17 05			
Kings Sutton	d																16 49	16 49					
Bicester North 8	d	16 02	16 02	16 18	16 18												17 01	17 01	17 18	17 18			
Oxford	d						16 11	16 11							16 42	16 42							17 11
Oxford Parkway 116	d						16 17	16 17							16 48	16 48							17 17
Islip	d																						
Bicester Village	d						16 26	16 26							16 57	16 57							17 26
Haddenham & Thame Parkway	d	16 14	16 14				16 38	16 38									17 13	17 13					17 38
Aylesbury	d										16 29	16 29											
Little Kimble	d										16 37	16 37											
Monks Risborough	d										16 41	16 41											
Princes Risborough 2	d	16 21	16 21								16 45	16 45					17 20	17 20					
Saunderton	d										16 50	16 50											
High Wycombe 1	d	16 31	16 31				16 51	16 51			16 57	16 57	17 14	17 14			17 30	17 30					17 51
Beaconsfield	d	16 37	16 37								17 03	17 03					17 36	17 36					
Seer Green	d										17 06	17 06											
Gerrards Cross 1	d	16 43	16 43						16 50	16 50	17 11	17 11					17 42	17 42					
Denham Golf Club	d								16 53	16 53													
Denham	d								16 56	16 56	17 15	17 15											
West Ruislip 8 § ⊖	d								17 05	17 05													
South Ruislip § ⊖	d								17 09	17 09													
Northolt Park	d								17 13	17 13													
Sudbury Hill Harrow	d																						
Sudbury & Harrow Road	d																						
Wembley Stadium	d	16 55	16 55						17 18	17 18							17 54	17 54					
London Paddington 15 ⊖	a																						
London Marylebone 15 ⊖	a	17 07	17 10	17 11	17 14		17 18	17 21	17 32	17 35	17 36	17 39	17 41	17 44	17 47	17 50	18 07	18 10	18 11	18 14			18 18

§ London Underground Limited (Central Line) also operate services between South Ruislip and West Ruislip at frequent intervals

A until 6 October
B from 13 October
C To Stourbridge Junction

For complete services between Banbury and Birmingham, refer to Table T71

For principal services between London and Aylesbury refer to Table T114

Please note, Network Rail have stated that further updates to this timetable are possible during the validity period.

Table T115-R

Saturdays
26 May to 8 December

Kidderminster, Birmingham Snow Hill, Stratford-upon-Avon, Banbury, Oxford Parkway, Aylesbury, High Wycombe - London

		CH ◇ A	CH B	CH A	CH B	CH A	CH ◇ B	CH ◇ A	CH ◇ B	CH ◇ A	CH B	CH A	CH ◇ B	CH ◇ A	CH ◇ B	CH ◇ A	CH B	CH A	CH B	CH A	CH ◇ B	CH ◇ A	CH ◇ B
Kidderminster	d																						
Stourbridge Junction 2	d																						
Cradley Heath	d																						
Rowley Regis	d																						
Birmingham Snow Hill	d												17 12	17 12									
Birmingham Moor Street	d						16 55	16 55					17 15	17 15							17 55	17 55	
Solihull	d						17 04	17 04					17 24	17 24							18 04	18 04	
Dorridge	d												17 29	17 29									
Lapworth	d																						
Stratford-upon-Avon	d																						
Stratford-upon-Avon Parkway	d																						
Wilmcote	d																						
Bearley	d																						
Claverdon	d																						
Hatton	d																						
Warwick Parkway	d						17 16	17 16					17 39	17 39							18 16	18 16	
Warwick	d												17 42	17 42									
Leamington Spa 8	d						17 22	17 22					17 46	17 46							18 22	18 22	
Banbury	d						17 41	17 41			17 45	17 45	18 05	18 05							18 41	18 41	
Kings Sutton	d																						
Bicester North 3	d										18 01	18 01	18 18	18 18									
Oxford	d	17 11							17 41	17 41					18 07	18 07							18 42
Oxford Parkway 116	d	17 17							17 48	17 48					18 15	18 15							18 48
Islip	d														18 18	18 18							
Bicester Village	d	17 26							17 57	17 57					18 26	18 26							18 57
Haddenham & Thame Parkway	d	17 38									18 13	18 13			18 38	18 38							
Aylesbury	d				17 29	17 29													18 29	18 29			
Little Kimble	d				17 37	17 37													18 37	18 37			
Monks Risborough	d				17 41	17 41													18 41	18 41			
Princes Risborough 2	d				17 45	17 45					18 20	18 20							18 45	18 45			
Saunderton	d				17 50	17 50													18 50	18 50			
High Wycombe 1	d	17 51			17 57	17 57	18 14	18 14			18 30	18 30			18 51	18 51			18 57	18 57	19 14	19 14	
Beaconsfield	d				18 03	18 03					18 36	18 36							19 03	19 03			
Seer Green	d				18 06	18 06													19 06	19 06			
Gerrards Cross 1	d		17 49	17 49	18 11	18 11					18 42	18 42					18 49	18 49	19 11	19 11			
Denham Golf Club	d		17 52	17 52													18 52	18 52					
Denham	d		17 55	17 55	18 15	18 15											18 55	18 55	19 15	19 15			
West Ruislip 3 § ⊖	d		18 05	18 05													19 05	19 05					
South Ruislip § ⊖	d		18 09	18 09													19 09	19 09					
Northolt Park	d		18 13	18 13													19 13	19 13					
Sudbury Hill Harrow	d																						
Sudbury & Harrow Road	d																						
Wembley Stadium	d		18 18	18 18							18 54	18 54					19 18	19 18					
London Paddington 15 ⊖	a																						
London Marylebone 10 ⊖	a	18 21	18 32	18 35	18 36	18 39	18 41	18 44	18 47	18 50	19 07	19 10	19 11	19 14	19 18	19 21	19 32	19 35	19 36	19 39	19 41	19 44	19 47

§ London Underground Limited (Central Line) also operate services between South Ruislip and West Ruislip at frequent intervals

A from 13 October
B until 6 October

For complete services between Banbury and Birmingham, refer to Table T71

For principal services between London and Aylesbury refer to Table T114

Table T115-R

Saturdays
26 May to 8 December

Kidderminster, Birmingham Snow Hill, Stratford-upon-Avon, Banbury, Oxford Parkway, Aylesbury, High Wycombe - London

		CH ◇ A	CH B	CH A	CH ◇ B	CH ◇ A	CH	CH ◇ B	CH ◇ A	CH B	CH A	CH B	CH A	CH ◇ B	CH ◇ A	CH ◇ B	CH ◇ A	CH B	CH A	CH ◇ B	CH ◇ A	CH ◇ B	CH ◇ A
Kidderminster	d																						
Stourbridge Junction 2	d																						
Cradley Heath	d																						
Rowley Regis	d																						
Birmingham Snow Hill	d				18 12	18 12														19 12	19 12		
Birmingham Moor Street	d				18 15	18 15								18 55	18 55					19 15	19 15		
Solihull	d				18 24	18 24								19 04	19 04					19 24	19 24		
Dorridge	d				18 29	18 29														19 29	19 29		
Lapworth	d																						
Stratford-upon-Avon	d						18 41																
Stratford-upon-Avon Parkway	d						18 45																
Wilmcote	d						18 48																
Bearley	d						18 52																
Claverdon	d						18 57																
Hatton	d						19 03																
Warwick Parkway	d				18 39	18 39								19 16	19 16					19 39	19 39		
Warwick	d				18 42	18 42	19 09													19 42	19 42		
Leamington Spa 8	d				18 46	18 46	19a17							19 22	19 22					19 46	19 46		
Banbury	d		18 44	18 44	19 05	19 05								19 41	19 41			19 46	19 46	20 05	20 05		
Kings Sutton	d		18 49	18 49																			
Bicester North 3	d		19 01	19 01	19 18	19 18												20 01	20 01	20 18	20 18		
Oxford	d	18 42						19 11	19 11							19 42	19 42					20 11	20 11
Oxford Parkway 116	d	18 48						19 17	19 17							19 48	19 48					20 17	20 17
Islip	d																						
Bicester Village	d	18 57						19 26	19 26							19 57	19 57					20 26	20 26
Haddenham & Thame Parkway	d		19 13	19 13				19 38	19 38									20 13	20 13			20 38	20 38
Aylesbury	d											19 29	19 29										
Little Kimble	d											19 37	19 37										
Monks Risborough	d											19 41	19 41										
Princes Risborough 2	d		19 20	19 20								19 45	19 45					20 20	20 20				
Saunderton	d											19 50	19 50										
High Wycombe 1	d		19 30	19 30				19 51	19 51			19 57	19 57	20 14	20 14			20 30	20 30			20 51	20 51
Beaconsfield	d		19 36	19 36								20 03	20 03					20 36	20 36				
Seer Green	d											20 06	20 06										
Gerrards Cross 1	d		19 42	19 42						19 49	19 49	20 11	20 11					20 42	20 42				
Denham Golf Club	d									19 52	19 52												
Denham	d									19 55	19 55	20 15	20 15										
West Ruislip 3 § ⊖	d									20 05	20 05												
South Ruislip § ⊖	d									20 09	20 09												
Northolt Park	d									20 13	20 13												
Sudbury Hill Harrow	d																						
Sudbury & Harrow Road	d																						
Wembley Stadium	d		19 54	19 54						20 18	20 18							20 54	20 54				
London Paddington 15 ⊖	a																						
London Marylebone 10 ⊖	a	19 50	20 07	20 10	20 11	20 14		20 18	20 21	20 32	20 35	20 36	20 39	20 41	20 44	20 48	20 51	21 07	21 10	21 11	21 14	21 18	21 21

§ London Underground Limited (Central Line) also operate services between South Ruislip and West Ruislip at frequent intervals

A from 13 October
B until 6 October

For complete services between Banbury and Birmingham, refer to Table T71

For principal services between London and Aylesbury refer to Table T114

Table T115-R

Saturdays
26 May to 8 December

Kidderminster, Birmingham Snow Hill, Stratford-upon-Avon, Banbury, Oxford Parkway, Aylesbury, High Wycombe - London

		CH	CH	CH	CH	CH	CH	CH	CH	CH	CH	CH	CH	CH	CH	CH	CH	CH	CH	CH	CH	CH	CH
						◇	◇	◇	◇			◇	◇		◇	◇							◇
		A	B	A	B	A	B	A	B	A	B	A	B		A	B	A	B	A	B	A	B	A
Kidderminster	d																						
Stourbridge Junction	d																						
Cradley Heath	d																						
Rowley Regis	d																						
Birmingham Snow Hill	d											20 12	20 12										
Birmingham Moor Street	d					19 55	19 55					20 15	20 15								20 45	20 45	
Solihull	d					20 04	20 04					20 24	20 24								20 55	20 55	
Dorridge	d											20 29	20 29								21 01	21 01	
Lapworth	d																						
Stratford-upon-Avon	d													20 42									
Stratford-upon-Avon Parkway	d													20 46									
Wilmcote	d													20 49									
Bearley	d													20 52									
Claverdon	d													20 57									
Hatton	d													21 02									
Warwick Parkway	d					20 16	20 16					20 39	20 39								21 13	21 13	
Warwick	d											20 42	20 42	21 09							21 17	21 17	
Leamington Spa	d					20 23	20 23					20 46	20 46	21a17							21 22	21 22	
Banbury	d					20 41	20 41			20 45	20 45	21 05	21 05								21 40	21 40	
Kings Sutton	d									20 50	20 50												
Bicester North	d									21 01	21 01	21 18	21 18								21 52	21 52	
Oxford	d							20 42	20 42						21 09	21 09							21 42
Oxford Parkway 116	d							20 48	20 48						21 15	21 15							21 48
Islip	d														21 18	21 18							
Bicester Village	d							20 57	20 57						21 26	21 26							21 57
Haddenham & Thame Parkway	d									21 13	21 13				21 38	21 38							22 09
Aylesbury	d			20 29	20 29														21 29	21 29			
Little Kimble	d			20 37	20 37														21 37	21 37			
Monks Risborough	d			20 41	20 41														21 41	21 41			
Princes Risborough	d			20 45	20 45					21 20	21 20								21 45	21 45			
Saunderton	d			20 50	20 50														21 50	21 50			
High Wycombe	d			20 57	20 57	21 14	21 14			21 30	21 30				21 51	21 51			21 57	21 57	22 14	22 14	22 22
Beaconsfield	d			21 03	21 03					21 36	21 36								22 03	22 03			
Seer Green	d			21 06	21 06														22 06	22 06			
Gerrards Cross	d	20 49	20 49	21 11	21 11					21 42	21 42						21 49	21 49	22 11	22 11			
Denham Golf Club	d	20 52	20 52														21 52	21 52					
Denham	d	20 55	20 55	21 15	21 15												21 55	21 55	22 15	22 15			
West Ruislip § ⊖	d	21 05	21 05														22 05	22 05					
South Ruislip § ⊖	d	21 09	21 09														22 09	22 09					
Northolt Park	d	21 13	21 13														22 13	22 13					
Sudbury Hill Harrow	d																						
Sudbury & Harrow Road	d																						
Wembley Stadium	d	21 18	21 18							21 54	21 54						22 18	22 18					
London Paddington ⊖	a																						
London Marylebone ⊖	a	21 32	21 35	21 36	21 39	21 41	21 44	21 47	21 50	22 07	22 10	22 11	22 14		22 18	22 21	22 31	22 34	22 36	22 39	22 41	22 44	22 49

§ London Underground Limited (Central Line) also operate services between South Ruislip and West Ruislip at frequent intervals

A until 6 October
B from 13 October

For complete services between Banbury and Birmingham, refer to Table T71

For principal services between London and Aylesbury refer to Table T114

Table T115-R

Saturdays
26 May to 8 December

Kidderminster, Birmingham Snow Hill, Stratford-upon-Avon, Banbury, Oxford Parkway, Aylesbury, High Wycombe - London

		CH	CH	CH	CH	CH	CH	CH	CH	CH	CH	CH	LM
		◇						◇	◇	◇	◇		
		A	B	A	B		A	B	A	B	A		C
Kidderminster	d												
Stourbridge Junction	d												
Cradley Heath	d												
Rowley Regis	d												
Birmingham Snow Hill	d									21 15	21 15		
Birmingham Moor Street	d									21 18	21 18		
Solihull	d									21 27	21 27		
Dorridge	d									21 34	21 34		
Lapworth	d									21 38	21 38		
Stratford-upon-Avon	d											22 15	23 30
Stratford-upon-Avon Parkway	d												23a33
Wilmcote	d												
Bearley	d												
Claverdon	d												
Hatton	d									21 44	21 44		
Warwick Parkway	d									21 49	21 49		
Warwick	d									21 52	21 52	22 35	
Leamington Spa	d									21 57	21 57	22 41	
Banbury	d		21 46	21 46						22 16	22 16	23a02	
Kings Sutton	d									22 21	22 21		
Bicester North	d		22 02	22 02						22 32	22 32		
Oxford	d	21 42						22 09	22 09				
Oxford Parkway 116	d	21 48						22 15	22 15				
Islip	d							22 18	22 18				
Bicester Village	d	21 57						22 26	22 26				
Haddenham & Thame Parkway	d	22 09	22 15	22 15				22 38	22 38	22 43	22 43		
Aylesbury	d					22 29							
Little Kimble	d					22 37							
Monks Risborough	d					22 41							
Princes Risborough	d		22 22	22 22		22a45				22 50	22 50		
Saunderton	d									22 55	22 55		
High Wycombe	d	22 22	22 32	22 32				22 52	22 52	23 02	23 02		
Beaconsfield	d		22 38	22 38				22 58	22 58	23 08	23 08		
Seer Green	d									23 11	23 11		
Gerrards Cross	d		22 44	22 44	22 48		22 48	23 04	23 04	23 15	23 15		
Denham Golf Club	d				22 51		22 51						
Denham	d				22 54		22 54			23 19	23 19		
West Ruislip § ⊖	d				22 58		22 58			23 24	23 24		
South Ruislip § ⊖	d				23 02		23 02			23 28	23 28		
Northolt Park	d				23 06		23 06			23 32	23 32		
Sudbury Hill Harrow	d												
Sudbury & Harrow Road	d												
Wembley Stadium	d		22 56	22 56	23 11		23 11			23 37	23 37		
London Paddington ⊖	a												
London Marylebone ⊖	a	22 52	23 10	23 13	23 24		23 27	23 28	23 31	23 48	23 51		

§ London Underground Limited (Central Line) also operate services between South Ruislip and West Ruislip at frequent intervals

A from 13 October
B until 6 October
C To Birmingham Snow Hill

For complete services between Banbury and Birmingham, refer to Table T71

For principal services between London and Aylesbury refer to Table T114

Please note, Network Rail have stated that further updates to this timetable are possible during the validity period.

Table T115-R

Sundays
20 May to 2 December

Kidderminster, Birmingham Snow Hill, Stratford-upon-Avon, Banbury, Oxford Parkway, Aylesbury, High Wycombe - London

		CH A	CH B	CH ◇ A	CH ◇ B	CH A	CH B	CH ◇ A	CH ◇ B	CH A	CH B	CH ◇ A	CH ◇ B	CH A	CH B	CH A	CH B	CH ◇ A	CH ◇ B	CH ◇ A	CH ◇ B	CH A	CH B
Kidderminster	d																						
Stourbridge Junction 2	d																						
Cradley Heath	d																						
Rowley Regis	d																						
Birmingham Snow Hill ⇌	d																						
Birmingham Moor Street	d																			08 25	08 25		
Solihull	d																			08 34	08 34		
Dorridge	d																			08 39	08 39		
Lapworth	d																						
Stratford-upon-Avon	d																						
Stratford-upon-Avon Parkway	d																						
Wilmcote	d																						
Bearley	d																						
Claverdon	d																						
Hatton	d																						
Warwick Parkway	d																			08 49	08 49		
Warwick	d																			08 52	08 52		
Leamington Spa 8	d																			08 58	08 58		
Banbury	d					07 50	07 50									08 49	08 49			09 16	09 16		
Kings Sutton	d																						
Bicester North 3	d					08 04	08 04									09 03	09 03			09 29	09 29		
Oxford	d			07 43	07 43			08 10	08 10			08 38	08 38					09 01	09 01				
Oxford Parkway 116	d			07 49	07 49			08 16	08 16			08 44	08 44					09 07	09 07				
Islip	d																	09 11	09 11				
Bicester Village	d			07 58	07 58			08 25	08 25			08 53	08 53					09 18	09 18				
Haddenham & Thame Parkway	d			08 10	08 10	08 16	08 16	08 37	08 37			09 05	09 05			09 15	09 15	09 31	09 31	09 40	09 40		
Aylesbury	d	07 23	07 23							08 29	08 29											09 32	09 32
Little Kimble	d	07 31	07 31							08 37	08 37											09 40	09 40
Monks Risborough	d	07 35	07 35							08 41	08 41											09 44	09 44
Princes Risborough 2	d	07 39	07 39			08 23	08 23			08 45	08 45					09 22	09 22					09 48	09 48
Saunderton	d	07 44	07 44							08 51	08 51											09 53	09 53
High Wycombe 1	d	07 51	07 51	08 23	08 23	08 33	08 33	08 50	08 50	09 00	09 00					09 32	09 32	09 44	09 44			10 00	10 00
Beaconsfield	d	07 57	07 57			08 39	08 39	08 56	08 56	09 06	09 06					09 38	09 38					10 06	10 06
Seer Green	d	08 00	08 00			08 42	08 42			09 09	09 09											10 09	10 09
Gerrards Cross 1	d	08 05	08 05			08 47	08 47	09 02	09 02	09 14	09 14			09 29	09 29	09 44	09 44					10 14	10 14
Denham Golf Club	d	08 08	08 08			08 50	08 50																
Denham	d	08 11	08 11			08 53	08 53							09 33	09 33								
West Ruislip 3 § ⊖	d	08 16	08 16			08 57	08 57							09 37	09 37								
South Ruislip § ⊖	d	08 20	08 20			09 01	09 01							09 41	09 41								
Northolt Park	d	08 24	08 24			09 05	09 05							09 45	09 45								
Sudbury Hill Harrow	d																						
Sudbury & Harrow Road	d																						
Wembley Stadium	d	08 29	08 29			09 10	09 10			09 26	09 26			09 50	09 50							10 26	10 26
London Paddington 15 ⊖	a																						
London Marylebone 15 ⊖	a	08 42	08 45	08 51	08 54	09 23	09 26	09 26	09 29	09 38	09 41	09 42	09 45	10 03	10 06	10 06	10 09	10 11	10 14	10 18	10 21	10 38	10 41

§ London Underground Limited (Central Line) also operate services between South Ruislip and West Ruislip at frequent intervals

A until 30 September
B from 7 October

For complete services between Banbury and Birmingham, refer to Table T71

For principal services between London and Aylesbury refer to Table T114

Table T115-R

Sundays
20 May to 2 December

Kidderminster, Birmingham Snow Hill, Stratford-upon-Avon, Banbury, Oxford Parkway, Aylesbury, High Wycombe - London

		CH ◇ A	CH ◇ B	CH ◇ A	CH ◇ B	CH A	CH B	CH A	CH B	CH ◇ A	CH ◇ B	CH ◇ A	CH ◇ B	CH A	CH B	CH ◇ A	CH ◇ B	CH ◇ A	CH ◇ B	CH ◇ A	CH ◇ B	CH A	CH B
Kidderminster	d																						
Stourbridge Junction 2	d																						
Cradley Heath	d																						
Rowley Regis	d																						
Birmingham Snow Hill ⇌	d									09 12	09 12												
Birmingham Moor Street	d	08 55	08 55							09 15	09 15							09 55	09 55				
Solihull	d	09 04	09 04							09 24	09 24							10 04	10 04				
Dorridge	d									09 29	09 29												
Lapworth	d																						
Stratford-upon-Avon	d															09 38	09 38						
Stratford-upon-Avon Parkway	d															09 41	09 41						
Wilmcote	d															09 44	09 44						
Bearley	d																						
Claverdon	d																						
Hatton	d															09 55	09 55						
Warwick Parkway	d	09 16	09 16							09 39	09 39							10 16	10 16				
Warwick	d									09 42	09 42					10 01	10 01						
Leamington Spa 8	d	09 22	09 22							09 46	09 46					10 06	10 06	10 22	10 22				
Banbury	d	09 40	09 40					09 44	09 44	10 07	10 07					10 24	10 24	10 40	10 40				
Kings Sutton	d							09 50	09 50														
Bicester North 3	d							10 02	10 02	10 19	10 19					10 36	10 36						
Oxford	d			09 42	09 42							10 11	10 11							10 42	10 42		
Oxford Parkway 116	d			09 48	09 48							10 17	10 17							10 48	10 48		
Islip	d																						
Bicester Village	d			09 57	09 57							10 26	10 26							10 57	10 57		
Haddenham & Thame Parkway	d							10 14	10 14			10 38	10 38			10 47	10 47						
Aylesbury	d													10 29	10 29								
Little Kimble	d													10 37	10 37								
Monks Risborough	d													10 41	10 41								
Princes Risborough 2	d							10 21	10 21					10 45	10 45	10 54	10 54						
Saunderton	d													10 50	10 50								
High Wycombe 1	d	10 13	10 13					10 31	10 31			10 51	10 51	10 57	10 57	11 03	11 03	11 14	11 14				
Beaconsfield	d							10 37	10 37					11 03	11 03	11 09	11 09						
Seer Green	d													11 06	11 06								
Gerrards Cross 1	d					10 29	10 29	10 43	10 43					11 11	11 11	11 15	11 15					11 29	11 29
Denham Golf Club	d					10 32	10 32																
Denham	d					10 35	10 35															11 33	11 33
West Ruislip 3 § ⊖	d																					11 37	11 37
South Ruislip § ⊖	d					10 40	10 40															11 41	11 41
Northolt Park	d					10 44	10 44															11 45	11 45
Sudbury Hill Harrow	d																						
Sudbury & Harrow Road	d																						
Wembley Stadium	d					10 49	10 49							11 23	11 23							11 50	11 50
London Paddington 15 ⊖	a																						
London Marylebone 15 ⊖	a	10 41	10 44	10 45	10 48	11 02	11 05	11 06	11 09	11 09	11 12	11 18	11 21	11 36	11 39	11 39	11 42	11 42	11 45	11 45	11 48	12 02	12 05

§ London Underground Limited (Central Line) also operate services between South Ruislip and West Ruislip at frequent intervals

A until 30 September
B from 7 October

For complete services between Banbury and Birmingham, refer to Table T71

For principal services between London and Aylesbury refer to Table T114

Table T115-R

Sundays

20 May to 2 December

Kidderminster, Birmingham Snow Hill, Stratford-upon-Avon, Banbury, Oxford Parkway, Aylesbury, High Wycombe - London

		CH	CH	CH	CH	CH	CH	CH	CH	CH	CH	CH	CH	CH	CH	CH	CH	CH	CH	CH	CH	CH	CH
				◇	◇	◇	◇			◇	◇	◇	◇					◇	◇	◇	◇		
		A	B	A	B	A	B	A	B	A	B	A	B	A	B	A	B	A	B	A	B	A	B
Kidderminster	d			09 40	09 40																		
Stourbridge Junction	d			09 48	09 48																		
Cradley Heath	d			09 54	09 54																		
Rowley Regis	d			10 00	10 00																		
Birmingham Snow Hill	d			10 12	10 12													11 12	11 12				
Birmingham Moor Street	d			10 15	10 15					10 55	10 55							11 15	11 15				
Solihull	d			10 24	10 24					11 04	11 04							11 24	11 24				
Dorridge	d			10 29	10 29													11 29	11 29				
Lapworth	d																						
Stratford-upon-Avon	d																						
Stratford-upon-Avon Parkway	d																						
Wilmcote	d																						
Bearley	d																						
Claverdon	d																						
Hatton	d																						
Warwick Parkway	d			10 39	10 39					11 16	11 16							11 39	11 39				
Warwick	d			10 42	10 42													11 42	11 42				
Leamington Spa	d			10 46	10 46					11 22	11 22							11 46	11 46				
Banbury	d	10 44	10 44	11 07	11 07					11 40	11 40					11 44	11 44	12 07	12 07				
Kings Sutton	d	10 50	10 50																				
Bicester North	d	11 02	11 02	11 19	11 19											12 02	12 02	12 19	12 19				
Oxford	d					11 09	11 09					11 42	11 42							12 11	12 11		
Oxford Parkway 116	d					11 15	11 15					11 48	11 48							12 17	12 17		
Islip	d					11 18	11 18																
Bicester Village	d					11 26	11 26					11 57	11 57							12 26	12 26		
Haddenham & Thame Parkway	d	11 14	11 14			11 38	11 38									12 14	12 14			12 38	12 38		
Aylesbury	d							11 29	11 29													12 29	12 29
Little Kimble	d							11 37	11 37													12 37	12 37
Monks Risborough	d							11 41	11 41													12 41	12 41
Princes Risborough	d	11 21	11 21					11 45	11 45							12 21	12 21					12 45	12 45
Saunderton	d							11 50	11 50													12 50	12 50
High Wycombe	d	11 31	11 31			11 51	11 51	11 57	11 57	12 13	12 13					12 31	12 31			12 51	12 51	12 57	12 57
Beaconsfield	d	11 37	11 37	11 45	11 45			12 03	12 03							12 37	12 37	12 45	12 45			13 03	13 03
Seer Green	d							12 06	12 06													13 06	13 06
Gerrards Cross	d	11 43	11 43					12 11	12 11					12 29	12 29	12 43	12 43					13 11	13 11
Denham Golf Club	d													12 32	12 32								
Denham	d													12 35	12 35								
West Ruislip § ⊖	d																						
South Ruislip § ⊖	d													12 40	12 40								
Northolt Park	d													12 44	12 44								
Sudbury Hill Harrow	d																						
Sudbury & Harrow Road	d																						
Wembley Stadium	d							12 23	12 23					12 49	12 49							13 23	13 23
London Paddington ⊖	a																						
London Marylebone ⊖	a	12 06	12 09	12 10	12 13	12 18	12 21	12 36	12 39	12 40	12 43	12 43	12 46	13 02	13 05	13 06	13 09	13 10	13 13	13 18	13 21	13 36	13 39

§ London Underground Limited (Central Line) also operate services between South Ruislip and West Ruislip at frequent intervals

A until 30 September
B from 7 October

For complete services between Banbury and Birmingham, refer to Table T71

For principal services between London and Aylesbury refer to Table T114

Table T115-R

Sundays

20 May to 2 December

Kidderminster, Birmingham Snow Hill, Stratford-upon-Avon, Banbury, Oxford Parkway, Aylesbury, High Wycombe - London

		CH	CH	CH	CH	CH	CH	CH	CH	CH	CH	CH	CH	CH	CH	CH	CH	CH	CH	CH	CH	CH	CH
		◇	◇	◇	◇					◇	◇		◇	◇			◇	◇	◇	◇			
		A	B	A	B	A	B	A	B	A	B		A	B	A	B	A	B	A	B	A	B	A
Kidderminster	d	11 13	11 13																				
Stourbridge Junction	d	11 22	11 22																				
Cradley Heath	d																						
Rowley Regis	d	11 33	11 33																				
Birmingham Snow Hill	d	11 49	11 49							12 12	12 12												
Birmingham Moor Street	d	11 55	11 55							12 15	12 15						12 55	12 55					
Solihull	d	12 04	12 04							12 24	12 24						13 04	13 04					
Dorridge	d									12 29	12 29												
Lapworth	d																						
Stratford-upon-Avon	d											12 19											
Stratford-upon-Avon Parkway	d											12 23											
Wilmcote	d											12 26											
Bearley	d																						
Claverdon	d																						
Hatton	d											12 38											
Warwick Parkway	d	12 16	12 16							12 39	12 39						13 16	13 16					
Warwick	d									12 42	12 42	12 47											
Leamington Spa	d	12 22	12 22							12 46	12 46	12a54					13 22	13 22					
Banbury	d	12 40	12 40					12 44	12 44	13 07	13 07						13 40	13 40					13 44
Kings Sutton	d							12 50	12 50														
Bicester North	d							13 02	13 02	13 19	13 19												14 02
Oxford	d			12 42	12 42								13 09	13 09					13 40	13 40			
Oxford Parkway 116	d			12 48	12 48								13 15	13 15					13 48	13 48			
Islip	d												13 18	13 18									
Bicester Village	d			12 57	12 57								13 26	13 26					13 57	13 57			
Haddenham & Thame Parkway	d							13 14	13 14				13 38	13 38									14 14
Aylesbury	d														13 29	13 29							
Little Kimble	d														13 37	13 37							
Monks Risborough	d														13 41	13 41							
Princes Risborough	d							13 21	13 21						13 45	13 45							14 21
Saunderton	d														13 50	13 50							
High Wycombe	d	13 13	13 13					13 31	13 31				13 51	13 51	13 57	13 57	14 13	14 13					14 31
Beaconsfield	d							13 37	13 37	13 45	13 45				14 03	14 03							14 37
Seer Green	d														14 06	14 06							
Gerrards Cross	d					13 29	13 29	13 43	13 43						14 11	14 11					14 29	14 29	14 43
Denham Golf Club	d																				14 32	14 32	
Denham	d					13 33	13 33														14 35	14 35	
West Ruislip § ⊖	d					13 37	13 37																
South Ruislip § ⊖	d					13 41	13 41														14 40	14 40	
Northolt Park	d					13 45	13 45														14 44	14 44	
Sudbury Hill Harrow	d																						
Sudbury & Harrow Road	d																						
Wembley Stadium	d					13 50	13 50								14 23	14 23					14 49	14 49	
London Paddington ⊖	a																						
London Marylebone ⊖	a	13 40	13 43	13 45	13 48	14 03	14 06	14 06	14 09	14 10	14 13		14 18	14 21	14 36	14 39	14 40	14 43	14 43	14 46	15 02	15 05	15 06

§ London Underground Limited (Central Line) also operate services between South Ruislip and West Ruislip at frequent intervals

A until 30 September
B from 7 October

For complete services between Banbury and Birmingham, refer to Table T71

For principal services between London and Aylesbury refer to Table T114

Table T115-R

Sundays
20 May to 2 December

Kidderminster, Birmingham Snow Hill, Stratford-upon-Avon, Banbury, Oxford Parkway, Aylesbury, High Wycombe - London

		CH A	CH ◇ B	CH ◇ A	CH ◇ B	CH ◇ A	CH B	CH A	CH ◇ B	CH ◇ A	CH ◇ B	CH ◇ A	CH B	CH A	CH B	CH A	CH ◇ B	CH ◇ A	CH	CH ◇ B	CH ◇ A	CH B	CH A
Kidderminster	d																						
Stourbridge Junction 2	d																						
Cradley Heath	d																						
Rowley Regis	d																						
Birmingham Snow Hill	d		13 12	13 12													14 12	14 12					
Birmingham Moor Street	d		13 15	13 15					13 55	13 55							14 15	14 15					
Solihull	d		13 24	13 24					14 04	14 04							14 24	14 24					
Dorridge	d		13 29	13 29													14 29	14 29					
Lapworth	d																						
Stratford-upon-Avon	d																		14 46				
Stratford-upon-Avon Parkway	d																		14 50				
Wilmcote	d																		14 53				
Bearley	d																						
Claverdon	d																						
Hatton	d																		15 04				
Warwick Parkway	d		13 39	13 39					14 16	14 16							14 39	14 39					
Warwick	d		13 42	13 42													14 42	14 42	15 11				
Leamington Spa 3	d		13 46	13 46					14 22	14 22							14 46	14 46	15a17				
Banbury	d	13 44	14 07	14 07					14 40	14 40					14 44	14 44	15 07	15 07					
Kings Sutton	d														14 50	14 50							
Bicester North 3	d	14 02	14 19	14 19											15 01	15 01	15 19	15 19					
Oxford	d				14 11	14 11					14 41	14 41								15 09	15 09		
Oxford Parkway 116	d				14 17	14 17					14 47	14 47								15 15	15 15		
Islip	d																			15 18	15 18		
Bicester Village	d				14 26	14 26					14 56	14 56								15 26	15 26		
Haddenham & Thame Parkway	d	14 14			14 38	14 38									15 13	15 13				15 38	15 38		
Aylesbury	d						14 29	14 29														15 29	15 29
Little Kimble	d						14 37	14 37														15 37	15 37
Monks Risborough	d						14 41	14 41														15 41	15 41
Princes Risborough 2	d	14 21					14 45	14 45							15 20	15 20						15 45	15 45
Saunderton	d						14 50	14 50														15 50	15 50
High Wycombe 1	d	14 31			14 51	14 51	14 57	14 57	15 13	15 13					15 30	15 30				15 51	15 51	15 57	15 57
Beaconsfield	d	14 37	14 45	14 45			15 03	15 03							15 36	15 36	15 45	15 45				16 03	16 03
Seer Green	d						15 06	15 06														16 06	16 06
Gerrards Cross 1	d	14 43					15 11	15 11					15 29	15 29	15 42	15 42						16 11	16 11
Denham Golf Club	d																						
Denham	d												15 33	15 33									
West Ruislip 5 § ⊖	d												15 37	15 37									
South Ruislip § ⊖	d												15 41	15 41									
Northolt Park	d												15 45	15 45									
Sudbury Hill Harrow	d																						
Sudbury & Harrow Road	d																						
Wembley Stadium	d						15 23	15 23					15 50	15 50								16 23	16 23
London Paddington 15 ⊖	a																						
London Marylebone 15 ⊖	a	15 09	15 10	15 13	15 18	15 21	15 36	15 39	15 40	15 43	15 43	15 46	16 03	16 06	16 06	16 09	16 10	16 13		16 18	16 21	16 36	16 39

§ London Underground Limited (Central Line) also operate services between South Ruislip and West Ruislip at frequent intervals

A from 7 October
B until 30 September

For complete services between Banbury and Birmingham, refer to Table T71

For principal services between London and Aylesbury refer to Table T114

Table T115-R

Sundays
20 May to 2 December

Kidderminster, Birmingham Snow Hill, Stratford-upon-Avon, Banbury, Oxford Parkway, Aylesbury, High Wycombe - London

		CH ◇ A	CH ◇ B	CH ◇ A	CH ◇ B	CH A	CH B	CH A	CH B	CH ◇ A	CH ◇ B	CH ◇ A	CH ◇ B	CH A	CH B	CH ◇ A	CH ◇ B	CH ◇ A	CH ◇ B	CH A	CH B	CH A	CH B
Kidderminster	d																						
Stourbridge Junction 2	d																						
Cradley Heath	d																						
Rowley Regis	d																						
Birmingham Snow Hill	d									15 12	15 12												
Birmingham Moor Street	d	14 55	14 55							15 15	15 15					15 55	15 55						
Solihull	d	15 04	15 04							15 24	15 24					16 04	16 04						
Dorridge	d									15 29	15 29												
Lapworth	d																						
Stratford-upon-Avon	d																						
Stratford-upon-Avon Parkway	d																						
Wilmcote	d																						
Bearley	d																						
Claverdon	d																						
Hatton	d																						
Warwick Parkway	d	15 16	15 16							15 39	15 39					16 16	16 16						
Warwick	d									15 42	15 42												
Leamington Spa 3	d	15 22	15 22							15 46	15 46					16 22	16 22						
Banbury	d	15 40	15 40					15 44	15 44	16 07	16 07					16 40	16 40					16 44	16 44
Kings Sutton	d																					16 50	16 50
Bicester North 3	d							16 01	16 01	16 19	16 19											17 01	17 01
Oxford	d			15 41	15 41							16 11	16 11					16 41	16 41				
Oxford Parkway 116	d			15 47	15 47							16 17	16 17					16 47	16 47				
Islip	d																						
Bicester Village	d			15 56	15 56							16 26	16 26					16 56	16 56				
Haddenham & Thame Parkway	d							16 13	16 13			16 38	16 38									17 13	17 13
Aylesbury	d													16 29	16 29								
Little Kimble	d													16 37	16 37								
Monks Risborough	d													16 41	16 41								
Princes Risborough 2	d							16 20	16 20					16 45	16 45							17 20	17 20
Saunderton	d													16 50	16 50								
High Wycombe 1	d	16 13	16 13					16 30	16 30			16 51	16 51	16 57	16 57	17 13	17 13					17 30	17 30
Beaconsfield	d							16 36	16 36	16 45	16 45			17 03	17 03							17 36	17 36
Seer Green	d													17 06	17 06								
Gerrards Cross 1	d					16 29	16 29	16 42	16 42					17 11	17 11					17 29	17 29	17 42	17 42
Denham Golf Club	d					16 32	16 32																
Denham	d					16 35	16 35													17 33	17 33		
West Ruislip 5 § ⊖	d																			17 37	17 37		
South Ruislip § ⊖	d					16 40	16 40													17 41	17 41		
Northolt Park	d					16 44	16 44													17 45	17 45		
Sudbury Hill Harrow	d																						
Sudbury & Harrow Road	d																						
Wembley Stadium	d					16 49	16 49							17 23	17 23					17 50	17 50		
London Paddington 15 ⊖	a																						
London Marylebone 15 ⊖	a	16 40	16 43	16 45	16 48	17 02	17 05	17 05	17 08	17 10	17 13	17 18	17 21	17 36	17 39	17 40	17 43	17 43	17 46	18 03	18 06	18 06	18 09

§ London Underground Limited (Central Line) also operate services between South Ruislip and West Ruislip at frequent intervals

A until 30 September
B from 7 October

For complete services between Banbury and Birmingham, refer to Table T71

For principal services between London and Aylesbury refer to Table T114

Please note, Network Rail have stated that further updates to this timetable are possible during the validity period.

Table T115-R

Sundays

20 May to 2 December

Kidderminster, Birmingham Snow Hill, Stratford-upon-Avon, Banbury, Oxford Parkway, Aylesbury, High Wycombe - London

		CH ◇ A	CH ◇ B	CH	CH ◇ A	CH ◇ B	CH A	CH B	CH ◇ A	CH ◇ B	CH ◇ A	CH ◇ B	CH A	CH B	CH A	CH B	CH ◇ A	CH ◇ B	CH ◇ A	CH ◇ B	CH A	CH B	CH ◇ A
Kidderminster	d																						
Stourbridge Junction	d																						
Cradley Heath	d																						
Rowley Regis	d																						
Birmingham Snow Hill	d	16 12	16 12														17 12	17 12					
Birmingham Moor Street	d	16 15	16 15						16 55	16 55							17 15	17 15					17 55
Solihull	d	16 24	16 24						17 04	17 04							17 24	17 24					18 04
Dorridge	d	16 29	16 29														17 29	17 29					
Lapworth	d																						
Stratford-upon-Avon	d			16 46																			
Stratford-upon-Avon Parkway	d			16 50																			
Wilmcote	d			16 53																			
Bearley	d																						
Claverdon	d																						
Hatton	d			17 04																			
Warwick Parkway	d	16 39	16 39						17 16	17 16							17 39	17 39					18 16
Warwick	d	16 42	16 42	17 11													17 42	17 42					
Leamington Spa	d	16 46	16 46	17a17					17 22	17 22							17 46	17 46					18 22
Banbury	d	17 07	17 07						17 40	17 40					17 44	17 44	18 07	18 07					18 40
Kings Sutton	d																						
Bicester North	d	17 19	17 19												18 01	18 01	18 19	18 19					
Oxford	d				17 09	17 09					17 40	17 40							18 11	18 11			
Oxford Parkway 116	d				17 15	17 15					17 47	17 47							18 17	18 17			
Islip	d				17 18	17 18																	
Bicester Village	d				17 26	17 26					17 56	17 56							18 26	18 26			
Haddenham & Thame Parkway	d				17 38	17 38									18 13	18 13			18 38	18 38			
Aylesbury	d						17 29	17 29													18 29	18 29	
Little Kimble	d						17 37	17 37													18 37	18 37	
Monks Risborough	d						17 41	17 41													18 41	18 41	
Princes Risborough	d						17 45	17 45							18 20	18 20					18 45	18 45	
Saunderton	d						17 50	17 50													18 50	18 50	
High Wycombe	d				17 51	17 51	17 57	17 57	18 12	18 12					18 30	18 30			18 51	18 51	18 57	18 57	19 13
Beaconsfield	d	17 45	17 45				18 03	18 03							18 36	18 36	18 45	18 45			19 03	19 03	
Seer Green	d						18 06	18 06													19 06	19 06	
Gerrards Cross	d						18 11	18 11					18 29	18 29	18 42	18 42					19 11	19 11	
Denham Golf Club	d												18 32	18 32									
Denham	d												18 35	18 35									
West Ruislip §	⊖ d																						
South Ruislip §	⊖ d												18 40	18 40									
Northolt Park	d												18 44	18 44									
Sudbury Hill Harrow	d																						
Sudbury & Harrow Road	d																						
Wembley Stadium	d						18 23	18 23					18 49	18 49							19 23	19 23	
London Paddington	⊖ a																						
London Marylebone	⊖ a	18 10	18 13		18 17	18 20	18 36	18 39	18 40	18 43	18 43	18 46	19 02	19 05	19 05	19 08	19 10	19 13	19 18	19 21	19 36	19 39	19 40

§ London Underground Limited (Central Line) also operate services between South Ruislip and West Ruislip at frequent intervals

A until 30 September
B from 7 October

For complete services between Banbury and Birmingham, refer to Table T71

For principal services between London and Aylesbury refer to Table T114

Table T115-R

Sundays

20 May to 2 December

Kidderminster, Birmingham Snow Hill, Stratford-upon-Avon, Banbury, Oxford Parkway, Aylesbury, High Wycombe - London

		CH ◇ A	CH ◇ B	CH ◇ A	CH B	CH A	CH B	CH A	CH ◇ B	CH ◇ A	CH	CH ◇ B	CH ◇ A	CH B	CH A	CH ◇ B	CH ◇ A	CH ◇ B	CH ◇ A	CH B	CH A	CH ◇ B	CH ◇ A
Kidderminster	d																						
Stourbridge Junction	d																						
Cradley Heath	d																						
Rowley Regis	d																						
Birmingham Snow Hill	d								18 12	18 12												19 12	19 12
Birmingham Moor Street	d	17 55							18 15	18 15						18 55	18 55					19 15	19 15
Solihull	d	18 04							18 24	18 24						19 04	19 04					19 24	19 24
Dorridge	d								18 29	18 29												19 29	19 29
Lapworth	d																						
Stratford-upon-Avon	d										18 46												
Stratford-upon-Avon Parkway	d										18 50												
Wilmcote	d										18 53												
Bearley	d																						
Claverdon	d																						
Hatton	d										19 04												
Warwick Parkway	d	18 16							18 39	18 39						19 16	19 16					19 39	19 39
Warwick	d								18 42	18 42	19 11											19 42	19 42
Leamington Spa	d	18 22							18 46	18 46	19a17					19 22	19 22					19 46	19 46
Banbury	d	18 40					18 44	18 44	19 07	19 07						19 41	19 41					20 07	20 07
Kings Sutton	d						18 50	18 50															
Bicester North	d						19 01	19 01	19 19	19 19						19 53	19 53					20 19	20 19
Oxford	d		18 41	18 41								19 09	19 09					19 41	19 41				
Oxford Parkway 116	d		18 47	18 47								19 15	19 15					19 48	19 48				
Islip	d											19 18	19 18										
Bicester Village	d		18 56	18 56								19 26	19 26					19 57	19 57				
Haddenham & Thame Parkway	d						19 13	19 13				19 38	19 38					20 09	20 09				
Aylesbury	d													19 29	19 29								
Little Kimble	d													19 37	19 37								
Monks Risborough	d													19 41	19 41								
Princes Risborough	d						19 20	19 20						19 45	19 45	20 07	20 07						
Saunderton	d													19 50	19 50								
High Wycombe	d	19 13					19 30	19 30				19 51	19 51	19 57	19 57	20 16	20 16						
Beaconsfield	d						19 36	19 36	19 45	19 45				20 03	20 03							20 45	20 45
Seer Green	d													20 06	20 06								
Gerrards Cross	d				19 29	19 29	19 42	19 42						20 11	20 11					20 32	20 32		
Denham Golf Club	d																			20 35	20 35		
Denham	d				19 33	19 33														20 38	20 38		
West Ruislip §	⊖ d				19 37	19 37																	
South Ruislip §	⊖ d				19 41	19 41														20 43	20 43		
Northolt Park	d				19 45	19 45														20 47	20 47		
Sudbury Hill Harrow	d																						
Sudbury & Harrow Road	d																						
Wembley Stadium	d				19 50	19 50								20 23	20 23					20 52	20 52		
London Paddington	⊖ a																						
London Marylebone	⊖ a	19 43	19 45	19 48	20 03	20 06	20 06	20 09	20 10	20 13		20 17	20 20	20 36	20 39	20 45	20 48	20 48	20 51	21 05	21 08	21 10	21 13

§ London Underground Limited (Central Line) also operate services between South Ruislip and West Ruislip at frequent intervals

A from 7 October
B until 30 September

For complete services between Banbury and Birmingham, refer to Table T71

For principal services between London and Aylesbury refer to Table T114

Table T115-R

Sundays
20 May to 2 December

Kidderminster, Birmingham Snow Hill, Stratford-upon-Avon, Banbury, Oxford Parkway, Aylesbury, High Wycombe - London

	CH	CH	CH	CH	CH	CH	CH	CH	CH	CH	CH	CH	CH	CH	CH	CH	CH	CH	CH	CH	CH	CH
	◇	◇			◇	◇	◇	◇			◇	◇	◇	◇			◇	◇	◇	◇	◇	◇
	A	B	A	B	A	B	A	B	A	B	A	B	A	B	A	B	A	B	A	B	A	B
Kidderminster d																						
Stourbridge Junction 2 d																						
Cradley Heath d																						
Rowley Regis d																						
Birmingham Snow Hill d											20 12	20 12										
Birmingham Moor Street d					19 39	19 39					20 15	20 15										
Solihull d					19 48	19 48					20 24	20 24										
Dorridge d					19 56	19 56					20 29	20 29										
Lapworth d					20 00	20 00																
Stratford-upon-Avon d																	20 38	20 38				
Stratford-upon-Avon Parkway d																	20 42	20 42				
Wilmcote d																	20 45	20 45				
Bearley d																						
Claverdon d																						
Hatton d					20 06	20 06											20 56	20 56				
Warwick Parkway d											20 39	20 39										
Warwick d					20 11	20 11					20 42	20 42					21 03	21 03				
Leamington Spa 8 d					20 17	20 17					20 46	20 46					21 08	21 08				
Banbury d			20 13	20 13	20 36	20 36					21 07	21 07			21 14	21 14	21 28	21 28				
Kings Sutton d			20 20	20 20																		
Bicester North 8 d			20 32	20 32	20 52	20 52					21 19	21 19			21 30	21 30	21 42	21 42				
Oxford d	20 11	20 11					20 49	20 49					21 08	21 08					21 54	21 54	22 07	22 07
Oxford Parkway 116 d	20 17	20 17					20 55	20 55					21 14	21 14					22 00	22 00	22 14	22 14
Islip d													21 17	21 17								
Bicester Village d	20 26	20 26					21 04	21 04					21 25	21 25					22 09	22 09	22 23	22 23
Haddenham & Thame Parkway d	20 38	20 38	20 44	20 44									21 37	21 37	21 43	21 43	21 55	21 55			22 36	22 36
Aylesbury d																						
Little Kimble d																						
Monks Risborough d																						
Princes Risborough 2 d			20 51	20 51											21 50	21 50						
Saunderton d			20 56	20 56											21 55	21 55						
High Wycombe 1 d	20 51	20 51	21 03	21 03	21 16	21 16							21 50	21 50	22 02	22 02	22 13	22 13			22 51	22 51
Beaconsfield d			21 09	21 09	21 22	21 22									22 08	22 08	22 19	22 19				
Seer Green d			21 12	21 12													22 22	22 22				
Gerrards Cross 1 d			21 17	21 17	21 28	21 28			21 35	21 35					22 14	22 14	22 27	22 27				
Denham Golf Club d															22 17	22 17						
Denham d									21 39	21 39					22 20	22 20						
West Ruislip 3 § ⊖ d									21 43	21 43							22 33	22 33				
South Ruislip § ⊖ d									21 47	21 47					22 25	22 25						
Northolt Park d									21 51	21 51					22 29	22 29						
Sudbury Hill Harrow d																						
Sudbury & Harrow Road d																						
Wembley Stadium d			21 29	21 29					21 56	21 56					22 34	22 34						
London Paddington 15 ⊖ a																						
London Marylebone 15 ⊖ a	21 18	21 21	21 41	21 44	21 53	21 56	21 56	21 59	22 09	22 12	22 13	22 16	22 16	22 19	22 47	22 50	22 53	22 56	22 56	22 59	23 16	23 19

§ London Underground Limited (Central Line) also operate services between South Ruislip and West Ruislip at frequent intervals

A until 30 September
B from 7 October

For complete services between Banbury and Birmingham, refer to Table T71

For principal services between London and Aylesbury refer to Table T114

Table T115-R

Sundays
20 May to 2 December

Kidderminster, Birmingham Snow Hill, Stratford-upon-Avon, Banbury, Oxford Parkway, Aylesbury, High Wycombe - London

	CH	CH	CH
		◇	◇
		A	B
Kidderminster d			
Stourbridge Junction 2 d			
Cradley Heath d			
Rowley Regis d			
Birmingham Snow Hill d		21 15	21 15
Birmingham Moor Street d		21 18	21 18
Solihull d		21 27	21 27
Dorridge d		21 34	21 34
Lapworth d			
Stratford-upon-Avon d			
Stratford-upon-Avon Parkway d			
Wilmcote d			
Bearley d			
Claverdon d			
Hatton d			
Warwick Parkway d		21 44	21 44
Warwick d		21 47	21 47
Leamington Spa 8 d		21 52	21 52
Banbury d		22 15	22 15
Kings Sutton d		22 20	22 20
Bicester North 8 d		22 31	22 31
Oxford d			
Oxford Parkway 116 d			
Islip d			
Bicester Village d			
Haddenham & Thame Parkway d		22 42	22 42
Aylesbury d	22 21		
Little Kimble d	22 29		
Monks Risborough d	22 33		
Princes Risborough 2 d	22a40	22 49	22 49
Saunderton d		22 54	22 54
High Wycombe 1 d		23 01	23 01
Beaconsfield d		23 07	23 07
Seer Green d		23 10	23 10
Gerrards Cross 1 d		23 13	23 13
Denham Golf Club d			
Denham d		23 17	23 17
West Ruislip 3 § ⊖ d			
South Ruislip § ⊖ d		23 23	23 23
Northolt Park d			
Sudbury Hill Harrow d			
Sudbury & Harrow Road d			
Wembley Stadium d		23 29	23 29
London Paddington 15 ⊖ a			
London Marylebone 15 ⊖ a		23 42	23 45

§ London Underground Limited (Central Line) also operate services between South Ruislip and West Ruislip at frequent intervals

A until 30 September
B from 7 October

For complete services between Banbury and Birmingham, refer to Table T71

For principal services between London and Aylesbury refer to Table T114

Please note, Network Rail have stated that further updates to this timetable are possible during the validity period.

Table T116-F

Mondays to Fridays

21 May to 7 December

London and Reading - Bedwyn, Oxford, Banbury and Birmingham

Miles	Miles		GW MX A	CH MX B	GW MX C	CH MX D	GW MO A	GW MX ◇■ E ☕	GW MO A	GW MX A	GW MX	GW MO ◇■ F ☕	GW MO ◇■ G ☕	GW MO 🚌	GW MX A	GW MX	GW MO A	GW MX H	GW MO I	GW MX A	GW MX	GW	GW MO J
0	—	**London Paddington** ⊖ d																			00 25		00 05
5¾	—	Ealing Broadway ⊖ d																	00 02	00 02			00 14
18½	—	Slough d										00 01					00 10		00 26	00 30	00 43		00 38
24¼	—	Maidenhead d								00 01					00 07		00 17		00 36	00 41			00 48
31	—	Twyford d							00 04	00 09					00 15			00 32	00 44	00 49			00 56
36	0	**Reading** a							00 13	00 16		00 16			00 23		00 32	00 39	00 51	00 58	01 01		01 03
—	—	d	00 04					00 10			00 18	00 20	00 20		00 24						01 03		
—	1	Reading West d									00s21												
—	5¼	Theale d									00s27												
—	8¾	Aldermaston d									00s32												
—	10¾	Midgham d									00s35												
—	13½	Thatcham d									00s40												
—	16½	Newbury Racecourse d									00s45												
—	17	**Newbury** a									00 48												
—	—	d																					
—	22½	Kintbury d																					
—	25½	Hungerford d																					
—	30½	**Bedwyn** a																					
38½	—	Tilehurst d													00 28								
41½	—	Pangbourne d					00 01								00 32								
44¾	—	Goring & Streatley d					00 06								00 37								
48½	—	Cholsey d			00 03		00 11								00 42								
53¼	—	**Didcot Parkway** a			00 14		00 20	00 26				00s35	00s35		00 50						01 19		
—	—	d			00 24									00 45		01 11					01 19		
55¼	—	Appleford d														01 15							
56¾	—	Culham d														01 18							
58½	—	Radley d			00 31									01 00		01 22							
63½	—	**Oxford** 115 a	00 32		00 39									01 15		01 30					01 35		
—	—	d		00 39		00 39																05 18	
72½	—	Tackley d		00 49		00 49																05 27	
75¼	—	Heyford d		00 54		00 54																05 32	
82¾	—	Kings Sutton d																				05 40	
86¼	—	**Banbury** 71 a		01 08		01 11																05 45	
106¼	—	Leamington Spa a																					
115¾	—	Coventry a																					
126½	—	Birmingham International a																					
135	—	**Birmingham New Street** 71 a																					

	GW MX	GW MO	GW	GW	GW	GW	GW	GW	GW K	GW MX ◇■ L	GW MO ◇■ L	GW M	GW ◇■ N ☕	GW	XC ◇■ O 🍴	GW	GW	GW ◇■ P	GW	GW	GW	XC ◇■ Q 🍴	GW
London Paddington ⊖ d	00 34	00 42	01 34	03 34						05 12	05 12		05 19				05 15	05 47		05 39			06 20
Ealing Broadway ⊖ d	00 42	00 50	01 42	03 42													05 23			05 47			
Slough d	01 07	01 13	02 04	04 05						05 30	05 30						05 50	06 03		06 15			06 36
Maidenhead d	01 18	01 20	02 12	04 13					05 28								05 57			06 26			
Twyford d	01 26	01 28	02 20	04 21					05 37			←					06 05			06 34			
Reading a	01 34	01 36	02 28	04 28					05 45	05 49	05 49	05 45	05 53				06 13	06 17		06 42			06 50
d					05 16			05 49	05 52	05 50	05 51	05 52	05 54	06 12	06 15		06 18	06 19	06 23		06 42	06 45	06 51
Reading West d					05 19				→					06 15							06 46		
Theale d					05 25			05 57						06 21							06 52		
Aldermaston d					05 30									06 26							06 57		
Midgham d					05 33									06 29							07 00		
Thatcham d					05 38			06 05						06 34							07 05		
Newbury Racecourse d					05 43									06 39							07 10		
Newbury a					05 45			06 11						06 42							07 12		
d					05 46			06 25													07 22		
Kintbury d					05 52			06 31													07 28		
Hungerford d					05 57			06 36													07 33		
Bedwyn a					06 04			06 43													07 40		
Tilehurst d												05 56					06 22		06 27				
Pangbourne d												06 00					06 27		06 31				
Goring & Streatley d												06 05					06 32		06 36				
Cholsey d												06 10					06 37		06 41				
Didcot Parkway a												06 22	06 08				06 45	06 34	06 48				07 06
d						05 27	05 49									06 29		06 35	06 49				07 07
Appleford d																							
Culham d																06 34							
Radley d																06 38							
Oxford 115 a						05 38	06 05			06 16	06 16				06 37	06 46		06 50	07 01			07 06	07 22
d						05 40									06 38	06 47						07 08	
Tackley d						05 49										06 56							
Heyford d						05 53										07 00							
Kings Sutton d						06 02										07 09							
Banbury 71 a						06 07									06 54	07 14						07 25	
Leamington Spa a															07 13							07 42	
Coventry a															07 25								
Birmingham International a															07 37								
Birmingham New Street 71 a															07 48							08 12	

A From London Paddington
B until 5 October
C From Reading
D from 9 October
E From London Paddington to Cardiff Central
F from 17 September. From London Paddington to Bristol Temple Meads
G until 10 September. From London Paddington to Bristol Temple Meads
H From Henley-on-Thames
I from 17 September. From London Paddington
J until 10 September
K To Didcot Parkway
L To Moreton-in-Marsh
M From Maidenhead
N To Swansea
O From Southampton Central to Manchester Piccadilly
P To Worcester Foregate Street
Q From Guildford to Newcastle

For complete services between Banbury and Birmingham, refer to Table T71

Table T116-F

Mondays to Fridays

21 May to 7 December

London and Reading - Bedwyn, Oxford, Banbury and Birmingham

	GW	GW ◇■ A ☕	GW ◇■ B ☕	GW	GW	GW ◇■ C ☕	XC ◇■ D 🍴	GW	GW ◇■ E	GW	GW ◇■ A ☕	GW ◇■ F ☕	GW	GW	GW	GW ◇■ G ☕	XC ◇■ H 🍴	GW	GW	GW ◇■ B ☕	GW	GW ◇■ I ☕
London Paddington ⊖ d	05 57	06 30	06 35	06 12		06 45			06 52	06 27	07 00	07 03		07 06	06 42	07 15		07 21	06 55	07 30	07 09	07 36
Ealing Broadway ⊖ d	06 06			06 20						06 36					06 50				07 03		07 17	
Slough d	06 31			06 42					07 08	07 01					07 13			07 37	07 28			
Maidenhead d	06 38			06 53						07 08					07 24				07 37		07 43	
Twyford d	06 46			07 01						07 16					07 32				07 45		07 51	
Reading a	06 54	06 55	07 00	07 09		07 10			07 21	07 26	07 26	07 28		07 37	07 40	07 40		07 51	07 53	07 55	07 59	08 01
d	06 54	06 57		07 09	07 10		07 15		07 22	07 27	07 28	07 30	07 39	07 42		07 42	07 46	07 52	07 53			08 03
Reading West d					07 13																	
Theale d					07 19									07 50								
Aldermaston d					07 24																	
Midgham d					07 27																	
Thatcham d					07 32									07 58								
Newbury Racecourse d					07 37																	
Newbury a					07 40							07 47		08 04								
d														08 04								
Kintbury d														08 11								
Hungerford d														08 15								
Bedwyn a														08 23								
Tilehurst d	06 58									07 31			07 43						07 58			
Pangbourne d	07 03									07 35			07 47						08 03			
Goring & Streatley d	07 08									07 40			07 52						08 08			
Cholsey d	07 13									07 45			07 57						08 14			
Didcot Parkway a	07 20	07 10		07 25					07 40	07 52	07 43		08 04			07 55			08 21			08 16
d								07 30	07 43				08 08									
Appleford d								07 34					08 13									
Culham d								07 37					08 15									
Radley d								07 41					08 19									
Oxford 115 a							07 36	07 49	07 56				08 27				08 10	08 17				
d							07 39										08 12					
Tackley d																						
Heyford d																						
Kings Sutton d																						
Banbury 71 a							07 55										08 29					
Leamington Spa a							08 13										08 46					
Coventry a							08 25															
Birmingham International a							08 37															
Birmingham New Street 71 a							08 48										09 18					

	GW	GW ◇■ J ☕	GW	XC ◇■ K 🍴	GW	GW L	GW ◇ E	GW M	GW ◇■ N ☕	GW	GW O	GW P	GW	GW Q	GW ◇■ G ☕	GW P	GW	XC ◇■ R 🍴	GW ◇■ S 🍴	GW	GW ◇■ A ☕	GW	GW
London Paddington ⊖ d	07 12	07 45					07 50	07 25	08 00					08 06	08 15		07 42		08 21	07 52	08 30	08 09	
Ealing Broadway ⊖ d	07 20							07 33									07 50			08 01		08 17	
Slough d	07 41						08 07	07 58									08 14		08 37	08 28		08 35	
Maidenhead d	07 52							08 07									08 25			08 36		08 43	
Twyford d	08 00							08 15				←				←	08 33			08 45		08 51	
Reading a	08 08	08 10					08 23	08 25	08 26			08 25		08 31	08 40	08 31	08 41		08 52	08 52	08 55	08 58	
d			08 12	08 15		08 19	08 23	08 34	08 27			08 34	08 35	08 43	08 42	08 43		08 50	08 53	08 54			09 10
Reading West d			08 15					→						→									09 13
Theale d			08 21										08 43			08 51							09 19
Aldermaston d			08 26										08 48										09 24
Midgham d			08 29																				09 27
Thatcham d			08 34										08 54			09 01							09 32
Newbury Racecourse d			08 39																				09 37
Newbury a			08 42										09 00			09 07							09 40
d													09 00										
Kintbury d													09 07										
Hungerford d													09 11										
Bedwyn a													09 19										
Tilehurst d						08 23						08 38								08 58			
Pangbourne d						08 27						08 42								09 02			
Goring & Streatley d						08 32						08 47								09 07			
Cholsey d						08 37					←	08 52								09 12			
Didcot Parkway a						08 44			08 42		08 44	09 00			08 55					09 22			
d					08 30	08 48				08 44	08 48												
Appleford d						→					08 52												
Culham d											08 55												
Radley d					08 37						08 59												
Oxford 115 a				08 37	08 45		08 48			08 55	09 07							09 13	09 18				
d				08 39						08 58								09 15					
Tackley d										09 07													
Heyford d										09 11													
Kings Sutton d										09 20													
Banbury 71 a				08 55						09 25								09 33					
Leamington Spa a				09 13														09 50					
Coventry a				09 25																			
Birmingham International a				09 37																			
Birmingham New Street 71 a				09 49														10 18					

A To Bristol Temple Meads
B To Penzance
C To Swansea
D From Southampton Central to Manchester Piccadilly
E To Great Malvern
F To Paignton. The Devon Express
G To Cardiff Central
H To Newcastle
I To Cheltenham Spa
J To Swansea. The St. David
K From Bournemouth to Manchester Piccadilly
L To Oxford
M To Didcot Parkway
N To Bristol Temple Meads. The Merchant Venturer
O From Reading
P From London Paddington
Q To Newbury
R From Winchester to Newcastle
S To Hereford

For complete services between Banbury and Birmingham, refer to Table T71

London and Reading - Bedwyn, Oxford, Banbury and Birmingham

	GW		GW	XC	GW	GW	GW	GW	GW	GW	GW FX	GW	GW	GW	XC	XC	GW		GW	GW	GW	GW	GW	GW
			◇ A	◇ B					◇ C		◇ D			◇ E	◇ F	◇ G			◇ H	◇ C	◇ I			◇ A
London Paddington ⊖ d	08 12		08 45			08 21	08 51	08 29	09 00		09 03	09 06	08 43	09 15			08 51		09 21	09 30	09 36	09 12		09 45
Ealing Broadway ⊖ d	08 21					08 29		08 38					08 51				08 59					09 20		
Slough d	08 41					08 56	09 07	09 00					09 12				09 26		09 37			09 41		
Maidenhead d	08 53					09 04		09 10					09 23				09 34					09 52		
Twyford d	09 01					09 12		09 18					09 31				09 42					10 00		
Reading a	09 10		09 10			09 19	09 21	09 25	09 25		09 27	09 36	09 39	09 40			09 49		09 51	09 55	10 01	10 08		10 10
Reading d				09 15		09 21	09 22		09 27			09 38		09 42	09 45	09 45	09 52		09 52		10 03		10 10	
Reading West d																							10 13	
Theale d												09 46											10 20	
Aldermaston d																							10 25	
Midgham d																							10 28	
Thatcham d												09 55											10 33	
Newbury Racecourse d																							10 38	
Newbury a												10 00											10 41	
Newbury d												10 01												
Kintbury d												10 07												
Hungerford d												10 12												
Bedwyn a												10 19												
Tilehurst d						09 25											09 56							
Pangbourne d						09 29											10 00							
Goring & Streatley d						09 34											10 05							
Cholsey d						09 39											10 10							
Didcot Parkway a						09 48	09 37		09 40					09 55			10 20				10 16			
Didcot Parkway d					09 29		09 38			09 54														
Appleford d																								
Culham d																								
Radley d					09 36					10 01														
Oxford 115 a				09 37	09 44		09 51			10 09					10 13	10 13			10 17					
Oxford d				09 39											10 15	10 15								
Tackley d																								
Heyford d																								
Kings Sutton d																								
Banbury 71 a				09 56											10 31	10 31								
Leamington Spa a				10 12											10 49	10 49								
Coventry a				10 24																				
Birmingham International a				10 37																				
Birmingham New Street 71 a				10 48											11 18	11 18								

	XC	GW	GW	GW	GW	GW FX	GW	GW	GW		XC	GW	GW	GW	GW	GW	GW	GW	XC	GW	GW	GW	GW	GW
	B				◇ C	◇ J			◇ E		◇ K			◇ L	◇ M	◇ N		◇ O	◇ B					◇ C
London Paddington ⊖ d			09 27	09 50	10 00	10 03	10 06	09 42	10 15				09 57	10 22	10 30	10 33	10 12	10 45				10 52	10 27	11 00
Ealing Broadway ⊖ d			09 35					09 52					10 05				10 20						10 35	
Slough d			09 57	10 06				10 12					10 27	10 38			10 41					11 08	10 57	
Maidenhead d			10 05					10 24					10 35				10 52						11 05	
Twyford d			10 13					10 32					10 43				11 00						11 13	
Reading a			10 20	10 20	10 25	10 28	10 36	10 39	10 40				10 50	10 52	10 56	10 58	11 08	11 10				11 22	11 22	11 26
Reading d	10 15		10 21	10 21	10 27		10 39		10 42		10 45		10 51	10 53		11 00			11 15	11 15		11 23	11 23	11 27
Reading West d																				11 18				
Theale d							10 48													11 24				
Aldermaston d																				11 29				
Midgham d																				11 32				
Thatcham d							10 59													11 37				
Newbury Racecourse d																				11 42				
Newbury a							11 05									11 17				11 45				
Newbury d							11 08																	
Kintbury d							11 14																	
Hungerford d							11 19																	
Bedwyn a							11 26																	
Tilehurst d			10 25										10 55										11 27	
Pangbourne d			10 30										11 00										11 31	
Goring & Streatley d			10 36										11 06										11 36	
Cholsey d			10 41										11 11										11 41	
Didcot Parkway a			10 50		10 40				10 55				11 20									11 38	11 50	11 41
Didcot Parkway d		10 28										11 03									11 30	11 39		
Appleford d																								
Culham d		10 35																						
Radley d												11 10												
Oxford 115 a	10 38	10 44		10 49							11 10	11 18		11 22					11 38		11 43	11 52		
Oxford d	10 39										11 13								11 39		11 46			
Tackley d																					11 55			
Heyford d																					11 59			
Kings Sutton d																					12 08			
Banbury 71 a	10 55										11 29								11 56		12 13			
Leamington Spa a	11 13										11 46								12 13					
Coventry a	11 25																		12 25					
Birmingham International a	11 37																		12 37					
Birmingham New Street 71 a	11 48										12 18								12 48					

A To Swansea
B From Bournemouth to Manchester Piccadilly
C To Bristol Temple Meads
D To Plymouth
E To Cardiff Central
F until 20 July, from 8 October. To Newcastle
G from 23 July until 5 October. To Glasgow Central
H To Worcester Foregate Street
I To Cheltenham Spa
J To Penzance. The Cornish Riviera- Restaurant for customers joining to Reading
K From Southampton Central to Newcastle
L To Hereford
M To Weston-super-Mare
N To Paignton. The Torbay Express
O To Swansea. Restaurant available for customers joining until Bristol Parkway

For complete services between Banbury and Birmingham, refer to Table T71

Table T116-F

Mondays to Fridays

21 May to 7 December

London and Reading - Bedwyn, Oxford, Banbury and Birmingham

	GW		GW	GW	GW	XC	XC	GW	GW	GW	GW	GW	GW	GW	GW	XC	GW		GW	GW	GW	GW FX	GW	GW
	◇ A			◇ B		◇ C	D			◇ E	◇ F	◇ G		◇ H		◇ I					◇ F	◇ J		
London Paddington ⊖ d	11 03		11 06	11 15	10 42				10 57	11 22	11 30	11 36	11 12	11 45					11 26	11 50	12 00	12 03	12 06	11 42
Ealing Broadway ⊖ d					10 51				11 05				11 20						11 34					11 50
Slough d					11 15				11 27	11 38			11 41						11 56	12 07				12 11
Maidenhead d					11 27				11 35				11 52						12 04					12 22
Twyford d					11 35				11 43				12 00						12 12					12 30
Reading a	11 28		11 36	11 40	11 42				11 50	11 52	11 56	12 01	12 08	12 10					12 19	12 23	12 26	12 29	12 36	12 38
Reading d			11 37	11 42		11 45	11 45		11 53	11 53		12 03			12 11	12 15			12 21	12 23	12 27		12 38	
Reading West d															12 14									
Theale d			11 45												12 20								12 46	
Aldermaston d															12 25									
Midgham d															12 28									
Thatcham d			11 58												12 33								12 55	
Newbury Racecourse d															12 38									
Newbury a			12 03												12 41								13 00	
Newbury d			12 04																				13 01	
Kintbury d			12 10																				13 07	
Hungerford d			12 15																				13 12	
Bedwyn a			12 22																				13 19	
Tilehurst d									11 57										12 25					
Pangbourne d									12 01										12 29					
Goring & Streatley d									12 06										12 34					
Cholsey d									12 11										12 39					
Didcot Parkway a				11 55					12 19			12 16							12 50		12 42			
Didcot Parkway d								12 00									12 30							
Appleford d																	12 34							
Culham d																								
Radley d								12 07																
Oxford 115 a						12 10	12 10	12 16		12 20						12 38	12 44			12 48				
Oxford d						12 13	12 13									12 39								
Tackley d																								
Heyford d																								
Kings Sutton d																								
Banbury 71 a						12 30	12 30									12 56								
Leamington Spa a						12 48	12 48									13 13								
Coventry a																13 25								
Birmingham International a																13 37								
Birmingham New Street 71 a						13 18	13 18									13 48								

A To Plymouth. The Mayflower
B To Cardiff Central
C until 20 July, from 8 October. To Newcastle
D from 23 July until 5 October. To Glasgow Central
E To Worcester Foregate Street
F To Bristol Temple Meads
G To Cheltenham Spa
H To Swansea
I From Bournemouth to Manchester Piccadilly
J To Penzance. The Royal Duchy - Restaurant for customers joining to Reading

For complete services between Banbury and Birmingham, refer to Table T71

<u>T116 UPDATE:</u> The route between Theale and Bedwyn will be CLOSED TO ALL TRAINS. Rail replacement buses on 4-7 June; 9-12 July; 16 July to 05 August; 28-30 August; 08-11 October and 19-22 November.

Table T116-F

Mondays to Fridays

21 May to 7 December

London and Reading - Bedwyn, Oxford, Banbury and Birmingham

Station		GW A	XC B	XC C	GW	GW D	GW E	GW F	GW G	GW H	GW	GW I	GW	XC J	GW	GW	GW	GW G	GW FX K	GW	GW	GW A	XC L
London Paddington	d	12 15				11 57	12 21		12 30	12 33	12 12	12 45				12 50	12 27	13 00	13 03	13 06	12 42	13 15	
Ealing Broadway	d					12 05					12 20						12 35				12 50		
Slough	d					12 27	12 37				12 41					13 06	12 57				13 13		
Maidenhead	d					12 35					12 52						13 05				13 25		
Twyford	d					12 43		←			13 00						13 13				13 33		
Reading	a	12 40				12 50	12 51	12 50	12 55	12 58	13 08	13 10				13 20	13 20	13 25	13 28	13 37	13 40	13 40	
	d	12 42	12 45	12 45		12 53	12 52	12 53		13 00			13 12	13 15		13 21	13 22	13 27		13 42		13 42	13 45
Reading West	d					→							13 15										
Theale	d												13 21							13 51			
Aldermaston	d												13 26										
Midgham	d												13 29										
Thatcham	d												13 34							14 02			
Newbury Racecourse	d												13 45										
Newbury	a									13 14			13 48							14 07			
	d																			14 11			
Kintbury	d																			14 17			
Hungerford	d																			14 22			
Bedwyn	a																			14 29			
Tilehurst	d							12 57									13 26						
Pangbourne	d							13 01									13 30						
Goring & Streatley	d							13 06									13 35						
Cholsey	d							13 11									13 40						
Didcot Parkway	a	12 55						13 21								13 36	13 49	13 40				13 55	
	d				13 01										13 29	13 38							
Appleford	d																						
Culham	d														13 35								
Radley	d				13 09																		
Oxford 115	a		13 11	13 11	13 17		13 20							13 38	13 44	13 51							14 11
	d		13 13	13 13										13 39									14 13
Tackley	d																						
Heyford	d																						
Kings Sutton	d																						
Banbury 71	a		13 30	13 30										13 56									14 30
Leamington Spa	a		13 47	13 47										14 13									14 49
Coventry	a													14 25									
Birmingham International	a													14 37									
Birmingham New Street 71	a		14 18	14 18										14 48									15 18

Station		GW	GW	GW M	GW G	GW N	GW	GW I	GW	XC J	GW	GW	GW	GW G	GW FX O	GW	GW	GW A	XC P	GW	GW M	GW	GW Q	GW
London Paddington	d		12 57	13 22	13 30	13 36	13 11	13 45				13 27	13 50	14 00	14 03	14 06	13 42	14 15			14 21	13 57	14 30	
Ealing Broadway	d		13 05				13 19					13 36					13 50					14 06		
Slough	d		13 27	13 38			13 43					13 58	14 07				14 11				14 37	14 28		
Maidenhead	d		13 35				13 54					14 06					14 22					14 36		
Twyford	d		13 43				14 02					14 14					14 30					14 44		
Reading	a		13 50	13 52	13 57	14 01	14 10	14 10				14 21	14 23	14 25	14 28	14 36	14 38	14 40			14 51	14 51	14 55	
	d		13 51	13 53	13 58	14 03			14 14	14 15		14 23	14 23			14 41		14 42	14 45		14 52	14 53	14 57	15 10
Reading West	d								14 17															15 14
Theale	d								14 23							14 49								15 20
Aldermaston	d								14 28															15 25
Midgham	d								14 31															15 28
Thatcham	d								14 36							14 58								15 33
Newbury Racecourse	d								14 41															15 38
Newbury	a								14 44							15 03								15 41
	d															15 04								
Kintbury	d															15 10								
Hungerford	d															15 15								
Bedwyn	a															15 22								
Tilehurst	d		13 57									14 27										14 57		
Pangbourne	d		14 01									14 31										15 01		
Goring & Streatley	d		14 06									14 36										15 06		
Cholsey	d		14 11									14 41										15 11		
Didcot Parkway	a		14 20		14 12	14 17						14 50						14 55				15 20	15 10	
	d	14 09									14 30									15 01				
Appleford	d																							
Culham	d																							
Radley	d	14 16																		15 08				
Oxford 115	a	14 24		14 16						14 38	14 43		14 48						15 09	15 16	15 20			
	d	14 25								14 39									15 13					
Tackley	d	14 34																						
Heyford	d	14 38																						
Kings Sutton	d	14 47																						
Banbury 71	a	14 52								14 56									15 30					
Leamington Spa	a									15 13									15 48					
Coventry	a									15 25														
Birmingham International	a									15 37														
Birmingham New Street 71	a									15 48									16 18					

A To Cardiff Central
B until 20 July, from 8 October. From Southampton Central to Newcastle
C from 23 July until 5 October. From Southampton Central to Dundee
D To Didcot Parkway
E To Worcester Shrub Hill
F From London Paddington
G To Bristol Temple Meads
H To Taunton. Restaurant available for customers joining to Reading
I To Swansea
J From Bournemouth to Manchester Piccadilly
K To Plymouth. Restaurant available for customers joining to Reading
L To Newcastle
M To Worcester Foregate Street
N To Cheltenham Spa
O To Penzance
P From Southampton Central to Edinburgh
Q To Weston-super-Mare

For complete services between Banbury and Birmingham, refer to Table T71

Table T116-F

Mondays to Fridays

21 May to 7 December

London and Reading - Bedwyn, Oxford, Banbury and Birmingham

Station		GW	GW A	XC B	GW	GW C	GW	GW D	GW E	GW FX F	GW G	GW	GW H	GW D	XC I	GW	GW	GW J	GW	GW K	GW	GW L	GW
London Paddington	d	14 12	14 45			14 27	14 50		15 00	15 03	15 06	14 41	15 15					15 22	14 57	15 30		15 36	15 12
Ealing Broadway	d	14 20				14 35						14 50							15 06				15 20
Slough	d	14 43				14 57	15 07					15 12						15 38	15 30				15 41
Maidenhead	d	14 54				15 05						15 24							15 37				15 52
Twyford	d	15 02				15 13		←				15 32		←					15 45				16 00
Reading	a	15 10	15 10			15 20	15 22	15 20	15 26	15 29	15 36	15 40	15 40	15 36				15 52	15 53	15 56		16 00	16 08
	d			15 15		15 23	15 22	15 23			15 45		15 42	15 45	15 45		15 52	15 53	15 56	15 58	16 01	16 03	
Reading West	d					→					→										16 04		
Theale	d													15 53							16 10		
Aldermaston	d																				16 15		
Midgham	d																				16 18		
Thatcham	d													16 01							16 23		
Newbury Racecourse	d																				16 28		
Newbury	a													16 07							16 31		
	d													16 11									
Kintbury	d													16 17									
Hungerford	d													16 22									
Bedwyn	a													16 29									
Tilehurst	d							15 27									15 56		16 00				
Pangbourne	d							15 31									16 00		16 04				
Goring & Streatley	d							15 36									16 05		16 09				
Cholsey	d							15 41									16 10		16 14				
Didcot Parkway	a						15 37	15 50					15 55				16 17		16 23	16 11		16 16	
	d				15 30		15 37									16 00	16 18						
Appleford	d															16 05							
Culham	d															16 07							
Radley	d															16 11	16 25						
Oxford 115	a			15 37	15 42		15 50								16 11	16 19	16 33	16 23					
	d			15 39											16 13	16 20							
Tackley	d															16 29							
Heyford	d															16 34							
Kings Sutton	d															16 42							
Banbury 71	a			15 56											16 29	16 49							
Leamington Spa	a			16 13											16 47								
Coventry	a			16 25																			
Birmingham International	a			16 37																			
Birmingham New Street 71	a			16 48											17 18								

Station		GW A	XC B	GW M	GW	GW E	GW FX N	GW	GW	GW A	XC O	GW	GW G	GW	GW J	GW P	GW Q	GW R	GW S	GW	GW	GW T	GW	XC B
London Paddington	d	15 45		15 52	15 27	16 00	16 03	16 06	15 42	16 15				15 57	16 22	16 30		16 33		16 36	16 12	16 45		
Ealing Broadway	d				15 35				15 50					16 05							16 20			
Slough	d			16 08	16 01				16 11					16 27	16u38						16 41			
Maidenhead	d				16 09				16 22					16 35							16 52			
Twyford	d				16 17				16 30					16 43							17 00			
Reading	a	16 10		16 22	16 24	16 25	16 28	16 36	16 38	16 40				16 51		16 55		16 57		17 03	17 08	17 10		
	d		16 15	16 23	16 25			16 42		16 42	16 45		16 49	16 53	16u53	16 57	17 01	17 01		17 05			17 12	17 15
Reading West	d																						17 15	
Theale	d							16 50					16 56										17 21	
Aldermaston	d												17 01										17 26	
Midgham	d																						17 29	
Thatcham	d							16 58					17 08										17 34	
Newbury Racecourse	d																		←				17 39	
Newbury	a							17 04					17 14					17 18	17 14				17 42	
	d							17 04					17 25					17 20	17 25					
Kintbury	d							17 11					→						17 31					
Hungerford	d							17 15										17a28	17 36					
Bedwyn	a							17 23											17 43					
Tilehurst	d				16 29									16 57			17 07							
Pangbourne	d				16 33									17 01			17 11							
Goring & Streatley	d				16 38									17 06			17 16							
Cholsey	d				16 43									17 11			17 21							
Didcot Parkway	a				16 52					16 55				17 23		17 11	17 31			17 20				
	d											16 59					17 34							
Appleford	d											17 04					→							
Culham	d											17 06												
Radley	d											17 10												
Oxford 115	a		16 38	16 46							17 08	17 18			17 22									17 37
	d		16 39								17 13													17 39
Tackley	d																							
Heyford	d																							
Kings Sutton	d																							
Banbury 71	a		16 55								17 31													17 56
Leamington Spa	a		17 13								17 50													18 13
Coventry	a		17 25																					18 25
Birmingham International	a		17 37																					18 37
Birmingham New Street 71	a		17 48								18 18													18 48

A To Swansea
B From Bournemouth to Manchester Piccadilly
C To Didcot Parkway
D From London Paddington
E To Bristol Temple Meads
F To Penzance. The Cornishman
G To Bedwyn
H To Cardiff Central
I To Newcastle
J To Great Malvern
K To Weston-super-Mare
L To Cheltenham Spa
M To Moreton-in-Marsh
N To Penzance
O From Southampton Central to Leeds
P To Taunton
Q To Banbury
R To Exeter St Davids
S From Reading
T To Swansea. The Capitals United

For complete services between Banbury and Birmingham, refer to Table T71

T116 UPDATE: The route between Theale and Bedwyn will be CLOSED TO ALL TRAINS. Rail replacement buses on 4-7 June; 9-12 July; 16 July to 05 August; 28-30 August; 08-11 October and 19-22 November.

Table T116-F

Mondays to Fridays

21 May to 7 December

London and Reading - Bedwyn, Oxford, Banbury and Birmingham

	GW		GW	GW	GW	GW FX	GW FO	GW	GW	GW	GW	XC	GW	GW	GW	GW	GW		GW	GW	GW	GW	GW	GW
			A		■ B ☕	◇■ C ☕	◇■ C ☕		◇■ D ☕	■ E ☕		◇■ F ☕	◇■ G ☕			■ H ☕	◇■ I ☕					◇■ J ☕		■ K ☕
London Paddington ⊖ d	16 52			16 49	17 00	17 03	17 03	16 28	17 07	17 15	16 42		17 22		17 18	17 30	17 33			16 58	17 12	17 36		17 45
Ealing Broadway ⊖ d								16 36			16 50									17 07	17 20			
Slough d								17 08			17 15									17 32	17 45			
Maidenhead d				17 10				17 15			17 26				17 40					17 43	17 52			
Twyford d				17 17				17 23	17 31		17 34				17 48					17 51	18 00			
Reading a	17 17			17 24	17 25	17 28		17 31	17 38	17 40	17 42		17 50		17 55	17 55	17 58			17 59	18 08			18 10
d	17 19			17 25	17 27	17 30	17u30		17 40	17 42		17 45	17 52		17 56	17 57	18 00						18 08	
Reading West d																								
Theale d									17 48															
Aldermaston d																								
Midgham d																								
Thatcham d									17 58															
Newbury Racecourse d																								
Newbury a						17 45	17 45		18 04								18 14							
d									18 05										18 26					
Kintbury d									18 13										18 32					
Hungerford d									18 20										18 37					
Bedwyn a									18 26										18 44					
Tilehurst d				17 29											18 00								18 12	
Pangbourne d				17 33											18 04								18 16	
Goring & Streatley d				17 37											18 09								18 21	
Cholsey d			←	17 41											18 14								18 26	
Didcot Parkway a			17 31	17 50	17 40					17 55					18 21	18 11						18 17	18 33	
d			17 34											18 08	18 29								18 39	
Appleford d			17 38																					
Culham d			17 41											18 13										
Radley d			17 45											18 17	18 36									
Oxford 115 a	17 43		17 53									18 08	18 15	18 25	18 44								18 54	
d			17 53									18 10												
Tackley d			18 02																					
Heyford d			18 07																					
Kings Sutton d			18 15																					
Banbury 71 a			18 23									18 26												
Leamington Spa a												18 44												
Coventry a																								
Birmingham International a																								
Birmingham New Street 71 a												19 18												

	GW	XC	GW	GW	GW	GW FX	GW	GW FO	GW		GW	GW	GW	XC	GW	GW	GW	GW	GW	GW	GW	GW	GW	GW
		◇■ L ☕	◇■ M ☕		■ N ☕	◇■ O ✕		◇■ O ✕	◇■ D ☕			■ K ☕	P	◇■ Q ☕		◇■ R ☕		■ S ☕		◇■ T ☕				■ U ☕
London Paddington ⊖ d			17 52	17 48	18 00	18 03	17 29	18 03	18 07		17 42	18 14	17 57			18 22	18 19	18 30	17 56	18 33		18 27		18 45
Ealing Broadway ⊖ d							17 37				17 50								18 04					
Slough d							18 02				18 13		18 17						18 29			18 43		
Maidenhead d				18 10			18 13				18 22		18 26				18 39		18 43			18 52		
Twyford d				18 17			18 21		18 30		18 30		18 35				18 46		18 51			18 59		
Reading a			18 20	18 24	18 26	18 28	18 29		18 37		18 38	18 40	18 42			18 50	18 53	18 55	18 58	18 58		19 06		19 10
d	18 12	18 15	18 21	18 28	18 28	18 30		18u30	18 39			18 42		18 45		18 51	18 57	18 57		19 00			19 10	
Reading West d	18 15																						19 13	
Theale d	18 21								18 47														19 21	
Aldermaston d	18 26																						19 26	
Midgham d	18 29																						19 29	
Thatcham d	18 34								18 57														19 34	
Newbury Racecourse d	18 39																						19 39	
Newbury a	18 42					18 45		18 45	19 03											19 14			19 42	
d									19 04											19 16	19 27			
Kintbury d									19 12												19 33			
Hungerford d									19 19											19 26	19 38			
Bedwyn a									19 25											19 32	19 45			
Tilehurst d				18 32													19 01							
Pangbourne d				18 36													19 05							
Goring & Streatley d				18 40													19 09							
Cholsey d				18 45													19 14							
Didcot Parkway a				18 55	18 40							18 55					19 23	19 11						
d															19 02									
Appleford d																								
Culham d																								
Radley d															19 09									
Oxford 115 a		18 37	18 48											19 11	19 17	19 20								
d		18 39												19 13	19 18									
Tackley d															19 28									
Heyford d															19 32									
Kings Sutton d															19 41									
Banbury 71 a		18 56												19 29	19 46									
Leamington Spa a		19 13												19 47										
Coventry a		19 26																						
Birmingham International a		19 37																						
Birmingham New Street 71 a		19 48												20 18										

A From Reading
B To Bristol Temple Meads
C To Penzance
D To Frome
E To Carmarthen. The Red Dragon
F To Leeds
G To Hereford
H To Taunton
I To Paignton
J To Cheltenham Spa. The Cheltenham Spa Express
K To Swansea
L From Bournemouth to Manchester Piccadilly
M To Worcester Shrub Hill
N To Bristol Temple Meads. The Bristolian
O To Penzance. The Golden Hind
P not from 4 June until 7 June
Q From Southampton Central
R To Hereford. The Cathedrals Express
S To Weston-super-Mare
T To Exeter St Davids
U To Swansea. Y Cymro - The Welshman

For complete services between Banbury and Birmingham, refer to Table T71

Table T116-F

Mondays to Fridays

21 May to 7 December

London and Reading - Bedwyn, Oxford, Banbury and Birmingham

	GW		XC	GW	GW	GW	GW	GW	GW	GW FX	GW	GW FO	GW FO	GW	GW FX	GW	GW FO		XC	GW	GW	GW	GW	GW
			◇■ A ☕	◇■ B ☕				■ C ☕		■ D ✕		■ E ✕	■ C ☕		■ F ☕		■ F ☕		◇■	◇■ G ☕			■ H ☕	
London Paddington ⊖ d	18 11			18 37	18 52			19 00	18 48	19 03	18 29	19 03	19 12	19 06	19 15	18 42	19 15			19 22		19 20	19 30	18 59
Ealing Broadway ⊖ d	18 19										18 37					18 50								19 07
Slough d	18 46										19 02					19 13				19 38				19 32
Maidenhead d	18 56								19 08		19 13					19 22						19 40		19 44
Twyford d	19 04								19 17		19 21			19 32		19 36						19 47		19 52
Reading a	19 11				19 17			19 25	19 26	19 28	19 30		19 38	19 39	19 41	19 43	19 43			19 52		19 54	19 55	19 59
d			19 15		19 19		19 19	19 27	19 30	19 30		19u30	19 39	19 40	19 42				19 45	19 53		19 54	19 59	
Reading West d														19 43										
Theale d														19 49										
Aldermaston d														19 54										
Midgham d														19 57										
Thatcham d														20 02										
Newbury Racecourse d														20 07										
Newbury a										19 46		19 46		20 09										
d														20 10										
Kintbury d														20 16										
Hungerford d														20 21										
Bedwyn a														20 28										
Tilehurst d							19 25		19 34													19 58		
Pangbourne d							19 29		19 38													20 02		
Goring & Streatley d							19 34		19 42													20 06		
Cholsey d							19 39		19 47													20 11		
Didcot Parkway a				19 15			19 46	19 40	19 55				19 53		19 56							20 18	20 12	
d						19 35	19 48														20 09			
Appleford d																					20 14			
Culham d							19 53																	
Radley d						19 42															20 19			
Oxford 115 a			19 38		19 43	19 52	20 03												20 09	20 20	20 27			
d			19 39																20 13					
Tackley d																								
Heyford d																								
Kings Sutton d																								
Banbury 71 a			19 56																20 30					
Leamington Spa a			20 13																20 48					
Coventry a			20 26																					
Birmingham International a			20 37																					
Birmingham New Street 71 a			20 48																21 23					

	GW	GW	XC	GW	GW	GW	GW	GW	GW		GW	GW	GW	XC	GW	GW	GW	GW	GW	XC	GW	GW	GW	GW
			◇■ A		◇■ I ☕				◇■ C ☕		◇■ J ☕		◇■ F ☕	◇■			◇■ K ☕			◇■ L		◇■ C ☕		M
London Paddington ⊖ d		19 35		19 12	19 48		19 27	19 52	20 00		20 03	19 42	20 15		19 57		20 22	20 18	20 12			20 45		20 27
Ealing Broadway ⊖ d				19 20			19 35					19 50			20 05				20 20					20 35
Slough d				19 42			19 58	20 08				20 11			20 27		20 38		20 42					20 57
Maidenhead d		19 54		19 53	20 07		20 06					20 22			20 35			20 41	20 53					21 05
Twyford d		20 01		20 03			20 14					20 30			20 43			20 48	21 01					21 13
Reading a		20 09		20 13	20 19		20 22	20 22	20 25		20 27	20 38	20 40		20 52		20 52	20 55	21 10			21 10		21 22
d	20 07	20 10	20 12		20 20		20 22	20 23	20 27		20 30		20 42	20 45			20 53	20 57		21 11	21 11	21 12		21 26
Reading West d	20 13																				21 14			→
Theale d	20 19																				21 20			
Aldermaston d	20 24																				21 25			
Midgham d	20 28																				21 28			
Thatcham d	20 33																				21 33			
Newbury Racecourse d	20 37																				21 50			
Newbury a	20 40										20 45										21 53			
d	20 52																							
Kintbury d	20 58																							
Hungerford d	21 03																							
Bedwyn a	21 10																							
Tilehurst d		20 14					20 26											21 02						
Pangbourne d		20 18					20 31											21 06						
Goring & Streatley d		20 22					20 36											21 10						
Cholsey d		20 26					20 42											21 14						
Didcot Parkway a		20 34			20 34		20 50		20 42				20 55					21 22				21 25		
d						20 42										21 01							21 26	
Appleford d																								
Culham d																								
Radley d						20 49										21 09							21 33	
Oxford 115 a			20 36			20 58		20 53						21 12		21 20	21 21			21 34			21 41	
d			20 39			20 59								21 14						21 36			21 42	
Tackley d						21 08																	21 51	
Heyford d						21 12																	21 55	
Kings Sutton d						21 21																	22 04	
Banbury 71 a			20 56			21 26								21 31						21 52			22 09	
Leamington Spa a			21 13											21 52						22 10				
Coventry a			21 26																	22 23				
Birmingham International a			21 37																	22 34				
Birmingham New Street 71 a			21 48											22 18						22 45				

A From Bournemouth to Manchester Piccadilly
B To Cheltenham Spa
C To Bristol Temple Meads
D To Plymouth. The Armada
E To Penzance. The Armada
F To Swansea
G To Hereford
H To Weston-super-Mare
I To Worcester Shrub Hill
J To Plymouth
K To Great Malvern
L From Bournemouth
M To Didcot Parkway

For complete services between Banbury and Birmingham, refer to Table T71

Table T116-F

London and Reading - Bedwyn, Oxford, Banbury and Birmingham

Mondays to Fridays

21 May to 7 December

		GW		GW A	GW	GW ◇■ B	GW	GW	GW ◇■ C	XC ◇■	GW	GW	GW	GW	GW	GW ◇■ D	GW ◇■ E	GW		GW	GW	GW FO ◇■ F	GW	GW FO	GW FX ◇■ F
London Paddington ⊖	d	20 50				21 03		20 42	21 15		21 18	20 57			21 12	21 45	21 48			21 27	21 42	22 15		22 18	22 15
Ealing Broadway ⊖	d							20 50				21 05			21 20					21 35	21 52				
Slough	d	21 07						21 13			21 34	21 27			21 41		22 04			21 57	22 12				
Maidenhead	d							21 24				21 35			21 52					22 10	22 24				
Twyford	d			←				21 32				21 43			22 00					22 18	22 32				
Reading	a	21 23		21 22		21 28		21 40	21 40		21 48	21 55			22 08	22 12	22 19			22 27	22 39	22 42		22 48	22 54
	d	21 23		21 26		21 30			21 43	21 45	21 49	21 58		22 07		22 13	22 20			22 28		22 44		22 50	22 56
Reading West	d													22 10											
Theale	d													22 16											
Aldermaston	d													22 21											
Midgham	d													22 24											
Thatcham	d													22 29											
Newbury Racecourse	d													22 34											
Newbury	a					21 44								22 36											
	d						21 55							22 37											
Kintbury	d						22 01							22 43											
Hungerford	d						22 06							22 48											
Bedwyn	a						22 13							22 55											
Tilehurst	d			21 30								22 02								22 36					
Pangbourne	d			21 35								22 06								22 40					
Goring & Streatley	d			21 40								22 11								22 45					
Cholsey	d			21 45								22 16								22 50					
Didcot Parkway	a			21 52					22 02			22 23				22 31				22 57		23 00			23 12
	d				21 58								22 31										23 05		
Appleford	d																						23 09		
Culham	d																						23 12		
Radley	d				22 05																		23 16		
Oxford 115	a	21 53			22 13					22 25	22 18		22 47				22 53						23 24	23 30	
	d									22 30								23 11							
Tackley	d																	23 20							
Heyford	d																	23 24							
Kings Sutton	d																	23 33							
Banbury 71	a									22 47								23 38							
Leamington Spa	a									23 04															
Coventry	a									23 16															
Birmingham International	a									23 26															
Birmingham New Street 71	a									23 56															

		GW FO	GW FX	GW FO	GW FX	GW FO ◇■ C	GW	GW FX	GW FX ◇■ C	GW FO		GW FO	GW FX	GW FX	GW	GW	GW FO G	GW FX	GW ◇■ H	GW FO	GW FX	GW FO	GW FX	GW FO	GW
London Paddington ⊖	d	21 57	22 18	22 21	22 21	22 45		21 57	22 45	22 27		22 50	22 50	22 27		22 59	23 20	23 20	23 30	23 12	23 14	23 42	23 27	23 27	23 51
Ealing Broadway ⊖	d	22 05						22 05		22 35				22 35		23 09				23 20	23 22		23 35	23 35	00 02
Slough	d	22 34		22 38	22 44			22 46		23 00		23 07	23 10	23 14		23 34	23 37	23 40		23 46	23 49	23 59	23 59	00 03	00 30
Maidenhead	d	22 42		22 45	22 51			22 57		23 11		23 14	23 17	23 25		23 41	23 46	23 47		23 58	00 01	00 07	00 07	00 10	00 41
Twyford	d	22 50		22 53	22 59			23 05		23 19		23 22	23 25	23 33		23 49	23 54	23 55		00 06	00 09	00 15	00 15	00 18	00 49
Reading	a	22 57	22 57	23 00	23 07	23 11		23 13	23 18	23 27		23 29	23 33	23 40		23 57	00 01	00 03	00 07	00 16	00 16	00 23	00 23	00 26	00 58
	d	22 58	22 59	23 02	23 08	23 13		23 13	23 20			23 30	23 33		23 45		00 03	00 04	00 10			00 23	00 24	00 27	
Reading West	d																								
Theale	d			23 10	23 16																				
Aldermaston	d			23 15	23 21																				
Midgham	d			23 18	23 24																				
Thatcham	d			23 23	23 29																				
Newbury Racecourse	d			23 28	23 34																				
Newbury	a			23 30	23 36																				
	d			23 31	23 37																				
Kintbury	d			23 37	23 43																				
Hungerford	d			23 42	23 48																				
Bedwyn	a			23 49	23 55																				
Tilehurst	d	23 02						23 17							23 49								00 28	00 32	
Pangbourne	d	23 06						23 22							23 53								00 32	00 37	
Goring & Streatley	d	23 11						23 27							23 58								00 37	00 42	
Cholsey	d	23 16						23 32							00 03								00 42	00 48	
Didcot Parkway	a	23 23				23 29		23 39	23 42						00 14				00 26			00 47	00 50	00 56	
	d						23 30								00 24							00 47			
Appleford	d																								
Culham	d																								
Radley	d														00 31										
Oxford 115	a		23 29				23 41					23 55	23 58		00 39		00 34	00 32				01 01			
	d																								
Tackley	d																								
Heyford	d																								
Kings Sutton	d																								
Banbury 71	a																								
Leamington Spa	a																								
Coventry	a																								
Birmingham International	a																								
Birmingham New Street 71	a																								

A From London Paddington
B To Plymouth
C To Swansea
D To Exeter St Davids
E To Worcester Shrub Hill
F To Bristol Temple Meads
G To Moreton-in-Marsh
H To Cardiff Central

For complete services between Banbury and Birmingham, refer to Table T71

Table T116-F

London and Reading - Bedwyn, Oxford, Banbury and Birmingham

Saturdays

26 May to 8 December

		GW A	GW B	CH	GW ◇■ C	GW D	GW	GW D	GW D	GW	GW ■ E	GW D	GW ■	GW	GW	GW		GW	GW	GW	GW ◇■ F	GW	GW	XC ◇■ G	GW
London Paddington ⊖	d												00 22		00 34	01 34		03 34			05 18				
Ealing Broadway ⊖	d											00 02			00 42	01 42		03 42							
Slough	d								00 03			00 30	00 43		01 07	02 04		04 04			05 34				
Maidenhead	d							00 07	00 10			00 41			01 18	02 12		04 11							
Twyford	d					00 06		00 15	00 18		00 32	00 49			01 26	02 20		04 19							
Reading	a					00 16		00 23	00 26		00 40	00 58	01 01		01 34	02 27		04 27			05 51				
	d	00 03			00 10		00 20	00 23	00 27				01 02						05 08	05 41	05 54	05 57	06 12	06 15	
Reading West	d						00s23												05 10	05 43			06 14		
Theale	d						00s29												05 16	05 49			06 20		
Aldermaston	d						00s34												05 21	05 54			06 25		
Midgham	d						00s37												05 25	05 58			06 29		
Thatcham	d						00s42												05 30	06 03			06 34		
Newbury Racecourse	d						00s47												05 34	06 07			06 38		
Newbury	a						00 50												05 37	06 10			06 44		
	d																		05 38	06 11					
Kintbury	d																		05 44	06 17					
Hungerford	d																		05 48	06 21					
Bedwyn	a																		05 57	06 31					
Tilehurst	d								00 32													06 00			
Pangbourne	d								00 37													06 05			
Goring & Streatley	d								00 42													06 10			
Cholsey	d		00 03						00 48													06 15			
Didcot Parkway	a		00 14		00 26			00 47	00 56				01 17								06 08	06 24			
	d		00 24					00 47		01 07			01 18	05 57							06 10				06 30
Appleford	d									01 11				06 01											
Culham	d									01 14				06 03											
Radley	d		00 31							01 18				06 07											06 37
Oxford 115	a	00 34	00 39					01 01		01 26			01 31	06 16							06 22			06 37	06 45
	d			00 40										06 18										06 39	
Tackley	d			00 50										06 27											
Heyford	d			00 55										06 30											
Kings Sutton	d			01 03										06 40											
Banbury 71	a			01 12										06 46										06 55	
Leamington Spa	a																							07 13	
Coventry	a																							07 25	
Birmingham International	a																							07 37	
Birmingham New Street 71	a																							07 48	

		GW	GW ◇■	GW	XC ◇■ H	GW	GW ◇■ F	GW ◇■ I		GW	GW ◇■ J	GW	GW	XC ◇■ G	GW	GW	GW ◇■	GW ◇■ I	GW	GW	XC ◇■ K	GW	GW	GW ◇■ F	
London Paddington ⊖	d	05 25	05 52				06 22	06 30		05 55		06 14				06 27	06 52	07 00		06 42			06 57	07 22	
Ealing Broadway ⊖	d	05 33								06 03		06 22				06 35				06 50			07 05		
Slough	d	05 51	06 08				06 38			06 28		06 43				06 57	07 08			07 12			07 27	07 38	
Maidenhead	d	06 02								06 39		06 54				07 04				07 24			07 34		
Twyford	d	06 10								06 47	←	07 02				07 12				07 32			07 42		
Reading	a	06 18	06 21				06 51	06 54		06 55	06 54	07 10				07 20	07 21	07 24		07 40			07 50	07 51	
	d	06 20	06 23	06 38	06 47		06 53	06 58		06 55	06 58		07 12	07 15		07 21	07 23		07 38		07 47		07 51	07 53	
Reading West	d							→					07 14												
Theale	d			06 46									07 20						07 46						
Aldermaston	d												07 25												
Midgham	d												07 29												
Thatcham	d			06 54									07 34						07 54						
Newbury Racecourse	d												07 38												
Newbury	a			07 00									07 43						08 00						
	d			07 01															08 01						
Kintbury	d			07 07															08 07						
Hungerford	d			07 11															08 12						
Bedwyn	a			07 21															08 20						
Tilehurst	d	06 24								06 59						07 25							07 55		
Pangbourne	d	06 28								07 03						07 29							07 59		
Goring & Streatley	d	06 33								07 08						07 34							08 04		
Cholsey	d	06 38								07 13						07 39							08 09		
Didcot Parkway	a	06 47	06 38							07 22	07 12					07 48							08 20		
	d		06 39			07 03									07 30							08 03			
Appleford	d																								
Culham	d														07 35										
Radley	d														07 39										
Oxford 115	a		06 52		07 10	07 15	07 19							07 38	07 47		07 52				08 10	08 15		08 19	
	d				07 12									07 40							08 12	08 17			
Tackley	d																					08 25			
Heyford	d																					08 30			
Kings Sutton	d																					08 38			
Banbury 71	a				07 29									07 56							08 29	08 45			
Leamington Spa	a				07 47									08 13							08 47				
Coventry	a													08 25											
Birmingham International	a													08 37											
Birmingham New Street 71	a				08 18									08 48							09 18				

A From London Paddington to Moreton-in-Marsh
B From Reading
C From London Paddington to Cardiff Central
D From London Paddington
E From Henley-on-Thames
F To Great Malvern
G From Southampton Central to Manchester Piccadilly
H From Guildford to Newcastle
I To Bristol Temple Meads
J From London Paddington to Bristol Temple Meads
K From Bournemouth to Newcastle

For complete services between Banbury and Birmingham, refer to Table T71

T116 UPDATE: The route between Theale and Bedwyn will be CLOSED TO ALL TRAINS. Rail replacement buses on 4-7 June; 9-12 July; 16 July to 05 August; 28-30 August; 08-11 October and 19-22 November.

London and Reading - Bedwyn, Oxford, Banbury and Birmingham

	GW	GW	GW	GW	XC	GW	GW	GW	GW	GW	GW	GW	GW	XC	GW		GW	GW	GW	GW	GW	GW	GW	GW
	■1 A		◇1 B		◇1 C			◇	◇1 D	◇1 E		◇1 F		◇1 G				◇1 H	◇1 D	■1 I		◇1 J	◇1 K	
London Paddington 15 ⊖ d	07 30	07 12	07 45				07 26	07 52	08 00	08 03	08 07	08 15	07 44				07 56	08 22	08 30	08 35	08 12	08 45	08 45	
Ealing Broadway ⊖ d		07 20					07 35						07 52				08 05				08 20			
Slough 3 d		07 41					07 57	08 09					08 15				08 27	08 38			08 41			
Maidenhead 3 d		07 52					08 04						08 26				08 34				08 52			
Twyford 3 d		08 00					08 12						08 34				08 42				09 00			
Reading 7 a	07 54	08 08	08 09				08 20	08 24	08 27	08 30	08 37	08 39	08 42				08 50	08 51	08 54		09 08	09 09	09 09	
d	07 58			08 14	08 15		08 21	08 25		08 33	08 41	08 42		08 45			08 51	08 54	08 58	09u03				09 10
Reading West d				08 16																				09 12
Theale d				08 22							08 48													09 18
Aldermaston d				08 27																				09 23
Midgham d				08 31																				09 27
Thatcham d				08 36							08 57													09 32
Newbury Racecourse d				08 40																				09 36
Newbury a				08 45						08 49	09 03									09 18				09 42
d											09 03													
Kintbury d											09 09													
Hungerford d											09 14													
Bedwyn a											09 24													
Tilehurst d							08 25										08 55							
Pangbourne d							08 29										08 59							
Goring & Streatley d							08 34										09 04							
Cholsey d							08 39										09 09							
Didcot Parkway a	08 11						08 48					08 55					09 18		09 12					
d						08 30									09 03									
Appleford d															09 07									
Culham d																								
Radley d						08 37																		
Oxford 115 a					08 38	08 46		08 51						09 10	09 17			09 21						
d					08 40									09 12										
Tackley d																								
Heyford d																								
Kings Sutton d																								
Banbury 71 a					08 56									09 28										
Leamington Spa 3 a					09 13									09 46										
Coventry a					09 25																			
Birmingham International a					09 37																			
Birmingham New Street 12 71 a					09 48									10 18										

	XC	GW	GW	GW	GW	GW	GW		GW	XC	XC	GW	GW	GW	GW	GW	GW	GW	GW	XC	GW	GW	GW
	◇1 C			◇1	◇1 D	◇1 L				◇1 M	◇1 N		O	◇1 P	Q	◇1 D		◇1 B		◇1 C			◇1
London Paddington 15 ⊖ d			08 27	08 52	09 00	09 03	09 07		08 42				08 57	09 22		09 30	09 14	09 45				09 27	09 52
Ealing Broadway ⊖ d			08 35						08 50				09 05				09 22					09 35	
Slough 3 d			08 57	09 08					09 10				09 27	09 38			09 43					09 57	10 08
Maidenhead 3 d			09 04						09 22				09 34				09 54					10 04	
Twyford 3 d			09 12						09 30				09 42		←		10 02					10 12	
Reading 7 a			09 20	09 21	09 24	09 27	09 37		09 38				09 50	09 51	09 50	09 55	10 10	10 10				10 20	10 21
d	09 15		09 21	09 23			09 40			09 45	09 45		09 55	09 53	09 55	09 58			10 12	10 15		10 22	10 23
Reading West d													→						10 14				
Theale d							09 48												10 20				
Aldermaston d																			10 25				
Midgham d																			10 29				
Thatcham d							09 56												10 34				
Newbury Racecourse d																			10 38				
Newbury a							10 02												10 44				
d							10 03																
Kintbury d							10 09																
Hungerford d							10 13																
Bedwyn a							10 23																
Tilehurst d			09 25												09 58							10 26	
Pangbourne d			09 29												10 03							10 30	
Goring & Streatley d			09 34												10 08							10 35	
Cholsey d			09 39												10 13							10 40	
Didcot Parkway a			09 48												10 21	10 12						10 49	
d		09 30										10 00									10 31		
Appleford d																					10 35		
Culham d		09 35																					
Radley d		09 39										10 07											
Oxford 115 a	09 38	09 47		09 52						10 10	10 10	10 15		10 19						10 38	10 45		10 50
d	09 40									10 12	10 12	10 17								10 40			
Tackley d												10 25											
Heyford d												10 30											
Kings Sutton d												10 38											
Banbury 71 a	09 56									10 28	10 28	10 45								10 56			
Leamington Spa 3 a	10 13									10 46	10 46									11 13			
Coventry a	10 26																			11 25			
Birmingham International a	10 37																			11 37			
Birmingham New Street 12 71 a	10 48									11 18	11 18									11 48			

A To Penzance
B To Swansea
C From Bournemouth to Manchester Piccadilly
D To Bristol Temple Meads
E from 15 September. To Exeter St Davids
F To Cheltenham Spa
G From Southampton Central to Newcastle
H To Hereford
I until 8 September. To Paignton
J from 15 September. To Swansea
K until 8 September. To Pembroke Dock. The Pembroke Coast Express
L from 15 September. To Plymouth
M until 21 July, from 13 October. To Newcastle
N from 28 July until 6 October. To Glasgow Central
O To Didcot Parkway
P To Worcester Foregate Street
Q From London Paddington

For complete services between Banbury and Birmingham, refer to Table T71

London and Reading - Bedwyn, Oxford, Banbury and Birmingham

	GW	GW	GW	GW	GW	XC	GW	GW	GW	GW	GW	GW	GW	GW	XC		GW	GW	GW	GW	GW	GW	GW	XC
	◇1 A	◇1 B			◇1 C	◇1 D		E	◇1 F	G	◇1 A		◇1 H		◇1 I				◇1	◇1 A	◇1 J			◇1 K
London Paddington 15 ⊖ d	10 00	10 03	10 07	09 42	10 15			09 57	10 22		10 30	10 12	10 45					10 27	10 52	11 00	11 03	11 07	10 42	
Ealing Broadway ⊖ d				09 50				10 05				10 20						10 35					10 50	
Slough 3 d				10 11				10 27	10 38			10 41						10 57	11 08				11 11	
Maidenhead 3 d				10 22				10 34				10 52						11 04					11 22	
Twyford 3 d				10 30				10 42		←		11 00						11 12					11 30	
Reading 7 a	10 24	10 27	10 37	10 38	10 39			10 50	10 51	10 50	10 54	11 08	11 09					11 20	11 21	11 24	11 27	11 37	11 38	
d			10 38		10 42	10 45		10 56	10 54	10 56	10 58			11 10	11 15			11 22	11 23			11 38		11 45
Reading West d								→						11 12										
Theale d			10 45											11 18								11 45		
Aldermaston d														11 23										
Midgham d														11 27										
Thatcham d			10 54											11 32								11 54		
Newbury Racecourse d														11 36										
Newbury a			11 00											11 42								12 00		
d			11 00																			12 00		
Kintbury d			11 06																			12 06		
Hungerford d			11 11																			12 11		
Bedwyn a			11 20																			12 20		
Tilehurst d										11 00								11 26						
Pangbourne d										11 04								11 30						
Goring & Streatley d										11 09								11 35						
Cholsey d										11 14								11 40						
Didcot Parkway a					10 55					11 24	11 12							11 50						
d							11 01										11 30							
Appleford d																								
Culham d																								
Radley d							11 08																	
Oxford 115 a						11 10	11 16		11 20						11 38		11 43		11 48					12 06
d						11 12									11 40									12 12
Tackley d																								
Heyford d																								
Kings Sutton d																								
Banbury 71 a						11 28									11 56									12 28
Leamington Spa 3 a						11 46									12 13									12 46
Coventry a															12 26									
Birmingham International a															12 37									
Birmingham New Street 12 71 a						12 18									12 48									13 18

	XC	GW	GW	GW	GW	GW	GW		GW	GW	XC	GW	GW	GW	GW	GW	GW	GW	GW	XC	GW	GW	GW
	◇1 L			◇1 M	◇1 N	◇1 O			◇1 H		◇1 I			◇	◇1 A	◇1 P			◇1 C	◇1 D			◇1 Q
London Paddington 15 ⊖ d			10 57	11 22	11 30	11 30	11 12		11 45				11 27	11 51	12 00	12 03	12 07	11 42	12 15			11 57	12 22
Ealing Broadway ⊖ d			11 05				11 20						11 35					11 50				12 05	
Slough 3 d			11 27	11 38			11 41						11 57	12 08				12 11				12 27	12 38
Maidenhead 3 d			11 34				11 52						12 04					12 22				12 34	
Twyford 3 d			11 42				12 00						12 12					12 30				12 42	
Reading 7 a			11 50	11 51	11 55	11 56	12 08		12 09				12 20	12 23	12 26	12 29	12 37	12 38	12 39			12 51	12 51
d	11 45		11 51	11 53	11 58	11 58				12 10	12 15		12 21	12 25			12 39		12 42	12 45		12 53	12 53
Reading West d										12 12													
Theale d										12 18							12 46						
Aldermaston d										12 23													
Midgham d										12 27													
Thatcham d										12 32							12 55						
Newbury Racecourse d										12 36													
Newbury a										12 42							13 01						
d																	13 01						
Kintbury d																	13 07						
Hungerford d																	13 12						
Bedwyn a																	13 21						
Tilehurst d			11 55										12 25									12 57	
Pangbourne d			11 59										12 29									13 01	
Goring & Streatley d			12 04										12 34									13 06	
Cholsey d			12 09										12 39									13 11	
Didcot Parkway a			12 18		12 12	12 12							12 48						12 55			13 20	
d		12 01										12 31									13 01		
Appleford d												12 35											
Culham d																							
Radley d		12 08																			13 08		
Oxford 115 a	12 06	12 16		12 20							12 38	12 45		12 50						13 10	13 16		13 20
d	12 12	12 18									12 40									13 12			
Tackley d		12 26																					
Heyford d		12 31																					
Kings Sutton d		12 39																					
Banbury 71 a	12 28	12 46									12 56									13 28			
Leamington Spa 3 a	12 46										13 13									13 46			
Coventry a											13 25												
Birmingham International a											13 37												
Birmingham New Street 12 71 a	13 18										13 48									14 18			

A To Bristol Temple Meads
B from 15 September. To Penzance. The Cornish Riviera
C To Cheltenham Spa
D From Southampton Central to Newcastle
E To Didcot Parkway
F To Hereford
G From London Paddington
H To Swansea
I From Bournemouth to Manchester Piccadilly
J from 15 September. To Plymouth
K until 21 July, from 13 October. To Newcastle
L from 28 July until 6 October. To Glasgow Central
M To Great Malvern
N from 15 September. To Bristol Temple Meads
O until 8 September. To Bristol Temple Meads
P from 15 September. To Penzance. The Royal Duchy
Q To Moreton-in-Marsh

For complete services between Banbury and Birmingham, refer to Table T71

Table T116-F

Saturdays

26 May to 8 December

London and Reading - Bedwyn, Oxford, Banbury and Birmingham

	GW ◇ A	GW ◇ B	GW ◇ C	GW	GW ◇ D	GW	XC ◇ E	GW	GW	GW ◇	GW ◇ A	GW F	GW	GW	XC ◇ G		GW	GW	GW ◇ H	GW ◇ A	GW ◇ D	GW	GW	XC ◇ E
London Paddington ⊖ d	12 30	12 33	12 33	12 12	12 45				12 27	12 52	13 00	13 03	13 07	12 42				12 57	13 22	13 30	13 45		13 12	
Ealing Broadway ⊖ d				12 20					12 35					12 50				13 05					13 20	
Slough d				12 41					12 57	13 08				13 11				13 27	13 38				13 43	
Maidenhead d				12 52					13 04					13 22				13 34					13 54	
Twyford d				13 00					13 12					13 30				13 42					14 02	
Reading a	12 54	12 57		13 08	13 09				13 20	13 21	13 24	13 27	13 37	13 38				13 50	13 51	13 55	14 09		14 10	
Reading d	12 58	13 00	13u00			13 10	13 15		13 23	13 23			13 38		13 45			13 51	13 53	13 58		14 10		14 15
Reading West d						13 12																14 12		
Theale d						13 18							13 45									14 18		
Aldermaston d						13 23																14 23		
Midgham d						13 27																14 27		
Thatcham d						13 32							13 54									14 32		
Newbury Racecourse d						13 36																14 36		
Newbury a		13 14	13 14			13 42							14 00									14 42		
Newbury d													14 00											
Kintbury d													14 06											
Hungerford d													14 11											
Bedwyn a													14 20											
Tilehurst d									13 27									13 55						
Pangbourne d									13 31									13 59						
Goring & Streatley d									13 36									14 04						
Cholsey d									13 41									14 09						
Didcot Parkway a	13 11								13 50									14 18		14 12				
Didcot Parkway d								13 31									13 59							
Appleford d																								
Culham d								13 36																
Radley d																	14 06							
Oxford 115 a							13 38	13 46		13 51					14 06		14 15		14 19					14 38
Oxford d							13 40								14 11		14 17							14 40
Tackley d																	14 25							
Heyford d																	14 30							
Kings Sutton d																	14 38							
Banbury 71 a							13 56								14 28		14 45							14 56
Leamington Spa a							14 13								14 46									15 13
Coventry a							14 25																	15 25
Birmingham International a							14 37																	15 37
Birmingham New Street 71 a							14 48								15 18									15 48

	GW	GW	GW ◇	GW ◇ A	GW ◇ F	GW	GW		GW ◇ I	XC ◇ J	GW	GW	GW ◇ H	GW ◇ K	GW ◇ L	GW	GW ◇ D	GW	XC ◇ E	GW	GW	GW ◇	GW ◇ A
London Paddington ⊖ d		13 27	13 52	14 00	14 03	14 07	13 42		14 15			13 57	14 22	14 30	14 30	14 12	14 45				14 27	14 52	15 00
Ealing Broadway ⊖ d		13 35					13 50					14 05				14 20					14 35		
Slough d		13 57	14 08				14 12					14 27	14 38			14 41					14 57	15 08	
Maidenhead d		14 04					14 23					14 34				14 52					15 04		
Twyford d		14 12					14 31					14 42				15 00					15 12		
Reading a		14 20	14 21	14 24	14 27	14 37	14 39		14 39			14 50	14 51	14 54	14 55	15 08	15 09				15 20	15 21	15 24
Reading d		14 22	14 23			14 38			14 42	14 45		14 51	14 53	14 58	14 58			15 10	15 15		15 21	15 23	
Reading West d																		15 12					
Theale d						14 45												15 18					
Aldermaston d																		15 23					
Midgham d																		15 27					
Thatcham d						14 54												15 32					
Newbury Racecourse d																		15 36					
Newbury a						15 00												15 42					
Newbury d						15 00																	
Kintbury d						15 06																	
Hungerford d						15 11																	
Bedwyn a						15 20																	
Tilehurst d		14 26										14 55									15 25		
Pangbourne d		14 30										14 59									15 29		
Goring & Streatley d		14 35										15 04									15 34		
Cholsey d		14 40										15 09									15 39		
Didcot Parkway a		14 49							14 55			15 21		15 12	15 12						15 48		
Didcot Parkway d	14 31										15 00									15 30			
Appleford d	14 35																						
Culham d																				15 35			
Radley d											15 07												
Oxford 115 a	14 46		14 51							15 10	15 16		15 20						15 38	15 45		15 50	
Oxford d										15 12									15 40				
Tackley d																							
Heyford d																							
Kings Sutton d																							
Banbury 71 a										15 28									15 56				
Leamington Spa a										15 46									16 13				
Coventry a																			16 25				
Birmingham International a																			16 37				
Birmingham New Street 71 a										16 18									16 48				

A To Bristol Temple Meads
B from 15 September. To Taunton
C until 8 September. To Paignton
D To Swansea
E From Bournemouth to Manchester Piccadilly
F from 15 September. To Penzance
G To Newcastle
H To Great Malvern
I To Cheltenham Spa
J From Southampton Central to Newcastle
K from 15 September. To Bristol Temple Meads
L until 8 September. To Weston-super-Mare

For complete services between Banbury and Birmingham, refer to Table T71

Table T116-F

Saturdays

26 May to 8 December

London and Reading - Bedwyn, Oxford, Banbury and Birmingham

	GW ◇ A	GW	GW	XC ◇ B	GW	GW	GW ◇ C	GW ◇ D	GW	GW ◇ E	GW	XC ◇ F	GW	GW	GW ◇		GW ◇ G	GW ◇ H	GW ◇ I	GW	GW	GW ◇ J	XC ◇ K	GW
London Paddington ⊖ d	15 03	15 07	14 42			14 57	15 20	15 30	15 12	15 45				15 27	15 52		16 00	16 00	16 03	16 07	15 42	16 15		
Ealing Broadway ⊖ d			14 50			15 05			15 20					15 35							15 50			
Slough d			15 13			15 27	15 37		15 41					15 57	16 08						16 11			
Maidenhead d			15 24			15 34			15 52					16 04							16 22			
Twyford d			15 32			15 42			16 00					16 12							16 30			
Reading a	15 27	15 37	15 40			15 50	15 52	15 55	16 08	16 09				16 20	16 21		16 24	16 25	16 27	16 37	16 38	16 39		
Reading d		15 38		15 45		15 53	15 54	15 58			16 10	16 15		16 21	16 23					16 38		16 42	16 45	
Reading West d											16 12													
Theale d		15 45									16 18									16 45				
Aldermaston d											16 23													
Midgham d											16 27													
Thatcham d		15 54									16 32									16 54				
Newbury Racecourse d											16 36													
Newbury a		16 00									16 42									17 00				
Newbury d		16 00																		17 00				
Kintbury d		16 06																		17 06				
Hungerford d		16 11																		17 11				
Bedwyn a		16 20																		17 20				
Tilehurst d						15 57								16 25										
Pangbourne d						16 01								16 29										
Goring & Streatley d						16 06								16 34										
Cholsey d						16 11								16 39										
Didcot Parkway a						16 20		16 12						16 48								16 55		
Didcot Parkway d					15 59								16 30											17 01
Appleford d													16 34											
Culham d																								
Radley d					16 06																			17 08
Oxford 115 a				16 06	16 15		16 19					16 38	16 44		16 49								17 10	17 16
Oxford d				16 11	16 17							16 40											17 12	
Tackley d					16 25																			
Heyford d					16 30																			
Kings Sutton d					16 38																			
Banbury 71 a				16 28	16 45							16 56											17 28	
Leamington Spa a				16 46								17 13											17 46	
Coventry a												17 25												
Birmingham International a												17 37												
Birmingham New Street 71 a				17 18								17 48											18 18	

	GW	GW ◇ L	GW ◇ M	GW	GW ◇ E	GW	XC ◇ F		GW	GW	GW ◇	GW ◇ D	GW ◇ A	GW	GW	XC ◇ N	GW	GW	GW ◇ O	GW ◇ P	GW	GW ◇ Q	GW
London Paddington ⊖ d	15 57	16 22	16 30	16 12	16 45					16 27	16 52	17 00	17 03	17 07	16 42			16 57	17 22	17 30	17 12	17 45	
Ealing Broadway ⊖ d	16 05			16 20						16 35					16 50			17 05			17 20		
Slough d	16 27	16 38		16 41						16 57	17 08				17 11			17 27	17 38		17 41		
Maidenhead d	16 34			16 52						17 04					17 22			17 34			17 52		
Twyford d	16 42			17 00						17 12					17 30			17 42			18 00		
Reading a	16 50	16 51	16 54	17 08	17 09					17 20	17 21	17 24	17 27	17 37	17 38			17 50	17 51	17 54	18 08	18 09	
Reading d	16 51	16 54	16 58			17 10	17 15			17 21	17 23			17 38		17 45		17 51	17 54	17 58			18 10
Reading West d						17 12																	18 12
Theale d						17 18								17 45									18 18
Aldermaston d						17 23																	18 23
Midgham d						17 27																	18 27
Thatcham d						17 32								17 54									18 32
Newbury Racecourse d						17 36																	18 36
Newbury a						17 42								18 00									18 41
Newbury d														18 00									
Kintbury d														18 06									
Hungerford d														18 11									
Bedwyn a														18 20									
Tilehurst d	16 55									17 25								17 55					
Pangbourne d	16 59									17 29								17 59					
Goring & Streatley d	17 04									17 34								18 04					
Cholsey d	17 09									17 39								18 09					
Didcot Parkway a	17 18		17 11							17 48								18 18		18 12			
Didcot Parkway d									17 31								18 01						
Appleford d																							
Culham d									17 36														
Radley d																	18 08						
Oxford 115 a		17 20					17 38		17 46		17 51					18 10	18 16		18 20				
Oxford d							17 40									18 12	18 18						
Tackley d																	18 26						
Heyford d																	18 31						
Kings Sutton d																	18 39						
Banbury 71 a							17 56									18 28	18 46						
Leamington Spa a							18 13									18 46							
Coventry a							18 25																
Birmingham International a							18 37																
Birmingham New Street 71 a							18 48									19 18							

A from 15 September. To Penzance
B To Newcastle
C To Great Malvern
D To Bristol Temple Meads
E To Swansea
F From Bournemouth to Manchester Piccadilly
G from 15 September. To Bristol Temple Meads
H until 8 September. To Bristol Temple Meads
I from 15 September. To Plymouth
J To Cheltenham Spa
K From Southampton Central to Newcastle
L To Hereford
M To Paignton. The Torbay Express
N To Leeds
O To Worcester Foregate Street
P To Weston-super-Mare
Q To Carmarthen

For complete services between Banbury and Birmingham, refer to Table T71

T116 UPDATE: The route between Theale and Bedwyn will be CLOSED TO ALL TRAINS. Rail replacement buses on 4-7 June; 9-12 July; 16 July to 05 August; 28-30 August; 08-11 October and 19-22 November.

Table T116-F

Saturdays

26 May to 8 December

London and Reading - Bedwyn, Oxford, Banbury and Birmingham

		XC	GW	GW	GW	GW	GW	GW	GW	GW	XC	GW	GW	GW	GW	GW	GW	GW	XC	GW	GW	GW	GW	GW
		◇1 A ✕			◇1	◇1 B ☕	◇1 C ☕			◇1 D ☕	◇1 E ✕			◇1 F ☕	◇1 G ☕		◇1 H ☕		◇1 A ✕			◇1	◇1 G ☕	◇1 I ☕
London Paddington [15] ⊖	d			17 27	17 52	18 00	18 03	18 07	17 42	18 15			17 57	18 22	18 30	18 12	18 45				18 27	18 52	19 00	19 03
Ealing Broadway ⊖	d			17 35					17 50				18 05			18 20					18 35			
Slough [3]	d			17 57	18 08				18 11				18 27	18 38		18 41					18 57	19 08		
Maidenhead [3]	d			18 04					18 22				18 34			18 52					19 04			
Twyford [3]	d			18 12					18 30				18 42			19 00					19 12			
Reading [7]	a			18 20	18 21	18 24	18 27	18 37	18 38	18 39			18 50	18 51	18 54	19 08	19 09				19 20	19 21	19 24	19 27
	d	18 15		18 21	18 23			18 38		18 42	18 45		18 51	18 54	18 58			19 10	19 15		19 21	19 23		19 31
Reading West	d																	19 12						
Theale	d							18 45										19 18						
Aldermaston	d																	19 23						
Midgham	d																	19 27						
Thatcham	d							18 54										19 32						
Newbury Racecourse	d																	19 36						
Newbury	a							19 00										19 41						19 47
	d							19 00																
Kintbury	d							19 06																
Hungerford	d							19 11																
Bedwyn	a							19 20																
Tilehurst	d			18 25									18 55								19 25			
Pangbourne	d			18 29									18 59								19 29			
Goring & Streatley	d			18 34									19 04								19 34			
Cholsey	d			18 39									19 09								19 39			
Didcot Parkway	a			18 48						18 55			19 18		19 11						19 48			
	d		18 30									19 01								19 30				
Appleford	d		18 34																					
Culham	d																			19 35				
Radley	d											19 08												
Oxford 115	a	18 38	18 45		18 50						19 10	19 16		19 20					19 38	19 45		19 50		
	d	18 40									19 12								19 40	19 47				
Tackley	d																			19 55				
Heyford	d																			20 00				
Kings Sutton	d																			20 08				
Banbury 71	a	18 56									19 28								19 56	20 15				
Leamington Spa [8]	a	19 13									19 46								20 13					
Coventry	a	19 25																	20 26					
Birmingham International	a	19 37																	20 37					
Birmingham New Street [12] 71	a	19 48									20 18								20 48					

		GW	GW	GW	GW	XC	GW	GW	GW	GW	GW	GW	GW	XC	GW	GW	GW	GW	GW	GW	GW	GW	XC
		◇1 J ☕			◇1 K ☕	◇1			◇1	◇1 B ☕		◇1 H ☕		◇1 A			◇1 L ☕	◇1 B ☕	◇1 I ☕	◇1 J ☕		◇1 D ☕	◇1
London Paddington [15] ⊖	d	19 03		18 42	19 15			18 57	19 22	19 30	19 12	19 45				19 27	19 52	20 00	20 03	20 03	19 42	20 15	
Ealing Broadway ⊖	d			18 50				19 05			19 20					19 35					19 50		
Slough [3]	d			19 11				19 27	19 38		19 41					19 57	20 08				20 11		
Maidenhead [3]	d			19 22				19 34			19 52					20 04					20 22		
Twyford [3]	d			19 30				19 42			20 00					20 12					20 30		
Reading [7]	a	19 28		19 38	19 39			19 50	19 51	19 55	20 08	20 09				20 20	20 21	20 24	20 27	20 28	20 38	20 39	
	d	19 31			19 42	19 45		19 51	19 53	19 58			20 10	20 15		20 21	20 23	20 28	20 30	20 30		20 42	20 45
Reading West	d												20 12										
Theale	d												20 18										
Aldermaston	d												20 23										
Midgham	d												20 27										
Thatcham	d												20 32										
Newbury Racecourse	d												20 36										
Newbury	a	19 47											20 39						20 44	20 44			
	d		20 03										20 51										
Kintbury	d		20 10										20 57										
Hungerford	d		20 13										21 01										
Bedwyn	a		20 23										21 10										
Tilehurst	d							19 55								20 25							
Pangbourne	d							19 59								20 29							
Goring & Streatley	d							20 04								20 34							
Cholsey	d							20 09								20 39							
Didcot Parkway	a				19 55			20 18		20 11						20 48		20 41				20 55	
	d						20 01								20 39								
Appleford	d														20 43								
Culham	d																						
Radley	d						20 08																
Oxford 115	a					20 10	20 16		20 21					20 38	20 54		20 46						21 10
	d					20 12								20 40									21 12
Tackley	d																						
Heyford	d																						
Kings Sutton	d																						
Banbury 71	a					20 29								20 56									21 28
Leamington Spa [8]	a					20 47								21 13									21 46
Coventry	a													21 26									22 00
Birmingham International	a													21 37									22 10
Birmingham New Street [12] 71	a					21 16								21 48									22 21

A From Bournemouth to Manchester Piccadilly
B To Bristol Temple Meads
C from 15 September. To Penzance
D To Cheltenham Spa
E From Southampton Central
F To Hereford
G To Taunton
H To Swansea
I from 15 September. To Plymouth
J until 8 September. To Plymouth
K from 15 September. To Swansea
L To Great Malvern

For complete services between Banbury and Birmingham, refer to Table T71

Table T116-F

Saturdays

26 May to 8 December

London and Reading - Bedwyn, Oxford, Banbury and Birmingham

		GW	GW	GW	GW	GW	GW	GW	GW	XC	GW	GW	GW	GW	XC	GW	GW	GW	GW	GW	GW	GW	GW	GW
			A	◇1	B	◇1 C ☕		◇1 D ☕		◇1 E		◇1			◇1		A	◇1	◇1 F ☕	B			◇ G	◇1 H ☕
London Paddington [15] ⊖	d		19 57	20 22		20 30	20 12	20 45				20 50	20 27	20 42			20 57	21 20	21 32			21 12	21 50	22 00
Ealing Broadway ⊖	d		20 05				20 20						20 35	20 50			21 05					21 20		
Slough [3]	d		20 27	20 38			20 41					21 06	20 57	21 11			21 27	21 36				21 45	22 06	
Maidenhead [3]	d		20 34				20 52						21 04	21 22			21 34	21 43				21 56		
Twyford [3]	d		20 42		←		21 00						21 12	21 30			21 42			←		22 04		
Reading [7]	a		20 50	20 51	20 50	20 54	21 08	21 09				21 19	21 20	21 38			21 50	21 54	21 57	21 50		22 12	22 22	22 26
	d		20 56	20 53	20 56	20 58			21 10	21 15		21 21	21 30		21 45		22 05	21 57	21 59	22 05	22 10		22 24	22 29
Reading West	d		→						21 12								→				22 12			
Theale	d								21 18												22 18			
Aldermaston	d								21 23												22 23			
Midgham	d								21 27												22 27			
Thatcham	d								21 32												22 32			
Newbury Racecourse	d								21 36												22 36			
Newbury	a								21 39												22 39			
	d								21 40												22 40			
Kintbury	d								21 46												22 45			
Hungerford	d								21 50												22 51			
Bedwyn	a								21 59												22 59			
Tilehurst	d				20 59								21 33							22 08				
Pangbourne	d				21 04								21 38							22 13				
Goring & Streatley	d				21 09								21 43							22 18				
Cholsey	d				21 14								21 48							22 23				
Didcot Parkway	a				21 23	21 11						21 36	21 57					22 12	22 13	22 32			22 38	22 42
	d	21 00									21 30	21 38				22 06		22 13					22 39	
Appleford	d																							
Culham	d										21 35													
Radley	d	21 07									21 39					22 13								
Oxford 115	a	21 15		21 20						21 38	21 48	21 53			22 10	22 21		22 26					22 50	
	d	21 17								21 39					22 12									
Tackley	d	21 25																						
Heyford	d	21 30																						
Kings Sutton	d	21 38																						
Banbury 71	a	21 45								21 56					22 28									
Leamington Spa [8]	a									22 13					22 46									
Coventry	a									22 25														
Birmingham International	a									22 36														
Birmingham New Street [12] 71	a									22 47					23 17									

		GW	GW	GW	GW	GW	GW	GW	GW	GW	GW	GW	GW	GW	GW
					◇1	🚌	◇1 F ☕			◇		◇1 F ☕	◇		
London Paddington [15] ⊖	d			21 42	22 20		22 35		22 12	22 50	22 43	23 30	23 33	23 20	23 43
Ealing Broadway ⊖	d			21 51					22 20		22 52			23 28	23 51
Slough [3]	d			22 16	22 36				22 45	23 08	23 18		23 51	23 55	00 15
Maidenhead [3]	d			22 28	22 43				22 56	23 15	23 29		23 58	00 06	00 26
Twyford [3]	d			22 36					23 04		23 37			00 14	00 34
Reading [7]	a			22 43	22 54		22 59		23 12	23 28	23 45	00 03	00 11	00 22	00 42
	d		22 35		22 56		23 02	23 13	23 13	23 30	23 46	00 05	00 13	00 23	
Reading West	d							23 15							
Theale	d							23 21							
Aldermaston	d							23 26							
Midgham	d							23 30							
Thatcham	d							23 35							
Newbury Racecourse	d							23 39							
Newbury	a							23 42							
	d							23 43							
Kintbury	d							23 49							
Hungerford	d							23 53							
Bedwyn	a							00 01							
Tilehurst	d		22 38						23 17		23 49			00 27	
Pangbourne	d		22 43						23 21		23 54			00 31	
Goring & Streatley	d		22 48						23 26		23 59			00 36	
Cholsey	d		22 53						23 31		00 04			00 41	
Didcot Parkway	a		23 00		23 11		23 17		23 40	23 45	00 13	00 20	00 28	00 50	
	d	22 45	23 01		23 13					23 46			00 29		
Appleford	d														
Culham	d														
Radley	d	22 52													
Oxford 115	a	23 00	23 13		23 27					00 01			00 43		
	d					23 41									
Tackley	d					00s01									
Heyford	d					00s16									
Kings Sutton	d														
Banbury 71	a					00 41									
Leamington Spa [8]	a														
Coventry	a														
Birmingham International	a														
Birmingham New Street [12] 71	a														

A To Didcot Parkway
B From London Paddington
C To Exeter St Davids
D To Swansea
E From Bournemouth
F To Bristol Temple Meads
G To Worcester Shrub Hill
H To Cardiff Central

For complete services between Banbury and Birmingham, refer to Table T71

Table T116-F

London and Reading - Bedwyn, Oxford, Banbury and Birmingham

Sundays

20 May to 2 December

		GW	GW	GW	GW	GW	GW	GW	GW	GW	GW	GW	GW	GW	GW	GW		GW	GW	GW	GW	GW	GW	GW	GW
		A		◇■ B	◇ A		A	bus	A						C	D		◇■ E	◇■ F		◇■ G	◇■ H	I	J	C
London Paddington ⊖	d									00 05	00 30	01 00	06 45		07 29	07 29		07 57	08 00		08 00	08 03			08 02
Ealing Broadway ⊖	d									00 13	00 38	01 08	06 53		07 37	07 37									08 10
Slough	d								00 15	00 38	01 03	01 26	07 16		08 04	08 04					08 21	08 26			08 34
Maidenhead	d						00 06		00 26	00 49	01 10	01 33	07 26		08 14	08 14					08 28	08 34			08 42
Twyford	d						00 14		00 34	00 57	01 18	01 41	07 34		08 22	08 22							←	←	08 50
Reading	a						00 22		00 42	01 05	01 26	01 49	07 41		08 29	08 29		08 35	08 39		08 44	08 46	08 29	08 29	08 57
	d			00 05	00 13	00 15	00 23							08 12	08 49	08 51		08 38	08 39	08 42	08 46	08 47	08 49	08 51	09 16
Reading West	d					00s18								08 15	→	→									→
Theale	d					00s24								08 21						08 50					
Aldermaston	d					00s29								08 26											
Midgham	d					00s32								08 29											
Thatcham	d					00s37								08 34						08 58					
Newbury Racecourse	d					00s42																			
Newbury	a					00 45								08 41						09 04					
	d																			09 04					
Kintbury	d																			09 11					
Hungerford	d																			09 15					
Bedwyn	a																			09 23					
Tilehurst	d						00 27																08 53	08 55	
Pangbourne	d						00 31																08 57	08 59	
Goring & Streatley	d						00 36																09 02	09 04	
Cholsey	d	00 04					00 41																09 07	09 09	
Didcot Parkway	a	00 13		00 20	00 28		00 50											08 53	08 57		09 01	09 02	09 14	09 16	
	d		00 18		00 29			01 00													09 02	09 03			
Appleford	d							01s10																	
Culham	d							01s20																	
Radley	d		00 25					01s30																	
Oxford 115	a		00 35		00 43			01 45													09 13	09 15			
	d																								
Tackley	d																								
Heyford	d																								
Kings Sutton	d																								
Banbury 71	a																								
Leamington Spa	a																								
Coventry	a																								
Birmingham International	a																								
Birmingham New Street 71	a																								

		GW	GW	XC	GW	GW	GW	GW		GW	GW	GW	GW	GW	GW	GW	GW	GW	GW	GW	GW	GW	GW	GW
		◇■ K	◇■ L	◇■ M	◇■ N		◇■ O	P		Q	◇■ R	I	◇■ S	◇■ T	U	V	◇■ W	◇■ E	X	◇■ Y	◇■ Z	X	V	V
London Paddington ⊖	d	08 27	08 30		08 33		08 33	08 15		08 15	08 34		08 37	08 37		08 30	08 57	08 57		09 00	09 03	08 45	09 04	
Ealing Broadway ⊖	d							08 23		08 23						08 38						08 53		
Slough	d							08 47		08 46	08 52		08 59	08 59		09 01						09 16	09 24	
Maidenhead	d							08 55		08 54						09 11						09 26	09 31	
Twyford	d							09 03		09 02		←			←	09 19						09 34		
Reading	a	09 02	09 06		09 10		09 10	09 11		09 13	09 13	08 57	09 18	09 19	09 13	09 27	09 31	09 34		09 37	09 39	09 42	09 46	
	d		09 10	09 12	09 15		09 15	09 15		09 23	09 15	09 16	09 19	09 20	09 23		09 32	09 37	09 37	09 39	09 39		09 46	
Reading West	d									→									09 40				09 50	
Theale	d																		09 46				09 56	
Aldermaston	d																		09 51				10 01	
Midgham	d																		09 54				10 04	
Thatcham	d																		09 59				10 09	
Newbury Racecourse	d																							
Newbury	a																09 47	09 51	10 05				10 16	
	d																		10 05				10 17	
Kintbury	d																		10 11				10 24	
Hungerford	d																		10 16				10 28	
Bedwyn	a																		10 25				10 36	
Tilehurst	d							09 19				09 20			09 27									
Pangbourne	d							09 23				09 25			09 31									
Goring & Streatley	d							09 28				09 30			09 36									
Cholsey	d							09 33				09 35			09 41									
Didcot Parkway	a		09 25		09 28		09 31	09 40			09 31	09 42	09 34	09 35	09 48					09 50	09 53			
	d					09 28					09 32		09 35	09 36										
Appleford	d																							
Culham	d																							
Radley	d					09 35																		
Oxford 115	a			09 35		09 43					09 46		09 44	09 45										
	d			09 37																				10 00
Tackley	d																							10 09
Heyford	d																							10 13
Kings Sutton	d																							10 23
Banbury 71	a			09 54																				10 30
Leamington Spa	a			10 11																				
Coventry	a			10 25																				
Birmingham International	a			10 38																				
Birmingham New Street 71	a			10 50																				

- **A** not 20 May. From London Paddington
- **B** not 20 May. From London Paddington to Bristol Temple Meads
- **C** until 9 September. To Didcot Parkway
- **D** from 16 September. To Didcot Parkway
- **E** until 9 September. To Penzance
- **F** from 16 September. To Penzance
- **G** until 9 September. To Great Malvern
- **H** from 16 September. To Great Malvern
- **I** until 9 September. From London Paddington
- **J** from 16 September. From London Paddington
- **K** To Cheltenham Spa
- **L** until 9 September. To Swansea
- **M** To Manchester Piccadilly
- **N** from 16 September until 21 October. To Swansea
- **O** from 28 October. To Swansea
- **P** from 16 September until 21 October
- **Q** from 28 October. To Didcot Parkway
- **R** until 9 September. To Hereford
- **S** from 16 September until 21 October. To Hereford
- **T** from 28 October. To Hereford
- **U** from 28 October. From London Paddington
- **V** until 9 September
- **W** from 16 September. To Plymouth
- **X** from 16 September
- **Y** until 9 September. To Weston-super-Mare
- **Z** from 16 September. To Bristol Temple Meads

For complete services between Banbury and Birmingham, refer to Table T71

Table T116-F

London and Reading - Bedwyn, Oxford, Banbury and Birmingham

Sundays

20 May to 2 December

		GW	GW	GW	GW	XC	GW	GW	GW	GW	GW	GW	GW	GW	GW	GW		GW	GW	GW	GW	GW	GW	GW	XC
			A	◇■ B	◇■ C	◇■ D	E	◇■ F	G	◇■ H	◇■ I	J	◇■ K	◇■ L	◇■ M			G	G	J	A	◇■ N	◇■ O	◇■ P	◇■ Q
London Paddington ⊖	d		09 07	09 30	09 33			09 34	09 15		09 37	09 30	09 57	10 00	10 03			09 45		10 04	10 02	10 27	10 33	10 30	
Ealing Broadway ⊖	d		09 15						09 23			09 38						09 53			10 10				
Slough	d		09 39					09 56	09 48		10 01	10 01						10 16		10 24	10 33				
Maidenhead	d		09 46						09 54			10 11						10 26		10 31	10 41				
Twyford	d		09 54				←		10 02	←		10 19						10 34			10 49				
Reading	a		10 02	10 07	10 09		10 02	10 10	10 12	10 10	10 16	10 26	10 31	10 39	10 39			10 40		10 46	10 57	11 03	11 08	11 08	
	d		10 14			10 11	10 14	10 15	10 14	10 15	10 18			10 39	10 39				10 44	10 46	11 14		11 08	11 09	11 11
Reading West	d		→					→											10 47	10 50	→				
Theale	d																		10 53	10 56					
Aldermaston	d																		10 58	11 01					
Midgham	d																		11 01	11 04					
Thatcham	d																		11 06	11 09					
Newbury Racecourse	d																		11 11	11 14					
Newbury	a																		11 15	11 19					
	d																								
Kintbury	d																								
Hungerford	d																								
Bedwyn	a																								
Tilehurst	d						10 18		10 18																
Pangbourne	d						10 22		10 22																
Goring & Streatley	d						10 27		10 27																
Cholsey	d						10 32		10 32																
Didcot Parkway	a						10 41		10 42	10 29	10 32			10 53	10 53								11 22	11 23	
	d	10 03								10 31	10 33					11 00									
Appleford	d																								
Culham	d																								
Radley	d	10 10														11 07									
Oxford 115	a	10 18				10 34				10 44	10 47					11 15									11 35
	d					10 37																			11 37
Tackley	d																								
Heyford	d																								
Kings Sutton	d																								
Banbury 71	a					10 54																			11 54
Leamington Spa	a					11 11																			12 11
Coventry	a					11 25																			12 25
Birmingham International	a					11 39																			12 38
Birmingham New Street 71	a					11 51																			12 50

		GW	GW	GW	GW	GW	GW	GW		GW	GW	GW	GW	GW	GW	GW	GW	GW	GW	XC	GW	GW	GW	GW
		G	E	◇■ R	◇■ S	J	◇■ T	◇■ U		◇■ V		G	G	J	A	◇■ W	◇■ X	◇■ C	◇■ B	◇■ Q	◇ J	G	E	◇■ G
London Paddington ⊖	d	10 15		10 34	10 37	10 30	10 57	11 00		11 03		10 45		11 04	11 02	11 27	11 30	11 33	11 30		11 34	11 15		11 37
Ealing Broadway ⊖	d	10 23				10 38						10 53			11 10							11 23		
Slough	d	10 46		10 54	10 59	11 01						11 16		11 24	11 33						11 54	11 46		11 57
Maidenhead	d	10 54				11 11						11 26		11 31	11 41							11 54		
Twyford	d	11 02	←			11 19						11 34			11 49							12 02	←	
Reading	a	11 12	10 57	11 14	11 16	11 26	11 31	11 39		11 39		11 41		11 46	11 57	12 05	12 05	12 08	12 08		12 12	12 12	11 57	12 14
	d	11 14	11 14	11 16	11 17			11 39		11 39			11 44	11 46	12 14			12 08	12 08	12 11	12 13	12 14	12 14	12 15
Reading West	d														→									
Theale	d												11 51	11 53										
Aldermaston	d																							
Midgham	d																							
Thatcham	d												12 00	12 02										
Newbury Racecourse	d																							
Newbury	a												12 05	12 07										
	d												12 06	12 08										
Kintbury	d												12 12	12 14										
Hungerford	d												12 17	12 19										
Bedwyn	a												12 24	12 26										
Tilehurst	d	11 18	11 18																			12 18	12 18	
Pangbourne	d	11 22	11 23																			12 22	12 23	
Goring & Streatley	d	11 27	11 28																			12 27	12 28	
Cholsey	d	11 32	11 33																			12 32	12 33	
Didcot Parkway	a	11 42	11 42	11 31	11 32			11 53		11 53								12 22	12 23		12 29	12 42	12 42	12 31
	d			11 32	11 32						11 58										12 30			12 33
Appleford	d																							
Culham	d																							
Radley	d										12 05													
Oxford 115	a			11 44	11 45						12 13									12 35	12 43			12 46
	d																			12 37				
Tackley	d																							
Heyford	d																							
Kings Sutton	d																							
Banbury 71	a																			12 54				
Leamington Spa	a																			13 11				
Coventry	a																			13 23				
Birmingham International	a																			13 36				
Birmingham New Street 71	a																			13 48				

- **A** until 9 September. To Didcot Parkway
- **B** until 9 September. To Carmarthen
- **C** from 16 September. To Carmarthen
- **D** From Southampton Central to Manchester Piccadilly
- **E** until 9 September. From London Paddington
- **F** until 9 September. To Great Malvern
- **G** from 16 September
- **H** until 9 September. From London Paddington to Great Malvern
- **I** from 16 September. To Great Malvern
- **J** until 9 September
- **K** To Plymouth
- **L** until 9 September. To Weston-super-Mare
- **M** from 16 September. To Weston-super-Mare
- **N** To Cheltenham Spa
- **O** from 16 September. To Swansea
- **P** until 9 September. To Swansea
- **Q** From Bournemouth to Manchester Piccadilly
- **R** until 9 September. To Hereford
- **S** from 16 September. To Hereford
- **T** To Penzance
- **U** until 9 September. To Bristol Temple Meads
- **V** from 16 September. To Bristol Temple Meads
- **W** until 9 September. To Paignton
- **X** from 16 September. To Paignton

For complete services between Banbury and Birmingham, refer to Table T71

T116 UPDATE: The route between Theale and Bedwyn will be CLOSED TO ALL TRAINS. Rail replacement buses on 4-7 June; 9-12 July; 16 July to 05 August; 28-30 August; 08-11 October and 19-22 November.

Table T116-F

Sundays

20 May to 2 December

London and Reading - Bedwyn, Oxford, Banbury and Birmingham

	GW	GW	GW	GW	GW	GW	GW	GW	GW	XC	XC	GW	GW	GW	GW	XC	GW	GW	GW	GW	GW	GW	GW
	A	◇■ B	◇■ C	◇■ D	◇■ E		F	F	A	◇■ G	◇■ H	I	◇■ J	◇■ K	◇■ L	◇■ M	N	F	◇■ O	◇■ P	A	◇■ Q	◇■ R
London Paddington ⊖ d	11 30	11 57	11 57	12 00	12 03		11 45		12 04			12 02	12 27	12 33	12 30			12 15	12 34	12 37	12 30	12 57	13 00
Ealing Broadway ⊖ d	11 38						11 53					12 10						12 23			12 38		
Slough d	12 01						12 16		12 24			12 33						12 46	12 53	12 59	13 01		
Maidenhead d	12 11						12 26		12 31			12 41						12 54			13 11		
Twyford d	12 19						12 34					12 49					←	13 02			13 19		
Reading a	12 26	12 31	12 31	12 39	12 39		12 42		12 46			12 57	13 03	13 07	13 08		12 57	13 12	13 15	13 16	13 26	13 31	13 39
d		12 32	12 33	12 39	12 39			12 44	12 46	12 54	12 54	13 14		13 09	13 09	13 11	13 14	13 14	13 16	13 17			13 39
Reading West d								12 47	12 50			→											
Theale d								12 53	12 56														
Aldermaston d								12 58	13 01														
Midgham d								13 01	13 04														
Thatcham d								13 06	13 09														
Newbury Racecourse d								13 11	13 14														
Newbury a		12 47	12 47					13 15	13 17														
d																							
Kintbury d																							
Hungerford d																							
Bedwyn a																							
Tilehurst d																	13 18	13 18					
Pangbourne d																	13 23	13 23					
Goring & Streatley d																	13 28	13 28					
Cholsey d																	13 33	13 33					
Didcot Parkway a				12 53	12 53									13 23	13 22		13 42	13 42	13 31	13 32			13 53
d						12 55													13 32	13 32			
Appleford d																							
Culham d																							
Radley d						13 02																	
Oxford 115 a						13 10				13 15	13 15					13 35			13 43	13 44			
d										13 17	13 17					13 37							
Tackley d																							
Heyford d																							
Kings Sutton d																							
Banbury 71 a										13 34	13 34					13 54							
Leamington Spa a										13 51	13 51					14 11							
Coventry a																14 23							
Birmingham International a																14 36							
Birmingham New Street 71 a										14 18	14 19					14 48							

	GW	XC	GW	GW	GW	GW	GW	GW	GW	GW	XC	GW	GW	GW	GW	GW	GW	GW	GW	GW	XC	GW
	◇■ S	◇■	F	F	A		A	I	◇■ T	◇■ U	◇■ M	F	N	◇■ V	◇■ W	◇■ X	A	◇■ Y	■ Z	■ AA	◇■	F
London Paddington ⊖ d	13 03		12 45		13 04			13 02	13 30	13 33		13 15		13 34	13 37		13 30	13 57	14 00	14 03		13 45
Ealing Broadway ⊖ d			12 53					13 10				13 23					13 38					13 53
Slough d			13 16		13 24			13 33				13 46		13 54	13 59		14 01					14 16
Maidenhead d			13 26		13 31			13 41				13 54					14 11					14 26
Twyford d			13 34					13 49				14 02	←				14 19					14 34
Reading a	13 39		13 42		13 46			13 56	14 07	14 08		14 12	13 56	14 15	14 16		14 26	14 31	14 39	14 39		14 42
d	13 39	13 41		13 44	13 46			14 15	14 08	14 10	14 10	14 14	14 15	14 16	14 17			14 32	14 39	14 39	14 41	
Reading West d								→														
Theale d				13 52	13 53																	
Aldermaston d																						
Midgham d																						
Thatcham d				14 00	14 02																	
Newbury Racecourse d																						
Newbury a				14 06	14 07													14 47				
d				14 06	14 08																	
Kintbury d				14 13	14 14																	
Hungerford d				14 17	14 19																	
Bedwyn a				14 25	14 26																	
Tilehurst d												14 18	14 19									
Pangbourne d												14 23	14 24									
Goring & Streatley d												14 28	14 29									
Cholsey d												14 33	14 34			←						
Didcot Parkway a	13 53								14 21	14 23		14 42	14 42	14 33	14 32	14 33			14 53	14 53		
d						13 58								14 34	14 32	14 34						
Appleford d														→								
Culham d																						
Radley d						14 05																
Oxford 115 a		14 04				14 13					14 35				14 44	14 45					15 04	
d		14 06					14 20				14 37										15 06	
Tackley d							14 29															
Heyford d							14 33															
Kings Sutton d							14 43															
Banbury 71 a		14 23					14 50				14 54										15 23	
Leamington Spa a		14 40									15 11										15 40	
Coventry a		14 52									15 23										15 52	
Birmingham International a		15 03									15 37										16 03	
Birmingham New Street 71 a		15 14									15 48										16 14	

- **A** until 9 September
- **B** from 16 September. To Penzance
- **C** until 9 September. To Penzance
- **D** until 9 September. To Weston-super-Mare
- **E** from 16 September. To Weston-super-Mare
- **F** from 16 September
- **G** from 22 July until 7 October. From Guildford
- **H** until 15 July, from 14 October. From Guildford to Newcastle
- **I** until 9 September. To Didcot Parkway
- **J** To Cheltenham Spa
- **K** from 16 September. To Swansea
- **L** until 9 September. To Swansea
- **M** From Bournemouth to Manchester Piccadilly
- **N** until 9 September. From London Paddington
- **O** until 9 September. To Hereford
- **P** from 16 September. To Hereford
- **Q** To Penzance
- **R** until 9 September. To Plymouth
- **S** from 16 September. To Plymouth
- **T** until 9 September. To Carmarthen
- **U** from 16 September. To Carmarthen
- **V** until 9 September. To Worcester Foregate Street
- **W** from 16 September. To Worcester Foregate Street
- **X** until 9 September. From London Paddington to Worcester Foregate Street
- **Y** To Plymouth
- **Z** until 9 September. To Bristol Temple Meads
- **AA** from 16 September. To Bristol Temple Meads

For complete services between Banbury and Birmingham, refer to Table T71

Table T116-F

Sundays

20 May to 2 December

London and Reading - Bedwyn, Oxford, Banbury and Birmingham

	GW	GW	GW	GW	GW	GW	GW	GW	GW	GW	GW	XC	GW	GW	GW	GW	GW	GW	GW	GW	XC	GW	GW
	A	B	A	B	C	◇■ D	■ E	◇■ F	◇■ G	◇■ H	◇■ I	◇■ J	A	◇■ K	L	◇■ M	B	◇■ N	■ O	■ P	◇■	A	A
London Paddington ⊖ d		14 04			14 00	14 22	14 27	14 30	14 27	14 30	14 33		14 15	14 34		14 37	14 30	14 57	15 00	15 03		14 45	
Ealing Broadway ⊖ d					14 09								14 23				14 38					14 53	
Slough d		14 24			14 31								14 46	14 53		14 59	15 01					15 16	
Maidenhead d		14 31			14 40								14 54				15 11					15 26	
Twyford d					14 48								15 02		←		15 19					15 34	
Reading a		14 46			14 56	14 58	14 59	15 04	15 05	15 08	15 08		15 10	15 12	14 56	15 13	15 26	15 31	15 39	15 39		15 42	
d	14 44	14 46			15 14					15 10	15 10	15 11	15 14	15 14	15 14	15 17			15 39	15 39	15 41		15 44
Reading West d	14 47	14 50			→																		
Theale d	14 53	14 56																					15 51
Aldermaston d	14 58	15 01																					
Midgham d	15 01	15 04																					
Thatcham d	15 06	15 09																					16 00
Newbury Racecourse d	15 11	15 14																					
Newbury a	15 15	15 18																					16 05
d																							16 06
Kintbury d																							16 12
Hungerford d																							16 17
Bedwyn a																							16 24
Tilehurst d													15 18		15 18								
Pangbourne d													15 22		15 22								
Goring & Streatley d													15 27		15 27								
Cholsey d													15 32		15 32								
Didcot Parkway a										15 24	15 24		15 41	15 29	15 39	15 29			15 53	15 53			
d			14 58	15 04										15 30		15 32							
Appleford d																							
Culham d																							
Radley d			15 05	15 11																			
Oxford 115 a			15 13	15 19								15 34		15 42		15 44					16 04		
d												15 37									16 06		
Tackley d																							
Heyford d																							
Kings Sutton d																							
Banbury 71 a												15 54									16 23		
Leamington Spa a												16 11									16 40		
Coventry a												16 23									16 52		
Birmingham International a												16 36									17 03		
Birmingham New Street 71 a												16 48									17 14		

	GW	GW	GW	GW	GW	GW	GW	GW	XC	XC	GW	GW	GW	GW	GW	GW	GW	GW	XC	GW	GW	GW
	B	A	B	C	■ E	◇■ G	◇■ H	◇■ I	◇■ Q	◇■ R	L	◇ S	A	◇■ T	B	◇■ U	■ G	■ E	◇■	A	A	B
London Paddington ⊖ d	15 04			15 00	15 27	15 27	15 30	15 33				15 34	15 15	15 37	15 30	15 57	16 00	16 03		15 45		16 04
Ealing Broadway ⊖ d				15 09									15 23		15 38					15 53		
Slough d	15 24			15 31								15 54	15 46	15 59	16 02					16 16		16 24
Maidenhead d	15 31			15 40									15 56		16 11					16 26		16 31
Twyford d				15 48							←		16 04		16 20					16 34		
Reading a	15 45			15 56	15 59	16 05	16 07	16 08			15 56	16 11	16 11	16 16	16 28	16 31	16 37	16 37		16 42		16 46
d	15 46			16 12			16 07	16 09	16 11	16 11	16 12	16 14	16 14	16 17		16 32	16 39	16 39	16 41		16 44	16 46
Reading West d				→																	16 47	16 50
Theale d	15 53																				16 53	16 56
Aldermaston d																					16 58	17 01
Midgham d																					17 01	17 04
Thatcham d	16 02																				17 06	17 09
Newbury Racecourse d																					17 11	17 14
Newbury a	16 07															16 47					17 15	17 17
d	16 08																					
Kintbury d	16 14																					
Hungerford d	16 19																					
Bedwyn a	16 26																					
Tilehurst d											16 16		16 18									
Pangbourne d											16 20		16 22									
Goring & Streatley d											16 25		16 27									
Cholsey d											16 31		16 32									
Didcot Parkway a							16 21	16 22			16 41	16 30	16 41	16 32			16 53	16 53				
d		16 02	16 04									16 30		16 33								
Appleford d																						
Culham d																						
Radley d		16 09	16 11																			
Oxford 115 a		16 17	16 19						16 34	16 35		16 42		16 44					17 04			
d									16 37	16 37									17 06			
Tackley d																						
Heyford d																						
Kings Sutton d																						
Banbury 71 a									16 54	16 54									17 23			
Leamington Spa a									17 11	17 11									17 40			
Coventry a									17 23	17 23									17 52			
Birmingham International a									17 36	17 36									18 03			
Birmingham New Street 71 a									17 48	17 48									18 14			

- **A** from 16 September
- **B** until 9 September
- **C** until 9 September. To Didcot Parkway
- **D** until 9 September. To Cheltenham Spa
- **E** from 16 September. To Bristol Temple Meads
- **F** from 16 September. To Cheltenham Spa
- **G** until 9 September. To Bristol Temple Meads
- **H** until 9 September. To Swansea
- **I** from 16 September. To Swansea
- **J** From Bournemouth to Manchester Piccadilly
- **K** until 9 September. To Hereford
- **L** until 9 September. From London Paddington
- **M** from 16 September. To Hereford
- **N** To Penzance
- **O** until 9 September. To Taunton
- **P** from 16 September. To Taunton
- **Q** until 9 September. From Bournemouth to Manchester Piccadilly
- **R** from 16 September. From Bournemouth to Manchester Piccadilly
- **S** until 9 September. To Worcester Foregate Street
- **T** from 16 September. To Worcester Foregate Street. ■ from Reading
- **U** To Plymouth

For complete services between Banbury and Birmingham, refer to Table T71

Table T116-F

Sundays

20 May to 2 December

London and Reading - Bedwyn, Oxford, Banbury and Birmingham

		GW	GW	GW	GW	GW	GW	GW	GW	GW	XC	XC	GW	GW	GW	GW	GW	GW	GW	GW	XC	GW	GW	GW
			A	B	C	D	E	F	G	H	I	J	K	L	M	N	A	O	F	D		L	L	A
London Paddington ⊖	d			16 00	16 22	16 27	16 30	16 27	16 30	16 33				16 15	16 34	16 37	16 30	16 57	17 00	17 03		16 45		17 04
Ealing Broadway ⊖	d			16 09										16 23			16 38					16 53		
Slough	d			16 31										16 46	16 54	16 59	17 01					17 16		17 24
Maidenhead	d			16 41										16 56	17 02	17 07	17 11					17 26		17 31
Twyford	d			16 49									←	17 04			17 19					17 34		
Reading	a			16 56	16 58	16 59	17 01	17 05	17 07	17 08			16 56	17 11	17 15	17 20	17 26	17 31	17 37	17 37		17 42		17 45
	d			17 12					17 07	17 10	17 11	17 11	17 12	17 14	17 15	17 20			17 39	17 39	17 41		17 44	17 46
Reading West	d			→																				
Theale	d																						17 51	17 53
Aldermaston	d																							
Midgham	d																							
Thatcham	d																						18 00	18 02
Newbury Racecourse	d																							
Newbury	a																						18 05	18 07
	d																						18 06	18 08
Kintbury	d																						18 12	18 14
Hungerford	d																						18 17	18 19
Bedwyn	a																						18 24	18 27
Tilehurst	d												17 17	17 18										
Pangbourne	d												17 21	17 23										
Goring & Streatley	d												17 26	17 27										
Cholsey	d												17 31	17 32										
Didcot Parkway	a								17 22	17 24			17 42	17 41	17 31	17 36			17 53	17 53				
	d	16 58													17 32	17 37								
Appleford	d																							
Culham	d																							
Radley	d	17 05																						
Oxford 115	a	17 12									17 34	17 35			17 44	17 50					18 04			
	d			17 19							17 37	17 37									18 06			
Tackley	d			17 28																				
Heyford	d			17 32																				
Kings Sutton	d			17 42																				
Banbury 71	a			17 48							17 54	17 54									18 23			
Leamington Spa	a										18 11	18 11									18 40			
Coventry	a										18 23	18 23									18 52			
Birmingham International	a										18 36	18 36									19 03			
Birmingham New Street 71	a										18 48	18 48									19 14			

		GW	GW	GW	GW	GW	GW	XC	XC	GW	GW	GW	GW	GW	GW	GW	GW	XC	GW	GW	GW	GW	GW
			B	P	Q	G	H	J	I	K	L	R	S	A	O	F	D		L	L	A		B
London Paddington ⊖	d		17 00	17 27	17 27	17 30	17 33				17 15	17 34	17 37	17 30	17 57	18 00	18 03		17 45		18 04		18 00
Ealing Broadway ⊖	d		17 09								17 23			17 38					17 53				18 09
Slough	d		17 31								17 46	17 53	17 59	18 01					18 16		18 24		18 31
Maidenhead	d		17 41								17 56	18 01	18 09	18 11					18 26		18 31		18 41
Twyford	d		17 49							←	18 04			18 19					18 34				18 49
Reading	a		17 57	17 59	18 05	18 07	18 08			17 57	18 11	18 18	18 19	18 26	18 31	18 37	18 37		18 42		18 45		18 56
	d		18 12			18 07	18 10	18 11	18 11	18 12	18 14	18 19	18 20		18 32	18 39	18 39	18 41		18 44	18 46		19 12
Reading West	d		→																	18 47	18 49		→
Theale	d																			18 53	18 55		
Aldermaston	d																			18 58	18 59		
Midgham	d																			19 01	19 04		
Thatcham	d																			19 06	19 09		
Newbury Racecourse	d																			19 11	19 12		
Newbury	a														18 47					19 15	19 17		
	d																						
Kintbury	d																						
Hungerford	d																						
Bedwyn	a																						
Tilehurst	d									18 17	18 18												
Pangbourne	d									18 21	18 22												
Goring & Streatley	d									18 26	18 27												
Cholsey	d									18 31	18 32												
Didcot Parkway	a					18 23	18 26			18 42	18 42	18 36	18 36			18 53	18 53						
	d	17 58										18 37	18 37									18 58	
Appleford	d																						
Culham	d																						
Radley	d	18 05																				19 05	
Oxford 115	a	18 12						18 32	18 34			18 49	18 49					19 03				19 12	
	d							18 37	18 37									19 06					
Tackley	d																						
Heyford	d																						
Kings Sutton	d																						
Banbury 71	a							18 54	18 54									19 23					
Leamington Spa	a							19 11	19 11									19 40					
Coventry	a							19 23	19 23									19 52					
Birmingham International	a							19 36	19 36									20 03					
Birmingham New Street 71	a							19 48	19 48									20 14					

A until 9 September
B until 9 September. To Didcot Parkway
C until 9 September. To Cheltenham Spa
D from 16 September. To Bristol Temple Meads
E from 16 September. To Cheltenham Spa
F until 9 September. To Bristol Temple Meads
G until 9 September. To Swansea
H from 16 September. To Swansea
I until 9 September. From Bournemouth to Manchester Piccadilly
J from 16 September. From Bournemouth to Manchester Piccadilly
K until 9 September. From London Paddington
L from 16 September
M until 9 September. To Great Malvern
N from 16 September. To Great Malvern
O To Penzance
P from 16 September. To Weston-super-Mare
Q until 9 September. To Weston-super-Mare
R until 9 September. To Hereford
S from 16 September. To Hereford

For complete services between Banbury and Birmingham, refer to Table T71

Table T116-F

Sundays

20 May to 2 December

London and Reading - Bedwyn, Oxford, Banbury and Birmingham

		GW	GW	GW	GW	GW	GW	XC	XC	GW	GW	GW	GW	GW	GW	GW	GW	GW	GW	XC	GW	GW	GW	GW
		A	B	C	D	E	F	G	H	I	J	K	L	M	N	F	E	O	J		J	M		P
London Paddington ⊖	d	18 22	18 27	18 30	18 27	18 30	18 33				18 15	18 34	18 37	18 30	18 57	19 00	19 00	19 03	18 45			19 04		19 00
Ealing Broadway ⊖	d										18 23			18 38					18 53					19 09
Slough	d										18 46	18 54	18 59	19 01					19 16			19 24		19 31
Maidenhead	d										18 56	19 02	19 05	19 11					19 26			19 31		19 41
Twyford	d									←	19 04			19 19					19 33					19 49
Reading	a	18 58	18 59	19 01	19 05	19 07	19 08			18 56	19 11	19 16	19 20	19 27	19 31	19 34	19 37	19 37	19 41			19 47		19 56
	d					19 07	19 10	19 11	19 11	19 12	19 14	19 18	19 20					19 39		19 41	19 44	19 47		20 12
Reading West	d																							→
Theale	d																				19 51	19 54		
Aldermaston	d																							
Midgham	d																							
Thatcham	d																				20 00	20 02		
Newbury Racecourse	d																							
Newbury	a																				20 05	20 07		
	d																				20 06	20 08		
Kintbury	d																				20 12	20 14		
Hungerford	d																				20 17	20 19		
Bedwyn	a																				20 24	20 29		
Tilehurst	d									19 16	19 18													
Pangbourne	d									19 20	19 22													
Goring & Streatley	d									19 25	19 27													
Cholsey	d									19 30	19 32													
Didcot Parkway	a					19 22	19 24			19 39	19 41	19 34	19 36					19 53						
	d											19 36	19 37										19 58	
Appleford	d																							
Culham	d																							
Radley	d																						20 05	
Oxford 115	a							19 34	19 35			19 46	19 49							20 03			20 12	
	d							19 37	19 37											20 06				
Tackley	d																							
Heyford	d																							
Kings Sutton	d																							
Banbury 71	a							19 54	19 54											20 23				
Leamington Spa	a							20 11	20 11											20 39				
Coventry	a							20 23	20 23											20 52				
Birmingham International	a							20 36	20 36											21 03				
Birmingham New Street 71	a							20 48	20 48											21 15				

		GW	GW	GW	GW	XC	XC	GW	GW	GW	GW	GW	GW	GW	GW	GW	GW	XC	GW	GW	GW	GW	GW
		B	D	E	F	G	H	I	J	Q	R	S	M	N	T	U	J			M	J	M	C
London Paddington ⊖	d	19 27	19 27	19 30	19 33				19 15	19 34	19 37		19 30	19 57	20 00	20 03	19 45					20 00	20 27
Ealing Broadway ⊖	d								19 23				19 38				19 53					20 09	
Slough	d								19 46	19 54	19 59		20 01				20 16					20 31	
Maidenhead	d								19 56				20 11				20 26					20 41	
Twyford	d							←	20 04				20 19				20 33					20 49	
Reading	a	19 59	20 05	20 07	20 08			19 56	20 11	20 15	20 16		20 26	20 31	20 37	20 37	20 41					20 57	20 58
	d			20 07	20 10	20 11	20 11	20 12	20 14	20 17	20 18			20 32	20 39	20 39		20 41	20 44			20 57	
Reading West	d																		20 47				
Theale	d																		20 53				
Aldermaston	d																		20 58				
Midgham	d																		21 01				
Thatcham	d																		21 06				
Newbury Racecourse	d																		21 11				
Newbury	a													20 47					21 16				
	d																						
Kintbury	d																						
Hungerford	d																						
Bedwyn	a																						
Tilehurst	d							20 16	20 18													21 01	
Pangbourne	d							20 21	20 22													21 06	
Goring & Streatley	d							20 26	20 27													21 11	
Cholsey	d							20 32	20 32			←										21 19	
Didcot Parkway	a			20 22	20 24			20 40	20 40	20 35	20 33	20 35			20 53	20 53						21 30	
	d									20 36	20 33	20 36								20 58	21 05		
Appleford	d									→													
Culham	d																						
Radley	d																			21 05	21 12		
Oxford 115	a					20 34	20 35				20 47	20 50						21 04		21 12	21 19		
	d					20 37	20 37											21 06					
Tackley	d																						
Heyford	d																						
Kings Sutton	d																						
Banbury 71	a					20 54	20 54											21 23					
Leamington Spa	a					21 11	21 11											21 40					
Coventry	a					21 23	21 23											21 52					
Birmingham International	a					21 36	21 36											22 02					
Birmingham New Street 71	a					21 48	21 48											22 14					

A until 9 September. To Cheltenham Spa
B from 16 September. To Bristol Temple Meads
C from 16 September. To Cheltenham Spa
D until 9 September. To Bristol Temple Meads
E until 9 September. To Swansea
F from 16 September. To Swansea
G until 9 September. From Bournemouth to Manchester Piccadilly
H from 16 September. From Bournemouth to Manchester Piccadilly
I until 9 September. From London Paddington
J from 16 September
K until 9 September. To Worcester Shrub Hill
L from 16 September. To Worcester Shrub Hill. from Reading
M until 9 September
N To Plymouth
O To Exeter St Davids
P until 9 September. To Didcot Parkway
Q until 9 September. To Great Malvern
R from 16 September. To Great Malvern
S until 9 September. From London Paddington to Great Malvern
T until 9 September. To Weston-super-Mare
U from 16 September. To Weston-super-Mare

For complete services between Banbury and Birmingham, refer to Table T71

Table T116-F

Sundays
20 May to 2 December

London and Reading - Bedwyn, Oxford, Banbury and Birmingham

		GW	GW	XC	GW	GW	GW	GW	GW	GW	GW	GW	GW	GW	GW	XC		GW	GW	GW	GW	GW	GW	GW	GW
		◇■	◇■	◇■	◇■		◇	◇■		◇		◇■	◇■	◇■		◇■					◇■	◇■	◇■		◇■
		A	B	C	D	E	F	G	H	I	F	J	K	L	I					F	B	D	M	I	N
		☕	☕		☕			☕				☕	☕	☕							☕	☕			
London Paddington ⊖	d	20 22	20 30		20 34	20 15	20 34			20 37	20 30	20 57	21 00	21 03	20 45					21 00	21 30	21 33	21 34	21 15	
Ealing Broadway ⊖	d					20 23					20 38				20 53					21 09				21 23	
Slough	d					20 46	20 55			20 58	21 02				21 16					21 31			21 53	21 46	
Maidenhead	d					20 56					21 11				21 26					21 41				21 56	
Twyford	d					21 04		←	←		21 19				21 33					21 49				22 04	←
Reading	a	21 00	21 07		21 09	21 11	21 13	21 09	21 11	21 14	21 27	21 31	21 37	21 37	21 41					21 55	22 07	22 09	22 10	22 11	22 10
	d		21 09	21 11	21 15	21 16	21 14	21 15	21 16	21 17			21 39	21 39		21 41		21 44		22 01	22 09	22 11	22 15	22 12	22 15
Reading West	d				↪	↪																	↪		
Theale	d																	21 51							
Aldermaston	d																								
Midgham	d																								
Thatcham	d																	22 00							
Newbury Racecourse	d																								
Newbury	a																	22 05							
	d																	22 06							
Kintbury	d																	22 12							
Hungerford	d																	22 17							
Bedwyn	a																	22 24							
Tilehurst	d								21 20											22 05				22 16	
Pangbourne	d								21 26											22 10				22 20	
Goring & Streatley	d								21 31											22 15				22 25	
Cholsey	d								21 42											22 21				22 30	
Didcot Parkway	a		21 21				21 31	21 28	21 51	21 33			21 53	21 53						22 29	22 22	22 24		22 38	22 30
	d						21 32			21 34									22 06						22 36
Appleford	d																								
Culham	d																								
Radley	d																		22 13						
Oxford 115	a			21 34			21 45			21 48						22 02			22 20						22 47
	d			21 37												22 06									
Tackley	d																								
Heyford	d																								
Kings Sutton	d																								
Banbury 71	a			21 53												22 22									
Leamington Spa	a			22 11												22 40									
Coventry	a			22 23												22 52									
Birmingham International	a			22 33												23 03									
Birmingham New Street 71	a			22 43												23 14									

		GW	GW	GW	GW	GW	GW	GW		GW	GW	GW	GW	GW	GW	GW	GW	GW	GW	GW	GW	GW	GW	GW	
		◇■		◇■				◇■				◇	◇■						◇■				◇■	◇■	
		O	F	K	I	F	I	L		🚌	P	F	Q	🚌	R		S	E	T	U	H		K	L	
				☕				☕					☕						☕				☕	☕	
London Paddington ⊖	d	21 37	21 30	22 00	21 45			22 03			22 15	22 36	22 37				22 45	22 45	23 03			23 15	23 37	23 37	
Ealing Broadway ⊖	d		21 38		21 53						22 23						22 53	22 53				23 23			
Slough	d	22 03	22 01		22 16						22 46	22 55					23 15	23 15				23 46	23 57	00 01	
Maidenhead	d		22 11		22 26						22 56						23 23	23 24				23 56			
Twyford	d		22 19		22 33						23 04				←		23 31	23 32		←	←	00 04			
Reading	a	22 20	22 26	22 37	22 42			22 43			23 11	23 12	23 12		23 11		23 40	23 41	23 42	23 40	23 41	00 13	00 16	00 16	
	d	22 21		22 39		22 44	22 44	22 45			23 20	23 13	23 15		23 20	23 22	23 52	23 52	23 46	23 52	23 52		00 20	00 20	
Reading West	d					22 47	22 47				↪					23 26	↪	↪							
Theale	d					22 53	22 53									23 32									
Aldermaston	d					22 58	22 58																		
Midgham	d					23 01	23 01																		
Thatcham	d					23 06	23 06									23 40									
Newbury Racecourse	d					23 11	23 11																		
Newbury	a					23 14	23 15									23 47									
	d																								
Kintbury	d																								
Hungerford	d																								
Bedwyn	a																								
Tilehurst	d														23 24					23 56	23 56				
Pangbourne	d														23 28					00 01	00 01				
Goring & Streatley	d														23 33					00 06	00 06				
Cholsey	d														23 38					00 11	00 11				
Didcot Parkway	a	22 36		22 53				23 00				23 31	23s32		23 47				00s02	00 20	00 20		00s35	00s35	
	d	22 43								23 10				23 45											
Appleford	d																								
Culham	d																								
Radley	d									23 25				23 59											
Oxford 115	a	22 57								23 50				00 15											
	d																								
Tackley	d																								
Heyford	d																								
Kings Sutton	d																								
Banbury 71	a																								
Leamington Spa	a																								
Coventry	a																								
Birmingham International	a																								
Birmingham New Street 71	a																								

- **A** until 9 September. To Cheltenham Spa
- **B** until 9 September. To Swansea
- **C** From Bournemouth
- **D** from 16 September. To Swansea
- **E** from 16 September. To Didcot Parkway
- **F** until 9 September
- **G** from 16 September. From London Paddington to Swansea
- **H** from 16 September. From London Paddington
- **I** from 16 September
- **J** To Exeter St Davids
- **K** until 9 September. To Bristol Temple Meads
- **L** from 16 September. To Bristol Temple Meads
- **M** until 9 September. To Worcester Shrub Hill
- **N** until 9 September. From London Paddington to Worcester Shrub Hill
- **O** from 16 September. To Worcester Shrub Hill
- **P** To Didcot Parkway
- **Q** from 16 September. To Bristol Parkway
- **R** From London Paddington
- **S** until 9 September. To Didcot Parkway
- **T** To Bristol Temple Meads
- **U** until 9 September. From London Paddington

For complete services between Banbury and Birmingham, refer to Table T71

Table T116-F

Sundays
20 May to 2 December

London and Reading - Bedwyn, Oxford, Banbury and Birmingham

		GW	GW
			A
London Paddington ⊖	d	23 47	23 53
Ealing Broadway ⊖	d	23 55	00 02
Slough	d	00 10	00 26
Maidenhead	d	00 17	00 36
Twyford	d		00 44
Reading	a	00 32	00 51
	d		
Reading West	d		
Theale	d		
Aldermaston	d		
Midgham	d		
Thatcham	d		
Newbury Racecourse	d		
Newbury	a		
	d		
Kintbury	d		
Hungerford	d		
Bedwyn	a		
Tilehurst	d		
Pangbourne	d		
Goring & Streatley	d		
Cholsey	d		
Didcot Parkway	a		
	d		
Appleford	d		
Culham	d		
Radley	d		
Oxford 115	a		
	d		
Tackley	d		
Heyford	d		
Kings Sutton	d		
Banbury 71	a		
Leamington Spa	a		
Coventry	a		
Birmingham International	a		
Birmingham New Street 71	a		

- **A** from 16 September

For complete services between Banbury and Birmingham, refer to Table T71

T116 UPDATE: The route between Theale and Bedwyn will be CLOSED TO ALL TRAINS. Rail replacement buses on 4-7 June; 9-12 July; 16 July to 05 August; 28-30 August; 08-11 October and 19-22 November.

Table T116-R

Mondays to Fridays

21 May to 7 December

Birmingham, Banbury, Oxford and Bedwyn - Reading and London

Miles	Miles		GW MX	GW MX	GW MO	GW MO	GW MO	GW MO	GW MX	GW MO	GW MX		GW MX	GW	GW MO	GW	GW MO	GW	GW	GW	GW	GW	GW	GW
			A		🚌	B	C	D	◇■ E	◇	F				G 🚌		G	H						
0	—	**Birmingham New Street** 71 d																						
8½	—	Birmingham International d																						
19¼	—	Coventry d																						
28¾	—	Leamington Spa d																						
48¾	—	**Banbury** 71 d																						
52¼	—	Kings Sutton d																						
59¾	—	Heyford d																						
62½	—	Tackley d									00 03													
71½	—	**Oxford** 115 a									00 12													
—	—	d			00 05				00 07		00 27				03 32			03 54		04 54				
76½	—	Radley d									00 33									05 00				
78¾	—	Culham d																						
79¾	—	Appleford d																						
81½	—	**Didcot Parkway** a			00 30				00 19		00 42				03 57			04 06		05 09				
—	—	d							00 23	00 35	00 47						04 07	04 10						05 17
86¾	—	Cholsey d									00 54						04 13	04 16						05 23
90¼	—	Goring & Streatley d				00 05	00 05				00 59						04 18	04 21						05 28
93½	—	Pangbourne d				00 09	00 09				01 04						04 22	04 25						05 32
96¼	—	Tilehurst d				00 14	00 14				01 08						04 27	04 30						05 37
—	0	**Bedwyn** d																						
—	5	Hungerford d																						
—	8	Kintbury d																						
—	13½	**Newbury** a																						
—	—	d																						
—	14	Newbury Racecourse d																						
—	17	Thatcham d						00 02																
—	19¾	Midgham d						00 07																
—	21¾	Aldermaston d						00 10																
—	25¾	Theale d						00 15																
—	29½	Reading West d	00 03					00s23																
99	30½	**Reading** a	00 06			00 19	00 19	00 26	00 37	00 50	01 14						04 32	04 35						05 42
—	—	d		00 14		00 20	00 20		00 39	00 51			01 15	02 24		03 54			04 40		05 02	05 18	05 36	05 44
104	—	Twyford a		00 21		00 26	00 26			00 58			01 21	02 30		04 00			04 46		05 08	05 24	05 42	05 53
110¾	—	Maidenhead a		00 29		00 34	00 34			01 06			01 29	02 38		04 08			04 54		05 17	05 32	05 50	06 01
116½	—	Slough a		00 40		00 42	00 42		00 56	01 14			01 36	02 45		04 15			05 01		05 28	05 44	05 57	06 13
129¾	—	Ealing Broadway ⊖ a		01 03		01 04	01 05			01 32			01 52	03 06		04 36			05 32		05 53	06 04	06 22	06 35
135	—	**London Paddington** ⊖ a		01 12		01 13	01 13		01 17	01 41			02 01	03 15		04 49			05 48		06 02	06 16	06 32	06 46

	GW	GW	GW		GW	GW	GW	GW	GW	GW	GW	GW	GW	GW	GW	GW	GW	GW	GW		GW	GW	GW	GW
	I				◇■ J									I					K		◇■ J	L	◇■ M	
Birmingham New Street 71 d																								
Birmingham International d																								
Coventry d																								
Leamington Spa d																								
Banbury 71 d																								
Kings Sutton d																								
Heyford d																								
Tackley d																								
Oxford 115 a																								
d		05 17	05 23											05 50	05 57	06 08							06 28	
Radley d														05 56		06 14								
Culham d														06 00										
Appleford d														06 03					←					
Didcot Parkway a		05 31	05 35											06 09	06 13	06 24			06 09					
d		05 38			05 40					05 47	06 01			06 17	06 14				06 17		06 30			
Cholsey d		05 44								05 53				→					06 23					
Goring & Streatley d		05 49								05 58									06 28					
Pangbourne d		05 53								06 02									06 33					
Tilehurst d		05 58								06 07									06 37					
Bedwyn d												05 42												
Hungerford d												05 48												
Kintbury d												05 52												
Newbury a												05 59												
d							05 30					05 59					06 09							
Newbury Racecourse d							05 32																	
Thatcham d							05 37					06 04					06 14							
Midgham d							05 42																	
Aldermaston d							05 45																	
Theale d							05 50					06 12					06 24							
Reading West d						←	05 57					06 19					06 32					←		
Reading a		06 03			05 54		06 01			06 13	06 16	06 22			06 27		06 36		06 46		06 43	06 46	06 51	
d	05 59				05 56	05 59		06 03	06 15	06 18	06 19	06 24	06 29		06 30		06 37	06 42	06 47		06 46	06 47	06 53	06 57
Twyford a	→							06 09		06 24	06 24		06 35				06 44	06 48	→			06 53		07 02
Maidenhead a						06 10		06 17		06 32	06 31		06 45		06 40			06 57				07 01	07 04	07 09
Slough a						06 18		06 24		06 43		06 40	06 54		06 48			07 08			06 59			07 16
Ealing Broadway ⊖ a								06 49		07 06			07 19					07 33						
London Paddington ⊖ a					06 22	06 36		06 59	06 44	07 16	06 53	07 00	07 29		07 06		07 10	07 46			07 17	07 24	07 25	07 36

A From Bedwyn
B until 10 September. From Didcot Parkway
C from 17 September. From Didcot Parkway
D From Newbury
E From Hereford
F From Banbury
G from 18 June
H until 15 June, MX from 19 June
I To London Paddington
J From Bristol Temple Meads
K From Oxford to London Paddington
L From Oxford
M From Worcester Shrub Hill

For complete services between Banbury and Birmingham, refer to Table T71

Table T116-R

Mondays to Fridays

21 May to 7 December

Birmingham, Banbury, Oxford and Bedwyn - Reading and London

	GW	GW	GW	GW	GW	GW	GW	GW	GW	GW	GW		GW	GW	GW	GW	GW	GW	GW	GW	XC	GW	GW	GW
			A	◇■ B	C		A	■ D	C	◇■ D	■ E			◇■ F	■ B				◇■ G	◇■ H	◇■ I		■ D	A
Birmingham New Street 71 d																					06 04			
Birmingham International d																					06 14			
Coventry d																					06 25			
Leamington Spa d																					06 37			
Banbury 71 d													06 08			06 28					06 54			
Kings Sutton d													06 13			06 33								
Heyford d													06 21			06 41								
Tackley d													06 26			06 46								
Oxford 115 a													06 35			06 58					07 14			
d													06 38	06 54		06 59					07 16			
Radley d													06 44			07 05								
Culham d													06 48			07 09								
Appleford d													06 51			07 12								
Didcot Parkway a													06 57	07 06		07 18								
d		06 33	06 41	06 48			06 52	06 59					07 02	07 08					07 20					07 20
Cholsey d		06 39	06 46				06 57						07 09											07 27
Goring & Streatley d		06 44	06 51				07 03						07 14											07 32
Pangbourne d		06 48	06 55				07 07						07 18											07 36
Tilehurst d		06 55	06 59				07 11						07 23											07 40
Bedwyn d	06 12									06 29										06 45				
Hungerford d	06 18									06 37										06 53				
Kintbury d	06 22									06 43										06 59				
Newbury a	06 29									06 50										07 06				
d	06 29									06 51							06 56			07 07				
Newbury Racecourse d	06 32																06 58							
Thatcham d	06 37									06 58							07 03			07 14				
Midgham d	06 41																07 08							
Aldermaston d	06 45																07 11							
Theale d	06 50									07 08							07 16			07 24				
Reading West d	06 57				←				←						←		07 23			07 33				
Reading a	07 00	07 00	07 04	07 02	07 04		07 16	07 14	07 16	07 18			07 28	07 20			07 27		07 34	07 37	07 40			07 45
d		07 01	07 07	07 04	07 07	07 12	07 18	07 16	07 18	07 19	07 27			07 24	07 27			07 32	07 35	07 40		07 42	07 48	07 53
Twyford a		07 07	→			07 18	→		07 23		→							07 38				07 48		→
Maidenhead a		07 15			07 17	07 27			07 30									07 46				07 56		
Slough a		07 24				07 38												07 56				08 07		
Ealing Broadway ⊖ a		07 48				08 03												08 19				08 32		
London Paddington ⊖ a		07 58		07 30	07 38	08 16		07 44	07 55	07 47				07 52	07 59			08 28	08 06	08 08		08 42	08 14	

	GW	GW	GW		GW	GW	GW	GW	GW	GW	GW	XC	GW	GW	GW	GW	GW	GW	GW		GW	GW	GW	GW
		C				A		◇■ F	C	■ B	◇■ J	◇■ K		A	◇■ L	C	■ M	◇■ N				◇■ O	A	
Birmingham New Street 71 d												06 33												
Birmingham International d																								
Coventry d																								
Leamington Spa d												07 00												
Banbury 71 d												07 20												07 28
Kings Sutton d																								07 33
Heyford d																								07 41
Tackley d																								07 46
Oxford 115 a												07 41												07 57
d							07 21	07 31				07 43						07 54						07 59
Radley d							07 27																	08 05
Culham d							07 31																	08 09
Appleford d							07 34																	
Didcot Parkway a							07 40																	08 16
d	07 30					07 34	07 44			07 47				07 50	07 56		08 01						08 08	
Cholsey d						07 40	07 50							07 55									08 13	
Goring & Streatley d						07 45	07 55							08 00									08 18	
Pangbourne d						07 49	07 59							08 04									08 22	
Tilehurst d						07 54	08 04							08 08									08 26	
Bedwyn d			07 05		07 05																			
Hungerford d			07 11		07 11						07 37													
Kintbury d			07 15		07 15																			
Newbury a			07 22		07 22						07 45													
d			07 22		07 22						07 47								07 53					
Newbury Racecourse d			07 25		07 25														07 55					
Thatcham d			07 30		07 30														08 00					
Midgham d			07 34		07 34														08 05					
Aldermaston d			07 38		07 38														08 08					
Theale d			07 43		07 43														08 13					
Reading West d		←	07 50		07 50				←							←			08 20					
Reading a	07 49	07 45	07 53		07 53	07 59	08 09	07 54	07 59	08 02	08 07	08 09		08 13	08 12	08 13	08 16	08 19	08 24				08 31	
d	07 50	07 53			07 57	08 02		07 58	08 02	08 03	08 09		08 12	08 16	08 14	08 16	08 17	08 21			08 33	08 34	08 53	
Twyford a		07 59			08 03	→			08 08				08 18	→		08 21					08 39		→	
Maidenhead a		08 06			08 11				08 16				08 26			08 30					08 47			
Slough a					08 18				08 25				08 38								08 58			
Ealing Broadway ⊖ a									08 48				09 03								09 23			
London Paddington ⊖ a	08 20	08 31			08 41			08 28	08 58	08 32	08 37		09 16		08 42	08 53	08 44	08 51			09 33	09 00		

A To London Paddington
B From Swansea
C From Didcot Parkway
D From Bristol Temple Meads
E From Swansea to London Paddington
F From Hereford
G From Worcester Shrub Hill
H From Frome
I To Bournemouth
J From Plymouth
K To Southampton Central
L From Cheltenham Spa
M From Weston-super-Mare
N From Moreton-in-Marsh. ☕ from Reading 🍴 to Reading
O From Plymouth. The Armada - Restaurant for customers joining until Taunton

For complete services between Banbury and Birmingham, refer to Table T71

T116 UPDATE: The route between Theale and Bedwyn will be CLOSED TO ALL TRAINS. Rail replacement buses on 4-7 June; 9-12 July; 16 July to 05 August; 28-30 August; 08-11 October and 19-22 November.

Birmingham, Banbury, Oxford and Bedwyn - Reading and London

	GW	GW	XC	GW	GW	GW	GW	GW	GW	GW	GW	GW	XC	GW	GW	GW	GW	GW	GW	GW	GW	GW	GW
		A	◇1 B 🛒	R 1 C ☕		D		◇1 E ☕	◇1 F ☕		◇1 G ☕		◇1 H 🛒	◇1 I ☕		◇1 J ☕			◇1 F ☕	K		D	
Birmingham New Street 71 d			07 04										07 33										
Birmingham International d			07 14																				
Coventry d			07 25																				
Leamington Spa d			07 38										08 00										
Banbury 71 d			07 55										08 17										
Kings Sutton d																							
Heyford d																							
Tackley d																							
Oxford 115 a			08 14										08 39										
Oxford d	08 07	08 11	08 16									08 35	08 43			08 54					09 01		09 06
Radley d												08 41											09 12
Culham d																							09 16
Appleford d												08 46											
Didcot Parkway a	08 19	08 28										08 54									09 13		09 23
Didcot Parkway d	08 21			08 30						08 35	08 55	08 57		09 01						09 08	09 17		
Cholsey d										08 41		09 03								09 14			
Goring & Streatley d										08 46		09 08								09 19			
Pangbourne d										08 50		09 12								09 23			
Tilehurst d										08 55		09 17								09 28			
Bedwyn d							07 56										08 41						
Hungerford d							08 02										08 47						
Kintbury d							08 06										08 51						
Newbury a							08 13										08 58						
Newbury d							08 21	08 34									08 58						
Newbury Racecourse d							08 23																
Thatcham d							08 28										09 03						
Midgham d							08 33																
Aldermaston d							08 36																
Theale d							08 41										09 11						
Reading West d						←	08 48															←	
Reading a	08 34		08 40	08 45		08 31	08 52	08 54		09 00	09 08	09 22	09 08	09 15		09 17	09 20			09 33	09 31	09 33	
Reading d	08 37			08 46	08 50	08 53		08 57	08 59	09 06	09 10			09 17	09 18	09 20	09 23	09 23	09 28	09 34	09 33	09 34	
Twyford a					08 56	09 00				09 13					09 24			09 29		→		09 40	
Maidenhead a					09 04	09 08				09 21					09 32			09 37				09 48	
Slough a					09 15					09 28					09 43			09 48				09 55	
Ealing Broadway ⊖ a					09 35					09 53					10 04							10 22	
London Paddington ⊖ a	09 07			09 12	09 46	09 30		09 23	09 25	10 02	09 37			09 43	10 16	09 46	09 53	10 08	09 55		09 59	10 31	

	GW	XC	GW	GW	GW	GW	GW	GW	GW	GW	XC	GW	GW	GW	GW	GW	GW	GW	GW	GW	XC	GW
	◇1 L ☕	◇1 M 🛒	◇1 N ☕				◇1 O ☕				◇1 P 🛒	◇1 Q ☕		K	◇1 R ☕		◇1 A 🛒	D	◇1 F ☕		R 1 B 🛒	◇1 Q ☕
Birmingham New Street 71 d		08 04									08 33										09 04	
Birmingham International d		08 14																			09 14	
Coventry d		08 25																			09 25	
Leamington Spa d		08 38									09 00										09 39	
Banbury 71 d		08 55									09 20									09 37	09 56	
Kings Sutton d																				09 42		
Heyford d																				09 50		
Tackley d																				09 55		
Oxford 115 a		09 15									09 41									10 04	10 14	
Oxford d		09 17				09 31				09 37	09 43						10 01			10 05	10 16	
Radley d																				10 12		
Culham d																						
Appleford d																						
Didcot Parkway a										09 50										10 22		
Didcot Parkway d			09 30					09 35						10 03	10 04				10 18			10 30
Cholsey d								09 41						10 09								
Goring & Streatley d								09 46						10 14								
Pangbourne d								09 50						10 18								
Tilehurst d								09 55						10 23								
Bedwyn d																09 41						
Hungerford d																09 47						
Kintbury d																09 51						
Newbury a																09 58						
Newbury d					09 23				09 32							09 58						
Newbury Racecourse d									09 35													
Thatcham d					09 31				09 40							10 03						
Midgham d									09 44													
Aldermaston d									09 48													
Theale d					09 40				09 53							10 11						
Reading West d									10 00									←				
Reading a		09 42	09 45		09 49	09 56		10 00	10 03		10 10			10 28	10 17	10 20	10 24	10 28	10 32		10 42	10 43
Reading d	09 36		09 46	09 48	09 51	09 57	10 01	10 03				10 12	10 18	10 33	10 19	10 22	10 26	10 33	10 34			10 46
Twyford a				09 54				10 09					10 24	→				10 39				
Maidenhead a				10 02				10 17					10 32					10 47				
Slough a				10 13		10 12		10 24					10 43				10 39	10 54				
Ealing Broadway ⊖ a				10 33				10 52					11 07					11 19				
London Paddington ⊖ a	10 02		10 14	10 46	10 21	10 31	10 37	11 01				10 39	11 16		10 45	10 53	10 57	11 31	11 00			11 12

A From Worcester Foregate Street
B From Manchester Piccadilly to Bournemouth
C From Weston-super-Mare. The Bristolian
D From Didcot Parkway
E From Plymouth
F From Swansea
G From Worcester Shrub Hill
H From Sheffield
I From Exeter St Davids
J From Hereford. The Cathedrals Express
K To London Paddington
L From Penzance. The Golden Hind
M From Nottingham to Bournemouth
N From Taunton
O From Swansea. Y Cymro - The Welshman
P From Leeds to Southampton Central
Q From Bristol Temple Meads
R From Cheltenham Spa

For complete services between Banbury and Birmingham, refer to Table T71

Table T116-R

Mondays to Fridays

21 May to 7 December

Birmingham, Banbury, Oxford and Bedwyn - Reading and London

	GW	GW	GW	GW	GW	GW	GW	XC	GW	GW	GW	GW	GW	GW	GW	XC	GW	GW	GW	GW	GW	GW	GW
			◇1 A ☕	B		◇1 C ☕		◇1 D 🛒	◇1 E ☕					◇1 F ☕		◇1 G 🛒	◇1 H ☕			◇1 A ☕	◇1 I 🛒	◇1 J ☕	
Birmingham New Street 71 d								09 33								10 04							
Birmingham International d																10 14							
Coventry d																10 25							
Leamington Spa d								10 00								10 38							
Banbury 71 d								10 19								10 55							
Kings Sutton d																							
Heyford d																							
Tackley d																							
Oxford 115 a								10 40								11 13							
Oxford d				10 31			10 37	10 43				11 01			11 07	11 16					11 31		
Radley d															11 13								
Culham d																							
Appleford d																							
Didcot Parkway a							10 57								11 22								
Didcot Parkway d					10 32	10 48							11 02	11 18			11 30						11 31
Cholsey d					10 38								11 08										11 37
Goring & Streatley d					10 43								11 13										11 42
Pangbourne d					10 47								11 17										11 46
Tilehurst d					10 52								11 22										11 51
Bedwyn d											10 41												
Hungerford d											10 47												
Kintbury d											10 51												
Newbury a											10 58												
Newbury d	10 14										10 58							11 12					
Newbury Racecourse d	10 17																	11 15					
Thatcham d	10 22										11 03							11 20					
Midgham d	10 26																	11 24					
Aldermaston d	10 30																	11 28					
Theale d	10 35										11 11							11 33					
Reading West d	10 42																	11 40					
Reading a	10 45			10 54	10 57	11 02		11 09			11 21	11 24	11 27	11 32		11 40	11 43	11 44			11 55		11 56
Reading d		10 49	10 53	10 56	11 03	11 05			11 11	11 19	11 22	11 26	11 33	11 34			11 46		11 49	11 52	11 57	12 01	12 03
Twyford a		10 57			11 09					11 26			11 39						11 55				12 09
Maidenhead a		11 05			11 17					11 34			11 47						12 03				12 17
Slough a		11 16		11 11	11 24					11 45		11 39	11 54						12 14		12 10		12 24
Ealing Broadway ⊖ a		11 35			11 49					12 07			12 19						12 33				12 49
London Paddington ⊖ a		11 46	11 21	11 30	12 01	11 32			11 37	12 17	11 52	11 58	12 32	12 00			12 14		12 46	12 21	12 28	12 30	13 01

	GW	XC	GW	GW	GW	GW	GW	GW	GW	GW	GW	XC	GW	GW	GW	GW	GW	GW	GW	GW	XC	GW
		◇1 K 🛒	◇1 H ☕		L	◇1 M ☕			N	◇1 F ☕		◇1 G 🛒	◇1 H ☕		◇1 A ☕	◇ I 🛒		◇1 J ☕			◇1 O 🛒	◇1 H ☕
Birmingham New Street 71 d		10 33										11 04									11 33	
Birmingham International d												11 14										
Coventry d												11 25										
Leamington Spa d		11 00										11 38									12 01	
Banbury 71 d		11 19										11 55									12 19	
Kings Sutton d																						
Heyford d																						
Tackley d																						
Oxford 115 a		11 41										12 14									12 40	
Oxford d	11 37	11 43						12 01			12 07	12 16				12 31				12 37	12 44	
Radley d											12 13											
Culham d																						
Appleford d											12 18											
Didcot Parkway a	11 49										12 24									12 49		
Didcot Parkway d					12 02	12 03				12 17			12 30				12 33	12 48				
Cholsey d					12 08												12 39					
Goring & Streatley d					12 13												12 44					
Pangbourne d					12 17												12 48					
Tilehurst d					12 22												12 53					
Bedwyn d							11 41															
Hungerford d							11 47															
Kintbury d							11 51															
Newbury a							11 58															
Newbury d							11 58												12 32			
Newbury Racecourse d																			12 34			
Thatcham d							12 03												12 39			
Midgham d																			12 44			
Aldermaston d																			12 47			
Theale d							12 11												12 52			
Reading West d									←										12 59			
Reading a		12 08			12 27	12 16	12 20	12 24	12 27	12 31		12 42	12 43			12 54	12 58	13 02	13 03		13 08	
Reading d			12 10	12 18	12 33	12 18	12 22	12 26	12 33	12 35			12 46	12 48	12 49	12 55	13 03	13 05				13 11
Twyford a				12 24	→				12 39					12 54			13 09					
Maidenhead a				12 32					12 47					13 02			13 17					
Slough a				12 43				12 39	12 54					13 13		13 10	13 24					
Ealing Broadway ⊖ a				13 03					13 20					13 32			13 49					
London Paddington ⊖ a			12 37	13 15		12 44	12 54	12 59	13 31	13 01			13 12	13 42	13 15	13 29	14 01	13 32				13 37

A From Penzance
B From Moreton-in-Marsh
C From Carmarthen. The Red Dragon
D From Newcastle
E From Paignton
F From Cardiff Central
G From Manchester Piccadilly to Bournemouth
H From Bristol Temple Meads
I From Great Malvern
J From Swansea
K From Newcastle to Southampton Central
L To London Paddington
M From Cheltenham Spa
N From Didcot Parkway
O From Edinburgh

For complete services between Banbury and Birmingham, refer to Table T71

Table T116-R

Birmingham, Banbury, Oxford and Bedwyn - Reading and London

Mondays to Fridays

21 May to 7 December

	GW	GW	GW	GW	GW	GW	GW	XC	GW	GW	GW		GW	GW	GW	GW	XC	GW	GW	GW	GW	GW	GW	GW
				A		◇ B		◇ C	◇ D		◇ E		◇ F				◇ G	◇ D			◇ H	◇ I		
Birmingham New Street 71 d								12 04									12 33							
Birmingham International d								12 14																
Coventry d								12 25																
Leamington Spa d								12 38									13 00							
Banbury 71 d							12 34	12 55									13 19							
Kings Sutton d							12 39																	
Heyford d							12 47																	
Tackley d							12 52																	
Oxford 115 a							13 04	13 14									13 41							
d			13 01				13 06	13 16			13 31					13 37	13 43						14 01	
Radley d							13 12																	
Culham d							13 16																	
Appleford d																								
Didcot Parkway a							13 23									13 51								
d					13 02	13 18			13 30					13 32							14 03			14 03
Cholsey d					13 09									13 38										14 09
Goring & Streatley d					13 14									13 43										14 14
Pangbourne d					13 18									13 47										14 18
Tilehurst d					13 23									13 52										14 23
Bedwyn d		12 36																	13 35					
Hungerford d		12 42																	13 41					
Kintbury d		12 46																	13 45					
Newbury a		12 53																	13 52					
d		12 53													13 31				13 52			14 05		
Newbury Racecourse d															13 33									
Thatcham d		12 58													13 38				13 57					
Midgham d															13 43									
Aldermaston d															13 46									
Theale d		13 06													13 51				14 05					
Reading West d															13 59									
Reading a		13 15	13 24		13 31	13 32		13 40	13 44		13 54			13 57	14 03		14 09		14 14		14 17	14 23	14 24	14 28
d	13 18	13 22	13 26	13 32	13 33	13 36			13 46	13 48	13 56		13 59	14 03				14 11	14 15	14 18	14 20	14 24	14 27	14 33
Twyford a	13 24				13 39					13 55				14 09						14 24				14 39
Maidenhead a	13 32				13 47					14 03				14 17						14 32				14 47
Slough a	13 43		13 39		13 55					14 14	14 09			14 24						14 43			14 41	14 54
Ealing Broadway ⊖ a	14 09				14 20					14 33				14 51						15 03				15 19
London Paddington ⊖ a	14 18	13 53	13 58	14 00	14 31	14 07			14 14	14 45	14 27		14 30	15 01				14 37	14 51	15 16	14 46	14 54	15 00	15 31

	GW	GW	XC		GW	GW	GW	GW	GW	GW	GW	GW	XC	GW	GW	GW	GW	GW	GW		GW	XC	GW	GW
	◇ B		◇ C		◇ J			K	◇ L		◇ M		◇ N	◇ D					◇ B			◇ C		◇ D
Birmingham New Street 71 d			13 04										13 33									14 04		
Birmingham International d			13 14																			14 14		
Coventry d			13 25																			14 25		
Leamington Spa d			13 38										14 00									14 38		
Banbury 71 d			13 55										14 19									14 55		
Kings Sutton d																								
Heyford d																								
Tackley d																								
Oxford 115 a			14 13										14 40									15 14		
d		14 07	14 16						14 31			14 37	14 43				15 01				15 07	15 16		
Radley d		14 13																			15 13			
Culham d																					15 17			
Appleford d																								
Didcot Parkway a		14 22										14 49									15 24			
d	14 18				14 30					14 32	14 48							15 02	15 18					15 30
Cholsey d										14 39								15 08						
Goring & Streatley d										14 44								15 13						
Pangbourne d										14 49								15 17						
Tilehurst d										14 53								15 22						
Bedwyn d																14 40								
Hungerford d																14 46								
Kintbury d																14 50								
Newbury a																14 57								
d						14 12										14 57							15 12	
Newbury Racecourse d						14 14																	15 14	
Thatcham d						14 19										15 02							15 19	
Midgham d						14 24																	15 24	
Aldermaston d						14 27																	15 27	
Theale d						14 32										15 10							15 32	
Reading West d						14 39																	15 40	
Reading a	14 32		14 40		14 44	14 45			14 54	14 59	15 02		15 08			15 19	15 25	15 27	15 32			15 41	15 44	15 44
d	14 35				14 46		14 48	14 53	14 56	15 03	15 04			15 12	15 18	15 22	15 27	15 33	15 34					15 46
Twyford a							14 54			15 09					15 24			15 39						
Maidenhead a							15 02			15 17					15 32			15 47						
Slough a							15 13		15 09	15 24					15 43		15 40	15 54						
Ealing Broadway ⊖ a							15 33			15 49					16 07			16 22						
London Paddington ⊖ a	15 02				15 14		15 46	15 21	15 27	15 59	15 30			15 40	16 16	15 52	15 59	16 32	16 01					16 14

A From Penzance. The Cornish Riviera
B From Cardiff Central
C From Manchester Piccadilly to Bournemouth
D From Bristol Temple Meads
E From Worcester Foregate Street
F From Swansea. The St. David
G From Glasgow Central to Southampton Central
H From Cheltenham Spa
I From Paignton
J From Weston-super-Mare
K From Penzance. The Cornishman
L From Hereford
M From Swansea
N From Dundee

For complete services between Banbury and Birmingham, refer to Table T71

Table T116-R

Birmingham, Banbury, Oxford and Bedwyn - Reading and London

Mondays to Fridays

21 May to 7 December

	GW	GW	GW	GW	GW	GW	XC	GW	GW	GW	GW		GW	GW	GW	GW	GW	GW	GW	GW	XC	GW	GW	GW
		◇ A	◇ B	◇ C			◇ D	◇ E		F	F		◇ G	H		I			◇ J		◇ K	◇ E		◇ L
Birmingham New Street 71 d							14 33														15 04			
Birmingham International d																					15 14			
Coventry d																					15 25			
Leamington Spa d							15 00														15 38			
Banbury 71 d						15 07	15 19														15 55			
Kings Sutton d						15 12																		
Heyford d						15 20																		
Tackley d						15 25																		
Oxford 115 a						15 34	15 40														16 14			
d			15 31			15 36	15 43								16 01					16 07	16 16			
Radley d						15 42														16 13				
Culham d																								
Appleford d																				16 18				
Didcot Parkway a						15 52														16 27				
d					15 32						16 03		16 04						16 18	16 29		16 30		
Cholsey d					15 38						16 08									16 35				
Goring & Streatley d					15 43						16 13									16 40				
Pangbourne d					15 47						16 17									16 44				
Tilehurst d					15 52						16 21									16 49				
Bedwyn d										15 33														
Hungerford d										15 39														
Kintbury d										15 43														
Newbury a										15 50														
d										15 50							15 55							
Newbury Racecourse d																	15 57							
Thatcham d										15 55							16 02							
Midgham d																	16 07							
Aldermaston d																	16 10							
Theale d										16 03							16 15							
Reading West d														←		←	16 22							
Reading a			15 54		15 57		16 11			16 12	16 26		16 16	16 12	16 24	16 26	16 26		16 32	16 54	16 40	16 44		
d	15 48	15 52	15 56	16 02	16 06			16 11	16 18	16 22	16 28		16 19	16 22	16 25	16 28		16 32	16 35			16 46	16 48	16 49
Twyford a	15 54				16 12				16 24	→	→					16 33		16 38					16 54	
Maidenhead a	16 02				16 20				16 32							16 40		16 46					17 02	
Slough a	16 13		16 09		16 28				16 43						16 40			16 53					17 13	
Ealing Broadway ⊖ a	16 33				16 53				17 08									17 19					17 40	
London Paddington ⊖ a	16 46	16 21	16 27	16 29	17 02			16 40	17 20				16 44	16 52	17 00	17 07		17 30	17 02			17 12	17 52	17 15

	GW	GW	GW		GW	XC	GW	GW	GW	GW	GW	GW	GW	GW	GW	GW	GW	GW	XC		GW	GW	GW	GW
	◇ M		◇ C			◇ N	◇ O		◇ P		F	◇ B	I	◇ J			◇ Q		◇ K		◇ E	R		◇ S
Birmingham New Street 71 d						15 33													16 04					
Birmingham International d																			16 14					
Coventry d																			16 25					
Leamington Spa d						16 01													16 38					
Banbury 71 d						16 19													16 55					
Kings Sutton d																								
Heyford d																								
Tackley d																								
Oxford 115 a						16 40													17 13					
d	16 31				16 37	16 43						17 01						17 07	17 16					17 31
Radley d					16 43													17 13						
Culham d																		17 17						
Appleford d																								
Didcot Parkway a					16 54													17 25						
d		16 33	16 48								17 02			17 19				17 29			17 30			
Cholsey d		16 39									17 07							17 35						
Goring & Streatley d		16 44									17 12							17 40						
Pangbourne d		16 48									17 16							17 44						
Tilehurst d		16 53									17 20							17 49						
Bedwyn d															16 45									
Hungerford d															16 51									
Kintbury d															16 55									
Newbury a															17 02									
d								16 48	16 53						17 02									
Newbury Racecourse d															17 05									
Thatcham d								16 53							17 10									
Midgham d															17 14									
Aldermaston d															17 18									
Theale d								17 01							17 23									
Reading West d													←		17 30									
Reading a	16 55	17 00	17 02			17 08		17 10	17 16		17 25	17 26	17 25	17 34	17 36			17 54	17 40		17 44			17 54
d	16 57	17 03	17 04				17 11	17 14	17 18	17 18	17 33	17 28	17 33	17 36		17 37	17 39				17 46	17 49	17 51	17 56
Twyford a		17 09								17 24	→		17 38			17 43							17 57	
Maidenhead a		17 17								17 32			17 45			17 51							18 05	
Slough a	17 10	17 24								17 43		17 41				17 58							18 16	18 09
Ealing Broadway ⊖ a		17 49								18 07						18 24							18 38	
London Paddington ⊖ a	17 28	18 02	17 30				17 39	17 46	17 54	18 17		17 59	18 10	18 03		18 36	18 07				18 14	18 16	18 51	18 28

A From Penzance. Restaurant available for customers joining until Castle Cary
B From Worcester Foregate Street
C From Swansea
D From Glasgow Central to Southampton Central
E From Bristol Temple Meads
F To London Paddington
G From Cheltenham Spa. The Cheltenham Spa Express
H From Bedwyn
I From Didcot Parkway
J From Cardiff Central
K From Manchester Piccadilly to Bournemouth
L From Penzance. The Royal Duchy
M From Worcester Shrub Hill
N From Glasgow Central
O From Bristol Temple Meads. The Merchant Venturer
P From Taunton
Q From Paignton. The Torbay Express
R From Plymouth. The Mayflower
S From Hereford

For complete services between Banbury and Birmingham, refer to Table T71

T116 UPDATE: The route between Theale and Bedwyn will be CLOSED TO ALL TRAINS. Rail replacement buses on 4-7 June; 9-12 July; 16 July to 05 August; 28-30 August; 08-11 October and 19-22 November.

Table T116-R

Mondays to Fridays

21 May to 7 December

Birmingham, Banbury, Oxford and Bedwyn - Reading and London

		GW ◇1 A ☕	GW	GW	GW ◇1 B ☕	XC ◇1 C 🛒	GW ◇1 D ☕	GW	GW	GW E	GW ◇1 F ☕	GW G		GW ◇1 H ☕	GW	GW ◇1 I ☕	GW	XC ◇1 J 🛒	GW	GW ◇1 K ☕	GW	GW E	GW ◇1 A ☕	GW G	GW
Birmingham New Street 12 71	d					16 33												17 04							
Birmingham International	d																	17 14							
Coventry	d																	17 25							
Leamington Spa 3	d					17 00												17 38							
Banbury 71	d					17 19											17 35	17 55							
Kings Sutton	d																17 40								
Heyford	d																17 49								
Tackley	d																17 53								
Oxford 115	a					17 40											18 09	18 14							
	d			17 35		17 43					18 06						18 10	18 16			18 31				18 36
Radley	d			17 41													18 16								18 42
Culham	d			17 45																					
Appleford	d			17 48																					18 47
Didcot Parkway	a			17 54													18 25								18 52
	d		17 32				18 00			18 01				18 20		18 31	18 32					18 40	18 48		
Cholsey	d		17 39							18 07							18 38					18 46			
Goring & Streatley	d		17 44							18 12							18 43					18 51			
Pangbourne	d		17 48							18 16							18 47					18 55			
Tilehurst	d		17 53							18 21							18 52					19 00			
Bedwyn	d								17 38						17 52										
Hungerford	d								17 44						17 58										
Kintbury	d								17 48						18 02										
Newbury	a								17 55						18 09										
	d								17 55						18 10										
Newbury Racecourse	d														18 12										
Thatcham	d								18 00						18 17										
Midgham	d														18 22										
Aldermaston	d								18 06						18 25										
Theale	d								18 11						18 30										
Reading West	d											←			18 37									←	
Reading 7	a		17 58			18 09	18 14		18 20	18 26	18 29	18 26		18 34	18 43	18 46	18 57	18 44			18 56	19 05	19 02	19 05	
	d	18 02	18 07		18 08		18 16	18 18	18 22	18 33	18 31	18 33		18 38		18 47			18 52	18 53	18 59	19 07	19 05	19 07	
Twyford 3	a		18 13					18 24		→		18 39							18 58			→		19 13	
Maidenhead 3	a		18 21					18 32				18 47							19 06					19 21	
Slough 3	a		18 28					18 43			18 44	18 54							19 17		19 12			19 28	
Ealing Broadway ⊖	a		18 53					19 06				19 19							19 36					19 53	
London Paddington 15 ⊖	a	18 30	19 06		18 39		18 44	19 15	18 52		19 03	19 31		19 07		19 13			19 46	19 20	19 30		19 33	20 06	

		XC ◇1 L 🛒	GW ◇1 D ☕	GW		GW	GW ◇1 M 🛒	GW	GW	GW ◇1 H ☕	GW	XC ◇1 J 🛒	GW ◇1 I ☕	GW	GW	GW	GW	GW ◇1 A ☕	GW ◇1 N ☕	XC ◇1 O 🛒		GW ◇1 B ☕	GW	GW E	GW
Birmingham New Street 12 71	d	17 33										18 04								18 33					
Birmingham International	d											18 14													
Coventry	d											18 25													
Leamington Spa 3	d	18 01										18 38								19 01					
Banbury 71	d	18 19									18 37	18 56								19 19					
Kings Sutton	d										18 42														
Heyford	d										18 52														
Tackley	d										18 56														
Oxford 115	a	18 40									19 05	19 13								19 41					
	d	18 43					19 02				19 06	19 16			19 32		19 37			19 43					19 57
Radley	d										19 13														20 03
Culham	d																								20 07
Appleford	d																								
Didcot Parkway	a										19 21						19 49								20 14
	d							19 02		19 18			19 30			19 34						20 00		20 08	
Cholsey	d							19 08								19 40								20 14	
Goring & Streatley	d							19 13								19 45								20 19	
Pangbourne	d							19 17								19 49								20 23	
Tilehurst	d							19 22								19 54								20 28	
Bedwyn	d								19 03																
Hungerford	d								19 09																
Kintbury	d								19 13																
Newbury	a								19 20																
	d					18 52													19 49						
Newbury Racecourse	d					18 54																			
Thatcham	d					18 59																			
Midgham	d					19 04																			
Aldermaston	d					19 07																			
Theale	d					19 12																			
Reading West	d					19 19																			
Reading 7	a	19 10				19 22	19 25	19 27		19 32		19 41	19 44		19 56	19 59			20 08	20 09		20 14		20 33	
	d		19 11	19 19		19 23	19 27	19 33		19 34			19 46	19 52	19 56	20 01		20 02	20 10			20 17	20 20	20 34	
Twyford 3	a			19 25				19 39						19 58		20 07							20 26	→	
Maidenhead 3	a			19 33				19 47						20 06		20 15							20 34		
Slough 3	a			19 45			19 40	19 56						20 17	20 11	20 23							20 45		
Ealing Broadway ⊖	a			20 03				20 22						20 36		20 49							21 07		
London Paddington 15 ⊖	a		19 38	20 16		19 54	19 59	20 31		20 01			20 14	20 46	20 30	21 01		20 32	20 37			20 43	21 16		

- **A** From Swansea
- **B** From Cheltenham Spa
- **C** From Aberdeen to Guildford
- **D** From Bristol Temple Meads
- **E** To London Paddington
- **F** From Moreton-in-Marsh
- **G** From Didcot Parkway
- **H** From Cardiff Central
- **I** From Weston-super-Mare
- **J** From Manchester Piccadilly to Bournemouth
- **K** From Penzance
- **L** From Glasgow Central
- **M** From Worcester Foregate Street
- **N** From Newquay
- **O** From Edinburgh

For complete services between Banbury and Birmingham, refer to Table T71

Table T116-R

Mondays to Fridays

21 May to 7 December

Birmingham, Banbury, Oxford and Bedwyn - Reading and London

		GW ◇1 A 🛒	GW B	XC ◇1 C 🛒	GW	GW ◇1 D ☕	GW	GW ◇1 E ☕	GW	GW F	GW	GW ◇1 G ☕		GW B	XC ◇1 H 🛒	GW	GW	GW	GW	GW	XC ◇1 C	GW	GW	GW ◇1 D ☕	GW
Birmingham New Street 12 71	d			19 04											19 33						20 04				
Birmingham International	d			19 14																	20 14				
Coventry	d			19 25																	20 25				
Leamington Spa 3	d			19 38											20 02						20 38				
Banbury 71	d			19 55							20 04				20 22						20 56				
Kings Sutton	d										20 09														
Heyford	d										20 17														
Tackley	d										20 22														
Oxford 115	a			20 13							20 32				20 40						21 14				
	d	20 06		20 16					20 31		20 34				20 42		21 01			21 07	21 16				21 25
Radley	d																			21 13					21 31
Culham	d																								
Appleford	d																								
Didcot Parkway	a										20 46									21 22					21 40
	d					20 30				20 30		20 48							21 02					21 30	
Cholsey	d									20 36									21 08						
Goring & Streatley	d									20 41									21 13						
Pangbourne	d									20 45									21 17						
Tilehurst	d									20 50									21 22						
Bedwyn	d				19 54											20 36							21 18		
Hungerford	d				20 00											20 42							21 24		
Kintbury	d				20 04											20 46							21 28		
Newbury	a				20 11											20 53							21 35		
	d				20 11											20 53						21 12			
Newbury Racecourse	d				20 14																	21 14			
Thatcham	d				20 19											20 58						21 19			
Midgham	d				20 23																	21 24			
Aldermaston	d				20 27																	21 27			
Theale	d				20 32											21 06						21 32			
Reading West	d		←		20 39									←								21 39			
Reading 7	a	20 29	20 33	20 41	20 42	20 44			20 54	20 58		21 02		20 58	21 07	21 16	21 26		21 27		21 42	21 43		21 45	
	d	20 31	20 34			20 46	20 48	20 54	20 56	21 07		21 04		21 07		21 21	21 29	21 29	21 37					21 46	
Twyford 3	a		20 40				20 54			→				21 13				21 35	21 43						
Maidenhead 3	a		20 48				21 02							21 21				21 43	21 51						
Slough 3	a	20 44	20 55				21 13		21 09					21 28			21 43	21 54	21 58						
Ealing Broadway ⊖	a		21 20				21 34							21 53				22 19	22 23						
London Paddington 15 ⊖	a	21 05	21 31			21 12	21 46	21 22	21 29			21 31		22 02		22 00	22 06	22 28	22 31					22 13	

		GW FO ◇1 A 🛒	GW FX ◇1 A 🛒	GW FO		GW FX	GW ◇1 I ☕	GW FO ◇1 G ☕	GW FX ◇1 G ☕	GW	XC ◇1 J	GW	GW	GW FX F	GW FO	GW FX K	GW	XC ◇1 L	GW FO	GW FX		GW FO ◇1 M	GW FX ◇1 M	GW FX ◇1 G ☕	GW FO ◇1 G ☕
Birmingham New Street 12 71	d										20 34							21 04							
Birmingham International	d																	21 14							
Coventry	d																	21 25							
Leamington Spa 3	d										21 00							21 38							
Banbury 71	d										21 19						21 37	21 55							
Kings Sutton	d																21 42								
Heyford	d																21 50								
Tackley	d																21 55								
Oxford 115	a										21 40						22 06	22 14							
	d	21 31	21 31								21 43			22 01	22 01		22 09	22 16				22 31	22 31		
Radley	d																22 15								
Culham	d																								
Appleford	d																								
Didcot Parkway	a													22 13	22 13		22 24								
	d							21 53	21 53				22 02	22 14	22 14		22 29								
Cholsey	d												22 08				22 35								
Goring & Streatley	d												22 13				22 40								
Pangbourne	d												22 17				22 44								
Tilehurst	d												22 22				22 49								
Bedwyn	d																								
Hungerford	d																								
Kintbury	d																								
Newbury	a																								
	d						21 44					21 51													
Newbury Racecourse	d											21 53													
Thatcham	d											21 58													
Midgham	d											22 03													
Aldermaston	d											22 06													
Theale	d											22 11													
Reading West	d											22 19				←									
Reading 7	a	21 55	21 55				22 02	22 09	22 09		22 16	22 24	22 27	22 29	22 31	22 29	22 54	22 42				22 56	22 56		
	d	21 57	21 57	22 01		22 01	22 03	22 10	22 12	22 15				22 37	22 34	22 37			22 48	22 48		22 59	22 59	23 02	23 04
Twyford 3	a			22 07		22 07				22 21				→					22 54	22 54					
Maidenhead 3	a			22 15		22 15				22 29									23 02	23 02					
Slough 3	a	22 11	22 11	22 26		22 27				22 40					22 50	23 02			23 13	23 14		23 12	23 16		
Ealing Broadway ⊖	a			22 59		22 59				23 05									23 52	23 52					
London Paddington 15 ⊖	a	22 29	22 31	23 08		23 08	22 37	22 39	22 51	23 16					23 08	23 23			00 01	00 01		23 30	23 36	23 40	23 37

- **A** From Great Malvern
- **B** From Didcot Parkway
- **C** From Manchester Piccadilly to Bournemouth
- **D** From Bristol Temple Meads
- **E** From Penzance. Restaurant available after PLY for customers joining until TAU
- **F** To London Paddington
- **G** From Swansea
- **H** From Glasgow Central
- **I** From Exeter St Davids
- **J** From Edinburgh to Southampton Central
- **K** From Oxford
- **L** From Manchester Piccadilly to Southampton Central
- **M** From Worcester Foregate Street

For complete services between Banbury and Birmingham, refer to Table T71

Birmingham, Banbury, Oxford and Bedwyn - Reading and London

Mondays to Fridays

21 May to 7 December

Station		GW FX ◇■ A ⊡	GW FO ◇■ A ⊡	GW	GW	GW	GW	GW FX	GW FO	GW	GW	XC ◇■	GW ◇■ B ⊡	GW	GW	CH C
Birmingham New Street ■ 71	d											22 04				
Birmingham International	d											22 14				
Coventry	d											22 25				
Leamington Spa ■	d											22 38				23 39
Banbury 71	d										22 36	22 55			23 45	23 58
Kings Sutton	d										22 42				23 50	
Heyford	d										22 50				23 58	
Tackley	d										22 55				00 03	
Oxford 115	a										23 05	23 14			00 12	00 22
	d					22 39	22 52	23 01	23 01			23 16			00 27	
Radley	d					22 45	23 00								00 33	
Culham	d						23 04									
Appleford	d						23 06									
Didcot Parkway	a					22 54	23 12	23 16	23 16						00 42	
	d	22 52	22 52					23 17	23 17	23 21			23 37		00 47	
Cholsey	d									23 27					00 54	
Goring & Streatley	d									23 32					00 59	
Pangbourne	d									23 36					01 04	
Tilehurst	d									23 41					01 08	
Bedwyn	d			22 22										23 17		
Hungerford	d			22 28										23 23		
Kintbury	d			22 32										23 27		
Newbury	a			22 39										23 34		
	d			22 39										23 34		
Newbury Racecourse	d			22 42										23 37		
Thatcham	d			22 47										23 42		
Midgham	d			22 51										23 46		
Aldermaston	d			22 55										23 50		
Theale	d			23 00										23 55		
Reading West	d			23 07										00 03		
Reading ■	a	23 07	23 07	23 10				23 31	23 31	23 46		23 49	23 52	00 06	01 14	
	d	23 08	23 10		23 14			23 37	23 37				23 54			
Twyford ■	a				23 20											
Maidenhead ■	a				23 28			23 48	23 48							
Slough ■	a				23 39			23 55	23 55							
Ealing Broadway ⊖	a				00 05											
London Paddington ■ ⊖	a	23 42	23 39		00 14			00 21	00 22				00 31			

Saturdays

26 May to 8 December

Station		GW D	GW	GW ◇■ E	GW F	GW	GW	GW G	GW	GW	GW	GW	GW	GW	GW	GW	GW	GW	GW ◇■ H ⊡	GW	GW	GW ◇	GW	GW
Birmingham New Street ■ 71	d																							
Birmingham International	d																							
Coventry	d																							
Leamington Spa ■	d																							
Banbury 71	d																							
Kings Sutton	d																							
Heyford	d																							
Tackley	d				00 03																			
Oxford 115	a				00 12																			
	d			00 07	00 27			04 00					05 14		05 40			06 01				06 31		06 37
Radley	d				00 33								05 20					06 07						
Culham	d												05 24											
Appleford	d																	06 11						
Didcot Parkway	a			00 20	00 42			04 12					05 31		05 52			06 18						06 50
	d			00 22	00 47			04 13					05 32				06 05		06 30				06 33	
Cholsey	d				00 54								05 37				06 10						06 38	
Goring & Streatley	d				00 59								05 42				06 15						06 43	
Pangbourne	d				01 04								05 47				06 20						06 48	
Tilehurst	d				01 08								05 51				06 24						06 52	
Bedwyn	d																				06 05			
Hungerford	d																				06 10			
Kintbury	d																				06 15			
Newbury	a																				06 22			
	d																				06 22			
Newbury Racecourse	d																				06 24			
Thatcham	d																				06 29			
Midgham	d																				06 34			
Aldermaston	d																				06 37			
Theale	d																				06 42			
Reading West	d	00 03																			06 49			
Reading ■	a	00 06		00 38	01 14			04 29					05 57				06 30		06 43		06 53	06 56	06 58	
	d		00 14	00 41		01 15	04 12		04 40	05 10	05 33	05 48		06 05		06 18	06 33		06 45	06 48		06 57	07 03	
Twyford ■	a		00 20			01 21	04 18		04 46	05 16	05 39	05 54		06 11		06 24	06 39			06 54			07 09	
Maidenhead ■	a		00 28			01 29	04 26		04 54	05 24	05 47	06 02		06 19		06 32	06 47			07 02			07 17	
Slough ■	a		00 39	00 57		01 36	04 33		05 01	05 35	05 54	06 13		06 26		06 43	06 54			07 13		07 11	07 24	
Ealing Broadway ⊖	a		01 02			01 52	04 54		05 19	06 03	06 19	06 33		06 51		07 03	07 19			07 35			07 49	
London Paddington ■ ⊖	a		01 11	01 18		02 01	05 06		05 32	06 14	06 29	06 46		07 01		07 16	07 31		07 14	07 43		07 30	08 01	

A From Penzance
B From Taunton
C From Stratford-upon-Avon
D From Bedwyn
E From Hereford
F From Banbury
G To Gatwick Airport
H From Bristol Temple Meads

For complete services between Banbury and Birmingham, refer to Table T71

Table T116-R

Birmingham, Banbury, Oxford and Bedwyn - Reading and London

Saturdays

26 May to 8 December

Station		GW ◇■ A ⊡	GW	GW	GW ◇■	GW ◇■ A ⊡	GW	GW	XC ◇■ B ✕	GW ◇■ C ⊡	GW	GW	GW ◇■ D	GW ◇■ A ⊡	GW	GW	XC ◇■ E	GW ◇■ F ⊡	GW	GW	GW ◇■	GW	GW ◇■ A ⊡
Birmingham New Street ■ 71	d								06 04								06 33						
Birmingham International	d								06 14														
Coventry	d								06 25														
Leamington Spa ■	d								06 38								07 00						
Banbury 71	d								06 55							07 05	07 19						
Kings Sutton	d															07 10							
Heyford	d															07 18							
Tackley	d															07 23							
Oxford 115	a								07 14							07 34	07 40						
	d				07 01			07 07	07 16				07 31			07 37	07 43				08 01		
Radley	d							07 13															
Culham	d							07 17															
Appleford	d																						
Didcot Parkway	a							07 25								07 51							
	d	07 00					07 02			07 30					07 32			08 01				08 02	08 16
Cholsey	d						07 07								07 37							08 07	
Goring & Streatley	d						07 12								07 42							08 12	
Pangbourne	d						07 17								07 47							08 17	
Tilehurst	d						07 21								07 51							08 21	
Bedwyn	d			06 41																07 41			
Hungerford	d			06 46																07 46			
Kintbury	d			06 51																07 51			
Newbury	a			06 58																07 58			
	d			06 58							07 16									07 58			
Newbury Racecourse	d										07 18												
Thatcham	d			07 03							07 23									08 03			
Midgham	d										07 27												
Aldermaston	d										07 31												
Theale	d			07 11							07 36									08 11			
Reading West	d										07 43												
Reading ■	a	07 13		07 20	07 24		07 27		07 41	07 43	07 47		07 54		07 57		08 09	08 14		08 20	08 24	08 27	08 32
	d	07 15	07 18	07 21	07 25	07 33	07 33			07 46		07 48	07 55	08 02	08 03			08 16	08 18	08 21	08 25	08 33	08 33
Twyford ■	a		07 24				07 39					07 54			08 09				08 24			08 39	
Maidenhead ■	a		07 32				07 47					08 02			08 17				08 32			08 47	
Slough ■	a		07 43		07 38		07 54					08 13	08 08		08 24				08 43		08 38	08 54	
Ealing Broadway ⊖	a		08 05				08 19					08 35			08 49				09 03			09 19	
London Paddington ■ ⊖	a	07 41	08 16	07 52	07 56	07 59	08 31			08 14		08 46	08 27	08 30	09 01			08 44	09 13	08 52	08 56	09 31	08 59

Station		GW	XC ◇■ G ✕	GW ◇■ C ⊡	GW	GW	GW ◇■ H ⊡	GW ◇■ I ⊡	GW	GW	GW ◇■ A ⊡	XC ◇■ J ✕	GW ◇■ K ⊡	GW ◇■ L ⊡	GW	GW	GW ◇■	GW	GW ◇■ A ⊡	GW	GW	XC ◇■ M	XC ◇■ N ✕	GW ◇■ H ⊡
Birmingham New Street ■ 71	d		07 04									07 33										08 04	08 04	
Birmingham International	d		07 14																			08 14	08 14	
Coventry	d		07 25																			08 25	08 25	
Leamington Spa ■	d		07 38									08 01										08 38	08 38	
Banbury 71	d		07 55									08 19										08 55	08 55	
Kings Sutton	d																							
Heyford	d																							
Tackley	d																							
Oxford 115	a		08 14									08 39										09 14	09 14	
	d	08 07	08 16					08 30		08 36		08 43					08 58			09 07		09 16	09 16	
Radley	d	08 13																		09 13				
Culham	d																			09 17				
Appleford	d	08 17																						
Didcot Parkway	a	08 24								08 51										09 25				
	d			08 30					08 32				08 55	09 01				09 02	09 18					
Cholsey	d								08 37									09 07						
Goring & Streatley	d								08 42									09 12						
Pangbourne	d								08 47									09 17						
Tilehurst	d								08 51									09 21						
Bedwyn	d															08 41								
Hungerford	d															08 46								
Kintbury	d															08 51								
Newbury	a															08 58								
	d				08 16		08 35									08 58					09 07			
Newbury Racecourse	d				08 18																09 09			
Thatcham	d				08 23											09 03					09 14			
Midgham	d				08 27																09 18			
Aldermaston	d				08 31																09 22			
Theale	d				08 36											09 11					09 27			
Reading West	d				08 43																09 34			
Reading ■	a		08 41	08 44	08 47		08 51	08 53	08 57			09 09	09 09	09 15		09 20	09 21	09 27	09 32		09 38	09 40	09 40	
	d			08 46		08 48	08 54	08 57	09 03		09 04		09 11	09 17	09 18	09 21	09 25	09 33	09 33					09 44
Twyford ■	a					08 54			09 09						09 24			09 39						
Maidenhead ■	a					09 02			09 17						09 32			09 47						
Slough ■	a					09 13		09 10	09 24						09 43		09 38	09 54						
Ealing Broadway ⊖	a					09 33			09 49						10 03			10 19						
London Paddington ■ ⊖	a			09 14		09 46	09 21	09 28	10 01		09 30		09 41	09 44	10 16	09 52	09 56	10 31	09 59					10 10

A From Swansea
B To Bournemouth
C From Bristol Temple Meads
D From Great Malvern
E To Southampton Central
F From Weston-super-Mare
G From Manchester Piccadilly to Bournemouth
H From Plymouth
I From Hereford
J From Sheffield
K From Cheltenham Spa
L From Taunton
M from 28 July until 1 September. From Nottingham to Bournemouth
N until 21 July, from 8 September. From Nottingham to Bournemouth

For complete services between Banbury and Birmingham, refer to Table T71

T116 UPDATE: The route between Theale and Bedwyn will be CLOSED TO ALL TRAINS. Rail replacement buses on 4-7 June; 9-12 July; 16 July to 05 August; 28-30 August; 08-11 October and 19-22 November.

Table T116-R

Saturdays
26 May to 8 December

Birmingham, Banbury, Oxford and Bedwyn - Reading and London

	GW ◇1 A	GW	GW ◇1 B	GW ◇1 C	GW	GW	XC ◇1 D	XC ◇1 E	GW ◇1 F	GW	GW	GW ◇	GW	GW ◇1 G	GW ◇1 H	GW	XC ◇1 I	GW ◇1 A	GW	GW	GW ◇1 J	GW ◇1 K
Birmingham New Street 71 d							08 33	08 33									09 04					
Birmingham International d																	09 14					
Coventry d																	09 25					
Leamington Spa d							09 00	09 00									09 38					
Banbury 71 d						09 08	09 19	09 19									09 55					
Kings Sutton d						09 12																
Heyford d						09 21																
Tackley d						09 25																
Oxford 115 a						09 36	09 40	09 41									10 15					
d			09 29			09 37	09 43	09 43				10 00				10 07	10 16					10 31
Radley d																10 13						
Culham d																						
Appleford d																10 17						
Didcot Parkway a						09 51										10 24						
d	09 30				09 32								10 03	10 18	10 23			10 31				
Cholsey d					09 37								10 09									
Goring & Streatley d					09 42								10 14									
Pangbourne d					09 47								10 18									
Tilehurst d					09 51								10 23									
Bedwyn d											09 41											
Hungerford d											09 46											
Kintbury d											09 51											
Newbury a											09 58											
d											09 58								10 16			
Newbury Racecourse d																			10 18			
Thatcham d											10 03								10 23			
Midgham d																			10 27			
Aldermaston d																			10 31			
Theale d											10 11								10 36			
Reading West d																			10 43			
Reading a	09 43		09 52		09 57		10 08	10 08			10 21	10 24	10 30	10 32	10 37		10 41	10 45	10 47			10 56
d	09 47	09 48	09 53	10 01	10 03				10 13	10 18	10 22	10 25	10 33	10 34	10 41			10 48		10 48	10 54	10 57
Twyford a		09 54			10 09					10 24			10 39							10 54		
Maidenhead a		10 02			10 17					10 32			10 47							11 02		
Slough a		10 13	10 06		10 24					10 43		10 39	10 54							11 13		11 10
Ealing Broadway ⊖ a		10 33			10 49					11 03			11 19							11 33		
London Paddington ⊖ a	10 14	10 46	10 24	10 29	11 01				10 39	11 16	10 53	10 58	11 31	11 01	11 07			11 14		11 46	11 21	11 28

	GW ◇1 L	GW	GW	GW ◇1 C	XC ◇1 M	GW ◇1 A	GW	GW	GW ◇1	GW	GW	XC ◇1 I	GW ◇1 A	GW	GW	GW 1 N	GW ◇1 O	GW ◇1 C	GW	GW	XC ◇1 P	GW ◇1 A	GW
Birmingham New Street 71 d					09 33							10 04									10 33		
Birmingham International d												10 14											
Coventry d												10 25											
Leamington Spa d					10 00							10 38									11 00		
Banbury 71 d					10 19							10 55								11 08	11 19		
Kings Sutton d																				11 12			
Heyford d																				11 21			
Tackley d																				11 25			
Oxford 115 a					10 41							11 14								11 35	11 41		
d	10 31		10 37		10 43				11 01		11 09	11 16					11 31			11 38	11 43		
Radley d											11 15												
Culham d																							
Appleford d																							
Didcot Parkway a			10 51								11 26									11 52			
d		10 32								11 02			11 30						11 32				
Cholsey d		10 37								11 07									11 37				
Goring & Streatley d		10 42								11 12									11 42				
Pangbourne d		10 47								11 17									11 47				
Tilehurst d		10 51								11 21									11 51				
Bedwyn d								10 41															
Hungerford d								10 46															
Kintbury d								10 51															
Newbury a								10 58															
d								10 58						11 16									
Newbury Racecourse d														11 18									
Thatcham d								11 03						11 23									
Midgham d														11 27									
Aldermaston d														11 31									
Theale d								11 11						11 36									
Reading West d														11 43									
Reading a	10 56	10 58			11 10			11 20	11 24	11 27		11 38	11 44	11 47			11 54		11 57		12 06		
d	10 57	11 03		11 05		11 13	11 18	11 21	11 25	11 33			11 46		11 48	11 52	11 55	12 03	12 03			12 12	12 18
Twyford a		11 09					11 24			11 39					11 54				12 09				12 24
Maidenhead a		11 17					11 32			11 47					12 02				12 17				12 32
Slough a	11 10	11 24					11 43		11 38	11 54					12 13		12 08		12 24				12 43
Ealing Broadway ⊖ a		11 49					12 05			12 19					12 33				12 49				13 03
London Paddington ⊖ a	11 29	12 01		11 31		11 40	12 16	11 52	11 59	12 31			12 14		12 46	12 21	12 26	12 29	13 01			12 38	13 16

A From Bristol Temple Meads
B From Hereford
C From Swansea
D from 28 July until 6 October. From Derby to Southampton Central
E until 21 July, from 13 October. From Leeds to Southampton Central
F From Exeter St Davids
G from 15 September. From Swansea
H From Worcester Shrub Hill
I From Manchester Piccadilly to Bournemouth
J From Plymouth
K until 8 September. From Great Malvern
L from 15 September. From Great Malvern
M From York
N From Penzance
O From Great Malvern
P From Newcastle to Southampton Central

For complete services between Banbury and Birmingham, refer to Table T71

Table T116-R

Saturdays
26 May to 8 December

Birmingham, Banbury, Oxford and Bedwyn - Reading and London

	GW	GW ◇1	GW	GW ◇1 A	GW	XC ◇1 B	GW ◇1 C	GW	GW	GW 1 D	GW ◇1 E	GW ◇1 F	GW	GW	GW ◇1 G	XC ◇1 H	GW ◇1 I	GW	GW	GW ◇1	GW	GW
Birmingham New Street 71 d						11 04										11 33						
Birmingham International d						11 14																
Coventry d						11 25																
Leamington Spa d						11 38										12 00						
Banbury 71 d						11 55										12 19						
Kings Sutton d																						
Heyford d																						
Tackley d																						
Oxford 115 a						12 15										12 41						
d		12 01			12 07	12 17						12 31		12 37		12 43				13 01		13 07
Radley d					12 13																	13 13
Culham d																						13 17
Appleford d					12 17																	
Didcot Parkway a					12 24									12 51								13 24
d			12 03	12 23			12 31						12 32								13 02	
Cholsey d			12 08										12 37								13 07	
Goring & Streatley d			12 13										12 42								13 12	
Pangbourne d			12 18										12 47								13 17	
Tilehurst d			12 22										12 51								13 21	
Bedwyn d	11 41																		12 41			
Hungerford d	11 46																		12 46			
Kintbury d	11 51																		12 51			
Newbury a	11 58																		12 58			
d	11 58							12 16											12 58			
Newbury Racecourse d								12 18														
Thatcham d	12 03							12 23											13 03			
Midgham d								12 27														
Aldermaston d								12 31														
Theale d	12 11							12 36											13 11			
Reading West d								12 43														
Reading a	12 20	12 24	12 29	12 37		12 42	12 46	12 47				12 54	12 57			13 09			13 20	13 24	13 27	
d	12 21	12 25	12 33	12 41			12 48		12 48	12 54	12 54	12 57	13 03		13 05		13 12	13 18	13 21	13 25	13 33	
Twyford a			12 39						12 54				13 09					13 24			13 39	
Maidenhead a			12 47						13 02				13 17					13 32			13 47	
Slough a		12 38	12 54						13 13			13 10	13 24					13 43		13 38	13 54	
Ealing Broadway ⊖ a			13 19						13 33				13 49					14 03			14 19	
London Paddington ⊖ a	12 52	12 56	13 31	13 07			13 14		13 46	13 21	13 21	13 28	14 01		13 31		13 38	14 16	13 52	13 56	14 31	

	GW 1 J	GW ◇1 K	XC ◇1 B	GW ◇1 L	GW	GW	GW ◇1 M	GW ◇1 N	GW	GW	XC ◇1 O	GW ◇1 P	GW ◇1 L	GW	GW	GW ◇	GW	GW ◇1 A	GW	XC ◇1 B	GW ◇1 I	GW Q	GW R
Birmingham New Street 71 d			12 04								12 33									13 04			
Birmingham International d			12 14																	13 14			
Coventry d			12 25																	13 25			
Leamington Spa d			12 38								13 00									13 38			
Banbury 71 d			12 55							13 08	13 19									13 55			
Kings Sutton d										13 12													
Heyford d										13 21													
Tackley d										13 25													
Oxford 115 a			13 14							13 36	13 41									14 14			
d			13 16				13 30			13 37	13 43					14 03			14 08	14 16			
Radley d																			14 14				
Culham d																							
Appleford d																			14 18				
Didcot Parkway a										13 52									14 25				
d				13 30					13 32								14 02	14 24			14 30		
Cholsey d									13 37								14 07						
Goring & Streatley d									13 42								14 12						
Pangbourne d									13 47								14 17						
Tilehurst d									13 51								14 21						
Bedwyn d															13 45								
Hungerford d															13 50								
Kintbury d															13 55								
Newbury a															14 02								
d						13 21						13 52			14 02							14 13	14 16
Newbury Racecourse d						13 23																14 15	14 18
Thatcham d						13 28									14 07							14 20	14 23
Midgham d						13 32																14 24	14 27
Aldermaston d						13 36																14 28	14 31
Theale d						13 41									14 15							14 33	14 36
Reading West d						13 48																14 40	14 43
Reading a			13 40	13 43		13 52	13 52		13 57		14 08	14 11			14 24	14 27	14 27	14 37		14 41	14 43	14 44	14 47
d	13 34	13 34		13 45	13 48		13 54	14 02	14 03			14 12	14 15	14 18	14 25	14 28	14 33	14 40			14 45		
Twyford a					13 54				14 09					14 24			14 39						
Maidenhead a					14 02				14 17					14 32			14 47						
Slough a					14 13		14 07		14 24					14 43		14 42	14 54						
Ealing Broadway ⊖ a					14 33				14 49					15 03			15 19						
London Paddington ⊖ a	14 00	14 00		14 14	14 46		14 25	14 29	15 01			14 38	14 41	15 16	14 58	15 01	15 31	15 07			15 14		

A From Cheltenham Spa
B From Manchester Piccadilly to Bournemouth
C From Paignton. The Torbay Express
D until 8 September. From Penzance
E from 15 September. From Penzance
F From Great Malvern
G From Carmarthen
H From Edinburgh
I From Weston-super-Mare
J until 8 September. From Penzance. The Cornish Riviera
K from 15 September. From Penzance. The Cornish Riviera
L From Bristol Temple Meads
M From Worcester Foregate Street
N From Swansea
O From Glasgow Central to Southampton Central
P from 15 September. From Exeter St Davids
Q until 8 September
R from 15 September

For complete services between Banbury and Birmingham, refer to Table T71

Birmingham, Banbury, Oxford and Bedwyn - Reading and London

		GW	GW	GW	GW	GW	GW	GW	GW	GW	GW	XC	GW	GW	GW	GW	GW	GW	XC	GW	GW	GW	GW
			A	B	A	C	D	E			F	G	H						I	H			B
Birmingham New Street 71	d											13 33							14 04				
Birmingham International	d																		14 14				
Coventry	d																		14 25				
Leamington Spa	d											14 00							14 38				
Banbury 71	d											14 19							14 56				
Kings Sutton	d																						
Heyford	d																						
Tackley	d																						
Oxford 115	a											14 40							15 15				
	d					14 30	14 30			14 37		14 43				15 01		15 07	15 16				
Radley	d																	15 13					
Culham	d																	15 17					
Appleford	d																						
Didcot Parkway	a									14 52								15 24					
	d								14 32								15 02			15 30			
Cholsey	d								14 37								15 07						
Goring & Streatley	d								14 42								15 12						
Pangbourne	d								14 47								15 17						
Tilehurst	d								14 51								15 21						
Bedwyn	d														14 41								
Hungerford	d														14 46								
Kintbury	d														14 51								
Newbury	a														14 58								
	d														14 58						15 13		
Newbury Racecourse	d																				15 15		
Thatcham	d														15 03						15 20		
Midgham	d																				15 24		
Aldermaston	d																				15 28		
Theale	d														15 11						15 33		
Reading West	d																				15 40		
Reading	a					14 53	14 56		14 57			15 08			15 20	15 24	15 27		15 40	15 43	15 44		
	d	14 48	14 50	14 52	14 55	14 55	14 58	15 03	15 03		15 06		15 13	15 18	15 21	15 25	15 33			15 45		15 48	15 52
Twyford	a	14 54							15 09					15 24			15 39					15 54	
Maidenhead	a	15 02							15 17					15 32			15 47					16 02	
Slough	a	15 13				15 08	15 11		15 24					15 43		15 38	15 54					16 13	
Ealing Broadway	a	15 35							15 49					16 03			16 19					16 33	
London Paddington	a	15 46	15 16	15 21	15 22	15 26	15 29	15 29	16 01		15 32		15 41	16 16	15 52	15 59	16 31			16 14		16 46	16 21

		GW	GW	GW	GW	GW	GW	XC	GW	GW	GW	GW	GW	GW	GW	GW	GW	XC	GW	GW	GW	GW	GW	GW
		A	J	K			L	M	H				N	O	P	Q		I	R	S	T	U		A
Birmingham New Street 71	d							14 33										15 04						
Birmingham International	d																	15 14						
Coventry	d																	15 25						
Leamington Spa	d							15 00										15 38						
Banbury 71	d					15 08		15 22										15 55						
Kings Sutton	d					15 12																		
Heyford	d					15 21																		
Tackley	d					15 25																		
Oxford 115	a					15 36		15 41										16 14						
	d		15 31			15 37		15 43				16 01					16 07	16 16						
Radley	d																16 13							
Culham	d																							
Appleford	d																16 17							
Didcot Parkway	a					15 51											16 24							
	d				15 34								16 02			16 23						16 31		
Cholsey	d				15 39								16 07											
Goring & Streatley	d				15 44								16 12											
Pangbourne	d				15 49								16 17											
Tilehurst	d				15 53								16 21											
Bedwyn	d										15 41													
Hungerford	d										15 46													
Kintbury	d										15 51													
Newbury	a										15 58													
	d										15 58			16 08					16 08		16 13			
Newbury Racecourse	d																		16 10		16 15			
Thatcham	d										16 03								16 15		16 20			
Midgham	d																		16 19		16 24			
Aldermaston	d																		16 23		16 28			
Theale	d										16 11								16 28		16 33			
Reading West	d														←				16 35		16 40			
Reading	a		15 54		15 59			16 09			16 20	16 24	16 27	16 29	16 27	16 37		16 42	16 42		16 44	16 46		
	d	15 52	15 55	16 03	16 03		16 06		16 12	16 18	16 21	16 25	16 33	16 32	16 33	16 40				16 44		16 48	16 48	16 52
Twyford	a				16 09					16 24			→		16 39								16 54	
Maidenhead	a				16 17					16 32					16 47								17 02	
Slough	a		16 08		16 24					16 43		16 38			16 54								17 13	
Ealing Broadway	a				16 49					17 03					17 19								17 33	
London Paddington	a	16 21	16 26	16 29	17 01		16 32		16 38	17 16	16 52	16 57		17 00	17 31	17 07				17 10		17 14	17 46	17 21

A until 8 September. From Penzance
B from 15 September. From Penzance
C from 15 September. From Hereford
D until 8 September. From Hereford
E from 15 September. From Swansea
F until 8 September. From Pembroke Dock. The Pembroke Coast Express
G From Dundee
H From Bristol Temple Meads
I From Manchester Piccadilly to Bournemouth
J From Moreton-in-Marsh
K From Swansea
L until 8 September. From Newquay. The Atlantic Coast Express
M From Glasgow Central to Southampton Central
N To London Paddington
O until 8 September. From Paignton
P From Didcot Parkway
Q From Cheltenham Spa
R from 15 September
S from 15 September. From Plymouth
T until 8 September
U From Weston-super-Mare

For complete services between Banbury and Birmingham, refer to Table T71

Please check the 'Additional Notes to Individual Tables' section for any other general notes that apply to this Table

Birmingham, Banbury, Oxford and Bedwyn - Reading and London

		GW	GW	GW	GW	XC	GW	GW	GW	GW	GW	GW	GW	XC	GW	GW	GW	GW	GW	GW	GW	GW	GW
		A	B			C	D	E						F	G	H	I	J	K		L	M	N
Birmingham New Street 71	d					15 33								16 04									
Birmingham International	d													16 14									
Coventry	d													16 25									
Leamington Spa	d					16 02								16 38									
Banbury 71	d					16 20								16 55									
Kings Sutton	d																						
Heyford	d																						
Tackley	d																						
Oxford 115	a					16 40								17 14									
	d	16 31			16 37	16 43					17 02		17 07	17 16									
Radley	d												17 13										
Culham	d												17 17										
Appleford	d																						
Didcot Parkway	a				16 51								17 24										
	d			16 32								17 02				17 30		17 30					
Cholsey	d			16 37								17 07											
Goring & Streatley	d			16 42								17 12											
Pangbourne	d			16 47								17 17											
Tilehurst	d			16 51								17 21											
Bedwyn	d									16 45													
Hungerford	d									16 50													
Kintbury	d									16 55													
Newbury	a									17 02													
	d							16 52		17 02					17 10				17 16				
Newbury Racecourse	d														17 12				17 18				
Thatcham	d									17 07					17 17				17 23				
Midgham	d														17 21				17 27				
Aldermaston	d														17 25				17 31				
Theale	d									17 15					17 30				17 36				
Reading West	d														17 37				17 43		←		
Reading	a	16 54		16 57		17 10		17 10		17 24	17 25	17 27		17 39	17 43	17 43		17 43	17 47		17 43		
	d	16 55	17 03	17 03			17 10	17 14	17 18	17 25	17 29	17 33				17 45	17 46	17 49		17 48	17 49	17 53	17 55
Twyford	a			17 09					17 24			17 39						→		17 54			
Maidenhead	a			17 17					17 32			17 47								18 02			
Slough	a	17 08		17 24					17 43		17 42	17 54								18 13			
Ealing Broadway	a			17 49					18 03			18 19								18 33			
London Paddington	a	17 26	17 29	18 01			17 38	17 44	18 16	17 56	18 00	18 31				18 14	18 12			18 46	18 15	18 21	18 21

		GW	GW	GW	GW	GW	GW	XC	GW	GW	GW	GW	GW	GW	GW	GW	XC	GW	GW	GW	GW	GW	GW	GW
		O	P			Q	R	S	D		K	G				T	F	U			V	A	B	
Birmingham New Street 71	d							16 33									17 04							
Birmingham International	d																17 14							
Coventry	d																17 25							
Leamington Spa	d							17 00									17 38							
Banbury 71	d				17 08			17 19									17 55							
Kings Sutton	d				17 12																			
Heyford	d				17 21																			
Tackley	d				17 25																			
Oxford 115	a				17 36			17 40									18 14							
	d	17 31	17 31		17 37			17 43					18 01		18 07		18 16					18 31		
Radley	d														18 13									
Culham	d																							
Appleford	d														18 17									
Didcot Parkway	a				17 51										18 24									
	d			17 32										18 03		18 24		18 32						18 32
Cholsey	d			17 37										18 08										18 37
Goring & Streatley	d			17 42										18 13										18 42
Pangbourne	d			17 47										18 18										18 47
Tilehurst	d			17 51										18 22										18 51
Bedwyn	d										17 41	17 41												
Hungerford	d										17 46	17 46												
Kintbury	d										17 51	17 51												
Newbury	a										17 58	17 58												
	d										17 58	17 58							18 16					
Newbury Racecourse	d																		18 18					
Thatcham	d										18 03	18 03							18 23					
Midgham	d																		18 27					
Aldermaston	d																		18 31					
Theale	d										18 11	18 11							18 36					
Reading West	d																		18 43					
Reading	a	17 54	17 54	17 57				18 10			18 20	18 20	18 24	18 28		18 37	18 43	18 45	18 47			18 54		18 57
	d	17 56	17 58	18 03		18 04	18 04		18 11	18 18	18 21	18 21	18 25	18 33		18 39		18 47		18 48	18 52	18 55	19 03	19 03
Twyford	a			18 09						18 24				18 39						18 54				19 09
Maidenhead	a			18 17						18 32				18 47						19 02				19 17
Slough	a	18 09	18 11	18 24						18 43			18 38	18 54						19 13		19 08		19 24
Ealing Broadway	a			18 49						19 03				19 19						19 33				19 49
London Paddington	a	18 27	18 29	19 01		18 30	18 31		18 37	19 16	18 52	18 56	18 59	19 31		19 06		19 14		19 46	19 22	19 26	19 29	20 01

A From Great Malvern
B From Swansea
C From Glasgow Central
D From Bristol Temple Meads
E from 15 September. From Taunton
F From Manchester Piccadilly to Bournemouth
G until 8 September
H from 15 September. From Bristol Temple Meads
I until 8 September. From Paignton
J until 8 September. From Bristol Temple Meads to London Paddington
K from 15 September
L until 8 September. From Bristol Temple Meads
M from 15 September. From Plymouth
N until 8 September. From Penzance
O from 15 September. From Hereford
P until 8 September. From Hereford
Q from 15 September. From Swansea
R until 8 September. From Swansea
S From Aberdeen to Guildford
T From Cheltenham Spa
U From Weston-super-Mare
V From Penzance. The Royal Duchy

For complete services between Banbury and Birmingham, refer to Table T71

T116 UPDATE: The route between Theale and Bedwyn will be CLOSED TO ALL TRAINS. Rail replacement buses on 4-7 June; 9-12 July; 16 July to 05 August; 28-30 August; 08-11 October and 19-22 November.

Table T116-R

Birmingham, Banbury, Oxford and Bedwyn - Reading and London

Saturdays 26 May to 8 December

	GW	XC ◇1 A	GW ◇1 B	GW	GW	GW ◇1	GW	GW	XC ◇1 C	GW ◇1 D	GW	GW	GW ◇1 E	GW ◇1 F	GW	GW	GW ◇1 G	XC ◇1 H	GW	GW	GW ◇1	GW
Birmingham New Street 71 d		17 33							18 04									18 33				
Birmingham International d									18 14													
Coventry d									18 25													
Leamington Spa d		18 02							18 38									19 00				
Banbury 71 d		18 19							18 55							19 08		19 19				
Kings Sutton d																19 12						
Heyford d																19 21						
Tackley d																19 25						
Oxford 115 a		18 41							19 14							19 35		19 41				
d	18 37	18 43				19 01		19 07	19 16				19 31			19 37		19 43			20 01	
Radley d								19 13														
Culham d								19 17														
Appleford d																						
Didcot Parkway a	18 51							19 24								19 51						
d							19 03			19 30					19 32							20 02
Cholsey d							19 08								19 37							20 07
Goring & Streatley d							19 13								19 42							20 12
Pangbourne d							19 17								19 47							20 17
Tilehurst d							19 22								19 51							20 21
Bedwyn d					18 41															19 42		
Hungerford d					18 46															19 48		
Kintbury d					18 51															19 52		
Newbury a					18 58															19 59		
d					18 58						19 16						19 48					
Newbury Racecourse d											19 18											
Thatcham d					19 03						19 23											
Midgham d											19 27											
Aldermaston d											19 31											
Theale d					19 11						19 36											
Reading West d											19 43											
Reading a		19 10			19 20	19 24	19 28		19 41	19 43	19 47		19 54		19 57		20 05	20 08			20 24	20 27
d			19 10	19 18	19 21	19 25	19 33			19 45		19 48	19 55	20 03	20 03		20 10		20 18		20 25	20 33
Twyford a				19 24			19 39					19 54			20 09				20 24			20 39
Maidenhead a				19 32			19 47					20 02			20 17				20 32			20 47
Slough a				19 43		19 38	19 54					20 13	20 08		20 24				20 43		20 38	20 54
Ealing Broadway ⊖ a				20 03			20 19					20 33			20 49				21 03			21 19
London Paddington ⊖ a			19 37	20 16	19 52	19 56	20 31			20 14		20 46	20 27	20 30	21 01		20 37		21 17		20 56	21 29

	GW	GW ◇1 I	GW	XC ◇1 C	GW ◇1 B	GW	GW ◇1 E	GW ◇1 J	GW	GW	GW ◇1 K	XC ◇1 A	GW	GW ◇1	GW	GW	GW	XC ◇1 C	GW ◇1 D	GW ◇1 L	GW	GW ◇1 J	XC ◇1 M
Birmingham New Street 71 d				19 04								19 33						20 04					20 33
Birmingham International d				19 14														20 14					
Coventry d				19 25														20 25					
Leamington Spa d				19 38								20 03						20 38					21 00
Banbury 71 d				19 55								20 20				20 36		20 55					21 20
Kings Sutton d																20 40							
Heyford d																20 49							
Tackley d																20 54							
Oxford 115 a				20 14								20 40				21 04		21 14					21 41
d	20 07			20 16			20 27			20 37		20 43		21 01		21 05		21 16		21 29			21 43
Radley d	20 13															21 11							
Culham d																							
Appleford d	20 17																						
Didcot Parkway a	20 24									20 51						21 20				21 41			
d		20 24			20 30				20 32						21 02				21 33	21 43		21 48	
Cholsey d									20 37						21 07								
Goring & Streatley d									20 42						21 12								
Pangbourne d									20 47						21 17								
Tilehurst d									20 51						21 21								
Bedwyn d																	20 47						
Hungerford d																	20 52						
Kintbury d																	20 57						
Newbury a																	21 04						
d			20 08														21 04						
Newbury Racecourse d			20 10														21 06						
Thatcham d			20 15														21 11						
Midgham d			20 19														21 16						
Aldermaston d			20 23														21 19						
Theale d			20 28														21 24						
Reading West d			20 35														21 31						
Reading a		20 38	20 39	20 41	20 44		20 51		20 57			21 08		21 24	21 27		21 35	21 42	21 46	21 56		22 02	22 14
d		20 40			20 46	20 48	20 52	21 02	21 03		21 05		21 18	21 25	21 33		21 36		21 48	21 58	22 03	22 09	
Twyford a						20 54			21 09				21 24		21 39						22 09		
Maidenhead a						21 02			21 17				21 32		21 47						22 17		
Slough a						21 13	21 06		21 24				21 43	21 38	21 58					22 11	22 28		
Ealing Broadway ⊖ a						21 33			21 49				22 04		22 23						22 49		
London Paddington ⊖ a		21 06			21 14	21 46	21 25	21 28	21 59		21 31		22 16	21 56	22 32		22 06		22 14	22 29	22 58	22 38	

A From Glasgow Central
B From Bristol Temple Meads
C From Manchester Piccadilly to Bournemouth
D From Weston-super-Mare
E From Great Malvern
F From Pembroke Dock
G From Plymouth
H From Edinburgh
I From Cheltenham Spa
J From Swansea
K From Penzance
L From Worcester Foregate Street
M From Edinburgh to Southampton Central

For complete services between Banbury and Birmingham, refer to Table T71

Table T116-R

Birmingham, Banbury, Oxford and Bedwyn - Reading and London

Saturdays 26 May to 8 December

	GW ◇1 A	GW B	GW	GW C	GW ◇1	GW D	GW E	XC ◇1 F	GW	GW	GW ◇1 G	GW ◇1 H	GW	GW	GW ◇1	GW	GW ◇1 I	GW	GW
Birmingham New Street 71 d								21 04											
Birmingham International d								21 14											
Coventry d								21 25											
Leamington Spa d								21 38											
Banbury 71 d								21 55		22 00									
Kings Sutton d										22 04									
Heyford d										22 13									
Tackley d										22 17									
Oxford 115 a								22 14		22 28									
d			21 47		22 01			22 18		22 29		22 35			23 01	23 10			
Radley d			21 53													23 16			
Culham d																23 20			
Appleford d																23 22			
Didcot Parkway a			22 02		22 13					22 41		22 49			23 14	23 29			
d				22 07	22 14						22 50	22 52		22 56	23 16		23 34		23 49
Cholsey d				22 12										23 01					23 54
Goring & Streatley d				22 17										23 06					23 59
Pangbourne d				22 22										23 11					00 04
Tilehurst d				22 26										23 15					00 08
Bedwyn d		21 35				21 35							22 19					23 22	
Hungerford d		21 40				21 40							22 24					23 27	
Kintbury d		21 45				21 45							22 29					23 32	
Newbury a		21 52				21 52							22 36					23 39	
d		21 52				22 00							22 36					23 39	
Newbury Racecourse d		21 54				22 02							22 38					23 41	
Thatcham d		21 59				22 07							22 43					23 46	
Midgham d		22 04				22 11							22 48					23 51	
Aldermaston d		22 07				22 15							22 51					23 54	
Theale d		22 12				22 20							22 56					23 59	
Reading West d		22 19				22 27	←						23 03					00 06	
Reading a		22 23		22 32	22 27	22 31	22 32	22 45			23 03	23 06	23 07	23 21	23 30		23 48	00 10	00 14
d	22 15			22 34	22 29		22 34		22 52		23 05	23 14		23 22	23 32		23 51		00 20
Twyford a				→			22 40		22 58					23 28					00 26
Maidenhead a							22 48		23 06					23 36					00 34
Slough a					22 42		22 59		23 17			23 31		23 47	23 51				00 45
Ealing Broadway ⊖ a							23 24		23 38					00 05					01 10
London Paddington ⊖ a	22 41				23 00		23 33		23 47		23 43	23 51		00 15	00 17		00 33		01 19

Sundays 20 May to 2 December

	GW J	GW K	GW L	GW M	GW (bus)	GW M	GW L	GW 1 M	GW M	GW 1 L	GW L	GW M	GW L	GW ◇1 N	GW ◇1 O	GW ◇ M	GW M	GW L	GW M	GW L	GW ◇ L	GW ◇1 O	GW L
Birmingham New Street 71 d																							
Birmingham International d																							
Coventry d																							
Leamington Spa d																							
Banbury 71 d																							
Kings Sutton d																							
Heyford d																							
Tackley d																							
Oxford 115 a																							
d					07 15											08 40		08 42	08 47		08 55		
Radley d					07 30											08 47		08 49	08 54				
Culham d																							
Appleford d																							
Didcot Parkway a					07 50											08 55		08 57	09 02		09 05		
d								08 00		08 08		08 29	08 30	08 46	08 46	08 56					09 06		
Cholsey d												08 35	08 36										
Goring & Streatley d								08 08		08 16		08 40	08 41										
Pangbourne d		00 04										08 44	08 45										
Tilehurst d		00 08										08 49	08 50										
Bedwyn d																							
Hungerford d																							
Kintbury d																							
Newbury a																							
d																				08 48			
Newbury Racecourse d																				08 50			
Thatcham d																				08 55			
Midgham d																				09 00			
Aldermaston d																				09 03			
Theale d																				09 08			
Reading West d	00 06																			09 16			
Reading a	00 10	00 14						08 19		08 27		08 53	08 54	09 01	09 01	09 12				09 20	09 21		
d		00 20	06 20	06 22		07 22	07 32	08 20	08 25	08 28	08 32	08 53	09 00	09 03	09 03	09 12	09 20				09 22	09 26	09 30
Twyford a		00 26	06 26	06 28		07 28	07 38		08 31		08 38	08 59	09 04				09 26						09 35
Maidenhead a		00 34	06 34	06 36		07 36	07 46		08 38		08 46	09 07	09 14				09 34						09 46
Slough a		00 45	06 44	06 47		07 47	07 55	08 38	08 47	08 44	08 55	09 15	09 24			09 29	09 45				09 40		09 55
Ealing Broadway ⊖ a		01 10	07 07	07 12		08 12	08 20		09 12		09 20	09 38	09 50				10 11						10 20
London Paddington ⊖ a		01 19	07 16	07 21		08 21	08 28	09 00	09 21	09 07	09 28	09 48	09 58	09 39	09 41	09 51	10 20				10 04	10 05	10 28

A until 8 September. From Newquay
B from 15 September
C To London Paddington
D until 8 September
E From Didcot Parkway
F From Manchester Piccadilly to Southampton Central
G From Penzance
H From Hereford
I From Taunton
J not 20 May. From Bedwyn
K not 20 May. From Didcot Parkway
L from 16 September
M until 9 September
N from 16 September. From Bristol Temple Meads
O until 9 September. From Bristol Temple Meads

For complete services between Banbury and Birmingham, refer to Table T71

Table T116-R

Sundays

20 May to 2 December

Birmingham, Banbury, Oxford and Bedwyn - Reading and London

Station		GW ◇■ A	GW B	GW ◇■ C	GW B	GW ◇■ D	GW E	GW		GW F	GW ◇■ G	GW ◇■ H	GW I	GW J	GW ◇ K	GW ◇ L	GW E	GW M	GW ◇■ N	GW B	GW ◇■ O	XC ◇■ P	GW ◇■ Q	GW ◇■ R
Birmingham New Street 71	d																					09 04		
Birmingham International	d																					09 14		
Coventry	d																					09 25		
Leamington Spa	d																					09 38		
Banbury 71	d																					09 55		
Kings Sutton	d																							
Heyford	d																							
Tackley	d																							
Oxford 115	a																					10 14		
	d							09 29							09 55	09 55						10 16		
Radley	d							09 36																
Culham	d																							
Appleford	d																							
Didcot Parkway	a							09 44							10 06	10 06								
	d				09 21		09 34			09 52	09 53	09 56		10 04	10 07	10 07								
Cholsey	d				09 27		09 40			09 58				10 10										
Goring & Streatley	d				09 32		09 45			10 02				10 14										
Pangbourne	d				09 37		09 50			10 07				10 19										
Tilehurst	d				09 41		09 54			10 12				10 24										
Bedwyn	d																09 35			09 45				
Hungerford	d																09 41			09 51				
Kintbury	d																09 46			09 56				
Newbury	a																09 52			10 02				
	d		09 03														09 53			10 03	10 18			10 32
Newbury Racecourse	d		09 05														09 55			10 05				
Thatcham	d		09 10														10 00			10 10				
Midgham	d		09 15														10 05			10 15				
Aldermaston	d		09 18														10 08			10 18				
Theale	d		09 23														10 13			10 23				
Reading West	d		09 31										←				10 21	←		10 31				
Reading	a		09 34		09 47		10 00			10 17	10 08	10 15	10 17	10 29	10 23	10 23	10 25	10 29		10 33	10 35	10 42		10 49
	d	09 33	09 36	09 48	09 53	09 55	10 00			10 19	10 09	10 16	10 19	10 30	10 25	10 25		10 30	10 33	10 33	10 36		10 44	10 51
Twyford	a				09 59		10 05			→			10 24	→				10 35						
Maidenhead	a		09 47		10 07		10 14						10 34					10 46		10 45				
Slough	a		09 55		10 15		10 24						10 41		10 39	10 44		10 55		10 52				
Ealing Broadway ⊖	a				10 38		10 50						11 10					11 20						
London Paddington ⊖	a	10 10	10 15	10 25	10 48	10 35	10 58				10 46	10 54	11 19		11 05	11 05		11 28	11 11	11 15	11 14		11 21	11 30

Station		GW B	GW E	GW ◇■ S	GW	GW ◇■ A	GW E	GW B	GW J	GW ◇■ T	GW ◇■ U	GW M	GW B	GW ◇■ G	GW ◇■ V	XC ◇■ W		GW B	GW ◇■ X	GW ◇■ H	GW B	GW	GW E	GW ◇■ N	GW ◇■ Q
Birmingham New Street 71	d															10 04									
Birmingham International	d															10 14									
Coventry	d															10 25									
Leamington Spa	d															10 38									
Banbury 71	d															10 55		11 00							
Kings Sutton	d																	11 05							
Heyford	d																	11 14							
Tackley	d																	11 19							
Oxford 115	a															11 14		11 29							
	d				10 32					10 55	11 00					11 16						11 32			
Radley	d				10 39																	11 39			
Culham	d																								
Appleford	d																								
Didcot Parkway	a				10 47					11 07	11 12											11 47			
	d			10 46		10 52		10 52	11 02	11 08	11 13									11 28					11 47
Cholsey	d							10 58	11 08																
Goring & Streatley	d							11 02	11 12																
Pangbourne	d							11 07	11 17																
Tilehurst	d							11 12	11 22																
Bedwyn	d						10 35						10 54												
Hungerford	d						10 41						11 00												
Kintbury	d						10 45						11 04												
Newbury	a						10 52						11 11												
	d						10 53						11 11		11 17				11 20						
Newbury Racecourse	d																								
Thatcham	d						10 58						11 16												
Midgham	d																								
Aldermaston	d																								
Theale	d						11 06						11 24												
Reading West	d											←													
Reading	a			11 02		11 08	11 15	11 17	11 27	11 23	11 27	11 27	11 33		11 36	11 40			11 40	11 46					12 02
	d	10 54	11 00	11 03		11 09		11 18	11 30	11 24	11 28	11 30	11 33	11 34	11 37				11 43	11 48	11 54		12 00	12 01	12 03
Twyford	a	11 00	11 05					11 24	→			11 35									12 00		12 05		
Maidenhead	a	11 08	11 16					11 32				11 46	11 45								12 08		12 16		
Slough	a	11 15	11 23					11 41		11 38	11 48	11 55	11 52								12 15		12 24		
Ealing Broadway ⊖	a	11 38	11 50					12 04				12 20									12 38		12 50		
London Paddington ⊖	a	11 47	11 58	11 40		11 45		12 13		12 05	12 08	12 28	12 14	12 10	12 14				12 21	12 26	12 47		12 58	12 38	12 40

- **A** from 16 September. From Bristol Temple Meads
- **B** until 9 September
- **C** until 9 September. From Cardiff Central
- **D** from 16 September. From Cardiff Central
- **E** from 16 September
- **F** until 9 September. To London Paddington
- **G** from 16 September. From Weston-super-Mare
- **H** until 9 September. From Weston-super-Mare
- **I** until 9 September. From Didcot Parkway
- **J** from 16 September. To London Paddington
- **K** from 16 September. From Worcester Foregate Street
- **L** until 9 September. From Worcester Foregate Street
- **M** from 16 September. From Didcot Parkway
- **N** from 16 September. From Swansea
- **O** from 16 September. From Exeter St Davids
- **P** To Bournemouth
- **Q** until 9 September. From Swansea
- **R** until 9 September. From Exeter St Davids
- **S** until 9 September. From Bristol Temple Meads
- **T** from 16 September. From Great Malvern
- **U** until 9 September. From Great Malvern
- **V** from 16 September. From Plymouth
- **W** From Manchester Piccadilly to Bournemouth
- **X** until 9 September. From Plymouth

For complete services between Banbury and Birmingham, refer to Table T71

Table T116-R

Sundays

20 May to 2 December

Birmingham, Banbury, Oxford and Bedwyn - Reading and London

Station		GW A	GW ◇■ B	GW ◇■ C	GW D	GW E	GW F	GW ◇ D		GW ◇ G	GW H	GW G	GW ◇■ B	XC ◇■ I	GW ◇■ C	GW	GW ◇■ J	GW ◇■ K	GW G	GW D	GW ◇■ L	GW ◇■ M	GW A	GW ◇■ B
Birmingham New Street 71	d													11 04										
Birmingham International	d													11 14										
Coventry	d													11 25										
Leamington Spa	d													11 38										
Banbury 71	d													11 55										
Kings Sutton	d																							
Heyford	d																							
Tackley	d																							
Oxford 115	a													12 14										
	d							11 55		12 00				12 16		12 32								
Radley	d															12 39								
Culham	d																							
Appleford	d																							
Didcot Parkway	a							12 07		12 12						12 47								
	d	11 52	11 53				12 04	12 08		12 13					12 29							12 47	12 52	12 53
Cholsey	d	11 58					12 10																12 58	
Goring & Streatley	d	12 02					12 14																13 02	
Pangbourne	d	12 07					12 19																13 08	
Tilehurst	d	12 12					12 24																13 13	
Bedwyn	d																							
Hungerford	d																							
Kintbury	d																							
Newbury	a																							
	d				11 45							12 03												
Newbury Racecourse	d				11 47							12 05												
Thatcham	d				11 52							12 10												
Midgham	d				11 57							12 15												
Aldermaston	d				12 00							12 18												
Theale	d				12 05							12 23												
Reading West	d				12 13	←					←	12 30												
Reading	a	12 17	12 08		12 16	12 17	12 29	12 22		12 27	12 29	12 33		12 41	12 45							13 02	13 18	13 08
	d	12 18	12 08	12 12		12 18	12 30	12 24		12 28	12 30	12 33	12 36		12 46		12 53	12 53	12 56	13 00	13 01	13 03	13 21	13 08
Twyford	a	→				12 24	→				12 35								13 00	13 05			→	
Maidenhead	a					12 32					12 46	12 45							13 07	13 16				
Slough	a					12 41		12 38		12 48	12 55	12 52							13 15	13 24				
Ealing Broadway ⊖	a					13 04					13 20								13 38	13 50				
London Paddington ⊖	a		12 45	12 50		13 13		13 05		13 09	13 28	13 14	13 13		13 24		13 30	13 35	13 49	13 58	13 40	13 43		13 45

Station		GW ◇■ C	GW D	GW ◇■ N	GW ◇■ O	GW E	GW F	GW ◇ P	GW ◇■ Q	GW H	GW G	GW ■ B	XC ◇■ I	GW ■ R	GW D	GW G		GW ◇■ S	GW ◇■ T	GW G	GW D	GW ◇■ L	GW ◇■ M	GW A	GW ■ B
Birmingham New Street 71	d												12 04												
Birmingham International	d												12 14												
Coventry	d												12 25												
Leamington Spa	d												12 38												
Banbury 71	d												12 55												
Kings Sutton	d																								
Heyford	d																								
Tackley	d																								
Oxford 115	a												13 14												
	d							13 00	13 00				13 16		13 28	13 29									
Radley	d														13 35	13 36									
Culham	d																								
Appleford	d																								
Didcot Parkway	a							13 12	13 12						13 43	13 44									
	d						13 01	13 13	13 13					13 29								13 47	13 47	13 49	13 53
Cholsey	d						13 07																	13 55	
Goring & Streatley	d						13 11																	13 59	
Pangbourne	d						13 16																	14 04	
Tilehurst	d						13 21																	14 09	
Bedwyn	d		12 34								12 54														
Hungerford	d		12 40								12 59														
Kintbury	d		12 44								13 03														
Newbury	a		12 51								13 10														
	d		12 52	12 59	12 59						13 11														
Newbury Racecourse	d																								
Thatcham	d		12 57								13 16														
Midgham	d																								
Aldermaston	d																								
Theale	d		13 05								13 24														
Reading West	d					←				←															
Reading	a		13 14	13 16	13 17	13 18	13 26	13 27	13 28	13 26	13 33		13 42	13 44								14 01	14 01	14 14	14 08
	d	13 12		13 16	13 19	13 21	13 30	13 28	13 30	13 30	13 33	13 36		13 46				13 51	13 54	13 56	14 00	14 02	14 02	14 18	14 08
Twyford	a					13 27	→			13 35										14 00	14 05			→	
Maidenhead	a					13 35				13 46	13 45									14 07	14 16				
Slough	a					13 44		13 48	13 44	13 55	13 52									14 15	14 24				
Ealing Broadway ⊖	a					14 07				14 20										14 38	14 50				
London Paddington ⊖	a	13 50		13 55	14 04	14 16		14 10	14 10	14 28	14 14	14 13		14 24				14 30	14 34	14 49	14 58	14 40	14 43		14 45

- **A** until 9 September. To London Paddington
- **B** from 16 September. From Bristol Temple Meads
- **C** until 9 September. From Bristol Temple Meads
- **D** from 16 September
- **E** until 9 September. From Didcot Parkway
- **F** from 16 September. To London Paddington
- **G** until 9 September
- **H** from 16 September. From Didcot Parkway
- **I** From Manchester Piccadilly to Bournemouth
- **J** until 9 September. From Cheltenham Spa
- **K** from 16 September. From Cheltenham Spa
- **L** from 16 September. From Swansea
- **M** until 9 September. From Swansea
- **N** until 9 September. From Penzance
- **O** from 16 September. From Penzance
- **P** until 9 September. From Great Malvern
- **Q** from 16 September. From Great Malvern
- **R** until 9 September. From Weston-super-Mare
- **S** until 9 September. From Plymouth
- **T** from 16 September. From Plymouth

For complete services between Banbury and Birmingham, refer to Table T71

T116 UPDATE: The route between Theale and Bedwyn will be CLOSED TO ALL TRAINS. Rail replacement buses on 4-7 June; 9-12 July; 16 July to 05 August; 28-30 August; 08-11 October and 19-22 November.

Table T116-R

Sundays
20 May to 2 December

Birmingham, Banbury, Oxford and Bedwyn - Reading and London

Station		XC	GW	GW	GW	GW	GW	GW	GW	GW	GW	GW	XC	GW	GW	GW	GW	GW	XC	GW	GW	GW	GW
			A	B	C	D	C	E	F	E	G	H	I	A		J	E	C		K	L	M	N
Birmingham New Street 71	d	12 33											13 04						13 33				
Birmingham International	d	12 44											13 14										
Coventry	d	12 55											13 25										
Leamington Spa	d	13 08											13 38						13 59				
Banbury 71	d	13 25											13 55						14 16				
Kings Sutton	d																						
Heyford	d																						
Tackley	d																						
Oxford 115	a	13 43											14 14						14 35				
	d	13 45					13 55	14 00					14 16		14 30				14 36				
Radley	d														14 37								
Culham	d																						
Appleford	d																						
Didcot Parkway	a						14 07	14 12							14 45								
	d					14 04	14 08	14 13						14 29						14 47		14 50	14 53
Cholsey	d					14 10																14 56	
Goring & Streatley	d					14 14																15 00	
Pangbourne	d					14 19																15 05	
Tilehurst	d					14 24																15 10	
Bedwyn	d																						
Hungerford	d																						
Kintbury	d																						
Newbury	a																						
	d				13 45					14 02													
Newbury Racecourse	d				13 47					14 04													
Thatcham	d				13 52					14 09													
Midgham	d				13 57					14 14													
Aldermaston	d				14 00					14 17													
Theale	d				14 05					14 22													
Reading West	d			←	14 13				←	14 28													
Reading	a	14 11		14 14	14 16	14 29	14 22	14 27	14 29	14 33			14 41	14 44					15 02	15 02		15 15	15 08
	d		14 13	14 18		14 30	14 25	14 28	14 30	14 33	14 36	14 39		14 45		14 50	14 54	15 00		15 03	15 06	15 20	15 09
Twyford	a			14 24		→			14 35								15 00	15 05				→	
Maidenhead	a			14 32					14 46	14 45							15 08	15 16					
Slough	a			14 41			14 41	14 47	14 55	14 52							15 15	15 24					
Ealing Broadway ⊖	a			15 04					15 20								15 38	15 50					
London Paddington ⊖	a		14 50	15 14			15 05	15 07	15 28	15 12	15 13	15 15		15 24		15 34	15 47	15 58		15 40	15 45		15 45

Station		GW	GW	GW	GW	GW	GW	GW	GW	GW	GW	XC	GW	GW	GW	GW	GW	GW	GW	GW	XC	XC	GW	GW
		C	O	P	B	D	Q	R	F	E	E	I	H		J	C	S	T	M	G	U	V	A	B
Birmingham New Street 71	d											14 04									14 33	14 33		
Birmingham International	d											14 14									14 44	14 44		
Coventry	d											14 25									14 55	14 55		
Leamington Spa	d											14 38									15 09	15 09		
Banbury 71	d											14 55									15 27	15 27		
Kings Sutton	d																							
Heyford	d																							
Tackley	d																							
Oxford 115	a											15 14									15 45	15 45		
	d						15 00	15 00				15 16		15 30							15 47	15 47		
Radley	d													15 37										
Culham	d																							
Appleford	d																							
Didcot Parkway	a						15 11	15 12						15 45										
	d		14 59			15 02	15 12	15 13									15 47	15 47	15 50	15 53			15 59	
Cholsey	d					15 08													15 56					
Goring & Streatley	d					15 12													16 00					
Pangbourne	d					15 17													16 05					
Tilehurst	d					15 22													16 10					
Bedwyn	d	14 35								14 54														
Hungerford	d	14 41								15 00														
Kintbury	d	14 45								15 04														
Newbury	a	14 52								15 11														
	d	14 53								15 12														
Newbury Racecourse	d																							
Thatcham	d	14 58								15 17														
Midgham	d																							
Aldermaston	d																							
Theale	d	15 06								15 25														
Reading West	d				←				←															←
Reading	a	15 15	15 15		15 15	15 27	15 27	15 27	15 27	15 35		15 40					16 02	16 02	16 15	16 08	16 11	16 12	16 15	16 15
	d		15 17	15 20	15 20	15 30	15 27	15 28	15 30	15 36	15 39		15 47		15 58	16 00	16 03	16 03	16 20	16 10			16 17	16 20
Twyford	a				15 26	→			15 35		15 44					16 05			→					16 26
Maidenhead	a				15 34				15 46	15 48	15 53					16 16								16 34
Slough	a				15 43		15 43	15 48	15 55	15 53	16 02					16 24								16 43
Ealing Broadway ⊖	a				16 06				16 20		16 30					16 50								17 06
London Paddington ⊖	a		15 54	16 05	16 16		16 10	16 09	16 28	16 14	16 39		16 26		16 38	16 58	16 40	16 41		16 45			16 54	17 16

A until 9 September. From Bristol Temple Meads
B until 9 September. From Didcot Parkway
C from 16 September
D from 16 September. To London Paddington
E until 9 September
F from 16 September. From Didcot Parkway
G from 16 September. From Bristol Temple Meads
H until 9 September. From Penzance
I From Manchester Piccadilly to Bournemouth
J from 16 September. From Penzance
K From Swansea
L until 9 September. From Cheltenham Spa
M until 9 September. To London Paddington
N from 16 September. From Weston-super-Mare
O until 9 September. From Weston-super-Mare
P from 16 September. From Cheltenham Spa
Q from 16 September. From Great Malvern
R until 9 September. From Great Malvern
S until 9 September. From Swansea
T from 16 September. From Swansea
U until 9 September. From Derby
V from 16 September. From Derby

For complete services between Banbury and Birmingham, refer to Table T71

Table T116-R

Sundays
20 May to 2 December

Birmingham, Banbury, Oxford and Bedwyn - Reading and London

Station		GW	GW	GW	GW	GW	GW	GW	GW	XC	GW	GW	GW	GW	GW	GW	GW	XC	GW	GW	GW	GW	GW
		A	B	C	D	E	F	G	F	H	I	J	K		F	L	A	M	N	O	P	Q	R
Birmingham New Street 71	d									15 04								15 33					
Birmingham International	d									15 14													
Coventry	d									15 25													
Leamington Spa	d									15 38								15 59					
Banbury 71	d									15 55					16 00			16 16					
Kings Sutton	d														16 05								
Heyford	d														16 14								
Tackley	d														16 19								
Oxford 115	a									16 14					16 31			16 35					
	d			16 00	16 00					16 16			16 23	16 30				16 36					
Radley	d													16 37									
Culham	d																						
Appleford	d																						
Didcot Parkway	a			16 12	16 12								16 35	16 45									
	d		16 04	16 13	16 13						16 29		16 36						16 47		16 50	16 53	
Cholsey	d		16 10																		16 56		
Goring & Streatley	d		16 14																		17 00		
Pangbourne	d		16 19																		17 05		
Tilehurst	d		16 24																		17 10		
Bedwyn	d																						
Hungerford	d																						
Kintbury	d																						
Newbury	a																						
	d	15 45					16 03					16 29				16 36							
Newbury Racecourse	d	15 47					16 05																
Thatcham	d	15 52					16 10																
Midgham	d	15 57					16 15																
Aldermaston	d	16 00					16 18																
Theale	d	16 05					16 23																
Reading West	d	16 13				←	16 30																
Reading	a	16 16	16 29	16 27	16 27	16 29	16 33			16 41	16 45	16 46	16 50			16 53		17 01	17 02		17 16	17 08	
	d		16 30	16 28	16 28	16 30	16 33	16 36	16 37		16 46	16 47	16 53			16 56	17 00		17 03	17 08	17 18	17 08	17 12
Twyford	a		→			16 35			16 43								17 05				→		
Maidenhead	a					16 46	16 45		16 51				17 04				17 16						
Slough	a			16 43	16 48	16 55	16 52		17 01				17 14				17 24						
Ealing Broadway ⊖	a					17 20			17 30								17 50						
London Paddington ⊖	a			17 09	17 11	17 28	17 15	17 12	17 43		17 24	17 29	17 36			17 37	17 58		17 40	17 45		17 45	17 50

Station		GW	GW	GW	GW	GW	GW	GW	GW	GW	GW	XC	GW	GW	GW	GW	GW	GW	GW	GW	GW	XC	XC	GW
		A	S	T	B	D	C	E	F	G	F	H	I	J	U	K	A		N	P	G	V	W	I
Birmingham New Street 71	d											16 04										16 33	16 33	
Birmingham International	d											16 14										16 44	16 44	
Coventry	d											16 25										16 55	16 55	
Leamington Spa	d											16 38										17 09	17 09	
Banbury 71	d											16 55										17 26	17 26	
Kings Sutton	d																							
Heyford	d																							
Tackley	d																							
Oxford 115	a											17 14										17 44	17 44	
	d					17 00	17 00					17 16				17 27		17 30				17 45	17 45	
Radley	d																	17 37						
Culham	d																							
Appleford	d																							
Didcot Parkway	a					17 12	17 12											17 45						
	d				17 04	17 13	17 13						17 29						17 47	17 50	17 54			
Cholsey	d				17 10															17 56				
Goring & Streatley	d				17 14															18 00				
Pangbourne	d				17 19															18 05				
Tilehurst	d				17 24															18 10				
Bedwyn	d	16 35							16 54															
Hungerford	d	16 41							17 00															
Kintbury	d	16 45							17 04															
Newbury	a	16 52							17 11															
	d	16 53							17 11															
Newbury Racecourse	d																							
Thatcham	d	16 58							17 16															
Midgham	d																							
Aldermaston	d																							
Theale	d	17 06							17 24															
Reading West	d		←					←																
Reading	a	17 15	17 16		17 29	17 27	17 27	17 29	17 33			17 41	17 45			17 51			18 02	18 15	18 09	18 10	18 12	
	d		17 18	17 27	17 30	17 28	17 29	17 30	17 33	17 35	17 37		17 46	17 47	17 54	17 55	18 00		18 03	18 18	18 10			18 13
Twyford	a		17 24		→			17 35			17 43						18 05			→				
Maidenhead	a		17 32					17 46	17 45		17 51					18 07	18 16							
Slough	a		17 41			17 48	17 43	17 55	17 52		18 01					18 16	18 24							
Ealing Broadway ⊖	a		18 04					18 20			18 30						18 50							
London Paddington ⊖	a		18 14	18 08		18 09	18 10	18 28	18 13	18 13	18 43		18 24	18 30	18 37	18 38	18 58		18 40		18 46			18 51

A from 16 September
B from 16 September. To London Paddington
C from 16 September. From Hereford
D until 9 September. From Hereford
E from 16 September. From Didcot Parkway
F until 9 September
G from 16 September. From Bristol Temple Meads
H From Manchester Piccadilly to Bournemouth
I until 9 September. From Bristol Temple Meads
J until 9 September. From Penzance
K from 1 July until 9 September
L from 16 September. From Plymouth
M From Sheffield
N From Swansea
O until 9 September. From Cheltenham Spa
P until 9 September. To London Paddington
Q from 16 September. From Weston-super-Mare
R until 9 September. From Weston-super-Mare
S until 9 September. From Didcot Parkway
T from 16 September. From Cheltenham Spa
U from 16 September. From Penzance
V until 9 September. From Newcastle
W from 16 September. From Newcastle

For complete services between Banbury and Birmingham, refer to Table T71

T116 UPDATE: The route between Theale and Bedwyn will be CLOSED TO ALL TRAINS. Rail replacement buses on 4-7 June; 9-12 July; 16 July to 05 August; 28-30 August; 08-11 October and 19-22 November.

Sundays

20 May to 2 December

Birmingham, Banbury, Oxford and Bedwyn - Reading and London

	GW	GW	GW	GW	GW	GW	GW	GW	GW	GW	GW	XC	GW	GW	GW	GW	GW	GW	XC	GW	GW	GW
				◇■	◇■		◇■	◇■	■	■■		◇■		■■		◇■	◇■		◇■	◇■		◇■
	A	B	C	D	E	F	G	H	I	J	I	K	I	L		L	J	B	M	N	O	P
				☕	☕		☕	☕		☕		✕		☕		☕	☕		✕	☕		☕
Birmingham New Street 71 d												17 04							17 33			
Birmingham International d												17 14										
Coventry d												17 25										
Leamington Spa d												17 38							17 59			
Banbury 71 d												17 55	18 00						18 17			
Kings Sutton d													18 05									
Heyford d													18 14									
Tackley d													18 19									
Oxford 115 a												18 14	18 29						18 35			
Oxford d				17 55	18 00							18 16			18 30				18 38			
Radley d															18 37							
Culham d																						
Appleford d																						
Didcot Parkway a				18 07	18 12										18 45							
Didcot Parkway d			18 04	18 08	18 13		18 17	18 17						18 29							18 50	18 53
Cholsey d			18 10																		18 56	
Goring & Streatley d			18 14																		19 00	
Pangbourne d			18 19																		19 05	
Tilehurst d			18 24																		19 10	
Bedwyn d																						
Hungerford d																						
Kintbury d																						
Newbury a																						
Newbury d		17 45							18 03							18 32	18 43					
Newbury Racecourse d		17 47							18 05													
Thatcham d		17 52							18 10													
Midgham d		17 57							18 15													
Aldermaston d		18 00							18 18													
Theale d		18 05							18 23													
Reading West d	←	18 13				←			18 30													
Reading a	18 15	18 16	18 29	18 22	18 27	18 29	18 32	18 32	18 36			18 41		18 46		18 48	18 59		19 05		19 15	19 08
Reading d	18 18		18 30	18 25	18 28	18 30	18 32	18 32		18 36	18 37			18 46		18 49	19 00	19 00		19 08	19 18	19 09
Twyford a	18 24		→			18 35					18 43							19 05			→	
Maidenhead a	18 32					18 46					18 51							19 16				
Slough a	18 41			18 46	18 43	18 55					19 01							19 24				
Ealing Broadway ⊖ a	19 04					19 20					19 34							19 49				
London Paddington ⊖ a	19 14			19 07	19 09	19 28	19 10	19 11		19 13	19 43			19 25		19 29	19 38	19 57		19 45		19 45

	GW	GW	GW	GW	GW	GW	GW	GW	GW	GW	GW	GW	GW	XC	GW	GW	GW	GW	GW	XC	GW	GW	GW
	◇■			◇■		◇■	◇■		■■	■■	■	◇■		◇■	◇■		■■	■■		◇■		◇■	
	Q	A	B	R	C	S	T	F	U	V	I	J	I	K	L		W	X	B	Y	O	Z	
	☕			☕		☕	☕		☕	☕		☕		✕	☕		☕	☕		✕		☕	
Birmingham New Street 71 d														18 04						18 33			
Birmingham International d														18 14						18 44			
Coventry d														18 25						18 55			
Leamington Spa d														18 38						19 09			
Banbury 71 d														18 55						19 26			
Kings Sutton d																							
Heyford d																							
Tackley d																							
Oxford 115 a														19 14						19 44			
Oxford d						18 55	18 55							19 16		19 30				19 45			
Radley d																19 37							
Culham d																							
Appleford d																							
Didcot Parkway a						19 07	19 07									19 45							
Didcot Parkway d					19 04	19 08	19 11		19 17	19 17					19 30						19 50	19 53	
Cholsey d					19 10																19 56		
Goring & Streatley d					19 14																20 00		
Pangbourne d					19 19																20 05		
Tilehurst d					19 24																20 10		
Bedwyn d			18 35								18 54												
Hungerford d			18 41								19 00												
Kintbury d			18 45								19 04												
Newbury a			18 53								19 11												
Newbury d			18 53								19 11												19 43
Newbury Racecourse d																							19 45
Thatcham d			18 58								19 16												19 50
Midgham d																							19 55
Aldermaston d																							19 58
Theale d			19 06								19 24												20 03
Reading West d		←						←															20 11
Reading a		19 15	19 15		19 29	19 23	19 27	19 29	19 32	19 32	19 35			19 40	19 45					20 08	20 15	20 08	20 14
Reading d	19 10	19 18		19 25	19 30	19 25	19 27	19 30	19 33	19 33		19 36	19 37		19 46		19 47	19 56	19 58		20 18	20 09	
Twyford a		19 24			→			19 35					19 43						20 05		→		
Maidenhead a		19 32						19 46					19 51						20 16				
Slough a		19 41				19 46	19 43	19 55					20 00						20 24				
Ealing Broadway ⊖ a		20 04						20 20					20 34						20 50				
London Paddington ⊖ a	19 50	20 14		20 07		20 08	20 10	20 28	20 10	20 13		20 15	20 44		20 25		20 28	20 37	20 58			20 45	

- **A** until 9 September. From Didcot Parkway
- **B** from 16 September
- **C** from 16 September. To London Paddington
- **D** until 9 September. From Worcester Foregate Street
- **E** from 16 September. From Worcester Foregate Street
- **F** from 16 September. From Didcot Parkway
- **G** until 9 September. From Carmarthen
- **H** from 16 September. From Carmarthen
- **I** until 9 September
- **J** from 16 September. From Plymouth
- **K** From Manchester Piccadilly to Bournemouth
- **L** until 9 September. From Plymouth
- **M** From Newcastle
- **N** until 9 September. From Cheltenham Spa
- **O** until 9 September. To London Paddington
- **P** from 16 September. From Paignton
- **Q** until 9 September. From Paignton
- **R** from 16 September. From Cheltenham Spa
- **S** until 9 September. From Hereford
- **T** from 16 September. From Hereford
- **U** until 9 September. From Swansea
- **V** from 16 September. From Swansea
- **W** until 9 September. From Penzance
- **X** from 16 September. From Penzance
- **Y** From Edinburgh
- **Z** from 16 September. From Bristol Temple Meads

For complete services between Banbury and Birmingham, refer to Table T71

Sundays

20 May to 2 December

Birmingham, Banbury, Oxford and Bedwyn - Reading and London

	GW	GW	GW	GW	GW	GW	GW	GW	GW	GW	XC	GW	GW	GW	GW	GW	GW	GW	GW	GW	GW	GW
	◇■			◇■	◇■		◇■	◇■	◇■	◇■	◇■	◇■	◇■	◇■				◇■	◇■	◇■		◇■
	A	B	C	D	E	F	G	H	I	J	K	L	A	M		N	O	P	Q	R	S	T
	☕						☕	☕	☕	☕	✕	☕	☕	☕				☕	☕	☕		☕
Birmingham New Street 71 d											19 04											
Birmingham International d											19 14											
Coventry d											19 25											
Leamington Spa d											19 38											
Banbury 71 d											19 55											
Kings Sutton d																						
Heyford d																						
Tackley d																						
Oxford 115 a											20 14											
Oxford d				19 55	19 55						20 16				20 30							
Radley d															20 37							
Culham d																						
Appleford d																						
Didcot Parkway a				20 07	20 07										20 45							
Didcot Parkway d			20 04	20 08	20 08		20 17	20 17					20 29								20 50	20 52
Cholsey d			20 10																		20 56	
Goring & Streatley d			20 14																		21 00	
Pangbourne d			20 19																		21 05	
Tilehurst d			20 24																		21 10	
Bedwyn d																						
Hungerford d																						
Kintbury d																						
Newbury a																						
Newbury d										20 20		20 28										
Newbury Racecourse d																						
Thatcham d																						
Midgham d																						
Aldermaston d																						
Theale d																						
Reading West d		←				←								←								
Reading a		20 15	20 29	20 23	20 23	20 29	20 32	20 32		20 38	20 41	20 45	20 46	20 45							21 15	21 08
Reading d	20 14	20 18	20 30	20 25	20 25	20 30	20 33	20 33	20 35	20 38		20 47	20 46	20 47		20 53	21 00	21 03	21 03	21 06	21 25	21 09
Twyford a		20 24	→			20 35						→				20 59	21 05				→	
Maidenhead a		20 32				20 44										21 07	21 16					
Slough a		20 41		20 43	20 46	20 53										21 16	21 24					
Ealing Broadway ⊖ a		21 04				21 18										21 39	21 50					
London Paddington ⊖ a	20 51	21 14		21 08	21 08	21 26	21 10	21 11	21 13	21 15			21 25	21 27		21 49	21 58	21 39	21 42	21 45		21 45

	XC	XC	GW	GW	GW	GW	GW	GW	GW	GW	GW	GW	GW	XC	GW	GW	GW	GW	XC	XC	GW	GW	GW
	◇■	◇■	◇■		◇■		◇■	◇■		◇■	◇■		◇■	◇■	◇■				◇■	◇	◇■	◇■	
	U	V	W	C	X	B	Y	Z	F	AA	BB		J	CC	DD		N	O	EE	FF	GG	HH	
	✕	✕	☕		☕		☕	☕		☕	☕		☕	✕	☕						☕	☕	
Birmingham New Street 71 d	19 33	19 33												20 04					20 33	20 33			
Birmingham International d	19 44	19 44												20 14									
Coventry d	19 55	19 55												20 25									
Leamington Spa d	20 09	20 09												20 38					21 00	21 00			
Banbury 71 d	20 26	20 26												20 55					21 19	21 19			
Kings Sutton d																							
Heyford d																							
Tackley d																							
Oxford 115 a	20 44	20 44												21 14					21 38	21 38			
Oxford d	20 45	20 45			20 53			20 55						21 16		21 30			21 40	21 40			
Radley d																21 37							
Culham d																							
Appleford d																							
Didcot Parkway a					21 06			21 10								21 45							
Didcot Parkway d			20 59	21 04	21 07			21 11			21 17										22 01	22 02	
Cholsey d				21 10																			
Goring & Streatley d				21 14																			
Pangbourne d				21 19																			
Tilehurst d				21 24																			
Bedwyn d												20 54											
Hungerford d												21 00											
Kintbury d												21 04											
Newbury a												21 11											
Newbury d												21 11											21 43
Newbury Racecourse d																							21 45
Thatcham d												21 16											21 50
Midgham d																							21 55
Aldermaston d																							21 58
Theale d												21 24											22 03
Reading West d						←			←														22 11
Reading a	21 12	21 13	21 15	21 29	21 20	21 15		21 27	21 29		21 32	21 34		21 38					22 06	22 06	22 16	22 13	22 14
Reading d			21 15	21 30	21 21	21 25	21 27	21 28	21 30	21 32	21 33		21 38		21 45		21 50	21 50			22 18	22 17	
Twyford a				→		21 31			21 35								21 56	21 56			→		
Maidenhead a					21 34	21 39		21 38	21 46								22 04	22 04					
Slough a					21 43	21 49		21 45	21 55								22 13	22 13					
Ealing Broadway ⊖ a						22 16			22 20								22 37	22 38					
London Paddington ⊖ a			21 53		22 07	22 26	22 07	22 12	22 28	22 09	22 13		22 15		22 28		22 46	22 46				23 03	

- **A** until 9 September. From Bristol Temple Meads
- **B** until 9 September. From Didcot Parkway
- **C** from 16 September. To London Paddington
- **D** from 16 September. From Worcester Foregate Street
- **E** until 9 September. From Worcester Foregate Street
- **F** from 16 September. From Didcot Parkway
- **G** until 9 September. From Carmarthen
- **H** from 16 September. From Carmarthen
- **I** from 16 September. From Bristol Temple Meads
- **J** from 16 September. From Plymouth
- **K** From Manchester Piccadilly to Bournemouth
- **L** until 9 September. From Newquay to London Paddington
- **M** until 9 September. From Newquay
- **N** until 9 September
- **O** from 16 September
- **P** from 16 September. From Penzance
- **Q** until 9 September. From Penzance
- **R** until 9 September. From Cheltenham Spa
- **S** until 9 September. To London Paddington
- **T** from 16 September. From Taunton
- **U** until 9 September. From Newcastle
- **V** from 16 September. From Newcastle
- **W** until 9 September. From Taunton
- **X** until 9 September. From Hereford
- **Y** from 16 September. From Cheltenham Spa
- **Z** from 16 September. From Hereford
- **AA** from 16 September. From Swansea
- **BB** until 9 September. From Swansea
- **CC** From Manchester Piccadilly to Southampton Central
- **DD** until 9 September. From Plymouth
- **EE** until 15 July, from 9 September. From Newcastle to Guildford
- **FF** from 22 July until 2 September. To Guildford
- **GG** from 16 September. From Weston-super-Mare to London Paddington
- **HH** until 9 September. From Weston-super-Mare

For complete services between Banbury and Birmingham, refer to Table T71

Table T116-R

Sundays

20 May to 2 December

Birmingham, Banbury, Oxford and Bedwyn - Reading and London

		GW	GW	GW	GW	GW	XC	GW		GW	GW	GW	GW	GW	GW	GW	GW	GW	GW	GW	GW	GW	GW	GW
		◇1	◇	◇			◇1	◇1		◇1	◇1			◇1	◇1		◇1	◇1						
		A	B	C	D	E	F	G		H	I	E	D	J	K		L	M	E	D			E	D
		☕						☕		☕	☕						☕	☕			🚌			
Birmingham New Street 12 71	d						21 04																	
Birmingham International	d						21 14																	
Coventry	d						21 24																	
Leamington Spa 8	d						21 36																	
Banbury 71	d						21 53																	
Kings Sutton	d																							
Heyford	d																							
Tackley	d																							
Oxford 115	a						22 11																	
	d		21 50	21 50			22 12							22 43	22 43						23 00			
Radley	d																				23 15			
Culham	d																							
Appleford	d																							
Didcot Parkway	a		22 01	22 02										22 56	22 56						23 40			
	d		22 03	22 03								22 24	22 24	22 56	22 56		23 11	23 11	23 15	23 15			23 53	23 53
Cholsey	d											22 30	22 30						23 21	23 21			23 59	23 59
Goring & Streatley	d											22 35	22 35						23 26	23 26			00 05	00 05
Pangbourne	d											22 39	22 39						23 30	23 30			00 09	00 09
Tilehurst	d											22 44	22 44						23 35	23 35			00 14	00 14
Bedwyn	d															22 35								
Hungerford	d															22 41								
Kintbury	d															22 45								
Newbury	a															22 52								
	d									22 22	22 23					22 53						23 23		
Newbury Racecourse	d																							
Thatcham	d															22 58						23 28		
Midgham	d																							
Aldermaston	d																							
Theale	d															23 06						23 36		
Reading West	d	←																						
Reading 7	a	22 16	22 18	22 19			22 38			22 42	22 44	22 50	22 50	23 12	23 13	23 15	23 26	23 26	23 40	23 40		23 45	00 19	00 19
	d	22 18	22 20	22 20	22 24	22 24		22 40		22 42	22 47	22 50	22 51	23 13	23 14		23 26	23 28	23 42	23 42			00 20	00 20
Twyford 3	a				22 30	22 30						22 56	22 57						23 48	23 48			00 26	00 26
Maidenhead 3	a				22 38	22 38						23 04	23 05						23 56	23 56			00 34	00 34
Slough 3	a		22 37	22 38	22 47	22 47						23 14	23 14	23 30	23 30				00 06	00 06			00 42	00 42
Ealing Broadway ⊖	a				23 08	23 07						23 37	23 37						00 30	00 30			01 04	01 05
London Paddington 15 ⊖	a	23 04	23 09	23 09	23 17	23 18		23 22		23 25	23 33	23 46	23 45	23 51	23 51		00 11	00 09	00 38	00 39			01 13	01 13

		GW
Birmingham New Street 12 71	d	
Birmingham International	d	
Coventry	d	
Leamington Spa 8	d	
Banbury 71	d	
Kings Sutton	d	
Heyford	d	
Tackley	d	
Oxford 115	a	
	d	
Radley	d	
Culham	d	
Appleford	d	
Didcot Parkway	a	
	d	
Cholsey	d	
Goring & Streatley	d	
Pangbourne	d	
Tilehurst	d	
Bedwyn	d	
Hungerford	d	
Kintbury	d	
Newbury	a	
	d	23 55
Newbury Racecourse	d	23 57
Thatcham	d	00 02
Midgham	d	00 07
Aldermaston	d	00 10
Theale	d	00 15
Reading West	d	00s23
Reading 7	a	00 26
	d	
Twyford 3	a	
Maidenhead 3	a	
Slough 3	a	
Ealing Broadway ⊖	a	
London Paddington 15 ⊖	a	

A from 16 September. From Weston-super-Mare
B until 9 September. From Great Malvern
C from 16 September. From Great Malvern
D from 16 September
E until 9 September
F From Manchester Piccadilly
G From Carmarthen
H until 9 September. From Penzance
I from 16 September. From Penzance
J from 16 September. From Worcester Shrub Hill
K until 9 September. From Worcester Shrub Hill
L from 16 September. From Plymouth
M until 9 September. From Plymouth

For complete services between Banbury and Birmingham, refer to Table T71

Table T116A

Leamington Spa - Kenilworth - Coventry

Mondays to Fridays

			XC		XC		XC		XC		XC		XC		XC		XC		XC		XC		XC		XC	
Leamington Spa	0608	0700	0714	0800	0814	0900	0914	1000	1014	1100	1114	1200	1214	1300	1314	1400	1414	1500	1514	1600	1614	1700	1714	1800	1814	1900
Kenilworth	0616	0708	▼	0808	▼	0908	▼	1008	▼	1108	▼	1208	▼	1308	▼	1408	▼	1508	▼	1608	▼	1708	▼	1808	▼	1908
Coventry	0625	0716	0725	0817	0825	0916	0925	1016	1024	1116	1125	1217	1225	1318	1326	1416	1425	1518	1525	1617	1625	1716	1725	1816	1825	1917
Birmingham New St	0701b	0745b	0748	0845b	0848	0945b	0949	1045b	1048	1145b	1148	1245b	1248		1348	1445b	1448		1548	1645b	1648	1745b	1748	1845b	1848	1945b

	XC		XC		XC	XC		XC
Leamington Spa	1914	2000	2014	2100	2114	2212	2217	2305
Kenilworth	▼	2008	▼	2108	▼	▼	2225	▼
Coventry	1926	2017	2026	2116	2126	2223	2240	2316
Birmingham New St	1948	2045b	2048	2146b	2148	2245	2316b	2356

Saturdays

			XC		XC		XC		XC		XC		XC		XC		XC		XC		XC		XC		XC
Leamington Spa	0608	0700	0714	0800	0814	0900	0914	1000	1014	1100	1114	1200	1214	1300	1314	1400	1414	1500	1514	1600	1614	1700	1714	1800	1814
Kenilworth	0616	0708	▼	0808	▼	0908	▼	1008	▼	1108	▼	1208	▼	1308	▼	1408	▼	1508	▼	1608	▼	1708	▼	1808	▼
Coventry	0625	0716	0725	0817	0825	0916	0925	1016	1026	1116	1125	1216	1226	1317	1325	1417	1425	1516	1525	1617	1625	1716	1725	1817	1825
Birmingham New St	0701b	0745b	0748	0845b	0848	0945b	0948	1045b	1048	1145b	1148	1245b	1248	1345b	1348	1445b	1448	1545b	1548	1645b	1648	1745b	1748	1845b	1848

		XC		XC		XC	XC	XC
Leamington Spa	1900	1914	2000	2015	2100	2115	2149	2214
Kenilworth	1908	▼	2008	▼	2108	▼	▼	▼
Coventry	1916	1925	2017	2026	2116	2126	2200	2225
Birmingham New St	1945b	1948	2045b	2048		2148	2221	2247

Sundays

	XC	XC	XC	XC	XC	XC	XC	XC	XC	XC	XC	XC	XC	XC
Leamington Spa	1012	1112	1212	1312	1412	1512	1612	1712	1812	1912	2012	2112	2212	2241
Coventry	1025	1125	1225	1323	1423	1523	1623	1723	1823	1923	2023	2123	2223	2252
Birmingham New St	1050	1151	1250	1348	1448	1548	1648	1748	1848	1948	2048	2148	2243	2314

Kenilworth is not served on a Sunday

Table T116A-R

Coventry - Kenilworth - Leamington Spa

Mondays to Fridays

	XC		XC		XC		XC		XC		XC		XC		XC		XC		XC		XC		XC		XC	
Birmingham New St	0604		0704	0710b	0804	0810b	0904	0910b	1004	1010b	1104	1110b	1204	1210b	1304	1310b	1404	1410b	1504	1510b	1604	1610b	1704	1710b	1804	1810b
Coventry	0625	0633	0725	0736	0825	0835	0925	0936	1025	1036	1125	1136	1225	1236	1325	1336	1425	1434	1525	1536	1625	1636	1725	1736	1825	1836
Kenilworth	▼	0644	▼	0744	▼	0844	▼	0944	▼	1044	▼	1144	▼	1244	▼	1344	▼	1442	▼	1544	▼	1644	▼	1744	▼	1844
Leamington Spa	0636	0655	0737	0755	0837	0855	0938	0955	1037	1055	1137	1155	1237	1256	1337	1355	1437	1454	1537	1555	1637	1655	1737	1755	1837	1855

	XC		XC		XC		XC	
Birmingham New St	1904	1910b	2004	2010b	2104	2110b	2204	2210b
Coventry	1925	1936	2025	2036	2125	2136	2225	2243
Kenilworth	▼	1944	▼	2044	▼	2144	▼	2253
Leamington Spa	1937	1955	2037	2055	2137	2156	2237	2303

Saturdays

	XC		XC		XC		XC		XC		XC		XC		XC		XC		XC		XC		XC		XC	
Birmingham New St	0604	0610b	0704	0710b	0804	0810b	0904	0910b	1004	1010b	1104	1110b	1204	1210b	1304	1310b	1404	1410b	1504	1510b	1604	1610b	1704	1710b	1804	1810b
Coventry	0625	0636	0725	0736	0825	0836	0925	0936	1025	1036	1125	1136	1225	1235	1325	1336	1425	1436	1525	1536	1625	1636	1725	1736	1825	1836
Kenilworth	▼	0644	▼	0744	▼	0844	▼	0944	▼	1044	▼	1144	▼	1244	▼	1344	▼	1444	▼	1544	▼	1644	▼	1744	▼	1844
Leamington Spa	0637	0655	0737	0755	0837	0855	0937	0955	1037	1055	1137	1155	1237	1256	1337	1356	1437	1455	1537	1555	1637	1655	1737	1755	1837	1855

	XC		XC		XC	
Birmingham New St	1904	1910b	2004	2010b	2104	2110b
Coventry	1925	1936	2025	2036	2125	2135
Kenilworth	▼	1944	▼	2044	▼	2143
Leamington Spa	1937	1955	2037	2055	2137	2155

Sundays

	XC	XC	XC	XC	XC	XC	XC	XC	XC	XC	XC	XC	XC
Birmingham New St	0904	1004	1104	1204	1304	1404	1504	1604	1704	1804	1904	2004	2104
Coventry	0925	1025	1125	1225	1325	1425	1525	1625	1725	1825	1925	2025	2124
Leamington Spa	0937	1037	1137	1237	1337	1437	1537	1637	1737	1837	1937	2037	2135

Kenilworth is not served on a Sunday

Table T117-F

Mondays to Fridays

21 May to 7 December

London - Greenford, Heathrow Airport and Reading

Stopping Services

Miles	Miles	Miles			GW MO	GW MX	GW MX	GW MO	GW MX	GW MO	GW MX	GW MO	GW MX		GW MX	GW MO	GW	GW	XR	HX	XR	HX	GW		GW
										A		B										◇1			◇1
0	0	0	London Paddington 15 ⊖	d								00 05	00 25		00 34	00 42	01 34	03 34	04 42		04 57	05 10			05 12
4¾	4¾	4¾	Acton Main Line	d																					
5¾	5¾	5¾	Ealing Broadway ⊖	d						00 02	00 02	00 14			00 42	00 50	01 42	03 42	04 50						
6½	6½	6½	West Ealing	d							00 04														
—	7¼	—	Drayton Green	d																					
—	7½	—	Castle Bar Park	d																					
—	8¼	—	South Greenford	d																					
—	9¼	—	Greenford ⊖	a																					
7¼	—	7¼	Hanwell	d							00 07														
9	—	9	Southall	d						00 07	00 11	00 19			00 48	00 56	01 47	03 48	04 54						
10¾	—	10¾	Hayes & Harlington	d						00 11	00 15	00 23			00 52	01 00	01 51	03 52	04 58						
—	—	14¾	Heathrow Termls 2 & 3 2 ⊖ ✈	a															05 05		05 16	05 26			
—	—	—		d															05 07	05 13	05 18	05 28			
—	—	16½	Heathrow Terminal 4 ⊖ ✈	a															05 11		05 22				
—	—	—		d																					
—	—	—	Heathrow Terminal 5 ⊖ ✈	a																05 17		05 32			
—	—	—		d																					
13¼	—	—	West Drayton	d						00 16	00 19	00 28			00 56	01 04	01 55	03 56							
14¾	—	—	Iver	d							00 22				00 59										
16¼	—	—	Langley	d						00 20	00 25	00 32			01 02	01 08									
18½	—	—	Slough 3	a						00 25	00 29	00 37	00 43		01 06	01 12	02 04	04 04							05 29
—	—	—		d				00 10		00 26	00 30	00 38	00 43		01 07	01 13	02 04	04 05							05 30
21	—	—	Burnham	d						00 30	00 34	00 42			01 11										
22½	—	—	Taplow	d							00 37				01 14										
24¼	—	—	Maidenhead 3	d		00 01	00 07	00 17		00 36	00 41	00 48			01 18	01 20	02 12	04 13					05 28		
31	—	—	Twyford 3	d	00 04	00 09	00 15		00 32	00 44	00 49	00 56			01 26	01 28	02 20	04 21					05 37		
36	—	—	Reading 7	a	00 13	00 16	00 23	00 32	00 39	00 51	00 58	01 03	01 01		01 34	01 36	02 28	04 28					05 45		05 49
—	—	—	Oxford	a									01 35												06 16

		GW	XR	HX	XR	XR	GW	HX	GW		XR	GW	GW	HX	XR	GW	XR	GW	HX		GW	XR	GW	GW	HX
				◇1				◇1				◇1		◇1					◇1						◇1
London Paddington 15 ⊖	d	05 15	05 17	05 25		05 32	05 39	05 40	05 42		05 44	05 47		05 55		05 57	06 02		06 10		06 12	06 16	06 20		06 25
Acton Main Line	d		05 23								05 50											06 22			
Ealing Broadway ⊖	d	05 23	05 27			05 41	05 47		05 50		05 54					06 06	06 11				06 20	06 25			
West Ealing	d					05 44			05 54		05 57						06 14	06 27				06 28			
Drayton Green	d								05 55									06 29							
Castle Bar Park	d								05 57									06 31							
South Greenford	d								06 01									06 34							
Greenford ⊖	a								06 06									06 39							
Hanwell	d					05 46											06 16								
Southall	d	05 29	05 33			05 50	05 56				06 03					06 12	06 20				06 27	06 33			
Hayes & Harlington	d	05 33	05a42			05 54	06 00				06a10					06 16	06 24				06 31	06a40			
Heathrow Termls 2 & 3 2 ⊖ ✈	a			05 40		06 00		05 55						06 10			06 30		06 25						06 40
	d			05 41	05 48	06 03		05 58						06 11	06 18		06 33		06 28						06 41
Heathrow Terminal 4 ⊖ ✈	a				05 52	06 07									06 22		06 37								
	d																								
Heathrow Terminal 5 ⊖ ✈	a			05 46				06 02						06 16					06 32						06 46
	d																								
West Drayton	d	05 39					06 04									06 20					06 35				
Iver	d	05 42					06 07									06 23									
Langley	d	05 45					06 10						←			06 26								←	
Slough 3	a	05 49					06 14					06 02	06 14			06 30					06 41		06 35	06 41	
	d	05 50					06 15					06 03	06 15			06 31					06 42		06 36	06 42	
Burnham	d						→						06 19								→			06 46	
Taplow	d												06 22											06 49	
Maidenhead 3	d	05 57											06 26			06 38								06 53	
Twyford 3	d	06 05											06 34			06 46								07 01	
Reading 7	a	06 13										06 17	06 42			06 54							06 50	07 09	
Oxford	a											06 50											07 22		

A from 17 September

B until 10 September

For non-stop services between London and Reading refer to Table T116

For Heathrow Express Services see Table T118

For non-stop services between London and Heathrow Airport see Table T118

Table T117-F

Mondays to Fridays

21 May to 7 December

London - Greenford, Heathrow Airport and Reading

Stopping Services

			XR	GW	XR	GW	HX	GW	XR	GW	GW		HX	XR	GW	XR	GW	GW	HX	GW	XR		GW	GW	HX
							◇1			◇1			◇1						◇1						◇1
London Paddington 15 ⊖	d			06 27	06 32		06 40	06 42	06 46	06 52			06 55		06 55	07 02		07 09	07 10	07 12	07 16		07 21		07 25
Acton Main Line	d								06 52												07 22				
Ealing Broadway ⊖	d			06 36	06 41			06 50	06 55						07 03	07 11		07 17		07 20	07 25				
West Ealing	d				06 44	06 56			06 58							07 14	07 27				07 28				
Drayton Green	d					06 58											07 29								
Castle Bar Park	d					07 00											07 31								
South Greenford	d					07 03											07 34								
Greenford ⊖	a					07 08											07 39								
Hanwell	d				06 46											07 16									
Southall	d			06 42	06 50			06 58	07 03						07 09	07 20				07 26	07 34				
Hayes & Harlington	d			06 46	06 54			07 02	07a10						07 13	07 24				07 30	07a41				
Heathrow Termls 2 & 3 2 ⊖ ✈	a				07 00		06 55						07 10			07 30			07 25						07 40
	d		06 48		07 03		06 58						07 11	07 18		07 33			07 28						07 41
Heathrow Terminal 4 ⊖ ✈	a		06 52		07 07									07 22		07 37									
	d																								
Heathrow Terminal 5 ⊖ ✈	a						07 02						07 16						07 32						07 46
	d																								
West Drayton	d			06 50				07 06							07 17					07 34					
Iver	d			06 53											07 20										
Langley	d			06 56							←				07 23									←	
Slough 3	a			07 00				07 12		07 07	07 12				07 27					07 40			07 36	07 40	
	d			07 01				07 13		07 08	07 13				07 28					07 41			07 37	07 41	
Burnham	d							→			07 17				07 32					→				07 45	
Taplow	d										07 20													07 48	
Maidenhead 3	d			07 08							07 24				07 37			07 43						07 52	
Twyford 3	d			07 16							07 32				07 45			07 51						08 00	
Reading 7	a			07 26						07 21	07 40				07 53			07 59					07 51	08 08	
Oxford	a									07 56													08 17		

		XR	GW	XR	GW	HX	GW		XR	GW	GW	GW	HX	XR	XR	GW	GW		GW	HX	GW	XR	GW	GW	GW
						◇1				◇			◇1							◇1			◇1 🍴		
London Paddington 15 ⊖	d		07 25	07 32		07 40	07 42		07 47	07 50		07 52	07 55		08 02		08 06		08 09	08 10	08 12	08 16	08 21		08 21
Acton Main Line	d								07 53													08 22			
Ealing Broadway ⊖	d		07 33	07 41			07 50		07 56			08 01			08 11				08 17		08 21	08 25			08 29
West Ealing	d			07 44	07 57				07 59						08 14	08 27						08 28			
Drayton Green	d				07 59											08 29									
Castle Bar Park	d				08 01											08 31									
South Greenford	d				08 04											08 34									
Greenford ⊖	a				08 09											08 39									
Hanwell	d			07 46											08 16										
Southall	d		07 39	07 50			07 56		08 04			08 08			08 20						08 26	08 33			08 37
Hayes & Harlington	d		07 43	07 54			08 00		08a11			08 12			08 24						08 30	08a40			08 41
Heathrow Termls 2 & 3 2 ⊖ ✈	a			08 00		07 55							08 10		08 30					08 25					
	d	07 48		08 03		07 58							08 11	08 18	08 33					08 28					
Heathrow Terminal 4 ⊖ ✈	a	07 52		08 07										08 22	08 37										
	d																								
Heathrow Terminal 5 ⊖ ✈	a					08 02							08 16							08 32					
	d																								
West Drayton	d		07 47				08 04					08 16									08 34				08 45
Iver	d		07 50									08 19													08 48
Langley	d		07 53				08 08				←	08 23												←	08 52
Slough 3	a		07 57				08 12			08 06	08 12	08 27							08 35		08 41		08 36	08 41	08 56
	d		07 58				08 14			08 07	08 14	08 28							08 35		08 41		08 37	08 41	08 56
Burnham	d		08 02				→				08 18										→			08 45	
Taplow	d										08 21													08 49	
Maidenhead 3	d		08 07								08 25	08 36							08 43					08 53	09 04
Twyford 3	d		08 15								08 33	08 45							08 51					09 01	09 12
Reading 7	a		08 25							08 23	08 41	08 52					08 31		08 58				08 52	09 10	09 19
Oxford	a									08 48													09 18		

For non-stop services between London and Reading refer to Table T116

For Heathrow Express Services see Table T118

For non-stop services between London and Heathrow Airport see Table T118

Table T117-F

Mondays to Fridays
21 May to 7 December

London - Greenford, Heathrow Airport and Reading
Stopping Services

	HX ◇1	XR	GW	XR	GW	HX ◇1	GW	XR		GW	GW	GW	HX ◇1	XR	XR	GW	HX ◇1	GW		XR	GW ◇1 ✕	GW	HX ◇1	XR
London Paddington 15 ⊖ d	08 25		08 29	08 32		08 40	08 43	08 46		08 51		08 51	08 55		09 02		09 10	09 12		09 17	09 21		09 25	
Acton Main Line d								08 52												09 23				
Ealing Broadway ⊖ d			08 38	08 41			08 51	08 55				08 59			09 11			09 20		09 26				
West Ealing d				08 44	08 56			08 58							09 14	09 27				09 29				
Drayton Green d					08 58											09 29								
Castle Bar Park d					09 00											09 31								
South Greenford d					09 03											09 34								
Greenford ⊖ a					09 09											09 39								
Hanwell d				08 46											09 16									
Southall d			08 43	08 50			08 57	09 03				09 07			09 20			09 26		09 34				
Hayes & Harlington d			08 47	08 54			09 01	09a10				09 11			09 24			09 30		09a41				
Heathrow Termls 2 & 3 2 ⊖ ✈ a	08 40			09 00		08 55							09 10		09 30		09 25						09 40	
d	08 41	08 48		09 03		08 58							09 11	09 18	09 33		09 28						09 41	09 48
Heathrow Terminal 4 ⊖ ✈ a		08 52		09 07										09 22	09 37									09 52
d																								
Heathrow Terminal 5 ⊖ ✈ a	08 46					09 02							09 16				09 32						09 46	
d																								
West Drayton d			08 51				09 05					09 15						09 34						
Iver d												09 18												
Langley d			08 56								←	09 22										←		
Slough 3 a			09 00				09 11			09 06	09 11	09 26						09 40			09 36	09 40		
d			09 00				09 12			09 07	09 12	09 26						09 41			09 37	09 41		
Burnham d			09 04				→				09 16							→				09 45		
Taplow d											09 19											09 48		
Maidenhead 3 d			09 10								09 23	09 34										09 52		
Twyford 3 d			09 18								09 31	09 42										10 00		
Reading 7 a			09 25							09 21	09 39	09 49									09 51	10 08		
Oxford a										09 51											10 17			

	GW	XR	GW	GW ◇1 ⊐		HX ◇1	GW	XR	GW	GW	HX ◇1	XR	GW	XR		GW	HX ◇1	GW	XR	GW ◇1 ⊐	GW	HX ◇1	XR	GW
London Paddington 15 ⊖ d	09 27	09 32		09 36		09 40	09 42	09 46	09 50		09 55		09 57	10 02			10 10	10 12	10 17	10 22		10 25		10 27
Acton Main Line d								09 52											10 23					
Ealing Broadway ⊖ d	09 35	09 41					09 52	09 55					10 05	10 11				10 20	10 26					10 35
West Ealing d		09 44	09 57					09 58						10 14		10 26			10 29					
Drayton Green d			09 59													10 29								
Castle Bar Park d			10 01													10 31								
South Greenford d			10 04													10 33								
Greenford ⊖ a			10 09													10 39								
Hanwell d		09 46												10 16										
Southall d		09 50					09 57	10 03						10 20				10 26	10 34					
Hayes & Harlington d	09 42	09 54					10 01	10a10					10 12	10 24				10 30	10a42					10 42
Heathrow Termls 2 & 3 2 ⊖ ✈ a		10 00				09 55					10 10			10 30			10 25					10 40		
d		10 03				09 58					10 11	10 18		10 33			10 28					10 41	10 48	
Heathrow Terminal 4 ⊖ ✈ a		10 07										10 22		10 37									10 52	
d																								
Heathrow Terminal 5 ⊖ ✈ a						10 02					10 16						10 32					10 46		
d																								
West Drayton d	09 46						10 05						10 16					10 34						10 46
Iver d	09 49												10 19											10 49
Langley d	09 53									←			10 23								←			10 53
Slough 3 a	09 57						10 12		10 05	10 12			10 27					10 40		10 37	10 40			10 57
d	09 57						10 12		10 06	10 12			10 27					10 41		10 38	10 41			10 57
Burnham d							→			10 16								→			10 45			
Taplow d										10 20											10 48			
Maidenhead 3 d	10 05									10 24			10 35								10 52			11 05
Twyford 3 d	10 13									10 32			10 43								11 00			11 13
Reading 7 a	10 20			10 01					10 20	10 39			10 50							10 52	11 08			11 22
Oxford a									10 49											11 22				

For non-stop services between London and Reading refer to Table T116

For Heathrow Express Services see Table T118

For non-stop services between London and Heathrow Airport see Table T118

Table T117-F

Mondays to Fridays
21 May to 7 December

London - Greenford, Heathrow Airport and Reading
Stopping Services

	XR	GW	HX ◇1	GW	XR	GW		GW	HX ◇1	XR	GW	XR	GW	HX ◇1	GW	XR		GW ◇1 ✕	GW	HX ◇1	XR	GW	XR	GW
London Paddington 15 ⊖ d	10 32		10 40	10 42	10 46	10 52			10 55		10 57	11 02		11 10	11 12	11 16		11 22		11 25		11 26	11 32	
Acton Main Line d					10 52											11 22								
Ealing Broadway ⊖ d	10 41			10 51	10 55						11 05	11 11			11 20	11 25						11 34	11 41	
West Ealing d	10 44	10 57			10 58							11 14	11 27			11 28							11 44	11 57
Drayton Green d		10 59											11 29											11 58
Castle Bar Park d		11 01											11 31											12 00
South Greenford d		11 04											11 34											12 04
Greenford ⊖ a		11 09											11 39											12 09
Hanwell d	10 46											11 16											11 46	
Southall d	10 50			11 00	11 04							11 20			11 26	11 33							11 50	
Hayes & Harlington d	10 54			11 04	11a11						11 12	11 24			11 30	11a40						11 41	11 54	
Heathrow Termls 2 & 3 2 ⊖ ✈ a	11 00		10 55						11 10			11 30		11 25						11 40			12 00	
d	11 03		10 58						11 11	11 18		11 33		11 28						11 41	11 48		12 03	
Heathrow Terminal 4 ⊖ ✈ a	11 07									11 22		11 37									11 52		12 07	
d																								
Heathrow Terminal 5 ⊖ ✈ a			11 02						11 16					11 32						11 46				
d																								
West Drayton d				11 08							11 16				11 34							11 45		
Iver d											11 19											11 48		
Langley d								←			11 23								←			11 52		
Slough 3 a				11 15		11 07		11 15			11 27				11 40			11 37	11 40			11 56		
d				11 15		11 08		11 15			11 27				11 41			11 38	11 41			11 56		
Burnham d				→				11 19							→				11 45					
Taplow d								11 23											11 48					
Maidenhead 3 d								11 27			11 35								11 52			12 04		
Twyford 3 d								11 35			11 43								12 00			12 12		
Reading 7 a						11 22		11 42			11 50							11 52	12 08			12 19		
Oxford a						11 52												12 20						

	GW ◇1 ⊐	HX ◇1		GW	XR	GW	GW	HX ◇1	XR	GW	XR	HX ◇1		GW	XR	GW	GW ◇1 ⊐	GW	HX ◇1	XR	GW	XR		GW ◇1 A ✕
London Paddington 15 ⊖ d	11 36	11 40		11 42	11 46	11 50		11 55		11 57	12 02	12 10		12 12	12 16		12 21		12 25		12 27	12 32		12 33
Acton Main Line d					11 52										12 22									
Ealing Broadway ⊖ d				11 50	11 55					12 05	12 11			12 20	12 25						12 35	12 41		
West Ealing d					11 58						12 14				12 28	12 32						12 44		
Drayton Green d																12 34								
Castle Bar Park d																12 36								
South Greenford d																12 39								
Greenford ⊖ a																12 44								
Hanwell d											12 16											12 46		
Southall d				11 56	12 03						12 20			12 26	12 33							12 50		
Hayes & Harlington d				12 00	12a10					12 12	12 24			12 30	12a40						12 42	12 54		
Heathrow Termls 2 & 3 2 ⊖ ✈ a		11 55						12 10			12 30	12 25							12 40			13 00		
d		11 58						12 11	12 18		12 33	12 28							12 41	12 48		13 03		
Heathrow Terminal 4 ⊖ ✈ a									12 22		12 37									12 52		13 07		
d																								
Heathrow Terminal 5 ⊖ ✈ a		12 02						12 16				12 32							12 46					
d																								
West Drayton d				12 04						12 16				12 34							12 46			
Iver d										12 19											12 49			
Langley d							←			12 23								←			12 53			
Slough 3 a				12 10		12 06	12 10			12 27				12 40			12 36	12 40			12 57			
d				12 11		12 07	12 11			12 27				12 41			12 37	12 41			12 57			
Burnham d				→			12 15							→				12 45						
Taplow d							12 18											12 48						
Maidenhead 3 d							12 22			12 35								12 52			13 05			
Twyford 3 d							12 30			12 43								13 00			13 13			
Reading 7 a	12 01					12 23	12 38			12 50							12 51	13 08			13 20			12 58
Oxford a						12 48											13 20							

A Restaurant available for customers joining to Reading

For non-stop services between London and Reading refer to Table T116

For Heathrow Express Services see Table T118

For non-stop services between London and Heathrow Airport see Table T118

Table T117-F

Mondays to Fridays

21 May to 7 December

London - Greenford, Heathrow Airport and Reading

Stopping Services

		HX ◇1	GW	XR	GW		GW	GW	HX ◇1	XR	GW	XR	HX ◇1	GW	XR		GW	GW ◇1	GW	HX ◇1	XR	GW	XR	GW ◇1	HX ◇1
London Paddington ⊖	d	12 40	12 42	12 46			12 50		12 55		12 57	13 02	13 10	13 11	13 16			13 22		13 25		13 27	13 32	13 36	13 40
Acton Main Line	d			12 52											13 22										
Ealing Broadway ⊖	d		12 50	12 55							13 05	13 11		13 19	13 25							13 36	13 41		
West Ealing	d			12 58	13 00							13 14			13 28		13 31						13 44		
Drayton Green	d				13 02												13 33								
Castle Bar Park	d				13 04												13 35								
South Greenford	d				13 07												13 38								
Greenford ⊖	a				13 13												13 43								
Hanwell	d											13 16											13 46		
Southall	d		12 58	13 03								13 20		13 28	13 33								13 50		
Hayes & Harlington	d		13 02	13a10							13 12	13 24		13 32	13a40							13 43	13 54		
HeathrowTermls 2 & 3 ⊖ ✈	a	12 55							13 10			13 30	13 25							13 40			14 00		13 55
	d	12 58							13 11	13 18		13 33	13 28							13 41	13 48		14 03		13 58
Heathrow Terminal 4 ⊖ ✈	a									13 22		13 37									13 52		14 07		
	d																								
Heathrow Terminal 5 ⊖ ✈	a	13 02							13 16				13 32							13 46					14 02
	d																								
West Drayton	d		13 06								13 16			13 36								13 47			
Iver	d										13 19											13 50			
Langley	d							←			13 23								←			13 54			
Slough	a		13 13				13 05	13 13			13 27			13 42				13 37	13 42			13 58			
	d		13 13				13 06	13 13			13 27			13 43				13 38	13 43			13 58			
Burnham	d		→					13 17						→					13 47						
Taplow	d							13 21											13 50						
Maidenhead	d							13 25			13 35								13 54			14 06			
Twyford	d							13 33			13 43								14 02			14 14			
Reading	a						13 20	13 40			13 50							13 52	14 10			14 21		14 01	
Oxford	a						13 51											14 16							

			GW	XR	GW	GW	GW	HX ◇1	XR	GW	XR		HX ◇1	GW	XR	GW	GW ◇1	GW	HX ◇1	XR	GW		XR	HX ◇1	GW
London Paddington ⊖	d		13 42	13 46		13 50		13 55		13 57	14 02		14 10	14 12	14 16		14 21		14 25		14 27		14 32	14 40	14 41
Acton Main Line	d			13 52											14 22										
Ealing Broadway ⊖	d		13 50	13 55						14 06	14 11			14 20	14 25						14 35		14 41		14 50
West Ealing	d			13 58	14 01						14 14				14 28	14 31							14 44		
Drayton Green	d				14 02											14 33									
Castle Bar Park	d				14 04											14 35									
South Greenford	d				14 08											14 38									
Greenford ⊖	a				14 13											14 43									
Hanwell	d										14 16												14 46		
Southall	d		13 56	14 03							14 20			14 27	14 34								14 50		14 57
Hayes & Harlington	d		14 00	14a10						14 13	14 24			14 31	14a41						14 42		14 54		15 01
HeathrowTermls 2 & 3 ⊖ ✈	a							14 10			14 30		14 25						14 40				15 00	14 55	
	d							14 11	14 18		14 33		14 28						14 41	14 48			15 03	14 58	
Heathrow Terminal 4 ⊖ ✈	a								14 22		14 37									14 52			15 07		
	d																								
Heathrow Terminal 5 ⊖ ✈	a							14 16					14 32						14 46					15 02	
	d																								
West Drayton	d		14 04							14 17				14 36							14 46				15 05
Iver	d									14 20											14 49				
Langley	d						←			14 24								←			14 53				
Slough	a		14 10			14 06	14 10			14 28				14 42			14 36	14 42			14 57				15 12
	d		14 11			14 07	14 11			14 28				14 43			14 37	14 43			14 57				15 12
Burnham	d		→				14 15							→				14 47							→
Taplow	d						14 18											14 50							
Maidenhead	d						14 22			14 36								14 54			15 05				
Twyford	d						14 30			14 44								15 02			15 13				
Reading	a					14 23	14 38			14 51							14 51	15 10			15 20				
Oxford	a					14 48											15 20								

For non-stop services between London and Reading refer to Table T116

For Heathrow Express Services see Table T118

For non-stop services between London and Heathrow Airport see Table T118

Table T117-F

Mondays to Fridays

21 May to 7 December

London - Greenford, Heathrow Airport and Reading

Stopping Services

		XR	GW		GW	GW	HX ◇1	XR	GW	XR	HX ◇1	GW	XR		GW	GW ◇1	GW	HX ◇1	XR	GW	XR	GW ◇1	HX ◇1		GW
London Paddington ⊖	d	14 46			14 50		14 55		14 57	15 02	15 10	15 12	15 17			15 22		15 25		15 27	15 32	15 36	15 40		15 42
Acton Main Line	d	14 52											15 23												
Ealing Broadway ⊖	d	14 55							15 06	15 11		15 20	15 26							15 35	15 41				15 50
West Ealing	d	14 58	15 01							15 14			15 29		15 31						15 44				
Drayton Green	d		15 03												15 33										
Castle Bar Park	d		15 05												15 35										
South Greenford	d		15 08												15 38										
Greenford ⊖	a		15 13												15 43										
Hanwell	d									15 16											15 46				
Southall	d	15 03								15 20		15 26	15 34								15 50				15 56
Hayes & Harlington	d	15a10							15 15	15 24		15 30	15a41							15 46	15 54				16 00
HeathrowTermls 2 & 3 ⊖ ✈	a						15 10			15 30	15 25							15 40			16 00		15 55		
	d						15 11	15 18		15 33	15 28							15 41	15 48		16 03		15 58		
Heathrow Terminal 4 ⊖ ✈	a							15 22		15 37									15 52		16 07				
	d																								
Heathrow Terminal 5 ⊖ ✈	a						15 16				15 32							15 46					16 02		
	d																								
West Drayton	d								15 19			15 34								15 50					16 04
Iver	d								15 22											15 53					
Langley	d					←			15 25								←			15 57					
Slough	a				15 06	15 12			15 29			15 40				15 37	15 40			16 01					16 10
	d				15 07	15 12			15 30			15 41				15 38	15 41			16 01					16 11
Burnham	d					15 16						→					15 45								→
Taplow	d					15 20											15 48								
Maidenhead	d					15 24			15 37								15 52			16 09					
Twyford	d					15 32			15 45								16 00			16 17					
Reading	a				15 22	15 40			15 53							15 52	16 08			16 24		16 00			
Oxford	a				15 50											16 23									

		XR	GW	GW ◇1	GW	HX ◇1	XR	GW	XR		GW	HX ◇1	GW	XR	GW	GW ◇1	GW	HX ◇1	XR		GW	XR	GW ◇1	GW	HX ◇1
London Paddington ⊖	d	15 47		15 52		15 55		15 57	16 02		16 09	16 10	16 12	16 16		16 22		16 25			16 28	16 32	16 33	16 36	16 40
Acton Main Line	d	15 53												16 22											
Ealing Broadway ⊖	d	15 56						16 05	16 11				16 20	16 25							16 36	16 41			
West Ealing	d	15 59	16 02						16 14					16 28	16 31							16 44			
Drayton Green	d		16 04												16 33										
Castle Bar Park	d		16 06												16 35										
South Greenford	d		16 09												16 38										
Greenford ⊖	a		16 14												16 43										
Hanwell	d								16 16													16 46			
Southall	d	16 03							16 20				16 26	16 33							16 43	16 50			
Hayes & Harlington	d	16a10						16 12	16 24				16 30	16a40							16 47	16 54			
HeathrowTermls 2 & 3 ⊖ ✈	a					16 10			16 30			16 25						16 40				17 00			16 55
	d					16 11	16 18		16 33			16 28						16 41	16 48			17 03			16 58
Heathrow Terminal 4 ⊖ ✈	a						16 22		16 37										16 52			17 07			
	d																								
Heathrow Terminal 5 ⊖ ✈	a					16 16						16 32						16 46							17 02
	d																								
West Drayton	d							16 16					16 34								16 51				
Iver	d							16 19													16 54				
Langley	d				←			16 23									←				17 02				
Slough	a			16 07	16 10			16 27			16 34		16 40				16 40				17 07				
	d			16 08	16 11			16 27			16 35		16 41			16u38	16 41				17 08				
Burnham	d				16 15								→				16 45				→				
Taplow	d				16 18												16 48								
Maidenhead	d				16 22			16 35			16a42						16 52								
Twyford	d				16 30			16 43									17 00								
Reading	a			16 22	16 38			16 51								16b53	17 08						16 57	17 03	
Oxford	a			16 46												17 22									

b Stops to pick up only

For non-stop services between London and Reading refer to Table T116

For Heathrow Express Services see Table T118

For non-stop services between London and Heathrow Airport see Table T118

Table T117-F

Mondays to Fridays
21 May to 7 December

London - Greenford, Heathrow Airport and Reading

Stopping Services

		GW	XR	GW	GW	GW	GW	GW	HX	XR	GW	GW	XR	HX	GW	XR	GW	GW	GW	GW	GW	GW
									◇1					◇1					◇1			
London Paddington 15 ⊖	d	16 42	16 46		16 49	16 52			16 55		16 56	16 58	17 02	17 10	17 12	17 16		17 18	17 22			
Acton Main Line	d		16 52													17 22						
Ealing Broadway ⊖	d	16 50	16 55									17 07	17 11		17 20	17 25						
West Ealing	d		16 58	17 02									17 14			17 28	17 32					
Drayton Green	d			17 04													17 34					
Castle Bar Park	d			17 06													17 36					
South Greenford	d			17 09													17 39					
Greenford ⊖	a			17 14													17 44					
Hanwell	d												17 16									
Southall	d	16 56	17 03									17 13	17 20		17 25	17 33						
Hayes & Harlington	d	17 00	17a10									17 17	17 24		17 29	17a40						
Heathrow Termls 2 & 3 2 ⊖ ✈	a								17 10				17 30	17 25								
	d								17 11	17 18			17 33	17 28								
Heathrow Terminal 4 ⊖ ✈	a									17 22			17 37									
	d																					
Heathrow Terminal 5 ⊖ ✈	a								17 16					17 32								
	d																					
West Drayton	d	17 04										17 21			17 33							
Iver	d	17 07										17 24			17 37							
Langley	d	17 10					←	←				17 27			17 40						←	←
Slough 3	a	17 14					17 07	17 14			17 22	17 31			17 44						17 31	17 44
	d	17 15					17 08	17 15			17 23	17 32			17 45						17 32	17 45
Burnham	d	→						17 19			17 27	→			→						17 36	
Taplow	d							17 22			17 30										17 39	
Maidenhead 3	d				17 10		17 15	17 26			17a36							17 40		←	17 43	17 52
Twyford 3	d				17 17		17 23	17 34										17 48		17 48	17 51	18 00
Reading 7	a				17 24	17 17	17 31	17 42										→	17 50	17 55	17 59	18 08
Oxford	a					17 43													18 15	18 44		

		HX	XR	GW	GW	XR	HX	GW	XR	GW	GW	GW	GW	GW	HX	XR	GW	GW	XR	HX	GW	XR	GW
		◇1					◇1					◇1			◇1			A		◇1			
London Paddington 15 ⊖	d	17 25		17 26	17 29	17 32	17 40	17 42	17 46		17 48	17 52			17 55		17 56	17 57	18 02	18 10	18 11	18 16	
Acton Main Line	d								17 52													18 22	
Ealing Broadway ⊖	d				17 37	17 41		17 50	17 55								18 04		18 11		18 19	18 25	
West Ealing	d					17 44			17 58	18 02									18 14			18 28	18 36
Drayton Green	d									18 04													18 38
Castle Bar Park	d									18 06													18 40
South Greenford	d									18 09													18 43
Greenford ⊖	a									18 14													18 48
Hanwell	d					17 46													18 16				
Southall	d				17 43	17 50		17 56	18 03								18 10		18 20		18 25	18 33	
Hayes & Harlington	d				17 47	17 54		18 00	18a10								18 14		18 24		18 29	18a44	
Heathrow Termls 2 & 3 2 ⊖ ✈	a	17 40				18 00	17 55								18 10				18 30	18 25			
	d	17 41	17 48			18 03	17 58								18 11	18 18			18 33	18 28			
Heathrow Terminal 4 ⊖ ✈	a		17 52			18 07										18 22			18 37				
	d																						
Heathrow Terminal 5 ⊖ ✈	a	17 46					18 02								18 16					18 32			
	d																						
West Drayton	d				17 51			18 04									18 18				18 37		
Iver	d				17 54												18 21						
Langley	d				17 57			18 08					←	←			18 24				18 42		
Slough 3	a			17 48	18 01			18 12					18 01	18 12			18 28	18 16			18 46		
	d			17 48	18 02			18 13					18 02	18 13			18 29	18 17			18 46		
Burnham	d			17 52	→			→					18 06	18 17			→	18 21			→		
Taplow	d			17 56									18 09										
Maidenhead 3	d			17a59							18 10		18 13	18 22				18 26					
Twyford 3	d										18 17		18 21	18 30				18 35					
Reading 7	a										18 24	18 20	18 29	18 38				18 42					
Oxford	a											18 48											

A not from 4 June until 7 June

For non-stop services between London and Reading refer to Table T116

For Heathrow Express Services see Table T118

For non-stop services between London and Heathrow Airport see Table T118

Table T117-F

Mondays to Fridays
21 May to 7 December

London - Greenford, Heathrow Airport and Reading

Stopping Services

		GW	GW	GW	HX	XR	GW	GW	GW	XR	HX	GW	XR	GW	GW	GW	GW	GW	HX	XR	GW	GW	XR
			◇1 A		◇1						◇1								◇1				
London Paddington 15 ⊖	d	18 19	18 22		18 25		18 27		18 29	18 32	18 40	18 42	18 46		18 48	18 52			18 55		18 55	18 59	19 02
Acton Main Line	d												18 52										
Ealing Broadway ⊖	d								18 37	18 41		18 50	18 55									19 07	19 11
West Ealing	d									18 44			18 58	19 06									19 14
Drayton Green	d													19 08									
Castle Bar Park	d													19 10									
South Greenford	d													19 13									
Greenford ⊖	a													19 18									
Hanwell	d									18 46													19 16
Southall	d								18 43	18 50		18 56	19 03									19 13	19 20
Hayes & Harlington	d								18 47	18 54		19 00	19a10									19 17	19 24
Heathrow Termls 2 & 3 2 ⊖ ✈	a				18 40					19 00	18 55								19 10				19 30
	d				18 41	18 48				19 03	18 58								19 11	19 18			19 33
Heathrow Terminal 4 ⊖ ✈	a					18 52				19 07										19 22			19 37
	d																						
Heathrow Terminal 5 ⊖ ✈	a				18 46						19 02								19 16				
	d																						
West Drayton	d								18 51			19 04										19 21	
Iver	d								18 54													19 24	
Langley	d			←				←	18 57			19 08					←	←				19 27	
Slough 3	a			18 28			18 43	18 46	19 01			19 12					19 01	19 12			19 19	19 31	
	d			18 29			18 43	18 46	19 02			19 13					19 02	19 13			19 20	19 32	
Burnham	d			18 33			18 47	18 50	→			→					19 06	19 17			19 24	→	
Taplow	d			18 36													19 09						
Maidenhead 3	d	18 39		18 43			18 52	18 56							19 08		19 13	19 22			19a30		
Twyford 3	d	18 46		18 51			18 59	19 04							19 17		19 21	19 36					
Reading 7	a	18 53	18 50	18 58			19 06	19 11							19 26	19 17	19 30	19 43					
Oxford	a		19 20													19 43							

		HX	GW	XR	GW	GW	GW	GW	GW	HX	XR	GW	XR	GW	GW	GW	HX	GW	XR	GW	GW	GW	HX
		◇1					◇1			◇1							◇1			◇1			◇1
London Paddington 15 ⊖	d	19 10	19 12	19 16		19 20	19 22			19 25		19 27	19 32	19 35			19 40	19 42	19 46	19 48	19 52		19 55
Acton Main Line	d			19 22															19 52				
Ealing Broadway ⊖	d		19 20	19 25								19 35	19 41					19 50	19 55				
West Ealing	d			19 28	19 36								19 44						19 58				
Drayton Green	d				19 38																		
Castle Bar Park	d				19 40																		
South Greenford	d				19 43																		
Greenford ⊖	a				19 48																		
Hanwell	d												19 46										
Southall	d		19 27	19 33									19 50					19 56	20 03				
Hayes & Harlington	d		19 31	19a40								19 43	19 54					20 00	20a10				
Heathrow Termls 2 & 3 2 ⊖ ✈	a	19 25								19 40			20 00				19 55						20 10
	d	19 28								19 41	19 48		20 03				19 58						20 11
Heathrow Terminal 4 ⊖ ✈	a										19 52		20 07										
	d																						
Heathrow Terminal 5 ⊖ ✈	a	19 32								19 46							20 02						20 16
	d																						
West Drayton	d		19 35									19 47						20 04					
Iver	d											19 50											
Langley	d							←	←			19 54				←						←	
Slough 3	a		19 41				19 37	19 31	19 41			19 58				19 58		20 10			20 07	20 10	
	d		19 42				19 38	19 32	19 42			19 58				19 58		20 11			20 08	20 11	
Burnham	d		→					19 36	19 46			→						→				20 15	
Taplow	d							19 39	19 49													20 18	
Maidenhead 3	d					19 40		19 44	19 53					19 54	←	20 06				20 07		20 22	
Twyford 3	d					19 47		19 52	20 03					20 01	20 03	20 14						20 30	
Reading 7	a					19 54	19 52	19 59	→					20 09	20 13	20 22				20 19	20 22	20 38	
Oxford	a						20 20														20 53		

A The Cathedrals Express

For non-stop services between London and Reading refer to Table T116

For Heathrow Express Services see Table T118

For non-stop services between London and Heathrow Airport see Table T118

London - Greenford, Heathrow Airport and Reading
Stopping Services

		XR	GW	XR	GW	HX ◇1	GW		XR	GW	GW ◇1	GW	HX ◇1	XR	GW	XR	GW		HX ◇1	GW	XR	GW	GW	HX ◇1	XR
London Paddington 15 ⊖	d		19 57	20 02		20 10	20 12		20 16	20 18	20 22		20 25		20 27	20 32			20 40	20 42	20 46	20 50		20 55	
Acton Main Line	d								20 22												20 52				
Ealing Broadway ⊖	d		20 05	20 11			20 20		20 25						20 35	20 41				20 50	20 55				
West Ealing	d			20 14	20 16				20 28							20 44	20 46				20 58				
Drayton Green	d				20 18												20 48								
Castle Bar Park	d				20 20												20 50								
South Greenford	d				20 23												20 54								
Greenford ⊖	a				20 28												21 00								
Hanwell	d			20 16												20 46									
Southall	d			20 20			20 27		20 33							20 50				20 58	21 03				
Hayes & Harlington	d		20 12	20 24			20 31		20a40						20 42	20 54				21 02	21a10				
Heathrow Termls 2 & 3 2 ⊖ ✈	a			20 30		20 25							20 40			21 00			20 55					21 10	
	d	20 18		20 33		20 28							20 41	20 48		21 03			20 58					21 11	21 18
Heathrow Terminal 4 ⊖ ✈	a	20 22		20 37										20 52		21 07									21 22
	d																								
Heathrow Terminal 5 ⊖ ✈	a					20 32							20 46						21 02					21 16	
	d																								
West Drayton	d		20 16				20 35								20 46					21 06					
Iver	d		20 19												20 49										
Langley	d		20 23									←			20 53								←		
Slough 3	a		20 27				20 41				20 37	20 41			20 57					21 12		21 06	21 12		
	d		20 27				20 42				20 38	20 42			20 57					21 13		21 07	21 13		
Burnham	d						→					20 46								→			21 17		
Taplow	d											20 49											21 20		
Maidenhead 3	d		20 35							20 41		20 53			21 05								21 24		
Twyford 3	d		20 43							20 48		21 01			21 13								21 32		
Reading 7	a		20 52							20 55	20 52	21 10			21 22							21 23	21 40		
Oxford	a										21 21											21 53			

		GW	XR		GW	HX ◇1	GW	XR	GW	GW	HX ◇1	XR	GW		XR	GW	HX ◇1	GW	XR	GW ◇1	GW	HX ◇1	XR		GW FX
London Paddington 15 ⊖	d	20 57	21 02			21 10	21 12	21 16	21 18		21 25		21 27		21 32		21 40	21 42	21 46	21 48		21 55			21 57
Acton Main Line	d							21 22										21 48	21 52						
Ealing Broadway ⊖	d	21 05	21 11				21 20	21 25					21 35		21 41			21 52	21 55						22 05
West Ealing	d		21 14		21 18			21 28							21 44	21 49			21 58						
Drayton Green	d				21 20											21 51									
Castle Bar Park	d				21 22											21 53									
South Greenford	d				21 25											21 56									
Greenford ⊖	a				21 30											22 01									
Hanwell	d		21 16												21 46										
Southall	d		21 20				21 26	21 33							21 50			21 57	22 03						
Hayes & Harlington	d	21 12	21 24				21 30	21a40					21 42		21 54			22 01	22a10						22 19
Heathrow Termls 2 & 3 2 ⊖ ✈	a		21 30			21 25					21 40				22 00		21 55					22 10			
	d		21 33			21 28					21 41	21 48			22 03		21 58					22 11	22 18		
Heathrow Terminal 4 ⊖ ✈	a		21 37									21 52			22 07								22 22		
	d																								
Heathrow Terminal 5 ⊖ ✈	a					21 32					21 46						22 02					22 16			
	d																								
West Drayton	d	21 16					21 34						21 46					22 05							22 23
Iver	d	21 19											21 49												22 26
Langley	d	21 23								←			21 53								←				22 30
Slough 3	a	21 27					21 40		21 33	21 40			21 57					22 12		22 03	22 12				22 33
	d	21 27					21 41		21 34	21 41			21 57					22 12		22 04	22 12				22 46
Burnham	d						→			21 45								→			22 16				→
Taplow	d									21 48											22 20				
Maidenhead 3	d	21 35								21 52			22 10								22 24				
Twyford 3	d	21 43								22 00			22 18								22 32				
Reading 7	a	21 55							21 48	22 08			22 27							22 19	22 39				
Oxford	a								22 18											22 53					

For non-stop services between London and Reading refer to Table T116

For Heathrow Express Services see Table T118

For non-stop services between London and Heathrow Airport see Table T118

Table T117-F

Mondays to Fridays
21 May to 7 December

London - Greenford, Heathrow Airport and Reading
Stopping Services

		GW FO	XR	HX ◇1	XR		GW FO	GW FX	GW FX	HX ◇1	XR	GW FO	GW FX	XR	HX ◇1		XR	GW FO	GW FX	GW FX	HX ◇1	XR	GW	XR	HX ◇1
London Paddington 15 ⊖	d	21 57	22 03	22 10	22 16		22 18	22 18		22 25		22 27	22 27	22 32	22 40		22 48	22 50	22 50		22 55		22 59	23 02	23 10
Acton Main Line	d				22 22												22 54						23 05		
Ealing Broadway ⊖	d	22 05	22 11		22 25							22 35	22 35	22 41			22 57						23 09	23 11	
West Ealing	d		22 14		22 28									22 44			23 01							23 14	
Drayton Green	d																								
Castle Bar Park	d																								
South Greenford	d																								
Greenford ⊖	a																								
Hanwell	d		22 16											22 46										23 16	
Southall	d		22 20		22 33							22 41	22 41	22 50			23 06							23 20	
Hayes & Harlington	d	22 19	22 24		22a40							22 45	22 45	22 54			23a13						23 19	23 24	
Heathrow Termls 2 & 3 2 ⊖ ✈	a		22 30	22 25						22 40				23 00	22 55						23 10			23 30	23 25
	d		22 33	22 28						22 41	22 48			23 03	22 58						23 11	23 18		23 33	23 28
Heathrow Terminal 4 ⊖ ✈	a		22 37								22 52			23 07								23 22		23 37	
	d																								
Heathrow Terminal 5 ⊖ ✈	a			22 32						22 46					23 02						23 16				23 32
	d																								
West Drayton	d	22 23										22 49	22 49										23 23		
Iver	d	22 26										22 52	22 52										23 26		
Langley	d	22 30							←			22 55	22 55							←			23 29		
Slough 3	a	22 34							22 33			22 59	22 59					23 06	23 09	22 59			23 33		
	d	22 34							22 46			23 00	23 14					23 07	23 10	23 14			23 34		
Burnham	d								22 50			23 04	→							23 17					
Taplow	d								22 53			23 07								23 21					
Maidenhead 3	d	22 42							22 57			23 11						23 14	23 17	23 25			23 41		
Twyford 3	d	22 50							23 05			23 19						23 22	23 25	23 33			23 49		
Reading 7	a	22 57					22 48	22 57	23 13			23 27						23 29	23 33	23 40			23 57		
Oxford	a						23 30	23 29										23 55	23 58						

			GW FO	GW FX	XR	GW FO	GW FX	GW FO	GW FX	HX ◇1	XR		GW FX	GW FO	GW FO	GW FO	GW
London Paddington 15 ⊖	d		23 12	23 14	23 18	23 20	23 20			23 25			23 27	23 27	23 42		23 51
Acton Main Line	d				23 24												23 57
Ealing Broadway ⊖	d		23 20	23 22	23 27								23 35	23 35			00 02
West Ealing	d				23 30												00 04
Drayton Green	d																
Castle Bar Park	d																
South Greenford	d																
Greenford ⊖	a																
Hanwell	d																00 07
Southall	d		23 26	23 28	23 35								23 41	23 41			00 11
Hayes & Harlington	d		23 30	23 32	23a42								23 45	23 45			00 15
Heathrow Termls 2 & 3 2 ⊖ ✈	a									23 40							
	d									23 41	23 48						
Heathrow Terminal 4 ⊖ ✈	a										23 52						
	d																
Heathrow Terminal 5 ⊖ ✈	a									23 46							
	d																
West Drayton	d		23 34	23 36									23 49	23 49			00 19
Iver	d												23 52	23 52			00 22
Langley	d							←	←				23 55	23 55		←	00 25
Slough 3	a		23 40	23 43		23 36	23 39	23 40	23 43				23 58	23 58	23 58	23 58	00 29
	d		23 46	23 49		23 37	23 40	23 46	23 49				23 59	00 03	23 59	00 03	00 30
Burnham	d		→	→				23 50	23 52					→			00 34
Taplow	d							23 54	23 56								00 37
Maidenhead 3	d					23 46	23 47	23 58	00 01				00 07		00 07	00 10	00 41
Twyford 3	d					23 54	23 55	00 06	00 09				00 15		00 15	00 18	00 49
Reading 7	a					00 01	00 03	00 16	00 16				00 23		00 23	00 26	00 58
Oxford	a					00 34	00 32								01 01		

For non-stop services between London and Reading refer to Table T116

For Heathrow Express Services see Table T118

For non-stop services between London and Heathrow Airport see Table T118

Table T117-F

London - Greenford, Heathrow Airport and Reading

Stopping Services

		GW	GW	GW	GW	GW		GW	GW	GW	GW	XR	HX	XR	XR	HX		XR	GW	HX	XR	GW	XR	HX	GW
					1			1								◇1			◇1	◇1				◇1	
London Paddington 15 ⊖	d							00 22	00 34	01 34	03 34	04 42			05 02	05 10		05 16	05 18	05 25		05 25	05 32	05 40	05 42
Acton Main Line	d																	05 22							
Ealing Broadway ⊖	d					00 02			00 42	01 42	03 42	04 50			05 11			05 25				05 33	05 41		05 50
West Ealing	d					00 04									05 14			05 28					05 44		05 53
Drayton Green	d																								05 56
Castle Bar Park	d																								05 58
South Greenford	d																								06 00
Greenford ⊖	a																								06 06
Hanwell	d					00 07									05 16								05 46		
Southall	d					00 11			00 48	01 47	03 47	04 54			05 20			05 33				05 38	05 50		
Hayes & Harlington	d					00 15			00 52	01 51	03 51	04 58			05 24			05a40				05 42	05 54		
HeathrowTermls 2 & 3 2 ⊖ ✈	a											05 05			05 30	05 26				05 40			06 00	05 55	
	d											05 07	05 13	05 18	05 33	05 28				05 41	05 48		06 03	05 58	
Heathrow Terminal 4 ⊖ ✈	a											05 11		05 22	05 37						05 52		06 07		
	d																								
Heathrow Terminal 5 ⊖ ✈	a												05 17			05 32				05 46				06 02	
	d																								
West Drayton	d					00 19			00 56	01 55	03 55														
Iver	d					00 22			00 59																
Langley	d					00 25			01 02																
Slough 3	a					00 29		00 43	01 06	02 04	04 03								05 33			05 51			
	d			00 03		00 30		00 43	01 07	02 04	04 04								05 34			05 51			
Burnham	d					00 34			01 11													05 55			
Taplow	d					00 37			01 14													05 58			
Maidenhead 3	d		00 07	00 10		00 41			01 18	02 12	04 11											06 02			
Twyford 3	d	00 06	00 15	00 18	00 32	00 49			01 26	02 20	04 19											06 10			
Reading 7	a	00 16	00 23	00 26	00 40	00 58		01 01	01 34	02 27	04 27								05 51			06 18			
Oxford	a		01 01					01 31											06 22						

		XR		GW	HX	XR	GW	XR	GW	HX	GW	XR		GW	GW	HX	XR	GW	XR	GW	HX	GW		XR	GW
				◇1	◇1					◇1				◇1 ☕		◇1					◇1				◇1
London Paddington 15 ⊖	d	05 46		05 52	05 55		05 55	06 02		06 10	06 14	06 16		06 22		06 25		06 27	06 32		06 40	06 42		06 46	06 52
Acton Main Line	d	05 52										06 23												06 52	
Ealing Broadway ⊖	d	05 55					06 03	06 11			06 22	06 26						06 35	06 41			06 50		06 55	
West Ealing	d	05 58						06 14	06 27			06 29							06 44	06 57				06 58	
Drayton Green	d								06 29											06 59					
Castle Bar Park	d								06 31											07 01					
South Greenford	d								06 34											07 04					
Greenford ⊖	a								06 39											07 09					
Hanwell	d							06 16											06 46						
Southall	d	06 03					06 08	06 20			06 27	06 33							06 50			06 56		07 03	
Hayes & Harlington	d	06a10					06 12	06 24			06 31	06a40						06 42	06 54			07 01		07a10	
HeathrowTermls 2 & 3 2 ⊖ ✈	a				06 10			06 30		06 25						06 40			07 00		06 55				
	d				06 11	06 18		06 33		06 28						06 41	06 48		07 03		06 58				
Heathrow Terminal 4 ⊖ ✈	a					06 22		06 37									06 52		07 07						
	d																								
Heathrow Terminal 5 ⊖ ✈	a				06 16					06 32						06 46					07 02				
	d																								
West Drayton	d						06 16				06 35							06 46				07 05			
Iver	d						06 19											06 49							
Langley	d						06 23								←			06 52							
Slough 3	a			06 07			06 27				06 42			06 37	06 42			06 57				07 12			07 07
	d			06 08			06 28				06 43			06 38	06 43			06 57				07 12			07 08
Burnham	d						06 31				→				06 46							→			
Taplow	d						06 35								06 50										
Maidenhead 3	d						06 39								06 54			07 04							
Twyford 3	d						06 47								07 02			07 12							
Reading 7	a			06 21			06 55							06 51	07 10			07 20							07 21
Oxford	a			06 52										07 19											07 52

For non-stop services between London and Reading refer to Table T116

For Heathrow Express Services see Table T118

For non-stop services between London and Heathrow Airport see Table T118

Table T117-F

London - Greenford, Heathrow Airport and Reading

Stopping Services

		GW	HX	XR		GW	XR	GW	HX	GW	XR	GW	GW	HX		XR	GW	XR	GW	HX	GW	XR	GW	GW	
			◇1						◇1			◇1 ☕		◇1						◇1			◇		
London Paddington 15 ⊖	d		06 55			06 57	07 02		07 10	07 12	07 16	07 22		07 25			07 26	07 32		07 40	07 44	07 46	07 52		
Acton Main Line	d										07 22											07 52			
Ealing Broadway ⊖	d					07 05	07 10			07 20	07 25						07 35	07 41			07 52	07 56			
West Ealing	d						07 13	07 27			07 28							07 44	07 57			07 58			
Drayton Green	d							07 29											07 59						
Castle Bar Park	d							07 31											08 01						
South Greenford	d							07 34											08 04						
Greenford ⊖	a							07 39											08 09						
Hanwell	d						07 15											07 46							
Southall	d						07 19			07 25	07 33							07 50			07 57	08 04			
Hayes & Harlington	d					07 12	07 23			07 29	07a40						07 42	07 54			08 01	08a10			
HeathrowTermls 2 & 3 2 ⊖ ✈	a		07 10				07 30		07 25					07 40				08 00		07 55					
	d		07 11	07 18			07 33		07 28					07 41		07 48		08 03		07 58					
Heathrow Terminal 4 ⊖ ✈	a			07 22			07 37									07 52		08 07							
	d																								
Heathrow Terminal 5 ⊖ ✈	a		07 16						07 32					07 46						08 02					
	d																								
West Drayton	d					07 16				07 33							07 46				08 05				
Iver	d					07 19											07 49								
Langley	d	←				07 22							←				07 52							←	
Slough 3	a	07 12				07 27				07 40		07 37	07 40				07 57				08 15		08 08	08 15	
	d	07 12				07 27				07 41		07 38	07 41				07 57				08 15		08 09	08 15	
Burnham	d	07 16								→			07 44								→			08 19	
Taplow	d	07 20											07 48											08 22	
Maidenhead 3	d	07 24				07 34							07 52				08 04							08 26	
Twyford 3	d	07 32				07 42							08 00				08 12							08 34	
Reading 7	a	07 40				07 50						07 51	08 08				08 20						08 24	08 42	
Oxford	a											08 19											08 51		

		HX	XR	GW	XR	GW	GW	HX	GW	GW		XR	GW	GW	HX	XR	GW	XR	GW	HX		GW	XR	GW	GW
		◇1					◇1 A ☕	◇1		◇1 ☕			◇1 ☕		◇1					◇1				◇1	
London Paddington 15 ⊖	d	07 55		07 56	08 02		08 03	08 10	08 12	08 15		08 16	08 22		08 25		08 27	08 32		08 40		08 42	08 46	08 52	
Acton Main Line	d											08 22											08 52		
Ealing Broadway ⊖	d			08 05	08 11				08 20			08 25					08 35	08 41				08 50	08 55		
West Ealing	d				08 14	08 27						08 28						08 44	08 57				08 58		
Drayton Green	d					08 29													08 59						
Castle Bar Park	d					08 31													09 01						
South Greenford	d					08 34													09 04						
Greenford ⊖	a					08 39													09 09						
Hanwell	d				08 16													08 46							
Southall	d				08 20				08 25			08 33						08 50				08 55	09 03		
Hayes & Harlington	d			08 12	08 24				08 29			08a40					08 42	08 54				08 59	09a10		
HeathrowTermls 2 & 3 2 ⊖ ✈	a	08 10			08 30			08 25							08 40			09 00		08 55					
	d	08 11	08 18		08 33			08 28							08 41	08 48		09 03		08 58					
Heathrow Terminal 4 ⊖ ✈	a		08 22		08 37											08 52		09 07							
	d																								
Heathrow Terminal 5 ⊖ ✈	a	08 16						08 32							08 46					09 02					
	d																								
West Drayton	d			08 16					08 33								08 46					09 03			
Iver	d			08 19													08 49								
Langley	d			08 22										←			08 52								←
Slough 3	a			08 27					08 40				08 37	08 40			08 57					09 10		09 07	09 10
	d			08 27					08 41				08 38	08 41			08 57					09 10		09 08	09 10
Burnham	d								→					08 44								→			09 14
Taplow	d													08 48											09 18
Maidenhead 3	d			08 34										08 52			09 04								09 22
Twyford 3	d			08 42										09 00			09 12								09 30
Reading 7	a			08 50			08 30			08 39			08 51	09 08			09 20							09 21	09 38
Oxford	a												09 21											09 52	

A from 15 September

For non-stop services between London and Reading refer to Table T116

For Heathrow Express Services see Table T118

For non-stop services between London and Heathrow Airport see Table T118

Table T117-F

Saturdays
26 May to 8 December

London - Greenford, Heathrow Airport and Reading
Stopping Services

	HX ◇1		XR	GW	XR	GW	HX ◇1	GW	XR	GW ◇1 ⊡	GW		HX ◇1	XR	GW	XR	GW	HX ◇1	GW	XR	GW ◇1		GW	HX ◇1
London Paddington 15 ⊖ d	08 55			08 57	09 02		09 10	09 14	09 16	09 22			09 25		09 27	09 32		09 40	09 42	09 46	09 52			09 55
Acton Main Line d									09 22											09 53				
Ealing Broadway ⊖ d				09 05	09 11			09 22	09 26						09 35	09 41			09 50	09 56				
West Ealing d					09 14	09 27			09 28							09 44	09 57			09 59				
Drayton Green d						09 29											09 59							
Castle Bar Park d						09 31											10 01							
South Greenford d						09 34											10 04							
Greenford ⊖ a						09 39											10 09							
Hanwell d					09 16											09 46								
Southall d					09 20			09 27	09 33							09 50			09 55	10 03				
Hayes & Harlington d				09 12	09 24			09 31	09a41						09 42	09 54			09 59	10a10				
Heathrow Termls 2 & 3 2 ⊖ ✈ a	09 10				09 30		09 25						09 40			10 00		09 55						10 10
d	09 11		09 18		09 33		09 28						09 41	09 48		10 03		09 58						10 11
Heathrow Terminal 4 ⊖ ✈ a			09 22		09 37									09 52		10 07								
d																								
Heathrow Terminal 5 ⊖ ✈ a	09 16						09 32						09 46					10 02						10 16
d																								
West Drayton d				09 16				09 35							09 46				10 03					
Iver d				09 19											09 49									
Langley d				09 22							←				09 52								←	
Slough 3 a				09 27				09 43		09 37	09 43				09 57				10 10		10 07		10 10	
d				09 27				09 43		09 38	09 43				09 57				10 11		10 08		10 11	
Burnham d								→			09 46								→				10 14	
Taplow d											09 50												10 18	
Maidenhead 3 d				09 34							09 54				10 04								10 22	
Twyford 3 d				09 42							10 02				10 12								10 30	
Reading 7 a				09 50						09 51	10 10				10 20						10 21		10 38	
Oxford a										10 19											10 50			

	XR	GW	XR	GW	HX ◇1	GW	GW ◇1 ⊡		XR	GW ◇1 ⊡	GW	HX ◇1	XR	GW	XR	GW	HX ◇1		GW	XR	GW ◇1	GW	HX ◇1	XR
London Paddington 15 ⊖ d		09 57	10 02		10 10	10 12	10 15		10 16	10 22		10 25		10 27	10 32		10 40		10 42	10 46	10 52		10 55	
Acton Main Line d									10 22											10 52				
Ealing Broadway ⊖ d		10 05	10 11			10 20			10 25					10 35	10 41				10 50	10 55				
West Ealing d			10 14	10 27					10 28						10 44	10 57				10 58				
Drayton Green d				10 29												10 59								
Castle Bar Park d				10 31												11 01								
South Greenford d				10 34												11 04								
Greenford ⊖ a				10 39												11 09								
Hanwell d			10 16												10 46									
Southall d			10 20			10 25			10 33						10 50				10 55	11 03				
Hayes & Harlington d		10 12	10 24			10 29			10a40					10 42	10 54				10 59	11a10				
Heathrow Termls 2 & 3 2 ⊖ ✈ a			10 30		10 25							10 40			11 00		10 55						11 10	
d	10 18		10 33		10 28							10 41	10 48		11 03		10 58						11 11	11 18
Heathrow Terminal 4 ⊖ ✈ a	10 22		10 37										10 52		11 07									11 22
d																								
Heathrow Terminal 5 ⊖ ✈ a					10 32							10 46					11 02						11 16	
d																								
West Drayton d		10 16				10 33								10 46					11 03					
Iver d		10 19												10 49										
Langley d		10 22									←			10 52								←		
Slough 3 a		10 27				10 40				10 37	10 40			10 57					11 10		11 07	11 10		
d		10 27				10 41				10 38	10 41			10 57					11 11		11 08	11 11		
Burnham d						→					10 44								→			11 14		
Taplow d											10 48											11 18		
Maidenhead 3 d		10 34									10 52			11 04								11 22		
Twyford 3 d		10 42									11 00			11 12								11 30		
Reading 7 a		10 50					10 39			10 51	11 08			11 20							11 21	11 38		
Oxford a										11 20											11 48			

For non-stop services between London and Reading refer to Table T116

For Heathrow Express Services see Table T118

For non-stop services between London and Heathrow Airport see Table T118

Table T117-F

Saturdays
26 May to 8 December

London - Greenford, Heathrow Airport and Reading
Stopping Services

	GW	XR	GW	HX ◇1	GW	XR	GW ◇1 ⊡	GW	HX ◇1		XR	GW	XR	GW	HX ◇1	GW	XR	GW ◇	GW		HX ◇1	XR	GW	XR
London Paddington 15 ⊖ d	10 57	11 02		11 10	11 12	11 16	11 22		11 25			11 27	11 32		11 40	11 42	11 46	11 51			11 55		11 57	12 02
Acton Main Line d						11 22											11 52							
Ealing Broadway ⊖ d	11 05	11 11			11 20	11 27						11 35	11 41			11 50	11 55						12 05	12 11
West Ealing d		11 14	11 27			11 30							11 44	11 57			11 58							12 14
Drayton Green d			11 29											11 59										
Castle Bar Park d			11 31											12 01										
South Greenford d			11 34											12 04										
Greenford ⊖ a			11 39											12 09										
Hanwell d		11 16											11 46											12 16
Southall d		11 20			11 25	11 35							11 50			11 55	12 03							12 20
Hayes & Harlington d	11 12	11 24			11 29	11a42						11 42	11 54			11 59	12a10						12 12	12 24
Heathrow Termls 2 & 3 2 ⊖ ✈ a		11 30		11 25					11 40				12 00		11 55						12 10			12 30
d		11 33		11 28					11 41		11 48		12 03		11 58						12 11	12 18		12 33
Heathrow Terminal 4 ⊖ ✈ a		11 37									11 52		12 07									12 22		12 37
d																								
Heathrow Terminal 5 ⊖ ✈ a				11 32					11 46						12 02						12 16			
d																								
West Drayton d	11 16				11 33							11 46				12 03							12 16	
Iver d	11 19											11 49											12 19	
Langley d	11 22							←				11 52							←				12 22	
Slough 3 a	11 27				11 40		11 37	11 40				11 57				12 10		12 07	12 10				12 27	
d	11 27				11 41		11 38	11 41				11 57				12 11		12 08	12 11				12 27	
Burnham d					→			11 44								→			12 14					
Taplow d								11 48											12 18					
Maidenhead 3 d	11 34							11 52				12 04							12 22				12 34	
Twyford 3 d	11 42							12 00				12 12							12 30				12 42	
Reading 7 a	11 50						11 51	12 08				12 20						12 23	12 38				12 51	
Oxford a							12 20											12 50						

	HX ◇1	GW	GW ◇1 ⊡	XR	GW		GW ◇1 ⊡	GW	HX ◇1	XR	GW	XR	GW ◇1 A ⊡	HX ◇1	GW		XR	GW	GW ◇1	GW	HX ◇1	XR	GW	XR
London Paddington 15 ⊖ d	12 10	12 12	12 15	12 16			12 22		12 25		12 27	12 32	12 33	12 40	12 42		12 46		12 52		12 55		12 57	13 02
Acton Main Line d				12 22													12 52							
Ealing Broadway ⊖ d		12 20		12 25							12 35	12 41			12 50		12 55						13 05	13 11
West Ealing d				12 28	12 31							12 44					12 58	13 01						13 14
Drayton Green d					12 33													13 03						
Castle Bar Park d					12 35													13 05						
South Greenford d					12 38													13 08						
Greenford ⊖ a					12 43													13 13						
Hanwell d												12 46												13 16
Southall d		12 25		12 33								12 50			12 55		13 03							13 20
Hayes & Harlington d		12 29		12a40							12 42	12 54			12 59		13a10						13 12	13 24
Heathrow Termls 2 & 3 2 ⊖ ✈ a	12 25								12 40			13 00		12 55							13 10			13 30
d	12 28								12 41	12 48		13 03		12 58							13 11	13 18		13 33
Heathrow Terminal 4 ⊖ ✈ a										12 52		13 07										13 22		13 37
d																								
Heathrow Terminal 5 ⊖ ✈ a	12 32								12 46					13 02							13 16			
d																								
West Drayton d		12 33									12 46				13 03								13 16	
Iver d											12 49												13 19	
Langley d								←			12 52									←			13 22	
Slough 3 a		12 40					12 37	12 40			12 57				13 10				13 07	13 10			13 27	
d		12 41					12 38	12 41			12 57				13 11				13 08	13 11			13 27	
Burnham d		→						12 44							→					13 14				
Taplow d								12 48												13 18				
Maidenhead 3 d								12 52			13 04									13 22			13 34	
Twyford 3 d								13 00			13 12									13 30			13 42	
Reading 7 a			12 39				12 51	13 08			13 20		12 57						13 21	13 38			13 50	
Oxford a							13 20												13 51					

A from 15 September

For non-stop services between London and Reading refer to Table T116

For Heathrow Express Services see Table T118

For non-stop services between London and Heathrow Airport see Table T118

London - Greenford, Heathrow Airport and Reading
Stopping Services

		HX	GW	XR	GW	GW	GW	HX		XR	GW	XR	HX	GW	XR	GW	GW	GW		HX	XR	GW	XR	HX	GW
		◇■				◇■ ☕		◇■					◇■				◇■			◇■				◇■	
London Paddington ⊖	d	13 10	13 12	13 16		13 22		13 25			13 27	13 32	13 40	13 42	13 46		13 52			13 55		13 57	14 02	14 10	14 12
Acton Main Line	d			13 22											13 52										
Ealing Broadway ⊖	d		13 20	13 25							13 35	13 41		13 50	13 55							14 05	14 11		14 20
West Ealing	d			13 28	13 31							13 44			13 58	14 01							14 14		
Drayton Green	d				13 33											14 03									
Castle Bar Park	d				13 35											14 05									
South Greenford	d				13 38											14 08									
Greenford ⊖	a				13 43											14 13									
Hanwell	d											13 46											14 16		
Southall	d		13 27	13 33								13 50		13 55	14 03								14 20		14 25
Hayes & Harlington	d		13 31	13a40							13 42	13 54		14 00	14a10							14 12	14 24		14 29
Heathrow Termls 2 & 3 ⊖ ✈	a	13 25						13 40				14 00	13 55							14 10			14 30	14 25	
	d	13 28						13 41		13 48		14 03	13 58							14 11	14 18		14 33	14 28	
Heathrow Terminal 4 ⊖ ✈	a									13 52		14 07									14 22		14 37		
	d																								
Heathrow Terminal 5 ⊖ ✈	a	13 32						13 46					14 02							14 16				14 32	
	d																								
West Drayton	d		13 35								13 46			14 04								14 16			14 33
Iver	d										13 49											14 19			
Langley	d						←				13 52							←				14 22			
Slough	a		13 42			13 37	13 42				13 57			14 11			14 07	14 11				14 27			14 40
	d		13 43			13 38	13 43				13 57			14 12			14 08	14 12				14 27			14 41
Burnham	d		→				13 46							→				14 15							→
Taplow	d						13 50											14 19							
Maidenhead	d						13 54				14 04							14 23				14 34			
Twyford	d						14 02				14 12							14 31				14 42			
Reading	a					13 51	14 10				14 20						14 21	14 39				14 50			
Oxford	a					14 19											14 51								

		GW	XR	GW		GW	GW	HX	XR	GW	XR	HX	GW	XR		GW	GW	GW	HX	XR	GW	XR	HX	GW	
		◇■ ☕				◇■ ☕		◇■				◇■					◇■		◇■				◇■		
London Paddington ⊖	d	14 15	14 16			14 22		14 25		14 27	14 32	14 40	14 42	14 46			14 52		14 55		14 57	15 02	15 10	15 12	
Acton Main Line	d		14 22											14 52											
Ealing Broadway ⊖	d		14 25							14 35	14 40		14 50	14 55							15 05	15 11		15 20	
West Ealing	d		14 28	14 31							14 42			14 58		15 01						15 14			
Drayton Green	d			14 33												15 03									
Castle Bar Park	d			14 35												15 05									
South Greenford	d			14 38												15 08									
Greenford ⊖	a			14 43												15 13									
Hanwell	d										14 44											15 16			
Southall	d		14 33								14 48		14 56	15 03								15 20		15 25	
Hayes & Harlington	d		14a40							14 42	14 52		15 01	15a10							15 12	15 24		15 29	
Heathrow Termls 2 & 3 ⊖ ✈	a							14 40			15 00	14 55							15 10			15 30	15 25		
	d							14 41	14 48		15 03	14 58							15 11	15 18		15 33	15 28		
Heathrow Terminal 4 ⊖ ✈	a								14 52		15 07									15 22		15 37			
	d																								
Heathrow Terminal 5 ⊖ ✈	a							14 46				15 02							15 16				15 32		
	d																								
West Drayton	d									14 46			15 05								15 16			15 33	
Iver	d									14 49											15 19				
Langley	d						←			14 52								←			15 22				
Slough	a					14 37	14 40			14 57			15 12				15 07	15 12			15 27			15 40	
	d					14 38	14 41			14 57			15 13				15 08	15 13			15 27			15 41	
Burnham	d						14 44						→					15 16						→	
Taplow	d						14 48											15 20							
Maidenhead	d						14 52			15 04								15 24			15 34				
Twyford	d						15 00			15 12								15 32			15 42				
Reading	a	14 39				14 51	15 08			15 20							15 21	15 40			15 50				
Oxford	a					15 20											15 50								

For non-stop services between London and Reading refer to Table T116

For Heathrow Express Services see Table T118

For non-stop services between London and Heathrow Airport see Table T118

London - Greenford, Heathrow Airport and Reading
Stopping Services

		XR	GW	GW	GW	HX		XR	GW	XR	HX	GW	XR	GW	GW	GW		HX	XR	GW	XR	HX	GW	GW	XR
				◇ 🚲		◇■					◇■				◇■			◇■				◇■		◇■ ☕	
London Paddington ⊖	d	15 16		15 20		15 25			15 27	15 32	15 40	15 42	15 46		15 52			15 55		15 57	16 02	16 10	16 12	16 15	16 16
Acton Main Line	d	15 22											15 52												16 22
Ealing Broadway ⊖	d	15 25							15 35	15 41		15 50	15 55							16 05	16 10		16 20		16 25
West Ealing	d	15 28	15 31							15 44			15 58	16 01							16 12				16 28
Drayton Green	d		15 33											16 03											
Castle Bar Park	d		15 35											16 05											
South Greenford	d		15 38											16 08											
Greenford ⊖	a		15 43											16 13											
Hanwell	d									15 46											16 14				
Southall	d	15 33								15 50		15 55	16 03								16 20		16 25		16 33
Hayes & Harlington	d	15a40							15 42	15 54		15 59	16a10							16 12	16 24		16 29		16a40
Heathrow Termls 2 & 3 ⊖ ✈	a					15 40				16 00	15 55							16 10			16 30	16 25			
	d					15 41		15 48		16 03	15 58							16 11	16 18		16 33	16 28			
Heathrow Terminal 4 ⊖ ✈	a							15 52		16 07									16 22		16 37				
	d																								
Heathrow Terminal 5 ⊖ ✈	a					15 46					16 02							16 16				16 32			
	d																								
West Drayton	d								15 46			16 03								16 16			16 33		
Iver	d								15 49											16 19					
Langley	d				←				15 52							←				16 22					
Slough	a			15 36	15 40				15 57			16 10			16 07	16 10				16 27			16 40		
	d			15 37	15 41				15 57			16 11			16 08	16 11				16 27			16 41		
Burnham	d				15 44							→				16 14							→		
Taplow	d				15 48											16 18									
Maidenhead	d				15 52				16 04							16 22				16 34					
Twyford	d				16 00				16 12							16 30				16 42					
Reading	a			15 52	16 08				16 20						16 21	16 38				16 50				16 39	
Oxford	a			16 19											16 49										

		GW		GW	GW	HX	XR	GW	XR	HX	GW	XR		GW	GW	GW	HX	XR	GW	XR	HX	GW		XR	GW
				◇■ ☕		◇■				◇■					◇■		◇■				◇■				
London Paddington ⊖	d			16 22		16 25		16 27	16 32	16 40	16 42	16 46			16 52		16 55		16 57	17 02	17 10	17 12		17 16	
Acton Main Line	d											16 52												17 22	
Ealing Broadway ⊖	d							16 35	16 41		16 50	16 55							17 05	17 11		17 20		17 25	
West Ealing	d	16 31							16 44			16 58		17 01						17 14				17 28	17 31
Drayton Green	d	16 33												17 03											17 33
Castle Bar Park	d	16 35												17 05											17 35
South Greenford	d	16 38												17 08											17 38
Greenford ⊖	a	16 43												17 13											17 43
Hanwell	d								16 46											17 16					
Southall	d								16 50		16 55	17 03								17 20		17 25		17 33	
Hayes & Harlington	d							16 42	16 54		16 59	17a10							17 12	17 24		17 29		17a40	
Heathrow Termls 2 & 3 ⊖ ✈	a					16 40			17 00	16 55							17 10			17 30	17 25				
	d					16 41	16 48		17 03	16 58							17 11	17 18		17 33	17 28				
Heathrow Terminal 4 ⊖ ✈	a						16 52		17 07									17 22		17 37					
	d																								
Heathrow Terminal 5 ⊖ ✈	a					16 46				17 02							17 16				17 32				
	d																								
West Drayton	d							16 46			17 03								17 16			17 33			
Iver	d							16 49											17 19						
Langley	d				←			16 52								←			17 22						
Slough	a			16 37	16 40			16 57			17 10				17 07	17 10			17 27			17 40			
	d			16 38	16 41			16 57			17 11				17 08	17 11			17 27			17 41			
Burnham	d				16 44						→					17 14						→			
Taplow	d				16 48											17 18									
Maidenhead	d				16 52			17 04								17 22			17 34						
Twyford	d				17 00			17 12								17 30			17 42						
Reading	a			16 51	17 08			17 20							17 21	17 38			17 50						
Oxford	a			17 20											17 51										

For non-stop services between London and Reading refer to Table T116

For Heathrow Express Services see Table T118

For non-stop services between London and Heathrow Airport see Table T118

Table T117-F

London - Greenford, Heathrow Airport and Reading

Stopping Services

Saturdays
26 May to 8 December

		GW ◇1 ⊏	GW	HX ◇1		XR	GW	XR	HX ◇1	GW	XR	GW	GW ◇1	GW		HX ◇1	XR	GW	XR	HX ◇1	GW	GW ◇1 ⊏	XR	GW	
London Paddington 15 ⊖	d	17 22		17 25			17 27	17 32	17 40	17 42	17 46		17 52			17 55		17 57	18 02	18 10	18 12	18 15	18 16		
Acton Main Line	d										17 52												18 22		
Ealing Broadway ⊖	d						17 35	17 41		17 50	17 55							18 05	18 11		18 20		18 25		
West Ealing	d							17 44			17 58	18 01							18 14				18 28	18 31	
Drayton Green	d											18 03												18 33	
Castle Bar Park	d											18 05												18 35	
South Greenford	d											18 08												18 38	
Greenford ⊖	a											18 13												18 43	
Hanwell	d							17 46											18 16						
Southall	d							17 50		17 55	18 03								18 20		18 25		18 33		
Hayes & Harlington	d						17 42	17 54		17 59	18a10							18 12	18 24		18 29		18a40		
HeathrowTermls 2 & 3 2 ⊖ ✈	a			17 40				18 00	17 55							18 10			18 30	18 25					
	d			17 41		17 48		18 03	17 58							18 11	18 18		18 33	18 28					
Heathrow Terminal 4 ⊖ ✈	a					17 52		18 07									18 22		18 37						
	d																								
Heathrow Terminal 5 ⊖ ✈	a			17 46					18 02							18 16				18 32					
	d																								
West Drayton	d						17 46			18 03								18 16			18 33				
Iver	d						17 49											18 19							
Langley	d		←				17 52							←				18 22							
Slough 3	a	17 37	17 40				17 57			18 10			18 07	18 10				18 27			18 40				
	d	17 38	17 41				17 57			18 11			18 08	18 11				18 27			18 41				
Burnham	d		17 44							→				18 14							→				
Taplow	d		17 48											18 18											
Maidenhead 8	d		17 52				18 04							18 22				18 34							
Twyford 3	d		18 00				18 12							18 30				18 42							
Reading 7	a	17 51	18 08				18 20						18 21	18 38				18 50				18 39			
Oxford	a	18 20											18 50												

		GW ◇1 ⊏	GW	HX ◇1	XR	GW	XR	HX ◇1	GW	XR		GW	GW ◇1	GW	HX ◇1	XR	GW	XR	HX ◇1	GW		XR	GW	GW ◇1	GW
London Paddington 15 ⊖	d	18 22		18 25		18 27	18 32	18 40	18 42	18 46			18 52		18 55		18 57	19 02	19 10	19 12		19 16		19 22	
Acton Main Line	d									18 52												19 22			
Ealing Broadway ⊖	d					18 35	18 41		18 50	18 55							19 05	19 11		19 20		19 25			
West Ealing	d						18 44			18 58		19 01						19 14				19 28	19 31		
Drayton Green	d											19 03											19 33		
Castle Bar Park	d											19 05											19 35		
South Greenford	d											19 08											19 38		
Greenford ⊖	a											19 13											19 43		
Hanwell	d						18 46											19 16							
Southall	d						18 50		18 55	19 03								19 20		19 25		19 33			
Hayes & Harlington	d					18 42	18 54		18 59	19a10							19 12	19 24		19 29		19a40			
HeathrowTermls 2 & 3 2 ⊖ ✈	a			18 40			19 00	18 55							19 10			19 30	19 25						
	d			18 41	18 48		19 03	18 58							19 11	19 18		19 33	19 28						
Heathrow Terminal 4 ⊖ ✈	a				18 52		19 07									19 22		19 37							
	d																								
Heathrow Terminal 5 ⊖ ✈	a			18 46				19 02							19 16				19 32						
	d																								
West Drayton	d					18 46			19 03								19 16			19 33					
Iver	d					18 49											19 19								
Langley	d		←			18 52								←			19 22								←
Slough 3	a	18 37	18 40			18 57			19 10				19 07	19 10			19 27			19 40				19 37	19 40
	d	18 38	18 41			18 57			19 11				19 08	19 11			19 27			19 41				19 38	19 41
Burnham	d		18 44						→					19 14						→					19 44
Taplow	d		18 48											19 18											19 48
Maidenhead 8	d		18 52			19 04								19 22			19 34								19 52
Twyford 3	d		19 00			19 12								19 30			19 42								20 00
Reading 7	a	18 51	19 08			19 20							19 21	19 38			19 50							19 51	20 08
Oxford	a	19 20											19 50											20 21	

For non-stop services between London and Reading refer to Table T116

For Heathrow Express Services see Table T118

For non-stop services between London and Heathrow Airport see Table T118

Table T117-F

London - Greenford, Heathrow Airport and Reading

Stopping Services

Saturdays
26 May to 8 December

		HX ◇1		XR	GW	XR	HX ◇1	GW	XR	GW	GW ◇1 ⊏	GW		HX ◇1	XR	GW	XR	HX ◇1	GW	GW ◇1 ⊏	XR	GW		GW ◇1	GW
London Paddington 15 ⊖	d	19 25			19 27	19 32	19 40	19 42	19 46		19 52			19 55		19 57	20 02	20 10	20 12	20 15	20 16			20 22	
Acton Main Line	d								19 52												20 22				
Ealing Broadway ⊖	d				19 35	19 41		19 50	19 55							20 05	20 11		20 20		20 25				
West Ealing	d					19 44			19 58	20 01							20 14				20 28	20 31			
Drayton Green	d									20 03												20 33			
Castle Bar Park	d									20 05												20 35			
South Greenford	d									20 08												20 38			
Greenford ⊖	a									20 13												20 43			
Hanwell	d					19 46											20 16								
Southall	d					19 50		19 55	20 03								20 20		20 25		20 33				
Hayes & Harlington	d				19 42	19 54		19 59	20a10							20 12	20 24		20 29		20a40				
HeathrowTermls 2 & 3 2 ⊖ ✈	a	19 40				20 00	19 55							20 10			20 30	20 25							
	d	19 41		19 48		20 03	19 58							20 11	20 18		20 33	20 28							
Heathrow Terminal 4 ⊖ ✈	a			19 52		20 07									20 22		20 37								
	d																								
Heathrow Terminal 5 ⊖ ✈	a	19 46					20 02							20 16				20 32							
	d																								
West Drayton	d				19 46			20 03								20 16			20 33						
Iver	d				19 49											20 19									
Langley	d				19 52							←				20 22									←
Slough 3	a				19 57			20 10			20 07	20 10				20 27			20 40					20 37	20 40
	d				19 57			20 11			20 08	20 11				20 27			20 41					20 38	20 41
Burnham	d							→				20 14							→						20 44
Taplow	d											20 18													20 48
Maidenhead 8	d				20 04							20 22				20 34									20 52
Twyford 3	d				20 12							20 30				20 42									21 00
Reading 7	a				20 20						20 21	20 38				20 50				20 39				20 51	21 08
Oxford	a										20 46													21 20	

		HX ◇1	XR	GW	XR	HX ◇1	GW	XR		GW	GW ◇1	GW	HX ◇1	XR	GW	XR	HX ◇1	GW		XR	GW	GW ◇1	GW	HX ◇1	XR
London Paddington 15 ⊖	d	20 25		20 27	20 32	20 40	20 42	20 46			20 50		20 55		20 57	21 02	21 10	21 12		21 16		21 20		21 25	
Acton Main Line	d							20 52												21 22					
Ealing Broadway ⊖	d			20 35	20 41		20 50	20 55							21 05	21 11		21 20		21 25					
West Ealing	d				20 44			20 58		21 01						21 14				21 28	21 31				
Drayton Green	d									21 03											21 33				
Castle Bar Park	d									21 05											21 35				
South Greenford	d									21 08											21 38				
Greenford ⊖	a									21 13											21 43				
Hanwell	d				20 46											21 16									
Southall	d				20 50		20 55	21 03								21 20		21 25		21 33					
Hayes & Harlington	d			20 42	20 54		20 59	21a10							21 12	21 24		21 29		21a40					
HeathrowTermls 2 & 3 2 ⊖ ✈	a	20 40			21 00	20 55							21 10			21 30	21 25							21 40	
	d	20 41	20 48		21 03	20 58							21 11	21 18		21 33	21 28							21 41	21 48
Heathrow Terminal 4 ⊖ ✈	a		20 52		21 07									21 22		21 37									21 52
	d																								
Heathrow Terminal 5 ⊖ ✈	a	20 46				21 02							21 16				21 32							21 46	
	d																								
West Drayton	d			20 46			21 03								21 16			21 33							
Iver	d			20 49											21 19			21 36							
Langley	d			20 52								←			21 22			21 40					←		
Slough 3	a			20 57			21 10				21 05	21 10			21 27			21 44				21 35	21 44		
	d			20 57			21 11				21 06	21 11			21 27			21 45				21 36	21 45		
Burnham	d						→					21 14						→					21 48		
Taplow	d											21 18											21 52		
Maidenhead 8	d			21 04								21 22			21 34							21 43	21 56		
Twyford 3	d			21 12								21 30			21 42								22 04		
Reading 7	a			21 20							21 19	21 38			21 50							21 54	22 12		
Oxford	a										21 53											22 26			

For non-stop services between London and Reading refer to Table T116

For Heathrow Express Services see Table T118

For non-stop services between London and Heathrow Airport see Table T118

Table T117-F

Saturdays
26 May to 8 December

London - Greenford, Heathrow Airport and Reading

Stopping Services

		XR	HX ◇1	GW	XR	GW ◇	GW	HX ◇1	XR	XR		HX ◇1	GW	XR	GW ◇1	GW	HX ◇1	XR	XR	HX ◇1		GW	XR	GW ◇	GW
London Paddington ⊖	d	21 32	21 40	21 42	21 47	21 50		21 55		22 02		22 10	22 12	22 16	22 20		22 25		22 32	22 40		22 43	22 46	22 50	
Acton Main Line	d			21 48	21 53									22 22								22 49	22 53		
Ealing Broadway ⊖	d	21 41		21 51	21 56					22 11			22 20	22 25					22 41			22 52	22 56		
West Ealing	d	21 44			21 59					22 14				22 28					22 44				22 59		
Drayton Green	d																								
Castle Bar Park	d																								
South Greenford	d																								
Greenford ⊖	a																								
Hanwell	d	21 46								22 16									22 46						
Southall	d	21 50		21 57	22 04					22 20			22 25	22 33					22 50			22 58	23 03		
Hayes & Harlington	d	21 54		22 01	22a11					22 24			22 29	22a40					22 54			23 02	23a10		
HeathrowTermls 2 & 3 ⊖ ✈	a	22 00	21 55					22 10		22 30		22 25					22 40		23 00	22 55					
	d	22 03	21 58					22 11	22 18	22 33		22 28					22 41	22 48	23 03	22 58					
Heathrow Terminal 4 ⊖ ✈	a	22 07							22 22	22 37								22 52	23 07						
	d																								
Heathrow Terminal 5 ⊖ ✈	a		22 02					22 16				22 32					22 46			23 02					
	d																								
West Drayton	d			22 05									22 33									23 06			
Iver	d			22 08									22 36									23 09			
Langley	d			22 11			←						22 40			←						23 13			←
Slough	a			22 16		22 06	22 16						22 44		22 35	22 44						23 17		23 08	23 17
	d			22 16		22 06	22 16						22 45		22 36	22 45						23 18		23 08	23 18
Burnham	d			→			22 19						→			22 48						→			23 21
Taplow	d						22 23									22 52									23 25
Maidenhead	d						22 28								22 43	22 56								23 15	23 29
Twyford	d						22 36									23 04									23 37
Reading	a					22 22	22 43								22 54	23 12								23 28	23 45
Oxford	a					22 50									23 27									00 01	

		HX ◇1	XR	XR	HX ◇1	GW		XR	HX ◇1	XR	GW ◇	GW	GW
London Paddington ⊖	d	22 55		23 02	23 10	23 20		23 22	23 25		23 33		23 43
Acton Main Line	d							23 29					
Ealing Broadway ⊖	d			23 11		23 28		23 32					23 51
West Ealing	d			23 14				23 35					
Drayton Green	d												
Castle Bar Park	d												
South Greenford	d												
Greenford ⊖	a												
Hanwell	d			23 16									
Southall	d			23 20		23 33		23 40					23 56
Hayes & Harlington	d			23 24		23 37		23a47					00 01
HeathrowTermls 2 & 3 ⊖ ✈	a	23 10		23 30	23 25				23 40				
	d	23 11	23 18	23 33	23 28				23 41	23 48			
Heathrow Terminal 4 ⊖ ✈	a		23 22	23 37						23 52			
	d												
Heathrow Terminal 5 ⊖ ✈	a	23 16			23 32				23 46				
	d												
West Drayton	d					23 41							00 05
Iver	d					23 44							
Langley	d					23 48						←	
Slough	a					23 55					23 51	23 55	00 12
	d					23 55					23 51	23 55	00 15
Burnham	d					→						23 59	00 18
Taplow	d											00 02	00 22
Maidenhead	d										23 58	00 06	00 26
Twyford	d											00 14	00 34
Reading	a										00 11	00 22	00 42
Oxford	a										00 43		

For non-stop services between London and Reading refer to Table T116

For Heathrow Express Services see Table T118

For non-stop services between London and Heathrow Airport see Table T118

Table T117-F

Sundays
20 May to 9 September

London - Greenford, Heathrow Airport and Reading

Stopping Services

		GW A	GW A	GW	GW	GW		HX	HX ◇1	XR	HX ◇1	XR	HX ◇1	XR	HX ◇1	XR		HX ◇	XR	HX ◇1	XR	HX ◇1	XR	GW	HX ◇1
London Paddington ⊖	d			00 05	00 30	01 00			05 10	05 11	05 25	05 27	05 40	05 41	05 55			06 10	06 11	06 25		06 40	06 41	06 45	06 55
Acton Main Line	d																								
Ealing Broadway ⊖	d			00 13	00 38	01 08				05 20		05 35		05 50					06 20				06 50	06 53	
West Ealing	d																								
Drayton Green	d																								
Castle Bar Park	d																								
South Greenford	d																								
Greenford ⊖	a																								
Hanwell	d																								
Southall	d			00 18	00 43	01 13				05 24		05 39		05 54					06 24				06 54	06 59	
Hayes & Harlington	d		00 01	00 22	00 47	01 17				05 28		05 43		05 58					06 28				06 58	07 03	
HeathrowTermls 2 & 3 ⊖ ✈	a								05 26	05 35	05 41	05 50	05 56	06 05	06 11			06 26	06 35	06 41		06 56	07 05		07 11
	d							05 13	05 28	05 37	05 43	05 53	05 58	06 07	06 13	06 23		06 28	06 37	06 43	06 53	06 58	07 07		07 13
Heathrow Terminal 4 ⊖ ✈	a									05 45		06 00		06 15		06 27			06 45		06 57		07 15		
	d																								
Heathrow Terminal 5 ⊖ ✈	a							05 17	05 32		05 47		06 02		06 17			06 32		06 47		07 02			07 17
	d																								
West Drayton	d		00 05	00 26	00 51																			07 07	
Iver	d			00 29	00 54																				
Langley	d			00 33	00 58																			07 12	
Slough	a		00 12	00 37	01 02	01 26																		07 16	
	d		00 15	00 38	01 03	01 26																		07 16	
Burnham	d		00 18	00 41																				07 20	
Taplow	d	00 02	00 22	00 45																					
Maidenhead	d	00 06	00 26	00 49	01 10	01 33																		07 26	
Twyford	d	00 14	00 34	00 57	01 18	01 41																		07 34	
Reading	a	00 22	00 42	01 05	01 26	01 49																		07 41	
Oxford	a																								

		XR		HX ◇1	XR	HX ◇1	XR	GW	HX ◇1	XR	HX ◇1	XR		GW ◇1 ☕	GW	HX ◇1	XR	HX ◇1	XR	GW ◇1 ☕	GW	GW ◇1 ☕		GW	HX ◇1
London Paddington ⊖	d			07 10	07 11	07 25		07 29	07 40	07 41	07 55			08 00	08 02	08 10	08 11	08 25		08 27	08 30	08 34			08 40
Acton Main Line	d																								
Ealing Broadway ⊖	d				07 20			07 37		07 50					08 10		08 20				08 38				
West Ealing	d																								
Drayton Green	d																								
Castle Bar Park	d																								
South Greenford	d																								
Greenford ⊖	a																								
Hanwell	d																								
Southall	d				07 24			07 43		07 54					08 16		08 24				08 44				
Hayes & Harlington	d				07 28			07 47		07 58					08 20		08 28				08 48				
HeathrowTermls 2 & 3 ⊖ ✈	a			07 26	07 35	07 41			07 56	08 05	08 11					08 26	08 35	08 41							08 55
	d	07 23		07 28	07 37	07 43	07 53		07 58	08 07	08 13	08 23				08 28	08 37	08 43	08 53						08 56
Heathrow Terminal 4 ⊖ ✈	a	07 27			07 45		07 57			08 15		08 27					08 45		08 57						
	d																								
Heathrow Terminal 5 ⊖ ✈	a			07 32		07 47			08 02		08 17					08 32		08 47							09 01
	d																								
West Drayton	d							07 51							08 24						08 52				
Iver	d																								
Langley	d							07 56							08 29						08 57			←	
Slough	a							08 00						08 20	08 34						09 01	08 51		09 01	
	d							08 04						08 21	08 34						09 01	08 52		09 01	
Burnham	d							08 08													→			09 05	
Taplow	d																								
Maidenhead	d							08 14						08 28	08 42									09 11	
Twyford	d							08 22							08 50									09 19	
Reading	a							08 29						08 44	08 57					09 02		09 13		09 27	
Oxford	a													09 13								09 46			

A not 20 May

For non-stop services between London and Reading refer to Table T116

For Heathrow Express Services see Table T118

For non-stop services between London and Heathrow Airport see Table T118

Table T117-F

Sundays
20 May to 9 September

London - Greenford, Heathrow Airport and Reading
Stopping Services

		XR	HX ◇1	XR		GW	HX ◇1	XR	HX ◇1	XR	GW	GW ◇1 🍴	GW	HX ◇1		XR	HX ◇1	XR	GW	GW	GW	HX ◇1	XR	HX ◇1	
London Paddington 15 ⊖	d	08 41	08 55			09 07	09 10	09 11	09 25		09 30	09 34		09 40		09 41	09 55		10 02	10 04		10 10	10 11	10 25	
Acton Main Line	d																								
Ealing Broadway ⊖	d	08 50				09 15		09 20			09 38					09 50			10 10				10 20		
West Ealing	d																								
Drayton Green	d																								
Castle Bar Park	d																								
South Greenford	d																								
Greenford ⊖	a																								
Hanwell	d																								
Southall	d	08 54				09 21		09 24			09 44					09 54			10 15				10 24		
Hayes & Harlington	d	08 58				09 25		09 28			09 48					09 58			10 19				10 28		
HeathrowTermls 2 & 3 2 ⊖ ✈	a	09 05	09 10				09 25	09 35	09 40					09 55		10 05	10 10					10 25	10 35	10 40	
	d	09 07	09 11	09 23			09 26	09 37	09 41	09 53				09 56		10 07	10 11	10 23				10 26	10 37	10 41	
Heathrow Terminal 4 ⊖ ✈	a	09 15		09 27				09 45		09 57						10 15		10 27					10 45		
	d																								
Heathrow Terminal 5 ⊖ ✈	a		09 16				09 31		09 46					10 01			10 16					10 31		10 46	
	d																								
West Drayton	d					09 29					09 52								10 23						
Iver	d																								
Langley	d					09 34					09 57		←						10 28		←				
Slough 3	a					09 39					10 01	09 55	10 01						10 33	10 23	10 33				
	d					09 39					10 01	09 56	10 01						10 33	10 24	10 33				
Burnham	d										→		10 05						→						
Taplow	d																								
Maidenhead 3	d					09 46							10 11							10 31	10 41				
Twyford 3	d					09 54							10 19								10 49				
Reading 7	a					10 02						10 10	10 26							10 46	10 57				
Oxford	a											10 44													

		XR	GW ◇1 🍴	GW	GW ◇1 🍴	GW	HX ◇1	XR	HX ◇1	XR		GW	HX ◇1	XR	HX ◇1	XR	GW	GW ◇	GW	HX ◇1		XR	HX ◇1	XR	GW
London Paddington 15 ⊖	d		10 27	10 30	10 34		10 40	10 41	10 55			11 02	11 10	11 11	11 25		11 30	11 34		11 40		11 41	11 55		12 02
Acton Main Line	d																								
Ealing Broadway ⊖	d			10 38				10 50				11 10		11 20			11 38					11 50			12 10
West Ealing	d																								
Drayton Green	d																								
Castle Bar Park	d																								
South Greenford	d																								
Greenford ⊖	a																								
Hanwell	d																								
Southall	d			10 44				10 54				11 15		11 24			11 44					11 54			12 15
Hayes & Harlington	d			10 48				10 58				11 19		11 28			11 48					11 58			12 19
HeathrowTermls 2 & 3 2 ⊖ ✈	a						10 55	11 05	11 10				11 25	11 35	11 40					11 55		12 05	12 10		
	d	10 53					10 56	11 07	11 11	11 23			11 26	11 37	11 41	11 53				11 56		12 07	12 11	12 23	
Heathrow Terminal 4 ⊖ ✈	a	10 57						11 15		11 27				11 45		11 57						12 15		12 27	
	d																								
Heathrow Terminal 5 ⊖ ✈	a						11 01		11 16				11 31		11 46					12 01			12 16		
	d																								
West Drayton	d			10 52								11 23					11 52								12 23
Iver	d																								
Langley	d			10 57		←						11 28					11 57		←						12 28
Slough 3	a			11 01	10 53	11 01						11 33					12 01	11 54	12 01						12 33
	d			11 01	10 54	11 01						11 33					12 01	11 54	12 01						12 33
Burnham	d			→		11 05											→		12 05						→
Taplow	d																								
Maidenhead 3	d					11 11						11 41							12 11						
Twyford 3	d					11 19						11 49							12 19						
Reading 7	a		11 03		11 14	11 26						11 57						12 12	12 26						
Oxford	a				11 44													12 43							

For non-stop services between London and Reading refer to Table T116

For Heathrow Express Services see Table T118

For non-stop services between London and Heathrow Airport see Table T118

Table T117-F

Sundays
20 May to 9 September

London - Greenford, Heathrow Airport and Reading
Stopping Services

		GW		GW	HX ◇	XR	HX ◇	XR	GW ◇1 🍴	GW	GW ◇1 🍴	GW		HX ◇1	XR	HX ◇1	XR	GW	HX ◇1	XR	HX ◇1	XR		GW	GW ◇1 🍴
London Paddington 15 ⊖	d	12 04			12 10	12 11	12 25		12 27	12 30	12 34			12 40	12 41	12 55		13 02	13 10	13 11	13 25			13 30	13 34
Acton Main Line	d																								
Ealing Broadway ⊖	d					12 20				12 38					12 50			13 10		13 20				13 38	
West Ealing	d																								
Drayton Green	d																								
Castle Bar Park	d																								
South Greenford	d																								
Greenford ⊖	a																								
Hanwell	d																								
Southall	d					12 24				12 44					12 54			13 15		13 24				13 44	
Hayes & Harlington	d					12 28				12 48					12 58			13 19		13 28				13 48	
HeathrowTermls 2 & 3 2 ⊖ ✈	a				12 25	12 35	12 40							12 55	13 05	13 10			13 25	13 35	13 40				
	d				12 26	12 37	12 41	12 53						12 56	13 07	13 11	13 23		13 26	13 37	13 41	13 53			
Heathrow Terminal 4 ⊖ ✈	a					12 45		12 57							13 15		13 27			13 45		13 57			
	d																								
Heathrow Terminal 5 ⊖ ✈	a				12 31		12 46							13 01		13 16			13 31		13 46				
	d																								
West Drayton	d									12 52								13 24						13 52	
Iver	d																								
Langley	d			←						12 57		←						13 28						13 57	
Slough 3	a	12 23		12 33						13 01	12 52	13 01						13 33						14 01	13 53
	d	12 24		12 33						13 01	12 53	13 01						13 33						14 01	13 54
Burnham	d									→		13 05												→	
Taplow	d																								
Maidenhead 3	d	12 31		12 41								13 11						13 41							
Twyford 3	d			12 49								13 19						13 49							
Reading 7	a	12 46		12 57					13 03		13 15	13 26						13 56							14 15
Oxford	a										13 43														14 45

		GW	HX ◇1	XR	HX ◇1	XR	GW	GW		GW	HX ◇1	XR	GW ◇1 🍴	HX ◇1	XR	GW	GW ◇1 🍴	GW		HX ◇1	XR	HX ◇1	XR	GW	HX ◇1
London Paddington 15 ⊖	d		13 40	13 41	13 55		14 00	14 04			14 10	14 11	14 22	14 25		14 30	14 34			14 40	14 41	14 55		15 00	15 10
Acton Main Line	d																								
Ealing Broadway ⊖	d			13 50			14 09					14 20				14 38					14 50			15 09	
West Ealing	d																								
Drayton Green	d																								
Castle Bar Park	d																								
South Greenford	d																								
Greenford ⊖	a																								
Hanwell	d																								
Southall	d			13 54			14 14					14 24				14 44					14 54			15 14	
Hayes & Harlington	d			13 58			14 18					14 28				14 48					14 58			15 18	
HeathrowTermls 2 & 3 2 ⊖ ✈	a		13 55	14 05	14 10						14 25	14 35		14 40						14 55	15 05	15 10			15 25
	d		13 56	14 07	14 11	14 23					14 26	14 37		14 41	14 53					14 56	15 07	15 11	15 23		15 26
Heathrow Terminal 4 ⊖ ✈	a			14 15		14 27						14 45			14 57						15 15		15 27		
	d																								
Heathrow Terminal 5 ⊖ ✈	a		14 01		14 16						14 31			14 46						15 01		15 16			15 31
	d																								
West Drayton	d						14 23									14 52								15 22	
Iver	d																								
Langley	d	←					14 28			←						14 57		←						15 27	
Slough 3	a	14 01					14 31	14 23		14 31						15 01	14 52	15 01						15 31	
	d	14 01					14 31	14 24		14 31						15 01	14 53	15 01						15 31	
Burnham	d	14 05					→									→		15 05						15 35	
Taplow	d																								
Maidenhead 3	d	14 11						14 31		14 40								15 11						15 40	
Twyford 3	d	14 19								14 48								15 19						15 48	
Reading 7	a	14 26						14 46		14 56			14 58				15 12	15 26						15 56	
Oxford	a																15 42								

For non-stop services between London and Reading refer to Table T116

For Heathrow Express Services see Table T118

For non-stop services between London and Heathrow Airport see Table T118

Table T117-F

Sundays
20 May to 9 September

London - Greenford, Heathrow Airport and Reading
Stopping Services

		XR	HX	XR	GW	GW	GW	HX	XR	HX		XR	GW	GW	GW	HX	XR	GW	HX	XR		GW	GW	GW	HX
			◇1			◇		◇1		◇1						◇1		◇1 ☕	◇1				◇1		◇1
London Paddington 15 ⊖	d	15 11	15 25		15 30	15 34		15 40	15 41	15 55			16 00	16 04		16 10	16 11	16 22	16 25			16 30	16 34		16 40
Acton Main Line	d																								
Ealing Broadway ⊖	d	15 20			15 38				15 50				16 09				16 20					16 38			
West Ealing	d																								
Drayton Green	d																								
Castle Bar Park	d																								
South Greenford	d																								
Greenford ⊖	a																								
Hanwell	d																								
Southall	d	15 24			15 44				15 54				16 14				16 24					16 44			
Hayes & Harlington	d	15 28			15 48				15 58				16 18				16 28					16 48			
HeathrowTermls 2 & 3 2 ⊖ ✈	a	15 35	15 40					15 55	16 05	16 10						16 25	16 35		16 40						16 55
	d	15 37	15 41	15 53				15 56	16 07	16 11		16 23				16 26	16 37		16 41	16 53					16 56
Heathrow Terminal 4 ⊖ ✈	a	15 45		15 57					16 15			16 27					16 45			16 57					
	d																								
Heathrow Terminal 5 ⊖ ✈	a		15 46					16 01		16 16						16 31			16 46						17 01
	d																								
West Drayton	d				15 52								16 22									16 52			
Iver	d																								
Langley	d				15 57		←						16 27		←							16 57		←	
Slough 5	a				16 01	15 54	16 01						16 31	16 23	16 31							17 00	16 54	17 00	
	d				16 02	15 54	16 02						16 31	16 24	16 31							17 01	16 54	17 01	
Burnham	d				→		16 07						→		16 35							→		17 05	
Taplow	d																								
Maidenhead 3	d						16 11							16 31	16 41								17 02	17 11	
Twyford 3	d						16 20								16 49									17 19	
Reading 7	a					16 11	16 28							16 46	16 56			16 58					17 15	17 26	
Oxford	a					16 42																	17 44		

		XR	HX	XR	GW	HX		XR	HX	XR	GW	GW	GW	HX	XR	HX		XR	GW	GW	GW	HX	XR	GW	HX
			◇1			◇			◇			◇1 ☕		◇		◇						◇		◇1 ☕	◇
London Paddington 15 ⊖	d	16 41	16 55		17 00	17 10		17 11	17 25		17 30	17 34		17 40	17 41	17 55			18 00	18 04		18 10	18 11	18 22	18 25
Acton Main Line	d																								
Ealing Broadway ⊖	d	16 50			17 09			17 20			17 38				17 50				18 09				18 20		
West Ealing	d																								
Drayton Green	d																								
Castle Bar Park	d																								
South Greenford	d																								
Greenford ⊖	a																								
Hanwell	d																								
Southall	d	16 54			17 14			17 24			17 44				17 54				18 14				18 24		
Hayes & Harlington	d	16 58			17 18			17 28			17 48				17 58				18 18				18 28		
HeathrowTermls 2 & 3 2 ⊖ ✈	a	17 05	17 10			17 25		17 35	17 40					17 55	18 05	18 10						18 25	18 35		18 40
	d	17 07	17 11	17 23		17 26		17 37	17 41	17 53				17 56	18 07	18 11		18 23				18 26	18 37		18 41
Heathrow Terminal 4 ⊖ ✈	a	17 15		17 27				17 45		17 57					18 15			18 27					18 45		
	d																								
Heathrow Terminal 5 ⊖ ✈	a		17 16			17 31			17 46					18 01		18 16						18 31			18 46
	d																								
West Drayton	d				17 22						17 52								18 22						
Iver	d																								
Langley	d				17 27						17 57		←						18 27		←				
Slough 5	a				17 31						18 01	17 53	18 01						18 31	18 23	18 31				
	d				17 31						18 01	17 53	18 01						18 31	18 24	18 31				
Burnham	d				17 35						→		18 05						→		18 35				
Taplow	d																								
Maidenhead 3	d				17 41							18 01	18 11							18 31	18 41				
Twyford 3	d				17 49								18 19								18 49				
Reading 7	a				17 57							18 18	18 26							18 45	18 56			18 58	
Oxford	a											18 49													

For non-stop services between London and Reading refer to Table T116

For Heathrow Express Services see Table T118

For non-stop services between London and Heathrow Airport see Table T118

Table T117-F

Sundays
20 May to 9 September

London - Greenford, Heathrow Airport and Reading
Stopping Services

		XR	GW	GW	GW	HX	XR	HX		XR	GW	HX	XR	HX	XR	GW	GW	GW		HX	XR	HX	XR	GW	HX
				◇		◇		◇				◇		◇			◇1 ☕			◇		◇			◇
London Paddington 15 ⊖	d		18 30	18 34		18 40	18 41	18 55			19 00	19 10	19 11	19 25		19 30	19 34			19 40	19 41	19 55		20 00	20 10
Acton Main Line	d																								
Ealing Broadway ⊖	d		18 38				18 50				19 09		19 20			19 38					19 50			20 09	
West Ealing	d																								
Drayton Green	d																								
Castle Bar Park	d																								
South Greenford	d																								
Greenford ⊖	a																								
Hanwell	d																								
Southall	d		18 44				18 54				19 15		19 24			19 44					19 54			20 15	
Hayes & Harlington	d		18 48				18 58				19 18		19 28			19 48					19 58			20 18	
HeathrowTermls 2 & 3 2 ⊖ ✈	a					18 55	19 05	19 10				19 25	19 35	19 40						19 55	20 05	20 10			20 25
	d	18 53				18 56	19 07	19 11		19 23		19 26	19 37	19 41	19 53					19 56	20 07	20 11	20 23		20 26
Heathrow Terminal 4 ⊖ ✈	a	18 57					19 15			19 27			19 45		19 57						20 15		20 27		
	d																								
Heathrow Terminal 5 ⊖ ✈	a					19 01		19 16				19 31		19 46						20 01		20 16			20 31
	d																								
West Drayton	d		18 52								19 22					19 52								20 22	
Iver	d																								
Langley	d		18 57		←						19 28					19 57		←						20 27	
Slough 5	a		19 01	18 54	19 01						19 31					20 01	19 52	20 01						20 31	
	d		19 01	18 54	19 01						19 31					20 01	19 54	20 01						20 31	
Burnham	d		→		19 05						19 35					→		20 05						20 35	
Taplow	d																								
Maidenhead 3	d			19 02	19 11						19 41							20 11						20 41	
Twyford 3	d				19 19						19 49							20 19						20 49	
Reading 7	a			19 16	19 27						19 56						20 15	20 26						20 57	
Oxford	a			19 46													20 50								

		XR	GW	HX		XR	GW	GW	GW	HX	XR	HX	XR	GW		GW	HX	XR	HX	XR	GW	GW	GW	HX	
			◇1 ☕	◇				◇		◇		◇		◇1 ☕			◇		◇			◇1		◇	
London Paddington 15 ⊖	d	20 11	20 22	20 25			20 30	20 34		20 40	20 41	20 55		20 57		21 00	21 10	21 11	21 25		21 30	21 34		21 40	
Acton Main Line	d																								
Ealing Broadway ⊖	d	20 20					20 38				20 50					21 09		21 20			21 38				
West Ealing	d																								
Drayton Green	d																								
Castle Bar Park	d																								
South Greenford	d																								
Greenford ⊖	a																								
Hanwell	d																								
Southall	d	20 24					20 44				20 54					21 15		21 24			21 44				
Hayes & Harlington	d	20 28					20 48				20 58					21 18		21 28			21 48				
HeathrowTermls 2 & 3 2 ⊖ ✈	a	20 35		20 40						20 55	21 05	21 10					21 25	21 35	21 40					21 56	
	d	20 37		20 41		20 53				20 56	21 07	21 11	21 23				21 26	21 37	21 41	21 53				21 58	
Heathrow Terminal 4 ⊖ ✈	a	20 45				20 57					21 15		21 27					21 45		21 57					
	d																								
Heathrow Terminal 5 ⊖ ✈	a			20 46						21 01		21 16					21 31		21 46					22 02	
	d																								
West Drayton	d						20 52									21 22					21 52				
Iver	d																								
Langley	d						20 57		←							21 27					21 57		←		
Slough 5	a						21 01	20 55	21 01							21 31					22 00	21 52	22 00		
	d						21 02	20 55	21 02							21 31					22 01	21 53	22 01		
Burnham	d						→		21 05							21 35					→		22 05		
Taplow	d																								
Maidenhead 3	d								21 11							21 41							22 11		
Twyford 3	d								21 19							21 49							22 19		
Reading 7	a		21 00					21 13	21 27					21 31		21 55						22 10	22 26		
Oxford	a							21 45														22 47			

For non-stop services between London and Reading refer to Table T116

For Heathrow Express Services see Table T118

For non-stop services between London and Heathrow Airport see Table T118

Table T117-F

Sundays

20 May to 9 September

London - Greenford, Heathrow Airport and Reading

Stopping Services

		XR	HX	XR	HX	XR	GW	HX	XR		GW	HX	XR	GW	HX	XR	HX	XR	GW		HX	GW
			◇		◇			◇			◇	◇			◇		◇				◇	
London Paddington 15 ⊖	d	21 41	21 55		22 10	22 11	22 15	22 25			22 36	22 40	22 41	22 45	22 55		23 10	23 11	23 15		23 25	23 47
Acton Main Line	d																					
Ealing Broadway ⊖	d	21 51				22 20	22 23						22 50	22 53				23 20	23 23			23 55
West Ealing	d																					
Drayton Green	d																					
Castle Bar Park	d																					
South Greenford	d																					
Greenford ⊖	a																					
Hanwell	d																					
Southall	d	21 55				22 24	22 28						22 54	22 59				23 24	23 29			
Hayes & Harlington	d	21 59				22 28	22 33						22 58	23 03				23 28	23 33			
HeathrowTermls 2 & 3 2 ⊖ ✈	a	22 06	22 11		22 26	22 35		22 41				22 56	23 05		23 11		23 26	23 35			23 41	
	d	22 08	22 13	22 23	22 28	22 37		22 43	22 53			22 58	23 07		23 13	23 23	23 28	23 37			23 43	
Heathrow Terminal 4 ⊖ ✈	a	22 16		22 27		22 45			22 57				23 15			23 27		23 45				
	d																					
Heathrow Terminal 5 ⊖ ✈	a		22 17		22 32			22 47				23 02			23 17		23 32				23 47	
	d																					
West Drayton	d						22 37							23 07					23 37			
Iver	d																					
Langley	d						22 42							23 11					23 42			
Slough 3	a						22 46				22 53			23 14					23 46			00 09
	d						22 46				22 55			23 15					23 46			00 10
Burnham	d						22 50							23 18					23 50			
Taplow	d																					
Maidenhead 3	d						22 56							23 23					23 56			00 17
Twyford 3	d						23 04							23 31					00 04			
Reading 7	a						23 11				23 12			23 40					00 13			00 32
Oxford	a																					

Sundays

16 September to 21 October

		GW	GW	GW	GW	GW	HX	HX	XR	HX		XR	HX	XR	HX	XR	HX	XR	HX	XR		HX	XR	GW	HX
								◇1		◇1			◇1		◇1		◇		◇1			◇1			◇1
London Paddington 15 ⊖	d			00 05	00 30	01 00		05 10	05 11	05 25		05 27	05 40	05 41	05 55		06 10	06 11	06 25			06 40	06 41	06 45	06 55
Acton Main Line	d																								
Ealing Broadway ⊖	d			00 13	00 38	01 08			05 20			05 35		05 50				06 20					06 50	06 53	
West Ealing	d																								
Drayton Green	d																								
Castle Bar Park	d																								
South Greenford	d																								
Greenford ⊖	a																								
Hanwell	d																								
Southall	d			00 18	00 43	01 13			05 24			05 39		05 54				06 24					06 54	06 59	
Hayes & Harlington	d		00 01	00 22	00 47	01 17			05 28			05 43		05 58				06 28					06 58	07 03	
HeathrowTermls 2 & 3 2 ⊖ ✈	a							05 26	05 35	05 41		05 50	05 56	06 05	06 11		06 26	06 35	06 41			06 56	07 05		07 11
	d						05 13	05 28	05 37	05 43		05 53	05 58	06 07	06 13	06 23	06 28	06 37	06 43	06 53		06 58	07 07		07 13
Heathrow Terminal 4 ⊖ ✈	a								05 45			06 00		06 15		06 27		06 45		06 57			07 15		
	d																								
Heathrow Terminal 5 ⊖ ✈	a						05 17	05 32		05 47			06 02		06 17		06 32		06 47			07 02			07 17
	d																								
West Drayton	d		00 05	00 26	00 51																			07 07	
Iver	d			00 29	00 54																				
Langley	d			00 33	00 58																			07 12	
Slough 3	a		00 12	00 37	01 02	01 26																		07 16	
	d		00 15	00 38	01 03	01 26																		07 16	
Burnham	d		00 18	00 41																				07 20	
Taplow	d	00 02	00 22	00 45																					
Maidenhead 3	d	00 06	00 26	00 49	01 10	01 33																		07 26	
Twyford 3	d	00 14	00 34	00 57	01 18	01 41																		07 34	
Reading 7	a	00 22	00 42	01 05	01 26	01 49																		07 41	
Oxford	a																								

For non-stop services between London and Reading refer to Table T116

For Heathrow Express Services see Table T118

For non-stop services between London and Heathrow Airport see Table T118

Table T117-F

Sundays

16 September to 21 October

London - Greenford, Heathrow Airport and Reading

Stopping Services

		XR		HX	XR	HX	XR	GW	HX	XR	HX	XR		GW	HX	XR	GW	HX	XR	GW	GW	HX		XR	GW
				◇1		◇1			◇1		◇1			◇1 ☕	◇1			◇1		◇1 ☕	◇1 ☕	◇1			
London Paddington 15 ⊖	d			07 10	07 11	07 25		07 29	07 40	07 41	07 55			08 03	08 10	08 11	08 15	08 25		08 27	08 37	08 40		08 41	08 45
Acton Main Line	d																								
Ealing Broadway ⊖	d				07 20			07 37		07 50						08 20	08 23							08 50	08 53
West Ealing	d																								
Drayton Green	d																								
Castle Bar Park	d																								
South Greenford	d																								
Greenford ⊖	a																								
Hanwell	d																								
Southall	d				07 24			07 43		07 54						08 24	08 29							08 54	08 59
Hayes & Harlington	d				07 28			07 47		07 58						08 28	08 33							08 58	09 03
HeathrowTermls 2 & 3 2 ⊖ ✈	a			07 26	07 35	07 41			07 56	08 05	08 11				08 26	08 35		08 41				08 56		09 05	
	d	07 23		07 28	07 37	07 43	07 53		07 58	08 07	08 13	08 23			08 28	08 37		08 43	08 53			08 58		09 07	
Heathrow Terminal 4 ⊖ ✈	a	07 27			07 45		07 57			08 15		08 27				08 45			08 57					09 15	
	d																								
Heathrow Terminal 5 ⊖ ✈	a			07 32		07 47			08 02		08 17				08 32			08 47				09 02			
	d																								
West Drayton	d							07 51									08 37								09 07
Iver	d																								
Langley	d							07 56									08 42								09 12
Slough 3	a							08 00						08 25			08 47				08 59				09 16
	d							08 04						08 26			08 47				08 59				09 16
Burnham	d							08 08																	09 20
Taplow	d																								
Maidenhead 3	d							08 14						08 34			08 55								09 26
Twyford 3	d							08 22									09 03								09 34
Reading 7	a							08 29						08 46			09 11			09 02	09 18				09 42
Oxford	a													09 15							09 44				

		HX	XR	HX	XR	GW	HX	XR		GW	HX	XR	GW	HX	XR	HX	XR	GW		HX	XR	GW	GW	HX	XR
		◇1		◇1			◇1			◇1 ☕	◇1			◇1		◇1				◇1		◇1 ☕	◇1 ☕	◇1	
London Paddington 15 ⊖	d	08 55		09 10	09 11	09 15	09 25			09 37	09 40	09 41	09 45	09 55		10 10	10 11	10 15		10 25		10 27	10 37	10 40	10 41
Acton Main Line	d																								
Ealing Broadway ⊖	d				09 20	09 23						09 50	09 53				10 20	10 23							10 50
West Ealing	d																								
Drayton Green	d																								
Castle Bar Park	d																								
South Greenford	d																								
Greenford ⊖	a																								
Hanwell	d																								
Southall	d				09 24	09 29						09 54	09 59				10 24	10 29							10 54
Hayes & Harlington	d				09 28	09 33						09 58	10 03				10 28	10 33							10 58
HeathrowTermls 2 & 3 2 ⊖ ✈	a	09 11		09 26	09 35		09 41				09 56	10 05		10 11		10 26	10 35			10 41				10 56	11 05
	d	09 13	09 23	09 28	09 37		09 43	09 53			09 58	10 07		10 13	10 23	10 28	10 37			10 43	10 53			10 58	11 07
Heathrow Terminal 4 ⊖ ✈	a		09 27		09 45			09 57				10 15			10 27		10 45				10 57				11 15
	d																								
Heathrow Terminal 5 ⊖ ✈	a	09 17		09 32			09 47				10 02			10 17		10 32				10 47				11 02	
	d																								
West Drayton	d					09 37							10 07					10 37							
Iver	d																								
Langley	d					09 42							10 12					10 42							
Slough 3	a					09 46				10 00			10 16					10 46					10 59		
	d					09 48				10 01			10 16					10 46					10 59		
Burnham	d												10 20												
Taplow	d																								
Maidenhead 3	d					09 54							10 26					10 54							
Twyford 3	d					10 02							10 34					11 02							
Reading 7	a					10 12				10 16			10 40					11 12				11 03	11 16		
Oxford	a									10 47													11 45		

For non-stop services between London and Reading refer to Table T116

For Heathrow Express Services see Table T118

For non-stop services between London and Heathrow Airport see Table T118

Table T117-F

Sundays

16 September to 21 October

London - Greenford, Heathrow Airport and Reading

Stopping Services

		GW	HX	XR	HX	XR	GW	HX	XR	GW		HX	XR	GW	HX	XR	HX	XR	GW	HX		XR	GW	GW	HX
			◇■		◇■			◇■		◇■		◇■			◇■		◇			◇			◇■ ☕	◇■ ☕	◇■
London Paddington ⊖	d	10 45	10 55		11 10	11 11	11 15	11 25		11 37		11 40	11 41	11 45	11 55		12 10	12 11	12 15	12 25			12 27	12 37	12 40
Acton Main Line	d																								
Ealing Broadway ⊖	d	10 53				11 20	11 23						11 50	11 53				12 20	12 23						
West Ealing	d																								
Drayton Green	d																								
Castle Bar Park	d																								
South Greenford	d																								
Greenford ⊖	a																								
Hanwell	d																								
Southall	d	10 59				11 24	11 29						11 54	11 59				12 24	12 29						
Hayes & Harlington	d	11 03				11 28	11 33						11 58	12 03				12 28	12 33						
Heathrow Termls 2 & 3 ⊖ ✈	a		11 11		11 26	11 35		11 41				11 56	12 05		12 11		12 26	12 35		12 41					12 56
	d		11 13	11 23	11 28	11 37		11 43	11 53			11 58	12 07		12 13	12 23	12 28	12 37		12 43		12 53			12 58
Heathrow Terminal 4 ⊖ ✈	a			11 27		11 45			11 57				12 15			12 27		12 45				12 57			
	d																								
Heathrow Terminal 5 ⊖ ✈	a		11 17		11 32			11 47				12 02			12 17		12 32			12 47					13 02
	d																								
West Drayton	d	11 07					11 37							12 07					12 37						
Iver	d																								
Langley	d	11 12					11 42							12 12					12 42						
Slough	a	11 16					11 46			11 56				12 16					12 46					12 59	
	d	11 16					11 46			11 57				12 16					12 46					12 59	
Burnham	d	11 20												12 20											
Taplow	d																								
Maidenhead	d	11 26					11 54							12 26					12 54						
Twyford	d	11 34					12 02							12 34					13 02						
Reading	a	11 41					12 12			12 14				12 42					13 12				13 03	13 16	
Oxford	a									12 46														13 44	

		XR	GW	HX	XR	HX		XR	GW	HX	XR	GW	HX	XR	GW	HX		XR	HX	XR	GW	HX	XR	GW	GW
				◇■		◇■				◇■		◇■ ☕	◇■			◇■			◇■			◇■		◇■ ☕	◇■ ☕
London Paddington ⊖	d	12 41	12 45	12 55		13 10		13 11	13 15	13 25		13 37	13 40	13 41	13 45	13 55			14 10	14 11	14 15	14 25		14 30	14 37
Acton Main Line	d																								
Ealing Broadway ⊖	d	12 50	12 53					13 20	13 23					13 50	13 53					14 20	14 23				
West Ealing	d																								
Drayton Green	d																								
Castle Bar Park	d																								
South Greenford	d																								
Greenford ⊖	a																								
Hanwell	d																								
Southall	d	12 54	12 59					13 24	13 29					13 54	13 59					14 24	14 29				
Hayes & Harlington	d	12 58	13 03					13 28	13 33					13 58	14 03					14 28	14 33				
Heathrow Termls 2 & 3 ⊖ ✈	a	13 05		13 11		13 26		13 35		13 41			13 56	14 05		14 11			14 26	14 35		14 41			
	d	13 07		13 13	13 23	13 28		13 37		13 43	13 53		13 58	14 07		14 13		14 23	14 28	14 37		14 43	14 53		
Heathrow Terminal 4 ⊖ ✈	a	13 15			13 27			13 45			13 57			14 15				14 27		14 45			14 57		
	d																								
Heathrow Terminal 5 ⊖ ✈	a			13 17		13 32				13 47			14 02			14 17			14 32			14 47			
	d																								
West Drayton	d		13 07						13 37						14 07						14 37				
Iver	d																								
Langley	d		13 12						13 42						14 12						14 42				
Slough	a		13 16						13 46			13 59			14 16						14 46				14 59
	d		13 16						13 46			13 59			14 16						14 46				14 59
Burnham	d		13 20												14 20										
Taplow	d																								
Maidenhead	d		13 26						13 54						14 26						14 54				
Twyford	d		13 34						14 02						14 34						15 02				
Reading	a		13 42						14 12			14 16			14 42						15 10			15 04	15 13
Oxford	a											14 44													15 44

For non-stop services between London and Reading refer to Table T116

For Heathrow Express Services see Table T118

For non-stop services between London and Heathrow Airport see Table T118

Table T117-F

Sundays

16 September to 21 October

London - Greenford, Heathrow Airport and Reading

Stopping Services

		HX	XR	GW	HX	XR	HX	XR		GW	HX	XR	GW	HX	XR	GW	HX	XR		HX	XR	GW	HX	XR	GW
		◇■			◇■		◇■				◇■		◇■ A	◇■			◇■			◇■			◇■		◇■ ☕
London Paddington ⊖	d	14 40	14 41	14 45	14 55		15 10	15 11		15 15	15 25		15 37	15 40	15 41	15 45	15 55			16 10	16 11	16 15	16 25		16 30
Acton Main Line	d																								
Ealing Broadway ⊖	d		14 50	14 53				15 20		15 23					15 50	15 53					16 20	16 23			
West Ealing	d																								
Drayton Green	d																								
Castle Bar Park	d																								
South Greenford	d																								
Greenford ⊖	a																								
Hanwell	d																								
Southall	d		14 54	14 59				15 24		15 29					15 54	15 59					16 24	16 29			
Hayes & Harlington	d		14 58	15 03				15 28		15 33					15 58	16 03					16 28	16 33			
Heathrow Termls 2 & 3 ⊖ ✈	a	14 56	15 05		15 11		15 26	15 35			15 41			15 56	16 05		16 11			16 26	16 35		16 41		
	d	14 58	15 07		15 13	15 23	15 28	15 37			15 43	15 53		15 58	16 07		16 13	16 23		16 28	16 37		16 43	16 53	
Heathrow Terminal 4 ⊖ ✈	a		15 15			15 27		15 45				15 57			16 15			16 27			16 45			16 57	
	d																								
Heathrow Terminal 5 ⊖ ✈	a	15 02			15 17		15 32				15 47			16 02			16 17			16 32			16 47		
	d																								
West Drayton	d			15 07						15 37						16 07						16 37			
Iver	d																								
Langley	d			15 12						15 42						16 12						16 42			
Slough	a			15 16						15 46			15 59			16 16						16 46			
	d			15 16						15 46			15 59			16 16						16 46			
Burnham	d			15 20						15 50						16 20						16 50			
Taplow	d																								
Maidenhead	d			15 26						15 56						16 26						16 56			
Twyford	d			15 34						16 04						16 34						17 04			
Reading	a			15 42						16 11			16 16			16 42						17 11			17 01
Oxford	a												16 44												

		GW	HX	XR		GW	HX	XR	HX	XR	GW	HX	XR	GW		HX	XR	GW	HX	XR	HX	XR	GW	HX	
		◇■	◇■				◇■		◇			◇		◇■ ☕		◇			◇		◇			◇	
London Paddington ⊖	d	16 37	16 40	16 41		16 45	16 55		17 10	17 11	17 15	17 25		17 37		17 40	17 41	17 45	17 55		18 10	18 11	18 15	18 25	
Acton Main Line	d																								
Ealing Broadway ⊖	d			16 50		16 53				17 20	17 23						17 50	17 53				18 20	18 23		
West Ealing	d																								
Drayton Green	d																								
Castle Bar Park	d																								
South Greenford	d																								
Greenford ⊖	a																								
Hanwell	d																								
Southall	d			16 54		16 59				17 24	17 29						17 54	17 59				18 24	18 29		
Hayes & Harlington	d			16 58		17 03				17 28	17 33						17 58	18 03				18 28	18 33		
Heathrow Termls 2 & 3 ⊖ ✈	a		16 56	17 05			17 11		17 26	17 35		17 41				17 56	18 05		18 11		18 26	18 35		18 41	
	d		16 58	17 07			17 13	17 23	17 28	17 37		17 43	17 53			17 58	18 07		18 13	18 23	18 28	18 37		18 43	
Heathrow Terminal 4 ⊖ ✈	a			17 15				17 27		17 45			17 57				18 15			18 27		18 45			
	d																								
Heathrow Terminal 5 ⊖ ✈	a		17 02				17 17		17 32			17 47				18 02			18 17		18 32			18 47	
	d																								
West Drayton	d					17 07					17 37							18 07					18 37		
Iver	d																								
Langley	d					17 12					17 42							18 12					18 42		
Slough	a	16 59				17 15					17 46			17 59				18 16					18 46		
	d	16 59				17 16					17 46			17 59				18 16					18 46		
Burnham	d					17 20					17 50							18 20					18 50		
Taplow	d																								
Maidenhead	d	17 07				17 26					17 56			18 09				18 26					18 56		
Twyford	d					17 34					18 04							18 34					19 04		
Reading	a	17 20				17 42					18 11			18 19				18 42					19 11		
Oxford	a	17 50												18 49											

A ■ from Reading

For non-stop services between London and Reading refer to Table T116

For Heathrow Express Services see Table T118

For non-stop services between London and Heathrow Airport see Table T118

Table T117-F

Sundays

16 September to 21 October

London - Greenford, Heathrow Airport and Reading

Stopping Services

	XR	GW	GW	HX	XR		GW	HX	XR	HX	XR	GW	HX	XR	GW		HX	XR	GW	HX	XR	HX	XR	GW
		◇1 ☕	◇1 A	◇				◇		◇			◇		◇1 ☕		◇			◇		◇		
London Paddington 15 ⊖ d		18 30	18 37	18 40	18 41		18 45	18 55		19 10	19 11	19 15	19 25		19 37		19 40	19 41	19 45	19 55		20 10	20 11	20 15
Acton Main Line d																								
Ealing Broadway ⊖ d					18 50		18 53				19 20	19 23						19 50	19 53				20 20	20 23
West Ealing d																								
Drayton Green d																								
Castle Bar Park d																								
South Greenford d																								
Greenford ⊖ a																								
Hanwell d																								
Southall d					18 54		18 59				19 24	19 29						19 54	19 59				20 24	20 29
Hayes & Harlington d					18 58		19 03				19 28	19 33						19 58	20 03				20 28	20 33
Heathrow Termls 2 & 3 2 ⊖ ✈ a				18 56	19 05			19 11		19 26	19 35		19 41				19 56	20 05		20 11		20 26	20 35	
d	18 53			18 58	19 07			19 13	19 23	19 28	19 37		19 43	19 53			19 58	20 07		20 13	20 23	20 28	20 37	
Heathrow Terminal 4 ⊖ ✈ a	18 57				19 15				19 27		19 45			19 57				20 15			20 27		20 45	
d																								
Heathrow Terminal 5 ⊖ ✈ a				19 02				19 17		19 32			19 47				20 02			20 17		20 32		
d																								
West Drayton d							19 07					19 37							20 07					20 37
Iver d																								
Langley d							19 12					19 42							20 12					20 42
Slough 8 a			18 59				19 16					19 46			19 59				20 16					20 46
d			18 59				19 16					19 46			19 59				20 16					20 46
Burnham d							19 20					19 50							20 20					20 50
Taplow d																								
Maidenhead 8 d			19 05				19 26					19 56							20 26					20 56
Twyford 8 d							19 33					20 04							20 33					21 04
Reading 7 a		19 01	19 20				19 41					20 11			20 16				20 41					21 11
Oxford a			19 49												20 47									

	HX		XR	GW	GW	HX	XR	GW	HX	XR	GW		HX	XR	GW	HX	XR	GW	HX	XR	GW		HX	XR
	◇			◇1 ☕	◇	◇			◇		◇1 ☕		◇			◇		◇1	◇				◇	
London Paddington 15 ⊖ d	20 25			20 27	20 37	20 40	20 41	20 45	20 55		20 57		21 10	21 11	21 15	21 25		21 37	21 40	21 41	21 45		21 55	
Acton Main Line d																								
Ealing Broadway ⊖ d							20 50	20 53						21 20	21 23					21 50	21 53			
West Ealing d																								
Drayton Green d																								
Castle Bar Park d																								
South Greenford d																								
Greenford ⊖ a																								
Hanwell d																								
Southall d							20 54	20 59						21 24	21 29					21 54	21 59			
Hayes & Harlington d							20 58	21 03						21 28	21 33					21 58	22 03			
Heathrow Termls 2 & 3 2 ⊖ ✈ a	20 41					20 56	21 05		21 11				21 26	21 35		21 41			21 56	22 05			22 11	
d	20 43		20 53			20 58	21 07		21 13	21 23			21 28	21 37		21 43	21 53		21 58	22 07			22 13	22 23
Heathrow Terminal 4 ⊖ ✈ a			20 57				21 15			21 27				21 45			21 57			22 15				22 27
d																								
Heathrow Terminal 5 ⊖ ✈ a	20 47					21 02			21 17				21 32			21 47			22 02				22 17	
d																								
West Drayton d								21 07							21 37						22 07			
Iver d																								
Langley d								21 12							21 42						22 12			
Slough 8 a					20 57			21 16							21 46			22 01			22 15			
d					20 58			21 16							21 46			22 03			22 16			
Burnham d								21 20							21 50						22 20			
Taplow d																								
Maidenhead 8 d								21 26							21 56						22 26			
Twyford 8 d								21 33							22 04						22 33			
Reading 7 a				20 58	21 14			21 41			21 31				22 11			22 20			22 42			
Oxford a					21 48													22 57						

A 1 from Reading

For non-stop services between London and Reading refer to Table T116

For Heathrow Express Services see Table T118

For non-stop services between London and Heathrow Airport see Table T118

Table T117-F

Sundays

16 September to 21 October

London - Greenford, Heathrow Airport and Reading

Stopping Services

	HX	XR	GW	HX	XR	GW	HX	XR		GW	HX	XR	HX	XR	GW	HX	GW	GW
	◇			◇		◇1 ☕	◇				◇		◇			◇		
London Paddington 15 ⊖ d	22 10	22 11	22 15	22 25		22 37	22 40	22 41		22 45	22 55		23 10	23 11	23 15	23 25	23 47	23 53
Acton Main Line d																		
Ealing Broadway ⊖ d		22 20	22 23					22 50		22 53				23 20	23 23		23 55	00 02
West Ealing d																		
Drayton Green d																		
Castle Bar Park d																		
South Greenford d																		
Greenford ⊖ a																		
Hanwell d																		
Southall d		22 24	22 29					22 54		22 58				23 24	23 29			00 07
Hayes & Harlington d		22 28	22 33					22 58		23 02				23 28	23 33			00 11
Heathrow Termls 2 & 3 2 ⊖ ✈ a	22 26	22 35		22 41			22 56	23 05			23 11		23 26	23 35		23 41		
d	22 28	22 37		22 43	22 53		22 58	23 07			23 13	23 23	23 28	23 37		23 43		
Heathrow Terminal 4 ⊖ ✈ a		22 45			22 57			23 15				23 27		23 45				
d																		
Heathrow Terminal 5 ⊖ ✈ a	22 32			22 47			23 02				23 17		23 32			23 47		
d																		
West Drayton d			22 37							23 06					23 37			00 16
Iver d																		
Langley d			22 42							23 11					23 42			00 20
Slough 8 a			22 46							23 15					23 46		00 09	00 25
d			22 46							23 15					23 46		00 10	00 26
Burnham d			22 50							23 19					23 50			00 30
Taplow d																		
Maidenhead 8 d			22 56							23 24					23 56		00 17	00 36
Twyford 8 d			23 04							23 32					00 04			00 44
Reading 7 a			23 11			23 12				23 41					00 13		00 32	00 51
Oxford a																		

Sundays

28 October to 2 December

	GW	GW	GW	GW	GW	HX	HX	XR	HX		XR	HX	XR	HX	XR	HX	XR	HX	XR		HX	XR	GW	HX
							◇1		◇1			◇1		◇1		◇		◇1			◇1			◇1
London Paddington 15 ⊖ d			00 05	00 30	01 00		05 10	05 11	05 25		05 27	05 40	05 41	05 55		06 10	06 11	06 25			06 40	06 41	06 45	06 55
Acton Main Line d																								
Ealing Broadway ⊖ d			00 13	00 38	01 08			05 20			05 35		05 50				06 20					06 50	06 53	
West Ealing d																								
Drayton Green d																								
Castle Bar Park d																								
South Greenford d																								
Greenford ⊖ a																								
Hanwell d																								
Southall d			00 18	00 43	01 13			05 24			05 39		05 54				06 24					06 54	06 59	
Hayes & Harlington d		00 01	00 22	00 47	01 17			05 28			05 43		05 58				06 28					06 58	07 03	
Heathrow Termls 2 & 3 2 ⊖ ✈ a							05 26	05 35	05 41		05 50	05 56	06 05	06 11		06 26	06 35	06 41			06 56	07 05		07 11
d						05 13	05 28	05 37	05 43		05 53	05 58	06 07	06 13	06 23	06 28	06 37	06 43	06 53		06 58	07 07		07 13
Heathrow Terminal 4 ⊖ ✈ a								05 45			06 00		06 15		06 27		06 45		06 57			07 15		
d																								
Heathrow Terminal 5 ⊖ ✈ a						05 17	05 32		05 47			06 02		06 17		06 32		06 47			07 02			07 17
d																								
West Drayton d		00 05	00 26	00 51																			07 07	
Iver d			00 29	00 54																				
Langley d			00 33	00 58																			07 12	
Slough 8 a		00 12	00 37	01 02	01 26																		07 16	
d		00 15	00 38	01 03	01 26																		07 16	
Burnham d		00 18	00 41																				07 20	
Taplow d	00 02	00 22	00 45																					
Maidenhead 8 d	00 06	00 26	00 49	01 10	01 33																		07 26	
Twyford 8 d	00 14	00 34	00 57	01 18	01 41																		07 34	
Reading 7 a	00 22	00 42	01 05	01 26	01 49																		07 41	
Oxford a																								

For non-stop services between London and Reading refer to Table T116

For Heathrow Express Services see Table T118

For non-stop services between London and Heathrow Airport see Table T118

Table T117-F

Sundays

28 October to 2 December

London - Greenford, Heathrow Airport and Reading

Stopping Services

		XR		HX ◇1	XR	HX ◇1	XR	GW	HX ◇1	XR	HX ◇1	XR		GW ◇1 ☕	HX ◇1	XR	GW	HX ◇1	XR	GW ◇1 ☕	GW ◇1 ☕	HX ◇1		XR	GW
London Paddington 15 ⊖	d			07 10	07 11	07 25		07 29	07 40	07 41	07 55			08 03	08 10	08 11	08 15	08 25		08 27	08 37	08 40		08 41	08 45
Acton Main Line	d																								
Ealing Broadway ⊖	d				07 20			07 37		07 50						08 20	08 23							08 50	08 53
West Ealing	d																								
Drayton Green	d																								
Castle Bar Park	d																								
South Greenford	d																								
Greenford ⊖	a																								
Hanwell	d																								
Southall	d				07 24			07 43		07 54						08 24	08 29							08 54	08 59
Hayes & Harlington	d				07 28			07 47		07 58						08 28	08 33							08 58	09 03
HeathrowTermls 2 & 3 4 ⊖ ✈	a			07 26	07 35	07 41			07 56	08 05	08 11				08 26	08 35		08 41				08 56		09 05	
	d	07 23		07 28	07 37	07 43	07 53		07 58	08 07	08 13	08 23			08 28	08 37		08 43	08 53			08 58		09 07	
Heathrow Terminal 4 ⊖ ✈	a	07 27			07 45		07 57			08 15		08 27				08 45			08 57					09 15	
	d																								
Heathrow Terminal 5 ⊖ ✈	a			07 32		07 47			08 02		08 17				08 32			08 47				09 02			
	d																								
West Drayton	d							07 51									08 37								09 07
Iver	d																								
Langley	d							07 56									08 42								09 12
Slough 3	a							08 00						08 25			08 46				08 59				09 16
	d							08 04						08 26			08 46				08 59				09 16
Burnham	d							08 08																	09 20
Taplow	d																								
Maidenhead 3	d							08 14						08 34			08 54								09 26
Twyford 3	d							08 22									09 02								09 34
Reading 7	a							08 29						08 46			09 13			09 02	09 19				09 42
Oxford	a													09 15							09 45				

		HX ◇1	XR	HX ◇1	XR	GW	HX ◇1	XR		GW ◇1 ☕	HX ◇1	XR	GW	HX ◇1	XR	HX ◇1	XR	GW		HX ◇1	XR	GW ◇1 ☕	GW ◇1 ☕	HX ◇1	XR
London Paddington 15 ⊖	d	08 55		09 10	09 11	09 15	09 25			09 37	09 40	09 41	09 45	09 55		10 10	10 11	10 15		10 25		10 27	10 37	10 40	10 41
Acton Main Line	d																								
Ealing Broadway ⊖	d				09 20	09 23						09 50	09 53				10 20	10 23							10 50
West Ealing	d																								
Drayton Green	d																								
Castle Bar Park	d																								
South Greenford	d																								
Greenford ⊖	a																								
Hanwell	d																								
Southall	d				09 24	09 29						09 54	09 59				10 24	10 29							10 54
Hayes & Harlington	d				09 28	09 33						09 58	10 03				10 28	10 33							10 58
HeathrowTermls 2 & 3 4 ⊖ ✈	a	09 11		09 26	09 35		09 41				09 56	10 05		10 11		10 26	10 35			10 41				10 56	11 05
	d	09 13	09 23	09 28	09 37		09 43	09 53			09 58	10 07		10 13	10 23	10 28	10 37			10 43	10 53			10 58	11 07
Heathrow Terminal 4 ⊖ ✈	a		09 27		09 45			09 57				10 15			10 27		10 45				10 57				11 15
	d																								
Heathrow Terminal 5 ⊖ ✈	a	09 17		09 32			09 47				10 02			10 17		10 32				10 47				11 02	
	d																								
West Drayton	d					09 37							10 07					10 37							
Iver	d																								
Langley	d					09 42							10 12					10 42							
Slough 3	a					09 46				10 00			10 16					10 46					10 59		
	d					09 48				10 01			10 16					10 46					10 59		
Burnham	d												10 20												
Taplow	d																								
Maidenhead 3	d					09 54							10 26					10 54							
Twyford 3	d					10 02							10 34					11 02							
Reading 7	a					10 12				10 16			10 40					11 12				11 03	11 16		
Oxford	a									10 47													11 45		

For non-stop services between London and Reading refer to Table T116

For Heathrow Express Services see Table T118

For non-stop services between London and Heathrow Airport see Table T118

Table T117-F

Sundays

28 October to 2 December

London - Greenford, Heathrow Airport and Reading

Stopping Services

		GW	HX ◇1	XR	HX ◇1	XR	GW	HX ◇1	XR	GW ◇1		HX ◇1	XR	GW	HX ◇1	XR	HX ◇	XR	GW	HX ◇		XR	GW ◇1 ☕	GW ◇1 ☕	HX ◇1
London Paddington 15 ⊖	d	10 45	10 55		11 10	11 11	11 15	11 25		11 37		11 40	11 41	11 45	11 55		12 10	12 11	12 15	12 25			12 27	12 37	12 40
Acton Main Line	d																								
Ealing Broadway ⊖	d	10 53				11 20	11 23						11 50	11 53				12 20	12 23						
West Ealing	d																								
Drayton Green	d																								
Castle Bar Park	d																								
South Greenford	d																								
Greenford ⊖	a																								
Hanwell	d																								
Southall	d	10 59				11 24	11 29						11 54	11 59				12 24	12 29						
Hayes & Harlington	d	11 03				11 28	11 33						11 58	12 03				12 28	12 33						
HeathrowTermls 2 & 3 4 ⊖ ✈	a		11 11		11 26	11 35		11 41				11 56	12 05		12 11		12 26	12 35		12 41					12 56
	d		11 13	11 23	11 28	11 37		11 43	11 53			11 58	12 07		12 13	12 23	12 28	12 37		12 43		12 53			12 58
Heathrow Terminal 4 ⊖ ✈	a			11 27		11 45			11 57				12 15			12 27		12 45				12 57			
	d																								
Heathrow Terminal 5 ⊖ ✈	a		11 17		11 32			11 47				12 02			12 17		12 32			12 47					13 02
	d																								
West Drayton	d	11 07					11 37							12 07					12 37						
Iver	d																								
Langley	d	11 12					11 42							12 12					12 42						
Slough 3	a	11 16					11 46			11 56				12 16					12 46					12 59	
	d	11 16					11 46			11 57				12 16					12 46					12 59	
Burnham	d	11 20												12 20											
Taplow	d																								
Maidenhead 3	d	11 26					11 54							12 26					12 54						
Twyford 3	d	11 34					12 02							12 34					13 02						
Reading 7	a	11 41					12 12			12 14				12 42					13 12				13 03	13 16	
Oxford	a									12 46														13 44	

		XR	GW	HX ◇1	XR	HX ◇1		XR	GW	HX ◇1	XR	GW ◇1 ☕	HX ◇1	XR	GW	HX ◇1		XR	HX ◇1	XR	GW	HX ◇1	XR	GW ◇1 ☕	GW ◇1 ☕
London Paddington 15 ⊖	d	12 41	12 45	12 55		13 10		13 11	13 15	13 25		13 37	13 40	13 41	13 45	13 55			14 10	14 11	14 15	14 25		14 30	14 37
Acton Main Line	d																								
Ealing Broadway ⊖	d	12 50	12 53					13 20	13 23					13 50	13 53					14 20	14 23				
West Ealing	d																								
Drayton Green	d																								
Castle Bar Park	d																								
South Greenford	d																								
Greenford ⊖	a																								
Hanwell	d																								
Southall	d	12 54	12 59					13 24	13 29					13 54	13 59					14 24	14 29				
Hayes & Harlington	d	12 58	13 03					13 28	13 33					13 58	14 03					14 28	14 33				
HeathrowTermls 2 & 3 4 ⊖ ✈	a	13 05		13 11		13 26		13 35		13 41			13 56	14 05		14 11			14 26	14 35		14 41			
	d	13 07		13 13	13 23	13 28		13 37		13 43	13 53		13 58	14 07		14 13		14 23	14 28	14 37		14 43	14 53		
Heathrow Terminal 4 ⊖ ✈	a	13 15			13 27			13 45			13 57			14 15				14 27		14 45			14 57		
	d																								
Heathrow Terminal 5 ⊖ ✈	a			13 17		13 32				13 47			14 02			14 17			14 32			14 47			
	d																								
West Drayton	d		13 07						13 37						14 07						14 37				
Iver	d																								
Langley	d		13 12						13 42						14 12						14 42				
Slough 3	a		13 16						13 46			13 59			14 16						14 46				14 59
	d		13 16						13 46			13 59			14 16						14 46				14 59
Burnham	d		13 20												14 20										
Taplow	d																								
Maidenhead 3	d		13 26						13 54						14 26						14 54				
Twyford 3	d		13 34						14 02						14 34						15 02				
Reading 7	a		13 42						14 12			14 16			14 42						15 10			15 04	15 13
Oxford	a											14 44													15 44

For non-stop services between London and Reading refer to Table T116

For Heathrow Express Services see Table T118

For non-stop services between London and Heathrow Airport see Table T118

Table T117-F

Sundays

28 October to 2 December

London - Greenford, Heathrow Airport and Reading

Stopping Services

	HX	XR	GW	HX	XR	HX	XR		GW	HX	XR	GW	HX	XR	GW	HX	XR		HX	XR	GW	HX	XR	GW
	◇1			◇1		◇1				◇1		◇1 A	◇1			◇1			◇1			◇1		◇1 ☕
London Paddington 15 ⊖ d	14 40	14 41	14 45	14 55		15 10	15 11		15 15	15 25		15 37	15 40	15 41	15 45	15 55			16 10	16 11	16 15	16 25		16 30
Acton Main Line d																								
Ealing Broadway ⊖ d		14 50	14 53				15 20		15 23					15 50	15 53					16 20	16 23			
West Ealing d																								
Drayton Green d																								
Castle Bar Park d																								
South Greenford d																								
Greenford ⊖ a																								
Hanwell d																								
Southall d		14 54	14 59				15 24		15 29					15 54	15 59					16 24	16 29			
Hayes & Harlington d		14 58	15 03				15 28		15 33					15 58	16 03					16 28	16 33			
Heathrow Termls 2 & 3 2 ⊖ ✈ a	14 56	15 05		15 11		15 26	15 35			15 41			15 56	16 05		16 11			16 26	16 35		16 41		
d	14 58	15 07		15 13	15 23	15 28	15 37			15 43	15 53		15 58	16 07		16 13	16 23		16 28	16 37		16 43	16 53	
Heathrow Terminal 4 ⊖ ✈ a		15 15			15 27		15 45				15 57			16 15			16 27			16 45			16 57	
d																								
Heathrow Terminal 5 ⊖ ✈ a	15 02			15 17		15 32				15 47			16 02			16 17			16 32			16 47		
d																								
West Drayton d			15 07						15 37						16 07						16 37			
Iver d																								
Langley d			15 12						15 42						16 12						16 42			
Slough 3 a			15 16						15 46			15 59			16 16						16 46			
d			15 16						15 46			15 59			16 16						16 46			
Burnham d			15 20						15 50						16 20						16 50			
Taplow d																								
Maidenhead 3 d			15 26						15 56						16 26						16 56			
Twyford 3 d			15 34						16 04						16 34						17 04			
Reading 7 a			15 42						16 11			16 16			16 42						17 11			17 01
Oxford a												16 44												

	GW	HX	XR		GW	HX	XR	HX	XR	GW	HX	XR	GW		HX	XR	GW	HX	XR	HX	XR	GW	HX	
	◇1	◇1				◇1		◇			◇		◇1 ☕		◇			◇		◇			◇	
London Paddington 15 ⊖ d	16 37	16 40	16 41		16 45	16 55		17 10	17 11	17 15	17 25		17 37		17 40	17 41	17 45	17 55		18 10	18 11	18 15	18 25	
Acton Main Line d																								
Ealing Broadway ⊖ d			16 50		16 53				17 20	17 23						17 50	17 53				18 20	18 23		
West Ealing d																								
Drayton Green d																								
Castle Bar Park d																								
South Greenford d																								
Greenford ⊖ a																								
Hanwell d																								
Southall d			16 54		16 59				17 24	17 29						17 54	17 59				18 24	18 29		
Hayes & Harlington d			16 58		17 03				17 28	17 33						17 58	18 03				18 28	18 33		
Heathrow Termls 2 & 3 2 ⊖ ✈ a		16 56	17 05			17 11		17 26	17 35		17 41				17 56	18 05		18 11		18 26	18 35		18 41	
d		16 58	17 07			17 13	17 23	17 28	17 37		17 43	17 53			17 58	18 07		18 13	18 23	18 28	18 37		18 43	
Heathrow Terminal 4 ⊖ ✈ a			17 15				17 27		17 45			17 57				18 15			18 27		18 45			
d																								
Heathrow Terminal 5 ⊖ ✈ a		17 02				17 17		17 32			17 47				18 02			18 17		18 32			18 47	
d																								
West Drayton d					17 07					17 37							18 07					18 37		
Iver d																								
Langley d					17 12					17 42							18 12					18 42		
Slough 3 a	16 59				17 15					17 46			17 59				18 16					18 46		
d	16 59				17 16					17 46			17 59				18 16					18 46		
Burnham d					17 20					17 50							18 20					18 50		
Taplow d																								
Maidenhead 3 d	17 07				17 26					17 56			18 09				18 26					18 56		
Twyford 3 d					17 34					18 04							18 34					19 04		
Reading 7 a	17 20				17 42					18 11			18 19				18 42					19 11		
Oxford a	17 50												18 49											

A 1 from Reading

For non-stop services between London and Reading refer to Table T116

For Heathrow Express Services see Table T118

For non-stop services between London and Heathrow Airport see Table T118

Table T117-F

Sundays

28 October to 2 December

London - Greenford, Heathrow Airport and Reading

Stopping Services

	XR	GW	GW	HX	XR		GW	HX	XR	HX	XR	GW	HX	XR	GW		HX	XR	GW	HX	XR	HX	XR	GW
		◇1 ☕	◇1 A	◇				◇		◇			◇		◇1 ☕		◇			◇		◇		
London Paddington 15 ⊖ d		18 30	18 37	18 40	18 41		18 45	18 55		19 10	19 11	19 15	19 25		19 37		19 40	19 41	19 45	19 55		20 10	20 11	20 15
Acton Main Line d																								
Ealing Broadway ⊖ d					18 50		18 53				19 20	19 23						19 50	19 53				20 20	20 23
West Ealing d																								
Drayton Green d																								
Castle Bar Park d																								
South Greenford d																								
Greenford ⊖ a																								
Hanwell d																								
Southall d					18 54		18 59				19 24	19 29						19 54	19 59				20 24	20 29
Hayes & Harlington d					18 58		19 03				19 28	19 33						19 58	20 03				20 28	20 33
Heathrow Termls 2 & 3 2 ⊖ ✈ a				18 56	19 05			19 11		19 26	19 35		19 41				19 56	20 05		20 11		20 26	20 35	
d	18 53			18 58	19 07			19 13	19 23	19 28	19 37		19 43	19 53			19 58	20 07		20 13	20 23	20 28	20 37	
Heathrow Terminal 4 ⊖ ✈ a	18 57				19 15				19 27		19 45			19 57				20 15			20 27		20 45	
d																								
Heathrow Terminal 5 ⊖ ✈ a				19 02				19 17		19 32			19 47				20 02			20 17		20 32		
d																								
West Drayton d							19 07					19 37							20 07					20 37
Iver d																								
Langley d							19 12					19 42							20 12					20 42
Slough 3 a			18 59				19 16					19 46			19 59				20 16					20 46
d			18 59				19 16					19 46			19 59				20 16					20 46
Burnham d							19 20					19 50							20 20					20 50
Taplow d																								
Maidenhead 3 d			19 05				19 26					19 56							20 26					20 56
Twyford 3 d							19 33					20 04							20 33					21 04
Reading 7 a		19 01	19 20				19 41					20 11			20 16				20 41					21 11
Oxford a			19 49												20 47									

	HX		XR	GW	GW	HX	XR	GW	HX	XR	GW		HX	XR	GW	HX	XR	GW	HX	XR	GW		HX	XR
	◇			◇1 ☕	◇	◇			◇		◇1 ☕		◇			◇		◇1	◇				◇	
London Paddington 15 ⊖ d	20 25			20 27	20 37	20 40	20 41	20 45	20 55		20 57		21 10	21 11	21 15	21 25		21 37	21 40	21 41	21 45		21 55	
Acton Main Line d																								
Ealing Broadway ⊖ d							20 50	20 53						21 20	21 23					21 50	21 53			
West Ealing d																								
Drayton Green d																								
Castle Bar Park d																								
South Greenford d																								
Greenford ⊖ a																								
Hanwell d																								
Southall d							20 54	20 59						21 24	21 29					21 54	21 59			
Hayes & Harlington d							20 58	21 03						21 28	21 33					21 58	22 03			
Heathrow Termls 2 & 3 2 ⊖ ✈ a	20 41					20 56	21 05		21 11				21 26	21 35		21 41			21 56	22 05			22 11	
d	20 43		20 53			20 58	21 07		21 13	21 23			21 28	21 37		21 43	21 53		21 58	22 07			22 13	22 23
Heathrow Terminal 4 ⊖ ✈ a			20 57				21 15			21 27				21 45			21 57			22 15				22 27
d																								
Heathrow Terminal 5 ⊖ ✈ a	20 47					21 02			21 17				21 32			21 47			22 02				22 17	
d																								
West Drayton d								21 07							21 37						22 07			
Iver d																								
Langley d								21 12							21 42						22 12			
Slough 3 a					20 57			21 16							21 46			22 01			22 15			
d					20 58			21 16							21 46			22 03			22 16			
Burnham d								21 20							21 50						22 20			
Taplow d																								
Maidenhead 3 d								21 26							21 56						22 26			
Twyford 3 d								21 33							22 04						22 33			
Reading 7 a				20 58	21 14			21 41			21 31				22 11			22 20			22 42			
Oxford a					21 48													22 57						

A 1 from Reading

For non-stop services between London and Reading refer to Table T116

For Heathrow Express Services see Table T118

For non-stop services between London and Heathrow Airport see Table T118

Table T117-F

Sundays

28 October to 2 December

London - Greenford, Heathrow Airport and Reading

Stopping Services

	HX	XR	GW	HX	XR	GW	HX	XR		GW	HX	XR	HX	XR	GW	HX	GW	GW
	◇			◇		◇1	◇				◇		◇			◇		
London Paddington 15 ⊖ d	22 10	22 11	22 15	22 25		22 37	22 40	22 41		22 45	22 55		23 10	23 11	23 15	23 25	23 47	23 53
Acton Main Line d																		
Ealing Broadway ⊖ d		22 20	22 23					22 50		22 53				23 20	23 23		23 55	00 02
West Ealing d																		
Drayton Green d																		
Castle Bar Park d																		
South Greenford d																		
Greenford ⊖ a																		
Hanwell d																		
Southall d		22 24	22 29					22 54		22 58				23 24	23 29			00 07
Hayes & Harlington d		22 28	22 33					22 58		23 02				23 28	23 33			00 11
HeathrowTermls 2 & 3 2 ⊖ ✈ a	22 26	22 35		22 41			22 56	23 05			23 11		23 26	23 35		23 41		
d	22 28	22 37		22 43	22 53		22 58	23 07			23 13	23 23	23 28	23 37		23 43		
Heathrow Terminal 4 ⊖ ✈ a		22 45			22 57			23 15				23 27		23 45				
d																		
Heathrow Terminal 5 ⊖ ✈ a	22 32			22 47			23 02				23 17		23 32			23 47		
d																		
West Drayton d			22 37							23 06					23 37			00 16
Iver d																		
Langley d			22 42							23 11					23 42			00 20
Slough 3 a			22 46							23 15					23 46		00 09	00 25
d			22 46							23 15					23 46		00 10	00 26
Burnham d			22 50							23 19					23 50			00 30
Taplow d																		
Maidenhead 3 d			22 56							23 24					23 56		00 17	00 36
Twyford 3 d			23 04							23 32					00 04			00 44
Reading 7 a			23 11			23 12				23 41					00 13		00 32	00 51
Oxford a																		

For non-stop services between London and Reading refer to Table T116

For Heathrow Express Services see Table T118

For non-stop services between London and Heathrow Airport see Table T118

Table T117-R

Mondays to Fridays

21 May to 7 December

Reading, Heathrow Airport and Greenford - London

Stopping Services

Miles	Miles	Miles		XR MX	GW MX	XR MO	XR MO	XR MX	XR MO	XR MX	GW MO		GW MO	GW MX	GW MO	GW MO	GW MX	GW MO	GW MX	GW MX	GW		GW	GW
																	◇1	◇						
						A	B				A		B		A	B								C
—	—	—	Oxford d														00 07		00 27					03 54
0	—	—	**Reading 7** d											00 14	00 20	00 20	00 39	00 51	01a14	01 15	02 24		03 54	04a35
5	—	—	**Twyford 3** d											00 21	00 27	00 27		00 59		01 21	02 30		04 00	
11¾	—	—	**Maidenhead 3** d											00 29	00 35	00 35		01 07		01 29	02 38		04 08	
13½	—	—	Taplow d											00 33										
15	—	—	Burnham d								00 01		00 01	00 36										
17½	—	—	**Slough 3** a								00 06		00 06	00 40	00 42	00 42	00 56	01 14		01 36	02 45		04 15	
—	—	—	d								00 07		00 07	00 41	00 42	00 42	00 57	01 14		01 37	02 46		04 16	
19¾	—	—	Langley d								00 11		00 11	00 45	00 46	00 47								
21¼	—	—	Iver d																					
22¾	—	—	West Drayton d								00 17		00 17	00 50	00 51	00 52					02 53		04 23	
—	—	—	**Heathrow Terminal 5** ⊖ ✈ a																					
—	—	—	d																					
—	—	0	**Heathrow Terminal 4** ⊖ ✈ a																					
—	—	—	d						00 01	00 07														
—	—	1¾	**Heathrow Termls 2 & 3 2** ⊖ ✈ a						00 05	00 11														
—	—	—	d					00 03	00 07	00 13														
25¼	—	5¾	Hayes & Harlington d					00 08	00 13	00 18	00 21		00 21	00 54	00 56	00 56		01 23		01 46	02 57		04 27	
27	—	7½	Southall d			00 02	00 03	00 12	00 17	00 22	00 25		00 25	00 58	00 59	01 00		01 27			03 01		04 31	
28¾	—	9¼	Hanwell d																					
—	0	—	**Greenford** ⊖ d																					
—	1	—	South Greenford d																					
—	1¾	—	Castle Bar Park d																					
—	2	—	Drayton Green d																					
29½	2¾	10	West Ealing d																					
30¼	3½	10¾	**Ealing Broadway** ⊖ d		00 05	00 07	00 08	00 17	00 22	00 27	00 30		00 30	01 03	01 05	01 05		01 32		01 52	03 06		04 36	
31¾	5	12¼	Acton Main Line d	00 02																				
36	9¼	16½	**London Paddington 15** ⊖ a	00 12	00 14	00 20	00 20	00 26	00 33	00 39	00 38		00 39	01 12	01 13	01 13	01 17	01 41		02 01	03 15		04 49	

	HX	GW	HX	XR MW FO	GW	XR	HX		XR	GW	HX	XR	GW	XR	HX	GW	XR		GW	GW	GW	XR	GW	GW
	◇1		◇1				◇1				◇1				◇1									
Oxford d																					05 17			
Reading 7 d		04 40			05 02					05 18			05 36						05 44	05 59	06a03		06 03	06 15
Twyford 3 d		04 46			05 08					05 24			05 42						05 54				06 09	
Maidenhead 3 d		04 54			05 17					05 33			05 50						06 02	06 11			06 17	
Taplow d					05 21					05 36									06 05					
Burnham d					05 24					05 39									06 08					
Slough 3 a		05 01			05 28					05 44			05 57						06 13	06 18			06 24	
d		05 05			05 29					05 44			05 58						06 14	06 19			06 25	
Langley d		05 09			05 33								06 02										06 29	
Iver d		05 13			05 36								06 05										06 32	
West Drayton d		05 17			05 40					05 51			06 09						06 21				06 36	
Heathrow Terminal 5 ⊖ ✈ a																								
d	05 12		05 27				05 42				05 57				06 12									
Heathrow Terminal 4 ⊖ ✈ a																								
d				05 22		05 41						05 52		06 11								06 22		
Heathrow Termls 2 & 3 2 ⊖ ✈ a	05 16		05 31	05 26		05 45	05 46				06 01	05 56		06 15	06 16							06 26		
d	05 17		05 33	05 28			05 48				06 03	05 58			06 18							06 28		
Hayes & Harlington d		05 23		05 33	05 44				05 47	05 56		06 03	06 13				06 17		06 26			06 33	06 40	
Southall d		05 27		05 37	05 48				05 51	05 59		06 07	06 17				06 21		06 30			06 37	06 44	
Hanwell d				05 40								06 10										06 40		
Greenford ⊖ d																06 13								
South Greenford d																06 16								
Castle Bar Park d																06 20								
Drayton Green d																06 22								
West Ealing d				05 44					05 56			06 12				06a24	06 26					06 42		
Ealing Broadway ⊖ d		05 32		05 47	05 53				05 59	06 05		06 15	06 23				06 29		06 35			06 45	06 50	
Acton Main Line d		05 36							06 02	06 08							06 32		06 39					
London Paddington 15 ⊖ a	05 33	05 48	05 49	05 56	06 02		06 04		06 12	06 16	06 19	06 26	06 32		06 34		06 42		06 46	06 36		06 56	06 59	06 44

A until 10 September
B from 17 September
C until 15 June, MX from 19 June

For non-stop services between Reading and London refer to Table T116

For non-stop services between London and Heathrow Airport see Table T118

For Heathrow Express Services see Table T118

Table T117-R

Mondays to Fridays

21 May to 7 December

Reading, Heathrow Airport and Greenford - London

Stopping Services

		HX	XR	GW	XR	GW	GW	HX	GW	GW		GW	HX	XR	GW	XR	GW	XR	GW	GW		GW	HX	GW	XR
		◇1						◇1					◇1									◇1 🛒	◇1		
Oxford	d									05 57										05 50		06 28			
Reading 7	d					06 18	06 19		06 29	06 30		06 37			←				06 42	06 47		06 53		06 57	
Twyford 3	d					06 24	06 25		06 37			06 45			06 37				06 49	06 53				07 03	
Maidenhead 3	d					06 32	06 32		→	06 42					06 45				06 57	07 01		07 06		07 10	
Taplow	d					06 36													07 01						
Burnham	d					06 39									06 50				07 04						
Slough 3	a					06 43				06 48					06 54				07 08					07 16	
	d					06 44				06 49					06 55				07 09					07 16	
Langley	d					06 48									06 59				07 13						
Iver	d														07 02				07 16						
West Drayton	d					06 53									07 06				07 20						
Heathrow Terminal 5 ⊖ ✈	a																								
	d	06 27						06 42					06 57										07 12		
Heathrow Terminal 4 ⊖ ✈	a																								
	d		06 41											06 52		07 11									07 22
Heathrow Termls 2 & 3 2 ⊖ ✈	a	06 31	06 45					06 46					07 01	06 56		07 15							07 16		07 26
	d	06 33						06 48					07 03	06 58									07 18		07 28
Hayes & Harlington	d				06 47	06 57								07 03	07 10			07 17	07 24						07 33
Southall	d				06 51	07 01								07 08	07 14			07 21	07 28						07 37
Hanwell	d													07 11											07 40
Greenford ⊖	d			06 42													07 12								
South Greenford	d			06 45													07 15								
Castle Bar Park	d			06 48													07 18								
Drayton Green	d			06 50													07 20								
West Ealing	d			06a53	06 56									07 13			07a23	07 26							07 42
Ealing Broadway ⊖	d				06 59	07 07								07 16	07 20			07 29	07 34						07 45
Acton Main Line	d				07 02													07 32							
London Paddington 15 ⊖	a	06 49			07 12	07 16	06 53	07 04		07 06		07 10	07 19	07 25	07 29			07 42	07 46	07 24		07 25	07 34	07 36	07 57

		GW	GW	HX	XR	GW		XR	GW	GW	GW	GW	HX	GW	XR	GW		GW	XC	HX	XR	GW	XR	GW	GW
				◇1								◇1 🛒	◇1					◇1 🛒	◇1 🍴	◇1					
Oxford	d										06 38	06 54							07 16						
Reading 7	d	07 01	07 07						07 12	07 18	07a28	07 24				07 32		07 35	07a40					07 42	07 50
Twyford 3	d	07 07							07 19	07 24						07 38								07 48	
Maidenhead 3	d	07 15	07 18						07 27	07 33				07 44		07 47								07 56	
Taplow	d								07 31															08 00	
Burnham	d	07 20							07 34							07 51								08 03	
Slough 3	a	07 24							07 38					07 51		07 56								08 07	
	d	07 26							07 39					07 51		07 56								08 08	
Langley	d	07 30							07 43							08 00								08 12	
Iver	d								07 46															08 15	
West Drayton	d	07 35							07 50							08 05								08 19	
Heathrow Terminal 5 ⊖ ✈	a																								
	d			07 27									07 42							07 57					
Heathrow Terminal 4 ⊖ ✈	a																								
	d				07 41										07 52						08 11				
Heathrow Termls 2 & 3 2 ⊖ ✈	a			07 31	07 45								07 46		07 56					08 01	08 15				
	d			07 33									07 48		07 58					08 03					
Hayes & Harlington	d	07 39						07 47	07 54						08 03	08 10							08 17	08 23	
Southall	d	07 43						07 51	07 58					08 02	08 07	08 14							08 21	08 27	
Hanwell	d														08 10										
Greenford ⊖	d					07 42																08 12			
South Greenford	d					07 45																08 15			
Castle Bar Park	d					07 48																08 18			
Drayton Green	d					07 50																08 20			
West Ealing	d					07a53		07 56							08 13							08a23	08 26		
Ealing Broadway ⊖	d	07 49						07 59	08 04						08 16	08 19							08 29	08 33	
Acton Main Line	d							08 02															08 32		
London Paddington 15 ⊖	a	07 58	07 38	07 49				08 12	08 16	07 55		07 52	08 04	08 18	08 26	08 28		08 06		08 19			08 42	08 42	08 20

For non-stop services between Reading and London refer to Table T116

For non-stop services between London and Heathrow Airport see Table T118

For Heathrow Express Services see Table T118

Table T117-R

Mondays to Fridays

21 May to 7 December

Reading, Heathrow Airport and Greenford - London

Stopping Services

		GW	GW	GW	GW	HX	XR	GW		XC	GW	XR	GW	GW	HX	GW	GW	XR		HX	GW	XR	GW	GW	XC
					◇1 🛒	◇1				◇1				◇1 🛒	◇1		◇1 A 🛒🍴			◇1					◇1 🍴
Oxford	d			07 21	07 31					07 43							07 54							08 07	08 16
Reading 7	d		07 53	08a09	07 58			08 02		08a09			08 12	08 14		08 16	08 21						08 33	08 37	08a40
Twyford 3	d	07 53	07 59					08 08					08 18			08 22							08 39		
Maidenhead 3	d	08 02	08 06					08 16					08 27			08 32					08 44		08 47		
Taplow	d												08 31										08 51		
Burnham	d							08 21					08 34										08 54		
Slough 3	a							08 25					08 38								08 51		08 58		
	d							08 26					08 39								08 51		08 59		
Langley	d							08 30					08 43										09 03		
Iver	d												08 46										09 06		
West Drayton	d							08 35					08 50										09 10		
Heathrow Terminal 5 ⊖ ✈	a																								
	d					08 12									08 27					08 42					
Heathrow Terminal 4 ⊖ ✈	a																								
	d						08 22											08 41				08 52			
Heathrow Termls 2 & 3 2 ⊖ ✈	a					08 16	08 26								08 31			08 45		08 46		08 56			
	d					08 18	08 28								08 33					08 48		08 58			
Hayes & Harlington	d						08 33	08 39				08 47	08 54									09 03	09 14		
Southall	d						08 37	08 43				08 51	08 58								09 01	09 07	09 18		
Hanwell	d						08 40															09 10			
Greenford ⊖	d										08 42														
South Greenford	d										08 45														
Castle Bar Park	d										08 48														
Drayton Green	d										08 50														
West Ealing	d						08 42				08a53	08 56										09 12			
Ealing Broadway ⊖	d						08 45	08 49				08 59	09 04									09 15	09 24		
Acton Main Line	d											09 02													
London Paddington 15 ⊖	a	08 24	08 31		08 28	08 35	08 56	08 58				09 12	09 16	08 42	08 49	08 53	08 51			09 04	09 21	09 26	09 33	09 07	

		HX	XR	GW		XR	GW	GW	HX	XR	GW	GW	XC	GW		GW	XR	GW	GW	HX	GW	GW	XR	HX	
		◇1							◇1				◇1 🍴	◇1 🛒					◇1 B 🛒	◇1				◇1	
Oxford	d											08 35	08 43						08 54			09 01			
Reading 7	d						08 50	08 53			09 06	09a22	09a08	09 10				09 18	09 20		09 23	09 33			
Twyford 3	d						08 56	09 00			09 13							09 24			09 29				
Maidenhead 3	d						09 04	09 09			09 21							09 32			09 41				
Taplow	d						09 08											09 36							
Burnham	d						09 11											09 39							
Slough 3	a						09 15				09 28							09 43			09 48				
	d						09 16				09 29							09 44			09 49				
Langley	d										09 33														
Iver	d										09 36														
West Drayton	d						09 23				09 40							09 51							
Heathrow Terminal 5 ⊖ ✈	a																								
	d	08 57							09 12											09 27				09 42	
Heathrow Terminal 4 ⊖ ✈	a																								
	d		09 11							09 22													09 41		
Heathrow Termls 2 & 3 2 ⊖ ✈	a	09 01	09 15						09 16	09 26										09 31			09 45	09 46	
	d	09 03							09 18	09 28										09 33				09 48	
Hayes & Harlington	d					09 17	09 27			09 33	09 44						09 47	09 55							
Southall	d					09 22				09 37	09 48						09 51	09 59							
Hanwell	d									09 40															
Greenford ⊖	d			09 12												09 42									
South Greenford	d			09 15												09 45									
Castle Bar Park	d			09 18												09 48									
Drayton Green	d			09 20												09 50									
West Ealing	d			09a23		09 26				09 42						09a53	09 56								
Ealing Broadway ⊖	d					09 29	09 37			09 45	09 53						09 59	10 07							
Acton Main Line	d					09 32											10 02								
London Paddington 15 ⊖	a	09 19				09 42	09 46	09 30	09 35	09 56	10 02			09 37			10 12	10 16	09 46	09 49	10 08	09 59		10 04	

A 🛒 from Reading 🍴 to Reading

B The Cathedrals Express

For non-stop services between Reading and London refer to Table T116

For non-stop services between London and Heathrow Airport see Table T118

For Heathrow Express Services see Table T118

Reading, Heathrow Airport and Greenford - London

Stopping Services

Station		HX	XR	GW	XC	GW		GW	GW	XR	GW	HX	XR	GW	XR	GW		XC	GW	GW	HX	GW	XR	GW	HX
		◇■			◇■							◇■						◇■		◇■	◇■	◇■			◇■
Oxford	d				09 17				09 31									09 43				10 01			
Reading ■	d			09 34	09a42	09 48		09 51	09 57							10 03		10a10	10 18	10 19		10 26			
Twyford ■	d			09 40		09 54										10 09			10 24						
Maidenhead ■	d			09 48		10 02										10 17			10 32						
Taplow	d					10 06													10 36						
Burnham	d					10 09								←					10 39						
Slough ■	a			09 55		10 13			10 12					10 13		10 24			10 43			10 39			
	d			09 56		10 14			10 12					10 14		10 25			10 44			10 40			
Langley	d			10 00		→										10 29			→						
Iver	d			10 03												10 32									
West Drayton	d			10 07										10 21		10 39									
Heathrow Terminal 5 ⊖ ✈	a																								
	d	09 57										10 12									10 27				10 42
Heathrow Terminal 4 ⊖ ✈	a																								
	d		09 52							10 11					10 22								10 41		
Heathrow Termls 2 & 3 ■ ⊖ ✈	a	10 01	09 56							10 15		10 16			10 26						10 31		10 45		10 46
	d	10 03	09 58									10 18			10 28						10 33				10 48
Hayes & Harlington	d		10 03	10 11									10 17	10 25	10 33	10 43									
Southall	d		10 07	10 15									10 21		10 37	10 47									
Hanwell	d		10 10												10 40										
Greenford ⊖	d										10 12													10 42	
South Greenford	d										10 15													10 45	
Castle Bar Park	d										10 18													10 48	
Drayton Green	d										10 20													10 50	
West Ealing	d		10 12								10a23		10 26		10 42									10a53	
Ealing Broadway ⊖	d		10 15	10 22									10 29	10 33	10 45	10 52									
Acton Main Line	d												10 32												
London Paddington ■■ ⊖	a	10 19	10 26	10 31				10 21	10 31			10 34	10 43	10 46	10 56	11 01				10 45	10 49	10 57			11 04

Station		XR		GW	HX	XR	GW	XC	GW	GW	XR	GW		HX	XR	GW	HX	XR	GW	XC	GW	GW		XR	GW
					◇■			■						◇■			◇■			◇■					
Oxford	d							10 16		10 31										10 43		11 01			
Reading ■	d						10 33	10a42	10 49	10 56									11 03	11a09	11 19	11 26			
Twyford ■	d						10 39		10 57										11 09		11 26				
Maidenhead ■	d						10 47		11 05										11 17		11 34				
Taplow	d								11 09												11 38				
Burnham	d			←					11 12							←					11 41				
Slough ■	a			10 43			10 54		11 16	11 11						11 16			11 24		11 45	11 39			
	d			10 44			10 55		11 17	11 11						11 17			11 25		11 46	11 41			
Langley	d						10 59		→										11 29		→				
Iver	d						11 02												11 32						
West Drayton	d			10 54			11 06									11 24			11 36						
Heathrow Terminal 5 ⊖ ✈	a																								
	d				10 57									11 12			11 27								
Heathrow Terminal 4 ⊖ ✈	a																								
	d					10 52					11 11							11 22						11 41	
Heathrow Termls 2 & 3 ■ ⊖ ✈	a				11 01	10 56					11 15			11 16			11 31	11 26						11 45	
	d				11 03	10 58								11 18			11 33	11 28							
Hayes & Harlington	d	10 47		10 59		11 03	11 10								11 17	11 28		11 33	11 40						
Southall	d	10 51				11 07	11 14								11 21			11 38	11 44						
Hanwell	d					11 10												11 41							
Greenford ⊖	d											11 12													11 42
South Greenford	d											11 15													11 45
Castle Bar Park	d											11 18													11 48
Drayton Green	d											11 20													11 50
West Ealing	d	10 56				11 12						11a23			11 26			11 43							11a53
Ealing Broadway ⊖	d	10 59		11 07		11 15	11 19								11 29	11 36		11 46	11 49						
Acton Main Line	d	11 02													11 32										
London Paddington ■■ ⊖	a	11 12		11 16	11 19	11 26	11 31			11 30				11 34	11 42	11 46	11 49	11 56	12 01			11 58			

For non-stop services between Reading and London refer to Table T116

For non-stop services between London and Heathrow Airport see Table T118

For Heathrow Express Services see Table T118

Table T117-R

Mondays to Fridays

21 May to 7 December

Reading, Heathrow Airport and Greenford - London

Stopping Services

Station		HX	XR	GW		HX	XR	GW	XC	GW	GW	XR	HX	XR		GW	GW	XR	GW	XC	GW	HX	XR	GW	
		◇■				◇■			◇■		◇■		◇■							◇■	◇■	◇■			
Oxford	d								11 16		11 31									11 43					
Reading ■	d							11 33	11a40	11 49	11 57								12 03	12a08	12 18			12 18	
Twyford ■	d							11 39		11 55									12 09					12 24	
Maidenhead ■	d							11 47		12 03									12 17					12 32	
Taplow	d									12 07														12 36	
Burnham	d			←						12 10						←								12 39	
Slough ■	a			11 45				11 54		12 14	12 10					12 14			12 24					12 43	
	d			11 46				11 55		12 15	12 11					12 15			12 25					12 44	
Langley	d							11 59		→									12 29					→	
Iver	d							12 02											12 32						
West Drayton	d			11 53				12 06								12 22			12 36						
Heathrow Terminal 5 ⊖ ✈	a																								
	d	11 42				11 57							12 12									12 27			
Heathrow Terminal 4 ⊖ ✈	a																								
	d						11 52					12 11						12 22					12 41		
Heathrow Termls 2 & 3 ■ ⊖ ✈	a	11 46				12 01	11 56					12 15	12 16					12 26				12 31	12 45		
	d	11 48				12 03	11 58						12 18					12 28				12 33			
Hayes & Harlington	d		11 47	11 57			12 03	12 10						12 17		12 27		12 33	12 40						
Southall	d		11 51				12 07	12 14						12 21				12 37	12 44						
Hanwell	d						12 10											12 40							
Greenford ⊖	d																12 16								
South Greenford	d																12 19								
Castle Bar Park	d																12 22								
Drayton Green	d																12 24								
West Ealing	d		11 56				12 12							12 26			12a29	12 42							
Ealing Broadway ⊖	d		11 59	12 08			12 15	12 19						12 29		12 37		12 45	12 49						
Acton Main Line	d		12 02											12 32											
London Paddington ■■ ⊖	a	12 04	12 12	12 17		12 19	12 26	12 32			12 28		12 35	12 42		12 46		12 56	13 01		12 44	12 49			

Station		GW	HX	XR	GW	GW	HX	XR	GW	XC		GW	GW	XR	HX	XR	GW	GW	HX	XR		GW	XC	GW	GW
			◇■				◇■			◇■			◇		◇■				◇■				◇■		
Oxford	d	12 01								12 16			12 31										12 44		13 01
Reading ■	d	12 26							12 33	12a42		12 48	12 55									13 03	13a08	13 18	13 26
Twyford ■	d								12 39			12 54										13 09		13 24	
Maidenhead ■	d								12 47			13 02										13 17		13 32	
Taplow	d											13 06												13 36	
Burnham	d				←							13 09					←							13 39	
Slough ■	a	12 39			12 43				12 54			13 13	13 10				13 13					13 24		13 43	13 39
	d	12 41			12 44				12 55			13 14	13 10				13 14					13 25		13 44	13 41
Langley	d								12 59			→										13 29		→	
Iver	d								13 02													13 32			
West Drayton	d				12 51				13 06								13 21					13 36			
Heathrow Terminal 5 ⊖ ✈	a																								
	d		12 42				12 57								13 12				13 27						
Heathrow Terminal 4 ⊖ ✈	a																								
	d							12 52						13 11						13 22					
Heathrow Termls 2 & 3 ■ ⊖ ✈	a		12 46				13 01	12 56						13 15	13 16				13 31	13 26					
	d		12 48				13 03	12 58							13 18				13 33	13 28					
Hayes & Harlington	d			12 47	12 55			13 03	13 10							13 17	13 25			13 33		13 40			
Southall	d			12 51				13 07	13 14							13 21				13 37		13 44			
Hanwell	d							13 10												13 40					
Greenford ⊖	d					12 47												13 16							
South Greenford	d					12 50												13 19							
Castle Bar Park	d					12 53												13 22							
Drayton Green	d					12 55												13 24							
West Ealing	d			12 56		12a58		13 12								13 26		13a27		13 42					
Ealing Broadway ⊖	d			12 59	13 05			13 15	13 22							13 29	13 33			13 45		13 49			
Acton Main Line	d			13 02												13 32									
London Paddington ■■ ⊖	a	12 59	13 04	13 12	13 15		13 19	13 26	13 31				13 29		13 35	13 42	13 42		13 49	13 56		14 01			13 58

For non-stop services between Reading and London refer to Table T116

For non-stop services between London and Heathrow Airport see Table T118

For Heathrow Express Services see Table T118

Table T117-R

Mondays to Fridays

21 May to 7 December

Reading, Heathrow Airport and Greenford - London

Stopping Services

	XR		HX ◇1	XR	GW	GW	HX ◇1	XR	GW	XC ◇1 🛒	GW		GW ◇1 🛒	XR	HX ◇1	XR	GW	GW	XR	GW	XC ◇1 🛒		GW	GW ◇1 ☕
Oxford d										13 16			13 31								13 43			
Reading 7 d									13 33	13a40	13 48		13 56							14 03	14a09		14 18	14 20
Twyford 3 d									13 39		13 55									14 09			14 24	
Maidenhead 3 d									13 47		14 03									14 17			14 32	
Taplow d											14 07												14 36	
Burnham d					←						14 10						←						14 39	
Slough 3 a					13 43				13 55		14 14		14 09				14 14			14 24			14 43	
d					13 44				13 56		14 15		14 10				14 15			14 25			14 44	
Langley d									14 00		→									14 29			→	
Iver d									14 03											14 32				
West Drayton d					13 51				14 07								14 22			14 36				
Heathrow Terminal 5 ⊖ ✈ a																								
d			13 42				13 57								14 12									
Heathrow Terminal 4 ⊖ ✈ a																								
d	13 41							13 52						14 11					14 22					
Heathrow Termls 2 & 3 ⊖ ✈ a	13 45		13 46				14 01	13 56						14 15	14 16				14 26					
d			13 48				14 03	13 58							14 18				14 28					
Hayes & Harlington d				13 47	13 55			14 03	14 11							14 17	14 26		14 33	14 40				
Southall d				13 51				14 07	14 15							14 21			14 37	14 44				
Hanwell d								14 10											14 40					
Greenford ⊖ d						13 46												14 16						
South Greenford d						13 49												14 19						
Castle Bar Park d						13 52												14 22						
Drayton Green d						13 54												14 24						
West Ealing d				13 56		13a57		14 12								14 26		14a27	14 42					
Ealing Broadway ⊖ d				13 59	14 09			14 15	14 20							14 29	14 36		14 45	14 51				
Acton Main Line d				14 02												14 32								
London Paddington 15 ⊖ a			14 04	14 12	14 18		14 19	14 26	14 31				14 27		14 35	14 42	14 45		14 56	15 01				14 46

	HX ◇1	GW	XR	HX ◇1	XR	GW	GW		HX ◇1	XR	GW	XC ◇1 🛒	GW	GW ◇1 🛒	XR	HX ◇1	XR		GW	GW	HX ◇1	XR	GW	XC ◇1 🛒
Oxford d		14 01										14 16		14 31										14 43
Reading 7 d		14 27									14 33	14a40	14 48	14 56									15 03	15a08
Twyford 3 d											14 39		14 54										15 09	
Maidenhead 3 d											14 47		15 02										15 17	
Taplow d													15 06											
Burnham d						←							15 09						←					
Slough 3 a		14 41				14 43					14 54		15 13	15 09					15 13				15 24	
d		14 42				14 44					14 55		15 14	15 10					15 14				15 25	
Langley d											14 59		→										15 29	
Iver d											15 02												15 32	
West Drayton d						14 51					15 06								15 21				15 36	
Heathrow Terminal 5 ⊖ ✈ a																								
d	14 27			14 42					14 57							15 12					15 27			
Heathrow Terminal 4 ⊖ ✈ a																								
d			14 41							14 52					15 11							15 22		
Heathrow Termls 2 & 3 ⊖ ✈ a	14 31		14 45	14 46					15 01	14 56					15 15	15 16					15 31	15 26		
d	14 33			14 48					15 03	14 58						15 18					15 33	15 28		
Hayes & Harlington d					14 47	14 55				15 03	15 10						15 17		15 25			15 33	15 40	
Southall d					14 51					15 08	15 14						15 21					15 37	15 44	
Hanwell d										15 11												15 40		
Greenford ⊖ d							14 46													15 16				
South Greenford d							14 49													15 19				
Castle Bar Park d							14 52													15 22				
Drayton Green d							14 54													15 24				
West Ealing d					14 56		14a57			15 13							15 26			15a27		15 42		
Ealing Broadway ⊖ d					14 59	15 07				15 16	15 22						15 29		15 33			15 45	15 49	
Acton Main Line d					15 02												15 32							
London Paddington 15 ⊖ a	14 49	15 00		15 04	15 12	15 16			15 19	15 26	15 31			15 27		15 35	15 42		15 46		15 49	15 56	15 59	

For non-stop services between Reading and London refer to Table T116

For non-stop services between London and Heathrow Airport see Table T118

For Heathrow Express Services see Table T118

Table T117-R

Mondays to Fridays

21 May to 7 December

Reading, Heathrow Airport and Greenford - London

Stopping Services

	GW	GW	XR	HX ◇1	XR	GW	GW	HX ◇1	XR		GW	XC ◇1 🛒	GW	GW ◇1 🛒	XR	HX ◇1	XR	GW	GW		XR	GW	XC ◇1 🛒	GW
Oxford d		15 01										15 16		15 31									15 43	
Reading 7 d	15 18	15 27									15 33	15a41	15 48	15 56								16 06	16a11	16 18
Twyford 3 d	15 24										15 39		15 54									16 13		16 24
Maidenhead 3 d	15 32										15 47		16 02									16 21		16 32
Taplow d	15 36												16 06											16 36
Burnham d	15 39					←							16 09					←						16 39
Slough 3 a	15 43	15 40				15 43					15 54		16 13	16 09				16 13				16 28		16 43
d	15 44	15 42				15 44					15 55		16 14	16 10				16 14				16 28		16 44
Langley d	→										15 59		→									16 32		→
Iver d											16 02											16 35		
West Drayton d						15 51					16 06							16 21				16 39		
Heathrow Terminal 5 ⊖ ✈ a																								
d				15 42				15 57								16 12								
Heathrow Terminal 4 ⊖ ✈ a																								
d			15 41						15 52						16 11						16 22			
Heathrow Termls 2 & 3 ⊖ ✈ a			15 45	15 46				16 01	15 56						16 15	16 16					16 26			
d				15 48				16 03	15 58							16 18					16 28			
Hayes & Harlington d					15 47	15 58			16 03		16 10						16 17	16 25			16 33	16 44		
Southall d					15 51				16 07		16 14						16 21				16 37	16 48		
Hanwell d									16 10												16 40			
Greenford ⊖ d							15 46												16 17					
South Greenford d							15 49												16 20					
Castle Bar Park d							15 52												16 23					
Drayton Green d							15 54												16 25					
West Ealing d					15 56		15a57		16 12								16 26		16a28		16 42			
Ealing Broadway ⊖ d					15 59	16 07			16 15		16 22						16 29	16 33			16 45	16 53		
Acton Main Line d					16 02												16 32							
London Paddington 15 ⊖ a		15 59		16 05	16 12	16 16		16 19	16 26		16 32			16 27		16 35	16 42	16 46			16 56	17 02		

	GW ◇1 A ☕	HX ◇1	GW	XR	HX ◇1		GW	XR	GW	HX ◇1	GW	XR	GW	GW	XC ◇1 🛒		GW	GW ◇1 ☕	XR	HX ◇1	XR	GW	GW	XR
Oxford d			16 01											16 07	16 16			16 31						
Reading 7 d	16 19		16 25				16 28						16 32	16a54	16a40		16 48	16 57						
Twyford 3 d							16 34						16 38				16 54							
Maidenhead 3 d							16 42						16 46				17 02							
Taplow d																	17 06							
Burnham d											←						17 09					←		
Slough 3 a			16 40								16 43		16 53				17 13	17 10				17 13		
d			16 40								16 44		16 54				17 14	17 11				17 14		
Langley d											16 48		16 58				→					17 18		
Iver d											16 51		17 01									17 21		
West Drayton d											16 55		17 05									17 25		
Heathrow Terminal 5 ⊖ ✈ a																								
d		16 27			16 42					16 57										17 12				
Heathrow Terminal 4 ⊖ ✈ a																								
d				16 41								16 52							17 11					17 22
Heathrow Termls 2 & 3 ⊖ ✈ a		16 31		16 45	16 46					17 01		16 56							17 15	17 16				17 26
d		16 33			16 48					17 03		16 58								17 18				17 28
Hayes & Harlington d								16 47			16 59	17 03	17 09								17 17	17 29		17 33
Southall d								16 51			17 03	17 07	17 13								17 21	17 33		17 37
Hanwell d												17 10												17 40
Greenford ⊖ d									16 46														17 17	
South Greenford d									16 49														17 20	
Castle Bar Park d									16 52														17 23	
Drayton Green d									16 54														17 25	
West Ealing d								16 56	16a57			17 12									17 26		17a28	17 42
Ealing Broadway ⊖ d								16 59			17 10	17 15	17 20								17 29	17 41		17 45
Acton Main Line d								17 02													17 32			
London Paddington 15 ⊖ a	16 44	16 49	17 00		17 05		17 07	17 12		17 19	17 20	17 26	17 30					17 28		17 35	17 42	17 52		17 56

A The Cheltenham Spa Express

For non-stop services between Reading and London refer to Table T116

For non-stop services between London and Heathrow Airport see Table T118

For Heathrow Express Services see Table T118

Table T117-R

Mondays to Fridays

21 May to 7 December

Reading, Heathrow Airport and Greenford - London

Stopping Services

	GW	XC	GW	HX	GW	XR	GW		GW	HX	XR	GW	GW	XR	GW	GW	HX		GW	GW	XC	GW	GW	XR
		◇■		◇■	◇■				◇■	◇■							◇■				◇■		◇■	
Oxford d		16 43							17 01											17 07	17 16		17 31	
Reading d	17 03	17a08	17 14		17 18		17 18		17 28							17 33			17 37	17a54	17a40	17 51	17 56	
Twyford d	17 09						17 24									17 39			17 43			17 57		
Maidenhead d	17 17						17 32								17 42	17 47			17 51			18 05		
Taplow d							17 36															18 09		
Burnham d							17 39					←			17 46							18 12		
Slough a	17 24						17 43		17 41			17 43			17 51				17 58			18 16	18 09	
Slough d	17 25						17 46		17 42			17 46			17 51				17 59			18 17	18 10	
Langley d	17 29						→								17 55				18 03			→		
Iver d	17 32																		18 06					
West Drayton d	17 36											17 53			18 00				18 10					
Heathrow Terminal 5 a																								
d				17 27						17 42							17 57							
Heathrow Terminal 4 a																								
d						17 41								17 52										18 11
Heathrow Termls 2 & 3 a				17 31		17 45				17 46				17 56			18 01							18 15
d				17 33						17 48				17 58			18 03							
Hayes & Harlington d	17 40										17 47	17 58		18 03	18 09				18 14					
Southall d	17 44										17 51	18 02		18 07	18 13				18 18					
Hanwell d														18 10										
Greenford d													17 47											
South Greenford d													17 50											
Castle Bar Park d													17 53											
Drayton Green d													17 55											
West Ealing d											17 56		17a58	18 12										
Ealing Broadway d	17 50										17 59	18 08		18 15	18 18				18 25					
Acton Main Line d											18 02													
London Paddington a	18 02		17 46	17 49	17 54				17 59	18 05	18 12	18 17		18 26	18 27	18 10	18 19		18 36				18 28	

	HX	XR	GW		GW	XR	GW	GW	GW	XC	GW	HX	GW		XR	HX	XR	GW	GW	HX	XR	GW	GW	
	◇■								◇■	◇■		◇■	◇■			◇■				◇■				
Oxford d										17 43			18 06										18 10	
Reading d								18 07	18 08	18a09	18 18		18 31									18 33	18a57	
Twyford d								18 13			18 24											18 39		
Maidenhead d							18 12	18 21			18 32											18 47		
Taplow d											18 36													
Burnham d			←				18 16				18 39							←						
Slough a			18 16				18 21	18 28			18 43		18 44					18 43				18 54		
Slough d			18 17				18 21	18 29			18 48		18 45					18 48				18 55		
Langley d							18 25	18 33			→											18 59		
Iver d								18 36														19 02		
West Drayton d			18 24				18 30	18 40										18 55				19 06		
Heathrow Terminal 5 a																								
d	18 12											18 27				18 42				18 57				
Heathrow Terminal 4 a																								
d						18 22									18 41						18 52			
Heathrow Termls 2 & 3 a	18 16					18 26						18 31			18 45	18 46				19 01	18 56			
d	18 18					18 28						18 33				18 48				19 03	18 58			
Hayes & Harlington d		18 17	18 28			18 33	18 38	18 44									18 47	18 59			19 03	19 10		
Southall d		18 22	18 33			18 37	18 42	18 48									18 52				19 07	19 14		
Hanwell d						18 40															19 10			
Greenford d					18 22														18 51					
South Greenford d					18 25														18 54					
Castle Bar Park d					18 28														18 57					
Drayton Green d					18 30														18 59					
West Ealing d		18 26			18a33	18 42											18 56		19a02		19 12			
Ealing Broadway d		18 29	18 38			18 45	18 49	18 54									18 59	19 06			19 15	19 20		
Acton Main Line d		18 32															19 02							
London Paddington a	18 34	18 42	18 51			18 55	18 59	19 06	18 39			18 49	19 03			19 05	19 10	19 15		19 19	19 26	19 31		

For non-stop services between Reading and London refer to Table T116

For non-stop services between London and Heathrow Airport see Table T118

For Heathrow Express Services see Table T118

Table T117-R

Mondays to Fridays

21 May to 7 December

Reading, Heathrow Airport and Greenford - London

Stopping Services

	XC	GW	GW	XR	HX		XR	GW	GW	HX	XR	GW	XC	GW	GW		GW	XR	HX	XR	GW	HX	XR	GW
	◇■				◇■					◇■			◇■				◇■		◇■			◇■		
Oxford d	18 16		18 31										18 43				19 02							
Reading d	18a44	18 52	18 59									19 07	19a10	19 19	19 23		19 27							19 33
Twyford d		18 58										19 13		19 25										19 39
Maidenhead d		19 06										19 21		19 34										19 48
Taplow d		19 10												19 37										
Burnham d		19 13						←						19 40							←			
Slough a		19 17	19 12					19 17				19 28		19 45			19 40				19 45			19 56
Slough d		19 18	19 13					19 18				19 29		19 45			19 41				19 45			19 57
Langley d		→										19 33		→										20 01
Iver d												19 36												20 04
West Drayton d								19 25				19 40									19 52			20 08
Heathrow Terminal 5 a																								
d					19 12					19 27									19 42			19 57		
Heathrow Terminal 4 a																								
d				19 11							19 22							19 41					19 52	
Heathrow Termls 2 & 3 a				19 15	19 16					19 31	19 26							19 45	19 46			20 01	19 56	
d					19 18					19 33	19 28								19 48			20 03	19 58	
Hayes & Harlington d							19 17	19 29			19 33	19 44								19 47	19 57		20 03	20 13
Southall d							19 21				19 38	19 48								19 52			20 07	20 17
Hanwell d											19 41												20 10	
Greenford d									19 21															
South Greenford d									19 24															
Castle Bar Park d									19 27															
Drayton Green d									19 29															
West Ealing d							19 26		19a32		19 43									19 56			20 12	
Ealing Broadway d							19 29	19 37			19 46	19 54								19 59	20 04		20 15	20 22
Acton Main Line d							19 32													20 02				
London Paddington a			19 30		19 35		19 42	19 46		19 49	19 56	20 06			19 54		19 59		20 04	20 12	20 16	20 19	20 26	20 31

	XC		GW	GW	GW	XR	HX	XR	GW	XR	GW		XC	GW	HX	GW	XR	HX	GW	GW	XR		GW	HX
	◇■						◇■						◇■	◇■	◇■			◇■		◇■				◇■
Oxford d	19 16			19 32									19 43							20 06				
Reading d	19a41		19 52	19 56							20 01		20a09	20 17					20 20	20 31				
Twyford d			19 58								20 08								20 26					
Maidenhead d			20 06								20 16								20 34					
Taplow d			20 10																20 38					
Burnham d			20 13						←										20 41				←	
Slough a			20 17	20 11					20 17		20 23								20 45	20 44			20 45	
Slough d			20 18	20 11					20 18		20 23								20 46	20 45			20 46	
Langley d			→								20 27								→					
Iver d											20 30													
West Drayton d									20 25		20 34												20 53	
Heathrow Terminal 5 a																								
d							20 12								20 27			20 42						20 57
Heathrow Terminal 4 a																								
d						20 11				20 22							20 41							
Heathrow Termls 2 & 3 a						20 15	20 16			20 26					20 31		20 45	20 46						21 01
d							20 18			20 28					20 33			20 48						21 03
Hayes & Harlington d								20 17	20 29	20 33	20 39										20 47		20 57	
Southall d								20 21		20 37	20 42										20 51			
Hanwell d										20 40														
Greenford d					20 02											20 32								
South Greenford d					20 05											20 35								
Castle Bar Park d					20 08											20 38								
Drayton Green d					20 10											20 40								
West Ealing d					20a13			20 26		20 42						20a43					20 56			
Ealing Broadway d								20 29	20 36	20 45	20 52										20 59		21 07	
Acton Main Line d								20 32													21 02			
London Paddington a				20 30			20 34	20 42	20 46	20 56	21 01			20 43	20 49			21 04		21 05	21 12		21 16	21 19

For non-stop services between Reading and London refer to Table T116

For non-stop services between London and Heathrow Airport see Table T118

For Heathrow Express Services see Table T118

Table T117-R

Mondays to Fridays

21 May to 7 December

Reading, Heathrow Airport and Greenford - London

Stopping Services

		XR	GW	XC		GW	GW	XC	GW	XR	HX	XR	GW	HX		XR	GW	GW	XR	HX	GW	XR	HX	XR	
				◇1 🛒				◇1 🛒			◇1			◇1						◇1			◇1		
Oxford	d			20 16			20 31	20 42													21 01				
Reading [7]	d		20 34	20a41		20 48	20 56	21a07									21 07				21 29				
Twyford [3]	d		20 40			20 54											21 13								
Maidenhead [3]	d		20 48			21 02											21 21								
Taplow	d					21 06																			
Burnham	d					21 09							←												
Slough [3]	a		20 55			21 13	21 09						21 13				21 28				21 43				
	d		20 56			21 16	21 11						21 16				21 29				21 45				
Langley	d		21 00			→											21 33								
Iver	d		21 03														21 36								
West Drayton	d		21 07										21 23				21 40								
Heathrow Terminal 5 ⊖ ✈	a																								
	d										21 12			21 27						21 42			21 57		
Heathrow Terminal 4 ⊖ ✈	a																								
	d	20 52								21 11						21 22			21 41					21 52	
Heathrow Termls 2 & 3 [2] ⊖ ✈	a	20 56								21 15	21 16			21 31		21 26			21 45	21 46			22 01	21 56	
	d	20 58									21 18			21 33		21 28				21 48			22 03	21 58	
Hayes & Harlington	d	21 03	21 11									21 19	21 27			21 33	21 44					21 47		22 03	
Southall	d	21 07	21 15									21 23				21 37	21 48					21 51		22 07	
Hanwell	d	21 10														21 40								22 10	
Greenford ⊖	d								21 04									21 35							
South Greenford	d								21 07									21 38							
Castle Bar Park	d								21 10									21 41							
Drayton Green	d								21 12									21 43							
West Ealing	d	21 12							21a15			21 28				21 42		21a46				21 56		22 12	
Ealing Broadway ⊖	d	21 15	21 20									21 31	21 34			21 45	21 53					21 59		22 15	
Acton Main Line	d											21 34										22 02			
London Paddington [15] ⊖	a	21 26	21 31				21 29				21 34	21 44	21 46	21 49		21 56	22 02			22 04	22 06	22 12	22 19	22 26	

		GW	GW	XC	GW	GW	XR	HX	XR	GW		XR	GW	GW	GW	HX	XR	HX	XR	GW		XC	GW	HX	GW
					FO	FX							FO	FX									FO		FX
				◇1	◇1 🛒	◇1 🛒		◇1							◇1 ☕	◇1		◇1				◇1		◇1	
Oxford	d			21 16	21 31	21 31																21 43	22 01		22 01
Reading [7]	d	21 29	21 37	21a42	21 57	21 57							22 01	22 01	22 03					22 15		22a16	22 34		22 37
Twyford [3]	d	21 35	21 43										22 07	22 07						22 21					
Maidenhead [3]	d	21 43	21 51										22 15	22 15						22 29					
Taplow	d	21 47											22 19	22 19						22 33					
Burnham	d	21 50											22 22	22 22						22 36					
Slough [3]	a	21 54	21 58		22 11	22 11							22 26	22 27						22 40			22 50		23 02
	d	21 55	21 59		22 12	22 12							22 35	22 35						22 41			22 51		23 03
Langley	d		22 03										22 39	22 39						22 45					
Iver	d		22 06										22 42	22 42						22 48					
West Drayton	d	22 04	22 10										22 46	22 46						22 52					
Heathrow Terminal 5 ⊖ ✈	a																								
	d							22 12								22 27		22 42						22 57	
Heathrow Terminal 4 ⊖ ✈	a																								
	d						22 11					22 22					22 41								
Heathrow Termls 2 & 3 [2] ⊖ ✈	a						22 15	22 16				22 26				22 31	22 45	22 46						23 01	
	d							22 18				22 28				22 33		22 48						23 03	
Hayes & Harlington	d	22 10	22 14						22 21			22 33	22 50	22 50					22 53	22 56					
Southall	d		22 18						22 24			22 37	22 54	22 54						23 00					
Hanwell	d											22 40													
Greenford ⊖	d									22 17															
South Greenford	d									22 20															
Castle Bar Park	d									22 24															
Drayton Green	d									22 27															
West Ealing	d									22 30		22 42													
Ealing Broadway ⊖	d	22 19	22 23						22 31	22 33		22 45	22 59	22 59						23 05					
Acton Main Line	d								22 34											23 09					
London Paddington [15] ⊖	a	22 28	22 31		22 29	22 31		22 34	22 44	22 44		22 56	23 08	23 08	22 37	22 49		23 04	23 14	23 16			23 08	23 19	23 23

For non-stop services between Reading and London refer to Table T116

For non-stop services between London and Heathrow Airport see Table T118

For Heathrow Express Services see Table T118

Table T117-R

Mondays to Fridays

21 May to 7 December

Reading, Heathrow Airport and Greenford - London

Stopping Services

		GW		XC	GW	GW	XR	GW	XR	HX	GW	XR		HX	XR	GW	GW	XR	HX	XR	GW	GW		GW	XC
					FO	FX		FO			FX					FX	FO					FX		FO	
				◇1				◇1		◇1	◇1			◇1					◇1						◇1
Oxford	d	22 09		22 16				22 31			22 31											23 01		23 01	23 16
Reading [7]	d	22a54		22a42	22 48	22 48		22 59			22 59										23 14	23 37		23 37	23a49
Twyford [3]	d				22 54	22 54															23 20				
Maidenhead [3]	d				23 02	23 02															23 28	23 49		23 49	
Taplow	d				23 06	23 06															23 32				
Burnham	d				23 09	23 09										←	←				23 35				
Slough [3]	a				23 13	23 14		23 12			23 16					23 14	23 13				23 39	23 55		23 55	
	d				23 27	23 27		23 13			23 17					23 27	23 27				23 40	23 57		23 57	
Langley	d				→	→										23 31	23 31				23 44				
Iver	d															23 34	23 34				23 47				
West Drayton	d															23 38	23 38				23 51				
Heathrow Terminal 5 ⊖ ✈	a																								
	d									23 12				23 27					23 42						
Heathrow Terminal 4 ⊖ ✈	a																								
	d						22 52		23 11						23 22			23 41							
Heathrow Termls 2 & 3 [2] ⊖ ✈	a						22 56		23 15	23 16				23 31	23 26			23 45	23 46						
	d						22 58			23 18				23 33	23 28				23 48						
Hayes & Harlington	d						23 03					23 18			23 33	23 42	23 43			23 47	23 55				
Southall	d						23 07					23 22			23 37	23 46	23 46			23 51	23 59				
Hanwell	d						23 10								23 40										
Greenford ⊖	d																								
South Greenford	d																								
Castle Bar Park	d																								
Drayton Green	d																								
West Ealing	d						23 12					23 26			23 42					23 56					
Ealing Broadway ⊖	d						23 15					23 29			23 45	23 52	23 52			23 59	00 05				
Acton Main Line	d											23 32								00 02					
London Paddington [15] ⊖	a						23 26	23 30		23 34	23 36	23 42		23 49	23 56	00 01	00 01		00 05	00 12	00 14	00 21		00 22	

		HX	XR
Oxford	d		
Reading [7]	d		
Twyford [3]	d		
Maidenhead [3]	d		
Taplow	d		
Burnham	d		
Slough [3]	a		
	d		
Langley	d		
Iver	d		
West Drayton	d		
Heathrow Terminal 5 ⊖ ✈	a		
	d	23 51	
Heathrow Terminal 4 ⊖ ✈	a		
	d		23 57
Heathrow Termls 2 & 3 [2] ⊖ ✈	a	23 55	00 01
	d		00 03
Hayes & Harlington	d		00 08
Southall	d		00 12
Hanwell	d		
Greenford ⊖	d		
South Greenford	d		
Castle Bar Park	d		
Drayton Green	d		
West Ealing	d		
Ealing Broadway ⊖	d		00 17
Acton Main Line	d		
London Paddington [15] ⊖	a		00 26

For non-stop services between Reading and London refer to Table T116

For non-stop services between London and Heathrow Airport see Table T118

For Heathrow Express Services see Table T118

Table T117-R

Saturdays
26 May to 8 December

Reading, Heathrow Airport and Greenford - London

Stopping Services

		XR	GW	XR	XR	GW		GW ◇1	GW	GW	GW	GW	GW	HX ◇1	HX ◇1	XR		XR	HX ◇1	XR	GW	HX ◇1	XR	GW	XR
Oxford	d							00 07	00 27			04 00													
Reading	d					00 14		00 41	01a14	01 15	04 12	04a29	04 40								05 10			05 33	
Twyford	d					00 20				01 21	04 18		04 46								05 16			05 39	
Maidenhead	d					00 28				01 29	04 26		04 54								05 24			05 47	
Taplow	d					00 32															05 27				
Burnham	d					00 35															05 30				
Slough	a					00 39		00 57		01 36	04 33		05 01								05 35			05 54	
	d					00 40		00 58		01 37	04 34		05 02								05 36			05 55	
Langley	d					00 44															05 39			05 58	
Iver	d																				05 42			06 01	
West Drayton	d					00 49					04 40										05 46			06 05	
Heathrow Terminal 5 ⊖ ✈	a																								
	d													05 12	05 27				05 42			05 57			
Heathrow Terminal 4 ⊖ ✈	a																								
	d				00 07											05 22		05 41					05 52		06 11
Heathrow Termls 2 & 3 ⊖ ✈	a				00 11									05 16	05 31	05 26		05 45	05 46			06 01	05 56		06 15
	d			00 03	00 13									05 17	05 33	05 28			05 48			06 03	05 58		
Hayes & Harlington	d			00 08	00 18	00 53				01 46	04 45		05 10			05 33				05 47	05 51		06 03	06 10	
Southall	d			00 12	00 22	00 57					04 49		05 14			05 37				05 51	05 55		06 07	06 14	
Hanwell	d															05 40							06 10		
Greenford ⊖	d																								
South Greenford	d																								
Castle Bar Park	d																								
Drayton Green	d																								
West Ealing	d															05 42				05 56			06 12		
Ealing Broadway ⊖	d		00 05	00 17	00 27	01 02				01 52	04 54		05 19			05 45				05 59	06 03		06 15	06 19	
Acton Main Line	d	00 02											05 23							06 02	06 06				
London Paddington ⊖	a	00 12	00 14	00 26	00 39	01 11		01 18		02 01	05 06		05 32	05 33	05 49	05 55			06 04	06 12	06 14	06 19	06 26	06 29	

		GW		HX ◇1	XR	GW	GW	HX ◇1	XR	GW	XR	GW		HX ◇1	XR	GW	HX ◇1	XR	GW	XR	GW	GW		GW ◇	HX ◇1
Oxford	d						05 14																	06 31	
Reading	d					05 48	05a57			06 05						06 18			06 33			06 48		06 57	
Twyford	d					05 54				06 11						06 24			06 39			06 54			
Maidenhead	d					06 02				06 19						06 32			06 47			07 02			
Taplow	d					06 05										06 35						07 05			
Burnham	d					06 08										06 38						07 08			
Slough	a					06 13				06 26						06 43			06 54			07 13		07 11	
	d					06 14				06 27						06 44			06 55			07 17		07 12	
Langley	d									06 30									06 58			→			
Iver	d									06 33									07 01						
West Drayton	d					06 20				06 37						06 50			07 05						
Heathrow Terminal 5 ⊖ ✈	a																								
	d			06 12				06 27						06 42			06 57								07 12
Heathrow Terminal 4 ⊖ ✈	a																								
	d								06 22		06 41							06 52		07 11					
Heathrow Termls 2 & 3 ⊖ ✈	a			06 16				06 31	06 26		06 45			06 46			07 01	06 56		07 15					07 16
	d			06 18				06 33	06 28					06 48			07 03	06 58							07 18
Hayes & Harlington	d				06 17	06 25			06 33	06 42					06 47	06 55		07 03	07 10						
Southall	d				06 21				06 37	06 45					06 51			07 08	07 14						
Hanwell	d								06 40									07 11							
Greenford ⊖	d	06 12										06 42									07 12				
South Greenford	d	06 15										06 45									07 15				
Castle Bar Park	d	06 18										06 48									07 18				
Drayton Green	d	06 20										06 50									07 20				
West Ealing	d	06a23			06 26				06 42			06a53			06 56			07 13			07a23				
Ealing Broadway ⊖	d				06 29	06 33			06 45	06 51					06 59	07 03		07 16	07 19						
Acton Main Line	d				06 32										07 02										
London Paddington ⊖	a			06 34	06 42	06 46		06 49	06 56	07 01				07 04	07 12	07 16	07 19	07 26	07 31					07 30	07 34

For non-stop services between Reading and London refer to Table T116

For non-stop services between London and Heathrow Airport see Table T118

For Heathrow Express Services see Table T118

Table T117-R

Saturdays
26 May to 8 December

Reading, Heathrow Airport and Greenford - London

Stopping Services

		XR	GW	HX ◇1		XR	GW	XR	GW	GW	GW ◇1	HX ◇1	XR	GW		HX ◇1	XR	GW	XC ◇1	GW	GW ◇1	XR	GW	HX ◇1	
Oxford	d										07 01								07 16		07 31				
Reading	d						07 03			07 18	07 25							07 33	07a41	07 48	07 55				
Twyford	d						07 09			07 24								07 39		07 54					
Maidenhead	d						07 17			07 32								07 47		08 02					
Taplow	d									07 35										08 05					
Burnham	d		←							07 38				←						08 08					
Slough	a		07 13				07 24			07 43	07 38			07 43				07 54		08 13	08 08				
	d		07 17				07 25			07 47	07 39			07 47				07 55		08 17	08 09				
Langley	d						07 28			→								07 58		→					
Iver	d						07 31											08 01							
West Drayton	d		07 23				07 35							07 53				08 05							
Heathrow Terminal 5 ⊖ ✈	a																								
	d			07 27								07 42				07 57								08 12	
Heathrow Terminal 4 ⊖ ✈	a																								
	d					07 22		07 41									07 52					08 11			
Heathrow Termls 2 & 3 ⊖ ✈	a			07 31		07 26		07 45				07 46				08 01	07 56					08 15		08 16	
	d			07 33		07 28						07 48				08 03	07 58							08 18	
Hayes & Harlington	d	07 17	07 28			07 33	07 40						07 47	07 58			08 03	08 10							
Southall	d	07 21				07 37	07 44						07 51				08 07	08 14							
Hanwell	d					07 40											08 10								
Greenford ⊖	d								07 42														08 12		
South Greenford	d								07 45														08 15		
Castle Bar Park	d								07 48														08 18		
Drayton Green	d								07 50														08 20		
West Ealing	d	07 26				07 42			07a53				07 56				08 12						08a23		
Ealing Broadway ⊖	d	07 29	07 35			07 45	07 49						07 59	08 05			08 15	08 19							
Acton Main Line	d	07 32											08 02												
London Paddington ⊖	a	07 42	07 43	07 49		07 56	08 01				07 56	08 04	08 12	08 16		08 19	08 26	08 31			08 27			08 34	

		XR	GW	HX ◇1	XR	GW	XC ◇1	GW	GW ◇1	XR		GW	HX ◇1	XR	GW	HX ◇1	XR	GW	XC ◇1	GW		GW ◇1	XR	GW	HX ◇1
Oxford	d						07 43		08 01										08 16			08 30			
Reading	d					08 03	08a09	08 18	08 25									08 33	08a41	08 48		08 57			
Twyford	d					08 09		08 24										08 39		08 54					
Maidenhead	d					08 17		08 32										08 47		09 02					
Taplow	d							08 35												09 05					
Burnham	d		←					08 38							←					09 08					
Slough	a		08 13			08 24		08 43	08 38						08 43			08 54		09 13		09 10			
	d		08 17			08 25		08 44	08 39						08 44			08 55		09 14		09 11			
Langley	d					08 28		→										08 58		→					
Iver	d					08 31												09 01							
West Drayton	d		08 23			08 35									08 50			09 05							
Heathrow Terminal 5 ⊖ ✈	a																								
	d			08 27									08 42			08 57									09 12
Heathrow Terminal 4 ⊖ ✈	a																								
	d				08 22					08 41							08 52						09 11		
Heathrow Termls 2 & 3 ⊖ ✈	a			08 31	08 26					08 45			08 46			09 01	08 56						09 15		09 16
	d			08 33	08 28								08 48			09 03	08 58								09 18
Hayes & Harlington	d	08 17	08 28		08 33	08 40								08 47	08 55		09 03	09 10							
Southall	d	08 21			08 37	08 44								08 51			09 07	09 14							
Hanwell	d				08 40												09 10								
Greenford ⊖	d											08 42												09 12	
South Greenford	d											08 45												09 15	
Castle Bar Park	d											08 48												09 18	
Drayton Green	d											08 50												09 20	
West Ealing	d	08 26			08 42							08a53		08 56			09 12							09a23	
Ealing Broadway ⊖	d	08 29	08 35		08 45	08 49								08 59	09 03		09 15	09 19							
Acton Main Line	d	08 32												09 02											
London Paddington ⊖	a	08 42	08 46	08 49	08 56	09 01			08 56				09 04	09 12	09 13	09 19	09 26	09 31				09 28			09 34

For non-stop services between Reading and London refer to Table T116

For non-stop services between London and Heathrow Airport see Table T118

For Heathrow Express Services see Table T118

Table T117-R

Reading, Heathrow Airport and Greenford - London

Stopping Services

		XR		GW	XR	GW	XC ◇1 ✕	GW ◇1 ⊏	HX ◇1	XR	GW	GW		GW ◇1	HX ◇1	XR	GW	HX ◇1	XR	GW	XC ◇1 A ✕	XC ◇1 B		GW	GW ◇1 ⊏
Oxford	d						08 43							08 58							09⟆16	09⟆16			09 29
Reading 7	d					09 03	09a09	09 11				09 18		09 25						09 33	09a40	09a40		09 48	09 53
Twyford 3	d					09 09						09 24								09 39				09 54	
Maidenhead 3	d					09 17						09 32								09 47				10 02	
Taplow	d											09 35												10 05	
Burnham	d			←								09 38					←							10 08	
Slough 3	a			09 13		09 24						09 43		09 38			09 43			09 54				10 13	10 06
	d			09 14		09 25						09 44		09 39			09 44			09 55				10 14	10 07
Langley	d					09 28						→								09 58				→	
Iver	d					09 31														10 01					
West Drayton	d			09 20		09 35											09 50			10 05					
Heathrow Terminal 5 ⊖ ✈	a																								
	d								09 27						09 42			09 57							
Heathrow Terminal 4 ⊖ ✈	a																								
	d				09 22					09 41									09 52						
Heathrow Termls 2 & 3 2 ⊖ ✈	a				09 26				09 31	09 45					09 46			10 01	09 56						
	d				09 28				09 33						09 48			10 03	09 58						
Hayes & Harlington	d	09 17		09 25	09 33	09 40										09 47	09 55		10 03	10 10					
Southall	d	09 21			09 37	09 44										09 51			10 07	10 14					
Hanwell	d				09 40														10 10						
Greenford ⊖	d										09 42														
South Greenford	d										09 45														
Castle Bar Park	d										09 48														
Drayton Green	d										09 50														
West Ealing	d	09 26			09 42						09a53					09 56			10 12						
Ealing Broadway ⊖	d	09 29		09 33	09 46	09 49										09 59	10 03		10 16	10 19					
Acton Main Line	d	09 32														10 02									
London Paddington 15 ⊖	a	09 42		09 46	09 56	10 01		09 41	09 49					09 56	10 04	10 12	10 16	10 19	10 26	10 31					10 24

		XR	GW	HX ◇1	XR	GW	HX ◇1	XR		GW	XC ◇1 ✕	GW	GW ◇	XR	GW	HX ◇1	XR	GW		XR	GW	XC ◇1 ✕	GW ◇1 ⊏	HX ◇1	XR
Oxford	d										09 43		10 00									10 16			
Reading 7	d									10 03	10a08	10 18	10 25								10 33	10a41	10 41		
Twyford 3	d									10 09		10 24									10 39				
Maidenhead 3	d									10 17		10 32									10 47				
Taplow	d											10 35													
Burnham	d					←						10 38						←							
Slough 3	a					10 13				10 24		10 43	10 39					10 43			10 54				
	d					10 14				10 25		10 44	10 40					10 44			10 55				
Langley	d									10 28		→									10 58				
Iver	d									10 31											11 01				
West Drayton	d					10 20				10 35								10 50			11 05				
Heathrow Terminal 5 ⊖ ✈	a																								
	d			10 12			10 27									10 42								10 57	
Heathrow Terminal 4 ⊖ ✈	a																								
	d	10 11						10 22						10 41						10 52					11 11
Heathrow Termls 2 & 3 2 ⊖ ✈	a	10 15		10 16			10 31	10 26						10 45		10 46				10 56				11 01	11 15
	d			10 18			10 33	10 28								10 48				10 58				11 03	
Hayes & Harlington	d				10 17	10 25		10 33		10 40							10 47	10 55		11 03	11 10				
Southall	d				10 21			10 37		10 44							10 51			11 07	11 14				
Hanwell	d							10 40												11 10					
Greenford ⊖	d		10 12												10 42										
South Greenford	d		10 15												10 45										
Castle Bar Park	d		10 18												10 48										
Drayton Green	d		10 20												10 50										
West Ealing	d		10a23		10 26			10 42							10a53		10 56			11 12					
Ealing Broadway ⊖	d				10 29	10 33		10 45		10 49							10 59	11 03		11 16	11 19				
Acton Main Line	d				10 32												11 02								
London Paddington 15 ⊖	a			10 34	10 42	10 46	10 49	10 56		11 01			10 58			11 05	11 12	11 16		11 26	11 31		11 07	11 19	

A until 21 July, from 8 September   B from 28 July until 1 September

For non-stop services between Reading and London refer to Table T116

For non-stop services between London and Heathrow Airport see Table T118

For Heathrow Express Services see Table T118

Table T117-R

Reading, Heathrow Airport and Greenford - London

Stopping Services

		GW	GW	GW ◇1 A ⊏	GW ◇1 B ⊏	HX ◇1	XR	GW	HX ◇1	XR		GW	XC ◇1 ✕	GW	GW ◇1	XR	GW	HX ◇1	XR	GW		HX ◇1	XR	GW	XC ◇1 ✕
Oxford	d			10⟆31	10⟆31								10 43		11 01										11 16
Reading 7	d		10 48	10⟆57	10⟆57							11 03	11a10	11 18	11 25									11 33	11a38
Twyford 3	d		10 54									11 09		11 24										11 39	
Maidenhead 3	d		11 02									11 17		11 32										11 47	
Taplow	d		11 05											11 35											
Burnham	d		11 08					←						11 38						←					
Slough 3	a		11 13	11⟆10	11⟆10			11 13				11 24		11 43	11 38					11 43				11 54	
	d		11 14	11⟆11	11⟆11			11 14				11 25		11 47	11 39					11 47				11 55	
Langley	d		→									11 28		→										11 58	
Iver	d											11 31												12 01	
West Drayton	d							11 20				11 35								11 53				12 05	
Heathrow Terminal 5 ⊖ ✈	a																								
	d					11 12			11 27									11 42				11 57			
Heathrow Terminal 4 ⊖ ✈	a																								
	d									11 22						11 41							11 52		
Heathrow Termls 2 & 3 2 ⊖ ✈	a					11 16			11 31	11 26						11 45		11 46				12 01	11 56		
	d					11 18			11 33	11 28								11 48				12 03	11 58		
Hayes & Harlington	d						11 17	11 25		11 33		11 40							11 47	11 58			12 03	12 10	
Southall	d						11 21			11 37		11 44							11 51				12 08	12 14	
Hanwell	d									11 40													12 11		
Greenford ⊖	d	11 12															11 42								
South Greenford	d	11 15															11 45								
Castle Bar Park	d	11 18															11 48								
Drayton Green	d	11 20															11 50								
West Ealing	d	11a23					11 26			11 42							11a53		11 56				12 13		
Ealing Broadway ⊖	d						11 29	11 33		11 45		11 49							11 59	12 05			12 16	12 19	
Acton Main Line	d						11 32												12 02						
London Paddington 15 ⊖	a			11⟆28	11⟆29	11 35	11 42	11 46	11 49	11 56		12 01			11 59			12 04	12 12	12 16		12 19	12 26	12 31	

		GW	GW ◇1 ⊏	XR	GW	HX ◇1		XR	GW	HX ◇1	XR	GW	XC ◇1 ✕	GW	GW ◇1	XR		HX ◇1	XR	GW	GW	XR	GW	GW ◇1 ⊏	XC ◇1 ✕
Oxford	d		11 31										11 43		12 01										12 17
Reading 7	d	11 48	11 55									12 03	12a06	12 18	12 25								12 33	12 41	12a42
Twyford 3	d	11 54										12 09		12 24									12 39		
Maidenhead 3	d	12 02										12 17		12 32									12 47		
Taplow	d	12 05												12 35											
Burnham	d	12 08							←					12 38						←					
Slough 3	a	12 13	12 08						12 13			12 24		12 43	12 38					12 43			12 54		
	d	12 14	12 09						12 14			12 25		12 44	12 39					12 44			12 55		
Langley	d	→										12 28		→									12 58		
Iver	d											12 31											13 01		
West Drayton	d								12 20			12 35								12 50			13 05		
Heathrow Terminal 5 ⊖ ✈	a																								
	d					12 12				12 27								12 42							
Heathrow Terminal 4 ⊖ ✈	a																								
	d			12 11							12 22					12 41						12 52			
Heathrow Termls 2 & 3 2 ⊖ ✈	a			12 15		12 16				12 31	12 26					12 45		12 46				12 56			
	d					12 18				12 33	12 28							12 48				12 58			
Hayes & Harlington	d							12 17	12 25		12 33	12 40							12 47	12 55		13 03	13 10		
Southall	d							12 21			12 37	12 44							12 51			13 07	13 14		
Hanwell	d										12 40											13 10			
Greenford ⊖	d				12 12																12 46				
South Greenford	d				12 15																12 49				
Castle Bar Park	d				12 18																12 52				
Drayton Green	d				12 20																12 54				
West Ealing	d				12a23			12 26			12 42								12 56		12a57	13 12			
Ealing Broadway ⊖	d							12 29	12 33		12 45	12 49							12 59	13 03		13 15	13 19		
Acton Main Line	d							12 32											13 02						
London Paddington 15 ⊖	a		12 26			12 34		12 42	12 46	12 49	12 56	13 01			12 56			13 04	13 12	13 16		13 26	13 31	13 07	

A until 8 September   B from 15 September

For non-stop services between Reading and London refer to Table T116

For non-stop services between London and Heathrow Airport see Table T118

For Heathrow Express Services see Table T118

Reading, Heathrow Airport and Greenford - London

Stopping Services

		GW	HX	GW	XR	HX	XR	GW		GW	HX	XR	GW	XC	GW	GW	XR	HX		XR	GW	GW	HX	XR	GW
			◇■	◇■		◇■					◇■			◇■		◇■		◇■					◇■		
				🛒										✠											
Oxford	d			12 31										12 43		13 01									
Reading ■	d	12 48		12 57									13 03	13a09	13 18	13 25									13 33
Twyford ■	d	12 54											13 09		13 24										13 39
Maidenhead ■	d	13 02											13 17		13 32										13 47
Taplow	d	13 05													13 35										
Burnham	d	13 08						←							13 38						←				
Slough ■	a	13 13		13 10				13 13					13 24		13 43	13 38					13 43				13 54
	d	13 14		13 11				13 14					13 25		13 44	13 39					13 44				13 55
Langley	d	→											13 28		→										13 58
Iver	d												13 31												14 01
West Drayton	d							13 20					13 35								13 50				14 05
Heathrow Terminal 5 ⊖ ✈	a																								
	d		12 57			13 12					13 27							13 42					13 57		
Heathrow Terminal 4 ⊖ ✈	a																								
	d				13 11							13 22					13 41							13 52	
Heathrow Termls 2 & 3 ■ ⊖ ✈	a		13 01		13 15	13 16					13 31	13 26					13 45	13 46					14 01	13 56	
	d		13 03			13 18					13 33	13 28						13 48					14 03	13 58	
Hayes & Harlington	d						13 17	13 25				13 33	13 40							13 47	13 55			14 03	14 10
Southall	d						13 21					13 37	13 44							13 51				14 07	14 14
Hanwell	d											13 40												14 10	
Greenford ⊖	d									13 16												13 46			
South Greenford	d									13 19												13 49			
Castle Bar Park	d									13 22												13 52			
Drayton Green	d									13 24												13 54			
West Ealing	d						13 26			13a27		13 42								13 56		13a57		14 12	
Ealing Broadway ⊖	d						13 29	13 33				13 46	13 49							13 59	14 03			14 15	14 19
Acton Main Line	d						13 32													14 02					
London Paddington ■ ⊖	a		13 19	13 28		13 35	13 42	13 46			13 49	13 56	14 01			13 56		14 04		14 12	14 16		14 19	14 26	14 31

		XC	GW	GW		XR	HX	XR	GW	GW	XR	GW	XC	GW		HX	XR	GW	GW	HX	XR	GW	GW	XR	
		◇■		◇■			◇■						◇■	◇■		◇■			◇	◇■					
														A											
		✠		🛒									✠	🛒											
Oxford	d	13 16		13 30									13 43						14 03						
Reading ■	d	13a40	13 48	13 54								14 03	14a08	14 12				14 18	14 28						
Twyford ■	d		13 54									14 09						14 24							
Maidenhead ■	d		14 02									14 17						14 32							
Taplow	d		14 05															14 35							
Burnham	d		14 08						←									14 38				←			
Slough ■	a		14 13	14 07					14 13			14 24						14 43	14 42			14 43			
	d		14 14	14 08					14 14			14 25						14 44	14 43			14 44			
Langley	d		→									14 28						→							
Iver	d											14 31													
West Drayton	d								14 20			14 35										14 50			
Heathrow Terminal 5 ⊖ ✈	a																								
	d						14 12									14 27				14 42					
Heathrow Terminal 4 ⊖ ✈	a																								
	d					14 11					14 22						14 41							14 52	
Heathrow Termls 2 & 3 ■ ⊖ ✈	a					14 15	14 16				14 26					14 31	14 45			14 46				14 56	
	d						14 18				14 28					14 33				14 48				14 58	
Hayes & Harlington	d							14 17	14 25		14 33	14 40									14 47	14 55		15 03	
Southall	d							14 21			14 37	14 44									14 51			15 07	
Hanwell	d										14 40													15 10	
Greenford ⊖	d									14 16													14 46		
South Greenford	d									14 19													14 49		
Castle Bar Park	d									14 22													14 52		
Drayton Green	d									14 24													14 54		
West Ealing	d							14 26		14a27	14 42										14 56		14a57	15 12	
Ealing Broadway ⊖	d							14 29	14 33		14 45	14 49									14 59	15 03		15 15	
Acton Main Line	d							14 32													15 02				
London Paddington ■ ⊖	a			14 25			14 34	14 42	14 46		14 56	15 01		14 38		14 49			15 01	15 04	15 12	15 16		15 26	

A from 15 September

For non-stop services between Reading and London refer to Table T116

For non-stop services between London and Heathrow Airport see Table T118

For Heathrow Express Services see Table T118

Table T117-R

Saturdays
26 May to 8 December

Reading, Heathrow Airport and Greenford - London

Stopping Services

		GW	GW	XC	GW	HX		GW	GW	XR	HX	XR	GW	GW	HX	XR		GW	XC	GW	GW	XR	HX	XR	GW
			◇■	◇■		◇■		◇■	◇■		◇■				◇■				◇■		◇■		◇■		
								A	B																
			🛒	✠				🛒	🛒										✠						
Oxford	d			14 16				14 30	14 30										14 43		15 01				
Reading ■	d	14 33	14 40	14a41	14 48			14 55	14 58									15 03	15a08	15 18	15 25				
Twyford ■	d	14 39			14 54													15 09		15 24					
Maidenhead ■	d	14 47			15 02													15 17		15 32					
Taplow	d				15 05															15 35					
Burnham	d				15 08								←							15 38					←
Slough ■	a	14 54			15 13			15 08	15 11				15 13					15 24		15 43	15 38				15 43
	d	14 55			15 17			15 09	15 12				15 17					15 25		15 44	15 39				15 44
Langley	d	14 58			→													15 28		→					
Iver	d	15 01																15 31							
West Drayton	d	15 05											15 23					15 35							15 50
Heathrow Terminal 5 ⊖ ✈	a																								
	d					14 57					15 12				15 27								15 42		
Heathrow Terminal 4 ⊖ ✈	a																								
	d									15 11						15 22						15 41			
Heathrow Termls 2 & 3 ■ ⊖ ✈	a					15 01				15 15	15 16				15 31	15 26						15 45	15 46		
	d					15 03					15 18				15 33	15 28							15 48		
Hayes & Harlington	d	15 10										15 17	15 28			15 33		15 40						15 47	15 55
Southall	d	15 14										15 21				15 37		15 44						15 51	
Hanwell	d															15 40									
Greenford ⊖	d													15 16											
South Greenford	d													15 19											
Castle Bar Park	d													15 22											
Drayton Green	d													15 24											
West Ealing	d											15 26		15a27		15 42								15 56	
Ealing Broadway ⊖	d	15 19										15 29	15 35			15 45		15 49						15 59	16 03
Acton Main Line	d											15 32												16 02	
London Paddington ■ ⊖	a	15 31	15 07			15 19		15 26	15 29		15 34	15 42	15 46		15 49	15 56		16 01			15 59		16 04	16 12	16 16

		GW		HX	XR	GW	XC	GW	GW	XR	HX	XR		GW	GW	HX	XR	GW	XC	GW	GW	XR		HX	XR
				◇■			◇■		◇■		◇■					◇■			◇■		◇■			◇■	
							✠		🛒										✠						
Oxford	d						15 16		15 31										15 43		16 01				
Reading ■	d					15 33	15a40	15 48	15 55									16 03	16a09	16 18	16 25				
Twyford ■	d					15 39		15 54										16 09		16 24					
Maidenhead ■	d					15 47		16 02										16 17		16 32					
Taplow	d							16 05												16 35					
Burnham	d							16 08						←						16 38					
Slough ■	a					15 54		16 13	16 08					16 13				16 24		16 43	16 38				
	d					15 55		16 14	16 09					16 14				16 25		16 44	16 39				
Langley	d					15 58		→										16 28		→					
Iver	d					16 01												16 31							
West Drayton	d					16 05								16 20				16 35							
Heathrow Terminal 5 ⊖ ✈	a																								
	d			15 57							16 12					16 27								16 42	
Heathrow Terminal 4 ⊖ ✈	a																								
	d				15 52					16 11							16 22					16 41			
Heathrow Termls 2 & 3 ■ ⊖ ✈	a			16 01	15 56					16 15	16 16					16 31	16 26					16 45		16 46	
	d			16 03	15 58						16 18					16 33	16 28							16 48	
Hayes & Harlington	d				16 03	16 10						16 17		16 25			16 33	16 40							16 47
Southall	d				16 07	16 14						16 21					16 37	16 44							16 51
Hanwell	d				16 10												16 40								
Greenford ⊖	d	15 46													16 16										
South Greenford	d	15 49													16 19										
Castle Bar Park	d	15 52													16 22										
Drayton Green	d	15 54													16 24										
West Ealing	d	15a57			16 12							16 26			16a27		16 42								16 56
Ealing Broadway ⊖	d				16 15	16 19						16 29		16 33			16 45	16 49							16 59
Acton Main Line	d											16 32													17 02
London Paddington ■ ⊖	a			16 19	16 26	16 31			16 26		16 35	16 42		16 46		16 49	16 56	17 01			16 57			17 04	17 12

A from 15 September
B until 8 September

For non-stop services between Reading and London refer to Table T116

For non-stop services between London and Heathrow Airport see Table T118

For Heathrow Express Services see Table T118

Table T117-R

Saturdays
26 May to 8 December

Reading, Heathrow Airport and Greenford - London
Stopping Services

	GW	GW	XR		GW	GW	XC	GW	HX	GW	XR	HX	XR		GW	GW	XR	GW	XC	GW	HX	XR	GW
						◇1	◇1		◇1	◇1		◇1							◇1	◇1 A	◇1		
Oxford d							16 16			16 31									16 43				
Reading d					16 33	16 40	16a42	16 48		16 55								17 03	17a10	17 14			17 18
Twyford d					16 39			16 54										17 09					17 24
Maidenhead d					16 47			17 02										17 17					17 32
Taplow d								17 05															17 35
Burnham d	←							17 08							←								17 38
Slough a	16 43				16 54			17 13		17 08					17 13			17 24					17 43
Slough d	16 44				16 55			17 14		17 09					17 14			17 25					17 44
Langley d					16 58			→										17 28					→
Iver d					17 01													17 31					
West Drayton d	16 50				17 05										17 20			17 35					
Heathrow Terminal 5 a																							
Heathrow Terminal 5 d									16 57			17 12									17 27		
Heathrow Terminal 4 a																							
Heathrow Terminal 4 d			16 52								17 11						17 22					17 41	
Heathrow Termls 2 & 3 a			16 56						17 01		17 15	17 16					17 26				17 31	17 45	
Heathrow Termls 2 & 3 d			16 58						17 03			17 18					17 28				17 33		
Hayes & Harlington d	16 55		17 03		17 10								17 17		17 25		17 33	17 40					
Southall d			17 07		17 14								17 21				17 37	17 44					
Hanwell d			17 10														17 40						
Greenford d		16 46														17 16							
South Greenford d		16 49														17 19							
Castle Bar Park d		16 52														17 22							
Drayton Green d		16 54														17 24							
West Ealing d		16a57	17 12										17 26			17a27	17 42						
Ealing Broadway d	17 03		17 15		17 19								17 29		17 33		17 45	17 49					
Acton Main Line d													17 32										
London Paddington a	17 16		17 26		17 31	17 07			17 19	17 26		17 34	17 42		17 46		17 56	18 01		17 44	17 49		

	GW	HX	XR	GW	GW	HX	XR	GW	XC		GW	GW	GW	XR	HX	XR	GW	GW	HX		XR	GW	XC	GW
	◇1	◇1				◇1			◇1			◇1 A	◇1 B		◇1				◇1				◇1	
Oxford d	17 02								17 16			17 31	17 31										17 43	
Reading d	17 29							17 33	17a39		17 48	17 56	17 58									18 03	18a10	18 18
Twyford d								17 39			17 54											18 09		18 24
Maidenhead d								17 47			18 02											18 17		18 32
Taplow d											18 05													18 35
Burnham d				←							18 08						←							18 38
Slough a	17 42			17 43				17 54			18 13	18 09	18 11				18 13					18 24		18 43
Slough d	17 43			17 44				17 55			18 14	18 10	18 12				18 14					18 25		18 44
Langley d								17 58			→											18 28		→
Iver d								18 01														18 31		
West Drayton d				17 50				18 05									18 20					18 35		
Heathrow Terminal 5 a																								
Heathrow Terminal 5 d		17 42				17 57									18 12				18 27					
Heathrow Terminal 4 a																								
Heathrow Terminal 4 d							17 52							18 11							18 22			
Heathrow Termls 2 & 3 a		17 46				18 01	17 56							18 15	18 16				18 31		18 26			
Heathrow Termls 2 & 3 d		17 48				18 03	17 58								18 18				18 33		18 28			
Hayes & Harlington d			17 47	17 55			18 03	18 10								18 17	18 25				18 33	18 40		
Southall d			17 51				18 07	18 14								18 21					18 37	18 44		
Hanwell d							18 10														18 40			
Greenford d					17 46													18 16						
South Greenford d					17 49													18 19						
Castle Bar Park d					17 52													18 22						
Drayton Green d					17 54													18 24						
West Ealing d			17 56		17a57		18 12									18 26		18a27			18 42			
Ealing Broadway d			17 59	18 03			18 15	18 19								18 29	18 33				18 45	18 49		
Acton Main Line d			18 02													18 32								
London Paddington a	18 00	18 04	18 12	18 16		18 19	18 26	18 31				18 27	18 29		18 34	18 42	18 46		18 49		18 56	19 01		

A from 15 September **B** until 8 September

For non-stop services between Reading and London refer to Table T116

For non-stop services between London and Heathrow Airport see Table T118

For Heathrow Express Services see Table T118

Table T117-R

Saturdays
26 May to 8 December

Reading, Heathrow Airport and Greenford - London
Stopping Services

	GW		XR	HX	XR	GW	GW	XR	GW	GW	XC		GW	HX	GW	XR	HX	GW	XR	GW	HX		XR	GW
	◇1			◇1						◇1	◇1			◇1	◇1		◇1				◇1			
Oxford d	18 01										18 16				18 31									
Reading d	18 25								18 33	18 39	18a43		18 48		18 55									19 03
Twyford d									18 39				18 54											19 09
Maidenhead d									18 47				19 02											19 17
Taplow d													19 05											
Burnham d						←							19 08							←				
Slough a	18 38					18 43			18 54				19 13		19 08					19 13				19 24
Slough d	18 39					18 44			18 55				19 14		19 09					19 14				19 25
Langley d									18 58				→											19 28
Iver d									19 01															19 31
West Drayton d						18 50			19 05											19 20				19 35
Heathrow Terminal 5 a																								
Heathrow Terminal 5 d				18 42										18 57			19 12				19 27			
Heathrow Terminal 4 a																								
Heathrow Terminal 4 d			18 41					18 52								19 11							19 22	
Heathrow Termls 2 & 3 a			18 45	18 46				18 56						19 01		19 15	19 16				19 31		19 26	
Heathrow Termls 2 & 3 d				18 48				18 58						19 03			19 18				19 33		19 28	
Hayes & Harlington d					18 47	18 55		19 03	19 10										19 17	19 25			19 33	19 40
Southall d					18 51			19 07	19 14										19 21				19 37	19 44
Hanwell d								19 10															19 40	
Greenford d							18 46											19 16						
South Greenford d							18 49											19 19						
Castle Bar Park d							18 52											19 22						
Drayton Green d							18 54											19 24						
West Ealing d					18 56		18a57	19 12										19a26	19 26				19 42	
Ealing Broadway d					18 59	19 03		19 15	19 19										19 29	19 33			19 45	19 49
Acton Main Line d					19 02														19 32					
London Paddington a	18 59			19 04	19 12	19 16		19 26	19 31	19 06				19 19	19 26		19 34		19 42	19 46	19 49		19 56	20 01

	XC	GW	GW	XR	HX	XR	GW		GW	HX	XR	GW	XC	GW	GW	XR	HX		XR	GW	GW	HX	XR	GW
	◇1		◇1		◇1					◇1			◇1		◇1		◇1					◇1		
Oxford d	18 43		19 01										19 16		19 31									
Reading d	19a10	19 18	19 25									19 33	19a41	19 48	19 55									20 03
Twyford d		19 24										19 39		19 54										20 09
Maidenhead d		19 32										19 47		20 02										20 17
Taplow d		19 35												20 05										
Burnham d		19 38					←							20 08						←				
Slough a		19 43	19 38				19 43					19 54		20 13	20 08					20 13				20 24
Slough d		19 44	19 39				19 44					19 55		20 14	20 09					20 14				20 25
Langley d		→										19 58		→										20 28
Iver d												20 01												20 31
West Drayton d							19 50					20 05								20 20				20 35
Heathrow Terminal 5 a																								
Heathrow Terminal 5 d					19 42					19 57							20 12					20 27		
Heathrow Terminal 4 a																								
Heathrow Terminal 4 d				19 41							19 52					20 11							20 22	
Heathrow Termls 2 & 3 a				19 45	19 46					20 01	19 56					20 15	20 16					20 31	20 26	
Heathrow Termls 2 & 3 d					19 48					20 03	19 58						20 18					20 33	20 28	
Hayes & Harlington d						19 47	19 55				20 03	20 10							20 17	20 25			20 33	20 40
Southall d						19 51					20 07	20 14							20 21				20 37	20 44
Hanwell d											20 10												20 40	
Greenford d									19 46												20 16			
South Greenford d									19 49												20 19			
Castle Bar Park d									19 52												20 22			
Drayton Green d									19 54												20 24			
West Ealing d						19 56			19a57		20 12								20 26		20a27		20 42	
Ealing Broadway d						19 59	20 03				20 15	20 19							20 29	20 33			20 45	20 49
Acton Main Line d						20 02													20 32					
London Paddington a			19 56		20 04	20 12	20 16			20 19	20 26	20 31			20 27		20 34		20 42	20 46		20 49	20 56	21 01

For non-stop services between Reading and London refer to Table T116

For non-stop services between London and Heathrow Airport see Table T118

For Heathrow Express Services see Table T118

Table T117-R

Saturdays
26 May to 8 December

Reading, Heathrow Airport and Greenford - London

Stopping Services

	XC ◇1	GW	GW ◇1	XR	HX ◇1	XR	GW	GW	XR		GW	GW ◇1	XC ◇1	GW	HX ◇1	GW ◇1	XR	HX ◇1	XR		GW	GW	HX ◇1	XR
Oxford d	19 43		20 01										20 16			20 27								
Reading d	20a08	20 18	20 25								20 33	20 40	20a41	20 48		20 52								
Twyford d		20 24									20 39			20 54										
Maidenhead d		20 32									20 47			21 02										
Taplow d		20 35												21 05										
Burnham d		20 38					←							21 08							←			
Slough a		20 43	20 38				20 43				20 54			21 13		21 06					21 13			
Slough d		20 44	20 39				20 44				20 55			21 14		21 07					21 14			
Langley d		→									20 58			→										
Iver d											21 01													
West Drayton d							20 50				21 05										21 20			
Heathrow Terminal 5 a																								
Heathrow Terminal 5 d					20 42										20 57			21 12					21 27	
Heathrow Terminal 4 a																								
Heathrow Terminal 4 d				20 41					20 52								21 11							21 22
Heathrow Termls 2 & 3 a				20 45	20 46				20 56						21 01		21 15	21 16					21 31	21 26
Heathrow Termls 2 & 3 d					20 48				20 58						21 03			21 18					21 33	21 28
Hayes & Harlington d						20 47	20 55		21 03		21 10								21 17		21 25			21 33
Southall d						20 51			21 07		21 14								21 21					21 37
Hanwell d									21 10															21 40
Greenford d								20 46														21 16		
South Greenford d								20 49														21 19		
Castle Bar Park d								20 52														21 22		
Drayton Green d								20 54														21 24		
West Ealing d						20 56		20a57	21 12										21 26			21a27		21 42
Ealing Broadway d						20 59	21 03		21 15		21 19								21 29		21 33			21 45
Acton Main Line d						21 02													21 32					
London Paddington a			20 56		21 04	21 12	21 17		21 26		21 29	21 06			21 19	21 25		21 34	21 42		21 46		21 49	21 56

	GW	XC ◇1	GW	GW ◇1	XR		HX ◇1	XR	GW	HX ◇1	GW	XR	GW	XC ◇1	GW ◇1		XR	HX ◇1	XR	HX ◇1	XR	GW	XC ◇1	GW ◇1
Oxford d		20 43		21 01										21 16	21 29								21 43	22 01
Reading d	21 03	21a08	21 18	21 25									21 33	21a42	21 58							22 03	22a14	22 29
Twyford d	21 09		21 24										21 39									22 09		
Maidenhead d	21 17		21 32										21 47									22 17		
Taplow d			21 35										21 50									22 20		
Burnham d			21 38						←				21 53									22 23		
Slough a	21 24		21 43	21 38					21 43				21 58		22 11							22 28		22 42
Slough d	21 25		21 44	21 39					21 44				21 59		22 12							22 29		22 43
Langley d	21 28		→										22 02											
Iver d	21 31												22 05											
West Drayton d	21 35								21 50				22 09									22 35		
Heathrow Terminal 5 a																								
Heathrow Terminal 5 d							21 42			21 57								22 12		22 27				
Heathrow Terminal 4 a																								
Heathrow Terminal 4 d					21 41							21 52					22 11				22 22			
Heathrow Termls 2 & 3 a					21 45		21 46			22 01		21 56					22 15	22 16		22 31	22 26			
Heathrow Termls 2 & 3 d							21 48			22 03		21 58						22 18		22 33	22 28			
Hayes & Harlington d	21 40							21 47	21 55			22 03	22 14						22 17		22 33	22 40		
Southall d	21 44							21 51				22 07	22 17						22 21		22 37	22 43		
Hanwell d												22 10									22 40			
Greenford d											21 56													
South Greenford d											21 59													
Castle Bar Park d											22 02													
Drayton Green d											22 04													
West Ealing d								21 56			22 08	22 12							22 26		22 42			
Ealing Broadway d	21 49							21 59	22 04		22 11	22 15	22 23						22 29		22 45	22 49		
Acton Main Line d								22 02											22 32					
London Paddington a	21 59			21 56			22 04	22 12	22 16	22 19	22 21	22 26	22 32		22 29			22 35	22 42	22 49	22 56	22 58		23 00

For non-stop services between Reading and London refer to Table T116

For non-stop services between London and Heathrow Airport see Table T118

For Heathrow Express Services see Table T118

Table T117-R

Saturdays
26 May to 8 December

Reading, Heathrow Airport and Greenford - London

Stopping Services

	XR	HX ◇1	XR	HX ◇1	XR	GW	XC ◇1		XR	HX ◇1	XR	GW	HX ◇1	GW ◇1	XR	XR	HX ◇1		XR	GW	GW ◇1	HX	XR
Oxford d							22 18							22 35							23 01		
Reading d						22 34	22a45					22 52		23 14						23 22	23 32		
Twyford d						22 40						22 58								23 28			
Maidenhead d						22 48						23 06								23 36			
Taplow d						22 51						23 09								23 39			
Burnham d						22 54						23 12								23 42			
Slough a						22 59						23 17		23 31						23 47	23 51		
Slough d						23 00						23 18		23 33						23 47	23 52		
Langley d						23 03																	
Iver d						23 06																	
West Drayton d						23 10						23 24								23 54			
Heathrow Terminal 5 a																							
Heathrow Terminal 5 d		22 42		22 57						23 12			23 27				23 42					23 51	
Heathrow Terminal 4 a																							
Heathrow Terminal 4 d	22 41				22 52				23 11						23 22	23 41							23 57
Heathrow Termls 2 & 3 a	22 45	22 46		23 01	22 56				23 15	23 16			23 31		23 26	23 45	23 46					23 55	00 01
Heathrow Termls 2 & 3 d		22 48		23 03	22 58					23 18			23 33		23 28		23 48						00 03
Hayes & Harlington d			22 47		23 03	23 15					23 18	23 29			23 33				23 51	23 58			00 08
Southall d			22 51		23 07	23 18					23 23	23 32			23 37				23 55				00 12
Hanwell d					23 10										23 40								
Greenford d																							
South Greenford d																							
Castle Bar Park d																							
Drayton Green d																							
West Ealing d			22 56		23 12						23 27				23 42				23 59				
Ealing Broadway d			22 59		23 15	23 24					23 30	23 38			23 45				00 02	00 05			00 17
Acton Main Line d			23 02								23 33								00 05				
London Paddington a		23 05	23 12	23 19	23 26	23 33				23 34	23 43	23 47	23 49	23 51	23 56		00 05		00 14	00 15	00 17		00 27

Sundays
20 May to 9 September

	XR	GW	XR	XR	GW	HX ◇1		HX ◇1	XR		XR	HX ◇1	HX ◇1	XR	XR	HX ◇1	GW	HX ◇1	XR		XR	HX ◇1	HX ◇1
	A	A	A		A																		
Oxford d																							
Reading d					00 20												06 22						
Twyford d					00 26												06 29						
Maidenhead d					00 34												06 38						
Taplow d					00 37																		
Burnham d					00 40												06 42						
Slough a					00 45												06 47						
Slough d					00 46												06 49						
Langley d					00 49												06 54						
Iver d					00 52																		
West Drayton d					00 56												06 59						
Heathrow Terminal 5 a																							
Heathrow Terminal 5 d						05 12	and every 15 minutes until	06 12				06 27	06 42			06 57		07 12				07 27	07 42
Heathrow Terminal 4 a																							
Heathrow Terminal 4 d				00 07					06 01		06 16			06 31	06 46				07 01		07 16		
Heathrow Termls 2 & 3 a				00 11		05 16		06 16	06 05		06 20	06 31	06 46	06 35	06 50	07 01		07 16	07 05		07 20	07 31	07 46
Heathrow Termls 2 & 3 d			00 03	00 13		05 17		06 17	06 07			06 32	06 47	06 37		07 02		07 17	07 07			07 32	07 47
Hayes & Harlington d			00 08	00 21	01 01				06 14					06 44			07 03		07 14				
Southall d			00 12	00 25	01 04				06 18					06 48			07 07		07 18				
Hanwell d																							
Greenford d																							
South Greenford d																							
Castle Bar Park d																							
Drayton Green d																							
West Ealing d																							
Ealing Broadway d	00 02	00 05	00 17	00 30	01 10				06 23					06 53			07 12		07 23				
Acton Main Line d	00 05																						
London Paddington a	00 14	00 15	00 27	00 39	01 19	05 33		06 33	06 34			06 48	07 03	07 04		07 18	07 21	07 33	07 34			07 48	08 03

A not 20 May

For non-stop services between Reading and London refer to Table T116

For non-stop services between London and Heathrow Airport see Table T118

For Heathrow Express Services see Table T118

Table T117-R

Sundays

20 May to 9 September

Reading, Heathrow Airport and Greenford - London

Stopping Services

Station		XR	XR		HX	GW	HX	XR	XR	HX	GW	HX	XR		XR	HX	GW	HX	XR	GW	XR	HX	GW		HX
					◇1		◇1			◇1	1	◇1				◇1		◇1				◇1	◇		◇1
Oxford	d																						08 40		
Reading 7	d					07 22					08 20						08 25			08 53			09 12		
Twyford 3	d					07 29											08 31			08 59					
Maidenhead 3	d					07 38											08 38			09 08					
Taplow	d																								
Burnham	d					07 42											08 42								
Slough 3	a					07 47					08 38						08 47			09 15			09 29		
	d					07 49					08 38						08 49			09 16			09 30		
Langley	d					07 54											08 54			09 20					
Iver	d																								
West Drayton	d					07 59											08 59			09 25					
Heathrow Terminal 5 ⊖ ✈	a																								
	d				07 57		08 12			08 27		08 42				08 57		09 12				09 27			09 42
Heathrow Terminal 4 ⊖ ✈	a																								
	d	07 31	07 46					08 01	08 16				08 31		08 46				09 01		09 16				
Heathrow Termls 2 & 3 2 ⊖ ✈	a	07 35	07 50		08 01		08 16	08 05	08 20	08 31		08 46	08 35		08 50	09 01		09 16	09 05		09 20	09 31			09 46
	d	07 37			08 02		08 17	08 07		08 32		08 47	08 37			09 02		09 17	09 07			09 32			09 47
Hayes & Harlington	d	07 44				08 03		08 14					08 44				09 03		09 14	09 29					
Southall	d	07 48				08 07		08 18					08 48				09 07		09 18	09 33					
Hanwell	d																								
Greenford ⊖	d																								
South Greenford	d																								
Castle Bar Park	d																								
Drayton Green	d																								
West Ealing	d																								
Ealing Broadway ⊖	d	07 53				08 12		08 23					08 53				09 12		09 23	09 38					
Acton Main Line	d																								
London Paddington 15 ⊖	a	08 04			08 18	08 21	08 33	08 34		08 48	09 00	09 03	09 04			09 18	09 21	09 33	09 34	09 48		09 48	09 51		10 03

Station		XR	GW	GW	XR	HX	HX	XR	GW		XR	HX	HX	XR	XR	GW	GW	XC	HX		GW	GW	HX	XR	GW
						◇1	◇1					◇1	◇1				◇	◇1	◇1			◇1	◇1		
Oxford	d																09 55	10 16							
Reading 7	d		09 20	09 36					09 53							10 19	10 25	10a42				10 51			10 54
Twyford 3	d		09 26						09 59							10 24									11 00
Maidenhead 3	d		09 34	09 48					10 08							10 34									11 08
Taplow	d																								
Burnham	d		09 39													10 38					←				
Slough 3	a		09 45	09 55					10 15							10 41	10 44				10 41				11 15
	d		09 49	09 55					10 16							10 48	10 45				10 48				11 16
Langley	d		09 53						10 20							→					10 52				11 20
Iver	d																								
West Drayton	d		09 58						10 25												10 57				11 25
Heathrow Terminal 5 ⊖ ✈	a																								
	d					09 57	10 12					10 27	10 42						10 57				11 12		
Heathrow Terminal 4 ⊖ ✈	a																								
	d	09 31			09 46			10 01			10 16			10 31	10 46									11 01	
Heathrow Termls 2 & 3 2 ⊖ ✈	a	09 35			09 50	10 01	10 16	10 05			10 20	10 31	10 46	10 35	10 50				11 01				11 16	11 05	
	d	09 37				10 02	10 17	10 07				10 32	10 47	10 37					11 02				11 17	11 07	
Hayes & Harlington	d	09 44	10 02					10 14	10 29					10 44							11 02			11 14	11 29
Southall	d	09 48	10 06					10 18	10 33					10 48							11 05			11 18	11 33
Hanwell	d																								
Greenford ⊖	d																								
South Greenford	d																								
Castle Bar Park	d																								
Drayton Green	d																								
West Ealing	d																								
Ealing Broadway ⊖	d	09 53	10 11					10 23	10 38					10 53							11 11			11 23	11 38
Acton Main Line	d																								
London Paddington 15 ⊖	a	10 04	10 20	10 15		10 18	10 33	10 34	10 48			10 48	11 03	11 04			11 05		11 18		11 19	11 30	11 33	11 34	11 47

For non-stop services between Reading and London refer to Table T116

For non-stop services between London and Heathrow Airport see Table T118

For Heathrow Express Services see Table T118

Table T117-R

Sundays

20 May to 9 September

Reading, Heathrow Airport and Greenford - London

Stopping Services

Station			XR	HX	HX	XR	GW	GW	XC	XR	HX		HX	XR	GW	XR	HX	HX	XR	GW	GW		GW	XC	XR
				◇1	◇1			◇1	◇1		◇1		◇1				◇1	◇1			◇			◇1	
Oxford	d							11 00	11 16												12 00			12 16	
Reading 7	d						11 18	11 28	11a40						11 54					12 18	12 28		12 33	12a41	
Twyford 3	d						11 24								12 00					12 24					
Maidenhead 3	d						11 32								12 08					12 32			12 45		
Taplow	d																								
Burnham	d						11 37													12 37					
Slough 3	a						11 41	11 48							12 15					12 41	12 48		12 52		
	d						11 42	11 49							12 16					12 42	12 49		12 53		
Langley	d						11 46								12 20					12 46					
Iver	d																								
West Drayton	d						11 51								12 25					12 51					
Heathrow Terminal 5 ⊖ ✈	a																								
	d			11 27	11 42						11 57		12 12				12 27	12 42							
Heathrow Terminal 4 ⊖ ✈	a																								
	d		11 16			11 31				11 46				12 01		12 16			12 31						12 46
Heathrow Termls 2 & 3 2 ⊖ ✈	a		11 20	11 31	11 46	11 35				11 50	12 01		12 16	12 05		12 20	12 31	12 46	12 35						12 50
	d			11 32	11 47	11 37					12 02		12 17	12 07			12 32	12 47	12 37						
Hayes & Harlington	d					11 44	11 55							12 14	12 29				12 44	12 55					
Southall	d					11 48	11 59							12 18	12 33				12 48	12 59					
Hanwell	d																								
Greenford ⊖	d																								
South Greenford	d																								
Castle Bar Park	d																								
Drayton Green	d																								
West Ealing	d																								
Ealing Broadway ⊖	d					11 53	12 04							12 23	12 38				12 53	13 04					
Acton Main Line	d																								
London Paddington 15 ⊖	a			11 48	12 03	12 04	12 13	12 08			12 18		12 33	12 34	12 47		12 48	13 03	13 04	13 13	13 09		13 14		

Station		HX	GW	HX	XR	XR	HX		GW	HX	XR	GW	GW	XC	XR	HX	HX		XR	XR	HX	GW	XC	HX	XR
		◇1	◇1	◇1			◇1			◇1			◇	◇1		◇1	◇1				◇1		◇1	◇1	
Oxford	d												13 00	13 16									13 45		
Reading 7	d		12 53						12 56			13 21	13 28	13a42								13 56	14a11		
Twyford 3	d								13 00			13 27										14 00			
Maidenhead 3	d								13 08			13 35										14 08			
Taplow	d																								
Burnham	d											13 40													
Slough 3	a								13 15			13 44	13 48									14 15			
	d								13 16			13 45	13 49									14 16			
Langley	d								13 20			13 49										14 20			
Iver	d																								
West Drayton	d								13 25			13 54										14 25			
Heathrow Terminal 5 ⊖ ✈	a																								
	d	12 57		13 12			13 27			13 42						13 57	14 12				14 27			14 42	
Heathrow Terminal 4 ⊖ ✈	a																								
	d				13 01	13 16					13 31				13 46				14 01	14 16					14 31
Heathrow Termls 2 & 3 2 ⊖ ✈	a	13 01		13 16	13 05	13 20	13 31			13 46	13 35				13 50	14 01	14 16		14 05	14 20	14 31			14 46	14 35
	d	13 02		13 17	13 07		13 32			13 47	13 37					14 02	14 17		14 07		14 32			14 47	14 37
Hayes & Harlington	d				13 14				13 29		13 44	13 58							14 14			14 29			14 44
Southall	d				13 18				13 33		13 48	14 02							14 18			14 33			14 48
Hanwell	d																								
Greenford ⊖	d																								
South Greenford	d																								
Castle Bar Park	d																								
Drayton Green	d																								
West Ealing	d																								
Ealing Broadway ⊖	d				13 23				13 38		13 53	14 07							14 23			14 38			14 53
Acton Main Line	d																								
London Paddington 15 ⊖	a	13 18	13 30	13 33	13 34		13 48		13 49	14 03	14 04	14 16	14 10			14 18	14 33		14 34		14 48	14 49		15 03	15 04

For non-stop services between Reading and London refer to Table T116

For non-stop services between London and Heathrow Airport see Table T118

For Heathrow Express Services see Table T118

Table T117-R

Sundays

20 May to 9 September

Reading, Heathrow Airport and Greenford - London

Stopping Services

		GW	GW ◇	GW	XC ◇1 ⌶	XR	HX ◇1	HX ◇1	XR		GW	XC ◇1 ⌶	GW ◇1 ☕	XR	HX ◇1	HX ◇1	XR	GW	GW ◇1 ☕		XR	HX ◇1	HX ◇1	XR	GW
Oxford	d		14 00		14 16							14 36							15 00						
Reading [7]	d	14 18	14 28	14 33	14a41						14 54	15a02	15 06					15 20	15 28						15 39
Twyford [3]	d	14 24									15 00							15 26							15 44
Maidenhead [3]	d	14 32		14 45							15 08							15 34							15 53
Taplow	d																								
Burnham	d	14 37																15 39							15 56
Slough [3]	a	14 41	14 47	14 52							15 15							15 43	15 48						16 02
	d	14 42	14 47	14 53							15 16							15 44	15 49						16 08
Langley	d	14 46									15 20							15 48							16 12
Iver	d																								
West Drayton	d	14 51									15 25							15 53							16 17
Heathrow Terminal 5 ⊖ ✈	a																								
	d						14 57	15 12							15 27	15 42						15 57	16 12		
Heathrow Terminal 4 ⊖ ✈	a																								
	d					14 46			15 01					15 16			15 31				15 46			16 01	
Heathrow Termls 2 & 3 [2] ⊖ ✈	a					14 50	15 01	15 16	15 05					15 20	15 31	15 46	15 35				15 50	16 01	16 16	16 05	
	d						15 02	15 17	15 07						15 32	15 47	15 37					16 02	16 17	16 07	
Hayes & Harlington	d	14 55							15 14		15 29						15 44	15 57						16 14	16 21
Southall	d	14 59							15 18		15 33						15 48	16 01						16 18	16 25
Hanwell	d																								
Greenford ⊖	d																								
South Greenford	d																								
Castle Bar Park	d																								
Drayton Green	d																								
West Ealing	d																								
Ealing Broadway ⊖	d	15 04							15 23		15 38						15 53	16 06						16 23	16 30
Acton Main Line	d																								
London Paddington [15] ⊖	a	15 14	15 07	15 12			15 18	15 33	15 34		15 47		15 45		15 48	16 03	16 04	16 16	16 09			16 18	16 33	16 34	16 39

		XC ◇1 ⌶	XC ◇1 ⌶	XR	HX ◇1		HX ◇1	XR	GW	GW ◇1 ☕	GW	XR	HX ◇1	HX ◇1	XR		GW	XC ◇1 ⌶	GW ◇ A	XC ◇1 ⌶	GW ◇1 ☕	XR	HX ◇1	HX ◇1	XR
Oxford	d	15 16	15 47							16 00								16 16	16 23	16 36					
Reading [7]	d	15a40	16a11						16 20	16 28	16 33						16 37	16a41	16 53	17a01	17 08				
Twyford [3]	d								16 26								16 43								
Maidenhead [3]	d								16 34		16 45						16 51		17 05						
Taplow	d																								
Burnham	d								16 39								16 56								
Slough [3]	a								16 43	16 48	16 52						17 01		17 14						
	d								16 44	16 49	16 53						17 08		17 17						
Langley	d								16 48								17 12								
Iver	d																								
West Drayton	d								16 53								17 17								
Heathrow Terminal 5 ⊖ ✈	a																								
	d				16 27		16 42						16 57	17 12									17 27	17 42	
Heathrow Terminal 4 ⊖ ✈	a																								
	d			16 16				16 31				16 46			17 01							17 16			17 31
Heathrow Termls 2 & 3 [2] ⊖ ✈	a			16 20	16 31		16 46	16 35				16 50	17 01	17 16	17 05							17 20	17 31	17 46	17 35
	d				16 32		16 47	16 37					17 02	17 17	17 07								17 32	17 47	17 37
Hayes & Harlington	d							16 44	16 57						17 14		17 21								17 44
Southall	d							16 48	17 01						17 18		17 25								17 48
Hanwell	d																								
Greenford ⊖	d																								
South Greenford	d																								
Castle Bar Park	d																								
Drayton Green	d																								
West Ealing	d																								
Ealing Broadway ⊖	d							16 53	17 06						17 23		17 30								17 53
Acton Main Line	d																								
London Paddington [15] ⊖	a				16 48		17 03	17 04	17 16	17 11	17 15		17 18	17 33	17 34		17 43		17 36		17 45		17 48	18 03	18 04

A from 1 July

For non-stop services between Reading and London refer to Table T116

For non-stop services between London and Heathrow Airport see Table T118

For Heathrow Express Services see Table T118

Table T117-R

Sundays

20 May to 9 September

Reading, Heathrow Airport and Greenford - London

Stopping Services

		GW	GW ◇1 ☕	XR	HX ◇1	HX ◇1	XR		GW	XC ◇1 ⌶	GW ◇ A	XC ◇1 ⌶	XR	HX ◇1	HX ◇1	XR	GW		GW ◇1 ☕	XR	HX ◇1	HX ◇1	XR	GW	XC ◇1 ⌶
Oxford	d		17 00							17 16	17 27	17 45							17 55						18 16
Reading [7]	d	17 18	17 28						17 37	17a41	17 55	18a10					18 18		18 25					18 37	18a41
Twyford [3]	d	17 24							17 43								18 24							18 43	
Maidenhead [3]	d	17 32							17 51		18 08						18 32							18 51	
Taplow	d																								
Burnham	d	17 37							17 56								18 37							18 56	
Slough [3]	a	17 41	17 48						18 01		18 16						18 41		18 46					19 01	
	d	17 42	17 49						18 08		18 16						18 42		18 47					19 12	
Langley	d	17 46							18 12								18 46							19 16	
Iver	d																								
West Drayton	d	17 51							18 17								18 51							19 21	
Heathrow Terminal 5 ⊖ ✈	a																								
	d				17 57	18 12								18 27	18 42						18 57	19 12			
Heathrow Terminal 4 ⊖ ✈	a																								
	d			17 46			18 01						18 16			18 31				18 46			19 01		
Heathrow Termls 2 & 3 [2] ⊖ ✈	a			17 50	18 01	18 16	18 05						18 20	18 31	18 46	18 35				18 50	19 01	19 16	19 05		
	d				18 02	18 17	18 07							18 32	18 47	18 37					19 02	19 17	19 07		
Hayes & Harlington	d	17 55					18 14		18 21							18 45	18 55						19 14	19 25	
Southall	d	17 59					18 18		18 25							18 50	18 59						19 18	19 29	
Hanwell	d																								
Greenford ⊖	d																								
South Greenford	d																								
Castle Bar Park	d																								
Drayton Green	d																								
West Ealing	d																								
Ealing Broadway ⊖	d	18 04					18 23		18 30							18 56	19 04						19 23	19 34	
Acton Main Line	d																								
London Paddington [15] ⊖	a	18 14	18 09		18 18	18 33	18 34		18 43		18 38			18 48	19 03	19 07	19 14		19 07		19 18	19 33	19 34	19 43	

		XC ◇1 ⌶	GW ◇1 ☕		XR	HX ◇1	HX ◇1	XR	GW	GW ◇1 ☕	XR	HX ◇1	HX ◇1		XR	GW	XC ◇1 ⌶	XC ◇1 ⌶	XR	HX ◇1	HX ◇1	XR	GW		GW ◇1
Oxford	d	18 38								18 55							19 16	19 45							19 55
Reading [7]	d	19a05	19 08						19 18	19 25						19 37	19a40	20a08					20 18		20 25
Twyford [3]	d								19 24							19 43							20 24		
Maidenhead [3]	d								19 32							19 51							20 32		
Taplow	d																								
Burnham	d								19 37							19 56							20 37		
Slough [3]	a								19 41	19 46						20 00							20 41		20 46
	d								19 42	19 47						20 12							20 42		20 47
Langley	d								19 46							20 17							20 46		
Iver	d																								
West Drayton	d								19 51							20 21							20 51		
Heathrow Terminal 5 ⊖ ✈	a																								
	d					19 27	19 42					19 57	20 12							20 27	20 42				
Heathrow Terminal 4 ⊖ ✈	a																								
	d				19 16			19 31			19 46				20 01				20 16			20 31			
Heathrow Termls 2 & 3 [2] ⊖ ✈	a				19 20	19 31	19 46	19 35			19 50	20 01	20 16		20 05				20 20	20 31	20 46	20 35			
	d					19 32	19 47	19 37				20 02	20 17		20 07					20 32	20 47	20 37			
Hayes & Harlington	d							19 44	19 55						20 14	20 26						20 44	20 55		
Southall	d							19 48	19 59						20 18	20 29						20 48	20 59		
Hanwell	d																								
Greenford ⊖	d																								
South Greenford	d																								
Castle Bar Park	d																								
Drayton Green	d																								
West Ealing	d																								
Ealing Broadway ⊖	d							19 53	20 04						20 23	20 35						20 53	21 04		
Acton Main Line	d																								
London Paddington [15] ⊖	a		19 45			19 48	20 03	20 04	20 14	20 08		20 18	20 33		20 34	20 44				20 48	21 03	21 04	21 14		21 08

A from 1 July

For non-stop services between Reading and London refer to Table T116

For non-stop services between London and Heathrow Airport see Table T118

For Heathrow Express Services see Table T118

Table T117-R

Sundays

20 May to 9 September

Reading, Heathrow Airport and Greenford - London

Stopping Services

	XC	XR	HX	HX		XR	GW	GW	XC	XR	HX	HX	XR	GW		XR	HX	GW	XC	HX	XR	GW	XC	XC
	◇■		◇■	◇■				◇■	◇■		◇■	◇■		◇■			◇■		◇■	◇■			◇■ A	◇ B
Oxford d	20 16								20 45					20 53					21 16				21§40	21§40
Reading d	20a41						20 53	21 06	21a12					21 21				21 25	21a38			21 50	22a06	22a06
Twyford d							20 59											21 31				21 56		
Maidenhead d							21 07							21 35				21 39				22 04		
Taplow d																								
Burnham d							21 12											21 44				22 09		
Slough a							21 16							21 43				21 49				22 13		
d							21 17							21 45				21 53				22 14		
Langley d							21 21											21 56				22 18		
Iver d																								
West Drayton d							21 26											22 04				22 24		
Heathrow Terminal 5 a																								
d			20 57	21 12							21 27	21 42					21 57			22 12				
Heathrow Terminal 4 a																								
d		20 46				21 01				21 16			21 31			21 46					22 01			
Heathrow Termls 2 & 3 a		20 50	21 01	21 16		21 05				21 20	21 31	21 46	21 35			21 50	22 01			22 16	22 05			
d			21 02	21 17		21 07					21 32	21 47	21 37				22 02			22 17	22 07			
Hayes & Harlington d						21 14	21 31						21 44					22 08			22 15	22 28		
Southall d						21 18	21 34						21 48								22 19	22 32		
Hanwell d																								
Greenford d																								
South Greenford d																								
Castle Bar Park d																								
Drayton Green d																								
West Ealing d																								
Ealing Broadway d						21 23	21 40						21 53					22 16			22 24	22 37		
Acton Main Line d																								
London Paddington a			21 18	21 33		21 34	21 49	21 45			21 48	22 03	22 04	22 07			22 18	22 26		22 33	22 35	22 46		

		XR	HX	XR	HX	GW	GW	XC	XR	HX		HX	XR	GW	XR	HX	GW	XR	HX	XR		GW	HX	
			◇■		◇■	◇		◇■		◇■		◇■				◇■	◇■		◇■					
Oxford d						21 50		22 12									22 43							
Reading d						22 20	22 24	22a38						22 50			23 14					23 42		
Twyford d							22 30							22 57								23 49		
Maidenhead d							22 38							23 05								23 57		
Taplow d																								
Burnham d							22 43							23 09								00 01		
Slough a						22 37	22 47							23 14			23 30					00 06		
d						22 41	22 48							23 14			23 31					00 07		
Langley d							22 51							23 19								00 11		
Iver d																								
West Drayton d							22 56							23 24								00 17		
Heathrow Terminal 5 a																								
d			22 27		22 42					22 57		23 12				23 27			23 42				23 57	
Heathrow Terminal 4 a																								
d		22 16		22 31					22 46				23 01		23 16			23 31		23 46				
Heathrow Termls 2 & 3 a		22 20	22 31	22 35	22 46				22 50	23 01		23 16	23 05		23 20	23 31		23 35	23 46	23 50			00 01	
d			22 32	22 37	22 47					23 02		23 17	23 07			23 32		23 37	23 47	23 52				
Hayes & Harlington d				22 44			22 59						23 15	23 28				23 44		23 58		00 21		
Southall d				22 48									23 19	23 32				23 48		00 02		00 25		
Hanwell d																								
Greenford d																								
South Greenford d																								
Castle Bar Park d																								
Drayton Green d																								
West Ealing d																								
Ealing Broadway d				22 53			23 07						23 24	23 37				23 53		00 07		00 30		
Acton Main Line d																								
London Paddington a			22 48	23 04	23 05	23 09	23 18			23 19		23 35	23 36	23 46		23 48	23 51	00 04	00 05	00 20		00 38		

A until 15 July, also 9 September B from 22 July until 2 September

For non-stop services between Reading and London refer to Table T116

For non-stop services between London and Heathrow Airport see Table T118

For Heathrow Express Services see Table T118

Table T117-R

Sundays

16 September to 2 December

Reading, Heathrow Airport and Greenford - London

Stopping Services

	XR	GW	XR	XR	GW	HX		HX		XR	XR	HX	HX	XR	GW	XR	HX	HX		XR	XR	HX	HX
						◇■		◇■				◇■	◇■				◇■	◇■				◇■	◇■
Oxford d																							
Reading d					00 20										06 20								
Twyford d					00 26										06 26								
Maidenhead d					00 34										06 35								
Taplow d					00 37																		
Burnham d					00 40										06 39								
Slough a					00 45										06 44								
d					00 46										06 44								
Langley d					00 49										06 48								
Iver d					00 52																		
West Drayton d					00 56										06 53								
Heathrow Terminal 5 a																							
d						05 12	and every 15 minutes until	06 12				06 27	06 42				06 57	07 12				07 27	07 42
Heathrow Terminal 4 a																							
d				00 07						06 01	06 16			06 31		06 46				07 01	07 16		
Heathrow Termls 2 & 3 a				00 11		05 16		06 16		06 05	06 20	06 31	06 46	06 35		06 50	07 01	07 16		07 05	07 20	07 31	07 46
d			00 03	00 13		05 17		06 17		06 07		06 32	06 47	06 37			07 02	07 17		07 07		07 32	07 47
Hayes & Harlington d			00 08	00 21	01 01					06 14				06 44	06 58					07 15			
Southall d			00 12	00 25	01 04					06 18				06 48	07 02					07 19			
Hanwell d																							
Greenford d																							
South Greenford d																							
Castle Bar Park d																							
Drayton Green d																							
West Ealing d																							
Ealing Broadway d	00 02	00 05	00 17	00 30	01 10					06 23				06 53	07 07					07 24			
Acton Main Line d	00 05																						
London Paddington a	00 14	00 15	00 27	00 39	01 19	05 33		06 33		06 34		06 48	07 03	07 04	07 16		07 18	07 34		07 35		07 48	08 03

	XR	XR	HX	GW	HX		XR	XR	HX	HX	XR	GW	XR	HX	GW		HX	XR	XR	HX	GW	GW	XR	HX
			◇■		◇■				◇■	◇■		■		◇■			◇■			◇■		◇		◇■
Oxford d																						08 55		
Reading d				07 32								08 28			08 32						09 00	09 22		
Twyford d				07 38											08 38						09 08			
Maidenhead d				07 46											08 46						09 16			
Taplow d																								
Burnham d				07 51											08 51									
Slough a				07 55								08 44			08 55						09 24	09 40		
d				07 56								08 45			08 56						09 24	09 41		
Langley d				08 00											09 00						09 30			
Iver d																								
West Drayton d				08 06											09 06						09 36			
Heathrow Terminal 5 a																								
d			07 57		08 12				08 27	08 42				08 57			09 12			09 27				09 42
Heathrow Terminal 4 a																								
d	07 31	07 46					08 01	08 16			08 31		08 46					09 01	09 16				09 31	
Heathrow Termls 2 & 3 a	07 35	07 50	08 01		08 16		08 05	08 20	08 31	08 46	08 35		08 50	09 01			09 16	09 05	09 20	09 31			09 35	09 46
d	07 37		08 02		08 17		08 07		08 32	08 47	08 37			09 02			09 17	09 07		09 32			09 37	09 47
Hayes & Harlington d	07 44			08 11			08 15				08 44				09 11			09 15			09 41		09 45	
Southall d	07 48			08 15			08 19				08 48				09 15			09 19			09 45		09 49	
Hanwell d																								
Greenford d																								
South Greenford d																								
Castle Bar Park d																								
Drayton Green d																								
West Ealing d																								
Ealing Broadway d	07 53			08 20			08 24				08 53				09 20			09 24			09 50		09 54	
Acton Main Line d																								
London Paddington a	08 04		08 18	08 28	08 34		08 36		08 48	09 03	09 04	09 07		09 18	09 28		09 34	09 35		09 48	09 58	10 04	10 05	10 07

For non-stop services between Reading and London refer to Table T116

For non-stop services between London and Heathrow Airport see Table T118

For Heathrow Express Services see Table T118

Reading, Heathrow Airport and Greenford - London

Stopping Services

		XR	HX	GW	XR	HX	XR	HX		GW	GW	XR	HX	GW	GW	XC	XR	HX		XR	HX	XR	HX	GW	GW
			◇■			◇■		◇■			◇		◇■		◇■	◇■		◇■			◇■		◇■		◇■
Oxford	d										09 55					10 16									10 55
Reading ■	d			09 30						10 00	10 25			10 30	10 36	10a42								11 00	11 24
Twyford ■	d			09 38						10 08				10 38										11 08	
Maidenhead ■	d			09 46						10 16				10 46										11 16	
Taplow	d																								
Burnham	d			09 51										10 51											
Slough ■	a			09 55						10 24	10 39			10 55										11 23	11 38
	d			09 56						10 25	10 41			10 56										11 26	11 39
Langley	d			10 00						10 30				11 00										11 30	
Iver	d																								
West Drayton	d			10 06						10 36				11 06										11 36	
Heathrow Terminal 5 ⊖ ✈	a																								
	d		09 57			10 12		10 27					10 42					10 57			11 12		11 27		
Heathrow Terminal 4 ⊖ ✈	a																								
	d	09 46			10 01		10 16					10 31					10 46			11 01		11 16			
Heathrow Termls 2 & 3 ■ ⊖ ✈	a	09 50	10 01		10 05	10 16	10 20	10 31				10 35	10 46				10 50	11 01		11 05	11 16	11 20	11 31		
	d		10 02		10 07	10 17		10 32				10 37	10 47					11 02		11 07	11 17		11 32		
Hayes & Harlington	d			10 11	10 15					10 41		10 45		11 11						11 15				11 41	
Southall	d			10 15	10 19					10 45		10 49		11 15						11 19				11 45	
Hanwell	d																								
Greenford ⊖	d																								
South Greenford	d																								
Castle Bar Park	d																								
Drayton Green	d																								
West Ealing	d																								
Ealing Broadway ⊖	d			10 20	10 24					10 50		10 54		11 20						11 24				11 50	
Acton Main Line	d																								
London Paddington ■ ⊖	a		10 18	10 28	10 35	10 37		10 48		10 58	11 05	11 05	11 07	11 28	11 14			11 18		11 35	11 35		11 48	11 58	12 05

		XR	HX	XR		HX	GW	XC	XR	HX	XR	HX	GW	GW		XR	HX	XR	HX	GW	XC	GW	XR	HX	
			◇■			◇■		◇■		◇■		◇■		◇			◇■		◇■		◇■	◇■		◇■	
Oxford	d							11 16						11 55							12 16				
Reading ■	d						11 30	11a40					12 00	12 24						12 30	12a41	12 53			
Twyford ■	d						11 38						12 08							12 38					
Maidenhead ■	d						11 46						12 16							12 46					
Taplow	d																								
Burnham	d						11 51													12 51					
Slough ■	a						11 55						12 24	12 38						12 55					
	d						11 56						12 25	12 39						12 56					
Langley	d						12 00						12 30							13 00					
Iver	d																								
West Drayton	d						12 06						12 36							13 06					
Heathrow Terminal 5 ⊖ ✈	a																								
	d		11 42			11 57				12 12		12 27					12 42		12 57					13 12	
Heathrow Terminal 4 ⊖ ✈	a																								
	d	11 31		11 46					12 01		12 16					12 31		12 46					13 01		
Heathrow Termls 2 & 3 ■ ⊖ ✈	a	11 35	11 46	11 50		12 01			12 05	12 16	12 20	12 31				12 35	12 46	12 50	13 01				13 05	13 16	
	d	11 37	11 47			12 02			12 07	12 17		12 32				12 37	12 47		13 02				13 07	13 17	
Hayes & Harlington	d	11 45					12 11		12 15				12 41			12 45				13 11			13 15		
Southall	d	11 49					12 15		12 19				12 45			12 49				13 15			13 19		
Hanwell	d																								
Greenford ⊖	d																								
South Greenford	d																								
Castle Bar Park	d																								
Drayton Green	d																								
West Ealing	d																								
Ealing Broadway ⊖	d	11 54					12 20		12 24				12 50			12 54				13 20			13 24		
Acton Main Line	d																								
London Paddington ■ ⊖	a	12 05	12 07			12 18	12 28		12 35	12 35		12 48	12 58	13 05		13 05	13 07		13 18	13 28		13 35	13 35	13 37	

For non-stop services between Reading and London refer to Table T116

For non-stop services between London and Heathrow Airport see Table T118

For Heathrow Express Services see Table T118

Reading, Heathrow Airport and Greenford - London

Stopping Services

		XR	HX	GW	XR	HX		GW	XR	HX	GW	XC	XR	HX	XR	HX		GW	XC	GW	XR	HX	XR	HX	GW
			◇■			◇■		◇■		◇■		◇■		◇■		◇■			◇■	◇■		◇■		◇■	
Oxford	d							13 00				13 16							13 45	13 55					
Reading ■	d			13 00				13 30			13 30	13a42						14 00	14a11	14 25					14 30
Twyford ■	d			13 08							13 38							14 08							14 38
Maidenhead ■	d			13 16							13 46							14 16							14 46
Taplow	d																								
Burnham	d										13 51														14 51
Slough ■	a			13 24				13 44			13 55							14 24		14 41					14 55
	d			13 25				13 46			13 56							14 25		14 41					14 56
Langley	d			13 30							14 00							14 30							15 00
Iver	d																								
West Drayton	d			13 36							14 06							14 36							15 06
Heathrow Terminal 5 ⊖ ✈	a																								
	d		13 27			13 42				13 57				14 12		14 27						14 42		14 57	
Heathrow Terminal 4 ⊖ ✈	a																								
	d	13 16			13 31				13 46				14 01		14 16						14 31		14 46		
Heathrow Termls 2 & 3 ■ ⊖ ✈	a	13 20	13 31		13 35	13 46			13 50	14 01			14 05	14 16	14 20	14 31					14 35	14 46	14 50	15 01	
	d		13 32		13 37	13 47				14 02			14 07	14 17		14 32					14 37	14 47		15 02	
Hayes & Harlington	d			13 41	13 45						14 11		14 15					14 41			14 45				15 11
Southall	d			13 45	13 49						14 15		14 19					14 45			14 49				15 15
Hanwell	d																								
Greenford ⊖	d																								
South Greenford	d																								
Castle Bar Park	d																								
Drayton Green	d																								
West Ealing	d																								
Ealing Broadway ⊖	d			13 50	13 54						14 20		14 24					14 50			14 54				15 20
Acton Main Line	d																								
London Paddington ■ ⊖	a		13 48	13 58	14 05	14 07		14 10		14 18	14 28		14 35	14 37		14 48		14 58		15 05	15 05	15 07		15 18	15 28

		XC		XR	HX	XR	HX	GW	XC	GW	XR	HX		GW	XR	HX	GW	XC	HX	XR	XR	HX		GW	XC
		◇■			◇■		◇■		◇■	◇■		◇■		◇■		◇■		◇■	◇■			◇■			◇■
Oxford	d	14 16							14 36					15 00				15 16							15 47
Reading ■	d	14a41						15 00	15a02	15 20				15 27			15 30	15a40						16 00	16a12
Twyford ■	d							15 08									15 38							16 08	
Maidenhead ■	d							15 16									15 46							16 16	
Taplow	d																								
Burnham	d																15 51							16 21	
Slough ■	a							15 24						15 43			15 55							16 24	
	d							15 25						15 44			15 56							16 25	
Langley	d							15 30									16 00							16 30	
Iver	d																								
West Drayton	d							15 36									16 06							16 36	
Heathrow Terminal 5 ⊖ ✈	a																								
	d				15 12		15 27					15 42				15 57			16 12			16 27			
Heathrow Terminal 4 ⊖ ✈	a																								
	d			15 01		15 16					15 31				15 46					16 01	16 16				
Heathrow Termls 2 & 3 ■ ⊖ ✈	a			15 05	15 16	15 20	15 31				15 35	15 46			15 50	16 01			16 16	16 05	16 20	16 31			
	d			15 07	15 17		15 32				15 37	15 47				16 02			16 17	16 07		16 32			
Hayes & Harlington	d			15 15				15 41			15 45						16 11			16 15				16 41	
Southall	d			15 19				15 45			15 49						16 15			16 19				16 45	
Hanwell	d																								
Greenford ⊖	d																								
South Greenford	d																								
Castle Bar Park	d																								
Drayton Green	d																								
West Ealing	d																								
Ealing Broadway ⊖	d			15 24				15 50			15 54						16 20			16 24				16 50	
Acton Main Line	d																								
London Paddington ■ ⊖	a			15 35	15 37		15 48	15 58		16 05	16 05	16 07		16 10		16 18	16 28		16 34	16 35		16 48		16 58	

For non-stop services between Reading and London refer to Table T116

For non-stop services between London and Heathrow Airport see Table T118

For Heathrow Express Services see Table T118

Table T117-R

Sundays
16 September to 2 December

Reading, Heathrow Airport and Greenford - London

Stopping Services

		HX ◇1	XR	GW ◇1	XR	HX ◇1	GW	XC ◇1	HX ◇1	XR	XR	HX ◇1	GW	XC ◇1	HX ◇1	XR	GW ◇1	GW ◇1	XR	HX ◇1	GW	XC ◇1
Oxford	d			16 00				16 16						16 36				17 00				17 16
Reading	d			16 28			16 30	16a41					17 00	17a01			17 27	17 29			17 30	17a41
Twyford	d						16 38						17 08								17 38	
Maidenhead	d						16 46						17 16								17 46	
Taplow	d																					
Burnham	d						16 51						17 21								17 51	
Slough	a			16 43			16 55						17 24					17 43			17 55	
	d			16 44			16 56						17 25					17 44			17 56	
Langley	d						17 00						17 30								18 00	
Iver	d																					
West Drayton	d						17 06						17 36								18 06	
Heathrow Terminal 5	a																					
	d	16 42				16 57			17 12			17 27			17 42					17 57		
Heathrow Terminal 4	a																					
	d		16 31		16 46					17 01	17 16					17 31			17 46			
Heathrow Termls 2 & 3	a	16 46	16 35		16 50	17 01			17 16	17 05	17 20	17 31			17 46	17 35			17 50	18 01		
	d	16 47	16 37			17 02			17 17	17 07		17 32			17 47	17 37				18 02		
Hayes & Harlington	d		16 45				17 11			17 15			17 41			17 45					18 11	
Southall	d		16 49				17 15			17 19			17 45			17 49					18 15	
Hanwell	d																					
Greenford	d																					
South Greenford	d																					
Castle Bar Park	d																					
Drayton Green	d																					
West Ealing	d																					
Ealing Broadway	d		16 54				17 20			17 24			17 50			17 54					18 20	
Acton Main Line	d																					
London Paddington	a	17 04	17 05	17 09		17 18	17 28		17 34	17 35		17 48	17 58		18 04	18 05	18 08	18 10		18 18	18 28	

		HX ◇1	XR	XR	HX ◇1	GW	XC ◇1	HX ◇1	XR	GW ◇1	XR	HX ◇1	GW	XC ◇1	HX ◇1	XR	XR	HX ◇1	GW	XC ◇1	HX ◇1	XR	GW ◇1
Oxford	d						17 45			18 00				18 16						18 38			
Reading	d					18 00	18a12			18 28			18 30	18a41					19 00	19a05			19 25
Twyford	d					18 08							18 38						19 08				
Maidenhead	d					18 16							18 46						19 16				
Taplow	d																						
Burnham	d					18 21							18 51						19 21				
Slough	a					18 24				18 43			18 55						19 24				
	d					18 25				18 44			18 56						19 25				
Langley	d					18 30							19 00						19 30				
Iver	d																						
West Drayton	d					18 36							19 06						19 35				
Heathrow Terminal 5	a																						
	d	18 12			18 27			18 42				18 57			19 12			19 27			19 42		
Heathrow Terminal 4	a																						
	d		18 01	18 16					18 31		18 46					19 01	19 16					19 31	
Heathrow Termls 2 & 3	a	18 16	18 05	18 20	18 31			18 46	18 35		18 50	19 01			19 16	19 05	19 20	19 31			19 46	19 35	
	d	18 17	18 07		18 32			18 47	18 37			19 02			19 17	19 07		19 32			19 47	19 37	
Hayes & Harlington	d		18 15			18 41			18 45				19 11			19 15			19 40			19 45	
Southall	d		18 19			18 45			18 49				19 15			19 19			19 44			19 49	
Hanwell	d																						
Greenford	d																						
South Greenford	d																						
Castle Bar Park	d																						
Drayton Green	d																						
West Ealing	d																						
Ealing Broadway	d		18 24			18 50			18 54				19 20			19 24			19 49			19 54	
Acton Main Line	d																						
London Paddington	a	18 34	18 35		18 48	18 58		19 04	19 05	19 09		19 18	19 28		19 34	19 35		19 48	19 57		20 04	20 05	20 07

For non-stop services between Reading and London refer to Table T116

For non-stop services between London and Heathrow Airport see Table T118

For Heathrow Express Services see Table T118

Table T117-R

Sundays
16 September to 2 December

Reading, Heathrow Airport and Greenford - London

Stopping Services

		GW ◇1	XR	HX ◇1	GW	XC ◇1	HX ◇1	XR	XR	HX ◇1	GW	XC ◇1	HX ◇1	XR	GW ◇1	XR	HX ◇1	GW	XC ◇1	HX ◇1	XR	XR
Oxford	d	18 55				19 16						19 45			19 55				20 16			
Reading	d	19 27			19 30	19a40					19 58	20a08			20 25			20 30	20a41			
Twyford	d				19 38						20 08							20 36				
Maidenhead	d				19 46						20 16							20 44				
Taplow	d																					
Burnham	d				19 51						20 21							20 49				
Slough	a	19 43			19 55						20 24				20 43			20 53				
	d	19 44			19 56						20 25				20 44			20 54				
Langley	d				20 00						20 30							20 58				
Iver	d																					
West Drayton	d				20 06						20 36							21 04				
Heathrow Terminal 5	a																					
	d			19 57			20 12			20 27			20 42				20 57			21 12		
Heathrow Terminal 4	a																					
	d		19 46					20 01	20 16					20 31		20 46					21 01	21 16
Heathrow Termls 2 & 3	a		19 50	20 01			20 16	20 05	20 20	20 31			20 46	20 35		20 50	21 01			21 16	21 05	21 20
	d			20 02			20 17	20 07		20 32			20 47	20 37			21 02			21 17	21 07	
Hayes & Harlington	d				20 11			20 15			20 41			20 45				21 09			21 15	
Southall	d				20 15			20 19			20 45			20 49				21 13			21 19	
Hanwell	d																					
Greenford	d																					
South Greenford	d																					
Castle Bar Park	d																					
Drayton Green	d																					
West Ealing	d																					
Ealing Broadway	d				20 20			20 24			20 50			20 54				21 18			21 24	
Acton Main Line	d																					
London Paddington	a	20 10		20 18	20 28		20 34	20 35		20 48	20 58		21 04	21 05	21 08		21 18	21 26		21 34	21 35	

		HX ◇1	GW	XC ◇1	HX ◇1	XR	GW ◇1	GW ◇1	XR	HX ◇1	GW	XC ◇1	HX ◇1	XR	GW	XC ◇1	XR	HX ◇1	XR	HX ◇1	GW ◇	GW	XC ◇1
Oxford	d			20 45				20 55				21 16				21 40					21 50		22 12
Reading	d		21 00	21a13			21 27	21 28			21 30	21a38			21 50	22a06					22 20	22 24	22a38
Twyford	d		21 08								21 38				21 56							22 30	
Maidenhead	d		21 16					21 40			21 46				22 04							22 38	
Taplow	d																						
Burnham	d		21 21								21 51				22 09							22 43	
Slough	a		21 24					21 45			21 55				22 13						22 38	22 47	
	d		21 25					21 47			21 56				22 14						22 43	22 48	
Langley	d		21 30								22 00				22 18							22 52	
Iver	d																						
West Drayton	d		21 36								22 06				22 24							22 57	
Heathrow Terminal 5	a																						
	d	21 27			21 42					21 57			22 12					22 27		22 42			
Heathrow Terminal 4	a																						
	d					21 31			21 46					22 01			22 16		22 31				
Heathrow Termls 2 & 3	a	21 31			21 46	21 35			21 50	22 01			22 16	22 05			22 20	22 31	22 35	22 46			
	d	21 32			21 47	21 37				22 02			22 17	22 07				22 32	22 37	22 47			
Hayes & Harlington	d		21 41			21 45					22 11			22 15	22 29				22 45			23 01	
Southall	d		21 45			21 49					22 15			22 19	22 33				22 49				
Hanwell	d																						
Greenford	d																						
South Greenford	d																						
Castle Bar Park	d																						
Drayton Green	d																						
West Ealing	d																						
Ealing Broadway	d		21 50			21 54					22 20			22 24	22 38				22 54			23 08	
Acton Main Line	d																						
London Paddington	a	21 48	21 58		22 04	22 05	22 07	22 12		22 18	22 28		22 34	22 35	22 46			22 48	23 05	23 06	23 09	23 17	

For non-stop services between Reading and London refer to Table T116

For non-stop services between London and Heathrow Airport see Table T118

For Heathrow Express Services see Table T118

Table T117-R

Sundays
16 September to 2 December

Reading, Heathrow Airport and Greenford - London

Stopping Services

		XR	HX ◇1	XR	HX ◇1	GW	XR	HX ◇1	GW ◇1		XR	HX ◇1	XR	GW	HX
Oxford	d								22 43						
Reading 7	d					22 51			23 13					23 42	
Twyford 3	d					22 57								23 49	
Maidenhead 3	d					23 05								23 57	
Taplow	d														
Burnham	d					23 10								00 01	
Slough 3	a					23 14			23 30					00 06	
	d					23 15			23 32					00 07	
Langley	d					23 20								00 11	
Iver	d														
West Drayton	d					23 25								00 17	
Heathrow Terminal 5 ⊖ ✈	a														
	d		22 57		23 12			23 27				23 42			23 57
Heathrow Terminal 4 ⊖ ✈	a														
	d	22 46		23 01			23 16				23 31		23 46		
Heathrow Termls 2 & 3 2 ⊖ ✈	a	22 50	23 01	23 05	23 16		23 20	23 31			23 35	23 46	23 50		00 01
	d		23 02	23 07	23 17			23 32			23 37	23 47	23 52		
Hayes & Harlington	d			23 14		23 30					23 45		23 58	00 21	
Southall	d			23 18							23 49		00 03	00 25	
Hanwell	d														
Greenford ⊖	d														
South Greenford	d														
Castle Bar Park	d														
Drayton Green	d														
West Ealing	d														
Ealing Broadway ⊖	d			23 23		23 37					23 54		00 08	00 30	
Acton Main Line	d														
London Paddington 15 ⊖	a		23 19	23 34	23 35	23 45		23 48	23 51		00 04	00 06	00 20	00 39	

For non-stop services between Reading and London refer to Table T116

For non-stop services between London and Heathrow Airport see Table T118

For Heathrow Express Services see Table T118

NRT MAY 2018 EDITION

Table T118-F

Mondays to Fridays
21 May to 7 December

London - Heathrow Airport (Heathrow Express Services)

Miles	Miles			XR	HX	XR	HX ◇1	HX ◇1	XR	HX ◇1	XR	HX ◇1	XR	HX ◇1	XR		HX ◇1	XR	HX ◇1	XR	HX ◇1	XR	HX ◇1	XR
0	—	London Paddington 15 ⊖	d	04 42		04 57	05 10	05 25		05 40	05 32	05 55		06 10	06 02	and at the same minutes past each hour until	20 25		20 40	20 32	20 55		21 10	21 02
14¾	0	Heathrow Terminals 2 & 3 2 ⊖ ✈	a	05 05		05 16	05 26	05 40		05 55	06 00	06 10		06 25	06 30		20 40		20 55	21 00	21 10		21 25	21 30
—	—		d	05 07	05 13	05 18	05 28	05 41	05 48	05 58	06 03	06 11	06 18	06 28	06 33		20 41	20 48	20 58	21 03	21 11	21 18	21 28	21 33
—	1¾	Heathrow Terminal 4 ⊖ ✈	a	05 11		05 22			05 52		06 07		06 22		06 37			20 52		21 07		21 22		21 37
16¼	—	Heathrow Terminal 5 ⊖ ✈	a		05 17		05 32	05 46		06 02		06 16		06 32			20 46		21 02		21 16		21 32	

		HX ◇1	XR	HX ◇1	XR	HX ◇1	XR	HX ◇1	XR	HX ◇1	XR	HX ◇1	XR	HX ◇1	XR	HX ◇1	XR	HX ◇1	XR
London Paddington 15 ⊖	d	21 25		21 40	21 32	21 55		22 10	22 03	22 25		22 40	22 32	22 55		23 10	23 02	23 25	
Heathrow Terminals 2 & 3 2 ⊖ ✈	a	21 40		21 55	22 00	22 10		22 25	22 30	22 40		22 55	23 00	23 10		23 25	23 30	23 40	
	d	21 41	21 48	21 58	22 03	22 11	22 18	22 28	22 33	22 41	22 48	22 58	23 03	23 11	23 18	23 28	23 33	23 41	23 48
Heathrow Terminal 4 ⊖ ✈	a		21 52		22 07		22 22		22 37		22 52		23 07		23 22		23 37		23 52
Heathrow Terminal 5 ⊖ ✈	a	21 46		22 02		22 16		22 32		22 46		23 02		23 16		23 32		23 46	

Saturdays
26 May to 8 December

		XR	HX	XR	HX ◇1	XR	HX ◇1	XR	HX ◇1	XR	HX ◇1	XR	HX ◇1		XR	HX ◇1	XR	HX ◇1	XR	HX ◇1	XR	HX ◇1		XR
London Paddington 15 ⊖	d	04 42			05 10	05 02	05 25		05 40	05 32	05 55		06 10	and at the same minutes past each hour until	22 02	22 25		22 40	22 32	22 55		23 10		23 02
Heathrow Terminals 2 & 3 2 ⊖ ✈	a	05 05			05 26	05 30	05 40		05 55	06 00	06 10		06 25		22 30	22 40		22 55	23 00	23 10		23 25		23 30
	d	05 07	05 13	05 18	05 28	05 33	05 41	05 48	05 58	06 03	06 11	06 18	06 28		22 33	22 41	22 48	22 58	23 03	23 11	23 18	23 28		23 33
Heathrow Terminal 4 ⊖ ✈	a	05 11		05 22		05 37		05 52		06 07		06 22			22 37		22 52		23 07		23 22			23 37
Heathrow Terminal 5 ⊖ ✈	a		05 17		05 32		05 46		06 02		06 16		06 32			22 46		23 02		23 16		23 32		

		HX ◇1	XR
London Paddington 15 ⊖	d	23 25	
Heathrow Terminals 2 & 3 2 ⊖ ✈	a	23 40	
	d	23 41	23 48
Heathrow Terminal 4 ⊖ ✈	a		23 52
Heathrow Terminal 5 ⊖ ✈	a	23 46	

Sundays
20 May to 9 September

		HX	HX ◇1	XR	HX ◇1	XR	HX ◇1	XR	HX ◇1	XR		HX ◇	XR	HX ◇1	XR	HX ◇1	XR	HX ◇1	XR	HX ◇1		XR	HX ◇1	XR	HX ◇1
London Paddington 15 ⊖	d		05 10	05 11	05 25	05 27	05 40	05 41	05 55			06 10	06 11	06 25		06 40	06 41	06 55		07 10		07 11	07 25		07 40
Heathrow Terminals 2 & 3 2 ⊖ ✈	a		05 26	05 35	05 41	05 50	05 56	06 05	06 11			06 26	06 35	06 41		06 56	07 05	07 11		07 26		07 35	07 41		07 56
	d	05 13	05 28	05 37	05 43	05 53	05 58	06 07	06 13	06 23		06 28	06 37	06 43	06 53	06 58	07 07	07 13	07 23	07 28		07 37	07 43	07 53	07 58
Heathrow Terminal 4 ⊖ ✈	a			05 45		06 00		06 15		06 27			06 45		06 57		07 15		07 27			07 45		07 57	
Heathrow Terminal 5 ⊖ ✈	a	05 17	05 32		05 47		06 02		06 17			06 32		06 47		07 02		07 17		07 32			07 47		08 02

		XR	HX ◇1	XR	HX ◇1	XR		HX ◇1	XR	HX ◇1	XR	HX ◇1	XR	HX ◇1	XR	HX ◇1		XR	HX ◇	XR	HX ◇	XR	HX ◇	XR
London Paddington 15 ⊖	d	07 41	07 55		08 10	08 11		08 25		08 40	08 41	08 55		09 10	09 11	09 25	and at the same minutes past each hour until		20 40	20 41	20 55		21 10	21 11
Heathrow Terminals 2 & 3 2 ⊖ ✈	a	08 05	08 11		08 26	08 35		08 41		08 55	09 05	09 10		09 25	09 35	09 40			20 55	21 05	21 10		21 25	21 35
	d	08 07	08 13	08 23	08 28	08 37		08 43	08 53	08 56	09 07	09 11	09 23	09 26	09 37	09 41		20 53	20 56	21 07	21 11	21 23	21 26	21 37
Heathrow Terminal 4 ⊖ ✈	a	08 15		08 27		08 45			08 57		09 15		09 27		09 45			20 57		21 15		21 27		21 45
Heathrow Terminal 5 ⊖ ✈	a		08 17		08 32			08 47		09 01		09 16		09 31		09 46			21 01		21 16		21 31	

		HX ◇		XR	HX ◇	XR	HX ◇	XR	HX ◇	XR	HX ◇	XR		HX ◇	XR	HX ◇	XR	HX ◇	XR	HX ◇
London Paddington 15 ⊖	d	21 25			21 40	21 41	21 55		22 10	22 11	22 25			22 40	22 41	22 55		23 10	23 11	23 25
Heathrow Terminals 2 & 3 2 ⊖ ✈	a	21 40			21 56	22 06	22 11		22 26	22 35	22 41			22 56	23 05	23 11		23 26	23 35	23 41
	d	21 41		21 53	21 58	22 08	22 13	22 23	22 28	22 37	22 43	22 53		22 58	23 07	23 13	23 23	23 28	23 37	23 43
Heathrow Terminal 4 ⊖ ✈	a			21 57		22 16		22 27		22 45		22 57			23 15		23 27		23 45	
Heathrow Terminal 5 ⊖ ✈	a	21 46			22 02		22 17		22 32		22 47			23 02		23 17		23 32		23 47

Sundays
16 September to 2 December

		HX	HX ◇1	XR	HX ◇1	XR	HX ◇1	XR	HX ◇1	XR	HX ◇	XR	HX ◇1	XR		HX ◇	XR	HX ◇	XR	HX ◇	XR	HX ◇	XR
London Paddington 15 ⊖	d		05 10	05 11	05 25	05 27	05 40	05 41	05 55		06 10	06 11	06 25		and at the same minutes past each hour until	21 40	21 41	21 55		22 10	22 11	22 25	
Heathrow Terminals 2 & 3 2 ⊖ ✈	a		05 26	05 35	05 41	05 50	05 56	06 05	06 11		06 26	06 35	06 41			21 56	22 05	22 11		22 26	22 35	22 41	
	d	05 13	05 28	05 37	05 43	05 53	05 58	06 07	06 13	06 23	06 28	06 37	06 43	06 53		21 58	22 07	22 13	22 23	22 28	22 37	22 43	22 53
Heathrow Terminal 4 ⊖ ✈	a			05 45		06 00		06 15		06 27		06 45		06 57			22 15		22 27		22 45		22 57
Heathrow Terminal 5 ⊖ ✈	a	05 17	05 32		05 47		06 02		06 17		06 32		06 47			22 02		22 17		22 32		22 47	

For Heathrow Connect services see Table T117

Table T118-F

Sundays

16 September to 2 December

London - Heathrow Airport (Heathrow Express Services)

	HX	XR		HX	XR	HX	XR	HX
	◇			◇		◇		◇
London Paddington [15] ⊖ d	22 40	22 41		22 55		23 10	23 11	23 25
Heathrow Terminals 2 & 3 [2] ⊖ ✈ a	22 56	23 05		23 11		23 26	23 35	23 41
d	22 58	23 07		23 13	23 23	23 28	23 37	23 43
Heathrow Terminal 4 ⊖ ✈ a		23 15			23 27		23 45	
Heathrow Terminal 5 ⊖ ✈ a	23 02			23 17		23 32		23 47

For Heathrow Connect services see Table T117

Table T118-R

Mondays to Fridays

21 May to 7 December

Heathrow Airport (Heathrow Express Services) - London

Miles	Miles		XR MX	XR MO	XR MX	HX	XR MW FO	HX	XR		HX	XR	HX	XR	HX	XR	HX	XR	HX		XR	HX	XR	HX
						◇1		◇1			◇1		◇1		◇1		◇1		◇1			◇1		◇1
0	—	Heathrow Terminal 5 ⊖ ✈ d				05 12		05 27			05 42		05 57		06 12		06 27		06 42			06 57		07 12
—	0	Heathrow Terminal 4 ⊖ ✈ d		00 01	00 07		05 22		05 41			05 52		06 11		06 22		06 41			06 52		07 11	
1½	1¾	Heathrow Terminals 2 & 3 [2] ⊖ ✈ a		00 05	00 11	05 16	05 26	05 31	05 45		05 46	05 56	06 01	06 15	06 16	06 26	06 31	06 45	06 46		06 56	07 01	07 15	07 16
—	—	d	00 03	00 07	00 13	05 17	05 28	05 33			05 48	05 58	06 03		06 18	06 28	06 33		06 48		06 58	07 03		07 18
16¼	—	London Paddington [15] ⊖ a	00 26	00 33	00 39	05 33	05 56	05 49			06 04	06 26	06 19		06 34	06 56	06 49		07 04		07 25	07 19		07 34

	XR	HX	XR	HX	XR		HX	XR	HX	XR	HX	XR	HX	XR	HX		XR	HX	XR	HX	XR	HX	XR	HX
		◇1		◇1			◇1		◇1		◇1		◇1		◇1			◇1		◇1		◇1		◇1
Heathrow Terminal 5 ⊖ ✈ d		07 27		07 42			07 57		08 12		08 27		08 42		08 57			09 12		09 27		09 42		09 57
Heathrow Terminal 4 ⊖ ✈ d	07 22		07 41		07 52			08 11		08 22		08 41		08 52			09 11		09 22		09 41		09 52	
Heathrow Terminals 2 & 3 [2] ⊖ ✈ a	07 26	07 31	07 45	07 46	07 56		08 01	08 15	08 16	08 26	08 31	08 45	08 46	08 56	09 01		09 15	09 16	09 26	09 31	09 45	09 46	09 56	10 01
d	07 28	07 33		07 48	07 58		08 03		08 18	08 28	08 33		08 48	08 58	09 03			09 18	09 28	09 33		09 48	09 58	10 03
London Paddington [15] ⊖ a	07 57	07 49		08 04	08 26		08 19		08 35	08 56	08 49		09 04	09 26	09 19			09 35	09 56	09 49		10 04	10 26	10 19

	XR		HX	XR	HX	XR	HX	XR	HX	XR	HX	XR	HX	XR	HX	XR	HX	XR	HX				
			◇1		◇1		◇1		◇1		◇1		◇1		◇1		◇1		◇1	and at the same minutes past each hour until			
Heathrow Terminal 5 ⊖ ✈ d			10 12		10 27		10 42		10 57		11 12		11 27		11 42		11 57		12 12				
Heathrow Terminal 4 ⊖ ✈ d	10 11			10 22		10 41		10 52		11 11		11 22		11 41		11 52		12 11					
Heathrow Terminals 2 & 3 [2] ⊖ ✈ a	10 15		10 16	10 26	10 31	10 45	10 46	10 56	11 01	11 15	11 16	11 26	11 31	11 45	11 46	11 56	12 01	12 15	12 16				
d			10 18	10 28	10 33		10 48	10 58	11 03		11 18	11 28	11 33		11 48	11 58	12 03		12 18				
London Paddington [15] ⊖ a			10 34	10 56	10 49		11 04	11 26	11 19		11 34	11 56	11 49		12 04	12 26	12 19		12 35				

	XR	HX	XR	HX	XR	HX	XR	HX		XR	HX	XR	HX	XR	HX	XR	HX	XR		HX	XR	HX	XR	HX
		◇1		◇1		◇1		◇1			◇1		◇1		◇1		◇1			◇1		◇1		◇1
Heathrow Terminal 5 ⊖ ✈ d		14 27		14 42		14 57		15 12			15 27		15 42		15 57		16 12			16 27		16 42		16 57
Heathrow Terminal 4 ⊖ ✈ d	14 22		14 41		14 52		15 11			15 22		15 41		15 52		16 11		16 22			16 41		16 52	
Heathrow Terminals 2 & 3 [2] ⊖ ✈ a	14 26	14 31	14 45	14 46	14 56	15 01	15 15	15 16		15 26	15 31	15 45	15 46	15 56	16 01	16 15	16 16	16 26		16 31	16 45	16 46	16 56	17 01
d	14 28	14 33		14 48	14 58	15 03		15 18		15 28	15 33		15 48	15 58	16 03		16 18	16 28		16 33		16 48	16 58	17 03
London Paddington [15] ⊖ a	14 56	14 49		15 04	15 26	15 19		15 35		15 56	15 49		16 05	16 26	16 19		16 35	16 56		16 49		17 05	17 26	17 19

	XR	HX	XR	HX		XR	HX	XR	HX	XR	HX	XR	HX	XR		HX	XR	HX	XR	HX	XR	HX	XR	HX
		◇1		◇1			◇1		◇1		◇1		◇1			◇1		◇1		◇1		◇1		◇1
Heathrow Terminal 5 ⊖ ✈ d		17 12		17 27			17 42		17 57		18 12		18 27			18 42		18 57		19 12		19 27		19 42
Heathrow Terminal 4 ⊖ ✈ d	17 11		17 22			17 41		17 52		18 11		18 22		18 41			18 52		19 11		19 22		19 41	
Heathrow Terminals 2 & 3 [2] ⊖ ✈ a	17 15	17 16	17 26	17 31		17 45	17 46	17 56	18 01	18 15	18 16	18 26	18 31	18 45		18 46	18 56	19 01	19 15	19 16	19 26	19 31	19 45	19 46
d		17 18	17 28	17 33			17 48	17 58	18 03		18 18	18 28	18 33			18 48	18 58	19 03		19 18	19 28	19 33		19 48
London Paddington [15] ⊖ a		17 35	17 56	17 49			18 05	18 26	18 19		18 34	18 55	18 49			19 05	19 26	19 19		19 35	19 56	19 49		20 04

	XR	HX	XR	HX		XR	HX	XR	HX	XR	HX	XR	HX		XR	HX	XR	HX	HX	XR			
		◇1		◇1	and at the same minutes past each hour until		◇1		◇1		◇1		◇1			◇1		◇1					
Heathrow Terminal 5 ⊖ ✈ d		19 57		20 12			22 27		22 42		22 57		23 12			23 27		23 42	23 51				
Heathrow Terminal 4 ⊖ ✈ d	19 52		20 11			22 22		22 41		22 52		23 11			23 22		23 41			23 57			
Heathrow Terminals 2 & 3 [2] ⊖ ✈ a	19 56	20 01	20 15	20 16		22 26	22 31	22 45	22 46	22 56	23 01	23 15	23 16		23 26	23 31	23 45	23 46	23 55	00 01			
d	19 58	20 03		20 18		22 28	22 33		22 48	22 58	23 03		23 18		23 28	23 33		23 48		00 03			
London Paddington [15] ⊖ a	20 26	20 19		20 34		22 56	22 49		23 04	23 26	23 19		23 34		23 56	23 49		00 05		00 26			

Saturdays

26 May to 8 December

	XR	XR	HX	XR	HX	XR	HX	XR	HX	XR	HX	XR		HX	XR	HX	XR	HX	XR	HX	XR		HX
			◇1		◇1		◇1		◇1		◇1		and at the same minutes past each hour until	◇1		◇1		◇1		◇1			◇1
Heathrow Terminal 5 ⊖ ✈ d			05 12		05 27		05 42		05 57		06 12			09 27		09 42		09 57		10 12			10 27
Heathrow Terminal 4 ⊖ ✈ d		00 07		05 22		05 41		05 52		06 11		06 22			09 41		09 52		10 11		10 22		
Heathrow Terminals 2 & 3 [2] ⊖ ✈ a		00 11	05 16	05 26	05 31	05 45	05 46	05 56	06 01	06 15	06 16	06 26		09 31	09 45	09 46	09 56	10 01	10 15	10 16	10 26		10 31
d	00 03	00 13	05 17	05 28	05 33		05 48	05 58	06 03		06 18	06 28		09 33		09 48	09 58	10 03		10 18	10 28		10 33
London Paddington [15] ⊖ a	00 26	00 39	05 33	05 55	05 49		06 04	06 26	06 19		06 34	06 56		09 49		10 04	10 26	10 19		10 34	10 56		10 49

	XR	HX	XR	HX	XR	HX	XR	HX		XR	HX	XR	HX	XR	HX	XR	HX	XR		HX	XR	HX	XR	HX
		◇1		◇1		◇1		◇1			◇1		◇1		◇1		◇1			◇1		◇1		◇1
Heathrow Terminal 5 ⊖ ✈ d		10 42		10 57		11 12		11 27			11 42		11 57		12 12		12 27			12 42		12 57		13 12
Heathrow Terminal 4 ⊖ ✈ d	10 41		10 52		11 11		11 22			11 41		11 52		12 11		12 22		12 41			12 52		13 11	
Heathrow Terminals 2 & 3 [2] ⊖ ✈ a	10 45	10 46	10 56	11 01	11 15	11 16	11 26	11 31		11 45	11 46	11 56	12 01	12 15	12 16	12 26	12 31	12 45		12 46	12 56	13 01	13 15	13 16
d		10 48	10 58	11 03		11 18	11 28	11 33			11 48	11 58	12 03		12 18	12 28	12 33			12 48	12 58	13 03		13 18
London Paddington [15] ⊖ a		11 05	11 26	11 19		11 35	11 56	11 49			12 04	12 26	12 19		12 34	12 56	12 49			13 04	13 26	13 19		13 35

For Heathrow Connect services see Table T117

Table T118-R

Heathrow Airport (Heathrow Express Services) - London

Saturdays

26 May to 8 December

		XR	HX	XR	HX	XR	HX	XR	HX	XR		HX	XR	HX	XR	HX	XR	HX	XR	HX		XR	HX	XR
			◇1		◇1		◇1		◇1			◇1		◇1		◇1		◇1		◇1			◇1	
Heathrow Terminal 5 ⊖ ✈ d			13 27		13 42		13 57		14 12			14 27		14 42		14 57		15 12		15 27			15 42	
Heathrow Terminal 4 ⊖ ✈ d		13 22		13 41		13 52		14 11		14 22			14 41		14 52		15 11		15 22			15 41		15 52
Heathrow Terminals 2 & 3 ⊖ ✈ a		13 26	13 31	13 45	13 46	13 56	14 01	14 15	14 16	14 26		14 31	14 45	14 46	14 56	15 01	15 15	15 16	15 26	15 31		15 45	15 46	15 56
d		13 28	13 33		13 48	13 58	14 03		14 18	14 28		14 33		14 48	14 58	15 03		15 18	15 28	15 33			15 48	15 58
London Paddington ⊖ a		13 56	13 49		14 04	14 26	14 19		14 34	14 56		14 49		15 04	15 26	15 19		15 34	15 56	15 49			16 04	16 26

	HX	XR	HX	XR	HX	XR	HX	XR	HX	XR	HX		XR	HX	XR	HX	XR	HX	XR	HX		XR	HX
	◇1		◇1		◇1		◇1		◇1		◇1			◇1		◇1		◇1		◇1			◇1
Heathrow Terminal 5 ⊖ ✈ d	15 57		16 12		16 27		16 42		16 57		17 12	and at the same minutes past each hour until		20 27		20 42		20 57		21 12			21 27
Heathrow Terminal 4 ⊖ ✈ d		16 11		16 22		16 41		16 52		17 11			20 22		20 41		20 52		21 11			21 22	
Heathrow Terminals 2 & 3 ⊖ ✈ a	16 01	16 15	16 16	16 26	16 31	16 45	16 46	16 56	17 01	17 15	17 16		20 26	20 31	20 45	20 46	20 56	21 01	21 15	21 16		21 26	21 31
d	16 03		16 18	16 28	16 33		16 48	16 58	17 03		17 18		20 28	20 33		20 48	20 58	21 03		21 18		21 28	21 33
London Paddington ⊖ a	16 19		16 35	16 56	16 49		17 04	17 26	17 19		17 34		20 56	20 49		21 04	21 26	21 19		21 34		21 56	21 49

	XR	HX	XR	HX	XR	HX	XR		HX	XR	HX	XR	HX	XR	HX	XR	HX		XR	HX	HX	XR
		◇1		◇1		◇1			◇1		◇1		◇1		◇1		◇1			◇1		
Heathrow Terminal 5 ⊖ ✈ d		21 42		21 57		22 12			22 27		22 42		22 57		23 12		23 27			23 42	23 51	
Heathrow Terminal 4 ⊖ ✈ d	21 41		21 52		22 11		22 22			22 41		22 52		23 11		23 22			23 41			23 57
Heathrow Terminals 2 & 3 ⊖ ✈ a	21 45	21 46	21 56	22 01	22 15	22 16	22 26		22 31	22 45	22 46	22 56	23 01	23 15	23 16	23 26	23 31		23 45	23 46	23 55	00 01
d		21 48	21 58	22 03		22 18	22 28		22 33		22 48	22 58	23 03		23 18	23 28	23 33			23 48		00 03
London Paddington ⊖ a		22 04	22 26	22 19		22 35	22 56		22 49		23 05	23 26	23 19		23 34	23 56	23 49			00 05		00 27

Sundays

20 May to 9 September

	XR	XR	HX		HX		XR	HX	XR	HX	XR	HX	XR	HX		XR	HX	XR	HX	XR	HX	XR
	A		◇1		◇1			◇1		◇1		◇1		◇1			◇1		◇1		◇1	
Heathrow Terminal 5 ⊖ ✈ d			05 12	and every 15 minutes until	05 57			06 12		06 27		06 42		06 57	and at the same minutes past each hour until		17 12		17 27		17 42	
Heathrow Terminal 4 ⊖ ✈ d		00 07					06 01		06 16		06 31		06 46			17 01		17 16		17 31		17 46
Heathrow Terminals 2 & 3 ⊖ ✈ a		00 11	05 16		06 01		06 05	06 16	06 20	06 31	06 35	06 46	06 50	07 01		17 05	17 16	17 20	17 31	17 35	17 46	17 50
d	00 03	00 13	05 17		06 02		06 07	06 17		06 32	06 37	06 47		07 02		17 07	17 17		17 32	17 37	17 47	
London Paddington ⊖ a	00 27	00 39	05 33		06 18		06 34	06 33		06 48	07 04	07 03		07 18		17 34	17 33		17 48	18 04	18 03	

	HX		XR	HX	XR	HX	XR	HX	XR	HX	XR		HX	XR	HX	XR	HX	XR	HX	XR	HX		XR	HX
	◇1			◇1		◇1		◇1		◇1			◇1		◇1		◇1		◇1		◇1			◇1
Heathrow Terminal 5 ⊖ ✈ d	17 57			18 12		18 27		18 42		18 57			19 12		19 27		19 42		19 57		20 12			20 27
Heathrow Terminal 4 ⊖ ✈ d			18 01		18 16		18 31		18 46		19 01			19 16		19 31		19 46		20 01			20 16	
Heathrow Terminals 2 & 3 ⊖ ✈ a	18 01		18 05	18 16	18 20	18 31	18 35	18 46	18 50	19 01	19 05		19 16	19 20	19 31	19 35	19 46	19 50	20 01	20 05	20 16		20 20	20 31
d	18 02		18 07	18 17		18 32	18 37	18 47		19 02	19 07		19 17		19 32	19 37	19 47		20 02	20 07	20 17			20 32
London Paddington ⊖ a	18 18		18 34	18 33		18 48	19 07	19 03		19 18	19 34		19 33		19 48	20 04	20 03		20 18	20 34	20 33			20 48

	XR	HX	XR	HX	XR	HX	XR		HX	XR	HX	XR	HX	XR	HX	XR	HX		XR	HX	XR	HX	XR	HX
		◇1		◇1		◇1			◇1		◇1		◇1		◇1		◇1			◇1		◇1		◇1
Heathrow Terminal 5 ⊖ ✈ d		20 42		20 57		21 12			21 27		21 42		21 57		22 12		22 27			22 42		22 57		23 12
Heathrow Terminal 4 ⊖ ✈ d	20 31		20 46		21 01		21 16			21 31		21 46		22 01		22 16			22 31		22 46		23 01	
Heathrow Terminals 2 & 3 ⊖ ✈ a	20 35	20 46	20 50	21 01	21 05	21 16	21 20		21 31	21 35	21 46	21 50	22 01	22 05	22 16	22 20	22 31		22 35	22 46	22 50	23 01	23 05	23 16
d	20 37	20 47		21 02	21 07	21 17			21 32	21 37	21 47		22 02	22 07	22 17		22 32		22 37	22 47		23 02	23 07	23 17
London Paddington ⊖ a	21 04	21 03		21 18	21 34	21 33			21 48	22 04	22 03		22 18	22 35	22 33		22 48		23 04	23 05		23 19	23 36	23 35

	XR	HX	XR		HX	XR	HX
		◇1			◇1		
Heathrow Terminal 5 ⊖ ✈ d		23 27			23 42		23 57
Heathrow Terminal 4 ⊖ ✈ d	23 16		23 31			23 46	
Heathrow Terminals 2 & 3 ⊖ ✈ a	23 20	23 31	23 35		23 46	23 50	00 01
d		23 32	23 37		23 47	23 52	
London Paddington ⊖ a		23 48	00 04		00 05	00 20	

Sundays

16 September to 2 December

	XR	XR	HX		HX	XR	HX	XR	HX		XR	HX	XR	HX	XR	HX	XR	HX	XR		HX	XR	HX
			◇1		◇1		◇1		◇1			◇1		◇1		◇1		◇1			◇1		◇1
Heathrow Terminal 5 ⊖ ✈ d			05 12	and every 15 minutes until	05 57		06 12		06 27			06 42		06 57		07 12		07 27			07 42		07 57
Heathrow Terminal 4 ⊖ ✈ d		00 07				06 01		06 16			06 31		06 46		07 01		07 16		07 31			07 46	
Heathrow Terminals 2 & 3 ⊖ ✈ a		00 11	05 16		06 01	06 05	06 16	06 20	06 31		06 35	06 46	06 50	07 01	07 05	07 16	07 20	07 31	07 35		07 46	07 50	08 01
d	00 03	00 13	05 17		06 02	06 07	06 17		06 32		06 37	06 47		07 02	07 07	07 17		07 32	07 37		07 47		08 02
London Paddington ⊖ a	00 27	00 39	05 33		06 18	06 34	06 33		06 48		07 04	07 03		07 18	07 35	07 34		07 48	08 04		08 03		08 18

A not 20 May

For Heathrow Connect services see Table T117

Table T118-R

Heathrow Airport (Heathrow Express Services) - London

Sundays

16 September to 2 December

	XR	HX		XR	HX	XR	HX	XR	HX	XR	HX	XR		HX	XR	HX	XR	HX	XR	HX	XR	HX		XR
		◇1			◇1		◇1		◇1		◇1			◇1		◇1		◇1		◇1		◇1		
Heathrow Terminal 5 ⊖ ✈ d		08 12			08 27		08 42		08 57		09 12			09 27		09 42		09 57		10 12		10 27		
Heathrow Terminal 4 ⊖ ✈ d	08 01			08 16		08 31		08 46		09 01		09 16			09 31		09 46		10 01		10 16			10 31
Heathrow Terminals 2 & 3 ⊖ ✈ a	08 05	08 16		08 20	08 31	08 35	08 46	08 50	09 01	09 05	09 16	09 20		09 31	09 35	09 46	09 50	10 01	10 05	10 16	10 20	10 31		10 35
d	08 07	08 17			08 32	08 37	08 47		09 02	09 07	09 17			09 32	09 37	09 47		10 02	10 07	10 17		10 32		10 37
London Paddington ⊖ a	08 36	08 34			08 48	09 04	09 03		09 18	09 35	09 34			09 48	10 05	10 07		10 18	10 35	10 37		10 48		11 05

	HX	XR	HX	XR	HX	XR	HX	XR		HX	XR	HX	XR	HX	XR	HX	XR	HX		XR	HX	XR	HX	XR
	◇1		◇1		◇1		◇1			◇1		◇1		◇1		◇1		◇1			◇1		◇1	
Heathrow Terminal 5 ⊖ ✈ d	10 42		10 57		11 12		11 27			11 42		11 57		12 12		12 27		12 42			12 57		13 12	
Heathrow Terminal 4 ⊖ ✈ d		10 46		11 01		11 16		11 31			11 46		12 01		12 16		12 31			12 46		13 01		13 16
Heathrow Terminals 2 & 3 ⊖ ✈ a	10 46	10 50	11 01	11 05	11 16	11 20	11 31	11 35		11 46	11 50	12 01	12 05	12 16	12 20	12 31	12 35	12 46		12 50	13 01	13 05	13 16	13 20
d	10 47		11 02	11 07	11 17		11 32	11 37		11 47		12 02	12 07	12 17		12 32	12 37	12 47			13 02	13 07	13 17	
London Paddington ⊖ a	11 07		11 18	11 35	11 35		11 48	12 05		12 07		12 18	12 35	12 35		12 48	13 05	13 07			13 18	13 35	13 37	

	HX	XR	HX	XR		HX	XR	HX	XR	HX	XR	HX	XR	HX		XR	HX	XR	HX	XR	HX
	◇1		◇1			◇1		◇1		◇1		◇1		◇1			◇1		◇1		◇1
Heathrow Terminal 5 ⊖ ✈ d	13 27		13 42			13 57		14 12		14 27		14 42		14 57			15 12		15 27		15 42
Heathrow Terminal 4 ⊖ ✈ d		13 31		13 46			14 01		14 16		14 31		14 46			15 01		15 16		15 31	
Heathrow Terminals 2 & 3 ⊖ ✈ a	13 31	13 35	13 46	13 50		14 01	14 05	14 16	14 20	14 31	14 35	14 46	14 50	15 01		15 05	15 16	15 20	15 31	15 35	15 46
d	13 32	13 37	13 47			14 02	14 07	14 17		14 32	14 37	14 47		15 02		15 07	15 17		15 32	15 37	15 47
London Paddington ⊖ a	13 48	14 05	14 07			14 18	14 35	14 37		14 48	15 05	15 07		15 18		15 35	15 37		15 48	16 05	16 07

	XR	HX	XR	HX	XR	HX	XR	HX		XR	HX	XR	HX	XR	HX	XR	HX		XR	HX	XR	HX	XR
		◇1		◇1		◇1		◇1			◇1		◇1		◇1		◇1			◇1		◇1	
Heathrow Terminal 5 ⊖ ✈ d		15 57		16 12		16 27		16 42	and at the same minutes past each hour until		20 57		21 12		21 27		21 42			21 57		22 12	
Heathrow Terminal 4 ⊖ ✈ d	15 46		16 01		16 16		16 31			20 46		21 01		21 16		21 31			21 46		22 01		22 16
Heathrow Terminals 2 & 3 ⊖ ✈ a	15 50	16 01	16 05	16 16	16 20	16 31	16 35	16 46		20 50	21 01	21 05	21 16	21 20	21 31	21 35	21 46		21 50	22 01	22 05	22 16	22 20
d		16 02	16 07	16 17		16 32	16 37	16 47			21 02	21 07	21 17		21 32	21 37	21 47			22 02	22 07	22 17	
London Paddington ⊖ a		16 18	16 35	16 34		16 48	17 05	17 04			21 18	21 35	21 34		21 48	22 05	22 04			22 18	22 35	22 34	

	HX	XR	HX	XR		HX	XR	HX	XR	HX	XR	HX	XR	HX
	◇1		◇1			◇1		◇1		◇1		◇1		
Heathrow Terminal 5 ⊖ ✈ d	22 27		22 42			22 57		23 12		23 27		23 42		23 57
Heathrow Terminal 4 ⊖ ✈ d		22 31		22 46			23 01		23 16		23 31		23 46	
Heathrow Terminals 2 & 3 ⊖ ✈ a	22 31	22 35	22 46	22 50		23 01	23 05	23 16	23 20	23 31	23 35	23 46	23 50	00 01
d	22 32	22 37	22 47			23 02	23 07	23 17		23 32	23 37	23 47	23 52	
London Paddington ⊖ a	22 48	23 05	23 06			23 19	23 34	23 35		23 48	00 04	00 06	00 20	

For Heathrow Connect services see Table T117

Table T119-F

Slough - Windsor & Eton

Mondays to Fridays

21 May to 7 December

Miles			GW	GW	GW	GW	GW	GW	GW	GW	GW	GW	GW	GW	and at the same minutes past each hour until	GW	GW	GW		GW	GW
0	Slough ■	d	05 30	05 50	06 10	06 30	06 50	07 08	07 30	07 50	08 08	08 30	08 50	09 10		16 30	16 50	17 10		17 30	17 51
2¾	Windsor & Eton Central	a	05 36	05 56	06 16	06 36	06 56	07 14	07 36	07 56	08 14	08 36	08 56	09 16		16 36	16 56	17 16		17 36	17 57

		GW	GW	GW	and at the same minutes past each hour until	GW	GW	GW		GW	GW
Slough ■	d	18 10	18 30	18 50		22 10	22 30	22 50		23 12	23 36
Windsor & Eton Central	a	18 16	18 36	18 56		22 16	22 36	22 56		23 18	23 42

Saturdays

26 May to 8 December

		GW	and every 30 minutes until	GW	GW	GW	GW	GW	and at the same minutes past each hour until	GW	GW	GW		GW	GW	GW	and every 30 minutes until	GW	GW	GW
Slough ■	d	06 17		09 47	10 11	10 30	10 50	11 10		17 30	17 50	18 10		18 30	18 50	19 17		22 47	23 22	23 56
Windsor & Eton Central	a	06 23		09 53	10 17	10 36	10 56	11 16		17 36	17 56	18 16		18 36	18 56	19 23		22 53	23 28	00 02

Sundays

20 May to 2 December

		GW	and every 30 minutes until	GW		GW	GW	GW	and at the same minutes past each hour until	GW	GW	GW			GW	and every 30 minutes until	GW
Slough ■	d	08 22		09 52		10 12	10 32	10 52		18 12	18 32	18 52			19 22		23 22
Windsor & Eton Central	a	08 28		09 58		10 18	10 38	10 58		18 18	18 38	18 58			19 28		23 28

Table T119-R

Windsor & Eton - Slough

Mondays to Fridays

21 May to 7 December

Miles			GW	GW ■	GW ■	GW ■	GW ■	GW ■	GW ■		GW ■	GW ■	GW ■	GW ■	GW ■	and at the same minutes past each hour until	GW ■	GW ■	GW ■		GW ■	GW ■
0	Windsor & Eton Central	d	05 39	05 59	06 19	06 39	06 59	07 17	07 39		07 59	08 17	08 39	08 59	09 19		16 39	16 59	17 19		17 39	18 00
2¾	Slough ■	a	05 45	06 05	06 25	06 45	07 05	07 23	07 45		08 05	08 23	08 45	09 05	09 25		16 45	17 05	17 25		17 45	18 06

		GW ■	GW ■	GW ■	and at the same minutes past each hour until	GW ■	GW ■	GW ■		GW ■	GW ■
Windsor & Eton Central	d	18 19	18 39	18 59		22 19	22 39	22 59		23 21	23 46
Slough ■	a	18 25	18 45	19 05		22 25	22 45	23 05		23 27	23 52

Saturdays

26 May to 8 December

		GW	and every 30 minutes until	GW	GW	GW	GW	GW	and at the same minutes past each hour until	GW	GW	GW		GW	GW	GW	and every 30 minutes until	GW	GW
Windsor & Eton Central	d	06 27		09 57	10 21	10 39	10 59	11 19		17 39	17 59	18 19		18 39	18 59	19 27		22 57	23 31
Slough ■	a	06 33		10 03	10 27	10 45	11 05	11 25		17 45	18 05	18 25		18 45	19 05	19 33		23 03	23 37

Sundays

20 May to 2 December

		GW	GW	and every 30 minutes until	GW		GW	GW	GW	and at the same minutes past each hour until	GW	GW	GW			GW	and every 30 minutes until	GW
Windsor & Eton Central	d	00 05	08 32		10 02		10 22	10 42	11 02		18 22	18 42	19 02			19 32		23 32
Slough ■	a	00 11	08 38		10 08		10 28	10 48	11 08		18 28	18 48	19 08			19 38		23 38

Table T120-F

Maidenhead - Marlow

Mondays to Fridays

21 May to 7 December

Miles			GW MX	GW	GW	GW	GW	GW	GW	GW	GW		GW	GW	GW	GW	GW	GW	GW	GW	GW		GW	GW	GW
0	Maidenhead ■	d		05 25	05 44		06 31		07 01		07 31			08 01		08 31		09 39	10 39	11 39	12 39		13 39	14 39	15 39
1¼	Furze Platt	d		05 29	05 48		06 35		07 05		07 35			08 05		08 35		09 43	10 43	11 43	12 43		13 43	14 43	15 43
3	Cookham	d		05 32	05 51		06 38		07 08		07 38			08 08		08 38		09 46	10 46	11 46	12 46		13 46	14 46	15 46
4½	Bourne End ■	a		05 36	05 55		06 42		07 12		07 42			08 12		08 42		09 50	10 50	11 50	12 50		13 50	14 50	15 50
—		d	00 07	05 40		06 16		06 46		07 16			07 46		08 16		08 46	09 54	10 54	11 54	12 54		13 54	14 54	15 54
7¼	Marlow	a	00 14	05 48		06 23		06 53		07 23			07 53		08 23		08 53	10 02	11 02	12 02	13 02		14 02	15 02	16 02

		GW	GW	GW	GW	GW	GW		GW	GW	GW	GW	GW	GW	GW	GW	GW		GW	GW	GW	GW	GW
Maidenhead ■	d	16 45	17 13		17 43		18 13			18 43		19 13		19 43		20 13			20 43		21 46	22 55	23 51
Furze Platt	d	16 49	17 17		17 47		18 17			18 47		19 17		19 47		20 17			20 47		21 50	22 59	23 55
Cookham	d	16 52	17 20		17 50		18 20			18 50		19 20		19 50		20 20			20 50		21 53	23 02	23 58
Bourne End ■	a	16 56	17 24		17 54		18 24			18 54		19 24		19 54		20 24			20 54		21 57	23 06	00 02
	d	17 00		17 27		17 57			18 27		18 57		19 27		19 57		20 27			20 57	22 01	23 10	00 07
Marlow	a	17 08		17 34		18 04			18 34		19 04		19 34		20 04		20 34			21 04	22 09	23 18	00 14

Saturdays

26 May to 8 December

		GW	GW	GW	GW	GW	GW	GW	GW	GW		GW	GW	GW	GW	GW	GW	GW	GW	GW		GW
Maidenhead ■	d		06 38	07 38	08 38	09 38	10 38	11 38	12 38	13 38		14 38	15 38	16 38	17 38	18 38	19 38	20 40	21 50	22 51		23 44
Furze Platt	d		06 42	07 42	08 42	09 42	10 42	11 42	12 42	13 42		14 42	15 42	16 42	17 42	18 42	19 42	20 44	21 54	22 55		23 48
Cookham	d		06 45	07 45	08 45	09 45	10 45	11 45	12 45	13 45		14 45	15 45	16 45	17 45	18 45	19 45	20 47	21 57	22 58		23 51
Bourne End ■	a		06 49	07 49	08 49	09 49	10 49	11 49	12 49	13 49		14 49	15 49	16 49	17 49	18 49	19 49	20 51	22 01	23 02		23 55
	d	00 07	06 53	07 53	08 53	09 53	10 53	11 53	12 53	13 53		14 53	15 53	16 53	17 53	18 53	19 53	20 55	22 05	23 06		23 59
Marlow	a	00 14	07 01	08 01	09 01	10 01	11 01	12 01	13 01	14 01		15 01	16 01	17 01	18 01	19 01	20 01	21 03	22 13	23 14		00 07

Sundays

20 May to 9 September

		GW	GW	GW	GW	GW	GW	GW	GW	GW		GW	GW	GW	GW	GW
Maidenhead ■	d	08 35	09 38	10 38	11 38	12 38	13 38	14 38	15 38	16 38		17 38	18 38	19 38	20 45	21 45
Furze Platt	d	08 39	09 42	10 42	11 42	12 42	13 42	14 42	15 42	16 42		17 42	18 42	19 42	20 49	21 49
Cookham	d	08 42	09 45	10 45	11 45	12 45	13 45	14 45	15 45	16 45		17 45	18 45	19 45	20 52	21 52
Bourne End ■	a	08 47	09 50	10 50	11 50	12 50	13 50	14 50	15 50	16 50		17 50	18 50	19 50	20 57	21 57
	d	08 51	09 54	10 54	11 54	12 54	13 54	14 54	15 54	16 54		17 54	18 54	19 54	21 01	22 01
Marlow	a	08 58	10 01	11 01	12 01	13 01	14 01	15 01	16 01	17 01		18 01	19 01	20 01	21 08	22 08

Sundays

16 September to 2 December

		GW	GW	GW	GW	GW	GW	GW	GW	GW		GW	GW	GW	GW	GW
Maidenhead ■	d	08 35	09 35	10 35	11 35	12 35	13 35	14 35	15 35	16 35		17 35	18 35	19 35	20 35	21 50
Furze Platt	d	08 39	09 39	10 39	11 39	12 39	13 39	14 39	15 39	16 39		17 39	18 39	19 39	20 39	21 54
Cookham	d	08 42	09 42	10 42	11 42	12 42	13 42	14 42	15 42	16 42		17 42	18 42	19 42	20 42	21 57
Bourne End ■	a	08 47	09 47	10 47	11 47	12 47	13 47	14 47	15 47	16 47		17 47	18 47	19 47	20 47	22 02
	d	08 51	09 51	10 51	11 51	12 51	13 51	14 51	15 51	16 51		17 51	18 51	19 51	20 51	22 06
Marlow	a	08 58	09 58	10 58	11 58	12 58	13 58	14 58	15 58	16 58		17 58	18 58	19 58	20 58	22 13

Table T120-R

Mondays to Fridays

21 May to 7 December

Marlow - Maidenhead

Miles			GW MX	GW	GW	GW	GW	GW		GW	GW	GW	GW	GW	GW	GW	GW	GW		GW	GW	GW	GW	GW	GW
0	**Marlow**	d	00 17	06 06		06 36		07 06			07 36		08 06		08 36		09 12	10 05		11 05	12 05	13 05	14 05	15 05	16 05
2¾	Bourne End ■	a	00 24	06 13		06 43		07 13			07 43		08 13		08 43		09 19	10 12		11 12	12 12	13 12	14 12	15 12	16 12
—		d	00 28		06 16		06 46			07 16		07 46		08 16		08 46	09 23	10 16		11 16	12 16	13 16	14 16	15 16	16 16
4¼	Cookham	d	00 32		06 19		06 49			07 19		07 49		08 19		08 49	09 27	10 20		11 20	12 20	13 20	14 20	15 20	16 20
6	Furze Platt	d	00 35		06 23		06 53			07 23		07 53		08 23		08 53	09 30	10 23		11 23	12 23	13 23	14 23	15 23	16 23
7¾	**Maidenhead ■**	a	00 40		06 27		06 57			07 27		07 57		08 27		08 57	09 35	10 28		11 28	12 28	13 28	14 28	15 28	16 28

		GW	GW	GW		GW	GW	GW	GW	GW	GW	GW	GW	GW		GW	GW	GW	GW	GW	GW	GW
Marlow	d	17 17		17 47			18 17		18 47		19 17		19 47			20 17		20 47		21 08	22 12	23 21
Bourne End ■	a	17 24		17 54			18 24		18 54		19 24		19 54			20 24		20 54		21 15	22 19	23 28
	d		17 28			17 58		18 28		18 58		19 28		19 58			20 28		20 58	21 19	22 23	23 32
Cookham	d		17 31			18 01		18 31		19 01		19 31		20 01			20 31		21 01	21 23	22 27	23 36
Furze Platt	d		17 35			18 05		18 35		19 05		19 35		20 05			20 35		21 05	21 26	22 30	23 39
Maidenhead ■	a		17 39			18 09		18 39		19 09		19 39		20 09			20 39		21 09	21 31	22 35	23 44

Saturdays

26 May to 8 December

		GW	GW	GW	GW	GW	GW	GW	GW	GW		GW	GW	GW	GW	GW	GW	GW	GW	GW
Marlow	d	00 17	07 06	08 06	09 06	10 06	11 06	12 06	13 06	14 06		15 06	16 06	17 06	18 06	19 06	20 06	21 06	22 16	23 17
Bourne End ■	a	00 24	07 13	08 13	09 13	10 13	11 13	12 13	13 13	14 13		15 13	16 13	17 13	18 13	19 13	20 13	21 13	22 23	23 24
	d	00 28	07 17	08 17	09 17	10 17	11 17	12 17	13 17	14 17		15 17	16 17	17 17	18 17	19 17	20 17	21 17	22 27	23 28
Cookham	d	00 32	07 21	08 21	09 21	10 21	11 21	12 21	13 21	14 21		15 21	16 21	17 21	18 21	19 21	20 21	21 21	22 31	23 32
Furze Platt	d	00 35	07 24	08 24	09 24	10 24	11 24	12 24	13 24	14 24		15 24	16 24	17 24	18 24	19 24	20 24	21 24	22 34	23 35
Maidenhead ■	a	00 40	07 29	08 29	09 29	10 29	11 29	12 29	13 29	14 29		15 29	16 29	17 29	18 29	19 29	20 29	21 29	22 39	23 40

Sundays

20 May to 9 September

		GW	GW	GW	GW	GW	GW	GW	GW	GW		GW	GW	GW	GW	GW	GW
Marlow	d	00 10	09 01	10 04	11 04	12 04	13 04	14 04	15 04	16 04		17 04	18 04	19 04	20 04	21 11	22 16
Bourne End ■	a	00 17	09 08	10 11	11 11	12 11	13 11	14 11	15 11	16 11		17 11	18 11	19 11	20 11	21 18	22 23
	d	00 21	09 12	10 15	11 15	12 15	13 15	14 15	15 15	16 15		17 15	18 15	19 15	20 15	21 22	22 27
Cookham	d	00 25	09 16	10 19	11 19	12 19	13 19	14 19	15 19	16 19		17 19	18 19	19 19	20 19	21 26	22 30
Furze Platt	d	00 28	09 20	10 23	11 23	12 23	13 23	14 23	15 23	16 23		17 23	18 23	19 23	20 23	21 30	22 34
Maidenhead ■	a	00 33	09 24	10 27	11 27	12 27	13 27	14 27	15 27	16 27		17 27	18 27	19 27	20 27	21 34	22 38

Sundays

16 September to 2 December

		GW	GW	GW	GW	GW	GW	GW	GW	GW		GW	GW	GW	GW	GW	GW
Marlow	d	00 10	09 01	10 09	11 09	12 09	13 09	14 09	15 09	16 09		17 09	18 09	19 09	20 09	21 09	22 16
Bourne End ■	a	00 17	09 08	10 16	11 16	12 16	13 16	14 16	15 16	16 16		17 16	18 16	19 16	20 16	21 16	22 23
	d	00 21	09 12	10 20	11 20	12 20	13 20	14 20	15 20	16 20		17 20	18 20	19 20	20 20	21 20	22 27
Cookham	d	00 25	09 16	10 24	11 24	12 24	13 24	14 24	15 24	16 24		17 24	18 24	19 24	20 24	21 24	22 30
Furze Platt	d	00 28	09 20	10 28	11 28	12 28	13 28	14 28	15 28	16 28		17 28	18 28	19 28	20 28	21 28	22 34
Maidenhead ■	a	00 33	09 24	10 32	11 32	12 32	13 32	14 32	15 32	16 32		17 32	18 32	19 32	20 32	21 32	22 38

Table T121-F

Mondays to Fridays

21 May to 7 December

Twyford - Henley-on-Thames

Miles			GW MX	GW	GW	GW	GW	GW	GW	GW	GW		GW	GW		GW	GW	GW		GW	GW		GW
0	**Twyford ■**	d	00 03	05 49	06 20	06 51	07 21	07 52	08 22	08 54	09 24		10 04	10 38	and every 30 minutes until	16 08	16 45	17 23	and every 30 minutes until	18 53	19 24		20 24
1¾	Wargrave	d	00 07	05 53	06 24	06 55	07 25	07 56	08 26	08 58	09 28		10 08	10 42		16 12	16 49	17 27		18 57	19 28		20 28
2¾	Shiplake	d	00 10	05 56	06 27	06 58	07 28	07 59	08 29	09 01	09 31		10 11	10 45		16 15	16 52	17 30		19 00	19 31		20 31
4½	**Henley-on-Thames**	a	00 15	06 01	06 32	07 03	07 33	08 04	08 34	09 06	09 36		10 16	10 50		16 20	16 57	17 35		19 05	19 36		20 36

		GW	GW	GW	GW	GW
Twyford ■	d	20 54	21 47	22 26	23 03	23 33
Wargrave	d	20 58	21 51	22 30	23 07	23 37
Shiplake	d	21 01	21 54	22 33	23 10	23 40
Henley-on-Thames	a	21 06	21 59	22 38	23 15	23 45

Saturdays

26 May to 8 December

		GW ■	GW	GW	GW		GW	GW	GW		GW		GW
Twyford ■	d	00 03	06 57	07 50	08 38	and every 30 minutes until	18 38	19 15	19 50	and hourly until	22 50		23 40
Wargrave	d	00 07	07 01	07 54	08 42		18 42	19 19	19 54		22 54		23 44
Shiplake	d	00 10	07 04	07 57	08 45		18 45	19 22	19 57		22 57		23 47
Henley-on-Thames	a	00 15	07 09	08 02	08 50		18 50	19 27	20 02		23 02		23 52

Sundays

20 May to 9 September

		GW	GW		GW	GW	GW	GW
Twyford ■	d	08 45	09 53	and every 30 minutes until	18 53	19 53	20 53	21 53
Wargrave	d	08 49	09 57		18 57	19 57	20 57	21 57
Shiplake	d	08 52	10 00		19 00	20 00	21 00	22 00
Henley-on-Thames	a	08 57	10 05		19 05	20 05	21 05	22 05

Sundays

16 September to 2 December

		GW	GW		GW	GW	GW	GW
Twyford ■	d	08 45	09 38	and every 30 minutes until	18 38	19 38	20 38	21 53
Wargrave	d	08 49	09 42		18 42	19 42	20 42	21 57
Shiplake	d	08 52	09 45		18 45	19 45	20 45	22 00
Henley-on-Thames	a	08 57	09 50		18 50	19 50	20 50	22 05

Table T121-R

Henley-on-Thames - Twyford

Mondays to Fridays
21 May to 7 December

Miles			GW MX	GW	GW	GW	GW	GW	GW	GW	GW	GW		GW	GW	GW		GW	GW	GW	GW
0	Henley-on-Thames	d	00 17	06 05	06 35	07 06	07 36	08 07	08 37	09 09	09 39	10 23	and every 30 minutes until	16 23	17 05	17 38	and every 30 minutes until	19 08	19 39	20 39	21 12
1¾	Shiplake	d	00 21	06 09	06 39	07 10	07 40	08 11	08 41	09 13	09 43	10 27		16 27	17 09	17 42		19 12	19 43	20 43	21 16
2¾	Wargrave	d	00 24	06 12	06 42	07 13	07 43	08 14	08 44	09 16	09 46	10 30		16 30	17 12	17 45		19 15	19 46	20 46	21 19
4½	Twyford	a	00 29	06 17	06 47	07 18	07 48	08 19	08 49	09 21	09 51	10 35		16 35	17 17	17 50		19 20	19 51	20 51	21 24

		GW	GW	GW	GW
Henley-on-Thames	d	22 03	22 41	23 18	23 48
Shiplake	d	22 07	22 45	23 22	23 52
Wargrave	d	22 10	22 48	23 25	23 55
Twyford	a	22 15	22 53	23 30	00 01

Saturdays
26 May to 8 December

		GW	GW	GW		GW	GW	GW	GW	GW	GW	GW
Henley-on-Thames	d	00 17	07 23	08 23	and every 30 minutes until	18 53	19 35	20 23	21 23	22 21	23 11	23 55
Shiplake	d	00 21	07 27	08 27		18 57	19 39	20 27	21 27	22 25	23 15	23 59
Wargrave	d	00 24	07 30	08 30		19 00	19 42	20 30	21 30	22 28	23 18	00 02
Twyford	a	00 29	07 35	08 35		19 05	19 47	20 35	21 35	22 33	23 23	00 07

Sundays
20 May to 9 September

		GW A	GW	GW		GW	GW	GW	GW
Henley-on-Thames	d		09 08	10 08	and every 30 minutes until	19 08	20 08	21 08	22 08
Shiplake	d		09 12	10 12		19 12	20 12	21 12	22 12
Wargrave	d	00 02	09 15	10 15		19 15	20 15	21 15	22 15
Twyford	a	00 07	09 20	10 20		19 20	20 20	21 20	22 20

Sundays
16 September to 2 December

		GW	GW	GW		GW	GW	GW	GW
Henley-on-Thames	d		09 17	09 53	and every 30 minutes until	18 53	19 53	20 53	22 08
Shiplake	d		09 21	09 57		18 57	19 57	20 57	22 12
Wargrave	d	00 02	09 24	10 00		19 00	20 00	21 00	22 15
Twyford	a	00 07	09 29	10 05		19 05	20 05	21 05	22 20

A not 20 May

Table T122-F

Reading - Basingstoke

Mondays to Fridays
21 May to 7 December

Miles			GW	GW	GW	GW	GW	XC	GW	XC	GW	XC	GW	GW	XC	GW	XC	GW	XC	GW	GW	XC	GW
0	Reading	d	05 39	06 05	06 38	07 05	07 37	07 52	08 05	08 20	08 38	08 49	09 05	09 34	09 47	10 04	10 20	10 36	10 52	11 03	11 33	11 52	12 03
1	Reading West	d	05 42	06 08	06 41	07 08	07 40		08 08		08 41		09 08	09 37		10 07		10 39		11 06	11 36		12 06
7¼	Mortimer	d	05 50	06 16	06 49	07 16	07 48		08 16		08 49		09 16	09 45		10 15		10 47		11 15	11 44		12 14
10½	Bramley (Hants)	d	05 55	06 21	06 54	07 21	07 53		08 21		08 54		09 21	09 50		10 20		10 52		11 20	11 49		12 19
15½	Basingstoke	a	06 05	06 31	07 04	07 31	08 03	08 08	08 33	08 41	09 04	09 10	09 31	10 04	10 09	10 29	10 39	11 03	11 09	11 30	11 59	12 09	12 29

		XC	GW	XC	GW	GW	XC	GW	XC	GW	XC	GW	GW	XC	GW	XC	GW	XC	GW	GW	XC	GW	GW
Reading	d	12 20	12 34	12 50	13 06	13 39	13 49	14 06	14 18	14 36	14 52	15 07	15 39	15 52	16 07	16 20	16 36	16 52	17 04	17 33	17 52	18 03	18 33
Reading West	d		12 37		13 09	13 42		14 09		14 39		15 10	15 42		16 10		16 39		17 07	17 36		18 06	18 36
Mortimer	d		12 45		13 17	13 50		14 17		14 47		15 18	15 50		16 18		16 47		17 15	17 44		18 14	18 44
Bramley (Hants)	d		12 50		13 22	13 55		14 22		14 52		15 23	15 55		16 23		16 52		17 20	17 49		18 19	18 49
Basingstoke	a	12 39	13 02	13 09	13 32	14 04	14 09	14 32	14 40	15 02	15 09	15 33	16 05	16 09	16 33	16 40	17 02	17 09	17 30	17 59	18 09	18 29	19 03

		XC	GW	GW	XC	GW	GW	XC	GW	GW	XC	GW	XC	XC	GW	GW
Reading	d	18 52	19 03	19 35	19 52	20 01	20 34	20 52	21 07	21 39	21 52	22 03	22 22	22 48	22 55	23 34
Reading West	d		19 06	19 38		20 04	20 37		21 10	21 42		22 06			22 58	23 37
Mortimer	d		19 14	19 46		20 12	20 45		21 18	21 50		22 14			23 07	23 45
Bramley (Hants)	d		19 19	19 51		20 17	20 50		21 23	21 55		22 19			23 12	23 50
Basingstoke	a	19 09	19 29	20 04	20 09	20 32	21 00	21 09	21 31	22 03	22 09	22 27	22 39	23 06	23 20	23 58

Saturdays
26 May to 8 December

		GW	GW	GW	GW	XC	GW	XC	GW	XC	GW A	GW B	GW	XC C	XC D	GW	XC	GW	XC	GW	GW	XC	GW A
Reading	d	06 05	06 33	07 06	07 33	07 52	08 03	08 20	08 35	08 52	09 03	09 05	09 34	09 52	09 52	10 03	10 20	10 34	10 48	11 05	11 34	11 52	12 03
Reading West	d	06 08	06 36	07 09	07 36		08 06		08 38		09 06	09 08	09 37			10 06		10 37		11 08	11 37		12 06
Mortimer	d	06 16	06 44	07 17	07 44		08 14		08 46		09 14	09 16	09 45			10 14		10 45		11 16	11 45		12 14
Bramley (Hants)	d	06 21	06 49	07 22	07 49		08 19		08 51		09 19	09 21	09 50			10 19		10 50		11 21	11 50		12 19
Basingstoke	a	06 30	06 57	07 30	07 57	08 08	08 27	08 39	09 00	09 09	09 28	09 30	09 58	10 09	10 09	10 27	10 40	10 58	11 09	11 30	11 58	12 09	12 27

		GW B	XC	GW	XC	GW	GW	XC	GW	XC	GW	XC	GW	GW	XC	GW	XC	GW	XC	GW	GW	XC	GW
Reading	d	12 06	12 20	12 35	12 52	13 04	13 34	13 46	14 04	14 20	14 34	14 52	15 03	15 34	15 52	16 03	16 20	16 34	16 52	17 03	17 34	17 52	18 03
Reading West	d	12 09		12 38		13 07	13 37		14 07		14 37		15 06	15 37		16 06		16 37		17 06	17 37		18 06
Mortimer	d	12 17		12 46		13 15	13 45		14 15		14 45		15 14	15 45		16 14		16 45		17 14	17 45		18 14
Bramley (Hants)	d	12 22		12 51		13 20	13 50		14 20		14 50		15 19	15 50		16 19		16 50		17 19	17 50		18 19
Basingstoke	a	12 31	12 40	12 59	13 09	13 28	13 58	14 09	14 28	14 40	14 58	15 09	15 27	15 58	16 09	16 27	16 40	16 58	17 09	17 27	17 58	18 09	18 27

		GW	XC	GW	GW	XC	GW	GW	XC	GW	GW	XC	GW	XC	GW A	GW B	XC	GW
Reading	d	18 34	18 52	19 03	19 34	19 52	20 03	20 33	20 52	21 03	21 33	21 52	22 05	22 22	22 35	22 36	22 50	23 08
Reading West	d	18 37		19 06	19 37		20 06	20 36		21 06	21 36		22 08		22 38	22 39		23 11
Mortimer	d	18 45		19 14	19 45		20 14	20 44		21 14	21 44		22 16		22 46	22 47		23 19
Bramley (Hants)	d	18 50		19 19	19 50		20 19	20 49		21 19	21 49		22 21		22 51	22 52		23 24
Basingstoke	a	18 58	19 09	19 27	19 59	20 09	20 27	20 57	21 09	21 27	21 57	22 08	22 29	22 39	22 59	23 00	23 07	23 32

Sundays
20 May to 2 December

		GW	GW	GW	XC	GW	XC		GW	XC	GW	XC	GW	XC	GW	XC	GW	XC	GW	GW
Reading	d	07 37	08 37	09 40	09 52	10 38	10 52	and at the same minutes past each hour until	17 38	17 52	18 38	18 51	19 38	19 52	20 38	20 52	21 38	21 52	22 38	23 38
Reading West	d	07 40	08 40	09 43		10 41			17 41		18 41		19 41		20 41		21 41		22 41	23 41
Mortimer	d	07 48	08 48	09 51		10 49			17 49		18 49		19 49		20 49		21 49		22 49	23 49
Bramley (Hants)	d	07 53	08 53	09 56		10 54			17 54		18 54		19 54		20 54		21 54		22 54	23 54
Basingstoke	a	08 01	09 01	10 05	10 11	11 02	11 09		18 02	18 09	19 02	19 09	20 02	20 09	21 02	21 08	22 02	22 09	23 02	00 02

A from 15 September
B until 8 September
C until 21 July, from 8 September
D from 28 July until 1 September

Table T122-R

Mondays to Fridays

21 May to 7 December

Basingstoke - Reading

Miles			GW	XC	GW	GW	XC	GW	GW	XC	GW	XC	XC	GW	XC	GW	GW	XC	GW	XC	GW	XC	GW
				◇1			◇1			◇1		◇1	◇1		◇1			■ 1		◇1		◇1	
												A	B										
										✕			✕		✕			✕		✕		✕	
0	**Basingstoke**	d	00 07	05 47	06 07	06 33	06 47	07 08	07 33	07 47	08 05	08 28	08 28	08 36	08 47	09 06	09 36	09 49	10 07	10 19	10 33	10 49	11 06
5	Bramley (Hants)	d	00 14		06 14	06 40		07 14	07 40		08 12			08 43		09 13	09 43		10 14		10 40		11 13
8¼	Mortimer	d	00 19		06 19	06 45		07 19	07 45		08 17			08 48		09 18	09 48		10 19		10 45		11 18
14½	Reading West	d	00 27		06 27	06 53		07 27	07 53		08 25			08 56		09 26	09 56		10 27		10 53		11 24
15½	**Reading** 7	a	00 30	06 05	06 31	06 57	07 05	07 33	07 57	08 04	08 29	08 44	08 44	09 00	09 04	09 30	10 00	10 07	10 31	10 37	10 57	11 06	11 28

		GW	XC	GW	XC	XC	GW	XC	GW	GW	XC	GW	XC	GW	XC	GW	GW	XC	GW	XC	GW	XC
			◇1		■ 1	◇1		◇1			◇1		◇1		◇1			◇1		◇1		◇1
					A	B																
			✕		✕	✕		✕			✕		✕		✕			✕		✕		✕
Basingstoke	d	11 33	11 49	12 04	12 18	12 18	12 33	12 49	13 11	13 35	13 49	14 08	14 19	14 38	14 49	15 05	15 35	15 48	16 07	16 18	16 36	16 49
Bramley (Hants)	d	11 40		12 11			12 40		13 18	13 42		14 15		14 45		15 12	15 42		16 14		16 43	
Mortimer	d	11 45		12 16			12 45		13 23	13 47		14 20		14 50		15 16	15 47		16 19		16 48	
Reading West	d	11 53		12 25			12 53		13 31	13 55		14 28		14 58		15 25	15 55		16 27		16 56	
Reading 7	a	11 57	12 05	12 29	12 37	12 37	12 57	13 06	13 35	13 59	14 05	14 33	14 36	15 02	15 05	15 28	15 59	16 04	16 33	16 34	17 00	17 08

		GW	GW	XC	GW	XC	GW	XC	GW	GW	XC	GW	GW	XC	GW	GW	GW	GW	GW
				◇1		◇1		◇1			◇1			◇1					
				✕		✕		✕			✕								
Basingstoke	d	17 04	17 33	17 49	18 04	18 18	18 33	18 47	19 06	19 33	19 49	20 06	20 35	20 49	21 03	21 34	22 14	22 55	23 24
Bramley (Hants)	d	17 11	17 40		18 11		18 40		19 13	19 40		20 13	20 42		21 10	21 41	22 21	23 02	23 31
Mortimer	d	17 16	17 45		18 16		18 45		19 18	19 45		20 18	20 47		21 15	21 46	22 26	23 07	23 36
Reading West	d	17 24	17 53		18 24		18 53		19 26	19 53		20 26	20 55		21 23	21 54	22 34	23 16	23 44
Reading 7	a	17 28	17 57	18 04	18 28	18 35	18 57	19 04	19 30	19 57	20 05	20 30	20 59	21 06	21 27	21 57	22 38	23 19	23 47

Saturdays

26 May to 8 December

		GW	XC	GW	XC	GW	XC	XC	GW	XC	GW	XC	XC	GW	XC	GW	GW	XC	GW	XC	GW	XC	GW
			◇1		◇1		◇1	◇1		◇1		◇1	◇1		◇1			◇1		◇1		◇1	
							C	D				C	D										
					✕			✕		✕			✕		✕			✕		✕		✕	
Basingstoke	d	00 02	05 41	06 34	06 52	07 03	07 25	07 25	07 35	07 52	08 03	08 19	08 19	08 34	08 52	09 04	09 33	09 52	10 03	10 19	10 37	10 52	11 05
Bramley (Hants)	d	00 09		06 41		07 10			07 42		08 10			08 41		09 11	09 40		10 10		10 44		11 12
Mortimer	d	00 14		06 46		07 15			07 47		08 15			08 46		09 16	09 45		10 15		10 49		11 17
Reading West	d	00 22		06 54		07 23			07 55		08 23			08 54		09 24	09 53		10 23		10 57		11 25
Reading 7	a	00 26	06 00	06 57	07 08	07 26	07 42	07 42	07 58	08 08	08 26	08 35	08 35	08 57	09 08	09 27	09 56	10 08	10 26	10 35	11 01	11 07	11 29

		GW	XC	GW	XC	GW	XC	GW	GW	XC	GW	XC	GW	GW	XC	GW	GW	XC	GW	XC	GW	XC	GW
			◇1		◇1		◇1			◇1		◇1			◇1			◇1		◇1		◇1	
													E	F									
			✕		✕		✕			✕		✕			✕			✕		✕		✕	
Basingstoke	d	11 33	11 52	12 03	12 19	12 34	12 52	13 06	13 35	13 52	14 06	14 19	14 33	14 34	14 52	15 03	15 33	15 52	16 03	16 18	16 33	16 52	17 05
Bramley (Hants)	d	11 40		12 10		12 41		13 13	13 42		14 13		14 40	14 41		15 10	15 40		16 10		16 40		17 12
Mortimer	d	11 45		12 15		12 46		13 18	13 47		14 18		14 45	14 46		15 15	15 45		16 15		16 45		17 17
Reading West	d	11 53		12 23		12 54		13 26	13 55		14 26		14 53	14 54		15 23	15 53		16 23		16 53		17 25
Reading 7	a	11 56	12 08	12 26	12 35	12 57	13 08	13 29	13 59	14 08	14 29	14 35	14 56	14 57	15 07	15 26	15 56	16 07	16 26	16 35	16 56	17 08	17 29

		GW	GW	XC	GW	XC	GW	XC	GW	GW	XC	GW	GW	XC	GW	GW	GW	GW	GW	GW
				◇1		◇1		◇1			◇1			◇1						
		E	F																	
				✕		✕		✕			✕									
Basingstoke	d	17 33	17 34	17 52	18 03	18 18	18 33	18 52	19 03	19 33	19 52	20 03	20 33	20 52	21 03	21 33	22 04	22 34	23 04	23 37
Bramley (Hants)	d	17 40	17 41		18 10		18 40		19 10	19 40		20 10	20 40		21 10	21 40	22 11	22 41	23 11	23 44
Mortimer	d	17 45	17 46		18 15		18 45		19 15	19 45		20 15	20 45		21 15	21 45	22 16	22 46	23 16	23 49
Reading West	d	17 53	17 54		18 23		18 53		19 23	19 53		20 23	20 53		21 23	21 53	22 24	22 54	23 24	23 57
Reading 7	a	17 56	17 58	18 07	18 26	18 35	18 56	19 08	19 26	19 56	20 09	20 26	20 56	21 08	21 26	21 56	22 27	22 57	23 27	00 01

Sundays

20 May to 2 December

		GW	GW	XC	GW	XC	GW	XC	GW	XC	GW	XC	GW	XC	GW	XC	GW	XC	GW	XC	GW	XC	GW
				◇1		◇1		◇1		◇1		◇1		◇1		◇1		◇1		◇1		◇1	
				✕		✕		✕		✕		✕		✕		✕		✕		✕		✕	
Basingstoke	d	08 07	09 07	09 47	10 07	10 47	11 07	11 47	12 07	12 47	13 07	13 47	14 06	14 47	15 07	15 47	16 07	16 47	17 07	17 47	18 07	18 47	19 07
Bramley (Hants)	d	08 14	09 14		10 14		11 14		12 14		13 14		14 13		15 14		16 14		17 14		18 14		19 14
Mortimer	d	08 19	09 19		10 19		11 19		12 19		13 19		14 18		15 19		16 19		17 19		18 19		19 19
Reading West	d	08 27	09 27		10 27		11 27		12 27		13 27		14 26		15 27		16 27		17 27		18 27		19 27
Reading 7	a	08 31	09 31	10 04	10 31	11 03	11 31	12 03	12 31	13 04	13 31	14 03	14 30	15 05	15 31	16 03	16 30	17 03	17 30	18 03	18 31	19 03	19 31

		XC	GW	XC	GW	GW	GW
		◇1		◇1			
		✕					
Basingstoke	d	19 47	20 07	20 47	21 07	22 07	23 07
Bramley (Hants)	d		20 14		21 14	22 15	23 14
Mortimer	d		20 19		21 19	22 20	23 19
Reading West	d		20 27		21 27	22 28	23 27
Reading 7	a	20 03	20 31	21 03	21 30	22 31	23 31

A until 20 July, from 8 October
B from 23 July until 5 October
C until 21 July, from 13 October
D from 28 July until 6 October
E from 15 September
F until 8 September

Table T123-F

Mondays to Fridays

21 May to 7 December

Brighton, Portsmouth and Weymouth - Bristol, Cardiff, Gloucester and Great Malvern

Miles	Miles	Miles	Miles	Miles			GW	GW	GW	GW	GW	GW	GW	GW	SW	GW	GW	GW	GW	GW	GW	GW	GW	GW
								◇1	◇1		◇	◇	◇1		1	◇			◇1	■	◇		◇	◇
								A				B	C			D			C					
								☕	☕				☕						☕	✕			✕	
—	—	0	—	—	Brighton 10	d																		
—	—	1½	—	—	Hove 2	d																		
—	—	6	—	—	Shoreham-by-Sea	d																		
—	—	10½	—	—	Worthing 4	d																		
—	—	22½	—	—	Barnham	d																		
—	—	28¾	—	—	**Chichester** 4	d																		
—	—	37½	—	—	Havant 10	d																		
0	—	—	—	—	**Portsmouth Harbour** ⛴	d														06 00			07 05	
0¾	—	—	—	—	Portsmouth & Southsea	d														06 04			07 09	
1¾	—	—	—	—	Fratton 8	d														06 08			07 13	
5½	—	41¾	—	—	Cosham	d														06 15			07 21	
11¼	—	47½	—	—	Fareham	a														06 23			07 28	
—	—	—	—	—		d														06 24			07 29	
25¾	—	62½	—	—	**Southampton Central** 8 ⛴	d														06 46			07 53	08 23
34	—	70¼	—	—	Romsey	d														07 00			08 11	08 35
50½	—	86¾	—	—	**Salisbury** 8	a														07 18			08 29	09 00
—	—	—	—	—		d				06 10					06 40					07 19			08 30	09 03
70¼	—	106½	—	—	Warminster	d				06 30					07 00			07 23		07 39			08 52	09 25
73½	—	109¾	—	—	Dilton Marsh	d				06x35								07x28		07x44				09x29
—	0	—	0	—	**Weymouth**	d						05 33									06 44			
—	2½	—	2½	—	Upwey	d						05 38									06 49			
—	7	—	7	—	Dorchester West	d						05 46									06 57			
—	14¾	—	14¾	—	Maiden Newton	d						05 58									07 09			
—	21¼	—	21¼	—	Chetnole	d						06x07									07x17			
—	23¼	—	23¼	—	Yetminster	d						06x10									07x20			
—	24¼	—	24¼	—	Thornford	d						06x12									07x22			
—	27½	—	27½	—	Yeovil Pen Mill	d						06 21									07 34			
—	39¼	—	39¼	—	Castle Cary	a						06 34									07 48			
—	—	—	—	—		d						06 35	06 44						07 27		07 48			
—	42¾	—	42¾	—	Bruton	d						06 40									07 54			
—	53¼	—	53¼	—	Frome	d			06 05		06 45	06 56				←					08 07			
75	59	111¼	59	0	**Westbury** 2	a			06 15	06 39	06 54	07 08	07 02		07 08	07 08		07 32	07 45	07 49	08 16		09 01	09 35
—	—	—	—	—		d	05 58	06 00	06 16	06 41	06 55	07 17	07 03	07 04	07 09	07 17	07 33	07 38	07 52	07 54	08 17	08 45	09 10	09 38
—	—	—	—	—	London Paddington 15 ⊖	a		07 47	08 08			→	08 37						09 23					
79	63	115¼	63	4	Trowbridge	d	06 04			06 47	07 02			07 10	07 15	07 23	07 39	07 44		08 00	08 24	08 51	09 16	09 44
82¼	66¼	118½	66¼	—	Bradford-on-Avon	d	06 10			06 53	07 08				07 21	07 29		07 50		08 06	08 30	08 57	09 22	09 50
83½	67¾	119¾	67¾	—	Avoncliff	d	06 13			06 56	07 11					07 32		07 54			08 33	09 00		09 53
84½	68½	120¾	68½	—	Freshford	d	06 16			06 59	07 13					07 35		07 57		08 10	08 35	09 03		09 56
91½	75¾	128	75¾	—	Bath Spa 7	a	06 26			07 09	07 24				07 33	07 45		08 07		08 21	08 46	09 13	09 34	10 06
—	—	—	—	9½	Melksham	d								07 20			07 49							
—	—	—	—	15¾	Chippenham	a								07 30			07 59							
—	—	—	—	32½	Swindon	a								07 48			08 15							
92½	76¾	129	76¾	—	Oldfield Park	a	06 30			07 13	07 28				07 37	07 49		08 12		08 25	08 49	09 17		10 10
98½	82¾	134¾	82¾	—	Keynsham	a	06 37			07 21	07 35				07 44	07 57		08 20		08 33	08 56	09 25	09 43	10 18
103	87¼	139½	87¼	—	**Bristol Temple Meads** 10	a	06 46			07 29	07 47				07 52	08 06		08 29		08 43	09 05	09 35	09 51	10 28
107½	91¾	144	91¾	—	Filton Abbey Wood	a	07 02			07 43	08 01					08 21		08 50		09 01	09 20	09 48	10 02	10 48
—	—	145½	93¼	—	Bristol Parkway	d				07 49						08a27		08 55			09a26	09 52		10 53
—	—	151¾	99½	—	Yate	d				07 59								09 04				10 02		11 03
—	—	162¼	110	—	Cam & Dursley	d				08 13								09 17				10 16		11 17
—	—	175¼	123	—	Gloucester	d				08a30				08 52				09 38				10a32		11 37
—	—	181¾	129½	—	Cheltenham Spa	d								09a05				09 48						11 48
—	—	189	137	—	Ashchurch for Tewkesbury	d												09 56						11 56
—	—	203¾	151½	—	Worcester Shrub Hill	d												10 16						12 14
—	—	204½	152¼	—	Worcester Foregate Street	d												10 19						12 17
—	—	211¼	159	—	Malvern Link	d												10 28						12 26
—	—	212½	160¼	—	Great Malvern	a												10 31						12 30
119½	119½	—	—	—	Severn Tunnel Jn	a	07 15																	
129½	113½	—	—	—	Newport (South Wales) 2	a	07 25				08 26									09 24			10 27	
141¼	125¼	—	—	—	**Cardiff Central** 7	a	07 41				08 43									09 42			10 43	

A From Bristol Temple Meads
B To Bristol Parkway
C From Plymouth
D From Weymouth

For connections from Bristol Parkway and Cardiff Central to Swansea refer to Table T128

For connections from Castle Cary, Westbury and Bristol Temple Meads to Exeter and Plymouth refer to Table T135

For connections from Salisbury to Yeovil Junction and Exeter refer to Table T160

For connections from Bournemouth to Southampton Central, Weymouth and Upwey refer to Table T158

For additional bus connections between Yeovil Junction and Yeovil Pen Mill refer to Table T123A

T123 UPDATE: Due to major engineering work in connection with electrification work taking place between Reading and Newbury and subsequent diversion of West of England trains, LOCAL TRAINS between Swindon and Westbury via Melksham will be subject to significant alteration on 4-7 June; 9-12 July; 16 July to 05 August; 28-30 August; 08-11 October and 19-22 November.

Table T123-F

Mondays to Fridays

21 May to 7 December

Brighton, Portsmouth and Weymouth - Bristol, Cardiff, Gloucester and Great Malvern

		GW	GW ◇■ A 🍴	GW ◇ ✕	GW ◇	GW	GW ◇■ A 🍴	GW ◇ B ✕	SW ◇■	GW ◇ C ✕	GW	GW ◇ ✕	GW	GW ◇	GW ◇ ✕	GW ◇■ D 🍴	GW ◇	GW ◇ ✕	GW E	SW ◇■ F	GW G	GW H
Brighton ■	d									08 59												
Hove ■	d									09 03												
Shoreham-by-Sea	d									09 13												
Worthing ■	d									09 22												
Barnham	d									09 37												
Chichester ■	d									09 46												
Havant ■	d									09 58												
Portsmouth Harbour ⛴	d			08 23				09 23				10 23			11 23			12 23				
Portsmouth & Southsea	d			08 27				09 27				10 27			11 27			12 27				
Fratton ■	d			08 31				09 31				10 31			11 31			12 31				
Cosham	d			08 39				09 39		10 05		10 39			11 39			12 39				
Fareham	a			08 46				09 46		10 12		10 46			11 46			12 46				
	d			08 47				09 47		10 13		10 47			11 47			12 47				
Southampton Central ■ ⛴	d			09 10				10 10		10 42		11 10			12 10		12 27	13 10				
Romsey	d			09 21				10 21		10 54		11 21			12 21		12 39	13 21				
Salisbury ■	a			09 39				10 39		11 12		11 39			12 39		13 04	13 39				
	d			09 40				10 40	10 52	11 13		11 40			12 40		13 07	13 39		13 52		
Warminster	d			10 01		10 26		11 01	11 12	11 32		12 01			13 01		13 34	14 00		14 12		
Dilton Marsh	d					10x30											13x39					
Weymouth	d				08 53									11 10								
Upwey	d				08 58									11 15								
Dorchester West	d				09 06									11 23								
Maiden Newton	d				09 18									11 41								
Chetnole	d				09x27									11x49								
Yetminster	d				09x30									11x52								
Thornford	d				09x32									11x55								
Yeovil Pen Mill	d				09 41									12 03								
Castle Cary	a				09 54									12 17								
	d		09 41		09 55									12 18		13 07						
Bruton	d				10 01									12 24								
Frome	d				10 15									12 37					14 10		←	
Westbury ■	a		09 59	10 09	10 24	10 34		11 09	11 20	11 40		12 09		12 46	13 09	13 25	13 42	14 08	14 19	14 20	14 19	
	d	09 46	10 01	10 10	10 38		11 05	11 10	11 23	11 41	11 47	12 10	12 20	12 47	13 10	13 27	13 44	14 10	14 24	14 21	14 24	14 38
London Paddington ■ ⊖	a		11 21				12 21									14 54			→			
Trowbridge	d	09 52		10 16	10 44			11 16	11 29	11 48	11 53	12 16	12 26	12 53	13 16		13 50	14 16		14 27	14 31	14 44
Bradford-on-Avon	d			10 22	10 50			11 22	11 35	11 54		12 22		12 59	13 22		13 56	14 22		14 33		14 50
Avoncliff	d				10 53					11 57				13 02			13 59					14 53
Freshford	d				10 56					11 59				13 05			14 02					14 56
Bath Spa ■	a			10 34	11 06			11 34	11 47	12 10		12 34		13 15	13 36		14 12	14 35		14 46		15 06
Melksham	d	10 02									12 03		12 36								14 40	
Chippenham	a	10 11									12 12		12 45								14 49	
Swindon	a	10 32									12 32		13 02								15 07	
Oldfield Park	a				11 10					12 14				13 19			14 16					15 10
Keynsham	a				11 18				11 56	12 21				13 27			14 24			14 54		15 18
Bristol Temple Meads ■	a			10 48	11 28			11 48	12 06	12 29		12 48		13 35	13 50		14 35	14 49		15 05		15 26
Filton Abbey Wood	a			11 01	11 48			12 01		12 48		13 01		13 48	14 01		14 48	15 01				
Bristol Parkway	d				11 52					12 52				13 52			14 53					15a44
Yate	d				12 02					13 01				14 02			15 03					
Cam & Dursley	d				12 16					13 14				14 16			15 17					
Gloucester	d				12a33					13 37				14a31			15 37					
Cheltenham Spa	d									13 48							15 48					
Ashchurch for Tewkesbury	d									13 56							15 56					
Worcester Shrub Hill	d									14 15							16 14					
Worcester Foregate Street	d									14 18							16 17					
Malvern Link	d									14 27							16 26					
Great Malvern	a									14 30							16 29					
Severn Tunnel Jn.	a																					
Newport (South Wales) ■	a			11 25				12 26				13 25			14 26			15 25				
Cardiff Central ■	a			11 43				12 42				13 42			14 41			15 42				

A From Penzance
B ✕ to Salisbury
C ✕ from Salisbury to Bristol Temple Meads
D From Paignton
E To Swindon
F From London Waterloo
G From Frome
H until 31 August

For connections from Bristol Parkway and Cardiff Central to Swansea refer to Table T128

For connections from Castle Cary, Westbury and Bristol Temple Meads to Exeter and Plymouth refer to Table T135

For connections from Salisbury to Yeovil Junction and Exeter refer to Table T160

For connections from Bournemouth to Southampton Central, Weymouth and Upwey refer to Table T158

For additional bus connections between Yeovil Junction and Yeovil Pen Mill refer to Table T123A

Table T123-F

Mondays to Fridays

21 May to 7 December

Brighton, Portsmouth and Weymouth - Bristol, Cardiff, Gloucester and Great Malvern

		GW A	GW ◇	SW ◇■ B ✕	GW ◇■ C 🍴	GW ◇ ✕	GW D	GW	GW ■ ✕	GW ◇■ E 🍴	GW	GW ◇	GW ◇■ F 🍴	GW ■ ✕	SW ◇■ G	GW	GW ■ ✕	GW	GW	GW ◇ H	GW ◇ ✕	GW ◇■ I 🍴	GW ◇ J
Brighton ■	d																						
Hove ■	d																						
Shoreham-by-Sea	d																						
Worthing ■	d																						
Barnham	d																						
Chichester ■	d																						
Havant ■	d																						
Portsmouth Harbour ⛴	d					13 23			14 23					15 23			16 23				17 23		
Portsmouth & Southsea	d					13 27			14 27					15 27			16 27				17 27		
Fratton ■	d					13 31			14 31					15 31			16 31				17 31		
Cosham	d					13 39			14 39					15 39			16 39				17 39		
Fareham	a					13 46			14 46					15 46			16 46				17 46		
	d					13 47			14 47					15 47			16 47				17 47		
Southampton Central ■ ⛴	d					14 10			15 10					16 10			17 10				18 10		
Romsey	d					14 21			15 21					16 21			17 21				18 21		
Salisbury ■	a					14 39			15 39					16 43			17 39				18 39		
	d			14 24		14 40			15 40					16 44			17 40				18 40		
Warminster	d			14 44		15 01		15 28	16 00					17 03		17 28	18 01		18 18		18 59		
Dilton Marsh	d							15x32								17x33			18x23				
Weymouth	d		13 10									15 08								17 30			
Upwey	d		13 15									15 13								17 35			
Dorchester West	d		13 22									15 21								17 43			
Maiden Newton	d		13 47									15 33								17 54			
Chetnole	d		13x55									15x42								18x03			
Yetminster	d		13x58									15x45								18x06			
Thornford	d		14x00									15x47								18x08			
Yeovil Pen Mill	d		14 10									15 56			16 53					18 23			
Castle Cary	a		14 23									16 09			17 06					18 36			
	d		14 24							15 55		16 10	16 25		17 07					18 37		18 52	
Bruton	d		14 29									16 16			17 12					18 43			
Frome	d		14 42				15 00					16 29			17 24					18 56			←
Westbury ■	a		14 51	14 51		15 09	15 09	15 36	16 09	16 13		16 38	16 44	17 11	17 33	17 36	18 09		18 26	19 04	19 08	19 11	19 04
	d	14 38	14 52		15 04	15 10		15 38	16 13	16 14	16 21	16 42	16 45	17 12		17 38	18 10	18 32	18 38	19 21	19 09	19 12	19 21
London Paddington ■ ⊖	a				16 21					17 54			18 07							→		20 37	
Trowbridge	d	14 44	14 59			15 16		15 44	16 20		16 27	16 47		17 19		17 44	18 16	18 38	18 44		19 17		19 27
Bradford-on-Avon	d	14 50	15 05			15 22		15 50	16 26			16 53		17 25		17 50	18 22		18 50		19 24		19 33
Avoncliff	d	14 53	15 08					15 53				16 56				17 53			18 53				19 36
Freshford	d	14 56	15 10					15 56				17 00				17 56			18 56				19 39
Bath Spa ■	a	15 07	15 21			15 34		16 07	16 38			17 09		17 37		18 06	18 35		19 06		19 36		19 49
Melksham	d										16 37							18 48					
Chippenham	a										16 46							19 01					
Swindon	a										17 03							19 21					
Oldfield Park	a	15 11						16 11				17 13				18 10			19 10				19 53
Keynsham	a	15 19						16 18				17 21				18 18			19 18				20 01
Bristol Temple Meads ■	a	15 29	15 35			15 48		16 28	16 52			17 31		17 51		18 28	18 49		19 29		19 49		20 09
Filton Abbey Wood	a		15 48			16 01		16 48	17 02			17 48		18 01		18 43	19 01		19 48		20 01		
Bristol Parkway	d	15a44	15 52					16 52				17 53				18 48			19 52				
Yate	d		16 02					17 01				18 01				18 57			20 02				
Cam & Dursley	d		16 16					17 14				18 14				19 11			20 16				
Gloucester	d		16a34					17 37				18a33				19 35			20 37				
Cheltenham Spa	d							17 48								19 46			20a48				
Ashchurch for Tewkesbury	d							17 56								19 55							
Worcester Shrub Hill	d							18 19								20 19							
Worcester Foregate Street	d							18 22								20 23							
Malvern Link	d							18 31								20 32							
Great Malvern	a							18 35								20 35							
Severn Tunnel Jn.	a								17 16					18 14			19 13				20 14		
Newport (South Wales) ■	a					16 25			17 26					18 24			19 24				20 24		
Cardiff Central ■	a					16 41			17 43					18 42			19 42				20 47		

A from 3 September
B From London Waterloo to Yeovil Pen Mill
C From Penzance. Restaurant available for customers joining until Castle Cary
D To Warminster
E From Taunton
F From Paignton. The Torbay Express
G From Yeovil Junction to Salisbury
H To Bristol Temple Meads
I From Newquay
J From Weymouth

For connections from Bristol Parkway and Cardiff Central to Swansea refer to Table T128

For connections from Castle Cary, Westbury and Bristol Temple Meads to Exeter and Plymouth refer to Table T135

For connections from Salisbury to Yeovil Junction and Exeter refer to Table T160

For connections from Bournemouth to Southampton Central, Weymouth and Upwey refer to Table T158

For additional bus connections between Yeovil Junction and Yeovil Pen Mill refer to Table T123A

Table T123-F

Mondays to Fridays
21 May to 7 December

Brighton, Portsmouth and Weymouth - Bristol, Cardiff, Gloucester and Great Malvern

		GW	GW	SW	GW	GW	GW	GW	GW	GW	GW	SW	GW	GW	GW	SW	GW	GW	GW
		◇	◇ ⌶	◇1 A	◇ ⌶	1		◇1 B ⊡	FO ◇	FX ◇		◇1 A		FO ◇	FX ◇	◇1 A ⌶			
Brighton 10	d		17 02																
Hove 2	d		17 06																
Shoreham-by-Sea	d		17 12																
Worthing 4	d		17 23																
Barnham	d		17 38																
Chichester 4	d		17 46																
Havant 30	d		17 58																
Portsmouth Harbour	d				18 23				19 23	19 23				20 23	20 23				21 23
Portsmouth & Southsea	d				18 27				19 27	19 27				20 27	20 27				21 27
Fratton 8	d				18 31				19 31	19 31				20 31	20 31				21 31
Cosham	d		18 05		18 39				19 38	19 38									
Fareham	a		18 12		18 46				19 46	19 46				20 45	20 45				21 43
	d		18 14		18 47				19 47	19 47				20 46	20 46				21 44
Southampton Central 8	d		18 42		19 10				20 10	20 10				21 11	21 11		21 20		22 23
Romsey	d		18 53		19 21				20 21	20 21				21 22	21 22		21 31		22 34
Salisbury 8	a		19 11		19 39				20 39	20 39				21 39	21 39		21 51		22 58
	d		19 13	18 23	19 40				20 40	20 40		20 57		21 40	21 40	20 25	21 53		23 00
Warminster	d		19 32		20 01				21 01	21 01		21 17		22 01	22 01		22 15		23 20
Dilton Marsh	d				20x06												22x19		23x24
Weymouth	d												20 21						
Upwey	d												20 26						
Dorchester West	d												20 34						
Maiden Newton	d												20 45						
Chetnole	d												20x52						
Yetminster	d												20x56						
Thornford	d												20x58						
Yeovil Pen Mill	d			19 27									21 06			21 27			
Castle Cary	a			19 39									21 18			21 40			
	d			19 40				20 47					21 18			21 41			
Bruton	d			19 45									21 24			21 46			
Frome	d			19 57		20 17					21 02		21 37			21 58			
Westbury 2	a		19 40	20 06	20 10	20 26		21 05	21 08	21 08	21 11	21 25	21 49	22 09	22 09	22 12	22 30		23 29
	d	19 32	19 41		20 11		20 38	21 07	21 10	21 10		21 25	21 55	22 10	22 10			22 35	
London Paddington 15 ⊖	a							22 37											
Trowbridge	d	19 38	19 48		20 18		20 44		21 17	21 17		21 31	22 02	22 16	22 16			22 41	
Bradford-on-Avon	d		19 54		20 24		20 50		21 23	21 23		21 37	22 08	22 22	22 22			22 47	
Avoncliff	d						20 53						22 11					22 49	
Freshford	d						20 56						22 13					22 53	
Bath Spa 7	a		20 06		20 36		21 07		21 34	21 34		21 50	22 24	22 34	22 34			23 03	
Melksham	d	19 47																	
Chippenham	a	20 00																	
Swindon	a	20 20																	
Oldfield Park	a		20 10				21 11						22 28					23 07	
Keynsham	a		20 17				21 19					21 58	22 35					23 15	
Bristol Temple Meads 10	a		20 26		20 50		21 28		21 48	21 48		22 06	22 43	22 48	22 48			23 25	
Filton Abbey Wood	a				21 01				22 01	22 01				23 01	23 01				
Bristol Parkway	d																		
Yate	d																		
Cam & Dursley	d																		
Gloucester	d	21 23																	
Cheltenham Spa	d	21a33																	
Ashchurch for Tewkesbury	d																		
Worcester Shrub Hill	d																		
Worcester Foregate Street	d																		
Malvern Link	d																		
Great Malvern	a																		
Severn Tunnel Jn.	a				21 13				22 16	22 16				23 16	23 16				
Newport (South Wales) 2	a				21 24				22 27	22 33				23 33	23 33				
Cardiff Central 7	a				21 44				22 43	22 56				23 49	23 55				

A From London Waterloo
B From Exeter St Davids

For connections from Bristol Parkway and Cardiff Central to Swansea refer to Table T128

For connections from Castle Cary, Westbury and Bristol Temple Meads to Exeter and Plymouth refer to Table T135

For connections from Salisbury to Yeovil Junction and Exeter refer to Table T160

For connections from Bournemouth to Southampton Central, Weymouth and Upwey refer to Table T158

For additional bus connections between Yeovil Junction and Yeovil Pen Mill refer to Table T123A

Table T123-F

Saturdays
26 May to 8 September

Brighton, Portsmouth and Weymouth - Bristol, Cardiff, Gloucester and Great Malvern

		GW	GW	SW	GW	GW	GW	GW	GW	GW	GW	GW	GW	GW	GW	GW	GW	GW	GW	GW	SW	GW	GW
			A	1			◇1 B ⊡	◇	◇			◇ C ⌶		◇		◇1 B ⊡	■ C ⌶	◇	■ 1 D ⊡	◇ C ⌶	◇1 E		◇
Brighton 10	d																						09 00
Hove 2	d																						09 04
Shoreham-by-Sea	d																						09 13
Worthing 4	d																						09 22
Barnham	d																						09 43
Chichester 4	d																						09 51
Havant 30	d																						10 02
Portsmouth Harbour	d							06 08				07 23					08 23			09 23			
Portsmouth & Southsea	d							06 12				07 27					08 27			09 27			
Fratton 8	d							06 16				07 31					08 31			09 31			
Cosham	d							06 23				07 39					08 39			09 39			10 08
Fareham	a							06 31				07 46					08 46			09 46			10 16
	d							06 32				07 47					08 47			09 47			10 17
Southampton Central 8	d							06 57				08 10		08 30			09 10			10 10			10 42
Romsey	d							07 11				08 21		08 41			09 21			10 21			10 54
Salisbury 8	a							07 29				08 39		09 00			09 39			10 39			11 12
	d	06 07		06 40				07 30				08 40		09 05			09 40			10 40	10 52		11 13
Warminster	d	06 28		07 00		07 23		07 50				09 01		09 27			10 01			11 01	11 12		11 33
Dilton Marsh	d	06x32				07x27		07x54						09x31									11x37
Weymouth	d								06 44									08 53					
Upwey	d								06 49									08 58					
Dorchester West	d								06 57									09 06					
Maiden Newton	d								07 09									09 18					
Chetnole	d								07x17									09x26					
Yetminster	d								07x20									09x29					
Thornford	d								07x22									09x31					
Yeovil Pen Mill	d								07 34									09 41					
Castle Cary	a								07 47									09 54					
	d						07 34		07 48							09 42		09 55					
Bruton	d								07 54									10 01					
Frome	d		06 49						08 07									10 16					
Westbury 2	a	06 37	06 58	07 08		07 31	07 52	08 00	08 16			09 09		09 37		10 00	10 09	10 25		11 09	11 20		11 42
	d	06 38		07 09	07 33	07 38	07 56	08 06	08 17	08 22	08 38	09 10	09 30	09 39	09 51	10 02	10 10	10 38	11 03	11 10	11 21	11 32	11 44
London Paddington 15 ⊖	a						09 21									11 21			12 21				
Trowbridge	d	06 44		07 15	07 39	07 44		08 12	08 24	08 29	08 44	09 16	09 36	09 45	09 57		10 16	10 44		11 16	11 27	11 38	11 51
Bradford-on-Avon	d	06 50		07 21		07 50		08 18	08 30		08 50	09 22		09 51	10 03		10 22	10 50		11 22	11 33		11 57
Avoncliff	d	06 53				07 53			08 33		08 53			09 54				10 53					12 00
Freshford	d	06 56				07 56			08 36		08 56			09 57				10 56					12 03
Bath Spa 7	a	07 06		07 33		08 06		08 31	08 46		09 06	09 34		10 06	10 15		10 34	11 06		11 34	11 46		12 13
Melksham	d				07 49					08 38			09 46									11 48	
Chippenham	a				08 00					08 48			10 00									12 00	
Swindon	a				08 20					09 07			10 20									12 20	
Oldfield Park	a	07 10		07 37		08 10			08 50		09 10			10 11				11 11					12 17
Keynsham	a	07 18		07 44		08 17			08 58		09 18			10 19				11 19			11 54		12 24
Bristol Temple Meads 10	a	07 28		07 52		08 28		08 45	09 06		09 27	09 48		10 27			10 48	11 27		11 48	12 05		12 35
Filton Abbey Wood	a	07 48				08 48		09 02			09 48	10 00		10 48			11 02	11 48		12 02			12 50
Bristol Parkway	d	07 53				08 53					09 52			10 52				11 52					12 55
Yate	d	08 02				09 02					10 02			11 02				12 02					13 04
Cam & Dursley	d	08 16				09 14					10 15			11 16				12 16					13 16
Gloucester	d	08a32				09 38					10a33			11 37				12a31					13 37
Cheltenham Spa	d					09 48								11 48									13 48
Ashchurch for Tewkesbury	d					09 56								11 57									13 56
Worcester Shrub Hill	d					10 16								12 14									14 15
Worcester Foregate Street	d					10 19								12a17									14 18
Malvern Link	d					10 28																	14 27
Great Malvern	a					10 33																	14 32
Severn Tunnel Jn.	a																						
Newport (South Wales) 2	a							09 25				10 23					11 25			12 24			
Cardiff Central 7	a							09 42				10 40					11 42			12 44			

A To Southampton Central
B From Plymouth
C ⌶ to Bristol Temple Meads
D From Penzance
E From London Waterloo

For connections from Bristol Parkway and Cardiff Central to Swansea refer to Table T128

For connections from Castle Cary, Westbury and Bristol Temple Meads to Exeter and Plymouth refer to Table T135

For connections from Salisbury to Yeovil Junction and Exeter refer to Table T160

For connections from Bournemouth to Southampton Central, Weymouth and Upwey refer to Table T158

For additional bus connections between Yeovil Junction and Yeovil Pen Mill refer to Table T123A

T123 UPDATE: Due to major engineering work in connection with electrification work taking place between Reading and Newbury and subsequent diversion of West of England trains, LOCAL TRAINS between Swindon and Westbury via Melksham will be subject to significant alteration on 4-7 June; 9-12 July; 16 July to 05 August; 28-30 August; 08-11 October and 19-22 November.

Table T123-F

Saturdays

26 May to 8 September

Brighton, Portsmouth and Weymouth - Bristol, Cardiff, Gloucester and Great Malvern

		GW ◇ A ✠	GW ◇	GW ◇	GW	GW ◇	GW ■ 1 B ⊡	GW ◇	SW ◇1 C	GW	GW ◇	GW	GW ◇	GW D	GW ■ 1 E ⊡	GW	GW ◇	GW	GW ◇	GW ■ 1 E ⊡	GW ◇	GW	GW ■
Brighton 10	d																						
Hove 2	d																						
Shoreham-by-Sea	d																						
Worthing 4	d																						
Barnham	d																						
Chichester 4	d																						
Havant 10	d																						
Portsmouth Harbour ⛴	d	10 23		11 23				12 23					13 23				14 23				15 23		16 23
Portsmouth & Southsea	d	10 27		11 27				12 27					13 27				14 27				15 27		16 27
Fratton 8	d	10 31		11 31				12 31					13 31				14 31				15 31		16 31
Cosham	d	10 39		11 39				12 39					13 39				14 39				15 39		16 39
Fareham	a	10 46		11 46				12 46					13 46				14 46				15 46		16 46
	d	10 47		11 47				12 47					13 47				14 47				15 47		16 47
Southampton Central 8 ⛴	d	11 10		12 10		12 27		13 10					14 10				15 10				16 10		17 10
Romsey	d	11 21		12 21		12 38		13 21					14 21				15 21				16 21		17 21
Salisbury 8	a	11 39		12 39		12 59		13 39					14 39				15 39				16 39		17 39
	d	11 40		12 40		13 03		13 40	13 52				14 40				15 40				16 40		17 40
Warminster	d	12 01		13 01		13 25		14 01	14 12				15 01			15 28	16 01		16 28		17 01		18 01
Dilton Marsh	d					13x29										15x32			16x32				
Weymouth	d		11 14								13 10											16 08	
Upwey	d		11 19								13 15											16 13	
Dorchester West	d		11 27								13 23											16 21	
Maiden Newton	d		11 43								13 47											16 40	
Chetnole	d		11x51								13x55											16x48	
Yetminster	d		11x54								13x58											16x51	
Thornford	d		11x56								14x00											16x53	
Yeovil Pen Mill	d		12 06								14 10											17 03	
Castle Cary	a		12 19								14 23											17 16	
	d		12 20				13 36				14 27				15 08					16 33		17 17	
Bruton	d		12 25								14 32											17 23	
Frome	d		12 38								14 45			15 00								17 36	
Westbury 8	a	12 09	12 47	13 09		13 34	13 54	14 09	14 20		14 55		15 09	15 09	15 26	15 37	16 09		16 38	16 51	17 09	17 45	18 09
	d	12 10	12 48	13 10	13 32	13 38	13 55	14 10	14 21	14 38	14 56	15 06	15 11		15 28	15 38	16 10	16 32	16 39	16 53	17 10	17 48	18 10
London Paddington 15 ⊖	a						15 16								17 00					18 12			
Trowbridge	d	12 16	12 55	13 16	13 38	13 44		14 16	14 27	14 44	15 03	15 12	15 17			15 44	16 16	16 38	16 46		17 16	17 54	18 16
Bradford-on-Avon	d	12 22	13 01	13 22		13 50		14 22	14 33	14 50	15 09		15 23			15 50	16 22		16 52		17 22	18 00	18 22
Avoncliff	d		13 04			13 53				14 53						15 53			16 55			18 03	
Freshford	d		13 06			13 56				14 56						15 56			16 58			18 06	
Bath Spa 7	a	12 34	13 17	13 34		14 06		14 34	14 46	15 06	15 21		15 35			16 06	16 34		17 08		17 34	18 16	18 34
Melksham	d				13 48							15 22						16 48					
Chippenham	a				14 00							15 31						17 00					
Swindon	a				14 20							15 50						17 22					
Oldfield Park	a		13 21			14 10				15 10						16 10			17 12			18 20	
Keynsham	a		13 28			14 18			14 54	15 18						16 18			17 20			18 28	
Bristol Temple Meads 10	a	12 48	13 37	13 49		14 27		14 49	15 05	15 28	15 36		15 49			16 28	16 48		17 28		17 48	18 36	18 48
Filton Abbey Wood	a	13 00	13 48	14 01		14 48		15 00			15 48		16 02			16 48	17 02		17 48		18 01	18 48	19 01
Bristol Parkway	d		13 52			14 53					15 52					16 52			17 52			18 52	
Yate	d		14 02			15 03					16 02					17 02			18 02			19 02	
Cam & Dursley	d		14 15			15 17					16 16					17 16			18 15			19 16	
Gloucester	d		14a34			15 37					16a33					17 37			18a32			19 38	
Cheltenham Spa	d					15 48										17 48						19 48	
Ashchurch for Tewkesbury	d					15 56										17 56						19 56	
Worcester Shrub Hill	d					16 14										18 20						20 20	
Worcester Foregate Street	d					16 17										18 23						20 23	
Malvern Link	d					16 26										18 32						20 32	
Great Malvern	a					16 32										18 36						20 35	
Severn Tunnel Jn.	a																17 14				18 13		
Newport (South Wales) 2	a	13 24		14 24				15 24					16 24				17 26				18 25		19 23
Cardiff Central 7	a	13 42		14 41				15 46					16 42				17 42				18 43		19 40

A ✠ to Bristol Temple Meads
B From Penzance
C From London Waterloo
D To Warminster
E From Paignton

For connections from Bristol Parkway and Cardiff Central to Swansea refer to Table T128

For connections from Castle Cary, Westbury and Bristol Temple Meads to Exeter and Plymouth refer to Table T135

For connections from Salisbury to Yeovil Junction and Exeter refer to Table T160

For connections from Bournemouth to Southampton Central, Weymouth and Upwey refer to Table T158

For additional bus connections between Yeovil Junction and Yeovil Pen Mill refer to Table T123A

Table T123-F

Saturdays

26 May to 8 September

Brighton, Portsmouth and Weymouth - Bristol, Cardiff, Gloucester and Great Malvern

		GW	GW	GW ◇ A	GW ◇	GW ◇1 B ⊡	GW ◇ C	GW ◇	GW A	GW ◇1 D ⊡	GW ◇	GW ◇1 E ⊡	GW C	GW	GW	GW ◇	SW ◇1 F	GW	GW ◇	GW
Brighton 10	d							17 00												
Hove 2	d							17 04												
Shoreham-by-Sea	d							17 13												
Worthing 4	d							17 22												
Barnham	d							17 42												
Chichester 4	d							17 50												
Havant 10	d							18 02												
Portsmouth Harbour ⛴	d				17 23						18 23					19 23			20 23	
Portsmouth & Southsea	d				17 27						18 27					19 27			20 27	
Fratton 8	d				17 31						18 31					19 31			20 31	
Cosham	d				17 39			18 08			18 39					19 39				
Fareham	a				17 46			18 16			18 46					19 46			20 45	
	d				17 47			18 17			18 47					19 47			20 47	
Southampton Central 8 ⛴	d				18 10			18 45			19 10					20 10			21 12	21 32
Romsey	d				18 21			18 56			19 21					20 21			21 23	21 43
Salisbury 8	a				18 39			19 14			19 39					20 39			21 41	22 02
	d				18 40			19 15			19 40					20 40	20 57		21 42	22 04
Warminster	d				19 01			19 35			20 01					21 01	21 17		22 03	22 25
Dilton Marsh	d							19x39												22x29
Weymouth	d			17 30					18 30									20 23		
Upwey	d			17 35					18 35									20 28		
Dorchester West	d			17 43					18 43									20 36		
Maiden Newton	d			17 55					18 54									20 48		
Chetnole	d			18x03					19x02									20x56		
Yetminster	d			18x06					19x05									20x59		
Thornford	d			18x08					19x07									21x02		
Yeovil Pen Mill	d			18 20					19 20									21 11		
Castle Cary	a			18 34					19 33									21 25		
	d			18 40		18 53			19 34	19 50								21 25		
Bruton	d			18 45					19 39									21 31		
Frome	d			18 58			←		19 51			←	←		20 53			21 44		
Westbury 8	a			19 07	19 09	19 12	19 07	19 44	20 00	20 08	20 09	20 08	20 00		21 02	21 09	21 25	21 54	22 11	22 35
	d	18 32	18 46	19 21	19 10	19 14	19 21	19 45	20 14	20 13	20 10	20 13	20 14	20 38		21 10	21 25	21 55	22 12	22 40
London Paddington 15 ⊖	a			→		20 37			→	→		21 31								
Trowbridge	d	18 38	18 52		19 16		19 27	19 51			20 16		20 22	20 44		21 16	21 31	22 02	22 18	22 46
Bradford-on-Avon	d		18 58		19 22		19 33	19 57			20 22		20 29	20 50		21 22	21 37	22 08	22 24	22 52
Avoncliff	d		19 01				19 36							20 53				22 11		22 55
Freshford	d		19 04				19 39							20 56				22 13		22 58
Bath Spa 7	a		19 14		19 34		19 49	20 09			20 34		20 41	21 06		21 36	21 50	22 24	22 36	23 08
Melksham	d	18 48																		
Chippenham	a	19 00																		
Swindon	a	19 22																		
Oldfield Park	a		19 18				19 53	20 13					20 45	21 10				22 28		23 12
Keynsham	a		19 25				20 01	20 20					20 52	21 18			21 58	22 35		23 20
Bristol Temple Meads 10	a		19 35		19 48		20 09	20 28			20 48		21 02	21 27		21 50	22 06	22 45	22 50	23 29
Filton Abbey Wood	a		19 48		20 01						21 00					22 04			23 02	
Bristol Parkway	d		19 52																	
Yate	d		20 02																	
Cam & Dursley	d		20 16																	
Gloucester	d		20 38																	
Cheltenham Spa	d		20a48																	
Ashchurch for Tewkesbury	d																			
Worcester Shrub Hill	d																			
Worcester Foregate Street	d																			
Malvern Link	d																			
Great Malvern	a																			
Severn Tunnel Jn.	a															22 19			23 17	
Newport (South Wales) 2	a				20 23						21 23					22 37			23 35	
Cardiff Central 7	a				20 42						21 42					23 00			23 56	

A To Bristol Temple Meads
B From Paignton
C From Weymouth
D From Penzance to London Paddington
E From Penzance
F From London Waterloo

For connections from Bristol Parkway and Cardiff Central to Swansea refer to Table T128

For connections from Castle Cary, Westbury and Bristol Temple Meads to Exeter and Plymouth refer to Table T135

For connections from Salisbury to Yeovil Junction and Exeter refer to Table T160

For connections from Bournemouth to Southampton Central, Weymouth and Upwey refer to Table T158

For additional bus connections between Yeovil Junction and Yeovil Pen Mill refer to Table T123A

Brighton, Portsmouth and Weymouth - Bristol, Cardiff, Gloucester and Great Malvern

		GW	GW	SW	GW	GW	GW	GW	GW	GW	GW	GW	GW	GW	GW	GW	GW	GW	GW	GW	SW	GW	GW
			A	■			◇■ B	◇	◇			◇ C		◇		◇■ B	■ C	◇	■ ■ D	◇ C	◇■ E		◇
Brighton	d																						09 00
Hove	d																						09 04
Shoreham-by-Sea	d																						09 13
Worthing	d																						09 22
Barnham	d																						09 43
Chichester	d																						09 51
Havant	d																						10 02
Portsmouth Harbour	d							06 08				07 23					08 23			09 23			
Portsmouth & Southsea	d							06 12				07 27					08 27			09 27			
Fratton	d							06 16				07 31					08 31			09 31			
Cosham	d							06 23				07 39					08 39			09 39			10 08
Fareham	a							06 31				07 46					08 46			09 46			10 16
	d							06 32				07 47					08 47			09 47			10 17
Southampton Central	d							06 57				08 10		08 30			09 10			10 10			10 42
Romsey	d							07 11				08 21		08 41			09 21			10 21			10 54
Salisbury	a							07 29				08 39		09 00			09 39			10 39			11 12
	d	06 07		06 40				07 30				08 40		09 05			09 40			10 40	10 52		11 13
Warminster	d	06 28		07 00		07 23		07 50				09 01		09 27			10 01			11 01	11 12		11 33
Dilton Marsh	d	06x32				07x27		07x54						09x31									11x37
Weymouth	d								06 44									08 53					
Upwey	d								06 49									08 58					
Dorchester West	d								06 57									09 06					
Maiden Newton	d								07 09									09 18					
Chetnole	d								07x17									09x26					
Yetminster	d								07x20									09x29					
Thornford	d								07x22									09x31					
Yeovil Pen Mill	d								07 34									09 41					
Castle Cary	a								07 47									09 54					
	d						07 34		07 48							09 42		09 55					
Bruton	d								07 54									10 01					
Frome	d		06 49						08 07									10 15					
Westbury	a	06 37	06 58	07 08		07 31	07 52	08 00	08 16			09 09		09 37		10 00	10 09	10 24		11 09	11 20		11 42
	d	06 38		07 09	07 33	07 38	07 56	08 06	08 17	08 22	08 38	09 10	09 32	09 39	09 51	10 02	10 10	10 38	11 03	11 10	11 21	11 32	11 44
London Paddington ⊖	a						09 21									11 21			12 21				
Trowbridge	d	06 44		07 15	07 39	07 44		08 12	08 24	08 29	08 44	09 16	09 38	09 45	09 57		10 16	10 44		11 16	11 27	11 38	11 51
Bradford-on-Avon	d	06 50		07 21		07 50		08 18	08 30		08 50	09 22		09 51	10 03		10 22	10 50		11 22	11 33		11 57
Avoncliff	d	06 53				07 53			08 33		08 53			09 54				10 53					12 00
Freshford	d	06 56				07 56			08 36		08 56			09 57				10 56					12 03
Bath Spa	a	07 06		07 33		08 06		08 31	08 46		09 06	09 34		10 06	10 15		10 34	11 06		11 34	11 46		12 13
Melksham	d				07 49					08 38			09 48									11 48	
Chippenham	a				08 00					08 48			10 00									12 00	
Swindon	a				08 20					09 07			10 20									12 20	
Oldfield Park	a	07 10		07 37		08 10			08 50		09 10			10 11				11 11					12 17
Keynsham	a	07 18		07 44		08 17			08 58		09 18			10 19				11 19			11 54		12 24
Bristol Temple Meads	a	07 28		07 52		08 28		08 47	09 06		09 27	09 48		10 27			10 48	11 27		11 48	12 05		12 35
Filton Abbey Wood	a	07 48				08 48		09 02			09 48	10 00		10 48			11 02	11 48		12 02			12 50
Bristol Parkway	d	07 53				08 53					09 52			10 52				11 52					12 55
Yate	d	08 02				09 02					10 02			11 02				12 02					13 04
Cam & Dursley	d	08 16				09 14					10 15			11 16				12 16					13 16
Gloucester	d	08a32				09 38					10a33			11 37				12a31					13 37
Cheltenham Spa	d					09 48								11 48									13 48
Ashchurch for Tewkesbury	d					09 56								11 57									13 56
Worcester Shrub Hill	d					10 16								12 14									14 15
Worcester Foregate Street	d					10 19								12a17									14 18
Malvern Link	d					10 28																	14 27
Great Malvern	a					10 33																	14 32
Severn Tunnel Jn.	a																						
Newport (South Wales)	a							09 25				10 23					11 25			12 24			
Cardiff Central	a							09 42				10 40					11 42			12 44			

A To Southampton Central
B From Plymouth
C to Bristol Temple Meads
D From Penzance
E From London Waterloo

For connections from Bristol Parkway and Cardiff Central to Swansea refer to Table T128

For connections from Castle Cary, Westbury and Bristol Temple Meads to Exeter and Plymouth refer to Table T135

For connections from Salisbury to Yeovil Junction and Exeter refer to Table T160

For connections from Bournemouth to Southampton Central, Weymouth and Upwey refer to Table T158

For additional bus connections between Yeovil Junction and Yeovil Pen Mill refer to Table T123A

Brighton, Portsmouth and Weymouth - Bristol, Cardiff, Gloucester and Great Malvern

		GW	GW	GW	GW	GW	GW	GW	SW	GW	GW	GW	GW	GW	GW	GW	GW	GW	GW	GW	GW	GW	GW
		◇ A	◇	◇	◇■ B		◇	◇	◇■ C		◇	◇■ D		◇	E		◇	◇■ F		◇	◇		■
Brighton	d																						
Hove	d																						
Shoreham-by-Sea	d																						
Worthing	d																						
Barnham	d																						
Chichester	d																						
Havant	d																						
Portsmouth Harbour	d	10 23		11 23				12 23						13 23			14 23				15 23		16 23
Portsmouth & Southsea	d	10 27		11 27				12 27						13 27			14 27				15 27		16 27
Fratton	d	10 31		11 31				12 31						13 31			14 31				15 31		16 31
Cosham	d	10 39		11 39				12 39						13 39			14 39				15 39		16 39
Fareham	a	10 46		11 46				12 46						13 46			14 46				15 46		16 46
	d	10 47		11 47				12 47						13 47			14 47				15 47		16 47
Southampton Central	d	11 10		12 10			12 27	13 10						14 10			15 10				16 10		17 10
Romsey	d	11 21		12 21			12 38	13 21						14 21			15 21				16 21		17 21
Salisbury	a	11 39		12 39			12 59	13 39						14 39			15 39				16 39		17 39
	d	11 40		12 40			13 03	13 40	13 52					14 40			15 40				16 40		17 40
Warminster	d	12 01		13 01			13 25	14 01	14 12					15 01		15 28	16 01				17 01	17 28	18 01
Dilton Marsh	d						13x29									15x32						17x32	
Weymouth	d		11 14								13 10									15 08			
Upwey	d		11 19								13 15									15 13			
Dorchester West	d		11 27								13 23									15 21			
Maiden Newton	d		11 43								13 47									15 33			
Chetnole	d		11x51								13x55									15x41			
Yetminster	d		11x54								13x58									15x44			
Thornford	d		11x56								14x00									15x46			
Yeovil Pen Mill	d		12 06								14 10									15 56			
Castle Cary	a		12 19								14 23									16 09			
	d		12 20		12 52						14 27	14 43						15 53		16 10			
Bruton	d		12 25								14 32									16 16			
Frome	d		12 38								14 45				15 00					16 29			
Westbury	a	12 09	12 47	13 09	13 10		13 34	14 09	14 20		14 55	15 01		15 09	15 09	15 37	16 09	16 11		16 38	17 09	17 37	18 09
	d	12 10	12 48	13 10	13 13	13 32	13 38	14 10	14 21	14 38	14 56	15 03	15 06	15 11		15 38	16 10	16 13	16 32	16 39	17 10	17 48	18 10
London Paddington ⊖	a				14 38							16 21						17 44					
Trowbridge	d	12 16	12 55	13 16		13 38	13 44	14 16	14 27	14 44	15 03		15 12	15 17		15 44	16 16		16 38	16 46	17 16	17 54	18 16
Bradford-on-Avon	d	12 22	13 01	13 22			13 50	14 22	14 33	14 50	15 09			15 23		15 50	16 22			16 52	17 22	18 00	18 22
Avoncliff	d		13 04				13 53			14 53						15 53				16 55		18 03	
Freshford	d		13 06				13 56			14 56						15 56				16 58		18 06	
Bath Spa	a	12 34	13 17	13 34			14 06	14 34	14 46	15 06	15 21			15 35		16 06	16 34			17 08	17 34	18 16	18 34
Melksham	d					13 48							15 22						16 48				
Chippenham	a					14 00							15 31						17 00				
Swindon	a					14 20							15 50						17 22				
Oldfield Park	a		13 21				14 10			15 10						16 10				17 12		18 20	
Keynsham	a		13 28				14 18		14 54	15 18						16 18				17 20		18 28	
Bristol Temple Meads	a	12 48	13 37	13 49			14 27	14 49	15 05	15 28	15 36			15 49		16 28	16 48			17 28	17 48	18 36	18 48
Filton Abbey Wood	a	13 00	13 48	14 01			14 48	15 00			15 48			16 02		16 48	17 02			17 48	18 01	18 48	19 01
Bristol Parkway	d		13 52				14 53				15 52					16 52				17 52		18 52	
Yate	d		14 02				15 03				16 02					17 02				18 02		19 02	
Cam & Dursley	d		14 15				15 17				16 16					17 16				18 15		19 16	
Gloucester	d		14a34				15 37				16a33					17 37				18a32		19 38	
Cheltenham Spa	d						15 48									17 48						19 48	
Ashchurch for Tewkesbury	d						15 56									17 56						19 56	
Worcester Shrub Hill	d						16 14									18 20						20 20	
Worcester Foregate Street	d						16 17									18 23						20 23	
Malvern Link	d						16 26									18 32						20 32	
Great Malvern	a						16 32									18 36						20 35	
Severn Tunnel Jn.	a																17 14				18 13		
Newport (South Wales)	a	13 24		14 24				15 24						16 24			17 26				18 25		19 23
Cardiff Central	a	13 42		14 41				15 46						16 42			17 42				18 43		19 40

A to Bristol Temple Meads
B From Exeter St Davids
C From London Waterloo
D From Penzance
E To Warminster
F From Taunton

For connections from Bristol Parkway and Cardiff Central to Swansea refer to Table T128

For connections from Castle Cary, Westbury and Bristol Temple Meads to Exeter and Plymouth refer to Table T135

For connections from Salisbury to Yeovil Junction and Exeter refer to Table T160

For connections from Bournemouth to Southampton Central, Weymouth and Upwey refer to Table T158

For additional bus connections between Yeovil Junction and Yeovil Pen Mill refer to Table T123A

T123 UPDATE: Due to major engineering work in connection with electrification work taking place between Reading and Newbury and subsequent diversion of West of England trains, LOCAL TRAINS between Swindon and Westbury via Melksham will be subject to significant alteration on 4-7 June; 9-12 July; 16 July to 05 August; 28-30 August; 08-11 October and 19-22 November.

Table T123-F

Saturdays
15 September to 8 December

Brighton, Portsmouth and Weymouth - Bristol, Cardiff, Gloucester and Great Malvern

		GW	GW	GW ◇ A	GW ◇	GW ◇■ B	GW ◇ C	GW ◇	GW ◇■ D	GW ◇	GW	GW	GW ◇	SW ◇■ E	GW	GW ◇	GW
Brighton	d							17 00									
Hove	d							17 04									
Shoreham-by-Sea	d							17 13									
Worthing	d							17 22									
Barnham	d							17 42									
Chichester	d							17 50									
Havant	d							18 02									
Portsmouth Harbour	d				17 23					18 23			19 23			20 23	
Portsmouth & Southsea	d				17 27					18 27			19 27			20 27	
Fratton	d				17 31					18 31			19 31			20 31	
Cosham	d				17 39			18 08		18 39			19 39				
Fareham	a				17 46			18 16		18 46			19 46			20 45	
	d				17 47			18 17		18 47			19 47			20 47	
Southampton Central	d				18 10			18 45		19 10			20 10			21 12	21 32
Romsey	d				18 21			18 56		19 21			20 21			21 23	21 43
Salisbury	a				18 39			19 14		19 39			20 39			21 41	22 02
	d				18 40			19 15		19 40			20 40	20 57		21 42	22 04
Warminster	d				19 01			19 35		20 01			21 01	21 17		22 03	22 25
Dilton Marsh	d							19x39									22x29
Weymouth	d			17 30											20 23		
Upwey	d			17 35											20 28		
Dorchester West	d			17 43											20 36		
Maiden Newton	d			17 55											20 48		
Chetnole	d			18x03											20x56		
Yetminster	d			18x06											20x59		
Thornford	d			18x08											21x02		
Yeovil Pen Mill	d			18 20											21 11		
Castle Cary	a			18 34											21 25		
	d			18 40		18 53			19 47						21 25		
Bruton	d			18 45											21 31		
Frome	d			18 58			←					20 53			21 44		
Westbury	a			19 07	19 09	19 12	19 07	19 44	20 05	20 09		21 02	21 09	21 25	21 54	22 11	22 35
	d	18 32	18 46	19 21	19 10	19 14	19 21	19 45	20 07	20 10	20 38		21 10	21 25	21 55	22 12	22 40
London Paddington ⊖	a			→		20 37			21 31								
Trowbridge	d	18 38	18 52		19 16		19 27	19 51		20 16	20 44		21 16	21 31	22 02	22 18	22 46
Bradford-on-Avon	d		18 58		19 22		19 33	19 57		20 22	20 50		21 22	21 37	22 08	22 24	22 52
Avoncliff	d		19 01				19 36				20 53				22 11		22 55
Freshford	d		19 04				19 39				20 56				22 13		22 58
Bath Spa	a		19 14		19 34		19 49	20 09		20 34	21 06		21 36	21 50	22 24	22 36	23 08
Melksham	d	18 48															
Chippenham	a	19 00															
Swindon	a	19 22															
Oldfield Park	a		19 18				19 53	20 13			21 10				22 28		23 12
Keynsham	a		19 25				20 01	20 20			21 18			21 58	22 35		23 20
Bristol Temple Meads	a		19 35		19 48		20 09	20 28		20 48	21 27		21 50	22 06	22 45	22 50	23 29
Filton Abbey Wood	a		19 48		20 01					21 00			22 04			23 02	
Bristol Parkway	d		19 52														
Yate	d		20 02														
Cam & Dursley	d		20 16														
Gloucester	d		20 38														
Cheltenham Spa	d		20a48														
Ashchurch for Tewkesbury	d																
Worcester Shrub Hill	d																
Worcester Foregate Street	d																
Malvern Link	d																
Great Malvern	a																
Severn Tunnel Jn.	a												22 19			23 17	
Newport (South Wales)	a				20 23					21 23			22 37			23 35	
Cardiff Central	a				20 42					21 42			23 00			23 56	

A To Bristol Temple Meads
B From Plymouth
C From Weymouth
D From Penzance
E From London Waterloo

For connections from Bristol Parkway and Cardiff Central to Swansea refer to Table T128

For connections from Castle Cary, Westbury and Bristol Temple Meads to Exeter and Plymouth refer to Table T135

For connections from Salisbury to Yeovil Junction and Exeter refer to Table T160

For connections from Bournemouth to Southampton Central, Weymouth and Upwey refer to Table T158

For additional bus connections between Yeovil Junction and Yeovil Pen Mill refer to Table T123A

Table T123-F

Sundays
20 May to 9 September

Brighton, Portsmouth and Weymouth - Bristol, Cardiff, Gloucester and Great Malvern

		GW	GW	GW ◇ A	GW ◇■ B	GW ◇ C	GW	GW ◇■ D	GW ■	GW	GW ◇■ E	GW ◇	GW ◇	GW ◇■ D	GW ■ E	GW ◇	SW ◇■ F	GW	GW ◇	GW ◇	GW ◇■ E	GW ◇	GW
Brighton	d															11 10							
Hove	d															11 14							
Shoreham-by-Sea	d															11 21							
Worthing	d															11 31							
Barnham	d															11 56							
Chichester	d															12 04							
Havant	d															12 15							
Portsmouth Harbour	d								09 08				11 08						13 08			14 08	
Portsmouth & Southsea	d								09 12				11 12						13 12			14 12	
Fratton	d								09 15				11 15						13 16			14 16	
Cosham	d								09 23				11 23			12 25			13 24			14 23	
Fareham	a								09 31				11 31			12 33			13 31			14 31	
	d								09 33				11 33			12 34			13 32			14 34	
Southampton Central	d								09 55				11 56			12 56			13 56			14 56	
Romsey	d								10 07				12 07			13 07			14 07			15 07	
Salisbury	a								10 24				12 25			13 25			14 25			15 25	
	d								10 26				12 27			13 25	13 55		14 27			15 27	
Warminster	d		08 47						10 49				12 42			13 44	14 15		14 45			15 44	
Dilton Marsh	d		08x52						10x54										14x50			15x50	
Weymouth	d											11 00								14 14			
Upwey	d											11 05								14 19			
Dorchester West	d											11 13								14 27			
Maiden Newton	d											11 32								14 39			
Chetnole	d											11x39								14x47			
Yetminster	d											11x42								14x50			
Thornford	d											11x45								14x52			
Yeovil Pen Mill	d											11 54								15 04			
Castle Cary	a											12 07								15 16			
	d				09 34						12 00	12 09		12 51						15 18	15 33		
Bruton	d											12 14								15 24			
Frome	d			09 39		←				11 40		12 27								15 37			
Westbury	a		08 55	09 48	09 51	09 48			10 58	11 49	12 19	12 36	12 53			13 56	14 24		14 56	15 46	15 50	15 56	
	d	08 28	08 55	09 57	09 54	09 57	10 30	10 46	10 58	11 50	12 21	12 37	12 58		13 50	13 56	14 25	14 35	15 00	15 47	15 50	16 04	16 20
London Paddington ⊖	a			→	11 30			12 21			13 55			14 30	15 15						17 29		
Trowbridge	d	08 33	09 02			10 03	10 35		11 05	11 56		12 43	13 05			14 02	14 31	14 40	15 06	15 53		16 10	16 25
Bradford-on-Avon	d		09 07			10 09			11 11	12 02			13 11			14 08	14 37		15 12	15 59		16 16	
Avoncliff	d		09 10			10 12				12 05						14 11				16 02			
Freshford	d		09 13			10 15				12 07						14 14				16 05			
Bath Spa	a		09 24			10 26			11 24	12 19			13 25			14 24	14 50		15 24	16 16		16 28	
Melksham	d	08 44					10 46					12 53						14 50					16 35
Chippenham	a	08 53					11 01					13 02						15 00					16 45
Swindon	a	09 12					11 20					13 20						15 19					17 04
Oldfield Park	a		09 28			10 29			11 27	12 23			13 28			14 27				16 19			
Keynsham	a		09 35			10 36			11 34	12 30			13 35			14 35	14 58			16 27			
Bristol Temple Meads	a		09 44			10 45			11 44	12 40			13 44			14 44	15 06		15 40	16 35		16 43	
Filton Abbey Wood	a					10 55			11 54				13 55			14 55			15 55			16 55	
Bristol Parkway	d																						
Yate	d																						
Cam & Dursley	d																						
Gloucester	d																						
Cheltenham Spa	d																						
Ashchurch for Tewkesbury	d																						
Worcester Shrub Hill	d																						
Worcester Foregate Street	d																						
Malvern Link	d																						
Great Malvern	a																						
Severn Tunnel Jn.	a					11 11			12 08				14 08			15 05			16 08			17 10	
Newport (South Wales)	a					11 21			12 21				14 20			15 20			16 19			17 21	
Cardiff Central	a					11 43			12 41				14 42			15 44			16 42			17 43	

A To Cardiff Central
B From Exeter St Davids
C From Frome
D From Plymouth
E From Penzance
F From London Waterloo

For connections from Bristol Parkway and Cardiff Central to Swansea refer to Table T128

For connections from Castle Cary, Westbury and Bristol Temple Meads to Exeter and Plymouth refer to Table T135

For connections from Salisbury to Yeovil Junction and Exeter refer to Table T160

For connections from Bournemouth to Southampton Central, Weymouth and Upwey refer to Table T158

For additional bus connections between Yeovil Junction and Yeovil Pen Mill refer to Table T123A

Table T123-F

Sundays

20 May to 9 September

Brighton, Portsmouth and Weymouth - Bristol, Cardiff, Gloucester and Great Malvern

		GW	GW	SW	GW	GW	SW	GW	GW	GW	GW	GW	GW	GW	SW	GW	GW	GW	GW	GW	GW	GW	GW
		■	◇	◇■ A	◇■ B ☕	◇	◇■ C	◇		◇	◇		◇■ D ☕	◇	◇■	◇	◇■ B ☕	◇	E	◇■ F ☕	G	◇	
Brighton	d							15 47								17 46							
Hove	d							15 51								17 50							
Shoreham-by-Sea	d							15 57								17 56							
Worthing	d							16 09								18 08							
Barnham	d							16 27								18 27							
Chichester	d							16 35								18 35							
Havant	d							16 45								18 50							
Portsmouth Harbour	d	15 08				16 10				17 08				18 08				19 08				20 08	22 08
Portsmouth & Southsea	d	15 12				16 14				17 12				18 12				19 12				20 12	22 12
Fratton	d	15 16				16 18				17 16				18 16				19 16				20 16	22 15
Cosham	d	15 23				16 25		16 52		17 23				18 23		18 57		19 23					
Fareham	a	15 31				16 33		16 59		17 31				18 31		19 04		19 31				20 31	22 31
	d	15 34				16 34		17 00		17 34				18 34		19 05		19 33				20 34	22 32
Southampton Central	d	15 56				16 56		17 22		17 56				18 56		19 28		19 56				20 56	22 57
Romsey	d	16 07				17 07		17 35		18 07				19 08		19 40		20 07				21 07	23 08
Salisbury	a	16 25				17 24		17 53		18 25				19 26		19 58		20 25				21 25	23 27
	d	16 27		17 10		17 25		17 54		18 27				19 27	19 55	20 01		20 26				21 26	23 28
Warminster	d	16 44		17 36		17 44		18 14		18 44				19 46	20 15	20 22		20 44				21 46	23 50
Dilton Marsh	d	16x50						18x19								20x27						21x53	23x55
Weymouth	d		16 10								17 56								20 09				
Upwey	d		16 15								18 01								20 14				
Dorchester West	d		16 23								18 09								20 22				
Maiden Newton	d		16 35								18 21								20 34				
Chetnole	d		16x43								18x29								20x42				
Yetminster	d		16x46								18x32								20x45				
Thornford	d		16x48								18x34								20x47				
Yeovil Pen Mill	d		16 58								18 44								20 57				
Castle Cary	a		17 10								18 56								21 09				
	d		17 13		17 34						19 00						20 37		21 10	21 27			
Bruton	d		17 18								19 05								21 16				
Frome	d		17 31				18 04				19 18								21 29		←		
Westbury	a	16 56	17 40	17 44	17 51	17 55	18 12	18 22		18 56	19 26			19 57	20 23	20 31	20 54	20 56	21 39	21 44	21 39	21 56	23 59
	d	17 00	17 41		17 54	18 00		18 25	18 39	19 01	19 26	19 41	19 54	20 00	20 23	20 39	20 56	21 00	21 47	21 46	21 47	22 00	
London Paddington ⊖	a				19 29								21 27				22 28		→	23 25			
Trowbridge	d	17 06	17 48			18 06		18 31	18 45	19 06	19 33	19 46		20 06	20 29	20 45		21 06			21 55	22 06	
Bradford-on-Avon	d	17 12	17 54			18 12		18 37		19 12	19 40			20 12	20 35	20 51		21 12			22 01	22 12	
Avoncliff	d					18 16					19 43					20 54					22 04		
Freshford	d					18 19					19 46					20 57					22 07		
Bath Spa	a	17 24	18 09			18 29		18 48		19 25	19 56			20 25	20 50	21 09		21 25			22 18	22 25	
Melksham	d								18 54			19 57											
Chippenham	a								19 04			20 07											
Swindon	a								19 21			20 24											
Oldfield Park	a	17 28	18 12					18 53			19 59					21 13					22 22		
Keynsham	a	17 35	18 20					19 00			20 07				20 59	21 19					22 29		
Bristol Temple Meads	a	17 44	18 29			18 44		19 09		19 39	20 18			20 39	21 07	21 29		21 41			22 37	22 41	
Filton Abbey Wood	a	17 55				18 55				19 55				20 55				21 55				22 56	
Bristol Parkway	d																						
Yate	d																						
Cam & Dursley	d																						
Gloucester	d											21 20											
Cheltenham Spa	d											21a28											
Ashchurch for Tewkesbury	d																						
Worcester Shrub Hill	d																						
Worcester Foregate Street	d																						
Malvern Link	d																						
Great Malvern	a																						
Severn Tunnel Jn.	a	18 08				19 08				20 10				21 07				22 11				23 09	
Newport (South Wales)	a	18 20				19 20				20 22				21 20				22 24				23 21	
Cardiff Central	a	18 42				19 42				20 43				21 40				22 45				23 41	

A To Frome
B From Plymouth
C To London Waterloo
D From Newquay
E To Bristol Temple Meads
F From Penzance
G From Weymouth

For connections from Bristol Parkway and Cardiff Central to Swansea refer to Table T128

For connections from Castle Cary, Westbury and Bristol Temple Meads to Exeter and Plymouth refer to Table T135

For connections from Salisbury to Yeovil Junction and Exeter refer to Table T160

For connections from Bournemouth to Southampton Central, Weymouth and Upwey refer to Table T158

For additional bus connections between Yeovil Junction and Yeovil Pen Mill refer to Table T123A

Table T123-F

Sundays

16 September to 21 October

Brighton, Portsmouth and Weymouth - Bristol, Cardiff, Gloucester and Great Malvern

		GW	GW	GW	GW	GW	GW	GW	GW	GW	GW	GW	GW	GW	GW	GW	GW	SW	GW	GW	GW	GW	GW
					A	◇■ B ☕	C		◇■ D ☕	■		◇■ E ☕	◇	◇	◇	◇■ D ☕	■ ■ E ☕	◇■ F		◇	◇	◇■ D ☕	◇
Brighton	d														11 10								
Hove	d														11 14								
Shoreham-by-Sea	d														11 21								
Worthing	d														11 31								
Barnham	d														11 56								
Chichester	d														12 04								
Havant	d														12 15								
Portsmouth Harbour	d									09 08				11 08						13 08			14 08
Portsmouth & Southsea	d									09 12				11 12						13 12			14 12
Fratton	d									09 15				11 15						13 16			14 16
Cosham	d									09 23				11 23	12 25					13 24			14 23
Fareham	a									09 31				11 31	12 33					13 31			14 31
	d									09 33				11 33	12 34					13 32			14 34
Southampton Central	d									09 55				11 56	12 56					13 56			14 56
Romsey	d									10 07				12 07	13 07					14 07			15 07
Salisbury	a									10 24				12 25	13 25					14 25			15 25
	d									10 26				12 27	13 25			13 55		14 27			15 27
Warminster	d			08 47						10 49				12 44	13 44			14 15		14 45			15 44
Dilton Marsh	d			08x52						10x54										14x50			15x50
Weymouth	d												11 05								14 14		
Upwey	d												11 10								14 19		
Dorchester West	d												11 18								14 27		
Maiden Newton	d												11 32								14 39		
Chetnole	d												11x39								14x47		
Yetminster	d												11x42								14x50		
Thornford	d												11x45								14x52		
Yeovil Pen Mill	d												11 54								15 04		
Castle Cary	a												12 07								15 16		
	d					09 20						12 01	12 08			12 51					15 18	15 39	
Bruton	d												12 14								15 24		
Frome	d				09 25		←				11 40		12 27								15 37		
Westbury	a			08 55	09 34	09 38	09 34			10 58	11 49	12 20	12 36	12 54	13 56			14 24		14 56	15 46	15 56	15 56
	d	08 28	08 48	08 56	09 43	09 40	09 43	10 30	10 43	10 58	11 50	12 21	12 37	12 56	13 56		13 59	14 25	14 35	15 00	15 47	15 57	16 04
London Paddington ⊖	a				→	11 14			12 14			14 04				14 34	15 34					17 37	
Trowbridge	d	08 33	08 54	09 02			09 49	10 35		11 05	11 56		12 43	13 03	14 02			14 31	14 40	15 06	15 53		16 10
Bradford-on-Avon	d		09 00	09 08			09 55			11 11	12 02			13 09	14 08			14 37		15 12	15 59		16 16
Avoncliff	d		09 03	09 11			09 58				12 05				14 11						16 02		
Freshford	d		09 05	09 14			10 00				12 07				14 14						16 05		
Bath Spa	a		09 17	09 23			10 11			11 24	12 19			13 23	14 24			14 50		15 24	16 15		16 28
Melksham	d	08 44						10 46					12 53						14 50				
Chippenham	a	08 53						10 55					13 02						15 00				
Swindon	a	09 12						11 14					13 20						15 19				
Oldfield Park	a		09 21	09 27			10 15			11 27	12 23			13 26	14 27						16 18		
Keynsham	a		09 28	09 34			10 22			11 34	12 30			13 33	14 35			14 58			16 26		
Bristol Temple Meads	a		09 36	09 44			10 31			11 44	12 40			13 41	14 44			15 06		15 40	16 35		16 41
Filton Abbey Wood	a			09 57			10 47			11 54				13 55	14 55					15 55			16 55
Bristol Parkway	d																						
Yate	d																						
Cam & Dursley	d																						
Gloucester	d																						
Cheltenham Spa	d																						
Ashchurch for Tewkesbury	d																						
Worcester Shrub Hill	d																						
Worcester Foregate Street	d																						
Malvern Link	d																						
Great Malvern	a																						
Severn Tunnel Jn.	a			10 10			11 03			12 08				14 07	15 05					16 08			17 10
Newport (South Wales)	a			10 21			11 14			12 21				14 19	15 20					16 19			17 21
Cardiff Central	a			10 42			11 36			12 41				14 41	15 41					16 42			17 43

A To Cardiff Central
B From Exeter St Davids
C From Frome
D From Plymouth
E From Penzance
F From London Waterloo

For connections from Bristol Parkway and Cardiff Central to Swansea refer to Table T128

For connections from Castle Cary, Westbury and Bristol Temple Meads to Exeter and Plymouth refer to Table T135

For connections from Salisbury to Yeovil Junction and Exeter refer to Table T160

For connections from Bournemouth to Southampton Central, Weymouth and Upwey refer to Table T158

For additional bus connections between Yeovil Junction and Yeovil Pen Mill refer to Table T123A

T123 UPDATE: Due to major engineering work in connection with electrification work taking place between Reading and Newbury and subsequent diversion of West of England trains, LOCAL TRAINS between Swindon and Westbury via Melksham will be subject to significant alteration on 4-7 June; 9-12 July; 16 July to 05 August; 28-30 August; 08-11 October and 19-22 November.

Table T123-F

Sundays

16 September to 21 October

Brighton, Portsmouth and Weymouth - Bristol, Cardiff, Gloucester and Great Malvern

		GW	GW	GW	SW	GW	GW	SW	GW	GW	GW	GW	GW	GW	GW	SW	GW	GW	GW	GW	GW	GW	GW
			■	◇	◇■ A	◇	◇■ B ☕	◇■ C	◇		◇	◇		◇■ B ☕	◇	◇■	◇	◇■ B ☕	◇		◇■ D ☕	◇	
Brighton	d								15 47								17 46						
Hove	d								15 51								17 50						
Shoreham-by-Sea	d								15 57								17 56						
Worthing	d								16 09								18 08						
Barnham	d								16 27								18 27						
Chichester	d								16 35								18 35						
Havant	d								16 46								18 50						
Portsmouth Harbour	d		15 08			16 10					17 08				18 08				19 08			20 08	22 08
Portsmouth & Southsea	d		15 12			16 14					17 12				18 12				19 12			20 12	22 12
Fratton	d		15 16			16 18					17 16				18 16				19 16			20 16	22 15
Cosham	d		15 23			16 25			16 53		17 23				18 23		18 57		19 23				
Fareham	a		15 31			16 33			16 59		17 31				18 31		19 04		19 31			20 31	22 31
	d		15 34			16 34			16 59		17 34				18 34		19 05		19 33			20 34	22 32
Southampton Central	d		15 56			16 56			17 22		17 56				18 56		19 28		19 56			20 56	22 57
Romsey	d		16 07			17 07			17 35		18 07				19 08		19 40		20 07			21 07	23 08
Salisbury	a		16 25			17 25			17 53		18 25				19 26		19 58		20 25			21 25	23 27
	d		16 27		17 10	17 27			17 54		18 27				19 27	19 55	20 01		20 26			21 26	23 28
Warminster	d		16 44		17 36	17 44			18 14		18 44				19 46	20 15	20 22		20 44			21 46	23 50
Dilton Marsh	d		16x50						18x19								20x27					21x53	23x55
Weymouth	d			16 10								17 56								20 09			
Upwey	d			16 15								18 01								20 14			
Dorchester West	d			16 23								18 09								20 22			
Maiden Newton	d			16 35								18 21								20 34			
Chetnole	d			16x43								18x29								20x42			
Yetminster	d			16x46								18x32								20x45			
Thornford	d			16x48								18x34								20x47			
Yeovil Pen Mill	d			16 58								18 44								20 57			
Castle Cary	a			17 10								18 56								21 09			
	d			17 13			17 45					19 00						20 32		21 10	21 28		
Bruton	d			17 18								19 05								21 16			
Frome	d			17 31				18 04				19 18								21 29			
Westbury	a		16 56	17 40	17 44	17 56	18 03	18 12	18 22		18 56	19 27			19 57	20 23	20 31	20 50	20 56	21 39	21 46	21 56	23 59
	d	16 52	17 00	17 41		18 00	18 05		18 25	18 45	19 01	19 34	19 41	19 46	20 00	20 23	20 36	20 52	21 00	21 47	21 47	22 00	
London Paddington ⊖	a						19 38							21 15				22 15			23 33		
Trowbridge	d	16 57	17 06	17 48		18 06			18 31	18 51	19 06	19 40	19 46		20 06	20 29	20 42		21 06	21 55		22 06	
Bradford-on-Avon	d		17 12	17 54		18 12			18 37		19 12	19 48			20 12	20 35	20 48		21 12	22 01		22 12	
Avoncliff	d					18 16						19 51					20 51			22 04			
Freshford	d					18 19						19 53					20 54			22 07			
Bath Spa	a		17 24	18 06		18 29			18 48		19 25	20 04			20 25	20 49	21 05		21 25	22 18		22 25	
Melksham	d	17 07								19 00			19 57										
Chippenham	a	17 24								19 10			20 07										
Swindon	a	17 41								19 27			20 24										
Oldfield Park	a		17 28	18 11					18 53			20 07					21 09			22 22			
Keynsham	a		17 35	18 19					19 00			20 15				20 57	21 15			22 29			
Bristol Temple Meads	a		17 44	18 28		18 43			19 09		19 39	20 25			20 39	21 05	21 24		21 41	22 37		22 41	
Filton Abbey Wood	a		17 55			18 55					19 55				20 55				21 55			22 56	
Bristol Parkway	d																						
Yate	d																						
Cam & Dursley	d																						
Gloucester	d												21 26										
Cheltenham Spa	d												21a34										
Ashchurch for Tewkesbury	d																						
Worcester Shrub Hill	d																						
Worcester Foregate Street	d																						
Malvern Link	d																						
Great Malvern	a																						
Severn Tunnel Jn.	a		18 08			19 08					20 10				21 07				22 11			23 09	
Newport (South Wales)	a		18 20			19 20					20 22				21 20				22 24			23 21	
Cardiff Central	a		18 42			19 40					20 43				21 40				22 49			23 41	

A To Frome
B From Plymouth
C To London Waterloo
D From Penzance

For connections from Bristol Parkway and Cardiff Central to Swansea refer to Table T128

For connections from Castle Cary, Westbury and Bristol Temple Meads to Exeter and Plymouth refer to Table T135

For connections from Salisbury to Yeovil Junction and Exeter refer to Table T160

For connections from Bournemouth to Southampton Central, Weymouth and Upwey refer to Table T158

For additional bus connections between Yeovil Junction and Yeovil Pen Mill refer to Table T123A

Table T123-F

Sundays

28 October to 2 December

Brighton, Portsmouth and Weymouth - Bristol, Cardiff, Gloucester and Great Malvern

		GW	GW	GW	GW	GW	GW	GW	GW	GW	GW	GW	GW	GW	GW	GW	GW	SW	GW	GW	GW	GW	GW
					A	◇■ B ☕	C		◇■ D ☕	■		◇■ E ☕	◇	◇	◇	◇■ D ☕	■ ■ E ☕	◇■ F		◇	◇	◇■ D ☕	◇
Brighton	d														11 10								
Hove	d														11 14								
Shoreham-by-Sea	d														11 21								
Worthing	d														11 31								
Barnham	d														11 56								
Chichester	d														12 04								
Havant	d														12 15								
Portsmouth Harbour	d									09 08				11 08						13 08			14 08
Portsmouth & Southsea	d									09 12				11 12						13 12			14 12
Fratton	d									09 15				11 15						13 16			14 16
Cosham	d									09 23				11 23	12 25					13 24			14 23
Fareham	a									09 31				11 31	12 33					13 31			14 31
	d									09 33				11 33	12 34					13 32			14 34
Southampton Central	d									09 55				11 56	12 56					13 56			14 56
Romsey	d									10 07				12 07	13 07					14 07			15 07
Salisbury	a									10 24				12 25	13 25					14 25			15 25
	d									10 26				12 27	13 25			13 55		14 27			15 27
Warminster	d			08 47						10 49				12 44	13 44			14 15		14 45			15 44
Dilton Marsh	d			08x52						10x54										14x50			15x50
Weymouth	d												11 05								14 14		
Upwey	d												11 10								14 19		
Dorchester West	d												11 18								14 27		
Maiden Newton	d												11 32								14 39		
Chetnole	d												11x39								14x47		
Yetminster	d												11x42								14x50		
Thornford	d												11x45								14x52		
Yeovil Pen Mill	d												11 54								15 04		
Castle Cary	a												12 07								15 17		
	d					09 20						12 01	12 08			12 51					15 19	15 39	
Bruton	d												12 14								15 24		
Frome	d				09 25		←				11 40		12 27								15 37		
Westbury	a			08 55	09 34	09 38	09 34			10 58	11 49	12 20	12 36	12 54	13 56			14 24		14 56	15 46	15 56	15 56
	d	08 28	08 48	08 56	09 43	09 40	09 43	10 30	10 43	10 58	11 50	12 21	12 37	12 56	13 56		13 59	14 25	14 35	15 00	15 47	15 57	16 04
London Paddington ⊖	a				→	11 14			12 14			14 04				14 34	15 34					17 37	
Trowbridge	d	08 33	08 54	09 02			09 49	10 35		11 05	11 56		12 43	13 03	14 02			14 31	14 40	15 06	15 53		16 10
Bradford-on-Avon	d		09 00	09 08			09 55			11 11	12 02			13 09	14 08			14 37		15 12	15 59		16 16
Avoncliff	d		09 03	09 11			09 58				12 05				14 11						16 02		
Freshford	d		09 05	09 14			10 00				12 07				14 14						16 05		
Bath Spa	a		09 17	09 23			10 11			11 24	12 19			13 23	14 24			14 50		15 24	16 15		16 28
Melksham	d	08 44						10 46					12 53						14 50				
Chippenham	a	08 53						10 55					13 02						15 00				
Swindon	a	09 12						11 14					13 20						15 19				
Oldfield Park	a		09 21	09 27			10 15			11 27	12 23			13 26	14 27						16 18		
Keynsham	a		09 28	09 34			10 22			11 34	12 30			13 33	14 35			14 58			16 26		
Bristol Temple Meads	a		09 36	09 44			10 31			11 44	12 40			13 41	14 44			15 06		15 40	16 35		16 41
Filton Abbey Wood	a			09 57			10 47			11 54				13 55	14 55					15 55			16 55
Bristol Parkway	d																						
Yate	d																						
Cam & Dursley	d																						
Gloucester	d																						
Cheltenham Spa	d																						
Ashchurch for Tewkesbury	d																						
Worcester Shrub Hill	d																						
Worcester Foregate Street	d																						
Malvern Link	d																						
Great Malvern	a																						
Severn Tunnel Jn.	a			10 10			11 03			12 08				14 07	15 05					16 08			17 10
Newport (South Wales)	a			10 21			11 14			12 21				14 19	15 20					16 19			17 21
Cardiff Central	a			10 42			11 36			12 41				14 41	15 41					16 42			17 43

A To Cardiff Central
B From Exeter St Davids
C From Frome
D From Plymouth
E From Penzance
F From London Waterloo

For connections from Bristol Parkway and Cardiff Central to Swansea refer to Table T128

For connections from Castle Cary, Westbury and Bristol Temple Meads to Exeter and Plymouth refer to Table T135

For connections from Salisbury to Yeovil Junction and Exeter refer to Table T160

For connections from Bournemouth to Southampton Central, Weymouth and Upwey refer to Table T158

For additional bus connections between Yeovil Junction and Yeovil Pen Mill refer to Table T123A

Table T123-F

Sundays

28 October to 2 December

Brighton, Portsmouth and Weymouth - Bristol, Cardiff, Gloucester and Great Malvern

		GW	GW	GW	SW	GW	GW	SW	GW	GW	GW	GW	GW	GW	GW	SW	GW	GW	GW	GW	GW	GW	GW
			■	◇	◇■ A	◇	◇■ B ☕	◇■ C	◇		◇	◇		◇■ B ☕	◇	◇■	◇	◇■ B ☕	◇		◇■ D ☕	◇	
Brighton ■	d								15 47								17 46						
Hove ■	d								15 51								17 50						
Shoreham-by-Sea	d								15 57								17 56						
Worthing ■	d								16 09								18 08						
Barnham	d								16 27								18 27						
Chichester ■	d								16 35								18 35						
Havant ■	d								16 46								18 50						
Portsmouth Harbour ⛴	d		15 08			16 10					17 08				18 08				19 08			20 08	22 08
Portsmouth & Southsea	d		15 12			16 14					17 12				18 12				19 12			20 12	22 12
Fratton ■	d		15 16			16 18					17 16				18 16				19 16			20 16	22 15
Cosham	d		15 23			16 25			16 53		17 23				18 23		18 57		19 23				
Fareham	a		15 31			16 33			16 59		17 31				18 31		19 04		19 31			20 31	22 31
	d		15 34			16 34			16 59		17 34				18 34		19 05		19 33			20 34	22 32
Southampton Central ■ ⛴	d		15 56			16 56			17 22		17 56				18 56		19 28		19 56			20 56	22 57
Romsey	d		16 07			17 07			17 35		18 07				19 08		19 40		20 07			21 07	23 08
Salisbury ■	a		16 25			17 25			17 53		18 25				19 26		19 58		20 25			21 25	23 27
	d		16 27		17 10	17 27			17 54		18 27				19 27	19 55	20 01		20 26			21 26	23 28
Warminster	d		16 44		17 36	17 44			18 14		18 44				19 46	20 15	20 22		20 44			21 46	23 50
Dilton Marsh	d		16x50						18x19								20x27					21x53	23x55
Weymouth	d			16 10								17 56								20 09			
Upwey	d			16 15								18 01								20 14			
Dorchester West	d			16 23								18 09								20 22			
Maiden Newton	d			16 35								18 21								20 34			
Chetnole	d			16x43								18x29								20x42			
Yetminster	d			16x46								18x32								20x45			
Thornford	d			16x48								18x34								20x47			
Yeovil Pen Mill	d			16 58								18 44								20 57			
Castle Cary	a			17 10								18 56								21 09			
	d			17 13			17 45					19 00						20 32		21 10	21 28		
Bruton	d			17 18								19 05								21 16			
Frome	d			17 31				18 04				19 18								21 29			
Westbury ■	a		16 56	17 40	17 44	17 56	18 03	18 12	18 22		18 56	19 27			19 57	20 23	20 31	20 50	20 56	21 39	21 46	21 56	23 59
	d	16 52	17 00	17 41		18 00	18 05		18 25	18 45	19 01	19 34	19 41	19 46	20 00	20 23	20 36	20 52	21 00	21 47	21 47	22 00	
London Paddington ■ ⊖	a						19 38							21 15				22 15			23 33		
Trowbridge	d	16 57	17 06	17 48		18 06			18 31	18 51	19 06	19 40	19 46		20 06	20 29	20 42		21 06	21 55		22 06	
Bradford-on-Avon	d		17 12	17 54		18 12			18 37		19 12	19 48			20 12	20 35	20 48		21 12	22 01		22 12	
Avoncliff	d					18 16						19 51					20 51			22 04			
Freshford	d					18 19						19 53					20 54			22 07			
Bath Spa ■	a		17 24	18 06		18 29			18 48		19 25	20 04			20 25	20 49	21 05		21 25	22 18		22 25	
Melksham	d	17 07								19 00			19 57										
Chippenham	a	17 24								19 10			20 07										
Swindon	a	17 41								19 27			20 24										
Oldfield Park	a		17 28	18 11					18 53			20 07					21 09			22 22			
Keynsham	a		17 35	18 19					19 00			20 15				20 57	21 15			22 29			
Bristol Temple Meads ■	a		17 44	18 27		18 43			19 09		19 39	20 25			20 39	21 05	21 24		21 41	22 37		22 41	
Filton Abbey Wood	a		17 55			18 55					19 55				20 55				21 55			22 56	
Bristol Parkway	d																						
Yate	d																						
Cam & Dursley	d																						
Gloucester	d												21 26										
Cheltenham Spa	d												21a34										
Ashchurch for Tewkesbury	d																						
Worcester Shrub Hill	d																						
Worcester Foregate Street	d																						
Malvern Link	d																						
Great Malvern	a																						
Severn Tunnel Jn	a		18 08			19 08					20 10				21 07				22 11			23 09	
Newport (South Wales) ■	a		18 20			19 20					20 22				21 20				22 24			23 21	
Cardiff Central ■	a		18 42			19 40					20 43				21 40				22 49			23 41	

A To Frome
B From Plymouth
C To London Waterloo
D From Penzance

For connections from Bristol Parkway and Cardiff Central to Swansea refer to Table T128

For connections from Castle Cary, Westbury and Bristol Temple Meads to Exeter and Plymouth refer to Table T135

For connections from Salisbury to Yeovil Junction and Exeter refer to Table T160

For connections from Bournemouth to Southampton Central, Weymouth and Upwey refer to Table T158

For additional bus connections between Yeovil Junction and Yeovil Pen Mill refer to Table T123A

Table T123-R

Mondays to Fridays

21 May to 7 December

Great Malvern, Gloucester, Cardiff and Bristol - Weymouth, Portsmouth and Brighton

Miles	Miles	Miles	Miles	Miles			GW MX	GW	GW	GW	GW	GW	GW	GW	GW	GW	GW	GW	GW	GW	SW	GW	GW	GW
							A			◇■ B ☕		◇				◇ 🍴	◇■ C ☕		■ 🍴	◇	◇■			◇ 🍴
0	0	—	—	—	**Cardiff Central** ■	d										06 30			07 30					08 30
11¾	11¾	—	—	—	Newport (South Wales) ■	d										06 44			07 44					08 44
21¾	21¾	—	—	—	Severn Tunnel Jn	d										06 55			07 56					08 55
—	—	0	0	—	Great Malvern	d																		
—	—	1¼	1¼	—	Malvern Link	d																		
—	—	8	8	—	Worcester Foregate Street	d																		
—	—	8½	8½	—	Worcester Shrub Hill	d														06 49				
—	—	23¼	23¼	—	Ashchurch for Tewkesbury	d														07 05				
—	—	30½	30½	—	Cheltenham Spa	d												06 24		07 16				
—	—	37	37	—	Gloucester	d								05 17				06 42		07 41				
—	—	50	50	—	Cam & Dursley	d												06 57		07 56				
—	—	60¾	60¾	—	Yate	d												07 12		08 10				
—	—	67	67	—	Bristol Parkway	d												07 24		08 20			08 45	
33¾	33¾	68½	68½	—	Filton Abbey Wood	d										07 12		07 28	08 11	08 23			08 49	09 09
38¼	38¼	73	73	—	**Bristol Temple Meads** ■	d				05 15		05 44			06 48	07 24		07 47	08 23	08 41	08 51		09 07	09 22
42¾	42¾	77½	77½	—	Keynsham	d						05 51			06 55			07 55		08 48	08 58		09 14	
48¾	48¾	83½	83½	—	Oldfield Park	d						05 59			07 02			08 03		08 55			09 21	
—	—	—	—	0	Swindon	d								06 10								08 53		
—	—	—	—	16¾	Chippenham	d								06 27								09 08		
—	—	—	—	23	Melksham	d								06 36								09 18		
49¾	49¾	84½	84½	—	**Bath Spa** ■	d						06 03			07 06	07 37		08 07	08 37	08 59	09 07		09 25	09 36
56¾	56¾	91¾	91¾	—	Freshford	d						06 12			07 15			08 16		09 08				
57¾	57¾	92½	92½	—	Avoncliff	d						06 15			07 18			08 19		09 11				
59	59	94	94	—	Bradford-on-Avon	d				05 39		06 19			07 22	07 50		08 23	08 48	09 15	09 22		09 37	09 48
62¼	62¼	97¼	97¼	28½	Trowbridge	d				05 46		06 26		06 46	07 28	07 57		08 29	08 54	09 21	09 29	09 34	09 44	09 54
—	—	—	—	—	London Paddington ■ ⊖	d											07 03							
66¼	66¼	101¼	101¼	32½	**Westbury** ■	a				05 54		06 33		06 53	07 35	08 04	08 26	08 36	09 01	09 28	09 35	09 41	09 51	10 01
—	—	—	—	—		d	00 09	05 24	05 49		06 25	06 40	06 54	07 01		08 05			09 02	09 32	09 39			10 02
—	72	—	107	—	Frome	d	00a18				06a34		07 04							09 42				
—	82½	—	117½	—	Bruton	d							07 16							09 54				
—	86	—	121	—	Castle Cary	a							07 21							09 59				
—	—	—	—	—		d							07 21							10 00				
—	97¾	—	132¾	—	Yeovil Pen Mill	d							07 35							10 14				
—	101	—	135¾	—	Thornford	d							07x40							10x18				
—	102	—	137	—	Yetminster	d							07x43							10x21				
—	104	—	139	—	Chetnole	d							07x47							10x25				
—	110½	—	145½	—	Maiden Newton	d							07 59							10 37				
—	118¼	—	153¼	—	Dorchester West	d							08 09							10 48				
—	122¾	—	157¾	—	Upwey	a							08 17							10 55				
—	125¼	—	160¼	—	**Weymouth**	a							08 23							11 03				
67¾	—	102½	—	—	Dilton Marsh	d								07x04										
71	—	105¾	—	—	Warminster	d		05 32	05 57			06 48		07 12		08 13					09 46			10 10
90¾	—	125½	—	—	**Salisbury** ■	a		05 53	06 18			07 10		07 36		08 32			09 31		10 09			10 31
—	—	—	—	—		d			06 19			07 11		07 36		08 33			09 33					10 32
107¼	—	142¼	—	—	Romsey	d			06 38			07 30		07 56		08 54			09 50					10 50
115½	—	150¼	—	—	**Southampton Central** ■	a			06 49			07 40		08 09		09 04			10 02					11 04
130	—	165	—	—	Fareham	a			07 15			08 05				09 27			10 25					11 27
—	—	—	—	—		d			07 16			08 06				09 28			10 25					11 27
135¾	—	170¾	—	—	Cosham	a			07 25			08 13				09 35			10 32					11 35
139½	—	—	—	—	Fratton ■	a			07 34			08 20				09 43			10 39					11 42
140½	—	—	—	—	Portsmouth & Southsea	a			07 38			08 24				09 47			10 44					11 46
141¼	—	—	—	—	**Portsmouth Harbour**	a			07 42			08 28				09 51			10 50					11 52
—	—	174¾	—	—	Havant ■	a																		
—	—	183¾	—	—	**Chichester** ■	a																		
—	—	190	—	—	Barnham	a																		
—	—	201¾	—	—	Worthing ■	a																		
—	—	206½	—	—	Shoreham-by-Sea	a																		
—	—	211	—	—	Hove ■	a																		
—	—	212½	—	—	Brighton ■	a																		

A From Bristol Temple Meads
B To London Paddington
C To Paignton. The Devon Express

For connections from Swansea to Cardiff Central and Bristol Parkway refer to Table T128

For connections from Plymouth and Exeter to Bristol Temple Meads, Westbury and Castle Cary, refer to Table T135

For connections from Exeter and Yeovil Junction to Salisbury refer to Table T160

For connections from Upwey, Weymouth and Southampton Central to Bournemouth refer to Table T158

For additional bus connections between Yeovil Junction and Yeovil Pen Mill refer to Table T123A

T123 UPDATE: Due to major engineering work in connection with electrification work taking place between Reading and Newbury and subsequent diversion of West of England trains, LOCAL TRAINS between Swindon and Westbury via Melksham will be subject to significant alteration on 4-7 June; 9-12 July; 16 July to 05 August; 28-30 August; 08-11 October and 19-22 November.

Table T123-R

Mondays to Fridays

21 May to 7 December

Great Malvern, Gloucester, Cardiff and Bristol - Weymouth, Portsmouth and Brighton

		GW	GW	GW	GW	GW	GW	GW	GW	GW	GW	GW	GW	GW	SW	GW	GW	GW	GW	SW	GW	GW
			◇■ A 💺	◇	◇ 🛒			◇	◇■ B 💺	◇ 🛒	◇	◇ 🛒	■ C 🛒		◇■ 🛒	◇■ D ✕	◇ 🛒			◇■ E 🛒	◇ 🛒	F
Cardiff Central [7]	d				09 30					10 30		11 30					12 30				13 30	
Newport (South Wales) [3]	d				09 44					10 45		11 44					12 44				13 44	
Severn Tunnel Jn.	d				09 55																	
Great Malvern	d							08 50					10 48									
Malvern Link	d							08 53					10 51									
Worcester Foregate Street	d							09 03					11 03									
Worcester Shrub Hill	d							09 06					11 06									
Ashchurch for Tewkesbury	d							09 24					11 24									
Cheltenham Spa	d							09 33					11 33									
Gloucester	d			08 41				09 44			10 41		11 47						12 42			
Cam & Dursley	d			08 56				09 59			10 56		12 00						12 56			
Yate	d			09 10				10 13			11 09		12 14						13 10			
Bristol Parkway	d			09 19				10 22			11 19		12 23						13 19			
Filton Abbey Wood	d			09 23	10 09			10 25		11 10	11 22	12 09	12 26				13 09		13 25		14 09	
Bristol Temple Meads [10]	d			09 46	10 22			10 47		11 22	11 49	12 22	12 39		12 49		13 22		13 49		14 22	
Keynsham	d			09 53				10 54			11 56				12 56				13 56			
Oldfield Park	d			10 01				11 02			12 03				13 03				14 03			
Swindon	d						10 47							12 49				13 29				
Chippenham	d						11 02							13 04				13 44				
Melksham	d						11 12							13 14				13 55				
Bath Spa [7]	d			10 05	10 35			11 06		11 35	12 07	12 35	12 56		13 07		13 35		14 07		14 35	
Freshford	d			10 14				11 15			12 16		13 05						14 16			
Avoncliff	d			10 16				11 17			12 19		13 08						14 19			
Bradford-on-Avon	d			10 20	10 47			11 21		11 47	12 23	12 47	13 12		13 19		13 47		14 23		14 47	
Trowbridge	d			10 27	10 53		11 22	11 28		11 53	12 29	12 53	13 18	13 23	13 28		13 53	14 04	14 29		14 53	
London Paddington [15] ⊖	d		09 03						10 33							12 33						
Westbury [3]	a			10 34	11 00		11 28	11 35	11 59	12 00	12 36	13 00	13 25	13 31	13 34	13 53	14 00	14 10	14 36		15 00	
	d	10 10		10 35	11 01	11 11			12 00	12 01	12 39	13 01	13 30	13 31	13 39	13 55	14 01		14 40	14 57	15 01	15 12
Frome	d			10 44							12 48			13a40					14a49	15 07		
Bruton	d			10 56							13 00									15 18		
Castle Cary	a		10 26	11 01					12 17		13 05					14 12				15 23		
	d			11 01							13 05									15 24		
Yeovil Pen Mill	d			11 15							13 19									15a35		
Thornford	d			11x20							13x24											
Yetminster	d			11x23							13x27											
Chetnole	d			11x27							13x31											
Maiden Newton	d			11 39							13 45											
Dorchester West	d			11 49							13 56											
Upwey	a			12 02							14 03											
Weymouth	a			12 09							14 10											
Dilton Marsh	d	10x12				11x13							13x32									15x14
Warminster	d	10a19			11 09	11 21				12 09		13 09	13 39		13 46		14 09				15 09	15a21
Salisbury [3]	a				11 32	11 42				12 32		13 31	14 01		14 12		14 32				15 32	
	d				11 32	11 43				12 32		13 31	14 02				14 32				15 32	
Romsey	d				11 50	12 04				12 50		13 50	14 21				14 50				15 50	
Southampton Central [8]	a				12 02	12 17				13 04		14 04	14 32				15 04				16 04	
Fareham	a				12 28					13 27		14 27	14 55				15 26				16 27	
	d				12 28					13 27		14 27	14 56				15 26				16 27	
Cosham	a				12 35					13 35		14 35	15 04				15 35				16 35	
Fratton [3]	a				12 42					13 42		14 42					15 42				16 42	
Portsmouth & Southsea	a				12 46					13 46		14 46					15 46				16 46	
Portsmouth Harbour	a				12 52					13 52		14 52					15 52				16 52	
Havant [3]	a												15 10									
Chichester [4]	a												15 23									
Barnham	a												15 35									
Worthing [4]	a												15 53									
Shoreham-by-Sea	a												16 00									
Hove [2]	a												16 08									
Brighton [10]	a												16 14									

A To Plymouth
B To Paignton. The Torbay Express
C 🛒 from Bristol Temple Meads
D To Taunton. Restaurant available for customers joining to Reading
E From London Waterloo
F From Frome

For connections from Swansea to Cardiff Central and Bristol Parkway refer to Table T128

For connections from Plymouth and Exeter to Bristol Temple Meads, Westbury and Castle Cary, refer to Table T135

For connections from Exeter and Yeovil Junction to Salisbury refer to Table T160

For connections from Upwey, Weymouth and Southampton Central to Bournemouth refer to Table T158

For additional bus connections between Yeovil Junction and Yeovil Pen Mill refer to Table T123A

Table T123-R

Mondays to Fridays

21 May to 7 December

Great Malvern, Gloucester, Cardiff and Bristol - Weymouth, Portsmouth and Brighton

		GW	GW	GW	GW	GW	SW	GW	GW	GW	SW	GW	GW	GW	GW	GW	GW	GW	GW	GW	GW	GW	GW
		◇		◇ 🛒	◇■ A 💺		◇■	◇ 🛒		◇	◇■ B		◇■ C 💺	■ 🛒		◇	◇■ 💺		◇■ D 💺	■ 🛒	◇		◇■ E 💺
Cardiff Central [7]	d			14 30				15 30						16 30						17 30			
Newport (South Wales) [3]	d			14 44				15 44						16 45						17 44			
Severn Tunnel Jn.	d													16 56						17 55			
Great Malvern	d	12 51								14 50												16 48	
Malvern Link	d	12 54								14 53												16 51	
Worcester Foregate Street	d	13 03								15 03												17 02	
Worcester Shrub Hill	d	13 06								15 06												17 06	
Ashchurch for Tewkesbury	d	13 24								15 24												17 24	
Cheltenham Spa	d	13 33								15 33											17 41	17 33	
Gloucester	d	13 46				14 41				15 46						16 40					17 54	17 46	
Cam & Dursley	d	14 00				14 56				16 00						16 56						18 00	
Yate	d	14 14				15 10				16 14						17 10						18 14	
Bristol Parkway	d	14 23				15 20				16 24		16 46				17 20		17 44				18 23	
Filton Abbey Wood	d	14 27		15 09		15 23		16 09		16 27		16 50		17 11		17 23		17 49		18 10		18 27	
Bristol Temple Meads [10]	d	14 48		15 22		15 44	15 51	16 22		16 48		17 06		17 23		17 49		18 04		18 22		18 51	
Keynsham	d	14 55				15 51	15 58			16 55		17 13				17 56		18 11				18 59	
Oldfield Park	d	15 02				15 58				17 02		17 20				18 03		18 19				19 06	
Swindon	d		15 19												17 36						18 48		
Chippenham	d		15 34												17 51						19 05		
Melksham	d		15 45												18 02						19 15		
Bath Spa [7]	d	15 06		15 35		16 02	16 08	16 35		17 06		17 24		17 37		18 07		18 23		18 36		19 10	
Freshford	d	15 15				16 11				17 17		17 34				18 16		18 34				19 19	
Avoncliff	d	15 18				16 14				17 19						18 19		18 36				19 22	
Bradford-on-Avon	d	15 22		15 48		16 18	16 24	16 47		17 24		17 38		17 50		18 23		18 40		18 48		19 26	
Trowbridge	d	15 28	15 54	15 58		16 24	16 30	16 53		17 31		17 45		17 57	18 11	18 29		18 47		18 54	19 24	19 32	
London Paddington [15] ⊖	d				15 03								16 33				17 07		17 33				18 07
Westbury [3]	a	15 35	16 00	16 04	16 21	16 31	16 37	17 00		17 36		17 52	18 03	18 04	18 17	18 36	18 52	18 54	19 00	19 01	19 31	19 39	19 55
	d	15 38		16 06	16 23		16 39	17 01	17 11	17 39	17 45	17 53	18 05	18 07		18 40	18 53		19 02	19 05	19 40		19 58
Frome	d	15 47								17 49						18 49	19a02						20a07
Bruton	d	15 58								18 01						19 01							
Castle Cary	a	16 04			16 40					18 06			18 22			19 06			19 19				
	d	16 09								18 06						19 06							
Yeovil Pen Mill	d	16 24								18 21						19 19							
Thornford	d	16x28								18x25						19x25							
Yetminster	d	16x31								18x28						19x28							
Chetnole	d	16x35								18x32						19x32							
Maiden Newton	d	16 47								18 44						19 44							
Dorchester West	d	16 58								19 02						19 54							
Upwey	a	17 05								19 10						20 02							
Weymouth	a	17 10								19 16						20 10							
Dilton Marsh	d								17x13			17x56									19x42		
Warminster	d			16 13			16 47	17 09	17a20		17 52	18a02		18 15						19 13	19 50		
Salisbury [3]	a			16 34			17 09	17 32			18 17			18 36						19 33	20 10		
	d			16 34				17 32						18 37						19 34	20 11		
Romsey	d			16 52				17 50						18 55						19 52	20 30		
Southampton Central [8]	a			17 04				18 04						19 05						20 04	20 44		
Fareham	a			17 26				18 27						19 27						20 28			
	d			17 27				18 27						19 28						20 29			
Cosham	a			17 35				18 35						19 36									
Fratton [3]	a			17 42				18 45						19 43						20 44			
Portsmouth & Southsea	a			17 46				18 52						19 47						20 49			
Portsmouth Harbour	a			17 52				18 58						19 51						20 54			
Havant [3]	a																						
Chichester [4]	a																						
Barnham	a																						
Worthing [4]	a																						
Shoreham-by-Sea	a																						
Hove [2]	a																						
Brighton [10]	a																						

A To Penzance. The Cornishman
B From Yeovil Junction
C To Exeter St Davids
D To Paignton
E 💺 to Westbury

For connections from Swansea to Cardiff Central and Bristol Parkway refer to Table T128

For connections from Plymouth and Exeter to Bristol Temple Meads, Westbury and Castle Cary, refer to Table T135

For connections from Exeter and Yeovil Junction to Salisbury refer to Table T160

For connections from Upwey, Weymouth and Southampton Central to Bournemouth refer to Table T158

For additional bus connections between Yeovil Junction and Yeovil Pen Mill refer to Table T123A

Table T123-R

Mondays to Fridays
21 May to 7 December

Great Malvern, Gloucester, Cardiff and Bristol - Weymouth, Portsmouth and Brighton

		GW ◇■ A ⊡	GW ◇ ⌶	SW ◇■	GW	GW	GW ◇	GW ◇■ B ⊡	GW	GW ◇	SW ■	GW ◇■ B ⊡	GW	SW ■	GW
Cardiff Central ■	d		18 30				19 30			20 30			21 00		
Newport (South Wales) ■	d		18 44				19 44			20 44			21 15		
Severn Tunnel Jn.	d		18 55										21 26		
Great Malvern	d														
Malvern Link	d														
Worcester Foregate Street	d														
Worcester Shrub Hill	d														
Ashchurch for Tewkesbury	d														
Cheltenham Spa	d														
Gloucester	d														
Cam & Dursley	d														
Yate	d														
Bristol Parkway	d														
Filton Abbey Wood	d		19 10				20 09			21 08			21 43		
Bristol Temple Meads ■	d		19 23		19 49		20 22		20 48	21 23			22 04	22 23	23 20
Keynsham	d				19 56				20 56				22 11		23 27
Oldfield Park	d				20 03				21 03				22 18		23 34
Swindon	d					20 08									
Chippenham	d					20 23									
Melksham	d					20 33									
Bath Spa ■	d		19 37		20 07		20 36		21 07	21 36			22 21	22 36	23 38
Freshford	d				20 16				21 16				22 30		23 48
Avoncliff	d				20 19				21 19				22 33		23 50
Bradford-on-Avon	d		19 50		20 23		20 47		21 23	21 48			22 37	22 47	23 54
Trowbridge	d		19 57		20 29	20 42	20 53		21 29	21 55			22 43	22 53	23 59
London Paddington ■ ⊖	d	18 33						20 03				21 03			
Westbury ■	a	20 03	20 06		20 36	20 49	21 00	21 24	21 36	22 03		22 23	22 50	23 00	00 08
	d	20 04	20 09	20 15	20 37		21 01	21 27	21 40	22 03	22 18	22 27		23 05	00 09
Frome	d				20a46				21 50						00a18
Bruton	d								22 02						
Castle Cary	a	20 21						21 44	22 07			22 44			
	d								22 08						
Yeovil Pen Mill	d								22 23						
Thornford	d								22x28						
Yetminster	d								22x31						
Chetnole	d								22x35						
Maiden Newton	d								22 47						
Dorchester West	d								22 58						
Upwey	a								23 05						
Weymouth	a								23 13						
Dilton Marsh	d									22x06					
Warminster	d		20 17	20 23			21 09			22 11	22 26			23 12	
Salisbury ■	a		20 38	20 44			21 32			22 32	22 48			23 38	
	d		20 39				21 32			22 32					
Romsey	d		20 57				21 50			22 53					
Southampton Central ■	a		21 07				22 02			23 04					
Fareham	a		21 31				22 41			23 27					
	d		21 32				22 41			23 27					
Cosham	a														
Fratton ■	a		21 48				22 54			23 44					
Portsmouth & Southsea	a		21 51				22 57			23 48					
Portsmouth Harbour	a		21 55				23 02			23 52					
Havant ■	a														
Chichester ■	a														
Barnham	a														
Worthing ■	a														
Shoreham-by-Sea	a														
Hove ■	a														
Brighton ■	a														

A To Exeter St Davids
B To Plymouth

For connections from Swansea to Cardiff Central and Bristol Parkway refer to Table T128

For connections from Plymouth and Exeter to Bristol Temple Meads, Westbury and Castle Cary, refer to Table T135

For connections from Exeter and Yeovil Junction to Salisbury refer to Table T160

For connections from Upwey, Weymouth and Southampton Central to Bournemouth refer to Table T158

For additional bus connections between Yeovil Junction and Yeovil Pen Mill refer to Table T123A

Table T123-R

Saturdays
26 May to 8 September

Great Malvern, Gloucester, Cardiff and Bristol - Weymouth, Portsmouth and Brighton

		GW A	GW	GW	GW ◇	GW	GW B	GW C	GW ◇ D	GW	GW ◇
Cardiff Central ■	d								06 30		07 30
Newport (South Wales) ■	d								06 44		07 44
Severn Tunnel Jn.	d								06 55		07 55
Great Malvern	d										
Malvern Link	d										
Worcester Foregate Street	d										
Worcester Shrub Hill	d										
Ashchurch for Tewkesbury	d										
Cheltenham Spa	d										
Gloucester	d										
Cam & Dursley	d										
Yate	d										
Bristol Parkway	d										
Filton Abbey Wood	d								07 10		08 10
Bristol Temple Meads ■	d				05 48			06 49	07 22	07 49	08 22
Keynsham	d				05 55			06 56		07 56	
Oldfield Park	d				06 02			07 03		08 03	
Swindon	d										
Chippenham	d										
Melksham	d										
Bath Spa ■	d				06 06			07 07	07 36	08 07	08 36
Freshford	d				06 15			07 16		08 16	
Avoncliff	d				06 18			07 19		08 19	
Bradford-on-Avon	d				06 22			07 23	07 48	08 23	08 48
Trowbridge	d				06 28			07 29	07 54	08 29	08 54
London Paddington ■ ⊖	d										
Westbury ■	a				06 35			07 36	08 01	08 36	09 01
	d	00 09	05 24	06 02	06 43	06 54	07 03		08 02		09 02
Frome	d	00a18				07 03					
Bruton	d					07 15					
Castle Cary	a					07 20					
	d					07 21					
Yeovil Pen Mill	d					07 35					
Thornford	d					07x40					
Yetminster	d					07x43					
Chetnole	d					07x47					
Maiden Newton	d					07 59					
Dorchester West	d					08 13					
Upwey	a					08 21					
Weymouth	a					08 26					
Dilton Marsh	d						07x05				09x05
Warminster	d		05 32	06 10	06 51		07 12		08 10		09 12
Salisbury ■	a		05 55	06 31	07 12		07 34		08 32		09 32
	d			06 32	07 24		07 36		08 33		09 33
Romsey	d			06 51	07 43		07 54		08 52		09 52
Southampton Central ■	a			07 02	07 55		08 07		09 02		10 03
Fareham	a			07 27	08 23				09 27		10 27
	d			07 28	08 24				09 28		10 28
Cosham	a			07 35	08 32				09 35		10 35
Fratton ■	a			07 42	08 39				09 43		10 42
Portsmouth & Southsea	a			07 46	08 45				09 46		10 46
Portsmouth Harbour	a			07 52	08 51				09 52		10 52
Havant ■	a										
Chichester ■	a										
Barnham	a										
Worthing ■	a										
Shoreham-by-Sea	a										
Hove ■	a										
Brighton ■	a										

		GW	GW ◇	SW ◇■ E	GW	GW ■ F ⊡	GW ◇	GW ◇	GW ◇ G ⌶	GW	GW	GW	GW ■ F ⊡
Cardiff Central ■	d						08 30		09 30				
Newport (South Wales) ■	d						08 44		09 44				
Severn Tunnel Jn.	d						08 55		09 55				
Great Malvern	d												
Malvern Link	d												
Worcester Foregate Street	d												
Worcester Shrub Hill	d		06 49									09 10	
Ashchurch for Tewkesbury	d		07 05									09 27	
Cheltenham Spa	d		07 16									09 36	
Gloucester	d		07 41					08 41				09 48	
Cam & Dursley	d		07 56					08 56				10 01	
Yate	d		08 10					09 10				10 14	
Bristol Parkway	d		08 20					09 19				10 23	
Filton Abbey Wood	d		08 23				09 10	09 22	10 10			10 27	
Bristol Temple Meads ■	d		08 40	08 51	09 08		09 22	09 49	10 22			10 49	
Keynsham	d		08 47	08 58	09 15			09 56				10 56	
Oldfield Park	d		08 54		09 22			10 03				11 03	
Swindon	d	08 36									10 36		
Chippenham	d	08 53									10 53		
Melksham	d	09 02									11 02		
Bath Spa ■	d		08 58	09 07	09 26		09 35	10 07	10 36			11 07	
Freshford	d		09 07					10 16				11 16	
Avoncliff	d		09 10					10 19				11 19	
Bradford-on-Avon	d		09 14	09 21	09 38		09 47	10 23	10 48			11 23	
Trowbridge	d	09 12	09 21	09 27	09 45		09 54	10 29	10 54		11 12	11 29	
London Paddington ■ ⊖	d					08 35							10 35
Westbury ■	a	09 20	09 27	09 34	09 52	09 57	10 00	10 36	11 01		11 20	11 36	11 52
	d		09 33	09 39	09 54	09 59	10 02	10 37	11 02	11 11			11 54
Frome	d		09 42		10 05			10 47					
Bruton	d		09 54					10 58					
Castle Cary	a		10 00		10 21	10 16		11 03					12 11
	d		10 01		10 23			11 04					
Yeovil Pen Mill	d		10 15		10 40			11 18					
Thornford	d		10x19					11x22					
Yetminster	d		10x22					11x25					
Chetnole	d		10x26					11x29					
Maiden Newton	d		10 38		11 00			11 41					
Dorchester West	d		10 54		11 13			11 54					
Upwey	a		11 01					12 01					
Weymouth	a		11 09		11 25			12 09					
Dilton Marsh	d									11x13			
Warminster	d			09 46			10 10		11 10	11 21			
Salisbury ■	a			10 09			10 32		11 32	11 42			
	d						10 33		11 33	11 43			
Romsey	d						10 51		11 51	12 04			
Southampton Central ■	a						11 03		12 03	12 21			
Fareham	a						11 27		12 27				
	d						11 28		12 28				
Cosham	a						11 35		12 35				
Fratton ■	a						11 42		12 42				
Portsmouth & Southsea	a						11 46		12 46				
Portsmouth Harbour	a						11 52		12 52				
Havant ■	a												
Chichester ■	a												
Barnham	a												
Worthing ■	a												
Shoreham-by-Sea	a												
Hove ■	a												
Brighton ■	a												

A From Bristol Temple Meads
B From Frome
C From Taunton
D From Cardiff Canton Sidings
E To London Waterloo
F To Paignton
G ⌶ from Bristol Temple Meads

For connections from Swansea to Cardiff Central and Bristol Parkway refer to Table T128

For connections from Plymouth and Exeter to Bristol Temple Meads, Westbury and Castle Cary, refer to Table T135

For connections from Exeter and Yeovil Junction to Salisbury refer to Table T160

For connections from Upwey, Weymouth and Southampton Central to Bournemouth refer to Table T158

For additional bus connections between Yeovil Junction and Yeovil Pen Mill refer to Table T123A

T123 UPDATE: Due to major engineering work in connection with electrification work taking place between Reading and Newbury and subsequent diversion of West of England trains, LOCAL TRAINS between Swindon and Westbury via Melksham will be subject to significant alteration on 4-7 June; 9-12 July; 16 July to 05 August; 28-30 August; 08-11 October and 19-22 November.

Table T123-R

Saturdays

26 May to 8 September

Great Malvern, Gloucester, Cardiff and Bristol - Weymouth, Portsmouth and Brighton

		GW	GW	GW	GW	GW	GW	SW	GW	GW	GW	GW	GW	GW	GW	GW	GW	GW	GW	SW	GW	GW	GW
		◇ A	◇	B	◇ A			◇1 C	◇1 D	◇ A		◇	E		◇	◇		◇1 F		◇1 C	◇	◇	
Cardiff Central 7	d	10 30			11 30					12 30		13 30				14 30					15 30		16 30
Newport (South Wales) 2	d	10 46			11 44					12 44		13 44				14 44					15 44		16 44
Severn Tunnel Jn.	d																						16 55
Great Malvern	d						10 57															14 50	
Malvern Link	d						11 00															14 53	
Worcester Foregate Street	d						11 10								12 41							15 03	
Worcester Shrub Hill	d						11 13								12 54							15 07	
Ashchurch for Tewkesbury	d						11 29								13 11							15 24	
Cheltenham Spa	d						11 38								13 20							15 34	
Gloucester	d		10 41				11 50				12 42				13 42				14 41			15 47	
Cam & Dursley	d		10 56				12 03				12 56				13 56				14 56			16 02	
Yate	d		11 10				12 16				13 10				14 11				15 10			16 15	
Bristol Parkway	d		11 20				12 25				13 19				14 20				15 19			16 24	
Filton Abbey Wood	d	11 10	11 23		12 10		12 29			13 10	13 23	14 10			14 24	15 10			15 23		16 10	16 28	17 10
Bristol Temple Meads 10	d	11 22	11 49		12 22		12 43	12 51		13 22	13 44	14 22			14 44	15 22			15 44	15 51	16 22	16 49	17 22
Keynsham	d		11 56				12 50	12 58			13 51				14 51				15 51	15 58		16 56	
Oldfield Park	d		12 03				12 57				13 58				14 58				15 58			17 03	
Swindon	d					12 36								14 36			15 22						
Chippenham	d					12 53								14 53			15 39						
Melksham	d					13 02								15 02			15 48						
Bath Spa 7	d	11 36	12 07		12 36		13 01	13 07		13 36	14 02	14 36			15 02	15 36			16 02	16 07	16 36	17 07	17 36
Freshford	d		12 16								14 11				15 11				16 11			17 16	
Avoncliff	d		12 19								14 14				15 14				16 14			17 19	
Bradford-on-Avon	d	11 48	12 23		12 48		13 13	13 20		13 48	14 18	14 48			15 18	15 48			16 18	16 24	16 48	17 23	17 48
Trowbridge	d	11 54	12 29		12 54	13 12	13 19	13 27		13 54	14 24	14 54		15 12	15 24	15 54	15 59		16 24	16 30	16 54	17 29	17 54
London Paddington 15 ⊖	d			11 35					12 33									15 03					
Westbury 2	a	12 01	12 36	12 48	13 01	13 20	13 26	13 33	13 53	14 01	14 31	15 01		15 20	15 31	16 01	16 07	16 19	16 33	16 37	17 01	17 36	18 01
	d	12 02	12 39		13 02		13 29	13 39	13 55	14 02	14 35	15 02	15 12		15 34	16 02	16 10	16 20		16 39	17 02	17 40	18 02
Frome	d		12 50								14a53				15 43							17 49	
Bruton	d		13 02												15 55							18 01	
Castle Cary	a		13 07						14 12						16 00			16 37				18 06	
	d		13 08												16 01							18 07	
Yeovil Pen Mill	d		13 22												16 15							18 21	
Thornford	d		13x26												16x19							18x25	
Yetminster	d		13x29												16x22							18x28	
Chetnole	d		13x33												16x26							18x32	
Maiden Newton	d		13 45												16 38							18 54	
Dorchester West	d		13 56												16 55							19 13	
Upwey	a		14 03												17 02							19 21	
Weymouth	a		14 10												17 08							19 27	
Dilton Marsh	d						13x31						15x14				16x12						
Warminster	d	12 10			13 10		13 38	13 46		14 10		15 10	15a23			16 10	16a21			16 47	17 10		18 10
Salisbury 8	a	12 32			13 32		14 01	14 10		14 32		15 32				16 32				17 09	17 32		18 32
	d	12 33			13 33		14 02			14 33		15 33				16 33					17 33		18 33
Romsey	d	12 51			13 51		14 21			14 51		15 51				16 51					17 51		18 51
Southampton Central 8	a	13 03			14 03		14 32			15 03		16 03				17 03					18 03		19 03
Fareham	a	13 27			14 27		14 55			15 27		16 27				17 27					18 27		19 27
	d	13 28			14 28		14 56			15 28		16 28				17 28					18 28		19 28
Cosham	a	13 35			14 35		15 03			15 35		16 35				17 35					18 35		19 35
Fratton 8	a	13 42			14 42					15 42		16 42				17 42					18 42		19 42
Portsmouth & Southsea	a	13 46			14 46					15 46		16 46				17 46					18 46		19 46
Portsmouth Harbour	a	13 52			14 52					15 52		16 52				17 52					18 52		19 52
Havant 8	a						15 10																
Chichester 4	a						15 21																
Barnham	a						15 29																
Worthing 4	a						15 51																
Shoreham-by-Sea	a						16 00																
Hove 2	a						16 12																
Brighton 10	a						16 18																

A from Bristol Temple Meads
B To Newquay. The Atlantic Coast Express
C To London Waterloo
D To Paignton
E From Frome
F To Plymouth

For connections from Swansea to Cardiff Central and Bristol Parkway refer to Table T128

For connections from Plymouth and Exeter to Bristol Temple Meads, Westbury and Castle Cary, refer to Table T135

For connections from Exeter and Yeovil Junction to Salisbury refer to Table T160

For connections from Upwey, Weymouth and Southampton Central to Bournemouth refer to Table T158

For additional bus connections between Yeovil Junction and Yeovil Pen Mill refer to Table T123A

Table T123-R

Saturdays

26 May to 8 September

Great Malvern, Gloucester, Cardiff and Bristol - Weymouth, Portsmouth and Brighton

		GW	GW	GW	GW	GW	GW	GW	GW	GW	GW	GW	GW	GW	GW	GW	GW	SW	GW
		◇1 A		◇	◇			◇		◇1 A		◇	◇1 A			◇		1	
Cardiff Central 7	d				17 30			18 30				19 30				20 30	21 00		
Newport (South Wales) 2	d				17 44			18 44				19 44				20 44	21 15		
Severn Tunnel Jn.	d				17 55												21 26		
Great Malvern	d						16 50												
Malvern Link	d						16 53												
Worcester Foregate Street	d						17 04												
Worcester Shrub Hill	d						17 08												
Ashchurch for Tewkesbury	d						17 24												
Cheltenham Spa	d						17 34								20 02				
Gloucester	d			16 42			17 47				18 41				20 14				
Cam & Dursley	d			16 56			18 02				18 56								
Yate	d			17 11			18 16				19 10								
Bristol Parkway	d			17 20			18 25				19 20								
Filton Abbey Wood	d			17 23	18 10		18 28	19 10			19 24	20 10				21 08	21 43		
Bristol Temple Meads 10	d			17 49	18 22		18 49	19 22			19 49	20 22		20 49		21 22	22 02	22 23	23 10
Keynsham	d			17 56			18 56				19 56			20 56			22 09		23 17
Oldfield Park	d			18 03			19 03				20 03			21 03			22 16		23 23
Swindon	d		17 36						19 36						21 06				
Chippenham	d		17 53						19 53						21 23				
Melksham	d		18 02						20 02						21 32				
Bath Spa 7	d			18 07	18 36		19 07	19 36			20 07	20 36		21 07		21 36	22 20	22 36	23 27
Freshford	d			18 16			19 16				20 16			21 16			22 29		23 36
Avoncliff	d			18 19			19 19				20 19			21 19			22 32		23 39
Bradford-on-Avon	d			18 23	18 48		19 23	19 48			20 23	20 48		21 23		21 48	22 36	22 47	23 43
Trowbridge	d		18 12	18 29	18 54		19 29	19 54	20 12		20 29	20 54		21 29	21 42	21 54	22 42	22 53	23 49
London Paddington 15 ⊖	d	17 03								19 03			20 03						
Westbury 2	a	18 19	18 20	18 36	19 01		19 36	20 01	20 20	20 25	20 36	21 01	21 23	21 36	21 50	22 01	22 49	23 00	23 56
	d	18 21		18 40	19 02	19 20		20 02		20 26	20 37	21 02	21 26	21 40		22 02		23 05	23 57
Frome	d			18 49							20a48			21 52					00a08
Bruton	d			19 01										22 04					
Castle Cary	a	18 38		19 06						20 44			21 43	22 09					
	d			19 06										22 10					
Yeovil Pen Mill	d			19 20										22 24					
Thornford	d			19x25										22x28					
Yetminster	d			19x28										22x31					
Chetnole	d			19x32										22x35					
Maiden Newton	d			19 44										22 47					
Dorchester West	d			19 54										22 58					
Upwey	a			20 02										23 05					
Weymouth	a			20 10										23 14					
Dilton Marsh	d					19x22										22x05			
Warminster	d				19 10	19 30		20 10				21 10				22 13		23 12	
Salisbury 8	a				19 32	19 51		20 32				21 32				22 33		23 35	
	d				19 33	19 52		20 33				21 33				22 34			
Romsey	d				19 51	20 11		20 51				21 51				22 54			
Southampton Central 8	a				20 03	20 22		21 03				22 02				23 04			
Fareham	a				20 27			21 27				22 26				23 27			
	d				20 28			21 28				22 27				23 28			
Cosham	a																		
Fratton 8	a				20 40			21 42				22 41				23 41			
Portsmouth & Southsea	a				20 44			21 46				22 45				23 45			
Portsmouth Harbour	a				20 50			21 52				22 52				23 52			
Havant 8	a																		
Chichester 4	a																		
Barnham	a																		
Worthing 4	a																		
Shoreham-by-Sea	a																		
Hove 2	a																		
Brighton 10	a																		

A To Plymouth

For connections from Swansea to Cardiff Central and Bristol Parkway refer to Table T128

For connections from Plymouth and Exeter to Bristol Temple Meads, Westbury and Castle Cary, refer to Table T135

For connections from Exeter and Yeovil Junction to Salisbury refer to Table T160

For connections from Upwey, Weymouth and Southampton Central to Bournemouth refer to Table T158

For additional bus connections between Yeovil Junction and Yeovil Pen Mill refer to Table T123A

Table T123-R

Saturdays

15 September to 8 December

Great Malvern, Gloucester, Cardiff and Bristol - Weymouth, Portsmouth and Brighton

		GW	GW	GW	GW	GW	GW	GW	GW	GW		GW	GW	GW	GW	GW	SW	GW	GW	GW		GW	GW	GW	GW
		A			◇		B	C	◇ D			◇		◇ E	◇■ F	◇ G	◇■ H	◇	◇	◇ I					◇ I
Cardiff Central ■	d								06 30			07 30						08 30		09 30					10 30
Newport (South Wales) ■	d								06 44			07 44						08 44		09 44					10 46
Severn Tunnel Jn	d								06 55			07 55						08 55		09 55					
Great Malvern	d																								
Malvern Link	d																								
Worcester Foregate Street	d																								
Worcester Shrub Hill	d													06 49										09 10	
Ashchurch for Tewkesbury	d													07 05										09 27	
Cheltenham Spa	d													07 16										09 36	
Gloucester	d													07 41					08 41					09 48	
Cam & Dursley	d													07 56					08 56					10 01	
Yate	d													08 10					09 10					10 14	
Bristol Parkway	d													08 20					09 19					10 23	
Filton Abbey Wood	d								07 10			08 10		08 23				09 10	09 22	10 10				10 27	11 10
Bristol Temple Meads ■	d				05 48			06 49	07 22	07 49		08 22		08 39			08 51	09 22	09 49	10 22				10 49	11 22
Keynsham	d				05 55			06 56		07 56				08 46			08 58		09 56					10 56	
Oldfield Park	d				06 02			07 03		08 03				08 53					10 03					11 03	
Swindon	d												08 36										10 36		
Chippenham	d												08 53										10 53		
Melksham	d												09 02										11 02		
Bath Spa ■	d				06 06			07 07	07 36	08 07		08 36		08 57			09 07	09 35	10 07	10 36				11 07	11 36
Freshford	d				06 15			07 16		08 16				09 06					10 16					11 16	
Avoncliff	d				06 18			07 19		08 19				09 09					10 19					11 19	
Bradford-on-Avon	d				06 22			07 23	07 48	08 23		08 48		09 13			09 21	09 47	10 23	10 48				11 23	11 48
Trowbridge	d				06 28			07 29	07 54	08 29		08 54	09 12	09 19			09 27	09 54	10 29	10 54			11 12	11 29	11 54
London Paddington ■ ⊖	d														08 03	←									
Westbury ■	a				06 35			07 36	08 01	08 36		09 01	09 20	09 26	09 27	09 26	09 34	10 00	10 36	11 01			11 20	11 36	12 01
	d	00 09	05 24	06 02	06 43	06 54	07 03		08 02			09 02		09 33	09 29	09 33	09 39	10 02	10 37	11 02		11 11			12 02
Frome	d	00a18				07 03								→		09 42			10 47						
Bruton	d					07 15										09 54			10 58						
Castle Cary	a					07 20									09 46	10 00			11 03						
	d					07 21										10 01			11 04						
Yeovil Pen Mill	d					07 35										10 15			11 18						
Thornford	d					07x40										10x19			11x22						
Yetminster	d					07x43										10x22			11x25						
Chetnole	d					07x47										10x26			11x29						
Maiden Newton	d					07 59										10 38			11 41						
Dorchester West	d					08 13										10 54			11 54						
Upwey	a					08 21										11 01			12 01						
Weymouth	a					08 26										11 09			12 09						
Dilton Marsh	d						07x05					09x05										11x13			
Warminster	d		05 32	06 10	06 51		07 12		08 10			09 12					09 46	10 10		11 10		11 21			12 10
Salisbury ■	a		05 55	06 31	07 12		07 34		08 32			09 32					10 09	10 32		11 32		11 42			12 32
	d			06 32	07 24		07 36		08 33			09 33						10 33		11 33		11 43			12 33
Romsey	d			06 51	07 43		07 54		08 52			09 52						10 51		11 51		12 04			12 51
Southampton Central ■	a			07 02	07 55		08 07		09 02			10 03						11 03		12 03		12 21			13 03
Fareham	a			07 27	08 23				09 27			10 27						11 27		12 27					13 27
	d			07 28	08 24				09 28			10 28						11 28		12 28					13 28
Cosham	a			07 35	08 32				09 35			10 35						11 35		12 35					13 35
Fratton ■	a			07 42	08 39				09 43			10 42						11 42		12 42					13 42
Portsmouth & Southsea	a			07 46	08 45				09 46			10 46						11 46		12 46					13 46
Portsmouth Harbour	a			07 52	08 51				09 52			10 52						11 52		12 52					13 52
Havant ■	a																								
Chichester ■	a																								
Barnham	a																								
Worthing ■	a																								
Shoreham-by-Sea	a																								
Hove ■	a																								
Brighton ■	a																								

A From Bristol Temple Meads
B From Frome
C From Taunton
D From Cardiff Canton Sidings
E To Weymouth
F To Exeter St Davids
G From Worcester Shrub Hill
H To London Waterloo
I from Bristol Temple Meads

For connections from Swansea to Cardiff Central and Bristol Parkway refer to Table T128

For connections from Plymouth and Exeter to Bristol Temple Meads, Westbury and Castle Cary, refer to Table T135

For connections from Exeter and Yeovil Junction to Salisbury refer to Table T160

For connections from Upwey, Weymouth and Southampton Central to Bournemouth refer to Table T158

For additional bus connections between Yeovil Junction and Yeovil Pen Mill refer to Table T123A

Table T123-R

Saturdays

15 September to 8 December

Great Malvern, Gloucester, Cardiff and Bristol - Weymouth, Portsmouth and Brighton

		GW	GW	GW	GW	GW		SW	GW	GW	GW	GW	GW	GW	GW	GW		GW	GW	GW	SW	GW	GW	GW	GW
		◇■ A	◇	◇ B		■		◇■ C	◇■ D	◇ B		◇	E		◇	◇			◇■ F		◇■ C	◇		◇	■
Cardiff Central ■	d			11 30						12 30		13 30				14 30						15 30			16 30
Newport (South Wales) ■	d			11 44						12 44		13 44				14 44						15 44			16 44
Severn Tunnel Jn.	d																								16 55
Great Malvern	d					10 57																		14 50	
Malvern Link	d					11 00																		14 53	
Worcester Foregate Street	d					11 10									12 41									15 03	
Worcester Shrub Hill	d					11 13									12 54									15 07	
Ashchurch for Tewkesbury	d					11 29									13 11									15 24	
Cheltenham Spa	d					11 38									13 20									15 34	
Gloucester	d		10 41			11 50					12 42				13 42					14 41				15 47	
Cam & Dursley	d		10 56			12 03					12 56				13 56					14 56				16 02	
Yate	d		11 10			12 16					13 10				14 11					15 10				16 15	
Bristol Parkway	d		11 20			12 25					13 19				14 20					15 19				16 24	
Filton Abbey Wood	d		11 23	12 10		12 29				13 10	13 23	14 10			14 24	15 10				15 23		16 10		16 28	17 10
Bristol Temple Meads ■	d		11 49	12 22		12 43		12 51		13 22	13 44	14 22			14 49	15 22				15 44	15 51	16 22		16 49	17 22
Keynsham	d		11 56			12 50		12 58			13 51				14 56					15 51	15 58			16 56	
Oldfield Park	d		12 03			12 57					13 58				15 03					15 58				17 03	
Swindon	d				12 36									14 36				15 22							
Chippenham	d				12 53									14 53				15 39							
Melksham	d				13 02									15 02				15 48							
Bath Spa ■	d		12 07	12 36		13 01		13 07		13 36	14 02	14 36			15 07	15 36				16 02	16 07	16 36		17 07	17 36
Freshford	d		12 16								14 11				15 16					16 11				17 16	
Avoncliff	d		12 19								14 14				15 19					16 14				17 19	
Bradford-on-Avon	d		12 23	12 48		13 13		13 20		13 48	14 18	14 48			15 23	15 48				16 18	16 24	16 48		17 23	17 48
Trowbridge	d		12 29	12 54	13 12	13 19		13 27		13 54	14 24	14 54		15 12	15 29	15 54		15 59		16 24	16 30	16 54		17 29	17 54
London Paddington ■ ⊖	d	11 03							12 33										15 03						
Westbury ■	a	12 19	12 36	13 01	13 20	13 26		13 33	13 53	14 01	14 31	15 01		15 20	15 36	16 01		16 07	16 19	16 33	16 37	17 01		17 36	18 01
	d	12 21	12 39	13 02		13 29		13 39	13 55	14 02	14 35	15 02	15 12		15 41	16 02			16 20		16 39	17 02	17 10	17 38	18 02
Frome	d		12 50								14a53				15 50									17 47	
Bruton	d		13 02												16 02									17 59	
Castle Cary	a	12 38	13 07						14 12						16 08				16 37					18 04	
	d		13 08												16 09									18 05	
Yeovil Pen Mill	d		13 22												16 24									18 21	
Thornford	d		13x26												16x28									18x25	
Yetminster	d		13x29												16x31									18x28	
Chetnole	d		13x33												16x35									18x32	
Maiden Newton	d		13 45												16 47									18 44	
Dorchester West	d		13 56												16 58									18 55	
Upwey	a		14 03												17 05									19 02	
Weymouth	a		14 10												17 10									19 10	
Dilton Marsh	d					13x31							15x14										17x12		
Warminster	d			13 10		13 38		13 46		14 10		15 10	15a23			16 10					16 47	17 10	17a21		18 10
Salisbury ■	a			13 32		14 01		14 10		14 32		15 32				16 32					17 09	17 32			18 32
	d			13 33		14 02				14 33		15 33				16 33						17 33			18 33
Romsey	d			13 51		14 21				14 51		15 51				16 51						17 51			18 51
Southampton Central ■	a			14 03		14 32				15 03		16 03				17 03						18 03			19 03
Fareham	a			14 27		14 55				15 27		16 27				17 27						18 27			19 27
	d			14 28		14 56				15 28		16 28				17 28						18 28			19 28
Cosham	a			14 35		15 03				15 35		16 35				17 35						18 35			19 35
Fratton ■	a			14 42						15 42		16 42				17 42						18 42			19 42
Portsmouth & Southsea	a			14 46						15 46		16 46				17 46						18 46			19 46
Portsmouth Harbour	a			14 52						15 52		16 52				17 52						18 52			19 52
Havant ■	a					15 10																			
Chichester ■	a					15 21																			
Barnham	a					15 29																			
Worthing ■	a					15 51																			
Shoreham-by-Sea	a					16 00																			
Hove ■	a					16 12																			
Brighton ■	a					16 18																			

A To Plymouth
B from Bristol Temple Meads
C To London Waterloo
D To Taunton
E From Frome
F To Penzance

For connections from Swansea to Cardiff Central and Bristol Parkway refer to Table T128

For connections from Plymouth and Exeter to Bristol Temple Meads, Westbury and Castle Cary, refer to Table T135

For connections from Exeter and Yeovil Junction to Salisbury refer to Table T160

For connections from Upwey, Weymouth and Southampton Central to Bournemouth refer to Table T158

For additional bus connections between Yeovil Junction and Yeovil Pen Mill refer to Table T123A

T123 UPDATE: Due to major engineering work in connection with electrification work taking place between Reading and Newbury and subsequent diversion of West of England trains, LOCAL TRAINS between Swindon and Westbury via Melksham will be subject to significant alteration on 4-7 June; 9-12 July; 16 July to 05 August; 28-30 August; 08-11 October and 19-22 November.

Table T123-R

Saturdays

15 September to 8 December

Great Malvern, Gloucester, Cardiff and Bristol - Weymouth, Portsmouth and Brighton

		GW ◇1 A	GW	GW ◇	GW ◇	GW	GW	GW ◇	GW	GW ◇1 B	GW	GW ◇	GW ◇1 B	GW	GW	GW ◇	GW	SW 1	GW
Cardiff Central 7	d				17 30			18 30				19 30				20 30	21 00		
Newport (South Wales) 2	d				17 44			18 44				19 44				20 44	21 15		
Severn Tunnel Jn.	d				17 55												21 26		
Great Malvern	d						16 50												
Malvern Link	d						16 53												
Worcester Foregate Street	d						17 04												
Worcester Shrub Hill	d						17 08												
Ashchurch for Tewkesbury	d						17 24												
Cheltenham Spa	d						17 34								20 02				
Gloucester	d			16 42			17 47				18 41				20 14				
Cam & Dursley	d			16 56			18 02				18 56								
Yate	d			17 11			18 16				19 10								
Bristol Parkway	d			17 20			18 25				19 20								
Filton Abbey Wood	d			17 23	18 10		18 28	19 10			19 24	20 10				21 08	21 43		
Bristol Temple Meads 10	d			17 49	18 22		18 49	19 22			19 49	20 22		20 49		21 22	22 02	22 23	23 10
Keynsham	d			17 56			18 56				19 56			20 56			22 09		23 17
Oldfield Park	d			18 03			19 03				20 03			21 03			22 16		23 23
Swindon	d		17 36						19 36						21 06				
Chippenham	d		17 53						19 53						21 23				
Melksham	d		18 02						20 02						21 32				
Bath Spa 7	d			18 07	18 36		19 07	19 36			20 07	20 36		21 07		21 36	22 20	22 36	23 27
Freshford	d			18 16			19 16				20 16			21 16			22 29		23 36
Avoncliff	d			18 19			19 19				20 19			21 19			22 32		23 39
Bradford-on-Avon	d			18 23	18 48		19 23	19 48			20 23	20 48		21 23		21 48	22 36	22 47	23 43
Trowbridge	d		18 12	18 29	18 54		19 29	19 54	20 12		20 29	20 54		21 29	21 42	21 54	22 42	22 53	23 49
London Paddington 15 ⊖	d	17 03								19 03			20 03						
Westbury 2	a	18 19	18 20	18 36	19 01		19 36	20 01	20 20	20 25	20 36	21 01	21 23	21 36	21 50	22 01	22 49	23 00	23 56
	d	18 21		18 40	19 02	19 20		20 02		20 26	20 37	21 02	21 26	21 40		22 02		23 05	23 57
Frome	d			18 49							20a48			21 52					00a08
Bruton	d			19 01										22 04					
Castle Cary	a	18 38		19 06						20 44			21 43	22 09					
	d			19 06										22 10					
Yeovil Pen Mill	d			19 20										22 24					
Thornford	d			19x25										22x28					
Yetminster	d			19x28										22x31					
Chetnole	d			19x32										22x35					
Maiden Newton	d			19 44										22 47					
Dorchester West	d			19 54										22 58					
Upwey	a			20 02										23 05					
Weymouth	a			20 10										23 14					
Dilton Marsh	d					19x22										22x05			
Warminster	d				19 10	19 30		20 10				21 10				22 13		23 12	
Salisbury 8	a				19 32	19 51		20 32				21 32				22 33		23 35	
	d				19 33	19 52		20 33				21 33				22 34			
Romsey	d				19 51	20 11		20 51				21 51				22 54			
Southampton Central 8	a				20 03	20 22		21 03				22 02				23 04			
Fareham	a				20 27			21 27				22 26				23 27			
	d				20 28			21 28				22 27				23 28			
Cosham	a																		
Fratton 8	a				20 40			21 42				22 41				23 41			
Portsmouth & Southsea	a				20 44			21 46				22 45				23 45			
Portsmouth Harbour	a				20 50			21 52				22 52				23 52			
Havant 8	a																		
Chichester 4	a																		
Barnham	a																		
Worthing 4	a																		
Shoreham-by-Sea	a																		
Hove 2	a																		
Brighton 10	a																		

A To Penzance

B To Plymouth

For connections from Swansea to Cardiff Central and Bristol Parkway refer to Table T128

For connections from Plymouth and Exeter to Bristol Temple Meads, Westbury and Castle Cary, refer to Table T135

For connections from Exeter and Yeovil Junction to Salisbury refer to Table T160

For connections from Upwey, Weymouth and Southampton Central to Bournemouth refer to Table T158

For additional bus connections between Yeovil Junction and Yeovil Pen Mill refer to Table T123A

Table T123-R

Sundays

20 May to 9 September

Great Malvern, Gloucester, Cardiff and Bristol - Weymouth, Portsmouth and Brighton

		GW	GW	GW ◇	GW	GW	GW ◇1 A	GW ◇	GW	GW ◇1 B	GW ◇	GW	GW ■ ◇ C	GW ◇1 D	GW ◇	GW	GW ◇1 A	GW ◇	GW ◇1 E	GW ◇	GW	SW ◇1 F	GW ◇
Cardiff Central 7	d			08 10				09 13			10 08		11 08		12 08			13 08		14 08			15 08
Newport (South Wales) 2	d			08 28				09 31			10 26		11 29		12 25			13 27		14 28			15 28
Severn Tunnel Jn.	d			08 45				09 42			10 36		11 39		12 36			13 37		14 39			15 39
Great Malvern	d																						
Malvern Link	d																						
Worcester Foregate Street	d																						
Worcester Shrub Hill	d																						
Ashchurch for Tewkesbury	d																						
Cheltenham Spa	d																						
Gloucester	d																						
Cam & Dursley	d																						
Yate	d																						
Bristol Parkway	d																						
Filton Abbey Wood	d			09 00				09 58			10 51		11 54		12 51			13 52		14 54			15 54
Bristol Temple Meads 10	d		08 23	09 10		09 20		10 15			11 10		12 10		13 10			14 10		15 10		16 04	16 10
Keynsham	d		08 30	09 18		09 27					11 16		12 17		13 17			14 17		15 17		16 11	
Oldfield Park	d		08 38	09 25		09 34					11 23		12 24		13 24			14 24		15 23			
Swindon	d				09 22							11 28				13 30					15 28		
Chippenham	d				09 37							11 43				13 47					15 43		
Melksham	d				09 47							11 53				13 56					15 53		
Bath Spa 7	d		08 42	09 28		09 38		10 28			11 26		12 27		13 27			14 27		15 27		16 20	16 24
Freshford	d		08 51			09 47		10 37					12 38					14 38					16 33
Avoncliff	d		08 54			09 50		10 41					12 40					14 40					16 37
Bradford-on-Avon	d		08 58	09 41		09 55		10 45			11 39		12 44		13 40			14 44		15 40		16 31	16 41
Trowbridge	d		09 04	09 50	09 56	10 02		10 51			11 47	12 02	12 51		13 47	14 06		14 51		15 47	16 02	16 37	16 46
London Paddington 15 ⊖	d						08 57			09 57				11 27			12 57		13 57				
Westbury 2	a		09 10	09 58	10 02	10 08	10 25	10 58			11 54	12 08	12 57	13 04	13 55	14 12	14 15	14 58		15 54	16 08	16 44	16 54
	d	08 30	09 12	10 00		10 10		11 02	11 25		12 01		13 01	13 06	14 01	14 25		15 02		16 03		16 46	17 01
Frome	d		09 22			10 20			11a34							14 34							
Bruton	d		09 34			10 31										14 46							
Castle Cary	a		09 39			10 35				11 34				13 25		14 51			15 36				
	d		09 40			10 40										14 51							
Yeovil Pen Mill	d		09 54			10 54										15 05							
Thornford	d		09x59			11x00										15x11							
Yetminster	d		10x02			11x03										15x14							
Chetnole	d		10x06			11x06										15x18							
Maiden Newton	d		10 18			11 23										15 29							
Dorchester West	d		10 29			11 34										15 40							
Upwey	a		10 36			11 41										15 49							
Weymouth	a		10 42			11 45										15 54							
Dilton Marsh	d	08x33		10x03							12x04				14x04					16x06			17x04
Warminster	d	08a39		10 09				11 09			12 10		13 09		14 10			15 09		16 12		16 53	17 10
Salisbury 8	a			10 31				11 31			12 32		13 31		14 34			15 31		16 32		17 16	17 31
	d			10 32				11 32			12 32		13 32		14 36			15 32		16 32			17 32
Romsey	d			10 50				11 50			12 50		13 50		14 54			15 50		16 50			17 50
Southampton Central 8	a			11 03				12 03			13 03		14 03		15 03			16 03		17 03			18 03
Fareham	a			11 26				12 26			13 29		14 26		15 27			16 26		17 26			18 26
	d			11 26				12 26			13 30		14 26		15 28			16 26		17 26			18 26
Cosham	a			11 34				12 34			13 37		14 34		15 36			16 34		17 34			18 34
Fratton 8	a			11 42				12 42					14 42					16 42		17 42			18 42
Portsmouth & Southsea	a			11 46				12 46					14 46					16 46		17 46			18 46
Portsmouth Harbour	a			11 51				12 53					14 53					16 52		17 51			18 52
Havant 8	a										13 45				15 42								
Chichester 4	a										13 57				15 53								
Barnham	a										14 08				16 01								
Worthing 4	a										14 26				16 19								
Shoreham-by-Sea	a										14 35				16 29								
Hove 2	a										14 47				16 40								
Brighton 10	a										14 53				16 47								

A To Penzance

B To Newquay

C ◇ from Bristol Temple Meads ■ to Bristol Temple Meads

D To Paignton

E To Plymouth

F To London Waterloo

For connections from Swansea to Cardiff Central and Bristol Parkway refer to Table T128

For connections from Plymouth and Exeter to Bristol Temple Meads, Westbury and Castle Cary, refer to Table T135

For connections from Exeter and Yeovil Junction to Salisbury refer to Table T160

For connections from Upwey, Weymouth and Southampton Central to Bournemouth refer to Table T158

For additional bus connections between Yeovil Junction and Yeovil Pen Mill refer to Table T123A

Table T123-R

Sundays

20 May to 9 September

Great Malvern, Gloucester, Cardiff and Bristol - Weymouth, Portsmouth and Brighton

		GW	SW	GW	GW	SW	GW	GW	GW	GW	GW	GW	GW	GW	GW	GW	GW	GW	SW	GW	GW
		◇1	◇1	◇		◇1	◇	◇	◇	◇1	◇	◇	◇1		◇	◇1		◇	1		
		A 🍴	B			C		D		E 🍴			A 🍴			A 🍴					
Cardiff Central 7	d			16 08			16 35		17 08		17 40	18 10			19 08			20 18			22 10
Newport (South Wales) 2	d			16 27			16 51		17 28		17 58	18 27			19 29			20 38			22 28
Severn Tunnel Jn.	d			16 39					17 39			18 39			19 39			20 50			22 43
Great Malvern	d																				
Malvern Link	d																				
Worcester Foregate Street	d																				
Worcester Shrub Hill	d																				
Ashchurch for Tewkesbury	d																				
Cheltenham Spa	d																				
Gloucester	d																				
Cam & Dursley	d																				
Yate	d																				
Bristol Parkway	d																				
Filton Abbey Wood	d			16 54			17 14		17 54		18 25	18 53			19 54			21 04			22 59
Bristol Temple Meads 10	d			17 10			17 35	17 43	18 10		18 49	19 10			20 15		20 48	21 25	21 35	22 15	23 15
Keynsham	d			17 17				17 51	18 16			19 17					20 55			22 22	
Oldfield Park	d			17 24				17 58	18 23			19 22					21 03			22 30	
Swindon	d				17 18									19 55							
Chippenham	d				17 33									20 10							
Melksham	d				17 43									20 20							
Bath Spa 7	d			17 28			17 49	18 01	18 27		19 02	19 26			20 27		21 06	21 38	21 49	22 33	23 28
Freshford	d							18 11							20 38		21 16			22 43	
Avoncliff	d							18 13							20 40		21 19			22 46	
Bradford-on-Avon	d			17 40			18 02	18 17	18 39		19 15	19 38			20 44		21 23	21 50	22 00	22 50	23 40
Trowbridge	d			17 47	17 52		18 09	18 24	18 47		19 21	19 46		20 29	20 51		21 30	21 57	22 06	22 56	23 47
London Paddington 15 ⊖	d	15 57								17 57			18 57			19 57					
Westbury 2	a	17 24		17 54	17 59		18 16	18 31	18 54	19 25	19 29	19 53		20 35	20 58	21 26	21 37	22 04	22 13	23 03	23 54
	d	17 25	17 48	18 01		18 16	18 17	18 31	19 01		19 31	19 59			21 01	21 28	21 38	22 05	22 15		23 55
Frome	d		17a57					18 39									21 48				
Bruton	d							18 52									21 59				
Castle Cary	a	17 42						18 56					20 30			21 44	22 04				
	d							18 58									22 05				
Yeovil Pen Mill	d							19 12									22 21				
Thornford	d							19x17									22x25				
Yetminster	d							19x20									22x28				
Chetnole	d							19x24									22x32				
Maiden Newton	d							19 36									22 44				
Dorchester West	d							19 47									22 55				
Upwey	a							19 55									23 02				
Weymouth	a							20 01									23 07				
Dilton Marsh	d						18x20					20x02									23x58
Warminster	d			18 08		18 23	18 26		19 08		19 38	20 08			21 08			22 13	22 22		00a04
Salisbury 8	a			18 31		18 43	18 52		19 31		20 01	20 31			21 31			22 34	22 45		
	d			18 32			18 55		19 32		20 02	20 32			21 32			22 36			
Romsey	d			18 50			19 14		19 50		20 20	20 50			21 50			22 54			
Southampton Central 8	a			19 03			19 26		20 03		20 30	21 03			22 03			23 05			
Fareham	a			19 26			19 53		20 26		20 58	21 26			22 26			23 29			
	d			19 26			19 54		20 26		20 59	21 26			22 26			23 30			
Cosham	a			19 34			20 02														
Fratton 8	a			19 42					20 40		21 13	21 40			22 42			23 43			
Portsmouth & Southsea	a			19 46					20 47		21 17	21 43			22 46			23 46			
Portsmouth Harbour	a			19 52					20 52		21 21	21 51			22 52			23 50			
Havant 8	a						20 10														
Chichester 4	a						20 21														
Barnham	a						20 29														
Worthing 4	a						20 50														
Shoreham-by-Sea	a						20 57														
Hove 2	a						21 05														
Brighton 10	a						21 10														

A To Plymouth
B From Salisbury
C From Frome to London Waterloo
D From Weston-super-Mare
E To Penzance

For connections from Swansea to Cardiff Central and Bristol Parkway refer to Table T128

For connections from Plymouth and Exeter to Bristol Temple Meads, Westbury and Castle Cary, refer to Table T135

For connections from Exeter and Yeovil Junction to Salisbury refer to Table T160

For connections from Upwey, Weymouth and Southampton Central to Bournemouth refer to Table T158

For additional bus connections between Yeovil Junction and Yeovil Pen Mill refer to Table T123A

Table T123-R

Sundays

16 September to 21 October

Great Malvern, Gloucester, Cardiff and Bristol - Weymouth, Portsmouth and Brighton

		GW	GW	GW	GW	GW	GW	GW	GW	GW	GW	GW	GW	GW	GW	GW	GW	GW	GW	GW	GW	SW	GW
				◇			◇1	◇		◇1	◇		◇	◇1	◇	◇1		◇	◇1	◇		◇1	◇
							A 🍴			A 🍴			B	C 🍴		D 🍴			A 🍴			E	
Cardiff Central 7	d			08 10				09 13			10 08		11 08		12 08			13 08		14 08			15 08
Newport (South Wales) 2	d			08 28				09 31			10 29		11 29		12 28			13 29		14 28			15 28
Severn Tunnel Jn.	d			08 45				09 42			10 39		11 39		12 39			13 39		14 39			15 39
Great Malvern	d																						
Malvern Link	d																						
Worcester Foregate Street	d																						
Worcester Shrub Hill	d																						
Ashchurch for Tewkesbury	d																						
Cheltenham Spa	d																						
Gloucester	d																						
Cam & Dursley	d																						
Yate	d																						
Bristol Parkway	d																						
Filton Abbey Wood	d			09 00				09 58			10 54		11 54		12 54			13 54		14 54			15 54
Bristol Temple Meads 10	d		08 19	09 15		09 25		10 15			11 10		12 10		13 10			14 10		15 10		16 04	16 15
Keynsham	d		08 26	09 21		09 32					11 16		12 17		13 17			14 17		15 17		16 11	
Oldfield Park	d		08 34	09 28		09 40					11 23		12 24		13 24			14 24		15 23			
Swindon	d				09 26							11 28					13 38				15 28		
Chippenham	d				09 41							11 43					13 55				15 43		
Melksham	d				09 51							11 53					14 04				15 53		
Bath Spa 7	d		08 38	09 31		09 44		10 28			11 26		12 27		13 27			14 27		15 27		16 20	16 27
Freshford	d		08 47			09 53		10 37					12 38					14 38					16 37
Avoncliff	d		08 50			09 55		10 41					12 40					14 40					16 40
Bradford-on-Avon	d		08 54	09 44		10 00		10 45			11 39		12 44		13 40			14 44		15 40		16 31	16 44
Trowbridge	d		09 00	09 52	10 00	10 07		10 51			11 47	12 02	12 51		13 47		14 14	14 51		15 47	16 02	16 37	16 50
London Paddington 15 ⊖	d						08 57			09 57				11 30		12 57			13 57				
Westbury 2	a		09 06	09 59	10 06	10 13	10 21	10 58			11 54	12 08	12 57	13 01	13 55	14 15	14 20	14 58		15 54	16 08	16 44	16 58
	d	08 30	09 07	10 00		10 18		11 02	11 25		12 01		13 01	13 02	14 01		14 25	15 02		16 05		16 46	17 01
Frome	d		09 18			10 34			11a34								14 34						
Bruton	d		09 30			10 46											14 46						
Castle Cary	a		09 35			10 50				11 34				13 21			14 51		15 36				
	d		09 35			10 51											14 51						
Yeovil Pen Mill	d		09 53			11 06											15 05						
Thornford	d		09x58			11x12											15x11						
Yetminster	d		10x01			11x15											15x14						
Chetnole	d		10x05			11x19											15x18						
Maiden Newton	d		10 17			11 30											15 29						
Dorchester West	d		10 29			11 41											15 40						
Upwey	a		10 36			11 49											15 49						
Weymouth	a		10 42			11 54											15 54						
Dilton Marsh	d	08x33		10x03							12x04				14x04					16x06			17x04
Warminster	d	08a39		10 09				11 09			12 10		13 09		14 10			15 09		16 12		16 53	17 10
Salisbury 8	a			10 31				11 31			12 32		13 31		14 34			15 31		16 32		17 16	17 31
	d			10 32				11 32			12 32		13 32		14 36			15 32		16 32			17 32
Romsey	d			10 50				11 50			12 50		13 50		14 54			15 50		16 50			17 50
Southampton Central 8	a			11 03				12 03			13 03		14 03		15 03			16 03		17 03			18 03
Fareham	a			11 26				12 26			13 29		14 26		15 27			16 26		17 26			18 26
	d			11 26				12 26			13 30		14 26		15 28			16 26		17 26			18 26
Cosham	a			11 34				12 34			13 37		14 34		15 36			16 34		17 34			18 34
Fratton 8	a			11 42				12 42					14 42					16 42		17 42			18 42
Portsmouth & Southsea	a			11 46				12 46					14 46					16 46		17 46			18 46
Portsmouth Harbour	a			11 51				12 53					14 53					16 52		17 51			18 52
Havant 8	a										13 45				15 42								
Chichester 4	a										13 57				15 53								
Barnham	a										14 08				16 01								
Worthing 4	a										14 26				16 19								
Shoreham-by-Sea	a										14 35				16 29								
Hove 2	a										14 47				16 40								
Brighton 10	a										14 53				16 47								

A To Plymouth
B ◇ from Bristol Temple Meads 1 to Bristol Temple Meads
C To Paignton
D To Penzance
E To London Waterloo

For connections from Swansea to Cardiff Central and Bristol Parkway refer to Table T128

For connections from Plymouth and Exeter to Bristol Temple Meads, Westbury and Castle Cary, refer to Table T135

For connections from Exeter and Yeovil Junction to Salisbury refer to Table T160

For connections from Upwey, Weymouth and Southampton Central to Bournemouth refer to Table T158

For additional bus connections between Yeovil Junction and Yeovil Pen Mill refer to Table T123A

T123 UPDATE: Due to major engineering work in connection with electrification work taking place between Reading and Newbury and subsequent diversion of West of England trains, LOCAL TRAINS between Swindon and Westbury via Melksham will be subject to significant alteration on 4-7 June; 9-12 July; 16 July to 05 August; 28-30 August; 08-11 October and 19-22 November.

Table T123-R

Sundays

16 September to 21 October

Great Malvern, Gloucester, Cardiff and Bristol - Weymouth, Portsmouth and Brighton

		GW	SW	GW	SW	GW	GW	GW	GW	GW	GW	GW	GW	GW	GW	GW	GW	GW	SW	GW	GW
		◇■ A 🍴	◇■ B	◇	◇■ C	◇	◇ D		◇	◇■ E 🍴	◇	◇	◇■ A 🍴		◇	◇■ A 🍴		◇	■		
Cardiff Central	d			16 08		16 35			17 08		17 40	18 08			19 08			20 18			22 10
Newport (South Wales)	d			16 27		16 53			17 28		17 58	18 27			19 29			20 38			22 28
Severn Tunnel Jn.	d			16 38					17 39			18 39			19 39			20 50			22 43
Great Malvern	d																				
Malvern Link	d																				
Worcester Foregate Street	d																				
Worcester Shrub Hill	d																				
Ashchurch for Tewkesbury	d																				
Cheltenham Spa	d																				
Gloucester	d																				
Cam & Dursley	d																				
Yate	d																				
Bristol Parkway	d																				
Filton Abbey Wood	d			16 54		17 19			17 54		18 26	18 53			19 54			21 04			22 59
Bristol Temple Meads	d			17 10		17 35	17 43		18 10		18 45	19 10			20 15		20 48	21 25	21 35	22 15	23 15
Keynsham	d			17 17		17 42			18 16			19 17					20 55			22 22	
Oldfield Park	d			17 24		17 49			18 23			19 22					21 03			22 30	
Swindon	d							17 52						19 53							
Chippenham	d							18 07						20 08							
Melksham	d							18 17						20 18							
Bath Spa	d			17 28		17 52	17 58		18 27		18 58	19 26			20 27		21 06	21 38	21 49	22 33	23 28
Freshford	d						18 08								20 38		21 16			22 43	
Avoncliff	d						18 09								20 40		21 19			22 46	
Bradford-on-Avon	d			17 40		18 04	18 13		18 39		19 10	19 38			20 44		21 23	21 50	22 00	22 50	23 40
Trowbridge	d			17 47		18 12	18 21	18 28	18 47		19 17	19 46		20 27	20 51		21 30	21 57	22 06	22 56	23 47
London Paddington ⊖	d	15 57								17 57			18 57			19 57					
Westbury	a	17 24		17 54		18 19	18 28	18 34	18 54	19 25	19 26	19 53		20 34	20 58	21 26	21 37	22 04	22 13	23 03	23 54
	d	17 25	17 48	18 01	18 16	18 20	18 31		19 01		19 30	19 59			21 01	21 28	21 38	22 05	22 15		23 55
Frome	d		17a57				18 39										21 48				
Bruton	d						18 52										21 59				
Castle Cary	a	17 42					18 56						20 30			21 44	22 04				
	d						18 58										22 05				
Yeovil Pen Mill	d						19 12										22 21				
Thornford	d						19x17										22x25				
Yetminster	d						19x20										22x28				
Chetnole	d						19x24										22x32				
Maiden Newton	d						19 36										22 44				
Dorchester West	d						19 47										22 55				
Upwey	a						19 55										23 02				
Weymouth	a						20 01										23 07				
Dilton Marsh	d					18x23						20x02									23x58
Warminster	d			18 08	18 23	18 29			19 08		19 38	20 08			21 08			22 13	22 22		00a04
Salisbury	a			18 31	18 43	18 52			19 31		20 01	20 31			21 31			22 34	22 45		
	d			18 32		18 56			19 32		20 02	20 32			21 32			22 36			
Romsey	d			18 50		19 14			19 50		20 20	20 50			21 50			22 54			
Southampton Central	a			19 03		19 27			20 03		20 30	21 03			22 03			23 05			
Fareham	a			19 26		19 53			20 26		20 58	21 26			22 26			23 29			
	d			19 26		19 54			20 26		20 59	21 26			22 26			23 30			
Cosham	a			19 34		20 02															
Fratton	a			19 42					20 40		21 13	21 40			22 42			23 43			
Portsmouth & Southsea	a			19 46					20 47		21 17	21 43			22 46			23 46			
Portsmouth Harbour	a			19 52					20 52		21 21	21 51			22 52			23 50			
Havant	a					20 10															
Chichester	a					20 21															
Barnham	a					20 29															
Worthing	a					20 50															
Shoreham-by-Sea	a					20 57															
Hove	a					21 05															
Brighton	a					21 10															

A To Plymouth
B From Salisbury
C From Frome to London Waterloo
D From Weston-super-Mare
E To Penzance

For connections from Swansea to Cardiff Central and Bristol Parkway refer to Table T128

For connections from Plymouth and Exeter to Bristol Temple Meads, Westbury and Castle Cary, refer to Table T135

For connections from Exeter and Yeovil Junction to Salisbury refer to Table T160

For connections from Upwey, Weymouth and Southampton Central to Bournemouth refer to Table T158

For additional bus connections between Yeovil Junction and Yeovil Pen Mill refer to Table T123A

Table T123-R

Sundays

28 October to 2 December

Great Malvern, Gloucester, Cardiff and Bristol - Weymouth, Portsmouth and Brighton

		GW	GW	GW	GW	GW	GW	GW	GW	GW	GW	GW	GW	GW	GW	GW	GW	GW	GW	GW	GW	SW	GW
				◇			◇■ A 🍴	◇		◇■ A 🍴	◇		■ ◇ B	◇■ C 🍴	◇	◇■ D 🍴		◇	◇■ A 🍴	◇		◇■ E	◇
Cardiff Central	d			08 10				09 08			10 08		11 08		12 08			13 08		14 08			15 08
Newport (South Wales)	d			08 28				09 26			10 29		11 29		12 28			13 29		14 28			15 28
Severn Tunnel Jn.	d			08 45				09 44			10 39		11 39		12 39			13 39		14 39			15 39
Great Malvern	d																						
Malvern Link	d																						
Worcester Foregate Street	d																						
Worcester Shrub Hill	d																						
Ashchurch for Tewkesbury	d																						
Cheltenham Spa	d																						
Gloucester	d																						
Cam & Dursley	d																						
Yate	d																						
Bristol Parkway	d																						
Filton Abbey Wood	d			09 00				10 00			10 54		11 54		12 54			13 54		14 54			15 54
Bristol Temple Meads	d		08 19	09 15		09 25		10 15			11 10		12 10		13 10			14 10		15 10		16 04	16 15
Keynsham	d		08 26	09 21		09 32					11 16		12 17		13 17			14 17		15 17		16 11	
Oldfield Park	d		08 34	09 28		09 40					11 23		12 24		13 24			14 24		15 23			
Swindon	d				09 26							11 28					13 38				15 28		
Chippenham	d				09 41							11 43					13 55				15 43		
Melksham	d				09 51							11 53					14 04				15 53		
Bath Spa	d		08 38	09 31		09 44		10 28			11 26		12 27		13 27			14 27		15 27		16 20	16 27
Freshford	d		08 47			09 53		10 37					12 38					14 38					16 37
Avoncliff	d		08 50			09 55		10 41					12 40					14 40					16 40
Bradford-on-Avon	d		08 54	09 44		10 00		10 45			11 39		12 44		13 40			14 44		15 40		16 31	16 44
Trowbridge	d		09 00	09 52	10 00	10 07		10 51			11 47	12 02	12 51		13 47		14 14	14 51		15 47	16 02	16 37	16 50
London Paddington ⊖	d						08 57			09 57				11 30		12 57			13 57				
Westbury	a		09 06	09 59	10 06	10 13	10 21	10 58			11 54	12 08	12 57	13 01	13 55	14 15	14 20	14 58		15 54	16 08	16 44	16 58
	d	08 30	09 07	10 00		10 18		11 02	11 25		12 01		13 01	13 02	14 01		14 25	15 02		16 05		16 46	17 01
Frome	d		09 18			10 34			11a34								14 33						
Bruton	d		09 30			10 46											14 45						
Castle Cary	a		09 35			10 50				11 34				13 21			14 49		15 36				
	d		09 35			10 51											14 50						
Yeovil Pen Mill	d		09 53			11 06											15 05						
Thornford	d		09x58			11x12											15 11						
Yetminster	d		10x01			11x15											15 14						
Chetnole	d		10x05			11x19											15 18						
Maiden Newton	d		10 17			11 30											15 29						
Dorchester West	d		10 29			11 41											15 40						
Upwey	a		10 36			11 49											15 49						
Weymouth	a		10 42			11 54											15 54						
Dilton Marsh	d	08x33		10x03							12x04				14x04					16x06			17x04
Warminster	d	08a39		10 09				11 09			12 10		13 09		14 10			15 09		16 12		16 53	17 10
Salisbury	a			10 31				11 31			12 32		13 31		14 34			15 31		16 32		17 16	17 31
	d			10 32				11 32			12 32		13 32		14 36			15 32		16 32			17 32
Romsey	d			10 50				11 50			12 50		13 50		14 54			15 50		16 50			17 50
Southampton Central	a			11 03				12 03			13 03		14 03		15 03			16 03		17 03			18 03
Fareham	a			11 26				12 26			13 29		14 26		15 27			16 26		17 26			18 26
	d			11 26				12 26			13 30		14 26		15 28			16 26		17 26			18 26
Cosham	a			11 34				12 34			13 37		14 34		15 36			16 34		17 34			18 34
Fratton	a			11 42				12 42					14 42					16 42		17 42			18 42
Portsmouth & Southsea	a			11 46				12 46					14 46					16 46		17 46			18 46
Portsmouth Harbour	a			11 51				12 53					14 53					16 52		17 51			18 52
Havant	a										13 45				15 42								
Chichester	a										13 57				15 53								
Barnham	a										14 08				16 01								
Worthing	a										14 26				16 19								
Shoreham-by-Sea	a										14 35				16 29								
Hove	a										14 47				16 40								
Brighton	a										14 53				16 47								

A To Plymouth
B ◇ from Bristol Temple Meads ■ to Bristol Temple Meads
C To Paignton
D To Penzance
E To London Waterloo

For connections from Swansea to Cardiff Central and Bristol Parkway refer to Table T128

For connections from Plymouth and Exeter to Bristol Temple Meads, Westbury and Castle Cary, refer to Table T135

For connections from Exeter and Yeovil Junction to Salisbury refer to Table T160

For connections from Upwey, Weymouth and Southampton Central to Bournemouth refer to Table T158

For additional bus connections between Yeovil Junction and Yeovil Pen Mill refer to Table T123A

Table T123-R

Sundays

28 October to 2 December

Great Malvern, Gloucester, Cardiff and Bristol - Weymouth, Portsmouth and Brighton

		GW	SW	GW	SW	GW	GW	GW	GW	GW	GW	GW	GW	GW	GW	GW	GW	GW	SW	GW	GW
		◇■	◇■	◇	◇■	◇	◇		◇	◇■	◇	◇	◇■		◇	◇■		◇	■		
		A	B		C		D			E			A			A					
Cardiff Central ■	d			16 08		16 35			17 08		17 40	18 08			19 08			20 18			22 10
Newport (South Wales) ■	d			16 27		16 53			17 28		17 58	18 27			19 29			20 38			22 28
Severn Tunnel Jn.	d			16 38					17 39			18 39			19 39			20 50			22 43
Great Malvern	d																				
Malvern Link	d																				
Worcester Foregate Street	d																				
Worcester Shrub Hill	d																				
Ashchurch for Tewkesbury	d																				
Cheltenham Spa	d																				
Gloucester	d																				
Cam & Dursley	d																				
Yate	d																				
Bristol Parkway	d																				
Filton Abbey Wood	d			16 54		17 19			17 54		18 26	18 53			19 54			21 04			22 59
Bristol Temple Meads ■	d			17 10		17 35	17 43		18 10		18 45	19 10			20 15		20 48	21 25	21 35	22 15	23 15
Keynsham	d			17 17		17 42			18 16			19 17					20 55			22 22	
Oldfield Park	d			17 24		17 49			18 23			19 22					21 03			22 30	
Swindon	d							17 52						19 53							
Chippenham	d							18 07						20 08							
Melksham	d							18 17						20 18							
Bath Spa ■	d			17 28		17 52	17 58		18 27		18 58	19 26			20 27		21 06	21 38	21 49	22 33	23 28
Freshford	d						18 08								20 38		21 16			22 43	
Avoncliff	d						18 09								20 40		21 19			22 46	
Bradford-on-Avon	d			17 40		18 04	18 13		18 39		19 10	19 38			20 44		21 23	21 50	22 00	22 50	23 40
Trowbridge	d			17 47		18 12	18 21	18 28	18 47		19 17	19 46		20 27	20 51		21 30	21 57	22 06	22 56	23 47
London Paddington ■ ⊖	d	15 57								17 57			18 57			19 57					
Westbury ■	a	17 24		17 54		18 19	18 28	18 34	18 54	19 25	19 26	19 53		20 34	20 58	21 26	21 37	22 04	22 13	23 03	23 54
	d	17 25	17 48	18 01	18 16	18 20	18 31		19 01		19 30	19 59			21 01	21 28	21 38	22 05	22 15		23 55
Frome	d		17a57				18 39										21 48				
Bruton	d						18 52										21 59				
Castle Cary	a	17 42					18 56						20 30			21 44	22 04				
	d						18 58										22 05				
Yeovil Pen Mill	d						19 12										22 21				
Thornford	d						19x17										22x25				
Yetminster	d						19x20										22x28				
Chetnole	d						19x24										22x32				
Maiden Newton	d						19 36										22 44				
Dorchester West	d						19 47										22 55				
Upwey	a						19 55										23 02				
Weymouth	a						20 01										23 07				
Dilton Marsh	d					18x23						20x02									23x58
Warminster	d			18 08	18 23	18 29			19 08		19 38	20 08			21 08			22 13	22 22		00a04
Salisbury ■	a			18 31	18 43	18 52			19 31		20 01	20 31			21 31			22 34	22 45		
	d			18 32		18 56			19 32		20 02	20 32			21 32			22 36			
Romsey	d			18 50		19 14			19 50		20 20	20 50			21 50			22 54			
Southampton Central ■	a			19 03		19 27			20 03		20 30	21 03			22 03			23 05			
Fareham	a			19 26		19 53			20 26		20 58	21 26			22 26			23 29			
	d			19 26		19 54			20 26		20 59	21 26			22 26			23 30			
Cosham	a			19 34		20 02															
Fratton ■	a			19 42					20 40		21 13	21 40			22 42			23 43			
Portsmouth & Southsea	a			19 46					20 47		21 17	21 43			22 46			23 46			
Portsmouth Harbour	a			19 52					20 52		21 21	21 51			22 52			23 50			
Havant ■	a					20 10															
Chichester ■	a					20 21															
Barnham	a					20 29															
Worthing ■	a					20 50															
Shoreham-by-Sea	a					20 57															
Hove ■	a					21 05															
Brighton ■	a					21 10															

A To Plymouth
B From Salisbury
C From Frome to London Waterloo
D From Weston-super-Mare
E To Penzance

For connections from Swansea to Cardiff Central and Bristol Parkway refer to Table T128

For connections from Plymouth and Exeter to Bristol Temple Meads, Westbury and Castle Cary, refer to Table T135

For connections from Exeter and Yeovil Junction to Salisbury refer to Table T160

For connections from Upwey, Weymouth and Southampton Central to Bournemouth refer to Table T158

For additional bus connections between Yeovil Junction and Yeovil Pen Mill refer to Table T123A

T123 UPDATE: Due to major engineering work in connection with electrification work taking place between Reading and Newbury and subsequent diversion of West of England trains, LOCAL TRAINS between Swindon and Westbury via Melksham will be subject to significant alteration on 4-7 June; 9-12 July; 16 July to 05 August; 28-30 August; 08-11 October and 19-22 November.

Table T123A-F

Mondays to Saturdays

21 May to 8 December

Yeovil Pen Mill - Yeovil Junction

Miles			SW	SW	SW	SW	SW	SW
			SX	SO	SX	SX	SO	SX
			◇■	◇■	◇■	■	◇■	■
				A			A	
0	Yeovil Pen Mill	d	05 41	12 58	15 44	16 31	17 38	20 30
—	Yeovil Bus Station	d						
1¾	Yeovil Junction	a	05 46	13 04	15 49	16 36	17 44	20 35
—		d						

A until 8 September

No Sunday Service

Table T123A-R

Mondays to Saturdays

21 May to 8 December

Yeovil Junction - Yeovil Pen Mill

Miles			SW	SW	SW	SW	SW	SW	SW
			SO	SO	SX	SX	SX	SX	SX
			◇■	◇■	◇■	◇■	◇■	◇■	◇■
			A	A					
0	Yeovil Junction	d	09 23	14 12	16 20	16 46	19 17	20 20	21 17
—	Yeovil Bus Station	d							
1¾	Yeovil Pen Mill	a	09 45	14 17	16 27	16 51	19 25	20 25	21 23

A until 8 September

No Sunday Service

Table T124-F

Mondays to Saturdays

21 May to 8 December

Cardiff Queen Street to Cardiff Bay

Miles			AW	AW	AW	AW	AW	and at the same minutes past each hour until	AW	AW	AW	AW	AW	AW	AW
0	Cardiff Queen Street [3]	d	06 36	06 48	07 00	07 12	07 24		22 36	22 48	23 00	23 12	23 24	23 36	23 48
1	Cardiff Bay	a	06 40	06 52	07 04	07 16	07 28		22 40	22 52	23 04	23 16	23 28	23 40	23 52

Sundays

20 May to 2 December

		AW	AW	AW	AW	AW	and at the same minutes past each hour until	AW	AW	AW	AW	AW
Cardiff Queen Street [3]	d	09 00	09 12	09 24	09 36	09 48		18 00	18 12	18 24	18 36	18 48
Cardiff Bay	a	09 04	09 16	09 28	09 40	09 52		18 04	18 16	18 28	18 40	18 52

When events are being held at the Principality Stadium, services are subject to alteration. Please check times before travelling.

Table T124-R

Mondays to Saturdays

21 May to 8 December

Cardiff Bay to Cardiff Queen Street

Miles			AW	AW	AW	AW	AW	and at the same minutes past each hour until	AW	AW	AW	AW	AW	AW	AW
0	Cardiff Bay	d	06 42	06 54	07 06	07 18	07 30		22 42	22 54	23 06	23 18	23 30	23 42	23 54
1	Cardiff Queen Street [3]	a	06 46	06 58	07 10	07 22	07 34		22 46	22 58	23 10	23 22	23 34	23 46	23 58

Sundays

20 May to 2 December

		AW	AW	AW	AW	AW	and at the same minutes past each hour until	AW	AW	AW	AW	AW
Cardiff Bay	d	09 06	09 18	09 30	09 42	09 54		18 06	18 18	18 30	18 42	18 54
Cardiff Queen Street [3]	a	09 10	09 22	09 34	09 46	09 58		18 10	18 22	18 34	18 46	18 58

When events are being held at the Principality Stadium, services are subject to alteration. Please check times before travelling.

Table T125-F

Mondays to Fridays

21 May to 7 December

London - Swindon, Cheltenham Spa, Bristol, Weston-super-Mare and South Wales

Miles	Miles	Miles			GW MX ◇1 A ☕	GW MX B	GW MX ◇1 C ☕	GW MX ◇1 D ☕	GW MO ◇1 E ☕	GW MO ◇1 F ☕	GW G	GW ◇1 ☕	GW ◇1 ☕		GW ◇1 ☕	GW ◇1 ☕	GW H	GW ◇1 ☕	GW ◇1 ☕	GW ◇1 I ☕	GW ◇1 ☕	GW ◇1 J ☕	GW K		GW ◇1 L ☕
0	0	0	LonPaddington [15] ⊖117,116	d								05 19			06 30	06 45		07 00	07 15	07 30	07 36	07 45			08 00
18½	18½	18½	Slough [3] 117,116	d					00 01																
36	36	36	Reading [7] 117,116	d			00 10	00 10	00 20	00 20		05 54			06 57	07 12		07 28	07 42	07 57	08 03	08 12			08 27
53¼	53¼	53¼	Didcot Parkway 116	d			00 29	00 29	00s35	00s35		06 09			07 12			07 44	07 56		08 17				08 43
77¼	77¼	77¼	Swindon	a			00 45	00 45	00s55	00s55		06 26			07 28	07 38		08 01	08 13	08 23	08 35	08 39			08 59
—	—	—		d	00 01		00 47	00 47			06 10	06 28	06 40		07 30	07 39	07 50	08 02	08 14	08 24	08 36	08 40	08 53		09 01
—	—	91	Kemble	d									06 54				08 05				08 51				
—	—	102¼	Stroud	d		00 06							07 09				08 20				09 07				
—	—	105	Stonehouse	d		00 11							07 15				08 25				09 12				
—	—	113¾	Gloucester [7]	a		00 27							07 31				08 48				09 30				
—	—	120¼	Cheltenham Spa [4]	a		00 40							07 47				09 05				09 52				
—	—	—	Worcester Shrub Hill	a																					
—	94	—	Chippenham	d			01 02	01 02	01s10	01s10	06a26	06 42			07 45			08 17		08 39			09a08		09 16
—	107	—	Bath Spa [7]	a			01 16	01 16	01s24	01s24		06 56			07 59			08 31		08 53					09 30
111¾	—	—	Bristol Parkway [7]	a	00 26											08 05			08 40			09 06			
—	—	—		d	00 28											08 10			08 41			09 09			
117¾	118½	—	Bristol Temple Meads [10]	a			01 30	01 30	01 39	01 39		07 10			08 18			08 47		09 10					09 44
—	137½	—	Weston-super-Mare	a																					
—	164¼	—	Taunton	a																09 44					
133½	—	—	Newport (South Wales)	a	00 55		02s10	02s10				07 48				08 31			09 04			09 30			
145¼	—	—	Cardiff Central [7] 128	a	01 16		02 31	02 32				08 02				08 50			09 20			09 49			
165½	—	—	Bridgend 128	a	01 41							08 24				09 14						10 11			
177¾	—	—	Port Talbot Parkway 128	a	01 54							08 36				09 26						10 23			
183¼	—	—	Neath 128	a	02 03							08 45				09 34						10 32			
192¾	—	—	Swansea 128	a	02 17							08 58				09 48						10 45			

		GW ◇1 ☕	GW ◇1 ☕	GW	GW ◇1 ☕	GW ◇1 ☕	GW ◇1 ☕	GW ◇1 ☕	GW ◇1 ☕		GW ◇1 ☕	GW K	GW ◇1 ☕	GW ◇1 ☕	GW ◇1 ☕	GW	GW ◇1 M ✕☕	GW ◇1 ☕	GW ◇1 ☕		GW ◇1 ☕	GW ◇1 ☕	GW ◇1 ☕	GW N	GW ◇1 ☕
LonPaddington [15] ⊖117,116	d	08 15	08 30		08 45	09 00	09 15	09 30	09 36		09 45		10 00	10 15	10 30		10 45	11 00	11 15		11 30	11 36	11 45		12 00
Slough [3] 117,116	d																								
Reading [7] 117,116	d	08 42	08 57		09 12	09 27	09 42	09 57	10 03		10 12		10 27	10 42	10 59		11 12	11 27	11 42		11 58	12 03	12 12		12 27
Didcot Parkway 116	d	08 56				09 41	09 56		10 17				10 41	10 56				11 42	11 56			12 17			12 43
Swindon	a	09 13	09 28		09 38	09 58	10 13	10 24	10 35		10 39		10 59	11 13	11 27		11 38	11 58	12 13		12 24	12 35	12 39		12 59
	d	09 14	09 30	09 36	09 39	09 59	10 14	10 26	10 36		10 40	10 47	11 00	11 14	11 29	11 36	11 39	12 00	12 14		12 30	12 36	12 40	12 49	13 01
Kemble	d			09 50					10 51							11 50						12 51			
Stroud	d			10 05					11 07							12 05						13 07			
Stonehouse	d			10 10					11 12							12 10						13 12			
Gloucester [7]	a			10 28					11 29							12 30						13 29			
Cheltenham Spa [4]	a			10 46					11 52							12 46						13 52			
Worcester Shrub Hill	a																								
Chippenham	d		09 45			10 14		10 41				11a02	11 14		11 43			12 15			12 45			13a04	13 16
Bath Spa [7]	a		09 59			10 28		10 55					11 28		11 57			12 29			12 59				13 30
Bristol Parkway [7]	a	09 40			10 05		10 40				11 06			11 40			12 05		12 40				13 06		
	d	09 45			10 09		10 41				11 09			11 41			12 09		12 41				13 09		
Bristol Temple Meads [10]	a		10 13			10 43		11 09					11 43		12 11			12 43			13 16				13 44
Weston-super-Mare	a														12 33										
Taunton	a																								
Newport (South Wales)	a	10 06			10 32		11 04				11 30			12 03			12 31		13 03				13 30		
Cardiff Central [7] 128	a	10 21			10 48		11 23				11 46			12 21			12 47		13 22				13 46		
Bridgend 128	a				11 10						12 08						13 09						14 09		
Port Talbot Parkway 128	a				11 22						12 20						13 21						14 23		
Neath 128	a				11 30						12 28						13 30						14 30		
Swansea 128	a				11 44						12 42						13 43						14 44		

A From London Paddington
B From Swindon
C from 31 July. From London Paddington
D until 27 July. From London Paddington
E from 17 September. From London Paddington
F until 10 September. From London Paddington
G From Gloucester to Southampton Central
H From Westbury
I To Penzance
J The St. David
K To Westbury
L The Merchant Venturer
M Restaurant available for customers joining until Bristol Parkway. ☕ from Bristol Parkway ✕ to Bristol Parkway
N To Frome

For connections to/from:
Oxford - refer to Table T116; Gatwick Airport - refer to Table T148; Table T117 for Services via London Paddington

For principal services between: London & Taunton - refer to Table T135; London & Worcester - refer to Table T126

Table T125-F

Mondays to Fridays

21 May to 7 December

London - Swindon, Cheltenham Spa, Bristol, Weston-super-Mare and South Wales

	GW	GW	GW	GW	GW	GW	GW	GW	GW	GW	GW	GW	GW	GW	GW	GW	GW	GW	GW	GW	GW
																	FO				
	◇■	◇■			◇■	◇■	◇■	◇■	◇■	◇■	◇■	◇■		◇■		◇■	◇■	◇■	◇■	◇■	◇■
			A										A			B	C				
	🍴	🍴			🍴	🍴	🍴	🍴	🍴	🍴	🍴	🍴		🍴		🍴	🍴	🍴	🍴	🍴	🍴
LonPaddington ■ ⊖117,116 d	12 15	12 30			12 45	13 00	13 15	13 30	13 36	13 45	14 00	14 15		14 30		14 45	14 45	15 00	15 15	15 30	15 36
Slough ■ 117,116 d																					
Reading ■ 117,116 d	12 42	12 57			13 12	13 27	13 42	13 58	14 03	14 12	14 27	14 42		14 57		15 12	15 12	15 28	15 42	15 58	16 03
Didcot Parkway 116 d	12 56					13 41	13 56	14 13	14 18			14 56		15 11					15 56	16 12	16 17
Swindon a	13 13	13 23			13 38	13 58	14 13	14 29	14 36	14 39	14 55	15 13		15 31		15 38	15 40	15 55	16 13	16 29	16 35
d	13 14	13 25	13 29	13 36	13 39	13 59	14 14	14 31	14 37	14 40	14 56	15 14	15 19	15 33	15 36	15 39	15 42	15 57	16 14	16 30	16 36
Kemble d				13 50					14 52						15 50						16 51
Stroud d				14 05					15 08						16 05						17 07
Stonehouse d				14 10					15 13						16 10						17 12
Gloucester ■ a				14 28					15 29						16 27						17 30
Cheltenham Spa ■ a				14 45					15 52						16 45						17 52
Worcester Shrub Hill a																					
Chippenham d		13 40	13a44			14 14		14 46			15 11		15a34	15 47				16 12		16 45	
Bath Spa ■ a		13 54				14 28		15 00			15 27			16 00				16 26		16 59	
Bristol Parkway ■ a	13 42				14 06		14 40			15 06		15 40				16 06	16 06		16 40		
d	13 44				14 09		14 41			15 09		15 41				16 10	16 10		16 41		
Bristol Temple Meads ■ a		14 08				14 43		15 15			15 41			16 15				16 40		17 14	
Weston-super-Mare a														16 50						17 50	
Taunton a																					
Newport (South Wales) a	14 05				14 31		15 07			15 30		16 03				16 31	16 31		17 06		
Cardiff Central ■ 128 a	14 21				14 47		15 23			15 44		16 22				16 45	16 45		17 23		
Bridgend 128 a					15 09					16 07						17 08	17 08				
Port Talbot Parkway 128 a					15 21					16 19						17 20	17 20				
Neath 128 a					15 29					16 28						17 29	17 29				
Swansea 128 a					15 43					16 41						17 42	17 42				

	GW	GW	GW	GW	GW	GW	GW	GW	GW	GW	GW	GW	GW	GW	GW	XC	GW	GW	GW	GW	GW	GW
																					FX	
	◇■	◇■	■	■		■	◇	■	■	■	◇■	■	◇	■	■	◇■	■	◇■	■	■	■	
					A	D			E		F		G	H		I			J			A
	🍴	🍴	🍴	🍴		🍴		🍴	🍴	🍴	🍴	🍴		🍴	🍴	🛒	🍴	🍴	🍴	🍴	🍴	
LonPaddington ■ ⊖117,116 d	15 45	16 00	16 15	16 30		16 45		17 00	17 15	17 30	17 36	17 45		18 00	18 14		18 30	18 37	18 45	19 00	19 12	
Slough ■ 117,116 d																						
Reading ■ 117,116 d	16 12	16 27	16 42	16 57		17 12		17 27	17 42	17 57		18 12		18 28	18 42		18 57		19 12	19 27		
Didcot Parkway 116 d			16 56	17 13				17 42	17 56	18 12	18 18			18 42	18 56		19 13	19 17		19 42		
Swindon a	16 39	16 54	17 13	17 29		17 38		17 58	18 13	18 29	18 37	18 43		18 59	19 13		19 29	19 35	19 39	19 58	20 03	
d	16 40	16 56	17 14	17 31	17 36	17 40	17 54	18 00	18 14	18 30	18 38	18 44	18 48	19 01	19 14		19 31	19 37	19 41	20 00	20 05	20 08
Kemble d							18 08				18 52							19 51				
Stroud d							18 23				19 08							20 06				
Stonehouse d							18 28				19 14							20 12				
Gloucester ■ a							18 47				19 31							20 27				
Cheltenham Spa ■ a							19 03				19 49							20 43				
Worcester Shrub Hill a																						
Chippenham d		17 11		17 46	17a51			18 15		18 45			19a05	19 16			19 46			20 15		20a23
Bath Spa ■ a		17 25		18 00				18 29		18 59				19 30			19 59			20 29		
Bristol Parkway ■ a	17 07		17 40			18 06			18 40			19 10			19 40				20 06		20 35	
d	17 10		17 41			18 10			18 41			19 12			19 41	19 57			20 09		20 37	
Bristol Temple Meads ■ a		17 39		18 15				18 46		19 14				19 44		20 09	20 14			20 43	20 48	
Weston-super-Mare a				18 52						19 52							20 53					
Taunton a				19 30						20 31												
Newport (South Wales) a	17 32		18 02			18 31			19 10			19 33			20 04	20 47			20 32			
Cardiff Central ■ 128 a	17 47		18 22			18 49			19 25			19 48			20 18	21 03			20 51			
Bridgend 128 a	18 10		18 49			19 12			19 49			20 11			20 44				21 15			
Port Talbot Parkway 128 a	18 22		19 01			19 24			20 01			20 24			20 56				21 27			
Neath 128 a	18 31		19 10			19 32			20 10			20 32			21 05				21 35			
Swansea 128 a	18 44		19 23			19 46			20 23			20 46			21 18				21 50			

A To Westbury
B until 5 July, FX from 9 July until 30 August, from 3 September
C from 6 July until 31 August
D The Capitals United
E To Carmarthen. The Red Dragon
F The Cheltenham Spa Express
G From Cheltenham Spa to Southampton Central
H The Bristolian
I From Manchester Piccadilly. 🛒 to Bristol Temple Meads
J Y Cymro - The Welshman

For connections to/from:
Oxford - refer to Table T116; Gatwick Airport - refer to Table T148; Table T117 for Services via London Paddington

For principal services between: London & Taunton - refer to Table T135; London & Worcester - refer to Table T126

Table T125-F

Mondays to Fridays

21 May to 7 December

London - Swindon, Cheltenham Spa, Bristol, Weston-super-Mare and South Wales

	GW	GW	GW	GW	GW	GW	GW	GW	GW	GW	GW	GW	GW	GW	GW	GW	GW	GW	GW	GW	GW	GW
	FO	FX	FO					FO	FX			FX	FO		FO	FX	FO	FX	FO	FX		FX
	■	■	■	◇	■	◇■	◇■	◇■	◇■	◇■		◇■	◇■	◇■	◇■	◇■			◇■	◇■	◇■	◇■
				A										B							C	D
	🍴	🍴	🍴		🍴	🍴	🍴	🍴	🍴	🍴		🍴	🍴	🍴	🍴	🍴			🍴	🍴	🍴	🍴
LonPaddington ■ ⊖117,116 d	19 12	19 15	19 15		19 30	19 48	20 00	20 15	20 15	20 45		21 15	21 15	21 45	22 15	22 15			22 45	22 45	23 30	23 30
Slough ■ 117,116 d																						
Reading ■ 117,116 d	19 39	19 42	19 48		19 59	20 20	20 27	20 42	20 42	21 12		21 43	21 43	22 13	22 44	22 56			23 13	23 20	00 10	00 10
Didcot Parkway 116 d	19 54	19 57			20 13	20 35	20 43	20 56	20 56	21 26		22 03	22 03	22 33	23 01	23 13			23 30	23 43	00 29	00 29
Swindon a	20 11	20 13	20 17		20 31	20 53	20 59	21 13	21 13	21 43		22 20	22 20	22 49	23 18	23 31			23 47	23 59	00 45	00 45
d	20 12	20 15	20 18	20 25	20 32	20 55	21 01	21 14	21 14	21 44	21 54	22 21	22 21	22 51	23 19	23 32	23 36	23 36	23 48	00 01	00 47	00 47
Kemble d				20 38		21 09					22 08						23 50	23 50				
Stroud d				20 53		21 24					22 23						00 05	00 06				
Stonehouse d				20 59		21 30					22 28						00 10	00 11				
Gloucester ■ a				21 15		21 45					22 46						00 28	00 27				
Cheltenham Spa ■ a				21 33		22 00					23 02						00 43	00 40				
Worcester Shrub Hill a						22 22																
Chippenham d					20 47		21 16			21 59				23 06	23 34	23 46					01 02	01 02
Bath Spa ■ a					21 01		21 30			22 13				23 20	23 48	23 59					01 16	01 16
Bristol Parkway ■ a	20 38	20 40	20 44					21 40	21 40			22 47	22 47						00 14	00 26		
d	20 39	20 42	20 45					21 41	21 41			22 48	22 48						00 15	00 28		
Bristol Temple Meads ■ a	20 59				21 15		21 44			22 28				23 34	00 03	00 14					01 30	01 30
Weston-super-Mare a					21 48									00b07								
Taunton a														00b36								
Newport (South Wales) a		21 03	21 06					22 04	22 04			23 16	23 17						00 36	00 55	02s10	02s10
Cardiff Central ■ 128 a		21 17	21 21					22 18	22 24			23 41	23 39						00 51	01 16	02 31	02 32
Bridgend 128 a		21 45	21 44					22 41	22 48			00 03	00 03						01 16	01 41		
Port Talbot Parkway 128 a		21 57	21 56					22 53	23 02			00 16	00 16						01 28	01 54		
Neath 128 a		22 06	22 04					23 02	23 10			00 25	00 25						01 37	02 03		
Swansea 128 a		22 20	22 18					23 15	23 24			00 39	00 39						01 50	02 17		

Saturdays

26 May to 8 September

	GW	GW	GW	GW	GW	GW	GW	GW	GW	GW	GW	GW	GW	GW	GW	GW	GW	GW	GW	GW	GW	GW
		◇■	◇■		◇■	◇■	◇■	■		◇■	◇■	◇■	◇■	◇■	◇■		◇■		◇■	◇■	◇■	◇■
	E	F	F				G	H	I					J				I				
		🍴	🍴		🍴	🍴		🍴		🍴	🍴	🍴	🍴	🍴	🍴		🍴		🍴	🍴	🍴	🍴
LonPaddington ■ ⊖117,116 d					06 30	07 00		07 30		07 45	08 00	08 15	08 30	08 45	09 00		09 30		09 45	10 00	10 15	10 30
Slough ■ 117,116 d																						
Reading ■ 117,116 d			00 10		06 58	07 28		07 58		08 12	08 30	08 42	08 58	09 12	09 28		09 58		10 12	10 28	10 42	10 58
Didcot Parkway 116 d			00 29		07 13			08 13				08 57	09 13				10 14				10 57	11 13
Swindon a			00 45		07 29	07 54		08 29		08 39	08 56	09 14	09 29	09 39	09 54		10 30		10 39	10 54	11 14	11 29
d			00 47	07 16	07 31	07 56		08 31	08 36	08 41	08 58	09 16	09 31	09 40	09 56	10 14	10 32	10 36	10 41	10 56	11 16	11 31
Kemble d				07 30								09 30				10 28					11 30	
Stroud d	00 05			07 45								09 45				10 43					11 45	
Stonehouse d	00 10			07 50								09 51				10 48					11 51	
Gloucester ■ a	00 28			08 05								10 06				11 04					12 06	
Cheltenham Spa ■ a	00 43			08 20								10 22				11 20					12 22	
Worcester Shrub Hill a																						
Chippenham d			01 02		07 46	08 11		08 46	08a52		09 13		09 46		10 11		10 47	10a52		11 11		11 46
Bath Spa ■ a			01 16		07 59	08 24		08 59			09 26		09 59		10 24		11 00			11 24		11 59
Bristol Parkway ■ a										09 04				10 05					11 04			
d		00 15					07 10			09 09				10 09					11 09			
Bristol Temple Meads ■ a			01 30		08 14	08 40		09 14			09 41		10 14		10 39		11 15			11 39		12 14
Weston-super-Mare a															11 10							12 38
Taunton a								09 48														
Newport (South Wales) a		00 36	02s10				07 31			09 29				10 30					11 30			
Cardiff Central ■ 128 a		00 51	02 31				07 47			09 46				10 45					11 45			
Bridgend 128 a		01 16					08 09			10 09				11 09					12 09			
Port Talbot Parkway 128 a		01 28					08 22			10 21				11 21					12 21			
Neath 128 a		01 37					08 30			10 29				11 29					12 29			
Swansea 128 a		01 50					08 44			10 43				11 43					12 43			

A From Westbury
B To Exeter St Davids
C FO until 20 July, from 27 July
D until 26 July
E From Swindon
F From London Paddington
G From Bristol Temple Meads
H To Penzance
I To Westbury
J To Pembroke Dock. The Pembroke Coast Express
b Stops to set down only, stops on request

For connections to/from:
Oxford - refer to Table T116; Gatwick Airport - refer to Table T148; Table T117 for Services via London Paddington

For principal services between: London & Taunton - refer to Table T135; London & Worcester - refer to Table T126

Table T125-F

Saturdays
26 May to 8 September

London - Swindon, Cheltenham Spa, Bristol, Weston-super-Mare and South Wales

	GW	GW	GW	GW	GW	GW	GW	GW	GW	GW	GW
	◇1	◇1		◇1		◇1	◇1	◇1	◇1	◇1	◇1
					A						
	☕	☕		☕		☕	☕	☕	☕	☕	☕
LonPaddington ⊖117,116 d	10 45	11 00		11 30		11 45	12 00	12 15	12 30	12 45	13 00
Slough 117,116 d											
Reading 117,116 d	11 12	11 28		11 58		12 12	12 29	12 42	12 58	13 12	13 28
Didcot Parkway 116 d				12 13				12 57	13 13		
Swindon a	11 39	11 54		12 29		12 39	12 56	13 14	13 29	13 39	13 54
d	11 40	11 56	12 14	12 31	12 36	12 41	12 57	13 16	13 31	13 40	13 56
Kemble d			12 28					13 30			
Stroud d			12 43					13 45			
Stonehouse d			12 48					13 51			
Gloucester a			13 04					14 06			
Cheltenham Spa a			13 20					14 22			
Worcester Shrub Hill a											
Chippenham d		12 11		12 46	12a52		13 12		13 46		14 11
Bath Spa a		12 24		12 59			13 25		13 59		14 24
Bristol Parkway a	12 04					13 04				14 04	
d	12 09					13 09				14 09	
Bristol Temple Meads a		12 40		13 14			13 41		14 14		14 39
Weston-super-Mare a									14 36		
Taunton a											
Newport (South Wales) a	12 30					13 30				14 30	
Cardiff Central 128 a	12 45					13 45				14 45	
Bridgend 128 a	13 09					14 09				15 09	
Port Talbot Parkway 128 a	13 21					14 21				15 21	
Neath 128 a	13 29					14 29				15 29	
Swansea 128 a	13 43					14 43				15 43	

	GW	GW	GW	GW	GW	GW	GW	GW	GW	GW
		◇1		◇1	◇1	◇1		◇1	◇1	◇1
			A				B			
		☕		☕	☕	☕		☕	☕	☕
LonPaddington ⊖117,116 d		13 30		13 45	14 00	14 15		14 30	14 45	15 00
Slough 117,116 d										
Reading 117,116 d		13 58		14 12	14 28	14 42		14 58	15 12	15 28
Didcot Parkway 116 d		14 13				14 57		15 13		
Swindon a		14 29		14 39	14 54	15 14		15 29	15 39	15 54
d	14 14	14 31	14 36	14 41	14 56	15 16	15 22	15 31	15 40	15 56
Kemble d	14 28					15 30				
Stroud d	14 43					15 45				
Stonehouse d	14 48					15 51				
Gloucester a	15 03					16 06				
Cheltenham Spa a	15 20					16 22				
Worcester Shrub Hill a										
Chippenham d		14 46	14a52		15 11		15a38	15 46		16 11
Bath Spa a		15 00			15 27			15 59		16 24
Bristol Parkway a				15 04					16 04	
d				15 09					16 09	
Bristol Temple Meads a		15 14			15 41			16 14		16 39
Weston-super-Mare a								16 38		
Taunton a										
Newport (South Wales) a				15 30					16 30	
Cardiff Central 128 a				15 45					16 44	
Bridgend 128 a				16 09					17 09	
Port Talbot Parkway 128 a				16 21					17 21	
Neath 128 a				16 29					17 29	
Swansea 128 a				16 43					17 43	

	GW	GW	GW	GW	GW	GW	GW	GW	GW	GW	GW
		◇1	◇1	◇1	◇1	◇1		◇1	◇1		◇1
						C	A				
		☕	☕	☕	☕	☕		☕	☕		☕
LonPaddington ⊖117,116 d		15 30	15 45	16 00	16 15	16 30		16 45	17 00		17 30
Slough 117,116 d											
Reading 117,116 d		15 58	16 12	16 28	16 42	16 58		17 12	17 28		17 58
Didcot Parkway 116 d		16 14			16 56	17 13					18 13
Swindon a		16 30	16 39	16 54	17 15	17 29		17 39	17 54		18 29
d	16 14	16 32	16 40	16 56	17 16	17 31	17 36	17 41	17 56	18 14	18 31
Kemble d	16 28				17 30					18 28	
Stroud d	16 43				17 45					18 43	
Stonehouse d	16 48				17 50					18 48	
Gloucester a	17 04				18 06					19 04	
Cheltenham Spa a	17 20				18 22					19 20	
Worcester Shrub Hill a											
Chippenham d		16 47		17 11		17 46	17a52		18 11		18 46
Bath Spa a		17 00		17 24		17 59			18 24		18 59
Bristol Parkway a			17 04					18 04			
d			17 09					18 09			
Bristol Temple Meads a		17 15		17 39		18 14			18 41		19 14
Weston-super-Mare a		17 40				18 36					19 50
Taunton a						19 05					
Newport (South Wales) a			17 31					18 30			
Cardiff Central 128 a			17 46					18 47			
Bridgend 128 a			18 09					19 09			
Port Talbot Parkway 128 a			18 21					19 21			
Neath 128 a			18 29					19 29			
Swansea 128 a			18 46					19 43			

	GW	GW	GW	XC	GW	GW	GW	GW	GW	GW	GW
	◇1	◇1	◇1	◇1	◇1		◇1	◇1		◇1	◇1
	D			E		A					
	☕	☕	☕	🍴	☕		☕	☕		☕	☕
LonPaddington ⊖117,116 d	17 45	18 00	18 15		18 30		18 45	19 00		19 30	19 45
Slough 117,116 d											
Reading 117,116 d	18 12	18 28	18 42		18 58		19 12	19 28		19 58	20 12
Didcot Parkway 116 d			18 56		19 13					20 13	
Swindon a	18 39	18 54	19 15		19 29		19 39	19 54		20 29	20 39
d	18 40	18 56	19 16		19 31	19 36	19 41	19 56	20 00	20 31	20 41
Kemble d			19 30						20 14		
Stroud d			19 45						20 29		
Stonehouse d			19 50						20 34		
Gloucester a			20 06						20 50		
Cheltenham Spa a			20 22						21 04		
Worcester Shrub Hill a											
Chippenham d		19 11			19 46	19a52		20 11		20 46	
Bath Spa a		19 24			20 00			20 24		20 59	
Bristol Parkway a	19 04						20 04				21 04
d	19 08			19 56			20 09				21 09
Bristol Temple Meads a		19 40		20 05	20 14			20 40		21 14	
Weston-super-Mare a					20 36			21 27			
Taunton a					21 01			21 59			
Newport (South Wales) a	19 30			20 44			20 30				21 30
Cardiff Central 128 a	19 44			21 00			20 44				21 48
Bridgend 128 a	20 09						21 09				22 10
Port Talbot Parkway 128 a	20 21						21 21				22 22
Neath 128 a	20 29						21 29				22 30
Swansea 128 a	20 42						21 43				22 44

A To Westbury
B To Warminster
C To Paignton. The Torbay Express
D To Carmarthen
E From Manchester Piccadilly. 🍴 to Bristol Temple Meads

For connections to/from:
Oxford - refer to Table T116; Gatwick Airport - refer to Table T148; Table T117 for Services via London Paddington

For principal services between: London & Taunton - refer to Table T135; London & Worcester - refer to Table T126

Table T125-F

Saturdays
26 May to 8 September

London - Swindon, Cheltenham Spa, Bristol, Weston-super-Mare and South Wales

	GW	GW	GW	GW	GW	GW	GW	GW	GW	GW
	◇1		◇1	◇1	◇1	◇1		◇1	◇1	◇1
		A		B						
	☕		☕	☕	☕	☕		☕	☕	☕
LonPaddington ⊖117,116 d	20 00		20 15	20 30	20 45	21 32		22 00	22 35	23 30
Slough 117,116 d										
Reading 117,116 d	20 28		20 42	20 58	21 12	21 59		22 29	23 02	00 05
Didcot Parkway 116 d	20 43		20 57	21 13		22 14		22 44	23 18	00 22
Swindon a	20 59		21 14	21 29	21 39	22 30		23 01	23 35	00 39
d	21 01	21 06	21 18	21 31	21 40	22 32	22 41	23 05	23 37	00 41
Kemble d			21 31				22 55			
Stroud d			21 46				23 10			
Stonehouse d			21 52				23 15			
Gloucester a			22 07				23 31			
Cheltenham Spa a			22 22							
Worcester Shrub Hill a										
Chippenham d	21 16	21a22		21 46		22 47			23 52	00 56
Bath Spa a	21 29			21 59		23 00			00 05	01 09
Bristol Parkway a					22 04			23 29		
d					22 12			23 34		
Bristol Temple Meads a	21 44			22 14		23 15			00 20	01 24
Weston-super-Mare a				22s47						
Taunton a				23 16						
Newport (South Wales) a					22 44			00 01		
Cardiff Central 128 a					23 05			00 23		
Bridgend 128 a					23 28					
Port Talbot Parkway 128 a					23 40					
Neath 128 a					23 48					
Swansea 128 a					00 03					

Saturdays
15 September to 8 December

	GW	GW	GW	GW	GW	GW	GW	GW	GW	GW	GW
		◇1	◇1		◇1	◇1	◇1	■ 1		◇1	◇1
	C	D	D				E	F	G		
		☕	☕		☕	☕		☕		☕	☕
LonPaddington ⊖117,116 d					06 30	07 00		07 30		07 45	08 00
Slough 117,116 d											
Reading 117,116 d			00 10		06 58	07 28		07 58		08 12	08 30
Didcot Parkway 116 d			00 29		07 13			08 13			
Swindon a			00 45		07 29	07 54		08 29		08 39	08 56
d			00 47	07 16	07 31	07 56		08 31	08 36	08 41	08 58
Kemble d				07 30							
Stroud d	00 05			07 45							
Stonehouse d	00 10			07 50							
Gloucester a	00 28			08 05							
Cheltenham Spa a	00 43			08 20							
Worcester Shrub Hill a											
Chippenham d			01 02		07 46	08 11		08 46	08a52		09 13
Bath Spa a			01 16		07 59	08 24		08 59			09 26
Bristol Parkway a										09 04	
d		00 15					07 10			09 09	
Bristol Temple Meads a			01 30		08 14	08 40		09 14			09 41
Weston-super-Mare a											
Taunton a								09 48			
Newport (South Wales) a		00 36	02s10				07 31			09 29	
Cardiff Central 128 a		00 51	02 31				07 47			09 46	
Bridgend 128 a		01 16					08 09			10 09	
Port Talbot Parkway 128 a		01 28					08 22			10 21	
Neath 128 a		01 37					08 30			10 29	
Swansea 128 a		01 50					08 44			10 43	

	GW	GW	GW	GW	GW	GW	GW	GW	GW	GW	GW
	◇1	◇1	◇1	◇1		◇1		◇1	◇1	◇1	◇1
							G				
	☕	☕	☕	☕		☕		☕	☕	☕	☕
LonPaddington ⊖117,116 d	08 15	08 30	08 45	09 00		09 30		09 45	10 00	10 15	10 30
Slough 117,116 d											
Reading 117,116 d	08 42	08 58	09 12	09 28		09 58		10 12	10 28	10 42	10 58
Didcot Parkway 116 d	08 57	09 13				10 14				10 57	11 13
Swindon a	09 14	09 29	09 39	09 54		10 30		10 39	10 54	11 14	11 29
d	09 16	09 31	09 40	09 56	10 14	10 32	10 36	10 41	10 56	11 16	11 31
Kemble d	09 30				10 28					11 30	
Stroud d	09 45				10 43					11 45	
Stonehouse d	09 51				10 48					11 51	
Gloucester a	10 06				11 04					12 06	
Cheltenham Spa a	10 22				11 20					12 22	
Worcester Shrub Hill a											
Chippenham d		09 46		10 11		10 47	10a52		11 11		11 46
Bath Spa a		09 59		10 24		11 00			11 24		11 59
Bristol Parkway a			10 05					11 04			
d			10 09					11 09			
Bristol Temple Meads a		10 14		10 39		11 15			11 39		12 14
Weston-super-Mare a											
Taunton a											
Newport (South Wales) a			10 30					11 30			
Cardiff Central 128 a			10 45					11 45			
Bridgend 128 a			11 09					12 09			
Port Talbot Parkway 128 a			11 21					12 21			
Neath 128 a			11 29					12 29			
Swansea 128 a			11 43					12 43			

A From Cheltenham Spa to Westbury
B To Exeter St Davids
C From Swindon
D From London Paddington
E From Bristol Temple Meads
F To Penzance
G To Westbury

For connections to/from:
Oxford - refer to Table T116; Gatwick Airport - refer to Table T148; Table T117 for Services via London Paddington

For principal services between: London & Taunton - refer to Table T135; London & Worcester - refer to Table T126

London - Swindon, Cheltenham Spa, Bristol, Weston-super-Mare and South Wales

	GW ◇1 ⊡	GW ◇1 ⊡	GW	GW ◇1 ⊡	GW A	GW ◇1 ⊡	GW ◇1 ⊡	GW ◇1 ⊡	GW ◇1 ⊡	GW ◇1 ⊡
LonPaddington ⊖117,116 d	10 45	11 00		11 30		11 45	12 00	12 15	12 30	12 45
Slough 117,116 d										
Reading 117,116 d	11 12	11 28		11 58		12 12	12 29	12 42	12 58	13 12
Didcot Parkway 116 d				12 13				12 57	13 13	
Swindon a	11 39	11 54		12 29		12 39	12 56	13 14	13 29	13 39
d	11 40	11 56	12 14	12 31	12 36	12 41	12 57	13 16	13 31	13 40
Kemble d			12 28					13 30		
Stroud d			12 43					13 45		
Stonehouse d			12 48					13 51		
Gloucester a			13 04					14 06		
Cheltenham Spa a			13 20					14 22		
Worcester Shrub Hill a										
Chippenham d		12 11		12 46	12a52		13 12		13 46	
Bath Spa a		12 24		12 59			13 25		13 59	
Bristol Parkway a	12 04					13 04				14 04
d	12 09					13 09				14 09
Bristol Temple Meads a		12 40		13 14			13 41		14 14	
Weston-super-Mare a										
Taunton a										
Newport (South Wales) a	12 30					13 30				14 30
Cardiff Central 128 a	12 45					13 45				14 45
Bridgend 128 a	13 09					14 09				15 09
Port Talbot Parkway 128 a	13 21					14 21				15 21
Neath 128 a	13 29					14 29				15 29
Swansea 128 a	13 43					14 43				15 43

	GW ◇1 ⊡	GW	GW ◇1 ⊡	GW A	GW ◇1 ⊡	GW ◇1 ⊡	GW ◇1 ⊡	GW A	GW ◇1 ⊡	GW ◇1 ⊡	GW ◇1 ⊡
LonPaddington ⊖117,116 d	13 00		13 30		13 45	14 00	14 15		14 30	14 45	15 00
Slough 117,116 d											
Reading 117,116 d	13 28		13 58		14 12	14 28	14 42		14 58	15 12	15 28
Didcot Parkway 116 d			14 13				14 57		15 13		
Swindon a	13 54		14 29		14 39	14 54	15 14		15 29	15 39	15 54
d	13 56	14 14	14 31	14 36	14 41	14 56	15 16	15 22	15 31	15 40	15 56
Kemble d		14 28					15 30				
Stroud d		14 43					15 45				
Stonehouse d		14 48					15 51				
Gloucester a		15 03					16 06				
Cheltenham Spa a		15 20					16 22				
Worcester Shrub Hill a											
Chippenham d	14 11		14 46	14a52		15 11		15a38	15 46		16 11
Bath Spa a	14 24		15 00			15 27			15 59		16 24
Bristol Parkway a					15 04					16 04	
d					15 09					16 09	
Bristol Temple Meads a	14 39		15 14			15 41			16 14		16 39
Weston-super-Mare a											
Taunton a											
Newport (South Wales) a					15 30					16 30	
Cardiff Central 128 a					15 45					16 44	
Bridgend 128 a					16 09					17 09	
Port Talbot Parkway 128 a					16 21					17 21	
Neath 128 a					16 29					17 29	
Swansea 128 a					16 43					17 43	

	GW	GW ◇1 ⊡	GW ◇1 ⊡	GW ◇1 ⊡	GW ◇1 ⊡	GW ◇1 B ⊡	GW A	GW ◇1 ⊡	GW ◇1 ⊡	GW	GW ◇1 ⊡
LonPaddington ⊖117,116 d		15 30	15 45	16 00	16 15	16 30		16 45	17 00		17 30
Slough 117,116 d											
Reading 117,116 d		15 58	16 12	16 28	16 42	16 58		17 12	17 28		17 58
Didcot Parkway 116 d		16 14			16 56	17 13					18 13
Swindon a		16 30	16 39	16 54	17 15	17 29		17 39	17 54		18 29
d	16 14	16 32	16 40	16 56	17 16	17 31	17 36	17 41	17 56	18 14	18 31
Kemble d	16 28				17 30					18 28	
Stroud d	16 43				17 45					18 43	
Stonehouse d	16 48				17 50					18 48	
Gloucester a	17 04				18 06					19 04	
Cheltenham Spa a	17 20				18 22					19 20	
Worcester Shrub Hill a											
Chippenham d		16 47		17 11		17 46	17a52		18 11		18 46
Bath Spa a		17 00		17 24		17 59			18 24		18 59
Bristol Parkway a			17 04					18 04			
d			17 09					18 09			
Bristol Temple Meads a		17 15		17 39		18 14			18 41		19 14
Weston-super-Mare a						18 36					19 50
Taunton a						19 05					
Newport (South Wales) a			17 31					18 30			
Cardiff Central 128 a			17 46					18 47			
Bridgend 128 a			18 09					19 09			
Port Talbot Parkway 128 a			18 21					19 21			
Neath 128 a			18 29					19 29			
Swansea 128 a			18 46					19 43			

	GW ◇1 C ⊡	GW ◇1 ⊡	GW ◇1 ⊡	XC ◇1 D	GW ◇1 ⊡	GW A	GW ◇1 ⊡	GW ◇1 ⊡	GW	GW ◇1 ⊡	GW ◇1 ⊡
LonPaddington ⊖117,116 d	17 45	18 00	18 15		18 30		18 45	19 00		19 15	19 30
Slough 117,116 d											
Reading 117,116 d	18 12	18 28	18 42		18 58		19 12	19 28		19 42	19 58
Didcot Parkway 116 d			18 56		19 13					19 57	20 13
Swindon a	18 39	18 54	19 15		19 29		19 39	19 54		20 14	20 29
d	18 40	18 56	19 16		19 31	19 36	19 41	19 56	20 00	20 16	20 31
Kemble d			19 30						20 14		
Stroud d			19 45						20 29		
Stonehouse d			19 50						20 34		
Gloucester a			20 06						20 50		
Cheltenham Spa a			20 22						21 04		
Worcester Shrub Hill a											
Chippenham d		19 11			19 46	19a52		20 11			20 46
Bath Spa a		19 24			20 00			20 24			20 59
Bristol Parkway a	19 04						20 04			20 39	
d	19 08			19 56			20 09			20 43	
Bristol Temple Meads a		19 40		20 05	20 14			20 40			21 14
Weston-super-Mare a					20 36			21 27			
Taunton a					21 01			21 59			
Newport (South Wales) a	19 30			20 44			20 30			21 04	
Cardiff Central 128 a	19 44			21 00			20 44			21 18	
Bridgend 128 a	20 09						21 09			21 45	
Port Talbot Parkway 128 a	20 21						21 21			21 58	
Neath 128 a	20 29						21 29			22 05	
Swansea 128 a	20 42						21 43			22 20	

A To Westbury
B To Paignton. The Torbay Express
C To Carmarthen
D From Manchester Piccadilly. ⊼ to Bristol Temple Meads

For connections to/from:
Oxford - refer to Table T116; Gatwick Airport - refer to Table T148; Table T117 for Services via London Paddington

For principal services between: London & Taunton - refer to Table T135; London & Worcester - refer to Table T126

London - Swindon, Cheltenham Spa, Bristol, Weston-super-Mare and South Wales

	GW ◇1 ⊡	GW ◇1 ⊡	GW A	GW ◇1 ⊡	GW ◇1 B ⊡	GW ◇1 ⊡	GW ◇1 ⊡	GW	GW ◇1 ⊡	GW ◇1 ⊡	GW ◇1 ⊡
LonPaddington ⊖117,116 d	19 45	20 00		20 15	20 30	20 45	21 32		22 00	22 35	23 30
Slough 117,116 d											
Reading 117,116 d	20 12	20 28		20 42	20 58	21 12	21 59		22 29	23 02	00 05
Didcot Parkway 116 d		20 43		20 57	21 13		22 14		22 44	23 18	00 22
Swindon a	20 39	20 59		21 14	21 29	21 39	22 30		23 01	23 35	00 39
d	20 41	21 01	21 06	21 18	21 31	21 40	22 32	22 41	23 05	23 37	00 41
Kemble d				21 31				22 55			
Stroud d				21 46				23 10			
Stonehouse d				21 52				23 15			
Gloucester a				22 07				23 31			
Cheltenham Spa a				22 22							
Worcester Shrub Hill a											
Chippenham d		21 16	21a22		21 46		22 47			23 52	00 56
Bath Spa a		21 29			21 59		23 00			00 05	01 09
Bristol Parkway a	21 04					22 04			23 29		
d	21 09					22 12			23 34		
Bristol Temple Meads a		21 44			22 14		23 15			00 20	01 24
Weston-super-Mare a					22s47						
Taunton a					23 16						
Newport (South Wales) a	21 30					22 44			00 01		
Cardiff Central 128 a	21 48					23 05			00 23		
Bridgend 128 a	22 10					23 28					
Port Talbot Parkway 128 a	22 22					23 40					
Neath 128 a	22 30					23 48					
Swansea 128 a	22 44					00 03					

Sundays
20 May to 9 September

	GW ◇1 C ⊡	GW ◇1 D ⊡	GW E	GW ◇1 ⊡	GW ◇1 ⊡	GW ◇1 ⊡	GW ◇1 F ⊡	GW	GW ◇1 ⊡	GW E	GW ◇1 ⊡
LonPaddington ⊖117,116 d		07 57		08 27	08 30	09 00	09 30		10 00		10 27
Slough 117,116 d											
Reading 117,116 d	00 05	08 38		09 03	09 10	09 39	10 09		10 39		11 04
Didcot Parkway 116 d	00 22	08 54			09 26	09 51			10 54		
Swindon a	00 39	09 12		09 36	09 43	10 08	10 35		11 11		11 36
d	00 41	09 13	09 22	09 37	09 44	10 10	10 37	10 44	11 12	11 28	11 37
Kemble d				09 50				10 58			11 50
Stroud d				10 06				11 13			12 05
Stonehouse d				10 11				11 18			12 09
Gloucester a				10 27				11 33			12 27
Cheltenham Spa a				10 43				11 47			12 45
Worcester Shrub Hill a											
Chippenham d	00 56	09 28	09a37			10 25			11 27	11a43	
Bath Spa a	01 09	09 41				10 38			11 41		
Bristol Parkway a					10 09		11 01				
d					10 10		11 02				
Bristol Temple Meads a	01 24	09 55				10 54			11 57		
Weston-super-Mare a						11 18			12 33		
Taunton a		10 34									
Newport (South Wales) a					10 29		11 24				
Cardiff Central 128 a					10 52		11 48				
Bridgend 128 a					11 14		12 10				
Port Talbot Parkway 128 a					11 27		12 23				
Neath 128 a					11 36		12 30				
Swansea 128 a					11 49		12 44				

	GW ◇1 ⊡	GW ◇1 ⊡	GW ◇1 F ⊡	GW ◇1 ⊡	GW G	GW ◇1 ⊡	GW ◇1 ⊡	GW ◇1 H ⊡	GW	GW ◇1 F ⊡	GW 1 ⊡
LonPaddington ⊖117,116 d	10 30	11 00	11 30	12 00		12 27	12 30	13 00		13 30	14 00
Slough 117,116 d											
Reading 117,116 d	11 09	11 39	12 08	12 39		13 04	13 09	13 39		14 08	14 39
Didcot Parkway 116 d	11 24	11 54	12 24	12 54			13 23	13 54		14 24	14 54
Swindon a	11 43	12 11	12 39	13 11		13 36	13 38	14 11		14 39	15 11
d	11 43	12 12	12 42	13 12	13 30	13 37	13 40	14 12	14 29	14 42	15 12
Kemble d						13 50			14 44		
Stroud d						14 05			14 59		
Stonehouse d						14 09			15 04		
Gloucester a						14 27			15 19		
Cheltenham Spa a						14 46			15 33		
Worcester Shrub Hill a											
Chippenham d		12 27		13 27	13a46			14 26			15 27
Bath Spa a		12 41		13 41				14 40			15 41
Bristol Parkway a	12 08		13 05				14 06			15 06	
d	12 10		13 09				14 07			15 09	
Bristol Temple Meads a		12 57		13 57				14 55			15 56
Weston-super-Mare a				14 37							
Taunton a								15 29			
Newport (South Wales) a	12 29		13 32				14 30			15 30	
Cardiff Central 128 a	12 49		13 56				14 52			15 53	
Bridgend 128 a	13 11		14 16				15 16			16 16	
Port Talbot Parkway 128 a	13 23		14 30				15 28			16 28	
Neath 128 a	13 31		14 38				15 36			16 36	
Swansea 128 a	13 46		14 53				15 51			16 49	

A From Cheltenham Spa to Westbury
B To Exeter St Davids
C not 20 May. From London Paddington
D To Penzance
E To Westbury
F To Carmarthen
G To Weymouth
H To Plymouth

For connections to/from:
Oxford - refer to Table T116; Gatwick Airport - refer to Table T148; Table T117 for Services via London Paddington

For principal services between: London & Taunton - refer to Table T135; London & Worcester - refer to Table T126

Sundays

20 May to 9 September

London - Swindon, Cheltenham Spa, Bristol, Weston-super-Mare and South Wales

	GW	GW	GW	GW	GW	GW	GW	GW	GW	GW	GW	GW	GW	GW	GW	GW	GW	GW	GW	GW	GW
		◇■	◇■	◇■	■ ■	◇■	◇■	■ ■		◇■	◇■	◇■	■ ■	■ ■		◇■	■ ■	◇■	◇■	◇■	
	A								A												A
		⊡	⊡	⊡	⊡	⊡	⊡	⊡		⊡	⊡	⊡	⊡	⊡		⊡	⊡	⊡	⊡	⊡	
LonPaddington ■ ⊖117,116 d		14 22	14 27	14 30	15 00	15 27	15 30	16 00		16 22	16 27	16 30	17 00	17 27		17 30	18 00	18 22	18 27	18 30	
Slough ■ 117,116 d																					
Reading ■ 117,116 d		14 59	15 06	15 10	15 39	16 06	16 07	16 39		16 59	17 06	17 07	17 39	18 06		18 07	18 39	18 59	19 06	19 07	
Didcot Parkway 116 d				15 25	15 54		16 22	16 54				17 23	17 54			18 24	18 54			19 23	
Swindon a		15 29	15 31	15 41	16 11	16 31	16 39	17 11		17 28	17 31	17 41	18 11	18 31		18 43	19 11	19 28	19 31	19 41	
d	15 28	15 33	15 33	15 44	16 12	16 33	16 43	17 12	17 18	17 33	17 33	17 43	18 12	18 33	18 42	18 43	19 12	19 32	19 33	19 43	19 55
Kemble d		15 46								17 46					18 56			19 46			
Stroud d		16 00								18 00					19 10			20 00			
Stonehouse d		16 05								18 05					19 15			20 05			
Gloucester ■ a		16 27								18 25					19 34			20 27			
Cheltenham Spa ■ a		16 47								18 40								20 45			
Worcester Shrub Hill a																					
Chippenham d	15a43		15 47		16 27	16 47		17 27	17a33		17 47		18 27	18 47			19 27		19 47		20a10
Bath Spa ■ a			16 02		16 41	17 02		17 41			18 02		18 41	19 02			19 41		20 02		
Bristol Parkway ■ a				16 08			17 07					18 07				19 07				20 07	
d				16 10			17 09					18 09				19 09				20 09	
Bristol Temple Meads ■ a			16 18		16 55	17 18		17 58			18 18		18 56	19 20			19 56		20 21		
Weston-super-Mare a					17 25									19 57							
Taunton a					18 01																
Newport (South Wales) a				16 35			17 38					18 30				19 31				20 31	
Cardiff Central ■ 128 a				16 57			18 00					18 51				19 51				20 53	
Bridgend 128 a				17 20			18 22					19 14				20 13				21 17	
Port Talbot Parkway 128 a				17 31			18 36					19 28				20 26				21 30	
Neath 128 a				17 40			18 44					19 36				20 33				21 37	
Swansea 128 a				17 54			18 57					19 50				20 48				21 50	

	GW	GW	GW	GW	GW	GW	GW	GW	GW	GW	GW	GW	GW	GW
	◇■	◇■		◇■	◇■	◇■	◇■	◇■	◇■	◇■		◇■	◇■	◇■
		B	C											
	⊡	⊡		⊡	⊡	⊡	⊡	⊡	⊡	⊡		⊡	⊡	⊡
LonPaddington ■ ⊖117,116 d	19 00	19 03		19 27	19 30	20 00	20 22	20 30	21 00	21 30		22 00	23 03	23 37
Slough ■ 117,116 d														23 57
Reading ■ 117,116 d	19 38	19 39		20 06	20 07	20 39	21 00	21 09	21 39	22 09		22 39	23 46	00 20
Didcot Parkway 116 d		19 54			20 23	20 54		21 22	21 54	22 23		22 54	00s02	00s35
Swindon a	20 02	20 10		20 31	20 40	21 11	21 28	21 40	22 11	22 41		23 11	00s21	00s55
d	20 06	20 12	20 28	20 33	20 42	21 12	21 30	21 42	22 12	22 42	22 57	23 12		
Kemble d			20 41				21 44				23 11			
Stroud d			20 56				21 59				23 26			
Stonehouse d			21 00				22 05				23 31			
Gloucester ■ a			21 15				22 20				23 46			
Cheltenham Spa ■ a			21 28				22 35				00 05			
Worcester Shrub Hill a														
Chippenham d		20 27		20 47		21 27			22 27			23 27	00s35	01s10
Bath Spa ■ a		20 40		21 02		21 39			22 41			23 41	00s50	01s24
Bristol Parkway ■ a	20 34				21 08			22 07		23 09				
d	20 35				21 09			22 09		23 11				
Bristol Temple Meads ■ a		20 55		21 17		21 54			22 57			23 57	01 06	01 39
Weston-super-Mare a		21 28				22 32								
Taunton a		21 51												
Newport (South Wales) a	20 52				21 28			22 31		23 34				
Cardiff Central ■ 128 a	21 16				21 52			22 58		23 56				
Bridgend 128 a	21 38				22 15			23 19		00 18				
Port Talbot Parkway 128 a	21 51				22 28			23 33		00 31				
Neath 128 a	22 00				22 35			23 41		00 39				
Swansea 128 a	22 13				22 49			23 55		00 53				

A To Westbury
B To Exeter St Davids
C From Westbury

For connections to/from:
Oxford - refer to Table T116; Gatwick Airport - refer to Table T148; Table T117 for Services via London Paddington

For principal services between: London & Taunton - refer to Table T135; London & Worcester - refer to Table T126

Sundays

16 September to 2 December

London - Swindon, Cheltenham Spa, Bristol, Weston-super-Mare and South Wales

	GW	GW	GW	GW	GW	GW	GW	GW	GW	GW	GW	GW	GW	GW	GW	GW	GW	GW	GW	GW	GW	GW
	◇■	◇■		◇■	◇■	◇■	◇■		◇■		◇■	◇■	◇■	◇■	◇■	◇■		◇■	◇■			◇■
	A	B	C				D			C				D			E		F	G	H	D
	⊡	⊡		⊡	⊡	⊡	⊡		⊡		⊡	⊡	⊡	⊡	⊡	⊡		⊡	⊡			⊡
LonPaddington ■ ⊖117,116 d		08 00		08 27	08 33	09 03	09 33		10 03		10 27	10 33	11 03	11 33	12 03	12 27		12 33	13 03			13 33
Slough ■ 117,116 d																						
Reading ■ 117,116 d	00 05	08 39		09 03	09 15	09 39	10 10		10 39		11 04	11 08	11 39	12 08	12 39	13 03		13 09	13 39			14 10
Didcot Parkway 116 d	00 22	08 58			09 32	09 54			10 54			11 23	11 54	12 23	12 54			13 24	13 54			14 26
Swindon a	00 39	09 17		09 36	09 49	10 11	10 36		11 11		11 36	11 42	12 11	12 39	13 11	13 32		13 40	14 11			14 41
d	00 41	09 17	09 26	09 37	09 50	10 12	10 38	10 44	11 12	11 28	11 37	11 42	12 12	12 41	13 12	13 33	13 38	13 41	14 12	14 25	14 25	14 44
Kemble d				09 50				10 58			11 50					13 46				14 40	14 40	
Stroud d				10 05				11 13			12 05					13 59				14 55	14 55	
Stonehouse d				10 11				11 18			12 09					14 05				15 00	15 00	
Gloucester ■ a				10 27				11 33			12 27					14 27				15 16	15 18	
Cheltenham Spa ■ a				10 43				11 47			12 45					14 45				15 33	15 33	
Worcester Shrub Hill a																						
Chippenham d	00 56	09 32	09a41			10 27			11 28	11a43			12 27		13 27		13a54		14 27			
Bath Spa ■ a	01 09	09 46				10 41			11 41				12 41		13 41				14 41			
Bristol Parkway ■ a					10 15		11 01					12 07		13 05				14 08				15 08
d					10 16		11 03					12 09		13 09				14 08				15 10
Bristol Temple Meads ■ a	01 24	10 00				10 58			11 56				12 56		13 57				14 55			
Weston-super-Mare a									12 33						14 32							
Taunton a		10 34																	15 29			
Newport (South Wales) a					10 35		11 24					12 28		13 32				14 31				15 31
Cardiff Central ■ 128 a					10 59		11 46					12 50		13 56				14 53				15 55
Bridgend 128 a					11 22		12 09					13 13		14 17				15 18				16 19
Port Talbot Parkway 128 a					11 35		12 22					13 25		14 31				15 30				16 31
Neath 128 a					11 44		12 29					13 32		14 39				15 38				16 39
Swansea 128 a					11 57		12 43					13 48		14 54				15 53				16 54

	GW	GW	GW	GW	GW	GW	GW	GW	GW	GW	GW	GW	GW	GW	GW	GW	GW	GW	GW	GW	GW
	■ ■		■ ■	◇■	◇■	■ ■	■ ■	◇■	■ ■	■ ■	◇■	◇■		■ ■	■ ■		◇■	■ ■	■ ■	◇■	◇■
		C											C								
	⊡		⊡	⊡	⊡	⊡	⊡	⊡	⊡	⊡	⊡	⊡		⊡	⊡		⊡	⊡	⊡	⊡	⊡
LonPaddington ■ ⊖117,116 d	14 03		14 27	14 30	14 33	15 03	15 27	15 33	16 03	16 27	16 30	16 33		17 03	17 27		17 33	18 03	18 27	18 30	18 33
Slough ■ 117,116 d																					
Reading ■ 117,116 d	14 39		15 01	15 04	15 10	15 39	16 01	16 09	16 39	17 01	17 03	17 10		17 39	18 01		18 10	18 39	19 01	19 03	19 10
Didcot Parkway 116 d	14 54				15 25	15 54		16 23	16 54			17 25		17 54			18 27	18 54			19 25
Swindon a	15 11		15 27	15 32	15 41	16 11	16 27	16 39	17 11	17 27	17 34	17 41		18 11	18 27		18 43	19 11	19 27	19 34	19 41
d	15 12	15 28	15 30	15 33	15 44	16 12	16 28	16 44	17 12	17 28	17 36	17 44	17 52	18 12	18 28	18 42	18 46	19 12	19 28	19 36	19 44
Kemble d				15 46							17 50					18 56				19 50	
Stroud d				16 00							18 05					19 10				20 05	
Stonehouse d				16 05							18 10					19 15				20 10	
Gloucester ■ a				16 27							18 27					19 34				20 27	
Cheltenham Spa ■ a				16 47							18 46									20 45	
Worcester Shrub Hill a																					
Chippenham d	15 27	15a43	15 47			16 27	16 44		17 27	17 44			18a07	18 27	18 44			19 27	19 44		
Bath Spa ■ a	15 41		16 01			16 41	16 58		17 41	17 58				18 41	18 58			19 41	19 58		
Bristol Parkway ■ a					16 08			17 08				18 08					19 09				20 08
d					16 10			17 10				18 10					19 12				20 10
Bristol Temple Meads ■ a	15 56		16 18			16 56	17 14		17 56	18 14				18 56	19 17			20 00	20 14		
Weston-super-Mare a						17 29									19 57						
Taunton a						18 02															
Newport (South Wales) a					16 35			17 39				18 30					19 34				20 30
Cardiff Central ■ 128 a					16 59			18 01				18 52					19 55				20 53
Bridgend 128 a					17 23			18 24				19 15					20 18				21 18
Port Talbot Parkway 128 a					17 34			18 38				19 28					20 31				21 31
Neath 128 a					17 42			18 46				19 37					20 38				21 39
Swansea 128 a					17 57			18 59				19 50					20 53				21 51

A From London Paddington
B To Penzance
C To Westbury
D To Carmarthen
E To Weymouth
F To Plymouth
G from 28 October
H until 21 October

For connections to/from:
Oxford - refer to Table T116; Gatwick Airport - refer to Table T148; Table T117 for Services via London Paddington

For principal services between: London & Taunton - refer to Table T135; London & Worcester - refer to Table T126

Table T125-F

Sundays

16 September to 2 December

London - Swindon, Cheltenham Spa, Bristol, Weston-super-Mare and South Wales

		GW	GW	GW	GW	GW	GW	GW	GW	GW	GW	GW	GW	GW	GW	GW	GW	GW
		A	◇1 ⎍	◇1 B ⎍	◇1 ⎍	C	◇1 ⎍	◇1 ⎍	◇1 ⎍	◇1 ⎍	◇1 ⎍	◇1 ⎍	D	E	◇1 ⎍	◇1 ⎍	◇1 ⎍	◇1 ⎍
LonPaddington 15 ⊖117,116	d		19 00	19 03	19 27		19 33	20 03	20 27	20 34	21 03	21 33			22 03	22 37	23 03	23 37
Slough 3 117,116	d																	00 01
Reading 7 117,116	d		19 36	19 39	20 01		20 10	20 39	20 59	21 15	21 39	22 11			22 45	23 15	23 46	00 20
Didcot Parkway 116	d			19 54			20 25	20 54		21 29	21 54	22 25			23 02	23s32	00s02	00s35
Swindon	a		20 00	20 11	20 27		20 40	21 11	21 31	21 46	22 11	22 42			23 19	23s50	00s21	00s55
	d	19 53	20 02	20 12	20 28	20 33	20 43	21 12	21 33	21 47	22 12	22 43	22 57	22 57	23 20			
Kemble	d					20 47			21 47				23 11	23 11				
Stroud	d					21 01			22 02				23 26	23 26				
Stonehouse	d					21 06			22 08				23 31	23 31				
Gloucester 7	a					21 20			22 23				23 46	23 46				
Cheltenham Spa 4	a					21 34			22 38				00 06	00 07				
Worcester Shrub Hill	a																	
Chippenham	d	20a08		20 27	20 44			21 27			22 27				23 33		00s35	01s10
Bath Spa 7	a			20 41	20 58			21 41			22 40				23 48		00s50	01s24
Bristol Parkway 7	a		20 29				21 09			22 13		23 09				00 17		
	d		20 29				21 10			22 14		23 10						
Bristol Temple Meads 10	a			20 55	21 14			21 56			22 57				00 04		01 06	01 39
Weston-super-Mare	a			21 25				22 32										
Taunton	a			21 48														
Newport (South Wales)	a		20 46				21 29			22 36		23 34						
Cardiff Central 7 128	a		21 12				21 54			22 58		23 56						
Bridgend 128	a		21 35				22 18			23 19		00 18						
Port Talbot Parkway 128	a		21 48				22 31			23 33		00 31						
Neath 128	a		21 57				22 39			23 41		00 38						
Swansea 128	a		22 10				22 52			23 55		00 52						

A To Westbury
B To Exeter St Davids
C From Westbury
D until 21 October
E from 28 October

For connections to/from:
Oxford - refer to Table T116; Gatwick Airport - refer to Table T148; Table T117 for Services via London Paddington

For principal services between: London & Taunton - refer to Table T135; London & Worcester - refer to Table T126

Table T125-R

Mondays to Fridays

21 May to 7 December

South Wales, Weston-super-Mare, Bristol, Cheltenham Spa and Swindon - London

Miles	Miles	Miles			GW	GW	GW	GW	GW	GW	GW	GW	GW	GW	GW	GW	GW	GW	GW	GW	GW	GW	GW
					◇1 ⎍	A	◇1 ⎍	◇1 ⎍	1 ⎍	1 ⎍	◇1 ⎍	1 ⎍	1 ⎍	◇1 ⎍	1 ⎍	B	1 C ✕	1 D ⎍	E	◇1 F ⎍	◇1 ⎍	◇1 G ⎍	◇1 ⎍
0	—	—	**Swansea** 128	d				03 54		04 58			05 29				05 59			06 29			06 59
9½	—	—	Neath 128	d				04 06		05 10			05 41				06 11			06 41			07 11
15	—	—	Port Talbot Parkway 128	d				04 14		05 18			05 49				06 19			06 49			07 19
27¼	—	—	Bridgend 128	d				04 27		05 31			06 02				06 32			07 02			07 32
47½	—	—	**Cardiff Central** 7 128	d				05 15		05 55			06 26				06 56			07 26			07 56
59¼	—	—	Newport (South Wales)	d				05 33		06 09			06 40				07 10			07 40			08 10
—	0	—	Taunton	d																		06 57	
—	26¾	—	Weston-super-Mare	d											06 20			06 48				07 26	
—	45¾	—	**Bristol Temple Meads** 10	d	04 45		05 30		06 00			06 33			07 00			07 30				08 00	
81	—	—	Bristol Parkway 7	a	04 54			06 01		06 30			07 01				07 32			08 01			08 31
—	—	—		d	04 55			06 03		06 31			07 02				07 33			08 03			08 32
—	57¼	—	Bath Spa 7	d			05 43		06 13			06 46			07 13			07 43				08 13	
—	70	—	Chippenham	d			05 56		06 26			06 59			07 26	07 31		07 56	08 00			08 25	
—	—	—	Worcester Shrub Hill	d							05 28										07 08		
—	—	0	**Cheltenham Spa** 4	d							05 54			06 30							07 31		
—	—	6½	Gloucester 7	d		05 17					06 10			06 46							07 46		
—	—	15½	Stonehouse	d		05 30					06 24			07 00							08 00		
—	—	18	Stroud	d		05 35					06 31			07 06							08 06		
—	—	29¼	Kemble	d		05 49					06 46			07 21							08 21		
115½	86¾	43	**Swindon**	a	05 20	06 05	06 10	06 28	06 40	06 56	07 00	07 13	07 27	07 35	07 40	07 48	07 58	08 10	08 15	08 28	08 35	08 40	08 57
—	—	—		d	05 22		06 12	06 30	06 42	06 58	07 02	07 15	07 29	07 36	07 42		08 00	08 12		08 30	08 36	08 41	08 59
139½	110¾	67	Didcot Parkway 116	a	05 39		06 29	06 47	06 59		07 19		07 46	07 55	08 00			08 29			08 53	08 59	
156¾	128	84½	**Reading** 7 117,116	a	05 54		06 43	07 02	07 14	07 25	07 34	07 46	08 02	08 12	08 16			08 45		08 57	09 08	09 15	09 25
174¼	145½	101¾	Slough 3 117,116	a			06 59																
192¾	164	120¼	**LonPaddington** 15 ⊖117,116	a	06 22		07 17	07 30	07 44	07 59	08 06	08 14	08 32	08 42	08 44		08 55	09 12		09 25	09 37	09 43	09 55

		GW	GW	GW	GW	GW	GW	GW	GW	GW	GW	GW	GW	GW	GW	GW	GW	GW	GW	GW	GW	GW	GW
		H	◇1 ⎍	◇1 I ⎍	◇1 ⎍	◇1 ⎍	◇1 ⎍	◇1 ⎍		◇1 J ⎍	E	◇1 K ⎍	◇1 ⎍	◇1 ⎍	◇1 ⎍	◇1 ⎍	◇1 ⎍	◇1 ⎍	◇1 ⎍		◇1 ⎍	E	◇1 ⎍
Swansea 128	d			07 29			07 59			08 29					09 29						10 29		
Neath 128	d			07 41			08 11			08 41					09 41						10 41		
Port Talbot Parkway 128	d			07 49			08 19			08 49					09 49						10 49		
Bridgend 128	d			08 02			08 32			09 02					10 02						11 02		
Cardiff Central 7 128	d			08 26			08 56			09 26			09 56		10 26			10 56			11 26		
Newport (South Wales)	d			08 40			09 10			09 40			10 10		10 40			11 10			11 40		
Taunton	d		07 12									09 07											
Weston-super-Mare	d		07 49									09 29											
Bristol Temple Meads 10	d	08 12	08 30		09 00			09 30				10 00		10 30		11 00			11 30				12 00
Bristol Parkway 7	a			09 01			09 31			10 01			10 31		11 01			11 31			12 01		
	d			09 03			09 33			10 03			10 33		11 03			11 32			12 03		
Bath Spa 7	d	08 30	08 43		09 13			09 43				10 13		10 43		11 13			11 43				12 13
Chippenham	d	08 45	08 56		09 26			09 56			10 12	10 26		10 56		11 25			11 56			12 13	12 26
Worcester Shrub Hill	d																						
Cheltenham Spa 4	d					08 31			09 18								10 36			11 20			
Gloucester 7	d					08 48			09 32								10 51			11 34			
Stonehouse	d					09 01			09 47								11 06			11 50			
Stroud	d					09 08			09 52								11 13			11 55			
Kemble	d					09 22			10 07								11 27			12 09			
Swindon	a	09 02	09 10	09 28	09 40	09 41	09 58	10 10	10 23	10 28	10 32	10 41	10 58	11 10	11 28	11 40	11 42	11 57	12 10	12 23	12 28	12 32	12 41
	d		09 12	09 30	09 42	09 46	10 00	10 12		10 30		10 42	11 00	11 12	11 30	11 41	11 45	11 59	12 12		12 30		12 42
Didcot Parkway 116	a		09 29			10 03	10 17	10 29		10 47			11 17	11 29			12 02	12 16	12 29		12 47		
Reading 7 117,116	a		09 45	10 00	10 09	10 17	10 32	10 43		11 02		11 10	11 32	11 43	11 59	12 09	12 16	12 31	12 43		13 02		13 10
Slough 3 117,116	a																						
LonPaddington 15 ⊖117,116	a		10 14	10 37	10 39	10 45	11 00	11 12		11 32		11 37	12 00	12 14	12 30	12 37	12 44	13 01	13 12		13 32		13 37

A To Southampton Central
B From Westbury to Cheltenham Spa
C The Capitals United- Restaurant for customers joining to Swindon
D The Bristolian
E From Westbury
F ◇ from Reading ■ to Reading
G From Exeter St Davids
H From Gloucester
I Y Cymro - The Welshman
J From Carmarthen. The Red Dragon
K From Paignton

For connections to/from:
Oxford - refer to Table T116; Gatwick Airport - refer to Table T148; Table T117 for Services via London Paddington

For principal services between: London & Taunton - refer to Table T135; London & Worcester - refer to Table T126

Table T125-R

Mondays to Fridays

21 May to 7 December

South Wales, Weston-super-Mare, Bristol, Cheltenham Spa and Swindon - London

	GW ◇■ 🍴	GW A	GW ◇■ 🍴	GW ◇■ B 🍴	GW ◇■ 🍴	GW ◇■ 🍴	GW ◇■ 🍴	GW ◇■ 🍴	GW	GW ◇■ 🍴	GW ◇■ 🍴	GW ◇■ 🍴	GW C	GW ◇■ 🍴	GW ◇■ 🍴	GW ◇■ 🍴	GW ◇■ D 🍴	GW ◇■ 🍴	GW ◇■ 🍴	GW	GW ◇■ 🍴	GW ◇■ E 🍴
Swansea 128 d				11 29						12 29					13 29						14 29	
Neath 128 d				11 41						12 41					13 41						14 41	
Port Talbot Parkway 128 d				11 49						12 49					13 49						14 49	
Bridgend 128 d				12 02						13 02					14 02						15 02	
Cardiff Central ■ 128 d	11 56			12 26			12 56			13 26		13 56			14 26			14 56			15 26	
Newport (South Wales) d	12 10			12 40			13 10			13 40		14 10			14 40			15 10			15 40	
Taunton d																						
Weston-super-Mare d								13 01														
Bristol Temple Meads ■ d			12 30		13 00			13 30			14 00			14 30		15 00			15 30			16 00
Bristol Parkway ■ a	12 31			13 01			13 31			14 01		14 31			15 01			15 31			16 01	
d	12 33			13 03			13 33			14 03		14 33			15 03			15 33			16 03	
Bath Spa ■ d			12 43		13 13			13 43			14 13			14 43		15 13			15 43			16 13
Chippenham d		12 46	12 56		13 26			13 56			14 26		14 50	14 56		15 26			15 56			16 26
Worcester Shrub Hill d																						
Cheltenham Spa ■ d						12 36			13 20								14 36			15 20		
Gloucester ■ d						12 52			13 33								14 52			15 33		
Stonehouse d						13 07			13 47								15 07			15 47		
Stroud d						13 14			13 52								15 14			15 52		
Kemble d						13 29			14 07								15 29			16 07		
Swindon a	12 58	13 02	13 10	13 28	13 40	13 43	13 58	14 10	14 22	14 28	14 41	14 58	15 07	15 10	15 28	15 40	15 43	15 58	16 10	16 22	16 28	16 41
d	13 00		13 12	13 30	13 42	13 46	14 00	14 12		14 30	14 42	15 00		15 12	15 30	15 42	15 46	16 00	16 12		16 30	16 42
Didcot Parkway 116 a	13 17		13 29			14 02	14 17	14 29		14 47		15 17		15 29			16 03	16 17	16 29		16 47	
Reading ■ 117,116 a	13 32		13 44	13 57	14 08	14 17	14 32	14 44		15 02	15 11	15 32		15 44	15 57	16 09	16 16	16 32	16 44		17 02	17 10
Slough ■ 117,116 a																						
LonPaddington ■ ⊖117,116 a	14 07		14 14	14 30	14 37	14 46	15 02	15 14		15 30	15 40	16 01		16 14	16 29	16 40	16 44	17 02	17 12		17 30	17 39

	GW ◇■ 🍴	GW A	GW ◇■ 🍴	GW ◇■ 🍴	GW ◇■ 🍴	GW ◇■ 🍴	GW ◇■ 🍴	GW ◇■ 🍴	GW ◇■ 🍴	GW ◇■ 🍴	GW ◇ F	GW ◇■ 🍴	GW ◇■ 🍴	GW A	GW ◇■ 🍴	GW ◇■ 🍴	GW ◇■ 🍴	GW ◇ G	GW ◇■ 🍴	GW	GW ◇■ 🍴	GW FO ◇■ 🍴
Swansea 128 d				15 29					16 29						17 29				18 29			19 29
Neath 128 d				15 41					16 41						17 41				18 41			19 41
Port Talbot Parkway 128 d				15 49					16 49						17 49				18 49			19 49
Bridgend 128 d				16 02					17 02						18 02				19 02			20 02
Cardiff Central ■ 128 d	15 56			16 26			16 56		17 26			17 56			18 26				19 26			20 26
Newport (South Wales) d	16 10			16 40			17 10		17 40			18 10			18 40				19 40			20 40
Taunton d																						
Weston-super-Mare d								17 10					18 08									
Bristol Temple Meads ■ d			16 30			17 00		17 31		18 00			18 30				19 30				20 30	
Bristol Parkway ■ a	16 31			17 01			17 31		18 01			18 31			19 01				20 01			21 01
d	16 33			17 03			17 33		18 03			18 33			19 03				20 03			21 03
Bath Spa ■ d			16 43			17 13		17 44		18 13			18 43				19 43				20 43	
Chippenham d		16 47	16 56			17 26		17 57		18 26			18 56	19 01			19 56	20 01			20 56	
Worcester Shrub Hill d																						
Cheltenham Spa ■ d					16 20						17 41					18 33				20 01		
Gloucester ■ d					16 43						17 54					18 50				20 13		
Stonehouse d					16 58						18 07					19 05				20 26		
Stroud d					17 04						18 12					19 11				20 31		
Kemble d					17 19						18 27					19 25				20 46		
Swindon a	16 58	17 03	17 10	17 28	17 33	17 40	17 58	18 12	18 28	18 41	18 42	18 58	19 10	19 21	19 28	19 39	20 10	20 20	20 28	21 02	21 10	21 28
d	17 00		17 12	17 30	17 35	17 42	18 00	18 13	18 30	18 42		19 00	19 12		19 30	19 41	20 12		20 30		21 12	21 35
Didcot Parkway 116 a	17 17		17 29			17 59	18 18	18 30	18 47			19 17	19 29			19 58	20 29		20 47		21 29	21 52
Reading ■ 117,116 a	17 34		17 44	17 57	18 03	18 14	18 34	18 46	19 02	19 10		19 32	19 44		19 57	20 14	20 44		21 02		21 45	22 09
Slough ■ 117,116 a																						
LonPaddington ■ ⊖117,116 a	18 03		18 14	18 30	18 39	18 44	19 07	19 13	19 33	19 38		20 01	20 14		20 32	20 43	21 12		21 31		22 13	22 39

A From Westbury
B The St. David
C From Frome
D The Cheltenham Spa Express
E The Merchant Venturer
F To Southampton Central
G From Westbury to Cheltenham Spa

For connections to/from:
Oxford - refer to Table T116; Gatwick Airport - refer to Table T148; Table T117 for Services via London Paddington

For principal services between: London & Taunton - refer to Table T135; London & Worcester - refer to Table T126

Table T125-R

Mondays to Fridays

21 May to 7 December

South Wales, Weston-super-Mare, Bristol, Cheltenham Spa and Swindon - London

	GW FX ◇■ 🍴	GW	GW FX ◇■ 🍴	GW FO ◇■ 🍴	GW FX ◇■ A 🍴	GW FO ◇■ A 🍴	GW	GW ◇■ 🍴	LM FO B
Swansea 128 d	19 29		20 29	20 29					
Neath 128 d	19 41		20 41	20 41					
Port Talbot Parkway 128 d	19 49		20 49	20 49					
Bridgend 128 d	20 02		21 02	21 02					
Cardiff Central ■ 128 d	20 26		21 26	21 26					
Newport (South Wales) d	20 40		21 40	21 40					
Taunton d					21 15	21 15		21 28	
Weston-super-Mare d								21 58	
Bristol Temple Meads ■ d					21 50	21 51		22 35	
Bristol Parkway ■ a	21 01		22 01	22 01					
d	21 03		22 03	22 03					
Bath Spa ■ d					22 04	22 04		22 48	
Chippenham d					22 17	22 17		23 01	
Worcester Shrub Hill d									23 46
Cheltenham Spa ■ d		21 02					22 01		00 08
Gloucester ■ d		21 21					22 13		00a19
Stonehouse d		21 33					22 26		
Stroud d		21 38					22 32		
Kemble d		21 53					22 46		
Swindon a	21 28	22 09	22 28	22 28	22 32	22 32	23 03	23 15	
d	21 35		22 30	22 30	22 34	22 34		23 17	
Didcot Parkway 116 a	21 52				22 51	22 51		23 35	
Reading ■ 117,116 a	22 09		23 00	23 02	23 07	23 07		23 52	
Slough ■ 117,116 a									
LonPaddington ■ ⊖117,116 a	22 51		23 40	23 37	23 42	23 39		00 31	

Saturdays

26 May to 8 September

	LM B	GW ◇■ 🍴	GW	GW ◇■ 🍴	GW ◇■ 🍴	GW ◇■ 🍴	GW ◇■ 🍴	GW ◇■ 🍴	GW ◇■ 🍴	GW ◇■ 🍴	GW C	GW ◇■ 🍴	GW ◇■ 🍴	GW ◇■ 🍴	GW ◇■ 🍴	GW C	GW ◇■ 🍴	GW ◇■ 🍴	GW ◇■ D 🍴	GW ◇■ 🍴	GW ◇■ 🍴	GW C
Swansea 128 d				03 59	04 59		05 29		05 59			06 29			06 59			07 29				
Neath 128 d				04 11	05 11		05 41		06 11			06 41			07 11			07 41				
Port Talbot Parkway 128 d				04 19	05 19		05 49		06 19			06 49			07 19			07 49				
Bridgend 128 d				04 31	05 32		06 02		06 32			07 02			07 32			08 02				
Cardiff Central ■ 128 d				04 55	05 56		06 26		06 56			07 26			07 56			08 26				
Newport (South Wales) d				05 09	06 10		06 40		07 10			07 40			08 10			08 40				
Taunton d														06 54					07 59			
Weston-super-Mare d								06 23						07 24					08 29			
Bristol Temple Meads ■ d		05 30		06 00		06 30		07 00		07 30				08 00			08 30		09 00		09 30	
Bristol Parkway ■ a					06 30		07 00		07 30			08 00			08 30			09 00				
d					06 34		07 04		07 33			08 04			08 33			09 04				
Bath Spa ■ d		05 43		06 13		06 43		07 13		07 43				08 13			08 43		09 13		09 43	
Chippenham d		05 56		06 26		06 56		07 26		07 56	08 01			08 26		08 48	08 56		09 26		09 56	10 01
Worcester Shrub Hill d																				08 37		
Cheltenham Spa ■ d	00 08		05 30										07 31							09 00		
Gloucester ■ d	00a19		05 43										07 47							09 15		
Stonehouse d			05 56										08 01							09 29		
Stroud d			06 01										08 07							09 35		
Kemble d			06 16										08 21							09 49		
Swindon a		06 10	06 32	06 40	06 59	07 10	07 29	07 41	07 58	08 09	08 20	08 29	08 35	08 41	08 58	09 07	09 09	09 29	09 41	10 03	10 09	10 20
d		06 12		06 42	07 01	07 12	07 31	07 42	08 00	08 12		08 31	08 37	08 42	09 00		09 12	09 31	09 42	10 05	10 12	
Didcot Parkway 116 a		06 29		06 59		07 29		07 59	08 16	08 29			08 54	09 00	09 17		09 29			10 22	10 29	
Reading ■ 117,116 a		06 43		07 13	07 28	07 43	07 58	08 14	08 32	08 44		08 58	09 09	09 15	09 32		09 43	09 57	10 11	10 37	10 45	
Slough ■ 117,116 a																						
LonPaddington ■ ⊖117,116 a		07 14		07 41	07 59	08 14	08 30	08 44	08 59	09 14		09 30	09 41	09 44	09 59		10 14	10 29	10 39	11 07	11 14	

A From Penzance
B From Birmingham New Street
C From Westbury
D From Exeter St Davids

For connections to/from:
Oxford - refer to Table T116; Gatwick Airport - refer to Table T148; Table T117 for Services via London Paddington

For principal services between: London & Taunton - refer to Table T135; London & Worcester - refer to Table T126

Table T125-R

Saturdays
26 May to 8 September

South Wales, Weston-super-Mare, Bristol, Cheltenham Spa and Swindon - London

		GW	GW	GW	GW	GW	GW	GW	GW	GW	GW	GW	GW	GW	GW	GW	GW	GW	GW	GW	GW	GW
		◇■	◇■		◇■	◇■	◇■	◇■	◇■		◇■	◇■		◇■	◇■	◇■	◇■	◇■		◇■	◇■	
									A	B	C								B	D		
		☕	☕		☕	☕	☕	☕	☕		☕	☕		☕	☕	☕	☕	☕		☕	☕	
Swansea	128 d	08 29				09 29					10 29				11 29					12 29		
Neath	128 d	08 41				09 41					10 41				11 41					12 41		
Port Talbot Parkway	128 d	08 49				09 49					10 49				11 49					12 49		
Bridgend	128 d	09 02				10 02					11 02				12 02					13 02		
Cardiff Central ■	128 d	09 26				10 26					11 26				12 26					13 26		
Newport (South Wales)	d	09 40				10 40					11 40				12 40					13 40		
Taunton	d								10 45													
Weston-super-Mare	d											11 30						13 00				
Bristol Temple Meads ■	d		10 00		10 30		11 00		11 30			12 00		12 30		13 00		13 30			14 00	
Bristol Parkway ■	a	10 00				11 00					12 00				13 00					14 00		
	d	10 04				11 04					12 04				13 04					14 04		
Bath Spa ■	d		10 13		10 43		11 13		11 43			12 13		12 43		13 13		13 43			14 13	
Chippenham	d		10 26		10 56		11 26		11 56	12 01		12 26		12 56		13 26		13 56	14 01		14 26	
Worcester Shrub Hill	d																					
Cheltenham Spa ■	d			10 01				11 00					12 01				13 00					14 01
Gloucester ■	d			10 14				11 15					12 14				13 16					14 14
Stonehouse	d			10 27				11 29					12 27				13 30					14 27
Stroud	d			10 32				11 35					12 32				13 36					14 32
Kemble	d			10 47				11 49					12 47				13 50					14 47
Swindon	a	10 29	10 41	11 04	11 09	11 29	11 40	12 03	12 09	12 20	12 29	12 41	13 04	13 09	13 29	13 40	14 04	14 09	14 20	14 29	14 40	15 04
	d	10 31	10 42		11 12	11 31	11 42	12 05	12 12		12 31	12 42		13 12	13 31	13 42	14 05	14 12		14 31	14 42	
Didcot Parkway	116 a				11 29			12 22	12 29					13 29			14 23	14 29				
Reading ■	117,116 a	11 00	11 09		11 44	11 58	12 10	12 37	12 46		12 58	13 10		13 43	13 57	14 12	14 37	14 43		14 59	15 08	
Slough ■	117,116 a																					
LonPaddington ■	⊖117,116 a	11 31	11 40		12 14	12 29	12 38	13 07	13 14		13 31	13 38		14 14	14 29	14 41	15 07	15 14		15 32	15 41	

		GW	GW	GW	GW	GW	GW	GW	GW	GW	GW	GW	GW	GW	GW	GW	GW	GW	GW	GW	GW	GW	GW
		◇■	◇■	◇■		◇■	◇■	◇■	◇■		◇■		◇■	◇■	◇■	◇■	◇■	◇■		◇■		◇■	◇■
					B							B									B	E	
		☕	☕	☕		☕	☕	☕	☕		☕		☕	☕	☕	☕	☕	☕		☕		☕	☕
Swansea	128 d		13 29					14 29					15 29				16 29					17 29	
Neath	128 d		13 41					14 41					15 41				16 41					17 41	
Port Talbot Parkway	128 d		13 49					14 49					15 49				16 49					17 49	
Bridgend	128 d		14 02					15 02					16 02				17 02					18 02	
Cardiff Central ■	128 d		14 26					15 26					16 26				17 26					18 26	
Newport (South Wales)	d		14 40					15 40					16 40				17 40					18 40	
Taunton	d																						
Weston-super-Mare	d						15 00									17 00				18 00			
Bristol Temple Meads ■	d	14 30		15 00			15 30		16 00		16 30			17 00		17 30		18 00		18 30			
Bristol Parkway ■	a		15 01					16 00					17 00				18 00					19 00	
	d		15 04					16 04					17 04				18 04					19 03	
Bath Spa ■	d	14 43		15 13			15 43		16 13		16 43			17 13		17 43		18 13		18 43			
Chippenham	d	14 56		15 26	15 32		15 56		16 26		16 56	17 01		17 26		17 56		18 26		18 56	19 01		
Worcester Shrub Hill	d																						
Cheltenham Spa ■	d					15 00				16 01					17 00				18 01				19 00
Gloucester ■	d					15 15				16 14					17 16				18 14				19 16
Stonehouse	d					15 29				16 27					17 30				18 27				19 30
Stroud	d					15 35				16 32					17 36				18 32				19 36
Kemble	d					15 49				16 47					17 50				18 47				19 50
Swindon	a	15 09	15 29	15 40	15 50	16 03	16 09	16 29	16 40	17 04	17 09	17 22	17 29	17 41	18 04	18 09	18 29	18 40	19 04	19 09	19 22	19 29	20 04
	d	15 12	15 31	15 42		16 05	16 12	16 31	16 42		17 12		17 31	17 42	18 06	18 12	18 31	18 42		19 12		19 29	20 06
Didcot Parkway	116 a	15 29				16 22	16 29				17 29				18 23	18 29				19 29			20 23
Reading ■	117,116 a	15 43	15 59	16 10		16 37	16 46	16 58	17 09		17 43		17 58	18 09	18 37	18 45	18 58	19 09		19 43		19 58	20 38
Slough ■	117,116 a																						
LonPaddington ■	⊖117,116 a	16 14	16 29	16 38		17 07	17 14	17 29	17 38		18 15		18 31	18 37	19 06	19 14	19 29	19 37		20 14		20 30	21 06

A From Paignton. The Torbay Express
B From Westbury
C From Carmarthen
D From Pembroke Dock. The Pembroke Coast Express
E From Pembroke Dock

For connections to/from:
Oxford - refer to Table T116; Gatwick Airport - refer to Table T148; Table T117 for Services via London Paddington

For principal services between: London & Taunton - refer to Table T135; London & Worcester - refer to Table T126

Table T125-R

Saturdays
26 May to 8 September

South Wales, Weston-super-Mare, Bristol, Cheltenham Spa and Swindon - London

		GW	GW	GW	GW	GW	GW	GW	GW
		◇■	◇■		◇■	◇■		◇■	◇■
				A				B	
		☕	☕		☕	☕		☕	☕
Swansea	128 d		18 29			19 29			
Neath	128 d		18 41			19 41			
Port Talbot Parkway	128 d		18 49			19 49			
Bridgend	128 d		19 02			20 02			
Cardiff Central ■	128 d		19 26			20 26			
Newport (South Wales)	d		19 40			20 40			
Taunton	d							21 14	21 30
Weston-super-Mare	d				20 10				21 53
Bristol Temple Meads ■	d	19 30			20 33			21 47	22 30
Bristol Parkway ■	a		20 00			21 00			
	d		20 04			21 03			
Bath Spa ■	d	19 43			20 46			22 03	22 45
Chippenham	d	19 56			20 59			22 16	22 58
Worcester Shrub Hill	d								
Cheltenham Spa ■	d			20 02			21 20		
Gloucester ■	d			20 14			21 35		
Stonehouse	d			20 27			21 48		
Stroud	d			20 32			21 53		
Kemble	d			20 47			22 08		
Swindon	a	20 09	20 29	21 03	21 12	21 28	22 25	22 30	23 13
	d	20 12	20 31		21 15	21 30		22 32	23 14
Didcot Parkway	116 a	20 29			21 32	21 47		22 49	23 32
Reading ■	117,116 a	20 44	20 57		21 46	22 02		23 03	23 48
Slough ■	117,116 a								
LonPaddington ■	⊖117,116 a	21 14	21 28		22 14	22 38		23 43	00 33

Saturdays
15 September to 8 December

		LM	GW	GW	GW	GW	GW	GW	GW	GW	GW	GW	GW	GW	GW	GW	GW	GW	GW	GW	GW	GW	GW
			◇■		◇■	◇■	◇■	◇■	◇■	◇■	◇■		◇■	◇■	◇■	◇■		◇■	◇■	◇■	◇■	◇■	◇■
		C										D					D			E			
			☕		☕	☕	☕	☕	☕	☕	☕		☕	☕	☕	☕		☕	☕	☕	☕	☕	☕
Swansea	128 d				03 59	04 59		05 29		05 59			06 29			06 59			07 29		07 59		
Neath	128 d				04 11	05 11		05 41		06 11			06 41			07 11			07 41		08 11		
Port Talbot Parkway	128 d				04 19	05 19		05 49		06 19			06 49			07 19			07 49		08 19		
Bridgend	128 d				04 31	05 32		06 02		06 32			07 02			07 32			08 02		08 32		
Cardiff Central ■	128 d				04 55	05 56		06 26		06 56			07 26			07 56			08 26		08 56		
Newport (South Wales)	d				05 09	06 10		06 40		07 10			07 40			08 10			08 40		09 10		
Taunton	d														06 54					07 59			
Weston-super-Mare	d								06 23						07 24					08 29			
Bristol Temple Meads ■	d		05 30		06 00		06 30		07 00		07 30				08 00			08 30		09 00			09 30
Bristol Parkway ■	a					06 30		07 00		07 30			08 00			08 30			09 00		09 30		
	d					06 34		07 04		07 33			08 04			08 33			09 04		09 33		
Bath Spa ■	d		05 43		06 13		06 43		07 13		07 43				08 13			08 43		09 13			09 43
Chippenham	d		05 56		06 26		06 56		07 26		07 56	08 01			08 26		08 48	08 56		09 26			09 56
Worcester Shrub Hill	d																					08 37	
Cheltenham Spa ■	d	00 08		05 30										07 31								09 00	
Gloucester ■	d	00a19		05 43										07 47								09 15	
Stonehouse	d			05 56										08 01								09 29	
Stroud	d			06 01										08 07								09 35	
Kemble	d			06 16										08 21								09 49	
Swindon	a		06 10	06 32	06 40	06 59	07 10	07 29	07 41	07 58	08 09	08 20	08 29	08 35	08 41	08 58	09 07	09 09	09 29	09 41	09 58	10 03	10 09
	d		06 12		06 42	07 01	07 12	07 31	07 42	08 00	08 12		08 31	08 37	08 42	09 00		09 12	09 31	09 42	10 00	10 05	10 12
Didcot Parkway	116 a		06 29		06 59		07 29		07 59	08 16	08 29			08 54	09 00	09 17		09 29			10 17	10 22	10 29
Reading ■	117,116 a		06 43		07 13	07 28	07 43	07 58	08 14	08 32	08 44		08 58	09 09	09 15	09 32		09 43	09 57	10 11	10 32	10 37	10 45
Slough ■	117,116 a																						
LonPaddington ■	⊖117,116 a		07 14		07 41	07 59	08 14	08 30	08 44	08 59	09 14		09 30	09 41	09 44	09 59		10 14	10 29	10 39	11 01	11 07	11 14

A To Westbury
B From Penzance
C From Birmingham New Street
D From Westbury
E From Exeter St Davids

For connections to/from:
Oxford - refer to Table T116; Gatwick Airport - refer to Table T148; Table T117 for Services via London Paddington

For principal services between: London & Taunton - refer to Table T135; London & Worcester - refer to Table T126

Table T125-R

South Wales, Weston-super-Mare, Bristol, Cheltenham Spa and Swindon - London

Saturdays

15 September to 8 December

		GW	GW	GW	GW	GW	GW	GW	GW	GW	GW	GW	GW	GW	GW	GW	GW	GW	GW	GW	GW	GW
			◇1	◇1		◇1	◇1	◇1	◇1	◇1		◇1	◇1		◇1	◇1	◇1	◇1	◇1		◇1	◇1
		A								B	A	C								A		
			☕	☕		☕	☕	☕	☕	☕		☕	☕		☕	☕	☕	☕	☕		☕	☕
Swansea	128 d		08 29				09 29					10 29				11 29					12 29	
Neath	128 d		08 41				09 41					10 41				11 41					12 41	
Port Talbot Parkway	128 d		08 49				09 49					10 49				11 49					12 49	
Bridgend	128 d		09 02				10 02					11 02				12 02					13 02	
Cardiff Central 7	128 d		09 26				10 26					11 26				12 26					13 26	
Newport (South Wales)	d		09 40				10 40					11 40				12 40					13 40	
Taunton	d									10 45												
Weston-super-Mare	d									11 07												
Bristol Temple Meads 10	d			10 00		10 30		11 00		11 30			12 00		12 30		13 00		13 30			14 00
Bristol Parkway 7	a		10 00				11 00					12 00				13 00					14 00	
	d		10 04				11 04					12 04				13 04					14 04	
Bath Spa 7	d			10 13		10 43		11 13		11 43			12 13		12 43		13 13		13 43			14 13
Chippenham	d	10 01		10 26		10 56		11 26		11 56	12 01		12 26		12 56		13 26		13 56	14 01		14 26
Worcester Shrub Hill	d																					
Cheltenham Spa 4	d				10 01				11 00					12 01				13 00				
Gloucester 7	d				10 14				11 15					12 14				13 16				
Stonehouse	d				10 27				11 29					12 27				13 30				
Stroud	d				10 32				11 35					12 32				13 36				
Kemble	d				10 47				11 49					12 47				13 50				
Swindon	a	10 20	10 29	10 41	11 04	11 09	11 29	11 40	12 03	12 09	12 20	12 29	12 41	13 04	13 09	13 29	13 40	14 04	14 09	14 20	14 29	14 40
	d		10 31	10 42		11 12	11 31	11 42	12 05	12 12		12 31	12 42		13 12	13 31	13 42	14 05	14 12		14 31	14 42
Didcot Parkway	116 a					11 29			12 22	12 29					13 29			14 23	14 29			
Reading 7	117,116 a		11 00	11 09		11 44	11 58	12 10	12 37	12 46		12 58	13 10		13 43	13 57	14 12	14 37	14 43		14 57	15 08
Slough 3	117,116 a																					
LonPaddington 15	⊖117,116 a		11 31	11 40		12 14	12 29	12 38	13 07	13 14		13 31	13 38		14 14	14 29	14 41	15 07	15 14		15 29	15 41

		GW	GW	GW	GW	GW	GW	GW	GW	GW	GW	GW	GW	GW	GW	GW	GW	GW	GW	GW	GW	GW	GW
			◇1	◇1	◇1		◇1	◇1	◇1	◇1		◇1		◇1	◇1	◇1	◇1	◇1	◇1		◇1		◇1
						A							A									A	
			☕	☕	☕		☕	☕	☕	☕		☕		☕	☕	☕	☕	☕	☕		☕		☕
Swansea	128 d			13 29					14 29					15 29				16 29					17 29
Neath	128 d			13 41					14 41					15 41				16 41					17 41
Port Talbot Parkway	128 d			13 49					14 49					15 49				16 49					17 49
Bridgend	128 d			14 02					15 02					16 02				17 02					18 02
Cardiff Central 7	128 d			14 26					15 26					16 26				17 26					18 26
Newport (South Wales)	d			14 40					15 40					16 40				17 40					18 40
Taunton	d																						
Weston-super-Mare	d																						
Bristol Temple Meads 10	d		14 30		15 00			15 30		16 00		16 30			17 00		17 30		18 00		18 30		
Bristol Parkway 7	a			15 01					16 00					17 00				18 00					19 00
	d			15 04					16 04					17 04				18 04					19 03
Bath Spa 7	d		14 43		15 13			15 43		16 13		16 43			17 13		17 43		18 13		18 43		
Chippenham	d		14 56		15 26	15 32		15 56		16 26		16 56	17 01		17 26		17 56		18 26		18 56	19 01	
Worcester Shrub Hill	d																						
Cheltenham Spa 4	d	14 01					15 00				16 01					17 00				18 01			
Gloucester 7	d	14 14					15 15				16 14					17 16				18 14			
Stonehouse	d	14 27					15 29				16 27					17 30				18 27			
Stroud	d	14 32					15 35				16 32					17 36				18 32			
Kemble	d	14 47					15 49				16 47					17 50				18 47			
Swindon	a	15 04	15 09	15 29	15 40	15 50	16 03	16 09	16 29	16 40	17 04	17 09	17 22	17 29	17 41	18 04	18 09	18 29	18 40	19 04	19 09	19 22	19 29
	d		15 12	15 31	15 42		16 05	16 12	16 31	16 42		17 12		17 31	17 42	18 06	18 12	18 31	18 42		19 12		19 29
Didcot Parkway	116 a		15 29				16 22	16 29				17 29				18 23	18 29				19 29		
Reading 7	117,116 a		15 43	15 58	16 10		16 37	16 46	16 58	17 09		17 43		17 58	18 09	18 37	18 45	18 58	19 09		19 43		19 58
Slough 3	117,116 a																						
LonPaddington 15	⊖117,116 a		16 14	16 29	16 38		17 07	17 14	17 29	17 38		18 14		18 30	18 37	19 06	19 14	19 29	19 37		20 14		20 30

A From Westbury

B From Paignton. The Torbay Express

C From Carmarthen

For connections to/from:
Oxford - refer to Table T116; Gatwick Airport - refer to Table T148; Table T117 for Services via London Paddington

For principal services between: London & Taunton - refer to Table T135; London & Worcester - refer to Table T126

Table T125-R

South Wales, Weston-super-Mare, Bristol, Cheltenham Spa and Swindon - London

Saturdays

15 September to 8 December

		GW	GW	GW	GW	GW	GW	GW	GW	GW
		◇1	◇1	◇1		◇1	◇1		◇1	◇1
					A				B	
		☕	☕	☕		☕	☕		☕	☕
Swansea	128 d			18 29			19 29			
Neath	128 d			18 41			19 41			
Port Talbot Parkway	128 d			18 49			19 49			
Bridgend	128 d			19 02			20 02			
Cardiff Central 7	128 d			19 26			20 26			
Newport (South Wales)	d			19 40			20 40			
Taunton	d								21 14	21 30
Weston-super-Mare	d					20 10				21 53
Bristol Temple Meads 10	d		19 30			20 33			21 47	22 30
Bristol Parkway 7	a			20 00			21 00			
	d			20 04			21 03			
Bath Spa 7	d		19 43			20 46			22 03	22 45
Chippenham	d		19 56			20 59			22 16	22 58
Worcester Shrub Hill	d									
Cheltenham Spa 4	d	19 00			20 02			21 20		
Gloucester 7	d	19 16			20 14			21 35		
Stonehouse	d	19 30			20 27			21 48		
Stroud	d	19 36			20 32			21 53		
Kemble	d	19 50			20 47			22 08		
Swindon	a	20 04	20 09	20 29	21 03	21 12	21 28	22 25	22 30	23 13
	d	20 06	20 12	20 31		21 15	21 30		22 32	23 14
Didcot Parkway	116 a	20 23	20 29			21 32	21 47		22 49	23 32
Reading 7	117,116 a	20 38	20 44	20 57		21 46	22 02		23 03	23 48
Slough 3	117,116 a									
LonPaddington 15	⊖117,116 a	21 06	21 14	21 28		22 14	22 38		23 43	00 33

Sundays

20 May to 9 September

		GW	GW	GW	GW	GW	GW	GW	GW	GW	GW	GW	GW	GW	GW	GW	GW	GW	GW	GW	GW	GW	GW
		◇1	◇1		◇1	◇1	◇1		◇1	◇1		◇1	◇1	◇1	◇1	◇1	◇1	1	◇	◇1		1	1
				C							C								D				
		☕	☕		☕	☕	☕		☕	☕		☕	☕	☕	☕	☕	☕	☕		☕		☕	☕
Swansea	128 d						08 10					09 24				10 24				11 24			
Neath	128 d						08 22					09 36				10 36				11 36			
Port Talbot Parkway	128 d						08 29					09 43				10 43				11 43			
Bridgend	128 d						08 43					09 56				10 56				11 56			
Cardiff Central 7	128 d				08 05		09 05					10 20				11 20				12 20			
Newport (South Wales)	d				08 23		09 26					10 39				11 39				12 39			
Taunton	d																						
Weston-super-Mare	d					08 23				09 51								11 54					
Bristol Temple Meads 10	d	07 45	08 15			09 00			09 47	10 30			11 00	11 30			12 00	12 30				13 00	13 30
Bristol Parkway 7	a				08 50		09 46					11 00				12 00				13 00			
	d				08 52		09 48					11 01				12 01				13 01			
Bath Spa 7	d	07 58	08 28			09 13			10 00	10 44			11 13	11 43			12 13	12 43				13 13	13 43
Chippenham	d	08 11	08 41	08 55		09 26			10 13	10 57	11 02		11 25	11 55			12 25	12 55	13 03			13 25	13 55
Worcester Shrub Hill	d																						
Cheltenham Spa 4	d							09 24							11 18						12 32		
Gloucester 7	d							09 37							11 34						12 45		
Stonehouse	d							09 50							11 48						12 58		
Stroud	d							09 55							11 54						13 03		
Kemble	d							10 09							12 08						13 17		
Swindon	a	08 26	08 56	09 12	09 17	09 41	10 14	10 24	10 28	11 12	11 20	11 28	11 40	12 11	12 22	12 28	12 41	13 11	13 20	13 28	13 32	13 41	14 11
	d	08 26	08 57		09 20	09 42	10 15		10 29	11 13		11 29	11 41	12 11	12 22	12 29	12 41	13 11		13 29		13 41	14 11
Didcot Parkway	116 a	08 45				09 56			10 45	11 27		11 46		12 28		12 46		13 28		13 46			14 27
Reading 7	117,116 a	09 01	09 25		09 46	10 15	10 43		11 02	11 46		12 02	12 10	12 45	12 51	13 02	13 12	13 44		14 01		14 11	14 44
Slough 3	117,116 a																						
LonPaddington 15	⊖117,116 a	09 41	10 05		10 25	10 54	11 21		11 40	12 26		12 40	12 50	13 24	13 30	13 43	13 50	14 24		14 43		14 50	15 24

A To Westbury

B From Penzance

C From Westbury

D From Weymouth

For connections to/from:
Oxford - refer to Table T116; Gatwick Airport - refer to Table T148; Table T117 for Services via London Paddington

For principal services between: London & Taunton - refer to Table T135; London & Worcester - refer to Table T126

Table T125-R

Sundays

20 May to 9 September

South Wales, Weston-super-Mare, Bristol, Cheltenham Spa and Swindon - London

	GW	GW	GW	GW	GW	GW	GW	GW	GW	GW	GW	GW	GW	GW	GW	GW	GW	GW	GW	GW	GW
	■	◇■	■		■	◇■	■	■	◇■	◇■		◇■	■		◇■	◇■	■	◇■	◇■	■	◇■
				A							A					B	C		D		C
	☕	☕	☕		☕	☕	☕	☕	☕	☕		☕	☕		☕	☕	☕	☕	☕	☕	☕
Swansea 128 d	12 24				13 24			14 24					15 24			15 51				16 51	
Neath 128 d	12 36				13 36			14 36					15 36			16 03				17 03	
Port Talbot Parkway 128 d	12 43				13 43			14 43					15 43			16 10				17 11	
Bridgend 128 d	12 56				13 56			14 56					15 56			16 23				17 24	
Cardiff Central 128 d	13 20				14 20			15 20					16 20			16 50				17 50	
Newport (South Wales) d	13 39				14 39			15 39					16 39			17 10				18 10	
Taunton d																	16 39		16 58		17 46
Weston-super-Mare d			13 20							15 20							17 01		17 30		
Bristol Temple Meads d			14 00			15 00	15 30			16 00		16 30			17 00		17 30		18 00		18 30
Bristol Parkway a	14 00				15 00			16 00					17 00			17 30				18 30	
d	14 01				15 01			16 01					17 01			17 30				18 30	
Bath Spa d			14 13			15 13	15 43			16 13		16 43			17 13		17 43		18 13		18 43
Chippenham d			14 25	15 01		15 25	15 55			16 25	16 46	16 55			17 25		17 55		18 25		18 56
Worcester Shrub Hill d																					
Cheltenham Spa d		13 33							15 33					16 32				17 33			
Gloucester d		13 49							15 46					16 45				17 49			
Stonehouse d		14 02							16 01					16 57				18 03			
Stroud d		14 09							16 06					17 02				18 09			
Kemble d		14 22							16 20					17 17				18 23			
Swindon a	14 28	14 37	14 40	15 19	15 28	15 41	16 11	16 28	16 34	16 41	17 04	17 11	17 28	17 33	17 41	17 57	18 10	18 38	18 40	18 58	19 11
d	14 29	14 37	14 41		15 29	15 41	16 11	16 29	16 36	16 41		17 11	17 29		17 41	17 59	18 11	18 39	18 41	18 59	19 12
Didcot Parkway 116 a	14 46		14 58		15 46	15 58	16 29	16 46				17 29	17 46			18 17	18 28			19 17	19 29
Reading 117,116 a	15 02	15 05	15 15		16 02	16 15	16 45	17 02	17 06	17 09		17 45	18 02		18 12	18 32	18 46	19 06	19 09	19 32	19 45
Slough 117,116 a																					
LonPaddington ⊖117,116 a	15 40	15 45	15 54		16 40	16 54	17 24	17 40	17 45	17 50		18 24	18 40		18 51	19 10	19 25	19 45	19 50	20 10	20 25

	GW	GW	GW	GW	GW	GW	GW	GW	GW	GW	GW	GW	GW
		◇■	◇■	◇■		◇■	◇■	◇■		◇■	◇■		◇■
	A		B		E						B		C
		☕	☕	☕		☕	☕	☕		☕	☕		☕
Swansea 128 d			17 51					18 51			19 55		
Neath 128 d			18 03					19 03			20 07		
Port Talbot Parkway 128 d			18 10					19 10			20 14		
Bridgend 128 d			18 23					19 23			20 28		
Cardiff Central 128 d			18 50					19 50			20 50		
Newport (South Wales) d			19 09					20 09			21 09		
Taunton d							18 56						21 31
Weston-super-Mare d							19 25			20 26			
Bristol Temple Meads d		19 00		19 30			20 00			21 00			22 10
Bristol Parkway a			19 30					20 30			21 32		
d			19 30					20 30			21 34		
Bath Spa d		19 13		19 43			20 13			21 15			22 22
Chippenham d	19 04	19 25		19 55	20 08		20 25			21 28			22 35
Worcester Shrub Hill d													
Cheltenham Spa d						19 32						21 47	
Gloucester d						19 46			20 17			21 59	
Stonehouse d						20 00			20 30			22 12	
Stroud d						20 06			20 35			22 17	
Kemble d						20 20			20 49			22 32	
Swindon a	19 21	19 41	19 57	20 11	20 24	20 34	20 41	20 57	21 04	21 42	22 00	22 47	22 49
d		19 41	19 59	20 11		20 35	20 41	20 59		21 44	22 00		22 52
Didcot Parkway 116 a			20 16	20 29			20 58	21 16		22 01			23 10
Reading 117,116 a		20 12	20 32	20 46		21 03	21 15	21 32		22 13	22 34		23 26
Slough 117,116 a													
LonPaddington ⊖117,116 a		20 51	21 10	21 25		21 45	21 53	22 13		23 03	23 22		00 09

A From Westbury
B From Carmarthen
C From Plymouth
D From Paignton
E From Westbury to Cheltenham Spa

For connections to/from:
Oxford - refer to Table T116; Gatwick Airport - refer to Table T148; Table T117 for Services via London Paddington

For principal services between: London & Taunton - refer to Table T135; London & Worcester - refer to Table T126

Table T125-R

Sundays

16 September to 2 December

South Wales, Weston-super-Mare, Bristol, Cheltenham Spa and Swindon - London

	GW	GW	GW	GW	GW	GW	GW	GW	GW	GW	GW	GW	GW	GW	GW	GW	GW	GW	GW	GW	GW	GW
	◇■	◇■		◇■	◇■	◇■	◇■		◇■	◇■		◇■	◇■	◇■	◇■	◇■	◇■	■	◇	◇■	■	
			A			B	C				A								D			
	☕	☕		☕	☕	☕	☕		☕	☕		☕	☕	☕	☕	☕	☕	☕		☕	☕	
Swansea 128 d						07 53	08 00					09 24				10 24				11 24		
Neath 128 d						08 05	08 12					09 36				10 36				11 36		
Port Talbot Parkway 128 d						08 12	08 19					09 43				10 43				11 43		
Bridgend 128 d						08 26	08 33					09 56				10 56				11 56		
Cardiff Central 128 d				08 05		08 49	08 55					10 20				11 20				12 20		
Newport (South Wales) d				08 23		09 08	09 15					10 39				11 39				12 39		
Taunton d																						
Weston-super-Mare d					08 15					09 46												
Bristol Temple Meads d	07 45	08 15			08 53				09 53	10 23			10 53	11 25			11 53	12 25			12 53	
Bristol Parkway a				08 50		09 35	09 35					11 00				12 00				13 00		
d				08 52		09 37	09 37					11 01				12 01				13 01		
Bath Spa d	07 58	08 28			09 06				10 06	10 36			11 06	11 38			12 06	12 38			13 06	
Chippenham d	08 11	08 41	08 55		09 19				10 19	10 49	10 57		11 19	11 51			12 19	12 51	13 03		13 19	
Worcester Shrub Hill d																						
Cheltenham Spa d								09 24							11 18							12 46
Gloucester d								09 37							11 34							13 04
Stonehouse d								09 50							11 48							13 17
Stroud d								09 55							11 54							13 22
Kemble d								10 09							12 08							13 36
Swindon a	08 26	08 56	09 12	09 17	09 34	10 03	10 03	10 24	10 34	11 04	11 14	11 28	11 33	12 06	12 22	12 28	12 34	13 06	13 20	13 28	13 34	13 51
d	08 26	08 57		09 19	09 35	10 04	10 04		10 35	11 05		11 29	11 35	12 07	12 22	12 29	12 34	13 07		13 29	13 35	
Didcot Parkway 116 a	08 45				09 52				10 51				11 52				12 52			13 46	13 52	
Reading 117,116 a	09 01	09 29		09 48	10 08	10 32	10 32		11 08	11 33		11 57	12 08	12 36	12 51	12 57	13 08	13 35		14 01	14 08	
Slough 117,116 a																						
LonPaddington ⊖117,116 a	09 39	10 10		10 35	10 46	11 11	11 11		11 45	12 10		12 38	12 45	13 13	13 35	13 40	13 45	14 13		14 40	14 45	

	GW	GW	GW	GW	GW	GW	GW	GW	GW	GW	GW	GW	GW	GW	GW	GW	GW	GW	GW	GW	GW
	■	■	■	◇■		■	◇■	◇■	■	■	◇■	◇■	■	◇■			◇■	■	◇■	◇■	■
					A										A		E	F	G		
	☕	☕	☕	☕		☕	☕	☕	☕	☕	☕	☕	☕	☕			☕	☕	☕	☕	☕
Swansea 128 d		12 24				13 24			14 24				15 24				15 51				16 51
Neath 128 d		12 36				13 36			14 36				15 36				16 03				17 03
Port Talbot Parkway 128 d		12 43				13 43			14 43				15 43				16 10				17 10
Bridgend 128 d		12 56				13 56			14 56				15 56				16 23				17 23
Cardiff Central 128 d		13 20				14 20			15 20				16 20				16 50				17 50
Newport (South Wales) d		13 39				14 39			15 40				16 39				17 09				18 09
Taunton d																		16 39	16 58		
Weston-super-Mare d			13 16							15 15								17 01	17 31		
Bristol Temple Meads d	13 25		13 53				14 53	15 25		15 53		16 25		16 53				17 25	17 53		
Bristol Parkway a		14 00				15 00			16 00				17 00				17 30				18 30
d		14 01				15 01			16 02				17 01				17 30				18 30
Bath Spa d	13 38		14 06				15 07	15 38		16 06		16 38		17 07				17 38	18 04		
Chippenham d	13 51		14 19		15 01		15 20	15 51		16 19		16 51		17 20	17 24			17 51	18 17		
Worcester Shrub Hill d																					
Cheltenham Spa d				13 46							15 46					16 46				17 46	
Gloucester d				14 02							16 02					16 59				18 02	
Stonehouse d				14 15							16 17					17 11				18 16	
Stroud d				14 22							16 22					17 16				18 22	
Kemble d				14 35							16 36					17 31				18 36	
Swindon a	14 06	14 28	14 34	14 50	15 19	15 28	15 34	16 06	16 27	16 34	16 50	17 06	17 28	17 35	17 41	17 47	17 57	18 06	18 33	18 51	18 57
d	14 06	14 29	14 34	14 50		15 29	15 36	16 07	16 29	16 35	16 52	17 07	17 29	17 35			17 59	18 07	18 33	18 52	18 59
Didcot Parkway 116 a		14 46	14 52			15 46	15 52		16 46	16 52			17 46	17 53			18 16		18 52		19 16
Reading 117,116 a	14 35	15 02	15 08	15 18		16 02	16 08	16 35	17 02	17 08	17 21	17 35	18 02	18 09			18 32	18 36	19 08	19 19	19 32
Slough 117,116 a																					
LonPaddington ⊖117,116 a	15 13	15 40	15 45	16 05		16 41	16 45	17 12	17 40	17 45	18 08	18 13	18 40	18 46			19 11	19 13	19 45	20 07	20 13

A From Westbury
B from 28 October
C until 21 October
D From Weymouth
E From Carmarthen
F From Plymouth
G From Paignton

For connections to/from:
Oxford - refer to Table T116; Gatwick Airport - refer to Table T148; Table T117 for Services via London Paddington

For principal services between: London & Taunton - refer to Table T135; London & Worcester - refer to Table T126

Table T125-R

Sundays
16 September to 2 December

South Wales, Weston-super-Mare, Bristol, Cheltenham Spa and Swindon - London

	GW	GW	GW	GW	GW	GW	GW	GW	GW	GW	GW	GW	GW
	◇1		◇1	◇1	◇1		◇1	◇1	◇1	◇1	◇1		◇1
	A	B		C		D					C		A
	☕		☕	☕	☕		☕	☕	☕	☕	☕		☕
Swansea 128 d				17 51					18 51		19 55		
Neath 128 d				18 03					19 03		20 07		
Port Talbot Parkway 128 d				18 10					19 10		20 14		
Bridgend 128 d				18 23					19 23		20 28		
Cardiff Central 7 128 d				18 50					19 50		20 50		
Newport (South Wales) d				19 09					20 09		21 09		
Taunton d	17 41						18 38						21 31
Weston-super-Mare d							19 17			20 26			
Bristol Temple Meads 10 d	18 25		18 53		19 25		19 53			21 00			22 10
Bristol Parkway 7 a				19 30					20 30		21 32		
d				19 30					20 30		21 34		
Bath Spa 7 d	18 38		19 06		19 38		20 06			21 16			22 23
Chippenham d	18 51	19 10	19 19		19 50	20 08	20 19			21 29			22 35
Worcester Shrub Hill d													
Cheltenham Spa 4 d								19 46				21 47	
Gloucester 7 d								20 01				21 59	
Stonehouse d								20 15				22 12	
Stroud d								20 21				22 17	
Kemble d								20 35				22 32	
Swindon a	19 06	19 27	19 34	19 57	20 06	20 24	20 34	20 49	20 57	21 43	22 00	22 47	22 50
d	19 07		19 35	19 59	20 06		20 34	20 50	20 59	21 45	22 00		22 52
Didcot Parkway 116 a			19 52	20 16			20 51			22 00			23 10
Reading 7 117,116 a	19 36		20 08	20 32	20 35		21 08	21 19	21 30	22 16	22 34		23 26
Slough 3 117,116 a													
LonPaddington 15 ⊖117,116 a	20 15		20 45	21 11	21 13		21 45	22 07	22 09	23 04	23 22		00 11

A From Plymouth
B From Westbury
C From Carmarthen
D From Westbury to Cheltenham Spa

For connections to/from:
Oxford - refer to Table T116; Gatwick Airport - refer to Table T148; Table T117 for Services via London Paddington

For principal services between: London & Taunton - refer to Table T135; London & Worcester - refer to Table T126

Table T126-F

Mondays to Fridays
21 May to 5 October

London and Oxford - Worcester and Hereford

Miles		GW	GW	GW	GW	GW	GW	GW	GW	GW
			MX		MX	MO				
		◇1	◇1		◇1	◇1	◇1	◇1	◇	◇1
		A	B				C	C		
			☕				🛒	🛒		🛒
0	**London Paddington** 15 ⊖116,125,135 d				05 12	05 12	05 47	06 52	07 50	08 21
18½	Slough 3 116,125,135 d				05 30	05 30	06 03	07 08	08 07	08 37
36	Reading 7 116,125,135 d				05 50	05 51	06 19	07 22	08 23	08 53
53¼	Didcot Parkway 116,125 d						06 35	07 43		
63½	**Oxford** 116 d			05 14	06 21	06 21	06 52	08 01	08 51	09 23
70½	Hanborough d						07 02	08 14	09 00	09 33
71½	Combe d									
75	Finstock d									
76¾	Charlbury a						07 09	08 21	09 07	09 40
—	d						07 10	08 22	09 08	09 41
80½	Ascott-under-Wychwood d									
81¾	Shipton d									
84¾	Kingham d						07 19	08 32	09 17	09 51
91¾	Moreton-in-Marsh a			05 39	06 45	06 45	07 28	08 40	09 25	09 59
—	d			05 42			07 29	08 41	09 29	10 00
101¼	Honeybourne d			05 53			07 40	08 53		10 12
106¾	Evesham a			05 59			07 48	09 01	09 44	10 20
—	d			05 59			07 52	09 02	09 44	10 30
112¾	Pershore d	00 02	00 05	06 07			07 59	09 09		10 37
120½	**Worcester Shrub Hill** 7 a	00 16	00 15	06 19			08 10	09 20	09 59	10 48
121¼	**Worcester Foregate Street** 7 a			06 22			08 15	09 24	10 03	10 52
128	Malvern Link a							09 33	10 12	11 01
128¾	Great Malvern a							09 37	10 15	11 05
131¾	Colwall a									11 12
136	Ledbury a									11 19
149¾	**Hereford** 7 a									11 40

	GW	GW	GW	GW	GW	GW	GW	GW	GW	GW	GW	GW
	◇1	◇1	◇1	◇1	◇1	◇1	◇1	◇1	◇1	◇1	◇1	◇1
					D	E						F
	🛒	☕	🛒	☕	☕🛒	🛒	🛒	🛒	🛒	☕	☕	☕
London Paddington 15 ⊖116,125,135 d	09 21	10 22	11 22	12 21	13 22	14 21	15 22	15 52	16 22	17 22	17 52	18 22
Slough 3 116,125,135 d	09 37	10 38	11 38	12 37	13 38	14 37	15 38	16 08	16u38			
Reading 7 116,125,135 d	09 52	10 53	11 53	12 52	13 53	14 52	15 53	16 23	16u53	17 52	18 21	18 51
Didcot Parkway 116,125 d												
Oxford 116 d	10 20	11 25	12 24	13 23	14 19	15 23	16 25	16 50	17 25	18 17	18 50	19 23
Hanborough d	10 30	11 35	12 35	13 33	14 29	15 33	16 35	17 00	17 35	18 27	19 00	19 34
Combe d									17 39			
Finstock d									17 46			
Charlbury a	10 37	11 42	12 42	13 40	14 36	15 40	16 42	17 07	17 50	18 34	19 07	19 41
d	10 38	11 43	12 43	13 41	14 37	15 41	16 43	17 08	17 52	18 35	19 08	19 42
Ascott-under-Wychwood d									17 58			
Shipton d									18 02		19 16	
Kingham d	10 47	11 52	12 52	13 50	14 46	15 50	16 53	17 18	18 09	18 45	19 22	19 52
Moreton-in-Marsh a	10 56	12 01	13 01	13 59	14 55	15 59	17 01	17 26	18 17	18 53	19 30	20 01
d	10 57	12 02	13 02	14 00	14 56	16 00	17 02		18 18	18 54	19 31	20 02
Honeybourne d		12 13	13 13	14 11		16 11	17 14		18 30	19 06		20 13
Evesham a	11 12	12 21	13 21	14 19	15 12	16 18	17 22		18 37	19 14	19 47	20 21
d	11 13	12 22	13 22	14 20	15 13	16 23	17 23		18 38	19 15	19 48	20 22
Pershore d		12 30	13 30	14 28		16 30	17 30		18 45	19 22	19 56	20 30
Worcester Shrub Hill 7 a	11 27	12 40	13 40	14 38	15 27	16 41	17 41		18 57	19 33	20 06	20 40
Worcester Foregate Street 7 a	11 31	12 46	13 44		15 41	16 44	17 45		19 10	19 38		20 44
Malvern Link a		12 55					17 54		19 19	19 47		20 54
Great Malvern a		12 59					17 58		19 24	19 51		20 58
Colwall a		13 13								19 57		21 04
Ledbury a		13 20								20 05		21 13
Hereford 7 a		13 47								20 26		21 32

	GW	GW	GW	GW
				FO
	◇1	◇1	◇1	
		E		
	☕	🛒	☕	
London Paddington 15 ⊖116,125,135 d	19 22	20 22	21 48	23 20
Slough 3 116,125,135 d	19 38	20 38	22 04	23 37
Reading 7 116,125,135 d	19 53	20 53	22 20	00 03
Didcot Parkway 116,125 d				
Oxford 116 d	20 23	21 24	22 56	00 36
Hanborough d	20 33	21 34	23 06	00 45
Combe d				
Finstock d				
Charlbury a	20 40	21 41	23 13	00 52
d	20 43	21 42	23 14	00 53
Ascott-under-Wychwood d				
Shipton d			23 21	
Kingham d	20 53	21 51	23 27	01 02
Moreton-in-Marsh a	21 01	22 00	23 36	01 11
d	21 06	22 01	23 37	
Honeybourne d	21 18	22 12	23 48	
Evesham a	21 26	22 20	23 56	
d	21 31	22 21	23 57	
Pershore d	21 39	22 29	00 05	
Worcester Shrub Hill 7 a	21 49	22 39	00 15	
Worcester Foregate Street 7 a	22 01	22 43		
Malvern Link a	22 10	22 53		
Great Malvern a	22 15	22 57		
Colwall a	22 25			
Ledbury a	22 32			
Hereford 7 a	22 52			

A 17 September, 24 September, 1 October. From London Paddington
B From London Paddington
C 🛒 from Oxford
D ☕ to Oxford 🛒 from Oxford
E 🛒 to Oxford
F The Cathedrals Express

For additional services between London and Worcester refer to Table T125

Table T126-F

Mondays to Fridays
8 October to 7 December

London and Oxford - Worcester and Hereford

	GW MO ◇■ A	GW MX ◇■ A 🍴	GW	GW MX ◇■	GW MO ◇■	GW ◇■ B 🛒	GW ◇■ B 🛒	GW ◇	GW ◇■ 🛒	GW ◇■ 🛒	GW ◇■ 🍴	GW ◇■ 🛒	GW ◇■ 🍴	GW ◇■ C 🍴🛒	GW ◇■ D 🛒	GW ◇■ 🛒	GW ◇■ 🛒	GW ◇■ 🛒	GW ◇■ 🍴	GW ◇■ 🍴	GW ◇■ E 🍴	GW ◇■ 🍴
London Paddington ■ ⊖116,125,135 d				05 12	05 12	05 47	06 52	07 50	08 21	09 21	10 22	11 22	12 21	13 22	14 21	15 22	15 52	16 22	17 22	17 52	18 22	19 22
Slough ■ 116,125,135 d				05 30	05 30	06 03	07 08	08 07	08 37	09 37	10 38	11 38	12 37	13 38	14 37	15 38	16 08	16u38				19 38
Reading ■ 116,125,135 d				05 50	05 51	06 19	07 22	08 23	08 53	09 52	10 53	11 53	12 52	13 53	14 52	15 53	16 23	16u53	17 52	18 21	18 51	19 53
Didcot Parkway 116,125 d						06 35	07 43															
Oxford 116 d			05 14	06 21	06 21	06 52	08 01	08 51	09 23	10 20	11 25	12 24	13 23	14 19	15 23	16 25	16 50	17 25	18 17	18 50	19 23	20 23
Hanborough d						07 02	08 14	09 00	09 33	10 30	11 35	12 35	13 33	14 29	15 33	16 35	17 00	17 35	18 27	19 00	19 34	20 33
Combe d																		17 39				
Finstock d																		17 46				
Charlbury a						07 09	08 21	09 07	09 40	10 37	11 42	12 42	13 40	14 36	15 40	16 42	17 07	17 50	18 34	19 07	19 41	20 40
d						07 10	08 22	09 08	09 41	10 38	11 43	12 43	13 41	14 37	15 41	16 43	17 08	17 52	18 35	19 08	19 42	20 43
Ascott-under-Wychwood d																		17 58				
Shipton d																		18 02		19 16		
Kingham d						07 19	08 32	09 17	09 51	10 47	11 52	12 52	13 50	14 46	15 50	16 53	17 18	18 09	18 45	19 22	19 52	20 53
Moreton-in-Marsh a			05 39	06 45	06 45	07 28	08 40	09 25	09 59	10 56	12 01	13 01	13 59	14 55	15 59	17 01	17 26	18 17	18 53	19 30	20 01	21 01
d			05 42			07 29	08 41	09 29	10 00	10 57	12 02	13 02	14 00	14 56	16 00	17 02		18 18	18 54	19 31	20 02	21 06
Honeybourne d			05 53			07 40	08 53		10 12		12 13	13 13	14 11		16 11	17 14		18 30	19 06		20 13	21 18
Evesham a			05 59			07 48	09 01	09 44	10 20	11 12	12 21	13 21	14 19	15 12	16 18	17 22		18 37	19 14	19 47	20 21	21 26
d			05 59			07 52	09 02	09 44	10 30	11 13	12 22	13 22	14 20	15 13	16 23	17 23		18 38	19 15	19 48	20 22	21 31
Pershore d	00 02	00 05	06 07			07 59	09 09		10 37		12 30	13 30	14 28		16 30	17 30		18 45	19 22	19 56	20 30	21 39
Worcester Shrub Hill ■ a	00 16	00 17	06 19			08 10	09 20	09 59	10 48	11 27	12 40	13 40	14 38	15 27	16 41	17 41		18 57	19 33	20 06	20 40	21 49
Worcester Foregate Street ■ a			06 22			08 15	09 24	10 03	10 52	11 31	12 46	13 44		15 41	16 44	17 45		19 10	19 38		20 44	22 01
Malvern Link a							09 33	10 12	11 01		12 55					17 54		19 19	19 47		20 54	22 10
Great Malvern a							09 37	10 15	11 05		12 59					17 58		19 24	19 51		20 58	22 15
Colwall a									11 12		13 13								19 57		21 04	22 25
Ledbury a									11 19		13 20								20 06		21 13	22 32
Hereford ■ a									11 40		13 47								20 28		21 34	22 54

	GW ◇■ D 🛒	GW ◇■ 🍴	GW FO
London Paddington ■ ⊖116,125,135 d	20 22	21 48	23 20
Slough ■ 116,125,135 d	20 38	22 04	23 37
Reading ■ 116,125,135 d	20 53	22 20	00 03
Didcot Parkway 116,125 d			
Oxford 116 d	21 24	22 56	00 36
Hanborough d	21 34	23 06	00 45
Combe d			
Finstock d			
Charlbury a	21 41	23 13	00 52
d	21 42	23 14	00 53
Ascott-under-Wychwood d			
Shipton d		23 21	
Kingham d	21 51	23 27	01 02
Moreton-in-Marsh a	22 00	23 36	01 11
d	22 01	23 37	
Honeybourne d	22 12	23 48	
Evesham a	22 20	23 56	
d	22 21	23 57	
Pershore d	22 29	00 05	
Worcester Shrub Hill ■ a	22 39	00 17	
Worcester Foregate Street ■ a	22 43		
Malvern Link a	22 53		
Great Malvern a	22 59		
Colwall a			
Ledbury a			
Hereford ■ a			

A From London Paddington
B 🛒 from Oxford
C 🍴 to Oxford 🛒 from Oxford
D 🛒 to Oxford
E The Cathedrals Express

For additional services between London and Worcester refer to Table T125

Table T126-F

Saturdays
26 May to 8 December

London and Oxford - Worcester and Hereford

	GW A	GW ◇■ B 🍴	GW ◇■ C 🍴	GW ◇■	GW ◇■ 🍴	GW ◇■ 🍴	GW ◇■ 🍴	GW ◇■ 🍴	GW ◇■ 🍴	GW ◇■ 🍴	GW ◇■ 🍴	GW ◇■ 🍴	GW ◇■ 🍴	GW ◇■ D 🛒	GW ◇■ 🍴	GW ◇■ 🍴	GW ◇■ 🍴	GW ◇■ 🍴	GW ◇■ D
London Paddington ■ ⊖116,125,135 d				05 18	06 22	07 22	08 22	09 22	10 22	11 22	12 22	13 22	14 22	15 20	16 22	17 22	18 22	19 52	21 50
Slough ■ 116,125,135 d				05 34	06 38	07 38	08 38	09 38	10 38	11 38	12 38	13 38	14 38	15 37	16 38	17 38	18 38	20 08	22 06
Reading ■ 116,125,135 d	00 03			05 54	06 53	07 53	08 54	09 53	10 54	11 53	12 53	13 53	14 53	15 54	16 54	17 54	18 54	20 23	22 24
Didcot Parkway 116,125 d				06 10															22 39
Oxford 116 d	00 36			06 24	07 23	08 23	09 24	10 23	11 23	12 23	13 23	14 23	15 23	16 25	17 23	18 23	19 23	20 49	22 53
Hanborough d	00 45			06 34	07 33	08 33	09 34	10 33	11 33	12 33	13 33	14 33	15 33	16 34	17 33	18 33	19 33	20 59	23 02
Combe d																			
Finstock d																			
Charlbury a	00 52			06 41	07 40	08 40	09 41	10 40	11 40	12 40	13 40	14 40	15 40	16 41	17 40	18 40	19 40	21 06	23 09
d	00 53			06 42	07 41	08 41	09 42	10 41	11 41	12 41	13 41	14 41	15 41	16 42	17 41	18 41	19 41	21 07	23 10
Ascott-under-Wychwood d																			
Shipton d												14 48			17 48		19 48		23 16
Kingham d	01 02			06 52	07 50	08 50	09 51	10 50	11 50	12 50	13 50	14 54	15 50	16 51	17 54	18 50	19 54	21 16	23 21
Moreton-in-Marsh a	01 11			07 00	07 59	08 59	10 00	10 59	11 59	12 59	14 00	15 03	15 59	16 59	18 03	18 59	20 03	21 25	23 29
d				07 01	08 00	09 00	10 01	11 00	12 00	13 00		15 04	16 00	16 59	18 04	19 00	20 04	21 26	23 30
Honeybourne d				07 13	08 11	09 11	10 12	11 11	12 11	13 11		15 15	16 11	17 10	18 15	19 11	20 15	21 37	23 41
Evesham a				07 21	08 19	09 19	10 20	11 19	12 19	13 19		15 23	16 19	17 17	18 23	19 19	20 23	21 44	23 47
d				07 24	08 20	09 20	10 22	11 20	12 27	13 23		15 24	16 21	17 20	18 24	19 20	20 25	21 45	23 48
Pershore d		00 05	00 05	07 32	08 28	09 28	10 29	11 28	12 34	13 30		15 32	16 28	17 28	18 32	19 28	20 33	21 53	23 55
Worcester Shrub Hill ■ a		00 15	00 17	07 43	08 40	09 40	10 40	11 40	12 46	13 42		15 44	16 40	17 40	18 44	19 40	20 45	22 05	00 10
Worcester Foregate Street ■ a				07 48	08 44	09 44	10 45	11 47	12 50	13 46		15 48	16 44	17 44	18 56	19 44	20 49	22 08	
Malvern Link a				07 57	08 53	09 53	10 55		13 00	13 56		15 57	16 54	17 55	19 06		20 58	22 17	
Great Malvern a				08 02	09 00	10 00	10 59		13 04	14 03		16 04	17 00	18 01	19 10		21 02	22 24	
Colwall a							11 13		13 13						19 16		21 08		
Ledbury a							11 21		13 21						19 24		21 16		
Hereford ■ a							11 41		13 40						19 45		21 35		

Sundays
20 May to 9 September

	GW ◇■ 🍴	GW ◇■ 🍴	GW ◇■ 🍴	GW ◇■ 🍴	GW ◇■ 🍴	GW ◇■ 🍴	GW ◇■ 🍴	GW ◇	GW ◇■	GW ◇■ 🍴	GW ◇■ D	GW ◇■ 🍴	GW ◇■
London Paddington ■ ⊖116,125,135 d	08 00	08 34	09 34	10 34	12 34	13 34	14 34	15 34	16 34	17 34	18 34	19 34	21 34
Slough ■ 116,125,135 d	08 21	08 52	09 56	10 54	12 53	13 54	14 53	15 54	16 54	17 53	18 54	19 54	21 53
Reading ■ 116,125,135 d	08 46	09 15	10 15	11 16	13 16	14 16	15 14	16 14	17 15	18 19	19 18	20 17	22 15
Didcot Parkway 116,125 d	09 02	09 32	10 31	11 32	13 32	14 34	15 30	16 30	17 32	18 37	19 36	20 36	22 36
Oxford 116 d	09 17	09 48	10 48	11 48	13 48	14 48	15 48	16 48	17 48	18 51	19 51	20 51	22 51
Hanborough d	09 26		10 59	11 57	13 57		16 00		17 58	19 01	20 01	21 01	22 58
Combe d													
Finstock d													
Charlbury a	09 33	10 01	11 05	12 05	14 05	15 03	16 05	17 03	18 06	19 08	20 08	21 08	23 04
d	09 34	10 02	11 06	12 06	14 06	15 04	16 06	17 03	18 06	19 08	20 08	21 08	23 05
Ascott-under-Wychwood d													
Shipton d													
Kingham d	09 44	10 09	11 14	12 14	14 14	15 12	16 14	17 12	18 15	19 19	20 19	21 19	23 15
Moreton-in-Marsh a	09 52	10 19	11 23	12 23	14 23	15 23	16 23	17 20	18 23	19 27	20 27	21 27	23 24
d	09 52	10 20	11 24	12 24	14 24	15 24	16 24	17 21	18 24	19 27	20 27	21 27	23 25
Honeybourne d	10 03		11 35	12 35	14 35		16 38		18 35	19 38	20 38	21 40	23 36
Evesham a	10 11	10 36	11 42	12 42	14 42	15 42	16 46	17 36	18 41	19 48	20 44	21 48	23 44
d	10 11	10 39	11 48	12 44	14 44	15 44	16 47	17 44	18 47	19 48	20 48	21 48	23 45
Pershore d	10 19		11 54	12 52	14 52	15 52	16 55	17 52	18 55	19 56	20 56	21 56	23 52
Worcester Shrub Hill ■ a	10 33	10 59	12 07	13 04	15 04	16 04	17 06	18 03	19 06	20 08	21 08	22 08	00 08
Worcester Foregate Street ■ a	10 37	11 03	12 10	13 08	15 08	16 07	17 10	18 06	19 10	20 14		22 12	
Malvern Link a	10 50	11 13	12 19	13 17	15 17		17 20		19 19	20 24		22 21	
Great Malvern a	10 54	11 17	12 25	13 21	15 21		17 24		19 22	20 28		22 25	
Colwall a		11 24		13 32	15 28		17 30			20 34			
Ledbury a		11 32		13 41	15 36		17 38			20 42			
Hereford ■ a		11 51		14 07	15 55		17 56			21 00			

A From London Paddington
B until 6 October. From London Paddington
C from 13 October. From London Paddington
D ■ from Oxford

For additional services between London and Worcester refer to Table T125

Table T126-F

Sundays

16 September to 2 December

London and Oxford - Worcester and Hereford

		GW	GW	GW	GW	GW	GW	GW	GW	GW	GW	GW	GW	GW	GW
		◇1	◇1	◇1	◇1	◇1	◇1	◇1	◇1	◇1	◇1	◇1	◇1	◇1	◇1
			A	B						C			C		
		[buffet]	[buffet]	[buffet]	[buffet]	[buffet]	[buffet]	[buffet]	[buffet]			[buffet]		[buffet]	
London Paddington 15 ⊖116,125,135	d	08 03	08 37	08 37	09 37	10 37	12 37	13 37	14 37	15 37	16 37	17 37	18 37	19 37	21 37
Slough 3 116,125,135	d	08 26	08 59	08 59	10 01	10 59	12 59	13 59	14 59	15 59	16 59	17 59	18 59	19 59	22 03
Reading 7 116,125,135	d	08 47	09 19	09 20	10 18	11 17	13 17	14 17	15 17	16 17	17 20	18 20	19 20	20 18	22 21
Didcot Parkway 116,125	d	09 03	09 35	09 36	10 33	11 32	13 32	14 32	15 32	16 33	17 37	18 37	19 37	20 33	22 43
Oxford 116	d	09 16	09 55	09 55	10 48	11 54	13 50	14 47	15 46	16 51	17 55	18 51	19 51	20 49	22 57
Hanborough	d	09 27			10 57	12 03	13 58		15 56		18 04	19 01	20 03	20 59	23 07
Combe	d														
Finstock	d														
Charlbury	a	09 34	10 06	10 06	11 03	12 11	14 06	15 01	16 01	17 05	18 12	19 08	20 11	21 05	23 13
	d	09 35	10 07	10 07	11 04	12 12	14 07	15 02	16 02	17 06	18 13	19 08	20 11	21 06	23 14
Ascott-under-Wychwood	d														
Shipton	d														
Kingham	d	09 44	10 15	10 15	11 13	12 20	14 15	15 10	16 12	17 15	18 22	19 19	20 21	21 17	23 24
Moreton-in-Marsh	a	09 53	10 24	10 24	11 23	12 29	14 24	15 21	16 20	17 23	18 30	19 27	20 29	21 25	23 33
	d	09 54	10 25	10 25	11 25	12 30	14 25	15 21	16 21	17 23	18 30	19 27	20 29	21 26	23 34
Honeybourne	d	10 05			11 35	12 41	14 36		16 35		18 41	19 38	20 40	21 38	23 45
Evesham	a	10 12	10 41	10 41	11 42	12 49	14 44	15 39	16 43	17 39	18 48	19 48	20 46	21 46	23 53
	d	10 13	10 45	10 45	11 49	12 50	14 45	15 45	16 48	17 44	18 48	19 48	20 47	21 47	23 54
Pershore	d	10 21			11 56	12 58	14 53	15 52	16 56	17 52	18 56	19 56	20 54	21 54	00 02
Worcester Shrub Hill 7	a	10 32	10 59	10 59	12 08	13 10	15 05	16 04	17 07	18 03	19 07	20 08	21 07	22 06	00 16
Worcester Foregate Street 7	a	10 37	11 03	11 03	12 12	13 14	15 08	16 07	17 11	18 06	19 11	20 15		22 09	
Malvern Link	a	10 50	11 13	11 13	12 21	13 23	15 18		17 21		19 20	20 25		22 19	
Great Malvern	a	10 54	11 17	11 17	12 25	13 27	15 22		17 25		19 23	20 29		22 23	
Colwall	a		11 24	11 24		13 34	15 29		17 31			20 35			
Ledbury	a		11 32	11 32		13 42	15 37		17 39			20 43			
Hereford 7	a		11 51	11 51		14 07	15 56		17 57			21 01			

A until 21 October
B from 28 October
C 1 from Reading to Oxford

For additional services between London and Worcester refer to Table T125

Table T126-R

Mondays to Fridays

21 May to 7 December

Hereford and Worcester - Oxford and London

Miles			GW	GW	GW	GW	GW	GW	GW	GW	GW	GW	GW	GW	GW	GW	GW	GW	GW	GW	GW	GW	GW
																						FO	FX
			◇1	◇1	◇1	◇1		◇1	◇1		◇1	◇	◇1	◇1	◇1	◇1	◇1	◇1	◇1	◇1	◇1	◇1	◇1
						A		B															
			[buffet]	[buffet]	[buffet]	[buffet][trolley]		[buffet]	[trolley]		[trolley]	[trolley]	[trolley]	[trolley]	[trolley]	[buffet]	[buffet]	[buffet]	[buffet]	[trolley]	[trolley]	[trolley]	[trolley]
0	**Hereford** 7	d		04 47	05 28			06 42						12 09				15 14					
13¾	Ledbury	d		05 04	05 45			07 02						12 27				15 31					
18	Colwall	d		05 12	05 53			07 09						12 34				15 39					
20¾	Great Malvern	d		05 17	05 59			07 15			09 54	10 59		12 40				15 45			18 29	19 42	19 42
21¾	Malvern Link	d		05 21	06 03			07 20			09 58	11 02		12 44				15 50			18 33	19 46	19 46
28½	**Worcester Foregate Street** 7	d		05 32	06 14		06 53	07 31	08 25		10 09	11 15	12 00	12 55	13 55		15 51	16 01		17 26	18 43	19 57	19 57
29¼	**Worcester Shrub Hill** 7	d	05 11	05 37	06 19		06 56	07 35	08 39		10 14	11 22	12 05	12 59	13 59	15 22	15 55	16 07		17 33	18 50	20 02	20 02
37	Pershore	d		05 46	06 27		07 05	07 45	08 48		10 23		12 14	13 08	14 08			16 16		17 44	18 59	20 11	20 11
43	Evesham	a	05 25	05 53	06 35		07 12	07 52	08 56		10 30	11 36	12 21	13 16	14 16	15 36	16 09	16 23		17 51	19 06	20 18	20 18
—		d	05 26	05 58	06 37		07 13	07 54	09 02		10 32	11 37	12 26	13 17	14 25	15 37	16 10	16 24		17 52	19 07	20 23	20 23
48	Honeybourne	d	05 34		06 43			08 02	09 09		10 40		12 33	13 24	14 32			16 32		18 00	19 15	20 31	20 31
58	Moreton-in-Marsh	a	05 45	06 13	06 56		07 27	08 13	09 21		10 51	11 51	12 45	13 36	14 44	15 52	16 25	16 43		18 11	19 26	20 43	20 43
—		d	05 46	06 14	06 56	07 10	07 28	08 15	09 22	09 50	10 52	11 52	12 46	13 46	14 45	15 53	16 26	16 46	17 38	18 12	19 27	20 44	20 44
65	Kingham	d	05 55	06 23		07 20	07 36	08 24	09 30	09 58	11 01	12 00	12 54	13 54	14 53	16 01		16 55		18 21	19 36	20 53	20 53
68	Shipton	d					07 40													18 26			
69½	Ascott-under-Wychwood	d					07 43																
73	Charlbury	a	06 04	06 32	07 12	07 29	07 49	08 33	09 40	10 07	11 10	12 09	13 04	14 04	15 03	16 11	16 40	17 04		18 33	19 45	21 03	21 03
—		d	06 05	06 33	07 12	07 31	07 49	08 35	09 41	10 08	11 11	12 09	13 05	14 05	15 04	16 12	16 43	17 10		18 35	19 46	21 05	21 05
74¾	Finstock	d					07 53																
78¼	Combe	d					07 58																
79¼	Hanborough	d	06 13	06 41	07 21	07 39	08 01	08 43	09 49	10 15	11 19	12 17	13 13	14 13	15 12	16 20		17 18		18 43	19 54	21 14	21 14
86¼	**Oxford** 116	a	06 23	06 51	07 30	07 49	08 11	08 53	09 59	10 25	11 29	12 30	13 24	14 24	15 24	16 30	16 57	17 28	18 04	19 00	20 04	21 28	21 28
96½	Didcot Parkway 125,116	a		07 06			08 28																
113¾	Reading 7 135,125,116	a	06 51	07 20	07 54	08 19		09 17	10 24	10 54	11 55	12 54	13 54	14 54	15 54	16 55	17 26	17 54	18 29	19 25	20 29	21 55	21 55
131¼	Slough 3 135,125,116	a							10 39	11 11	12 10	13 10	14 09	15 09	16 09	17 10	17 41	18 09	18 44	19 40	20 44	22 11	22 11
149¾	**London Paddington** 15 ⊖135,125,116	a	07 25	07 52	08 28	08 51		09 46	10 57	11 30	12 28	13 29	14 27	15 27	16 27	17 28	17 59	18 28	19 03	19 59	21 05	22 29	22 31

		GW	GW	GW	GW
		FO	FX	FX	FO
		◇1	◇1	◇1	◇1
Hereford 7	d			21 51	21 51
Ledbury	d			22 11	22 11
Colwall	d			22 18	22 18
Great Malvern	d			22 24	22 24
Malvern Link	d				
Worcester Foregate Street 7	d	20 59	20 59	22 36	22 36
Worcester Shrub Hill 7	d	21 03	21 03	22 44	22 44
Pershore	d	21 12	21 12	22 53	22 53
Evesham	a	21 20	21 20	23 00	23 00
	d	21 21	21 21	23 01	23 01
Honeybourne	d	21 28	21 28	23 09	23 09
Moreton-in-Marsh	a	21 40	21 40	23 20	23 20
	d	21 41	21 41	23 22	23 22
Kingham	d	21 49	21 49	23 31	23 31
Shipton	d				
Ascott-under-Wychwood	d				
Charlbury	a	21 59	21 59	23 40	23 40
	d	22 07	22 07	23 41	23 41
Finstock	d				
Combe	d				
Hanborough	d	22 15	22 15	23 49	23 49
Oxford 116	a	22 25	22 25	23 59	23 59
Didcot Parkway 125,116	a			00 19	00 20
Reading 7 135,125,116	a	22 56	22 56	00 37	00 38
Slough 3 135,125,116	a	23 12	23 16	00 56	00 57
London Paddington 15 ⊖135,125,116	a	23 30	23 36	01 17	01 18

A [buffet] from Reading [trolley] to Reading
B The Cathedrals Express

For additional services between Worcester and London refer to Table T125

Table T126-R

Hereford and Worcester - Oxford and London

Saturdays 26 May to 8 September

		GW	GW	GW	GW	GW	GW	GW	GW	GW	GW	GW	GW	GW	GW	GW	GW	GW
		◇■	◇■ ⊡	◇■ ⊡	◇■ ⊡	◇■ ⊡	◇■ ⊡	◇■ ⊡	◇■ ⊡	◇■ ⊡	◇■ ⊡	◇■ ⊡	◇■ ⊡	◇■ ⊡	◇■ A	◇■	◇■	■
Hereford ■	d		06 17	07 13					12 13			15 13					20 20	
Ledbury	d		06 34	07 30					12 30			15 30					20 41	
Colwall	d		06 42	07 38					12 38			15 38					20 48	
Great Malvern	d	05 54	06 48	07 44	08 43	09 45	10 45		12 46		14 35	15 44	16 35	17 45	18 35		20 54	22 41
Malvern Link	d	05 58	06 52	07 48	08 47	09 49	10 49		12 50		14 39	15 48	16 39	17 49	18 38		20 58	22 45
Worcester Foregate Street ■	d	06 09	07 03	07 59	08 58	10 00	11 00	12 06	13 01		14 57	15 59	16 57	18 00	18 48	20 04	21 11	22 56
Worcester Shrub Hill ■	d	06 13	07 08	08 04	09 04	10 04	11 04	12 10	13 06		15 02	16 04	17 02	18 06	19 02	20 08	21 18	23 00
Pershore	d	06 22	07 17	08 13	09 13	10 14	11 13	12 20	13 15		15 11	16 13	17 11	18 15	19 11	20 18	21 27	23 10
Evesham	a	06 30	07 25	08 21	09 20	10 21	11 21	12 27	13 23		15 19	16 21	17 19	18 23	19 18	20 26	21 35	23 19
	d	06 31	07 26	08 26	09 22	10 25	11 25	12 28	13 26		15 28	16 22	17 25	18 28	19 28	20 28	21 36	
Honeybourne	d	06 38	07 33	08 33	09 30	10 32	11 32	12 36	13 33		15 35	16 29	17 32	18 35	19 35	20 35	21 43	
Moreton-in-Marsh	a	06 50	07 45	08 45	09 41	10 44	11 44	12 47	13 45		15 47	16 41	17 44	18 47	19 46	20 47	21 55	
	d	06 51	07 46	08 46	09 42	10 45	11 45	12 48	13 46	14 50	15 48	16 42	17 45	18 48	19 47	20 48	21 56	
Kingham	d	06 59	07 54	08 54	09 51	10 53	11 53	12 57	13 54	14 59	15 56	16 50	17 53	18 56	19 55	20 56	22 04	
Shipton	d		08 00		09 56				14 00			16 56						
Ascott-under-Wychwood	d																	
Charlbury	a	07 09	08 07	09 04	10 03	11 03	12 03	13 06	14 07	15 08	16 06	17 03	18 03	19 06	20 04	21 06	22 14	
	d	07 10	08 08	09 05	10 04	11 04	12 04	13 07	14 08	15 09	16 07	17 04	18 04	19 07	20 04	21 08	22 15	
Finstock	d																	
Combe	d																	
Hanborough	d	07 18	08 16	09 13	10 12	11 12	12 12	13 15	14 16	15 17	16 15	17 12	18 12	19 15	20 12	21 16	22 23	
Oxford 116	a	07 28	08 27	09 24	10 26	11 22	12 25	13 25	14 27	15 28	16 27	17 22	18 22	19 25	20 21	21 27	22 34	
Didcot Parkway 125,116	a															21 41	22 49	
Reading ■ 135,125,116	a	07 54	08 53	09 52	10 56	11 54	12 54	13 52	14 56	15 54	16 54	17 54	18 54	19 54	20 51	21 56	23 06	
Slough ■ 135,125,116	a	08 08	09 10	10 06	11 10	12 08	13 10	14 07	15 11	16 08	17 08	18 11	19 08	20 08	21 06	22 11	23 31	
London Paddington ■ ⊖135,125,116	a	08 27	09 28	10 24	11 28	12 26	13 28	14 25	15 29	16 26	17 26	18 29	19 26	20 27	21 25	22 29	23 51	

Saturdays 15 September to 8 December

		GW	GW	GW	GW	GW	GW	GW	GW	GW	GW	GW	GW	GW	GW	GW	GW	GW
		◇■	◇■ ⊡	◇■ ⊡	◇■ ⊡	◇■ ⊡	◇■ ⊡	◇■ ⊡	◇■ ⊡	◇■ ⊡	◇■ ⊡	◇■ ⊡	◇■ ⊡	◇■ ⊡	◇■ A	◇■	◇■	■
Hereford ■	d		06 17	07 13					12 13			15 13					20 20	
Ledbury	d		06 34	07 30					12 30			15 30					20 41	
Colwall	d		06 42	07 38					12 38			15 38					20 48	
Great Malvern	d	05 54	06 48	07 44	08 43	09 45	10 45		12 46		14 35	15 44	16 35	17 45	18 35		20 54	22 41
Malvern Link	d	05 58	06 52	07 48	08 47	09 49	10 49		12 50		14 39	15 48	16 39	17 49	18 38		20 58	22 45
Worcester Foregate Street ■	d	06 09	07 03	07 59	08 58	10 00	11 00	12 06	13 01		14 57	15 59	16 57	18 00	18 48	20 04	21 11	22 56
Worcester Shrub Hill ■	d	06 13	07 08	08 04	09 04	10 04	11 04	12 10	13 06		15 02	16 04	17 02	18 06	19 02	20 08	21 18	23 00
Pershore	d	06 22	07 17	08 13	09 13	10 14	11 13	12 20	13 15		15 11	16 13	17 11	18 15	19 11	20 18	21 27	23 10
Evesham	a	06 30	07 25	08 21	09 20	10 21	11 21	12 27	13 23		15 19	16 21	17 19	18 23	19 18	20 26	21 35	23 19
	d	06 31	07 26	08 26	09 22	10 25	11 25	12 28	13 26		15 28	16 22	17 25	18 28	19 28	20 28	21 36	
Honeybourne	d	06 38	07 33	08 33	09 30	10 32	11 32	12 36	13 33		15 35	16 29	17 32	18 35	19 35	20 35	21 43	
Moreton-in-Marsh	a	06 50	07 45	08 45	09 41	10 44	11 44	12 47	13 45		15 47	16 41	17 44	18 47	19 46	20 47	21 55	
	d	06 51	07 46	08 46	09 42	10 45	11 45	12 48	13 46	14 50	15 48	16 42	17 45	18 48	19 47	20 48	21 56	
Kingham	d	06 59	07 54	08 54	09 51	10 53	11 53	12 57	13 54	14 59	15 56	16 50	17 53	18 56	19 55	20 56	22 04	
Shipton	d		08 00		09 56				14 00			16 56						
Ascott-under-Wychwood	d																	
Charlbury	a	07 09	08 07	09 04	10 03	11 03	12 03	13 06	14 07	15 08	16 06	17 03	18 03	19 06	20 04	21 06	22 14	
	d	07 10	08 08	09 05	10 04	11 04	12 04	13 07	14 08	15 09	16 07	17 04	18 04	19 07	20 04	21 08	22 15	
Finstock	d																	
Combe	d																	
Hanborough	d	07 18	08 16	09 13	10 12	11 12	12 12	13 15	14 16	15 17	16 15	17 12	18 12	19 15	20 12	21 16	22 23	
Oxford 116	a	07 28	08 27	09 24	10 26	11 22	12 25	13 25	14 27	15 28	16 27	17 22	18 22	19 25	20 21	21 27	22 34	
Didcot Parkway 125,116	a															21 41	22 49	
Reading ■ 135,125,116	a	07 54	08 53	09 52	10 56	11 54	12 54	13 52	14 53	15 54	16 54	17 54	18 54	19 54	20 51	21 56	23 06	
Slough ■ 135,125,116	a	08 08	09 10	10 06	11 10	12 08	13 10	14 07	15 08	16 08	17 08	18 09	19 08	20 08	21 06	22 11	23 31	
London Paddington ■ ⊖135,125,116	a	08 27	09 28	10 24	11 29	12 26	13 28	14 25	15 26	16 26	17 26	18 27	19 26	20 27	21 25	22 29	23 51	

A ■ from Oxford

For additional services between Worcester and London refer to Table T125

Table T126-R

Hereford and Worcester - Oxford and London

Sundays 20 May to 9 September

		GW	GW	GW	GW	GW	GW	GW	GW	GW	GW	GW	GW
		◇	◇■ ⊡	◇ ⊡	◇■ ⊡	◇■ ⊡	◇■ ⊡	◇■ ⊡	◇■ ⊡	◇■ A	◇■ ⊡	◇	◇■ A
Hereford ■	d					13 32	14 32		16 34		18 38		
Ledbury	d					13 51	14 52		16 52		18 57		
Colwall	d					13 58	14 59		17 00		19 04		
Great Malvern	d		09 24	11 13	13 20	14 07	15 09		17 05		19 11	20 15	
Malvern Link	d		09 28	11 17	13 24	14 11	15 13		17 09		19 15	20 18	
Worcester Foregate Street ■	d	08 30	09 38	11 28	13 33	14 22	15 24	16 28	17 24	18 26	19 30	20 28	
Worcester Shrub Hill ■	d	08 39	09 42	11 32	13 38	14 28	15 28	16 32	17 28	18 30	19 34	20 32	21 28
Pershore	d	08 48	09 51	11 41	13 47	14 39	15 37	16 41	17 37	18 40	19 43	20 42	21 37
Evesham	a	08 55	09 59	11 48	13 54	14 46	15 46	16 46	17 47	18 48	19 49	20 49	21 45
	d	08 55	10 00	11 55	13 55	14 55	15 55	16 55	17 55	18 55	19 55	20 50	21 49
Honeybourne	d	09 02	10 07	12 02	14 02		16 02	17 02	18 02	19 02	20 02	20 57	21 56
Moreton-in-Marsh	a	09 14	10 19	12 14	14 14	15 10	16 14	17 14	18 14	19 14	20 14	21 08	22 07
	d	09 14	10 20	12 14	14 14	15 11	16 14	17 14	18 14	19 14	20 14	21 09	22 08
Kingham	d	09 22	10 28	12 22	14 22	15 19	16 22	17 22	18 22	19 22	20 22	21 17	22 16
Shipton	d												
Ascott-under-Wychwood	d												
Charlbury	a	09 32	10 38	12 32	14 32	15 29	16 32	17 32	18 34	19 32	20 32	21 26	22 25
	d	09 32	10 39	12 32	14 32	15 29	16 32	17 32	18 36	19 32	20 32	21 26	22 25
Finstock	d												
Combe	d												
Hanborough	d	09 40	10 47	12 40	14 40	15 36	16 40	17 40		19 40	20 42	21 34	22 34
Oxford 116	a	09 51	10 55	12 51	14 49	15 49	16 54	17 54	18 51	19 51	20 52	21 48	22 43
Didcot Parkway 125,116	a	10 06	11 12	13 12	15 12	16 12	17 12	18 07	19 07	20 07	21 06	22 01	22 56
Reading ■ 135,125,116	a	10 23	11 27	13 27	15 27	16 27	17 27	18 22	19 23	20 23	21 20	22 18	23 13
Slough ■ 135,125,116	a	10 44	11 48	13 48	15 48	16 48	17 48	18 46	19 46	20 46	21 43	22 37	23 30
London Paddington ■ ⊖135,125,116	a	11 05	12 08	14 10	16 09	17 11	18 09	19 07	20 08	21 08	22 07	23 09	23 51

Sundays 16 September to 2 December

		GW	GW	GW	GW	GW	GW	GW	GW	GW	GW	GW	GW
		◇	◇■ ⊡	◇■	◇■ ⊡	◇■ ⊡	◇■ ⊡	◇■ ⊡	◇■ ⊡	◇■	◇■ ⊡	◇	◇■
Hereford ■	d					13 32	14 32		16 34		18 38		
Ledbury	d					13 51	14 51		16 51		18 57		
Colwall	d					13 58	14 58		17 00		19 04		
Great Malvern	d		09 20	11 13	13 20	14 07	15 09		17 05		19 12	20 15	
Malvern Link	d		09 24	11 17	13 23	14 11	15 13		17 09		19 16	20 18	
Worcester Foregate Street ■	d	08 30	09 34	11 28	13 32	14 22	15 24	16 28	17 24	18 26	19 30	20 28	
Worcester Shrub Hill ■	d	08 39	09 38	11 32	13 37	14 28	15 28	16 32	17 28	18 30	19 35	20 31	21 28
Pershore	d	08 48	09 47	11 41	13 45	14 39	15 37	16 41	17 37	18 40	19 44	20 41	21 37
Evesham	a	08 55	09 55	11 48	13 53	14 46	15 46	16 46	17 47	18 48	19 50	20 48	21 45
	d	08 55	09 55	11 55	13 55	14 55	15 50	16 55	17 55	18 55	19 55	20 54	21 49
Honeybourne	d	09 02	10 02	12 01	14 02		15 56	17 02	18 02	19 02	20 02	21 01	21 56
Moreton-in-Marsh	a	09 14	10 14	12 13	14 14	15 10	16 07	17 14	18 14	19 14	20 14	21 12	22 07
	d	09 14	10 14	12 14	14 14	15 11	16 08	17 14	18 16	19 14	20 14	21 13	22 08
Kingham	d	09 22	10 22	12 22	14 22	15 19	16 16	17 22	18 22	19 22	20 22	21 21	22 16
Shipton	d												
Ascott-under-Wychwood	d												
Charlbury	a	09 32	10 32	12 32	14 32	15 29	16 26	17 32	18 34	19 32	20 32	21 30	22 25
	d	09 32	10 32	12 32	14 32	15 29	16 26	17 32	18 36	19 32	20 32	21 30	22 25
Finstock	d												
Combe	d												
Hanborough	d	09 40	10 40	12 40	14 40	15 36	16 36	17 40		19 40	20 40	21 38	22 34
Oxford 116	a	09 51	10 51	12 52	14 49	15 49	16 49	17 54	18 51	19 51	20 51	21 48	22 43
Didcot Parkway 125,116	a	10 06	11 07	13 12	15 11	16 12	17 12	18 12	19 07	20 07	21 10	22 02	22 56
Reading ■ 135,125,116	a	10 23	11 23	13 28	15 27	16 27	17 27	18 27	19 27	20 23	21 27	22 19	23 12
Slough ■ 135,125,116	a	10 39	11 38	13 44	15 43	16 43	17 43	18 43	19 43	20 43	21 45	22 38	23 30
London Paddington ■ ⊖135,125,116	a	11 05	12 05	14 10	16 10	17 09	18 10	19 09	20 10	21 08	22 12	23 09	23 51

A ■ from Oxford

For additional services between Worcester and London refer to Table T125

Table T127-F

Mondays to Fridays

21 May to 7 December

Cardiff Central - Ebbw Vale Town

Miles			AW	AW	AW	AW	AW	AW	AW	AW	AW	AW	AW	AW	AW	AW	AW	AW	AW FO	AW FX
—	Newport (South Wales)	d																		
0	**Cardiff Central 7**	d	06 34	07 38	08 34	09 34	10 34	11 34	12 34	13 34	14 34	15 34	16 34	17 37	18 34	19 35	20 34	21 34	23 05	23 05
—	Pye Corner	d	06 53	07 57	08 54	09 53	10 53	11 53	12 53	13 53	14 53	15 53	16 53	17 56	18 53	19 54	20 53	21 53	23 27	23 28
14	Rogerstone	d	06 57	08 00	08 58	09 57	10 57	11 57	12 57	13 57	14 57	15 57	16 57	18 00	18 57	19 58	20 57	21 57	23 29	23 30
15¼	Risca & Pontymister	d	07 01	08 03	09 01	10 00	11 00	12 00	13 00	14 00	15 00	16 00	17 00	18 03	19 00	20 01	21 01	22 01	23 32	23 33
17¼	Cross Keys	d	07 06	08 09	09 07	10 06	11 06	12 06	13 06	14 06	15 06	16 06	17 06	18 09	19 06	20 07	21 06	22 06	23 38	23 39
20¾	Newbridge (Ebbw Vale)	d	07 14	08 17	09 15	10 14	11 14	12 14	13 14	14 14	15 14	16 14	17 14	18 17	19 14	20 15	21 14	22 14	23 46	23 47
23½	Llanhilleth	d	07 20	08 23	09 21	10 20	11 20	12 20	13 20	14 20	15 20	16 20	17 20	18 23	19 20	20 21	21 20	22 20	23 52	23 53
28¾	**Ebbw Vale Parkway**	a	07 29	08 32	09 29	10 28	11 28	12 28	13 28	14 28	15 28	16 28	17 28	18 31	19 28	20 29	21 29	22 29	00 02	00 01
—	Ebbw Vale Town	a	07 35	08 39	09 35	10 35	11 35	12 35	13 35	14 35	15 35	16 35	17 35	18 36	19 35	20 37	21 35	22 35	00 08	00 09

Saturdays

26 May to 8 December

		AW	AW	AW	AW	AW	AW	AW	AW	AW	AW	AW	AW	AW	AW	AW	AW	AW
Newport (South Wales)	d																	
Cardiff Central 7	d	06 34	07 37	08 34	09 34	10 34	11 34	12 34	13 34	14 34	15 34	16 34	17 34	18 34	19 35	20 34	21 34	23 02
Pye Corner	d	06 53	07 56	08 53	09 53	10 53	11 53	12 53	13 53	14 53	15 53	16 53	17 53	18 53	19 53	20 53	21 53	23 24
Rogerstone	d	06 57	08 00	08 57	09 57	10 57	11 57	12 57	13 57	14 57	15 57	16 57	17 57	18 57	19 58	20 57	21 57	23 26
Risca & Pontymister	d	07 00	08 04	09 00	10 00	11 01	12 01	13 01	14 01	15 01	16 01	17 01	18 01	19 01	20 01	21 01	22 01	23 29
Cross Keys	d	07 06	08 09	09 06	10 06	11 06	12 06	13 06	14 06	15 06	16 06	17 06	18 06	19 06	20 10	21 06	22 06	23 37
Newbridge (Ebbw Vale)	d	07 14	08 17	09 14	10 14	11 14	12 14	13 14	14 14	15 14	16 14	17 14	18 14	19 14	20 14	21 14	22 14	23 43
Llanhilleth	d	07 20	08 23	09 20	10 20	11 20	12 20	13 20	14 20	15 20	16 20	17 20	18 20	19 20	20 20	21 20	22 20	23 49
Ebbw Vale Parkway	a	07 28	08 32	09 28	10 28	11 29	12 29	13 29	14 29	15 29	16 29	17 29	18 29	19 29	20 29	21 29	22 29	23 57
Ebbw Vale Town	a	07 35	08 38	09 35	10 35	11 35	12 35	13 35	14 35	15 35	16 35	17 35	18 35	19 35	20 37	21 35	22 35	00 07

Sundays

20 May to 2 December

		AW	AW	AW	AW	AW	AW	AW
Newport (South Wales)	d							
Cardiff Central 7	d	07 38	09 22	11 30	13 53	16 29	19 02	21 28
Pye Corner	d	07 58	09 43	11 50	14 14	16 49	19 22	21 48
Rogerstone	d	08 02	09 47	11 54	14 18	16 53	19 26	21 52
Risca & Pontymister	d	08 06	09 50	11 57	14 22	16 57	19 30	21 56
Cross Keys	d	08 12	09 56	12 02	14 27	17 03	19 36	22 02
Newbridge (Ebbw Vale)	d	08 20	10 04	12 10	14 36	17 11	19 44	22 10
Llanhilleth	d	08 27	10 10	12 16	14 42	17 18	19 51	22 17
Ebbw Vale Parkway	a	08 35	10 18	12 25	14 50	17 26	19 59	22 25
Ebbw Vale Town	a	08 41	10 26	12 32	14 58	17 34	20 07	22 32

Table T127-R

Mondays to Fridays

21 May to 7 December

Ebbw Vale Town - Cardiff Central

Miles			AW	AW	AW	AW	AW	AW	AW	AW	AW	AW	AW	AW	AW	AW	AW	AW	AW
—	Ebbw Vale Town	d	06 35	07 37	08 40	09 38	10 37	11 37	12 37	13 37	14 37	15 37	16 37	17 37	18 40	19 37	20 41	21 37	22 37
0	**Ebbw Vale Parkway**	d	06 38	07 40	08 43	09 41	10 40	11 40	12 40	13 40	14 40	15 40	16 40	17 40	18 43	19 40	20 44	21 40	22 40
5¼	Llanhilleth	d	06 46	07 48	08 51	09 49	10 48	11 48	12 48	13 48	14 48	15 48	16 48	17 48	18 51	19 48	20 52	21 48	22 48
8	Newbridge (Ebbw Vale)	d	06 52	07 54	08 57	09 55	10 54	11 54	12 54	13 54	14 54	15 54	16 54	17 54	18 57	19 54	20 58	21 54	22 54
11½	Cross Keys	d	07 00	08 02	09 05	10 03	11 02	12 02	13 02	14 02	15 02	16 02	17 02	18 02	19 05	20 02	21 06	22 02	23 02
13½	Risca & Pontymister	d	07 05	08 07	09 10	10 08	11 07	12 07	13 07	14 07	15 07	16 07	17 07	18 07	19 10	20 07	21 11	22 07	23 07
14¾	Rogerstone	d	07 09	08 11	09 14	10 12	11 11	12 11	13 11	14 11	15 11	16 11	17 11	18 11	19 14	20 11	21 15	22 11	23 11
—	Pye Corner	d	07 13	08 15	09 18	10 16	11 15	12 15	13 15	14 15	15 15	16 15	17 15	18 15	19 18	20 15	21 19	22 15	23 15
28¾	**Cardiff Central 7**	a	07 35	08 37	09 39	10 38	11 38	12 37	13 37	14 36	15 37	16 36	17 37	18 37	19 40	20 37	21 43	22 40	23 40
—	Newport (South Wales)	a																	

Saturdays

26 May to 8 December

		AW	AW	AW	AW	AW	AW	AW	AW	AW	AW	AW	AW	AW	AW	AW	AW	AW
Ebbw Vale Town	d	06 37	07 37	08 40	09 37	10 37	11 37	12 37	13 37	14 37	15 37	16 37	17 37	18 37	19 37	20 41	21 37	22 37
Ebbw Vale Parkway	d	06 40	07 40	08 43	09 40	10 40	11 40	12 40	13 40	14 40	15 40	16 40	17 40	18 40	19 40	20 44	21 40	22 40
Llanhilleth	d	06 48	07 48	08 51	09 48	10 48	11 48	12 48	13 48	14 48	15 48	16 48	17 48	18 48	19 48	20 52	21 48	22 48
Newbridge (Ebbw Vale)	d	06 54	07 54	08 57	09 54	10 54	11 54	12 54	13 54	14 54	15 54	16 54	17 54	18 54	19 55	20 58	21 54	22 54
Cross Keys	d	07 02	08 02	09 05	10 02	11 02	12 02	13 02	14 02	15 02	16 02	17 02	18 02	19 02	20 03	21 06	22 02	23 02
Risca & Pontymister	d	07 07	08 07	09 10	10 07	11 07	12 07	13 07	14 07	15 07	16 07	17 07	18 07	19 07	20 07	21 11	22 07	23 07
Rogerstone	d	07 11	08 11	09 14	10 11	11 11	12 11	13 11	14 11	15 11	16 11	17 11	18 11	19 11	20 11	21 15	22 11	23 11
Pye Corner	d	07 15	08 15	09 18	10 15	11 15	12 15	13 15	14 15	15 15	16 15	17 15	18 15	19 15	20 15	21 19	22 15	23 15
Cardiff Central 7	a	07 36	08 38	09 40	10 37	11 37	12 37	13 38	14 37	15 37	16 36	17 38	18 37	19 37	20 37	21 41	22 37	23 38
Newport (South Wales)	a																	

Sundays

20 May to 2 December

		AW	AW	AW	AW	AW	AW	AW
Ebbw Vale Town	d	08 49	10 27	12 33	15 01	17 35	20 08	22 32
Ebbw Vale Parkway	d	08 52	10 30	12 36	15 04	17 38	20 11	22 35
Llanhilleth	d	09 01	10 39	12 45	15 13	17 47	20 19	22 44
Newbridge (Ebbw Vale)	d	09 07	10 45	12 51	15 19	17 53	20 25	22 50
Cross Keys	d	09 15	10 53	12 59	15 27	18 01	20 33	22 58
Risca & Pontymister	d	09 20	10 58	13 04	15 32	18 06	20 38	23 03
Rogerstone	d	09 24	11 02	13 08	15 36	18 10	20 41	23 07
Pye Corner	d	09 28	11 05	13 11	15 40	18 13	20 45	23 10
Cardiff Central 7	a	09 53	11 30	13 36	16 08	18 42	21 11	23 35
Newport (South Wales)	a							

Table T128-F

Mondays to Fridays

21 May to 7 December

Cardiff - Maesteg, Swansea and West Wales

Miles	Miles			AW MO ◇ A	AW MX ◇	AW MX	AW MX ◇	AW	GW MX ◇1 ☕	GW MO ◇1 B ☕	GW MO ◇1 C ☕	GW MX ◇1 ☕	AW	AW	AW	AW	AW ◇	AW	AW ◇ 🛒	AW	AW ◇	AW	AW ◇
—	—	London Paddington 15 ⊖	d																				
—	—	Reading 7	d																				
—	—	Manchester Piccadilly 10	d																				
—	—	Gloucester 7	d																			05 50	
—	—	Bristol Parkway 7	d									00 28											
—	—	Newport (South Wales)	d									00 57										06 44	
0	—	**Cardiff Central 7**	d									01 19							05 35	05 53	06 42	07 03	
11	—	Pontyclun	d																05 51			07 15	
14	—	Llanharan	d																05 56			07 20	
16¾	—	Pencoed	d																06 01			07 24	
20¼	0	Bridgend	d						00 05	00 19	00 19	01 43							06 07	06 15	07 05	07 33	
—	1	Wildmill	d																	06 17		07 35	
—	2¼	Sarn	d																	06 20		07 38	
—	3	Tondu	d																	06 24		07 42	
—	7	Garth (Mid Glamorgan)	d																	06 33		07 51	
—	7¾	Maesteg (Ewenny Road)	d																	06 36		07 54	
—	8¼	Maesteg	a																	06 41		07 56	
26¼	—	Pyle	d																06 15		07 14		
32½	—	Port Talbot Parkway	d				00 01		00 18	00 32	00 32	01 56							06 23		07 22		
34½	—	Baglan	d				00 05												06 27		07 26		
36¼	—	Briton Ferry	d				00 09												06 30		07 30		
38	—	Neath	d				00 13		00 26	00 39	00 40	02 04							06 34		07 34		
41¾	—	Skewen	d				00 16												06 38		07 37		
43½	—	Llansamlet	d				00 20												06 42		07 42		
47½	—	**Swansea**	a				00 28		00 39	00 52	00 53	02 17							06 51		07 50		
—	—		d			00 13	00 45									05 45	06 04		06 53		07 54		08 14
53	—	Gowerton	d			00 24	00s55									05 55	06 15		07 03		08 05		
53¾	—	Llanelli	a			00 29	01s02									06 02	06 22		07 11		08 11		08 30
—	—		d			00 30										06 04			07 11		08 12		08 31
62¾	—	Pembrey & Burry Port	d	00 04		00 35	01s09									06 10			07 17		08 17		
68	—	Kidwelly	d	00x11		00x42	01s15									06x18			07x23		08x24		
72¼	—	Ferryside	d	00x17		00x48	01s21									06x24			07x29		08x30		
79¼	—	**Carmarthen**	a	00 33		01 05	01 40									06 38			07 43		08 43		
—	—		d					04 50					05 30	05 50	05 58	06 39			07 46		08 44		
93¼	0	Whitland	a					05 03					05 46	06 05	06 13	06 56			08 00		08 59		09 09
—	—		d					05 03					05 47	06 05	06 13	06 56			08 00		09 02		09 10
—	5¼	Narberth	d										05x56			07x05					09x11		
—	10¾	Kilgetty	d										06x05			07x15					09x21		
—	11½	Saundersfoot	d										06x07			07x17					09x23		
—	15¾	**Tenby**	a										06 14			07 24					09 30		
—	—		d										06 24			07 32					09 43		
—	17	Penally	d										06x27			07x35					09x46		
—	20¼	Manorbier	d										06 33			07 42					09 53		
—	23¾	Lamphey	d										06x41			07x49					10x00		
—	25¼	Pembroke	d										06 44			07 52					10 03		
—	27¼	**Pembroke Dock**	a										06 54			08 07					10 18		
98¾	—	Clunderwen	d					05x10						06x12	06x19				08x07				09x17
105¼	0	Clarbeston Road	d					05x18						06x20	06x27			07 20	08x14				09x25
—	5¼	Haverfordwest	d					05 29							06 35				08 23				
—	10	Johnston	d		00x06			05x37							06x43				08x31				
—	14	**Milford Haven**	a		00 21			05 52							06 58				08 43				
—	—	Fishguard & Goodwick	a											06 38				07 38					09 44
121	—	**Fishguard Harbour 30** ⛴	a											06 44				07 44					09 50
—	—		d																				
—	—	Rosslare Harbour ⛴	a																				

A not 4 June **B** from 17 September **C** until 10 September

When events are being held at the Principality Stadium, services are subject to alteration. Please check times before travelling.

Ferry service between Fishguard Harbour and Rosslare Harbour is operated by Stena Line

Table T128-F

Mondays to Fridays

21 May to 7 December

Cardiff - Maesteg, Swansea and West Wales

		AW	AW ◇ A 🛒	GW ◇1 ☕	AW ◇	AW ◇	GW ◇1 ☕	AW ◇ 🛒	AW	AW	AW	GW ◇1 B ☕	AW ◇ 🛒	AW R	AW ◇ A 🛒	AW	AW ◇ 🛒	GW ◇1 ☕	AW 🛒	AW	AW	AW ◇ 🛒	GW ◇1 ☕
London Paddington 15 ⊖	d			05 19			06 45					07 45						08 45					09 45
Reading 7	d			05 54			07 12					08 12						09 12					10 12
Manchester Piccadilly 10	d														06 29		07 30					08 31	
Gloucester 7	d										07 58					08 58							
Bristol Parkway 7	d						08 10					09 09						10 09					11 09
Newport (South Wales)	d		07 32	07 49		08 01	08 33	08 38			08 52	09 31			09 36	09 52	10 24	10 34				11 22	11 32
Cardiff Central 7	d	07 14	07 50	08 05		08 21	08 53	09 04		09 12	09 18	09 52			10 04	10 18	10 41	10 50		11 12	11 18	11 38	11 48
Pontyclun	d					08 33					09 30					10 30					11 30		
Llanharan	d					08 38					09 35					10 35					11 35		
Pencoed	d					08 42					09 39					10 39					11 39		
Bridgend	d	07 38	08 09	08 25		08 50	09 15	09 24		09 32	09 46	10 12			10 23	10 46	11 00	11 11		11 32	11 46	11 59	12 09
Wildmill	d					08 52					09 49					10 49					11 49		
Sarn	d					08 55					09 52					10 52					11 52		
Tondu	d					08 59					09 55					10 55					11 55		
Garth (Mid Glamorgan)	d					09 08					10 05					11 05					12 04		
Maesteg (Ewenny Road)	d					09 11					10 07					11 07					12 07		
Maesteg	a					09 16					10 10					11 10					12 11		
Pyle	d	07 46	08 17							09 40										11 40			
Port Talbot Parkway	d	07 55	08 25	08 38			09 28	09 37		09 48		10 25			10 36		11 12	11 24		11 48		12 11	12 22
Baglan	d	07 58	08 28							09 52										11 52			
Briton Ferry	d	08 02	08 31							09 55										11 55			
Neath	d	08 06	08 35	08 46			09 35	09 44		09 59		10 33			10 43		11 19	11 31		11 59		12 18	12 29
Skewen	d	08 09	08 39							10 03										12 03			
Llansamlet	d	08 13	08 43							10 07										12 07			
Swansea	a	08 25	08 52	08 58			09 48	09 56		10 18		10 45			10 55		11 33	11 44		12 18		12 35	12 42
	d		09 06		09 34			10 03					11 00		11 04		11 37		12 00	12 22		12 40	
Gowerton	d		09 17		09 45			10 14							11 17				12 10	12 33		12 51	
Llanelli	a		09 23		09 52			10 20					11 15		11 22		11 51		12 17	12 40		12 57	
	d		09 25					10 22					11 17		11 23		11 53		12 19			12 59	
Pembrey & Burry Port	d		09 31					10 28							11 28		11 59		12 25			13 05	
Kidwelly	d		09x37					10x34									12x05						
Ferryside	d		09x42					10x39									12x10						
Carmarthen	a		09 55					10 54							11 49		12 25		12 48			13 24	
	d		09 59						10 58						11 53				12 51			13 30	
Whitland	a		10 13						11 12				11 51		12 06				13 06			13 45	
	d		10 14						11 13				11 51		12 06				13 06			13 45	
Narberth	d								11x22										13x15				
Kilgetty	d								11x32										13x25				
Saundersfoot	d								11x34										13x27				
Tenby	a								11 41										13 34				
	d								11 49										13 45				
Penally	d								11x52										13x48				
Manorbier	d								11 58										13 54				
Lamphey	d								12x06										14x02				
Pembroke	d								12 09										14 05				
Pembroke Dock	a								12 23										14 19				
Clunderwen	d		10x20												12x12							13x52	
Clarbeston Road	d		10x28												12x20							13x59	
Haverfordwest	d		10 36												12 28							14 08	
Johnston	d		10x44												12x36							14x16	
Milford Haven	a		10 57												12 53							14 31	
Fishguard & Goodwick	a												12 23										
Fishguard Harbour 30 ⛴	a												12 30										
	d													13 10									
Rosslare Harbour ⛴	a													16 25									

A not from 26 June until 29 June **B** The St. David

When events are being held at the Principality Stadium, services are subject to alteration. Please check times before travelling.

Ferry service between Fishguard Harbour and Rosslare Harbour is operated by Stena Line

Table T128-F

Mondays to Fridays

21 May to 7 December

Cardiff - Maesteg, Swansea and West Wales

		AW	AW	GW	AW	AW	AW	AW	AW	GW	AW	AW	GW	AW	AW	AW	AW	GW	AW	AW	AW	AW
			◇ ⊥	◇1 A ✕⊐			◇		◇ ⊥	◇1 ⊐		◇ ⊥	◇1 ⊐		■ ⊥		■ ⊥	◇1 ⊐	◇ ⊥			
London Paddington 15 ⊖	d			10 45						11 45			12 45					13 45				
Reading 7	d			11 12						12 12			13 12					14 12				
Manchester Piccadilly 10	d		09 31						10 31			11 31					12 31					
Gloucester 7	d	10 58														13 58			14 48			
Bristol Parkway 7	d			12 09						13 09			14 09					15 09				
Newport (South Wales)	d	11 52	12 23	12 33					13 23	13 32		14 22	14 33		14 56	14 59	15 22	15 31	15 42			
Cardiff Central 7	d	12 18	12 40	12 50		13 13		13 18	13 40	13 49	14 21	14 43	14 49		15 13	15 19	15 39	15 48	16 04	16 18	16 38	
Pontyclun	d	12 30						13 30			14 33					15 31				16 30	16 50	
Llanharan	d	12 35						13 35			14 38					15 36				16 35		
Pencoed	d	12 39						13 39			14 42					15 40				16 39	16 57	
Bridgend	d	12 46	12 59	13 10		13 34		13 46	14 04	14 10	14 49	15 02	15 10		15 32	15 47	16 01	16 08	16 24	16 45	17a04	
Wildmill	d	12 49						13 49			14 52					15 50				16 48		
Sarn	d	12 52						13 52			14 55					15 53				16 51		
Tondu	d	12 55						13 55			14 58					15 56				16 54		
Garth (Mid Glamorgan)	d	13 05						14 05			15 08					16 06				17 04		
Maesteg (Ewenny Road)	d	13 07						14 07			15 10					16 08				17 06		
Maesteg	a	13 10						14 10			15 13					16 11				17 09		
Pyle	d					13 42									15 40				16 32			
Port Talbot Parkway	d		13 12	13 23		13 50			14 18	14 24		15 15	15 23		15 49		16 14	16 21	16 39			
Baglan	d					13 54									15 52							
Briton Ferry	d					13 57									15 55							
Neath	d		13 19	13 31		14 01			14 25	14 31		15 22	15 30		15 59		16 21	16 29	16 46			
Skewen	d					14 05									16 03							
Llansamlet	d					14 09									16 07							
Swansea	a		13 34	13 43		14 20			14 35	14 44		15 35	15 43		16 15		16 35	16 41	17 00			
	d		13 37		14 00		14 35		14 37			15 37		16 00	16 20		16 40		17 05			17 38
Gowerton	d		13 48						14 51			15 48		16 11	16 31		16 51		17 16			17 48
Llanelli	a		13 54		14 15		14 51		14 55			15 55		16 17	16 38		16 57		17 23			17 55
	d		13 56		14 16				14 56			15 56		16 18			16 59		17 24			17 57
Pembrey & Burry Port	d		14 02		14 22				15 02			16 02		16 24			17 05		17 30			18 03
Kidwelly	d		14x08									16x08					17x11		17x36			18x11
Ferryside	d		14x13									16x14					17x16		17x42			18x17
Carmarthen	a		14 30		14 47				15 22			16 30		16 47			17 28		17 54			18 33
	d				14 51				15 28					16 51			17 31		17 59			
Whitland	a				15 05				15 43					17 05			17 45		18 13			
	d				15 06				15 43					17 06			17 46		18 14			
Narberth	d				15x15									17x15								
Kilgetty	d				15x25									17x25								
Saundersfoot	d				15x27									17x27								
Tenby	a				15 34									17 34								
	d				15 45									17 45								
Penally	d				15x48									17x48								
Manorbier	d				15 54									17 54								
Lamphey	d				16x02									18x02								
Pembroke	d				16 05									18 05								
Pembroke Dock	a				16 19									18 19								
Clunderwen	d								15x50								17x52		18x20			
Clarbeston Road	d								15x57								18x00		18x28			
Haverfordwest	d								16 06								18 08					
Johnston	d								16x14								18x16					
Milford Haven	a								16 25								18 31					
Fishguard & Goodwick	a																		18 46			
Fishguard Harbour 30 ⛴	a																		18 56			
	d																					
Rosslare Harbour ⛴	a																					

A Restaurant available for customers joining until Bristol Parkway. ⊐ from Bristol Parkway ✕ to Bristol Parkway

When events are being held at the Principality Stadium, services are subject to alteration. Please check times before travelling.

Ferry service between Fishguard Harbour and Rosslare Harbour is operated by Stena Line

Table T128-F

Mondays to Fridays

21 May to 7 December

Cardiff - Maesteg, Swansea and West Wales

		GW	AW	AW	AW	AW	AW	GW	AW	AW	GW	AW	GW	AW	AW	AW	AW	AW	GW	AW	GW	AW	GW
		◇1 ⊐	■ ⊥		■ ⊥	◇	■ ⊥	◇1 ⊐			■ 1 ⊐		■ 1 A ⊐	■ ⊥		R			■ 1 B ⊐	■ ⊥	■ 1 ⊐		■ 1 ⊐
London Paddington 15 ⊖	d	14 45						15 45			16 15		16 45						17 15		17 45		18 14
Reading 7	d	15 12						16 12			16 42		17 12						17 42		18 12		18 42
Manchester Piccadilly 10	d		13 31				14 31							15 31						16 31			
Gloucester 7	d									16 58							17 58					19 00	
Bristol Parkway 7	d	16 10						17 10			17 41		18 10						18 41		19 12		19 41
Newport (South Wales)	d	16 32	16 40		17 01		17 22	17 33		17 52	18 04		18 32	18 41			18 53		19 11	19 24	19 35	19 54	20 05
Cardiff Central 7	d	16 48	17 04		17 19		17 39	17 51	18 06	18 12	18 25		18 52	19 04			19 10		19 30	19 46	19 52	20 13	20 25
Pontyclun	d				17 34				18 18	18 24							19 26					20 25	
Llanharan	d		17 19		17 38					18 29							19 31					20 30	
Pencoed	d				17 42				18 25	18 33							19 35					20 34	
Bridgend	d	17 09	17 27		17 48		18 00	18 11	18 30	18 44	18 50		19 13	19 23			19 45		19 50	20 05	20 12	20 41	20 45
Wildmill	d				17 50					18 47							19 48					20 44	
Sarn	d				17 53					18 50							19 51					20 47	
Tondu	d				17 57					18 53							19 54					20 50	
Garth (Mid Glamorgan)	d				18 06					19 03							20 04					21 00	
Maesteg (Ewenny Road)	d				18 09					19 05							20 06					21 02	
Maesteg	a				18 15					19 08							20 09					21 05	
Pyle	d		17 34				18 09		18 39					19 30									
Port Talbot Parkway	d	17 22	17 42				18 18	18 24	18 47		19 03		19 26	19 38					20 03	20 21	20 26		20 58
Baglan	d		17 44						18 51					19 41									
Briton Ferry	d		17 48						18 54					19 44									
Neath	d	17 30	17 52				18 26	18 32	18 58		19 11		19 33	19 48					20 11	20 28	20 33		21 06
Skewen	d		17 56						19 02					19 53									
Llansamlet	d		18 00						19 06					19 57									
Swansea	a	17 42	18 07				18 39	18 44	19 14		19 23		19 46	20 04					20 23	20 42	20 46		21 18
	d		18 14			18 21	18 42					19 34		20 11					20 34	20 48			
Gowerton	d		18 25			18 32	18 53					19 45		20 22						20 59			
Llanelli	a		18 31			18 39	19 00					19 52		20 29					20 50	21 06			
	d		18 33				19 01					19 54		20 30					20 51	21 07			
Pembrey & Burry Port	d		18 38				19 07					20 00		20 36					20 58	21 13			
Kidwelly	d		18x44									20x07								21x20			
Ferryside	d		18x50									20x13								21x26			
Carmarthen	a		19 02				19 28					20 29		20 58					21 20	21 37			
	d		19 05				19 30								21 03			21 10		21 41			
Whitland	a		19 21				19 45								21 18			21 25		21 56			
	d		19 21				19 46								21 18			21 25		21 56			
Narberth	d		19x31															21x34					
Kilgetty	d		19x41															21x43					
Saundersfoot	d		19x43															21x45					
Tenby	a		19 55															21 52					
	d			20 05														21 54					
Penally	d			20x08														21x57					
Manorbier	d			20 14														22 03					
Lamphey	d			20x22														22x10					
Pembroke	d			20 25														22 13					
Pembroke Dock	a			20 36														22 26					
Clunderwen	d						19x53								21x25					22x03			
Clarbeston Road	d						20x00								21x33					22x10			
Haverfordwest	d						20 09													22 23			
Johnston	d						20x17													22x31			
Milford Haven	a						20 32													22 46			
Fishguard & Goodwick	a														21 52								
Fishguard Harbour 30 ⛴	a														22 00								
	d															23 45							
Rosslare Harbour ⛴	a															04 00							

A The Capitals United

B The Red Dragon

When events are being held at the Principality Stadium, services are subject to alteration. Please check times before travelling.

Ferry service between Fishguard Harbour and Rosslare Harbour is operated by Stena Line

Table T128-F

Mondays to Fridays

21 May to 7 December

Cardiff - Maesteg, Swansea and West Wales

		GW	AW FX	AW FO	AW FX	AW	GW FO	GW FX	AW FO	AW FX	AW FO	GW FO	GW FX	AW	AW	GW	GW FO	GW FX
		■ ■ A ☕	◇	◇	◇		■ ■ ☕	■ ■ ☕	◇	◇	◇	◇■ ☕	◇■ ☕		◇	◇■ ☕	◇■ ☕	◇■ ☕
London Paddington ■ ⊖	d	18 45					19 15	19 15				20 15	20 15			21 15	22 45	22 45
Reading ■	d	19 12					19 48	19 42				20 42	20 42			21 43	23 13	23 20
Manchester Piccadilly ■	d								18 31	18 29					19 31			
Gloucester ■	d					19 58												
Bristol Parkway ■	d	20 09					20 45	20 42				21 41	21 41			22 48	00 15	00 28
Newport (South Wales)	d	20 34				20 52	21 08	21 04	21 52	21 55		22 05	22 05		22 41	23 20	00 38	00 57
Cardiff Central ■	d	20 54	21 06	21 06		21 10	21 24	21 24	22 08	22 16		22 22	22 28	22 36	23 15	23 44	00 54	01 19
Pontyclun	d					21 22			22 21	22 27					23 29			
Llanharan	d					21 27			22 25	22 32					23 34			
Pencoed	d					21 32			22 29	22 36					23 39			
Bridgend	d	21 16	21 27	21 27		21 40	21 45	21 46	22 35	22 41		22 42	22 49	22 59	23 45	00 05	01 17	01 43
Wildmill	d					21 42								23 01				
Sarn	d					21 45								23 04				
Tondu	d					21 49								23 08				
Garth (Mid Glamorgan)	d					21 58								23 17				
Maesteg (Ewenny Road)	d					22 01								23 20				
Maesteg	a					22 05								23 23				
Pyle	d		21 35	21 35											23 53			
Port Talbot Parkway	d	21 29	21 45	21 45			21 58	21 59	22 47	22 54		22 55	23 04		00 01	00 18	01 30	01 56
Baglan	d														00 05			
Briton Ferry	d														00 09			
Neath	d	21 36	21 52	21 52			22 05	22 07	22 54			23 03	23 11		00 13	00 26	01 38	02 04
Skewen	d														00 16			
Llansamlet	d														00 20			
Swansea	a	21 50	22 05	22 05			22 18	22 20	23 07			23 15	23 24		00 28	00 39	01 50	02 17
	d		22 27	22 27					23 11						00 45			
Gowerton	d		22 38	22 38					23 22		←				00s55			
Llanelli	a		22 44	22 44					23 29	23 22	23 29				01s02			
	d		22 45	22 46					23 31	23 24	23 31							
Pembrey & Burry Port	d		22 51	22 51					→	23 30	23 37				01s09			
Kidwelly	d		22x57	22x57						23x36	23x43				01s15			
Ferryside	d		23x03	23x03	←					23x41	23x48				01s21			
Carmarthen	a		23 15	23 18	23 15					23 59	00 07				01 40			
	d		23 20	23 19	23 20													
Whitland	a		→	23 33	23 35													
	d			23 34	23 35													
Narberth	d																	
Kilgetty	d																	
Saundersfoot	d																	
Tenby	a																	
	d																	
Penally	d																	
Manorbier	d																	
Lamphey	d																	
Pembroke	d																	
Pembroke Dock	a																	
Clunderwen	d			23x40	23x42													
Clarbeston Road	d			23x49	23x50													
Haverfordwest	d			23 56	23 58													
Johnston	d			00x04	00x06													
Milford Haven	a			00 19	00 21													
Fishguard & Goodwick	a																	
Fishguard Harbour ■ ⛴	a																	
	d																	
Rosslare Harbour ⛴	a																	

A Y Cymro - The Welshman

When events are being held at the Principality Stadium, services are subject to alteration. Please check times before travelling.

Ferry service between Fishguard Harbour and Rosslare Harbour is operated by Stena Line

Table T128-F

Saturdays

26 May to 8 September

Cardiff - Maesteg, Swansea and West Wales

		AW	AW	AW	AW	GW	GW	AW	AW	AW	AW	AW	AW	AW	AW	GW	AW	AW	GW	AW	AW	GW	AW
		◇		◇		◇■ ☕	◇■ ☕	◇						◇ 🚲		◇■	◇		◇■			◇■	◇ 🚲
London Paddington ■ ⊖	d																						
Reading ■	d																						
Manchester Piccadilly ■	d																						
Gloucester ■	d																	05 50					
Bristol Parkway ■	d						00 15															07 10	
Newport (South Wales)	d						00 38											06 44				07 33	07 38
Cardiff Central ■	d						00 54							05 33	05 51		06 42	07 04			07 14	07 51	07 58
Pontyclun	d													05 47	06 03			07 16					
Llanharan	d													05 53	06 08			07 21					
Pencoed	d													05 57	06 13			07 25					
Bridgend	d					00 05	01 17							06 03	06 20		07 02	07 32			07 38	08 11	08 17
Wildmill	d														06 22			07 35					
Sarn	d														06 25			07 38					
Tondu	d														06 29			07 41					
Garth (Mid Glamorgan)	d														06 38			07 51					
Maesteg (Ewenny Road)	d														06 41			07 53					
Maesteg	a														06 43			07 56					
Pyle	d													06 11			07 10				07 46		
Port Talbot Parkway	d			00 01		00 18	01 30							06 20			07 18				07 54	08 24	08 30
Baglan	d			00 05										06 23			07 22				07 58		
Briton Ferry	d			00 09										06 27			07 25				08 01		
Neath	d			00 13		00 26	01 38							06 31			07 29				08 05	08 32	08 37
Skewen	d			00 16										06 34			07 33				08 09		
Llansamlet	d			00 20										06 38			07 37				08 13		
Swansea	a			00 28		00 39	01 50							06 47			07 45				08 22	08 44	08 51
	d		00 13	00 45				04 31				05 45		06 53		07 23	07 50		08 15				09 05
Gowerton	d		00 24	00s55				04 42				05 55		07 03			08 00						09 16
Llanelli	a		00 29	01s02				04 49				06 02		07 11		07 39	08 07		08 31				09 22
	d		00 30									06 04		07 11		07 40	08 08		08 36				09 24
Pembrey & Burry Port	d		00 35	01s09								06 10		07 17		07 47	08 14		08 43				09 30
Kidwelly	d		00x42	01s15								06x17		07x23			08x20						09x36
Ferryside	d		00x48	01s21								06x23		07x29			08x26						09x41
Carmarthen	a		01 05	01 40								06 38		07 43		08 08	08 40		09 08				09 53
	d				04 50				05 30	05 50	05 58	06 39		07 46		08 16	08 45			09 40			09 57
Whitland	a				05 03				05 46	06 05	06 13	06 56		08 00		08 34	09 01			09 54			10 13
	d				05 03				05 46	06 06	06 13	06 56		08 00		08 35	09 01			09 54			10 14
Narberth	d								05x55			07x05				08x44				10x03			
Kilgetty	d								06x05			07x15				08x53				10x13			
Saundersfoot	d								06x07			07x17				08 58				10x15			
Tenby	a								06 14			07 24				09 07				10 26			
	d								06 24			07 32				09 08							
Penally	d								06x27			07x35				09x11							
Manorbier	d								06 33			07 42				09 20							
Lamphey	d								06x41			07x49				09x29							
Pembroke	d								06 44			07 52				09 35							
Pembroke Dock	a								06 59			08 07				09 44							
Clunderwen	d				05x10					06x13	06x19			08x07			09x07						10x20
Clarbeston Road	d				05x18					06x21	06x27		07 20	08x15			09x15						10x28
Haverfordwest	d				05 30						06 35			08 23									10 36
Johnston	d	00x04			05x38						06x43			08x31									10x44
Milford Haven	a	00 19			05 53						06 58			08 48									10 58
Fishguard & Goodwick	a									06 39			07 38				09 33						
Fishguard Harbour ■ ⛴	a									06 46			07 44				09 43						
	d																						
Rosslare Harbour ⛴	a																						

When events are being held at the Principality Stadium, services are subject to alteration. Please check times before travelling.

Ferry service between Fishguard Harbour and Rosslare Harbour is operated by Stena Line

Table T128-F

Saturdays
26 May to 8 September

Cardiff - Maesteg, Swansea and West Wales

		AW	AW	AW	AW	AW	AW	AW	GW	AW	AW	AW	AW	GW	AW	AW	AW	AW	GW	AW	AW	AW	AW
		◇	◇	◇				◇	◇1	◇		◇		◇2 A	◇			◇	◇1			◇	
London Paddington 15 ⊖	d								07 45					08 45					09 45				
Reading 7	d								08 12					09 12					10 12				
Manchester Piccadilly 10	d											06 30			07 30					08 30			
Gloucester 7	d						07 58						08 58								10 58		
Bristol Parkway 7	d								09 09					10 09					11 09				
Newport (South Wales)	d	08 02		08 33			08 52	09 01	09 32			09 39	09 52	10 31	10 44			10 59	11 31	11 37	11 52		
Cardiff Central 7	d	08 21		09 04		09 14	09 18	09 18	09 50			10 00	10 18	10 50	11 05	11 14		11 18	11 50	12 04	12 18		
Pontyclun	d	08 33					09 30	09 30					10 30					11 30			12 30		
Llanharan	d	08 38					09 35	09 35					10 35					11 35			12 35		
Pencoed	d	08 42					09 39	09 39					10 39					11 39			12 39		
Bridgend	d	08 50		09 23		09 34	09 46	09 46	10 10			10 19	10 46	11 10	11 24	11 34		11 46	12 10	12 23	12 46		
Wildmill	d	08 52					09 49	09 49					10 49					11 49			12 49		
Sarn	d	08 55					09 52	09 52					10 52					11 52			12 52		
Tondu	d	08 59					09 55	09 55					10 55					11 55			12 55		
Garth (Mid Glamorgan)	d	09 08					10 05	10 05					11 05					12 05			13 05		
Maesteg (Ewenny Road)	d	09 11					10 07	10 07					11 07					12 07			13 07		
Maesteg	a	09 15					10 10	10 10					11 10					12 10			13 10		
Pyle	d					09 43										11 42							
Port Talbot Parkway	d			09 36		09 52			10 23			10 31		11 23	11 38	11 50			12 23	12 36			
Baglan	d					09 55										11 54							
Briton Ferry	d					09 59										11 57							
Neath	d			09 43		10 03			10 31			10 38		11 31	11 46	12 01			12 31	12 43			
Skewen	d					10 06										12 05							
Llansamlet	d					10 10										12 09							
Swansea	a			09 55		10 21			10 43			10 51		11 43	11 59	12 20			12 43	12 55			
	d		09 15	10 04						11 00		11 04		11 50	12 05		12 35			13 02		13 12	13 35
Gowerton	d		09 26	10 15								11 17			12 16					13 14		13 23	
Llanelli	a		09 33	10 21						11 15		11 23		12 06	12 22		12 50			13 20		13 30	13 50
	d			10 22						11 17		11 23		12 07	12 24		12 51			13 22			13 51
Pembrey & Burry Port	d			10 28								11 31		12 14	12 30		12 57			13 28			13 57
Kidwelly	d			10x34											12x36								
Ferryside	d			10x40											12x41								
Carmarthen	a			10 51								11 51		12 40	12 53		13 23			13 47			14 20
	d				10 56							11 53		12 47						13 51			14 38
Whitland	a				11 10					11 51		12 08		13 04						14 06			14 54
	d				11 11					11 51		12 08		13 06						14 15			14 54
Narberth	d				11x20																		15x03
Kilgetty	d				11x30																		15x13
Saundersfoot	d				11x32									13 26									15x15
Tenby	a				11 39									13 34									15 22
	d				11 45									13 40									15 34
Penally	d				11x48																		15x37
Manorbier	d				11 54									13 50									15 43
Lamphey	d				12x02																		15x51
Pembroke	d				12 05									14 02									15 54
Pembroke Dock	a				12 20									14 13									16 09
Clunderwen	d											12x15								14x21			
Clarbeston Road	d											12x22								14x29			
Haverfordwest	d											12 31								14 37			
Johnston	d											12x39								14x45			
Milford Haven	a											12 54								15 00			
Fishguard & Goodwick	a									12 23													
Fishguard Harbour 30 ⛴	a									12 30													
	d										13 10												
Rosslare Harbour ⛴	a										16 25												

A The Pembroke Coast Express

When events are being held at the Principality Stadium, services are subject to alteration. Please check times before travelling.

Ferry service between Fishguard Harbour and Rosslare Harbour is operated by Stena Line

Table T128-F

Saturdays
26 May to 8 September

Cardiff - Maesteg, Swansea and West Wales

		GW	AW	AW	AW	GW	AW	AW	GW	AW	AW	AW	AW	AW	GW	AW	AW	GW	AW	AW	AW	AW
		◇1	◇			◇1			◇1	◇					◇1	◇		◇1			◇	◇
London Paddington 15 ⊖	d	10 45				11 45			12 45						13 45			14 45				
Reading 7	d	11 12				12 12			13 12						14 12			15 12				
Manchester Piccadilly 10	d		09 30				10 31			11 31				12 31						13 31		
Gloucester 7	d												13 58			14 42						
Bristol Parkway 7	d	12 09				13 09			14 09						15 09			16 09				
Newport (South Wales)	d	12 31	12 40			13 32	13 37		14 31	14 39		14 55	14 52	15 22	15 31	15 37		16 31		16 38	16 56	
Cardiff Central 7	d	12 50	13 04	13 10	13 18	13 50	14 04	14 21	14 50	15 04		15 14	15 18	15 40	15 50	16 04	16 18	16 50		17 04	17 17	
Pontyclun	d				13 30			14 33					15 30				16 30				17 27	
Llanharan	d				13 35			14 38					15 35				16 35				17 32	
Pencoed	d				13 39			14 42					15 39				16 39				17 36	
Bridgend	d	13 10	13 23	13 32	13 46	14 10	14 23	14 49	15 10	15 23		15 34	15 46	15 59	16 10	16 24	16 46	17 10		17 25	17 43	
Wildmill	d				13 49			14 52					15 49				16 49				17 45	
Sarn	d				13 52			14 55					15 52				16 52				17 48	
Tondu	d				13 55			14 58					15 55				16 55				17 52	
Garth (Mid Glamorgan)	d				14 05			15 08					16 05				17 05				18 01	
Maesteg (Ewenny Road)	d				14 07			15 10					16 07				17 07				18 04	
Maesteg	a				14 10			15 13					16 10				17 10				18 08	
Pyle	d			13 40								15 42				16 32				17 32		
Port Talbot Parkway	d	13 23	13 36	13 48		14 23	14 36		15 23	15 36		15 50		16 17	16 23	16 40		17 23		17 40		
Baglan	d			13 52								15 54								17 42		
Briton Ferry	d			13 55								15 57								17 46		
Neath	d	13 31	13 43	13 59		14 31	14 43		15 31	15 43		16 01		16 24	16 31	16 48		17 31		17 50		
Skewen	d			14 03								16 05								17 54		
Llansamlet	d			14 07								16 09								17 58		
Swansea	a	13 43	13 57	14 18		14 43	14 55		15 43	15 55		16 17		16 36	16 43	17 01		17 43		18 05		
	d		14 05				15 00			16 00	16 09	16 23		16 40		17 06			17 59	18 11		18 17
Gowerton	d		14 16				15 12			16 11	16 21	16 34		16 51		17 16			18 09	18 22		18 28
Llanelli	a		14 22				15 18			16 17	16 27	16 41		16 57		17 23			18 16	18 28		18 34
	d		14 24				15 20			16 19	16 28			16 59		17 24			18 18	18 32		
Pembrey & Burry Port	d		14 30				15 26			16 25	16 35			17 05		17 30			18 24	18 38		
Kidwelly	d		14x36							16x31	16x43			17x11		17x36			18x32	18x44		
Ferryside	d		14x41							16x36	16x49			17x16		17x42			18x38	18x53		
Carmarthen	a		14 53				15 45			16 53	17 02			17 28		17 55			18 54	19 05		
	d						15 49				17 17			17 31		17 57				19 09		
Whitland	a						16 03				17 31			17 45		18 12				19 25		
	d						16 04				17 32			17 46		18 13				19 25		
Narberth	d										17x41									19x35		
Kilgetty	d										17x51									19x45		
Saundersfoot	d										17x53									19x47		
Tenby	a										18 00									19 57		
	d										18 05									19 57		
Penally	d										18x08									20x00		
Manorbier	d										18 14									20 07		
Lamphey	d										18x22									20x14		
Pembroke	d										18 25									20 17		
Pembroke Dock	a										18 40									20 29		
Clunderwen	d						16x10							17x52		18x20						
Clarbeston Road	d						16x18							18x00		18x27						
Haverfordwest	d						16 26							18 08								
Johnston	d						16x34							18x16								
Milford Haven	a						16 49							18 31								
Fishguard & Goodwick	a															18 46						
Fishguard Harbour 30 ⛴	a															18 54						
	d																					
Rosslare Harbour ⛴	a																					

When events are being held at the Principality Stadium, services are subject to alteration. Please check times before travelling.

Ferry service between Fishguard Harbour and Rosslare Harbour is operated by Stena Line

Table T128-F

Saturdays

26 May to 8 September

Cardiff - Maesteg, Swansea and West Wales

Station		AW	GW	AW	AW	AW	GW	AW	AW	AW	AW	GW	AW	GW	AW	GW	AW	AW	GW	AW	AW	GW
			◇■ ☕	■ A 🚲			◇■ ☕	■ 🚲			■	◇■ ☕	■ 🚲	◇■ ☕		◇■ ☕	◇		◇■ ☕	◇		◇■ ☕
London Paddington ⊖	d		15 45				16 45					17 45				18 45			19 45			20 45
Reading	d		16 12				17 12					18 12				19 12			20 12			21 12
Manchester Piccadilly	d			14 31				15 31					16 31							18 31		
Gloucester	d				16 58				17 58						18 58			19 58				
Bristol Parkway	d		17 09				18 09					19 08				20 09			21 09			22 12
Newport (South Wales)	d		17 32	17 37	17 52		18 31	18 39	18 52			19 31	19 41		19 52	20 31		20 52	21 31	21 45		22 46
Cardiff Central	d	17 38	17 50	18 04	18 18		18 50	19 04	19 15			19 50	20 01		20 13	20 50	21 04	21 12	21 51	22 08	22 35	23 08
Pontyclun	d				18 30				19 28						20 26			21 24		22 21	22 47	
Llanharan	d				18 35				19 33						20 31			21 29		22 25	22 52	
Pencoed	d				18 39				19 37						20 35			21 32		22 29	22 56	
Bridgend	d	17 58	18 10	18 25	18 46		19 10	19 24	19 45			20 10	20 20		20 42	21 10	21 23	21 41	22 11	22 35	23 02	23 29
Wildmill	d				18 49				19 48						20 45			21 43				
Sarn	d				18 52				19 51						20 48			21 46				
Tondu	d				18 55				19 54						20 51			21 50				
Garth (Mid Glamorgan)	d				19 05				20 04						21 01			21 59				
Maesteg (Ewenny Road)	d				19 07				20 06						21 03			22 02				
Maesteg	a				19 11				20 09						21 06			22 04				
Pyle	d	18 06		18 33				19 31									21 31				23 10	
Port Talbot Parkway	d	18 14	18 23	18 41			19 23	19 39				20 23	20 33			21 23	21 39		22 24	22 47	23 19	23 42
Baglan	d	18 18						19 42													23 24	
Briton Ferry	d	18 21						19 45													23 26	
Neath	d	18 25	18 32	18 49			19 31	19 49				20 31				21 31	21 46		22 32	22 54	23 31	23 50
Skewen	d	18 29						19 54													23 35	
Llansamlet	d	18 33						19 58													23 39	
Swansea	a	18 44	18 46	19 02			19 43	20 05				20 42				21 43	21 57		22 44	23 07	23 47	00 03
	d			19 05		19 34		20 13				21 00					22 25			23 10	23 53	
Gowerton	d			19 16		19 45		20 24						←			22 36			23 21	00 04	
Llanelli	a			19 23		19 52		20 30				21 16	21 02	21 16			22 42			23 28	00 11	
	d			19 24		19 54		20 32				21 17	21 03	21 17			22 44			23 29	00 12	
Pembrey & Burry Port	d			19 30		20 00		20 37				→	21 09	21 24			22 50			23 35	00 17	
Kidwelly	d					20x07							21x14				22x56			23x41	00x24	
Ferryside	d					20x13							21x19				23x01			23x46	00x30	
Carmarthen	a			19 51		20 29		20 57					21 31	21 48			23 23			00 03	00 47	
	d			19 58				21 00		21 07			22 05									
Whitland	a			20 13				21 15		21 23			22 19									
	d			20 13				21 15		21 23			22 20									
Narberth	d							21x24														
Kilgetty	d							21x33														
Saundersfoot	d							21x35														
Tenby	a							21 42														
	d							21 43														
Penally	d							21x46														
Manorbier	d							21 52														
Lamphey	d							22x00														
Pembroke	d							22 03														
Pembroke Dock	a							22 18														
Clunderwen	d			20x20									22x26									
Clarbeston Road	d			20x28						21x37			22x34									
Haverfordwest	d			20 36									22 42									
Johnston	d			20x44									22x50									
Milford Haven	a			20 59									23 05									
Fishguard & Goodwick	a									21 56												
Fishguard Harbour ⛴	a									22 04												
	d										23 45											
Rosslare Harbour ⛴	a										04 00											

A not 23 June

When events are being held at the Principality Stadium, services are subject to alteration. Please check times before travelling.

Ferry service between Fishguard Harbour and Rosslare Harbour is operated by Stena Line

Table T128-F

Saturdays

15 September to 8 December

Cardiff - Maesteg, Swansea and West Wales

Station		AW	AW	AW	AW	GW	GW	AW	AW	AW	AW	AW	AW	AW	AW	AW	AW	GW	AW	GW	AW	AW	AW
		◇		◇		◇■ ☕	◇■ ☕	◇						◇ 🚲		◇		◇■		◇■	◇	◇ 🚲	◇
London Paddington ⊖	d																						
Reading	d																						
Manchester Piccadilly	d																						
Gloucester	d																05 50						
Bristol Parkway	d						00 15													07 10			
Newport (South Wales)	d						00 38										06 44			07 33		07 38	08 02
Cardiff Central	d						00 54							05 33	05 51	06 42	07 04		07 14	07 51		07 58	08 21
Pontyclun	d													05 47	06 03		07 16						08 33
Llanharan	d													05 53	06 08		07 21						08 38
Pencoed	d													05 57	06 13		07 25						08 42
Bridgend	d					00 05	01 17							06 03	06 20	07 03	07 32		07 38	08 11		08 17	08 50
Wildmill	d														06 22		07 35						08 52
Sarn	d														06 25		07 38						08 55
Tondu	d														06 29		07 41						08 59
Garth (Mid Glamorgan)	d														06 38		07 51						09 08
Maesteg (Ewenny Road)	d														06 41		07 53						09 11
Maesteg	a														06 43		07 56						09 15
Pyle	d													06 11		07 11			07 46				
Port Talbot Parkway	d			00 01		00 18	01 30							06 20		07 19			07 54	08 24		08 30	
Baglan	d			00 05										06 23		07 23			07 58				
Briton Ferry	d			00 09										06 27		07 26			08 01				
Neath	d			00 13		00 26	01 38							06 31		07 30			08 05	08 32		08 37	
Skewen	d			00 16										06 34		07 34			08 09				
Llansamlet	d			00 20										06 38		07 38			08 13				
Swansea	a			00 28		00 39	01 50							06 47		07 46			08 22	08 44		08 51	
	d		00 13	00 45				04 31				05 45		06 53		07 50		08 15				09 05	
Gowerton	d		00 24	00s55				04 42				05 55		07 03		08 00						09 16	
Llanelli	a		00 29	01s02				04 49				06 02		07 11		08 07		08 31				09 22	
	d		00 30									06 04		07 11		08 08		08 36				09 24	
Pembrey & Burry Port	d		00 35	01s09								06 10		07 17		08 14		08 43				09 30	
Kidwelly	d		00x42	01s15								06x17		07x23		08x20						09x36	
Ferryside	d		00x48	01s21								06x23		07x29		08x26						09x41	
Carmarthen	a		01 05	01 40								06 38		07 43		08 40		09 08				09 53	
	d				04 50				05 30	05 50	05 58	06 39		07 46		08 43						09 57	
Whitland	a				05 03				05 46	06 05	06 13	06 56		08 00		08 59						10 13	
	d				05 03				05 46	06 06	06 13	06 56		08 00		09 02					09 07	10 14	
Narberth	d								05x55			07x05				09x11							
Kilgetty	d								06x05			07x15				09x21							
Saundersfoot	d								06x07			07x17				09x23							
Tenby	a								06 14			07 24				09 30							
	d								06 24			07 32				09 43							
Penally	d								06x27			07x35				09x46							
Manorbier	d								06 33			07 42				09 53							
Lamphey	d								06x41			07x49				10x00							
Pembroke	d								06 44			07 52				10 03							
Pembroke Dock	a								06 59			08 07				10 17							
Clunderwen	d				05x10					06x13	06x19			08x07							09x14	10x20	
Clarbeston Road	d				05x18					06x21	06x27		07 20	08x15							09x22	10x28	
Haverfordwest	d				05 30						06 35			08 23								10 36	
Johnston	d	00x04			05x38						06x43			08x31								10x44	
Milford Haven	a	00 19			05 53						06 58			08 48								10 58	
Fishguard & Goodwick	a									06 39			07 38								09 41		
Fishguard Harbour ⛴	a									06 46			07 44								09 47		
	d																						
Rosslare Harbour ⛴	a																						

When events are being held at the Principality Stadium, services are subject to alteration. Please check times before travelling.

Ferry service between Fishguard Harbour and Rosslare Harbour is operated by Stena Line

Table T128-F

Saturdays

15 September to 8 December

Cardiff - Maesteg, Swansea and West Wales

		AW	AW	AW	AW	AW	AW	GW	AW	AW	AW	AW	GW	AW	AW	AW	AW	GW	AW	AW	AW	GW	AW
		◇	◇ 🛒				◇ 🛒	◇**1** 🍽	◇ 🛒	R	◇ 🛒		◇**1** 🍽		◇ 🛒		◇ 🛒	◇**1** 🍽	■ 🛒		◇	◇**1** 🍽	
London Paddington ⊖	d							07 45					08 45					09 45				10 45	
Reading	d							08 12					09 12					10 12				11 12	
Manchester Piccadilly	d										06 30				07 30				08 30				
Gloucester	d					07 58						08 58								10 58			
Bristol Parkway	d							09 09					10 09					11 09				12 09	
Newport (South Wales)	d		08 33			08 52	09 01	09 32			09 39	09 52	10 31		10 44		10 59	11 31	11 37	11 52		12 31	
Cardiff Central	d		09 04		09 14	09 18	09 18	09 50			10 00	10 18	10 50		11 05	11 14	11 18	11 50	12 04	12 18		12 50	
Pontyclun	d					09 30	09 30					10 30					11 30			12 30			
Llanharan	d					09 35	09 35					10 35					11 35			12 35			
Pencoed	d					09 39	09 39					10 39					11 39			12 39			
Bridgend	d		09 23		09 34	09 46	09 46	10 10			10 19	10 46	11 10		11 24	11 34	11 46	12 10	12 23	12 46		13 10	
Wildmill	d					09 49	09 49					10 49					11 49			12 49			
Sarn	d					09 52	09 52					10 52					11 52			12 52			
Tondu	d					09 55	09 55					10 55					11 55			12 55			
Garth (Mid Glamorgan)	d					10 05	10 05					11 05					12 05			13 05			
Maesteg (Ewenny Road)	d					10 07	10 07					11 07					12 07			13 07			
Maesteg	a					10 10	10 10					11 10					12 10			13 10			
Pyle	d				09 43											11 42							
Port Talbot Parkway	d		09 36		09 52			10 23			10 31		11 23		11 38	11 50		12 23	12 36			13 23	
Baglan	d				09 55											11 54							
Briton Ferry	d				09 59											11 57							
Neath	d		09 43		10 03			10 31			10 38		11 31		11 46	12 01		12 31	12 43			13 31	
Skewen	d				10 06											12 05							
Llansamlet	d				10 10											12 09							
Swansea	a		09 55		10 21			10 43			10 51		11 43		11 59	12 20		12 43	12 55			13 43	
	d	09 15	10 04						11 00		11 04			11 50	12 05				13 02		13 12		13 50
Gowerton	d	09 26	10 15								11 17				12 16				13 14		13 23		
Llanelli	a	09 33	10 21						11 15		11 23			12 06	12 22				13 20		13 30		14 05
	d		10 22						11 17		11 23			12 11	12 24				13 22				14 06
Pembrey & Burry Port	d		10 28								11 31			12 17	12 30				13 28				14 13
Kidwelly	d		10x34												12x36								
Ferryside	d		10x40												12x41								
Carmarthen	a		10 51								11 51			12 40	12 53				13 47				14 40
	d			10 56							11 53			12 58					13 51				14 58
Whitland	a			11 10					11 51		12 08			13 12					14 06				15 12
	d			11 11					11 51		12 08			13 12					14 06				15 12
Narberth	d			11x20										13x21									15x21
Kilgetty	d			11x30										13x31									15x31
Saundersfoot	d			11x32										13x33									15x33
Tenby	a			11 39										13 40									15 40
	d			11 45										13 45									15 45
Penally	d			11x48										13x48									15x48
Manorbier	d			11 54										13 54									15 54
Lamphey	d			12x02										14x02									16x02
Pembroke	d			12 05										14 05									16 05
Pembroke Dock	a			12 20										14 19									16 19
Clunderwen	d										12x15								14x13				
Clarbeston Road	d										12x22								14x20				
Haverfordwest	d										12 31								14 29				
Johnston	d										12x39								14x37				
Milford Haven	a										12 54								14 52				
Fishguard & Goodwick	a								12 23														
Fishguard Harbour	a								12 30														
	d									13 10													
Rosslare Harbour	a									16 25													

When events are being held at the Principality Stadium, services are subject to alteration. Please check times before travelling.

Ferry service between Fishguard Harbour and Rosslare Harbour is operated by Stena Line

Table T128-F

Saturdays

15 September to 8 December

Cardiff - Maesteg, Swansea and West Wales

		AW	AW	AW	GW	AW	AW	GW	AW	AW	AW	AW	AW	GW	AW	AW	GW	AW	AW	AW	AW	AW
		◇ 🛒			◇**1** 🍽	■ 🛒		◇**1** 🍽	◇ 🛒				■ 🛒	◇**1** 🍽	◇ 🛒	🛒	◇**1** 🍽		■ 🛒	◇ 🛒	◇	
London Paddington ⊖	d				11 45			12 45						13 45			14 45					
Reading	d				12 12			13 12						14 12			15 12					
Manchester Piccadilly	d	09 30				10 31			11 31				12 31						13 31			
Gloucester	d											13 58			14 42							
Bristol Parkway	d				13 09			14 09						15 09			16 09					
Newport (South Wales)	d	12 40			13 32	13 37		14 31	14 39		14 55	14 52	15 22	15 31	15 37		16 31		16 38	16 56		
Cardiff Central	d	13 04	13 10	13 18	13 50	14 04	14 21	14 50	15 04		15 14	15 18	15 40	15 50	16 04	16 18	16 50		17 04	17 17		17 38
Pontyclun	d			13 30			14 33					15 30				16 30				17 27		
Llanharan	d			13 35			14 38					15 35				16 35				17 32		
Pencoed	d			13 39			14 42					15 39				16 39				17 36		
Bridgend	d	13 23	13 32	13 46	14 10	14 23	14 49	15 10	15 23		15 34	15 46	15 59	16 10	16 24	16 46	17 10		17 25	17 43		17 58
Wildmill	d			13 49			14 52					15 49				16 49				17 45		
Sarn	d			13 52			14 55					15 52				16 52				17 48		
Tondu	d			13 55			14 58					15 55				16 55				17 52		
Garth (Mid Glamorgan)	d			14 05			15 08					16 05				17 05				18 01		
Maesteg (Ewenny Road)	d			14 07			15 10					16 07				17 07				18 04		
Maesteg	a			14 10			15 13					16 10				17 10				18 08		
Pyle	d		13 40								15 42				16 32				17 32			18 06
Port Talbot Parkway	d	13 36	13 48		14 23	14 36		15 23	15 36		15 50		16 17	16 23	16 40		17 23		17 40			18 14
Baglan	d		13 52								15 54								17 42			18 18
Briton Ferry	d		13 55								15 57								17 46			18 21
Neath	d	13 43	13 59		14 31	14 43		15 31	15 43		16 01		16 24	16 31	16 48		17 31		17 50			18 25
Skewen	d		14 03								16 05								17 54			18 29
Llansamlet	d		14 07								16 09								17 58			18 33
Swansea	a	13 57	14 18		14 43	14 55		15 43	15 55		16 17		16 36	16 43	17 01		17 43		18 05			18 44
	d	14 05				15 00			16 00	16 09	16 23		16 40		17 06			17 50	18 09		18 17	
Gowerton	d	14 16				15 12			16 11	16 21	16 34		16 51		17 16			18 00	18 20		18 28	
Llanelli	a	14 22				15 18			16 17	16 27	16 41		16 57		17 23			18 07	18 26		18 35	
	d	14 24				15 20			16 19	16 28			16 59		17 24			18 09	18 28			
Pembrey & Burry Port	d	14 30				15 26			16 25	16 35			17 05		17 30			18 15	18 34			
Kidwelly	d	14x36							16x31				17x11		17x36			18x23	18x40			
Ferryside	d	14x41							16x36				17x16		17x42			18x29	18x46			
Carmarthen	a	14 53				15 45			16 53	16 57			17 28		17 55			18 47	19 01			
	d					15 49				16 59			17 31		17 57				19 05			
Whitland	a					16 03				17 13			17 45		18 12				19 21			
	d					16 04				17 14			17 46		18 13				19 21			
Narberth	d									17x23									19x31			
Kilgetty	d									17x32									19x41			
Saundersfoot	d									17x34									19x43			
Tenby	a									17 41									19 53			
	d									17 46									19 53			
Penally	d									17x49									19x56			
Manorbier	d									17 56									20 03			
Lamphey	d									18x03									20x10			
Pembroke	d									18 06									20 13			
Pembroke Dock	a									18 21									20 25			
Clunderwen	d					16x10							17x52		18x20							
Clarbeston Road	d					16x18							18x00		18x27							
Haverfordwest	d					16 26							18 08									
Johnston	d					16x34							18x16									
Milford Haven	a					16 49							18 31									
Fishguard & Goodwick	a														18 46							
Fishguard Harbour	a														18 54							
	d																					
Rosslare Harbour	a																					

When events are being held at the Principality Stadium, services are subject to alteration. Please check times before travelling.

Ferry service between Fishguard Harbour and Rosslare Harbour is operated by Stena Line

Table T128-F

Saturdays

15 September to 8 December

Cardiff - Maesteg, Swansea and West Wales

		GW	AW	AW	AW	GW	AW	AW	AW	AW	GW	AW	GW	AW	GW	AW	AW	GW	GW	AW	AW	GW
		◇1 ☕	▣ 🛒			◇1 ☕	▣ 🛒			⛴	◇1 ☕	▣ 🛒	◇1 ☕		◇1 ☕	◇		◇1 ☕	◇1 ☕	◇		◇1 ☕
London Paddington 15 ⊖	d	15 45				16 45					17 45				18 45			19 15	19 45			20 45
Reading 7	d	16 12				17 12					18 12				19 12			19 42	20 12			21 12
Manchester Piccadilly 10	d		14 31				15 31					16 31								18 31		
Gloucester 7	d			16 58				17 58						18 58			19 58					
Bristol Parkway 7	d	17 09				18 09					19 08				20 09			20 43	21 09			22 12
Newport (South Wales)	d	17 32	17 37	17 52		18 31	18 39	18 52			19 31	19 41		19 52	20 31		20 52	21 05	21 31	21 45		22 46
Cardiff Central 7	d	17 50	18 04	18 18		18 50	19 04	19 15			19 50	20 01		20 13	20 50	21 04	21 12	21 23	21 51	22 08	22 35	23 08
Pontyclun	d			18 30				19 28						20 26			21 24			22 21	22 47	
Llanharan	d			18 35				19 33						20 31			21 29			22 25	22 52	
Pencoed	d			18 39				19 37						20 35			21 32			22 29	22 56	
Bridgend	d	18 10	18 25	18 46		19 10	19 24	19 45			20 10	20 20		20 42	21 10	21 23	21 41	21 47	22 11	22 35	23 02	23 29
Wildmill	d			18 49				19 48						20 45			21 43					
Sarn	d			18 52				19 51						20 48			21 46					
Tondu	d			18 55				19 54						20 51			21 50					
Garth (Mid Glamorgan)	d			19 05				20 04						21 01			21 59					
Maesteg (Ewenny Road)	d			19 07				20 06						21 03			22 02					
Maesteg	a			19 11				20 09						21 06			22 04					
Pyle	d		18 33				19 31									21 31					23 10	
Port Talbot Parkway	d	18 23	18 41			19 23	19 39				20 23	20 33			21 23	21 39		22 00	22 24	22 47	23 19	23 42
Baglan	d						19 42														23 24	
Briton Ferry	d						19 45														23 26	
Neath	d	18 32	18 49			19 31	19 49				20 31				21 31	21 46		22 08	22 32	22 54	23 31	23 50
Skewen	d						19 54														23 35	
Llansamlet	d						19 58														23 39	
Swansea	a	18 46	19 02			19 43	20 05				20 42				21 43	21 57		22 20	22 44	23 07	23 47	00 03
	d		19 05		19 34		20 13				21 00					22 25				23 10	23 53	
Gowerton	d		19 16		19 45		20 24						←			22 36				23 21	00 04	
Llanelli	a		19 23		19 52		20 30				21 16	21 02	21 16			22 42				23 28	00 11	
	d		19 24		19 54		20 32				21 17	21 03	21 17			22 44				23 29	00 12	
Pembrey & Burry Port	d		19 30		20 00		20 37				→	21 09	21 24			22 50				23 35	00 17	
Kidwelly	d				20x07							21x14				22x56				23x41	00x24	
Ferryside	d				20x13							21x19				23x01				23x46	00x30	
Carmarthen	a		19 51		20 29		20 57					21 31	21 48			23 23				00 03	00 47	
	d		19 58				21 00		21 07			22 05										
Whitland	a		20 13				21 15		21 23			22 19										
	d		20 13				21 15		21 23			22 20										
Narberth	d						21x24															
Kilgetty	d						21x33															
Saundersfoot	d						21x35															
Tenby	a						21 42															
	d						21 43															
Penally	d						21x46															
Manorbier	d						21 52															
Lamphey	d						22x00															
Pembroke	d						22 03															
Pembroke Dock	a						22 18															
Clunderwen	d		20x20									22x26										
Clarbeston Road	d		20x28						21x37			22x34										
Haverfordwest	d		20 36									22 42										
Johnston	d		20x44									22x50										
Milford Haven	a		20 59									23 05										
Fishguard & Goodwick	a								21 56													
Fishguard Harbour 30 ⛴	a								22 04													
	d									23 45												
Rosslare Harbour ⛴	a									04 00												

When events are being held at the Principality Stadium, services are subject to alteration. Please check times before travelling.

Ferry service between Fishguard Harbour and Rosslare Harbour is operated by Stena Line

Table T128-F

Sundays

20 May to 2 December

Cardiff - Maesteg, Swansea and West Wales

		AW	AW	AW	AW	AW	AW	AW	AW	AW	AW	AW	AW	GW	GW	AW	GW	GW	AW	AW	GW	GW	AW
		A	🚌		B	◇ B		🛒	◇ C 🛒	B 🛒	⛴	◇ 🛒	◇	◇1 B ☕	◇1 C ☕	◇	◇1 C ☕	◇1 B ☕	◇ C 🛒	◇ B 🛒	◇1 B ☕	◇1 C ☕	
London Paddington 15 ⊖	d													08 30	08 33		09 33	09 30			10 30	10 33	
Reading 7	d													09 10	09 15		10 10	10 09			11 09	11 08	
Manchester Piccadilly 10	d																						
Gloucester 7	d																						
Bristol Parkway 7	d													10 10	10 16		11 03	11 02			12 10	12 09	
Newport (South Wales)	d											09 33		10 30	10 36	10 58	11 25	11 25			12 29	12 28	
Cardiff Central 7	d					07 10						09 56		10 54	11 03	11 19	11 49	11 50	12 05	12 05	12 52	12 53	
Pontyclun	d											10 08							12 18	12 18			
Llanharan	d											10 13							12 23	12 23			
Pencoed	d											10 18							12 28	12 28			
Bridgend	d					07 32						10 25		11 15	11 23	11 39	12 10	12 11	12 35	12 35	13 11	13 13	
Wildmill	d																						
Sarn	d																						
Tondu	d																						
Garth (Mid Glamorgan)	d																						
Maesteg (Ewenny Road)	d																						
Maesteg	a																						
Pyle	d											10 33							12 43	12 43			
Port Talbot Parkway	d					07 46						10 40		11 28	11 36	11 53	12 23	12 24	12 51	12 54	13 24	13 26	
Baglan	d																						
Briton Ferry	d																						
Neath	d					07 54						10 48		11 37	11 45	12 01	12 30	12 31			13 32	13 33	
Skewen	d																						
Llansamlet	d																						
Swansea	a					08 07						11 00		11 49	11 57	12 14	12 43	12 44			13 46	13 48	
	d			00 10		08 15			10 45			11 04	11 12			12 16	12 49	12 50					14 02
Gowerton	d	00 04		00s21		08 26						11 15	11 20			12 27							14 13
Llanelli	a	00 11		00s28		08 33			11 00			11 22	11 27			12 34	13 05	13 06	13 23	13 23			14 20
	d	00 12				08 35			11 02			11 24				12 35	13 07	13 08	13 24	13 26			14 22
Pembrey & Burry Port	d	00 17		00s34		08 41			11 08			11 30				12 41	13 13	13 14	13 30	13 33			14 28
Kidwelly	d	00x24		00s41		08x48						11x37				12x47							14x34
Ferryside	d	00x30		00s47		08x54						11x43				12x53							14x40
Carmarthen	a	00 47		01 03		09 07			11 27			11 56				13 09	13 36	13 37	13 54	13 59			14 55
	d		00 57		08 20	09 10	09 55	10 19	11 32	11 32		12 06				13 09			13 57	14 05			14 57
Whitland	a		01 17		08 36	09 26	10 11	10 34	11 46	11 48		12 22				13 24			14 12	14 21			15 11
	d		01 17		08 36	09 26	10 11	10 34	11 47	11 48		12 22				13 25			14 13	14 21			15 12
Narberth	d					09x35		10x43															15x21
Kilgetty	d					09x45		10x52															15x31
Saundersfoot	d					09x47		10x54															15x33
Tenby	a					09 54		11 01															15 40
	d					09 56		11 11															15 44
Penally	d					09x59		11x14															15x47
Manorbier	d					10 06		11 20															15 53
Lamphey	d					10x14		11x28															16x01
Pembroke	d					10 17		11 31															16 04
Pembroke Dock	a					10 27		11 41															16 17
Clunderwen	d				08x44		10x19					12x30							14x20	14x29			
Clarbeston Road	d				08x52		10x27					12x39							14x27	14x37			
Haverfordwest	d				09 00		10 35					12 47							14 36	14 45			
Johnston	d				09x09		10x44					12x56							14x44	14x54			
Milford Haven	a				09 20		10 55					13 07							14 59	15 09			
Fishguard & Goodwick	a		02 07						12 18	12 21						13 56							
Fishguard Harbour 30 ⛴	a		02 14						12 27	12 28						14 05							
	d										13 10												
Rosslare Harbour ⛴	a										16 25												

A not 20 May **B** until 9 September **C** from 16 September

When events are being held at the Principality Stadium, services are subject to alteration. Please check times before travelling.

Ferry service between Fishguard Harbour and Rosslare Harbour is operated by Stena Line

Table T128-F

Sundays

20 May to 2 December

Cardiff - Maesteg, Swansea and West Wales

		GW	GW	GW	AW	AW	AW	AW	GW	GW	AW	GW	GW	AW	GW	GW	AW	GW	GW	AW	AW	GW	GW
		◇■	◇■	◇■	◇	■	■	■	◇■	◇■		◇■	◇■	■	◇■	◇■	◇	◇■	◇■	■		◇■	◇■
		A	B	A		A	B	A	A	B		A	B		A	B		A	B			A	B
London Paddington ⊖	d	11 30	11 33						12 30	12 33		13 30	13 33		14 30	14 33		15 30	15 33			16 30	16 33
Reading	d	12 08	12 08						13 09	13 09		14 08	14 10		15 10	15 10		16 07	16 09			17 07	17 10
Manchester Piccadilly	d					10 31	10 31							12 32						14 30			
Gloucester	d																						
Bristol Parkway	d	13 09	13 09						14 07	14 08		15 09	15 10		16 10	16 10		17 09	17 10			18 09	18 10
Newport (South Wales)	d	13 35	13 35			13 31	13 31		14 30	14 31		15 34	15 35	15 49	16 36	16 36		17 38	17 39	17 37		18 31	18 32
Cardiff Central	d	13 59	14 00			14 05	14 05		14 54	14 56		15 56	15 59	16 14	17 00	17 02		18 03	18 05	18 10		18 54	18 54
Pontyclun	d					14 18	14 19							16 26						18 23			
Llanharan	d					14 23	14 24							16 31						18 28			
Pencoed	d					14 27	14 28							16 36						18 32			
Bridgend	d	14 17	14 18			14 34	14 35		15 16	15 18		16 17	16 20	16 43	17 21	17 24		18 23	18 25	18 39		19 15	19 15
Wildmill	d																						
Sarn	d																						
Tondu	d																						
Garth (Mid Glamorgan)	d																						
Maesteg (Ewenny Road)	d																						
Maesteg	a																						
Pyle	d					14 42	14 43							16 51						18 47			
Port Talbot Parkway	d	14 30	14 31			14 51	14 52		15 29	15 31		16 28	16 31	16 59	17 32	17 35		18 36	18 38	18 56		19 28	19 28
Baglan	d																						
Briton Ferry	d																						
Neath	d	14 38	14 39			14 59	15 00		15 36	15 38		16 36	16 39	17 07	17 41	17 43		18 44	18 46	19 04		19 36	19 37
Skewen	d																						
Llansamlet	d			←																			
Swansea	a	14 53	14 54	14 53		15 11	15 12		15 51	15 53		16 49	16 54	17 20	17 54	17 57		18 57	18 59	19 17		19 50	19 50
	d	15 04	15 03	15 04	15 29	15 44	15 44				16 38	16 56	17 07	17 25			18 37			19 22			
Gowerton	d	→			15 39	15 56	15 55	←			16 49			17 37			18 48			19 33			
Llanelli	a		15 19	15 20	15 46	16 03	16 02	16 03			16 56	17 13	17 24	17 44			18 55			19 40			
	d		15 20	15 21		16 03	16 03	16 03			16 58	17 14	17 25	17 45			18 57			19 41			
Pembrey & Burry Port	d		15 27	15 28		→	16 09	16 10			17 04	17 20	17 31	17 52			19 03			19 47			
Kidwelly	d										17x11						19x10						
Ferryside	d										17x17						19x16						
Carmarthen	a		15 48	15 49			16 32	16 33			17 30	17 45	17 55	18 15			19 29			20 09			
	d						16 35	16 35			17 35			18 20			19 32			20 10			
Whitland	a						16 51	16 51			17 52			18 36			19 48			20 26			
	d						16 52	16 53			17 52			18 37			19 48			20 30	20 37		
Narberth	d										18x01										20x44		
Kilgetty	d										18x11										20x53		
Saundersfoot	d										18x13										20x55		
Tenby	a										18 20										21 02		
	d										18 23										21 06		
Penally	d										18x26										21x09		
Manorbier	d										18 33										21 15		
Lamphey	d										18x40										21x23		
Pembroke	d										18 44										21 26		
Pembroke Dock	a										18 59										21 36		
Clunderwen	d						17x00	17x00						18x45			19x56			20x38			
Clarbeston Road	d						17x08	17x08						18x53			20x04			20x46			
Haverfordwest	d						17 16	17 17						19 01			20a12			20 54			
Johnston	d						17x25	17x25						19x10						21x03			
Milford Haven	a						17 37	17 37						19 25						21 20			
Fishguard & Goodwick	a																						
Fishguard Harbour	a																						
	d																						
Rosslare Harbour	a																						

A until 9 September

B from 16 September

When events are being held at the Principality Stadium, services are subject to alteration. Please check times before travelling.

Ferry service between Fishguard Harbour and Rosslare Harbour is operated by Stena Line

Table T128-F

Sundays

20 May to 2 December

Cardiff - Maesteg, Swansea and West Wales

		GW	AW	GW	AW	AW	AW	GW	GW	GW	GW	GW	GW	AW	GW	GW	GW	GW
		◇■		◇■		■	◇	◇■	◇■	◇■	◇■	◇■	◇■	◇	◇■	◇■	◇■	◇■
		A	A	B	B			A	B	B	A	A	B	C	A	B	B	A
London Paddington ⊖	d	17 30		17 33				18 30	18 33	19 00	19 00	19 30	19 33		20 30	20 34	21 33	21 30
Reading	d	18 07		18 10				19 07	19 10	19 36	19 38	20 07	20 10		21 09	21 15	22 11	22 09
Manchester Piccadilly	d																	
Gloucester	d																	
Bristol Parkway	d	19 09		19 12				20 09	20 10	20 29	20 35	21 09	21 10		22 09	22 14	23 10	23 11
Newport (South Wales)	d	19 32		19 34				20 32	20 31	20 48	20 53	21 29	21 30		22 36	22 37	23 36	23 36
Cardiff Central	d	19 53		19 58			20 13	20 55	20 57	21 16	21 19	21 54	21 58	22 30	23 00	23 00	23 58	23 59
Pontyclun	d																	
Llanharan	d																	
Pencoed	d																	
Bridgend	d	20 14		20 19			20 33	21 17	21 18	21 37	21 40	22 16	22 19	22 51	23 21	23 21	00 19	00 19
Wildmill	d																	
Sarn	d																	
Tondu	d																	
Garth (Mid Glamorgan)	d																	
Maesteg (Ewenny Road)	d																	
Maesteg	a																	
Pyle	d						20 41											
Port Talbot Parkway	d	20 27		20 32			20 49	21 30	21 31	21 49	21 52	22 29	22 32	23 05	23 34	23 34	00 32	00 32
Baglan	d																	
Briton Ferry	d																	
Neath	d	20 34		20 39			20 57	21 37	21 39	21 58	22 01	22 36	22 40	23 13	23 42	23 42	00 39	00 40
Skewen	d																	
Llansamlet	d																	
Swansea	a	20 48		20 53			21 10	21 50	21 51	22 10	22 13	22 49	22 52	23 25	23 55	23 55	00 52	00 53
	d		20 53		20 58		21 18							23 38				
Gowerton	d		21 05		21 09		21 29							23 49				
Llanelli	a		21 12		21 16		21 36							23 56				
	d		21 13		21 18		21 37							23 58				
Pembrey & Burry Port	d		21 19		21 23		21 43							00 04				
Kidwelly	d		21x26		21x30									00x11				
Ferryside	d		21x32		21x36									00x17				
Carmarthen	a		21 44		21 48		22 06							00 33				
	d		21 48		21 51		22 10											
Whitland	a		22 03		22 06		22 26											
	d		22 04		22 07		22 26											
Narberth	d																	
Kilgetty	d																	
Saundersfoot	d																	
Tenby	a																	
	d																	
Penally	d																	
Manorbier	d																	
Lamphey	d																	
Pembroke	d																	
Pembroke Dock	a																	
Clunderwen	d						22x34											
Clarbeston Road	d						22x42											
Haverfordwest	d						22 50											
Johnston	d						22x59											
Milford Haven	a						23 10											
Fishguard & Goodwick	a		22 36		22 39													
Fishguard Harbour	a		22 44		22 47													
	d					23 45												
Rosslare Harbour	a					04 00												

A until 9 September

B from 16 September

C not 3 June

When events are being held at the Principality Stadium, services are subject to alteration. Please check times before travelling.

Ferry service between Fishguard Harbour and Rosslare Harbour is operated by Stena Line

West Wales, Swansea and Maesteg - Cardiff

Miles	Miles			AW MO	AW MX	AW	GW	AW MX	AW	GW	GW	AW		GW	GW	AW	AW	GW	AW	GW	AW	AW		AW	AW
						◇	◇■ ⊡		◇	■ ■ ⊡	■ ■ ⊡	◇ ⊼		■ ■ A ✕	■ ◇■ B ⊡		◇ ⊼	◇■ ⊡	■ ⊼	◇■ C ⊡		◇ ⊼			
—	—	Rosslare Harbour	d																						
0	—	**Fishguard Harbour**	a																						
—	—		d					02 37																06 50	
—	—	Fishguard & Goodwick	d					02 40																06 53	
—	0	**Milford Haven**	d		00 18																	05 55			
—	4	Johnston	d		00x26																	06x03			
—	8¾	Haverfordwest	d		00 33																	06 10			
15¾	14	Clarbeston Road	d		00x41			02 59														06x18		07a14	
22¼	—	Clunderwen	d		00x48																	06x25			
—	0	**Pembroke Dock**	d																						
—	2	Pembroke	d																						
—	3½	Lamphey	d																						
—	7	Manorbier	d																						
—	10¼	Penally	d																						
—	11½	**Tenby**	a																						
—	—		d																						
—	15¾	Saundersfoot	d																						
—	16½	Kilgetty	d																						
—	22	Narberth	d																						
27¼	27¼	Whitland	a		00 54			03 11														06 31			
—	—		d		00 54			03 11														06 31			
41¾	—	**Carmarthen**	a		01 16			03 29														06 47			
—	—		d			02 59			04 53			05 03					05 46		06 15			06 50			
48¾	—	Ferryside	d														05x56		06x25			07x00			
53	—	Kidwelly	d														06x01		06x30			07x05			
58¼	—	Pembrey & Burry Port	d						05 12			05 21					06 08		06 37			07 12			
62¼	—	Llanelli	a			03 21			05 18			05 26					06 13		06 42			07 17			
—	—		d			03 21						05 28					06 15		06 44			07 19			
68	—	Gowerton	d														06 21		06 50			07 25			
73½	—	**Swansea**	a			03 42											06 35		07 05			07 38			
—	—		d				03 54			04 58	05 29			05 59	06 29		06 38	06 59	07 07	07 29		07 42			
77½	—	Llansamlet	d														06 45								
79¼	—	Skewen	d														06 49								
83	—	Neath	d				04 06			05 10	05 41			06 11	06 41		06 53	07 11	07 18	07 41		07 53			
84¾	—	Briton Ferry	d														06 57								
86½	—	Baglan	d														07 00								
88½	—	Port Talbot Parkway	d				04 14			05 18	05 49	06 01		06 19	06 49		07 04	07 19	07 25	07 49		08 00			
94¼	—	Pyle	d									06 09					07 12		07 33			08 07			
—	0	Maesteg	d													06 44									07 59
—	0½	Maesteg (Ewenny Road)	d													06 46									08 01
—	1¼	Garth (Mid Glamorgan)	d													06 49									08 04
—	5¼	Tondu	d													06 57									08 13
—	6	Sarn	d													07 00									08 16
—	7¼	Wildmill	d													07 03									08 18
100¼	8¼	Bridgend	d	00 07			04 27			05 31	06 02	06 16		06 32	07 02	07 07	07 20	07 32	07 41	08 02	08 07	08 15			08 22
104¾	—	Pencoed	d									06 22				07 13	07 26				08 13				08 28
107	—	Llanharan	d									06 26				07 18			07 48			08 22			
110	—	Pontyclun	d									06 31				07 23	07 35				08 21				08 35
121	—	**Cardiff Central**	a	00 34			05 12			05 52	06 22	06 45		06 53	07 23	07 37	07 49	07 53	08 04	08 23	08 34	08 38			08 48
—	—	Newport (South Wales)	a				05 31			06 07	06 38	07 02		07 08	07 38			08 08	08 17	08 38		09 03			
—	—	Bristol Parkway	a				06 01			06 30	07 01			07 32	08 01			08 31		09 01					
—	—	Gloucester	a																						
—	—	Manchester Piccadilly	a									10 13							11 13			12 13			
—	—	Reading	a				07 02			07 25	08 02				08 57			09 25		10 00					
—	—	London Paddington ⊖	a				07 30			07 59	08 32			08 55	09 25			09 55		10 37					

A The Capitals United- Restaurant for customers joining to Swindon

B ◇ from Reading ■ to Reading

C Y Cymro - The Welshman

When events are being held at the Principality Stadium, services are subject to alteration. Please check times before travelling.

Ferry service between Fishguard Harbour and Rosslare Harbour is operated by Stena Line

Table T128-R

Mondays to Fridays

21 May to 7 December

West Wales, Swansea and Maesteg - Cardiff

		AW	GW	AW	GW	AW	AW	AW		AW	GW	AW	AW	AW	GW	AW	AW	AW		AW	GW	AW	AW	AW	AW
		◇ A ⊼	◇■ ⊡	◇	◇■ B ⊡	■ ⊼	◇ ⊼				◇■ ⊡	■ ⊼	◇		◇■ ⊡	■ ⊼				⊼	◇■ C ⊡		◇ ⊼	■	
Rosslare Harbour	d																							08 00	
Fishguard Harbour	a																							11 15	
	d											07 50										09 54			
Fishguard & Goodwick	d											07 53										09 57			
Milford Haven	d					07 05										09 08									
Johnston	d					07x13										09x16									
Haverfordwest	d					07 20										09 23									
Clarbeston Road	d					07x28						08x11				09x31						10x17			
Clunderwen	d					07x35						08x19				09x38						10x25			
Pembroke Dock	d						06 59													09 09					
Pembroke	d						07 07													09 17					
Lamphey	d						07x10													09x20					
Manorbier	d						07 18													09 29					
Penally	d						07x23													09x34					
Tenby	a						07 26													09 37					
	d						07 29													09 38					
Saundersfoot	d						07x34													09x46					
Kilgetty	d						07x36													09x48					
Narberth	d						07x45													09x58					
Whitland	a					07 41	07 53					08 23				09 44				10 06		10 31			
	d					07 41	07 53					08 24				09 44				10 07		10 32			
Carmarthen	a					07 55	08 12					08 43				10 03				10 24		10 49			
	d				07 30	08 01	08 15					09 00				10 06				10 31			11 03		
Ferryside	d				07 43	08x11	08x24					09x10											11x13		
Kidwelly	d				07 50	08x16	08x29					09x15											11x18		
Pembrey & Burry Port	d				07 58	08 23	08 35					09 18				10 25				10 50			11 24		
Llanelli	a				08 03	08 28	08 40					09 24				10 31				10 56			11 30		
	d			07 45	08 05	08 30	08 41					09 25	09 39			10 32				10 57			11 31		
Gowerton	d			07 54		08 36						09 35	09 46							11 04			11 38		
Swansea	a			08 08	08 22	08 49	09 03					09 51	10 01			10 49				11 23			11 50		
	d		07 59		08 29	08 53				09 10	09 29	09 55	10 08		10 29	10 55		11 10			11 29		11 55		
Llansamlet	d									09 17								11 17							
Skewen	d									09 21								11 21							
Neath	d		08 11		08 41	09 04				09 25	09 41	10 06			10 41	11 06		11 25			11 41		12 06		
Briton Ferry	d									09 29								11 28							
Baglan	d									09 32								11 32							
Port Talbot Parkway	d		08 19		08 49	09 11				09 36	09 49	10 13			10 49	11 13		11 36			11 49		12 13		
Pyle	d									09 45								11 44							
Maesteg	d	07 59						09 16						10 16			11 15								12 17
Maesteg (Ewenny Road)	d	08 01						09 18						10 18			11 17								12 19
Garth (Mid Glamorgan)	d	08 04						09 21						10 21			11 20								12 22
Tondu	d	08 13						09 30						10 30			11 29								12 31
Sarn	d	08 16						09 33						10 33			11 32								12 34
Wildmill	d	08 18						09 35						10 35			11 34								12 36
Bridgend	d	08 22	08 32		09 02	09 24		09 39		09 53	10 02	10 26		10 39	11 02	11 26	11 38	11 55			12 02		12 26		12 40
Pencoed	d	08 28						09 45						10 45			11 44								12 46
Llanharan	d							09 49						10 49			11 48								12 50
Pontyclun	d	08 35						09 53						10 53			11 52								12 54
Cardiff Central	a	08 48	08 52		09 22	09 45		10 07		10 18	10 22	10 48	11 10	11 12	11 22	11 48	12 08	12 18			12 22		12 48		13 08
Newport (South Wales)	a	09 34	09 08		09 38	10 17		10 23		10 34	10 38	11 02			11 38	12 17	12 27				12 38		13 02		13 28
Bristol Parkway	a		09 31		10 01						11 01				12 01						13 01				
Gloucester	a							11 20									13 20								14 22
Manchester Piccadilly	a					13 13						14 13				15 13							16 13		
Reading	a		10 32		11 02						11 59				13 02						13 57				
London Paddington ⊖	a		11 00		11 32						12 30				13 32						14 30				

A ⊼ ◇ from Cardiff Central

B The Red Dragon

C The St. David

When events are being held at the Principality Stadium, services are subject to alteration. Please check times before travelling.

Ferry service between Fishguard Harbour and Rosslare Harbour is operated by Stena Line

Table T128-R

Mondays to Fridays

21 May to 7 December

West Wales, Swansea and Maesteg - Cardiff

		GW	AW	AW	AW	AW	GW	AW	AW	AW	AW	GW	AW	AW	AW	AW	GW	AW	AW	GW	AW	AW
		◇1	■				◇1	■	◇		■	◇1	■		■		◇1	■		◇1		■
Rosslare Harbour	d																					
Fishguard Harbour	a																					
	d										12 50											
Fishguard & Goodwick	d										12 53											
Milford Haven	d		11 08										13 08									15 08
Johnston	d		11x16										13x16									15x16
Haverfordwest	d		11 23										13 23									15 23
Clarbeston Road	d		11x31										13x31									15x31
Clunderwen	d		11x38										13x38									15x38
Pembroke Dock	d					11 09										13 09						
Pembroke	d					11 17										13 17						
Lamphey	d					11x20										13x20						
Manorbier	d					11 29										13 29						
Penally	d					11x34										13x34						
Tenby	a					11 37										13 37						
	d					11 43										13 41						
Saundersfoot	d					11x51										13x49						
Kilgetty	d					11x53										13x51						
Narberth	d					12x03										14x01						
Whitland	a		11 44			12 11					13 24		13 44			14 09						15 44
	d		11 44			12 11					13 24		13 44			14 09						15 44
Carmarthen	a		12 00			12 29					13 40		14 00			14 27						16 00
	d		12 05			12 33		13 02			13 47		14 05			14 40		15 03				16 05
Ferryside	d							13x12										15x13				
Kidwelly	d							13x17										15x18				
Pembrey & Burry Port	d		12 23			12 52		13 23					14 23			14 59		15 25				16 23
Llanelli	a		12 28			12 58		13 29			14 09		14 28			15 05		15 30				16 28
	d		12 30		12 45	12 59		13 30	14 04		14 09		14 30			15 05		15 32				16 30
Gowerton	d		12 36		12 52			13 37	14 11				14 36					15 38				16 36
Swansea	a		12 49		13 04	13 22		13 51	14 25				14 49			15 24		15 51				16 49
	d	12 29	12 54		13 10		13 29	13 55				14 29	14 55		15 10		15 29	15 55		16 29		16 55
Llansamlet	d				13 17										15 17							
Skewen	d				13 21										15 21							
Neath	d	12 41	13 05		13 25		13 41	14 06				14 41	15 06		15 25		15 41	16 06		16 41		17 06
Briton Ferry	d				13 29										15 28							
Baglan	d				13 32										15 32							
Port Talbot Parkway	d	12 49	13 12		13 36		13 49	14 13			14 43	14 49	15 13		15 36		15 49	16 13		16 49		17 13
Pyle	d				13 45										15 44							
Maesteg	d			13 15						14 15				15 17					16 15			
Maesteg (Ewenny Road)	d			13 17						14 17				15 19					16 17			
Garth (Mid Glamorgan)	d			13 20						14 20				15 22					16 20			
Tondu	d			13 29						14 29				15 31					16 29			
Sarn	d			13 32						14 32				15 34					16 32			
Wildmill	d			13 34						14 34				15 36					16 34			
Bridgend	d	13 02	13 25	13 38	13 53		14 02	14 26		14 38		15 02	15 26	15 41	15 53		16 02	16 26	16 38	17 02	17 14	17 26
Pencoed	d			13 44						14 44				15 47					16 44			
Llanharan	d			13 48						14 48				15 51					16 48			
Pontyclun	d			13 52						14 52				15 55					16 52			
Cardiff Central 7	a	13 22	13 48	14 07	14 15		14 23	14 47		15 06	15 19	15 22	15 47	16 09	16 14		16 22	16 47	17 06	17 23	17 35	17 46
Newport (South Wales)	a	13 38	14 17				14 38	15 02		15 27		15 38	16 02	16 24	16 33		16 38	17 02	17 26	17 38		18 03
Bristol Parkway 7	a	14 01					15 01					16 01					17 01			18 01		
Gloucester 7	a									16 21				17 19					18 20			
Manchester Piccadilly 10	a		17 13					18 13					19 13					20 19				21 09
Reading 7	a	15 02					15 57					17 02					17 57			19 02		
London Paddington 15 ⊖	a	15 30					16 29					17 30					18 30			19 33		

When events are being held at the Principality Stadium, services are subject to alteration. Please check times before travelling.

Ferry service between Fishguard Harbour and Rosslare Harbour is operated by Stena Line

Table T128-R

Mondays to Fridays

21 May to 7 December

West Wales, Swansea and Maesteg - Cardiff

		AW	AW	AW	GW	AW	AW	AW	GW	AW	AW	AW	AW	GW	GW	AW	AW	AW	AW	GW	GW	AW	AW
														FO	FX					FX	FO		
			■		◇1	◇	◇		◇1	◇				◇1	◇1	◇		R		◇1	◇1	◇	
Rosslare Harbour	d																	18 10					
Fishguard Harbour	a																	21 25					
	d																19 08						
Fishguard & Goodwick	d																19 11						
Milford Haven	d									17 11												19 12	
Johnston	d									17x19												19x20	
Haverfordwest	d									17 26												19 27	
Clarbeston Road	d									17x34							19x30					19x37	
Clunderwen	d									17x41												19x44	
Pembroke Dock	d			15 09							17 09	19 19											
Pembroke	d			15 17							17 17	19 27											
Lamphey	d			15x20							17x20	19x31											
Manorbier	d			15 29							17 29	19 39											
Penally	d			15x34							17x34	19x44											
Tenby	a			15 37							17 37	19 47											
	d			15 41							17 38												
Saundersfoot	d			15x49							17x46												
Kilgetty	d			15x51							17x48												
Narberth	d			16x01							17x58												
Whitland	a			16 09						17 47	18 06						19 42					19 50	
	d			16 09						17 47	18 07						19 42					19 50	
Carmarthen	a			16 27						18 03	18 24						20 02					20 06	
	d			16 31		16 58				18 08	18 31					18 50						20 11	
Ferryside	d					17x08				18x18						19x00							
Kidwelly	d					17x13				18x23						19x06							
Pembrey & Burry Port	d			16 50		17 19				18 30	18 50					19 14						20 29	
Llanelli	a			16 56		17 25				18 35	18 56					19 20						20 34	
	d		16 45	16 57		17 26	17 52			18 36	18 57					19 21						20 35	
Gowerton	d			17 04		17 33	17 59			18 43	19 05					19 29						20 42	
Swansea	a		17 02	17 22		17 46	18 14			18 56	19 22					19 43						20 55	
	d		17 12		17 29	17 49			18 29	19 00				19 29	19 29	19 51				20 29	20 29	21 00	
Llansamlet	d		17 19			17 55				19 06													
Skewen	d		17 23			17 59				19 10													
Neath	d		17 27		17 41	18 03			18 41	19 14				19 41	19 41	20 02				20 41	20 41	21 11	
Briton Ferry	d		17 30			18 07				19 18													
Baglan	d		17 34			18 10				19 21													
Port Talbot Parkway	d		17 38		17 49	18 14			18 49	19 25				19 49	19 49	20 09				20 49	20 49	21 18	
Pyle	d		17 46			18 22				19 33													
Maesteg	d	17 15						18 20					19 20						20 15				21 15
Maesteg (Ewenny Road)	d	17 17						18 22					19 22						20 17				21 17
Garth (Mid Glamorgan)	d	17 20						18 25					19 25						20 20				21 20
Tondu	d	17 29						18 34					19 34						20 29				21 29
Sarn	d	17 32						18 37					19 37						20 32				21 32
Wildmill	d	17 34						18 39					19 39						20 34				21 34
Bridgend	d	17 38	17 56		18 02	18 29		18 43	19 02	19 40			19 43	20 02	20 02	20 23			20 38	21 02	21 02	21 31	21 38
Pencoed	d	17 44						18 49					19 49						20 44				21 44
Llanharan	d	17 48						18 52					19 52						20 48				21 48
Pontyclun	d	17 52						18 57					19 58						20 52				21 52
Cardiff Central 7	a	18 06	18 15		18 22	18 50		19 12	19 23	20 03			20 13	20 22	20 22	20 45			21 08	21 22	21 22	22 03	22 10
Newport (South Wales)	a	18 22	18 33		18 38	19 06			19 38					20 38	20 38				21 26	21 38	21 38		
Bristol Parkway 7	a				19 01				20 01					21 01	21 01					22 01	22 01		
Gloucester 7	a	19 17																	22 22				
Manchester Piccadilly 10	a					22 15																	
Reading 7	a				19 57				21 02					22 09	22 09					23 00	23 02		
London Paddington 15 ⊖	a				20 32				21 31					22 39	22 51					23 40	23 37		

When events are being held at the Principality Stadium, services are subject to alteration. Please check times before travelling.

Ferry service between Fishguard Harbour and Rosslare Harbour is operated by Stena Line

Table T128-R

Mondays to Fridays

21 May to 7 December

West Wales, Swansea and Maesteg - Cardiff

		AW ◇	AW	AW	AW	AW ◇	AW	AW	AW
Rosslare Harbour	d								
Fishguard Harbour	a								
	d						22 14		
Fishguard & Goodwick	d						22 17		
Milford Haven	d		20 36						23 18
Johnston	d		20x44						23x26
Haverfordwest	d		20 51						23 33
Clarbeston Road	d		20x59				22x36		23x41
Clunderwen	d		21x06				22x43		23x48
Pembroke Dock	d			21 09				22 28	
Pembroke	d			21 17				22 36	
Lamphey	d			21x20				22x39	
Manorbier	d			21 29				22 47	
Penally	d			21x34				22x53	
Tenby	a			21 37				22 55	
	d	19 57		21 53				22 55	
Saundersfoot	d	20x05		22x01				23x03	
Kilgetty	d	20x07		22x03				23x05	
Narberth	d	20x17		22x13				23x14	
Whitland	a	20 25	21 12	22 21			22 50	23 22	23 54
	d	20 27	21 12	22 21			22 50	23 25	23 54
Carmarthen	a	20 44	21 34	22 43			23 08	23 44	00 16
	d	20 49					23 10		
Ferryside	d	20x59					23x21		
Kidwelly	d	21x04					23x27		
Pembrey & Burry Port	d	21 11					23 34		
Llanelli	a	21 16					23 40		
	d	21 17				22 01	23 40		
Gowerton	d	21 26				22 08	23 48		
Swansea	a	21 40				22 25	00 08		
	d	21 45				22 32			
Llansamlet	d	21 52				22 39			
Skewen	d	21 56				22 43			
Neath	d	22 00				22 47			
Briton Ferry	d	22 03				22 51			
Baglan	d	22 07				22 54			
Port Talbot Parkway	d	22 11				22 58			
Pyle	d	22 19				23 07			
Maesteg	d				22 15				
Maesteg (Ewenny Road)	d				22 17				
Garth (Mid Glamorgan)	d				22 20				
Tondu	d				22 29				
Sarn	d				22 32				
Wildmill	d				22 34				
Bridgend	d	22 27			22 38	23 15			
Pencoed	d				22 44				
Llanharan	d				22 48				
Pontyclun	d				22 52				
Cardiff Central	a	22 55			23 08	23 40			
Newport (South Wales)	a				23 38				
Bristol Parkway	a								
Gloucester	a				00 39				
Manchester Piccadilly	a								
Reading	a								
London Paddington ⊖	a								

When events are being held at the Principality Stadium, services are subject to alteration. Please check times before travelling.

Ferry service between Fishguard Harbour and Rosslare Harbour is operated by Stena Line

Table T128-R

Saturdays

26 May to 8 September

West Wales, Swansea and Maesteg - Cardiff

		AW	AW ◇	GW ◇1 ☕	AW	GW ◇1 ☕	GW ◇1 ☕	AW ◇ 🛒	GW ◇1 ☕	GW ◇1 ☕	AW	AW ▣ 🛒	GW ◇1 ☕	AW	GW ◇1 ☕	AW ▣ 🛒	AW	AW	GW ◇1 ☕	AW ◇ 🛒	AW ◇ 🛒	AW	AW
Rosslare Harbour	d																						
Fishguard Harbour	a																						
	d				02 37												06 50						
Fishguard & Goodwick	d				02 40												06 53						
Milford Haven	d	00 18														05 55				07 05			
Johnston	d	00x26														06x03				07x13			
Haverfordwest	d	00 33														06 10				07 20			
Clarbeston Road	d	00x41			02 58											06x18	07a14			07x28			
Clunderwen	d	00x48														06x25				07x35			
Pembroke Dock	d																				06 59		
Pembroke	d																				07 07		
Lamphey	d																				07x10		
Manorbier	d																				07 17		
Penally	d																				07x23		
Tenby	a																				07 26		
	d																				07 29		
Saundersfoot	d																				07x34		
Kilgetty	d																				07x36		
Narberth	d																				07x45		
Whitland	a	00 54			03 10											06 31				07 41	07 53		
	d	00 54			03 10											06 31				07 41	07 53		
Carmarthen	a	01 16			03 28											06 47				07 55	08 11		
	d		02 44					05 04				05 55		06 20		06 50				08 01	08 14		
Ferryside	d											06x05		06x30		07x00				08x11	08x24		
Kidwelly	d											06x10		06x35		07x05				08x16	08x30		
Pembrey & Burry Port	d							05 22				06 17		06 42		07 12				08 23	08 36		
Llanelli	a		03 06					05 27				06 22		06 47		07 17				08 28	08 40		
	d		03 06					05 29				06 24		06 48		07 19				08 30	08 42		
Gowerton	d											06 30		06 55		07 25				08 36			
Swansea	a		03 29									06 43		07 08		07 38				08 49	09 02		
	d			03 59		04 59	05 29		05 59	06 29		06 47	06 59	07 11	07 29	07 44			08 29	08 54			09 10
Llansamlet	d													07 18									09 17
Skewen	d													07 22									09 21
Neath	d			04 11		05 11	05 41		06 11	06 41		06 58	07 11	07 26	07 41	07 55			08 41	09 06			09 25
Briton Ferry	d													07 29									09 29
Baglan	d													07 33									09 32
Port Talbot Parkway	d			04 19		05 19	05 49	06 02	06 19	06 49		07 05	07 19	07 37	07 49	08 02			08 49	09 13			09 36
Pyle	d							06 09				07 12		07 45		08 09				09 21			09 45
Maesteg	d										06 46							08 00				09 17	
Maesteg (Ewenny Road)	d										06 48							08 02				09 19	
Garth (Mid Glamorgan)	d										06 51							08 05				09 22	
Tondu	d										07 00							08 14				09 31	
Sarn	d										07 03							08 17				09 34	
Wildmill	d										07 05							08 19				09 36	
Bridgend	d			04 31		05 32	06 02	06 17	06 32	07 02	07 09	07 20	07 32	07 53	08 02	08 17		08 23	09 02	09 32		09 40	09 53
Pencoed	d							06 23			07 15			08 08		08 23						09 46	
Llanharan	d							06 26				07 27		08 12				08 30				09 50	
Pontyclun	d							06 31			07 22			08 16		08 30						09 54	
Cardiff Central	a			04 52		05 52	06 22	06 44	06 52	07 23	07 36	07 43	07 52	08 36	08 22	08 44		08 46	09 22	09 53		10 07	10 16
Newport (South Wales)	a			05 07		06 08	06 38	07 02	07 08	07 38		08 02	08 08		08 38	09 02		09 23	09 38	10 07		10 24	10 34
Bristol Parkway	a			05 36		06 30	07 00		07 30	08 00			08 30		09 00				10 00				
Gloucester	a																	10 19				11 20	
Manchester Piccadilly	a							10 13				11 13				12 13				13 13			
Reading	a			07 13		07 28	07 58		08 32	08 58			09 32		09 57				11 00				
London Paddington ⊖	a			07 41		07 59	08 30		08 59	09 30			09 59		10 29				11 31				

When events are being held at the Principality Stadium, services are subject to alteration. Please check times before travelling.

Ferry service between Fishguard Harbour and Rosslare Harbour is operated by Stena Line

Table T128-R

Saturdays

26 May to 8 September

West Wales, Swansea and Maesteg - Cardiff

		GW	AW	AW	AW	AW	GW	AW	AW	AW	AW	GW	AW	AW	AW	AW	GW	AW	AW	AW	AW	GW	AW
		◇■	◇	◇		■	◇■	■				◇■		■	■	◇	◇■ A	■		◇		◇■	◇
Rosslare Harbour	d														08 00								
Fishguard Harbour	a														11 15								
	d			07 50									09 53										
Fishguard & Goodwick	d			07 53									09 56										
Milford Haven	d							09 08										11 08					
Johnston	d							09x16										11x16					
Haverfordwest	d							09 23										11 23					
Clarbeston Road	d			08x11				09x31					10x14					11x31					
Clunderwen	d			08x19				09x38					10x22					11x38					
Pembroke Dock	d				08 35												10 01						
Pembroke	d				08 43												10 11						
Lamphey	d				08x46																		
Manorbier	d				08 55												10 24						
Penally	d				09x00																		
Tenby	a				09 03												10 33						
	d				09 08												10 38				11 41		
Saundersfoot	d				09x16												10 48				11x49		
Kilgetty	d				09x18																11x51		
Narberth	d				09x28																12x01		
Whitland	a			08 23	09 38			09 44					10 28				11 07	11 44			12 09		
	d			08 24				09 44			10 05		10 29				11 09	11 44			12 09		
Carmarthen	a			08 43				10 02			10 25		10 46				11 26	12 00			12 27		
	d			09 00			09 38	10 04			10 27			11 09			11 35	12 05			12 33		13 02
Ferryside	d			09x10										11x19									13x12
Kidwelly	d			09x15										11x24									13x17
Pembrey & Burry Port	d			09 21			09 59	10 24			10 47			11 30			11 56	12 23			12 52		13 23
Llanelli	a			09 27			10 04	10 29			10 53			11 36			12 01	12 28			12 58		13 29
	d		08 55	09 28			10 06	10 31			10 53			11 37			12 03	12 30		12 42	12 59		13 30
Gowerton	d		09 04	09 35							11 01			11 44				12 36					13 37
Swansea	a		09 22	09 50			10 22	10 48			11 19			11 56			12 19	12 49		13 01	13 19		13 49
	d	09 29	09 33	09 54			10 29	10 55		11 10		11 29		12 00			12 29	12 53		13 07		13 29	14 00
Llansamlet	d									11 17										13 14			
Skewen	d									11 21										13 18			
Neath	d	09 41	09 45	10 06			10 41	11 06		11 25		11 41		12 11			12 41	13 04		13 22		13 41	14 11
Briton Ferry	d									11 28										13 25			
Baglan	d									11 32										13 29			
Port Talbot Parkway	d	09 49	09 52	10 13			10 49	11 13		11 36		11 49		12 18			12 49	13 11		13 33		13 49	14 18
Pyle	d		10 01	10 20				11 21		11 44								13 19		13 41			
Maesteg	d					10 15			11 15							12 18			13 15				
Maesteg (Ewenny Road)	d					10 17			11 17							12 20			13 17				
Garth (Mid Glamorgan)	d					10 20			11 20							12 23			13 20				
Tondu	d					10 29			11 29							12 32			13 29				
Sarn	d					10 32			11 32							12 35			13 32				
Wildmill	d					10 34			11 34							12 37			13 34				
Bridgend	d	10 02	10 10	10 28		10 38	11 02	11 28	11 38	11 52		12 02		12 31		12 41	13 02	13 26	13 38	13 52		14 02	14 31
Pencoed	d					10 44			11 44							12 47			13 44				
Llanharan	d					10 48			11 48							12 51			13 48				
Pontyclun	d					10 52			11 52							12 55			13 52				
Cardiff Central	a	10 22	10 33	10 48		11 06	11 22	11 48	12 06	12 15		12 22		12 52		13 09	13 22	13 48	14 07	14 13		14 22	14 52
Newport (South Wales)	a	10 38		11 07		11 33	11 38	12 07	12 23			12 38		13 07		13 34	13 38	14 07		14 32		14 38	15 07
Bristol Parkway	a	11 00					12 00					13 00					14 00					15 01	
Gloucester	a								13 21														
Manchester Piccadilly	a			14 14				15 15						16 15				17 14					18 15
Reading	a	11 58					12 58					13 57					14 59					15 59	
London Paddington ⊖	a	12 29					13 31					14 29					15 32					16 29	

A The Pembroke Coast Express

When events are being held at the Principality Stadium, services are subject to alteration. Please check times before travelling.

Ferry service between Fishguard Harbour and Rosslare Harbour is operated by Stena Line

Table T128-R

Saturdays

26 May to 8 September

West Wales, Swansea and Maesteg - Cardiff

		AW	AW	GW	AW	AW	AW	AW	GW	AW	AW	GW	AW	AW	AW	GW	AW	AW	AW	GW	AW	AW
			■	◇■	■				◇■	■		◇■	■			◇■	◇	◇		◇■		◇
Rosslare Harbour	d																					
Fishguard Harbour	a																					
	d		12 43																			
Fishguard & Goodwick	d		12 46																			
Milford Haven	d				13 08								15 08									17 08
Johnston	d				13x16								15x16									17x16
Haverfordwest	d				13 23								15 23									17 23
Clarbeston Road	d				13x31								15x31									17x31
Clunderwen	d				13x38								15x38									17x38
Pembroke Dock	d							13 09								14 55					16 25	
Pembroke	d							13 17								15 05					16 33	
Lamphey	d							13x20								15x08					16x36	
Manorbier	d							13 29								15 20					16 45	
Penally	d							13x34								15x26					16x50	
Tenby	a							13 37								15 30					16 53	
	d							13 42								15 35					16 55	
Saundersfoot	d							13x50								15 45					17x03	
Kilgetty	d							13x52								15x47					17x05	
Narberth	d							14x02								15x56					17x15	
Whitland	a		13 17		13 44			14 10					15 44			16 08					17 26	17 44
	d		13 17		13 44			14 11					15 44			16 09					17 26	17 45
Carmarthen	a		13 32		14 00			14 28					16 00			16 27					17 44	18 03
	d		13 37		14 05			14 33		15 03			16 05			16 33	17 02				18 33	18 07
Ferryside	d		13x48							15x13						16 46	17x12				→	18x17
Kidwelly	d		13x53							15x18						16 52	17x17					18x23
Pembrey & Burry Port	d		14 00		14 23			14 52		15 25			16 23			17 00	17 23					18 30
Llanelli	a		14 05		14 28			14 58		15 30			16 28			17 05	17 29					18 35
	d		14 06		14 30			14 58		15 32			16 30		16 47	17 07	17 30	17 40				18 36
Gowerton	d				14 36					15 38			16 36				17 37	17 47				18 44
Swansea	a				14 49			15 20		15 51			16 49		17 04	17 23	17 49	18 09				18 56
	d			14 29	14 55		15 10		15 29	15 55		16 29	16 58		17 11	17 29	17 54			18 29		19 00
Llansamlet	d						15 17								17 18							
Skewen	d						15 21								17 22							
Neath	d			14 41	15 06		15 25		15 41	16 06		16 41	17 09		17 26	17 41	18 05			18 41		19 11
Briton Ferry	d						15 28								17 29							
Baglan	d						15 32								17 33							
Port Talbot Parkway	d		14 38	14 49	15 13		15 36		15 49	16 13		16 49	17 16		17 37	17 49	18 12			18 49		19 19
Pyle	d						15 44			16 21			17 24		17 45		18 19					
Maesteg	d	14 15				15 17					16 15			17 15					18 20			
Maesteg (Ewenny Road)	d	14 17				15 19					16 17			17 17					18 22			
Garth (Mid Glamorgan)	d	14 20				15 22					16 20			17 20					18 25			
Tondu	d	14 29				15 30					16 29			17 29					18 34			
Sarn	d	14 32				15 33					16 32			17 32					18 37			
Wildmill	d	14 34				15 36					16 34			17 34					18 39			
Bridgend	d	14 38		15 02	15 26	15 39	15 53		16 02	16 28	16 38	17 02	17 31	17 38	17 53	18 02	18 27		18 43	19 02		19 33
Pencoed	d	14 44				15 45					16 44			17 44					18 49			
Llanharan	d	14 48				15 49					16 48			17 48					18 53			
Pontyclun	d	14 52				15 53					16 52			17 52					18 57			
Cardiff Central	a	15 05	15 13	15 22	15 51	16 06	16 16		16 22	16 49	17 06	17 22	17 52	18 05	18 20	18 22	18 47		19 13	19 22		19 56
Newport (South Wales)	a	15 22		15 38	16 07	16 22	16 32		16 38	17 07	17 25	17 38	18 08	18 22		18 38	19 03			19 38		
Bristol Parkway	a			16 00					17 00			18 00				19 00				20 00		
Gloucester	a	16 19				17 19					18 18			19 20								
Manchester Piccadilly	a				19 15					20 15			21 15				22 14					
Reading	a			16 58					17 58			18 58				19 58				20 57		
London Paddington ⊖	a			17 29					18 31			19 29				20 30				21 28		

When events are being held at the Principality Stadium, services are subject to alteration. Please check times before travelling.

Ferry service between Fishguard Harbour and Rosslare Harbour is operated by Stena Line

Table T128-R

Saturdays

26 May to 8 September

West Wales, Swansea and Maesteg - Cardiff

		AW	AW	AW	GW	AW	AW	AW	AW	AW	AW	AW	AW	AW	AW	AW	AW	AW	AW	AW
		◇			◇1 ☕	◇		R		◇		◇			◇					
Rosslare Harbour ⛴	d							18 10												
Fishguard Harbour 30 ⛴	a							21 25												
	d						19 00											22 15		
Fishguard & Goodwick	d						19 03											22 18		
Milford Haven	d									19 08			21 16							23 18
Johnston	d									19x16			21x24							23x26
Haverfordwest	d									19 23			21 31							23 33
Clarbeston Road	d						19x22			19x31			21x39					22x37		23x41
Clunderwen	d									19x38			21x46					22x45		23x48
Pembroke Dock	d											19 13		21 09					22 18	
Pembroke	d											19 21		21 17					22 26	
Lamphey	d											19x25		21x20					22x29	
Manorbier	d											19 33		21 29					22 37	
Penally	d											19x38		21x34					22x43	
Tenby	a											19 41		21 37					22 45	
	d											19 55		21 42					22 45	
Saundersfoot	d											20x03		21x50					22x53	
Kilgetty	d											20x05		21x52					22x55	
Narberth	d											20x15		22x02					23x04	
Whitland	a			←			19 34			19 44		20 25	21 52	22 10				22 51	23 12	23 54
	d						19 34			19 44		20 25	21 52	22 11				22 52	23 15	23 54
Carmarthen	a			17 44			19 54			20 04		20 43	22 14	22 32				23 08	23 34	00 16
	d			18 33		18 54				20 07		20 47						23 11		
Ferryside	d					19x04						20x58						23x21		
Kidwelly	d					19x10						21x04						23x26		
Pembrey & Burry Port	d			18 52		19 18				20 25		21 11						23 33		
Llanelli	a			18 58		19 24				20 30		21 17						23 38		
	d			18 59		19 25				20 31		21 17			21 38			23 39		
Gowerton	d			19 07		19 33				20 38		21 26			21 46			23 46		
Swansea	a			19 21		19 47				20 51		21 42			22 06			00 02		
	d		19 10		19 29	19 52				20 55		21 43					22 20			
Llansamlet	d		19 17									21 50					22 27			
Skewen	d		19 21									21 54					22 31			
Neath	d		19 25		19 41	20 03				21 06		21 59					22 35			
Briton Ferry	d		19 28									22 02					22 38			
Baglan	d		19 32									22 06					22 42			
Port Talbot Parkway	d		19 36		19 49	20 10				21 13		22 10					22 46			
Pyle	d		19 44									22 18					22 54			
Maesteg	d	19 15							20 15		21 15					22 15				
Maesteg (Ewenny Road)	d	19 17							20 17		21 17					22 17				
Garth (Mid Glamorgan)	d	19 20							20 20		21 20					22 20				
Tondu	d	19 29							20 29		21 29					22 29				
Sarn	d	19 32							20 32		21 32					22 32				
Wildmill	d	19 34							20 34		21 34					22 34				
Bridgend	d	19 38	19 52		20 02	20 24			20 38	21 26	21 38	22 26				22 38	23 02			
Pencoed	d	19 44							20 44		21 44					22 44				
Llanharan	d	19 47							20 48		21 48					22 48				
Pontyclun	d	19 52							20 52		21 52					22 52				
Cardiff Central 7	a	20 06	20 17		20 22	20 47			21 07	21 47	22 13	22 50				23 09	23 26			
Newport (South Wales)	a	20 24			20 38				21 25	22 10						23 35				
Bristol Parkway 7	a				21 00															
Gloucester 7	a								22 19							00 40				
Manchester Piccadilly 10	a	23 49																		
Reading 7	a				22 02															
London Paddington 15 ⊖	a				22 38															

When events are being held at the Principality Stadium, services are subject to alteration. Please check times before travelling.

Ferry service between Fishguard Harbour and Rosslare Harbour is operated by Stena Line

Table T128-R

Saturdays

15 September to 8 December

West Wales, Swansea and Maesteg - Cardiff

		AW	AW	GW	AW	GW	GW	AW	GW	GW	AW	AW	GW	AW	GW	AW	AW	AW	GW	GW	AW	AW	AW
			◇	◇1 ☕		◇1 ☕	◇1 ☕	◇ 🛒	◇1 ☕	◇1 ☕		R 🛒	◇1 ☕		◇1 ☕	R 🛒			◇1 ☕	◇1 ☕	◇ 🛒	◇ 🛒	
Rosslare Harbour ⛴	d																						
Fishguard Harbour 30 ⛴	a																						
	d				02 37												06 50						
Fishguard & Goodwick	d				02 40												06 53						
Milford Haven	d	00 18														05 55					07 05		
Johnston	d	00x26														06x03					07x13		
Haverfordwest	d	00 33														06 10					07 20		
Clarbeston Road	d	00x41			02 58											06x18	07a14				07x28		
Clunderwen	d	00x48														06x25					07x35		
Pembroke Dock	d																					06 59	
Pembroke	d																					07 07	
Lamphey	d																					07x10	
Manorbier	d																					07 17	
Penally	d																					07x23	
Tenby	a																					07 26	
	d																					07 29	
Saundersfoot	d																					07x34	
Kilgetty	d																					07x36	
Narberth	d																					07x45	
Whitland	a	00 54			03 10											06 31					07 41	07 53	
	d	00 54			03 10											06 31					07 41	07 53	
Carmarthen	a	01 16			03 28											06 47					07 55	08 11	
	d		02 44					05 04				05 55		06 20		06 50					08 01	08 14	
Ferryside	d											06x05		06x30		07x00					08x11	08x24	
Kidwelly	d											06x10		06x35		07x05					08x16	08x30	
Pembrey & Burry Port	d							05 22				06 17		06 42		07 12					08 23	08 36	
Llanelli	a		03 06					05 27				06 22		06 47		07 17					08 28	08 40	
	d		03 06					05 29				06 24		06 48		07 19					08 30	08 42	
Gowerton	d											06 30		06 55		07 25					08 36		
Swansea	a		03 29									06 43		07 08		07 38					08 49	09 02	
	d			03 59		04 59	05 29		05 59	06 29		06 47	06 59	07 11	07 29	07 44			07 59	08 29	08 54		
Llansamlet	d													07 18									
Skewen	d													07 22									
Neath	d			04 11		05 11	05 41		06 11	06 41		06 58	07 11	07 26	07 41	07 55			08 11	08 41	09 06		
Briton Ferry	d													07 29									
Baglan	d													07 33									
Port Talbot Parkway	d			04 19		05 19	05 49	06 02	06 19	06 49		07 05	07 19	07 37	07 49	08 02			08 19	08 49	09 13		
Pyle	d							06 09				07 12		07 45		08 09					09 21		
Maesteg	d										06 46							08 00					09 17
Maesteg (Ewenny Road)	d										06 48							08 02					09 19
Garth (Mid Glamorgan)	d										06 51							08 05					09 22
Tondu	d										07 00							08 14					09 31
Sarn	d										07 03							08 17					09 34
Wildmill	d										07 05							08 19					09 36
Bridgend	d			04 31		05 32	06 02	06 17	06 32	07 02	07 09	07 20	07 32	07 53	08 02	08 17		08 23	08 32	09 02	09 32		09 40
Pencoed	d							06 23			07 15			08 08		08 23							09 46
Llanharan	d							06 26				07 27		08 12				08 30					09 50
Pontyclun	d							06 31			07 22			08 16		08 30							09 54
Cardiff Central 7	a			04 52		05 52	06 22	06 44	06 52	07 23	07 36	07 43	07 52	08 36	08 22	08 44		08 46	08 52	09 22	09 53		10 07
Newport (South Wales)	a			05 07		06 08	06 38	07 02	07 08	07 38		08 02	08 08		08 38	09 02		09 23	09 08	09 38	10 07		10 24
Bristol Parkway 7	a			05 36		06 30	07 00		07 30	08 00			08 30		09 00				09 30	10 00			
Gloucester 7	a																	10 19					11 20
Manchester Piccadilly 10	a							10 13				11 13				12 13					13 13		
Reading 7	a			07 13		07 28	07 58		08 32	08 58			09 32		09 57				10 32	11 00			
London Paddington 15 ⊖	a			07 41		07 59	08 30		08 59	09 30			09 59		10 29				11 01	11 31			

When events are being held at the Principality Stadium, services are subject to alteration. Please check times before travelling.

Ferry service between Fishguard Harbour and Rosslare Harbour is operated by Stena Line

Table T128-R

West Wales, Swansea and Maesteg - Cardiff

Saturdays

15 September to 8 December

		AW	GW	AW	AW	AW		GW	AW	AW	AW	AW	GW	AW	AW	AW		AW	GW	AW	AW	AW	AW	GW	AW
			◇1	◇	◇	■		◇1	■				◇1		■	■		◇	◇1	■		◇		◇1	◇
Rosslare Harbour	d															08 00									
Fishguard Harbour	a															11 15									
	d				07 50									09 53											
Fishguard & Goodwick	d				07 53									09 56											
Milford Haven	d								09 08											11 08					
Johnston	d								09x16											11x16					
Haverfordwest	d								09 23											11 23					
Clarbeston Road	d				08x11				09x31					10x14						11x31					
Clunderwen	d				08x19				09x38					10x22						11x38					
Pembroke Dock	d											09 09											11 09		
Pembroke	d											09 17											11 17		
Lamphey	d											09x20											11x20		
Manorbier	d											09 29											11 29		
Penally	d											09x34											11x34		
Tenby	a											09 37											11 37		
	d											09 37											11 41		
Saundersfoot	d											09x45											11x49		
Kilgetty	d											09x47											11x51		
Narberth	d											09x57											12x01		
Whitland	a				08 23				09 44			10 05		10 28						11 44			12 09		
	d				08 24				09 44			10 05		10 29						11 44			12 09		
Carmarthen	a				08 43				10 02			10 23		10 46						12 00			12 27		
	d				09 00			09 38	10 04			10 27			11 09					12 05			12 33		13 02
Ferryside	d				09x10										11x19										13x12
Kidwelly	d				09x15										11x24										13x17
Pembrey & Burry Port	d				09 21			09 59	10 24			10 47			11 30					12 23			12 52		13 23
Llanelli	a				09 27			10 04	10 29			10 53			11 36					12 28			12 58		13 29
	d			08 55	09 28			10 06	10 31			10 53			11 37					12 30		12 42	12 59		13 30
Gowerton	d			09 04	09 35							11 01			11 44					12 36					13 37
Swansea	a			09 22	09 50			10 22	10 48			11 19			11 56					12 49		13 01	13 19		13 49
	d	09 10	09 29	09 33	09 54			10 29	10 55		11 10		11 29		12 00				12 29	12 53		13 07		13 29	14 00
Llansamlet	d	09 17									11 17											13 14			
Skewen	d	09 21									11 21											13 18			
Neath	d	09 25	09 41	09 45	10 06			10 41	11 06		11 25		11 41		12 11				12 41	13 04		13 22		13 41	14 11
Briton Ferry	d	09 29									11 28											13 25			
Baglan	d	09 32									11 32											13 29			
Port Talbot Parkway	d	09 36	09 49	09 52	10 13			10 49	11 13		11 36		11 49		12 18				12 49	13 11		13 33		13 49	14 18
Pyle	d	09 45		10 01	10 20				11 21		11 44									13 19		13 41			
Maesteg	d					10 15				11 15								12 18			13 15				
Maesteg (Ewenny Road)	d					10 17				11 17								12 20			13 17				
Garth (Mid Glamorgan)	d					10 20				11 20								12 23			13 20				
Tondu	d					10 29				11 29								12 32			13 29				
Sarn	d					10 32				11 32								12 35			13 32				
Wildmill	d					10 34				11 34								12 37			13 34				
Bridgend	d	09 53	10 02	10 10	10 28	10 38		11 02	11 28	11 38	11 52		12 02		12 31			12 41	13 02	13 26	13 38	13 52		14 02	14 31
Pencoed	d					10 44				11 44								12 47			13 44				
Llanharan	d					10 48				11 48								12 51			13 48				
Pontyclun	d					10 52				11 52								12 55			13 52				
Cardiff Central 7	a	10 16	10 22	10 33	10 48	11 06		11 22	11 48	12 06	12 15		12 22		12 52			13 09	13 22	13 48	14 07	14 13		14 22	14 52
Newport (South Wales)	a	10 34	10 38		11 07	11 33		11 38	12 07	12 23			12 38		13 07			13 34	13 38	14 07		14 32		14 38	15 07
Bristol Parkway 7	a		11 00					12 00					13 00						14 00					15 01	
Gloucester 7	a									13 21															
Manchester Piccadilly 10	a				14 14				15 15						16 15					17 14					18 15
Reading 7	a		11 58					12 58					13 57						14 57					15 58	
London Paddington 15 ⊖	a		12 29					13 31					14 29						15 29					16 29	

When events are being held at the Principality Stadium, services are subject to alteration. Please check times before travelling.

Ferry service between Fishguard Harbour and Rosslare Harbour is operated by Stena Line

Table T128-R

West Wales, Swansea and Maesteg - Cardiff

Saturdays

15 September to 8 December

		AW		AW	GW	AW	AW	AW	AW	GW	AW	AW		GW	AW	AW	AW	AW	GW	AW	AW	AW		GW	AW
				■	◇1	■				◇1	■			◇1	■				◇1	◇	◇			◇1	◇
Rosslare Harbour	d																								
Fishguard Harbour	a																								
	d			12 43																					
Fishguard & Goodwick	d			12 46																					
Milford Haven	d					13 08									15 08										17 08
Johnston	d					13x16									15x16										17x16
Haverfordwest	d					13 23									15 23										17 23
Clarbeston Road	d					13x31									15x31										17x31
Clunderwen	d					13x38									15x38										17x38
Pembroke Dock	d								13 09									15 09							
Pembroke	d								13 17									15 17							
Lamphey	d								13x20									15x20							
Manorbier	d								13 29									15 29							
Penally	d								13x34									15x34							
Tenby	a								13 37									15 37							
	d								13 42									15 44							
Saundersfoot	d								13x50									15x52							
Kilgetty	d								13x52									15x54							
Narberth	d								14x02									16x04							
Whitland	a			13 17		13 44			14 10						15 44			16 12							17 44
	d			13 17		13 44			14 11						15 44			16 12							17 45
Carmarthen	a			13 32		14 00			14 28						16 00			16 30							18 03
	d			13 37		14 05			14 33		15 03				16 05			16 32		17 02					18 07
Ferryside	d			13x48							15x13									17x12					18x17
Kidwelly	d			13x53							15x18									17x17					18x23
Pembrey & Burry Port	d			14 00		14 23			14 52		15 25				16 23			16 52		17 23					18 30
Llanelli	a			14 05		14 28			14 58		15 30				16 28			16 58		17 29					18 35
	d			14 06		14 30			14 58		15 32				16 30		16 47	16 58		17 30	17 40				18 36
Gowerton	d					14 36					15 38				16 36			17 05		17 37	17 47				18 44
Swansea	a					14 49			15 20		15 51				16 49		17 04	17 20		17 49	18 09				18 56
	d				14 29	14 55		15 10		15 29	15 55			16 29	16 58		17 11		17 29	17 54				18 29	19 00
Llansamlet	d							15 17									17 18								
Skewen	d							15 21									17 22								
Neath	d				14 41	15 06		15 25		15 41	16 06			16 41	17 09		17 26		17 41	18 05				18 41	19 11
Briton Ferry	d							15 28									17 29								
Baglan	d							15 32									17 33								
Port Talbot Parkway	d			14 38	14 49	15 13		15 36		15 49	16 13			16 49	17 16		17 37		17 49	18 12				18 49	19 19
Pyle	d							15 44			16 21				17 24		17 45			18 19					
Maesteg	d	14 15					15 17					16 15				17 15						18 20			
Maesteg (Ewenny Road)	d	14 17					15 19					16 17				17 17						18 22			
Garth (Mid Glamorgan)	d	14 20					15 22					16 20				17 20						18 25			
Tondu	d	14 29					15 30					16 29				17 29						18 34			
Sarn	d	14 32					15 33					16 32				17 32						18 37			
Wildmill	d	14 34					15 36					16 34				17 34						18 39			
Bridgend	d	14 38			15 02	15 26	15 39	15 53		16 02	16 28	16 38		17 02	17 31	17 38	17 53		18 02	18 27		18 43		19 02	19 33
Pencoed	d	14 44					15 45					16 44				17 44						18 49			
Llanharan	d	14 48					15 49					16 48				17 48						18 53			
Pontyclun	d	14 52					15 53					16 52				17 52						18 57			
Cardiff Central 7	a	15 05		15 13	15 22	15 51	16 06	16 16		16 22	16 49	17 06		17 22	17 52	18 05	18 20		18 22	18 47		19 13		19 22	19 56
Newport (South Wales)	a	15 22			15 38	16 07	16 22	16 32		16 38	17 07	17 25		17 38	18 08	18 22			18 38	19 03				19 38	
Bristol Parkway 7	a				16 00					17 00				18 00					19 00					20 00	
Gloucester 7	a	16 19					17 19					18 18				19 20									
Manchester Piccadilly 10	a					19 15					20 15				21 15					22 14					
Reading 7	a				16 58					17 58				18 58					19 58					20 57	
London Paddington 15 ⊖	a				17 29					18 30				19 29					20 30					21 28	

When events are being held at the Principality Stadium, services are subject to alteration. Please check times before travelling.

Ferry service between Fishguard Harbour and Rosslare Harbour is operated by Stena Line

Saturdays

15 September to 8 December

West Wales, Swansea and Maesteg - Cardiff

		AW	AW	AW	GW	AW	AW	AW	AW	AW	AW	AW	AW	AW	AW	AW	AW	AW	AW	AW
		◇			◇1 ☕	◇		R		◇		◇			◇					
Rosslare Harbour 🚢	d							18 10												
Fishguard Harbour 🚢	a							21 25												
	d						19 00											22 15		
Fishguard & Goodwick	d						19 03											22 18		
Milford Haven	d									19 08			21 16							23 18
Johnston	d									19x16			21x24							23x26
Haverfordwest	d									19 23			21 31							23 33
Clarbeston Road	d						19x22			19x31			21x39					22x37		23x41
Clunderwen	d									19x38			21x46					22x45		23x48
Pembroke Dock	d			17 12								19 09		21 09					22 18	
Pembroke	d			17 20								19 17		21 17					22 26	
Lamphey	d			17x23								19x21		21x20					22x29	
Manorbier	d			17 32								19 29		21 29					22 37	
Penally	d			17x37								19x34		21x34					22x43	
Tenby	a			17 40								19 37		21 37					22 45	
	d			17 43								19 51		21 42					22 45	
Saundersfoot	d			17x51								19x59		21x50					22x53	
Kilgetty	d			17x53								20x01		21x52					22x55	
Narberth	d			18x03								20x11		22x02					23x04	
Whitland	a			18 11			19 34			19 44		20 21	21 52	22 10				22 51	23 12	23 54
	d			18 11			19 34			19 44		20 21	21 52	22 11				22 52	23 15	23 54
Carmarthen	a			18 29			19 54			20 04		20 39	22 14	22 32				23 08	23 34	00 16
	d			18 33		18 54				20 07		20 47						23 11		
Ferryside	d					19x04						20x58						23x21		
Kidwelly	d					19x10						21x04						23x26		
Pembrey & Burry Port	d			18 52		19 18				20 25		21 11						23 33		
Llanelli	a			18 58		19 24				20 30		21 17						23 38		
	d			18 59		19 25				20 31		21 17			21 38			23 39		
Gowerton	d			19 07		19 33				20 38		21 26			21 46			23 46		
Swansea	a			19 21		19 47				20 51		21 42			22 06			00 02		
	d		19 10		19 29	19 52				20 55		21 43					22 20			
Llansamlet	d		19 17									21 50					22 27			
Skewen	d		19 21									21 54					22 31			
Neath	d		19 25		19 41	20 03				21 06		21 59					22 35			
Briton Ferry	d		19 28									22 02					22 38			
Baglan	d		19 32									22 06					22 42			
Port Talbot Parkway	d		19 36		19 49	20 10				21 13		22 10					22 46			
Pyle	d		19 44									22 18					22 54			
Maesteg	d	19 15							20 15		21 15					22 15				
Maesteg (Ewenny Road)	d	19 17							20 17		21 17					22 17				
Garth (Mid Glamorgan)	d	19 20							20 20		21 20					22 20				
Tondu	d	19 29							20 29		21 29					22 29				
Sarn	d	19 32							20 32		21 32					22 32				
Wildmill	d	19 34							20 34		21 34					22 34				
Bridgend	d	19 38	19 52		20 02	20 24			20 38	21 26	21 38	22 26				22 38	23 02			
Pencoed	d	19 44							20 44		21 44					22 44				
Llanharan	d	19 47							20 48		21 48					22 48				
Pontyclun	d	19 52							20 52		21 52					22 52				
Cardiff Central 7	a	20 06	20 17		20 22	20 47			21 07	21 47	22 13	22 50				23 09	23 26			
Newport (South Wales)	a	20 24			20 38				21 25	22 10						23 35				
Bristol Parkway 7	a				21 00															
Gloucester 7	a								22 19							00 40				
Manchester Piccadilly 10	a	23 49																		
Reading 7	a				22 02															
London Paddington 15 ⊖	a				22 38															

When events are being held at the Principality Stadium, services are subject to alteration. Please check times before travelling.

Ferry service between Fishguard Harbour and Rosslare Harbour is operated by Stena Line

Table T128-R

Sundays

20 May to 2 December

West Wales, Swansea and Maesteg - Cardiff

		AW	GW	GW	AW	GW	GW	GW	AW	AW	GW	GW	AW	AW	GW	GW	AW	AW	AW	AW	AW	GW	AW
		🚌	◇1 A ☕	◇1 B ☕	R	◇1 C ☕	◇1 D ☕	◇1 C ☕	■ C 🛒	D	◇1 D ☕	◇1 C ☕	C 🛒	D 🛒	◇1 D ☕	◇1 C ☕	◇ D 🛒	■ C 🛒	◇ D 🛒	■ C 🛒		■ 1 ☕	C
Rosslare Harbour 🚢	d				08 00																		
Fishguard Harbour 🚢	a				11 15																		
	d	02 17																					
Fishguard & Goodwick	d	02 22																					
Milford Haven	d																	09 28					
Johnston	d																	09x36					
Haverfordwest	d																	09 43					
Clarbeston Road	d																	09x52					
Clunderwen	d																	09x59					
Pembroke Dock	d																						10 40
Pembroke	d																						10 48
Lamphey	d																						10x51
Manorbier	d																						11 00
Penally	d																						11x05
Tenby	a																						11 08
	d																						11 16
Saundersfoot	d																						11x24
Kilgetty	d																						11x26
Narberth	d																						11x36
Whitland	a	03 12																10 06					11 44
	d	03 12																10 06					11 45
Carmarthen	a	03 32																10 24					12 01
	d								08 45	09 34			09 40	09 43			10 30	10 30			10 53		
Ferryside	d												09x50	09x53							11x03		
Kidwelly	d												09x56	09x59							11x09		
Pembrey & Burry Port	d								09 04	09 52			10 03	10 06			10 49	10 49			11 17		
Llanelli	a								09 10	09 57			10 09	10 12			10 54	10 55			11 23		
	d								09 12	09 58			10 10	10 13			10 56	10 57			11 23		
Gowerton	d												10 17	10 20			11 04	11 04	←	←	11 31		
Swansea	a								09 30	10 16			10 32	10 36			11 18	11 16	11 18	11 16	11 47		
	d		07 53	08 00		08 10	09 24	09 24	09 34		10 24	10 24			11 24	11 24	11 31	11 32	11 31	11 32		12 24	
Llansamlet	d																→	→					
Skewen	d																						
Neath	d		08 05	08 12		08 22	09 36	09 36	09 45		10 36	10 36			11 36	11 36			11 42	11 43		12 36	
Briton Ferry	d																						
Baglan	d																						
Port Talbot Parkway	d		08 12	08 19		08 29	09 43	09 43	09 52		10 43	10 43			11 43	11 43			11 49	11 50		12 43	
Pyle	d								09 59										11 56	11 57			
Maesteg	d																						
Maesteg (Ewenny Road)	d																						
Garth (Mid Glamorgan)	d																						
Tondu	d																						
Sarn	d																						
Wildmill	d																						
Bridgend	d		08 26	08 33		08 43	09 56	09 56	10 07		10 56	10 56			11 56	11 56			12 04	12 05		12 56	
Pencoed	d																		12 10	12 11			
Llanharan	d																		12 14	12 15			
Pontyclun	d																		12 19	12 20			
Cardiff Central 7	a		08 47	08 54		09 04	10 18	10 18	10 30		11 18	11 18			12 18	12 18			12 33	12 34		13 18	
Newport (South Wales)	a		09 06	09 13		09 24	10 38	10 38	10 51		11 38	11 38			12 38	12 38			12 52	12 52		13 38	
Bristol Parkway 7	a		09 35	09 35		09 46	11 00	11 00			12 00	12 00			13 00	13 00						14 00	
Gloucester 7	a																						
Manchester Piccadilly 10	a								14 17										16 14	16 14			
Reading 7	a		10 32	10 32		10 43	11 57	12 02			12 57	13 02			14 01	14 01						15 02	
London Paddington 15 ⊖	a		11 11	11 11		11 21	12 38	12 40			13 40	13 43			14 40	14 43						15 40	

A from 28 October
B from 16 September until 21 October
C until 9 September
D from 16 September

When events are being held at the Principality Stadium, services are subject to alteration. Please check times before travelling.

Ferry service between Fishguard Harbour and Rosslare Harbour is operated by Stena Line

Table T128-R

Sundays
20 May to 2 December

West Wales, Swansea and Maesteg - Cardiff

		GW	GW	AW	AW	AW	GW	GW	AW	GW	GW	AW	AW	GW	GW	AW	GW	GW	AW	GW	AW	AW	GW
		A	B			◇				◇ A	◇ B	◇	◇	B	A		◇ A	◇ B		◇ B		R	◇ A
Rosslare Harbour	d																					18 10	
Fishguard Harbour	a																					21 25	
	d					12 40							14 22										
Fishguard & Goodwick	d					12 43							14 25										
Milford Haven	d			11 23					13 18							15 13					17 40		
Johnston	d			11x31					13x24							15x21					17x48		
Haverfordwest	d			11 38					13 31							15 28					17 55		
Clarbeston Road	d			11x47					13x40							15x37					18x03		
Clunderwen	d			11x54					13x47							15x44					18x10		
Pembroke Dock	d				12 00														16 25				
Pembroke	d				12 08														16 33				
Lamphey	d				12x11														16x36				
Manorbier	d				12 20														16 45				
Penally	d				12x25														16x50				
Tenby	a				12 28														16 53				
	d				12 28														16 53				
Saundersfoot	d				12x36														17x01				
Kilgetty	d				12x38														17x03				
Narberth	d				12x48														17x13				
Whitland	a			12 01	12 56	13 14			13 54				14 56			15 51			17 21		18 16		
	d			12 03	13 00	13 14			13 57				14 57			15 54			17 24		18 16		
Carmarthen	a			12 21	13 17	13 30			14 15				15 14			16 11			17 42		18 35		
	d			12 24	13 20	13 38			14 25	14 58	14 58		15 40			16 16	16 55	16 55	17 47				
Ferryside	d				13x30								15x51			16x26			17x57				
Kidwelly	d				13x36								15x57			16x32			18x03				
Pembrey & Burry Port	d			12 44	13 43				14 44	15 18	15 18		16 04			16 40	17 15	17 15	18 11				
Llanelli	a			12 50	13 49	14 00			14 50	15 25	15 25		16 10			16 46	17 21	17 21	18 17				
	d			12 50	13 50	14 00			14 51	15 27	15 27	15 41	16 10			16 49	17 22	17 22	18 18				
Gowerton	d			12 59	13 58				14 59			15 50	16 16			16 58			18 26				
Swansea	a			13 13	14 16				15 16	15 43	15 43	16 03	16 35			17 15	17 39	17 39	18 46				
	d	13 24	13 24	13 43			14 24	15 24	15 34	15 51	15 51			16 51	16 51	17 30	17 51	17 51		18 51			18 51
Llansamlet	d																						
Skewen	d																						
Neath	d	13 36	13 36	13 54			14 36	15 36	15 45	16 03	16 03			17 03	17 03	17 41	18 03	18 03		19 03			19 03
Briton Ferry	d																						
Baglan	d																						
Port Talbot Parkway	d	13 43	13 43	14 01			14 43	15 43	15 52	16 10	16 10			17 10	17 11	17 48	18 10	18 10		19 10			19 10
Pyle	d			14 09					15 59							17 55							
Maesteg	d																						
Maesteg (Ewenny Road)	d																						
Garth (Mid Glamorgan)	d																						
Tondu	d																						
Sarn	d																						
Wildmill	d																						
Bridgend	d	13 56	13 56	14 17		14 44	14 56	15 56	16 07	16 23	16 23			17 23	17 24	18 03	18 23	18 23		19 23			19 23
Pencoed	d			14 23					16 13							18 09							
Llanharan	d			14 27					16 17							18 13							
Pontyclun	d			14 31					16 22							18 18							
Cardiff Central	a	14 18	14 18	14 48		15 10	15 18	16 18	16 37	16 45	16 45			17 45	17 46	18 32	18 45	18 45		19 45			19 45
Newport (South Wales)	a	14 38	14 38	15 12			15 38	16 38	16 56	17 07	17 07			18 07	18 07	18 53	19 07	19 07		20 08			20 08
Bristol Parkway	a	15 00	15 00				16 00	17 00		17 30	17 30			18 30	18 30		19 30	19 30		20 30			20 30
Gloucester	a																						
Manchester Piccadilly	a			18 18					20 16							22 19							
Reading	a	16 02	16 02				17 02	18 02		18 32	18 32			19 32	19 32		20 32	20 32		21 30			21 32
London Paddington ⊖	a	16 40	16 41				17 40	18 40		19 10	19 11			20 13	20 10		21 10	21 11		22 09			22 13

A until 9 September

B from 16 September

When events are being held at the Principality Stadium, services are subject to alteration. Please check times before travelling.

Ferry service between Fishguard Harbour and Rosslare Harbour is operated by Stena Line

Table T128-R

Sundays
20 May to 2 December

West Wales, Swansea and Maesteg - Cardiff

		GW	AW	AW	AW	AW	AW	AW	AW	AW	AW
		◇	◇								
Rosslare Harbour	d										
Fishguard Harbour	a										
	d									23 03	
Fishguard & Goodwick	d									23 06	
Milford Haven	d				19 38			21 35			23 15
Johnston	d				19x46			21x42			23x23
Haverfordwest	d				19 53			21 50			23 30
Clarbeston Road	d				20x01			21x58		23x25	23x39
Clunderwen	d				20x08			22x06			23x46
Pembroke Dock	d			19 01					21 46		
Pembroke	d			19 09					21 54		
Lamphey	d			19x12					21x57		
Manorbier	d			19 21					22 06		
Penally	d			19x26					22x11		
Tenby	a			19 29					22 14		
	d			19 29					22 14		
Saundersfoot	d			19x37					22x22		
Kilgetty	d			19x39					22x24		
Narberth	d			19x49					22x34		
Whitland	a			19 57	20 14			22 12	22 42	23 37	23 53
	d			20 00	20 17			22 13	22 45	23 38	23 53
Carmarthen	a			20 17	20 36			22 30	23 06	23 54	00 14
	d	19 05		20 21		21 15	21 15	22 35		23 57	
Ferryside	d			20x31				22x44			
Kidwelly	d			20x37				22x50			
Pembrey & Burry Port	d	19 25		20 45		21 34	21 34	22 57			
Llanelli	a	19 31		20 51		21 40	21 40	23 03			
	d	19 32	20 04	20 52		21 41	21 41	23 04			
Gowerton	d		20 11	21 00		21 48	21 48	23 12			
Swansea	a	19 49	20 25	21 19		22 04	22 04	23 26		00 37	
	d	19 55	20 40			22 10	22 10	23 31			
Llansamlet	d										
Skewen	d										
Neath	d	20 07	20 51			22 21	22 21	23 43			
Briton Ferry	d										
Baglan	d										
Port Talbot Parkway	d	20 14	20 58			22 28	22 28	23 50			
Pyle	d					22 37	22 37	23 58			
Maesteg	d										
Maesteg (Ewenny Road)	d										
Garth (Mid Glamorgan)	d										
Tondu	d										
Sarn	d										
Wildmill	d										
Bridgend	d	20 28	21 14			22 45	22 45	00 07			
Pencoed	d										
Llanharan	d										
Pontyclun	d										
Cardiff Central	a	20 49	21 37			23 10	23 10	00 34			
Newport (South Wales)	a	21 07				23 36					
Bristol Parkway	a	21 32									
Gloucester	a										
Manchester Piccadilly	a										
Reading	a	22 34									
London Paddington ⊖	a	23 22									

When events are being held at the Principality Stadium, services are subject to alteration. Please check times before travelling.

Ferry service between Fishguard Harbour and Rosslare Harbour is operated by Stena Line

Table T129-F

Mondays to Fridays

21 May to 7 December

Shrewsbury - Swansea

Miles			AW ◇	AW ◇	AW ◇	AW ◇	AW ◇	AW ◇
0	**Shrewsbury**	d	04 49		05 56	10 09	14 05	18 24
12¾	Church Stretton	d	05 07		06 14	10 27	14 23	18 42
20	Craven Arms	d	05 18		06 26	10 37	14 34	18 54
22½	Broome	d			06x32	10x43	14x40	19x00
25	Hopton Heath	d			06x36	10x47	14x44	19x04
28	Bucknell	d			06x41	10x52	14x49	19x09
32¼	Knighton	a	05 37		06 47	10 59	14 55	19 15
—		d	05 40		06 56	11 01	14 58	19 18
34¾	Knucklas	d			07x02	11x07	15x03	19x23
38¾	Llangynllo	d			07x10	11x15	15x11	19x31
41¾	Llanbister Road	d			07x15	11x20	15x16	19x36
45¼	Dolau	d			07x21	11x26	15x22	19x42
48½	Pen-y-bont	d			07x25	11x30	15x27	19x47
51¾	Llandrindod	a	06 14		07 34	11 39	15 36	19 56
—		d			07 35	12 00	15 41	19 56
57½	Builth Road	d			07x44	12x09	15x50	20x06
59½	Cilmeri	d			07x48	12x13	15x54	20x09
63	Garth (Powys)	d			07x53	12x18	15x59	20x15
64¾	Llangammarch	d			07x57	12x22	16x03	20x19
68	Llanwrtyd	a			08 03	12 28	16 09	20 25
—		d			08 09	12 31	16 23	20 30
70¾	Sugar Loaf	d			08x15	12x37	16x29	20x37
74¾	Cynghordy	d			08x22	12x44	16x36	20x44
79½	Llandovery	a			08 32	12 54	16 46	20 53
—		d		06 42	08 34	12 56	16 48	20 56
83¼	Llanwrda	d		06x48	08x40	13x02	16x54	21x02
85	Llangadog	d		06x52	08x44	13x06	16x58	21x06
90¾	Llandeilo	a		07 01	08 53	13 15	17 07	21 15
—		d		07 03	08 56	13 18	17 10	21 17
91½	Ffairfach	d		07 06	08 58	13 20	17 12	21 20
95½	Llandybie	d		07x13	09x06	13x28	17x20	21x27
97¼	Ammanford	d		07x18	09x10	13x32	17x24	21x32
98½	Pantyffynnon	d		07 21	09 13	13 35	17 27	21 35
103¼	Pontarddulais	d		07x28	09x20	13x42	17x34	21x42
105½	Llangennech	d		07x32	09x25	13x47	17x39	21x46
107½	Bynea	d		07x36	09x28	13x50	17x42	21x50
110¼	Llanelli	a		07 41	09 33	13 58	17 47	21 55
116	Gowerton	a		07 54	09 46	14 11	17 59	22 08
121½	**Swansea**	a		08 08	10 01	14 25	18 14	22 25

Saturdays

26 May to 8 December

		AW ◇	AW ◇	AW ◇	AW ◇
Shrewsbury	d	05 16	09 00	13 58	17 57
Church Stretton	d	05 33	09 19	14 16	18 13
Craven Arms	d	05 47	09 29	14 26	18 24
Broome	d	05x52	09x35	14x37	18x30
Hopton Heath	d	05x56	09x39	14x41	18x34
Bucknell	d	06x00	09x44	14x46	18x39
Knighton	a	06 07	09 51	14 53	18 46
	d	06 12	09 53	14 55	18 48
Knucklas	d	06x17	09x59	15x01	18x54
Llangynllo	d	06x25	10x07	15x09	19x02
Llanbister Road	d	06x30	10x12	15x14	19x07
Dolau	d	06x35	10x18	15x20	19x13
Pen-y-bont	d	06x39	10x22	15x24	19x17
Llandrindod	a	06 46	10 31	15 33	19 26
	d	06 54	10 34	15 40	19 27
Builth Road	d	07x03	10x41	15x49	19x36
Cilmeri	d	07x06	10x45	15x53	19x40
Garth (Powys)	d	07x11	10x50	15x58	19x45
Llangammarch	d	07x14	10x54	16x02	19x49
Llanwrtyd	a	07 20	11 00	16 08	19 55
	d	07 23	11 07	16 11	20 08
Sugar Loaf	d	07x29	11x13	16x17	20x15
Cynghordy	d	07x35	11x20	16x24	20x22
Llandovery	a	07 45	11 30	16 34	20 31
	d	07 47	11 32	16 36	20 34
Llanwrda	d	07x53	11x38	16x42	20x40
Llangadog	d	07x56	11x42	16x46	20x44
Llandeilo	a	08 05	11 51	16 55	20 53
	d	08 08	11 54	16 58	20 55
Ffairfach	d	08 10	11 56	17 00	20 58
Llandybie	d	08x18	12x04	17x08	21x05
Ammanford	d	08x22	12x08	17x12	21x10
Pantyffynnon	d	08 25	12 11	17 15	21 13
Pontarddulais	d	08x32	12x18	17x22	21x20
Llangennech	d	08x37	12x23	17x27	21x24
Bynea	d	08x40	12x26	17x30	21x28
Llanelli	a	08 48	12 35	17 35	21 33
Gowerton	a	09 04		17 47	21 46
Swansea	a	09 22	13 01	18 09	22 06

When events are being held at the Principality Stadium, services are subject to alteration. Please check times before travelling.

Table T129-F

Sundays

20 May to 2 December

Shrewsbury - Swansea

		AW ◇	AW ◇
Shrewsbury	d	12 04	16 18
Church Stretton	d	12 22	16 36
Craven Arms	d	12 33	16 47
Broome	d	12x39	16x53
Hopton Heath	d	12x43	16x57
Bucknell	d	12x48	17x02
Knighton	a	12 55	17 08
	d	12 57	17 11
Knucklas	d	13x03	17x16
Llangynllo	d	13x11	17x24
Llanbister Road	d	13x16	17x29
Dolau	d	13x22	17x35
Pen-y-bont	d	13x26	17x40
Llandrindod	a	13 35	17 49
	d	13 41	18 03
Builth Road	d	13x50	18x13
Cilmeri	d	13x54	18x16
Garth (Powys)	d	13x59	18x22
Llangammarch	d	14x03	18x26
Llanwrtyd	a	14 09	18 32
	d	14 12	18 34
Sugar Loaf	d	14x18	18x41
Cynghordy	d	14x25	18x48
Llandovery	a	14 35	18 57
	d	14 37	19 00
Llanwrda	d	14x43	19x06
Llangadog	d	14x47	19x10
Llandeilo	a	14 56	19 19
	d	14 59	19 21
Ffairfach	d	15 01	19 24
Llandybie	d	15x09	19x31
Ammanford	d	15x13	19x36
Pantyffynnon	d	15 16	19 39
Pontarddulais	d	15x23	19x46
Llangennech	d	15x28	19x50
Bynea	d	15x31	19x54
Llanelli	a	15 37	19 59
Gowerton	a	15 50	20 11
Swansea	a	16 03	20 25

When events are being held at the Principality Stadium, services are subject to alteration. Please check times before travelling.

Table T129-R

Swansea - Shrewsbury

Mondays to Fridays
21 May to 7 December

Miles			AW ◇	AW ◇	AW ◇	AW ◇	AW ◇	AW ◇
0	**Swansea**	d			06 04	09 34	14 35	18 21
5½	Gowerton	d			06 15	09 45		18 32
11¼	Llanelli	d	05 20		06 25	09 55	14 53	18 42
14	Bynea	d	05x23		06x28	09x58	14x56	18x45
16	Llangennech	d	05x27		06x32	10x02	15x00	18x49
18¼	Pontarddulais	d	05x31		06x37	10x06	15x05	18x53
23	Pantyffynnon	d	05 39		06 44	10 14	15 12	19 01
24¼	Ammanford	d	05 42		06 47	10 17	15 15	19 04
26	Llandybie	d	05 46		06 52	10 21	15 20	19 08
30	Ffairfach	d	05x54		06x59	10x29	15x27	19x16
30¾	Llandeilo	a	05 56		07 02	10 31	15 30	19 18
—		d	05 59		07 06	10 34	15 32	19 21
36½	Llangadog	d	06 08		07 16	10 43	15 42	19 30
38¾	Llanwrda	d	06 12		07 19	10 47	15 45	19 34
42	Llandovery	a	06 22		07 26	10 53	15 52	19 40
—		d			07 28	10 56	15 54	19 43
46¾	Cynghordy	d			07x37	11x04	16x03	19x51
49½	Sugar Loaf	d			07x45	11x13	16x11	20x00
53½	Llanwrtyd	a			07 51	11 19	16 17	20 06
—		d			08 08	11 21	16 24	20 31
56¾	Llangammarch	d			08x14	11x27	16x30	20x37
58½	Garth (Powys)	d			08x18	11x31	16x34	20x41
62	Cilmeri	d			08x23	11x37	16x39	20x47
64	Builth Road	d			08x27	11x40	16x43	20x50
69¾	Llandrindod	a			08 38	11 52	16 54	21 02
—		d		06 18	08 45	12 01	16 59	21 19
73¼	Pen-y-bont	d		06x25	08x52	12x09	17x06	21x27
76¾	Dolau	d		06 30	08 57	12 14	17 11	21 32
79¾	Llanbister Road	d		06x36	09x03	12x20	17x17	21x38
82¾	Llangynllo	d		06x42	09x09	12x25	17x23	21x43
86¾	Knucklas	d		06x48	09x15	12x32	17x29	21x50
89¾	Knighton	a		06 54	09 21	12 37	17 35	21 55
—		d		07 03	09 23	12 40	17 37	21 58
93½	Bucknell	d		07 09	09 29	12 46	17 43	22 04
96½	Hopton Heath	d		07x14	09x34	12x50	17x48	22x08
99	Broome	d		07x18	09x38	12x55	17x52	22x13
101½	Craven Arms	a		07 27	09 46	13 02	17 59	22 20
108¾	Church Stretton	a		07 42	09 58	13 17	18 12	22 35
121½	**Shrewsbury**	a		07 57	10 14	13 32	18 28	22 54

Saturdays
26 May to 8 December

		AW ◇	AW ◇	AW ◇	AW ◇
Swansea	d	04 31	09 15	13 12	18 17
Gowerton	d	04 42	09 26	13 23	18 28
Llanelli	d	04 50	09 34	13 32	18 40
Bynea	d	04x55	09x39	13x37	18x44
Llangennech	d	04x58	09x43	13x41	18x48
Pontarddulais	d	05x02	09x47	13x46	18x52
Pantyffynnon	d	05 10	09 55	13 53	18 59
Ammanford	d	05 13	09 58	13 56	19 02
Llandybie	d	05 17	10 02	14 01	19 07
Ffairfach	d	05x24	10x10	14x08	19x14
Llandeilo	a	05 27	10 12	14 11	19 16
	d	05 29	10 15	14 13	19 19
Llangadog	d	05 39	10 24	14 23	19 28
Llanwrda	d	05 42	10 28	14 26	19 32
Llandovery	a	05 49	10 34	14 33	19 38
	d	05 51	10 37	14 35	19 41
Cynghordy	d	05x59	10x45	14x44	19x49
Sugar Loaf	d	06x07	10x54	14x52	19x57
Llanwrtyd	a	06 13	11 00	14 58	20 03
	d	06 16	11 05	15 01	20 08
Llangammarch	d	06x21	11x11	15x07	20x14
Garth (Powys)	d	06x25	11x15	15x11	20x18
Cilmeri	d	06x30	11x21	15x16	20x23
Builth Road	d	06x33	11x24	15x20	20x26
Llandrindod	a	06 44	11 36	15 31	20 37
	d	06 55	11 40	15 42	20 42
Pen-y-bont	d	07x02	11x48	15x50	20x49
Dolau	d	07x07	11 53	15 55	20 54
Llanbister Road	d	07x13	11x59	16x01	20x59
Llangynllo	d	07x18	12x05	16x06	21x04
Knucklas	d	07x24	12x11	16x13	21x10
Knighton	a	07 29	12 16	16 18	21 16
	d	07 32	12 18	16 21	21 18
Bucknell	d	07 38	12 24	16 27	21 24
Hopton Heath	d	07x42	12x28	16x31	21x28
Broome	d	07x46	12x32	16x36	21x32
Craven Arms	a	07 53	12 40	16 42	21 39
Church Stretton	a	08 06	12 53	16 55	21 52
Shrewsbury	a	08 22	13 09	17 11	22 08

When events are being held at the Principality Stadium, services are subject to alteration. Please check times before travelling.

Table T129-R

Swansea - Shrewsbury

Sundays
20 May to 2 December

		AW ◇	AW ◇
Swansea	d	11 12	15 29
Gowerton	d	11 20	15 39
Llanelli	d	11 32	15 49
Bynea	d	11x37	15x54
Llangennech	d	11x41	15x58
Pontarddulais	d	11x45	16x05
Pantyffynnon	d	11 53	16 12
Ammanford	d	11 56	16 15
Llandybie	d	12 00	16 20
Ffairfach	d	12x08	16x27
Llandeilo	a	12 10	16 30
	d	12 13	16 32
Llangadog	d	12 22	16 42
Llanwrda	d	12 26	16 45
Llandovery	a	12 32	16 52
	d	12 35	16 54
Cynghordy	d	12x43	17x03
Sugar Loaf	d	12x52	17x11
Llanwrtyd	a	12 58	17 17
	d	13 00	17 20
Llangammarch	d	13x06	17x26
Garth (Powys)	d	13x10	17x30
Cilmeri	d	13x16	17x35
Builth Road	d	13x19	17x39
Llandrindod	a	13 31	17 50
	d	13 43	18 01
Pen-y-bont	d	13x51	18x09
Dolau	d	13 56	18 14
Llanbister Road	d	14x02	18x20
Llangynllo	d	14x07	18x25
Knucklas	d	14x14	18x32
Knighton	a	14 19	18 37
	d	14 22	18 40
Bucknell	d	14 28	18 46
Hopton Heath	d	14x32	18x50
Broome	d	14x37	18x55
Craven Arms	a	14 44	19 02
Church Stretton	a	14 57	19 17
Shrewsbury	a	15 12	19 38

When events are being held at the Principality Stadium, services are subject to alteration. Please check times before travelling.

Table T130-F

Mondays to Fridays

21 May to 7 September

Treherbert, Aberdare, Merthyr, Pontypridd, Rhymney and Coryton - Cardiff, Penarth, Barry, Barry Island and Bridgend

Miles	Miles	Miles	Miles	Miles			AW MX A	AW	AW B	AW	AW	AW C	AW	AW D	AW E	AW F	AW	AW G	AW H	AW E	AW I	AW J	AW	AW H
0	—	—	—	—	**Treherbert**	d							05 46											
0½	—	—	—	—	Ynyswen	d							05 48											
1¼	—	—	—	—	Treorchy	d							05 50											
2¼	—	—	—	—	Ton Pentre	d							05 52											
3¼	—	—	—	—	Ystrad Rhondda	a							05 55											
—	—	—	—	—		d							05 58											
4½	—	—	—	—	Llwynypia	d							06 00											
5½	—	—	—	—	Tonypandy	d							06 03											
6	—	—	—	—	Dinas Rhondda	d							06 05											
7½	—	—	—	—	Porth	a							06 08											
—	—	—	—	—		d							06 09											
8¾	—	—	—	—	Trehafod	d							06 12											
—	—	0	—	—	**Merthyr Tydfil**	d																		
—	—	1½	—	—	Pentre-bach	d																		
—	—	2¾	—	—	Troed Y Rhiw	d																		
—	—	4½	—	—	Merthyr Vale	a																		
—	—	—	—	—		d																		
—	—	6¾	—	—	Quakers Yard	d																		
—	—	—	—	0	**Aberdare**	d																		
—	—	—	—	1½	Cwmbach	d																		
—	—	—	—	2¾	Fernhill	d																		
—	—	—	—	3¾	Mountain Ash	a																		
—	—	—	—	—		d																		
—	—	—	—	5	Penrhiwceiber	d																		
—	—	8¾	—	7¾	Abercynon	d																		
10¾	—	11½	—	11	**Pontypridd** 3	a							06 17											
—	—	—	—	—		d				05 18			06 18											
11½	—	—	—	—	Trefforest	d				05 21			06 21											
14	—	—	—	—	Trefforest Estate	d				05 25														
16¼	—	—	—	—	Taffs Well	d				05 28			06 28									06 53	06 53	
18¼	—	—	0	—	Radyr 3	a				05 31			06 31									06 56	06 56	
—	—	—	—	—		d				05 31			06 31									07 04	07 04	
—	—	—	1½	—	Danescourt	d																→	→	
—	—	—	2	—	Fairwater	d																		
—	—	—	2¼	—	Waun-gron Park	d																		
—	—	—	3¾	—	Ninian Park	d																		
19¾	—	—	—	—	Llandaf	d				05 34			06 34											
21¾	—	—	—	—	Cathays	d				05 39			06 39											
—	0	—	—	—	**Rhymney** 3	d											06 08	06 08	06 32	06 32				07 00
—	1	—	—	—	Pontlottyn	d											06 11	06 11	06 35	06 35				07 03
—	3½	—	—	—	Tir-phil	d											06 16	06 16	06 40	06 40				07 08
—	4½	—	—	—	Brithdir	d											06 18	06 18	06 42	06 42				07 10
—	6	—	—	—	Bargoed	a											06 22	06 22	06 46	06 46				07 14
—	—	—	—	—		d											06 25	06 25	06 46	06 46	07 02			07 15
—	6½	—	—	—	Gilfach Fargoed	d											06 28	06 28			07 04			07 18
—	7½	—	—	—	Pengam	d											06 30	06 30	06 51	06 51	07 07			07 20
—	9¼	—	—	—	Hengoed	d											06 34	06 34	06 54	06 54	07 10			07 24
—	10½	—	—	—	Ystrad Mynach	d											06 37	06 37	06 57	06 57	07 13			07 27
—	13	—	—	—	Llanbradach	d											06 41	06 41	07 01	07 01	07 18			07 31
—	14¼	—	—	—	Energlyn & Churchill Park	d											06 45	06 45	07 05	07 05				07 35
—	15	—	—	—	Aber	d											06 47	06 47	07 08	07 08	07 23			07 38
—	15¾	—	—	—	Caerphilly	d						06 10					06 50	06 50	07 10	07 10	07 25			07 40
—	18¼	—	—	—	Lisvane & Thornhill	d						06 14					06 54	06 54	07 15	07 15	07 30			07 45
—	19¼	—	—	—	Llanishen	d						06 16					06 56	06 56	07 17	07 17	07 32			07 47
—	20¼	—	—	—	Heath High Level	d						06 19					06 59	06 59	07 20	07 20	07 35			07 50
—	—	0	—	—	**Coryton**	d										06 45								
—	—	0½	—	—	Whitchurch (Cardiff)	d										06 46								
—	—	0¾	—	—	Rhiwbina	d										06 48								
—	—	1¼	—	—	Birchgrove	d										06 50								
—	—	1½	—	—	Ty Glas	d										06 51								
—	—	2¼	—	—	Heath Low Level	d										06 54								
22½	22¾	4¾	—	—	**Cardiff Queen Street** 3	a				05 43		06 25	06 43			06 59	07 04	07 04	07 25	07 25	07 40			07 55
—	—	—	—	—		d	00 01			05 45		06 26	06 45			07 01	07 05	07 05	07 26	07 26	07 41			07 56
23	23¼	—	4¾	—	**Cardiff Central** 7	a	00 05			05 48		06 29	06 49			07 04	07 08	07 08	→	→	→			→
—	—	—	—	—		d		05 20	05 41	05 55	06 25	06 41		06 55	07 01		07 10							
24	24¼	—	—	—	Grangetown	d		05 24	05 45	05 59	06 29	06 45		06 59	07 05		07 14							
—	26¾	—	—	—	Dingle Road	d									07 11									
—	27	—	—	—	**Penarth**	a									07 16									
25¾	—	—	—	—	Cogan	d		05 28	05 48	06 03	06 33	06 48		07 03			07 18							
26½	—	—	—	—	Eastbrook	d		05 30	05 51	06 05	06 35	06 51		07 05			07 20							
27½	—	—	—	—	Dinas Powys	d		05 32	05 53	06 07	06 37	06 53		07 07			07 22							
29½	—	—	—	—	Cadoxton	d		05 37	05 57	06 12	06 42	06 57		07 12			07 27							
30¼	—	—	—	—	Barry Docks	d		05 39	06 00	06 14	06 44	07 00		07 14			07 29							
31½	—	0	—	—	**Barry** 3	d		05 44	06 05	06 19	06 49	07 05		07 19			07 34							
32¼	—	—	—	—	**Barry Island**	a		05 50		06 25	06 55			07 25			07 40							
—	—	3¼	—	—	Rhoose Cardiff Int Airport ✈	d			06 12			07 12												
—	—	9¾	—	—	Llantwit Major	d			06 23			07 22												
—	—	19	—	—	**Bridgend**	a			06 40			07 39												

A From Cardiff Bay
B From Cardiff Canton Sidings
C From Barry Island
D From Hereford
E To Rhymney
F From Barry Island to Radyr
G To Aberdare
H To Treherbert
I From Cardiff Canton Sidings to Rhymney
J To Coryton

When events are being held at the Principality Stadium, services are subject to alteration. Please check times before travelling.

For connections to Cardiff Bay please refer to Table T124

Table T130-F

Mondays to Fridays

21 May to 7 September

Treherbert, Aberdare, Merthyr, Pontypridd, Rhymney and Coryton - Cardiff, Penarth, Barry, Barry Island and Bridgend

		AW A	AW B	AW C	AW D	AW B	AW A	AW E	AW F	AW	AW G	AW H	AW I	AW J	AW K	AW	AW L	AW M	AW	AW G	AW N	AW F
Treherbert	d						06 16									06 46						
Ynyswen	d						06 18									06 48						
Treorchy	d						06 20									06 50						
Ton Pentre	d						06 22									06 52						
Ystrad Rhondda	a						06 25									06 55						
	d						06 28									06 58						
Llwynypia	d						06 30									07 00						
Tonypandy	d						06 33									07 03						
Dinas Rhondda	d						06 35									07 05						
Porth	a						06 38									07 08						
	d						06 39									07 09						
Trehafod	d						06 42									07 12						
Merthyr Tydfil	d													06 38								
Pentre-bach	d													06 42								
Troed Y Rhiw	d													06 45								
Merthyr Vale	a													06 48								
	d													06 50								
Quakers Yard	d													06 55								
Aberdare	d									06 22									06 52			
Cwmbach	d									06 25									06 55			
Fernhill	d									06 28									06 58			
Mountain Ash	a									06 31									07 01			
	d									06 34									07 04			
Penrhiwceiber	d									06 37									07 07			
Abercynon	d									06 45				07 00					07 15			
Pontypridd 3	a						06 47			06 53				07 07		07 17			07 22			
	d						06 48			06 54				07 08		07 18			07 24			
Trefforest	d						06 51			06 57				07 11		07 21			07 27			
Trefforest Estate	d													07 15								
Taffs Well	d						06 58	←	←	07 04				07 19		07 28			07 34			
Radyr 3	a						07 01	06 56	06 56	07 08				07 23		07 31			07 38			
	d						07 01	07 04	07 04	07 08				07 23		07 31		07 34	07 38			
Danescourt	d							07 08	07 08									07 38				
Fairwater	d							07 10	07 10									07 40				
Waun-gron Park	d							07 12	07 12									07 42				
Ninian Park	d							07 15	07 15									07 45				
Llandaf	d						07 04			07 11				07 26		07 35			07 41			
Cathays	d						07 09			07 16				07 31		07 40			07 46			
Rhymney 3	d	07 00		07 24	07 42																	
Pontlottyn	d	07 03		07 27	07 45																	
Tir-phil	d	07 08		07 32	07 50																	
Brithdir	d	07 10		07 34	07 52																	
Bargoed	a	07 14		07 38	07 59		08 31															
	d	07 15	07 32	07 42	08 00	08 15	08 32															
Gilfach Fargoed	d	07 18		07 45		08 18																
Pengam	d	07 20	07 37	07 48	08 05	08 20	08 37															
Hengoed	d	07 24	07 40	07 52	08 09	08 24	08 40															
Ystrad Mynach	d	07 27	07 43	07 55	08 12	08 27	08 43															
Llanbradach	d	07 31	07 48	08 00	08 16	08 31	08 48															
Energlyn & Churchill Park	d	07 35		08 04	08 20	08 35																
Aber	d	07 38	07 53	08 07	08 22	08 37	08 52															
Caerphilly	d	07 40	07 55	08 10	08 25	08 40	08 55															
Lisvane & Thornhill	d	07 45	08 00	08 15	08 29	08 44	08 59															
Llanishen	d	07 47	08 02	08 18	08 31	08 46	09 01															
Heath High Level	d	07 50	08 05	08 21	08 34	08 49	09 04															
Coryton	d								07 45				07 15					08 15				
Whitchurch (Cardiff)	d								07 46				07 16					08 16				
Rhiwbina	d								07 48				07 18					08 18				
Birchgrove	d								07 50				07 20					08 20				
Ty Glas	d								07 51				07 21					08 21				
Heath Low Level	d								07 54		←	←	07 24		←			08 24		←	←	←
Cardiff Queen Street 3	a	07 55	08 09	08 25	08 39	08 54	09 09		07 59	07 19	07 25	07 25	07 29	07 34	07 40	07 45		08 32	07 49	07 55	07 55	07 59
	d	07 56	08 11	08 26	08 41	08 56	09 11		08 01	07 21	07 26	07 26	07 31	07 36	07 41	07 46		08 33	07 51	07 56	07 56	08 01
Cardiff Central 7	a	→	→	→	→	→	→	07 20	→	07 24	07 29	07 29	07 34	07 38	07 44	07 51		→	07 54	07 59	07 59	08 04
	d									07 25		07 31		07 41	07 46		07 52		07 55		08 01	
Grangetown	d									07 29		07 35		07 45	07 50				07 59		08 06	
Dingle Road	d											07 41			07 56						08 12	
Penarth	a											07 46			08 01						08 16	
Cogan	d									07 33				07 48					08 03			
Eastbrook	d									07 35				07 51					08 05			
Dinas Powys	d									07 37				07 53					08 07			
Cadoxton	d									07 42				07 57					08 12			
Barry Docks	d									07 44				08 00					08 14			
Barry 3	d									07 49				08 05			08a11		08 19			
Barry Island	a									07 55									08 25			
Rhoose Cardiff Int Airport ✈	d													08 12								
Llantwit Major	d													08 22								
Bridgend	a													08 39								

A To Bargoed
B From Cardiff Central to Bargoed
C To Penarth
D To Cardiff Central
E From Taffs Well to Coryton
F From Taffs Well to Radyr
G From Rhymney to Treherbert
H From Rhymney to Penarth continues to Rhymney
I From Cardiff Central to Radyr
J From Cardiff Central
K From Cardiff Canton Sidings to Rhymney
L From Carmarthen
M To Radyr
N From Rhymney to Bargoed

When events are being held at the Principality Stadium, services are subject to alteration. Please check times before travelling.

For connections to Cardiff Bay please refer to Table T124

Table T130-F

Mondays to Fridays
21 May to 7 September

Treherbert, Aberdare, Merthyr, Pontypridd, Rhymney and Coryton - Cardiff, Penarth, Barry, Barry Island and Bridgend

		AW A	AW B	AW C	AW	AW A	AW		AW	AW D	AW E	AW A	AW B	AW D	AW	AW A	AW		AW C	AW E	AW F	AW G	AW	AW A	AW
Treherbert	d				07 16										07 45								08 16		
Ynyswen	d				07 18										07 47								08 18		
Treorchy	d				07 20										07 49								08 20		
Ton Pentre	d				07 22										07 51								08 22		
Ystrad Rhondda	a				07 25										07 54								08 25		
	d				07 28										07 58								08 28		
Llwynypia	d				07 30										08 00								08 30		
Tonypandy	d				07 33										08 03								08 33		
Dinas Rhondda	d				07 36										08 05								08 35		
Porth	a				07 39										08 08								08 38		
	d				07 40										08 09								08 39		
Trehafod	d				07 43										08 12								08 42		
Merthyr Tydfil	d		07 08										07 38								08 08				
Pentre-bach	d		07 12										07 42								08 12				
Troed Y Rhiw	d		07 15										07 45								08 15				
Merthyr Vale	a		07 18										07 48								08 18				
	d		07 20										07 50								08 20				
Quakers Yard	d		07 25										07 55								08 25				
Aberdare	d						07 22										07 52								08 22
Cwmbach	d						07 25										07 55								08 25
Fernhill	d						07 28										07 58								08 28
Mountain Ash	a						07 31										08 01								08 31
	d						07 34										08 04								08 34
Penrhiwceiber	d						07 37										08 07								08 37
Abercynon	d		07 30				07 45						08 00				08 15				08 30				08 45
Pontypridd ■	a		07 37		07 48		07 53						08 07		08 17		08 23				08 37		08 47		08 53
	d		07 38		07 49		07 54						08 08		08 18		08 24				08 38		08 48		08 54
Trefforest	d		07 41		07 52		07 57						08 11		08 21		08 27				08 41		08 51		08 57
Trefforest Estate	d		07 45										08 15								08 45				
Taffs Well	d		07 49		07 59		08 04						08 19		08 28		08 34				08 49		08 58		09 04
Radyr ■	a		07 53		08 03		08 08						08 23		08 31		08 38				08 53		09 01		09 08
	d		07 53		08 03	08 04	08 08		08 13				08 23		08 31	08 34	08 38				08 53		09 01	09 04	09 08
Danescourt	d					08 08										08 38								09 08	
Fairwater	d					08 10										08 40								09 10	
Waun-gron Park	d					08 12										08 42								09 12	
Ninian Park	d					08 15										08 45								09 15	
Llandaf	d		07 56		08 06				08 16				08 26		08 34		08 41				08 56		09 04		09 11
Cathays	d		08 01		08 11		08 15		08 20				08 31		08 39		08 46				09 01		09 09		09 16
Rhymney ■	d																								
Pontlottyn	d																								
Tir-phil	d																								
Brithdir	d																								
Bargoed	a																								
	d																								
Gilfach Fargoed	d																								
Pengam	d																								
Hengoed	d																								
Ystrad Mynach	d																								
Llanbradach	d																								
Energlyn & Churchill Park	d																								
Aber	d																								
Caerphilly	d																								
Lisvane & Thornhill	d																								
Llanishen	d																								
Heath High Level	d																								
Coryton	d	07 45				08 45						08 15				09 15								09 45	
Whitchurch (Cardiff)	d	07 46				08 46						08 16				09 16								09 46	
Rhiwbina	d	07 48				08 48						08 18				09 18								09 48	
Birchgrove	d	07 50				08 50						08 20				09 20								09 50	
Ty Glas	d	07 51				08 51						08 21				09 21								09 51	
Heath Low Level	d	07 54		←		08 54				←	←	08 24		←		09 24			←	←		←		09 54	
Cardiff Queen Street ■	a	07 59	08 04	08 09	08 14	08 59	08 18		08 23	08 25	08 32	08 32	08 34	08 39	08 44	09 29	08 49		08 54	08 59	09 04	09 09	09 14	09 59	09 19
	d	08 01	08 06	08 11	08 15	09 01	08 19		08 24	08 26	08 33	08 33	08 36	08 41	08 46	09 31	08 51		08 56	09 01	09 06	09 11	09 16	10 01	09 21
Cardiff Central ■	a	08 04	08 09	08 14	08 21	→	08 22		08 30	08 29	08 36	08 36	08 39	08 47	08 52	→	08 54		08 59	09 04	09 09	09 14	09 21	→	09 24
	d		08 10	08 16			08 25			08 31			08 41				08 55		09 01		09 10	09 16			09 25
Grangetown	d		08 14	08 20			08 29			08 35			08 45				08 59		09 05		09 14	09 20			09 29
Dingle Road	d			08 26						08 41									09 11			09 26			
Penarth	a			08 32						08 46									09 17			09 31			
Cogan	d		08 18				08 33						08 48				09 03				09 18				09 33
Eastbrook	d		08 20				08 35						08 51				09 05				09 20				09 35
Dinas Powys	d		08 22				08 37						08 53				09 07				09 22				09 37
Cadoxton	d		08 27				08 42						08 57				09 12				09 27				09 42
Barry Docks	d		08 29				08 44						08 59				09 14				09 29				09 44
Barry ■	d		08 34				08 49						09 03				09 19				09 34				09 49
Barry Island	a		08 40				08 55										09 25				09 40				09 55
Rhoose Cardiff Int Airport ✈	d												09 10												
Llantwit Major	d												09 19												
Bridgend	a												09 36												

A To Radyr
B From Cardiff Canton Sidings
C From Cardiff Central to Bargoed
D From Rhymney
E From Radyr to Cardiff Central continues to Radyr
F From Barry Island
G From Treherbert to Bargoed

When events are being held at the Principality Stadium, services are subject to alteration. Please check times before travelling.

For connections to Cardiff Bay please refer to Table T124

Table T130-F

Mondays to Fridays
21 May to 7 September

Treherbert, Aberdare, Merthyr, Pontypridd, Rhymney and Coryton - Cardiff, Penarth, Barry, Barry Island and Bridgend

		AW A	AW B		AW C	AW	AW B	AW	AW D	AW E	AW A	AW B	AW C		AW E	AW	AW B	AW	AW	AW A	AW B	AW C	AW F		AW
Treherbert	d					08 46										09 16									09 46
Ynyswen	d					08 48										09 18									09 48
Treorchy	d					08 50										09 20									09 50
Ton Pentre	d					08 52										09 22									09 52
Ystrad Rhondda	a					08 55										09 25									09 55
	d					08 58										09 28									09 58
Llwynypia	d					09 00										09 30									10 00
Tonypandy	d					09 03										09 33									10 03
Dinas Rhondda	d					09 05										09 35									10 05
Porth	a					09 08										09 38									10 08
	d					09 09										09 39									10 09
Trehafod	d					09 12										09 42									10 12
Merthyr Tydfil	d				08 38								09 08									09 38			
Pentre-bach	d				08 42								09 12									09 42			
Troed Y Rhiw	d				08 45								09 15									09 45			
Merthyr Vale	a				08 48								09 18									09 48			
	d				08 50								09 20									09 50			
Quakers Yard	d				08 55								09 25									09 55			
Aberdare	d							08 52										09 22							
Cwmbach	d							08 55										09 25							
Fernhill	d							08 58										09 28							
Mountain Ash	a							09 01										09 31							
	d							09 04										09 34							
Penrhiwceiber	d							09 07										09 37							
Abercynon	d				09 00			09 15					09 30					09 45				10 00			
Pontypridd ■	a				09 07	09 17		09 23					09 37			09 47		09 53				10 07			10 17
	d				09 08	09 18		09 24					09 38			09 48		09 54				10 08			10 18
Trefforest	d				09 11	09 21		09 27					09 41			09 51		09 57				10 11			10 21
Trefforest Estate	d				09 15								09 45									10 15			
Taffs Well	d				09 19	09 28		09 34					09 49			09 58		10 04				10 19			10 28
Radyr ■	a				09 23	09 31		09 38					09 53			10 01		10 08				10 23			10 31
	d				09 23	09 31	09 34	09 38					09 53			10 01	10 04	10 08				10 23			10 31
Danescourt	d						09 38										10 08								
Fairwater	d						09 40										10 10								
Waun-gron Park	d						09 42										10 12								
Ninian Park	d						09 45										10 15								
Llandaf	d				09 26	09 34		09 41					09 56			10 04		10 11				10 26			10 34
Cathays	d				09 31	09 39		09 46					10 01			10 09		10 16				10 31			10 39
Rhymney ■	d								08 32										09 27						
Pontlottyn	d								08 35										09 30						
Tir-phil	d								08 39										09 35						
Brithdir	d								08 42										09 37						
Bargoed	a								08 46										09 41						
	d								08 47	09 17					09 32				09 45				10 00		
Gilfach Fargoed	d								10 43	09 19															
Pengam	d								→	09 22					09 37				09 50				10 05		
Hengoed	d									09 25					09 40				09 54				10 09		
Ystrad Mynach	d									09 28					09 43				09 57				10 12		
Llanbradach	d									09 33					09 48				10 01				10 16		
Energlyn & Churchill Park	d																		10 05				10 20		
Aber	d									09 37					09 52				10 07				10 22		
Caerphilly	d									09 40					09 55				10 10				10 25		
Lisvane & Thornhill	d									09 44					09 59				10 14				10 29		
Llanishen	d									09 46					10 01				10 16				10 31		
Heath High Level	d									09 49					10 04				10 19				10 34		
Coryton	d		09 15				10 15					09 45					10 45				10 15				
Whitchurch (Cardiff)	d		09 16				10 16					09 46					10 46				10 16				
Rhiwbina	d		09 18				10 18					09 48					10 48				10 18				
Birchgrove	d		09 20				10 20					09 50					10 50				10 20				
Ty Glas	d		09 21				10 21					09 51					10 51				10 21				
Heath Low Level	d	←	09 24				10 24				←	09 54					10 54			←	10 24				
Cardiff Queen Street ■	a	09 29	09 29		09 34	09 44	10 29	09 49		09 54	09 59	09 59	10 04		10 09	10 14	10 59	10 19	10 24	10 29	10 29	10 34	10 39		10 44
	d	09 31	09 31		09 36	09 46	10 31	09 51		09 56	10 01	10 01	10 06		10 11	10 16	11 01	10 21	10 26	10 31	10 31	10 36	10 41		10 46
Cardiff Central ■	a	09 34	09 34		09 39	09 51	→	09 54		09 59	10 04	10 04	10 09		10 14	10 21	→	10 24	10 29	10 34	10 34	10 39	10 44		10 51
	d				09 41			09 55		10 01			10 10		10 16			10 25	10 31			10 41	10 46		
Grangetown	d				09 45			09 59		10 05			10 14		10 20			10 29	10 35			10 45	10 50		
Dingle Road	d									10 11					10 26				10 41				10 56		
Penarth	a									10 16					10 31				10 46				11 01		
Cogan	d				09 48			10 03					10 18					10 33				10 48			
Eastbrook	d				09 51			10 05					10 20					10 35				10 51			
Dinas Powys	d				09 53			10 07					10 22					10 37				10 53			
Cadoxton	d				09 57			10 12					10 27					10 42				10 57			
Barry Docks	d				09 59			10 14					10 29					10 44				11 00			
Barry ■	d				10 03			10 19					10 34					10 49				11 05			
Barry Island	a							10 25					10 40					10 55							
Rhoose Cardiff Int Airport ✈	d				10 10																	11 12			
Llantwit Major	d				10 19																	11 22			
Bridgend	a				10 36																	11 39			

A From Radyr to Cardiff Central continues to Radyr
B To Radyr
C From Barry Island
D To Rhymney
E From Penarth
F From Penarth to Rhymney

When events are being held at the Principality Stadium, services are subject to alteration. Please check times before travelling.

For connections to Cardiff Bay please refer to Table T124

Table T130-F

Mondays to Fridays

21 May to 7 September

Treherbert, Aberdare, Merthyr, Pontypridd, Rhymney and Coryton - Cardiff, Penarth, Barry, Barry Island and Bridgend

		AW A	AW	AW B	AW C	AW D	AW A	AW	AW C		AW A	AW	AW E	AW D	AW A	AW	AW B	AW F	AW		AW A	AW	AW C	AW D	AW A
Treherbert	d															10 16			10 46						
Ynyswen	d															10 18			10 48						
Treorchy	d															10 20			10 50						
Ton Pentre	d															10 22			10 52						
Ystrad Rhondda	a															10 25			10 55						
	d															10 28			10 58						
Llwynypia	d															10 30			11 00						
Tonypandy	d															10 33			11 03						
Dinas Rhondda	d															10 35			11 05						
Porth	a															10 38			11 08						
	d															10 52			11 09						
Trehafod	d															10 55			11 12						
Merthyr Tydfil	d			10 04													10 38								
Pentre-bach	d			10 08													10 42								
Troed Y Rhiw	d			10 11													10 45								
Merthyr Vale	a			10 14													10 48								
	d			10 15													10 50								
Quakers Yard	d			10 21													10 55								
Aberdare	d		09 52									10 22										10 52			
Cwmbach	d		09 55									10 25										10 55			
Fernhill	d		09 58									10 28										10 58			
Mountain Ash	a		10 01									10 31										11 01			
	d		10 04									10 34										11 04			
Penrhiwceiber	d		10 07									10 37										11 07			
Abercynon	d		10 15	10 25								10 45					11 00					11 15			
Pontypridd 3	a		10 23	10 33								10 53				11 00	11 06		11 17			11 23			
	d		10 24					10 38				10 54				11 04	11 08		11 18			11 24			
Trefforest	d		10 27					10 41				10 57				11 07	11 11		11 21			11 27			
Trefforest Estate	d																11 15								
Taffs Well	d		10 34					10 49				11 04				11 14	11 19		11 28			11 34			
Radyr 3	a		10 38					10 53				11 08				11 17	11 23		11 31			11 38			
	d	10 34	10 38					10 53			11 04	11 08				11 21	11 23		11 31		11 34	11 38			
Danescourt	d	10 38									11 08										11 38				
Fairwater	d	10 40									11 10										11 40				
Waun-gron Park	d	10 42									11 12										11 42				
Ninian Park	d	10 45									11 15										11 45				
Llandaf	d		10 41					10 56				11 11					11 26		11 34			11 41			
Cathays	d		10 46					11 01				11 16					11 31		11 39			11 46			
Rhymney 3	d												10 27												
Pontlottyn	d												10 30												
Tir-phil	d												10 35												
Brithdir	d												10 37												
Bargoed	a												10 41					←							
	d				10 17				10 32				10 45										11 17		
Gilfach Fargoed	d				10 19													10 43					11 19		
Pengam	d				10 22				10 37				10 50					11 05					11 22		
Hengoed	d				10 25				10 40				10 54					11 09					11 25		
Ystrad Mynach	d				10 28				10 43				10 57					11 12					11 28		
Llanbradach	d				10 33				10 48				11 01					11 16					11 33		
Energlyn & Churchill Park	d												11 05					11 20							
Aber	d				10 37				10 52				11 07					11 22					11 37		
Caerphilly	d				10 40				10 55				11 10					11 25					11 40		
Lisvane & Thornhill	d				10 44				10 59				11 14					11 29					11 44		
Llanishen	d				10 46				11 01				11 16					11 31					11 46		
Heath High Level	d				10 49				11 04				11 19					11 34					11 49		
Coryton	d	11 15					10 45				11 45				11 15						12 15				11 45
Whitchurch (Cardiff)	d	11 16					10 46				11 46				11 16						12 16				11 46
Rhiwbina	d	11 18					10 48				11 48				11 18						12 18				11 48
Birchgrove	d	11 20					10 50				11 50				11 20						12 20				11 50
Ty Glas	d	11 21					10 51				11 51				11 21						12 21				11 51
Heath Low Level	d	11 24				←	10 54				11 54			←	11 24						12 24			←	11 54
Cardiff Queen Street 3	a	11 29	10 49		10 54	10 59	10 59	11 04	11 09		11 59	11 19	11 24	11 29	11 29		11 34	11 39	11 44		12 29	11 49	11 54	11 59	11 59
	d	11 31	10 51		10 56	11 01	11 01	11 06	11 11		12 01	11 21	11 26	11 31	11 31		11 36	11 41	11 46		12 31	11 51	11 56	12 01	12 01
Cardiff Central 7	a	→	10 54		10 59	11 04	11 04	11 09	11 14		→	11 24	11 29	11 34	11 34	11 36	11 39	11 44	11 51		→	11 54	11 59	12 04	12 04
	d		10 55		11 01			11 10	11 16			11 25	11 31				11 41	11 46				11 55	12 01		
Grangetown	d		10 59		11 05			11 14	11 20			11 29	11 35				11 45	11 50				11 59	12 05		
Dingle Road	d				11 11				11 26				11 41					11 56					12 11		
Penarth	a				11 16				11 31				11 46					12 01					12 16		
Cogan	d		11 03					11 18				11 33					11 48					12 03			
Eastbrook	d		11 05					11 20				11 35					11 51					12 05			
Dinas Powys	d		11 07					11 22				11 37					11 53					12 07			
Cadoxton	d		11 12					11 27				11 42					11 57					12 12			
Barry Docks	d		11 14					11 29				11 44					12 00					12 14			
Barry 3	d		11 19					11 34				11 49					12 05					12 19			
Barry Island	a		11 25					11 40				11 55										12 25			
Rhoose Cardiff Int Airport ✈	d																12 12								
Llantwit Major	d																12 22								
Bridgend	a																12 39								

A To Radyr
B From Barry Island
C From Penarth
D From Radyr to Cardiff Central continues to Radyr
E To Rhymney
F From Rhymney to Penarth continues to Rhymney

When events are being held at the Principality Stadium, services are subject to alteration. Please check times before travelling.

For connections to Cardiff Bay please refer to Table T124

Table T130-F

Mondays to Fridays

21 May to 7 September

Treherbert, Aberdare, Merthyr, Pontypridd, Rhymney and Coryton - Cardiff, Penarth, Barry, Barry Island and Bridgend

		AW A	AW B	AW	AW C		AW	AW D	AW E	AW C	AW F	AW G	AW	AW	AW B		AW E	AW C	AW C	AW	AW B	AW	AW C	AW	AW D
Treherbert	d			11 16									11 46									12 16			
Ynyswen	d			11 18									11 48									12 18			
Treorchy	d			11 20									11 50									12 20			
Ton Pentre	d			11 22									11 52									12 22			
Ystrad Rhondda	a			11 25									11 55									12 25			
	d			11 28									11 58									12 28			
Llwynypia	d			11 30									12 00									12 30			
Tonypandy	d			11 33									12 03									12 33			
Dinas Rhondda	d			11 35									12 05									12 35			
Porth	a			11 38									12 08									12 38			
	d			11 39									12 09									12 39			
Trehafod	d			11 42									12 12									12 42			
Merthyr Tydfil	d	11 08									11 38									12 08					
Pentre-bach	d	11 12									11 42									12 12					
Troed Y Rhiw	d	11 15									11 45									12 15					
Merthyr Vale	a	11 18									11 48									12 18					
	d	11 20									11 50									12 20					
Quakers Yard	d	11 25									11 55									12 25					
Aberdare	d						11 22																	12 22	
Cwmbach	d						11 25																	12 25	
Fernhill	d						11 28																	12 28	
Mountain Ash	a						11 31																	12 31	
	d						11 34																	12 34	
Penrhiwceiber	d						11 37																	12 37	
Abercynon	d	11 30					11 45				12 00									12 30				12 45	
Pontypridd 3	a	11 37		11 47			11 53				12 07		12 17							12 37		12 48		12 53	
	d	11 38		11 48			11 54				12 08		12 18							12 38		12 48		12 54	
Trefforest	d	11 41		11 51			11 57				12 11		12 21							12 41		12 51		12 57	
Trefforest Estate	d	11 45									12 15									12 45					
Taffs Well	d	11 49		11 58			12 04				12 19		12 28							12 49		12 58		13 04	
Radyr 3	a	11 53		12 01			12 08				12 23		12 31							12 53		13 00		13 08	
	d	11 53		12 01	12 04		12 08				12 23		12 31						12 34	12 53		13 01	13 04	13 08	
Danescourt	d				12 08														12 38				13 08		
Fairwater	d				12 10														12 40				13 10		
Waun-gron Park	d				12 12														12 42				13 12		
Ninian Park	d				12 15														12 45				13 15		
Llandaf	d	11 56		12 04			12 11				12 26		12 34							12 56		13 04		13 11	
Cathays	d	12 01		12 09			12 16				12 31		12 39							13 01		13 09		13 16	
Rhymney 3	d							11 27																	12 27
Pontlottyn	d							11 30																	12 30
Tir-phil	d							11 35																	12 35
Brithdir	d							11 37																	12 37
Bargoed	a							11 41																	12 41
	d		11 32					11 45				12 00			12 17						12 32				12 45
Gilfach Fargoed	d														12 19										
Pengam	d		11 37					11 50				12 05			12 22						12 37				12 50
Hengoed	d		11 40					11 54				12 09			12 25						12 40				12 54
Ystrad Mynach	d		11 43					11 57				12 12			12 28						12 43				12 57
Llanbradach	d		11 48					12 01				12 16			12 33						12 48				13 01
Energlyn & Churchill Park	d							12 05				12 20													13 05
Aber	d		11 52					12 07				12 22			12 37						12 52				13 07
Caerphilly	d		11 55					12 10				12 25			12 40						12 55				13 10
Lisvane & Thornhill	d		11 59					12 14				12 29			12 44						12 59				13 14
Llanishen	d		12 01					12 16				12 31			12 46						13 01				13 16
Heath High Level	d		12 04					12 19				12 34			12 49						13 04				13 19
Coryton	d				12 45					12 15								12 45	13 15				13 45		
Whitchurch (Cardiff)	d				12 46					12 16								12 46	13 16				13 46		
Rhiwbina	d				12 48					12 18								12 48	13 18				13 48		
Birchgrove	d				12 50					12 20								12 50	13 20				13 50		
Ty Glas	d				12 51					12 21								12 51	13 21				13 51		
Heath Low Level	d				12 54				←	12 24							←	12 54	13 24				13 54		
Cardiff Queen Street 3	a	12 04	12 09	12 14	12 59		12 19	12 24	12 29	12 29	12 34	12 39	12 44		12 54		12 59	12 59	13 29	13 04	13 09	13 14	13 59	13 19	13 24
	d	12 06	12 11	12 16	13 01		12 21	12 26	12 31	12 31	12 36	12 41	12 46		12 56		13 01	13 01	13 31	13 06	13 11	13 16	14 01	13 21	13 26
Cardiff Central 7	a	12 09	12 14	12 21	→		12 24	12 29	12 34	12 34	12 39	12 44	12 51		12 59		13 04	13 04	→	13 12	13 14	13 21	→	13 24	13 29
	d	12 10	12 16				12 25	12 31			12 41	12 46		12 55	13 01						13 16			13 25	13 31
Grangetown	d	12 14	12 20				12 29	12 35			12 45	12 50		12 59	13 05						13 20			13 29	13 35
Dingle Road	d		12 26					12 41				12 56			13 11						13 26				13 41
Penarth	a		12 31					12 46				13 01			13 16						13 31				13 46
Cogan	d	12 18					12 33				12 48			13 03										13 33	
Eastbrook	d	12 20					12 35				12 51			13 05										13 35	
Dinas Powys	d	12 22					12 37				12 53			13 07										13 37	
Cadoxton	d	12 27					12 42				12 57			13 12										13 42	
Barry Docks	d	12 29					12 44				13 00			13 14										13 44	
Barry 3	d	12 34					12 49				13 05			13 19										13 49	
Barry Island	a	12 40					12 55							13 25										13 55	
Rhoose Cardiff Int Airport ✈	d										13 12														
Llantwit Major	d										13 22														
Bridgend	a										13 39														

A From Pontypridd
B From Penarth
C To Radyr
D To Rhymney
E From Radyr to Cardiff Central continues to Radyr
F From Barry Island
G From Penarth to Rhymney

When events are being held at the Principality Stadium, services are subject to alteration. Please check times before travelling.

For connections to Cardiff Bay please refer to Table T124

Table T130-F

Mondays to Fridays
21 May to 7 September

Treherbert, Aberdare, Merthyr, Pontypridd, Rhymney and Coryton - Cardiff, Penarth, Barry, Barry Island and Bridgend

		AW A	AW B	AW C	AW	AW B	AW	AW D	AW A	AW B	AW E	AW F	AW D	AW	AW B	AW	AW D	AW A	AW B	AW C	AW	AW B
Treherbert	d				12 46									13 16							13 43	
Ynyswen	d				12 48									13 18							13 45	
Treorchy	d				12 50									13 20							13 51	
Ton Pentre	d				12 52									13 22							13 53	
Ystrad Rhondda	a				12 55									13 25							13 56	
	d				12 58									13 28							13 58	
Llwynypia	d				13 00									13 30							14 00	
Tonypandy	d				13 03									13 33							14 03	
Dinas Rhondda	d				13 05									13 35							14 05	
Porth	a				13 08									13 38							14 08	
	d				13 09									13 39							14 09	
Trehafod	d				13 12									13 42							14 12	
Merthyr Tydfil	d			12 38							13 08									13 38		
Pentre-bach	d			12 42							13 12									13 42		
Troed Y Rhiw	d			12 45							13 15									13 45		
Merthyr Vale	a			12 48							13 18									13 48		
	d			12 50							13 20									13 50		
Quakers Yard	d			12 55							13 25									13 55		
Aberdare	d						12 52															
Cwmbach	d						12 55															
Fernhill	d						12 58															
Mountain Ash	a						13 01															
	d						13 04															
Penrhiwceiber	d						13 07															
Abercynon	d			13 00			13 15				13 30					13 45				14 00		
Pontypridd	a			13 07	13 17		13 23				13 37			13 47		13 52				14 07	14 17	
	d			13 08	13 18		13 24				13 38			13 48		13 54				14 08	14 18	
Trefforest	d			13 11	13 21		13 27				13 41			13 51		13 57				14 11	14 21	
Trefforest Estate	d			13 15							13 45									14 15		
Taffs Well	d			13 19	13 28		13 34				13 49			13 58		14 04				14 19	14 28	
Radyr	a			13 23	13 31		13 38				13 53			14 01		14 08				14 23	14 31	
	d			13 23	13 31	13 34	13 38				13 53			14 01	14 04	14 08				14 23	14 31	14 34
Danescourt	d					13 38									14 08							14 38
Fairwater	d					13 40									14 10							14 40
Waun-gron Park	d					13 42									14 12							14 42
Ninian Park	d					13 45									14 15							14 45
Llandaf	d			13 26	13 34		13 41				13 56			14 04		14 11				14 26	14 34	
Cathays	d			13 31	13 39		13 46				14 01			14 09		14 16				14 31	14 39	
Rhymney	d																13 27					
Pontlottyn	d																13 30					
Tir-phil	d																13 35					
Brithdir	d																13 37					
Bargoed	a																13 41					
	d							13 17					13 32				13 45					
Gilfach Fargoed	d							13 19														
Pengam	d							13 22					13 37				13 50					
Hengoed	d							13 25					13 40				13 54					
Ystrad Mynach	d							13 28					13 43				13 57					
Llanbradach	d							13 33					13 48				14 01					
Energlyn & Churchill Park	d																14 05					
Aber	d							13 37					13 52				14 07					
Caerphilly	d							13 40					13 55				14 10					
Lisvane & Thornhill	d							13 44					13 59				14 14					
Llanishen	d							13 46					14 01				14 16					
Heath High Level	d							13 49					14 04				14 19					
Coryton	d		13 15			14 15				13 45					14 45				14 15			15 15
Whitchurch (Cardiff)	d		13 16			14 16				13 46					14 46				14 16			15 16
Rhiwbina	d		13 18			14 18				13 48					14 48				14 18			15 18
Birchgrove	d		13 20			14 20				13 50					14 50				14 20			15 20
Ty Glas	d		13 21			14 21				13 51					14 51				14 21			15 21
Heath Low Level	d	←	13 24			14 24			←	13 54					14 54			←	14 24			15 24
Cardiff Queen Street	a	13 29	13 29	13 34	13 44	14 29	13 49	13 54	13 59	13 59	14 04		14 09	14 14	14 59	14 19	14 24	14 29	14 29	14 34	14 44	15 29
	d	13 31	13 31	13 36	13 46	14 31	13 51	13 56	14 01	14 01	14 06		14 11	14 16	15 01	14 21	14 25	14 31	14 31	14 36	14 46	15 31
Cardiff Central	a	13 34	13 34	13 39	13 51	→	13 54	13 59	14 04	14 04	14 09		14 14	14 21	→	14 24	14 31	14 34	14 34	14 39	14 50	→
	d			13 41			13 55	14 01				14 10	14 16			14 25	14 34			14 41		
Grangetown	d			13 45			13 59	14 05				14 14	14 20			14 29	16 05			14 45		
Dingle Road	d							14 11					14 26				16 11					
Penarth	a							14 16					14 31				16 16					
Cogan	d			13 48			14 03					14 18				14 33				14 48		
Eastbrook	d			13 51			14 05					14 20				14 35				14 51		
Dinas Powys	d			13 53			14 07					14 22				14 37				14 53		
Cadoxton	d			13 57			14 12					14 27				14 42				14 57		
Barry Docks	d			14 00			14 14					14 29				14 44				15 00		
Barry	d			14 05			14 19					14 34				14 49				15 05		
Barry Island	a						14 25					14 40				14 55						
Rhoose Cardiff Int Airport ✈	d			14 12																15 12		
Llantwit Major	d			14 22																15 22		
Bridgend	a			14 39																15 39		

A From Radyr to Cardiff Central continues to Radyr
B To Radyr
C From Barry Island
D From Penarth
E From Barry Island to Aberdare
F From Maesteg

When events are being held at the Principality Stadium, services are subject to alteration. Please check times before travelling.

For connections to Cardiff Bay please refer to Table T124

Table T130-F

Mondays to Fridays
21 May to 7 September

Treherbert, Aberdare, Merthyr, Pontypridd, Rhymney and Coryton - Cardiff, Penarth, Barry, Barry Island and Bridgend

		AW	AW A	AW B	AW C	AW D	AW B	AW	AW E	AW A	AW B	AW	AW C	AW	AW B	AW	AW D	AW A	AW C	AW D	AW	AW B	AW
Treherbert	d											14 16		14 46							15 16		
Ynyswen	d											14 18		14 48							15 18		
Treorchy	d											14 20		14 50							15 20		
Ton Pentre	d											14 22		14 52							15 22		
Ystrad Rhondda	a											14 25		14 55							15 25		
	d											14 28		14 58							15 28		
Llwynypia	d											14 30		15 00							15 30		
Tonypandy	d											14 33		15 03							15 33		
Dinas Rhondda	d											14 35		15 05							15 35		
Porth	a											14 38		15 08							15 38		
	d											14 52		15 09							15 39		
Trehafod	d											14 55		15 12							15 42		
Merthyr Tydfil	d				14 08								14 38						15 08				
Pentre-bach	d				14 12								14 42						15 12				
Troed Y Rhiw	d				14 15								14 45						15 15				
Merthyr Vale	a				14 18								14 48						15 18				
	d				14 20								14 50						15 20				
Quakers Yard	d				14 25								14 55						15 25				
Aberdare	d	13 52						14 22								14 52							15 22
Cwmbach	d	13 55						14 25								14 55							15 25
Fernhill	d	13 58						14 28								14 58							15 28
Mountain Ash	a	14 01						14 31								15 01							15 31
	d	14 04						14 34								15 04							15 34
Penrhiwceiber	d	14 07						14 37								15 07							15 37
Abercynon	d	14 15			14 30			14 45					15 00			15 15			15 30				15 45
Pontypridd	a	14 23			14 37			14 53				15 01	15 07	15 17		15 23			15 37		15 47		15 53
	d	14 24			14 38			14 54				15 04	15 08	15 18		15 24			15 38		15 48		15 54
Trefforest	d	14 27			14 41			14 57				15 07	15 11	15 21		15 27			15 41		15 51		15 57
Trefforest Estate	d				14 45								15 15						15 45				
Taffs Well	d	14 34			14 49			15 04				15 14	15 19	15 28		15 34			15 49		15 58		16 04
Radyr	a	14 38			14 53			15 08				15 17	15 23	15 31		15 38			15 53		16 01		16 08
	d	14 38			14 53		15 04	15 08				15 21	15 23	15 31	15 34	15 38			15 53		16 01	16 04	16 08
Danescourt	d						15 08								15 38							16 08	
Fairwater	d						15 10								15 40							16 10	
Waun-gron Park	d						15 12								15 42							16 12	
Ninian Park	d						15 15								15 45							16 15	
Llandaf	d	14 41			14 56			15 11					15 26	15 34		15 41			15 56		16 04		16 11
Cathays	d	14 46			15 01			15 16					15 31	15 39		15 46			16 01		16 09		16 16
Rhymney	d								14 27														
Pontlottyn	d								14 30														
Tir-phil	d								14 35														
Brithdir	d								14 37														
Bargoed	a								14 41														
	d					14 32			14 45								15 17			15 32			
Gilfach Fargoed	d																15 19						
Pengam	d					14 37			14 50								15 22			15 37			
Hengoed	d					14 40			14 54								15 25			15 40			
Ystrad Mynach	d					14 43			14 57								15 28			15 43			
Llanbradach	d					14 48			15 01								15 33			15 48			
Energlyn & Churchill Park	d								15 05														
Aber	d					14 52			15 07								15 37			15 52			
Caerphilly	d					14 55			15 10								15 40			15 55			
Lisvane & Thornhill	d					14 59			15 14								15 44			15 59			
Llanishen	d					15 01			15 16								15 46			16 01			
Heath High Level	d					15 04			15 19								15 49			16 04			
Coryton	d			14 45			15 45				15 15				16 15							16 45	
Whitchurch (Cardiff)	d			14 46			15 46				15 16				16 16							16 46	
Rhiwbina	d			14 48			15 48				15 18				16 18							16 48	
Birchgrove	d			14 50			15 50				15 20				16 20							16 50	
Ty Glas	d			14 51			15 51				15 21				16 21							16 51	
Heath Low Level	d		←	14 54			15 54			←	15 24				16 24			←				16 54	
Cardiff Queen Street	a	14 49	14 59	14 59	15 04	15 09	15 59	15 19	15 24	15 29	15 29		15 34	15 44	16 29	15 49	15 54	15 59	16 04	16 09	16 14	16 59	16 19
	d	14 51	15 01	15 01	15 06	15 11	16 01	15 21	15 26	15 31	15 31		15 36	15 46	16 31	15 51	15 56	16 01	16 06	16 11	16 16	17 01	16 21
Cardiff Central	a	14 54	15 05	15 05	15 09	15 14	→	15 24	15 29	15 34	15 34	15 36	15 39	15 51	→	15 54	15 59	16 04	16 09	16 14	16 21	→	16 24
	d	14 55			15 10	15 16		15 25	15 31				15 41			15 55	16 01		16 10	16 16			16 25
Grangetown	d	14 59			15 14	15 20		15 29	15 35				15 45			15 59	16 05		16 14	16 20			16 29
Dingle Road	d					15 26			15 41								16 11			16 26			
Penarth	a					15 31			15 46								16 16			16 31			
Cogan	d	15 03			15 18			15 33					15 48			16 03			16 18				16 33
Eastbrook	d	15 05			15 20			15 35					15 51			16 05			16 20				16 35
Dinas Powys	d	15 07			15 22			15 37					15 53			16 07			16 22				16 37
Cadoxton	d	15 12			15 27			15 42					15 57			16 12			16 27				16 42
Barry Docks	d	15 14			15 29			15 44					16 00			16 14			16 29				16 44
Barry	d	15 19			15 34			15 49					16 05			16 19			16 34				16 49
Barry Island	a	15 25			15 40			15 55								16 25			16 40				16 55
Rhoose Cardiff Int Airport ✈	d												16 12										
Llantwit Major	d												16 22										
Bridgend	a												16 39										

A From Radyr to Cardiff Central continues to Radyr
B To Radyr
C From Barry Island
D From Penarth
E To Ystrad Mynach

When events are being held at the Principality Stadium, services are subject to alteration. Please check times before travelling.

For connections to Cardiff Bay please refer to Table T124

Treherbert, Aberdare, Merthyr, Pontypridd, Rhymney and Coryton - Cardiff, Penarth, Barry, Barry Island and Bridgend

		AW	AW A	AW B	AW C	AW	AW B	AW	AW D	AW A	AW B	AW C	AW E	AW	AW B	AW	AW F	AW A	AW B	AW C	AW G	AW
Treherbert	d					15 43								16 16								16 46
Ynyswen	d					15 45								16 18								16 48
Treorchy	d					15 51								16 20								16 50
Ton Pentre	d					15 53								16 22								16 52
Ystrad Rhondda	a					15 56								16 25								16 55
	d					15 58								16 28								16 58
Llwynypia	d					16 00								16 30								17 00
Tonypandy	d					16 03								16 33								17 03
Dinas Rhondda	d					16 05								16 35								17 05
Porth	a					16 08								16 38								17 08
	d					16 09								16 39								17 09
Trehafod	d					16 12								16 42								17 12
Merthyr Tydfil	d				15 38							16 08								16 38		
Pentre-bach	d				15 42							16 12								16 42		
Troed Y Rhiw	d				15 45							16 15								16 45		
Merthyr Vale	a				15 48							16 18								16 48		
	d				15 50							16 20								16 50		
Quakers Yard	d				15 55							16 25								16 55		
Aberdare	d							15 52								16 22						
Cwmbach	d							15 55								16 25						
Fernhill	d							15 58								16 28						
Mountain Ash	a							16 01								16 31						
	d							16 04								16 34						
Penrhiwceiber	d							16 07								16 37						
Abercynon	d				16 00			16 15				16 30				16 45				17 00		
Pontypridd 3	a				16 07	16 17		16 23				16 37		16 47		16 53				17 07		17 17
	d				16 08	16 18		16 24				16 38		16 48		16 54				17 08		17 18
Trefforest	d				16 11	16 21		16 27				16 41		16 51		16 57				17 11		17 21
Trefforest Estate	d				16 15							16 45								17 15		
Taffs Well	d				16 19	16 28		16 34				16 49		16 58		17 04				17 19		17 28
Radyr 3	a				16 23	16 31		16 38				16 53		17 01		17 08				17 23		17 31
	d				16 23	16 31	16 34	16 38				16 53		17 01	17 04	17 08				17 23		17 31
Danescourt	d						16 38								17 08							
Fairwater	d						16 40								17 10							
Waun-gron Park	d						16 42								17 12							
Ninian Park	d						16 45								17 15							
Llandaf	d				16 26	16 34		16 41				16 56		17 04		17 11				17 26		17 34
Cathays	d				16 31	16 39		16 46				17 01		17 09		17 16				17 31		17 39
Rhymney 3	d	15 27															16 27					
Pontlottyn	d	15 30															16 30					
Tir-phil	d	15 35															16 35					
Brithdir	d	15 37															16 37					
Bargoed	a	15 41															16 41					
	d	15 45							16 17				16 32				16 45				17 00	
Gilfach Fargoed	d								16 19													
Pengam	d	15 50							16 22				16 37				16 50				17 05	
Hengoed	d	15 54							16 25				16 40				16 54				17 09	
Ystrad Mynach	d	15 57							16 28				16 43				16 57				17 12	
Llanbradach	d	16 01							16 33				16 48				17 01				17 16	
Energlyn & Churchill Park	d	16 05															17 05				17 20	
Aber	d	16 07							16 37				16 52				17 07				17 22	
Caerphilly	d	16 10							16 40				16 55				17 10				17 25	
Lisvane & Thornhill	d	16 14							16 44				16 59				17 14				17 29	
Llanishen	d	16 16							16 46				17 01				17 16				17 31	
Heath High Level	d	16 19							16 49				17 04				17 19				17 34	
Coryton	d			16 15			17 15				16 45				17 45				17 15			
Whitchurch (Cardiff)	d			16 16			17 16				16 46				17 46				17 16			
Rhiwbina	d			16 18			17 18				16 48				17 48				17 18			
Birchgrove	d			16 20			17 20				16 50				17 50				17 20			
Ty Glas	d			16 21			17 21				16 51				17 51				17 21			
Heath Low Level	d		←	16 24			17 24			←	16 54				17 54			←	17 24			
Cardiff Queen Street 3	a	16 24	16 29	16 29	16 34	16 44	17 29	16 49	16 54	16 59	16 59	17 04	17 09	17 14	17 59	17 19	17 24	17 29	17 29	17 34	17 39	17 44
	d	16 26	16 31	16 31	16 36	16 46	17 31	16 51	16 56	17 01	17 01	17 06	17 11	17 16	18 01	17 21	17 26	17 31	17 31	17 36	17 41	17 46
Cardiff Central 7	a	16 32	16 34	16 34	16 39	16 50	→	16 54	16 59	17 04	17 04	17 09	17 14	17 21	→	17 24	17 29	17 34	17 34	17 39	17 44	17 51
	d				16 41			16 55	17 01			17 10	17 16			17 25	17 31			17 41	17 46	
Grangetown	d				16 45			16 59	17 05			17 14	17 20			17 29	17 35			17 45	17 50	
Dingle Road	d								17 11				17 26				17 41				17 56	
Penarth	a								17 16				17 31				17 46				18 01	
Cogan	d				16 48			17 03				17 18				17 33				17 48		
Eastbrook	d				16 51			17 05				17 20				17 35				17 51		
Dinas Powys	d				16 53			17 07				17 22				17 37				17 53		
Cadoxton	d				16 57			17 12				17 27				17 42				17 57		
Barry Docks	d				17 00			17 14				17 29				17 44				18 00		
Barry 3	d				17 05			17 19				17 34				17 49				18 05		
Barry Island	a							17 25				17 40				17 55						
Rhoose Cardiff Int Airport ✈	d				17 12															18 12		
Llantwit Major	d				17 22															18 22		
Bridgend	a				17 37															18 39		

A From Radyr to Cardiff Central continues to Radyr
B To Radyr
C From Barry Island
D From Penarth to Rhymney
E From Penarth
F To Treherbert
G From Penarth to Cardiff Central

When events are being held at the Principality Stadium, services are subject to alteration. Please check times before travelling.

For connections to Cardiff Bay please refer to Table T124

Treherbert, Aberdare, Merthyr, Pontypridd, Rhymney and Coryton - Cardiff, Penarth, Barry, Barry Island and Bridgend

		AW A	AW	AW B	AW A	AW C	AW D	AW	AW E	AW	AW F	AW B	AW A	AW C	AW	AW A	AW	AW G	AW H	AW C	AW	AW	AW
Treherbert	d							17 16							17 46						18 16		
Ynyswen	d							17 18							17 48						18 18		
Treorchy	d							17 20							17 50						18 20		
Ton Pentre	d							17 22							17 52						18 22		
Ystrad Rhondda	a							17 25							17 55						18 25		
	d							17 28							17 58						18 28		
Llwynypia	d							17 30							18 00						18 30		
Tonypandy	d							17 33							18 03						18 33		
Dinas Rhondda	d							17 35							18 05						18 35		
Porth	a							17 38							18 08						18 38		
	d							17 39							18 09						18 39		
Trehafod	d							17 42							18 12						18 42		
Merthyr Tydfil	d					17 08								17 38						18 08			
Pentre-bach	d					17 12								17 42						18 12			
Troed Y Rhiw	d					17 15								17 45						18 15			
Merthyr Vale	a					17 18								17 48						18 18			
	d					17 20								17 50						18 20			
Quakers Yard	d					17 25								17 55						18 25			
Aberdare	d		16 52							17 22							17 52						18 22
Cwmbach	d		16 55							17 25							17 55						18 25
Fernhill	d		16 58							17 28							17 58						18 28
Mountain Ash	a		17 01							17 31							18 01						18 31
	d		17 04							17 34							18 04						18 34
Penrhiwceiber	d		17 07							17 37							18 07						18 37
Abercynon	d		17 15			17 30				17 45				18 00			18 15			18 30			18 45
Pontypridd 3	a		17 22			17 37		17 47		17 52				18 07	18 17		18 23			18 37	18 47		18 53
	d		17 24			17 38		17 48		17 54				18 08	18 18		18 24			18 38	18 48		18 54
Trefforest	d		17 27			17 41		17 51		17 57				18 11	18 21		18 27			18 41	18 51		18 57
Trefforest Estate	d					17 45								18 15						18 45			
Taffs Well	d		17 34			17 49		17 58		18 04				18 19	18 28		18 34			18 49	18 58		19 04
Radyr 3	a		17 38			17 53		18 01		18 08				18 23	18 31		18 38			18 53	19 01		19 08
	d	17 34	17 38			17 53		18 01	18 04	18 08				18 23	18 31	18 34	18 38			18 53	19 01	19 04	19 08
Danescourt	d	17 38							18 08							18 38						19 08	
Fairwater	d	17 40							18 10							18 40						19 10	
Waun-gron Park	d	17 42							18 12							18 42						19 12	
Ninian Park	d	17 45							18 15							18 45						19 15	
Llandaf	d		17 41			17 56		18 04		18 11				18 26	18 34		18 41			18 56	19 04		19 11
Cathays	d		17 46			18 01		18 09		18 16				18 31	18 39		18 46			19 01	19 09		19 16
Rhymney 3	d										17 27												
Pontlottyn	d										17 30												
Tir-phil	d										17 35												
Brithdir	d										17 37												
Bargoed	a										17 41												
	d						17 32				17 45							18 15					
Gilfach Fargoed	d																	18 18					
Pengam	d						17 37				17 50							18 20					
Hengoed	d						17 40				17 54							18 24					
Ystrad Mynach	d						17 43				17 57							18 27					
Llanbradach	d						17 48				18 01							18 31					
Energlyn & Churchill Park	d										18 05							18 35					
Aber	d						17 52				18 07							18 37					
Caerphilly	d						17 55				18 10							18 40					
Lisvane & Thornhill	d						17 59				18 14							18 44					
Llanishen	d						18 01				18 16							18 46					
Heath High Level	d						18 04				18 19							18 49					
Coryton	d	18 15			17 45				18 45				18 15			19 15							
Whitchurch (Cardiff)	d	18 16			17 46				18 46				18 16			19 16							
Rhiwbina	d	18 18			17 48				18 48				18 18			19 18							
Birchgrove	d	18 20			17 50				18 50				18 20			19 20							
Ty Glas	d	18 21			17 51				18 51				18 21			19 21							
Heath Low Level	d	18 24		←	17 54				18 54			←	18 24			19 24			←				
Cardiff Queen Street 3	a	18 29	17 49	17 59	17 59	18 04	18 09	18 14	18 59	18 19	18 24	18 29	18 29	18 34	18 44	19 29	18 49	18 54	18 59	19 04	19 14		19 19
	d	18 31	17 51	18 01	18 01	18 06	18 11	18 16	19 01	18 21	18 26	18 31	18 31	18 36	18 46	19 31	18 51	18 56	19 01	19 06	19 16		19 20
Cardiff Central 7	a	→	17 54	18 04	18 04	18 09	18 14	18 21	→	18 24	18 29	18 34	18 34	18 39	18 51	→	18 54	18 59	19 06	19 12	19 21	19 22	19 23
	d		17 55			18 10	18 16			18 25	18 31			18 41			18 55	19 01					19 25
Grangetown	d		17 59			18 14	18 20			18 29	18 35			18 45			18 59	19 05					19 29
Dingle Road	d						18 26				18 41							19 11					
Penarth	a						18 31				18 46							19 16					
Cogan	d		18 03			18 18				18 33				18 48			19 03						19 33
Eastbrook	d		18 05			18 20				18 35				18 51			19 05						19 35
Dinas Powys	d		18 07			18 22				18 37				18 53			19 07						19 37
Cadoxton	d		18 12			18 27				18 42				18 57			19 12						19 42
Barry Docks	d		18 14			18 29				18 44				19 00			19 14						19 44
Barry 3	d		18 19			18 34				18 49				19 05			19 19						19 49
Barry Island	a		18 25			18 40				18 55							19 25						19 55
Rhoose Cardiff Int Airport ✈	d													19 12									
Llantwit Major	d													19 22									
Bridgend	a													19 39									

A To Radyr
B From Radyr to Cardiff Central continues to Radyr
C From Barry Island
D From Penarth
E To Cardiff Central
F To Caerphilly
G From Cardiff Central
H From Radyr

When events are being held at the Principality Stadium, services are subject to alteration. Please check times before travelling.

For connections to Cardiff Bay please refer to Table T124

Table T130-F

Mondays to Fridays

21 May to 7 September

Treherbert, Aberdare, Merthyr, Pontypridd, Rhymney and Coryton - Cardiff, Penarth, Barry, Barry Island and Bridgend

Station		AW A	AW B	AW C	AW	AW D	AW	AW C	AW	AW E	AW F	AW G	AW F	AW	AW	AW H	AW C	AW C	AW	AW G	AW I	AW	AW
Treherbert	d				18 46				19 16				19 16						19 46			20 16	
Ynyswen	d				18 48				19 18				19 18						19 48			20 18	
Treorchy	d				18 50				19 20				19 20						19 50			20 20	
Ton Pentre	d				18 52				19 22				19 22						19 52			20 22	
Ystrad Rhondda	a				18 55				19 25				19 25						19 55			20 25	
	d				18 58				19 28				19 28						19 58			20 28	
Llwynypia	d				19 00				19 30				19 30						20 00			20 30	
Tonypandy	d				19 03				19 33				19 33						20 03			20 33	
Dinas Rhondda	d				19 05				19 35				19 35						20 05			20 35	
Porth	a				19 08				19 38				19 38						20 08			20 38	
	d				19 09				19 39				19 39						20 09			20 39	
Trehafod	d				19 12				19 42				19 42						20 12			20 42	
Merthyr Tydfil	d			18 38				19 08									19 38						
Pentre-bach	d			18 42				19 12									19 42						
Troed Y Rhiw	d			18 45				19 15									19 45						
Merthyr Vale	a			18 48				19 18									19 48						
	d			18 50				19 20									19 50						
Quakers Yard	d			18 55				19 25									19 55						
Aberdare	d					18 52														19 52			
Cwmbach	d					18 55														19 55			
Fernhill	d					18 58														19 58			
Mountain Ash	a					19 01														20 01			
	d					19 04														20 04			
Penrhiwceiber	d					19 07														20 07			
Abercynon	d			19 00		19 15		19 30							19 43		20 00			20 15			
Pontypridd	a			19 07	19 17	19 23		19 37	19 47				19 47		19 52		20 07		20 18	20 23		20 47	
	d			19 08	19 18	19 24		19 38	19 48				19 48		19 54		20 08		20 18	20 24		20 48	
Trefforest	d			19 11	19 21	19 27		19 41	19 51				19 51		19 57		20 11		20 21	20 27		20 51	
Trefforest Estate	d			19 15				19 45									20 15						
Taffs Well	d			19 19	19 28	19 34		19 49	19 58				19 58		20 04		20 19		20 28	20 34		20 58	
Radyr	a			19 23	19 31	19 38		19 53	20 01				20 01		20 08		20 23		20 31	20 38		21 01	
	d			19 23	19 31	19 38		19 53	20 01				20 01	20 04	20 08		20 23		20 31	20 38		21 01	21 04
Danescourt	d													20 08									21 08
Fairwater	d													20 10									21 10
Waun-gron Park	d													20 12									21 12
Ninian Park	d													20 15									21 15
Llandaf	d			19 26	19 34	19 41		19 56	20 04				20 04		20 11		20 26		20 34	20 41		21 04	
Cathays	d			19 31	19 39	19 46		20 01	20 09				20 09		20 16		20 31		20 39	20 46		21 09	
Rhymney	d										20 00	20 46											
Pontlottyn	d										20 03	20 49											
Tir-phil	d										20 08	20 54											
Brithdir	d										20 10	20 56											
Bargoed	a										20 14	21 00											
	d										20 15	21 00											
Gilfach Fargoed	d										20 18	21 03											
Pengam	d										20 20	21 05											
Hengoed	d										20 24	21 09											
Ystrad Mynach	d										20 27	21 12	21 39										
Llanbradach	d										20 31	21 16	21 44										
Energlyn & Churchill Park	d										20 35	21 20											
Aber	d										20 37	21 22	21 48										
Caerphilly	d						19 40			20 25	20 40	21 25	21 51										
Lisvane & Thornhill	d						19 44			20 29	20 44	21 29	21 55										
Llanishen	d						19 46			20 31	20 46	21 31	21 57										
Heath High Level	d						19 49			20 34	20 49	21 34	22 00										
Coryton	d		19 15													20 15							
Whitchurch (Cardiff)	d		19 16													20 16							
Rhiwbina	d		19 18													20 18							
Birchgrove	d		19 20													20 20							
Ty Glas	d		19 21													20 21							
Heath Low Level	d	←	19 24													20 24		←			←		
Cardiff Queen Street	a	19 29	19 29	19 34	19 44	19 49	19 54	20 04	20 14	20 39	20 54	21 42	22 05		20 19	20 29	20 34	20 39	20 44	20 49	20 54	21 14	
	d	19 31	19 31	19 36	19 46	19 51	19 56	20 06	20 16	20 41	20 56	21 44	22 06		20 21	20 31	20 36	20 41	20 46	20 51	20 56	21 16	
Cardiff Central	a	19 34	19 34	19 39	19 51	19 57	19 59	20 09	20 21	→	→	→	→	20 24	20 27	20 34	20 39	20 46	20 51	20 57	20 59	21 21	21 20
	d			19 41		20 06		20 10									20 41			21 06	21 10		
Grangetown	d			19 45		20 10		20 14									20 45			21 10	21 14		
Dingle Road	d					20 14														21 14			
Penarth	a					20 19														21 19			
Cogan	d			19 48				20 18									20 48				21 18		
Eastbrook	d			19 51				20 20									20 51				21 20		
Dinas Powys	d			19 53				20 22									20 53				21 22		
Cadoxton	d			19 57				20 27									20 57				21 27		
Barry Docks	d			20 00				20 29									21 00				21 29		
Barry	d			20 05				20 34									21 05				21 34		
Barry Island	a							20 40													21 40		
Rhoose Cardiff Int Airport ✈	d			20 12													21 12						
Llantwit Major	d			20 22													21 22						
Bridgend	a			20 39													21 39						

A From Radyr to Cardiff Central continues to Radyr
B To Radyr
C From Barry Island
D To Rhymney
E From Barry Island to Cardiff Central
F To Barry Island
G To Cardiff Central
H From Bridgend to Radyr
I From Rhymney

When events are being held at the Principality Stadium, services are subject to alteration. Please check times before travelling.

For connections to Cardiff Bay please refer to Table T124

Table T130-F

Mondays to Fridays

21 May to 7 September

Treherbert, Aberdare, Merthyr, Pontypridd, Rhymney and Coryton - Cardiff, Penarth, Barry, Barry Island and Bridgend

Station		AW A	AW	AW A	AW B	AW C	AW D	AW	AW FX E	AW F	AW	AW	AW G	AW A	AW C	AW	AW A	AW H	AW	AW C	AW
Treherbert	d											21 16									
Ynyswen	d											21 18									
Treorchy	d											21 20									
Ton Pentre	d											21 22									
Ystrad Rhondda	a											21 25									
	d											21 28									
Llwynypia	d											21 30									
Tonypandy	d											21 33									
Dinas Rhondda	d											21 35									
Porth	a											21 38									
	d											21 39									
Trehafod	d											21 42									
Merthyr Tydfil	d					20 38									21 38					22 38	
Pentre-bach	d					20 42									21 42					22 42	
Troed Y Rhiw	d					20 45									21 45					22 45	
Merthyr Vale	a					20 48									21 48					22 48	
	d					20 50									21 50					22 50	
Quakers Yard	d					20 55									21 55					22 55	
Aberdare	d		20 22					20 54	20 54								21 54				22 54
Cwmbach	d		20 25					20 57	20 57								21 57				22 57
Fernhill	d		20 28					21 00	21 00								22 00				23 00
Mountain Ash	a		20 31					21 03	21 03								22 03				23 03
	d		20 34					21 04	21 04								22 04				23 04
Penrhiwceiber	d		20 37					21 07	21 07								22 07				23 07
Abercynon	d		20 45			21 00		21 15	21 15						22 00		22 15			23 00	23 13
Pontypridd	a		20 53			21 07		21 22	21 22			21 47			22 07		22 23			23 07	23 24
	d		20 54			21 08		21 24	21 24			21 48			22 08		22 24			23 08	
Trefforest	d		20 57			21 11		21 27	21 27			21 51			22 11		22 27			23 11	
Trefforest Estate	d					21 15									22 15					23 15	
Taffs Well	d		21 04			21 19		21 34	21 34			21 58			22 19		22 34			23 19	
Radyr	a		21 08			21 23		21 38	21 38			22 01			22 23		22 38			23 23	
	d	21 04	21 08			21 23		21 38	21 38			22 01		22 04	22 23		22 38		23 14	23 23	
Danescourt	d	21 08												22 08							
Fairwater	d	21 10												22 10							
Waun-gron Park	d	21 12												22 12							
Ninian Park	d	21 15												22 15							
Llandaf	d		21 11			21 26		21 41	21 41			22 04			22 26		22 41		23 16	23 26	
Cathays	d		21 16			21 31		21 46	21 46			22 09			22 31		22 46		23 20	23 31	
Rhymney	d												21 36								
Pontlottyn	d												21 39								
Tir-phil	d												21 44								
Brithdir	d												21 46								
Bargoed	a												21 50								
	d												21 50								
Gilfach Fargoed	d												21 53								
Pengam	d												21 55								
Hengoed	d												21 59								
Ystrad Mynach	d										21 39		22 02								
Llanbradach	d										21 44		22 06								
Energlyn & Churchill Park	d												22 10								
Aber	d										21 48		22 12								
Caerphilly	d										21 51		22 15			22 28					
Lisvane & Thornhill	d										21 55		22 19								
Llanishen	d										21 57		22 21								
Heath High Level	d										22 00		22 24								
Coryton	d				21 15									22 45							
Whitchurch (Cardiff)	d				21 16									22 46							
Rhiwbina	d				21 18									22 48							
Birchgrove	d				21 20									22 50							
Ty Glas	d				21 21									22 51							
Heath Low Level	d				21 24		←			←				22 54				←			
Cardiff Queen Street	a		21 19		21 29	21 34	21 42	21 49	21 49	22 05	22 05	22 14	22 29	22 59	22 34	22 39	22 49	22 59	23 24	23 34	
	d		21 21		21 31	21 36	21 44	21 51	21 51	22 06	22 06	22 16	22 31	23 01	22 36	22 41	22 54	23 01	23 25	23 36	
Cardiff Central	a	21 20	21 27		21 34	21 39	21 48	21 54	21 54	22 09	22 09	22 21	22 34	→	22 39	22 46	23 04	23 06	23 28	23 42	
	d	21 31		21 31		21 41		21 56	21 56	22 10	22 10		22 36		22 43		23 12		23 31		
Grangetown	d	21 35		21 35		21 45		22 00	22 00	22 14	22 14		22 40		22 47		23 16		23 35		
Dingle Road	d	21 41		21 41				22 04	22 04				22 44				23 20				
Penarth	a	21 46		21 46				22 09	22 09				22 49				23 25				
Cogan	d					21 48				22 18	22 18				22 50				23 38		
Eastbrook	d					21 51				22 20	22 20				22 53				23 41		
Dinas Powys	d					21 53				22 22	22 22				22 55				23 43		
Cadoxton	d					21 57				22 27	22 27				22 59				23 47		
Barry Docks	d					22 00				22 29	22 29				23 02				23 50		
Barry	d					22 05				22 34	22 34				23 06				23 54		
Barry Island	a									22 40	22 40								00 01		
Rhoose Cardiff Int Airport ✈	d					22 12									23 13						
Llantwit Major	d					22 22									23 23						
Bridgend	a					22 39			22 58						23 40						

A To Cardiff Central
B From Cardiff Central to Radyr
C From Barry Island
D From Rhymney
E To Maesteg
F From Treherbert
G To Ystrad Mynach
H From Radyr

When events are being held at the Principality Stadium, services are subject to alteration. Please check times before travelling.

For connections to Cardiff Bay please refer to Table T124

Table T130-F

Mondays to Fridays

10 September to 7 December

Treherbert, Aberdare, Merthyr, Pontypridd, Rhymney and Coryton - Cardiff, Penarth, Barry, Barry Island and Bridgend

		AW MX A	AW	AW	AW	AW	AW B	AW	AW C	AW D	AW E	AW	AW F	AW G	AW D	AW H	AW I	AW	AW G	AW J	AW K	AW L	AW M
Treherbert	d							05 47															
Ynyswen	d							05 49															
Treorchy	d							05 51															
Ton Pentre	d							05 53															
Ystrad Rhondda	a							05 56															
	d							05 58															
Llwynypia	d							06 00															
Tonypandy	d							06 03															
Dinas Rhondda	d							06 05															
Porth	a							06 08															
	d							06 09															
Trehafod	d							06 12															
Merthyr Tydfil	d																						
Pentre-bach	d																						
Troed Y Rhiw	d																						
Merthyr Vale	a																						
	d																						
Quakers Yard	d																						
Aberdare	d																						
Cwmbach	d																						
Fernhill	d																						
Mountain Ash	a																						
	d																						
Penrhiwceiber	d																						
Abercynon	d																						
Pontypridd ■	a							06 17															
	d				05 18			06 18															
Trefforest	d				05 21			06 21															
Trefforest Estate	d				05 25																		
Taffs Well	d				05 28			06 28									06 53	06 53					
Radyr ■	a				05 31			06 31									06 56	06 56					
	d				05 31			06 31									07 04	07 04					
Danescourt	d																→	→					
Fairwater	d																						
Waun-gron Park	d																						
Ninian Park	d																						
Llandaf	d				05 34			06 34															
Cathays	d				05 39			06 39															
Rhymney ■	d											06 08	06 08	06 32	06 32				07 00	07 00		07 24	07 42
Pontlottyn	d											06 11	06 11	06 35	06 35				07 03	07 03		07 27	07 45
Tir-phil	d											06 16	06 16	06 40	06 40				07 08	07 08		07 32	07 50
Brithdir	d											06 18	06 18	06 42	06 42				07 10	07 10		07 34	07 52
Bargoed	a											06 22	06 22	06 46	06 46				07 14	07 14		07 38	07 59
	d											06 25	06 25	06 46	06 46	07 02			07 15	07 15	07 32	07 43	08 00
Gilfach Fargoed	d											06 28	06 28			07 04			07 18	07 18		07 46	
Pengam	d											06 30	06 30	06 51	06 51	07 07			07 20	07 20	07 37	07 49	08 05
Hengoed	d											06 34	06 34	06 54	06 54	07 10			07 24	07 24	07 40	07 53	08 09
Ystrad Mynach	d											06 37	06 37	06 57	06 57	07 13			07 27	07 27	07 43	07 56	08 12
Llanbradach	d											06 41	06 41	07 01	07 01	07 18			07 31	07 31	07 48	08 01	08 16
Energlyn & Churchill Park	d											06 45	06 45	07 05	07 05				07 35	07 35		08 05	08 20
Aber	d											06 47	06 47	07 07	07 07	07 22			07 37	07 37	07 52	08 08	08 22
Caerphilly	d						06 10					06 50	06 50	07 10	07 10	07 25			07 40	07 40	07 55	08 11	08 25
Lisvane & Thornhill	d						06 14					06 54	06 54	07 14	07 14	07 29			07 44	07 44	07 59	08 16	08 29
Llanishen	d						06 16					06 56	06 56	07 16	07 16	07 31			07 46	07 46	08 01	08 18	08 31
Heath High Level	d						06 19					06 59	06 59	07 19	07 19	07 34			07 49	07 49	08 04	08 21	08 34
Coryton	d										06 45												
Whitchurch (Cardiff)	d										06 46												
Rhiwbina	d										06 48												
Birchgrove	d										06 50												
Ty Glas	d										06 51												
Heath Low Level	d										06 54												
Cardiff Queen Street ■	a				05 45		06 25	06 43			06 59	07 04	07 04	07 24	07 24	07 39			07 54	07 54	08 09	08 25	08 39
	d	00 01			05 45		06 26	06 45			07 01	07 05	07 05	07 26	07 26	07 41			07 56	07 56	08 11	08 26	08 41
Cardiff Central ■	a	00 05			05 48		06 29	06 49			07 04	07 08	07 08	→	→	→			→	→	→	→	→
	d		05 20	05 41	05 55	06 25	06 41		06 55	07 01		07 10											
Grangetown	d		05 24	05 45	05 59	06 29	06 45		06 59	07 05		07 14											
Dingle Road	d									07 11													
Penarth	a									07 17													
Cogan	d		05 28	05 48	06 03	06 33	06 48		07 03			07 18											
Eastbrook	d		05 30	05 51	06 05	06 35	06 51		07 05			07 20											
Dinas Powys	d		05 32	05 53	06 07	06 37	06 53		07 07			07 22											
Cadoxton	d		05 37	05 57	06 12	06 42	06 57		07 12			07 27											
Barry Docks	d		05 39	06 00	06 14	06 44	07 00		07 14			07 29											
Barry ■	d		05 44	06 04	06 19	06 49	07 05		07 19			07 34											
Barry Island	a		05 51		06 26	06 56			07 26			07 41											
Rhoose Cardiff Int Airport ✈	d			06 11			07 12																
Llantwit Major	d			06 22			07 22																
Bridgend	a			06 40			07 40																

A From Cardiff Bay
B From Barry Island
C From Hereford
D To Rhymney
E From Barry Island to Radyr
F To Aberdare
G To Treherbert
H From Cardiff Central to Rhymney
I To Coryton
J To Ystrad Mynach
K From Cardiff Central to Ystrad Mynach
L To Penarth
M To Cardiff Central

When events are being held at the Principality Stadium, services are subject to alteration. Please check times before travelling.

For connections to Cardiff Bay please refer to Table T124

Table T130-F

Mondays to Fridays

10 September to 7 December

Treherbert, Aberdare, Merthyr, Pontypridd, Rhymney and Coryton - Cardiff, Penarth, Barry, Barry Island and Bridgend

		AW A	AW B	AW C	AW D	AW	AW E	AW F	AW G	AW H	AW I	AW	AW J	AW K	AW	AW E	AW L	AW D	AW K	AW H	AW M	AW	AW K
Treherbert	d		06 17									06 47										07 17	
Ynyswen	d		06 19									06 49										07 19	
Treorchy	d		06 21									06 51										07 21	
Ton Pentre	d		06 23									06 53										07 23	
Ystrad Rhondda	a		06 26									06 56										07 26	
	d		06 28									06 58										07 28	
Llwynypia	d		06 30									07 00										07 30	
Tonypandy	d		06 33									07 03										07 33	
Dinas Rhondda	d		06 35									07 05										07 36	
Porth	a		06 38									07 08										07 39	
	d		06 39									07 09										07 40	
Trehafod	d		06 42									07 12										07 43	
Merthyr Tydfil	d									06 38										07 08			
Pentre-bach	d									06 42										07 12			
Troed Y Rhiw	d									06 45										07 15			
Merthyr Vale	a									06 48										07 18			
	d									06 50										07 20			
Quakers Yard	d									06 55										07 25			
Aberdare	d					06 21									06 51								
Cwmbach	d					06 24									06 54								
Fernhill	d					06 28									06 58								
Mountain Ash	a					06 31									07 01								
	d					06 34									07 04								
Penrhiwceiber	d					06 37									07 07								
Abercynon	d					06 45				07 00					07 15					07 30			
Pontypridd ■	a		06 47			06 53				07 07		07 17			07 23					07 37		07 48	
	d		06 48			06 54				07 08		07 18			07 24					07 38		07 49	
Trefforest	d		06 51			06 57				07 11		07 21			07 27					07 41		07 52	
Trefforest Estate	d									07 15										07 45			
Taffs Well	d		06 58	←	←	07 04				07 19		07 28			07 34					07 49		07 59	
Radyr ■	a		07 01	06 56	06 56	07 08				07 23		07 31			07 38					07 53		08 03	
	d		07 01	07 04	07 04	07 08				07 23		07 31		07 34	07 38					07 53		08 03	08 04
Danescourt	d			07 08	07 08									07 38									08 08
Fairwater	d			07 10	07 10									07 40									08 10
Waun-gron Park	d			07 12	07 12									07 42									08 12
Ninian Park	d			07 15	07 15									07 45									08 15
Llandaf	d		07 04			07 11				07 26		07 34			07 41					07 56		08 06	
Cathays	d		07 09			07 16				07 31		07 39			07 46					08 01		08 11	
Rhymney ■	d																						
Pontlottyn	d																						
Tir-phil	d																						
Brithdir	d																						
Bargoed	a		08 32																				
	d	08 15	08 32																				
Gilfach Fargoed	d	08 18																					
Pengam	d	08 20	08 37																				
Hengoed	d	08 24	08 40																				
Ystrad Mynach	d	08 27	08 43																				
Llanbradach	d	08 31	08 48																				
Energlyn & Churchill Park	d	08 35																					
Aber	d	08 37	08 52																				
Caerphilly	d	08 40	08 55																				
Lisvane & Thornhill	d	08 44	08 59																				
Llanishen	d	08 46	09 01																				
Heath High Level	d	08 49	09 04																				
Coryton	d				07 45				07 15					08 15					07 45				08 45
Whitchurch (Cardiff)	d				07 46				07 16					08 16					07 46				08 46
Rhiwbina	d				07 48				07 18					08 18					07 48				08 48
Birchgrove	d				07 50				07 20					08 20					07 50				08 50
Ty Glas	d				07 51				07 21					08 21					07 51				08 51
Heath Low Level	d				07 54		←	←	07 24		←			08 24		←	←	←	07 54		←		08 54
Cardiff Queen Street ■	a	08 54	09 09		07 59	07 19	07 24	07 24	07 30	07 33	07 39	07 44		08 29	07 49	07 54	07 54	07 59	07 59	08 04	08 09	08 14	08 59
	d	08 56	09 11		08 01	07 21	07 26	07 26	07 31	07 35	07 41	07 46		08 31	07 51	07 56	07 56	08 01	08 01	08 06	08 11	08 15	09 01
Cardiff Central ■	a	→	→	07 20	→	07 24	07 29	07 29	07 34	07 38	07 44	07 52		→	07 54	07 59	07 59	08 04	08 04	08 09	08 14	08 22	→
	d					07 25		07 31		07 41	07 46		07 52		07 55		08 01			08 10	08 16		
Grangetown	d					07 29		07 35		07 45	07 50				07 59		08 05			08 14	08 20		
Dingle Road	d							07 41			07 56						08 11				08 26		
Penarth	a							07 47			08 02						08 17				08 32		
Cogan	d					07 33				07 48					08 03					08 18			
Eastbrook	d					07 35				07 51					08 05					08 20			
Dinas Powys	d					07 37				07 53					08 07					08 22			
Cadoxton	d					07 42				07 57					08 12					08 27			
Barry Docks	d					07 44				08 00					08 14					08 29			
Barry ■	d					07 49				08 05			08a11		08 19					08 34			
Barry Island	a					07 56									08 26					08 41			
Rhoose Cardiff Int Airport ✈	d									08 12													
Llantwit Major	d									08 22													
Bridgend	a									08 40													

A From Cardiff Central to Bargoed
B To Ystrad Mynach
C From Taffs Well to Coryton
D From Taffs Well to Radyr
E From Rhymney to Treherbert
F From Rhymney to Penarth continues to Rhymney
G From Cardiff Central to Radyr
H From Cardiff Central
I From Cardiff Central to Rhymney
J From Carmarthen
K To Radyr
L From Rhymney to Ystrad Mynach
M From Cardiff Central to Ystrad Mynach

When events are being held at the Principality Stadium, services are subject to alteration. Please check times before travelling.

For connections to Cardiff Bay please refer to Table T124

Table T130-F

Mondays to Fridays
10 September to 7 December

Treherbert, Aberdare, Merthyr, Pontypridd, Rhymney and Coryton - Cardiff, Penarth, Barry, Barry Island and Bridgend

		AW		AW A	AW B	AW C	AW D	AW A	AW	AW C	AW		AW E	AW B	AW F	AW G	AW H	AW	AW C	AW	AW I		AW B	AW C
Treherbert	d									07 45									08 17						
Ynyswen	d									07 47									08 19						
Treorchy	d									07 49									08 21						
Ton Pentre	d									07 51									08 23						
Ystrad Rhondda	a									07 54									08 26						
	d									07 58									08 28						
Llwynypia	d									08 00									08 30						
Tonypandy	d									08 03									08 33						
Dinas Rhondda	d									08 05									08 35						
Porth	a									08 08									08 38						
	d									08 09									08 39						
Trehafod	d									08 12									08 42						
Merthyr Tydfil	d							07 38								08 08									
Pentre-bach	d							07 42								08 12									
Troed Y Rhiw	d							07 45								08 15									
Merthyr Vale	a							07 48								08 18									
	d							07 50								08 20									
Quakers Yard	d							07 55								08 25									
Aberdare	d	07 21										07 51									08 21				
Cwmbach	d	07 24										07 54									08 24				
Fernhill	d	07 28										07 58									08 28				
Mountain Ash	a	07 31										08 01									08 31				
	d	07 34										08 04									08 34				
Penrhiwceiber	d	07 37										08 07									08 37				
Abercynon	d	07 45						08 00				08 15				08 30					08 45				
Pontypridd	a	07 53						08 07		08 17		08 23				08 37			08 47		08 53				
	d	07 54						08 08		08 18		08 24				08 38			08 48		08 54				
Trefforest	d	07 57						08 11		08 21		08 27				08 41			08 51		08 57				
Trefforest Estate	d							08 15								08 45									
Taffs Well	d	08 04						08 19		08 28		08 34				08 49			08 58		09 04				
Radyr	a	08 08						08 23		08 31		08 38				08 53			09 01		09 08				
	d	08 08		08 13				08 23		08 31	08 34	08 38				08 53			09 01	09 04	09 08				
Danescourt	d										08 38									09 08					
Fairwater	d										08 40									09 10					
Waun-gron Park	d										08 42									09 12					
Ninian Park	d										08 45									09 15					
Llandaf	d			08 16				08 26		08 34		08 41				08 56			09 04		09 11				
Cathays	d	08 15		08 20				08 31		08 39		08 46				09 01			09 09		09 16				
Rhymney	d																					08 32			
Pontlottyn	d																					08 35			
Tir-phil	d																					08 39			
Brithdir	d																					08 42			
Bargoed	a																					08 46			
	d																	08 32				08 47			
Gilfach Fargoed	d																							
Pengam	d																	08 37				08 52			
Hengoed	d																	08 40				08 55			
Ystrad Mynach	d																	08 43				08 58			
Llanbradach	d																	08 48				09 03			
Energlyn & Churchill Park	d																							
Aber	d																	08 52				09 07			
Caerphilly	d																	08 55				09 10			
Lisvane & Thornhill	d																	08 59				09 14			
Llanishen	d																	09 01				09 16			
Heath High Level	d																	09 04				09 19			
Coryton	d						08 15				09 15									09 45					09 15
Whitchurch (Cardiff)	d						08 16				09 16									09 46					09 16
Rhiwbina	d						08 18				09 18									09 48					09 18
Birchgrove	d						08 20				09 20									09 50					09 20
Ty Glas	d						08 21				09 21									09 51					09 21
Heath Low Level	d				←	←	08 24		←		09 24			←	←		←			09 54				←	09 24
Cardiff Queen Street	a	08 19		08 24	08 25	08 29	08 29	08 34	08 39	08 44	09 29	08 49		08 54	08 59	09 04	09 09	09 09	09 14	09 59	09 19	09 24		09 29	09 29
	d	08 20		08 25	08 26	08 31	08 31	08 36	08 41	08 46	09 31	08 51		08 56	09 01	09 06	09 11	09 11	09 16	10 01	09 21	09 26		09 31	09 31
Cardiff Central	a	08 23		08 30	08 29	08 34	08 34	08 39	08 47	08 52	→	08 54		08 59	09 04	09 09	09 14	09 14	09 22	→	09 24	09 29		09 34	09 34
	d	08 25			08 31			08 41				08 55		09 01		09 10	09 16	09 16			09 25	09 31			
Grangetown	d	08 29			08 35			08 45				08 59		09 05		09 14	09 20	09 20			09 29	09 35			
Dingle Road	d				08 41									09 11			09 26	09 26				09 41			
Penarth	a				08 47									09 17			09 32	09 32				09 47			
Cogan	d	08 33						08 48				09 03				09 18					09 33				
Eastbrook	d	08 35						08 51				09 05				09 20					09 35				
Dinas Powys	d	08 37						08 53				09 07				09 22					09 37				
Cadoxton	d	08 42						08 57				09 12				09 27					09 42				
Barry Docks	d	08 44						08 59				09 14				09 29					09 44				
Barry	d	08 49						09 03				09 19				09 34					09 49				
Barry Island	a	08 56										09 26				09 41					09 56				
Rhoose Cardiff Int Airport ✈	d							09 10																	
Llantwit Major	d							09 19																	
Bridgend	a							09 37																	

A From Rhymney
B From Radyr to Cardiff Central continues to Radyr
C To Radyr
D From Cardiff Central
E From Cardiff Central to Bargoed
F From Barry Island
G From Treherbert to Ystrad Mynach
H From Penarth
I To Cardiff Central

When events are being held at the Principality Stadium, services are subject to alteration. Please check times before travelling.

For connections to Cardiff Bay please refer to Table T124

Table T130-F

Mondays to Fridays
10 September to 7 December

Treherbert, Aberdare, Merthyr, Pontypridd, Rhymney and Coryton - Cardiff, Penarth, Barry, Barry Island and Bridgend

		AW A	AW	AW B	AW	AW C	AW B	AW A		AW D	AW	AW B	AW	AW	AW C	AW B	AW A	AW E		AW	AW B	AW	AW C	AW B	AW A
Treherbert	d		08 47								09 17									09 47					
Ynyswen	d		08 49								09 19									09 49					
Treorchy	d		08 51								09 21									09 51					
Ton Pentre	d		08 53								09 23									09 53					
Ystrad Rhondda	a		08 56								09 26									09 56					
	d		08 58								09 28									09 58					
Llwynypia	d		09 00								09 30									10 00					
Tonypandy	d		09 03								09 33									10 03					
Dinas Rhondda	d		09 05								09 35									10 05					
Porth	a		09 08								09 38									10 08					
	d		09 09								09 39									10 09					
Trehafod	d		09 12								09 42									10 12					
Merthyr Tydfil	d	08 38						09 08									09 38								10 04
Pentre-bach	d	08 42						09 12									09 42								10 08
Troed Y Rhiw	d	08 45						09 15									09 45								10 11
Merthyr Vale	a	08 48						09 18									09 48								10 14
	d	08 50						09 20									09 50								10 15
Quakers Yard	d	08 55						09 25									09 55								10 21
Aberdare	d				08 51								09 21									09 51			
Cwmbach	d				08 54								09 24									09 54			
Fernhill	d				08 58								09 28									09 58			
Mountain Ash	a				09 01								09 31									10 01			
	d				09 04								09 34									10 04			
Penrhiwceiber	d				09 07								09 37									10 07			
Abercynon	d	09 00			09 15			09 30					09 45				10 00					10 15			10 25
Pontypridd	a	09 07	09 17		09 23			09 37			09 47		09 53				10 07			10 17		10 23			10 34
	d	09 08	09 18		09 24			09 38			09 48		09 54				10 08			10 18		10 24			
Trefforest	d	09 11	09 21		09 27			09 41			09 51		09 57				10 11			10 21		10 27			
Trefforest Estate	d	09 15						09 45									10 15								
Taffs Well	d	09 19	09 28		09 34			09 49			09 58		10 04				10 19			10 28		10 34			
Radyr	a	09 23	09 31		09 38			09 53			10 01		10 08				10 23			10 31		10 38			
	d	09 23	09 31	09 34	09 38			09 53			10 01	10 04	10 08				10 23			10 31	10 34	10 38			
Danescourt	d			09 38								10 08									10 38				
Fairwater	d			09 40								10 10									10 40				
Waun-gron Park	d			09 42								10 12									10 42				
Ninian Park	d			09 45								10 15									10 45				
Llandaf	d	09 26	09 34		09 41			09 56			10 04		10 11				10 26			10 34		10 41			
Cathays	d	09 31	09 39		09 46			10 01			10 09		10 16				10 31			10 39		10 46			
Rhymney	d													09 27											
Pontlottyn	d													09 30											
Tir-phil	d													09 35											
Brithdir	d													09 37											
Bargoed	a													09 41											
	d									09 25				09 45				10 00							
Gilfach Fargoed	d									09 27															
Pengam	d									09 30				09 50				10 05							
Hengoed	d									09 33				09 54				10 09							
Ystrad Mynach	d									09 43				09 57				10 12							
Llanbradach	d									09 48				10 01				10 16							
Energlyn & Churchill Park	d													10 05				10 20							
Aber	d									09 52				10 07				10 22							
Caerphilly	d									09 55				10 10				10 25							
Lisvane & Thornhill	d									09 59				10 14				10 29							
Llanishen	d									10 01				10 16				10 31							
Heath High Level	d									10 04				10 19				10 34							
Coryton	d			10 15			09 45					10 45				10 15					11 15			10 45	
Whitchurch (Cardiff)	d			10 16			09 46					10 46				10 16					11 16			10 46	
Rhiwbina	d			10 18			09 48					10 48				10 18					11 18			10 48	
Birchgrove	d			10 20			09 50					10 50				10 20					11 20			10 50	
Ty Glas	d			10 21			09 51					10 51				10 21					11 21			10 51	
Heath Low Level	d			10 24		←	09 54					10 54			←	10 24					11 24		←	10 54	
Cardiff Queen Street	a	09 34	09 44	10 29	09 49	09 59	09 59	10 04		10 09	10 14	10 59	10 19	10 24	10 29	10 29	10 34	10 39		10 44	11 29	10 49	10 59	10 59	
	d	09 36	09 46	10 31	09 51	10 01	10 01	10 06		10 11	10 16	11 01	10 21	10 26	10 31	10 31	10 36	10 41		10 46	11 31	10 51	11 01	11 01	
Cardiff Central	a	09 39	09 52	→	09 54	10 04	10 04	10 09		10 14	10 22	→	10 24	10 29	10 34	10 34	10 39	10 44		10 52	→	10 54	11 04	11 04	
	d	09 41			09 55			10 10		10 16			10 25	10 31			10 41	10 46				10 55			
Grangetown	d	09 45			09 59			10 14		10 20			10 29	10 35			10 45	10 50				10 59			
Dingle Road	d									10 26				10 41				10 56							
Penarth	a									10 32				10 47				11 02							
Cogan	d	09 48			10 03			10 18					10 33				10 48					11 03			
Eastbrook	d	09 51			10 05			10 20					10 35				10 51					11 05			
Dinas Powys	d	09 53			10 07			10 22					10 37				10 53					11 07			
Cadoxton	d	09 57			10 12			10 27					10 42				10 57					11 12			
Barry Docks	d	09 59			10 14			10 29					10 44				11 00					11 14			
Barry	d	10 03			10 19			10 34					10 49				11 05					11 19			
Barry Island	a				10 26			10 41					10 56									11 26			
Rhoose Cardiff Int Airport ✈	d	10 10															11 12								
Llantwit Major	d	10 19															11 22								
Bridgend	a	10 37															11 40								

A From Barry Island
B To Radyr
C From Radyr to Cardiff Central continues to Radyr
D From Penarth
E From Penarth to Rhymney

When events are being held at the Principality Stadium, services are subject to alteration. Please check times before travelling.

For connections to Cardiff Bay please refer to Table T124

Treherbert, Aberdare, Merthyr, Pontypridd, Rhymney and Coryton - Cardiff, Penarth, Barry, Barry Island and Bridgend

		AW	AW A	AW B	AW	AW C	AW D	AW B	AW	AW E	AW	AW B	AW	AW D	AW B	AW F	AW A	AW B	AW	AW C	AW D	AW B
Treherbert	d								10 17		10 47											
Ynyswen	d								10 19		10 49											
Treorchy	d								10 21		10 51											
Ton Pentre	d								10 23		10 53											
Ystrad Rhondda	a								10 26		10 56											
	d								10 28		10 58											
Llwynypia	d								10 30		11 00											
Tonypandy	d								10 33		11 03											
Dinas Rhondda	d								10 35		11 05											
Porth	a								10 38		11 08											
	d								10 52		11 09											
Trehafod	d								10 55		11 12											
Merthyr Tydfil	d									10 38						11 08						
Pentre-bach	d									10 42						11 12						
Troed Y Rhiw	d									10 45						11 15						
Merthyr Vale	a									10 48						11 18						
	d									10 50						11 20						
Quakers Yard	d									10 55						11 25						
Aberdare	d				10 21								10 51						11 21			
Cwmbach	d				10 24								10 54						11 24			
Fernhill	d				10 28								10 58						11 28			
Mountain Ash	a				10 31								11 01						11 31			
	d				10 34								11 04						11 34			
Penrhiwceiber	d				10 37								11 07						11 37			
Abercynon	d				10 45					11 00			11 15			11 30			11 45			
Pontypridd	a				10 53				11 00	11 06	11 17		11 23			11 37			11 53			
	d	10 38			10 54				11 04	11 08	11 18		11 24			11 38			11 54			
Trefforest	d	10 41			10 57				11 07	11 11	11 21		11 27			11 41			11 57			
Trefforest Estate	d									11 15						11 45						
Taffs Well	d	10 49			11 04				11 14	11 19	11 28		11 34			11 49			12 04			
Radyr	a	10 53			11 08				11 17	11 23	11 31		11 38			11 53			12 08			
	d	10 53		11 04	11 08				11 21	11 23	11 31	11 34	11 38			11 53		12 04	12 08			
Danescourt	d			11 08								11 38						12 08				
Fairwater	d			11 10								11 40						12 10				
Waun-gron Park	d			11 12								11 42						12 12				
Ninian Park	d			11 15								11 45						12 15				
Llandaf	d	10 56			11 11					11 26	11 34		11 41			11 56			12 11			
Cathays	d	11 01			11 16					11 31	11 39		11 46			12 01			12 16			
Rhymney	d					10 27														11 27		
Pontlottyn	d					10 30														11 30		
Tir-phil	d					10 35														11 35		
Brithdir	d					10 37														11 37		
Bargoed	a					10 41														11 41		
	d		10 25			10 45											11 25			11 45		
Gilfach Fargoed	d		10 27														11 27					
Pengam	d		10 30			10 50											11 30			11 50		
Hengoed	d		10 33			10 54											11 33			11 54		
Ystrad Mynach	d		10 43			10 57											11 39			11 57		
Llanbradach	d		10 48			11 01											11 43			12 01		
Energlyn & Churchill Park	d					11 05														12 05		
Aber	d		10 52			11 07											11 48			12 07		
Caerphilly	d		10 55			11 10											11 55			12 10		
Lisvane & Thornhill	d		10 59			11 14											11 59			12 14		
Llanishen	d		11 01			11 16											12 01			12 16		
Heath High Level	d		11 04			11 19											12 04			12 19		
Coryton	d			11 45				11 15				12 15			11 45			12 45				12 15
Whitchurch (Cardiff)	d			11 46				11 16				12 16			11 46			12 46				12 16
Rhiwbina	d			11 48				11 18				12 18			11 48			12 48				12 18
Birchgrove	d			11 50				11 20				12 20			11 50			12 50				12 20
Ty Glas	d			11 51				11 21				12 21			11 51			12 51				12 21
Heath Low Level	d			11 54			←	11 24				12 24		←	11 54			12 54			←	12 24
Cardiff Queen Street	a	11 04	11 09	11 59	11 19	11 24	11 29	11 29		11 34	11 44	12 29	11 49	11 59	11 59	12 04	12 09	12 59	12 19	12 24	12 29	12 29
	d	11 06	11 11	12 01	11 21	11 26	11 31	11 31		11 36	11 46	12 31	11 51	12 01	12 01	12 06	12 11	13 01	12 21	12 26	12 31	12 31
Cardiff Central	a	11 09	11 14	→	11 24	11 29	11 34	11 34	11 36	11 39	11 52	→	11 54	12 04	12 04	12 09	12 14	→	12 24	12 29	12 34	12 34
	d	11 10	11 16		11 25	11 31				11 41			11 55			12 10	12 16		12 25	12 31		
Grangetown	d	11 14	11 20		11 29	11 35				11 45			11 59			12 14	12 20		12 29	12 35		
Dingle Road	d		11 26			11 41											12 26			12 41		
Penarth	a		11 32			11 47											12 32			12 47		
Cogan	d	11 18			11 33					11 48			12 03			12 18			12 33			
Eastbrook	d	11 20			11 35					11 51			12 05			12 20			12 35			
Dinas Powys	d	11 22			11 37					11 53			12 07			12 22			12 37			
Cadoxton	d	11 27			11 42					11 57			12 12			12 27			12 42			
Barry Docks	d	11 29			11 44					12 00			12 14			12 29			12 44			
Barry	d	11 34			11 49					12 05			12 19			12 34			12 49			
Barry Island	a	11 41			11 56								12 26			12 41			12 56			
Rhoose Cardiff Int Airport ✈	d									12 12												
Llantwit Major	d									12 22												
Bridgend	a									12 40												

A From Penarth
B To Radyr
C To Rhymney
D From Radyr to Cardiff Central continues to Radyr
E From Barry Island
F From Pontypridd

When events are being held at the Principality Stadium, services are subject to alteration. Please check times before travelling.

For connections to Cardiff Bay please refer to Table T124

Treherbert, Aberdare, Merthyr, Pontypridd, Rhymney and Coryton - Cardiff, Penarth, Barry, Barry Island and Bridgend

		AW	AW A	AW B	AW	AW	AW C	AW D	AW D	AW	AW E	AW	AW D	AW	AW F	AW C	AW D	AW A	AW	AW D	AW	AW C	AW D
Treherbert	d	11 17			11 47							12 17							12 47				
Ynyswen	d	11 19			11 49							12 19							12 49				
Treorchy	d	11 21			11 51							12 21							12 51				
Ton Pentre	d	11 23			11 53							12 23							12 53				
Ystrad Rhondda	a	11 26			11 56							12 26							12 56				
	d	11 28			11 58							12 28							12 58				
Llwynypia	d	11 30			12 00							12 30							13 00				
Tonypandy	d	11 33			12 03							12 33							13 03				
Dinas Rhondda	d	11 35			12 05							12 35							13 05				
Porth	a	11 38			12 08							12 38							13 08				
	d	11 52			12 09							12 39							13 09				
Trehafod	d	11 55			12 12							12 42							13 12				
Merthyr Tydfil	d		11 38							12 08								12 38					
Pentre-bach	d		11 42							12 12								12 42					
Troed Y Rhiw	d		11 45							12 15								12 45					
Merthyr Vale	a		11 48							12 18								12 48					
	d		11 50							12 20								12 50					
Quakers Yard	d		11 55							12 25								12 55					
Aberdare	d													12 21							12 51		
Cwmbach	d													12 24							12 54		
Fernhill	d													12 28							12 58		
Mountain Ash	a													12 31							13 01		
	d													12 34							13 04		
Penrhiwceiber	d													12 37							13 07		
Abercynon	d		12 00							12 30				12 45				13 00			13 15		
Pontypridd	a	12 00	12 07		12 17					12 37		12 48		12 53				13 07	13 17		13 23		
	d	12 04	12 08		12 18					12 38		12 48		12 54				13 08	13 18		13 24		
Trefforest	d	12 07	12 11		12 21					12 41		12 51		12 57				13 11	13 21		13 27		
Trefforest Estate	d		12 15							12 45								13 15					
Taffs Well	d	12 14	12 19		12 28					12 49		12 58		13 04				13 19	13 28		13 34		
Radyr	a	12 17	12 23		12 31					12 53		13 00		13 08				13 23	13 31		13 38		
	d	12 21	12 23		12 31				12 34	12 53		13 01	13 04	13 08				13 23	13 31	13 34	13 38		
Danescourt	d								12 38				13 08							13 38			
Fairwater	d								12 40				13 10							13 40			
Waun-gron Park	d								12 42				13 12							13 42			
Ninian Park	d								12 45				13 15							13 45			
Llandaf	d		12 26		12 34					12 56		13 04		13 11				13 26	13 34		13 41		
Cathays	d		12 31		12 39					13 01		13 09		13 16				13 31	13 39		13 46		
Rhymney	d														12 27								
Pontlottyn	d														12 30								
Tir-phil	d														12 35								
Brithdir	d														12 37								
Bargoed	a														12 41								
	d			12 00							12 25				12 45								
Gilfach Fargoed	d										12 27												
Pengam	d			12 05							12 30				12 50								
Hengoed	d			12 09							12 33				12 54								
Ystrad Mynach	d			12 12							12 43				12 57								
Llanbradach	d			12 16							12 48				13 01								
Energlyn & Churchill Park	d			12 20											13 05								
Aber	d			12 22							12 52				13 07								
Caerphilly	d			12 25							12 55				13 10								
Lisvane & Thornhill	d			12 29							12 59				13 14								
Llanishen	d			12 31							13 01				13 16								
Heath High Level	d			12 34							13 04				13 19								
Coryton	d							12 45	13 15				13 45				13 15			14 15			13 45
Whitchurch (Cardiff)	d							12 46	13 16				13 46				13 16			14 16			13 46
Rhiwbina	d							12 48	13 18				13 48				13 18			14 18			13 48
Birchgrove	d							12 50	13 20				13 50				13 20			14 20			13 50
Ty Glas	d							12 51	13 21				13 51				13 21			14 21			13 51
Heath Low Level	d						←	12 54	13 24				13 54			←	13 24			14 24		←	13 54
Cardiff Queen Street	a		12 34	12 39	12 44		12 59	12 59	13 29	13 04	13 09	13 14	13 59	13 19	13 24	13 29	13 29	13 34	13 44	14 29	13 49	13 59	13 59
	d		12 36	12 41	12 46		13 01	13 01	13 31	13 06	13 11	13 16	14 01	13 21	13 26	13 31	13 31	13 36	13 46	14 31	13 51	14 01	14 01
Cardiff Central	a	12 42	12 39	12 44	12 52		13 04	13 04	→	13 12	13 14	13 22	→	13 24	13 29	13 34	13 34	13 39	13 52	→	13 54	14 04	14 04
	d		12 41	12 46		12 55					13 16			13 25	13 31			13 41			13 55		
Grangetown	d		12 45	12 50		12 59					13 20			13 29	13 35			13 45			13 59		
Dingle Road	d			12 56							13 26				13 41								
Penarth	a			13 02							13 32				13 47								
Cogan	d		12 48			13 03								13 33				13 48			14 03		
Eastbrook	d		12 51			13 05								13 35				13 51			14 05		
Dinas Powys	d		12 53			13 07								13 37				13 53			14 07		
Cadoxton	d		12 57			13 12								13 42				13 57			14 12		
Barry Docks	d		13 00			13 14								13 44				14 00			14 14		
Barry	d		13 05			13 19								13 49				14 05			14 19		
Barry Island	a					13 25								13 56							14 26		
Rhoose Cardiff Int Airport ✈	d		13 12															14 12					
Llantwit Major	d		13 22															14 22					
Bridgend	a		13 40															14 40					

A From Barry Island
B From Penarth to Rhymney
C From Radyr to Cardiff Central continues to Radyr
D To Radyr
E From Penarth
F To Rhymney

When events are being held at the Principality Stadium, services are subject to alteration. Please check times before travelling.

For connections to Cardiff Bay please refer to Table T124

Table T130-F

Mondays to Fridays

10 September to 7 December

Treherbert, Aberdare, Merthyr, Pontypridd, Rhymney and Coryton - Cardiff, Penarth, Barry, Barry Island and Bridgend

		AW A	AW	AW B	AW	AW C		AW	AW D	AW E	AW C	AW F	AW G	AW	AW C	AW		AW	AW E	AW C	AW F	AW B	AW C	AW	AW H
Treherbert	d				13 17									13 43											
Ynyswen	d				13 19									13 45											
Treorchy	d				13 21									13 51											
Ton Pentre	d				13 23									13 53											
Ystrad Rhondda	a				13 26									13 56											
	d				13 28									13 58											
Llwynypia	d				13 30									14 00											
Tonypandy	d				13 33									14 03											
Dinas Rhondda	d				13 35									14 05											
Porth	a				13 38									14 08											
	d				13 39									14 09											
Trehafod	d				13 42									14 12											
Merthyr Tydfil	d	13 08										13 38									14 08				
Pentre-bach	d	13 12										13 42									14 12				
Troed Y Rhiw	d	13 15										13 45									14 15				
Merthyr Vale	a	13 18										13 48									14 18				
	d	13 20										13 50									14 20				
Quakers Yard	d	13 25										13 55									14 25				
Aberdare	d															13 51								14 21	
Cwmbach	d															13 54								14 24	
Fernhill	d															13 58								14 28	
Mountain Ash	a															14 01								14 31	
	d															14 04								14 34	
Penrhiwceiber	d															14 07								14 37	
Abercynon	d	13 30						13 45				14 00				14 15					14 30			14 45	
Pontypridd	a	13 37			13 47			13 52				14 07		14 17		14 23					14 37			14 52	
	d	13 38			13 48			13 54				14 08		14 18		14 24					14 38			14 54	
Trefforest	d	13 41			13 51			13 57				14 11		14 21		14 27					14 41			14 57	
Trefforest Estate	d	13 45										14 15									14 45				
Taffs Well	d	13 49			13 58			14 04				14 19		14 28		14 34					14 49			15 04	
Radyr	a	13 53			14 01			14 08				14 23		14 31		14 38					14 53			15 08	
	d	13 53			14 01	14 04		14 08				14 23		14 31	14 34	14 38					14 53		15 04	15 08	
Danescourt	d					14 08									14 38								15 08		
Fairwater	d					14 10									14 40								15 10		
Waun-gron Park	d					14 12									14 42								15 12		
Ninian Park	d					14 15									14 45								15 15		
Llandaf	d	13 56			14 04			14 11				14 26		14 34		14 41					14 56			15 11	
Cathays	d	14 01			14 09			14 16				14 31		14 39		14 46					15 01			15 16	
Rhymney	d								13 27																14 27
Pontlottyn	d								13 30																14 30
Tir-phil	d								13 35																14 35
Brithdir	d								13 37																14 37
Bargoed	a								13 41																14 41
	d			13 25					13 45													14 25			14 45
Gilfach Fargoed	d			13 27																		14 27			
Pengam	d			13 30					13 50													14 30			14 50
Hengoed	d			13 33					13 54													14 33			14 54
Ystrad Mynach	d			13 43					13 57									14 28				14 43			14 57
Llanbradach	d			13 48					14 01									14 33				14 48			15 01
Energlyn & Churchill Park	d								14 05																15 05
Aber	d			13 52					14 07									14 37				14 52			15 07
Caerphilly	d			13 55					14 10									14 40				14 55			15 10
Lisvane & Thornhill	d			13 59					14 14									14 44				14 59			15 14
Llanishen	d			14 01					14 16									14 46				15 01			15 16
Heath High Level	d			14 04					14 19									14 49				15 04			15 19
Coryton	d					14 45					14 15				15 15					14 45			15 45		
Whitchurch (Cardiff)	d					14 46					14 16				15 16					14 46			15 46		
Rhiwbina	d					14 48					14 18				15 18					14 48			15 48		
Birchgrove	d					14 50					14 20				15 20					14 50			15 50		
Ty Glas	d					14 51					14 21				15 21					14 51			15 51		
Heath Low Level	d					14 54				←	14 24				15 24				←	14 54			15 54		
Cardiff Queen Street	a	14 04		14 09	14 14	14 59		14 19	14 24	14 29	14 29	14 34	←	14 44	15 29	14 49		14 54	14 59	14 59	15 04	15 09	15 59	15 19	15 24
	d	14 06		14 11	14 16	15 01		14 21	14 25	14 31	14 31	14 36		14 46	15 31	14 51		14 56	15 01	15 01	15 06	15 11	16 01	15 21	15 26
Cardiff Central	a	14 09		14 14	14 21	→		14 24	14 31	14 34	14 34	14 39	14 31	14 50	→	14 54		14 59	15 04	15 04	15 09	15 14	→	15 24	15 29
	d		14 10	14 16				14 25	14 46			14 41	14 46			14 55		15 01			15 10	15 16		15 25	15 31
Grangetown	d		14 14	14 20				14 29	→			14 45	16 05			14 59		15 05			15 14	15 20		15 29	15 35
Dingle Road	d			14 26									16 11					15 11				15 26			15 41
Penarth	a			14 32									16 17					15 17				15 32			15 47
Cogan	d		14 18					14 33				14 48				15 03					15 18			15 33	
Eastbrook	d		14 20					14 35				14 51				15 05					15 20			15 35	
Dinas Powys	d		14 22					14 37				14 53				15 07					15 22			15 37	
Cadoxton	d		14 27					14 42				14 57				15 12					15 27			15 42	
Barry Docks	d		14 29					14 44				15 00				15 14					15 29			15 44	
Barry	d		14 34					14 49				15 05				15 19					15 34			15 49	
Barry Island	a		14 40					14 56								15 26					15 41			15 56	
Rhoose Cardiff Int Airport	d											15 12													
Llantwit Major	d											15 22													
Bridgend	a											15 40													

A From Barry Island to Aberdare
B From Penarth
C To Radyr
D From Ebbw Vale Town to Penarth
E From Radyr to Cardiff Central continues to Radyr
F From Barry Island
G From Ebbw Vale Town
H To Ystrad Mynach

When events are being held at the Principality Stadium, services are subject to alteration. Please check times before travelling.

For connections to Cardiff Bay please refer to Table T124

Table T130-F

Mondays to Fridays

10 September to 7 December

Treherbert, Aberdare, Merthyr, Pontypridd, Rhymney and Coryton - Cardiff, Penarth, Barry, Barry Island and Bridgend

		AW A		AW B	AW	AW C	AW	AW B	AW	AW A	AW C	AW D		AW	AW B	AW	AW	AW A	AW B	AW C	AW	AW B		AW	AW E
Treherbert	d				14 17		14 47							15 17							15 43				
Ynyswen	d				14 19		14 49							15 19							15 45				
Treorchy	d				14 21		14 51							15 21							15 51				
Ton Pentre	d				14 23		14 53							15 23							15 53				
Ystrad Rhondda	a				14 26		14 56							15 26							15 56				
	d				14 28		14 58							15 28							15 58				
Llwynypia	d				14 30		15 00							15 30							16 00				
Tonypandy	d				14 33		15 03							15 33							16 03				
Dinas Rhondda	d				14 35		15 05							15 35							16 05				
Porth	a				14 38		15 08							15 38							16 08				
	d				14 52		15 09							15 39							16 09				
Trehafod	d				14 55		15 12							15 42							16 12				
Merthyr Tydfil	d					14 38					15 08									15 38					
Pentre-bach	d					14 42					15 12									15 42					
Troed Y Rhiw	d					14 45					15 15									15 45					
Merthyr Vale	a					14 48					15 18									15 48					
	d					14 50					15 20									15 50					
Quakers Yard	d					14 55					15 25									15 55					
Aberdare	d								14 51							15 21								15 51	
Cwmbach	d								14 54							15 24								15 54	
Fernhill	d								14 58							15 28								15 58	
Mountain Ash	a								15 01							15 31								16 01	
	d								15 04							15 34								16 04	
Penrhiwceiber	d								15 07							15 37								16 07	
Abercynon	d					15 00			15 15		15 30					15 45				16 00				16 15	
Pontypridd	a				15 01	15 07	15 17		15 23		15 37			15 47		15 53				16 07	16 17			16 22	
	d				15 04	15 08	15 18		15 24		15 38			15 48		15 54				16 08	16 18			16 24	
Trefforest	d				15 07	15 11	15 21		15 27		15 41			15 51		15 57				16 11	16 21			16 27	
Trefforest Estate	d					15 15					15 45									16 15					
Taffs Well	d				15 14	15 19	15 28		15 34		15 49			15 58		16 04				16 19	16 28			16 34	
Radyr	a				15 17	15 23	15 31		15 38		15 53			16 01		16 08				16 23	16 31			16 38	
	d				15 21	15 23	15 31	15 34	15 38		15 53			16 01	16 04	16 08				16 23	16 31	16 34		16 38	
Danescourt	d							15 38							16 08							16 38			
Fairwater	d							15 40							16 10							16 40			
Waun-gron Park	d							15 42							16 12							16 42			
Ninian Park	d							15 45							16 15							16 45			
Llandaf	d					15 26	15 34		15 41		15 56			16 04		16 11				16 26	16 34			16 41	
Cathays	d					15 31	15 39		15 46		16 01			16 09		16 16				16 31	16 39			16 46	
Rhymney	d																15 27								
Pontlottyn	d																15 30								
Tir-phil	d																15 35								
Brithdir	d																15 37								
Bargoed	a																15 41								
	d											15 25					15 45								16 17
Gilfach Fargoed	d											15 27													16 19
Pengam	d											15 30					15 50								16 22
Hengoed	d											15 33					15 54								16 25
Ystrad Mynach	d											15 43					15 57								16 28
Llanbradach	d											15 48					16 01								16 33
Energlyn & Churchill Park	d																16 05								
Aber	d											15 52					16 07								16 37
Caerphilly	d											15 55					16 10								16 40
Lisvane & Thornhill	d											15 59					16 14								16 44
Llanishen	d											16 01					16 16								16 46
Heath High Level	d											16 04					16 19								16 49
Coryton	d			15 15				16 15							16 45				16 15			17 15			
Whitchurch (Cardiff)	d			15 16				16 16							16 46				16 16			17 16			
Rhiwbina	d			15 18				16 18							16 48				16 18			17 18			
Birchgrove	d			15 20				16 20							16 50				16 20			17 20			
Ty Glas	d			15 21				16 21							16 51				16 21			17 21			
Heath Low Level	d	←		15 24				16 24		←					16 54			←	16 24			17 24			
Cardiff Queen Street	a	15 29		15 29		15 34	15 44	16 29	15 49	15 59	16 04	16 09		16 14	16 59	16 19	16 24	16 29	16 29	16 34	16 44	17 29		16 49	16 54
	d	15 31		15 31		15 36	15 46	16 31	15 51	16 01	16 06	16 11		16 16	17 01	16 21	16 26	16 31	16 31	16 36	16 46	17 31		16 51	16 56
Cardiff Central	a	15 34		15 34	15 37	15 39	15 52	→	15 54	16 04	16 09	16 14		16 22	→	16 24	16 32	16 34	16 34	16 39	16 50	→		16 54	16 59
	d					15 41			15 55		16 10	16 16				16 25				16 41				16 55	17 01
Grangetown	d					15 45			15 59		16 14	16 20				16 29				16 45				16 59	17 05
Dingle Road	d											16 26													17 11
Penarth	a											16 32													17 17
Cogan	d					15 48			16 03		16 18					16 33				16 48				17 03	
Eastbrook	d					15 51			16 05		16 20					16 35				16 51				17 05	
Dinas Powys	d					15 53			16 07		16 22					16 37				16 53				17 07	
Cadoxton	d					15 57			16 12		16 27					16 42				16 57				17 12	
Barry Docks	d					16 00			16 14		16 29					16 44				17 00				17 14	
Barry	d					16 05			16 19		16 34					16 49				17 05				17 19	
Barry Island	a								16 26		16 41					16 56								17 26	
Rhoose Cardiff Int Airport	d					16 12														17 12					
Llantwit Major	d					16 22														17 22					
Bridgend	a					16 40														17 40					

A From Radyr to Cardiff Central continues to Radyr
B To Radyr
C From Barry Island
D From Penarth
E From Penarth to Rhymney

When events are being held at the Principality Stadium, services are subject to alteration. Please check times before travelling.

For connections to Cardiff Bay please refer to Table T124

Table T130-F

Mondays to Fridays

10 September to 7 December

Treherbert, Aberdare, Merthyr, Pontypridd, Rhymney and Coryton - Cardiff, Penarth, Barry, Barry Island and Bridgend

		AW A	AW B	AW C	AW	AW B	AW	AW D	AW A	AW B	AW C	AW E	AW	AW B	AW	AW F	AW A	AW B	AW C	AW	AW G	AW	AW D
Treherbert	d				16 17								16 47							17 17			
Ynyswen	d				16 19								16 49							17 19			
Treorchy	d				16 21								16 51							17 21			
Ton Pentre	d				16 23								16 53							17 23			
Ystrad Rhondda	a				16 26								16 56							17 26			
	d				16 28								16 58							17 28			
Llwynypia	d				16 30								17 00							17 30			
Tonypandy	d				16 33								17 03							17 33			
Dinas Rhondda	d				16 35								17 05							17 35			
Porth	a				16 38								17 08							17 38			
	d				16 39								17 09							17 39			
Trehafod	d				16 42								17 12							17 42			
Merthyr Tydfil	d			16 08							16 38								17 08				
Pentre-bach	d			16 12							16 42								17 12				
Troed Y Rhiw	d			16 15							16 45								17 15				
Merthyr Vale	a			16 18							16 48								17 18				
	d			16 20							16 50								17 20				
Quakers Yard	d			16 25							16 55								17 25				
Aberdare	d						16 21								16 51							17 21	
Cwmbach	d						16 24								16 54							17 24	
Fernhill	d						16 28								16 58							17 28	
Mountain Ash	a						16 31								17 01							17 31	
	d						16 34								17 04							17 34	
Penrhiwceiber	d						16 37								17 07							17 37	
Abercynon	d			16 30			16 45				17 00				17 15				17 30			17 45	
Pontypridd 3	a			16 37	16 47		16 53				17 07		17 17		17 23				17 37	17 47		17 53	
	d			16 38	16 48		16 54				17 08		17 18		17 24				17 38	17 48		17 54	
Trefforest	d			16 41	16 51		16 57				17 11		17 21		17 27				17 41	17 51		17 57	
Trefforest Estate	d			16 45							17 15								17 45				
Taffs Well	d			16 49	16 58		17 04				17 19		17 28		17 34				17 49	17 58		18 04	
Radyr 3	a			16 53	17 01		17 08				17 23		17 31		17 38				17 53	18 01		18 08	
	d			16 53	17 01	17 04	17 08				17 23		17 31	17 34	17 38				17 53	18 01	18 04	18 08	
Danescourt	d					17 08								17 38							18 08		
Fairwater	d					17 10								17 40							18 10		
Waun-gron Park	d					17 12								17 42							18 12		
Ninian Park	d					17 15								17 45							18 15		
Llandaf	d			16 56	17 04		17 11				17 26		17 34		17 41				17 56	18 04		18 11	
Cathays	d			17 01	17 09		17 16				17 31		17 39		17 46				18 01	18 09		18 16	
Rhymney 3	d							16 27															17 27
Pontlottyn	d							16 30															17 30
Tir-phil	d							16 35															17 35
Brithdir	d							16 37															17 37
Bargoed	a							16 41															17 41
	d							16 45				17 00				17 17							17 45
Gilfach Fargoed	d															17 19							
Pengam	d							16 50				17 05				17 22							17 50
Hengoed	d							16 54				17 09				17 25							17 54
Ystrad Mynach	d							16 57				17 12				17 28							17 57
Llanbradach	d							17 01				17 16				17 33							18 01
Energlyn & Churchill Park	d							17 05				17 20											18 05
Aber	d							17 07				17 22				17 37							18 07
Caerphilly	d							17 10				17 25				17 40							18 10
Lisvane & Thornhill	d							17 14				17 29				17 44							18 14
Llanishen	d							17 16				17 31				17 46							18 16
Heath High Level	d							17 19				17 34				17 49							18 19
Coryton	d		16 45			17 45				17 15				18 15				17 45			18 45		
Whitchurch (Cardiff)	d		16 46			17 46				17 16				18 16				17 46			18 46		
Rhiwbina	d		16 48			17 48				17 18				18 18				17 48			18 48		
Birchgrove	d		16 50			17 50				17 20				18 20				17 50			18 50		
Ty Glas	d		16 51			17 51				17 21				18 21				17 51			18 51		
Heath Low Level	d	←	16 54			17 54			←	17 24				18 24			←	17 54			18 54		
Cardiff Queen Street 3	a	16 59	16 59	17 04	17 14	17 59	17 19	17 24	17 29	17 29	17 34	17 39	17 44	18 29	17 49	17 54	17 59	17 59	18 04	18 14	18 59	18 19	18 24
	d	17 01	17 01	17 06	17 16	18 01	17 21	17 26	17 31	17 31	17 36	17 41	17 46	18 31	17 51	17 56	18 01	18 01	18 06	18 16	19 01	18 21	18 26
Cardiff Central 7	a	17 04	17 04	17 09	17 22	→	17 24	17 29	17 34	17 34	17 39	17 44	17 52	→	17 54	17 59	18 04	18 04	18 09	18 22	→	18 24	18 29
	d			17 10			17 25	17 31			17 41	17 46			17 55	18 01			18 10			18 25	18 31
Grangetown	d			17 14			17 29	17 35			17 45	17 50			17 59	18 05			18 14			18 29	18 35
Dingle Road	d							17 41				17 56				18 11							18 41
Penarth	a							17 47				18 02				18 17							18 47
Cogan	d			17 18			17 33				17 48				18 03				18 18			18 33	
Eastbrook	d			17 20			17 35				17 51				18 05				18 20			18 35	
Dinas Powys	d			17 22			17 37				17 53				18 07				18 22			18 37	
Cadoxton	d			17 27			17 42				17 57				18 12				18 27			18 42	
Barry Docks	d			17 29			17 44				18 00				18 14				18 29			18 44	
Barry 3	d			17 34			17 49				18 05				18 19				18 34			18 49	
Barry Island	a			17 41			17 56								18 26				18 41			18 56	
Rhoose Cardiff Int Airport ✈	d										18 12												
Llantwit Major	d										18 22												
Bridgend	a										18 40												

A From Radyr to Cardiff Central continues to Radyr
B To Radyr
C From Barry Island
D To Treherbert
E From Penarth to Cardiff Central
F From Penarth
G To Cardiff Central

When events are being held at the Principality Stadium, services are subject to alteration. Please check times before travelling.

For connections to Cardiff Bay please refer to Table T124

Table T130-F

Mondays to Fridays

10 September to 7 December

Treherbert, Aberdare, Merthyr, Pontypridd, Rhymney and Coryton - Cardiff, Penarth, Barry, Barry Island and Bridgend

		AW A	AW B	AW C	AW	AW B	AW	AW D	AW E	AW C	AW	AW	AW	AW A	AW B	AW C	AW	AW F	AW	AW C	AW	AW G
Treherbert	d				17 47						18 17						18 47				19 17	
Ynyswen	d				17 49						18 19						18 49				19 19	
Treorchy	d				17 51						18 21						18 51				19 21	
Ton Pentre	d				17 53						18 23						18 53				19 23	
Ystrad Rhondda	a				17 56						18 26						18 56				19 26	
	d				17 58						18 28						18 58				19 28	
Llwynypia	d				18 00						18 30						19 00				19 30	
Tonypandy	d				18 03						18 33						19 03				19 33	
Dinas Rhondda	d				18 05						18 35						19 05				19 35	
Porth	a				18 08						18 38						19 08				19 38	
	d				18 09						18 39						19 09				19 39	
Trehafod	d				18 12						18 42						19 12				19 42	
Merthyr Tydfil	d			17 38						18 08						18 38				19 08		
Pentre-bach	d			17 42						18 12						18 42				19 12		
Troed Y Rhiw	d			17 45						18 15						18 45				19 15		
Merthyr Vale	a			17 48						18 18						18 48				19 18		
	d			17 50						18 20						18 50				19 20		
Quakers Yard	d			17 55						18 25						18 55				19 25		
Aberdare	d						17 51						18 21					18 51				
Cwmbach	d						17 54						18 24					18 54				
Fernhill	d						17 58						18 28					18 58				
Mountain Ash	a						18 01						18 31					19 01				
	d						18 04						18 34					19 04				
Penrhiwceiber	d						18 07						18 37					19 07				
Abercynon	d			18 00			18 15			18 30			18 45			19 00		19 15		19 30		
Pontypridd 3	a			18 07	18 17		18 22			18 37	18 47		18 52			19 07	19 17	19 23		19 37	19 47	
	d			18 08	18 18		18 24			18 38	18 48		18 54			19 08	19 18	19 24		19 38	19 48	
Trefforest	d			18 11	18 21		18 27			18 41	18 51		18 57			19 11	19 21	19 27		19 41	19 51	
Trefforest Estate	d			18 15						18 45						19 15				19 45		
Taffs Well	d			18 19	18 28		18 34			18 49	18 58		19 04			19 19	19 28	19 34		19 49	19 58	
Radyr 3	a			18 23	18 31		18 38			18 53	19 01		19 08			19 23	19 31	19 38		19 53	20 01	
	d			18 23	18 31	18 34	18 38			18 53	19 01	19 04	19 08			19 23	19 31	19 38		19 53	20 01	
Danescourt	d					18 38						19 08										
Fairwater	d					18 40						19 10										
Waun-gron Park	d					18 42						19 12										
Ninian Park	d					18 45						19 15										
Llandaf	d			18 26	18 34		18 41			18 56	19 04		19 11			19 26	19 34	19 41		19 56	20 04	
Cathays	d			18 31	18 39		18 46			19 01	19 09		19 16			19 31	19 39	19 46		20 01	20 09	
Rhymney 3	d																					
Pontlottyn	d																					
Tir-phil	d																					
Brithdir	d																					
Bargoed	a																					
	d							18 15														
Gilfach Fargoed	d							18 18														
Pengam	d							18 20														
Hengoed	d							18 24														
Ystrad Mynach	d							18 27														
Llanbradach	d							18 31														
Energlyn & Churchill Park	d							18 35														
Aber	d							18 37														
Caerphilly	d							18 40											19 40			20 25
Lisvane & Thornhill	d							18 44											19 44			20 29
Llanishen	d							18 46											19 46			20 31
Heath High Level	d							18 49											19 49			20 34
Coryton	d		18 15			19 15									19 15							
Whitchurch (Cardiff)	d		18 16			19 16									19 16							
Rhiwbina	d		18 18			19 18									19 18							
Birchgrove	d		18 20			19 20									19 20							
Ty Glas	d		18 21			19 21									19 21							
Heath Low Level	d	←	18 24			19 24			←					←	19 24							
Cardiff Queen Street 3	a	18 29	18 29	18 34	18 44	19 29	18 49	18 54	18 59	19 04	19 15		19 19	19 29	19 29	19 34	19 44	19 49	19 54	20 04	20 14	20 39
	d	18 31	18 31	18 36	18 46	19 31	18 51	18 56	19 01	19 06	19 16		19 20	19 31	19 31	19 36	19 46	19 51	19 56	20 06	20 16	20 41
Cardiff Central 7	a	18 34	18 34	18 39	18 52	→	18 54	18 59	19 06	19 12	19 22	19 22	19 23	19 34	19 34	19 39	19 52	19 57	19 59	20 09	20 22	→
	d			18 41			18 55	19 01					19 25			19 41			20 06	20 10		
Grangetown	d			18 45			18 59	19 05					19 29			19 45			20 10	20 14		
Dingle Road	d							19 11											20 14			
Penarth	a							19 17											20 20			
Cogan	d			18 48			19 03						19 33			19 48				20 18		
Eastbrook	d			18 51			19 05						19 35			19 51				20 20		
Dinas Powys	d			18 53			19 07						19 37			19 53				20 22		
Cadoxton	d			18 57			19 12						19 42			19 57				20 27		
Barry Docks	d			19 00			19 14						19 44			20 00				20 29		
Barry 3	d			19 05			19 19						19 49			20 05				20 34		
Barry Island	a						19 26						19 56							20 41		
Rhoose Cardiff Int Airport ✈	d			19 12												20 12						
Llantwit Major	d			19 22												20 22						
Bridgend	a			19 40												20 40						

A From Radyr to Cardiff Central continues to Radyr
B To Radyr
C From Barry Island
D From Cardiff Central
E From Radyr
F To Rhymney
G From Barry Island to Cardiff Central

When events are being held at the Principality Stadium, services are subject to alteration. Please check times before travelling.

For connections to Cardiff Bay please refer to Table T124

Treherbert, Aberdare, Merthyr, Pontypridd, Rhymney and Coryton - Cardiff, Penarth, Barry, Barry Island and Bridgend

		AW A	AW B	AW A	AW	AW	AW C	AW D	AW D	AW	AW B	AW E	AW	AW	AW B	AW	AW B	AW C	AW D	AW E	AW	AW FX F	AW G
Treherbert	d			19 17						19 47			20 17										
Ynyswen	d			19 19						19 49			20 19										
Treorchy	d			19 21						19 51			20 21										
Ton Pentre	d			19 23						19 53			20 23										
Ystrad Rhondda	a			19 26						19 56			20 26										
	d			19 28						19 58			20 28										
Llwynypia	d			19 30						20 00			20 30										
Tonypandy	d			19 33						20 03			20 33										
Dinas Rhondda	d			19 35						20 05			20 35										
Porth	a			19 38						20 08			20 38										
	d			19 39						20 09			20 39										
Trehafod	d			19 42						20 12			20 42										
Merthyr Tydfil	d							19 38											20 38				
Pentre-bach	d							19 42											20 42				
Troed Y Rhiw	d							19 45											20 45				
Merthyr Vale	a							19 48											20 48				
	d							19 50											20 50				
Quakers Yard	d							19 55											20 55				
Aberdare	d										19 51					20 21					20 51	20 51	
Cwmbach	d										19 54					20 24					20 54	20 54	
Fernhill	d										19 58					20 28					20 58	20 58	
Mountain Ash	a										20 01					20 31					21 01	21 01	
	d										20 04					20 34					21 04	21 04	
Penrhiwceiber	d										20 07					20 37					21 07	21 07	
Abercynon	d					19 43		20 00			20 15					20 45			21 00		21 15	21 15	
Pontypridd 3	a			19 47		19 52		20 07		20 17	20 22		20 47			20 53			21 07		21 23	21 23	
	d			19 48		19 54		20 08		20 18	20 24		20 48			20 54			21 08		21 24	21 24	
Trefforest	d			19 51		19 57		20 11		20 21	20 27		20 51			20 57			21 11		21 27	21 27	
Trefforest Estate	d							20 15											21 15				
Taffs Well	d			19 58		20 04		20 19		20 28	20 34		20 58			21 04			21 19		21 34	21 34	
Radyr 3	a			20 01		20 08		20 23		20 31	20 38		21 01			21 08			21 23		21 38	21 38	
	d			20 01	20 04	20 08		20 23		20 31	20 38		21 01	21 04	21 04	21 08			21 23		21 38	21 38	
Danescourt	d				20 08									21 08	21 08								
Fairwater	d				20 10									21 10	21 10								
Waun-gron Park	d				20 12									21 12	21 12								
Ninian Park	d				20 15									21 15	21 15								
Llandaf	d			20 04		20 11		20 26		20 34	20 41		21 04			21 11			21 26		21 41	21 41	
Cathays	d			20 09		20 16		20 31		20 39	20 46		21 09			21 16			21 31		21 46	21 46	
Rhymney 3	d	20 00	20 46																				
Pontlottyn	d	20 03	20 49																				
Tir-phil	d	20 08	20 54																				
Brithdir	d	20 10	20 56																				
Bargoed	a	20 14	21 00																				
	d	20 15	21 00																				
Gilfach Fargoed	d	20 18	21 03																				
Pengam	d	20 20	21 05																				
Hengoed	d	20 24	21 09																				
Ystrad Mynach	d	20 27	21 12	21 39																			
Llanbradach	d	20 31	21 16	21 44																			
Energlyn & Churchill Park	d	20 35	21 20																				
Aber	d	20 37	21 22	21 48																			
Caerphilly	d	20 40	21 25	21 51																			
Lisvane & Thornhill	d	20 44	21 29	21 55																			
Llanishen	d	20 46	21 31	21 57																			
Heath High Level	d	20 49	21 34	22 00																			
Coryton	d						20 15											21 15					
Whitchurch (Cardiff)	d						20 16											21 16					
Rhiwbina	d						20 18											21 18					
Birchgrove	d						20 20											21 20					
Ty Glas	d						20 21											21 21					
Heath Low Level	d						20 24		←			←						21 24		←			←
Cardiff Queen Street 3	a	20 54	21 42	22 05		20 19	20 29	20 34	20 39	20 44	20 49	20 54	21 14			21 19		21 29	21 34	21 42	21 49	21 49	22 05
	d	20 56	21 44	22 06		20 21	20 31	20 36	20 41	20 46	20 51	20 56	21 16			21 21		21 31	21 36	21 44	21 51	21 51	22 06
Cardiff Central 7	a	→	→	→	20 24	20 27	20 34	20 39	20 46	20 52	20 57	20 59	21 22	21 20	21 20	21 27		21 34	21 39	21 48	21 54	21 54	22 09
	d							20 41			21 06	21 10			21 31		21 31		21 41		21 56	21 56	22 10
Grangetown	d							20 45			21 10	21 14			21 35		21 35		21 45		22 00	22 00	22 14
Dingle Road	d										21 14				21 41		21 41				22 04	22 04	
Penarth	a										21 20				21 47		21 47				22 10	22 10	
Cogan	d							20 48				21 18							21 48				22 18
Eastbrook	d							20 51				21 20							21 51				22 20
Dinas Powys	d							20 53				21 22							21 53				22 22
Cadoxton	d							20 57				21 27							21 57				22 27
Barry Docks	d							21 00				21 29							22 00				22 29
Barry 3	d							21 05				21 34							22 05				22 34
Barry Island	a											21 41											22 41
Rhoose Cardiff Int Airport ✈	d							21 12											22 12				
Llantwit Major	d							21 22											22 22				
Bridgend	a							21 42											22 40			22 58	

A To Barry Island
B To Cardiff Central
C From Cardiff Central to Radyr
D From Barry Island
E From Rhymney
F To Maesteg
G From Treherbert

When events are being held at the Principality Stadium, services are subject to alteration. Please check times before travelling.

For connections to Cardiff Bay please refer to Table T124

Table T130-F

Mondays to Fridays

10 September to 7 December

Treherbert, Aberdare, Merthyr, Pontypridd, Rhymney and Coryton - Cardiff, Penarth, Barry, Barry Island and Bridgend

		AW	AW	AW A	AW B	AW C	AW	AW B	AW D	AW	AW C	AW
Treherbert	d		21 17									
Ynyswen	d		21 19									
Treorchy	d		21 21									
Ton Pentre	d		21 23									
Ystrad Rhondda	a		21 26									
	d		21 28									
Llwynypia	d		21 30									
Tonypandy	d		21 33									
Dinas Rhondda	d		21 35									
Porth	a		21 38									
	d		21 39									
Trehafod	d		21 42									
Merthyr Tydfil	d					21 38					22 38	
Pentre-bach	d					21 42					22 42	
Troed Y Rhiw	d					21 45					22 45	
Merthyr Vale	a					21 48					22 48	
	d					21 50					22 50	
Quakers Yard	d					21 55					22 55	
Aberdare	d							21 51				22 51
Cwmbach	d							21 54				22 54
Fernhill	d							21 58				22 58
Mountain Ash	a							22 01				23 01
	d							22 04				23 04
Penrhiwceiber	d							22 07				23 08
Abercynon	d					22 00		22 15			23 00	23 14
Pontypridd 3	a		21 47			22 07		22 23			23 07	23 24
	d		21 48			22 08		22 24			23 08	
Trefforest	d		21 51			22 11		22 27			23 11	
Trefforest Estate	d					22 15					23 15	
Taffs Well	d		21 58			22 19		22 34			23 19	
Radyr 3	a		22 01			22 23		22 38			23 23	
	d		22 01		22 04	22 23		22 38		23 14	23 23	
Danescourt	d				22 08							
Fairwater	d				22 10							
Waun-gron Park	d				22 12							
Ninian Park	d				22 15							
Llandaf	d		22 04			22 26		22 41		23 16	23 26	
Cathays	d		22 09			22 31		22 46		23 20	23 31	
Rhymney 3	d			21 36								
Pontlottyn	d			21 39								
Tir-phil	d			21 44								
Brithdir	d			21 46								
Bargoed	a			21 50								
	d			21 50								
Gilfach Fargoed	d			21 53								
Pengam	d			21 55								
Hengoed	d			21 59								
Ystrad Mynach	d	21 39		22 02								
Llanbradach	d	21 44		22 06								
Energlyn & Churchill Park	d			22 10								
Aber	d	21 48		22 12								
Caerphilly	d	21 51		22 15			22 28					
Lisvane & Thornhill	d	21 55		22 19								
Llanishen	d	21 57		22 21								
Heath High Level	d	22 00		22 24								
Coryton	d				22 45							
Whitchurch (Cardiff)	d				22 46							
Rhiwbina	d				22 48							
Birchgrove	d				22 50							
Ty Glas	d				22 51							
Heath Low Level	d				22 54				←			
Cardiff Queen Street 3	a	22 05	22 14	22 29	22 59	22 34	22 39	22 49	22 59	23 24	23 34	
	d	22 06	22 16	22 31	23 01	22 36	22 41	22 54	23 01	23 25	23 36	
Cardiff Central 7	a	22 09	22 22	22 34	→	22 39	22 46	23 04	23 06	23 28	23 42	
	d	22 10		22 36		22 43		23 12		23 31		
Grangetown	d	22 14		22 40		22 47		23 16		23 35		
Dingle Road	d			22 44				23 20				
Penarth	a			22 50				23 26				
Cogan	d	22 18				22 50				23 38		
Eastbrook	d	22 20				22 53				23 41		
Dinas Powys	d	22 22				22 55				23 43		
Cadoxton	d	22 27				22 59				23 47		
Barry Docks	d	22 29				23 02				23 50		
Barry 3	d	22 34				23 06				23 54		
Barry Island	a	22 41								00 01		
Rhoose Cardiff Int Airport ✈	d					23 13						
Llantwit Major	d					23 23						
Bridgend	a					23 41						

A To Ystrad Mynach
B To Cardiff Central
C From Barry Island
D From Radyr

When events are being held at the Principality Stadium, services are subject to alteration. Please check times before travelling.

For connections to Cardiff Bay please refer to Table T124

Table T130-F

Saturdays

26 May to 8 September

Treherbert, Aberdare, Merthyr, Pontypridd, Rhymney and Coryton - Cardiff, Penarth, Barry, Barry Island and Bridgend

		AW A	AW	AW	AW	AW	AW	AW	AW	AW B		AW C	AW	AW D	AW	AW E	AW	AW	AW F	AW G		AW	AW	AW H	AW I
Treherbert	d												05 46					06 16							
Ynyswen	d												05 48					06 18							
Treorchy	d												05 50					06 20							
Ton Pentre	d												05 52					06 22							
Ystrad Rhondda	a												05 55					06 25							
	d												05 58					06 28							
Llwynypia	d												06 00					06 30							
Tonypandy	d												06 03					06 33							
Dinas Rhondda	d												06 05					06 35							
Porth	a												06 08					06 38							
	d												06 09					06 39							
Trehafod	d												06 12					06 42							
Merthyr Tydfil	d																								06 38
Pentre-bach	d																								06 42
Troed Y Rhiw	d																								06 45
Merthyr Vale	a																								06 48
	d																								06 50
Quakers Yard	d																								06 55
Aberdare	d																					06 22			
Cwmbach	d																					06 25			
Fernhill	d																					06 28			
Mountain Ash	a																					06 31			
	d																					06 34			
Penrhiwceiber	d																					06 37			
Abercynon	d																					06 45			07 00
Pontypridd 3	a												06 17					06 47				06 52			07 07
	d					05 18							06 18					06 48				06 54			07 08
Trefforest	d					05 21							06 21					06 51				06 57			07 11
Trefforest Estate	d					05 25																			07 15
Taffs Well	d					05 28							06 28			06 53	06 53	06 58	←	←		07 04			07 19
Radyr 3	a					05 31							06 31			06 56	06 56	07 01	06 56	06 56		07 08			07 23
	d					05 31							06 31			07 04	07 04	07 01	07 04	07 04		07 08			07 23
Danescourt	d															→	→		07 08	07 08					
Fairwater	d																		07 10	07 10					
Waun-gron Park	d																		07 12	07 12					
Ninian Park	d																		07 15	07 15					
Llandaf	d					05 34							06 34					07 04				07 11			07 26
Cathays	d					05 39							06 39					07 09				07 16			07 31
Rhymney 3	d														06 08								06 32		
Pontlottyn	d														06 11								06 35		
Tir-phil	d														06 16								06 40		
Brithdir	d														06 18								06 42		
Bargoed	a														06 22								06 46		
	d														06 25								06 46		
Gilfach Fargoed	d														06 28										
Pengam	d														06 30								06 51		
Hengoed	d														06 34								06 54		
Ystrad Mynach	d														06 37								06 57		
Llanbradach	d														06 41								07 01		
Energlyn & Churchill Park	d														06 45								07 05		
Aber	d														06 47								07 08		
Caerphilly	d									06 10					06 50								07 10		
Lisvane & Thornhill	d									06 14					06 54								07 15		
Llanishen	d									06 16					06 56								07 17		
Heath High Level	d									06 19					06 59								07 20		
Coryton	d													06 45						07 45				07 15	
Whitchurch (Cardiff)	d													06 46						07 46				07 16	
Rhiwbina	d													06 48						07 48				07 18	
Birchgrove	d													06 50						07 50				07 20	
Ty Glas	d													06 51						07 51				07 21	
Heath Low Level	d													06 54						07 54				07 24	
Cardiff Queen Street 3	a					05 43				06 25			06 43	06 59	07 04			07 12		07 59		07 20	07 25	07 29	07 34
	d	00 01				05 45				06 26			06 44	07 01	07 06			07 13		08 01		07 21	07 26	07 31	07 36
Cardiff Central 7	a	00 05				05 48				06 29			06 48	07 04	07 09			07 16	07 20	→		07 24	07 29	07 34	07 39
	d		05 20	05 41	05 46	05 55	06 16	06 25	06 36	06 41		06 55	07 01		07 10			07 16				07 25	07 31		07 41
Grangetown	d		05 24	05 45	05 50	05 59	06 20	06 29	06 40	06 45		06 59	07 05		07 14			07 20				07 29	07 35		07 45
Dingle Road	d				05 54		06 24		06 44				07 11					07 26					07 41		
Penarth	a				05 59		06 29		06 49				07 16					07 31					07 46		
Cogan	d		05 28	05 48		06 03		06 33		06 48		07 03			07 18							07 33			07 48
Eastbrook	d		05 30	05 51		06 05		06 35		06 51		07 05			07 20							07 35			07 51
Dinas Powys	d		05 32	05 53		06 07		06 37		06 53		07 07			07 22							07 37			07 53
Cadoxton	d		05 37	05 57		06 12		06 42		06 57		07 12			07 27							07 42			07 57
Barry Docks	d		05 39	06 00		06 14		06 44		07 00		07 14			07 29							07 44			08 00
Barry 3	d		05 44	06 05		06 19		06 49		07 05		07 19			07 34							07 49			08 05
Barry Island	a		05 50			06 25		06 55				07 25			07 40							07 55			
Rhoose Cardiff Int Airport ✈	d			06 12						07 12															08 12
Llantwit Major	d			06 22						07 22															08 22
Bridgend	a			06 39						07 39															08 39

A From Cardiff Bay
B From Barry Island
C From Hereford
D From Barry Island to Radyr
E To Coryton
F From Taffs Well to Coryton
G From Taffs Well to Radyr
H From Cardiff Central to Radyr
I From Cardiff Central

When events are being held at the Principality Stadium, services are subject to alteration. Please check times before travelling.

For connections to Cardiff Bay please refer to Table T124

Table T130-F

Saturdays

26 May to 8 September

Treherbert, Aberdare, Merthyr, Pontypridd, Rhymney and Coryton - Cardiff, Penarth, Barry, Barry Island and Bridgend

		AW A	AW	AW B	AW	AW		AW C	AW B	AW	AW D	AW	AW B	AW	AW	AW E		AW B	AW F	AW G	AW	AW B	AW	AW A	AW E
Treherbert	d		06 46									07 16									07 45				
Ynyswen	d		06 48									07 18									07 47				
Treorchy	d		06 50									07 20									07 49				
Ton Pentre	d		06 52									07 22									07 51				
Ystrad Rhondda	a		06 55									07 25									07 54				
	d		06 58									07 28									07 58				
Llwynypia	d		07 00									07 30									08 00				
Tonypandy	d		07 03									07 33									08 03				
Dinas Rhondda	d		07 05									07 36									08 05				
Porth	a		07 08									07 39									08 08				
	d		07 09									07 40									08 09				
Trehafod	d		07 12									07 43									08 12				
Merthyr Tydfil	d									07 08									07 38						
Pentre-bach	d									07 12									07 42						
Troed Y Rhiw	d									07 15									07 45						
Merthyr Vale	a									07 18									07 48						
	d									07 20									07 50						
Quakers Yard	d									07 25									07 55						
Aberdare	d				06 52									07 22									07 52		
Cwmbach	d				06 55									07 25									07 55		
Fernhill	d				06 58									07 28									07 58		
Mountain Ash	a				07 01									07 31									08 01		
	d				07 04									07 34									08 04		
Penrhiwceiber	d				07 07									07 37									08 07		
Abercynon	d				07 15					07 30				07 45					08 00				08 15		
Pontypridd 3	a		07 17		07 22					07 37		07 48		07 52					08 07		08 17		08 22		
	d		07 18		07 24					07 38		07 49		07 54					08 08		08 18		08 24		
Trefforest	d		07 21		07 27					07 41		07 52		07 57					08 11		08 21		08 27		
Trefforest Estate	d									07 45									08 15						
Taffs Well	d		07 28		07 34					07 49		07 59		08 04					08 19		08 28		08 34		
Radyr 3	a		07 31		07 38					07 53		08 03		08 08					08 23		08 31		08 38		
	d		07 31	07 34	07 38					07 53		08 03	08 04	08 08					08 23		08 31	08 34	08 38		
Danescourt	d			07 38									08 08									08 38			
Fairwater	d			07 40									08 10									08 40			
Waun-gron Park	d			07 42									08 12									08 42			
Ninian Park	d			07 45									08 15									08 45			
Llandaf	d		07 35		07 41					07 56		08 06		08 11					08 26		08 34		08 41		
Cathays	d		07 40		07 46					08 01		08 11		08 16					08 31		08 39		08 46		
Rhymney 3	d					07 00									07 24					07 42					
Pontlottyn	d					07 03									07 27					07 45					
Tir-phil	d					07 08									07 32					07 50					
Brithdir	d					07 10									07 34					07 52					
Bargoed	a					07 14									07 38					07 59					
	d	07 02				07 15					07 32				07 43					08 00				08 15	
Gilfach Fargoed	d	07 04				07 18									07 46									08 18	
Pengam	d	07 07				07 20					07 37				07 48					08 05				08 20	
Hengoed	d	07 10				07 24					07 40				07 52					08 09				08 24	
Ystrad Mynach	d	07 13				07 27					07 43				07 55					08 12				08 27	
Llanbradach	d	07 18				07 31					07 48				08 00					08 16				08 31	
Energlyn & Churchill Park	d					07 35									08 04					08 20				08 35	
Aber	d	07 23				07 38					07 53				08 07					08 22				08 37	
Caerphilly	d	07 25				07 40					07 55				08 10					08 25				08 40	
Lisvane & Thornhill	d	07 30				07 45					08 00				08 14					08 29				08 44	
Llanishen	d	07 32				07 47					08 02				08 16					08 31				08 46	
Heath High Level	d	07 35				07 50					08 05				08 19					08 34				08 49	
Coryton	d			08 15					07 45				08 45					08 15				09 15			
Whitchurch (Cardiff)	d			08 16					07 46				08 46					08 16				09 16			
Rhiwbina	d			08 18					07 48				08 48					08 18				09 18			
Birchgrove	d			08 20					07 50				08 50					08 20				09 20			
Ty Glas	d			08 21					07 51				08 51					08 21				09 21			
Heath Low Level	d			08 24				←	07 54				08 54			←		08 24				09 24			←
Cardiff Queen Street 3	a	07 39	07 45	08 29	07 49	07 55		07 59	07 59	08 04	08 10	08 15	08 59	08 19	08 24	08 29		08 29	08 34	08 39	08 44	09 29	08 49	08 54	08 59
	d	07 41	07 46	08 31	07 51	07 56		08 01	08 01	08 06	08 11	08 16	09 01	08 21	08 26	08 31		08 31	08 36	08 41	08 46	09 31	08 51	08 56	09 01
Cardiff Central 7	a	07 44	07 51	→	07 54	07 59		08 04	08 04	08 09	08 14	08 21	→	08 24	08 29	08 34		08 34	08 39	08 47	08 52	→	08 54	08 59	09 04
	d	07 46			07 55	07 59				08 10	08 16			08 25	08 31				08 41	09 14			08 55	09 01	
Grangetown	d	07 50			07 59	08 03				08 14	08 20			08 29	08 35				08 45	→			08 59	09 05	
Dingle Road	d	07 56				08 11					08 26				08 41									09 11	
Penarth	a	08 01				08 16					08 31				08 46									09 16	
Cogan	d				08 03					08 18				08 33					08 48				09 03		
Eastbrook	d				08 05					08 20				08 35					08 51				09 05		
Dinas Powys	d				08 07					08 22				08 37					08 53				09 07		
Cadoxton	d				08 12					08 27				08 42					08 57				09 12		
Barry Docks	d				08 14					08 29				08 44					09 00				09 14		
Barry 3	d				08 19					08 34				08 49					09 05				09 19		
Barry Island	a				08 25					08 40				08 55									09 25		
Rhoose Cardiff Int Airport ✈	d																		09 12						
Llantwit Major	d																		09 22						
Bridgend	a																		09 39						

A From Penarth
B To Radyr
C From Taffs Well to Radyr
D From Penarth to Bargoed
E From Radyr to Cardiff Central continues to Radyr
F From Cardiff Central
G To Swansea

When events are being held at the Principality Stadium, services are subject to alteration. Please check times before travelling.

For connections to Cardiff Bay please refer to Table T124

Table T130-F

Saturdays
26 May to 8 September

Treherbert, Aberdare, Merthyr, Pontypridd, Rhymney and Coryton - Cardiff, Penarth, Barry, Barry Island and Bridgend

		AW A	AW B	AW C	AW	AW	AW A	AW	AW D	AW E	AW A	AW B	AW D	AW	AW A	AW	AW	AW E	AW A	AW B	AW	AW A
Treherbert	d					08 16								08 46							09 16	
Ynyswen	d					08 18								08 48							09 18	
Treorchy	d					08 20								08 50							09 20	
Ton Pentre	d					08 22								08 52							09 22	
Ystrad Rhondda	a					08 25								08 55							09 25	
	d					08 28								08 58							09 28	
Llwynypia	d					08 30								09 00							09 30	
Tonypandy	d					08 33								09 03							09 33	
Dinas Rhondda	d					08 35								09 05							09 35	
Porth	a					08 38								09 08							09 38	
	d					08 39								09 09							09 39	
Trehafod	d					08 42								09 12							09 42	
Merthyr Tydfil	d		08 08									08 38								09 08		
Pentre-bach	d		08 12									08 42								09 12		
Troed Y Rhiw	d		08 15									08 45								09 15		
Merthyr Vale	a		08 18									08 48								09 18		
	d		08 20									08 50								09 20		
Quakers Yard	d		08 25									08 55								09 25		
Aberdare	d							08 22								08 52						
Cwmbach	d							08 25								08 55						
Fernhill	d							08 28								08 58						
Mountain Ash	a							08 31								09 01						
	d							08 34								09 04						
Penrhiwceiber	d							08 37								09 07						
Abercynon	d		08 30					08 45				09 00				09 15				09 30		
Pontypridd	a		08 37			08 47		08 52				09 07		09 17		09 22				09 37	09 47	
	d		08 38			08 48		08 54				09 08		09 18		09 24				09 38	09 48	
Trefforest	d		08 41			08 51		08 57				09 11		09 21		09 27				09 41	09 51	
Trefforest Estate	d		08 45									09 15								09 45		
Taffs Well	d		08 49			08 58		09 04				09 19		09 28		09 34				09 49	09 58	
Radyr	a		08 53			09 01		09 08				09 23		09 31		09 38				09 53	10 01	
	d		08 53			09 01	09 04	09 08				09 23		09 31	09 34	09 38				09 53	10 01	10 04
Danescourt	d						09 08								09 38							10 08
Fairwater	d						09 10								09 40							10 10
Waun-gron Park	d						09 12								09 42							10 12
Ninian Park	d						09 15								09 45							10 15
Llandaf	d		08 56			09 04		09 11				09 26		09 34		09 41				09 56	10 04	
Cathays	d		09 01			09 09		09 16				09 31		09 39		09 46				10 01	10 09	
Rhymney	d								08 32													
Pontlottyn	d								08 35													
Tir-phil	d								08 39													
Brithdir	d								08 42													
Bargoed	a								08 46													
	d				08 32				08 47				09 00				09 17					
Gilfach Fargoed	d																09 19					
Pengam	d				08 37				08 52				09 05				09 22					
Hengoed	d				08 40				08 55				09 09				09 25					
Ystrad Mynach	d				08 43				08 58				09 12				09 28					
Llanbradach	d				08 48				09 03				09 16				09 33					
Energlyn & Churchill Park	d												09 20									
Aber	d				08 52				09 07				09 22				09 37					
Caerphilly	d				08 55				09 10				09 25				09 40					
Lisvane & Thornhill	d				08 59				09 14				09 29				09 44					
Llanishen	d				09 01				09 16				09 31				09 46					
Heath High Level	d				09 04				09 19				09 34				09 49					
Coryton	d	08 45					09 45				09 15				10 15				09 45			10 45
Whitchurch (Cardiff)	d	08 46					09 46				09 16				10 16				09 46			10 46
Rhiwbina	d	08 48					09 48				09 18				10 18				09 48			10 48
Birchgrove	d	08 50					09 50				09 20				10 20				09 50			10 50
Ty Glas	d	08 51					09 51				09 21				10 21				09 51			10 51
Heath Low Level	d	08 54					09 54			←	09 24				10 24			←	09 54			10 54
Cardiff Queen Street	a	08 59	09 04	←	09 09	09 14	09 59	09 19	09 24	09 29	09 29	09 34	09 39	09 44	10 29	09 49	09 54	09 59	09 59	10 04	10 14	10 59
	d	09 01	09 06		09 11	09 16	10 01	09 21	09 26	09 31	09 31	09 36	09 41	09 46	10 31	09 51	09 56	10 01	10 01	10 06	10 16	11 01
Cardiff Central	a	09 04	09 09	08 47	09 14	09 21	→	09 24	09 29	09 34	09 34	09 39	09 44	09 51	→	09 54	09 59	10 04	10 04	10 09	10 21	→
	d		09 10	09 14	09 16			09 25	09 31			09 41	09 46			09 55	10 01			10 10		
Grangetown	d		09 14		09 20			09 29	09 35			09 45	09 50			09 59	10 05			10 14		
Dingle Road	d				09 26				09 41				09 56				10 11					
Penarth	a				09 31				09 46				10 01				10 16					
Cogan	d		09 18					09 33				09 48				10 03				10 18		
Eastbrook	d		09 20					09 35				09 51				10 05				10 20		
Dinas Powys	d		09 22					09 37				09 53				10 07				10 22		
Cadoxton	d		09 27					09 42				09 57				10 12				10 27		
Barry Docks	d		09 29					09 44				10 00				10 14				10 29		
Barry	d		09 34					09 49				10 05				10 19				10 34		
Barry Island	a		09 40					09 55								10 25				10 40		
Rhoose Cardiff Int Airport ✈	d											10 12										
Llantwit Major	d											10 22										
Bridgend	a			09 33								10 39										

A To Radyr
B From Barry Island
C From Rhymney to Swansea
D From Penarth
E From Radyr to Cardiff Central continues to Radyr

When events are being held at the Principality Stadium, services are subject to alteration. Please check times before travelling.

For connections to Cardiff Bay please refer to Table T124

Table T130-F

Saturdays
26 May to 8 September

Treherbert, Aberdare, Merthyr, Pontypridd, Rhymney and Coryton - Cardiff, Penarth, Barry, Barry Island and Bridgend

		AW	AW A	AW B	AW C	AW D	AW	AW	AW C	AW	AW	AW	AW B	AW	AW A	AW C	AW	AW E	AW B	AW C	AW	AW	AW
Treherbert	d							09 46													10 16		
Ynyswen	d							09 48													10 18		
Treorchy	d							09 50													10 20		
Ton Pentre	d							09 52													10 22		
Ystrad Rhondda	a							09 55													10 25		
	d							09 58													10 28		
Llwynypia	d							10 00													10 30		
Tonypandy	d							10 03													10 33		
Dinas Rhondda	d							10 05													10 35		
Porth	a							10 08													10 38		
	d							10 09													10 52		
Trehafod	d							10 12													10 55		
Merthyr Tydfil	d					09 38					10 04											10 38	
Pentre-bach	d					09 42					10 08											10 42	
Troed Y Rhiw	d					09 45					10 11											10 45	
Merthyr Vale	a					09 48					10 14											10 48	
	d					09 50					10 15											10 50	
Quakers Yard	d					09 55					10 21											10 55	
Aberdare	d	09 22								09 52							10 22						
Cwmbach	d	09 25								09 55							10 25						
Fernhill	d	09 28								09 58							10 28						
Mountain Ash	a	09 31								10 01							10 31						
	d	09 34								10 04							10 34						
Penrhiwceiber	d	09 37								10 07							10 37						
Abercynon	d	09 45				10 00				10 15	10 25						10 43					10 59	
Pontypridd	a	09 52				10 07		10 17		10 22	10 33						10 52				11 00	11 07	
	d	09 54				10 08		10 18		10 24				10 38			10 54				11 04	11 09	
Trefforest	d	09 57				10 11		10 21		10 27				10 41			10 57				11 07	11 12	
Trefforest Estate	d					10 15																11 16	
Taffs Well	d	10 04				10 19		10 28		10 34				10 49			11 04				11 14	11 20	
Radyr	a	10 08				10 23		10 31		10 38				10 53			11 08				11 17	11 23	
	d	10 08				10 23		10 31	10 34	10 38				10 53		11 04	11 08				11 21	11 23	
Danescourt	d								10 38							11 08							
Fairwater	d								10 40							11 10							
Waun-gron Park	d								10 42							11 12							
Ninian Park	d								10 45							11 15							
Llandaf	d	10 11				10 26		10 34		10 41				10 56			11 11					11 26	
Cathays	d	10 16				10 31		10 39		10 46				11 01			11 16					11 31	
Rhymney	d		09 27															10 27					
Pontlottyn	d		09 30															10 30					
Tir-phil	d		09 35															10 35					
Brithdir	d		09 37															10 37					
Bargoed	a		09 41															10 41					
	d		09 45				10 00					10 17			10 32			10 45					11 00
Gilfach Fargoed	d											10 19											
Pengam	d		09 50				10 05					10 22			10 37			10 50					11 05
Hengoed	d		09 54				10 09					10 25			10 40			10 54					11 09
Ystrad Mynach	d		09 57				10 12					10 28			10 43			10 57					11 12
Llanbradach	d		10 01				10 16					10 33			10 48			11 01					11 16
Energlyn & Churchill Park	d		10 05				10 20											11 05					11 20
Aber	d		10 07				10 22					10 37			10 52			11 07					11 22
Caerphilly	d		10 10				10 25					10 40			10 55			11 10					11 25
Lisvane & Thornhill	d		10 14				10 29					10 44			10 59			11 14					11 29
Llanishen	d		10 16				10 31					10 46			11 01			11 16					11 31
Heath High Level	d		10 19				10 34					10 49			11 04			11 19					11 34
Coryton	d				10 15				11 15							11 45				11 15			
Whitchurch (Cardiff)	d				10 16				11 16							11 46				11 16			
Rhiwbina	d				10 18				11 18							11 48				11 18			
Birchgrove	d				10 20				11 20							11 50				11 20			
Ty Glas	d				10 21				11 21							11 51				11 21			
Heath Low Level	d			←	10 24				11 24				←			11 54			←	11 24			
Cardiff Queen Street	a	10 19	10 24	10 29	10 29	10 34	10 39	10 44	11 29	10 49		10 54	10 59	11 04	11 09	11 59	11 19	11 24	11 29	11 29		11 34	11 39
	d	10 21	10 26	10 31	10 31	10 36	10 41	10 46	11 31	10 51		10 56	11 01	11 06	11 11	12 01	11 21	11 26	11 31	11 31		11 36	11 41
Cardiff Central	a	10 24	10 29	10 34	10 34	10 39	10 44	10 51	→	10 54		10 59	11 04	11 09	11 14	→	11 24	11 29	11 34	11 34	11 36	11 39	11 44
	d	10 25	10 31			10 41	10 46			10 55		11 01		11 10	11 16		11 25	11 31				11 41	11 46
Grangetown	d	10 29	10 35			10 45	10 50			10 59		11 05		11 14	11 20		11 29	11 35				11 45	11 50
Dingle Road	d		10 41				10 56					11 11			11 26			11 41					11 56
Penarth	a		10 46				11 01					11 16			11 31			11 46					12 01
Cogan	d	10 33				10 48				11 03				11 18			11 33					11 48	
Eastbrook	d	10 35				10 51				11 05				11 20			11 35					11 51	
Dinas Powys	d	10 37				10 53				11 07				11 22			11 37					11 53	
Cadoxton	d	10 42				10 57				11 12				11 27			11 42					11 57	
Barry Docks	d	10 44				11 00				11 14				11 29			11 44					12 00	
Barry	d	10 49				11 05				11 19				11 34			11 49					12 05	
Barry Island	a	10 55								11 25				11 40			11 55						
Rhoose Cardiff Int Airport ✈	d					11 12																12 12	
Llantwit Major	d					11 22																12 22	
Bridgend	a					11 39																12 39	

A From Penarth
B From Radyr to Cardiff Central continues to Radyr
C To Radyr
D From Barry Island
E From Cardiff Central

When events are being held at the Principality Stadium, services are subject to alteration. Please check times before travelling.

For connections to Cardiff Bay please refer to Table T124

Table T130-F

Saturdays

26 May to 8 September

Treherbert, Aberdare, Merthyr, Pontypridd, Rhymney and Coryton - Cardiff, Penarth, Barry, Barry Island and Bridgend

		AW	AW A	AW		AW	AW B	AW A	AW	AW C	AW	AW A	AW	AW C		AW B	AW A	AW	AW	AW	AW	AW B	AW A	AW A
Treherbert	d	10 46									11 16									11 46				
Ynyswen	d	10 48									11 18									11 48				
Treorchy	d	10 50									11 20									11 50				
Ton Pentre	d	10 52									11 22									11 52				
Ystrad Rhondda	a	10 55									11 25									11 55				
	d	10 58									11 28									11 58				
Llwynypia	d	11 00									11 30									12 00				
Tonypandy	d	11 03									11 33									12 03				
Dinas Rhondda	d	11 05									11 35									12 05				
Porth	a	11 08									11 38									12 08				
	d	11 09									11 39									12 09				
Trehafod	d	11 12									11 42									12 12				
Merthyr Tydfil	d								11 08									11 38						
Pentre-bach	d								11 12									11 42						
Troed Y Rhiw	d								11 15									11 45						
Merthyr Vale	a								11 18									11 48						
	d								11 20									11 50						
Quakers Yard	d								11 25									11 55						
Aberdare	d			10 52									11 22											
Cwmbach	d			10 55									11 25											
Fernhill	d			10 58									11 28											
Mountain Ash	a			11 01									11 31											
	d			11 04									11 34											
Penrhiwceiber	d			11 07									11 37											
Abercynon	d			11 15					11 30				11 45					12 00						
Pontypridd 3	a	11 17		11 22					11 37		11 47		11 52					12 07		12 17				
	d	11 18		11 24					11 38		11 48		11 54					12 08		12 18				
Trefforest	d	11 21		11 27					11 41		11 51		11 57					12 11		12 21				
Trefforest Estate	d								11 45									12 15						
Taffs Well	d	11 28		11 34					11 49		11 58		12 04					12 19		12 28				
Radyr 3	a	11 31		11 38					11 53		12 01		12 08					12 23		12 31				
	d	11 31	11 34	11 38					11 53		12 01	12 04	12 08					12 23		12 31				12 34
Danescourt	d		11 38									12 08												12 38
Fairwater	d		11 40									12 10												12 40
Waun-gron Park	d		11 42									12 12												12 42
Ninian Park	d		11 45									12 15												12 45
Llandaf	d	11 34		11 41					11 56		12 04		12 11					12 26		12 34				
Cathays	d	11 39		11 46					12 01		12 09		12 16					12 31		12 39				
Rhymney 3	d													11 27										
Pontlottyn	d													11 30										
Tir-phil	d													11 35										
Brithdir	d													11 37										
Bargoed	a													11 41										
	d					11 17				11 32				11 45					12 00		12 17			
Gilfach Fargoed	d					11 19															12 19			
Pengam	d					11 22				11 37				11 50					12 05		12 22			
Hengoed	d					11 25				11 40				11 54					12 09		12 25			
Ystrad Mynach	d					11 28				11 43				11 57					12 12		12 28			
Llanbradach	d					11 33				11 48				12 01					12 16		12 33			
Energlyn & Churchill Park	d													12 05					12 20					
Aber	d					11 37				11 52				12 07					12 22		12 37			
Caerphilly	d					11 40				11 55				12 10					12 25		12 40			
Lisvane & Thornhill	d					11 44				11 59				12 14					12 29		12 44			
Llanishen	d					11 46				12 01				12 16					12 31		12 46			
Heath High Level	d					11 49				12 04				12 19					12 34		12 49			
Coryton	d		12 15					11 45				12 45					12 15						12 45	13 15
Whitchurch (Cardiff)	d		12 16					11 46				12 46					12 16						12 46	13 16
Rhiwbina	d		12 18					11 48				12 48					12 18						12 48	13 18
Birchgrove	d		12 20					11 50				12 50					12 20						12 50	13 20
Ty Glas	d		12 21					11 51				12 51					12 21						12 51	13 21
Heath Low Level	d		12 24				←	11 54				12 54				←	12 24					←	12 54	13 24
Cardiff Queen Street 3	a	11 44	12 29	11 49		11 54	11 59	11 59	12 04	12 09	12 14	12 59	12 19	12 24		12 29	12 29	12 34	12 39	12 44	12 54	12 59	12 59	13 29
	d	11 46	12 31	11 51		11 56	12 01	12 01	12 06	12 11	12 16	13 01	12 21	12 26		12 31	12 31	12 36	12 41	12 46	12 56	13 01	13 01	13 31
Cardiff Central 7	a	11 51	→	11 54		11 59	12 04	12 04	12 09	12 14	12 21	→	12 24	12 29		12 34	12 34	12 39	12 44	12 51	12 59	13 04	13 04	→
	d			11 55		12 01			12 10	12 16			12 25	12 31				12 41	12 46	12 55	13 01			
Grangetown	d			11 59		12 05			12 14	12 20			12 29	12 35				12 45	12 50	12 59	13 05			
Dingle Road	d					12 11				12 26				12 41					12 56		13 11			
Penarth	a					12 16				12 31				12 46					13 01		13 16			
Cogan	d			12 03					12 18				12 33					12 48		13 03				
Eastbrook	d			12 05					12 20				12 35					12 51		13 05				
Dinas Powys	d			12 07					12 22				12 37					12 53		13 07				
Cadoxton	d			12 12					12 27				12 42					12 57		13 12				
Barry Docks	d			12 14					12 29				12 44					13 00		13 14				
Barry 3	d			12 19					12 34				12 49					13 05		13 19				
Barry Island	a			12 25					12 40				12 55							13 25				
Rhoose Cardiff Int Airport ✈	d																	13 12						
Llantwit Major	d																	13 22						
Bridgend	a																	13 39						

A To Radyr

B From Radyr to Cardiff Central continues to Radyr

C From Penarth

When events are being held at the Principality Stadium, services are subject to alteration. Please check times before travelling.

For connections to Cardiff Bay please refer to Table T124

Table T130-F

Saturdays

26 May to 8 September

Treherbert, Aberdare, Merthyr, Pontypridd, Rhymney and Coryton - Cardiff, Penarth, Barry, Barry Island and Bridgend

		AW	AW A	AW	AW B	AW	AW A	AW C	AW B	AW		AW	AW	AW B	AW	AW	AW C	AW B	AW	AW A		AW	AW B	AW	AW
Treherbert	d			12 16									12 46									13 16			
Ynyswen	d			12 18									12 48									13 18			
Treorchy	d			12 20									12 50									13 20			
Ton Pentre	d			12 22									12 52									13 22			
Ystrad Rhondda	a			12 25									12 55									13 25			
	d			12 28									12 58									13 28			
Llwynypia	d			12 30									13 00									13 30			
Tonypandy	d			12 33									13 03									13 33			
Dinas Rhondda	d			12 35									13 05									13 35			
Porth	a			12 38									13 08									13 38			
	d			12 39									13 09									13 39			
Trehafod	d			12 42									13 12									13 42			
Merthyr Tydfil	d	12 08								12 38									13 08						
Pentre-bach	d	12 12								12 42									13 12						
Troed Y Rhiw	d	12 15								12 45									13 15						
Merthyr Vale	a	12 18								12 48									13 18						
	d	12 20								12 50									13 20						
Quakers Yard	d	12 25								12 55									13 25						
Aberdare	d					12 22									12 52										
Cwmbach	d					12 25									12 55										
Fernhill	d					12 28									12 58										
Mountain Ash	a					12 31									13 01										
	d					12 34									13 04										
Penrhiwceiber	d					12 37									13 07										
Abercynon	d	12 30				12 45				13 00					13 15				13 30					13 45	
Pontypridd 3	a	12 37		12 48		12 52				13 07			13 17		13 22				13 37			13 47		13 52	
	d	12 38		12 48		12 54				13 08			13 18		13 24				13 38			13 48		13 54	
Trefforest	d	12 41		12 51		12 57				13 11			13 21		13 27				13 41			13 51		13 57	
Trefforest Estate	d	12 45								13 15									13 45						
Taffs Well	d	12 49		12 58		13 04				13 19			13 28		13 34				13 49			13 58		14 04	
Radyr 3	a	12 53		13 00		13 08				13 23			13 31		13 38				13 53			14 01		14 08	
	d	12 53		13 01	13 04	13 08				13 23			13 31	13 34	13 38				13 53			14 01	14 04	14 08	
Danescourt	d				13 08									13 38									14 08		
Fairwater	d				13 10									13 40									14 10		
Waun-gron Park	d				13 12									13 42									14 12		
Ninian Park	d				13 15									13 45									14 15		
Llandaf	d	12 56		13 04		13 11				13 26			13 34		13 41				13 56			14 04		14 11	
Cathays	d	13 01		13 09		13 16				13 31			13 39		13 46				14 01			14 09		14 16	
Rhymney 3	d						12 27																		13 27
Pontlottyn	d						12 30																		13 30
Tir-phil	d						12 35																		13 35
Brithdir	d						12 37																		13 37
Bargoed	a						12 41																		13 41
	d		12 32				12 45					13 00				13 17				13 32					13 45
Gilfach Fargoed	d															13 19									
Pengam	d		12 37				12 50					13 05				13 22				13 37					13 50
Hengoed	d		12 40				12 54					13 09				13 25				13 40					13 54
Ystrad Mynach	d		12 43				12 57					13 12				13 28				13 43					13 57
Llanbradach	d		12 48				13 01					13 16				13 33				13 48					14 01
Energlyn & Churchill Park	d						13 05					13 20													14 05
Aber	d		12 52				13 07					13 22				13 37				13 52					14 07
Caerphilly	d		12 55				13 10					13 25				13 40				13 55					14 10
Lisvane & Thornhill	d		12 59				13 14					13 29				13 44				13 59					14 14
Llanishen	d		13 01				13 16					13 31				13 46				14 01					14 16
Heath High Level	d		13 04				13 19					13 34				13 49				14 04					14 19
Coryton	d				13 45				13 15					14 15				13 45					14 45		
Whitchurch (Cardiff)	d				13 46				13 16					14 16				13 46					14 46		
Rhiwbina	d				13 48				13 18					14 18				13 48					14 48		
Birchgrove	d				13 50				13 20					14 20				13 50					14 50		
Ty Glas	d				13 51				13 21					14 21				13 51					14 51		
Heath Low Level	d				13 54			←	13 24					14 24			←	13 54					14 54		
Cardiff Queen Street 3	a	13 04	13 09	13 14	13 59	13 19	13 24	13 29	13 29	13 34		13 39	13 44	14 29	13 49	13 54	13 59	13 59	14 04	14 09		14 14	14 59	14 19	14 24
	d	13 06	13 11	13 16	14 01	13 21	13 26	13 31	13 31	13 36		13 41	13 46	14 31	13 51	13 56	14 01	14 01	14 06	14 11		14 16	15 01	14 21	14 26
Cardiff Central 7	a	13 09	13 14	13 21	→	13 24	13 29	13 34	13 34	13 39		13 44	13 51	→	13 54	13 59	14 04	14 04	14 09	14 14		14 21	→	14 24	14 29
	d	13 10	13 16			13 25	13 31			13 41		13 46			13 55	14 01			14 10	14 16				14 25	14 31
Grangetown	d	13 14	13 20			13 29	13 35			13 45		13 50			13 59	14 05			14 14	14 20				14 29	14 35
Dingle Road	d		13 26				13 41					13 56				14 11				14 26					14 41
Penarth	a		13 31				13 46					14 01				14 16				14 31					14 46
Cogan	d	13 18				13 33				13 48					14 03				14 18					14 33	
Eastbrook	d	13 20				13 35				13 51					14 05				14 20					14 35	
Dinas Powys	d	13 22				13 37				13 53					14 07				14 22					14 37	
Cadoxton	d	13 27				13 42				13 57					14 12				14 27					14 42	
Barry Docks	d	13 29				13 44				14 00					14 14				14 29					14 44	
Barry 3	d	13 34				13 49				14 05					14 19				14 34					14 49	
Barry Island	a	13 40				13 55									14 25				14 40					14 55	
Rhoose Cardiff Int Airport ✈	d									14 12															
Llantwit Major	d									14 22															
Bridgend	a									14 39															

A From Penarth

B To Radyr

C From Radyr to Cardiff Central continues to Radyr

When events are being held at the Principality Stadium, services are subject to alteration. Please check times before travelling.

For connections to Cardiff Bay please refer to Table T124

Treherbert, Aberdare, Merthyr, Pontypridd, Rhymney and Coryton - Cardiff, Penarth, Barry, Barry Island and Bridgend

		AW A	AW B	AW	AW	AW	AW B	AW	AW	AW A	AW B	AW	AW C	AW B	AW	AW C	AW A	AW B	AW	AW	AW	AW	AW B
Treherbert	d					13 46													14 16			14 46	
Ynyswen	d					13 48													14 18			14 48	
Treorchy	d					13 50													14 20			14 50	
Ton Pentre	d					13 52													14 22			14 52	
Ystrad Rhondda	a					13 55													14 25			14 55	
	d					13 58													14 28			14 58	
Llwynypia	d					14 00													14 30			15 00	
Tonypandy	d					14 03													14 33			15 03	
Dinas Rhondda	d					14 05													14 35			15 05	
Porth	a					14 08													14 38			15 08	
	d					14 09													14 52			15 09	
Trehafod	d					14 12													14 55			15 12	
Merthyr Tydfil	d			13 38								14 08								14 38			
Pentre-bach	d			13 42								14 12								14 42			
Troed Y Rhiw	d			13 45								14 15								14 45			
Merthyr Vale	a			13 48								14 18								14 48			
	d			13 50								14 20								14 50			
Quakers Yard	d			13 55								14 25								14 55			
Aberdare	d							13 52							14 22								
Cwmbach	d							13 55							14 25								
Fernhill	d							13 58							14 28								
Mountain Ash	a							14 01							14 31								
	d							14 04							14 34								
Penrhiwceiber	d							14 07							14 37								
Abercynon	d			14 00				14 15				14 30			14 45					15 00			
Pontypridd 3	a			14 07		14 17		14 22				14 37			14 52				15 00	15 07		15 17	
	d			14 08		14 18		14 24				14 38			14 54				15 04	15 08		15 18	
Trefforest	d			14 11		14 21		14 27				14 41			14 57				15 07	15 11		15 21	
Trefforest Estate	d			14 15								14 45								15 15			
Taffs Well	d			14 19		14 28		14 34				14 49			15 04				15 14	15 19		15 28	
Radyr 3	a			14 23		14 31		14 38				14 53			15 08				15 17	15 23		15 31	
	d			14 23		14 31	14 34	14 38				14 53		15 04	15 08				15 21	15 23		15 31	15 34
Danescourt	d						14 38							15 08									15 38
Fairwater	d						14 40							15 10									15 40
Waun-gron Park	d						14 42							15 12									15 42
Ninian Park	d						14 45							15 15									15 45
Llandaf	d			14 26		14 34		14 41				14 56			15 11					15 26		15 34	
Cathays	d			14 31		14 39		14 46				15 01			15 16					15 31		15 39	
Rhymney 3	d															14 27							
Pontlottyn	d															14 30							
Tir-phil	d															14 35							
Brithdir	d															14 37							
Bargoed	a															14 41							
	d				14 00				14 17				14 32			14 45					15 00		
Gilfach Fargoed	d								14 19														
Pengam	d				14 05				14 22				14 37			14 50					15 05		
Hengoed	d				14 09				14 25				14 40			14 54					15 09		
Ystrad Mynach	d				14 12				14 28				14 43			14 57					15 12		
Llanbradach	d				14 16				14 33				14 48			15 01					15 16		
Energlyn & Churchill Park	d				14 20											15 05					15 20		
Aber	d				14 22				14 37				14 52			15 07					15 22		
Caerphilly	d				14 25				14 40				14 55			15 10					15 25		
Lisvane & Thornhill	d				14 29				14 44				14 59			15 14					15 29		
Llanishen	d				14 31				14 46				15 01			15 16					15 31		
Heath High Level	d				14 34				14 49				15 04			15 19					15 34		
Coryton	d		14 15				15 15				14 45			15 45				15 15					16 15
Whitchurch (Cardiff)	d		14 16				15 16				14 46			15 46				15 16					16 16
Rhiwbina	d		14 18				15 18				14 48			15 48				15 18					16 18
Birchgrove	d		14 20				15 20				14 50			15 50				15 20					16 20
Ty Glas	d		14 21				15 21				14 51			15 51				15 21					16 21
Heath Low Level	d	←	14 24				15 24			←	14 54			15 54			←	15 24					16 24
Cardiff Queen Street 3	a	14 29	14 29	14 34	14 39	14 44	15 29	14 49	14 54	14 59	14 59	15 04	15 09	15 59	15 19	15 24	15 29	15 29		15 34	15 39	15 44	16 29
	d	14 31	14 31	14 36	14 41	14 46	15 31	14 51	14 56	15 01	15 01	15 06	15 11	16 01	15 21	15 26	15 31	15 31		15 36	15 41	15 46	16 31
Cardiff Central 7	a	14 34	14 34	14 39	14 44	14 51	→	14 54	14 59	15 04	15 04	15 09	15 14	→	15 24	15 29	15 34	15 34	15 36	15 39	15 44	15 51	→
	d			14 41	14 46			14 55	15 01			15 10	15 16		15 25	15 31				15 41	15 46		
Grangetown	d			14 45	14 50			14 59	15 05			15 14	15 20		15 29	15 35				15 45	15 50		
Dingle Road	d				14 56				15 11				15 26			15 41					15 56		
Penarth	a				15 01				15 16				15 31			15 46					16 01		
Cogan	d			14 48				15 03				15 18			15 33					15 48			
Eastbrook	d			14 51				15 05				15 20			15 35					15 51			
Dinas Powys	d			14 53				15 07				15 22			15 37					15 53			
Cadoxton	d			14 57				15 12				15 27			15 42					15 57			
Barry Docks	d			15 00				15 14				15 29			15 44					16 00			
Barry 3	d			15 05				15 19				15 34			15 49					16 05			
Barry Island	a							15 25				15 40			15 55								
Rhoose Cardiff Int Airport ✈	d			15 12																16 12			
Llantwit Major	d			15 22																16 22			
Bridgend	a			15 39																16 39			

A From Radyr to Cardiff Central continues to Radyr
B To Radyr
C From Penarth

When events are being held at the Principality Stadium, services are subject to alteration. Please check times before travelling.

For connections to Cardiff Bay please refer to Table T124

Table T130-F

Saturdays

26 May to 8 September

Treherbert, Aberdare, Merthyr, Pontypridd, Rhymney and Coryton - Cardiff, Penarth, Barry, Barry Island and Bridgend

		AW	AW	AW A	AW	AW B	AW	AW C	AW	AW B	AW A	AW C	AW	AW	AW	AW C	AW	AW	AW A	AW C	AW	AW
Treherbert	d						15 16								15 46							
Ynyswen	d						15 18								15 48							
Treorchy	d						15 20								15 50							
Ton Pentre	d						15 22								15 52							
Ystrad Rhondda	a						15 25								15 55							
	d						15 28								15 58							
Llwynypia	d						15 30								16 00							
Tonypandy	d						15 33								16 03							
Dinas Rhondda	d						15 35								16 05							
Porth	a						15 38								16 08							
	d						15 39								16 09							
Trehafod	d						15 42								16 12							
Merthyr Tydfil	d				15 08								15 38								16 08	
Pentre-bach	d				15 12								15 42								16 12	
Troed Y Rhiw	d				15 15								15 45								16 15	
Merthyr Vale	a				15 18								15 48								16 18	
	d				15 20								15 50								16 20	
Quakers Yard	d				15 25								15 55								16 25	
Aberdare	d	14 52							15 22								15 52					
Cwmbach	d	14 55							15 25								15 55					
Fernhill	d	14 58							15 28								15 58					
Mountain Ash	a	15 01							15 31								16 01					
	d	15 04							15 34								16 04					
Penrhiwceiber	d	15 07							15 37								16 07					
Abercynon	d	15 15			15 30				15 45				16 00				16 15				16 30	
Pontypridd 3	a	15 22			15 37		15 47		15 52				16 07		16 17		16 22				16 37	
	d	15 24			15 38		15 48		15 54				16 08		16 18		16 24				16 38	
Trefforest	d	15 27			15 41		15 51		15 57				16 11		16 21		16 27				16 41	
Trefforest Estate	d				15 45								16 15								16 45	
Taffs Well	d	15 34			15 49		15 58		16 04				16 19		16 28		16 34				16 49	
Radyr 3	a	15 38			15 53		16 01		16 08				16 23		16 31		16 38				16 53	
	d	15 38			15 53		16 01	16 04	16 08				16 23		16 31	16 34	16 38				16 53	
Danescourt	d							16 08								16 38						
Fairwater	d							16 10								16 40						
Waun-gron Park	d							16 12								16 42						
Ninian Park	d							16 15								16 45						
Llandaf	d	15 41			15 56		16 04		16 11				16 26		16 34		16 41				16 56	
Cathays	d	15 46			16 01		16 09		16 16				16 31		16 39		16 46				17 01	
Rhymney 3	d									15 27												
Pontlottyn	d									15 30												
Tir-phil	d									15 35												
Brithdir	d									15 37												
Bargoed	a									15 41												
	d		15 17			15 32				15 45				16 00				16 17				16 32
Gilfach Fargoed	d		15 19															16 19				
Pengam	d		15 22			15 37				15 50				16 05				16 22				16 37
Hengoed	d		15 25			15 40				15 54				16 09				16 25				16 40
Ystrad Mynach	d		15 28			15 43				15 57				16 12				16 28				16 43
Llanbradach	d		15 33			15 48				16 01				16 16				16 33				16 48
Energlyn & Churchill Park	d									16 05				16 20								
Aber	d		15 37			15 52				16 07				16 22				16 37				16 52
Caerphilly	d		15 40			15 55				16 10				16 25				16 40				16 55
Lisvane & Thornhill	d		15 44			15 59				16 14				16 29				16 44				16 59
Llanishen	d		15 46			16 01				16 16				16 31				16 46				17 01
Heath High Level	d		15 49			16 04				16 19				16 34				16 49				17 04
Coryton	d							16 45				16 15				17 15				16 45		
Whitchurch (Cardiff)	d							16 46				16 16				17 16				16 46		
Rhiwbina	d							16 48				16 18				17 18				16 48		
Birchgrove	d							16 50				16 20				17 20				16 50		
Ty Glas	d							16 51				16 21				17 21				16 51		
Heath Low Level	d			←				16 54			←	16 24				17 24			←	16 54		
Cardiff Queen Street 3	a	15 49	15 54	15 59	16 04	16 09	16 14	16 59	16 19	16 24	16 29	16 29	16 34	16 39	16 44	17 29	16 49	16 54	16 59	16 59	17 04	17 09
	d	15 51	15 56	16 01	16 06	16 11	16 16	17 01	16 21	16 26	16 31	16 31	16 36	16 41	16 46	17 31	16 51	16 56	17 01	17 01	17 06	17 11
Cardiff Central 7	a	15 54	15 59	16 04	16 09	16 14	16 21	→	16 24	16 32	16 34	16 34	16 39	16 44	16 51	→	16 54	16 59	17 04	17 04	17 09	17 14
	d	15 55	16 01		16 10	16 16			16 25				16 41	16 46			16 55	17 01			17 10	17 16
Grangetown	d	15 59	16 05		16 14	16 20			16 29				16 45	16 50			16 59	17 05			17 14	17 20
Dingle Road	d		16 11			16 26								16 56				17 11				17 26
Penarth	a		16 16			16 31								17 01				17 16				17 31
Cogan	d	16 03			16 18				16 33				16 48				17 03				17 18	
Eastbrook	d	16 05			16 20				16 35				16 51				17 05				17 20	
Dinas Powys	d	16 07			16 22				16 37				16 53				17 07				17 22	
Cadoxton	d	16 12			16 27				16 42				16 57				17 12				17 27	
Barry Docks	d	16 14			16 29				16 44				17 00				17 14				17 29	
Barry 3	d	16 19			16 34				16 49				17 05				17 19				17 34	
Barry Island	a	16 25			16 40				16 55								17 25				17 40	
Rhoose Cardiff Int Airport ✈	d												17 12									
Llantwit Major	d												17 22									
Bridgend	a												17 39									

A From Radyr to Cardiff Central continues to Radyr
B From Penarth
C To Radyr

When events are being held at the Principality Stadium, services are subject to alteration. Please check times before travelling.

For connections to Cardiff Bay please refer to Table T124

Table T130-F

Saturdays
26 May to 8 September

Treherbert, Aberdare, Merthyr, Pontypridd, Rhymney and Coryton - Cardiff, Penarth, Barry, Barry Island and Bridgend

		AW	AW A	AW	AW B	AW C	AW D	AW		AW	AW	AW D	AW	AW	AW D	AW	AW	AW		AW E	AW	AW B	AW C	AW D	AW
Treherbert	d	16 16									16 46							17 16							
Ynyswen	d	16 18									16 48							17 18							
Treorchy	d	16 20									16 50							17 20							
Ton Pentre	d	16 22									16 52							17 22							
Ystrad Rhondda	a	16 25									16 55							17 25							
	d	16 28									16 58							17 28							
Llwynypia	d	16 30									17 00							17 30							
Tonypandy	d	16 33									17 03							17 33							
Dinas Rhondda	d	16 35									17 05							17 35							
Porth	a	16 38									17 08							17 38							
	d	16 39									17 09							17 39							
Trehafod	d	16 42									17 12							17 42							
Merthyr Tydfil	d							16 38								17 08									17 38
Pentre-bach	d							16 42								17 12									17 42
Troed Y Rhiw	d							16 45								17 15									17 45
Merthyr Vale	a							16 48								17 18									17 48
	d							16 50								17 20									17 50
Quakers Yard	d							16 55								17 25									17 55
Aberdare	d			16 22									16 52								17 22				
Cwmbach	d			16 25									16 55								17 25				
Fernhill	d			16 28									16 58								17 28				
Mountain Ash	a			16 31									17 01								17 31				
	d			16 34									17 04								17 34				
Penrhiwceiber	d			16 37									17 07								17 37				
Abercynon	d			16 45				17 00					17 15			17 30					17 45				18 00
Pontypridd	a	16 47		16 52				17 07			17 17		17 22			17 37		17 47			17 52				18 07
	d	16 48		16 54				17 08			17 18		17 24			17 38		17 48			17 54				18 08
Trefforest	d	16 51		16 57				17 11			17 21		17 27			17 41		17 51			17 57				18 11
Trefforest Estate	d							17 15								17 45									18 15
Taffs Well	d	16 58		17 04				17 19			17 28		17 34			17 49		17 58			18 04				18 19
Radyr	a	17 01		17 08				17 23			17 31		17 38			17 53		18 01			18 08				18 23
	d	17 01	17 04	17 08				17 23			17 31	17 34	17 38			17 53		18 01		18 04	18 08				18 23
Danescourt	d		17 08									17 38								18 08					
Fairwater	d		17 10									17 40								18 10					
Waun-gron Park	d		17 12									17 42								18 12					
Ninian Park	d		17 15									17 45								18 15					
Llandaf	d	17 04		17 11				17 26			17 34		17 41			17 56		18 04			18 11				18 26
Cathays	d	17 09		17 16				17 31			17 39		17 46			18 01		18 09			18 16				18 31
Rhymney	d				16 27																	17 27			
Pontlottyn	d				16 30																	17 30			
Tir-phil	d				16 35																	17 35			
Brithdir	d				16 37																	17 37			
Bargoed	a				16 41																	17 41			
	d				16 45					17 00				17 17			17 32					17 45			
Gilfach Fargoed	d													17 19											
Pengam	d				16 50					17 05				17 22			17 37					17 50			
Hengoed	d				16 54					17 09				17 25			17 40					17 54			
Ystrad Mynach	d				16 57					17 12				17 28			17 43					17 57			
Llanbradach	d				17 01					17 16				17 33			17 48					18 01			
Energlyn & Churchill Park	d				17 05					17 20												18 05			
Aber	d				17 07					17 22				17 37			17 52					18 07			
Caerphilly	d				17 10					17 25				17 40			17 55					18 10			
Lisvane & Thornhill	d				17 14					17 29				17 44			17 59					18 14			
Llanishen	d				17 16					17 31				17 46			18 01					18 16			
Heath High Level	d				17 19					17 34				17 49			18 04					18 19			
Coryton	d						17 15					18 15			17 45					18 45				18 15	
Whitchurch (Cardiff)	d						17 16					18 16			17 46					18 46				18 16	
Rhiwbina	d						17 18					18 18			17 48					18 48				18 18	
Birchgrove	d						17 20					18 20			17 50					18 50				18 20	
Ty Glas	d						17 21					18 21			17 51					18 51				18 21	
Heath Low Level	d					←	17 24					18 24			17 54					18 54			←	18 24	
Cardiff Queen Street	a	17 14		17 19	17 24	17 29	17 29	17 34		17 39	17 44	18 29	17 49	17 54	17 59	18 04	18 09	18 14		18 59	18 19	18 24	18 29	18 29	18 34
	d	17 16		17 21	17 26	17 31	17 31	17 36		17 41	17 46	18 31	17 51	17 56	18 01	18 06	18 11	18 16		19 01	18 21	18 26	18 31	18 31	18 36
Cardiff Central	a	17 21	17 20	17 24	17 29	17 34	17 34	17 39		17 44	17 51	→	17 54	17 59	18 04	18 09	18 14	18 21		→	18 24	18 29	18 34	18 34	18 39
	d			17 25	17 31			17 41		17 46			17 55	18 01		18 10	18 16				18 25	18 31			18 41
Grangetown	d			17 29	17 35			17 45		17 50			17 59	18 05		18 14	18 20				18 29	18 35			18 45
Dingle Road	d				17 41					17 56				18 11			18 26					18 41			
Penarth	a				17 46					18 01				18 16			18 31					18 46			
Cogan	d			17 33				17 48					18 03			18 18					18 33				18 48
Eastbrook	d			17 35				17 51					18 05			18 20					18 35				18 51
Dinas Powys	d			17 37				17 53					18 07			18 22					18 37				18 53
Cadoxton	d			17 42				17 57					18 12			18 27					18 42				18 57
Barry Docks	d			17 44				18 00					18 14			18 29					18 44				19 00
Barry	d			17 49				18 05					18 19			18 34					18 49				19 05
Barry Island	a			17 55									18 25			18 40					18 55				
Rhoose Cardiff Int Airport	d							18 12																	19 12
Llantwit Major	d							18 22																	19 22
Bridgend	a							18 39																	19 39

A To Coryton
B From Penarth
C From Radyr to Cardiff Central continues to Radyr
D To Radyr
E To Cardiff Central

When events are being held at the Principality Stadium, services are subject to alteration. Please check times before travelling.

For connections to Cardiff Bay please refer to Table T124

Table T130-F

Saturdays
26 May to 8 September

Treherbert, Aberdare, Merthyr, Pontypridd, Rhymney and Coryton - Cardiff, Penarth, Barry, Barry Island and Bridgend

		AW	AW A	AW		AW B	AW	AW C	AW	AW	AW	AW	AW	AW D		AW A	AW	AW	AW	AW B	AW	AW	AW	AW
Treherbert	d	17 46								18 16								18 46				19 16		
Ynyswen	d	17 48								18 18								18 48				19 18		
Treorchy	d	17 50								18 20								18 50				19 20		
Ton Pentre	d	17 52								18 22								18 52				19 22		
Ystrad Rhondda	a	17 55								18 25								18 55				19 25		
	d	17 58								18 28								18 58				19 28		
Llwynypia	d	18 00								18 30								19 00				19 30		
Tonypandy	d	18 03								18 33								19 03				19 33		
Dinas Rhondda	d	18 05								18 35								19 05				19 35		
Porth	a	18 08								18 38								19 08				19 38		
	d	18 09								18 39								19 09				19 39		
Trehafod	d	18 12								18 42								19 12				19 42		
Merthyr Tydfil	d								18 08								18 38				19 08			
Pentre-bach	d								18 12								18 42				19 12			
Troed Y Rhiw	d								18 15								18 45				19 15			
Merthyr Vale	a								18 18								18 48				19 18			
	d								18 20								18 50				19 20			
Quakers Yard	d								18 25								18 55				19 25			
Aberdare	d			17 52								18 22							18 52					
Cwmbach	d			17 55								18 25							18 55					
Fernhill	d			17 58								18 28							18 58					
Mountain Ash	a			18 01								18 31							19 01					
	d			18 04								18 34							19 04					
Penrhiwceiber	d			18 07								18 37							19 07					
Abercynon	d			18 15					18 30			18 45					19 00		19 15		19 30			19 43
Pontypridd	a	18 17		18 22					18 37	18 47		18 52					19 07	19 17	19 22		19 37	19 47		19 52
	d	18 18		18 24					18 38	18 48		18 54					19 08	19 18	19 24		19 38	19 48		19 54
Trefforest	d	18 21		18 27					18 41	18 51		18 57					19 11	19 21	19 27		19 41	19 51		19 57
Trefforest Estate	d								18 45								19 15				19 45			
Taffs Well	d	18 28		18 34					18 49	18 58		19 04					19 19	19 28	19 34		19 49	19 58		20 04
Radyr	a	18 31		18 38					18 53	19 01		19 08					19 23	19 31	19 38		19 53	20 01		20 08
	d	18 31	18 34	18 38					18 53	19 01	19 04	19 08					19 23	19 31	19 38		19 53	20 01	20 04	20 08
Danescourt	d		18 38								19 08												20 08	
Fairwater	d		18 40								19 10												20 10	
Waun-gron Park	d		18 42								19 12												20 12	
Ninian Park	d		18 45								19 15												20 15	
Llandaf	d	18 34		18 41					18 56	19 04		19 11					19 26	19 34	19 41		19 56	20 04		20 11
Cathays	d	18 39		18 46					19 01	19 09		19 16					19 31	19 39	19 46		20 01	20 09		20 16
Rhymney	d																							
Pontlottyn	d																							
Tir-phil	d																							
Brithdir	d																							
Bargoed	a																							
	d						18 15						18 48											
Gilfach Fargoed	d						18 18						18 50											
Pengam	d						18 20						18 53											
Hengoed	d						18 24						18 56											
Ystrad Mynach	d						18 27						18 59											
Llanbradach	d						18 31						19 04											
Energlyn & Churchill Park	d						18 35																	
Aber	d						18 37						19 08											
Caerphilly	d					18 36	18 40						19 11							19 40				
Lisvane & Thornhill	d						18 44						19 15							19 44				
Llanishen	d						18 46						19 17							19 46				
Heath High Level	d						18 49						19 20							19 49				
Coryton	d		19 15													19 15								
Whitchurch (Cardiff)	d		19 16													19 16								
Rhiwbina	d		19 18													19 18								
Birchgrove	d		19 20													19 20								
Ty Glas	d		19 21													19 21								
Heath Low Level	d		19 24					←						←		19 24								
Cardiff Queen Street	a	18 44	19 29	18 49			18 54	18 59	19 04	19 14		19 19	19 24	19 29		19 29	19 34	19 44	19 49	19 54	20 04	20 14		20 19
	d	18 46	19 31	18 51			18 56	19 01	19 06	19 16		19 21	19 26	19 31		19 31	19 36	19 46	19 51	19 56	20 06	20 16		20 21
Cardiff Central	a	18 51	→	18 54		19 16	18 59	19 06	19 12	19 21	19 22	19 24	19 29	19 34		19 34	19 39	19 51	19 57	19 59	20 09	20 21	20 24	20 24
	d			18 55			19 01					19 25	19 31				19 41			20 06	20 10			20 31
Grangetown	d			18 59			19 05					19 29	19 35				19 45			20 10	20 14			20 35
Dingle Road	d						19 11						19 41							20 14				20 41
Penarth	a						19 16						19 46							20 19				20 46
Cogan	d			19 03								19 33					19 48				20 18			
Eastbrook	d			19 05								19 35					19 51				20 20			
Dinas Powys	d			19 07								19 37					19 53				20 22			
Cadoxton	d			19 12								19 42					19 57				20 27			
Barry Docks	d			19 14								19 44					20 00				20 29			
Barry	d			19 19								19 49					20 05				20 34			
Barry Island	a			19 25								19 55									20 40			
Rhoose Cardiff Int Airport	d																20 12							
Llantwit Major	d																20 22							
Bridgend	a																20 39							

A To Radyr
B From Penarth
C From Radyr
D From Radyr to Cardiff Central continues to Radyr

When events are being held at the Principality Stadium, services are subject to alteration. Please check times before travelling.

For connections to Cardiff Bay please refer to Table T124

Table T130-F

Saturdays

26 May to 8 September

Treherbert, Aberdare, Merthyr, Pontypridd, Rhymney and Coryton - Cardiff, Penarth, Barry, Barry Island and Bridgend

		AW A	AW	AW B	AW	AW	AW C	AW	AW	AW		AW	AW A	AW	AW C	AW	AW C	AW	AW C	AW D		AW	AW C	AW	AW E
Treherbert	d				19 46			20 16										21 16							
Ynyswen	d				19 48			20 18										21 18							
Treorchy	d				19 50			20 20										21 20							
Ton Pentre	d				19 52			20 22										21 22							
Ystrad Rhondda	a				19 55			20 25										21 25							
	d				19 58			20 28										21 28							
Llwynypia	d				20 00			20 30										21 30							
Tonypandy	d				20 03			20 33										21 33							
Dinas Rhondda	d				20 05			20 35										21 35							
Porth	a				20 08			20 38										21 38							
	d				20 09			20 39										21 39							
Trehafod	d				20 12			20 42										21 42							
Merthyr Tydfil	d		19 38											20 38								21 38			
Pentre-bach	d		19 42											20 42								21 42			
Troed Y Rhiw	d		19 45											20 45								21 45			
Merthyr Vale	a		19 48											20 48								21 48			
	d		19 50											20 50								21 50			
Quakers Yard	d		19 55											20 55								21 55			
Aberdare	d					19 52				20 22						20 54								21 54	
Cwmbach	d					19 55				20 25						20 57								21 57	
Fernhill	d					19 58				20 28						21 00								22 00	
Mountain Ash	a					20 01				20 31						21 03								22 03	
	d					20 04				20 34						21 04								22 04	
Penrhiwceiber	d					20 07				20 37						21 07								22 07	
Abercynon	d		20 00			20 15				20 45				21 00		21 15						22 00		22 15	
Pontypridd ■	a		20 07		20 18	20 22		20 47		20 52				21 07		21 22		21 47				22 07		22 23	
	d		20 08		20 18	20 24		20 48		20 54				21 08		21 24		21 48				22 08		22 24	
Trefforest	d		20 11		20 21	20 27		20 51		20 57				21 11		21 27		21 51				22 11		22 27	
Trefforest Estate	d		20 15											21 15								22 15			
Taffs Well	d		20 19		20 28	20 34		20 58		21 04				21 19		21 34		21 58				22 19		22 34	
Radyr ■	a		20 23		20 31	20 38		21 01		21 08				21 23		21 38		22 01				22 23		22 38	
	d		20 23		20 31	20 38		21 01	21 04	21 08				21 23		21 38		22 01		22 04		22 23		22 38	
Danescourt	d								21 08											22 08					
Fairwater	d								21 10											22 10					
Waun-gron Park	d								21 12											22 12					
Ninian Park	d								21 15											22 15					
Llandaf	d		20 26		20 34	20 41		21 04		21 11				21 26		21 41		22 04				22 26		22 41	
Cathays	d		20 31		20 39	20 46		21 09		21 16				21 31		21 46		22 09				22 31		22 46	
Rhymney ■	d						20 00								20 46				21 36						
Pontlottyn	d						20 03								20 49				21 39						
Tir-phil	d						20 08								20 54				21 44						
Brithdir	d						20 10								20 56				21 46						
Bargoed	a						20 14								21 00				21 50						
	d						20 15								21 00				21 50						
Gilfach Fargoed	d						20 18								21 03				21 53						
Pengam	d						20 20								21 05				21 55						
Hengoed	d						20 24								21 09				21 59						
Ystrad Mynach	d						20 27								21 12		21 39		22 02						
Llanbradach	d						20 31								21 16		21 44		22 06						
Energlyn & Churchill Park	d						20 35								21 20				22 10						
Aber	d						20 37								21 22		21 48		22 12						
Caerphilly	d			20 25			20 40								21 25		21 51		22 15				22 28		
Lisvane & Thornhill	d			20 29			20 44								21 29		21 55		22 19						
Llanishen	d			20 31			20 46								21 31		21 57		22 21						
Heath High Level	d			20 34			20 49								21 34		22 00		22 24						
Coryton	d	20 15											21 15							22 45					
Whitchurch (Cardiff)	d	20 16											21 16							22 46					
Rhiwbina	d	20 18											21 18							22 48					
Birchgrove	d	20 20											21 20							22 50					
Ty Glas	d	20 21											21 21							22 51					
Heath Low Level	d	20 24											21 24							22 54					←
Cardiff Queen Street ■	a	20 29	20 34	20 39	20 44	20 49	20 54	21 14		21 19			21 29	21 34	21 42	21 50	22 05	22 14	22 29	22 59		22 34	22 39	22 50	22 59
	d	20 31	20 36	20 41	20 46	20 51	20 56	21 16		21 21			21 31	21 36	21 42	21 51	22 06	22 16	22 31	23 01		22 36	22 40	22 54	23 01
Cardiff Central ■	a	20 34	20 39	20 46	20 51	20 57	20 59	21 21	21 20	21 27			21 34	21 39	21 48	21 54	22 09	22 21	22 34	→		22 42	22 44	23 00	23 06
	d		20 41			21 06	21 10					21 31		21 41		22 06	22 10		22 36					23 12	
Grangetown	d		20 45			21 10	21 14					21 35		21 45		22 10	22 14		22 40					23 16	
Dingle Road	d					21 14						21 41				22 14			22 44					23 20	
Penarth	a					21 19						21 46				22 19			22 49					23 25	
Cogan	d		20 48				21 18							21 48			22 18								
Eastbrook	d		20 51				21 20							21 51			22 20								
Dinas Powys	d		20 53				21 22							21 53			22 22								
Cadoxton	d		20 57				21 27							21 57			22 27								
Barry Docks	d		21 00				21 29							22 00			22 29								
Barry ■	d		21 05				21 34							22 05			22 34								
Barry Island	a						21 40										22 40								
Rhoose Cardiff Int Airport ✈	d		21 12											22 12											
Llantwit Major	d		21 22											22 22											
Bridgend	a		21 39											22 39											

A From Cardiff Central to Radyr
B From Barry Island
C From Penarth
D To Cardiff Central
E From Radyr

When events are being held at the Principality Stadium, services are subject to alteration. Please check times before travelling.

For connections to Cardiff Bay please refer to Table T124

Table T130-F

Saturdays

26 May to 8 September

Treherbert, Aberdare, Merthyr, Pontypridd, Rhymney and Coryton - Cardiff, Penarth, Barry, Barry Island and Bridgend

		AW	AW	AW
Treherbert	d			
Ynyswen	d			
Treorchy	d			
Ton Pentre	d			
Ystrad Rhondda	a			
	d			
Llwynypia	d			
Tonypandy	d			
Dinas Rhondda	d			
Porth	a			
	d			
Trehafod	d			
Merthyr Tydfil	d		22 38	
Pentre-bach	d		22 42	
Troed Y Rhiw	d		22 45	
Merthyr Vale	a		22 48	
	d		22 50	
Quakers Yard	d		22 55	
Aberdare	d			22 54
Cwmbach	d			22 57
Fernhill	d			23 00
Mountain Ash	a			23 03
	d			23 04
Penrhiwceiber	d			23 07
Abercynon	d		23 00	23 13
Pontypridd ■	a		23 07	23 24
	d		23 08	
Trefforest	d		23 11	
Trefforest Estate	d		23 15	
Taffs Well	d		23 19	
Radyr ■	a		23 23	
	d	23 14	23 23	
Danescourt	d			
Fairwater	d			
Waun-gron Park	d			
Ninian Park	d			
Llandaf	d	23 16	23 26	
Cathays	d	23 20	23 31	
Rhymney ■	d			
Pontlottyn	d			
Tir-phil	d			
Brithdir	d			
Bargoed	a			
	d			
Gilfach Fargoed	d			
Pengam	d			
Hengoed	d			
Ystrad Mynach	d			
Llanbradach	d			
Energlyn & Churchill Park	d			
Aber	d			
Caerphilly	d			
Lisvane & Thornhill	d			
Llanishen	d			
Heath High Level	d			
Coryton	d			
Whitchurch (Cardiff)	d			
Rhiwbina	d			
Birchgrove	d			
Ty Glas	d			
Heath Low Level	d			
Cardiff Queen Street ■	a	23 24	23 34	
	d	23 25	23 36	
Cardiff Central ■	a	23 28	23 42	
	d	23 30		
Grangetown	d	23 34		
Dingle Road	d			
Penarth	a			
Cogan	d	23 37		
Eastbrook	d	23 40		
Dinas Powys	d	23 42		
Cadoxton	d	23 46		
Barry Docks	d	23 49		
Barry ■	d	23 53		
Barry Island	a	00 01		
Rhoose Cardiff Int Airport ✈	d			
Llantwit Major	d			
Bridgend	a			

When events are being held at the Principality Stadium, services are subject to alteration. Please check times before travelling.

For connections to Cardiff Bay please refer to Table T124

Table T130-F

Saturdays

15 September to 8 December

Treherbert, Aberdare, Merthyr, Pontypridd, Rhymney and Coryton - Cardiff, Penarth, Barry, Barry Island and Bridgend

		AW A	AW	AW	AW	AW	AW	AW	AW	AW B	AW C	AW	AW D	AW	AW E	AW	AW F	AW	AW	AW G	AW H	AW I	AW
Treherbert	d											05 47				06 17							06 47
Ynyswen	d											05 49				06 19							06 49
Treorchy	d											05 51				06 21							06 51
Ton Pentre	d											05 53				06 23							06 53
Ystrad Rhondda	a											05 56				06 26							06 56
	d											05 58				06 28							06 58
Llwynypia	d											06 00				06 30							07 00
Tonypandy	d											06 03				06 33							07 03
Dinas Rhondda	d											06 05				06 35							07 05
Porth	a											06 08				06 38							07 08
	d											06 09				06 39							07 09
Trehafod	d											06 12				06 42							07 12
Merthyr Tydfil	d																				06 38		
Pentre-bach	d																				06 42		
Troed Y Rhiw	d																				06 45		
Merthyr Vale	a																				06 48		
	d																				06 50		
Quakers Yard	d																				06 55		
Aberdare	d																	06 21					
Cwmbach	d																	06 24					
Fernhill	d																	06 28					
Mountain Ash	a																	06 31					
	d																	06 34					
Penrhiwceiber	d																	06 37					
Abercynon	d																	06 45			07 00		
Pontypridd ■	a											06 17				06 47		06 52			07 07		07 17
	d					05 18						06 18				06 48		06 54			07 08		07 18
Trefforest	d					05 21						06 21				06 51		06 57			07 11		07 21
Trefforest Estate	d					05 25															07 15		
Taffs Well	d					05 28						06 28			06 53	06 58	←	07 04			07 19		07 28
Radyr ■	a					05 31						06 31			06 56	07 01	06 56	07 08			07 23		07 31
	d					05 31						06 31			07 04	07 01	07 04	07 08			07 23		07 31
Danescourt	d														→		07 08						
Fairwater	d																07 10						
Waun-gron Park	d																07 12						
Ninian Park	d																07 15						
Llandaf	d					05 34						06 34				07 04		07 11			07 26		07 34
Cathays	d					05 39						06 39				07 09		07 16			07 31		07 39
Rhymney ■	d													06 08					06 32				
Pontlottyn	d													06 11					06 35				
Tir-phil	d													06 16					06 40				
Brithdir	d													06 18					06 42				
Bargoed	a													06 22					06 46				
	d													06 25					06 46			07 02	
Gilfach Fargoed	d													06 28								07 04	
Pengam	d													06 30					06 51			07 07	
Hengoed	d													06 34					06 54			07 10	
Ystrad Mynach	d													06 37					06 57			07 13	
Llanbradach	d													06 41					07 01			07 18	
Energlyn & Churchill Park	d													06 45					07 05				
Aber	d													06 47					07 07			07 22	
Caerphilly	d									06 10				06 50					07 10			07 25	
Lisvane & Thornhill	d									06 14				06 54					07 14			07 29	
Llanishen	d									06 16				06 56					07 16			07 31	
Heath High Level	d									06 19				06 59					07 19			07 34	
Coryton	d												06 45							07 15			
Whitchurch (Cardiff)	d												06 46							07 16			
Rhiwbina	d												06 48							07 18			
Birchgrove	d												06 50							07 20			
Ty Glas	d												06 51							07 21			
Heath Low Level	d												06 54							07 24			
Cardiff Queen Street ■	a					05 45				06 25		06 42	06 59	07 04		07 12		07 20	07 24	07 29	07 33	07 39	07 44
	d	00 01				05 45				06 26		06 44	07 01	07 06		07 13		07 21	07 26	07 31	07 36	07 41	07 46
Cardiff Central ■	a	00 05				05 48				06 29		06 48	07 04	07 09		07 16	07 20	07 24	07 29	07 34	07 39	07 44	07 52
	d		05 20	05 41	05 46	05 55	06 16	06 25	06 36	06 41	06 55	07 01		07 10		07 16		07 25	07 31		07 41	07 46	
Grangetown	d		05 24	05 45	05 50	05 59	06 20	06 29	06 40	06 45	06 59	07 05		07 14		07 20		07 29	07 35		07 45	07 50	
Dingle Road	d				05 54		06 24		06 44			07 11				07 26			07 41			07 56	
Penarth	a				06 00		06 30		06 50			07 17				07 32			07 47			08 02	
Cogan	d		05 28	05 48		06 03		06 33		06 48	07 03			07 18				07 33			07 48		
Eastbrook	d		05 30	05 51		06 05		06 35		06 51	07 05			07 20				07 35			07 51		
Dinas Powys	d		05 32	05 53		06 07		06 37		06 53	07 07			07 22				07 37			07 53		
Cadoxton	d		05 37	05 57		06 12		06 42		06 57	07 12			07 27				07 42			07 57		
Barry Docks	d		05 39	06 00		06 14		06 44		07 00	07 14			07 29				07 44			08 00		
Barry ■	d		05 44	06 05		06 19		06 49		07 05	07 19			07 34				07 49			08 05		
Barry Island	a		05 51			06 26		06 56			07 26			07 41				07 56					
Rhoose Cardiff Int Airport ✈	d			06 12						07 12											08 12		
Llantwit Major	d			06 22						07 22											08 22		
Bridgend	a			06 40						07 40											08 40		

A From Cardiff Bay
B From Barry Island
C From Hereford
D From Barry Island to Radyr
E To Coryton
F From Taffs Well to Coryton
G To Radyr
H From Cardiff Central
I From Penarth

When events are being held at the Principality Stadium, services are subject to alteration. Please check times before travelling.

For connections to Cardiff Bay please refer to Table T124

Table T130-F

Saturdays

15 September to 8 December

Treherbert, Aberdare, Merthyr, Pontypridd, Rhymney and Coryton - Cardiff, Penarth, Barry, Barry Island and Bridgend

		AW A	AW	AW B	AW C	AW	AW D	AW	AW A	AW	AW	AW C	AW E	AW F	AW	AW A	AW	AW D	AW C	AW G	AW H	AW	AW
Treherbert	d							07 17							07 45								08 17
Ynyswen	d							07 19							07 47								08 19
Treorchy	d							07 21							07 49								08 21
Ton Pentre	d							07 23							07 51								08 23
Ystrad Rhondda	a							07 26							07 54								08 26
	d							07 28							07 58								08 28
Llwynypia	d							07 30							08 00								08 30
Tonypandy	d							07 33							08 03								08 33
Dinas Rhondda	d							07 35							08 05								08 35
Porth	a							07 38							08 08								08 38
	d							07 39							08 09								08 39
Trehafod	d							07 42							08 12								08 42
Merthyr Tydfil	d					07 08							07 38							08 08			
Pentre-bach	d					07 12							07 42							08 12			
Troed Y Rhiw	d					07 15							07 45							08 15			
Merthyr Vale	a					07 18							07 48							08 18			
	d					07 20							07 50							08 20			
Quakers Yard	d					07 25							07 55							08 25			
Aberdare	d		06 51							07 21							07 51						
Cwmbach	d		06 54							07 24							07 54						
Fernhill	d		06 58							07 28							07 58						
Mountain Ash	a		07 01							07 31							08 01						
	d		07 04							07 34							08 04						
Penrhiwceiber	d		07 07							07 37							08 07						
Abercynon	d		07 15			07 30				07 45			08 00				08 15			08 30			
Pontypridd ■	a		07 22			07 37		07 47		07 52			08 07		08 17		08 22			08 37			08 47
	d		07 24			07 38		07 48		07 54			08 08		08 18		08 24			08 38			08 48
Trefforest	d		07 27			07 41		07 51		07 57			08 11		08 21		08 27			08 41			08 51
Trefforest Estate	d					07 45							08 15							08 45			
Taffs Well	d		07 34			07 49		07 58		08 04			08 19		08 28		08 34			08 49			08 58
Radyr ■	a		07 38			07 53		08 01		08 08			08 23		08 31		08 38			08 53			09 01
	d	07 34	07 38			07 53		08 01	08 04	08 08			08 23		08 31	08 34	08 38			08 53			09 01
Danescourt	d	07 38							08 08							08 38							
Fairwater	d	07 40							08 10							08 40							
Waun-gron Park	d	07 42							08 12							08 42							
Ninian Park	d	07 45							08 15							08 45							
Llandaf	d		07 41			07 56		08 04		08 11			08 26		08 34		08 41			08 56			09 04
Cathays	d		07 46			08 01		08 09		08 16			08 31		08 40		08 46			09 01			09 09
Rhymney ■	d			07 00							07 24			07 42									
Pontlottyn	d			07 03							07 27			07 45									
Tir-phil	d			07 08							07 32			07 50									
Brithdir	d			07 10							07 34			07 52									
Bargoed	a			07 14							07 38			07 59									
	d			07 15			07 32				07 43			08 00				08 15				08 32	
Gilfach Fargoed	d			07 18							07 46							08 18					
Pengam	d			07 20			07 37				07 48			08 05				08 20				08 37	
Hengoed	d			07 24			07 40				07 52			08 09				08 24				08 40	
Ystrad Mynach	d			07 27			07 43				07 55			08 12				08 27				08 43	
Llanbradach	d			07 31			07 48				08 00			08 16				08 31				08 48	
Energlyn & Churchill Park	d			07 35							08 04			08 20				08 35					
Aber	d			07 37			07 52				08 07			08 22				08 37				08 52	
Caerphilly	d			07 40			07 55				08 10			08 25				08 40				08 55	
Lisvane & Thornhill	d			07 44			07 59				08 14			08 29				08 44				08 59	
Llanishen	d			07 46			08 01				08 16			08 31				08 46				09 01	
Heath High Level	d			07 49			08 04				08 19			08 34				08 49				09 04	
Coryton	d				07 45							08 15							08 45				
Whitchurch (Cardiff)	d				07 46							08 16							08 46				
Rhiwbina	d				07 48							08 18							08 48				
Birchgrove	d				07 50							08 20							08 50				
Ty Glas	d				07 51							08 21							08 51				
Heath Low Level	d				07 54							08 24							08 54				
Cardiff Queen Street ■	a		07 49	07 54	07 59	08 04	08 09	08 14		08 19	08 24	08 29	08 34	08 39	08 44		08 49	08 54	08 59	09 04	←	09 09	09 14
	d		07 51	07 56	08 01	08 06	08 11	08 16		08 21	08 26	08 31	08 36	08 41	08 46		08 51	08 56	09 01	09 06		09 11	09 16
Cardiff Central ■	a	07 50	07 54	07 59	08 04	08 09	08 14	08 22	08 19	08 24	08 29	08 34	08 39	08 47	08 52	08 50	08 54	08 59	09 04	09 09	08 47	09 14	09 22
	d		07 55	08 01		08 10	08 16			08 25	08 31		08 41	09 14			08 55	09 01		09 10	09 14	09 16	
Grangetown	d		07 59	08 05		08 14	08 20			08 29	08 35		08 45	→			08 59	09 05		09 14		09 20	
Dingle Road	d			08 11			08 26				08 41							09 11				09 26	
Penarth	a			08 17			08 32				08 47							09 17				09 32	
Cogan	d		08 03			08 18				08 33			08 48				09 03			09 18			
Eastbrook	d		08 05			08 20				08 35			08 51				09 05			09 20			
Dinas Powys	d		08 07			08 22				08 37			08 53				09 07			09 22			
Cadoxton	d		08 12			08 27				08 42			08 57				09 12			09 27			
Barry Docks	d		08 14			08 29				08 44			09 00				09 14			09 29			
Barry ■	d		08 19			08 34				08 49			09 05				09 19			09 34			
Barry Island	a		08 26			08 41				08 56							09 26			09 41			
Rhoose Cardiff Int Airport ✈	d												09 12										
Llantwit Major	d												09 22										
Bridgend	a												09 40								09 33		

A To Coryton
B To Ystrad Mynach
C To Radyr
D From Penarth
E From Cardiff Central
F To Swansea
G From Barry Island
H From Rhymney to Swansea

When events are being held at the Principality Stadium, services are subject to alteration. Please check times before travelling.

For connections to Cardiff Bay please refer to Table T124

Table T130-F

Saturdays
15 September to 8 December

Treherbert, Aberdare, Merthyr, Pontypridd, Rhymney and Coryton - Cardiff, Penarth, Barry, Barry Island and Bridgend

		AW A	AW	AW B	AW C	AW D	AW B	AW	AW A	AW	AW	AW C	AW D	AW B	AW	AW A	AW	AW B	AW C	AW D	AW	AW
Treherbert	d							08 47							09 17							09 47
Ynyswen	d							08 49							09 19							09 49
Treorchy	d							08 51							09 21							09 51
Ton Pentre	d							08 53							09 23							09 53
Ystrad Rhondda	a							08 56							09 26							09 56
	d							08 58							09 28							09 58
Llwynypia	d							09 00							09 30							10 00
Tonypandy	d							09 03							09 33							10 03
Dinas Rhondda	d							09 05							09 35							10 05
Porth	a							09 08							09 38							10 08
	d							09 09							09 39							10 09
Trehafod	d							09 12							09 42							10 12
Merthyr Tydfil	d					08 38							09 08							09 38		
Pentre-bach	d					08 42							09 12							09 42		
Troed Y Rhiw	d					08 45							09 15							09 45		
Merthyr Vale	a					08 48							09 18							09 48		
	d					08 50							09 20							09 50		
Quakers Yard	d					08 55							09 25							09 55		
Aberdare	d		08 21							08 51							09 21					
Cwmbach	d		08 24							08 54							09 24					
Fernhill	d		08 28							08 58							09 28					
Mountain Ash	a		08 31							09 01							09 31					
	d		08 34							09 04							09 34					
Penrhiwceiber	d		08 37							09 07							09 37					
Abercynon	d		08 45			09 00				09 15			09 30				09 45			10 00		
Pontypridd	a		08 52			09 07		09 17		09 22			09 37		09 47		09 52			10 07		10 17
	d		08 54			09 08		09 18		09 24			09 38		09 48		09 54			10 08		10 18
Trefforest	d		08 57			09 11		09 21		09 27			09 41		09 51		09 57			10 11		10 21
Trefforest Estate	d					09 15							09 45							10 15		
Taffs Well	d		09 04			09 19		09 28		09 34			09 49		09 58		10 04			10 19		10 28
Radyr	a		09 08			09 23		09 31		09 38			09 53		10 01		10 08			10 23		10 31
	d	09 04	09 08			09 23		09 31	09 34	09 38			09 53		10 01	10 04	10 08			10 23		10 31
Danescourt	d	09 08							09 38							10 08						
Fairwater	d	09 10							09 40							10 10						
Waun-gron Park	d	09 12							09 42							10 12						
Ninian Park	d	09 15							09 45							10 15						
Llandaf	d		09 11			09 26		09 34		09 41			09 56		10 04		10 11			10 26		10 34
Cathays	d		09 16			09 31		09 40		09 46			10 01		10 09		10 16			10 31		10 39
Rhymney	d			08 32														09 27				
Pontlottyn	d			08 35														09 30				
Tir-phil	d			08 39														09 35				
Brithdir	d			08 42														09 37				
Bargoed	a			08 46														09 41				
	d			08 47			09 00							09 25				09 45			10 00	
Gilfach Fargoed	d													09 27								
Pengam	d			08 52			09 05							09 30				09 50			10 05	
Hengoed	d			08 55			09 09							09 33				09 54			10 09	
Ystrad Mynach	d			08 58			09 12				09 28			09 43				09 57			10 12	
Llanbradach	d			09 03			09 16				09 33			09 48				10 01			10 16	
Energlyn & Churchill Park	d						09 20											10 05			10 20	
Aber	d			09 07			09 22				09 37			09 52				10 07			10 22	
Caerphilly	d			09 10			09 25				09 40			09 55				10 10			10 25	
Lisvane & Thornhill	d			09 14			09 29				09 44			09 59				10 14			10 29	
Llanishen	d			09 16			09 31				09 46			10 01				10 16			10 31	
Heath High Level	d			09 19			09 34				09 49			10 04				10 19			10 34	
Coryton	d				09 15							09 45							10 15			
Whitchurch (Cardiff)	d				09 16							09 46							10 16			
Rhiwbina	d				09 18							09 48							10 18			
Birchgrove	d				09 20							09 50							10 20			
Ty Glas	d				09 21							09 51							10 21			
Heath Low Level	d				09 24							09 54							10 24			
Cardiff Queen Street	a		09 19	09 24	09 29	09 34	09 39	09 44		09 49	09 54	09 59	10 04	10 09	10 14		10 19	10 24	10 29	10 34	10 39	10 44
	d		09 21	09 26	09 31	09 36	09 41	09 46		09 51	09 56	10 01	10 06	10 11	10 16		10 21	10 26	10 31	10 36	10 41	10 46
Cardiff Central	a	09 20	09 24	09 29	09 34	09 39	09 44	09 52	09 50	09 54	09 59	10 04	10 09	10 14	10 22	10 20	10 24	10 29	10 34	10 39	10 44	10 52
	d		09 25	09 31		09 41	09 46			09 55	10 01		10 10	10 16			10 25	10 31		10 41	10 46	
Grangetown	d		09 29	09 35		09 45	09 50			09 59	10 05		10 14	10 20			10 29	10 35		10 45	10 50	
Dingle Road	d			09 41			09 56				10 11			10 26				10 41			10 56	
Penarth	a			09 47			10 02				10 17			10 32				10 47			11 02	
Cogan	d		09 33			09 48				10 03			10 18				10 33			10 48		
Eastbrook	d		09 35			09 51				10 05			10 20				10 35			10 51		
Dinas Powys	d		09 37			09 53				10 07			10 22				10 37			10 53		
Cadoxton	d		09 42			09 57				10 12			10 27				10 42			10 57		
Barry Docks	d		09 44			10 00				10 14			10 29				10 44			11 00		
Barry	d		09 49			10 05				10 19			10 34				10 49			11 05		
Barry Island	a		09 56							10 26			10 41				10 56					
Rhoose Cardiff Int Airport	d					10 12														11 12		
Llantwit Major	d					10 22														11 22		
Bridgend	a					10 40														11 40		

A To Coryton
B From Penarth
C To Radyr
D From Barry Island

When events are being held at the Principality Stadium, services are subject to alteration. Please check times before travelling.

For connections to Cardiff Bay please refer to Table T124

Table T130-F

Saturdays
15 September to 8 December

Treherbert, Aberdare, Merthyr, Pontypridd, Rhymney and Coryton - Cardiff, Penarth, Barry, Barry Island and Bridgend

		AW A	AW	AW	AW	AW B	AW	AW C	AW A	AW	AW D	AW	AW B	AW	AW	AW	AW A	AW	AW	AW B	AW	AW C	AW
Treherbert	d											10 17				10 47							11 17
Ynyswen	d											10 19				10 49							11 19
Treorchy	d											10 21				10 51							11 21
Ton Pentre	d											10 23				10 53							11 23
Ystrad Rhondda	a											10 26				10 56							11 26
	d											10 28				10 58							11 28
Llwynypia	d											10 30				11 00							11 30
Tonypandy	d											10 33				11 03							11 33
Dinas Rhondda	d											10 35				11 05							11 35
Porth	a											10 38				11 08							11 38
	d											10 52				11 09							11 39
Trehafod	d											10 55				11 12							11 42
Merthyr Tydfil	d			10 04										10 38							11 08		
Pentre-bach	d			10 08										10 42							11 12		
Troed Y Rhiw	d			10 11										10 45							11 15		
Merthyr Vale	a			10 14										10 48							11 18		
	d			10 15										10 50							11 20		
Quakers Yard	d			10 21										10 55							11 25		
Aberdare	d		09 51							10 21								10 51					
Cwmbach	d		09 54							10 24								10 54					
Fernhill	d		09 58							10 28								10 58					
Mountain Ash	a		10 01							10 31								11 01					
	d		10 04							10 34								11 04					
Penrhiwceiber	d		10 07							10 37								11 07					
Abercynon	d		10 15	10 25						10 44				10 59				11 15			11 30		
Pontypridd	a		10 22	10 34						10 52		11 00		11 07		11 17		11 22			11 37		11 47
	d		10 24				10 38			10 54		11 04		11 09		11 18		11 24			11 38		11 48
Trefforest	d		10 27				10 41			10 57		11 07		11 12		11 21		11 27			11 41		11 51
Trefforest Estate	d													11 16							11 45		
Taffs Well	d		10 34				10 49			11 04		11 14		11 20		11 28		11 34			11 49		11 58
Radyr	a		10 38				10 53			11 08		11 17		11 23		11 31		11 38			11 53		12 01
	d	10 34	10 38				10 53		11 04	11 08		11 21		11 23		11 31	11 34	11 38			11 53		12 01
Danescourt	d	10 38							11 08								11 38						
Fairwater	d	10 40							11 10								11 40						
Waun-gron Park	d	10 42							11 12								11 42						
Ninian Park	d	10 45							11 15								11 45						
Llandaf	d		10 41				10 56			11 11				11 26		11 34		11 41			11 56		12 04
Cathays	d		10 46				11 01			11 16				11 31		11 39		11 46			12 01		12 09
Rhymney	d										10 27												
Pontlottyn	d										10 30												
Tir-phil	d										10 35												
Brithdir	d										10 37												
Bargoed	a										10 41												
	d							10 25			10 45				11 00							11 25	
Gilfach Fargoed	d							10 27														11 27	
Pengam	d							10 30			10 50				11 05							11 30	
Hengoed	d							10 33			10 54				11 09							11 33	
Ystrad Mynach	d				10 28			10 43			10 57				11 12				11 28			11 43	
Llanbradach	d				10 33			10 48			11 01				11 16				11 33			11 48	
Energlyn & Churchill Park	d										11 05				11 20								
Aber	d				10 37			10 52			11 07				11 22				11 37			11 52	
Caerphilly	d				10 40			10 55			11 10				11 25				11 40			11 55	
Lisvane & Thornhill	d				10 44			10 59			11 14				11 29				11 44			11 59	
Llanishen	d				10 46			11 01			11 16				11 31				11 46			12 01	
Heath High Level	d				10 49			11 04			11 19				11 34				11 49			12 04	
Coryton	d					10 45							11 15							11 45			
Whitchurch (Cardiff)	d					10 46							11 16							11 46			
Rhiwbina	d					10 48							11 18							11 48			
Birchgrove	d					10 50							11 20							11 50			
Ty Glas	d					10 51							11 21							11 51			
Heath Low Level	d					10 54							11 24							11 54			
Cardiff Queen Street	a		10 49		10 54	10 59	11 04	11 09		11 19	11 24		11 29	11 34	11 39	11 44		11 49	11 54	11 59	12 04	12 09	12 14
	d		10 51		10 56	11 01	11 06	11 11		11 21	11 26		11 31	11 36	11 41	11 46		11 51	11 56	12 01	12 06	12 11	12 16
Cardiff Central	a	10 50	10 54		10 59	11 04	11 09	11 14	11 20	11 24	11 29	11 34	11 34	11 39	11 44	11 52	11 50	11 54	11 59	12 04	12 09	12 14	12 22
	d		10 55		11 01		11 10	11 16		11 25	11 31			11 41	11 46			11 55	12 01		12 10	12 16	
Grangetown	d		10 59		11 05		11 14	11 20		11 29	11 35			11 45	11 50			11 59	12 05		12 14	12 20	
Dingle Road	d				11 11			11 26			11 41				11 56				12 11			12 26	
Penarth	a				11 17			11 32			11 47				12 02				12 17			12 32	
Cogan	d		11 03				11 18			11 33				11 48				12 03			12 18		
Eastbrook	d		11 05				11 20			11 35				11 51				12 05			12 20		
Dinas Powys	d		11 07				11 22			11 37				11 53				12 07			12 22		
Cadoxton	d		11 12				11 27			11 42				11 57				12 12			12 27		
Barry Docks	d		11 14				11 29			11 44				12 00				12 14			12 29		
Barry	d		11 19				11 34			11 49				12 05				12 19			12 34		
Barry Island	a		11 26				11 41			11 56								12 26			12 41		
Rhoose Cardiff Int Airport	d													12 12									
Llantwit Major	d													12 22									
Bridgend	a													12 40									

A To Coryton
B To Radyr
C From Penarth
D From Cardiff Central

When events are being held at the Principality Stadium, services are subject to alteration. Please check times before travelling.

For connections to Cardiff Bay please refer to Table T124

Treherbert, Aberdare, Merthyr, Pontypridd, Rhymney and Coryton - Cardiff, Penarth, Barry, Barry Island and Bridgend

		AW A	AW	AW B	AW C	AW	AW	AW	AW A	AW	AW C	AW	AW B	AW	AW A	AW	AW D	AW C	AW	AW	AW	AW A
Treherbert	d							11 47						12 17							12 47	
Ynyswen	d							11 49						12 19							12 49	
Treorchy	d							11 51						12 21							12 51	
Ton Pentre	d							11 53						12 23							12 53	
Ystrad Rhondda	a							11 56						12 26							12 56	
	d							11 58						12 28							12 58	
Llwynypia	d							12 00						12 30							13 00	
Tonypandy	d							12 03						12 33							13 03	
Dinas Rhondda	d							12 05						12 35							13 05	
Porth	a							12 08						12 38							13 08	
	d							12 09						12 39							13 09	
Trehafod	d							12 12						12 42							13 12	
Merthyr Tydfil	d					11 38						12 08							12 38			
Pentre-bach	d					11 42						12 12							12 42			
Troed Y Rhiw	d					11 45						12 15							12 45			
Merthyr Vale	a					11 48						12 18							12 48			
	d					11 50						12 20							12 50			
Quakers Yard	d					11 55						12 25							12 55			
Aberdare	d		11 21													12 21						
Cwmbach	d		11 24													12 24						
Fernhill	d		11 28													12 28						
Mountain Ash	a		11 31													12 31						
	d		11 34													12 34						
Penrhiwceiber	d		11 37													12 37						
Abercynon	d		11 45			12 00						12 30				12 45			13 00			
Pontypridd	a		11 52			12 07		12 17				12 37		12 48		12 52			13 07		13 17	
	d		11 54			12 08		12 18				12 38		12 48		12 54			13 08		13 18	
Trefforest	d		11 57			12 11		12 21				12 41		12 51		12 57			13 11		13 21	
Trefforest Estate	d					12 15						12 45							13 15			
Taffs Well	d		12 04			12 19		12 28				12 49		12 58		13 04			13 19		13 28	
Radyr	a		12 08			12 23		12 31				12 53		13 00		13 08			13 23		13 31	
	d	12 04	12 08			12 23		12 31	12 34			12 53		13 01	13 04	13 08			13 23		13 31	13 34
Danescourt	d	12 08							12 38						13 08							13 38
Fairwater	d	12 10							12 40						13 10							13 40
Waun-gron Park	d	12 12							12 42						13 12							13 42
Ninian Park	d	12 15							12 45						13 15							13 45
Llandaf	d		12 11			12 26		12 34				12 56		13 04		13 11			13 26		13 34	
Cathays	d		12 16			12 31		12 39				13 01		13 09		13 16			13 31		13 39	
Rhymney	d			11 27													12 27					
Pontlottyn	d			11 30													12 30					
Tir-phil	d			11 35													12 35					
Brithdir	d			11 37													12 37					
Bargoed	a			11 41													12 41					
	d			11 45			12 00						12 25				12 45			13 00		
Gilfach Fargoed	d												12 27									
Pengam	d			11 50			12 05						12 30				12 50			13 05		
Hengoed	d			11 54			12 09						12 33				12 54			13 09		
Ystrad Mynach	d			11 57			12 12			12 28			12 43				12 57			13 12		
Llanbradach	d			12 01			12 16			12 33			12 48				13 01			13 16		
Energlyn & Churchill Park	d			12 05			12 20										13 05			13 20		
Aber	d			12 07			12 22			12 37			12 52				13 07			13 22		
Caerphilly	d			12 10			12 25			12 40			12 55				13 10			13 25		
Lisvane & Thornhill	d			12 14			12 29			12 44			12 59				13 14			13 29		
Llanishen	d			12 16			12 31			12 46			13 01				13 16			13 31		
Heath High Level	d			12 19			12 34			12 49			13 04				13 19			13 34		
Coryton	d				12 15						12 45							13 15				
Whitchurch (Cardiff)	d				12 16						12 46							13 16				
Rhiwbina	d				12 18						12 48							13 18				
Birchgrove	d				12 20						12 50							13 20				
Ty Glas	d				12 21						12 51							13 21				
Heath Low Level	d				12 24						12 54							13 24				
Cardiff Queen Street	a		12 19	12 24	12 29	12 34	12 39	12 44		12 54	12 59	13 04	13 09	13 14		13 19	13 24	13 29	13 34	13 39	13 44	
	d		12 21	12 26	12 31	12 36	12 41	12 46		12 56	13 01	13 06	13 11	13 16		13 21	13 26	13 31	13 36	13 41	13 46	
Cardiff Central	a	12 20	12 24	12 29	12 34	12 39	12 44	12 52	12 50	12 59	13 04	13 09	13 14	13 22	13 20	13 24	13 29	13 34	13 39	13 44	13 52	13 50
	d		12 25	12 31		12 41	12 46	12 55		13 01		13 10	13 16			13 25	13 31		13 41	13 46		
Grangetown	d		12 29	12 35		12 45	12 50	12 59		13 05		13 14	13 20			13 29	13 35		13 45	13 50		
Dingle Road	d			12 41			12 56			13 11			13 26				13 41			13 56		
Penarth	a			12 47			13 02			13 17			13 32				13 47			14 02		
Cogan	d		12 33			12 48		13 03				13 18				13 33			13 48			
Eastbrook	d		12 35			12 51		13 05				13 20				13 35			13 51			
Dinas Powys	d		12 37			12 53		13 07				13 22				13 37			13 53			
Cadoxton	d		12 42			12 57		13 12				13 27				13 42			13 57			
Barry Docks	d		12 44			13 00		13 14				13 29				13 44			14 00			
Barry	d		12 49			13 05		13 19				13 34				13 49			14 05			
Barry Island	a		12 56					13 26				13 41				13 56						
Rhoose Cardiff Int Airport ✈	d					13 12													14 12			
Llantwit Major	d					13 22													14 22			
Bridgend	a					13 40													14 40			

A To Coryton
B From Penarth
C To Radyr
D From Penarth to Bargoed

When events are being held at the Principality Stadium, services are subject to alteration. Please check times before travelling.

For connections to Cardiff Bay please refer to Table T124

Table T130-F

Saturdays

15 September to 8 December

Treherbert, Aberdare, Merthyr, Pontypridd, Rhymney and Coryton - Cardiff, Penarth, Barry, Barry Island and Bridgend

		AW	AW	AW A	AW	AW B	AW C	AW	AW	AW A	AW	AW	AW	AW	AW C	AW	AW	AW A	AW	AW B	AW C	AW	AW B
Treherbert	d										13 17			13 47									
Ynyswen	d										13 19			13 49									
Treorchy	d										13 21			13 51									
Ton Pentre	d										13 23			13 53									
Ystrad Rhondda	a										13 26			13 56									
	d										13 28			13 58									
Llwynypia	d										13 30			14 00									
Tonypandy	d										13 33			14 03									
Dinas Rhondda	d										13 35			14 05									
Porth	a										13 38			14 08									
	d										13 52			14 09									
Trehafod	d										13 55			14 12									
Merthyr Tydfil	d				13 08							13 38							14 08				
Pentre-bach	d				13 12							13 42							14 12				
Troed Y Rhiw	d				13 15							13 45							14 15				
Merthyr Vale	a				13 18							13 48							14 18				
	d				13 20							13 50							14 20				
Quakers Yard	d				13 25							13 55							14 25				
Aberdare	d	12 51														13 51						14 21	
Cwmbach	d	12 54														13 54						14 24	
Fernhill	d	12 58														13 58						14 28	
Mountain Ash	a	13 01														14 01						14 31	
	d	13 04														14 04						14 34	
Penrhiwceiber	d	13 07														14 07						14 37	
Abercynon	d	13 15			13 30			13 45				14 00				14 15			14 30			14 45	
Pontypridd	a	13 22			13 37			13 52			14 00	14 07		14 17		14 22			14 37			14 52	
	d	13 24			13 38			13 54			14 04	14 08		14 18		14 24			14 38			14 54	
Trefforest	d	13 27			13 41			13 57			14 07	14 11		14 21		14 27			14 41			14 57	
Trefforest Estate	d				13 45							14 15							14 45				
Taffs Well	d	13 34			13 49			14 04			14 14	14 19		14 28		14 34			14 49			15 04	
Radyr	a	13 38			13 53			14 08			14 17	14 23		14 31		14 38			14 53			15 08	
	d	13 38			13 53		14 04	14 08			14 21	14 23		14 31	14 34	14 38			14 53		15 04	15 08	
Danescourt	d						14 08								14 38						15 08		
Fairwater	d						14 10								14 40						15 10		
Waun-gron Park	d						14 12								14 42						15 12		
Ninian Park	d						14 15								14 45						15 15		
Llandaf	d	13 41			13 56			14 11				14 26		14 34		14 41			14 56			15 11	
Cathays	d	13 46			14 01			14 16				14 31		14 39		14 46			15 01			15 16	
Rhymney	d								13 27														14 27
Pontlottyn	d								13 30														14 30
Tir-phil	d								13 35														14 35
Brithdir	d								13 37														14 37
Bargoed	a								13 41														14 41
	d					13 25			13 45				14 00							14 25			14 45
Gilfach Fargoed	d					13 27														14 27			
Pengam	d					13 30			13 50				14 05							14 30			14 50
Hengoed	d					13 33			13 54				14 09							14 33			14 54
Ystrad Mynach	d		13 28			13 39			13 57				14 12				14 28			14 43			14 57
Llanbradach	d		13 33			13 43			14 01				14 16				14 33			14 48			15 01
Energlyn & Churchill Park	d								14 05				14 20										15 05
Aber	d		13 37			13 48			14 07				14 22				14 37			14 52			15 07
Caerphilly	d		13 40			13 55			14 10				14 25				14 40			14 55			15 10
Lisvane & Thornhill	d		13 44			13 59			14 14				14 29				14 44			14 59			15 14
Llanishen	d		13 46			14 01			14 16				14 31				14 46			15 01			15 16
Heath High Level	d		13 49			14 04			14 19				14 34				14 49			15 04			15 19
Coryton	d			13 45						14 15								14 45					
Whitchurch (Cardiff)	d			13 46						14 16								14 46					
Rhiwbina	d			13 48						14 18								14 48					
Birchgrove	d			13 50						14 20								14 50					
Ty Glas	d			13 51						14 21								14 51					
Heath Low Level	d			13 54						14 24								14 54					
Cardiff Queen Street	a	13 49	13 54	13 59	14 04	14 09		14 19	14 24	14 29		14 34	14 39	14 44		14 49	14 54	14 59	15 04	15 09		15 19	15 24
	d	13 51	13 56	14 01	14 06	14 11		14 21	14 26	14 31		14 36	14 41	14 46		14 51	14 56	15 01	15 06	15 11		15 21	15 26
Cardiff Central	a	13 54	13 59	14 04	14 09	14 14	14 20	14 24	14 29	14 34	14 36	14 39	14 44	14 52	14 50	14 54	14 59	15 04	15 09	15 14	15 20	15 24	15 29
	d	13 55	14 01		14 10	14 16		14 25	14 31			14 41	14 46			14 55	15 01		15 10	15 16		15 25	15 31
Grangetown	d	13 59	14 05		14 14	14 20		14 29	14 35			14 45	14 50			14 59	15 05		15 14	15 20		15 29	15 35
Dingle Road	d		14 11			14 26			14 41				14 56				15 11			15 26			15 41
Penarth	a		14 17			14 32			14 47				15 02				15 17			15 32			15 47
Cogan	d	14 03			14 18			14 33				14 48				15 03			15 18			15 33	
Eastbrook	d	14 05			14 20			14 35				14 51				15 05			15 20			15 35	
Dinas Powys	d	14 07			14 22			14 37				14 53				15 07			15 22			15 37	
Cadoxton	d	14 12			14 27			14 42				14 57				15 12			15 27			15 42	
Barry Docks	d	14 14			14 29			14 44				15 00				15 14			15 29			15 44	
Barry	d	14 19			14 34			14 49				15 05				15 19			15 34			15 49	
Barry Island	a	14 26			14 41			14 56								15 26			15 41			15 56	
Rhoose Cardiff Int Airport ✈	d											15 12											
Llantwit Major	d											15 22											
Bridgend	a											15 40											

A To Radyr
B From Penarth
C To Coryton

When events are being held at the Principality Stadium, services are subject to alteration. Please check times before travelling.

For connections to Cardiff Bay please refer to Table T124

Table T130-F

Saturdays
15 September to 8 December

Treherbert, Aberdare, Merthyr, Pontypridd, Rhymney and Coryton - Cardiff, Penarth, Barry, Barry Island and Bridgend

		AW	AW	AW	AW	AW		AW	AW	AW	AW	AW	AW	AW	AW	AW		AW	AW	AW	AW	AW	AW	AW	AW
			A					B			A		C		B			C	A				B		
Treherbert	d	14 17				14 47								15 17								15 47			
Ynyswen	d	14 19				14 49								15 19								15 49			
Treorchy	d	14 21				14 51								15 21								15 51			
Ton Pentre	d	14 23				14 53								15 23								15 53			
Ystrad Rhondda	a	14 26				14 56								15 26								15 56			
	d	14 28				14 58								15 28								15 58			
Llwynypia	d	14 30				15 00								15 30								16 00			
Tonypandy	d	14 33				15 03								15 33								16 03			
Dinas Rhondda	d	14 35				15 05								15 35								16 05			
Porth	a	14 38				15 08								15 38								16 08			
	d	14 52				15 09								15 39								16 09			
Trehafod	d	14 55				15 12								15 42								16 12			
Merthyr Tydfil	d			14 38								15 08								15 38					
Pentre-bach	d			14 42								15 12								15 42					
Troed Y Rhiw	d			14 45								15 15								15 45					
Merthyr Vale	a			14 48								15 18								15 48					
	d			14 50								15 20								15 50					
Quakers Yard	d			14 55								15 25								15 55					
Aberdare	d								14 51							15 21								15 51	
Cwmbach	d								14 54							15 24								15 54	
Fernhill	d								14 58							15 28								15 58	
Mountain Ash	a								15 01							15 31								16 01	
	d								15 04							15 34								16 04	
Penrhiwceiber	d								15 07							15 37								16 07	
Abercynon	d			15 00					15 15			15 30				15 44				16 00				16 15	
Pontypridd	a	15 00		15 07		15 17			15 22			15 37		15 47		15 52				16 07		16 17		16 22	
	d	15 04		15 08		15 18			15 24			15 38		15 48		15 54				16 08		16 18		16 24	
Trefforest	d	15 07		15 11		15 21			15 27			15 41		15 51		15 57				16 11		16 21		16 27	
Trefforest Estate	d			15 15								15 45								16 15					
Taffs Well	d	15 14		15 19		15 28			15 34			15 49		15 58		16 04				16 19		16 28		16 34	
Radyr	a	15 17		15 23		15 31			15 38			15 53		16 01		16 08				16 23		16 31		16 38	
	d	15 21		15 23		15 31		15 34	15 38			15 53		16 01	16 04	16 08				16 23		16 31	16 34	16 38	
Danescourt	d							15 38							16 08								16 38		
Fairwater	d							15 40							16 10								16 40		
Waun-gron Park	d							15 42							16 12								16 42		
Ninian Park	d							15 45							16 15								16 45		
Llandaf	d			15 26		15 34			15 41			15 56		16 04		16 11				16 26		16 34		16 41	
Cathays	d			15 31		15 39			15 46			16 01		16 09		16 16				16 31		16 39		16 46	
Rhymney	d																	15 27							
Pontlottyn	d																	15 30							
Tir-phil	d																	15 35							
Brithdir	d																	15 37							
Bargoed	a																	15 41							
	d				15 00								15 25					15 45			16 00				16 17
Gilfach Fargoed	d												15 27												16 19
Pengam	d				15 05								15 30					15 50			16 05				16 22
Hengoed	d				15 09								15 33					15 54			16 09				16 25
Ystrad Mynach	d				15 12					15 28			15 43					15 57			16 12				16 28
Llanbradach	d				15 16					15 33			15 48					16 01			16 16				16 33
Energlyn & Churchill Park	d				15 20													16 05			16 20				
Aber	d				15 22					15 37			15 52					16 07			16 22				16 37
Caerphilly	d				15 25					15 40			15 55					16 10			16 25				16 40
Lisvane & Thornhill	d				15 29					15 44			15 59					16 14			16 29				16 44
Llanishen	d				15 31					15 46			16 01					16 16			16 31				16 46
Heath High Level	d				15 34					15 49			16 04					16 19			16 34				16 49
Coryton	d		15 15								15 45								16 15						
Whitchurch (Cardiff)	d		15 16								15 46								16 16						
Rhiwbina	d		15 18								15 48								16 18						
Birchgrove	d		15 20								15 50								16 20						
Ty Glas	d		15 21								15 51								16 21						
Heath Low Level	d		15 24								15 54								16 24						
Cardiff Queen Street	a		15 29	15 34	15 39	15 44			15 49	15 54	15 59	16 04	16 09	16 14		16 19		16 24	16 29	16 34	16 39	16 44		16 49	16 54
	d		15 31	15 36	15 41	15 46			15 51	15 56	16 01	16 06	16 11	16 16		16 21		16 26	16 31	16 36	16 41	16 46		16 51	16 56
Cardiff Central	a	15 34	15 34	15 39	15 44	15 52		15 50	15 54	15 59	16 04	16 09	16 14	16 22	16 20	16 24		16 32	16 34	16 39	16 44	16 52	16 50	16 54	16 59
	d			15 41	15 46				15 55	16 01		16 10	16 16			16 25				16 41	16 46			16 55	17 01
Grangetown	d			15 45	15 50				15 59	16 05		16 14	16 20			16 29				16 45	16 50			16 59	17 05
Dingle Road	d				15 56					16 11			16 26								16 56				17 11
Penarth	a				16 02					16 17			16 32								17 02				17 17
Cogan	d			15 48					16 03			16 18				16 33				16 48				17 03	
Eastbrook	d			15 51					16 05			16 20				16 35				16 51				17 05	
Dinas Powys	d			15 53					16 07			16 22				16 37				16 53				17 07	
Cadoxton	d			15 57					16 12			16 27				16 42				16 57				17 12	
Barry Docks	d			16 00					16 14			16 29				16 44				17 00				17 14	
Barry	d			16 05					16 19			16 34				16 49				17 05				17 19	
Barry Island	a								16 26			16 41				16 56								17 26	
Rhoose Cardiff Int Airport	d			16 12																17 12					
Llantwit Major	d			16 22																17 22					
Bridgend	a			16 40																17 40					

A To Radyr B To Coryton C From Penarth

When events are being held at the Principality Stadium, services are subject to alteration. Please check times before travelling.

For connections to Cardiff Bay please refer to Table T124

Table T130-F

Saturdays
15 September to 8 December

Treherbert, Aberdare, Merthyr, Pontypridd, Rhymney and Coryton - Cardiff, Penarth, Barry, Barry Island and Bridgend

		AW		AW	AW	AW	AW	AW	AW	AW	AW	AW		AW	AW	AW	AW	AW	AW	AW	AW	AW		AW	AW
		A					B		C	A					B			A				B			C
Treherbert	d					16 17								16 47							17 17				
Ynyswen	d					16 19								16 49							17 19				
Treorchy	d					16 21								16 51							17 21				
Ton Pentre	d					16 23								16 53							17 23				
Ystrad Rhondda	a					16 26								16 56							17 26				
	d					16 28								16 58							17 28				
Llwynypia	d					16 30								17 00							17 30				
Tonypandy	d					16 33								17 03							17 33				
Dinas Rhondda	d					16 35								17 05							17 35				
Porth	a					16 38								17 08							17 38				
	d					16 39								17 09							17 39				
Trehafod	d					16 42								17 12							17 42				
Merthyr Tydfil	d			16 08							16 38								17 08						
Pentre-bach	d			16 12							16 42								17 12						
Troed Y Rhiw	d			16 15							16 45								17 15						
Merthyr Vale	a			16 18							16 48								17 18						
	d			16 20							16 50								17 20						
Quakers Yard	d			16 25							16 55								17 25						
Aberdare	d							16 21								16 51								17 21	
Cwmbach	d							16 24								16 54								17 24	
Fernhill	d							16 28								16 58								17 28	
Mountain Ash	a							16 31								17 01								17 31	
	d							16 34								17 04								17 34	
Penrhiwceiber	d							16 37								17 07								17 37	
Abercynon	d			16 30				16 45			17 00					17 15			17 30					17 45	
Pontypridd	a			16 37		16 47		16 52			17 07			17 17		17 22			17 37		17 47			17 52	
	d			16 38		16 48		16 54			17 08			17 18		17 24			17 38		17 48			17 54	
Trefforest	d			16 41		16 51		16 57			17 11			17 21		17 27			17 41		17 51			17 57	
Trefforest Estate	d			16 45							17 15								17 45						
Taffs Well	d			16 49		16 58		17 04			17 19			17 28		17 34			17 49		17 58			18 04	
Radyr	a			16 53		17 01		17 08			17 23			17 31		17 38			17 53		18 01			18 08	
	d			16 53		17 01	17 04	17 08			17 23			17 31	17 34	17 38			17 53		18 01	18 04		18 08	
Danescourt	d						17 08								17 38							18 08			
Fairwater	d						17 10								17 40							18 10			
Waun-gron Park	d						17 12								17 42							18 12			
Ninian Park	d						17 15								17 45							18 15			
Llandaf	d			16 56		17 04		17 11			17 26			17 34		17 41			17 56		18 04			18 11	
Cathays	d			17 01		17 09		17 16			17 31			17 39		17 46			18 01		18 09			18 16	
Rhymney	d								16 27																17 27
Pontlottyn	d								16 30																17 30
Tir-phil	d								16 35																17 35
Brithdir	d								16 37																17 37
Bargoed	a								16 41																17 41
	d				16 32				16 45			17 00					17 17			17 32					17 45
Gilfach Fargoed	d																17 19								
Pengam	d				16 37				16 50			17 05					17 22			17 37					17 50
Hengoed	d				16 40				16 54			17 09					17 25			17 40					17 54
Ystrad Mynach	d				16 43				16 57			17 12					17 28			17 43					17 57
Llanbradach	d				16 48				17 01			17 16					17 33			17 48					18 01
Energlyn & Churchill Park	d								17 05			17 20													18 05
Aber	d				16 52				17 07			17 22					17 37			17 52					18 07
Caerphilly	d				16 55				17 10			17 25					17 40			17 55					18 10
Lisvane & Thornhill	d				16 59				17 14			17 29					17 44			17 59					18 14
Llanishen	d				17 01				17 16			17 31					17 46			18 01					18 16
Heath High Level	d				17 04				17 19			17 34					17 49			18 04					18 19
Coryton	d	16 45								17 15								17 45							
Whitchurch (Cardiff)	d	16 46								17 16								17 46							
Rhiwbina	d	16 48								17 18								17 48							
Birchgrove	d	16 50								17 20								17 50							
Ty Glas	d	16 51								17 21								17 51							
Heath Low Level	d	16 54								17 24								17 54							
Cardiff Queen Street	a	16 59		17 04	17 09	17 14		17 19	17 24	17 29	17 34	17 39		17 44		17 49	17 54	17 59	18 04	18 09	18 14			18 19	18 24
	d	17 01		17 06	17 11	17 16		17 21	17 26	17 31	17 36	17 41		17 46		17 51	17 56	18 01	18 06	18 11	18 16			18 21	18 26
Cardiff Central	a	17 04		17 09	17 14	17 22	17 20	17 24	17 29	17 34	17 39	17 44		17 52	17 50	17 54	17 59	18 04	18 09	18 14	18 22	18 20		18 24	18 29
	d			17 10	17 16			17 25	17 31		17 41	17 46				17 55	18 01		18 10	18 16				18 25	18 31
Grangetown	d			17 14	17 20			17 29	17 35		17 45	17 50				17 59	18 05		18 14	18 20				18 29	18 35
Dingle Road	d				17 26				17 41			17 56					18 11			18 26					18 41
Penarth	a				17 32				17 47			18 02					18 17			18 32					18 47
Cogan	d			17 18				17 33			17 48					18 03			18 18					18 33	
Eastbrook	d			17 20				17 35			17 51					18 05			18 20					18 35	
Dinas Powys	d			17 22				17 37			17 53					18 07			18 22					18 37	
Cadoxton	d			17 27				17 42			17 57					18 12			18 27					18 42	
Barry Docks	d			17 29				17 44			18 00					18 14			18 29					18 44	
Barry	d			17 34				17 49			18 05					18 19			18 34					18 49	
Barry Island	a			17 41				17 56								18 26			18 41					18 56	
Rhoose Cardiff Int Airport	d										18 12														
Llantwit Major	d										18 22														
Bridgend	a										18 40														

A To Radyr B To Coryton C From Penarth

When events are being held at the Principality Stadium, services are subject to alteration. Please check times before travelling.

For connections to Cardiff Bay please refer to Table T124

Table T130-F

Saturdays

15 September to 8 December

Treherbert, Aberdare, Merthyr, Pontypridd, Rhymney and Coryton - Cardiff, Penarth, Barry, Barry Island and Bridgend

		AW A	AW	AW	AW B	AW	AW C	AW		AW	AW	AW	AW	AW	AW	AW A	AW	AW		AW	AW C	AW	AW	AW	AW
Treherbert	d			17 47								18 17						18 47					19 17		
Ynyswen	d			17 49								18 19						18 49					19 19		
Treorchy	d			17 51								18 21						18 51					19 21		
Ton Pentre	d			17 53								18 23						18 53					19 23		
Ystrad Rhondda	a			17 56								18 26						18 56					19 26		
	d			17 58								18 28						18 58					19 28		
Llwynypia	d			18 00								18 30						19 00					19 30		
Tonypandy	d			18 03								18 33						19 03					19 33		
Dinas Rhondda	d			18 05								18 35						19 05					19 35		
Porth	a			18 08								18 38						19 08					19 38		
	d			18 09								18 39						19 09					19 39		
Trehafod	d			18 12								18 42						19 12					19 42		
Merthyr Tydfil	d		17 38								18 08						18 38					19 08			
Pentre-bach	d		17 42								18 12						18 42					19 12			
Troed Y Rhiw	d		17 45								18 15						18 45					19 15			
Merthyr Vale	a		17 48								18 18						18 48					19 18			
	d		17 50								18 20						18 50					19 20			
Quakers Yard	d		17 55								18 25						18 55					19 25			
Aberdare	d					17 51								18 21						18 51					
Cwmbach	d					17 54								18 24						18 54					
Fernhill	d					17 58								18 28						18 58					
Mountain Ash	a					18 01								18 31						19 01					
	d					18 04								18 34						19 04					
Penrhiwceiber	d					18 07								18 37						19 07					
Abercynon	d		18 00			18 15					18 30			18 45			19 00			19 15		19 30			19 43
Pontypridd	a		18 07	18 17		18 22					18 37	18 47		18 52			19 07	19 17		19 22		19 37	19 47		19 52
	d		18 08	18 18		18 24					18 38	18 48		18 54			19 08	19 18		19 24		19 38	19 48		19 54
Trefforest	d		18 11	18 21		18 27					18 41	18 51		18 57			19 11	19 21		19 27		19 41	19 51		19 57
Trefforest Estate	d		18 15								18 45						19 15					19 45			
Taffs Well	d		18 19	18 28		18 34					18 49	18 58		19 04			19 19	19 28		19 34		19 49	19 58		20 04
Radyr	a		18 23	18 31		18 38					18 53	19 01		19 08			19 23	19 31		19 38		19 53	20 01		20 08
	d		18 23	18 31	18 34	18 38					18 53	19 01	19 04	19 08			19 23	19 31		19 38		19 53	20 01	20 04	20 08
Danescourt	d				18 38								19 08											20 08	
Fairwater	d				18 40								19 10											20 10	
Waun-gron Park	d				18 42								19 12											20 12	
Ninian Park	d				18 45								19 15											20 15	
Llandaf	d		18 26	18 34		18 41					18 56	19 04		19 11			19 26	19 34		19 41		19 56	20 04		20 11
Cathays	d		18 31	18 39		18 46					19 01	19 09		19 16			19 31	19 39		19 46		20 01	20 09		20 16
Rhymney	d																								
Pontlottyn	d																								
Tir-phil	d																								
Brithdir	d																								
Bargoed	a																								
	d							18 15							18 48										
Gilfach Fargoed	d							18 18							18 50										
Pengam	d							18 20							18 53										
Hengoed	d							18 24							18 56										
Ystrad Mynach	d							18 27							18 59										
Llanbradach	d							18 31							19 04										
Energlyn & Churchill Park	d							18 35																	
Aber	d							18 37							19 08										
Caerphilly	d						18 36	18 40							19 11						19 40				
Lisvane & Thornhill	d							18 44							19 15						19 44				
Llanishen	d							18 46							19 17						19 46				
Heath High Level	d							18 49							19 20						19 49				
Coryton	d	18 15								18 45						19 15									
Whitchurch (Cardiff)	d	18 16								18 46						19 16									
Rhiwbina	d	18 18								18 48						19 18									
Birchgrove	d	18 20								18 50						19 20									
Ty Glas	d	18 21								18 51						19 21									
Heath Low Level	d	18 24								18 54						19 24									
Cardiff Queen Street	a	18 29	18 34	18 44		18 49		18 54		18 59	19 04	19 14		19 19	19 24	19 29	19 34	19 44		19 49	19 54	20 04	20 14		20 19
	d	18 31	18 36	18 46		18 51		18 56		19 01	19 06	19 16		19 21	19 26	19 31	19 36	19 46		19 51	19 56	20 06	20 16		20 21
Cardiff Central	a	18 34	18 39	18 52	18 50	18 54	19 16	18 59		19 06	19 12	19 22	19 22	19 24	19 29	19 34	19 39	19 52		19 57	19 59	20 09	20 21	20 24	20 24
	d		18 41			18 55		19 01						19 25	19 31		19 41				20 06	20 10			20 31
Grangetown	d		18 45			18 59		19 05						19 29	19 35		19 45				20 10	20 14			20 35
Dingle Road	d							19 11							19 41						20 14				20 41
Penarth	a							19 17							19 47						20 20				20 47
Cogan	d		18 48			19 03								19 33			19 48					20 18			
Eastbrook	d		18 51			19 05								19 35			19 51					20 20			
Dinas Powys	d		18 53			19 07								19 37			19 53					20 22			
Cadoxton	d		18 57			19 12								19 42			19 57					20 27			
Barry Docks	d		19 00			19 14								19 44			20 00					20 29			
Barry	d		19 05			19 19								19 49			20 05					20 34			
Barry Island	a					19 26								19 56								20 41			
Rhoose Cardiff Int Airport ✈	d		19 12														20 12								
Llantwit Major	d		19 22														20 22								
Bridgend	a		19 40														20 40								

A To Radyr **B** To Coryton **C** From Penarth

When events are being held at the Principality Stadium, services are subject to alteration. Please check times before travelling.

For connections to Cardiff Bay please refer to Table T124

Table T130-F

Saturdays

15 September to 8 December

Treherbert, Aberdare, Merthyr, Pontypridd, Rhymney and Coryton - Cardiff, Penarth, Barry, Barry Island and Bridgend

		AW A	AW	AW B		AW	AW	AW C	AW	AW	AW	AW	AW A	AW		AW C	AW	AW D	AW	AW E	AW C	AW	AW C	AW	
Treherbert	d					19 47			20 17										21 17						
Ynyswen	d					19 49			20 19										21 19						
Treorchy	d					19 51			20 21										21 21						
Ton Pentre	d					19 53			20 23										21 23						
Ystrad Rhondda	a					19 56			20 26										21 26						
	d					19 58			20 28										21 28						
Llwynypia	d					20 00			20 30										21 30						
Tonypandy	d					20 03			20 33										21 33						
Dinas Rhondda	d					20 05			20 35										21 35						
Porth	a					20 08			20 38										21 38						
	d					20 09			20 39										21 39						
Trehafod	d					20 12			20 42										21 42						
Merthyr Tydfil	d		19 38											20 38								21 38			
Pentre-bach	d		19 42											20 42								21 42			
Troed Y Rhiw	d		19 45											20 45								21 45			
Merthyr Vale	a		19 48											20 48								21 48			
	d		19 50											20 50								21 50			
Quakers Yard	d		19 55											20 55								21 55			
Aberdare	d						19 51				20 21						20 51							21 51	
Cwmbach	d						19 54				20 24						20 54							21 54	
Fernhill	d						19 58				20 28						20 58							21 58	
Mountain Ash	a						20 01				20 31						21 01							22 01	
	d						20 04				20 34						21 04							22 04	
Penrhiwceiber	d						20 07				20 37						21 07							22 07	
Abercynon	d		20 00				20 15				20 45			21 00			21 15					22 00		22 15	
Pontypridd	a		20 07			20 17	20 22		20 47		20 52			21 07			21 22		21 47			22 07		22 23	
	d		20 08			20 18	20 24		20 48		20 54			21 08			21 24		21 48			22 08		22 24	
Trefforest	d		20 11			20 21	20 27		20 51		20 57			21 11			21 27		21 51			22 11		22 27	
Trefforest Estate	d		20 15											21 15								22 15			
Taffs Well	d		20 19			20 28	20 34		20 58		21 04			21 19			21 34		21 58			22 19		22 34	
Radyr	a		20 23			20 31	20 38		21 01		21 08			21 23			21 38		22 01			22 23		22 38	
	d		20 23			20 31	20 38		21 01	21 04	21 08			21 23			21 38		22 01	22 04		22 23		22 38	
Danescourt	d									21 08										22 08					
Fairwater	d									21 10										22 10					
Waun-gron Park	d									21 12										22 12					
Ninian Park	d									21 15										22 15					
Llandaf	d		20 26			20 34	20 41		21 04		21 11			21 26			21 41		22 04			22 26		22 41	
Cathays	d		20 31			20 39	20 46		21 09		21 16			21 31			21 46		22 09			22 31		22 46	
Rhymney	d							20 00								20 46					21 36				
Pontlottyn	d							20 03								20 49					21 39				
Tir-phil	d							20 08								20 54					21 44				
Brithdir	d							20 10								20 56					21 46				
Bargoed	a							20 14								21 00					21 50				
	d							20 15								21 00					21 50				
Gilfach Fargoed	d							20 18								21 03					21 53				
Pengam	d							20 20								21 05					21 55				
Hengoed	d							20 24								21 09					21 59				
Ystrad Mynach	d							20 27								21 12		21 39			22 02				
Llanbradach	d							20 31								21 16		21 44			22 06				
Energlyn & Churchill Park	d							20 35								21 20					22 10				
Aber	d							20 37								21 22		21 48			22 12				
Caerphilly	d			20 25				20 40								21 25		21 51			22 15		22 28		
Lisvane & Thornhill	d			20 29				20 44								21 29		21 55			22 19				
Llanishen	d			20 31				20 46								21 31		21 57			22 21				
Heath High Level	d			20 34				20 49								21 34		22 00			22 24				
Coryton	d	20 15											21 15												
Whitchurch (Cardiff)	d	20 16											21 16												
Rhiwbina	d	20 18											21 18												
Birchgrove	d	20 20											21 20												
Ty Glas	d	20 21											21 21												
Heath Low Level	d	20 24											21 24												
Cardiff Queen Street	a	20 29	20 34	20 39		20 44	20 49	20 54	21 14		21 19		21 29	21 34		21 42	21 50	22 05	22 14		22 29	22 34	22 39	22 49	
	d	20 31	20 36	20 41		20 46	20 51	20 56	21 16		21 21		21 31	21 36		21 42	21 51	22 06	22 16		22 31	22 36	22 40	22 54	
Cardiff Central	a	20 34	20 39	20 46		20 52	20 57	20 59	21 22	21 20	21 27		21 34	21 39		21 48	21 54	22 09	22 22	22 20	22 34	22 42	22 44	22 57	
	d		20 41				21 06	21 10				21 31		21 41			22 06	22 10			22 36			23 12	
Grangetown	d		20 45				21 10	21 14				21 35		21 45			22 10	22 14			22 40			23 16	
Dingle Road	d						21 14					21 41					22 14				22 44			23 20	
Penarth	a						21 20					21 47					22 20				22 50			23 26	
Cogan	d		20 48					21 18						21 48				22 18							
Eastbrook	d		20 51					21 20						21 51				22 20							
Dinas Powys	d		20 53					21 22						21 53				22 22							
Cadoxton	d		20 57					21 27						21 57				22 27							
Barry Docks	d		21 00					21 29						22 00				22 29							
Barry	d		21 05					21 34						22 05				22 34							
Barry Island	a							21 41										22 41							
Rhoose Cardiff Int Airport ✈	d		21 12											22 12											
Llantwit Major	d		21 22											22 22											
Bridgend	a		21 40											22 40											

A To Radyr **C** From Penarth **E** To Coryton
B From Barry Island **D** From Penarth to Pontypridd

When events are being held at the Principality Stadium, services are subject to alteration. Please check times before travelling.

For connections to Cardiff Bay please refer to Table T124

Table T130-F

Saturdays

15 September to 8 December

Treherbert, Aberdare, Merthyr, Pontypridd, Rhymney and Coryton - Cardiff, Penarth, Barry, Barry Island and Bridgend

		AW	AW	AW	AW
Treherbert	d				
Ynyswen	d				
Treorchy	d				
Ton Pentre	d				
Ystrad Rhondda	a				
	d				
Llwynypia	d				
Tonypandy	d				
Dinas Rhondda	d				
Porth	a				
	d				
Trehafod	d				
Merthyr Tydfil	d			22 38	
Pentre-bach	d			22 42	
Troed Y Rhiw	d			22 45	
Merthyr Vale	a			22 48	
	d			22 50	
Quakers Yard	d			22 55	
Aberdare	d				22 51
Cwmbach	d				22 54
Fernhill	d				22 58
Mountain Ash	a				23 01
	d				23 04
Penrhiwceiber	d				23 08
Abercynon	d			23 00	23 14
Pontypridd	a			23 07	23 24
	d			23 08	
Trefforest	d			23 11	
Trefforest Estate	d			23 15	
Taffs Well	d			23 19	
Radyr	a			23 23	
	d		23 14	23 23	
Danescourt	d				
Fairwater	d				
Waun-gron Park	d				
Ninian Park	d				
Llandaf	d		23 16	23 26	
Cathays	d		23 20	23 31	
Rhymney	d				
Pontlottyn	d				
Tir-phil	d				
Brithdir	d				
Bargoed	a				
	d				
Gilfach Fargoed	d				
Pengam	d				
Hengoed	d				
Ystrad Mynach	d				
Llanbradach	d				
Energlyn & Churchill Park	d				
Aber	d				
Caerphilly	d				
Lisvane & Thornhill	d				
Llanishen	d				
Heath High Level	d				
Coryton	d	22 45			
Whitchurch (Cardiff)	d	22 46			
Rhiwbina	d	22 48			
Birchgrove	d	22 50			
Ty Glas	d	22 51			
Heath Low Level	d	22 54			
Cardiff Queen Street	a	22 59	23 24	23 34	
	d	23 01	23 25	23 36	
Cardiff Central	a	23 06	23 28	23 43	
	d		23 30		
Grangetown	d		23 34		
Dingle Road	d				
Penarth	a				
Cogan	d		23 37		
Eastbrook	d		23 40		
Dinas Powys	d		23 42		
Cadoxton	d		23 46		
Barry Docks	d		23 49		
Barry	d		23 53		
Barry Island	a		00 01		
Rhoose Cardiff Int Airport ✈	d				
Llantwit Major	d				
Bridgend	a				

When events are being held at the Principality Stadium, services are subject to alteration. Please check times before travelling.

For connections to Cardiff Bay please refer to Table T124

Table T130-F

Sundays

20 May to 9 September

Treherbert, Aberdare, Merthyr, Pontypridd, Rhymney and Coryton - Cardiff, Penarth, Barry, Barry Island and Bridgend

		AW A	AW	AW	AW	AW	AW	AW	AW B	AW		AW C	AW B	AW	AW	AW D	AW E	AW	AW D	AW		AW	AW F	AW E	AW
Treherbert	d					08 17								10 12						12 12					
Ynyswen	d					08 19								10 14						12 14					
Treorchy	d					08 21								10 16						12 16					
Ton Pentre	d					08 23								10 18						12 18					
Ystrad Rhondda	a					08 26								10 21						12 21					
	d					08 28								10 23						12 23					
Llwynypia	d					08 30								10 25						12 25					
Tonypandy	d					08 33								10 28						12 28					
Dinas Rhondda	d					08 35								10 30						12 30					
Porth	a					08 38								10 33						12 33					
	d					08 39								10 34						12 34					
Trehafod	d					08 42								10 37						12 37					
Merthyr Tydfil	d								09 38								11 38							13 38	
Pentre-bach	d								09 42								11 42							13 42	
Troed Y Rhiw	d								09 45								11 45							13 45	
Merthyr Vale	a								09 48								11 48							13 48	
	d								09 50								11 50							13 50	
Quakers Yard	d								09 55								11 55							13 55	
Aberdare	d									09 54					10 54							12 54			
Cwmbach	d									09 57					10 57							12 57			
Fernhill	d									10 00					11 00							13 00			
Mountain Ash	a									10 03					11 03							13 03			
	d									10 04					11 04							13 04			
Penrhiwceiber	d									10 07					11 07							13 07			
Abercynon	d								09 59	10 13					11 13		11 59					13 13		13 59	
Pontypridd	a					08 47			10 07	10 22				10 42	11 22		12 07			12 42		13 22		14 07	
	d					08 48			10 09	10 24				10 43	11 24		12 09			12 43		13 24		14 09	
Trefforest	d					08 51			10 12	10 27				10 46	11 27		12 12			12 46		13 27		14 12	
Trefforest Estate	d																								
Taffs Well	d					08 58			10 20	10 34				10 53	11 34		12 20			12 53		13 34		14 20	
Radyr	a					09 01			10 23	10 37				10 56	11 37		12 23			12 56		13 37		14 23	
	d					09 01			10 23	10 37				10 56	11 37		12 23			12 56		13 37		14 23	
Danescourt	d																								
Fairwater	d																								
Waun-gron Park	d																								
Ninian Park	d																								
Llandaf	d					09 04			10 26	10 40				10 59	11 40		12 26			12 59		13 40		14 26	
Cathays	d					09 09			10 31	10 45				11 04	11 45		12 31			13 04		13 45		14 31	
Rhymney	d							09 08					10 09			11 09							13 09		
Pontlottyn	d							09 11					10 12			11 12							13 12		
Tir-phil	d							09 16					10 16			11 17							13 17		
Brithdir	d							09 18					10 19			11 19							13 19		
Bargoed	a							09 22					10 22			11 23							13 23		
	d							09 23					10 23			11 23							13 23		
Gilfach Fargoed	d							09 26					10 25			11 26							13 26		
Pengam	d							09 28					10 28			11 28							13 28		
Hengoed	d							09 32					10 31			11 32							13 32		
Ystrad Mynach	d							09 35					10 35			11 35			12 33				13 35		
Llanbradach	d							09 39					10 39			11 39			12 37				13 39		
Energlyn & Churchill Park	d							09 43					10 43			11 43			12 41				13 43		
Aber	d							09 45					10 45			11 45			12 43				13 45		
Caerphilly	d							09 48					10 48			11 48			12 48				13 48		
Lisvane & Thornhill	d							09 52					10 52			11 52			12 52				13 52		
Llanishen	d							09 54					10 54			11 54			12 54				13 54		
Heath High Level	d							09 57					10 57			11 57			12 57				13 57		
Coryton	d																								
Whitchurch (Cardiff)	d																								
Rhiwbina	d																								
Birchgrove	d																								
Ty Glas	d																								
Heath Low Level	d																								
Cardiff Queen Street	a					09 12		10 02	10 34	10 49			11 02	11 07	11 49	12 02	12 34		13 02	13 07		13 49	14 02	14 34	
	d	00 01				09 14		10 04	10 36	10 51			11 04	11 09	11 51	12 04	12 36		13 04	13 09		13 51	14 04	14 36	
Cardiff Central	a	00 05				09 16		10 07	10 39	10 54			11 07	11 12	11 54	12 07	12 39		13 07	13 11		13 54	14 07	14 39	
	d		08 25	08 41	09 16	09 25	09 55	10 25	10 41	10 55		11 14	11 17	11 25	11 55	12 25	12 41	12 55	13 16	13 25		13 55	14 25	14 41	14 55
Grangetown	d		08 29	08 45	09 20	09 29	09 59	10 29	10 45	10 59			11 20	11 29	11 59	12 29	12 45	12 59	13 20	13 29		13 59	14 29	14 45	14 59
Dingle Road	d				09 26								11 25						13 26						
Penarth	a				09 31								11 30						13 31						
Cogan	d		08 33	08 48		09 33	10 03	10 33	10 48	11 03				11 33	12 03	12 33	12 48	13 03		13 33		14 03	14 33	14 48	15 03
Eastbrook	d		08 35	08 51		09 35	10 05	10 35	10 51	11 05				11 35	12 05	12 35	12 51	13 05		13 35		14 05	14 35	14 51	15 05
Dinas Powys	d		08 37	08 53		09 37	10 07	10 37	10 53	11 07				11 37	12 07	12 37	12 53	13 07		13 37		14 07	14 37	14 53	15 07
Cadoxton	d		08 42	08 57		09 42	10 12	10 42	10 57	11 12				11 42	12 12	12 42	12 57	13 12		13 42		14 12	14 42	14 57	15 12
Barry Docks	d		08 44	09 00		09 44	10 14	10 44	11 00	11 14				11 44	12 14	12 44	13 00	13 14		13 44		14 14	14 44	15 00	15 14
Barry	d		08 49	09 05		09 49	10 19	10 49	11 05	11 19		11 32		11 49	12 19	12 49	13 05	13 19		13 49		14 19	14 49	15 05	15 19
Barry Island	a		08 56			09 55	10 25	10 55		11 25		11 38		11 55	12 25	12 55		13 26		13 55		14 25	14 55		15 25
Rhoose Cardiff Int Airport ✈	d			09 12					11 12								13 12							15 12	
Llantwit Major	d			09 22					11 22								13 22							15 22	
Bridgend	a			09 37					11 39								13 39							15 39	

A not 20 May. From Cardiff Bay
B From Cardiff Central
C From Newport (South Wales)
D From Penarth
E From Barry Island
F From Barry Island to Aberdare

When events are being held at the Principality Stadium, services are subject to alteration. Please check times before travelling.

For connections to Cardiff Bay please refer to Table T124

Table T130-F

Sundays

20 May to 9 September

Treherbert, Aberdare, Merthyr, Pontypridd, Rhymney and Coryton - Cardiff, Penarth, Barry, Barry Island and Bridgend

		AW A	AW	AW	AW	AW B		AW B	AW	AW A	AW	AW	AW B	AW B	AW	AW C		AW	AW	AW B	AW	AW	AW	AW	AW
Treherbert	d		14 17								16 17							18 17						20 17	
Ynyswen	d		14 19								16 19							18 19						20 19	
Treorchy	d		14 21								16 21							18 21						20 21	
Ton Pentre	d		14 23								16 23							18 23						20 23	
Ystrad Rhondda	a		14 26								16 26							18 26						20 26	
	d		14 28								16 28							18 28						20 28	
Llwynypia	d		14 30								16 30							18 30						20 30	
Tonypandy	d		14 33								16 33							18 33						20 33	
Dinas Rhondda	d		14 35								16 35							18 35						20 35	
Porth	a		14 38								16 38							18 38						20 38	
	d		14 39								16 39							18 39						20 39	
Trehafod	d		14 42								16 42							18 42						20 42	
Merthyr Tydfil	d							15 38						17 38								19 38			
Pentre-bach	d							15 42						17 42								19 42			
Troed Y Rhiw	d							15 45						17 45								19 45			
Merthyr Vale	a							15 48						17 48								19 48			
	d							15 50						17 50								19 50			
Quakers Yard	d							15 55						17 55								19 55			
Aberdare	d			14 54								16 54							18 54						20 54
Cwmbach	d			14 57								16 57							18 57						20 57
Fernhill	d			15 00								17 00							19 00						21 00
Mountain Ash	a			15 03								17 03							19 03						21 03
	d			15 04								17 04							19 04						21 04
Penrhiwceiber	d			15 07								17 07							19 07						21 07
Abercynon	d			15 13				15 59				17 13		17 59					19 13			19 59			21 13
Pontypridd 3	a		14 47	15 22				16 07			16 47	17 22		18 07				18 47	19 22			20 07		20 47	21 22
	d		14 48	15 24				16 09			16 48	17 24		18 09				18 48	19 24			20 09		20 48	21 24
Trefforest	d		14 51	15 27				16 12			16 51	17 27		18 12				18 51	19 27			20 12		20 51	21 27
Trefforest Estate	d																								
Taffs Well	d		14 58	15 34				16 20			16 58	17 34		18 20				18 58	19 34			20 20		20 58	21 34
Radyr 3	a		15 01	15 37				16 23			17 01	17 37		18 23				19 01	19 37			20 23		21 01	21 37
	d		15 01	15 37				16 23			17 01	17 37		18 23				19 01	19 37			20 23		21 01	21 37
Danescourt	d																								
Fairwater	d																								
Waun-gron Park	d																								
Ninian Park	d																								
Llandaf	d		15 04	15 40				16 26			17 04	17 40		18 26				19 04	19 40			20 26		21 04	21 40
Cathays	d		15 09	15 45				16 31			17 09	17 45		18 31				19 09	19 45			20 31		21 09	21 45
Rhymney 3	d					15 20							17 20							19 20					
Pontlottyn	d					15 23							17 23							19 23					
Tir-phil	d					15 28							17 28							19 28					
Brithdir	d					15 30							17 30							19 30					
Bargoed	a					15 34							17 34							19 34					
	d					15 35							17 35							19 35					
Gilfach Fargoed	d					15 38							17 38							19 38					
Pengam	d					15 40							17 40							19 40					
Hengoed	d					15 44							17 44							19 44					
Ystrad Mynach	d	14 33				15 47				16 33			17 47			18 33				19 47					
Llanbradach	d	14 37				15 51				16 37			17 51			18 37				19 51					
Energlyn & Churchill Park	d	14 41				15 55				16 41			17 55			18 41				19 55					
Aber	d	14 43				15 57				16 43			17 57			18 43				19 57					
Caerphilly	d	14 48				16 00				16 48			18 00			18 48				20 00					
Lisvane & Thornhill	d	14 52				16 04				16 52			18 04			18 52				20 04					
Llanishen	d	14 54				16 06				16 54			18 06			18 54				20 06					
Heath High Level	d	14 57				16 09				16 57			18 09			18 57				20 09					
Coryton	d																								
Whitchurch (Cardiff)	d																								
Rhiwbina	d																								
Birchgrove	d																								
Ty Glas	d																								
Heath Low Level	d																								
Cardiff Queen Street 3	a	15 02	15 14	15 49		16 14		16 34		17 02	17 14	17 49	18 14	18 34		19 02		19 14	19 49	20 14		20 34		21 14	21 49
	d	15 04	15 16	15 51		16 16		16 36		17 04	17 16	17 51	18 16	18 36		19 04		19 16	19 51	20 16		20 36		21 16	21 51
Cardiff Central 7	a	15 07	15 18	15 54		16 18		16 39		17 07	17 18	17 54	18 18	18 39		19 07		19 18	19 54	20 18		20 39		21 18	21 56
	d	15 16	15 25	15 55	16 10	16 25		16 41	16 55	17 16	17 25	17 55	18 25	18 41	18 55	19 16		19 25	19 55	20 25	20 31	20 41	20 55	21 25	
Grangetown	d	15 20	15 29	15 59	16 14	16 29		16 45	16 59	17 20	17 29	17 59	18 29	18 45	18 59	19 20		19 29	19 59	20 29	20 35	20 45	20 59	21 29	
Dingle Road	d	15 24								17 24						19 24					20 41				
Penarth	a	15 29								17 29						19 29					20 46				
Cogan	d		15 33	16 03	16 18	16 33		16 48	17 03		17 33	18 03	18 33	18 48	19 03			19 33	20 03	20 33		20 48	21 03	21 33	
Eastbrook	d		15 35	16 05	16 20	16 35		16 51	17 05		17 35	18 05	18 35	18 51	19 05			19 35	20 05	20 35		20 51	21 05	21 35	
Dinas Powys	d		15 37	16 07	16 22	16 37		16 53	17 07		17 37	18 07	18 37	18 53	19 07			19 37	20 07	20 37		20 53	21 07	21 37	
Cadoxton	d		15 42	16 12	16 27	16 42		16 57	17 12		17 42	18 12	18 42	18 57	19 12			19 42	20 12	20 42		20 57	21 12	21 42	
Barry Docks	d		15 44	16 14	16 29	16 44		17 00	17 14		17 44	18 14	18 44	19 00	19 14			19 44	20 14	20 44		21 00	21 14	21 44	
Barry 3	d		15 49	16 19	16 34	16 49		17 05	17 19		17 49	18 19	18 49	19 05	19 19			19 49	20 19	20 49		21 05	21 19	21 49	
Barry Island	a		15 55	16 25	16 40	16 55			17 25		17 55	18 25	18 55		19 25			19 55	20 25	20 55			21 26	21 55	
Rhoose Cardiff Int Airport ✈	d							17 12						19 12								21 12			
Llantwit Major	d							17 22						19 22								21 22			
Bridgend	a							17 39						19 41								21 39			

A From Penarth **B** From Barry Island **C** From Penarth to Cardiff Central

When events are being held at the Principality Stadium, services are subject to alteration. Please check times before travelling.

For connections to Cardiff Bay please refer to Table T124

Table T130-F

Sundays

20 May to 9 September

Treherbert, Aberdare, Merthyr, Pontypridd, Rhymney and Coryton - Cardiff, Penarth, Barry, Barry Island and Bridgend

		AW		AW	AW A
Treherbert	d				
Ynyswen	d				
Treorchy	d				
Ton Pentre	d				
Ystrad Rhondda	a				
	d				
Llwynypia	d				
Tonypandy	d				
Dinas Rhondda	d				
Porth	a				
	d				
Trehafod	d				
Merthyr Tydfil	d				21 38
Pentre-bach	d				21 42
Troed Y Rhiw	d				21 45
Merthyr Vale	a				21 48
	d				21 50
Quakers Yard	d				21 55
Aberdare	d	20 54			
Cwmbach	d	20 57			
Fernhill	d	21 00			
Mountain Ash	a	21 03			
	d	21 04			
Penrhiwceiber	d	21 07			
Abercynon	d	21 13			21 59
Pontypridd 3	a	21 22			22 07
	d	21 24			22 09
Trefforest	d	21 27			22 12
Trefforest Estate	d				
Taffs Well	d	21 34			22 20
Radyr 3	a	21 37			22 23
	d	21 37			22 23
Danescourt	d				
Fairwater	d				
Waun-gron Park	d				
Ninian Park	d				
Llandaf	d	21 40			22 26
Cathays	d	21 45			22 31
Rhymney 3	d				
Pontlottyn	d				
Tir-phil	d				
Brithdir	d				
Bargoed	a				
	d				
Gilfach Fargoed	d				
Pengam	d				
Hengoed	d				
Ystrad Mynach	d				
Llanbradach	d				
Energlyn & Churchill Park	d				
Aber	d				
Caerphilly	d				
Lisvane & Thornhill	d				
Llanishen	d				
Heath High Level	d				
Coryton	d				
Whitchurch (Cardiff)	d				
Rhiwbina	d				
Birchgrove	d				
Ty Glas	d				
Heath Low Level	d				
Cardiff Queen Street 3	a	21 49			22 34
	d	21 51			22 36
Cardiff Central 7	a	21 56			22 42
	d	22 25		22 25	
Grangetown	d	22 29		22 29	
Dingle Road	d				
Penarth	a				
Cogan	d	22 33		22 33	
Eastbrook	d	22 35		22 35	
Dinas Powys	d	22 37		22 37	
Cadoxton	d	22 42		22 42	
Barry Docks	d	22 44		22 44	
Barry 3	d	22 49		22 49	
Barry Island	a	22 55		22 55	
Rhoose Cardiff Int Airport ✈	d				
Llantwit Major	d				
Bridgend	a				

A From Barry Island

When events are being held at the Principality Stadium, services are subject to alteration. Please check times before travelling.

For connections to Cardiff Bay please refer to Table T124

Table T130-F

Sundays

16 September to 2 December

Treherbert, Aberdare, Merthyr, Pontypridd, Rhymney and Coryton - Cardiff, Penarth, Barry, Barry Island and Bridgend

		AW A	AW	AW	AW	AW	AW	AW	AW B	AW	AW	AW	AW	AW B	AW C	AW	AW	AW	AW	AW D	AW C	AW	AW
Treherbert	d					08 17						10 12						12 12					
Ynyswen	d					08 19						10 14						12 14					
Treorchy	d					08 21						10 16						12 16					
Ton Pentre	d					08 23						10 18						12 18					
Ystrad Rhondda	a					08 26						10 21						12 21					
	d					08 28						10 23						12 23					
Llwynypia	d					08 30						10 25						12 25					
Tonypandy	d					08 33						10 28						12 28					
Dinas Rhondda	d					08 35						10 30						12 30					
Porth	a					08 38						10 33						12 33					
	d					08 39						10 34						12 34					
Trehafod	d					08 42						10 37						12 37					
Merthyr Tydfil	d								09 38						11 38						13 38		
Pentre-bach	d								09 42						11 42						13 42		
Troed Y Rhiw	d								09 45						11 45						13 45		
Merthyr Vale	a								09 48						11 48						13 48		
	d								09 50						11 50						13 50		
Quakers Yard	d								09 55						11 55						13 55		
Aberdare	d									09 53			10 53						12 53				
Cwmbach	d									09 56			10 56						12 56				
Fernhill	d									10 00			11 00						13 00				
Mountain Ash	a									10 03			11 03						13 03				
	d									10 03			11 03						13 03				
Penrhiwceiber	d									10 07			11 07						13 07				
Abercynon	d								09 59	10 13			11 13		11 59				13 13		13 59		
Pontypridd 3	a					08 47			10 07	10 22		10 42	11 22		12 07			12 42	13 22		14 07		
	d					08 48			10 09	10 24		10 43	11 24		12 09			12 43	13 24		14 09		
Trefforest	d					08 51			10 12	10 27		10 46	11 27		12 12			12 46	13 27		14 12		
Trefforest Estate	d																						
Taffs Well	d					08 58			10 20	10 34		10 53	11 34		12 20			12 53	13 34		14 20		
Radyr 3	a					09 01			10 23	10 37		10 56	11 37		12 23			12 56	13 37		14 23		
	d					09 01			10 23	10 37		10 56	11 37		12 23			12 56	13 37		14 23		
Danescourt	d																						
Fairwater	d																						
Waun-gron Park	d																						
Ninian Park	d																						
Llandaf	d					09 04			10 26	10 40		10 59	11 40		12 26			12 59	13 40		14 26		
Cathays	d					09 09			10 31	10 45		11 04	11 45		12 31			13 04	13 45		14 31		
Rhymney 3	d							09 08			10 09			11 09						13 09			
Pontlottyn	d							09 11			10 12			11 12						13 12			
Tir-phil	d							09 16			10 16			11 17						13 17			
Brithdir	d							09 18			10 19			11 19						13 19			
Bargoed	a							09 22			10 22			11 23						13 23			
	d							09 23			10 23			11 23						13 23			
Gilfach Fargoed	d							09 26			10 25			11 26						13 26			
Pengam	d							09 28			10 28			11 28						13 28			
Hengoed	d							09 32			10 31			11 32						13 32			
Ystrad Mynach	d							09 35			10 35			11 35			12 33			13 35			14 33
Llanbradach	d							09 39			10 39			11 39			12 37			13 39			14 37
Energlyn & Churchill Park	d							09 43			10 43			11 43			12 41			13 43			14 41
Aber	d							09 45			10 45			11 45			12 43			13 45			14 43
Caerphilly	d							09 48			10 48			11 48			12 48			13 48			14 48
Lisvane & Thornhill	d							09 52			10 52			11 52			12 52			13 52			14 52
Llanishen	d							09 54			10 54			11 54			12 54			13 54			14 54
Heath High Level	d							09 57			10 57			11 57			12 57			13 57			14 57
Coryton	d																						
Whitchurch (Cardiff)	d																						
Rhiwbina	d																						
Birchgrove	d																						
Ty Glas	d																						
Heath Low Level	d																						
Cardiff Queen Street 3	a					09 14		10 02	10 34	10 49	11 02	11 07	11 49	12 02	12 34		13 02	13 09	13 49	14 02	14 34		15 02
	d	00 01				09 16		10 04	10 36	10 51	11 04	11 09	11 51	12 04	12 36		13 04	13 09	13 51	14 04	14 36		15 04
Cardiff Central 7	a	00 05				09 18		10 06	10 39	10 54	11 07	11 12	11 54	12 07	12 39		13 07	13 11	13 54	14 07	14 39		15 07
	d		08 25	08 41	09 16	09 25	09 55	10 25	10 41	10 55	11 16	11 25	11 55	12 25	12 41	12 55	13 16	13 25	13 55	14 25	14 41	14 55	15 16
Grangetown	d		08 29	08 45	09 20	09 29	09 59	10 29	10 45	10 59	11 19	11 29	11 59	12 29	12 45	12 59	13 20	13 29	13 59	14 29	14 45	14 59	15 20
Dingle Road	d				09 26						11 24						13 26						15 24
Penarth	a				09 31						11 29						13 32						15 30
Cogan	d		08 33	08 48		09 33	10 03	10 33	10 48	11 03		11 33	12 03	12 33	12 48	13 03		13 33	14 03	14 33	14 48	15 03	
Eastbrook	d		08 35	08 51		09 35	10 05	10 35	10 51	11 05		11 35	12 05	12 35	12 51	13 05		13 35	14 05	14 35	14 51	15 05	
Dinas Powys	d		08 37	08 53		09 37	10 07	10 37	10 53	11 07		11 37	12 07	12 37	12 53	13 07		13 37	14 07	14 37	14 53	15 07	
Cadoxton	d		08 42	08 57		09 42	10 12	10 42	10 57	11 12		11 42	12 12	12 42	12 57	13 12		13 42	14 12	14 42	14 57	15 12	
Barry Docks	d		08 44	09 00		09 44	10 14	10 44	11 00	11 14		11 44	12 14	12 44	13 00	13 14		13 44	14 14	14 44	15 00	15 14	
Barry 3	d		08 49	09 05		09 49	10 19	10 49	11 05	11 19		11 49	12 19	12 49	13 05	13 19		13 49	14 19	14 49	15 05	15 19	
Barry Island	a		08 56			09 56	10 26	10 56		11 26		11 56	12 26	12 56		13 26		13 56	14 26	14 56		15 26	
Rhoose Cardiff Int Airport ✈	d			09 12					11 12						13 12						15 12		
Llantwit Major	d			09 22					11 22						13 22						15 22		
Bridgend	a			09 37					11 40						13 40						15 40		

A From Cardiff Bay
B From Cardiff Central
C From Barry Island
D From Barry Island to Aberdare

When events are being held at the Principality Stadium, services are subject to alteration. Please check times before travelling.

For connections to Cardiff Bay please refer to Table T124

Table T130-F

Sundays

16 September to 2 December

Treherbert, Aberdare, Merthyr, Pontypridd, Rhymney and Coryton - Cardiff, Penarth, Barry, Barry Island and Bridgend

		AW	AW	AW A	AW A	AW	AW	AW	AW	AW A	AW A		AW	AW	AW	AW A	AW	AW	AW	AW	AW	AW	AW
Treherbert	d	14 17						16 17						18 17						20 17			
Ynyswen	d	14 19						16 19						18 19						20 19			
Treorchy	d	14 21						16 21						18 21						20 21			
Ton Pentre	d	14 23						16 23						18 23						20 23			
Ystrad Rhondda	a	14 26						16 26						18 26						20 26			
	d	14 28						16 28						18 28						20 28			
Llwynypia	d	14 30						16 30						18 30						20 30			
Tonypandy	d	14 33						16 33						18 33						20 33			
Dinas Rhondda	d	14 35						16 35						18 35						20 35			
Porth	a	14 38						16 38						18 38						20 38			
	d	14 39						16 39						18 39						20 39			
Trehafod	d	14 42						16 42						18 42						20 42			
Merthyr Tydfil	d				15 38						17 38							19 38					
Pentre-bach	d				15 42						17 42							19 42					
Troed Y Rhiw	d				15 45						17 45							19 45					
Merthyr Vale	a				15 48						17 48							19 48					
	d				15 50						17 50							19 50					
Quakers Yard	d				15 55						17 55							19 55					
Aberdare	d		14 53						16 53						18 53						20 53	20 53	
Cwmbach	d		14 56						16 56						18 56						20 56	20 56	
Fernhill	d		15 00						17 00						19 00						21 00	21 00	
Mountain Ash	a		15 03						17 03						19 03						21 03	21 03	
	d		15 03						17 03						19 03						21 03	21 03	
Penrhiwceiber	d		15 07						17 07						19 07						21 07	21 07	
Abercynon	d		15 13		15 59				17 13		17 59				19 13			19 59			21 13	21 13	
Pontypridd 3	a	14 47	15 22		16 07			16 47	17 22		18 07			18 47	19 22			20 07		20 47	21 22	21 22	
	d	14 48	15 24		16 09			16 48	17 24		18 09			18 48	19 24			20 09		20 48	21 24	21 24	
Trefforest	d	14 51	15 27		16 12			16 51	17 27		18 12			18 51	19 27			20 12		20 51	21 27	21 27	
Trefforest Estate	d																						
Taffs Well	d	14 58	15 34		16 20			16 58	17 34		18 20			18 58	19 34			20 20		20 58	21 34	21 34	
Radyr 3	a	15 01	15 37		16 23			17 01	17 37		18 23			19 01	19 37			20 23		21 01	21 37	21 37	
	d	15 01	15 37		16 23			17 01	17 37		18 23			19 01	19 37			20 23		21 01	21 37	21 37	
Danescourt	d																						
Fairwater	d																						
Waun-gron Park	d																						
Ninian Park	d																						
Llandaf	d	15 04	15 40		16 26			17 04	17 40		18 26			19 04	19 40			20 26		21 04	21 40	21 40	
Cathays	d	15 09	15 45		16 31			17 09	17 45		18 31			19 09	19 45			20 31		21 09	21 45	21 45	
Rhymney 3	d			15 20						17 20						19 20							
Pontlottyn	d			15 23						17 23						19 23							
Tir-phil	d			15 28						17 28						19 28							
Brithdir	d			15 30						17 30						19 30							
Bargoed	a			15 34						17 34						19 34							
	d			15 35						17 35						19 35							
Gilfach Fargoed	d			15 38						17 38						19 38							
Pengam	d			15 40						17 40						19 40							
Hengoed	d			15 44						17 44						19 44							
Ystrad Mynach	d			15 47			16 33			17 47			18 33			19 47							
Llanbradach	d			15 51			16 37			17 51			18 37			19 51							
Energlyn & Churchill Park	d			15 55			16 41			17 55			18 41			19 55							
Aber	d			15 57			16 43			17 57			18 43			19 57							
Caerphilly	d			16 00			16 48			18 00			18 48			20 00							
Lisvane & Thornhill	d			16 04			16 52			18 04			18 52			20 04							
Llanishen	d			16 06			16 54			18 06			18 54			20 06							
Heath High Level	d			16 09			16 57			18 09			18 57			20 09							
Coryton	d																						
Whitchurch (Cardiff)	d																						
Rhiwbina	d																						
Birchgrove	d																						
Ty Glas	d																						
Heath Low Level	d																						
Cardiff Queen Street 3	a	15 14	15 49	16 14	16 34		17 02	17 14	17 49	18 14	18 34		19 02	19 14	19 49	20 14		20 34		21 14	21 49	21 49	
	d	15 16	15 51	16 16	16 36		17 04	17 16	17 51	18 16	18 36		19 04	19 16	19 51	20 16		20 36		21 16	21 51	21 51	
Cardiff Central 7	a	15 18	15 54	16 18	16 39		17 07	17 18	17 54	18 18	18 39		19 07	19 18	19 54	20 18		20 39		21 18	21 57	21 57	
	d	15 25	15 55	16 25	16 41	16 55	17 16	17 25	17 55	18 25	18 41	18 55	19 16	19 25	19 55	20 25	20 31	20 41	20 55	21 25		22 25	22 25
Grangetown	d	15 29	15 59	16 29	16 45	16 59	17 20	17 29	17 59	18 29	18 45	18 59	19 20	19 29	19 59	20 29	20 35	20 45	20 59	21 29		22 29	22 29
Dingle Road	d						17 24						19 24				20 41						
Penarth	a						17 30						19 30				20 47						
Cogan	d	15 33	16 03	16 33	16 48	17 03		17 33	18 03	18 33	18 48	19 03		19 33	20 03	20 33		20 48	21 03	21 33		22 33	22 33
Eastbrook	d	15 35	16 05	16 35	16 51	17 05		17 35	18 05	18 35	18 51	19 05		19 35	20 05	20 35		20 51	21 05	21 35		22 35	22 35
Dinas Powys	d	15 37	16 07	16 37	16 53	17 07		17 37	18 07	18 37	18 53	19 07		19 37	20 07	20 37		20 53	21 07	21 37		22 37	22 37
Cadoxton	d	15 42	16 12	16 42	16 57	17 12		17 42	18 12	18 42	18 57	19 12		19 42	20 12	20 42		20 57	21 12	21 42		22 42	22 42
Barry Docks	d	15 44	16 14	16 44	17 00	17 14		17 44	18 14	18 44	19 00	19 14		19 44	20 14	20 44		21 00	21 14	21 44		22 44	22 44
Barry 3	d	15 49	16 19	16 49	17 05	17 19		17 49	18 19	18 49	19 05	19 19		19 49	20 19	20 49		21 05	21 19	21 49		22 49	22 49
Barry Island	a	15 56	16 26	16 56		17 26		17 56	18 26	18 56		19 26		19 56	20 26	20 56			21 26	21 56		22 56	22 56
Rhoose Cardiff Int Airport ✈	d				17 12						19 12							21 12					
Llantwit Major	d				17 22						19 22							21 22					
Bridgend	a				17 40						19 41							21 40					

A From Barry Island

When events are being held at the Principality Stadium, services are subject to alteration. Please check times before travelling.

For connections to Cardiff Bay please refer to Table T124

Table T130-F

Sundays

16 September to 2 December

Treherbert, Aberdare, Merthyr, Pontypridd, Rhymney and Coryton - Cardiff, Penarth, Barry, Barry Island and Bridgend

		AW A
Treherbert	d	
Ynyswen	d	
Treorchy	d	
Ton Pentre	d	
Ystrad Rhondda	a	
	d	
Llwynypia	d	
Tonypandy	d	
Dinas Rhondda	d	
Porth	a	
	d	
Trehafod	d	
Merthyr Tydfil	d	21 38
Pentre-bach	d	21 42
Troed Y Rhiw	d	21 45
Merthyr Vale	a	21 48
	d	21 50
Quakers Yard	d	21 55
Aberdare	d	
Cwmbach	d	
Fernhill	d	
Mountain Ash	a	
	d	
Penrhiwceiber	d	
Abercynon	d	21 59
Pontypridd 3	a	22 07
	d	22 09
Trefforest	d	22 12
Trefforest Estate	d	
Taffs Well	d	22 20
Radyr 3	a	22 23
	d	22 23
Danescourt	d	
Fairwater	d	
Waun-gron Park	d	
Ninian Park	d	
Llandaf	d	22 26
Cathays	d	22 31
Rhymney 3	d	
Pontlottyn	d	
Tir-phil	d	
Brithdir	d	
Bargoed	a	
	d	
Gilfach Fargoed	d	
Pengam	d	
Hengoed	d	
Ystrad Mynach	d	
Llanbradach	d	
Energlyn & Churchill Park	d	
Aber	d	
Caerphilly	d	
Lisvane & Thornhill	d	
Llanishen	d	
Heath High Level	d	
Coryton	d	
Whitchurch (Cardiff)	d	
Rhiwbina	d	
Birchgrove	d	
Ty Glas	d	
Heath Low Level	d	
Cardiff Queen Street 3	a	22 34
	d	22 36
Cardiff Central 7	a	22 42
	d	
Grangetown	d	
Dingle Road	d	
Penarth	a	
Cogan	d	
Eastbrook	d	
Dinas Powys	d	
Cadoxton	d	
Barry Docks	d	
Barry 3	d	
Barry Island	a	
Rhoose Cardiff Int Airport ✈	d	
Llantwit Major	d	
Bridgend	a	

A From Barry Island

When events are being held at the Principality Stadium, services are subject to alteration. Please check times before travelling.

For connections to Cardiff Bay please refer to Table T124

Table T130-R

Mondays to Fridays

21 May to 7 September

Bridgend, Barry Island, Barry, Penarth and Cardiff - Coryton, Rhymney, Pontypridd, Merthyr, Aberdare and Treherbert

Miles	Miles	Miles	Miles	Miles			AW	AW	AW	AW	AW	AW	AW	AW	AW		AW	AW	AW	AW	AW	AW	AW	AW	AW
—	—	0	—	—	**Bridgend**	d												05 42							
—	—	9¼	—	—	Llantwit Major	d												05 56							
—	—	15¾	—	—	Rhoose Cardiff Int Airport ✈	d												06 06							
0	—	—	—	—	**Barry Island**	d		05 14					05 50							06 25					
0¾	—	19	—	—	**Barry** 3	d		05 19					05 55					06 15		06 30					
2	—	—	—	—	Barry Docks	d		05 22					05 58					06 18		06 33					
2¾	—	—	—	—	Cadoxton	d		05 25					06 01					06 21		06 36					
4¾	—	—	—	—	Dinas Powys	d		05 29					06 05					06 25		06 40					
5¾	—	—	—	—	Eastbrook	d		05 32					06 08					06 28		06 43					
6½	—	—	—	—	Cogan	d		05 34					06 10					06 30		06 45					
—	0	—	—	—	**Penarth**	d																		07 02	
—	0¾	—	—	—	Dingle Road	d																		07 04	
8¼	2¾	—	—	—	Grangetown	d		05 38					06 14					06 34		06 49				07 08	
9¼	3¾	—	0	—	**Cardiff Central** 7	a		05 43					06 19					06 39		06 54				07 14	
—	—	—	—	—		d	05 26	05 46	05 51		05 56	06 11	06 21	06 26	06 31		06 36	06 41	06 51	06 56	07 05	07 06	07 11	07 16	07 21
9¾	4¼	0½	—	—	**Cardiff Queen Street** 3	a	05 29	05 49	05 55		05 59	06 14	06 24	06 29	06 34		06 39	06 44	06 54	06 59	07 08		07 14	07 19	07 24
—	—	—	—	—		d	05 30	05 50	05 55		06 00	06 15	06 25	06 30	06 35		06 40	06 45	06 55	07 00	07 09		07 15	07 20	07 25
—	—	3	—	—	Heath Low Level	d			06 00				06 30						07 00						07 30
—	4½	—	—	—	Ty Glas	d			06 03				06 33						07 03						07 33
—	—	4¼	—	—	Birchgrove	d			06 04				06 34						07 04						07 34
—	—	4¾	—	—	Rhiwbina	d			06 06				06 36						07 06						07 36
—	—	5	—	—	Whitchurch (Cardiff)	d			06 08				06 38						07 08						07 38
—	—	5½	—	—	**Coryton**	a			06 12				06 43						07 13						07 43
—	6¾	—	—	—	Heath High Level	d		05 55																07 25	
—	7¾	—	—	—	Llanishen	d		05 58																07 28	
—	8¾	—	—	—	Lisvane & Thornhill	d		06 00																07 30	
—	11¼	—	—	—	Caerphilly	d		06a08																07 36	
—	12	—	—	—	Aber	d																		07 38	
—	12¾	—	—	—	Energlyn & Churchill Park	d																		07 40	
—	14	—	—	—	Llanbradach	d																		07 44	
—	16¾	—	—	—	Ystrad Mynach	d																		07 49	
—	17¾	—	—	—	Hengoed	d																		07 52	
—	19½	—	—	—	Pengam	d																		07 55	
—	20½	—	—	—	Gilfach Fargoed	d																			
—	21	—	—	—	Bargoed	a																		08 04	
—	—	—	—	—		d																			
—	22½	—	—	—	Brithdir	d																			
—	23½	—	—	—	Tir-phil	d																			
—	26	—	—	—	Pontlottyn	d																			
—	27	—	—	—	**Rhymney** 3	a																			
10½	—	—	—	—	Cathays	d	05 33				06 03	06 18		06 33	06 37		06 43	06 48		07 03	07 12		07 18		
13	—	—	—	—	Llandaf	d	05 37				06 07	06 22		06 37			06 47	06 52		07 07	07 16		07 22		
—	—	—	1	—	Ninian Park	d							07 10						07 40			07 10			
—	—	—	2½	—	Waun-gron Park	d							07 13						07 43			07 13			
—	—	—	2¾	—	Fairwater	d							07 15						07 45			07 15			
—	—	—	3¼	—	Danescourt	d							07 17						07 47			07 17			
14	—	—	4¾	—	Radyr 3	a	05 40				06 10	06 25	07 24	06 40	06 43		06 50	06 55	07 54	07 10	07 19	07 24	07 25		
—	—	—	—	—		d	05 41				06 11	06 25		06 41	06 43		06 51	06 55		07 11	07 20		07 26		
16	—	—	—	—	Taffs Well	d	05 45				06 15	06 29		06 45	06a50		06 55	06 59		07 15	07 24		07 30		
18¼	—	—	—	—	Trefforest Estate	d	05 49				06 19			06 49						07 19					
20¼	—	—	—	—	Trefforest	d	05 53				06 23	06 36		06 53			07 02	07 06		07 23	07 31		07 37		
21¾	—	0	—	0	**Pontypridd** 3	a	05 56				06 26	06 39		06 56			07 05	07 09		07 26	07 34		07 40		
—	—	—	—	—		d	05 58			06 11	06 27	06 42		06 57			07 06	07 12		07 27	07 35		07 42		
—	—	3¼	—	3¼	Abercynon	d	06 05			06 19	06 34	06 49		07 04				07 19		07 34			07 49		
—	—	—	—	6	Penrhiwceiber	d				06 24		06 54						07 24					07 54		
—	—	—	—	7¼	Mountain Ash	a				06 28		06 58						07 28					07 58		
—	—	—	—	—		d				06 33		07 03						07 33					08 03		
—	—	—	—	8¼	Fernhill	d				06 35		07 05						07 35					08 05		
—	—	—	—	9½	Cwmbach	d				06 39		07 09						07 39					08 09		
—	—	—	—	11	**Aberdare**	a				06 46		07 16						07 46					08 16		
—	—	4¾	—	—	Quakers Yard	d	06 09				06 39			07 09						07 39					
—	—	7	—	—	Merthyr Vale	a	06 14				06 44			07 14						07 44					
—	—	—	—	—		d	06 17				06 47			07 17						07 47					
—	—	8¾	—	—	Troed Y Rhiw	d	06 20				06 50			07 20						07 50					
—	—	10	—	—	Pentre-bach	d	06 23				06 53			07 23						07 53					
—	—	11½	—	—	**Merthyr Tydfil**	a	06 31				07 01			07 31						08 01					
23½	—	—	—	—	Trehafod	d											07 11				07 40				
24¾	—	—	—	—	Porth	a											07 14				07 43				
—	—	—	—	—		d											07 15				07 44				
26¼	—	—	—	—	Dinas Rhondda	d											07 19				07 48				
26¾	—	—	—	—	Tonypandy	d											07 21				07 50				
27¾	—	—	—	—	Llwynypia	d											07 23				07 52				
29	—	—	—	—	Ystrad Rhondda	a											07 26				07 55				
—	—	—	—	—		d											07 29				07 59				
29½	—	—	—	—	Ton Pentre	d											07 31				08 02				
30¾	—	—	—	—	Treorchy	d											07 34				08 06				
31¾	—	—	—	—	Ynyswen	d											07 37				08 09				
32¼	—	—	—	—	**Treherbert**	a											07 43				08 12				

When events are being held at the Principality Stadium, services are subject to alteration. Please check times before travelling.

For connections to Cardiff Bay please refer to Table T124

Table T130-R

Mondays to Fridays

21 May to 7 September

Bridgend, Barry Island, Barry, Penarth and Cardiff - Coryton, Rhymney, Pontypridd, Merthyr, Aberdare and Treherbert

		AW	AW	AW	AW	AW	AW	AW	AW	AW	AW	AW	AW	AW	AW	AW	AW	AW	AW	AW	AW	AW
Bridgend	d						06 42										07 20				07 42	
Llantwit Major	d						06 56														07 56	
Rhoose Cardiff Int Airport ✈	d						07 06														08 06	
Barry Island	d		06 55						07 25				07 40			07 55						
Barry 3	d		07 00				07 15		07 30				07 45			08 00	08a11			08 13	08 21	
Barry Docks	d		07 03				07 18		07 33				07 48			08 03				08 16	08 24	
Cadoxton	d		07 06				07 21		07 36				07 51			08 06				08 19	08 27	
Dinas Powys	d		07 10				07 25		07 40				07 55			08 10				08 23		
Eastbrook	d		07 13				07 28		07 43				07 58			08 13				08 26		
Cogan	d		07 15				07 30		07 45				08 00			08 15				08 29		
Penarth	d			07 17										08 02								08 32
Dingle Road	d			07 19										08 04								08 34
Grangetown	d		07 19	07 23			07 34		07 49				08 04	08 08		08 19						08 38
Cardiff Central 7	a		07 24	07 29			07 39		07 54				08 09	08 14		08 24				08 40	08 39	08 44
	d	07 21	07 26	07 31	07 35	07 36	07 41	07 51	07 56	07 57	08 05	08 06	08 11	08 16	08 21	08 26		08 35	08 36		08 41	08 46
Cardiff Queen Street 3	a	07 24	07 29	07 34	07 38		07 44	07 54	07 59		08 08		08 14	08 19	08 24	08 29		08 38			08 44	08 49
	d	07 25	07 30	07 35	07 39		07 45	07 55	08 00		08 09		08 15	08 20	08 25	08 30		08 39			08 45	08 50
Heath Low Level	d	07 30						08 00							08 30							
Ty Glas	d	07 33						08 03							08 33							
Birchgrove	d	07 34						08 04							08 34							
Rhiwbina	d	07 36						08 06							08 36							
Whitchurch (Cardiff)	d	07 38						08 08							08 38							
Coryton	a	07 43						08 13							08 43							
Heath High Level	d			07 40										08 25								08 55
Llanishen	d			07 43										08 28								08 58
Lisvane & Thornhill	d			07 45										08 30								09 00
Caerphilly	d			07 51										08 36								09 06
Aber	d			07 53										08 38								09 08
Energlyn & Churchill Park	d													08 40								
Llanbradach	d			07 57										08 44								09 12
Ystrad Mynach	d			08 02										08 49								09 17
Hengoed	d			08 05										08 52								09 20
Pengam	d			08 08										08 55								09 23
Gilfach Fargoed	d																					
Bargoed	a			08 13										09 00								09 31
	d			08 14										09 01								
Brithdir	d			08 18										09 05								
Tir-phil	d			08 21										09 08								
Pontlottyn	d			08 25										09 12								
Rhymney 3	a			08 31										09 18								
Cathays	d		07 33		07 42		07 48		08 03		08 12		08 18			08 33		08 42			08 48	
Llandaf	d		07 37		07 46		07 52		08 08		08 16		08 22			08 37		08 46			08 52	
Ninian Park	d	08 10				07 40		08 40				08 10			09 10				08 40			
Waun-gron Park	d	08 13				07 43		08 43				08 13			09 13				08 43			
Fairwater	d	08 15				07 45		08 45				08 15			09 15				08 45			
Danescourt	d	08 17				07 47		08 47				08 17			09 17				08 47			
Radyr 3	a	08 26	07 40		07 49	07 54	07 55	08 54	08 10	08 10	08 19	08 26	08 25		09 24	08 40		08 49	08 54		08 55	
	d		07 41		07 50		07 56		08 11		08 20		08 26			08 41		08 50			08 56	
Taffs Well	d		07 45		07 54		08 00		08 15		08 24		08 30			08 45		08 54			09 00	
Trefforest Estate	d		07 49						08 19							08 49						
Trefforest	d		07 53		08 01		08 07		08 23		08 31		08 37			08 53		09 01			09 07	
Pontypridd 3	a		07 56		08 04		08 10		08 26		08 34		08 40			08 56		09 04			09 10	
	d		07 57		08 05		08 12		08 27		08 35		08 42			08 57		09 05			09 12	
Abercynon	d		08 04				08 19		08 34				08 49			09 04					09 19	
Penrhiwceiber	d						08 24						08 54								09 24	
Mountain Ash	a						08 28						08 58								09 28	
	d						08 33						09 03								09 33	
Fernhill	d						08 35						09 05								09 35	
Cwmbach	d						08 39						09 09								09 39	
Aberdare	a						08 46						09 16								09 46	
Quakers Yard	d		08 09						08 39							09 09						
Merthyr Vale	a		08 14						08 44							09 14						
	d		08 17						08 47							09 17						
Troed Y Rhiw	d		08 20						08 50							09 20						
Pentre-bach	d		08 23						08 53							09 23						
Merthyr Tydfil	a		08 31						09 01							09 31						
Trehafod	d				08 10						08 40							09 10				
Porth	a				08 13						08 43							09 13				
	d				08 14						08 44							09 14				
Dinas Rhondda	d				08 18						08 48							09 18				
Tonypandy	d				08 20						08 50							09 20				
Llwynypia	d				08 22						08 52							09 22				
Ystrad Rhondda	a				08 25						08 55							09 25				
	d				08 29						08 59							09 29				
Ton Pentre	d				08 31						09 01							09 31				
Treorchy	d				08 34						09 04							09 34				
Ynyswen	d				08 37						09 07							09 37				
Treherbert	a				08 42						09 12							09 42				

When events are being held at the Principality Stadium, services are subject to alteration. Please check times before travelling.

For connections to Cardiff Bay please refer to Table T124

Table T130-R

Mondays to Fridays

21 May to 7 September

Bridgend, Barry Island, Barry, Penarth and Cardiff - Coryton, Rhymney, Pontypridd, Merthyr, Aberdare and Treherbert

		AW	AW	AW	AW	AW	AW	AW	AW	AW	AW	AW	AW	AW	AW	AW	AW	AW	AW	AW	AW	AW	AW
Bridgend	d										08 42												
Llantwit Major	d										08 56												
Rhoose Cardiff Int Airport ✈	d										09 06												
Barry Island	d		08 25		08 40			08 55						09 25				09 40			09 55		
Barry 3	d		08 30		08 45			09 00			09 15			09 30				09 45			10 00		
Barry Docks	d		08 33		08 48			09 03			09 18			09 33				09 48			10 03		
Cadoxton	d		08 36		08 51			09 06			09 21			09 36				09 51			10 06		
Dinas Powys	d		08 40		08 55			09 10			09 25			09 40				09 55			10 10		
Eastbrook	d		08 43		08 58			09 13			09 28			09 43				09 58			10 13		
Cogan	d		08 45		09 00			09 15			09 30			09 45				10 00			10 15		
Penarth	d											09 32							10 02			10 17	
Dingle Road	d											09 34							10 04			10 19	
Grangetown	d		08 49		09 04			09 19			09 34	09 38		09 49				10 04	10 08		10 19	10 23	
Cardiff Central 7	a		08 54		09 09			09 24			09 39	09 44		09 54				10 09	10 14		10 24	10 29	
	d	08 51	08 56	09 05	09 11	09 16	09 21	09 26	09 35	09 36	09 41	09 46	09 51	09 56		10 05	10 06	10 11	10 16	10 21	10 26	10 31	10 35
Cardiff Queen Street 3	a	08 54	08 59	09 08	09 14	09 19	09 24	09 29	09 38		09 44	09 49	09 54	09 59		10 08		10 14	10 19	10 24	10 29	10 34	10 38
	d	08 55	09 00	09 09	09 15	09 20	09 25	09 30	09 39		09 45	09 50	09 55	10 00		10 09		10 15	10 20	10 25	10 30	10 35	10 39
Heath Low Level	d	09 00					09 30						10 00							10 30			
Ty Glas	d	09 03					09 33						10 03							10 33			
Birchgrove	d	09 04					09 34						10 04							10 34			
Rhiwbina	d	09 06					09 36						10 06							10 36			
Whitchurch (Cardiff)	d	09 08					09 38						10 08							10 38			
Coryton	a	09 13					09 43						10 13							10 43			
Heath High Level	d					09 25						09 55							10 25			10 40	
Llanishen	d					09 28						09 58							10 28			10 43	
Lisvane & Thornhill	d					09 30						10 00							10 30			10 45	
Caerphilly	d					09 36						10 06							10 36			10 51	
Aber	d					09 38						10 08							10 38			10 53	
Energlyn & Churchill Park	d					09 40													10 40				
Llanbradach	d					09 44						10 12							10 44			10 57	
Ystrad Mynach	d					09 49						10 17							10 49			11 02	
Hengoed	d					09 52						10 20							10 52			11 05	
Pengam	d					09 55						10 23							10 55			11 08	
Gilfach Fargoed	d																						
Bargoed	a					10 00						10 31							11 00			11 16	
	d					10 01													11 01				
Brithdir	d					10 05													11 05				
Tir-phil	d					10 08													11 08				
Pontlottyn	d					10 12													11 12				
Rhymney 3	a					10 18													11 18				
Cathays	d		09 03	09 12	09 18			09 33	09 42		09 48			10 03		10 12		10 18			10 33		10 42
Llandaf	d		09 07	09 16	09 22			09 37	09 46		09 52			10 07		10 16		10 22			10 37		10 46
Ninian Park	d	09 40					10 10			09 40			10 40				10 10			11 10			
Waun-gron Park	d	09 43					10 13			09 43			10 43				10 13			11 13			
Fairwater	d	09 45					10 15			09 45			10 45				10 15			11 15			
Danescourt	d	09 47					10 17			09 47			10 47				10 17			11 17			
Radyr 3	a	09 54	09 10	09 19	09 25		10 24	09 40	09 49	09 54	09 55		10 54	10 10		10 19	10 24	10 25		11 24	10 40		10 49
	d		09 11	09 20	09 26			09 41	09 50		09 56			10 11		10 20		10 26			10 41		10 50
Taffs Well	d		09 15	09 24	09 30			09 45	09 54		10 00			10 15		10 24		10 30			10 45		10 54
Trefforest Estate	d		09 19					09 49													10 49		
Trefforest	d		09 23	09 31	09 37			09 53	10 01		10 07			10 22		10 31		10 37			10 53		11 01
Pontypridd 3	a		09 26	09 34	09 40			09 56	10 04		10 10			10 31		10 34		10 40			10 56		11 04
	d		09 27	09 35	09 42			09 57	10 05		10 12				10 34	10 35		10 42			10 57		11 05
Abercynon	d		09 34		09 49			10 04			10 19				10 40			10 49			11 04		
Penrhiwceiber	d				09 54						10 24							10 54					
Mountain Ash	a				09 58						10 28							10 58					
	d				10 03						10 33							11 03					
Fernhill	d				10 05						10 35							11 05					
Cwmbach	d				10 09						10 39							11 09					
Aberdare	a				10 16						10 46							11 16					
Quakers Yard	d		09 39					10 09							10 44						11 09		
Merthyr Vale	a		09 44					10 14							10 49						11 14		
	d		09 47					10 17							10 52						11 17		
Troed Y Rhiw	d		09 50					10 20							10 55						11 20		
Pentre-bach	d		09 53					10 23							10 58						11 23		
Merthyr Tydfil	a		10 01					10 31							11 06						11 31		
Trehafod	d			09 40					10 10							10 40							11 10
Porth	a			09 43					10 13							10 43							11 13
	d			09 44					10 14							10 44							11 14
Dinas Rhondda	d			09 48					10 18							10 48							11 18
Tonypandy	d			09 50					10 20							10 50							11 20
Llwynypia	d			09 52					10 22							10 52							11 22
Ystrad Rhondda	a			09 55					10 25							10 55							11 25
	d			09 59					10 29							10 59							11 29
Ton Pentre	d			10 01					10 31							11 01							11 31
Treorchy	d			10 04					10 34							11 04							11 34
Ynyswen	d			10 07					10 37							11 07							11 37
Treherbert	a			10 12					10 42							11 12							11 42

When events are being held at the Principality Stadium, services are subject to alteration. Please check times before travelling.

For connections to Cardiff Bay please refer to Table T124

Table T130-R

Mondays to Fridays

21 May to 7 September

Bridgend, Barry Island, Barry, Penarth and Cardiff - Coryton, Rhymney, Pontypridd, Merthyr, Aberdare and Treherbert

		AW	AW	AW	AW	AW	AW	AW	AW	AW	AW	AW	AW	AW	AW	AW	AW	AW	AW	AW	AW	AW
Bridgend	d		09 45														10 45					
Llantwit Major	d		09 58														10 58					
Rhoose Cardiff Int Airport ✈	d		10 08														11 08					
Barry Island	d						10 25			10 40			10 55							11 25		
Barry 3	d		10 16				10 30			10 45			11 00				11 16			11 30		
Barry Docks	d		10 19				10 33			10 48			11 03				11 19			11 33		
Cadoxton	d		10 22				10 36			10 51			11 06				11 22			11 36		
Dinas Powys	d		10 26				10 40			10 55			11 10				11 26			11 40		
Eastbrook	d		10 28				10 43			10 58			11 13				11 28			11 43		
Cogan	d		10 30				10 45			11 00			11 15				11 30			11 45		
Penarth	d			10 32							11 02			11 17				11 32				
Dingle Road	d			10 34							11 04			11 19				11 34				
Grangetown	d		10 34	10 38			10 49			11 04	11 08		11 19	11 23			11 34	11 38		11 49		
Cardiff Central 7	a		10 41	10 44			10 54			11 09	11 14		11 24	11 29			11 39	11 44		11 54		
	d	10 36		10 46	10 51	10 55	10 56		11 06	11 11	11 16	11 21	11 26	11 31	11 35	11 36	11 41	11 46	11 51	11 56	12 05	12 06
Cardiff Queen Street 3	a			10 49	10 54		10 59			11 14	11 19	11 24	11 29	11 34	11 38		11 44	11 49	11 54	11 59	12 08	
	d			10 50	10 55		11 00			11 15	11 20	11 25	11 30	11 35	11 39		11 45	11 50	11 55	12 00	12 09	
Heath Low Level	d				11 00							11 30							12 00			
Ty Glas	d				11 03							11 33							12 03			
Birchgrove	d				11 04							11 34							12 04			
Rhiwbina	d				11 06							11 36							12 06			
Whitchurch (Cardiff)	d				11 08							11 38							12 08			
Coryton	a				11 13							11 43							12 13			
Heath High Level	d			10 55							11 25			11 40				11 55				
Llanishen	d			10 58							11 28			11 43				11 58				
Lisvane & Thornhill	d			11 00							11 30			11 45				12 00				
Caerphilly	d			11 06							11 36			11 51				12 06				
Aber	d			11 08							11 38			11 53				12 08				
Energlyn & Churchill Park	d										11 40											
Llanbradach	d			11 12							11 44			11 57				12 12				
Ystrad Mynach	d			11 17							11 49			12 02				12 17				
Hengoed	d			11 20							11 52			12 05				12 20				
Pengam	d			11 23							11 55			12 08				12 23				
Gilfach Fargoed	d																					
Bargoed	a			11 31							12 00			12 16				12 31				
	d										12 01											
Brithdir	d										12 05											
Tir-phil	d										12 08											
Pontlottyn	d										12 12											
Rhymney 3	a										12 18											
Cathays	d						11 03			11 18			11 33		11 42		11 48			12 03	12 12	
Llandaf	d						11 07			11 22			11 37		11 46		11 52			12 07	12 16	
Ninian Park	d	10 40			11 40				11 10			12 10				11 40			12 40			12 10
Waun-gron Park	d	10 43			11 43				11 13			12 13				11 43			12 43			12 13
Fairwater	d	10 45			11 45				11 15			12 15				11 45			12 45			12 15
Danescourt	d	10 47			11 47			←	11 17			12 17				11 47			12 47			12 17
Radyr 3	a	10 54			11 54	11 03	11 10	11 03	11 24	11 25		12 24	11 40		11 49	11 54	11 55		12 54	12 10	12 19	12 24
	d					11 20	11 11	11 20		11 26			11 41		11 50		11 56			12 11	12 20	
Taffs Well	d					→	11 15	11 24		11 30			11 45		11 54		12 00			12 15	12 24	
Trefforest Estate	d						11 19						11 49							12 19		
Trefforest	d						11 23	11 31		11 37			11 53		12 01		12 07			12 23	12 31	
Pontypridd 3	a						11 26	11 34		11 40			11 56		12 04		12 10			12 26	12 34	
	d						11 27	11 36		11 42			11 57		12 05		12 12			12 27	12 35	
Abercynon	d						11 34			11 49			12 04				12 19			12 34		
Penrhiwceiber	d									11 54							12 24					
Mountain Ash	a									11 58							12 28					
	d									12 03							12 33					
Fernhill	d									12 05							12 35					
Cwmbach	d									12 09							12 39					
Aberdare	a									12 16							12 46					
Quakers Yard	d						11 39						12 09							12 39		
Merthyr Vale	a						11 44						12 14							12 44		
	d						11 47						12 17							12 47		
Troed Y Rhiw	d						11 50						12 20							12 50		
Pentre-bach	d						11 53						12 23							12 53		
Merthyr Tydfil	a						12 01						12 31							13 01		
Trehafod	d							11 41							12 10						12 40	
Porth	a							11 44							12 13						12 43	
	d							11 45							12 14						12 44	
Dinas Rhondda	d							11 49							12 18						12 48	
Tonypandy	d							11 51							12 20						12 50	
Llwynypia	d							11 53							12 22						12 52	
Ystrad Rhondda	a							11 56							12 25						12 55	
	d							11 59							12 29						12 59	
Ton Pentre	d							12 01							12 31						13 01	
Treorchy	d							12 04							12 34						13 04	
Ynyswen	d							12 07							12 37						13 07	
Treherbert	a							12 13							12 42						13 12	

When events are being held at the Principality Stadium, services are subject to alteration. Please check times before travelling.

For connections to Cardiff Bay please refer to Table T124

Table T130-R

Mondays to Fridays

21 May to 7 September

Bridgend, Barry Island, Barry, Penarth and Cardiff - Coryton, Rhymney, Pontypridd, Merthyr, Aberdare and Treherbert

		AW	AW	AW	AW	AW	AW	AW	AW	AW	AW	AW	AW	AW	AW	AW	AW	AW	AW	AW	AW	AW	AW
Bridgend	d								11 42														12 42
Llantwit Major	d								11 56														12 56
Rhoose Cardiff Int Airport ✈	d								12 06														13 06
Barry Island	d	11 40			11 55								12 25			12 40			12 55				
Barry 3	d	11 45			12 00				12 15				12 30			12 45			13 00				13 15
Barry Docks	d	11 48			12 03				12 18				12 33			12 48			13 03				13 18
Cadoxton	d	11 51			12 06				12 21				12 36			12 51			13 06				13 21
Dinas Powys	d	11 55			12 10				12 25				12 40			12 55			13 10				13 25
Eastbrook	d	11 58			12 13				12 28				12 43			12 58			13 13				13 28
Cogan	d	12 00			12 15				12 30				12 45			13 00			13 15				13 30
Penarth	d		12 02			12 17					12 32						13 02			13 17			
Dingle Road	d		12 04			12 19					12 34						13 04			13 19			
Grangetown	d	12 04	12 08		12 19	12 23			12 34		12 38		12 49			13 04	13 08		13 19	13 23			13 34
Cardiff Central 7	a	12 09	12 14		12 24	12 29			12 40		12 44		12 54			13 09	13 14		13 24	13 29			13 39
	d	12 11	12 16	12 21	12 26	12 31	12 35	12 36		12 41	12 46	12 51	12 56	13 05	13 06	13 11	13 16	13 21	13 26	13 31	13 35	13 36	13 41
Cardiff Queen Street 3	a	12 14	12 19	12 24	12 29	12 34	12 38			12 44	12 49	12 54	12 59	13 08		13 14	13 19	13 24	13 29	13 34	13 38		13 44
	d	12 15	12 20	12 25	12 30	12 35	12 39			12 45	12 50	12 55	13 00	13 09		13 15	13 20	13 25	13 30	13 35	13 39		13 45
Heath Low Level	d			12 30								13 00						13 30					
Ty Glas	d			12 33								13 03						13 33					
Birchgrove	d			12 34								13 04						13 34					
Rhiwbina	d			12 36								13 06						13 36					
Whitchurch (Cardiff)	d			12 38								13 08						13 38					
Coryton	a			12 43								13 13						13 43					
Heath High Level	d		12 25			12 40					12 55						13 25			13 40			
Llanishen	d		12 28			12 43					12 58						13 28			13 43			
Lisvane & Thornhill	d		12 30			12 45					13 00						13 30			13 45			
Caerphilly	d		12 36			12 51					13 06						13 36			13 51			
Aber	d		12 38			12 53					13 08						13 38			13 53			
Energlyn & Churchill Park	d		12 40														13 40						
Llanbradach	d		12 44			12 57					13 12						13 44			13 57			
Ystrad Mynach	d		12 49			13 02					13 17						13 49			14 02			
Hengoed	d		12 52			13 05					13 20						13 52			14 05			
Pengam	d		12 55			13 08					13 23						13 55			14 08			
Gilfach Fargoed	d																						
Bargoed	a		13 00			13 16					13 31						14 00			14 16			
	d		13 01														14 01						
Brithdir	d		13 05														14 05						
Tir-phil	d		13 08														14 08						
Pontlottyn	d		13 12														14 12						
Rhymney 3	a		13 18														14 18						
Cathays	d	12 18			12 33		12 42			12 48			13 03	13 12		13 18			13 33		13 42		13 48
Llandaf	d	12 22			12 37		12 46			12 52			13 07	13 16		13 22			13 37		13 46		13 52
Ninian Park	d			13 10				12 40				13 40			13 10			14 10				13 40	
Waun-gron Park	d			13 13				12 43				13 43			13 13			14 13				13 43	
Fairwater	d			13 15				12 45				13 45			13 15			14 15				13 45	
Danescourt	d			13 17				12 47				13 47			13 17			14 17				13 47	
Radyr 3	a	12 25		13 24	12 40		12 49	12 54		12 55		13 54	13 10	13 19	13 24	13 25		14 24	13 40		13 49	13 54	13 55
	d	12 25			12 41		12 50			12 56			13 11	13 20		13 26			13 41		13 50		13 56
Taffs Well	d	12 29			12 45		12 54			13 00			13 15	13 24		13 30			13 45		13 54		14 00
Trefforest Estate	d				12 49								13 19						13 49				
Trefforest	d	12 36			12 53		13 01			13 07			13 23	13 31		13 37			13 53		14 01		14 07
Pontypridd 3	a	12 41			12 56		13 04			13 10			13 26	13 34		13 40			13 56		14 04		14 10
	d				12 57		13 05			13 12			13 27	13 35		13 42			13 57		14 05		14 12
Abercynon	d				13 04					13 19			13 34			13 49			14 04				14 19
Penrhiwceiber	d									13 24						13 54							14 24
Mountain Ash	a									13 28						13 58							14 28
	d									13 33						14 03							14 33
Fernhill	d									13 35						14 05							14 35
Cwmbach	d									13 39						14 09							14 39
Aberdare	a									13 46						14 16							14 46
Quakers Yard	d				13 09								13 39						14 09				
Merthyr Vale	a				13 14								13 44						14 14				
	d				13 17								13 47						14 17				
Troed Y Rhiw	d				13 20								13 50						14 20				
Pentre-bach	d				13 23								13 53						14 23				
Merthyr Tydfil	a				13 31								14 01						14 31				
Trehafod	d						13 10							13 40							14 10		
Porth	a						13 13							13 43							14 13		
	d						13 14							13 44							14 14		
Dinas Rhondda	d						13 18							13 48							14 18		
Tonypandy	d						13 20							13 50							14 20		
Llwynypia	d						13 22							13 52							14 22		
Ystrad Rhondda	a						13 25							13 55							14 25		
	d						13 29							13 59							14 29		
Ton Pentre	d						13 31							14 01							14 31		
Treorchy	d						13 34							14 04							14 34		
Ynyswen	d						13 37							14 07							14 37		
Treherbert	a						13 42							14 12							14 42		

When events are being held at the Principality Stadium, services are subject to alteration. Please check times before travelling.

For connections to Cardiff Bay please refer to Table T124

Table T130-R

Mondays to Fridays

21 May to 7 September

Bridgend, Barry Island, Barry, Penarth and Cardiff - Coryton, Rhymney, Pontypridd, Merthyr, Aberdare and Treherbert

Station		AW	AW	AW	AW		AW	AW	AW	AW	AW	AW	AW	AW	AW		AW	AW	AW	AW	AW	AW	AW	AW	AW
Bridgend	d													13 42							13 38				
Llantwit Major	d													13 56											
Rhoose Cardiff Int Airport ✈	d													14 06											
Barry Island	d			13 25							13 55								14 25				14 40		
Barry 3	d			13 30							14 00			14 15					14 30		14a33		14 45		
Barry Docks	d			13 33							14 03			14 18					14 33				14 48		
Cadoxton	d			13 36							14 06			14 21					14 36				14 51		
Dinas Powys	d			13 40							14 10			14 25					14 40				14 55		
Eastbrook	d			13 43							14 13			14 28					14 43				14 58		
Cogan	d			13 45							14 15			14 30					14 45				15 00		
Penarth	d	13 32							14 02						14 32									15 02	
Dingle Road	d	13 34							14 04						14 34									15 04	
Grangetown	d	13 38		13 49					14 08		14 19			14 34	14 38				14 49				15 04	15 08	
Cardiff Central 7	a	13 44		13 54					14 14		14 24			14 39	14 44				14 54				15 10	15 14	
	d	13 46	13 51	13 56	14 05		14 06	14 11	14 16	14 21	14 26	14 36	14 36	14 41	14 46		14 51	14 53	14 56			15 06	15 11	15 16	15 21
Cardiff Queen Street 3	a	13 49	13 54	13 59	14 08			14 14	14 19	14 24	14 29	14 39		14 44	14 49		14 54		14 58				15 14	15 19	15 24
	d	13 50	13 55	14 00	14 09			14 15	14 20	14 25	14 30	14 40		14 45	14 50		14 55		15 00				15 15	15 20	15 25
Heath Low Level	d		14 00							14 30							15 00								15 30
Ty Glas	d		14 03							14 33							15 03								15 33
Birchgrove	d		14 04							14 34							15 04								15 34
Rhiwbina	d		14 06							14 36							15 06								15 36
Whitchurch (Cardiff)	d		14 08							14 38							15 08								15 38
Coryton	a		14 13							14 43							15 13								15 43
Heath High Level	d	13 55							14 25						14 55									15 25	
Llanishen	d	13 58							14 28						14 58									15 28	
Lisvane & Thornhill	d	14 00							14 30						15 00									15 30	
Caerphilly	d	14 06							14 36						15 06									15 36	
Aber	d	14 08							14 38						15 08									15 38	
Energlyn & Churchill Park	d								14 40															15 40	
Llanbradach	d	14 12							14 44						15 12									15 44	
Ystrad Mynach	d	14 17							14 49						15 17									15 49	
Hengoed	d	14 20							14 52						15 20									15 52	
Pengam	d	14 23							14 55						15 23									15 55	
Gilfach Fargoed	d																								
Bargoed	a	14 31							15 00						15 31									16 00	
	d								15 01															16 01	
Brithdir	d								15 05															16 05	
Tir-phil	d								15 08															16 08	
Pontlottyn	d								15 12															16 12	
Rhymney 3	a								15 18															16 18	
Cathays	d			14 03	14 12			14 18			14 33	14 43		14 48					15 03				15 18		
Llandaf	d			14 07	14 16			14 22			14 37	14 47		14 52					15 07				15 22		
Ninian Park	d		14 40				14 10			15 10			14 40				15 40					15 10			16 10
Waun-gron Park	d		14 43				14 13			15 13			14 43				15 43					15 13			16 13
Fairwater	d		14 45				14 15			15 15			14 45				15 45					15 15			16 15
Danescourt	d		14 47				14 17			15 17			14 47				15 47			←		15 17			16 17
Radyr 3	a		14 54	14 10	14 19		14 24	14 25		15 24	14 40	14 50	14 54	14 55			15 54	15 08	15 10	15 08		15 24	15 25		16 24
	d			14 11	14 20			14 26			14 41	14 51		14 56				15 21	15 11	15 21			15 26		
Taffs Well	d			14 15	14 24			14 30			14 45	14 55		15 00				→	15 15	15 25			15 30		
Trefforest Estate	d			14 19							14 49								15 19						
Trefforest	d			14 23	14 31			14 37			14 53	15 02		15 07					15 23	15 32			15 37		
Pontypridd 3	a			14 26	14 34			14 41			14 56	15 04		15 10					15 26	15 35			15 40		
	d			14 27	14 35			14 42			14 57	15 06		15 12					15 27	15 36			15 42		
Abercynon	d			14 34				14 49			15 04			15 19					15 34				15 49		
Penrhiwceiber	d							14 54						15 24									15 54		
Mountain Ash	a							14 58						15 28									15 58		
	d							15 03						15 33									16 03		
Fernhill	d							15 05						15 35									16 05		
Cwmbach	d							15 09						15 39									16 09		
Aberdare	a							15 16						15 46									16 16		
Quakers Yard	d			14 39							15 09								15 39						
Merthyr Vale	a			14 44							15 14								15 44						
	d			14 47							15 17								15 47						
Troed Y Rhiw	d			14 50							15 20								15 50						
Pentre-bach	d			14 53							15 23								15 53						
Merthyr Tydfil	a			15 01							15 31								16 01						
Trehafod	d				14 40							15 11								15 41					
Porth	a				14 43							15 14								15 44					
	d				14 44							15 15								15 45					
Dinas Rhondda	d				14 48							15 19								15 49					
Tonypandy	d				14 50							15 21								15 51					
Llwynypia	d				14 52							15 23								15 53					
Ystrad Rhondda	a				14 55							15 26								15 56					
	d				14 59							15 29								15 59					
Ton Pentre	d				15 01							15 31								16 01					
Treorchy	d				15 04							15 34								16 04					
Ynyswen	d				15 07							15 37								16 07					
Treherbert	a				15 12							15 43								16 13					

When events are being held at the Principality Stadium, services are subject to alteration. Please check times before travelling.

For connections to Cardiff Bay please refer to Table T124

Table T130-R

Mondays to Fridays

21 May to 7 September

Bridgend, Barry Island, Barry, Penarth and Cardiff - Coryton, Rhymney, Pontypridd, Merthyr, Aberdare and Treherbert

Station			AW	AW	AW	AW	AW	AW	AW	AW	AW		AW	AW	AW	AW	AW	AW	AW	AW	AW		AW	AW	AW
Bridgend	d					14 42													15 42						
Llantwit Major	d					14 56													15 56						
Rhoose Cardiff Int Airport ✈	d					15 06													16 06						
Barry Island	d		14 55						15 25				15 40			15 55								16 25	
Barry 3	d		15 00			15 15			15 30				15 45			16 00				16 15				16 30	
Barry Docks	d		15 04			15 18			15 33				15 48			16 03				16 18				16 33	
Cadoxton	d		15 07			15 21			15 36				15 51			16 06				16 21				16 36	
Dinas Powys	d		15 11			15 25			15 40				15 55			16 10				16 25				16 40	
Eastbrook	d		15 13			15 28			15 43				15 58			16 13				16 28				16 43	
Cogan	d		15 15			15 30			15 45				16 00			16 15				16 30				16 45	
Penarth	d						15 32			15 47				16 02			16 17				16 32				
Dingle Road	d						15 34			15 49				16 04			16 19				16 34				
Grangetown	d		15 19			15 34	15 38		15 49	15 53			16 04	16 08		16 19	16 23			16 34	16 38			16 49	
Cardiff Central 7	a		15 24			15 39	15 44		15 54	15 59			16 09	16 14		16 24	16 29			16 39	16 44			16 54	
	d		15 26	15 35	15 36	15 41	15 46	15 51	15 56	16 01	16 05		16 11	16 16	16 21	16 26	16 31	16 35	16 36	16 41	16 46		16 51	16 56	17 01
Cardiff Queen Street 3	a		15 29	15 38		15 44	15 49	15 54	15 59	16 04	16 08		16 14	16 19	16 24	16 29	16 34	16 38		16 44	16 49		16 54	16 59	17 04
	d		15 30	15 39		15 45	15 50	15 55	16 00	16 05	16 09		16 15	16 20	16 25	16 30	16 35	16 39		16 45	16 50		16 55	17 00	17 05
Heath Low Level	d							16 00							16 30								17 00		
Ty Glas	d							16 03							16 33								17 03		
Birchgrove	d							16 04							16 34								17 04		
Rhiwbina	d							16 06							16 36								17 06		
Whitchurch (Cardiff)	d							16 08							16 38								17 08		
Coryton	a							16 13							16 43								17 13		
Heath High Level	d						15 55			16 10				16 25			16 40				16 55				17 10
Llanishen	d						15 58			16 13				16 28			16 43				16 58				17 13
Lisvane & Thornhill	d						16 00			16 15				16 30			16 45				17 00				17 15
Caerphilly	d						16 06			16 21				16 36			16 51				17 06				17 21
Aber	d						16 08			16 23				16 38			16 53				17 08				17 23
Energlyn & Churchill Park	d									16 25				16 40											17 26
Llanbradach	d						16 12			16 29				16 44			16 57				17 12				17 29
Ystrad Mynach	d						16 17			16 34				16 49			17 02				17 17				17 35
Hengoed	d						16 20			16 37				16 52			17 05				17 20				17 37
Pengam	d						16 23			16 40				16 55			17 08				17 23				17 41
Gilfach Fargoed	d									16 43															17 44
Bargoed	a						16 31			16 52				17 00			17 16				17 31				17 47
	d													17 01			17 17								17 49
Brithdir	d													17 05											17 52
Tir-phil	d													17 08											17 55
Pontlottyn	d													17 12											18 00
Rhymney 3	a													17 18											18 06
Cathays	d		15 33	15 42		15 48			16 03		16 12		16 18			16 33	18 43	16 42		16 48				17 03	
Llandaf	d		15 37	15 46		15 52			16 07		16 16		16 22			16 37	18 47	16 46		16 52				17 07	
Ninian Park	d				15 40			16 40							17 10				16 40				17 40		
Waun-gron Park	d				15 43			16 43							17 13				16 43				17 43		
Fairwater	d				15 45			16 45							17 15				16 45				17 45		
Danescourt	d				15 47			16 47							17 17				16 47				17 47		
Radyr 3	a		15 40	15 49	15 54	15 55		16 54	16 10		16 19		16 25		17 24	16 40	18 51	16 49	16 54	16 55			17 54	17 10	
	d		15 41	15 50		15 56			16 11		16 20		16 26			16 41	18 51	16 50		16 56				17 11	
Taffs Well	d		15 45	15 54		16 00			16 15		16 24		16 30			16 45	→	16 54		17 00				17 15	
Trefforest Estate	d		15 49						16 19							16 49								17 19	
Trefforest	d		15 53	16 01		16 07			16 23		16 31		16 37			16 53		17 01		17 07				17 23	
Pontypridd 3	a		15 56	16 04		16 10			16 26		16 34		16 40			16 56		17 04		17 10				17 26	
	d		15 57	16 05		16 12			16 27		16 35		16 42			16 57		17 05		17 12				17 27	
Abercynon	d		16 04			16 19			16 34				16 49			17 04				17 19				17 34	
Penrhiwceiber	d					16 24							16 54							17 24					
Mountain Ash	a					16 28							16 58							17 28					
	d					16 33							17 03							17 33					
Fernhill	d					16 35							17 05							17 35					
Cwmbach	d					16 39							17 09							17 39					
Aberdare	a					16 46							17 16							17 46					
Quakers Yard	d		16 09						16 39							17 09								17 39	
Merthyr Vale	a		16 14						16 44							17 14								17 44	
	d		16 17						16 47							17 17								17 47	
Troed Y Rhiw	d		16 20						16 50							17 20								17 50	
Pentre-bach	d		16 23						16 53							17 23								17 53	
Merthyr Tydfil	a		16 31						17 01							17 31								18 01	
Trehafod	d			16 10							16 40							17 10							
Porth	a			16 13							16 43							17 13							
	d			16 14							16 44							17 14							
Dinas Rhondda	d			16 18							16 48							17 18							
Tonypandy	d			16 20							16 50							17 20							
Llwynypia	d			16 22							16 52							17 22							
Ystrad Rhondda	a			16 25							16 55							17 25							
	d			16 29							16 59							17 29							
Ton Pentre	d			16 31							17 01							17 31							
Treorchy	d			16 34							17 04							17 34							
Ynyswen	d			16 37							17 07							17 37							
Treherbert	a			16 42							17 12							17 42							

When events are being held at the Principality Stadium, services are subject to alteration. Please check times before travelling.

For connections to Cardiff Bay please refer to Table T124

Bridgend, Barry Island, Barry, Penarth and Cardiff - Coryton, Rhymney, Pontypridd, Merthyr, Aberdare and Treherbert

		AW	AW	AW	AW	AW	AW	AW	AW	AW	AW	AW	AW	AW	AW	AW	AW	AW	AW	AW	AW	AW	AW
Bridgend	d										16 42												
Llantwit Major	d										16 56												
Rhoose Cardiff Int Airport ✈	d										17 06												
Barry Island	d			16 40			16 55							17 25				17 40			17 55		
Barry	d			16 45			17 00				17 15			17 30				17 45			18 00		
Barry Docks	d			16 48			17 03				17 18			17 33				17 48			18 03		
Cadoxton	d			16 51			17 06				17 21			17 36				17 51			18 06		
Dinas Powys	d			16 55			17 10				17 25			17 40				17 55			18 10		
Eastbrook	d			16 58			17 13				17 28			17 43				17 58			18 13		
Cogan	d			17 00			17 15				17 30			17 45				18 00			18 15		
Penarth	d				17 02			17 17				17 32			17 47				18 02				18 17
Dingle Road	d				17 04			17 19				17 34			17 49				18 04				18 19
Grangetown	d			17 04	17 08		17 19	17 23			17 34	17 38		17 49	17 53			18 04	18 08		18 19		18 23
Cardiff Central	a			17 09	17 14		17 24	17 29			17 39	17 44		17 54	17 59			18 09	18 14		18 24		18 29
	d	17 05	17 06	17 11	17 16	17 21	17 26	17 31	17 35	17 36	17 41	17 46	17 51	17 56	18 01	18 05	18 06	18 11	18 16	18 21	18 26		18 31
Cardiff Queen Street	a	17 08		17 14	17 19	17 24	17 29	17 34	17 38		17 44	17 49	17 54	17 59	18 04	18 08		18 14	18 19	18 24	18 29		18 34
	d	17 09		17 15	17 20	17 25	17 30	17 35	17 39		17 45	17 50	17 55	18 00	18 05	18 09		18 15	18 20	18 25	18 30		18 35
Heath Low Level	d					17 30							18 00							18 30			
Ty Glas	d					17 33							18 03							18 33			
Birchgrove	d					17 34							18 04							18 34			
Rhiwbina	d					17 36							18 06							18 36			
Whitchurch (Cardiff)	d					17 38							18 08							18 38			
Coryton	a					17 43							18 13							18 43			
Heath High Level	d				17 25			17 40				17 55			18 10				18 25				18 40
Llanishen	d				17 28			17 43				17 59			18 13				18 28				18 43
Lisvane & Thornhill	d				17 31			17 45				18 02			18 15				18 30				18 45
Caerphilly	d				17 37			17 51				18 07			18 21				18 36				18 51
Aber	d				17 39			17 53				18 10			18 23				18 38				18 53
Energlyn & Churchill Park	d				17 41			17 55				18 13							18 40				18 55
Llanbradach	d				17 45			17 59				18 17			18 27				18 44				18 59
Ystrad Mynach	d				17 50			18 04				18 22			18 32				18a53				19 04
Hengoed	d				17 53			18 07				18 25			18 35								19 07
Pengam	d				17 56			18 10				18 29			18 38								19 10
Gilfach Fargoed	d							18 13				18 33			18 41								19 13
Bargoed	a				18 03			18 16				18 36			18 48								19 16
	d							18 18				18 38			18 48								19 18
Brithdir	d							18 22				18 41											19 22
Tir-phil	d							18 25				18 44											19 25
Pontlottyn	d							18 29				18 49											19 29
Rhymney	a							18 35				18 55											19 36
Cathays	d	17 12		17 18			17 33		17 42		17 48			18 03	20 12	18 12		18 18			18 33		
Llandaf	d	17 16		17 22			17 37		17 46		17 52			18 07	20 16	18 16		18 22			18 37		
Ninian Park	d		17 10			18 10				17 40			18 40				18 10						
Waun-gron Park	d		17 13			18 13				17 43			18 43				18 13						
Fairwater	d		17 15			18 15				17 45			18 45				18 15						
Danescourt	d		17 17			18 17				17 47			18 47				18 17					←	
Radyr	a	17 19	17 24	17 25		18 24	17 40		17 49	17 54	17 55		18 54	18 10	20 19	18 19	18 24	18 25			18 40	18 51	
	d	17 20		17 26			17 41		17 50		17 56			18 11	20 20	18 20		18 25			18 41	18 51	
Taffs Well	d	17 24		17 30			17 45		17 54		18 00			18 15	→	18 24		18 29			18 45	18 55	
Trefforest Estate	d						17 49							18 19							18 49		
Trefforest	d	17 31		17 37			17 53		18 01		18 07			18 23		18 31		18 36			18 53	19 02	
Pontypridd	a	17 34		17 40			17 56		18 04		18 10			18 26		18 34		18 41			18 56	19 05	
	d	17 35		17 42			17 57		18 05		18 12			18 27		18 35					18 57	19 06	
Abercynon	d			17 49			18 04				18 19			18 34							19 04		
Penrhiwceiber	d			17 54							18 24												
Mountain Ash	a			17 58							18 28												
	d			18 03							18 33												
Fernhill	d			18 05							18 35												
Cwmbach	d			18 09							18 39												
Aberdare	a			18 16							18 46												
Quakers Yard	d						18 09							18 39							19 09		
Merthyr Vale	a						18 14							18 44							19 14		
	d						18 17							18 47							19 17		
Troed Y Rhiw	d						18 20							18 50							19 20		
Pentre-bach	d						18 23							18 53							19 23		
Merthyr Tydfil	a						18 31							19 01							19 31		
Trehafod	d	17 40							18 10							18 40						19 11	
Porth	a	17 43							18 13							18 43						19 14	
	d	17 44							18 14							18 44						19 15	
Dinas Rhondda	d	17 48							18 18							18 48						19 19	
Tonypandy	d	17 50							18 20							18 50						19 21	
Llwynypia	d	17 52							18 22							18 52						19 23	
Ystrad Rhondda	a	17 55							18 25							18 55						19 26	
	d	17 59							18 29							18 59						19 29	
Ton Pentre	d	18 01							18 31							19 01						19 31	
Treorchy	d	18 04							18 34							19 04						19 34	
Ynyswen	d	18 07							18 37							19 07						19 37	
Treherbert	a	18 12							18 43							19 12						19 43	

When events are being held at the Principality Stadium, services are subject to alteration. Please check times before travelling.

For connections to Cardiff Bay please refer to Table T124

Table T130-R

Mondays to Fridays

21 May to 7 September

Bridgend, Barry Island, Barry, Penarth and Cardiff - Coryton, Rhymney, Pontypridd, Merthyr, Aberdare and Treherbert

		AW	AW	AW	AW	AW		AW	AW	AW	AW	AW	AW		AW	AW	AW	AW	AW	AW	AW	AW
Bridgend	d		17 42										18 42						19 42			
Llantwit Major	d		17 56										18 56						19 56			
Rhoose Cardiff Int Airport ✈	d		18 06										19 06						20 06			
Barry Island	d				18 25			18 40	18 55						19 25	19 55						
Barry	d		18 15		18 30			18 45	19 00				19 15		19 30	20 00			20 15			
Barry Docks	d		18 18		18 33			18 48	19 03				19 18		19 33	20 03			20 18			
Cadoxton	d		18 21		18 36			18 51	19 06				19 21		19 36	20 06			20 21			
Dinas Powys	d		18 25		18 40			18 55	19 10				19 25		19 40	20 10			20 25			
Eastbrook	d		18 28		18 43			18 58	19 13				19 28		19 43	20 13			20 28			
Cogan	d		18 30		18 45			19 00	19 15				19 30		19 45	20 15			20 30			
Penarth	d					18 47				19 17							20 20				20 47	
Dingle Road	d					18 49				19 19							20 22				20 49	
Grangetown	d		18 34		18 49	18 53		19 04	19 19	19 23			19 34		19 49	20 19	20 26		20 34		20 53	
Cardiff Central	a		18 39		18 56	18 59		19 09	19 24	19 29			19 39		19 56	20 24	20 31		20 39		21 00	
	d	18 36	18 41	18 51		19 01	19 05	19 11	19 26	19 31	19 36		19 41	19 51	20 01	20 26	20 31	20 36	20 41	20 51	21 01	21 05
Cardiff Queen Street	a		18 44	18 54		19 04	19 08	19 14	19 29	19 34			19 44	19 54	20 04	20 29	20 34		20 44	20 54	21 04	21 08
	d		18 47	18 55		19 05	19 09	19 15	19 30	19 35			19 45	19 55	20 05	20 30	20 35		20 45	20 55	21 05	21 09
Heath Low Level	d			19 00										20 00						21 00		
Ty Glas	d			19 03										20 03						21 03		
Birchgrove	d			19 04										20 04						21 04		
Rhiwbina	d			19 06										20 06						21 06		
Whitchurch (Cardiff)	d			19 08										20 08						21 08		
Coryton	a			19 13										20 13						21 13		
Heath High Level	d					19 10				19 40					20 11		20 40				21 11	
Llanishen	d					19 13				19 43					20 14		20 43				21 14	
Lisvane & Thornhill	d					19 15				19 45					20 15		20 45				21 16	
Caerphilly	d					19a21				19 51					20a24		20 51				21 23	
Aber	d									19 53							20 53				21 25	
Energlyn & Churchill Park	d									19 56							20 55					
Llanbradach	d									19 59							20 59				21 30	
Ystrad Mynach	d									20 04							21 04				21a39	
Hengoed	d									20 07							21 07					
Pengam	d									20 10							21 10					
Gilfach Fargoed	d									20 13							21 13					
Bargoed	a									20 17							21 17					
	d									20 18							21 18					
Brithdir	d									20 22							21 22					
Tir-phil	d									20 25							21 25					
Pontlottyn	d									20 29							21 29					
Rhymney	a									20 35							21 36					
Cathays	d		18 50				19 12	19 18	19 33				19 48			20 33			20 48			21 12
Llandaf	d		18 54				19 16	19 22	19 37				19 52			20 37			20 52			21 16
Ninian Park	d	18 40		19 40							19 40			20 40				20 40		21 40		
Waun-gron Park	d	18 43		19 43							19 43			20 43				20 43		21 43		
Fairwater	d	18 45		19 45							19 45			20 45				20 45		21 45		
Danescourt	d	18 47		19 47							19 47	←		20 47				20 47		21 47		
Radyr	a	18 54	18 57	19 54			19 19	19 25	19 40		19 54	20 19	19 55	20 54		20 40		20 54	20 55	21 54		21 19
	d		18 58				19 20	19 26	19 41			20 20	19 56			20 41			20 56			21 20
Taffs Well	d		19 02				19 24	19 30	19 45			20 24	20 00			20 45			21 00			21 24
Trefforest Estate	d								19 49							20 49						
Trefforest	d		19 09				19 31	19 37	19 53			20 31	20 07			20 53			21 07			21 31
Pontypridd	a		19 12				19 34	19 40	19 56			20 34	20 10			20 56			21 10			21 34
	d		19 12				19 35	19 42	19 57			20 35	20 12			20 57			21 12			21 35
Abercynon	d		19 19					19 49	20 04				20 21			21 04			21 19			
Penrhiwceiber	d		19 24					19 54					20 26						21 24			
Mountain Ash	a		19 28					19 56					20 30						21 28			
	d		19 33					20 03					20 33						21 29			
Fernhill	d		19 35					20 05					20 35						21 31			
Cwmbach	d		19 39					20 09					20 39						21 35			
Aberdare	a		19 46					20 16					20 46						21 42			
Quakers Yard	d								20 09							21 09						
Merthyr Vale	a								20 14							21 14						
	d								20 15							21 15						
Troed Y Rhiw	d								20 19							21 19						
Pentre-bach	d								20 22							21 22						
Merthyr Tydfil	a								20 30							21 31						
Trehafod	d						19 40					20 40										21 40
Porth	a						19 43					20 43										21 43
	d						19 44					20 44										21 44
Dinas Rhondda	d						19 48					20 48										21 48
Tonypandy	d						19 50					20 50										21 50
Llwynypia	d						19 52					20 52										21 52
Ystrad Rhondda	a						19 55					20 55										21 55
	d						19 59					20 59										21 59
Ton Pentre	d						20 01					21 01										22 01
Treorchy	d						20 04					21 04										22 04
Ynyswen	d						20 07					21 07										22 07
Treherbert	a						20 12					21 12										22 12

When events are being held at the Principality Stadium, services are subject to alteration. Please check times before travelling.

For connections to Cardiff Bay please refer to Table T124

Table T130-R

Mondays to Fridays

21 May to 7 September

Bridgend, Barry Island, Barry, Penarth and Cardiff - Coryton, Rhymney, Pontypridd, Merthyr, Aberdare and Treherbert

		AW	AW	AW	AW	AW	AW	AW	AW	AW	AW	AW	AW	AW	AW	AW	AW	AW	AW
Bridgend	d					20 42							21 42						22 42
Llantwit Major	d					20 56							21 56						22 56
Rhoose Cardiff Int Airport ✈	d					21 06							22 06						23 06
Barry Island	d	20 55								21 55							22 44		
Barry 3	d	21 00				21 15				22 00			22 15				22 49		23 15
Barry Docks	d	21 03				21 18				22 03			22 18				22 52		23 18
Cadoxton	d	21 06				21 21				22 06			22 21				22 55		23 21
Dinas Powys	d	21 10				21 25				22 10			22 25				22 59		23 25
Eastbrook	d	21 13				21 28				22 13			22 28				23 02		23 28
Cogan	d	21 15				21 30				22 15			22 30				23 04		23 30
Penarth	d			21 24			21 47				22 20					22 48		23 26	
Dingle Road	d			21 26			21 49				22 22					22 50		23 28	
Grangetown	d	21 19		21 30		21 34	21 53			22 19	22 26		22 34			22 54	23 08	23 32	23 34
Cardiff Central 7	a	21 24		21 36		21 39	21 59			22 24	22 33		22 39			23 01	23 13	23 39	23 43
	d	21 27	21 31		21 36	21 41	22 01	22 05	22 21	22 26		22 35	22 41	22 46	22 55	23 16	23 26		
Cardiff Queen Street 3	a	21 30	21 34			21 44	22 04	22 08	22 24	22 29		22 38	22 44	22 49		23 19	23 29		
	d	21 31	21 35			21 45	22 05	22 09	22 25	22 30		22 39	22 45	22 50		23 20	23 30		
Heath Low Level	d								22 30										
Ty Glas	d								22 33										
Birchgrove	d								22 34										
Rhiwbina	d								22 36										
Whitchurch (Cardiff)	d								22 38										
Coryton	a								22 43										
Heath High Level	d		21 40				22 10					22 44				23 25			
Llanishen	d		21 43				22 13					22 47				23 28			
Lisvane & Thornhill	d		21 45				22 15					22 49				23 30			
Caerphilly	d		21 51				22a23					22 55				23 36			
Aber	d		21 53									22 57				23 38			
Energlyn & Churchill Park	d		21 55									22 59				23 40			
Llanbradach	d		21 59									23 03				23 44			
Ystrad Mynach	d		22 04									23 08				23a53			
Hengoed	d		22 07									23 11							
Pengam	d		22 10									23 14							
Gilfach Fargoed	d		22 13									23 17							
Bargoed	a		22 17									23 21							
	d		22 18									23 22							
Brithdir	d		22 22									23 26							
Tir-phil	d		22 25									23 29							
Pontlottyn	d		22 29									23 33							
Rhymney 3	a		22 36									23 39							
Cathays	d	21 34				21 48		22 12		22 33			22 48	22 53			23 33		
Llandaf	d	21 38				21 52		22 16		22 37			22 52	22 57			23 37		
Ninian Park	d				21 40										22 59				
Waun-gron Park	d				21 43										23 02				
Fairwater	d				21 45										23 04				
Danescourt	d				21 47										23 06				
Radyr 3	a	21 41			21 54	21 55		22 19		22 40			22 55	23 00	23 13		23 40		
	d	21 42				21 56		22 20		22 41			22 56	23 00			23 41		
Taffs Well	d	21 46				22 00		22 24		22 45			23 00	23 04			23 45		
Trefforest Estate	d	21 50								22 49									
Trefforest	d	21 54				22 07		22 31		22 53			23 07	23 11			23 52		
Pontypridd 3	a	21 57				22 10		22 34		22 56			23 10	23 14			23 59		
	d	21 58				22 12		22 35		22 57			23 12	23 15					
Abercynon	d	22 05				22 19				23 04			23 19						
Penrhiwceiber	d					22 24							23 24						
Mountain Ash	a					22 28							23 28						
	d					22 29							23 29						
Fernhill	d					22 31							23 31						
Cwmbach	d					22 35							23 35						
Aberdare	a					22 42							23 42						
Quakers Yard	d	22 10								23 09									
Merthyr Vale	a	22 15								23 14									
	d	22 16								23 15									
Troed Y Rhiw	d	22 20								23 19									
Pentre-bach	d	22 23								23 22									
Merthyr Tydfil	a	22 31								23 30									
Trehafod	d							22 40						23 20					
Porth	a							22 43						23 23					
	d							22 44						23 24					
Dinas Rhondda	d							22 48						23 28					
Tonypandy	d							22 50						23 30					
Llwynypia	d							22 52						23 32					
Ystrad Rhondda	a							22 55						23 35					
	d							22 59						23 38					
Ton Pentre	d							23 01						23 40					
Treorchy	d							23 04						23 43					
Ynyswen	d							23 07						23 46					
Treherbert	a							23 12						23 52					

When events are being held at the Principality Stadium, services are subject to alteration. Please check times before travelling.

For connections to Cardiff Bay please refer to Table T124

Table T130-R

Mondays to Fridays

10 September to 7 December

Bridgend, Barry Island, Barry, Penarth and Cardiff - Coryton, Rhymney, Pontypridd, Merthyr, Aberdare and Treherbert

		AW	AW	AW	AW	AW	AW	AW	AW	AW	AW	AW	AW	AW	AW	AW	AW	AW	AW	AW	AW	AW	AW
Bridgend	d											05 42											
Llantwit Major	d											05 56											
Rhoose Cardiff Int Airport ✈	d											06 06											
Barry Island	d		05 14					05 50							06 25							06 55	
Barry 3	d		05 19					05 55				06 15			06 30							07 00	
Barry Docks	d		05 22					05 58				06 18			06 33							07 03	
Cadoxton	d		05 25					06 01				06 21			06 36							07 06	
Dinas Powys	d		05 29					06 05				06 25			06 40							07 10	
Eastbrook	d		05 32					06 08				06 28			06 43							07 13	
Cogan	d		05 34					06 10				06 30			06 45							07 15	
Penarth	d												06 32						07 02				07 18
Dingle Road	d												06 34						07 04				07 20
Grangetown	d		05 38					06 14				06 34	06 38		06 49				07 08			07 19	07 23
Cardiff Central 7	a		05 43					06 19				06 39	06 44		06 54				07 14			07 24	07 29
	d	05 26	05 46	05 51		05 56	06 11	06 21	06 26	06 31	06 36	06 41	06 46	06 51	06 56	07 06	07 06	07 11	07 16	07 21	07 21	07 26	07 31
Cardiff Queen Street 3	a	05 29	05 49	05 55		05 59	06 14	06 24	06 29	06 34	06 39	06 44	06 49	06 54	06 59	07 09		07 14	07 19	07 24	07 24	07 29	07 34
	d	05 30	05 50	05 55		06 00	06 15	06 25	06 30	06 35	06 40	06 45	06 50	06 55	07 00	07 10		07 15	07 20	07 25	07 25	07 30	07 35
Heath Low Level	d			06 00				06 30						07 00						07 30	07 30		
Ty Glas	d			06 03				06 33						07 03						07 33	07 33		
Birchgrove	d			06 04				06 34						07 04						07 34	07 34		
Rhiwbina	d			06 06				06 36						07 06						07 36	07 36		
Whitchurch (Cardiff)	d			06 08				06 38						07 08						07 38	07 38		
Coryton	a			06 13				06 43						07 13						07 43	07 43		
Heath High Level	d		05 55										06 55						07 25				07 40
Llanishen	d		05 58										06 58						07 28				07 43
Lisvane & Thornhill	d		06 00										07 00						07 30				07 45
Caerphilly	d		06a09										07 06						07 36				07 51
Aber	d												07 08						07 38				07 53
Energlyn & Churchill Park	d																		07 40				
Llanbradach	d												07 12						07 44				07 57
Ystrad Mynach	d												07 17						07 49				08 02
Hengoed	d												07 20						07 52				08 05
Pengam	d												07 23						07 55				08 08
Gilfach Fargoed	d																						
Bargoed	a												07 32						08 04				08 13
	d																						08 14
Brithdir	d																						08 18
Tir-phil	d																						08 21
Pontlottyn	d																						08 25
Rhymney 3	a																						08 32
Cathays	d	05 33				06 03	06 18		06 33	06 37	06 43	06 48			07 03	07 13		07 18				07 33	
Llandaf	d	05 37				06 07	06 22		06 37		06 47	06 52			07 07	07 17		07 22				07 37	
Ninian Park	d							07 10						07 40			07 10				08 10		
Waun-gron Park	d							07 14						07 44			07 14				08 14		
Fairwater	d							07 16						07 46			07 16				08 16		
Danescourt	d							07 19						07 49			07 19				08 19		
Radyr 3	a	05 40				06 10	06 25	07 26	06 40	06 43	06 50	06 55		07 56	07 10	07 20	07 26	07 26			08 28	07 40	
	d	05 41				06 11	06 25		06 41	06 43	06 51	06 55			07 11	07 21		07 26				07 41	
Taffs Well	d	05 45				06 15	06 29		06 45	06a50	06 55	06 59			07 15	07 25		07 30				07 45	
Trefforest Estate	d	05 49				06 19			06 49						07 19							07 49	
Trefforest	d	05 53				06 23	06 36		06 53		07 02	07 06			07 23	07 32		07 37				07 53	
Pontypridd 3	a	05 56				06 26	06 39		06 56		07 05	07 09			07 26	07 35		07 40				07 56	
	d	05 57			06 11	06 27	06 42		06 57		07 06	07 12			07 27	07 36		07 42				07 57	
Abercynon	d	06 04			06 19	06 34	06 49		07 04			07 19			07 34			07 49				08 04	
Penrhiwceiber	d				06 25		06 55					07 25						07 55					
Mountain Ash	a				06 28		06 58					07 28						07 58					
	d				06 34		07 04					07 34						08 04					
Fernhill	d				06 37		07 07					07 37						08 07					
Cwmbach	d				06 41		07 11					07 41						08 11					
Aberdare	a				06 48		07 18					07 48						08 18					
Quakers Yard	d	06 09				06 39			07 09						07 39							08 09	
Merthyr Vale	a	06 14				06 44			07 14						07 44							08 14	
	d	06 17				06 47			07 17						07 47							08 17	
Troed Y Rhiw	d	06 21				06 51			07 21						07 51							08 21	
Pentre-bach	d	06 24				06 54			07 24						07 54							08 24	
Merthyr Tydfil	a	06 33				07 03			07 33						08 03							08 33	
Trehafod	d										07 11					07 41							
Porth	a										07 14					07 44							
	d										07 15					07 45							
Dinas Rhondda	d										07 19					07 49							
Tonypandy	d										07 21					07 51							
Llwynypia	d										07 23					07 53							
Ystrad Rhondda	a										07 26					07 56							
	d										07 29					07 59							
Ton Pentre	d										07 31					08 02							
Treorchy	d										07 34					08 06							
Ynyswen	d										07 37					08 09							
Treherbert	a										07 43					08 13							

When events are being held at the Principality Stadium, services are subject to alteration. Please check times before travelling.

For connections to Cardiff Bay please refer to Table T124

Bridgend, Barry Island, Barry, Penarth and Cardiff - Coryton, Rhymney, Pontypridd, Merthyr, Aberdare and Treherbert

		AW	AW	AW	AW	AW	AW	AW	AW	AW	AW	AW	AW	AW	AW	AW	AW	AW	AW	AW	AW	AW	AW
Bridgend	d			06 42											07 20					07 42			
Llantwit Major	d			06 56																07 56			
Rhoose Cardiff Int Airport ✈	d			07 06																08 06			
Barry Island	d						07 25				07 40			07 55									08 25
Barry	d			07 15			07 30				07 45			08 00	08a11				08 13	08 21			08 30
Barry Docks	d			07 18			07 33				07 48			08 03					08 16	08 24			08 33
Cadoxton	d			07 21			07 36				07 51			08 06					08 19	08 27			08 36
Dinas Powys	d			07 25			07 40				07 55			08 10					08 23				08 40
Eastbrook	d			07 28			07 43				07 58			08 13					08 26				08 43
Cogan	d			07 30			07 45				08 00			08 15					08 29				08 45
Penarth	d				07 32							08 02				08 17					08 32		
Dingle Road	d				07 34							08 04				08 19					08 34		
Grangetown	d			07 34	07 38		07 49				08 04	08 08		08 19		08 23					08 38		08 49
Cardiff Central	a			07 39	07 44		07 54				08 09	08 14		08 24		08 29			08 40	08 39	08 44		08 54
	d	07 36	07 36	07 41	07 46	07 51	07 56	07 57	08 06	08 06	08 11	08 16	08 21	08 26		08 31	08 36	08 36		08 41	08 46	08 51	08 56
Cardiff Queen Street	a	07 39		07 44	07 49	07 54	07 59		08 09		08 14	08 19	08 24	08 29		08 34	08 39			08 43	08 49	08 54	08 59
	d	07 40		07 45	07 50	07 55	08 00		08 10		08 15	08 20	08 25	08 30		08 35	08 40			08 45	08 50	08 55	09 00
Heath Low Level	d					08 00							08 30									09 00	
Ty Glas	d					08 03							08 33									09 03	
Birchgrove	d					08 04							08 34									09 04	
Rhiwbina	d					08 06							08 36									09 06	
Whitchurch (Cardiff)	d					08 08							08 38									09 08	
Coryton	a					08 13							08 43									09 13	
Heath High Level	d				07 55							08 25				08 40					08 55		
Llanishen	d				07 58							08 28				08 43					08 58		
Lisvane & Thornhill	d				08 00							08 30				08 45					09 00		
Caerphilly	d				08 06							08 36				08 51					09 06		
Aber	d				08 08							08 38				08 53					09 08		
Energlyn & Churchill Park	d											08 40											
Llanbradach	d				08 12							08 44				08 57					09 12		
Ystrad Mynach	d				08 17							08 49				09 07					09a20		
Hengoed	d				08 20							08 52				09 10							
Pengam	d				08 23							08 55				09 13							
Gilfach Fargoed	d																						
Bargoed	a				08 32							09 00				09 22							
	d											09 01											
Brithdir	d											09 05											
Tir-phil	d											09 08											
Pontlottyn	d											09 12											
Rhymney	a											09 19											
Cathays	d	07 43		07 48			08 03		08 13		08 18			08 33			08 43			08 48			09 03
Llandaf	d	07 47		07 52			08 08		08 17		08 22			08 37			08 47			08 52			09 07
Ninian Park	d		07 40			08 40				08 10			09 10					08 40				09 40	
Waun-gron Park	d		07 44			08 44				08 14			09 14					08 44				09 44	
Fairwater	d		07 46			08 46				08 16			09 16					08 46				09 46	
Danescourt	d		07 49			08 49				08 19			09 19					08 49				09 49	
Radyr	a	07 50	07 56	07 55		08 56	08 10	08 10	08 20	08 28	08 25		09 26	08 40			08 50	08 56		08 55		09 56	09 10
	d	07 51		07 56			08 11		08 21		08 26			08 41			08 51			08 56			09 11
Taffs Well	d	07 55		08 00			08 15		08 25		08 30			08 45			08 55			09 00			09 15
Trefforest Estate	d						08 19							08 49									09 19
Trefforest	d	08 02		08 07			08 23		08 32		08 37			08 53			09 02			09 07			09 23
Pontypridd	a	08 05		08 10			08 26		08 35		08 40			08 56			09 05			09 10			09 26
	d	08 06		08 12			08 27		08 36		08 42			08 57			09 06			09 12			09 27
Abercynon	d			08 19			08 34				08 49			09 04						09 19			09 34
Penrhiwceiber	d			08 25							08 55									09 25			
Mountain Ash	a			08 28							08 58									09 28			
	d			08 34							09 04									09 34			
Fernhill	d			08 37							09 07									09 37			
Cwmbach	d			08 41							09 11									09 41			
Aberdare	a			08 48							09 18									09 48			
Quakers Yard	d						08 39							09 09									09 39
Merthyr Vale	a						08 45							09 14									09 44
	d						08 47							09 17									09 47
Troed Y Rhiw	d						08 51							09 21									09 51
Pentre-bach	d						08 54							09 24									09 54
Merthyr Tydfil	a						09 03							09 33									10 03
Trehafod	d	08 11							08 41								09 11						
Porth	a	08 14							08 44								09 14						
	d	08 15							08 45								09 15						
Dinas Rhondda	d	08 19							08 49								09 19						
Tonypandy	d	08 21							08 51								09 21						
Llwynypia	d	08 23							08 53								09 23						
Ystrad Rhondda	a	08 26							08 56								09 26						
	d	08 29							08 59								09 29						
Ton Pentre	d	08 31							09 01								09 31						
Treorchy	d	08 34							09 04								09 34						
Ynyswen	d	08 37							09 07								09 37						
Treherbert	a	08 43							09 13								09 43						

When events are being held at the Principality Stadium, services are subject to alteration. Please check times before travelling.

For connections to Cardiff Bay please refer to Table T124

Bridgend, Barry Island, Barry, Penarth and Cardiff - Coryton, Rhymney, Pontypridd, Merthyr, Aberdare and Treherbert

		AW	AW	AW	AW	AW	AW	AW	AW	AW	AW	AW	AW	AW	AW	AW	AW	AW	AW	AW	AW	AW
Bridgend	d									08 42												
Llantwit Major	d									08 56												
Rhoose Cardiff Int Airport ✈	d									09 06												
Barry Island	d		08 40			08 55							09 25						09 40			09 55
Barry	d		08 45			09 00				09 15			09 30						09 45			10 00
Barry Docks	d		08 48			09 03				09 18			09 33						09 48			10 03
Cadoxton	d		08 51			09 06				09 21			09 36						09 51			10 06
Dinas Powys	d		08 55			09 10				09 25			09 40						09 55			10 10
Eastbrook	d		08 58			09 13				09 28			09 43						09 58			10 13
Cogan	d		09 00			09 15				09 30			09 45						10 00			10 15
Penarth	d						09 17				09 32				09 47	09 47				10 02		
Dingle Road	d						09 19				09 34				09 49	09 49				10 04		
Grangetown	d		09 04			09 19	09 23			09 34	09 38		09 49		09 53	09 53			10 04	10 08		10 19
Cardiff Central	a		09 09			09 24	09 29			09 39	09 44		09 54		09 58	09 58			10 09	10 14		10 24
	d	09 06	09 11	09 16	09 21	09 26	09 31	09 36	09 36	09 41	09 46	09 51	09 56			10 06	10 06	10 06	10 11	10 16	10 21	10 26
Cardiff Queen Street	a	09 09	09 14	09 19	09 24	09 29	09 34	09 39		09 44	09 49	09 54	09 59			10 09	10 09		10 14	10 19	10 24	10 29
	d	09 10	09 15	09 20	09 25	09 30	09 35	09 40		09 45	09 50	09 55	10 00			10 10	10 10		10 15	10 20	10 25	10 30
Heath Low Level	d				09 30							10 00									10 30	
Ty Glas	d				09 33							10 03									10 33	
Birchgrove	d				09 34							10 04									10 34	
Rhiwbina	d				09 36							10 06									10 36	
Whitchurch (Cardiff)	d				09 38							10 08									10 38	
Coryton	a				09 43							10 14									10 44	
Heath High Level	d			09 25			09 40				09 55									10 25		
Llanishen	d			09 28			09 43				09 58									10 28		
Lisvane & Thornhill	d			09 30			09 45				10 00									10 30		
Caerphilly	d			09 36			09 51				10 06									10 36		
Aber	d			09 38			09 53				10 08									10 38		
Energlyn & Churchill Park	d			09 40																10 40		
Llanbradach	d			09 44			09 57				10 12									10 44		
Ystrad Mynach	d			09 49			10 07				10a21									10 49		
Hengoed	d			09 52			10 10													10 52		
Pengam	d			09 55			10 13													10 55		
Gilfach Fargoed	d																					
Bargoed	a			10 00			10 22													11 00		
	d			10 01																11 01		
Brithdir	d			10 05																11 05		
Tir-phil	d			10 08																11 08		
Pontlottyn	d			10 12																11 12		
Rhymney	a			10 19																11 19		
Cathays	d	09 13	09 18			09 33		09 43		09 48			10 03			10 13	10 13		10 18			10 33
Llandaf	d	09 17	09 22			09 37		09 47		09 52			10 07			10 17	10 17		10 22			10 37
Ninian Park	d				10 10				09 40			10 40						10 10			11 10	
Waun-gron Park	d				10 14				09 44			10 44						10 14			11 14	
Fairwater	d				10 16				09 46			10 46						10 16			11 16	
Danescourt	d				10 19				09 49			10 49						10 19			11 19	
Radyr	a	09 20	09 25		10 26	09 40		09 50	09 56	09 55		10 56	10 10			10 20	10 20	10 26	10 25		11 26	10 40
	d	09 21	09 26			09 41		09 51		09 56			10 11			10 21	10 21		10 26			10 41
Taffs Well	d	09 25	09 30			09 45		09 55		10 00			10 15			10 25	10 25		10 30			10 45
Trefforest Estate	d					09 49																10 49
Trefforest	d	09 32	09 37			09 53		10 02		10 07			10 21			10 32	10 32		10 37			10 53
Pontypridd	a	09 35	09 40			09 56		10 05		10 10			10 32			10 35	10 35		10 40			10 56
	d	09 36	09 42			09 57		10 06		10 12				10 34		10 36	10 36		10 42			10 57
Abercynon	d		09 49			10 04				10 19				10 40					10 49			11 04
Penrhiwceiber	d		09 55							10 25									10 55			
Mountain Ash	a		09 58							10 28									10 58			
	d		10 04							10 34									11 04			
Fernhill	d		10 07							10 37									11 07			
Cwmbach	d		10 11							10 41									11 11			
Aberdare	a		10 18							10 48									11 18			
Quakers Yard	d					10 09								10 44								11 09
Merthyr Vale	a					10 14								10 49								11 14
	d					10 17								10 52								11 17
Troed Y Rhiw	d					10 21								10 56								11 21
Pentre-bach	d					10 24								10 59								11 24
Merthyr Tydfil	a					10 33								11 07								11 33
Trehafod	d	09 41						10 11								10 41	10 41					
Porth	a	09 44						10 14								10 44	10 44					
	d	09 45						10 15								10 45	10 45					
Dinas Rhondda	d	09 49						10 19								10 49	10 49					
Tonypandy	d	09 51						10 21								10 51	10 51					
Llwynypia	d	09 53						10 23								10 53	10 53					
Ystrad Rhondda	a	09 56						10 26								10 56	10 56					
	d	09 59						10 29								10 59	10 59					
Ton Pentre	d	10 01						10 31								11 01	11 01					
Treorchy	d	10 04						10 34								11 04	11 04					
Ynyswen	d	10 07						10 37								11 07	11 07					
Treherbert	a	10 13						10 43								11 13	11 13					

When events are being held at the Principality Stadium, services are subject to alteration. Please check times before travelling.

For connections to Cardiff Bay please refer to Table T124

Table T130-R

Mondays to Fridays

10 September to 7 December

Bridgend, Barry Island, Barry, Penarth and Cardiff - Coryton, Rhymney, Pontypridd, Merthyr, Aberdare and Treherbert

		AW	AW	AW	AW	AW	AW	AW	AW	AW	AW	AW	AW	AW	AW	AW	AW	AW	AW	AW	AW	AW	AW
Bridgend	d				09 45														10 45				
Llantwit Major	d				09 58														10 58				
Rhoose Cardiff Int Airport ✈	d				10 08														11 08				
Barry Island	d								10 25			10 40			10 55							11 25	
Barry	d				10 16				10 30			10 45			11 00				11 16			11 30	
Barry Docks	d				10 19				10 33			10 48			11 03				11 19			11 33	
Cadoxton	d				10 22				10 36			10 51			11 06				11 22			11 36	
Dinas Powys	d				10 26				10 40			10 55			11 10				11 26			11 40	
Eastbrook	d				10 28				10 43			10 58			11 13				11 28			11 43	
Cogan	d				10 30				10 45			11 00			11 15				11 30			11 45	
Penarth	d	10 17				10 32							11 02			11 17				11 32			
Dingle Road	d	10 19				10 34							11 04			11 19				11 34			
Grangetown	d	10 23			10 34	10 38			10 49			11 04	11 08		11 19	11 23			11 34	11 38		11 49	
Cardiff Central	a	10 29			10 41	10 44			10 54			11 09	11 14		11 24	11 29			11 39	11 44		11 54	
	d	10 31	10 31	10 36		10 46	10 51	10 55	10 56		11 06	11 11	11 16	11 21	11 26	11 31	11 36	11 36	11 41	11 46	11 51	11 56	12 06
Cardiff Queen Street	a	10 34				10 49	10 54		10 59			11 14	11 19	11 24	11 29	11 34	11 39		11 44	11 49	11 54	11 59	12 09
	d	10 35				10 50	10 55		11 00			11 15	11 20	11 25	11 30	11 35	11 40		11 45	11 50	11 55	12 00	12 10
Heath Low Level	d						11 00							11 30							12 00		
Ty Glas	d						11 03							11 33							12 03		
Birchgrove	d						11 04							11 34							12 04		
Rhiwbina	d						11 06							11 36							12 06		
Whitchurch (Cardiff)	d						11 08							11 38							12 08		
Coryton	a						11 13							11 44							12 14		
Heath High Level	d	10 40				10 55							11 25			11 40				11 55			
Llanishen	d	10 43				10 58							11 28			11 43				11 58			
Lisvane & Thornhill	d	10 45				11 00							11 30			11 45				12 00			
Caerphilly	d	10 51				11 06							11 36			11 51				12 06			
Aber	d	10 53				11 08							11 38			11 53				12 08			
Energlyn & Churchill Park	d												11 40										
Llanbradach	d	10 57				11 12							11 44			11 57				12 12			
Ystrad Mynach	d	11 07				11a21							11 49			12 07				12a21			
Hengoed	d	11 10											11 52			12 10							
Pengam	d	11 13											11 55			12 13							
Gilfach Fargoed	d																						
Bargoed	a	11 22											12 00			12 22							
	d												12 01										
Brithdir	d												12 05										
Tir-phil	d												12 08										
Pontlottyn	d												12 12										
Rhymney	a												12 19										
Cathays	d								11 03			11 18			11 33		11 43		11 48			12 03	12 13
Llandaf	d								11 07			11 22			11 37		11 47		11 52			12 07	12 17
Ninian Park	d			10 40			11 40				11 10			12 10				11 40			12 40		
Waun-gron Park	d			10 44			11 44				11 14			12 14				11 44			12 44		
Fairwater	d			10 46			11 46				11 16			12 16				11 46			12 46		
Danescourt	d			10 49			11 49			←	11 19			12 19				11 49			12 49		
Radyr	a		10 43	10 56			11 56	11 03	11 10	11 03	11 26	11 25		12 26	11 40		11 50	11 56	11 55		12 56	12 10	12 20
	d		10 51					11 20	11 11	11 20		11 26			11 41		11 51		11 56			12 11	12 21
Taffs Well	d		10 55					→	11 15	11 24		11 30			11 45		11 55		12 00			12 15	12 25
Trefforest Estate	d								11 19						11 49							12 19	
Trefforest	d		11 02						11 23	11 31		11 37			11 53		12 02		12 07			12 23	12 32
Pontypridd	a		11 05						11 26	11 34		11 40			11 56		12 05		12 10			12 26	12 35
	d		11 06						11 27	11 36		11 42			11 57		12 06		12 12			12 27	12 36
Abercynon	d								11 34			11 49			12 04				12 19			12 34	
Penrhiwceiber	d											11 55							12 25				
Mountain Ash	a											11 58							12 28				
	d											12 04							12 34				
Fernhill	d											12 07							12 37				
Cwmbach	d											12 11							12 41				
Aberdare	a											12 18							12 48				
Quakers Yard	d								11 39						12 09							12 39	
Merthyr Vale	a								11 44						12 14							12 44	
	d								11 47						12 17							12 47	
Troed Y Rhiw	d								11 51						12 21							12 51	
Pentre-bach	d								11 54						12 24							12 54	
Merthyr Tydfil	a								12 03						12 33							13 03	
Trehafod	d		11 11							11 41							12 11						12 41
Porth	a		11 14							11 44							12 14						12 44
	d		11 15							11 45							12 15						12 45
Dinas Rhondda	d		11 19							11 49							12 19						12 49
Tonypandy	d		11 21							11 51							12 21						12 51
Llwynypia	d		11 23							11 53							12 23						12 53
Ystrad Rhondda	a		11 26							11 56							12 26						12 56
	d		11 29							11 59							12 29						12 59
Ton Pentre	d		11 31							12 01							12 31						13 01
Treorchy	d		11 34							12 04							12 34						13 04
Ynyswen	d		11 37							12 07							12 37						13 07
Treherbert	a		11 43							12 13							12 43						13 13

When events are being held at the Principality Stadium, services are subject to alteration. Please check times before travelling.

For connections to Cardiff Bay please refer to Table T124

Table T130-R

Mondays to Fridays

10 September to 7 December

Bridgend, Barry Island, Barry, Penarth and Cardiff - Coryton, Rhymney, Pontypridd, Merthyr, Aberdare and Treherbert

		AW	AW	AW	AW	AW	AW	AW	AW	AW	AW	AW	AW	AW	AW	AW	AW	AW	AW	AW	AW	AW
Bridgend	d									11 42												
Llantwit Major	d									11 56												
Rhoose Cardiff Int Airport ✈	d									12 06												
Barry Island	d		11 40			11 55								12 25			12 40			12 55		
Barry	d		11 45			12 00				12 15				12 30			12 45			13 00		
Barry Docks	d		11 48			12 03				12 18				12 33			12 48			13 03		
Cadoxton	d		11 51			12 06				12 21				12 36			12 51			13 06		
Dinas Powys	d		11 55			12 10				12 25				12 40			12 55			13 10		
Eastbrook	d		11 58			12 13				12 28				12 43			12 58			13 13		
Cogan	d		12 00			12 15				12 30				12 45			13 00			13 15		
Penarth	d			12 02			12 17					12 32						13 02			13 17	
Dingle Road	d			12 04			12 19					12 34						13 04			13 19	
Grangetown	d		12 04	12 08		12 19	12 23			12 34		12 38		12 49			13 04	13 08		13 19	13 23	
Cardiff Central	a		12 09	12 14		12 24	12 29			12 40		12 44		12 54			13 09	13 14		13 24	13 29	
	d	12 06	12 11	12 16	12 21	12 26	12 31	12 36	12 36		12 41	12 46	12 51	12 56	13 06	13 06	13 11	13 16	13 21	13 26	13 31	13 36
Cardiff Queen Street	a		12 14	12 19	12 24	12 29	12 34	12 39			12 44	12 49	12 54	12 59	13 09		13 14	13 19	13 24	13 29	13 34	13 39
	d		12 15	12 20	12 25	12 30	12 35	12 40			12 45	12 50	12 55	13 00	13 10		13 15	13 20	13 25	13 30	13 35	13 40
Heath Low Level	d				12 30								13 00						13 30			
Ty Glas	d				12 33								13 03						13 33			
Birchgrove	d				12 34								13 04						13 34			
Rhiwbina	d				12 36								13 06						13 36			
Whitchurch (Cardiff)	d				12 38								13 08						13 38			
Coryton	a				12 44								13 14						13 44			
Heath High Level	d			12 25			12 40					12 55						13 25			13 40	
Llanishen	d			12 28			12 43					12 58						13 28			13 43	
Lisvane & Thornhill	d			12 30			12 45					13 00						13 30			13 45	
Caerphilly	d			12 36			12 51					13 06						13 36			13 51	
Aber	d			12 38			12 53					13 08						13 38			13 53	
Energlyn & Churchill Park	d			12 40														13 40				
Llanbradach	d			12 44			12 57					13 12						13 44			13 57	
Ystrad Mynach	d			12 49			13 07					13a21						13 49			14 07	
Hengoed	d			12 52			13 10											13 52			14 10	
Pengam	d			12 55			13 13											13 55			14 13	
Gilfach Fargoed	d																					
Bargoed	a			13 00			13 22											14 00			14 22	
	d			13 01														14 01				
Brithdir	d			13 05														14 05				
Tir-phil	d			13 08														14 08				
Pontlottyn	d			13 12														14 12				
Rhymney	a			13 19														14 19				
Cathays	d		12 18			12 33		12 43			12 48			13 03	13 13		13 18			13 33		13 43
Llandaf	d		12 22			12 37		12 47			12 52			13 07	13 17		13 22			13 37		13 47
Ninian Park	d	12 10			13 10				12 40				13 40			13 10			14 10			
Waun-gron Park	d	12 14			13 14				12 44				13 44			13 14			14 14			
Fairwater	d	12 16			13 16				12 46				13 46			13 16			14 16			
Danescourt	d	12 19			13 19				12 49				13 49			13 19			14 19			
Radyr	a	12 26	12 25		13 26	12 40		12 50	12 56		12 55		13 56	13 10	13 20	13 26	13 25		14 26	13 40		13 50
	d		12 25			12 41		12 51			12 56			13 11	13 21		13 26			13 41		13 51
Taffs Well	d		12 29			12 45		12 55			13 00			13 15	13 25		13 30			13 45		13 55
Trefforest Estate	d					12 49								13 19						13 49		
Trefforest	d		12 36			12 53		13 02			13 07			13 23	13 32		13 37			13 53		14 02
Pontypridd	a		12 42			12 56		13 05			13 10			13 26	13 35		13 40			13 56		14 05
	d					12 57		13 06			13 12			13 27	13 36		13 42			13 57		14 06
Abercynon	d					13 04					13 19			13 34			13 49			14 04		
Penrhiwceiber	d										13 25						13 55					
Mountain Ash	a										13 28						13 58					
	d										13 34						14 04					
Fernhill	d										13 37						14 07					
Cwmbach	d										13 41						14 11					
Aberdare	a										13 48						14 18					
Quakers Yard	d					13 09								13 39						14 09		
Merthyr Vale	a					13 14								13 44						14 14		
	d					13 17								13 47						14 17		
Troed Y Rhiw	d					13 21								13 51						14 21		
Pentre-bach	d					13 24								13 54						14 24		
Merthyr Tydfil	a					13 33								14 03						14 33		
Trehafod	d							13 11							13 41							14 11
Porth	a							13 14							13 44							14 14
	d							13 15							13 45							14 15
Dinas Rhondda	d							13 19							13 49							14 19
Tonypandy	d							13 21							13 51							14 21
Llwynypia	d							13 23							13 53							14 23
Ystrad Rhondda	a							13 26							13 56							14 26
	d							13 29							13 59							14 29
Ton Pentre	d							13 31							14 01							14 31
Treorchy	d							13 34							14 04							14 34
Ynyswen	d							13 37							14 07							14 37
Treherbert	a							13 43							14 13							14 43

When events are being held at the Principality Stadium, services are subject to alteration. Please check times before travelling.

For connections to Cardiff Bay please refer to Table T124

Table T130-R

Mondays to Fridays

10 September to 7 December

Bridgend, Barry Island, Barry, Penarth and Cardiff - Coryton, Rhymney, Pontypridd, Merthyr, Aberdare and Treherbert

		AW	AW	AW	AW	AW	AW	AW	AW	AW	AW	AW	AW	AW	AW	AW	AW	AW	AW	AW	AW	AW	AW
Bridgend	d		12 42													13 42							
Llantwit Major	d		12 56													13 56							
Rhoose Cardiff Int Airport ✈	d		13 06													14 06							
Barry Island	d					13 25						13 55								14 25			14 40
Barry	d		13 15			13 30						14 00				14 15				14 30			14 45
Barry Docks	d		13 18			13 33						14 03				14 18				14 33			14 48
Cadoxton	d		13 21			13 36						14 06				14 21				14 36			14 51
Dinas Powys	d		13 25			13 40						14 10				14 25				14 40			14 55
Eastbrook	d		13 28			13 43						14 13				14 28				14 43			14 58
Cogan	d		13 30			13 45						14 15				14 30				14 45			15 00
Penarth	d			13 32						14 02			14 17				14 32						
Dingle Road	d			13 34						14 04			14 19				14 34						
Grangetown	d		13 34	13 38		13 49				14 08		14 19	14 23			14 34				14 49			15 04
Cardiff Central	a		13 39	13 44		13 54				14 14		14 24	14 29			14 39	14 42			14 54			15 10
	d	13 36	13 41	13 46	13 51	13 56	14 06	14 06	14 11	14 16	14 21	14 26	14 31	14 36	14 36	14 41	14 46	14 51	14 51	14 56		15 06	15 11
Cardiff Queen Street	a		13 44	13 49	13 54	13 59	14 09		14 14	14 19	14 24	14 29	14 34	14 39		14 44	14 49		14 54	14 58			15 14
	d		13 45	13 50	13 55	14 00	14 10		14 15	14 20	14 25	14 30	14 35	14 40		14 45	14 50		14 55	15 00			15 15
Heath Low Level	d				14 00						14 30								15 00				
Ty Glas	d				14 03						14 33								15 03				
Birchgrove	d				14 04						14 34								15 04				
Rhiwbina	d				14 06						14 36								15 06				
Whitchurch (Cardiff)	d				14 08						14 38								15 08				
Coryton	a				14 14						14 44								15 14				
Heath High Level	d			13 55						14 25			14 40				14 55						
Llanishen	d			13 58						14 28			14 43				14 58						
Lisvane & Thornhill	d			14 00						14 30			14 45				15 00						
Caerphilly	d			14 06						14 36			14 51				15 06						
Aber	d			14 08						14 38			14 53				15 08						
Energlyn & Churchill Park	d									14 40													
Llanbradach	d			14 12						14 44			14 57				15 12						
Ystrad Mynach	d			14a21						14 49			15 07				15a21						
Hengoed	d									14 52			15 10										
Pengam	d									14 55			15 13										
Gilfach Fargoed	d																						
Bargoed	a									15 00			15 22										
	d									15 01													
Brithdir	d									15 05													
Tir-phil	d									15 08													
Pontlottyn	d									15 12													
Rhymney	a									15 19													
Cathays	d		13 48			14 03	14 13		14 18			14 33		14 43		14 48				15 03			15 18
Llandaf	d		13 52			14 07	14 17		14 22			14 37		14 47		14 52				15 07			15 22
Ninian Park	d	13 40			14 40			14 10			15 10				14 40				15 40			15 10	
Waun-gron Park	d	13 44			14 44			14 14			15 15				14 44				15 44			15 15	
Fairwater	d	13 46			14 46			14 16			15 16				14 46				15 46			15 16	
Danescourt	d	13 49			14 49			14 19			15 20				14 49				15 49		←	15 20	
Radyr	a	13 56	13 55		14 56	14 10	14 20	14 26	14 25		15 26	14 40		14 50	14 56	14 55		15 09	15 56	15 10	15 09	15 26	15 25
	d		13 56			14 11	14 21		14 26			14 41		14 51		14 56		15 21		15 11	15 21		15 26
Taffs Well	d		14 00			14 15	14 25		14 30			14 45		14 55		15 00		→		15 15	15 25		15 30
Trefforest Estate	d					14 19						14 49								15 19			
Trefforest	d		14 07			14 23	14 32		14 37			14 53		15 02		15 07				15 23	15 32		15 37
Pontypridd	a		14 10			14 26	14 35		14 41			14 56		15 05		15 10				15 26	15 35		15 40
	d		14 12			14 27	14 36		14 42			14 57		15 06		15 12				15 27	15 36		15 42
Abercynon	d		14 19			14 34			14 49			15 04				15 19				15 34			15 49
Penrhiwceiber	d		14 25						14 55							15 25							15 55
Mountain Ash	a		14 28						14 58							15 28							15 58
	d		14 34						15 04							15 34							16 04
Fernhill	d		14 37						15 07							15 37							16 07
Cwmbach	d		14 41						15 11							15 41							16 11
Aberdare	a		14 48						15 18							15 48							16 18
Quakers Yard	d					14 39						15 09								15 39			
Merthyr Vale	a					14 44						15 14								15 44			
	d					14 47						15 17								15 47			
Troed Y Rhiw	d					14 51						15 21								15 51			
Pentre-bach	d					14 54						15 24								15 54			
Merthyr Tydfil	a					15 03						15 33								16 03			
Trehafod	d						14 41							15 11							15 41		
Porth	a						14 44							15 14							15 44		
	d						14 45							15 15							15 45		
Dinas Rhondda	d						14 49							15 19							15 49		
Tonypandy	d						14 51							15 21							15 51		
Llwynypia	d						14 53							15 23							15 53		
Ystrad Rhondda	a						14 56							15 26							15 56		
	d						14 59							15 29							15 59		
Ton Pentre	d						15 01							15 31							16 01		
Treorchy	d						15 04							15 34							16 04		
Ynyswen	d						15 07							15 37							16 07		
Treherbert	a						15 13							15 43							16 13		

When events are being held at the Principality Stadium, services are subject to alteration. Please check times before travelling.

For connections to Cardiff Bay please refer to Table T124

Table T130-R

Mondays to Fridays

10 September to 7 December

Bridgend, Barry Island, Barry, Penarth and Cardiff - Coryton, Rhymney, Pontypridd, Merthyr, Aberdare and Treherbert

		AW	AW	AW	AW	AW	AW	AW	AW	AW	AW	AW	AW	AW	AW	AW	AW	AW	AW	AW	AW	AW	AW
Bridgend	d						14 42													15 42			
Llantwit Major	d						14 56													15 56			
Rhoose Cardiff Int Airport ✈	d						15 06													16 06			
Barry Island	d			14 55						15 25			15 40			15 55							16 25
Barry	d			15 00			15 15			15 30			15 45			16 00				16 15			16 30
Barry Docks	d			15 04			15 18			15 33			15 48			16 03				16 18			16 33
Cadoxton	d			15 07			15 21			15 36			15 51			16 06				16 21			16 36
Dinas Powys	d			15 11			15 25			15 40			15 55			16 10				16 25			16 40
Eastbrook	d			15 13			15 28			15 43			15 58			16 13				16 28			16 43
Cogan	d			15 15			15 30			15 45			16 00			16 15				16 30			16 45
Penarth	d	15 02						15 32			15 47			16 02			16 17				16 32		
Dingle Road	d	15 04						15 34			15 49			16 04			16 19				16 34		
Grangetown	d	15 08		15 19			15 34	15 38		15 49	15 53		16 04	16 08		16 19	16 23			16 34	16 38		16 49
Cardiff Central	a	15 14		15 24			15 39	15 44		15 54	15 59		16 09	16 14		16 24	16 29			16 39	16 44		16 54
	d	15 16	15 21	15 26	15 36	15 36	15 41	15 46	15 51	15 56	16 01	16 06	16 11	16 16	16 21	16 26	16 31	16 36	16 36	16 41	16 46	16 51	16 56
Cardiff Queen Street	a	15 19	15 24	15 29	15 39		15 44	15 49	15 54	15 59	16 04	16 09	16 14	16 19	16 24	16 29	16 34	16 39		16 44	16 49	16 54	16 59
	d	15 20	15 25	15 30	15 40		15 45	15 50	15 55	16 00	16 05	16 10	16 15	16 20	16 25	16 30	16 35	16 40		16 45	16 50	16 55	17 00
Heath Low Level	d		15 30						16 00						16 30							17 00	
Ty Glas	d		15 33						16 03						16 33							17 03	
Birchgrove	d		15 34						16 04						16 34							17 04	
Rhiwbina	d		15 36						16 06						16 36							17 06	
Whitchurch (Cardiff)	d		15 38						16 08						16 38							17 08	
Coryton	a		15 44						16 14						16 44							17 14	
Heath High Level	d	15 25						15 55			16 10			16 25			16 40				16 55		
Llanishen	d	15 28						15 58			16 13			16 28			16 43				16 58		
Lisvane & Thornhill	d	15 30						16 00			16 15			16 30			16 45				17 00		
Caerphilly	d	15 36						16 06			16 21			16 36			16 51				17 06		
Aber	d	15 38						16 08			16 23			16 38			16 53				17 08		
Energlyn & Churchill Park	d	15 40									16 25			16 40									
Llanbradach	d	15 44						16 12			16 29			16 44			16 57				17 12		
Ystrad Mynach	d	15 49						16 17			16 34			16 49			17 02				17 17		
Hengoed	d	15 52						16 20			16 37			16 52			17 05				17 20		
Pengam	d	15 55						16 23			16 40			16 55			17 08				17 23		
Gilfach Fargoed	d										16 43												
Bargoed	a	16 00						16 32			16 53			17 00			17 17				17 32		
	d	16 01												17 01			17 17						
Brithdir	d	16 05												17 05									
Tir-phil	d	16 08												17 08									
Pontlottyn	d	16 12												17 12									
Rhymney	a	16 19												17 19									
Cathays	d			15 33	15 43		15 48			16 03		16 13	16 18			16 33	18 43	16 43		16 48			17 03
Llandaf	d			15 37	15 47		15 52			16 07		16 17	16 22			16 37	18 47	16 47		16 52			17 07
Ninian Park	d		16 10			15 40			16 40						17 10				16 40			17 40	
Waun-gron Park	d		16 14			15 44			16 44						17 14				16 44			17 44	
Fairwater	d		16 16			15 46			16 46						17 16				16 46			17 46	
Danescourt	d		16 19			15 49			16 49						17 19				16 49			17 49	
Radyr	a		16 26	15 40	15 50	15 56	15 55		16 56	16 10		16 20	16 25		17 26	16 40	18 51	16 50	16 56	16 55		17 56	17 10
	d			15 41	15 51		15 56			16 11		16 21	16 26			16 41	18 51	16 51		16 56			17 11
Taffs Well	d			15 45	15 55		16 00			16 15		16 25	16 30			16 45	→	16 55		17 00			17 15
Trefforest Estate	d			15 49						16 19						16 49							17 19
Trefforest	d			15 53	16 02		16 07			16 23		16 32	16 37			16 53		17 02		17 07			17 23
Pontypridd	a			15 56	16 05		16 10			16 26		16 35	16 40			16 56		17 05		17 10			17 26
	d			15 57	16 06		16 12			16 27		16 36	16 42			16 57		17 06		17 12			17 27
Abercynon	d			16 04			16 19			16 34			16 49			17 04				17 19			17 34
Penrhiwceiber	d						16 25						16 55							17 25			
Mountain Ash	a						16 28						16 58							17 28			
	d						16 34						17 04							17 34			
Fernhill	d						16 37						17 07							17 37			
Cwmbach	d						16 41						17 11							17 41			
Aberdare	a						16 48						17 18							17 48			
Quakers Yard	d			16 09						16 39						17 09							17 39
Merthyr Vale	a			16 14						16 44						17 14							17 44
	d			16 17						16 47						17 17							17 47
Troed Y Rhiw	d			16 21						16 51						17 21							17 51
Pentre-bach	d			16 24						16 54						17 24							17 54
Merthyr Tydfil	a			16 33						17 03						17 33							18 03
Trehafod	d				16 11							16 41						17 11					
Porth	a				16 14							16 44						17 14					
	d				16 15							16 45						17 15					
Dinas Rhondda	d				16 19							16 49						17 19					
Tonypandy	d				16 21							16 51						17 21					
Llwynypia	d				16 23							16 53						17 23					
Ystrad Rhondda	a				16 26							16 56						17 26					
	d				16 29							16 59						17 29					
Ton Pentre	d				16 31							17 01						17 31					
Treorchy	d				16 34							17 04						17 34					
Ynyswen	d				16 37							17 07						17 37					
Treherbert	a				16 43							17 13						17 43					

When events are being held at the Principality Stadium, services are subject to alteration. Please check times before travelling.

For connections to Cardiff Bay please refer to Table T124

Table T130-R

Mondays to Fridays
10 September to 7 December

Bridgend, Barry Island, Barry, Penarth and Cardiff - Coryton, Rhymney, Pontypridd, Merthyr, Aberdare and Treherbert

		AW		AW	AW	AW	AW	AW	AW	AW	AW	AW		AW	AW	AW	AW	AW	AW	AW	AW	AW		AW	AW
Bridgend	d													16 42											
Llantwit Major	d													16 56											
Rhoose Cardiff Int Airport ✈	d													17 06											
Barry Island	d					16 40			16 55								17 25				17 40				17 55
Barry 3	d					16 45			17 00					17 15			17 30				17 45				18 00
Barry Docks	d					16 48			17 03					17 18			17 33				17 48				18 03
Cadoxton	d					16 51			17 06					17 21			17 36				17 51				18 06
Dinas Powys	d					16 55			17 10					17 25			17 40				17 55				18 10
Eastbrook	d					16 58			17 13					17 28			17 43				17 58				18 13
Cogan	d					17 00			17 15					17 30			17 45				18 00				18 15
Penarth	d						17 02			17 17					17 32			17 47				18 02			
Dingle Road	d						17 04			17 19					17 34			17 49				18 04			
Grangetown	d					17 04	17 08		17 19	17 23				17 34	17 38		17 49	17 53			18 04	18 08			18 19
Cardiff Central 7	a					17 09	17 14		17 24	17 29				17 39	17 44		17 54	17 59			18 09	18 14			18 24
	d	17 01		17 06	17 06	17 11	17 16	17 21	17 26	17 31	17 36	17 36		17 41	17 46	17 51	17 56	18 01	18 06	18 06	18 11	18 16		18 21	18 26
Cardiff Queen Street 3	a	17 04		17 09		17 14	17 19	17 24	17 29	17 34	17 39			17 44	17 49	17 54	17 59	18 04	18 09		18 14	18 19		18 24	18 29
	d	17 05		17 10		17 15	17 20	17 25	17 30	17 35	17 40			17 45	17 50	17 55	18 00	18 05	18 10		18 15	18 20		18 25	18 30
Heath Low Level	d							17 30								18 00								18 30	
Ty Glas	d							17 33								18 03								18 33	
Birchgrove	d							17 34								18 04								18 34	
Rhiwbina	d							17 36								18 06								18 36	
Whitchurch (Cardiff)	d							17 38								18 08								18 38	
Coryton	a							17 44								18 14								18 44	
Heath High Level	d	17 10					17 25			17 40					17 55			18 10				18 25			
Llanishen	d	17 13					17 28			17 43					17 59			18 13				18 28			
Lisvane & Thornhill	d	17 15					17 31			17 45					18 02			18 15				18 30			
Caerphilly	d	17 21					17 37			17 51					18 07			18 21				18 36			
Aber	d	17 23					17 39			17 53					18 10			18 23				18 38			
Energlyn & Churchill Park	d	17 26					17 41			17 55					18 13							18 40			
Llanbradach	d	17 29					17 45			17 59					18 17			18 27				18 44			
Ystrad Mynach	d	17 35					17 50			18 04					18 22			18 32				18a54			
Hengoed	d	17 37					17 53			18 07					18 25			18 35							
Pengam	d	17 41					17 56			18 10					18 29			18 38							
Gilfach Fargoed	d	17 44								18 13					18 33			18 41							
Bargoed	a	17 47					18 04			18 16					18 36			18 49							
	d	17 49								18 18					18 38			18 48							
Brithdir	d	17 52								18 22					18 41										
Tir-phil	d	17 55								18 25					18 44										
Pontlottyn	d	18 00								18 29					18 49										
Rhymney 3	a	18 07								18 36					18 56										
Cathays	d			17 13		17 18			17 33		17 43			17 48			18 03	20 13	18 13		18 18				18 33
Llandaf	d			17 17		17 22			17 37		17 47			17 52			18 07	20 17	18 17		18 22				18 37
Ninian Park	d				17 10			18 10				17 40				18 40				18 10					
Waun-gron Park	d				17 14			18 14				17 44				18 44				18 14					
Fairwater	d				17 16			18 16				17 46				18 46				18 16					
Danescourt	d				17 19			18 19				17 49				18 49				18 19					
Radyr 3	a			17 20	17 26	17 25		18 26	17 40		17 50	17 56		17 55		18 56	18 10	20 20	18 20	18 26	18 25				18 40
	d			17 21		17 26			17 41		17 51			17 56			18 11	20 21	18 21		18 25				18 41
Taffs Well	d			17 25		17 30			17 45		17 55			18 00			18 15	→	18 25		18 29				18 45
Trefforest Estate	d								17 49								18 19								18 49
Trefforest	d			17 32		17 37			17 53		18 02			18 07			18 23		18 32		18 36				18 53
Pontypridd 3	a			17 35		17 40			17 56		18 05			18 10			18 26		18 35		18 42				18 56
	d			17 36		17 42			17 57		18 06			18 12			18 27		18 36						18 57
Abercynon	d					17 49			18 04					18 19			18 34								19 04
Penrhiwceiber	d					17 55								18 25											
Mountain Ash	a					17 58								18 28											
	d					18 04								18 34											
Fernhill	d					18 07								18 37											
Cwmbach	d					18 11								18 41											
Aberdare	a					18 18								18 48											
Quakers Yard	d								18 09								18 39								19 09
Merthyr Vale	a								18 14								18 44								19 14
	d								18 17								18 47								19 17
Troed Y Rhiw	d								18 21								18 51								19 21
Pentre-bach	d								18 24								18 54								19 24
Merthyr Tydfil	a								18 33								19 00								19 33
Trehafod	d			17 41							18 11								18 41						
Porth	a			17 44							18 14								18 44						
	d			17 45							18 15								18 45						
Dinas Rhondda	d			17 49							18 19								18 49						
Tonypandy	d			17 51							18 21								18 51						
Llwynypia	d			17 53							18 23								18 53						
Ystrad Rhondda	a			17 56							18 26								18 56						
	d			17 59							18 29								18 59						
Ton Pentre	d			18 01							18 31								19 01						
Treorchy	d			18 04							18 34								19 04						
Ynyswen	d			18 07							18 37								19 07						
Treherbert	a			18 13							18 43								19 13						

When events are being held at the Principality Stadium, services are subject to alteration. Please check times before travelling.

For connections to Cardiff Bay please refer to Table T124

Table T130-R

Mondays to Fridays
10 September to 7 December

Bridgend, Barry Island, Barry, Penarth and Cardiff - Coryton, Rhymney, Pontypridd, Merthyr, Aberdare and Treherbert

		AW	AW	AW	AW	AW	AW	AW		AW	AW	AW	AW	AW	AW	AW	AW	AW		AW	AW	AW	AW	AW	AW
Bridgend	d				17 42									18 42								19 42			
Llantwit Major	d				17 56									18 56								19 56			
Rhoose Cardiff Int Airport ✈	d				18 06									19 06								20 06			
Barry Island	d						18 25			18 40	18 55						19 25	19 55							
Barry 3	d				18 15		18 30			18 45	19 00			19 15			19 30	20 00				20 15			
Barry Docks	d				18 18		18 33			18 48	19 03			19 18			19 33	20 03				20 18			
Cadoxton	d				18 21		18 36			18 51	19 06			19 21			19 36	20 06				20 21			
Dinas Powys	d				18 25		18 40			18 55	19 10			19 25			19 40	20 10				20 25			
Eastbrook	d				18 28		18 43			18 58	19 13			19 28			19 43	20 13				20 28			
Cogan	d				18 30		18 45			19 00	19 15			19 30			19 45	20 15				20 30			
Penarth	d		18 17					18 47				19 17								20 20				20 47	
Dingle Road	d		18 19					18 49				19 19								20 22				20 49	
Grangetown	d		18 23		18 34		18 49	18 53		19 04	19 19	19 23		19 34			19 49	20 19		20 26		20 34		20 53	
Cardiff Central 7	a		18 29		18 39		18 56	18 59		19 09	19 24	19 29		19 39			19 54	20 24		20 31		20 39		20 58	
	d		18 31	18 36	18 41	18 51		19 06		19 11	19 26	19 31	19 36	19 41		19 51	20 01	20 26		20 31	20 36	20 41	20 51	21 01	21 06
Cardiff Queen Street 3	a		18 34		18 44	18 54		19 09		19 14	19 29	19 34		19 44		19 54	20 04	20 28		20 34		20 44	20 54	21 04	21 09
	d		18 35		18 47	18 55		19 10		19 15	19 30	19 35		19 45		19 55	20 05	20 30		20 35		20 45	20 55	21 05	21 10
Heath Low Level	d					19 00										20 00							21 00		
Ty Glas	d					19 03										20 03							21 03		
Birchgrove	d					19 04										20 04							21 04		
Rhiwbina	d					19 06										20 06							21 06		
Whitchurch (Cardiff)	d					19 08										20 08							21 08		
Coryton	a					19 14										20 14							21 14		
Heath High Level	d		18 40									19 40					20 11			20 40				21 11	
Llanishen	d		18 43									19 43					20 14			20 43				21 14	
Lisvane & Thornhill	d		18 45									19 45					20 16			20 45				21 16	
Caerphilly	d		18 51									19 51					20a25			20 51				21 23	
Aber	d		18 53									19 53								20 53				21 25	
Energlyn & Churchill Park	d		18 55									19 56								20 55					
Llanbradach	d		18 59									19 59								20 59				21 30	
Ystrad Mynach	d		19 04									20 04								21 04				21a40	
Hengoed	d		19 07									20 07								21 07					
Pengam	d		19 10									20 10								21 10					
Gilfach Fargoed	d		19 13									20 13								21 13					
Bargoed	a		19 16									20 17								21 17					
	d		19 18									20 18								21 18					
Brithdir	d		19 22									20 22								21 22					
Tir-phil	d		19 25									20 25								21 25					
Pontlottyn	d		19 29									20 29								21 29					
Rhymney 3	a		19 37									20 36								21 37					
Cathays	d				18 50			19 13		19 18	19 33			19 48				20 33				20 48			21 13
Llandaf	d				18 54			19 17		19 22	19 37			19 52				20 37				20 52			21 17
Ninian Park	d			18 40		19 40							19 40			20 40					20 40		21 40		
Waun-gron Park	d			18 44		19 44							19 44			20 44					20 44		21 44		
Fairwater	d			18 46		19 46							19 46			20 46					20 46		21 46		
Danescourt	d	←		18 49		19 49							19 49		←	20 49					20 49		21 49		
Radyr 3	a	18 51		18 56	18 57	19 56		19 20		19 25	19 40		19 56	19 55	20 20	20 56		20 40			20 56	20 55	21 56		21 20
	d	18 51			18 58			19 21		19 26	19 41			19 56	20 21			20 42				20 56			21 21
Taffs Well	d	18 55			19 02			19 25		19 30	19 45			20 00	20 25			20 46				21 00			21 25
Trefforest Estate	d										19 49							20 50							
Trefforest	d	19 02			19 09			19 32		19 37	19 53			20 07	20 32			20 53				21 07			21 32
Pontypridd 3	a	19 05			19 12			19 35		19 40	19 56			20 10	20 35			20 56				21 10			21 35
	d	19 06			19 12			19 36		19 42	19 57			20 12	20 36			20 58				21 12			21 36
Abercynon	d				19 19					19 49	20 04			20 21				21 05				21 19			
Penrhiwceiber	d				19 24					19 55				20 27								21 25			
Mountain Ash	a				19 28					19 59				20 31								21 28			
	d				19 33					20 04				20 34								21 29			
Fernhill	d				19 35					20 07				20 37								21 32			
Cwmbach	d				19 39					20 11				20 41								21 36			
Aberdare	a				19 46					20 18				20 48								21 43			
Quakers Yard	d										20 09							21 10							
Merthyr Vale	a										20 14							21 15							
	d										20 14							21 15							
Troed Y Rhiw	d										20 18							21 19							
Pentre-bach	d										20 22							21 23							
Merthyr Tydfil	a										20 30							21 31							
Trehafod	d	19 11						19 41							20 41										21 41
Porth	a	19 14						19 44							20 44										21 44
	d	19 15						19 45							20 45										21 45
Dinas Rhondda	d	19 19						19 49							20 49										21 49
Tonypandy	d	19 21						19 51							20 51										21 51
Llwynypia	d	19 23						19 53							20 53										21 53
Ystrad Rhondda	a	19 26						19 56							20 56										21 56
	d	19 29						19 59							20 59										21 59
Ton Pentre	d	19 31						20 01							21 01										22 01
Treorchy	d	19 34						20 04							21 04										22 04
Ynyswen	d	19 37						20 07							21 07										22 07
Treherbert	a	19 43						20 13							21 13										22 13

When events are being held at the Principality Stadium, services are subject to alteration. Please check times before travelling.

For connections to Cardiff Bay please refer to Table T124

Table T130-R

Mondays to Fridays
10 September to 7 December

Bridgend, Barry Island, Barry, Penarth and Cardiff - Coryton, Rhymney, Pontypridd, Merthyr, Aberdare and Treherbert

		AW	AW	AW	AW	AW	AW	AW	AW	AW	AW	AW	AW	AW	AW	AW	AW	AW	AW
Bridgend	d					20 42							21 42						22 42
Llantwit Major	d					20 56							21 56						22 56
Rhoose Cardiff Int Airport ✈	d					21 06							22 06						23 06
Barry Island	d	20 55								21 55							22 44		
Barry 3	d	21 00				21 15				22 00			22 15				22 49		23 15
Barry Docks	d	21 03				21 18				22 03			22 18				22 52		23 18
Cadoxton	d	21 06				21 21				22 06			22 21				22 55		23 21
Dinas Powys	d	21 10				21 25				22 10			22 25				22 59		23 25
Eastbrook	d	21 13				21 28				22 13			22 28				23 02		23 28
Cogan	d	21 15				21 30				22 15			22 30				23 04		23 30
Penarth	d			21 24			21 47				22 20					22 48		23 26	
Dingle Road	d			21 26			21 49				22 22					22 50		23 28	
Grangetown	d	21 19		21 30		21 34	21 53			22 19	22 26		22 34			22 54	23 08	23 32	23 34
Cardiff Central 7	a	21 24		21 36		21 39	21 59			22 24	22 33		22 39			23 01	23 13	23 39	23 43
	d	21 27	21 31		21 36	21 41	22 01	22 06	22 21	22 26		22 35	22 41	22 46	22 55	23 16	23 26		
Cardiff Queen Street 3	a	21 30	21 34			21 44	22 04	22 09	22 24	22 29		22 38	22 44	22 49		23 19	23 29		
	d	21 31	21 35			21 45	22 05	22 10	22 25	22 30		22 39	22 45	22 50		23 20	23 30		
Heath Low Level	d								22 30										
Ty Glas	d								22 33										
Birchgrove	d								22 34										
Rhiwbina	d								22 36										
Whitchurch (Cardiff)	d								22 38										
Coryton	a								22 44										
Heath High Level	d		21 40				22 10					22 44				23 25			
Llanishen	d		21 43				22 13					22 47				23 28			
Lisvane & Thornhill	d		21 45				22 15					22 49				23 30			
Caerphilly	d		21 51				22a23					22 55				23 36			
Aber	d		21 53									22 57				23 38			
Energlyn & Churchill Park	d		21 55									22 59				23 40			
Llanbradach	d		21 59									23 03				23 44			
Ystrad Mynach	d		22 04									23 08				23a54			
Hengoed	d		22 07									23 11							
Pengam	d		22 10									23 14							
Gilfach Fargoed	d		22 13									23 17							
Bargoed	a		22 17									23 21							
	d		22 18									23 22							
Brithdir	d		22 22									23 26							
Tir-phil	d		22 25									23 29							
Pontlottyn	d		22 29									23 33							
Rhymney 3	a		22 37									23 40							
Cathays	d	21 34				21 48		22 13		22 33			22 48	22 53			23 33		
Llandaf	d	21 38				21 52		22 17		22 37			22 52	22 57			23 37		
Ninian Park	d				21 40										22 59				
Waun-gron Park	d				21 44										23 02				
Fairwater	d				21 46										23 04				
Danescourt	d				21 49										23 06				
Radyr 3	a	21 41			21 56	21 55		22 20		22 40			22 55	23 00	23 13		23 40		
	d	21 42				21 56		22 21		22 41			22 56	23 00			23 41		
Taffs Well	d	21 46				22 00		22 25		22 45			23 00	23 04			23 45		
Trefforest Estate	d	21 50								22 49									
Trefforest	d	21 54				22 07		22 32		22 53			23 07	23 11			23 52		
Pontypridd 3	a	21 57				22 10		22 35		22 56			23 10	23 14			23 59		
	d	21 58				22 12		22 36		22 57			23 12	23 15					
Abercynon	d	22 05				22 19				23 04			23 19						
Penrhiwceiber	d					22 25							23 25						
Mountain Ash	a					22 28							23 28						
	d					22 29							23 34						
Fernhill	d					22 32							23 37						
Cwmbach	d					22 36							23 41						
Aberdare	a					22 43							23 48						
Quakers Yard	d	22 10								23 09									
Merthyr Vale	a	22 15								23 14									
	d	22 15								23 14									
Troed Y Rhiw	d	22 19								23 18									
Pentre-bach	d	22 23								23 22									
Merthyr Tydfil	a	22 31								23 30									
Trehafod	d							22 41						23 20					
Porth	a							22 44						23 23					
	d							22 45						23 24					
Dinas Rhondda	d							22 49						23 28					
Tonypandy	d							22 51						23 30					
Llwynypia	d							22 53						23 32					
Ystrad Rhondda	a							22 56						23 35					
	d							22 59						23 38					
Ton Pentre	d							23 01						23 40					
Treorchy	d							23 04						23 43					
Ynyswen	d							23 07						23 46					
Treherbert	a							23 13						23 52					

When events are being held at the Principality Stadium, services are subject to alteration. Please check times before travelling.

For connections to Cardiff Bay please refer to Table T124

Table T130-R

Saturdays
26 May to 8 September

Bridgend, Barry Island, Barry, Penarth and Cardiff - Coryton, Rhymney, Pontypridd, Merthyr, Aberdare and Treherbert

		AW	AW		AW	AW	AW	AW	AW	AW	AW	AW	AW	AW	AW	AW	AW	AW	AW	AW	AW	AW	AW
Bridgend	d												05 42										
Llantwit Major	d												05 56										
Rhoose Cardiff Int Airport ✈	d												06 06										
Barry Island	d		05 14						05 50						06 25							06 55	
Barry 3	d		05 19						05 55				06 15		06 30							07 00	
Barry Docks	d		05 22						05 58				06 18		06 33							07 03	
Cadoxton	d		05 25						06 01				06 21		06 36							07 06	
Dinas Powys	d		05 29						06 05				06 25		06 40							07 10	
Eastbrook	d		05 32						06 08				06 28		06 43							07 13	
Cogan	d		05 34						06 10				06 30		06 45							07 15	
Penarth	d							06 02											07 02				07 17
Dingle Road	d							06 04											07 04				07 19
Grangetown	d		05 38					06 08	06 14				06 34		06 49				07 08			07 19	07 23
Cardiff Central 7	a		05 43					06 13	06 19				06 39		06 54				07 14			07 24	07 29
	d	05 26	05 46	05 51		05 56	06 11	06 15	06 21	06 26	06 31	06 36	06 41	06 51	06 56	07 05	07 06	07 11	07 16	07 21	07 21	07 26	07 31
Cardiff Queen Street 3	a	05 29	05 50	05 55		05 59	06 14	06 19	06 24	06 29	06 34	06 39	06 44	06 54	06 59	07 08		07 14	07 19	07 24	07 24	07 29	07 34
	d	05 30	05 50	05 56		06 00	06 15	06 20	06 25	06 30	06 35	06 40	06 45	06 55	07 00	07 09		07 15	07 20	07 25	07 25	07 30	07 35
Heath Low Level	d			06 01					06 30					07 00						07 30	07 30		
Ty Glas	d			06 04					06 33					07 03						07 33	07 33		
Birchgrove	d			06 05					06 34					07 04						07 34	07 34		
Rhiwbina	d			06 07					06 36					07 06						07 36	07 36		
Whitchurch (Cardiff)	d			06 09					06 38					07 08						07 38	07 38		
Coryton	a			06 14					06 43					07 13						07 43	07 43		
Heath High Level	d		05 55					06 25											07 25				07 40
Llanishen	d		05 58					06 28											07 28				07 43
Lisvane & Thornhill	d		06 00					06 30											07 30				07 45
Caerphilly	d		06a08					06 36											07 36				07 51
Aber	d							06 38											07 38				07 53
Energlyn & Churchill Park	d																		07 40				
Llanbradach	d							06 42											07 44				07 57
Ystrad Mynach	d							06 47											07 49				08 02
Hengoed	d							06 50											07 52				08 05
Pengam	d							06 53											07 55				08 08
Gilfach Fargoed	d																						
Bargoed	a							07 01											08 03				08 13
	d																						08 14
Brithdir	d																						08 18
Tir-phil	d																						08 21
Pontlottyn	d																						08 25
Rhymney 3	a																						08 31
Cathays	d	05 33				06 03	06 18			06 33	06 37	06 43	06 48		07 03	07 12		07 18				07 33	
Llandaf	d	05 37				06 07	06 22			06 37		06 47	06 52		07 07	07 16		07 22				07 37	
Ninian Park	d								07 10					07 40			07 10				08 10		
Waun-gron Park	d								07 13					07 43			07 13				08 13		
Fairwater	d								07 15					07 45			07 15				08 15		
Danescourt	d								07 17					07 47			07 17				08 17		
Radyr 3	a	05 40				06 10	06 25		07 24	06 40	06 43	06 50	06 55	07 54	07 10	07 19	07 24	07 25			08 24	07 40	
	d	05 41				06 11	06 25			06 41	06 44	06 51	06 55		07 11	07 20		07 26				07 41	
Taffs Well	d	05 45				06 15	06 29			06 45	06a50	06 55	06 59		07 15	07 24		07 30				07 45	
Trefforest Estate	d	05 49				06 19				06 49					07 19							07 49	
Trefforest	d	05 53				06 23	06 36			06 53		07 02	07 06		07 23	07 31		07 37				07 53	
Pontypridd 3	a	05 56				06 26	06 39			06 56		07 05	07 09		07 26	07 34		07 40				07 56	
	d	05 57			06 11	06 27	06 42			06 57		07 06	07 12		07 27	07 35		07 42				07 57	
Abercynon	d	06 04			06 19	06 34	06 49			07 04			07 19		07 34			07 49				08 04	
Penrhiwceiber	d				06 24		06 54						07 24					07 54					
Mountain Ash	a				06 28		06 58						07 28					07 58					
	d				06 33		07 03						07 33					08 03					
Fernhill	d				06 35		07 05						07 35					08 05					
Cwmbach	d				06 39		07 09						07 39					08 09					
Aberdare	a				06 46		07 16						07 46					08 16					
Quakers Yard	d	06 09				06 39				07 09					07 39							08 09	
Merthyr Vale	a	06 14				06 44				07 14					07 44							08 14	
	d	06 17				06 47				07 17					07 47							08 17	
Troed Y Rhiw	d	06 20				06 50				07 20					07 50							08 20	
Pentre-bach	d	06 23				06 53				07 23					07 53							08 23	
Merthyr Tydfil	a	06 31				07 01				07 31					08 01							08 31	
Trehafod	d											07 11				07 40							
Porth	a											07 14				07 43							
	d											07 15				07 44							
Dinas Rhondda	d											07 19				07 48							
Tonypandy	d											07 21				07 50							
Llwynypia	d											07 23				07 52							
Ystrad Rhondda	a											07 26				07 55							
	d											07 29				07 59							
Ton Pentre	d											07 31				08 01							
Treorchy	d											07 34				08 04							
Ynyswen	d											07 37				08 07							
Treherbert	a											07 43				08 12							

When events are being held at the Principality Stadium, services are subject to alteration. Please check times before travelling.

For connections to Cardiff Bay please refer to Table T124

Table T130-R

Saturdays
26 May to 8 September

Bridgend, Barry Island, Barry, Penarth and Cardiff - Coryton, Rhymney, Pontypridd, Merthyr, Aberdare and Treherbert

		AW	AW	AW	AW	AW	AW	AW	AW	AW	AW	AW	AW	AW	AW	AW	AW	AW	AW	AW	AW	AW	AW
Bridgend	d			06 42														07 42					
Llantwit Major	d			06 56														07 56					
Rhoose Cardiff Int Airport ✈	d			07 06														08 06					
Barry Island	d						07 25				07 40			07 55							08 25		
Barry ■	d			07 15			07 30				07 45			08 00				08 15			08 30		
Barry Docks	d			07 18			07 33				07 48			08 03				08 18			08 33		
Cadoxton	d			07 21			07 36				07 51			08 06				08 21			08 36		
Dinas Powys	d			07 25			07 40				07 55			08 10				08 25			08 40		
Eastbrook	d			07 28			07 43				07 58			08 13				08 28			08 43		
Cogan	d			07 30			07 45				08 00			08 15				08 30			08 45		
Penarth	d				07 32			07 47				08 02			08 17				08 32			08 47	
Dingle Road	d				07 34			07 49				08 04			08 19				08 34			08 49	
Grangetown	d			07 34	07 38		07 49	07 53			08 05	08 08		08 19	08 23			08 34	08 38		08 49	08 53	
Cardiff Central ■	a			07 39	07 44		07 54	07 59			08 09	08 14		08 24	08 29			08 39	08 44		08 54	08 59	
	d	07 35	07 36	07 41	07 46	07 51	07 56	08 01	08 05	08 06	08 11	08 16	08 21	08 26	08 31	08 35	08 36	08 41	08 46	08 51	08 56	09 01	09 05
Cardiff Queen Street ■	a	07 38		07 44	07 49	07 54	07 59	08 04	08 08		08 14	08 19	08 24	08 29	08 34	08 38		08 44	08 49	08 54	08 59	09 04	09 08
	d	07 39		07 45	07 50	07 55	08 00	08 05	08 09		08 15	08 20	08 25	08 30	08 35	08 39		08 45	08 50	08 55	09 00	09 05	09 09
Heath Low Level	d					08 00							08 30							09 00			
Ty Glas	d					08 03							08 33							09 03			
Birchgrove	d					08 04							08 34							09 04			
Rhiwbina	d					08 06							08 36							09 06			
Whitchurch (Cardiff)	d					08 08							08 38							09 08			
Coryton	a					08 13							08 43							09 13			
Heath High Level	d				07 55			08 10				08 25			08 40				08 55			09 10	
Llanishen	d				07 58			08 13				08 28			08 43				08 58			09 13	
Lisvane & Thornhill	d				08 00			08 15				08 30			08 45				09 00			09 15	
Caerphilly	d				08 06			08 21				08 36			08 51				09 06			09 21	
Aber	d				08 08			08 23				08 38			08 53				09 08			09 23	
Energlyn & Churchill Park	d							08 25				08 40										09 25	
Llanbradach	d				08 12			08 29				08 44			08 57				09 12			09 29	
Ystrad Mynach	d				08 17			08 34				08 49			09 02				09 17			09 34	
Hengoed	d				08 20			08 37				08 52			09 05				09 20			09 37	
Pengam	d				08 23			08 40				08 55			09 08				09 23			09 40	
Gilfach Fargoed	d							08 43														09 43	
Bargoed	a				08 31			08 52				09 00			09 16				09 31			09 52	
	d											09 01											
Brithdir	d											09 05											
Tir-phil	d											09 08											
Pontlottyn	d											09 12											
Rhymney ■	a											09 18											
Cathays	d	07 42		07 48			08 03		08 12		08 18			08 33		08 42		08 48			09 03		09 12
Llandaf	d	07 46		07 52			08 07		08 16		08 22			08 37		08 46		08 52			09 07		09 16
Ninian Park	d		07 40			08 40				08 10			09 10				08 40			09 40			
Waun-gron Park	d		07 43			08 43				08 13			09 13				08 43			09 43			
Fairwater	d		07 45			08 45				08 15			09 15				08 45			09 45			
Danescourt	d		07 47			08 47				08 17			09 17				08 47			09 47			
Radyr ■	a	07 49	07 54	07 55		08 54	08 10		08 19	08 24	08 25		09 24	08 40		08 49	08 54	08 55		09 54	09 10		09 19
	d	07 50		07 56			08 11		08 20		08 26			08 41		08 50		08 56			09 11		09 20
Taffs Well	d	07 54		08 00			08 15		08 24		08 30			08 45		08 54		09 00			09 15		09 24
Trefforest Estate	d						08 19							08 49							09 19		
Trefforest	d	08 01		08 07			08 23		08 31		08 37			08 53		09 01		09 07			09 23		09 31
Pontypridd ■	a	08 04		08 10			08 26		08 34		08 40			08 56		09 04		09 10			09 26		09 34
	d	08 05		08 12			08 27		08 35		08 42			08 57		09 05		09 12			09 27		09 35
Abercynon	d			08 19			08 34				08 49			09 04				09 19			09 34		
Penrhiwceiber	d			08 24							08 54							09 24					
Mountain Ash	a			08 28							08 58							09 28					
	d			08 33							09 03							09 33					
Fernhill	d			08 35							09 05							09 35					
Cwmbach	d			08 39							09 09							09 39					
Aberdare	a			08 46							09 16							09 46					
Quakers Yard	d						08 39							09 09							09 39		
Merthyr Vale	a						08 44							09 14							09 44		
	d						08 47							09 17							09 47		
Troed Y Rhiw	d						08 50							09 20							09 50		
Pentre-bach	d						08 53							09 23							09 53		
Merthyr Tydfil	a						09 01							09 31							10 01		
Trehafod	d	08 10							08 40							09 10							09 40
Porth	a	08 13							08 43							09 13							09 43
	d	08 14							08 44							09 14							09 44
Dinas Rhondda	d	08 18							08 48							09 18							09 48
Tonypandy	d	08 20							08 50							09 20							09 50
Llwynypia	d	08 22							08 52							09 22							09 52
Ystrad Rhondda	a	08 25							08 55							09 25							09 55
	d	08 29							08 59							09 29							09 59
Ton Pentre	d	08 31							09 01							09 31							10 01
Treorchy	d	08 34							09 04							09 34							10 04
Ynyswen	d	08 37							09 07							09 37							10 07
Treherbert	a	08 42							09 12							09 42							10 12

When events are being held at the Principality Stadium, services are subject to alteration. Please check times before travelling.

For connections to Cardiff Bay please refer to Table T124

Table T130-R

Saturdays
26 May to 8 September

Bridgend, Barry Island, Barry, Penarth and Cardiff - Coryton, Rhymney, Pontypridd, Merthyr, Aberdare and Treherbert

		AW	AW	AW	AW	AW	AW	AW	AW	AW	AW	AW	AW	AW	AW	AW	AW	AW	AW	AW	AW	AW
Bridgend	d									08 42												
Llantwit Major	d									08 56												
Rhoose Cardiff Int Airport ✈	d									09 06												
Barry Island	d		08 40			08 55							09 25					09 40			09 55	
Barry ■	d		08 45			09 00				09 15			09 30					09 45			10 00	
Barry Docks	d		08 48			09 03				09 18			09 33					09 48			10 03	
Cadoxton	d		08 51			09 06				09 21			09 36					09 51			10 06	
Dinas Powys	d		08 55			09 10				09 25			09 40					09 55			10 10	
Eastbrook	d		08 58			09 13				09 28			09 43					09 58			10 13	
Cogan	d		09 00			09 15				09 30			09 45					10 00			10 15	
Penarth	d						09 17				09 32				09 47				10 02			10 17
Dingle Road	d						09 19				09 34				09 49				10 04			10 19
Grangetown	d		09 04			09 19	09 23			09 34	09 38		09 49		09 53			10 04	10 08		10 19	10 23
Cardiff Central ■	a		09 09			09 24	09 29			09 39	09 44		09 54		09 59			10 09	10 14		10 24	10 29
	d	09 06	09 11	09 16	09 21	09 26	09 31	09 35	09 36	09 41	09 46	09 51	09 56		10 01	10 05	10 06	10 11	10 16	10 21	10 26	10 31
Cardiff Queen Street ■	a		09 14	09 19	09 24	09 29	09 34	09 38		09 44	09 49	09 54	09 59		10 04	10 08		10 14	10 19	10 24	10 29	10 34
	d		09 15	09 20	09 25	09 30	09 35	09 39		09 45	09 50	09 55	10 00		10 05	10 09		10 15	10 20	10 25	10 30	10 35
Heath Low Level	d				09 30							10 00								10 30		
Ty Glas	d				09 33							10 03								10 33		
Birchgrove	d				09 34							10 04								10 34		
Rhiwbina	d				09 36							10 06								10 36		
Whitchurch (Cardiff)	d				09 38							10 08								10 38		
Coryton	a				09 43							10 13								10 43		
Heath High Level	d			09 25			09 40				09 55				10 10				10 25			10 40
Llanishen	d			09 28			09 43				09 58				10 13				10 28			10 43
Lisvane & Thornhill	d			09 30			09 45				10 00				10 15				10 30			10 45
Caerphilly	d			09 36			09 51				10 06				10 21				10 36			10 51
Aber	d			09 38			09 53				10 08				10 23				10 38			10 53
Energlyn & Churchill Park	d			09 40											10 25				10 40			
Llanbradach	d			09 44			09 57				10 12				10 29				10 44			10 57
Ystrad Mynach	d			09 49			10 02				10 17				10 34				10 49			11 02
Hengoed	d			09 52			10 05				10 20				10 37				10 52			11 05
Pengam	d			09 55			10 08				10 23				10 40				10 55			11 08
Gilfach Fargoed	d														10 43							
Bargoed	a			10 00			10 16				10 31				10 52				11 00			11 16
	d			10 01															11 01			
Brithdir	d			10 05															11 05			
Tir-phil	d			10 08															11 08			
Pontlottyn	d			10 12															11 12			
Rhymney ■	a			10 18															11 18			
Cathays	d		09 18			09 33		09 42		09 48			10 03			10 12		10 18			10 33	
Llandaf	d		09 22			09 37		09 46		09 52			10 07			10 16		10 22			10 37	
Ninian Park	d	09 10			10 10				09 40			10 40					10 10			11 10		
Waun-gron Park	d	09 13			10 13				09 43			10 43					10 13			11 13		
Fairwater	d	09 15			10 15				09 45			10 45					10 15			11 15		
Danescourt	d	09 17			10 17				09 47			10 47					10 17			11 17		
Radyr ■	a	09 24	09 25		10 24	09 40		09 49	09 54	09 55		10 55	10 10			10 19	10 24	10 25		11 24	10 40	
	d		09 26			09 41		09 50		09 56			10 11			10 20		10 26			10 41	
Taffs Well	d		09 30			09 45		09 54		10 00			10 15			10 24		10 30			10 45	
Trefforest Estate	d					09 49															10 49	
Trefforest	d		09 37			09 53		10 01		10 07			10 22			10 31		10 37			10 53	
Pontypridd ■	a		09 40			09 56		10 04		10 10			10 31			10 34		10 40			10 56	
	d		09 42			09 57		10 05		10 12				10 34		10 35		10 42			10 57	
Abercynon	d		09 49			10 04				10 19				10 40				10 49			11 04	
Penrhiwceiber	d		09 54							10 24								10 54				
Mountain Ash	a		09 58							10 28								10 58				
	d		10 03							10 33								11 03				
Fernhill	d		10 05							10 35								11 05				
Cwmbach	d		10 09							10 39								11 09				
Aberdare	a		10 16							10 46								11 16				
Quakers Yard	d					10 09								10 44							11 09	
Merthyr Vale	a					10 14								10 49							11 14	
	d					10 17								10 52							11 17	
Troed Y Rhiw	d					10 20								10 55							11 20	
Pentre-bach	d					10 23								10 58							11 23	
Merthyr Tydfil	a					10 31								11 06							11 31	
Trehafod	d							10 10								10 40						
Porth	a							10 13								10 43						
	d							10 14								10 44						
Dinas Rhondda	d							10 18								10 48						
Tonypandy	d							10 20								10 50						
Llwynypia	d							10 22								10 52						
Ystrad Rhondda	a							10 25								10 55						
	d							10 29								10 59						
Ton Pentre	d							10 31								11 01						
Treorchy	d							10 34								11 04						
Ynyswen	d							10 37								11 07						
Treherbert	a							10 42								11 12						

When events are being held at the Principality Stadium, services are subject to alteration. Please check times before travelling.

For connections to Cardiff Bay please refer to Table T124

Table T130-R

Saturdays

26 May to 8 September

Bridgend, Barry Island, Barry, Penarth and Cardiff - Coryton, Rhymney, Pontypridd, Merthyr, Aberdare and Treherbert

		AW	AW	AW	AW	AW	AW	AW	AW	AW	AW	AW	AW	AW	AW	AW	AW	AW	AW	AW	AW	AW	AW
Bridgend	d			09 42														10 42					
Llantwit Major	d			09 56														10 56					
Rhoose Cardiff Int Airport ✈	d			10 06														11 06					
Barry Island	d							10 25			10 40			10 55									11 25		
Barry 3	d			10 15				10 30			10 45			11 00				11 15			11 30		
Barry Docks	d			10 18				10 33			10 48			11 03				11 18			11 33		
Cadoxton	d			10 21				10 36			10 51			11 06				11 21			11 36		
Dinas Powys	d			10 25				10 40			10 55			11 10				11 25			11 40		
Eastbrook	d			10 28				10 43			10 58			11 13				11 28			11 43		
Cogan	d			10 30				10 45			11 00			11 15				11 30			11 45		
Penarth	d				10 32					10 47		11 04			11 17				11 32			11 47	
Dingle Road	d				10 34					10 49		11 06			11 19				11 34			11 49	
Grangetown	d			10 34	10 38			10 49		10 53	11 04	11 10		11 19	11 23			11 34	11 38		11 49	11 53	
Cardiff Central 7	a			10 41	10 44			10 54		10 59	11 09	11 15		11 24	11 29			11 39	11 44		11 54	11 59	
	d	10 35	10 36		10 46	10 51	10 51	10 56		11 01	11 11	11 16	11 21	11 26	11 31	11 35	11 36	11 41	11 46	11 51	11 56	12 01	12 05
Cardiff Queen Street 3	a	10 38			10 49		10 54	10 59		11 04	11 14	11 19	11 24	11 29	11 34	11 38		11 44	11 49	11 54	11 59	12 04	12 08
	d	10 39			10 50		10 55	11 00		11 05	11 15	11 20	11 25	11 30	11 35	11 39		11 45	11 50	11 55	12 00	12 05	12 09
Heath Low Level	d						11 00						11 30								12 00			
Ty Glas	d						11 03						11 33								12 03			
Birchgrove	d						11 04						11 34								12 04			
Rhiwbina	d						11 06						11 36								12 06			
Whitchurch (Cardiff)	d						11 08						11 38								12 08			
Coryton	a						11 13						11 43								12 13			
Heath High Level	d				10 55					11 10		11 25			11 40				11 55			12 10	
Llanishen	d				10 58					11 13		11 28			11 43				11 58			12 13	
Lisvane & Thornhill	d				11 00					11 15		11 30			11 45				12 00			12 15	
Caerphilly	d				11 06					11 21		11 36			11 51				12 06			12 21	
Aber	d				11 08					11 23		11 38			11 53				12 08			12 23	
Energlyn & Churchill Park	d									11 25		11 40										12 25	
Llanbradach	d				11 12					11 29		11 44			11 57				12 12			12 29	
Ystrad Mynach	d				11 17					11 34		11 49			12 02				12 17			12 34	
Hengoed	d				11 20					11 37		11 52			12 05				12 20			12 37	
Pengam	d				11 23					11 40		11 55			12 08				12 23			12 40	
Gilfach Fargoed	d									11 43												12 43	
Bargoed	a				11 31					11 52		12 00			12 16				12 31			12 52	
	d											12 01												
Brithdir	d											12 05												
Tir-phil	d											12 08												
Pontlottyn	d											12 12												
Rhymney 3	a											12 18												
Cathays	d	10 42						11 03			11 18			11 33		11 42		11 48			12 03		12 12
Llandaf	d	10 46						11 07			11 22			11 37		11 46		11 52			12 07		12 16
Ninian Park	d		10 40				11 40						12 10				11 40			12 40			
Waun-gron Park	d		10 43				11 43						12 13				11 43			12 43			
Fairwater	d		10 45				11 45						12 15				11 45			12 45			
Danescourt	d		10 47				11 47		←				12 17				11 47			12 47			
Radyr 3	a	10 49	10 55			11 02	11 54	11 10	11 02		11 25		12 24	11 40		11 49	11 54	11 55		12 54	12 10		12 19
	d	10 50				11 21		11 11	11 21		11 26			11 41		11 50		11 56			12 11		12 20
Taffs Well	d	10 54				→		11 15	11 25		11 30			11 45		11 54		12 00			12 15		12 24
Trefforest Estate	d							11 19						11 49								12 19		
Trefforest	d	11 01						11 23	11 32		11 37			11 53		12 01		12 07			12 23		12 31
Pontypridd 3	a	11 04						11 26	11 35		11 40			11 56		12 04		12 10			12 26		12 34
	d	11 05						11 27	11 36		11 42			11 57		12 05		12 12			12 27		12 35
Abercynon	d							11 34			11 49			12 04				12 19			12 34		
Penrhiwceiber	d										11 54							12 24					
Mountain Ash	a										11 58							12 28					
	d										12 03							12 33					
Fernhill	d										12 05							12 35					
Cwmbach	d										12 09							12 39					
Aberdare	a										12 16							12 46					
Quakers Yard	d							11 39						12 09							12 39		
Merthyr Vale	a							11 44						12 14							12 44		
	d							11 47						12 17							12 47		
Troed Y Rhiw	d							11 50						12 20							12 50		
Pentre-bach	d							11 53						12 23							12 53		
Merthyr Tydfil	a							12 01						12 31							13 01		
Trehafod	d	11 10							11 41							12 10							12 40
Porth	a	11 13							11 44							12 13							12 43
	d	11 14							11 45							12 14							12 44
Dinas Rhondda	d	11 18							11 49							12 18							12 48
Tonypandy	d	11 20							11 51							12 20							12 50
Llwynypia	d	11 22							11 53							12 22							12 52
Ystrad Rhondda	a	11 25							11 56							12 25							12 55
	d	11 29							11 59							12 29							12 59
Ton Pentre	d	11 31							12 01							12 31							13 01
Treorchy	d	11 34							12 04							12 34							13 04
Ynyswen	d	11 37							12 07							12 37							13 07
Treherbert	a	11 42							12 13							12 42							13 12

When events are being held at the Principality Stadium, services are subject to alteration. Please check times before travelling.

For connections to Cardiff Bay please refer to Table T124

Table T130-R

Saturdays

26 May to 8 September

Bridgend, Barry Island, Barry, Penarth and Cardiff - Coryton, Rhymney, Pontypridd, Merthyr, Aberdare and Treherbert

		AW	AW	AW	AW	AW	AW	AW	AW	AW	AW	AW	AW	AW	AW	AW	AW	AW	AW	AW	AW	AW
Bridgend	d										11 42												
Llantwit Major	d										11 56												
Rhoose Cardiff Int Airport ✈	d										12 06												
Barry Island	d		11 40			11 55							12 25				12 40			12 55		
Barry 3	d		11 45			12 00				12 15			12 30				12 45			13 00		
Barry Docks	d		11 48			12 03				12 18			12 33				12 48			13 03		
Cadoxton	d		11 51			12 06				12 21			12 36				12 51			13 06		
Dinas Powys	d		11 55			12 10				12 25			12 40				12 55			13 10		
Eastbrook	d		11 58			12 13				12 28			12 43				12 58			13 13		
Cogan	d		12 00			12 15				12 30			12 45				13 00			13 15		
Penarth	d			12 02			12 17				12 32			12 47				13 02			13 17	
Dingle Road	d			12 04			12 19				12 34			12 49				13 04			13 19	
Grangetown	d		12 04	12 08		12 19	12 23			12 34	12 38		12 49	12 53			13 04	13 08		13 19	13 23	
Cardiff Central 7	a		12 09	12 14		12 24	12 29			12 39	12 44		12 54	12 59			13 09	13 14		13 24	13 29	
	d	12 06	12 11	12 16	12 21	12 26	12 31	12 35	12 36	12 41	12 46	12 51	12 56	13 01	13 05	13 06	13 11	13 16	13 21	13 26	13 31	13 35
Cardiff Queen Street 3	a		12 14	12 19	12 24	12 29	12 34	12 38		12 44	12 49	12 54	12 59	13 04	13 08		13 14	13 19	13 24	13 29	13 34	13 38
	d		12 15	12 20	12 25	12 30	12 35	12 39		12 45	12 50	12 55	13 00	13 05	13 09		13 15	13 20	13 25	13 30	13 35	13 39
Heath Low Level	d				12 30							13 00							13 30			
Ty Glas	d				12 33							13 03							13 33			
Birchgrove	d				12 34							13 04							13 34			
Rhiwbina	d				12 36							13 06							13 36			
Whitchurch (Cardiff)	d				12 38							13 08							13 38			
Coryton	a				12 43							13 13							13 43			
Heath High Level	d			12 25			12 40				12 55			13 10				13 25			13 40	
Llanishen	d			12 28			12 43				12 58			13 13				13 28			13 43	
Lisvane & Thornhill	d			12 30			12 45				13 00			13 15				13 30			13 45	
Caerphilly	d			12 36			12 51				13 06			13 21				13 36			13 51	
Aber	d			12 38			12 53				13 08			13 23				13 38			13 53	
Energlyn & Churchill Park	d			12 40										13 25				13 40				
Llanbradach	d			12 44			12 57				13 12			13 29				13 44			13 57	
Ystrad Mynach	d			12 49			13 02				13 17			13 34				13 49			14 02	
Hengoed	d			12 52			13 05				13 20			13 37				13 52			14 05	
Pengam	d			12 55			13 08				13 23			13 40				13 55			14 08	
Gilfach Fargoed	d													13 43								
Bargoed	a			13 00			13 16				13 31			13 52				14 00			14 16	
	d			13 01														14 01				
Brithdir	d			13 05														14 05				
Tir-phil	d			13 08														14 08				
Pontlottyn	d			13 12														14 12				
Rhymney 3	a			13 18														14 18				
Cathays	d		12 18			12 33		12 42		12 48			13 03		13 12		13 18			13 33		13 42
Llandaf	d		12 22			12 37		12 46		12 52			13 07		13 16		13 22			13 37		13 46
Ninian Park	d	12 10			13 10				12 40			13 40				13 10			14 10			
Waun-gron Park	d	12 13			13 13				12 43			13 43				13 13			14 13			
Fairwater	d	12 15			13 15				12 45			13 45				13 15			14 15			
Danescourt	d	12 17			13 17				12 47			13 47				13 17			14 17			
Radyr 3	a	12 24	12 25		13 24	12 40		12 49	12 54	12 55		13 54	13 10		13 19	13 24	13 25		14 24	13 40		13 49
	d		12 25			12 41		12 50		12 56			13 11		13 20		13 26			13 41		13 50
Taffs Well	d		12 29			12 45		12 54		13 00			13 15		13 24		13 30			13 45		13 54
Trefforest Estate	d					12 49							13 19							13 49		
Trefforest	d		12 36			12 53		13 01		13 07			13 23		13 31		13 37			13 53		14 01
Pontypridd 3	a		12 41			12 56		13 04		13 10			13 26		13 34		13 40			13 56		14 04
	d					12 57		13 05		13 12			13 27		13 35		13 42			13 57		14 05
Abercynon	d					13 04				13 19			13 34				13 49			14 04		
Penrhiwceiber	d									13 24								13 54					
Mountain Ash	a									13 28								13 58					
	d									13 33								14 03					
Fernhill	d									13 35								14 05					
Cwmbach	d									13 39								14 09					
Aberdare	a									13 46								14 16					
Quakers Yard	d					13 09							13 39							14 09		
Merthyr Vale	a					13 14							13 44							14 14		
	d					13 17							13 47							14 17		
Troed Y Rhiw	d					13 20							13 50							14 20		
Pentre-bach	d					13 23							13 53							14 23		
Merthyr Tydfil	a					13 31							14 01							14 31		
Trehafod	d							13 10								13 40							14 10
Porth	a							13 13								13 43							14 13
	d							13 14								13 44							14 14
Dinas Rhondda	d							13 18								13 48							14 18
Tonypandy	d							13 20								13 50							14 20
Llwynypia	d							13 22								13 52							14 22
Ystrad Rhondda	a							13 25								13 55							14 25
	d							13 29								13 59							14 29
Ton Pentre	d							13 31								14 01							14 31
Treorchy	d							13 34								14 04							14 34
Ynyswen	d							13 37								14 07							14 37
Treherbert	a							13 42								14 12							14 42

When events are being held at the Principality Stadium, services are subject to alteration. Please check times before travelling.

For connections to Cardiff Bay please refer to Table T124

Table T130-R

Saturdays
26 May to 8 September

Bridgend, Barry Island, Barry, Penarth and Cardiff - Coryton, Rhymney, Pontypridd, Merthyr, Aberdare and Treherbert

		AW	AW	AW	AW	AW	AW	AW	AW	AW	AW	AW	AW	AW	AW	AW	AW	AW	AW	AW	AW	AW	AW
Bridgend	d		12 42														13 42						
Llantwit Major	d		12 56														13 56						
Rhoose Cardiff Int Airport ✈	d		13 06														14 06						
Barry Island	d					13 25				13 40			13 55								14 25		
Barry	d		13 15			13 30				13 45			14 00				14 15				14 30		
Barry Docks	d		13 18			13 34				13 48			14 03				14 18				14 33		
Cadoxton	d		13 21			13 37				13 51			14 06				14 21				14 36		
Dinas Powys	d		13 25			13 41				13 55			14 10				14 25				14 40		
Eastbrook	d		13 28			13 43				13 58			14 13				14 28				14 43		
Cogan	d		13 30			13 45				14 00			14 15				14 30				14 45		
Penarth	d			13 32			13 47				14 02			14 17				14 32					14 47
Dingle Road	d			13 34			13 49				14 04			14 19				14 34					14 49
Grangetown	d		13 34	13 38		13 49	13 53			14 04	14 08		14 19	14 23			14 34	14 38			14 49		14 53
Cardiff Central	a		13 39	13 44		13 54	13 59			14 09	14 14		14 24	14 29			14 39	14 44			14 54		14 59
	d	13 36	13 41	13 46	13 51	13 56	14 01	14 05	14 06	14 11	14 16	14 21	14 26	14 31	14 35	14 36	14 41	14 46	14 51	14 53	14 56		15 01
Cardiff Queen Street	a		13 44	13 49	13 54	13 59	14 04	14 08		14 14	14 19	14 24	14 29	14 34	14 38		14 44	14 49	14 54		14 59		15 04
	d		13 45	13 50	13 55	14 00	14 05	14 09		14 15	14 20	14 25	14 30	14 35	14 39		14 45	14 50	14 55		15 00		15 05
Heath Low Level	d				14 00							14 30							15 00				
Ty Glas	d				14 03							14 33							15 03				
Birchgrove	d				14 04							14 34							15 04				
Rhiwbina	d				14 06							14 36							15 06				
Whitchurch (Cardiff)	d				14 08							14 38							15 08				
Coryton	a				14 13							14 43							15 13				
Heath High Level	d			13 55			14 10				14 25			14 40				14 55					15 10
Llanishen	d			13 58			14 13				14 28			14 43				14 58					15 13
Lisvane & Thornhill	d			14 00			14 15				14 30			14 45				15 00					15 15
Caerphilly	d			14 06			14 21				14 36			14 51				15 06					15 21
Aber	d			14 08			14 23				14 38			14 53				15 08					15 23
Energlyn & Churchill Park	d						14 25				14 40												15 25
Llanbradach	d			14 12			14 29				14 44			14 57				15 12					15 29
Ystrad Mynach	d			14 17			14 34				14 49			15 02				15 17					15 34
Hengoed	d			14 20			14 37				14 52			15 05				15 20					15 37
Pengam	d			14 23			14 40				14 55			15 08				15 23					15 40
Gilfach Fargoed	d						14 43																15 43
Bargoed	a			14 31			14 52				15 00			15 16				15 31					15 52
	d										15 01												
Brithdir	d										15 05												
Tir-phil	d										15 08												
Pontlottyn	d										15 12												
Rhymney	a										15 18												
Cathays	d		13 48			14 03		14 12		14 18			14 33		14 42		14 48				15 03		
Llandaf	d		13 52			14 07		14 16		14 22			14 37		14 46		14 52				15 07		
Ninian Park	d	13 40			14 40				14 10			15 10				14 40			15 40				
Waun-gron Park	d	13 43			14 43				14 13			15 13				14 43			15 43				
Fairwater	d	13 45			14 45				14 15			15 15				14 45			15 45				
Danescourt	d	13 47			14 47				14 17			15 17				14 47			15 47			←	
Radyr	a	13 54	13 55		14 54	14 10		14 19	14 24	14 25		15 25	14 40		14 49	14 54	14 55		15 54	15 08	15 10	15 08	
	d		13 56			14 11		14 20		14 26			14 41		14 50		14 56			15 21	15 11	15 21	
Taffs Well	d		14 00			14 15		14 24		14 30			14 45		14 54		15 00			→	15 15	15 25	
Trefforest Estate	d					14 19							14 49								15 19		
Trefforest	d		14 07			14 23		14 31		14 37			14 53		15 01		15 07				15 23	15 32	
Pontypridd	a		14 10			14 26		14 34		14 40			14 56		15 04		15 10				15 26	15 35	
	d		14 12			14 27		14 35		14 42			14 57		15 05		15 12				15 27	15 36	
Abercynon	d		14 19			14 34				14 49			15 04				15 19				15 34		
Penrhiwceiber	d		14 24							14 54							15 24						
Mountain Ash	a		14 28							14 58							15 28						
	d		14 33							15 03							15 33						
Fernhill	d		14 35							15 05							15 35						
Cwmbach	d		14 39							15 09							15 39						
Aberdare	a		14 46							15 16							15 46						
Quakers Yard	d					14 39							15 09								15 39		
Merthyr Vale	a					14 44							15 14								15 44		
	d					14 47							15 17								15 47		
Troed Y Rhiw	d					14 50							15 20								15 50		
Pentre-bach	d					14 53							15 23								15 53		
Merthyr Tydfil	a					15 01							15 31								16 01		
Trehafod	d							14 40							15 10							15 41	
Porth	a							14 43							15 13							15 44	
	d							14 44							15 14							15 45	
Dinas Rhondda	d							14 48							15 18							15 49	
Tonypandy	d							14 50							15 20							15 51	
Llwynypia	d							14 52							15 22							15 53	
Ystrad Rhondda	a							14 55							15 25							15 56	
	d							14 59							15 29							15 59	
Ton Pentre	d							15 01							15 31							16 01	
Treorchy	d							15 04							15 34							16 04	
Ynyswen	d							15 07							15 37							16 07	
Treherbert	a							15 12							15 42							16 13	

When events are being held at the Principality Stadium, services are subject to alteration. Please check times before travelling.

For connections to Cardiff Bay please refer to Table T124

Table T130-R

Saturdays
26 May to 8 September

Bridgend, Barry Island, Barry, Penarth and Cardiff - Coryton, Rhymney, Pontypridd, Merthyr, Aberdare and Treherbert

		AW	AW	AW	AW	AW	AW	AW	AW	AW	AW	AW	AW	AW	AW	AW	AW	AW	AW	AW	AW	AW	AW
Bridgend	d									14 42													15 42
Llantwit Major	d									14 56													15 56
Rhoose Cardiff Int Airport ✈	d									15 06													16 06
Barry Island	d		14 40			14 55							15 25			15 40			15 55				
Barry	d		14 45			15 00				15 15			15 30			15 45			16 00				16 15
Barry Docks	d		14 48			15 03				15 18			15 33			15 48			16 03				16 18
Cadoxton	d		14 51			15 06				15 21			15 36			15 51			16 06				16 21
Dinas Powys	d		14 55			15 10				15 25			15 40			15 55			16 10				16 25
Eastbrook	d		14 58			15 13				15 28			15 43			15 58			16 13				16 28
Cogan	d		15 00			15 15				15 30			15 45			16 00			16 15				16 30
Penarth	d			15 02			15 17				15 32			15 47			16 02			16 17			
Dingle Road	d			15 04			15 19				15 34			15 49			16 04			16 19			
Grangetown	d		15 04	15 08		15 19	15 23			15 34	15 38		15 49	15 53		16 04	16 08		16 19	16 23			16 34
Cardiff Central	a		15 09	15 14		15 24	15 29			15 39	15 44		15 54	15 59		16 09	16 14		16 24	16 29			16 39
	d	15 06	15 11	15 16	15 21	15 26	15 31	15 35	15 36	15 41	15 46	15 51	15 56	16 01	16 05	16 11	16 16	16 21	16 26	16 31	16 35	16 36	16 41
Cardiff Queen Street	a		15 14	15 19	15 24	15 29	15 34	15 38		15 44	15 49	15 54	15 59	16 04	16 08	16 14	16 19	16 24	16 29	16 34	16 38		16 44
	d		15 15	15 20	15 25	15 30	15 35	15 39		15 45	15 50	15 55	16 00	16 05	16 09	16 15	16 20	16 25	16 30	16 35	16 39		16 45
Heath Low Level	d				15 30							16 00						16 30					
Ty Glas	d				15 33							16 03						16 33					
Birchgrove	d				15 34							16 04						16 34					
Rhiwbina	d				15 36							16 06						16 36					
Whitchurch (Cardiff)	d				15 38							16 08						16 38					
Coryton	a				15 43							16 13						16 43					
Heath High Level	d			15 25			15 40				15 55			16 10			16 25			16 40			
Llanishen	d			15 28			15 43				15 58			16 13			16 28			16 43			
Lisvane & Thornhill	d			15 30			15 45				16 00			16 15			16 30			16 45			
Caerphilly	d			15 36			15 51				16 06			16 21			16 36			16 51			
Aber	d			15 38			15 53				16 08			16 23			16 38			16 53			
Energlyn & Churchill Park	d			15 40										16 25			16 40						
Llanbradach	d			15 44			15 57				16 12			16 29			16 44			16 57			
Ystrad Mynach	d			15 49			16 02				16 17			16 34			16 49			17 02			
Hengoed	d			15 52			16 05				16 20			16 37			16 52			17 05			
Pengam	d			15 55			16 08				16 23			16 40			16 55			17 08			
Gilfach Fargoed	d													16 43									
Bargoed	a			16 00			16 16				16 31			16 52			17 00			17 16			
	d			16 01													17 01						
Brithdir	d			16 05													17 05						
Tir-phil	d			16 08													17 08						
Pontlottyn	d			16 12													17 12						
Rhymney	a			16 18													17 18						
Cathays	d		15 18			15 33		15 42		15 48			16 03		16 12	16 18			16 33		16 42		16 48
Llandaf	d		15 22			15 37		15 46		15 52			16 07		16 16	16 22			16 37		16 46		16 52
Ninian Park	d	15 10			16 10				15 40			16 40						17 10				16 40	
Waun-gron Park	d	15 13			16 13				15 43			16 43						17 13				16 43	
Fairwater	d	15 15			16 15				15 45			16 45						17 15				16 45	
Danescourt	d	15 17			16 17				15 47			16 47						17 17				16 47	
Radyr	a	15 25	15 25		16 24	15 40		15 49	15 54	15 55		16 54	16 10		16 19	16 25		17 24	16 40		16 49	16 54	16 55
	d		15 26			15 41		15 50		15 56			16 11		16 20	16 26			16 41		16 50		16 56
Taffs Well	d		15 30			15 45		15 54		16 00			16 15		16 24	16 30			16 45		16 54		17 00
Trefforest Estate	d					15 49							16 19						16 49				
Trefforest	d		15 37			15 53		16 01		16 07			16 23		16 31	16 37			16 53		17 01		17 07
Pontypridd	a		15 40			15 56		16 04		16 10			16 26		16 34	16 40			16 56		17 04		17 10
	d		15 42			15 57		16 05		16 12			16 27		16 35	16 42			16 57		17 05		17 12
Abercynon	d		15 49			16 04				16 19			16 34			16 49			17 04				17 19
Penrhiwceiber	d		15 54							16 24						16 54							17 24
Mountain Ash	a		15 58							16 28						16 58							17 28
	d		16 03							16 33						17 03							17 33
Fernhill	d		16 05							16 35						17 05							17 35
Cwmbach	d		16 09							16 39						17 09							17 39
Aberdare	a		16 16							16 46						17 16							17 46
Quakers Yard	d					16 09							16 39						17 09				
Merthyr Vale	a					16 14							16 44						17 14				
	d					16 17							16 47						17 17				
Troed Y Rhiw	d					16 20							16 50						17 20				
Pentre-bach	d					16 23							16 53						17 23				
Merthyr Tydfil	a					16 31							17 01						17 31				
Trehafod	d							16 10							16 40						17 10		
Porth	a							16 13							16 43						17 13		
	d							16 14							16 44						17 14		
Dinas Rhondda	d							16 18							16 48						17 18		
Tonypandy	d							16 20							16 50						17 20		
Llwynypia	d							16 22							16 52						17 22		
Ystrad Rhondda	a							16 25							16 55						17 25		
	d							16 29							16 59						17 29		
Ton Pentre	d							16 31							17 01						17 31		
Treorchy	d							16 34							17 04						17 34		
Ynyswen	d							16 37							17 07						17 37		
Treherbert	a							16 42							17 12						17 42		

When events are being held at the Principality Stadium, services are subject to alteration. Please check times before travelling.

For connections to Cardiff Bay please refer to Table T124

Table T130-R

Saturdays
26 May to 8 September

Bridgend, Barry Island, Barry, Penarth and Cardiff - Coryton, Rhymney, Pontypridd, Merthyr, Aberdare and Treherbert

		AW		AW	AW	AW	AW	AW	AW	AW	AW	AW		AW	AW	AW	AW	AW	AW	AW	AW	AW		AW	AW
Bridgend	d																16 42								
Llantwit Major	d																16 56								
Rhoose Cardiff Int Airport ✈	d																17 06								
Barry Island	d				16 25				16 40			16 55								17 25					17 40
Barry	d				16 30				16 45			17 00					17 15			17 30					17 45
Barry Docks	d				16 33				16 48			17 03					17 18			17 33					17 48
Cadoxton	d				16 36				16 51			17 06					17 21			17 36					17 51
Dinas Powys	d				16 40				16 55			17 10					17 25			17 40					17 55
Eastbrook	d				16 43				16 58			17 13					17 28			17 43					17 58
Cogan	d				16 45				17 00			17 15					17 30			17 45					18 00
Penarth	d	16 32								17 02				17 17				17 32			17 47				
Dingle Road	d	16 34								17 04				17 19				17 34			17 49				
Grangetown	d	16 38			16 49				17 04	17 08		17 19		17 23			17 34	17 38		17 49	17 53				18 04
Cardiff Central	a	16 44			16 54				17 09	17 14		17 24		17 29			17 39	17 44		17 54	17 59				18 09
	d	16 46		16 51	16 56	17 01	17 05	17 06	17 11	17 16	17 21	17 26		17 31	17 35	17 36	17 41	17 46	17 51	17 56	18 01	18 05		18 06	18 11
Cardiff Queen Street	a	16 49		16 54	16 59	17 04	17 08		17 14	17 19	17 24	17 29		17 34	17 38		17 44	17 49	17 54	17 59	18 04	18 08			18 14
	d	16 50		16 55	17 00	17 05	17 09		17 15	17 20	17 25	17 30		17 35	17 39		17 45	17 50	17 55	18 00	18 05	18 09			18 15
Heath Low Level	d			17 00							17 30								18 00						
Ty Glas	d			17 03							17 33								18 03						
Birchgrove	d			17 04							17 34								18 04						
Rhiwbina	d			17 06							17 36								18 06						
Whitchurch (Cardiff)	d			17 08							17 38								18 08						
Coryton	a			17 13							17 43								18 13						
Heath High Level	d	16 55				17 10				17 25				17 40				17 55			18 10				
Llanishen	d	16 58				17 13				17 28				17 43				17 59			18 13				
Lisvane & Thornhill	d	17 00				17 15				17 31				17 45				18 02			18 15				
Caerphilly	d	17 06				17 21				17 37				17 51				18 07			18 21				
Aber	d	17 08				17 23				17 39				17 53				18 10			18 23				
Energlyn & Churchill Park	d					17 26				17 41				17 55				18 13							
Llanbradach	d	17 12				17 29				17 45				17 59				18 17			18 27				
Ystrad Mynach	d	17 17				17 35				17 50				18 04				18 22			18 32				
Hengoed	d	17 20				17 37				17 53				18 07				18 25			18 35				
Pengam	d	17 23				17 41				17 56				18 10				18 29			18 38				
Gilfach Fargoed	d					17 44								18 13				18 33			18 41				
Bargoed	a	17 31				17 47				18 03				18 16				18 36			18 48				
	d					17 49								18 18				18 38							
Brithdir	d					17 52								18 22				18 41							
Tir-phil	d					17 55								18 25				18 44							
Pontlottyn	d					18 00								18 29				18 49							
Rhymney	a					18 06								18 35				18 55							
Cathays	d				17 03		17 12		17 18			17 33			17 42		17 48			18 03		18 12			18 18
Llandaf	d				17 07		17 16		17 22			17 37			17 46		17 52			18 07		18 16			18 22
Ninian Park	d			17 40				17 10								17 40			18 40					18 10	
Waun-gron Park	d			17 43				17 13								17 43			18 43					18 13	
Fairwater	d			17 45				17 15								17 45			18 45					18 15	
Danescourt	d			17 47				17 17								17 47			18 47					18 17	
Radyr	a			17 54	17 10		17 19	17 24	17 25			17 40			17 49	17 54	17 55		18 54	18 10		18 19		18 24	18 25
	d				17 11		17 20		17 26			17 41			17 50		17 56			18 11		18 20			18 25
Taffs Well	d				17 15		17 24		17 30			17 45			17 54		18 00			18 15		18 24			18 29
Trefforest Estate	d				17 19							17 49								18 19					
Trefforest	d				17 23		17 31		17 37			17 53			18 01		18 07			18 23		18 31			18 36
Pontypridd	a				17 26		17 34		17 40			17 56			18 04		18 10			18 26		18 34			18 41
	d				17 27		17 35		17 42			17 57			18 05		18 12			18 27		18 35			
Abercynon	d				17 34				17 49			18 04					18 19			18 34					
Penrhiwceiber	d								17 54								18 24								
Mountain Ash	a								17 58								18 28								
	d								18 03								18 33								
Fernhill	d								18 05								18 35								
Cwmbach	d								18 09								18 39								
Aberdare	a								18 16								18 46								
Quakers Yard	d				17 39							18 09								18 39					
Merthyr Vale	a				17 44							18 14								18 44					
	d				17 47							18 17								18 47					
Troed Y Rhiw	d				17 50							18 20								18 50					
Pentre-bach	d				17 53							18 23								18 53					
Merthyr Tydfil	a				18 01							18 31								19 01					
Trehafod	d						17 40								18 10							18 40			
Porth	a						17 43								18 13							18 43			
	d						17 44								18 14							18 44			
Dinas Rhondda	d						17 48								18 18							18 48			
Tonypandy	d						17 50								18 20							18 50			
Llwynypia	d						17 52								18 22							18 52			
Ystrad Rhondda	a						17 55								18 25							18 55			
	d						17 59								18 29							18 59			
Ton Pentre	d						18 01								18 31							19 01			
Treorchy	d						18 04								18 34							19 04			
Ynyswen	d						18 07								18 37							19 07			
Treherbert	a						18 12								18 42							19 12			

When events are being held at the Principality Stadium, services are subject to alteration. Please check times before travelling.

For connections to Cardiff Bay please refer to Table T124

Table T130-R

Saturdays
26 May to 8 September

Bridgend, Barry Island, Barry, Penarth and Cardiff - Coryton, Rhymney, Pontypridd, Merthyr, Aberdare and Treherbert

		AW	AW	AW	AW		AW	AW		AW	AW	AW	AW		AW	AW	AW	AW		AW	AW	AW	AW	AW	AW
Bridgend	d							17 42												18 42					
Llantwit Major	d							17 56												18 56					
Rhoose Cardiff Int Airport ✈	d							18 06												19 06					
Barry Island	d			17 55								18 25			18 40	18 55						19 25		19 55	
Barry	d			18 00				18 15				18 30			18 45	19 00				19 15		19 30		20 00	
Barry Docks	d			18 03				18 18				18 33			18 48	19 03				19 18		19 33		20 03	
Cadoxton	d			18 06				18 21				18 36			18 51	19 06				19 21		19 36		20 06	
Dinas Powys	d			18 10				18 25				18 40			18 55	19 10				19 25		19 40		20 10	
Eastbrook	d			18 13				18 28				18 43			18 58	19 13				19 28		19 43		20 13	
Cogan	d			18 15				18 30				18 45			19 00	19 15				19 30		19 45		20 15	
Penarth	d	18 02			18 17					18 32			18 47				19 17						19 47		20 20
Dingle Road	d	18 04			18 19					18 34			18 49				19 19						19 49		20 22
Grangetown	d	18 08		18 19	18 23			18 34		18 38		18 49	18 53		19 04	19 19	19 23			19 34		19 49	19 53	20 19	20 26
Cardiff Central	a	18 14		18 25	18 29			18 39		18 47		18 55	18 59		19 09	19 24	19 29			19 39		19 56	19 59	20 24	20 31
	d	18 16	18 21	18 26	18 31	18 36	18 36	18 41			18 51		19 01	19 05	19 11	19 26	19 31	19 36		19 41	19 51	20 01	20 05	20 26	20 31
Cardiff Queen Street	a	18 19	18 24	18 29	18 34	18 38		18 44			18 54		19 04	19 08	19 14	19 29	19 34			19 44	19 54	20 04	20 09	20 29	20 34
	d	18 20	18 25	18 30	18 35	18 40		18 47			18 55		19 05	19 09	19 15	19 30	19 35			19 45	19 55	20 05	20 09	20 30	20 35
Heath Low Level	d		18 30								19 00										20 00				
Ty Glas	d		18 33								19 03										20 03				
Birchgrove	d		18 34								19 04										20 04				
Rhiwbina	d		18 36								19 06										20 06				
Whitchurch (Cardiff)	d		18 38								19 08										20 08				
Coryton	a		18 43								19 13										20 13				
Heath High Level	d	18 25			18 40								19 10				19 40					20 11			20 40
Llanishen	d	18 28			18 43								19 13				19 43					20 14			20 43
Lisvane & Thornhill	d	18 30			18 45								19 15				19 45					20 15			20 45
Caerphilly	d	18 36			18 51								19a23				19 51					20a24			20 51
Aber	d	18 38			18 53												19 53								20 53
Energlyn & Churchill Park	d	18 40			18 55												19 56								20 55
Llanbradach	d	18 44			18 59												19 59								20 59
Ystrad Mynach	d	18a53			19 04												20 04								21 04
Hengoed	d				19 07												20 07								21 07
Pengam	d				19 10												20 10								21 10
Gilfach Fargoed	d				19 13												20 13								21 13
Bargoed	a				19 16												20 17								21 17
	d				19 18												20 18								21 18
Brithdir	d				19 22												20 22								21 22
Tir-phil	d				19 25												20 25								21 25
Pontlottyn	d				19 29												20 29								21 29
Rhymney	a				19 36												20 35								21 36
Cathays	d			18 33		18 43		18 50						19 12	19 18	19 33				19 48			20 12	20 33	
Llandaf	d			18 37		18 47		18 54						19 16	19 22	19 37				19 52			20 16	20 37	
Ninian Park	d						18 40				19 40							19 40			20 40				
Waun-gron Park	d						18 43				19 43							19 43			20 43				
Fairwater	d						18 45				19 45							19 45			20 45				
Danescourt	d						18 47				19 47							19 47			20 47				
Radyr	a			18 40		18 50	18 54	18 57			19 54			19 19	19 25	19 40		19 54		19 55	20 54		20 19	20 40	
	d			18 41		18 50		18 58						19 20	19 26	19 41				19 56			20 20	20 41	
Taffs Well	d			18 45		18 54		19 02						19 24	19 30	19 45				20 00			20 24	20 45	
Trefforest Estate	d			18 49												19 49								20 49	
Trefforest	d			18 53		19 01		19 09						19 31	19 37	19 53				20 07			20 31	20 53	
Pontypridd	a			18 56		19 04		19 12						19 34	19 40	19 56				20 10			20 34	20 56	
	d			18 57		19 06		19 12						19 35	19 42	19 57				20 11			20 35	20 57	
Abercynon	d			19 04				19 19							19 49	20 04				20 21				21 04	
Penrhiwceiber	d							19 24							19 54					20 26					
Mountain Ash	a							19 28							19 56					20 30					
	d							19 33							20 03					20 33					
Fernhill	d							19 35							20 05					20 35					
Cwmbach	d							19 39							20 09					20 39					
Aberdare	a							19 46							20 16					20 46					
Quakers Yard	d			19 09												20 09								21 09	
Merthyr Vale	a			19 14												20 14								21 14	
	d			19 17												20 15								21 15	
Troed Y Rhiw	d			19 20												20 19								21 19	
Pentre-bach	d			19 23												20 22								21 22	
Merthyr Tydfil	a			19 31												20 30								21 30	
Trehafod	d					19 11								19 40									20 40		
Porth	a					19 14								19 43									20 43		
	d					19 15								19 44									20 44		
Dinas Rhondda	d					19 19								19 48									20 48		
Tonypandy	d					19 21								19 50									20 50		
Llwynypia	d					19 23								19 52									20 52		
Ystrad Rhondda	a					19 26								19 55									20 55		
	d					19 29								19 59									20 59		
Ton Pentre	d					19 31								20 01									21 01		
Treorchy	d					19 34								20 04									21 04		
Ynyswen	d					19 37								20 07									21 07		
Treherbert	a					19 42								20 12									21 12		

When events are being held at the Principality Stadium, services are subject to alteration. Please check times before travelling.

For connections to Cardiff Bay please refer to Table T124

Table T130-R

Saturdays
26 May to 8 September

Bridgend, Barry Island, Barry, Penarth and Cardiff - Coryton, Rhymney, Pontypridd, Merthyr, Aberdare and Treherbert

Station		AW	AW	AW	AW	AW	AW	AW	AW	AW	AW	AW	AW	AW	AW	AW	AW	AW	AW	AW	AW	AW
Bridgend	d		19 42								20 42						21 42					
Llantwit Major	d		19 56								20 56						21 56					
Rhoose Cardiff Int Airport ✈	d		20 06								21 06						22 06					
Barry Island	d						20 55								21 55						22 44	
Barry 3	d		20 15				21 00				21 15				22 00		22 15				22 49	
Barry Docks	d		20 18				21 03				21 18				22 03		22 18				22 52	
Cadoxton	d		20 21				21 06				21 21				22 06		22 21				22 55	
Dinas Powys	d		20 25				21 10				21 25				22 10		22 25				22 59	
Eastbrook	d		20 28				21 13				21 28				22 13		22 28				23 02	
Cogan	d		20 30				21 15				21 30				22 15		22 30				23 04	
Penarth	d				20 47					21 24		21 47				22 20				22 48		23 26
Dingle Road	d				20 49					21 26		21 49				22 22				22 50		23 28
Grangetown	d		20 34		20 53		21 19			21 30	21 34	21 53			22 19	22 26	22 34			22 54	23 08	23 32
Cardiff Central 7	a		20 39		20 59		21 24			21 37	21 39	21 58			22 24	22 33	22 39			23 01	23 13	23 37
	d	20 36	20 41	20 51	21 01	21 05	21 27	21 31	21 36		21 41	22 01	22 05	22 21	22 26	22 35	22 41	22 46	22 55	23 16	23 26	
Cardiff Queen Street 3	a		20 44	20 54	21 04	21 08	21 30	21 34			21 44	22 04	22 08	22 24	22 29	22 38	22 44	22 49		23 19	23 29	
	d		20 45	20 55	21 05	21 09	21 31	21 35			21 45	22 05	22 09	22 25	22 30	22 39	22 45	22 50		23 20	23 30	
Heath Low Level	d			21 00										22 30								
Ty Glas	d			21 03										22 33								
Birchgrove	d			21 04										22 34								
Rhiwbina	d			21 06										22 36								
Whitchurch (Cardiff)	d			21 08										22 38								
Coryton	a			21 13										22 43								
Heath High Level	d				21 11			21 40				22 10				22 44				23 25		
Llanishen	d				21 14			21 43				22 13				22 47				23 28		
Lisvane & Thornhill	d				21 17			21 45				22 15				22 49				23 30		
Caerphilly	d				21 23			21 51				22a23				22 55				23 36		
Aber	d				21 25			21 53								22 57				23 38		
Energlyn & Churchill Park	d							21 55								22 59				23 40		
Llanbradach	d				21 30			21 59								23 03				23 44		
Ystrad Mynach	d				21a39			22 04								23 08				23a53		
Hengoed	d							22 07								23 11						
Pengam	d							22 10								23 14						
Gilfach Fargoed	d							22 13								23 17						
Bargoed	a							22 17								23 21						
	d							22 18								23 22						
Brithdir	d							22 22								23 26						
Tir-phil	d							22 25								23 29						
Pontlottyn	d							22 29								23 33						
Rhymney 3	a							22 36								23 39						
Cathays	d		20 48			21 12	21 34				21 48		22 12		22 33		22 48	22 53			23 33	
Llandaf	d		20 52			21 16	21 38				21 52		22 16		22 37		22 52	22 57			23 37	
Ninian Park	d	20 40		21 40					21 40										22 59			
Waun-gron Park	d	20 43		21 43					21 43										23 02			
Fairwater	d	20 45		21 45					21 45										23 04			
Danescourt	d	20 47		21 47					21 47										23 06			
Radyr 3	a	20 54	20 55	21 54		21 19	21 41		21 54		21 55		22 19		22 40		22 55	23 00	23 12		23 40	
	d		20 56			21 20	21 42				21 56		22 20		22 41		22 56	23 00			23 40	
Taffs Well	d		21 00			21 24	21 46				22 00		22 24		22 45		23 00	23 04			23 44	
Trefforest Estate	d						21 50								22 49							
Trefforest	d		21 07			21 31	21 54				22 07		22 31		22 53		23 07	23 11			23 52	
Pontypridd 3	a		21 10			21 34	21 57				22 10		22 34		22 56		23 10	23 14			23 59	
	d		21 12			21 35	21 58				22 12		22 35		22 57		23 11	23 15				
Abercynon	d		21 19				22 05				22 19				23 04		23 19					
Penrhiwceiber	d		21 24								22 24						23 24					
Mountain Ash	a		21 28								22 28						23 28					
	d		21 29								22 29						23 29					
Fernhill	d		21 31								22 31						23 31					
Cwmbach	d		21 35								22 35						23 35					
Aberdare	a		21 42								22 42						23 42					
Quakers Yard	d						22 10								23 09							
Merthyr Vale	a						22 15								23 14							
	d						22 16								23 15							
Troed Y Rhiw	d						22 20								23 19							
Pentre-bach	d						22 23								23 22							
Merthyr Tydfil	a						22 31								23 30							
Trehafod	d					21 40							22 40					23 20				
Porth	a					21 43							22 43					23 23				
	d					21 44							22 44					23 24				
Dinas Rhondda	d					21 48							22 48					23 28				
Tonypandy	d					21 50							22 50					23 30				
Llwynypia	d					21 52							22 52					23 32				
Ystrad Rhondda	a					21 55							22 55					23 35				
	d					21 59							22 59					23 38				
Ton Pentre	d					22 01							23 01					23 40				
Treorchy	d					22 04							23 04					23 43				
Ynyswen	d					22 07							23 07					23 46				
Treherbert	a					22 12							23 12					23 52				

When events are being held at the Principality Stadium, services are subject to alteration. Please check times before travelling.

For connections to Cardiff Bay please refer to Table T124

Table T130-R

Saturdays
26 May to 8 September

Bridgend, Barry Island, Barry, Penarth and Cardiff - Coryton, Rhymney, Pontypridd, Merthyr, Aberdare and Treherbert

Station		AW
Bridgend	d	22 42
Llantwit Major	d	22 56
Rhoose Cardiff Int Airport ✈	d	23 06
Barry Island	d	
Barry 3	d	23 15
Barry Docks	d	23 18
Cadoxton	d	23 21
Dinas Powys	d	23 25
Eastbrook	d	23 28
Cogan	d	23 30
Penarth	d	
Dingle Road	d	
Grangetown	d	23 34
Cardiff Central 7	a	23 42
	d	
Cardiff Queen Street 3	a	
	d	
Heath Low Level	d	
Ty Glas	d	
Birchgrove	d	
Rhiwbina	d	
Whitchurch (Cardiff)	d	
Coryton	a	
Heath High Level	d	
Llanishen	d	
Lisvane & Thornhill	d	
Caerphilly	d	
Aber	d	
Energlyn & Churchill Park	d	
Llanbradach	d	
Ystrad Mynach	d	
Hengoed	d	
Pengam	d	
Gilfach Fargoed	d	
Bargoed	a	
	d	
Brithdir	d	
Tir-phil	d	
Pontlottyn	d	
Rhymney 3	a	
Cathays	d	
Llandaf	d	
Ninian Park	d	
Waun-gron Park	d	
Fairwater	d	
Danescourt	d	
Radyr 3	a	
	d	
Taffs Well	d	
Trefforest Estate	d	
Trefforest	d	
Pontypridd 3	a	
	d	
Abercynon	d	
Penrhiwceiber	d	
Mountain Ash	a	
	d	
Fernhill	d	
Cwmbach	d	
Aberdare	a	
Quakers Yard	d	
Merthyr Vale	a	
	d	
Troed Y Rhiw	d	
Pentre-bach	d	
Merthyr Tydfil	a	
Trehafod	d	
Porth	a	
	d	
Dinas Rhondda	d	
Tonypandy	d	
Llwynypia	d	
Ystrad Rhondda	a	
	d	
Ton Pentre	d	
Treorchy	d	
Ynyswen	d	
Treherbert	a	

When events are being held at the Principality Stadium, services are subject to alteration. Please check times before travelling.

For connections to Cardiff Bay please refer to Table T124

Table T130-R

Saturdays

15 September to 8 December

Bridgend, Barry Island, Barry, Penarth and Cardiff - Coryton, Rhymney, Pontypridd, Merthyr, Aberdare and Treherbert

		AW	AW		AW	AW	AW	AW	AW	AW		AW	AW	AW	AW	AW	AW	AW	AW	AW		AW	AW	AW	AW
Bridgend	d													05 42											
Llantwit Major	d													05 56											
Rhoose Cardiff Int Airport ✈	d													06 06											
Barry Island	d		05 14						05 50								06 25							06 55	
Barry 3	d		05 19						05 55					06 15			06 30							07 00	
Barry Docks	d		05 22						05 58					06 18			06 33							07 03	
Cadoxton	d		05 25						06 01					06 21			06 36							07 06	
Dinas Powys	d		05 29						06 05					06 25			06 40							07 10	
Eastbrook	d		05 32						06 08					06 28			06 43							07 13	
Cogan	d		05 34						06 10					06 30			06 45							07 15	
Penarth	d							06 02							06 32							07 02			07 17
Dingle Road	d							06 04							06 34							07 04			07 19
Grangetown	d		05 38					06 08	06 14					06 34	06 38		06 49					07 08		07 19	07 23
Cardiff Central 7	a		05 43					06 13	06 19					06 39	06 44		06 54					07 14		07 24	07 29
	d	05 26	05 46	05 51		05 56	06 11	06 15	06 21	06 26		06 31	06 36	06 41	06 46	06 51	06 56	07 06	07 06	07 11		07 16	07 21	07 26	07 31
Cardiff Queen Street 3	a	05 29	05 50	05 55		05 59	06 14	06 19	06 24	06 29		06 34	06 39	06 44	06 49	06 54	06 59	07 09		07 14		07 19	07 25	07 29	07 34
	d	05 30	05 50	05 56		06 00	06 15	06 20	06 25	06 30		06 35	06 40	06 45	06 50	06 55	07 00	07 10		07 15		07 20	07 26	07 30	07 35
Heath Low Level	d			06 01					06 30							07 00							07 30		
Ty Glas	d			06 04					06 33							07 03							07 33		
Birchgrove	d			06 05					06 34							07 04							07 34		
Rhiwbina	d			06 07					06 36							07 06							07 36		
Whitchurch (Cardiff)	d			06 09					06 38							07 08							07 38		
Coryton	a			06 14					06 44							07 14							07 44		
Heath High Level	d		05 55					06 25							06 55							07 25			07 40
Llanishen	d		05 58					06 28							06 58							07 28			07 43
Lisvane & Thornhill	d		06 00					06 30							07 00							07 30			07 45
Caerphilly	d		06a09					06 36							07 06							07 36			07 51
Aber	d							06 38							07 08							07 38			07 53
Energlyn & Churchill Park	d																					07 40			
Llanbradach	d							06 42							07 12							07 44			07 57
Ystrad Mynach	d							06 47							07 17							07 49			08 02
Hengoed	d							06 50							07 20							07 52			08 05
Pengam	d							06 53							07 23							07 55			08 08
Gilfach Fargoed	d																								
Bargoed	a							07 02							07 32							08 07			08 13
	d																								08 14
Brithdir	d																								08 18
Tir-phil	d																								08 21
Pontlottyn	d																								08 25
Rhymney 3	a																								08 32
Cathays	d	05 33				06 03	06 18			06 33		06 37	06 43	06 48			07 03	07 13		07 18				07 33	
Llandaf	d	05 37				06 07	06 22			06 37			06 47	06 52			07 07	07 17		07 22				07 37	
Ninian Park	d								07 10										07 10						
Waun-gron Park	d								07 14										07 14						
Fairwater	d								07 16										07 16						
Danescourt	d								07 19										07 19						
Radyr 3	a	05 40				06 10	06 25		07 26	06 40		06 43	06 50	06 55			07 10	07 20	07 26	07 25				07 40	
	d	05 41				06 11	06 25			06 41		06 44	06 51	06 55			07 11	07 21		07 26				07 41	
Taffs Well	d	05 45				06 15	06 29			06 45		06a50	06 55	06 59			07 15	07 25		07 30				07 45	
Trefforest Estate	d	05 49				06 19				06 49							07 19							07 49	
Trefforest	d	05 53				06 23	06 36			06 53			07 02	07 06			07 23	07 32		07 37				07 53	
Pontypridd 3	a	05 56				06 26	06 39			06 56			07 05	07 09			07 26	07 35		07 40				07 56	
	d	05 57			06 11	06 27	06 42			06 57			07 06	07 12			07 27	07 36		07 42				07 57	
Abercynon	d	06 04			06 19	06 34	06 49			07 04				07 19			07 34			07 49				08 04	
Penrhiwceiber	d				06 25		06 55							07 25						07 54					
Mountain Ash	a				06 28		06 58							07 28						07 58					
	d				06 34		07 04							07 34						08 03					
Fernhill	d				06 37		07 07							07 37						08 05					
Cwmbach	d				06 41		07 11							07 41						08 09					
Aberdare	a				06 49		07 19							07 49						08 17					
Quakers Yard	d	06 09				06 39				07 09							07 39							08 09	
Merthyr Vale	a	06 14				06 44				07 14							07 44							08 14	
	d	06 17				06 47				07 17							07 47							08 17	
Troed Y Rhiw	d	06 21				06 51				07 21							07 51							08 21	
Pentre-bach	d	06 24				06 54				07 24							07 54							08 24	
Merthyr Tydfil	a	06 33				07 03				07 33							08 03							08 33	
Trehafod	d												07 11					07 41							
Porth	a												07 14					07 44							
	d												07 15					07 45							
Dinas Rhondda	d												07 19					07 49							
Tonypandy	d												07 21					07 51							
Llwynypia	d												07 23					07 53							
Ystrad Rhondda	a												07 26					07 56							
	d												07 29					07 59							
Ton Pentre	d												07 31					08 01							
Treorchy	d												07 34					08 04							
Ynyswen	d												07 37					08 07							
Treherbert	a												07 43					08 13							

When events are being held at the Principality Stadium, services are subject to alteration. Please check times before travelling.

For connections to Cardiff Bay please refer to Table T124

Table T130-R

Saturdays

15 September to 8 December

Bridgend, Barry Island, Barry, Penarth and Cardiff - Coryton, Rhymney, Pontypridd, Merthyr, Aberdare and Treherbert

		AW	AW	AW	AW	AW		AW	AW	AW	AW	AW	AW	AW	AW	AW		AW	AW	AW	AW	AW	AW	AW	AW
Bridgend	d			06 42																07 42					
Llantwit Major	d			06 56																07 56					
Rhoose Cardiff Int Airport ✈	d			07 06																08 06					
Barry Island	d							07 25				07 40			07 55								08 25		
Barry 3	d			07 15				07 30				07 45			08 00					08 15			08 30		
Barry Docks	d			07 18				07 33				07 48			08 03					08 18			08 33		
Cadoxton	d			07 21				07 36				07 51			08 06					08 21			08 36		
Dinas Powys	d			07 25				07 40				07 55			08 10					08 25			08 40		
Eastbrook	d			07 28				07 43				07 58			08 13					08 28			08 43		
Cogan	d			07 30				07 45				08 00			08 15					08 30			08 45		
Penarth	d				07 32				07 47				08 02			08 17					08 32			08 47	
Dingle Road	d				07 34				07 49				08 04			08 19					08 34			08 49	
Grangetown	d			07 34	07 38			07 49	07 53			08 04	08 08		08 19	08 23				08 34	08 38		08 49	08 53	
Cardiff Central 7	a			07 39	07 44			07 54	07 59			08 09	08 14		08 24	08 29				08 39	08 44		08 54	08 59	
	d	07 36	07 36	07 41	07 46	07 51		07 56	08 01	08 06	08 06	08 11	08 16	08 21	08 26	08 31		08 36	08 36	08 41	08 46	08 51	08 56	09 01	09 06
Cardiff Queen Street 3	a	07 39		07 44	07 49	07 54		07 59	08 04	08 09		08 14	08 19	08 24	08 29	08 34		08 39		08 44	08 49	08 54	08 59	09 04	09 09
	d	07 40		07 45	07 50	07 55		08 00	08 05	08 10		08 15	08 20	08 25	08 30	08 35		08 40		08 45	08 50	08 55	09 00	09 05	09 10
Heath Low Level	d					08 00								08 30								09 00			
Ty Glas	d					08 03								08 33								09 03			
Birchgrove	d					08 04								08 34								09 04			
Rhiwbina	d					08 06								08 36								09 06			
Whitchurch (Cardiff)	d					08 08								08 38								09 08			
Coryton	a					08 14								08 44								09 14			
Heath High Level	d				07 55				08 10				08 25			08 40					08 55			09 10	
Llanishen	d				07 58				08 13				08 28			08 43					08 58			09 13	
Lisvane & Thornhill	d				08 00				08 15				08 30			08 45					09 00			09 15	
Caerphilly	d				08 06				08 21				08 36			08 51					09 06			09 21	
Aber	d				08 08				08 23				08 38			08 53					09 08			09 23	
Energlyn & Churchill Park	d								08 25				08 40											09 25	
Llanbradach	d				08 12				08 29				08 44			08 57					09 12			09 29	
Ystrad Mynach	d				08 17				08 34				08 49			09 07					09a21			09 34	
Hengoed	d				08 20				08 37				08 52			09 10								09 37	
Pengam	d				08 23				08 40				08 55			09 13								09 40	
Gilfach Fargoed	d								08 43															09 43	
Bargoed	a				08 32				08 53				09 00			09 22								09 53	
	d												09 01												
Brithdir	d												09 05												
Tir-phil	d												09 08												
Pontlottyn	d												09 12												
Rhymney 3	a												09 19												
Cathays	d	07 43		07 48				08 03		08 13		08 18			08 33			08 43		08 48			09 03		09 13
Llandaf	d	07 47		07 52				08 07		08 17		08 22			08 37			08 47		08 52			09 07		09 17
Ninian Park	d		07 40								08 10								08 40						
Waun-gron Park	d		07 44								08 14								08 44						
Fairwater	d		07 46								08 16								08 46						
Danescourt	d		07 49								08 19								08 49						
Radyr 3	a	07 50	07 56	07 55				08 10		08 20	08 26	08 25			08 40			08 50	08 56	08 55			09 10		09 20
	d	07 51		07 56				08 11		08 21		08 26			08 41			08 51		08 56			09 11		09 21
Taffs Well	d	07 55		08 00				08 15		08 25		08 30			08 45			08 55		09 00			09 15		09 25
Trefforest Estate	d							08 19							08 49								09 19		
Trefforest	d	08 02		08 07				08 23		08 32		08 37			08 53			09 02		09 07			09 23		09 32
Pontypridd 3	a	08 05		08 10				08 26		08 35		08 40			08 56			09 05		09 10			09 26		09 35
	d	08 06		08 12				08 27		08 36		08 42			08 57			09 06		09 12			09 27		09 36
Abercynon	d			08 19				08 34				08 49			09 04					09 19			09 34		
Penrhiwceiber	d			08 25								08 55								09 25					
Mountain Ash	a			08 28								08 58								09 28					
	d			08 34								09 04								09 34					
Fernhill	d			08 37								09 07								09 37					
Cwmbach	d			08 41								09 11								09 41					
Aberdare	a			08 49								09 19								09 49					
Quakers Yard	d							08 39							09 09								09 39		
Merthyr Vale	a							08 44							09 14								09 44		
	d							08 47							09 17								09 47		
Troed Y Rhiw	d							08 51							09 21								09 51		
Pentre-bach	d							08 54							09 24								09 54		
Merthyr Tydfil	a							09 03							09 33								10 03		
Trehafod	d	08 11								08 41								09 11							09 41
Porth	a	08 14								08 44								09 14							09 44
	d	08 15								08 45								09 15							09 45
Dinas Rhondda	d	08 19								08 49								09 19							09 49
Tonypandy	d	08 21								08 51								09 21							09 51
Llwynypia	d	08 23								08 53								09 23							09 53
Ystrad Rhondda	a	08 26								08 56								09 26							09 56
	d	08 29								08 59								09 29							09 59
Ton Pentre	d	08 31								09 01								09 31							10 01
Treorchy	d	08 34								09 04								09 34							10 04
Ynyswen	d	08 37								09 07								09 37							10 07
Treherbert	a	08 43								09 13								09 43							10 13

When events are being held at the Principality Stadium, services are subject to alteration. Please check times before travelling.

For connections to Cardiff Bay please refer to Table T124

Table T130-R

Saturdays

15 September to 8 December

Bridgend, Barry Island, Barry, Penarth and Cardiff - Coryton, Rhymney, Pontypridd, Merthyr, Aberdare and Treherbert

		AW	AW	AW	AW	AW	AW	AW	AW	AW	AW	AW	AW	AW	AW	AW	AW	AW	AW	AW	AW	AW
Bridgend	d									08 42												
Llantwit Major	d									08 56												
Rhoose Cardiff Int Airport ✈	d									09 06												
Barry Island	d		08 40			08 55							09 25					09 40			09 55	
Barry	d		08 45			09 00				09 15			09 30					09 45			10 00	
Barry Docks	d		08 48			09 03				09 18			09 33					09 48			10 03	
Cadoxton	d		08 51			09 06				09 21			09 36					09 51			10 06	
Dinas Powys	d		08 55			09 10				09 25			09 40					09 55			10 10	
Eastbrook	d		08 58			09 13				09 28			09 43					09 58			10 13	
Cogan	d		09 00			09 15				09 30			09 45					10 00			10 15	
Penarth	d						09 17				09 32				09 47				10 02			10 17
Dingle Road	d						09 19				09 34				09 49				10 04			10 19
Grangetown	d		09 04			09 19	09 23			09 34	09 38		09 49		09 53			10 04	10 08		10 19	10 23
Cardiff Central	a		09 09			09 24	09 29			09 39	09 44		09 54		09 59			10 09	10 14		10 24	10 29
	d	09 06	09 11	09 16	09 21	09 26	09 31	09 36	09 36	09 41	09 46	09 51	09 56		10 01	10 06	10 06	10 11	10 16	10 21	10 26	10 31
Cardiff Queen Street	a		09 14	09 19	09 24	09 29	09 34	09 39		09 44	09 49	09 54	09 59		10 04	10 09		10 14	10 19	10 24	10 29	10 34
	d		09 15	09 20	09 25	09 30	09 35	09 40		09 45	09 50	09 55	10 00		10 05	10 10		10 15	10 20	10 25	10 30	10 35
Heath Low Level	d				09 30							10 00								10 30		
Ty Glas	d				09 33							10 03								10 33		
Birchgrove	d				09 34							10 04								10 34		
Rhiwbina	d				09 36							10 06								10 36		
Whitchurch (Cardiff)	d				09 38							10 08								10 38		
Coryton	a				09 44							10 14								10 44		
Heath High Level	d			09 25			09 40				09 55				10 10				10 25			10 40
Llanishen	d			09 28			09 43				09 58				10 13				10 28			10 43
Lisvane & Thornhill	d			09 30			09 45				10 00				10 15				10 30			10 45
Caerphilly	d			09 36			09 51				10 06				10 21				10 36			10 51
Aber	d			09 38			09 53				10 08				10 23				10 38			10 53
Energlyn & Churchill Park	d			09 40											10 25				10 40			
Llanbradach	d			09 44			09 57				10 12				10 29				10 44			10 57
Ystrad Mynach	d			09 49			10 07				10a21				10 34				10 49			11 07
Hengoed	d			09 52			10 10								10 37				10 52			11 10
Pengam	d			09 55			10 13								10 40				10 55			11 13
Gilfach Fargoed	d														10 43							
Bargoed	a			10 00			10 22								10 53				11 00			11 22
	d			10 01															11 01			
Brithdir	d			10 05															11 05			
Tir-phil	d			10 08															11 08			
Pontlottyn	d			10 12															11 12			
Rhymney	a			10 19															11 19			
Cathays	d		09 18			09 33		09 43		09 48			10 03			10 13		10 18			10 33	
Llandaf	d		09 22			09 37		09 47		09 52			10 07			10 17		10 22			10 37	
Ninian Park	d	09 10							09 40								10 10					
Waun-gron Park	d	09 14							09 44								10 14					
Fairwater	d	09 16							09 46								10 16					
Danescourt	d	09 19							09 49								10 19					
Radyr	a	09 26	09 25			09 40		09 50	09 56	09 55			10 10			10 20	10 26	10 25			10 40	
	d		09 26			09 41		09 51		09 56			10 11			10 21		10 26			10 41	
Taffs Well	d		09 30			09 45		09 55		10 00			10 15			10 25		10 30			10 45	
Trefforest Estate	d					09 49															10 49	
Trefforest	d		09 37			09 53		10 02		10 07			10 21			10 32		10 37			10 53	
Pontypridd	a		09 40			09 56		10 05		10 10			10 32			10 35		10 40			10 56	
	d		09 42			09 57		10 06		10 12				10 34		10 36		10 42			10 57	
Abercynon	d		09 49			10 04				10 19				10 40				10 49			11 04	
Penrhiwceiber	d		09 55							10 25								10 55				
Mountain Ash	a		09 58							10 28								10 58				
	d		10 04							10 34								11 04				
Fernhill	d		10 07							10 37								11 07				
Cwmbach	d		10 11							10 41								11 11				
Aberdare	a		10 19							10 49								11 19				
Quakers Yard	d					10 09								10 44							11 09	
Merthyr Vale	a					10 14								10 49							11 14	
	d					10 17								10 52							11 17	
Troed Y Rhiw	d					10 21								10 56							11 21	
Pentre-bach	d					10 24								10 59							11 24	
Merthyr Tydfil	a					10 33								11 08							11 33	
Trehafod	d							10 11								10 41						
Porth	a							10 14								10 44						
	d							10 15								10 45						
Dinas Rhondda	d							10 19								10 49						
Tonypandy	d							10 21								10 51						
Llwynypia	d							10 23								10 53						
Ystrad Rhondda	a							10 26								10 56						
	d							10 29								10 59						
Ton Pentre	d							10 31								11 01						
Treorchy	d							10 34								11 04						
Ynyswen	d							10 37								11 07						
Treherbert	a							10 43								11 13						

When events are being held at the Principality Stadium, services are subject to alteration. Please check times before travelling.

For connections to Cardiff Bay please refer to Table T124

Table T130-R

Saturdays

15 September to 8 December

Bridgend, Barry Island, Barry, Penarth and Cardiff - Coryton, Rhymney, Pontypridd, Merthyr, Aberdare and Treherbert

		AW	AW	AW	AW	AW	AW	AW	AW	AW	AW	AW	AW	AW	AW	AW	AW	AW	AW	AW	AW	AW	AW
Bridgend	d			09 42															10 42				
Llantwit Major	d			09 56															10 56				
Rhoose Cardiff Int Airport ✈	d			10 06															11 06				
Barry Island	d							10 25				10 40			10 55							11 25	
Barry	d			10 15				10 30				10 45			11 00				11 15			11 30	
Barry Docks	d			10 18				10 33				10 48			11 03				11 18			11 33	
Cadoxton	d			10 21				10 36				10 51			11 06				11 21			11 36	
Dinas Powys	d			10 25				10 40				10 55			11 10				11 25			11 40	
Eastbrook	d			10 28				10 43				10 58			11 13				11 28			11 43	
Cogan	d			10 30				10 45				11 00			11 15				11 30			11 45	
Penarth	d				10 32					10 47			11 04			11 17				11 32			11 47
Dingle Road	d				10 34					10 49			11 06			11 19				11 34			11 49
Grangetown	d			10 34	10 38			10 49		10 53		11 04	11 10		11 19	11 23			11 34	11 38		11 49	11 53
Cardiff Central	a			10 42	10 44			10 54		10 59		11 09	11 15		11 24	11 29			11 39	11 44		11 54	11 59
	d	10 36	10 36		10 46	10 51	10 51	10 56		11 01	11 06	11 11	11 16	11 21	11 26	11 31	11 36	11 36	11 41	11 46	11 51	11 56	12 01
Cardiff Queen Street	a	10 39			10 49	10 54		10 59		11 04		11 14	11 19	11 24	11 29	11 34	11 39		11 44	11 49	11 54	11 59	12 04
	d	10 40			10 50	10 55		11 00		11 05		11 15	11 20	11 25	11 30	11 35	11 40		11 45	11 50	11 55	12 00	12 05
Heath Low Level	d					11 00								11 30							12 00		
Ty Glas	d					11 03								11 33							12 03		
Birchgrove	d					11 04								11 34							12 04		
Rhiwbina	d					11 06								11 36							12 06		
Whitchurch (Cardiff)	d					11 08								11 38							12 08		
Coryton	a					11 14								11 44							12 14		
Heath High Level	d				10 55					11 10			11 25			11 40				11 55			12 10
Llanishen	d				10 58					11 13			11 28			11 43				11 58			12 13
Lisvane & Thornhill	d				11 00					11 15			11 30			11 45				12 00			12 15
Caerphilly	d				11 06					11 21			11 36			11 51				12 06			12 21
Aber	d				11 08					11 23			11 38			11 53				12 08			12 23
Energlyn & Churchill Park	d									11 25			11 40										12 25
Llanbradach	d				11 12					11 29			11 44			11 57				12 12			12 29
Ystrad Mynach	d				11a21					11 34			11 49			12 07				12a21			12 35
Hengoed	d									11 37			11 52			12 10							12 37
Pengam	d									11 40			11 55			12 13							12 41
Gilfach Fargoed	d									11 43													12 44
Bargoed	a									11 53			12 00			12 22							12 53
	d												12 01										
Brithdir	d												12 05										
Tir-phil	d												12 08										
Pontlottyn	d												12 12										
Rhymney	a												12 19										
Cathays	d	10 43						11 03				11 18			11 33		11 43		11 48			12 03	
Llandaf	d	10 47						11 07				11 22			11 37		11 47		11 52			12 07	
Ninian Park	d		10 40								11 10							11 40					
Waun-gron Park	d		10 44								11 14							11 44					
Fairwater	d		10 46								11 16							11 46					
Danescourt	d		10 49						←		11 19							11 49					
Radyr	a	10 50	10 55				11 02	11 10	11 02		11 25	11 25			11 40		11 50	11 56	11 55			12 10	
	d	10 51					11 21	11 11	11 21			11 26			11 41		11 51		11 56			12 11	
Taffs Well	d	10 55					→	11 15	11 25			11 30			11 45		11 55		12 00			12 15	
Trefforest Estate	d							11 19							11 49							12 19	
Trefforest	d	11 02						11 23	11 32			11 37			11 53		12 02		12 07			12 23	
Pontypridd	a	11 05						11 26	11 35			11 40			11 56		12 05		12 10			12 26	
	d	11 06						11 27	11 36			11 42			11 57		12 06		12 12			12 27	
Abercynon	d							11 34				11 49			12 04				12 19			12 34	
Penrhiwceiber	d											11 55							12 25				
Mountain Ash	a											11 58							12 28				
	d											12 04							12 34				
Fernhill	d											12 07							12 37				
Cwmbach	d											12 11							12 41				
Aberdare	a											12 19							12 49				
Quakers Yard	d							11 39							12 09							12 39	
Merthyr Vale	a							11 44							12 14							12 44	
	d							11 47							12 17							12 47	
Troed Y Rhiw	d							11 51							12 21							12 51	
Pentre-bach	d							11 54							12 24							12 54	
Merthyr Tydfil	a							12 03							12 33							13 03	
Trehafod	d	11 11							11 41								12 11						
Porth	a	11 14							11 44								12 14						
	d	11 15							11 45								12 15						
Dinas Rhondda	d	11 19							11 49								12 19						
Tonypandy	d	11 21							11 51								12 21						
Llwynypia	d	11 23							11 53								12 23						
Ystrad Rhondda	a	11 26							11 56								12 26						
	d	11 29							11 59								12 29						
Ton Pentre	d	11 31							12 01								12 31						
Treorchy	d	11 34							12 04								12 34						
Ynyswen	d	11 37							12 07								12 37						
Treherbert	a	11 43							12 13								12 43						

When events are being held at the Principality Stadium, services are subject to alteration. Please check times before travelling.

For connections to Cardiff Bay please refer to Table T124

Table T130-R

Saturdays

15 September to 8 December

Bridgend, Barry Island, Barry, Penarth and Cardiff - Coryton, Rhymney, Pontypridd, Merthyr, Aberdare and Treherbert

Station		AW	AW	AW	AW	AW	AW	AW	AW	AW	AW	AW	AW	AW	AW	AW	AW	AW	AW	AW	AW	AW
Bridgend	d										11 42											
Llantwit Major	d										11 56											
Rhoose Cardiff Int Airport ✈	d										12 06											
Barry Island	d			11 40			11 55							12 25				12 40			12 55	
Barry 3	d			11 45			12 00				12 15			12 30				12 45			13 00	
Barry Docks	d			11 48			12 03				12 18			12 33				12 48			13 03	
Cadoxton	d			11 51			12 06				12 21			12 36				12 51			13 06	
Dinas Powys	d			11 55			12 10				12 25			12 40				12 55			13 10	
Eastbrook	d			11 58			12 13				12 28			12 43				12 58			13 13	
Cogan	d			12 00			12 15				12 30			12 45				13 00			13 15	
Penarth	d				12 02				12 17			12 32			12 47				13 02			13 17
Dingle Road	d				12 04				12 19			12 34			12 49				13 04			13 19
Grangetown	d			12 04	12 08		12 19		12 23		12 34	12 38		12 49	12 53			13 04	13 08		13 19	13 23
Cardiff Central 7	a			12 09	12 14		12 24		12 29		12 39	12 44		12 54	12 59			13 09	13 14		13 24	13 29
	d	12 06	12 06	12 11	12 16	12 21	12 26	12 26	12 31	12 36	12 41	12 46	12 51	12 56	13 01	13 06	13 06	13 11	13 16	13 21	13 26	13 31
Cardiff Queen Street 3	a	12 09		12 14	12 19	12 24	12 29		12 34		12 44	12 49	12 54	12 59	13 04	13 09		13 14	13 19	13 24	13 29	13 34
	d	12 10		12 15	12 20	12 25	12 30		12 35		12 45	12 50	12 55	13 00	13 05	13 10		13 15	13 20	13 25	13 30	13 35
Heath Low Level	d					12 30							13 00							13 30		
Ty Glas	d					12 33							13 03							13 33		
Birchgrove	d					12 34							13 04							13 34		
Rhiwbina	d					12 36							13 06							13 36		
Whitchurch (Cardiff)	d					12 38							13 08							13 38		
Coryton	a					12 44							13 14							13 44		
Heath High Level	d				12 25				12 40			12 55			13 10				13 25			13 40
Llanishen	d				12 28				12 43			12 58			13 13				13 28			13 43
Lisvane & Thornhill	d				12 30				12 45			13 00			13 15				13 30			13 45
Caerphilly	d				12 36				12 51			13 06			13 21				13 36			13 51
Aber	d				12 38				12 53			13 08			13 23				13 38			13 53
Energlyn & Churchill Park	d				12 40										13 25				13 40			
Llanbradach	d				12 44				12 57			13 12			13 29				13 44			13 57
Ystrad Mynach	d				12 49				13 07			13a24			13 34				13 49			14 07
Hengoed	d				12 52				13 10						13 37				13 52			14 10
Pengam	d				12 55				13 13						13 40				13 55			14 13
Gilfach Fargoed	d														13 43							
Bargoed	a				13 00				13 22						13 53				14 00			14 22
	d				13 01														14 01			
Brithdir	d				13 05														14 05			
Tir-phil	d				13 08														14 08			
Pontlottyn	d				13 12														14 12			
Rhymney 3	a				13 19														14 19			
Cathays	d	12 13		12 18			12 33				12 48			13 03		13 13		13 18			13 33	
Llandaf	d	12 17		12 22			12 37				12 52			13 07		13 17		13 22			13 37	
Ninian Park	d		12 10							12 40							13 10					
Waun-gron Park	d		12 14							12 44							13 14					
Fairwater	d		12 16							12 46							13 16					
Danescourt	d		12 19							12 49							13 19					
Radyr 3	a	12 20	12 26	12 25			12 40	12 43		12 56	12 55			13 10		13 20	13 26	13 25			13 40	
	d	12 21		12 25			12 41	12 50			12 56			13 11		13 21		13 26			13 41	
Taffs Well	d	12 25		12 29			12 45	12 54			13 00			13 15		13 25		13 30			13 45	
Trefforest Estate	d						12 49							13 19							13 49	
Trefforest	d	12 32		12 36			12 53	13 01			13 07			13 23		13 32		13 37			13 53	
Pontypridd 3	a	12 35		12 42			12 56	13 04			13 10			13 26		13 35		13 40			13 56	
	d	12 36					12 57	13 06			13 12			13 27		13 36		13 42			13 57	
Abercynon	d						13 04				13 19			13 34				13 49			14 04	
Penrhiwceiber	d										13 25							13 55				
Mountain Ash	a										13 28							13 58				
	d										13 34							14 04				
Fernhill	d										13 37							14 07				
Cwmbach	d										13 41							14 11				
Aberdare	a										13 49							14 19				
Quakers Yard	d						13 09							13 39							14 09	
Merthyr Vale	a						13 14							13 44							14 14	
	d						13 17							13 47							14 17	
Troed Y Rhiw	d						13 21							13 51							14 21	
Pentre-bach	d						13 24							13 54							14 24	
Merthyr Tydfil	a						13 33							14 03							14 33	
Trehafod	d	12 41						13 11								13 41						
Porth	a	12 44						13 14								13 44						
	d	12 45						13 15								13 45						
Dinas Rhondda	d	12 49						13 19								13 49						
Tonypandy	d	12 51						13 21								13 51						
Llwynypia	d	12 53						13 23								13 53						
Ystrad Rhondda	a	12 56						13 26								13 56						
	d	12 59						13 29								13 59						
Ton Pentre	d	13 01						13 31								14 01						
Treorchy	d	13 04						13 34								14 04						
Ynyswen	d	13 07						13 37								14 07						
Treherbert	a	13 13						13 43								14 13						

When events are being held at the Principality Stadium, services are subject to alteration. Please check times before travelling.

For connections to Cardiff Bay please refer to Table T124

Table T130-R

Saturdays

15 September to 8 December

Bridgend, Barry Island, Barry, Penarth and Cardiff - Coryton, Rhymney, Pontypridd, Merthyr, Aberdare and Treherbert

Station		AW	AW	AW	AW	AW	AW	AW	AW	AW	AW	AW	AW	AW	AW	AW	AW	AW	AW	AW	AW	AW	AW
Bridgend	d			12 42													13 42						
Llantwit Major	d			12 56													13 56						
Rhoose Cardiff Int Airport ✈	d			13 06													14 06						
Barry Island	d						13 25			13 40			13 55								14 25		
Barry 3	d			13 15			13 30			13 45			14 00				14 15				14 30		
Barry Docks	d			13 18			13 34			13 48			14 03				14 18				14 33		
Cadoxton	d			13 21			13 37			13 51			14 06				14 21				14 36		
Dinas Powys	d			13 25			13 41			13 55			14 10				14 25				14 40		
Eastbrook	d			13 28			13 43			13 58			14 13				14 28				14 43		
Cogan	d			13 30			13 45			14 00			14 15				14 30				14 45		
Penarth	d				13 32						14 02			14 17				14 32					14 47
Dingle Road	d				13 34						14 04			14 19				14 34					14 49
Grangetown	d			13 34	13 38		13 49			14 04	14 08		14 19	14 23			14 34	14 38			14 49		14 53
Cardiff Central 7	a			13 39	13 44		13 54			14 09	14 14		14 24	14 29			14 39	14 44			14 54		14 59
	d	13 36	13 36	13 41	13 46	13 51	13 56	14 06	14 06	14 11	14 16	14 21	14 26	14 31	14 36	14 36	14 41	14 46	14 51	14 51	14 56		15 01
Cardiff Queen Street 3	a	13 39		13 44	13 49	13 54	13 59	14 09		14 14	14 19	14 24	14 29	14 34	14 39		14 44	14 49	14 54		14 59		15 04
	d	13 40		13 45	13 50	13 55	14 00	14 10		14 15	14 20	14 25	14 30	14 35	14 40		14 45	14 50	14 55		15 00		15 05
Heath Low Level	d					14 00						14 30							15 00				
Ty Glas	d					14 03						14 33							15 03				
Birchgrove	d					14 04						14 34							15 04				
Rhiwbina	d					14 06						14 36							15 06				
Whitchurch (Cardiff)	d					14 08						14 38							15 08				
Coryton	a					14 14						14 44							15 14				
Heath High Level	d				13 55						14 25			14 40				14 55					15 10
Llanishen	d				13 58						14 28			14 43				14 58					15 13
Lisvane & Thornhill	d				14 00						14 30			14 45				15 00					15 15
Caerphilly	d				14 06						14 36			14 51				15 06					15 21
Aber	d				14 08						14 38			14 53				15 08					15 23
Energlyn & Churchill Park	d										14 40												15 25
Llanbradach	d				14 12						14 44			14 57				15 12					15 29
Ystrad Mynach	d				14a21						14 49			15 07				15a21					15 34
Hengoed	d										14 52			15 10									15 37
Pengam	d										14 55			15 13									15 40
Gilfach Fargoed	d																						15 43
Bargoed	a										15 00			15 22									15 53
	d										15 01												
Brithdir	d										15 05												
Tir-phil	d										15 08												
Pontlottyn	d										15 12												
Rhymney 3	a										15 19												
Cathays	d	13 43		13 48			14 03	14 13		14 18			14 33		14 43		14 48				15 03		
Llandaf	d	13 47		13 52			14 07	14 17		14 22			14 37		14 47		14 52				15 07		
Ninian Park	d		13 40						14 10							14 40							
Waun-gron Park	d		13 44						14 14							14 44							
Fairwater	d		13 46						14 16							14 46							
Danescourt	d		13 49						14 19							14 49						←	
Radyr 3	a	13 50	13 56	13 55			14 10	14 20	14 24	14 25			14 40		14 50	14 56	14 55			15 09	15 10	15 09	
	d	13 51		13 56			14 11	14 21		14 26			14 41		14 51		14 56			15 21	15 11	15 21	
Taffs Well	d	13 55		14 00			14 15	14 25		14 30			14 45		14 55		15 00			→	15 15	15 25	
Trefforest Estate	d						14 19						14 49								15 19		
Trefforest	d	14 02		14 07			14 23	14 32		14 37			14 53		15 02		15 07				15 23	15 32	
Pontypridd 3	a	14 05		14 10			14 26	14 35		14 40			14 56		15 05		15 10				15 26	15 35	
	d	14 06		14 12			14 27	14 36		14 42			14 57		15 06		15 12				15 27	15 36	
Abercynon	d			14 19			14 34			14 49			15 04				15 19				15 34		
Penrhiwceiber	d			14 25						14 55							15 25						
Mountain Ash	a			14 28						14 58							15 28						
	d			14 34						15 04							15 34						
Fernhill	d			14 37						15 07							15 37						
Cwmbach	d			14 41						15 11							15 41						
Aberdare	a			14 49						15 19							15 49						
Quakers Yard	d						14 39						15 09								15 39		
Merthyr Vale	a						14 44						15 14								15 44		
	d						14 47						15 17								15 47		
Troed Y Rhiw	d						14 51						15 21								15 51		
Pentre-bach	d						14 54						15 24								15 54		
Merthyr Tydfil	a						15 03						15 33								16 03		
Trehafod	d	14 11						14 41							15 11							15 41	
Porth	a	14 14						14 44							15 14							15 44	
	d	14 15						14 45							15 15							15 45	
Dinas Rhondda	d	14 19						14 49							15 19							15 49	
Tonypandy	d	14 21						14 51							15 21							15 51	
Llwynypia	d	14 23						14 53							15 23							15 53	
Ystrad Rhondda	a	14 26						14 56							15 26							15 56	
	d	14 29						14 59							15 29							15 59	
Ton Pentre	d	14 31						15 01							15 31							16 01	
Treorchy	d	14 34						15 04							15 34							16 04	
Ynyswen	d	14 37						15 07							15 37							16 07	
Treherbert	a	14 43						15 13							15 43							16 13	

When events are being held at the Principality Stadium, services are subject to alteration. Please check times before travelling.

For connections to Cardiff Bay please refer to Table T124

Table T130-R

Saturdays

15 September to 8 December

Bridgend, Barry Island, Barry, Penarth and Cardiff - Coryton, Rhymney, Pontypridd, Merthyr, Aberdare and Treherbert

		AW	AW	AW	AW	AW	AW	AW	AW	AW	AW	AW	AW	AW	AW	AW	AW	AW	AW	AW	AW	AW	AW
Bridgend	d									14 42													
Llantwit Major	d									14 56													
Rhoose Cardiff Int Airport ✈	d									15 06													
Barry Island	d		14 40			14 55							15 25				15 40			15 55			
Barry 3	d		14 45			15 00				15 15			15 30				15 45			16 00			
Barry Docks	d		14 48			15 03				15 18			15 33				15 48			16 03			
Cadoxton	d		14 51			15 06				15 21			15 36				15 51			16 06			
Dinas Powys	d		14 55			15 10				15 25			15 40				15 55			16 10			
Eastbrook	d		14 58			15 13				15 28			15 43				15 58			16 13			
Cogan	d		15 00			15 15				15 30			15 45				16 00			16 15			
Penarth	d			15 02			15 17				15 32			15 47				16 02			16 17		
Dingle Road	d			15 04			15 19				15 34			15 49				16 04			16 19		
Grangetown	d		15 04	15 08		15 19	15 23			15 34	15 38		15 49	15 53			16 04	16 08		16 19	16 23		
Cardiff Central 7	a		15 09	15 14		15 24	15 29			15 39	15 44		15 54	15 59			16 09	16 14		16 24	16 29		
	d	15 06	15 11	15 16	15 21	15 26	15 31	15 36	15 36	15 41	15 46	15 51	15 56	16 01	16 06	16 06	16 11	16 16	16 21	16 26	16 31	16 36	16 36
Cardiff Queen Street 3	a		15 14	15 19	15 24	15 29	15 34	15 39		15 44	15 49	15 54	15 59	16 04	16 09		16 14	16 19	16 24	16 29	16 34	16 39	
	d		15 15	15 20	15 25	15 30	15 35	15 40		15 45	15 50	15 55	16 00	16 05	16 10		16 15	16 20	16 25	16 30	16 35	16 40	
Heath Low Level	d				15 30							16 00							16 30				
Ty Glas	d				15 33							16 03							16 33				
Birchgrove	d				15 34							16 04							16 34				
Rhiwbina	d				15 36							16 06							16 36				
Whitchurch (Cardiff)	d				15 38							16 08							16 38				
Coryton	a				15 44							16 14							16 44				
Heath High Level	d			15 25			15 40				15 55			16 10				16 25			16 40		
Llanishen	d			15 28			15 43				15 58			16 13				16 28			16 43		
Lisvane & Thornhill	d			15 30			15 45				16 00			16 15				16 30			16 45		
Caerphilly	d			15 36			15 51				16 06			16 21				16 36			16 51		
Aber	d			15 38			15 53				16 08			16 23				16 38			16 53		
Energlyn & Churchill Park	d			15 40										16 25				16 40					
Llanbradach	d			15 44			15 57				16 12			16 29				16 44			16 57		
Ystrad Mynach	d			15 49			16 02				16 17			16 34				16 49			17 02		
Hengoed	d			15 52			16 05				16 20			16 37				16 52			17 05		
Pengam	d			15 55			16 08				16 23			16 40				16 55			17 08		
Gilfach Fargoed	d													16 43									
Bargoed	a			16 00			16 17				16 32			16 53				17 00			17 17		
	d			16 01														17 01					
Brithdir	d			16 05														17 05					
Tir-phil	d			16 08														17 08					
Pontlottyn	d			16 12														17 12					
Rhymney 3	a			16 19														17 19					
Cathays	d		15 18			15 33		15 43		15 48			16 03		16 13		16 18			16 33		16 43	
Llandaf	d		15 22			15 37		15 47		15 52			16 07		16 17		16 22			16 37		16 47	
Ninian Park	d	15 10							15 40							16 10							16 40
Waun-gron Park	d	15 14							15 44							16 14							16 44
Fairwater	d	15 16							15 46							16 16							16 46
Danescourt	d	15 19							15 49							16 19							16 49
Radyr 3	a	15 24	15 25			15 40		15 50	15 56	15 55			16 10		16 20	16 26	16 25			16 40		16 50	16 56
	d		15 26			15 41		15 51		15 56			16 11		16 21		16 26			16 41		16 51	
Taffs Well	d		15 30			15 45		15 55		16 00			16 15		16 25		16 30			16 45		16 55	
Trefforest Estate	d					15 49							16 19							16 49			
Trefforest	d		15 37			15 53		16 02		16 07			16 23		16 32		16 37			16 52		17 02	
Pontypridd 3	a		15 40			15 56		16 05		16 10			16 26		16 35		16 40			16 55		17 05	
	d		15 42			15 57		16 06		16 12			16 27		16 36		16 42			16 57		17 06	
Abercynon	d		15 49			16 04				16 19			16 34				16 49			17 04			
Penrhiwceiber	d		15 55							16 25							16 55						
Mountain Ash	a		15 58							16 28							16 58						
	d		16 04							16 34							17 04						
Fernhill	d		16 07							16 37							17 07						
Cwmbach	d		16 11							16 41							17 11						
Aberdare	a		16 19							16 49							17 19						
Quakers Yard	d					16 09							16 39							17 09			
Merthyr Vale	a					16 14							16 44							17 14			
	d					16 17							16 47							17 17			
Troed Y Rhiw	d					16 21							16 51							17 21			
Pentre-bach	d					16 24							16 54							17 24			
Merthyr Tydfil	a					16 33							17 03							17 33			
Trehafod	d							16 11							16 41							17 11	
Porth	a							16 14							16 44							17 14	
	d							16 15							16 45							17 15	
Dinas Rhondda	d							16 19							16 49							17 19	
Tonypandy	d							16 21							16 51							17 21	
Llwynypia	d							16 23							16 53							17 23	
Ystrad Rhondda	a							16 26							16 56							17 26	
	d							16 29							16 59							17 29	
Ton Pentre	d							16 31							17 01							17 31	
Treorchy	d							16 34							17 04							17 34	
Ynyswen	d							16 37							17 07							17 37	
Treherbert	a							16 43							17 13							17 43	

When events are being held at the Principality Stadium, services are subject to alteration. Please check times before travelling.

For connections to Cardiff Bay please refer to Table T124

Table T130-R

Saturdays

15 September to 8 December

Bridgend, Barry Island, Barry, Penarth and Cardiff - Coryton, Rhymney, Pontypridd, Merthyr, Aberdare and Treherbert

		AW	AW	AW	AW	AW	AW	AW	AW	AW	AW	AW	AW	AW	AW	AW	AW	AW	AW	AW	AW	AW
Bridgend	d	15 42														16 42						
Llantwit Major	d	15 56														16 56						
Rhoose Cardiff Int Airport ✈	d	16 06														17 06						
Barry Island	d				16 25				16 40			16 55							17 25			
Barry 3	d	16 15			16 30				16 45			17 00				17 15			17 30			
Barry Docks	d	16 18			16 33				16 48			17 03				17 18			17 33			
Cadoxton	d	16 21			16 36				16 51			17 06				17 21			17 36			
Dinas Powys	d	16 25			16 40				16 55			17 10				17 25			17 40			
Eastbrook	d	16 28			16 43				16 58			17 13				17 28			17 43			
Cogan	d	16 30			16 45				17 00			17 15				17 30			17 45			
Penarth	d		16 32							17 02			17 17				17 32			17 47		
Dingle Road	d		16 34							17 04			17 19				17 34			17 49		
Grangetown	d	16 34	16 38		16 49				17 04	17 08		17 19	17 23			17 34	17 38		17 49	17 53		
Cardiff Central 7	a	16 39	16 44		16 54				17 09	17 14		17 24	17 29			17 39	17 44		17 54	17 59		
	d	16 41	16 46	16 51	16 56	17 01	17 06	17 06	17 11	17 16	17 21	17 26	17 31	17 36	17 36	17 41	17 46	17 51	17 56	18 01	18 06	18 06
Cardiff Queen Street 3	a	16 44	16 49	16 54	16 59	17 04	17 09		17 14	17 19	17 24	17 29	17 34	17 39		17 44	17 49	17 54	17 59	18 04	18 09	
	d	16 45	16 50	16 55	17 00	17 05	17 10		17 15	17 20	17 25	17 30	17 35	17 40		17 45	17 50	17 55	18 00	18 05	18 10	
Heath Low Level	d			17 00							17 30							18 00				
Ty Glas	d			17 03							17 33							18 03				
Birchgrove	d			17 04							17 34							18 04				
Rhiwbina	d			17 06							17 36							18 06				
Whitchurch (Cardiff)	d			17 08							17 38							18 08				
Coryton	a			17 14							17 44							18 14				
Heath High Level	d		16 55			17 10				17 25			17 40				17 55			18 10		
Llanishen	d		16 58			17 13				17 28			17 43				17 59			18 13		
Lisvane & Thornhill	d		17 00			17 15				17 31			17 45				18 02			18 15		
Caerphilly	d		17 06			17 21				17 37			17 51				18 07			18 21		
Aber	d		17 08			17 23				17 39			17 53				18 10			18 23		
Energlyn & Churchill Park	d					17 26				17 41			17 55				18 13					
Llanbradach	d		17 12			17 29				17 45			17 59				18 17			18 27		
Ystrad Mynach	d		17 17			17 35				17 50			18 04				18 22			18 32		
Hengoed	d		17 20			17 37				17 53			18 07				18 25			18 35		
Pengam	d		17 23			17 41				17 56			18 10				18 29			18 38		
Gilfach Fargoed	d					17 44							18 13				18 33			18 41		
Bargoed	a		17 32			17 47				18 03			18 16				18 36			18 49		
	d					17 49							18 18				18 38					
Brithdir	d					17 52							18 22				18 41					
Tir-phil	d					17 55							18 25				18 44					
Pontlottyn	d					18 00							18 29				18 49					
Rhymney 3	a					18 07							18 36				18 56					
Cathays	d	16 48			17 03		17 13		17 18			17 33		17 43		17 48			18 03		18 13	
Llandaf	d	16 52			17 07		17 17		17 22			17 37		17 47		17 52			18 07		18 17	
Ninian Park	d							17 10							17 40							18 10
Waun-gron Park	d							17 14							17 44							18 14
Fairwater	d							17 16							17 46							18 16
Danescourt	d							17 19							17 49							18 19
Radyr 3	a	16 55			17 10		17 20	17 26	17 25			17 40		17 50	17 56	17 55			18 10		18 20	18 26
	d	16 56			17 11		17 21		17 26			17 41		17 51		17 56			18 11		18 21	
Taffs Well	d	17 00			17 15		17 25		17 30			17 45		17 55		18 00			18 15		18 25	
Trefforest Estate	d				17 19							17 49							18 19			
Trefforest	d	17 07			17 23		17 32		17 37			17 53		18 02		18 07			18 23		18 32	
Pontypridd 3	a	17 10			17 26		17 35		17 40			17 56		18 05		18 10			18 26		18 35	
	d	17 12			17 27		17 36		17 42			17 57		18 06		18 12			18 27		18 36	
Abercynon	d	17 19			17 34				17 49			18 04				18 19			18 34			
Penrhiwceiber	d	17 25							17 55							18 25						
Mountain Ash	a	17 28							17 58							18 28						
	d	17 34							18 04							18 34						
Fernhill	d	17 37							18 07							18 37						
Cwmbach	d	17 41							18 11							18 41						
Aberdare	a	17 49							18 19							18 49						
Quakers Yard	d				17 39							18 09							18 39			
Merthyr Vale	a				17 44							18 14							18 44			
	d				17 47							18 17							18 47			
Troed Y Rhiw	d				17 51							18 21							18 51			
Pentre-bach	d				17 54							18 24							18 54			
Merthyr Tydfil	a				18 03							18 33							19 03			
Trehafod	d						17 41							18 11							18 41	
Porth	a						17 44							18 14							18 44	
	d						17 45							18 15							18 45	
Dinas Rhondda	d						17 49							18 19							18 49	
Tonypandy	d						17 51							18 21							18 51	
Llwynypia	d						17 53							18 23							18 53	
Ystrad Rhondda	a						17 56							18 26							18 56	
	d						17 59							18 29							18 59	
Ton Pentre	d						18 01							18 31							19 01	
Treorchy	d						18 04							18 34							19 04	
Ynyswen	d						18 07							18 37							19 07	
Treherbert	a						18 13							18 43							19 13	

When events are being held at the Principality Stadium, services are subject to alteration. Please check times before travelling.

For connections to Cardiff Bay please refer to Table T124

Table T130-R

Saturdays

15 September to 8 December

Bridgend, Barry Island, Barry, Penarth and Cardiff - Coryton, Rhymney, Pontypridd, Merthyr, Aberdare and Treherbert

		AW	AW	AW	AW	AW		AW	AW	AW	AW	AW	AW		AW	AW	AW	AW	AW	AW	AW	AW	AW
Bridgend	d								17 42										18 42				
Llantwit Major	d								17 56										18 56				
Rhoose Cardiff Int Airport ✈	d								18 06										19 06				
Barry Island	d	17 40			17 55							18 25			18 40	18 55					19 25		19 55
Barry	d	17 45			18 00				18 15			18 30			18 45	19 00			19 15		19 30		20 00
Barry Docks	d	17 48			18 03				18 18			18 33			18 48	19 03			19 18		19 33		20 03
Cadoxton	d	17 51			18 06				18 21			18 36			18 51	19 06			19 21		19 36		20 06
Dinas Powys	d	17 55			18 10				18 25			18 40			18 55	19 10			19 25		19 40		20 10
Eastbrook	d	17 58			18 13				18 28			18 43			18 58	19 13			19 28		19 43		20 13
Cogan	d	18 00			18 15				18 30			18 45			19 00	19 15			19 30		19 45		20 15
Penarth	d		18 02			18 18				18 32			18 47				19 17					19 47	
Dingle Road	d		18 04			18 20				18 34			18 49				19 19					19 49	
Grangetown	d	18 04	18 08		18 19	18 24			18 34	18 38		18 49	18 53		19 04	19 19	19 23		19 34		19 49	19 53	20 19
Cardiff Central	a	18 09	18 14		18 25	18 29			18 39	18 47		18 57	18 59		19 09	19 24	19 29		19 39		19 54	19 59	20 24
	d	18 11	18 16	18 21	18 26	18 31	18 36	18 36	18 41		18 51		19 01	19 06	19 11	19 26	19 31	19 36	19 41	19 51	20 01	20 06	20 26
Cardiff Queen Street	a	18 14	18 19	18 24	18 29	18 34	18 38		18 44		18 54		19 04	19 09	19 14	19 29	19 34		19 44	19 54	20 04	20 09	20 29
	d	18 15	18 20	18 25	18 30	18 35	18 40		18 47		18 55		19 05	19 10	19 15	19 30	19 35		19 45	19 55	20 05	20 10	20 30
Heath Low Level	d			18 30							19 00									20 00			
Ty Glas	d			18 33							19 03									20 03			
Birchgrove	d			18 34							19 04									20 04			
Rhiwbina	d			18 36							19 06									20 06			
Whitchurch (Cardiff)	d			18 38							19 08									20 08			
Coryton	a			18 44							19 14									20 14			
Heath High Level	d		18 25			18 40							19 10				19 40				20 11		
Llanishen	d		18 28			18 43							19 13				19 43				20 14		
Lisvane & Thornhill	d		18 30			18 45							19 15				19 45				20 15		
Caerphilly	d		18 36			18 51							19a23				19 51				20a25		
Aber	d		18 38			18 53											19 53						
Energlyn & Churchill Park	d		18 40			18 55											19 56						
Llanbradach	d		18 44			18 59											19 59						
Ystrad Mynach	d		18a54			19 04											20 04						
Hengoed	d					19 07											20 07						
Pengam	d					19 10											20 10						
Gilfach Fargoed	d					19 13											20 13						
Bargoed	a					19 16											20 17						
	d					19 18											20 18						
Brithdir	d					19 22											20 22						
Tir-phil	d					19 25											20 25						
Pontlottyn	d					19 29											20 29						
Rhymney	a					19 37											20 36						
Cathays	d	18 18			18 33		18 43		18 50					19 13	19 18	19 33			19 48			20 13	20 33
Llandaf	d	18 22			18 37		18 47		18 54					19 17	19 22	19 37			19 52			20 17	20 37
Ninian Park	d							18 40										19 40					
Waun-gron Park	d							18 44										19 44					
Fairwater	d							18 46										19 46					
Danescourt	d							18 49										19 49					
Radyr	a	18 25			18 40		18 50	18 56	18 57					19 20	19 25	19 40		19 56	19 55			20 20	20 40
	d	18 25			18 41		18 50		18 58					19 21	19 26	19 41			19 56			20 21	20 41
Taffs Well	d	18 29			18 45		18 54		19 02					19 25	19 30	19 45			20 00			20 25	20 45
Trefforest Estate	d				18 49											19 49							20 49
Trefforest	d	18 36			18 53		19 01		19 09					19 32	19 37	19 53			20 07			20 32	20 53
Pontypridd	a	18 42			18 56		19 04		19 12					19 35	19 40	19 56			20 10			20 35	20 56
	d				18 57		19 06		19 12					19 36	19 42	19 57			20 12			20 36	20 57
Abercynon	d				19 04				19 19						19 49	20 04			20 21				21 04
Penrhiwceiber	d								19 24						19 55				20 27				
Mountain Ash	a								19 28						19 58				20 31				
	d								19 33						20 04				20 34				
Fernhill	d								19 35						20 07				20 37				
Cwmbach	d								19 39						20 11				20 41				
Aberdare	a								19 47						20 19				20 49				
Quakers Yard	d				19 09											20 09							21 09
Merthyr Vale	a				19 14											20 14							21 14
	d				19 17											20 14							21 14
Troed Y Rhiw	d				19 21											20 18							21 18
Pentre-bach	d				19 24											20 22							21 22
Merthyr Tydfil	a				19 33											20 30							21 30
Trehafod	d						19 11							19 41								20 41	
Porth	a						19 14							19 44								20 44	
	d						19 15							19 45								20 45	
Dinas Rhondda	d						19 19							19 49								20 49	
Tonypandy	d						19 21							19 51								20 51	
Llwynypia	d						19 23							19 53								20 53	
Ystrad Rhondda	a						19 26							19 56								20 56	
	d						19 29							19 59								20 59	
Ton Pentre	d						19 31							20 01								21 01	
Treorchy	d						19 34							20 04								21 04	
Ynyswen	d						19 37							20 07								21 07	
Treherbert	a						19 43							20 13								21 13	

When events are being held at the Principality Stadium, services are subject to alteration. Please check times before travelling.

For connections to Cardiff Bay please refer to Table T124

Table T130-R

Saturdays

15 September to 8 December

Bridgend, Barry Island, Barry, Penarth and Cardiff - Coryton, Rhymney, Pontypridd, Merthyr, Aberdare and Treherbert

		AW	AW	AW	AW	AW	AW	AW	AW	AW	AW	AW	AW	AW	AW	AW	AW	AW	AW	AW	AW	AW
Bridgend	d			19 42								20 42						21 42				
Llantwit Major	d			19 56								20 56						21 56				
Rhoose Cardiff Int Airport ✈	d			20 06								21 06						22 06				
Barry Island	d							20 55								21 55						22 44
Barry	d			20 15				21 00				21 15				22 00		22 15				22 49
Barry Docks	d			20 18				21 03				21 18				22 03		22 18				22 52
Cadoxton	d			20 21				21 06				21 21				22 06		22 21				22 55
Dinas Powys	d			20 25				21 10				21 25				22 10		22 25				22 59
Eastbrook	d			20 28				21 13				21 28				22 13		22 28				23 02
Cogan	d			20 30				21 15				21 30				22 15		22 30				23 04
Penarth	d	20 20				20 47					21 24		21 47				22 20				22 48	
Dingle Road	d	20 22				20 49					21 26		21 49				22 22				22 50	
Grangetown	d	20 26		20 34		20 53		21 19			21 30	21 34	21 53			22 19	22 26	22 34			22 54	23 08
Cardiff Central	a	20 31		20 39		20 57		21 25			21 38	21 39	21 58			22 24	22 31	22 39			23 01	23 13
	d	20 31	20 36	20 41	20 51	21 01	21 06	21 27	21 31	21 36		21 41	22 01	22 06	22 21	22 26	22 35	22 41	22 46	22 55	23 16	23 26
Cardiff Queen Street	a	20 34		20 44	20 54	21 04	21 09	21 30	21 34			21 44	22 04	22 09	22 24	22 29	22 38	22 44	22 49		23 19	23 29
	d	20 35		20 45	20 55	21 05	21 10	21 31	21 35			21 45	22 05	22 10	22 25	22 30	22 39	22 45	22 50		23 20	23 30
Heath Low Level	d				21 00										22 30							
Ty Glas	d				21 03										22 33							
Birchgrove	d				21 04										22 34							
Rhiwbina	d				21 06										22 36							
Whitchurch (Cardiff)	d				21 08										22 38							
Coryton	a				21 14										22 44							
Heath High Level	d	20 40				21 11			21 40				22 10				22 44				23 25	
Llanishen	d	20 43				21 14			21 43				22 13				22 47				23 28	
Lisvane & Thornhill	d	20 45				21 17			21 45				22 15				22 49				23 30	
Caerphilly	d	20 51				21 23			21 51				22a23				22 55				23 36	
Aber	d	20 53				21 25			21 53								22 57				23 38	
Energlyn & Churchill Park	d	20 55							21 55								22 59				23 40	
Llanbradach	d	20 59				21 30			21 59								23 03				23 44	
Ystrad Mynach	d	21 04				21a40			22 04								23 08				23a54	
Hengoed	d	21 07							22 07								23 11					
Pengam	d	21 10							22 10								23 14					
Gilfach Fargoed	d	21 13							22 13								23 17					
Bargoed	a	21 17							22 17								23 21					
	d	21 18							22 18								23 22					
Brithdir	d	21 22							22 22								23 26					
Tir-phil	d	21 25							22 25								23 29					
Pontlottyn	d	21 29							22 29								23 33					
Rhymney	a	21 36							22 37								23 40					
Cathays	d			20 48			21 13	21 34				21 48		22 13		22 33		22 48	22 53			23 33
Llandaf	d			20 52			21 17	21 38				21 52		22 17		22 37		22 52	22 57			23 37
Ninian Park	d		20 40							21 40										22 59		
Waun-gron Park	d		20 44							21 44										23 02		
Fairwater	d		20 46							21 46										23 04		
Danescourt	d		20 49							21 49										23 06		
Radyr	a		20 56	20 55			21 20	21 41		21 56		21 55		22 20		22 40		22 55	23 00	23 12		23 40
	d			20 56			21 21	21 42				21 56		22 21		22 41		22 56	23 00			23 40
Taffs Well	d			21 00			21 25	21 46				22 00		22 25		22 45		23 00	23 04			23 44
Trefforest Estate	d							21 50								22 49						
Trefforest	d			21 07			21 32	21 54				22 07		22 32		22 53		23 07	23 11			23 52
Pontypridd	a			21 10			21 35	21 57				22 10		22 35		22 56		23 10	23 14			23 59
	d			21 12			21 36	21 58				22 12		22 36		22 57		23 11	23 15			
Abercynon	d			21 19				22 05				22 19				23 04		23 19				
Penrhiwceiber	d			21 25								22 25						23 25				
Mountain Ash	a			21 28								22 28						23 28				
	d			21 29								22 29						23 34				
Fernhill	d			21 32								22 32						23 37				
Cwmbach	d			21 36								22 36						23 41				
Aberdare	a			21 44								22 44						23 49				
Quakers Yard	d							22 10								23 09						
Merthyr Vale	a							22 15								23 14						
	d							22 15								23 14						
Troed Y Rhiw	d							22 19								23 18						
Pentre-bach	d							22 23								23 22						
Merthyr Tydfil	a							22 31								23 30						
Trehafod	d						21 41							22 41					23 20			
Porth	a						21 44							22 44					23 23			
	d						21 45							22 45					23 24			
Dinas Rhondda	d						21 49							22 49					23 28			
Tonypandy	d						21 51							22 51					23 30			
Llwynypia	d						21 53							22 53					23 32			
Ystrad Rhondda	a						21 56							22 56					23 35			
	d						21 59							22 59					23 38			
Ton Pentre	d						22 01							23 01					23 40			
Treorchy	d						22 04							23 04					23 43			
Ynyswen	d						22 07							23 07					23 46			
Treherbert	a						22 13							23 13					23 52			

When events are being held at the Principality Stadium, services are subject to alteration. Please check times before travelling.

For connections to Cardiff Bay please refer to Table T124

Table T130-R

Saturdays
15 September to 8 December

Bridgend, Barry Island, Barry, Penarth and Cardiff - Coryton, Rhymney, Pontypridd, Merthyr, Aberdare and Treherbert

Station		AW	AW
Bridgend	d		22 42
Llantwit Major	d		22 56
Rhoose Cardiff Int Airport ✈	d		23 06
Barry Island	d		
Barry 3	d		23 15
Barry Docks	d		23 18
Cadoxton	d		23 21
Dinas Powys	d		23 25
Eastbrook	d		23 28
Cogan	d		23 30
Penarth	d	23 26	
Dingle Road	d	23 28	
Grangetown	d	23 32	23 34
Cardiff Central 7	a	23 37	23 42
	d		
Cardiff Queen Street 3	a		
	d		
Heath Low Level	d		
Ty Glas	d		
Birchgrove	d		
Rhiwbina	d		
Whitchurch (Cardiff)	d		
Coryton	a		
Heath High Level	d		
Llanishen	d		
Lisvane & Thornhill	d		
Caerphilly	d		
Aber	d		
Energlyn & Churchill Park	d		
Llanbradach	d		
Ystrad Mynach	d		
Hengoed	d		
Pengam	d		
Gilfach Fargoed	d		
Bargoed	a		
	d		
Brithdir	d		
Tir-phil	d		
Pontlottyn	d		
Rhymney 3	a		
Cathays	d		
Llandaf	d		
Ninian Park	d		
Waun-gron Park	d		
Fairwater	d		
Danescourt	d		
Radyr 3	a		
	d		
Taffs Well	d		
Trefforest Estate	d		
Trefforest	d		
Pontypridd 3	a		
	d		
Abercynon	d		
Penrhiwceiber	d		
Mountain Ash	a		
	d		
Fernhill	d		
Cwmbach	d		
Aberdare	a		
Quakers Yard	d		
Merthyr Vale	a		
	d		
Troed Y Rhiw	d		
Pentre-bach	d		
Merthyr Tydfil	a		
Trehafod	d		
Porth	a		
	d		
Dinas Rhondda	d		
Tonypandy	d		
Llwynypia	d		
Ystrad Rhondda	a		
	d		
Ton Pentre	d		
Treorchy	d		
Ynyswen	d		
Treherbert	a		

When events are being held at the Principality Stadium, services are subject to alteration. Please check times before travelling.

For connections to Cardiff Bay please refer to Table T124

Table T130-R

Sundays
20 May to 9 September

Bridgend, Barry Island, Barry, Penarth and Cardiff - Coryton, Rhymney, Pontypridd, Merthyr, Aberdare and Treherbert

Station		AW	AW	AW	AW	AW	AW	AW	AW	AW	AW	AW	AW	AW	AW	AW	AW	AW	AW	AW	AW	AW	AW
Bridgend	d											09 42									11 42	11 42	
Llantwit Major	d											09 56									11 56	11 56	
Rhoose Cardiff Int Airport ✈	d											10 06									12 06	12 06	
Barry Island	d						08 55				09 55		10 25	10 25		10 55		11 25	11 44	11 55			12 25
Barry 3	d						09 00				10 00	10 15	10 30	10 30		11 00		11 30	11 49	12 00	12 15	12 15	12 30
Barry Docks	d						09 03				10 03	10 18	10 33	10 33		11 03		11 33	11 52	12 03	12 18	12 18	12 33
Cadoxton	d						09 06				10 06	10 21	10 36	10 36		11 06		11 36	11 55	12 06	12 21	12 21	12 36
Dinas Powys	d						09 10				10 10	10 25	10 40	10 40		11 10		11 40	11 59	12 10	12 25	12 25	12 40
Eastbrook	d						09 13				10 13	10 28	10 43	10 43		11 13		11 43	12 02	12 13	12 28	12 28	12 43
Cogan	d						09 15				10 15	10 30	10 45	10 45		11 15		11 45	12 04	12 15	12 30	12 30	12 45
Penarth	d							09 32	09 32								11 32						
Dingle Road	d							09 34	09 34								11 34						
Grangetown	d						09 19	09 38	09 38		10 19	10 34	10 49	10 49		11 19	11 38	11 49	12 08	12 19	12 34	12 34	12 49
Cardiff Central 7	a						09 24	09 43	09 43		10 24	10 41	10 56	10 56		11 24	11 43	11 54	12 15	12 24	12 41	12 41	12 56
	d	08 26	08 41	08 54	09 00	09 05	09 41		10 06	10 06	10 26			11 00	11 00	11 41	11 46	12 06		12 26		13 06	
Cardiff Queen Street 3	a	08 29	08 44	08 57	09 03	09 08	09 44		10 09	10 09	10 29			11 03	11 03	11 44	11 49	12 09		12 29		13 09	
	d	08 30	08 45		09 04	09 09	09 45		10 10	10 10	10 30			11 04	11 04	11 45	11 50	12 10		12 30		13 10	
Heath Low Level	d																						
Ty Glas	d																						
Birchgrove	d																						
Rhiwbina	d																						
Whitchurch (Cardiff)	d																						
Coryton	a																						
Heath High Level	d					09 14			10 15	10 15							11 55	12 15					
Llanishen	d					09 17			10 18	10 18							11 58	12 18					
Lisvane & Thornhill	d					09 19			10 20	10 20							12 00	12 20					
Caerphilly	d					09 25			10 26	10 26							12 06	12 26					
Aber	d					09 27			10 28	10 28							12 08	12 28					
Energlyn & Churchill Park	d					09 29			10 30	10 30							12 10	12 30					
Llanbradach	d					09 33			10 34	10 34							12 14	12 34					
Ystrad Mynach	d					09 38			10 39	10 39							12a23	12 39					
Hengoed	d					09 41			10 42	10 42								12 42					
Pengam	d					09 44			10 45	10 45								12 45					
Gilfach Fargoed	d					09 47			10 48	10 48								12 48					
Bargoed	a					09 51			10 51	10 51								12 51					
	d					09 52			10 51	10 51								12 51					
Brithdir	d					09 56			10 55	10 55								12 55					
Tir-phil	d					09 59			10 58	10 58								12 58					
Pontlottyn	d					10 03			11 02	11 02								13 02					
Rhymney 3	a					10 09			11 09	11 09								13 09					
Cathays	d	08 33	08 48		09 07		09 48				10 33			11 07	11 07	11 48		15 48		12 33		13 13	
Llandaf	d	08 37	08 52		09 11		09 52				10 37			11 11	11 11	11 52		15 52		12 37		13 17	
Ninian Park	d																						
Waun-gron Park	d																						
Fairwater	d																						
Danescourt	d																						
Radyr 3	a	08 40	08 55		09 14		09 55				10 40			11 14	11 14	11 55		15 55		12 40		13 20	
	d	08 40	08 55		09 14		09 55				10 40			11 14	11 14	11 55		15 55		12 40		13 20	
Taffs Well	d	08 44	08 59		09 18		09 59				10 44			11 18	11 18	11 59		→		12 44		13 24	
Trefforest Estate	d																						
Trefforest	d	08 52	09 06		09 25		10 06				10 52			11 25	11 25	12 06				12 52		13 31	
Pontypridd 3	a	08 55	09 09		09 28		10 09				10 55			11 28	11 28	12 09				12 55		13 34	
	d	08 57	09 11		09 30		10 11				10 57			11 30	11 30	12 11				12 57		13 36	
Abercynon	d	09 05	09 19				10 19				11 05					12 19				13 05			
Penrhiwceiber	d		09 24				10 24									12 24							
Mountain Ash	a		09 28				10 28									12 28							
	d		09 29				10 29									12 29							
Fernhill	d		09 31				10 31									12 31							
Cwmbach	d		09 35				10 35									12 35							
Aberdare	a		09 42				10 42									12 42							
Quakers Yard	d	09 09									11 09									13 09			
Merthyr Vale	a	09 14									11 14									13 14			
	d	09 16									11 16									13 16			
Troed Y Rhiw	d	09 20									11 20									13 20			
Pentre-bach	d	09 23									11 23									13 23			
Merthyr Tydfil	a	09 31									11 31									13 31			
Trehafod	d				09 35									11 35	11 35							13 41	
Porth	a				09 38									11 38	11 38							13 44	
	d				09 39									11 39	11 39							13 45	
Dinas Rhondda	d				09 43									11 43	11 43							13 49	
Tonypandy	d				09 45									11 45	11 45							13 51	
Llwynypia	d				09 47									11 47	11 47							13 53	
Ystrad Rhondda	a				09 50									11 50	11 50							13 56	
	d				09 53									11 53	11 53							13 59	
Ton Pentre	d				09 55									11 55	11 55							14 01	
Treorchy	d				09 58									11 58	11 58							14 04	
Ynyswen	d				10 01									12 01	12 01							14 07	
Treherbert	a				10 07									12 07	12 07							14 13	

When events are being held at the Principality Stadium, services are subject to alteration. Please check times before travelling.

For connections to Cardiff Bay please refer to Table T124

Table T130-R

Sundays
20 May to 9 September

Bridgend, Barry Island, Barry, Penarth and Cardiff - Coryton, Rhymney, Pontypridd, Merthyr, Aberdare and Treherbert

		AW	AW	AW	AW	AW		AW	AW	AW	AW	AW	AW	AW	AW	AW		AW	AW	AW	AW	AW	AW	AW	AW
Bridgend	d							13 42										15 42							
Llantwit Major	d							13 56										15 56							
Rhoose Cardiff Int Airport ✈	d							14 06										16 06							
Barry Island	d		12 55		13 25	13 55			14 25	14 25			14 55		15 25	15 55			16 25	16 41		16 55		17 25	17 55
Barry [3]	d		13 00		13 30	14 00		14 15	14 30	14 30			15 00		15 30	16 00		16 15	16 30	16 45		17 00		17 30	18 00
Barry Docks	d		13 03		13 33	14 03		14 18	14 33	14 33			15 03		15 33	16 03		16 18	16 33			17 03		17 33	18 03
Cadoxton	d		13 06		13 36	14 06		14 21	14 36	14 36			15 06		15 36	16 06		16 21	16 36			17 06		17 36	18 06
Dinas Powys	d		13 10		13 40	14 10		14 25	14 40	14 40			15 10		15 40	16 10		16 25	16 40			17 10		17 40	18 10
Eastbrook	d		13 13		13 43	14 13		14 28	14 43	14 43			15 13		15 43	16 13		16 28	16 43			17 13		17 43	18 13
Cogan	d		13 15		13 45	14 15		14 30	14 45	14 45			15 15		15 45	16 15		16 30	16 45			17 15		17 45	18 15
Penarth	d			13 32										15 32									17 32		
Dingle Road	d			13 34										15 34									17 34		
Grangetown	d		13 19	13 38	13 49	14 19		14 34	14 49	14 49			15 19	15 38	15 49	16 19		16 34	16 49			17 19	17 38	17 49	18 19
Cardiff Central [7]	a		13 24	13 43	13 54	14 24		14 41	14 56	14 56			15 25	15 43	15 54	16 24		16 41	16 56	17 01		17 24	17 43	17 54	18 24
	d	13 06	13 41	13 46	14 06	14 26				15 06	15 06		15 41	15 46	16 06	16 26					17 06	17 41	17 46	18 06	18 26
Cardiff Queen Street [3]	a	13 09	13 44	13 49	14 09	14 29				15 09	15 09		15 44	15 49	16 09	16 29					17 09	17 44	17 49	18 09	18 29
	d	13 10	13 45	13 50	14 10	14 30				15 10	15 10		15 45	15 50	16 10	16 30					17 10	17 45	17 50	18 10	18 30
Heath Low Level	d																								
Ty Glas	d																								
Birchgrove	d																								
Rhiwbina	d																								
Whitchurch (Cardiff)	d																								
Coryton	a																								
Heath High Level	d			13 55	14 15									15 55	16 15								17 55	18 15	
Llanishen	d			13 58	14 18									15 58	16 18								17 58	18 18	
Lisvane & Thornhill	d			14 00	14 20									16 00	16 20								18 00	18 20	
Caerphilly	d			14 06	14 26									16 06	16 26								18 06	18 26	
Aber	d			14 08	14 28									16 08	16 28								18 08	18 28	
Energlyn & Churchill Park	d			14 10	14 30									16 10	16 30								18 10	18 30	
Llanbradach	d			14 14	14 34									16 14	16 34								18 14	18 34	
Ystrad Mynach	d			14a23	14 39									16a23	16 39								18a23	18 39	
Hengoed	d				14 42										16 42									18 42	
Pengam	d				14 45										16 45									18 45	
Gilfach Fargoed	d				14 48										16 48									18 48	
Bargoed	a				14 51										16 51									18 51	
	d				14 51										16 51									18 51	
Brithdir	d				14 55										16 55									18 55	
Tir-phil	d				14 58										16 58									18 58	
Pontlottyn	d				15 02										17 02									19 02	
Rhymney [3]	a				15 09										17 09									19 09	
Cathays	d	13 13	13 48			14 33				15 13	15 13		15 48			16 33					17 13	17 48			18 33
Llandaf	d	13 17	13 52			14 37				15 17	15 17		15 52			16 37					17 17	17 52			18 37
Ninian Park	d																								
Waun-gron Park	d																								
Fairwater	d																								
Danescourt	d											←													
Radyr [3]	a	13 20	13 55			14 40				15 20	15 20	15 55	15 55			16 40					17 20	17 55			18 40
	d	13 20	13 55			14 40				15 20	15 20	15 55	15 55			16 40					17 20	17 55			18 40
Taffs Well	d	13 24	13 59			14 44				15 24	15 24	15 59	15 59			16 44					17 24	17 59			18 44
Trefforest Estate	d																								
Trefforest	d	13 31	14 06			14 52				15 31	15 31	16 06	16 06			16 52					17 31	18 06			18 52
Pontypridd [3]	a	13 34	14 09			14 55				15 34	15 34	16 09	16 09			16 55					17 34	18 09			18 55
	d	13 36	14 11			14 57				15 36	15 36	16 11	16 11			16 57					17 36	18 11			18 57
Abercynon	d		14 19			15 05						16 19	16 19			17 05						18 19			19 05
Penrhiwceiber	d		14 24									16 24	16 24									18 24			
Mountain Ash	a		14 28									16 28	16 28									18 28			
	d		14 29									16 29	16 29									18 29			
Fernhill	d		14 31									16 31	16 31									18 31			
Cwmbach	d		14 35									16 35	16 35									18 35			
Aberdare	a		14 42									16 42	16 42									18 42			
Quakers Yard	d					15 09										17 09									19 09
Merthyr Vale	a					15 14										17 14									19 14
	d					15 16										17 16									19 16
Troed Y Rhiw	d					15 20										17 20									19 20
Pentre-bach	d					15 23										17 23									19 23
Merthyr Tydfil	a					15 31										17 31									19 31
Trehafod	d	13 41								15 41	15 41										17 41				
Porth	a	13 44								15 44	15 44										17 44				
	d	13 45								15 45	15 45										17 45				
Dinas Rhondda	d	13 49								15 49	15 49										17 49				
Tonypandy	d	13 51								15 51	15 51										17 51				
Llwynypia	d	13 53								15 53	15 53										17 53				
Ystrad Rhondda	a	13 56								15 56	15 56										17 56				
	d	13 59								15 59	15 59										17 59				
Ton Pentre	d	14 01								16 01	16 01										18 01				
Treorchy	d	14 04								16 04	16 04										18 04				
Ynyswen	d	14 07								16 07	16 07										18 07				
Treherbert	a	14 13								16 13	16 13										18 13				

When events are being held at the Principality Stadium, services are subject to alteration. Please check times before travelling.

For connections to Cardiff Bay please refer to Table T124

Table T130-R

Sundays
20 May to 9 September

Bridgend, Barry Island, Barry, Penarth and Cardiff - Coryton, Rhymney, Pontypridd, Merthyr, Aberdare and Treherbert

		AW		AW	AW	AW	AW	AW	AW	AW	AW	AW		AW	AW	AW	AW	AW							
Bridgend	d	17 42								19 42							21 42								
Llantwit Major	d	17 56								19 56							21 56								
Rhoose Cardiff Int Airport ✈	d	18 06								20 06							22 06								
Barry Island	d			18 25	18 25		18 55	19 25	19 55		20 25			20 55	21 25	21 55		22 55							
Barry [3]	d	18 15		18 30	18 30		19 00	19 30	20 00	20 15	20 30			21 00	21 30	22 00	22 15	23 00							
Barry Docks	d	18 18		18 33	18 33		19 03	19 33	20 03	20 18	20 33			21 03	21 33	22 03	22 18	23 03							
Cadoxton	d	18 21		18 36	18 36		19 06	19 36	20 06	20 21	20 36			21 06	21 36	22 06	22 21	23 06							
Dinas Powys	d	18 25		18 40	18 40		19 10	19 40	20 10	20 25	20 40			21 10	21 40	22 10	22 25	23 10							
Eastbrook	d	18 28		18 43	18 43		19 13	19 43	20 13	20 28	20 43			21 13	21 43	22 13	22 28	23 13							
Cogan	d	18 30		18 45	18 45		19 15	19 45	20 15	20 30	20 45			21 15	21 45	22 15	22 30	23 15							
Penarth	d											20 47													
Dingle Road	d											20 49													
Grangetown	d	18 34		18 49	18 49		19 19	19 49	20 19	20 34	20 49	20 53		21 19	21 49	22 19	22 34	23 19							
Cardiff Central [7]	a	18 41		18 56	18 56		19 24	19 54	20 24	20 41	20 54	20 58		21 26	21 54	22 26	22 41	23 26							
	d				19 06	19 06	19 41	20 06	20 26		21 06	21 16			22 06										
Cardiff Queen Street [3]	a				19 09	19 09	19 44	20 09	20 29		21 09	21 19			22 09										
	d				19 10	19 10	19 45	20 10	20 30		21 10	21 20			22 10										
Heath Low Level	d																								
Ty Glas	d																								
Birchgrove	d																								
Rhiwbina	d																								
Whitchurch (Cardiff)	d																								
Coryton	a																								
Heath High Level	d							20 15				21 25													
Llanishen	d							20 18				21 28													
Lisvane & Thornhill	d							20 20				21 30													
Caerphilly	d							20 26				21 36													
Aber	d							20 28				21 38													
Energlyn & Churchill Park	d							20 30				21 40													
Llanbradach	d							20 34				21 44													
Ystrad Mynach	d							20 39				21 49													
Hengoed	d							20 42				21 52													
Pengam	d							20 45				21 55													
Gilfach Fargoed	d							20 48				21 58													
Bargoed	a							20 51				22 01													
	d							20 51				22 01													
Brithdir	d							20 55				22 05													
Tir-phil	d							20 58				22 08													
Pontlottyn	d							21 02				22 12													
Rhymney [3]	a							21 09				22 19													
Cathays	d				19 13	19 13	19 48		20 33		21 13				22 13										
Llandaf	d				19 17	19 17	19 52		20 37		21 17				22 17										
Ninian Park	d																								
Waun-gron Park	d																								
Fairwater	d																								
Danescourt	d																								
Radyr [3]	a				19 20	19 20	19 55		20 40		21 20				22 20										
	d				19 20	19 20	19 55		20 40		21 20				22 20										
Taffs Well	d				19 24	19 24	19 59		20 44		21 24				22 24										
Trefforest Estate	d																								
Trefforest	d				19 31	19 31	20 06		20 52		21 31				22 31										
Pontypridd [3]	a				19 34	19 34	20 09		20 55		21 34				22 34										
	d				19 36	19 36	20 11		20 57		21 36				22 36										
Abercynon	d						20 19		21 05																
Penrhiwceiber	d						20 24																		
Mountain Ash	a						20 28																		
	d						20 29																		
Fernhill	d						20 31																		
Cwmbach	d						20 35																		
Aberdare	a						20 42																		
Quakers Yard	d								21 09																
Merthyr Vale	a								21 14																
	d								21 16																
Troed Y Rhiw	d								21 20																
Pentre-bach	d								21 23																
Merthyr Tydfil	a								21 31																
Trehafod	d				19 41	19 41					21 41				22 41										
Porth	a				19 44	19 44					21 44				22 44										
	d				19 45	19 45					21 45				22 45										
Dinas Rhondda	d				19 49	19 49					21 49				22 49										
Tonypandy	d				19 51	19 51					21 51				22 51										
Llwynypia	d				19 53	19 53					21 53				22 53										
Ystrad Rhondda	a				19 56	19 56					21 56				22 56										
	d				19 59	19 59					21 59				22 59										
Ton Pentre	d				20 01	20 01					22 01				23 01										
Treorchy	d				20 04	20 04					22 04				23 04										
Ynyswen	d				20 07	20 07					22 07				23 07										
Treherbert	a				20 13	20 13					22 13				23 13										

When events are being held at the Principality Stadium, services are subject to alteration. Please check times before travelling.

For connections to Cardiff Bay please refer to Table T124

Table T130-R

Sundays

16 September to 2 December

Bridgend, Barry Island, Barry, Penarth and Cardiff - Coryton, Rhymney, Pontypridd, Merthyr, Aberdare and Treherbert

		AW	AW	AW	AW	AW	AW	AW	AW	AW	AW	AW	AW	AW	AW	AW	AW	AW	AW	AW	AW	AW	AW
Bridgend	d										09 42	09 42							11 42				
Llantwit Major	d										09 56	09 56							11 56				
Rhoose Cardiff Int Airport ✈	d										10 06	10 06							12 06				
Barry Island	d						08 55			09 55			10 25		10 55		11 25	11 55		12 25		12 55	
Barry	d						09 00			10 00	10 15	10 15	10 30		11 00		11 30	12 00	12 15	12 30		13 00	
Barry Docks	d						09 03			10 03	10 18	10 18	10 33		11 03		11 33	12 03	12 18	12 33		13 03	
Cadoxton	d						09 06			10 06	10 21	10 21	10 36		11 06		11 36	12 06	12 21	12 36		13 06	
Dinas Powys	d						09 10			10 10	10 25	10 25	10 40		11 10		11 40	12 10	12 25	12 40		13 10	
Eastbrook	d						09 13			10 13	10 28	10 28	10 43		11 13		11 43	12 13	12 28	12 43		13 13	
Cogan	d						09 15			10 15	10 30	10 30	10 45		11 15		11 45	12 15	12 30	12 45		13 15	
Penarth	d							09 32								11 32							13 32
Dingle Road	d							09 34								11 34							13 34
Grangetown	d						09 19	09 38		10 19	10 34	10 34	10 49		11 19	11 38	11 49	12 19	12 34	12 49		13 19	13 38
Cardiff Central	a						09 24	09 43		10 24	10 41	10 41	10 57		11 24	11 43	11 54	12 24	12 41	12 57		13 24	13 43
	d	08 26	08 41	08 54	09 00	09 05	09 41		10 06	10 26		11 00		11 00	11 41	11 46	12 06	12 26			13 06	13 41	13 46
Cardiff Queen Street	a	08 29	08 44	08 57	09 03	09 08	09 44		10 09	10 29		11 03		11 03	11 44	11 49	12 09	12 29			13 09	13 44	13 49
	d	08 30	08 45		09 04	09 09	09 45		10 10	10 30		11 04		11 04	11 45	11 50	12 10	12 30			13 10	13 45	13 50
Heath Low Level	d																						
Ty Glas	d																						
Birchgrove	d																						
Rhiwbina	d																						
Whitchurch (Cardiff)	d																						
Coryton	a																						
Heath High Level	d					09 14			10 15							11 55	12 15						13 55
Llanishen	d					09 17			10 18							11 58	12 18						13 58
Lisvane & Thornhill	d					09 19			10 20							12 00	12 20						14 00
Caerphilly	d					09 25			10 26							12 06	12 26						14 06
Aber	d					09 27			10 28							12 08	12 28						14 08
Energlyn & Churchill Park	d					09 29			10 30							12 10	12 30						14 10
Llanbradach	d					09 33			10 34							12 14	12 34						14 14
Ystrad Mynach	d					09 38			10 39							12a23	12 39						14a23
Hengoed	d					09 41			10 42								12 42						
Pengam	d					09 44			10 45								12 45						
Gilfach Fargoed	d					09 47			10 48								12 48						
Bargoed	a					09 51			10 51								12 51						
	d					09 52			10 51								12 51						
Brithdir	d					09 56			10 55								12 55						
Tir-phil	d					09 59			10 58								12 58						
Pontlottyn	d					10 03			11 02								13 02						
Rhymney	a					10 09			11 10								13 10						
Cathays	d	08 33	08 48		09 07		09 48			10 33		11 07		11 07	11 48		15 48	12 33			13 13	13 48	
Llandaf	d	08 37	08 52		09 11		09 52			10 37		11 11		11 11	11 52		15 52	12 37			13 17	13 52	
Ninian Park	d																						
Waun-gron Park	d																						
Fairwater	d																						
Danescourt	d																						
Radyr	a	08 40	08 55		09 14		09 55			10 40		11 14		11 14	11 55		15 55	12 40			13 20	13 55	
	d	08 40	08 55		09 14		09 55			10 40		11 14		11 14	11 55		15 55	12 40			13 20	13 55	
Taffs Well	d	08 44	08 59		09 18		09 59			10 44		11 18		11 18	11 59		→	12 44			13 24	13 59	
Trefforest Estate	d																						
Trefforest	d	08 52	09 06		09 25		10 06			10 52		11 25		11 25	12 06			12 52			13 31	14 06	
Pontypridd	a	08 55	09 09		09 28		10 09			10 55		11 28		11 28	12 09			12 55			13 34	14 09	
	d	08 57	09 11		09 30		10 11			10 57		11 30		11 30	12 11			12 57			13 36	14 11	
Abercynon	d	09 05	09 19				10 19			11 05					12 19			13 05				14 19	
Penrhiwceiber	d		09 25				10 25								12 25							14 25	
Mountain Ash	a		09 28				10 28								12 28							14 28	
	d		09 29				10 29								12 29							14 29	
Fernhill	d		09 32				10 32								12 32							14 32	
Cwmbach	d		09 36				10 36								12 36							14 36	
Aberdare	a		09 44				10 44								12 44							14 44	
Quakers Yard	d	09 09								11 09								13 09					
Merthyr Vale	a	09 14								11 14								13 14					
	d	09 16								11 16								13 16					
Troed Y Rhiw	d	09 20								11 20								13 20					
Pentre-bach	d	09 23								11 23								13 23					
Merthyr Tydfil	a	09 32								11 32								13 32					
Trehafod	d				09 35							11 35		11 35							13 41		
Porth	a				09 38							11 38		11 38							13 44		
	d				09 39							11 39		11 39							13 45		
Dinas Rhondda	d				09 43							11 43		11 43							13 49		
Tonypandy	d				09 45							11 45		11 45							13 51		
Llwynypia	d				09 47							11 47		11 47							13 53		
Ystrad Rhondda	a				09 50							11 50		11 50							13 56		
	d				09 53							11 53		11 53							13 59		
Ton Pentre	d				09 55							11 55		11 55							14 01		
Treorchy	d				09 58							11 58		11 58							14 04		
Ynyswen	d				10 01							12 01		12 01							14 07		
Treherbert	a				10 07							12 07		12 07							14 13		

When events are being held at the Principality Stadium, services are subject to alteration. Please check times before travelling.

For connections to Cardiff Bay please refer to Table T124

Table T130-R

Sundays

16 September to 2 December

Bridgend, Barry Island, Barry, Penarth and Cardiff - Coryton, Rhymney, Pontypridd, Merthyr, Aberdare and Treherbert

		AW	AW	AW	AW	AW	AW	AW	AW	AW	AW	AW	AW	AW	AW	AW	AW	AW	AW	AW	AW	AW	AW
Bridgend	d			13 42								15 42						17 42	17 42				
Llantwit Major	d			13 56								15 56						17 56	17 56				
Rhoose Cardiff Int Airport ✈	d			14 06								16 06						18 06	18 06				
Barry Island	d	13 25	13 55		14 25			14 55		15 25	15 55		16 25	16 55		17 25	17 55			18 25		18 55	
Barry	d	13 30	14 00	14 15	14 30			15 00		15 30	16 00	16 15	16 30	17 00		17 30	18 00	18 15	18 15	18 30		19 00	
Barry Docks	d	13 33	14 03	14 18	14 33			15 03		15 33	16 03	16 18	16 33	17 03		17 33	18 03	18 18	18 18	18 33		19 03	
Cadoxton	d	13 36	14 06	14 21	14 36			15 06		15 36	16 06	16 21	16 36	17 06		17 36	18 06	18 21	18 21	18 36		19 06	
Dinas Powys	d	13 40	14 10	14 25	14 40			15 10		15 40	16 10	16 25	16 40	17 10		17 40	18 10	18 25	18 25	18 40		19 10	
Eastbrook	d	13 43	14 13	14 28	14 43			15 13		15 43	16 13	16 28	16 43	17 13		17 43	18 13	18 28	18 28	18 43		19 13	
Cogan	d	13 45	14 15	14 30	14 45			15 15		15 45	16 15	16 30	16 45	17 15		17 45	18 15	18 30	18 30	18 45		19 15	
Penarth	d								15 32						17 32								19 32
Dingle Road	d								15 34						17 34								19 34
Grangetown	d	13 49	14 19	14 34	14 49			15 19	15 38	15 49	16 19	16 34	16 49	17 19	17 38	17 49	18 19	18 34	18 34	18 49		19 19	19 38
Cardiff Central	a	13 54	14 24	14 41	14 57			15 25	15 43	15 54	16 24	16 41	16 57	17 24	17 43	17 54	18 24	18 41	18 41	18 57		19 24	19 44
	d	14 06	14 26			15 06		15 41	15 46	16 06	16 26	17 06		17 41	17 46	18 06	18 26		19 06		19 06	19 41	
Cardiff Queen Street	a	14 09	14 29			15 09		15 44	15 49	16 09	16 29	17 09		17 44	17 49	18 09	18 29		19 09		19 09	19 44	
	d	14 10	14 30			15 10		15 45	15 50	16 10	16 30	17 10		17 45	17 50	18 10	18 30		19 10		19 10	19 45	
Heath Low Level	d																						
Ty Glas	d																						
Birchgrove	d																						
Rhiwbina	d																						
Whitchurch (Cardiff)	d																						
Coryton	a																						
Heath High Level	d	14 15							15 55	16 15					17 55	18 15							
Llanishen	d	14 18							15 58	16 18					17 58	18 18							
Lisvane & Thornhill	d	14 20							16 00	16 20					18 00	18 20							
Caerphilly	d	14 26							16 06	16 26					18 06	18 26							
Aber	d	14 28							16 08	16 28					18 08	18 28							
Energlyn & Churchill Park	d	14 30							16 10	16 30					18 10	18 30							
Llanbradach	d	14 34							16 14	16 34					18 14	18 34							
Ystrad Mynach	d	14 39							16a23	16 39					18a23	18 39							
Hengoed	d	14 42								16 42						18 42							
Pengam	d	14 45								16 45						18 45							
Gilfach Fargoed	d	14 48								16 48						18 48							
Bargoed	a	14 51								16 51						18 51							
	d	14 51								16 51						18 51							
Brithdir	d	14 55								16 55						18 55							
Tir-phil	d	14 58								16 58						18 58							
Pontlottyn	d	15 02								17 02						19 02							
Rhymney	a	15 10								17 10						19 10							
Cathays	d		14 33			15 13		15 48			16 33	17 13		17 48			18 33		19 13		19 13	19 48	
Llandaf	d		14 37			15 17		15 52			16 37	17 17		17 52			18 37		19 17		19 17	19 52	
Ninian Park	d																						
Waun-gron Park	d																						
Fairwater	d																						
Danescourt	d						←																
Radyr	a		14 40			15 20	15 55	15 55			16 40	17 20		17 55			18 40		19 20		19 20	19 55	
	d		14 40			15 20	15 55	15 55			16 40	17 20		17 55			18 40		19 20		19 20	19 55	
Taffs Well	d		14 44			15 24	15 59	15 59			16 44	17 24		17 59			18 44		19 24		19 24	19 59	
Trefforest Estate	d																						
Trefforest	d		14 52			15 31	16 06	16 06			16 52	17 31		18 06			18 52		19 31		19 31	20 06	
Pontypridd	a		14 55			15 34	16 09	16 09			16 55	17 34		18 09			18 55		19 34		19 34	20 09	
	d		14 57			15 36	16 11	16 11			16 57	17 36		18 11			18 57		19 36		19 36	20 11	
Abercynon	d		15 05				16 19	16 19			17 05			18 19			19 05					20 19	
Penrhiwceiber	d						16 25	16 25						18 25								20 25	
Mountain Ash	a						16 28	16 28						18 28								20 28	
	d						16 29	16 29						18 29								20 29	
Fernhill	d						16 32	16 32						18 32								20 32	
Cwmbach	d						16 36	16 36						18 36								20 36	
Aberdare	a						16 44	16 44						18 44								20 44	
Quakers Yard	d		15 09								17 09						19 09						
Merthyr Vale	a		15 14								17 14						19 14						
	d		15 16								17 16						19 16						
Troed Y Rhiw	d		15 20								17 20						19 20						
Pentre-bach	d		15 23								17 23						19 23						
Merthyr Tydfil	a		15 32								17 32						19 32						
Trehafod	d					15 41						17 41							19 41		19 41		
Porth	a					15 44						17 44							19 44		19 44		
	d					15 45						17 45							19 45		19 45		
Dinas Rhondda	d					15 49						17 49							19 49		19 49		
Tonypandy	d					15 51						17 51							19 51		19 51		
Llwynypia	d					15 53						17 53							19 53		19 53		
Ystrad Rhondda	a					15 56						17 56							19 56		19 56		
	d					15 59						17 59							19 59		19 59		
Ton Pentre	d					16 01						18 01							20 01		20 01		
Treorchy	d					16 04						18 04							20 04		20 04		
Ynyswen	d					16 07						18 07							20 07		20 07		
Treherbert	a					16 13						18 13							20 13		20 13		

When events are being held at the Principality Stadium, services are subject to alteration. Please check times before travelling.

For connections to Cardiff Bay please refer to Table T124

Please note, Network Rail have stated that further updates to this timetable are possible during the validity period.

Table T130-R

Sundays

16 September to 2 December

Bridgend, Barry Island, Barry, Penarth and Cardiff - Coryton, Rhymney, Pontypridd, Merthyr, Aberdare and Treherbert

		AW		AW	AW	AW	AW	AW	AW	AW	AW	AW
Bridgend	d				19 42						21 42	
Llantwit Major	d				19 56						21 56	
Rhoose Cardiff Int Airport ✈	d				20 06						22 06	
Barry Island	d	19 25		19 55		20 25		20 55	21 25	21 55		22 55
Barry	d	19 30		20 00	20 15	20 30		21 00	21 30	22 00	22 15	23 00
Barry Docks	d	19 33		20 03	20 18	20 33		21 03	21 33	22 03	22 18	23 03
Cadoxton	d	19 36		20 06	20 21	20 36		21 06	21 36	22 06	22 21	23 06
Dinas Powys	d	19 40		20 10	20 25	20 40		21 10	21 40	22 10	22 25	23 10
Eastbrook	d	19 43		20 13	20 28	20 43		21 13	21 43	22 13	22 28	23 13
Cogan	d	19 45		20 15	20 30	20 45		21 15	21 45	22 15	22 30	23 15
Penarth	d						20 47					
Dingle Road	d						20 49					
Grangetown	d	19 49		20 19	20 34	20 49	20 53	21 19	21 49	22 19	22 34	23 19
Cardiff Central	a	19 54		20 24	20 41	20 54	21 00	21 26	21 54	22 26	22 41	23 26
	d	20 06		20 26		21 06	21 16		22 06			
Cardiff Queen Street	a	20 09		20 29		21 09	21 19		22 09			
	d	20 10		20 30		21 10	21 20		22 10			
Heath Low Level	d											
Ty Glas	d											
Birchgrove	d											
Rhiwbina	d											
Whitchurch (Cardiff)	d											
Coryton	a											
Heath High Level	d	20 15					21 25					
Llanishen	d	20 18					21 28					
Lisvane & Thornhill	d	20 20					21 30					
Caerphilly	d	20 26					21 36					
Aber	d	20 28					21 38					
Energlyn & Churchill Park	d	20 30					21 40					
Llanbradach	d	20 34					21 44					
Ystrad Mynach	d	20 39					21 49					
Hengoed	d	20 42					21 52					
Pengam	d	20 45					21 55					
Gilfach Fargoed	d	20 48					21 58					
Bargoed	a	20 51					22 01					
	d	20 51					22 01					
Brithdir	d	20 55					22 05					
Tir-phil	d	20 58					22 08					
Pontlottyn	d	21 02					22 12					
Rhymney	a	21 10					22 20					
Cathays	d			20 33		21 13			22 13			
Landaf	d			20 37		21 17			22 17			
Ninian Park	d											
Waun-gron Park	d											
Fairwater	d											
Danescourt	d											
Radyr	a			20 40		21 20			22 20			
	d			20 40		21 20			22 20			
Taffs Well	d			20 44		21 24			22 24			
Trefforest Estate	d											
Trefforest	d			20 52		21 31			22 31			
Pontypridd	a			20 55		21 34			22 34			
	d			20 57		21 36			22 36			
Abercynon	d			21 05								
Penrhiwceiber	d											
Mountain Ash	a											
	d											
Fernhill	d											
Cwmbach	d											
Aberdare	a											
Quakers Yard	d			21 09								
Merthyr Vale	a			21 14								
	d			21 16								
Troed Y Rhiw	d			21 20								
Pentre-bach	d			21 23								
Merthyr Tydfil	a			21 32								
Trehafod	d					21 41			22 41			
Porth	a					21 44			22 44			
	d					21 45			22 45			
Dinas Rhondda	d					21 49			22 49			
Tonypandy	d					21 51			22 51			
Llwynypia	d					21 53			22 53			
Ystrad Rhondda	a					21 56			22 56			
	d					21 59			22 59			
Ton Pentre	d					22 01			23 01			
Treorchy	d					22 04			23 04			
Ynyswen	d					22 07			23 07			
Treherbert	a					22 13			23 13			

When events are being held at the Principality Stadium, services are subject to alteration. Please check times before travelling.

For connections to Cardiff Bay please refer to Table T124

Table T131-F

Mondays to Fridays

21 May to 7 December

Manchester, Holyhead and Crewe - Cardiff

Miles	Miles			AW MO	AW ◇	AW MX ◇	AW	AW ◇ A ⚒	AW ◇	AW ◇	AW ◇ ⚒	AW ◇ ⚒		AW	AW ◇ A ⚒	AW BHX ■ ☒	AW ◇ ⚒	AW ◇ ⚒	AW ◇ ⚒	AW ◇ ⚒	AW ◇	AW ◇ ⚒		AW ◇ ⚒	AW ◇ ⚒
0	—	**Manchester Piccadilly**	d												06 29			07 30		08 31		09 31			10 31
6	—	Stockport	d												06 39			07 39		08 39		09 39			10 39
12	—	Wilmslow	d												06 47			07 47		08 47		09 47			10 47
—	0	Holyhead	d									04 25				05 34			06 28					08 05	
—	25	Bangor (Gwynedd)	d									04 57				06 02			07 06					09 02	
—	40	Llandudno Junction	d									05 15				06 20			07 25					09 25	
—	85	Chester	d									06 18				07 16			08 19					10 21	
—	97	Wrexham General	d									06 34				07 34			08 35					10 36	
—	102	Ruabon	d									06 41							08 42					10 43	
—	106	Chirk	d									06 48							08 49					10 49	
—	109	Gobowen	d									06 54							08 54					10 55	
31	—	**Crewe**	d					04 49			05 58			06 40	07 08		07 34	08 08		09 08	09 14	10 08			11 08
35½	—	Nantwich	d					04 57			06 06			06 46	07 17		07 40				09 22				
40	—	Wrenbury	d								06x12						07x46				09x29				
44¾	—	Whitchurch (Shrops)	d					05 08			06 19			06 58			07 54				09 37				
49¾	—	Prees	d								06x25						07x59				09x43				
53	—	Wem	d					05 17			06 30			07 08			08 05				09 49				
56½	—	Yorton	d	00x02							06x35						08x10				09x55				
63¾	126	**Shrewsbury**	a	00 14				05 28			06 45	07 12		07 25	07 42	08 03	08 25	08 37	09 12	09 37	10 06	10 37		11 13	11 37
—	—		d		04 49			05 30	05 56	06 10	06 47	07 17			07 44	08 10		08 40	09 14	09 40	10 09	10 39		11 16	11 39
76½	—	Church Stretton	d		05 07			05 45	06 14	06 26	07 02				07 59				09 30		10 27	10 54			11 54
83¾	—	Craven Arms	d		05a17			05 53	06 26	06 34	07 10				08 07				09 38		10 37			11 37	
91	154	Ludlow	d					06 01		06 43	07 17	07 43			08 15			09 06	09 45	10 06		11 08		11 44	12 08
102	—	Leominster	d					06 11		06 54	07 28	07 53			08 26			09 16		10 16		11 18			12 18
114½	177½	**Hereford**	a					06 30		07 09	07 43	08 09			08 40	08 55		09 32	10 09	10 32		11 34		12 06	12 34
—	—		d			00 09	05 26	06 41		07 10	07 45	08 10			08 42	09 00		09 33	10 10	10 33		11 35		12 08	12 35
138½	—	Abergavenny	d			00 33	05 51	07 04		07 34	08 08	08 33			09 05			09 58	10 33	10 56		11 58		12 31	12 58
148	211	Pontypool and New Inn	d				06 02	07 14		07 45	08 18	08 43							10 43					12 42	
151	214	Cwmbran	d			00 46	06 07	07 19		07 50	08 23	08 48			09 17			10 11	10 48	11 09		12 11		12 47	13 11
158	221	**Newport (South Wales)**	a			00 57	06 19	07 30		08 00	08 37	08 59			09 34	09 40		10 22	11 01	11 20		12 22		12 56	13 22
169¾	232	**Cardiff Central**	a			01 21	06 42	07 49		08 17	08 56	09 19			09 59	09 58		10 38	11 15	11 38		12 37		13 20	13 40
—	—	Swansea	a					08 52	10 01		09 56				10 55			11 33		12 35	14 25	13 34			14 35

		AW	AW ◇ ⚒	AW ■ ⚒	AW ■ ⚒	AW ◇	AW	AW ■ ⚒		AW ■ ⚒	AW ■ ⚒	AW	AW ■ ⚒	AW ◇ ⚒	AW ■ ⚒	AW ◇	AW ■ ⚒	AW ■ ⚒		AW FX ◇	AW FO ◇	AW FX ◇	AW FO ◇	AW ◇	AW ◇
Manchester Piccadilly	d		11 31		12 31			13 31			14 31		15 31		16 31		17 31			18 29	18 31	19 31	19 31	20 31	21 36
Stockport	d		11 39		12 39			13 39			14 39		15 39		16 39		17 39			18 37	18 39	19 40	19 40	20 40	21 45
Wilmslow	d		11 47		12 47			13 47			14 47		15 47		16 47		17 48			18 45	18 47	19 47	19 47	20 47	21 52
Holyhead	d			10 41						12 32				14 36				16 51							
Bangor (Gwynedd)	d			11 07						13 07				15 04				17 19							
Llandudno Junction	d			11 25						13 25				15 27				17 37							
Chester	d			12 19						14 20				16 22				18 30							
Wrexham General	d			12 34						14 34				16 37				18 46							
Ruabon	d			12 41						14 41				16 44				18 53							
Chirk	d			12 47						14 48				16 51				18 59							
Gobowen	d			12 53						14 53				16 56				19 05							
Crewe	d	11 20	12 08		13 08		13 20	14 08			15 08	15 22	16 08		17 08	17 20	18 09			19 08	19 08	20 10	20 10	21 21	22 12
Nantwich	d	11 28					13 28	14 17				15 32	16 17			17 28	18 18			19 17	19 17	20 18	20 18	21 29	22 20
Wrenbury	d	11x35					13x35					15x39				17x35				19x23	19x23			21x35	22x26
Whitchurch (Shrops)	d	11 43					13 43	14 28				15 47	16 28			17 43	18 29			19 29	19 29	20 29	20 29	21 42	22 33
Prees	d	11x49					13x49					15x53				17x50				19x35	19x35			21x48	22x39
Wem	d	11 55					13 55					15 59	16 36			17 56	18 37			19 40	19 40	20 37	20 37	21 53	22 44
Yorton	d	12x01					14x01					16x05				18x01				19x45	19x45			21x58	22x49
Shrewsbury	a	12 11	12 37	13 11	13 37		14 11	14 45		15 11	15 37	16 14	16 47	17 14	17 37	18 12	18 48	19 23		19 55	19 55	20 48	20 48	22 08	23 01
	d		12 39	13 15	13 40	14 05		14 50		15 15	15 40		16 50	17 16	17 40	18 24	18 50	19 25		19 56	19 56	20 50	20 50	22 09	
Church Stretton	d			13 30		14 23		15 05		15 30			17 06	17 31		18 42	19 05	19 40		20 11	20 11	21 05	21 05	22 24	
Craven Arms	d			13 38		14 34		15 13		15 38			17 14	17 39		18 54	19 13	19 48		20 19	20 19	21 13	21 13	22 32	
Ludlow	d		13 05	13 45	14 06			15 20		15 46	16 06		17 21	17 46	18 06		19 20	19 56		20 27	20 27	21 20	21 20	22 40	
Leominster	d		13 15		14 16			15 31			16 16		17 32	17 57	18 16		19 31			20 37	20 37	21 31	21 31	22 50	
Hereford	a		13 31	14 09	14 32			15 49		16 09	16 32		17 49	18 12	18 32		19 46	20 19		20 53	20 53	21 46	21 46	23 09	
	d		13 32	14 11	14 33			15 51		16 11	16 33		17 51	18 14	18 33		19 48	20 22		20 54	20 54	21 50	21 50	23 11	
Abergavenny	d		13 55	14 33	14 56			16 14		16 34	16 56		18 14	18 37	18 56		20 11	20 45		21 22	21 22	22 16	22 16	23 34	
Pontypool and New Inn	d		14 05					16 23		16 44			18 24				20 21			21 32	21 32			23 43	
Cwmbran	d		14 10		15 09			16 28		16 49	17 09		18 29	18 49	19 09		20 26	20 57		21 37	21 37	22 28	22 28	23 48	
Newport (South Wales)	a		14 20	14 54	15 21			16 39		16 59	17 21		18 39	19 00	19 22		20 37	21 15		21 51	21 50	22 39	22 40	23 59	
Cardiff Central	a		14 37	15 10	15 38			16 54		17 16	17 38		18 55	19 20	19 43		21 03	21 35		22 13	22 05	23 00	23 00	00 23	
Swansea	a		15 35	16 15	16 35	18 14		18 07			18 39		20 04		20 42	22 25					23 07	00 28	00 28		

A not from 26 June until 29 June

For connections from Liverpool Lime Street and Runcorn refer to Table T91. For connections to Bristol Temple Meads refer to Table T132

When events are being held at the Principality Stadium, services are subject to alteration. Please check times before travelling.

For other services between Shrewsbury and Chester refer to Table T75

For other stations served by AW trains from and to Cardiff between Chester and Holyhead refer to Table T81

For connections to Reading and London Paddington via Newport refer to Table T125

Table T131-F

Mondays to Fridays

21 May to 7 December

Manchester, Holyhead and Crewe - Cardiff

Station		AW	AW
		◇	◇
Manchester Piccadilly [10] ⇌	d		22 36
Stockport	d		22 44
Wilmslow	d		22 52
Holyhead	d		
Bangor (Gwynedd)	d		
Llandudno Junction	d		
Chester	d		
Wrexham General	d		
Ruabon	d		
Chirk	d		
Gobowen	d		
Crewe [10]	d		23 14
Nantwich	d		23 22
Wrenbury	d		23x27
Whitchurch (Shrops)	d		23 34
Prees	d		23x40
Wem	d		23 45
Yorton	d		23x50
Shrewsbury [5]	a		00 04
	d	23 08	
Church Stretton	d	23 24	
Craven Arms [3]	d	23 32	
Ludlow	d	23 41	
Leominster	d	23 52	
Hereford [7]	a	00 07	
	d	00 09	
Abergavenny	d	00 33	
Pontypool and New Inn	d		
Cwmbran	d	00 46	
Newport (South Wales) [6]	a	00 57	
Cardiff Central [7]	a	01 21	
Swansea	a		

Saturdays

26 May to 8 December

Station		AW	AW	AW	AW	AW	AW	AW	AW	AW	AW
		◇	◇		◇	◇	◇	◇	◇	◇	
								A	B		
					🛒		🛒	🛒		🛒	
Manchester Piccadilly [10] ⇌	d									06 30	
Stockport	d									06 39	
Wilmslow	d									06 47	
Holyhead	d							04 25			
Bangor (Gwynedd)	d							04 57			
Llandudno Junction	d							05 15			
Chester	d							06 20	06 20		
Wrexham General	d							06 35	06 35		
Ruabon	d							06 42	06 42		
Chirk	d							06 48	06 48		
Gobowen	d							06 54	06 54		
Crewe [10]	d				04 54		05 55			07 08	07 20
Nantwich	d				05 02		06 03			07 17	07 27
Wrenbury	d						06x09				07x34
Whitchurch (Shrops)	d				05 13		06 16			07 28	07 41
Prees	d						06x22				07x47
Wem	d				05 22		06 27			07 36	07 53
Yorton	d						06x32				07x58
Shrewsbury [5]	a				05 33		06 42	07 12	07 12	07 47	08 08
	d		05 16		05 40	06 13	06 44	07 18	07 18	07 50	
Church Stretton	d		05 33		05 55	06 28	06 59			08 05	
Craven Arms [3]	d		05 47		06 03	06 36	07 07			08 13	
Ludlow	d				06 10	06 44	07 14	07 44	07 44	08 20	
Leominster	d				06 21	06 55	07 25	07 54	07 54	08 31	
Hereford [7]	a				06 37	07 09	07 40	08 10	08 10	08 49	
	d	00 09		05 42	06 42	07 11	07 44	08 11	08 11	08 51	
Abergavenny	d	00 33		06 07	07 05	07 34	08 07	08 34	08 34	09 14	
Pontypool and New Inn	d			06 18	07 15	07 44	08 17	08 44	08 44		
Cwmbran	d	00 46		06 23	07 20	07 49	08 22	08 49	08 49	09 26	
Newport (South Wales) [6]	a	00 57		06 34	07 37	07 59	08 31	09 00	09 00	09 37	
Cardiff Central [7]	a	01 21		06 54	07 54	08 18	08 50	09 18	09 18	09 59	
Swansea	a		09 22		08 51		09 55			10 51	

Station		AW	AW	AW	AW	AW	AW	AW	AW	AW	AW	AW	AW
					■				■			■	■
		◇	◇	◇			◇	◇			◇		
		🛒		🛒	🛒		🛒	🛒	🛒		🛒	🛒	🛒
Manchester Piccadilly [10] ⇌	d	07 30			08 30		09 30		10 31		11 31		12 31
Stockport	d	07 40			08 39		09 40		10 40		11 39		12 39
Wilmslow	d	07 47			08 47		09 48		10 47		11 47		12 47
Holyhead	d			06 35				08 20				10 33	
Bangor (Gwynedd)	d			07 07				09 02				11 05	
Llandudno Junction	d			07 25				09 25				11 23	
Chester	d			08 20				10 19				12 19	
Wrexham General	d			08 34				10 34				12 33	
Ruabon	d			08 41				10 41				12 40	
Chirk	d			08 48				10 47				12 46	
Gobowen	d			08 53				10 53				12 52	
Crewe [10]	d	08 08			09 08	09 20	10 08		11 08	11 20	12 08		13 08
Nantwich	d	08 17				09 28				11 31	12 17		
Wrenbury	d					09x34				11x38			
Whitchurch (Shrops)	d	08 27				09 42				11 46	12 28		
Prees	d					09x48				11x53			
Wem	d					09 54				11 59			
Yorton	d					10x00				12x04			
Shrewsbury [5]	a	08 45		09 11	09 37	10 12	10 36	11 11	11 37	12 14	12 45	13 10	13 37
	d	08 50	09 00	09 17	09 40		10 38	11 15	11 40		12 50	13 15	13 40
Church Stretton	d	09 05	09 19		09 55		10 54		11 55		13 05	13 30	
Craven Arms [3]	d	09 13	09 29		10 03		11 02		12 03		13 13	13 38	
Ludlow	d	09 20		09 44	10 10		11 09	11 41	12 10		13 20	13 44	14 06
Leominster	d	09 31			10 21		11 20		12 21		13 31		14 16
Hereford [7]	a	09 48		10 07	10 36		11 36	12 04	12 36		13 49	14 09	14 32
	d	09 50		10 09	10 38		11 40	12 06	12 38		13 51	14 10	14 33
Abergavenny	d	10 13		10 32	11 01		12 03	12 29	13 01		14 14	14 32	14 56
Pontypool and New Inn	d			10 42				12 39				14 43	
Cwmbran	d	10 25		10 47	11 13		12 15	12 44	13 13		14 26	14 48	15 09
Newport (South Wales) [6]	a	10 36		10 57	11 27		12 27	12 54	13 28		14 36	15 04	15 21
Cardiff Central [7]	a	11 02		11 13	11 57		12 57	13 17	13 53		14 53	15 24	15 37
Swansea	a	11 59	13 01		12 55		13 57		14 55		15 55		16 36

A from 15 September B until 8 September

For connections from Liverpool Lime Street and Runcorn refer to Table T91. For connections to Bristol Temple Meads refer to Table T132

When events are being held at the Principality Stadium, services are subject to alteration. Please check times before travelling.

For other services between Shrewsbury and Chester refer to Table T75

For other stations served by AW trains from and to Cardiff between Chester and Holyhead refer to Table T81

For connections to Reading and London Paddington via Newport refer to Table T125

Table T131-F

Saturdays

26 May to 8 December

Manchester, Holyhead and Crewe - Cardiff

Station		AW	AW	AW	AW	AW	AW	AW	AW	AW	AW
				■		■		■		■	
		◇			◇				◇		◇
						A					
				🛒	🛒	🛒		🛒	🛒	🛒	
Manchester Piccadilly [10] ⇌	d			13 31		14 31		15 31		16 31	
Stockport	d			13 39		14 40		15 39		16 39	
Wilmslow	d			13 47		14 47		15 47		16 47	
Holyhead	d				12 38				14 27		
Bangor (Gwynedd)	d				13 07				14 55		
Llandudno Junction	d				13 25				15 18		
Chester	d				14 19				16 21		
Wrexham General	d				14 33				16 36		
Ruabon	d				14 40				16 43		
Chirk	d				14 47				16 50		
Gobowen	d				14 52				16 55		
Crewe [10]	d		13 20	14 08		15 09	15 20	16 08		17 08	
Nantwich	d		13 28	14 17			15 28	16 17		17 17	
Wrenbury	d		13x35				15x35				
Whitchurch (Shrops)	d		13 43	14 27			15 43	16 27		17 27	
Prees	d		13x49				15x49				
Wem	d		13 55				15 55				
Yorton	d		14x01				16x01				
Shrewsbury [5]	a		14 11	14 45	15 10	15 38	16 11	16 45	17 13	17 44	
	d	13 58		14 46	15 13	15 40		16 46	17 16	17 46	17 57
Church Stretton	d	14 16		15 01		15 55		17 01		18 01	18 13
Craven Arms [3]	d	14 26		15 09		16 03		17 09		18 09	18 24
Ludlow	d			15 17	15 39	16 10		17 17	17 42	18 16	
Leominster	d			15 27		16 21		17 27		18 27	
Hereford [7]	a			15 43	16 01	16 36		17 43	18 05	18 42	
	d			15 46	16 03	16 38		17 46	18 07	18 44	
Abergavenny	d			16 09	16 26	17 01		18 09	18 30	19 07	
Pontypool and New Inn	d				16 36				18 40		
Cwmbran	d			16 21	16 41	17 13		18 21	18 45	19 19	
Newport (South Wales) [6]	a			16 35	16 51	17 33		18 35	18 55	19 34	
Cardiff Central [7]	a			16 54	17 08	17 53		18 55	19 15	19 58	
Swansea	a	18 09		18 05		19 02		20 05			22 06

Station		AW	AW	AW	AW	AW	AW	AW	AW	AW
			■							
				◇	◇	◇	◇	◇	◇	
			🛒	🛒						
Manchester Piccadilly [10] ⇌	d		17 31		18 31	19 31	20 30	21 33	22 35	
Stockport	d		17 39		18 39	19 40	20 39	21 43	22 44	
Wilmslow	d		17 47		18 47	19 47	20 47	21 50	22 52	
Holyhead	d			16 52						
Bangor (Gwynedd)	d			17 20						
Llandudno Junction	d			17 38						
Chester	d			18 32						
Wrexham General	d			18 47						
Ruabon	d			18 54						
Chirk	d			19 01						
Gobowen	d			19 06						
Crewe [10]	d	17 20	18 09		19 10	20 09	21 09	22 12	23 14	
Nantwich	d	17 28	18 17		19 18	20 17	21 17	22 20	23 22	
Wrenbury	d	17x35			19x24		21x23	22x26	23x27	
Whitchurch (Shrops)	d	17 43	18 28		19 31	20 28	21 30	22 33	23 34	
Prees	d	17x49			19x37		21x36	22x39	23x43	
Wem	d	17 55			19 42	20 36	21 41	22 44	23 47	
Yorton	d	18x01			19x47		21x46	22x49	23x52	
Shrewsbury [5]	a	18 11	18 46	19 24	19 56	20 47	21 53	23 01	00 05	
	d		18 50	19 26	19 58	20 48	21 55			
Church Stretton	d		19 05	19 41	20 13	21 03	22 10			
Craven Arms [3]	d		19 13	19 49	20 21	21 11	22 18			
Ludlow	d		19 20	19 55	20 28	21 19	22 26			
Leominster	d		19 31		20 39	21 29	22 37			
Hereford [7]	a		19 50	20 20	20 54	21 45	22 51			
	d		19 52	20 21	20 56	21 46	22 53			23 15
Abergavenny	d		20 15	20 44	21 19	22 09	23 16			23 38
Pontypool and New Inn	d		20 24		21 28		23 26			
Cwmbran	d		20 29	20 57	21 33	22 22	23 31			23 50
Newport (South Wales) [6]	a		20 41	21 14	21 44	22 33	23 44			00 02
Cardiff Central [7]	a		21 00	21 35	22 05	23 00	00 10			00 34
Swansea	a				23 07					

A not 23 June

For connections from Liverpool Lime Street and Runcorn refer to Table T91. For connections to Bristol Temple Meads refer to Table T132

When events are being held at the Principality Stadium, services are subject to alteration. Please check times before travelling.

For other services between Shrewsbury and Chester refer to Table T75

For other stations served by AW trains from and to Cardiff between Chester and Holyhead refer to Table T81

For connections to Reading and London Paddington via Newport refer to Table T125

Please note, Network Rail have stated that further updates to this timetable are possible during the validity period.

Table T131-F

Sundays

20 May to 2 December

Manchester, Holyhead and Crewe - Cardiff

		AW 🚌	AW ◇	AW ■ 🍴	AW ■ A 🍴	AW ■ B 🍴	AW ◇	AW ■ 🍴	AW ■ 🍴	AW ■ 🍴	AW ■ 🍴	AW ■ 🍴	AW ◇	AW ■ 🍴	AW ■ 🍴	AW ■ 🍴	AW ■ 🍴	AW ■	AW ◇	AW ◇	AW
Manchester Piccadilly [10]	d			09 30	10 31	10 31		11 30		12 32	13 30	14 30		15 30	16 30	17 30		18 30	19 30	20 30	
Stockport	d			09 40	10 40	10 40		11 43		12 42	13 40	14 40		15 40	16 39	17 40		18 40	19 40	20 40	
Wilmslow	d			09 48	10 48	10 48		11 50		12 50	13 47	14 48		15 48	16 48	17 47		18 48	19 48	20 48	
Holyhead	d								10 20								16 25				
Bangor (Gwynedd)	d								10 59								17 04				
Llandudno Junction	d								11 22								17 25				
Chester	d								12 28								18 25				23 00
Wrexham General	d								12 44								18 40				
Ruabon	d								12 51								18 47				
Chirk	d								12 57								18 54				
Gobowen	d								13 03								18 59				
Crewe [10]	d			10 13	11 11	11 11		12 13		13 13	14 13	15 10		16 10	17 13	18 13		19 13	20 10	21 13	23 23
Nantwich	d			10 22						13 21					17 21			19 21		21 21	23 31
Wrenbury	d			10x27						13x26					17x26			19x26		21x26	23x37
Whitchurch (Shrops)	d			10 35						13 34					17 34			19 34		21 35	23 45
Prees	d			10x40						13x39					17x39			19x39		21x40	23x51
Wem	d			10 46						13 45					17 45			19 45		21 47	23 57
Yorton	d			10x50						13x49					17x49			19x49		21x51	00x02
Shrewsbury [6]	a			11 01	11 41	11 41		12 43	13 21	13 59	14 43	15 44		16 39	18 00	18 43	19 17	20 00	20 40	22 03	00 14
	d	07 50		11 03	11 45	11 45	12 04	12 44	13 22	14 01	14 44	15 47	16 18	16 40	18 01	18 44	19 21	20 01	20 42	22 04	
Church Stretton	d	08 15		11 19			12 22		13 38		15 00		16 36	16 56			19 37		20 57	22 20	
Craven Arms [3]	d	08 35		11 27			12 33		13 46		15 08		16 47	17 04			19 45		21 05	22 29	
Ludlow	d	08 55		11 36	12 13	12 13		13 13	13 54	14 28	15 16	16 17		17 12	18 29	19 12	19 53	20 29	21 13	22 37	
Leominster	d	09 20		11 47	12 23	12 23		13 24	14 05	14 39	15 26	16 28		17 22	18 39		20 04	20 39	21 24	22 49	
Hereford [7]	a	09 50		12 02	12 38	12 38		13 38	14 20	14 53	15 41	16 43		17 37	18 54	19 34	20 18	20 54	21 38	23 03	
	d		10 07	12 03	12 39	12 39		13 40	14 22	14 56	15 43	16 44		17 39	18 57	19 36	20 21	20 55	21 40	23 05	
Abergavenny	d		10 31	12 27	13 02	13 02		14 03	14 45	15 19	16 06	17 08		18 02	19 20	19 59	20 46	21 18	22 03	23 29	
Pontypool and New Inn	d		10 41		13 12	13 12			14 55		16 16			18 12			20 56		22 13	23 39	
Cwmbran	d		10 46	12 40	13 17	13 17		14 16	15 00	15 31	16 21	17 21		18 17	19 33	20 11	21 01	21 31	22 18	23 44	
Newport (South Wales) [6]	a		10 57	12 53	13 29	13 29		14 26	15 10	15 46	16 32	17 35		18 27	19 43	20 27	21 10	21 44	22 29	23 54	
Cardiff Central [7]	a		11 18	13 18	13 54	13 54		14 49	15 34	16 11	16 56	17 56		18 50	20 08	20 49	21 37	22 10	22 54	00 18	
Swansea	a		12 14		15 11	15 12	16 03			17 20		19 17	20 25								

A until 9 September

B from 16 September

For connections from Liverpool Lime Street and Runcorn refer to Table T91. For connections to Bristol Temple Meads refer to Table T132

When events are being held at the Principality Stadium, services are subject to alteration. Please check times before travelling.

For other services between Shrewsbury and Chester refer to Table T75

For other stations served by AW trains from and to Cardiff between Chester and Holyhead refer to Table T81

For connections to Reading and London Paddington via Newport refer to Table T125

Table T131-R

Mondays to Fridays

21 May to 7 December

Cardiff - Crewe, Holyhead and Manchester

Miles	Miles			AW MO	AW MX ◇	AW MX	AW	AW	AW MX ◇	AW MO ◇	AW ◇ 🍴	AW FO ◇ 🍴	AW FX ◇ 🍴	AW ◇	AW ◇ 🍴	AW ◇ 🍴	AW ■ 🍴	AW ◇	AW ◇ 🍴	AW ◇ 🍴	AW ◇ 🍴	AW ■ 🍴	AW
—	—	Swansea	d														07 07	06 04		07 42		08 53	
0	0	Cardiff Central [7]	d			00 30			04 35	04 35	05 08	05 38	05 39		06 50	07 21	08 05			08 50	09 21	10 05	
11¾	11¾	Newport (South Wales) [6]	d			01 00			04 53	04 54	05 27	05 57	05 57		07 04	07 36	08 19			09 05	09 35	10 19	
18¾	18¾	Cwmbran	d			01 12			05 05	05 05	05 39	06 08	06 08		07 14	07 46	08 29			09 15	09 46	10 29	
21¾	21¾	Pontypool and New Inn	d			01 18			05 11	05 11	05 45	06 14	06 14			07 52					09 51		
31¼	31¼	Abergavenny	d	00 05		01 29			05 22	05 22	05 54	06 23	06 23		07 27	08 01	08 42			09 28	10 01	10 42	
55¼	55¼	Hereford [7]	a	00 36		01 59			05 46	05 46	06 18	06 47	06 47		07 51	08 25	09 07			09 52	10 25	11 06	
—	—		d						05 47	05 47	06 25	06 49	06 49		07 53	08 27	09 08			09 54	10 27	11 08	
67¾	—	Leominster	d						06 00	06 00	06 38	07 02	07 02		08 06		09 21			10 07		11 21	
78¾	78¾	Ludlow	d						06 11	06 11	06 49	07 13	07 13		08 17	08 48	09 32			10 18	10 48	11 32	
86	86	Craven Arms [3]	d						06 20	06 20	06 57	07 21	07 21	07 28	08 25	08 56		09 47		10 26	10 57		
93¼	93¼	Church Stretton	d						06 29	06 29	07 08	07 30	07 30	07 42	08 34	09 05		09 59		10 39	11 06		
106	106	Shrewsbury [6]	a						06 43	06 43	07 22	07 44	07 44	07 57	08 48	09 19	09 58	10 14		10 52	11 21	11 58	
—	—		d		00 12		05 31		06 44	06 44	07 25	07 46	07 46	08 00	08 51	09 25	10 00	10 18	10 23	10 54	11 25	11 59	12 24
113¼	—	Yorton	d		00x21		05x38							08x09				10x28					12x34
116½	—	Wem	d		00 26		05 43		06 56	06 56		07 57	07 57	08 15				10 31					12 37
120	—	Prees	d		00x31		05x48							08x20				10x39					12x45
125	—	Whitchurch (Shrops)	d		00 38		05 55		07 04	07 04		08 06	08 06	08 28	09 08			10 46		11 12			12 52
129¾	—	Wrenbury	d		00x44		06x01							08x34				10x53					12x59
134¼	—	Nantwich	d		00 51		06 07		07 13	07 13		08 15	08 15	08 41	09 17			10 59		11 20			13 05
138¾	—	Crewe [10]	a		01 03		06 17		07 24	07 24		08 24	08 24	08 53	09 27		10 28	11 10		11 28		12 28	13 15
—	—		d					06 27	07 26	07 26		08 28	08 28		09 30		10 30			11 30		12 30	
—	123¾	Gobowen	a								07 42					09 42			10 42		11 42		
—	126¾	Chirk	a								07 48					09 48			10 48		11 47		
—	130¾	Ruabon	a								07 54					09 54			10 54		11 54		
—	135¾	Wrexham General	a								08 01					10 01			11 00		12 00		
—	147¾	Chester	a								08 20					10 20			11 20		12 19		
—	192¾	Llandudno Junction	a								09 17					11 15			12 16		13 11		
—	207¾	Bangor (Gwynedd)	a													11 39			12 33		13 29		
—	232¾	Holyhead	a													12 23			13 17		14 14		
157¾	—	Wilmslow	a					06 44	07 49	07 49		08 48	08 48		09 49		10 48			11 49		12 49	
163¾	—	Stockport	a					06 54	07 58	07 58		08 59	08 59		09 58		10 58			11 58		12 58	
169¾	—	Manchester Piccadilly [10]	a					07 09	08 10	08 10		09 13	09 13		10 13		11 13			12 13		13 13	

		AW ◇ 🍴	AW ■ 🍴	AW ■ 🍴	AW ◇	AW ■ 🍴	AW	AW ◇ 🍴	AW ◇ 🍴	AW ◇ 🍴	AW ■ 🍴	AW	AW ◇ 🍴	AW ■ 🍴	AW ■ 🍴	AW ■ 🍴	AW ■ 🍴	AW ◇	AW ■ 🍴	AW BHX ■ ⊠	AW ■ 🍴	AW ■ 🍴	AW
Swansea	d		09 55		09 34	10 55			11 55		12 54			13 55		14 55	15 10	14 35	15 55		16 55	17 12	
Cardiff Central [7]	d		10 50	11 21		12 05			12 50	13 21	14 05			14 50	15 21	15 50	16 21		16 50	17 16	17 50	18 21	
Newport (South Wales) [6]	d		11 04	11 36		12 19			13 04	13 35	14 19			15 04	15 36	16 04	16 35		17 04	17 31	18 04	18 35	
Cwmbran	d		11 14	11 46		12 29			13 14	13 46	14 29			15 14	15 46	16 14	16 44		17 14	17 42	18 15	18 45	
Pontypool and New Inn	d			11 52						13 51					15 52	16 19				17 49	18 20		
Abergavenny	d		11 27	12 01		12 42			13 26	14 01	14 43			15 27	16 01	16 29	16 57		17 27	18 00	18 29	18 59	
Hereford [7]	a		11 51	12 25		13 06			13 53	14 25	15 06			15 51	16 25	16 53	17 22		17 51	18 24	18 53	19 23	
	d		11 53	12 27		13 08			13 55	14 25	15 08			15 53	16 28	16 54	17 24		17 53	18 25	18 55	19 24	
Leominster	d		12 06			13 21			14 08		15 21			16 06	16 41	17 07			18 06		19 08		
Ludlow	d		12 17	12 48		13 32			14 19	14 46	15 32			16 17	16 52	17 18			18 17		19 19	19 45	
Craven Arms [3]	d		12 25	12 56	13 02				14 27	14 55				16 25	17 00	17 27		18 00	18 25		19 27		
Church Stretton	d		12 35	13 05	13 17				14 36	15 04					17 09	17 36		18 13	18 41		19 36		
Shrewsbury [6]	a		12 49	13 21	13 32	13 58			14 50	15 23	15 58			16 48	17 24	17 50	18 09	18 28	18 55	19 08	19 50	20 11	
	d	12 25	12 54	13 26		13 59	14 24	14 25	14 52	15 29	15 59	16 24	16 24	16 50	17 25	17 53	18 10	18 30	18 56	19 09	19 52	20 13	20 32
Yorton	d						14x34					16x34						18x40					20x39
Wem	d						14 37					16 37		17 01				18 45					20 44
Prees	d						14x45					16x45						18x50					20x49
Whitchurch (Shrops)	d		13 10				14 52		15 09			16 52		17 10		18 09		18 57	19 13				20 56
Wrenbury	d						14x57					16x59						19x04					21x02
Nantwich	d		13 20				15 05		15 18			17 05		17 19		18 19		19 10	19 23				21 08
Crewe [10]	a		13 28			14 28	15 15		15 28		16 28	17 15		17 27		18 27	18 43	19 20	19 33		20 22	20 43	21 19
	d		13 30			14 30			15 30		16 30			17 30		18 30	18 45		19 37		20 24	20 48	
Gobowen	a	12 40		13 43				14 42		15 46			16 42		17 42								
Chirk	a	12 48		13 48				14 48		15 51			16 48		17 48								
Ruabon	a	12 52		13 55				14 54		15 58			16 54		17 54								
Wrexham General	a	13 00		14 01				15 01		16 04			17 01		18 01					19 37			
Chester	a	13 19		14 19				15 18		16 23			17 21		18 19		19 05			19 57		21 08	
Llandudno Junction	a	14 11		15 12				16 12		17 15			18 19		19 17					20 49			
Bangor (Gwynedd)	a	14 34		15 30				16 42		17 37			18 46		19 34					21 06			
Holyhead	a	15 07		16 14				17 16		18 21			19 17		20 20					21 41			
Wilmslow	a		13 49			14 49			15 49		16 49			17 49		18 49			19 56		20 41		
Stockport	a		13 58			14 58			15 58		16 59			17 58		18 58			20 04		20 52		
Manchester Piccadilly [10]	a		14 13			15 13			16 13		17 13			18 13		19 13			20 19		21 09		

For connections from Bristol Temple Meads refer to Table T132. For connections to Runcorn and Liverpool Lime Street refer to Table T91

When events are being held at the Principality Stadium, services are subject to alteration. Please check times before travelling.

For other services between Shrewsbury and Chester refer to Table T75

For other stations served by AW trains from and to Cardiff between Chester and Holyhead refer to Table T81

For connections to Reading and London Paddington via Newport refer to Table T125

Please note, Network Rail have stated that further updates to this timetable are possible during the validity period.

Table T131-R

Cardiff - Crewe, Holyhead and Manchester

Mondays to Fridays
21 May to 7 December

		AW	AW	AW	AW	AW	AW
		◇ 🍴	◇	◇	◇	◇	◇
Swansea	d	17 49			18 21		
Cardiff Central 7	d	18 55	19 34	20 17		21 17	21 55
Newport (South Wales) 5	d	19 09	19 48	20 31		21 32	22 12
Cwmbran	d	19 19	19 58	20 41		21 43	22 23
Pontypool and New Inn	d	19 24	20 03	20 47			22 29
Abergavenny	d	19 34	20 12	20 56		21 56	22 39
Hereford 7	a	19 58	20 38	21 21		22 20	23 06
	d	19 59	20 39	21 22		22 21	23 08
Leominster	d	20 12	20 52	21 35		22 34	23 21
Ludlow	d	20 23	21 03	21 46		22 45	23 32
Craven Arms 3	d	20 32	21 12	21 54	22 20	22 54	23 42
Church Stretton	d	20 41	21 21	22 04	22 35	23 03	23 51
Shrewsbury 5	a	20 55	21 37	22 18	22 54	23 17	00 07
	d	20 56	21 39	22 20		23 18	00 12
Yorton	d			22x28		23x27	00x21
Wem	d			22 32		23 32	00 26
Prees	d			22x36		23x37	00x31
Whitchurch (Shrops)	d	21 13		22 43		23 44	00 38
Wrenbury	d			22x49		23x50	00x44
Nantwich	d	21 22		22 54		23 56	00 51
Crewe 10	a	21 33		23 04		00 05	01 03
	d	21 35		23 06		00 07	
Gobowen	a		21 56				
Chirk	a		22 01				
Ruabon	a		22 08				
Wrexham General	a		22 12				
Chester	a		22 36			00 31	
Llandudno Junction	a		23 49				
Bangor (Gwynedd)	a		00 13				
Holyhead	a		00 48				
Wilmslow	a	21 52		23 23			
Stockport	a	22 01		23 32			
Manchester Piccadilly 10 ⛴	a	22 15		23 50			

Saturdays
26 May to 8 December

		AW	AW	AW	AW	AW	AW	AW	AW	AW	AW	AW
											■	
		◇				◇	◇ 🍴	◇ 🍴		◇	🍴	◇ 🍴
Swansea	d									04 31		
Cardiff Central 7	d			00 30		04 35	05 21	05 37				06 50
Newport (South Wales) 5	d			00 46		04 52	05 35	05 56				07 04
Cwmbran	d			00 56		05 03	05 46	06 08				07 14
Pontypool and New Inn	d			01 02		05 09	05 51	06 13				
Abergavenny	d			01 13		05 18	06 01	06 23				07 27
Hereford 7	a			01 43		05 46	06 25	06 46				07 51
	d					05 47	06 25	06 49				07 53
Leominster	d					06 00	06 39	07 02				08 06
Ludlow	d					06 11	06 50	07 13				08 17
Craven Arms 3	d					06 20	06 59	07 21		07 54		08 25
Church Stretton	d					06 29	07 08	07 30		08 07		08 34
Shrewsbury 5	a					06 43	07 22	07 44		08 22		08 51
	d	00 12			05 44	06 46	07 25	07 46	07 57		08 22	08 52
Yorton	d	00x21			05x52				08x06			
Wem	d	00 26			05 58	06 57		07 57	08 12			
Prees	d	00x31			06x03				08x17			
Whitchurch (Shrops)	d	00 38			06 10	07 06		08 06	08 25			09 09
Wrenbury	d	00x44			06x17				08x31			
Nantwich	d	00 51			06 23	07 15		08 15	08 38			09 18
Crewe 10	a	01 03			06 35	07 25		08 24	08 50			09 27
	d		06 27			07 27		08 28				09 30
Gobowen	a						07 42				08 39	
Chirk	a						07 48				08 45	
Ruabon	a						07 54				08 51	
Wrexham General	a						08 01				08 59	
Chester	a						08 19				09 17	
Llandudno Junction	a						09 12				10 12	
Bangor (Gwynedd)	a						09 35				10 30	
Holyhead	a						10 15				11 05	
Wilmslow	a		06 44			07 44		08 45				09 47
Stockport	a		06 55			07 58		08 59				09 58
Manchester Piccadilly 10 ⛴	a		07 07			08 10		09 13				10 13

		AW	AW	AW	AW	AW	AW	AW	AW	AW	AW	AW
			■		■	■						
		◇ 🍴	🍴		🍴	🍴	◇ 🍴	◇ 🍴		◇ 🍴	◇ 🍴	◇
Swansea	d		06 47			07 44		08 54			09 54	09 15
Cardiff Central 7	d	07 21	07 50			08 50	09 21	09 55			10 55	
Newport (South Wales) 5	d	07 36	08 04			09 04	09 35	10 09			11 09	
Cwmbran	d	07 46	08 14			09 16	09 46	10 19			11 19	
Pontypool and New Inn	d	07 51					09 52					
Abergavenny	d	08 01	08 27			09 29	10 01	10 32			11 32	
Hereford 7	a	08 26	08 51			09 53	10 25	10 56			11 56	
	d	08 27	08 53			09 55	10 26	10 58			11 58	
Leominster	d		09 06			10 08		11 11			12 11	
Ludlow	d	08 48	09 17			10 19	10 48	11 22			12 22	
Craven Arms 3	d	08 56				10 27	10 57				12 30	12 40
Church Stretton	d	09 05				10 36	11 07				12 39	12 53
Shrewsbury 5	a	09 23	09 43			10 50	11 23	11 48			12 52	13 09
	d	09 25	09 47	10 18	10 22	10 52	11 25	11 49	12 24	12 25	12 54	
Yorton	d			10x28					12x34			
Wem	d			10 31					12 37			
Prees	d			10x39					12x45			
Whitchurch (Shrops)	d		10 04	10 46		11 09		12 06	12 52			
Wrenbury	d			10x53					12x59			
Nantwich	d		10 13	10 59		11 18		12 15	13 05			
Crewe 10	a		10 23	11 10		11 25		12 24	13 15		13 26	
	d		10 30			11 30		12 30			13 30	
Gobowen	a	09 42			10 40		11 42			12 43		
Chirk	a	09 48			10 46		11 47			12 48		
Ruabon	a	09 54			10 52		11 54			12 55		
Wrexham General	a	10 01			10 59		12 00			13 01		
Chester	a	10 19			11 21		12 18			13 20		
Llandudno Junction	a	11 11			12 14		13 14			14 13		
Bangor (Gwynedd)	a	11 35			12 32		13 32			14 37		
Holyhead	a	12 09			13 12		14 13			15 09		
Wilmslow	a		10 48			11 49		12 48			13 47	
Stockport	a		10 58			11 58		12 58			13 58	
Manchester Piccadilly 10 ⛴	a		11 13			12 13		13 13			14 14	

For connections from Bristol Temple Meads refer to Table T132. For connections to Runcorn and Liverpool Lime Street refer to Table T91

When events are being held at the Principality Stadium, services are subject to alteration. Please check times before travelling.

For other services between Shrewsbury and Chester refer to Table T75

For other stations served by AW trains from and to Cardiff between Chester and Holyhead refer to Table T81

For connections to Reading and London Paddington via Newport refer to Table T125

Table T131-R

Cardiff - Crewe, Holyhead and Manchester

Saturdays
26 May to 8 December

		AW	AW	AW	AW	AW	AW	AW	AW	AW	AW	AW
		■	■			■		■		■		
		🍴	🍴	◇ 🍴		🍴	◇ 🍴	🍴		🍴	◇ 🍴	◇
Swansea	d		10 55			12 00		12 53			14 00	13 12
Cardiff Central 7	d	11 21	11 55			12 55	13 21	13 55			14 55	
Newport (South Wales) 5	d	11 35	12 09			13 09	13 36	14 09			15 09	
Cwmbran	d	11 46	12 19			13 19	13 46	14 19			15 19	
Pontypool and New Inn	d	11 50					13 50					
Abergavenny	d	12 00	12 32			13 32	14 01	14 32			15 32	
Hereford 7	a	12 26	12 56			13 56	14 26	14 56			15 56	
	d	12 28	12 58			13 58	14 27	14 58			15 58	
Leominster	d		13 11			14 11		15 11			16 11	
Ludlow	d	12 49	13 22			14 22	14 48	15 22			16 22	
Craven Arms 3	d	12 57				14 32	14 56				16 30	16 42
Church Stretton	d	13 06				14 42	15 05				16 39	16 55
Shrewsbury 5	a	13 20	13 48			14 55	15 24	15 48			16 53	17 11
	d	13 25	13 49	14 22	14 24	14 57	15 30	15 49	16 24	16 25	16 55	
Yorton	d				14x34				16x34			
Wem	d				14 37				16 37			
Prees	d				14x45				16x45			
Whitchurch (Shrops)	d		14 06		14 52			16 06	16 52			
Wrenbury	d				14x57				16x59			
Nantwich	d		14 15		15 05			16 15	17 05			
Crewe 10	a		14 24		15 15	15 27		16 24	17 15		17 26	
	d		14 30			15 30		16 30			17 30	
Gobowen	a	13 42		14 40			15 47			16 43		
Chirk	a	13 47		14 45			15 52			16 48		
Ruabon	a	13 54		14 52			15 59			16 55		
Wrexham General	a	14 00		14 58			16 05			17 01		
Chester	a	14 19		15 20			16 23			17 19		
Llandudno Junction	a	15 14		16 11			17 16			18 17		
Bangor (Gwynedd)	a	15 32		16 34			17 39			18 41		
Holyhead	a	16 13		17 12			18 19			19 13		
Wilmslow	a		14 47			15 47		16 47			17 47	
Stockport	a		14 58			15 58		16 59			17 58	
Manchester Piccadilly 10 ⛴	a		15 15			16 15		17 14			18 15	

		AW	AW	AW	AW	AW	AW	AW	AW	AW	AW	AW
		■	■				■	■	■			
		🍴	🍴			◇	🍴		🍴		◇ 🍴	◇
Swansea	d		14 55		15 10		15 55		16 58		17 54	
Cardiff Central 7	d	15 21	15 55		16 18		16 55	17 21	17 55		18 50	19 34
Newport (South Wales) 5	d	15 36	16 09		16 34		17 09	17 35	18 09		19 04	19 48
Cwmbran	d	15 46	16 19		16 44		17 19	17 46	18 20		19 15	19 58
Pontypool and New Inn	d	15 52	16 24		16 50			17 52	18 25		19 20	20 03
Abergavenny	d	16 01	16 34		17a02		17 32	18 01	18 35		19 30	20 12
Hereford 7	a	16 25	16 58				17 56	18 25	18 59		19 54	20 38
	d	16 29	17 00				17 58	18 27	19 00		19 55	20 39
Leominster	d	16 42	17 13				18 11		19 13		20 08	20 52
Ludlow	d	16 54	17 24				18 22	18 48	19 24		20 19	21 03
Craven Arms 3	d						18 30	18 56			20 28	21 12
Church Stretton	d	17 08					18 39	19 05			20 37	21 21
Shrewsbury 5	a	17 22	17 50				18 53	19 19	19 50		20 53	21 35
	d	17 24	17 52	18 25		18 25	18 55	19 28	19 52	20 32	20 57	21 39
Yorton	d			18x35						20x39		
Wem	d			18 38						20 44		
Prees	d			18x46						20x49		
Whitchurch (Shrops)	d		18 08	18 53					20 08	20 56		
Wrenbury	d			19x00						21x02		
Nantwich	d		18 18	19 06					20 18	21 08		
Crewe 10	a		18 27	19 16			19 26		20 27	21 19	21 28	
	d		18 30				19 30		20 30		21 30	
Gobowen	a	17 41				18 42		19 45				21 56
Chirk	a	17 46				18 48		19 50				22 01
Ruabon	a	17 53				18 54		19 57				22 08
Wrexham General	a	17 59				19 01		20 03				22 14
Chester	a	18 17				19 21		20 23				22 33
Llandudno Junction	a	19 14				20 20		21 24				23 38
Bangor (Gwynedd)	a	19 32				20 47		21 42				
Holyhead	a	20 18				21 31		22 25				
Wilmslow	a		18 47				19 47		20 47		21 47	
Stockport	a		18 58				19 58		20 59		21 59	
Manchester Piccadilly 10 ⛴	a		19 15				20 15		21 15		22 14	

		AW	AW	AW	AW	AW
		◇	◇	◇	◇	◇
Swansea	d	18 17			20 55	
Cardiff Central 7	d		20 10	20 55	21 54	
Newport (South Wales) 5	d		20 26	21 10	22 12	
Cwmbran	d		20 37	21 21	22 24	
Pontypool and New Inn	d		20 42		22 29	
Abergavenny	d		20 52	21 34	22 39	
Hereford 7	a		21 17	21 58	23 03	
	d		21 20	22 00		
Leominster	d		21 33	22 14		
Ludlow	d		21 44	22 25		
Craven Arms 3	d	21 40	21 54	22 33		
Church Stretton	d	21 52	22 03	22 42		
Shrewsbury 5	a	22 08	22 17	22 57		
	d		22 19	23 06		23 30
Yorton	d		22x27	23x14		23x38
Wem	d		22 32	23 20		23 44
Prees	d		22x36	23x24		23x48
Whitchurch (Shrops)	d		22 44	23 32		23 55
Wrenbury	d		22x49	23x37		00x01
Nantwich	d		22 55	23 43		00 07
Crewe 10	a		23 04	23 54		00 16
	d		23 06	23 57		
Gobowen	a					
Chirk	a					
Ruabon	a					
Wrexham General	a					
Chester	a			00 22		
Llandudno Junction	a					
Bangor (Gwynedd)	a					
Holyhead	a					
Wilmslow	a		23 24			
Stockport	a		23 32			
Manchester Piccadilly 10 ⛴	a		23 49			

For connections from Bristol Temple Meads refer to Table T132. For connections to Runcorn and Liverpool Lime Street refer to Table T91

When events are being held at the Principality Stadium, services are subject to alteration. Please check times before travelling.

For other services between Shrewsbury and Chester refer to Table T75

For other stations served by AW trains from and to Cardiff between Chester and Holyhead refer to Table T81

For connections to Reading and London Paddington via Newport refer to Table T125

Lydney, Chepstow and Caldicot stations are still open, but train times have not been provided by Network Rail.

Table T131-R

Sundays

20 May to 2 December

Cardiff - Crewe, Holyhead and Manchester

		AW	AW	AW	AW	AW	AW	AW	AW	AW	AW	AW	AW	AW	AW	AW	AW	AW	AW	AW	AW	AW	AW
		◇ A			◇ ⌶	◇ ⌶	■ ⌶	■ B ⌶	◇ C ⌶	◇ ⌶	◇ C ⌶	■ B ⌶	◇	■ ⌶	■ ⌶	■ ⌶	■ ⌶	■ ⌶	◇ ⌶	■ ⌶	◇	■	■ ⌶
Swansea	d							09\34			11\31	11\32	11 12			13 43				15 34	15 29		17 30
Cardiff Central	d					08 30	09 17	10\34	10\34	11 35	12\36	12\36		13 14	13 40	14 56	15 15	15 56		16 40		17 35	18 36
Newport (South Wales)	d					08 49	09 40	10\54	10\54	11 54	12\54	12\54		13 35	13 58	15 14	15 34	16 14		16 58		17 53	18 58
Cwmbran	d					09 00	09 51	11\05	11\05	12 07	13\09	13\09		13 45	14 09	15 24	15 44	16 24		17 09		18 04	19 09
Pontypool and New Inn	d					09 06	09 57	11\11	11\11	12 13	13\15	13\15		13 51			15 50			17 15		18 10	
Abergavenny	d					09 15	10 08	11\21	11\21	12 24	13\25	13\25		14 00	14 22	15 38	15 59	16 37		17 25		18 20	19 22
Hereford	a					09 40	10 34	11\47	11\47	12 50	13\49	13\49		14 26	14 47	16 02	16 25	17 02		17 49		18 44	19 47
	d					09 41	10 36	11\50	11\50	12 54	13\55	13\55		14 26	14 48	16 04	16 28	17 04		17 53		18 49	19 49
Leominster	d					09 55	10 50	12\03	12\03	13 08	14\08	14\08		14 40	15 01		16 41			18 07		19 03	20 03
Ludlow	d					10 06	11 01	12\14	12\14	13 19	14\19	14\19		14 51	15 12	16 25	16 52	17 26		18 18		19 14	20 14
Craven Arms	d					10 14		12\24	12\24		14\28	14\28	14 44	15 00			17 00			18 26	19 04		20 22
Church Stretton	d					10 23		12\33	12\33		14\37	14\37	14 57				17 09			18 35	19 17		20 31
Shrewsbury	a					10 37	11 30	12\48	12\48	13 48	14\51	14\51	15 12	15 21	15 38	16 51	17 23	17 52		18 49	19 38	19 41	20 45
	d				09 55	10 39	11 31	12\51	12\51	13 50	14\53	14\53		15 24	15 40	16 53	17 30	17 54	18 20	18 54		19 42	20 48
Yorton	d						11x40								15x48							19x50	
Wem	d					10 51	11 43								15 51							19 53	
Prees	d						11x50								15x58							20x00	
Whitchurch (Shrops)	d					11 00	11 58								16 06							20 07	
Wrenbury	d	00x01					12x04								16x11							20x12	
Nantwich	d	00\07				11 09	12 11								16 18							20 19	
Crewe	a	00\16			10 25	11 22	12 22	13\26	13\26	14 25	15\25	15\25			16 27	17 25		18 25		19 24		20 28	21 21
	d		08 28	09 28	10 28	11 23	12 28	13\29	13\29	14 28	15\28	15\28			16 28	17 28		18 28		19 28		20 29	21 28
Gobowen	a													15 42			17 47		18 38				
Chirk	a													15 47			17 53		18 43				
Ruabon	a													15 54			17 59		18 49				
Wrexham General	a													16 00			18 06		18 56				
Chester	a													16 20			18 25		19 15				
Llandudno Junction	a													17 29			19 23		20 36				
Bangor (Gwynedd)	a													17 52			19 48		20 57				
Holyhead	a													18 37			20 18		21 34				
Wilmslow	a		08 46	09 49	10 46	11 41	12 48	13\49	13\49	14 48	15\46	15\46			16 46	17 45		18 46		19 46		20 46	21 48
Stockport	a				10 58		12 58	13\59	13\59	14 58	15\57	15\57			16 57	17 57		18 57		19 57		20 57	22 01
Manchester Piccadilly	a		09 14	10 12	11 17	12 03	13 13	14\17	14\17	15 15	16\14	16\14			17 14	18 18		19 15		20 16		21 15	22 19

		AW	AW	AW	AW
		◇	◇	◇	
Swansea	d				22 10
Cardiff Central	d	19 40		21 12	23 20
Newport (South Wales)	d	19 59		21 29	23 39
Cwmbran	d	20 10		21 40	23 49
Pontypool and New Inn	d	20 16		21 46	23 55
Abergavenny	d	20 26		21 55	00 05
Hereford	a	20 52		22 20	00 36
	d	20 54		22 21	
Leominster	d	21 08		22 34	
Ludlow	d	21 19		22 45	
Craven Arms	d	21 29		22 54	
Church Stretton	d	21 38		23 03	
Shrewsbury	a	21 56		23 19	
	d		22 32	23 19	
Yorton	d			23x28	
Wem	d			23 33	
Prees	d			23x38	
Whitchurch (Shrops)	d			23 45	
Wrenbury	d			23x51	
Nantwich	d			23 57	
Crewe	a		23 03	00 06	
	d		23 06	00 10	
Gobowen	a				
Chirk	a				
Ruabon	a				
Wrexham General	a				
Chester	a		23 31	00 34	
Llandudno Junction	a				
Bangor (Gwynedd)	a				
Holyhead	a				
Wilmslow	a				
Stockport	a				
Manchester Piccadilly	a				

A not 20 May
B until 9 September
C from 16 September

For connections from Bristol Temple Meads refer to Table T132. For connections to Runcorn and Liverpool Lime Street refer to Table T91

When events are being held at the Principality Stadium, services are subject to alteration. Please check times before travelling.

For other services between Shrewsbury and Chester refer to Table T75

For other stations served by AW trains from and to Cardiff between Chester and Holyhead refer to Table T81

For connections to Reading and London Paddington via Newport refer to Table T125

Table T132-F

Mondays to Fridays

21 May to 7 December

Bath Spa - Bristol - Cardiff

Miles	Miles			AW MX	GW MX	AW MX	GW MX	AW MX	GW MX	GW MX	XC MO	XC MX	AW	GW	AW	GW	XC	XC	GW	AW	GW	XC	AW
				◇	◇■ ☕		◇■ ☕	◇	◇■ A ☕	◇■ B ☕	◇■	◇■					◇■ C ⌶	◇■		◇ D ⌶	◇■ ☕	◇■	◇
0	—	**Bath Spa**	d		00 01				01\18	01\18							06 09		06 28		06 58		
1	—	Oldfield Park	d																06 31				
7	—	Keynsham	d																06 38				
11½	—	**Bristol Temple Meads**	a		00 14				01\30	01\30							06 20		06 46		07 10		
—	—		d						01\37	01\37	05 20	05 20		05 52		06 20	06 27		06 51		07 17		
16	—	Filton Abbey Wood	d											06 02		06 31			07 03		07 26		
—	0	**Bristol Parkway**	a								05 30	05 30					06 37						
—	—		d				00 28				05 38	05 38											
17½	—	Patchway	d											06 07		06 36							
21	4¾	Pilning	d																				
28	11¾	Severn Tunnel Jn	d											06 18	06 29	06 50		06 55	07 15			07 41	
38	21¾	Newport (South Wales)	a				00 55		02s10	02s10	05 58	06 07		06 35	06 41	07 01		07 06	07 25		07 48	07 52	
—	—		d	00 01		00 08	00 57	00 59			06 00	06 08	06 23	06 37	06 44	07 02		07 07	07 28	07\32	07 49	07 54	08 01
49¾	33½	**Cardiff Central**	a	00 23		00 34	01 16	01 21	02\31	02\32	06 16	06 23	06 42	06 51	07 00	07 19		07 22	07 41	07\49	08 02	08 08	08 17

		GW	GW	GW	SW	GW	GW	GW	AW	AW	AW	GW	GW	GW	XC	GW	GW	GW	GW	GW	AW	AW BHX	AW
				◇	■	◇■ ☕	◇	◇■ ☕	◇ ⌶		◇ ⌶	◇■ ☕			◇■ ⌶	■ ⌶	◇■ ☕	◇■ E ☕	◇	◇■ ☕	◇ D ⌶	■ ⊠	
Bath Spa	d		07 11	07 25	07 35		07 47	08 01						08 10		08 22	08 33		08 47	08 55			
Oldfield Park	d		07 14	07 28	07 38		07 50							08 13		08 26			08 50				
Keynsham	d		07 21	07 35	07 45		07 57	08 10						08 21		08 34			08 57				
Bristol Temple Meads	a		07 29	07 47	07 52		08 06	08 18						08 29		08 43	08 47		09 05	09 10			
	d	07 20	07 34	07 53			08 10						08 24	08 41		08 54			09 10				
Filton Abbey Wood	d	07 31	07 44	08 01			08 22						08 32	08 51		09 01			09 21				
Bristol Parkway	a	07 35	07 48				08 27							08 54					09 26				
	d	07 39				08 10						08 41						09 09					
Patchway	d	07 44		08 06									08 36										
Pilning	d																						
Severn Tunnel Jn	d	07 55								08 38			08 48										09 38
Newport (South Wales)	a	08 06		08 26		08 31				08 50		09 04	09 05			09 24		09 30					09 51
	d	08 08		08 28		08 33			08 38	08 52	09 00	09 06	09 06		09 14	09 25		09 31			09\36	09 42	09 52
Cardiff Central	a	08 23		08 43		08 50			08 56	09 07	09 19	09 20	09 26		09 29	09 42		09 49			09\59	09 58	10 11

		GW	GW	GW	GW	XC	AW	GW	GW	GW	AW	AW	GW	GW	GW	GW	XC	XC	AW	GW	GW	GW
			◇■ ☕		◇■ F ☕	◇■	◇ ⌶	◇ ⌶	◇■ ☕	◇■ ☕		◇ ⌶		◇■ ☕	◇	◇■ ☕	◇■ G ⌶	◇■ H ⌶	◇ ⌶	◇ ⌶	◇■ ☕	◇■ ☕
Bath Spa	d			09 15	09 32			09 35	10 01						10 08	10 30				10 36	10 57	
Oldfield Park	d			09 18											10 11							
Keynsham	d			09 25				09 43							10 18							
Bristol Temple Meads	a			09 35	09 44			09 51	10 13						10 28	10 43				10 48	11 09	
	d	09 21		09 41				09 55					10 24		10 41					10 54		
Filton Abbey Wood	d	09 30		09 48				10 02					10 32		10 48					11 02		
Bristol Parkway	a			09 52											10 53							
	d		09 45							10 09				10 41								11 09
Patchway	d	09 35											10 36									
Pilning	d																					
Severn Tunnel Jn	d	09 46											10 48									
Newport (South Wales)	a	09 58	10 06					10 27		10 32			11 00	11 04						11 25		11 30
	d	10 00	10 07			10 13	10 24	10 27		10 34	10 40	11 01	11 02	11 06			11\12	11\12	11 22	11 27		11 32
Cardiff Central	a	10 14	10 21			10 27	10 38	10 43		10 48	10 54	11 15	11 22	11 23			11\28	11\29	11 38	11 43		11 46

		AW	AW	GW	GW	GW	GW	XC	AW	GW	SW	GW	GW	AW	AW	GW	GW	GW	GW	XC	AW	GW	GW
			■ ⌶	◇	◇■ ☕	◇	◇■ ☕	◇■ ⌶	◇ ⌶	◇	◇■	◇■ ☕	◇■ I ☕		◇ ⌶		◇■ ☕	◇ J ⌶	◇■ ☕	◇■ ⌶	◇ ⌶	◇ ⌶	◇■ ☕
Bath Spa	d					11 08	11 30			11 36	11 49	11 59						12 11	12 31			12 36	13 01
Oldfield Park	d					11 11												12 14					
Keynsham	d					11 18					11 56							12 21					
Bristol Temple Meads	a					11 28	11 43			11 48	12 06	12 11						12 29	12 43			12 48	13 16
	d			11 21		11 41				11 54						12 21		12 41				12 54	
Filton Abbey Wood	d			11 30		11 48				12 01						12 30		12 48				13 01	
Bristol Parkway	a					11 52												12 52					
	d				11 41								12 09				12 41						
Patchway	d			11 35												12 35							
Pilning	d																						
Severn Tunnel Jn	d	11 38		11 46										12 39		12 46							
Newport (South Wales)	a	11 50		11 57	12 03					12 26			12 31	12 51		12 59	13 03					13 25	
	d	11 52	11 55	11 59	12 04			12 12	12 23	12 27			12 33	12 53	12 57	13 01	13 05			13 11	13 23	13 26	
Cardiff Central	a	12 13	12 10	12 19	12 21			12 26	12 37	12 42			12 47	13 08	13 20	13 22	13 22			13 26	13 40	13 42	

A from 31 July
B until 27 July
C ⌶ from Bristol Temple Meads
D not from 26 June until 29 June
E The St. David
F The Merchant Venturer
G from 23 July
H until 20 July
I Restaurant available for customers joining until Bristol Parkway
J ⌶ to Bristol Temple Meads

When events are being held at the Principality Stadium, services are subject to alteration. Please check times before travelling.

Table T132-F

Mondays to Fridays
21 May to 7 December

Bath Spa - Bristol - Cardiff

		GW		GW	GW	GW	GW	XC	AW	GW	GW	GW		AW	AW	GW	GW	GW	GW	XC	AW	GW		SW	GW
		◇■ ☕			◇■ ☕	◇	◇■ ☕	◇■ 🍴	◇ 🍴	◇ 🍴	◇■ ☕	◇■ ☕		■ 🍴			◇■ ☕	◇	◇■ ☕	◇■ 🍴	■ 🍴	◇ 🍴		◇■	◇■ ☕
Bath Spa 7	d					13 17	13 32			13 38	13 56							14 14	14 30			14 36		14 47	15 02
Oldfield Park	d					13 20												14 17							
Keynsham	d					13 27												14 24						14 55	
Bristol Temple Meads 10	a					13 35	13 44			13 50	14 08							14 35	14 43			14 49		15 05	15 15
	d			13 21		13 41				13 54						14 21		14 41				14 54			
Filton Abbey Wood	d			13 30		13 48				14 01						14 32		14 48				15 01			
Bristol Parkway 7	a					13 52												14 52							
	d	13 09			13 44							14 09					14 41								
Patchway	d			13 35												14 36									
Pilning	d																								
Severn Tunnel Jn.	d			13 46											14 38	14 48									
Newport (South Wales)	a	13 30		13 57	14 05					14 26		14 31			14 50	15 03	15 07					15 25			
	d	13 32		13 59	14 07			14 12	14 22	14 27		14 33		14 56	14 59	15 05	15 08			15 13	15 22	15 26			
Cardiff Central 7	a	13 46		14 13	14 21			14 26	14 37	14 41		14 47		15 10	15 15	15 26	15 23			15 30	15 38	15 42			

		GW	AW	GW	GW	GW	GW	GW		GW	XC	GW	GW	GW	AW	AW	GW	GW		GW	GW	XC	AW	GW	GW
		◇■ ☕	◇ 🍴	◇	◇■ ☕	A	B	◇		◇■ ☕	◇■ 🍴	◇ 🍴	◇■ ☕	◇■ ☕	■ 🍴	■ 🍴		◇■ ☕			◇■ ☕	◇■ 🍴	■ 🍴	■ 🍴	◇■ ☕
Bath Spa 7	d					15 08	15 09	15 22		15 29		15 36	16 02							16 08	16 28			16 39	
Oldfield Park	d					15 11	15 12													16 11					
Keynsham	d					15 18	15 19													16 19					
Bristol Temple Meads 10	a					15 26	15 29	15 35		15 41		15 48	16 15							16 28	16 40			16 52	
	d			15 21		15 33	15 33	15 41				15 54					16 24			16 41				16 55	
Filton Abbey Wood	d			15 30				15 48				16 01					16 32			16 48				17 03	
Bristol Parkway 7	a					15 44	15 44	15 52												16 52					
	d	15 09			15 41									16 10				16 41							17 10
Patchway	d			15 35													16 36								
Pilning	d																								
Severn Tunnel Jn.	d		15 28	15 46													16 48							17 16	
Newport (South Wales)	a	15 30	15 40	15 57	16 03							16 25		16 31			17 02	17 06						17 26	17 32
	d	15 31	15 42	15 59	16 08						16 13	16 25		16 32	16 40	17 01	17 05	17 07				17 12	17 22	17 29	17 33
Cardiff Central 7	a	15 44	15 58	16 15	16 22						16 30	16 41		16 45	16 54	17 16	17 27	17 23				17 30	17 38	17 43	17 47

		GW	GW	AW		GW	GW	GW	GW	XC	GW	GW	GW	AW		AW	AW	GW	GW	GW	GW	XC	AW	GW	
			◇■ ☕				■ ■ ☕	◇	◇■ ☕	◇■ 🍴	■ 🍴	■ ■ ☕	■ ■ C ☕	■ 🍴			◇ 🍴		■ ■ D ☕		■ ■ ☕	◇■	■ 🍴	■ 🍴	
Bath Spa 7	d	16 45	17 01					17 12	17 27		17 38	18 02								18 08	18 31			18 36	
Oldfield Park	d							17 15												18 11					
Keynsham	d	16 53						17 21												18 18					
Bristol Temple Meads 10	a	17 01	17 14					17 31	17 39		17 51	18 15								18 28	18 46			18 49	
	d	17 09				17 21		17 41			17 54							18 22		18 36				18 54	
Filton Abbey Wood	d	17 24				17 28		17 48			18 02							18 33		18 43				19 01	
Bristol Parkway 7	a	17 29						17 52												18 47					
	d						17 41						18 10						18 41						
Patchway	d					17 33												18 37							
Pilning	d																								
Severn Tunnel Jn.	d			17 38		17 44					18 14					18 38		18 50						19 14	
Newport (South Wales)	a			17 50		17 57	18 02				18 24		18 31			18 49		19 03	19 10					19 24	
	d			17 52		17 59	18 04			18 11	18 27		18 32	18 41		18 53	19 01	19 06	19 11			19 16	19 24	19 26	
Cardiff Central 7	a			18 10		18 13	18 22			18 27	18 42		18 49	18 55		19 09	19 20	19 23	19 25			19 33	19 43	19 42	

		GW	GW	AW	GW	GW	GW	GW	XC	GW		GW	GW	GW	AW	XC	GW	GW	AW	GW FX		GW FO	XC	AW	GW
		■ ■ ☕	■ ■ ☕			■ ■ ☕		■ ■ E ☕	◇■	◇ 🍴		◇	■ ■ ☕	■ ■ F ☕	■ 🍴	◇■	◇ 🍴	■ ■ ☕		■ ■ ☕		■ ■ ☕	◇■	■ 🍴	◇ 🍴
Bath Spa 7	d	19 01					19 08	19 32		19 37		19 51	20 01				20 07	20 31							20 37
Oldfield Park	d						19 11					19 54					20 10								
Keynsham	d						19 18					20 01					20 17								
Bristol Temple Meads 10	a	19 14					19 29	19 44		19 49		20 09	20 14				20 26	20 43							20 50
	d				19 21		19 41			19 54						20 15									20 54
Filton Abbey Wood	d				19 32		19 48			20 02						20 22									21 01
Bristol Parkway 7	a						19 52																		
	d		19 12			19 41								20 09						20 42		20 45			
Patchway	d				19 36											20 25									
Pilning	d																								
Severn Tunnel Jn.	d			19 40	19 47					20 14						20 37			20 38						21 14
Newport (South Wales)	a		19 33	19 53	19 58	20 04				20 24				20 32		20 47			20 50	21 03		21 06			21 24
	d		19 35	19 54	20 00	20 05			20 13	20 29				20 34	20 39	20 49			20 52	21 04		21 08	21 12	21 17	21 26
Cardiff Central 7	a		19 48	20 12	20 18	20 18			20 28	20 47				20 51	21 03	21 03			21 10	21 17		21 21	21 28	21 35	21 44

A until 31 August
B from 3 September
C The Capitals United
D The Red Dragon
E The Bristolian
F Y Cymro - The Welshman

When events are being held at the Principality Stadium, services are subject to alteration. Please check times before travelling.

Table T132-F

Mondays to Fridays
21 May to 7 December

Bath Spa - Bristol - Cardiff

		GW		AW FO	AW FX	GW FO	GW FX	GW	GW	GW FO	GW FX	XC FX		XC FO	GW FO	GW FX	SW	GW	GW	AW	GW FX	GW FO		GW FX	GW FO
		■ ■ ☕		◇	◇				◇■ ☕	◇■ ☕	◇■ ☕	◇■		◇■	◇	◇	◇■	◇■ ☕		◇	◇■ ☕	◇■ ☕		◇	◇
Bath Spa 7	d	21 03						21 09	21 32						21 36	21 36	21 51	22 15	22 25					22 36	22 36
Oldfield Park	d							21 12											22 28						
Keynsham	d							21 19									21 59		22 35						
Bristol Temple Meads 10	a	21 15						21 28	21 44						21 48	21 48	22 06	22 28	22 43					22 48	22 48
	d					21 19	21 21								21 54	21 54								22 54	22 54
Filton Abbey Wood	d					21 30	21 32								22 01	22 01								23 01	23 01
Bristol Parkway 7	a																								
	d									21 41	21 41										22 48	22 48			
Patchway	d					21 34	21 36								22 06	22 06								23 06	23 06
Pilning	d																								
Severn Tunnel Jn.	d					21 46	21 47					22 01		22 01	22 17	22 17								23 17	23 17
Newport (South Wales)	a					21 58	21 59			22 04	22 04	22 12		22 13	22 27	22 33					23 16	23 17		23 33	23 33
	d			21 52	21 55	21 59	22 00			22 05	22 05	22 14		22 14	22 29	22 36				22 41	23 20	23 20		23 33	23 34
Cardiff Central 7	a			22 05	22 13	22 13	22 14			22 18	22 24	22 35		22 30	22 43	22 56				23 00	23 41	23 39		23 55	23 49

		GW	GW	GW FO	AW FX	AW FO	AW FX
			◇■ ☕	◇■ ☕			
Bath Spa 7	d	23 05	23 22	23 50			
Oldfield Park	d	23 08					
Keynsham	d	23 15					
Bristol Temple Meads 10	a	23 25	23 34	00 03			
	d						
Filton Abbey Wood	d						
Bristol Parkway 7	a						
	d						
Patchway	d						
Pilning	d						
Severn Tunnel Jn.	d				23 54	23 54	←
Newport (South Wales)	a				00 05	00 06	00 05
	d				00 08	00 07	00 08
Cardiff Central 7	a				→	00 26	00 34

Saturdays
26 May to 8 December

		AW	AW	GW	AW	GW	AW	AW	XC	GW		GW	GW	AW	XC	GW	GW	SW	AW	GW		GW	AW	AW	AW
		◇		◇■ ☕	◇	◇■ ☕			◇■	◇■			◇■	◇ 🍴	◇■			■	◇			◇■ ☕	◇ 🍴		◇ A 🍴
Bath Spa 7	d					01 18											07 08	07 35				08 02			
Oldfield Park	d																07 11	07 38							
Keynsham	d																07 18	07 45							
Bristol Temple Meads 10	a					01 30											07 28	07 52				08 14			
	d					01 37				06 45		06 51				07 23	07 41			07 55					
Filton Abbey Wood	d									06 53		07 02	←			07 30	07 48			08 03					
Bristol Parkway 7	a									06 58			06 58				07 52								
	d			00 15						07 10			07 10												
Patchway	d									→						07 35									
Pilning	d																								
Severn Tunnel Jn.	d							06 30	06 54			07 15			07 37	07 46								08 38	
Newport (South Wales)	a			00 36		02s10		06 42	07 05			07 27	07 31		07 48	07 58				08 25				08 50	
	d	00 01	00 07	00 38	00 59		06 38	06 44	07 06			07 28	07 33	07 38	07 50	08 00			08 02	08 27			08 33	08 52	09 01
Cardiff Central 7	a	00 23	00 26	00 51	01 21	02 31	06 54	07 03	07 21			07 45	07 47	07 54	08 04	08 17			08 18	08 42			08 50	09 10	09 18

		AW	GW	GW	GW	XC		GW	GW	GW	GW	GW	AW	AW	GW	GW		GW	XC	GW	GW	GW	GW	AW	AW
		◇ B			◇■ ☕	◇■ 🍴		◇ B	◇ A	◇	■ ■ ☕	◇■ ☕	◇ 🍴					◇■ ☕	◇■	◇ C 🍴	◇■ ☕	◇■ A ☕	◇■ D ☕		◇ 🍴
Bath Spa 7	d			08 08	08 27			08 33	08 33	08 48	09 02					09 08		09 29		09 36	10 02				
Oldfield Park	d			08 11						08 51						09 11									
Keynsham	d			08 18						08 58						09 18									
Bristol Temple Meads 10	a			08 28	08 40			08 45	08 47	09 06	09 14					09 27		09 41		09 48	10 14				
	d		08 23	08 40				08 55	08 55						09 22	09 41				09 52					
Filton Abbey Wood	d		08 31	08 48				09 03	09 03						09 31	09 48				10 01					
Bristol Parkway 7	a			08 52												09 52									
	d											09 09										10 09	10 09		
Patchway	d		08 36												09 35										
Pilning	d																								
Severn Tunnel Jn.	d		08 47											09 38	09 46										
Newport (South Wales)	a		09 01					09 25	09 25			09 29		09 50	09 58					10 23		10 30	10 30		
	d	09 01	09 02			09 07		09 26	09 26			09 32	09 39	09 52	10 00				10 07	10 25		10 31	10 31	10 40	10 44
Cardiff Central 7	a	09 18	09 23			09 23		09 42	09 42			09 46	09 59	10 09	10 18				10 21	10 40		10 45	10 45	10 55	11 02

A from 15 September
B until 8 September
C 🍴 to Bristol Temple Meads
D until 8 September. The Pembroke Coast Express

When events are being held at the Principality Stadium, services are subject to alteration. Please check times before travelling.

Lydney, Chepstow and Caldicot stations are still open, but train times have not been provided by Network Rail.

Table T132-F

Bath Spa - Bristol - Cardiff

Saturdays

26 May to 8 December

		AW	GW	GW	GW	XC	GW	GW		GW	AW	AW	GW	GW	GW	XC	GW	SW		GW	GW	AW	AW	AW	GW
		◇ 🛒		◇	◇■ ☕	◇■ 🛒	▣ A 🛒	◇■ ☕		◇■ ☕	▣ 🛒			◇	◇■ ☕	◇■ 🛒	◇ A 🛒	◇■		◇■ ☕	◇■ ☕	◇ 🛒		◇ 🛒	
Bath Spa	d			10 09	10 27		10 36	11 03						11 09	11 27		11 36	11 47		12 02					
Oldfield Park	d			10 12										11 12											
Keynsham	d			10 19										11 19				11 55							
Bristol Temple Meads	a			10 27	10 39		10 48	11 15						11 27	11 39		11 48	12 05		12 14					
	d		10 23	10 41			10 55						11 22	11 41			11 54								12 21
Filton Abbey Wood	d		10 32	10 48			11 03						11 31	11 48			12 02								12 31
Bristol Parkway	a			10 52										11 52											
	d									11 09											12 09				
Patchway	d		10 36										11 35												12 35
Pilning	d																								
Severn Tunnel Jn.	d		10 48									11 38	11 46										12 38		12 46
Newport (South Wales)	a		11 01				11 25			11 30		11 50	11 58				12 24				12 30		12 50		13 00
	d	10 59	11 03			11 07	11 26			11 31	11 37	11 52	12 00			12 07	12 26				12 31	12 40	12 52	12 56	13 02
Cardiff Central	a	11 13	11 19			11 24	11 42			11 45	11 57	12 06	12 17			12 23	12 44				12 45	12 57	13 07	13 17	13 18

		GW	GW	XC		GW	GW	GW	AW	GW	GW	GW	XC	GW		GW	GW	AW	AW	AW	GW	GW	GW	AW	
		◇	◇■ ☕	◇■ 🛒		◇ A 🛒	◇■ ☕	◇■ ☕	▣ 🛒		◇	◇■ ☕	◇■ 🛒	◇		◇■ ☕	◇■ ☕	◇ 🛒				◇	◇■ ☕	▣ 🛒	
Bath Spa	d	12 15	12 27			12 36	13 02				13 18	13 28		13 36		14 02						14 08	14 27		
Oldfield Park	d	12 18									13 21											14 11			
Keynsham	d	12 25									13 29											14 18			
Bristol Temple Meads	a	12 35	12 40			12 48	13 14				13 37	13 41		13 49		14 14						14 27	14 39		
	d	12 41				12 53				13 20	13 41			13 54							14 21	14 41			
Filton Abbey Wood	d	12 50				13 01				13 30	13 48			14 01							14 32	14 48			
Bristol Parkway	a	12 54									13 52											14 52			
	d							13 09									14 09								
Patchway	d									13 35											14 36				
Pilning	d																								
Severn Tunnel Jn.	d									13 46									14 38		14 48				
Newport (South Wales)	a					13 24		13 30		13 58				14 24			14 30		14 50		14 59				
	d			13 07		13 26		13 32	13 37	13 59			14 07	14 25			14 31	14 39	14 52	14 55	15 01			15 06	
Cardiff Central	a			13 21		13 42		13 45	13 53	14 17			14 22	14 41			14 45	14 53	15 09	15 11	15 17			15 24	

		XC	AW	GW	SW	GW	GW	AW	GW	GW		GW	GW	XC	GW	GW	GW	AW	AW	GW		GW	GW	XC	GW
		◇■ 🛒	▣ 🛒	◇	◇■	◇■ ☕	◇■ ☕	◇ 🛒				◇	◇■ ☕	◇■ 🛒	◇	◇■ ☕	◇■ ☕	▣ 🛒	◇ 🛒				◇■ ☕	◇■ 🛒	◇
Bath Spa	d			14 36	14 47	15 02				15 08		15 22	15 29		15 37	16 02						16 08	16 27		16 36
Oldfield Park	d									15 11												16 11			
Keynsham	d				14 55					15 18												16 18			
Bristol Temple Meads	a			14 49	15 05	15 14				15 28		15 36	15 41		15 49	16 14						16 28	16 39		16 48
	d			14 53					15 21			15 41			15 55					16 21		16 41			16 54
Filton Abbey Wood	d			15 01					15 31			15 48			16 02					16 32		16 48			17 02
Bristol Parkway	a											15 52										16 52			
	d						15 09										16 09								
Patchway	d								15 35											16 36					
Pilning	d																								
Severn Tunnel Jn.	d							15 23	15 47											16 48					17 15
Newport (South Wales)	a			15 24			15 30	15 35	15 58						16 24		16 30			17 00					17 26
	d	15 11	15 22	15 25			15 31	15 37	16 00					16 07	16 26		16 31	16 38	16 56	17 02				17 09	17 27
Cardiff Central	a	15 26	15 37	15 46			15 45	15 53	16 15					16 25	16 42		16 44	16 54	17 08	17 17				17 24	17 42

		GW	GW	AW	AW	GW		GW	GW	XC	GW	GW	GW	AW	AW	AW		GW	GW	GW	XC	GW	GW	GW	AW
		◇■ ☕	◇■ ☕	▣ B 🛒				◇	◇■ ☕	◇■ 🛒	◇	◇■ C ☕	◇■ ☕	▣ 🛒		◇ 🛒				◇■ ☕	◇■	▣	◇■ ☕	◇■ ☕	▣ 🛒
Bath Spa	d	17 03						17 10	17 27		17 36	18 02							18 18	18 27		18 36	19 02		
Oldfield Park	d							17 13											18 21						
Keynsham	d							17 20											18 28						
Bristol Temple Meads	a	17 15						17 28	17 39		17 48	18 14							18 36	18 41		18 48	19 14		
	d					17 21		17 41			17 54							18 23	18 41			18 54			
Filton Abbey Wood	d					17 30		17 48			18 01							18 32	18 48			19 01			
Bristol Parkway	a							17 52											18 52						
	d		17 09										18 09											19 08	
Patchway	d					17 35												18 36							
Pilning	d																								
Severn Tunnel Jn.	d				17 38	17 46					18 14				18 38			18 48							
Newport (South Wales)	a		17 31		17 50	17 58					18 25		18 30		18 50			19 00				19 23		19 30	
	d		17 32	17 37	17 52	17 59				18 07	18 26		18 31	18 39	18 52	18 57		19 02			19 12	19 25		19 31	19 41
Cardiff Central	a		17 46	17 53	18 10	18 15				18 24	18 43		18 47	18 55	19 12	19 15		19 17			19 30	19 40		19 44	19 58

A 🛒 to Bristol Temple Meads B not 23 June C The Torbay Express

When events are being held at the Principality Stadium, services are subject to alteration. Please check times before travelling.

Table T132-F

Bath Spa - Bristol - Cardiff

Saturdays

26 May to 8 December

		AW	GW	GW	GW	XC	GW	GW		GW	AW	XC	GW	GW	GW	AW	GW	XC		AW	GW	GW	GW	GW	GW
					◇■ ☕	◇■	◇	◇		◇■ ☕	▣ 🛒	◇■	◇■ ☕	◇	◇■ ☕		◇■ A ☕	◇■		◇ 🛒	◇	B	◇■ ☕		◇■ ☕
Bath Spa	d			19 15	19 27		19 36	19 51					20 02	20 10	20 27						20 36	20 43	21 02	21 08	
Oldfield Park	d			19 18				19 54						20 13								20 46		21 11	
Keynsham	d			19 26				20 01						20 20								20 53		21 18	
Bristol Temple Meads	a			19 35	19 40		19 48	20 09					20 14	20 28	20 40						20 48	21 02	21 14	21 27	
	d		19 19	19 41			19 54					20 10									20 53				
Filton Abbey Wood	d		19 27	19 48			20 01					20 17									21 01				
Bristol Parkway	a			19 52																					
	d									20 09							20 43								21 09
Patchway	d		19 31									20 21													
Pilning	d																								
Severn Tunnel Jn.	d	19 37	19 43									20 31				20 38									
Newport (South Wales)	a	19 50	19 55				20 23			20 30		20 44				20 50	21 04				21 23				21 30
	d	19 52	19 57			20 05	20 25			20 31	20 41	20 46				20 52	21 05	21 10		21 15	21 26				21 31
Cardiff Central	a	20 11	20 13			20 20	20 42			20 44	21 00	21 00				21 07	21 18	21 26		21 35	21 42				21 48

		AW	GW	GW		XC	AW	GW	SW	GW	GW	GW	GW	GW		GW	AW	GW	AW
		◇		◇■ ☕		◇■	◇	◇	◇■	◇■ ☕	◇■ ☕		◇	◇■ ☕			◇	◇■ ☕	
Bath Spa	d			21 32				21 38	21 51	22 02		22 25	22 38	23 02		23 10			
Oldfield Park	d											22 28				23 13			
Keynsham	d								21 59			22 36				23 20			
Bristol Temple Meads	a			21 44				21 50	22 06	22 14		22 45	22 50	23 15		23 29			
	d		21 29					21 57					22 55						
Filton Abbey Wood	d		21 36					22 04					23 02						
Bristol Parkway	a																		
	d										22 12							23 34	
Patchway	d		21 41					22 09					23 07						
Pilning	d																		
Severn Tunnel Jn.	d		21 52			22 02		22 20					23 18						23 49
Newport (South Wales)	a		22 09			22 18		22 37			22 44		23 35					00 01	00 11
	d	21 45	22 11			22 21	22 34	22 39			22 46		23 36				23 45	00 02	00 12
Cardiff Central	a	22 05	22 32			22 42	23 00	23 00			23 05		23 56				00 10	00 23	00 38

Sundays

20 May to 2 December

		GW	GW	AW	AW	GW	GW	GW	GW	AW		GW	GW	GW	GW	GW	GW	GW	AW	AW		GW	GW	GW	GW
		◇■ C ☕	◇■ C ☕	C	C	◇■ C ☕	◇ D	◇ E	F	◇ 🛒		F	G	G	◇■ G ☕	◇■ F ☕	◇■ G ☕	◇■ F ☕	G	◇		F	◇ G	◇■ G ☕	◇■ F ☕
Bath Spa	d		00 08			01 12			09 18			09 25	09 26		09 42	09 46						10 12	10 27	10 40	10 43
Oldfield Park	d								09 21			09 28	09 28									10 15	10 29		
Keynsham	d								09 28			09 35	09 36									10 22	10 37		
Bristol Temple Meads	a		00 20			01 24			09 36			09 44	09 44		09 55	10 00						10 31	10 45	10 54	10 58
	d						08 48	08 48				09 49		09 54								10 40	10 48		
Filton Abbey Wood	d						08 55	08 55				09 58		10 01								10 47	10 56		
Bristol Parkway	a																								
	d																10 10	10 16							
Patchway	d																					10 52	11 00		
Pilning	d																								
Severn Tunnel Jn.	d						09 08	09 08				10 10		10 14								11 03	11 11		
Newport (South Wales)	a						09 18	09 24				10 21		10 25			10 29	10 35				11 14	11 21		
	d	00 02		00 08	00 12		09 19	09 25		09 33		10 23		10 26			10 30	10 36	10 53	10 58		11 15	11 23		
Cardiff Central	a	00 23		00 34	00 38		09 39	09 45		09 55		10 42		10 46			10 52	10 59	11 12	11 18		11 36	11 43		

		GW	GW	AW	XC	GW		GW	GW	GW	GW	GW	XC	AW	GW	GW		GW	GW	AW	AW	GW	XC	GW	GW
		◇■ G ☕	◇■ F ☕		◇■ 🛒	▣		◇■ F ☕	◇■ G ☕	◇■ F ☕	◇■ G ☕		◇■ 🛒	▣ 🛒	◇ F	◇ G		◇■ F ☕	◇■ G ☕		▣ 🛒	◇■ ☕	◇■ 🛒	◇ F	◇ G
Bath Spa	d					11 24		11 42	11 43			12 20						12 43	12 43					13 23	13 25
Oldfield Park	d					11 27						12 23												13 26	13 28
Keynsham	d					11 35						12 30												13 33	13 36
Bristol Temple Meads	a					11 44		11 56	11 57			12 40						12 56	12 57					13 41	13 44
	d					11 47									12 48	12 48								13 48	13 48
Filton Abbey Wood	d					11 55									12 55	12 57								13 55	13 55
Bristol Parkway	a																								
	d	11 02	11 03							12 09	12 10											13 09			
Patchway	d																								
Pilning	d																								
Severn Tunnel Jn.	d			11 27		12 09									13 08	13 09				13 13				14 08	14 08
Newport (South Wales)	a	11 24	11 24	11 39		12 21				12 28	12 29				13 19	13 20				13 25		13 32		14 19	14 20
	d	11 25	11 25	11 41	11 49	12 22				12 28	12 29		12 46	12 54	13 19	13 21				13 27	13 31	13 35	14 08	14 22	14 22
Cardiff Central	a	11 48	11 46	12 06	12 09	12 41				12 50	12 49		13 07	13 18	13 40	13 41				13 50	13 54	13 56	14 27	14 41	14 42

A from 15 September
B until 8 September
C not 20 May
D until 21 October
E from 28 October
F from 16 September
G until 9 September

When events are being held at the Principality Stadium, services are subject to alteration. Please check times before travelling.

Table T132-F

Sundays

20 May to 2 December

Bath Spa - Bristol - Cardiff

		GW	AW	GW	GW	GW	XC	XC		AW	GW	GW	GW	GW	SW	AW	GW	GW		AW	XC	GW	GW	AW	GW
				A	B		C	D			B	A	A	B			A	B							A
Bath Spa	d	13 43									14 25	14 25	14 42	14 43	14 51							15 25	15 43		
Oldfield Park	d										14 28	14 28													
Keynsham	d										14 36	14 36			14 59										
Bristol Temple Meads	a	13 57									14 44	14 44	14 55	14 55	15 06							15 40	15 56		
	d					14 16					14 48	14 48										15 48			
Filton Abbey Wood	d					14 23					14 55	14 55										15 55			
Bristol Parkway	a																								
	d			14 07	14 08												15 09	15 10							16 10
Patchway	d																								
Pilning	d																								
Severn Tunnel Jn.	d					14 36					15 08	15 08				15 14						16 08			
Newport (South Wales)	a			14 30	14 31	14 47					15 20	15 20				15 26	15 30	15 31				16 19			16 35
	d		14 28	14 30	14 31	14 47	15 04	15 04		15 10	15 21	15 21				15 28	15 34	15 35		15 49	16 08	16 20		16 32	16 36
Cardiff Central	a		14 49	14 52	14 53	15 08	15 27	15 28		15 34	15 41	15 44				15 50	15 53	15 55		16 11	16 29	16 42		16 56	16 57

		GW	GW	GW		GW	GW	GW	XC	GW	GW	GW	GW	GW		GW	AW	AW	GW	GW	XC	GW	GW	GW	
		B		B		A	B	A		B	A	A	B	B		A			A	B			B	A	
Bath Spa	d			16 03		16 04	16 17	16 17		16 29	16 29	16 43	16 43	16 59		17 04						17 25	17 43	17 43	
Oldfield Park	d						16 18	16 19														17 28			
Keynsham	d						16 27	16 27														17 36			
Bristol Temple Meads	a			16 18		16 18	16 35	16 35		16 41	16 43	16 55	16 56	17 14		17 18						17 44	17 56	17 58	
	d		16 12							16 48	16 48											17 48			
Filton Abbey Wood	d		16 19							16 55	16 55											17 55			
Bristol Parkway	a																								
	d	16 10																	17 09	17 10					
Patchway	d									17 00	17 00														
Pilning	d																								
Severn Tunnel Jn.	d		16 32							17 11	17 11						17 13					18 08			
Newport (South Wales)	a	16 35	16 44							17 21	17 21						17 26		17 38	17 39		18 20			
	d	16 36	16 45						17 06	17 22	17 22						17 27	17 37	17 38	17 39	18 08	18 20			
Cardiff Central	a	16 59	17 06						17 26	17 43	17 43						17 49	17 56	18 00	18 01	18 29	18 42			

		GW	GW	GW	GW	GW	AW	GW	GW	XC		GW	GW	GW	GW	GW	GW	GW	GW	AW		AW	XC	GW	GW
		B	A	E	F	A		A	B			B	A			B	A	A	B						A
Bath Spa	d	17 59	18 04	18 09	18 09	18 11						18 30	18 30	18 43	18 49	19 01	19 04							19 25	19 43
Oldfield Park	d			18 11	18 11	18 12									18 53										
Keynsham	d			18 19	18 19	18 21									19 00										
Bristol Temple Meads	a	18 14	18 18	18 27	18 28	18 29						18 43	18 44	18 56	19 09	19 17	19 20							19 39	19 56
	d											18 48	18 48											19 48	
Filton Abbey Wood	d											18 55	18 55											19 55	
Bristol Parkway	a																								
	d							18 09	18 10									19 09	19 12						
Patchway	d																							20 00	
Pilning	d																								
Severn Tunnel Jn.	d											19 08	19 08									19 31		20 11	
Newport (South Wales)	a							18 30	18 30			19 20	19 20					19 31	19 34			19 47		20 22	
	d						18 29	18 31	18 32	19 07		19 20	19 20					19 32	19 34	19 46		19 48	20 08	20 23	
Cardiff Central	a						18 50	18 51	18 52	19 27		19 40	19 42					19 51	19 55	20 08		20 14	20 30	20 43	

		GW	GW	GW	GW	GW		AW	GW	GW	GW	GW	GW	XC	AW	GW		GW	GW	SW	SW	GW	GW	GW	GW
		B	A	B	A	B			A	B	A	B	A					A	B	B	A	B	A	B	A
Bath Spa	d	19 43	19 58	19 59	20 04	20 05										20 25		20 42	20 43	20 50	20 52	20 59	21 04	21 06	21 11
Oldfield Park	d		19 59			20 07																		21 09	21 14
Keynsham	d		20 08			20 15														20 58	20 59			21 15	21 20
Bristol Temple Meads	a	20 00	20 18	20 14	20 21	20 25										20 39		20 55	20 55	21 05	21 07	21 14	21 17	21 24	21 29
	d															20 48									
Filton Abbey Wood	d															20 55									
Bristol Parkway	a																								
	d								20 09	20 10		20 29	20 35												
Patchway	d																								
Pilning	d																								
Severn Tunnel Jn.	d										←					21 08									
Newport (South Wales)	a								20 31	20 30	20 31	20 46	20 52			21 20									
	d							20 28	20 32	20 31	20 32	20 48	20 53	21 08	21 10	21 20									
Cardiff Central	a							20 49	→	20 53	20 53	21 12	21 16	21 27	21 37	21 40									

A until 9 September
B from 16 September
C until 15 July
D from 22 July
E from 28 October
F from 16 September until 21 October

When events are being held at the Principality Stadium, services are subject to alteration. Please check times before travelling.

Table T132-F

Sundays

20 May to 2 December

Bath Spa - Bristol - Cardiff

		AW	GW	GW	AW	GW	GW	GW		GW	GW	AW	GW	GW	GW	GW	GW	AW		GW	GW	GW	GW	AW	
			A	B		A	B	A		B			A	B		B	A			B	A	A	B		
Bath Spa	d					21 25	21 25	21 40		21 43	22 19				22 25	22 42	22 43					23 43	23 49		
Oldfield Park	d										22 22														
Keynsham	d										22 29														
Bristol Temple Meads	a					21 41	21 41	21 54		21 56	22 37				22 41	22 57	22 57					23 57	00 04		
	d					21 48	21 48								22 49										
Filton Abbey Wood	d					21 55	21 55								22 56										
Bristol Parkway	a																								
	d		21 09	21 10									22 09	22 14						23 10	23 11				
Patchway	d					22 00	22 00																		
Pilning	d																								
Severn Tunnel Jn.	d	21 13				22 11	22 11								23 09			23 13							
Newport (South Wales)	a	21 25	21 28	21 29		22 24	22 24						22 31	22 36	23 21			23 30		23 34	23 34				
	d	21 27	21 29	21 30	21 46	22 25	22 25					22 30	22 36	22 37	23 21			23 30		23 36	23 36			23 55	
Cardiff Central	a	21 48	21 52	21 54	22 10	22 45	22 49					22 54	22 58	22 58	23 41			23 51		23 56	23 56			00 18	

A until 9 September
B from 16 September

When events are being held at the Principality Stadium, services are subject to alteration. Please check times before travelling.

Lydney, Chepstow and Caldicot stations are still open, but train times have not been provided by Network Rail.

Table T132-R

Mondays to Fridays

21 May to 7 December

Cardiff - Bristol - Bath Spa

Miles	Miles			GW	GW	AW	AW	AW	AW	GW	AW	AW	GW	GW	GW	AW	GW	GW	GW	GW	GW	XC	AW
				MX		MX	MX	MO			FO	FX											
					◇■ ⊡		◇	◇	◇ ⌶	◇■ ⊡	◇ ⌶	◇ ⌶	◇	■ ■ ⊡	■ ■ ⊡		■ ■ ⊡	■ ■ ⊡		■ ■ ⊡	◇ ⌶	◇■	◇ ⌶
0	0	**Cardiff Central**	d			00 30	04 35	04 35	05 08	05 15	05 38	05 39		05 55		06 12	06 26				06 30	06 40	06 50
11¾	11¾	Newport (South Wales)	a			00 46	04 51	04 52	05 25	05 31	05 55	05 55		06 07		06 26	06 38				06 42	06 53	07 02
—	—		d							05 33				06 09		06 28	06 40				06 44	06 55	
21¾	21¾	Severn Tunnel Jn	d	00 03												06a38					06 55	07a05	
28¾	28¾	Pilning	d																				
32¼	32¼	Patchway	d	00 16																	07 08		
—	33½	**Bristol Parkway**	a							06 01				06 30			07 01						
—	—		d																				
35¾	—	Filton Abbey Wood	d	00 20																	07 12		
38¼	—	**Bristol Temple Meads**	a	00 33																	07 20		
—	—		d		05 30								05 44		06 00			06 33	06 48	07 00	07 24		
42¾	—	Keynsham	d										05 51						06 55				
48¾	—	Oldfield Park	d										05 59						07 02				
49¾	—	**Bath Spa**	a		05 41								06 01		06 11			06 44	07 05	07 11	07 36		

		GW	GW	GW	XC	GW	AW	AW	GW	GW	GW	XC	GW	GW	GW	GW	SW	AW	GW	GW	GW	GW	XC
		■ ■ A ⊡		■ ■ B ✕	◇■	◇■ ⊡		◇ ⌶		■ ■ ⊡	■ ⌶	◇■	◇■ ⊡	◇	◇■ ⊡	◇	◇■	■ ⌶	◇■ ⊡		◇■ C ⊡	◇ ⌶	◇■
Cardiff Central	d			06 56	07 00		07 05	07 21		07 26	07 30	07 45			07 56	08 00		08 05			08 26	08 30	08 45
Newport (South Wales)	a			07 08	07 13		07 19	07 34		07 38	07 44	07 59			08 08	08 13		08 17			08 38	08 42	08 58
	d			07 10	07 14		07 23			07 40	07 44				08 10	08 15					08 40	08 44	
Severn Tunnel Jn	d				07 25		07a38				07 56					08 26						08 55	
Pilning	d																						
Patchway	d				07 37											08 39							
Bristol Parkway	a			07 32						08 01					08 31						09 01		
	d		07 24						07 49					08 20						08 45			
Filton Abbey Wood	d		07 28		07 41				07 53		08 11			08 23		08 43				08 49		09 09	
Bristol Temple Meads	a		07 40		07 51				08 00		08 18			08 36		08 51				09 00		09 19	
	d	07 30	07 47			08 00			08 12		08 23		08 30	08 41			08 51		09 00	09 07		09 22	
Keynsham	d		07 55						08 19					08 48			08 58			09 14			
Oldfield Park	d		08 03						08 26					08 55						09 21			
Bath Spa	a	07 41	08 06			08 11			08 29		08 35		08 41	08 58			09 05		09 11	09 24		09 34	

		AW	GW	GW	GW	GW	GW	GW	AW	AW	GW	GW	XC	GW	GW	GW	GW	GW	AW	AW	AW	GW
		◇ ⌶	◇■ ⊡	◇	◇■ ⊡	◇ D	E	◇■ ⊡		◇ ⌶	◇■ F ⊡	◇ ⌶	◇■ ⌶	◇■ ⊡	◇	◇■ ⊡		◇■ ⊡	■ ⌶			◇■ ⊡
Cardiff Central	d	08 50			08 56	09 00	09 00		09 12	09 21	09 26	09 30	09 45			09 56	10 00		10 05	10 09	10 19	10 26
Newport (South Wales)	a	09 03			09 08	09 14	09 14		09 26	09 34	09 38	09 42	09 58			10 09	10 13		10 17	10 23	10 34	10 38
	d				09 10	09 15	09 15		09 28		09 40	09 44				10 10	10 15			10 27		10 40
Severn Tunnel Jn	d					09 26	09 26		09a36			09 55					10 26			10a37		
Pilning	d																					
Patchway	d					09 39	09 39										10 39					
Bristol Parkway	a				09 31						10 01					10 31						11 01
	d			09 19											10 22							
Filton Abbey Wood	d			09 23		09 43	09 43					10 09			10 25		10 42					
Bristol Temple Meads	a			09 35		09 54	09 54					10 19			10 39		10 52					
	d		09 30	09 46				10 00				10 22		10 30	10 47			11 00				
Keynsham	d			09 53											10 54							
Oldfield Park	d			10 01											11 02							
Bath Spa	a		09 41	10 03				10 11				10 34		10 41	11 04			11 11				

		GW	XC	AW	GW	GW	GW	GW	GW	AW	GW	GW	XC	GW	GW	SW	GW	GW	GW	AW	AW	GW	GW
		◇ ⌶	◇■	■ ⌶	◇■ ⊡	◇	◇■ ⊡		◇■ ⊡	■ ⌶	◇■ ⊡	◇ ⌶	◇■ ⌶	◇■ ⊡	■ G ⌶	◇■ ⌶	◇■ ⊡		◇■ ⊡	■ ⌶		◇■ H ⊡	◇ ⌶
Cardiff Central	d	10 30	10 45	10 50			10 56	11 00		11 21	11 26	11 30	11 45				11 56	12 00		12 05	12 12	12 26	12 30
Newport (South Wales)	a	10 42	10 58	11 02			11 08	11 13		11 34	11 38	11 42	11 59				12 08	12 13		12 17	12 27	12 38	12 42
	d	10 45					11 10	11 15			11 40	11 44					12 10	12 15			12 28	12 40	12 44
Severn Tunnel Jn	d							11 26										12 26			12a39		
Pilning	d																						
Patchway	d							11 39										12 39					
Bristol Parkway	a						11 31				12 01						12 31					13 01	
	d					11 19									12 23								
Filton Abbey Wood	d	11 10				11 22		11 42				12 09			12 26			12 42					13 09
Bristol Temple Meads	a	11 19				11 34		11 51				12 18			12 35			12 51					13 19
	d	11 22			11 30	11 49			12 00			12 22		12 30	12 39	12 49			13 00				13 22
Keynsham	d					11 56										12 56							
Oldfield Park	d					12 03										13 03							
Bath Spa	a	11 34			11 41	12 06			12 11			12 34		12 41	12 51	13 05			13 11				13 34

A The Bristolian
B The Capitals United- Restaurant for customers joining to Swindon
C Y Cymro - The Welshman
D from 2 July
E until 29 June
F The Red Dragon
G ⌶ from Bristol Temple Meads
H The St. David

When events are being held at the Principality Stadium, services are subject to alteration. Please check times before travelling.

		XC	AW	GW	GW	GW	GW	GW	AW	AW	GW	GW	XC	GW	GW	GW	GW	GW	AW	GW	GW	XC	AW
		◇■ ⌶	◇ ⌶	◇■ ⊡		◇■ ⊡	◇	◇■ ⊡		◇ ⌶	◇■ ⊡	◇ ⌶	◇■ ⌶	◇■ ⊡	◇	◇■ ⊡		◇■ ⊡	■ ⌶	◇■ ⊡	◇ ⌶	◇■ ⌶	■ ⌶
Cardiff Central	d	12 45	12 50			12 56	13 00		13 12	13 21	13 26	13 30	13 45			13 56	14 00		14 05	14 26	14 30	14 45	14 50
Newport (South Wales)	a	12 59	13 02			13 08	13 14		13 28	13 34	13 38	13 42	13 58			14 08	14 13		14 17	14 38	14 42	14 58	15 02
	d					13 10	13 16		13 28		13 40	13 44				14 10	14 15			14 40	14 44		
Severn Tunnel Jn	d						13 27		13a39								14 26						
Pilning	d																						
Patchway	d						13 40										14 39						
Bristol Parkway	a					13 31					14 01					14 31				15 01			
	d				13 19										14 23								
Filton Abbey Wood	d				13 25		13 43					14 09			14 27		14 42				15 09		
Bristol Temple Meads	a				13 36		13 53					14 18			14 39		14 51				15 18		
	d			13 30	13 49			14 00				14 22		14 30	14 48			15 00			15 22		
Keynsham	d				13 56										14 55								
Oldfield Park	d				14 03										15 02								
Bath Spa	a			13 41	14 06			14 11				14 34		14 41	15 05			15 11			15 34		

		GW	GW	GW	GW	SW	AW	AW	GW	GW	GW	GW	XC	AW	GW	GW	GW	GW	GW	AW	AW	GW	GW
		◇■ ⊡		◇■ ⊡		◇■		■ ⌶	◇■ A ⊡		◇■ ⊡	◇ ⌶	◇■ ⌶	■ ⌶	◇■ ⊡	◇	◇■ ⊡		◇■ ⊡		■ ⌶		◇■ ⊡
Cardiff Central	d			14 56	15 00		15 12	15 21			15 26	15 30	15 45	15 50			15 56	16 00		16 10	16 21		16 26
Newport (South Wales)	a			15 08	15 14		15 27	15 34			15 38	15 42	15 58	16 02			16 08	16 14		16 24	16 33		16 38
	d			15 10	15 15		15 28				15 40	15 44					16 10	16 15		16 27			16 40
Severn Tunnel Jn	d				15 26		15a37											16 26		16a37			
Pilning	d																						
Patchway	d				15 39													16 39					
Bristol Parkway	a			15 31							16 01						16 31						17 01
	d		15 20							15 54						16 24						16 46	
Filton Abbey Wood	d		15 23		15 42					15 58		16 09				16 27		16 43				16 50	
Bristol Temple Meads	a		15 38		15 51							16 19				16 39		16 52				17 02	
	d	15 30	15 44			15 51			16 00			16 22			16 30	16 48			17 00			17 06	
Keynsham	d		15 51			15 58				16 12						16 55						17 13	
Oldfield Park	d		15 58							16 20						17 02						17 20	
Bath Spa	a	15 41	16 00			16 06			16 11	16 22		16 34			16 41	17 05			17 11			17 23	

		GW	XC	AW	GW	GW	GW	GW	GW	AW	AW	GW	GW	GW	XC	AW	GW	GW	GW	GW	AW	AW
											BHX											
		■ ⌶	◇■ ⌶	■ ⌶	◇■ ⊡	◇	◇■ ⊡		◇■ ⊡		■ ⊠		◇■ ⊡	■ ⌶	◇■ ⌶	■ ⌶	◇■ ⊡		◇■ ⊡			■ ⌶
Cardiff Central	d	16 30	16 45	16 50			16 56	17 00		17 12	17 16		17 26	17 30	17 45	17 50			17 56	18 00	18 08	18 21
Newport (South Wales)	a	16 44	16 58	17 02			17 08	17 14		17 26	17 30		17 38	17 43	17 59	18 03			18 08	18 14	18 22	18 33
	d	16 45					17 10	17 15		17 28			17 40	17 44					18 10	18 16	18 24	
Severn Tunnel Jn	d	16 56						17 26		17a38				17 55						18 27	18a34	
Pilning	d																					
Patchway	d							17 39												18 40		
Bristol Parkway	a						17 31						18 01						18 31			
	d					17 20						17 44						18 23				
Filton Abbey Wood	d	17 11				17 23		17 43				17 49		18 10				18 27		18 47		
Bristol Temple Meads	a	17 19				17 35		17 53				18 00		18 19				18 38		18 54		
	d	17 23			17 31	17 49			18 00			18 04		18 22			18 30	18 51				
Keynsham	d					17 56						18 11						18 59				
Oldfield Park	d					18 03						18 19						19 06				
Bath Spa	a	17 35			17 42	18 06			18 11			18 21		18 34			18 41	19 09				

		GW	GW	XC	AW	GW	GW	GW	GW	GW	AW	XC	GW	GW	GW	AW	GW	GW	GW	GW	GW	XC	AW
																			FX	FO			
		◇■ ⊡	◇ ⌶	◇■ ⌶	◇ ⌶	◇■ ⊡			◇■ ⊡	◇	◇	◇■	◇■ ⊡			◇	◇■ ⊡	◇	◇■ ⊡	◇■ ⊡		◇■	
Cardiff Central	d	18 26	18 30	18 45	18 55			19 00	19 26	19 30	19 34	19 50			20 00	20 17	20 26	20 30			21 00	21 05	21 12
Newport (South Wales)	a	18 38	18 42	18 58	19 06			19 14	19 38	19 42	19 46	20 03			20 14	20 29	20 38	20 43			21 14	21 18	21 26
	d	18 40	18 44					19 15	19 40	19 44		20 05			20 16		20 40	20 44			21 15		21 27
Severn Tunnel Jn	d		18 55					19 26				20a15			20 27						21 26		21a38
Pilning	d																						
Patchway	d							19 39							20 40						21 39		
Bristol Parkway	a	19 01							20 01								21 01						
	d																						
Filton Abbey Wood	d		19 10					19 44		20 09					20 44			21 08			21 43		
Bristol Temple Meads	a		19 18					19 53		20 18					20 53			21 17			21 51		
	d		19 23			19 30	19 49			20 22			20 30	20 48				21 23	21 50	21 51	22 04		
Keynsham	d						19 56							20 56							22 11		
Oldfield Park	d						20 03							21 03							22 18		
Bath Spa	a		19 35			19 41	20 06			20 34			20 41	21 06				21 36	22 02	22 02	22 21		

A The Merchant Venturer

When events are being held at the Principality Stadium, services are subject to alteration. Please check times before travelling.

Table T132-R

Mondays to Fridays
21 May to 7 December

Cardiff - Bristol - Bath Spa

		AW ◇	GW ◇■ ☕	GW	SW ■	XC ◇■	AW ◇		GW ◇■ ☕	GW FO	GW FX	GW	GW FO	GW FX	AW	GW FX	GW FO
Cardiff Central	d	21 17	21 26	21 30		21 50	21 55			22 04	22 04		22 36	22 36	23 20	23 27	23 27
Newport (South Wales)	a	21 31	21 38	21 44		22 03	22 09			22 16	22 18		22 50	22 52	23 38	23 44	23 45
	d		21 40	21 45						22 18	22 20		22 51	22 54	23 38	23 45	23 45
Severn Tunnel Jn	d			21 56						22 28	22 37		23 02	23 11	23a57	00 03	00 03
Pilning	d																
Patchway	d									22 41	22 50					00 16	00 16
Bristol Parkway	a		22 01														
	d																
Filton Abbey Wood	d			22 11						22 45	22 54		23 17	23 26		00 20	00 20
Bristol Temple Meads	a			22 21						22 59	23 06		23 26	23 38		00 33	00 33
	d				22 23				22 35			23 20					
Keynsham	d											23 27					
Oldfield Park	d											23 34					
Bath Spa	a				22 34				22 46			23 37					

Saturdays
26 May to 8 December

		GW	GW ◇■ ☕	AW	AW ◇	GW ◇	GW ◇■ ☕	AW ◇ 🍴	AW ◇ 🍴	GW ◇■ ☕		AW	GW ◇■ ☕	GW ◇■ ☕	GW	GW ◇■ ☕	GW ◇	XC ◇■	AW ◇ 🍴	GW ◇■ ☕		GW ◇■ ☕	GW	XC ◇■	GW ◇■ ☕
Cardiff Central	d			00 30	04 35		04 55	05 21	05 37	05 56		06 10	06 26				06 30	06 40	06 50	06 56				07 00	
Newport (South Wales)	a			00 43	04 50		05 07	05 34	05 51	06 08		06 24	06 38				06 42	06 53	07 02	07 08				07 13	
	d						05 09			06 10		06 26	06 40				06 44	06 55		07 10				07 15	
Severn Tunnel Jn	d	00 03										06a36					06 55	07a05						07 25	
Pilning	d																								
Patchway	d	00 16																						07 37	
Bristol Parkway	a						05 36			06 30			07 00							07 30					
	d						05 42																		
Filton Abbey Wood	d	00 20															07 10							07 41	
Bristol Temple Meads	a	00 33					05 53										07 18							07 52	
	d		05 30			05 48	06 00							06 30	06 49	07 00	07 22					07 30	07 49		08 00
Keynsham	d					05 55									06 56								07 56		
Oldfield Park	d					06 02									07 03								08 03		
Bath Spa	a		05 41			06 04	06 11							06 41	07 05	07 11	07 34					07 41	08 05		08 11

		AW	AW ◇ 🍴	GW ◇■ ☕	GW ◇	XC ◇■		AW ■ 🍴	GW ◇■ ☕	GW ◇ A	GW ◇ B	GW ◇■ ☕	SW ◇■	GW	GW ◇■ ☕	GW ◇■ ☕		GW B	GW ◇	XC ◇■	AW ■ 🍴	GW ◇■ ☕	GW ◇	GW ◇■ A ☕	GW
Cardiff Central	d	07 07	07 21	07 26	07 30	07 45		07 50				07 56		08 00		08 26			08 30	08 45	08 50			08 56	09 00
Newport (South Wales)	a	07 21	07 34	07 38	07 42	07 58		08 02				08 08		08 14		08 38			08 42	08 58	09 02			09 08	09 14
	d	07 23		07 40	07 44							08 10		08 15		08 40			08 44					09 10	09 15
Severn Tunnel Jn	d	07a33			07 55									08 26					08 55						09 26
Pilning	d													08 34											
Patchway	d													08 41											09 39
Bristol Parkway	a			08 00								08 30				09 00								09 30	
	d									08 20	08 20												09 19		
Filton Abbey Wood	d				08 10					08 23	08 23			08 46					09 10				09 22		09 43
Bristol Temple Meads	a				08 18					08 34	08 34			08 54					09 18				09 34		09 52
	d				08 22				08 30	08 39	08 40		08 51		09 00			09 08	09 22			09 30	09 49		
Keynsham	d									08 46	08 47		08 58					09 15					09 56		
Oldfield Park	d									08 53	08 54							09 22					10 03		
Bath Spa	a				08 34				08 41	08 55	08 56		09 05		09 11			09 24	09 34			09 41	10 05		

		GW ◇■ ☕		AW	AW ◇ 🍴	GW ◇■ ☕	GW ◇ C 🍴	XC ◇■ 🍴	AW ◇ 🍴	GW ◇■ ☕	GW	GW		GW ◇■ ☕	AW	AW	GW ◇■ ☕	GW ◇ C 🍴	XC ◇■	AW ◇ 🍴	GW ◇■ D ☕	GW ◇		GW	GW ◇■ ☕
Cardiff Central	d			09 10	09 21	09 26	09 30	09 45	09 55			10 00			10 10	10 19	10 26	10 30	10 45	10 55				11 00	
Newport (South Wales)	a			09 23	09 33	09 38	09 42	09 58	10 07			10 14			10 24	10 34	10 38	10 44	10 58	11 07				11 14	
	d			09 25		09 40	09 44					10 15			10 27		10 40	10 46						11 15	
Severn Tunnel Jn	d			09a35			09 55					10 26			10a37									11 26	
Pilning	d																								
Patchway	d											10 39												11 39	
Bristol Parkway	a					10 00											11 00								
	d										10 23											11 20			
Filton Abbey Wood	d						10 10				10 27	10 43						11 10				11 23		11 43	
Bristol Temple Meads	a						10 18				10 39	10 51						11 18				11 35		11 52	
	d	10 00					10 22			10 30	10 49			11 00				11 22			11 30	11 49			12 00
Keynsham	d										10 56											11 56			
Oldfield Park	d										11 03											12 03			
Bath Spa	a	10 11					10 34			10 41	11 05			11 11				11 34			11 41	12 05			12 11

A from 15 September
B until 8 September
C 🍴 from Bristol Temple Meads
D The Torbay Express

When events are being held at the Principality Stadium, services are subject to alteration. Please check times before travelling.

Table T132-R

Saturdays
26 May to 8 December

Cardiff - Bristol - Bath Spa

		AW ■ 🍴	GW ◇■ ☕	GW ◇ A 🍴		XC ◇■ 🍴	AW ■ 🍴	GW ◇■ ☕	GW ■	SW ◇■ 🍴	GW	GW ◇■ ☕	AW	GW ◇■ ☕		GW ◇ A 🍴	XC ◇■ 🍴	AW ■ 🍴	GW ◇■ ☕	GW	GW	GW ◇■ ☕	AW 🍴	AW ◇ 🍴
Cardiff Central	d	11 21	11 26	11 30		11 45	11 55				12 00		12 09	12 26		12 30	12 45	12 55			13 00		13 12	13 21
Newport (South Wales)	a	11 33	11 38	11 42		11 58	12 07				12 14		12 23	12 38		12 42	12 59	13 07			13 14		13 26	13 34
	d		11 40	11 44							12 15		12 27	12 40		12 44					13 15		13 27	
Severn Tunnel Jn	d										12 26		12a37								13 26		13a38	
Pilning	d																							
Patchway	d										12 39										13 39			
Bristol Parkway	a		12 00											13 00										
	d								12 25											13 19				
Filton Abbey Wood	d			12 10					12 29		12 43					13 10				13 23	13 43			
Bristol Temple Meads	a			12 18					12 38		12 52					13 18				13 35	13 52			
	d			12 22				12 30	12 43	12 51		13 00				13 22			13 30	13 44		14 00		
Keynsham	d								12 50	12 58										13 51				
Oldfield Park	d								12 57											13 58				
Bath Spa	a			12 34				12 41	12 59	13 05		13 11				13 34			13 41	14 01		14 11		

		GW ◇■ B ☕	GW ◇■ C ☕	GW ◇	XC ◇■ 🍴	AW ■ 🍴	GW ◇■ ☕	GW ◇ D	GW ◇ C	GW		GW ◇■ ☕	AW ◇	GW ◇■ ☕	GW ◇	XC ◇■ 🍴	AW ◇ 🍴	GW ◇■ ☕	GW	SW ◇■		GW	GW ◇■ ☕	AW	AW ■ 🍴
Cardiff Central	d	13 26	13 26	13 30	13 45	13 55				14 00			14 17	14 26	14 30	14 45	14 55					15 00		15 08	15 21
Newport (South Wales)	a	13 38	13 38	13 42	13 58	14 07				14 14			14 32	14 38	14 42	14 58	15 07					15 14		15 22	15 34
	d	13 40	13 40	13 44						14 15				14 40	14 44							15 15		15 27	
Severn Tunnel Jn	d									14 26												15 26		15a35	
Pilning	d																					15 34			
Patchway	d									14 39												15 42			
Bristol Parkway	a	14 00	14 00											15 01											
	d							14 20	14 20										15 19						
Filton Abbey Wood	d			14 10				14 24	14 24	14 43					15 10				15 23			15 46			
Bristol Temple Meads	a			14 18				14 36	14 37	14 52					15 18				15 34			15 54			
	d			14 22			14 30	14 44	14 49			15 00			15 22			15 30	15 44	15 51			16 00		
Keynsham	d							14 51	14 56										15 51	15 58					
Oldfield Park	d							14 58	15 03										15 58						
Bath Spa	a			14 34			14 41	15 00	15 05			15 11			15 34			15 41	16 00	16 05			16 11		

		GW ◇■ ☕	GW ◇	XC ◇■ 🍴	AW ■ 🍴	GW ◇■ ☕		GW ◇	GW	GW ◇■ ☕	AW	AW	GW ◇■ ☕	GW ■	XC ◇■ 🍴	AW ■ 🍴		GW ◇■ ☕	GW ◇	GW	GW ◇■ ☕	AW	AW ■	GW ◇■ ☕	GW ◇
Cardiff Central	d	15 26	15 30	15 45	15 55				16 00		16 08	16 18	16 26	16 30	16 45	16 55				17 00		17 09	17 21	17 26	17 30
Newport (South Wales)	a	15 38	15 42	15 58	16 07				16 14		16 22	16 32	16 38	16 42	16 58	17 07				17 14		17 25	17 33	17 38	17 42
	d	15 40	15 44						16 15		16 24		16 40	16 44						17 15		17 25		17 40	17 44
Severn Tunnel Jn	d								16 26		16a34			16 55						17 26		17a35			17 55
Pilning	d																								
Patchway	d								16 39											17 39					
Bristol Parkway	a	16 00											17 00											18 00	
	d							16 24											17 20						
Filton Abbey Wood	d		16 10					16 28	16 43					17 10					17 23	17 43					18 10
Bristol Temple Meads	a		16 18					16 39	16 51					17 18					17 36	17 52					18 18
	d		16 22			16 30		16 49		17 00				17 22				17 30	17 49		18 00				18 22
Keynsham	d							16 56											17 56						
Oldfield Park	d							17 03											18 03						
Bath Spa	a		16 34			16 41		17 05		17 11				17 34				17 41	18 05		18 11				18 34

		XC ◇■ 🍴		AW ■ 🍴	GW ◇■ ☕	GW	GW	AW	GW ◇■ ☕	GW ◇	XC ◇■ 🍴	AW ◇ 🍴		GW ◇■ ☕	GW	GW	GW ◇■ ☕	GW ◇	AW ◇	GW ◇■ ☕	GW	GW		XC ◇■	AW ◇
Cardiff Central	d	17 45		17 55			18 00	18 08	18 26	18 30	18 45	18 50				19 00	19 26	19 30	19 34		19 54			20 00	20 10
Newport (South Wales)	a	17 58		18 08			18 14	18 22	18 38	18 42	18 59	19 03				19 14	19 38	19 42	19 46		20 08			20 13	20 24
	d						18 15	18 27	18 40	18 44						19 15	19 40	19 44			20 10			20 15	
Severn Tunnel Jn	d						18 26	18a37								19 26					20 21			20a25	
Pilning	d																								
Patchway	d						18 39									19 39					20 34				
Bristol Parkway	a								19 00								20 00								
	d					18 25									19 20										
Filton Abbey Wood	d					18 28	18 43			19 10					19 24	19 43		20 10			20 40				
Bristol Temple Meads	a					18 39	18 52			19 18					19 35	19 52		20 18			20 49				
	d				18 30	18 49				19 22				19 30	19 49			20 22		20 33		20 49			
Keynsham	d					18 56									19 56							20 56			
Oldfield Park	d					19 03									20 03							21 03			
Bath Spa	a				18 41	19 05				19 34				19 41	20 05			20 34		20 44		21 05			

A 🍴 from Bristol Temple Meads
B until 8 September. The Pembroke Coast Express
C from 15 September
D until 8 September

When events are being held at the Principality Stadium, services are subject to alteration. Please check times before travelling.

Table T132-R

Cardiff - Bristol - Bath Spa

Saturdays
26 May to 8 December

Station		GW	GW	XC	AW	GW	GW	AW	AW	SW	GW	GW	GW	GW	AW
		◇■ ☕	◇	◇■	◇	◇■ ☕			◇	■	◇■ ☕				
Cardiff Central	d	20 26	20 30	20 50	20 55		21 00	21 11	21 54			22 00		22 47	23 18
Newport (South Wales)	a	20 38	20 42	21 03	21 08		21 14	21 25	22 10			22 13		23 03	23 35
	d	20 40	20 44				21 15	21 27				22 15		23 03	23 37
Severn Tunnel Jn	d						21 26	21a37				22 35			23a56
Pilning	d														
Patchway	d						21 39					22 48			
Bristol Parkway	a	21 00													
	d														
Filton Abbey Wood	d		21 08				21 43					22 52			
Bristol Temple Meads	a		21 17				21 52					23 00		23 43	
	d		21 22			21 47	22 02			22 23	22 30		23 10		
Keynsham	d						22 09						23 17		
Oldfield Park	d						22 16						23 23		
Bath Spa	a		21 34			22 01	22 18			22 34	22 41		23 26		

Sundays
20 May to 2 December

Station		GW	GW	GW	GW	GW	GW	GW	GW	GW	AW	GW	GW	GW	GW	GW	GW	GW	GW	GW	GW	GW	AW
		◇■ ☕	◇■ ☕	◇■ ☕	A	B	◇■ A ☕	◇■ B ☕	◇ B	◇ A	◇ 🍴	◇■ C ☕	◇■ D ☕	◇■ B ☕	B	A	◇■ B ☕	◇■ A ☕	◇ C	◇ D	◇ B	◇ C	▪ 🍴
Cardiff Central	d		08 05						08 10	08 10	08 30	08 49	08 55	09 05					09 08	09 13	09 13		09 17
Newport (South Wales)	a		08 21						08 26	08 26	08 47	09 06	09 13	09 24					09 24	09 29	09 30	←	09 37
	d		08 23						08 28	08 28		09 08	09 15	09 26					09 26	09 31	09 31		
Severn Tunnel Jn	d								08 45	08 45									09 44	09 42	09 42	09 44	
Pilning	d																		↪				
Patchway	d																			09 55	09 55	09 57	
Bristol Parkway	a		08 50									09 35	09 35	09 46									
	d																						
Filton Abbey Wood	d								09 00	09 00										09 58	09 58	10 00	
Bristol Temple Meads	a								09 08	09 08										10 10	10 10	10 12	
	d	07 45		08 15	08 19	08 23	08 53	09 00	09 10	09 15					09 20	09 25	09 47	09 53		10 15	10 15	10 15	
Keynsham	d				08 26	08 30			09 18	09 21					09 27	09 32							
Oldfield Park	d				08 34	08 38			09 25	09 28					09 34	09 40							
Bath Spa	a	07 56		08 26	08 36	08 40	09 05	09 12	09 28	09 31					09 37	09 42	09 58	10 04		10 26	10 26	10 26	

Station		GW	GW	GW	GW	GW	GW	GW	AW	AW	AW	XC	GW	GW	GW	GW	GW	GW	AW	XC	GW	GW	GW
		◇■ A ☕	◇■ B ☕	◇■ A ☕	◇■ B ☕	◇ B	◇ A	◇■ ☕		▪ B 🍴	◇ A 🍴	◇■	◇■ A ☕	◇■ B ☕	◇■ A ☕	◇■ B ☕	▪ ◇ E	◇■ ☕	◇ 🍴	◇■	▪ ■ A ☕	▪ ■ B ☕	▪ ■ A ☕
Cardiff Central	d					10 08	10 08	10 20	10 30	10 34	10 34	10 45					11 08	11 20	11 35	11 45			
Newport (South Wales)	a					10 24	10 27	10 38	10 46	10 51	10 51	11 04					11 27	11 38	11 51	12 03			
	d					10 26	10 29	10 39	10 48								11 29	11 39					
Severn Tunnel Jn	d					10 36	10 39		10a58								11 39						
Pilning	d																						
Patchway	d																						
Bristol Parkway	a							11 00										12 00					
	d																						
Filton Abbey Wood	d					10 51	10 54										11 54						
Bristol Temple Meads	a					11 00	11 03										12 03						
	d	10 23	10 30	10 53	11 00	11 10	11 10						11 25	11 30	11 53	12 00	12 10				12 25	12 30	12 53
Keynsham	d					11 16	11 16										12 17						
Oldfield Park	d					11 23	11 23										12 24						
Bath Spa	a	10 34	10 42	11 04	11 11	11 26	11 26						11 36	11 41	12 04	12 11	12 26				12 36	12 41	13 04

Station		GW	GW	GW	GW	AW	AW	AW	XC	GW	GW	GW	GW	GW	GW	GW	AW	GW	AW	XC	GW	GW
		▪ ■ B ☕	◇ B	◇ A	◇■ ☕		▪ B 🍴	◇ A 🍴	◇■	▪ ■ A ☕	▪ ■ B ☕	▪ ■ A ☕	▪ ■ B ☕	◇ B	◇ A	◇ B	▪ 🍴	▪ ■ ☕	▪ 🍴	◇■	◇■ A ☕	◇■ B ☕
Cardiff Central	d		12 08	12 08	12 20	12 25	12 36	12 36	12 45					13 08	13 08		13 14	13 20	13 40	13 45		
Newport (South Wales)	a		12 24	12 27	12 38	12 45	12 52	12 52	13 03					13 26	13 27		13 33	13 38	13 56	14 01		
	d		12 25	12 28	12 39	12 47								13 27	13 29			13 39				
Severn Tunnel Jn	d		12 36	12 39		12a57								13 37	13 39							
Pilning	d																					
Patchway	d		12 49	12 52																		
Bristol Parkway	a				13 00													14 00				
	d																					
Filton Abbey Wood	d		12 51	12 54										13 52	13 54	←						
Bristol Temple Meads	a		13 01	13 04										14 04	14 03	14 04						
	d	13 00	13 10	13 10						13 25	13 30	13 53	14 00	14 10	14 10	14 10					14 53	15 00
Keynsham	d		13 17	13 17										↪	14 17	14 17						
Oldfield Park	d		13 24	13 24											14 24	14 24						
Bath Spa	a	13 11	13 27	13 27						13 36	13 41	14 04	14 11		14 26	14 26					15 05	15 11

A from 16 September
B until 9 September
C from 28 October
D from 16 September until 21 October
E ◇ from Bristol Temple Meads ▪ to Bristol Temple Meads

When events are being held at the Principality Stadium, services are subject to alteration. Please check times before travelling.

Table T132-R

Cardiff - Bristol - Bath Spa

Sundays
20 May to 2 December

Station		GW	GW	AW	XC	AW	GW	GW	GW	GW	SW	GW	GW	AW	GW	GW	XC	AW	GW	GW	GW	GW
		◇	▪ ■ ☕		◇■ 🍴	▪ 🍴	◇■ A ☕	▪ ■ B ☕	▪ ■ A ☕	◇■ B ☕	◇■	◇ B	◇ A	▪ 🍴	▪ ■ B ☕	▪ ■ A ☕	◇■ 🍴	▪ 🍴	◇■ A ☕	◇■ B ☕	◇■ A ☕	◇■ B ☕
Cardiff Central	d	14 08	14 20	14 25	14 45	14 56						15 08	15 08	15 15	15 20	15 20	15 45	15 56				
Newport (South Wales)	a	14 27	14 38	14 43	15 03	15 12						15 26	15 26	15 32	15 38	15 38	16 03	16 12				
	d	14 28	14 39	14 45								15 28	15 28		15 39	15 40						
Severn Tunnel Jn	d	14 39		14a55								15 39	15 39									
Pilning	d																					
Patchway	d											15 52	15 52									
Bristol Parkway	a		15 00												16 00	16 00						
	d																					
Filton Abbey Wood	d	14 54										15 54	15 54									
Bristol Temple Meads	a	15 03										16 04	16 04									
	d	15 10					15 25	15 30	15 53	16 00	16 04	16 10	16 15						16 25	16 30	16 53	17 00
Keynsham	d	15 17									16 11											
Oldfield Park	d	15 23																				
Bath Spa	a	15 27					15 36	15 41	16 04	16 11	16 18	16 22	16 26						16 36	16 41	17 05	17 11

Station		GW	GW	GW	AW	GW	GW	GW	GW	AW	XC	GW	GW	AW	GW	GW	GW	GW	GW	AW	GW	GW	GW
		◇ A	◇ B	▪ ■ ☕		▪ ■ A ☕	▪ ■ B ☕	◇ B	◇ A	▪ 🍴	◇■ 🍴	◇■ A ☕	◇■ B ☕	B	◇ A	◇ B	◇■ A ☕	◇■ B ☕	◇	▪	◇■ A ☕	◇■ B ☕	◇ B
Cardiff Central	d	16 08	16 08	16 20	16 25			16 35	16 35	16 40	16 45	16 50	16 50	17 03					17 08	17 35			17 40
Newport (South Wales)	a	16 26	16 26	16 38	16 43			16 49	16 51	16 56	17 01	17 07	17 07	17 22					17 26	17 51			17 56
	d	16 27	16 27	16 39	16 45			16 51	16 53			17 09	17 10						17 28				17 58
Severn Tunnel Jn	d	16 38	16 39		16a54														17 39				
Pilning	d																						
Patchway	d																						18 20
Bristol Parkway	a			17 00								17 30	17 30										
	d																						
Filton Abbey Wood	d	16 54	16 54					17 14	17 19										17 54				18 25
Bristol Temple Meads	a	17 03	17 03					17 23	17 28										18 02				18 39
	d	17 10	17 10			17 25	17 30	17 35	17 35						17 43	17 43	17 53	18 00	18 10		18 25	18 30	18 49
Keynsham	d	17 17	17 17						17 42							17 51			18 16				→
Oldfield Park	d	17 24	17 24						17 49							17 58			18 23				
Bath Spa	a	17 26	17 26			17 36	17 41	17 49	17 51						17 57	18 01	18 02	18 11	18 26		18 36	18 41	

Station		GW	GW	XC	GW	GW	GW	GW	GW	GW	AW	AW	XC	GW	GW	GW	GW	GW	GW	GW	GW	AW	XC
		◇ A	◇ B	◇■ 🍴	▪ ■ A ☕	▪ ■ B ☕	◇■ A ☕	◇■ B ☕	◇ A	◇ B		▪ 🍴	◇■ 🍴	◇■ ☕	◇■ A ☕	◇■ B ☕	◇■ A ☕	◇■ B ☕	◇ B	◇ A		◇	◇■
Cardiff Central	d	17 40		17 45	17 50	17 50			18 08	18 10	18 24	18 36	18 45	18 50					19 08	19 08		19 40	19 45
Newport (South Wales)	a	17 56		18 02	18 07	18 07			18 25	18 25	18 44	18 53	19 01	19 07					19 27	19 27		19 56	20 01
	d	17 58			18 09	18 10			18 27	18 27	18 46			19 09					19 29	19 29			
Severn Tunnel Jn	d								18 39	18 39	18a56								19 39	19 39			
Pilning	d																						
Patchway	d	18 22																					
Bristol Parkway	a				18 30	18 30								19 30									
	d																						
Filton Abbey Wood	d	18 26	←						18 53	18 53									19 54	19 54			
Bristol Temple Meads	a	18 39	18 39						19 04	19 04									20 05	20 07			
	d	18 45	18 49				18 53	19 00	19 10	19 10					19 25	19 30	19 53	20 00	20 15	20 15	20 48		
Keynsham	d								19 17	19 17											20 55		
Oldfield Park	d								19 22	19 22											21 03		
Bath Spa	a	18 57	19 01				19 04	19 11	19 26	19 26					19 36	19 41	20 04	20 11	20 27	20 27	21 05		

Station		GW	GW	GW	GW	AW	XC	GW	AW	SW	GW	GW	GW	GW	GW	AW	GW	AW
		◇■ ☕	◇■ B ☕	◇■ A ☕	◇		◇■	◇■ ☕	◇	■	◇■ ☕		A	B				
Cardiff Central	d	19 50			20 18	20 24	20 45	20 50	21 12				21 18	21 18	22 10	22 26	23 07	23 20
Newport (South Wales)	a	20 08			20 38	20 44	21 03	21 07	21 27				21 35	21 36	22 26	22 44	23 23	23 36
	d	20 09			20 38	20 46		21 09					21 37	21 38	22 28	22 46	23 25	
Severn Tunnel Jn	d				20 50	20a56							21 49	21 51	22 43	22a56		
Pilning	d																	
Patchway	d												22 02	22 04	22 56			
Bristol Parkway	a	20 30						21 32										
	d																	
Filton Abbey Wood	d				21 04								22 09	22 09	22 59			
Bristol Temple Meads	a				21 13								22 19	22 21	23 10		23 59	
	d		21 00	21 00	21 25					21 35	22 10	22 15			23 15			
Keynsham	d											22 22						
Oldfield Park	d											22 30						
Bath Spa	a		21 13	21 14	21 37					21 47	22 21	22 32			23 28			

A from 16 September
B until 9 September

When events are being held at the Principality Stadium, services are subject to alteration. Please check times before travelling.

Lydney, Chepstow and Caldicot stations are still open, but train times have not been provided by Network Rail.

Table T133-F

Bristol - Avonmouth and Severn Beach

Mondays to Fridays

21 May to 7 December

Miles			GW	GW	GW	GW	GW	GW	GW	GW	GW	GW	GW ◇	GW	GW	GW ◇	GW	GW	GW	GW	GW	GW	GW
0	**Bristol Temple Meads**	d	05 14	05 48	06 00	06 20	06 30	06 51	07 04	07 20	07 46	08 03	08 10	08 36	08 45	09 10	09 16	09 48	10 03	10 34	10 45	11 16	11 45
1	Lawrence Hill	d	05 17	05 51	06 03	06 23	06 33	06 55	07 07	07 23	07 49	08 06	08 13	08 39	08 48	09 13	09 19	09 51		10 37	10 49	11 19	11 48
1½	Stapleton Road	d	05 19	05 53	06a05	06a25	06 35	06a57	07 09	07a25	07a51	08 08	08a15	08 41	08a50	09a15	09 21	09a53	10 07	10 39	10a51	11 21	11a50
2¾	Montpelier	d	05 22	05 56			06 39		07 13			08 11		08 44			09 24		10 11	10 42		11 24	
3¼	Redland	d	05 24	05 58			06 41		07 15			08 13		08 46			09 26		10 13	10 44		11 26	
4	Clifton Down	d	05 27	06 01			06 44		07 17			08 16		08 50			09 29		10 17	10 48		11 29	
6	Sea Mills	d	05 32	06 05			06 49					08 21		08 55			09 33		10 22	10 53		11 33	
7¼	Shirehampton	d	05 36	06 09			06 53		07 23			08 25		08 59			09 37		10 26	10 57		11 37	
9	Avonmouth	d	05 40	06a12			06 57		07 27			08a28		09a02			09 41		10a29	11a00		11 40	
10	St Andrews Road	d	05 43				07 00		07 31								09 44						
13½	**Severn Beach**	a	05 50				07 07		07 38								09 51					11 49	

		GW	GW	GW	GW	GW	GW	GW	GW	GW	GW	GW	GW	GW	GW	GW	GW	GW	GW	GW	GW	GW	GW
Bristol Temple Meads	d	12 03	12 34	12 45	13 16	13 45	14 03	14 34	14 45	15 15	15 45	16 03	16 15	16 35	16 45	17 09	17 13	17 46	18 03	18 22	18 46	19 21	19 33
Lawrence Hill	d		12 37	12 47	13 19	13 47		14 37	14 47	15 18	15 47	16 06	16 18	16 38	16 49	17 12	17 16	17 49	18 06	18 25	18 49	19 24	19 36
Stapleton Road	d	12 07	12 39	12a50	13 21	13a50	14 07	14 39	14a49	15 20	15a50	16 08	16a20	16 40	16a51	17a14	17 19	17a51	18 09	18a27	18 52	19a26	19 38
Montpelier	d	12 10	12 42		13 24		14 10	14 42		15 24		16 12		16 43			17 23		18 12		18 57		19 42
Redland	d	12 12	12 44		13 26		14 12	14 44		15 26		16 14		16 45			17 25		18 14		18 59		19 44
Clifton Down	d	12 17	12 48		13 29		14 17	14 48		15 29		16 17		16 48			17 28		18 17		19 10		19 47
Sea Mills	d	12 22	12 53		13 33		14 22	14 53		15 33		16 22		16 53			17 33		18 22		19 14		19 51
Shirehampton	d	12 26	12 57		13 37		14 26	14 57		15 37		16 26		16 57			17 37		18 26		19 18		19 55
Avonmouth	d	12a29	13a00		13 41		14a29	15a00		15 40		16a29		17a00			17 41		18 30		19a22		19a59
St Andrews Road	d				13 44												17 44		18 33				
Severn Beach	a				13 51					15 49							17 51		18 40				

		GW	GW	GW FO	GW FX	GW	GW
Bristol Temple Meads	d	19 45	20 34	21 19	21 21	21 37	22 20
Lawrence Hill	d	19 47	20 37	21 22	21 24	21 40	22 23
Stapleton Road	d	19a50	20 40	21a24	21a26	21 42	22 25
Montpelier	d		20 44			21 45	22 28
Redland	d		20 46			21 47	22 30
Clifton Down	d		20 49			21 53	22 33
Sea Mills	d		20 54			21 57	22 37
Shirehampton	d		20 58			22 01	22 41
Avonmouth	d		21 02			22a05	22 44
St Andrews Road	d		21 05				
Severn Beach	a		21 12				22 53

Saturdays

26 May to 8 December

		GW	GW	GW	GW	GW	GW	GW	GW	GW	GW	GW	GW	GW	GW	GW	GW	GW	GW	GW	GW	GW	GW
Bristol Temple Meads	d	06 03	06 33	06 51	07 16	07 47	08 03	08 34	08 45	09 16	09 45	10 03	10 34	10 45	11 16	11 47	12 03	12 36	12 45	13 16	13 45	14 03	14 34
Lawrence Hill	d		06 36	06 54	07 19	07 50	08 06	08 37	08 48	09 19	09 48		10 37	10 48	11 19	11 50		12 39	12 48	13 19	13 48		14 37
Stapleton Road	d	06 06	06 38	06a56	07 21	07a52	08 08	08 39	08a50	09 21	09a50	10 07	10 39	10a50	11 21	11a52	12 07	12 41	12a50	13 21	13a50	14 07	14 39
Montpelier	d	06 10	06 41		07 24		08 11	08 42		09 24		10 10	10 42		11 24		12 10	12 44		13 24		14 10	14 42
Redland	d	06 12	06 43		07 26		08 13	08 44		09 26		10 12	10 44		11 26		12 12	12 46		13 26		14 12	14 44
Clifton Down	d	06 15	06 47		07 29		08 16	08 48		09 29		10 17	10 48		11 29		12 17	12 50		13 29		14 17	14 48
Sea Mills	d	06 19	06 51		07 33		08 21	08 52		09 33		10 21	10 52		11 33		12 21	12 54		13 33		14 21	14 52
Shirehampton	d	06 22	06 55		07 37		08 25	08 56		09 37		10 25	10 56		11 37		12 25	12 58		13 37		14 25	14 56
Avonmouth	d	06a29	07a01		07 41		08a31	09a02		09 41		10a31	11a02		11 41		12a31	13a04		13 41		14a31	15a02
St Andrews Road	d				07 44					09 44					11 44					13 44			
Severn Beach	a				07 53					09 53					11 53					13 53			

		GW	GW	GW	GW	GW	GW	GW	GW	GW	GW	GW	GW	GW	GW	GW
Bristol Temple Meads	d	14 45	15 16	15 45	16 03	16 34	16 45	17 16	17 45	18 03	18 45	19 03	19 45	20 34	21 40	22 16
Lawrence Hill	d	14 48	15 19	15 48	16 06	16 37	16 48	17 19	17 48	18 06	18 48	19 06	19 48	20 37	21 43	22 19
Stapleton Road	d	14a50	15 21	15a50	16 08	16 39	16a50	17 21	17a50	18 08	18a50	19 08	19a50	20 39	21 45	22 21
Montpelier	d		15 24		16 11	16 42		17 24		18 11		19 11		20 42	21 48	22 24
Redland	d		15 26		16 13	16 44		17 26		18 13		19 13		20 44	21 50	22 26
Clifton Down	d		15 29		16 17	16 48		17 29		18 17		19 17		20 48	21 54	22 29
Sea Mills	d		15 33		16 21	16 52		17 33		18 21		19 21		20 52	21 58	22 33
Shirehampton	d		15 37		16 25	16 56		17 37		18 25		19 24		20 56	22 01	22 37
Avonmouth	d		15 41		16a31	17a02		17 41		18 29		19 28		21 00	22a08	22 41
St Andrews Road	d		15 44					17 44		18 32		19 32		21 03		22 44
Severn Beach	a		15 53					17 53		18 40		19 40		21 11		22 53

Sundays

20 May to 9 September

		GW	GW	GW ◇	GW	GW	GW	GW	GW	GW	GW	GW	GW	GW
Bristol Temple Meads	d	09 01	10 23	11 23	12 23	13 23	14 23	15 23	16 23	16 53	17 53	18 50	19 53	20 53
Lawrence Hill	d	09 04	10 26	11 26	12 26	13 26	14 26	15 26	16 26	16 56	17 56	18 53	19 56	20 56
Stapleton Road	d	09 06	10 28	11 28	12 28	13 28	14 28	15 28	16 28	16 58	17 58	18 55	19 58	20 58
Montpelier	d	09 09	10 31	11 31	12 31	13 31	14 31	15 31	16 31	17 02	18 01	18 59	20 01	21 01
Redland	d	09 11	10 33	11 33	12 33	13 33	14 33	15 33	16 33	17 04	18 03	19 01	20 03	21 03
Clifton Down	d	09 14	10 36	11 36	12 36	13 36	14 36	15 36	16 36	17 06	18 06	19 06	20 06	21a06
Sea Mills	d	09 18	10 40	11 40	12 40	13 40	14 40	15 40	16 40	17 10	18 10	19 10	20 10	
Shirehampton	d	09 22	10 44	11 44	12 44	13 44	14 44	15 44	16 44	17 14	18 14	19 14	20 14	
Avonmouth	d	09 26	10 51	11 51	12 48	13 48	14 51	15 51	16 51	17 23	18 18	19 18	20a17	
St Andrews Road	d	09 29	10 55	11 55	12 51	13 52	14 55	15 55	16 55	17 27	18 22	19 21		
Severn Beach	a	09 36	11 02	12 02	12 58	13 59	15 02	16 02	17 02	17 34	18 29	19 29		

Table T133-F

Bristol - Avonmouth and Severn Beach

Sundays

16 September to 2 December

		GW	GW A	GW B		GW A	GW B	GW A	GW B	GW	GW A	GW B	GW B	GW B	GW B
Bristol Temple Meads	d	09 01	10 23	10 23	and at the same minutes past each hour until	15 23	15 23	16 23	16 23	16 53	17 53	17 53	18 50	19 53	20 53
Lawrence Hill	d	09 04	10 26	10 26		15 26	15 26	16 26	16 26	16 56	17 56	17 56	18 53	19 56	20 56
Stapleton Road	d	09 06	10 28	10 28		15 28	15 28	16 28	16 28	16 58	17 58	17 58	18 55	19 58	20 58
Montpelier	d	09 09	10 31	10 31		15 31	15 31	16 31	16 31	17 02	18 01	18 01	18 59	20 01	21 01
Redland	d	09 11	10 33	10 33		15 33	15 33	16 33	16 33	17 04	18 03	18 03	19 01	20 03	21 03
Clifton Down	d	09 14	10 36	10 36		15 36	15 36	16 36	16 36	17 06	18 06	18 06	19 06	20 06	21a07
Sea Mills	d	09 18	10 40	10 40		15 40	15 40	16 40	16 40	17 10	18 10	18 10	19 10	20 10	
Shirehampton	d	09 22	10 44	10 44		15 44	15 44	16 44	16 44	17 14	18 14	18 14	19 14	20 14	
Avonmouth	d	09 26	10a49	10 51		15a49	15 51	16a47	16 51	17 23	18a17	18 18	19 18	20a17	
St Andrews Road	d	09 29		10 55			15 55		16 55	17 27		18 22	19 21		
Severn Beach	a	09 36		11 02			16 02		17 02	17 34		18 30	19 29		

A from 28 October

B until 21 October

Table T133-R

Severn Beach and Avonmouth - Bristol

Sundays

16 September to 2 December

		GW	GW A	GW B	GW A	GW B	GW A	GW B	GW A	GW B	GW A	GW B	GW A	GW B	GW A	GW B	GW	GW	GW	GW B	GW B	GW B
Severn Beach	d	09 42		11 12		12 12		13 12		14 12		15 12		16 12		17 12	17 42		18 41	19 42		
St Andrews Road	d	09 48		11 18		12 18		13 18		14 18		15 18		16 18		17 18	17 48		18 47	19 48		
Avonmouth	d	09 52	10 52	11 22	11 52	12 22	12 52	13 22	13 52	14 22	14 52	15 22	15 52	16 22	16 52	17 22	17 52	18 22	18 52	19 52	20 22	
Shirehampton	d	09 56	10 55	11 26	11 55	12 26	12 55	13 26	13 55	14 26	14 55	15 26	15 55	16 26	16 55	17 26	17 56	18 25	18 56	19 55	20 25	
Sea Mills	d	10 00	10 59	11 30	11 59	12 30	12 59	13 30	13 59	14 30	14 59	15 30	15 59	16 30	16 59	17 30	18 00	18 29	19 00	19 59	20 29	
Clifton Down	d	10 05	11 04	11 42	12 04	12 41	13 04	13 37	14 04	14 37	15 04	15 37	16 04	16 37	17 07	17 35	18 06	18 37	19 06	20 05	20 34	21 23
Redland	d	10 07	11 07	11 44	12 07	12 43	13 07	13 39	14 07	14 39	15 07	15 39	16 07	16 39	17 10	17 37	18 09	18 40	19 09	20 08	20 37	21 25
Montpelier	d	10 09	11 09	11 46	12 09	12 45	13 09	13 41	14 09	14 41	15 09	15 41	16 09	16 41	17 12	17 39	18 11	18 42	19 11	20 10	20 39	21 27
Stapleton Road	d	10 15	11 13	11 51	12 13	12 52	13 13	13 47	14 13	14 48	15 13	15 47	16 13	16 48	17 16	17 44	18 15	18 48	19 15	20 16	20 43	21 33
Lawrence Hill	d	10 17	11 15	11 53	12 15	12 54	13 15	13 49	14 15	14 50	15 15	15 49	16 15	16 50	17 18	17 46	18 17	18 50	19 17	20 18	20 45	21 35
Bristol Temple Meads	a	10 21	11 20	11 57	12 20	12 58	13 20	13 55	14 20	14 54	15 20	15 55	16 20	16 54	17 22	17 49	18 22	18 54	19 21	20 21	20 50	21 38

A from 28 October

B until 21 October

Table T133-R

Mondays to Fridays

21 May to 7 December

Severn Beach and Avonmouth - Bristol

Miles			GW MX	GW	GW	GW	GW	GW	GW	GW	GW	GW ◇	GW	GW	GW	GW ◇	GW	GW ◇	GW	GW	GW	GW	GW
0	**Severn Beach**	d		06 00				07 16	07 51						09 56					11 54			
3½	St Andrews Road	d		06 06				07 22	07 57											12 00			
4½	Avonmouth ■	d		06 12	06 29			07 26	08 01		08 36		09 15		10 04		10 34		11 15	12 04	12 34		13 15
6	Shirehampton	d		06 16	06 33			07 30	08 05		08 40		09 19		10 07		10 38		11 19	12 07	12 38		13 19
7½	Sea Mills	d		06 20	06 37			07 35	08 10		08 44		09 23		10 11		10 42		11 23	12 11	12 42		13 23
9½	Clifton Down	d		06 25	06 43			07 40	08 16		08 49		09 28		10 16		10 49		11 30	12 16	12 48		13 30
10¼	Redland	d		06 28	06 45			07 44	08 19		08 52		09 31		10 19		10 52		11 33	12 19	12 51		13 33
10¾	Montpelier	d		06 30	06 47			07 46	08 21		08 55		09 33		10 21		10 55		11 36	12 21	12 54		13 36
12	Stapleton Road	d	00 25	06 36	06 53	07 07	07 33	07 52	08 26	08 54	09 01	09 29	09 39	09 53	10 25	10 32	11 01	11 28	11 40	12 25	13 01	13 31	13 42
12½	Lawrence Hill	d	00 27	06 38	06 55	07 09	07 35	07 54	08 28	08 56	09 04	09 31	09 41			10 34	11 03	11 30	11 42		13 03	13 33	13 44
13½	**Bristol Temple Meads** ■	a	00 33	06 41	06 58	07 13	07 40	07 58	08 32	09 00	09 08	09 35	09 47	10 01	10 32	10 39	11 08	11 34	11 49	12 32	13 06	13 36	13 50

		GW	GW ◇	GW	GW	GW	GW	GW ◇	GW	GW	GW ◇	GW	GW	GW	GW	GW	GW	GW	GW	GW	GW	GW
Severn Beach	d	13 56					15 54								17 54		18 45					21 29
St Andrews Road	d						16 00								18 00		18 51					21 35
Avonmouth ■	d	14 04		14 34		15 15	16 04			16 34		17 14			18 04		18 55		19 32		20 03	21 39
Shirehampton	d	14 07		14 38		15 19	16 07			16 38		17 18			18 07		18 59		19 36		20 07	21 43
Sea Mills	d	14 11		14 42		15 23	16 11			16 42		17 22			18 11		19 04		19 40		20 11	21 47
Clifton Down	d	14 16		14 48		15 31	16 16			16 47		17 29			18 16		19 11		19 46		20 16	21 52
Redland	d	14 19		14 51		15 34	16 19			16 50		17 32			18 19		19 14		19 48		20 19	21 54
Montpelier	d	14 21		14 54		15 36	16 21			16 53		17 35			18 22		19 16		19 50		20 22	21 56
Stapleton Road	d	14 26	14 32	15 00	15 30	15 42	16 26	16 33	16 55	16 59	17 29	17 41	17 54	18 20	18 28	18 33	19 22	19 29	19 56	20 21	20 28	22 02
Lawrence Hill	d		14 34	15 02	15 31	15 45		16 35	16 57	17 01	17 31	17 44	17 56		18 30	18 35	19 25	19 31	19 58	20 23	20 30	22 04
Bristol Temple Meads ■	a	14 32	14 39	15 07	15 38	15 51	16 32	16 39	17 02	17 05	17 35	17 47	18 00	18 25	18 35	18 38	19 28	19 34	20 04	20 27	20 34	22 07

		GW	GW FO	GW FX	GW
Severn Beach	d				23 08
St Andrews Road	d				23 15
Avonmouth ■	d	22 19			23 18
Shirehampton	d	22 23			23 22
Sea Mills	d	22 27			23 26
Clifton Down	d	22 32			23 38
Redland	d	22 35			23 40
Montpelier	d	22 38			23 42
Stapleton Road	d	22 44	22 51	23 00	23 48
Lawrence Hill	d	22 47	22 54	23 03	23 50
Bristol Temple Meads ■	a	22 53	22 59	23 06	23 54

Saturdays

26 May to 8 December

		GW	GW	GW	GW	GW	GW ◇	GW	GW	GW	GW	GW ◇	GW	GW	GW	GW	GW	GW	GW ◇ A	GW ◇ B	GW	GW	GW
Severn Beach	d				07 54				09 54					11 54				13 54					
St Andrews Road	d				08 00				10 00					12 00				14 00					
Avonmouth ■	d		06 34	07 16	08 04	08 35		09 16	10 04		10 35		11 16	12 04	12 35		13 16	14 04			14 35		15 16
Shirehampton	d		06 37	07 19	08 07	08 38		09 19	10 07		10 38		11 19	12 07	12 38		13 19	14 07			14 38		15 19
Sea Mills	d		06 41	07 23	08 11	08 42		09 23	10 11		10 42		11 23	12 11	12 42		13 23	14 11			14 42		15 23
Clifton Down	d		06 46	07 31	08 16	08 47		09 30	10 16		10 48		11 32	12 16	12 49		13 31	14 16			14 48		15 31
Redland	d		06 49	07 33	08 19	08 50		09 32	10 19		10 51		11 34	12 19	12 52		13 34	14 19			14 51		15 34
Montpelier	d		06 51	07 35	08 21	08 52		09 34	10 21		10 53		11 36	12 21	12 54		13 36	14 21			14 53		15 36
Stapleton Road	d	00 25	06 55	07 40	08 25	08 56	09 27	09 39	10 25	10 31	10 57	11 29	11 40	12 25	12 58	13 28	13 40	14 25	14 30	14 30	14 58	15 28	15 40
Lawrence Hill	d	00 27	06 57	07 42	08 27	08 58	09 29	09 41		10 33	10 59	11 31	11 42	12 27	13 00	13 30	13 42		14 32	14 32	15 00	15 30	15 42
Bristol Temple Meads ■	a	00 33	07 05	07 49	08 32	09 06	09 34	09 48	10 32	10 39	11 08	11 35	11 52	12 34	13 09	13 35	13 50	14 32	14 36	14 37	15 09	15 34	15 50

		GW	GW ◇	GW	GW ◇	GW	GW	GW	GW	GW	GW	GW	GW	GW	GW
Severn Beach	d	15 54					17 54			18 53	19 47		21 31		22 54
St Andrews Road	d	16 00					18 00			18 59	19 53		21 37		23 00
Avonmouth ■	d	16 04		16 35		17 16	18 04			19 03	19 57		21 41	22 16	23 04
Shirehampton	d	16 07		16 38		17 19	18 07			19 07	20 00		21 45	22 19	23 07
Sea Mills	d	16 11		16 42		17 23	18 11			19 11	20 04		21 49	22 23	23 11
Clifton Down	d	16 16		16 48		17 31	18 16			19 16	20 09		21 54	22 31	23 16
Redland	d	16 19		16 50		17 33	18 19			19 19	20 12		21 56	22 34	23 19
Montpelier	d	16 21		16 52		17 35	18 21			19 21	20 14		21 58	22 36	23 21
Stapleton Road	d	16 25	16 33	16 56	17 29	17 40	18 25	18 34	19 19	19 25	20 18	20 24	22 02	22 40	23 25
Lawrence Hill	d		16 35	16 58	17 31	17 42	18 27	18 36	19 21	19 27	20 20	20 26	22 04	22 42	23 27
Bristol Temple Meads ■	a	16 32	16 39	17 07	17 36	17 49	18 35	18 39	19 26	19 37	20 26	20 30	22 10	22 50	23 33

Sundays

20 May to 9 September

		GW	GW	GW	GW	GW	GW	GW	GW	GW	GW	GW	GW	GW
Severn Beach	d	09 42	11 12	12 12	13 12	14 12	15 12	16 12	17 12	17 42	18 41	19 42		
St Andrews Road	d	09 48	11 18	12 18	13 18	14 18	15 18	16 18	17 18	17 48	18 47	19 48		
Avonmouth ■	d	09 52	11 22	12 22	13 22	14 22	15 22	16 22	17 22	17 52	18 52	19 52	20 22	
Shirehampton	d	09 56	11 26	12 26	13 26	14 26	15 26	16 26	17 26	17 56	18 56	19 55	20 25	
Sea Mills	d	10 00	11 30	12 30	13 30	14 30	15 30	16 30	17 30	18 00	19 00	19 59	20 29	
Clifton Down	d	10 05	11 42	12 41	13 37	14 37	15 37	16 37	17 35	18 06	19 06	20 05	20 34	21 23
Redland	d	10 07	11 44	12 43	13 39	14 39	15 39	16 39	17 37	18 09	19 09	20 08	20 37	21 25
Montpelier	d	10 09	11 46	12 45	13 41	14 41	15 41	16 41	17 39	18 11	19 11	20 10	20 39	21 27
Stapleton Road	d	10 15	11 51	12 52	13 46	14 48	15 46	16 48	17 44	18 15	19 15	20 16	20 43	21 33
Lawrence Hill	d	10 17	11 53	12 54	13 48	14 50	15 48	16 50	17 46	18 17	19 17	20 18	20 45	21 35
Bristol Temple Meads ■	a	10 21	11 57	12 58	13 54	14 54	15 54	16 54	17 49	18 22	19 21	20 21	20 50	21 38

A until 8 September
B from 15 September

Table T134-F

Mondays to Fridays

21 May to 7 December

Gloucester - Taunton

Miles			GW MX	GW MX ◇■ ⊡	GW MX	GW A	GW ◇ B	GW ■	XC ◇■	GW ◇	GW	GW	GW ◇ ⊼	GW	GW	XC ◇■	GW	XC ◇■ ⊼	GW ■ ⊼	GW	GW ◇	XC ◇■ ⊼	GW ◇
—	Cardiff Central ■	d											06 30			07 00			07 30				08 00
0	**Gloucester** ■	d										06 16		06 42			07 05				07 41		
13	Cam & Dursley	d										06 32		06 57			07 23				07 56		
28	Yate	d										06 45		07 12			07 38				08 10		
34	**Bristol Parkway** ■	a										06 54		07 22			07 48				08 20		
—		d								06 24		06 57		07 24			07 49	07 55		08 12	08 20	08 28	
35¼	Filton Abbey Wood	d			00 20					06 28		07 01	07 12	07 28		07 41	07 53		08 11	08 16	08 23		08 43
38¼	Stapleton Road	d			00 25							07 07		07 33									
38¾	Lawrence Hill	d			00 27							07 09		07 35									
39¾	**Bristol Temple Meads** ■	a			00 33					06 36		07 13	07 20	07 40		07 51	08 00	08 06	08 18	08 24	08 36	08 40	08 51
—		d				05 24	05 24	06 03	06 34	06 43	06 48	07 18			07 48			08 10		08 26		08 44	08 55
40¾	Bedminster	d									06 50				07 50					08 28			
41½	Parson Street	d									06 53				07 52					08 30			
47¾	Nailsea & Backwell	d						06 14			07 02	07 28			08 01					08 39			09 05
51¾	Yatton	d						06 21			07 07	07 33			08 07					08 45			09 10
55¾	Worle	d		00b02				06 27			07 12	07 39			08 13					08 51			09 16
58½	Weston Milton	d									07 18				08 18					08 56			
59¾	**Weston-super-Mare**	a		00b07		05 45	05 45	06 34		07 02	07 21	07 47			08 23					08 59			09 23
—		d		00b08		05 47	05 47			07 06		07 49			08 25					09 01			09 29
67¼	Highbridge & Burnham	d		00b19		05 57	05 57			07 17		08 00			08 36					09 11			09 40
73½	Bridgwater	d	00 02	00b26		06 05	06 05			07 25		08 08			08 44					09 19			09 48
85¼	**Taunton**	a	00s14	00b36		06 18	06 18		07 06	07 38		08 23			08 57			08 42		09 32		09 14	10 01

		GW	XC ◇■ ⊼	GW ◇■ ⊡	GW ◇ ⊼	GW	GW ◇	XC ◇■ ⊼	GW ◇ C	GW D	GW	XC ◇■ ⊼	GW E	GW ◇ ⊼	GW	GW ◇	XC ◇■ ⊼	GW	XC ◇■ ⊼	GW ◇ ⊼	GW	GW ◇	XC ◇■ ⊼
Cardiff Central ■	d				08 30				09 00	09 00				09 30				10 00		10 30			
Gloucester ■	d						08 41									09 44						10 41	
Cam & Dursley	d						08 56									09 59						10 56	
Yate	d						09 10									10 13						11 09	
Bristol Parkway ■	a						09 19									10 22						11 18	
	d	08 45	08 57			09 12	09 19	09 27			09 41	09 57			10 12	10 22	10 32		10 58		11 12	11 19	11 32
Filton Abbey Wood	d	08 49			09 09	09 16	09 23		09 43	09 43	09 48			10 09	10 16	10 25		10 42		11 10	11 16	11 22	
Stapleton Road	d	08 54					09 29				09 53					10 32						11 28	
Lawrence Hill	d	08 56					09 31									10 34						11 30	
Bristol Temple Meads ■	a	09 00	09 11		09 19	09 24	09 35	09 39	09 54	09 54	10 01	10 08		10 19	10 24	10 39	10 43	10 52	11 10	11 19	11 24	11 34	11 42
	d			09 12		09 26		09 44	09 55	09 55			10 19		10 26		10 45	10 54	11 15		11 26		11 44
Bedminster	d					09 28									10 28						11 28		
Parson Street	d					09 30									10 30						11 30		
Nailsea & Backwell	d					09 39			10 05	10 05					10 39			11 04			11 39		
Yatton	d					09 45			10 11	10 11					10 45			11 09			11 45		
Worle	d					09 51			10 17	10 17					10 51			11 15			11 51		
Weston Milton	d					09 56									10 56						11 56		
Weston-super-Mare	a					10 01			10 22	10 22			10 37		11 00			11 21	11 32		12 00		
	d								10 24	10 24								11 22	11 36				
Highbridge & Burnham	d								10 35	10 35								11 33					
Bridgwater	d								10 43	10 43								11 41					
Taunton	a			09 44				10 15	10 59	10 59							11 16	11 55	11 58				12 14

		GW	XC ◇■ ⊼	GW ◇■ ⊡	GW ◇ ⊼	GW	GW ■	XC ◇■ ⊼	GW	XC ◇■ ⊼	GW ◇ ⊼	GW	GW	XC ◇■ F ⊼	XC ◇■ G ⊼	GW ◇	XC ◇■ ⊼	GW ◇ ⊼	GW	GW ◇	XC ◇■ H ⊼	XC ◇■ I ⊼
Cardiff Central ■	d	11 00			11 30				12 00		12 30					13 00		13 30				
Gloucester ■	d						11 47						12 42							13 46		
Cam & Dursley	d						12 00						12 56							14 00		
Yate	d						12 14						13 10							14 14		
Bristol Parkway ■	a						12 23						13 18							14 22		
	d		11 56			12 12	12 23	12 30		12 59		13 12	13 19	13 31	13 32		13 58		14 12	14 23	14 31	14 31
Filton Abbey Wood	d	11 42			12 09	12 16	12 26		12 42		13 09	13 16	13 25			13 43		14 09	14 16	14 27		
Stapleton Road	d												13 31							14 32		
Lawrence Hill	d												13 33							14 34		
Bristol Temple Meads ■	a	11 51	12 05		12 18	12 24	12 35	12 42	12 51	13 10	13 19	13 24	13 36	13 41	13 42	13 53	14 08	14 18	14 24	14 39	14 42	14 43
	d	11 53		12 14		12 26		12 45	12 53			13 26		13 45	13 45	13 58			14 26		14 45	14 45
Bedminster	d					12 29						13 29							14 28			
Parson Street	d					12 31						13 31							14 30			
Nailsea & Backwell	d	12 03				12 39			13 03			13 39				14 08			14 39			
Yatton	d	12 08				12 45			13 08			13 45				14 13			14 45			
Worle	d	12 14				12 51			13 14			13 51				14 19			14 51			
Weston Milton	d					12 56						13 56							14 56			
Weston-super-Mare	a	12 20		12 33		13 00			13 21			14 00				14 25			15 00			
	d	12 21							13 23							14 26						
Highbridge & Burnham	d	12 32							13 34							14 37						
Bridgwater	d	12 40							13 42							14 45						
Taunton	a	12 53						13 16	13 55					14 15	14 16	14 58					15 16	15 16

A from 2 July until 31 August
B until 29 June, from 3 September
C from 2 July
D until 29 June
E until 7 September
F until 20 July, from 8 October
G from 23 July until 5 October
H from 23 July
I until 20 July
b Stops to set down only, stops on request

For connections from London Paddington refer to Table T125

For full services to Brighton, Portsmouth Harbour, Westbury and Weymouth refer to Table T123

Table T134-F

Gloucester - Taunton

Mondays to Fridays
21 May to 7 December

		GW	XC	GW	GW	GW	XC	GW	GW	XC	GW	GW	GW	GW	XC	GW	GW	XC	GW	GW	GW	GW	XC
			◇1 ⌶	◇ ⌶			◇1 ⌶			◇1 ⌶	◇1 ⊒	◇ ⌶		◇	◇1 ⌶			◇1 A ⌶	◇1 ⊒	■ ⌶		◇	◇1 ⌶
Cardiff Central 7	d	14 00		14 30				15 00				15 30				16 00				16 30			
Gloucester 7	d					14 41								15 46								16 40	
Cam & Dursley	d					14 56								16 00								16 56	
Yate	d					15 10								16 14								17 10	
Bristol Parkway 7	a					15 20								16 23								17 19	
	d		14 58		15 12	15 20	15 31		15 54	15 58			16 12	16 24	16 31		16 46	16 57			17 12	17 20	17 26
Filton Abbey Wood	d	14 42		15 09	15 16	15 23		15 42	15a57			16 09	16 16	16 27		16 43	16 50			17 11	17 16	17 23	
Stapleton Road	d					15 30								16 33			16 55					17 29	
Lawrence Hill	d					15 31								16 35			16 57					17 31	
Bristol Temple Meads 10	a	14 51	15 10	15 18	15 24	15 38	15 41	15 51		16 11		16 19	16 24	16 39	16 43	16 52	17 02	17 10		17 19	17 24	17 35	17 40
	d	14 53	15 13		15 26		15 44	15 53			16 17		16 26		16 45	16 54		17 13	17 17		17 26		17 44
Bedminster	d				15 28			15 57					16 28			16 57					17 29		
Parson Street	d				15 30			15 59					16 30			17 00					17 32		
Nailsea & Backwell	d	15 03			15 39			16 07			16 29		16 39			17 08			17 29		17 40		
Yatton	d	15 08			15 45			16 12			16 36		16 45			17 14			17 36		17 46		
Worle	d	15 14			15 51			16 18			16 44		16 51			17 20			17 43		17 52		
Weston Milton	d				15 56			16 22					16 56			17 24					17 57		
Weston-super-Mare	a	15 22			16 00			16 26			16 50		17 00			17 27			17 50		18 01		
	d	15 29						16 27								17 28							
Highbridge & Burnham	d	15 39						16 38								17 39							
Bridgwater	d	15 47						16 46								17 47							
Taunton	a	16 02	15 44				16 14	16 59							17 16	18 01		17 44					18 15

		GW	GW	XC	GW	GW	GW	GW	XC	GW	XC	GW	GW	GW	XC	GW	XC	GW	GW	GW	GW	XC
				◇1 ⌶	■ ⌶	■ 1 ⊒			◇1 ⌶		◇1 ⌶	■ 1 ⊒	◇ ⌶		◇1 B ⌶		◇1 ⌶	◇	■ 1 ⊒			◇1 A ⌶
Cardiff Central 7	d	17 00			17 30					18 00			18 30			19 00		19 30				
Gloucester 7	d							17 46						18 42	19 06						19 45	
Cam & Dursley	d							18 00						18 56							20 00	
Yate	d							18 14						19 10							20 15	
Bristol Parkway 7	a							18 23						19 19	19 31						20 26	
	d		17 44	17 57			18 12	18 23	18 30		18 57			19 19	19 33		19 57			20 11	20 27	20 32
Filton Abbey Wood	d	17 43	17 49		18 10		18 16	18 27		18 47			19 10	19 24		19 44		20 09		20 15	20 30	
Stapleton Road	d		17 54				18 20	18 33						19 29						20 21		
Lawrence Hill	d		17 56					18 35						19 31						20 23		
Bristol Temple Meads 10	a	17 53	18 00	18 07	18 19		18 25	18 38	18 42	18 54	19 06		19 18	19 34	19 43	19 53	20 09	20 18		20 27	20 38	20 42
	d	17 55				18 20	18 27		18 45	18 56		19 17			19 46	19 55			20 19			20 49
Bedminster	d	17 58					18 30			18 59						19 57						
Parson Street	d	18 01					18 32			19 01						19 59						
Nailsea & Backwell	d	18 09				18 32	18 40			19 09		19 29				20 08			20 30			
Yatton	d	18 15				18 39	18 46			19 15		19 36				20 13			20 37			
Worle	d	18 21				18 46	18 52			19 21		19 43				20 19			20 45			
Weston Milton	d	18 25					18 57			19 25		19 49				20 23			20 50			
Weston-super-Mare	a	18 29				18 52	19 00			19 28		19 52				20 27			20 53			
	d	18 30				19 00				19 30		20 02				20 29						
Highbridge & Burnham	d	18 41				19 11				19 40		20 13				20 39						
Bridgwater	d	18 49				19 19				19 48		20 20				20 47						
Taunton	a	19 03				19 30			19 15	20 02		20 31			20 16	21 01						21 19

		GW FX	GW	GW FO	XC	GW	GW	GW	XC	GW	GW	XC	GW	GW	XC	GW FO	GW	GW FX	GW	GW FO	GW	GW FX	XC
		■ 1 ⊒		■ 1 ⊒	◇1 A ⌶	◇	■ 1 ⊒		◇1		◇	◇1		1	◇1						◇1 ⊒		◇1 C
Cardiff Central 7	d		20 00			20 30				21 00			21 30			22 04		22 04		22 36		22 36	
Gloucester 7	d							20 39						21 35	22 06				22 32				
Cam & Dursley	d							20 54						21 49									
Yate	d							21 09						22 01									
Bristol Parkway 7	a							21 17						22 10	22 33				23 04				
	d	20 37		20 39	20 56			21 19	21 26			22 03		22 11	22 34				23 04				23 23
Filton Abbey Wood	d		20 44			21 08		21 23		21 43			22 11	22 17		22 45		22 54		23 17		23 26	
Stapleton Road	d															22 51		23 00					
Lawrence Hill	d															22 54		23 03					
Bristol Temple Meads 10	a	20 48	20 53	20 59	21 05	21 17		21 31	21 36	21 51		22 14	22 21	22 24	22 43	22 59		23 06	23 14	23 26		23 38	23 41
	d		20 55		21 13		21 18		21 44		21 54						23 06				23 37		
Bedminster	d		20 58								21 57						23 10						
Parson Street	d		21 00								22 00						23 12						
Nailsea & Backwell	d		21 08				21 29				22 09						23 20				23b48		
Yatton	d		21 13				21 35				22 13						23 26				23b55		
Worle	d		21 19				21 42				22 19						23 32				00b02		
Weston Milton	d		21 23								22 23						23 37						
Weston-super-Mare	a		21 27				21 48				22 28						23 40				00b07		
	d		21 35								22 29						23 42				00b08		
Highbridge & Burnham	d		21 45								22 40						23 54				00b19		
Bridgwater	d		21 53								22 48						00 02				00b26		
Taunton	a		22 10		21 43				22 15		23 00						00s14				00b36		

A ⌶ to Bristol Temple Meads
B until 11 October, FX from 15 October
C until 20 July, from 8 October
b Stops to set down only, stops on request

For connections from London Paddington refer to Table T125

For full services to Brighton, Portsmouth Harbour, Westbury and Weymouth refer to Table T123

Table T134-F

Gloucester - Taunton

Mondays to Fridays
21 May to 7 December

		XC	GW
		◇1 A ⌶	
Cardiff Central 7	d		23 27
Gloucester 7	d		
Cam & Dursley	d		
Yate	d		
Bristol Parkway 7	a		
	d	23 23	
Filton Abbey Wood	d		00 20
Stapleton Road	d		00 25
Lawrence Hill	d		00 27
Bristol Temple Meads 10	a	23 41	00 33
	d		
Bedminster	d		
Parson Street	d		
Nailsea & Backwell	d		
Yatton	d		
Worle	d		
Weston Milton	d		
Weston-super-Mare	a		
	d		
Highbridge & Burnham	d		
Bridgwater	d		
Taunton	a		

Saturdays
26 May to 8 December

		GW	GW	GW	GW	GW	XC	GW	GW	GW	GW	GW	GW	GW	XC	GW	XC	GW	GW	GW	XC	GW	XC
			◇1 ⊒		◇	◇1 ⊒	◇1		◇ B	■ 1 C ⊒	◇ B			◇	◇1		◇1 ⌶	◇		◇	◇1 ⌶		◇1 ⌶
Cardiff Central 7	d					04 55								06 30	07 00			07 30				08 00	
Gloucester 7	d												06 21			07 02				07 41			
Cam & Dursley	d												06 36			07 16				07 56			
Yate	d												06 51			07 30				08 10			
Bristol Parkway 7	a					05 36							07 00			07 39				08 19			
	d					05 42							07 01			07 43	07 55		08 11	08 20	08 26		08 56
Filton Abbey Wood	d			00 20									07 04	07 10	07 41	07 46		08 10	08 15	08 23		08 46	
Stapleton Road	d			00 25																			
Lawrence Hill	d			00 27							←												
Bristol Temple Meads 10	a			00 33		05 53							07 13	07 18	07 52	07 55	08 05	08 18	08 23	08 34	08 38	08 54	09 07
	d				05 24		06 08	06 18	06 42	06 43	06 42	06 47	07 18			07 57	08 12		08 25		08 45	08 58	
Bedminster	d								→			06 49	07 21						08 27				
Parson Street	d											06 51	07 23						08 29				
Nailsea & Backwell	d							06 28				07 00	07 31			08 07			08 38			09 08	
Yatton	d							06 33				07 06	07 37			08 12			08 44			09 13	
Worle	d		00b02					06 39				07 12	07 43			08 18			08 50			09 19	
Weston Milton	d											07 17	07 47						08 55				
Weston-super-Mare	a		00b07		05 43			06 44		07 00	07 02	07 21	07 50			08 24			08 59			09 25	
	d		00b08		05 47			06 46		07 06	07 06		07 51									09 32	
Highbridge & Burnham	d		00b19		05 57			06 57					08 02									09 43	
Bridgwater	d	00 02	00b26		06 05			07 05					08 10									09 51	
Taunton	a	00s14	00b36		06 18		07 14	07 19		07 26	07 32		08 23				08 42				09 15	10 05	

		GW	GW	GW	GW	XC	GW	XC	XC	GW	GW	GW	XC	XC	GW	GW	XC	GW	GW	XC	GW	XC	XC
		■ 1 ⊒	◇		◇	◇1 ⌶		◇1 B ⌶	◇1 C ⌶	◇			◇1 D ⌶	◇1 E	◇1 C ⊒		◇1 ⌶	◇		◇1 F	◇	◇1 G ⌶	◇1 H
Cardiff Central 7	d		08 30				09 00			09 30						10 00		10 30					
Gloucester 7	d				08 41							09 48									10 41		
Cam & Dursley	d				08 56							10 01									10 56		
Yate	d				09 10							10 14									11 10		
Bristol Parkway 7	a				09 18							10 23									11 19		
	d			09 12	09 19	09 26		09 55	09 55		10 12	10 23	10 31	10 31			10 56		11 12	11 20	11 20	11 27	11 27
Filton Abbey Wood	d		09 10	09 16	09 22		09 43			10 10	10 16	10 27				10 43		11 10	11 16		11 23		
Stapleton Road	d				09 27							10 31									11 29		
Lawrence Hill	d				09 29							10 33									11 31		
Bristol Temple Meads 10	a		09 18	09 24	09 34	09 39	09 52	10 04	10 04	10 18	10 24	10 39	10 42	10 43		10 51	11 09	11 18	11 24	11 33	11 35	11 39	11 39
	d	09 17		09 26		09 44	09 55		10 20		10 26		10 45	10 45	10 48	10 55	11 12		11 26	11 37		11 44	11 44
Bedminster	d			09 28							10 28								11 28				
Parson Street	d			09 30							10 30								11 30				
Nailsea & Backwell	d			09 39			10 05				10 39					11 05			11 39				
Yatton	d			09 45			10 11				10 45					11 10			11 45				
Worle	d			09 51			10 17				10 51					11 16			11 51				
Weston Milton	d			09 56							10 56								11 56				
Weston-super-Mare	a			10 00			10 22				11 00				11 10	11 23	11 29		12 00				
	d						10 24									11 24	11 39						
Highbridge & Burnham	d						10 35									11 35							
Bridgwater	d						10 43									11 43							
Taunton	a	09 48				10 16	10 56		11 00				11 15	11 16		11 56	11 59			12 09		12 15	12 16

A from 23 July until 5 October
B from 15 September
C until 8 September
D until 21 July, from 13 October
E from 28 July until 6 October
F from 15 September until 6 October
G from 13 October
H from 28 July until 8 September
b Stops to set down only, stops on request

For connections from London Paddington refer to Table T125

For full services to Brighton, Portsmouth Harbour, Westbury and Weymouth refer to Table T123

Table T134-F

Gloucester - Taunton

Saturdays
26 May to 8 December

		XC ◇ A	GW	XC ◇	GW ◇	GW ◇ B	GW	GW	XC ◇	GW	XC ◇	GW ◇	GW	GW	XC ◇ C	XC ◇ D	GW	XC ◇	GW ◇ B	GW ◇	GW	GW ◇ B	GW ◇ E
Cardiff Central	d		11 00		11 30					12 00		12 30					13 00			13 30			
Gloucester	d							11 50						12 42								13 42	13 42
Cam & Dursley	d							12 03						12 56								13 56	13 56
Yate	d							12 16						13 10								14 11	14 11
Bristol Parkway	a							12 25						13 19								14 19	14 19
	d	11 27		11 54			12 12	12 25	12 31		12 55		13 12	13 19	13 25	13 25		13 55			14 12	14 20	14 20
Filton Abbey Wood	d		11 43		12 10		12 16	12 29		12 43		13 10	13 16	13 23			13 43			14 10	14 16	14 24	14 24
Stapleton Road	d													13 28								14 30	14 30
Lawrence Hill	d													13 30								14 32	14 32
Bristol Temple Meads	a	11 39	11 52	12 04	12 18		12 24	12 38	12 42	12 52	13 09	13 18	13 24	13 35	13 39	13 39	13 52	14 05		14 18	14 24	14 36	14 37
	d	11 44	11 53			12 20	12 26		12 44	12 53			13 26		13 45	13 45	13 54		14 18		14 26		
Bedminster	d						12 28						13 28								14 28		
Parson Street	d						12 30						13 30				13 58				14 31		
Nailsea & Backwell	d		12 03				12 39			13 03			13 39				14 06				14 40		
Yatton	d		12 09				12 45			13 08			13 45				14 11				14 45		
Worle	d		12 15				12 51			13 14			13 51				14 17				14 51		
Weston Milton	d						12 56						13 56								14 56		
Weston-super-Mare	a		12 20			12 38	13 00			13 20			14 00				14 23		14 36		15 01		
	d		12 22							13 23							14 24						
Highbridge & Burnham	d		12 33							13 34							14 35						
Bridgwater	d		12 41							13 42							14 43						
Taunton	a	12 16	12 55						13 16	13 57					14 16	14 16	14 57						

		XC ◇ B	XC ◇ E	GW	XC ◇	GW ◇	GW	GW	XC ◇ A	XC ◇ F	GW	XC ◇	GW ◇	GW ◇ B	GW	GW ◇	XC ◇	GW	XC ◇ E	XC ◇ B	GW	GW ◇ B
Cardiff Central	d			14 00		14 30					15 00		15 30					16 00			16 30	
Gloucester	d							14 41								15 47						
Cam & Dursley	d							14 56								16 02						
Yate	d							15 10								16 15						
Bristol Parkway	a							15 19								16 24						
	d	14 28	14 28		14 56		15 12	15 19	15 26	15 26		15 56			16 12	16 24	16 31		16 55	16 55		
Filton Abbey Wood	d			14 43		15 10	15 16	15 23			15 46		16 10		16 16	16 28		16 43			17 10	
Stapleton Road	d							15 28								16 33						
Lawrence Hill	d							15 30								16 35						
Bristol Temple Meads	a	14 40	14 41	14 52	15 09	15 18	15 24	15 34	15 38	15 38	15 54	16 07	16 18		16 24	16 39	16 43	16 51	17 07	17 08	17 18	
	d	14 44	14 44	14 53	15 12		15 26		15 43	15 44	15 55			16 20	16 26		16 45	16 54	17 10			17 21
Bedminster	d						15 28								16 28							
Parson Street	d						15 30								16 30							
Nailsea & Backwell	d			15 03			15 39				16 05				16 39			17 04				
Yatton	d			15 08			15 45				16 11				16 45			17 09				
Worle	d			15 14			15 51				16 17				16 51			17 15				
Weston Milton	d						15 56								16 56							
Weston-super-Mare	a			15 20			16 00				16 22			16 38	17 00			17 21				17 40
	d			15 28							16 23							17 25				
Highbridge & Burnham	d			15 38							16 34							17 36				
Bridgwater	d			15 46							16 42							17 44				
Taunton	a	15 15	15 16	16 00	15 42				16 14	16 14	16 56						17 17	17 58	17 40			

		GW	GW ◇	XC ◇	GW	XC ◇	GW ◇ G	GW ◇	GW	GW	XC ◇	GW	XC ◇ E	XC ◇ B	GW ◇	GW ◇	GW	GW	XC ◇	GW	XC ◇	GW ◇	GW ◇
Cardiff Central	d				17 00			17 30				18 00			18 30					19 00			19 30
Gloucester	d		16 42							17 47								18 41					
Cam & Dursley	d		16 56							18 02								18 56					
Yate	d		17 11							18 16								19 10					
Bristol Parkway	a		17 19							18 24								19 19					
	d	17 12	17 20	17 27		17 55			18 12	18 25	18 31		18 55	18 57			19 11	19 20	19 26		19 56		
Filton Abbey Wood	d	17 16	17 23		17 43			18 10	18 16	18 28		18 43			19 10		19 15	19 24		19 43			20 10
Stapleton Road	d		17 29							18 34							19 19						
Lawrence Hill	d		17 31							18 36							19 21						
Bristol Temple Meads	a	17 24	17 36	17 39	17 52	18 04		18 18	18 24	18 39	18 43	18 52	19 05	19 08	19 18		19 26	19 35	19 39	19 52	20 05		20 18
	d	17 25		17 44	17 54		18 18		18 26		18 44	18 53				19 19			19 44	19 53		20 18	
Bedminster	d	17 27							18 28														
Parson Street	d	17 30							18 30														
Nailsea & Backwell	d	17 40			18 04				18 39			19 03				19 30				20 03			
Yatton	d	17 46			18 09				18 45			19 09				19 37				20 09			
Worle	d	17 52			18 15				18 51			19 15				19 43				20 15			
Weston Milton	d	17 57							18 56			19 19								20 19			
Weston-super-Mare	a	18 03			18 21		18 36		19 00			19 22				19 50				20 22		20 36	
	d				18 22		18 42					19 24								20 23		20 40	
Highbridge & Burnham	d				18 33							19 35								20 34			
Bridgwater	d				18 41							19 43								20 42			
Taunton	a			18 15	18 56		19 05				19 15	19 57							20 15	20 57		21 01	

A until 21 July
B until 8 September
C until 21 July, from 13 October
D from 28 July until 6 October
E from 15 September
F from 28 July
G The Torbay Express

For connections from London Paddington refer to Table T125

For full services to Brighton, Portsmouth Harbour, Westbury and Weymouth refer to Table T123

Table T134-F

Gloucester - Taunton

Saturdays
26 May to 8 December

		GW	GW	XC ◇	GW	GW ◇	XC ◇ A	XC ◇ B	GW ◇	XC ◇	GW	GW	GW ◇	GW	XC ◇	GW ◇	XC ◇	GW
Cardiff Central	d				19 54				20 30			21 00						22 00
Gloucester	d		19 47											21 14			22 06	
Cam & Dursley	d		20 02											21 29				
Yate	d		20 16											21 43				
Bristol Parkway	a		20 25											21 52			22 32	
	d	20 15	20 26	20 31			20 55	20 55		21 25				21 52	22 00		22 33	
Filton Abbey Wood	d	20 19	20 29		20 40				21 08		21 36	21 43		21 56				22 52
Stapleton Road	d	20 24																
Lawrence Hill	d	20 26																
Bristol Temple Meads	a	20 30	20 40	20 42	20 49		21 04	21 04	21 17	21 34	23 43	21 52		22 07	22 12		22 42	23 00
	d			20 44		20 54		21 11		21 45			22 02			22 17		
Bedminster	d												22 05					
Parson Street	d												22 07					
Nailsea & Backwell	d					21 05							22 15			22s27		
Yatton	d					21 12							22 21			22s34		
Worle	d					21 18							22 27			22s40		
Weston Milton	d					21 23							22 31					
Weston-super-Mare	a					21 27							22 34			22s47		
	d					21 30							22 35					
Highbridge & Burnham	d					21 40							22 46			22s58		
Bridgwater	d					21 48							22 54			23s05		
Taunton	a			21 15		21 59		21 41		22 15			23 07			23 16		

Sundays
20 May to 2 December

		GW ◇	GW ◇	XC ◇	GW	GW ◇	XC ◇	GW ◇	GW ◇ C	GW ◇ D	GW	GW ◇ E	XC ◇	GW ◇ E	GW ◇ F	GW E	GW G	GW D	XC ◇	GW ◇	GW	XC ◇ H	XC ◇ I
Cardiff Central	d					08 10			09 13	09 08				10 08	10 08						11 08		
Gloucester	d															10 16	10 16	10 16					
Cam & Dursley	d															10 31	10 31	10 31					
Yate	d															10 45	10 45	10 45					
Bristol Parkway	a															10 54	10 54	10 54					
	d												10 38			10 55	10 55	10 55	11 41			12 39	12 40
Filton Abbey Wood	d					09 00			09 58	10 00				10 51	10 54	10 58	10 58	10 58			11 54		
Stapleton Road	d										10 15												
Lawrence Hill	d										10 17												
Bristol Temple Meads	a					09 08			10 10	10 12	10 21		10 48	11 00	11 03	11 06	11 07	11 07	11 51		12 03	12 51	12 50
	d	07 26	08 28	08 44	09 00		09 48	10 00			10 22	10 56	10 57			11 10	11 10	11 11	11 54	12 00		12 54	12 54
Bedminster	d										10 25					11 14	11 14	11 14				→	
Parson Street	d										10 27					11 17	11 17	11 17					
Nailsea & Backwell	d		08 38		09 08						10 35					11 23	11 23	11 23		12 11			
Yatton	d	07 39	08 43		09 15						10 40					11 28	11 28	11 28		12 17			
Worle	d		08 49		09 21						10 46					11 35	11 35	11 35		12 24			
Weston Milton	d																						
Weston-super-Mare	a	07 48	08 55		09 30						10 51	11 18				11 41	11 41	11 41		12 33			
	d	07 49	08 58								10 53					11 41	11 41	11 41					
Highbridge & Burnham	d		09 09								11 03					11 52	11 52	11 52					
Bridgwater	d	08 05	09 17								11 11					12 00	12 00	12 00					
Taunton	a	08 18	09 30	09 14			10 18	10 34			11 24		11 29			12 13	12 13	12 13	12 25				13 25

		XC ◇ H	GW ◇ E	GW ◇ F	GW	GW D	GW C	XC ◇	GW ◇ F	GW ◇ E	GW ◇ E	GW ◇ F	XC ◇	GW ◇	GW ◇	GW F	XC ◇	GW E	XC ◇	GW	GW ◇	XC ◇	GW
Cardiff Central	d		12 08	12 08							13 08	13 08			14 08						15 08		
Gloucester	d					12 18	12 18																15 13
Cam & Dursley	d					12 33	12 34																15 28
Yate	d					12 48	12 48																15 42
Bristol Parkway	a					12 56	12 57																15 52
	d					12 58	12 58	13 23					14 21				14 55		15 25			15 56	16 01
Filton Abbey Wood	d		12 51	12 54		13 01	13 01				13 52	13 54			14 54						15 54		16 04
Stapleton Road	d																						
Lawrence Hill	d	←																					
Bristol Temple Meads	a	12 51	13 01	13 04		13 09	13 09	13 32			14 04	14 03	14 31		15 03		15 08		15 34		16 04	16 09	16 13
	d	12 54			13 07			13 44	14 00	14 00			14 44	14 55		15 05		15 10	15 44	15 55		16 14	16 28
Bedminster	d															15 08		15 13		15 58			16 31
Parson Street	d															15 10		15 15		16 00			16 33
Nailsea & Backwell	d				13 16				14 12	14 12						15 18		15 23		16 08			16 41
Yatton	d				13 22				14 18	14 18						15 23		15 28		16 14			16 47
Worle	d				13 27				14 25	14 25						15 29		15 34		16 20			16 53
Weston Milton	d															15 34		15 39		16 24			16 58
Weston-super-Mare	a				13 33				14 32	14 37						15 38		15 43		16 27			17 01
	d				13 34															16 29			
Highbridge & Burnham	d				13 45															16 40			
Bridgwater	d				13 53															16 48			
Taunton	a	13 25			14 04			14 15					15 14	15 29					16 14	17 02		16 44	

A until 8 September
B from 15 September
C until 21 October
D from 28 October
E until 9 September
F from 16 September
G from 16 September until 21 October
H from 22 July until 7 October
I until 15 July, from 14 October

For connections from London Paddington refer to Table T125

For full services to Brighton, Portsmouth Harbour, Westbury and Weymouth refer to Table T123

Table T134-F

Sundays

20 May to 2 December

Gloucester - Taunton

		XC	GW	GW	GW	XC	GW	GW		GW	XC	GW	GW	XC	GW	GW	XC	GW		GW	GW	GW	GW	GW	XC
		◇1 ⊼	1 A ⊡	1 B ⊡	◇	◇1 ⊼	◇ A			◇ B	◇1 ⊼	◇		◇1 ⊼	◇ A	◇ B	◇1 ⊼	◇ A		◇ B	B	◇ B	◇ A	A	◇1 ⊼
Cardiff Central 7	d				16 08		16 35			16 35		17 08						17 40		17 40		18 08	18 10		
Gloucester 7	d												17 19												
Cam & Dursley	d												17 34												
Yate	d												17 48												
Bristol Parkway 7	a												17 56												
	d	16 21				16 56					17 22		17 57	18 03			18 22								18 56
Filton Abbey Wood	d				16 54		17 14			17 19		17 54	18 00					18 25		18 26		18 53	18 53		
Stapleton Road	d																				18 48				
Lawrence Hill	d																				18 50				
Bristol Temple Meads 10	a	16 32			17 03	17 08	17 23			17 28	17 31	18 02	18 09	18 14			18 35	18 39		18 39	18 54	19 04	19 04		19 08
	d	16 44	17 00	17 01				17 28			17 44				18 30	18 30	18 44				19 06			19 06	
Bedminster	d							17 31													19 09			19 09	
Parson Street	d							17 33							18 34	18 34					19 11			19 11	
Nailsea & Backwell	d		17 09	17 10				17 41							18 42	18 42					19 19			19 19	
Yatton	d		17 16	17 17				17 47							18 47	18 47					19 25			19 25	
Worle	d		17 22	17 23				17 53							18 53	18 53					19 31			19 31	
Weston Milton	d							17 58													19 34			19 34	
Weston-super-Mare	a		17 25	17 29				18 01							18 59	18 59					19 37			19 37	
	d		17 28	17 29											19 01	19 08					19 40			19 40	
Highbridge & Burnham	d		17 40	17 42											19 13	19 18					19 50			19 50	
Bridgwater	d		17 46	17 47											19 21	19 26					19 58			19 58	
Taunton	a	17 14	18 01	18 02							18 17				19 33	19 40	19 17				20 11			20 11	

		GW	XC	GW		GW	GW	XC	GW	GW	GW	XC	XC	GW		GW	XC	GW	XC	GW	GW	GW	XC	GW
		1 ⊡	◇1 ⊼	◇ A		◇ B		◇1 C ⊼	D	E	A	◇1 F ⊼	◇1 G	◇1 B ⊡		◇1 A ⊡	◇1	◇	◇1 C ⊼	◇1 ⊡	E	H	◇1	B
Cardiff Central 7	d			19 08		19 08												20 18						21 18
Gloucester 7	d						19 19														21 14	21 15		
Cam & Dursley	d						19 35														21 29	21 31		
Yate	d						19 49														21 43	21 45		
Bristol Parkway 7	a						19 57														21 53	21 53		
	d		19 23				19 58	20 05				20 22	20 22				20 57		21 22		21 54	21 54	21 59	
Filton Abbey Wood	d			19 54		19 54	20 01											21 04			21 57	21 58		22 09
Stapleton Road	d									20 16	20 16													
Lawrence Hill	d									20 18	20 18													
Bristol Temple Meads 10	a		19 32	20 05		20 07	20 10	20 14		20 21	20 21	20 31	20 31				21 06	21 13	21 30		22 06	22 06	22 10	22 19
	d	19 25	19 43					20 19	20 25	20 25	20 25	20 44	20 44	20 55		21 00			21 44	22 00				
Bedminster	d								20 28	20 28	20 28													
Parson Street	d								20 30	20 30	20 30													
Nailsea & Backwell	d	19 34							20 38	20 38	20 38			21 06		21 10				22 11				
Yatton	d	19 41							20 44	20 44	20 44			21 13		21 16				22 17				
Worle	d	19 46							20 50	20 50	20 50			21 19		21 23				22 24				
Weston Milton	d								20 54	20 54	20 54													
Weston-super-Mare	a	19 57						20 37	20 57	20 57	20 57			21 25		21 28				22 32				
	d							20 38	20 59	20 59	21 00			21 26		21 29								
Highbridge & Burnham	d								21 10	21 10	21 10													
Bridgwater	d								21 18	21 18	21 18													
Taunton	a		20 17					20 58	21 31	21 31	21 31	21 14	21 14	21 48		21 51			22 14					

		GW	XC	XC	GW	GW	XC	XC
		A	◇1	◇1			◇1 G ⊼	◇1 I
Cardiff Central 7	d	21 18				22 10		
Gloucester 7	d		22 08					
Cam & Dursley	d							
Yate	d							
Bristol Parkway 7	a		22 35					
	d		22 36	22 53			23 22	23 22
Filton Abbey Wood	d	22 09				22 59		
Stapleton Road	d							
Lawrence Hill	d							
Bristol Temple Meads 10	a	22 21	22 46	23 02		23 10	23 33	23 33
	d				23 10			
Bedminster	d				23 13			
Parson Street	d				23 15			
Nailsea & Backwell	d				23 23			
Yatton	d				23 28			
Worle	d				23 34			
Weston Milton	d				23 39			
Weston-super-Mare	a				23 43			
	d							
Highbridge & Burnham	d							
Bridgwater	d							
Taunton	a							

A until 9 September
B from 16 September
C ⊼ to Bristol Temple Meads
D from 28 October
E from 16 September until 21 October
F until 15 July, from 14 October. ⊼ to Bristol Temple Meads
G from 22 July until 7 October
H until 9 September, from 28 October
I until 15 July, from 14 October

For connections from London Paddington refer to Table T125

For full services to Brighton, Portsmouth Harbour, Westbury and Weymouth refer to Table T123

Table T134-R

Mondays to Fridays

21 May to 7 December

Taunton - Gloucester

Miles			GW MO	GW	XC MO	XC MX	GW	GW		GW	XC	GW	GW	XC	GW	GW	GW	GW		XC	GW	GW	GW	GW	XC
				◇1 ⊡	◇1	◇1					◇1 ⊼		1 ⊡	◇1 ⊼	◇1 ⊡		1 A ⊡			◇1 ⊼			◇	◇1 ⊡	◇1 ⊼
0	**Taunton**	d								05 12						06 02		06 34		06 51				06 57	
11¾	Bridgwater	d								05 24						06 14		06 46						07 07	
18	Highbridge & Burnham	d								05 32						06 21		06 54						07 15	
25¾	**Weston-super-Mare**	a								05 42						06 32		07 05						07 25	
—		d								05 46			06 20			06 36	06 48	07 08						07 26	
27	Weston Milton	d											06 26			06 39	06 54	07 11							
29½	Worle	d								05 51			06 33			06 43	06 59	07 15						07 34	
33½	Yatton	d								05 57			06 40			06 48	07 06	07 21						07 41	
37½	Nailsea & Backwell	d	00 06							06 03			06 47			06 54	07 13	07 27						07 48	
43¾	Parson Street	d	00 13							06 11						07 02		07 35							
44½	Bedminster	d	00 16							06 13						07 04		07 37				←			
45½	**Bristol Temple Meads 10**	a	00 20							06 18			06 57			07 08	07 24	07 41		07 26		07 41		07 58	
—		d		04 45	05 20	05 20	05 52	06 00		06 20	06 27	06 51		07 00	07 17	07 20		07 46		07 30	07 34	07 46	07 53		08 00
46½	Lawrence Hill	d						06 03		06 23		06 55				07 23		→				07 49			
47	Stapleton Road	d						06 05		06 26		06 57				07 25						07 51			
50	Filton Abbey Wood	d					06 02	06 11		06 31		07 03			07 26	07 31					07 44	07 58	08 01		
51¼	**Bristol Parkway 7**	a		04 54	05 30	05 30		06 16			06 37			07 08		07 35				07 38	07 48	08 03			08 08
—		d			05 38	05 38										07 39					07 49				
57½	Yate	d																			07 59				
72¼	Cam & Dursley	d																			08 13				
85¼	**Gloucester 7**	a																			08 30				
—	Cardiff Central 7	a			06 16	06 23	06 51			07 19		07 41			08 02	08 23							08 43		

		GW	GW	GW		GW	XC	XC	GW	GW	GW	XC	GW	GW		GW	XC	GW	GW	GW	GW	XC	GW	GW
		◇		◇1 ⊡			◇1 B	◇1 C ⊼			⊼	◇1 ⊼	◇				◇1 ⊼			◇ ⊼	◇1 ⊡	◇1 ⊼		
Taunton	d			07 12		07 35	07 51	07 51				08 12				08 36	08 51				09 07		09 16	09 35
Bridgwater	d			07 24		07 47										08 48							09 28	09 47
Highbridge & Burnham	d			07 32		07 55										08 56							09 36	09 54
Weston-super-Mare	a			07 42		08 05						08 34				09 09					09 27		09 46	10 05
	d		07 37	07 49		08 07						08 35		08 41		09 11					09 29		09 48	
Weston Milton	d		07 40	07 54		08 10								08 44		09 14								
Worle	d		07 44	07 59		08 16								08 48		09 19							09 54	
Yatton	d		07 49	08 06		08 22								08 54		09 25					09 40		10 04	
Nailsea & Backwell	d		07 55	08 13		08 28								09 01		09 31					09 47		10 10	
Parson Street	d		08 03			08 35								09 08		09 37								
Bedminster	d		08 05			08 38				←				09 11		09 40			←					
Bristol Temple Meads 10	a		08 09	08 25		08 42	08 27	08 27		08 42		08 55		09 15		09 44	09 26		09 44		09 57		10 21	
	d	08 10	08 24			08 45	08 30	08 30	08 41	08 45	08 54	09 00	09 10	09 21		09 48	09 30	09 41	09 48	09 55		10 00	10 24	
Lawrence Hill	d	08 13				→				08 48			09 13			→			09 51					
Stapleton Road	d	08 16								08 50			09 15						09 53					
Filton Abbey Wood	d	08 22	08 32						08 51	08 55	09 01		09 21	09 30				09 48	09 59	10 02			10 32	
Bristol Parkway 7	a	08 27					08 38	08 38	08 54	09 03		09 08	09 26				09 38	09 52	10 04			10 08		
	d								08 55									09 52						
Yate	d								09 04									10 02						
Cam & Dursley	d								09 17									10 16						
Gloucester 7	a								09 35									10 32						
Cardiff Central 7	a		09 26								09 42			10 14						10 43			11 22	

		XC	GW	GW	GW	XC	GW	XC	GW	GW		GW	GW	XC	GW	XC	GW	GW	GW	XC		GW	GW	XC	GW
		◇1 ⊼	◇		◇ ⊼	◇1 ⊼	◇	◇1 ⊼	◇			◇		◇1 ⊼		◇1 ⊼	◇		◇ ⊼	◇1 ⊼			◇1 ⊡	◇1 ⊼	◇
Taunton	d	09 51					10 11	10 51					11 04	11 17		11 51						12 04		12 51	
Bridgwater	d						10 23						11 16									12 18			
Highbridge & Burnham	d						10 31						11 24									12 26			
Weston-super-Mare	a						10 41						11 34									12 39			
	d			10 10			10 43			11 10			11 38					12 09				12 41	13 01		
Weston Milton	d			10 13						11 13								12 12							
Worle	d			10 17			10 48			11 17			11 44					12 16				12 46			
Yatton	d			10 23			10 54			11 23			11 50					12 22				12 52			
Nailsea & Backwell	d			10 29			11 00			11 29			11 56					12 28				12 58			
Parson Street	d			10 36						11 37								12 36							
Bedminster	d			10 39						11 40					←			12 39							
Bristol Temple Meads 10	a	10 25		10 42			11 11	11 24		11 43			12 04	11 52	12 04	12 24		12 42				13 10	13 21	13 24	
	d	10 30	10 41	10 45	10 54	11 00	11 21	11 30	11 41	11 45		11 54	12 21	12 00	12 21	12 30	12 41	12 45	12 54	13 00		13 21		13 30	13 41
Lawrence Hill	d			10 49						11 48			→					12 47							
Stapleton Road	d			10 52						11 50								12 50							
Filton Abbey Wood	d		10 48	10 57	11 02		11 30		11 48	11 56		12 01			12 30		12 48	12 55	13 01			13 30			13 48
Bristol Parkway 7	a	10 38	10 53	11 04		11 08		11 38	11 52	12 03				12 08		12 38	12 52	13 03		13 08				13 38	13 52
	d		10 53						11 52								12 52								13 52
Yate	d		11 03						12 02								13 01								14 02
Cam & Dursley	d		11 17						12 16								13 14								14 16
Gloucester 7	a		11 33						12 33								13 33								14 31
Cardiff Central 7	a				11 43		12 19					12 42			13 22				13 42			14 13			

A The Bristolian
B from 23 July until 5 October
C until 20 July, from 8 October

For connections to London Paddington refer to Table T125

For full services to Cardiff Central, Cheltenham Spa, Gloucester and Great Malvern refer to Table T123

Table T134-R

Taunton - Gloucester

Mondays to Fridays

21 May to 7 December

		GW		GW	GW	XC	GW	XC	GW	GW	GW	XC		GW	XC	GW	GW	GW	GW	GW	XC	GW		GW	XC
				◇ 🍴		◇1 🍴		◇1 🍴	◇		◇ 🍴	◇1 🍴		◇	◇1 🍴		◇		◇ 🍴		◇1 🍴				◇1 🍴
Taunton	d				13 08	13 22		13 51						14 11	14 51					14 57	15 15				15 51
Bridgwater	d				13 20									14 23						15 09					
Highbridge & Burnham	d				13 28									14 31						15 16				←	
Weston-super-Mare	a				13 38									14 42						15 27	15 37			15 27	
	d	13 10			13 41					14 10				14 45				15 10		15 44	15 39			15 44	
Weston Milton	d	13 13								14 13								15 13		→					
Worle	d	13 17			13 48					14 17				14 51				15 17						15 50	
Yatton	d	13 23			13 54					14 23				14 57				15 23						15 56	
Nailsea & Backwell	d	13 29			14 00					14 29				15 03				15 29						16 02	
Parson Street	d	13 37								14 36								15 36							
Bedminster	d	13 39					←			14 39								15 39							
Bristol Temple Meads 10	a	13 42			14 12	13 55	14 12	14 26		14 43				15 14	15 23			15 43			15 57			16 13	16 23
	d	13 45		13 54	14 21	14 00	14 21	14 30	14 41	14 45	14 54	15 00		15 21	15 30	15 33	15 41	15 45	15 54		16 00	16 15		16 24	16 30
Lawrence Hill	d	13 47			→					14 47								15 47				16 18			
Stapleton Road	d	13 50								14 50								15 50				16 20			
Filton Abbey Wood	d	13 55		14 01			14 32		14 48	14 55	15 01			15 30			15 48	15 55	16 01			16 26		16 32	
Bristol Parkway 7	a	14 03				14 08		14 39	14 52	15 03		15 08			15 39	15 44	15 52	16 04			16 08	16 34			16 38
	d								14 53								15 52								
Yate	d								15 03								16 02								
Cam & Dursley	d								15 17								16 16								
Gloucester 7	a								15 33								16 34								
Cardiff Central 7	a			14 41			15 26				15 42			16 15					16 41					17 27	

		GW	GW	GW	XC	GW	GW	XC		GW	GW	GW	GW	GW	XC	GW	XC	GW		GW	GW	GW	XC	GW	XC
				■ 🍴	◇1 🍴			◇1 🍴		◇1 ☕	◇		■ 🍴		◇1 🍴		◇1 🍴	◇1 ☕				■ 🍴	◇1 🍴		◇1 🍴
Taunton	d						16 07	16 51						17 06	17 22		17 50							18 08	18 52
Bridgwater	d						16 19							17 18										18 20	
Highbridge & Burnham	d						16 27							17 26										18 28	
Weston-super-Mare	a						16 37							17 37										18 39	
	d		16 10				16 39			17 10		17 15		17 38				18 08			18 15			18 40	
Weston Milton	d		16 13				16 42							17 41										18 43	
Worle	d		16 17				16 46					17 21		17 46							18 21			18 47	
Yatton	d		16 23				16 52					17 26		17 52							18 27			18 53	
Nailsea & Backwell	d		16 29				16 58					17 32		17 58							18 33			18 59	
Parson Street	d		16 37				17 06							18 06										19 07	
Bedminster	d		16 40				17 09							18 08		←								19 09	
Bristol Temple Meads 10	a		16 44				17 13	17 24		17 29		17 44		18 12	17 54	18 12	18 23	18 27			18 44			19 13	19 25
	d	16 41	16 45	16 55	17 00	17 09	17 21	17 30			17 41	17 46	17 54	18 22	18 00	18 22	18 30			18 36	18 46	18 54	19 00	19 21	19 30
Lawrence Hill	d		16 49			17 12						17 49		→		18 25					18 49			19 24	
Stapleton Road	d		16 51			17 15						17 52				18 27					18a51			19 26	
Filton Abbey Wood	d	16 48	16 57	17 03		17 24	17 28				17 48	17 57	18 02			18 33				18 43		19 01		19 32	
Bristol Parkway 7	a	16 52	17 04		17 08	17 29		17 39			17 52	18 04			18 08		18 38			18 47			19 08		19 39
	d	16 52									17 53									18 48					
Yate	d	17 01									18 01									18 57					
Cam & Dursley	d	17 14									18 14									19 11					
Gloucester 7	a	17 34									18 33									19 27					
Cardiff Central 7	a			17 43			18 13						18 42			19 23						19 42		20 18	

		GW	GW	GW		XC	XC	GW	XC	GW	GW	GW	GW	GW		GW	GW	GW	GW	XC	GW	GW	GW	GW	
													FO	FX				FO	FX					FO	
				◇ 🍴		◇1	◇1		◇1 A 🍴		◇	◇ 🍴					◇1 ☕	◇	◇	◇1	1	◇1 ☕		◇	
Taunton	d							19 17	19 51		20 10					20 35	21 15			21 19		21 28			
Bridgwater	d							19 29								20 47						21 39			
Highbridge & Burnham	d							19 36								20 55						21 47			
Weston-super-Mare	a							19 47								21 05						21 57			
	d		19 08					19 51								21 07					21 34	21 58			
Weston Milton	d		19 11													21 10					21 39				
Worle	d		19 15					19 56								21 14					21 44	22 05			
Yatton	d		19 21					20 02								21 19					21 51	22 12			
Nailsea & Backwell	d		19 27					20 08								21 25					21 58	22 18			
Parson Street	d		19 35													21 33									
Bedminster	d		19 37													21 35									
Bristol Temple Meads 10	a		19 40					20 20	20 25		20 54					21 39	21 47			21 52	22 11	22 29			
	d	19 41	19 45	19 54		20 00	20 15		20 30	20 41		20 54	21 19	21 21		21 41		21 54	21 54	22 00			22 42	22 54	
Lawrence Hill	d		19 47										21 22	21 24											
Stapleton Road	d		19 50										21 24	21 26											
Filton Abbey Wood	d	19 48	19 55	20 02			20 22			20 48		21 01	21 30	21 32		21 51		22 01	22 01				22 49	23 01	
Bristol Parkway 7	a	19 52	20 03			20 08			20 38	20 52						21 55				22 09			22 53		
	d	19 52				20 10				20 52						21 56							22 53		
Yate	d	20 02								21 01						22 05							23 02		
Cam & Dursley	d	20 16								21 14						22 19							23 15		
Gloucester 7	a	20 33				20 38				21 32						22 38							23 38		
Cardiff Central 7	a			20 47			21 03					21 44	22 13	22 14				22 43	22 56					23 49	

A 🍴 to Bristol Temple Meads

For connections to London Paddington refer to Table T125

For full services to Cardiff Central, Cheltenham Spa, Gloucester and Great Malvern refer to Table T123

Table T134-R

Taunton - Gloucester

Mondays to Fridays

21 May to 7 December

		GW	GW	GW
		FX		
		◇	◇	
Taunton	d		22 23	22 45
Bridgwater	d			22 57
Highbridge & Burnham	d			23 05
Weston-super-Mare	a		22 47	23 15
	d		22 49	23 17
Weston Milton	d			23 20
Worle	d			23 24
Yatton	d			23 30
Nailsea & Backwell	d			23 36
Parson Street	d			23 42
Bedminster	d			23 45
Bristol Temple Meads 10	a		23 13	23 51
	d	22 54		
Lawrence Hill	d			
Stapleton Road	d			
Filton Abbey Wood	d	23 01		
Bristol Parkway 7	a			
	d			
Yate	d			
Cam & Dursley	d			
Gloucester 7	a			
Cardiff Central 7	a	23 55		

Saturdays

26 May to 8 December

		XC	XC	GW	GW	GW	GW	XC	GW	GW		XC	XC	GW	GW	GW	GW	XC	GW	GW		XC	XC	GW	GW
		◇1 A	◇1 B 🍴		◇1		◇1 ☕	◇1 🍴				◇1 A	◇1 B 🍴			◇1 ☕		◇1 🍴				◇1 A	◇1 B 🍴		
Taunton	d			05 35						06 34		06 50	06 50			06 54				07 35		07 50	07 50		
Bridgwater	d			05 47						06 46		⌇	⌇			07 05				07 47		⌇	⌇		
Highbridge & Burnham	d			05 55						06 54		⌇	⌇			07 12				07 55		⌇	⌇		
Weston-super-Mare	a			06 05						07 04		⌇	⌇			07 22				08 06		⌇	⌇		
	d			06 06			06 23			07 08		⌇	⌇			07 24			07 37	08 07		⌇	⌇		
Weston Milton	d			06 09						07 11		⌇	⌇						07 40	08 10		⌇	⌇		
Worle	d			06 13			06 30			07 15		⌇	⌇			07 31			07 44	08 14		⌇	⌇		
Yatton	d			06 18			06 37			07 21		⌇	⌇			07 37			07 49	08 19		⌇	⌇		
Nailsea & Backwell	d			06 24			06 43			07 27		⌇	⌇			07 44			07 55	08 25		⌇	⌇		
Parson Street	d			06 32						07 34		⌇	⌇						08 03	08 33		⌇	⌇		
Bedminster	d			06 34						07 37		⌇	⌇		←				08 05	08 35		⌇	⌇		←
Bristol Temple Meads 10	a			06 40			06 54			07 43		07 22	07 22		07 43	07 54			08 10	08 39		08 24	08 24		08 39
	d	06 15	06 15		06 45	06 51		07 00	07 23	07 47		07 30	07 30	07 41	07 47		07 55	08 00	08 23	08 45		08 30	08 30	08 40	08 45
Lawrence Hill	d	⌇	⌇			06 54				→		⌇	⌇		07 50					→		⌇	⌇		08 48
Stapleton Road	d	⌇	⌇			06 56						⌇	⌇		07 52							⌇	⌇		08 50
Filton Abbey Wood	d	⌇	⌇		06 53	07 02			07 30			⌇	⌇	07 48	07 58		08 03		08 31			⌇	⌇	08 48	08 56
Bristol Parkway 7	a	06 23	06 23		06 58			07 08				07 38	07 38	07 52	08 04			08 08				08 38	08 38	08 52	09 04
	d	06 25	06 25		07 10									07 53										08 53	
Yate	d	⌇	⌇											08 02										09 02	
Cam & Dursley	d	⌇	⌇											08 16										09 14	
Gloucester 7	a	06 52	06 52											08 32										09 30	
Cardiff Central 7	a				07 47	07 45			08 17								08 42		09 23						

		GW	GW	XC	GW	XC		GW	GW	GW	XC	GW	XC	GW	GW	GW		XC	XC	GW	GW	GW	GW	XC	XC
		◇	◇1 ☕	◇1 🍴		◇1 🍴				◇	◇1 🍴		◇1 🍴	◇		■		◇1 C 🍴	◇1 D 🍴	D	C	◇1 E ☕	◇1 F ☕	◇1 D 🍴	◇1 C 🍴
Taunton	d		07 59	08 11		08 50						09 12	09 50					10 11		10 11	10 17	10 45	10 45	10 50	10 51
Bridgwater	d		08 09									09 24						⌇		10 23	10 29	⌇	⌇	⌇	⌇
Highbridge & Burnham	d		08 17									09 32						⌇		10 31	10 37	⌇	⌇	⌇	⌇
Weston-super-Mare	a		08 27									09 42						10 31		10 42	10 47	⌇	11 05	⌇	⌇
	d		08 29		08 40				09 10			09 44			10 10			10 33		10 43	10 48	⌇	11 07	⌇	⌇
Weston Milton	d								09 13						10 13			⌇		⌇	⌇	⌇	⌇	⌇	⌇
Worle	d				08 45				09 17			09 49			10 17			⌇		10 48	10 53	⌇	⌇	⌇	⌇
Yatton	d		08 40		08 51				09 23			09 55			10 23			⌇		10 54	10 59	⌇	⌇	⌇	⌇
Nailsea & Backwell	d		08 46		08 57				09 29			10 01			10 29			⌇		11 00	11 05	⌇	⌇	⌇	⌇
Parson Street	d								09 35						10 35			⌇		⌇	⌇	⌇	⌇	⌇	⌇
Bedminster	d								09 38						10 38			⌇		⌇	⌇	⌇	⌇	⌇	⌇
Bristol Temple Meads 10	a		08 56	08 49	09 08	09 25			09 43			10 12	10 25		10 43			10 51		11 11	11 16	11 20	11 26	11 24	11 25
	d	08 55		09 00	09 22	09 30		09 41	09 45	09 52	10 00	10 23	10 30	10 41	10 45	10 55		11 00	11 00	11 22	11 22			11 30	11 30
Lawrence Hill	d								09 48						10 48			⌇	⌇	⌇	⌇			⌇	⌇
Stapleton Road	d								09 50						10 50			⌇	⌇	⌇	⌇			⌇	⌇
Filton Abbey Wood	d	09 03			09 31			09 48	09 56	10 01		10 32		10 48	10 56	11 03		⌇	⌇	11 31	11 31			⌇	⌇
Bristol Parkway 7	a			09 08		09 38		09 52	10 04		10 08		10 38	10 52	11 04			11 08	11 08	⌇	⌇			11 38	11 38
	d							09 52						10 52						⌇	⌇				
Yate	d							10 02						11 02						⌇	⌇				
Cam & Dursley	d							10 15						11 16						⌇	⌇				
Gloucester 7	a							10 33						11 32						⌇	⌇				
Cardiff Central 7	a	09 42			10 18					10 40		11 19				11 42				12 17	12 17				

A from 28 July until 6 October
B until 21 July, from 13 October
C until 8 September
D from 15 September
E until 8 September. The Torbay Express
F from 15 September. The Torbay Express

For connections to London Paddington refer to Table T125

For full services to Cardiff Central, Cheltenham Spa, Gloucester and Great Malvern refer to Table T123

Table T134-R

Taunton - Gloucester

Saturdays

26 May to 8 December

		GW ◇	GW	GW ◇■ A ⊏	GW ◇	GW	XC ◇■ ⍑	GW		XC ◇■ ⍑	GW ◇	GW	GW ◇	XC ◇■ ⍑	GW B	GW A	GW ◇■ A ⊏	XC ◇■ ⍑		GW ◇	GW	GW ◇	XC ◇■ A ⍑	GW	XC ◇■ B ⍑
Taunton	d					11 04	11 17			11 50					12 07	12 07		12 50						13 07	13 15
Bridgwater	d					11 16									12 19	12 19								13 19	
Highbridge & Burnham	d					11 24									12 27	12 27								13 27	
Weston-super-Mare	a					11 34									12 38	12 41								13 38	
	d		11 13	11 30		11 40						12 10			12 39	12 43	13 00				13 10			13 41	
Weston Milton	d		11 16									12 13									13 13				
Worle	d		11 20			11 45						12 17			12 45	12 48					13 17			13 47	
Yatton	d		11 25			11 51						12 23			12 51	12 54					13 23			13 53	
Nailsea & Backwell	d		11 31			11 57						12 29			12 57	13 00					13 29			13 59	
Parson Street	d		11 38									12 35									13 36				
Bedminster	d		11 40					←				12 38									13 38				
Bristol Temple Meads 10	a		11 45	11 49		12 09	11 53	12 09		12 25		12 43			13 09	13 12	13 19	13 23			13 43			14 11	13 55
	d	11 41	11 47		11 54	12 21	12 00	12 21		12 30	12 41	12 45	12 53	13 00	13 20	13 20		13 30		13 41	13 45	13 54	14 00	14 21	14 00
Lawrence Hill	d		11 50			→						12 48									13 48			→	
Stapleton Road	d		11 52									12 50									13 51				
Filton Abbey Wood	d	11 48	11 58		12 02			12 31			12 50	12 56	13 01		13 30	13 30				13 48	13 57	14 01			
Bristol Parkway 7	a	11 52	12 04				12 08			12 38	12 54	13 04		13 08				13 38		13 52	14 04		14 08		14 08
	d	11 52									12 55									13 52					
Yate	d	12 02									13 04									14 02					
Cam & Dursley	d	12 16									13 16									14 15					
Gloucester 7	a	12 31									13 32									14 34					
Cardiff Central 7	a				12 44			13 18					13 42		14 17	14 17						14 41			

		GW	XC ◇■ ⍑	GW ◇		GW	GW ◇	XC ◇■ ⍑	GW B	GW A	GW ◇■ A ⊏	XC ◇■ C ⍑	XC ◇■ D ⍑	GW ◇		GW	GW ◇	XC ◇■ ⍑	GW	XC ◇■ ⍑	GW	GW	GW ◇	XC ◇■ ⍑	
Taunton	d		13 50						14 07	14 07		14 52	14 52					15 03	15 07	15 50					
Bridgwater	d								14 19	14 19									15 19						
Highbridge & Burnham	d								14 27	14 27									15 27						
Weston-super-Mare	a								14 38	14 38								15 23	15 38						
	d					14 10			14 39	14 40	15 00					15 10		15 29	15 39			16 10			
Weston Milton	d					14 13										15 13						16 13			
Worle	d					14 17			14 45	14 45						15 17			15 45			16 17			
Yatton	d					14 23			14 51	14 51						15 23			15 51			16 23			
Nailsea & Backwell	d					14 29			14 57	14 57						15 29			15 57			16 29			
Parson Street	d					14 37										15 35						16 35			
Bedminster	d	←				14 39										15 38						16 38			
Bristol Temple Meads 10	a	14 11	14 25			14 43			15 09	15 09	15 21	15 25	15 25			15 43		15 49	16 09	16 25		16 43			
	d	14 21	14 30	14 41		14 45	14 53	15 00	15 21	15 21		15 30	15 30	15 41		15 45	15 55	16 00	16 21	16 30	16 41	16 45	16 54	17 00	
Lawrence Hill	d					14 48										15 48						16 48			
Stapleton Road	d					14 50										15 50						16 50			
Filton Abbey Wood	d	14 32		14 48		14 56	15 01		15 31	15 31				15 48		15 56	16 02		16 32		16 48	16 56	17 02		
Bristol Parkway 7	a		14 39	14 52		15 04		15 08				15 38	15 39	15 52		16 04		16 08		16 38	16 52	17 04		17 08	
	d			14 53										15 52							16 52				
Yate	d			15 03										16 02							17 02				
Cam & Dursley	d			15 17										16 16							17 16				
Gloucester 7	a			15 33										16 33							17 33				
Cardiff Central 7	a	15 17					15 46		16 15	16 15							16 42		17 17				17 42		

		GW B	GW A	GW ◇■ A ⊏	XC ◇■ E ⍑	XC ◇■ F ⍑	GW ◇	GW	GW ◇	XC ◇■ A ⍑		GW	XC ◇■ B ⍑	GW	GW ◇■ A ⊏	XC ◇■ ⍑	GW	GW	GW ■	XC ◇■ ⍑		GW	XC ◇■ A ⍑	XC ◇■ B ⍑	GW
Taunton	d	16 07	16 07		16 51	16 51						17 06	17 21			17 51						18 08	18 50	18 51	
Bridgwater	d	16 19	16 19									17 18										18 20			
Highbridge & Burnham	d	16 27	16 27									17 26										18 28			
Weston-super-Mare	a	16 38	16 40									17 37										18 39			
	d	16 39	16 42	17 00				17 10				17 40			18 00			18 10				18 40			
Weston Milton	d							17 13										18 13							
Worle	d	16 45	16 47					17 17				17 46						18 17				18 46			
Yatton	d	16 51	16 53					17 23				17 52						18 23				18 52			
Nailsea & Backwell	d	16 57	16 59					17 29				17 58						18 29				18 58			
Parson Street	d	17 05	17 07					17 37										18 35							
Bedminster	d							17 40						←				18 38							
Bristol Temple Meads 10	a	17 11	17 12	17 21	17 25	17 25		17 44				18 10	17 55	18 10	18 22	18 26		18 43				19 09	19 23	19 24	
	d	17 21	17 21		17 30	17 30	17 41	17 45	17 54	18 00		18 23	18 00	18 23		18 30	18 41	18 45	18 54	19 00		19 19	19 30	19 30	19 41
Lawrence Hill	d							17 48				→						18 48							
Stapleton Road	d							17 51										18 50							
Filton Abbey Wood	d	17 30	17 30				17 48	17 57	18 01					18 32			18 48	18 56	19 01			19 27			19 48
Bristol Parkway 7	a				17 38	17 39	17 52	18 04		18 08			18 08			18 38	18 52	19 04		19 08			19 38	19 39	19 52
	d						17 52										18 52								19 52
Yate	d						18 02										19 02								20 02
Cam & Dursley	d						18 15										19 16								20 16
Gloucester 7	a						18 32										19 32								20 32
Cardiff Central 7	a	18 15	18 15						18 43					19 17					19 40			20 13			

A until 8 September
B from 15 September
C until 21 July, from 13 October
D from 28 July until 6 October
E from 28 July until 1 September
F until 21 July, from 8 September

For connections to London Paddington refer to Table T125

For full services to Cardiff Central, Cheltenham Spa, Gloucester and Great Malvern refer to Table T123

Table T134-R

Taunton - Gloucester

Saturdays

26 May to 8 December

		GW	GW ◇	XC ◇■ A	GW	XC ◇■ B		XC ◇■	XC ◇■ C ⍑	XC ◇■ D ⍑	GW ◇■ ⊏	GW	GW ◇	GW	GW ◇■ ⊏	GW ◇		GW	GW ◇■ ⊏	GW	GW ◇				
Taunton	d				19 06	19 18			19 50	19 51				20 17	21 14				21 30	21 35					
Bridgwater	d				19 17									20 29						21 47					
Highbridge & Burnham	d				19 25									20 37						21 55					
Weston-super-Mare	a				19 36									20 48					21 51	22 05					
	d	19 10			19 40						20 10			20 50					21 53	22 06					
Weston Milton	d	19 13												20 53						22 09					
Worle	d	19 17			19 45									20 57						22 13					
Yatton	d	19 23			19 51									21 03						22 19					
Nailsea & Backwell	d	19 29			19 57									21 09						22 25					
Parson Street	d	19 35												21 16						22 32					
Bedminster	d	19 38												21 19						22 35					
Bristol Temple Meads 10	a	19 43			20 10	19 53			20 22	20 24	20 30			21 24	21 46				22 12	22 41					
	d	19 45	19 54	20 00		20 00		20 10	20 30	20 30		20 41	20 53	21 29		21 57		22 11			22 55				
Lawrence Hill	d	19 48																							
Stapleton Road	d	19 50																							
Filton Abbey Wood	d	19 56	20 01					20 17				20 48	21 01	21 36		22 04		22 19			23 02				
Bristol Parkway 7	a	20 04		20 08		20 08			20 38	20 39		20 52						22 22							
	d											20 52						22 23							
Yate	d											21 02						22 32							
Cam & Dursley	d											21 16						22 46							
Gloucester 7	a											21 32						23 03							
Cardiff Central 7	a		20 42					21 00					21 42	22 32		23 00					23 56				

Sundays

20 May to 2 December

		GW ◇■ E ⊏	GW ◇ F	GW ◇ G	GW ◇■ H ⊏	XC ◇■ ⍑	GW	GW ◇	GW E	GW H		GW ◇■ E ⊏	GW ◇■ H ⊏	XC ◇■ ⍑	GW E	GW ◇ H	GW ◇ E	GW ◇ H	GW ◇ E	XC ◇■ ⍑		GW ■	GW	GW ■ ■ H ⊏	GW E
Taunton	d							08 35									10 03	10 07		10 50					11 36
Bridgwater	d							08 47									10 15	10 19							11 47
Highbridge & Burnham	d							08 55									10 23	10 26	←						11 54
Weston-super-Mare	a							09 06									10 32	10 36	10 32						12 04
	d	08 15			08 23			09 07				09 46	09 51				10 40	10 39	10 40					11 54	12 09
Weston Milton	d							09 10									→								12 12
Worle	d	08 22			08 30			09 14				09 53	09 58					10 44	10 46					12 01	12 16
Yatton	d	08 29			08 37			09 20				10 00	10 05					10 50	10 51					12 07	12 22
Nailsea & Backwell	d	08 35			08 43			09 26				10 06	10 11					10 56	10 57					12 14	12 28
Parson Street	d																	11 03	11 05						12 37
Bedminster	d																	11 06	11 07						12 39
Bristol Temple Meads 10	a	08 46			08 54			09 37				10 17	10 23					11 10	11 11	11 23				12 24	12 44
	d		08 48	08 48		09 15	09 20		09 49	09 54				10 30	10 40	10 48		11 23	11 23	11 30		11 47	12 11		
Lawrence Hill	d																	11 26	11 26						
Stapleton Road	d																	11a28	11a28						
Filton Abbey Wood	d		08 55	08 55			09 25		09 58	10 01					10 47	10 56						11 55	12 16		
Bristol Parkway 7	a					09 23	09 29							10 38						11 38			12 20		
	d					09 25	09 29																12 22		
Yate	d						09 40																12 32		
Cam & Dursley	d						09 53																12 46		
Gloucester 7	a					09 52	10 10																13 04		
Cardiff Central 7	a		09 39	09 45					10 42	10 46					11 36	11 43						12 41			

		XC ◇■ I ⍑	XC ◇■ J ⍑	GW ◇ E	GW ◇ H	XC ◇■ ⍑		GW ◇ H	XC ◇■ ⍑	GW ■ ■ E ⊏	GW ◇ E	GW ◇ H	GW ■ ■ H ⊏	XC ◇■ ⍑	GW ◇	GW		GW E	XC ◇■ I ⍑	XC ◇■ J ⍑	GW	GW ◇ E	GW ◇ H	GW H	XC ◇■ ⍑
Taunton	d	11 52	11 52			12 00		12 06	12 50					13 23				13 34	13 50	13 50				13 53	
Bridgwater	d							12 17										13 46						14 05	
Highbridge & Burnham	d							12 24										13 53						14 12	
Weston-super-Mare	a					12 19		12 34										14 04						14 23	
	d					12 21		12 36		13 16			13 20					14 07						14 25	
Weston Milton	d							12 39										14 10						14 28	
Worle	d							12 43		13 22			13 26					14 14						14 32	
Yatton	d							12 49		13 29			13 33					14 20						14 38	
Nailsea & Backwell	d							12 55		13 34			13 38					14 26						14 44	
Parson Street	d							13 03										14 33						14 51	
Bedminster	d							13 06										14 36			←			14 54	
Bristol Temple Meads 10	a	12 24	12 27			12 44		13 09	13 23	13 47			13 50	13 54				14 40	14 21	14 22				14 58	
	d	12 30	12 30	12 48	12 48	13 00			13 30		13 48	13 48		14 00	14 16	14 39			14 30	14 30	14 39	14 48	14 48		15 00
Lawrence Hill	d															→									
Stapleton Road	d																								
Filton Abbey Wood	d			12 55	12 57						13 55	13 55			14 23						14 46	14 55	14 55		
Bristol Parkway 7	a	12 38	12 38			13 08			13 38					14 08					14 38	14 39	14 50				15 08
	d																				14 51				
Yate	d																				15 02				
Cam & Dursley	d																				15 16				
Gloucester 7	a																				15 33				
Cardiff Central 7	a			13 40	13 41						14 41	14 42			15 08							15 41	15 44		

A from 15 September
B until 8 September
C from 15 September. ⍑ to Bristol Temple Meads
D until 8 September. ⍑ to Bristol Temple Meads
E from 16 September
F until 21 October
G from 28 October
H until 9 September
I from 22 July
J until 15 July

For connections to London Paddington refer to Table T125

For full services to Cardiff Central, Cheltenham Spa, Gloucester and Great Malvern refer to Table T123

Taunton - Gloucester

		XC	GW	GW	GW	XC	GW	GW		GW	XC	GW	GW	GW	GW	XC	GW	XC		GW	GW	GW	GW	XC	GW
		◇■ ⊥	■ ■ A ⊐	◇	◇■ B ⊐	◇■ ⊥	◇	A		B	◇■ ⊥		◇	A	B	◇■ ⊥	■ ■ ⊐	◇■ ⊥		◇	■	◇■ B ⊐	◇■ A ⊐	◇■ ⊥	A
Taunton	d	14 49						15 09		15 19	15 51					15 59	16 39	16 52				16 58	16 58		17 10
Bridgwater	d							15 21		15 31												17 09	17 09		17 21
Highbridge & Burnham	d							15 28		15 38												17 17	17 17		17 28
Weston-super-Mare	a							15 39		15 48						16 18	16 59					17 27	17 27		17 39
	d		15 15		15 20			15 45		15 50				16 10	16 10	16 29	17 01			17 09		17 30	17 31		17 45
Weston Milton	d							15 48		15 53				16 13	16 13					17 12					
Worle	d		15 21		15 27			15 52		15 57				16 18	16 18					17 16					17 51
Yatton	d		15 28		15 33			15 58		16 03				16 24	16 24					17 22		17 41			17 57
Nailsea & Backwell	d		15 34		15 40			16 04		16 09				16 30	16 30					17 28		17 47			18 03
Parson Street	d													16 37	16 37										
Bedminster	d													16 40	16 40					17 36					
Bristol Temple Meads ■	a	15 21	15 47		15 51			16 15		16 20	16 25			16 43	16 45	16 47	17 20	17 24		17 40		17 57	17 51		18 14
	d	15 30		15 48		16 00	16 12				16 30	16 41	16 48	16 53	16 53	17 00		17 30			17 48			18 00	
Lawrence Hill	d													16 56	16 56										
Stapleton Road	d													16a58	16a58										
Filton Abbey Wood	d			15 55			16 19					16 46	16 55								17 55				
Bristol Parkway ■	a	15 38				16 08					16 39	16 50				17 08		17 39						18 08	
	d											16 51													
Yate	d											17 02													
Cam & Dursley	d											17 16													
Gloucester ■	a											17 33													
Cardiff Central ■	a			16 42			17 06						17 43								18 42				

		GW	GW	GW		XC	XC	GW	GW	GW	GW	GW	GW	GW		XC	GW	GW	GW	XC	GW	GW	XC	XC
		B	◇■ A ⊐	◇■ B ⊐		◇■ C ⊥	◇■ D ⊥	E	F	G	◇ A	◇ B	F	B		◇■ ⊥	◇ A	◇ B	◇■ A ⊐	◇■ ⊥	◇	◇■ B ⊐	◇■ H ⊥	◇■ H ⊥
Taunton	d	17 19	17 41	17 46		17 51	17 52										18 15	18 18	18 38	18 50		18 56	19 24	19 52
Bridgwater	d	17 30															18 27	18 30	18 48			19 06		
Highbridge & Burnham	d	17 37															18 34	18 37	18 55			19 13		
Weston-super-Mare	a	17 48															18 45	18 48	19 06			19 24		
	d	17 50								18 09			18 09	18 16			18 45	18 49	19 17			19 25		
Weston Milton	d									18 12			18 12	18 19										
Worle	d	17 56								18 17			18 17	18 24			18 51	18 54						
Yatton	d	18 02	18 06							18 23			18 23	18 30			18 56	19 00	19 28			19 35		
Nailsea & Backwell	d	18 08	18 12							18 29			18 29	18 36			19 02	19 06	19 34			19 41		
Parson Street	d									18 35			18 36	18 43			19 10	19 14						
Bedminster	d									18 38			18 39	18 46										
Bristol Temple Meads ■	a	18 19	18 21	18 23		18 27	18 27			18 43			18 43	18 50			19 15	19 19	19 46	19 23		19 51	19 57	20 25
	d					18 30	18 30	18 37	18 37		18 48	18 48	18 50	18 50		19 00				19 30	19 48		20 00	20 30
Lawrence Hill	d												18 53	18 53										
Stapleton Road	d												18a55	18a55										
Filton Abbey Wood	d							18 42	18 42		18 55	18 55									19 55			
Bristol Parkway ■	a					18 39	18 39	18 46	18 46							19 08				19 38			20 08	20 39
	d							18 46	18 46															
Yate	d							18 58	18 58															
Cam & Dursley	d							19 12	19 12															
Gloucester ■	a							19 30	19 31															
Cardiff Central ■	a										19 40	19 42									20 43			

		GW	GW	GW	GW	GW	GW	GW	XC	GW		GW	GW	GW	GW
			◇	◇■ ⊐		◇ B	◇ A	◇■ ⊐	◇■				◇		
Taunton	d				20 25			21 31				21 36			
Bridgwater	d				20 37							21 48			
Highbridge & Burnham	d				20 44							21 55			
Weston-super-Mare	a				20 54							22 05			
	d			20 26	20 59							22 07		22 48	23 47
Weston Milton	d				21 02							22 10			23 50
Worle	d			20 33	21 06							22 14			23 54
Yatton	d			20 39	21 12							22 20			23 59
Nailsea & Backwell	d			20 46	21 18							22 26			00 06
Parson Street	d				21 25							22 33			00 13
Bedminster	d				21 28										00 16
Bristol Temple Meads ■	a			20 57	21 32			22 00				22 39		23 07	00 20
	d	20 41	20 48			21 48	21 48		22 10	22 30			22 49		
Lawrence Hill	d														
Stapleton Road	d														
Filton Abbey Wood	d	20 47	20 55			21 55	21 55			22 35			22 56		
Bristol Parkway ■	a	20 51							22 19	22 39					
	d	20 51								22 39					
Yate	d	21 03								22 50					
Cam & Dursley	d	21 17								23 03					
Gloucester ■	a	21 34								23 21					
Cardiff Central ■	a		21 40			22 45	22 49						23 41		

A from 16 September
B until 9 September
C until 15 July, from 9 September
D from 22 July until 2 September
E until 9 September, from 28 October
F from 16 September until 21 October
G from 28 October
H ⊥ to Bristol Temple Meads

For connections to London Paddington refer to Table T125

For full services to Cardiff Central, Cheltenham Spa, Gloucester and Great Malvern refer to Table T123

London and Birmingham - Devon and Cornwall

Miles	Miles	Miles			GW MX	GW MX	GW MX	GW MX	GW MX	XC MO	XC MX	GW	GW MO		GW	GW	GW	GW	GW	GW	GW	GW	GW		XC
					A	◇■ B ⊐	◇■ B ⊐	C	■ D 🛏 ⊐	◇■	◇■	E	■ D 🛏 ⊐		◇■ ⊐					■	◇				◇■
0	—	—	**London Paddington** ■ ⊖	d																					
18½	—	—	Slough ■	d																					
36	—	—	**Reading** ■	d					00u46				00u41												
41¼	—	—	Theale	d																					
49½	—	—	Thatcham	d																					
53	—	—	Newbury	d																					
61½	—	—	Hungerford	d																					
75¼	—	—	Pewsey	d																					
95½	—	—	Westbury 123	d																					
101¼	—	—	Frome 123	d																					
115¼	—	—	Castle Cary 123	d																					
—	0	—	**Birmingham New Street** ■	d																					
—	—	—	Cardiff Central ■	d																					
—	—	—	Newport (South Wales)	d																					
—	—	—	Swindon	d																					
—	87	—	Bristol Parkway ■	d																					
—	88¼	—	Filton Abbey Wood	d																					
—	—	—	Bath Spa ■	d																					
—	92¾	—	**Bristol Temple Meads** ■	d																	05 24				06 34
—	112¾	—	Weston-super-Mare	d		00b08															05 47				
—	126½	—	Bridgwater	d	00 02	00b26															06 05				
143	138¾	—	Taunton	d	00s14	00b38			02 38												06 20				07 07
157¼	—	—	Tiverton Parkway	d	00s31	00b51															06 35				07 19
173¾	—	—	**Exeter St Davids** ■	a	00 52	01 05			03 07				03 08								06 52				07 32
—	—	—	Exmouth	d																			06 43		
—	—	—	Exeter Central	d																			07 12		
—	—	—	**Exeter St Davids** ■	d					04 11				04 35				05 34	06 11	06 28		06 55		07 18		07 34
174¾	—	—	Exeter St Thomas	d													05 38	06 14			06 58		07 21		
182¼	—	—	Starcross	d													05 46	06 22			07 07		07 29		
184¼	—	—	Dawlish Warren	d													05 51	06 27			07 12		07 34		
185¾	—	—	Dawlish	d													05 55	06 31	06 41		07 16		07 38		
188¾	—	—	Teignmouth	d													06 00	06 36	06 46		07 21		07 43		
193¾	—	0	Newton Abbot	a					04 31				04 55				06 07	06 44	06 53		07 28		07 50		07 54
—	—	—		d					04 32				04 56			05 42	06 09	06 45	06 54	07 06	07 28		07 52		07 56
—	—	5¼	Torre	d												05 50	06 17	06 53		07 15			08 00		
—	—	6	Torquay	d												05 53	06 20	06 56		07 20			08 03		
—	—	8¼	Paignton	a												06 00	06 26	07 06		07 27			08 10		
202½	—	—	Totnes	d			00 10												07 07		07 42				08 07
214	—	—	Ivybridge	d			00 26												07 23		07 58				
225¾	—	—	**Plymouth**	a			00 40		05 11				05 35						07 36		08 11				08 33
—	—	—		d					05 49	06 00	06 28		06 28		07 02				07 53		08 14				
227	—	—	Devonport	d											07 07						08 17				
227½	—	—	Dockyard	d																					
228	—	—	Keyham	d																					
228¾	—	—	St Budeaux Ferry Road	d																					
230	—	—	Saltash	d											07 15				08 02		08 24				
235	—	—	St Germans	d											07 23				08 09		08 31				
240¼	—	—	Menheniot	d																					
243½	—	—	Liskeard ■	d					06 15	06 23	06 51		07 09		07 36				08 21		08 43				
252½	—	—	Bodmin Parkway	d					06 29	06 35	07 03		07 23		07 49				08 33		08 55				
256	—	—	Lostwithiel	d					06 35	06 41	07 08		07 29		07 55				08 45		09 00				
260½	—	—	Par	d					06 43	06 48	07 15		07 38		08 03				08a54		09 08	09 17			
—	—	—	Newquay	a																		10 09			
265	—	—	St Austell	d					06 52	06 55	07 21		07 46		08 11						09 16				
279½	—	—	Truro	d					07 10	07 11	07 38		08 06		08 29						09 34				
288½	—	—	Redruth	d				00 14	07 23	07 23	07 49		08 20		08 41						09 47				
292	—	—	Camborne	d				00 20	07 31	07 30	07 55		08 27		08 48						09 53				
298	—	—	Hayle	d				00 27	07 40	07 38	08 03		08 38		08 57						10 00				
299½	—	—	St Erth	d				00 31	07 45	07 43	08 07	08 28	08 45		09 02						10 08				
305¼	—	—	**Penzance**	a				00 41	07 55	07 52	08 16	08 38	08 59		09 12						10 16				

A From Bristol Temple Meads
B From London Paddington
C From Plymouth
D From London Paddington. The Night Riviera
E From St Ives
b Stops to set down only, stops on request

For connections from Heathrow Airport, Gatwick Airport and Oxford refer to Tables T148 and T116. Table T116 includes services to/from Bedwyn.

For the complete service between Westbury and Castle Cary refer to Table T123

T135 UPDATE: Major engineering work in connection with electrification works is taking place between Reading and Westbury. The route via Newbury will be closed to all trains on 4-7 June; 9-12 July; 16 July to 05 August; 28-30 August; 08-11 October and 19-22 November. Trains will be re-timed or cancelled and run to a special timetable during this period. Please check revised train times with *www.nationalrail.co.uk*. Rail replacement buses will operate between intermediate stations.

London and Birmingham - Devon and Cornwall

		GW	GW	GW	GW	GW	XC	GW	GW	GW	XC	GW	GW	GW	GW	GW	XC	GW	GW	GW	GW	GW	XC
			◇		◇1 ⊐	A	◇1 ⊥	B	◇	◇1 C ⊐	◇1 D ⊥		A	◇1 ⊐	B	◇	◇1 E ⊥		◇1 ⊐	◇	◇ F	G	◇1 H ⊥
London Paddington 15 ⊖	d				06 35					07 03				07 30					09 03				
Slough 3	d																						
Reading 7	d				07 02					07 30				07 57					09 31				
Theale	d																						
Thatcham	d																						
Newbury	d									07 48													
Hungerford	d																						
Pewsey	d									08 08													
Westbury 123	d									08 27													
Frome 123	d																						
Castle Cary 123	d																		10 27				
Birmingham New Street 12	d						06 42				07 12						08 12						09 17
Cardiff Central 7	d															08 00						09 00	
Newport (South Wales)	d															08 15						09 15	
Swindon	d													08 24									
Bristol Parkway 7	d		06 24				07 55				08 28						09 27						10 32
Filton Abbey Wood	d		06 28													08 43						09 43	
Bath Spa 7	d													08 55									
Bristol Temple Meads 10	d		06 43				08 10				08 44			09 12		08 55	09 44					09 55	10 45
Weston-super-Mare	d		07 06													09 29						10 24	
Bridgwater	d		07 25													09 48						10 43	
Taunton	d		07 39		08 18		08 43			09 04	09 15			09 45		10 01	10 16		10 50			11 00	11 17
Tiverton Parkway	d		07 55				08 55			09 17	09 27						10 29		11 03			11 16	11 30
Exeter St Davids 6	a		08 12		08 41		09 07			09 31	09 40			10 09		10 31	10 42		11 17			11 32	11 43
Exmouth	d	07 12				08 22							09 23					10 23					
Exeter Central	d	07 43				08 53							09 53					10 52					
Exeter St Davids 6	d	07 49	08 14	08 26	08 44	09 00	09 09		09 26	09 32	09 41		10 01	10 11		10 32	10 45	10 58	11 18			11 35	11 46
Exeter St Thomas	d	07 53		08 29		09 03							10 04					11 01				11 38	
Starcross	d	08 01		08 38		09 11		←					10 12		←			11 09					
Dawlish Warren	d	08 06		08 43		09 21		09 21					10 24		10 24	10 44		11 14				11 57	
Dawlish	d	08 10		08 47		→		09 25					→		10 28	10 48		11 18				→	
Teignmouth	d	08 15		08 52				09 30							10 33	10 53		11 23					
Newton Abbot	a	08 22	08 35	08 59			09 27	09 37	09 47	09 52	09 59			10 30	10 40	11 00	11 04	11 30	11 38				12 04
	d	08 24	08 35	09 01			09 29	09 38	09 47	09 53	10 04	10 07		10 32	10 41	11 01	11 05	11 32	11 39				12 07
Torre	d	08 33		09 09				09 46				10 15			10 49	11 10		11 40					
Torquay	d	08 36		09 12			09 40	09 49		10 05		10 18			10 52	11 13		11 43					
Paignton	a	08 44		09 19			09 47	09 56		10 11		10 25			10 59	11 20		11 50					
Totnes	d		08 49						10 00		10 17			10 44			11 18		11 52				12 20
Ivybridge	d		09 05						10 16														
Plymouth	a		09 18		09 34				10 29		10 42			11 10			11 44		12 19				12 47
	d		09 21		09 45				10 46					11 19							12 43		
Devonport	d		09 24																				
Dockyard	d																						
Keyham	d																						
St Budeaux Ferry Road	d								10 53														
Saltash	d		09 31						10 57												12 52		
St Germans	d		09 38						11 04												12 59		
Menheniot	d																						
Liskeard 6	d		09 50		10 10				11 18					11 44							13 11		
Bodmin Parkway	d		10 02		10 23				11 32					11 57							13 23		
Lostwithiel	d		10 07						11 37												13 29		
Par	d		10 15						11 44					12 08						12 11	13 36		
Newquay	a																			13 02			
St Austell	d		10 22		10 38				11 51					12 15							13 43		
Truro	d		10 40		10 56				12 08					12 33							14 00		
Redruth	d		10 53		11 09				12 21					12 46							14 13		
Camborne	d		10 59		11 16				12 27					12 53							14 19		
Hayle	d		11 06						12 34												14 26		
St Erth	d		11 10		11 26				12 38					13 03							14 30		
Penzance	a		11 20		11 36				12 47					13 13							14 39		

A To Paignton
B From Exmouth
C The Devon Express
D From Derby
E From Leeds
F From Gunnislake
G To Gunnislake
H From York

For connections from Heathrow Airport, Gatwick Airport and Oxford refer to Tables T148 and T116. Table T116 includes services to/from Bedwyn.

For the complete service between Westbury and Castle Cary refer to Table T123

Table T135-F

Mondays to Fridays

21 May to 29 June

London and Birmingham - Devon and Cornwall

		GW	GW	GW	GW	GW	XC	XC	GW	GW	GW	GW	GW	GW	GW	XC	GW	GW	GW	GW	GW	GW	XC
		A		B	◇1 C ⊐	D	◇1 E ⊥	◇1 F ⊥		◇	◇	B	◇1 G ⊐	D	◇1 H ⊐	◇1 I ⊥		B	◇1 J ✕⊐	◇1 K ✕⊐	D		◇1 L ⊥
London Paddington 15 ⊖	d				10 03								10 33		11 03				12 03	12 03			
Slough 3	d																						
Reading 7	d				10 32								11 00		11 30				12 30	12 30			
Theale	d																						
Thatcham	d																						
Newbury	d												11 21										
Hungerford	d																						
Pewsey	d												11 41										
Westbury 123	d												12 00										
Frome 123	d																						
Castle Cary 123	d												12 18										
Birmingham New Street 12	d						09 42	10 17								11 17							12 17
Cardiff Central 7	d																						
Newport (South Wales)	d																						
Swindon	d																						
Bristol Parkway 7	d						10 58	11 32								12 30							13 31
Filton Abbey Wood	d																						
Bath Spa 7	d																						
Bristol Temple Meads 10	d						11 15	11 44								12 45							13 45
Weston-super-Mare	d						11 36																
Bridgwater	d																						
Taunton	d						11 59	12 15					12 41		12 51	13 17							14 16
Tiverton Parkway	d						12 11	12 27							13 04	13 29							14 28
Exeter St Davids 6	a				12 03		12 24	12 40					13 04		13 18	13 43			14 03	14 03			14 40
Exmouth	d			11 23								12 23						13 23					
Exeter Central	d			11 52								12 52						13 52					
Exeter St Davids 6	d			11 58	12 08		12 25	12 41	12 49			12 57	13 06		13 19	13 44		13 58	14 08	14 08			14 42
Exeter St Thomas	d			12 01								13 00						14 01					
Starcross	d	←		12 09		←						13 09		←				14 09			←		
Dawlish Warren	d	11 57		12 22		12 22						13 20		13 20				14 23			14 23		
Dawlish	d	12 01		→		12 27	12 37					→	13 19	13 24				→			14 27		
Teignmouth	d	12 06				12 32	12 42						13 25	13 29							14 32		
Newton Abbot	a	12 13			12 27	12 39	12 48	12 59	13 09				13 32	13 36	13 39	14 03			14 27	14 27	14 39		15 00
	d	12 15	12 18		12 29	12 40	12 50	13 01	13 11				13 33	13 39	13 41	14 04	14 10		14 29	14 29	14 40	14 50	15 01
Torre	d		12 26			12 49			13 19					13 49			14 18				14 49		
Torquay	d		12 29			12 52	13 01		13 22				13 45	13 53			14 21				14 52		
Paignton	a		12 35			13 00	13 08		13 29				13 52	14 00			14 27				14 59		
Totnes	d	12 28						13 12							13 54	14 17						15 02	15 13
Ivybridge	d	12 45																				15 19	
Plymouth	a	12 59			13 04			13 38							14 21	14 43			15 03	15 03		15 34	15 40
	d	12 59			13 13						14 09								15 11	15 11			
Devonport	d	13 02																					
Dockyard	d	13x03																					
Keyham	d	13a05																					
St Budeaux Ferry Road	d																						
Saltash	d										14 18												
St Germans	d										14 25												
Menheniot	d																						
Liskeard 6	d				13 38						14 37								15 36	15 37			
Bodmin Parkway	d				13 51						14 49								15 49	15 50			
Lostwithiel	d										14 54												
Par	d				14 02					14 07	15 01								16 00	16 01			
Newquay	a									14 59													
St Austell	d				14 09						15 08								16 08	16 08			
Truro	d				14 27						15 26								16 25	16 26			
Redruth	d				14 39						15 39								16 38	16 38			
Camborne	d				14 47						15 45								16 45	16 46			
Hayle	d				14 56						15 52								16 54	16 54			
St Erth	d				15 01						15 57								16 59	16 59			
Penzance	a				15 11						16 09								17 09	17 09			

A From Cardiff Central to Gunnislake
B To Paignton
C The Cornish Riviera- Restaurant for customers joining to Reading
D From Exmouth
E From Manchester Piccadilly
F From Newcastle
G The Torbay Express
H The Mayflower
I From Edinburgh
J until 15 June. The Royal Duchy - Restaurant for customers joining to Reading. ⊐ from Newton Abbot ✕ to Newton Abbot
K from 18 June. The Royal Duchy - Restaurant for customers joining to Reading. ⊐ from Newton Abbot ✕ to Newton Abbot
L From Glasgow Central

For connections from Heathrow Airport, Gatwick Airport and Oxford refer to Tables T148 and T116. Table T116 includes services to/from Bedwyn.

For the complete service between Westbury and Castle Cary refer to Table T123

Table T135-F

Mondays to Fridays

21 May to 29 June

London and Birmingham - Devon and Cornwall

	GW	GW	GW	GW	GW	GW	GW	GW	GW	GW	XC	GW	XC	GW	GW	GW	GW	GW	XC	GW	GW
						FO	FX														
		◇1		◇		◇1	◇1	◇			◇1		◇1			◇1	◇		◇1		
		A				B	B				C		D						E		F
		✕				✕☕	✕☕				♨		♨			☕			♨		
London Paddington 15 ⊖ d		12 33				13 03	13 03									14 03					
Slough 3 d																					
Reading 7 d		13 00				13u31	13 31									14 30					
Theale d																					
Thatcham d																					
Newbury d		13 16																			
Hungerford d																					
Pewsey d		13 35																			
Westbury 123 d		13 55																			
Frome 123 d																					
Castle Cary 123 d		14 13																			
Birmingham New Street 12 d											13 17		13 42						14 17		
Cardiff Central 7 d								13 00													
Newport (South Wales) d								13 16													
Swindon d																					
Bristol Parkway 7 d											14 31		14 58						15 31		
Filton Abbey Wood d								13 43													
Bath Spa 7 d																					
Bristol Temple Meads 10 d								13 58			14 45		15 13						15 44		
Weston-super-Mare d								14 26													
Bridgwater d								14 45													
Taunton d		14a34				14 48	14 48	14 59			15 17		15 45			15 50			16 15		
Tiverton Parkway d						15 01	15 01	15 15			15 30		15 57			16 03			16 27		
Exeter St Davids 6 a						15 15	15 15	15 33			15 43		16 12			16 17			16 40		
Exmouth d			14 24												15 24			15 53			
Exeter Central d			14 52												15 53			16 22			16 46
Exeter St Davids 6 d			15 01			15 16	15 18				15 45			15 50	15 58	16 20		16 28	16 46		16 55
Exeter St Thomas d			15 04												16 01			16 31			16 58
Starcross d			15 12												16 10			16 39			17 06
Dawlish Warren d			15 17											16 03	16 15			16 44			17 11
Dawlish d			15 21											16 07	16 19			16 48			17 15
Teignmouth d			15 26											16 12	16 24			16 53			17 20
Newton Abbot a			15 33			15 37	15 37				16 03			16 20	16 31	16 39		17 00	17 04		17 28
d	15 05		15 35			15 39	15 39		15 55	15 59	16 05			16 21	16 32	16 41		17 02	17 06		17 29
Torre d	15 13		15 43							16 07					16 41			17 10			17 37
Torquay d	15 16		15 46							16 10					16 44			17 13			17 40
Paignton a	15 22		15 53							16 16					16 51			17 20			17 48
Totnes d						15 51	15 51		16 07		16 18			16 33		16 53			17 17		
Ivybridge d									16 24					16 50							
Plymouth a						16 18	16 18		16 38		16 45			17 05		17 19			17 42		
d					15 57							17 01				17 25				17 55	
Devonport d					16 00							17 04									
Dockyard d					16x02							17x05									
Keyham d					16 04							17 07									
St Budeaux Ferry Road d					16 08							17 10									
Saltash d					16 12							17 14				17 36				18 04	
St Germans d					16 19							17 21				17 44					
Menheniot d					16x26							17x29									
Liskeard 6 d					16 33							17a36				17 56				18 23	
Bodmin Parkway d					16 45											18 09				18 35	
Lostwithiel d					16 50											18 15				18 40	
Par d				16 10	16 58											18 23	18 29			18 47	
Newquay a				17 02													19 21				
St Austell d					17 06											18 31				18 55	
Truro d					17 23											18 48				19 11	
Redruth d					17 36											19 01				19 24	
Camborne d					17 42											19 08				19 30	
Hayle d					17 50											19 17				19 37	
St Erth d					17 54											19 22				19 42	
Penzance a					18 04											19 32				19 51	

A Restaurant available for customers joining to Reading
B Restaurant available for customers joining to Reading. ☕ from Exeter St Davids ✕ to Exeter St Davids
C From Dundee
D From Manchester Piccadilly
E From Glasgow Central
F From St James' Park

For connections from Heathrow Airport, Gatwick Airport and Oxford refer to Tables T148 and T116. Table T116 includes services to/from Bedwyn.

For the complete service between Westbury and Castle Cary refer to Table T123

Table T135-F

Mondays to Fridays

21 May to 29 June

London and Birmingham - Devon and Cornwall

	GW	GW	GW	GW	GW	XC	GW	XC	GW	GW	GW	XC	GW	GW	GW	GW	XC	GW	GW	GW	GW	GW
			FO	FX																		
			◇1	◇1		◇1		◇1	◇1			◇1		◇1	◇1		◇1			◇1	◇1	◇1
	A	B	C	C	D	E		F			B	G	D			B	E	D	H	B	I	J
			☕	☕		♨		♨	☕			♨		☕	☕		♨			☕	✕☕	☕
London Paddington 15 ⊖ d			15 03	15 03					16 03					16 33	17 03					17 33	18 03	
Slough 3 d																						
Reading 7 d			15u30	15 30					16 30					17 01	17 30					18 00	18 30	
Theale d																						
Thatcham d																						
Newbury d														17 20	17 47					18 16	18 47	
Hungerford d														17 30								
Pewsey d			16 03	16 03										17 45	18 06					18 42		
Westbury 123 d			16 23	16 23										18 05						19 02		
Frome 123 d																						
Castle Cary 123 d			16 41	16 41										18 23						19 20		
Birmingham New Street 12 d						15 17		15 42				16 12					17 12					
Cardiff Central 7 d																						
Newport (South Wales) d																						
Swindon d																						
Bristol Parkway 7 d						16 31		16 57				17 26					18 30					
Filton Abbey Wood d																						
Bath Spa 7 d																						
Bristol Temple Meads 10 d						16 45		17 13				17 44					18 45					
Weston-super-Mare d																						
Bridgwater d																						
Taunton d			17 03	17 05		17 17		17 45	17 52			18 16		18 46	18 55		19 16			19 43	19 51	
Tiverton Parkway d			17 16	17 18		17 29		17 57	18 05			18 28		18 59	19 08		19 28			19 56		
Exeter St Davids 6 a			17 30	17 32		17 42		18 11	18 19			18 41		19 13	19 22		19 42			20 10	20 14	
Exmouth d		16 53									18 01					18 59						
Exeter Central d		17 23					17 46				18 30					19 27						←
Exeter St Davids 6 d		17 28	17 37	17 37		17 45	17 51	18 12	18 24		18 36	18 46			19 25	19 33	19 44			20 20	20 16	20 20
Exeter St Thomas d		17 31					17 55				18 39					19 36				→		20 24
Starcross d		17 40			←		18 03				18 47		←			19 44		←				20 32
Dawlish Warren d		17 49			17 49		18 08				18 58		18 58			19 55		19 55				20 38
Dawlish d		→			17 53		18 12	18 24			→		19 02			→		19 59				20 43
Teignmouth d					17 58		18 17	18 29					19 07					20 04				20 50
Newton Abbot a			17 56	17 56	18 05	18 11	18 24	18 35	18 43			19 05	19 14		19 45		20 02	20 11			20 35	20 56
d			17 58	17 58	18 07	18 12	18 26	18 37	18 45			19 06	19 16		19 46		20 03	20 13			20 37	20 58
Torre d					18 15		18 34						19 24					20 21				21 08
Torquay d					18 18		18 37	18 48					19 27					20 24				21 12
Paignton a					18 25		18 44	18 55					19 34					20 30				21 19
Totnes d			18 10	18 10		18 24			18 58			19 18			19 59		20 15				20 50	
Ivybridge d									19 14													
Plymouth a			18 36	18 36		18 49			19 28			19 43			20 25		20 40				21 16	
d	18 17		18 40	18 40		19 01			19 31			19 49			20 28		20 50				21 21	
Devonport d	18 20																					
Dockyard d	18x21																					
Keyham d	18 23																					
St Budeaux Ferry Road d	18 25																					
Saltash d	18 31								19 42						20 39							
St Germans d	18 38														20 46							
Menheniot d	18x45																					
Liskeard 6 d	18a52		19 05	19 05		19 24			19 58			20 12			20 59		21 13				21 46	
Bodmin Parkway d			19 19	19 19		19 36			20 11			20 24			21 12		21 25				22 00	
Lostwithiel d																	21 31					
Par d			19 30	19 30		19 46			20 23	20 28		20 34			21 23		21 37				22 11	
Newquay a										21 20												
St Austell d			19 42	19 42		19 52			20 30			20 41			21 30		21 44				22 19	
Truro d			20 00	20 00		20 18			20 48			21 02			21 48		22 03				22 36	
Redruth d			20 12	20 12		20 29			21 00			21 18			22 00		22 14				22 49	
Camborne d			20 20	20 20		20 35			21 08			21 25					22 20					
Hayle d																	22 28					
St Erth d			20 30	20 30		20 46			21 19			21 35			22 15		22 32		22 45			
Penzance a			20 40	20 40		20 54			21 29			21 43			22 25		22 41		22 55		23 10	

A From Gunnislake
B To Paignton
C The Cornishman
D From Exmouth
E From Glasgow Central. ♨ to Plymouth
F From Manchester Piccadilly. ♨ to Bristol Temple Meads
G From Aberdeen. ♨ to Plymouth
H From St Ives
I The Golden Hind. ☕ from Taunton ✕ to Taunton
J From London Paddington

For connections from Heathrow Airport, Gatwick Airport and Oxford refer to Tables T148 and T116. Table T116 includes services to/from Bedwyn.

For the complete service between Westbury and Castle Cary refer to Table T123

T135 UPDATE: Major engineering work in connection with electrification works is taking place between Reading and Westbury. The route via Newbury will be closed to all trains on 4-7 June; 9-12 July; 16 July to 05 August; 28-30 August; 08-11 October and 19-22 November. Trains will be re-timed or cancelled and run to a special timetable during this period. Please check revised train times with *www.nationalrail.co.uk*. Rail replacement buses will operate between intermediate stations.

Table T135-F

Mondays to Fridays

21 May to 29 June

London and Birmingham - Devon and Cornwall

		GW	XC	GW	GW	GW	GW	GW	GW	XC	XC	GW	XC	GW	GW	GW	GW	GW	GW	GW	GW
				FX	FO	FX	FO		FX										FX	FO	FX
		◇■	◇■	◇■	◇■	■ ■	■ ■			◇■	◇■	◇■	◇■		◇■	◇		◇■	■	■	■
		A	B			C	C			D	E		B						F	G	H
		⊡	⊼	⊡	⊡	✕⊡	✕⊡			⊼	⊼	⊡			⊡			⊡	🛏 ⊡	🛏 ⊡	🛏 ⊡
London Paddington ■ ⊖	d	18 07		18 33	18 33	19 03	19 03					20 03			21 03			21 45	23 45	23 45	
Slough ■	d																				
Reading ■	d	18 39		19 00	19 00	19 30	19u30					20 30			21 30			22 13	00u46	00u46	
Theale	d	18 47																			
Thatcham	d	18 57																			
Newbury	d	19 04		19 16	19 16	19 48	19 48					20 46			21 46						
Hungerford	d	19 19		19 26	19 26																
Pewsey	d	19 37		19 44	19 44							21 06			22 05						
Westbury 123	d	19 58		20 04	20 04							21 27			22 27						
Frome 123	d	20a07																			
Castle Cary 123	d			20 22	20 22							21 45			22 45						
Birmingham New Street ■	d		18 12							19 12	19 42		20 12								
Cardiff Central ■	d																				
Newport (South Wales)	d																				
Swindon	d																	22 51			
Bristol Parkway ■	d		19 33							20 32	20 56		21 26								
Filton Abbey Wood	d																				
Bath Spa ■	d																	23 22			
Bristol Temple Meads ■	d		19 46							20 49	21 13		21 44			21 54	23 06	23 37			
Weston-super-Mare	d															22 29	23 42	00b08			
Bridgwater	d															22 48	00 02	00b26			
Taunton	d		20 17	20 45	20 45	20 53	20 53			21 20	21 44	22 07	22 16		23 08	23 12	00s14	00b38	02 38	02 38	
Tiverton Parkway	d		20 29	20 58	20 58	21 06	21 06			21 32	21 56	22 20	22 28		23 21	23 28	00s31	00b51			
Exeter St Davids ■	a		20 41	21 12	21 12	21 20	21 20			21 45	22 09	22 34	22 41		23 35	23 46	00 52	01 05	03 07	03 07	
Exmouth	d													22 07							
Exeter Central	d							21 21						22 35							
Exeter St Davids ■	d		20 43		21 14	21 22	21 23	21 29		21 47	22 10	22 36	22 42	22 46	23 37				04 11	04 11	
Exeter St Thomas	d							21 32						22 49							
Starcross	d							21 40						22 58							
Dawlish Warren	d							21 45						23 03							
Dawlish	d							21 49						23 07							
Teignmouth	d							21 54						23 12							
Newton Abbot	a		21 01		21 33	21 41	21 43	22 01		22 05	22 28	22 55	23 01	23 19	23 56				04 31	04 31	
	d		21 02		21 35	21 43	21 44	22 03		22 07	22 30	22 57	23 03	23 20	23 58				04 32	04 33	
Torre	d							22 11						23 27							
Torquay	d							22 14						23 30							
Paignton	a							22 21						23 37							
Totnes	d		21 14			21 55	21 57			22 18	22 41	23 09	23 19		00 10						
Ivybridge	d														00 26						←
Plymouth	a		21 39		22 11	22 22	22 24			22 45	23 07	23 36	23 44		00 40				05 11	05 11	05 11
	d						22 29		22 42										05 49	05 40	05 49
Devonport	d																		→		
Dockyard	d																				
Keyham	d																				
St Budeaux Ferry Road	d																				
Saltash	d						22 40		22 51												
St Germans	d						22 47		22 58												
Menheniot	d																				
Liskeard ■	d						23 00		23 10											06 06	06 15
Bodmin Parkway	d						23 14		23 24											06 20	06 29
Lostwithiel	d						23 20		23 29											06 27	06 35
Par	d						23 29		23 36											06 35	06 43
Newquay	a																				
St Austell	d						23 36		23 44											06 44	06 52
Truro	d						23 58		23 59											07 05	07 10
Redruth	d						00 13		00 14											07 18	07 23
Camborne	d						00 21		00 20											07 26	07 31
Hayle	d						00 30		00 27											07 35	07 40
St Erth	d						00 35		00 31											07 40	07 45
Penzance	a						00 45		00 41											07 50	07 55

A ⊡ to Westbury
B From Edinburgh
C The Armada. ⊡ from Taunton ✕ to Taunton
D From Glasgow Central. ⊼ to Bristol Temple Meads
E From Manchester Piccadilly. ⊼ to Bristol Temple Meads
F To Penzance. The Night Riviera
G The Night Riviera
H From London Paddington. The Night Riviera
b Stops to set down only, stops on request

For connections from Heathrow Airport, Gatwick Airport and Oxford refer to Tables T148 and T116. Table T116 includes services to/from Bedwyn.

For the complete service between Westbury and Castle Cary refer to Table T123

Table T135-F

Mondays to Fridays

2 July to 31 August

London and Birmingham - Devon and Cornwall

		GW	GW	GW	GW	GW	XC	XC	GW	GW	GW	GW	GW	GW	GW	GW	GW	GW	GW	XC	GW	GW	GW
		MX	MX	MX	MX	MX	MO	MX		MO													
			◇■	◇■		■	◇■	◇■		■	◇■					■		◇■		◇■		◇	
		A	B	B	C	D			E	D													
			⊡	⊡		🛏 ⊡				🛏 ⊡	⊡												
London Paddington ■ ⊖	d																						
Slough ■	d																						
Reading ■	d					00u46				00u41													
Theale	d																						
Thatcham	d																						
Newbury	d																						
Hungerford	d																						
Pewsey	d																						
Westbury 123	d																						
Frome 123	d																						
Castle Cary 123	d																						
Birmingham New Street ■	d																						
Cardiff Central ■	d																						
Newport (South Wales)	d																						
Swindon	d																						
Bristol Parkway ■	d																					06 24	
Filton Abbey Wood	d																					06 28	
Bath Spa ■	d																						
Bristol Temple Meads ■	d																05 24			06 34		06 43	
Weston-super-Mare	d		00b08														05 47					07 06	
Bridgwater	d	00 02	00b26														06 05					07 25	
Taunton	d	00s14	00b38			02 38											06 20			07 07		07 39	
Tiverton Parkway	d	00s31	00b51														06 35			07 19		07 55	
Exeter St Davids ■	a	00 52	01 05			03 07				03 08							06 52			07 32		08 12	
Exmouth	d																		06 43		07 12		
Exeter Central	d																		07 12		07 43		
Exeter St Davids ■	d					04 11				04 35			05 34	06 11	06 28		06 55		07 18	07 34	07 49	08 14	08 26
Exeter St Thomas	d												05 38	06 14			06 58		07 21		07 53		08 29
Starcross	d												05 46	06 22			07 07		07 29		08 01		08 38
Dawlish Warren	d												05 51	06 27			07 12		07 34		08 06		08 43
Dawlish	d												05 55	06 31	06 41		07 16		07 38		08 10		08 47
Teignmouth	d												06 00	06 36	06 46		07 21		07 43		08 15		08 52
Newton Abbot	a					04 31				04 55			06 07	06 44	06 53		07 28		07 50	07 54	08 22	08 35	08 59
	d					04 32				04 56		05 42	06 09	06 45	06 54	07 06	07 28		07 52	07 56	08 24	08 35	09 01
Torre	d											05 50	06 17	06 53		07 15			08 00		08 33		09 09
Torquay	d											05 53	06 20	06 56		07 20			08 03		08 36		09 12
Paignton	a											06 00	06 26	07 06		07 27			08 10		08 44		09 19
Totnes	d			00 10											07 07		07 42			08 07		08 49	
Ivybridge	d			00 26											07 23		07 58					09 05	
Plymouth	a			00 40		05 11				05 35					07 37		08 11			08 33		09 18	
	d					05 49	06 00	06 28		06 28	07 02						08 14	08 20				09 21	
Devonport	d										07 07							08 24				09 24	
Dockyard	d																						
Keyham	d																						
St Budeaux Ferry Road	d																						
Saltash	d										07 15							08 33				09 31	
St Germans	d										07 23							08 41				09 38	
Menheniot	d																						
Liskeard ■	d					06 15	06 23	06 51		07 09	07 36						08 38	08 53				09 50	
Bodmin Parkway	d					06 29	06 35	07 03		07 23	07 49						08 50					10 02	
Lostwithiel	d					06 35	06 41	07 08		07 29	07 55						08 55					10 07	
Par	d					06 43	06 48	07 15		07 38	08 03						09 17	09 15				10 15	
Newquay	a																10 09						
St Austell	d					06 52	06 55	07 21		07 46	08 11							09 22				10 22	
Truro	d					07 10	07 11	07 38		08 06	08 29							09 40				10 40	
Redruth	d				00 14	07 23	07 23	07 49		08 20	08 41							09 53				10 53	
Camborne	d				00 20	07 31	07 30	07 55		08 27	08 48							10 00				10 59	
Hayle	d				00 27	07 40	07 38	08 03		08 38	08 57							10 08				11 06	
St Erth	d				00 31	07 45	07 43	08 07	08 28	08 45	09 02							10 13				11 10	
Penzance	a				00 41	07 55	07 52	08 16	08 38	08 59	09 12							10 24				11 20	

A From Bristol Temple Meads
B From London Paddington
C From Plymouth
D From London Paddington. The Night Riviera
E From St Ives
b Stops to set down only, stops on request

For connections from Heathrow Airport, Gatwick Airport and Oxford refer to Tables T148 and T116. Table T116 includes services to/from Bedwyn.

For the complete service between Westbury and Castle Cary refer to Table T123

London and Birmingham - Devon and Cornwall

	GW ◇■ ☕	GW A	XC ◇■ ⊥	GW B	GW ◇		GW ◇	GW ◇■ C ☕	XC ◇■ D ⊥	GW	GW A	GW ◇■ ☕	GW B	GW ◇	XC ◇■ E ⊥		GW	GW ◇■ ☕	GW F	GW ◇ G	XC ◇■ E ⊥	GW ◇ H	GW	GW A
London Paddington ⊖ d	06 35							07 03				07 30						09 03						
Slough d																								
Reading d	07 02							07 30				07 57						09 31						
Theale d																								
Thatcham d																								
Newbury d								07 48																
Hungerford d																								
Pewsey d								08 08																
Westbury 123 d								08 27																
Frome 123 d																								
Castle Cary 123 d																		10 27						
Birmingham New Street d			06 42						07 12						08 12						09 17			
Cardiff Central d														08 00						09 00				
Newport (South Wales) d														08 15						09 15				
Swindon d												08 24												
Bristol Parkway d			07 55						08 28						09 27						10 32			
Filton Abbey Wood d														08 43						09 43				
Bath Spa d												08 55												
Bristol Temple Meads d			08 10						08 44			09 12		08 55	09 44					09 55	10 45			
Weston-super-Mare d														09 29						10 24				
Bridgwater d														09 48						10 43				
Taunton d	08 18		08 43					09 04	09 15			09 45		10 01	10 16			10 50		11 00	11 17			
Tiverton Parkway d			08 55					09 17	09 27						10 29			11 03		11 16	11 30			
Exeter St Davids a	08 41		09 07					09 31	09 40			10 09		10 31	10 42			11 17		11 32	11 43			
Exmouth d		08 22									09 23						10 23							11 23
Exeter Central d		08 53									09 53						10 52							11 52
Exeter St Davids d	08 44	09 00	09 09		09 26			09 32	09 41		10 01	10 11		10 32	10 45		10 58	11 18		11 35	11 46			11 58
Exeter St Thomas d		09 03									10 04						11 01			11 38				12 01
Starcross d		09 11		←							10 12		←				11 09					←		12 09
Dawlish Warren d		09 21		09 21							10 24		10 24	10 44			11 14			11 57		11 57		12 22
Dawlish d		→		09 25							→		10 28	10 48			11 18			→		12 01		→
Teignmouth d				09 30									10 33	10 53			11 23					12 06		
Newton Abbot a			09 27	09 37	09 47			09 52	09 59			10 30	10 40	11 00	11 04		11 30	11 38			12 04	12 13		
Newton Abbot d			09 29	09 38	09 47			09 53	10 04	10 07		10 32	10 41	11 01	11 05		11 32	11 39			12 07	12 15	12 18	
Torre d				09 46						10 15			10 49	11 10			11 40						12 26	
Torquay d			09 40	09 49				10 05		10 18			10 52	11 13			11 43						12 29	
Paignton a			09 47	09 56				10 11		10 25			10 59	11 20			11 50						12 35	
Totnes d					10 00				10 17			10 44			11 18			11 52			12 20	12 28		
Ivybridge d					10 16																	12 45		
Plymouth a	09 34				10 29				10 42			11 10			11 44			12 19			12 47	13 01		
Plymouth d	09 45				10 46							11 19						12 29						
Devonport d																								
Dockyard d																								
Keyham d																								
St Budeaux Ferry Road d					10 53																			
Saltash d					10 57													12 39						
St Germans d					11 04													12 47						
Menheniot d																								
Liskeard d	10 10				11 18							11 44						12 59						
Bodmin Parkway d	10 23				11 32							11 57						13 12						
Lostwithiel d					11 37													13 18						
Par d					11 44		11 47					12 08						13 28	13 38					
Newquay a							12 38											14 18						
St Austell d	10 38				11 51							12 15							13 45					
Truro d	10 56				12 08							12 33							14 02					
Redruth d	11 09				12 21							12 46							14 15					
Camborne d	11 16				12 27							12 53							14 21					
Hayle d					12 34														14 28					
St Erth d	11 26				12 38							13 03							14 32					
Penzance a	11 36				12 47							13 13							14 41					

A To Paignton
B From Exmouth
C The Devon Express
D From Derby
E From Leeds
F From Newquay
G To Plymouth
H From Cardiff Central

For connections from Heathrow Airport, Gatwick Airport and Oxford refer to Tables T148 and T116. Table T116 includes services to/from Bedwyn.

For the complete service between Westbury and Castle Cary refer to Table T123

Table T135-F

Mondays to Fridays

2 July to 31 August

London and Birmingham - Devon and Cornwall

	GW ◇■ A ☕		GW B	XC ◇■ C ⊥	XC ◇■ D ⊥	GW ◇	GW	GW E	GW ◇■ F ☕	GW B	GW ◇■ G ☕		XC ◇■ H ⊥	GW	GW E	GW ◇■ I ✕☕	GW B	GW	XC ◇■ J ⊥	XC ◇■ K ⊥	GW		GW ◇■ L ✕	GW
London Paddington ⊖ d	10 03								10 33		11 03					12 03							12 33	
Slough d																								
Reading d	10 32								11 00		11 30					12 30							13 00	
Theale d																								
Thatcham d																								
Newbury d									11 21														13 16	
Hungerford d																								
Pewsey d									11 41														13 35	
Westbury 123 d									12 00														13 55	
Frome 123 d																								
Castle Cary 123 d									12 18														14 13	
Birmingham New Street d				09 42	10 17								11 17						12 17	12 17				
Cardiff Central d																								
Newport (South Wales) d																								
Swindon d																								
Bristol Parkway d				10 58	11 32								12 30						13 31	13 32				
Filton Abbey Wood d																								
Bath Spa d																								
Bristol Temple Meads d				11 15	11 44								12 45						13 45	13 45				
Weston-super-Mare d				11 36																				
Bridgwater d																								
Taunton d				11 59	12 15				12 41		12 51		13 17						14 16	14 17			14a34	
Tiverton Parkway d				12 11	12 27						13 04		13 29						14 28	14 29				
Exeter St Davids a	12 03			12 24	12 40				13 04		13 18		13 43			14 03			14 40	14 43				
Exmouth d								12 23							13 23									
Exeter Central d								12 52							13 52									
Exeter St Davids d	12 08			12 25	12 41		12 49	12 57	13 06		13 19		13 44		13 58	14 08			14 42	14 44				
Exeter St Thomas d								13 00							14 01									
Starcross d			←					13 09		←					14 09		←							
Dawlish Warren d			12 22					13 20		13 20					14 23		14 23							
Dawlish d			12 27	12 37				→	13 19	13 24					→		14 27							
Teignmouth d			12 32	12 42					13 25	13 29							14 32							
Newton Abbot a	12 27		12 39	12 48	12 59		13 09		13 32	13 36	13 39		14 03			14 27	14 39		15 00	15 03				
Newton Abbot d	12 29		12 40	12 50	13 01		13 11		13 33	13 39	13 41		14 04	14 10		14 29	14 40	14 50	15 01	15 04				15 05
Torre d			12 49				13 19			13 49				14 18			14 49							15 13
Torquay d			12 52	13 01			13 22		13 45	13 53				14 21			14 52							15 16
Paignton a			13 00	13 08			13 29		13 52	14 00				14 27			14 59							15 22
Totnes d					13 12						13 54		14 17					15 02	15 13	15 17				
Ivybridge d																		15 19						
Plymouth a	13 03				13 38						14 21		14 43			15 03		15 34	15 40	15 43				
Plymouth d	13 13					14 09										15 11					15 57			
Devonport d																					16 00			
Dockyard d																					16x02			
Keyham d																					16 04			
St Budeaux Ferry Road d																					16 08			
Saltash d						14 18															16 12			
St Germans d						14 25															16 19			
Menheniot d																					16x26			
Liskeard d	13 38					14 37										15 37					16a33			
Bodmin Parkway d	13 51					14 49										15 50								
Lostwithiel d						14 54																		
Par d	14 02					15 01										16 01								
Newquay a																								
St Austell d	14 09					15 08										16 08								
Truro d	14 27					15 26										16 26								
Redruth d	14 39					15 39										16 38								
Camborne d	14 47					15 45										16 46								
Hayle d	14 56					15 52										16 54								
St Erth d	15 01					15 57										16 59								
Penzance a	15 11					16 09										17 09								

A The Cornish Riviera- Restaurant for customers joining to Reading
B From Exmouth
C From Manchester Piccadilly
D From Newcastle
E To Paignton
F The Torbay Express
G The Mayflower
H From Edinburgh
I The Royal Duchy - Restaurant for customers joining to Reading. ☕ from Newton Abbot ✕ to Newton Abbot
J until 20 July. From Glasgow Central
K from 23 July. From Edinburgh
L Restaurant available for customers joining to Reading

For connections from Heathrow Airport, Gatwick Airport and Oxford refer to Tables T148 and T116. Table T116 includes services to/from Bedwyn.

For the complete service between Westbury and Castle Cary refer to Table T123

T135 UPDATE: Major engineering work in connection with electrification works is taking place between Reading and Westbury. The route via Newbury will be closed to all trains on 4-7 June; 9-12 July; 16 July to 05 August; 28-30 August; 08-11 October and 19-22 November. Trains will be re-timed or cancelled and run to a special timetable during this period. Please check revised train times with *www.nationalrail.co.uk*. Rail replacement buses will operate between intermediate stations.

Table T135-F

Mondays to Fridays

2 July to 31 August

London and Birmingham - Devon and Cornwall

		GW	GW ◇	GW FO ◇1 A ✕⊐	GW FX ◇1 A ✕⊐	GW ◇	GW	GW	XC ◇1 B ⌶	XC ◇1 C ⌶	GW	XC ◇1 D ⌶	GW	GW	GW ◇1 ⊐	GW ◇	GW	XC ◇1 E ⌶	GW	GW F	GW	GW G	GW FO ◇1 H ⊐
London Paddington ⊖	d			13 03	13 03										14 03								15 03
Slough	d																						
Reading	d			13u31	13 31										14 30								15u30
Theale	d																						
Thatcham	d																						
Newbury	d																						
Hungerford	d																						
Pewsey	d																						16 03
Westbury 123	d																						16 23
Frome 123	d																						
Castle Cary 123	d																						16 41
Birmingham New Street	d								13 17	13 17		13 42						14 17					
Cardiff Central	d					13 00																	
Newport (South Wales)	d					13 16																	
Swindon	d																						
Bristol Parkway	d								14 31	14 31		14 58						15 31					
Filton Abbey Wood	d					13 43																	
Bath Spa	d																						
Bristol Temple Meads	d					13 58			14 45	14 45		15 13						15 44					
Weston-super-Mare	d					14 26																	
Bridgwater	d					14 45																	
Taunton	d			14 48	14 48	14 59			15 17	15 17		15 45			15 50			16 15					17 03
Tiverton Parkway	d			15 01	15 01	15 15			15 29	15 30		15 57			16 03			16 27					17 16
Exeter St Davids	a			15 15	15 15	15 33			15 43	15 43		16 12			16 17			16 40					17 30
Exmouth	d	14 24												15 24			15 53					16 53	
Exeter Central	d	14 52												15 53			16 22			16 46		17 23	
Exeter St Davids	d	15 01		15 16	15 18				15 44	15 45			15 50	15 58	16 20		16 28	16 46		16 55		17 28	17 37
Exeter St Thomas	d	15 04												16 01			16 31			16 58		17 31	
Starcross	d	15 12												16 10			16 39			17 06		17 40	
Dawlish Warren	d	15 17											16 03	16 15			16 44			17 11		17 49	
Dawlish	d	15 21											16 07	16 19			16 48			17 15		→	
Teignmouth	d	15 26											16 12	16 24			16 53			17 20			
Newton Abbot	a	15 33		15 37	15 37				16 03	16 03			16 20	16 31	16 39		17 00	17 04		17 28			17 56
	d	15 35		15 39	15 39		15 55	15 59	16 04	16 05			16 21	16 32	16 41		17 02	17 06		17 29			17 58
Torre	d	15 43						16 07						16 41			17 10			17 37			
Torquay	d	15 46						16 10						16 44			17 13			17 40			
Paignton	a	15 53						16 16						16 51			17 20			17 48			
Totnes	d			15 51	15 51		16 07		16 17	16 18			16 33		16 53			17 17					18 10
Ivybridge	d						16 24						16 50										
Plymouth	a			16 18	16 18		16 38		16 45	16 45			17 05		17 19			17 42					18 36
	d			16 26	16 26						17 01				17 25				17 55		18 17		18 40
Devonport	d										17 04										18 20		
Dockyard	d										17x05										18x21		
Keyham	d										17 07										18 23		
St Budeaux Ferry Road	d										17 10										18 25		
Saltash	d										17 14				17 36				18 04		18 31		
St Germans	d										17 21				17 44						18 38		
Menheniot	d										17x29										18x45		
Liskeard	d			16 54	16 54						17a36				17 56				18 23		18a52		19 05
Bodmin Parkway	d			17 07	17 07										18 09				18 35				19 19
Lostwithiel	d			17 13	17 13										18 15				18 40				
Par	d		16 10	17 21	17 21										18 23	18 29			18 47				19 30
Newquay	a		17 02													19 21							
St Austell	d			17 28	17 28										18 31				18 55				19 42
Truro	d			17 46	17 46										18 48				19 11				20 00
Redruth	d			17 59	17 59										19 01				19 24				20 12
Camborne	d			18 07	18 07										19 08				19 30				20 20
Hayle	d			18 15	18 15										19 17				19 37				
St Erth	d			18 20	18 20										19 22				19 42				20 30
Penzance	a			18 30	18 30										19 32				19 51				20 40

A Restaurant available for customers joining to Reading. ⊐ from Exeter St Davids ✕ to Exeter St Davids
B from 23 July. From Newcastle
C until 20 July. From Dundee
D From Manchester Piccadilly
E From Glasgow Central
F From St James' Park
G To Paignton
H The Cornishman

For connections from Heathrow Airport, Gatwick Airport and Oxford refer to Tables T148 and T116. Table T116 includes services to/from Bedwyn.

For the complete service between Westbury and Castle Cary refer to Table T123

Table T135-F

Mondays to Fridays

2 July to 31 August

London and Birmingham - Devon and Cornwall

		GW FX ◇1 A ⊐	GW B	XC ◇1 C ⌶	GW	XC ◇1 D ⌶	GW ◇1 ⊐	GW	GW E	XC ◇1 F ⌶	GW B	GW ◇1 ⊐	GW ◇1 ⊐	GW E	XC ◇1 C ⌶	GW B	GW G	GW ◇1 E ⊐	GW ◇1 H ✕⊐	GW ◇1 I ⊐	GW ◇1 J ⊐	XC ◇1 K ⌶
London Paddington ⊖	d	15 03					16 03					16 33	17 03					17 33	18 03		18 07	
Slough	d																					
Reading	d	15 30					16 30					17 01	17 30					18 00	18 30		18 39	
Theale	d																				18 47	
Thatcham	d																				18 57	
Newbury	d											17 20	17 47					18 16	18 47		19 04	
Hungerford	d											17 30									19 19	
Pewsey	d	16 03										17 45	18 06					18 42			19 37	
Westbury 123	d	16 23										18 05						19 02			19 58	
Frome 123	d																				20a07	
Castle Cary 123	d	16 41										18 23						19 20				
Birmingham New Street	d			15 17		15 42				16 12					17 12							18 12
Cardiff Central	d																					
Newport (South Wales)	d																					
Swindon	d																					
Bristol Parkway	d			16 31		16 57				17 26					18 30							19 33
Filton Abbey Wood	d																					
Bath Spa	d																					
Bristol Temple Meads	d			16 45		17 13				17 44					18 45							19 46
Weston-super-Mare	d																					
Bridgwater	d																					
Taunton	d	17 05		17 17		17 45	17 52			18 16		18 46	18 55		19 16			19 43	19 51			20 17
Tiverton Parkway	d	17 18		17 29		17 57	18 05			18 28		18 59	19 08		19 28			19 56				20 29
Exeter St Davids	a	17 32		17 42		18 11	18 19			18 41		19 13	19 22		19 42			20 10	20 14			20 41
Exmouth	d								18 01					18 59								
Exeter Central	d				17 46				18 30					19 27						←		
Exeter St Davids	d	17 37		17 45	17 51	18 12	18 24		18 36	18 46			19 25	19 33	19 44			20 20	20 16	20 20		20 43
Exeter St Thomas	d				17 55				18 39					19 36				→		20 24		
Starcross	d		←		18 03				18 47		←			19 44		←				20 32		
Dawlish Warren	d		17 49		18 08				18 58		18 58			19 55		19 55				20 38		
Dawlish	d		17 53		18 12	18 24			→		19 02			→		19 59				20 43		
Teignmouth	d		17 58		18 17	18 29					19 07					20 04				20 50		
Newton Abbot	a	17 56	18 05	18 11	18 24	18 35	18 43			19 05	19 14		19 45		20 02	20 11			20 35	20 56		21 01
	d	17 58	18 07	18 12	18 26	18 37	18 45			19 06	19 16		19 46		20 03	20 13			20 37	20 58		21 02
Torre	d		18 15		18 34						19 24					20 21				21 08		
Torquay	d		18 18		18 37	18 48					19 27					20 24				21 12		
Paignton	a		18 25		18 44	18 55					19 34					20 30				21 19		
Totnes	d	18 10		18 24			18 58			19 18			19 59		20 15				20 50			21 14
Ivybridge	d						19 14															
Plymouth	a	18 36		18 49			19 28			19 43			20 25		20 40				21 16			21 39
	d	18 40		19 01			19 31			19 49			20 28		20 50				21 21			
Devonport	d																					
Dockyard	d																					
Keyham	d																					
St Budeaux Ferry Road	d																					
Saltash	d						19 42						20 39									
St Germans	d												20 46									
Menheniot	d																					
Liskeard	d	19 05		19 24			19 58			20 12			20 59		21 13				21 46			
Bodmin Parkway	d	19 19		19 36			20 11			20 24			21 12		21 25				22 00			
Lostwithiel	d														21 31							
Par	d	19 30		19 46			20 23	20 28		20 34			21 23		21 37				22 11			
Newquay	a							21 20														
St Austell	d	19 42		19 52			20 30			20 41			21 30		21 44				22 19			
Truro	d	20 00		20 18			20 48			21 02			21 48		22 03				22 36			
Redruth	d	20 12		20 29			21 00			21 18			22 00		22 14				22 49			
Camborne	d	20 20		20 35			21 08			21 25					22 20							
Hayle	d														22 28							
St Erth	d	20 30		20 46			21 19			21 35			22 15		22 32		22 45					
Penzance	a	20 40		20 54			21 29			21 43			22 25		22 41		22 55		23 10			

A The Cornishman
B From Exmouth
C From Glasgow Central. ⌶ to Plymouth
D From Manchester Piccadilly. ⌶ to Bristol Temple Meads
E To Paignton
F From Aberdeen. ⌶ to Plymouth
G From St Ives
H The Golden Hind. ⊐ from Taunton ✕ to Taunton
I From London Paddington
J ⊐ to Westbury
K From Edinburgh

For connections from Heathrow Airport, Gatwick Airport and Oxford refer to Tables T148 and T116. Table T116 includes services to/from Bedwyn.

For the complete service between Westbury and Castle Cary refer to Table T123

2 July to 31 August

London and Birmingham - Devon and Cornwall

		GW FX	GW FO	GW FX	GW FO	GW	GW FX	XC	XC	GW	XC	GW	GW	GW	GW	GW	GW FX	GW FO	GW FX
		◇■	◇■	■ ■	■ ■			◇■	◇■	◇■	◇■		◇■	◇		◇■	■	■	■
				A	A			B	C		D						E	F	G
		☕	☕	✕☕	✕☕			🛒	🛒	☕			☕			☕	🛏 ☕	🛏 ☕	🛏 ☕
London Paddington ■ ⊖	d	18 33	18 33	19 03	19 03					20 03			21 03			21 45	23 45	23 45	
Slough ■	d																		
Reading ■	d	19 00	19 00	19 30	19u30					20 30			21 30			22 13	00u46	00u46	
Theale	d																		
Thatcham	d																		
Newbury	d	19 16	19 16	19 48	19 48					20 46			21 46						
Hungerford	d	19 26	19 26																
Pewsey	d	19 44	19 44							21 06			22 05						
Westbury 123	d	20 04	20 04							21 27			22 27						
Frome 123	d																		
Castle Cary 123	d	20 22	20 22							21 45			22 45						
Birmingham New Street ■	d							19 12	19 42		20 12								
Cardiff Central ■	d																		
Newport (South Wales)	d																		
Swindon	d															22 51			
Bristol Parkway ■	d							20 32	20 56		21 26								
Filton Abbey Wood	d																		
Bath Spa ■	d															23 22			
Bristol Temple Meads ■	d							20 49	21 13		21 44			21 54	23 06	23 37			
Weston-super-Mare	d													22 29	23 42	00b08			
Bridgwater	d													22 48	00 02	00b26			
Taunton	d	20 45	20 45	20 53	20 53			21 20	21 44	22 07	22 16		23 08	23 12	00s14	00b38	02 38	02 38	
Tiverton Parkway	d	20 58	20 58	21 06	21 06			21 32	21 56	22 20	22 28		23 21	23 28	00s31	00b51			
Exeter St Davids ■	a	21 12	21 12	21 20	21 20			21 45	22 09	22 34	22 41		23 35	23 46	00 52	01 05	03 07	03 07	
Exmouth	d											22 07							
Exeter Central	d					21 21						22 35							
Exeter St Davids ■	d		21 14	21 22	21 23	21 29		21 47	22 10	22 36	22 42	22 46	23 37				04 11	04 11	
Exeter St Thomas	d					21 32						22 49							
Starcross	d					21 40						22 58							
Dawlish Warren	d					21 45						23 03							
Dawlish	d					21 49						23 07							
Teignmouth	d					21 54						23 12							
Newton Abbot	a		21 33	21 41	21 43	22 01		22 05	22 28	22 55	23 01	23 19	23 56				04 31	04 31	
	d		21 35	21 43	21 44	22 03		22 07	22 30	22 57	23 03	23 20	23 58				04 32	04 33	
Torre	d					22 11						23 27							
Torquay	d					22 14						23 30							
Paignton	a					22 21						23 37							
Totnes	d			21 55	21 57			22 18	22 41	23 09	23 19		00 10						
Ivybridge	d												00 26						←
Plymouth	a		22 11	22 22	22 24			22 45	23 07	23 36	23 44		00 40				05 11	05 11	05 11
	d				22 29		22 42										05 49	05 40	05 49
Devonport	d																→		
Dockyard	d																		
Keyham	d																		
St Budeaux Ferry Road	d																		
Saltash	d				22 40		22 51												
St Germans	d				22 47		22 58												
Menheniot	d																		
Liskeard ■	d				23 00		23 10											06 06	06 15
Bodmin Parkway	d				23 14		23 24											06 20	06 29
Lostwithiel	d				23 20		23 29											06 27	06 35
Par	d				23 29		23 36											06 35	06 43
Newquay	a																		
St Austell	d				23 36		23 44											06 44	06 52
Truro	d				23 58		23 59											07 05	07 10
Redruth	d				00 13		00 14											07 18	07 23
Camborne	d				00 21		00 20											07 26	07 31
Hayle	d				00 30		00 27											07 35	07 40
St Erth	d				00 35		00 31											07 40	07 45
Penzance	a				00 45		00 41											07 50	07 55

- **A** The Armada. ☕ from Taunton ✕ to Taunton
- **B** From Glasgow Central. 🛒 to Bristol Temple Meads
- **C** From Manchester Piccadilly. 🛒 to Bristol Temple Meads
- **D** From Edinburgh
- **E** To Penzance. The Night Riviera
- **F** The Night Riviera
- **G** From London Paddington. The Night Riviera
- **b** Stops to set down only, stops on request

For connections from Heathrow Airport, Gatwick Airport and Oxford refer to Tables T148 and T116. Table T116 includes services to/from Bedwyn.

For the complete service between Westbury and Castle Cary refer to Table T123

3 September to 7 December

London and Birmingham - Devon and Cornwall

		GW MX	GW MX	GW MX	GW MX	GW MX	XC MO	XC MX	GW	GW MO	GW	GW	GW	GW	GW	GW	GW	GW	GW	GW	XC	GW	GW
			◇■	◇■		■	◇■	◇■		■	■	◇■					■	◇			◇■		◇
		A	B	B	C	D			E	F	G												
			☕	☕		🛏 ☕				🛏 ☕	🛏 ☕	☕											
London Paddington ■ ⊖	d																						
Slough ■	d																						
Reading ■	d					00u46				00u41	00u41												
Theale	d																						
Thatcham	d																						
Newbury	d																						
Hungerford	d																						
Pewsey	d																						
Westbury 123	d																						
Frome 123	d																						
Castle Cary 123	d																						
Birmingham New Street ■	d																						
Cardiff Central ■	d																						
Newport (South Wales)	d																						
Swindon	d																						
Bristol Parkway ■	d																						06 24
Filton Abbey Wood	d																						06 28
Bath Spa ■	d																						
Bristol Temple Meads ■	d																	05 24			06 34		06 43
Weston-super-Mare	d		00b08															05 47					07 06
Bridgwater	d	00 02	00b26															06 05					07 25
Taunton	d	00s14	00b38			02 38												06 20			07 07		07 39
Tiverton Parkway	d	00s31	00b51															06 35			07 19		07 55
Exeter St Davids ■	a	00 52	01 05			03 07				03 07	03 08							06 52			07 32		08 12
Exmouth	d																			06 43		07 12	
Exeter Central	d																			07 12		07 43	
Exeter St Davids ■	d					04 11				04 35	04 35			05 34	06 11	06 28		06 55		07 18	07 34	07 49	08 14
Exeter St Thomas	d													05 38	06 14			06 58		07 21		07 53	
Starcross	d													05 46	06 22			07 07		07 29		08 01	
Dawlish Warren	d													05 51	06 27			07 12		07 34		08 06	
Dawlish	d													05 55	06 31	06 41		07 16		07 38		08 10	
Teignmouth	d													06 00	06 36	06 46		07 21		07 43		08 15	
Newton Abbot	a					04 31				04 55	04 55			06 07	06 44	06 53		07 28		07 50	07 54	08 22	08 35
	d					04 32				04 56	04 56		05 42	06 09	06 45	06 54	07 06	07 28		07 52	07 56	08 24	08 35
Torre	d												05 50	06 17	06 53		07 15			08 00		08 33	
Torquay	d												05 53	06 20	06 56		07 20			08 03		08 36	
Paignton	a												06 00	06 26	07 06		07 27			08 10		08 44	
Totnes	d			00 10												07 07		07 42			08 07		08 49
Ivybridge	d			00 26												07 23		07 58					09 05
Plymouth	a			00 40		05 11				05 35	05 35					07 36		08 11			08 33		09 18
	d					05 49	06 00	06 28		06 28	06 28	07 02				07 53		08 14					09 21
Devonport	d											07 07						08 17					09 24
Dockyard	d																						
Keyham	d																						
St Budeaux Ferry Road	d																						
Saltash	d											07 15				08 02		08 24					09 31
St Germans	d											07 23				08 09		08 31					09 38
Menheniot	d																						
Liskeard ■	d					06 15	06 23	06 51		07 09	07 09	07 36				08 21		08 43					09 50
Bodmin Parkway	d					06 29	06 35	07 03		07 23	07 23	07 49				08 33		08 55					10 02
Lostwithiel	d					06 35	06 41	07 08		07 29	07 29	07 55				08 45		09 00					10 07
Par	d					06 43	06 48	07 15		07 38	07 38	08 03				08a54		09 08	09 17				10 15
Newquay	a																		10 09				
St Austell	d					06 52	06 55	07 21		07 46	07 46	08 11						09 16					10 22
Truro	d					07 10	07 11	07 38		08 06	08 06	08 29						09 34					10 40
Redruth	d				00 14	07 23	07 23	07 49		08 20	08 20	08 41						09 47					10 53
Camborne	d				00 20	07 31	07 30	07 55		08 27	08 27	08 48						09 53					10 59
Hayle	d				00 27	07 40	07 38	08 03		08 38	08 38	08 57						10 00					11 06
St Erth	d				00 31	07 45	07 43	08 07	08 28	08 45	08 45	09 02						10 08					11 10
Penzance	a				00 41	07 55	07 52	08 16	08 38	08 59	08 59	09 12						10 16					11 20

- **A** From Bristol Temple Meads
- **B** From London Paddington
- **C** From Plymouth
- **D** From London Paddington. The Night Riviera
- **E** From St Ives
- **F** from 17 September. From London Paddington. The Night Riviera
- **G** 3 September, 10 September. From London Paddington. The Night Riviera
- **b** Stops to set down only, stops on request

For connections from Heathrow Airport, Gatwick Airport and Oxford refer to Tables T148 and T116. Table T116 includes services to/from Bedwyn.

For the complete service between Westbury and Castle Cary refer to Table T123

T135 UPDATE: Major engineering work in connection with electrification works is taking place between Reading and Westbury. The route via Newbury will be closed to all trains on 4-7 June; 9-12 July; 16 July to 05 August; 28-30 August; 08-11 October and 19-22 November. Trains will be re-timed or cancelled and run to a special timetable during this period. Please check revised train times with *www.nationalrail.co.uk*. Rail replacement buses will operate between intermediate stations.

Table T135-F

Mondays to Fridays

3 September to 7 December

London and Birmingham - Devon and Cornwall

Station		GW	GW ◇1 🛒	GW A	XC ◇1 ☕	GW B	GW ◇	GW ◇1 C 🛒	XC ◇1 D ☕	GW	GW A	GW ◇1 🛒	GW B	GW ◇	XC ◇1 E ☕	GW	GW ◇1 🛒	GW ◇	GW ◇	XC ◇1 E ☕	GW F	GW G	GW A
London Paddington 15 ⊖	d		06 35					07 03				07 30					09 03						
Slough 3	d																						
Reading 7	d		07 02					07 30				07 57					09 31						
Theale	d																						
Thatcham	d																						
Newbury	d							07 48															
Hungerford	d																						
Pewsey	d							08 08															
Westbury 123	d							08 27															
Frome 123	d																						
Castle Cary 123	d																10 27						
Birmingham New Street 12	d				06 42				07 12						08 12					09 17			
Cardiff Central 7	d													08 00					09 00				
Newport (South Wales)	d													08 15					09 15				
Swindon	d											08 24											
Bristol Parkway 7	d				07 55				08 28						09 27					10 32			
Filton Abbey Wood	d													08 43					09 43				
Bath Spa 7	d											08 55											
Bristol Temple Meads 10	d				08 10				08 44			09 12		08 55	09 44				09 55	10 45			
Weston-super-Mare	d													09 29					10 24				
Bridgwater	d													09 48					10 43				
Taunton	d		08 18		08 43			09 04	09 15			09 45		10 01	10 16		10 50		11 00	11 17			
Tiverton Parkway	d				08 55			09 17	09 27						10 29		11 03		11 16	11 30			
Exeter St Davids 6	a		08 41		09 07			09 31	09 40			10 09		10 31	10 42		11 17		11 32	11 43			
Exmouth	d			08 22							09 23					10 23							11 23
Exeter Central	d			08 53							09 53					10 52							11 52
Exeter St Davids 6	d	08 26	08 44	09 00	09 09		09 26	09 32	09 41		10 01	10 11		10 32	10 45	10 58	11 18		11 35	11 46			11 58
Exeter St Thomas	d	08 29		09 03							10 04					11 01							12 01
Starcross	d	08 38		09 11		←					10 12		←			11 09							12 09
Dawlish Warren	d	08 43		09 21		09 21					10 24		10 24	10 44		11 14							12 22
Dawlish	d	08 47		→		09 25					→		10 28	10 48		11 18							→
Teignmouth	d	08 52				09 30							10 33	10 53		11 23							
Newton Abbot	a	08 59			09 27	09 37	09 47	09 52	09 59			10 30	10 40	11 00	11 04	11 30	11 38		11 55	12 04			
	d	09 01			09 29	09 38	09 47	09 53	10 04	10 07		10 32	10 41	11 01	11 05	11 32	11 39		11 57	12 07	12 09	12 18	
Torre	d	09 09				09 46				10 15			10 49	11 10		11 40					12 17	12 26	
Torquay	d	09 12			09 40	09 49		10 05		10 18			10 52	11 13		11 43					12 20	12 29	
Paignton	a	09 19			09 47	09 56		10 11		10 25			10 59	11 20		11 50					12 26	12 35	
Totnes	d						10 00		10 17			10 44			11 18		11 52		12 09	12 20			
Ivybridge	d						10 16												12 26				
Plymouth	a		09 34				10 29		10 42			11 10			11 44		12 19		12 40	12 47			
	d		09 45				10 46					11 19							12 43				
Devonport	d																						
Dockyard	d																						
Keyham	d																						
St Budeaux Ferry Road	d						10 53																
Saltash	d						10 57												12 52				
St Germans	d						11 04												12 59				
Menheniot	d																						
Liskeard 6	d		10 10				11 18					11 44							13 11				
Bodmin Parkway	d		10 23				11 32					11 57							13 23				
Lostwithiel	d						11 37												13 29				
Par	d						11 44					12 08						12 11	13 36				
Newquay	a																	13 02					
St Austell	d		10 38				11 51					12 15							13 43				
Truro	d		10 56				12 08					12 33							14 00				
Redruth	d		11 09				12 21					12 46							14 13				
Camborne	d		11 16				12 27					12 53							14 19				
Hayle	d						12 34												14 26				
St Erth	d		11 26				12 38					13 03							14 30				
Penzance	a		11 36				12 47					13 13							14 39				

A To Paignton
B From Exmouth
C The Devon Express
D From Derby
E From Leeds
F from 10 September
G until 7 September

For connections from Heathrow Airport, Gatwick Airport and Oxford refer to Tables T148 and T116. Table T116 includes services to/from Bedwyn.

For the complete service between Westbury and Castle Cary refer to Table T123

Table T135-F

Mondays to Fridays

3 September to 7 December

London and Birmingham - Devon and Cornwall

Station		GW ◇1 A 🛒	GW B	XC ◇1 C ☕	XC ◇1 D ☕	GW	GW ◇	GW ◇	GW E	GW ◇1 F 🛒	GW B	GW ◇1 G 🛒	XC ◇1 H ☕	GW	GW E	GW ◇1 I ✕🛒	GW B	GW	XC ◇1 J ☕	XC ◇1 K ☕	GW	GW ◇1 L ✕
London Paddington 15 ⊖	d	10 03								10 33		11 03				12 03						12 33
Slough 3	d																					
Reading 7	d	10 32								11 00		11 30				12 30						13 00
Theale	d																					
Thatcham	d																					
Newbury	d									11 21												13 16
Hungerford	d																					
Pewsey	d									11 41												13 35
Westbury 123	d									12 00												13 55
Frome 123	d																					
Castle Cary 123	d									12 18												14 13
Birmingham New Street 12	d			09 42	10 17								11 17						12 17	12 17		
Cardiff Central 7	d																					
Newport (South Wales)	d																					
Swindon	d																					
Bristol Parkway 7	d			10 58	11 32								12 30						13 31	13 32		
Filton Abbey Wood	d																					
Bath Spa 7	d																					
Bristol Temple Meads 10	d			11 15	11 44								12 45						13 45	13 45		
Weston-super-Mare	d			11 36																		
Bridgwater	d																					
Taunton	d			11 59	12 15					12 41		12 51	13 17						14 16	14 17		14a34
Tiverton Parkway	d			12 11	12 27							13 04	13 29						14 28	14 29		
Exeter St Davids 6	a	12 03		12 24	12 40					13 04		13 18	13 43			14 03			14 40	14 43		
Exmouth	d								12 23						13 23							
Exeter Central	d								12 52						13 52							
Exeter St Davids 6	d	12 08		12 25	12 41	12 49			12 57	13 06		13 19	13 44		13 58	14 08			14 42	14 44		
Exeter St Thomas	d								13 00						14 01							
Starcross	d		←						13 09		←				14 09		←					
Dawlish Warren	d		12 22						13 20		13 20				14 23		14 23					
Dawlish	d		12 27	12 37					→	13 19	13 24				→		14 27					
Teignmouth	d		12 32	12 42						13 25	13 29						14 32					
Newton Abbot	a	12 27	12 39	12 48	12 59	13 09				13 32	13 36	13 39	14 03			14 27	14 39		15 00	15 03		
	d	12 29	12 40	12 50	13 01	13 11				13 33	13 39	13 41	14 04	14 10		14 29	14 40	14 50	15 01	15 04	15 05	
Torre	d		12 49			13 19					13 49			14 18			14 49				15 13	
Torquay	d		12 52	13 01		13 22				13 45	13 53			14 21			14 52				15 16	
Paignton	a		13 00	13 08		13 29				13 52	14 00			14 27			14 59				15 22	
Totnes	d				13 12							13 54	14 17					15 02	15 13	15 17		
Ivybridge	d																	15 19				
Plymouth	a	13 04			13 38							14 21	14 43			15 03		15 34	15 40	15 43		
	d	13 13						14 09								15 11						
Devonport	d																					
Dockyard	d																					
Keyham	d																					
St Budeaux Ferry Road	d																					
Saltash	d							14 18														
St Germans	d							14 25														
Menheniot	d																					
Liskeard 6	d	13 38						14 37								15 37						
Bodmin Parkway	d	13 51						14 49								15 50						
Lostwithiel	d							14 54														
Par	d	14 02					14 07	15 01								16 01						
Newquay	a						14 59															
St Austell	d	14 09						15 08								16 08						
Truro	d	14 27						15 26								16 26						
Redruth	d	14 39						15 39								16 38						
Camborne	d	14 47						15 45								16 46						
Hayle	d	14 56						15 52								16 54						
St Erth	d	15 01						15 57								16 59						
Penzance	a	15 11						16 09								17 09						

A The Cornish Riviera- Restaurant for customers joining to Reading
B From Exmouth
C From Manchester Piccadilly
D From Newcastle
E To Paignton
F The Torbay Express
G The Mayflower
H From Edinburgh
I The Royal Duchy - Restaurant for customers joining to Reading. 🛒 from Newton Abbot ✕ to Newton Abbot
J from 8 October. From Glasgow Central
K until 5 October. From Edinburgh
L Restaurant available for customers joining to Reading

For connections from Heathrow Airport, Gatwick Airport and Oxford refer to Tables T148 and T116. Table T116 includes services to/from Bedwyn.

For the complete service between Westbury and Castle Cary refer to Table T123

Table T135-F

Mondays to Fridays

3 September to 7 December

London and Birmingham - Devon and Cornwall

		GW	GW	GW	GW	GW	GW	GW		GW	XC	GW	XC	GW	GW	GW	GW	GW		XC	GW	GW	GW	GW	GW
					FO	FX																			FO
			◇		◇■	◇■	◇				◇■		◇■			◇■	◇			◇■					◇■
					A	A					B		C							D		E	F	G	H
					✕⊏⊐	✕⊏⊐					⊥		⊥			⊏⊐				⊥					⊏⊐
London Paddington ⊖	d				13 03	13 03										14 03									15 03
Slough	d																								
Reading	d				13u31	13 31										14 30									15u30
Theale	d																								
Thatcham	d																								
Newbury	d																								
Hungerford	d																								
Pewsey	d																								16 03
Westbury 123	d																								16 23
Frome 123	d																								
Castle Cary 123	d																								16 41
Birmingham New Street	d										13 17		13 42							14 17					
Cardiff Central	d						13 00																		
Newport (South Wales)	d						13 16																		
Swindon	d																								
Bristol Parkway	d										14 31		14 58							15 31					
Filton Abbey Wood	d						13 43																		
Bath Spa	d																								
Bristol Temple Meads	d						13 58				14 45		15 13							15 44					
Weston-super-Mare	d						14 26																		
Bridgwater	d						14 45																		
Taunton	d				14 48	14 48	14 59				15 17		15 45			15 50				16 15					17 03
Tiverton Parkway	d				15 01	15 01	15 15				15 29		15 57			16 03				16 27					17 16
Exeter St Davids	a				15 15	15 15	15 33				15 43		16 12			16 17				16 40					17 30
Exmouth	d	14 24													15 24			15 53						16 53	
Exeter Central	d	14 52													15 53			16 22				16 46		17 23	
Exeter St Davids	d	15 01			15 16	15 18					15 44			15 50	15 58	16 20		16 28		16 46		16 55		17 28	17 37
Exeter St Thomas	d	15 04													16 01			16 31				16 58		17 31	
Starcross	d	15 12													16 10			16 39				17 06		17 40	
Dawlish Warren	d	15 17												16 03	16 15			16 44				17 11		17 49	
Dawlish	d	15 21												16 07	16 19			16 48				17 15		→	
Teignmouth	d	15 26												16 12	16 24			16 53				17 20			
Newton Abbot	a	15 33			15 37	15 37					16 03			16 20	16 31	16 39		17 00		17 04		17 28			17 56
	d	15 35			15 39	15 39		15 55		15 59	16 04			16 21	16 32	16 41		17 02		17 06		17 29			17 58
Torre	d	15 43								16 07					16 41			17 10				17 37			
Torquay	d	15 46								16 10					16 44			17 13				17 40			
Paignton	a	15 53								16 16					16 51			17 20				17 48			
Totnes	d				15 51	15 51		16 07			16 17			16 33		16 53				17 17					18 10
Ivybridge	d							16 24						16 50											
Plymouth	a				16 18	16 18		16 38			16 45			17 05		17 19				17 42					18 36
	d			15 57								17 01				17 25					17 55		18 17		18 40
Devonport	d			16 00								17 04											18 20		
Dockyard	d			16x02								17x05											18x21		
Keyham	d			16 04								17 07											18 23		
St Budeaux Ferry Road	d			16 08								17 10											18 25		
Saltash	d			16 12								17 14				17 36					18 04		18 31		
St Germans	d			16 19								17 21				17 44							18 38		
Menheniot	d			16x26								17x29											18x45		
Liskeard	d			16 33								17a36				17 56					18 23		18a52		19 05
Bodmin Parkway	d			16 45												18 09					18 35				19 19
Lostwithiel	d			16 50												18 15					18 40				
Par	d		16 10	16 58												18 23	18 29				18 47				19 30
Newquay	a		17 02														19 21								
St Austell	d			17 06												18 31					18 55				19 42
Truro	d			17 23												18 48					19 11				20 00
Redruth	d			17 36												19 01					19 24				20 12
Camborne	d			17 42												19 08					19 30				20 20
Hayle	d			17 50												19 17					19 37				
St Erth	d			17 54												19 22					19 42				20 30
Penzance	a			18 04												19 32					19 51				20 40

A Restaurant available for customers joining to Reading. ⊏⊐ from Exeter St Davids ✕ to Exeter St Davids
B From Dundee
C From Manchester Piccadilly
D From Glasgow Central
E From St James' Park
F From Gunnislake
G To Paignton
H The Cornishman

For connections from Heathrow Airport, Gatwick Airport and Oxford refer to Tables T148 and T116. Table T116 includes services to/from Bedwyn.

For the complete service between Westbury and Castle Cary refer to Table T123

Table T135-F

Mondays to Fridays

3 September to 7 December

London and Birmingham - Devon and Cornwall

		GW	GW	XC		GW	XC	GW	GW	GW	XC	GW	GW	GW		GW	XC	GW	GW	GW	GW	GW	GW	XC	
		FX																							
		◇■		◇■			◇■	◇■			◇■		◇■	◇■			◇■			◇■	◇■	◇■	◇■	◇■	
		A	B	C			D			E	F	B				E	C	B	G	E	H	I	J	K	
		⊏⊐		⊥			⊥	⊏⊐			⊥		⊏⊐	⊏⊐			⊥			⊏⊐	✕⊏⊐	⊏⊐	⊏⊐	⊥	
London Paddington ⊖	d	15 03						16 03					16 33	17 03						17 33	18 03		18 07		
Slough	d																								
Reading	d	15 30						16 30					17 01	17 30						18 00	18 30		18 39		
Theale	d																						18 47		
Thatcham	d																						18 57		
Newbury	d												17 20	17 47						18 16	18 47		19 04		
Hungerford	d												17 30										19 19		
Pewsey	d	16 03											17 45	18 06						18 42			19 37		
Westbury 123	d	16 23											18 05							19 02			19 58		
Frome 123	d																						20a07		
Castle Cary 123	d	16 41											18 23							19 20					
Birmingham New Street	d			15 17			15 42				16 12						17 12							18 12	
Cardiff Central	d																								
Newport (South Wales)	d																								
Swindon	d																								
Bristol Parkway	d			16 31			16 57				17 26						18 30							19 33	
Filton Abbey Wood	d																								
Bath Spa	d																								
Bristol Temple Meads	d			16 45			17 13				17 44						18 45							19 46	
Weston-super-Mare	d																								
Bridgwater	d																								
Taunton	d	17 05		17 17			17 45	17 52			18 16		18 46	18 55			19 16			19 43	19 51			20 17	
Tiverton Parkway	d	17 18		17 29			17 57	18 05			18 28		18 59	19 08			19 28			19 56				20 29	
Exeter St Davids	a	17 32		17 42			18 11	18 19			18 41		19 13	19 22			19 42			20 10	20 14			20 41	
Exmouth	d									18 01						18 59									
Exeter Central	d					17 46				18 30						19 27						←			
Exeter St Davids	d	17 37		17 45		17 51	18 12	18 24		18 36	18 46			19 25		19 33	19 44			20 20	20 16	20 20		20 43	
Exeter St Thomas	d					17 55				18 39						19 36				→		20 24			
Starcross	d		←			18 03				18 47		←				19 44		←				20 32			
Dawlish Warren	d		17 49			18 08				18 58		18 58				19 55		19 55				20 38			
Dawlish	d		17 53			18 12	18 24			→		19 02				→		19 59				20 43			
Teignmouth	d		17 58			18 17	18 29					19 07						20 04				20 50			
Newton Abbot	a	17 56	18 05	18 11		18 24	18 35	18 43			19 05	19 14		19 45			20 02	20 11			20 35	20 56		21 01	
	d	17 58	18 07	18 12		18 26	18 37	18 45			19 06	19 16		19 46			20 03	20 13			20 37	20 58		21 02	
Torre	d		18 15			18 34						19 24						20 21				21 08			
Torquay	d		18 18			18 37	18 48					19 27						20 24				21 12			
Paignton	a		18 25			18 44	18 55					19 34						20 30				21 19			
Totnes	d	18 10		18 24				18 58			19 18			19 59			20 15				20 50			21 14	
Ivybridge	d							19 14																	
Plymouth	a	18 36		18 49				19 28			19 43			20 25			20 40				21 16			21 39	
	d	18 40		19 01				19 31			19 49			20 28			20 50				21 21				
Devonport	d																								
Dockyard	d																								
Keyham	d																								
St Budeaux Ferry Road	d																								
Saltash	d							19 42						20 39											
St Germans	d													20 46											
Menheniot	d																								
Liskeard	d	19 05		19 24				19 58			20 12			20 59			21 13				21 46				
Bodmin Parkway	d	19 19		19 36				20 11			20 24			21 12			21 25				22 00				
Lostwithiel	d																21 31								
Par	d	19 30		19 46				20 23	20 28		20 34			21 23			21 37				22 11				
Newquay	a								21 20																
St Austell	d	19 42		19 52				20 30			20 41			21 30			21 44				22 19				
Truro	d	20 00		20 18				20 48			21 02			21 48			22 03				22 36				
Redruth	d	20 12		20 29				21 00			21 18			22 00			22 14				22 49				
Camborne	d	20 20		20 35				21 08			21 25						22 20								
Hayle	d																22 28								
St Erth	d	20 30		20 46				21 19			21 35			22 15			22 32		22 45						
Penzance	a	20 40		20 54				21 29			21 43			22 25			22 41		22 55		23 10				

A The Cornishman
B From Exmouth
C From Glasgow Central. ⊥ to Plymouth
D From Manchester Piccadilly. ⊥ to Bristol Temple Meads
E To Paignton
F From Aberdeen. ⊥ to Plymouth
G From St Ives
H The Golden Hind. ⊏⊐ from Taunton ✕ to Taunton
I From London Paddington
J ⊏⊐ to Westbury
K until 11 October, FX from 15 October. From Edinburgh

For connections from Heathrow Airport, Gatwick Airport and Oxford refer to Tables T148 and T116. Table T116 includes services to/from Bedwyn.

For the complete service between Westbury and Castle Cary refer to Table T123

T135 UPDATE: Major engineering work in connection with electrification works is taking place between Reading and Westbury. The route via Newbury will be closed to all trains on 4-7 June; 9-12 July; 16 July to 05 August; 28-30 August; 08-11 October and 19-22 November. Trains will be re-timed or cancelled and run to a special timetable during this period. Please check revised train times with *www.nationalrail.co.uk*. Rail replacement buses will operate between intermediate stations.

London and Birmingham - Devon and Cornwall

Mondays to Fridays
3 September to 7 December

		GW	GW	GW	GW	GW	GW	XC	XC	GW		XC	GW	GW	GW	GW	GW	GW	GW	GW
		FX	FO	FX	FO		FX											FX	FO	FX
		◇■	◇■	■ ■	■ ■			◇■	◇■	◇■		◇■		◇■	◇		◇■	■	■	■
				A	A			B	C			D						E	F	G
		☕	☕	✕☕	✕☕			⌶	⌶	☕				☕			☕	🛏 ☕	🛏 ☕	🛏 ☕
London Paddington 15 ⊖	d	18 33	18 33	19 03	19 03					20 03				21 03			21 45	23 45	23 45	
Slough 5	d																			
Reading 7	d	19 00	19 00	19 30	19u30					20 30				21 30			22 13	00u46	00u46	
Theale	d																			
Thatcham	d																			
Newbury	d	19 16	19 16	19 48	19 48					20 46				21 46						
Hungerford	d	19 26	19 26																	
Pewsey	d	19 44	19 44							21 06				22 05						
Westbury 123	d	20 04	20 04							21 27				22 27						
Frome 123	d																			
Castle Cary 123	d	20 22	20 22							21 45				22 45						
Birmingham New Street 12	d							19 12	19 42			20 12								
Cardiff Central 7	d																			
Newport (South Wales)	d																			
Swindon	d																22 51			
Bristol Parkway 7	d							20 32	20 56			21 26								
Filton Abbey Wood	d																			
Bath Spa 7	d																23 22			
Bristol Temple Meads 10	d							20 49	21 13			21 44			21 54	23 06	23 37			
Weston-super-Mare	d														22 29	23 42	00b08			
Bridgwater	d														22 48	00 02	00b26			
Taunton	d	20 45	20 45	20 53	20 53			21 20	21 44	22 07		22 16		23 08	23 12	00s14	00b38	02 38	02 38	
Tiverton Parkway	d	20 58	20 58	21 06	21 06			21 32	21 56	22 20		22 28		23 21	23 28	00s31	00b51			
Exeter St Davids 6	a	21 12	21 12	21 20	21 20			21 45	22 09	22 34		22 41		23 35	23 46	00 52	01 05	03 07	03 07	
Exmouth	d												22 07							
Exeter Central	d					21 21							22 35							
Exeter St Davids 6	d		21 14	21 22	21 23	21 29		21 47	22 10	22 36		22 42	22 46	23 37				04 11	04 11	
Exeter St Thomas	d					21 32							22 49							
Starcross	d					21 40							22 58							
Dawlish Warren	d					21 45							23 03							
Dawlish	d					21 49							23 07							
Teignmouth	d					21 54							23 12							
Newton Abbot	a		21 33	21 41	21 43	22 01		22 05	22 28	22 55		23 01	23 19	23 56				04 31	04 31	
	d		21 35	21 43	21 44	22 03		22 07	22 30	22 57		23 03	23 20	23 58				04 32	04 33	
Torre	d					22 11							23 27							
Torquay	d					22 14							23 30							
Paignton	a					22 21							23 37							
Totnes	d			21 55	21 57			22 18	22 41	23 09		23 19		00 10						
Ivybridge	d													00 26						←
Plymouth	a		22 11	22 22	22 24			22 45	23 07	23 36		23 44		00 40				05 11	05 11	05 11
	d				22 29		22 42											05 49	05 40	05 49
Devonport	d																	→		
Dockyard	d																			
Keyham	d																			
St Budeaux Ferry Road	d																			
Saltash	d				22 40		22 51													
St Germans	d				22 47		22 58													
Menheniot	d																			
Liskeard 5	d				23 00		23 10												06 06	06 15
Bodmin Parkway	d				23 14		23 24												06 20	06 29
Lostwithiel	d				23 20		23 29												06 27	06 35
Par	d				23 29		23 36												06 35	06 43
Newquay	a																			
St Austell	d				23 36		23 44												06 44	06 52
Truro	d				23 58		23 59												07 05	07 10
Redruth	d				00 13		00 14												07 18	07 23
Camborne	d				00 21		00 20												07 26	07 31
Hayle	d				00 30		00 27												07 35	07 40
St Erth	d				00 35		00 31												07 40	07 45
Penzance	a				00 45		00 41												07 50	07 55

A The Armada. ☕ from Taunton ✕ to Taunton
B From Glasgow Central. ⌶ to Bristol Temple Meads
C From Manchester Piccadilly. ⌶ to Bristol Temple Meads
D From Edinburgh
E To Penzance. The Night Riviera
F The Night Riviera
G From London Paddington. The Night Riviera
b Stops to set down only, stops on request

For connections from Heathrow Airport, Gatwick Airport and Oxford refer to Tables T148 and T116. Table T116 includes services to/from Bedwyn.

For the complete service between Westbury and Castle Cary refer to Table T123

London and Birmingham - Devon and Cornwall

Saturdays
26 May to 8 September

		GW	GW	GW	GW	GW	GW	GW	GW	XC		GW	GW	GW	GW	XC	GW	GW	GW	GW		GW	XC	GW	GW
			◇■	◇■	■ ■	■				◇■		◇			◇■	◇■	◇■		■ ■				◇■		■ ■
		A	B	B	C	D								E								F		G	
			☕	☕	☕	🛏 ☕									☕				☕				⌶		☕
London Paddington 15 ⊖	d																								07 03
Slough 5	d																								
Reading 7	d					00u46																			07u30
Theale	d																								
Thatcham	d																								
Newbury	d																								
Hungerford	d																								
Pewsey	d																								
Westbury 123	d																								
Frome 123	d																								
Castle Cary 123	d																								
Birmingham New Street 12	d																						06 42		
Cardiff Central 7	d																								
Newport (South Wales)	d																								
Swindon	d																								
Bristol Parkway 7	d																						07 55		
Filton Abbey Wood	d																								
Bath Spa 7	d																								
Bristol Temple Meads 10	d											05 24				06 08			06 43				08 12		
Weston-super-Mare	d		00b08									05 47							07 06						
Bridgwater	d	00 02	00b26									06 05													
Taunton	d	00s14	00b38			02 38						06 20				07 15			07 30				08 43		08 50
Tiverton Parkway	d	00s31	00b51									06 35				07 27			07 43				08 55		
Exeter St Davids 6	a	00 52	01 05			03 07						06 52				07 40			07 56				09 07		09 12
Exmouth	d																	07 18				08 23			
Exeter Central	d																	07 47				08 53			
Exeter St Davids 6	d					04 11	05 18	05 38	06 11			06 55				07 41		07 54	08 02	08 37		08 58	09 10		09 18
Exeter St Thomas	d						05 21	05 41	06 14			06 58						07 57	08 06			09 01			
Starcross	d						05 29	05 49	06 22			07 07						08 05				09 10		←	
Dawlish Warren	d						05 34	05 54	06 27			07 12						08 10				09 21		09 21	
Dawlish	d						05 38	05 58	06 31			07 16						08 14	08 20	08 50		→		09 25	09 32
Teignmouth	d						05 43	06 03	06 36			07 21						08 19	08 27	08 55				09 31	09 39
Newton Abbot	a					04 31	05 51	06 10	06 44			07 28				07 59		08 26	08 33	09 02			09 28	09 39	09 45
	d					04 33	05 52	06 11	06 45			07 28	07 40			08 01		08 28	08 35	09 06			09 29	09 40	09 47
Torre	d						06 00	06 19	06 53				07 48					08 36						09 49	
Torquay	d						06 03	06 22	06 56				07 51					08 39		09 16			09 41	09 52	
Paignton	a						06 11	06 31	07 06				07 59					08 48		09 25			09 47	10 00	
Totnes	d			00 10								07 42				08 12			08 48						10 00
Ivybridge	d			00 26								07 58							09 04						
Plymouth	a			00 40		05 11						08 13				08 38			09 17						10 26
	d					05 40				07 30					08 18		08 57		09 21						10 30
Devonport	d																								
Dockyard	d																								
Keyham	d																								
St Budeaux Ferry Road	d																								
Saltash	d														08 29		09 08		09 32						10 41
St Germans	d														08 36		09 15								10 49
Menheniot	d																								
Liskeard 5	d					06 06				07 53					08 49		09 28		09 48						11 02
Bodmin Parkway	d					06 20				08 05					09 02		09 41		10 01						11 15
Lostwithiel	d					06 27				08 11					09 08				10 08						11 21
Par	d					06 35				08 20					09 16		09 54		10 16						11 30
Newquay	a									09 10							10 47								
St Austell	d					06 44									09 23				10 23						11 37
Truro	d					07 05									09 42				10 42						11 56
Redruth	d				00 13	07 18									09 54				10 54						12 08
Camborne	d				00 21	07 26									10 02				11 02						12 16
Hayle	d				00 30	07 35									10 11				11 11						
St Erth	d				00 35	07 40								08 28	10 17				11 17						12 28
Penzance	a				00 45	07 50								08 40	10 27				11 27						12 38

A From Bristol Temple Meads
B From London Paddington
C From London Paddington. The Armada
D From London Paddington. The Night Riviera
E From St Ives
F To Paignton
G From Exmouth
b Stops to set down only, stops on request

For connections from Heathrow Airport, Gatwick Airport and Oxford refer to Tables T148 and T116. Table T116 includes services to/from Bedwyn.

For the complete service between Westbury and Castle Cary refer to Table T123

Table T135-F

Saturdays

26 May to 8 September

London and Birmingham - Devon and Cornwall

Station		XC ◇■ A 🛒	GW	GW	GW ■ 🍽	GW	GW	XC ◇■ B 🛒	GW	GW ■ C 🍽	GW ◇■ 🍽	GW ■ D 🍽	XC ◇■ E 🛒	XC ◇■ F 🛒	XC ◇■ G	GW C	GW ◇■ H 🍽	GW I	XC ◇■ J 🛒	XC ◇■ K	XC ◇■ L 🛒	GW	GW
London Paddington ■ ⊖	d				07 30					08 35	09 03						10 03						
Slough ■	d																						
Reading ■	d				07 58					09u03	09u31						10u31						
Theale	d																						
Thatcham	d																						
Newbury	d									09 20													
Hungerford	d																						
Pewsey	d									09 40													
Westbury 123	d									09 59													
Frome 123	d																						
Castle Cary 123	d									10 17													
Birmingham New Street ■	d	07 12						08 12					08 42	09 12	09 12				09 42	10 12	10 12		
Cardiff Central ■	d																						
Newport (South Wales)	d																						
Swindon	d				08 31																		
Bristol Parkway ■	d	08 26						09 26					09 55	10 31	10 31				10 56	11 27	11 27		
Filton Abbey Wood	d																						
Bath Spa ■	d				09 02																		
Bristol Temple Meads ■	d	08 45			09 17			09 44					10 20	10 45	10 45				11 12	11 44	11 44		
Weston-super-Mare	d																		11 39				
Bridgwater	d																						
Taunton	d	09 16			09 50			10 17		10 39	10 47		11 01	11 16	11 17				12 00	12 17	12 17		
Tiverton Parkway	d	09 28						10 30		10 52	11 00		11 13	11 28	11 30				12 12	12 30	12 30		
Exeter St Davids ■	a	09 40			10 13			10 43		11 06	11 14		11 26	11 41	11 43		12 04		12 25	12 43	12 43		
Exmouth	d			09 23					10 25							11 23							12 23
Exeter Central	d			09 52			10 30		10 53							11 52							12 52
Exeter St Davids ■	d	09 42	09 46	09 58	10 17	10 22	10 45	10 49	11 00	11 10	11 17		11 30	11 43	11 45	11 58	12 09		12 27	12 46	12 46	12 50	12 58
Exeter St Thomas	d			10 01					11 03							12 01							13 01
Starcross	d			10 10					11 12			←				12 10		←					13 10
Dawlish Warren	d			10 15		10 33			11 17	11 29		11 29				12 20		12 20				13 01	13 15
Dawlish	d			10 20		10 37		11 03	11 22	→		11 35				→		12 25	12 39			13 06	13 19
Teignmouth	d			10 25		10 42		11 09	11 28			11 42						12 31	12 44			13 11	13 24
Newton Abbot	a	10 00	10 06	10 32	10 36	10 49	11 05	11 15	11 35		11 39	11 48	11 52	12 01	12 03		12 28	12 38	12 50	13 04	13 04	13 18	13 31
	d	10 01	10 08	10 34	10 39	10 50	11 06	11 17	11 38		11 41	11 50	11 54	12 04	12 05		12 31	12 39	12 52	13 06	13 06	13 20	13 32
Torre	d			10 42			11 14		11 47									12 47					13 40
Torquay	d			10 45		11 00	11 17	11 29	11 50			12 03						12 50	13 03				13 43
Paignton	a			10 52		11 08	11 27	11 37	11 59			12 10						12 58	13 10				13 51
Totnes	d	10 13	10 21		10 52						11 54		12 07	12 15	12 17					13 18	13 18	13 33	
Ivybridge	d		10 37								12 10											13 49	
Plymouth	a	10 39	10 51		11 18						12 24		12 33	12 41	12 44		13 06			13 45	13 45	14 04	
	d		10 53		11 25						12 27		12 39				13 10			13 48	13 48		
Devonport	d		10 56																				
Dockyard	d																						
Keyham	d																						
St Budeaux Ferry Road	d		11 00																				
Saltash	d		11 05								12 38												
St Germans	d																						
Menheniot	d		11x16																				
Liskeard ■	d		11 23		11 50						12 54		13 05				13 35			14 11	14 11		
Bodmin Parkway	d		11 35		12 03						13 07		13 21				13 48			14 24	14 24		
Lostwithiel	d																						
Par	d		11 48		12 14								13 33				14 00			14 34	14 34		
Newquay	a		12 38										14 31										
St Austell	d				12 21						13 23						14 07			14 42	14 42		
Truro	d				12 40						13 42						14 25			15 00	15 00		
Redruth	d				12 52						13 54						14 37			15 12	15 12		
Camborne	d				13 00						14 02						14 45			15 19	15 19		
Hayle	d				13 09						14 11						14 54						
St Erth	d				13 15						14 17						15 01			15 29	15 29		
Penzance	a				13 25						14 27						15 11			15 38	15 38		

A From Derby
B From Leeds
C To Paignton
D From London Paddington
E From Manchester Piccadilly. 🛒 to Plymouth
F until 21 July. From York
G from 28 July. From Leeds
H The Cornish Riviera
I From Exmouth
J From Manchester Piccadilly
K from 28 July. From York
L until 21 July. From York. 🛒 to Plymouth

For connections from Heathrow Airport, Gatwick Airport and Oxford refer to Tables T148 and T116. Table T116 includes services to/from Bedwyn.

For the complete service between Westbury and Castle Cary refer to Table T123

Table T135-F

Saturdays

26 May to 8 September

London and Birmingham - Devon and Cornwall

Station		GW ■ A 🍽	GW ◇■ 🍽	GW ■ B 🍽	XC ◇■ C 🛒	GW ■ D 🍽	GW A	GW ◇■ E 🍽	GW F	GW	XC ◇■ G 🛒	XC ◇■ H	GW ◇■ 🍽	GW	GW A	GW ■ 🍽	GW F	XC ◇■ I 🛒	GW	GW	GW J	XC ◇■ K 🛒
London Paddington ■ ⊖	d	10 35	11 03			11 35		12 03					12 33			13 03						
Slough ■	d																					
Reading ■	d	11u03	11u31			12u03		12u32					13u00			13u31						
Theale	d																					
Thatcham	d																					
Newbury	d												13 16									
Hungerford	d																					
Pewsey	d	11 35											13 36									
Westbury 123	d	11 54				12 53							13 55									
Frome 123	d																					
Castle Cary 123	d	12 12											14 13									
Birmingham New Street ■	d				11 12						12 12	12 12						13 12				13 42
Cardiff Central ■	d																					
Newport (South Wales)	d																					
Swindon	d																					
Bristol Parkway ■	d				12 31						13 25	13 25						14 28				14 56
Filton Abbey Wood	d																					
Bath Spa ■	d																					
Bristol Temple Meads ■	d				12 44						13 45	13 45						14 44				15 12
Weston-super-Mare	d																					
Bridgwater	d																					
Taunton	d	12 35			13 17	13 32					14 17	14 17	14 36			14 46		15 16				15 43
Tiverton Parkway	d	12 48			13 30						14 30	14 30				14 59		15 28				15 55
Exeter St Davids ■	a	13 01	13 06		13 43	13 55		14 04			14 43	14 43	14 58			15 13		15 40				16 07
Exmouth	d						13 23								14 25					15 24		
Exeter Central	d						13 55								14 53					15 53		
Exeter St Davids ■	d	13 08	13 14		13 45	13 59	14 03	14 10		14 30	14 46	14 46	15 03		15 06	15 16		15 42		15 58		16 10
Exeter St Thomas	d						14 06								15 09					16 01		
Starcross	d			←			14 14		←						15 17		←			16 10		
Dawlish Warren	d	13 27		13 27			14 25		14 25	14 41			15 16		15 28		15 28	15 54		16 15		16 31
Dawlish	d	→		13 34			→		14 29	14 45	14 58	14 58	15 21		→		15 32			16 19		→
Teignmouth	d			13 42					14 34	14 50	15 04	15 04	15 28				15 37			16 24		
Newton Abbot	a		13 35	13 48	14 03			14 32	14 41	14 57	15 11	15 11	15 34			15 38	15 44	16 04		16 31		
	d		13 37	13 50	14 05			14 35	14 42	14 59	15 13	15 13	15 36			15 40	15 46	16 06	16 23	16 33		
Torre	d								14 51	15 07							15 54			16 41		
Torquay	d			14 03					14 54	15 10	15 25	15 25	15 49				15 57			16 44		
Paignton	a			14 12					15 01	15 18	15 33	15 33	15 58				16 06			16 52		
Totnes	d		13 50		14 19											15 53		16 17	16 36			
Ivybridge	d																		16 52			
Plymouth	a		14 16		14 45	14 54		15 11								16 19		16 43	17 09			
	d		14 22			14 58		15 16						15 58		16 23		16 50				
Devonport	d																					
Dockyard	d																					
Keyham	d																					
St Budeaux Ferry Road	d																					
Saltash	d													16 07								
St Germans	d													16 14								
Menheniot	d													16x21								
Liskeard ■	d		14 47					15 41						16 28		16 48		17 13				
Bodmin Parkway	d		15 00					15 54						16 40		17 01		17 29				
Lostwithiel	d					15 38								16 45								
Par	d					15 49		16 05						16 52				17 41				
Newquay	a					16 47												18 39				
St Austell	d		15 16					16 12						16 59		17 16						
Truro	d		15 35					16 31						17a18		17 35						
Redruth	d		15 47					16 43								17 47						
Camborne	d		15 55					16 51								17 55						
Hayle	d		16 04													18 04						
St Erth	d		16 10					17 02								18 10					18 32	
Penzance	a		16 20					17 12								18 20					18 44	

A To Paignton
B From London Paddington
C From Edinburgh
D The Atlantic Coast Express
E The Royal Duchy
F From Exmouth
G until 21 July. From Glasgow Central
H from 28 July. From Edinburgh
I From Dundee
J From St Ives
K From Manchester Piccadilly to Paignton

For connections from Heathrow Airport, Gatwick Airport and Oxford refer to Tables T148 and T116. Table T116 includes services to/from Bedwyn.

For the complete service between Westbury and Castle Cary refer to Table T123

T135 UPDATE: Major engineering work in connection with electrification works is taking place between Reading and Westbury. The route via Newbury will be closed to all trains on 4-7 June; 9-12 July; 16 July to 05 August; 28-30 August; 08-11 October and 19-22 November. Trains will be re-timed or cancelled and run to a special timetable during this period. Please check revised train times with *www.nationalrail.co.uk*. Rail replacement buses will operate between intermediate stations.

Table T135-F

Saturdays

26 May to 8 September

London and Birmingham - Devon and Cornwall

		GW	XC	XC	XC	GW	GW	GW	GW	XC	GW	GW	GW	GW	XC	GW	GW	GW	GW	GW	GW	XC	GW
		◇1	◇1	◇1	◇1	◇1		◇1		◇1			◇1		◇1			◇1	◇1			◇1	◇1
			A	B	C					D					E		F		G	H		I	
		⊒	⊥	⊥	⊥			⊒		⊥			⊒		⊥			⊒	⊒			⊥	⊒
London Paddington 15 ⊖	d	14 03						15 03					16 03					17 03	16 30				18 03
Slough 3	d																						
Reading 7	d	14u31						15u31					16u31					17u31	16 58				18u31
Theale	d																						
Thatcham	d																						
Newbury	d																						
Hungerford	d																						
Pewsey	d							16 01										18 02					
Westbury 123	d							16 20										18 21					
Frome 123	d																						
Castle Cary 123	d							16 38										18 39					
Birmingham New Street 12	d			14 12	14 12					15 12					16 12							17 12	
Cardiff Central 7	d																						
Newport (South Wales)	d																						
Swindon	d																		17 31				
Bristol Parkway 7	d			15 26	15 26					16 31					17 27							18 31	
Filton Abbey Wood	d																						
Bath Spa 7	d																		18 02				
Bristol Temple Meads 10	d			15 43	15 44					16 45					17 44				18 18			18 44	
Weston-super-Mare	d																		18 42				
Bridgwater	d																						
Taunton	d	15 48		16 15	16 15			17 01		17 18			17 46		18 16			19 02	19 08			19 16	19 46
Tiverton Parkway	d	16 01		16 27	16 27			17 14		17 31			17 59		18 28			19 15	19 21			19 28	
Exeter St Davids 6	a	16 15		16 40	16 40			17 28		17 44			18 12		18 41			19 29	19 35			19 44	20 09
Exmouth	d								16 53					17 53									
Exeter Central	d						16 48		17 24					18 21									
Exeter St Davids 6	d	16 18		16 42	16 42		16 55	17 30	17 34	17 47		17 51	18 16	18 27	18 46	19 03	19 18	19 34	19 40			19 45	20 13
Exeter St Thomas	d						16 58		17 37					18 30			19 21						
Starcross	d		←				17 06		17 45					18 38			19 29						
Dawlish Warren	d		16 31				17 11		17 50			18 03		18 43			19 34						
Dawlish	d		16 36				17 15		17 54			18 08		18 47		19 16	19 38						
Teignmouth	d		16 41				17 20		17 59			18 14		18 52		19 21	19 43						
Newton Abbot	a	16 37	16 47	17 00	17 00		17 27	17 49	18 06	18 10		18 22	18 35	18 59	19 04	19 28	19 50	19 54	19 59			20 05	20 32
	d	16 39	16 49	17 02	17 02		17 29	17 51	18 09	18 12		18 23	18 37	19 01	19 05	19 28	19 52	19 56	20 01			20 06	20 34
Torre	d						17 37		18 17					19 09			20 00		20 11				
Torquay	d		17 01				17 40		18 20					19 12		19 38	20 03		20 15				
Paignton	a		17 10				17 50		18 30					19 21		19 46	20 13		20 24				
Totnes	d	16 52		17 13	17 13			18 04		18 24		18 36	18 50		19 17			20 08				20 18	20 47
Ivybridge	d	17 08										18 52	19 06										
Plymouth	a	17 21		17 39	17 39			18 31		18 51		19 08	19 20		19 42			20 35				20 43	21 13
	d	17 26		17 42	17 42	17 52				18 55		19 10	19 30		19 48						20 42		21 21
Devonport	d					17 57															20 45		
Dockyard	d																				20x46		
Keyham	d																				20 48		
St Budeaux Ferry Road	d																				20 50		
Saltash	d					18 05						19 20									20 55		
St Germans	d					18 13						19 28									21 03		
Menheniot	d					18 21																	
Liskeard 8	d	17 51		18 05	18 05	18 28				19 21		19 40	19 55		20 11						21 15		21 47
Bodmin Parkway	d	18 04		18 17	18 17	18 41				19 33		19 54	20 08		20 23						21 27		22 01
Lostwithiel	d					18 47							20 14		20 28						21 32		
Par	d	18 15		18 28	18 28	18 55				19 44	19 48	20 05	20 22		20 35						21 39		22 12
Newquay	a										20 40												
St Austell	d	18 22		18 34	18 34	19 03				19 53		20 12	20 29		20 41						21 46		22 19
Truro	d	18 41		18 52	18 52	19 21				20 11		20 31	20 48		21 02						22 04		22 38
Redruth	d	18 53		19 08	19 08	19 34				20 24		20 44	21 00		21 13						22 17		22 51
Camborne	d	19 01		19 15	19 15	19 41				20 31		20 51	21 08		21 19						22 23		22 58
Hayle	d			19 23	19 23	19 50									21 27						22 30		23 07
St Erth	d	19 11		19 27	19 27	19 55				20 43		21 01	21 18		21 31					22 20	22 34		23 13
Penzance	a	19 21		19 36	19 36	20 05				20 52		21 12	21 28		21 40					22 30	22 43		23 23

A From Manchester Piccadilly
B until 21 July. From Glasgow Central. ⊥ to Plymouth
C from 28 July. From Newcastle. ⊥ to Plymouth
D From Glasgow Central. ⊥ to Plymouth
E From Aberdeen. ⊥ to Plymouth
F From Barnstaple
G The Torbay Express
H From St Ives
I From Glasgow Central

For connections from Heathrow Airport, Gatwick Airport and Oxford refer to Tables T148 and T116. Table T116 includes services to/from Bedwyn.

For the complete service between Westbury and Castle Cary refer to Table T123

Table T135-F

Saturdays

26 May to 8 September

London and Birmingham - Devon and Cornwall

		GW	XC	GW	XC	GW	GW	GW	XC	GW	GW
			◇1	◇1	◇1		◇1		◇1	◇	◇1
			A		B				A		
			⊥	⊒	⊥		⊒				⊒
London Paddington 15 ⊖	d			19 03			20 03				20 30
Slough 3	d										
Reading 7	d			19 31			20 30				20 58
Theale	d										
Thatcham	d										
Newbury	d			19 47			20 46				
Hungerford	d										
Pewsey	d			20 07			21 06				
Westbury 123	d			20 26			21 26				
Frome 123	d										
Castle Cary 123	d			20 44			21 44				
Birmingham New Street 12	d		18 12		19 12				20 12		
Cardiff Central 7	d										
Newport (South Wales)	d										
Swindon	d										21 31
Bristol Parkway 7	d		19 26		20 31				21 25		
Filton Abbey Wood	d										
Bath Spa 7	d										22 02
Bristol Temple Meads 10	d		19 44		20 44				21 45	22 02	22 17
Weston-super-Mare	d									22 35	22s47
Bridgwater	d									22 54	23s05
Taunton	d		20 16	21 07	21 16		22 07		22 18	23 07	23 17
Tiverton Parkway	d		20 28	21 20	21 28		22 20		22 30	23 23	23 30
Exeter St Davids 6	a		20 40	21 34	21 43		22 34		22 44	23 41	23 46
Exmouth	d	19 41				21 16					
Exeter Central	d	20 04				21 44					
Exeter St Davids 6	d	20 18	20 42	21 37	21 45	21 50	22 38		22 47		
Exeter St Thomas	d	20 21				21 53					
Starcross	d	20 29				22 01					
Dawlish Warren	d	20 34				22 06					
Dawlish	d	20 38				22 10	22 51				
Teignmouth	d	20 43				22 15	22 57				
Newton Abbot	a	20 50	21 00	21 56	22 04	22 22	23 03		23 11		
	d	20 52	21 01	21 58	22 06	22 23	23 06	23 08	23 13		
Torre	d	21 00				22 31		23 16			
Torquay	d	21 03				22 34		23 19			
Paignton	a	21 10				22 42		23 27			
Totnes	d		21 13	22 11	22 21		23 18		23 30		
Ivybridge	d										
Plymouth	a		21 38	22 38	22 50		23 45		23 56		
	d										
Devonport	d										
Dockyard	d										
Keyham	d										
St Budeaux Ferry Road	d										
Saltash	d										
St Germans	d										
Menheniot	d										
Liskeard 8	d										
Bodmin Parkway	d										
Lostwithiel	d										
Par	d										
Newquay	a										
St Austell	d										
Truro	d										
Redruth	d										
Camborne	d										
Hayle	d										
St Erth	d										
Penzance	a										

A From Edinburgh
B From Glasgow Central

For connections from Heathrow Airport, Gatwick Airport and Oxford refer to Tables T148 and T116. Table T116 includes services to/from Bedwyn.

For the complete service between Westbury and Castle Cary refer to Table T123

London and Birmingham - Devon and Cornwall

	GW	GW	GW	GW	GW	GW	GW	GW	GW		GW	XC	GW	GW	GW	GW	XC	GW	GW		GW	GW	GW	XC
		◇■	◇■	R ■		R						◇■		◇			◇■		◇					◇■
	A	B	B	C		D							E										F	
		⊡	⊡	⊡		🛏 ⊡																		⊼
London Paddington ⊖ d																								
Slough d																								
Reading d						00u46																		
Theale d																								
Thatcham d																								
Newbury d																								
Hungerford d																								
Pewsey d																								
Westbury 123 d																								
Frome 123 d																								
Castle Cary 123 d																								
Birmingham New Street d																								06 42
Cardiff Central d																								
Newport (South Wales) d																								
Swindon d																								
Bristol Parkway d																								07 55
Filton Abbey Wood d																								
Bath Spa d																								
Bristol Temple Meads d														05 24			06 08		06 42					08 12
Weston-super-Mare d		00b08												05 47					07 06					
Bridgwater d	00 02	00b26												06 05										
Taunton d	00s14	00b38				02 38								06 20			07 15		07 34					08 43
Tiverton Parkway d	00s31	00b51												06 35			07 27		07 49					08 55
Exeter St Davids a	00 52	01 05				03 07								06 52			07 40		08 06					09 07
Exmouth d																		07 18					08 23	
Exeter Central d																		07 47					08 53	
Exeter St Davids d						04 11		05 18	05 38		06 11			06 55			07 41	07 54	08 10			08 37	08 59	09 10
Exeter St Thomas d								05 21	05 41		06 14			06 58				07 57	08 13				09 02	
Starcross d								05 29	05 49		06 22			07 07				08 05					09 10	
Dawlish Warren d								05 34	05 54		06 27			07 12				08 10					09 22	
Dawlish d								05 38	05 58		06 31			07 16				08 14	08 25			08 50	→	
Teignmouth d								05 43	06 03		06 36			07 21				08 19	08 30			08 55		
Newton Abbot a						04 31		05 51	06 10		06 44			07 28			07 59	08 26	08 37			09 02		09 28
d						04 33		05 52	06 11		06 45			07 28		07 40	08 01	08 28	08 38			09 06		09 29
Torre d								06 00	06 19		06 53					07 48		08 36						
Torquay d								06 03	06 22		06 56					07 51		08 39				09 16		09 41
Paignton a								06 11	06 31		07 06					07 59		08 48				09 25		09 47
Totnes d			00 10											07 42			08 12		08 50					
Ivybridge d			00 26											07 58					09 07					
Plymouth a			00 40			05 11								08 11			08 38		09 21					
d						05 40						06 28		08 18					09 23		09 50			
Devonport d														08 21							09 53			
Dockyard d																								
Keyham d																								
St Budeaux Ferry Road d																								
Saltash d														08 28					09 32		10 00			
St Germans d														08 35					09 39		10 07			
Menheniot d																					10x14			
Liskeard d						06 06						06 51		08 47					09 51		10 21			
Bodmin Parkway d						06 20						07 03		08 59					10 03		10 33			
Lostwithiel d						06 27						07 08		09 04							10 39			
Par d					06 10	06 35	06 52					07 14		09 11	09 17				10 15		10 46			
Newquay a							07 44								10 09									
St Austell d					06 17	06 44						07 21		09 19					10 22		10 53			
Truro d					06 35	07 05						07 37		09 36					10 40		11 11			
Redruth d				00 13	06 48	07 18						07 48		09 49					10 53		11 24			
Camborne d				00 21	06 54	07 26						07 55		09 55					10 59		11 30			
Hayle d				00 30	07 01	07 35						08 03		10 02					11 06		11 37			
St Erth d				00 35	07 05	07 40						08 07	08 28	10 07					11 10		11 42			
Penzance a				00 45	07 15	07 50						08 15	08 40	10 17					11 22		11 52			

A From Bristol Temple Meads
B From London Paddington
C From London Paddington. The Armada
D From London Paddington. The Night Riviera
E From St Ives
F To Paignton
b Stops to set down only, stops on request

For connections from Heathrow Airport, Gatwick Airport and Oxford refer to Tables T148 and T116. Table T116 includes services to/from Bedwyn.

For the complete service between Westbury and Castle Cary refer to Table T123

London and Birmingham - Devon and Cornwall

	GW	GW	XC	GW	GW		GW	GW	GW	GW	XC	GW	GW	GW	XC		XC	GW	GW	GW	GW	XC	XC	XC
			◇■		R ■		◇	◇■			◇■		◇■		◇■		◇■	◇		◇■		◇■	◇■	◇■
	A		B								C	D		A	E		F		D	G	A	H	I	J
			⊼		⊡			⊡			⊼		⊡		⊼					⊡		⊼		⊼
London Paddington ⊖ d					07 30			08 03					09 03							10 03				
Slough d																								
Reading d					07 58			08 33					09 31							10 31				
Theale d																								
Thatcham d																								
Newbury d								08 50																
Hungerford d																								
Pewsey d								09 10																
Westbury 123 d								09 29																
Frome 123 d																								
Castle Cary 123 d								09 47																
Birmingham New Street d			07 12								08 12				09 12		09 12					09 42	10 05	10 12
Cardiff Central d																								
Newport (South Wales) d																								
Swindon d					08 31																			
Bristol Parkway d			08 26								09 26				10 31		10 31					10 56	11 20	11 27
Filton Abbey Wood d																								
Bath Spa d					09 02																			
Bristol Temple Meads d			08 45		09 17						09 44				10 45		10 45					11 12	11 37	11 44
Weston-super-Mare d																						11 39		
Bridgwater d																								
Taunton d			09 16		09 50			10 11			10 17		10 46		11 16		11 17					12 00	12 10	12 16
Tiverton Parkway d			09 28					10 24			10 30		10 59		11 28		11 30					12 12	12 22	12 28
Exeter St Davids a			09 40		10 13			10 39			10 43		11 13		11 41		11 43			12 04		12 25	12 34	12 41
Exmouth d				09 23								10 25							11 23					
Exeter Central d				09 52						10 33		10 53							11 52					
Exeter St Davids d		09 28	09 42	09 58	10 16				10 22	10 45	10 50	10 59	11 17		11 43		11 45		11 58	12 08		12 27	12 36	12 42
Exeter St Thomas d				10 01								11 02							12 01					
Starcross d	←			10 09								11 11							12 09		←			
Dawlish Warren d	09 22			10 14					10 33			11 16							12 19		12 19			
Dawlish d	09 26			10 18					10 37			11 20							→		12 24	12 39		
Teignmouth d	09 31			10 23					10 42			11 25		←							12 29	12 44		
Newton Abbot a	09 38	09 48	10 00	10 30	10 35				10 49	11 05	11 09	11 32	11 36	11 32	12 01		12 03			12 27	12 36	12 50	12 54	13 00
d	09 39	09 49	10 01	10 33	10 37				10 50	11 06	11 11	11 41	11 39	11 41	12 04		12 05			12 29	12 37	12 52	12 55	13 02
Torre d	09 47			10 41						11 14		→		11 49							12 46			
Torquay d	09 50			10 44					11 00	11 17				11 52							12 49	13 03		
Paignton a	09 58			10 51					11 08	11 26				12 01							12 57	13 10		
Totnes d		10 01	10 13		10 50						11 23		11 52		12 15		12 17						13 07	13 13
Ivybridge d		10 18											12 08											
Plymouth a		10 32	10 39		11 16						11 51		12 22		12 41		12 44			13 04			13 33	13 39
d		10 33			11 20													12 45		13 10				
Devonport d																								
Dockyard d																								
Keyham d																								
St Budeaux Ferry Road d		10 39																						
Saltash d		10 44																12 54						
St Germans d		10 51																13 01						
Menheniot d																								
Liskeard d		11 03			11 45													13 13		13 35				
Bodmin Parkway d		11 15			11 58													13 25		13 48				
Lostwithiel d		11 20																13 30						
Par d		11 28			12 09		12 12											13 37		14 00				
Newquay a							13 04																	
St Austell d		11 37			12 16													13 45		14 07				
Truro d		11 55			12 35													14 02		14 25				
Redruth d		12 08			12 47													14 15		14 37				
Camborne d		12 14			12 55													14 21		14 45				
Hayle d		12 21																14 28		14 54				
St Erth d		12 25			13 05													14 33		14 59				
Penzance a		12 36			13 15													14 43		15 09				

A From Exmouth
B From Derby
C From Leeds
D To Paignton
E from 13 October. From York
F until 6 October. From Leeds
G The Cornish Riviera
H From Manchester Piccadilly
I until 6 October. From York
J from 13 October. From Newcastle

For connections from Heathrow Airport, Gatwick Airport and Oxford refer to Tables T148 and T116. Table T116 includes services to/from Bedwyn.

For the complete service between Westbury and Castle Cary refer to Table T123

T135 UPDATE: Major engineering work in connection with electrification works is taking place between Reading and Westbury. The route via Newbury will be closed to all trains on 4-7 June; 9-12 July; 16 July to 05 August; 28-30 August; 08-11 October and 19-22 November. Trains will be re-timed or cancelled and run to a special timetable during this period. Please check revised train times with *www.nationalrail.co.uk*. Rail replacement buses will operate between intermediate stations.

Table T135-F

Saturdays

15 September to 8 December

London and Birmingham - Devon and Cornwall

		GW ◇	GW	GW	GW ◇■	XC ◇■ A	GW B	GW ◇■ C	GW D	GW	XC ◇■ E	XC ◇■ F	GW ◇■	GW ◇	GW	GW B	GW ■	GW D	XC ◇■ G	XC ◇■ H	GW	GW I
London Paddington ⊖	d				11 03			12 03					12 33				13 03					
Slough	d																					
Reading	d				11 31			12 32					13 00				13 31					
Theale	d																					
Thatcham	d																					
Newbury	d												13 16									
Hungerford	d																					
Pewsey	d				12 02								13 36									
Westbury 123	d				12 21								13 55									
Frome 123	d																					
Castle Cary 123	d				12 39								14 13									
Birmingham New Street	d					11 12					12 12	12 12							13 12	13 42		
Cardiff Central	d																					
Newport (South Wales)	d																					
Swindon	d																					
Bristol Parkway	d					12 31					13 25	13 25							14 28	14 56		
Filton Abbey Wood	d																					
Bath Spa	d																					
Bristol Temple Meads	d					12 44					13 45	13 45							14 44	15 12		
Weston-super-Mare	d																					
Bridgwater	d																					
Taunton	d				13 01	13 17					14 17	14 17	14a34				14 46		15 17	15 43		
Tiverton Parkway	d				13 14	13 30					14 30	14 30					14 59		15 29	15 55		
Exeter St Davids	a				13 28	13 43		14 04			14 43	14 43					15 13		15 43	16 09		
Exmouth	d			12 23			13 23									14 25						
Exeter Central	d			12 52			13 52									14 53						
Exeter St Davids	d		12 53	12 58	13 30	13 45	13 58	14 08		14 30	14 46	14 46				14 59	15 16		15 44			
Exeter St Thomas	d			13 01			14 01									15 02						
Starcross	d			13 10			14 09		←							15 10						
Dawlish Warren	d		13 04	13 15			14 20		14 20	14 41						15 15						
Dawlish	d		13 08	13 19			→		14 24	14 45						15 19						
Teignmouth	d		13 13	13 24					14 29	14 50						15 24		←				
Newton Abbot	a		13 20	13 31	13 50	14 03		14 27	14 36	14 57	15 04	15 04				15 31	15 35	15 31	16 03			
	d		13 22	13 32	13 51	14 05		14 29	14 37	14 59	15 06	15 06				15 40	15 37	15 40	16 04		16 23	
Torre	d			13 40					14 46	15 07						→		15 48				
Torquay	d			13 43					14 49	15 10								15 51				
Paignton	a			13 51					14 56	15 18								16 00				
Totnes	d		13 35		14 04	14 19					15 18	15 18					15 50		16 17		16 36	
Ivybridge	d		13 51																		16 52	
Plymouth	a		14 05		14 31	14 45		15 04			15 45	15 45					16 16		16 43		17 09	
	d		14 09					15 10							15 55		16 21					
Devonport	d																					
Dockyard	d																					
Keyham	d																					
St Budeaux Ferry Road	d																					
Saltash	d		14 18												16 04							
St Germans	d		14 25												16 10							
Menheniot	d														16x17							
Liskeard	d		14 37					15 35							16 24		16 46					
Bodmin Parkway	d		14 49					15 48							16 36		16 59					
Lostwithiel	d		14 54												16 41							
Par	d	14 05	15 01					15 59						16 10	16 48							
Newquay	a	14 57												17 02								
St Austell	d		15 08					16 06							16 56		17 14					
Truro	d		15 26					16 25							17 13		17 33					
Redruth	d		15 39					16 37							17 26		17 45					
Camborne	d		15 45					16 45							17 32		17 53					
Hayle	d														17 39		18 02					
St Erth	d		15 55					16 55							17 44		18 07					18 32
Penzance	a		16 06					17 05							17 54		18 17					18 44

A From Edinburgh
B To Paignton
C The Royal Duchy
D From Exmouth
E from 13 October. From Glasgow Central
F until 6 October. From Edinburgh
G From Dundee
H From Manchester Piccadilly
I From St Ives

For connections from Heathrow Airport, Gatwick Airport and Oxford refer to Tables T148 and T116. Table T116 includes services to/from Bedwyn.

For the complete service between Westbury and Castle Cary refer to Table T123

Table T135-F

Saturdays

15 September to 8 December

London and Birmingham - Devon and Cornwall

		GW A	GW ◇■	GW B	XC ◇■ C	GW	GW ◇	GW	GW ◇■	GW	XC ◇■ D	GW	GW	XC ◇■ E	GW ◇■	GW	XC ◇■ F	GW	GW G	GW H	GW ◇■	GW ◇■ I	XC ◇■ D
London Paddington ⊖	d		14 03						15 03						16 03						17 03	16 30	
Slough	d																						
Reading	d		14 31						15 31						16 31						17 31	16 58	
Theale	d																						
Thatcham	d																						
Newbury	d																						
Hungerford	d																						
Pewsey	d								16 01												18 02		
Westbury 123	d								16 20												18 21		
Frome 123	d																						
Castle Cary 123	d								16 38												18 39		
Birmingham New Street	d				14 12						15 12			15 42			16 12						17 12
Cardiff Central	d																						
Newport (South Wales)	d																						
Swindon	d																					17 31	
Bristol Parkway	d				15 26						16 31			16 55			17 27						18 31
Filton Abbey Wood	d																						
Bath Spa	d																					18 02	
Bristol Temple Meads	d				15 44						16 45			17 10			17 44					18 18	18 44
Weston-super-Mare	d																					18 42	
Bridgwater	d																						
Taunton	d		15 48		16 15				17 01		17 18			17 41	17 46		18 16				19 02	19 08	19 16
Tiverton Parkway	d		16 01		16 27				17 14		17 31			17 53	17 59		18 28				19 15	19 21	19 28
Exeter St Davids	a		16 15		16 40				17 28		17 44			18 05	18 12		18 41				19 29	19 35	19 44
Exmouth	d	15 24								16 53						17 53							
Exeter Central	d	15 53				16 48				17 24						18 21							
Exeter St Davids	d	16 01	16 18		16 42	16 55			17 30	17 34	17 47	17 53		18 07	18 16	18 27	18 46	19 00	19 18		19 34	19 40	19 45
Exeter St Thomas	d	16 04				16 58				17 37						18 30			19 21				
Starcross	d	16 12				17 06				17 45						18 38			19 29				
Dawlish Warren	d	16 17				17 11				17 50		18 04				18 43			19 34				
Dawlish	d	16 21				17 15				17 54		18 08		18 19		18 47		19 13	19 38				
Teignmouth	d	16 26		←		17 20				17 59		18 13		18 24		18 52		19 18	19 43				
Newton Abbot	a	16 33	16 37	16 33	17 00	17 27			17 49	18 06	18 10	18 20		18 30	18 35	18 59	19 04	19 25	19 50		19 54	19 59	20 05
	d	16 42	16 39	16 42	17 02	17 29			17 51	18 09	18 12	18 22		18 31	18 37	19 01	19 05	19 25	19 52		19 56	20 01	20 06
Torre	d	→		16 50		17 37				18 17						19 09			20 00			20 11	
Torquay	d			16 53		17 40				18 20				18 43		19 12		19 35	20 03			20 15	
Paignton	a			17 01		17 50				18 30				18 49		19 21		19 43	20 13			20 24	
Totnes	d		16 52		17 13				18 04		18 24	18 35			18 50		19 17				20 08		20 18
Ivybridge	d		17 08									18 51			19 06								
Plymouth	a		17 21		17 39				18 30		18 51	19 05			19 20		19 42				20 34		20 43
	d		17 26					17 52	18 39		18 55	19 10					19 48				20 40		20 58
Devonport	d							17 55															
Dockyard	d							17x57															
Keyham	d							17 59															
St Budeaux Ferry Road	d							18 01															
Saltash	d							18 06				19 19									20 50		
St Germans	d							18 12				19 26									20 58		
Menheniot	d							18x19															
Liskeard	d		17 51					18 26	19 04		19 21	19 38					20 11				21 10		21 25
Bodmin Parkway	d		18 04					18 38	19 17		19 33	19 50					20 23				21 24		21 37
Lostwithiel	d							18 43				19 55					20 28						
Par	d		18 15				18 20	18 50	19 28		19 44	20 03	20 15				20 35				21 36		21 47
Newquay	a						19 12						21 07										
St Austell	d		18 22					18 58	19 35		19 53	20 10					20 41				21 44		22 01
Truro	d		18 41					19 15	19 54		20 11	20 28					21 02				22 03		22 18
Redruth	d		18 53					19 28	20 06		20 24	20 41					21 13				22 15		22 29
Camborne	d		19 01					19 34	20 14		20 31	20 47					21 19						22 35
Hayle	d							19 41									21 27						
St Erth	d		19 11					19 46	20 24		20 43	21 00					21 31			22 20	22 32		22 45
Penzance	a		19 21					19 56	20 34		20 52	21 10					21 40			22 30	22 42		22 54

A To Paignton
B From Exmouth
C From Glasgow Central
D From Glasgow Central. to Plymouth
E From Manchester Piccadilly
F From Aberdeen. to Plymouth
G From Barnstaple
H From St Ives
I The Torbay Express

For connections from Heathrow Airport, Gatwick Airport and Oxford refer to Tables T148 and T116. Table T116 includes services to/from Bedwyn.

For the complete service between Westbury and Castle Cary refer to Table T123

Table T135-F

Saturdays
15 September to 8 December

London and Birmingham - Devon and Cornwall

		GW	GW	XC	GW	XC	GW	XC	GW	GW	XC	GW	GW
		◇1		◇1	◇1	◇1		◇1	◇1		◇1	◇	◇1
				A		B		C			A		
		☕		🛒	☕	🛒			☕				☕
London Paddington ⊖	d	18 03			19 03				20 03				20 30
Slough	d												
Reading	d	18 31			19 31				20 30				20 58
Theale	d												
Thatcham	d												
Newbury	d				19 47				20 46				
Hungerford	d												
Pewsey	d				20 07				21 06				
Westbury 123	d				20 26				21 26				
Frome 123	d												
Castle Cary 123	d				20 44				21 44				
Birmingham New Street	d			18 12		19 12		19 42			20 12		
Cardiff Central	d												
Newport (South Wales)	d												
Swindon	d												21 31
Bristol Parkway	d			19 26		20 31		20 55			21 25		
Filton Abbey Wood	d												
Bath Spa	d												22 02
Bristol Temple Meads	d			19 44		20 44		21 11			21 45	22 02	22 17
Weston-super-Mare	d											22 35	22s47
Bridgwater	d											22 54	23s05
Taunton	d	19 46		20 16	21 07	21 16		21 42	22 07		22 18	23 07	23 17
Tiverton Parkway	d			20 28	21 20	21 28		21 54	22 20		22 30	23 23	23 30
Exeter St Davids	a	20 09		20 40	21 34	21 43		22 07	22 34		22 44	23 41	23 46
Exmouth	d		19 41				21 16						
Exeter Central	d		20 04				21 44						
Exeter St Davids	d	20 13	20 18	20 42	21 37	21 45	21 50	22 08	22 38		22 47		
Exeter St Thomas	d		20 21				21 53						
Starcross	d		20 29				22 01						
Dawlish Warren	d		20 34				22 06						
Dawlish	d		20 38				22 10		22 51				
Teignmouth	d		20 43				22 15		22 57				
Newton Abbot	a	20 32	20 50	21 00	21 56	22 04	22 22	22 26	23 03		23 11		
	d	20 34	20 52	21 01	21 58	22 06	22 23	22 28	23 06	23 08	23 13		
Torre	d		21 00				22 31			23 16			
Torquay	d		21 03				22 34			23 19			
Paignton	a		21 10				22 42			23 27			
Totnes	d	20 47		21 13	22 11	22 21		22 39	23 18		23 30		
Ivybridge	d												
Plymouth	a	21 13		21 38	22 38	22 50		23 05	23 45		23 56		
	d	21 21											
Devonport	d												
Dockyard	d												
Keyham	d												
St Budeaux Ferry Road	d												
Saltash	d												
St Germans	d												
Menheniot	d												
Liskeard	d	21 46											
Bodmin Parkway	d	22 00											
Lostwithiel	d												
Par	d	22 11											
Newquay	a												
St Austell	d	22 19											
Truro	d	22 38											
Redruth	d	22 50											
Camborne	d	22 58											
Hayle	d	23 06											
St Erth	d	23 12											
Penzance	a	23 22											

A From Edinburgh
B From Glasgow Central
C From Manchester Piccadilly

For connections from Heathrow Airport, Gatwick Airport and Oxford refer to Tables T148 and T116. Table T116 includes services to/from Bedwyn.

For the complete service between Westbury and Castle Cary refer to Table T123

Table T135-F

Sundays
20 May to 9 September

London and Birmingham - Devon and Cornwall

		GW	GW	XC	GW	GW	GW	XC	GW	GW	GW	GW	XC	GW	GW	GW	XC	GW	GW	GW	XC	GW	GW
				◇1		◇		◇1			◇		◇1		◇1	◇1	◇1			◇1	◇1		◇1
					A		B			A		C					D				E		
								🛒					🛒		☕	☕	🛒			☕	🛒		☕
London Paddington ⊖	d														07 57	08 57				09 57			10 57
Slough	d																						
Reading	d														08 38	09 37				10 32			11 32
Theale	d																						
Thatcham	d																						
Newbury	d															09 52							
Hungerford	d																						
Pewsey	d																			11 06			
Westbury 123	d															10 27							
Frome 123	d																						
Castle Cary 123	d																			11 35			
Birmingham New Street	d																09 30				10 30		
Cardiff Central	d																						
Newport (South Wales)	d																						
Swindon	d														09 13								
Bristol Parkway	d																10 38				11 41		
Filton Abbey Wood	d																						
Bath Spa	d														09 42								
Bristol Temple Meads	d					07 26		08 44			08 28		09 48		10 00		10 57				11 54		
Weston-super-Mare	d					07 49					08 58												
Bridgwater	d					08 05					09 17												
Taunton	d					08 20		09 15			09 32		10 19		10 34	11 01	11 30			11 56	12 25		12 48
Tiverton Parkway	d					08 35		09 27			09 47		10 31		10 48	11 15	11 42				12 36		
Exeter St Davids	a					08 52		09 39			10 04		10 44		11 02	11 29	11 54			12 21	12 52		13 14
Exmouth	d									09 10				10 19				11 24				12 28	
Exeter Central	d									09 38				10 48				11 52				12 56	
Exeter St Davids	d				08 45	08 53		09 41		09 54	10 05		10 45	10 53	11 05	11 32	11 56	11 58	12 15	12 23	12 53	13 02	13 15
Exeter St Thomas	d				08 47					09 57				10 56				12 00					
Starcross	d				08 56		←			10 05				11 04				12 09					
Dawlish Warren	d				09 08		09 08			10 10				11 09				12 14				13 13	
Dawlish	d				→	09 05	09 12			10 14	10 18			11 13	11 20			12 18				13 17	
Teignmouth	d					09 09	09 19			10 19	10 23	←		11 18	11 26			12 23				13 22	
Newton Abbot	a					09 16	09 26	09 59		10 26	10 30	10 26	11 03	11 25	11 33	11 49	12 14	12 30	12 35	12 43	13 12	13 29	13 35
	d					09 17	09 26	10 00		10 37	10 31	10 37	11 05	11 27	11 33	11 50	12 15	12 32	12 36	12 44	13 13	13 30	13 37
Torre	d						09 35			→		10 45		11 35				12 40				13 38	
Torquay	d						09 38					10 48		11 38				12 43				13 41	
Paignton	a						09 45					10 54		11 45				12 51				13 48	
Totnes	d					09 32		10 12			10 43		11 16		11 46	12 03	12 27		12 48	12 57	13 26		
Ivybridge	d					09 48													13 04				
Plymouth	a					10 02		10 37			11 11		11 42		12 14	12 32	12 52		13 18	13 26	13 52		14 14
	d		08 57	09 20		10 05					11 13				12 15	12 35	12 55			13 29			14 15
Devonport	d		09 00								11 16												
Dockyard	d		09x02																				
Keyham	d		09 04																				
St Budeaux Ferry Road	d		09 06																				
Saltash	d		09 11			10 12					11 23												
St Germans	d		09 18			10 19					11 30												
Menheniot	d					10x27																	
Liskeard	d		09 30	09 44		10 33					11 42				12 42	13 00	13 18			13 54			14 41
Bodmin Parkway	d		09 42	09 57		10 45					11 54				12 55	13 14	13 30			14 06			14 55
Lostwithiel	d		09 47			10 50					11 59									14 12			
Par	d	09 00	09 54	10 12		10 58			11 49		12 06				13 07	13 26	13 40			14 23			
Newquay	a	09 50		11 06					12 47											15 13			
St Austell	d		10 02			11 09					12 16				13 16	13 33	13 51						15 11
Truro	d		10 19			11 31					12 34				13 36	13 52	14 09						15 29
Redruth	d		10 32			11 44					12 47				13 47	14 04	14 20						15 40
Camborne	d		10 38			11 50					12 53				13 55	14 12	14 27						15 48
Hayle	d		10 46			11 57					13 00												
St Erth	d		10 49			12 01					13 03				14 06	14 23	14 37						15 59
Penzance	a		10 59			12 10					13 14				14 16	14 33	14 47						16 11

A To Paignton
B From Exeter St Davids
C From Exmouth
D 🛒 to Plymouth
E From Leeds

For connections from Heathrow Airport, Gatwick Airport and Oxford refer to Tables T148 and T116. Table T116 includes services to/from Bedwyn.

For the complete service between Westbury and Castle Cary refer to Table T123

T135 UPDATE: Major engineering work in connection with electrification works is taking place between Reading and Westbury. The route via Newbury will be closed to all trains on 4-7 June; 9-12 July; 16 July to 05 August; 28-30 August; 08-11 October and 19-22 November. Trains will be re-timed or cancelled and run to a special timetable during this period. Please check revised train times with *www.nationalrail.co.uk*. Rail replacement buses will operate between intermediate stations.

Table T135-F

Sundays
20 May to 9 September

London and Birmingham - Devon and Cornwall

		GW	GW	XC	XC	GW	GW	GW	GW	XC	GW	GW	GW	XC	GW	GW	GW	GW	XC	GW	XC	GW	GW
				◇■	◇■		◇■	◇■	◇	◇■		◇■		◇■	◇■		◇	◇■	◇■		◇■		◇■
				A	B					C				D					E		F	G	
				⊥	⊥		🍽	🍽		⊥		🍽		⊥	🍽			🍽	⊥		⊥		🍽
London Paddington ■ ⊖	d						11 27	11 57				12 57			13 00			13 57					14 57
Slough ■	d																						
Reading ■	d						12 09	12 33				13 32			13 39			14 32					15 32
Theale	d																						
Thatcham	d																						
Newbury	d							12 48										14 48					
Hungerford	d																						
Pewsey	d						12 43																
Westbury 123	d						13 06					14 18											
Frome 123	d																						
Castle Cary 123	d						13 25											15 37					
Birmingham New Street ■	d			11 30	11 30					12 12				13 12					14 12		14 42		
Cardiff Central ■	d																						
Newport (South Wales)	d																						
Swindon	d														14 12								
Bristol Parkway ■	d			12 39	12 40					13 23				14 21					15 25		15 56		
Filton Abbey Wood	d																						
Bath Spa ■	d														14 42								
Bristol Temple Meads ■	d			12 54	12 54					13 44				14 44	14 55				15 44		16 14		
Weston-super-Mare	d																						
Bridgwater	d																						
Taunton	d			13 25	13 25		13 46	13 56		14 16		14 55		15 15	15 30			15 58	16 15		16 45		16 50
Tiverton Parkway	d			13 37	13 37		14 00	14 09		14 28				15 27					16 27		16 57		17 03
Exeter St Davids ■	a			13 52	13 52		14 14	14 23		14 42		15 18		15 39	15 54			16 23	16 40		17 09		17 18
Exmouth	d		12 55			13 24					14 27					15 23				16 23			
Exeter Central	d		13 20			13 52					14 56		15 20			15 51				16 51			
Exeter St Davids ■	d		13 26	13 53	13 53	13 59	14 16	14 25		14 43	15 05	15 21	15 31	15 42	15 56	16 01	16 04	16 25	16 43	16 57	17 13		17 20
Exeter St Thomas	d					14 02											16 07						
Starcross	d					14 10											16 16						
Dawlish Warren	d					14 15										16 12	16 21			17 08			
Dawlish	d		13 39			14 19	14 30				15 17		15 43			16 16	16 25			17 12	17 25		
Teignmouth	d		13 44			14 24	14 36				15 22		15 48			16 21	16 30			17 17	17 30		
Newton Abbot	a		13 51	14 12	14 12	14 31	14 42	14 48		15 02	15 29	15 41	15 55	16 00	16 16	16 28	16 36	16 45	17 01	17 24	17 36		17 40
	d		13 52	14 13	14 13	14 33	14 43	14 48		15 03	15 30	15 42	15 56	16 01	16 18	16 29	16 36	16 45	17 03	17 26	17 38		17 41
Torre	d		14 01			14 41					15 39		16 04			16 37				17 34			
Torquay	d		14 04			14 44	14 54				15 42		16 07			16 40				17 37	17 49		
Paignton	a		14 11			14 51	15 03				15 50		16 15			16 47				17 44	17 56		
Totnes	d			14 26	14 26			15 01		15 16		15 54		16 13			16 50	16 59	17 16				17 55
Ivybridge	d																17 06						
Plymouth	a			14 52	14 52			15 29		15 42		16 22		16 38	16 55		17 20	17 29	17 42				18 21
	d	14 50						15 31				16 25					17 35						18 25
Devonport	d																						
Dockyard	d																						
Keyham	d																						
St Budeaux Ferry Road	d																						
Saltash	d	14 59															17 43						
St Germans	d	15 06															17 50						
Menheniot	d																17x58						
Liskeard ■	d	15 18						15 57				16 50					18 04						18 50
Bodmin Parkway	d	15 30						16 11				17 03					18 16						19 03
Lostwithiel	d	15 36															18 21						
Par	d	15 44						16 23	16 47			17 14					18 28						19 13
Newquay	a								17 39														
St Austell	d	15 51						16 31				17 22					18 35						19 21
Truro	d	16 10						16 49				17 40					18 53						19 37
Redruth	d	16 23						17 01				17 53					19 05						19 50
Camborne	d	16 29						17 09				18 01					19 11						19 59
Hayle	d																19 18						
St Erth	d	16 39						17 21				18 13					19 21					20 00	20 11
Penzance	a	16 50						17 30				18 24					19 33					20 09	20 23

A from 22 July. From Leeds
B until 15 July. From Leeds
C From York
D From Newcastle
E From Edinburgh
F From Manchester Piccadilly
G From St Ives

For connections from Heathrow Airport, Gatwick Airport and Oxford refer to Tables T148 and T116. Table T116 includes services to/from Bedwyn.

For the complete service between Westbury and Castle Cary refer to Table T123

Table T135-F

Sundays
20 May to 9 September

London and Birmingham - Devon and Cornwall

		GW	XC	GW	GW	GW	XC	GW	GW	XC	GW	GW	GW	XC	GW	GW	XC	XC	XC	GW	GW	GW
		◇	◇■		◇■		◇■		◇■	◇■	◇		◇■	◇■		◇■	◇■	◇■	◇■	◇■		◇■
			A				B			A				C			D	E	F			
			⊥		🍽		⊥		🍽	⊥			🍽	⊥		🍽	⊥		⊥	🍽		🍽
London Paddington ■ ⊖	d				15 57				16 57				17 57			18 57				19 03		19 57
Slough ■	d																					
Reading ■	d				16 32				17 32				18 32			19 32				19 39		20 32
Theale	d																					
Thatcham	d																					
Newbury	d				16 48								18 48									20 48
Hungerford	d																					
Pewsey	d												19 08									21 09
Westbury 123	d				17 25								19 27									21 28
Frome 123	d																					
Castle Cary 123	d				17 43											20 31						21 45
Birmingham New Street ■	d		15 12				16 12			17 12				18 12			18 42	19 12	19 12			
Cardiff Central ■	d																					
Newport (South Wales)	d																					
Swindon	d																			20 12		
Bristol Parkway ■	d		16 21				17 22			18 22				19 23			20 05	20 22	20 22			
Filton Abbey Wood	d																					
Bath Spa ■	d																			20 42		
Bristol Temple Meads ■	d		16 44				17 44			18 44	18 30			19 43			20 19	20 44	20 44	21 00		
Weston-super-Mare	d										19 01						20 38			21 29		
Bridgwater	d										19 21											
Taunton	d		17 15		18 05		18 18		18 50	19 18	19 35		20 03	20 18		20 52	20 59	21 15	21 15	21 52		22 06
Tiverton Parkway	d		17 27		18 18		18 30		19 03	19 30	19 51		20 16	20 30		21 06	21 14	21 27	21 27	22 06		22 19
Exeter St Davids ■	a		17 40		18 35		18 45		19 18	19 45	20 08		20 30	20 43		21 21	21 29	21 39	21 40	22 21		22 35
Exmouth	d			17 23				18 23				19 23			20 28						21 30	
Exeter Central	d			17 51				18 50				19 51			20 56						21 57	
Exeter St Davids ■	d		17 42	17 57	18 36		18 47	18 57	19 20	19 49		19 57	20 31	20 43	21 02	21 22	21 30	21 41	21 41		22 04	22 36
Exeter St Thomas	d			18 00				19 00				20 00									22 07	
Starcross	d			18 08				19 08				20 08									22 14	
Dawlish Warren	d			18 13				19 13				20 13			21 13						22 20	
Dawlish	d			18 17				19 17				20 17			21 17	21 35	21 42				22 24	
Teignmouth	d			18 22				19 22				20 22			21 22	21 41	21 48				22 29	
Newton Abbot	a		18 00	18 29	18 56		19 05	19 29	19 39	20 07		20 29	20 52	21 01	21 29	21 48	21 54	21 59	21 59		22 36	22 57
	d		18 00	18 31	18 58		19 06	19 31	19 40	20 08		20 31	20 53	21 04	21 31	21 48	21 55	22 00	22 01		22 37	22 57
Torre	d			18 39				19 39				20 39			21 39						22 45	
Torquay	d			18 42				19 42				20 42			21 42		22 08				22 48	
Paignton	a			18 49				19 49				20 49			21 49		22 14				22 56	
Totnes	d		18 13				19 18		19 54	20 20			21 06	21 14		22 02		22 12	22 13			23 10
Ivybridge	d																					
Plymouth	a		18 38		19 35		19 43		20 21	20 45			21 33	21 41		22 31		22 38	22 38			23 40
	d		18 53			19 42			20 25	20 50			21 35									
Devonport	d																					
Dockyard	d																					
Keyham	d																					
St Budeaux Ferry Road	d																					
Saltash	d					19 51																
St Germans	d					19 58																
Menheniot	d																					
Liskeard ■	d		19 16			20 10			20 49	21 13			22 01									
Bodmin Parkway	d		19 28			20 22			21 02	21 25			22 14									
Lostwithiel	d					20 27																
Par	d	19 22	19 38			20 34			21 13	21 35			22 26									
Newquay	a	20 13																				
St Austell	d		19 45			20 42			21 20	21 43			22 34									
Truro	d		20 01			20 58			21 38	22 00			22 49									
Redruth	d		20 12			21 12			21 52	22 11			23 04									
Camborne	d		20 21			21 18			21 58	22 20			23 12									
Hayle	d					21 26																
St Erth	d		20 31			21 29			22 10	22 30			23 23									
Penzance	a		20 39			21 40			22 22	22 42			23 35									

A From Edinburgh. ⊥ to Plymouth
B From Edinburgh
C From Motherwell
D From Manchester Piccadilly. ⊥ to Bristol Temple Meads
E from 22 July. From Motherwell
F until 15 July. From Aberdeen. ⊥ to Bristol Temple Meads

For connections from Heathrow Airport, Gatwick Airport and Oxford refer to Tables T148 and T116. Table T116 includes services to/from Bedwyn.

For the complete service between Westbury and Castle Cary refer to Table T123

London and Birmingham - Devon and Cornwall

Sundays

20 May to 9 September

		XC	GW	GW
		◇1 A	◇1	B
London Paddington ⊖	d		20 57	23 50
Slough	d			
Reading	d		21 32	00u41
Theale	d			
Thatcham	d			
Newbury	d			
Hungerford	d			
Pewsey	d			
Westbury 123	d			
Frome 123	d			
Castle Cary 123	d			
Birmingham New Street	d	20 12		
Cardiff Central	d			
Newport (South Wales)	d			
Swindon	d			
Bristol Parkway	d	21 22		
Filton Abbey Wood	d			
Bath Spa	d			
Bristol Temple Meads	d	21 44		
Weston-super-Mare	d			
Bridgwater	d			
Taunton	d	22 15	22s47	
Tiverton Parkway	d	22 28	23s01	
Exeter St Davids	a	22 46	23 19	03 08
Exmouth	d			
Exeter Central	d			
Exeter St Davids	d	22 48		04 35
Exeter St Thomas	d			
Starcross	d			
Dawlish Warren	d			
Dawlish	d			
Teignmouth	d			
Newton Abbot	a	23 06		04 55
	d	23 07		04 56
Torre	d			
Torquay	d			
Paignton	a			
Totnes	d	23 20		
Ivybridge	d			
Plymouth	a	23 46		05 35
	d			06 28
Devonport	d			
Dockyard	d			
Keyham	d			
St Budeaux Ferry Road	d			
Saltash	d			
St Germans	d			
Menheniot	d			
Liskeard	d			07 09
Bodmin Parkway	d			07 23
Lostwithiel	d			07 29
Par	d			07 38
Newquay	a			
St Austell	d			07 46
Truro	d			08 06
Redruth	d			08 20
Camborne	d			08 27
Hayle	d			08 38
St Erth	d			08 45
Penzance	a			08 59

A From Aberdeen. to Bristol Temple Meads
B The Night Riviera

For connections from Heathrow Airport, Gatwick Airport and Oxford refer to Tables T148 and T116. Table T116 includes services to/from Bedwyn.

For the complete service between Westbury and Castle Cary refer to Table T123

London and Birmingham - Devon and Cornwall

Sundays

16 September to 2 December

		GW	GW	GW	GW	GW	XC	GW	GW	GW		XC	GW	GW	GW	GW	XC	GW	GW	GW		XC	GW	GW	GW
				A	◇	B	◇1	A	◇	C		◇1		◇1		◇1	◇1 D			◇1		◇1 E		◇1	
London Paddington ⊖	d													08 00		08 57				09 57				10 57	
Slough	d																								
Reading	d													08 39		09 32				10 32				11 32	
Theale	d																								
Thatcham	d																								
Newbury	d															09 48									
Hungerford	d																								
Pewsey	d																			11 06					
Westbury 123	d															10 22									
Frome 123	d																								
Castle Cary 123	d																			11 35					
Birmingham New Street	d																09 30					10 30			
Cardiff Central	d																								
Newport (South Wales)	d																								
Swindon	d													09 17											
Bristol Parkway	d																10 38					11 41			
Filton Abbey Wood	d																								
Bath Spa	d													09 46											
Bristol Temple Meads	d				07 26		08 44		08 28			09 48		10 00			10 57					11 54			
Weston-super-Mare	d				07 49				08 58																
Bridgwater	d				08 05				09 17																
Taunton	d				08 20		09 15		09 32			10 19		10 34		10 58	11 30			11 56		12 25		12 48	
Tiverton Parkway	d				08 35		09 27		09 47			10 31		10 47		11 12	11 42					12 36			
Exeter St Davids	a				08 52		09 39		10 04			10 44		11 01		11 26	11 54			12 21		12 52		13 14	
Exmouth	d							09 10					10 19					11 24					12 28		
Exeter Central	d							09 38					10 48					11 52					12 56		
Exeter St Davids	d			08 45	08 53		09 41	09 54	10 05			10 45	10 53	11 05		11 26	11 56	11 58	12 15	12 23		12 53	13 02	13 15	
Exeter St Thomas	d			08 47				09 57					10 56					12 00							
Starcross	d			08 56		←		10 05					11 04					12 09							
Dawlish Warren	d			09 08		09 08		10 10					11 09					12 14					13 13		
Dawlish	d			→	09 05	09 12		10 14	10 18				11 13	11 19				12 18					13 17		
Teignmouth	d				09 09	09 19		10 19	10 23	←			11 18	11 25				12 23					13 22		
Newton Abbot	a				09 16	09 26	09 59	10 26	10 30	10 26		11 03	11 25	11 32		11 47	12 14	12 30	12 35	12 43		13 12	13 29	13 35	
	d				09 17	09 26	10 00	10 37	10 31	10 37		11 05	11 27	11 33		11 47	12 15	12 32	12 36	12 44		13 13	13 30	13 37	
Torre	d					09 35		→		10 45			11 35					12 40					13 38		
Torquay	d					09 38				10 48			11 38					12 43					13 41		
Paignton	a					09 45				10 54			11 45					12 51					13 48		
Totnes	d				09 32		10 12		10 43			11 16		11 45		12 01	12 27		12 48	12 57		13 26			
Ivybridge	d				09 48														13 04						
Plymouth	a				10 02		10 37		11 11			11 42		12 13		12 30	12 52		13 18	13 26		13 52		14 14	
	d	09 00			10 05				11 13					12 15			12 55		13 31					14 15	14 50
Devonport	d	09 04																							
Dockyard	d																								
Keyham	d																								
St Budeaux Ferry Road	d	09 08																							
Saltash	d	09 12			10 12				11 22										13 39						14 59
St Germans	d	09 18			10 19				11 29										13 46						15 06
Menheniot	d				10x27																				
Liskeard	d	09 30			10 33				11 41					12 40			13 18		13 58					14 39	15 18
Bodmin Parkway	d	09 42			10 45				11 53					12 53			13 30		14 10					14 53	15 30
Lostwithiel	d	09 48			10 50				11 58																15 36
Par	d	09 55	10 10		10 57				12 06					13 04	13 15		13 40		14 21						15 44
Newquay	a		11 02												14 07										
St Austell	d	10 02			11 06				12 15					13 15			13 51		14 29					15 10	15 51
Truro	d	10 20			11 23				12 34					13 36			14 09		14 45					15 27	16 10
Redruth	d	10 33			11 36				12 47					13 47			14 20		14 59					15 39	16 23
Camborne	d	10 39			11 42				12 53					13 55			14 27		15 06					15 47	16 29
Hayle	d	10 46			11 49				13 00																
St Erth	d	10 50			11 52				13 05					14 06			14 37		15 17					15 58	16 39
Penzance	a	10 59			12 02				13 14					14 16			14 47		15 26					16 11	16 50

A To Paignton
B From Exeter St Davids
C From Exmouth
D to Plymouth
E From Leeds

For connections from Heathrow Airport, Gatwick Airport and Oxford refer to Tables T148 and T116. Table T116 includes services to/from Bedwyn.

For the complete service between Westbury and Castle Cary refer to Table T123

T135 UPDATE: Major engineering work in connection with electrification works is taking place between Reading and Westbury. The route via Newbury will be closed to all trains on 4-7 June; 9-12 July; 16 July to 05 August; 28-30 August; 08-11 October and 19-22 November. Trains will be re-timed or cancelled and run to a special timetable during this period. Please check revised train times with *www.nationalrail.co.uk*. Rail replacement buses will operate between intermediate stations.

Table T135-F

Sundays

16 September to 2 December

London and Birmingham - Devon and Cornwall

		GW	XC	XC	GW	GW	GW	GW	XC	GW	GW	GW	XC	GW	GW	GW	GW	XC	GW	XC	GW	GW	XC
			◇1 A 🚲	◇1 B 🚲		◇1 ☕	◇1 ☕	◇	◇1 C 🚲		◇1 ☕		◇1 D 🚲	◇1 ☕		◇	◇1 ☕	◇1 E 🚲		◇1 F 🚲	G	◇1 ☕	◇1 H 🚲
London Paddington ⊖	d					11 30	11 57				12 57			13 03			13 57					14 57	
Slough	d																						
Reading	d					12 09	12 32				13 32			13 39			14 32					15 32	
Theale	d																						
Thatcham	d																						
Newbury	d						12 48										14 48						
Hungerford	d																						
Pewsey	d					12 38																	
Westbury 123	d					13 02					14 18												
Frome 123	d																						
Castle Cary 123	d					13 21											15 37						
Birmingham New Street	d		11 30	11 30					12 12				13 12					14 12		14 42			15 12
Cardiff Central	d																						
Newport (South Wales)	d																						
Swindon	d													14 12									
Bristol Parkway	d		12 39	12 40					13 23				14 21					15 25		15 56			16 21
Filton Abbey Wood	d																						
Bath Spa	d													14 43									
Bristol Temple Meads	d		12 54	12 54					13 44				14 44	14 55				15 44		16 14			16 44
Weston-super-Mare	d																						
Bridgwater	d																						
Taunton	d		13 25	13 25		13 42	13 54		14 16		14 55		15 15	15 30			15 58	16 15		16 45		16 50	17 15
Tiverton Parkway	d		13 37	13 37		13 56	14 07		14 28				15 27					16 27		16 57		17 03	17 27
Exeter St Davids	a		13 52	13 52		14 12	14 21		14 42		15 18		15 39	15 54			16 23	16 40		17 09		17 18	17 40
Exmouth	d	12 55			13 24					14 27					15 23				16 23				
Exeter Central	d	13 20			13 52					14 56		15 20			15 51				16 51				
Exeter St Davids	d	13 26	13 53	13 53	13 59	14 13	14 24		14 43	15 05	15 21	15 31	15 42	15 56	16 01	16 05	16 25	16 43	16 57	17 13		17 20	17 42
Exeter St Thomas	d				14 02											16 07							
Starcross	d				14 10											16 16							
Dawlish Warren	d				14 15										16 12	16 21			17 08				
Dawlish	d	13 39			14 19	14 27				15 17		15 43			16 16	16 25			17 12	17 25			
Teignmouth	d	13 44			14 24	14 33				15 22		15 48			16 21	16 30			17 17	17 30			
Newton Abbot	a	13 51	14 12	14 12	14 31	14 39	14 43		15 02	15 29	15 41	15 55	16 00	16 16	16 28	16 36	16 45	17 01	17 24	17 36		17 40	18 00
	d	13 52	14 13	14 13	14 33	14 40	14 45		15 03	15 30	15 42	15 56	16 01	16 18	16 29	16 36	16 45	17 03	17 26	17 38		17 41	18 00
Torre	d	14 01			14 41					15 39		16 04			16 37				17 34				
Torquay	d	14 04			14 44	14 52				15 42		16 07			16 40				17 37	17 49			
Paignton	a	14 11			14 51	15 01				15 50		16 15			16 47				17 44	17 56			
Totnes	d		14 26	14 26			14 57		15 16		15 54		16 13			16 50	16 59	17 16				17 55	18 13
Ivybridge	d															17 06							
Plymouth	a		14 52	14 52			15 25		15 42		16 22		16 38	16 55		17 20	17 29	17 42				18 21	18 38
	d						15 30				16 25					17 35						18 25	18 53
Devonport	d																						
Dockyard	d																						
Keyham	d																						
St Budeaux Ferry Road	d																						
Saltash	d															17 43							
St Germans	d															17 50							
Menheniot	d															17x58							
Liskeard	d						15 55				16 50					18 04						18 50	19 16
Bodmin Parkway	d						16 09				17 03					18 16						19 03	19 28
Lostwithiel	d															18 21							
Par	d						16 21	16 34			17 14					18 28						19 13	19 38
Newquay	a							17 26															
St Austell	d						16 29				17 22					18 35						19 21	19 45
Truro	d						16 47				17 40					18 53						19 37	20 01
Redruth	d						16 59				17 53					19 05						19 50	20 12
Camborne	d						17 07				18 01					19 11						19 59	20 21
Hayle	d															19 18							
St Erth	d						17 20				18 12					19 21					20 00	20 11	20 31
Penzance	a						17 29				18 24					19 33					20 09	20 23	20 39

A until 7 October. From Leeds
B from 14 October. From Leeds
C From York
D From Newcastle
E From Edinburgh
F From Manchester Piccadilly
G From St Ives
H From Edinburgh. 🚲 to Plymouth

For connections from Heathrow Airport, Gatwick Airport and Oxford refer to Tables T148 and T116. Table T116 includes services to/from Bedwyn.

For the complete service between Westbury and Castle Cary refer to Table T123

Table T135-F

Sundays

16 September to 2 December

London and Birmingham - Devon and Cornwall

		GW	GW	GW	XC	GW	GW	XC	GW	GW	GW	XC	GW	GW	XC	XC	XC	GW	GW	GW	XC	GW
			◇1 ☕		◇1 A 🚲		◇1 ☕	◇1 B 🚲	◇		◇1 ☕	◇1 C 🚲		◇1 ☕	◇1 D 🚲	◇1 E 🚲	◇1 F	◇1 ☕		◇1 ☕	◇1 G 🚲	◇1 ☕
London Paddington ⊖	d		15 57				16 57				17 57			18 57				19 03		19 57		20 57
Slough	d																					
Reading	d		16 32				17 32				18 32			19 32				19 39		20 32		21 32
Theale	d																					
Thatcham	d																					
Newbury	d		16 48								18 48									20 48		
Hungerford	d																					
Pewsey	d										19 08									21 09		
Westbury 123	d		17 25								19 27									21 28		
Frome 123	d																					
Castle Cary 123	d		17 43											20 31						21 45		
Birmingham New Street	d				16 12			17 12				18 12			18 42	19 12	19 12				20 12	
Cardiff Central	d																					
Newport (South Wales)	d																					
Swindon	d																	20 12				
Bristol Parkway	d				17 22			18 22				19 23			20 05	20 22	20 22				21 22	
Filton Abbey Wood	d																					
Bath Spa	d																	20 43				
Bristol Temple Meads	d				17 44			18 44	18 30			19 43			20 19	20 44	20 44	20 55			21 44	
Weston-super-Mare	d								19 08						20 38			21 26				
Bridgwater	d								19 26													
Taunton	d		18 05		18 18		18 50	19 18	19 41		20 03	20 18		20 52	20 59	21 15	21 15	21 49		22 06	22 15	22s47
Tiverton Parkway	d		18 18		18 30		19 03	19 30	19 56		20 16	20 30		21 06	21 12	21 27	21 27	22 03		22 19	22 28	23s01
Exeter St Davids	a		18 35		18 45		19 18	19 45	20 14		20 30	20 43		21 21	21 27	21 39	21 39	22 19		22 35	22 46	23 20
Exmouth	d	17 23				18 23				19 23			20 28						21 30			
Exeter Central	d	17 51				18 50				19 51			20 56						21 57			
Exeter St Davids	d	17 57	18 36		18 47	18 57	19 20	19 49		19 57	20 31	20 43	21 02	21 22	21 30	21 41	21 41		22 04	22 36	22 48	
Exeter St Thomas	d	18 00				19 00				20 00									22 07			
Starcross	d	18 08				19 08				20 08									22 14			
Dawlish Warren	d	18 13				19 13				20 13			21 13						22 20			
Dawlish	d	18 17				19 17				20 17			21 17	21 35	21 42				22 24			
Teignmouth	d	18 22				19 22				20 22			21 22	21 41	21 47				22 29			
Newton Abbot	a	18 29	18 56		19 05	19 29	19 38	20 07		20 29	20 52	21 01	21 29	21 48	21 53	21 59	21 59		22 36	22 57	23 06	
	d	18 31	18 58		19 06	19 31	19 39	20 08		20 31	20 53	21 04	21 31	21 48	21 55	22 01	22 01		22 37	22 57	23 07	
Torre	d	18 39				19 39				20 39			21 39						22 45			
Torquay	d	18 42				19 42				20 42			21 42						22 48			
Paignton	a	18 49				19 49				20 49			21 49						22 56			
Totnes	d				19 18		19 53	20 20			21 06	21 14		22 02		22 19	22 19			23 10	23 20	
Ivybridge	d																					
Plymouth	a		19 35		19 43		20 20	20 45			21 33	21 41		22 29	22 37	22 45	22 45			23 40	23 46	
	d			19 42			20 25	20 50			21 35											
Devonport	d																					
Dockyard	d																					
Keyham	d																					
St Budeaux Ferry Road	d																					
Saltash	d			19 51																		
St Germans	d			19 58																		
Menheniot	d																					
Liskeard	d			20 10			20 49	21 13			22 00											
Bodmin Parkway	d			20 22			21 02	21 25			22 14											
Lostwithiel	d			20 27																		
Par	d			20 34			21 13	21 35			22 26											
Newquay	a																					
St Austell	d			20 42			21 20	21 43			22 34											
Truro	d			20 58			21 37	22 00			22 49											
Redruth	d			21 12			21 51	22 11			23 04											
Camborne	d			21 18			21 57	22 20			23 12											
Hayle	d			21 26																		
St Erth	d			21 29			22 10	22 30			23 24											
Penzance	a			21 40			22 22	22 42			23 35											

A From Edinburgh
B From Glasgow Central. 🚲 to Plymouth
C From Glasgow Central
D From Manchester Piccadilly. 🚲 to Bristol Temple Meads
E from 14 October. From Aberdeen. 🚲 to Bristol Temple Meads
F until 7 October. From Glasgow Central
G From Aberdeen. 🚲 to Bristol Temple Meads

For connections from Heathrow Airport, Gatwick Airport and Oxford refer to Tables T148 and T116. Table T116 includes services to/from Bedwyn.

For the complete service between Westbury and Castle Cary refer to Table T123

Sundays

16 September to 2 December

London and Birmingham - Devon and Cornwall

		GW
		■
		A
		🛏 ☕
London Paddington 15 ⊖	d	23 50
Slough 3	d	
Reading 7	d	00u41
Theale	d	
Thatcham	d	
Newbury	d	
Hungerford	d	
Pewsey	d	
Westbury 123	d	
Frome 123	d	
Castle Cary 123	d	
Birmingham New Street 12	d	
Cardiff Central 7	d	
Newport (South Wales)	d	
Swindon	d	
Bristol Parkway 7	d	
Filton Abbey Wood	d	
Bath Spa 7	d	
Bristol Temple Meads 10	d	
Weston-super-Mare	d	
Bridgwater	d	
Taunton	d	
Tiverton Parkway	d	
Exeter St Davids 6	a	03 07
Exmouth	d	
Exeter Central	d	
Exeter St Davids 6	d	04 35
Exeter St Thomas	d	
Starcross	d	
Dawlish Warren	d	
Dawlish	d	
Teignmouth	d	
Newton Abbot	a	04 55
	d	04 56
Torre	d	
Torquay	d	
Paignton	a	
Totnes	d	
Ivybridge	d	
Plymouth	a	05 35
	d	06 28
Devonport	d	
Dockyard	d	
Keyham	d	
St Budeaux Ferry Road	d	
Saltash	d	
St Germans	d	
Menheniot	d	
Liskeard 6	d	07 09
Bodmin Parkway	d	07 23
Lostwithiel	d	07 29
Par	d	07 38
Newquay	a	
St Austell	d	07 46
Truro	d	08 06
Redruth	d	08 20
Camborne	d	08 27
Hayle	d	08 38
St Erth	d	08 45
Penzance	a	08 59

A The Night Riviera

For connections from Heathrow Airport, Gatwick Airport and Oxford refer to Tables T148 and T116. Table T116 includes services to/from Bedwyn.

For the complete service between Westbury and Castle Cary refer to Table T123

Mondays to Fridays

21 May to 29 June

Cornwall and Devon - Birmingham and London

Miles	Miles	Miles			GW MO	GW MX	GW MX	GW	GW	GW	GW	XC	GW	GW	GW	GW	GW	GW	XC	GW	XC	GW	GW
					■		■																
								◇1	◇1	◇1		◇1	◇1	◇1		◇1			◇1		◇1		◇1
					A	B	A					C			D	E	B	D	F	B	G	D	H
					🛏 ☕		🛏 ☕	☕	☕	☕		trolley	☕	☕		☕			trolley		trolley		✕ ☕
0	—	—	**Penzance**	d																			05 05
5¾	—	—	St Erth	d																			
7¼	—	—	Hayle	d																			
13¼	—	—	Camborne	d																			
16¾	—	—	Redruth	d																			05 26
25¾	—	—	Truro	d																			05 38
40¼	—	—	St Austell	d																			05 56
—	—	—	Newquay	d																			
44¾	—	—	Par	d																			
49¼	—	—	Lostwithiel	d																			
52¾	—	—	Bodmin Parkway	d																			06 12
61¾	—	—	Liskeard 6	d																			06 25
65	—	—	Menheniot	d																			
70¼	—	—	St Germans	d																			
75¼	—	—	Saltash	d																			
76½	—	—	St Budeaux Ferry Road	d																			
77¼	—	—	Keyham	d																			
77¾	—	—	Dockyard	d																			
78¼	—	—	Devonport	d																			
79½	—	—	**Plymouth**	a																			06 49
—	—	—		d						04 51		05 20		05 29		05 53			06 25				06 53
90¼	—	—	Ivybridge	d																			
102¾	—	—	Totnes	d			00 22					05 45		05 56					06 50				
—	—	0	Paignton	d											06 03			06 34			07 01	07 10	
—	—	2¼	Torquay	d											06 08			06 39			07 07	07 15	
—	—	3	Torre	d		00 03									06 11			06 42				07 18	
111½	—	8¾	Newton Abbot	a		00 11	00 34			05 26		05 56		06 07	06 19	06 28		06 50	07 01		07 17	07 26	07 28
—	—	—		d	00 01	00 13	00 36			05 27		06 02		06 09	06 21	06 29		06 52	07 03		07 18	07 34	07 31
116½	—	—	Teignmouth	d		00 20								06 16	06 28			06 59			07 25	→	
119¾	—	—	Dawlish	d		00 25								06 22	06 33		←	07 04		←	07 30		
121	—	—	Dawlish Warren	d		00 30									06 45		06 45	07 15		07 15			
123	—	—	Starcross	d		00 34									→		06 49	→		07 19			
130½	—	—	Exeter St Thomas	d		00 43											06 58			07 28			
131½	—	—	**Exeter St Davids** 6	a	00 23	00 48	00 57			05 46		06 19		06 34		06 50	07 03		07 20	07 33	07 42		07 50
—	—	—	Exeter Central	a													07 10			07 39			
—	—	—	Exmouth	a													07 41			08 16			
—	—	—	**Exeter St Davids** 6	d	00 59		01 06			05 52	06 00	06 24	06 28	06 36		06 52			07 24		07 44		07 52
148	—	—	Tiverton Parkway	d						06 07	06 17	06 37	06 43	06 51					07 37		07 57		
162¼	0	—	Taunton	d			01 42			06 22	06 34	06 51	06 57	07 05		07 17			07 51		08 12		08 16
—	11¾	—	Bridgwater	a							06 46		07 06										
—	25¾	—	Weston-super-Mare	a							07 05		07 25								08 34		
—	45½	—	**Bristol Temple Meads** 10	a							07 41	07 26	07 58						08 27		08 55		
—	—	—		d				05 15			07 46	07 30	08 00						08 30		09 00		
—	—	—	Bath Spa 7	a									08 11										
—	—	—	Filton Abbey Wood	a							07 57												
—	51¼	—	Bristol Parkway 7	a							08 03	07 38							08 38		09 08		
—	—	—	Swindon	a									08 40										
—	—	—	Newport (South Wales)	a																			
—	—	—	Cardiff Central 7	a																			
—	138¼	—	**Birmingham New Street** 12	a								08 56							09 58		10 23		
190	—	—	Castle Cary 123	d						06 44				07 27									
204	—	—	Frome 123	d					06 05														
209¼	—	—	Westbury 123	d				06 00	06 16	07 03				07 52									
230	—	—	Pewsey	d				06 18	06 34	07 22				08 10									
243¾	—	—	Hungerford	a				06 35	06 51	07 34													
252¼	—	—	Newbury	a				06 50	07 06	07 45				08 30									
255¾	—	—	Thatcham	a				06 57	07 13														
264½	—	—	Theale	a				07 06	07 22														
269¼	—	—	**Reading** 7	a	04s06		03s58	07 18	07 37	08 07			09 15	08 54		08 33							09 33
286¾	—	—	Slough 3	a																			
305¾	—	—	**London Paddington** 15 ⊖	a	05 02		05 03	07 47	08 08	08 37			09 43	09 23		09 00							10 02

A From Penzance. The Night Riviera
B From Paignton
C To Edinburgh
D To Exmouth
E The Armada - Restaurant for customers joining until Taunton
F To Glasgow Central
G To Manchester Piccadilly. trolley from Newton Abbot
H The Golden Hind. ☕ to Plymouth ☕ from Reading ✕ from Plymouth to Reading

For connections to Oxford, Gatwick Airport and Heathrow Airport refer to Tables T116 and T148

For connections from Swansea refer to Table T128

T135 UPDATE: Major engineering work in connection with electrification works is taking place between Reading and Westbury. The route via Newbury will be closed to all trains on 4-7 June; 9-12 July; 16 July to 05 August; 28-30 August; 08-11 October and 19-22 November. Trains will be re-timed or cancelled and run to a special timetable during this period. Please check revised train times with *www.nationalrail.co.uk*. Rail replacement buses will operate between intermediate stations.

Table T135-R

Mondays to Fridays

21 May to 29 June

Cornwall and Devon - Birmingham and London

		GW A	GW	XC ◇1 B ⊼	GW ◇1 ⊡	GW ◇1 ⊡	GW	GW ◇ C	XC ◇1 D ⊼	GW ◇ E	GW F	GW ◇1 ⊡	GW A	GW G	GW	XC ◇1 H ⊼	XC ◇1 I ⊼	GW ◇1 ⊡	GW	GW	XC ◇1 J ⊼	GW G	GW 1 K ⊡
Penzance	d		05 19			05 41		06 00	06 28			06 47		06 58				07 41			08 28	08 44	09 00
St Erth	d							06 09	06 36			06 57		07a06				07 51			08 36	08a52	09 10
Hayle	d		05 29					06 12										07 55					
Camborne	d		05 38			05 58		06 21	06 46			07 08						08 05			08 46		09 21
Redruth	d					06 05		06 27	06 52			07 15						08 12			08 52		09 28
Truro	d		05a53			06 18		06 39	07 04			07 28						08 25			09 04		09 41
St Austell	d					06 35		06 56	07 20			07 45						08 43			09 20		09 58
Newquay	d																						
Par	d					06 43		07 02	07 27			07 53						08 50			09 27		10 05
Lostwithiel	d					06 51		07 09				08 00											
Bodmin Parkway	d					06 57		07 15	07 37			08 07						09 02			09 37		10 17
Liskeard 8	d					07 11		07 28	07 53			08 20						09 15			09 50		10 30
Menheniot	d							07x32															
St Germans	d					07 23		07 40				08 31						09 27					
Saltash	d					07 31		07 46				08 39						09 35					
St Budeaux Ferry Road	d							07 50															
Keyham	d							07 53															
Dockyard	d							07x55															
Devonport	d							07 58															
Plymouth	a					07 41		08 03	08 20			08 49						09 45			10 18		10 54
	d			07 25		07 45		08 09	08 25			08 51				09 25		09 49			10 25		11 00
Ivybridge	d							08 24				09 06						10 04					
Totnes	d			07 50		08 15		08 39	08 50			09 21				09 50		10 19			10 50		
Paignton	d				07 48		08 20				09 12				09 34		10 07		10 21	10 33			
Torquay	d				07 55		08 25				09 17				09 39		10 13		10 26	10 38			
Torre	d	←			07 59		08 28				09 20		←		09 42				10 29	10 41			
Newton Abbot	a	07 26		08 01	08 07	08 27	08 36	08 51	09 01		09 28	09 33	09 28		09 50	10 01	10 23	10 31	10 36	10 49	11 01		
	d	07 34		08 03	08 08	08 28	08 38	08 52	09 03		09 39	09 34	09 39			10 03	10 24	10 32	10 39	10 51	11 03		
Teignmouth	d	07 41			08 15		08 45	08 59			→		09 45				10 31		10 46	10 58			
Dawlish	d	07 46			08 22		08 50	09 04					09 50				10 36		10 51	11 03			
Dawlish Warren	d	07 52					08 55						09 55						10 56	11 15			
Starcross	d	07 55			08 28		08 59						09 59						11 00				
Exeter St Thomas	d	08 06			08 36		09 08						10 08						11 09				
Exeter St Davids 6	a	08 10		08 20	08 40	08 48	09 12	09 16	09 22			09 53	10 14			10 20	10 48	10 53	11 13	11 28	11 20		11 52
Exeter Central	a	08 18					09 19						10 19						11 19				
Exmouth	a	08 47					09 48						10 48						11 48				
Exeter St Davids 6	d			08 24	08 42	08 51			09 24	09 33		09 55				10 23	10 50	10 55			11 24		11 55
Tiverton Parkway	d			08 37		09 06			09 38	09 50		10 10				10 37	11 03	11 11			11 37		
Taunton	d			08 51	09 07	09 20			09 51	10 11		10 28				10 51	11 17	11 25			11 51		
Bridgwater	a									10 22													
Weston-super-Mare	a				09 27					10 41													
Bristol Temple Meads 10	a			09 26	09 57				10 25	11 11						11 24	11 52				12 24		
	d			09 30	10 00				10 30	11 21						11 30	12 00				12 30		
Bath Spa 7	a				10 11																		
Filton Abbey Wood	a									11 30													
Bristol Parkway 7	a			09 38					10 38							11 38	12 08				12 38		
Swindon	a				10 41																		
Newport (South Wales)	a									11 57													
Cardiff Central 7	a									12 19													
Birmingham New Street 12	a			10 56					11 58							12 56	13 26				13 56		
Castle Cary 123	d					09 41																	
Frome 123	d																						
Westbury 123	d					10 01						11 05											
Pewsey	d					10 18																	
Hungerford	a																						
Newbury	a																						
Thatcham	a																						
Theale	a																						
Reading 7	a				11 10	10 52						11 51						12 42					13 31
Slough 3	a																						
London Paddington 15 ⊖	a				11 37	11 21						12 21						13 15					14 00

A From Paignton
B To Edinburgh
C ◇ from Plymouth
D To Glasgow Central. ⊼ from Plymouth
E From St James' Park
F To Exmouth
G To St Ives
H To Aberdeen
I To Manchester Piccadilly
J To Glasgow Central. ⊼ ◇ from Plymouth 1 to Plymouth
K The Cornish Riviera

For connections to Oxford, Gatwick Airport and Heathrow Airport refer to Tables T116 and T148

For connections from Swansea refer to Table T128

Table T135-R

Mondays to Fridays

21 May to 29 June

Cornwall and Devon - Birmingham and London

		GW	GW ◇1 ⊡	GW	XC ◇1 A ⊼	XC ◇1 B ⊼	GW ◇	GW C	GW 1 D ✕⊡	GW E	XC ◇1 F ⊼	GW	GW ◇	GW C	GW ◇1 G ✕⊡	GW E	GW	XC ◇1 H ⊼	XC ◇1 I ⊼	GW ◇	GW ◇1 J ⊡	GW ◇1 ⊡	GW ◇
Penzance	d					09 35			10 00			10 51								11 41	12 04		
St Erth	d					09 43			10 10			11 00								11 50	12 14		
Hayle	d					09 47						11 03								11 53			
Camborne	d					09 56			10 21			11 12								12 02			
Redruth	d					10 03			10 28			11 18								12 08	12 28		
Truro	d					10 15			10 41			11 30								12 19	12 41		
St Austell	d					10 31			10 58			11 47								12 36	12 59		
Newquay	d						10 13																13 05
Par	d					10 38	11a02		11 06			11 53								12 43			13a54
Lostwithiel	d					10 45						12 00								12 49			
Bodmin Parkway	d					10 51			11 17			12 06								12 55	13 15		
Liskeard 8	d					11 04			11 30			12 19								13 08	13 28		
Menheniot	d																			13x13			
St Germans	d											12 30								13 21			
Saltash	d											12 37								13 28			
St Budeaux Ferry Road	d																						
Keyham	d																						
Dockyard	d																						
Devonport	d																						
Plymouth	a					11 27			11 55			12 46								13 37	13 52		
	d				11 25	11 50			12 01		12 25				12 55			13 25		13 43	13 56		
Ivybridge	d																			13 58			
Totnes	d				11 50	12 15			12 28		12 51				13 22			13 51		14 12			
Paignton	d	11 20	11 32	11 42				12 13					12 53	13 08			13 40		14 04				
Torquay	d	11 25	11 38	11 47				12 18					12 59	13 13			13 45		14 10				
Torre	d	11 28		11 50				12 21					13 02	13 16			13 48						
Newton Abbot	a	11 37	11 48	11 58	12 01	12 26		12 30	12 40		13 02		13 10	13 25	13 34		13 56	14 02	14 20	14 24	14 31		
	d	11 37	11 50		12 03	12 28		12 31	12 41		13 04		13 12	13 25	13 35			14 04	14 21		14 32		
Teignmouth	d	11 45	11 57					12 38					13 19	13 33					14 28				
Dawlish	d	11 50	12 03					12 43		←			13 24	13 38		←			14 33				
Dawlish Warren	d	11 54						12 54		12 54				13 50		13 50							
Starcross	d	11 58						→		12 58				→		13 54							
Exeter St Thomas	d	12 08								13 07						14 03							
Exeter St Davids 6	a	12 11	12 15		12 22	12 45			13 00	13 13	13 22		13 36		13 54	14 08		14 22	14 45		14 52		
Exeter Central	a	12 19								13 19						14 19							
Exmouth	a	12 48								13 48						14 48							
Exeter St Davids 6	d		12 17		12 24	12 50			13 02		13 24		13 38		13 59			14 24	14 48		14 55		
Tiverton Parkway	d		12 32		12 38	13 06			13 17		13 38		13 55		14 14			14 38	15 02		15 10		
Taunton	d		12 46		12 51	13 22			13 31		13 51		14 11		14 28			14 51	15 15		15 24	15 33	
Bridgwater	a												14 23										
Weston-super-Mare	a												14 42						15 37				
Bristol Temple Meads 10	a				13 24	13 55					14 26		15 14					15 23	15 57				
	d				13 30	14 00					14 30		15 21					15 30	16 00				
Bath Spa 7	a																						
Filton Abbey Wood	a												15 29										
Bristol Parkway 7	a				13 38	14 08					14 39							15 39	16 08				
Swindon	a																						
Newport (South Wales)	a												15 57										
Cardiff Central 7	a												16 15										
Birmingham New Street 12	a				14 56	15 23					15 56							16 56	17 23				
Castle Cary 123	d		13 07																			15 55	
Frome 123	d																						
Westbury 123	d		13 27												15 04							16 14	
Pewsey	d		13 45																			16 32	
Hungerford	a																						
Newbury	a		14 04																			16 51	
Thatcham	a																						
Theale	a																						
Reading 7	a		14 23						14 51						15 50						16 46	17 16	
Slough 3	a																						
London Paddington 15 ⊖	a		14 54						15 21						16 21						17 15	17 54	

A To Dundee
B To Manchester Piccadilly. ⊼ ◇ from Plymouth 1 to Plymouth
C To Exmouth
D The Cornishman. ⊡ to Plymouth ⊡ from Reading ✕ from Plymouth to Reading
E From Paignton
F To Glasgow Central
G Restaurant available for customers joining until Castle Cary. ⊡ from Westbury ✕ to Westbury
H To Edinburgh
I To Manchester Piccadilly
J The Royal Duchy

For connections to Oxford, Gatwick Airport and Heathrow Airport refer to Tables T116 and T148

For connections from Swansea refer to Table T128

Table T135-R

Mondays to Fridays

21 May to 29 June

Cornwall and Devon - Birmingham and London

Station		GW	GW	XC ◇■ A ⊼	GW ◇■ B ☕	GW C	GW ■ D ☕	GW E	GW	GW	XC ◇■ F ⊼	XC ◇■ G ⊼	GW C	GW ◇■ ☕	GW E	GW ◇	GW	XC ◇■ F ⊼	GW ◇	GW	GW ◇■ ☕	GW
Penzance	d									12 57				14 00					14 49			
St Erth	d									13 06				14 10					14 58			
Hayle	d									13 09									15 01			
Camborne	d									13 18				14 21					15 11			
Redruth	d									13 24				14 28					15 17			
Truro	d									13 35				14 41					15 28			
St Austell	d									13 52				14 58					15 45			
Newquay	d															15 01						
Par	d									13 59				15 06		15a47			15 52			
Lostwithiel	d									14 05									15 58			
Bodmin Parkway	d									14 11				15 17					16 04			
Liskeard ■	d									14 24				15 30					16 17			
Menheniot	d									14x29									16 22			
St Germans	d									14 37									16 30			
Saltash	d									14 44									16 37			
St Budeaux Ferry Road	d																		16 41			
Keyham	d																		16 43			
Dockyard	d																		16x45			
Devonport	d																		16 47			
Plymouth	a									14 53				15 55					16 51			
	d			14 25			15 00			15 08	15 25			16 00				16 25			16 57	
Ivybridge	d									15 23											17 13	
Totnes	d			14 50			15 27			15 37	15 51			16 27				16 50			17 28	
Paignton	d	14 21	14 40		14 54	15 13			15 32				16 12				16 29			16 57		17 26
Torquay	d	14 26	14 45		15 00	15 18			15 37				16 17				16 34			17 02		17 31
Torre	d	14 29	14 48			15 21			15 40				16 21				16 37			17 05		17 34
Newton Abbot	a	14 37	14 56	15 01	15 10	15 29	15 38		15 48	15 49	16 02		16 29	16 39			16 46	17 01		17 13	17 39	17 42
	d	14 39		15 03	15 12	15 31	15 40				16 04		16 31	16 40			16 47	17 03		17 15	17 41	17 44
Teignmouth	d	14 46			15 19	15 38							16 38				16 55			17 22		17 51
Dawlish	d	14 51			15 25	15 43		←					16 43		←		17 00			17 27		17 56
Dawlish Warren	d	14 56				15 54		15 54					16 53		16 53		17 04			17 32		18 01
Starcross	d	15 00				→		15 58					→		16 57					17 36		18 05
Exeter St Thomas	d	15 09						16 07							17 07					17 45		18 14
Exeter St Davids ■	a	15 13		15 20	15 37		15 59	16 12			16 22			16 59	17 11		17 17	17 20		17 51	18 00	18 19
Exeter Central	a	15 19						16 18							17 18					17 56		18 24
Exmouth	a	15 48						16 49							17 51					18 27		18 54
Exeter St Davids ■	d			15 24	15 39		16 01				16 24	16 54		17 02				17 24			18 02	
Tiverton Parkway	d			15 37			16 16				16 38	17 08		17 17				17 37			18 17	
Taunton	d			15 51	16 04		16 30				16 51	17 22		17 31				17 50			18 31	
Bridgwater	a																					
Weston-super-Mare	a																					
Bristol Temple Meads ■	a			16 23							17 24	17 54						18 23				
	d			16 30							17 30	18 00						18 30				
Bath Spa ■	a																					
Filton Abbey Wood	a																					
Bristol Parkway ■	a			16 38							17 39	18 08						18 38				
Swindon	a																					
Newport (South Wales)	a																					
Cardiff Central ■	a																					
Birmingham New Street ■	a			17 56							18 56	19 23						19 56				
Castle Cary 123	d				16 25																18 52	
Frome 123	d																					
Westbury 123	d				16 45																19 12	
Pewsey	d				17 02																19 29	
Hungerford	a																					
Newbury	a																				19 48	
Thatcham	a																					
Theale	a																					
Reading ■	a				17 37		17 46							18 52							20 08	
Slough ■	a																					
London Paddington ■ ⊖	a				18 07		18 16							19 20							20 37	

A To Edinburgh
B The Torbay Express
C To Exmouth
D The Mayflower
E From Paignton
F To Leeds
G To Manchester Piccadilly

For connections to Oxford, Gatwick Airport and Heathrow Airport refer to Tables T116 and T148

For connections from Swansea refer to Table T128

Table T135-R

Mondays to Fridays

21 May to 29 June

Cornwall and Devon - Birmingham and London

Station		XC ◇■ A ⊼	GW	GW	GW ◇■ B ✕☕	GW C	GW	XC ◇■ D ⊼	GW ◇	GW ◇■ ☕	GW ◇	GW ◇	GW	GW FX ◇■ ☕	GW FO ◇■ ☕	GW	GW	XC ◇■	GW	GW ■	GW	GW FX	GW FO ◇■ ☕
Penzance	d				16 00						16 44			17 42	17 42		19 16					20 18	20 18
St Erth	d				16 10						16 53			17 52	17 52		19 25					20 28	20 28
Hayle	d										16 56			17 56	17 56		19 28					20 32	20 32
Camborne	d				16 21						17 06			18 07	18 07		19 38					20 42	20 42
Redruth	d				16 28						17 12			18 14	18 14		19 44					20 49	20 49
Truro	d				16 41						17 25			18 26	18 26		19 56					21 01	21 01
St Austell	d				16 59						17 42			18 44	18 44		20 13					21 18	21 18
Newquay	d											17 22				19 24							
Par	d				17 06						17 48	18a11		18 51	18 51	20a13	20 19					21 25	21 25
Lostwithiel	d				17 14						17 55						20 26					21 32	21 32
Bodmin Parkway	d				17 20						18 01			19 03	19 03		20 32					21 38	21 38
Liskeard ■	d				17 33	17 49					18 14			19 16	19 16		20 45					21 51	21 51
Menheniot	d																20 49						
St Germans	d					18 00					18 25						20 58					22 02	22 02
Saltash	d					18 06					18 32						21 04					22 09	22 09
St Budeaux Ferry Road	d					18 10											21 08						
Keyham	d																21 10						
Dockyard	d																21x12						
Devonport	d																21 14						
Plymouth	a				17 58	18 18					18 42			19 40	19 40		21 19					22 22	22 22
	d	17 25		17 35	18 03			18 25			18 44			19 44	19 44						21 25		
Ivybridge	d			17 52							18 59										21 40		
Totnes	d	17 51		18 06	18 31			18 50			19 13			20 12	20 12						21 54		
Paignton	d		17 52				18 34		18 52				19 37					20 14	20 35	21 35			
Torquay	d		17 57				18 39		18 57				19 42					20 20	20 40	21 41			
Torre	d		18 00				18 42						19 45						20 43	21 45			
Newton Abbot	a	18 02	18 08	18 18	18 42		18 49	19 01	19 07		19 25		19 53	20 23	20 23			20 30	20 51	21 53	22 06		
	d	18 04	18 10	18 19	18 44		18 52	19 03	19 09		19 26		19 54	20 25	20 25			20 31	20 53		22 06		
Teignmouth	d		18 17	18 26			18 59		19 16				20 02						21 00		22 13		
Dawlish	d		18 22	18 32			19 04		19 21				20 07						21 05		22 18		
Dawlish Warren	d		18 27	18 36			19 15		19 25				20 11						21 10		22 23		
Starcross	d		18 31				19 19						20 15						21 14		22 27		
Exeter St Thomas	d		18 40				19 28						20 25						21 23		22 36		
Exeter St Davids ■	a	18 22	18 44	18 48	19 03		19 32	19 20	19 39		19 48		20 29	20 44	20 44			20 50	21 28		22 40		
Exeter Central	a		18 53										20 37						21 34				
Exmouth	a		19 24										21 06						22 03				
Exeter St Davids ■	d	18 25			19 05			19 24	19 39	19 55				20 46	20 46			20 52					
Tiverton Parkway	d	18 39			19 20			19 37		20 10				21 01	21 01			21 05					
Taunton	d	18 52			19 34			19 51	20 10	20 26				21 15	21 15			21 19					
Bridgwater	a																						
Weston-super-Mare	a																						
Bristol Temple Meads ■	a	19 25						20 25	20 54					21 47	21 47			21 52					
	d	19 30						20 30						21 50	21 51			22 00					
Bath Spa ■	a													22 02	22 02								
Filton Abbey Wood	a																						
Bristol Parkway ■	a	19 39						20 38										22 09					
Swindon	a													22 32	22 32								
Newport (South Wales)	a																						
Cardiff Central ■	a																						
Birmingham New Street ■	a	20 51						22 02										23 43					
Castle Cary 123	d									20 47													
Frome 123	d																						
Westbury 123	d									21 07													
Pewsey	d									21 24													
Hungerford	a																						
Newbury	a									21 43													
Thatcham	a																						
Theale	a																						
Reading ■	a				20 53					22 02				23 07	23 07								
Slough ■	a																						
London Paddington ■ ⊖	a				21 22					22 37				23 42	23 39								

A To Leeds
B Restaurant available after PLY for customers joining until TAU. ☕ to Plymouth ☕ from Reading ✕ from Plymouth to Reading
C To Gunnislake
D ⊼ to Bristol Temple Meads

For connections to Oxford, Gatwick Airport and Heathrow Airport refer to Tables T116 and T148

For connections from Swansea refer to Table T128

T135 UPDATE: Major engineering work in connection with electrification works is taking place between Reading and Westbury. The route via Newbury will be closed to all trains on 4-7 June; 9-12 July; 16 July to 05 August; 28-30 August; 08-11 October and 19-22 November. Trains will be re-timed or cancelled and run to a special timetable during this period. Please check revised train times with *www.nationalrail.co.uk*. Rail replacement buses will operate between intermediate stations.

Table T135-R

Mondays to Fridays

21 May to 29 June

Cornwall and Devon - Birmingham and London

		GW	GW	GW	GW	GW	GW	GW	XC
							FX	FO	
			◇		A		B	B	◇1
Penzance	d						21 45	21 45	22 10
St Erth	d						21 55	21 55	22 18
Hayle	d								22 22
Camborne	d						22 08	22 08	22 31
Redruth	d						22 16	22 16	22 38
Truro	d						22 29	22 29	22 49
St Austell	d						22 47	22 47	23 05
Newquay	d	21 26							
Par	d	22a16					22 56	22 56	23 12
Lostwithiel	d								23 19
Bodmin Parkway	d						23 08	23 08	23 25
Liskeard 6	d						23 24	23 24	23 37
Menheniot	d								
St Germans	d								
Saltash	d								
St Budeaux Ferry Road	d								
Keyham	d				22 57				
Dockyard	d				22x59				
Devonport	d				23 01				
Plymouth	a				23 06		23 47	23 47	00 01
	d				23 10		23 54	23 54	
Ivybridge	d				23 26				
Totnes	d				23 40		00 22	00 22	
Paignton	d			22 45		23 55			
Torquay	d			22 50		23 59			
Torre	d			22 53		00 03			
Newton Abbot	a			23 01	23 51	00 11	00 34	00 34	
	d			23 03	23 52	00 13	00 36	00 36	
Teignmouth	d			23 10		00 20			
Dawlish	d			23 15		00 25			
Dawlish Warren	d			23 20		00 30			
Starcross	d			23 24		00 34			
Exeter St Thomas	d			23 33		00 43			
Exeter St Davids 6	a			23 37	00 12	00 48	00 57	00 57	
Exeter Central	a								
Exmouth	a								
Exeter St Davids 6	d		21 49				01 06	01 06	
Tiverton Parkway	d		22 06						
Taunton	d		22 23				01 42	01 42	
Bridgwater	a								
Weston-super-Mare	a		22 47						
Bristol Temple Meads 10	a		23 13						
	d								
Bath Spa 7	a								
Filton Abbey Wood	a								
Bristol Parkway 7	a								
Swindon	a								
Newport (South Wales)	a								
Cardiff Central 7	a								
Birmingham New Street 12	a								
Castle Cary 123	d								
Frome 123	d								
Westbury 123	d								
Pewsey	d								
Hungerford	a								
Newbury	a								
Thatcham	a								
Theale	a								
Reading 7	a						03s58	04s00	
Slough 3	a								
London Paddington 15 ⊖	a						05 03	05 07	

A From Gunnislake

B The Night Riviera

For connections to Oxford, Gatwick Airport and Heathrow Airport refer to Tables T116 and T148

For connections from Swansea refer to Table T128

Table T135-R

Mondays to Fridays

2 July to 31 August

Cornwall and Devon - Birmingham and London

		GW	GW	GW	GW	GW	GW	GW	XC	GW	GW	GW	GW	GW	GW	XC	XC	GW	XC	GW	GW	GW	GW
		MO	MX	MX																			
		A	B	A	◇1	◇1	◇1		◇1 C	◇1	◇1	D	◇1 E	B	D	◇1 F	◇1 G	B	◇1 H	D	◇1 I	B	
Penzance	d																				05 05		05 19
St Erth	d																						
Hayle	d																						05 29
Camborne	d																						05 38
Redruth	d																				05 26		
Truro	d																				05 38		05a53
St Austell	d																				05 56		
Newquay	d																						
Par	d																						
Lostwithiel	d																						
Bodmin Parkway	d																				06 12		
Liskeard 6	d																				06 25		
Menheniot	d																						
St Germans	d																						
Saltash	d																						
St Budeaux Ferry Road	d																						
Keyham	d																						
Dockyard	d																						
Devonport	d																						
Plymouth	a																				06 49		
	d						04 51		05 20		05 29		05 53			06 25	06 25				06 53		
Ivybridge	d																						
Totnes	d			00 22					05 45		05 56					06 50	06 50						
Paignton	d											06 03			06 34				07 01	07 10			
Torquay	d											06 08			06 39				07 07	07 15			
Torre	d		00 03									06 11			06 42					07 18		←	
Newton Abbot	a		00 11	00 34			05 26		05 56		06 07	06 19	06 28		06 50	07 01	07 01		07 17	07 26	07 28	07 26	
	d	00 01	00 13	00 36			05 27		06 02		06 09	06 21	06 29		06 52	07 03	07 03		07 18	07 34	07 31	07 34	
Teignmouth	d		00 20								06 16	06 28			06 59				07 25	→		07 41	
Dawlish	d		00 25								06 22	06 33		←	07 04			←	07 30			07 46	
Dawlish Warren	d		00 30									06 45		06 45	07 15			07 15				07 52	
Starcross	d		00 34									→		06 49	→			07 19				07 55	
Exeter St Thomas	d		00 43											06 58				07 28				08 06	
Exeter St Davids 6	a	00 23	00 48	00 57			05 46		06 19		06 34		06 50	07 03		07 20	07 20	07 33	07 42		07 50	08 10	
Exeter Central	a													07 10				07 39				08 18	
Exmouth	a													07 41				08 16				08 47	
Exeter St Davids 6	d	00 59		01 06			05 52	06 00	06 24	06 28	06 36		06 52			07 24	07 24		07 44		07 52		
Tiverton Parkway	d						06 07	06 17	06 37	06 43	06 51					07 37	07 37		07 57				
Taunton	d			01 42			06 22	06 34	06 51	06 57	07 05		07 17			07 51	07 51		08 12		08 16		
Bridgwater	a							06 46		07 06													
Weston-super-Mare	a							07 05		07 25									08 34				
Bristol Temple Meads 10	a							07 41	07 26	07 58						08 27	08 27		08 55				
	d				05 15			07 46	07 30	08 00						08 30	08 30		09 00				
Bath Spa 7	a									08 11													
Filton Abbey Wood	a							07 57															
Bristol Parkway 7	a							08 03	07 38							08 38	08 38		09 08				
Swindon	a									08 40													
Newport (South Wales)	a																						
Cardiff Central 7	a																						
Birmingham New Street 12	a								08 56							09 58	09 58		10 23				
Castle Cary 123	d						06 44				07 27												
Frome 123	d					06 05																	
Westbury 123	d				06 00	06 16	07 03				07 52												
Pewsey	d				06 18	06 34	07 22				08 10												
Hungerford	a				06 35	06 51	07 34																
Newbury	a				06 50	07 06	07 45				08 30												
Thatcham	a				06 57	07 13																	
Theale	a				07 06	07 22																	
Reading 7	a	04s06		03s58	07 18	07 37	08 07			09 15	08 54		08 33								09 33		
Slough 3	a																						
London Paddington 15 ⊖	a	05 02		05 03	07 47	08 08	08 37			09 43	09 23		09 00								10 02		

A From Penzance. The Night Riviera

B From Paignton

C To Newcastle

D To Exmouth

E The Armada - Restaurant for customers joining until Taunton

F from 23 July. To Newcastle

G until 20 July. To Glasgow Central

H To Manchester Piccadilly. Trolley service from Newton Abbot

I The Golden Hind. Buffet to Plymouth, buffet from Reading; restaurant from Plymouth to Reading

For connections to Oxford, Gatwick Airport and Heathrow Airport refer to Tables T116 and T148

For connections from Swansea refer to Table T128

Table T135-R

Mondays to Fridays

2 July to 31 August

Cornwall and Devon - Birmingham and London

		XC	GW	GW	GW	GW	XC	XC	GW	GW	GW	GW	GW	GW	XC	XC	GW	GW	GW	XC	XC	GW	GW
		◇1 A	◇1	◇1		◇ B	◇1 C	◇1 D	◇ E	F	◇1	G	H		◇1 A	◇1 I	◇1			■ ◇1 J	■ ◇1 K	H	■ 1 L
Penzance	d			05 41		06 00	06 28	06 28			06 47		06 58				07 41			08 28	08 28	08 44	09 00
St Erth	d					06 09	06 36	06 36			06 57		07a06				07 51			08 36	08 36	08a52	09 10
Hayle	d					06 12											07 55						
Camborne	d			05 58		06 21	06 46	06 46			07 08						08 05			08 46	08 46		09 21
Redruth	d			06 05		06 27	06 52	06 52			07 15						08 12			08 52	08 52		09 28
Truro	d			06 18		06 39	07 04	07 04			07 28						08 25			09 04	09 04		09 41
St Austell	d			06 35		06 56	07 20	07 20			07 45						08 43			09 20	09 20		09 58
Newquay	d																						
Par	d			06 43		07 02	07 27	07 27			07 53						08 50			09 27	09 27		10 05
Lostwithiel	d			06 51		07 09					08 00												
Bodmin Parkway	d			06 57		07 15	07 37	07 37			08 07						09 02			09 37	09 37		10 17
Liskeard 6	d			07 11		07 28	07 53	07 53			08 20						09 15			09 50	09 50		10 30
Menheniot	d					07x32																	
St Germans	d			07 23		07 40					08 31						09 27						
Saltash	d			07 31		07 46					08 39						09 35						
St Budeaux Ferry Road	d					07 50																	
Keyham	d					07 53																	
Dockyard	d					07x55																	
Devonport	d					07 58																	
Plymouth	a			07 41		08 03	08 20	08 20			08 49						09 45			10 18	10 19		10 54
	d	07 25		07 45		08 09	08 25	08 25			08 51				09 25		09 49			10 25	10 25		11 00
Ivybridge	d					08 24					09 06						10 04						
Totnes	d	07 50		08 15		08 39	08 50	08 50			09 21				09 50		10 19			10 50	10 50		
Paignton	d		07 48		08 20					09 12				09 34		10 07		10 21	10 33				
Torquay	d		07 55		08 25					09 17				09 39		10 13		10 26	10 38				
Torre	d		07 59		08 28					09 20		←		09 42				10 29	10 41				
Newton Abbot	a	08 01	08 07	08 27	08 36	08 51	09 01	09 01		09 28	09 33	09 28		09 50	10 01	10 23	10 31	10 36	10 49	11 01	11 01		
	d	08 03	08 08	08 28	08 38	08 52	09 03	09 03		09 39	09 34	09 39			10 03	10 24	10 32	10 39	10 51	11 03	11 03		
Teignmouth	d		08 15		08 45	08 59				→		09 45				10 31		10 46	10 58				
Dawlish	d		08 22		08 50	09 04						09 50				10 36		10 51	11 03				
Dawlish Warren	d				08 55							09 55						10 56	11 15				
Starcross	d		08 28		08 59							09 59						11 00					
Exeter St Thomas	d		08 36		09 08							10 08						11 09					
Exeter St Davids 6	a	08 20	08 40	08 48	09 12	09 16	09 22	09 22			09 53	10 14			10 20	10 48	10 53	11 13	11 28	11 20	11 20		11 52
Exeter Central	a				09 19							10 19						11 19					
Exmouth	a				09 48							10 48						11 48					
Exeter St Davids 6	d	08 24	08 42	08 51			09 24	09 24	09 33		09 55				10 23	10 50	10 55			11 24	11 24		11 55
Tiverton Parkway	d	08 37		09 06			09 38	09 38	09 50		10 10				10 37	11 03	11 11			11 37	11 37		
Taunton	d	08 51	09 07	09 20			09 51	09 51	10 11		10 28				10 51	11 17	11 25			11 51	11 51		
Bridgwater	a								10 22														
Weston-super-Mare	a		09 27						10 41														
Bristol Temple Meads 10	a	09 26	09 57				10 25	10 25	11 11						11 24	11 52				12 24	12 24		
	d	09 30	10 00				10 30	10 30	11 21						11 30	12 00				12 30	12 30		
Bath Spa 7	a		10 11																				
Filton Abbey Wood	a								11 30														
Bristol Parkway 7	a	09 38					10 38	10 38							11 38	12 08				12 38	12 38		
Swindon	a		10 41																				
Newport (South Wales)	a								11 57														
Cardiff Central 7	a								12 19														
Birmingham New Street 12	a	10 56					11 58	11 58							12 56	13 26				13 56	13 56		
Castle Cary 123	d			09 41																			
Frome 123	d																						
Westbury 123	d			10 01							11 05												
Pewsey	d			10 18																			
Hungerford	a																						
Newbury	a																						
Thatcham	a																						
Theale	a																						
Reading 7	a		11 10	10 52							11 51						12 42						13 31
Slough 3	a																						
London Paddington 15 ⊖	a		11 37	11 21							12 21						13 15						14 00

A To Newcastle
B ◇ from Plymouth
C from 23 July. To Newcastle
D until 20 July. To Glasgow Central. trolley from Plymouth
E From St James' Park
F To Exmouth
G From Paignton
H To St Ives
I To Manchester Piccadilly
J until 20 July. To Glasgow Central. trolley ◇ from Plymouth ■ to Plymouth
K from 23 July. To Newcastle. ◇ from Plymouth ■ to Plymouth
L The Cornish Riviera

For connections to Oxford, Gatwick Airport and Heathrow Airport refer to Tables T116 and T148

For connections from Swansea refer to Table T128

Table T135-R

Mondays to Fridays

2 July to 31 August

Cornwall and Devon - Birmingham and London

		GW	GW	GW	XC	XC	GW	GW	GW	GW	XC	GW	GW	GW	GW	GW	XC	XC	GW	GW	GW	GW
			◇1		◇1 A	■ ◇1 B	◇	C	■ 1 D	E	◇1 F	◇	C	◇1 G	E		◇1 A	◇1 H	◇	◇1 I	◇1	J
Penzance	d					09 35			10 00					10 49					11 41	12 04		
St Erth	d					09 43			10 10					10 59					11 50	12 14		
Hayle	d					09 47								11 04					11 53			
Camborne	d					09 56			10 21					11 14					12 02			
Redruth	d					10 03			10 28					11 21					12 08	12 28		
Truro	d					10 15			10 41					11 34					12 19	12 41		
St Austell	d					10 31			10 58					11 51					12 36	12 59		
Newquay	d						10 13															12 41
Par	d					10 38	11a02		11 06					11 58					12 43			13a35
Lostwithiel	d					10 45													12 49			
Bodmin Parkway	d					10 51			11 17					12 10					12 55	13 15		
Liskeard 6	d					11 04			11 30					12 23					13 08	13 28		
Menheniot	d																		13x13			
St Germans	d													12 34					13 21			
Saltash	d													12 42					13 28			
St Budeaux Ferry Road	d																					
Keyham	d																					
Dockyard	d																					
Devonport	d																					
Plymouth	a					11 27			11 55					12 52					13 37	13 52		
	d				11 25	11 50			12 01		12 25			12 55			13 25		13 43	13 56		
Ivybridge	d																		13 58			
Totnes	d				11 50	12 15			12 28		12 51			13 22			13 51		14 12			
Paignton	d	11 20	11 32	11 42				12 13				12 53	13 08			13 40		14 04				
Torquay	d	11 25	11 38	11 47				12 18				12 59	13 13			13 45		14 10				
Torre	d	11 28		11 50				12 21				13 02	13 16			13 48						
Newton Abbot	a	11 37	11 48	11 58	12 01	12 26		12 30	12 40		13 02	13 10	13 25	13 34		13 56	14 02	14 20	14 24	14 31		
	d	11 37	11 50		12 03	12 28		12 31	12 41		13 04	13 12	13 25	13 35			14 04	14 21		14 32		
Teignmouth	d	11 45	11 57					12 38				13 19	13 33					14 28				
Dawlish	d	11 50	12 03					12 43		←		13 24	13 38		←			14 33				
Dawlish Warren	d	11 54						12 54		12 54			13 50		13 50							
Starcross	d	11 58						→		12 58			→		13 54							
Exeter St Thomas	d	12 08								13 07					14 03							
Exeter St Davids 6	a	12 11	12 15		12 22	12 45			13 00	13 13	13 22	13 36		13 54	14 08		14 22	14 45		14 52		
Exeter Central	a	12 19								13 19					14 19							
Exmouth	a	12 48								13 48					14 48							
Exeter St Davids 6	d		12 17		12 24	12 50			13 02		13 24	13 38		13 59			14 24	14 48		14 55		
Tiverton Parkway	d		12 32		12 38	13 06			13 17		13 38	13 55		14 14			14 38	15 02		15 10		
Taunton	d		12 46		12 51	13 22			13 31		13 51	14 11		14 28			14 51	15 15		15 24	15 33	
Bridgwater	a											14 23										
Weston-super-Mare	a											14 42						15 37				
Bristol Temple Meads 10	a				13 24	13 55					14 26	15 14					15 23	15 57				
	d				13 30	14 00					14 30	15 21					15 30	16 00				
Bath Spa 7	a																					
Filton Abbey Wood	a											15 29										
Bristol Parkway 7	a				13 38	14 08					14 39						15 39	16 08				
Swindon	a																					
Newport (South Wales)	a											15 57										
Cardiff Central 7	a											16 15										
Birmingham New Street 12	a				14 56	15 23					15 56						16 56	17 23				
Castle Cary 123	d		13 07																		15 55	
Frome 123	d																					
Westbury 123	d		13 27											15 04							16 14	
Pewsey	d		13 45																		16 32	
Hungerford	a																					
Newbury	a		14 04																		16 51	
Thatcham	a																					
Theale	a																					
Reading 7	a		14 23						14 51					15 50						16 46	17 16	
Slough 3	a																					
London Paddington 15 ⊖	a		14 54						15 21					16 21						17 15	17 54	

A To Newcastle
B To Manchester Piccadilly. trolley ◇ from Plymouth ■ to Plymouth
C To Exmouth
D The Cornishman. to Plymouth from Reading ✕ from Plymouth to Reading
E From Paignton
F To Edinburgh
G Restaurant available for customers joining until Castle Cary. from Westbury ✕ to Westbury
H To Manchester Piccadilly
I The Royal Duchy
J To Penzance

For connections to Oxford, Gatwick Airport and Heathrow Airport refer to Tables T116 and T148

For connections from Swansea refer to Table T128

T135 UPDATE: Major engineering work in connection with electrification works is taking place between Reading and Westbury. The route via Newbury will be closed to all trains on 4-7 June; 9-12 July; 16 July to 05 August; 28-30 August; 08-11 October and 19-22 November. Trains will be re-timed or cancelled and run to a special timetable during this period. Please check revised train times with *www.nationalrail.co.uk*. Rail replacement buses will operate between intermediate stations.

Table T135-R

Mondays to Fridays

2 July to 31 August

Cornwall and Devon - Birmingham and London

	GW	GW	XC	GW	GW	GW	GW	GW	GW	XC	XC	GW	GW	GW	GW	GW	XC	XC	GW	GW	GW	GW
			◇■	◇■		■				◇■	◇■		◇■		◇		◇■	◇■		◇■		
			A	B	C	D	E			F	G	C		E			H	I				
			⊥	☕		☕				⊥	⊥		☕				⊥	⊥		☕		
Penzance d									12 57				14 00		14 49							
St Erth d									13 06				14 10		14 58							
Hayle d									13 09						15 01							
Camborne d									13 18				14 21		15 11							
Redruth d									13 24				14 28		15 17							
Truro d									13 35				14 41		15 28							
St Austell d									13 52				14 58		15 45							
Newquay d																				15 07		
Par d									13 59				15 06		15a51					16 01		
Lostwithiel d									14 05											16 10		
Bodmin Parkway d									14 11				15 17							16 17		
Liskeard ■ d									14 24				15 30							16 30	16 44	
Menheniot d									14x29												16x48	
St Germans d									14 37												16 56	
Saltash d									14 44												17 03	
St Budeaux Ferry Road d																					17 07	
Keyham d																					17 09	
Dockyard d																					17x10	
Devonport d																					17 13	
Plymouth a									14 53				15 55							16 54	17 18	
d			14 25			15 00			15 08	15 25			16 00				16 25	16 25		16 57		
Ivybridge d									15 23											17 13		
Totnes d			14 50			15 27			15 37	15 51			16 27				16 50	16 50		17 28		
Paignton d	14 21	14 40		14 54	15 13			15 32				16 12				16 29			16 57			17 26
Torquay d	14 26	14 45		15 00	15 18			15 37				16 17				16 34			17 02			17 31
Torre d	14 29	14 48			15 21			15 40				16 21				16 37			17 05			17 34
Newton Abbot a	14 37	14 56	15 01	15 10	15 29	15 38		15 48	15 49	16 02		16 29	16 39			16 46	17 01	17 02	17 13	17 39		17 42
d	14 39		15 03	15 12	15 31	15 40				16 04		16 31	16 40			16 47	17 03	17 03	17 15	17 41		17 44
Teignmouth d	14 46			15 19	15 38							16 38				16 55			17 22			17 51
Dawlish d	14 51			15 25	15 43		←					16 43		←		17 00			17 27			17 56
Dawlish Warren d	14 56				15 54		15 54					16 53		16 53		17 04			17 32			18 01
Starcross d	15 00				→		15 58					→		16 57					17 36			18 05
Exeter St Thomas d	15 09						16 07							17 07					17 45			18 14
Exeter St Davids ■ a	15 13		15 20	15 37		15 59	16 12			16 22			16 59	17 11		17 17	17 20	17 22	17 51	18 00		18 19
Exeter Central a	15 19						16 18							17 18					17 56			18 24
Exmouth a	15 48						16 49							17 51					18 27			18 54
Exeter St Davids ■ d			15 24	15 39		16 01				16 24	16 54		17 02				17 24	17 24		18 02		
Tiverton Parkway d			15 37			16 16				16 38	17 08		17 17				17 37	17 37		18 17		
Taunton d			15 51	16 04		16 30				16 51	17 22		17 31				17 50	17 50		18 31		
Bridgwater a																						
Weston-super-Mare a																						
Bristol Temple Meads ■ a			16 23							17 24	17 54						18 23	18 23				
d			16 30							17 30	18 00						18 30	18 30				
Bath Spa ■ a																						
Filton Abbey Wood a																						
Bristol Parkway ■ a			16 38							17 39	18 08						18 38	18 38				
Swindon a																						
Newport (South Wales) a																						
Cardiff Central ■ a																						
Birmingham New Street ■ a			17 56							18 56	19 23						19 56	19 56				
Castle Cary 123 d				16 25																18 52		
Frome 123 d																						
Westbury 123 d				16 45																19 12		
Pewsey d				17 02																19 29		
Hungerford a																						
Newbury a																				19 48		
Thatcham a																						
Theale a																						
Reading ■ a				17 37		17 46							18 52							20 08		
Slough ■ a																						
London Paddington ■ ⊖ a				18 07		18 16							19 20							20 37		

A To Newcastle
B The Torbay Express
C To Exmouth
D The Mayflower
E From Paignton
F To Leeds
G To Manchester Piccadilly
H until 20 July. To Leeds
I from 23 July. To York

For connections to Oxford, Gatwick Airport and Heathrow Airport refer to Tables T116 and T148

For connections from Swansea refer to Table T128

Table T135-R

Mondays to Fridays

2 July to 31 August

Cornwall and Devon - Birmingham and London

	XC	GW	GW	GW	GW	GW	XC	GW	GW	GW	GW	GW	GW	GW	GW	GW	XC	GW	GW	GW	GW
													FX	FO							
	◇■			◇■			◇■	◇	◇■	◇	◇		◇■	◇■		■	◇■		■		
	A			B	C		D														
	⊥			✕☕			⊥		☕				☕	☕							
Penzance d				16 00						16 44			17 42	17 42		19 16					
St Erth d				16 10						16 53			17 52	17 52		19 26					
Hayle d										16 56			17 56	17 56		19 30					
Camborne d				16 21						17 06			18 07	18 07		19 41					
Redruth d				16 28						17 12			18 14	18 14		19 48					
Truro d				16 41						17 25			18 26	18 26		20 01					
St Austell d				16 59						17 42			18 44	18 44		20 18					
Newquay d											17 22				19 24						
Par d				17 06						17 48	18a11		18 51	18 51	20a13	20 26					
Lostwithiel d				17 14						17 55						20 33					
Bodmin Parkway d				17 20						18 01			19 03	19 03		20 40					
Liskeard ■ d				17 33	17 49					18 14			19 16	19 16		20 52					21 04
Menheniot d																					21x08
St Germans d					18 00					18 25											21 16
Saltash d					18 06					18 32											21 23
St Budeaux Ferry Road d					18 10																21 27
Keyham d																					21 29
Dockyard d																					21x30
Devonport d																					21 33
Plymouth a				17 58	18 18					18 42			19 40	19 40		21 17					21 38
d	17 25		17 35	18 03			18 25			18 44			19 44	19 44						21 25	
Ivybridge d			17 52							18 59										21 40	
Totnes d	17 51		18 06	18 31			18 50			19 13			20 12	20 12						21 54	
Paignton d		17 52				18 34		18 52				19 37					20 14	20 35	21 35		
Torquay d		17 57				18 39		18 57				19 42					20 20	20 40	21 41		
Torre d		18 00				18 42						19 45						20 43	21 45		
Newton Abbot a	18 02	18 08	18 18	18 42		18 49	19 01	19 07		19 25		19 53	20 23	20 23			20 30	20 51	21 53	22 06	
d	18 04	18 10	18 19	18 44		18 52	19 03	19 09		19 26		19 54	20 25	20 25			20 31	20 53		22 06	
Teignmouth d		18 17	18 26			18 59		19 16				20 02						21 00		22 13	
Dawlish d		18 22	18 32			19 04		19 21				20 07						21 05		22 18	
Dawlish Warren d		18 27	18 36			19 15		19 25				20 11						21 10		22 23	
Starcross d		18 31				19 19						20 15						21 14		22 27	
Exeter St Thomas d		18 40				19 28						20 25						21 23		22 36	
Exeter St Davids ■ a	18 22	18 44	18 48	19 03		19 32	19 20	19 39		19 48		20 29	20 44	20 44			20 50	21 28		22 40	
Exeter Central a		18 53										20 37						21 34			
Exmouth a		19 24										21 06						22 03			
Exeter St Davids ■ d	18 25			19 05			19 24	19 39	19 55				20 46	20 46			20 52				
Tiverton Parkway d	18 39			19 20			19 37		20 10				21 01	21 01			21 05				
Taunton d	18 52			19 34			19 51	20 10	20 26				21 15	21 15			21 19				
Bridgwater a																					
Weston-super-Mare a																					
Bristol Temple Meads ■ a	19 25						20 25	20 54					21 47	21 47			21 52				
d	19 30						20 30						21 50	21 51			22 00				
Bath Spa ■ a													22 02	22 02							
Filton Abbey Wood a																					
Bristol Parkway ■ a	19 39						20 38										22 09				
Swindon a													22 32	22 32							
Newport (South Wales) a																					
Cardiff Central ■ a																					
Birmingham New Street ■ a	20 51						22 02										23 43				
Castle Cary 123 d									20 47												
Frome 123 d																					
Westbury 123 d									21 07												
Pewsey d									21 24												
Hungerford a																					
Newbury a									21 43												
Thatcham a																					
Theale a																					
Reading ■ a				20 53					22 02				23 07	23 07							
Slough ■ a																					
London Paddington ■ ⊖ a				21 22					22 37				23 42	23 39							

A To Leeds
B Restaurant available after PLY for customers joining until TAU. ☕ to Plymouth ☕ from Reading ✕ from Plymouth to Reading
C To Gunnislake
D ⊥ to Bristol Temple Meads

For connections to Oxford, Gatwick Airport and Heathrow Airport refer to Tables T116 and T148

For connections from Swansea refer to Table T128

Cornwall and Devon - Birmingham and London

Station		GW FX	GW FO ◇1	GW	GW ◇	GW	GW A	GW	GW FX B	GW FO B	XC ◇1
Penzance	d	20 18	20 18						21 45	21 45	22 10
St Erth	d	20 28	20 28						21 55	21 55	22 18
Hayle	d	20 32	20 32								22 22
Camborne	d	20 42	20 42						22 08	22 08	22 31
Redruth	d	20 49	20 49						22 16	22 16	22 38
Truro	d	21 01	21 01						22 29	22 29	22 49
St Austell	d	21 18	21 18						22 47	22 47	23 05
Newquay	d			21 26							
Par	d	21 25	21 25	22a16					22 56	22 56	23 12
Lostwithiel	d	21 32	21 32								23 19
Bodmin Parkway	d	21 38	21 38						23 08	23 08	23 25
Liskeard	d	21 51	21 51						23 24	23 24	23 37
Menheniot	d										
St Germans	d	22 02	22 02								
Saltash	d	22 09	22 09								
St Budeaux Ferry Road	d										
Keyham	d						22 57				
Dockyard	d						22x59				
Devonport	d						23 01				
Plymouth	a	22 22	22 22				23 06		23 47	23 47	00 01
	d						23 10		23 54	23 54	
Ivybridge	d						23 26				
Totnes	d						23 40		00 22	00 22	
Paignton	d					22 45		23 55			
Torquay	d					22 50		23 59			
Torre	d					22 53		00 03			
Newton Abbot	a					23 01	23 51	00 11	00 34	00 34	
	d					23 03	23 52	00 13	00 36	00 36	
Teignmouth	d					23 10		00 20			
Dawlish	d					23 15		00 25			
Dawlish Warren	d					23 20		00 30			
Starcross	d					23 24		00 34			
Exeter St Thomas	d					23 33		00 43			
Exeter St Davids	a					23 37	00 12	00 48	00 57	00 57	
Exeter Central	a										
Exmouth	a										
Exeter St Davids	d				21 49				01 06	01 06	
Tiverton Parkway	d				22 06						
Taunton	d				22 23				01 42	01 42	
Bridgwater	a										
Weston-super-Mare	a				22 47						
Bristol Temple Meads	a				23 13						
	d										
Bath Spa	a										
Filton Abbey Wood	a										
Bristol Parkway	a										
Swindon	a										
Newport (South Wales)	a										
Cardiff Central	a										
Birmingham New Street	a										
Castle Cary 123	d										
Frome 123	d										
Westbury 123	d										
Pewsey	d										
Hungerford	a										
Newbury	a										
Thatcham	a										
Theale	a										
Reading	a								03s58	04s00	
Slough	a										
London Paddington ⊖	a								05 03	05 07	

A From Gunnislake
B The Night Riviera

For connections to Oxford, Gatwick Airport and Heathrow Airport refer to Tables T116 and T148

For connections from Swansea refer to Table T128

Cornwall and Devon - Birmingham and London

Station		GW MO A	GW MX B	GW MX A	GW ◇1	GW ◇1	GW ◇1	GW	XC ◇1 C	GW ◇1	GW ◇1	GW D
Penzance	d											
St Erth	d											
Hayle	d											
Camborne	d											
Redruth	d											
Truro	d											
St Austell	d											
Newquay	d											
Par	d											
Lostwithiel	d											
Bodmin Parkway	d											
Liskeard	d											
Menheniot	d											
St Germans	d											
Saltash	d											
St Budeaux Ferry Road	d											
Keyham	d											
Dockyard	d											
Devonport	d											
Plymouth	a											
	d						04 51		05 20		05 29	
Ivybridge	d											
Totnes	d			00 22					05 45		05 56	
Paignton	d											06 03
Torquay	d											06 08
Torre	d		00 03									06 11
Newton Abbot	a		00 11	00 34			05 26		05 56		06 07	06 19
	d	00 01	00 13	00 36			05 27		06 02		06 09	06 21
Teignmouth	d		00 20								06 16	06 28
Dawlish	d		00 25								06 22	06 33
Dawlish Warren	d		00 30									06 45
Starcross	d		00 34									→
Exeter St Thomas	d		00 43									
Exeter St Davids	a	00 23	00 48	00 57			05 46		06 19		06 34	
Exeter Central	a											
Exmouth	a											
Exeter St Davids	d	00 59		01 06			05 52	06 00	06 24	06 28	06 36	
Tiverton Parkway	d						06 07	06 17	06 37	06 43	06 51	
Taunton	d			01 42			06 22	06 34	06 51	06 57	07 05	
Bridgwater	a							06 46		07 06		
Weston-super-Mare	a							07 05		07 25		
Bristol Temple Meads	a							07 41	07 26	07 58		
	d				05 15			07 46	07 30	08 00		
Bath Spa	a									08 11		
Filton Abbey Wood	a							07 57				
Bristol Parkway	a							08 03	07 38			
Swindon	a									08 40		
Newport (South Wales)	a											
Cardiff Central	a											
Birmingham New Street	a								08 56			
Castle Cary 123	d						06 44				07 27	
Frome 123	d					06 05						
Westbury 123	d				06 00	06 16	07 03				07 52	
Pewsey	d				06 18	06 34	07 22				08 10	
Hungerford	a				06 35	06 51	07 34					
Newbury	a				06 50	07 06	07 45				08 30	
Thatcham	a				06 57	07 13						
Theale	a				07 06	07 22						
Reading	a	04s06		03s58	07 18	07 37	08 07			09 15	08 54	
Slough	a											
London Paddington ⊖	a	05 02		05 03	07 47	08 08	08 37			09 43	09 23	

Station		GW ◇1 E	GW B	GW D	XC ◇1 F	XC ◇1 G	GW B	XC ◇1 H	GW D	GW ◇1 I	GW B	GW
Penzance	d									05 05		05 19
St Erth	d											
Hayle	d											05 29
Camborne	d											05 38
Redruth	d									05 26		
Truro	d									05 38		05a53
St Austell	d									05 56		
Newquay	d											
Par	d											
Lostwithiel	d											
Bodmin Parkway	d									06 12		
Liskeard	d									06 25		
Menheniot	d											
St Germans	d											
Saltash	d											
St Budeaux Ferry Road	d											
Keyham	d											
Dockyard	d											
Devonport	d											
Plymouth	a									06 49		
	d	05 53			06 25	06 25				06 53		
Ivybridge	d											
Totnes	d				06 50	06 50						
Paignton	d			06 34				07 01	07 10			
Torquay	d			06 39				07 07	07 15			
Torre	d			06 42					07 18		←	
Newton Abbot	a	06 28		06 50	07 01	07 01		07 17	07 26	07 28	07 26	
	d	06 29		06 52	07 03	07 03		07 18	07 34	07 31	07 34	
Teignmouth	d			06 59				07 25	→		07 41	
Dawlish	d		←	07 04			←	07 30			07 46	
Dawlish Warren	d		06 45	07 15			07 15				07 52	
Starcross	d		06 49	→			07 19				07 55	
Exeter St Thomas	d		06 58				07 28				08 06	
Exeter St Davids	a	06 50	07 03		07 20	07 20	07 33	07 42		07 50	08 10	
Exeter Central	a		07 10				07 39				08 18	
Exmouth	a		07 41				08 16				08 47	
Exeter St Davids	d	06 52			07 24	07 24		07 44		07 52		
Tiverton Parkway	d				07 37	07 37		07 57				
Taunton	d	07 17			07 51	07 51		08 12		08 16		
Bridgwater	a											
Weston-super-Mare	a							08 34				
Bristol Temple Meads	a				08 27	08 27		08 55				
	d				08 30	08 30		09 00				
Bath Spa	a											
Filton Abbey Wood	a											
Bristol Parkway	a				08 38	08 38		09 08				
Swindon	a											
Newport (South Wales)	a											
Cardiff Central	a											
Birmingham New Street	a				09 58	09 58		10 23				
Castle Cary 123	d											
Frome 123	d											
Westbury 123	d											
Pewsey	d											
Hungerford	a											
Newbury	a											
Thatcham	a											
Theale	a											
Reading	a	08 33								09 33		
Slough	a											
London Paddington ⊖	a	09 00								10 02		

A From Penzance. The Night Riviera
B From Paignton
C To Newcastle
D To Exmouth
E The Armada - Restaurant for customers joining until Taunton
F until 5 October. To Newcastle
G from 8 October. To Glasgow Central
H To Manchester Piccadilly. Trolley from Newton Abbot
I The Golden Hind. Buffet to Plymouth, buffet from Reading. ✕ from Plymouth to Reading

For connections to Oxford, Gatwick Airport and Heathrow Airport refer to Tables T116 and T148

For connections from Swansea refer to Table T128

T135 UPDATE: Major engineering work in connection with electrification works is taking place between Reading and Westbury. The route via Newbury will be closed to all trains on 4-7 June; 9-12 July; 16 July to 05 August; 28-30 August; 08-11 October and 19-22 November. Trains will be re-timed or cancelled and run to a special timetable during this period. Please check revised train times with *www.nationalrail.co.uk*. Rail replacement buses will operate between intermediate stations.

Table T135-R

Mondays to Fridays

3 September to 7 December

Cornwall and Devon - Birmingham and London

		XC ◇■ A 🛒	GW ◇■ ☕	GW ◇■ ☕	GW	GW ◇ B	XC ◇■ C 🛒	XC ◇■ D 🛒	GW ◇ E	GW F	GW ◇■ ☕	GW G	GW H	GW	XC ◇■ A 🛒	XC ◇■ I 🛒	GW ◇■ ☕	GW	GW	XC ■ ◇■ J 🛒	XC ■ ◇■ K 🛒	GW H	GW ■ ■ L ☕
Penzance	d			05 41		06 00	06 28	06 28			06 47		06 58				07 41			08 28	08 28	08 44	09 00
St Erth	d					06 09	06 36	06 36			06 57		07a06				07 51			08 36	08 36	08a52	09 10
Hayle	d					06 12											07 55						
Camborne	d			05 58		06 21	06 46	06 46			07 08						08 05			08 46	08 46		09 21
Redruth	d			06 05		06 27	06 52	06 52			07 15						08 12			08 52	08 52		09 28
Truro	d			06 18		06 39	07 04	07 04			07 28						08 25			09 04	09 04		09 41
St Austell	d			06 35		06 56	07 20	07 20			07 45						08 43			09 20	09 20		09 58
Newquay	d																						
Par	d			06 43		07 02	07 27	07 27			07 53						08 50			09 27	09 27		10 05
Lostwithiel	d			06 51		07 09					08 00												
Bodmin Parkway	d			06 57		07 15	07 37	07 37			08 07						09 02			09 37	09 37		10 17
Liskeard ■	d			07 11		07 28	07 53	07 53			08 20						09 15			09 50	09 50		10 30
Menheniot	d					07x32																	
St Germans	d			07 23		07 40					08 31						09 27						
Saltash	d			07 31		07 46					08 39						09 35						
St Budeaux Ferry Road	d					07 50																	
Keyham	d					07 53																	
Dockyard	d					07x55																	
Devonport	d					07 58																	
Plymouth	a			07 41		08 03	08 20	08 20			08 49						09 45			10 18	10 18		10 54
	d	07 25		07 45		08 09	08 25	08 25			08 51				09 25		09 49			10 25	10 25		11 00
Ivybridge	d					08 24					09 06						10 04						
Totnes	d	07 50		08 15		08 39	08 50	08 50			09 21				09 50		10 19			10 50	10 50		
Paignton	d		07 48		08 20					09 12				09 34		10 07		10 21	10 33				
Torquay	d		07 55		08 25					09 17				09 39		10 13		10 26	10 38				
Torre	d		07 59		08 28					09 20		←		09 42				10 29	10 41				
Newton Abbot	a	08 01	08 07	08 27	08 36	08 51	09 01	09 01		09 28	09 33	09 28		09 50	10 01	10 23	10 31	10 36	10 49	11 01	11 01		
	d	08 03	08 08	08 28	08 38	08 52	09 03	09 03		09 39	09 34	09 39			10 03	10 24	10 32	10 39	10 51	11 03	11 03		
Teignmouth	d		08 15		08 45	08 59				→		09 45				10 31		10 46	10 58				
Dawlish	d		08 22		08 50	09 04						09 50				10 36		10 51	11 03				
Dawlish Warren	d				08 55							09 55						10 56	11 15				
Starcross	d		08 28		08 59							09 59						11 00					
Exeter St Thomas	d		08 36		09 08							10 08						11 09					
Exeter St Davids ■	a	08 20	08 40	08 48	09 12	09 16	09 22	09 22			09 53	10 14			10 20	10 48	10 53	11 13	11 28	11 20	11 20		11 52
Exeter Central	a				09 19							10 19						11 19					
Exmouth	a				09 48							10 48						11 48					
Exeter St Davids ■	d	08 24	08 42	08 51			09 24	09 24	09 33		09 55				10 23	10 50	10 55			11 24	11 24		11 55
Tiverton Parkway	d	08 37		09 06			09 38	09 38	09 50		10 10				10 37	11 03	11 11			11 37	11 37		
Taunton	d	08 51	09 07	09 20			09 51	09 51	10 11		10 28				10 51	11 17	11 25			11 51	11 51		
Bridgwater	a								10 22														
Weston-super-Mare	a		09 27						10 41														
Bristol Temple Meads ■	a	09 26	09 57				10 25	10 25	11 11						11 24	11 52				12 24	12 24		
	d	09 30	10 00				10 30	10 30	11 21						11 30	12 00				12 30	12 30		
Bath Spa ■	a		10 11																				
Filton Abbey Wood	a								11 30														
Bristol Parkway ■	a	09 38					10 38	10 38							11 38	12 08				12 38	12 38		
Swindon	a		10 41																				
Newport (South Wales)	a								11 57														
Cardiff Central ■	a								12 19														
Birmingham New Street ■	a	10 56					11 58	11 58							12 56	13 26				13 56	13 56		
Castle Cary 123	d			09 41																			
Frome 123	d																						
Westbury 123	d			10 01							11 05												
Pewsey	d			10 18																			
Hungerford	a																						
Newbury	a																						
Thatcham	a																						
Theale	a																						
Reading ■	a		11 10	10 52							11 51						12 42						13 31
Slough ■	a																						
London Paddington ■ ⊖	a		11 37	11 21							12 21						13 15						14 00

A To Newcastle
B ◇ from Plymouth
C until 5 October. To Newcastle
D from 8 October. To Glasgow Central. 🛒 from Plymouth
E From St James' Park
F To Exmouth
G From Paignton
H To St Ives
I To Manchester Piccadilly
J until 5 October. To Newcastle. ◇ from Plymouth ■ to Plymouth
K from 8 October. To Glasgow Central. 🛒 ◇ from Plymouth ■ to Plymouth
L The Cornish Riviera

For connections to Oxford, Gatwick Airport and Heathrow Airport refer to Tables T116 and T148

For connections from Swansea refer to Table T128

Table T135-R

Mondays to Fridays

3 September to 7 December

Cornwall and Devon - Birmingham and London

		GW	GW ◇■ ☕	GW	XC ◇■ A 🛒	XC ■ ◇■ B 🛒	GW ◇	GW C	GW ■ ■ D ✕☕	GW E	XC ◇■ F 🛒	GW	GW ◇	GW C	GW ◇■ G ✕☕	GW E	GW	XC ◇■ A 🛒	XC ◇■ H 🛒	GW ◇	GW ◇■ I ☕	GW ◇■ ☕
Penzance	d					09 35			10 00			10 51								11 41	12 04	
St Erth	d					09 43			10 10			11 00								11 50	12 14	
Hayle	d					09 47						11 03								11 53		
Camborne	d					09 56			10 21			11 12								12 02		
Redruth	d					10 03			10 28			11 18								12 08	12 28	
Truro	d					10 15			10 41			11 30								12 19	12 41	
St Austell	d					10 31			10 58			11 47								12 36	12 59	
Newquay	d						10 13															
Par	d					10 38	11a02		11 06			11 53								12 43		
Lostwithiel	d					10 45						12 00								12 49		
Bodmin Parkway	d					10 51			11 17			12 06								12 55	13 15	
Liskeard ■	d					11 04			11 30			12 19								13 08	13 28	
Menheniot	d																			13x13		
St Germans	d											12 30								13 21		
Saltash	d											12 37								13 28		
St Budeaux Ferry Road	d																					
Keyham	d																					
Dockyard	d																					
Devonport	d																					
Plymouth	a					11 27			11 55			12 46								13 37	13 52	
	d				11 25	11 50			12 01		12 25				12 55			13 25		13 43	13 56	
Ivybridge	d																			13 58		
Totnes	d				11 50	12 15			12 28		12 51				13 22			13 51		14 12		
Paignton	d	11 20	11 32	11 42				12 13					12 53	13 08			13 40		14 04			
Torquay	d	11 25	11 38	11 47				12 18					12 59	13 13			13 45		14 10			
Torre	d	11 28		11 50				12 21					13 02	13 16			13 48					
Newton Abbot	a	11 37	11 48	11 58	12 01	12 26		12 30	12 40		13 02		13 10	13 25	13 34		13 56	14 02	14 20	14 24	14 31	
	d	11 37	11 50		12 03	12 28		12 31	12 41		13 04		13 12	13 25	13 35			14 04	14 21		14 32	
Teignmouth	d	11 45	11 57					12 38					13 19	13 33					14 28			
Dawlish	d	11 50	12 03					12 43		←			13 24	13 38		←			14 33			
Dawlish Warren	d	11 54						12 54		12 54				13 50		13 50						
Starcross	d	11 58						→		12 58				→		13 54						
Exeter St Thomas	d	12 08								13 07						14 03						
Exeter St Davids ■	a	12 11	12 15		12 22	12 45			13 00	13 13	13 22		13 36		13 54	14 08		14 22	14 45		14 52	
Exeter Central	a	12 19								13 19						14 19						
Exmouth	a	12 48								13 48						14 48						
Exeter St Davids ■	d		12 17		12 24	12 50			13 02		13 24		13 38		13 59			14 24	14 48		14 55	
Tiverton Parkway	d		12 32		12 38	13 06			13 17		13 38		13 55		14 14			14 38	15 02		15 10	
Taunton	d		12 46		12 51	13 22			13 31		13 51		14 11		14 28			14 51	15 15		15 24	15 33
Bridgwater	a												14 23									
Weston-super-Mare	a												14 42						15 37			
Bristol Temple Meads ■	a				13 24	13 55					14 26		15 14					15 23	15 57			
	d				13 30	14 00					14 30		15 21					15 30	16 00			
Bath Spa ■	a																					
Filton Abbey Wood	a												15 29									
Bristol Parkway ■	a				13 38	14 08					14 39							15 39	16 08			
Swindon	a																					
Newport (South Wales)	a												15 57									
Cardiff Central ■	a												16 15									
Birmingham New Street ■	a				14 56	15 23					15 56							16 56	17 23			
Castle Cary 123	d		13 07																			15 55
Frome 123	d																					
Westbury 123	d		13 27												15 04							16 14
Pewsey	d		13 45																			16 32
Hungerford	a																					
Newbury	a		14 04																			16 51
Thatcham	a																					
Theale	a																					
Reading ■	a		14 23						14 51						15 50						16 46	17 16
Slough ■	a																					
London Paddington ■ ⊖	a		14 54						15 21						16 21						17 15	17 54

A To Newcastle
B To Manchester Piccadilly. 🛒 ◇ from Plymouth ■ to Plymouth
C To Exmouth
D The Cornishman. ☕ to Plymouth ☕ from Reading ✕ from Plymouth to Reading
E From Paignton
F To Edinburgh
G Restaurant available for customers joining until Castle Cary. ☕ from Westbury ✕ to Westbury
H To Manchester Piccadilly
I The Royal Duchy

For connections to Oxford, Gatwick Airport and Heathrow Airport refer to Tables T116 and T148

For connections from Swansea refer to Table T128

Table T135-R

Mondays to Fridays

3 September to 7 December

Cornwall and Devon - Birmingham and London

		GW ◇	GW	GW	XC ◇1 A	GW ◇1 B	GW C	GW 1 D	GW E	GW	GW	XC ◇1 F	XC ◇1 G	GW C	GW ◇1	GW E	GW ◇	GW	XC ◇1 H	XC ◇1 I	GW ◇	GW	GW ◇1
Penzance	d										12 57				14 00						14 49		
St Erth	d										13 06				14 10						14 58		
Hayle	d										13 09										15 01		
Camborne	d										13 18				14 21						15 11		
Redruth	d										13 24				14 28						15 17		
Truro	d										13 35				14 41						15 28		
St Austell	d										13 52				14 58						15 45		
Newquay	d	13 05															15 01						
Par	d	13a54									13 59				15 06		15a47				15 52		
Lostwithiel	d										14 05										15 58		
Bodmin Parkway	d										14 11				15 17						16 04		
Liskeard 4	d										14 24				15 30						16 17		
Menheniot	d										14x29										16 22		
St Germans	d										14 37										16 30		
Saltash	d										14 44										16 37		
St Budeaux Ferry Road	d																				16 41		
Keyham	d																				16 43		
Dockyard	d																				16x45		
Devonport	d																				16 47		
Plymouth	a										14 53				15 55						16 51		
	d				14 25			15 00			15 08	15 25			16 00				16 25	16 25			16 57
Ivybridge	d										15 23												17 13
Totnes	d				14 50			15 27			15 37	15 51			16 27				16 50	16 50			17 28
Paignton	d		14 21	14 40		14 54	15 13			15 32				16 12				16 29				16 57	
Torquay	d		14 26	14 45		15 00	15 18			15 37				16 17				16 34				17 02	
Torre	d		14 29	14 48			15 21			15 40				16 21				16 37				17 05	
Newton Abbot	a		14 37	14 56	15 01	15 10	15 29	15 38		15 48	15 49	16 02		16 29	16 39			16 46	17 01	17 02		17 13	17 39
	d		14 39		15 03	15 12	15 31	15 40				16 04		16 31	16 40			16 47	17 03	17 03		17 15	17 41
Teignmouth	d		14 46			15 19	15 38							16 38				16 55				17 22	
Dawlish	d		14 51			15 25	15 43		←					16 43		←		17 00				17 27	
Dawlish Warren	d		14 56				15 54		15 54					16 53		16 53		17 04				17 32	
Starcross	d		15 00				→		15 58					→		16 57						17 36	
Exeter St Thomas	d		15 09						16 07							17 07						17 45	
Exeter St Davids 6	a		15 13		15 20	15 37		15 59	16 12			16 22			16 59	17 11		17 17	17 20	17 22		17 51	18 00
Exeter Central	a		15 19						16 18							17 18						17 56	
Exmouth	a		15 48						16 49							17 51						18 27	
Exeter St Davids 6	d				15 24	15 39		16 01				16 24	16 54		17 02				17 24	17 24			18 02
Tiverton Parkway	d				15 37			16 16				16 38	17 08		17 17				17 37	17 37			18 17
Taunton	d				15 51	16 04		16 30				16 51	17 22		17 31				17 50	17 50			18 31
Bridgwater	a																						
Weston-super-Mare	a																						
Bristol Temple Meads 10	a				16 23							17 24	17 54						18 23	18 23			
	d				16 30							17 30	18 00						18 30	18 30			
Bath Spa 7	a																						
Filton Abbey Wood	a																						
Bristol Parkway 7	a				16 38							17 39	18 08						18 38	18 38			
Swindon	a																						
Newport (South Wales)	a																						
Cardiff Central 7	a																						
Birmingham New Street 12	a				17 56							18 56	19 23						19 56	19 56			
Castle Cary 123	d					16 25																	18 52
Frome 123	d																						
Westbury 123	d					16 45																	19 12
Pewsey	d					17 02																	19 29
Hungerford	a																						
Newbury	a																						19 48
Thatcham	a																						
Theale	a																						
Reading 7	a					17 37		17 46							18 52								20 08
Slough 3	a																						
London Paddington 15 ⊖	a					18 07		18 16							19 20								20 37

A To Newcastle
B The Torbay Express
C To Exmouth
D The Mayflower
E From Paignton
F To Leeds
G To Manchester Piccadilly
H from 8 October. To Leeds
I until 5 October. To York

For connections to Oxford, Gatwick Airport and Heathrow Airport refer to Tables T116 and T148

For connections from Swansea refer to Table T128

Table T135-R

Mondays to Fridays

3 September to 7 December

Cornwall and Devon - Birmingham and London

		GW	XC ◇1 A	GW	GW	GW ◇1 B	GW C	GW	XC ◇1 D	GW ◇	GW ◇1	GW ◇	GW ◇	GW	GW FX ◇1	GW FO ◇1	GW	GW	XC ◇1	GW	GW 1	GW
Penzance	d					16 00						16 44			17 42	17 42		19 16				
St Erth	d					16 10						16 53			17 52	17 52		19 25				
Hayle	d											16 56			17 56	17 56		19 28				
Camborne	d					16 21						17 06			18 07	18 07		19 38				
Redruth	d					16 28						17 12			18 14	18 14		19 44				
Truro	d					16 41						17 25			18 26	18 26		19 56				
St Austell	d					16 59						17 42			18 44	18 44		20 13				
Newquay	d												17 22				19 24					
Par	d					17 06						17 48	18a11		18 51	18 51	20a13	20 19				
Lostwithiel	d					17 14						17 55						20 26				
Bodmin Parkway	d					17 20						18 01			19 03	19 03		20 32				
Liskeard 4	d					17 33	17 49					18 14			19 16	19 16		20 45				
Menheniot	d																	20 49				
St Germans	d						18 00					18 25						20 58				
Saltash	d						18 06					18 32						21 04				
St Budeaux Ferry Road	d						18 10											21 08				
Keyham	d																	21 10				
Dockyard	d																	21x12				
Devonport	d																	21 14				
Plymouth	a					17 58	18 18					18 42			19 40	19 40		21 19				
	d		17 25		17 35	18 03			18 25			18 44			19 44	19 44						21 25
Ivybridge	d				17 52							18 59										21 40
Totnes	d		17 51		18 06	18 31			18 50			19 13			20 12	20 12						21 54
Paignton	d	17 26		17 52				18 34		18 52				19 37					20 14	20 35	21 35	
Torquay	d	17 31		17 57				18 39		18 57				19 42					20 20	20 40	21 41	
Torre	d	17 34		18 00				18 42						19 45						20 43	21 45	
Newton Abbot	a	17 42	18 02	18 08	18 18	18 42		18 49	19 01	19 07		19 25		19 53	20 23	20 23			20 30	20 51	21 53	22 06
	d	17 44	18 04	18 10	18 19	18 44		18 52	19 03	19 09		19 26		19 54	20 25	20 25			20 31	20 53		22 06
Teignmouth	d	17 51		18 17	18 26			18 59		19 16				20 02						21 00		22 13
Dawlish	d	17 56		18 22	18 32			19 04		19 21				20 07						21 05		22 18
Dawlish Warren	d	18 01		18 27	18 36			19 15		19 25				20 11						21 10		22 23
Starcross	d	18 05		18 31				19 19						20 15						21 14		22 27
Exeter St Thomas	d	18 14		18 40				19 28						20 25						21 23		22 36
Exeter St Davids 6	a	18 19	18 22	18 44	18 48	19 03		19 32	19 20	19 39		19 48		20 29	20 44	20 44			20 50	21 28		22 40
Exeter Central	a	18 24		18 53										20 37						21 34		
Exmouth	a	18 54		19 24										21 06						22 03		
Exeter St Davids 6	d		18 25			19 05			19 24	19 39	19 55				20 46	20 46			20 52			
Tiverton Parkway	d		18 39			19 20			19 37		20 10				21 01	21 01			21 05			
Taunton	d		18 52			19 34			19 51	20 10	20 26				21 15	21 15			21 19			
Bridgwater	a																					
Weston-super-Mare	a																					
Bristol Temple Meads 10	a		19 25						20 25	20 54					21 47	21 47			21 52			
	d		19 30						20 30						21 50	21 51			22 00			
Bath Spa 7	a														22 02	22 02						
Filton Abbey Wood	a																					
Bristol Parkway 7	a		19 39						20 38										22 09			
Swindon	a														22 32	22 32						
Newport (South Wales)	a																					
Cardiff Central 7	a																					
Birmingham New Street 12	a		20 51						22 02										23 43			
Castle Cary 123	d										20 47											
Frome 123	d																					
Westbury 123	d										21 07											
Pewsey	d										21 24											
Hungerford	a																					
Newbury	a										21 43											
Thatcham	a																					
Theale	a																					
Reading 7	a					20 53					22 02				23 07	23 07						
Slough 3	a																					
London Paddington 15 ⊖	a					21 22					22 37				23 42	23 39						

A To Leeds
B Restaurant available after PLY for customers joining until TAU. to Plymouth from Reading from Plymouth to Reading
C To Gunnislake
D to Bristol Temple Meads

For connections to Oxford, Gatwick Airport and Heathrow Airport refer to Tables T116 and T148

For connections from Swansea refer to Table T128

T135 UPDATE: Major engineering work in connection with electrification works is taking place between Reading and Westbury. The route via Newbury will be closed to all trains on 4-7 June; 9-12 July; 16 July to 05 August; 28-30 August; 08-11 October and 19-22 November. Trains will be re-timed or cancelled and run to a special timetable during this period. Please check revised train times with *www.nationalrail.co.uk*. Rail replacement buses will operate between intermediate stations.

Table T135-R

Cornwall and Devon - Birmingham and London

Mondays to Fridays
3 September to 7 December

		GW FX	GW FO	GW	GW	GW	GW	GW	GW FX	GW FO	XC
			◇1		◇		A		B	B	◇1
Penzance	d	20 18	20 18						21 45	21 45	22 10
St Erth	d	20 28	20 28						21 55	21 55	22 18
Hayle	d	20 32	20 32								22 22
Camborne	d	20 42	20 42						22 08	22 08	22 31
Redruth	d	20 49	20 49						22 16	22 16	22 38
Truro	d	21 01	21 01						22 29	22 29	22 49
St Austell	d	21 18	21 18						22 47	22 47	23 05
Newquay	d			21 26							
Par	d	21 25	21 25	22a16					22 56	22 56	23 12
Lostwithiel	d	21 32	21 32								23 19
Bodmin Parkway	d	21 38	21 38						23 08	23 08	23 25
Liskeard 6	d	21 51	21 51						23 24	23 24	23 37
Menheniot	d										
St Germans	d	22 02	22 02								
Saltash	d	22 09	22 09								
St Budeaux Ferry Road	d										
Keyham	d						22 57				
Dockyard	d						22x59				
Devonport	d						23 01				
Plymouth	a	22 22	22 22				23 06		23 47	23 47	00 01
	d						23 10		23 54	23 54	
Ivybridge	d						23 26				
Totnes	d						23 40		00 22	00 22	
Paignton	d					22 45		23 55			
Torquay	d					22 50		23 59			
Torre	d					22 53		00 03			
Newton Abbot	a					23 01	23 51	00 11	00 34	00 34	
	d					23 03	23 52	00 13	00 36	00 36	
Teignmouth	d					23 10		00 20			
Dawlish	d					23 15		00 25			
Dawlish Warren	d					23 20		00 30			
Starcross	d					23 24		00 34			
Exeter St Thomas	d					23 33		00 43			
Exeter St Davids 6	a					23 37	00 12	00 48	00 57	00 57	
Exeter Central	a										
Exmouth	a										
Exeter St Davids 6	d				21 49				01 06	01 06	
Tiverton Parkway	d				22 06						
Taunton	d				22 23				01 42	01 42	
Bridgwater	a										
Weston-super-Mare	a				22 47						
Bristol Temple Meads 10	a				23 13						
	d										
Bath Spa 7	a										
Filton Abbey Wood	a										
Bristol Parkway 7	a										
Swindon	a										
Newport (South Wales)	a										
Cardiff Central 7	a										
Birmingham New Street 12	a										
Castle Cary 123	d										
Frome 123	d										
Westbury 123	d										
Pewsey	d										
Hungerford	a										
Newbury	a										
Thatcham	a										
Theale	a										
Reading 7	a								03s58	04s00	
Slough 3	a										
London Paddington 15 ⊖	a								05 03	05 07	

A From Gunnislake
B The Night Riviera

For connections to Oxford, Gatwick Airport and Heathrow Airport refer to Tables T116 and T148

For connections from Swansea refer to Table T128

Table T135-R

Cornwall and Devon - Birmingham and London

Saturdays
26 May to 8 September

		GW	GW	GW	GW	XC	XC	GW	GW	GW	XC	XC	GW	GW	XC	GW	GW	XC	GW	GW	GW	GW	GW
			■			◇1	◇1	◇1			◇1	◇1		◇1	◇1		◇1	◇1			◇1		
		A	B			C	D			E	C	F	A		G			H		E		A	
Penzance	d				05 20														05 40				
St Erth	d																		05 49				
Hayle	d																		05 52				
Camborne	d				05 38														06 02				
Redruth	d				05 44														06 08				
Truro	d				05a56														06 19				
St Austell	d																		06 36				
Newquay	d																						
Par	d																		06 43				
Lostwithiel	d																		06 50				
Bodmin Parkway	d																		06 56				
Liskeard 6	d																		07 10				
Menheniot	d																		07x14				
St Germans	d																		07 21				
Saltash	d																		07 28				
St Budeaux Ferry Road	d																		07 32				
Keyham	d																		07 34				
Dockyard	d																		07x35				
Devonport	d																		07 37				
Plymouth	a																		07 45				
	d					05 25	05 25	05 40			06 25	06 25					06 57	07 25			07 50		08 08
Ivybridge	d																						08 23
Totnes	d		00 22			05 50	05 50	06 07			06 50	06 50						07 50			08 17		08 38
Paignton	d								06 13	06 34					07 02	07 11				08 06			
Torquay	d								06 18	06 39					07 08	07 16				08 11			
Torre	d	00 03							06 21	06 42						07 19				08 14		←	
Newton Abbot	a	00 11	00 34			06 01	06 01	06 19	06 29	06 50	07 01	07 01			07 18	07 27	07 32	08 01		08 22	08 28	08 22	08 49
	d	00 13	00 36			06 03	06 03	06 20	06 30	06 52	07 03	07 03			07 19		07 33	08 03		08 34	08 30	08 34	08 51
Teignmouth	d	00 20							06 38	06 59					07 26					→		08 41	08 58
Dawlish	d	00 25							06 43	07 04			←		07 31							08 46	09 03
Dawlish Warren	d	00 30							06 47	07 15			07 15									08 51	
Starcross	d	00 34							06 51	→			07 19									08 55	
Exeter St Thomas	d	00 43							07 01				07 28									09 04	
Exeter St Davids 6	a	00 48	00 57			06 20	06 20	06 39	07 05		07 20	07 20	07 33		07 42		07 52	08 20			08 49	09 09	09 16
Exeter Central	a								07 13				07 47									09 19	
Exmouth	a								07 44				08 16									09 50	
Exeter St Davids 6	d		01 06	06 00		06 23	06 23	06 43			07 23	07 23		07 29	07 45		07 56	08 23			08 52		
Tiverton Parkway	d			06 17		06 37	06 37	06 59			07 37	07 37		07 45	07 58		08 11	08 37			09 07		
Taunton	d		01 42	06 34		06 50	06 50	07 13			07 50	07 50		07 59	08 11		08 25	08 50			09 21		
Bridgwater	a			06 45										08 08									
Weston-super-Mare	a			07 04										08 27									
Bristol Temple Meads 10	a			07 43		07 22	07 22				08 24	08 24		08 56	08 49			09 25					
	d			07 47		07 30	07 30				08 30	08 30		09 00	09 00			09 30					
Bath Spa 7	a													09 11									
Filton Abbey Wood	a			07 58																			
Bristol Parkway 7	a			08 04		07 38	07 38				08 38	08 38			09 08			09 38					
Swindon	a													09 41									
Newport (South Wales)	a																						
Cardiff Central 7	a																						
Birmingham New Street 12	a					08 56	08 56				09 56	09 56			10 25			10 56					
Castle Cary 123	d							07 34													09 42		
Frome 123	d																						
Westbury 123	d							07 56													10 02		
Pewsey	d							08 14													10 19		
Hungerford	a																						
Newbury	a							08 34															
Thatcham	a																						
Theale	a																						
Reading 7	a		04s00					08 51						10 11			09 40				10 52		
Slough 3	a																						
London Paddington 15 ⊖	a		05 07					09 21						10 39			10 10				11 21		

A From Paignton
B From Penzance. The Night Riviera
C from 28 July. To Newcastle
D until 21 July. To Edinburgh
E To Exmouth
F until 21 July. To Glasgow Central
G To Manchester Piccadilly. from Newton Abbot
H To Newcastle

For connections to Oxford, Gatwick Airport and Heathrow Airport refer to Tables T116 and T148

For connections from Swansea refer to Table T128

Table T135-R

Saturdays

26 May to 8 September

Cornwall and Devon - Birmingham and London

		XC A	XC B	GW C	XC D	GW E	GW	GW F	GW G	GW	XC H	XC D	GW E	GW	GW F	XC A	XC B	GW C	GW	GW I	GW	XC H	GW
Penzance	d	06 30	06 30	06 41			06 50							07 39		08 28	08 28	08 45		08 55			09 30
St Erth	d	06 38	06 38	06a49			07 00							07 50		08 36	08 36	08a53		09 06			09 41
Hayle	d	06 41	06 41											07 55						09 11			09 46
Camborne	d	06 51	06 51				07 12							08 06		08 46	08 46			09 22			09 56
Redruth	d	06 57	06 57				07 19							08 13		08 52	08 52			09 29			10 03
Truro	d	07 09	07 09				07 32							08 27		09 04	09 04			09 43			10 16
St Austell	d	07 25	07 25				07 49							08 44		09 20	09 20			10 00			10 35
Newquay	d																					09 35	
Par	d	07 32	07 32				07 56							08 52		09 27	09 27			10 07		10 31	10 43
Lostwithiel	d	07 39	07 39				08 04							09 00									
Bodmin Parkway	d	07 46	07 46				08 10							09 06		09 37	09 37			10 19		10 43	10 56
Liskeard	d	07 58	07 58				08 23							09 19		09 50	09 50			10 32		10 55	11 09
Menheniot	d																						
St Germans	d													09 31									
Saltash	d													09 39									
St Budeaux Ferry Road	d																						
Keyham	d																						
Dockyard	d																						
Devonport	d																						
Plymouth	a	08 21	08 21				08 47							09 48		10 17	10 17			10 55		11 18	11 32
	d	08 25	08 25		08 39		08 51				09 18			10 01		10 25	10 25			11 00		11 25	11 39
Ivybridge	d													10 16									11 54
Totnes	d	08 50	08 50		09 04		09 19				09 43			10 31		10 50	10 50					11 50	12 10
Paignton	d					09 04			09 18	09 30		10 06	10 16						11 00		11 21		
Torquay	d					09 09			09 25	09 35		10 12	10 21						11 05		11 26		
Torre	d					09 12			09 29	09 38			10 24						11 08		11 29		
Newton Abbot	a	09 01	09 01		09 15	09 20	09 30		09 37	09 46	09 54	10 22	10 32	10 43		11 01	11 01		11 16		11 39	12 01	12 21
	d	09 03	09 03		09 17	09 22	09 32		09 39	09 48	09 56	10 23	10 33	10 44		11 03	11 03		11 18		11 39	12 03	12 23
Teignmouth	d					09 29			09 47	09 55	10 03	10 30	10 40						11 25		11 47		
Dawlish	d					09 34		←	09 54	10 00	10 09	10 35	10 45		←				11 30		11 52		
Dawlish Warren	d				09 29	09 46		09 46	10 00	10 05	10 13		10 56		10 56				11 35		11 56		
Starcross	d					→		09 50					→		11 00						12 00		
Exeter St Thomas	d							09 59							11 09						12 10		
Exeter St Davids	a	09 20	09 20		09 39		09 51	10 04	10 11	10 17	10 23	10 46		11 03	11 14	11 20	11 20		11 47	11 52	12 14	12 20	12 42
Exeter Central	a							10 21							11 19				11 52		12 20		
Exmouth	a							10 52							11 50				12 20		12 51		
Exeter St Davids	d	09 23	09 23		09 45		09 54		10 15		10 25	10 49		11 07		11 23	11 23			11 56		12 23	12 45
Tiverton Parkway	d	09 37	09 37		09 58		10 10		10 30		10 38	11 02		11 22		11 36	11 36					12 36	13 01
Taunton	d	09 50	09 50		10 11		10 24		10 45		10 51	11 17		11 36		11 50	11 50					12 50	13 15
Bridgwater	a																						
Weston-super-Mare	a				10 31																		
Bristol Temple Meads	a	10 25	10 25		10 51				11 20		11 25	11 53				12 25	12 25					13 23	
	d	10 30	10 30		11 00				11 30		11 30	12 00				12 30	12 30					13 30	
Bath Spa	a								11 41														
Filton Abbey Wood	a																						
Bristol Parkway	a	10 38	10 38		11 08						11 38	12 08				12 38	12 38					13 38	
Swindon	a								12 09														
Newport (South Wales)	a																						
Cardiff Central	a																						
Birmingham New Street	a	11 56	11 56		12 26						12 56	13 26				13 56	13 56					14 56	
Castle Cary 123	d																						13 36
Frome 123	d																						
Westbury 123	d						11 03																13 55
Pewsey	d																						14 13
Hungerford	a																						
Newbury	a																						
Thatcham	a																						
Theale	a																						
Reading	a						11 49		12 46					12 51						13 31			14 47
Slough	a																						
London Paddington ⊖	a						12 21		13 14					13 21						14 00			15 16

A from 28 July. To Newcastle
B until 21 July. To Glasgow Central. from Plymouth
C To St Ives
D To Manchester Piccadilly
E To Exmouth
F From Paignton
G The Torbay Express
H To Newcastle
I The Cornish Riviera

For connections to Oxford, Gatwick Airport and Heathrow Airport refer to Tables T116 and T148

For connections from Swansea refer to Table T128

Table T135-R

Saturdays

26 May to 8 September

Cornwall and Devon - Birmingham and London

		GW A	GW	GW B	XC C	GW	GW	GW	GW	GW	GW D	XC E	XC F	XC G	GW A	GW	GW B	XC H	GW	GW	GW	GW I
Penzance	d		09 57					10 58								12 00					13 07	
St Erth	d		10 08			10 26		11 09								12 11					13 18	
Hayle	d					10 30		11 14								12 16					13 23	
Camborne	d		10 19			10 41		11 25								12 27					13 33	
Redruth	d		10 26			10 48		11 32								12 34					13 40	
Truro	d		10 39			11 00		11 46								12 48					13 53	
St Austell	d		10 57			11 17		12 03								13 06					14 10	
Newquay	d										11 30											
Par	d		11 05			11 25					12 24										14 18	
Lostwithiel	d					11 33																
Bodmin Parkway	d		11 17			11 39		12 19								13 22					14 29	
Liskeard	d		11 31			11 54		12 32								13 35					14 42	
Menheniot	d					12 00																
St Germans	d					12 09																
Saltash	d					12 17																
St Budeaux Ferry Road	d																					
Keyham	d																					
Dockyard	d																					
Devonport	d																					
Plymouth	a		11 54			12 28		12 58			13 07					13 58					15 06	
	d		12 05			12 30		13 03			13 14	13 25	13 25			14 03		14 25			15 10	
Ivybridge	d					12 45																
Totnes	d					13 00					13 41	13 51	13 51					14 50				
Paignton	d	12 13			12 35		12 58		13 08	13 26				13 55	14 08				14 50	15 07		15 44
Torquay	d	12 18			12 42		13 03		13 15	13 31				14 01	14 13				14 58	15 12		15 49
Torre	d	12 21					13 06								14 16					15 15		
Newton Abbot	a	12 29	12 40		12 53	13 12	13 14		13 25	13 41	13 53	14 01	14 02	14 11	14 24	14 38		15 01	15 08	15 23	15 45	15 59
	d	12 31	12 42		12 54	13 13	13 20		13 27	13 43	13 54	14 03	14 03	14 12	14 26	14 40		15 03	15 10	15 25	15 46	16 08
Teignmouth	d	12 38			13 02	13 21	13 28		13 36	13 51				14 19	14 34				15 18	15 33		→
Dawlish	d	12 43		←	13 09	13 27	13 33		13 44	13 56				14 24	14 40		←		15 25	15 38		
Dawlish Warren	d	12 54		12 54		13 32	13 38		13 55	14 07					14 52		14 52		15 32	15 43		
Starcross	d	→		12 58			13 43								→		14 56			15 48		
Exeter St Thomas	d			13 07			13 52										15 06			15 57		
Exeter St Davids	a		13 01	13 13	13 22	13 50	13 57	14 00	14 08	14 20	14 15	14 22	14 22	14 35		14 59	15 11	15 21	15 42	16 02	16 05	
Exeter Central	a			13 19			14 05										15 19			16 19		
Exmouth	a			13 50													15 50			16 50		
Exeter St Davids	d		13 10		13 23			14 04	14 11		14 18	14 25	14 25	14 37		15 03		15 23	15 46		16 08	
Tiverton Parkway	d				13 37							14 38	14 38	14 50		15 19		15 37			16 23	
Taunton	d		13 36		13 50			14 30	14 45			14 52	14 52	15 03		15 34		15 50	16 12		16 37	
Bridgwater	a																					
Weston-super-Mare	a													15 23								
Bristol Temple Meads	a				14 25							15 25	15 25	15 49				16 25				
	d				14 30							15 30	15 30	16 00				16 30				
Bath Spa	a																					
Filton Abbey Wood	a																					
Bristol Parkway	a				14 39							15 38	15 39	16 08				16 38				
Swindon	a																					
Newport (South Wales)	a																					
Cardiff Central	a																					
Birmingham New Street	a				15 56							16 56	16 56	17 26				17 56				
Castle Cary 123	d								15 08										16 33			
Frome 123	d																					
Westbury 123	d								15 28										16 53			
Pewsey	d								15 46										17 11			
Hungerford	a																					
Newbury	a								16 06													
Thatcham	a																					
Theale	a																					
Reading	a		14 52					15 49	16 29		15 59					16 49			17 44		17 52	
Slough	a																					
London Paddington ⊖	a		15 22					16 21	17 00		16 32					17 21			18 12		18 21	

A To Exmouth
B From Paignton
C To Edinburgh
D The Atlantic Coast Express
E until 21 July. To Edinburgh
F from 28 July. To Newcastle
G To Manchester Piccadilly
H To Newcastle
I To Exeter Central

For connections to Oxford, Gatwick Airport and Heathrow Airport refer to Tables T116 and T148

For connections from Swansea refer to Table T128

T135 UPDATE: Major engineering work in connection with electrification works is taking place between Reading and Westbury. The route via Newbury will be closed to all trains on 4-7 June; 9-12 July; 16 July to 05 August; 28-30 August; 08-11 October and 19-22 November. Trains will be re-timed or cancelled and run to a special timetable during this period. Please check revised train times with *www.nationalrail.co.uk*. Rail replacement buses will operate between intermediate stations.

Table T135-R

Saturdays

26 May to 8 September

Cornwall and Devon - Birmingham and London

		XC	XC	XC	GW	GW	GW	GW		GW	GW	XC	GW	GW	XC	GW	GW	XC		GW	XC	GW	GW	GW	GW
		◇■	◇■	◇■				◇■			◇■	◇■	◇■		◇■			◇■		◇■	◇■	◇■			◇■
		A	B	C	D		E	F		D		G			H						I				
		⌶	⌶	⌶				☕			☕	⌶	☕		⌶					☕	⌶				☕
Penzance	d							14 00			15 00									15 52	16 25	16 55			
St Erth	d							14 10			15 10									16 02	16 34	17 05			
Hayle	d										15 15											17 10			
Camborne	d							14 22			15 25									16 14	16 45	17 20			
Redruth	d							14 29			15 33									16 21	16 52	17 27			
Truro	d							14 42			15 46									16 34	17 05	17 40			
St Austell	d							14 59			16 03									16 52	17 22	17 58			
Newquay	d					13 23									15 30										17 28
Par	d					14 28		15 06			16 11				16 27					16 59	17 29	18 05			18 24
Lostwithiel	d					14 36					16 19									17 06		18 13			
Bodmin Parkway	d					14 42		15 18			16 25				16 38					17 13	17 41	18 19			18 37
Liskeard ■	d					14 55		15 31			16 38				16 51					17 26	17 54	18 32			18 50
Menheniot	d					14x59																			
St Germans	d					15 07					16 50											18 44			
Saltash	d					15 14					16 59											18 51			
St Budeaux Ferry Road	d																								
Keyham	d																								
Dockyard	d																								
Devonport	d					15 20																			
Plymouth	a					15 25		15 54			17 10				17 14					17 49	18 18	19 01			19 14
	d	15 25	15 25	15 25		15 32		16 00							17 25		17 36			17 55	18 25				19 20
Ivybridge	d					15 47											17 51								19 36
Totnes	d	15 51	15 51	15 51		16 02		16 27							17 50		18 05			18 22	18 51				19 51
Paignton	d						16 11					16 37	17 00	17 11		17 51		18 08					18 52	19 30	
Torquay	d						16 16					16 44	17 07	17 16		17 56		18 15					18 57	19 35	
Torre	d				←		16 19							17 19		17 59							19 00	19 38	
Newton Abbot	a	16 02	16 02	16 02	15 59	16 15	16 28	16 39				16 55	17 17	17 27	18 01	18 07	18 17	18 25		18 33	19 02		19 08	19 46	20 02
	d	16 04	16 04	16 04	16 08		16 30	16 40				16 56	17 19	17 30	18 03	18 08	18 17	18 27		18 35	19 04		19 10	19 48	20 04
Teignmouth	d				16 15		16 38					17 04	17 27	17 38		18 15	18 24						19 17	19 55	
Dawlish	d				16 20		16 43			←		17 10	17 34	17 43		18 20	18 29						19 22	20 00	
Dawlish Warren	d						16 53			16 53			17 40	17 48		18 25	18 40						19 27	20 05	
Starcross	d						→			16 58				17 53		18 29							19 31	20 09	
Exeter St Thomas	d									17 08				18 02		18 38							19 40	20 18	
Exeter St Davids ■	a	16 21	16 21	16 22	16 34			16 59		17 13		17 22	17 50	18 07	18 21	18 43	18 54	18 47		18 57	19 22		19 45	20 24	20 28
Exeter Central	a				16 40					17 19				18 17		18 48								20 36	
Exmouth	a									17 50				18 48		19 21								21 07	
Exeter St Davids ■	d	16 24	16 24	16 24				17 03				17 24	18 02		18 23			18 49		19 00	19 24				20 30
Tiverton Parkway	d	16 38	16 38	16 38				17 18				17 38	18 17		18 37			19 05		19 15	19 38				
Taunton	d	16 51	16 51	16 51				17 33				17 51	18 31		18 50			19 18		19 29	19 51				20 55
Bridgwater	a																								
Weston-super-Mare	a																								
Bristol Temple Meads ■	a	17 25	17 25	17 25								18 26			19 23			19 53			20 24				
	d	17 30	17 30	17 30								18 30			19 30			20 00			20 30				
Bath Spa ■	a																								
Filton Abbey Wood	a																								
Bristol Parkway ■	a	17 38	17 39	17 39								18 38			19 38			20 08			20 39				
Swindon	a																								
Newport (South Wales)	a																								
Cardiff Central ■	a																								
Birmingham New Street ■	a	18 55	18 55	18 56								19 58			20 49			21 38			21 51				
Castle Cary 123	d												18 53							19 50					
Frome 123	d																								
Westbury 123	d												19 14							20 13					
Pewsey	d																			20 30					
Hungerford	a																								
Newbury	a												19 47												
Thatcham	a																								
Theale	a																								
Reading ■	a							18 49					20 05							21 03					22 13
Slough ■	a																								
London Paddington ■ ⊖	a							19 22					20 37							21 31					22 41

A from 28 July until 1 September. To Newcastle
B 8 September. To Newcastle
C until 21 July. To York
D From Paignton
E To Exmouth
F The Royal Duchy
G To Leeds
H To Manchester Piccadilly
I To Leeds. ⌶ to Bristol Temple Meads

For connections to Oxford, Gatwick Airport and Heathrow Airport refer to Tables T116 and T148

For connections from Swansea refer to Table T128

Table T135-R

Saturdays

26 May to 8 September

Cornwall and Devon - Birmingham and London

		GW	GW	GW		GW	XC	GW	GW	GW	GW	XC	GW	GW
			◇■				◇■					◇■		
						A								
			☕											
Penzance	d		17 40			18 50				19 06		21 29		
St Erth	d		17 50			18a58				19 15		21 38		
Hayle	d		17 54							19 18				
Camborne	d		18 05							19 28		21 49		
Redruth	d		18 12							19 35		21 56		
Truro	d		18 25							19 46		22 09		
St Austell	d		18 42							20 03		22 26		
Newquay	d						19 00				20 45			
Par	d		18 49	19 00			19 53			20 10	21 37	22 33		
Lostwithiel	d			19 08						20 16	21 44			
Bodmin Parkway	d		19 01	19 14			20 05			20 22	21 50	22 44		
Liskeard ■	d		19 14	19 27			20 18			20 35	22 03	22 58		
Menheniot	d									20x39	22x07			
St Germans	d			19 38						20 48	22 16			
Saltash	d			19 45						20 55	22 23			
St Budeaux Ferry Road	d									20 59	22 27			
Keyham	d									21 01	22 29			
Dockyard	d									21x02	22x30			
Devonport	d			19 51						21 05	22 33			
Plymouth	a		19 37	19 55			20 41			21 09	22 38	23 22		
	d		19 40							21 15				
Ivybridge	d									21 30				
Totnes	d		20 09							21 44				
Paignton	d	19 51						20 20	21 20				22 45	23 30
Torquay	d	19 56						20 25	21 25				22 50	23 35
Torre	d							20 28	21 28				22 53	23 38
Newton Abbot	a	20 06	20 20					20 36	21 36	21 56			23 01	23 46
	d	20 08	20 22					20 37	21 38	21 57				23 47
Teignmouth	d	20 15						20 45	21 45	22 04				23 54
Dawlish	d	20 20						20 50	21 50	22 09				23 59
Dawlish Warren	d	20 25						20 54	21 55					00 04
Starcross	d							20 58	21 59					00 08
Exeter St Thomas	d							21 08	22 08					00 17
Exeter St Davids ■	a	20 37	20 41					21 12	22 12	22 23				00 22
Exeter Central	a													
Exmouth	a													
Exeter St Davids ■	d		20 45											
Tiverton Parkway	d		21 00											
Taunton	d		21 14											
Bridgwater	a													
Weston-super-Mare	a													
Bristol Temple Meads ■	a		21 46											
	d		21 47											
Bath Spa ■	a		22 01											
Filton Abbey Wood	a													
Bristol Parkway ■	a													
Swindon	a		22 30											
Newport (South Wales)	a													
Cardiff Central ■	a													
Birmingham New Street ■	a													
Castle Cary 123	d													
Frome 123	d													
Westbury 123	d													
Pewsey	d													
Hungerford	a													
Newbury	a													
Thatcham	a													
Theale	a													
Reading ■	a		23 03											
Slough ■	a													
London Paddington ■ ⊖	a		23 43											

A To St Ives

For connections to Oxford, Gatwick Airport and Heathrow Airport refer to Tables T116 and T148

For connections from Swansea refer to Table T128

Cornwall and Devon - Birmingham and London

		GW	GW	GW	GW	XC	XC	GW	GW	GW	XC	XC	GW	GW	XC	GW	GW	XC	GW	GW	GW	GW	GW
						◇1	◇1	◇1			◇1	◇1		◇1	◇1		◇1	◇1			◇1		
		A	B			C	D			E	C	F	A		G			H		E		A	
Penzance	d				05 20														05 40				
St Erth	d																		05 49				
Hayle	d																		05 52				
Camborne	d				05 38														06 02				
Redruth	d				05 44														06 08				
Truro	d				05a56														06 19				
St Austell	d																		06 36				
Newquay	d																						
Par	d																		06 43				
Lostwithiel	d																		06 50				
Bodmin Parkway	d																		06 56				
Liskeard 6	d																		07 10				
Menheniot	d																		07x14				
St Germans	d																		07 21				
Saltash	d																		07 28				
St Budeaux Ferry Road	d																		07 32				
Keyham	d																		07 34				
Dockyard	d																		07x35				
Devonport	d																		07 37				
Plymouth	a																		07 45				
	d					05 25	05 25	05 40			06 25	06 25					06 57	07 25			07 50		08 08
Ivybridge	d																						08 23
Totnes	d		00 22			05 50	05 50	06 07			06 50	06 50						07 50			08 17		08 38
Paignton	d								06 13	06 34					07 02	07 11				08 06			
Torquay	d								06 18	06 39					07 08	07 16				08 11			
Torre	d	00 03							06 21	06 42						07 19				08 14		←	
Newton Abbot	a	00 11	00 34			06 01	06 01	06 19	06 29	06 50	07 01	07 01			07 18	07 27	07 32	08 01		08 22	08 28	08 22	08 49
	d	00 13	00 36			06 03	06 03	06 20	06 30	06 52	07 03	07 03			07 19		07 33	08 03		08 34	08 30	08 34	08 51
Teignmouth	d	00 20							06 38	06 59					07 26					→		08 41	08 58
Dawlish	d	00 25							06 43	07 04			←		07 31							08 46	09 03
Dawlish Warren	d	00 30							06 47	07 15			07 15									08 51	
Starcross	d	00 34							06 51	→			07 19									08 55	
Exeter St Thomas	d	00 43							07 01				07 28									09 04	
Exeter St Davids 6	a	00 48	00 57			06 20	06 20	06 39	07 05		07 20	07 20	07 33		07 42		07 52	08 20			08 49	09 09	09 16
Exeter Central	a								07 13				07 47									09 19	
Exmouth	a								07 44				08 16									09 50	
Exeter St Davids 6	d		01 06	06 00		06 23	06 23	06 43			07 23	07 23		07 29	07 45		07 56	08 23			08 52		
Tiverton Parkway	d			06 17		06 37	06 37	06 59			07 37	07 37		07 45	07 58		08 11	08 37			09 07		
Taunton	d		01 42	06 34		06 50	06 50	07 13			07 50	07 50		07 59	08 11		08 25	08 50			09 21		
Bridgwater	a			06 45										08 08									
Weston-super-Mare	a			07 04										08 27									
Bristol Temple Meads 10	a			07 43		07 22	07 22				08 24	08 24		08 56	08 49			09 25					
	d			07 47		07 30	07 30				08 30	08 30		09 00	09 00			09 30					
Bath Spa 7	a													09 11									
Filton Abbey Wood	a			07 58																			
Bristol Parkway 7	a			08 04		07 38	07 38				08 38	08 38			09 08			09 38					
Swindon	a													09 41									
Newport (South Wales)	a																						
Cardiff Central 7	a																						
Birmingham New Street 12	a					08 56	08 56				09 56	09 56			10 25			10 56					
Castle Cary 123	d							07 34													09 42		
Frome 123	d																						
Westbury 123	d							07 56													10 02		
Pewsey	d							08 14													10 19		
Hungerford	a																						
Newbury	a							08 34															
Thatcham	a																						
Theale	a																						
Reading 7	a		04s00					08 51						10 11			09 40				10 52		
Slough 3	a																						
London Paddington 15 ⊖	a		05 07					09 21						10 39			10 10				11 21		

A From Paignton
B From Penzance. The Night Riviera
C until 6 October. To Newcastle
D from 13 October. To Edinburgh
E To Exmouth
F from 13 October. To Glasgow Central
G To Manchester Piccadilly. from Newton Abbot
H To Newcastle

For connections to Oxford, Gatwick Airport and Heathrow Airport refer to Tables T116 and T148

For connections from Swansea refer to Table T128

Table T135-R

Saturdays

15 September to 8 December

Cornwall and Devon - Birmingham and London

		XC	XC	GW	GW	GW	GW	GW	GW	GW	XC	GW	XC	GW	GW	GW	XC	XC	GW	GW	GW	GW	GW
		◇1	◇1			1		◇	◇1		◇1		◇1		◇1		◇1	◇1			◇1	◇1	
		A	B	C	D		E		F		G		H	D		E	A	B	C		I		
Penzance	d	06 30	06 30	06 41		06 50						07 39			07 59		08 28	08 28	08 50		09 00		
St Erth	d	06 38	06 38	06a49		07 00						07 48			08 09		08 36	08 36	08a58		09 10		
Hayle	d	06 41	06 41									07 51			08 14								
Camborne	d	06 51	06 51			07 12						08 02			08 24		08 46	08 46			09 21		
Redruth	d	06 57	06 57			07 19						08 08			08 31		08 52	08 52			09 29		
Truro	d	07 09	07 09			07 32						08 20			08 44		09 04	09 04			09 42		
St Austell	d	07 25	07 25			07 49						08 37			09 01		09 20	09 20			10 00		
Newquay	d							07 47															
Par	d	07 32	07 32			07 56		08a38				08 44			09 09		09 27	09 27			10 07		
Lostwithiel	d	07 39	07 39			08 04						08 51											
Bodmin Parkway	d	07 46	07 46			08 10						08 57			09 20		09 37	09 37			10 18		
Liskeard 6	d	07 58	07 58			08 23						09 10			09 33		09 50	09 50			10 31		
Menheniot	d																						
St Germans	d											09 21											
Saltash	d											09 31											
St Budeaux Ferry Road	d																						
Keyham	d																						
Dockyard	d																						
Devonport	d																						
Plymouth	a	08 21	08 21			08 47						09 42			09 57		10 17	10 17			10 55		
	d	08 25	08 25			08 51					09 25				10 01		10 25	10 25			11 00		
Ivybridge	d														10 16								
Totnes	d	08 50	08 50			09 19					09 50				10 31		10 50	10 50					
Paignton	d				09 04				09 18	09 30			10 06	10 16						11 00			11 21
Torquay	d				09 09				09 25	09 35			10 12	10 21						11 05			11 26
Torre	d				09 12				09 29	09 38				10 24						11 08			11 29
Newton Abbot	a	09 01	09 01		09 20	09 30			09 37	09 46	10 01		10 22	10 32	10 43		11 01	11 01		11 16			11 39
	d	09 03	09 03		09 22	09 32			09 39	09 48	10 03		10 23	10 33	10 44		11 03	11 03		11 18			11 39
Teignmouth	d				09 29				09 47	09 55			10 30	10 40						11 25			11 47
Dawlish	d				09 34		←		09 54	10 00			10 35	10 45		←				11 30			11 52
Dawlish Warren	d				09 46		09 46		10 00	10 05				10 56		10 56				11 35			11 56
Starcross	d				→		09 50							→		11 00							12 00
Exeter St Thomas	d						09 59									11 09							12 10
Exeter St Davids 6	a	09 20	09 20			09 51	10 04		10 11	10 17	10 21		10 46		11 03	11 14	11 20	11 20		11 47	11 52		12 14
Exeter Central	a						10 21									11 19				11 52			12 20
Exmouth	a						10 52									11 50				12 20			12 51
Exeter St Davids 6	d	09 23	09 23			09 54			10 15		10 24		10 49		11 07		11 23	11 23			11 56	12 01	
Tiverton Parkway	d	09 37	09 37			10 10			10 30		10 37		11 02		11 22		11 36	11 36				12 17	
Taunton	d	09 50	09 50			10 24			10 45		10 50		11 17		11 36		11 50	11 50				12 31	
Bridgwater	a																						
Weston-super-Mare	a								11 05														
Bristol Temple Meads 10	a	10 25	10 25						11 26		11 24		11 53				12 25	12 25					
	d	10 30	10 30						11 30		11 30		12 00				12 30	12 30					
Bath Spa 7	a								11 41														
Filton Abbey Wood	a																						
Bristol Parkway 7	a	10 38	10 38								11 38		12 08				12 38	12 38					
Swindon	a								12 09														
Newport (South Wales)	a																						
Cardiff Central 7	a																						
Birmingham New Street 12	a	11 56	11 56								12 56		13 26				13 56	13 56					
Castle Cary 123	d																					12 52	
Frome 123	d																						
Westbury 123	d					11 03																13 13	
Pewsey	d																					13 31	
Hungerford	a																						
Newbury	a																					13 51	
Thatcham	a																						
Theale	a																						
Reading 7	a					11 49			12 46						12 51						13 31	14 11	
Slough 3	a																						
London Paddington 15 ⊖	a					12 21			13 14						13 21						14 00	14 38	

A until 6 October. To Newcastle
B from 13 October. To Glasgow Central. from Plymouth
C To St Ives
D To Exmouth
E From Paignton
F The Torbay Express
G To Newcastle
H To Manchester Piccadilly
I The Cornish Riviera

For connections to Oxford, Gatwick Airport and Heathrow Airport refer to Tables T116 and T148

For connections from Swansea refer to Table T128

T135 UPDATE: Major engineering work in connection with electrification works is taking place between Reading and Westbury. The route via Newbury will be closed to all trains on 4-7 June; 9-12 July; 16 July to 05 August; 28-30 August; 08-11 October and 19-22 November. Trains will be re-timed or cancelled and run to a special timetable during this period. Please check revised train times with *www.nationalrail.co.uk*. Rail replacement buses will operate between intermediate stations.

Table T135-R

Saturdays

15 September to 8 December

Cornwall and Devon - Birmingham and London

		XC ◇1 A 🍴	XC ◇1 B 🍴	GW ◇	GW C	GW ◇1 🛒	GW D	GW E	XC ◇1 F 🍴	GW D	GW	GW C	GW ◇1 🛒	GW D	XC ◇1 G 🍴	XC ◇1 H 🍴	GW ◇	GW ◇	XC ◇1 I 🍴	GW C	GW ◇1 🛒	GW D
Penzance	d		09 43			10 00					10 36		10 58				11 41					
St Erth	d		09 51			10 10					10 46		11 08				11 50					
Hayle	d										10 49						11 53					
Camborne	d		10 01			10 21					11 00		11 19				12 03					
Redruth	d		10 07			10 29					11 06		11 27				12 09					
Truro	d		10 19			10 42					11 17		11 40				12 22					
St Austell	d		10 35			10 59					11 34		11 57				12 39					
Newquay	d			10 13														13 06				
Par	d		10 41	11a02		11 07					11 41						12 45	13a55				
Lostwithiel	d		10 48								11 48						12 52					
Bodmin Parkway	d		10 55			11 18					11 54		12 13				12 58					
Liskeard 4	d		11 15			11 31					12 07		12 26				13 11					
Menheniot	d										12x11						13x15					
St Germans	d										12 19						13 23					
Saltash	d										12 26						13 30					
St Budeaux Ferry Road	d																					
Keyham	d																					
Dockyard	d																					
Devonport	d																					
Plymouth	a		11 40			11 55					12 36		12 50				13 41					
	d	11 25	11 48			11 59			12 25				12 54		13 25	13 25					13 55	
Ivybridge	d					12 14																
Totnes	d	11 50	12 13			12 29			12 51				13 22		13 51	13 51						
Paignton	d				12 13			12 42				13 13							13 55	14 08		
Torquay	d				12 18			12 47				13 18							14 01	14 13		
Torre	d				12 21					←		13 21		←						14 16		←
Newton Abbot	a	12 01	12 24		12 29	12 41		12 57	13 02	12 57		13 29	13 33	13 29	14 01	14 02			14 11	14 24	14 30	14 24
	d	12 03	12 25		12 31	12 42		13 07	13 03	13 07		13 39	13 35	13 39	14 03	14 03			14 12	14 38	14 31	14 38
Teignmouth	d				12 38			→		13 15		→		13 46					14 19	→		14 45
Dawlish	d				12 43		←			13 20				13 51					14 24			14 50
Dawlish Warren	d				12 54		12 54			13 24				13 55								14 55
Starcross	d				→		12 58							13 59								14 59
Exeter St Thomas	d						13 07							14 09								15 08
Exeter St Davids 6	a	12 20	12 43			13 01	13 13		13 22	13 36			13 54	14 13	14 22	14 22			14 35		14 50	15 13
Exeter Central	a						13 19							14 19								15 19
Exmouth	a						13 50							14 50								15 50
Exeter St Davids 6	d	12 23	12 48			13 05			13 23				13 57		14 25	14 25			14 37		14 53	
Tiverton Parkway	d	12 36	13 02			13 20			13 37						14 38	14 38			14 50		15 09	
Taunton	d	12 50	13 15			13 34			13 50				14 22		14 52	14 52			15 03		15 23	
Bridgwater	a																					
Weston-super-Mare	a																		15 23			
Bristol Temple Meads 10	a	13 23	13 55						14 25						15 25	15 25			15 49			
	d	13 30	14 00						14 30						15 30	15 30			16 00			
Bath Spa 7	a																					
Filton Abbey Wood	a																					
Bristol Parkway 7	a	13 38	14 08						14 39						15 38	15 39			16 08			
Swindon	a																					
Newport (South Wales)	a																					
Cardiff Central 7	a																					
Birmingham New Street 12	a	14 56	15 26						15 56						16 56	16 56			17 26			
Castle Cary 123	d												14 43									
Frome 123	d																					
Westbury 123	d												15 03									
Pewsey	d																					
Hungerford	a																					
Newbury	a																					
Thatcham	a																					
Theale	a																					
Reading 7	a					14 49							15 49								16 41	
Slough 3	a																					
London Paddington 15 ⊖	a					15 21							16 21								17 10	

A To Newcastle
B To Manchester Piccadilly. 🍴 from Plymouth
C To Exmouth
D From Paignton
E To Exeter St Davids
F To Edinburgh
G from 13 October. To Edinburgh
H until 6 October. To Newcastle
I To Manchester Piccadilly

For connections to Oxford, Gatwick Airport and Heathrow Airport refer to Tables T116 and T148

For connections from Swansea refer to Table T128

Table T135-R

Saturdays

15 September to 8 December

Cornwall and Devon - Birmingham and London

		GW ◇1 🛒	XC ◇1 A 🍴	GW ◇	GW B	GW ◇1 🛒	GW C	GW D	XC ◇1 E 🍴	XC ◇1 F 🍴	GW C	GW	XC ◇1 G 🍴	GW B	GW ◇1 H 🛒	GW C	GW ◇	XC ◇1 I 🍴	GW ◇	GW B	GW ◇1 🛒	GW C	XC ◇1 I 🍴
Penzance	d			12 55											14 00				14 52				
St Erth	d			13 04											14 10				15 01				
Hayle	d			13 07															15 04				
Camborne	d			13 17											14 22				15 14				
Redruth	d			13 23											14 29				15 20				
Truro	d			13 36											14 42				15 31				
St Austell	d			13 53											14 59				15 48				
Newquay	d																15 00						
Par	d			14 00											15 06		15a50		15 55				
Lostwithiel	d			14 07															16 01				
Bodmin Parkway	d			14 13											15 18				16 07				
Liskeard 4	d			14 26											15 31				16 20				
Menheniot	d																		16x24				
St Germans	d			14 36															16 33				
Saltash	d			14 43															16 40				
St Budeaux Ferry Road	d																						
Keyham	d																						
Dockyard	d																						
Devonport	d			14 49																			
Plymouth	a			14 55											15 54				16 50				
	d		14 25			15 00			15 25	15 25		15 32			16 00			16 25			16 56		17 25
Ivybridge	d											15 47									17 11		
Totnes	d		14 50			15 27			15 51	15 51		16 01			16 27			16 51			17 27		17 51
Paignton	d				15 13			15 44						16 13						17 11			
Torquay	d				15 18			15 49						16 18						17 16			
Torre	d				15 21						←			16 21						17 19			
Newton Abbot	a		15 01		15 29	15 39		15 59	16 02	16 02	15 59	16 15		16 29	16 39			17 02		17 27	17 38		18 02
	d		15 03		15 31	15 40		16 08	16 04	16 04	16 08			16 31	16 40			17 04		17 29	17 40		18 04
Teignmouth	d				15 38			→			16 15			16 38						17 36			
Dawlish	d				15 43		←				16 20			16 43		←				17 41		←	
Dawlish Warren	d				15 54		15 54							16 54		16 54				17 52		17 52	
Starcross	d				→		15 58							→		16 58				→		17 56	
Exeter St Thomas	d						16 07									17 07						18 06	
Exeter St Davids 6	a		15 21			16 00	16 12		16 21	16 22	16 34				16 59	17 13		17 22			17 59	18 10	18 22
Exeter Central	a						16 19				16 40					17 19						18 17	
Exmouth	a						16 50									17 50						18 48	
Exeter St Davids 6	d		15 23			16 03			16 24	16 24			16 53		17 03			17 24			18 02		18 24
Tiverton Parkway	d		15 37			16 19			16 38	16 38			17 07		17 18			17 38			18 17		18 38
Taunton	d	15 30	15 50			16 33			16 51	16 51			17 21		17 33			17 51			18 31		18 51
Bridgwater	a																						
Weston-super-Mare	a																						
Bristol Temple Meads 10	a		16 25						17 25	17 25			17 55					18 26					19 24
	d		16 30						17 30	17 30			18 00					18 30					19 30
Bath Spa 7	a																						
Filton Abbey Wood	a																						
Bristol Parkway 7	a		16 38						17 39	17 39			18 08					18 38					19 39
Swindon	a																						
Newport (South Wales)	a																						
Cardiff Central 7	a																						
Birmingham New Street 12	a		17 56						18 55	18 56			19 26					19 58					20 51
Castle Cary 123	d	15 53																			18 53		
Frome 123	d																						
Westbury 123	d	16 13																			19 14		
Pewsey	d	16 31																					
Hungerford	a																						
Newbury	a	16 51																			19 47		
Thatcham	a																						
Theale	a																						
Reading 7	a	17 10				17 49									18 49						20 05		
Slough 3	a																						
London Paddington 15 ⊖	a	17 44				18 21									19 22						20 37		

A To Newcastle
B To Exmouth
C From Paignton
D To Exeter Central
E until 6 October. To Newcastle
F from 13 October. To York
G To Manchester Piccadilly
H The Royal Duchy
I To Leeds

For connections to Oxford, Gatwick Airport and Heathrow Airport refer to Tables T116 and T148

For connections from Swansea refer to Table T128

Table T135-R

Saturdays
15 September to 8 December

Cornwall and Devon - Birmingham and London

		GW	GW	GW ◇1 ⊡	XC ◇1 A ⚒	GW	GW	GW ◇	GW	GW	GW ◇1 ⊡	GW B	GW	GW	GW 1	GW	GW	GW	XC ◇1	GW	GW
Penzance	d			15 52			16 44				17 40	18 50					19 06		21 29		
St Erth	d			16 02			16 53				17 50	18a58					19 15		21 38		
Hayle	d						16 56				17 54						19 18				
Camborne	d			16 14			17 06				18 05						19 28		21 49		
Redruth	d			16 21			17 12				18 12						19 35		21 56		
Truro	d			16 34			17 25				18 25						19 46		22 09		
St Austell	d			16 52			17 42				18 42						20 03		22 26		
Newquay	d							17 20					19 15					21 20			
Par	d			16 59			17 48	18a10			18 49		20a05				20 10	22 12	22 33		
Lostwithiel	d			17 06			17 55										20 16	22 19			
Bodmin Parkway	d			17 13			18 01				19 01						20 22	22 25	22 44		
Liskeard ■	d			17 26			18 14				19 14						20 35	22 38	22 58		
Menheniot	d																20x39	22x42			
St Germans	d						18 25										20 48	22 51			
Saltash	d						18 32										20 55	22 58			
St Budeaux Ferry Road	d																20 59	23 02			
Keyham	d																21 01	23 04			
Dockyard	d																21x02	23x05			
Devonport	d																21 05	23 08			
Plymouth	a			17 49			18 41				19 37						21 09	23 13	23 22		
	d		17 40	17 55	18 25		18 44				19 40						21 15				
Ivybridge	d		17 55				18 59										21 30				
Totnes	d		18 09	18 22	18 50		19 13				20 09						21 44				
Paignton	d	17 52				18 52			19 24	19 51				20 20	20 44	21 20				22 45	23 30
Torquay	d	17 57				18 57			19 29	19 56				20 25	20 50	21 25				22 50	23 35
Torre	d	18 00				19 00			19 32					20 28		21 28				22 53	23 38
Newton Abbot	a	18 08	18 21	18 33	19 01	19 08	19 25		19 40	20 06	20 20			20 36	21 00	21 36	21 56			23 01	23 46
	d	18 10	18 21	18 35	19 03	19 10	19 26		19 42	20 08	20 22			20 37	21 02	21 38	21 57				23 47
Teignmouth	d	18 17	18 28			19 17	19 33		19 49	20 15				20 45		21 45	22 04				23 54
Dawlish	d	18 22	18 33			19 22	19 38		19 54	20 20				20 50		21 50	22 09				23 59
Dawlish Warren	d	18 27	18 38			19 27	19 42		20 03	20 25				20 54		21 55					00 04
Starcross	d	18 31				19 31			20 07					20 58		21 59					00 08
Exeter St Thomas	d	18 40				19 40			20 16					21 08		22 08					00 17
Exeter St Davids ■	a	18 45	18 50	18 54	19 21	19 45	19 55		20 25	20 37	20 41			21 12	21 22	22 12	22 23				00 22
Exeter Central	a	18 51							20 36												
Exmouth	a	19 21							21 07												
Exeter St Davids ■	d			18 57	19 23						20 45										
Tiverton Parkway	d			19 12	19 37						21 00										
Taunton	d			19 26	19 50						21 14										
Bridgwater	a																				
Weston-super-Mare	a																				
Bristol Temple Meads ■	a				20 22						21 46										
	d				20 30						21 47										
Bath Spa ■	a										22 01										
Filton Abbey Wood	a																				
Bristol Parkway ■	a				20 38																
Swindon	a										22 30										
Newport (South Wales)	a																				
Cardiff Central ■	a																				
Birmingham New Street ■	a				21 52																
Castle Cary 123	d			19 47																	
Frome 123	d																				
Westbury 123	d			20 07																	
Pewsey	d			20 25																	
Hungerford	a																				
Newbury	a																				
Thatcham	a																				
Theale	a																				
Reading ■	a			20 59							23 03										
Slough ■	a																				
London Paddington ■ ⊖	a			21 31							23 43										

A ⚒ to Bristol Temple Meads
B To St Ives

For connections to Oxford, Gatwick Airport and Heathrow Airport refer to Tables T116 and T148

For connections from Swansea refer to Table T128

Table T135-R

Sundays
20 May to 9 September

Cornwall and Devon - Birmingham and London

		GW A	GW ◇	GW ◇1 ⊡	GW ◇ B	GW ◇1 ⊡	XC ◇1 C ⚒	GW	GW ◇1 ⊡	GW D	XC ◇1 E ⚒	XC ◇1 F ⚒	XC ◇1 G ⚒	GW	GW ◇1 ⊡	XC ◇1 H ⚒	GW ◇	GW	GW 1 ⊡	XC ◇1 G ⚒	XC ◇1 E ⚒	XC ◇1 F ⚒	GW
Penzance	d								08 05	08 45						09 30			09 47				
St Erth	d								08 14	08a53						09 38			09 56				
Hayle	d								08 19														
Camborne	d								08 31							09 48			10 08				
Redruth	d								08 37							09 54			10 14				
Truro	d								08 50							10 08			10 27				
St Austell	d								09 07							10 24			10 44				
Newquay	d																09 58						
Par	d								09 15							10 31	10a45		10 54				
Lostwithiel	d																						
Bodmin Parkway	d								09 26							10 41			11 05				
Liskeard ■	d								09 39							10 54			11 18				
Menheniot	d																						
St Germans	d																		11 30				
Saltash	d								09 56														
St Budeaux Ferry Road	d																						
Keyham	d																						
Dockyard	d																						
Devonport	d																						
Plymouth	a								10 04							11 17			11 43				
	d					08 37	09 25		10 10		10 25	10 25			11 00	11 25			11 45	12 00	12 25	12 24	
Ivybridge	d																						
Totnes	d					09 03	09 50		10 37		10 50	10 50			11 27	11 50			12 14		12 50	12 50	
Paignton	d							09 49					10 50	10 58				11 49					12 56
Torquay	d							09 54					10 56	11 03				11 54					13 01
Torre	d							09 57						11 06				11 57					13 04
Newton Abbot	a					09 16	10 01	10 05	10 49		11 01	11 01	11 06	11 14	11 39	12 01		12 05	12 27	12 34	13 01	13 01	13 12
	d					09 17	10 03	10 07	10 50		11 03	11 03	11 08	11 15	11 40	12 03		12 08	12 27	12 36	13 03	13 03	13 13
Teignmouth	d					09 25		10 14					11 15	11 21				12 16					13 20
Dawlish	d					09 31		10 19					11 20	11 26				12 21					13 25
Dawlish Warren	d	00 04						10 24						11 32				12 25					13 30
Starcross	d	00 08						10 28						11 36				12 29					
Exeter St Thomas	d	00 17						10 37						11 45				12 39					
Exeter St Davids ■	a	00 22				09 43	10 20	10 40	11 09		11 21	11 21	11 30	11 48	11 59	12 20		12 42	12 46	12 54	13 20	13 21	13 41
Exeter Central	a							10 47						11 54				12 50					13 52
Exmouth	a							11 17						12 24				13 20					14 21
Exeter St Davids ■	d		08 01	08 43	09 34	09 45	10 23		11 11		11 23	11 23	11 33		12 01	12 23			12 47	12 56	13 23	13 23	
Tiverton Parkway	d		08 18	08 58	09 51		10 37		11 26		11 37	11 37	11 47		12 17	12 37				13 10	13 37	13 37	
Taunton	d		08 35	09 11	10 07	10 09	10 50		11 39		11 52	11 52	12 00		12 30	12 50			13 13	13 23	13 50	13 50	
Bridgwater	a		08 46		10 18																		
Weston-super-Mare	a		09 06		10 36								12 19										
Bristol Temple Meads ■	a		09 37		11 10		11 23				12 24	12 27	12 44			13 23				13 54	14 21	14 22	
	d						11 30				12 30	12 30	13 00			13 30				14 00	14 30	14 30	
Bath Spa ■	a																						
Filton Abbey Wood	a																						
Bristol Parkway ■	a						11 38				12 38	12 38	13 08			13 38				14 08	14 38	14 39	
Swindon	a																						
Newport (South Wales)	a																						
Cardiff Central ■	a																						
Birmingham New Street ■	a						12 49				13 48	13 48	14 27			14 48				15 27	15 48	15 49	
Castle Cary 123	d			09 34					12 00						12 51								
Frome 123	d																						
Westbury 123	d			09 54		10 46			12 21										13 50				
Pewsey	d			10 11					12 38														
Hungerford	a																						
Newbury	a			10 31		11 20			12 58														
Thatcham	a																						
Theale	a																						
Reading ■	a			10 49		11 40			13 16						13 51				14 37				
Slough ■	a																						
London Paddington ■ ⊖	a			11 30		12 21			13 55						14 30				15 15				

A not 20 May. From Paignton
B To Severn Beach
C To Motherwell
D To St Ives
E from 22 July. To Edinburgh
F until 15 July. To Motherwell
G To Manchester Piccadilly
H To Edinburgh. ⚒ from Plymouth

For connections to Oxford, Gatwick Airport and Heathrow Airport refer to Tables T116 and T148

For connections from Swansea refer to Table T128

T135 UPDATE: Major engineering work in connection with electrification works is taking place between Reading and Westbury. The route via Newbury will be closed to all trains on 4-7 June; 9-12 July; 16 July to 05 August; 28-30 August; 08-11 October and 19-22 November. Trains will be re-timed or cancelled and run to a special timetable during this period. Please check revised train times with *www.nationalrail.co.uk*. Rail replacement buses will operate between intermediate stations.

Cornwall and Devon - Birmingham and London

Sundays
20 May to 9 September

		XC	GW	XC	GW	GW	GW	GW	XC	XC	GW	GW	GW	GW	XC	GW	GW	GW	GW	GW	GW	XC	XC
		◇■ A 🛒	■ ■ ☕	◇■ B 🛒		◇■ ☕			◇■ C 🛒	◇■ D 🛒	◇		■ ■ ☕	■ ■ ☕	◇■ C 🛒	◇■ ☕		◇■ ☕	◇		◇■ ☕	◇■ E 🛒	◇■ F 🛒
Penzance	d		11 00			11 40		12 01		12 30			13 00						13 37				
St Erth	d		11 09			11 49		12 12		12 38			13 09						13 48				
Hayle	d									12 42									13 51				
Camborne	d		11 22			12 01		12 24		12 51			13 23						14 01				
Redruth	d		11 28			12 07		12 30		12 58			13 29						14 07				
Truro	d		11 42			12 21		12 41		13 09			13 41						14 18				
St Austell	d		11 58			12 37		12 57		13 26			14 00						14 35				
Newquay	d			11 32							13 10												
Par	d		12 05	12 23		12 45		13 03		13 32	13a57		14 06						14 42				
Lostwithiel	d							13 11		13 39									14 48				
Bodmin Parkway	d		12 18	12 35		12 58		13 17		13 46			14 18						14 54				
Liskeard ■	d		12 31	12 48		13 11		13 33		13 58			14 31						15 07				
Menheniot	d							13x38															
St Germans	d							13 45											15 18				
Saltash	d							13 53											15 25				
St Budeaux Ferry Road	d																						
Keyham	d																						
Dockyard	d																						
Devonport	d																						
Plymouth	a		12 57	13 11		13 36		14 03		14 23			14 56						15 33				
	d	12 52	13 00	13 25		13 45		14 07	14 25	14 35			15 00	15 12	15 24			15 42	15 51		16 10	16 25	16 25
Ivybridge	d							14 23											16 06				
Totnes	d		13 28	13 50		14 13		14 37	14 51	15 01			15 27		15 50			16 09	16 20		16 39	16 51	16 51
Paignton	d				13 52		14 18					14 57				15 45	15 55			16 19			
Torquay	d				13 57		14 23					15 01				15 50	16 00			16 24			
Torre	d				14 00		14 26					15 04				15 55	16 03			16 27			
Newton Abbot	a	13 26	13 39	14 01	14 08	14 25	14 34	14 49	15 02	15 11		15 12	15 38	15 45	16 01	16 04	16 11	16 20	16 32	16 36	16 51	17 02	17 02
	d	13 27	13 41	14 03	14 09	14 26	14 37	14 50	15 04	15 13		15 16	15 40	15 47	16 03	16 05	16 12	16 23	16 33	16 37	16 55	17 04	17 04
Teignmouth	d				14 16		14 44	14 57				15 23				16 13	16 19			16 44			
Dawlish	d				14 21		14 49	15 02				15 28				16 18	16 24			16 49			
Dawlish Warren	d				14 26		14 54										16 29			16 54			
Starcross	d				14 30		14 58													16 58			
Exeter St Thomas	d				14 39		15 07													17 07			
Exeter St Davids ■	a	13 45	14 00	14 20	14 41	14 45	15 12	15 15	15 22	15 30		15 41	15 58	16 07	16 21	16 31	16 40	16 43	16 54	17 11	17 15	17 22	17 22
Exeter Central	a				14 49		15 21					15 49					16 49			17 19			
Exmouth	a				15 18		15 46					16 19					17 19			17 45			
Exeter St Davids ■	d	13 47	14 02	14 23		14 47			15 24	15 32			16 01	16 09	16 25	16 33		16 44			17 17	17 25	17 25
Tiverton Parkway	d		14 16	14 36					15 37	15 46			16 16	16 24	16 39			17 00			17 32	17 39	17 39
Taunton	d		14 30	14 49		15 11			15 51	15 59			16 30	16 39	16 52	16 58		17 12			17 46	17 51	17 52
Bridgwater	a															17 08							
Weston-super-Mare	a									16 18				16 59		17 27							
Bristol Temple Meads ■	a	14 40		15 21					16 25	16 47				17 20	17 24	17 57					18 23	18 27	18 27
	d	15 00		15 30					16 30	17 00				17 30	17 30	18 00					18 30	18 30	18 30
Bath Spa ■	a													17 41		18 11					18 41		
Filton Abbey Wood	a																						
Bristol Parkway ■	a	15 08		15 38					16 39	17 08					17 39							18 39	18 39
Swindon	a													18 10		18 40					19 11		
Newport (South Wales)	a																						
Cardiff Central ■	a																						
Birmingham New Street ■	a	16 27		16 49					17 49	18 27					18 50							19 50	19 50
Castle Cary 123	d					15 33												17 34					
Frome 123	d																						
Westbury 123	d					15 50												17 54					
Pewsey	d					16 08												18 11					
Hungerford	a																						
Newbury	a					16 29												18 31					
Thatcham	a																						
Theale	a																						
Reading ■	a		15 46			16 46							17 46	18 46		19 09		18 48			19 45		
Slough ■	a																						
London Paddington ■ ⊖	a		16 26			17 29							18 30	19 25		19 50		19 29			20 25		

A To Manchester Piccadilly
B To Edinburgh
C To Leeds
D To Manchester Piccadilly. 🛒 from Plymouth
E until 15 July, also 9 September. To Leeds
F from 22 July until 2 September. To Leeds

For connections to Oxford, Gatwick Airport and Heathrow Airport refer to Tables T116 and T148

For connections from Swansea refer to Table T128

Cornwall and Devon - Birmingham and London

Sundays
20 May to 9 September

		GW	GW	GW	XC	GW	GW	XC	GW	XC	GW	GW	GW	GW	GW	GW	GW	GW	GW	GW	GW	GW
			◇	■ ■ ☕	◇■ A 🛒		◇■ ☕	◇■ B 🛒	◇■ ☕	◇■ C 🛒	◇		◇■ ☕	D	◇■ ☕	E		◇■ ☕				
Penzance	d		14 37	15 00	15 30				16 13						17 35		17 55			19 00		20 12
St Erth	d		14 48	15 10	15 38				16 23						17 44		18 04			19 09		20 22
Hayle	d		14 51														18 07					20 25
Camborne	d		15 01	15 23	15 49				16 37						17 57		18 17			19 21		20 35
Redruth	d		15 07	15 30	15 55				16 43						18 04		18 23			19 27		20 41
Truro	d		15 18	15 42	16 07				16 57						18 17		18 34			19 39		20 53
St Austell	d		15 35	16 00	16 23				17 13						18 35		18 51			19 56		21 10
Newquay	d						15 59				17 45										20 20	
Par	d		15 41	16 07	16 30		16 53		17 21		18a34				18 42		18 58			20 03	21a07	21 16
Lostwithiel	d		15 48														19 04			20 09		21 23
Bodmin Parkway	d		15 54	16 18	16 40		17 05		17 33						18 53		19 10			20 15		21 29
Liskeard ■	d		16 08	16 31	16 52		17 18		17 46						19 06		19 23			20 28		21 42
Menheniot	d																			20x33		
St Germans	d		16 18																	20 41		21 53
Saltash	d		16 25						18 02								19 40			20 47		22 00
St Budeaux Ferry Road	d																19 44			20 52		
Keyham	d																19 46					
Dockyard	d																19 48					
Devonport	d																19 50			20 55		
Plymouth	a		16 35	16 57	17 15		17 41		18 10						19 30		19 55			21 00		22 09
	d		16 36	17 00	17 25		17 50		18 15	18 25			18 45		19 34			20 04		21 15		
Ivybridge	d		16 52																	21 30		
Totnes	d		17 06	17 28	17 50		18 17			18 52			19 12		20 01					21 44		
Paignton	d	16 53				17 50		18 20				18 54		19 53					20 53			
Torquay	d	16 58				17 55		18 26				18 59		19 58					20 58			
Torre	d	17 01				17 58						19 02		20 01		←			21 01			
Newton Abbot	a	17 09	17 17	17 39	18 01	18 06	18 29	18 36		19 03		19 10	19 24	20 09	20 12	20 09		20 39	21 09	21 56		
	d	17 11	17 18	17 40	18 03	18 07	18 31	18 37		19 05		19 11	19 26	20 16	20 14	20 16		20 41	21 11	21 57		
Teignmouth	d	17 18	17 25			18 14						19 18		→		20 24			21 18	22 04		
Dawlish	d	17 23	17 30			18 19						19 23				20 29			21 23	22 09		
Dawlish Warren	d	17 28				18 24						19 28				20 34			21 28			
Starcross	d					18 28										20 38						
Exeter St Thomas	d					18 37										20 47						
Exeter St Davids ■	a	17 39	17 44	18 00	18 20	18 39	18 50	18 56	19 08	19 23		19 39	19 45		20 34	20 52		21 00	21 39	22 22		
Exeter Central	a	17 49				18 49						19 54				20 57			21 51			
Exmouth	a	18 19				19 18						20 24				21 25			22 21			
Exeter St Davids ■	d		17 48	18 01	18 23		18 52	18 58	19 13	19 25			19 47		20 35			21 02				
Tiverton Parkway	d			18 18	18 37			19 11		19 38			20 02		20 51			21 17				
Taunton	d		18 18	18 33	18 50		19 16	19 24	19 39	19 52			20 15		21 04			21 31				
Bridgwater	a		18 29																			
Weston-super-Mare	a		18 48																			
Bristol Temple Meads ■	a		19 19		19 23			19 57		20 25								22 00				
	d				19 30			20 00		20 30								22 10				
Bath Spa ■	a																	22 21				
Filton Abbey Wood	a																					
Bristol Parkway ■	a				19 38			20 08		20 39												
Swindon	a																	22 49				
Newport (South Wales)	a																					
Cardiff Central ■	a																					
Birmingham New Street ■	a				20 52			21 18		21 48												
Castle Cary 123	d												20 37		21 27							
Frome 123	d																					
Westbury 123	d						19 54						20 56		21 46							
Pewsey	d														22 01							
Hungerford	a																					
Newbury	a						20 27								22 21							
Thatcham	a																					
Theale	a																					
Reading ■	a			19 47			20 45		20 57				21 43		22 42			23 26				
Slough ■	a																					
London Paddington ■ ⊖	a			20 28			21 27		21 42				22 28		23 25			00 09				

A To Leeds. 🛒 from Plymouth
B 🛒 to Bristol Temple Meads
C To Leeds. 🛒 to Bristol Temple Meads
D To Exmouth
E From Paignton

For connections to Oxford, Gatwick Airport and Heathrow Airport refer to Tables T116 and T148

For connections from Swansea refer to Table T128

Sundays
20 May to 9 September

Cornwall and Devon - Birmingham and London

		GW	GW	GW
				1 A
Penzance	d			21 15
St Erth	d			21 25
Hayle	d			
Camborne	d			21 39
Redruth	d			21 46
Truro	d			22 01
St Austell	d			22 19
Newquay	d			
Par	d			
Lostwithiel	d			
Bodmin Parkway	d			22 35
Liskeard	d			22 50
Menheniot	d			
St Germans	d			
Saltash	d			
St Budeaux Ferry Road	d			
Keyham	d			
Dockyard	d			
Devonport	d			
Plymouth	a			23 13
	d			23 20
Ivybridge	d			
Totnes	d			23 48
Paignton	d	21 53	23 00	
Torquay	d	21 58	23 05	
Torre	d	22 01	23 08	
Newton Abbot	a	22 09	23 16	00 01
	d	22 10	23 18	00 01
Teignmouth	d	22 17	23 25	
Dawlish	d	22 22	23 30	
Dawlish Warren	d	22 27	23 35	
Starcross	d	22 31	23 39	
Exeter St Thomas	d	22 40	23 48	
Exeter St Davids	a	22 42	23 52	00 23
Exeter Central	a	22 51		
Exmouth	a	23 20		
Exeter St Davids	d			00 59
Tiverton Parkway	d			
Taunton	d			
Bridgwater	a			
Weston-super-Mare	a			
Bristol Temple Meads	a			
	d			
Bath Spa	a			
Filton Abbey Wood	a			
Bristol Parkway	a			
Swindon	a			
Newport (South Wales)	a			
Cardiff Central	a			
Birmingham New Street	a			
Castle Cary 123	d			
Frome 123	d			
Westbury 123	d			
Pewsey	d			
Hungerford	a			
Newbury	a			
Thatcham	a			
Theale	a			
Reading	a			04s06
Slough	a			
London Paddington ⊖	a			05 02

A The Night Riviera

For connections to Oxford, Gatwick Airport and Heathrow Airport refer to Tables T116 and T148

For connections from Swansea refer to Table T128

Table T135-R

Sundays
16 September to 2 December

Cornwall and Devon - Birmingham and London

		GW	GW	GW	GW	GW	XC	GW	GW	XC	XC	GW	GW	XC	XC	GW	GW	GW	GW	XC	XC	GW	XC
		A	◇	◇1	◇ B	◇1	◇1 C		◇1	◇1 D	◇1 E		◇1	◇1 F	◇1 G		1	H	◇	◇1 E	◇1 D		◇1 E
Penzance	d								08 05					09 30	09 30		09 47	10 19					
St Erth	d								08 14					09 38	09 38		09 56	10a27					
Hayle	d								08 19														
Camborne	d								08 31					09 48	09 48		10 09						
Redruth	d								08 37					09 54	09 54		10 15						
Truro	d								08 50					10 06	10 08		10 28						
St Austell	d								09 07					10 22	10 24		10 45						
Newquay	d																		11 12				
Par	d								09 15					10 29	10 31		10 53		12a01				
Lostwithiel	d																						
Bodmin Parkway	d								09 26					10 39	10 41		11 06						
Liskeard	d								09 39					10 52	10 54		11 19						
Menheniot	d																						
St Germans	d																11 30						
Saltash	d								09 56														
St Budeaux Ferry Road	d																						
Keyham	d																						
Dockyard	d																						
Devonport	d																						
Plymouth	a								10 04					11 15	11 17		11 43						
	d					08 35	09 25		10 10	10 25			11 00	11 25	11 25		11 45			12 00	12 25		12 52
Ivybridge	d																						
Totnes	d					09 02	09 50		10 37	10 50			11 27	11 50	11 50		12 14				12 50		
Paignton	d							09 49			10 50	10 58				11 49						12 56	
Torquay	d							09 54			10 56	11 03				11 54						13 01	
Torre	d							09 57				11 06				11 57						13 04	
Newton Abbot	a					09 14	10 01	10 05	10 49	11 01	11 06	11 14	11 39	12 01	12 01	12 05	12 27			12 34	13 01	13 12	13 26
	d					09 16	10 03	10 07	10 51	11 03	11 08	11 15	11 40	12 03	12 03	12 08	12 28			12 36	13 03	13 13	13 27
Teignmouth	d					09 23		10 14			11 15	11 21				12 16						13 20	
Dawlish	d					09 29		10 19			11 20	11 26				12 21						13 25	
Dawlish Warren	d	00 04						10 24				11 32				12 25						13 30	
Starcross	d	00 08						10 28				11 36				12 29							
Exeter St Thomas	d	00 17						10 37				11 45				12 39							
Exeter St Davids	a	00 22				09 41	10 20	10 40	11 10	11 21	11 30	11 48	11 59	12 20	12 20	12 42	12 48			12 54	13 20	13 41	13 45
Exeter Central	a							10 47				11 54				12 50						13 52	
Exmouth	a							11 17				12 24				13 20						14 21	
Exeter St Davids	d		08 01	08 30	09 31	09 43	10 23		11 11	11 23	11 33		12 01	12 23	12 23		12 49			12 56	13 23		13 47
Tiverton Parkway	d		08 18	08 45	09 48		10 37		11 27	11 37	11 47		12 17	12 37	12 37					13 10	13 37		
Taunton	d		08 35	08 58	10 03	10 07	10 50		11 40	11 52	12 00		12 30	12 50	12 50		13 15			13 23	13 50		
Bridgwater	a		08 46		10 15																		
Weston-super-Mare	a		09 06		10 32						12 19												
Bristol Temple Meads	a		09 37		11 11		11 23			12 24	12 44			13 23	13 23					13 54	14 21		14 43
	d						11 30			12 30	13 00			13 30	13 30					14 00	14 30		15 00
Bath Spa	a																						
Filton Abbey Wood	a																						
Bristol Parkway	a						11 38			12 38	13 08			13 38	13 38					14 08	14 38		15 08
Swindon	a																						
Newport (South Wales)	a																						
Cardiff Central	a																						
Birmingham New Street	a						12 49			13 48	14 27			14 48	14 48					15 27	15 48		16 27
Castle Cary 123	d			09 20					12 01				12 51										
Frome 123	d																						
Westbury 123	d			09 40		10 43			12 21								13 59						
Pewsey	d			09 57					12 38														
Hungerford	a																						
Newbury	a			10 17		11 17			12 58														
Thatcham	a																						
Theale	a																						
Reading	a			10 35		11 36			13 17				13 51				14 46						
Slough	a																						
London Paddington ⊖	a			11 14		12 14			14 04				14 34				15 34						

A From Paignton
B To Avonmouth
C To Glasgow Central
D To Edinburgh
E To Manchester Piccadilly
F from 14 October. To Edinburgh. from Plymouth
G until 7 October. To Glasgow Central. from Plymouth
H until 21 October. To St Ives

For connections to Oxford, Gatwick Airport and Heathrow Airport refer to Tables T116 and T148

For connections from Swansea refer to Table T128

T135 UPDATE: Major engineering work in connection with electrification works is taking place between Reading and Westbury. The route via Newbury will be closed to all trains on 4-7 June; 9-12 July; 16 July to 05 August; 28-30 August; 08-11 October and 19-22 November. Trains will be re-timed or cancelled and run to a special timetable during this period. Please check revised train times with *www.nationalrail.co.uk*. Rail replacement buses will operate between intermediate stations.

Table T135-R

Sundays

16 September to 2 December

Cornwall and Devon - Birmingham and London

		GW	GW	XC	GW	GW	GW	GW	XC	XC	GW	GW	GW	XC	GW	GW	GW	GW	GW	GW	XC	GW	GW
		■ ⊡	A	◇■ B ✕		◇■ ⊡			◇■ C ✕	◇■ D ✕		■ ⊡	■ ⊡	◇■ C ✕	◇■ ⊡		◇	◇■ ⊡		◇■ ⊡	◇■ C ✕		◇
Penzance	d	11 00	11 45					12 04		12 30		13 00					13 37						14 37
St Erth	d	11 10	11a53					12 13		12 38		13 09					13 48						14 48
Hayle	d									12 42							13 51						14 51
Camborne	d	11 24						12 24		12 51		13 23					14 01						15 01
Redruth	d	11 30						12 30		12 58		13 29					14 07						15 07
Truro	d	11 43						12 41		13 09		13 41					14 18						15 18
St Austell	d	12 00						12 57		13 26		14 00					14 35						15 35
Newquay	d																						
Par	d	12 07						13 03		13 32		14 06					14 42						15 41
Lostwithiel	d							13 12		13 39							14 48						15 48
Bodmin Parkway	d	12 19						13 17		13 46		14 18					14 54						15 54
Liskeard ■	d	12 33						13 33		13 58		14 31					15 07						16 08
Menheniot	d							13x38															
St Germans	d							13 45									15 18						16 18
Saltash	d							13 53									15 25						16 25
St Budeaux Ferry Road	d																						
Keyham	d																						
Dockyard	d																						
Devonport	d																						
Plymouth	a	12 57						14 03		14 23		14 56					15 33						16 35
	d	13 00		13 25		13 50		14 07	14 25	14 35		15 00	15 12	15 24			15 40	15 54		16 10	16 25		16 36
Ivybridge	d							14 23									15 55						16 52
Totnes	d	13 28		13 50		14 17		14 37	14 51	15 01		15 27		15 50			16 09	16 20		16 37	16 51		17 06
Paignton	d				13 52		14 18				14 57				15 45	15 55			16 19			16 53	
Torquay	d				13 57		14 23				15 01				15 50	16 00			16 24			16 58	
Torre	d				14 00		14 26				15 04				15 55	16 03			16 27			17 01	
Newton Abbot	a	13 40		14 01	14 08	14 29	14 34	14 49	15 02	15 11	15 12	15 38	15 45	16 01	16 04	16 11	16 21	16 31	16 36	16 49	17 02	17 09	17 17
	d	13 41		14 03	14 09	14 30	14 37	14 50	15 04	15 13	15 16	15 40	15 47	16 03	16 05	16 12	16 22	16 34	16 37	16 55	17 04	17 11	17 18
Teignmouth	d				14 16		14 44	14 57			15 23				16 13	16 19			16 44			17 18	17 25
Dawlish	d				14 21		14 49	15 02			15 28				16 18	16 24			16 49			17 23	17 30
Dawlish Warren	d				14 26		14 54									16 28			16 54			17 28	
Starcross	d				14 30		14 58												16 58				
Exeter St Thomas	d				14 39		15 07												17 07				
Exeter St Davids ■	a	14 01		14 20	14 41	14 49	15 12	15 16	15 22	15 30	15 41	15 59	16 07	16 21	16 31	16 40	16 43	16 53	17 11	17 15	17 22	17 39	17 44
Exeter Central	a				14 49		15 21				15 49					16 49			17 19			17 49	
Exmouth	a				15 18		15 46				16 19					17 19			17 45			18 19	
Exeter St Davids ■	d	14 03		14 23		14 53			15 24	15 32		16 01	16 09	16 25	16 33			16 54		17 17	17 25		17 45
Tiverton Parkway	d	14 17		14 36					15 37	15 46		16 16	16 24	16 39				17 10			17 39		
Taunton	d	14 32		14 49		15 17			15 51	15 59		16 30	16 39	16 52	16 58			17 23		17 41	17 51		18 15
Bridgwater	a														17 08								18 26
Weston-super-Mare	a									16 18			16 59		17 27								18 45
Bristol Temple Meads ■	a			15 21					16 25	16 47			17 20	17 24	17 51					18 21	18 27		19 15
	d			15 30					16 30	17 00			17 25	17 30	17 53					18 25	18 30		
Bath Spa ■	a												17 36		18 02					18 36			
Filton Abbey Wood	a																						
Bristol Parkway ■	a			15 38					16 39	17 08				17 39							18 39		
Swindon	a												18 06		18 33					19 06			
Newport (South Wales)	a																						
Cardiff Central ■	a																						
Birmingham New Street ■	a			16 49					17 49	18 27				18 50							19 50		
Castle Cary 123	d					15 39												17 45					
Frome 123	d																						
Westbury 123	d					15 57												18 05					
Pewsey	d					16 15												18 22					
Hungerford	a																						
Newbury	a					16 36												18 42					
Thatcham	a																						
Theale	a																						
Reading ■	a	15 48				16 53						17 47	18 36		19 08			18 59		19 36			
Slough ■	a																						
London Paddington ■ ⊖	a	16 38				17 37						18 37	19 13		19 45			19 38		20 15			

A from 28 October. To St Ives
B To Edinburgh
C To Leeds
D To Manchester Piccadilly. ✕ from Plymouth

For connections to Oxford, Gatwick Airport and Heathrow Airport refer to Tables T116 and T148

For connections from Swansea refer to Table T128

Table T135-R

Sundays

16 September to 2 December

Cornwall and Devon - Birmingham and London

		GW	GW	XC	GW	GW	XC	GW	XC	GW	GW	GW	GW	GW	GW	GW	GW	GW	GW	GW	GW	GW
		◇	■ ⊡	◇■ A ✕		◇■ ⊡	◇■ B ✕	◇■ ⊡	◇■ C ✕		D	◇■ ⊡	E	D	◇■ ⊡	E	◇■ ⊡					
Penzance	d		15 00	15 30				16 13							17 35				19 00	20 12		
St Erth	d		15 10	15 38				16 24							17 44				19 09	20 22		
Hayle	d																			20 25		
Camborne	d		15 23	15 49				16 37							17 57				19 21	20 35		
Redruth	d		15 30	15 55				16 44							18 04				19 27	20 41		
Truro	d		15 42	16 07				16 57							18 16				19 39	20 53		
St Austell	d		16 00	16 23				17 14							18 35				19 56	21 10		
Newquay	d	15 10								17 45												
Par	d	15a59	16 07	16 30				17 20		18a34					18 42				20 03	21 17		
Lostwithiel	d																		20 09	21 23		
Bodmin Parkway	d		16 18	16 40				17 32							18 53				20 15	21 29		
Liskeard ■	d		16 31	16 52				17 46							19 06				20 28	21 42		
Menheniot	d																		20x33			
St Germans	d																		20 41	21 53		
Saltash	d							18 02											20 47	22 00		
St Budeaux Ferry Road	d																		20 52			
Keyham	d																					
Dockyard	d																					
Devonport	d																		20 55			
Plymouth	a		16 56	17 15				18 11							19 30				21 00	22 10		
	d		17 00	17 25		17 40		18 15	18 25			18 40			19 34		20 04		21 15			
Ivybridge	d																		21 30			
Totnes	d		17 28	17 50		18 07			18 52			19 07			20 01				21 44			
Paignton	d				17 50		18 20				18 54			19 53				20 53			21 53	23 00
Torquay	d				17 55		18 26				18 59			19 58				20 58			21 58	23 05
Torre	d				17 58						19 02			20 01		←		21 01			22 01	23 08
Newton Abbot	a		17 39	18 01	18 06	18 19	18 36		19 03		19 10	19 19		20 09	20 12	20 09	20 39	21 09	21 56		22 09	23 16
	d		17 40	18 03	18 07	18 21	18 37		19 05		19 11	19 21		20 16	20 14	20 16	20 41	21 11	21 57		22 10	23 18
Teignmouth	d				18 14						19 18			→		20 24		21 18	22 04		22 17	23 25
Dawlish	d				18 19						19 23		←			20 29		21 23	22 09		22 22	23 30
Dawlish Warren	d				18 24						19 35		19 35			20 34		21 28			22 27	23 35
Starcross	d				18 28						→					20 38					22 31	23 39
Exeter St Thomas	d				18 37											20 47					22 40	23 48
Exeter St Davids ■	a		18 01	18 20	18 39	18 42	18 56	19 08	19 23			19 40	19 48		20 34	20 52	21 00	21 39	22 22		22 42	23 52
Exeter Central	a				18 49								19 54			20 57		21 51			22 51	
Exmouth	a				19 18								20 24			21 25		22 21			23 20	
Exeter St Davids ■	d		18 01	18 23		18 44	18 58	19 13	19 25			19 42			20 35		21 02					
Tiverton Parkway	d		18 19	18 37			19 11		19 38			19 57			20 51		21 17					
Taunton	d		18 34	18 50		19 08	19 24	19 40	19 52			20 10			21 04		21 31					
Bridgwater	a																					
Weston-super-Mare	a																					
Bristol Temple Meads ■	a			19 23			19 57		20 25								22 00					
	d			19 30			20 00		20 30								22 10					
Bath Spa ■	a																22 21					
Filton Abbey Wood	a																					
Bristol Parkway ■	a			19 38			20 08		20 39													
Swindon	a																22 50					
Newport (South Wales)	a																					
Cardiff Central ■	a																					
Birmingham New Street ■	a			20 52			21 18		21 48													
Castle Cary 123	d											20 32			21 28							
Frome 123	d																					
Westbury 123	d					19 46						20 52			21 47							
Pewsey	d														22 02							
Hungerford	a																					
Newbury	a					20 19									22 22							
Thatcham	a																					
Theale	a																					
Reading ■	a		19 49			20 38		20 56				21 38			22 44		23 26					
Slough ■	a																					
London Paddington ■ ⊖	a		20 37			21 15		21 39				22 15			23 33		00 11					

A To Leeds. ✕ from Plymouth
B ✕ to Bristol Temple Meads
C To Leeds. ✕ to Bristol Temple Meads
D To Exmouth
E From Paignton

For connections to Oxford, Gatwick Airport and Heathrow Airport refer to Tables T116 and T148

For connections from Swansea refer to Table T128

Cornwall and Devon - Birmingham and London

		GW ■ A
Penzance	d	21 15
St Erth	d	21 25
Hayle	d	
Camborne	d	21 39
Redruth	d	21 46
Truro	d	22 01
St Austell	d	22 19
Newquay	d	
Par	d	
Lostwithiel	d	
Bodmin Parkway	d	22 35
Liskeard ■	d	22 50
Menheniot	d	
St Germans	d	
Saltash	d	
St Budeaux Ferry Road	d	
Keyham	d	
Dockyard	d	
Devonport	d	
Plymouth	a	23 13
	d	23 20
Ivybridge	d	
Totnes	d	23 48
Paignton	d	
Torquay	d	
Torre	d	
Newton Abbot	a	00 01
	d	00 01
Teignmouth	d	
Dawlish	d	
Dawlish Warren	d	
Starcross	d	
Exeter St Thomas	d	
Exeter St Davids ■	a	00 23
Exeter Central	a	
Exmouth	a	
Exeter St Davids ■	d	00 59
Tiverton Parkway	d	
Taunton	d	
Bridgwater	a	
Weston-super-Mare	a	
Bristol Temple Meads ■	a	
	d	
Bath Spa ■	a	
Filton Abbey Wood	a	
Bristol Parkway ■	a	
Swindon	a	
Newport (South Wales)	a	
Cardiff Central ■	a	
Birmingham New Street ■	a	
Castle Cary 123	d	
Frome 123	d	
Westbury 123	d	
Pewsey	d	
Hungerford	a	
Newbury	a	
Thatcham	a	
Theale	a	
Reading ■	a	04s06
Slough ■	a	
London Paddington ■ ⊖	a	05 02

A The Night Riviera

For connections to Oxford, Gatwick Airport and Heathrow Airport refer to Tables T116 and T148

For connections from Swansea refer to Table T128

T135 UPDATE: Major engineering work in connection with electrification works is taking place between Reading and Westbury. The route via Newbury will be closed to all trains on 4-7 June; 9-12 July; 16 July to 05 August; 28-30 August; 08-11 October and 19-22 November. Trains will be re-timed or cancelled and run to a special timetable during this period. Please check revised train times with *www.nationalrail.co.uk*. Rail replacement buses will operate between intermediate stations.

Exmouth - Exeter - Barnstaple

Miles	Miles			GW MO A	GW MO	GW MX	GW	SW ■ B	GW	GW C	SW ■ D	GW C		SW ■ E	GW	GW C	GW	GW ◇ F	SW ◇■ E	GW C	GW	SW ◇■ G		GW C	GW
0	—	**Exmouth**	d		00 01	00 04			06 14	06 43		07 12			07 51	08 22	08 52			09 23	09 53			10 23	10 53
2	—	Lympstone Village	d		00 05	00 08			06 18	06 47		07 16			07 55	08 26	08 56			09 27	09 57			10 27	10 57
3	—	Lympstone Commando	d		00x06	00x09			06x19	06x50		07x18			07x56	08x28	08x58			09x29				10x28	
3½	—	Exton	d		00x08	00x11			06x21	06x51		07x19			07x58	08x29	08x59			09x30				10x30	
5	—	Topsham	d		00 13	00 16			06 26	06 56		07 27			08 06	08 35	09 05			09 36	10 06			10 36	11 06
—	—	Newcourt	d		00 17	00 20			06 30	07 00		07 31			08 09	08 39	09 09			09 39	10 09			10 40	11 09
7	—	Digby & Sowton	d		00 19	00 23			06 33	07 03		07 34			08 13	08 43	09 12			09 42	10 12			10 43	11 12
9	—	Polsloe Bridge	d		00 23	00 26			06 36	07 06		07 38			08 17	08 47	09 16			09 46				10 46	
10	—	St James' Park	d		00 25	00 29			06 39	07 09		07 40			08 20	08 49	09 17	09 25		09 49				10 49	
10½	—	**Exeter Central**	a		00 28	00s31			06 41	07 11		07 42			08 23	08 52	09 20	09 27		09 51	10 18			10 51	11 18
—	—		d	00 01	00 29			06 32	06 42	07 12	07 39	07 43		08 18	08 25	08 53	09 21	09 28	09 41	09 53	10 20	10 39		10 52	11 19
11¼	—	**Exeter St Davids** ■	a	00 04	00 32	00 35		06 35	06 45	07 15	07 42	07 46		08 21	08 28	08 56	09 25	09 31	09 44	09 56	10 23	10 42		10 55	11 22
—	—		d				05 48		06 48						08 31		09 27				10 27				11 27
15½	—	Newton St Cyres	d																						
18¼	0	Crediton	d				06 01		06 59						08 42		09 38				10 38				11 38
21¾	3½	Yeoford	d				06x07		07x05						08x48		09x44				10x44				11x44
—	14¼	Sampford Courtenay	d																						
—	18	Okehampton	a																						
24½	—	Copplestone	d				06x12		07x10						08x53		09x49				10x49				11x49
26¼	—	Morchard Road	d						07x13						08x56		09x52				10x52				11x52
28¾	—	Lapford	d						07x17																
32½	—	Eggesford	d				06 27		07 33						09 11		10 08				11 08				12 08
36½	—	Kings Nympton	d						07x38						09x17										
39¼	—	Portsmouth Arms	d						07x43																
43½	—	Umberleigh	d				06x41		07x49						09x27		10x23				11x23				12x23
45¾	—	Chapelton	d						07x53																
50¼	—	**Barnstaple**	a				06 51		08 01						09 37		10 33				11 33				12 33

		SW ◇■ G	GW C	GW	SW ◇■ G	GW C	GW	SW ◇■ G		GW C	GW	SW ◇■ G	GW C	GW	SW ◇■ G	GW C	GW C	SW ◇■ G		GW C	GW	GW C	SW ◇■ H	SW ◇■ G	GW C
Exmouth	d		11 23	11 53		12 23	12 53			13 23	13 53		14 24	14 53		15 24	15 53				16 23	16 53			
Lympstone Village	d		11 27	11 57		12 27	12 57			13 27	13 57		14 28	14 57		15 28	15 57				16 27	16 57			
Lympstone Commando	d		11x28			12x28				13x28			14x30			15x29	15x58				16x28	16x58			
Exton	d		11x30			12x30				13x30			14x32			15x31	16x00				16x30	17x00			
Topsham	d		11 36	12 05		12 36	13 06			13 36	14 09		14 36	15 09		15 37	16 06				16 35	17 07			
Newcourt	d		11 39	12 09		12 39	13 09			13 39	14 12		14 40	15 13		15 40	16 10				16 40	17 11			
Digby & Sowton	d		11 41	12 12		12 42	13 11			13 42	14 15		14 43	15 16		15 43	16 12				16 43	17 14			
Polsloe Bridge	d		11 46			12 46				13 46			14 46			15 47	16 16				16 46	17 17			
St James' Park	d		11 48			12 48				13 48			14 49			15 49	16 19			16 43	16 49	17 20			
Exeter Central	a		11 51	12 19		12 51	13 18			13 51	14 21		14 51	15 22		15 52	16 21			16 45	16 51	17 22			
	d	11 39	11 52	12 20	12 39	12 52	13 19	13 39		13 52	14 22	14 39	14 52	15 23	15 41	15 53	16 22	16 37		16 46	16 52	17 23	17 30	17 39	17 46
Exeter St Davids ■	a	11 43	11 55	12 23	12 43	12 55	13 22	13 43		13 55	14 26	14 43	14 55	15 26	15 44	15 56	16 25	16 43		16 49	16 55	17 26	17 33	17 42	17 49
	d			12 27			13 27				14 27			15 28							16 57				
Newton St Cyres	d																								
Crediton	d			12 38			13 38				14 38			15 39							17 08				
Yeoford	d			12x44			13x44				14x44			15x45							17x15				
Sampford Courtenay	d																								
Okehampton	a																								
Copplestone	d			12x49			13x49				14x49			15x50							17x19				
Morchard Road	d			12x52			13x52				14x52			15x53							17x22				
Lapford	d																				17x27				
Eggesford	d			13 08			14 08				15 08			16 08							17 42				
Kings Nympton	d						14x15														17x49				
Portsmouth Arms	d																								
Umberleigh	d			13x23			14x23				15x23			16x23							17x59				
Chapelton	d																								
Barnstaple	a			13 37			14 35				15 33			16 33							18 09				

		GW	GW C	SW ◇■ G		GW	GW	GW C	SW ◇■ G	GW	SW ◇■ G	GW	GW	GW C		GW	SW ◇■ G	GW	GW C	SW ◇■ G	GW FO	GW	SW ◇■ G		
Exmouth	d	17 25	18 01			18 32		18 59		19 39		20 15				21 11			22 07			23 07			
Lympstone Village	d	17 29	18 05			18 36		19 03		19 45		20 19				21 15			22 11			23 11			
Lympstone Commando	d	17x30	18x07					19x04				20x20				21x16			22x12			23x12			
Exton	d	17x32	18x09					19x06				20x22				21x18			22x14			23x14			
Topsham	d	17 36	18 14			18 42		19 11		19 54		20 27				21 23			22 19			23 19			
Newcourt	d	17 40	18 18			18 46		19 15		19 57		20 31				21 27			22 23			23 23			
Digby & Sowton	d	17 44	18 21			18 49		19 18		20 00		20 34				21 30			22 26			23 26			
Polsloe Bridge	d	17 46	18 24					19 21				20 37				21 33			22 29			23 29			
St James' Park	d	17 50	18 27					19 24				20 42				21 36			22 32			23 32			
Exeter Central	a	17 51	18 29			18 55		19 26		20 06		20 44				21 38			22 34			23 35			
	d	17 52	18 30	18 39		18 56	19 03	19 27	19 42	20 07	20 39	20 45	20 53	21 21		21 38	21 44	21 55	22 35	22 44	22 49	23 36	23 57		
Exeter St Davids ■	a	17 56	18 33	18 43		18 58	19 07	19 30	19 46	20 10	20 43	20 48	20 56	21 25		21 42	21 47	21 58	22 38	22 47	22 52	23 40	00 01		
	d	17 58				19 00							21 00								22 53				
Newton St Cyres	d	18x05				19x07							21x07												
Crediton	d	18 12				19 14							21 14								23 05				
Yeoford	d	18x18				19x20							21x20								23x11				
Sampford Courtenay	d																								
Okehampton	a																								
Copplestone	d	18x23				19x26							21x26								23x16				
Morchard Road	d	18x26				19x29							21x29								23x19				
Lapford	d	18x30											21x33								23x23				
Eggesford	d	18 42				19 43							21 43								23 33				
Kings Nympton	d	18x49											21x48								23x39				
Portsmouth Arms	d	18x53																							
Umberleigh	d	19x00				19x57							21x58								23x49				
Chapelton	d	19x04																							
Barnstaple	a	19 12				20 07							22 09								23 59				

A From Exmouth
B From Axminster
C To Paignton
D From Gillingham (Dorset)
E From Salisbury
F To Cardiff Central
G From London Waterloo
H From Honiton

For connections at Exeter St Davids refer to Table T135

Table T136-F

Exmouth - Exeter - Barnstaple

Saturdays

26 May to 8 December

Station		GW	GW	SW ■ A	GW	SW ■ B	GW C	SW ■ D	GW	GW C	GW	SW ◇■ D	GW C	GW	GW E	GW F	SW ◇■ G	GW C	GW	SW ◇■ G	GW C	GW	SW ◇■ G
Exmouth	d	00 04			06 14		07 18		07 51	08 23	08 52		09 23	09 53				10 25	10 54		11 23	11 53	
Lympstone Village	d	00 08			06 18		07 22		07 55	08 27	08 56		09 27	09 57				10 29	10 58		11 27	11 57	
Lympstone Commando	d	00x09			06x19		07x23		07x56	08x29	08x58		09x29	09x58				10x30	10x59		11x28	11x58	
Exton	d	00x11			06x21		07x25		07x58	08x30	08x59		09x30					10x32			11x30		
Topsham	d	00 16			06 26		07 31		08 06	08 36	09 05		09 36	10 08				10 37	11 08		11 36	12 06	
Newcourt	d	00 20			06 30		07 34		08 09	08 40	09 09		09 39	10 11				10 41	11 11		11 39	12 09	
Digby & Sowton	d	00 23			06 33		07 37		08 13	08 43	09 12		09 42	10 14				10 44	11 14		11 42	12 12	
Polsloe Bridge	d	00 26			06 36		07 41		08 17	08 47	09 16		09 46					10 47			11 46		
St James' Park	d	00 29			06 39		07 44		08 20	08 49	09 17		09 49					10 50			11 48		
Exeter Central	a	00s31			06 41		07 46		08 23	08 52	09 20		09 51	10 21				10 53	11 20		11 51	12 19	
	d			06 32	06 42	07 39	07 47	08 19	08 26	08 53	09 21	09 41	09 52	10 21	10 30	10 33	10 39	10 53	11 21	11 39	11 52	12 20	12 39
Exeter St Davids ■	a	00 35		06 35	06 45	07 42	07 50	08 22	08 29	08 56	09 25	09 44	09 55	10 25	10 33	10 36	10 42	10 57	11 24	11 42	11 55	12 23	12 42
	d		05 54		06 54				08 31		09 27			10 27					11 27			12 27	
Newton St Cyres	d																						
Crediton	d		06 05		07 05				08 42		09 38			10 38					11 38			12 38	
Yeoford	d		06x11		07x11				08x48		09x44			10x44					11x44			12x44	
Sampford Courtenay	d																						
Okehampton	a																						
Copplestone	d		06x16		07x16				08x53		09x49			10x50					11x49			12x49	
Morchard Road	d				07x19				08x56		09x52			10x53					11x52			12x52	
Lapford	d				07x23																		
Eggesford	d		06 31		07 36				09 11		10 08			11 10					12 08			13 10	
Kings Nympton	d				07x41				09x17														
Portsmouth Arms	d				07x46																		
Umberleigh	d		06x45		07x52				09x27		10x23			11x25					12x23			13x25	
Chapelton	d				07x56																		
Barnstaple	a		06 59		08 06				09 39		10 35			11 37					12 35			13 37	

Station		GW C	GW	SW ◇■ G	GW F	GW E	GW H	GW	SW ◇■ G	GW C	GW	SW ◇■ G	GW C	GW	SW ◇■ G	GW C	GW	GW	GW C	SW ◇■ G	GW	GW C	SW ◇■ I
Exmouth	d	12 23	12 53		13 23	13 23		13 55		14 25	14 55		15 24	15 53			16 23		16 53		17 24	17 53	
Lympstone Village	d	12 27	12 57		13 27	13 27		13 59		14 29	14 59		15 28	15 57			16 27		16 57		17 28	17 57	
Lympstone Commando	d	12x28	12x58		13x28	13x28		14x00		14x30	15x00		15x29	15x58			16x28		16x58		17x29	17x58	
Exton	d	12x30			13x30	13x30				14x32			15x31	16x00			16x30		17x00		17x31	18x00	
Topsham	d	12 36	13 06		13 36	13 36		14 09		14 37	15 07		15 37	16 06			16 36		17 06		17 36	18 05	
Newcourt	d	12 39	13 09		13 39	13 39		14 12		14 41	15 11		15 40	16 09			16 39		17 10		17 39	18 09	
Digby & Sowton	d	12 42	13 12		13 42	13 42		14 15		14 44	15 14		15 43	16 12			16 42		17 13		17 42	18 12	
Polsloe Bridge	d	12 46			13 46	13 46				14 47			15 47	16 16			16 45		17 16		17 46	18 15	
St James' Park	d	12 48			13 48	13 48		14 22		14 50			15 49	16 19			16 49	17 04	17 20		17 49	18 18	
Exeter Central	a	12 52	13 19		13 51	13 51		14 24		14 52	15 20		15 52	16 21			16 51	17 06	17 23		17 52	18 20	
	d	12 52	13 20	13 39	13 52	13 55	14 08	14 25	14 39	14 53	15 21	15 39	15 53	16 22	16 39	16 48	16 53	17 07	17 24	17 39	17 52	18 21	18 38
Exeter St Davids ■	a	12 56	13 23	13 42	13 55	13 58	14 12	14 28	14 42	14 56	15 25	15 42	15 56	16 26	16 42	16 51	16 56	17 10	17 27	17 42	17 56	18 24	18 42
	d		13 30					14 30			15 27						16 57				17 57		
Newton St Cyres	d																				18x04		
Crediton	d		13 40					14 41			15 38						17 09				18 11		
Yeoford	d		13x46					14x47			15x44						17x15				18x17		
Sampford Courtenay	d																						
Okehampton	a																						
Copplestone	d		13x51					14x52			15x50						17x21				18x23		
Morchard Road	d		13x54					14x55			15x53						17x24				18x26		
Lapford	d																17x27				18x30		
Eggesford	d		14 08					15 08			16 08						17 40				18 41		
Kings Nympton	d		14x13														17x46				18x48		
Portsmouth Arms	d																				18x52		
Umberleigh	d		14x23					15x23			16x23						17x55				18x59		
Chapelton	d																				19x03		
Barnstaple	a		14 37					15 35			16 35						18 08				19 13		

Station		SW ◇■ J	GW K	GW H	GW	SW ◇■ G	GW C	GW	SW ◇■ G	GW	SW ◇■ G	GW C	SW ◇■ G	GW	GW	GW
Exmouth	d		18 23	18 23	18 54		19 41	20 07				21 16		22 19	23 17	23 45
Lympstone Village	d		18 27	18 27	18 58		19 45	20 11				21 20		22 23	23 21	23 49
Lympstone Commando	d				18x59			20x13				21x21		22x24	23x22	23x50
Exton	d				19x01			20x14				21x23		22x26	23x24	23x52
Topsham	d		18 34	18 34	19 08		19 51	20 19				21 28		22 31	23 29	23 58
Newcourt	d		18 37	18 37	19 11		19 54	20 23				21 32		22 35	23 33	00 01
Digby & Sowton	d		18 40	18 40	19 14		19 57	20 26				21 35		22 38	23 36	00 04
Polsloe Bridge	d				19 18			20 29				21 38		22 41	23 39	00 07
St James' Park	d				19 20			20 32				21 41		22 44	23 42	00 09
Exeter Central	a		18 46	18 47	19 23		20 04	20 34				21 43		22 47	23 45	00 12
	d	18 43	18 47	18 49	19 24	19 39	20 04	20 35	20 42	20 52	21 39	21 44	22 42	22 48	23 46	00 13
Exeter St Davids ■	a	18 47	18 50	18 52	19 27	19 42	20 07	20 39	20 45	20 55	21 42	21 47	22 45	22 51	23 50	00 18
	d		18 52	18 53						21 00						
Newton St Cyres	d		18x59	19x00						21x07						
Crediton	d		19 08	19 09						21 14						
Yeoford	d		19x14	19x15						21x20						
Sampford Courtenay	d															
Okehampton	a															
Copplestone	d		19x19	19x21						21x26						
Morchard Road	d		19x22	19x24						21x29						
Lapford	d									21x33						
Eggesford	d		19 43	19 43						21 43						
Kings Nympton	d									21x48						
Portsmouth Arms	d															
Umberleigh	d		19x57	19x57						21x58						
Chapelton	d															
Barnstaple	a		20 09	20 09						22 11						

A From Axminster
B From Yeovil Junction
C To Paignton
D From Salisbury
E until 8 September. To Paignton
F from 15 September. To Paignton
G From London Waterloo
H until 8 September
I from 15 September. From London Waterloo
J until 8 September. From London Waterloo
K from 15 September

For connections at Exeter St Davids refer to Table T135

Table T136-F

Exmouth - Exeter - Barnstaple

Sundays

20 May to 2 December

Station		GW A	GW	SW ■ B	GW C	GW D	GW	SW ◇■ E	GW D	GW C	GW	SW ◇■ F	GW D	GW	GW	SW ◇■ F	GW D	GW D	SW ◇■ F	GW D	GW	GW	GW C
Exmouth	d					09 10			10 19		10 54		11 24		12 00		12 28	12 55		13 24		13 58	
Lympstone Village	d					09 14			10 23		10 58		11 28		12 04		12 32	12 59		13 28		14 02	
Lympstone Commando	d					09x15			10x24				11x29				12x33			13x29			
Exton	d					09x17			10x26				11x31				12x35			13x31			
Topsham	d					09 22			10 31		11 04		11 36		12 11		12 40	13 07		13 36		14 08	
Newcourt	d	00 01				09 26			10 35		11 08		11 40		12 14		12 44	13 10		13 40		14 12	
Digby & Sowton	d	00 04				09 29			10 38		11 11		11 43		12 17		12 47	13 13		13 43		14 15	
Polsloe Bridge	d	00 07				09 32			10 41				11 46				12 50			13 46			
St James' Park	d	00 09			09 01	09 35			10 44	11 00			11 49				12 53			13 49			14 27
Exeter Central	a	00 12			09 03	09 38			10 46	11 02	11 17		11 51		12 23		12 55	13 19		13 51		14 21	14 29
	d	00 13		08 56	09 04	09 38		10 42	10 48	11 03		11 42	11 52	11 59		12 42	12 56	13 20	13 42	13 52	14 04	14 22	14 30
Exeter St Davids ■	a	00 18		08 59	09 07	09 42		10 45	10 51	11 06		11 45	11 55	12 02		12 45	12 59	13 23	13 45	13 55	14 07	14 25	14 33
	d		08 39		09 08		09 49			11 08				12 05							14 08		14 35
Newton St Cyres	d		08x47											12x13									14x43
Crediton	d		08 53		09 18		10 00			11 19				12 19							14 20		14 49
Yeoford	d		09x00				10x07							12x26							14x27		
Sampford Courtenay	d				09 44					11 43													15 13
Okehampton	a				09 52					11 51													15 20
Copplestone	d		09x05				10x12							12x32							14x33		
Morchard Road	d		09 08				10x15							12x35									
Lapford	d		09x12											12x39									
Eggesford	d		09 21				10 29							12 48							14 46		
Kings Nympton	d		09x27											12x54									
Portsmouth Arms	d		09x32											12x59									
Umberleigh	d		09x38				10x44							13x05							15x01		
Chapelton	d		09x42											13x09									
Barnstaple	a		09 50				10 54							13 16							15 11		

Station		SW ◇■ F	GW D	GW D	SW ◇■ F	GW D	GW	GW	GW C	SW ◇■ F	GW D	GW	SW ◇■ F	GW D	GW	GW	SW ◇■ F	GW D	SW ◇■ F	GW D	GW	SW ◇■ F	GW D
Exmouth	d		14 27			15 23		15 55			16 23	16 55		17 23		17 55		18 23		19 23			20 28
Lympstone Village	d		14 31			15 27		15 59			16 27	16 59		17 27		17 59		18 27		19 27			20 32
Lympstone Commando	d		14x32			15x28					16x28			17x28				18x28		19x28			20x33
Exton	d		14x34			15x30					16x30			17x30				18x30		19x30			20x35
Topsham	d		14 39			15 35		16 05			16 35	17 06		17 35		18 06		18 34		19 35			20 40
Newcourt	d		14 43			15 39		16 09			16 39	17 10		17 39		18 10		18 39		19 39			20 44
Digby & Sowton	d		14 46			15 42		16 12			16 42	17 13		17 42		18 13		18 41		19 42			20 47
Polsloe Bridge	d		14 49			15 45					16 45	17 16		17 45		18 16		18 44		19 45			20 50
St James' Park	d		14 52			15 48			16 29		16 48			17 48				18 47		19 48			20 53
Exeter Central	a		14 55			15 50		16 18	16 31		16 50	17 20		17 50		18 20		18 49		19 50			20 55
	d	14 42	14 56	15 20	15 41	15 51	15 59		16 32	16 42	16 51	17 21	17 42	17 51	18 03	18 21	18 42	18 50	19 42	19 51	19 56	20 42	20 56
Exeter St Davids ■	a	14 45	15 00	15 23	15 44	15 54	16 02		16 35	16 45	16 54	17 24	17 45	17 54	18 06	18 24	18 45	18 54	19 45	19 54	19 59	20 45	20 59
	d						16 05		16 37						18 07						20 01		
Newton St Cyres	d						16x13														20x08		
Crediton	d						16 19		16 47						18 18						20 18		
Yeoford	d						16x26								18x25						20x24		
Sampford Courtenay	d								17 11														
Okehampton	a								17 19														
Copplestone	d						16x31								18x30						20x30		
Morchard Road	d						16x34														20x33		
Lapford	d						16x38														20x37		
Eggesford	d						16 45								18 44						20 47		
Kings Nympton	d						16x53														20x52		
Portsmouth Arms	d						16x56														20x57		
Umberleigh	d						17x04								18x58						21x03		
Chapelton	d						17x08														21x07		
Barnstaple	a						17 17								19 09						21 15		

Station		SW ◇■ F	GW D	SW ◇■ F	GW	GW
Exmouth	d		21 30		22 27	23 29
Lympstone Village	d		21 34		22 31	23 34
Lympstone Commando	d		21x35		22x32	23x35
Exton	d		21x37		22x34	23x37
Topsham	d		21 42		22 39	23 45
Newcourt	d		21 46		22 44	23 48
Digby & Sowton	d		21 49		22 46	23 51
Polsloe Bridge	d		21 52		22 49	23 55
St James' Park	d		21 55		22 53	23 57
Exeter Central	a		21 57		22 55	23 59
	d	21 43	21 57	22 45	22 56	00 01
Exeter St Davids ■	a	21 46	22 00	22 48	22 59	00 04
	d					
Newton St Cyres	d					
Crediton	d					
Yeoford	d					
Sampford Courtenay	d					
Okehampton	a					
Copplestone	d					
Morchard Road	d					
Lapford	d					
Eggesford	d					
Kings Nympton	d					
Portsmouth Arms	d					
Umberleigh	d					
Chapelton	d					
Barnstaple	a					

A not 20 May. From Exmouth
B From Salisbury
C until 9 September
D To Paignton
E From Basingstoke
F From London Waterloo

For connections at Exeter St Davids refer to Table T135

Barnstaple - Exeter - Exmouth

Mondays to Fridays
21 May to 7 December

Miles	Miles		SW ◇■ A	GW	GW	GW	SW ◇■ A	GW B	SW ◇■ A	GW B	GW	GW B	SW ◇■ A	GW	GW	GW B	SW ◇■ A	GW	GW B	SW ◇■ A	GW	GW B
0	—	**Barnstaple** d									06 58							08 43			09 43	
4¼	—	Chapelton d									07x03											
6¾	—	Umberleigh d									07x07							08x51			09x51	
10¾	—	Portsmouth Arms d									07x14											
13¾	—	Kings Nympton d									07x19							09x03				
17½	—	Eggesford d									07 28							09 10			10 07	
21½	—	Lapford d									07x33							09x16				
23¾	—	Morchard Road d									07x38							09x20			10x16	
25½	—	Copplestone d									07x41							09x24			10x20	
—	0	Okehampton d																				
—	3¾	Sampford Courtenay d																				
28½	14½	Yeoford d									07x46							09x28			10x24	
32	18	Crediton d									07 53							09 37			10 37	
34¾	—	Newton St Cyres d									07x56											
39	—	**Exeter St Davids** ■ a									08 05							09 47			10 47	
—	—	d	05 10	05 44	06 06	06 29	06 41	07 07	07 25	07 36	08 07	08 15	08 23	08 45	08 59	09 16	09 25	09 49	10 16	10 25	10 49	11 16
39¾	—	**Exeter Central** a	05 13	05 47	06 09	06 32	06 44	07 10	07 28	07 39	08 10	08 18	08 26	08 48	09 02	09 19	09 28	09 52	10 19	10 28	10 52	11 19
—	—	d		05 48	06 10	06 37		07 11		07 48		08 19		08 49	09 03	09 20		09 53	10 20		10 53	11 20
40¼	—	St James' Park d			06 12	06 39		07 13		07 50		08 21		08 51	09a05	09 22			10 22			11 22
41¼	—	Polsloe Bridge d			06 15	06 42		07 16		07 53		08 24		08 54		09 25			10 25			11 25
43¼	—	Digby & Sowton d		05 54	06 19	06 46		07 20		07 57		08 28		08 58		09 29		09 59	10 29		10 59	11 29
—	—	Newcourt d		05 57	06 22	06 49		07 23		08 00		08 31		09 01		09 32		10 02	10 32		11 02	11 32
45¼	—	Topsham d		06 01	06 26	06 55		07 28		08 03		08 34		09 04		09 35		10 05	10 35		11 05	11 35
46¾	—	Exton d			06x28	06x58		07x30		08x06		08x37		09x07		09x38			10x38			11x38
47¼	—	Lympstone Commando d			06x30	07x00		07x32		08x08		08x39		09x09		09x40			10x40			11x40
48¼	—	Lympstone Village d		06 06	06 33	07 02		07 34		08 11		08 43		09 12		09 43		10 11	10 43		11 11	11 43
50¼	—	**Exmouth** a		06 10	06 38	07 08		07 41		08 16		08 47		09 17		09 48		10 15	10 48		11 15	11 48

	SW ◇■ A	GW	GW B	SW ◇■ A	GW	GW B	SW ◇■ A	GW	GW B	SW ◇■ A	GW	GW B	SW ◇■ A	GW	GW	GW B	SW ◇■ A	SW ◇■ C	GW	GW B	SW ◇■ A	SW ■ D
Barnstaple d		10 43			11 43			12 43			13 43			14 43					15 43			
Chapelton d																						
Umberleigh d		10x51			11x51			12x51			13x51			14x51					15x51			
Portsmouth Arms d																						
Kings Nympton d								13x02														
Eggesford d		11 07			12 07			13 07			14 07			15 07					16 07			
Lapford d																						
Morchard Road d		11x16			12x16			13x16			14x16			15x16					16x16			
Copplestone d		11x20			12x20			13x20			14x20			15x20					16x20			
Okehampton d																						
Sampford Courtenay d																						
Yeoford d		11x24			12x24			13x24			14x24			15x24					16x24			
Crediton d		11 37			12 37			13 37			14 37			15 37					16 34			
Newton St Cyres d																						
Exeter St Davids ■ a		11 48			12 47			13 48			14 48			15 48					16 45			
d	11 25	11 49	12 16	12 25	12 49	13 16	13 25	13 52	14 16	14 25	14 52	15 16	15 25	15 49	16 08	16 15	16 24	16 36	16 47	17 15	17 25	17 46
Exeter Central a	11 28	11 52	12 19	12 28	12 52	13 19	13 28	13 55	14 19	14 28	14 55	15 19	15 28	15 52	16 11	16 18	16 27	16 39	16 50	17 18	17 28	17 49
d		11 53	12 20		12 53	13 20		13 56	14 20		14 56	15 20		15 53	16 12	16 19			16 51	17 19		
St James' Park d			12 22			13 22			14 22			15 22			16a14	16 21			16 53	17 21		
Polsloe Bridge d			12 25			13 25			14 25			15 25				16 24			16 56	17 25		
Digby & Sowton d		11 59	12 29		12 59	13 29		14 02	14 29		15 02	15 29		15 59		16 28			17 00	17 29		
Newcourt d		12 02	12 32		13 02	13 32		14 05	14 32		15 05	15 32		16 02		16 31			17 03	17 32		
Topsham d		12 05	12 35		13 05	13 35		14 08	14 35		15 08	15 35		16 05		16 34			17 07	17 37		
Exton d			12x38			13x38			14x38			15x38				16x37			17x10	17x39		
Lympstone Commando d			12x40			13x40			14x40			15x40				16x39			17x12	17x41		
Lympstone Village d		12 11	12 43		13 11	13 43		14 14	14 43		15 14	15 43		16 11		16 42			17 15	17 44		
Exmouth a		12 16	12 48		13 15	13 48		14 19	14 48		15 19	15 48		16 16		16 49			17 20	17 51		

	GW B	GW B	SW ◇■ A	GW	GW B	SW ◇■ A	GW	GW	SW ◇ E	GW B	GW	SW ■ F	GW B	GW	GW	SW ■ F	GW
Barnstaple d				17 13			18 14	19 17						20 24			22 16
Chapelton d				17x19													
Umberleigh d				17x23			18x22	19x25						20x32			22x24
Portsmouth Arms d							18x29										
Kings Nympton d				17x34			18x34										
Eggesford d				17 42			18 41	19 41						20 49			22 40
Lapford d				17x48			18x48										
Morchard Road d				17x51			18x52	19x50						20x58			22x48
Copplestone d				17x55			18x56	19x54						21x01			22x52
Okehampton d																	
Sampford Courtenay d																	
Yeoford d				17x59			19x00	19x58						21x05			22x56
Crediton d				18 15			19 18	20 09						21 21			23 05
Newton St Cyres d				18x18			19x23							21x24			23x08
Exeter St Davids ■ a				18 29			19 31	20 19						21 33			23 16
d	17 53	18 21	18 25	18 33	18 50	19 25	19 33	20 20	20 25	20 34	21 14	21 25	21 31	21 37	22 31	22 57	23 26
Exeter Central a	17 56	18 24	18 28	18 36	18 53	19 28	19 36	20 23	20 29	20 37	21 17	21 28	21 34	21 40	22 34	23 00	23 29
d	17 57	18 25			18 54		19 37			20 38			21 34		22 35		23 30
St James' Park d	17 59	18 27			18 56		19 39			20 40			21 36		22 37		23 32
Polsloe Bridge d	18 02	18 30			19 00		19 43			20 43			21 39		22 40		23 35
Digby & Sowton d	18 06	18 34			19 04		19 47			20 47			21 43		22 44		23 39
Newcourt d	18 09	18 37			19 07		19 50			20 50			21 46		22 47		23 42
Topsham d	18 13	18 41			19 11		19 54			20 54			21 50		22 51		23 46
Exton d	18x16	18x44			19x13		19x57			20x56			21x52		22x53		23x48
Lympstone Commando d	18x18	18x46			19x15		19x59			20x58			21x54		22x55		23x50
Lympstone Village d	18 21	18 49			19 18		20 01			21 00			21 58		22 58		23 52
Exmouth a	18 27	18 54			19 24		20 06			21 06			22 03		23 03		23 59

A To London Waterloo
B From Paignton
C To Honiton
D To Axminster
E To Basingstoke
F To Salisbury

For connections at Exeter St Davids refer to Table T135

Barnstaple - Exeter - Exmouth

Saturdays
26 May to 8 December

	GW	SW ◇■ A	GW	GW	SW ◇■ A	GW B	SW ◇■ A	GW B	GW	SW ◇■ A	GW	GW B	SW ◇■ A	GW	GW B	SW ◇■ A	GW	GW B	SW ◇■ A	GW B	GW	GW B
Barnstaple d	00 05								07 05					08 43			09 43				10 45	
Chapelton d									07x10													
Umberleigh d									07x14					08x51			09x51				10x53	
Portsmouth Arms d									07x21													
Kings Nympton d									07x26					09x02								
Eggesford d	00s27								07 35					09 11			10 08				11 10	
Lapford d									07x40					09x16								
Morchard Road d									07x45					09x20			10x16				11x18	
Copplestone d									07x48					09x24			10x20				11x22	
Okehampton d																						
Sampford Courtenay d																						
Yeoford d									07x54					09x28			10x24				11x26	
Crediton d	00s47								08 01					09 37			10 38				11 42	
Newton St Cyres d									08x04													
Exeter St Davids ■ a	01 00								08 13					09 47			10 49				11 54	
d		05 10	05 44	06 29	06 41	07 10	07 25	07 44	08 16	08 24	08 45	09 16	09 25	09 48	10 18	10 25	10 51	11 16	11 25	11 49	11 57	12 17
Exeter Central a		05 13	05 47	06 32	06 44	07 13	07 28	07 47	08 19	08 27	08 48	09 19	09 28	09 51	10 21	10 28	10 54	11 19	11 28	11 52	12 02	12 20
d			05 48	06 37		07 14		07 48	08 20		08 49	09 20		09 52	10 22		10 55	11 20		11 53		12 21
St James' Park d				06 39		07 16		07 50	08 22		08 51	09 22		09 54	10 24			11 22				12 23
Polsloe Bridge d				06 42		07 19		07 53	08 25		08 54	09 25		09 57	10 27			11 25				12 26
Digby & Sowton d			05 54	06 46		07 23		07 57	08 29		08 58	09 29		10 01	10 31		11 01	11 29		11 59		12 30
Newcourt d			05 57	06 49		07 26		08 00	08 32		09 01	09 32		10 04	10 34		11 04	11 32		12 02		12 33
Topsham d			06 01	06 53		07 31		08 03	08 35		09 04	09 35		10 08	10 38		11 08	11 36		12 06		12 36
Exton d				06x55		07x33		08x06	08x38		09x07	09x38		10x10	10x40			11x38				12x39
Lympstone Commando d				06x57		07x35		08x08	08x40		09x09	09x40		10x12	10x42		11x10	11x40		12x09		12x41
Lympstone Village d			06 06	06 59		07 38		08 11	08 44		09 12	09 43		10 15	10 44		11 14	11 43		12 12		12 43
Exmouth a			06 12	07 06		07 44		08 16	08 50		09 19	09 50		10 21	10 52		11 21	11 50		12 20		12 51

	SW ◇■ A	GW	GW B	SW ◇■ A	GW	GW C	GW B	SW ◇■ A	GW	GW B	SW ◇■ A	GW	GW B	SW ◇■ A	GW B	GW	GW B	SW ◇■ A	GW	GW B	SW ◇■ A	GW
Barnstaple d		11 43			12 43				13 43			14 43				15 43						17 10
Chapelton d																						17x15
Umberleigh d		11x51			12x51				13x51			14x51				15x51						17x19
Portsmouth Arms d																						
Kings Nympton d					13x02																	17x30
Eggesford d		12 08			13 11				14 08			15 08				16 08						17 40
Lapford d																						17x45
Morchard Road d		12x16			13x19				14x16			15x16				16x16						17x49
Copplestone d		12x20			13x22				14x20			15x20				16x20						17x53
Okehampton d																						
Sampford Courtenay d																						
Yeoford d		12x24			13x27				14x24			15x24				16x24						17x57
Crediton d		12 37			13 40				14 40			15 37				16 34						18 14
Newton St Cyres d																						18x17
Exeter St Davids ■ a		12 48			13 50				14 50			15 47				16 45						18 28
d	12 25	12 49	13 16	13 25	13 51	14 00	14 16	14 25	14 51	15 16	15 25	15 49	16 16	16 25	16 37	16 47	17 16	17 25	17 45	18 14	18 25	18 32
Exeter Central a	12 28	12 52	13 19	13 28	13 54	14 05	14 19	14 28	14 54	15 19	15 28	15 52	16 19	16 28	16 40	16 50	17 19	17 28	17 48	18 17	18 28	18 36
d		12 53	13 20		13 55		14 20		14 55	15 20		15 53	16 20			16 51	17 20		17 49	18 18		
St James' Park d			13 22		13 57		14 23			15 22		15 55	16 22			16 53	17 22		17 51	18 20		
Polsloe Bridge d			13 25				14 26			15 25			16 25			16 56	17 25		17 54	18 23		
Digby & Sowton d		12 59	13 29		14 03		14 30		15 01	15 29		15 59	16 29			17 00	17 29		17 58	18 27		
Newcourt d		13 02	13 32		14 06		14 33		15 04	15 32		16 02	16 32			17 03	17 32		18 01	18 30		
Topsham d		13 06	13 35		14 09		14 37		15 08	15 35		16 07	16 35			17 07	17 36		18 06	18 33		
Exton d			13x38				14x39			15x38			16x38			17x09	17x38		18x08	18x36		
Lympstone Commando d		13x09	13x40		14x12		14x41		15x11	15x40		16x09	16x40			17x11	17x40		18x10	18x38		
Lympstone Village d		13 12	13 43		14 15		14 44		15 14	15 43		16 13	16 43			17 14	17 43		18 12	18 40		
Exmouth a		13 20	13 50		14 22		14 50		15 21	15 50		16 20	16 50			17 21	17 50		18 20	18 48		

	GW C	GW D	GW E	SW ◇■ A	GW	GW	SW ◇■ F	GW B	SW ■ G	GW	GW	GW	SW ■ G	GW	GW
Barnstaple d			18 11			19 17				20 24					22 30
Chapelton d															
Umberleigh d			18x19			19x25				20x32					22x38
Portsmouth Arms d			18x26												
Kings Nympton d			18x31												
Eggesford d			18 40			19 42				20 49					22 55
Lapford d			18x45												
Morchard Road d			18x50			19x50				20x57					23x03
Copplestone d			18x53			19x54				21x01					23x07
Okehampton d															
Sampford Courtenay d															
Yeoford d			18x58			19x58				21x05					23x11
Crediton d			19 06			20 07				21 16					23 20
Newton St Cyres d						20x10				21x19					23x23
Exeter St Davids ■ a			19 16			20 19				21 29					23 31
d	18 45	18 48		19 25	19 32	20 20	20 25	20 33	21 25	21 32	21 40	22 40	22 57	23 09	
Exeter Central a	18 48	18 51		19 28	19 35	20 25	20 28	20 36	21 28	21 35	21 43	22 43	23 00	23 12	
d	18 52	18 52			19 36			20 38			21 44	22 44		23 13	
St James' Park d	18 54	18 54			19 38			20 40			21 46	22 46		23 15	
Polsloe Bridge d	18 57	18 57			19 41			20 43			21 49	22 49		23 18	
Digby & Sowton d	19 01	19 01			19 45			20 47			21 53	22 53		23 22	
Newcourt d	19 04	19 04			19 48			20 50			21 56	22 56		23 25	
Topsham d	19 08	19 08			19 52			20 54			22 00	23 00		23 29	
Exton d	19x10	19x10			19x54			20x56			22x02	23x02		23x31	
Lympstone Commando d	19x12	19x12			19x56			20x58			22x04	23x04		23x33	
Lympstone Village d	19 15	19 15			19 59			21 01			22 07	23 07		23 37	
Exmouth a	19 21	19 21			20 05			21 07			22 14	23 14		23 43	

A To London Waterloo
B From Paignton
C until 8 September. From Paignton
D from 15 September. From Paignton
E To Paignton
F To Basingstoke
G To Salisbury

For connections at Exeter St Davids refer to Table T135

Table T136-R

Sundays

20 May to 9 September

Barnstaple - Exeter - Exmouth

		GW	SW	GW	GW	SW	GW	GW	GW	GW		SW	GW	GW	SW	GW	GW	GW	GW	SW		GW	SW	GW	GW
			◇■			◇■						◇■			◇■					◇■			◇■		
			A			A		B				A	B		A		B			A		B	A		B
Barnstaple	d								09 58							11 29								13 22	
Chapelton	d								10x04															13x28	
Umberleigh	d								10x08							11x37								13x31	
Portsmouth Arms	d								10x15															13 39	
Kings Nympton	d								10x20															13x44	
Eggesford	d								10 28							11 54								13 52	
Lapford	d								10x33															13x58	
Morchard Road	d								10x38															14x02	
Copplestone	d								10x41							12x04								14x05	
Okehampton	d						09 55											12 12							
Sampford Courtenay	d						10 02											12 19							
Yeoford	d								10x46							12x09								14x11	
Crediton	d						10 25		10 53							12 18		12 42						14 18	
Newton St Cyres	d															12x21		12x46						14x22	
Exeter St Davids ■	a						10 35		11 04							12 32		12 58						14 31	
	d	08 30	09 25	09 40	10 13	10 25	10 36	10 44	11 07			11 25	11 51		12 25	12 32	12 47	12 59		13 25		13 49	14 25	14 32	14 46
Exeter Central	a	08 33	09 28	09 43	10 16	10 28	10 39	10 47	11 10			11 28	11 54		12 28	12 35	12 50	13 02		13 28		13 52	14 28	14 35	14 49
	d	08 34		09 44	10 17		10 39	10 48		11 22			11 55	12 26			12 51	13 02	13 22			13 53			14 50
St James' Park	d	08 36		09 46			10a41	10 50					11 57				12 53	13a04				13 55			14 52
Polsloe Bridge	d	08 39		09 49	10 20			10 53		11 25			12 00				12 56					13 58			14 55
Digby & Sowton	d	08 43		09 53	10 24			10 57		11 29			12 04	12 32			13 00		13 28			14 02			14 59
Newcourt	d	08 46		09 56	10 27			11 00		11 32			12 07	12 35			13 03		13 31			14 05			15 02
Topsham	d	08 50		10 00	10 32			11 04		11 37			12 11	12 41			13 07		13 36			14 09			15 06
Exton	d	08x52		10x02				11x06					12x13				13x09					14x11			15x08
Lympstone Commando	d	08x54		10x04				11x08					12x15				13x11					14x13			15x10
Lympstone Village	d	08 57		10 08	10 37			11 12		11 42			12 19	12 46			13 14		13 41			14 17			15 14
Exmouth	a	09 03		10 12	10 42			11 17		11 47			12 24	12 51			13 20		13 47			14 21			15 18

		GW	SW	GW	GW	GW		SW	GW	GW	GW	SW	GW	SW	GW	GW		GW	SW	GW	SW	GW	GW	SW	GW
			◇■					◇■				◇■		◇■					◇■		◇■			■	
		B	A	B				A		B	B	A	B	A				B	A	B	C		B	D	B
Barnstaple	d								15 28						17 21							19 26			
Chapelton	d														17x26										
Umberleigh	d								15x36						17x30							19x34			
Portsmouth Arms	d								15x44						17x37										
Kings Nympton	d														17x42										
Eggesford	d								15 55						17 51							19 51			
Lapford	d														17x56										
Morchard Road	d														18x01										
Copplestone	d								16x04						18x04							20x01			
Okehampton	d				15 23											17 59									
Sampford Courtenay	d				15 30											18 07									
Yeoford	d								16x10						18x10							20x06			
Crediton	d				15 54				16 18						18 18	18 30						20 15			
Newton St Cyres	d														18x22										
Exeter St Davids ■	a				16 08				16 29						18 31	18 41						20 26			
	d	15 18	15 25	15 46	16 10			16 25	16 32	16 46	17 16	17 25	17 46	18 25	18 32			18 46	19 25	19 51	20 25		20 54	21 25	21 48
Exeter Central	a	15 21	15 28	15 49	16 13			16 28	16 35	16 49	17 19	17 28	17 49	18 28	18 35			18 49	19 28	19 54	20 28		20 57	21 28	21 51
	d	15 22		15 50	16 14	16 22				16 50	17 20		17 49					18 50		19 55			20 58		21 51
St James' Park	d			15 52	16a16					16 52			17 51					18 52		19 57			21 00		21 53
Polsloe Bridge	d			15 55						16 55	17 23		17 54					18 55		20 00			21 03		21 56
Digby & Sowton	d	15 28		15 59		16 28				16 59	17 27		17 58					18 59		20 04			21 06		22 00
Newcourt	d	15 31		16 02		16 31				17 02	17 30		18 01					19 02		20 07			21 09		22 03
Topsham	d	15 36		16 06		16 36				17 06	17 36		18 06					19 06		20 11			21 13		22 08
Exton	d			16x08						17x08			18x08					19x08		20x13			21x15		22x10
Lympstone Commando	d			16x10						17x10			18x10					19x11		20x15			21x17		22x12
Lympstone Village	d	15 41		16 14		16 41				17 13	17 41		18 13					19 13		20 18			21 21		22 15
Exmouth	a	15 46		16 19		16 45				17 19	17 45		18 19					19 18		20 24			21 25		22 21

		GW		GW	SW	GW
					■	
				B	D	
Barnstaple	d	21 30				
Chapelton	d	21x36				
Umberleigh	d	21x39				
Portsmouth Arms	d	21x47				
Kings Nympton	d	21x52				
Eggesford	d	22 00				
Lapford	d	22x06				
Morchard Road	d	22x10				
Copplestone	d	22x13				
Okehampton	d					
Sampford Courtenay	d					
Yeoford	d	22x19				
Crediton	d	22 28				
Newton St Cyres	d	22x31				
Exeter St Davids ■	a	22 42				
	d			22 48	23 15	23 25
Exeter Central	a			22 51	23 18	23 28
	d			22 52		23 29
St James' Park	d			22 54		23 31
Polsloe Bridge	d			22 57		23 34
Digby & Sowton	d			23 01		23 38
Newcourt	d			23 04		23 41
Topsham	d			23 08		23 45
Exton	d			23x10		23x47
Lympstone Commando	d			23x13		23x49
Lympstone Village	d			23 16		23 52
Exmouth	a			23 20		23 57

A To London Waterloo
B From Paignton
C To Basingstoke
D To Salisbury

For connections at Exeter St Davids refer to Table T135

Table T136-R

Sundays

16 September to 2 December

Barnstaple - Exeter - Exmouth

		GW	SW	GW	GW	SW	GW	GW	GW	SW		GW	GW	SW	GW	GW	GW	SW	GW	SW		GW	GW	GW	SW
			◇■			◇■				◇■				◇■				◇■		◇■					◇■
			A			A	B			A		B		A		B		A	B	A			B	B	A
Barnstaple	d							09 58							11 29							13 22			
Chapelton	d							10x04														13x28			
Umberleigh	d							10x08							11x37							13x31			
Portsmouth Arms	d							10x15														13 39			
Kings Nympton	d							10x20														13x44			
Eggesford	d							10 28							11 54							13 52			
Lapford	d							10x33														13x58			
Morchard Road	d							10x38														14x02			
Copplestone	d							10x41							12x04							14x05			
Okehampton	d																								
Sampford Courtenay	d																								
Yeoford	d							10x46							12x09							14x11			
Crediton	d							10 53							12 18							14 18			
Newton St Cyres	d														12x21							14x22			
Exeter St Davids ■	a							11 04							12 32							14 31			
	d	08 30	09 25	09 40	10 13	10 25	10 44	11 07		11 25		11 51		12 25	12 32	12 47		13 25	13 49	14 25		14 32	14 46	15 18	15 25
Exeter Central	a	08 33	09 28	09 43	10 16	10 28	10 47	11 10		11 28		11 54		12 28	12 35	12 50		13 28	13 52	14 28		14 35	14 49	15 21	15 28
	d	08 34		09 44	10 17		10 48		11 22			11 55	12 26			12 51	13 22		13 53				14 50	15 22	
St James' Park	d	08 36		09 46			10 50					11 57				12 53			13 55				14 52		
Polsloe Bridge	d	08 39		09 49	10 20		10 53		11 25			12 00				12 56			13 58				14 55		
Digby & Sowton	d	08 43		09 53	10 24		10 57		11 29			12 04	12 32			13 00	13 28		14 02				14 59	15 28	
Newcourt	d	08 46		09 56	10 27		11 00		11 32			12 07	12 35			13 03	13 31		14 05				15 02	15 31	
Topsham	d	08 50		10 00	10 32		11 04		11 37			12 11	12 41			13 07	13 36		14 09				15 06	15 36	
Exton	d	08x52		10x02			11x06					12x13				13x09			14x11				15x08		
Lympstone Commando	d	08x54		10x04			11x08					12x15				13x11			14x13				15x10		
Lympstone Village	d	08 57		10 08	10 37		11 12		11 42			12 19	12 46			13 14	13 41		14 17				15 14	15 41	
Exmouth	a	09 03		10 12	10 42		11 17		11 47			12 24	12 51			13 20	13 47		14 21				15 18	15 46	

		GW	GW	SW	GW	GW		GW	SW	GW	SW	GW	GW	SW	GW	SW		GW	GW	SW	GW	GW	GW	SW	GW
				◇■					◇■		◇■			◇■		◇■				■				■	
		B		A		B		B	A	B	A		B	A	B	C			B	D	B		B	D	
Barnstaple	d				15 28							17 21						19 26				21 30			
Chapelton	d											17x26										21x36			
Umberleigh	d				15x36							17x30						19x34				21x39			
Portsmouth Arms	d				15x44							17x37										21x47			
Kings Nympton	d											17x42										21x52			
Eggesford	d				15 55							17 51						19 51				22 00			
Lapford	d											17x56										22x06			
Morchard Road	d											18x01										22x10			
Copplestone	d				16x04							18x04						20x01				22x13			
Okehampton	d																								
Sampford Courtenay	d																								
Yeoford	d				16x10							18x10						20x06				22x19			
Crediton	d				16 18							18 18						20 15				22 28			
Newton St Cyres	d											18x22										22x31			
Exeter St Davids ■	a				16 29							18 31						20 26				22 42			
	d	15 46		16 25	16 32	16 46		17 16	17 25	17 46	18 25	18 32	18 46	19 25	19 51	20 25			20 54	21 25	21 48		22 48	23 15	23 25
Exeter Central	a	15 49		16 28	16 35	16 49		17 19	17 28	17 49	18 28	18 35	18 49	19 28	19 54	20 28			20 57	21 28	21 51		22 51	23 18	23 28
	d	15 50	16 22			16 50		17 20		17 49			18 50		19 55				20 58		21 51		22 52		23 29
St James' Park	d	15 52				16 52				17 51			18 52		19 57				21 00		21 53		22 54		23 31
Polsloe Bridge	d	15 55				16 55		17 23		17 54			18 55		20 00				21 03		21 56		22 57		23 34
Digby & Sowton	d	15 59	16 28			16 59		17 27		17 58			18 59		20 04				21 06		22 00		23 01		23 38
Newcourt	d	16 02	16 31			17 02		17 30		18 01			19 02		20 07				21 09		22 03		23 04		23 41
Topsham	d	16 06	16 36			17 06		17 36		18 06			19 06		20 11				21 13		22 08		23 08		23 45
Exton	d	16x08				17x08				18x08			19x08		20x13				21x15		22x10		23x10		23x47
Lympstone Commando	d	16x10				17x10				18x10			19x11		20x15				21x17		22x12		23x13		23x49
Lympstone Village	d	16 14	16 41			17 13		17 41		18 13			19 13		20 18				21 21		22 15		23 16		23 52
Exmouth	a	16 19	16 45			17 19		17 45		18 19			19 18		20 24				21 25		22 21		23 20		23 57

A To London Waterloo
B From Paignton
C To Basingstoke
D To Salisbury

For connections at Exeter St Davids refer to Table T135

Table T139-F

Plymouth - Gunnislake

Mondays to Fridays

21 May to 29 June

Miles			GW	GW	GW ◇■ A ☕	GW ◇ B	GW	GW ◇ C	GW ◇ D	GW	GW E	GW	GW A	GW	GW F	GW G	GW H	GW
0	**Plymouth**	d	05 06	06 41	07 02	08 14	08 40	09 21	10 46	10 54	12 59	14 54	15 57	16 37	17 01	18 17	18 23	21 31
1¼	Devonport	d		06 44	07a06	08a17	08 43	09a24		10 57	13 02	14 57	16 00	16 40	17 04	18 20	18 26	21 34
1½	Dockyard	d		06x45			08x44			10x58	13x03	14x58	16x02	16x41	17x05	18x21	18x27	21x35
2¼	Keyham	d		06 47			08 46			11 00	13 05	15 00	16 04	16 43	17 07	18 23	18 29	21 37
—	St Budeaux Ferry Road	a							10 52				16 08		17 10	18 25		
3	St Budeaux Victoria Road	d	05 12	06 51			08 50			11 04	13 09	15 04		16 47			18 33	21 41
7¼	Bere Ferrers	d		06 58			08 57			11 11	13 16	15 11		16 54			18 40	21 48
10	Bere Alston	a	05 25	07 05			09 04			11 18	13 24	15 18		17 01			18 47	21 55
—		d	05 27	07 07			09 06			11 20	13 25	15 20		17 03			18 49	21 57
11¾	Calstock	d	05 34	07 14			09 13			11 27	13 32	15 27		17 10			18 56	22 04
14½	**Gunnislake**	a	05 48	07 27			09 26			11 40	13 46	15 40		17 23			19 09	22 17

Mondays to Fridays

2 July to 7 December

		GW	GW	GW ◇■ A ☕	GW ◇ I	GW ◇■ J	GW	GW ◇ C	GW ◇ D	GW	GW	GW	GW F	GW	GW F	GW G	GW H	GW
Plymouth	d	05 06	06 41	07 02	08§14	08§20	08 40	09 21	10 46	10 54	12 54	14 54	15 57	16 37	17 01	18 17	18 23	21 31
Devonport	d		06 44	07a06	08a17	08a24	08 43	09a24		10 57	12 57	14 57	16 00	16 40	17 04	18 20	18 26	21 34
Dockyard	d		06x45				08x44			10x58	12x58	14x58	16x02	16x41	17x05	18x21	18x27	21x35
Keyham	d		06 47				08 46			11 00	13 00	15 00	16 04	16 43	17 07	18 23	18 29	21 37
St Budeaux Ferry Road	a								10 52				16 08		17 10	18 25		
St Budeaux Victoria Road	d	05 12	06 51				08 50			11 04	13 04	15 04		16 47			18 33	21 41
Bere Ferrers	d		06 58				08 57			11 11	13 11	15 11		16 54			18 40	21 48
Bere Alston	a	05 25	07 05				09 04			11 18	13 19	15 18		17 01			18 47	21 55
	d	05 27	07 07				09 06			11 20	13 20	15 20		17 03			18 49	21 57
Calstock	d	05 34	07 14				09 13			11 27	13 27	15 27		17 10			18 56	22 04
Gunnislake	a	05 48	07 27				09 26			11 40	13 41	15 40		17 23			19 09	22 17

Saturdays

26 May to 8 September

		GW	GW	GW K	GW	GW	GW	GW	GW ◇■ A	GW	GW A	GW
Plymouth	d	06 41	08 37	10 53	10 59	12 50	14 48	16 38	17 52	18 23	20 42	21 31
Devonport	d	06 44	08 40	10 56	11 02	12 53	14 51	16 41	17a56	18 26	20 45	21 34
Dockyard	d	06x45	08x41		11x03	12x54	14x52	16x42		18x27	20x46	21x35
Keyham	d	06 47	08 43		11 05	12 56	14 54	16 44		18 29	20 48	21 37
St Budeaux Ferry Road	a			11 00							20 50	
St Budeaux Victoria Road	d	06 51	08 47		11 09	13 00	14 58	16 48		18 33		21 41
Bere Ferrers	d	06 58	08 54		11 16	13 07	15 05	16 55		18 40		21 48
Bere Alston	a	07 05	09 01		11 23	13 14	15 12	17 02		18 47		21 55
	d	07 07	09 03		11 25	13 16	15 14	17 04		18 49		21 57
Calstock	d	07 14	09 10		11 32	13 23	15 21	17 11		18 56		22 04
Gunnislake	a	07 27	09 23		11 45	13 37	15 34	17 24		19 09		22 17

Saturdays

15 September to 8 December

		GW	GW ◇ B	GW	GW A	GW D	GW	GW	GW	GW	GW A	GW	GW
Plymouth	d	06 41	08 18	08 37	09 50	10 33	10 54	12 54	14 54	16 38	17 52	18 23	21 31
Devonport	d	06 44	08a21	08 40	09a53		10 57	12 57	14 57	16 41	17 55	18 26	21 34
Dockyard	d	06x45		08x41			10x58	12x58	14x58	16x42	17x57	18x27	21x35
Keyham	d	06 47		08 43			11 00	13 00	15 00	16 44	17 59	18 29	21 37
St Budeaux Ferry Road	a					10 39					18 01		
St Budeaux Victoria Road	d	06 51		08 47			11 04	13 04	15 04	16 48		18 33	21 41
Bere Ferrers	d	06 58		08 54			11 11	13 11	15 11	16 55		18 40	21 48
Bere Alston	a	07 05		09 01			11 18	13 18	15 18	17 02		18 47	21 55
	d	07 07		09 03			11 20	13 20	15 20	17 04		18 49	21 57
Calstock	d	07 14		09 10			11 27	13 27	15 27	17 11		18 56	22 04
Gunnislake	a	07 27		09 23			11 40	13 41	15 40	17 24		19 09	22 17

A To Penzance
B From Bristol Temple Meads to Penzance
C From Bristol Parkway to Penzance
D From Exeter St Davids to Penzance
E From Cardiff Central
F To Liskeard
G From Gunnislake to Liskeard
H From Liskeard
I from 3 September. From Bristol Temple Meads to Penzance
J until 31 August. To Penzance
K From Exeter St Davids to Newquay

For connections at Plymouth refer to Table T135

Table T139-F

Plymouth - Gunnislake

Sundays

20 May to 9 September

		GW A	GW	GW ◇ B	GW	GW	GW	GW	GW
Plymouth	d	08 57	09 10	11 13	11 17	13 06	15 11	17 41	20 01
Devonport	d	09 00	09 13	11a16	11 20	13 09	15 14	17 44	20 04
Dockyard	d	09x02	09x14		11x21	13x10	15x15	17x45	20x05
Keyham	d	09 04	09 16		11 23	13 12	15 17	17 47	20 07
St Budeaux Ferry Road	a	09 06							
St Budeaux Victoria Road	d		09 20		11 27	13 16	15 21	17 51	20 11
Bere Ferrers	d		09 27		11 34	13 23	15 28	17 58	20 18
Bere Alston	a		09 34		11 41	13 30	15 35	18 05	20 25
	d		09 36		11 43	13 32	15 37	18 07	20 27
Calstock	d		09 43		11 50	13 39	15 44	18 14	20 34
Gunnislake	a		09 56		12 03	13 52	15 57	18 27	20 47

Sundays

16 September to 2 December

		GW A	GW	GW	GW	GW	GW
Plymouth	d	09 00	09 10	11 17	13 06	15 11	17 41
Devonport	d	09 04	09 13	11 20	13 09	15 14	17 44
Dockyard	d		09x14	11x21	13x10	15x15	17x45
Keyham	d		09 16	11 23	13 12	15 17	17 47
St Budeaux Ferry Road	a	09 08					
St Budeaux Victoria Road	d		09 20	11 27	13 16	15 21	17 51
Bere Ferrers	d		09 27	11 34	13 23	15 28	17 58
Bere Alston	a		09 34	11 41	13 30	15 35	18 05
	d		09 36	11 43	13 32	15 37	18 07
Calstock	d		09 43	11 50	13 39	15 44	18 14
Gunnislake	a		09 56	12 03	13 52	15 57	18 27

A To Penzance
B From Bristol Temple Meads to Penzance

For connections at Plymouth refer to Table T135

Table T139-R

Gunnislake - Plymouth

Mondays to Fridays

21 May to 29 June

Miles			GW	GW A	GW	GW	GW ◇ B	GW	GW	GW ◇ C	GW D	GW E	GW	GW C	GW F
0	**Gunnislake**	d	05 51		07 31	09 29	11 45	13 50	15 45		17 27		19 13		22 21
3	Calstock	d	06 02		07 42	09 40	11 56	14 02	15 56		17 39		19 24		22 32
4½	Bere Alston	a	06 08		07 49	09 47	12 03	14 08	16 03		17 45		19 31		22 39
—		d	06 11		07 51	09 49	12 05	14 10	16 05		17 47		19 33		22 41
7½	Bere Ferrers	d	06 16		07 56	09 54	12 10	14 16	16 10		17 53		19 38		22 46
11½	St Budeaux Victoria Road	d	06 25		08 05	10 03	12 19	14 24	16 19		18 01		19 47		22 55
—	St Budeaux Ferry Road	d		07 50						16 41		18 10		21 08	
12½	Keyham	d	06 27	07 53	08 07	10 05	12 21	14 27	16 21	16 43	18 04		19 49	21 10	22 57
13	Dockyard	d	06x29	07x55	08x09	10x07	12x23	14x29	16x23	16x45	18x05		19x51	21x12	22x59
13½	Devonport	d	06 31	07 58	08 11	10 09	12 25	14 30	16 25	16 47	18 08		19 53	21 14	23 01
14½	**Plymouth**	a	06 36	08 03	08 17	10 14	12 30	14 35	16 30	16 51	18 12	18 18	19 58	21 19	23 06

Mondays to Fridays

2 July to 7 December

		GW	GW A	GW	GW	GW	GW	GW	GW ◇ G	GW H	GW	GW E	GW	GW G	GW H	GW F
Gunnislake	d	05 51		07 31	09 29	11 45	13 45	15 45			17 27		19 13			22 21
Calstock	d	06 02		07 42	09 40	11 56	13 56	15 56			17 39		19 24			22 32
Bere Alston	a	06 08		07 49	09 47	12 03	14 03	16 03			17 45		19 31			22 39
	d	06 11		07 51	09 49	12 05	14 05	16 05			17 47		19 33			22 41
Bere Ferrers	d	06 16		07 56	09 54	12 10	14 10	16 10			17 53		19 38			22 46
St Budeaux Victoria Road	d	06 25		08 05	10 03	12 19	14 19	16 19			18 01		19 47			22 55
St Budeaux Ferry Road	d		07 50						16 41	17 07		18 10		21 08	21 27	
Keyham	d	06 27	07 53	08 07	10 05	12 21	14 21	16 21	16 43	17 09	18 04		19 49	21 10	21 29	22 57
Dockyard	d	06x29	07x55	08x09	10x07	12x23	14x23	16x23	16x45	17x10	18x05		19x51	21x12	21x30	22x59
Devonport	d	06 31	07 58	08 11	10 09	12 25	14 25	16 25	16 47	17 13	18 08		19 53	21 14	21 33	23 01
Plymouth	a	06 36	08 03	08 17	10 14	12 30	14 30	16 30	16 51	17 18	18 12	18 18	19 58	21 19	21 38	23 06

Saturdays

26 May to 8 September

		GW C	GW	GW	GW	GW	GW I	GW	GW	GW J	GW	GW A	GW K	GW
Gunnislake	d		07 31	09 27	11 51	13 45		15 45	17 29		19 18			22 21
Calstock	d		07 42	09 38	12 02	13 56		15 56	17 40		19 29			22 32
Bere Alston	a		07 49	09 45	12 09	14 03		16 03	17 47		19 36			22 39
	d		07 51	09 47	12 11	14 05		16 05	17 49		19 38			22 41
Bere Ferrers	d		07 56	09 52	12 16	14 10		16 10	17 54		19 43			22 46
St Budeaux Victoria Road	d		08 05	10 01	12 25	14 19		16 19	18 03		19 52			22 55
St Budeaux Ferry Road	d	07 32										20 59	22 27	
Keyham	d	07 34	08 07	10 03	12 27	14 21		16 21	18 05		19 54	21 01	22 29	22 57
Dockyard	d	07x35	08x09	10x05	12x29	14x23		16x23	18x07		19x56	21x02	22x30	22x59
Devonport	d	07 37	08 11	10 07	12 31	14 25	15 20	16 25	18 09	19 51	19 58	21 05	22 33	23 01
Plymouth	a	07 45	08 17	10 13	12 36	14 30	15 25	16 30	18 14	19 55	20 03	21 09	22 38	23 06

Saturdays

15 September to 8 December

		GW C	GW	GW	GW	GW	GW ◇ C	GW	GW	GW	GW A	GW	GW K
Gunnislake	d		07 31	09 27	11 45	13 45		15 45	17 29	19 13		22 21	
Calstock	d		07 42	09 38	11 56	13 56		15 56	17 40	19 24		22 32	
Bere Alston	a		07 49	09 45	12 03	14 03		16 03	17 47	19 31		22 39	
	d		07 51	09 47	12 05	14 05		16 05	17 49	19 33		22 41	
Bere Ferrers	d		07 56	09 52	12 10	14 10		16 10	17 54	19 38		22 46	
St Budeaux Victoria Road	d		08 05	10 01	12 19	14 19		16 19	18 03	19 47		22 55	
St Budeaux Ferry Road	d	07 32									20 59		23 02
Keyham	d	07 34	08 07	10 03	12 21	14 21		16 21	18 05	19 49	21 01	22 57	23 04
Dockyard	d	07x35	08x09	10x05	12x23	14x23		16x23	18x07	19x51	21x02	22x59	23x05
Devonport	d	07 37	08 11	10 07	12 25	14 25	14 49	16 25	18 09	19 53	21 05	23 01	23 08
Plymouth	a	07 45	08 17	10 13	12 30	14 30	14 55	16 30	18 14	19 58	21 09	23 06	23 13

Sundays

20 May to 9 September

		GW	GW	GW	GW	GW	GW C	GW A	GW
Gunnislake	d	10 10	12 07	13 58	16 04	18 35			20 50
Calstock	d	10 21	12 18	14 09	16 15	18 46			21 01
Bere Alston	a	10 28	12 25	14 16	16 22	18 53			21 08
	d	10 30	12 27	14 18	16 24	18 55			21 10
Bere Ferrers	d	10 35	12 32	14 23	16 29	19 00			21 15
St Budeaux Victoria Road	d	10 44	12 41	14 32	16 38	19 09			21 24
St Budeaux Ferry Road	d						19 44	20 52	
Keyham	d	10 46	12 43	14 34	16 40	19 11	19 46		21 26
Dockyard	d	10x48	12x45	14x36	16x42	19x13	19 48		21x28
Devonport	d	10 50	12 47	14 38	16 44	19 15	19 50	20 55	21 30
Plymouth	a	10 55	12 52	14 43	16 49	19 20	19 55	21 00	21 35

A From Penzance to Exeter St Davids
B To Penzance
C From Penzance
D To Liskeard
E From Liskeard to Gunnislake
F To Exeter St Davids
G from 3 September. From Penzance
H until 31 August. From Liskeard
I From Newquay to Newton Abbot
J From Par
K From Newquay

For connections at Plymouth refer to Table T135

Table T139-R

Gunnislake - Plymouth

Sundays

16 September to 2 December

		GW	GW	GW	GW	GW	GW A
Gunnislake	d	10 10	12 07	13 58	16 04	18 35	
Calstock	d	10 21	12 18	14 09	16 15	18 46	
Bere Alston	a	10 28	12 25	14 16	16 22	18 53	
	d	10 30	12 27	14 18	16 24	18 55	
Bere Ferrers	d	10 35	12 32	14 23	16 29	19 00	
St Budeaux Victoria Road	d	10 44	12 41	14 32	16 38	19 09	
St Budeaux Ferry Road	d						20 52
Keyham	d	10 46	12 43	14 34	16 40	19 11	
Dockyard	d	10x48	12x45	14x36	16x42	19x13	
Devonport	d	10 50	12 47	14 38	16 44	19 15	20 55
Plymouth	a	10 55	12 52	14 43	16 49	19 20	21 00

A From Penzance to Exeter St Davids

For connections at Plymouth refer to Table T135

Table T140-F

Mondays to Fridays
21 May to 7 December

Liskeard - Looe

Miles			GW	GW	GW	GW	GW	GW	GW	GW	GW		GW	GW	GW
0	**Liskeard** 8	d	06 05	07 14	08 50	10 14	11 15	12 16	13 19	14 24	15 41		16 41	18 06	19 20
2	Coombe Junction Halt	a			08 56					14 30					
—		d			08 59					14 33					
3¾	St Keyne Wishing Well Halt	d	06x17	07x26	09x05	10x27	11x28	12x28	13x31	14x40	15x53		16x53	18x19	19x33
5	Causeland	d	06x21	07x30	09x09	10x30	11x31	12x32	13x35	14x44	15x57		16x57	18x23	19x35
6½	Sandplace	d	06x24	07x33	09x13	10x34	11x35	12x35	13x38	14x47	16x00		17x00	18x26	19x40
8¾	**Looe**	a	06 34	07 43	09 21	10 41	11 44	12 45	13 48	14 55	16 10		17 10	18 37	19 49

Saturdays
26 May to 8 September

		GW	GW	GW	GW	GW	GW	GW	GW	GW		GW	GW	GW	GW
Liskeard 8	d	06 10	07 14	08 17	09 56	11 13	12 16	13 39	14 39	15 48		16 55	17 58	19 25	20 41
Coombe Junction Halt	a			08 23					14 45						
	d			08 25					14 47						
St Keyne Wishing Well Halt	d		07x26	08x31	10x08	11x25	12x28	13x51	14x53			17x07	18x10	19x38	20x53
Causeland	d		07x30	08x35	10x11	11x29	12x32	13x55	14x57			17x11	18x14	19x40	20x57
Sandplace	d		07x33	08x38	10x15	11x32	12x35	13x58	15x00			17x14	18x17	19x45	21x00
Looe	a	06 37	07 45	08 48	10 25	11 44	12 47	14 10	15 11	16 16		17 26	18 29	19 56	21 11

Saturdays
15 September to 8 December

		GW	GW	GW	GW	GW	GW	GW	GW	GW		GW	GW	GW
Liskeard 8	d	06 10	07 14	08 20	09 56	11 10	12 16	13 39	14 42	15 51		16 55	17 58	19 25
Coombe Junction Halt	a			08 26					14 48					
	d			08 28					14 50					
St Keyne Wishing Well Halt	d		07x26	08x34	10x08	11x22	12x28	13x51	14x56	16x03		17x07	18x10	19x38
Causeland	d		07x30	08x38	10x11	11x26	12x32	13x55	15x00	16x07		17x11	18x14	19x40
Sandplace	d		07x33	08x41	10x15	11x29	12x35	13x58	15x03	16x10		17x14	18x17	19x45
Looe	a	06 37	07 45	08 51	10 25	11 41	12 47	14 10	15 14	16 22		17 26	18 29	19 56

Sundays
20 May to 9 September

		GW	GW	GW	GW	GW	GW	GW	GW
Liskeard 8	d	10 12	11 25	12 48	13 59	15 02	16 10	17 35	20 15
Coombe Junction Halt	a								
	d								
St Keyne Wishing Well Halt	d	10x25	11x38	13x01	14x12	15x15	16x23	17x48	20x28
Causeland	d	10x28	11x41	13x04	14x15	15x18	16x26	17x51	20x31
Sandplace	d	10x32	11x45	13x08	14x19	15x22	16x30	17x55	20x35
Looe	a	10 41	11 54	13 17	14 28	15 31	16 39	18 04	20 44

Sundays
16 September to 2 December

		GW A	GW A	GW A	GW A	GW A	GW A	GW A	GW A
Liskeard 8	d	10 12	11 25	12 48	14 02	15 23	16 35	17 40	20 15
Coombe Junction Halt	a								
	d								
St Keyne Wishing Well Halt	d	10x25	11x38	13x01	14x15	15x36	16x48	17x53	20x28
Causeland	d	10x28	11x41	13x04	14x18	15x39	16x51	17x56	20x31
Sandplace	d	10x32	11x45	13x08	14x22	15x43	16x55	18x00	20x35
Looe	a	10 41	11 54	13 17	14 31	15 52	17 04	18 09	20 44

A until 21 October

For connections at Liskeard refer to Table T135

Table T140-R

Mondays to Fridays
21 May to 7 December

Looe - Liskeard

Miles			GW	GW	GW	GW	GW	GW		GW	GW	GW	GW	GW	GW
0	**Looe**	d	06 37	07 46	09 29	10 44	11 47	12 48		13 51	14 58	16 13	17 15	18 42	19 52
2¼	Sandplace	d	06x42	07x51	09x34	10x49		12x53		13x56	15x03		17x20	18x47	19x57
3¾	Causeland	d	06x46	07x55	09x38	10x53		12x57		14x00	15x07		17x24	18x51	20x01
5	St Keyne Wishing Well Halt	d	06x49	07x58	09x41	10x56		13x00		14x04	15x10		17x27	18x54	20x04
6¾	Coombe Junction Halt	a			09 47						15 19				
—		d			09 49						15 21				
8¾	**Liskeard** 8	a	07 05	08 14	10 00	11 12	12 13	13 16		14 18	15 29	16 37	17 43	19 10	20 20

Saturdays
26 May to 8 September

		GW	GW	GW	GW	GW	GW	GW	GW	GW		GW	GW	GW	GW
Looe	d	06 38	07 46	08 51	10 27	11 45	12 48	14 11	15 14	16 17		17 27	18 30	20 00	21 13
Sandplace	d		07x51	08x56	10x32	11x50	12x53		15x19			17x32	18x35	20x05	21x18
Causeland	d		07x55	09x00	10x36	11x54	12x57		15x23			17x36	18x39	20x09	21x22
St Keyne Wishing Well Halt	d		07x58	09x03	10x39	11x57	13x00		15x26			17x39	18x42	20x12	21x25
Coombe Junction Halt	a			09 09					15 32						
	d			09 11					15 34						
Liskeard 8	a	07 04	08 14	09 22	10 56	12 14	13 18	14 36	15 45	16 42		17 57	18 58	20 29	21 41

Saturdays
15 September to 8 December

		GW	GW	GW	GW	GW	GW	GW	GW	GW		GW	GW	GW
Looe	d	06 38	07 46	08 55	10 28	11 43	12 48	14 11	15 17	16 23		17 27	18 30	20 00
Sandplace	d		07x51	09x00	10x33	11x48	12x53	14x16	15x22	16x28		17x32	18x35	20x05
Causeland	d		07x55	09x04	10x37	11x52	12x57	14x20	15x26	16x32		17x36	18x39	20x09
St Keyne Wishing Well Halt	d		07x58	09x07	10x40	11x55	13x00	14x23	15x29	16x35		17x39	18x42	20x12
Coombe Junction Halt	a			09 13					15 35					
	d			09 15					15 37					
Liskeard 8	a	07 04	08 14	09 26	10 57	12 12	13 18	14 39	15 48	16 52		17 57	18 58	20 29

Sundays
20 May to 9 September

		GW	GW	GW	GW	GW	GW	GW	GW
Looe	d	10 44	11 57	13 20	14 31	15 34	16 42	18 15	20 50
Sandplace	d	10x49	12x02	13x25	14x36	15x39	16x47	18x20	20x55
Causeland	d	10x53	12x06	13x29	14x40	15x43	16x51	18x24	20x59
St Keyne Wishing Well Halt	d	10x57	12x10	13x33	14x44	15x47	16x55	18x28	21x03
Coombe Junction Halt	a								
	d								
Liskeard 8	a	11 12	12 25	13 48	14 59	16 02	17 10	18 43	21 18

Sundays
16 September to 2 December

		GW A	GW A	GW A	GW A	GW A	GW A	GW A	GW A
Looe	d	10 44	11 57	13 20	14 34	15 55	17 07	18 15	20 50
Sandplace	d	10x49	12x02	13x25	14x39	16x00	17x12	18x20	20x55
Causeland	d	10x53	12x06	13x29	14x43	16x04	17x16	18x24	20x59
St Keyne Wishing Well Halt	d	10x57	12x10	13x33	14x47	16x08	17x20	18x28	21x03
Coombe Junction Halt	a								
	d								
Liskeard 8	a	11 12	12 25	13 48	15 02	16 23	17 35	18 43	21 18

A until 21 October

For connections at Liskeard refer to Table T135

Table T142-F

Par - Newquay

Mondays to Fridays
21 May to 29 June

Miles			GW	GW	GW	GW	GW	GW
				◇	◇	◇	◇	
0	**Par**	d	09 17	12 11	14 07	16 10	18 29	20 28
4¼	Luxulyan	d	09x28	12x22	14x18	16x21	18x40	20x39
6¼	Bugle	d	09x34	12x27	14x24	16x26	18x46	20x45
8¾	Roche	d	09x38	12x33	14x29	16x32	18x50	20x49
14½	St Columb Road	d	09x50	12x44	14x40	16x43	19x02	21x01
18¼	Quintrell Downs	d	09 58	12 52	14 48	16 51	19 10	21 09
20¾	**Newquay**	a	10 09	13 02	14 59	17 02	19 21	21 20

Mondays to Fridays
2 July to 31 August

		GW	GW	GW	GW	GW	GW
			◇	◇■	◇	◇	
		A		B			
Par	d	09 17	11 47	13 28	16 10	18 29	20 28
Luxulyan	d	09x28	11x58	.	16x21	18x40	20x39
Bugle	d	09x34	12x03	.	16x26	18x46	20x45
Roche	d	09x38	12x09	.	16x32	18x50	20x49
St Columb Road	d	09x50	12x20	.	16x43	19x02	21x01
Quintrell Downs	d	09 58	12 28	.	16 51	19 10	21 09
Newquay	a	10 09	12 38	14 18	17 02	19 21	21 20

Mondays to Fridays
3 September to 7 December

		GW	GW	GW	GW	GW	GW
			◇	◇	◇	◇	
Par	d	09 17	12 11	14 07	16 10	18 29	20 28
Luxulyan	d	09x28	12x22	14x18	16x21	18x40	20x39
Bugle	d	09x34	12x27	14x24	16x26	18x46	20x45
Roche	d	09x38	12x33	14x29	16x32	18x50	20x49
St Columb Road	d	09x50	12x44	14x40	16x43	19x02	21x01
Quintrell Downs	d	09 58	12 52	14 48	16 51	19 10	21 09
Newquay	a	10 09	13 02	14 59	17 02	19 21	21 20

Saturdays
26 May to 8 September

		XC	GW	GW	XC	GW	XC	GW
		◇■	◇■		◇■	■	◇■	
		C	C	D	E	F	G	
Par	d	08 20	09 54	11 48	13 33	15 49	17 41	19 48
Luxulyan	d	.	.	.	.	.	.	19x59
Bugle	d	.	.	.	.	.	.	20x05
Roche	d	.	.	.	.	.	.	20x09
St Columb Road	d	.	.	.	.	.	.	20x21
Quintrell Downs	d	.	.	.	.	.	.	20 29
Newquay	a	09 10	10 47	12 38	14 31	16 47	18 39	20 40

Saturdays
15 September to 8 December

		GW	GW	GW	GW	GW	GW	GW
				◇	◇	◇	◇	
Par	d	06 52	09 17	12 12	14 05	16 10	18 20	20 15
Luxulyan	d	07x03	09x28	12x23	14x16	16x21	18x31	20x26
Bugle	d	07x09	09x34	12x29	14x22	16x27	18x37	20x32
Roche	d	07x13	09x38	12x33	14x26	16x31	18x41	20x36
St Columb Road	d	07x25	09x50	12x45	14x38	16x43	18x53	20x48
Quintrell Downs	d	07 33	09 58	12 53	14 46	16 51	19 01	20 56
Newquay	a	07 44	10 09	13 04	14 57	17 02	19 12	21 07

Sundays
20 May to 9 September

		GW	XC	GW	GW	GW	GW
			◇■		◇■	◇	◇
			C		B		
Par	d	09 00	10 12	11 49	14 23	16 47	19 22
Luxulyan	d	09x11	.	12x00	.	16x59	19x33
Bugle	d	09x17	.	12x13	.	17x05	19x39
Roche	d	09x22	.	12x17	.	17x09	19x44
St Columb Road	d	09x33	.	12x29	.	17x21	19x55
Quintrell Downs	d	09 41	.	12 37	.	17 29	20 03
Newquay	a	09 50	11 06	12 47	15 13	17 39	20 13

A From Bristol Temple Meads
B From London Paddington
C From Plymouth
D From Exeter St Davids
E From Manchester Piccadilly
F From London Paddington. The Atlantic Coast Express
G From Dundee

For connections at Par refer to Table T135

Table T142-F

Par - Newquay

Sundays
16 September to 2 December

		GW	GW	GW
				◇
Par	d	10 10	13 15	16 34
Luxulyan	d	10x21	13x26	16x45
Bugle	d	10x27	13x32	16x51
Roche	d	10x32	13x37	16x56
St Columb Road	d	10x43	13x48	17x07
Quintrell Downs	d	10 51	13 56	17 15
Newquay	a	11 02	14 07	17 26

For connections at Par refer to Table T135

Table T142-R

Mondays to Fridays

21 May to 7 December

Newquay - Par

Miles			GW	GW	GW	GW	GW	GW	GW	GW
			◇		◇	◇	◇■	◇		
				A	B	B	C			
0	**Newquay**	d	10 13	12 41	13 05	15 01	15 07	17 22	19 24	21 26
2½	Quintrell Downs	d	10 19	12 47	13 11	15 07	⌇	17 28	19 30	21 32
6½	St Columb Road	d	10x26	12x54	13x18	⌇	⌇	17x35	19x37	21x39
12	Roche	d	10x38	13x05	13x30	⌇	⌇	17x47	19x48	21x51
14½	Bugle	d	10x42	13x10	13x34	15x28	⌇	17x51	19x53	21x55
16½	Luxulyan	d	10x48	13x18	13x40	⌇	⌇	17x57	20x00	22x01
20¾	**Par**	a	11 02	13 35	13 54	15 47	15 59	18 11	20 13	22 16

Saturdays

26 May to 8 December

		GW	XC	GW	GW	GW	GW	GW	XC	GW	GW	XC	GW	GW	GW
		◇	◇■	◇	■	◇		◇	◇■	◇	◇■	◇■			
		D	E	D	F	D	G	D	H	D	I	J	D	J	K
Newquay	d	07 47	09 35	10 13	11 30	13 06	13 23	15 00	15 30	17 20	17 28	19 00	19 15	20 45	21 20
Quintrell Downs	d	07 53	⌇	10 19	⌇	13 12	⌇	15 06	⌇	17 26	⌇	⌇	19 21	20 51	21 26
St Columb Road	d	08x00	⌇	10x26	⌇	13x19	⌇	15x13	⌇	17x33	⌇	⌇	19x28	20x58	21x33
Roche	d	08x12	⌇	10x38	⌇	13x31	⌇	15x25	⌇	17x45	⌇	⌇	19x40	21x09	21x44
Bugle	d	08x16	⌇	10x42	⌇	13x35	⌇	15x29	⌇	17x49	⌇	⌇	19x44	21x14	21x49
Luxulyan	d	08x22	⌇	10x48	⌇	13x41	⌇	15x35	⌇	17x55	⌇	⌇	19x50	21x20	21x55
Par	a	08 38	10 29	11 02	12 22	13 55	14 08	15 50	16 24	18 10	18 23	19 52	20 05	21 34	22 09

Sundays

20 May to 2 December

		GW	GW	XC	GW	GW	GW	GW	GW	GW
		◇	◇	◇■	◇	◇	◇■	◇		
		L	M	N	L	M	O	L	M	L
Newquay	d	09 58	11 12	11 32	13 10	15 10	15 59	17 45	17 45	20 20
Quintrell Downs	d	10 04	11 18	⌇	13 16	15 16	⌇	17 51	17 51	20 26
St Columb Road	d	10x12	11x26	⌇	13x24	15x24	⌇	17x59	17x59	20x34
Roche	d	10x23	11x37	⌇	13x35	15x35	⌇	18x10	18x10	20x45
Bugle	d	10x28	11x42	⌇	13x40	15x40	⌇	18x15	18x15	20x50
Luxulyan	d	10x31	11x47	⌇	13x43	15x45	⌇	18x20	18x20	20x53
Par	a	10 45	12 01	12 22	13 57	15 59	16 51	18 34	18 34	21 07

A from 2 July until 31 August. To Penzance
B until 29 June, from 3 September
C from 2 July until 31 August. To London Paddington
D from 15 September
E until 8 September. To Newcastle
F until 8 September. To London Paddington. The Atlantic Coast Express
G until 8 September. To Newton Abbot
H until 8 September. To Manchester Piccadilly
I until 8 September. To London Paddington
J until 8 September. To Plymouth
K from 15 September. To Plymouth
L until 9 September
M from 16 September
N until 9 September. To Edinburgh
O until 9 September. To London Paddington

For connections at Par refer to Table T135

Table T143-F

Mondays to Fridays

21 May to 7 December

Truro - Falmouth

Miles			GW	GW	GW	GW	GW	GW		GW	GW	GW	GW	GW	GW	GW	GW	GW	GW	GW
0	**Truro**	d	06 04	06 31	07 16	07 47	08 20	08 51	and at the same minutes past each hour until	15 20	15 51	16 20	16 51	17 27	17 59	18 31	19 02	20 04	21 05	22 44
4¼	Perranwell	d	06x10	06x37	07x22	07x53	08x26			15x26		16x26	16x57	17x33	18x05	18x37	19x08	20x10	21x11	22x50
8¼	Penryn	d	06 18	06 45	07 30	08 01	08 34	09 04		15 34	16 04	16 34	17 05	17 41	18 13	18 45	19 16	20 18	21 19	22 58
10¼	Penmere	d	06 23	06 50	07 35	08 06	08 39	09 09		15 39	16 09	16 39	17 10	17 46	18 18	18 50	19 21	20 23	21 24	23 03
11¾	Falmouth Town	d	06 26	06 53	07 38	08 09	08 42	09 12		15 42	16 12	16 42	17 13	17 49	18 21	18 53	19 24	20 26	21 27	23 06
12¼	**Falmouth Docks**	a	06 28	06 55	07 40	08 11	08 44	09 14		15 44	16 14	16 47	17 15	17 51	18 23	18 55	19 26	20 28	21 29	23 08

Saturdays

26 May to 8 December

		GW	GW	GW	GW	GW	GW		GW	GW	GW	GW	GW	GW	GW	GW	GW	GW	GW
Truro	d	06 05	06 31	07 16	07 47	08 20	08 51	and at the same minutes past each hour until	15 20	15 51	16 20	16 52	17 28	17 59	18 31	19 02	20 04	21 05	22 12
Perranwell	d	06 11	06 37	07 22	07 53	08 26			15 26		16 26	16 58	17 34	18 05	18 37	19 08	20 10	21 11	22 18
Penryn	d	06 19	06 46	07 30	08 01	08 34	09 04		15 34	16 04	16 34	17 06	17 42	18 13	18 45	19 16	20 18	21 19	22 26
Penmere	d	06 24	06 51	07 35	08 06	08 39	09 09		15 39	16 09	16 39	17 11	17 47	18 18	18 50	19 21	20 23	21 24	22 31
Falmouth Town	d	06 27	06 54	07 38	08 09	08 42	09 12		15 42	16 12	16 42	17 14	17 50	18 21	18 53	19 24	20 26	21 27	22 34
Falmouth Docks	a	06 29	06 56	07 40	08 11	08 44	09 14		15 44	16 14	16 44	17 16	17 52	18 23	18 55	19 26	20 28	21 29	22 36

Sundays

20 May to 2 December

		GW	GW	GW	GW	GW	GW	GW	GW	GW	GW	GW	GW	GW
			A	B										
Truro	d	09 09	10 33	10 36	11 36	12 39	13 44	14 40	15 47	17 10	18 25	19 55	21 03	22 04
Perranwell	d	09 16	10 40	10 43	11 43	12 46	13 51	14 47	15 54	17x17	18x32	20x02	21 10	22 11
Penryn	d	09 23	10 47	10 50	11 50	12 53	13 58	14 54	16 01	17 24	18 39	20 09	21 17	22 18
Penmere	d	09 28	10 52	10 55	11 55	12 58	14 03	14 59	16 05	17 28	18 43	20 13	21 21	22 22
Falmouth Town	d	09 31	10 55	10 58	11 58	13 01	14 06	15 02	16 08	17 31	18 46	20 16	21 24	22 25
Falmouth Docks	a	09 33	10 57	11 00	12 00	13 03	14 08	15 04	16 11	17 34	18 49	20 19	21 27	22 28

A until 9 September
B from 16 September

For connections at Truro refer to Table T135

Table T143-R

Mondays to Fridays

21 May to 7 December

Falmouth - Truro

Miles			GW	GW	GW	GW	GW	GW	GW	GW	GW	GW	GW	GW	GW		GW	GW	GW	GW	GW	GW
0	**Falmouth Docks**	d	06 31	07 16	07 47	08 20	08 50	09 20	09 50	10 20	10 50	11 20	11 50	12 20	12 50	and at the same minutes past each hour until	15 20	15 50	16 20	16 50	17 27	17 59
0½	Falmouth Town	d	06 34	07 19	07 50	08 23	08 53	09 23	09 53	10 23	10 53	11 23	11 53	12 23	12 53		15 23	15 53	16 23	16 53	17 30	18 02
2	Penmere	d	06 37	07 22	07 53	08 26	08 56	09 26	09 56	10 26	10 56	11 26	11 56	12 26	12 56		15 26	15 56	16 26	16 56	17 33	18 05
4	Penryn	d	06 45	07 30	08 01	08 34	09 04	09 34	10 04	10 34	11 04	11 34	12 04	12 34	13 04		15 34	16 04	16 34	17 04	17 40	18 13
8	Perranwell	d	06x51	07x36	08x07	08x40		09x40		10x40		11x40		12x40			15x40		16x40	17x11	17x48	18x19
12¼	**Truro**	a	06 59	07 44	08 15	08 48	09 18	09 48	10 18	10 48	11 18	11 48	12 17	12 48	13 18		15 48	16 18	16 48	17 19	17 55	18 27

		GW	GW	GW	GW	GW	GW
Falmouth Docks	d	18 31	19 02	19 29	20 31	21 32	23 11
Falmouth Town	d	18 34	19 05	19 32	20 34	21 35	23 14
Penmere	d	18 37	19 08	19 35	20 37	21 38	23 17
Penryn	d	18 45	19 16	19 40	20 42	21 43	23 22
Perranwell	d	18x51	19x22	19x46	20x48	21x49	23x28
Truro	a	18 59	19 30	19 55	20 57	21 59	23 38

Saturdays

26 May to 8 December

		GW	GW	GW	GW	GW	GW	GW	GW	GW	GW	GW	GW	GW		GW	GW	GW	GW	GW	GW	GW
Falmouth Docks	d	06 32	07 16	07 47	08 20	08 50	09 20	09 50	10 20	10 50	11 20	11 50	12 20	12 50	and at the same minutes past each hour until	15 20	15 50	16 20	16 52	17 28	17 59	18 31
Falmouth Town	d	06 35	07 19	07 50	08 23	08 53	09 23	09 53	10 23	10 53	11 23	11 53	12 23	12 53		15 23	15 53	16 23	16 55	17 31	18 02	18 34
Penmere	d	06 38	07 22	07 53	08 26	08 56	09 26	09 56	10 26	10 56	11 26	11 56	12 26	12 56		15 26	15 56	16 26	16 58	17 34	18 05	18 37
Penryn	d	06 46	07 30	08 01	08 34	09 04	09 34	10 04	10 34	11 04	11 34	12 04	12 34	13 04		15 34	16 04	16 34	17 06	17 42	18 13	18 45
Perranwell	d	06 52	07 36	08 07	08 40		09 40		10 40		11 40		12 40			15 40		16 40	17 12	17 48	18 19	18 51
Truro	a	07 00	07 44	08 15	08 48	09 18	09 48	10 18	10 48	11 18	11 48	12 17	12 48	13 18		15 48	16 18	16 48	17 20	17 56	18 27	18 59

		GW	GW	GW	GW	GW
Falmouth Docks	d	19 02	19 34	20 31	21 32	22 39
Falmouth Town	d	19 05	19 37	20 34	21 35	22 42
Penmere	d	19 08	19 40	20 37	21 38	22 45
Penryn	d	19 16	19 45	20 42	21 43	22 50
Perranwell	d	19 22	19 51	20 48	21 49	22 56
Truro	a	19 30	20 00	20 57	21 58	23 06

Sundays

20 May to 2 December

		GW	GW	GW	GW A	GW B	GW	GW	GW	GW	GW	GW	GW	GW
Falmouth Docks	d	09 37	11 03	12 03	13 06	13 06	14 11	15 09	16 14	17 40	18 52	20 22	21 30	22 33
Falmouth Town	d	09 40	11 06	12 06	13 09	13 09	14 14	15 12	16 17	17 43	18 55	20 25	21 33	22 36
Penmere	d	09 43	11 09	12 09	13 12	13 12	14 17	15 15	16 20	17 46	18 58	20 28	21 36	22 39
Penryn	d	09 48	11 14	12 14	13 16	13 17	14 22	15 20	16 25	17 51	19 03	20 33	21 41	22 44
Perranwell	d	09x55	11 21	12 21	13 23	13 24	14 29	15 27	16 32	17x58	19 10	20 40	21 48	22 51
Truro	a	10 03	11 29	12 29	13 31	13 31	14 37	15 35	16 39	18 06	19 18	20 48	21 56	22 59

A until 9 September

B from 16 September

For connections at Truro refer to Table T135

Table T144-F

Mondays to Fridays

21 May to 7 December

St Erth - St Ives

Miles			GW	GW	GW	GW	GW	GW	GW	GW A	GW B	GW A	GW B
—	Penzance	d	06 58		08 44								
0	**St Erth**	d	07 06	07 59	08 52	09 38	10 18	10 48	11 18	11 48	11 52	12 18	
0¾	Lelant Saltings	d		08 01	08 55	09 41	10 21	10 51	11 21	11 51	11 55	12 21	12 21
1	Lelant	d	07x10	08x02	08x56								
3	Carbis Bay	d	07 15	08 08	09 02	09 47		10 57		11 57	12 01		
4¼	**St Ives**	a	07 18	08 12	09 06	09 50	10 29	11 00	11 29	12 00	12 04	12 29	12 29

Miles			GW	GW	GW	GW A	GW B	GW	GW	GW	GW A	GW B
—	Penzance	d										
0	**St Erth**	d	12 48	13 18	13 48	14 18		14 48	15 18	15 48	16 18	
0¾	Lelant Saltings	d	12 51	13 21	13 51	14 21	14 21	14 51	15 21	15 51	16 21	16 21
1	Lelant	d										
3	Carbis Bay	d	12 57		13 57			14 57		15 57		
4¼	**St Ives**	a	13 00	13 29	14 00	14 29	14 29	15 00	15 29	16 00	16 29	16 29

		GW	GW	GW	GW	GW	GW	GW	GW	GW	GW	GW
Penzance	d											
St Erth	d	16 48	17 17	17 48	18 18	18 48	19 18	19 48	20 18	20 48	21 23	21 58
Lelant Saltings	d		17 20		18 21		19 21		20 21			22 01
Lelant	d	16x50		17x50	18x23	18x53		19x51		20x51	21x26	22x02
Carbis Bay	d	16 56		17 56	18 28	18 56		19 56		20 56	21 31	22 08
St Ives	a	16 59	17 28	17 59	18 31	19 01	19 29	19 59	20 29	21 00	21 34	22 11

Saturdays

26 May to 8 September

		GW	GW	GW	GW	GW	GW	GW	GW	GW	GW	GW
Penzance	d	06 41		08 45								
St Erth	d	06 50	07 59	08 54	09 35	10 19	10 48	11 19	11 48	12 18	12 48	13 20
Lelant Saltings	d		08 01	08 57	09 38	10 22	10 51	11 22	11 51	12 21	12 51	13 23
Lelant	d	06x52	08x02	08x59								
Carbis Bay	d	06 58	08 08	09 04	09 44		10 57		11 57		12 57	
St Ives	a	07 03	08 14	09 09	09 49	10 32	11 02	11 32	12 02	12 31	13 02	13 33

		GW	GW	GW	GW	GW	GW	GW	GW	GW	GW	GW
Penzance	d										18 50	
St Erth	d		14 19	14 48	15 18	15 48	16 18	16 48	17 17	17 59	18 59	19 58
Lelant Saltings	d	13 51	14 22	14 51	15 21	15 51	16 21		17 20	18 02	19 02	20 01
Lelant	d							16x50		18x04	19x04	20x03
Carbis Bay	d	13 57		14 57		15 57		16 56	17 26	18 09	19 09	20 08
St Ives	a	14 02	14 32	15 02	15 31	16 02	16 31	17 01	17 31	18 13	19 14	20 13

		GW	GW	GW
Penzance	d			
St Erth	d	20 33	21 06	21 47
Lelant Saltings	d	20 36	21 09	21 50
Lelant	d	20x38	21x11	21x52
Carbis Bay	d	20 43	21 16	21 57
St Ives	a	20 47	21 20	22 00

Saturdays

15 September to 8 December

		GW	GW	GW	GW	GW	GW	GW	GW	GW	GW	GW
Penzance	d	06 41		08 50								
St Erth	d	06 50	07 59	08 59	09 35	10 14	10 48	11 19	11 48	12 18	12 48	13 18
Lelant Saltings	d		08 01	09 02	09 38	10 17	10 51	11 22	11 51	12 21	12 51	13 21
Lelant	d	06x52	08x02	09x04								
Carbis Bay	d	06 58	08 08	09 09	09 44		10 57		11 57		12 57	
St Ives	a	07 03	08 14	09 14	09 49	10 27	11 02	11 32	12 02	12 31	13 02	13 31

		GW	GW	GW	GW	GW	GW	GW	GW	GW	GW	GW
Penzance	d										18 50	
St Erth	d	13 48	14 19	14 48	15 18	15 48	16 18	16 48	17 17	17 59	18 59	19 52
Lelant Saltings	d	13 51	14 22	14 51	15 21	15 51	16 21		17 20	18 02	19 02	19 55
Lelant	d							16x50		18x04	19x04	19x56
Carbis Bay	d	13 57		14 57		15 57		16 56	17 26	18 09	19 09	20 02
St Ives	a	14 02	14 32	15 02	15 31	16 02	16 31	17 01	17 31	18 13	19 14	20 06

		GW	GW	GW
Penzance	d			
St Erth	d	20 33	21 06	21 47
Lelant Saltings	d	20 36	21 09	21 50
Lelant	d	20x38	21x11	21x52
Carbis Bay	d	20 43	21 16	21 57
St Ives	a	20 47	21 20	22 00

Sundays

20 May to 9 September

		GW	GW	GW	GW	GW	GW	GW	GW	GW	GW
Penzance	d	08 45									
St Erth	d	08 53	09 26	10 00	10 30	11 12	11 41	12 18		13 17	13 48
Lelant Saltings	d	08 57	09 29	10 03	10 33	11 15	11 44	12 21	12 51	13 20	13 51
Lelant	d	08 59									
Carbis Bay	d	09 04		10 09	10 39		11 50		12 57		13 57
St Ives	a	09 07	09 37	10 12	10 42	11 23	11 53	12 29	13 00	13 28	14 00

		GW	GW	GW	GW	GW	GW	GW	GW	GW	GW
Penzance	d										
St Erth	d	14 17	14 48		15 48	16 18	16 48	17 24	17 56	18 30	19 30
Lelant Saltings	d	14 20	14 51	15 21	15 51	16 21	16 50	17 27	17 59	18 33	19 33
Lelant	d							17 29	18 01	18 35	19x35
Carbis Bay	d		14 57		15 57		16 57	17 34	18 06	18 40	19 40
St Ives	a	14 28	15 00	15 29	16 00	16 29	17 01	17 38	18 10	18 44	19 44

Sundays

16 September to 21 October

		GW	GW	GW	GW	GW	GW	GW	GW	GW
Penzance	d	10 19								
St Erth	d	10 30	11 13	11 42	12 15	12 49	13 19	13 49	14 18	14 48
Lelant Saltings	d	10 33	11 16	11 45	12 18	12 52	13 22	13 52	14 21	14 51
Lelant	d	10x35			12 20					
Carbis Bay	d	10 40		11 51	12 25	12 58		13 58		14 57
St Ives	a	10 45	11 24	11 55	12 30	13 01	13 30	14 01	14 29	15 00

		GW	GW	GW	GW	GW	GW	GW	GW
Penzance	d								
St Erth	d	15 18	15 48	16 18	16 48	17 23	17 55	18 30	19 30
Lelant Saltings	d	15 21	15 51	16 21	16 51	17 26	17 58	18 33	19 33
Lelant	d						18 00	18 35	19x35
Carbis Bay	d		15 57		16 57		18 05	18 40	19 40
St Ives	a	15 29	16 00	16 29	17 00	17 34	18 09	18 43	19 43

A from 10 September

B until 7 September

For connections at St Erth refer to Table T135

Table T144-F

Sundays
28 October to 2 December

St Erth - St Ives

		GW	GW	GW	GW	GW	GW	GW	GW	GW	GW	GW	GW	GW	GW
Penzance	d	11 45													
St Erth	d	11 56	12 30	13 19	13 49	14 18	14 48	15 18	15 48	16 18	16 48	17 23	17 55	18 30	19 30
Lelant Saltings	d	11 59	12 33	13 22	13 52	14 21	14 51	15 21	15 51	16 21	16 51	17 26	17 58	18 33	19 33
Lelant	d	12x01											18 00	18 35	19x35
Carbis Bay	d	12 06	12 39		13 58		14 57		15 57		16 57		18 05	18 40	19 40
St Ives	a	12 11	12 42	13 30	14 01	14 29	15 00	15 29	16 00	16 29	17 00	17 34	18 09	18 43	19 43

For connections at St Erth refer to Table T135

Table T144-R

Sundays
28 October to 2 December

St Ives - St Erth

		GW	GW	GW	GW	GW	GW	GW	GW	GW	GW	GW	GW	GW	GW
St Ives	d	12 13	12 48	13 34	14 04	14 33	15 03	15 33	16 03	16 33	17 03	17 40	18 11	18 50	19 46
Carbis Bay	d	12 16	12 51	13 37		14 36		15 36		16 36		17 43		18 51	19 49
Lelant	d	12x21											18 18	18 58	19x54
Lelant Saltings	d	12 24	12 58	13 44	14 13	14 43	15 12	15 43	16 12	16 43	17 12	17 50	18 21	19 01	19 57
St Erth	a	12 26	13 00	13 46	14 15	14 45	15 14	15 45	16 14	16 45	17 14	17 52	18 24	19 03	20 00
Penzance	a														20 09

For connections at St Erth refer to Table T135

Table T144-R

St Ives - St Erth

Mondays to Fridays
21 May to 7 December

Miles			GW	GW	GW	GW	GW	GW	GW	GW A	GW B	GW	GW	GW	GW B	GW A	GW	GW	GW	GW B	GW A	GW	GW
0	**St Ives**	d	07 25	08 15	09 22	09 53	10 33	11 03	11 33	12 03	12 07	12 33	13 03	13 33	14 03	14 03	14 33	15 04	15 33	16 03	16 03	16 33	17 03
1¼	Carbis Bay	d	07 28	08 18	09 25		10 36		11 36			12 36		13 36			14 36		15 36			16 36	
3¼	Lelant	d	07x33	08x23	09x30																		
3½	Lelant Saltings	d			09 32		10 42		11 43		12a16	12 43		13 43	14a12	14 13	14 43	15 13	15 43	16a12	16 13	16 43	17 12
4¼	**St Erth**	a	07 37	08 28	09 35	10 03	10 45	11 14	11 45	12 14		12 45	13 14	13 45		14 15	14 45	15 14	15 45		16 15	16 45	17 14
—	Penzance	a		08 38																			

		GW	GW	GW	GW	GW	GW	GW	GW	GW	GW
St Ives	d	17 31	18 03	18 33	19 05	19 32	20 03	20 33	21 03	21 37	22 31
Carbis Bay	d	17 34		18 36		19 35		20 36	21 06	21 40	22 34
Lelant	d		18x10	18x41		19x40		20x41	21x11	21x45	22x39
Lelant Saltings	d	17 41	18 13	18 45		19 43	20 12	20 44	21 14		22 41
St Erth	a	17 44	18 15	18 48	19 16	19 45	20 14	20 47	21 16	21 50	22 45
Penzance	a										22 55

Saturdays
26 May to 8 September

		GW	GW	GW	GW	GW	GW	GW	GW	GW	GW	GW	GW	GW	GW	GW	GW	GW	GW	GW	GW	GW	GW
St Ives	d	07 12	08 15	09 18	09 50	10 33	11 03	11 33	12 03	12 33	13 03	13 35	14 03	14 33	15 03	15 33	16 03	16 33	17 03	17 32	18 17	19 25	20 15
Carbis Bay	d	07 15	08 18	09 21		10 36		11 36		12 36		13 38		14 36		15 36		16 36		17 35	18 20	19 28	20 18
Lelant	d	07x19	08x22	09x25																17x40	18x25	19x33	20x23
Lelant Saltings	d			09 27		10 43		11 43		12 43		13a46	14 12	14 43	15 12	15 43	16 12	16 43	17 12	17 43	18 28	19 36	20 26
St Erth	a	07 24	08 28	09 32	10 00	10 45	11 13	11 47	12 15	12 47	13 13		14 14	14 47	15 16	15 47	16 16	16 46	17 16	17 47	18 31	19 40	20 30
Penzance	a		08 40																		18 44		

		GW	GW	GW
St Ives	d	20 49	21 24	22 05
Carbis Bay	d	20 52	21 27	22 08
Lelant	d	20x57	21x32	22x13
Lelant Saltings	d	21 00	21 35	22 16
St Erth	a	21 02	21 37	22 19
Penzance	a			22 30

Saturdays
15 September to 8 December

		GW	GW	GW	GW	GW	GW	GW	GW	GW	GW	GW	GW	GW	GW	GW	GW	GW	GW	GW	GW	GW	GW
St Ives	d	07 12	08 15	09 18	09 50	10 28	11 03	11 33	12 03	12 33	13 03	13 33	14 03	14 33	15 03	15 33	16 03	16 33	17 03	17 32	18 17	19 25	20 10
Carbis Bay	d	07 15	08 18	09 21		10 31		11 36		12 36		13 36		14 36		15 36		16 36		17 35	18 20	19 28	20 13
Lelant	d	07x19	08x22	09x25																17x40	18x25	19x33	20x18
Lelant Saltings	d			09 27		10 38		11 43		12 43		13 43	14 12	14 43	15 12	15 43	16 12	16 43	17 12	17 43	18 28	19 36	20 21
St Erth	a	07 24	08 28	09 32	10 00	10 40	11 13	11 47	12 15	12 47	13 13	13 47	14 14	14 47	15 16	15 47	16 16	16 46	17 16	17 47	18 31	19 40	20 25
Penzance	a		08 40																		18 44		

		GW	GW	GW
St Ives	d	20 49	21 24	22 05
Carbis Bay	d	20 52	21 27	22 08
Lelant	d	20x57	21x32	22x13
Lelant Saltings	d	21 00	21 35	22 16
St Erth	a	21 02	21 37	22 19
Penzance	a			22 30

Sundays
20 May to 9 September

		GW	GW	GW	GW	GW	GW	GW	GW	GW	GW	GW	GW	GW	GW	GW	GW	GW	GW	GW	GW
St Ives	d	09 10	09 40	10 15	10 50	11 26	11 56	12 33	13 03	13 31	14 03	14 31	15 03	15 33	16 03	16 33	17 03	17 40	18 12	18 50	19 46
Carbis Bay	d	09 13		10 18		11 29		12 36		13 34		14 34		15 36		16 36		17 43	18 15	18 53	19 49
Lelant	d	09x18																17 48	18 20	18 58	19x54
Lelant Saltings	d	09 21	09 49	10 25	10 59	11 36	12 05	12a42	13 12	13 41	14 12	14 41	15a11	15 43	16 12	16 43	17 12	17 51	18 23	19 01	19 57
St Erth	a	09 23	09 51	10 27	11 01	11 38	12 07		13 14	13 43	14 14	14 43		15 45	16 14	16 45	17 14	17 53	18 25	19 03	20 00
Penzance	a																				20 09

Sundays
16 September to 21 October

		GW	GW	GW	GW	GW	GW	GW	GW	GW	GW	GW	GW	GW	GW	GW	GW	GW
St Ives	d	10 52	11 27	11 57	12 33	13 04	13 34	14 04	14 33	15 03	15 33	16 03	16 33	17 03	17 40	18 11	18 50	19 46
Carbis Bay	d	10 55	11 30		12 36	13 07	13 37		14 36		15 36		16 36		17 43		18 51	19 49
Lelant	d	11x00			12 41											18 18	18 58	19x54
Lelant Saltings	d	11 03	11 37	12 06	12 44	13 14	13 44	14 13	14 43	15 12	15 43	16 12	16 43	17 12	17 50	18 21	19 01	19 57
St Erth	a	11 05	11 39	12 08	12 46	13 16	13 46	14 15	14 45	15 14	15 45	16 14	16 45	17 14	17 52	18 24	19 03	20 00
Penzance	a																	20 09

A from 10 September
B until 7 September

For connections at St Erth refer to Table T135

Table T148-F

Reading - Guildford, Redhill and Gatwick Airport

Mondays to Fridays
21 May to 5 October

Miles	Station			GW MX	GW 🛒	GW 🛒	GW 🛒	GW 🛒	GW 🛒	GW	GW	GW 🛒	GW	GW	GW	GW	GW	GW	GW	GW	GW	GW	GW	GW
0	**Reading [7]**	149	d		04 31	05 32	05 54	06 05	06 32	07 04	07 34	08 04	08 20	08 32		09 04	09 32	10 04	10 32	11 04	11 32	12 04	12 32	13 04
6½	Wokingham	149	d		04 40	05 41	06 05	06 14	06 41	07 13	07 43	08 13	08 29	08 41		09 13	09 42	10 13	10 41	11 13	11 41	12 13	12 41	13 13
10	Crowthorne		d				06 11	06 21		07 18	07 48	08 18	08 35			09 18		10 19		11 18		12 18		13 18
11½	Sandhurst		d				06 15	06 25		07 22	07 52	08 22	08 38			09 22		10 22		11 22		12 22		13 22
13½	Blackwater		d		04 48	05 49	06 18	06 28	06 49	07 25	07 55	08 25	08 42	08 49		09 25	09 50	10 26	10 49	11 25	11 49	12 25	12 52	13 25
15½	Farnborough North		d	00 02			06 23	06 33		07 30	08 00	08 30	08 46			09 30		10 30		11 30		12 30		13 30
17½	North Camp		d	00 04	04 54	05 56	06 27	06 37	06 56	07 34	08 04	08 34	08 50	08 55		09 34	09 57	10 34	10 55	11 34	11 55	12 34	13 01	13 34
19½	Ash [5]	149	d	00 08			06 31	06 41		07 38	08 08	08 38	08 54			09 38		10 38		11 38		12 38		13 38
21½	Wanborough	149	d	00 12			06 35								←									
25¾	**Guildford**	149	a	00 19	05 06	06 07	06 42	06 50	07 07	07 47	08 17	08 47	09 03	09 07	09 03	09 47	10 08	10 47	11 06	11 47	12 07	12 47	13 12	13 47
—			d	00 21	05 10	06 08	06 44	06 57	07 08	07 48	08 18	08 49	09 12	09 08	09 12	09 48	10 09	10 48	11 08	11 48	12 09	12 48	13 13	13 48
27¾	Shalford		d				06 50	07a02		07 53		08 54	→		09 19	09 53		10 53		11 53		12 54		13 53
29¾	Chilworth		d				06 54			07 57		08 58			09 24	09 57				11 57				13 57
33½	Gomshall		d				07 00			08 04		09 04			09 31	10 04				12 04				14 04
38¼	Dorking West		d				07 08			08 11		09 12			09 38			11 06				13 06		
39	Dorking Deepdene		d	00 37	05 26	06 25	07 10		07 24	08 14	08 35	09 14		09 26	09 41	10 11	10 26	11 08	11 26	12 11	12 26	13 09	13 30	14 11
41¾	Betchworth		d				07 15			08 19		09 19			09 46			11 14				13 14		
44½	Reigate	186	d	00 45	05 35	06 32	07 20		07 32	08 24	08 42	09 24		09 36	09 51	10 19	10 34	11 19	11 34	12 19	12 34	13 19	13 38	14 19
46½	**Redhill**	186	a	00 49	05 39	06 37	07 24		07 37	08 28	08 46	09 28		09 41	09 55	10 23	10 38	11 25	11 38	12 23	12 38	13 23	13 42	14 23
52¾	**Gatwick Airport [10]**	186	a	01 07	05 51	06 54			07 51	08 51				09 51			10 53		11 51		12 51		13 53	

Station			GW	GW	GW	GW	GW	GW	GW	GW 🛒	GW	GW	GW	XC ◇[1]	GW	GW 🛒	GW 🛒	GW	GW 🛒	GW	GW	GW
Reading [7]	149	d	13 32	14 04	14 32	15 04	15 28	16 04	16 32	16 51	17 04	17 32	18 04	18 21	18 31	19 02	19 32	20 04	20 29	21 26	22 36	23 34
Wokingham	149	d	13 41	14 13	14 41	15 13	15 39	16 13	16 41	17 01	17 13	17 41	18 13		18 40	19 11	19 41	20 13	20 38	21 35	22 45	23 43
Crowthorne		d		14 18		15 18	15 44	16 18		17 06	17 18	17 46	18 18			19 16		20 18		21 40	22 50	23 48
Sandhurst		d		14 22		15 22	15 48	16 22		17 10	17 22	17 49	18 22			19 20		20 22		21 44	22 54	23 52
Blackwater		d	13 49	14 25	14 49	15 25	15 51	16 25	16 49	17 13	17 25	17 53	18 25		18 48	19 23	19 49	20 25	20 46	21 47	22 57	23 55
Farnborough North		d		14 30		15 30		16 30		17 18	17 30		18 30			19 28		20 30		21 52	23 02	00 02
North Camp		d	13 55	14 34	14 55	15 34	15 58	16 34	16 55	17 22	17 34	17 59	18 34		18 54	19 32	19 55	20 34	20 52	21 56	23 06	00 04
Ash [5]	149	d		14 38		15 38		16 38		17 26	17 38		18 38			19 36		20 38		22 00	23 10	00 08
Wanborough	149	d						16 42			17 42											00 12
Guildford	149	a	14 07	14 47	15 06	15 47	16 09	16 49	17 08	17 35	17 49	18 10	18 47	18 59	19 05	19 45	20 06	20 47	21 04	22 09	23 19	00 19
		d	14 08	14 47	15 08	15 48	16 10	16 50	17 09	17 36	17 50	18 11	18 50		19 06	19 50	20 07	20 47	21 08	22 10	23 20	00 21
Shalford		d		14 53		15 53		16 55		17a41	17 55		18 55			19a54		20 53	21 13	22 15	23 25	
Chilworth		d				15 57		16 59			17 59		18 59					20 57			23 29	
Gomshall		d				16 04		17 06			18 06		19 06		19 18			21 04	21 21		23 35	
Dorking West		d		15 06		16 11		17 13			18 14		19 13					21 11			23 43	
Dorking Deepdene		d	14 26	15 08	15 26	16 13	16 28	17 16	17 26		18 16	18 28	19 16		19 26		20 24	21 14	21 29	22 29	23 45	00 37
Betchworth		d		15 13		16 18		17 21			18 21		19 21					21 19			23 50	
Reigate	186	d	14 34	15 20	15 34	16 23	16 36	17 26	17 34		18 26	18 35	19 26		19 34		20 35	21 24	21 36	22 36	23 55	00 45
Redhill	186	a	14 39	15 26	15 38	16 27	16 40	17 32	17 40		18 30	18 39	19 32		19 40		20 39	21 28	21 40	22 40	00 01	00 49
Gatwick Airport [10]	186	a	14 51		15 51		16 52		17 51			18 50			19 50		20 54		21 53	22 52	00 20	01 07

Mondays to Fridays
8 October to 7 December

Station			GW MX	GW 🛒	GW 🛒	GW 🛒	GW 🛒	GW 🛒	GW	GW	GW 🛒	GW	GW	GW	GW	GW	GW	GW	GW	GW	GW	GW	GW	GW
Reading [7]	149	d		04 31	05 32	05 54	06 05	06 32	07 04	07 34	08 04	08 32	09 04	09 32	10 04	10 32	11 04	11 32	12 04	12 32	13 04	13 32	14 04	14 32
Wokingham	149	d		04 40	05 41	06 05	06 14	06 41	07 13	07 43	08 13	08 41	09 13	09 42	10 13	10 41	11 13	11 41	12 13	12 41	13 13	13 41	14 13	14 41
Crowthorne		d				06 11	06 21		07 18	07 48	08 18		09 18		10 19		11 18		12 18		13 18		14 18	
Sandhurst		d				06 15	06 25		07 22	07 52	08 22		09 22		10 22		11 22		12 22		13 22		14 22	
Blackwater		d		04 48	05 49	06 18	06 28	06 49	07 25	07 55	08 25	08 49	09 25	09 50	10 26	10 49	11 25	11 49	12 25	12 52	13 25	13 49	14 25	14 49
Farnborough North		d	00 02			06 23	06 33		07 30	08 00	08 30		09 30		10 30		11 30		12 30		13 30		14 30	
North Camp		d	00 04	04 54	05 56	06 27	06 37	06 56	07 34	08 04	08 34	08 55	09 34	09 57	10 34	10 55	11 34	11 55	12 34	13 01	13 34	13 55	14 34	14 55
Ash [5]	149	d	00 08			06 31	06 41		07 38	08 08	08 38		09 38		10 38		11 38		12 38		13 38		14 38	
Wanborough	149	d	00 12			06 35																		
Guildford	149	a	00 19	05 06	06 07	06 42	06 50	07 07	07 47	08 17	08 47	09 07	09 47	10 08	10 47	11 06	11 47	12 07	12 47	13 12	13 47	14 07	14 47	15 06
		d	00 21	05 10	06 08	06 44	06 57	07 08	07 48	08 18	08 49	09 08	09 48	10 09	10 48	11 08	11 48	12 09	12 48	13 13	13 48	14 08	14 47	15 08
Shalford		d				06 50	07a02		07 53		08 54		09 53		10 53		11 53		12 54		13 53		14 53	
Chilworth		d				06 54			07 57		08 58		09 57				11 57				13 57			
Gomshall		d				07 00			08 04		09 04		10 04				12 04				14 04			
Dorking West		d				07 08			08 11		09 12				11 06				13 06				15 06	
Dorking Deepdene		d	00 37	05 26	06 25	07 10		07 24	08 14	08 35	09 14	09 26	10 11	10 26	11 08	11 26	12 11	12 26	13 09	13 30	14 11	14 26	15 08	15 26
Betchworth		d				07 15			08 19		09 19				11 14				13 14				15 13	
Reigate	186	d	00 45	05 35	06 32	07 20		07 32	08 24	08 42	09 24	09 36	10 19	10 34	11 19	11 34	12 19	12 34	13 19	13 38	14 19	14 34	15 20	15 34
Redhill	186	a	00 49	05 39	06 37	07 24		07 37	08 28	08 46	09 28	09 41	10 23	10 38	11 25	11 38	12 23	12 38	13 23	13 42	14 23	14 39	15 26	15 38
Gatwick Airport [10]	186	a	01 07	05 51	06 54			07 51	08 51			09 51		10 53		11 51		12 51		13 53		14 51		15 51

Table T148-F

Reading - Guildford, Redhill and Gatwick Airport

Mondays to Fridays
8 October to 7 December

Station			GW	GW	GW	GW	GW 🛒	GW	GW	GW	XC ◇[1]	GW	GW 🛒	GW 🛒	GW	GW 🛒	GW	GW
Reading [7]	149	d	15 04	15 28	16 04	16 32	16 51	17 04	17 32	18 04	18 21	18 31	19 02	19 32	20 04	20 29	22 36	23 34
Wokingham	149	d	15 13	15 39	16 13	16 41	17 01	17 13	17 41	18 13		18 40	19 11	19 41	20 13	20 38	22 45	23 43
Crowthorne		d	15 18	15 44	16 18		17 06	17 18	17 46	18 18			19 16		20 18		22 50	23 48
Sandhurst		d	15 22	15 48	16 22		17 10	17 22	17 49	18 22			19 20		20 22		22 54	23 52
Blackwater		d	15 25	15 51	16 25	16 49	17 13	17 25	17 53	18 25		18 48	19 23	19 49	20 25	20 46	22 57	23 55
Farnborough North		d	15 30		16 30		17 18	17 30		18 30			19 28		20 30		23 02	00 02
North Camp		d	15 34	15 58	16 34	16 55	17 22	17 34	17 59	18 34		18 54	19 32	19 55	20 34	20 52	23 06	00 04
Ash [5]	149	d	15 38		16 38		17 26	17 38		18 38			19 36		20 38		23 10	00 08
Wanborough	149	d			16 42			17 42										00 12
Guildford	149	a	15 47	16 09	16 49	17 08	17 35	17 49	18 10	18 47	18 59	19 05	19 45	20 06	20 47	21 04	23 19	00 19
		d	15 48	16 10	16 50	17 09	17 36	17 50	18 11	18 50		19 06	19 50	20 07	20 47	21 08	23 20	00 21
Shalford		d	15 53		16 55		17a41	17 55		18 55			19a54		20 53	21 13	23 25	
Chilworth		d	15 57		16 59			17 59		18 59					20 57		23 29	
Gomshall		d	16 04		17 06			18 06		19 06		19 18			21 04	21 21	23 35	
Dorking West		d	16 11		17 13			18 14		19 13					21 11		23 43	
Dorking Deepdene		d	16 13	16 28	17 16	17 26		18 16	18 28	19 16		19 26		20 24	21 14	21 29	23 45	00 37
Betchworth		d	16 18		17 21			18 21		19 21					21 19		23 50	
Reigate	186	d	16 23	16 36	17 26	17 34		18 26	18 35	19 26		19 34		20 35	21 24	21 36	23 55	00 45
Redhill	186	a	16 27	16 40	17 32	17 40		18 30	18 39	19 32		19 40		20 39	21 28	21 40	00 01	00 49
Gatwick Airport [10]	186	a		16 52		17 51			18 50			19 50		20 54		21 53	00 20	01 07

Saturdays
26 May to 8 December

Station			GW	GW	GW	GW	GW	GW	GW	GW [1]	GW	GW [1]	GW	GW [1]	GW	GW [1]	GW	GW	GW [1]	GW	GW [1]	GW	GW [1]	GW
Reading [7]	149	d		04 31	05 16	05 35		06 01	06 19	06 51	07 20	07 51	08 20	09 01	09 20	10 01	10 20	11 20	12 01	12 20	13 01	14 20	15 01	15 20
Wokingham	149	d		04 40	05 25	05 45		06 10	06 29	07 00	07 29	08 00	08 29	09 10	09 29	10 10	10 29	11 31	12 10	12 29	13 10	14 29	15 10	15 29
Crowthorne		d			05 31				06 35	07 05	07 35	08 05	08 35		09 35		10 35	11 36		12 35		14 35		15 35
Sandhurst		d			05 35				06 38	07 09	07 38	08 09	08 38		09 38		10 38	11 40		12 38		14 38		15 38
Blackwater		d		04 48	05 38			06 18	06 42	07 12	07 42	08 12	08 42	09 19	09 42	10 19	10 42	11 43	12 18	12 42	13 18	14 42	15 18	15 42
Farnborough North		d	00 02		05 43				06 46	07 17	07 46	08 16	08 46		09 46		10 46	11 48		12 46		14 46		15 46
North Camp		d	00 04	04 54	05 47			06 24	06 50	07 21	07 50	08 20	08 50	09 25	09 50	10 26	10 50	11 52	12 25	12 50	13 25	14 50	15 24	15 50
Ash [5]	149	d	00 08		05 51				06 54	07 25	07 54	08 25	08 54		09 54		10 54	11 56		12 54		14 54		15 54
Wanborough	149	d	00 12		05 55		←																	
Guildford	149	a	00 19	05 06	06 02	06 07	06 02	06 38	07 03	07 34	08 03	08 34	09 03	09 38	10 03	10 38	11 03	12 05	12 38	13 03	13 37	15 03	15 37	16 03
		d	00 21	05 10	06 11	06 08	06 11	06 39	07 14	07 38	08 15	08 37	09 15	09 39	10 16	10 39	11 16	12 17	12 40	13 17	13 38	15 16	15 38	16 16
Shalford		d			→		06 17		07 20		08 21		09 20		10 22		11 21	12 22		13 23		15 22		16 21
Chilworth		d					06 21		07 24		08 25		09 24				11 26			13 27		15 26		16 25
Gomshall		d					06 27		07 30		08 31		09 31				11 32			13 33		15 33		16 31
Dorking West		d					06 35		07 38		08 39		09 38		10 35			12 35						16 39
Dorking Deepdene		d	00 37	05 26		06 26	06 37	06 55	07 40	07 56	08 41	08 56	09 41	09 55	10 37	10 56	11 39	12 37	12 56	13 41	13 55	15 40	15 55	16 41
Betchworth		d					06 42		07 45		08 46		09 46		10 42			12 42						16 46
Reigate	186	d	00 45	05 35		06 34	06 47	07 04	07 50	08 04	08 51	09 04	09 51	10 04	10 47	11 04	11 47	12 48	13 04	13 48	14 04	15 48	16 04	16 51
Redhill	186	a	00 49	05 39		06 38	06 51	07 09	07 54	08 08	08 56	09 09	09 55	10 08	10 52	11 08	11 52	12 52	13 08	13 52	14 08	15 52	16 08	16 56
Gatwick Airport [10]	186	a	01 07	05 51		06 54		07 20		08 20		09 21		10 20		11 20			13 20		14 20		16 21	

Station			GW [1]	GW	GW [1]	GW	GW [1]	XC ◇[1]	GW [1]	GW [1]	GW	GW [1]	GW [1]	GW [1]	GW [1]	GW [1]
Reading [7]	149	d	16 01	16 20	17 01	17 20	18 01	18 23	19 01	19 20	19 36	20 01	20 29	21 23	22 36	23 34
Wokingham	149	d	16 10	16 29	17 10	17 29	18 10		19 10	19 29	19 45	20 10	20 38	21 32	22 45	23 43
Crowthorne		d		16 35		17 35				19 35	19 50			21 37	22 50	23 48
Sandhurst		d		16 38		17 38				19 38	19 54			21 41	22 54	23 52
Blackwater		d	16 18	16 42	17 18	17 42	18 18		19 18	19 42	19 57	20 18	20 46	21 44	22 57	23 55
Farnborough North		d		16 46		17 46				19 46	20 02			21 49	23 02	23 59
North Camp		d	16 25	16 50	17 25	17 50	18 25		19 24	19 50	20 06	20 24	20 52	21 53	23 06	00 04
Ash [5]	149	d		16 54		17 54				19 54	20 10			21 57	23 10	00 08
Wanborough	149	d		16 58		17 59										00 12
Guildford	149	a	16 38	17 05	17 36	18 06	18 36	19 01	19 38	20 05	20 19	20 35	21 04	22 08	23 19	00 19
		d	16 39	17 16	17 37	18 15	18 38		19 39	20 07	20 19	20 38	21 08	22 10	23 20	00 21
Shalford		d		17 21	17 42	18 20				20 12	20 24		21 13	22 15	23 25	
Chilworth		d		17 25		18 24					20 28				23 29	
Gomshall		d		17 31		18 31					20 35	20 49	21 21		23 35	
Dorking West		d		17 39		18 39					20 42				23 43	
Dorking Deepdene		d	16 56	17 41	17 56	18 41	18 55		19 56	20 26	20 46	20 57	21 29	22 28	23 45	00 37
Betchworth		d		17 46		18 46					20 51				23 50	
Reigate	186	d	17 04	17 51	18 04	18 51	19 04		20 04	20 34	20 56	21 04	21 36	22 36	23 55	00 45
Redhill	186	a	17 09	17 55	18 08	18 55	19 08		20 08	20 38	21 00	21 08	21 40	22 40	23 59	00 49
Gatwick Airport [10]	186	a	17 21		18 20		19 20		20 20	20 50		21 20	21 51	22 51	00 20	01 05

20 May to 2 December

Reading - Guildford, Redhill and Gatwick Airport

			GW	GW	GW	GW	GW	GW	GW	GW	GW	GW	GW	GW	GW	GW	GW	GW	GW	GW	GW	GW	GW	GW
			■ A			■		■		■ B	■ C		■		■		■		■		■		■	
Reading 7	149	d		06 03	07 12	07 48	08 18	08 48	09 18	09 48	09 48	10 18	10 48	11 18	11 48	12 18	12 48	13 18	13 48	14 18	14 48	15 18	15 48	16 18
Wokingham	149	d		06 11	07 20	07 57	08 26	08 57	09 26	09 57	09 57	10 26	10 57	11 26	11 57	12 26	12 57	13 26	13 57	14 26	14 57	15 26	15 57	16 26
Crowthorne		d				08 02		09 02		10 02	10 03		11 02		12 02		13 02		14 02		15 02		16 02	
Sandhurst		d				08 05		09 05		10 05	10 06		11 05		12 05		13 05		14 05		15 05		16 05	
Blackwater		d		06 20	07 29	08 09	08 34	09 09	09 34	10 09	10 09	10 34	11 09	11 34	12 09	12 34	13 09	13 34	14 09	14 34	15 09	15 34	16 09	16 34
Farnborough North		d				08 13		09 13		10 13	10 13		11 13		12 13		13 13		14 13		15 13		16 13	
North Camp		d	00 04	06 27	07 36	08 17	08 41	09 17	09 41	10 17	10 17	10 41	11 17	11 41	12 17	12 41	13 17	13 41	14 17	14 41	15 17	15 41	16 17	16 41
Ash 5	149	d	00 08			08 21		09 21		10 21	10 21		11 21		12 21		13 21		14 21		15 21		16 21	
Wanborough	149	d	00 12																					
Guildford	149	a	00 19	06 38	07 47	08 30	08 52	09 30	09 52	10 30	10 30	10 52	11 30	11 52	12 30	12 52	13 30	13 52	14 30	14 52	15 30	15 52	16 30	16 52
		d	00 21	06 39	07 47	08 31	08 52	09 31	09 52	10 31	10 32	10 52	11 31	11 52	12 31	12 52	13 31	13 52	14 31	14 52	15 31	15 52	16 31	16 52
Shalford		d				08 36		09 36		10 36	10 37		11 36		12 36		13 36		14 36		15 36		16 36	
Chilworth		d				08 40				10 40	10 41				12 40				14 40				16 40	
Gomshall		d				08 47				10 47	10 47				12 47				14 47				16 47	
Dorking West		d						09 49					11 49				13 49				15 49			
Dorking Deepdene		d	00 37	06 56	08 05	08 54	09 09	09 52	10 09	10 54	10 55	11 09	11 52	12 09	12 54	13 09	13 52	14 09	14 54	15 09	15 52	16 09	16 54	17 09
Betchworth		d						09 57					11 57				13 57				15 57			
Reigate	186	d	00 45	07 04	08 13	09 02	09 17	10 02	10 17	11 02	11 02	11 17	12 02	12 17	13 02	13 17	14 02	14 17	15 02	15 17	16 02	16 17	17 02	17 17
Redhill	186	a	00 49	07 08	08 17	09 06	09 24	10 06	10 24	11 06	11 06	11 24	12 06	12 24	13 06	13 24	14 06	14 24	15 06	15 24	16 06	16 24	17 06	17 24
Gatwick Airport 10	186	a	01 05	07 27	08 28		09 35		10 35			11 35		12 35		13 35		14 35		15 35		16 35		17 35

			GW	GW	GW	GW	GW	GW	GW	GW	XC	XC	GW
			■		■		■		■		◇■ D	◇ E	■
Reading 7	149	d	16 48	17 18	17 48	18 18	18 48	19 18	20 18	21 18	22 14	22 14	22 17
Wokingham	149	d	16 57	17 26	17 57	18 26	18 57	19 26	20 26	21 26			22 26
Crowthorne		d	17 02		18 02		19 02		20 32	21 32			
Sandhurst		d	17 05		18 05		19 05		20 36	21 36			
Blackwater		d	17 09	17 34	18 09	18 34	19 09	19 35	20 39	21 39			22 34
Farnborough North		d	17 13		18 13		19 13		20 45	21 44			
North Camp		d	17 17	17 41	18 17	18 41	19 17	19 41	20 48	21 48			22 41
Ash 5	149	d	17 21		18 21		19 21		20 52	21 52			
Wanborough	149	d											
Guildford	149	a	17 30	17 52	18 30	18 52	19 30	19 52	21 01	22 01	22 42	22 42	22 52
		d	17 31	17 52	18 31	18 52	19 31	19 52	21 02	22 01			22 56
Shalford		d	17 36		18 36		19 36		21 07				23 01
Chilworth		d			18 40				21 11				23 05
Gomshall		d			18 47				21 18				23 11
Dorking West		d	17 49				19 49		21 25				23 18
Dorking Deepdene		d	17 52	18 09	18 54	19 09	19 52	20 10	21 27	22 19			23 19
Betchworth		d	17 57				19 57		21 33				23 26
Reigate	186	d	18 02	18 17	19 02	19 17	20 02	20 17	21 37	22 29			23 29
Redhill	186	a	18 06	18 24	19 06	19 24	20 06	20 24	21 43	22 35			23 35
Gatwick Airport 10	186	a		18 35		19 35		20 35	21 54	22 47			23 48

A not 20 May
B from 16 September
C until 9 September
D until 15 July, from 9 September
E from 22 July until 2 September

21 May to 5 October

Gatwick Airport, Redhill and Guildford - Reading

Miles				GW	GW	GW	XC	XC	GW	GW	GW	GW	GW	GW	GW	GW	GW	GW	GW	GW	GW	GW	GW	GW
				MO	MX	MO	◇■ A	◇■ B ✠																
0	**Gatwick Airport** 10	186	d						05 10	06 00			07 03		08 02			09 03			10 00		11 00	
5¾	**Redhill**	186	d						05 35	06 15	06 30		07 14	07 31	08 14		08 51	09 14		09 33	10 14	10 30	11 14	11 30
7¾	Reigate	186	d						05 39	06 19	06 40		07 18	07 39	08 18		08 56	09 18		09 38	10 18	10 38	11 18	11 39
10½	Betchworth		d											07 43			09 00			09 43		10 43		
13¼	Dorking Deepdene		d						05 46	06 26	06 47		07 25	07 48	08 25		09 05	09 25		09 47	10 25	10 47	11 25	11 46
14	Dorking West		d											07 50			09 07			09 50		10 50		
18¾	Gomshall		d											07 58			09 15			09 58				11 54
22½	Chilworth		d											08 03			09 21			10 04				12 00
24½	Shalford		d									07 21		08 07			09 30		←	10 08		11 03		12 04
26½	**Guildford**		a						06 05	06 42	07 03	07 25	07 41	08 12	08 41		09 36	09 42	09 36	10 13	10 42	11 08	11 42	12 08
—			d		00 03		06 01	06 01	06 06	06 43	07 04	07 27	07 43	08 13	08 43	09 10	09 48	09 44	09 48	10 15	10 44	11 09	11 44	12 10
30¾	Wanborough	149	d						06 13					08 20		09 18	→							
32¾	Ash 5	149	d	00 08					06 18	06 53	07 14	07 36	07 52	08 25		09 22			09 57	10 24		11 19		12 20
34¾	North Camp		d	00 12	00 15				06 22	06 57	07 18	07 41	07 56	08 29	08 55	09 26			10 01	10 28	10 56	11 23	11 56	12 24
36¾	Farnborough North		d	00 16					06 26	07 01	07 22	07 45	08 00	08 33					10 05	10 32		11 27		12 28
38¾	Blackwater		d	00 20	00 22	←			06 30	07 05	07 27	07 49	08 05	08 37	09 02	09 33			10 10	10 37	11 02	11 31	12 02	12 32
40¾	Sandhurst		d	00 23		00 23			06 34	07 09	07 30	07 53	08 08	08 41					10 13	10 40		11 35		12 36
42¼	Crowthorne		d	→		00 27			06 38	07 13	07 34	07 57	08 12	08 45					10 17	10 44		11 39		12 40
45½	Wokingham	149	d		00 30	00 33			06 43	07 18	07 39	08 02	08 17	08 50	09 10	09 41		10 06	10 22	10 49	11 10	11 44	12 10	12 45
52¼	**Reading** 7	149	a		00 42	00 43	06 33	06 33	06 51	07 26	07 48	08 16	08 29	08 59	09 18	09 49		10 15	10 31	10 58	11 19	11 52	12 19	12 53

			GW	GW	GW	GW	GW	GW	GW	GW	GW	GW	GW	GW	GW	GW	GW	GW	GW	GW	GW	GW	GW
Gatwick Airport 10	186	d	12 00		13 00		14 00		15 00		16 00		17 00			18 00		19 00		20 00		21 00	
Redhill	186	d	12 14	12 30	13 14	13 30	14 14	14 30	15 14	15 29	16 14	16 31	17 14		17 45	18 14	18 43	19 13		20 13	20 34	21 13	21 35
Reigate	186	d	12 18	12 38	13 18	13 38	14 18	14 38	15 18	15 34	16 18	16 35	17 18		17 49	18 18	18 47	19 17		20 18	20 38	21 18	21 39
Betchworth		d		12 43						15 38		16 40			17 54		18 52				20 43		21 44
Dorking Deepdene		d	12 25	12 47	13 25	13 45	14 25	14 45	15 25	15 43	16 25	16 44	17 25		17 58	18 25	18 56	19 24		20 25	20 47	21 25	21 48
Dorking West		d		12 50						15 45					18 01		18 59				20 50		21 51
Gomshall		d				13 53		14 53		15 53		16 52			18 09		19 07				20 58		21 59
Chilworth		d				13 59		14 59		15 59		16 58			18 15		19 13				21 04		22 05
Shalford		d		13 03		14 03		15 03		16 03		17 02		17 58	18 19		19 17		20 02		21 08		22 09
Guildford		a	12 42	13 08	13 42	14 08	14 42	15 08	15 42	16 08	16 43	17 07	17 42	18 02	18 23	18 42	19 22	19 42	20 06	20 42	21 12	21 42	22 13
		d	12 44	13 09	13 44	14 09	14 44	15 09	15 44	16 09	16 44	17 09	17 44	18 04	18 26	18 46	19 26	19 43	20 10	20 44	21 17	21 44	22 15
Wanborough	149	d																					
Ash 5	149	d		13 19		14 19		15 19		16 19		17 19	17 53	18 14	18 35		19 35		20 19		21 27		22 23
North Camp		d	12 56	13 23	13 56	14 23	14 56	15 23	15 56	16 23	16 56	17 23	17 57	18 18	18 39	19 01	19 39	19 56	20 23	20 56	21 31	21 56	22 28
Farnborough North		d		13 27		14 27		15 27		16 27		17 27	18 01	18 22	18 43		19 43		20 27		21 35		22 32
Blackwater		d	13 02	13 31	14 02	14 31	15 02	15 32	16 02	16 31	17 02	17 31	18 06	18 27	18 48	19 07	19 48	20 02	20 32	21 02	21 39	22 02	22 36
Sandhurst		d		13 35		14 35		15 35		16 35		17 35		18 30	18 51		19 51		20 35		21 43		22 40
Crowthorne		d		13 39		14 39		15 39		16 39		17 39		18 34	18 58		19 57		20 39		21 47		22 44
Wokingham	149	d	13 10	13 44	14 10	14 44	15 10	15 44	16 10	16 44	17 10	17 44	18 14	18 39	19 06	19 17	20 02	20 10	20 44	21 09	21 52	22 09	22 49
Reading 7	149	a	13 19	13 52	14 19	14 52	15 19	15 53	16 19	16 52	17 19	17 52	18 23	18 48	19 18	19 29	20 15	20 24	20 57	21 20	22 00	22 21	22 58

			GW	GW
Gatwick Airport 10	186	d	22 00	23 18
Redhill	186	d	22 12	23 32
Reigate	186	d	22 16	23 36
Betchworth		d	22 21	
Dorking Deepdene		d	22 25	23 43
Dorking West		d	22 28	
Gomshall		d	22 36	
Chilworth		d	22 42	
Shalford		d	22 46	
Guildford		a	22 50	00 02
		d	22 52	00 03
Wanborough	149	d	22 59	
Ash 5	149	d	23 03	
North Camp		d	23 07	00 15
Farnborough North		d	23 11	
Blackwater		d	23 15	00 22
Sandhurst		d	23 19	
Crowthorne		d	23 26	
Wokingham	149	d	23 35	00 30
Reading 7	149	a	23 49	00 42

A until 20 July
B from 23 July

Table T148-R

Gatwick Airport, Redhill and Guildford - Reading

Mondays to Fridays
8 October to 7 December

		GW MO	GW MX	GW MO	XC ◇■	GW	GW	GW	GW	GW	GW	GW	GW	GW	GW	GW	GW	GW	GW	GW	GW	GW	GW
Gatwick Airport ■	186 d					05 10	06 00		07 03		08 02		09 03		10 00		11 00		12 00		13 00		14 00
Redhill	186 d					05 35	06 15		07 14	07 31	08 14		09 14	09 33	10 14	10 30	11 14	11 30	12 14	12 30	13 14	13 30	14 14
Reigate	186 d					05 39	06 19		07 18	07 39	08 18		09 18	09 38	10 18	10 38	11 18	11 39	12 18	12 38	13 18	13 38	14 18
Betchworth	d									07 43				09 43		10 43				12 43			
Dorking Deepdene	d					05 46	06 26		07 25	07 48	08 25		09 25	09 47	10 25	10 47	11 25	11 46	12 25	12 47	13 25	13 45	14 25
Dorking West	d									07 50				09 50		10 50				12 50			
Gomshall	d									07 58				09 58				11 54				13 53	
Chilworth	d									08 03				10 04				12 00				13 59	
Shalford	d							07 21		08 07				10 08		11 03		12 04		13 03		14 03	
Guildford	a					06 05	06 42	07 25	07 41	08 12	08 41		09 42	10 13	10 42	11 08	11 42	12 08	12 42	13 08	13 42	14 08	14 42
	d		00 03		06 01	06 06	06 43	07 27	07 43	08 13	08 43	09 10	09 44	10 15	10 44	11 09	11 44	12 10	12 44	13 09	13 44	14 09	14 44
Wanborough	149 d					06 13				08 20		09 18											
Ash ■	149 d	00 08				06 18	06 53	07 36	07 52	08 25		09 22		10 24		11 19		12 20		13 19		14 19	
North Camp	d	00 12	00 15			06 22	06 57	07 41	07 56	08 29	08 55	09 26		10 28	10 56	11 23	11 56	12 24	12 56	13 23	13 56	14 23	14 56
Farnborough North	d	00 16				06 26	07 01	07 45	08 00	08 33				10 32		11 27		12 28		13 27		14 27	
Blackwater	d	00 20	00 22	←		06 30	07 05	07 49	08 05	08 37	09 02	09 33		10 37	11 02	11 31	12 02	12 32	13 02	13 31	14 02	14 31	15 02
Sandhurst	d	00 23		00 23		06 34	07 09	07 53	08 08	08 41				10 40		11 35		12 36		13 35		14 35	
Crowthorne	d	→		00 27		06 38	07 13	07 57	08 12	08 45				10 44		11 39		12 40		13 39		14 39	
Wokingham	149 d		00 30	00 33		06 43	07 18	08 02	08 17	08 50	09 10	09 41	10 06	10 49	11 10	11 44	12 10	12 45	13 10	13 44	14 10	14 44	15 10
Reading ■	149 a		00 42	00 43	06 33	06 51	07 26	08 16	08 29	08 59	09 18	09 49	10 15	10 58	11 19	11 52	12 19	12 53	13 19	13 52	14 19	14 52	15 19

		GW	GW	GW	GW	GW	GW	GW	GW	GW	GW	GW	GW	GW	GW	GW	GW
Gatwick Airport ■	186 d		15 00		16 00		17 00				19 00			21 00		22 00	23 18
Redhill	186 d	14 30	15 14	15 29	16 14	16 31	17 14		17 45	18 43	19 13		20 34	21 13	21 35	22 12	23 32
Reigate	186 d	14 38	15 18	15 34	16 18	16 35	17 18		17 49	18 47	19 17		20 38	21 18	21 39	22 16	23 36
Betchworth	d			15 38		16 40			17 54	18 52			20 43		21 44	22 21	
Dorking Deepdene	d	14 45	15 25	15 43	16 25	16 44	17 25		17 58	18 56	19 24		20 47	21 25	21 48	22 25	23 43
Dorking West	d			15 45					18 01	18 59			20 50		21 51	22 28	
Gomshall	d	14 53		15 53		16 52			18 09	19 07			20 58		21 59	22 36	
Chilworth	d	14 59		15 59		16 58			18 15	19 13			21 04		22 05	22 42	
Shalford	d	15 03		16 03		17 02		17 58	18 19	19 17		20 02	21 08		22 09	22 46	
Guildford	a	15 08	15 42	16 08	16 43	17 07	17 42	18 02	18 23	19 22	19 42	20 06	21 12	21 42	22 13	22 50	00 02
	d	15 09	15 44	16 09	16 44	17 09	17 44	18 04	18 26	19 26	19 43	20 10	21 17	21 44	22 15	22 52	00 03
Wanborough	149 d															22 59	
Ash ■	149 d	15 19		16 19		17 19	17 53	18 14	18 35	19 35		20 19	21 27		22 23	23 03	
North Camp	d	15 23	15 56	16 23	16 56	17 23	17 57	18 18	18 39	19 39	19 56	20 23	21 31	21 56	22 28	23 07	00 15
Farnborough North	d	15 27		16 27		17 27	18 01	18 22	18 43	19 43		20 27	21 35		22 32	23 11	
Blackwater	d	15 32	16 02	16 31	17 02	17 31	18 06	18 27	18 48	19 48	20 02	20 32	21 39	22 02	22 36	23 15	00 22
Sandhurst	d	15 35		16 35		17 35		18 30	18 51	19 51		20 35	21 43		22 40	23 19	
Crowthorne	d	15 39		16 39		17 39		18 34	18 58	19 57		20 39	21 47		22 44	23 26	
Wokingham	149 d	15 44	16 10	16 44	17 10	17 44	18 14	18 39	19 06	20 02	20 10	20 44	21 52	22 09	22 49	23 35	00 30
Reading ■	149 a	15 53	16 19	16 52	17 19	17 52	18 23	18 48	19 18	20 15	20 24	20 57	22 00	22 21	22 58	23 49	00 42

Saturdays
26 May to 8 December

		GW	XC ◇■ A	XC ◇■ B ✕	XC ◇■ C	GW ■	GW ■	GW	GW ■	GW	GW ■	GW	GW ■	GW	GW ■	GW	GW ■	GW	GW ■	GW	GW ■	GW	GW ■
Gatwick Airport ■	186 d					06 12	06 31		07 31		08 31		09 30		10 30		11 30		12 30		13 30		14 30
Redhill	186 d					06 27	06 44	06 58	07 44	07 58	08 44	09 00	09 42	10 01	10 43	11 02	11 44	12 02	12 44	13 02	13 44	14 02	14 44
Reigate	186 d					06 34	06 49	07 04	07 49	08 04	08 49	09 04	09 47	10 06	10 49	11 06	11 49	12 06	12 49	13 06	13 49	14 06	14 49
Betchworth	d							07 08		08 08		09 09		10 10				12 11				14 11	
Dorking Deepdene	d					06 43	06 56	07 13	07 56	08 13	08 56	09 13	09 54	10 15	10 56	11 13	11 56	12 15	12 56	13 13	13 56	14 15	14 56
Dorking West	d							07 15		08 15		09 16		10 18				12 18				14 18	
Gomshall	d					06 52		07 23		08 23		09 23				11 21				13 21			
Chilworth	d							07 29		08 28		09 29				11 27				13 27			
Shalford	d					07 03		07 33		08 32		09 32		10 31		11 31		12 31		13 31		14 31	
Guildford	a					07 07	07 19	07 37	08 12	08 36	09 12	09 37	10 12	10 36	11 12	11 36	12 12	12 36	13 12	13 36	14 12	14 36	15 12
	d	00 03	06 09	06 09	06 09	07 09	07 21	07 48	08 14	08 48	09 13	09 48	10 14	10 47	11 14	11 47	12 14	12 47	13 14	13 47	14 14	14 47	15 14
Wanborough	149 d							07 55		08 55													
Ash ■	149 d						07 30	07 59		08 59		09 57		10 57		11 57		12 57		13 57		14 57	
North Camp	d	00 15				07 21	07 34	08 03	08 26	09 03	09 25	10 01	10 26	11 01	11 26	12 01	12 26	13 01	13 26	14 01	14 26	15 01	15 26
Farnborough North	d							08 07		09 07		10 05		11 05		12 05		13 05		14 05		15 05	
Blackwater	d	00 22				07 27	07 41	08 12	08 32	09 12	09 32	10 10	10 32	11 09	11 32	12 09	12 32	13 09	13 32	14 09	14 32	15 09	15 32
Sandhurst	d							08 15		09 15		10 13		11 13		12 13		13 13		14 13		15 13	
Crowthorne	d							08 18		09 18		10 17		11 17		12 17		13 17		14 17		15 17	
Wokingham	149 d	00 30				07 35	07 49	08 23	08 40	09 23	09 40	10 22	10 40	11 22	11 40	12 22	12 40	13 22	13 40	14 22	14 40	15 22	15 40
Reading ■	149 a	00 42	06 44	06 44	06 46	07 45	07 57	08 34	08 49	09 32	09 48	10 31	10 49	11 31	11 49	12 30	12 49	13 30	13 49	14 30	14 49	15 30	15 49

A until 21 July B from 28 July until 6 October C from 13 October

Table T148-R

Gatwick Airport, Redhill and Guildford - Reading

Saturdays
26 May to 8 December

		GW	GW ■	GW	GW ■	GW	GW ■	GW	GW ■	GW	GW ■	GW	GW ■	GW ■	GW	GW ■	GW ■
Gatwick Airport ■	186 d		15 30		16 30		17 30		18 30		19 30		20 30	21 00		22 00	23 18
Redhill	186 d	14 59	15 44	15 59	16 44	16 59	17 44	17 59	18 44	18 59	19 44	19 59	20 44	21 14	21 35	22 12	23 31
Reigate	186 d	15 04	15 49	16 04	16 48	17 04	17 49	18 04	18 48	19 04	19 49	20 04	20 49	21 19	21 39	22 16	23 35
Betchworth	d	15 08		16 08		17 08		18 08		19 08		20 08			21 44	22 21	
Dorking Deepdene	d	15 13	15 56	16 13	16 55	17 13	17 56	18 13	18 55	19 13	19 56	20 13	20 56	21 26	21 48	22 25	23 42
Dorking West	d	15 15		16 15		17 15		18 15		19 15		20 15			21 51	22 28	
Gomshall	d	15 23		16 23		17 23		18 23		19 23		20 23			21 59	22 36	
Chilworth	d	15 28		16 28		17 28		18 28		19 28					22 05	22 42	
Shalford	d	15 32		16 32		17 32		18 32		19 32		20 31			22 09	22 46	
Guildford	a	15 37	16 12	16 37	17 12	17 36	18 12	18 36	19 12	19 36	20 12	20 35	21 12	21 42	22 13	22 50	00 01
	d	15 48	16 14	16 48	17 14	17 48	18 14	18 48	19 14	19 48	20 14	20 48	21 14	21 44	22 14	22 52	00 03
Wanborough	149 d															22 59	
Ash ■	149 d	15 57		16 58		17 58		18 57		19 57		20 57			22 23	23 03	
North Camp	d	16 01	16 26	17 02	17 26	18 02	18 26	19 01	19 26	20 01	20 26	21 01	21 26	21 56	22 27	23 07	
Farnborough North	d	16 05		17 06		18 06		19 05		20 05		21 05			22 31	23 12	
Blackwater	d	16 10	16 32	17 10	17 32	18 10	18 32	19 10	19 32	20 10	20 32	21 10	21 32	22 02	22 35	23 17	
Sandhurst	d	16 13		17 14		18 14		19 13		20 13		21 13			22 39	23 21	
Crowthorne	d	16 17		17 18		18 18		19 17		20 17		21 17			22 43	23 26	
Wokingham	149 d	16 22	16 40	17 23	17 40	18 23	18 40	19 22	19 40	20 22	20 40	21 22	21 40	22 09	22 48	23 34	00 24
Reading ■	149 a	16 31	16 49	17 31	17 49	18 31	18 49	19 31	19 49	20 31	20 50	21 31	21 50	22 20	22 58	23 49	00 33

Sundays
20 May to 2 December

		GW ■ A	GW	GW	GW ■	GW	GW ■	GW	GW ■	GW	XC ◇■	GW ■	GW	GW ■	GW	GW ■	GW	GW ■	GW	GW ■	GW	GW ■	GW
Gatwick Airport ■	186 d		07 11	08 18		09 17		10 17		11 17			12 17		13 17		14 17		15 17		16 17		17 17
Redhill	186 d		07 20	08 29	08 43	09 28	09 43	10 28	10 43	11 28		11 43	12 28	12 43	13 28	13 43	14 28	14 43	15 28	15 43	16 28	16 43	17 28
Reigate	186 d		07 23	08 33	08 47	09 32	09 47	10 32	10 47	11 32		11 47	12 32	12 48	13 32	13 48	14 32	14 48	15 32	15 48	16 32	16 48	17 32
Betchworth	d						09 52					11 52				13 53				15 53			
Dorking Deepdene	d		07 32	08 40	08 54	09 41	09 56	10 41	10 54	11 41		11 56	12 41	12 56	13 41	13 58	14 41	14 56	15 41	15 58	16 41	16 56	17 41
Dorking West	d						09 59					11 59				14 01				16 01			
Gomshall	d				09 02				11 02					13 04				15 04				17 04	
Chilworth	d				09 08				11 08					13 10				15 10				17 10	
Shalford	d				09 12		10 12		11 12			12 12		13 15		14 15		15 15		16 15		17 15	
Guildford	a		07 50	08 56	09 17	09 57	10 17	10 57	11 20	11 57		12 20	12 57	13 20	13 57	14 20	14 57	15 20	15 57	16 20	16 57	17 20	17 57
	d	00 03	07 52	08 59	09 23	10 00	10 23	11 00	11 23	12 00	12 14	12 23	13 00	13 23	14 00	14 23	15 00	15 23	16 00	16 23	17 00	17 23	18 00
Wanborough	149 d																						
Ash ■	149 d		08 02		09 33		10 33		11 33			12 33		13 33		14 33		15 33		16 33		17 33	
North Camp	d		08 06	09 11	09 37	10 11	10 37	11 11	11 37	12 11		12 37	13 11	13 37	14 11	14 37	15 11	15 37	16 11	16 37	17 11	17 37	18 11
Farnborough North	d		08 10		09 41		10 41		11 41			12 41		13 41		14 41		15 41		16 41		17 41	
Blackwater	d		08 14	09 17	09 45	10 17	10 45	11 17	11 45	12 17		12 45	13 17	13 45	14 17	14 45	15 17	15 45	16 17	16 45	17 17	17 45	18 17
Sandhurst	d		08 18		09 49		10 49		11 49			12 49		13 49		14 49		15 49		16 49		17 49	
Crowthorne	d		08 22		09 53		10 53		11 53			12 53		13 53		14 53		15 53		16 53		17 53	
Wokingham	149 d	00 24	08 26	09 26	09 58	10 26	10 58	11 26	11 58	12 26		12 58	13 26	13 58	14 26	14 58	15 26	15 58	16 26	16 58	17 26	17 58	18 26
Reading ■	149 a	00 33	08 35	09 38	10 06	10 35	11 06	11 35	12 06	12 35	12 48	13 06	13 35	14 06	14 35	15 06	15 35	16 06	16 35	17 06	17 35	18 06	18 35

		GW ■	GW	GW ■	GW	GW ■	GW	GW ■	GW	GW
Gatwick Airport ■	186 d		18 17		19 17		20 17	21 07	22 18	23 08
Redhill	186 d	17 43	18 28	18 43	19 28	19 43	20 30	21 19	22 29	23 19
Reigate	186 d	17 48	18 32	18 48	19 32	19 48	20 34	21 22	22 33	23 22
Betchworth	d	17 53				19 53		21 29		23 29
Dorking Deepdene	d	17 58	18 41	18 56	19 41	19 58	20 41	21 33	22 40	23 33
Dorking West	d	18 01				20 01		21 36		23 36
Gomshall	d			19 04				21 44		23 44
Chilworth	d			19 10				21 50		23 50
Shalford	d	18 15		19 15		20 15		21 54	22 54	23 54
Guildford	a	18 20	18 57	19 20	19 57	20 20	20 57	21 58	22 58	23 58
	d	18 23	19 00	19 23	20 00	20 23	21 00	22 00	23 00	23 59
Wanborough	149 d									
Ash ■	149 d	18 33		19 33		20 33		22 09		00 08
North Camp	d	18 37	19 11	19 37	20 11	20 37	21 11	22 13	23 11	00 12
Farnborough North	d	18 41		19 41		20 41		22 17		00 16
Blackwater	d	18 45	19 17	19 45	20 17	20 45	21 17	22 22	23 17	00 20
Sandhurst	d	18 49		19 49		20 49		22 25		00 23
Crowthorne	d	18 53		19 53		20 53		22 29		00 27
Wokingham	149 d	18 58	19 26	19 58	20 26	20 58	21 26	22 34	23 26	00 33
Reading ■	149 a	19 07	19 35	20 07	20 35	21 07	21 36	22 44	23 36	00 43

A not 20 May

Table T149-F

London - Hounslow, Richmond, Kingston, Windsor, Weybridge, Ascot, Guildford and Reading

Miles	Miles	Miles			SW MX ■	SW MX	SW MO ■	SW MX ■	SW MX ■	SW ■	SW MX	SW MO ■	SW MX		SW MO	SW MX	SW MO	SW MO	SW MX	SW MX	SW ■	SW MO	SW MX		SW
0	—	0	**London Waterloo** ■ ⊖	d																		00 18	00 18		
1¼	—	1¼	Vauxhall ⊖	d															00 02			00 22	00 22		
2¾	—	2¾	Queenstown Rd.(Battersea)	d																		00 25	00 25		
4	—	4	**Clapham Junction** ■	d															00 08	00 02		00 29	00 30		
4¾	—	4¾	Wandsworth Town	d																00 05		00 32	00 33		
5¾	—	5¾	Putney	d															00 12	00 08		00 35	00 36		
7	0	7	Barnes	d														00 03		00 12		00 38	00 39		
—	0½	—	Barnes Bridge	d																00 14					
—	1½	—	Chiswick	d																00 17					
—	2½	—	Kew Bridge	d																00 20					
—	3½	—	Brentford	d																00 23					
—	4¼	—	Syon Lane	d																00 25					
—	5	—	Isleworth	d																00 27					
—	6½	—	**Hounslow**	d							00 01									00 31					
8¾	—	8¾	Mortlake	d														00 05				00 40	00 41		
9	—	9	North Sheen	d														00 07				00 42	00 43		
9¾	—	9¾	**Richmond** ⊖	d												00 06		00 10	00 18			00 45	00 46		
10¾	—	10¾	St Margarets	d									00 01					00 12				00 47	00 48		
11¼	—	11¼	Twickenham	a									00 03			00 10		00 14	00 22			00 49	00 50		
—	—	—		d								00 03	00 04			00 10	00 12	00 15	00 22			00 50	00 51		04 52
12¼	—	—	Strawberry Hill	d									00 09				00 15					00s53	00s54		04 55
12½	—	—	Fulwell	a																					
13½	—	—	Teddington	a									00 12				00 18					00s56	00s57		04 58
14¾	—	—	Hampton Wick	a									00 14				00 21					00s59	01s00		05 01
15¼	—	—	**Kingston**	a									00 16				00 23					01 01	01 02		05 03
—	—	12½	Whitton	d														00 18	00 25						
—	—	14¾	Feltham	d							00 06	00 09				00 16		00 22	00 29	00 36					
—	—	17½	Ashford (Surrey)	d		00 03					00 10							00 26	00 33	00 40					
0	—	19	**Staines**	d		00 07					00 14	00 15			00 21	00 23		00a30	00a37	00a47	05 23				
2½	—	—	Wraysbury	d		00 11																			
3¾	—	—	Sunnymeads	d		00 14																			
4¾	—	—	Datchet	d		00 17																			
6¾	—	—	**Windsor & Eton Riverside**	a		00 22																			
—	—	21	Egham	d							00 19	00 20			00s25	00 27					05 27				
0	—	23¾	Virginia Water	a							00 23	00 24			00s30	00 31					05 31				
—	—	—		d				00 01			00 23	00 24				00 31					05 31				
2½	—	—	Chertsey	d							00 29				00s35										
4	—	—	Addlestone	d							00 32				00s38										
5¾	—	—	**Weybridge**	a							00 36														
—	—	25¼	Longcross	d																					
—	—	27	Sunningdale	d				00 08				00 30				00 37					05 37				
—	0	29	**Ascot** ■	d			00 05	00 13	00 23			00 35				00 42					05 43				
—	3¼	—	Bagshot	d					00 29																
—	6½	—	Camberley	a					00 35																
—	8¾	—	Frimley	d					00 40																
—	12	—	Ash Vale	d					00 47																
—	14½	—	**Aldershot**	a					00s52																
—	—	—		d						06 08															
—	17¼	—	Ash ■	d						06 15															
—	19¼	—	Wanborough	d						06 18															
—	23½	—	**Guildford**	a						06 25															
—	—	31¼	Martins Heron	d			00 09	00 17				00 39				00 46					05 47				
—	—	32¾	Bracknell	d			00 13	00 20				00 43				00 50					05 50				
—	—	36¼	**Wokingham**	d			00 19	00 32				00 49				00 56					05 57				
—	—	38¾	Winnersh	d			00 23	00 36				00 53									06 00				
—	—	39¾	Winnersh Triangle	d	00 02		00 25	00 38				00 55									06 02				
—	—	40½	Earley	d	00 05		00 27	00 40				00 57									06 05				
—	—	43½	**Reading** ■	a	00 12		00 32	00 45				01 02				01 05					06 12				

The xx15 and xx45 services from London Waterloo to Whitton continue to London Waterloo via Brentford

The xx03 and xx33 London Waterloo to Kingston services continue to London Waterloo via Wimbledon

The xx07 and xx37 services from London Waterloo to Whitton continue to London Waterloo via Richmond

For additional services between Wokingham and Reading refer to Table T148

Table T149-F

London - Hounslow, Richmond, Kingston, Windsor, Weybridge, Ascot, Guildford and Reading

		SW	SW ■	SW	SW	SW	SW ■	SW ■	SW ■		SW ■	SW	SW	SW	SW	SW ■	SW	SW ■	SW		SW ■	SW	SW	SW	SW
London Waterloo ■ ⊖	d		05 05		05 33				05 50				05 58	06 03			06 15	06 20				06 22	06 28		
Vauxhall ⊖	d		05 09		05 37								06 02	06 07			06 19					06 26	06 32		
Queenstown Rd.(Battersea)	d		05 12		05 40									06 10			06 22					06 29			
Clapham Junction ■	d		05 15		05 43				05 58				06 08	06 13			06 25	06 28				06 32	06 38		
Wandsworth Town	d		05 18		05 46									06 16			06 28					06 35			
Putney	d		05 21		05 49								06 12	06 19			06 31					06 38	06 42		
Barnes	d		05 24		05 52									06 22			06 35					06 42			
Barnes Bridge	d																					06 44			
Chiswick	d																					06 47			
Kew Bridge	d																					06 50			
Brentford	d																					06 53			
Syon Lane	d																					06 55			
Isleworth	d																					06 57			
Hounslow	d														06 31							07 01			06 48
Mortlake	d		05 26		05 54									06 24			06 37								
North Sheen	d		05 28		05 56									06 26			06 39		←						
Richmond ⊖	d		05 31		05 59				06 06				06 18	06 29			06 42	06 36	06 42				06 48		
St Margarets	d		05 33		06 01									06 31			→		06 44						
Twickenham	a		05 35		06 03				06 10				06 21	06 33				06 40	06 46				06 51		06 56
	d		05 36	05 53	06 04				06 10			06 17	06 22	06 34				06 40	06 47				06 52		
Strawberry Hill	d				06 07									06 37											
Fulwell	a																								
Teddington	a				06 10									06 40											
Hampton Wick	a				06 14									06 44											
Kingston	a				06 16									06 46											
Whitton	d		05 39	05 56								06a20	06 25						06a50				06 55	←	
Feltham	d		05 43	06 00					06 16				06 29		06 36			06 46				07 06	06 59	07 06	
Ashford (Surrey)	d		05 47	06 04									06 33		06 40							→	07 03	07 10	
Staines	d	05 44	05 53	06 08		06 14			06 23				06 37		06 44			06 53					07 07	07 14	
Wraysbury	d			06 12									06 41										07 11		
Sunnymeads	d			06 15									06 44										07 14		
Datchet	d			06 18									06 47										07 17		
Windsor & Eton Riverside	a			06 22									06 56										07 22		
Egham	d	05 49	05 57			06 19			06 27						06 49			06 57						07 19	
Virginia Water	a	05 53	06 01			06 23			06 31						06 53			07 01						07 23	
	d	05 53	06 01			06 23			06 31						06 53			07 01						07 23	
Chertsey	d	05 59				06 29									06 59									07 29	
Addlestone	d	06 02				06 32									07 02									07 32	
Weybridge	a	06 07				06 37									07 07									07 37	
Longcross	d								06 35									07 05							
Sunningdale	d		06 07						06 37									07 07							
Ascot ■	d		06 13					06 23	06 43		06 53					06 53		07 13			07 23				
Bagshot	d							06 29			06 59										07 29				
Camberley	a							06 35			07 05										07 35				
Frimley	d							06 43			07 13										07 43				
Ash Vale	d							06 49			07 19										07 49				
Aldershot	a							06 56			07 26										07 54				
	d						06 38	07 08			07 38										08 08				
Ash ■	d						06 45	07 15			07 46										08 15				
Wanborough	d						06 48	07 18			07 49										08 18				
Guildford	a						06 55	07 25			07 56										08 26				
Martins Heron	d		06 17						06 47									07 17							
Bracknell	d		06 20						06 50							06 58		07 20							
Wokingham	d		06 27						06 57							07 10		07 28							
Winnersh	d		06 30						07 00									07 31							
Winnersh Triangle	d		06 32						07 02									07 33							
Earley	d		06 35						07 05									07 36							
Reading ■	a		06 40						07 10							07 18		07 43							

The xx15 and xx45 services from London Waterloo to Whitton continue to London Waterloo via Brentford

The xx03 and xx33 London Waterloo to Kingston services continue to London Waterloo via Wimbledon

The xx07 and xx37 services from London Waterloo to Whitton continue to London Waterloo via Richmond

For additional services between Wokingham and Reading refer to Table T148

London - Hounslow, Richmond, Kingston, Windsor, Weybridge, Ascot, Guildford and Reading

		SW	SW	SW 1	SW	SW 1	SW	SW	SW	SW	SW	SW	SW	SW 1	SW	SW	SW	SW	SW 1	SW	SW	SW	SW
London Waterloo 15 ⊖	d	06 33	06 45	06 50			06 52	06 58			07 03		07 15	07 20		07 22	07 28	07 33	07 34			07 40	
Vauxhall ⊖	d	06 37	06 49				06 56	07 02			07 07		07 19			07 26	07 32	07 36	07 39			07 45	
Queenstown Rd.(Battersea)	d	06 40	06 52				06 59				07 10		07 22			07 29		07 39				07 48	
Clapham Junction 10	d	06 43	06 55	06 58			07 02	07 08			07 13		07 25	07 28		07 32	07 38	07 43	07 46			07 51	07 54
Wandsworth Town	d	06 46	06 58				07 05				07 16		07 28			07 35		07 45				07 54	
Putney	d	06 49	07 01				07 08	07 12			07 19		07 31			07 38	07 42	07 49				07 57	
Barnes	d	06 52	07 05				07 12				07 22		07 35			07 42		07 52				08 00	
Barnes Bridge	d						07 14									07 44						08 02	
Chiswick	d						07 17									07 47						08 05	
Kew Bridge	d						07 20									07 50						08 08	
Brentford	d						07 23									07 53						08 11	
Syon Lane	d						07 25									07 55						08 13	
Isleworth	d						07 27									07 57						08 15	
Hounslow	d						07 31									08 01						08 27	
Mortlake	d	06 54	07 07								07 24		07 37					07 54					
North Sheen	d	06 56	07 09		←						07 26		07 39		←			07 56			←		
Richmond ⊖	d	06 59	07 12	07 06	07 12			07 18			07 29		07 42	07 36	07 42		07 48	07 59	07 54		07 59		08 02
St Margarets	d	07 01	→		07 14						07 31		→		07 44			→			08 01		
Twickenham	a	07 03		07 10	07 16			07 21			07 33			07 40	07 46		07 51		07 58		08 03		08 06
	d	07 04		07 10	07 17			07 22		07 27	07 34	07 37		07 40	07 47		07 52		07 58		08 04		08 07
Strawberry Hill	d	07 07								07 30	07 37	07 46									08 07		08 16
Fulwell	a									07 33													
Teddington	a	07 10									07 40	07 49									08 10		08 19
Hampton Wick	a	07 14									07 44	07 51									08 14		08 21
Kingston	a	07 16									07 46	07 53									08 16		08 23
Whitton	d				07a20			07 25	←						07a50		07 55			←		08a33	
Feltham	d			07 16			07 36	07 29	07 36					07 46		08 08	07 59		08 04	08 08			
Ashford (Surrey)	d						→	07 33	07 40							→	08 03		08 08	08 12			
Staines	d			07 23				07 37	07 44					07 53			08 07		08 12	08 16			
Wraysbury	d							07 41									08 11						
Sunnymeads	d							07 44									08 14						
Datchet	d							07 47									08 17						
Windsor & Eton Riverside	a							07 52									08 22						
Egham	d			07 27					07 49					07 57					08 17	08 21			
Virginia Water	a			07 31					07 53					08 01						08 25			
	d			07 31					07 53					08 01						08 25			
Chertsey	d								07 59											08 31			
Addlestone	d								08 02											08 34			
Weybridge	a								08 07											08 39			
Longcross	d			07 35										08 05									
Sunningdale	d			07 37										08 07									
Ascot 3	d			07 43		07 53								08 13					08 27				
Bagshot	d					07 59													08 33				
Camberley	a					08 05													08 39				
Frimley	d					08 13													08 43				
Ash Vale	d					08 19													08 50				
Aldershot	a					08 24													08 55				
	d					08 38													09 08				
Ash 5	d					08 45													09 15				
Wanborough	d					08 48													09 18				
Guildford	a					08 55													09 25				
Martins Heron	d			07 47										08 17									
Bracknell	d			07 50										08 20									
Wokingham	d			07 57										08 28									
Winnersh	d			08 00										08 31									
Winnersh Triangle	d			08 02										08 33									
Earley	d			08 05										08 36									
Reading 7	a			08 12										08 43									

The xx15 and xx45 services from London Waterloo to Whitton continue to London Waterloo via Brentford

The xx03 and xx33 London Waterloo to Kingston services continue to London Waterloo via Wimbledon

The xx07 and xx37 services from London Waterloo to Whitton continue to London Waterloo via Richmond

For additional services between Wokingham and Reading refer to Table T148

London - Hounslow, Richmond, Kingston, Windsor, Weybridge, Ascot, Guildford and Reading

		SW	SW 1	SW	SW 1	SW	SW	SW	SW 1	SW	SW	SW	SW	SW 1	SW	SW 1	SW	SW	SW	SW 1	SW	SW
London Waterloo 15 ⊖	d	07 45	07 50			07 52	07 58	08 03	08 07			08 10	08 15	08 20			08 22	08 28	08 33	08 37		
Vauxhall ⊖	d	07 49				07 56	08 02	08 07				08 14	08 19				08 26	08 32	08 37			
Queenstown Rd.(Battersea)	d	07 52				07 59		08 10				08 17	08 22				08 29		08 40			
Clapham Junction 10	d	07 55	07 58			08 02	08 08	08 13	08 16			08 20	08 25	08 28			08 32	08 38	08 43	08 46		
Wandsworth Town	d	07 58				08 06		08 16				08 23	08 28				08 35		08 46			
Putney	d	08 01				08 09	08 12	08 19				08 26	08 31				08 38	08 42	08 49			
Barnes	d	08 05				08 12		08 23				08 29	08 35				08 42		08 53			
Barnes Bridge	d					08 14						08 31					08 44					
Chiswick	d					08 18						08 34					08 47					
Kew Bridge	d					08 20						08 36					08 50					
Brentford	d					08 23						08 39					08 53					
Syon Lane	d					08 25						08 41					08 55					
Isleworth	d					08 27						08 43					08 57					
Hounslow	d					08 31						08 48					09 01					
Mortlake	d	08 07						08 25					08 37						08 55			
North Sheen	d	08 09		←				08 27			←		08 39		←				08 57			←
Richmond ⊖	d	08 12	08 06	08 12			08 18	08 30	08 24		08 30		08 42	08 36	08 42			08 48	09 00	08 54		09 00
St Margarets	d	→		08 14				→			08 32		→		08 44				→			09 02
Twickenham	a		08 10	08 16			08 21		08 28		08 34			08 40	08 46			08 51		08 58		09 04
	d		08 10	08 17			08 22		08 28		08 35			08 40	08 47			08 52		08 58		09 05
Strawberry Hill	d										08 38											09 08
Fulwell	a																					
Teddington	a										08 41											09 11
Hampton Wick	a										08 44											09 14
Kingston	a										08 46											09 16
Whitton	d			08a20			08 25			←		08a53			08a50			08 55			←	
Feltham	d		08 16			08 38	08 29		08 34	08 38				08 46			09 08	08 59		09 04	09 08	
Ashford (Surrey)	d					→	08 33		08 38	08 42							→	09 03		09 08	09 12	
Staines	d		08 23				08 37		08 42	08 46				08 53				09 07		09 12	09 16	
Wraysbury	d						08 41											09 11				
Sunnymeads	d						08 44											09 14				
Datchet	d						08 47											09 17				
Windsor & Eton Riverside	a						08 52											09 22				
Egham	d		08 27						08 47	08 51				08 57						09 17	09 21	
Virginia Water	a		08 31						08 51	08 55				09 01						09 21	09 25	
	d		08 31						08 51	08 55				09 01						09 21	09 25	
Chertsey	d									09 01											09 31	
Addlestone	d									09 04											09 34	
Weybridge	a									09 09											09 39	
Longcross	d		08 35						08 54													
Sunningdale	d		08 37						08 58					09 07						09 26		
Ascot 3	d		08 43		08 53				09 02					09 13		09 23				09 31		
Bagshot	d				08 59											09 29						
Camberley	a				09 05											09 35						
Frimley	d				09 13											09 43						
Ash Vale	d				09 19											09 49						
Aldershot	a				09 25											09 54						
	d				09 38											10 08						
Ash 5	d				09 45											10 15						
Wanborough	d				09 48											10 18						
Guildford	a				09 55											10 25						
Martins Heron	d		08 47						09 06					09 17						09 35		
Bracknell	d		08 50						09 10					09 20						09 38		
Wokingham	d		08 57						09 17					09 27						09 45		
Winnersh	d		09 00						09 20					09 30								
Winnersh Triangle	d		09 02						09 22					09 32								
Earley	d		09 05						09 25					09 35								
Reading 7	a		09 12						09 30					09 42						09 54		

The xx15 and xx45 services from London Waterloo to Whitton continue to London Waterloo via Brentford

The xx03 and xx33 London Waterloo to Kingston services continue to London Waterloo via Wimbledon

The xx07 and xx37 services from London Waterloo to Whitton continue to London Waterloo via Richmond

For additional services between Wokingham and Reading refer to Table T148

Table T149-F

London - Hounslow, Richmond, Kingston, Windsor, Weybridge, Ascot, Guildford and Reading

		SW	SW	SW [1]	SW	SW [1]	GW	SW	SW	SW	SW	SW	SW	SW [1]	SW	SW [1]	SW	SW	SW	SW	SW	SW	SW [1]
London Waterloo [15] ⊖	d	08 40	08 43	08 50				08 52	08 58		09 03	09 07	09 15	09 20			09 22	09 28		09 33	09 37	09 45	09 50
Vauxhall ⊖	d	08 44	08 47					08 57	09 03		09 07	09 11	09 19				09 26	09 32		09 37	09 41	09 49	
Queenstown Rd.(Battersea)	d	08 47	08 50					09 00			09 10	09 14	09 22				09 29			09 40	09 44	09 52	
Clapham Junction [10]	d	08 50	08 55	08 58				09 03	09 08		09 13	09 17	09 25	09 28			09 32	09 38		09 43	09 47	09 55	09 58
Wandsworth Town	d	08 53	08 58					09 06			09 16	09 20	09 28				09 35			09 46	09 50	09 58	
Putney	d	08 56	09 01					09 09	09 12		09 19	09 23	09 31				09 38	09 42		09 49	09 53	10 01	
Barnes	d	08 59	09 05					09 12			09 22	09 27	09 35				09 42			09 52	09 57	10 05	
Barnes Bridge	d	09 01						09 15				09 29					09 44				09 59		
Chiswick	d	09 03						09 18				09 32					09 47				10 02		
Kew Bridge	d	09 06						09 20				09 35					09 50				10 05		
Brentford	d	09 09						09 23				09 38					09 53				10 08		
Syon Lane	d	09 11						09 25				09 40					09 55				10 10		
Isleworth	d	09 13						09 27				09 42					09 57				10 12		
Hounslow	d	09 18						09 31				09 48					10 01				10 18		
Mortlake	d		09 07								09 24		09 37							09 54		10 07	
North Sheen	d		09 09		←						09 26		09 39		←					09 56		10 09	
Richmond ⊖	d		09 12	09 06	09 12				09 18		09 29		09 42	09 36	09 42			09 48		09 59		10 12	10 06
St Margarets	d		→		09 14						09 31		→		09 44					10 01		→	
Twickenham	a			09 10	09 16				09 22		09 33			09 40	09 46			09 51		10 03			10 10
	d			09 10	09 17				09 22		09 34			09 40	09 47			09 52		10 04			10 10
Strawberry Hill	d										09 37									10 07			
Fulwell	a																						
Teddington	a										09 40									10 10			
Hampton Wick	a										09 44									10 14			
Kingston	a										09 46									10 16			
Whitton	d	09a23			09a20				09 25	←		09a53			09a50			09 55	←		10a26		
Feltham	d			09 16				09 36	09 30	09 36				09 46			10 06	09 59	10 06				10 16
Ashford (Surrey)	d							→	09 34	09 40							→	10 03	10 10				
Staines	d			09 23					09 38	09 44				09 53				10 07	10 14				10 23
Wraysbury	d								09 42									10 11					
Sunnymeads	d								09 44									10 14					
Datchet	d								09 47									10 17					
Windsor & Eton Riverside	a								09 53									10 22					
Egham	d			09 27						09 49				09 57					10 19				10 27
Virginia Water	a			09 31						09 53				10 01					10 23				10 31
	d			09 31						09 53				10 01					10 23				10 31
Chertsey	d									09 59									10 29				
Addlestone	d									10 02									10 32				
Weybridge	a									10 12									10 37				
Longcross	d																						
Sunningdale	d			09 37										10 07									10 37
Ascot [8]	d			09 43		09 53								10 13		10 23							10 43
Bagshot	d					09 59										10 29							
Camberley	a					10 05										10 35							
Frimley	d					10 13										10 43							
Ash Vale	d					10 19										10 49							
Aldershot	a					10 24										10 54							
	d					10 38										11 08							
Ash [5]	d					10 45										11 15							
Wanborough	d					10 48										11 18							
Guildford	a					10 55										11 25							
Martins Heron	d			09 47										10 17									10 47
Bracknell	d			09 50										10 20									10 50
Wokingham	d			09 57			10 06							10 27									10 57
Winnersh	d			10 00										10 30									11 00
Winnersh Triangle	d			10 02										10 32									11 02
Earley	d			10 05										10 35									11 05
Reading [7]	a			10 12			10 15							10 42									11 12

The xx15 and xx45 services from London Waterloo to Whitton continue to London Waterloo via Brentford

The xx03 and xx33 London Waterloo to Kingston services continue to London Waterloo via Wimbledon

The xx07 and xx37 services from London Waterloo to Whitton continue to London Waterloo via Richmond

For additional services between Wokingham and Reading refer to Table T148

Table T149-F

London - Hounslow, Richmond, Kingston, Windsor, Weybridge, Ascot, Guildford and Reading

		SW	SW [1]	SW	SW	SW	SW	SW	SW	SW [1]	SW	SW [1]	SW	SW	SW	SW	SW	SW	SW [1]	SW	SW [1]	SW
London Waterloo [15] ⊖	d			09 52	09 58		10 03	10 07	10 15	10 20			10 22	10 28		10 33	10 37	10 45	10 50			10 52
Vauxhall ⊖	d			09 56	10 02		10 07	10 11	10 19				10 26	10 32		10 37	10 41	10 49				10 56
Queenstown Rd.(Battersea)	d			09 59			10 10	10 14	10 22				10 29			10 40	10 44	10 52				10 59
Clapham Junction [10]	d			10 02	10 08		10 13	10 17	10 25	10 28			10 32	10 38		10 43	10 47	10 55	10 58			11 02
Wandsworth Town	d			10 05			10 16	10 20	10 28				10 35			10 46	10 50	10 58				11 05
Putney	d			10 08	10 12		10 19	10 23	10 31				10 38	10 42		10 49	10 53	11 01				11 08
Barnes	d			10 12			10 22	10 27	10 35				10 42			10 52	10 57	11 05				11 12
Barnes Bridge	d			10 14				10 29					10 44				10 59					11 14
Chiswick	d			10 17				10 32					10 47				11 02					11 17
Kew Bridge	d			10 20				10 35					10 50				11 05					11 20
Brentford	d			10 23				10 38					10 53				11 08					11 23
Syon Lane	d			10 25				10 40					10 55				11 10					11 25
Isleworth	d			10 27				10 42					10 57				11 12					11 27
Hounslow	d			10 31				10 48					11 01				11 18					11 31
Mortlake	d						10 24		10 37							10 54		11 07				
North Sheen	d	←					10 26		10 39		←					10 56		11 09		←		
Richmond ⊖	d	10 12			10 18		10 29		10 42	10 36	10 42			10 48		10 59		11 12	11 06	11 12		
St Margarets	d	10 14					10 31		→		10 44					11 01		→		11 14		
Twickenham	a	10 16			10 21		10 33			10 40	10 46			10 51		11 03			11 10	11 16		
	d	10 17			10 22		10 34			10 40	10 47			10 52		11 04			11 10	11 17		
Strawberry Hill	d						10 37									11 07						
Fulwell	a																					
Teddington	a						10 40									11 10						
Hampton Wick	a						10 44									11 14						
Kingston	a						10 46									11 16						
Whitton	d	10a20			10 25	←		10a55			10a50			10 55	←		11a23			11a20		
Feltham	d			10 36	10 29	10 36				10 46			11 06	10 59	11 06				11 16			11 36
Ashford (Surrey)	d			→	10 33	10 40							→	11 03	11 10							→
Staines	d				10 37	10 44				10 53				11 07	11 14				11 23			
Wraysbury	d				10 41									11 11								
Sunnymeads	d				10 44									11 14								
Datchet	d				10 47									11 17								
Windsor & Eton Riverside	a				10 52									11 22								
Egham	d					10 49				10 57					11 19				11 27			
Virginia Water	a					10 53				11 01					11 23				11 31			
	d					10 53				11 01					11 23				11 31			
Chertsey	d					10 59									11 29							
Addlestone	d					11 02									11 32							
Weybridge	a					11 07									11 37							
Longcross	d																					
Sunningdale	d									11 07									11 37			
Ascot [8]	d		10 53							11 13		11 23							11 43		11 53	
Bagshot	d		10 59									11 29									11 59	
Camberley	a		11 05									11 35									12 05	
Frimley	d		11 13									11 43									12 13	
Ash Vale	d		11 19									11 49									12 19	
Aldershot	a		11 24									11 54									12 24	
	d		11 38									12 08									12 38	
Ash [5]	d		11 45									12 15									12 45	
Wanborough	d		11 48									12 18									12 48	
Guildford	a		11 55									12 25									12 55	
Martins Heron	d									11 17									11 47			
Bracknell	d									11 20									11 50			
Wokingham	d									11 27									11 57			
Winnersh	d									11 30									12 00			
Winnersh Triangle	d									11 32									12 02			
Earley	d									11 35									12 05			
Reading [7]	a									11 42									12 12			

The xx15 and xx45 services from London Waterloo to Whitton continue to London Waterloo via Brentford

The xx03 and xx33 London Waterloo to Kingston services continue to London Waterloo via Wimbledon

The xx07 and xx37 services from London Waterloo to Whitton continue to London Waterloo via Richmond

For additional services between Wokingham and Reading refer to Table T148

Table T149-F

Mondays to Fridays

21 May to 5 October

London - Hounslow, Richmond, Kingston, Windsor, Weybridge, Ascot, Guildford and Reading

		SW	SW	SW	SW	SW	SW ■	SW	SW ■	SW	SW	SW	SW	SW	SW	SW ■	SW	SW ■	SW	SW	SW	SW	SW
London Waterloo 15 ⊖	d	10 58		11 03	11 07	11 15	11 20			11 22	11 28		11 33	11 37	11 45	11 50			11 52	11 58		12 03	12 07
Vauxhall ⊖	d	11 02		11 07	11 11	11 19				11 26	11 32		11 37	11 41	11 49				11 56	12 02		12 07	12 11
Queenstown Rd.(Battersea)	d			11 10	11 14	11 22				11 29			11 40	11 44	11 52				11 59			12 10	12 14
Clapham Junction 10	d	11 08		11 13	11 17	11 27	11 28			11 32	11 38		11 43	11 47	11 55	11 58			12 02	12 08		12 13	12 17
Wandsworth Town	d			11 16	11 20	11 29				11 35			11 46	11 50	11 58				12 05			12 16	12 20
Putney	d	11 12		11 19	11 23	11 32				11 38	11 42		11 49	11 53	12 01				12 08	12 12		12 19	12 23
Barnes	d			11 22	11 27	11 36				11 42			11 52	11 57	12 05				12 12			12 22	12 27
Barnes Bridge	d				11 29					11 44				11 59					12 14				12 29
Chiswick	d				11 32					11 47				12 02					12 17				12 32
Kew Bridge	d				11 35					11 50				12 05					12 20				12 35
Brentford	d				11 38					11 53				12 08					12 23				12 38
Syon Lane	d				11 40					11 55				12 10					12 25				12 40
Isleworth	d				11 42					11 57				12 12					12 27				12 42
Hounslow	d				11 48					12 01				12 18					12 31				12 48
Mortlake	d			11 24		11 39							11 54		12 07							12 24	
North Sheen	d			11 26		11 41		←					11 56		12 09		←					12 26	
Richmond ⊖	d	11 18		11 29		11 43	11 36	11 43			11 48		11 59		12 12	12 06	12 12			12 18		12 29	
St Margarets	d			11 31		→		11 46					12 01		→		12 14					12 31	
Twickenham	a	11 21		11 33			11 40	11 48			11 51		12 03			12 10	12 16			12 21		12 33	
	d	11 22		11 34			11 40	11 48			11 52		12 04			12 10	12 17			12 22		12 34	
Strawberry Hill	d			11 37									12 07									12 37	
Fulwell	a																						
Teddington	a			11 40									12 10									12 40	
Hampton Wick	a			11 44									12 14									12 44	
Kingston	a			11 46									12 16									12 46	
Whitton	d	11 25	←		11a53			11a51			11 55	←		12a23			12a20			12 25	←		12a53
Feltham	d	11 29	11 36				11 46			12 06	11 59	12 06				12 16			12 36	12 29	12 36		
Ashford (Surrey)	d	11 33	11 40							→	12 03	12 10							→	12 33	12 40		
Staines	d	11 37	11 44				11 53				12 07	12 14				12 23				12 37	12 44		
Wraysbury	d	11 41									12 11									12 41			
Sunnymeads	d	11 44									12 14									12 44			
Datchet	d	11 47									12 17									12 47			
Windsor & Eton Riverside	a	11 52									12 22									12 52			
Egham	d		11 49				11 57					12 19				12 27					12 49		
Virginia Water	a		11 53				12 01					12 23				12 31					12 53		
	d		11 53				12 01					12 23				12 31					12 53		
Chertsey	d		11 59									12 29									12 59		
Addlestone	d		12 02									12 32									13 02		
Weybridge	a		12 07									12 37									13 07		
Longcross	d																						
Sunningdale	d						12 07									12 37							
Ascot 8	d						12 13		12 23							12 43		12 53					
Bagshot	d								12 29									12 59					
Camberley	a								12 35									13 05					
Frimley	d								12 43									13 13					
Ash Vale	d								12 49									13 19					
Aldershot	a								12 54									13 24					
	d								13 08									13 38					
Ash 5	d								13 15									13 45					
Wanborough	d								13 18									13 48					
Guildford	a								13 25									13 55					
Martins Heron	d						12 17									12 47							
Bracknell	d						12 20									12 50							
Wokingham	d						12 27									12 57							
Winnersh	d						12 30									13 00							
Winnersh Triangle	d						12 32									13 02							
Earley	d						12 35									13 05							
Reading 7	a						12 42									13 12							

The xx15 and xx45 services from London Waterloo to Whitton continue to London Waterloo via Brentford

The xx03 and xx33 London Waterloo to Kingston services continue to London Waterloo via Wimbledon

The xx07 and xx37 services from London Waterloo to Whitton continue to London Waterloo via Richmond

For additional services between Wokingham and Reading refer to Table T148

Table T149-F

Mondays to Fridays

21 May to 5 October

London - Hounslow, Richmond, Kingston, Windsor, Weybridge, Ascot, Guildford and Reading

		SW	SW ■	SW	SW ■	SW	SW	SW	SW	SW	SW	SW ■	SW	SW ■	SW	SW	SW	SW	SW	SW	SW ■	SW	SW ■
London Waterloo 15 ⊖	d	12 15	12 20			12 22	12 28		12 33	12 37	12 45	12 50			12 52	12 58		13 03	13 07	13 15	13 20		
Vauxhall ⊖	d	12 19				12 26	12 32		12 37	12 41	12 49				12 56	13 02		13 07	13 11	13 19			
Queenstown Rd.(Battersea)	d	12 22				12 29			12 40	12 44	12 52				12 59			13 10	13 14	13 22			
Clapham Junction 10	d	12 25	12 28			12 32	12 38		12 43	12 47	12 55	12 58			13 02	13 08		13 13	13 17	13 25	13 28		
Wandsworth Town	d	12 28				12 35			12 46	12 50	12 58				13 05			13 16	13 20	13 28			
Putney	d	12 31				12 38	12 42		12 49	12 53	13 01				13 08	13 12		13 19	13 23	13 31			
Barnes	d	12 35				12 42			12 52	12 57	13 05				13 12			13 22	13 27	13 35			
Barnes Bridge	d					12 44				12 59					13 14				13 29				
Chiswick	d					12 47				13 02					13 17				13 32				
Kew Bridge	d					12 50				13 05					13 20				13 35				
Brentford	d					12 53				13 08					13 23				13 38				
Syon Lane	d					12 55				13 10					13 25				13 40				
Isleworth	d					12 57				13 12					13 27				13 42				
Hounslow	d					13 01				13 18					13 31				13 48				
Mortlake	d	12 37							12 54		13 07							13 24		13 37			
North Sheen	d	12 39		←					12 56		13 09		←					13 26		13 39		←	
Richmond ⊖	d	12 42	12 36	12 42			12 48		12 59		13 12	13 06	13 12			13 18		13 29		13 42	13 36	13 42	
St Margarets	d	→		12 44					13 01		→		13 14					13 31		→		13 44	
Twickenham	a		12 40	12 46			12 51		13 03			13 10	13 16			13 21		13 33			13 40	13 46	
	d		12 40	12 47			12 52		13 04			13 10	13 17			13 22		13 34			13 40	13 47	
Strawberry Hill	d								13 07									13 37					
Fulwell	a																						
Teddington	a								13 10									13 40					
Hampton Wick	a								13 14									13 44					
Kingston	a								13 16									13 46					
Whitton	d			12a50			12 55	←		13a23			13a20			13 25	←		13a53			13a50	
Feltham	d		12 46			13 06	12 59	13 06				13 16			13 36	13 29	13 36				13 46		
Ashford (Surrey)	d					→	13 03	13 10							→	13 33	13 40						
Staines	d		12 53				13 07	13 14				13 23				13 37	13 44				13 53		
Wraysbury	d						13 11									13 41							
Sunnymeads	d						13 14									13 44							
Datchet	d						13 17									13 47							
Windsor & Eton Riverside	a						13 23									13 52							
Egham	d		12 57					13 19				13 27					13 49				13 57		
Virginia Water	a		13 01					13 23				13 31					13 53				14 01		
	d		13 01					13 23				13 31					13 53				14 01		
Chertsey	d							13 29									13 59						
Addlestone	d							13 32									14 02						
Weybridge	a							13 37									14 07						
Longcross	d											13 35											
Sunningdale	d		13 07									13 37									14 07		
Ascot 8	d		13 13		13 23							13 43		13 53							14 13		14 23
Bagshot	d				13 29									13 59									14 29
Camberley	a				13 35									14 05									14 35
Frimley	d				13 43									14 13									14 43
Ash Vale	d				13 49									14 19									14 49
Aldershot	a				13 54									14 24									14 54
	d				14 08									14 38									15 08
Ash 5	d				14 15									14 45									15 15
Wanborough	d				14 18									14 48									15 18
Guildford	a				14 25									14 55									15 25
Martins Heron	d		13 17									13 47									14 17		
Bracknell	d		13 20									13 50									14 20		
Wokingham	d		13 27									13 57									14 27		
Winnersh	d		13 30									14 00									14 30		
Winnersh Triangle	d		13 32									14 02									14 32		
Earley	d		13 35									14 05									14 35		
Reading 7	a		13 42									14 12									14 42		

The xx15 and xx45 services from London Waterloo to Whitton continue to London Waterloo via Brentford

The xx03 and xx33 London Waterloo to Kingston services continue to London Waterloo via Wimbledon

The xx07 and xx37 services from London Waterloo to Whitton continue to London Waterloo via Richmond

For additional services between Wokingham and Reading refer to Table T148

London - Hounslow, Richmond, Kingston, Windsor, Weybridge, Ascot, Guildford and Reading

		SW	SW	SW	SW	SW	SW	SW ■	SW	SW ■	SW	SW	SW	SW	SW	SW	SW ■	SW	SW ■	SW	SW	SW
London Waterloo ■ ⊖	d	13 22	13 28		13 33	13 37	13 45	13 50			13 52	13 58		14 03	14 07	14 15	14 20			14 22	14 28	
Vauxhall ⊖	d	13 26	13 32		13 37	13 41	13 49				13 56	14 02		14 07	14 11	14 19				14 26	14 32	
Queenstown Rd.(Battersea)	d	13 29			13 40	13 44	13 52				13 59			14 10	14 14	14 22				14 29		
Clapham Junction ■	d	13 32	13 38		13 43	13 47	13 55	13 58			14 02	14 08		14 13	14 17	14 25	14 28			14 32	14 38	
Wandsworth Town	d	13 35			13 46	13 50	13 58				14 05			14 16	14 20	14 28				14 35		
Putney	d	13 38	13 42		13 49	13 53	14 01				14 08	14 12		14 19	14 23	14 31				14 38	14 42	
Barnes	d	13 42			13 52	13 57	14 05				14 12			14 22	14 27	14 35				14 42		
Barnes Bridge	d	13 44				13 59					14 14				14 29					14 44		
Chiswick	d	13 47				14 02					14 17				14 32					14 47		
Kew Bridge	d	13 50				14 05					14 20				14 35					14 50		
Brentford	d	13 53				14 08					14 23				14 38					14 53		
Syon Lane	d	13 55				14 10					14 25				14 40					14 55		
Isleworth	d	13 57				14 12					14 27				14 42					14 57		
Hounslow	d	14 01				14 18					14 31				14 48					15 01		
Mortlake	d				13 54		14 07							14 24		14 37						
North Sheen	d				13 56		14 09		←					14 26		14 39		←				
Richmond ⊖	d		13 48		13 59		14 12	14 06	14 12			14 18		14 29		14 42	14 36	14 42			14 48	
St Margarets	d				14 01		→		14 14					14 31		→		14 44				
Twickenham	a		13 51		14 03			14 10	14 16			14 21		14 33			14 40	14 46			14 51	
	d		13 52		14 04			14 10	14 17			14 22		14 34			14 40	14 47			14 52	
Strawberry Hill	d				14 07									14 37								
Fulwell	a																					
Teddington	a				14 10									14 40								
Hampton Wick	a				14 14									14 44								
Kingston	a				14 16									14 46								
Whitton	d		13 55	←		14a23			14a20			14 25	←		14a53			14a50			14 55	←
Feltham	d	14 06	13 59	14 06				14 16			14 36	14 29	14 36				14 46			15 06	14 59	15 06
Ashford (Surrey)	d	→	14 03	14 10							→	14 33	14 40							→	15 03	15 10
Staines	d		14 07	14 14				14 23				14 37	14 45				14 53				15 07	15 14
Wraysbury	d		14 11									14 41									15 11	
Sunnymeads	d		14 14									14 44									15 14	
Datchet	d		14 17									14 47									15 17	
Windsor & Eton Riverside	a		14 22									14 52									15 22	
Egham	d			14 19				14 27					14 49				14 57					15 19
Virginia Water	a			14 23				14 31					14 53				15 01					15 23
	d			14 23				14 31					14 53				15 01					15 23
Chertsey	d			14 29									14 59									15 29
Addlestone	d			14 32									15 02									15 32
Weybridge	a			14 37									15 07									15 37
Longcross	d																					
Sunningdale	d							14 37									15 07					
Ascot ■	d							14 43		14 53							15 13		15 23			
Bagshot	d									14 59									15 29			
Camberley	a									15 05									15 35			
Frimley	d									15 13									15 43			
Ash Vale	d									15 19									15 49			
Aldershot	a									15 24									15 55			
	d									15 38									16 08			
Ash ■	d									15 45									16 15			
Wanborough	d									15 48									16 18			
Guildford	a									15 55									16 25			
Martins Heron	d							14 47									15 17					
Bracknell	d							14 50									15 20					
Wokingham	d							14 57									15 27					
Winnersh	d							15 00									15 30					
Winnersh Triangle	d							15 02									15 32					
Earley	d							15 05									15 35					
Reading ■	a							15 12									15 42					

The xx15 and xx45 services from London Waterloo to Whitton continue to London Waterloo via Brentford

The xx03 and xx33 London Waterloo to Kingston services continue to London Waterloo via Wimbledon

The xx07 and xx37 services from London Waterloo to Whitton continue to London Waterloo via Richmond

For additional services between Wokingham and Reading refer to Table T148

London - Hounslow, Richmond, Kingston, Windsor, Weybridge, Ascot, Guildford and Reading

		SW	SW	SW	SW ■	SW	SW ■	SW	SW	SW	SW	SW	SW	SW ■	SW	SW ■	SW	SW	SW	SW	SW	SW	SW ■
London Waterloo ■ ⊖	d	14 33	14 37	14 45	14 50			14 52	14 58		15 03	15 07	15 15	15 20			15 22	15 28		15 33	15 37	15 45	15 50
Vauxhall ⊖	d	14 37	14 41	14 49				14 56	15 02		15 07	15 11	15 19				15 26	15 32		15 37	15 41	15 49	
Queenstown Rd.(Battersea)	d	14 40	14 44	14 52				15 00			15 10	15 14	15 22				15 29			15 40	15 44	15 52	
Clapham Junction ■	d	14 43	14 47	14 55	14 58			15 03	15 08		15 13	15 17	15 25	15 28			15 32	15 38		15 43	15 47	15 55	15 58
Wandsworth Town	d	14 46	14 50	14 58				15 05			15 16	15 20	15 28				15 35			15 46	15 50	15 58	
Putney	d	14 49	14 53	15 01				15 08	15 12		15 19	15 23	15 31				15 38	15 42		15 49	15 53	16 01	
Barnes	d	14 52	14 57	15 05				15 12			15 22	15 27	15 35				15 42			15 52	15 57	16 05	
Barnes Bridge	d		14 59					15 14				15 29					15 44				15 59		
Chiswick	d		15 02					15 17				15 32					15 47				16 02		
Kew Bridge	d		15 05					15 20				15 35					15 50				16 05		
Brentford	d		15 08					15 23				15 38					15 53				16 08		
Syon Lane	d		15 10					15 25				15 40					15 55				16 10		
Isleworth	d		15 12					15 27				15 42					15 57				16 12		
Hounslow	d		15 18					15 31				15 48					16 01				16 18		
Mortlake	d	14 54		15 07							15 24		15 37							15 54		16 07	
North Sheen	d	14 56		15 09		←					15 26		15 39		←					15 56		16 09	
Richmond ⊖	d	14 59		15 12	15 06	15 12			15 18		15 29		15 42	15 36	15 42			15 48		15 59		16 12	16 06
St Margarets	d	15 01		→		15 14					15 31		→		15 44					16 01		→	
Twickenham	a	15 03			15 10	15 16			15 21		15 33			15 40	15 46			15 51		16 03			16 10
	d	15 04			15 10	15 17			15 22		15 34			15 40	15 47			15 52		16 04			16 10
Strawberry Hill	d	15 07									15 37									16 07			
Fulwell	a																						
Teddington	a	15 10									15 40									16 10			
Hampton Wick	a	15 14									15 44									16 14			
Kingston	a	15 16									15 46									16 16			
Whitton	d		15a23			15a20			15 25	←		15a53			15a50			15 55	←		16a23		
Feltham	d				15 16			15 36	15 29	15 36				15 46			16 06	15 59	16 06				16 16
Ashford (Surrey)	d							→	15 33	15 40							→	16 03	16 10				
Staines	d				15 23				15 37	15 44				15 53				16 07	16 14				16 23
Wraysbury	d								15 41									16 11					
Sunnymeads	d								15 44									16 14					
Datchet	d								15 47									16 17					
Windsor & Eton Riverside	a								15 52									16 22					
Egham	d				15 27					15 49				15 57					16 19				16 27
Virginia Water	a				15 31					15 53				16 01					16 23				16 31
	d				15 31					15 53				16 01					16 23				16 31
Chertsey	d									16 00									16 29				
Addlestone	d									16 03									16 32				
Weybridge	a									16 07									16 37				
Longcross	d													16 05									
Sunningdale	d				15 37									16 08									16 37
Ascot ■	d				15 43		15 53							16 13		16 23							16 43
Bagshot	d						15 59									16 29							
Camberley	a						16 05									16 35							
Frimley	d						16 13									16 43							
Ash Vale	d						16 19									16 49							
Aldershot	a						16 24									16 54							
	d						16 38									17 08							
Ash ■	d						16 45									17 15							
Wanborough	d						16 48									17 18							
Guildford	a						16 55									17 25							
Martins Heron	d				15 47									16 17									16 47
Bracknell	d				15 50									16 20									16 50
Wokingham	d				15 57									16 27									16 57
Winnersh	d				16 00									16 30									17 00
Winnersh Triangle	d				16 02									16 32									17 02
Earley	d				16 05									16 35									17 05
Reading ■	a				16 12									16 42									17 12

The xx15 and xx45 services from London Waterloo to Whitton continue to London Waterloo via Brentford

The xx03 and xx33 London Waterloo to Kingston services continue to London Waterloo via Wimbledon

The xx07 and xx37 services from London Waterloo to Whitton continue to London Waterloo via Richmond

For additional services between Wokingham and Reading refer to Table T148

Table T149-F

Mondays to Fridays

21 May to 5 October

London - Hounslow, Richmond, Kingston, Windsor, Weybridge, Ascot, Guildford and Reading

		SW	SW ■	SW	SW	SW	SW ■	SW	SW	SW	SW	SW ■	SW	SW ■	SW ◇	SW ◇	SW	SW ■	SW ◇	SW	SW	SW
London Waterloo ■ ⊖	d			15 52	15 58	16 01	16 05			16 07	16 15	16 20			16 22	16 28	16 31	16 35			16 37	16 45
Vauxhall ⊖	d			15 56	16 02	16 05	16 09			16 12	16 19				16 26	16 32	16 35	16 39			16 42	16 49
Queenstown Rd.(Battersea)	d			15 59		16 08				16 15	16 22				16 29		16 38				16 45	16 52
Clapham Junction ■	d			16 02	16 08	16 11	16 15			16 18	16 25	16 28			16 32	16 38	16 41	16 45			16 48	16 55
Wandsworth Town	d			16 05		16 14				16 20	16 28				16 35		16 44				16 50	16 58
Putney	d			16 08	16 12	16 17				16 23	16 31				16 38	16 42	16 47				16 53	17 01
Barnes	d			16 12		16 22				16 27	16 35				16 42		16 52				16 57	17 05
Barnes Bridge	d			16 14						16 29					16 44						16 59	
Chiswick	d			16 17						16 32					16 47						17 02	
Kew Bridge	d			16 20						16 35					16 50						17 05	
Brentford	d			16 23						16 38					16 53						17 08	
Syon Lane	d			16 25						16 40					16 55						17 10	
Isleworth	d			16 27						16 42					16 57						17 12	
Hounslow	d			16 31						16 48					17 01						17 18	
Mortlake	d					16 24					16 37						16 54					17 07
North Sheen	d	←				16 26			←		16 39		←				16 56			←		17 09
Richmond ⊖	d	16 12			16 18	16 29	16 23		16 29		16 42	16 36	16 42			16 48	16 59	16 53		16 59		17 12
St Margarets	d	16 14				→			16 31		→		16 44				→			17 01		→
Twickenham	a	16 16			16 21		16 27		16 33			16 40	16 46			16 51		16 57		17 03		
	d	16 17			16 22		16 27		16 34			16 40	16 47			16 52		16 57		17 04		
Strawberry Hill	d								16 37											17 07		
Fulwell	a																					
Teddington	a								16 42											17 12		
Hampton Wick	a								16 46											17 16		
Kingston	a								16 48											17 18		
Whitton	d	16a20			16 25			←		16a53			16a50			16 55			←		17a23	
Feltham	d			16 38	16 29		16 33	16 38				16 46			17 08	16 59		17 03	17 08			
Ashford (Surrey)	d			→	16 33		16 37	16 42							→	17 03		17 07	17 12			
Staines	d				16 37		16 41	16 46				16 53				17 07		17 11	17 16			
Wraysbury	d				16 41											17 11						
Sunnymeads	d				16 44											17 14						
Datchet	d				16 47											17 17						
Windsor & Eton Riverside	a				16 52											17 23						
Egham	d						16 46	16 50				16 57						17 16	17 21			
Virginia Water	a						16 50	16 55				17 01						17 20	17 25			
	d						16 50	16 55				17 01						17 20	17 25			
Chertsey	d							17 00											17 31			
Addlestone	d							17 03											17 34			
Weybridge	a							17 08											17 40			
Longcross	d						16 53											17 23				
Sunningdale	d						16 57					17 07						17 27				
Ascot ■	d		16 53				17 01					17 13		17 23				17 31				
Bagshot	d		16 59											17 29								
Camberley	a		17 05											17 35								
Frimley	d		17 13											17 43								
Ash Vale	d		17 19											17 49								
Aldershot	a		17 24											17 54								
	d		17 38											18 08								
Ash ■	d		17 45											18 15								
Wanborough	d		17 48											18 18								
Guildford	a		17 55											18 25								
Martins Heron	d						17 05					17 17						17 35				
Bracknell	d						17 09					17 20						17 39				
Wokingham	d						17 15					17 27						17 45				
Winnersh	d											17 30										
Winnersh Triangle	d											17 32										
Earley	d											17 35										
Reading ■	a						17 28					17 42						18 01				

The xx15 and xx45 services from London Waterloo to Whitton continue to London Waterloo via Brentford

The xx03 and xx33 London Waterloo to Kingston services continue to London Waterloo via Wimbledon

The xx07 and xx37 services from London Waterloo to Whitton continue to London Waterloo via Richmond

For additional services between Wokingham and Reading refer to Table T148

Table T149-F

Mondays to Fridays

21 May to 5 October

London - Hounslow, Richmond, Kingston, Windsor, Weybridge, Ascot, Guildford and Reading

		SW ■	SW	SW ◇	SW ◇	SW	SW ◇■	SW ◇	SW	SW	SW	SW ■	SW	SW ■	SW	SW ■	SW ◇	SW ◇	SW	SW ■	SW ◇	SW	SW
London Waterloo ■ ⊖	d	16 50		16 52	16 58	17 01	17 05			17 07	17 13		17 15	17 20			17 22	17 28	17 31	17 35			17 37
Vauxhall ⊖	d			16 56	17 02	17 05	17 09			17 12	17 17		17 20				17 26	17 32	17 35	17 39			17 42
Queenstown Rd.(Battersea)	d			16 59		17 08				17 15			17 23				17 29		17 38				17 45
Clapham Junction ■	d	16 58		17 02	17 08	17 11	17 15			17 18	17 23		17 26	17 28			17 32	17 38	17 42	17 45			17 48
Wandsworth Town	d			17 05		17 14				17 20			17 28				17 35		17 44				17 50
Putney	d			17 08	17 12	17 17				17 23	17 27		17 31				17 38	17 42	17 47				17 53
Barnes	d			17 12		17 22				17 27			17 35				17 42		17 52				17 57
Barnes Bridge	d			17 14						17 29							17 44						17 59
Chiswick	d			17 17						17 32							17 47						18 02
Kew Bridge	d			17 20						17 35							17 50						18 05
Brentford	d			17 23						17 38							17 53						18 08
Syon Lane	d			17 25						17 40							17 55						18 10
Isleworth	d			17 27						17 42							17 57						18 12
Hounslow	d			17 31						17 48							18 01						18 16
Mortlake	d					17 24							17 37						17 54				
North Sheen	d		←			17 26			←				17 39		←				17 56			←	
Richmond ⊖	d	17 06	17 12		17 18	17 29	17 23		17 29		17 33		17 42	17 37	17 42			17 48	17 59	17 53		17 59	
St Margarets	d		17 14			→			17 31				→		17 44				→			18 01	
Twickenham	a	17 10	17 16		17 21		17 27		17 33		17 37			17 40	17 46			17 51		17 57		18 03	
	d	17 10	17 17		17 22		17 27		17 34		17 37			17 41	17 47			17 52		17 57		18 04	
Strawberry Hill	d								17 37		17 41											18 07	
Fulwell	a																						
Teddington	a								17 42		17 46											18 12	
Hampton Wick	a								17 46		17 54											18 16	
Kingston	a								17 48		17 56											18 18	
Whitton	d		17a20		17 25			←		17a53					17a50			17 55			←		18a23
Feltham	d	17 16		17 38	17 29		17 33	17 38						17 47			18 08	17 59		18 03	18 08		
Ashford (Surrey)	d			→	17 33		17 37	17 42									→	18 03		18 07	18 12		
Staines	d	17 23			17 37		17 41	17 46						17 53				18 07		18 11	18 16		
Wraysbury	d				17 41													18 11					
Sunnymeads	d				17 44													18 14					
Datchet	d				17 47													18 17					
Windsor & Eton Riverside	a				17 53													18 23					
Egham	d	17 27					17 46	17 51						17 58						18 16	18 21		
Virginia Water	a	17 31					17 50	17 55						18 02						18 20	18 25		
	d	17 31					17 50	17 55						18 02						18 20	18 25		
Chertsey	d							18 01													18 31		
Addlestone	d							18 04													18 34		
Weybridge	a							18 10													18 40		
Longcross	d													18 05									
Sunningdale	d	17 37					17 55							18 09						18 25			
Ascot ■	d	17 43					18 01							18 13		18 23				18 30			
Bagshot	d						18 07									18 29							
Camberley	a						18 13									18 35							
Frimley	d						18 17									18 43							
Ash Vale	d						18 24									18 49							
Aldershot	a						18 29									18 54							
	d											18 38				19 08							
Ash ■	d											18 45				19 15							
Wanborough	d											18 48				19 18							
Guildford	a											18 55				19 25							
Martins Heron	d	17 47												18 17						18 34			
Bracknell	d	17 50												18 21						18 37			
Wokingham	d	17 57												18 27						18 44			
Winnersh	d	18 00												18 31									
Winnersh Triangle	d	18 02												18 33									
Earley	d	18 05												18 35									
Reading ■	a	18 12												18 42						18 57			

The xx15 and xx45 services from London Waterloo to Whitton continue to London Waterloo via Brentford

The xx03 and xx33 London Waterloo to Kingston services continue to London Waterloo via Wimbledon

The xx07 and xx37 services from London Waterloo to Whitton continue to London Waterloo via Richmond

For additional services between Wokingham and Reading refer to Table T148

Table T149-F

London - Hounslow, Richmond, Kingston, Windsor, Weybridge, Ascot, Guildford and Reading

		SW	SW	SW	SW	SW	SW	SW	SW	SW	SW	SW	SW	SW	SW	SW	SW	SW	SW	SW	SW	SW	SW
				■		◇	◇■	■	◇		■	◇					■		■	◇	◇		■
London Waterloo ■ ⊖	d	17 43	17 45	17 50		17 52	17 54		17 58	18 01	18 05			18 07	18 13	18 15	18 20			18 22	18 28	18 31	18 35
Vauxhall ⊖	d	17 47	17 50			17 56	17 58		18 02	18 05	18 09			18 12	18 17	18 20				18 26	18 32	18 35	18 39
Queenstown Rd.(Battersea)	d		17 53			17 59				18 08				18 15		18 23				18 29		18 38	
Clapham Junction ■	d	17 53	17 56	17 58		18 02	18 04		18 08	18 11	18 15			18 18	18 23	18 26	18 28			18 32	18 38	18 41	18 45
Wandsworth Town	d		17 58			18 05				18 14				18 20		18 28				18 35		18 44	
Putney	d	17 57	18 01			18 08			18 12	18 17				18 23	18 27	18 31				18 38	18 42	18 47	
Barnes	d		18 05			18 12				18 22				18 27		18 35				18 42		18 52	
Barnes Bridge	d					18 14								18 29						18 44			
Chiswick	d					18 17								18 32						18 47			
Kew Bridge	d					18 20								18 35						18 50			
Brentford	d					18 23								18 38						18 53			
Syon Lane	d					18 25								18 40						18 55			
Isleworth	d					18 27								18 42						18 57			
Hounslow	d					18 31	18 19							18 48						19 01			
Mortlake	d		18 07							18 24						18 37						18 54	
North Sheen	d		18 09		←					18 26			←			18 39		←				18 56	
Richmond ⊖	d	18 03	18 12	18 07	18 12				18 18	18 29	18 23		18 29		18 33	18 42	18 37	18 42			18 48	18 59	18 53
St Margarets	d		→		18 14					→			18 31			→		18 44				→	
Twickenham	a	18 07		18 10	18 16				18 21		18 27		18 33		18 37		18 40	18 46			18 51		18 57
	d	18 07		18 11	18 17				18 22		18 27		18 34		18 37		18 41	18 47			18 52		18 57
Strawberry Hill	d	18 11											18 37		18 41								
Fulwell	a	18 13													18 43								
Teddington	a												18 42										
Hampton Wick	a												18 46										
Kingston	a												18 48										
Whitton	d				18a20				18 25			←		18a53				18a50			18 55		
Feltham	d			18 17		18 38	18 25		18 29		18 33	18 38					18 47			19 08	18 59		19 03
Ashford (Surrey)	d					→			18 33		18 37	18 42								→	19 03		19 07
Staines	d			18 23			18 31		18 37		18 41	18 46					18 53				19 07		19 11
Wraysbury	d								18 41												19 11		
Sunnymeads	d								18 44												19 14		
Datchet	d								18 47												19 17		
Windsor & Eton Riverside	a								18 53												19 23		
Egham	d			18 28			18 36				18 46	18 51					18 58						19 16
Virginia Water	a			18 32			18 40				18 50	18 55					19 02						19 20
	d			18 32			18 40				18 50	18 55					19 02						19 20
Chertsey	d											19 01											
Addlestone	d											19 04											
Weybridge	a											19 10											
Longcross	d			18 35													19 05						
Sunningdale	d			18 38			18 46				18 55						19 09						19 25
Ascot ■	d			18 43			18 53				19 00						19 13		19 23				19 30
Bagshot	d						18 59												19 29				
Camberley	a						19 05												19 35				
Frimley	d						19 09												19 43				
Ash Vale	d						19 16												19 49				
Aldershot	a						19 21												19 54				
	d							19 38											20 08				
Ash ■	d							19 45											20 15				
Wanborough	d							19 48											20 18				
Guildford	a							19 55											20 25				
Martins Heron	d			18 47							19 04						19 17						19 34
Bracknell	d			18 51							19 07						19 21						19 37
Wokingham	d			18 57							19 14						19 27						19 47
Winnersh	d			19 01													19 31						
Winnersh Triangle	d			19 03													19 33						
Earley	d			19 05													19 35						
Reading ■	a			19 12							19 28						19 47						20 01

The xx15 and xx45 services from London Waterloo to Whitton continue to London Waterloo via Brentford

The xx03 and xx33 London Waterloo to Kingston services continue to London Waterloo via Wimbledon

The xx07 and xx37 services from London Waterloo to Whitton continue to London Waterloo via Richmond

For additional services between Wokingham and Reading refer to Table T148

Table T149-F

London - Hounslow, Richmond, Kingston, Windsor, Weybridge, Ascot, Guildford and Reading

		SW	SW	SW	SW	SW	SW	SW	SW	SW	SW	SW	SW	SW	SW	SW	SW	SW	SW	SW	SW	SW
		◇					■		■	◇	◇		■	◇				■		■		
London Waterloo ■ ⊖	d			18 37	18 43	18 45	18 50			18 52	18 58	19 01	19 05			19 07	19 15	19 20			19 22	19 28
Vauxhall ⊖	d			18 42	18 47	18 50				18 56	19 02	19 05	19 09			19 12	19 19				19 26	19 32
Queenstown Rd.(Battersea)	d			18 45		18 53				18 59		19 08				19 15	19 22				19 29	
Clapham Junction ■	d			18 48	18 53	18 56	18 58			19 02	19 08	19 11	19 15			19 18	19 25	19 28			19 32	19 38
Wandsworth Town	d			18 51		18 58				19 05		19 14				19 21	19 28				19 35	
Putney	d			18 54	18 57	19 01				19 08	19 12	19 17				19 24	19 31				19 38	19 42
Barnes	d			18 57		19 05				19 12		19 22				19 27	19 35				19 42	
Barnes Bridge	d			18 59						19 14						19 29					19 44	
Chiswick	d			19 02						19 17						19 32					19 47	
Kew Bridge	d			19 05						19 20						19 35					19 50	
Brentford	d			19 08						19 23						19 38					19 53	
Syon Lane	d			19 10						19 25						19 40					19 55	
Isleworth	d			19 12						19 27						19 42					19 57	
Hounslow	d			19 18						19 31						19 48					20 01	
Mortlake	d					19 07						19 24					19 37					
North Sheen	d		←			19 09		←				19 26			←		19 39		←			
Richmond ⊖	d		18 59		19 03	19 12	19 07	19 12			19 18	19 29	19 23		19 29		19 42	19 36	19 42			19 48
St Margarets	d		19 01			→		19 14				→			19 31		→		19 44			
Twickenham	a		19 03		19 07		19 10	19 16			19 21		19 27		19 33			19 40	19 46			19 51
	d		19 04		19 07		19 11	19 17			19 22		19 27		19 34			19 40	19 47			19 52
Strawberry Hill	d		19 07		19 11										19 37							
Fulwell	a				19 13																	
Teddington	a		19 12												19 42							
Hampton Wick	a		19 16												19 46							
Kingston	a		19 18												19 48							
Whitton	d	←		19a23				19a20			19 25			←		19a53			19a50			19 55
Feltham	d	19 08					19 17			19 38	19 29		19 33	19 38				19 46			20 08	19 59
Ashford (Surrey)	d	19 12								→	19 33		19 37	19 42							→	20 03
Staines	d	19 16					19 23				19 37		19 41	19 46				19 53				20 07
Wraysbury	d										19 41											20 11
Sunnymeads	d										19 44											20 14
Datchet	d										19 47											20 17
Windsor & Eton Riverside	a										19 53											20 22
Egham	d	19 21					19 28						19 46	19 51				19 57				
Virginia Water	a	19 25					19 32						19 50	19 55				20 01				
	d	19 25					19 32						19 50	19 55				20 01				
Chertsey	d	19 31												20 01								
Addlestone	d	19 34												20 04								
Weybridge	a	19 46												20 10								
Longcross	d																					
Sunningdale	d						19 37						19 55					20 07				
Ascot ■	d						19 43		19 53				20 00					20 13		20 23		
Bagshot	d								19 59											20 29		
Camberley	a								20 05											20 35		
Frimley	d								20 13											20 43		
Ash Vale	d								20 19											20 49		
Aldershot	a								20 24											20 54		
	d								20 38											21 08		
Ash ■	d								20 45											21 15		
Wanborough	d								20 48											21 18		
Guildford	a								20 55											21 25		
Martins Heron	d						19 47						20 04					20 17				
Bracknell	d						19 50						20 07					20 20				
Wokingham	d						19 57						20 17					20 27				
Winnersh	d						20 00											20 30				
Winnersh Triangle	d						20 02											20 32				
Earley	d						20 05											20 35				
Reading ■	a						20 12						20 25					20 42				

The xx15 and xx45 services from London Waterloo to Whitton continue to London Waterloo via Brentford

The xx03 and xx33 London Waterloo to Kingston services continue to London Waterloo via Wimbledon

The xx07 and xx37 services from London Waterloo to Whitton continue to London Waterloo via Richmond

For additional services between Wokingham and Reading refer to Table T148

Table T149-F

Mondays to Fridays
21 May to 5 October

London - Hounslow, Richmond, Kingston, Windsor, Weybridge, Ascot, Guildford and Reading

		SW	SW	SW	SW	SW	SW		SW ■	SW	SW ■	SW	SW	SW	SW	SW	SW		SW ■	SW	SW ■	SW ■	SW	SW	SW
London Waterloo 15 ⊖	d	19 33	19 35			19 37	19 45		19 50			19 52	19 58		20 03	20 07	20 15		20 20				20 22	20 28	
Vauxhall ⊖	d	19 37	19 40			19 41	19 49					19 56	20 02		20 07	20 11	20 19						20 26	20 32	
Queenstown Rd.(Battersea)	d	19 40				19 44	19 52					19 59			20 10	20 14	20 22						20 29		
Clapham Junction 10	d	19 43	19 46			19 47	19 55		19 58			20 02	20 08		20 13	20 17	20 25		20 28				20 32	20 38	
Wandsworth Town	d	19 46				19 50	19 58					20 05			20 16	20 20	20 28						20 35		
Putney	d	19 49				19 53	20 01					20 08	20 12		20 19	20 23	20 31						20 38	20 42	
Barnes	d	19 52				19 57	20 05					20 12			20 22	20 27	20 35						20 42		
Barnes Bridge	d					19 59						20 14				20 29							20 44		
Chiswick	d					20 02						20 17				20 32							20 47		
Kew Bridge	d					20 05						20 20				20 35							20 50		
Brentford	d					20 08						20 23				20 38							20 53		
Syon Lane	d					20 10						20 25				20 40							20 55		
Isleworth	d					20 12						20 27				20 42							20 57		
Hounslow	d					20 18						20 31				20 48							21 01		
Mortlake	d	19 55					20 07								20 24		20 37								
North Sheen	d	19 57			←		20 09			←					20 26		20 39			←					
Richmond ⊖	d	19 59	19 54		19 59		20 12		20 06	20 12			20 18		20 29		20 42		20 36	20 42				20 48	
St Margarets	d	→			20 02		→			20 14					20 31		→			20 44					
Twickenham	a		19 58		20 04				20 10	20 16			20 21		20 33				20 40	20 46				20 51	
	d		19 58		20 04				20 10	20 17			20 22		20 34				20 40	20 47				20 52	
Strawberry Hill	d				20 08										20 37										
Fulwell	a																								
Teddington	a				20 11										20 40										
Hampton Wick	a				20 14										20 44										
Kingston	a				20 16										20 46										
Whitton	d			←		20a23				20a20			20 25	←		20a53				20a50				20 55	←
Feltham	d		20 04	20 08					20 16			20 36	20 29	20 36					20 46				21 06	20 59	21 06
Ashford (Surrey)	d		20 08	20 12								→	20 33	20 40									→	21 03	21 10
Staines	d		20 12	20 16					20 23				20 37	20 44					20 53					21 07	21 14
Wraysbury	d												20 41											21 11	
Sunnymeads	d												20 44											21 14	
Datchet	d												20 47											21 17	
Windsor & Eton Riverside	a												20 52											21 22	
Egham	d		20 17	20 21					20 27					20 49					20 57						21 19
Virginia Water	a		20 21	20 25					20 31					20 53					21 01						21 23
	d		20 21	20 25					20 31					20 53					21 01						21 23
Chertsey	d			20 31										20 59											21 29
Addlestone	d			20 34										21 02											21 32
Weybridge	a			20 39										21 07											21 37
Longcross	d																								
Sunningdale	d		20 26						20 37										21 07						
Ascot 8	d		20 31						20 43		20 53								21 13		21 23				
Bagshot	d										20 59										21 29				
Camberley	a										21 05										21 35				
Frimley	d										21 13										21 43				
Ash Vale	d										21 19										21 49				
Aldershot	a										21 24										21 54				
	d										21 38										22 08	22 38			
Ash 5	d										21 45										22 15	22 45			
Wanborough	d										21 48										22 18	22 48			
Guildford	a										21 55										22 25	22 56			
Martins Heron	d		20 35						20 47										21 17						
Bracknell	d		20 38						20 50										21 20						
Wokingham	d		20 49						20 57										21 27						
Winnersh	d								21 00										21 31						
Winnersh Triangle	d								21 02										21 33						
Earley	d								21 05										21 35						
Reading 7	a		20 59						21 12										21 42						

The xx15 and xx45 services from London Waterloo to Whitton continue to London Waterloo via Brentford

The xx03 and xx33 London Waterloo to Kingston services continue to London Waterloo via Wimbledon

The xx07 and xx37 services from London Waterloo to Whitton continue to London Waterloo via Richmond

For additional services between Wokingham and Reading refer to Table T148

Table T149-F

Mondays to Fridays
21 May to 5 October

London - Hounslow, Richmond, Kingston, Windsor, Weybridge, Ascot, Guildford and Reading

		SW	SW		SW	SW ■	SW	SW	SW	SW	SW	SW	SW		SW ■	SW	SW ■	SW	SW	SW	SW	SW	SW		SW ■
London Waterloo 15 ⊖	d	20 33	20 37		20 45	20 50		20 52	20 58		21 03	21 07	21 15		21 20			21 22	21 28		21 33	21 37	21 45		21 50
Vauxhall ⊖	d	20 37	20 41		20 49			20 56	21 02		21 07	21 11	21 19					21 27	21 32		21 37	21 41	21 49		
Queenstown Rd.(Battersea)	d	20 40	20 44		20 52			20 59			21 10	21 14	21 22					21 30			21 40	21 44	21 52		
Clapham Junction 10	d	20 43	20 47		20 55	20 58		21 02	21 08		21 13	21 17	21 25		21 28			21 33	21 38		21 43	21 47	21 55		21 58
Wandsworth Town	d	20 46	20 50		20 58			21 05			21 16	21 20	21 28					21 36			21 46	21 50	21 58		
Putney	d	20 49	20 53		21 01			21 08	21 12		21 19	21 23	21 31					21 39	21 42		21 49	21 53	22 01		
Barnes	d	20 52	20 57		21 05			21 12			21 22	21 27	21 35					21 42			21 52	21 57	22 05		
Barnes Bridge	d		20 59					21 14				21 29						21 44				21 59			
Chiswick	d		21 02					21 17				21 32						21 47				22 02			
Kew Bridge	d		21 05					21 20				21 35						21 50				22 05			
Brentford	d		21 08					21 23				21 38						21 53				22 08			
Syon Lane	d		21 10					21 25				21 40						21 55				22 10			
Isleworth	d		21 12					21 27				21 42						21 57				22 12			
Hounslow	d		21 18					21 31				21 48						22 01				22 18			
Mortlake	d	20 54			21 07						21 24		21 37								21 54		22 07		
North Sheen	d	20 56			21 09		←				21 26		21 39			←					21 56		22 09		
Richmond ⊖	d	20 59			21 12	21 06	21 12		21 18		21 29		21 42		21 36	21 42			21 48		21 59		22 12		22 06
St Margarets	d	21 01			→		21 14				21 31		→			21 44					22 01		→		
Twickenham	a	21 03				21 10	21 16		21 21		21 33				21 40	21 46			21 51		22 03				22 10
	d	21 04				21 10	21 17		21 22		21 34				21 40	21 47			21 52		22 04				22 10
Strawberry Hill	d	21 07									21 37										22 07				
Fulwell	a																								
Teddington	a	21 10									21 40										22 10				
Hampton Wick	a	21 14									21 44										22 14				
Kingston	a	21 16									21 46										22 16				
Whitton	d		21a23				21a20		21 25	←		21a53				21a50			21 55	←		22a23			
Feltham	d					21 16		21 36	21 29	21 36					21 46			22 06	21 59	22 06					22 16
Ashford (Surrey)	d							→	21 33	21 40								→	22 03	22 10					
Staines	d					21 23			21 37	21 44					21 53				22 07	22 14					22 23
Wraysbury	d								21 41										22 11						
Sunnymeads	d								21 44										22 14						
Datchet	d								21 47										22 17						
Windsor & Eton Riverside	a								21 52										22 22						
Egham	d					21 27				21 49					21 57					22 19					22 27
Virginia Water	a					21 31				21 53					22 01					22 23					22 31
	d					21 31				21 53					22 01					22 23					22 31
Chertsey	d									21 59										22 29					
Addlestone	d									22 02										22 32					
Weybridge	a									22 07										22 37					
Longcross	d																								
Sunningdale	d					21 37									22 07										22 37
Ascot 8	d					21 43									22 13		22 23								22 43
Bagshot	d																22 29								
Camberley	a																22 35								
Frimley	d																22 43								
Ash Vale	d																22 49								
Aldershot	a																22 54								
	d																23 08								
Ash 5	d																23 15								
Wanborough	d																23 18								
Guildford	a																23 25								
Martins Heron	d					21 47									22 17										22 47
Bracknell	d					21 50									22 20										22 50
Wokingham	d					21 57									22 27										22 57
Winnersh	d					22 00									22 30										23 00
Winnersh Triangle	d					22 02									22 32										23 02
Earley	d					22 05									22 35										23 05
Reading 7	a					22 12									22 42										23 12

The xx15 and xx45 services from London Waterloo to Whitton continue to London Waterloo via Brentford

The xx03 and xx33 London Waterloo to Kingston services continue to London Waterloo via Wimbledon

The xx07 and xx37 services from London Waterloo to Whitton continue to London Waterloo via Richmond

For additional services between Wokingham and Reading refer to Table T148

Table T149-F

London - Hounslow, Richmond, Kingston, Windsor, Weybridge, Ascot, Guildford and Reading

Mondays to Fridays

21 May to 5 October

		SW	SW	SW	SW	SW	SW [1]	SW [1]	SW		SW	SW	SW	SW [1]	SW	SW	SW	SW	SW [1]		SW	SW	SW	SW	SW
London Waterloo [15]	⊖ d		21 52	21 58		22 03	22 20		22 22		22 28		22 33	22 50	22 52	22 58		23 03	23 20		23 22	23 28		23 33	23 50
Vauxhall	⊖ d		21 56	22 02		22 07			22 26		22 32		22 37		22 56	23 02		23 07			23 26	23 32		23 37	
Queenstown Rd.(Battersea)	d		21 59			22 10			22 29				22 40		22 59			23 10			23 29			23 40	
Clapham Junction [10]	d		22 02	22 08		22 13	22 28		22 32		22 38		22 43	22 58	23 02	23 08		23 13	23 28		23 32	23 38		23 43	23 58
Wandsworth Town	d		22 05			22 16			22 35				22 46		23 05			23 16			23 35			23 46	
Putney	d		22 08	22 12		22 19			22 38		22 42		22 49		23 08	23 12		23 19			23 38	23 42		23 49	
Barnes	d		22 12			22 22			22 42				22 52		23 12			23 22			23 42			23 52	
Barnes Bridge	d		22 14						22 44						23 14						23 44				
Chiswick	d		22 17						22 47						23 17						23 47				
Kew Bridge	d		22 20						22 50						23 20						23 50				
Brentford	d		22 23						22 53						23 23						23 53				
Syon Lane	d		22 25						22 55						23 25						23 55				
Isleworth	d		22 27						22 57						23 27						23 57				
Hounslow	d		22 31						23 01						23 31						00 01				
Mortlake	d					22 24							22 54					23 24						23 54	
North Sheen	d	←				22 26							22 56					23 26						23 56	
Richmond	⊖ d	22 12		22 18		22 29	22 36				22 48		22 59	23 06		23 18		23 29	23 36			23 48		23 59	00 06
St Margarets	d	22 14				22 31							23 01					23 31						00 01	
Twickenham	a	22 16		22 21		22 33	22 40				22 51		23 03	23 10		23 21		23 33	23 40			23 51		00 03	00 10
	d			22 22		22 34	22 40				22 52		23 04	23 10		23 22		23 34	23 40			23 52		00 04	00 10
Strawberry Hill	d					22 37							23 07					23 37						00 09	
Fulwell	a																								
Teddington	a					22 40							23 10					23 40						00 12	
Hampton Wick	a					22 44							23 14					23 44						00 14	
Kingston	a					22 46							23 16					23 46						00 16	
Whitton	d			22 25	←						22 55	←				23 25	←					23 55	←		
Feltham	d		22 36	22 29	22 36		22 46		23 06		22 59	23 06		23 16	23 36	23 29	23 36		23 46		00 06	23 59	00 06		00 16
Ashford (Surrey)	d		→	22 33	22 40				→		23 03	23 10			→	23 33	23 40				→	00 03	00 10		
Staines	d			22 37	22 44		22 53				23 07	23 14		23 23		23 37	23 44		23 53			00 07	00 14		00 23
Wraysbury	d			22 41							23 11					23 41						00 11			
Sunnymeads	d			22 44							23 14					23 44						00 14			
Datchet	d			22 47							23 17					23 47						00 17			
Windsor & Eton Riverside	a			22 52							23 22					23 52						00 22			
Egham	d				22 49		22 57					23 19		23 27			23 49		23 57				00 19		00 27
Virginia Water	a				22 53		23 01					23 23		23 31			23 53		00 01				00 23		00 31
	d				22 53		23 01					23 23		23 31			23 53		00 01				00 23		00 31
Chertsey	d				22 59							23 29					23 59						00 29		
Addlestone	d				23 02							23 32					00a02						00 32		
Weybridge	a				23 07							23 37											00 36		
Longcross	d																								
Sunningdale	d						23 07							23 37					00 08						00 37
Ascot [3]	d						23 13	23 23						23 43					00 13						00 42
Bagshot	d							23 29																	
Camberley	a							23 35																	
Frimley	d							23 43																	
Ash Vale	d							23 49																	
Aldershot	a							23 54																	
	d																								
Ash [5]	d																								
Wanborough	d																								
Guildford	a																								
Martins Heron	d						23 17							23 47					00 17						00 46
Bracknell	d						23 20							23 50					00 20						00 50
Wokingham	d						23 27							23 57					00 32						00 56
Winnersh	d						23 30							23 59					00 36						
Winnersh Triangle	d						23 32							00 02					00 38						
Earley	d						23 35							00 05					00 40						
Reading [7]	a						23 42							00 12					00 45						01 05

The xx15 and xx45 services from London Waterloo to Whitton continue to London Waterloo via Brentford

The xx03 and xx33 London Waterloo to Kingston services continue to London Waterloo via Wimbledon

The xx07 and xx37 services from London Waterloo to Whitton continue to London Waterloo via Richmond

For additional services between Wokingham and Reading refer to Table T148

Table T149-F

London - Hounslow, Richmond, Kingston, Windsor, Weybridge, Ascot, Guildford and Reading

Mondays to Fridays

21 May to 5 October

		SW	SW	SW
London Waterloo [15]	⊖ d	23 52	23 58	
Vauxhall	⊖ d	23 56	00 02	
Queenstown Rd.(Battersea)	d	23 59		
Clapham Junction [10]	d	00 02	00 08	
Wandsworth Town	d	00 05		
Putney	d	00 08	00 12	
Barnes	d	00 12		
Barnes Bridge	d	00 14		
Chiswick	d	00 17		
Kew Bridge	d	00 20		
Brentford	d	00 23		
Syon Lane	d	00 25		
Isleworth	d	00 27		
Hounslow	d	00 31		
Mortlake	d			
North Sheen	d			
Richmond	⊖ d		00 18	
St Margarets	d			
Twickenham	a		00 22	
	d		00 22	
Strawberry Hill	d			
Fulwell	a			
Teddington	a			
Hampton Wick	a			
Kingston	a			
Whitton	d		00 25	←
Feltham	d	00 36	00 29	00 36
Ashford (Surrey)	d	→	00 33	00 40
Staines	d		00a37	00a47
Wraysbury	d			
Sunnymeads	d			
Datchet	d			
Windsor & Eton Riverside	a			
Egham	d			
Virginia Water	a			
	d			
Chertsey	d			
Addlestone	d			
Weybridge	a			
Longcross	d			
Sunningdale	d			
Ascot [3]	d			
Bagshot	d			
Camberley	a			
Frimley	d			
Ash Vale	d			
Aldershot	a			
	d			
Ash [5]	d			
Wanborough	d			
Guildford	a			
Martins Heron	d			
Bracknell	d			
Wokingham	d			
Winnersh	d			
Winnersh Triangle	d			
Earley	d			
Reading [7]	a			

The xx15 and xx45 services from London Waterloo to Whitton continue to London Waterloo via Brentford

The xx03 and xx33 London Waterloo to Kingston services continue to London Waterloo via Wimbledon

The xx07 and xx37 services from London Waterloo to Whitton continue to London Waterloo via Richmond

For additional services between Wokingham and Reading refer to Table T148

Table T149-F

London - Hounslow, Richmond, Kingston, Windsor, Weybridge, Ascot, Guildford and Reading

		SW MX ■	SW MX	SW MO ■	SW MX ■	SW MX ■	SW ■	SW MX	SW MO ■	SW MX	SW MO	SW MX	SW MO	SW MO	SW MX	SW MX	SW ■	SW MO	SW MX	SW	SW	SW ■	SW
London Waterloo ■ ⊖	d																	00 18	00 18			05 05	
Vauxhall ⊖	d														00 02			00 22	00 22			05 09	
Queenstown Rd.(Battersea)	d																	00 25	00 25			05 12	
Clapham Junction ■	d														00 08	00 02		00 29	00 30			05 15	
Wandsworth Town	d															00 05		00 32	00 33			05 18	
Putney	d														00 12	00 08		00 35	00 36			05 21	
Barnes	d													00 03		00 12		00 38	00 39			05 24	
Barnes Bridge	d															00 14							
Chiswick	d															00 17							
Kew Bridge	d															00 20							
Brentford	d															00 23							
Syon Lane	d															00 25							
Isleworth	d															00 27							
Hounslow	d							00 01								00 31							
Mortlake	d													00 05				00 40	00 41			05 26	
North Sheen	d													00 07				00 42	00 43			05 28	
Richmond ⊖	d											00 06		00 10	00 18			00 45	00 46			05 31	
St Margarets	d									00 01				00 12				00 47	00 48			05 33	
Twickenham	a									00 03		00 10		00 14	00 22			00 49	00 50			05 35	
	d								00 03	00 04		00 10	00 12	00 15	00 22			00 50	00 51	04 52		05 36	05 53
Strawberry Hill	d									00 09			00 15					00s53	00s54	04 55			
Fulwell	a																						
Teddington	a									00 12			00 18					00s56	00s57	04 58			
Hampton Wick	a									00 14			00 21					00s59	01s00	05 01			
Kingston	a									00 16			00 23					01 01	01 02	05 03			
Whitton	d													00 18	00 25							05 39	05 56
Feltham	d							00 06	00 09			00 16		00 22	00 29	00 36						05 43	06 00
Ashford (Surrey)	d		00 03					00 10						00 26	00 33	00 40						05 47	06 04
Staines	d		00 07					00 14	00 15		00 21	00 23		00a30	00a37	00a47	05 23				05 44	05 53	06 08
Wraysbury	d		00 11																				06 13
Sunnymeads	d		00 14																				06 16
Datchet	d		00 17																				06 20
Windsor & Eton Riverside	a		00 25																				06 25
Egham	d							00 19	00 20		00s25	00 27					05 27				05 49	05 57	
Virginia Water	a							00 23	00 24		00s30	00 31					05 31				05 53	06 01	
	d				00 01			00 23	00 24			00 31					05 31				05 53	06 01	
Chertsey	d							00 29			00s35										05 59		
Addlestone	d							00 32			00s38										06 02		
Weybridge	a							00 36													06 07		
Longcross	d																						
Sunningdale	d				00 08				00 30			00 37					05 37					06 07	
Ascot ■	d			00 05	00 13	00 23			00 35			00 42					05 43					06 13	
Bagshot	d					00 29																	
Camberley	a					00 35																	
Frimley	d					00 40																	
Ash Vale	d					00 47																	
Aldershot	a					00s52																	
	d						06 08																
Ash ■	d						06 15																
Wanborough	d						06 18																
Guildford	a						06 25																
Martins Heron	d			00 09	00 17				00 39			00 46					05 47					06 17	
Bracknell	d			00 13	00 20				00 43			00 50					05 50					06 20	
Wokingham	d			00 19	00 32				00 49			00 56					05 57					06 27	
Winnersh	d			00 23	00 36				00 53								06 00					06 30	
Winnersh Triangle	d	00 02		00 25	00 38				00 55								06 02					06 32	
Earley	d	00 05		00 27	00 40				00 57								06 07					06 37	
Reading ■	a	00 15		00 35	00 48				01 05			01 08					06 13					06 43	

The xx15 and xx45 services from London Waterloo to Whitton continue to London Waterloo via Brentford

The xx03 and xx33 London Waterloo to Kingston services continue to London Waterloo via Wimbledon

The xx07 and xx37 services from London Waterloo to Whitton continue to London Waterloo via Richmond

For additional services between Wokingham and Reading refer to Table T148

Table T149-F

London - Hounslow, Richmond, Kingston, Windsor, Weybridge, Ascot, Guildford and Reading

		SW	SW	SW ■	SW ■	SW ■	SW ■	SW	SW	SW	SW	SW ■	SW	SW ■	SW	SW ■	SW	SW	SW	SW	SW	SW	SW ■
London Waterloo ■ ⊖	d	05 33				05 50			05 58	06 03			06 15	06 20			06 22	06 28			06 33	06 45	06 50
Vauxhall ⊖	d	05 37							06 02	06 07			06 19				06 26	06 32			06 37	06 49	
Queenstown Rd.(Battersea)	d	05 40								06 10			06 22				06 29				06 40	06 52	
Clapham Junction ■	d	05 43				05 58			06 08	06 13			06 25	06 28			06 32	06 38			06 43	06 55	06 58
Wandsworth Town	d	05 46								06 16			06 28				06 35				06 46	06 58	
Putney	d	05 49							06 12	06 19			06 31				06 38	06 42			06 49	07 01	
Barnes	d	05 52								06 22			06 35				06 42				06 52	07 05	
Barnes Bridge	d																06 44						
Chiswick	d																06 47						
Kew Bridge	d																06 50						
Brentford	d																06 53						
Syon Lane	d																06 55						
Isleworth	d																06 57						
Hounslow	d										06 31						07 01			06 48			
Mortlake	d	05 54								06 24			06 37								06 54	07 07	
North Sheen	d	05 56								06 26			06 39		←						06 56	07 09	
Richmond ⊖	d	05 59				06 06			06 18	06 29			06 42	06 36	06 42			06 48			06 59	07 12	07 06
St Margarets	d	06 01								06 31			→		06 44						07 01	→	
Twickenham	a	06 03				06 10			06 21	06 33				06 40	06 46			06 51		06 56	07 03		07 10
	d	06 04				06 10		06 17	06 22	06 34				06 40	06 47			06 52			07 04		07 10
Strawberry Hill	d	06 07								06 37											07 07		
Fulwell	a																						
Teddington	a	06 10								06 40											07 10		
Hampton Wick	a	06 14								06 44											07 14		
Kingston	a	06 16								06 46											07 16		
Whitton	d							06a20	06 25						06a50			06 55	←				
Feltham	d					06 16			06 29		06 36			06 46			07 06	06 59	07 06				07 16
Ashford (Surrey)	d								06 33		06 40						→	07 03	07 10				
Staines	d		06 14			06 23			06 37		06 44			06 53				07 07	07 14				07 23
Wraysbury	d								06 41									07 12					
Sunnymeads	d								06 44									07 15					
Datchet	d								06 47									07 19					
Windsor & Eton Riverside	a								06 56									07 25					
Egham	d		06 19			06 27					06 49			06 57					07 19				07 27
Virginia Water	a		06 23			06 31					06 53			07 01					07 23				07 31
	d		06 23			06 31					06 53			07 01					07 23				07 31
Chertsey	d		06 29								06 59								07 29				
Addlestone	d		06 32								07 02								07 32				
Weybridge	a		06 37								07 07								07 37				
Longcross	d					06 35								07 05									07 35
Sunningdale	d					06 37								07 07									07 37
Ascot ■	d				06 23	06 43	06 53					06 53		07 13		07 23							07 43
Bagshot	d				06 29		06 59									07 29							
Camberley	a				06 35		07 05									07 35							
Frimley	d				06 43		07 13									07 43							
Ash Vale	d				06 49		07 19									07 49							
Aldershot	a				06 56		07 26									07 54							
	d			06 38	07 08		07 38									08 08							
Ash ■	d			06 45	07 15		07 46									08 15							
Wanborough	d			06 48	07 18		07 49									08 18							
Guildford	a			06 55	07 25		07 56									08 26							
Martins Heron	d					06 47								07 17									07 47
Bracknell	d					06 50						06 58		07 20									07 50
Wokingham	d					06 57						07 10		07 27									07 57
Winnersh	d					07 00								07 31									08 00
Winnersh Triangle	d					07 02								07 33									08 02
Earley	d					07 07								07 37									08 07
Reading ■	a					07 13						07 21		07 45									08 15

The xx15 and xx45 services from London Waterloo to Whitton continue to London Waterloo via Brentford

The xx03 and xx33 London Waterloo to Kingston services continue to London Waterloo via Wimbledon

The xx07 and xx37 services from London Waterloo to Whitton continue to London Waterloo via Richmond

For additional services between Wokingham and Reading refer to Table T148

Table T149-F

Mondays to Fridays

8 October to 7 December

London - Hounslow, Richmond, Kingston, Windsor, Weybridge, Ascot, Guildford and Reading

		SW		SW ■	SW	SW	SW	SW	SW	SW	SW	SW ■	
London Waterloo ⊖	d				06 52	06 58			07 03		07 15	07 20	
Vauxhall ⊖	d				06 56	07 02			07 07		07 19		
Queenstown Rd.(Battersea)	d				06 59				07 10		07 22		
Clapham Junction	d				07 02	07 08			07 13		07 25	07 28	
Wandsworth Town	d				07 05				07 16		07 28		
Putney	d				07 08	07 12			07 19		07 31		
Barnes	d				07 12				07 22		07 35		
Barnes Bridge	d				07 14								
Chiswick	d				07 17								
Kew Bridge	d				07 20								
Brentford	d				07 23								
Syon Lane	d				07 25								
Isleworth	d				07 27								
Hounslow	d				07 31								
Mortlake	d								07 24		07 37		
North Sheen	d	←							07 26		07 39		
Richmond ⊖	d	07 12				07 18			07 29		07 42	07 36	
St Margarets	d	07 14							07 31		→		
Twickenham	a	07 16				07 21			07 33			07 40	
	d	07 17				07 22		07 27	07 34	07 37		07 40	
Strawberry Hill	d							07 30	07 37	07 46			
Fulwell	a							07 33					
Teddington	a								07 40	07 49			
Hampton Wick	a								07 44	07 51			
Kingston	a								07 46	07 53			
Whitton	d	07a20				07 25	←						
Feltham	d				07 36	07 29	07 36					07 46	
Ashford (Surrey)	d				→	07 33	07 40						
Staines	d					07 37	07 44					07 53	
Wraysbury	d					07 42							
Sunnymeads	d					07 45							
Datchet	d					07 49							
Windsor & Eton Riverside	a					07 55							
Egham	d						07 49					07 57	
Virginia Water	a						07 53					08 01	
	d						07 53					08 01	
Chertsey	d						07 59						
Addlestone	d						08 02						
Weybridge	a						08 07						
Longcross	d											08 05	
Sunningdale	d											08 07	
Ascot	d			07 53								08 13	
Bagshot	d			07 59									
Camberley	a			08 05									
Frimley	d			08 13									
Ash Vale	d			08 19									
Aldershot	a			08 24									
	d			08 38									
Ash	d			08 45									
Wanborough	d			08 48									
Guildford	a			08 55									
Martins Heron	d											08 17	
Bracknell	d											08 20	
Wokingham	d											08 27	
Winnersh	d											08 30	
Winnersh Triangle	d											08 32	
Earley	d											08 37	
Reading	a											08 45	

		SW	SW	SW	SW	SW ■	SW	SW	SW	SW		SW	SW ■
London Waterloo ⊖	d		07 22	07 28	07 33	07 34			07 40			07 45	07 50
Vauxhall ⊖	d		07 26	07 32	07 36	07 39			07 45			07 49	
Queenstown Rd.(Battersea)	d		07 29		07 39				07 48			07 52	
Clapham Junction	d		07 32	07 38	07 43	07 46			07 51	07 54		07 55	07 58
Wandsworth Town	d		07 35		07 45				07 54			07 58	
Putney	d		07 38	07 42	07 49				07 57			08 01	
Barnes	d		07 42		07 52				08 00			08 05	
Barnes Bridge	d		07 44						08 02				
Chiswick	d		07 47						08 05				
Kew Bridge	d		07 50						08 08				
Brentford	d		07 53						08 11				
Syon Lane	d		07 55						08 13				
Isleworth	d		07 57						08 15				
Hounslow	d		08 01						08 27				
Mortlake	d				07 54							08 07	
North Sheen	d	←			07 56			←				08 09	
Richmond ⊖	d	07 42		07 48	07 59	07 54		07 59		08 02		08 12	08 06
St Margarets	d	07 44			→			08 01				→	
Twickenham	a	07 46		07 51		07 58		08 03		08 06			08 10
	d	07 47		07 52		07 58		08 04		08 07			08 10
Strawberry Hill	d							08 07		08 16			
Fulwell	a												
Teddington	a							08 10		08 19			
Hampton Wick	a							08 14		08 21			
Kingston	a							08 16		08 23			
Whitton	d	07a50		07 55			←		08a33				
Feltham	d		08 08	07 59		08 04	08 08						08 16
Ashford (Surrey)	d		→	08 03		08 08	08 12						
Staines	d			08 07		08 12	08 16						08 23
Wraysbury	d			08 12									
Sunnymeads	d			08 15									
Datchet	d			08 19									
Windsor & Eton Riverside	a			08 25									
Egham	d					08 17	08 21						08 27
Virginia Water	a						08 25						08 31
	d						08 25						08 31
Chertsey	d						08 31						
Addlestone	d						08 34						
Weybridge	a						08 39						
Longcross	d												08 35
Sunningdale	d												08 37
Ascot	d					08 27							08 43
Bagshot	d					08 33							
Camberley	a					08 39							
Frimley	d					08 43							
Ash Vale	d					08 50							
Aldershot	a					08 55							
	d					09 08							
Ash	d					09 15							
Wanborough	d					09 18							
Guildford	a					09 25							
Martins Heron	d												08 47
Bracknell	d												08 50
Wokingham	d												08 57
Winnersh	d												09 00
Winnersh Triangle	d												09 02
Earley	d												09 06
Reading	a												09 14

The xx15 and xx45 services from London Waterloo to Whitton continue to London Waterloo via Brentford

The xx03 and xx33 London Waterloo to Kingston services continue to London Waterloo via Wimbledon

The xx07 and xx37 services from London Waterloo to Whitton continue to London Waterloo via Richmond

For additional services between Wokingham and Reading refer to Table T148

Table T149-F

Mondays to Fridays

8 October to 7 December

London - Hounslow, Richmond, Kingston, Windsor, Weybridge, Ascot, Guildford and Reading

		SW	SW ■	SW	SW	SW	SW ■	SW		SW	SW	SW	SW ■
London Waterloo ⊖	d			07 52	07 58	08 03	08 07				08 10	08 15	08 20
Vauxhall ⊖	d			07 56	08 02	08 07					08 14	08 19	
Queenstown Rd.(Battersea)	d			07 59		08 10					08 17	08 22	
Clapham Junction	d			08 02	08 08	08 13	08 16				08 20	08 25	08 28
Wandsworth Town	d			08 06		08 16					08 23	08 28	
Putney	d			08 09	08 12	08 19					08 26	08 31	
Barnes	d			08 12		08 23					08 29	08 35	
Barnes Bridge	d			08 14							08 31		
Chiswick	d			08 18							08 34		
Kew Bridge	d			08 20							08 36		
Brentford	d			08 23							08 39		
Syon Lane	d			08 25							08 41		
Isleworth	d			08 27							08 43		
Hounslow	d			08 31							08 48		
Mortlake	d					08 25						08 37	
North Sheen	d	←				08 27				←		08 39	
Richmond ⊖	d	08 12			08 18	08 30	08 24			08 30		08 42	08 36
St Margarets	d	08 14				→				08 32		→	
Twickenham	a	08 16			08 21		08 28			08 34			08 40
	d	08 17			08 22		08 28			08 35			08 40
Strawberry Hill	d									08 38			
Fulwell	a												
Teddington	a									08 41			
Hampton Wick	a									08 44			
Kingston	a									08 46			
Whitton	d	08a20			08 25			←			08a53		
Feltham	d			08 38	08 29		08 34	08 38					08 46
Ashford (Surrey)	d			→	08 33		08 38	08 42					
Staines	d				08 37		08 42	08 46					08 53
Wraysbury	d				08 42								
Sunnymeads	d				08 45								
Datchet	d				08 49								
Windsor & Eton Riverside	a				08 55								
Egham	d						08 47	08 51					08 57
Virginia Water	a						08 51	08 55					09 01
	d						08 51	08 55					09 01
Chertsey	d							09 01					
Addlestone	d							09 04					
Weybridge	a							09 09					
Longcross	d						08 54						
Sunningdale	d						08 58						09 07
Ascot	d		08 53				09 02						09 13
Bagshot	d		08 59										
Camberley	a		09 05										
Frimley	d		09 13										
Ash Vale	d		09 19										
Aldershot	a		09 25										
	d		09 38										
Ash	d		09 45										
Wanborough	d		09 48										
Guildford	a		09 55										
Martins Heron	d						09 06						09 17
Bracknell	d						09 10						09 20
Wokingham	d						09 17						09 27
Winnersh	d						09 20						09 30
Winnersh Triangle	d						09 22						09 32
Earley	d						09 25						09 37
Reading	a						09 33						09 45

		SW	SW ■	SW	SW	SW		SW ■	SW	SW	SW	SW	SW ■
London Waterloo ⊖	d			08 22	08 28	08 33		08 37			08 40	08 43	08 50
Vauxhall ⊖	d			08 26	08 32	08 37					08 44	08 47	
Queenstown Rd.(Battersea)	d			08 29		08 40					08 47	08 50	
Clapham Junction	d			08 32	08 38	08 43		08 46			08 50	08 55	08 58
Wandsworth Town	d			08 35		08 46					08 53	08 58	
Putney	d			08 38	08 42	08 49					08 56	09 01	
Barnes	d			08 42		08 53					08 59	09 05	
Barnes Bridge	d			08 44							09 01		
Chiswick	d			08 47							09 03		
Kew Bridge	d			08 50							09 06		
Brentford	d			08 53							09 09		
Syon Lane	d			08 55							09 11		
Isleworth	d			08 57							09 13		
Hounslow	d			09 01							09 18		
Mortlake	d					08 55						09 07	
North Sheen	d	←				08 57				←		09 09	
Richmond ⊖	d	08 42			08 48	09 00		08 54		09 00		09 12	09 06
St Margarets	d	08 44				→				09 02		→	
Twickenham	a	08 46			08 51			08 58		09 04			09 10
	d	08 47			08 52			08 58		09 05			09 10
Strawberry Hill	d									09 08			
Fulwell	a												
Teddington	a									09 11			
Hampton Wick	a									09 14			
Kingston	a									09 16			
Whitton	d	08a50			08 55				←		09a23		
Feltham	d			09 08	08 59			09 04	09 08				09 16
Ashford (Surrey)	d			→	09 03			09 08	09 12				
Staines	d				09 07			09 12	09 16				09 23
Wraysbury	d				09 12								
Sunnymeads	d				09 15								
Datchet	d				09 19								
Windsor & Eton Riverside	a				09 25								
Egham	d							09 17	09 21				09 27
Virginia Water	a							09 21	09 25				09 31
	d							09 21	09 25				09 31
Chertsey	d								09 31				
Addlestone	d								09 34				
Weybridge	a								09 39				
Longcross	d												
Sunningdale	d							09 26					09 37
Ascot	d		09 23					09 31					09 43
Bagshot	d		09 29										
Camberley	a		09 35										
Frimley	d		09 43										
Ash Vale	d		09 49										
Aldershot	a		09 54										
	d		10 08										
Ash	d		10 15										
Wanborough	d		10 18										
Guildford	a		10 25										
Martins Heron	d							09 35					09 47
Bracknell	d							09 38					09 50
Wokingham	d							09 45					09 57
Winnersh	d												10 00
Winnersh Triangle	d												10 02
Earley	d												10 07
Reading	a							09 58					10 15

The xx15 and xx45 services from London Waterloo to Whitton continue to London Waterloo via Brentford

The xx03 and xx33 London Waterloo to Kingston services continue to London Waterloo via Wimbledon

The xx07 and xx37 services from London Waterloo to Whitton continue to London Waterloo via Richmond

For additional services between Wokingham and Reading refer to Table T148

Table T149-F

Mondays to Fridays

8 October to 7 December

London - Hounslow, Richmond, Kingston, Windsor, Weybridge, Ascot, Guildford and Reading

		SW	SW 1	GW	SW	SW	SW	SW	SW	SW	SW 1	SW	SW 1	SW	SW	SW	SW	SW	SW	SW 1	SW	SW 1
London Waterloo ⊖	d				08 52	08 58		09 03	09 07	09 15	09 20			09 22	09 28		09 33	09 37	09 45	09 50		
Vauxhall ⊖	d				08 57	09 03		09 07	09 11	09 19				09 26	09 32		09 37	09 41	09 49			
Queenstown Rd.(Battersea)	d				09 00			09 10	09 14	09 22				09 29			09 40	09 44	09 52			
Clapham Junction	d				09 03	09 08		09 13	09 17	09 25	09 28			09 32	09 38		09 43	09 47	09 55	09 58		
Wandsworth Town	d				09 06			09 16	09 20	09 28				09 35			09 46	09 50	09 58			
Putney	d				09 09	09 12		09 19	09 23	09 31				09 38	09 42		09 49	09 53	10 01			
Barnes	d				09 12			09 22	09 27	09 35				09 42			09 52	09 57	10 05			
Barnes Bridge	d				09 15				09 29					09 44				09 59				
Chiswick	d				09 18				09 32					09 47				10 02				
Kew Bridge	d				09 20				09 35					09 50				10 05				
Brentford	d				09 23				09 38					09 53				10 08				
Syon Lane	d				09 25				09 40					09 55				10 10				
Isleworth	d				09 27				09 42					09 57				10 12				
Hounslow	d				09 31				09 48					10 01				10 18				
Mortlake	d							09 24		09 37							09 54		10 07			
North Sheen	d	←						09 26		09 39		←					09 56		10 09		←	
Richmond ⊖	d	09 12				09 18		09 29		09 42	09 36	09 42			09 48		09 59		10 12	10 06	10 12	
St Margarets	d	09 14						09 31		→		09 44					10 01		→		10 14	
Twickenham	a	09 16				09 22		09 33			09 40	09 46			09 51		10 03			10 10	10 16	
	d	09 17				09 22		09 34			09 40	09 47			09 52		10 04			10 10	10 17	
Strawberry Hill	d							09 37									10 07					
Fulwell	a																					
Teddington	a							09 40									10 10					
Hampton Wick	a							09 44									10 14					
Kingston	a							09 46									10 16					
Whitton	d	09a20				09 25	←		09a53			09a50			09 55	←		10a26			10a20	
Feltham	d				09 36	09 30	09 36				09 46			10 06	09 59	10 06				10 16		
Ashford (Surrey)	d				→	09 34	09 40							→	10 03	10 10						
Staines	d					09 38	09 44				09 53				10 07	10 14				10 23		
Wraysbury	d					09 42									10 12							
Sunnymeads	d					09 45									10 15							
Datchet	d					09 49									10 19							
Windsor & Eton Riverside	a					09 56									10 25							
Egham	d						09 49				09 57					10 19				10 27		
Virginia Water	a						09 53				10 01					10 23				10 31		
	d						09 53				10 01					10 23				10 31		
Chertsey	d						09 59									10 29						
Addlestone	d						10 02									10 32						
Weybridge	a						10 17									10 37						
Longcross	d																					
Sunningdale	d										10 07									10 37		
Ascot	d		09 53								10 13		10 23							10 43		10 53
Bagshot	d		09 59										10 29									10 59
Camberley	a		10 05										10 35									11 05
Frimley	d		10 13										10 43									11 13
Ash Vale	d		10 19										10 49									11 19
Aldershot	a		10 24										10 54									11 24
	d		10 38										11 08									11 38
Ash	d		10 45										11 15									11 45
Wanborough	d		10 48										11 18									11 48
Guildford	a		10 55										11 25									11 55
Martins Heron	d										10 17									10 47		
Bracknell	d										10 20									10 50		
Wokingham	d			10 06							10 27									10 57		
Winnersh	d										10 30									11 00		
Winnersh Triangle	d										10 32									11 02		
Earley	d										10 37									11 07		
Reading	a			10 15							10 45									11 15		

The xx15 and xx45 services from London Waterloo to Whitton continue to London Waterloo via Brentford

The xx03 and xx33 London Waterloo to Kingston services continue to London Waterloo via Wimbledon

The xx07 and xx37 services from London Waterloo to Whitton continue to London Waterloo via Richmond

For additional services between Wokingham and Reading refer to Table T148

Table T149-F

Mondays to Fridays

8 October to 7 December

London - Hounslow, Richmond, Kingston, Windsor, Weybridge, Ascot, Guildford and Reading

		SW	SW	SW	SW	SW	SW	SW 1	SW	SW 1	SW	SW	SW	SW	SW	SW	SW 1	SW	SW 1	SW	SW	SW	SW
London Waterloo ⊖	d	09 52	09 58		10 03	10 07	10 15	10 20			10 22	10 28		10 33	10 37	10 45	10 50			10 52	10 58		11 03
Vauxhall ⊖	d	09 56	10 02		10 07	10 11	10 19				10 26	10 32		10 37	10 41	10 49				10 56	11 02		11 07
Queenstown Rd.(Battersea)	d	09 59			10 10	10 14	10 22				10 29			10 40	10 44	10 52				10 59			11 10
Clapham Junction	d	10 02	10 08		10 13	10 17	10 25	10 28			10 32	10 38		10 43	10 47	10 55	10 58			11 02	11 08		11 13
Wandsworth Town	d	10 05			10 16	10 20	10 28				10 35			10 46	10 50	10 58				11 05			11 16
Putney	d	10 08	10 12		10 19	10 23	10 31				10 38	10 42		10 49	10 53	11 01				11 08	11 12		11 19
Barnes	d	10 12			10 22	10 27	10 35				10 42			10 52	10 57	11 05				11 12			11 22
Barnes Bridge	d	10 14				10 29					10 44				10 59					11 14			
Chiswick	d	10 17				10 32					10 47				11 02					11 17			
Kew Bridge	d	10 20				10 35					10 50				11 05					11 20			
Brentford	d	10 23				10 38					10 53				11 08					11 23			
Syon Lane	d	10 25				10 40					10 55				11 10					11 25			
Isleworth	d	10 27				10 42					10 57				11 12					11 27			
Hounslow	d	10 31				10 48					11 01				11 18					11 31			
Mortlake	d				10 24		10 37							10 54		11 07							11 24
North Sheen	d				10 26		10 39		←					10 56		11 09		←					11 26
Richmond ⊖	d		10 18		10 29		10 42	10 36	10 42			10 48		10 59		11 12	11 06	11 12			11 18		11 29
St Margarets	d				10 31		→		10 44					11 01		→		11 14					11 31
Twickenham	a		10 21		10 33			10 40	10 46			10 51		11 03			11 10	11 16			11 21		11 33
	d		10 22		10 34			10 40	10 47			10 52		11 04			11 10	11 17			11 22		11 34
Strawberry Hill	d				10 37									11 07									11 37
Fulwell	a																						
Teddington	a				10 40									11 10									11 40
Hampton Wick	a				10 44									11 14									11 44
Kingston	a				10 46									11 16									11 46
Whitton	d		10 25	←		10a55			10a50			10 55	←		11a23			11a20			11 25	←	
Feltham	d	10 36	10 29	10 36				10 46			11 06	10 59	11 06				11 16			11 36	11 29	11 36	
Ashford (Surrey)	d	→	10 33	10 40							→	11 03	11 10							→	11 33	11 40	
Staines	d		10 37	10 44				10 53				11 07	11 14				11 23				11 37	11 44	
Wraysbury	d		10 42									11 12									11 42		
Sunnymeads	d		10 45									11 15									11 45		
Datchet	d		10 49									11 19									11 49		
Windsor & Eton Riverside	a		10 55									11 25									11 55		
Egham	d			10 49				10 57					11 19				11 27					11 49	
Virginia Water	a			10 53				11 01					11 23				11 31					11 53	
	d			10 53				11 01					11 23				11 31					11 53	
Chertsey	d			10 59									11 29									11 59	
Addlestone	d			11 02									11 32									12 02	
Weybridge	a			11 07									11 37									12 07	
Longcross	d																						
Sunningdale	d							11 07									11 37						
Ascot	d							11 13		11 23							11 43		11 53				
Bagshot	d									11 29									11 59				
Camberley	a									11 35									12 05				
Frimley	d									11 43									12 13				
Ash Vale	d									11 49									12 19				
Aldershot	a									11 54									12 24				
	d									12 08									12 38				
Ash	d									12 15									12 45				
Wanborough	d									12 18									12 48				
Guildford	a									12 25									12 55				
Martins Heron	d							11 17									11 47						
Bracknell	d							11 20									11 50						
Wokingham	d							11 27									11 57						
Winnersh	d							11 30									12 00						
Winnersh Triangle	d							11 32									12 02						
Earley	d							11 37									12 07						
Reading	a							11 45									12 15						

The xx15 and xx45 services from London Waterloo to Whitton continue to London Waterloo via Brentford

The xx03 and xx33 London Waterloo to Kingston services continue to London Waterloo via Wimbledon

The xx07 and xx37 services from London Waterloo to Whitton continue to London Waterloo via Richmond

For additional services between Wokingham and Reading refer to Table T148

Table T149-F

Mondays to Fridays

8 October to 7 December

London - Hounslow, Richmond, Kingston, Windsor, Weybridge, Ascot, Guildford and Reading

		SW	SW	SW ■	SW	SW ■	SW	SW	SW	SW	SW	SW	SW ■	SW	SW ■	SW	SW	SW	SW	SW	SW	SW ■	SW
London Waterloo ■ ⊖	d	11 07	11 15	11 20			11 22	11 28		11 33	11 37	11 45	11 50			11 52	11 58		12 03	12 07	12 15	12 20	
Vauxhall ⊖	d	11 11	11 19				11 26	11 32		11 37	11 41	11 49				11 56	12 02		12 07	12 11	12 19		
Queenstown Rd.(Battersea)	d	11 14	11 22				11 29			11 40	11 44	11 52				11 59			12 10	12 14	12 22		
Clapham Junction ■	d	11 17	11 27	11 28			11 32	11 38		11 43	11 47	11 55	11 58			12 02	12 08		12 13	12 17	12 25	12 28	
Wandsworth Town	d	11 20	11 29				11 35			11 46	11 50	11 58				12 05			12 16	12 20	12 28		
Putney	d	11 23	11 32				11 38	11 42		11 49	11 53	12 01				12 08	12 12		12 19	12 23	12 31		
Barnes	d	11 27	11 36				11 42			11 52	11 57	12 05				12 12			12 22	12 27	12 35		
Barnes Bridge	d	11 29					11 44				11 59					12 14				12 29			
Chiswick	d	11 32					11 47				12 02					12 17				12 32			
Kew Bridge	d	11 35					11 50				12 05					12 20				12 35			
Brentford	d	11 38					11 53				12 08					12 23				12 38			
Syon Lane	d	11 40					11 55				12 10					12 25				12 40			
Isleworth	d	11 42					11 57				12 12					12 27				12 42			
Hounslow	d	11 48					12 01				12 18					12 31				12 48			
Mortlake	d		11 39							11 54		12 07							12 24		12 37		
North Sheen	d		11 41		←					11 56		12 09		←					12 26		12 39		←
Richmond ⊖	d		11 43	11 36	11 43			11 48		11 59		12 12	12 06	12 12			12 18		12 29		12 42	12 36	12 42
St Margarets	d		→		11 46					12 01		→		12 14					12 31		→		12 44
Twickenham	a			11 40	11 48			11 51		12 03			12 10	12 16			12 21		12 33			12 40	12 46
	d			11 40	11 48			11 52		12 04			12 10	12 17			12 22		12 34			12 40	12 47
Strawberry Hill	d									12 07									12 37				
Fulwell	a																						
Teddington	a									12 10									12 40				
Hampton Wick	a									12 14									12 44				
Kingston	a									12 16									12 46				
Whitton	d	11a53			11a51			11 55	←		12a23			12a20			12 25	←		12a53			12a50
Feltham	d			11 46			12 06	11 59	12 06				12 16			12 36	12 29	12 36				12 46	
Ashford (Surrey)	d						→	12 03	12 10							→	12 33	12 40					
Staines	d			11 53				12 07	12 14				12 23				12 37	12 44				12 53	
Wraysbury	d							12 12									12 42						
Sunnymeads	d							12 15									12 45						
Datchet	d							12 19									12 49						
Windsor & Eton Riverside	a							12 25									12 55						
Egham	d			11 57					12 19				12 27					12 49				12 57	
Virginia Water	a			12 01					12 23				12 31					12 53				13 01	
	d			12 01					12 23				12 31					12 53				13 01	
Chertsey	d								12 29									12 59					
Addlestone	d								12 32									13 02					
Weybridge	a								12 37									13 07					
Longcross	d																						
Sunningdale	d			12 07									12 37									13 07	
Ascot ■	d			12 13		12 23							12 43		12 53							13 13	
Bagshot	d					12 29									12 59								
Camberley	a					12 35									13 05								
Frimley	d					12 43									13 13								
Ash Vale	d					12 49									13 19								
Aldershot	a					12 54									13 24								
	d					13 08									13 38								
Ash ■	d					13 15									13 45								
Wanborough	d					13 18									13 48								
Guildford	a					13 25									13 55								
Martins Heron	d			12 17									12 47									13 17	
Bracknell	d			12 20									12 50									13 20	
Wokingham	d			12 27									12 57									13 27	
Winnersh	d			12 30									13 00									13 30	
Winnersh Triangle	d			12 32									13 02									13 32	
Earley	d			12 37									13 07									13 37	
Reading ■	a			12 45									13 15									13 45	

The xx15 and xx45 services from London Waterloo to Whitton continue to London Waterloo via Brentford

The xx03 and xx33 London Waterloo to Kingston services continue to London Waterloo via Wimbledon

The xx07 and xx37 services from London Waterloo to Whitton continue to London Waterloo via Richmond

For additional services between Wokingham and Reading refer to Table T148

Table T149-F

Mondays to Fridays

8 October to 7 December

London - Hounslow, Richmond, Kingston, Windsor, Weybridge, Ascot, Guildford and Reading

		SW ■	SW	SW	SW	SW	SW	SW	SW ■	SW	SW ■	SW	SW	SW	SW	SW	SW	SW ■	SW	SW ■	SW	SW
London Waterloo ■ ⊖	d		12 22	12 28		12 33	12 37	12 45	12 50			12 52	12 58		13 03	13 07	13 15	13 20			13 22	13 28
Vauxhall ⊖	d		12 26	12 32		12 37	12 41	12 49				12 56	13 02		13 07	13 11	13 19				13 26	13 32
Queenstown Rd.(Battersea)	d		12 29			12 40	12 44	12 52				12 59			13 10	13 14	13 22				13 29	
Clapham Junction ■	d		12 32	12 38		12 43	12 47	12 55	12 58			13 02	13 08		13 13	13 17	13 25	13 28			13 32	13 38
Wandsworth Town	d		12 35			12 46	12 50	12 58				13 05			13 16	13 20	13 28				13 35	
Putney	d		12 38	12 42		12 49	12 53	13 01				13 08	13 12		13 19	13 23	13 31				13 38	13 42
Barnes	d		12 42			12 52	12 57	13 05				13 12			13 22	13 27	13 35				13 42	
Barnes Bridge	d		12 44				12 59					13 14				13 29					13 44	
Chiswick	d		12 47				13 02					13 17				13 32					13 47	
Kew Bridge	d		12 50				13 05					13 20				13 35					13 50	
Brentford	d		12 53				13 08					13 23				13 38					13 53	
Syon Lane	d		12 55				13 10					13 25				13 40					13 55	
Isleworth	d		12 57				13 12					13 27				13 42					13 57	
Hounslow	d		13 01				13 18					13 31				13 48					14 01	
Mortlake	d					12 54		13 07							13 24		13 37					
North Sheen	d					12 56		13 09		←					13 26		13 39		←			
Richmond ⊖	d			12 48		12 59		13 12	13 06	13 12			13 18		13 29		13 42	13 36	13 42			13 48
St Margarets	d					13 01		→		13 14					13 31		→		13 44			
Twickenham	a			12 51		13 03			13 10	13 16			13 21		13 33			13 40	13 46			13 51
	d			12 52		13 04			13 10	13 17			13 22		13 34			13 40	13 47			13 52
Strawberry Hill	d					13 07									13 37							
Fulwell	a																					
Teddington	a					13 10									13 40							
Hampton Wick	a					13 14									13 44							
Kingston	a					13 16									13 46							
Whitton	d			12 55	←		13a23			13a20			13 25	←		13a53			13a50			13 55
Feltham	d		13 06	12 59	13 06				13 16			13 36	13 29	13 36				13 46			14 06	13 59
Ashford (Surrey)	d		→	13 03	13 10							→	13 33	13 40							→	14 03
Staines	d			13 07	13 14				13 23				13 37	13 44				13 53				14 07
Wraysbury	d			13 12									13 42									14 12
Sunnymeads	d			13 15									13 45									14 15
Datchet	d			13 19									13 49									14 19
Windsor & Eton Riverside	a			13 25									13 55									14 25
Egham	d				13 19				13 27					13 49				13 57				
Virginia Water	a				13 23				13 31					13 53				14 01				
	d				13 23				13 31					13 53				14 01				
Chertsey	d				13 29									13 59								
Addlestone	d				13 32									14 02								
Weybridge	a				13 37									14 07								
Longcross	d								13 35													
Sunningdale	d								13 37									14 07				
Ascot ■	d	13 23							13 43		13 53							14 13		14 23		
Bagshot	d	13 29									13 59									14 29		
Camberley	a	13 35									14 05									14 35		
Frimley	d	13 43									14 13									14 43		
Ash Vale	d	13 49									14 19									14 49		
Aldershot	a	13 54									14 24									14 54		
	d	14 08									14 38									15 08		
Ash ■	d	14 15									14 45									15 15		
Wanborough	d	14 18									14 48									15 18		
Guildford	a	14 25									14 55									15 25		
Martins Heron	d								13 47									14 17				
Bracknell	d								13 50									14 20				
Wokingham	d								13 57									14 27				
Winnersh	d								14 00									14 30				
Winnersh Triangle	d								14 02									14 32				
Earley	d								14 07									14 37				
Reading ■	a								14 15									14 45				

The xx15 and xx45 services from London Waterloo to Whitton continue to London Waterloo via Brentford

The xx03 and xx33 London Waterloo to Kingston services continue to London Waterloo via Wimbledon

The xx07 and xx37 services from London Waterloo to Whitton continue to London Waterloo via Richmond

For additional services between Wokingham and Reading refer to Table T148

Table T149-F

Mondays to Fridays

8 October to 7 December

London - Hounslow, Richmond, Kingston, Windsor, Weybridge, Ascot, Guildford and Reading

		SW	SW	SW	SW	SW ■	SW	SW ■	SW	SW	SW	SW	SW	SW	SW ■	SW	SW ■	SW	SW	SW	SW	SW	SW
London Waterloo 15 ⊖	d		13 33	13 37	13 45	13 50			13 52	13 58		14 03	14 07	14 15	14 20			14 22	14 28		14 33	14 37	14 45
Vauxhall ⊖	d		13 37	13 41	13 49				13 56	14 02		14 07	14 11	14 19				14 26	14 32		14 37	14 41	14 49
Queenstown Rd.(Battersea)	d		13 40	13 44	13 52				13 59			14 10	14 14	14 22				14 29			14 40	14 44	14 52
Clapham Junction 10	d		13 43	13 47	13 55	13 58			14 02	14 08		14 13	14 17	14 25	14 28			14 32	14 38		14 43	14 47	14 55
Wandsworth Town	d		13 46	13 50	13 58				14 05			14 16	14 20	14 28				14 35			14 46	14 50	14 58
Putney	d		13 49	13 53	14 01				14 08	14 12		14 19	14 23	14 31				14 38	14 42		14 49	14 53	15 01
Barnes	d		13 52	13 57	14 05				14 12			14 22	14 27	14 35				14 42			14 52	14 57	15 05
Barnes Bridge	d			13 59					14 14				14 29					14 44				14 59	
Chiswick	d			14 02					14 17				14 32					14 47				15 02	
Kew Bridge	d			14 05					14 20				14 35					14 50				15 05	
Brentford	d			14 08					14 23				14 38					14 53				15 08	
Syon Lane	d			14 10					14 25				14 40					14 55				15 10	
Isleworth	d			14 12					14 27				14 42					14 57				15 12	
Hounslow	d			14 18					14 31				14 48					15 01				15 18	
Mortlake	d		13 54		14 07							14 24		14 37							14 54		15 07
North Sheen	d		13 56		14 09		←					14 26		14 39		←					14 56		15 09
Richmond ⊖	d		13 59		14 12	14 06	14 12			14 18		14 29		14 42	14 36	14 42			14 48		14 59		15 12
St Margarets	d		14 01		→		14 14					14 31		→		14 44					15 01		→
Twickenham	a		14 03			14 10	14 16			14 21		14 33			14 40	14 46			14 51		15 03		
	d		14 04			14 10	14 17			14 22		14 34			14 40	14 47			14 52		15 04		
Strawberry Hill	d		14 07									14 37									15 07		
Fulwell	a																						
Teddington	a		14 10									14 40									15 10		
Hampton Wick	a		14 14									14 44									15 14		
Kingston	a		14 16									14 46									15 16		
Whitton	d	←		14a23			14a20			14 25	←		14a53			14a50			14 55	←		15a23	
Feltham	d	14 06				14 16			14 36	14 29	14 36				14 46			15 06	14 59	15 06			
Ashford (Surrey)	d	14 10							→	14 33	14 40							→	15 03	15 10			
Staines	d	14 14				14 23				14 37	14 45				14 53				15 07	15 14			
Wraysbury	d									14 42									15 12				
Sunnymeads	d									14 45									15 15				
Datchet	d									14 49									15 19				
Windsor & Eton Riverside	a									14 55									15 25				
Egham	d	14 19				14 27					14 49				14 57					15 19			
Virginia Water	a	14 23				14 31					14 53				15 01					15 23			
	d	14 23				14 31					14 53				15 01					15 23			
Chertsey	d	14 29									14 59									15 29			
Addlestone	d	14 32									15 02									15 32			
Weybridge	a	14 37									15 07									15 37			
Longcross	d																						
Sunningdale	d					14 37									15 07								
Ascot 8	d					14 43		14 53							15 13		15 23						
Bagshot	d							14 59									15 29						
Camberley	a							15 05									15 35						
Frimley	d							15 13									15 43						
Ash Vale	d							15 19									15 49						
Aldershot	a							15 24									15 55						
	d							15 38									16 08						
Ash 5	d							15 45									16 15						
Wanborough	d							15 48									16 18						
Guildford	a							15 55									16 25						
Martins Heron	d					14 47									15 17								
Bracknell	d					14 50									15 20								
Wokingham	d					14 57									15 27								
Winnersh	d					15 00									15 30								
Winnersh Triangle	d					15 02									15 32								
Earley	d					15 07									15 37								
Reading 7	a					15 15									15 45								

The xx15 and xx45 services from London Waterloo to Whitton continue to London Waterloo via Brentford

The xx03 and xx33 London Waterloo to Kingston services continue to London Waterloo via Wimbledon

The xx07 and xx37 services from London Waterloo to Whitton continue to London Waterloo via Richmond

For additional services between Wokingham and Reading refer to Table T148

Table T149-F

Mondays to Fridays

8 October to 7 December

London - Hounslow, Richmond, Kingston, Windsor, Weybridge, Ascot, Guildford and Reading

		SW ■	SW	SW ■	SW	SW	SW	SW	SW	SW	SW ■	SW	SW ■	SW	SW	SW	SW	SW	SW	SW ■	SW	SW ■
London Waterloo 15 ⊖	d	14 50			14 52	14 58		15 03	15 07	15 15	15 20			15 22	15 28		15 33	15 37	15 45	15 50		
Vauxhall ⊖	d				14 56	15 02		15 07	15 11	15 19				15 26	15 32		15 37	15 41	15 49			
Queenstown Rd.(Battersea)	d				15 00			15 10	15 14	15 22				15 29			15 40	15 44	15 52			
Clapham Junction 10	d	14 58			15 03	15 08		15 13	15 17	15 25	15 28			15 32	15 38		15 43	15 47	15 55	15 58		
Wandsworth Town	d				15 05			15 16	15 20	15 28				15 35			15 46	15 50	15 58			
Putney	d				15 08	15 12		15 19	15 23	15 31				15 38	15 42		15 49	15 53	16 01			
Barnes	d				15 12			15 22	15 27	15 35				15 42			15 52	15 57	16 05			
Barnes Bridge	d				15 14				15 29					15 44				15 59				
Chiswick	d				15 17				15 32					15 47				16 02				
Kew Bridge	d				15 20				15 35					15 50				16 05				
Brentford	d				15 23				15 38					15 53				16 08				
Syon Lane	d				15 25				15 40					15 55				16 10				
Isleworth	d				15 27				15 42					15 57				16 12				
Hounslow	d				15 31				15 48					16 01				16 18				
Mortlake	d							15 24		15 37							15 54		16 07			
North Sheen	d		←					15 26		15 39		←					15 56		16 09		←	
Richmond ⊖	d	15 06	15 12			15 18		15 29		15 42	15 36	15 42			15 48		15 59		16 12	16 06	16 12	
St Margarets	d		15 14					15 31		→		15 44					16 01		→		16 14	
Twickenham	a	15 10	15 16			15 21		15 33			15 40	15 46			15 51		16 03			16 10	16 16	
	d	15 10	15 17			15 22		15 34			15 40	15 47			15 52		16 04			16 10	16 17	
Strawberry Hill	d							15 37									16 07					
Fulwell	a																					
Teddington	a							15 40									16 10					
Hampton Wick	a							15 44									16 14					
Kingston	a							15 46									16 16					
Whitton	d		15a20			15 25	←		15a53			15a50			15 55	←		16a23			16a20	
Feltham	d	15 16			15 36	15 29	15 36				15 46			16 06	15 59	16 06				16 16		
Ashford (Surrey)	d				→	15 33	15 40							→	16 03	16 10						
Staines	d	15 23				15 37	15 44				15 53				16 07	16 14				16 23		
Wraysbury	d					15 42									16 12							
Sunnymeads	d					15 45									16 15							
Datchet	d					15 49									16 19							
Windsor & Eton Riverside	a					15 55									16 25							
Egham	d	15 27					15 49				15 57					16 19				16 27		
Virginia Water	a	15 31					15 53				16 01					16 23				16 31		
	d	15 31					15 53				16 01					16 23				16 31		
Chertsey	d						16 00									16 29						
Addlestone	d						16 03									16 32						
Weybridge	a						16 07									16 37						
Longcross	d										16 05											
Sunningdale	d	15 37									16 08									16 37		
Ascot 8	d	15 43		15 53							16 13		16 23							16 43		16 53
Bagshot	d			15 59									16 29									16 59
Camberley	a			16 05									16 35									17 05
Frimley	d			16 13									16 43									17 13
Ash Vale	d			16 19									16 49									17 19
Aldershot	a			16 24									16 54									17 24
	d			16 38									17 08									17 38
Ash 5	d			16 45									17 15									17 45
Wanborough	d			16 48									17 18									17 48
Guildford	a			16 55									17 25									17 55
Martins Heron	d	15 47									16 17									16 47		
Bracknell	d	15 50									16 20									16 50		
Wokingham	d	15 57									16 27									16 57		
Winnersh	d	16 00									16 30									17 00		
Winnersh Triangle	d	16 02									16 32									17 02		
Earley	d	16 07									16 37									17 07		
Reading 7	a	16 15									16 45									17 15		

The xx15 and xx45 services from London Waterloo to Whitton continue to London Waterloo via Brentford

The xx03 and xx33 London Waterloo to Kingston services continue to London Waterloo via Wimbledon

The xx07 and xx37 services from London Waterloo to Whitton continue to London Waterloo via Richmond

For additional services between Wokingham and Reading refer to Table T148

London - Hounslow, Richmond, Kingston, Windsor, Weybridge, Ascot, Guildford and Reading

		SW	SW	SW	SW	SW	SW	SW	SW	SW	SW	SW	SW	SW	SW	SW	SW	SW	SW	SW	SW	SW	SW
					■					■		■	◇	◇		■	◇				■		◇
London Waterloo 15 ⊖	d	15 52	15 58	16 01	16 05			16 07	16 15	16 20			16 22	16 28	16 31	16 35			16 37	16 45	16 50		16 52
Vauxhall ⊖	d	15 56	16 02	16 05	16 09			16 12	16 19				16 26	16 32	16 35	16 39			16 42	16 49			16 56
Queenstown Rd.(Battersea)	d	15 59		16 08				16 15	16 22				16 29		16 38				16 45	16 52			16 59
Clapham Junction 10	d	16 02	16 08	16 11	16 15			16 18	16 25	16 28			16 32	16 38	16 41	16 45			16 48	16 55	16 58		17 02
Wandsworth Town	d	16 05		16 14				16 20	16 28				16 35		16 44				16 50	16 58			17 05
Putney	d	16 08	16 12	16 17				16 23	16 31				16 38	16 42	16 47				16 53	17 01			17 08
Barnes	d	16 12		16 22				16 27	16 35				16 42		16 52				16 57	17 05			17 12
Barnes Bridge	d	16 14						16 29					16 44						16 59				17 14
Chiswick	d	16 17						16 32					16 47						17 02				17 17
Kew Bridge	d	16 20						16 35					16 50						17 05				17 20
Brentford	d	16 23						16 38					16 53						17 08				17 23
Syon Lane	d	16 25						16 40					16 55						17 10				17 25
Isleworth	d	16 27						16 42					16 57						17 12				17 27
Hounslow	d	16 31						16 48					17 01						17 18				17 31
Mortlake	d			16 24					16 37						16 54					17 07			
North Sheen	d			16 26			←		16 39		←				16 56			←		17 09		←	
Richmond ⊖	d		16 18	16 29	16 23		16 29		16 42	16 36	16 42			16 48	16 59	16 53		16 59		17 12	17 06	17 12	
St Margarets	d			→			16 31		→		16 44				→			17 01		→		17 14	
Twickenham	a		16 21		16 27		16 33			16 40	16 46			16 51		16 57		17 03			17 10	17 16	
	d		16 22		16 27		16 34			16 40	16 47			16 52		16 57		17 04			17 10	17 17	
Strawberry Hill	d						16 37											17 07					
Fulwell	a																						
Teddington	a						16 42											17 12					
Hampton Wick	a						16 46											17 16					
Kingston	a						16 48											17 18					
Whitton	d		16 25			←		16a53			16a50			16 55			←		17a23			17a20	
Feltham	d	16 38	16 29		16 33	16 38				16 46			17 08	16 59		17 03	17 08				17 16		17 38
Ashford (Surrey)	d	→	16 33		16 37	16 42							→	17 03		17 07	17 12						→
Staines	d		16 37		16 41	16 46				16 53				17 07		17 11	17 16				17 23		
Wraysbury	d		16 42											17 12									
Sunnymeads	d		16 45											17 15									
Datchet	d		16 49											17 19									
Windsor & Eton Riverside	a		16 55											17 26									
Egham	d				16 46	16 50				16 57						17 16	17 21				17 27		
Virginia Water	a				16 50	16 55				17 01						17 20	17 25				17 31		
	d				16 50	16 55				17 01						17 20	17 25				17 31		
Chertsey	d					17 00											17 31						
Addlestone	d					17 03											17 34						
Weybridge	a					17 08											17 40						
Longcross	d				16 53											17 23							
Sunningdale	d				16 57					17 07						17 27					17 37		
Ascot 3	d				17 01					17 13		17 23				17 31					17 43		
Bagshot	d											17 29											
Camberley	a											17 35											
Frimley	d											17 43											
Ash Vale	d											17 49											
Aldershot	a											17 54											
	d											18 08											
Ash 5	d											18 15											
Wanborough	d											18 18											
Guildford	a											18 25											
Martins Heron	d				17 05					17 17						17 35					17 47		
Bracknell	d				17 09					17 20						17 39					17 50		
Wokingham	d				17 15					17 27						17 45					17 57		
Winnersh	d									17 30											18 00		
Winnersh Triangle	d									17 32											18 02		
Earley	d									17 37											18 07		
Reading 7	a				17 31					17 45						18 04					18 15		

The xx15 and xx45 services from London Waterloo to Whitton continue to London Waterloo via Brentford

The xx03 and xx33 London Waterloo to Kingston services continue to London Waterloo via Wimbledon

The xx07 and xx37 services from London Waterloo to Whitton continue to London Waterloo via Richmond

For additional services between Wokingham and Reading refer to Table T148

London - Hounslow, Richmond, Kingston, Windsor, Weybridge, Ascot, Guildford and Reading

		SW	SW	SW	SW	SW	SW	SW	SW	SW	SW	SW	SW	SW	SW	SW	SW	SW	SW	SW	SW	SW	SW
		◇		◇■	◇				■		■		■	◇	◇		■	◇					■
London Waterloo 15 ⊖	d	16 58	17 01	17 05			17 07	17 13		17 15	17 20			17 22	17 28	17 31	17 35			17 37	17 43	17 45	17 50
Vauxhall ⊖	d	17 02	17 05	17 09			17 12	17 17		17 20				17 26	17 32	17 35	17 39			17 42	17 47	17 50	
Queenstown Rd.(Battersea)	d		17 08				17 15			17 23				17 29		17 38				17 45		17 53	
Clapham Junction 10	d	17 08	17 11	17 15			17 18	17 23		17 26	17 28			17 32	17 38	17 42	17 45			17 48	17 53	17 56	17 58
Wandsworth Town	d		17 14				17 20			17 28				17 35		17 44				17 50		17 58	
Putney	d	17 12	17 17				17 23	17 27		17 31				17 38	17 42	17 47				17 53	17 57	18 01	
Barnes	d		17 22				17 27			17 35				17 42		17 52				17 57		18 05	
Barnes Bridge	d						17 29							17 44						17 59			
Chiswick	d						17 32							17 47						18 02			
Kew Bridge	d						17 35							17 50						18 05			
Brentford	d						17 38							17 53						18 08			
Syon Lane	d						17 40							17 55						18 10			
Isleworth	d						17 42							17 57						18 12			
Hounslow	d						17 48							18 01						18 16			
Mortlake	d		17 24							17 37						17 54						18 07	
North Sheen	d		17 26			←				17 39		←				17 56			←			18 09	
Richmond ⊖	d	17 18	17 29	17 23		17 29		17 33		17 42	17 37	17 42			17 48	17 59	17 53		17 59		18 03	18 12	18 07
St Margarets	d		→			17 31				→		17 44				→			18 01			→	
Twickenham	a	17 21		17 27		17 33		17 37			17 40	17 46			17 51		17 57		18 03		18 07		18 10
	d	17 22		17 27		17 34		17 37			17 41	17 47			17 52		17 57		18 04		18 07		18 11
Strawberry Hill	d					17 37		17 41											18 07		18 11		
Fulwell	a																				18 13		
Teddington	a					17 42		17 46											18 12				
Hampton Wick	a					17 46		17 54											18 16				
Kingston	a					17 48		17 56											18 18				
Whitton	d	17 25			←		17a53					17a50			17 55			←		18a23			
Feltham	d	17 29		17 33	17 38						17 47			18 08	17 59		18 03	18 08					18 17
Ashford (Surrey)	d	17 33		17 37	17 42									→	18 03		18 07	18 12					
Staines	d	17 37		17 41	17 46						17 53				18 07		18 11	18 16					18 23
Wraysbury	d	17 42													18 12								
Sunnymeads	d	17 45													18 15								
Datchet	d	17 49													18 19								
Windsor & Eton Riverside	a	17 56													18 26								
Egham	d			17 46	17 51						17 58						18 16	18 21					18 28
Virginia Water	a			17 50	17 55						18 02						18 20	18 25					18 32
	d			17 50	17 55						18 02						18 20	18 25					18 32
Chertsey	d				18 01													18 31					
Addlestone	d				18 04													18 34					
Weybridge	a				18 10													18 40					
Longcross	d										18 05												18 35
Sunningdale	d			17 55							18 09						18 25						18 38
Ascot 3	d			18 01							18 13		18 23				18 30						18 43
Bagshot	d			18 07									18 29										
Camberley	a			18 13									18 35										
Frimley	d			18 17									18 43										
Ash Vale	d			18 24									18 49										
Aldershot	a			18 32									18 54										
	d								18 38				19 08										
Ash 5	d								18 45				19 15										
Wanborough	d								18 48				19 18										
Guildford	a								18 55				19 25										
Martins Heron	d										18 17						18 34						18 47
Bracknell	d										18 21						18 37						18 51
Wokingham	d										18 27						18 44						18 57
Winnersh	d										18 31												19 01
Winnersh Triangle	d										18 33												19 03
Earley	d										18 35												19 07
Reading 7	a										18 43						19 00						19 15

The xx15 and xx45 services from London Waterloo to Whitton continue to London Waterloo via Brentford

The xx03 and xx33 London Waterloo to Kingston services continue to London Waterloo via Wimbledon

The xx07 and xx37 services from London Waterloo to Whitton continue to London Waterloo via Richmond

For additional services between Wokingham and Reading refer to Table T148

London - Hounslow, Richmond, Kingston, Windsor, Weybridge, Ascot, Guildford and Reading

		SW		SW ◇	SW ◇ 1	SW 1	SW ◇	SW	SW 1	SW ◇	SW	SW		SW	SW	SW 1	SW	SW 1	SW ◇	SW ◇	SW	SW 1		SW ◇	SW
London Waterloo 15 ⊖	d			17 52	17 54		17 58	18 01	18 05			18 07		18 13	18 15	18 20			18 22	18 28	18 31	18 35			
Vauxhall ⊖	d			17 56	17 58		18 02	18 05	18 09			18 12		18 17	18 20				18 26	18 32	18 35	18 39			
Queenstown Rd.(Battersea)	d			17 59				18 08				18 15			18 23				18 29		18 38				
Clapham Junction 10	d			18 02	18 04		18 08	18 11	18 15			18 18		18 23	18 26	18 28			18 32	18 38	18 41	18 45			
Wandsworth Town	d			18 05				18 14				18 20			18 28				18 35		18 44				
Putney	d			18 08			18 12	18 17				18 23		18 27	18 31				18 38	18 42	18 47				
Barnes	d			18 12				18 22				18 27			18 35				18 42		18 52				
Barnes Bridge	d			18 14								18 29							18 44						
Chiswick	d			18 17								18 32							18 47						
Kew Bridge	d			18 20								18 35							18 50						
Brentford	d			18 23								18 38							18 53						
Syon Lane	d			18 25								18 40							18 55						
Isleworth	d			18 27								18 42							18 57						
Hounslow	d			18 31	18 19							18 48							19 01						
Mortlake	d							18 24							18 37						18 54				
North Sheen	d	←						18 26			←				18 39		←				18 56				←
Richmond ⊖	d	18 12					18 18	18 29	18 23		18 29			18 33	18 42	18 37	18 42			18 48	18 59	18 53			18 59
St Margarets	d	18 14						→			18 31				→		18 44				→				19 01
Twickenham	a	18 16					18 21		18 27		18 33			18 37		18 40	18 46			18 51		18 57			19 03
	d	18 17					18 22		18 27		18 34			18 37		18 41	18 47			18 52		18 57			19 04
Strawberry Hill	d										18 37			18 41											19 07
Fulwell	a													18 43											
Teddington	a										18 42														19 12
Hampton Wick	a										18 46														19 16
Kingston	a										18 48														19 18
Whitton	d	18a20					18 25			←		18a53					18a50			18 55				←	
Feltham	d			18 38	18 25		18 29		18 33	18 38						18 47			19 08	18 59		19 03		19 08	
Ashford (Surrey)	d			→			18 33		18 37	18 42									→	19 03		19 07		19 12	
Staines	d				18 31		18 37		18 41	18 46						18 53				19 07		19 11		19 16	
Wraysbury	d						18 42													19 12					
Sunnymeads	d						18 45													19 15					
Datchet	d						18 49													19 19					
Windsor & Eton Riverside	a						18 56													19 26					
Egham	d				18 36				18 46	18 51						18 58						19 16		19 21	
Virginia Water	a				18 40				18 50	18 55						19 02						19 20		19 25	
	d				18 40				18 50	18 55						19 02						19 20		19 25	
Chertsey	d									19 01														19 31	
Addlestone	d									19 04														19 34	
Weybridge	a									19 10														19 46	
Longcross	d															19 05									
Sunningdale	d				18 46				18 55							19 09						19 25			
Ascot 8	d				18 53				19 00							19 13		19 23				19 30			
Bagshot	d				18 59													19 29							
Camberley	a				19 05													19 35							
Frimley	d				19 09													19 43							
Ash Vale	d				19 16													19 49							
Aldershot	a				19 21													19 54							
	d					19 38												20 08							
Ash 5	d					19 45												20 15							
Wanborough	d					19 48												20 18							
Guildford	a					19 55												20 25							
Martins Heron	d								19 04							19 17						19 34			
Bracknell	d								19 07							19 21						19 37			
Wokingham	d								19 14							19 27						19 47			
Winnersh	d															19 31									
Winnersh Triangle	d															19 33									
Earley	d															19 37									
Reading 7	a								19 31							19 45						20 01			

The xx15 and xx45 services from London Waterloo to Whitton continue to London Waterloo via Brentford

The xx03 and xx33 London Waterloo to Kingston services continue to London Waterloo via Wimbledon

The xx07 and xx37 services from London Waterloo to Whitton continue to London Waterloo via Richmond

For additional services between Wokingham and Reading refer to Table T148

London - Hounslow, Richmond, Kingston, Windsor, Weybridge, Ascot, Guildford and Reading

		SW	SW	SW	SW 1	SW	SW 1	SW ◇		SW ◇	SW	SW 1	SW ◇	SW	SW	SW	SW 1	SW		SW 1	SW	SW	SW	SW	SW
London Waterloo 15 ⊖	d	18 37	18 43	18 45	18 50			18 52		18 58	19 01	19 05			19 07	19 15	19 20				19 22	19 28	19 33	19 35	
Vauxhall ⊖	d	18 42	18 47	18 50				18 56		19 02	19 05	19 09			19 12	19 19					19 26	19 32	19 37	19 40	
Queenstown Rd.(Battersea)	d	18 45		18 53				18 59			19 08				19 15	19 22					19 29		19 40		
Clapham Junction 10	d	18 48	18 53	18 56	18 58			19 02		19 08	19 11	19 15			19 18	19 25	19 28				19 32	19 38	19 43	19 46	
Wandsworth Town	d	18 51		18 58				19 05			19 14				19 21	19 28					19 35		19 46		
Putney	d	18 54	18 57	19 01				19 08		19 12	19 17				19 24	19 31					19 38	19 42	19 49		
Barnes	d	18 57		19 05				19 12			19 22				19 27	19 35					19 42		19 52		
Barnes Bridge	d	18 59						19 14							19 29						19 44				
Chiswick	d	19 02						19 17							19 32						19 47				
Kew Bridge	d	19 05						19 20							19 35						19 50				
Brentford	d	19 08						19 23							19 38						19 53				
Syon Lane	d	19 10						19 25							19 40						19 55				
Isleworth	d	19 12						19 27							19 42						19 57				
Hounslow	d	19 18						19 31							19 48						20 01				
Mortlake	d			19 07							19 24					19 37							19 55		
North Sheen	d			19 09		←					19 26			←		19 39		←					19 57		
Richmond ⊖	d		19 03	19 12	19 07	19 12				19 18	19 29	19 23		19 29		19 42	19 36	19 42				19 48	19 59	19 54	
St Margarets	d			→		19 14					→			19 31		→		19 44					→		
Twickenham	a		19 07		19 10	19 16				19 21		19 27		19 33			19 40	19 46				19 51		19 58	
	d		19 07		19 11	19 17				19 22		19 27		19 34			19 40	19 47				19 52		19 58	
Strawberry Hill	d		19 11											19 37											
Fulwell	a		19 13																						
Teddington	a													19 42											
Hampton Wick	a													19 46											
Kingston	a													19 48											
Whitton	d	19a23				19a20				19 25			←		19a53			19a50				19 55			←
Feltham	d				19 17			19 38		19 29		19 33	19 38				19 46				20 08	19 59		20 04	20 08
Ashford (Surrey)	d							→		19 33		19 37	19 42								→	20 03		20 08	20 12
Staines	d				19 23					19 37		19 41	19 46				19 53					20 07		20 12	20 16
Wraysbury	d									19 42												20 12			
Sunnymeads	d									19 45												20 15			
Datchet	d									19 49												20 19			
Windsor & Eton Riverside	a									19 56												20 25			
Egham	d				19 28							19 46	19 51				19 57							20 17	20 21
Virginia Water	a				19 32							19 50	19 55				20 01							20 21	20 25
	d				19 32							19 50	19 55				20 01							20 21	20 25
Chertsey	d												20 01												20 31
Addlestone	d												20 04												20 34
Weybridge	a												20 10												20 39
Longcross	d																								
Sunningdale	d				19 37							19 55					20 07							20 26	
Ascot 8	d				19 43		19 53					20 00					20 13			20 23				20 31	
Bagshot	d						19 59													20 29					
Camberley	a						20 05													20 35					
Frimley	d						20 13													20 43					
Ash Vale	d						20 19													20 49					
Aldershot	a						20 24													20 54					
	d						20 38													21 08					
Ash 5	d						20 45													21 15					
Wanborough	d						20 48													21 18					
Guildford	a						20 55													21 25					
Martins Heron	d				19 47							20 04					20 17							20 35	
Bracknell	d				19 50							20 07					20 20							20 38	
Wokingham	d				19 57							20 17					20 27							20 49	
Winnersh	d				20 00												20 30								
Winnersh Triangle	d				20 02												20 32								
Earley	d				20 07												20 37								
Reading 7	a				20 15							20 28					20 45							21 02	

The xx15 and xx45 services from London Waterloo to Whitton continue to London Waterloo via Brentford

The xx03 and xx33 London Waterloo to Kingston services continue to London Waterloo via Wimbledon

The xx07 and xx37 services from London Waterloo to Whitton continue to London Waterloo via Richmond

For additional services between Wokingham and Reading refer to Table T148

Table T149-F

London - Hounslow, Richmond, Kingston, Windsor, Weybridge, Ascot, Guildford and Reading

Station		SW	SW	SW	SW [1]	SW	SW [1]	SW	SW	SW	SW	SW	SW	SW [1]	SW	SW [1]	SW [1]	SW	SW	SW	SW	SW
London Waterloo [15] ⊖	d		19 37	19 45	19 50			19 52	19 58		20 03	20 07	20 15	20 20				20 22	20 28		20 33	20 37
Vauxhall ⊖	d		19 41	19 49				19 56	20 02		20 07	20 11	20 19					20 26	20 32		20 37	20 41
Queenstown Rd.(Battersea)	d		19 44	19 52				19 59			20 10	20 14	20 22					20 29			20 40	20 44
Clapham Junction [10]	d		19 47	19 55	19 58			20 02	20 08		20 13	20 17	20 25	20 28				20 32	20 38		20 43	20 47
Wandsworth Town	d		19 50	19 58				20 05			20 16	20 20	20 28					20 35			20 46	20 50
Putney	d		19 53	20 01				20 08	20 12		20 19	20 23	20 31					20 38	20 42		20 49	20 53
Barnes	d		19 57	20 05				20 12			20 22	20 27	20 35					20 42			20 52	20 57
Barnes Bridge	d		19 59					20 14				20 29						20 44				20 59
Chiswick	d		20 02					20 17				20 32						20 47				21 02
Kew Bridge	d		20 05					20 20				20 35						20 50				21 05
Brentford	d		20 08					20 23				20 38						20 53				21 08
Syon Lane	d		20 10					20 25				20 40						20 55				21 10
Isleworth	d		20 12					20 27				20 42						20 57				21 12
Hounslow	d		20 18					20 31				20 48						21 01				21 18
Mortlake	d			20 07							20 24		20 37								20 54	
North Sheen	d	←		20 09		←					20 26		20 39		←						20 56	
Richmond ⊖	d	19 59		20 12	20 06	20 12			20 18		20 29		20 42	20 36	20 42				20 48		20 59	
St Margarets	d	20 02		→		20 14					20 31		→		20 44						21 01	
Twickenham	a	20 04			20 10	20 16			20 21		20 33			20 40	20 46				20 51		21 03	
	d	20 04			20 10	20 17			20 22		20 34			20 40	20 47				20 52		21 04	
Strawberry Hill	d	20 08									20 37										21 07	
Fulwell	a																					
Teddington	a	20 11									20 40										21 10	
Hampton Wick	a	20 14									20 44										21 14	
Kingston	a	20 16									20 46										21 16	
Whitton	d		20a23			20a20			20 25	←		20a53			20a50				20 55	←		21a23
Feltham	d				20 16			20 36	20 29	20 36				20 46				21 06	20 59	21 06		
Ashford (Surrey)	d							→	20 33	20 40								→	21 03	21 10		
Staines	d				20 23				20 37	20 44				20 53					21 07	21 14		
Wraysbury	d								20 42										21 12			
Sunnymeads	d								20 45										21 15			
Datchet	d								20 49										21 19			
Windsor & Eton Riverside	a								20 55										21 25			
Egham	d				20 27					20 49				20 57						21 19		
Virginia Water	a				20 31					20 53				21 01						21 23		
	d				20 31					20 53				21 01						21 23		
Chertsey	d									20 59										21 29		
Addlestone	d									21 02										21 32		
Weybridge	a									21 07										21 37		
Longcross	d																					
Sunningdale	d				20 37									21 07								
Ascot [3]	d				20 43		20 53							21 13		21 23						
Bagshot	d						20 59									21 29						
Camberley	a						21 05									21 35						
Frimley	d						21 13									21 43						
Ash Vale	d						21 19									21 49						
Aldershot	a						21 24									21 54						
	d						21 38									22 08	22 38					
Ash [5]	d						21 45									22 15	22 45					
Wanborough	d						21 48									22 18	22 48					
Guildford	a						21 55									22 25	22 56					
Martins Heron	d				20 47									21 17								
Bracknell	d				20 50									21 20								
Wokingham	d				20 57									21 27								
Winnersh	d				21 00									21 30								
Winnersh Triangle	d				21 02									21 32								
Earley	d				21 07									21 35								
Reading [7]	a				21 15									21 43								

The xx15 and xx45 services from London Waterloo to Whitton continue to London Waterloo via Brentford

The xx03 and xx33 London Waterloo to Kingston services continue to London Waterloo via Wimbledon

The xx07 and xx37 services from London Waterloo to Whitton continue to London Waterloo via Richmond

For additional services between Wokingham and Reading refer to Table T148

Table T149-F

London - Hounslow, Richmond, Kingston, Windsor, Weybridge, Ascot, Guildford and Reading

Station		SW	SW [1]	SW	SW	SW	SW	SW	SW	SW	SW [1]	SW	SW [1]	SW	SW	SW	SW	SW	SW	SW [1]	SW	SW	SW
London Waterloo [15] ⊖	d	20 45	20 50		20 52	20 58		21 03	21 07	21 15	21 20			21 22	21 28		21 33	21 37	21 45	21 50		21 52	21 58
Vauxhall ⊖	d	20 49			20 56	21 02		21 07	21 11	21 19				21 27	21 32		21 37	21 41	21 49			21 56	22 02
Queenstown Rd.(Battersea)	d	20 52			20 59			21 10	21 14	21 22				21 30			21 40	21 44	21 52			21 59	
Clapham Junction [10]	d	20 55	20 58		21 02	21 08		21 13	21 17	21 25	21 28			21 33	21 38		21 43	21 47	21 55	21 58		22 02	22 08
Wandsworth Town	d	20 58			21 05			21 16	21 20	21 28				21 36			21 46	21 50	21 58			22 05	
Putney	d	21 01			21 08	21 12		21 19	21 23	21 31				21 39	21 42		21 49	21 53	22 01			22 08	22 12
Barnes	d	21 05			21 12			21 22	21 27	21 35				21 42			21 52	21 57	22 05			22 12	
Barnes Bridge	d				21 14				21 29					21 44				21 59				22 14	
Chiswick	d				21 17				21 32					21 47				22 02				22 17	
Kew Bridge	d				21 20				21 35					21 50				22 05				22 20	
Brentford	d				21 23				21 38					21 53				22 08				22 23	
Syon Lane	d				21 25				21 40					21 55				22 10				22 25	
Isleworth	d				21 27				21 42					21 57				22 12				22 27	
Hounslow	d				21 31				21 48					22 01				22 18				22 31	
Mortlake	d	21 07						21 24		21 37							21 54		22 07				
North Sheen	d	21 09		←				21 26		21 39		←					21 56		22 09		←		
Richmond ⊖	d	21 12	21 06	21 12		21 18		21 29		21 42	21 36	21 42			21 48		21 59		22 12	22 06	22 12		22 18
St Margarets	d	→		21 14				21 31		→		21 44					22 01		→		22 14		
Twickenham	a		21 10	21 16		21 21		21 33			21 40	21 46			21 51		22 03			22 10	22 16		22 21
	d		21 10	21 17		21 22		21 34			21 40	21 47			21 52		22 04			22 10			22 22
Strawberry Hill	d							21 37									22 07						
Fulwell	a																						
Teddington	a							21 40									22 10						
Hampton Wick	a							21 44									22 14						
Kingston	a							21 46									22 16						
Whitton	d			21a20		21 25	←		21a53			21a50			21 55	←		22a23					22 25
Feltham	d		21 16		21 36	21 29	21 36				21 46			22 06	21 59	22 06				22 16		22 36	22 29
Ashford (Surrey)	d				→	21 33	21 40							→	22 03	22 10						→	22 33
Staines	d		21 23			21 37	21 44				21 53				22 07	22 14				22 23			22 37
Wraysbury	d					21 42									22 11								22 41
Sunnymeads	d					21 45									22 14								22 44
Datchet	d					21 49									22 17								22 47
Windsor & Eton Riverside	a					21 55									22 22								22 52
Egham	d		21 27				21 49				21 57					22 19				22 27			
Virginia Water	a		21 31				21 53				22 01					22 23				22 31			
	d		21 31				21 53				22 01					22 23				22 31			
Chertsey	d						21 59									22 29							
Addlestone	d						22 02									22 32							
Weybridge	a						22 07									22 37							
Longcross	d																						
Sunningdale	d		21 37								22 07									22 37			
Ascot [3]	d		21 43								22 13		22 23							22 43			
Bagshot	d												22 29										
Camberley	a												22 35										
Frimley	d												22 43										
Ash Vale	d												22 49										
Aldershot	a												22 54										
	d												23 08										
Ash [5]	d												23 15										
Wanborough	d												23 18										
Guildford	a												23 25										
Martins Heron	d		21 47								22 17									22 47			
Bracknell	d		21 50								22 20									22 50			
Wokingham	d		21 57								22 27									22 57			
Winnersh	d		22 00								22 30									23 00			
Winnersh Triangle	d		22 02								22 32									23 02			
Earley	d		22 07								22 37									23 05			
Reading [7]	a		22 15								22 45									23 15			

The xx15 and xx45 services from London Waterloo to Whitton continue to London Waterloo via Brentford

The xx03 and xx33 London Waterloo to Kingston services continue to London Waterloo via Wimbledon

The xx07 and xx37 services from London Waterloo to Whitton continue to London Waterloo via Richmond

For additional services between Wokingham and Reading refer to Table T148

Table T149-F

Mondays to Fridays

8 October to 7 December

London - Hounslow, Richmond, Kingston, Windsor, Weybridge, Ascot, Guildford and Reading

		SW	SW	SW ■	SW ■	SW		SW	SW	SW	SW ■	SW	SW	SW	SW	SW ■		SW	SW	SW	SW	SW	SW	SW	SW
London Waterloo ■ ⊖	d		22 03	22 20		22 22		22 28		22 33	22 50	22 52	22 58		23 03	23 20		23 22	23 28		23 33	23 50	23 52	23 58	
Vauxhall ⊖	d		22 07			22 26		22 32		22 37		22 56	23 02		23 07			23 26	23 32		23 37		23 56	00 02	
Queenstown Rd.(Battersea)	d		22 10			22 29				22 40		22 59			23 10			23 29			23 40		23 59		
Clapham Junction ■	d		22 13	22 28		22 32		22 38		22 43	22 58	23 02	23 08		23 13	23 28		23 32	23 38		23 43	23 58	00 02	00 08	
Wandsworth Town	d		22 16			22 35				22 46		23 05			23 16			23 35			23 46		00 05		
Putney	d		22 19			22 38		22 42		22 49		23 08	23 12		23 19			23 38	23 42		23 49		00 08	00 12	
Barnes	d		22 22			22 42				22 52		23 12			23 22			23 42			23 52		00 12		
Barnes Bridge	d					22 44						23 14						23 44					00 14		
Chiswick	d					22 47						23 17						23 47					00 17		
Kew Bridge	d					22 50						23 20						23 50					00 20		
Brentford	d					22 53						23 23						23 53					00 23		
Syon Lane	d					22 55						23 25						23 55					00 25		
Isleworth	d					22 57						23 27						23 57					00 27		
Hounslow	d					23 01						23 31						00 01					00 31		
Mortlake	d		22 24							22 54					23 24						23 54				
North Sheen	d		22 26							22 56					23 26						23 56				
Richmond ⊖	d		22 29	22 36				22 48		22 59	23 06		23 18		23 29	23 36			23 48		23 59	00 06		00 18	
St Margarets	d		22 31							23 01					23 31						00 01				
Twickenham	a		22 33	22 40				22 51		23 03	23 10		23 21		23 33	23 40			23 51		00 03	00 10		00 22	
	d		22 34	22 40				22 52		23 04	23 10		23 22		23 34	23 40			23 52		00 04	00 10		00 22	
Strawberry Hill	d		22 37							23 07					23 37						00 09				
Fulwell	a																								
Teddington	a		22 40							23 10					23 40						00 12				
Hampton Wick	a		22 44							23 14					23 44						00 14				
Kingston	a		22 46							23 16					23 46						00 16				
Whitton	d	←						22 55	←				23 25	←					23 55	←				00 25	←
Feltham	d	22 36		22 46		23 06		22 59	23 06		23 16	23 36	23 29	23 36		23 46		00 06	23 59	00 06		00 16	00 36	00 29	00 36
Ashford (Surrey)	d	22 40				→		23 03	23 10			→	23 33	23 40				→	00 03	00 10			→	00 33	00 40
Staines	d	22 44		22 53				23 07	23 14		23 23		23 37	23 44		23 53			00 07	00 14		00 23		00a37	00a47
Wraysbury	d							23 11					23 41						00 11						
Sunnymeads	d							23 14					23 44						00 14						
Datchet	d							23 17					23 47						00 17						
Windsor & Eton Riverside	a							23 25					23 55						00 25						
Egham	d	22 49		22 57					23 19		23 27			23 49		23 57				00 19		00 27			
Virginia Water	a	22 53		23 01					23 23		23 31			23 53		00 01				00 23		00 31			
	d	22 53		23 01					23 23		23 31			23 53		00 01				00 23		00 31			
Chertsey	d	22 59							23 29					23 59						00 29					
Addlestone	d	23 02							23 32					00a02						00 32					
Weybridge	a	23 07							23 37											00 36					
Longcross	d																								
Sunningdale	d			23 07							23 37					00 08						00 37			
Ascot ■	d			23 13	23 23						23 43					00 13						00 42			
Bagshot	d				23 29																				
Camberley	a				23 35																				
Frimley	d				23 43																				
Ash Vale	d				23 49																				
Aldershot	a				23 54																				
	d																								
Ash ■	d																								
Wanborough	d																								
Guildford	a																								
Martins Heron	d			23 17							23 47					00 17						00 46			
Bracknell	d			23 20							23 50					00 20						00 50			
Wokingham	d			23 27							23 57					00 32						00 56			
Winnersh	d			23 30							23 59					00 36									
Winnersh Triangle	d			23 32							00 02					00 38									
Earley	d			23 37							00 05					00 40									
Reading ■	a			23 45							00 15					00 48						01 08			

The xx15 and xx45 services from London Waterloo to Whitton continue to London Waterloo via Brentford

The xx03 and xx33 London Waterloo to Kingston services continue to London Waterloo via Wimbledon

The xx07 and xx37 services from London Waterloo to Whitton continue to London Waterloo via Richmond

For additional services between Wokingham and Reading refer to Table T148

Table T149-F

Saturdays

26 May to 6 October

London - Hounslow, Richmond, Kingston, Windsor, Weybridge, Ascot, Guildford and Reading

		SW	SW ■	SW ■	SW	SW	SW	SW ■	SW ■	SW		SW	SW ■	SW	SW	SW	SW ■	SW	SW	SW		SW	SW ■	SW	SW
London Waterloo ■ ⊖	d													00 18			05 05			05 33			05 50	05 58	06 03
Vauxhall ⊖	d									00 02				00 22			05 09			05 37				06 02	06 07
Queenstown Rd.(Battersea)	d													00 25			05 12			05 40					06 10
Clapham Junction ■	d									00 08		00 02		00 30			05 15			05 43			05 58	06 08	06 13
Wandsworth Town	d											00 05		00 33			05 18			05 46					06 16
Putney	d									00 12		00 08		00 36			05 21			05 49				06 12	06 19
Barnes	d											00 12		00 39			05 24			05 52					06 22
Barnes Bridge	d											00 14													
Chiswick	d											00 17													
Kew Bridge	d											00 20													
Brentford	d											00 23													
Syon Lane	d											00 25													
Isleworth	d											00 27													
Hounslow	d					00 01						00 31													
Mortlake	d													00 41			05 26			05 54					06 24
North Sheen	d													00 43			05 28			05 56					06 26
Richmond ⊖	d						00 06			00 18				00 46			05 31			05 59			06 06	06 18	06 29
St Margarets	d	00 01												00 48			05 33			06 01					06 31
Twickenham	a	00 03					00 10			00 22				00 50			05 35			06 03			06 10	06 21	06 33
	d	00 04					00 10			00 22				00 51	04 52		05 36	05 38	05 53	06 04			06 10	06 22	06 34
Strawberry Hill	d	00 09												00s54	04 55					06 07					06 37
Fulwell	a																								
Teddington	a	00 12												00s57	04 58					06 10					06 40
Hampton Wick	a	00 14												01s00	05 01					06 14					06 44
Kingston	a	00 16												01 02	05 03					06 16					06 46
Whitton	d									00 25							05 39	05a41	05 56					06 25	
Feltham	d					00 06	00 16			00 29		00 36					05 43		06 00				06 16	06 29	
Ashford (Surrey)	d				00 03	00 10				00 33		00 40					05 47		06 04					06 33	
Staines	d				00 07	00 14	00 23			00a37		00a47	05 23			05 44	05 53		06 08			06 16	06 23	06 37	
Wraysbury	d				00 11														06 12					06 41	
Sunnymeads	d				00 14														06 15					06 44	
Datchet	d				00 17														06 18					06 47	
Windsor & Eton Riverside	a				00 22														06 22					06 51	
Egham	d					00 19	00 27						05 27			05 49	05 57					06 20	06 27		
Virginia Water	a					00 23	00 31						05 31			05 53	06 01					06 25	06 31		
	d			00 01		00 23	00 31						05 31			05 53	06 01					06 25	06 31		
Chertsey	d					00 29										05 59						06 30			
Addlestone	d					00 32										06 02						06 33			
Weybridge	a					00 36										06 07						06 38			
Longcross	d																								
Sunningdale	d			00 08			00 37						05 37				06 07						06 37		
Ascot ■	d			00 13			00 42	00 45					05 43				06 13						06 43		
Bagshot	d							00 51																	
Camberley	a							00 57																	
Frimley	d							01 01																	
Ash Vale	d							01 08																	
Aldershot	a							01s13																	
	d								06 08																
Ash ■	d								06 15																
Wanborough	d								06 18																
Guildford	a								06 25																
Martins Heron	d			00 17			00 46						05 47				06 17						06 47		
Bracknell	d			00 20			00 50						05 50				06 20						06 50		
Wokingham	d			00 32			00 56						05 57				06 27						06 57		
Winnersh	d			00 36									06 00				06 30						07 00		
Winnersh Triangle	d		00 02	00 38									06 02				06 32						07 02		
Earley	d		00 05	00 40									06 05				06 35						07 05		
Reading ■	a		00 12	00 45			01 05						06 10				06 40						07 10		

The xx15 and xx45 services from London Waterloo to Whitton continue to London Waterloo via Brentford

The xx03 and xx33 London Waterloo to Kingston services continue to London Waterloo via Wimbledon

The xx07 and xx37 services from London Waterloo to Whitton continue to London Waterloo via Richmond

For additional services between Wokingham and Reading refer to Table T148

Table T149-F

London - Hounslow, Richmond, Kingston, Windsor, Weybridge, Ascot, Guildford and Reading

Saturdays
26 May to 6 October

		SW 1	SW	SW 1	SW 1	SW 1		SW 1	SW	SW	SW	SW	SW 1	SW 1	SW	SW		SW	SW	SW	SW	SW 1	SW	SW 1	SW
London Waterloo 15 ⊖	d					06 20			06 22	06 28		06 33	06 50		06 52	06 58			07 03	07 07	07 15	07 20			07 22
Vauxhall ⊖	d								06 26	06 32		06 37			06 56	07 02			07 07	07 11	07 19				07 26
Queenstown Rd.(Battersea)	d								06 29			06 40			06 59				07 10	07 14	07 22				07 29
Clapham Junction 10	d					06 28			06 32	06 38		06 43	06 58		07 02	07 08			07 13	07 17	07 25	07 28			07 32
Wandsworth Town	d								06 35			06 46			07 05				07 16	07 20	07 28				07 35
Putney	d								06 38	06 42		06 49			07 08	07 12			07 19	07 23	07 31				07 38
Barnes	d								06 42			06 52			07 12				07 22	07 27	07 35				07 42
Barnes Bridge	d								06 44						07 14					07 29					07 44
Chiswick	d								06 47						07 17					07 32					07 47
Kew Bridge	d								06 50						07 20					07 35					07 50
Brentford	d								06 53						07 23					07 38					07 53
Syon Lane	d								06 55						07 25					07 40					07 55
Isleworth	d								06 57						07 27					07 42					07 57
Hounslow	d								07 01						07 31					07 48					08 01
Mortlake	d											06 54							07 24		07 37				
North Sheen	d											06 56							07 26		07 39		←		
Richmond ⊖	d					06 36				06 48		06 59	07 06			07 18			07 29		07 42	07 36	07 42		
St Margarets	d											07 01							07 31		→		07 44		
Twickenham	a					06 40				06 51		07 03	07 10			07 21			07 33			07 40	07 46		
	d					06 40				06 52		07 04	07 10			07 22			07 34			07 40	07 47		
Strawberry Hill	d											07 07							07 37						
Fulwell	a																								
Teddington	a											07 10							07 40						
Hampton Wick	a											07 14							07 44						
Kingston	a											07 16							07 46						
Whitton	d									06 55	←					07 25		←		07a53			07a50		
Feltham	d					06 46			07 06	06 59	07 06		07 16		07 36	07 29		07 36				07 46			08 06
Ashford (Surrey)	d								→	07 03	07 10				→	07 33		07 40							→
Staines	d		06 44			06 53				07 07	07 14		07 23			07 37		07 44				07 53			
Wraysbury	d									07 11						07 41									
Sunnymeads	d									07 14						07 44									
Datchet	d									07 17						07 47									
Windsor & Eton Riverside	a									07 21						07 51									
Egham	d		06 49			06 57					07 19		07 27					07 49				07 57			
Virginia Water	a		06 53			07 01					07 23		07 31					07 53				08 01			
	d		06 53			07 01					07 23		07 31					07 53				08 01			
Chertsey	d		06 59								07 29							07 59							
Addlestone	d		07 02								07 32							08 02							
Weybridge	a		07 07								07 37							08 07							
Longcross	d																								
Sunningdale	d					07 07							07 37									08 07			
Ascot 3	d				06 53	07 13							07 43	07 53								08 13		08 23	
Bagshot	d				06 59									07 59										08 29	
Camberley	a				07 05									08 05										08 35	
Frimley	d				07 13									08 13										08 43	
Ash Vale	d				07 19									08 19										08 49	
Aldershot	a				07 24									08 24										08 54	
	d	06 38		07 08	07 38			08 08						08 38										09 08	
Ash 5	d	06 45		07 15	07 45			08 15						08 45										09 15	
Wanborough	d	06 48		07 18	07 48			08 18						08 48										09 18	
Guildford	a	06 55		07 25	07 55			08 25						08 55										09 25	
Martins Heron	d					07 17							07 47									08 17			
Bracknell	d					07 20							07 50									08 20			
Wokingham	d					07 27							07 57									08 27			
Winnersh	d					07 30							08 00									08 30			
Winnersh Triangle	d					07 32							08 02									08 32			
Earley	d					07 35							08 05									08 35			
Reading 7	a					07 40							08 10									08 40			

The xx15 and xx45 services from London Waterloo to Whitton continue to London Waterloo via Brentford

The xx03 and xx33 London Waterloo to Kingston services continue to London Waterloo via Wimbledon

The xx07 and xx37 services from London Waterloo to Whitton continue to London Waterloo via Richmond

For additional services between Wokingham and Reading refer to Table T148

Table T149-F

London - Hounslow, Richmond, Kingston, Windsor, Weybridge, Ascot, Guildford and Reading

Saturdays
26 May to 6 October

		SW		SW	SW	SW	SW	SW 1	SW	SW 1	SW	SW		SW	SW	SW	SW	SW 1	SW	SW 1	SW	SW		SW	SW
London Waterloo 15 ⊖	d	07 28			07 33	07 37	07 45	07 50			07 52	07 58			08 03	08 07	08 15	08 20			08 22	08 28			08 33
Vauxhall ⊖	d	07 32			07 37	07 41	07 49				07 56	08 02			08 07	08 11	08 19				08 26	08 32			08 37
Queenstown Rd.(Battersea)	d				07 40	07 44	07 52				07 59				08 10	08 14	08 22				08 29				08 40
Clapham Junction 10	d	07 38			07 43	07 47	07 55	07 58			08 02	08 08			08 13	08 17	08 25	08 28			08 32	08 38			08 43
Wandsworth Town	d				07 46	07 50	07 58				08 05				08 16	08 20	08 28				08 35				08 46
Putney	d	07 42			07 49	07 53	08 01				08 08	08 12			08 19	08 23	08 31				08 38	08 42			08 49
Barnes	d				07 52	07 57	08 05				08 12				08 22	08 27	08 35				08 42				08 52
Barnes Bridge	d					07 59					08 14					08 29					08 44				
Chiswick	d					08 02					08 17					08 32					08 47				
Kew Bridge	d					08 05					08 20					08 35					08 50				
Brentford	d					08 08					08 23					08 38					08 53				
Syon Lane	d					08 10					08 25					08 40					08 55				
Isleworth	d					08 12					08 27					08 42					08 57				
Hounslow	d					08 18					08 31					08 48					09 01				
Mortlake	d				07 54		08 07								08 24		08 37								08 54
North Sheen	d				07 56		08 09		←						08 26		08 39		←						08 56
Richmond ⊖	d	07 48			07 59		08 12	08 06	08 12			08 18			08 29		08 42	08 36	08 42			08 48			08 59
St Margarets	d				08 01		→		08 14						08 31		→		08 44						09 01
Twickenham	a	07 51			08 03			08 10	08 16			08 21			08 33			08 40	08 46			08 51			09 03
	d	07 52			08 04			08 10	08 17			08 22			08 34			08 40	08 47			08 52			09 04
Strawberry Hill	d				08 07										08 37										09 07
Fulwell	a																								
Teddington	a				08 10										08 40										09 10
Hampton Wick	a				08 14										08 44										09 14
Kingston	a				08 16										08 46										09 16
Whitton	d	07 55		←		08a23			08a20			08 25		←		08a53			08a50			08 55		←	
Feltham	d	07 59		08 06				08 16			08 36	08 29		08 36				08 46			09 06	08 59		09 06	
Ashford (Surrey)	d	08 03		08 10							→	08 33		08 40							→	09 03		09 10	
Staines	d	08 07		08 14				08 23				08 37		08 44				08 53				09 07		09 14	
Wraysbury	d	08 11										08 41										09 11			
Sunnymeads	d	08 14										08 44										09 14			
Datchet	d	08 17										08 47										09 17			
Windsor & Eton Riverside	a	08 21										08 51										09 21			
Egham	d			08 19				08 27						08 49				08 57						09 19	
Virginia Water	a			08 23				08 31						08 53				09 01						09 23	
	d			08 23				08 31						08 53				09 01						09 23	
Chertsey	d			08 29										08 59										09 29	
Addlestone	d			08 32										09 02										09 32	
Weybridge	a			08 37										09 07										09 37	
Longcross	d																								
Sunningdale	d							08 37										09 07							
Ascot 3	d							08 43		08 53								09 13		09 23					
Bagshot	d									08 59										09 29					
Camberley	a									09 05										09 35					
Frimley	d									09 13										09 43					
Ash Vale	d									09 19										09 49					
Aldershot	a									09 24										09 54					
	d									09 38										10 08					
Ash 5	d									09 45										10 15					
Wanborough	d									09 48										10 18					
Guildford	a									09 55										10 25					
Martins Heron	d							08 47										09 17							
Bracknell	d							08 50										09 20							
Wokingham	d							08 57										09 27							
Winnersh	d							09 00										09 30							
Winnersh Triangle	d							09 02										09 32							
Earley	d							09 05										09 35							
Reading 7	a							09 10										09 40							

The xx15 and xx45 services from London Waterloo to Whitton continue to London Waterloo via Brentford

The xx03 and xx33 London Waterloo to Kingston services continue to London Waterloo via Wimbledon

The xx07 and xx37 services from London Waterloo to Whitton continue to London Waterloo via Richmond

For additional services between Wokingham and Reading refer to Table T148

Table T149-F

Saturdays
26 May to 6 October

London - Hounslow, Richmond, Kingston, Windsor, Weybridge, Ascot, Guildford and Reading

		SW	SW	SW ■	SW	SW ■	SW	SW		SW	SW	SW	SW	SW ■	SW	SW ■	SW	SW		SW	SW	SW	SW	SW ■	SW
London Waterloo ■ ⊖	d	08 37	08 45	08 50			08 52	08 58			09 03	09 07	09 15	09 20			09 22	09 28			09 33	09 37	09 45	09 50	
Vauxhall ⊖	d	08 41	08 49				08 56	09 02			09 07	09 11	09 19				09 26	09 32			09 37	09 41	09 49		
Queenstown Rd.(Battersea)	d	08 44	08 52				08 59				09 10	09 14	09 22				09 29				09 40	09 44	09 52		
Clapham Junction ■	d	08 47	08 55	08 58			09 02	09 08			09 13	09 17	09 25	09 28			09 32	09 38			09 43	09 47	09 55	09 58	
Wandsworth Town	d	08 50	08 58				09 05				09 16	09 20	09 28				09 35				09 46	09 50	09 58		
Putney	d	08 53	09 01				09 08	09 12			09 19	09 23	09 31				09 38	09 42			09 49	09 53	10 01		
Barnes	d	08 57	09 05				09 12				09 22	09 27	09 35				09 42				09 52	09 57	10 05		
Barnes Bridge	d	08 59					09 14					09 29					09 44					09 59			
Chiswick	d	09 02					09 17					09 32					09 47					10 02			
Kew Bridge	d	09 05					09 20					09 35					09 50					10 05			
Brentford	d	09 08					09 23					09 38					09 53					10 08			
Syon Lane	d	09 10					09 25					09 40					09 55					10 10			
Isleworth	d	09 12					09 27					09 42					09 57					10 12			
Hounslow	d	09 18					09 31					09 48					10 01					10 18			
Mortlake	d		09 07								09 24		09 37								09 54		10 07		
North Sheen	d		09 09		←						09 26		09 39		←						09 56		10 09		←
Richmond ⊖	d		09 12	09 06	09 12			09 18			09 29		09 42	09 36	09 42			09 48			09 59		10 12	10 06	10 12
St Margarets	d		→		09 14						09 31		→		09 44						10 01		→		10 14
Twickenham	a			09 10	09 16			09 21			09 33			09 40	09 46			09 51			10 03			10 10	10 16
	d			09 10	09 17			09 22			09 34			09 40	09 47			09 52			10 04			10 10	10 17
Strawberry Hill	d										09 37										10 07				
Fulwell	a																								
Teddington	a										09 40										10 10				
Hampton Wick	a										09 44										10 14				
Kingston	a										09 46										10 16				
Whitton	d	09a23			09a20			09 25		←		09a53			09a50			09 55		←		10a23			10a20
Feltham	d			09 16			09 36	09 29		09 36				09 46			10 06	09 59		10 06				10 16	
Ashford (Surrey)	d						→	09 33		09 40							→	10 03		10 10					
Staines	d			09 23				09 37		09 44				09 53				10 07		10 14				10 23	
Wraysbury	d							09 41										10 11							
Sunnymeads	d							09 44										10 14							
Datchet	d							09 47										10 17							
Windsor & Eton Riverside	a							09 51										10 21							
Egham	d			09 27						09 49				09 57						10 19				10 27	
Virginia Water	a			09 31						09 53				10 01						10 23				10 31	
	d			09 31						09 53				10 01						10 23				10 31	
Chertsey	d									09 59										10 29					
Addlestone	d									10 02										10 32					
Weybridge	a									10 07										10 37					
Longcross	d																								
Sunningdale	d			09 37										10 07										10 37	
Ascot ■	d			09 43		09 53								10 13		10 23								10 43	
Bagshot	d					09 59										10 29									
Camberley	a					10 05										10 35									
Frimley	d					10 13										10 43									
Ash Vale	d					10 19										10 49									
Aldershot	a					10 24										10 54									
	d					10 38										11 08									
Ash ■	d					10 45										11 15									
Wanborough	d					10 48										11 18									
Guildford	a					10 55										11 25									
Martins Heron	d			09 47										10 17										10 47	
Bracknell	d			09 50										10 20										10 50	
Wokingham	d			09 57										10 27										10 57	
Winnersh	d			10 00										10 30										11 00	
Winnersh Triangle	d			10 02										10 32										11 02	
Earley	d			10 05										10 35										11 05	
Reading ■	a			10 10										10 40										11 10	

The xx15 and xx45 services from London Waterloo to Whitton continue to London Waterloo via Brentford

The xx03 and xx33 London Waterloo to Kingston services continue to London Waterloo via Wimbledon

The xx07 and xx37 services from London Waterloo to Whitton continue to London Waterloo via Richmond

For additional services between Wokingham and Reading refer to Table T148

Table T149-F

Saturdays
26 May to 6 October

London - Hounslow, Richmond, Kingston, Windsor, Weybridge, Ascot, Guildford and Reading

		SW ■	SW	SW		SW	SW	SW	SW	SW ■	SW	SW ■	SW	SW		SW	SW	SW	SW	SW ■	SW	SW ■	SW	SW
London Waterloo ■ ⊖	d		09 52	09 58			10 03	10 07	10 15	10 20			10 22	10 28			10 33	10 37	10 45	10 50			10 52	10 58
Vauxhall ⊖	d		09 56	10 02			10 07	10 11	10 19				10 26	10 32			10 37	10 41	10 49				10 56	11 02
Queenstown Rd.(Battersea)	d		09 59				10 10	10 14	10 22				10 29				10 40	10 44	10 52				10 59	
Clapham Junction ■	d		10 02	10 08			10 13	10 17	10 25	10 28			10 32	10 38			10 43	10 47	10 55	10 58			11 02	11 08
Wandsworth Town	d		10 05				10 16	10 20	10 28				10 35				10 46	10 50	10 58				11 05	
Putney	d		10 08	10 12			10 19	10 23	10 31				10 38	10 42			10 49	10 53	11 01				11 08	11 12
Barnes	d		10 12				10 22	10 27	10 35				10 42				10 52	10 57	11 05				11 12	
Barnes Bridge	d		10 14					10 29					10 44					10 59					11 14	
Chiswick	d		10 17					10 32					10 47					11 02					11 17	
Kew Bridge	d		10 20					10 35					10 50					11 05					11 20	
Brentford	d		10 23					10 38					10 53					11 08					11 23	
Syon Lane	d		10 25					10 40					10 55					11 10					11 25	
Isleworth	d		10 27					10 42					10 57					11 12					11 27	
Hounslow	d		10 31					10 48					11 01					11 18					11 31	
Mortlake	d						10 24		10 37								10 54		11 07					
North Sheen	d						10 26		10 39		←						10 56		11 09		←			
Richmond ⊖	d			10 18			10 29		10 42	10 36	10 42			10 48			10 59		11 12	11 06	11 12			11 18
St Margarets	d						10 31		→		10 44						11 01		→		11 14			
Twickenham	a			10 21			10 33			10 40	10 46			10 51			11 03			11 10	11 16			11 21
	d			10 22			10 34			10 40	10 47			10 52			11 04			11 10	11 17			11 22
Strawberry Hill	d						10 37										11 07							
Fulwell	a																							
Teddington	a						10 40										11 10							
Hampton Wick	a						10 44										11 14							
Kingston	a						10 46										11 16							
Whitton	d			10 25		←		10a53			10a50			10 55		←		11a23			11a20			11 25
Feltham	d		10 36	10 29		10 36				10 46			11 06	10 59		11 06				11 16			11 36	11 29
Ashford (Surrey)	d		→	10 33		10 40							→	11 03		11 10							→	11 33
Staines	d			10 37		10 44				10 53				11 07		11 14				11 23				11 37
Wraysbury	d			10 41										11 11										11 41
Sunnymeads	d			10 44										11 14										11 44
Datchet	d			10 47										11 17										11 47
Windsor & Eton Riverside	a			10 51										11 21										11 51
Egham	d					10 49				10 57						11 19				11 27				
Virginia Water	a					10 53				11 01						11 23				11 31				
	d					10 53				11 01						11 23				11 31				
Chertsey	d					10 59										11 29								
Addlestone	d					11 02										11 32								
Weybridge	a					11 07										11 37								
Longcross	d																							
Sunningdale	d									11 07										11 37				
Ascot ■	d	10 53								11 13		11 23								11 43		11 53		
Bagshot	d	10 59										11 29										11 59		
Camberley	a	11 05										11 35										12 05		
Frimley	d	11 13										11 43										12 13		
Ash Vale	d	11 19										11 49										12 19		
Aldershot	a	11 24										11 54										12 24		
	d	11 38										12 08										12 38		
Ash ■	d	11 45										12 15										12 45		
Wanborough	d	11 48										12 18										12 48		
Guildford	a	11 55										12 25										12 55		
Martins Heron	d									11 17										11 47				
Bracknell	d									11 20										11 50				
Wokingham	d									11 27										11 57				
Winnersh	d									11 30										12 00				
Winnersh Triangle	d									11 32										12 02				
Earley	d									11 35										12 05				
Reading ■	a									11 40										12 10				

The xx15 and xx45 services from London Waterloo to Whitton continue to London Waterloo via Brentford

The xx03 and xx33 London Waterloo to Kingston services continue to London Waterloo via Wimbledon

The xx07 and xx37 services from London Waterloo to Whitton continue to London Waterloo via Richmond

For additional services between Wokingham and Reading refer to Table T148

Table T149-F

Saturdays
26 May to 6 October

London - Hounslow, Richmond, Kingston, Windsor, Weybridge, Ascot, Guildford and Reading

		SW	SW	SW	SW	SW ■	SW	SW ■	SW	SW	SW	SW	SW	SW	SW ■	SW	SW ■	SW	SW	SW	SW	SW	SW
London Waterloo ■ ⊖	d		11 03	11 07	11 15	11 20			11 22	11 28		11 33	11 37	11 45	11 50			11 52	11 58		12 03	12 07	12 15
Vauxhall ⊖	d		11 07	11 11	11 19				11 26	11 32		11 37	11 41	11 49				11 56	12 02		12 07	12 11	12 19
Queenstown Rd.(Battersea)	d		11 10	11 14	11 22				11 29			11 40	11 44	11 52				11 59			12 10	12 14	12 22
Clapham Junction ■	d		11 13	11 17	11 25	11 28			11 32	11 38		11 43	11 47	11 55	11 58			12 02	12 08		12 13	12 17	12 25
Wandsworth Town	d		11 16	11 20	11 28				11 35			11 46	11 50	11 58				12 05			12 16	12 20	12 28
Putney	d		11 19	11 23	11 31				11 38	11 42		11 49	11 53	12 01				12 08	12 12		12 19	12 23	12 31
Barnes	d		11 22	11 27	11 35				11 42			11 52	11 57	12 05				12 12			12 22	12 27	12 35
Barnes Bridge	d			11 29					11 44				11 59					12 14				12 29	
Chiswick	d			11 32					11 47				12 02					12 17				12 32	
Kew Bridge	d			11 35					11 50				12 05					12 20				12 35	
Brentford	d			11 38					11 53				12 08					12 23				12 38	
Syon Lane	d			11 40					11 55				12 10					12 25				12 40	
Isleworth	d			11 42					11 57				12 12					12 27				12 42	
Hounslow	d			11 48					12 01				12 18					12 31				12 48	
Mortlake	d		11 24		11 37							11 54		12 07							12 24		12 37
North Sheen	d		11 26		11 39		←					11 56		12 09		←					12 26		12 39
Richmond ⊖	d		11 29		11 42	11 36	11 42			11 48		11 59		12 12	12 06	12 12			12 18		12 29		12 42
St Margarets	d		11 31		→		11 44					12 01		→		12 14					12 31		→
Twickenham	a		11 33			11 40	11 46			11 51		12 03			12 10	12 16			12 21		12 33		
	d		11 34			11 40	11 47			11 52		12 04			12 10	12 17			12 22		12 34		
Strawberry Hill	d		11 37									12 07									12 37		
Fulwell	a																						
Teddington	a		11 40									12 10									12 40		
Hampton Wick	a		11 44									12 14									12 44		
Kingston	a		11 46									12 16									12 46		
Whitton	d	←		11a53			11a50			11 55	←		12a23			12a20			12 25	←		12a53	
Feltham	d	11 36				11 46			12 06	11 59	12 06				12 16			12 36	12 29	12 36			
Ashford (Surrey)	d	11 40							→	12 03	12 10							→	12 33	12 40			
Staines	d	11 44				11 53				12 07	12 14				12 23				12 37	12 44			
Wraysbury	d									12 11									12 41				
Sunnymeads	d									12 14									12 44				
Datchet	d									12 17									12 47				
Windsor & Eton Riverside	a									12 21									12 51				
Egham	d	11 49				11 57					12 19				12 27					12 49			
Virginia Water	a	11 53				12 01					12 23				12 31					12 53			
	d	11 53				12 01					12 23				12 31					12 53			
Chertsey	d	11 59									12 29									12 59			
Addlestone	d	12 02									12 32									13 02			
Weybridge	a	12 07									12 37									13 07			
Longcross	d																						
Sunningdale	d					12 07									12 37								
Ascot ■	d					12 13		12 23							12 43		12 53						
Bagshot	d							12 29									12 59						
Camberley	a							12 35									13 05						
Frimley	d							12 43									13 13						
Ash Vale	d							12 49									13 19						
Aldershot	a							12 54									13 24						
	d							13 08									13 38						
Ash ■	d							13 15									13 45						
Wanborough	d							13 18									13 48						
Guildford	a							13 25									13 55						
Martins Heron	d					12 17									12 47								
Bracknell	d					12 20									12 50								
Wokingham	d					12 27									12 57								
Winnersh	d					12 30									13 00								
Winnersh Triangle	d					12 32									13 02								
Earley	d					12 35									13 05								
Reading ■	a					12 40									13 10								

The xx15 and xx45 services from London Waterloo to Whitton continue to London Waterloo via Brentford

The xx03 and xx33 London Waterloo to Kingston services continue to London Waterloo via Wimbledon

The xx07 and xx37 services from London Waterloo to Whitton continue to London Waterloo via Richmond

For additional services between Wokingham and Reading refer to Table T148

Table T149-F

Saturdays
26 May to 6 October

London - Hounslow, Richmond, Kingston, Windsor, Weybridge, Ascot, Guildford and Reading

		SW ■	SW	SW ■	SW	SW	SW	SW	SW	SW	SW ■	SW	SW ■	SW	SW	SW	SW	SW	SW	SW ■	SW	SW ■	SW
London Waterloo ■ ⊖	d	12 20			12 22	12 28		12 33	12 37	12 45	12 50			12 52	12 58		13 03	13 07	13 15	13 20			13 22
Vauxhall ⊖	d				12 26	12 32		12 37	12 41	12 49				12 56	13 02		13 07	13 11	13 19				13 26
Queenstown Rd.(Battersea)	d				12 29			12 40	12 44	12 52				12 59			13 10	13 14	13 22				13 29
Clapham Junction ■	d	12 28			12 32	12 38		12 43	12 47	12 55	12 58			13 02	13 08		13 13	13 17	13 25	13 28			13 32
Wandsworth Town	d				12 35			12 46	12 50	12 58				13 05			13 16	13 20	13 28				13 35
Putney	d				12 38	12 42		12 49	12 53	13 01				13 08	13 12		13 19	13 23	13 31				13 38
Barnes	d				12 42			12 52	12 57	13 05				13 12			13 22	13 27	13 35				13 42
Barnes Bridge	d				12 44				12 59					13 14				13 29					13 44
Chiswick	d				12 47				13 02					13 17				13 32					13 47
Kew Bridge	d				12 50				13 05					13 20				13 35					13 50
Brentford	d				12 53				13 08					13 23				13 38					13 53
Syon Lane	d				12 55				13 10					13 25				13 40					13 55
Isleworth	d				12 57				13 12					13 27				13 42					13 57
Hounslow	d				13 01				13 18					13 31				13 48					14 01
Mortlake	d							12 54		13 07							13 24		13 37				
North Sheen	d		←					12 56		13 09		←					13 26		13 39		←		
Richmond ⊖	d	12 36	12 42			12 48		12 59		13 12	13 06	13 12			13 18		13 29		13 42	13 36	13 42		
St Margarets	d		12 44					13 01		→		13 14					13 31		→		13 44		
Twickenham	a	12 40	12 46			12 51		13 03			13 10	13 16			13 21		13 33			13 40	13 46		
	d	12 40	12 47			12 52		13 04			13 10	13 17			13 22		13 34			13 40	13 47		
Strawberry Hill	d							13 07									13 37						
Fulwell	a																						
Teddington	a							13 10									13 40						
Hampton Wick	a							13 14									13 44						
Kingston	a							13 16									13 46						
Whitton	d		12a50			12 55	←		13a23			13a20			13 25	←		13a53			13a50		
Feltham	d	12 46			13 06	12 59	13 06				13 16			13 36	13 29	13 36				13 46			14 06
Ashford (Surrey)	d				→	13 03	13 10							→	13 33	13 40							→
Staines	d	12 53				13 07	13 14				13 23				13 37	13 44				13 53			
Wraysbury	d					13 11									13 41								
Sunnymeads	d					13 14									13 44								
Datchet	d					13 17									13 47								
Windsor & Eton Riverside	a					13 21									13 51								
Egham	d	12 57					13 19				13 27					13 49				13 57			
Virginia Water	a	13 01					13 23				13 31					13 53				14 01			
	d	13 01					13 23				13 31					13 53				14 01			
Chertsey	d						13 29									13 59							
Addlestone	d						13 32									14 02							
Weybridge	a						13 37									14 07							
Longcross	d																						
Sunningdale	d	13 07									13 37									14 07			
Ascot ■	d	13 13		13 23							13 43		13 53							14 13		14 23	
Bagshot	d			13 29									13 59									14 29	
Camberley	a			13 35									14 05									14 35	
Frimley	d			13 43									14 13									14 43	
Ash Vale	d			13 49									14 19									14 49	
Aldershot	a			13 54									14 24									14 54	
	d			14 08									14 38									15 08	
Ash ■	d			14 15									14 45									15 15	
Wanborough	d			14 18									14 48									15 18	
Guildford	a			14 25									14 55									15 25	
Martins Heron	d	13 17									13 47									14 17			
Bracknell	d	13 20									13 50									14 20			
Wokingham	d	13 27									13 57									14 27			
Winnersh	d	13 30									14 00									14 30			
Winnersh Triangle	d	13 32									14 02									14 32			
Earley	d	13 35									14 05									14 35			
Reading ■	a	13 40									14 10									14 40			

The xx15 and xx45 services from London Waterloo to Whitton continue to London Waterloo via Brentford

The xx03 and xx33 London Waterloo to Kingston services continue to London Waterloo via Wimbledon

The xx07 and xx37 services from London Waterloo to Whitton continue to London Waterloo via Richmond

For additional services between Wokingham and Reading refer to Table T148

Table T149-F

London - Hounslow, Richmond, Kingston, Windsor, Weybridge, Ascot, Guildford and Reading

Saturdays
26 May to 6 October

		SW		SW	SW	SW	SW	SW ■	SW	SW ■	SW	SW		SW	SW	SW	SW	SW ■	SW	SW ■	SW	SW		SW	SW
London Waterloo ⊖	d	13 28			13 33	13 37	13 45	13 50			13 52	13 58			14 03	14 07	14 15	14 20			14 22	14 28			14 33
Vauxhall ⊖	d	13 32			13 37	13 41	13 49				13 56	14 02			14 07	14 11	14 19				14 26	14 32			14 37
Queenstown Rd.(Battersea)	d				13 40	13 44	13 52				13 59				14 10	14 14	14 22				14 29				14 40
Clapham Junction	d	13 38			13 43	13 47	13 55	13 58			14 02	14 08			14 13	14 17	14 25	14 28			14 32	14 38			14 43
Wandsworth Town	d				13 46	13 50	13 58				14 05				14 16	14 20	14 28				14 35				14 46
Putney	d	13 42			13 49	13 53	14 01				14 08	14 12			14 19	14 23	14 31				14 38	14 42			14 49
Barnes	d				13 52	13 57	14 05				14 12				14 22	14 27	14 35				14 42				14 52
Barnes Bridge	d					13 59					14 14					14 29					14 44				
Chiswick	d					14 02					14 17					14 32					14 47				
Kew Bridge	d					14 05					14 20					14 35					14 50				
Brentford	d					14 08					14 23					14 38					14 53				
Syon Lane	d					14 10					14 25					14 40					14 55				
Isleworth	d					14 12					14 27					14 42					14 57				
Hounslow	d					14 18					14 31					14 48					15 01				
Mortlake	d				13 54		14 07								14 24		14 37								14 54
North Sheen	d				13 56		14 09		←						14 26		14 39		←						14 56
Richmond ⊖	d	13 48			13 59		14 12	14 06	14 12			14 18			14 29		14 42	14 36	14 42			14 48			14 59
St Margarets	d				14 01		→		14 14						14 31		→		14 44						15 01
Twickenham	a	13 51			14 03			14 10	14 16			14 21			14 33			14 40	14 46			14 51			15 03
	d	13 52			14 04			14 10	14 17			14 22			14 34			14 40	14 47			14 52			15 04
Strawberry Hill	d				14 07										14 37										15 07
Fulwell	a																								
Teddington	a				14 10										14 40										15 10
Hampton Wick	a				14 14										14 44										15 14
Kingston	a				14 16										14 46										15 16
Whitton	d	13 55		←		14a23			14a20			14 25		←		14a53			14a50			14 55		←	
Feltham	d	13 59		14 06				14 16			14 36	14 29		14 36				14 46			15 06	14 59		15 06	
Ashford (Surrey)	d	14 03		14 10							→	14 33		14 40							→	15 03		15 10	
Staines	d	14 07		14 14				14 23				14 37		14 44				14 53				15 07		15 14	
Wraysbury	d	14 11										14 41										15 11			
Sunnymeads	d	14 14										14 44										15 14			
Datchet	d	14 17										14 47										15 17			
Windsor & Eton Riverside	a	14 21										14 51										15 21			
Egham	d			14 19				14 27						14 49				14 57						15 19	
Virginia Water	a			14 23				14 31						14 53				15 01						15 23	
	d			14 23				14 31						14 53				15 01						15 23	
Chertsey	d			14 29										14 59										15 29	
Addlestone	d			14 32										15 02										15 32	
Weybridge	a			14 37										15 07										15 37	
Longcross	d																								
Sunningdale	d							14 37										15 07							
Ascot	d							14 43		14 53								15 13		15 23					
Bagshot	d									14 59										15 29					
Camberley	a									15 05										15 35					
Frimley	d									15 13										15 43					
Ash Vale	d									15 19										15 49					
Aldershot	a									15 24										15 54					
	d									15 38										16 08					
Ash	d									15 45										16 15					
Wanborough	d									15 48										16 18					
Guildford	a									15 55										16 25					
Martins Heron	d							14 47										15 17							
Bracknell	d							14 50										15 20							
Wokingham	d							14 57										15 27							
Winnersh	d							15 00										15 30							
Winnersh Triangle	d							15 02										15 32							
Earley	d							15 05										15 35							
Reading	a							15 10										15 40							

The xx15 and xx45 services from London Waterloo to Whitton continue to London Waterloo via Brentford

The xx03 and xx33 London Waterloo to Kingston services continue to London Waterloo via Wimbledon

The xx07 and xx37 services from London Waterloo to Whitton continue to London Waterloo via Richmond

For additional services between Wokingham and Reading refer to Table T148

Table T149-F

London - Hounslow, Richmond, Kingston, Windsor, Weybridge, Ascot, Guildford and Reading

Saturdays
26 May to 6 October

		SW	SW	SW ■	SW	SW ■	SW	SW		SW	SW	SW	SW	SW ■	SW	SW ■	SW	SW		SW	SW	SW	SW	SW ■	SW
London Waterloo ⊖	d	14 37	14 45	14 50			14 52	14 58			15 03	15 07	15 15	15 20			15 22	15 28			15 33	15 37	15 45	15 50	
Vauxhall ⊖	d	14 41	14 49				14 56	15 02			15 07	15 11	15 19				15 26	15 32			15 37	15 41	15 49		
Queenstown Rd.(Battersea)	d	14 44	14 52				14 59				15 10	15 14	15 22				15 29				15 40	15 44	15 52		
Clapham Junction	d	14 47	14 55	14 58			15 02	15 08			15 13	15 17	15 25	15 28			15 32	15 38			15 43	15 47	15 55	15 58	
Wandsworth Town	d	14 50	14 58				15 05				15 16	15 20	15 28				15 35				15 46	15 50	15 58		
Putney	d	14 53	15 01				15 08	15 12			15 19	15 23	15 31				15 38	15 42			15 49	15 53	16 01		
Barnes	d	14 57	15 05				15 12				15 22	15 27	15 35				15 42				15 52	15 57	16 05		
Barnes Bridge	d	14 59					15 14					15 29					15 44					15 59			
Chiswick	d	15 02					15 17					15 32					15 47					16 02			
Kew Bridge	d	15 05					15 20					15 35					15 50					16 05			
Brentford	d	15 08					15 23					15 38					15 53					16 08			
Syon Lane	d	15 10					15 25					15 40					15 55					16 10			
Isleworth	d	15 12					15 27					15 42					15 57					16 12			
Hounslow	d	15 18					15 31					15 48					16 01					16 18			
Mortlake	d		15 07								15 24		15 37								15 54		16 07		
North Sheen	d		15 09		←						15 26		15 39		←						15 56		16 09		←
Richmond ⊖	d		15 12	15 06	15 12			15 18			15 29		15 42	15 36	15 42			15 48			15 59		16 12	16 06	16 12
St Margarets	d		→		15 14						15 31		→		15 44						16 01		→		16 14
Twickenham	a			15 10	15 16			15 21			15 33			15 40	15 46			15 51			16 03			16 10	16 16
	d			15 10	15 17			15 22			15 34			15 40	15 47			15 52			16 04			16 10	16 17
Strawberry Hill	d										15 37										16 07				
Fulwell	a																								
Teddington	a										15 40										16 10				
Hampton Wick	a										15 44										16 14				
Kingston	a										15 46										16 16				
Whitton	d	15a23			15a20			15 25		←		15a53			15a50			15 55		←		16a23			16a20
Feltham	d			15 16			15 36	15 29		15 36				15 46			16 06	15 59		16 06				16 16	
Ashford (Surrey)	d						→	15 33		15 40							→	16 03		16 10					
Staines	d			15 23				15 37		15 44				15 53				16 07		16 14				16 23	
Wraysbury	d							15 41										16 11							
Sunnymeads	d							15 44										16 14							
Datchet	d							15 47										16 17							
Windsor & Eton Riverside	a							15 51										16 21							
Egham	d			15 27						15 49				15 57						16 19				16 27	
Virginia Water	a			15 31						15 53				16 01						16 23				16 31	
	d			15 31						15 53				16 01						16 23				16 31	
Chertsey	d									15 59										16 29					
Addlestone	d									16 02										16 32					
Weybridge	a									16 07										16 37					
Longcross	d																								
Sunningdale	d			15 37										16 07										16 37	
Ascot	d			15 43		15 53								16 13		16 23								16 43	
Bagshot	d					15 59										16 29									
Camberley	a					16 05										16 35									
Frimley	d					16 13										16 43									
Ash Vale	d					16 19										16 49									
Aldershot	a					16 24										16 54									
	d					16 38										17 08									
Ash	d					16 45										17 15									
Wanborough	d					16 48										17 18									
Guildford	a					16 55										17 25									
Martins Heron	d			15 47										16 17										16 47	
Bracknell	d			15 50										16 20										16 50	
Wokingham	d			15 57										16 27										16 57	
Winnersh	d			16 00										16 30										17 00	
Winnersh Triangle	d			16 02										16 32										17 02	
Earley	d			16 05										16 35										17 05	
Reading	a			16 10										16 40										17 10	

The xx15 and xx45 services from London Waterloo to Whitton continue to London Waterloo via Brentford

The xx03 and xx33 London Waterloo to Kingston services continue to London Waterloo via Wimbledon

The xx07 and xx37 services from London Waterloo to Whitton continue to London Waterloo via Richmond

For additional services between Wokingham and Reading refer to Table T148

Table T149-F

Saturdays
26 May to 6 October

London - Hounslow, Richmond, Kingston, Windsor, Weybridge, Ascot, Guildford and Reading

		SW 1	SW	SW		SW	SW	SW	SW	SW 1	SW	SW 1	SW	SW		SW	SW	SW	SW	SW 1	SW	SW 1	SW	SW
London Waterloo 15 ⊖	d		15 52	15 58			16 03	16 07	16 15	16 20			16 22	16 28			16 33	16 37	16 45	16 50			16 52	16 58
Vauxhall ⊖	d		15 56	16 02			16 07	16 11	16 19				16 26	16 32			16 37	16 41	16 49				16 56	17 02
Queenstown Rd.(Battersea)	d		15 59				16 10	16 14	16 22				16 29				16 40	16 44	16 52				16 59	
Clapham Junction 10	d		16 02	16 08			16 13	16 17	16 25	16 28			16 32	16 38			16 43	16 47	16 55	16 58			17 02	17 08
Wandsworth Town	d		16 05				16 16	16 20	16 28				16 35				16 46	16 50	16 58				17 05	
Putney	d		16 08	16 12			16 19	16 23	16 31				16 38	16 42			16 49	16 53	17 01				17 08	17 12
Barnes	d		16 12				16 22	16 27	16 35				16 42				16 52	16 57	17 05				17 12	
Barnes Bridge	d		16 14					16 29					16 44					16 59					17 14	
Chiswick	d		16 17					16 32					16 47					17 02					17 17	
Kew Bridge	d		16 20					16 35					16 50					17 05					17 20	
Brentford	d		16 23					16 38					16 53					17 08					17 23	
Syon Lane	d		16 25					16 40					16 55					17 10					17 25	
Isleworth	d		16 27					16 42					16 57					17 12					17 27	
Hounslow	d		16 31					16 48					17 01					17 18					17 31	
Mortlake	d						16 24		16 37								16 54		17 07					
North Sheen	d						16 26		16 39		←						16 56		17 09		←			
Richmond ⊖	d			16 18			16 29		16 42	16 36	16 42			16 48			16 59		17 12	17 06	17 12			17 18
St Margarets	d						16 31		→		16 44						17 01		→		17 14			
Twickenham	a			16 21			16 33			16 40	16 46			16 51			17 03			17 10	17 16			17 21
	d			16 22			16 34			16 40	16 47			16 52			17 04			17 10	17 17			17 22
Strawberry Hill	d						16 37										17 07							
Fulwell	a																							
Teddington	a						16 40										17 10							
Hampton Wick	a						16 44										17 14							
Kingston	a						16 46										17 16							
Whitton	d			16 25		←		16a53			16a50			16 55		←		17a23			17a20			17 25
Feltham	d		16 36	16 29		16 36				16 46			17 06	16 59		17 06				17 16			17 36	17 29
Ashford (Surrey)	d		→	16 33		16 40							→	17 03		17 10							→	17 33
Staines	d			16 37		16 44				16 53				17 07		17 14				17 23				17 37
Wraysbury	d			16 41										17 11										17 41
Sunnymeads	d			16 44										17 14										17 44
Datchet	d			16 47										17 17										17 47
Windsor & Eton Riverside	a			16 51										17 21										17 51
Egham	d					16 49				16 57						17 19				17 27				
Virginia Water	a					16 53				17 01						17 23				17 31				
	d					16 53				17 01						17 23				17 31				
Chertsey	d					16 59										17 29								
Addlestone	d					17 02										17 32								
Weybridge	a					17 07										17 37								
Longcross	d																							
Sunningdale	d									17 07										17 37				
Ascot 8	d	16 53								17 13		17 23								17 43		17 53		
Bagshot	d	16 59										17 29										17 59		
Camberley	a	17 05										17 35										18 05		
Frimley	d	17 13										17 43										18 13		
Ash Vale	d	17 19										17 49										18 19		
Aldershot	a	17 24										17 54										18 24		
	d	17 38										18 08										18 38		
Ash 5	d	17 45										18 15										18 45		
Wanborough	d	17 48										18 18										18 48		
Guildford	a	17 55										18 25										18 55		
Martins Heron	d									17 17										17 47				
Bracknell	d									17 20										17 50				
Wokingham	d									17 27										17 57				
Winnersh	d									17 30										18 00				
Winnersh Triangle	d									17 32										18 02				
Earley	d									17 35										18 05				
Reading 7	a									17 40										18 10				

The xx15 and xx45 services from London Waterloo to Whitton continue to London Waterloo via Brentford

The xx03 and xx33 London Waterloo to Kingston services continue to London Waterloo via Wimbledon

The xx07 and xx37 services from London Waterloo to Whitton continue to London Waterloo via Richmond

For additional services between Wokingham and Reading refer to Table T148

Table T149-F

Saturdays
26 May to 6 October

London - Hounslow, Richmond, Kingston, Windsor, Weybridge, Ascot, Guildford and Reading

		SW	SW	SW	SW	SW 1	SW	SW 1	SW	SW		SW	SW	SW	SW	SW 1	SW	SW 1	SW	SW		SW	SW	SW	SW
London Waterloo 15 ⊖	d		17 03	17 07	17 15	17 20			17 22	17 28			17 33	17 37	17 45	17 50			17 52	17 58			18 03	18 07	18 15
Vauxhall ⊖	d		17 07	17 11	17 19				17 26	17 32			17 37	17 41	17 49				17 56	18 02			18 07	18 11	18 19
Queenstown Rd.(Battersea)	d		17 10	17 14	17 22				17 29				17 40	17 44	17 52				17 59				18 10	18 14	18 22
Clapham Junction 10	d		17 13	17 17	17 25	17 28			17 32	17 38			17 43	17 47	17 55	17 58			18 02	18 08			18 13	18 17	18 25
Wandsworth Town	d		17 16	17 20	17 28				17 35				17 46	17 50	17 58				18 05				18 16	18 20	18 28
Putney	d		17 19	17 23	17 31				17 38	17 42			17 49	17 53	18 01				18 08	18 12			18 19	18 23	18 31
Barnes	d		17 22	17 27	17 35				17 42				17 52	17 57	18 05				18 12				18 22	18 27	18 35
Barnes Bridge	d			17 29					17 44					17 59					18 14					18 29	
Chiswick	d			17 32					17 47					18 02					18 17					18 32	
Kew Bridge	d			17 35					17 50					18 05					18 20					18 35	
Brentford	d			17 38					17 53					18 08					18 23					18 38	
Syon Lane	d			17 40					17 55					18 10					18 25					18 40	
Isleworth	d			17 42					17 57					18 12					18 27					18 42	
Hounslow	d			17 48					18 01					18 18					18 31					18 48	
Mortlake	d		17 24		17 37								17 54		18 07								18 24		18 37
North Sheen	d		17 26		17 39		←						17 56		18 09		←						18 26		18 39
Richmond ⊖	d		17 29		17 42	17 36	17 42			17 48			17 59		18 12	18 06	18 12			18 18			18 29		18 42
St Margarets	d		17 31		→		17 44						18 01		→		18 14						18 31		→
Twickenham	a		17 33			17 40	17 46			17 51			18 03			18 10	18 16			18 21			18 33		
	d		17 34			17 40	17 47			17 52			18 04			18 10	18 17			18 22			18 34		
Strawberry Hill	d		17 37										18 07										18 37		
Fulwell	a																								
Teddington	a		17 40										18 10										18 40		
Hampton Wick	a		17 44										18 14										18 44		
Kingston	a		17 46										18 16										18 46		
Whitton	d	←		17a53			17a50			17 55		←		18a23			18a20			18 25		←		18a53	
Feltham	d	17 36				17 46			18 06	17 59		18 06				18 16			18 36	18 29		18 36			
Ashford (Surrey)	d	17 40							→	18 03		18 10							→	18 33		18 40			
Staines	d	17 44				17 53				18 07		18 14				18 23				18 37		18 44			
Wraysbury	d									18 11										18 41					
Sunnymeads	d									18 14										18 44					
Datchet	d									18 17										18 47					
Windsor & Eton Riverside	a									18 21										18 51					
Egham	d	17 49				17 57						18 19				18 27						18 49			
Virginia Water	a	17 53				18 01						18 23				18 31						18 53			
	d	17 53				18 01						18 23				18 31						18 53			
Chertsey	d	17 59										18 29										18 59			
Addlestone	d	18 02										18 32										19 02			
Weybridge	a	18 07										18 37										19 07			
Longcross	d																								
Sunningdale	d					18 07										18 37									
Ascot 8	d					18 13		18 23								18 43		18 53							
Bagshot	d							18 29										18 59							
Camberley	a							18 35										19 05							
Frimley	d							18 43										19 13							
Ash Vale	d							18 49										19 19							
Aldershot	a							18 54										19 24							
	d							19 08										19 38							
Ash 5	d							19 15										19 45							
Wanborough	d							19 18										19 48							
Guildford	a							19 25										19 55							
Martins Heron	d					18 17										18 47									
Bracknell	d					18 20										18 50									
Wokingham	d					18 27										18 57									
Winnersh	d					18 30										19 00									
Winnersh Triangle	d					18 32										19 02									
Earley	d					18 35										19 05									
Reading 7	a					18 40										19 10									

The xx15 and xx45 services from London Waterloo to Whitton continue to London Waterloo via Brentford

The xx03 and xx33 London Waterloo to Kingston services continue to London Waterloo via Wimbledon

The xx07 and xx37 services from London Waterloo to Whitton continue to London Waterloo via Richmond

For additional services between Wokingham and Reading refer to Table T148

Table T149-F

Saturdays
26 May to 6 October

London - Hounslow, Richmond, Kingston, Windsor, Weybridge, Ascot, Guildford and Reading

		SW ■	SW	SW ■	SW	SW		SW	SW	SW	SW	SW ■	SW	SW ■	SW	SW		SW	SW	SW	SW	SW ■	SW	SW ■	SW
London Waterloo ⊖	d	18 20			18 22	18 28			18 33	18 37	18 45	18 50			18 52	18 58			19 03	19 07	19 15	19 20			19 22
Vauxhall ⊖	d				18 26	18 32			18 37	18 41	18 49				18 56	19 02			19 07	19 11	19 19				19 26
Queenstown Rd.(Battersea)	d				18 29				18 40	18 44	18 52				18 59				19 10	19 14	19 22				19 29
Clapham Junction	d	18 28			18 32	18 38			18 43	18 47	18 55	18 58			19 02	19 08			19 13	19 17	19 25	19 28			19 32
Wandsworth Town	d				18 35				18 46	18 50	18 58				19 05				19 16	19 20	19 28				19 35
Putney	d				18 38	18 42			18 49	18 53	19 01				19 08	19 12			19 19	19 23	19 31				19 38
Barnes	d				18 42				18 52	18 57	19 05				19 12				19 22	19 27	19 35				19 42
Barnes Bridge	d				18 44					18 59					19 14					19 29					19 44
Chiswick	d				18 47					19 02					19 17					19 32					19 47
Kew Bridge	d				18 50					19 05					19 20					19 35					19 50
Brentford	d				18 53					19 08					19 23					19 38					19 53
Syon Lane	d				18 55					19 10					19 25					19 40					19 55
Isleworth	d				18 57					19 12					19 27					19 42					19 57
Hounslow	d				19 01					19 18					19 31					19 48					20 01
Mortlake	d								18 54		19 07								19 24		19 37				
North Sheen	d		←						18 56		19 09		←						19 26		19 39		←		
Richmond ⊖	d	18 36	18 42			18 48			18 59		19 12	19 06	19 12			19 18			19 29		19 42	19 36	19 42		
St Margarets	d		18 44						19 01		→		19 14						19 31		→		19 44		
Twickenham	a	18 40	18 46			18 51			19 03			19 10	19 16			19 21			19 33			19 40	19 46		
	d	18 40	18 47			18 52			19 04			19 10	19 17			19 22			19 34			19 40	19 47		
Strawberry Hill	d								19 07										19 37						
Fulwell	a																								
Teddington	a								19 10										19 40						
Hampton Wick	a								19 14										19 44						
Kingston	a								19 16										19 46						
Whitton	d		18a50			18 55		←		19a23			19a20			19 25		←		19a53			19a50		
Feltham	d	18 46			19 06	18 59		19 06				19 16			19 36	19 29		19 36				19 46			20 06
Ashford (Surrey)	d				→	19 03		19 10							→	19 33		19 40							→
Staines	d	18 53				19 07		19 14				19 23				19 37		19 44				19 53			
Wraysbury	d					19 11										19 41									
Sunnymeads	d					19 14										19 44									
Datchet	d					19 17										19 47									
Windsor & Eton Riverside	a					19 21										19 51									
Egham	d	18 57						19 19				19 27						19 49				19 57			
Virginia Water	a	19 01						19 23				19 31						19 53				20 01			
	d	19 01						19 23				19 31						19 53				20 01			
Chertsey	d							19 29										19 59							
Addlestone	d							19 32										20 02							
Weybridge	a							19 37										20 07							
Longcross	d																								
Sunningdale	d	19 07										19 37										20 07			
Ascot ■	d	19 13		19 23								19 43		19 53								20 13		20 23	
Bagshot	d			19 29										19 59										20 29	
Camberley	a			19 35										20 05										20 35	
Frimley	d			19 43										20 13										20 43	
Ash Vale	d			19 49										20 19										20 49	
Aldershot	a			19 54										20 24										20 54	
	d			20 08										20 38										21 08	
Ash ■	d			20 15										20 45										21 15	
Wanborough	d			20 18										20 48										21 18	
Guildford	a			20 25										20 55										21 25	
Martins Heron	d	19 17										19 47										20 17			
Bracknell	d	19 20										19 50										20 20			
Wokingham	d	19 27										19 57										20 27			
Winnersh	d	19 30										20 00										20 30			
Winnersh Triangle	d	19 32										20 02										20 32			
Earley	d	19 35										20 05										20 35			
Reading ■	a	19 40										20 10										20 40			

The xx15 and xx45 services from London Waterloo to Whitton continue to London Waterloo via Brentford

The xx03 and xx33 London Waterloo to Kingston services continue to London Waterloo via Wimbledon

The xx07 and xx37 services from London Waterloo to Whitton continue to London Waterloo via Richmond

For additional services between Wokingham and Reading refer to Table T148

Table T149-F

Saturdays
26 May to 6 October

London - Hounslow, Richmond, Kingston, Windsor, Weybridge, Ascot, Guildford and Reading

		SW		SW	SW	SW	SW	SW ■	SW	SW ■	SW	SW		SW	SW	SW	SW	SW ■	SW	SW ■	SW ■	SW		SW	SW
London Waterloo ⊖	d	19 28			19 33	19 37	19 45	19 50			19 52	19 58			20 03	20 07	20 15	20 20				20 22		20 28	
Vauxhall ⊖	d	19 32			19 37	19 41	19 49				19 56	20 02			20 07	20 11	20 19					20 26		20 32	
Queenstown Rd.(Battersea)	d				19 40	19 44	19 52				19 59				20 10	20 14	20 22					20 29			
Clapham Junction	d	19 38			19 43	19 47	19 55	19 58			20 02	20 08			20 13	20 17	20 26	20 28				20 32		20 38	
Wandsworth Town	d				19 46	19 50	19 58				20 05				20 16	20 20	20 29					20 35			
Putney	d	19 42			19 49	19 53	20 01				20 08	20 12			20 19	20 23	20 32					20 38		20 42	
Barnes	d				19 52	19 57	20 05				20 12				20 22	20 27	20 35					20 42			
Barnes Bridge	d					19 59					20 14					20 29						20 44			
Chiswick	d					20 02					20 17					20 32						20 47			
Kew Bridge	d					20 05					20 20					20 35						20 50			
Brentford	d					20 08					20 23					20 38						20 53			
Syon Lane	d					20 10					20 25					20 40						20 55			
Isleworth	d					20 12					20 27					20 42						20 57			
Hounslow	d					20 18					20 31					20 48						21 01			
Mortlake	d				19 54		20 07								20 24		20 37								
North Sheen	d				19 56		20 09		←						20 26		20 39		←						
Richmond ⊖	d	19 48			19 59		20 12	20 06	20 12			20 18			20 29		20 42	20 36	20 42					20 48	
St Margarets	d				20 01		→		20 14						20 31		→		20 44						
Twickenham	a	19 51			20 03			20 10	20 16			20 21			20 33			20 40	20 46					20 51	
	d	19 52			20 04			20 10	20 17			20 22			20 34			20 40	20 47					20 52	
Strawberry Hill	d				20 07										20 37										
Fulwell	a																								
Teddington	a				20 10										20 40										
Hampton Wick	a				20 14										20 44										
Kingston	a				20 16										20 46										
Whitton	d	19 55		←		20a23			20a20			20 25		←		20a53			20a50					20 55	←
Feltham	d	19 59		20 06				20 16			20 36	20 29		20 36				20 46				21 06		20 59	21 06
Ashford (Surrey)	d	20 03		20 10							→	20 33		20 40								→		21 03	21 10
Staines	d	20 07		20 14				20 23				20 37		20 44				20 53						21 07	21 14
Wraysbury	d	20 11										20 41												21 11	
Sunnymeads	d	20 14										20 44												21 14	
Datchet	d	20 17										20 47												21 17	
Windsor & Eton Riverside	a	20 21										20 51												21 21	
Egham	d			20 19				20 27						20 49				20 57							21 19
Virginia Water	a			20 23				20 31						20 53				21 01							21 23
	d			20 23				20 31						20 53				21 01							21 23
Chertsey	d			20 29										20 59											21 29
Addlestone	d			20 32										21 02											21 32
Weybridge	a			20 37										21 07											21 37
Longcross	d																								
Sunningdale	d							20 37										21 07							
Ascot ■	d							20 43		20 53								21 13		21 23					
Bagshot	d									20 59										21 29					
Camberley	a									21 05										21 35					
Frimley	d									21 13										21 43					
Ash Vale	d									21 19										21 49					
Aldershot	a									21 24										21 54					
	d									21 38										22 08	22 38				
Ash ■	d									21 45										22 15	22 45				
Wanborough	d									21 48										22 18	22 48				
Guildford	a									21 55										22 25	22 55				
Martins Heron	d							20 47										21 17							
Bracknell	d							20 50										21 20							
Wokingham	d							20 57										21 27							
Winnersh	d							21 00										21 30							
Winnersh Triangle	d							21 02										21 32							
Earley	d							21 05										21 35							
Reading ■	a							21 10										21 40							

The xx15 and xx45 services from London Waterloo to Whitton continue to London Waterloo via Brentford

The xx03 and xx33 London Waterloo to Kingston services continue to London Waterloo via Wimbledon

The xx07 and xx37 services from London Waterloo to Whitton continue to London Waterloo via Richmond

For additional services between Wokingham and Reading refer to Table T148

Table T149-F

Saturdays

26 May to 6 October

London - Hounslow, Richmond, Kingston, Windsor, Weybridge, Ascot, Guildford and Reading

		SW	SW	SW	SW ■	SW	SW	SW		SW	SW	SW	SW	SW ■	SW	SW ■	SW	SW		SW	SW	SW	SW	SW ■	SW
London Waterloo ⊖	d	20 33	20 37	20 45	20 50		20 52	20 58			21 03	21 07	21 15	21 20			21 22	21 28			21 33	21 37	21 45	21 50	
Vauxhall ⊖	d	20 37	20 41	20 49			20 56	21 02			21 07	21 11	21 19				21 26	21 32			21 37	21 41	21 49		
Queenstown Rd.(Battersea)	d	20 40	20 44	20 52			20 59				21 10	21 14	21 22				21 29				21 40	21 44	21 52		
Clapham Junction	d	20 43	20 47	20 55	20 58		21 02	21 08			21 13	21 17	21 25	21 28			21 32	21 38			21 43	21 47	21 55	21 58	
Wandsworth Town	d	20 46	20 50	20 58			21 05				21 16	21 20	21 28				21 35				21 46	21 50	21 58		
Putney	d	20 49	20 53	21 01			21 08	21 12			21 19	21 23	21 31				21 38	21 42			21 49	21 53	22 01		
Barnes	d	20 52	20 57	21 05			21 12				21 22	21 27	21 35				21 42				21 52	21 57	22 05		
Barnes Bridge	d		20 59				21 14					21 29					21 44					21 59			
Chiswick	d		21 02				21 17					21 32					21 47					22 02			
Kew Bridge	d		21 05				21 20					21 35					21 50					22 05			
Brentford	d		21 08				21 23					21 38					21 53					22 08			
Syon Lane	d		21 10				21 25					21 40					21 55					22 10			
Isleworth	d		21 12				21 27					21 42					21 57					22 12			
Hounslow	d		21 18				21 31					21 48					22 01					22 18			
Mortlake	d	20 54		21 07							21 24		21 37								21 54		22 07		
North Sheen	d	20 56		21 09		←					21 26		21 39		←						21 56		22 09		←
Richmond ⊖	d	20 59		21 12	21 06	21 12		21 18			21 29		21 42	21 36	21 42			21 48			21 59		22 12	22 06	22 12
St Margarets	d	21 01		→		21 14					21 31		→		21 44						22 01		→		22 14
Twickenham	a	21 03			21 10	21 16		21 21			21 33			21 40	21 46			21 51			22 03			22 10	22 16
	d	21 04			21 10	21 17		21 22			21 34			21 40	21 47			21 52			22 04			22 10	
Strawberry Hill	d	21 07									21 37										22 07				
Fulwell	a																								
Teddington	a	21 10									21 40										22 10				
Hampton Wick	a	21 14									21 44										22 14				
Kingston	a	21 16									21 46										22 16				
Whitton	d		21a23			21a20		21 25		←		21a53			21a50			21 55		←		22a23			
Feltham	d				21 16		21 36	21 29		21 36				21 46			22 06	21 59		22 06				22 16	
Ashford (Surrey)	d						→	21 33		21 40							→	22 03		22 10					
Staines	d				21 23			21 37		21 44				21 53				22 07		22 14				22 23	
Wraysbury	d							21 41										22 11							
Sunnymeads	d							21 44										22 14							
Datchet	d							21 47										22 17							
Windsor & Eton Riverside	a							21 51										22 21							
Egham	d				21 27					21 49				21 57						22 19				22 27	
Virginia Water	a				21 31					21 53				22 01						22 23				22 31	
	d				21 31					21 53				22 01						22 23				22 31	
Chertsey	d									21 59										22 29					
Addlestone	d									22 02										22 32					
Weybridge	a									22 07										22 37					
Longcross	d																								
Sunningdale	d				21 37									22 07										22 37	
Ascot	d				21 43									22 13		22 23								22 43	
Bagshot	d															22 29									
Camberley	a															22 35									
Frimley	d															22 43									
Ash Vale	d															22 49									
Aldershot	a															22 54									
	d															23 08									
Ash	d															23 15									
Wanborough	d															23 18									
Guildford	a															23 25									
Martins Heron	d				21 47									22 17										22 47	
Bracknell	d				21 50									22 20										22 50	
Wokingham	d				21 57									22 27										22 57	
Winnersh	d				22 00									22 30										23 00	
Winnersh Triangle	d				22 02									22 32										23 02	
Earley	d				22 05									22 35										23 05	
Reading	a				22 10									22 40										23 10	

The xx15 and xx45 services from London Waterloo to Whitton continue to London Waterloo via Brentford

The xx03 and xx33 London Waterloo to Kingston services continue to London Waterloo via Wimbledon

The xx07 and xx37 services from London Waterloo to Whitton continue to London Waterloo via Richmond

For additional services between Wokingham and Reading refer to Table T148

Table T149-F

Saturdays

26 May to 6 October

London - Hounslow, Richmond, Kingston, Windsor, Weybridge, Ascot, Guildford and Reading

		SW	SW	SW		SW	SW ■	SW ■	SW	SW	SW	SW	SW ■	SW		SW	SW	SW	SW ■	SW	SW	SW	SW	SW	
London Waterloo ⊖	d	21 52	21 58			22 03	22 20		22 22	22 28		22 33	22 50	22 52		22 58		23 03	23 20	23 22	23 28		23 33	23 50	
Vauxhall ⊖	d	21 56	22 02			22 07			22 26	22 32		22 37		22 56		23 02		23 07		23 26	23 32		23 37		
Queenstown Rd.(Battersea)	d	21 59				22 10			22 29			22 40		22 59				23 10		23 29			23 40		
Clapham Junction	d	22 02	22 08			22 13	22 28		22 32	22 38		22 43	22 58	23 02		23 08		23 13	23 28	23 32	23 38		23 43	23 58	
Wandsworth Town	d	22 05				22 16			22 35			22 46		23 05				23 16		23 35			23 46		
Putney	d	22 08	22 12			22 19			22 38	22 42		22 49		23 08		23 12		23 19		23 38	23 42		23 49		
Barnes	d	22 12				22 22			22 42			22 52		23 12				23 22		23 42			23 52		
Barnes Bridge	d	22 14							22 44					23 14						23 44					
Chiswick	d	22 17							22 47					23 17						23 47					
Kew Bridge	d	22 20							22 50					23 20						23 50					
Brentford	d	22 23							22 53					23 23						23 53					
Syon Lane	d	22 25							22 55					23 25						23 55					
Isleworth	d	22 27							22 57					23 27						23 57					
Hounslow	d	22 31							23 01					23 31						00 01					
Mortlake	d					22 24						22 54						23 24					23 54		
North Sheen	d					22 26						22 56						23 26					23 56		
Richmond ⊖	d		22 18			22 29	22 36			22 48		22 59	23 06			23 18		23 29	23 36		23 48		23 59	00 06	
St Margarets	d					22 31						23 01						23 31					00 01		
Twickenham	a		22 21			22 33	22 40			22 51		23 03	23 10			23 21		23 33	23 40		23 51		00 03	00 10	
	d		22 22			22 34	22 40			22 52		23 04	23 10			23 22		23 34	23 40		23 52		00 04	00 10	
Strawberry Hill	d					22 37						23 07						23 37					00 09		
Fulwell	a																								
Teddington	a					22 40						23 10						23 41					00 12		
Hampton Wick	a					22 44						23 14						23 44					00 14		
Kingston	a					22 46						23 16						23 46					00 16		
Whitton	d		22 25	←						22 55	←					23 25	←				23 55	←			
Feltham	d	22 36	22 29	22 36			22 46		23 06	22 59	23 06		23 16	23 36		23 29	23 36		23 46	00 06	23 59	00 06		00 16	
Ashford (Surrey)	d	→	22 33	22 40					→	23 03	23 10			→		23 33	23 40			→	00 03	00 10			
Staines	d		22 37	22 44			22 53			23 07	23 14		23 23			23 37	23 44		23 53		00 07	00 14		00 23	
Wraysbury	d		22 41							23 11						23 41					00 11				
Sunnymeads	d		22 44							23 14						23 44					00 14				
Datchet	d		22 47							23 17						23 47					00 17				
Windsor & Eton Riverside	a		22 51							23 21						23 51					00 21				
Egham	d			22 49			22 57				23 19		23 27				23 49		23 57			00 19		00 27	
Virginia Water	a			22 53			23 01				23 23		23 31				23 53		00 01			00 23		00 31	
	d			22 53			23 01				23 23		23 31				23 53		00 01			00 23		00 31	
Chertsey	d			22 59							23 29						23 59					00 29			
Addlestone	d			23 02							23 32						00a02					00 32			
Weybridge	a			23 07							23 37											00 36			
Longcross	d																								
Sunningdale	d						23 07						23 37						00 08					00 37	
Ascot	d						23 13	23 23					23 43						00 13					00 42	
Bagshot	d							23 29																	
Camberley	a							23 35																	
Frimley	d							23 43																	
Ash Vale	d							23 49																	
Aldershot	a							23 54																	
	d																								
Ash	d																								
Wanborough	d																								
Guildford	a																								
Martins Heron	d						23 17						23 47						00 17					00 46	
Bracknell	d						23 20						23 50						00 20					00 49	
Wokingham	d						23 27						23 57						00 32					00 56	
Winnersh	d						23 30						23 59						00 36						
Winnersh Triangle	d						23 32						00 02						00 38						
Earley	d						23 35						00 05						00 40						
Reading	a						23 40						00 10						00 45					01 04	

The xx15 and xx45 services from London Waterloo to Whitton continue to London Waterloo via Brentford

The xx03 and xx33 London Waterloo to Kingston services continue to London Waterloo via Wimbledon

The xx07 and xx37 services from London Waterloo to Whitton continue to London Waterloo via Richmond

For additional services between Wokingham and Reading refer to Table T148

Table T149-F

Saturdays
26 May to 6 October

London - Hounslow, Richmond, Kingston, Windsor, Weybridge, Ascot, Guildford and Reading

		SW	SW	SW
London Waterloo 15 ⊖	d	23 52	23 58	
Vauxhall ⊖	d	23 56	00 02	
Queenstown Rd.(Battersea)	d	23 59		
Clapham Junction 10	d	00 02	00 08	
Wandsworth Town	d	00 05		
Putney	d	00 08	00 12	
Barnes	d	00 12		
Barnes Bridge	d	00 14		
Chiswick	d	00 17		
Kew Bridge	d	00 20		
Brentford	d	00 23		
Syon Lane	d	00 25		
Isleworth	d	00 27		
Hounslow	d	00 31		
Mortlake	d			
North Sheen	d			
Richmond ⊖	d		00 18	
St Margarets	d			
Twickenham	a		00 22	
	d		00 22	
Strawberry Hill	d			
Fulwell	a			
Teddington	a			
Hampton Wick	a			
Kingston	a			
Whitton	d		00 25	←
Feltham	d	00 36	00 29	00 36
Ashford (Surrey)	d	→	00 33	00 40
Staines	d		00a37	00a47
Wraysbury	d			
Sunnymeads	d			
Datchet	d			
Windsor & Eton Riverside	a			
Egham	d			
Virginia Water	a			
	d			
Chertsey	d			
Addlestone	d			
Weybridge	a			
Longcross	d			
Sunningdale	d			
Ascot 3	d			
Bagshot	d			
Camberley	a			
Frimley	d			
Ash Vale	d			
Aldershot	a			
	d			
Ash 5	d			
Wanborough	d			
Guildford	a			
Martins Heron	d			
Bracknell	d			
Wokingham	d			
Winnersh	d			
Winnersh Triangle	d			
Earley	d			
Reading 7	a			

The xx15 and xx45 services from London Waterloo to Whitton continue to London Waterloo via Brentford

The xx03 and xx33 London Waterloo to Kingston services continue to London Waterloo via Wimbledon

The xx07 and xx37 services from London Waterloo to Whitton continue to London Waterloo via Richmond

For additional services between Wokingham and Reading refer to Table T148

Table T149-F

Saturdays
13 October to 8 December

London - Hounslow, Richmond, Kingston, Windsor, Weybridge, Ascot, Guildford and Reading

		SW	SW 1	SW 1	SW	SW	SW	SW 1	SW 1	SW	SW	SW 1	SW	SW	SW	SW 1	SW	SW	SW	SW	SW 1	SW	SW
London Waterloo 15 ⊖	d												00 18			05 05			05 33		05 50	05 58	06 03
Vauxhall ⊖	d									00 02			00 22			05 09			05 37			06 02	06 07
Queenstown Rd.(Battersea)	d												00 25			05 12			05 40				06 10
Clapham Junction 10	d									00 08	00 02		00 30			05 15			05 43		05 58	06 08	06 13
Wandsworth Town	d										00 05		00 33			05 18			05 46				06 16
Putney	d									00 12	00 08		00 36			05 21			05 49			06 12	06 19
Barnes	d										00 12		00 39			05 24			05 52				06 22
Barnes Bridge	d										00 14												
Chiswick	d										00 17												
Kew Bridge	d										00 20												
Brentford	d										00 23												
Syon Lane	d										00 25												
Isleworth	d										00 27												
Hounslow	d					00 01					00 31												
Mortlake	d												00 41			05 26			05 54				06 24
North Sheen	d												00 43			05 28			05 56				06 26
Richmond ⊖	d						00 06			00 18			00 46			05 31			05 59		06 06	06 18	06 29
St Margarets	d	00 01											00 48			05 33			06 01				06 31
Twickenham	a	00 03					00 10			00 22			00 50			05 35			06 03		06 10	06 21	06 33
	d	00 04					00 10			00 22			00 51	04 52		05 36	05 38	05 53	06 04		06 10	06 22	06 34
Strawberry Hill	d	00 09											00s54	04 55					06 07				06 37
Fulwell	a																						
Teddington	a	00 12											00s57	04 58					06 10				06 40
Hampton Wick	a	00 14											01s00	05 01					06 14				06 44
Kingston	a	00 16											01 02	05 03					06 16				06 46
Whitton	d									00 25						05 39	05a41	05 56				06 25	
Feltham	d					00 06	00 16			00 29	00 36					05 43		06 00			06 16	06 29	
Ashford (Surrey)	d				00 03	00 10				00 33	00 40					05 47		06 04				06 33	
Staines	d				00 07	00 14	00 23			00a37	00a47	05 23			05 44	05 53		06 08		06 16	06 23	06 37	
Wraysbury	d				00 11													06 13				06 42	
Sunnymeads	d				00 14													06 16				06 45	
Datchet	d				00 17													06 20				06 49	
Windsor & Eton Riverside	a				00 25													06 25				06 54	
Egham	d					00 19	00 27					05 27			05 49	05 57				06 20	06 27		
Virginia Water	a					00 23	00 31					05 31			05 53	06 01				06 25	06 31		
	d			00 01		00 23	00 31					05 31			05 53	06 01				06 25	06 31		
Chertsey	d					00 29									05 59					06 30			
Addlestone	d					00 32									06 02					06 33			
Weybridge	a					00 36									06 07					06 38			
Longcross	d																						
Sunningdale	d			00 08			00 37					05 37				06 07					06 37		
Ascot 3	d			00 13			00 42	00 45				05 43				06 13					06 43		
Bagshot	d							00 51															
Camberley	a							00 57															
Frimley	d							01 01															
Ash Vale	d							01 08															
Aldershot	a							01s13															
	d								06 08														
Ash 5	d								06 15														
Wanborough	d								06 18														
Guildford	a								06 25														
Martins Heron	d			00 17			00 46					05 47				06 17					06 47		
Bracknell	d			00 20			00 50					05 50				06 20					06 50		
Wokingham	d			00 32			00 56					05 57				06 27					06 57		
Winnersh	d			00 36								06 00				06 30					07 00		
Winnersh Triangle	d		00 02	00 38								06 02				06 32					07 02		
Earley	d		00 05	00 40								06 07				06 37					07 07		
Reading 7	a		00 15	00 48			01 08					06 13				06 43					07 13		

The xx15 and xx45 services from London Waterloo to Whitton continue to London Waterloo via Brentford

The xx03 and xx33 London Waterloo to Kingston services continue to London Waterloo via Wimbledon

The xx07 and xx37 services from London Waterloo to Whitton continue to London Waterloo via Richmond

For additional services between Wokingham and Reading refer to Table T148

Table T149-F

Saturdays
13 October to 8 December

London - Hounslow, Richmond, Kingston, Windsor, Weybridge, Ascot, Guildford and Reading

		SW ■	SW	SW ■	SW ■	SW ■	SW ■	SW	SW	SW	SW	SW ■	SW ■	SW	SW	SW	SW	SW	SW	SW ■	SW	SW ■	SW
London Waterloo [15] ⊖	d					06 20		06 22	06 28		06 33	06 50		06 52	06 58		07 03	07 07	07 15	07 20			07 22
Vauxhall ⊖	d							06 26	06 32		06 37			06 56	07 02		07 07	07 11	07 19				07 26
Queenstown Rd.(Battersea)	d							06 29			06 40			06 59			07 10	07 14	07 22				07 29
Clapham Junction [10]	d					06 28		06 32	06 38		06 43	06 58		07 02	07 08		07 13	07 17	07 25	07 28			07 32
Wandsworth Town	d							06 35			06 46			07 05			07 16	07 20	07 28				07 35
Putney	d							06 38	06 42		06 49			07 08	07 12		07 19	07 23	07 31				07 38
Barnes	d							06 42			06 52			07 12			07 22	07 27	07 35				07 42
Barnes Bridge	d							06 44						07 14				07 29					07 44
Chiswick	d							06 47						07 17				07 32					07 47
Kew Bridge	d							06 50						07 20				07 35					07 50
Brentford	d							06 53						07 23				07 38					07 53
Syon Lane	d							06 55						07 25				07 40					07 55
Isleworth	d							06 57						07 27				07 42					07 57
Hounslow	d							07 01						07 31				07 48					08 01
Mortlake	d										06 54						07 24		07 37				
North Sheen	d										06 56						07 26		07 39		←		
Richmond ⊖	d					06 36			06 48		06 59	07 06			07 18		07 29		07 42	07 36	07 42		
St Margarets	d										07 01						07 31		→		07 44		
Twickenham	a					06 40			06 51		07 03	07 10			07 21		07 33			07 40	07 46		
	d					06 40			06 52		07 04	07 10			07 22		07 34			07 40	07 47		
Strawberry Hill	d										07 07						07 37						
Fulwell	a																						
Teddington	a										07 10						07 40						
Hampton Wick	a										07 14						07 44						
Kingston	a										07 16						07 46						
Whitton	d								06 55	←					07 25	←		07a53			07a50		
Feltham	d					06 46		07 06	06 59	07 06		07 16		07 36	07 29	07 36				07 46			08 06
Ashford (Surrey)	d							→	07 03	07 10				→	07 33	07 40							→
Staines	d		06 44			06 53			07 07	07 14		07 23			07 37	07 44				07 53			
Wraysbury	d								07 12						07 42								
Sunnymeads	d								07 15						07 45								
Datchet	d								07 19						07 49								
Windsor & Eton Riverside	a								07 24						07 54								
Egham	d		06 49			06 57				07 19		07 27				07 49				07 57			
Virginia Water	a		06 53			07 01				07 23		07 31				07 53				08 01			
	d		06 53			07 01				07 23		07 31				07 53				08 01			
Chertsey	d		06 59							07 29						07 59							
Addlestone	d		07 02							07 32						08 02							
Weybridge	a		07 07							07 37						08 07							
Longcross	d																						
Sunningdale	d					07 07						07 37								08 07			
Ascot [5]	d				06 53	07 13						07 43	07 53							08 13		08 23	
Bagshot	d				06 59								07 59									08 29	
Camberley	a				07 05								08 05									08 35	
Frimley	d				07 13								08 13									08 43	
Ash Vale	d				07 19								08 19									08 49	
Aldershot	a				07 24								08 24									08 54	
	d	06 38		07 08	07 38		08 08						08 38									09 08	
Ash [5]	d	06 45		07 15	07 45		08 15						08 45									09 15	
Wanborough	d	06 48		07 18	07 48		08 18						08 48									09 18	
Guildford	a	06 55		07 25	07 55		08 25						08 55									09 25	
Martins Heron	d					07 17						07 47								08 17			
Bracknell	d					07 20						07 50								08 20			
Wokingham	d					07 27						07 57								08 27			
Winnersh	d					07 30						08 00								08 30			
Winnersh Triangle	d					07 32						08 02								08 32			
Earley	d					07 37						08 07								08 37			
Reading [7]	a					07 43						08 13								08 43			

The xx15 and xx45 services from London Waterloo to Whitton continue to London Waterloo via Brentford

The xx03 and xx33 London Waterloo to Kingston services continue to London Waterloo via Wimbledon

The xx07 and xx37 services from London Waterloo to Whitton continue to London Waterloo via Richmond

For additional services between Wokingham and Reading refer to Table T148

Table T149-F

Saturdays
13 October to 8 December

London - Hounslow, Richmond, Kingston, Windsor, Weybridge, Ascot, Guildford and Reading

		SW	SW	SW	SW	SW	SW ■	SW	SW ■	SW	SW	SW	SW	SW	SW	SW ■	SW	SW ■	SW	SW	SW	SW
London Waterloo [15] ⊖	d	07 28		07 33	07 37	07 45	07 50			07 52	07 58		08 03	08 07	08 15	08 20			08 22	08 28		08 33
Vauxhall ⊖	d	07 32		07 37	07 41	07 49				07 56	08 02		08 07	08 11	08 19				08 26	08 32		08 37
Queenstown Rd.(Battersea)	d			07 40	07 44	07 52				07 59			08 10	08 14	08 22				08 29			08 40
Clapham Junction [10]	d	07 38		07 43	07 47	07 55	07 58			08 02	08 08		08 13	08 17	08 25	08 28			08 32	08 38		08 43
Wandsworth Town	d			07 46	07 50	07 58				08 05			08 16	08 20	08 28				08 35			08 46
Putney	d	07 42		07 49	07 53	08 01				08 08	08 12		08 19	08 23	08 31				08 38	08 42		08 49
Barnes	d			07 52	07 57	08 05				08 12			08 22	08 27	08 35				08 42			08 52
Barnes Bridge	d				07 59					08 14				08 29					08 44			
Chiswick	d				08 02					08 17				08 32					08 47			
Kew Bridge	d				08 05					08 20				08 35					08 50			
Brentford	d				08 08					08 23				08 38					08 53			
Syon Lane	d				08 10					08 25				08 40					08 55			
Isleworth	d				08 12					08 27				08 42					08 57			
Hounslow	d				08 18					08 31				08 48					09 01			
Mortlake	d			07 54		08 07							08 24		08 37							08 54
North Sheen	d			07 56		08 09		←					08 26		08 39		←					08 56
Richmond ⊖	d	07 48		07 59		08 12	08 06	08 12			08 18		08 29		08 42	08 36	08 42			08 48		08 59
St Margarets	d			08 01		→		08 14					08 31		→		08 44					09 01
Twickenham	a	07 51		08 03			08 10	08 16			08 21		08 33			08 40	08 46			08 51		09 03
	d	07 52		08 04			08 10	08 17			08 22		08 34			08 40	08 47			08 52		09 04
Strawberry Hill	d			08 07									08 37									09 07
Fulwell	a																					
Teddington	a			08 10									08 40									09 10
Hampton Wick	a			08 14									08 44									09 14
Kingston	a			08 16									08 46									09 16
Whitton	d	07 55	←		08a23			08a20			08 25	←		08a53			08a50			08 55	←	
Feltham	d	07 59	08 06				08 16			08 36	08 29	08 36				08 46			09 06	08 59	09 06	
Ashford (Surrey)	d	08 03	08 10							→	08 33	08 40							→	09 03	09 10	
Staines	d	08 07	08 14				08 23				08 37	08 44				08 53				09 07	09 14	
Wraysbury	d	08 12									08 42									09 12		
Sunnymeads	d	08 15									08 45									09 15		
Datchet	d	08 19									08 49									09 19		
Windsor & Eton Riverside	a	08 24									08 54									09 24		
Egham	d		08 19				08 27					08 49				08 57					09 19	
Virginia Water	a		08 23				08 31					08 53				09 01					09 23	
	d		08 23				08 31					08 53				09 01					09 23	
Chertsey	d		08 29									08 59									09 29	
Addlestone	d		08 32									09 02									09 32	
Weybridge	a		08 37									09 07									09 37	
Longcross	d																					
Sunningdale	d						08 37									09 07						
Ascot [5]	d						08 43		08 53							09 13		09 23				
Bagshot	d								08 59									09 29				
Camberley	a								09 05									09 35				
Frimley	d								09 13									09 43				
Ash Vale	d								09 19									09 49				
Aldershot	a								09 24									09 54				
	d								09 38									10 08				
Ash [5]	d								09 45									10 15				
Wanborough	d								09 48									10 18				
Guildford	a								09 55									10 25				
Martins Heron	d						08 47									09 17						
Bracknell	d						08 50									09 20						
Wokingham	d						08 57									09 27						
Winnersh	d						09 00									09 30						
Winnersh Triangle	d						09 02									09 32						
Earley	d						09 07									09 37						
Reading [7]	a						09 13									09 43						

The xx15 and xx45 services from London Waterloo to Whitton continue to London Waterloo via Brentford

The xx03 and xx33 London Waterloo to Kingston services continue to London Waterloo via Wimbledon

The xx07 and xx37 services from London Waterloo to Whitton continue to London Waterloo via Richmond

For additional services between Wokingham and Reading refer to Table T148

Table T149-F

Saturdays

13 October to 8 December

London - Hounslow, Richmond, Kingston, Windsor, Weybridge, Ascot, Guildford and Reading

		SW	SW	SW ■	SW	SW ■	SW	SW		SW	SW	SW	SW	SW ■	SW	SW ■	SW	SW		SW	SW	SW	SW	SW ■	SW
London Waterloo ■ ⊖	d	08 37	08 45	08 50			08 52	08 58			09 03	09 07	09 15	09 20			09 22	09 28			09 33	09 37	09 45	09 50	
Vauxhall ⊖	d	08 41	08 49				08 56	09 02			09 07	09 11	09 19				09 26	09 32			09 37	09 41	09 49		
Queenstown Rd.(Battersea)	d	08 44	08 52				08 59				09 10	09 14	09 22				09 29				09 40	09 44	09 52		
Clapham Junction ■	d	08 47	08 55	08 58			09 02	09 08			09 13	09 17	09 25	09 28			09 32	09 38			09 43	09 47	09 55	09 58	
Wandsworth Town	d	08 50	08 58				09 05				09 16	09 20	09 28				09 35				09 46	09 50	09 58		
Putney	d	08 53	09 01				09 08	09 12			09 19	09 23	09 31				09 38	09 42			09 49	09 53	10 01		
Barnes	d	08 57	09 05				09 12				09 22	09 27	09 35				09 42				09 52	09 57	10 05		
Barnes Bridge	d	08 59					09 14					09 29					09 44					09 59			
Chiswick	d	09 02					09 17					09 32					09 47					10 02			
Kew Bridge	d	09 05					09 20					09 35					09 50					10 05			
Brentford	d	09 08					09 23					09 38					09 53					10 08			
Syon Lane	d	09 10					09 25					09 40					09 55					10 10			
Isleworth	d	09 12					09 27					09 42					09 57					10 12			
Hounslow	d	09 18					09 31					09 48					10 01					10 18			
Mortlake	d		09 07								09 24		09 37								09 54		10 07		
North Sheen	d		09 09		←						09 26		09 39		←						09 56		10 09		←
Richmond ⊖	d		09 12	09 06	09 12			09 18			09 29		09 42	09 36	09 42			09 48			09 59		10 12	10 06	10 12
St Margarets	d		→		09 14						09 31		→		09 44						10 01		→		10 14
Twickenham	a			09 10	09 16			09 21			09 33			09 40	09 46			09 51			10 03			10 10	10 16
	d			09 10	09 17			09 22			09 34			09 40	09 47			09 52			10 04			10 10	10 17
Strawberry Hill	d										09 37										10 07				
Fulwell	a																								
Teddington	a										09 40										10 10				
Hampton Wick	a										09 44										10 14				
Kingston	a										09 46										10 16				
Whitton	d	09a23			09a20			09 25		←		09a53			09a50			09 55		←		10a23			10a20
Feltham	d			09 16			09 36	09 29		09 36				09 46			10 06	09 59		10 06				10 16	
Ashford (Surrey)	d						→	09 33		09 40							→	10 03		10 10					
Staines	d			09 23				09 37		09 44				09 53				10 07		10 14				10 23	
Wraysbury	d							09 42										10 12							
Sunnymeads	d							09 45										10 15							
Datchet	d							09 49										10 19							
Windsor & Eton Riverside	a							09 54										10 24							
Egham	d			09 27						09 49				09 57						10 19				10 27	
Virginia Water	a			09 31						09 53				10 01						10 23				10 31	
	d			09 31						09 53				10 01						10 23				10 31	
Chertsey	d									09 59										10 29					
Addlestone	d									10 02										10 32					
Weybridge	a									10 07										10 37					
Longcross	d																								
Sunningdale	d			09 37										10 07										10 37	
Ascot ■	d			09 43		09 53								10 13		10 23								10 43	
Bagshot	d					09 59										10 29									
Camberley	a					10 05										10 35									
Frimley	d					10 13										10 43									
Ash Vale	d					10 19										10 49									
Aldershot	a					10 24										10 54									
	d					10 38										11 08									
Ash ■	d					10 45										11 15									
Wanborough	d					10 48										11 18									
Guildford	a					10 55										11 25									
Martins Heron	d			09 47										10 17										10 47	
Bracknell	d			09 50										10 20										10 50	
Wokingham	d			09 57										10 27										10 57	
Winnersh	d			10 00										10 30										11 00	
Winnersh Triangle	d			10 02										10 32										11 02	
Earley	d			10 07										10 37										11 07	
Reading ■	a			10 13										10 43										11 13	

The xx15 and xx45 services from London Waterloo to Whitton continue to London Waterloo via Brentford

The xx03 and xx33 London Waterloo to Kingston services continue to London Waterloo via Wimbledon

The xx07 and xx37 services from London Waterloo to Whitton continue to London Waterloo via Richmond

For additional services between Wokingham and Reading refer to Table T148

Table T149-F

Saturdays

13 October to 8 December

London - Hounslow, Richmond, Kingston, Windsor, Weybridge, Ascot, Guildford and Reading

		SW ■	SW	SW		SW	SW	SW	SW	SW ■	SW	SW ■	SW	SW		SW	SW	SW	SW	SW ■	SW	SW ■	SW	SW	
London Waterloo ■ ⊖	d		09 52	09 58			10 03	10 07	10 15	10 20			10 22	10 28			10 33	10 37	10 45	10 50			10 52	10 58	
Vauxhall ⊖	d		09 56	10 02			10 07	10 11	10 19				10 26	10 32			10 37	10 41	10 49				10 56	11 02	
Queenstown Rd.(Battersea)	d		09 59				10 10	10 14	10 22				10 29				10 40	10 44	10 52				10 59		
Clapham Junction ■	d		10 02	10 08			10 13	10 17	10 25	10 28			10 32	10 38			10 43	10 47	10 55	10 58			11 02	11 08	
Wandsworth Town	d		10 05				10 16	10 20	10 28				10 35				10 46	10 50	10 58				11 05		
Putney	d		10 08	10 12			10 19	10 23	10 31				10 38	10 42			10 49	10 53	11 01				11 08	11 12	
Barnes	d		10 12				10 22	10 27	10 35				10 42				10 52	10 57	11 05				11 12		
Barnes Bridge	d		10 14					10 29					10 44					10 59					11 14		
Chiswick	d		10 17					10 32					10 47					11 02					11 17		
Kew Bridge	d		10 20					10 35					10 50					11 05					11 20		
Brentford	d		10 23					10 38					10 53					11 08					11 23		
Syon Lane	d		10 25					10 40					10 55					11 10					11 25		
Isleworth	d		10 27					10 42					10 57					11 12					11 27		
Hounslow	d		10 31					10 48					11 01					11 18					11 31		
Mortlake	d						10 24		10 37								10 54		11 07						
North Sheen	d						10 26		10 39		←						10 56		11 09		←				
Richmond ⊖	d			10 18			10 29		10 42	10 36	10 42			10 48			10 59		11 12	11 06	11 12			11 18	
St Margarets	d						10 31		→		10 44						11 01		→		11 14				
Twickenham	a			10 21			10 33			10 40	10 46			10 51			11 03			11 10	11 16			11 21	
	d			10 22			10 34			10 40	10 47			10 52			11 04			11 10	11 17			11 22	
Strawberry Hill	d						10 37										11 07								
Fulwell	a																								
Teddington	a						10 40										11 10								
Hampton Wick	a						10 44										11 14								
Kingston	a						10 46										11 16								
Whitton	d			10 25		←		10a53			10a50			10 55		←		11a23			11a20			11 25	
Feltham	d		10 36	10 29		10 36				10 46			11 06	10 59		11 06				11 16			11 36	11 29	
Ashford (Surrey)	d		→	10 33		10 40							→	11 03		11 10							→	11 33	
Staines	d			10 37		10 44				10 53				11 07		11 14				11 23				11 37	
Wraysbury	d			10 42										11 12										11 42	
Sunnymeads	d			10 45										11 15										11 45	
Datchet	d			10 49										11 19										11 49	
Windsor & Eton Riverside	a			10 54										11 24										11 54	
Egham	d					10 49				10 57						11 19				11 27					
Virginia Water	a					10 53				11 01						11 23				11 31					
	d					10 53				11 01						11 23				11 31					
Chertsey	d					10 59										11 29									
Addlestone	d					11 02										11 32									
Weybridge	a					11 07										11 37									
Longcross	d																								
Sunningdale	d									11 07										11 37					
Ascot ■	d	10 53								11 13		11 23								11 43		11 53			
Bagshot	d	10 59										11 29										11 59			
Camberley	a	11 05										11 35										12 05			
Frimley	d	11 13										11 43										12 13			
Ash Vale	d	11 19										11 49										12 19			
Aldershot	a	11 24										11 54										12 24			
	d	11 38										12 08										12 38			
Ash ■	d	11 45										12 15										12 45			
Wanborough	d	11 48										12 18										12 48			
Guildford	a	11 55										12 25										12 55			
Martins Heron	d									11 17										11 47					
Bracknell	d									11 20										11 50					
Wokingham	d									11 27										11 57					
Winnersh	d									11 30										12 00					
Winnersh Triangle	d									11 32										12 02					
Earley	d									11 37										12 07					
Reading ■	a									11 43										12 13					

The xx15 and xx45 services from London Waterloo to Whitton continue to London Waterloo via Brentford

The xx03 and xx33 London Waterloo to Kingston services continue to London Waterloo via Wimbledon

The xx07 and xx37 services from London Waterloo to Whitton continue to London Waterloo via Richmond

For additional services between Wokingham and Reading refer to Table T148

Table T149-F

Saturdays
13 October to 8 December

London - Hounslow, Richmond, Kingston, Windsor, Weybridge, Ascot, Guildford and Reading

		SW	SW	SW	SW	SW ■	SW	SW ■	SW	SW		SW	SW	SW	SW	SW ■	SW	SW ■	SW	SW		SW	SW	SW	SW
London Waterloo 15 ⊖	d		11 03	11 07	11 15	11 20			11 22	11 28			11 33	11 37	11 45	11 50			11 52	11 58			12 03	12 07	12 15
Vauxhall ⊖	d		11 07	11 11	11 19				11 26	11 32			11 37	11 41	11 49				11 56	12 02			12 07	12 11	12 19
Queenstown Rd.(Battersea)	d		11 10	11 14	11 22				11 29				11 40	11 44	11 52				11 59				12 10	12 14	12 22
Clapham Junction 10	d		11 13	11 17	11 25	11 28			11 32	11 38			11 43	11 47	11 55	11 58			12 02	12 08			12 13	12 17	12 25
Wandsworth Town	d		11 16	11 20	11 28				11 35				11 46	11 50	11 58				12 05				12 16	12 20	12 28
Putney	d		11 19	11 23	11 31				11 38	11 42			11 49	11 53	12 01				12 08	12 12			12 19	12 23	12 31
Barnes	d		11 22	11 27	11 35				11 42				11 52	11 57	12 05				12 12				12 22	12 27	12 35
Barnes Bridge	d			11 29					11 44					11 59					12 14					12 29	
Chiswick	d			11 32					11 47					12 02					12 17					12 32	
Kew Bridge	d			11 35					11 50					12 05					12 20					12 35	
Brentford	d			11 38					11 53					12 08					12 23					12 38	
Syon Lane	d			11 40					11 55					12 10					12 25					12 40	
Isleworth	d			11 42					11 57					12 12					12 27					12 42	
Hounslow	d			11 48					12 01					12 18					12 31					12 48	
Mortlake	d		11 24		11 37								11 54		12 07								12 24		12 37
North Sheen	d		11 26		11 39		←						11 56		12 09		←						12 26		12 39
Richmond ⊖	d		11 29		11 42	11 36	11 42			11 48			11 59		12 12	12 06	12 12			12 18			12 29		12 42
St Margarets	d		11 31		→		11 44						12 01		→		12 14						12 31		→
Twickenham	a		11 33			11 40	11 46			11 51			12 03			12 10	12 16			12 21			12 33		
	d		11 34			11 40	11 47			11 52			12 04			12 10	12 17			12 22			12 34		
Strawberry Hill	d		11 37										12 07										12 37		
Fulwell	a																								
Teddington	a		11 40										12 10										12 40		
Hampton Wick	a		11 44										12 14										12 44		
Kingston	a		11 46										12 16										12 46		
Whitton	d	←		11a53			11a50			11 55		←		12a23			12a20			12 25		←		12a53	
Feltham	d	11 36				11 46			12 06	11 59		12 06				12 16			12 36	12 29		12 36			
Ashford (Surrey)	d	11 40							→	12 03		12 10							→	12 33		12 40			
Staines	d	11 44				11 53				12 07		12 14				12 23				12 37		12 44			
Wraysbury	d									12 12										12 42					
Sunnymeads	d									12 15										12 45					
Datchet	d									12 19										12 49					
Windsor & Eton Riverside	a									12 24										12 54					
Egham	d	11 49				11 57						12 19				12 27						12 49			
Virginia Water	a	11 53				12 01						12 23				12 31						12 53			
	d	11 53				12 01						12 23				12 31						12 53			
Chertsey	d	11 59										12 29										12 59			
Addlestone	d	12 02										12 32										13 02			
Weybridge	a	12 07										12 37										13 07			
Longcross	d																								
Sunningdale	d					12 07										12 37									
Ascot ■	d					12 13		12 23								12 43		12 53							
Bagshot	d							12 29										12 59							
Camberley	a							12 35										13 05							
Frimley	d							12 43										13 13							
Ash Vale	d							12 49										13 19							
Aldershot	a							12 54										13 24							
	d							13 08										13 38							
Ash ■	d							13 15										13 45							
Wanborough	d							13 18										13 48							
Guildford	a							13 25										13 55							
Martins Heron	d					12 17										12 47									
Bracknell	d					12 20										12 50									
Wokingham	d					12 27										12 57									
Winnersh	d					12 30										13 00									
Winnersh Triangle	d					12 32										13 02									
Earley	d					12 37										13 07									
Reading ■	a					12 43										13 13									

The xx15 and xx45 services from London Waterloo to Whitton continue to London Waterloo via Brentford

The xx03 and xx33 London Waterloo to Kingston services continue to London Waterloo via Wimbledon

The xx07 and xx37 services from London Waterloo to Whitton continue to London Waterloo via Richmond

For additional services between Wokingham and Reading refer to Table T148

Table T149-F

Saturdays
13 October to 8 December

London - Hounslow, Richmond, Kingston, Windsor, Weybridge, Ascot, Guildford and Reading

		SW ■	SW	SW ■	SW	SW		SW	SW	SW	SW	SW ■	SW	SW ■	SW	SW		SW	SW	SW	SW	SW ■	SW	SW ■	SW
London Waterloo 15 ⊖	d	12 20			12 22	12 28			12 33	12 37	12 45	12 50			12 52	12 58			13 03	13 07	13 15	13 20			13 22
Vauxhall ⊖	d				12 26	12 32			12 37	12 41	12 49				12 56	13 02			13 07	13 11	13 19				13 26
Queenstown Rd.(Battersea)	d				12 29				12 40	12 44	12 52				12 59				13 10	13 14	13 22				13 29
Clapham Junction 10	d	12 28			12 32	12 38			12 43	12 47	12 55	12 58			13 02	13 08			13 13	13 17	13 25	13 28			13 32
Wandsworth Town	d				12 35				12 46	12 50	12 58				13 05				13 16	13 20	13 28				13 35
Putney	d				12 38	12 42			12 49	12 53	13 01				13 08	13 12			13 19	13 23	13 31				13 38
Barnes	d				12 42				12 52	12 57	13 05				13 12				13 22	13 27	13 35				13 42
Barnes Bridge	d				12 44					12 59					13 14					13 29					13 44
Chiswick	d				12 47					13 02					13 17					13 32					13 47
Kew Bridge	d				12 50					13 05					13 20					13 35					13 50
Brentford	d				12 53					13 08					13 23					13 38					13 53
Syon Lane	d				12 55					13 10					13 25					13 40					13 55
Isleworth	d				12 57					13 12					13 27					13 42					13 57
Hounslow	d				13 01					13 18					13 31					13 48					14 01
Mortlake	d								12 54		13 07								13 24		13 37				
North Sheen	d		←						12 56		13 09		←						13 26		13 39		←		
Richmond ⊖	d	12 36	12 42			12 48			12 59		13 12	13 06	13 12			13 18			13 29		13 42	13 36	13 42		
St Margarets	d		12 44						13 01		→		13 14						13 31		→		13 44		
Twickenham	a	12 40	12 46			12 51			13 03			13 10	13 16			13 21			13 33			13 40	13 46		
	d	12 40	12 47			12 52			13 04			13 10	13 17			13 22			13 34			13 40	13 47		
Strawberry Hill	d								13 07										13 37						
Fulwell	a																								
Teddington	a								13 10										13 40						
Hampton Wick	a								13 14										13 44						
Kingston	a								13 16										13 46						
Whitton	d		12a50			12 55		←		13a23			13a20			13 25		←		13a53			13a50		
Feltham	d	12 46			13 06	12 59		13 06				13 16			13 36	13 29		13 36				13 46			14 06
Ashford (Surrey)	d				→	13 03		13 10							→	13 33		13 40							→
Staines	d	12 53				13 07		13 14				13 23				13 37		13 44				13 53			
Wraysbury	d					13 12										13 42									
Sunnymeads	d					13 15										13 45									
Datchet	d					13 19										13 49									
Windsor & Eton Riverside	a					13 24										13 54									
Egham	d	12 57						13 19				13 27						13 49				13 57			
Virginia Water	a	13 01						13 23				13 31						13 53				14 01			
	d	13 01						13 23				13 31						13 53				14 01			
Chertsey	d							13 29										13 59							
Addlestone	d							13 32										14 02							
Weybridge	a							13 37										14 07							
Longcross	d																								
Sunningdale	d	13 07										13 37										14 07			
Ascot ■	d	13 13		13 23								13 43		13 53								14 13		14 23	
Bagshot	d			13 29										13 59										14 29	
Camberley	a			13 35										14 05										14 35	
Frimley	d			13 43										14 13										14 43	
Ash Vale	d			13 49										14 19										14 49	
Aldershot	a			13 54										14 24										14 54	
	d			14 08										14 38										15 08	
Ash ■	d			14 15										14 45										15 15	
Wanborough	d			14 18										14 48										15 18	
Guildford	a			14 25										14 55										15 25	
Martins Heron	d	13 17										13 47										14 17			
Bracknell	d	13 20										13 50										14 20			
Wokingham	d	13 27										13 57										14 27			
Winnersh	d	13 30										14 00										14 30			
Winnersh Triangle	d	13 32										14 02										14 32			
Earley	d	13 37										14 07										14 37			
Reading ■	a	13 43										14 13										14 43			

The xx15 and xx45 services from London Waterloo to Whitton continue to London Waterloo via Brentford

The xx03 and xx33 London Waterloo to Kingston services continue to London Waterloo via Wimbledon

The xx07 and xx37 services from London Waterloo to Whitton continue to London Waterloo via Richmond

For additional services between Wokingham and Reading refer to Table T148

Table T149-F

Saturdays

13 October to 8 December

London - Hounslow, Richmond, Kingston, Windsor, Weybridge, Ascot, Guildford and Reading

		SW		SW	SW	SW	SW	SW ■	SW	SW ■	SW	SW		SW	SW	SW	SW	SW ■	SW	SW ■	SW	SW		SW	SW
London Waterloo ■ ⊖	d	13 28			13 33	13 37	13 45	13 50			13 52	13 58			14 03	14 07	14 15	14 20			14 22	14 28			14 33
Vauxhall ⊖	d	13 32			13 37	13 41	13 49				13 56	14 02			14 07	14 11	14 19				14 26	14 32			14 37
Queenstown Rd.(Battersea)	d				13 40	13 44	13 52				13 59				14 10	14 14	14 22				14 29				14 40
Clapham Junction ■	d	13 38			13 43	13 47	13 55	13 58			14 02	14 08			14 13	14 17	14 25	14 28			14 32	14 38			14 43
Wandsworth Town	d				13 46	13 50	13 58				14 05				14 16	14 20	14 28				14 35				14 46
Putney	d	13 42			13 49	13 53	14 01				14 08	14 12			14 19	14 23	14 31				14 38	14 42			14 49
Barnes	d				13 52	13 57	14 05				14 12				14 22	14 27	14 35				14 42				14 52
Barnes Bridge	d					13 59					14 14					14 29					14 44				
Chiswick	d					14 02					14 17					14 32					14 47				
Kew Bridge	d					14 05					14 20					14 35					14 50				
Brentford	d					14 08					14 23					14 38					14 53				
Syon Lane	d					14 10					14 25					14 40					14 55				
Isleworth	d					14 12					14 27					14 42					14 57				
Hounslow	d					14 18					14 31					14 48					15 01				
Mortlake	d				13 54		14 07								14 24		14 37								14 54
North Sheen	d				13 56		14 09		←						14 26		14 39		←						14 56
Richmond ⊖	d	13 48			13 59		14 12	14 06	14 12			14 18			14 29		14 42	14 36	14 42			14 48			14 59
St Margarets	d				14 01		→		14 14						14 31		→		14 44						15 01
Twickenham	a	13 51			14 03			14 10	14 16			14 21			14 33			14 40	14 46			14 51			15 03
	d	13 52			14 04			14 10	14 17			14 22			14 34			14 40	14 47			14 52			15 04
Strawberry Hill	d				14 07										14 37										15 07
Fulwell	a																								
Teddington	a				14 10										14 40										15 10
Hampton Wick	a				14 14										14 44										15 14
Kingston	a				14 16										14 46										15 16
Whitton	d	13 55		←		14a23			14a20			14 25		←		14a53			14a50			14 55		←	
Feltham	d	13 59		14 06				14 16			14 36	14 29		14 36				14 46			15 06	14 59		15 06	
Ashford (Surrey)	d	14 03		14 10							→	14 33		14 40							→	15 03		15 10	
Staines	d	14 07		14 14				14 23				14 37		14 44				14 53				15 07		15 14	
Wraysbury	d	14 12										14 42										15 12			
Sunnymeads	d	14 15										14 45										15 15			
Datchet	d	14 19										14 49										15 19			
Windsor & Eton Riverside	a	14 24										14 54										15 24			
Egham	d			14 19				14 27						14 49				14 57						15 19	
Virginia Water	a			14 23				14 31						14 53				15 01						15 23	
	d			14 23				14 31						14 53				15 01						15 23	
Chertsey	d			14 29										14 59										15 29	
Addlestone	d			14 32										15 02										15 32	
Weybridge	a			14 37										15 07										15 37	
Longcross	d																								
Sunningdale	d							14 37										15 07							
Ascot ■	d							14 43		14 53								15 13		15 23					
Bagshot	d									14 59										15 29					
Camberley	a									15 05										15 35					
Frimley	d									15 13										15 43					
Ash Vale	d									15 19										15 49					
Aldershot	a									15 24										15 54					
	d									15 38										16 08					
Ash ■	d									15 45										16 15					
Wanborough	d									15 48										16 18					
Guildford	a									15 55										16 25					
Martins Heron	d							14 47										15 17							
Bracknell	d							14 50										15 20							
Wokingham	d							14 57										15 27							
Winnersh	d							15 00										15 30							
Winnersh Triangle	d							15 02										15 32							
Earley	d							15 07										15 37							
Reading ■	a							15 13										15 43							

The xx15 and xx45 services from London Waterloo to Whitton continue to London Waterloo via Brentford

The xx03 and xx33 London Waterloo to Kingston services continue to London Waterloo via Wimbledon

The xx07 and xx37 services from London Waterloo to Whitton continue to London Waterloo via Richmond

For additional services between Wokingham and Reading refer to Table T148

Table T149-F

Saturdays

13 October to 8 December

London - Hounslow, Richmond, Kingston, Windsor, Weybridge, Ascot, Guildford and Reading

		SW	SW	SW ■	SW	SW ■	SW	SW		SW	SW	SW	SW	SW ■	SW	SW ■	SW	SW		SW	SW	SW	SW	SW ■	SW
London Waterloo ■ ⊖	d	14 37	14 45	14 50			14 52	14 58			15 03	15 07	15 15	15 20			15 22	15 28			15 33	15 37	15 45	15 50	
Vauxhall ⊖	d	14 41	14 49				14 56	15 02			15 07	15 11	15 19				15 26	15 32			15 37	15 41	15 49		
Queenstown Rd.(Battersea)	d	14 44	14 52				14 59				15 10	15 14	15 22				15 29				15 40	15 44	15 52		
Clapham Junction ■	d	14 47	14 55	14 58			15 02	15 08			15 13	15 17	15 25	15 28			15 32	15 38			15 43	15 47	15 55	15 58	
Wandsworth Town	d	14 50	14 58				15 05				15 16	15 20	15 28				15 35				15 46	15 50	15 58		
Putney	d	14 53	15 01				15 08	15 12			15 19	15 23	15 31				15 38	15 42			15 49	15 53	16 01		
Barnes	d	14 57	15 05				15 12				15 22	15 27	15 35				15 42				15 52	15 57	16 05		
Barnes Bridge	d	14 59					15 14					15 29					15 44					15 59			
Chiswick	d	15 02					15 17					15 32					15 47					16 02			
Kew Bridge	d	15 05					15 20					15 35					15 50					16 05			
Brentford	d	15 08					15 23					15 38					15 53					16 08			
Syon Lane	d	15 10					15 25					15 40					15 55					16 10			
Isleworth	d	15 12					15 27					15 42					15 57					16 12			
Hounslow	d	15 18					15 31					15 48					16 01					16 18			
Mortlake	d		15 07								15 24		15 37								15 54		16 07		
North Sheen	d		15 09		←						15 26		15 39		←						15 56		16 09		←
Richmond ⊖	d		15 12	15 06	15 12			15 18			15 29		15 42	15 36	15 42			15 48			15 59		16 12	16 06	16 12
St Margarets	d		→		15 14						15 31		→		15 44						16 01		→		16 14
Twickenham	a			15 10	15 16			15 21			15 33			15 40	15 46			15 51			16 03			16 10	16 16
	d			15 10	15 17			15 22			15 34			15 40	15 47			15 52			16 04			16 10	16 17
Strawberry Hill	d										15 37										16 07				
Fulwell	a																								
Teddington	a										15 40										16 10				
Hampton Wick	a										15 44										16 14				
Kingston	a										15 46										16 16				
Whitton	d	15a23			15a20			15 25		←		15a53			15a50			15 55		←		16a23			16a20
Feltham	d			15 16			15 36	15 29		15 36				15 46			16 06	15 59		16 06				16 16	
Ashford (Surrey)	d						→	15 33		15 40							→	16 03		16 10					
Staines	d			15 23				15 37		15 44				15 53				16 07		16 14				16 23	
Wraysbury	d							15 42										16 12							
Sunnymeads	d							15 45										16 15							
Datchet	d							15 49										16 19							
Windsor & Eton Riverside	a							15 54										16 24							
Egham	d			15 27						15 49				15 57						16 19				16 27	
Virginia Water	a			15 31						15 53				16 01						16 23				16 31	
	d			15 31						15 53				16 01						16 23				16 31	
Chertsey	d									15 59										16 29					
Addlestone	d									16 02										16 32					
Weybridge	a									16 07										16 37					
Longcross	d																								
Sunningdale	d			15 37										16 07										16 37	
Ascot ■	d			15 43		15 53								16 13		16 23								16 43	
Bagshot	d					15 59										16 29									
Camberley	a					16 05										16 35									
Frimley	d					16 13										16 43									
Ash Vale	d					16 19										16 49									
Aldershot	a					16 24										16 54									
	d					16 38										17 08									
Ash ■	d					16 45										17 15									
Wanborough	d					16 48										17 18									
Guildford	a					16 55										17 25									
Martins Heron	d			15 47										16 17										16 47	
Bracknell	d			15 50										16 20										16 50	
Wokingham	d			15 57										16 27										16 57	
Winnersh	d			16 00										16 30										17 00	
Winnersh Triangle	d			16 02										16 32										17 02	
Earley	d			16 07										16 37										17 07	
Reading ■	a			16 13										16 43										17 13	

The xx15 and xx45 services from London Waterloo to Whitton continue to London Waterloo via Brentford

The xx03 and xx33 London Waterloo to Kingston services continue to London Waterloo via Wimbledon

The xx07 and xx37 services from London Waterloo to Whitton continue to London Waterloo via Richmond

For additional services between Wokingham and Reading refer to Table T148

Table T149-F

Saturdays
13 October to 8 December

London - Hounslow, Richmond, Kingston, Windsor, Weybridge, Ascot, Guildford and Reading

		SW ■	SW	SW	SW	SW	SW	SW	SW ■	SW	SW ■	SW	SW	SW	SW	SW	SW	SW ■	SW	SW ■	SW	SW
London Waterloo ■ ⊖	d		15 52	15 58		16 03	16 07	16 15	16 20			16 22	16 28		16 33	16 37	16 45	16 50			16 52	16 58
Vauxhall ⊖	d		15 56	16 02		16 07	16 11	16 19				16 26	16 32		16 37	16 41	16 49				16 56	17 02
Queenstown Rd.(Battersea)	d		15 59			16 10	16 14	16 22				16 29			16 40	16 44	16 52				16 59	
Clapham Junction ■	d		16 02	16 08		16 13	16 17	16 25	16 28			16 32	16 38		16 43	16 47	16 55	16 58			17 02	17 08
Wandsworth Town	d		16 05			16 16	16 20	16 28				16 35			16 46	16 50	16 58				17 05	
Putney	d		16 08	16 12		16 19	16 23	16 31				16 38	16 42		16 49	16 53	17 01				17 08	17 12
Barnes	d		16 12			16 22	16 27	16 35				16 42			16 52	16 57	17 05				17 12	
Barnes Bridge	d		16 14				16 29					16 44				16 59					17 14	
Chiswick	d		16 17				16 32					16 47				17 02					17 17	
Kew Bridge	d		16 20				16 35					16 50				17 05					17 20	
Brentford	d		16 23				16 38					16 53				17 08					17 23	
Syon Lane	d		16 25				16 40					16 55				17 10					17 25	
Isleworth	d		16 27				16 42					16 57				17 12					17 27	
Hounslow	d		16 31				16 48					17 01				17 18					17 31	
Mortlake	d					16 24		16 37							16 54		17 07					
North Sheen	d					16 26		16 39		←					16 56		17 09		←			
Richmond ⊖	d			16 18		16 29		16 42	16 36	16 42			16 48		16 59		17 12	17 06	17 12			17 18
St Margarets	d					16 31		→		16 44					17 01		→		17 14			
Twickenham	a			16 21		16 33			16 40	16 46			16 51		17 03			17 10	17 16			17 21
	d			16 22		16 34			16 40	16 47			16 52		17 04			17 10	17 17			17 22
Strawberry Hill	d					16 37									17 07							
Fulwell	a																					
Teddington	a					16 40									17 10							
Hampton Wick	a					16 44									17 14							
Kingston	a					16 46									17 16							
Whitton	d			16 25	←		16a53			16a50			16 55	←		17a23			17a20			17 25
Feltham	d		16 36	16 29	16 36				16 46			17 06	16 59	17 06				17 16			17 36	17 29
Ashford (Surrey)	d		→	16 33	16 40							→	17 03	17 10							→	17 33
Staines	d			16 37	16 44				16 53				17 07	17 14				17 23				17 37
Wraysbury	d			16 42									17 12									17 42
Sunnymeads	d			16 45									17 15									17 45
Datchet	d			16 49									17 19									17 49
Windsor & Eton Riverside	a			16 54									17 24									17 54
Egham	d				16 49				16 57					17 19				17 27				
Virginia Water	a				16 53				17 01					17 23				17 31				
	d				16 53				17 01					17 23				17 31				
Chertsey	d				16 59									17 29								
Addlestone	d				17 02									17 32								
Weybridge	a				17 07									17 37								
Longcross	d																					
Sunningdale	d								17 07									17 37				
Ascot ■	d	16 53							17 13		17 23							17 43		17 53		
Bagshot	d	16 59									17 29									17 59		
Camberley	a	17 05									17 35									18 05		
Frimley	d	17 13									17 43									18 13		
Ash Vale	d	17 19									17 49									18 19		
Aldershot	a	17 24									17 54									18 24		
	d	17 38									18 08									18 38		
Ash ■	d	17 45									18 15									18 45		
Wanborough	d	17 48									18 18									18 48		
Guildford	a	17 55									18 25									18 55		
Martins Heron	d								17 17									17 47				
Bracknell	d								17 20									17 50				
Wokingham	d								17 27									17 57				
Winnersh	d								17 30									18 00				
Winnersh Triangle	d								17 32									18 02				
Earley	d								17 37									18 07				
Reading ■	a								17 43									18 13				

The xx15 and xx45 services from London Waterloo to Whitton continue to London Waterloo via Brentford

The xx03 and xx33 London Waterloo to Kingston services continue to London Waterloo via Wimbledon

The xx07 and xx37 services from London Waterloo to Whitton continue to London Waterloo via Richmond

For additional services between Wokingham and Reading refer to Table T148

Table T149-F

Saturdays
13 October to 8 December

London - Hounslow, Richmond, Kingston, Windsor, Weybridge, Ascot, Guildford and Reading

		SW	SW	SW	SW	SW ■	SW	SW ■	SW	SW	SW	SW	SW	SW	SW ■	SW	SW ■	SW	SW	SW	SW	SW	SW
London Waterloo ■ ⊖	d		17 03	17 07	17 15	17 20			17 22	17 28		17 33	17 37	17 45	17 50			17 52	17 58		18 03	18 07	18 15
Vauxhall ⊖	d		17 07	17 11	17 19				17 26	17 32		17 37	17 41	17 49				17 56	18 02		18 07	18 11	18 19
Queenstown Rd.(Battersea)	d		17 10	17 14	17 22				17 29			17 40	17 44	17 52				17 59			18 10	18 14	18 22
Clapham Junction ■	d		17 13	17 17	17 25	17 28			17 32	17 38		17 43	17 47	17 55	17 58			18 02	18 08		18 13	18 17	18 25
Wandsworth Town	d		17 16	17 20	17 28				17 35			17 46	17 50	17 58				18 05			18 16	18 20	18 28
Putney	d		17 19	17 23	17 31				17 38	17 42		17 49	17 53	18 01				18 08	18 12		18 19	18 23	18 31
Barnes	d		17 22	17 27	17 35				17 42			17 52	17 57	18 05				18 12			18 22	18 27	18 35
Barnes Bridge	d			17 29					17 44				17 59					18 14				18 29	
Chiswick	d			17 32					17 47				18 02					18 17				18 32	
Kew Bridge	d			17 35					17 50				18 05					18 20				18 35	
Brentford	d			17 38					17 53				18 08					18 23				18 38	
Syon Lane	d			17 40					17 55				18 10					18 25				18 40	
Isleworth	d			17 42					17 57				18 12					18 27				18 42	
Hounslow	d			17 48					18 01				18 18					18 31				18 48	
Mortlake	d		17 24		17 37							17 54		18 07							18 24		18 37
North Sheen	d		17 26		17 39		←					17 56		18 09		←					18 26		18 39
Richmond ⊖	d		17 29		17 42	17 36	17 42			17 48		17 59		18 12	18 06	18 12			18 18		18 29		18 42
St Margarets	d		17 31		→		17 44					18 01		→		18 14					18 31		→
Twickenham	a		17 33			17 40	17 46			17 51		18 03			18 10	18 16			18 21		18 33		
	d		17 34			17 40	17 47			17 52		18 04			18 10	18 17			18 22		18 34		
Strawberry Hill	d		17 37									18 07									18 37		
Fulwell	a																						
Teddington	a		17 40									18 10									18 40		
Hampton Wick	a		17 44									18 14									18 44		
Kingston	a		17 46									18 16									18 46		
Whitton	d	←		17a53			17a50			17 55	←		18a23			18a20			18 25	←		18a53	
Feltham	d	17 36				17 46			18 06	17 59	18 06				18 16			18 36	18 29	18 36			
Ashford (Surrey)	d	17 40							→	18 03	18 10							→	18 33	18 40			
Staines	d	17 44				17 53				18 07	18 14				18 23				18 37	18 44			
Wraysbury	d									18 12									18 42				
Sunnymeads	d									18 15									18 45				
Datchet	d									18 19									18 49				
Windsor & Eton Riverside	a									18 24									18 54				
Egham	d	17 49				17 57					18 19				18 27					18 49			
Virginia Water	a	17 53				18 01					18 23				18 31					18 53			
	d	17 53				18 01					18 23				18 31					18 53			
Chertsey	d	17 59									18 29									18 59			
Addlestone	d	18 02									18 32									19 02			
Weybridge	a	18 07									18 37									19 07			
Longcross	d																						
Sunningdale	d					18 07									18 37								
Ascot ■	d					18 13		18 23							18 43		18 53						
Bagshot	d							18 29									18 59						
Camberley	a							18 35									19 05						
Frimley	d							18 43									19 13						
Ash Vale	d							18 49									19 19						
Aldershot	a							18 54									19 24						
	d							19 08									19 38						
Ash ■	d							19 15									19 45						
Wanborough	d							19 18									19 48						
Guildford	a							19 25									19 55						
Martins Heron	d					18 17									18 47								
Bracknell	d					18 20									18 50								
Wokingham	d					18 27									18 57								
Winnersh	d					18 30									19 00								
Winnersh Triangle	d					18 32									19 02								
Earley	d					18 37									19 07								
Reading ■	a					18 43									19 13								

The xx15 and xx45 services from London Waterloo to Whitton continue to London Waterloo via Brentford

The xx03 and xx33 London Waterloo to Kingston services continue to London Waterloo via Wimbledon

The xx07 and xx37 services from London Waterloo to Whitton continue to London Waterloo via Richmond

For additional services between Wokingham and Reading refer to Table T148

Table T149-F

Saturdays
13 October to 8 December

London - Hounslow, Richmond, Kingston, Windsor, Weybridge, Ascot, Guildford and Reading

Station		SW ■	SW	SW ■	SW	SW	SW	SW	SW	SW	SW ■	SW	SW ■	SW	SW	SW	SW	SW	SW	SW ■	SW	SW ■	SW
London Waterloo ⊖	d	18 20			18 22	18 28		18 33	18 37	18 45	18 50			18 52	18 58		19 03	19 07	19 15	19 20			19 22
Vauxhall ⊖	d				18 26	18 32		18 37	18 41	18 49				18 56	19 02		19 07	19 11	19 19				19 26
Queenstown Rd.(Battersea)	d				18 29			18 40	18 44	18 52				18 59			19 10	19 14	19 22				19 29
Clapham Junction	d	18 28			18 32	18 38		18 43	18 47	18 55	18 58			19 02	19 08		19 13	19 17	19 25	19 28			19 32
Wandsworth Town	d				18 35			18 46	18 50	18 58				19 05			19 16	19 20	19 28				19 35
Putney	d				18 38	18 42		18 49	18 53	19 01				19 08	19 12		19 19	19 23	19 31				19 38
Barnes	d				18 42			18 52	18 57	19 05				19 12			19 22	19 27	19 35				19 42
Barnes Bridge	d				18 44				18 59					19 14				19 29					19 44
Chiswick	d				18 47				19 02					19 17				19 32					19 47
Kew Bridge	d				18 50				19 05					19 20				19 35					19 50
Brentford	d				18 53				19 08					19 23				19 38					19 53
Syon Lane	d				18 55				19 10					19 25				19 40					19 55
Isleworth	d				18 57				19 12					19 27				19 42					19 57
Hounslow	d				19 01				19 18					19 31				19 48					20 01
Mortlake	d							18 54		19 07							19 24		19 37				
North Sheen	d		←					18 56		19 09		←					19 26		19 39		←		
Richmond ⊖	d	18 36	18 42			18 48		18 59		19 12	19 06	19 12			19 18		19 29		19 42	19 36	19 42		
St Margarets	d		18 44					19 01		→		19 14					19 31		→		19 44		
Twickenham	a	18 40	18 46			18 51		19 03			19 10	19 16			19 21		19 33			19 40	19 46		
	d	18 40	18 47			18 52		19 04			19 10	19 17			19 22		19 34			19 40	19 47		
Strawberry Hill	d							19 07									19 37						
Fulwell	a																						
Teddington	a							19 10									19 40						
Hampton Wick	a							19 14									19 44						
Kingston	a							19 16									19 46						
Whitton	d		18a50			18 55	←		19a23			19a20			19 25	←		19a53			19a50		
Feltham	d	18 46			19 06	18 59	19 06				19 16			19 36	19 29	19 36				19 46			20 06
Ashford (Surrey)	d				→	19 03	19 10							→	19 33	19 40							→
Staines	d	18 53				19 07	19 14				19 23				19 37	19 44				19 53			
Wraysbury	d					19 12									19 42								
Sunnymeads	d					19 15									19 45								
Datchet	d					19 19									19 49								
Windsor & Eton Riverside	a					19 24									19 54								
Egham	d	18 57					19 19				19 27					19 49				19 57			
Virginia Water	a	19 01					19 23				19 31					19 53				20 01			
	d	19 01					19 23				19 31					19 53				20 01			
Chertsey	d						19 29									19 59							
Addlestone	d						19 32									20 02							
Weybridge	a						19 37									20 07							
Longcross	d																						
Sunningdale	d	19 07									19 37									20 07			
Ascot ■	d	19 13		19 23							19 43		19 53							20 13		20 23	
Bagshot	d			19 29									19 59									20 29	
Camberley	a			19 35									20 05									20 35	
Frimley	d			19 43									20 13									20 43	
Ash Vale	d			19 49									20 19									20 49	
Aldershot	a			19 54									20 24									20 54	
	d			20 08									20 38									21 08	
Ash ■	d			20 15									20 45									21 15	
Wanborough	d			20 18									20 48									21 18	
Guildford	a			20 25									20 55									21 25	
Martins Heron	d	19 17									19 47									20 17			
Bracknell	d	19 20									19 50									20 20			
Wokingham	d	19 27									19 57									20 27			
Winnersh	d	19 30									20 00									20 30			
Winnersh Triangle	d	19 32									20 02									20 32			
Earley	d	19 37									20 07									20 37			
Reading ■	a	19 43									20 13									20 43			

The xx15 and xx45 services from London Waterloo to Whitton continue to London Waterloo via Brentford

The xx03 and xx33 London Waterloo to Kingston services continue to London Waterloo via Wimbledon

The xx07 and xx37 services from London Waterloo to Whitton continue to London Waterloo via Richmond

For additional services between Wokingham and Reading refer to Table T148

Table T149-F

Saturdays
13 October to 8 December

London - Hounslow, Richmond, Kingston, Windsor, Weybridge, Ascot, Guildford and Reading

Station		SW	SW	SW	SW	SW	SW ■	SW	SW ■	SW	SW	SW	SW	SW	SW	SW ■	SW	SW ■	SW ■	SW	SW	SW
London Waterloo ⊖	d	19 28		19 33	19 37	19 45	19 50			19 52	19 58		20 03	20 07	20 15	20 20				20 22	20 28	
Vauxhall ⊖	d	19 32		19 37	19 41	19 49				19 56	20 02		20 07	20 11	20 19					20 26	20 32	
Queenstown Rd.(Battersea)	d			19 40	19 44	19 52				19 59			20 10	20 14	20 22					20 29		
Clapham Junction	d	19 38		19 43	19 47	19 55	19 58			20 02	20 08		20 13	20 17	20 26	20 28				20 32	20 38	
Wandsworth Town	d			19 46	19 50	19 58				20 05			20 16	20 20	20 29					20 35		
Putney	d	19 42		19 49	19 53	20 01				20 08	20 12		20 19	20 23	20 32					20 38	20 42	
Barnes	d			19 52	19 57	20 05				20 12			20 22	20 27	20 35					20 42		
Barnes Bridge	d				19 59					20 14				20 29						20 44		
Chiswick	d				20 02					20 17				20 32						20 47		
Kew Bridge	d				20 05					20 20				20 35						20 50		
Brentford	d				20 08					20 23				20 38						20 53		
Syon Lane	d				20 10					20 25				20 40						20 55		
Isleworth	d				20 12					20 27				20 42						20 57		
Hounslow	d				20 18					20 31				20 48						21 01		
Mortlake	d			19 54		20 07							20 24		20 37							
North Sheen	d			19 56		20 09		←					20 26		20 39		←					
Richmond ⊖	d	19 48		19 59		20 12	20 06	20 12			20 18		20 29		20 42	20 36	20 42				20 48	
St Margarets	d			20 01		→		20 14					20 31		→		20 44					
Twickenham	a	19 51		20 03			20 10	20 16			20 21		20 33			20 40	20 46				20 51	
	d	19 52		20 04			20 10	20 17			20 22		20 34			20 40	20 47				20 52	
Strawberry Hill	d			20 07									20 37									
Fulwell	a																					
Teddington	a			20 10									20 40									
Hampton Wick	a			20 14									20 44									
Kingston	a			20 16									20 46									
Whitton	d	19 55	←		20a23			20a20			20 25	←		20a53			20a50				20 55	←
Feltham	d	19 59	20 06				20 16			20 36	20 29	20 36				20 46				21 06	20 59	21 06
Ashford (Surrey)	d	20 03	20 10							→	20 33	20 40								→	21 03	21 10
Staines	d	20 07	20 14				20 23				20 37	20 44				20 53					21 07	21 14
Wraysbury	d	20 12									20 42										21 12	
Sunnymeads	d	20 15									20 45										21 15	
Datchet	d	20 19									20 49										21 19	
Windsor & Eton Riverside	a	20 24									20 54										21 24	
Egham	d		20 19				20 27					20 49				20 57						21 19
Virginia Water	a		20 23				20 31					20 53				21 01						21 23
	d		20 23				20 31					20 53				21 01						21 23
Chertsey	d		20 29									20 59										21 29
Addlestone	d		20 32									21 02										21 32
Weybridge	a		20 37									21 07										21 37
Longcross	d																					
Sunningdale	d						20 37									21 07						
Ascot ■	d						20 43		20 53							21 13		21 23				
Bagshot	d								20 59									21 29				
Camberley	a								21 05									21 35				
Frimley	d								21 13									21 43				
Ash Vale	d								21 19									21 49				
Aldershot	a								21 24									21 54				
	d								21 38									22 08	22 38			
Ash ■	d								21 45									22 15	22 45			
Wanborough	d								21 48									22 18	22 48			
Guildford	a								21 55									22 25	22 55			
Martins Heron	d						20 47									21 17						
Bracknell	d						20 50									21 20						
Wokingham	d						20 57									21 27						
Winnersh	d						21 00									21 30						
Winnersh Triangle	d						21 02									21 32						
Earley	d						21 07									21 37						
Reading ■	a						21 13									21 43						

The xx15 and xx45 services from London Waterloo to Whitton continue to London Waterloo via Brentford

The xx03 and xx33 London Waterloo to Kingston services continue to London Waterloo via Wimbledon

The xx07 and xx37 services from London Waterloo to Whitton continue to London Waterloo via Richmond

For additional services between Wokingham and Reading refer to Table T148

Table T149-F

Saturdays
13 October to 8 December

London - Hounslow, Richmond, Kingston, Windsor, Weybridge, Ascot, Guildford and Reading

Station		SW	SW	SW	SW 1	SW	SW	SW		SW	SW	SW	SW	SW 1	SW	SW 1	SW	SW		SW	SW	SW	SW	SW 1	SW
London Waterloo 15 ⊖	d	20 33	20 37	20 45	20 50		20 52	20 58			21 03	21 07	21 15	21 20			21 22	21 28			21 33	21 37	21 45	21 50	
Vauxhall ⊖	d	20 37	20 41	20 49			20 56	21 02			21 07	21 11	21 19				21 26	21 32			21 37	21 41	21 49		
Queenstown Rd.(Battersea)	d	20 40	20 44	20 52			20 59				21 10	21 14	21 22				21 29				21 40	21 44	21 52		
Clapham Junction 10	d	20 43	20 47	20 55	20 58		21 02	21 08			21 13	21 17	21 25	21 28			21 32	21 38			21 43	21 47	21 55	21 58	
Wandsworth Town	d	20 46	20 50	20 58			21 05				21 16	21 20	21 28				21 35				21 46	21 50	21 58		
Putney	d	20 49	20 53	21 01			21 08	21 12			21 19	21 23	21 31				21 38	21 42			21 49	21 53	22 01		
Barnes	d	20 52	20 57	21 05			21 12				21 22	21 27	21 35				21 42				21 52	21 57	22 05		
Barnes Bridge	d		20 59				21 14					21 29					21 44					21 59			
Chiswick	d		21 02				21 17					21 32					21 47					22 02			
Kew Bridge	d		21 05				21 20					21 35					21 50					22 05			
Brentford	d		21 08				21 23					21 38					21 53					22 08			
Syon Lane	d		21 10				21 25					21 40					21 55					22 10			
Isleworth	d		21 12				21 27					21 42					21 57					22 12			
Hounslow	d		21 18				21 31					21 48					22 01					22 18			
Mortlake	d	20 54		21 07							21 24		21 37								21 54		22 07		
North Sheen	d	20 56		21 09		←					21 26		21 39		←						21 56		22 09		←
Richmond ⊖	d	20 59		21 12	21 06	21 12		21 18			21 29		21 42	21 36	21 42			21 48			21 59		22 12	22 06	22 12
St Margarets	d	21 01		→		21 14					21 31		→		21 44						22 01		→		22 14
Twickenham	a	21 03			21 10	21 16		21 21			21 33			21 40	21 46			21 51			22 03			22 10	22 16
	d	21 04			21 10	21 17		21 22			21 34			21 40	21 47			21 52			22 04			22 10	
Strawberry Hill	d	21 07									21 37										22 07				
Fulwell	a																								
Teddington	a	21 10									21 40										22 10				
Hampton Wick	a	21 14									21 44										22 14				
Kingston	a	21 16									21 46										22 16				
Whitton	d		21a23			21a20		21 25		←		21a53			21a50			21 55		←		22a23			
Feltham	d				21 16		21 36	21 29		21 36				21 46			22 06	21 59		22 06				22 16	
Ashford (Surrey)	d						→	21 33		21 40							→	22 03		22 10					
Staines	d				21 23			21 37		21 44				21 53				22 07		22 14				22 23	
Wraysbury	d							21 42										22 12							
Sunnymeads	d							21 45										22 15							
Datchet	d							21 49										22 19							
Windsor & Eton Riverside	a							21 54										22 24							
Egham	d				21 27					21 49				21 57						22 19				22 27	
Virginia Water	a				21 31					21 53				22 01						22 23				22 31	
	d				21 31					21 53				22 01						22 23				22 31	
Chertsey	d									21 59										22 29					
Addlestone	d									22 02										22 32					
Weybridge	a									22 07										22 37					
Longcross	d																								
Sunningdale	d				21 37									22 07										22 37	
Ascot 8	d				21 43									22 13		22 23								22 43	
Bagshot	d															22 29									
Camberley	a															22 35									
Frimley	d															22 43									
Ash Vale	d															22 49									
Aldershot	a															22 54									
	d															23 08									
Ash 6	d															23 15									
Wanborough	d															23 18									
Guildford	a															23 25									
Martins Heron	d				21 47									22 17										22 47	
Bracknell	d				21 50									22 20										22 50	
Wokingham	d				21 57									22 27										22 57	
Winnersh	d				22 00									22 30										23 00	
Winnersh Triangle	d				22 02									22 32										23 02	
Earley	d				22 07									22 35										23 07	
Reading 7	a				22 13									22 41										23 13	

The xx15 and xx45 services from London Waterloo to Whitton continue to London Waterloo via Brentford

The xx03 and xx33 London Waterloo to Kingston services continue to London Waterloo via Wimbledon

The xx07 and xx37 services from London Waterloo to Whitton continue to London Waterloo via Richmond

For additional services between Wokingham and Reading refer to Table T148

Table T149-F

Saturdays
13 October to 8 December

London - Hounslow, Richmond, Kingston, Windsor, Weybridge, Ascot, Guildford and Reading

Station		SW	SW	SW		SW	SW 1	SW 1	SW	SW	SW	SW	SW 1	SW		SW	SW	SW	SW 1	SW	SW	SW	SW	SW	
London Waterloo 15 ⊖	d	21 52	21 58			22 03	22 20		22 22	22 28		22 33	22 50	22 52		22 58		23 03	23 20	23 22	23 28		23 33	23 50	
Vauxhall ⊖	d	21 56	22 02			22 07			22 26	22 32		22 37		22 56		23 02		23 07		23 26	23 32		23 37		
Queenstown Rd.(Battersea)	d	21 59				22 10			22 29			22 40		22 59				23 10		23 29			23 40		
Clapham Junction 10	d	22 02	22 08			22 13	22 28		22 32	22 38		22 43	22 58	23 02		23 08		23 13	23 28	23 32	23 38		23 43	23 58	
Wandsworth Town	d	22 05				22 16			22 35			22 46		23 05				23 16		23 35			23 46		
Putney	d	22 08	22 12			22 19			22 38	22 42		22 49		23 08		23 12		23 19		23 38	23 42		23 49		
Barnes	d	22 12				22 22			22 42			22 52		23 12				23 22		23 42			23 52		
Barnes Bridge	d	22 14							22 44					23 14						23 44					
Chiswick	d	22 17							22 47					23 17						23 47					
Kew Bridge	d	22 20							22 50					23 20						23 50					
Brentford	d	22 23							22 53					23 23						23 53					
Syon Lane	d	22 25							22 55					23 25						23 55					
Isleworth	d	22 27							22 57					23 27						23 57					
Hounslow	d	22 31							23 01					23 31						00 01					
Mortlake	d					22 24						22 54						23 24					23 54		
North Sheen	d					22 26						22 56						23 26					23 56		
Richmond ⊖	d		22 18			22 29	22 36			22 48		22 59	23 06			23 18		23 29	23 36		23 48		23 59	00 06	
St Margarets	d					22 31						23 01						23 31					00 01		
Twickenham	a		22 21			22 33	22 40			22 51		23 03	23 10			23 21		23 33	23 40		23 51		00 03	00 10	
	d		22 22			22 34	22 40			22 52		23 04	23 10			23 22		23 34	23 40		23 52		00 04	00 10	
Strawberry Hill	d					22 37						23 07						23 37					00 09		
Fulwell	a																								
Teddington	a					22 40						23 10						23 41					00 12		
Hampton Wick	a					22 44						23 14						23 44					00 14		
Kingston	a					22 46						23 16						23 46					00 16		
Whitton	d		22 25	←						22 55	←					23 25	←				23 55	←			
Feltham	d	22 36	22 29	22 36			22 46		23 06	22 59	23 06		23 16	23 36		23 29	23 36		23 46	00 06	23 59	00 06		00 16	
Ashford (Surrey)	d	→	22 33	22 40					→	23 03	23 10			→		23 33	23 40			→	00 03	00 10			
Staines	d		22 37	22 44			22 53			23 07	23 14		23 23			23 37	23 44		23 53		00 07	00 14		00 23	
Wraysbury	d		22 42							23 11						23 41					00 11				
Sunnymeads	d		22 45							23 14						23 44					00 14				
Datchet	d		22 49							23 17						23 47					00 17				
Windsor & Eton Riverside	a		22 56							23 24						23 54					00 21				
Egham	d			22 49			22 57				23 19		23 27				23 49		23 57			00 19		00 27	
Virginia Water	a			22 53			23 01				23 23		23 31				23 53		00 01			00 23		00 31	
	d			22 53			23 01				23 23		23 31				23 53		00 01			00 23		00 31	
Chertsey	d			22 59							23 29						23 59					00 29			
Addlestone	d			23 02							23 32						00a02					00 32			
Weybridge	a			23 07							23 37											00 36			
Longcross	d																								
Sunningdale	d						23 07						23 37						00 08					00 37	
Ascot 8	d						23 13	23 23					23 43						00 13					00 42	
Bagshot	d							23 29																	
Camberley	a							23 35																	
Frimley	d							23 43																	
Ash Vale	d							23 49																	
Aldershot	a							23 54																	
	d																								
Ash 6	d																								
Wanborough	d																								
Guildford	a																								
Martins Heron	d						23 17						23 47						00 17					00 46	
Bracknell	d						23 20						23 50						00 20					00 49	
Wokingham	d						23 27						23 57						00 32					00 56	
Winnersh	d						23 30						23 59						00 36						
Winnersh Triangle	d						23 32						00 02						00 38						
Earley	d						23 37						00 05						00 40						
Reading 7	a						23 43						00 13						00 48					01 07	

The xx15 and xx45 services from London Waterloo to Whitton continue to London Waterloo via Brentford

The xx03 and xx33 London Waterloo to Kingston services continue to London Waterloo via Wimbledon

The xx07 and xx37 services from London Waterloo to Whitton continue to London Waterloo via Richmond

For additional services between Wokingham and Reading refer to Table T148

Table T149-F

Saturdays
13 October to 8 December

London - Hounslow, Richmond, Kingston, Windsor, Weybridge, Ascot, Guildford and Reading

		SW	SW	SW
London Waterloo ■ ⊖	d	23 52	23 58	
Vauxhall ⊖	d	23 56	00 02	
Queenstown Rd.(Battersea)	d	23 59		
Clapham Junction ■	d	00 02	00 08	
Wandsworth Town	d	00 05		
Putney	d	00 08	00 12	
Barnes	d	00 12		
Barnes Bridge	d	00 14		
Chiswick	d	00 17		
Kew Bridge	d	00 20		
Brentford	d	00 23		
Syon Lane	d	00 25		
Isleworth	d	00 27		
Hounslow	d	00 31		
Mortlake	d			
North Sheen	d			
Richmond ⊖	d		00 18	
St Margarets	d			
Twickenham	a		00 22	
	d		00 22	
Strawberry Hill	d			
Fulwell	a			
Teddington	a			
Hampton Wick	a			
Kingston	a			
Whitton	d		00 25	←
Feltham	d	00 36	00 29	00 36
Ashford (Surrey)	d	→	00 33	00 40
Staines	d		00a37	00a47
Wraysbury	d			
Sunnymeads	d			
Datchet	d			
Windsor & Eton Riverside	a			
Egham	d			
Virginia Water	a			
	d			
Chertsey	d			
Addlestone	d			
Weybridge	a			
Longcross	d			
Sunningdale	d			
Ascot ■	d			
Bagshot	d			
Camberley	a			
Frimley	d			
Ash Vale	d			
Aldershot	a			
	d			
Ash ■	d			
Wanborough	d			
Guildford	a			
Martins Heron	d			
Bracknell	d			
Wokingham	d			
Winnersh	d			
Winnersh Triangle	d			
Earley	d			
Reading ■	a			

The xx15 and xx45 services from London Waterloo to Whitton continue to London Waterloo via Brentford

The xx03 and xx33 London Waterloo to Kingston services continue to London Waterloo via Wimbledon

The xx07 and xx37 services from London Waterloo to Whitton continue to London Waterloo via Richmond

For additional services between Wokingham and Reading refer to Table T148

Table T149-F

Sundays
20 May to 30 September

London - Hounslow, Richmond, Kingston, Windsor, Weybridge, Ascot, Guildford and Reading

		SW	SW	SW	GW	SW	SW	SW	SW	SW	SW	SW	SW	SW	SW	SW	SW	SW	SW	SW	SW	SW	SW
			■		■	■			■	■						■			■	■		■	
		A	A	A	A	A	A	A			A	A											
London Waterloo ■ ⊖	d													00 18	06 14		06 44		07 09		07 14		07 44
Vauxhall ⊖	d										00 02			00 22	06 18		06 48		07 13		07 18		07 48
Queenstown Rd.(Battersea)	d													00 28	06 21		06 51				07 21		07 51
Clapham Junction ■	d										00 08	00 02		00 31	06 24		06 54		07 19		07 24		07 54
Wandsworth Town	d											00 05		00 33	06 27		06 57				07 27		07 57
Putney	d										00 12	00 08		00 36	06 30		07 00		07 23		07 30		08 00
Barnes	d											00 12		00 39	06 33		07 03				07 33		08 03
Barnes Bridge	d											00 14											
Chiswick	d											00 17											
Kew Bridge	d											00 20											
Brentford	d											00 23											
Syon Lane	d											00 25											
Isleworth	d											00 27											
Hounslow	d						00 01					00 31											
Mortlake	d													00 42	06 35		07 05				07 35		08 05
North Sheen	d													00 44	06 37		07 07				07 37		08 07
Richmond ⊖	d							00 06			00 18			00 46	06 40		07 10		07 29		07 40		08 10
St Margarets	d	00 01												00 49	06 42		07 12				07 42		08 12
Twickenham	a	00 03						00 10			00 22			00 51	06 44		07 14		07 32		07 44		08 14
	d	00 04						00 10			00 22			00 51	06 45		07 15		07 33		07 45		08 15
Strawberry Hill	d	00 09												00s55	06 49						07 49		
Fulwell	a																						
Teddington	a	00 12												00s58	06 52						07 52		
Hampton Wick	a	00 14												01s00	06 57						07 57		
Kingston	a	00 16												01 03	06 59						07 59		
Whitton	d										00 25						07 18						08 18
Feltham	d						00 06	00 16			00 29	00 36					07 22		07 39				08 22
Ashford (Surrey)	d			00 03			00 10				00 33	00 40					07 26						08 26
Staines	d			00 07			00 14	00 23			00a37	00a47	06 32			07 15	07 30	07 40	07 45			08 15	08 30
Wraysbury	d			00 11													07 34						08 34
Sunnymeads	d			00 14													07 37						08 37
Datchet	d			00 17													07 40						08 40
Windsor & Eton Riverside	a			00 21													07 44						08 44
Egham	d						00 19	00 27					06 36			07 20		07 45	07 50			08 20	
Virginia Water	a						00 23	00 31					06 41			07 24		07 49	07 54			08 24	
	d					00 01	00 23	00 31					06 41			07 24		07 49	07 54			08 24	
Chertsey	d						00 29						06 46					07 55					
Addlestone	d						00 32						06 49					07a58					
Weybridge	a						00 36						06 53										
Longcross	d																						
Sunningdale	d					00 08		00 37								07 30			08 00			08 30	
Ascot ■	d					00 13		00 42	00 46							07 35			08 05	08 13		08 35	
Bagshot	d								00 52											08 19			
Camberley	a								00 58											08 25			
Frimley	d								01 02											08 29			
Ash Vale	d								01 09											08 36			
Aldershot	a								01s14											08 41			
	d									07 48										08 48			
Ash ■	d									07 55										08 55			
Wanborough	d									07 59										08 59			
Guildford	a									08 06										09 06			
Martins Heron	d					00 17		00 46								07 39			08 09			08 39	
Bracknell	d					00 20		00 49								07 43			08 13			08 43	
Wokingham	d				00 24	00 32		00 56								07 49			08 19			08 49	
Winnersh	d					00 36										07 53			08 23			08 53	
Winnersh Triangle	d		00 02			00 38										07 55			08 25			08 55	
Earley	d		00 05			00 40										07 57			08 27			08 57	
Reading ■	a		00 10		00 33	00 45		01 04								08 02			08 32			09 02	

A not 20 May

For additional services between Wokingham and Reading refer to Table T148

Table T149-F

Sundays

20 May to 30 September

London - Hounslow, Richmond, Kingston, Windsor, Weybridge, Ascot, Guildford and Reading

		SW	SW ■	SW ■	SW	SW	SW ■	SW	SW	SW ■	SW ■	SW	SW	SW ■	SW	SW	SW ■	SW ■	SW	SW	SW ■	SW	SW
London Waterloo ⊖	d	07 50	08 09		08 14	08 25	08 39	08 44	08 50	09 09		09 14	09 25	09 39	09 44	09 50	10 09		10 14	10 25	10 39	10 44	10 50
Vauxhall ⊖	d	07 54	08 13		08 18	08 29	08 43	08 48	08 54	09 13		09 18	09 29	09 43	09 48	09 54	10 13		10 18	10 29	10 43	10 48	10 54
Queenstown Rd.(Battersea)	d	07 57			08 21			08 51	08 57			09 21			09 51	09 57			10 21			10 51	10 57
Clapham Junction	d	08 00	08 19		08 24	08 35	08 49	08 54	09 00	09 19		09 24	09 35	09 49	09 54	10 00	10 19		10 24	10 35	10 49	10 54	11 00
Wandsworth Town	d	08 03			08 27			08 57	09 03			09 27			09 57	10 03			10 27			10 57	11 03
Putney	d	08 06	08 23		08 30	08 39	08 53	09 00	09 06	09 23		09 30	09 39	09 53	10 00	10 06	10 23		10 30	10 39	10 53	11 00	11 06
Barnes	d	08 09			08 33			09 03	09 09			09 33			10 03	10 09			10 33			11 03	11 09
Barnes Bridge	d	08 11							09 11							10 11							11 11
Chiswick	d	08 13							09 13							10 13							11 13
Kew Bridge	d	08 16							09 16							10 16							11 16
Brentford	d	08 19							09 19							10 19							11 19
Syon Lane	d	08 21							09 21							10 21							11 21
Isleworth	d	08 23							09 23							10 23							11 23
Hounslow	d	08 26							09 26							10 26							11 26
Mortlake	d				08 35			09 05				09 35			10 05				10 35			11 05	
North Sheen	d				08 37			09 07				09 37			10 07				10 37			11 07	
Richmond ⊖	d		08 29		08 40	08 45	08 59	09 10		09 29		09 40	09 45	09 59	10 10		10 29		10 40	10 45	10 59	11 10	
St Margarets	d				08 42			09 12				09 42			10 12				10 42			11 12	
Twickenham	a		08 32		08 44	08 48	09 02	09 14		09 32		09 44	09 48	10 02	10 14		10 32		10 44	10 48	11 02	11 14	
	d		08 33		08 45	08 49	09 03	09 15		09 33		09 45	09 49	10 03	10 15		10 33		10 45	10 49	11 03	11 15	
Strawberry Hill	d				08 49							09 49							10 49				
Fulwell	a																						
Teddington	a				08 52							09 52							10 52				
Hampton Wick	a				08 57							09 57							10 57				
Kingston	a				08 59							09 59							10 59				
Whitton	d					08 52		09 18					09 52		10 18					10 52		11 18	
Feltham	d	08 32	08 39			08 56	09 09	09 22	09 32	09 39			09 56	10 09	10 22	10 32	10 39			10 56	11 09	11 22	11 32
Ashford (Surrey)	d	08 36				09 00		09 26	09 36				10 00		10 26	10 36				11 00		11 26	11 36
Staines	d	08 40	08 45			09 04	09 15	09 30	09 40	09 45			10 04	10 15	10 30	10 40	10 45			11 04	11 15	11 30	11 40
Wraysbury	d							09 34							10 34							11 35	
Sunnymeads	d							09 37							10 37							11 38	
Datchet	d					09 12		09 40					10 12		10 40					11 12		11 42	
Windsor & Eton Riverside	a					09 16		09 44					10 16		10 44					11 16		11 46	
Egham	d	08 45	08 50				09 20		09 45	09 50				10 20		10 45	10 50				11 20		11 45
Virginia Water	a	08 49	08 54				09 24		09 49	09 54				10 24		10 49	10 54				11 24		11 49
	d	08 49	08 54				09 24		09 49	09 54				10 24		10 49	10 54				11 24		11 49
Chertsey	d	08 55							09 55							10 55							11 55
Addlestone	d	08a58							09a58							10a58							11a58
Weybridge	a																						
Longcross	d																						
Sunningdale	d		09 00				09 30			10 00				10 30			11 00				11 30		
Ascot ■	d		09 05	09 13			09 35			10 05	10 13			10 35			11 05	11 13			11 35		
Bagshot	d			09 19							10 19							11 19					
Camberley	a			09 25							10 25							11 25					
Frimley	d			09 29							10 29							11 29					
Ash Vale	d			09 36							10 36							11 36					
Aldershot	a			09 41							10 41							11 41					
	d			09 48							10 48							11 48					
Ash ■	d			09 55							10 55							11 55					
Wanborough	d			09 59							10 59							11 59					
Guildford	a			10 06							11 06							12 06					
Martins Heron	d		09 09				09 39			10 09				10 39			11 09				11 39		
Bracknell	d		09 13				09 43			10 13				10 43			11 13				11 43		
Wokingham	d		09 19				09 49			10 19				10 49			11 19				11 49		
Winnersh	d		09 23				09 53			10 23				10 53			11 23				11 53		
Winnersh Triangle	d		09 25				09 55			10 25				10 55			11 25				11 55		
Earley	d		09 27				09 57			10 27				10 57			11 27				11 57		
Reading ■	a		09 32				10 02			10 32				11 02			11 32				12 02		

For additional services between Wokingham and Reading refer to Table T148

Table T149-F

Sundays

20 May to 30 September

London - Hounslow, Richmond, Kingston, Windsor, Weybridge, Ascot, Guildford and Reading

		SW ■	SW ■	SW	SW	SW ■	SW	SW	SW ■	SW ■	SW	SW	SW	SW ■	SW	SW	SW ■	SW ■	SW	SW	SW	SW ■
London Waterloo ⊖	d	11 09		11 14	11 25	11 39	11 44	11 50	12 09		12 14	12 25		12 39	12 44	12 50	13 09		13 14	13 25		13 39
Vauxhall ⊖	d	11 13		11 19	11 29	11 43	11 48	11 54	12 13		12 19	12 29		12 43	12 48	12 54	13 13		13 18	13 29		13 43
Queenstown Rd.(Battersea)	d			11 22			11 51	11 57			12 22				12 51	12 57			13 21			
Clapham Junction	d	11 19		11 25	11 35	11 49	11 54	12 00	12 19		12 25	12 35		12 49	12 54	13 00	13 19		13 24	13 35		13 49
Wandsworth Town	d			11 28			11 57	12 03			12 28				12 57	13 03			13 27			
Putney	d	11 23		11 31	11 39	11 53	12 00	12 06	12 23		12 31	12 39		12 53	13 00	13 06	13 23		13 30	13 39		13 53
Barnes	d			11 34			12 03	12 09			12 34				13 03	13 09			13 33			
Barnes Bridge	d							12 11								13 11						
Chiswick	d							12 13								13 13						
Kew Bridge	d							12 16								13 16						
Brentford	d							12 19								13 19						
Syon Lane	d							12 21								13 21						
Isleworth	d							12 23								13 23						
Hounslow	d							12 26								13 26						
Mortlake	d			11 36			12 05				12 36				13 05				13 35			
North Sheen	d			11 38			12 07				12 38				13 07				13 37			
Richmond ⊖	d	11 29		11 41	11 45	11 59	12 10		12 29		12 41	12 45		12 59	13 10		13 29		13 40	13 45		13 59
St Margarets	d			11 43			12 12				12 43				13 12				13 42			
Twickenham	a	11 32		11 45	11 48	12 02	12 14		12 32		12 45	12 48		13 02	13 14		13 32		13 44	13 48		14 02
	d	11 33		11 46	11 49	12 03	12 15		12 33		12 46	12 49	12 56	13 03	13 15		13 33		13 45	13 49	13 56	14 03
Strawberry Hill	d			11 50							12 50								13 49			
Fulwell	a																					
Teddington	a			11 53							12 53								13 52			
Hampton Wick	a			11 57							12 57								13 57			
Kingston	a			11 59							12 59								13 59			
Whitton	d				11 52		12 18					12 52	12a59		13 18					13 52	13a59	
Feltham	d	11 39			11 56	12 09	12 22	12 32	12 39			12 56		13 09	13 22	13 32	13 39			13 56		14 09
Ashford (Surrey)	d				12 00		12 26	12 36				13 00			13 26	13 36				14 00		
Staines	d	11 45			12 04	12 15	12 30	12 40	12 45			13 04		13 15	13 30	13 40	13 45			14 04		14 15
Wraysbury	d						12 34								13 34							
Sunnymeads	d						12 37								13 37							
Datchet	d				12 12		12 40					13 12			13 40					14 12		
Windsor & Eton Riverside	a				12 16		12 44					13 16			13 44					14 16		
Egham	d	11 50				12 20		12 45	12 50					13 20		13 45	13 50					14 20
Virginia Water	a	11 54				12 24		12 49	12 54					13 24		13 49	13 54					14 24
	d	11 54				12 24		12 49	12 54					13 24		13 49	13 54					14 24
Chertsey	d							12 55								13 55						
Addlestone	d							12a58								13a58						
Weybridge	a																					
Longcross	d																					
Sunningdale	d	12 00				12 30			13 00					13 30			14 00					14 30
Ascot ■	d	12 05	12 13			12 35			13 05	13 13				13 35			14 05	14 13				14 35
Bagshot	d		12 19							13 19								14 19				
Camberley	a		12 25							13 25								14 25				
Frimley	d		12 29							13 29								14 29				
Ash Vale	d		12 36							13 36								14 36				
Aldershot	a		12 41							13 41								14 41				
	d		12 48							13 48								14 48				
Ash ■	d		12 55							13 55								14 55				
Wanborough	d		12 59							13 59								14 59				
Guildford	a		13 06							14 06								15 06				
Martins Heron	d	12 09				12 39			13 09					13 39			14 09					14 39
Bracknell	d	12 13				12 43			13 13					13 43			14 13					14 43
Wokingham	d	12 19				12 49			13 19					13 49			14 19					14 49
Winnersh	d	12 23				12 53			13 23					13 53			14 23					14 53
Winnersh Triangle	d	12 25				12 55			13 25					13 55			14 25					14 55
Earley	d	12 27				12 57			13 27					13 57			14 27					14 57
Reading ■	a	12 32				13 02			13 32					14 02			14 32					15 02

For additional services between Wokingham and Reading refer to Table T148

Table T149-F

Sundays
20 May to 30 September

London - Hounslow, Richmond, Kingston, Windsor, Weybridge, Ascot, Guildford and Reading

		SW	SW	SW ■	SW ■	SW	SW	SW	SW	SW ■	SW		SW	SW	SW ■	SW ■	SW	SW	SW	SW	SW ■	SW	SW
London Waterloo ■ ⊖	d	13 44	13 50	14 09		14 14	14 20	14 25		14 39			17 44	17 50	18 09		18 14	18 20	18 25		18 39		18 44
Vauxhall ⊖	d	13 48	13 54	14 13		14 18	14 24	14 29		14 43			17 48	17 54	18 13		18 18	18 24	18 29		18 43		18 48
Queenstown Rd.(Battersea)	d	13 51	13 57			14 21	14 27						17 51	17 57			18 21	18 27					18 51
Clapham Junction ■	d	13 54	14 00	14 19		14 24	14 30	14 35		14 49			17 54	18 00	18 19		18 24	18 30	18 35		18 49		18 54
Wandsworth Town	d	13 57	14 03			14 27	14 33						17 57	18 03			18 27	18 33					18 57
Putney	d	14 00	14 06	14 23		14 30	14 36	14 39		14 53	←		18 00	18 06	18 23		18 30	18 36	18 39		18 53	←	19 00
Barnes	d	14 03	14 09			14 33	14 39				14 39		18 03	18 09			18 33	18 39				18 39	19 03
Barnes Bridge	d		14 11				→				14 41			18 11				→				18 41	
Chiswick	d		14 13								14 44			18 13								18 44	
Kew Bridge	d		14 16								14 46			18 16								18 46	
Brentford	d		14 19								14 49			18 19								18 49	
Syon Lane	d		14 21								14 51			18 21								18 51	
Isleworth	d		14 23								14 53			18 23								18 53	
Hounslow	d		14 26								14 57			18 26								18 57	
Mortlake	d	14 05				14 35							18 05				18 35						19 05
North Sheen	d	14 07				14 37							18 07				18 37						19 07
Richmond ⊖	d	14 10		14 29		14 40		14 45		14 59			18 10		18 29		18 40		18 45		18 59		19 10
St Margarets	d	14 12				14 42							18 12				18 42						19 12
Twickenham	a	14 14		14 32		14 44		14 49		15 02	15 04		18 14		18 32		18 44		18 49		19 02	19 04	19 14
	d	14 15		14 33		14 45		14 49	14 56	15 03	15 11		18 15		18 33		18 45		18 49	18 56	19 03	19 11	19 15
Strawberry Hill	d					14 49					15 14						18 49					19 14	
Fulwell	a																						
Teddington	a					14 52					15 17						18 52					19 17	
Hampton Wick	a					14 57					15 20						18 57					19 20	
Kingston	a					14 59					15 22	and at					18 59					19 22	
Whitton	d	14 18						14 52	14a59			the same	18 18						18 52	18a59			19 18
Feltham	d	14 22	14 32	14 39				14 57		15 09		minutes	18 22	18 32	18 39				18 57		19 09		19 22
Ashford (Surrey)	d	14 26	14 36					15 01				past	18 26	18 36					19 01				19 26
Staines	d	14 30	14 40	14 45				15 05		15 15		each	18 30	18 40	18 45				19 05		19 15		19 30
Wraysbury	d	14 34										hour until	18 34										19 34
Sunnymeads	d	14 37											18 37										19 37
Datchet	d	14 40						15 12					18 40						19 12				19 40
Windsor & Eton Riverside	a	14 44						15 17					18 44						19 17				19 44
Egham	d		14 45	14 50						15 20				18 45	18 50						19 20		
Virginia Water	a		14 49	14 54						15 24				18 49	18 54						19 24		
	d		14 49	14 54						15 24				18 49	18 54						19 24		
Chertsey	d		14 55											18 55									
Addlestone	d		14a58											18a58									
Weybridge	a																						
Longcross	d																						
Sunningdale	d			15 00						15 30					19 00						19 30		
Ascot ■	d			15 05	15 13					15 35					19 05	19 13					19 35		
Bagshot	d				15 19											19 19							
Camberley	a				15 25											19 25							
Frimley	d				15 29											19 29							
Ash Vale	d				15 36											19 36							
Aldershot	a				15 41											19 41							
	d				15 48											19 48							
Ash ■	d				15 55											19 55							
Wanborough	d				15 59											19 59							
Guildford	a				16 06											20 06							
Martins Heron	d			15 09						15 39					19 09						19 39		
Bracknell	d			15 13						15 43					19 13						19 43		
Wokingham	d			15 19						15 49					19 19						19 49		
Winnersh	d			15 23						15 53					19 23						19 53		
Winnersh Triangle	d			15 25						15 55					19 25						19 55		
Earley	d			15 27						15 57					19 27						19 57		
Reading ■	a			15 32						16 02					19 32						20 02		

For additional services between Wokingham and Reading refer to Table T148

Table T149-F

Sundays
20 May to 30 September

London - Hounslow, Richmond, Kingston, Windsor, Weybridge, Ascot, Guildford and Reading

		SW	SW ■	SW ■	SW	SW	SW	SW	SW ■	SW	SW	SW	SW ■	SW ■	SW	SW	SW	SW	SW ■	SW	SW	SW	SW ■
London Waterloo ■ ⊖	d	18 50	19 09		19 14	19 20	19 25		19 39		19 44	19 50	20 09		20 14	20 20	20 25		20 39		20 44	20 50	21 09
Vauxhall ⊖	d	18 54	19 13		19 18	19 24	19 29		19 43		19 48	19 54	20 13		20 18	20 24	20 29		20 43		20 48	20 54	21 13
Queenstown Rd.(Battersea)	d	18 57			19 21	19 27					19 51	19 57			20 21	20 27					20 51	20 57	
Clapham Junction ■	d	19 00	19 19		19 24	19 30	19 35		19 49		19 54	20 00	20 19		20 24	20 30	20 35		20 49		20 54	21 00	21 19
Wandsworth Town	d	19 03			19 27	19 33					19 57	20 03			20 27	20 33					20 57	21 03	
Putney	d	19 06	19 23		19 30	19 36	19 39		19 53	←	20 00	20 06	20 23		20 30	20 36	20 39		20 53	←	21 00	21 06	21 23
Barnes	d	19 09			19 33	19 39				19 39	20 03	20 09			20 33	20 39				20 39	21 03	21 09	
Barnes Bridge	d	19 11				→				19 41		20 11				→				20 41		21 11	
Chiswick	d	19 13								19 44		20 13								20 44		21 13	
Kew Bridge	d	19 16								19 46		20 16								20 46		21 16	
Brentford	d	19 19								19 49		20 19								20 49		21 19	
Syon Lane	d	19 21								19 51		20 21								20 51		21 21	
Isleworth	d	19 23								19 53		20 23								20 53		21 23	
Hounslow	d	19 26								19 57		20 26								20 57		21 26	
Mortlake	d				19 35						20 05				20 35						21 05		
North Sheen	d				19 37						20 07				20 37						21 07		
Richmond ⊖	d		19 29		19 40		19 45		19 59		20 10		20 29		20 40		20 45		20 59		21 10		21 29
St Margarets	d				19 42						20 12				20 42						21 12		
Twickenham	a		19 32		19 44		19 49		20 02	20 04	20 14		20 32		20 44		20 49		21 02	21 04	21 14		21 32
	d		19 33		19 45		19 49	19 56	20 03	20 11	20 15		20 33		20 45		20 49	20 56	21 03	21 11	21 15		21 33
Strawberry Hill	d				19 49					20 14					20 49					21 14			
Fulwell	a																						
Teddington	a				19 52					20 17					20 52					21 17			
Hampton Wick	a				19 57					20 20					20 57					21 20			
Kingston	a				19 59					20 22					20 59					21 22			
Whitton	d						19 52	19a59			20 18						20 52	20a59			21 18		
Feltham	d	19 32	19 39				19 57		20 09		20 22	20 32	20 39				20 57		21 09		21 22	21 32	21 39
Ashford (Surrey)	d	19 36					20 01				20 26	20 36					21 01				21 26	21 36	
Staines	d	19 41	19 45				20 05		20 15		20 30	20 40	20 45				21 05		21 15		21 30	21 40	21 45
Wraysbury	d										20 34										21 34		
Sunnymeads	d										20 37										21 37		
Datchet	d						20 12				20 40						21 12				21 40		
Windsor & Eton Riverside	a						20 17				20 44						21 17				21 44		
Egham	d	19 45	19 50						20 20			20 45	20 50						21 20			21 45	21 50
Virginia Water	a	19 49	19 54						20 24			20 49	20 54						21 24			21 49	21 54
	d	19 49	19 54						20 24			20 49	20 54						21 24			21 49	21 54
Chertsey	d	19 55										20 55										21 55	
Addlestone	d	19a58										20a58										21a58	
Weybridge	a																						
Longcross	d																						
Sunningdale	d		20 00						20 30				21 00						21 31				22 00
Ascot ■	d		20 05	20 13					20 35				21 05	21 13					21 35				22 05
Bagshot	d			20 19										21 19									
Camberley	a			20 25										21 25									
Frimley	d			20 29										21 29									
Ash Vale	d			20 36										21 36									
Aldershot	a			20 42										21 41									
	d			20 48										21 48									
Ash ■	d			20 57										21 55									
Wanborough	d			21 00										21 59									
Guildford	a			21 07										22 06									
Martins Heron	d		20 09						20 39				21 09						21 39				22 09
Bracknell	d		20 13						20 43				21 13						21 43				22 13
Wokingham	d		20 19						20 49				21 19						21 49				22 19
Winnersh	d		20 23						20 53				21 23						21 53				22 23
Winnersh Triangle	d		20 25						20 55				21 25						21 55				22 25
Earley	d		20 27						20 57				21 27						21 57				22 27
Reading ■	a		20 32						21 02				21 32						22 02				22 32

For additional services between Wokingham and Reading refer to Table T148

Table T149-F

Sundays
20 May to 30 September

London - Hounslow, Richmond, Kingston, Windsor, Weybridge, Ascot, Guildford and Reading

		SW ■	SW	SW	SW	SW ■	SW	SW	SW	SW ■	SW ■	SW	SW	SW	SW ■	SW	SW	SW	SW ■	SW	SW	SW ■	SW
London Waterloo ⊖	d		21 14		21 20	21 39		21 44	21 50	22 09		22 14		22 20	22 39		22 44	22 50	23 09	23 14	23 20	23 39	
Vauxhall ⊖	d		21 18		21 24	21 43		21 48	21 54	22 13		22 18		22 24	22 43		22 48	22 54	23 13	23 18	23 24	23 43	
Queenstown Rd.(Battersea)	d		21 21		21 27			21 51	21 57			22 21		22 27			22 51	22 57		23 21	23 27		
Clapham Junction	d		21 24		21 30	21 49		21 54	22 00	22 19		22 24		22 30	22 49		22 54	23 00	23 19	23 24	23 30	23 49	
Wandsworth Town	d		21 27		21 33			21 57	22 03			22 27		22 33			22 57	23 03		23 27	23 33		
Putney	d		21 30		21 36	21 53	←	22 00	22 06	22 23		22 30		22 36	22 53	←	23 00	23 06	23 23	23 30	23 36	23 53	←
Barnes	d		21 33		21 39		21 39	22 03	22 09			22 33		22 39		22 39	23 03	23 09		23 33	23 39		23 39
Barnes Bridge	d				→		21 41		22 11					→		22 41		23 11			→		23 41
Chiswick	d						21 44		22 13							22 44		23 13					23 44
Kew Bridge	d						21 46		22 16							22 46		23 16					23 46
Brentford	d						21 49		22 19							22 49		23 19					23 49
Syon Lane	d						21 51		22 21							22 51		23 21					23 51
Isleworth	d						21 53		22 23							22 53		23 23					23 53
Hounslow	d						21 57		22 26							22 57		23 26					23 58
Mortlake	d		21 35					22 05				22 35					23 05			23 35			
North Sheen	d		21 37					22 07				22 37					23 07			23 37			
Richmond ⊖	d		21 40			21 59		22 10		22 29		22 40			22 59		23 10		23 29	23 40		23 59	
St Margarets	d		21 42					22 12				22 42					23 12			23 42			
Twickenham	a		21 44			22 02	22 04	22 14		22 32		22 44			23 02	23 04	23 14		23 32	23 44		00 02	00 05
	d		21 45	21 56		22 03	22 11	22 15		22 33		22 45	22 56		23 03	23 11	23 15		23 33	23 45		00 03	00 12
Strawberry Hill	d		21 49				22 14					22 49				23 14				23 48			00 15
Fulwell	a																						
Teddington	a		21 52				22 17					22 52				23 17				23 51			00 18
Hampton Wick	a		21 57				22 20					22 57				23 20				23 54			00 21
Kingston	a		21 59				22 22					22 59				23 22				23 56			00 23
Whitton	d			21a59				22 18					22a59				23 18						
Feltham	d					22 09		22 22	22 32	22 39					23 09		23 22	23 32	23 39			00 09	
Ashford (Surrey)	d							22 26	22 36								23 26	23 36					
Staines	d					22 15		22 30	22 40	22 45					23 15		23 30	23 40	23 45			00 15	
Wraysbury	d							22 34									23 34						
Sunnymeads	d							22 37									23 37						
Datchet	d							22 40									23 40						
Windsor & Eton Riverside	a							22 44									23 44						
Egham	d					22 20			22 45	22 50					23 20			23 45	23 50			00 20	
Virginia Water	a					22 24			22 49	22 54					23 24			23 49	23 54			00 24	
	d					22 24			22 49	22 54					23 24			23 49	23 54			00 24	
Chertsey	d								22 55									23 55					
Addlestone	d								22a58									23a58					
Weybridge	a																						
Longcross	d																						
Sunningdale	d					22 30				23 00					23 30				23 59			00 30	
Ascot	d	22 13				22 35				23 05	23 13				23 35				00 05			00 35	
Bagshot	d	22 19									23 19												
Camberley	a	22 25									23 25												
Frimley	d	22 29									23 29												
Ash Vale	d	22 36									23 36												
Aldershot	a	22 41									23 41												
	d	22 48																					
Ash	d	22 55																					
Wanborough	d	22 58																					
Guildford	a	23 06																					
Martins Heron	d					22 39				23 09					23 39				00 09			00 39	
Bracknell	d					22 43				23 13					23 43				00 13			00 43	
Wokingham	d					22 49				23 19					23 49				00 19			00 49	
Winnersh	d					22 53				23 23					23 53				00 23			00 53	
Winnersh Triangle	d					22 55				23 25					23 55				00 25			00 55	
Earley	d					22 57				23 27					23 57				00 27			00 57	
Reading	a					23 02				23 32					00 02				00 32			01 02	

For additional services between Wokingham and Reading refer to Table T148

Table T149-F

Sundays
20 May to 30 September

London - Hounslow, Richmond, Kingston, Windsor, Weybridge, Ascot, Guildford and Reading

		SW
London Waterloo ⊖	d	23 44
Vauxhall ⊖	d	23 48
Queenstown Rd.(Battersea)	d	23 51
Clapham Junction	d	23 54
Wandsworth Town	d	23 57
Putney	d	23 59
Barnes	d	00 03
Barnes Bridge	d	
Chiswick	d	
Kew Bridge	d	
Brentford	d	
Syon Lane	d	
Isleworth	d	
Hounslow	d	
Mortlake	d	00 05
North Sheen	d	00 07
Richmond ⊖	d	00 10
St Margarets	d	00 12
Twickenham	a	00 14
	d	00 15
Strawberry Hill	d	
Fulwell	a	
Teddington	a	
Hampton Wick	a	
Kingston	a	
Whitton	d	00 18
Feltham	d	00 22
Ashford (Surrey)	d	00 26
Staines	d	00a30
Wraysbury	d	
Sunnymeads	d	
Datchet	d	
Windsor & Eton Riverside	a	
Egham	d	
Virginia Water	a	
	d	
Chertsey	d	
Addlestone	d	
Weybridge	a	
Longcross	d	
Sunningdale	d	
Ascot	d	
Bagshot	d	
Camberley	a	
Frimley	d	
Ash Vale	d	
Aldershot	a	
	d	
Ash	d	
Wanborough	d	
Guildford	a	
Martins Heron	d	
Bracknell	d	
Wokingham	d	
Winnersh	d	
Winnersh Triangle	d	
Earley	d	
Reading	a	

For additional services between Wokingham and Reading refer to Table T148

Table T149-F

Sundays

7 October to 2 December

London - Hounslow, Richmond, Kingston, Windsor, Weybridge, Ascot, Guildford and Reading

		SW	SW	SW	SW	GW	SW	SW	SW	SW		SW	SW	SW	SW	SW	SW	SW	SW	SW		SW	SW	SW	SW
			■	■		■	■	■					■	■						■				■	■
			A	B			A	B		A		B													
London Waterloo ⊖	d																	00 18	06 14			06 44		07 09	
Vauxhall ⊖	d														00 02			00 22	06 18			06 48		07 13	
Queenstown Rd.(Battersea)	d																	00 28	06 21			06 51			
Clapham Junction	d														00 08	00 02		00 31	06 24			06 54		07 19	
Wandsworth Town	d															00 05		00 33	06 27			06 57			
Putney	d														00 12	00 08		00 36	06 30			07 00		07 23	
Barnes	d															00 12		00 39	06 33			07 03			
Barnes Bridge	d															00 14									
Chiswick	d															00 17									
Kew Bridge	d															00 20									
Brentford	d															00 23									
Syon Lane	d															00 25									
Isleworth	d															00 27									
Hounslow	d								00 01							00 31									
Mortlake	d																	00 42	06 35			07 05			
North Sheen	d																	00 44	06 37			07 07			
Richmond ⊖	d									00 06		00 06			00 18			00 46	06 40			07 10		07 29	
St Margarets	d	00 01																00 49	06 42			07 12			
Twickenham	a	00 03								00 10		00 10			00 22			00 51	06 44			07 14		07 32	
	d	00 04								00 10		00 10			00 22			00 51	06 45			07 15		07 33	
Strawberry Hill	d	00 09																00s55	06 49						
Fulwell	a																								
Teddington	a	00 12																00s58	06 52						
Hampton Wick	a	00 14																01s00	06 57						
Kingston	a	00 16																01 03	06 59						
Whitton	d														00 25							07 18			
Feltham	d								00 06	00 16		00 16			00 29	00 36						07 22		07 39	
Ashford (Surrey)	d				00 03				00 10						00 33	00 40						07 26			
Staines	d				00 07				00 14	00 23		00 23			00a37	00a47	06 32			07 15		07 30	07 40	07 45	
Wraysbury	d				00 11																	07 35			
Sunnymeads	d				00 14																	07 38			
Datchet	d				00 17																	07 42			
Windsor & Eton Riverside	a				00 21																	07 46			
Egham	d								00 19	00 27		00 27					06 36			07 20			07 45	07 50	
Virginia Water	a								00 23	00 31		00 31					06 41			07 24			07 49	07 54	
	d						00 01	00 01	00 23	00 31		00 31					06 41			07 24			07 49	07 54	
Chertsey	d								00 29								06 46						07 55		
Addlestone	d								00 32								06 49						07a58		
Weybridge	a								00 36								06 53								
Longcross	d																								
Sunningdale	d						00 08	00 08		00 37		00 37								07 30				08 00	
Ascot	d						00 13	00 13		00 42		00 42	00 46							07 35				08 05	08 13
Bagshot	d												00 52												08 19
Camberley	a												00 58												08 25
Frimley	d												01 02												08 29
Ash Vale	d												01 09												08 36
Aldershot	a												01s14												08 41
	d													07 48											08 48
Ash	d													07 55											08 55
Wanborough	d													07 59											08 59
Guildford	a													08 06											09 06
Martins Heron	d						00 17	00 17		00 46		00 46								07 39				08 09	
Bracknell	d						00 20	00 20		00 49		00 49								07 43				08 13	
Wokingham	d					00 24	00 32	00 32		00 56		00 56								07 49				08 19	
Winnersh	d						00 36	00 36												07 53				08 23	
Winnersh Triangle	d		00 02	00 02			00 38	00 38												07 55				08 25	
Earley	d		00 05	00 05			00 40	00 40												07 57				08 27	
Reading	a		00 10	00 13		00 33	00 45	00 48		01 04		01 07								08 05				08 35	

A 7 October B not 7 October

For additional services between Wokingham and Reading refer to Table T148

Table T149-F

Sundays

7 October to 2 December

London - Hounslow, Richmond, Kingston, Windsor, Weybridge, Ascot, Guildford and Reading

		SW	SW	SW	SW	SW		SW	SW	SW	SW	SW	SW	SW	SW	SW		SW	SW	SW	SW	SW	SW	SW	SW
			■			■		■			■			■	■				■			■	■		
London Waterloo ⊖	d	07 14		07 44	07 50	08 09			08 14	08 25	08 39	08 44	08 50	09 09		09 14		09 25	09 39	09 44	09 50	10 09		10 14	10 25
Vauxhall ⊖	d	07 18		07 48	07 54	08 13			08 18	08 29	08 43	08 48	08 54	09 13		09 18		09 29	09 43	09 48	09 54	10 13		10 18	10 29
Queenstown Rd.(Battersea)	d	07 21		07 51	07 57				08 21			08 51	08 57			09 21				09 51	09 57			10 21	
Clapham Junction	d	07 24		07 54	08 00	08 19			08 24	08 35	08 49	08 54	09 00	09 19		09 24		09 35	09 49	09 54	10 00	10 19		10 24	10 35
Wandsworth Town	d	07 27		07 57	08 03				08 27			08 57	09 03			09 27				09 57	10 03			10 27	
Putney	d	07 30		08 00	08 06	08 23			08 30	08 39	08 53	09 00	09 06	09 23		09 30		09 39	09 53	10 00	10 06	10 23		10 30	10 39
Barnes	d	07 33		08 03	08 09				08 33			09 03	09 09			09 33				10 03	10 09			10 33	
Barnes Bridge	d				08 11								09 11								10 11				
Chiswick	d				08 13								09 13								10 13				
Kew Bridge	d				08 16								09 16								10 16				
Brentford	d				08 19								09 19								10 19				
Syon Lane	d				08 21								09 21								10 21				
Isleworth	d				08 23								09 23								10 23				
Hounslow	d				08 26								09 26								10 26				
Mortlake	d	07 35		08 05					08 35			09 05				09 35				10 05				10 35	
North Sheen	d	07 37		08 07					08 37			09 07				09 37				10 07				10 37	
Richmond ⊖	d	07 40		08 10		08 29			08 40	08 45	08 59	09 10		09 29		09 40		09 45	09 59	10 10		10 29		10 40	10 45
St Margarets	d	07 42		08 12					08 42			09 12				09 42				10 12				10 42	
Twickenham	a	07 44		08 14		08 32			08 44	08 48	09 02	09 14		09 32		09 44		09 48	10 02	10 14		10 32		10 44	10 48
	d	07 45		08 15		08 33			08 45	08 49	09 03	09 15		09 33		09 45		09 49	10 03	10 15		10 33		10 45	10 49
Strawberry Hill	d	07 49							08 49							09 49								10 49	
Fulwell	a																								
Teddington	a	07 52							08 52							09 52								10 52	
Hampton Wick	a	07 57							08 57							09 57								10 57	
Kingston	a	07 59							08 59							09 59								10 59	
Whitton	d			08 18						08 52		09 18						09 52		10 18					10 52
Feltham	d			08 22	08 32	08 39				08 56	09 09	09 22	09 32	09 39				09 56	10 09	10 22	10 32	10 39			10 56
Ashford (Surrey)	d			08 26	08 36					09 00		09 26	09 36					10 00		10 26	10 36				11 00
Staines	d		08 15	08 30	08 40	08 45				09 04	09 15	09 30	09 40	09 45				10 04	10 15	10 30	10 40	10 45			11 04
Wraysbury	d			08 35								09 35								10 35					
Sunnymeads	d			08 38								09 38								10 38					
Datchet	d			08 42						09 13		09 42						10 13		10 42					11 13
Windsor & Eton Riverside	a			08 46						09 18		09 46						10 18		10 46					11 18
Egham	d		08 20		08 45	08 50					09 20		09 45	09 50					10 20		10 45	10 50			
Virginia Water	a		08 24		08 49	08 54					09 24		09 49	09 54					10 24		10 49	10 54			
	d		08 24		08 49	08 54					09 24		09 49	09 54					10 24		10 49	10 54			
Chertsey	d				08 55								09 55								10 55				
Addlestone	d				08a58								09a58								10a58				
Weybridge	a																								
Longcross	d																								
Sunningdale	d		08 30			09 00					09 30			10 00					10 30			11 00			
Ascot	d		08 35			09 05		09 13			09 35			10 05	10 13				10 35			11 05	11 13		
Bagshot	d							09 19							10 19								11 19		
Camberley	a							09 25							10 25								11 25		
Frimley	d							09 29							10 29								11 29		
Ash Vale	d							09 36							10 36								11 36		
Aldershot	a							09 41							10 41								11 41		
	d							09 48							10 48								11 48		
Ash	d							09 55							10 55								11 55		
Wanborough	d							09 59							10 59								11 59		
Guildford	a							10 06							11 06								12 06		
Martins Heron	d		08 39			09 09					09 39			10 09					10 39			11 09			
Bracknell	d		08 43			09 13					09 43			10 13					10 43			11 13			
Wokingham	d		08 49			09 19					09 49			10 19					10 49			11 19			
Winnersh	d		08 53			09 23					09 53			10 23					10 53			11 23			
Winnersh Triangle	d		08 55			09 25					09 55			10 25					10 55			11 25			
Earley	d		08 57			09 27					09 57			10 27					10 57			11 27			
Reading	a		09 05			09 35					10 05			10 35					11 05			11 35			

For additional services between Wokingham and Reading refer to Table T148

Table T149-F

Sundays
7 October to 2 December

London - Hounslow, Richmond, Kingston, Windsor, Weybridge, Ascot, Guildford and Reading

		SW ■	SW	SW	SW ■	SW ■	SW	SW	SW ■	SW	SW	SW ■	SW ■	SW	SW	SW	SW ■	SW	SW	SW ■	SW ■	SW
London Waterloo ⊖	d	10 39	10 44	10 50	11 09		11 14	11 25	11 39	11 44	11 50	12 09		12 14	12 25		12 39	12 44	12 50	13 09		13 14
Vauxhall ⊖	d	10 43	10 48	10 54	11 13		11 19	11 29	11 43	11 48	11 54	12 13		12 19	12 29		12 43	12 48	12 54	13 13		13 18
Queenstown Rd.(Battersea)	d		10 51	10 57			11 22			11 51	11 57			12 22				12 51	12 57			13 21
Clapham Junction	d	10 49	10 54	11 00	11 19		11 25	11 35	11 49	11 54	12 00	12 19		12 25	12 35		12 49	12 54	13 00	13 19		13 24
Wandsworth Town	d		10 57	11 03			11 28			11 57	12 03			12 28				12 57	13 03			13 27
Putney	d	10 53	11 00	11 06	11 23		11 31	11 39	11 53	12 00	12 06	12 23		12 31	12 39		12 53	13 00	13 06	13 23		13 30
Barnes	d		11 03	11 09			11 34			12 03	12 09			12 34				13 03	13 09			13 33
Barnes Bridge	d			11 11							12 11								13 11			
Chiswick	d			11 13							12 13								13 13			
Kew Bridge	d			11 16							12 16								13 16			
Brentford	d			11 19							12 19								13 19			
Syon Lane	d			11 21							12 21								13 21			
Isleworth	d			11 23							12 23								13 23			
Hounslow	d			11 26							12 26								13 26			
Mortlake	d		11 05				11 36			12 05				12 36				13 05				13 35
North Sheen	d		11 07				11 38			12 07				12 38				13 07				13 37
Richmond ⊖	d	10 59	11 10		11 29		11 41	11 45	11 59	12 10		12 29		12 41	12 45		12 59	13 10		13 29		13 40
St Margarets	d		11 12				11 43			12 12				12 43				13 12				13 42
Twickenham	a	11 02	11 14		11 32		11 45	11 48	12 02	12 14		12 32		12 45	12 48		13 02	13 14		13 32		13 44
	d	11 03	11 15		11 33		11 46	11 49	12 03	12 15		12 33		12 46	12 49	12 56	13 03	13 15		13 33		13 45
Strawberry Hill	d						11 50							12 50								13 49
Fulwell	a																					
Teddington	a						11 53							12 53								13 52
Hampton Wick	a						11 57							12 57								13 57
Kingston	a						11 59							12 59								13 59
Whitton	d		11 18					11 52		12 18					12 52	12a59		13 18				
Feltham	d	11 09	11 22	11 32	11 39			11 56	12 09	12 22	12 32	12 39			12 56		13 09	13 22	13 32	13 39		
Ashford (Surrey)	d		11 26	11 36				12 00		12 26	12 36				13 00			13 26	13 36			
Staines	d	11 15	11 30	11 40	11 45			12 04	12 15	12 30	12 40	12 45			13 04		13 15	13 30	13 40	13 45		
Wraysbury	d		11 35							12 35								13 35				
Sunnymeads	d		11 38							12 38								13 38				
Datchet	d		11 42					12 13		12 42					13 13			13 42				
Windsor & Eton Riverside	a		11 46					12 18		12 46					13 18			13 46				
Egham	d	11 20		11 45	11 50				12 20		12 45	12 50					13 20		13 45	13 50		
Virginia Water	a	11 24		11 49	11 54				12 24		12 49	12 54					13 24		13 49	13 54		
	d	11 24		11 49	11 54				12 24		12 49	12 54					13 24		13 49	13 54		
Chertsey	d			11 55							12 55								13 55			
Addlestone	d			11a58							12a58								13a58			
Weybridge	a																					
Longcross	d																					
Sunningdale	d	11 30			12 00				12 30			13 00					13 30			14 00		
Ascot	d	11 35			12 05	12 13			12 35			13 05	13 13				13 35			14 05	14 13	
Bagshot	d					12 19							13 19								14 19	
Camberley	a					12 25							13 25								14 25	
Frimley	d					12 29							13 29								14 29	
Ash Vale	d					12 36							13 36								14 36	
Aldershot	a					12 41							13 41								14 41	
	d					12 48							13 48								14 48	
Ash	d					12 55							13 55								14 55	
Wanborough	d					12 59							13 59								14 59	
Guildford	a					13 06							14 06								15 06	
Martins Heron	d	11 39			12 09				12 39			13 09					13 39			14 09		
Bracknell	d	11 43			12 13				12 43			13 13					13 43			14 13		
Wokingham	d	11 49			12 19				12 49			13 19					13 49			14 19		
Winnersh	d	11 53			12 23				12 53			13 23					13 53			14 23		
Winnersh Triangle	d	11 55			12 25				12 55			13 25					13 55			14 25		
Earley	d	11 57			12 27				12 57			13 27					13 57			14 27		
Reading	a	12 05			12 35				13 05			13 35					14 05			14 35		

For additional services between Wokingham and Reading refer to Table T148

Table T149-F

Sundays
7 October to 2 December

London - Hounslow, Richmond, Kingston, Windsor, Weybridge, Ascot, Guildford and Reading

		SW	SW	SW ■	SW	SW	SW ■	SW ■	SW	SW	SW	SW	SW ■	SW		SW	SW	SW ■	SW ■	SW	SW	SW	SW	SW ■
London Waterloo ⊖	d	13 25		13 39	13 44	13 50	14 09		14 14	14 20	14 25		14 39			17 44	17 50	18 09		18 14	18 20	18 25		18 39
Vauxhall ⊖	d	13 29		13 43	13 48	13 54	14 13		14 18	14 24	14 29		14 43			17 48	17 54	18 13		18 18	18 24	18 29		18 43
Queenstown Rd.(Battersea)	d				13 51	13 57			14 21	14 27						17 51	17 57			18 21	18 27			
Clapham Junction	d	13 35		13 49	13 54	14 00	14 19		14 24	14 30	14 35		14 49			17 54	18 00	18 19		18 24	18 30	18 35		18 49
Wandsworth Town	d				13 57	14 03			14 27	14 33						17 57	18 03			18 27	18 33			
Putney	d	13 39		13 53	14 00	14 06	14 23		14 30	14 36	14 39		14 53	←		18 00	18 06	18 23		18 30	18 36	18 39		18 53
Barnes	d				14 03	14 09			14 33	14 39				14 39		18 03	18 09			18 33	18 39			
Barnes Bridge	d					14 11				→				14 41			18 11				→			
Chiswick	d					14 13								14 44			18 13							
Kew Bridge	d					14 16								14 46			18 16							
Brentford	d					14 19								14 49			18 19							
Syon Lane	d					14 21								14 51			18 21							
Isleworth	d					14 23								14 53			18 23							
Hounslow	d					14 26								14 57			18 26							
Mortlake	d				14 05				14 35							18 05				18 35				
North Sheen	d				14 07				14 37							18 07				18 37				
Richmond ⊖	d	13 45		13 59	14 10		14 29		14 40		14 45		14 59			18 10		18 29		18 40		18 45		18 59
St Margarets	d				14 12				14 42							18 12				18 42				
Twickenham	a	13 48		14 02	14 14		14 32		14 44		14 49		15 02	15 04		18 14		18 32		18 44		18 49		19 02
	d	13 49	13 56	14 03	14 15		14 33		14 45		14 49	14 56	15 03	15 11		18 15		18 33		18 45		18 49	18 56	19 03
Strawberry Hill	d								14 49					15 14						18 49				
Fulwell	a																							
Teddington	a								14 52					15 17						18 52				
Hampton Wick	a								14 57					15 20						18 57				
Kingston	a								14 59					15 22	and at					18 59				
Whitton	d	13 52	13a59		14 18						14 52	14a59			the same	18 18						18 52	18a59	
Feltham	d	13 56		14 09	14 22	14 32	14 39				14 57		15 09		minutes	18 22	18 32	18 39				18 57		19 09
Ashford (Surrey)	d	14 00			14 26	14 36					15 01				past	18 26	18 36					19 01		
Staines	d	14 04		14 15	14 30	14 40	14 45				15 05		15 15		each	18 30	18 40	18 45				19 05		19 15
Wraysbury	d				14 35										hour until	18 35								
Sunnymeads	d				14 38											18 38								
Datchet	d	14 13			14 42						15 13					18 42						19 13		
Windsor & Eton Riverside	a	14 18			14 46						15 19					18 46						19 19		
Egham	d			14 20		14 45	14 50						15 20				18 45	18 50						19 20
Virginia Water	a			14 24		14 49	14 54						15 24				18 49	18 54						19 24
	d			14 24		14 49	14 54						15 24				18 49	18 54						19 24
Chertsey	d					14 55											18 55							
Addlestone	d					14a58											18a58							
Weybridge	a																							
Longcross	d																							
Sunningdale	d			14 30			15 00						15 30					19 00						19 30
Ascot	d			14 35			15 05	15 13					15 35					19 05	19 13					19 35
Bagshot	d							15 19											19 19					
Camberley	a							15 25											19 25					
Frimley	d							15 29											19 29					
Ash Vale	d							15 36											19 36					
Aldershot	a							15 41											19 41					
	d							15 48											19 48					
Ash	d							15 55											19 55					
Wanborough	d							15 59											19 59					
Guildford	a							16 06											20 06					
Martins Heron	d			14 39			15 09						15 39					19 09						19 39
Bracknell	d			14 43			15 13						15 43					19 13						19 43
Wokingham	d			14 49			15 19						15 49					19 19						19 49
Winnersh	d			14 53			15 23						15 53					19 23						19 53
Winnersh Triangle	d			14 55			15 25						15 55					19 25						19 55
Earley	d			14 57			15 27						15 57					19 27						19 57
Reading	a			15 05			15 35						16 05					19 35						20 05

For additional services between Wokingham and Reading refer to Table T148

Table T149-F

Sundays

7 October to 2 December

London - Hounslow, Richmond, Kingston, Windsor, Weybridge, Ascot, Guildford and Reading

Station		SW	SW	SW	SW ■	SW ■	SW	SW	SW	SW	SW ■	SW	SW	SW	SW ■	SW ■	SW	SW	SW	SW	SW ■	SW
London Waterloo ■ ⊖	d		18 44	18 50	19 09		19 14	19 20	19 25		19 39		19 44	19 50	20 09		20 14	20 20	20 25		20 39	
Vauxhall ⊖	d		18 48	18 54	19 13		19 18	19 24	19 29		19 43		19 48	19 54	20 13		20 18	20 24	20 29		20 43	
Queenstown Rd.(Battersea)	d		18 51	18 57			19 21	19 27					19 51	19 57			20 21	20 27				
Clapham Junction ■	d		18 54	19 00	19 19		19 24	19 30	19 35		19 49		19 54	20 00	20 19		20 24	20 30	20 35		20 49	
Wandsworth Town	d		18 57	19 03			19 27	19 33					19 57	20 03			20 27	20 33				
Putney	d	←	19 00	19 06	19 23		19 30	19 36	19 39		19 53	←	20 00	20 06	20 23		20 30	20 36	20 39		20 53	←
Barnes	d	18 39	19 03	19 09			19 33	19 39				19 39	20 03	20 09			20 33	20 39				20 39
Barnes Bridge	d	18 41		19 11				→				19 41		20 11				→				20 41
Chiswick	d	18 44		19 13								19 44		20 13								20 44
Kew Bridge	d	18 46		19 16								19 46		20 16								20 46
Brentford	d	18 49		19 19								19 49		20 19								20 49
Syon Lane	d	18 51		19 21								19 51		20 21								20 51
Isleworth	d	18 53		19 23								19 53		20 23								20 53
Hounslow	d	18 57		19 26								19 57		20 26								20 57
Mortlake	d		19 05				19 35						20 05				20 35					
North Sheen	d		19 07				19 37						20 07				20 37					
Richmond ⊖	d		19 10		19 29		19 40		19 45		19 59		20 10		20 29		20 40		20 45		20 59	
St Margarets	d		19 12				19 42						20 12				20 42					
Twickenham	a	19 04	19 14		19 32		19 44		19 49		20 02	20 04	20 14		20 32		20 44		20 49		21 02	21 04
	d	19 11	19 15		19 33		19 45		19 49	19 56	20 03	20 11	20 15		20 33		20 45		20 49	20 56	21 03	21 11
Strawberry Hill	d	19 14					19 49					20 14					20 49					21 14
Fulwell	a																					
Teddington	a	19 17					19 52					20 17					20 52					21 17
Hampton Wick	a	19 20					19 57					20 20					20 57					21 20
Kingston	a	19 22					19 59					20 22					20 59					21 22
Whitton	d		19 18						19 52	19a59			20 18						20 52	20a59		
Feltham	d		19 22	19 32	19 39				19 57		20 09		20 22	20 32	20 39				20 57		21 09	
Ashford (Surrey)	d		19 26	19 36					20 01				20 26	20 36					21 01			
Staines	d		19 30	19 41	19 45				20 05		20 15		20 30	20 40	20 45				21 05		21 15	
Wraysbury	d		19 35										20 34									
Sunnymeads	d		19 38										20 37									
Datchet	d		19 42						20 12				20 40						21 13			
Windsor & Eton Riverside	a		19 46						20 17				20 46						21 19			
Egham	d			19 45	19 50						20 20			20 45	20 50						21 20	
Virginia Water	a			19 49	19 54						20 24			20 49	20 54						21 24	
	d			19 49	19 54						20 24			20 49	20 54						21 24	
Chertsey	d			19 55										20 55								
Addlestone	d			19a58										20a58								
Weybridge	a																					
Longcross	d																					
Sunningdale	d				20 00						20 30				21 00						21 31	
Ascot ■	d				20 05	20 13					20 35				21 05	21 13					21 35	
Bagshot	d					20 19										21 19						
Camberley	a					20 25										21 25						
Frimley	d					20 29										21 29						
Ash Vale	d					20 36										21 36						
Aldershot	a					20 42										21 41						
	d					20 48										21 48						
Ash ■	d					20 57										21 55						
Wanborough	d					21 00										21 59						
Guildford	a					21 07										22 06						
Martins Heron	d				20 09						20 39				21 09						21 39	
Bracknell	d				20 13						20 43				21 13						21 43	
Wokingham	d				20 19						20 49				21 19						21 49	
Winnersh	d				20 23						20 53				21 23						21 53	
Winnersh Triangle	d				20 25						20 55				21 25						21 55	
Earley	d				20 27						20 57				21 27						21 57	
Reading ■	a				20 35						21 05				21 35						22 05	

For additional services between Wokingham and Reading refer to Table T148

Table T149-F

Sundays

7 October to 2 December

London - Hounslow, Richmond, Kingston, Windsor, Weybridge, Ascot, Guildford and Reading

Station		SW	SW	SW ■	SW ■	SW	SW	SW	SW ■	SW	SW	SW	SW ■	SW ■	SW	SW	SW	SW ■	SW	SW	SW	SW ■	SW
London Waterloo ■ ⊖	d	20 44	20 50	21 09		21 14		21 20	21 39		21 44	21 50	22 09		22 14		22 20	22 39		22 44	22 50	23 09	23 14
Vauxhall ⊖	d	20 48	20 54	21 13		21 18		21 24	21 43		21 48	21 54	22 13		22 18		22 24	22 43		22 48	22 54	23 13	23 18
Queenstown Rd.(Battersea)	d	20 51	20 57			21 21		21 27			21 51	21 57			22 21		22 27			22 51	22 57		23 21
Clapham Junction ■	d	20 54	21 00	21 19		21 24		21 30	21 49		21 54	22 00	22 19		22 24		22 30	22 49		22 54	23 00	23 19	23 24
Wandsworth Town	d	20 57	21 03			21 27		21 33			21 57	22 03			22 27		22 33			22 57	23 03		23 27
Putney	d	21 00	21 06	21 23		21 30		21 36	21 53	←	22 00	22 06	22 23		22 30		22 36	22 53	←	23 00	23 06	23 23	23 30
Barnes	d	21 03	21 09			21 33		21 39		21 39	22 03	22 09			22 33		22 39		22 39	23 03	23 09		23 33
Barnes Bridge	d		21 11					→		21 41		22 11					→		22 41		23 11		
Chiswick	d		21 13							21 44		22 13							22 44		23 13		
Kew Bridge	d		21 16							21 46		22 16							22 46		23 16		
Brentford	d		21 19							21 49		22 19							22 49		23 19		
Syon Lane	d		21 21							21 51		22 21							22 51		23 21		
Isleworth	d		21 23							21 53		22 23							22 53		23 23		
Hounslow	d		21 26							21 57		22 26							22 57		23 26		
Mortlake	d	21 05				21 35					22 05				22 35					23 05			23 35
North Sheen	d	21 07				21 37					22 07				22 37					23 07			23 37
Richmond ⊖	d	21 10		21 29		21 40			21 59		22 10		22 29		22 40			22 59		23 10		23 29	23 40
St Margarets	d	21 12				21 42					22 12				22 42					23 12			23 42
Twickenham	a	21 14		21 32		21 44			22 02	22 04	22 14		22 32		22 44			23 02	23 04	23 14		23 32	23 44
	d	21 15		21 33		21 45	21 56		22 03	22 11	22 15		22 33		22 45	22 56		23 03	23 11	23 15		23 33	23 45
Strawberry Hill	d					21 49				22 14					22 49				23 14				23 48
Fulwell	a																						
Teddington	a					21 52				22 17					22 52				23 17				23 51
Hampton Wick	a					21 57				22 20					22 57				23 20				23 54
Kingston	a					21 59				22 22					22 59				23 22				23 56
Whitton	d	21 18					21a59				22 18					22a59				23 18			
Feltham	d	21 22	21 32	21 39					22 09		22 22	22 32	22 39					23 09		23 22	23 32	23 39	
Ashford (Surrey)	d	21 26	21 36								22 26	22 36								23 26	23 36		
Staines	d	21 30	21 40	21 45					22 15		22 30	22 40	22 45					23 15		23 30	23 40	23 45	
Wraysbury	d	21 34									22 35									23 35			
Sunnymeads	d	21 37									22 38									23 38			
Datchet	d	21 40									22 42									23 42			
Windsor & Eton Riverside	a	21 46									22 46									23 46			
Egham	d		21 45	21 50					22 20			22 45	22 50					23 20			23 45	23 50	
Virginia Water	a		21 49	21 54					22 24			22 49	22 54					23 24			23 49	23 54	
	d		21 49	21 54					22 24			22 49	22 54					23 24			23 49	23 54	
Chertsey	d		21 55									22 55									23 55		
Addlestone	d		21a58									22a58									23a58		
Weybridge	a																						
Longcross	d																						
Sunningdale	d			22 00					22 30				23 00					23 30				23 59	
Ascot ■	d			22 05	22 13				22 35				23 05	23 13				23 35				00 05	
Bagshot	d				22 19									23 19									
Camberley	a				22 25									23 25									
Frimley	d				22 29									23 29									
Ash Vale	d				22 36									23 36									
Aldershot	a				22 41									23 41									
	d				22 48																		
Ash ■	d				22 55																		
Wanborough	d				22 58																		
Guildford	a				23 06																		
Martins Heron	d			22 09					22 39				23 09					23 39				00 09	
Bracknell	d			22 13					22 43				23 13					23 43				00 13	
Wokingham	d			22 19					22 49				23 19					23 49				00 19	
Winnersh	d			22 23					22 53				23 23					23 53				00 23	
Winnersh Triangle	d			22 25					22 55				23 25					23 55				00 25	
Earley	d			22 27					22 57				23 27					23 57				00 27	
Reading ■	a			22 35					23 05				23 35					00 05				00 35	

For additional services between Wokingham and Reading refer to Table T148

Table T149-F

Sundays

7 October to 2 December

London - Hounslow, Richmond, Kingston, Windsor, Weybridge, Ascot, Guildford and Reading

		SW	SW ■	SW		SW
London Waterloo ■ ⊖	d	23 20	23 39			23 44
Vauxhall ⊖	d	23 24	23 43			23 48
Queenstown Rd.(Battersea)	d	23 27				23 51
Clapham Junction ■	d	23 30	23 49			23 54
Wandsworth Town	d	23 33				23 57
Putney	d	23 36	23 53	←		23 59
Barnes	d	23 39		23 39		00 03
Barnes Bridge	d	→		23 41		
Chiswick	d			23 44		
Kew Bridge	d			23 46		
Brentford	d			23 49		
Syon Lane	d			23 51		
Isleworth	d			23 53		
Hounslow	d			23 58		
Mortlake	d					00 05
North Sheen	d					00 07
Richmond ⊖	d		23 59			00 10
St Margarets	d					00 12
Twickenham	a		00 02	00 05		00 14
	d		00 03	00 12		00 15
Strawberry Hill	d			00 15		
Fulwell	a					
Teddington	a			00 18		
Hampton Wick	a			00 21		
Kingston	a			00 23		
Whitton	d					00 18
Feltham	d		00 09			00 22
Ashford (Surrey)	d					00 26
Staines	d		00 15			00a30
Wraysbury	d					
Sunnymeads	d					
Datchet	d					
Windsor & Eton Riverside	a					
Egham	d		00 20			
Virginia Water	a		00 24			
	d		00 24			
Chertsey	d					
Addlestone	d					
Weybridge	a					
Longcross	d					
Sunningdale	d		00 30			
Ascot ■	d		00 35			
Bagshot	d					
Camberley	a					
Frimley	d					
Ash Vale	d					
Aldershot	a					
	d					
Ash ■	d					
Wanborough	d					
Guildford	a					
Martins Heron	d		00 39			
Bracknell	d		00 43			
Wokingham	d		00 49			
Winnersh	d		00 53			
Winnersh Triangle	d		00 55			
Earley	d		00 57			
Reading ■	a		01 05			

For additional services between Wokingham and Reading refer to Table T148

Table T149-R

Mondays to Fridays

21 May to 5 October

Reading, Guildford, Ascot, Weybridge, Windsor, Kingston, Richmond and Hounslow - London

Miles	Miles	Miles	Miles			SW MO	SW MX	SW MO	SW MX ■	SW MX	SW MO ■	SW MX ■	SW	SW		SW	SW	SW	SW	SW	SW ◇	SW ◇	SW ◇	SW ■
—	—	0	—	**Reading** ■	d																			05 42
—	—	3	—	Earley	d																			05 47
—	—	4¼	—	Winnersh Triangle	d																			05 49
—	—	4¾	—	Winnersh	d																			05 51
—	—	6¾	—	**Wokingham**	d				00 02															05 56
—	—	11¼	—	Bracknell	d				00 08															06 02
—	—	12¼	—	Martins Heron	d				00 11															06 05
—	0	—	—	**Guildford**	d																			
—	4¼	—	—	Wanborough	d																			
—	6¼	—	—	Ash ■	d																			
—	9	—	—	**Aldershot**	a																			
—	—	—	—		d																			
—	11½	—	—	Ash Vale	d																			
—	14¾	—	—	Frimley	d																			
—	17	—	—	Camberley	a																			
—	—	—	—		d																			
—	20¼	—	—	Bagshot	d																			
—	23½	14½	—	**Ascot** ■	d				00a17															06 10
—	—	16½	—	Sunningdale	d																			06 13
—	—	18¼	—	Longcross	d																			
0	—	—	—	**Weybridge**	d																			
1¾	—	—	—	Addlestone	d																05 39			
3¼	—	—	—	Chertsey	d																05 42			
11	—	5¾	—	Virginia Water	a																05 47			06 19
—	—	—	—		d																05 54			06 19
—	—	22½	—	Egham	d																05 57			06 23
—	—	—	0	**Windsor & Eton Riverside**	d																	05 53		
—	—	—	2	Datchet	d																	05 56		
—	—	—	3	Sunnymeads	d																	05 59		
—	—	—	4¼	Wraysbury	d																	06 02		
—	—	24½	6¾	**Staines**	d									04 53				05 37			06 03	06 08		06 29
—	—	26	—	Ashford (Surrey)	d									04 56				05 40			06 06	06 11		
—	—	28¾	—	Feltham	d							00 05		05 01				05 45			06 11	06 16		06 35
—	—	31	—	Whitton	d			00 02						05 05				05 49				06 20		
0	—	—	—	**Kingston**	d								01 17							05 59				
0½	—	—	—	Hampton Wick	d								01s22							06 01				
1¾	—	—	—	Teddington	d								01s25							06 05				
2¾	—	—	—	Fulwell	d												05 36							
3	—	—	—	Strawberry Hill	d					00 03			01a28				05 38			06 08				
4	—	32¼	—	Twickenham	a			00 05		00 06		00 10		05 08			05 42	05 52		06 12		06 23		06 40
—	—	—	—		d							00 11		05 08			05 43	05 53		06 13		06 23		06 41
4½	—	32¾	—	St Margarets	d									05 10			05 45			06 15				
5½	—	33¾	—	**Richmond** ⊖	d							00 15		05 14			05 49	05 58		06 19		06 28		06 45
6¼	—	34½	—	North Sheen	d									05 16			05 51			06 21				
7	—	35¼	—	Mortlake	d									05 18			05 53			06 23				
—	0	—	—	**Hounslow**	d											05 31			06 01		06 16			
—	—	—	—	Isleworth	d											05 34			06 04		06 19			
—	2¼	—	—	Syon Lane	d											05 36			06 06		06 21			
—	3	—	—	Brentford	d											05 39			06 09		06 24			
—	4	—	—	Kew Bridge	d											05 41			06 11		06 26			
—	5	—	—	Chiswick	d											05 44			06 14		06 29			
—	6	—	—	Barnes Bridge	d											05 46			06 16		06 31			
8¼	6½	36½	—	Barnes	d									05 21		05 49	05 56		06 19	06 26	06 34		←	
9½	—	37¾	—	Putney	d						00 05			05 24		05 52	05 59	06 04	06 22	06 29	06 37	06 34	06 37	06 52
10½	—	38¾	—	Wandsworth Town	d		00 02							05 27		05 55	06 02		06 25	06 32	→		06 40	
11¼	—	39½	—	Clapham Junction ■	d	00 02	00 05				00 09	00 24		05 30		05 58	06 05	06 09	06 28	06 35		06 39	06 43	06 56
12½	—	41¼	—	Queenstown Rd.(Battersea)	d	00 05	00 08							05 33		06 01	06 08		06 31	06 38			06 46	
14	—	42¼	—	Vauxhall ⊖	d	00 08	00 12				00 15			05 37		06 05	06 12	06 15	06 35	06 42		06 45	06 50	
15¼	—	43½	—	**London Waterloo** ■ ⊖	a	00 13	00 16				00 19	00 38		05 41		06 09	06 16	06 19	06 39	06 46		06 49	06 56	07 07

Table T149-R

Mondays to Fridays

21 May to 5 October

Reading, Guildford, Ascot, Weybridge, Windsor, Kingston, Richmond and Hounslow - London

		SW ■	SW	SW	SW	SW ◇	SW	SW	SW	SW ◇	SW ■	SW	SW	SW ■	SW	SW ◇	SW ◇	SW	SW	SW ◇■	SW ■	SW ◇	SW ■
Reading ■	d										06 09			06 23									06 41
Earley	d										06 14												06 46
Winnersh Triangle	d										06 16												06 48
Winnersh	d										06 18												06 50
Wokingham	d										06 23			06 32									06 55
Bracknell	d										06 29			06 39									07 02
Martins Heron	d										06 32			06 42									07 05
Guildford	d																				06 30		
Wanborough	d																				06 36		
Ash ■	d																				06 40		
Aldershot	a																				06 47		
	d	05 58																		06 28			
Ash Vale	d	06 02																		06 32			
Frimley	d	06 10																		06 40			
Camberley	a	06 14																		06 44			
	d	06 18																		06 47			
Bagshot	d	06 23																		06 52			
Ascot ■	d	06a30									06 40			06 46						06 59			07 10
Sunningdale	d										06 43			06 50						07 02			07 13
Longcross	d																			07 05			
Weybridge	d									06 32												07 02	
Addlestone	d									06 36												07 06	
Chertsey	d									06 39												07 09	
Virginia Water	a									06 44	06 49			06 55						07 08		07 14	07 19
	d									06 45	06 49			06 55						07 08		07 15	07 19
Egham	d									06 48	06 53			06 59						07 12		07 18	07 23
Windsor & Eton Riverside	d					06 23										06 53							
Datchet	d					06 26										06 56							
Sunnymeads	d					06 29										06 59							
Wraysbury	d					06 32										07 02							
Staines	d				06 33	06 38				06 54	06 59			07 04		07 08				07 18		07 24	07 29
Ashford (Surrey)	d				06 36	06 41				06 57						07 11				07 21		07 27	
Feltham	d				06 41	06 46				07 02	07 05			07 12		07 16				07 26		07 32	07 36
Whitton	d		06 20			06 50		06 50	06 53							07 20			07 20	07 30			
Kingston	d			06 29									06 59										
Hampton Wick	d			06 31									07 01										
Teddington	d			06 35									07 05										
Fulwell	d														07 12								
Strawberry Hill	d			06 38									07 08		07 14			←					
Twickenham	a			06 42		06 53			06 56		07 10		07 12	07 17	07 18	07 23		07 18		07 33			07 41
	d			06 43		06 53			06 58		07 11		07 13	07 18	07 27	07 23		07 27		07 33			07 41
St Margarets	d			06 45					07 00				07 15		→			07 29					
Richmond ⊖	d			06 49		06 58			07 04		07 15		07 19	07 24		07 28		07 32		07 38			07 46
North Sheen	d			06 51					07 06				07 21					07 34					
Mortlake	d			06 53					07 08				07 23					07 37					
Hounslow	d		06 31		06 46			06 59		07 14									07 29			07 44	
Isleworth	d		06 34		06 49			07 02		07 17									07 32			07 47	
Syon Lane	d		06 36		06 51			07 05		07 20									07 35			07 50	
Brentford	d		06 39		06 54			07 08		07 23									07 38			07 53	
Kew Bridge	d		06 41		06 56			07 10		07 25									07 40			07 55	
Chiswick	d		06 44		06 59			07 13		07 28									07 43			07 58	
Barnes Bridge	d		06 46		07 01			07 16		07 31		←					←		07 46			08 01	
Barnes	d		06 49	06 56	07 04		←	07 19	07 11	07 34		07 19	07 26				07 34	07 40	07 49			08 04	
Putney	d		06 52	06 59	07 07	07 04	07 07	→	07 14	→	07 22	07 22	07 29			07 34	07 37	07 43	07 52			→	
Wandsworth Town	d		06 55	07 02	→		07 10		07 17			07 25	07 32				07 40	07 46	07 55				
Clapham Junction ■	d		06 58	07 05		07 09	07 13		07 20		07 26	07 28	07 35	07 33		07 39	07 43	07 49	07 58	07 47			07 54
Queenstown Rd.(Battersea)	d		07 01	07 08			07 16		07 23			07 31	07 38				07 46	07 52	08 01				
Vauxhall ⊖	d		07 05	07 12		07 15	07 20		07 27			07 35	07 42	07 38		07 45	07 50	07 56	08 05	07 53			
London Waterloo ■ ⊖	a		07 11	07 18		07 21	07 28		07 34		07 37	07 42	07 48	07 46		07 51	07 57	08 04	08 10	07 59			08 04

Table T149-R

Mondays to Fridays

21 May to 5 October

Reading, Guildford, Ascot, Weybridge, Windsor, Kingston, Richmond and Hounslow - London

		SW	SW ■	SW	SW ◇	SW ◇	SW	SW	SW ◇■	SW ■	SW ■	SW	SW ◇	SW ■	SW	SW ◇	SW ◇	SW	SW	SW ◇■	SW	SW ◇	SW ■
Reading ■	d		06 54								07 12			07 23									07 42
Earley	d										07 17												07 47
Winnersh Triangle	d										07 19												07 49
Winnersh	d										07 21												07 51
Wokingham	d		07 03								07 26			07 34									07 56
Bracknell	d		07 10								07 32			07 40									08 02
Martins Heron	d		07 13								07 35			07 43									08 05
Guildford	d									07 00													
Wanborough	d									07 06													
Ash ■	d									07 10													
Aldershot	a									07 17													
	d								07 00											07 30			
Ash Vale	d								07 04											07 34			
Frimley	d								07 10											07 40			
Camberley	a								07 14											07 44			
	d								07 17											07 47			
Bagshot	d								07 22											07 52			
Ascot ■	d		07 17						07 29		07 40			07 48						07 59			08 10
Sunningdale	d		07 21						07 32		07 43			07 51						08 02			08 13
Longcross	d								07 35														08 16
Weybridge	d												07 33									08 03	
Addlestone	d												07 37									08 07	
Chertsey	d												07 40									08 11	
Virginia Water	a		07 26						07 38				07 45	07 56						08 08		08 16	08 19
	d		07 26						07 38				07 50	07 56						08 08		08 24	08 19
Egham	d		07 29						07 42		07 50		07 54	07 59						08 12		→	08 23
Windsor & Eton Riverside	d				07 23											07 53							
Datchet	d				07 26											07 56							
Sunnymeads	d				07 29											07 59							
Wraysbury	d				07 32											08 02							
Staines	d		07 35		07 38				07 48		07 56		07 59	08 05		08 08				08 18			08 29
Ashford (Surrey)	d				07 41				07 51				08 02			08 11				08 21			
Feltham	d		07 42		07 46				07 56		08 02		08 07	08 12		08 16				08 26			08 35
Whitton	d				07 50			07 50	08 00							08 20			08 20	08 30	08 33		
Kingston	d	07 29										07 59											
Hampton Wick	d	07 31										08 01											
Teddington	d	07 35										08 05											
Fulwell	d			07 42											08 12								
Strawberry Hill	d	07 38		07 44			←					08 08			08 14			←					
Twickenham	a	07 42	07 47	07 48	07 53		07 48		08 03		08 09	08 12		08 17	08 18	08 23		08 18		08 33	08 36		08 40
	d	07 43	07 48	07 57	07 54		07 57		08 03		08 09	08 13		08 18	08 27	08 24		08 27		08 33	08 37		08 41
St Margarets	d	07 45		→			07 59					08 15			→			08 29					
Richmond ⊖	d	07 49	07 54		07 58		08 02		08 08		08 14	08 19		08 24		08 28		08 32		08 38	08 42		08 45
North Sheen	d	07 51					08 04					08 21						08 34					
Mortlake	d	07 53					08 07					08 23						08 37					
Hounslow	d							07 59					08 14						08 31				
Isleworth	d							08 02					08 17						08 34				
Syon Lane	d							08 05					08 20						08 36				
Brentford	d							08 08					08 23						08 39				
Kew Bridge	d							08 10					08 25						08 41				
Chiswick	d							08 13					08 28						08 44				
Barnes Bridge	d					←		08 16					08 31						08 46				
Barnes	d	07 56				08 04	08 10	08 19				08 26	08 34				←	08 40	08 49				
Putney	d	07 59			08 05	08 07	08 13	08 22				08 29	08 37			08 35	08 37	08 43	08 52		08 48		
Wandsworth Town	d	08 02				08 10	08 16	08 25				08 32	→				08 40	08 46	→		08 51		
Clapham Junction ■	d	08 05	08 03		08 09	08 13	08 19	08 28	08 17		08 22	08 35		08 33		08 39	08 43	08 49		08 47	08 54		08 54
Queenstown Rd.(Battersea)	d	08 08				08 16	08 22	08 31				08 38					08 46	08 52					
Vauxhall ⊖	d	08 12	08 09		08 15	08 20	08 26	08 35	08 23			08 42		08 38		08 45	08 50	08 56		08 53	09 01		
London Waterloo ■ ⊖	a	08 18	08 16		08 21	08 27	08 34	08 42	08 29		08 36	08 49		08 46		08 51	08 58	09 04		09 00	09 13		09 06

Table T149-R

Mondays to Fridays

21 May to 5 October

Reading, Guildford, Ascot, Weybridge, Windsor, Kingston, Richmond and Hounslow - London

		SW	SW ■	SW	SW ◇	SW ◇	SW ◇	SW ◇	SW	SW	SW ■	SW	SW ■	SW	SW ◇	SW ◇	SW ◇	SW	SW	SW	SW ■	SW
Reading ■	d										08 12										08 42	
Earley	d										08 17										08 47	
Winnersh Triangle	d										08 19										08 49	
Winnersh	d										08 21										08 51	
Wokingham	d										08 26										08 56	
Bracknell	d										08 32										09 02	
Martins Heron	d										08 35										09 05	
Guildford	d		07 30										08 01									
Wanborough	d		07 36										08 07									
Ash ■	d		07 40										08 11									
Aldershot	a		07 47										08 18									
	d		08 00										08 30									
Ash Vale	d		08 04										08 34									
Frimley	d		08 10										08 40									
Camberley	a		08 14										08 44									
	d		08 18										08 48									
Bagshot	d		08 23										08 53									
Ascot ■	d		08a30								08 40		09a00								09 10	
Sunningdale	d										08 43										09 13	
Longcross	d										08 46										09 16	
Weybridge	d							08 33										09 03				
Addlestone	d							08 37										09 07				
Chertsey	d				←			08 40							←			09 10				
Virginia Water	a				08 16			08 45			08 49				08 45			09 15			09 19	
	d				08 24			08 54			08 49				08 54			09 24			09 19	
Egham	d				08 27			→			08 53				08 57			→			09 23	
Windsor & Eton Riverside	d					08 23										08 53						
Datchet	d					08 26										08 56						
Sunnymeads	d					08 29										08 59						
Wraysbury	d					08 32										09 02						
Staines	d				08 33	08 38					08 59				09 03	09 08					09 29	
Ashford (Surrey)	d				08 36	08 41									09 06	09 11						
Feltham	d				08 41	08 46					09 05				09 11	09 16					09 35	
Whitton	d					08 50			08 50	08 53						09 20			09 20	09 23		
Kingston	d			08 29										08 59								
Hampton Wick	d			08 31										09 01								
Teddington	d			08 35										09 05								
Fulwell	d																					
Strawberry Hill	d			08 38										09 08								
Twickenham	a			08 42		08 53				08 56	09 10			09 12		09 23				09 26	09 40	
	d			08 43		08 53				08 58	09 11			09 13		09 23				09 28	09 41	
St Margarets	d			08 45						09 00				09 15						09 30		
Richmond ⊖	d			08 49		08 58				09 04	09 15			09 19		09 28				09 34	09 45	
North Sheen	d			08 51						09 06				09 21						09 36		
Mortlake	d			08 53						09 08				09 23						09 38		
Hounslow	d				08 46				09 01						09 16				09 31			
Isleworth	d				08 49				09 04						09 19				09 34			
Syon Lane	d				08 51				09 06						09 21				09 36			
Brentford	d				08 54				09 09						09 24				09 39			
Kew Bridge	d				08 56				09 11						09 26				09 41			
Chiswick	d				08 59				09 14						09 29				09 44			
Barnes Bridge	d				09 01				09 16			←			09 31				09 46			←
Barnes	d	←		08 56	09 04		←		09 19	09 11		09 19		09 26	09 34		←		09 49	09 41		09 49
Putney	d	08 52		08 59	09 07	09 04	09 07		→	09 14		09 22		09 29	09 37	09 34	09 37		→	09 44		09 52
Wandsworth Town	d	08 55		09 02	→		09 10			09 17		09 25		09 32	→		09 40			09 47		09 55
Clapham Junction ■	d	08 58		09 05		09 09	09 13			09 20	09 24	09 28		09 35		09 39	09 43			09 50	09 54	09 58
Queenstown Rd.(Battersea)	d	09 01		09 08			09 16			09 23		09 31		09 38			09 46			09 53		10 01
Vauxhall ⊖	d	09 05		09 12		09 15	09 20			09 27		09 35		09 42		09 45	09 50			09 57		10 05
London Waterloo ■ ⊖	a	09 13		09 18		09 21	09 28			09 34	09 34	09 43		09 48		09 51	09 58			10 02	10 04	10 11

Table T149-R

Mondays to Fridays

21 May to 5 October

Reading, Guildford, Ascot, Weybridge, Windsor, Kingston, Richmond and Hounslow - London

		SW ■	SW	SW	SW	SW	SW	SW	SW	SW ■	SW	SW	SW	SW	SW ■	SW	SW ■	SW	SW	SW	SW ■	SW	SW
Reading ■	d									09 12					09 25						09 42		
Earley	d									09 17					09 30						09 47		
Winnersh Triangle	d									09 19					09 32						09 49		
Winnersh	d									09 21					09 34						09 51		
Wokingham	d									09 26					09 39						09 56		
Bracknell	d									09 32					09 46						10 02		
Martins Heron	d									09 35					09 49						10 05		
Guildford	d	08 30															09 00						
Wanborough	d	08 36															09 06						
Ash ■	d	08 40															09 10						
Aldershot	a	08 48															09 17						
	d	09 00															09 30						
Ash Vale	d	09 04															09 34						
Frimley	d	09 10															09 40						
Camberley	a	09 14															09 44						
	d	09 18															09 48						
Bagshot	d	09 23															09 53						
Ascot ■	d	09a30								09 40					09 55		10a00				10 10		
Sunningdale	d									09 43					09 58						10 13		
Longcross	d																				10 16		
Weybridge	d						09 33											10 03					
Addlestone	d						09 37											10 07					
Chertsey	d			←			09 40						←					10 10					
Virginia Water	a			09 15			09 45			09 49			09 45		10 03			10 15			10 20		
	d			09 24			09 54			09 49			09 54		10 03			10 24			10 20		
Egham	d			09 27			→			09 53			09 57		10 06			→			10 24		
Windsor & Eton Riverside	d				09 23									09 53									
Datchet	d				09 26									09 56									
Sunnymeads	d				09 29									09 59									
Wraysbury	d				09 32									10 02									
Staines	d			09 33	09 38					09 59			10 03	10 08	10 14						10 29		
Ashford (Surrey)	d			09 36	09 41								10 06	10 11									
Feltham	d			09 41	09 46					10 05			10 11	10 16	10 20						10 35		
Whitton	d				09 50			09 50	09 53					10 20					10 20	10 26			
Kingston	d		09 29									09 59											10 29
Hampton Wick	d		09 31									10 01											10 31
Teddington	d		09 35									10 05											10 35
Fulwell	d																						
Strawberry Hill	d		09 38									10 08											10 38
Twickenham	a		09 42		09 53				09 56	10 10		10 12		10 23	10 26					10 28	10 40		10 42
	d		09 43		09 53				09 58	10 11		10 13		10 23	10 27					10 28	10 41		10 43
St Margarets	d		09 45						10 00			10 15								10 30			10 45
Richmond ⊖	d		09 49		09 58				10 04	10 15		10 19		10 28	10 32					10 34	10 45		10 49
North Sheen	d		09 51						10 06			10 21								10 36			10 51
Mortlake	d		09 53						10 08			10 23								10 38			10 53
Hounslow	d			09 46				10 01					10 16						10 31				
Isleworth	d			09 49				10 04					10 19						10 34				
Syon Lane	d			09 51				10 06					10 21						10 36				
Brentford	d			09 54				10 09					10 24						10 39				
Kew Bridge	d			09 56				10 11					10 26						10 41				
Chiswick	d			09 59				10 14					10 29						10 44				
Barnes Bridge	d			10 01				10 16			←		10 31						10 46			←	
Barnes	d		09 56	10 04		←		10 19	10 11		10 19	10 26	10 34			←			10 49	10 41		10 49	10 56
Putney	d		09 59	10 07	10 04	10 07		→	10 14		10 22	10 29	10 37	10 34		10 37			→	10 44		10 52	10 59
Wandsworth Town	d		10 02	→		10 10			10 17		10 25	10 32	→			10 40				10 47		10 55	11 02
Clapham Junction ■	d		10 05		10 09	10 13			10 20	10 24	10 28	10 35		10 39	10 42	10 43				10 50	10 54	10 58	11 05
Queenstown Rd.(Battersea)	d		10 08			10 16			10 23		10 31	10 38				10 47				10 53		11 01	11 08
Vauxhall ⊖	d		10 12		10 15	10 20			10 27		10 35	10 42		10 45		10 50				10 57		11 05	11 12
London Waterloo ■ ⊖	a		10 16		10 19	10 26			10 32	10 37	10 41	10 46		10 49	10 51	10 56				11 02	11 04	11 11	11 16

Table T149-R

Mondays to Fridays

21 May to 5 October

Reading, Guildford, Ascot, Weybridge, Windsor, Kingston, Richmond and Hounslow - London

		SW	SW	SW ■	SW	SW ■	SW	SW	SW	SW ■	SW	SW ■	SW	SW	SW	SW	SW	SW	SW	SW ■	SW	SW ■
Reading ■	d			09 55						10 12										10 42		
Earley	d			10 00						10 17										10 47		
Winnersh Triangle	d			10 02						10 19										10 49		
Winnersh	d			10 04						10 21										10 51		
Wokingham	d			10 09						10 26										10 56		
Bracknell	d			10 15						10 32										11 02		
Martins Heron	d			10 18						10 35										11 05		
Guildford	d					09 30						10 00										10 30
Wanborough	d					09 36						10 06										10 36
Ash ■	d					09 40						10 10										10 40
Aldershot	a					09 47						10 17										10 47
	d					10 00						10 30										11 00
Ash Vale	d					10 04						10 34										11 04
Frimley	d					10 10						10 40										11 10
Camberley	a					10 14						10 44										11 14
	d					10 18						10 48										11 18
Bagshot	d					10 23						10 53										11 23
Ascot ■	d			10 25		10a30				10 40		11a00								11 10		11a30
Sunningdale	d			10 28						10 43										11 13		
Longcross	d																					
Weybridge	d						10 33										11 03					
Addlestone	d						10 37										11 07					
Chertsey	d	←					10 40							←			11 10					
Virginia Water	a	10 15		10 33			10 45			10 49				10 45			11 15			11 19		
	d	10 24		10 33			10 54			10 49				10 54			11 24			11 19		
Egham	d	10 27		10 36			→			10 53				10 57			→			11 23		
Windsor & Eton Riverside	d		10 23												10 53							
Datchet	d		10 26												10 56							
Sunnymeads	d		10 29												10 59							
Wraysbury	d		10 32												11 02							
Staines	d	10 33	10 38	10 42						10 59				11 03	11 08					11 29		
Ashford (Surrey)	d	10 36	10 41											11 06	11 11							
Feltham	d	10 41	10 46	10 49						11 05				11 11	11 16					11 35		
Whitton	d		10 50					10 50	10 55						11 20			11 20	11 23			
Kingston	d												10 59									
Hampton Wick	d												11 01									
Teddington	d												11 05									
Fulwell	d																					
Strawberry Hill	d												11 08									
Twickenham	a		10 53	10 55					10 57	11 10			11 12		11 23				11 26	11 40		
	d		10 53	10 56					10 58	11 11			11 13		11 23				11 28	11 41		
St Margarets	d								11 00				11 15						11 30			
Richmond ⊖	d		10 58	11 01					11 03	11 15			11 19		11 28				11 34	11 45		
North Sheen	d								11 05				11 21						11 36			
Mortlake	d								11 08				11 23						11 38			
Hounslow	d	10 46						11 01						11 16				11 31				
Isleworth	d	10 49						11 04						11 19				11 34				
Syon Lane	d	10 51						11 06						11 21				11 36				
Brentford	d	10 54						11 09						11 24				11 39				
Kew Bridge	d	10 56						11 11						11 26				11 41				
Chiswick	d	10 59						11 14						11 29				11 44				
Barnes Bridge	d	11 01						11 16			←			11 31				11 46			←	
Barnes	d	11 04			←			11 19	11 11		11 19		11 26	11 34		←		11 49	11 41		11 49	
Putney	d	11 07	11 04		11 07			→	11 14		11 22		11 29	11 37	11 34	11 37		→	11 44		11 52	
Wandsworth Town	d	→			11 10				11 17		11 25		11 32	→		11 40			11 47		11 55	
Clapham Junction ■	d		11 09	11 12	11 13				11 20	11 24	11 28		11 35		11 39	11 43			11 50	11 54	11 58	
Queenstown Rd.(Battersea)	d				11 17				11 23		11 31		11 38			11 46			11 53		12 01	
Vauxhall ⊖	d		11 15		11 20				11 27		11 35		11 42		11 45	11 50			11 57		12 05	
London Waterloo ■ ⊖	a		11 19	11 25	11 27				11 32	11 34	11 42		11 46		11 49	11 56			12 02	12 04	12 11	

Table T149-R

Mondays to Fridays

21 May to 5 October

Reading, Guildford, Ascot, Weybridge, Windsor, Kingston, Richmond and Hounslow - London

		SW	SW	SW	SW	SW	SW	SW	SW ■	SW	SW ■	SW	SW	SW	SW	SW	SW	SW	SW ■	SW	SW ■	SW	SW
Reading ■	d								11 12										11 42				
Earley	d								11 17										11 47				
Winnersh Triangle	d								11 19										11 49				
Winnersh	d								11 21										11 51				
Wokingham	d								11 26										11 56				
Bracknell	d								11 32										12 02				
Martins Heron	d								11 35										12 05				
Guildford	d										11 00										11 30		
Wanborough	d										11 06										11 36		
Ash ■	d										11 10										11 40		
Aldershot	a										11 17										11 47		
	d										11 30										12 00		
Ash Vale	d										11 34										12 04		
Frimley	d										11 40										12 10		
Camberley	a										11 44										12 14		
	d										11 48										12 18		
Bagshot	d										11 53										12 23		
Ascot ■	d								11 40		12a00								12 10		12a30		
Sunningdale	d								11 43										12 13				
Longcross	d																						
Weybridge	d					11 33										12 03							
Addlestone	d					11 37										12 07							
Chertsey	d		←			11 40							←			12 10							←
Virginia Water	a		11 15			11 45			11 49				11 45			12 15			12 19				12 15
	d		11 24			11 54			11 49				11 54			12 24			12 19				12 24
Egham	d		11 27			→			11 53				11 57			→			12 23				12 27
Windsor & Eton Riverside	d			11 23										11 53									
Datchet	d			11 26										11 56									
Sunnymeads	d			11 29										11 59									
Wraysbury	d			11 32										12 02									
Staines	d		11 33	11 38					11 59				12 03	12 08					12 29				12 33
Ashford (Surrey)	d		11 36	11 41									12 06	12 11									12 36
Feltham	d		11 41	11 46					12 05				12 11	12 16					12 35				12 41
Whitton	d			11 50			11 51	11 53						12 20			12 20	12 23					
Kingston	d	11 29										11 59										12 29	
Hampton Wick	d	11 31										12 01										12 31	
Teddington	d	11 35										12 05										12 35	
Fulwell	d																						
Strawberry Hill	d	11 38										12 08										12 38	
Twickenham	a	11 42		11 53				11 56	12 10			12 12		12 23				12 26	12 40			12 42	
	d	11 43		11 53				11 58	12 11			12 13		12 23				12 28	12 41			12 43	
St Margarets	d	11 45						12 00				12 15						12 30				12 45	
Richmond ⊖	d	11 49		11 58				12 04	12 15			12 19		12 28				12 34	12 45			12 49	
North Sheen	d	11 51						12 06				12 21						12 36				12 51	
Mortlake	d	11 53						12 08				12 23						12 38				12 53	
Hounslow	d		11 46				12 01						12 16				12 31						12 46
Isleworth	d		11 49				12 04						12 19				12 34						12 49
Syon Lane	d		11 51				12 06						12 21				12 36						12 51
Brentford	d		11 54				12 09						12 24				12 39						12 54
Kew Bridge	d		11 56				12 11						12 26				12 41						12 56
Chiswick	d		11 59				12 14						12 29				12 44						12 59
Barnes Bridge	d		12 01				12 16			←			12 31				12 46			←			13 01
Barnes	d	11 56	12 04		←		12 19	12 11		12 19		12 26	12 34		←		12 49	12 41		12 49		12 56	13 04
Putney	d	11 59	12 07	12 04	12 07		→	12 14		12 22		12 29	12 37	12 34	12 37		→	12 44		12 52		12 59	13 07
Wandsworth Town	d	12 02	→		12 10			12 17		12 25		12 32	→		12 40			12 47		12 55		13 02	→
Clapham Junction ■	d	12 05		12 09	12 13			12 20	12 24	12 28		12 35		12 39	12 43			12 50	12 54	12 58		13 05	
Queenstown Rd.(Battersea)	d	12 08			12 16			12 23		12 31		12 38			12 46			12 53		13 01		13 08	
Vauxhall ⊖	d	12 12		12 15	12 20			12 27		12 35		12 42		12 45	12 50			12 57		13 05		13 12	
London Waterloo ■ ⊖	a	12 16		12 19	12 26			12 32	12 34	12 42		12 46		12 49	12 56			13 02	13 04	13 11		13 16	

21 May to 5 October

Reading, Guildford, Ascot, Weybridge, Windsor, Kingston, Richmond and Hounslow - London

		SW	SW	SW	SW	SW		SW [1]	SW	SW [1]	SW	SW	SW	SW	SW	SW		SW	SW [1]	SW	SW [1]	SW	SW	SW	SW
Reading [7]	d							12 12											12 42						
Earley	d							12 17											12 47						
Winnersh Triangle	d							12 19											12 49						
Winnersh	d							12 21											12 51						
Wokingham	d							12 26											12 56						
Bracknell	d							12 32											13 02						
Martins Heron	d							12 35											13 05						
Guildford	d									12 00											12 30				
Wanborough	d									12 06											12 36				
Ash [5]	d									12 10											12 40				
Aldershot	a									12 17											12 47				
	d									12 30											13 00				
Ash Vale	d									12 34											13 04				
Frimley	d									12 40											13 10				
Camberley	a									12 44											13 14				
	d									12 48											13 18				
Bagshot	d									12 53											13 23				
Ascot [8]	d							12 40		13a00									13 10		13a30				
Sunningdale	d							12 43											13 13						
Longcross	d																		13 16						
Weybridge	d			12 33											13 03										
Addlestone	d			12 37											13 07										
Chertsey	d			12 40								←			13 10								←		
Virginia Water	a			12 45				12 49				12 45			13 15				13 19				13 15		
	d			12 54				12 49				12 54			13 24				13 19				13 24		
Egham	d			→				12 53				12 57			→				13 23				13 27		
Windsor & Eton Riverside	d	12 23											12 53											13 23	
Datchet	d	12 26											12 56											13 26	
Sunnymeads	d	12 29											12 59											13 29	
Wraysbury	d	12 32											13 02											13 32	
Staines	d	12 38						12 59				13 03	13 08						13 29				13 33	13 38	
Ashford (Surrey)	d	12 41										13 06	13 11										13 36	13 41	
Feltham	d	12 46						13 05				13 11	13 16						13 35				13 41	13 46	
Whitton	d	12 50			12 50	12 53							13 20			13 20		13 23						13 50	
Kingston	d										12 59											13 29			
Hampton Wick	d										13 01											13 31			
Teddington	d										13 05											13 35			
Fulwell	d																								
Strawberry Hill	d										13 08											13 38			
Twickenham	a	12 53				12 56		13 10			13 12		13 23					13 26	13 40			13 42		13 53	
	d	12 53				12 58		13 11			13 13		13 23					13 28	13 41			13 43		13 53	
St Margarets	d					13 00					13 15							13 30				13 45			
Richmond ⊖	d	12 58				13 04		13 15			13 19		13 28					13 34	13 45			13 49		13 58	
North Sheen	d					13 06					13 21							13 36				13 51			
Mortlake	d					13 08					13 23							13 38				13 53			
Hounslow	d				13 01							13 16				13 31							13 46		
Isleworth	d				13 04							13 19				13 34							13 49		
Syon Lane	d				13 06							13 21				13 36							13 51		
Brentford	d				13 09							13 24				13 39							13 54		
Kew Bridge	d				13 11							13 26				13 41							13 56		
Chiswick	d				13 14							13 29				13 44							13 59		
Barnes Bridge	d				13 16				←			13 31				13 46				←			14 01		
Barnes	d		←		13 19	13 11			13 19		13 26	13 34		←		13 49		13 41		13 49		13 56	14 04		←
Putney	d	13 04	13 07		→	13 14			13 22		13 29	13 37	13 34	13 37		→		13 44		13 52		13 59	14 07	14 04	14 07
Wandsworth Town	d		13 10			13 17			13 25		13 32	→		13 40				13 47		13 55		14 02	→		14 10
Clapham Junction [10]	d	13 09	13 13			13 20		13 24	13 28		13 35		13 39	13 43				13 50	13 54	13 58		14 05		14 09	14 13
Queenstown Rd.(Battersea)	d		13 16			13 23			13 31		13 38			13 46				13 53		14 01		14 08			14 16
Vauxhall ⊖	d	13 15	13 20			13 27			13 35		13 42		13 45	13 50				13 57		14 05		14 12		14 15	14 20
London Waterloo [15] ⊖	a	13 19	13 26			13 32		13 34	13 41		13 46		13 49	13 56				14 02	14 04	14 11		14 17		14 19	14 26

21 May to 5 October

Reading, Guildford, Ascot, Weybridge, Windsor, Kingston, Richmond and Hounslow - London

		SW		SW	SW	SW [1]	SW	SW [1]	SW	SW	SW	SW		SW	SW	SW	SW [1]	SW	SW [1]	SW	SW	SW		SW	SW
Reading [7]	d					13 12											13 42								
Earley	d					13 17											13 47								
Winnersh Triangle	d					13 19											13 49								
Winnersh	d					13 21											13 51								
Wokingham	d					13 26											13 56								
Bracknell	d					13 32											14 02								
Martins Heron	d					13 35											14 05								
Guildford	d							13 00											13 30						
Wanborough	d							13 06											13 36						
Ash [5]	d							13 10											13 40						
Aldershot	a							13 17											13 47						
	d							13 30											14 00						
Ash Vale	d							13 34											14 04						
Frimley	d							13 40											14 10						
Camberley	a							13 44											14 14						
	d							13 48											14 18						
Bagshot	d							13 53											14 23						
Ascot [8]	d					13 40		14a00									14 10		14a30						
Sunningdale	d					13 43											14 13								
Longcross	d																								
Weybridge	d	13 33												14 03											14 33
Addlestone	d	13 37												14 07											14 37
Chertsey	d	13 40								←				14 10							←				14 40
Virginia Water	a	13 45				13 49				13 45				14 15			14 19				14 15				14 45
	d	13 54				13 49				13 54				14 24			14 19				14 24				14 54
Egham	d	→				13 53				13 57				→			14 23				14 27				→
Windsor & Eton Riverside	d										13 53											14 23			
Datchet	d										13 56											14 26			
Sunnymeads	d										13 59											14 29			
Wraysbury	d										14 02											14 32			
Staines	d					13 59				14 03	14 08						14 29				14 33	14 38			
Ashford (Surrey)	d									14 06	14 11										14 36	14 41			
Feltham	d					14 05				14 11	14 16						14 35				14 41	14 46			
Whitton	d			13 50	13 53						14 20				14 20	14 23						14 50			
Kingston	d								13 59											14 29					
Hampton Wick	d								14 01											14 31					
Teddington	d								14 05											14 35					
Fulwell	d																								
Strawberry Hill	d								14 08											14 38					
Twickenham	a				13 56	14 10			14 12		14 23					14 26	14 40			14 42		14 53			
	d				13 58	14 11			14 13		14 23					14 28	14 41			14 43		14 53			
St Margarets	d				14 00				14 15							14 30				14 45					
Richmond ⊖	d				14 04	14 15			14 19		14 28					14 34	14 45			14 49		14 58			
North Sheen	d				14 06				14 21							14 36				14 51					
Mortlake	d				14 08				14 23							14 38				14 53					
Hounslow	d			14 01						14 16					14 31						14 46				
Isleworth	d			14 04						14 19					14 34						14 49				
Syon Lane	d			14 06						14 21					14 36						14 51				
Brentford	d			14 09						14 24					14 39						14 54				
Kew Bridge	d			14 11						14 26					14 41						14 56				
Chiswick	d			14 14						14 29					14 44						14 59				
Barnes Bridge	d			14 16			←			14 31					14 46			←			15 01				
Barnes	d			14 19	14 11		14 19		14 26	14 34		←			14 49	14 41		14 49		14 56	15 04			←	
Putney	d			→	14 14		14 22		14 29	14 37	14 34	14 37			→	14 44		14 52		14 59	15 07	15 04		15 07	
Wandsworth Town	d				14 17		14 25		14 32	→		14 40				14 47		14 55		15 02	→			15 10	
Clapham Junction [10]	d				14 20	14 24	14 28		14 35		14 39	14 43				14 50	14 54	14 58		15 05		15 09		15 13	
Queenstown Rd.(Battersea)	d				14 23		14 31		14 38			14 46				14 53		15 01		15 08				15 16	
Vauxhall ⊖	d				14 27		14 35		14 42		14 45	14 50				14 57		15 05		15 12		15 15		15 20	
London Waterloo [15] ⊖	a				14 32	14 34	14 41		14 46		14 49	14 56				15 02	15 04	15 11		15 16		15 19		15 26	

Table T149-R

Mondays to Fridays

21 May to 5 October

Reading, Guildford, Ascot, Weybridge, Windsor, Kingston, Richmond and Hounslow - London

		SW	SW	SW ■	SW	SW ■	SW	SW	SW	SW	SW	SW	SW	SW ■	SW	SW ■	SW	SW	SW	SW	SW	SW	SW
Reading 7	d			14 12										14 42									
Earley	d			14 17										14 47									
Winnersh Triangle	d			14 19										14 49									
Winnersh	d			14 21										14 51									
Wokingham	d			14 26										14 56									
Bracknell	d			14 32										15 02									
Martins Heron	d			14 35										15 05									
Guildford	d					14 00										14 30							
Wanborough	d					14 06										14 36							
Ash ■	d					14 10										14 40							
Aldershot	a					14 17										14 47							
	d					14 30										15 00							
Ash Vale	d					14 34										15 04							
Frimley	d					14 40										15 10							
Camberley	a					14 44										15 14							
	d					14 48										15 18							
Bagshot	d					14 53										15 23							
Ascot ■	d			14 40		15a00								15 10		15a30							
Sunningdale	d			14 43										15 13									
Longcross	d																						
Weybridge	d										15 03										15 33		
Addlestone	d										15 07										15 37		
Chertsey	d							←			15 10							←			15 40		
Virginia Water	a			14 49				14 45			15 15			15 19				15 15			15 45		
	d			14 49				14 54			15 24			15 19				15 24			15 54		
Egham	d			14 53				14 57			→			15 23				15 27			→		
Windsor & Eton Riverside	d								14 53										15 23				
Datchet	d								14 56										15 26				
Sunnymeads	d								14 59										15 29				
Wraysbury	d								15 02										15 32				
Staines	d			14 59				15 03	15 08					15 29				15 33	15 38				
Ashford (Surrey)	d							15 06	15 11									15 36	15 41				
Feltham	d			15 05				15 11	15 16					15 35				15 41	15 46				
Whitton	d	14 50	14 53						15 20			15 20	15 23						15 50			15 50	15 53
Kingston	d						14 59										15 29						
Hampton Wick	d						15 01										15 31						
Teddington	d						15 05										15 35						
Fulwell	d																						
Strawberry Hill	d						15 08										15 38						
Twickenham	a		14 56	15 10			15 12		15 23				15 26	15 40			15 42		15 53				15 56
	d		14 58	15 11			15 13		15 23				15 28	15 41			15 43		15 53				15 58
St Margarets	d		15 00				15 15						15 30				15 45						16 00
Richmond ⊖	d		15 04	15 15			15 19		15 28				15 34	15 45			15 49		15 58				16 04
North Sheen	d		15 06				15 21						15 36				15 51						16 06
Mortlake	d		15 08				15 23						15 38				15 53						16 08
Hounslow	d	15 01						15 16				15 31						15 46				16 01	
Isleworth	d	15 04						15 19				15 34						15 49				16 04	
Syon Lane	d	15 06						15 21				15 36						15 51				16 06	
Brentford	d	15 09						15 24				15 39						15 54				16 09	
Kew Bridge	d	15 11						15 26				15 41						15 56				16 11	
Chiswick	d	15 14						15 29				15 44						15 59				16 14	
Barnes Bridge	d	15 16			←			15 31				15 46			←			16 01				16 16	
Barnes	d	15 19	15 11		15 19		15 26	15 34		←		15 49	15 41		15 49		15 56	16 04		←		16 19	16 11
Putney	d	→	15 14		15 22		15 29	15 37	15 34	15 37		→	15 44		15 52		15 59	16 07	16 04	16 07		→	16 14
Wandsworth Town	d		15 17		15 25		15 32	→		15 40			15 47		15 55		16 02	→		16 10			16 17
Clapham Junction 10	d		15 20	15 24	15 28		15 35		15 39	15 43			15 50	15 54	15 58		16 05		16 09	16 13			16 20
Queenstown Rd.(Battersea)	d		15 23		15 31		15 38			15 46			15 53		16 01		16 08			16 16			16 23
Vauxhall ⊖	d		15 27		15 35		15 42		15 45	15 50			15 57		16 05		16 12		16 15	16 20			16 27
London Waterloo 15 ⊖	a		15 32	15 34	15 41		15 46		15 49	15 56			16 05	16 05	16 11		16 19		16 19	16 26			16 32

Table T149-R

Mondays to Fridays

21 May to 5 October

Reading, Guildford, Ascot, Weybridge, Windsor, Kingston, Richmond and Hounslow - London

		SW ■	SW	SW ■	SW	SW	SW	SW	SW	SW	SW	SW ■	SW	SW ■	SW	SW	SW	SW	SW	SW	SW	SW ■
Reading 7	d	15 12										15 42										16 12
Earley	d	15 17										15 47										16 17
Winnersh Triangle	d	15 19										15 49										16 19
Winnersh	d	15 21										15 51										16 21
Wokingham	d	15 26										15 56										16 26
Bracknell	d	15 32										16 02										16 32
Martins Heron	d	15 35										16 05										16 35
Guildford	d			15 00										15 30								
Wanborough	d			15 06										15 36								
Ash ■	d			15 10										15 40								
Aldershot	a			15 17										15 47								
	d			15 30										16 00								
Ash Vale	d			15 34										16 04								
Frimley	d			15 40										16 10								
Camberley	a			15 44										16 14								
	d			15 48										16 18								
Bagshot	d			15 53										16 23								
Ascot ■	d	15 40		16a00								16 10		16a30								16 40
Sunningdale	d	15 43										16 13										16 43
Longcross	d											16 16										
Weybridge	d								16 03										16 33			
Addlestone	d								16 07										16 37			
Chertsey	d					←			16 10							←			16 40			
Virginia Water	a	15 49				15 45			16 15			16 20				16 15			16 45			16 49
	d	15 49				15 54			16 24			16 20				16 24			16 54			16 49
Egham	d	15 53				15 57			→			16 24				16 27			→			16 53
Windsor & Eton Riverside	d						15 53										16 23					
Datchet	d						15 56										16 26					
Sunnymeads	d						15 59										16 29					
Wraysbury	d						16 02										16 32					
Staines	d	15 59				16 03	16 08					16 29				16 33	16 38					16 59
Ashford (Surrey)	d					16 06	16 11									16 36	16 41					
Feltham	d	16 05				16 11	16 16					16 35				16 41	16 46					17 05
Whitton	d						16 20			16 20	16 23						16 50			16 50	16 53	
Kingston	d				15 59										16 29							
Hampton Wick	d				16 01										16 31							
Teddington	d				16 05										16 35							
Fulwell	d																					
Strawberry Hill	d				16 08										16 38							
Twickenham	a	16 10			16 12		16 23				16 26	16 40			16 42		16 53				16 56	17 10
	d	16 11			16 13		16 23				16 28	16 41			16 43		16 53				16 58	17 11
St Margarets	d				16 15						16 30				16 45						17 00	
Richmond ⊖	d	16 15			16 19		16 28				16 34	16 45			16 49		16 58				17 04	17 15
North Sheen	d				16 21						16 36				16 51						17 06	
Mortlake	d				16 23						16 38				16 53						17 08	
Hounslow	d					16 16				16 31						16 46				17 01		
Isleworth	d					16 19				16 34						16 49				17 04		
Syon Lane	d					16 21				16 36						16 51				17 06		
Brentford	d					16 24				16 39						16 54				17 09		
Kew Bridge	d					16 26				16 41						16 56				17 11		
Chiswick	d					16 29				16 44						16 59				17 14		
Barnes Bridge	d		←			16 31				16 46			←			17 01				17 16		
Barnes	d		16 19		16 26	16 34		←		16 49	16 41		16 49		16 56	17 04		←		17 19	17 11	
Putney	d		16 22		16 29	16 37	16 34	16 37		→	16 44		16 52		16 59	17 07	17 05	17 07		→	17 14	
Wandsworth Town	d		16 25		16 32	→		16 40			16 47		16 55		17 02	→		17 10			17 17	
Clapham Junction 10	d	16 24	16 28		16 35		16 39	16 43			16 50	16 54	16 58		17 05		17 09	17 13			17 20	17 24
Queenstown Rd.(Battersea)	d		16 31		16 38			16 46			16 53		17 01		17 08			17 16			17 23	
Vauxhall ⊖	d		16 35		16 42		16 45	16 50			16 57		17 05		17 12		17 15	17 20			17 27	
London Waterloo 15 ⊖	a	16 34	16 41		16 49		16 49	16 56			17 02	17 04	17 11		17 19		17 19	17 26			17 32	17 35

Table T149-R

Mondays to Fridays

21 May to 5 October

Reading, Guildford, Ascot, Weybridge, Windsor, Kingston, Richmond and Hounslow - London

		SW	SW ■	SW	SW	SW	SW	SW	SW	SW	SW	SW ■	SW	SW ■	SW	SW	SW	SW	SW	SW	SW	SW ■	SW
Reading ■	d											16 42										17 12	
Earley	d											16 47										17 17	
Winnersh Triangle	d											16 49										17 19	
Winnersh	d											16 51										17 21	
Wokingham	d											16 56										17 26	
Bracknell	d											17 02										17 32	
Martins Heron	d											17 05										17 35	
Guildford	d		16 00											16 30									
Wanborough	d		16 06											16 36									
Ash ■	d		16 10											16 40									
Aldershot	a		16 17											16 47									
	d		16 30											17 00									
Ash Vale	d		16 34											17 04									
Frimley	d		16 40											17 10									
Camberley	a		16 44											17 14									
	d		16 48											17 18									
Bagshot	d		16 53											17 23									
Ascot ■	d		17a00									17 10		17a30								17 40	
Sunningdale	d											17 13										17 43	
Longcross	d											17 16											
Weybridge	d							17 03															
Addlestone	d							17 07															
Chertsey	d				←			17 10								←							
Virginia Water	a				16 45			17 15				17 19				17 15						17 49	
	d				16 54			17 24				17 19				17 24						17 49	
Egham	d				16 57			→				17 23				17 27						17 53	
Windsor & Eton Riverside	d					16 53											17 23						
Datchet	d					16 56											17 26						
Sunnymeads	d					16 59											17 29						
Wraysbury	d					17 02											17 32						
Staines	d				17 03	17 08						17 29				17 33	17 38					17 59	
Ashford (Surrey)	d				17 06	17 11										17 36	17 41						
Feltham	d				17 11	17 16						17 35				17 41	17 46					18 05	
Whitton	d					17 20			17 20	17 23							17 50		17 50	17 53			
Kingston	d			16 59											17 29								
Hampton Wick	d			17 01											17 31								
Teddington	d			17 05											17 35								
Fulwell	d																						
Strawberry Hill	d			17 08							17 31				17 38						17 59		
Twickenham	a			17 12		17 23				17 26	17 34	17 40			17 42		17 53			17 56	18 02	18 10	
	d			17 13		17 23				17 28	17 35	17 41			17 43		17 53			17 58	18 03	18 11	
St Margarets	d			17 15						17 30					17 45					18 00	18 05		
Richmond ⊖	d			17 19		17 28				17 34	17 40	17 45			17 49		17 58			18 04	18 08	18 15	
North Sheen	d			17 21						17 36					17 51					18 06	18 10		
Mortlake	d			17 23						17 38					17 53					18 08	18 13		
Hounslow	d				17 16				17 31							17 46			18 01				
Isleworth	d				17 19				17 34							17 49			18 04				
Syon Lane	d				17 21				17 36							17 51			18 06				
Brentford	d				17 24				17 39							17 54			18 09				
Kew Bridge	d				17 26				17 41							17 56			18 11				
Chiswick	d				17 29				17 44							17 59			18 14				
Barnes Bridge	d	←			17 31				17 46				←			18 01			18 16				←
Barnes	d	17 19		17 26	17 34		←		17 49	17 41			17 49		17 56	18 04		←	18 19	18 12	18 16		18 19
Putney	d	17 22		17 29	17 37	17 34	17 37		→	17 44			17 52		17 59	18 07	18 04	18 07	→	18 15	18 19		18 22
Wandsworth Town	d	17 25		17 32	→		17 40			17 47			17 55		18 02	→		18 10		18 18			18 25
Clapham Junction ■	d	17 28		17 35		17 39	17 43			17 51	17 49	17 54	17 58		18 05		18 09	18 13		18 21	18 24	18 26	18 28
Queenstown Rd.(Battersea)	d	17 31		17 38			17 46			17 54			18 01		18 08			18 16		18 24			18 31
Vauxhall ⊖	d	17 35		17 42		17 45	17 50			17 58	17 55		18 05		18 12		18 15	18 20		18 27	18 30		18 35
London Waterloo ■ ⊖	a	17 41		17 49		17 49	17 57			18 04	18 02	18 09	18 11		18 19		18 19	18 26		18 33	18 34	18 39	18 41

Table T149-R

Mondays to Fridays

21 May to 5 October

Reading, Guildford, Ascot, Weybridge, Windsor, Kingston, Richmond and Hounslow - London

		SW	SW	SW	SW	SW ■	SW ■	SW	SW	SW ■	SW	SW	SW	SW	SW	SW ■	SW ■	SW	SW	SW ■	SW	SW ■	SW
Reading ■	d					17 23				17 42						17 56				18 12			
Earley	d					17 28				17 47						18 01				18 17			
Winnersh Triangle	d					17 30				17 49						18 03				18 19			
Winnersh	d					17 32				17 51						18 05				18 21			
Wokingham	d					17 37				17 56						18 10				18 26			
Bracknell	d					17 43				18 02						18 16				18 32			
Martins Heron	d					17 46				18 05						18 19				18 35			
Guildford	d						17 00										17 30					18 00	
Wanborough	d						17 06										17 36					18 06	
Ash ■	d						17 10										17 40					18 10	
Aldershot	a						17 17										17 47					18 17	
	d						17 30										18 00					18 30	
Ash Vale	d						17 34										18 04					18 34	
Frimley	d						17 40										18 10					18 40	
Camberley	a						17 44										18 14					18 44	
	d						17 48										18 18					18 48	
Bagshot	d						17 53										18 23					18 53	
Ascot ■	d					17 55	18a00			18 10						18 25	18a30			18 40		19a02	
Sunningdale	d					17 58				18 13						18 28				18 43			
Longcross	d									18 16										18 46			
Weybridge	d		17 37										18 07										
Addlestone	d		17 41										18 11										
Chertsey	d		17 44										18 14										
Virginia Water	a		17 49			18 03				18 19			18 19			18 33				18 49			
	d		17 54			18 03				18 19			18 24			18 33				18 49			
Egham	d		17 57			18 06				18 23			18 27			18 37				18 53			
Windsor & Eton Riverside	d			17 53										18 23									
Datchet	d			17 56										18 26									
Sunnymeads	d			17 59										18 29									
Wraysbury	d			18 02										18 32									
Staines	d		18 03	18 08		18 14				18 29			18 33	18 38		18 44				18 59			
Ashford (Surrey)	d		18 06	18 11									18 36	18 41									
Feltham	d		18 11	18 16		18 20				18 35			18 41	18 46		18 50				19 05			
Whitton	d			18 20				18 20	18 23					18 50				18 50	18 53				
Kingston	d	17 59										18 29											18 59
Hampton Wick	d	18 01										18 31											19 01
Teddington	d	18 05										18 35											19 05
Fulwell	d																						
Strawberry Hill	d	18 08										18 38											19 08
Twickenham	a	18 12		18 23					18 26	18 40		18 42		18 53					18 56	19 10			19 12
	d	18 13		18 23					18 28	18 41		18 43		18 53					18 58	19 11			19 13
St Margarets	d	18 15							18 30			18 45							19 00				19 15
Richmond ⊖	d	18 19		18 28					18 34	18 45		18 49		18 58					19 04	19 15			19 19
North Sheen	d	18 21							18 36			18 51							19 06				19 21
Mortlake	d	18 23							18 38			18 53							19 08				19 23
Hounslow	d		18 16			18 26		18 31					18 46			18 56		19 01					
Isleworth	d		18 19					18 34					18 49					19 04					
Syon Lane	d		18 21					18 36					18 51					19 06					
Brentford	d		18 24			18 31		18 39					18 54			19 01		19 09					
Kew Bridge	d		18 26					18 41					18 56					19 11					
Chiswick	d		18 29					18 44					18 59					19 14					
Barnes Bridge	d		18 31					18 46			←		19 01					19 16			←		
Barnes	d	18 26	18 34		←			18 49	18 41		18 49	18 56	19 04		←			19 19	19 11		19 19		19 26
Putney	d	18 29	18 37	18 34	18 37	18 39		→	18 44		18 52	18 59	19 07	19 04	19 07	19 09		→	19 14		19 22		19 29
Wandsworth Town	d	18 32	→		18 40				18 47		18 55	19 02	→		19 10				19 17		19 25		19 32
Clapham Junction ■	d	18 35		18 39	18 43	18 44			18 50	18 54	18 58	19 05		19 09	19 13	19 14			19 20	19 24	19 28		19 35
Queenstown Rd.(Battersea)	d	18 38			18 46				18 53		19 01	19 08			19 16				19 23		19 31		19 38
Vauxhall ⊖	d	18 42		18 45	18 50				18 57		19 05	19 12		19 15	19 20				19 27		19 35		19 42
London Waterloo ■ ⊖	a	18 49		18 49	18 56	18 56			19 02	19 04	19 11	19 16		19 19	19 26	19 28			19 32	19 34	19 41		19 46

Table T149-R

Mondays to Fridays

21 May to 5 October

Reading, Guildford, Ascot, Weybridge, Windsor, Kingston, Richmond and Hounslow - London

		SW		SW	SW	SW	SW	SW ■	SW	SW	SW	SW		SW	SW ■	SW ■	SW	SW	SW ■	SW	SW ■	SW		SW	SW
Reading 7	d							18 42							18 52				19 12						
Earley	d							18 47							18 57				19 17						
Winnersh Triangle	d							18 49							18 59				19 19						
Winnersh	d							18 51							19 01				19 21						
Wokingham	d							18 56							19 06				19 26						
Bracknell	d							19 02							19 12				19 32						
Martins Heron	d							19 05							19 15				19 35						
Guildford	d															18 30					19 00				
Wanborough	d															18 36					19 06				
Ash 6	d															18 40					19 10				
Aldershot	a															18 47					19 17				
	d															19 00					19 30				
Ash Vale	d															19 04					19 34				
Frimley	d															19 10					19 40				
Camberley	a															19 14					19 44				
	d															19 18					19 48				
Bagshot	d															19 23					19 53				
Ascot 3	d							19 10							19 20	19a30			19 40		20a00				
Sunningdale	d							19 13							19 23				19 43						
Longcross	d							19 16											19 46						
Weybridge	d	18 37									19 07													19 37	
Addlestone	d	18 41									19 11													19 41	
Chertsey	d	18 44									19 14													19 44	
Virginia Water	a	18 49						19 19			19 19				19 28				19 49					19 49	
	d	18 54						19 19			19 24				19 28				19 49					19 54	
Egham	d	18 57						19 23			19 27				19 31				19 53					19 57	
Windsor & Eton Riverside	d			18 53								19 23													19 53
Datchet	d			18 56								19 26													19 56
Sunnymeads	d			18 59								19 29													19 59
Wraysbury	d			19 02								19 32													20 02
Staines	d	19 03		19 08				19 29			19 33	19 38			19a41				19 59					20 03	20 08
Ashford (Surrey)	d	19 06		19 11							19 36	19 41												20 06	20 11
Feltham	d	19 11		19 16				19 35			19 41	19 46							20 05					20 11	20 16
Whitton	d			19 20		19 20	19 23					19 50					19 50	19 53							20 20
Kingston	d									19 29												19 59			
Hampton Wick	d									19 31												20 01			
Teddington	d									19 35												20 05			
Fulwell	d																								
Strawberry Hill	d									19 38												20 08			
Twickenham	a			19 23			19 26	19 40		19 42		19 53						19 56	20 10			20 12			20 23
	d			19 23			19 28	19 41		19 43		19 53						19 58	20 11			20 13			20 23
St Margarets	d						19 30			19 45								20 00				20 15			
Richmond ⊖	d			19 28			19 34	19 45		19 49		19 58						20 04	20 15			20 19			20 28
North Sheen	d						19 36			19 51								20 06				20 21			
Mortlake	d						19 38			19 53								20 08				20 23			
Hounslow	d	19 16				19 31					19 46						20 01							20 16	
Isleworth	d	19 19				19 34					19 49						20 04							20 19	
Syon Lane	d	19 21				19 36					19 51						20 06							20 21	
Brentford	d	19 24				19 39					19 54						20 09							20 24	
Kew Bridge	d	19 26				19 41					19 56						20 11							20 26	
Chiswick	d	19 29				19 44					19 59						20 14							20 29	
Barnes Bridge	d	19 31				19 46			←		20 01						20 16			←				20 31	
Barnes	d	19 34			←	19 49	19 41		19 49	19 56	20 04			←			20 19	20 11		20 19		20 26		20 34	
Putney	d	19 37		19 34	19 37	→	19 44		19 52	19 59	20 07	20 04		20 07			→	20 14		20 22		20 29		20 37	20 34
Wandsworth Town	d	→			19 40		19 47		19 55	20 02	→			20 10				20 17		20 25		20 32		→	
Clapham Junction 10	d			19 39	19 43		19 50	19 54	19 58	20 05		20 09		20 13				20 20	20 24	20 28		20 35			20 39
Queenstown Rd.(Battersea)	d				19 46		19 53		20 01	20 08				20 16				20 23		20 31		20 38			
Vauxhall ⊖	d			19 45	19 50		19 57		20 05	20 12		20 15		20 20				20 27		20 35		20 42			20 45
London Waterloo 15 ⊖	a			19 49	19 56		20 02	20 04	20 11	20 16		20 19		20 27				20 32	20 34	20 41		20 46			20 49

Table T149-R

Mondays to Fridays

21 May to 5 October

Reading, Guildford, Ascot, Weybridge, Windsor, Kingston, Richmond and Hounslow - London

		SW	SW	SW	SW	SW ■	SW	SW ■		SW	SW	SW	SW	SW	SW	SW	SW ■	SW		SW ■	SW ■	SW	SW	SW	SW
Reading 7	d					19 42											20 12								
Earley	d					19 47											20 17								
Winnersh Triangle	d					19 49											20 19								
Winnersh	d					19 51											20 21								
Wokingham	d					19 56											20 26								
Bracknell	d					20 02											20 32								
Martins Heron	d					20 05											20 35								
Guildford	d							19 30												20 00	20 30				
Wanborough	d							19 36												20 06	20 36				
Ash 6	d							19 40												20 10	20 40				
Aldershot	a							19 47												20 17	20 47				
	d							20 00												20 30					
Ash Vale	d							20 04												20 34					
Frimley	d							20 10												20 40					
Camberley	a							20 14												20 44					
	d							20 18												20 48					
Bagshot	d							20 23												20 53					
Ascot 3	d					20 10		20a30									20 40			21a00					
Sunningdale	d					20 13											20 43								
Longcross	d					20 16											20 46								
Weybridge	d		20 05											20 33											
Addlestone	d		20 09											20 37											
Chertsey	d		20 12								←			20 40									←		
Virginia Water	a		20 17			20 19					20 17			20 45			20 49						20 45		
	d		20 24			20 19					20 24			20 54			20 49						20 54		
Egham	d		→			20 23					20 27			→			20 53						20 57		
Windsor & Eton Riverside	d											20 23												20 53	
Datchet	d											20 26												20 56	
Sunnymeads	d											20 29												20 59	
Wraysbury	d											20 32												21 02	
Staines	d					20 29					20 33	20 38					20 59						21 03	21 08	
Ashford (Surrey)	d										20 36	20 41											21 06	21 11	
Feltham	d					20 35					20 41	20 46					21 05						21 11	21 16	
Whitton	d			20 20	20 23							20 50			20 50	20 53								21 20	
Kingston	d									20 29												20 59			
Hampton Wick	d									20 31												21 01			
Teddington	d									20 35												21 05			
Fulwell	d																								
Strawberry Hill	d									20 38												21 08			
Twickenham	a				20 26	20 40				20 42		20 53				20 56	21 10					21 12		21 23	
	d				20 28	20 41				20 43		20 53				20 58	21 11					21 13		21 23	
St Margarets	d				20 30					20 45						21 00						21 15			
Richmond ⊖	d				20 34	20 45				20 49		20 58				21 04	21 15					21 19		21 28	
North Sheen	d				20 36					20 51						21 06						21 21			
Mortlake	d				20 38					20 53						21 08						21 23			
Hounslow	d			20 31							20 46				21 01								21 16		
Isleworth	d			20 34							20 49				21 04								21 19		
Syon Lane	d			20 36							20 51				21 06								21 21		
Brentford	d			20 39							20 54				21 09								21 24		
Kew Bridge	d			20 41							20 56				21 11								21 26		
Chiswick	d			20 44							20 59				21 14								21 29		
Barnes Bridge	d			20 46			←				21 01				21 16			←					21 31		
Barnes	d	←		20 49	20 41		20 49			20 56	21 04		←		21 19	21 11		21 19				21 26	21 34		←
Putney	d	20 37		→	20 44		20 52			20 59	21 07	21 04	21 07		→	21 14		21 22				21 29	21 37	21 34	21 37
Wandsworth Town	d	20 40			20 47		20 55			21 02	→		21 10			21 17		21 25				21 32	→		21 40
Clapham Junction 10	d	20 43			20 50	20 54	20 58			21 05		21 09	21 13			21 20	21 24	21 28				21 35		21 39	21 43
Queenstown Rd.(Battersea)	d	20 46			20 53		21 01			21 08			21 16			21 23		21 31				21 38			21 46
Vauxhall ⊖	d	20 50			20 57		21 05			21 12		21 15	21 20			21 27		21 35				21 42		21 45	21 50
London Waterloo 15 ⊖	a	20 56			21 02	21 04	21 11			21 16		21 19	21 26			21 32	21 34	21 41				21 46		21 49	21 56

Table T149-R

Mondays to Fridays

21 May to 5 October

Reading, Guildford, Ascot, Weybridge, Windsor, Kingston, Richmond and Hounslow - London

		SW	SW	SW	SW ■	SW	SW	SW	SW	SW	SW	SW	SW	SW ■	SW	SW ■	SW ■	SW	SW	SW	SW	SW
Reading ■	d				20 42									21 12								
Earley	d				20 47									21 17								
Winnersh Triangle	d				20 49									21 19								
Winnersh	d				20 51									21 21								
Wokingham	d				20 56									21 26								
Bracknell	d				21 02									21 32								
Martins Heron	d				21 05									21 35								
Guildford	d															21 00	21 30					
Wanborough	d															21 06	21 36					
Ash ■	d															21 10	21 40					
Aldershot	a															21 17	21 47					
	d															21 30						
Ash Vale	d															21 34						
Frimley	d															21 40						
Camberley	a															21 44						
	d															21 48						
Bagshot	d															21 53						
Ascot ■	d				21 10									21 40		22a00						
Sunningdale	d				21 13									21 43								
Longcross	d																					
Weybridge	d	21 03									21 33											
Addlestone	d	21 07									21 37											
Chertsey	d	21 10						←			21 40								←			
Virginia Water	a	21 15			21 19			21 15			21 45			21 49					21 45			
	d	21 24			21 19			21 24			21 54			21 49					21 54			
Egham	d	→			21 23			21 27			→			21 53					21 57			
Windsor & Eton Riverside	d								21 23											21 53		
Datchet	d								21 26											21 56		
Sunnymeads	d								21 29											21 59		
Wraysbury	d								21 32											22 02		
Staines	d				21 29			21 33	21 38					21 59					22 03	22 08		
Ashford (Surrey)	d							21 36	21 41										22 06	22 11		
Feltham	d				21 35			21 41	21 46					22 05					22 11	22 16		
Whitton	d		21 20	21 23					21 50			21 50	21 53							22 20		22 23
Kingston	d						21 29											21 59				
Hampton Wick	d						21 31											22 01				
Teddington	d						21 35											22 05				
Fulwell	d																					
Strawberry Hill	d						21 38											22 08				
Twickenham	a			21 26	21 40		21 42		21 53				21 56	22 10				22 12		22 23		22 26
	d			21 28	21 41		21 43		21 53				21 58	22 11				22 13		22 23		22 28
St Margarets	d			21 30			21 45						22 00					22 15				22 30
Richmond ⊖	d			21 34	21 45		21 49		21 58				22 04	22 15				22 19		22 28		22 34
North Sheen	d			21 36			21 51						22 06					22 21				22 36
Mortlake	d			21 38			21 53						22 08					22 23				22 38
Hounslow	d		21 31					21 46				22 01							22 16			
Isleworth	d		21 34					21 49				22 04							22 19			
Syon Lane	d		21 36					21 51				22 06							22 21			
Brentford	d		21 39					21 54				22 09							22 24			
Kew Bridge	d		21 41					21 56				22 11							22 26			
Chiswick	d		21 44					21 59				22 14							22 29			
Barnes Bridge	d		21 46			←		22 01				22 16			←				22 31			
Barnes	d		21 49	21 41		21 49	21 56	22 04		←		22 19	22 11		22 19			22 26	22 34		←	22 41
Putney	d		→	21 44		21 52	21 59	22 07	22 04	22 07		→	22 14		22 22			22 29	22 37	22 34	22 37	22 44
Wandsworth Town	d			21 47		21 55	22 02	→		22 10			22 17		22 25			22 32	→		22 40	22 47
Clapham Junction ■	d			21 50	21 54	21 58	22 05		22 09	22 13			22 20	22 24	22 28			22 35		22 39	22 43	22 50
Queenstown Rd.(Battersea)	d			21 53		22 01	22 08			22 16			22 23		22 31			22 38			22 46	22 53
Vauxhall ⊖	d			21 57		22 05	22 12		22 15	22 20			22 27		22 35			22 42		22 45	22 50	22 57
London Waterloo ■ ⊖	a			22 02	22 04	22 11	22 16		22 19	22 26			22 32	22 34	22 41			22 46		22 49	22 56	23 02

Table T149-R

Mondays to Fridays

21 May to 5 October

Reading, Guildford, Ascot, Weybridge, Windsor, Kingston, Richmond and Hounslow - London

		SW	SW ■	SW	SW	SW	SW	SW	SW MX ■	SW MO ■	SW ■	SW ■	SW	SW	SW	SW	SW	SW ■	SW	SW	SW	SW	SW
Reading ■	d		21 42						22 12	22 12								22 42					
Earley	d		21 47						22 17	22 17								22 47					
Winnersh Triangle	d		21 49						22 19	22 19								22 49					
Winnersh	d		21 51						22 21	22 21								22 51					
Wokingham	d		21 56						22 26	22 26								22 56					
Bracknell	d		22 02						22 32	22 32								23 02					
Martins Heron	d		22 05						22 35	22 35								23 05					
Guildford	d										22 00	22 30											
Wanborough	d										22 06	22 36											
Ash ■	d										22 10	22 40											
Aldershot	a										22 17	22 47											
	d										22 30												
Ash Vale	d										22 34												
Frimley	d										22 40												
Camberley	a										22 44												
	d										22 48												
Bagshot	d										22 53												
Ascot ■	d		22 10						22 40	22 40	23a00							23 10					
Sunningdale	d		22 13						22 43	22 43								23 13					
Longcross	d																						
Weybridge	d	22 03						22 33									23 03						23 33
Addlestone	d	22 07						22 37									23 07						23 37
Chertsey	d	22 10			←			22 40						←			23 10		←				23 40
Virginia Water	a	22 15	22 19		22 15			22 45	22 49	22 49				22 45			23 15	23 19	23 15				23 45
	d	22 24	22 19		22 24			22 54	22 49	22 49				22 54			23 24	23 19	23 24				23 54
Egham	d	→	22 23		22 27			→	22 53	22 53				22 57			→	23 23	23 27				→
Windsor & Eton Riverside	d					22 23									22 53					23 28			
Datchet	d					22 26									22 56					23 31			
Sunnymeads	d					22 29									22 59					23 34			
Wraysbury	d					22 32									23 02					23 37			
Staines	d		22 29		22 33	22 38			22 59	22 59				23 03	23 08			23 29	23a32	23a42			
Ashford (Surrey)	d				22 36	22 41								23 06	23 11								
Feltham	d		22 35		22 41	22 46			23 05	23 05				23 11	23 16			23 35					
Whitton	d					22 50									23 20								
Kingston	d			22 29									22 59								23 29	23 55	
Hampton Wick	d			22 31									23 01								23 31	23 57	
Teddington	d			22 35									23 05								23 35	23 59	
Fulwell	d																						
Strawberry Hill	d			22 38									23 08								23 38	00 03	
Twickenham	a		22 40	22 42		22 53			23 10	23 10			23 12		23 23			23 40			23 42	00 06	
	d		22 41	22 43		22 53			23 11	23 11			23 13		23 23			23 41			23 43		
St Margarets	d			22 45									23 15								23 45		
Richmond ⊖	d		22 45	22 49		22 58			23 15	23 15			23 19		23 28			23 45			23 49		
North Sheen	d			22 51									23 21								23 51		
Mortlake	d			22 53									23 23								23 53		
Hounslow	d				22 46									23 16									
Isleworth	d				22 49									23 19									
Syon Lane	d				22 51									23 21									
Brentford	d				22 54									23 24									
Kew Bridge	d				22 56									23 26									
Chiswick	d				22 59									23 29									
Barnes Bridge	d				23 01									23 31									
Barnes	d			22 56	23 04		←						23 26	23 34		←					23 56		
Putney	d			22 59	23 07	23 04	23 07						23 29	23 37	23 34	23 37					23 59		
Wandsworth Town	d			23 02	→		23 10						23 32	→		23 40					00 02		
Clapham Junction ■	d		22 54	23 05		23 10	23 13		23 24	23 24			23 35		23 39	23 43		23 54			00 05		
Queenstown Rd.(Battersea)	d			23 08			23 16						23 38			23 46					00 08		
Vauxhall ⊖	d			23 12		23 15	23 20						23 42		23 45	23 50					00 12		
London Waterloo ■ ⊖	a		23 04	23 16		23 20	23 26		23 34	23 36			23 47		23 49	23 56		00 04			00 16		

21 May to 5 October

Reading, Guildford, Ascot, Weybridge, Windsor, Kingston, Richmond and Hounslow - London

		SW ■	SW	SW ■	SW ■	SW ■
Reading ■	d	23 12				23 52
Earley	d	23 17				
Winnersh Triangle	d	23 19				
Winnersh	d	23 21				
Wokingham	d	23 26				00 02
Bracknell	d	23 32				00 08
Martins Heron	d	23 35				00 11
Guildford	d			23 00	23 30	
Wanborough	d			23 06	23 36	
Ash ■	d			23 10	23 40	
Aldershot	a			23 18	23 47	
	d			23 30		
Ash Vale	d			23 34		
Frimley	d			23 40		
Camberley	a			23 44		
	d			23 48		
Bagshot	d			23 53		
Ascot ■	d	23 40		00a01		00a17
Sunningdale	d	23 43				
Longcross	d					
Weybridge	d					
Addlestone	d					
Chertsey	d		←			
Virginia Water	a	23 49	23 45			
	d	23 49	23 54			
Egham	d	23 53	23 57			
Windsor & Eton Riverside	d					
Datchet	d					
Sunnymeads	d					
Wraysbury	d					
Staines	d	23 59	00a02			
Ashford (Surrey)	d					
Feltham	d	00 05				
Whitton	d					
Kingston	d					
Hampton Wick	d					
Teddington	d					
Fulwell	d					
Strawberry Hill	d					
Twickenham	a	00 10				
	d	00 11				
St Margarets	d					
Richmond	⊖ d	00 15				
North Sheen	d					
Mortlake	d					
Hounslow	d					
Isleworth	d					
Syon Lane	d					
Brentford	d					
Kew Bridge	d					
Chiswick	d					
Barnes Bridge	d					
Barnes	d					
Putney	d					
Wandsworth Town	d					
Clapham Junction ■	d	00 24				
Queenstown Rd.(Battersea)	d					
Vauxhall	⊖ d					
London Waterloo ■	⊖ a	00 38				

Table T149-R

Mondays to Fridays

8 October to 7 December

Reading, Guildford, Ascot, Weybridge, Windsor, Kingston, Richmond and Hounslow - London

		SW MO	SW MX	SW MO	SW MX ■	SW MX	SW MO ■	SW MX ■	SW	SW		SW	SW	SW	SW	SW	SW ◇	SW ◇	SW ◇	SW ■		SW ■	SW	SW	SW
Reading ■	d																			05 39					
Earley	d																			05 44					
Winnersh Triangle	d																			05 46					
Winnersh	d																			05 48					
Wokingham	d				00 02															05 53					
Bracknell	d				00 08															05 59					
Martins Heron	d				00 11															06 02					
Guildford	d																								
Wanborough	d																								
Ash ■	d																								
Aldershot	a																								
	d																					05 58			
Ash Vale	d																					06 02			
Frimley	d																					06 10			
Camberley	a																					06 14			
	d																					06 18			
Bagshot	d																					06 23			
Ascot ■	d				00a17															06 07		06a30			
Sunningdale	d																			06 10					
Longcross	d																								
Weybridge	d																								
Addlestone	d																05 39								
Chertsey	d																05 42								
Virginia Water	a																05 47			06 19					
	d																05 54			06 19					
Egham	d																05 57			06 23					
Windsor & Eton Riverside	d																	05 51							
Datchet	d																	05 55							
Sunnymeads	d																	05 58							
Wraysbury	d																	06 02							
Staines	d									04 53				05 37			06 03	06 08		06 29					06 33
Ashford (Surrey)	d									04 56				05 40			06 06	06 11							06 36
Feltham	d							00 05		05 01				05 45			06 11	06 16		06 35					06 41
Whitton	d			00 02						05 05				05 49				06 20					06 20		
Kingston	d								01 17							05 59								06 29	
Hampton Wick	d								01s22							06 01								06 31	
Teddington	d								01s25							06 05								06 35	
Fulwell	d												05 36												
Strawberry Hill	d					00 03			01a28				05 38			06 08								06 38	
Twickenham	a			00 05		00 06		00 10		05 08			05 42	05 52		06 12		06 23		06 40				06 42	
	d							00 11		05 08			05 43	05 53		06 13		06 23		06 41				06 43	
St Margarets	d									05 10			05 45			06 15								06 45	
Richmond	⊖ d							00 15		05 14			05 49	05 58		06 19		06 28		06 45				06 49	
North Sheen	d									05 16			05 51			06 21								06 51	
Mortlake	d									05 18			05 53			06 23								06 53	
Hounslow	d											05 31			06 01		06 16						06 31		06 46
Isleworth	d											05 34			06 04		06 19						06 34		06 49
Syon Lane	d											05 36			06 06		06 21						06 36		06 51
Brentford	d											05 39			06 09		06 24						06 39		06 54
Kew Bridge	d											05 41			06 11		06 26						06 41		06 56
Chiswick	d											05 44			06 14		06 29						06 44		06 59
Barnes Bridge	d											05 46			06 16		06 31						06 46		07 01
Barnes	d									05 21		05 49	05 56		06 19	06 26	06 34		←				06 49	06 56	07 04
Putney	d						00 05			05 24		05 52	05 59	06 04	06 22	06 29	06 37	06 34	06 37	06 52			06 52	06 59	07 07
Wandsworth Town	d		00 02							05 27		05 55	06 02		06 25	06 32	→		06 40				06 55	07 02	→
Clapham Junction ■	d	00 02	00 05				00 09	00 24		05 30		05 58	06 05	06 09	06 28	06 35		06 39	06 43	06 56			06 58	07 05	
Queenstown Rd.(Battersea)	d	00 05	00 08							05 33		06 01	06 08		06 31	06 38			06 46				07 01	07 08	
Vauxhall	⊖ d	00 08	00 12				00 15			05 37		06 05	06 12	06 15	06 35	06 42		06 45	06 50				07 05	07 12	
London Waterloo ■	⊖ a	00 13	00 16				00 19	00 38		05 41		06 09	06 16	06 19	06 39	06 46		06 49	06 56	07 07			07 11	07 18	

Reading, Guildford, Ascot, Weybridge, Windsor, Kingston, Richmond and Hounslow - London

		SW ◇	SW	SW	SW	SW ◇	SW ■	SW	SW	SW ■	SW	SW ◇	SW ◇	SW	SW	SW ◇■	SW ■	SW ◇	SW ■	SW	SW ■	SW	SW ◇
Reading ■	d						06 08			06 20									06 40		06 54		
Earley	d						06 14												06 45				
Winnersh Triangle	d						06 16												06 47				
Winnersh	d						06 18												06 49				
Wokingham	d						06 23			06 31									06 54		07 03		
Bracknell	d						06 29			06 37									07 00		07 10		
Martins Heron	d						06 32			06 40									07 03		07 13		
Guildford	d																06 30						
Wanborough	d																06 36						
Ash ■	d																06 40						
Aldershot	a																06 47						
	d															06 28							
Ash Vale	d															06 32							
Frimley	d															06 39							
Camberley	a															06 43							
	d															06 44							
Bagshot	d															06 49							
Ascot ■	d						06 37			06 45						06 57			07 08		07 17		
Sunningdale	d						06 40			06 48						07 00			07 11		07 21		
Longcross	d															07 03							
Weybridge	d					06 32												07 02					
Addlestone	d					06 36												07 06					
Chertsey	d					06 39												07 09					
Virginia Water	a					06 44	06 49			06 55						07 08		07 14	07 19		07 26		
	d					06 45	06 49			06 55						07 08		07 15	07 19		07 26		
Egham	d					06 48	06 53			06 59						07 12		07 18	07 23		07 29		
Windsor & Eton Riverside	d	06 21										06 51											07 21
Datchet	d	06 25										06 55											07 25
Sunnymeads	d	06 28										06 58											07 28
Wraysbury	d	06 32										07 02											07 32
Staines	d	06 38				06 54	06 59			07 04		07 08				07 18		07 24	07 29		07 35		07 38
Ashford (Surrey)	d	06 41				06 57						07 11				07 21		07 27					07 41
Feltham	d	06 46				07 02	07 05			07 12		07 16				07 26		07 32	07 36		07 42		07 46
Whitton	d	06 50		06 50	06 53							07 20			07 20	07 30							07 50
Kingston	d								06 59											07 29			
Hampton Wick	d								07 01											07 31			
Teddington	d								07 05											07 35			
Fulwell	d										07 12											07 42	
Strawberry Hill	d								07 08		07 14			←						07 38		07 44	
Twickenham	a	06 53			06 56		07 10		07 12	07 17	07 18	07 23		07 18		07 33			07 41	07 42	07 47	07 48	07 53
	d	06 53			06 58		07 11		07 13	07 18	07 27	07 23		07 27		07 33			07 41	07 43	07 48	07 57	07 54
St Margarets	d				07 00				07 15		→			07 29						07 45		→	
Richmond ⊖	d	06 58			07 04		07 15		07 19	07 24		07 28		07 32		07 38			07 46	07 49	07 54		07 58
North Sheen	d				07 06				07 21					07 34						07 51			
Mortlake	d				07 08				07 23					07 37						07 53			
Hounslow	d			06 59		07 14									07 29			07 44					
Isleworth	d			07 02		07 17									07 32			07 47					
Syon Lane	d			07 05		07 20									07 35			07 50					
Brentford	d			07 08		07 23									07 38			07 53					
Kew Bridge	d			07 10		07 25									07 40			07 55					
Chiswick	d			07 13		07 28									07 43			07 58					
Barnes Bridge	d			07 16		07 31		←					←		07 46			08 01					
Barnes	d		←	07 19	07 11	07 34		07 19	07 26				07 34	07 40	07 49			08 04		07 56			
Putney	d	07 04	07 07	→	07 14	→	07 22	07 22	07 29			07 34	07 37	07 43	07 52			→		07 59			08 05
Wandsworth Town	d		07 10		07 17			07 25	07 32				07 40	07 46	07 55					08 02			
Clapham Junction ■	d	07 09	07 13		07 20		07 26	07 28	07 35	07 33		07 39	07 43	07 49	07 58	07 47			07 54	08 05	08 03		08 09
Queenstown Rd.(Battersea)	d		07 16		07 23			07 31	07 38				07 46	07 52	08 01					08 08			
Vauxhall ⊖	d	07 15	07 20		07 27			07 35	07 42	07 38		07 45	07 50	07 56	08 05	07 53				08 12	08 09		08 15
London Waterloo ■ ⊖	a	07 21	07 28		07 34		07 37	07 42	07 48	07 46		07 51	07 57	08 04	08 10	07 59			08 04	08 18	08 16		08 21

Table T149-R

Mondays to Fridays

8 October to 7 December

Reading, Guildford, Ascot, Weybridge, Windsor, Kingston, Richmond and Hounslow - London

		SW ◇	SW	SW	SW ◇■	SW ■	SW ■	SW	SW ◇	SW ■	SW	SW ◇	SW ◇	SW	SW	SW ◇■	SW	SW ◇	SW ■	SW	SW ■	SW
Reading ■	d						07 09			07 22									07 39			
Earley	d						07 14												07 44			
Winnersh Triangle	d						07 16												07 46			
Winnersh	d						07 18												07 48			
Wokingham	d						07 23			07 32									07 53			
Bracknell	d						07 29			07 38									07 59			
Martins Heron	d						07 32			07 41									08 02			
Guildford	d					07 00															07 30	
Wanborough	d					07 06															07 36	
Ash ■	d					07 10															07 40	
Aldershot	a					07 17															07 47	
	d				06 59											07 29					08 00	
Ash Vale	d				07 03											07 33					08 04	
Frimley	d				07 09											07 39					08 10	
Camberley	a				07 13											07 43					08 14	
	d				07 14											07 44					08 18	
Bagshot	d				07 19											07 49					08 23	
Ascot ■	d				07 26		07 37			07 46						07 56			08 07		08a30	
Sunningdale	d				07 29		07 40			07 49						07 59			08 10			
Longcross	d				07 32														08 13			
Weybridge	d								07 33									08 03				
Addlestone	d								07 37									08 07				
Chertsey	d								07 40									08 11				
Virginia Water	a				07 38				07 45	07 55						08 08		08 16	08 19			
	d				07 38				07 50	07 55						08 08		08 24	08 19			
Egham	d				07 42		07 50		07 54	07 58						08 12		→	08 23			
Windsor & Eton Riverside	d											07 51										
Datchet	d											07 55										
Sunnymeads	d											07 58										
Wraysbury	d											08 02										
Staines	d				07 48		07 56		07 59	08 04		08 08				08 18			08 29			
Ashford (Surrey)	d				07 51				08 02			08 11				08 21						
Feltham	d				07 56		08 02		08 07	08 12		08 16				08 26			08 35			
Whitton	d			07 50	08 00							08 20			08 20	08 30	08 33					
Kingston	d							07 59														08 29
Hampton Wick	d							08 01														08 31
Teddington	d							08 05														08 35
Fulwell	d										08 12											
Strawberry Hill	d		←					08 08			08 14			←								08 38
Twickenham	a		07 48		08 03		08 09	08 12		08 17	08 18	08 23		08 18		08 33	08 36		08 40			08 42
	d		07 57		08 03		08 09	08 13		08 18	08 27	08 24		08 27		08 33	08 37		08 41			08 43
St Margarets	d		07 59					08 15			→			08 29								08 45
Richmond ⊖	d		08 02		08 08		08 14	08 19		08 24		08 28		08 32		08 38	08 42		08 45			08 49
North Sheen	d		08 04					08 21						08 34								08 51
Mortlake	d		08 07					08 23						08 37								08 53
Hounslow	d			07 59					08 14						08 31							
Isleworth	d			08 02					08 17						08 34							
Syon Lane	d			08 05					08 20						08 36							
Brentford	d			08 08					08 23						08 39							
Kew Bridge	d			08 10					08 25						08 41							
Chiswick	d			08 13					08 28						08 44							
Barnes Bridge	d	←		08 16					08 31						08 46							
Barnes	d	08 04	08 10	08 19				08 26	08 34				←	08 40	08 49					←		08 56
Putney	d	08 07	08 13	08 22				08 29	08 37			08 35	08 37	08 43	08 52		08 48			08 52		08 59
Wandsworth Town	d	08 10	08 16	08 25				08 32	→				08 40	08 46	→		08 51			08 55		09 02
Clapham Junction ■	d	08 13	08 19	08 28	08 17		08 22	08 35		08 33		08 39	08 43	08 49		08 47	08 54		08 54	08 58		09 05
Queenstown Rd.(Battersea)	d	08 16	08 22	08 31				08 38					08 46	08 52						09 01		09 08
Vauxhall ⊖	d	08 20	08 26	08 35	08 23			08 42		08 38		08 45	08 50	08 56		08 53	09 01			09 05		09 12
London Waterloo ■ ⊖	a	08 27	08 34	08 42	08 29		08 36	08 49		08 46		08 51	08 58	09 04		09 00	09 13		09 06	09 13		09 18

Table T149-R

Mondays to Fridays
8 October to 7 December

Reading, Guildford, Ascot, Weybridge, Windsor, Kingston, Richmond and Hounslow - London

Station		SW ◇	SW ◇	SW ◇	SW ◇	SW	SW	SW ■	SW	SW ■	SW	SW ◇	SW ◇	SW ◇	SW	SW	SW	SW ■	SW	SW ■	SW	SW	SW
Reading ■	d							08 09										08 39					
Earley	d							08 14										08 44					
Winnersh Triangle	d							08 16										08 46					
Winnersh	d							08 18										08 48					
Wokingham	d							08 23										08 53					
Bracknell	d							08 29										08 59					
Martins Heron	d							08 32										09 02					
Guildford	d									08 01										08 30			
Wanborough	d									08 07										08 36			
Ash ■	d									08 11										08 40			
Aldershot	a									08 18										08 48			
	d									08 30										09 00			
Ash Vale	d									08 34										09 04			
Frimley	d									08 40										09 10			
Camberley	a									08 44										09 14			
	d									08 48										09 18			
Bagshot	d									08 53										09 23			
Ascot ■	d							08 37		09a00								09 07		09a30			
Sunningdale	d							08 40										09 10					
Longcross	d							08 43										09 13					
Weybridge	d				08 33										09 03								
Addlestone	d				08 37										09 07								
Chertsey	d	←			08 40							←			09 10							←	
Virginia Water	a	08 16			08 45			08 49				08 45			09 15			09 19				09 15	
	d	08 24			08 54			08 49				08 54			09 24			09 19				09 24	
Egham	d	08 27			→			08 53				08 57			→			09 23				09 27	
Windsor & Eton Riverside	d		08 21										08 51										09 21
Datchet	d		08 25										08 55										09 25
Sunnymeads	d		08 28										08 58										09 28
Wraysbury	d		08 32										09 02										09 32
Staines	d	08 33	08 38					08 59				09 03	09 08					09 29				09 33	09 38
Ashford (Surrey)	d	08 36	08 41									09 06	09 11									09 36	09 41
Feltham	d	08 41	08 46					09 05				09 11	09 16					09 35				09 41	09 46
Whitton	d		08 50			08 50	08 53						09 20			09 20	09 23						09 50
Kingston	d										08 59										09 29		
Hampton Wick	d										09 01										09 31		
Teddington	d										09 05										09 35		
Fulwell	d																						
Strawberry Hill	d										09 08										09 38		
Twickenham	a		08 53				08 56	09 10			09 12		09 23				09 26	09 40			09 42		09 53
	d		08 53				08 58	09 11			09 13		09 23				09 28	09 41			09 43		09 53
St Margarets	d						09 00				09 15						09 30				09 45		
Richmond ⊖	d		08 58				09 04	09 15			09 19		09 28				09 34	09 45			09 49		09 58
North Sheen	d						09 06				09 21						09 36				09 51		
Mortlake	d						09 08				09 23						09 38				09 53		
Hounslow	d	08 46				09 01						09 16				09 31						09 46	
Isleworth	d	08 49				09 04						09 19				09 34						09 49	
Syon Lane	d	08 51				09 06						09 21				09 36						09 51	
Brentford	d	08 54				09 09						09 24				09 39						09 54	
Kew Bridge	d	08 56				09 11						09 26				09 41						09 56	
Chiswick	d	08 59				09 14						09 29				09 44						09 59	
Barnes Bridge	d	09 01				09 16			←			09 31				09 46			←			10 01	
Barnes	d	09 04		←		09 19	09 11		09 19		09 26	09 34		←		09 49	09 41		09 49		09 56	10 04	
Putney	d	09 07	09 04	09 07		→	09 14		09 22		09 29	09 37	09 34	09 37		→	09 44		09 52		09 59	10 07	10 04
Wandsworth Town	d	→		09 10			09 17		09 25		09 32	→		09 40			09 47		09 55		10 02	→	
Clapham Junction ■	d		09 09	09 13			09 20	09 24	09 28		09 35		09 39	09 43			09 50	09 54	09 58		10 05		10 09
Queenstown Rd.(Battersea)	d			09 16			09 23		09 31		09 38			09 46			09 53		10 01		10 08		
Vauxhall ⊖	d		09 15	09 20			09 27		09 35		09 42		09 45	09 50			09 57		10 05		10 12		10 15
London Waterloo ■ ⊖	a		09 21	09 28			09 34	09 34	09 43		09 48		09 51	09 58			10 02	10 04	10 11		10 16		10 19

Table T149-R

Mondays to Fridays
8 October to 7 December

Reading, Guildford, Ascot, Weybridge, Windsor, Kingston, Richmond and Hounslow - London

Station		SW	SW	SW	SW	SW ■	SW	SW	SW	SW	SW ■	SW	SW ■	SW	SW	SW	SW ■	SW	SW	SW	SW	SW ■
Reading ■	d					09 09					09 23						09 39					09 53
Earley	d					09 14					09 28						09 44					09 58
Winnersh Triangle	d					09 16					09 30						09 46					10 00
Winnersh	d					09 18					09 32						09 48					10 02
Wokingham	d					09 23					09 37						09 53					10 07
Bracknell	d					09 29					09 44						09 59					10 13
Martins Heron	d					09 32					09 47						10 02					10 16
Guildford	d												09 00									
Wanborough	d												09 06									
Ash ■	d												09 10									
Aldershot	a												09 17									
	d												09 30									
Ash Vale	d												09 34									
Frimley	d												09 40									
Camberley	a												09 44									
	d												09 48									
Bagshot	d												09 53									
Ascot ■	d					09 37					09 52		10a00				10 07					10 22
Sunningdale	d					09 40					09 55						10 10					10 25
Longcross	d																10 13					
Weybridge	d		09 33											10 03								
Addlestone	d		09 37											10 07								
Chertsey	d		09 40						←					10 10						←		
Virginia Water	a		09 45			09 49			09 45		10 03			10 15			10 20			10 15		10 33
	d		09 54			09 49			09 54		10 03			10 24			10 20			10 24		10 33
Egham	d		→			09 53			09 57		10 06			→			10 24			10 27		10 36
Windsor & Eton Riverside	d									09 51											10 21	
Datchet	d									09 55											10 25	
Sunnymeads	d									09 58											10 28	
Wraysbury	d									10 02											10 32	
Staines	d					09 59			10 03	10 08	10 14						10 29			10 33	10 38	10 42
Ashford (Surrey)	d								10 06	10 11										10 36	10 41	
Feltham	d					10 05			10 11	10 16	10 20						10 35			10 41	10 46	10 50
Whitton	d			09 50	09 53					10 20					10 20	10 26					10 50	
Kingston	d							09 59											10 29			
Hampton Wick	d							10 01											10 31			
Teddington	d							10 05											10 35			
Fulwell	d																					
Strawberry Hill	d							10 08											10 38			
Twickenham	a				09 56	10 10		10 12		10 23	10 26					10 28	10 40		10 42		10 53	10 56
	d				09 58	10 11		10 13		10 23	10 27					10 28	10 41		10 43		10 53	10 56
St Margarets	d				10 00			10 15								10 30			10 45			
Richmond ⊖	d				10 04	10 15		10 19		10 28	10 32					10 34	10 45		10 49		10 58	11 01
North Sheen	d				10 06			10 21								10 36			10 51			
Mortlake	d				10 08			10 23								10 38			10 53			
Hounslow	d			10 01					10 16						10 31					10 46		
Isleworth	d			10 04					10 19						10 34					10 49		
Syon Lane	d			10 06					10 21						10 36					10 51		
Brentford	d			10 09					10 24						10 39					10 54		
Kew Bridge	d			10 11					10 26						10 41					10 56		
Chiswick	d			10 14					10 29						10 44					10 59		
Barnes Bridge	d			10 16			←		10 31						10 46			←		11 01		
Barnes	d	←		10 19	10 11		10 19	10 26	10 34			←			10 49	10 41		10 49	10 56	11 04		
Putney	d	10 07		→	10 14		10 22	10 29	10 37	10 34		10 37			→	10 44		10 52	10 59	11 07	11 04	
Wandsworth Town	d	10 10			10 17		10 25	10 32	→			10 40				10 47		10 55	11 02	→		
Clapham Junction ■	d	10 13			10 20	10 24	10 28	10 35		10 39	10 42	10 43				10 50	10 54	10 58	11 05		11 09	11 12
Queenstown Rd.(Battersea)	d	10 16			10 23		10 31	10 38				10 47				10 53		11 01	11 08			
Vauxhall ⊖	d	10 20			10 27		10 35	10 42		10 45		10 50				10 57		11 05	11 12		11 15	
London Waterloo ■ ⊖	a	10 26			10 32	10 37	10 41	10 46		10 49	10 51	10 56				11 02	11 04	11 11	11 16		11 19	11 25

8 October to 7 December

Reading, Guildford, Ascot, Weybridge, Windsor, Kingston, Richmond and Hounslow - London

		SW	SW ■	SW	SW	SW	SW ■	SW	SW ■	SW	SW	SW	SW	SW	SW	SW	SW ■	SW	SW ■	SW	SW	SW	SW
Reading ■	d						10 09										10 39						
Earley	d						10 14										10 44						
Winnersh Triangle	d						10 16										10 46						
Winnersh	d						10 18										10 48						
Wokingham	d						10 23										10 53						
Bracknell	d						10 29										10 59						
Martins Heron	d						10 32										11 02						
Guildford	d		09 30						10 00										10 30				
Wanborough	d		09 36						10 06										10 36				
Ash ■	d		09 40						10 10										10 40				
Aldershot	a		09 47						10 17										10 47				
	d		10 00						10 30										11 00				
Ash Vale	d		10 04						10 34										11 04				
Frimley	d		10 10						10 40										11 10				
Camberley	a		10 14						10 44										11 14				
	d		10 18						10 48										11 18				
Bagshot	d		10 23						10 53										11 23				
Ascot ■	d		10a30				10 37		11a00								11 07		11a30				
Sunningdale	d						10 40										11 10						
Longcross	d																						
Weybridge	d			10 33										11 03									
Addlestone	d			10 37										11 07									
Chertsey	d			10 40							←			11 10							←		
Virginia Water	a			10 45			10 49				10 45			11 15			11 19				11 15		
	d			10 54			10 49				10 54			11 24			11 19				11 24		
Egham	d			→			10 53				10 57			→			11 23				11 27		
Windsor & Eton Riverside	d											10 51										11 21	
Datchet	d											10 55										11 25	
Sunnymeads	d											10 58										11 28	
Wraysbury	d											11 02										11 32	
Staines	d						10 59				11 03	11 08					11 29				11 33	11 38	
Ashford (Surrey)	d										11 06	11 11									11 36	11 41	
Feltham	d						11 05				11 11	11 16					11 35				11 41	11 46	
Whitton	d				10 50	10 55						11 20			11 20	11 23						11 50	
Kingston	d									10 59										11 29			
Hampton Wick	d									11 01										11 31			
Teddington	d									11 05										11 35			
Fulwell	d																						
Strawberry Hill	d									11 08										11 38			
Twickenham	a					10 57	11 10			11 12		11 23				11 26	11 40			11 42		11 53	
	d					10 58	11 11			11 13		11 23				11 28	11 41			11 43		11 53	
St Margarets	d					11 00				11 15						11 30				11 45			
Richmond ⊖	d					11 03	11 15			11 19		11 28				11 34	11 45			11 49		11 58	
North Sheen	d					11 05				11 21						11 36				11 51			
Mortlake	d					11 08				11 23						11 38				11 53			
Hounslow	d				11 01						11 16				11 31						11 46		
Isleworth	d				11 04						11 19				11 34						11 49		
Syon Lane	d				11 06						11 21				11 36						11 51		
Brentford	d				11 09						11 24				11 39						11 54		
Kew Bridge	d				11 11						11 26				11 41						11 56		
Chiswick	d				11 14						11 29				11 44						11 59		
Barnes Bridge	d				11 16			←			11 31				11 46			←			12 01		
Barnes	d	←			11 19	11 11		11 19		11 26	11 34		←		11 49	11 41		11 49		11 56	12 04		←
Putney	d	11 07			→	11 14		11 22		11 29	11 37	11 35	11 37		→	11 44		11 52		11 59	12 07	12 04	12 07
Wandsworth Town	d	11 10				11 17		11 25		11 32	→		11 40			11 47		11 55		12 02	→		12 10
Clapham Junction ■	d	11 13				11 20	11 24	11 28		11 35		11 39	11 43			11 50	11 54	11 58		12 05		12 09	12 13
Queenstown Rd.(Battersea)	d	11 17				11 23		11 31		11 38			11 46			11 53		12 01		12 08			12 16
Vauxhall ⊖	d	11 20				11 27		11 35		11 42		11 45	11 50			11 57		12 05		12 12		12 15	12 20
London Waterloo ■ ⊖	a	11 27				11 32	11 34	11 43		11 46		11 49	11 56			12 02	12 04	12 11		12 16		12 19	12 26

Table T149-R

Mondays to Fridays

8 October to 7 December

Reading, Guildford, Ascot, Weybridge, Windsor, Kingston, Richmond and Hounslow - London

		SW	SW	SW	SW ■	SW	SW ■	SW	SW	SW	SW	SW	SW	SW	SW ■	SW	SW ■	SW	SW	SW	SW	SW	SW
Reading ■	d				11 09										11 39								
Earley	d				11 14										11 44								
Winnersh Triangle	d				11 16										11 46								
Winnersh	d				11 18										11 48								
Wokingham	d				11 23										11 53								
Bracknell	d				11 29										11 59								
Martins Heron	d				11 32										12 02								
Guildford	d						11 00										11 30						
Wanborough	d						11 06										11 36						
Ash ■	d						11 10										11 40						
Aldershot	a						11 17										11 47						
	d						11 30										12 00						
Ash Vale	d						11 34										12 04						
Frimley	d						11 40										12 10						
Camberley	a						11 44										12 14						
	d						11 48										12 18						
Bagshot	d						11 53										12 23						
Ascot ■	d				11 37		12a00								12 07		12a30						
Sunningdale	d				11 40										12 10								
Longcross	d																						
Weybridge	d	11 33										12 03										12 33	
Addlestone	d	11 37										12 07										12 37	
Chertsey	d	11 40							←			12 10							←			12 40	
Virginia Water	a	11 45			11 49				11 45			12 15			12 19				12 15			12 45	
	d	11 54			11 49				11 54			12 24			12 19				12 24			12 54	
Egham	d	→			11 53				11 57			→			12 23				12 27			→	
Windsor & Eton Riverside	d									11 51										12 21			
Datchet	d									11 55										12 25			
Sunnymeads	d									11 58										12 28			
Wraysbury	d									12 02										12 32			
Staines	d				11 59				12 03	12 08					12 29				12 33	12 38			
Ashford (Surrey)	d								12 06	12 11									12 36	12 41			
Feltham	d				12 05				12 11	12 16					12 35				12 41	12 46			
Whitton	d		11 51	11 53						12 20			12 20	12 23						12 50			12 50
Kingston	d							11 59										12 29					
Hampton Wick	d							12 01										12 31					
Teddington	d							12 05										12 35					
Fulwell	d																						
Strawberry Hill	d							12 08										12 38					
Twickenham	a			11 56	12 10			12 12		12 23				12 26	12 40			12 42		12 53			
	d			11 58	12 11			12 13		12 23				12 28	12 41			12 43		12 53			
St Margarets	d			12 00				12 15						12 30				12 45					
Richmond ⊖	d			12 04	12 15			12 19		12 28				12 34	12 45			12 49		12 58			
North Sheen	d			12 06				12 21						12 36				12 51					
Mortlake	d			12 08				12 23						12 38				12 53					
Hounslow	d		12 01						12 16				12 31						12 46				13 01
Isleworth	d		12 04						12 19				12 34						12 49				13 04
Syon Lane	d		12 06						12 21				12 36						12 51				13 06
Brentford	d		12 09						12 24				12 39						12 54				13 09
Kew Bridge	d		12 11						12 26				12 41						12 56				13 11
Chiswick	d		12 14						12 29				12 44						12 59				13 14
Barnes Bridge	d		12 16			←			12 31				12 46			←			13 01				13 16
Barnes	d		12 19	12 11		12 19		12 26	12 34		←		12 49	12 41		12 49		12 56	13 04		←		13 19
Putney	d		→	12 14		12 22		12 29	12 37	12 34	12 37		→	12 44		12 52		12 59	13 07	13 04	13 07		→
Wandsworth Town	d			12 17		12 25		12 32	→		12 40			12 47		12 55		13 02	→		13 10		
Clapham Junction ■	d			12 20	12 24	12 28		12 35		12 39	12 43			12 50	12 54	12 58		13 05		13 09	13 13		
Queenstown Rd.(Battersea)	d			12 23		12 31		12 38			12 46			12 53		13 01		13 08			13 16		
Vauxhall ⊖	d			12 27		12 35		12 42		12 45	12 50			12 57		13 05		13 12		13 15	13 20		
London Waterloo ■ ⊖	a			12 32	12 34	12 42		12 46		12 49	12 56			13 02	13 04	13 11		13 16		13 19	13 26		

Table T149-R

Mondays to Fridays
8 October to 7 December

Reading, Guildford, Ascot, Weybridge, Windsor, Kingston, Richmond and Hounslow - London

		SW		SW ■	SW	SW ■	SW	SW	SW	SW	SW	SW		SW	SW ■	SW	SW ■	SW	SW	SW	SW	SW		SW	SW
Reading ■	d			12 09											12 39										
Earley	d			12 14											12 44										
Winnersh Triangle	d			12 16											12 46										
Winnersh	d			12 18											12 48										
Wokingham	d			12 23											12 53										
Bracknell	d			12 29											12 59										
Martins Heron	d			12 32											13 02										
Guildford	d					12 00											12 30								
Wanborough	d					12 06											12 36								
Ash ■	d					12 10											12 40								
Aldershot	a					12 17											12 47								
	d					12 30											13 00								
Ash Vale	d					12 34											13 04								
Frimley	d					12 40											13 10								
Camberley	a					12 44											13 14								
	d					12 48											13 18								
Bagshot	d					12 53											13 23								
Ascot ■	d			12 37		13a00									13 07		13a30								
Sunningdale	d			12 40											13 10										
Longcross	d														13 13										
Weybridge	d										13 03											13 33			
Addlestone	d										13 07											13 37			
Chertsey	d							←			13 10								←			13 40			
Virginia Water	a			12 49				12 45			13 15				13 19				13 15			13 45			
	d			12 49				12 54			13 24				13 19				13 24			13 54			
Egham	d			12 53				12 57			→				13 23				13 27			→			
Windsor & Eton Riverside	d								12 51											13 21					
Datchet	d								12 55											13 25					
Sunnymeads	d								12 58											13 28					
Wraysbury	d								13 02											13 32					
Staines	d			12 59				13 03	13 08						13 29				13 33	13 38					
Ashford (Surrey)	d							13 06	13 11										13 36	13 41					
Feltham	d			13 05				13 11	13 16						13 35				13 41	13 46					
Whitton	d	12 53							13 20			13 20		13 23						13 50				13 50	13 53
Kingston	d						12 59											13 29							
Hampton Wick	d						13 01											13 31							
Teddington	d						13 05											13 35							
Fulwell	d																								
Strawberry Hill	d						13 08											13 38							
Twickenham	a	12 56		13 10			13 12		13 23					13 26	13 40			13 42		13 53					13 56
	d	12 58		13 11			13 13		13 23					13 28	13 41			13 43		13 53					13 58
St Margarets	d	13 00					13 15							13 30				13 45							14 00
Richmond ⊖	d	13 04		13 15			13 19		13 28					13 34	13 45			13 49		13 58					14 04
North Sheen	d	13 06					13 21							13 36				13 51							14 06
Mortlake	d	13 08					13 23							13 38				13 53							14 08
Hounslow	d							13 16				13 31							13 46					14 01	
Isleworth	d							13 19				13 34							13 49					14 04	
Syon Lane	d							13 21				13 36							13 51					14 06	
Brentford	d							13 24				13 39							13 54					14 09	
Kew Bridge	d							13 26				13 41							13 56					14 11	
Chiswick	d							13 29				13 44							13 59					14 14	
Barnes Bridge	d				←			13 31				13 46				←			14 01					14 16	
Barnes	d	13 11			13 19		13 26	13 34		←		13 49		13 41		13 49		13 56	14 04		←			14 19	14 11
Putney	d	13 14			13 22		13 29	13 37	13 34	13 37		→		13 44		13 52		13 59	14 07	14 04	14 07			→	14 14
Wandsworth Town	d	13 17			13 25		13 32	→		13 40				13 47		13 55		14 02	→		14 10				14 17
Clapham Junction ■	d	13 20		13 24	13 28		13 35		13 39	13 43				13 50	13 54	13 58		14 05		14 09	14 13				14 20
Queenstown Rd.(Battersea)	d	13 23			13 31		13 38			13 46				13 53		14 01		14 08			14 16				14 23
Vauxhall ⊖	d	13 27			13 35		13 42		13 45	13 50				13 57		14 05		14 12		14 15	14 20				14 27
London Waterloo ■ ⊖	a	13 32		13 34	13 41		13 46		13 49	13 56				14 02	14 04	14 11		14 17		14 19	14 26				14 32

Table T149-R

Mondays to Fridays
8 October to 7 December

Reading, Guildford, Ascot, Weybridge, Windsor, Kingston, Richmond and Hounslow - London

		SW ■	SW	SW ■	SW	SW	SW	SW		SW	SW	SW	SW ■	SW	SW ■	SW	SW	SW		SW	SW	SW	SW	SW ■	SW
Reading ■	d	13 09											13 39											14 09	
Earley	d	13 14											13 44											14 14	
Winnersh Triangle	d	13 16											13 46											14 16	
Winnersh	d	13 18											13 48											14 18	
Wokingham	d	13 23											13 53											14 23	
Bracknell	d	13 29											13 59											14 29	
Martins Heron	d	13 32											14 02											14 32	
Guildford	d			13 00											13 30										
Wanborough	d			13 06											13 36										
Ash ■	d			13 10											13 40										
Aldershot	a			13 17											13 47										
	d			13 30											14 00										
Ash Vale	d			13 34											14 04										
Frimley	d			13 40											14 10										
Camberley	a			13 44											14 14										
	d			13 48											14 18										
Bagshot	d			13 53											14 23										
Ascot ■	d	13 37		14a00									14 07		14a30									14 37	
Sunningdale	d	13 40											14 10											14 40	
Longcross	d																								
Weybridge	d									14 03											14 33				
Addlestone	d									14 07											14 37				
Chertsey	d					←				14 10							←				14 40				
Virginia Water	a	13 49				13 45				14 15			14 19				14 15				14 45			14 49	
	d	13 49				13 54				14 24			14 19				14 24				14 54			14 49	
Egham	d	13 53				13 57				→			14 23				14 27				→			14 53	
Windsor & Eton Riverside	d						13 51											14 21							
Datchet	d						13 55											14 25							
Sunnymeads	d						13 58											14 28							
Wraysbury	d						14 02											14 32							
Staines	d	13 59				14 03	14 08						14 29				14 33	14 38						14 59	
Ashford (Surrey)	d					14 06	14 11										14 36	14 41							
Feltham	d	14 05				14 11	14 16						14 35				14 41	14 46						15 05	
Whitton	d						14 20				14 20	14 23						14 50				14 50	14 53		
Kingston	d				13 59											14 29									
Hampton Wick	d				14 01											14 31									
Teddington	d				14 05											14 35									
Fulwell	d																								
Strawberry Hill	d				14 08											14 38									
Twickenham	a	14 10			14 12		14 23					14 26	14 40			14 42		14 53					14 56	15 10	
	d	14 11			14 13		14 23					14 28	14 41			14 43		14 53					14 58	15 11	
St Margarets	d				14 15							14 30				14 45							15 00		
Richmond ⊖	d	14 15			14 19		14 28					14 34	14 45			14 49		14 58					15 04	15 15	
North Sheen	d				14 21							14 36				14 51							15 06		
Mortlake	d				14 23							14 38				14 53							15 08		
Hounslow	d					14 16					14 31						14 46					15 01			
Isleworth	d					14 19					14 34						14 49					15 04			
Syon Lane	d					14 21					14 36						14 51					15 06			
Brentford	d					14 24					14 39						14 54					15 09			
Kew Bridge	d					14 26					14 41						14 56					15 11			
Chiswick	d					14 29					14 44						14 59					15 14			
Barnes Bridge	d		←			14 31					14 46			←			15 01					15 16			←
Barnes	d		14 19		14 26	14 34		←			14 49	14 41		14 49		14 56	15 04			←		15 19	15 11		15 19
Putney	d		14 22		14 29	14 37	14 34	14 37			→	14 44		14 52		14 59	15 07	15 04		15 07		→	15 14		15 22
Wandsworth Town	d		14 25		14 32	→		14 40				14 47		14 55		15 02	→			15 10			15 17		15 25
Clapham Junction ■	d	14 24	14 28		14 35		14 39	14 43				14 50	14 54	14 58		15 05		15 09		15 13			15 20	15 24	15 28
Queenstown Rd.(Battersea)	d		14 31		14 38			14 46				14 53		15 01		15 08				15 16			15 23		15 31
Vauxhall ⊖	d		14 35		14 42		14 45	14 50				14 57		15 05		15 12		15 15		15 20			15 27		15 35
London Waterloo ■ ⊖	a	14 34	14 41		14 46		14 49	14 56				15 02	15 04	15 11		15 16		15 19		15 26			15 32	15 34	15 41

Table T149-R

Mondays to Fridays

8 October to 7 December

Reading, Guildford, Ascot, Weybridge, Windsor, Kingston, Richmond and Hounslow - London

		SW ■	SW	SW	SW	SW	SW	SW	SW	SW ■	SW	SW ■	SW	SW	SW	SW	SW	SW	SW	SW ■	SW	SW ■
Reading 7	d									14 39										15 09		
Earley	d									14 44										15 14		
Winnersh Triangle	d									14 46										15 16		
Winnersh	d									14 48										15 18		
Wokingham	d									14 53										15 23		
Bracknell	d									14 59										15 29		
Martins Heron	d									15 02										15 32		
Guildford	d	14 00										14 30										15 00
Wanborough	d	14 06										14 36										15 06
Ash 5	d	14 10										14 40										15 10
Aldershot	a	14 17										14 47										15 17
	d	14 30										15 00										15 30
Ash Vale	d	14 34										15 04										15 34
Frimley	d	14 40										15 10										15 40
Camberley	a	14 44										15 14										15 44
	d	14 48										15 18										15 48
Bagshot	d	14 53										15 23										15 53
Ascot 5	d	15a00								15 07		15a30								15 37		16a00
Sunningdale	d									15 10										15 40		
Longcross	d																					
Weybridge	d						15 03										15 33					
Addlestone	d						15 07										15 37					
Chertsey	d			←			15 10							←			15 40					
Virginia Water	a			14 45			15 15			15 19				15 15			15 45			15 49		
	d			14 54			15 24			15 19				15 24			15 54			15 49		
Egham	d			14 57			→			15 23				15 27			→			15 53		
Windsor & Eton Riverside	d				14 51										15 21							
Datchet	d				14 55										15 25							
Sunnymeads	d				14 58										15 28							
Wraysbury	d				15 02										15 32							
Staines	d			15 03	15 08					15 29				15 33	15 38					15 59		
Ashford (Surrey)	d			15 06	15 11									15 36	15 41							
Feltham	d			15 11	15 16					15 35				15 41	15 46					16 05		
Whitton	d				15 20			15 20	15 23						15 50			15 50	15 53			
Kingston	d		14 59										15 29									
Hampton Wick	d		15 01										15 31									
Teddington	d		15 05										15 35									
Fulwell	d																					
Strawberry Hill	d		15 08										15 38									
Twickenham	a		15 12		15 23				15 26	15 40			15 42		15 53				15 56	16 10		
	d		15 13		15 23				15 28	15 41			15 43		15 53				15 58	16 11		
St Margarets	d		15 15						15 30				15 45						16 00			
Richmond ⊖	d		15 19		15 28				15 34	15 45			15 49		15 58				16 04	16 15		
North Sheen	d		15 21						15 36				15 51						16 06			
Mortlake	d		15 23						15 38				15 53						16 08			
Hounslow	d			15 16				15 31						15 46				16 01				
Isleworth	d			15 19				15 34						15 49				16 04				
Syon Lane	d			15 21				15 36						15 51				16 06				
Brentford	d			15 24				15 39						15 54				16 09				
Kew Bridge	d			15 26				15 41						15 56				16 11				
Chiswick	d			15 29				15 44						15 59				16 14				
Barnes Bridge	d			15 31				15 46			←			16 01				16 16			←	
Barnes	d		15 26	15 34		←		15 49	15 41		15 49		15 56	16 04		←		16 19	16 11		16 19	
Putney	d		15 29	15 37	15 34	15 37		→	15 44		15 52		15 59	16 07	16 04	16 07		→	16 14		16 22	
Wandsworth Town	d		15 32	→		15 40			15 47		15 55		16 02	→		16 10			16 17		16 25	
Clapham Junction 10	d		15 35		15 39	15 43			15 50	15 54	15 58		16 05		16 09	16 13			16 20	16 24	16 28	
Queenstown Rd.(Battersea)	d		15 38			15 46			15 53		16 01		16 08			16 16			16 23		16 31	
Vauxhall ⊖	d		15 42		15 45	15 50			15 57		16 05		16 12		16 15	16 20			16 27		16 35	
London Waterloo 15 ⊖	a		15 46		15 49	15 56			16 05	16 05	16 11		16 19		16 19	16 26			16 32	16 34	16 41	

Table T149-R

Mondays to Fridays

8 October to 7 December

Reading, Guildford, Ascot, Weybridge, Windsor, Kingston, Richmond and Hounslow - London

		SW	SW	SW	SW	SW	SW	SW	SW ■	SW	SW ■	SW	SW	SW	SW	SW	SW	SW	SW ■	SW	SW ■	SW	SW
Reading 7	d								15 39										16 09				
Earley	d								15 44										16 14				
Winnersh Triangle	d								15 46										16 16				
Winnersh	d								15 48										16 18				
Wokingham	d								15 53										16 23				
Bracknell	d								15 59										16 29				
Martins Heron	d								16 02										16 32				
Guildford	d										15 30										16 00		
Wanborough	d										15 36										16 06		
Ash 5	d										15 40										16 10		
Aldershot	a										15 47										16 17		
	d										16 00										16 30		
Ash Vale	d										16 04										16 34		
Frimley	d										16 10										16 40		
Camberley	a										16 14										16 44		
	d										16 18										16 48		
Bagshot	d										16 23										16 53		
Ascot 5	d								16 07		16a30								16 37		17a00		
Sunningdale	d								16 10										16 40				
Longcross	d								16 13														
Weybridge	d					16 03										16 33							
Addlestone	d					16 07										16 37							
Chertsey	d		←			16 10							←			16 40							←
Virginia Water	a		15 45			16 15			16 20				16 15			16 45			16 49				16 45
	d		15 54			16 24			16 20				16 24			16 54			16 49				16 54
Egham	d		15 57			→			16 24				16 27			→			16 53				16 57
Windsor & Eton Riverside	d			15 51										16 21									
Datchet	d			15 55										16 25									
Sunnymeads	d			15 58										16 28									
Wraysbury	d			16 02										16 32									
Staines	d		16 03	16 08					16 29				16 33	16 38					16 59				17 03
Ashford (Surrey)	d		16 06	16 11									16 36	16 41									17 06
Feltham	d		16 11	16 16					16 35				16 41	16 46					17 05				17 11
Whitton	d			16 20			16 20	16 23						16 50			16 50	16 53					
Kingston	d	15 59										16 29										16 59	
Hampton Wick	d	16 01										16 31										17 01	
Teddington	d	16 05										16 35										17 05	
Fulwell	d																						
Strawberry Hill	d	16 08										16 38										17 08	
Twickenham	a	16 12		16 23				16 26	16 40			16 42		16 53				16 56	17 10			17 12	
	d	16 13		16 23				16 28	16 41			16 43		16 53				16 58	17 11			17 13	
St Margarets	d	16 15						16 30				16 45						17 00				17 15	
Richmond ⊖	d	16 19		16 28				16 34	16 45			16 49		16 58				17 04	17 15			17 19	
North Sheen	d	16 21						16 36				16 51						17 06				17 21	
Mortlake	d	16 23						16 38				16 53						17 08				17 23	
Hounslow	d		16 16				16 31						16 46				17 01						17 16
Isleworth	d		16 19				16 34						16 49				17 04						17 19
Syon Lane	d		16 21				16 36						16 51				17 06						17 21
Brentford	d		16 24				16 39						16 54				17 09						17 24
Kew Bridge	d		16 26				16 41						16 56				17 11						17 26
Chiswick	d		16 29				16 44						16 59				17 14						17 29
Barnes Bridge	d		16 31				16 46			←			17 01				17 16			←			17 31
Barnes	d	16 26	16 34		←		16 49	16 41		16 49		16 56	17 04		←		17 19	17 11		17 19		17 26	17 34
Putney	d	16 29	16 37	16 34	16 37		→	16 44		16 52		16 59	17 07	17 05	17 07		→	17 14		17 22		17 29	17 37
Wandsworth Town	d	16 32	→		16 40			16 47		16 55		17 02	→		17 10			17 17		17 25		17 32	→
Clapham Junction 10	d	16 35		16 39	16 43			16 50	16 54	16 58		17 05		17 09	17 13			17 20	17 24	17 28		17 35	
Queenstown Rd.(Battersea)	d	16 38			16 46			16 53		17 01		17 08			17 16			17 23		17 31		17 38	
Vauxhall ⊖	d	16 42		16 45	16 50			16 57		17 05		17 12		17 15	17 20			17 27		17 35		17 42	
London Waterloo 15 ⊖	a	16 49		16 49	16 56			17 02	17 04	17 11		17 19		17 19	17 26			17 32	17 35	17 41		17 49	

8 October to 7 December

Reading, Guildford, Ascot, Weybridge, Windsor, Kingston, Richmond and Hounslow - London

		SW	SW	SW	SW	SW	SW	SW ■	SW	SW ■	SW	SW	SW	SW	SW	SW	SW	SW ■	SW	SW	SW	SW	SW
Reading	d							16 39										17 09					
Earley	d							16 44										17 14					
Winnersh Triangle	d							16 46										17 16					
Winnersh	d							16 48										17 18					
Wokingham	d							16 53										17 23					
Bracknell	d							16 59										17 29					
Martins Heron	d							17 02										17 32					
Guildford	d									16 30													
Wanborough	d									16 36													
Ash	d									16 40													
Aldershot	a									16 47													
	d									17 00													
Ash Vale	d									17 04													
Frimley	d									17 10													
Camberley	a									17 14													
	d									17 18													
Bagshot	d									17 23													
Ascot	d							17 07		17a30								17 37					
Sunningdale	d							17 10										17 40					
Longcross	d							17 13															
Weybridge	d			17 03																	17 37		
Addlestone	d			17 07																	17 41		
Chertsey	d			17 10								←									17 44		
Virginia Water	a			17 15				17 19				17 15						17 49			17 49		
	d			17 24				17 19				17 24						17 49			17 54		
Egham	d			→				17 23				17 27						17 53			17 57		
Windsor & Eton Riverside	d	16 51											17 21									17 51	
Datchet	d	16 55											17 25									17 55	
Sunnymeads	d	16 58											17 28									17 58	
Wraysbury	d	17 02											17 32									18 02	
Staines	d	17 08						17 29				17 33	17 38					17 59			18 03	18 08	
Ashford (Surrey)	d	17 11										17 36	17 41								18 06	18 11	
Feltham	d	17 16						17 35				17 41	17 46					18 05			18 11	18 16	
Whitton	d	17 20			17 20	17 23							17 50		17 50	17 53						18 20	
Kingston	d										17 29									17 59			
Hampton Wick	d										17 31									18 01			
Teddington	d										17 35									18 05			
Fulwell	d																						
Strawberry Hill	d						17 31				17 38						17 59			18 08			
Twickenham	a	17 23				17 26	17 34	17 40			17 42		17 53			17 56	18 02	18 10		18 12		18 23	
	d	17 23				17 28	17 35	17 41			17 43		17 53			17 58	18 03	18 11		18 13		18 23	
St Margarets	d					17 30					17 45					18 00	18 05			18 15			
Richmond ⊖	d	17 28				17 34	17 40	17 45			17 49		17 58			18 04	18 08	18 15		18 19		18 28	
North Sheen	d					17 36					17 51					18 06	18 10			18 21			
Mortlake	d					17 38					17 53					18 08	18 13			18 23			
Hounslow	d				17 31							17 46			18 01						18 16		
Isleworth	d				17 34							17 49			18 04						18 19		
Syon Lane	d				17 36							17 51			18 06						18 21		
Brentford	d				17 39							17 54			18 09						18 24		
Kew Bridge	d				17 41							17 56			18 11						18 26		
Chiswick	d				17 44							17 59			18 14						18 29		
Barnes Bridge	d				17 46				←			18 01			18 16				←		18 31		
Barnes	d		←		17 49	17 41			17 49		17 56	18 04		←	18 19	18 12	18 16		18 19	18 26	18 34		←
Putney	d	17 34	17 37		→	17 44			17 52		17 59	18 07	18 04	18 07	→	18 15	18 19		18 22	18 29	18 37	18 34	18 37
Wandsworth Town	d		17 40			17 47			17 55		18 02	→		18 10		18 18			18 25	18 32	→		18 40
Clapham Junction	d	17 39	17 43			17 51	17 49	17 54	17 58		18 05		18 09	18 13		18 21	18 24	18 26	18 28	18 35		18 39	18 43
Queenstown Rd.(Battersea)	d		17 46			17 54			18 01		18 08			18 16		18 24			18 31	18 38			18 46
Vauxhall ⊖	d	17 45	17 50			17 58	17 55		18 05		18 12		18 15	18 20		18 27	18 30		18 35	18 42		18 45	18 50
London Waterloo ⊖	a	17 49	17 57			18 04	18 02	18 09	18 11		18 19		18 19	18 26		18 33	18 34	18 39	18 41	18 49		18 49	18 56

8 October to 7 December

Reading, Guildford, Ascot, Weybridge, Windsor, Kingston, Richmond and Hounslow - London

		SW ■	SW ■	SW	SW	SW ■	SW	SW	SW	SW	SW	SW ■	SW ■	SW	SW	SW ■	SW	SW ■	SW	SW	SW	SW
Reading	d	17 23				17 39						17 56				18 09						
Earley	d	17 28				17 44						18 01				18 14						
Winnersh Triangle	d	17 30				17 46						18 03				18 16						
Winnersh	d	17 32				17 48						18 05				18 18						
Wokingham	d	17 37				17 53						18 10				18 23						
Bracknell	d	17 43				17 59						18 16				18 29						
Martins Heron	d	17 46				18 02						18 19				18 32						
Guildford	d		17 00										17 30					18 00				
Wanborough	d		17 06										17 36					18 06				
Ash	d		17 10										17 40					18 10				
Aldershot	a		17 17										17 47					18 17				
	d		17 30										18 00					18 30				
Ash Vale	d		17 34										18 04					18 34				
Frimley	d		17 40										18 10					18 40				
Camberley	a		17 44										18 14					18 44				
	d		17 48										18 18					18 48				
Bagshot	d		17 53										18 23					18 53				
Ascot	d	17 55	18a00			18 07						18 25	18a30			18 37		19a02				
Sunningdale	d	17 58				18 10						18 28				18 40						
Longcross	d					18 13										18 43						
Weybridge	d								18 07											18 37		
Addlestone	d								18 11											18 41		
Chertsey	d								18 14											18 44		
Virginia Water	a	18 03				18 19			18 19			18 33				18 49				18 49		
	d	18 03				18 19			18 24			18 33				18 49				18 54		
Egham	d	18 06				18 23			18 27			18 37				18 53				18 57		
Windsor & Eton Riverside	d									18 21											18 51	
Datchet	d									18 25											18 55	
Sunnymeads	d									18 28											18 58	
Wraysbury	d									18 32											19 02	
Staines	d	18 14				18 29			18 33	18 38		18 44				18 59				19 03	19 08	
Ashford (Surrey)	d								18 36	18 41										19 06	19 11	
Feltham	d	18 20				18 35			18 41	18 46		18 50				19 05				19 11	19 16	
Whitton	d			18 20	18 23					18 50				18 50	18 53						19 20	
Kingston	d							18 29											18 59			
Hampton Wick	d							18 31											19 01			
Teddington	d							18 35											19 05			
Fulwell	d																					
Strawberry Hill	d							18 38											19 08			
Twickenham	a				18 26	18 40		18 42		18 53					18 56	19 10			19 12		19 23	
	d				18 28	18 41		18 43		18 53					18 58	19 11			19 13		19 23	
St Margarets	d				18 30			18 45							19 00				19 15			
Richmond ⊖	d				18 34	18 45		18 49		18 58					19 04	19 15			19 19		19 28	
North Sheen	d				18 36			18 51							19 06				19 21			
Mortlake	d				18 38			18 53							19 08				19 23			
Hounslow	d	18 26		18 31					18 46			18 56		19 01						19 16		
Isleworth	d			18 34					18 49					19 04						19 19		
Syon Lane	d			18 36					18 51					19 06						19 21		
Brentford	d	18 31		18 39					18 54			19 01		19 09						19 24		
Kew Bridge	d			18 41					18 56					19 11						19 26		
Chiswick	d			18 44					18 59					19 14						19 29		
Barnes Bridge	d			18 46			←		19 01					19 16			←			19 31		
Barnes	d			18 49	18 41		18 49	18 56	19 04		←			19 19	19 11		19 19		19 26	19 34		←
Putney	d	18 39		→	18 44		18 52	18 59	19 07	19 04	19 07	19 09		→	19 14		19 22		19 29	19 37	19 34	19 37
Wandsworth Town	d				18 47		18 55	19 02	→		19 10				19 17		19 25		19 32	→		19 40
Clapham Junction	d	18 44			18 50	18 54	18 58	19 05		19 09	19 13	19 14			19 20	19 24	19 28		19 35		19 39	19 43
Queenstown Rd.(Battersea)	d				18 53		19 01	19 08			19 16				19 23		19 31		19 38			19 46
Vauxhall ⊖	d				18 57		19 05	19 12		19 15	19 20				19 27		19 35		19 42		19 45	19 50
London Waterloo ⊖	a	18 56			19 02	19 04	19 11	19 16		19 19	19 26	19 28			19 32	19 34	19 41		19 46		19 49	19 56

Table T149-R

Mondays to Fridays

8 October to 7 December

Reading, Guildford, Ascot, Weybridge, Windsor, Kingston, Richmond and Hounslow - London

		SW	SW	SW 1	SW	SW	SW	SW	SW	SW 1	SW 1	SW	SW	SW 1	SW	SW 1	SW	SW	SW	SW	SW	SW	SW
Reading 7	d			18 39						18 49				19 09									
Earley	d			18 44						18 54				19 14									
Winnersh Triangle	d			18 46						18 56				19 16									
Winnersh	d			18 48						18 58				19 18									
Wokingham	d			18 53						19 03				19 23									
Bracknell	d			18 59						19 09				19 29									
Martins Heron	d			19 02						19 12				19 32									
Guildford	d										18 30					19 00							
Wanborough	d										18 36					19 06							
Ash 5	d										18 40					19 10							
Aldershot	a										18 47					19 17							
	d										19 00					19 30							
Ash Vale	d										19 04					19 34							
Frimley	d										19 10					19 40							
Camberley	a										19 14					19 44							
	d										19 18					19 48							
Bagshot	d										19 23					19 53							
Ascot 3	d			19 07						19 17	19a30			19 37		20a00							
Sunningdale	d			19 10						19 20				19 40									
Longcross	d			19 13										19 43									
Weybridge	d						19 07											19 37			20 05		
Addlestone	d						19 11											19 41			20 09		
Chertsey	d						19 14											19 44			20 12		
Virginia Water	a			19 19			19 19			19 28				19 49				19 49			20 17		
	d			19 19			19 24			19 28				19 49				19 54			20 24		
Egham	d			19 23			19 27			19 31				19 53				19 57			→		
Windsor & Eton Riverside	d							19 21											19 51				
Datchet	d							19 25											19 55				
Sunnymeads	d							19 28											19 58				
Wraysbury	d							19 32											20 02				
Staines	d			19 29			19 33	19 38		19a41				19 59				20 03	20 08				
Ashford (Surrey)	d						19 36	19 41										20 06	20 11				
Feltham	d			19 35			19 41	19 46						20 05				20 11	20 16				
Whitton	d	19 20	19 23					19 50				19 50	19 53						20 20			20 20	20 23
Kingston	d					19 29											19 59						
Hampton Wick	d					19 31											20 01						
Teddington	d					19 35											20 05						
Fulwell	d																						
Strawberry Hill	d					19 38											20 08						
Twickenham	a		19 26	19 40		19 42		19 53					19 56	20 10			20 12		20 23				20 26
	d		19 28	19 41		19 43		19 53					19 58	20 11			20 13		20 23				20 28
St Margarets	d		19 30			19 45							20 00				20 15						20 30
Richmond ⊖	d		19 34	19 45		19 49		19 58					20 04	20 15			20 19		20 28				20 34
North Sheen	d		19 36			19 51							20 06				20 21						20 36
Mortlake	d		19 38			19 53							20 08				20 23						20 38
Hounslow	d	19 31					19 46					20 01						20 16				20 31	
Isleworth	d	19 34					19 49					20 04						20 19				20 34	
Syon Lane	d	19 36					19 51					20 06						20 21				20 36	
Brentford	d	19 39					19 54					20 09						20 24				20 39	
Kew Bridge	d	19 41					19 56					20 11						20 26				20 41	
Chiswick	d	19 44					19 59					20 14						20 29				20 44	
Barnes Bridge	d	19 46			←		20 01					20 16			←			20 31				20 46	
Barnes	d	19 49	19 41		19 49	19 56	20 04		←			20 19	20 11		20 19		20 26	20 34		←		20 49	20 41
Putney	d	→	19 44		19 52	19 59	20 07	20 04	20 07			→	20 14		20 22		20 29	20 37	20 34	20 37		→	20 44
Wandsworth Town	d		19 47		19 55	20 02	→		20 10				20 17		20 25		20 32	→		20 40			20 47
Clapham Junction 10	d		19 50	19 54	19 58	20 05		20 09	20 13				20 20	20 24	20 28		20 35		20 39	20 43			20 50
Queenstown Rd.(Battersea)	d		19 53		20 01	20 08			20 16				20 23		20 31		20 38			20 46			20 53
Vauxhall ⊖	d		19 57		20 05	20 12		20 15	20 20				20 27		20 35		20 42		20 45	20 50			20 57
London Waterloo 15 ⊖	a		20 02	20 04	20 11	20 16		20 19	20 27				20 32	20 34	20 41		20 46		20 49	20 56			21 02

Table T149-R

Mondays to Fridays

8 October to 7 December

Reading, Guildford, Ascot, Weybridge, Windsor, Kingston, Richmond and Hounslow - London

		SW 1	SW	SW 1	SW	SW	SW	SW	SW	SW	SW	SW 1	SW	SW 1	SW 1	SW	SW	SW	SW	SW	SW	SW
Reading 7	d	19 39										20 09										
Earley	d	19 44										20 14										
Winnersh Triangle	d	19 46										20 16										
Winnersh	d	19 48										20 18										
Wokingham	d	19 53										20 23										
Bracknell	d	19 59										20 29										
Martins Heron	d	20 02										20 32										
Guildford	d			19 30										20 00	20 30							
Wanborough	d			19 36										20 06	20 36							
Ash 5	d			19 40										20 10	20 40							
Aldershot	a			19 47										20 17	20 47							
	d			20 00										20 30								
Ash Vale	d			20 04										20 34								
Frimley	d			20 10										20 40								
Camberley	a			20 14										20 44								
	d			20 18										20 48								
Bagshot	d			20 23										20 53								
Ascot 3	d	20 07		20a30								20 37		21a00								
Sunningdale	d	20 10										20 40										
Longcross	d	20 13										20 43										
Weybridge	d								20 33											21 03		
Addlestone	d								20 37											21 07		
Chertsey	d					←			20 40								←			21 10		
Virginia Water	a	20 19				20 17			20 45			20 49					20 45			21 15		
	d	20 19				20 24			20 54			20 49					20 54			21 24		
Egham	d	20 23				20 27			→			20 53					20 57			→		
Windsor & Eton Riverside	d						20 21											20 51				
Datchet	d						20 25											20 55				
Sunnymeads	d						20 28											20 58				
Wraysbury	d						20 32											21 02				
Staines	d	20 29				20 33	20 38					20 59					21 03	21 08				
Ashford (Surrey)	d					20 36	20 41										21 06	21 11				
Feltham	d	20 35				20 41	20 46					21 05					21 11	21 16				
Whitton	d						20 50			20 50	20 53							21 20			21 20	21 23
Kingston	d				20 29											20 59						
Hampton Wick	d				20 31											21 01						
Teddington	d				20 35											21 05						
Fulwell	d																					
Strawberry Hill	d				20 38											21 08						
Twickenham	a	20 40			20 42		20 53				20 56	21 10				21 12		21 23				21 26
	d	20 41			20 43		20 53				20 58	21 11				21 13		21 23				21 28
St Margarets	d				20 45						21 00					21 15						21 30
Richmond ⊖	d	20 45			20 49		20 58				21 04	21 15				21 19		21 28				21 34
North Sheen	d				20 51						21 06					21 21						21 36
Mortlake	d				20 53						21 08					21 23						21 38
Hounslow	d					20 46				21 01							21 16				21 31	
Isleworth	d					20 49				21 04							21 19				21 34	
Syon Lane	d					20 51				21 06							21 21				21 36	
Brentford	d					20 54				21 09							21 24				21 39	
Kew Bridge	d					20 56				21 11							21 26				21 41	
Chiswick	d					20 59				21 14							21 29				21 44	
Barnes Bridge	d		←			21 01				21 16			←				21 31				21 46	
Barnes	d		20 49		20 56	21 04		←		21 19	21 11		21 19			21 26	21 34		←		21 49	21 41
Putney	d		20 52		20 59	21 07	21 04	21 07		→	21 14		21 22			21 29	21 37	21 34	21 37		→	21 44
Wandsworth Town	d		20 55		21 02	→		21 10			21 17		21 25			21 32	→		21 40			21 47
Clapham Junction 10	d	20 54	20 58		21 05		21 09	21 13			21 20	21 24	21 28			21 35		21 39	21 43			21 50
Queenstown Rd.(Battersea)	d		21 01		21 08			21 16			21 23		21 31			21 38			21 46			21 53
Vauxhall ⊖	d		21 05		21 12		21 15	21 20			21 27		21 35			21 42		21 45	21 50			21 57
London Waterloo 15 ⊖	a	21 04	21 11		21 16		21 19	21 26			21 32	21 34	21 41			21 46		21 49	21 56			22 02

8 October to 7 December

Reading, Guildford, Ascot, Weybridge, Windsor, Kingston, Richmond and Hounslow - London

		SW	SW	SW	SW	SW	SW	SW	SW	SW	SW	SW	SW	SW	SW	SW	SW	SW	SW	SW	SW	SW	SW
		■									■		■	■							■		
Reading ■	d	20 39									21 09										21 39		
Earley	d	20 44									21 14										21 44		
Winnersh Triangle	d	20 46									21 16										21 46		
Winnersh	d	20 48									21 18										21 48		
Wokingham	d	20 53									21 23										21 53		
Bracknell	d	20 59									21 29										21 59		
Martins Heron	d	21 02									21 32										22 02		
Guildford	d												21 00	21 30									
Wanborough	d												21 06	21 36									
Ash ■	d												21 10	21 40									
Aldershot	a												21 17	21 47									
	d												21 30										
Ash Vale	d												21 34										
Frimley	d												21 40										
Camberley	a												21 44										
	d												21 48										
Bagshot	d												21 53										
Ascot ■	d	21 07									21 37		22a00								22 07		
Sunningdale	d	21 10									21 40										22 10		
Longcross	d																						
Weybridge	d							21 33												22 03			
Addlestone	d							21 37												22 07			
Chertsey	d				←			21 40								←				22 10			←
Virginia Water	a	21 19			21 15			21 45			21 49					21 45				22 15	22 19		22 15
	d	21 19			21 24			21 54			21 49					21 54				22 24	22 19		22 24
Egham	d	21 23			21 27			→			21 53					21 57				→	22 23		22 27
Windsor & Eton Riverside	d					21 21											21 51						
Datchet	d					21 25											21 55						
Sunnymeads	d					21 28											21 58						
Wraysbury	d					21 32											22 02						
Staines	d	21 29			21 33	21 38					21 59					22 03	22 08				22 29		22 33
Ashford (Surrey)	d				21 36	21 41										22 06	22 11						22 36
Feltham	d	21 35			21 41	21 46					22 05					22 11	22 16				22 35		22 41
Whitton	d					21 50			21 50	21 53							22 20		22 23				
Kingston	d			21 29											21 59							22 29	
Hampton Wick	d			21 31											22 01							22 31	
Teddington	d			21 35											22 05							22 35	
Fulwell	d																						
Strawberry Hill	d			21 38											22 08							22 38	
Twickenham	a	21 40		21 42		21 53				21 56	22 10				22 12		22 23		22 26		22 40	22 42	
	d	21 41		21 43		21 53				21 58	22 11				22 13		22 23		22 28		22 41	22 43	
St Margarets	d			21 45						22 00					22 15				22 30			22 45	
Richmond ⊖	d	21 45		21 49		21 58				22 04	22 15				22 19		22 28		22 34		22 45	22 49	
North Sheen	d			21 51						22 06					22 21				22 36			22 51	
Mortlake	d			21 53						22 08					22 23				22 38			22 53	
Hounslow	d				21 46				22 01							22 16							22 46
Isleworth	d				21 49				22 04							22 19							22 49
Syon Lane	d				21 51				22 06							22 21							22 51
Brentford	d				21 54				22 09							22 24							22 54
Kew Bridge	d				21 56				22 11							22 26							22 56
Chiswick	d				21 59				22 14							22 29							22 59
Barnes Bridge	d		←		22 01				22 16			←				22 31							23 01
Barnes	d		21 49	21 56	22 04		←		22 19	22 11		22 19			22 26	22 34		←	22 41			22 56	23 04
Putney	d		21 52	21 59	22 07	22 04	22 07		→	22 14		22 22			22 29	22 37	22 34	22 37	22 44			22 59	23 07
Wandsworth Town	d		21 55	22 02	→		22 10			22 17		22 25			22 32	→		22 40	22 47			23 02	→
Clapham Junction ■	d	21 54	21 58	22 05		22 09	22 13			22 20	22 24	22 28			22 35		22 39	22 43	22 50		22 54	23 05	
Queenstown Rd.(Battersea)	d		22 01	22 08			22 16			22 23		22 31			22 38			22 46	22 53			23 08	
Vauxhall ⊖	d		22 05	22 12		22 15	22 20			22 27		22 35			22 42		22 45	22 50	22 57			23 12	
London Waterloo ■ ⊖	a	22 04	22 11	22 16		22 19	22 26			22 32	22 34	22 41			22 46		22 49	22 56	23 02		23 04	23 16	

8 October to 7 December

Reading, Guildford, Ascot, Weybridge, Windsor, Kingston, Richmond and Hounslow - London

		SW	SW	SW	SW	SW	SW	SW	SW	SW	SW	SW	SW	SW	SW	SW	SW	SW	SW	SW	SW	SW	SW
					MX ■	MO ■	■	■						■						■		■	■
Reading ■	d				22 09	22 09								22 39						23 12			
Earley	d				22 14	22 14								22 44						23 17			
Winnersh Triangle	d				22 16	22 16								22 46						23 19			
Winnersh	d				22 18	22 18								22 48						23 21			
Wokingham	d				22 23	22 23								22 53						23 26			
Bracknell	d				22 29	22 29								22 59						23 32			
Martins Heron	d				22 32	22 32								23 02						23 35			
Guildford	d						22 00	22 30														23 00	23 30
Wanborough	d						22 06	22 36														23 06	23 36
Ash ■	d						22 10	22 40														23 10	23 40
Aldershot	a						22 17	22 47														23 18	23 47
	d						22 30															23 30	
Ash Vale	d						22 34															23 34	
Frimley	d						22 40															23 40	
Camberley	a						22 44															23 44	
	d						22 48															23 48	
Bagshot	d						22 53															23 53	
Ascot ■	d				22 37	22 37	23a00							23 07						23 40		00a01	
Sunningdale	d				22 40	22 40								23 10						23 43			
Longcross	d																						
Weybridge	d			22 33									23 03						23 33				
Addlestone	d			22 37									23 07						23 37				
Chertsey	d			22 40						←			23 10		←				23 40		←		
Virginia Water	a			22 45	22 49	22 49				22 45			23 15	23 19	23 15				23 45	23 49	23 45		
	d			22 54	22 49	22 49				22 54			23 24	23 19	23 24				23 54	23 49	23 54		
Egham	d			→	22 53	22 53				22 57			→	23 23	23 27				→	23 53	23 57		
Windsor & Eton Riverside	d	22 21									22 53					23 28							
Datchet	d	22 25									22 56					23 31							
Sunnymeads	d	22 28									22 59					23 34							
Wraysbury	d	22 32									23 02					23 37							
Staines	d	22 38			22 59	22 59				23 03	23 08			23 29	23a32	23a42				23 59	00a02		
Ashford (Surrey)	d	22 41								23 06	23 11												
Feltham	d	22 46			23 05	23 05				23 11	23 16			23 35						00 05			
Whitton	d	22 50									23 20												
Kingston	d								22 59								23 29	23 55					
Hampton Wick	d								23 01								23 31	23 57					
Teddington	d								23 05								23 35	23 59					
Fulwell	d																						
Strawberry Hill	d								23 08								23 38	00 03					
Twickenham	a	22 53			23 10	23 10			23 12		23 23			23 40			23 42	00 06		00 10			
	d	22 53			23 11	23 11			23 13		23 23			23 41			23 43			00 11			
St Margarets	d								23 15								23 45						
Richmond ⊖	d	22 58			23 15	23 15			23 19		23 28			23 45			23 49			00 15			
North Sheen	d								23 21								23 51						
Mortlake	d								23 23								23 53						
Hounslow	d									23 16													
Isleworth	d									23 19													
Syon Lane	d									23 21													
Brentford	d									23 24													
Kew Bridge	d									23 26													
Chiswick	d									23 29													
Barnes Bridge	d									23 31													
Barnes	d		←						23 26	23 34		←					23 56						
Putney	d	23 04	23 07						23 29	23 37	23 34	23 37					23 59						
Wandsworth Town	d		23 10						23 32	→		23 40					00 02						
Clapham Junction ■	d	23 10	23 13		23 24	23 24			23 35		23 39	23 43		23 54			00 05			00 24			
Queenstown Rd.(Battersea)	d		23 16						23 38			23 46					00 08						
Vauxhall ⊖	d	23 15	23 20						23 42		23 45	23 50					00 12						
London Waterloo ■ ⊖	a	23 20	23 26		23 34	23 36			23 47		23 49	23 56		00 04			00 16			00 38			

Table T149-R

Mondays to Fridays

8 October to 7 December

Reading, Guildford, Ascot, Weybridge, Windsor, Kingston, Richmond and Hounslow - London

		SW ■
Reading [7]	d	23 52
Earley	d	
Winnersh Triangle	d	
Winnersh	d	
Wokingham	d	00 02
Bracknell	d	00 08
Martins Heron	d	00 11
Guildford	d	
Wanborough	d	
Ash [5]	d	
Aldershot	a	
	d	
Ash Vale	d	
Frimley	d	
Camberley	a	
	d	
Bagshot	d	
Ascot [3]	d	00a17
Sunningdale	d	
Longcross	d	
Weybridge	d	
Addlestone	d	
Chertsey	d	
Virginia Water	a	
	d	
Egham	d	
Windsor & Eton Riverside	d	
Datchet	d	
Sunnymeads	d	
Wraysbury	d	
Staines	d	
Ashford (Surrey)	d	
Feltham	d	
Whitton	d	
Kingston	d	
Hampton Wick	d	
Teddington	d	
Fulwell	d	
Strawberry Hill	d	
Twickenham	a	
	d	
St Margarets	d	
Richmond ⊖	d	
North Sheen	d	
Mortlake	d	
Hounslow	d	
Isleworth	d	
Syon Lane	d	
Brentford	d	
Kew Bridge	d	
Chiswick	d	
Barnes Bridge	d	
Barnes	d	
Putney	d	
Wandsworth Town	d	
Clapham Junction [10]	d	
Queenstown Rd.(Battersea)	d	
Vauxhall ⊖	d	
London Waterloo [15] ⊖	a	

Table T149-R

Saturdays

26 May to 6 October

Reading, Guildford, Ascot, Weybridge, Windsor, Kingston, Richmond and Hounslow - London

		SW	SW ■	SW	SW ■	SW	SW	SW	GW	SW		SW	SW	SW	SW	SW	SW	SW ■	SW ■	SW		SW	SW	SW	SW
Reading [7]	d																	05 42							
Earley	d																	05 47							
Winnersh Triangle	d																	05 49							
Winnersh	d																	05 51							
Wokingham	d		00 02						05 45									05 56							
Bracknell	d		00 08															06 02							
Martins Heron	d		00 11															06 05							
Guildford	d								06a07																
Wanborough	d																								
Ash [5]	d																								
Aldershot	a																								
	d																		06 00						
Ash Vale	d																		06 04						
Frimley	d																		06 10						
Camberley	a																		06 14						
	d																		06 18						
Bagshot	d																		06 23						
Ascot [3]	d		00a17															06 10	06a30						
Sunningdale	d																	06 13							
Longcross	d																								
Weybridge	d																								06 33
Addlestone	d														05 39										06 37
Chertsey	d														05 42										06 40
Virginia Water	a														05 47			06 19							06 45
	d														05 54			06 19							06 54
Egham	d														05 57			06 23							→
Windsor & Eton Riverside	d															05 53							06 23		
Datchet	d															05 56							06 26		
Sunnymeads	d															05 59							06 29		
Wraysbury	d															06 02							06 32		
Staines	d						04 58					05 37			06 03	06 08		06 29				06 33	06 38		
Ashford (Surrey)	d						05 01					05 40			06 06	06 11						06 36	06 41		
Feltham	d				00 05		05 06					05 45			06 11	06 16		06 35				06 41	06 46		
Whitton	d						05 10			05 41		05 49				06 20							06 50		
Kingston	d					01 17								05 59						06 29					
Hampton Wick	d					01s19								06 01						06 31					
Teddington	d					01s22								06 05						06 35					
Fulwell	d																								
Strawberry Hill	d			00 03		01a28		05 38						06 08						06 38					
Twickenham	a			00 06	00 10		05 13	05 41				05 52		06 12		06 23		06 40		06 42			06 53		
	d				00 11		05 13	05 43				05 53		06 13		06 23		06 41		06 43			06 53		
St Margarets	d						05 15	05 45						06 15						06 45					
Richmond ⊖	d				00 15		05 19	05 49				05 58		06 19		06 28		06 45		06 49			06 58		
North Sheen	d						05 21	05 51						06 21						06 51					
Mortlake	d						05 23	05 53						06 23						06 53					
Hounslow	d									05 46					06 16							06 46			
Isleworth	d									05 49					06 19							06 49			
Syon Lane	d									05 51					06 21							06 51			
Brentford	d									05 54					06 24							06 54			
Kew Bridge	d									05 56					06 26							06 56			
Chiswick	d									05 59					06 29							06 59			
Barnes Bridge	d									06 01					06 31							07 01			
Barnes	d						05 26	05 56		06 04			←	06 26	06 34		←			06 56		07 04		←	
Putney	d						05 29	05 59		06 07		06 04	06 07	06 29	06 37	06 34	06 37			06 59		07 07	07 04	07 07	
Wandsworth Town	d	00 02					05 32	06 02		→			06 10	06 32	→		06 40			07 02		→		07 10	
Clapham Junction [10]	d	00 05			00 24		05 35	06 05				06 09	06 13	06 35		06 39	06 43	06 54		07 05			07 09	07 13	
Queenstown Rd.(Battersea)	d	00 08					05 38	06 08					06 16	06 38			06 46			07 08				07 16	
Vauxhall ⊖	d	00 12					05 42	06 12				06 15	06 20	06 42		06 45	06 50			07 12			07 15	07 20	
London Waterloo [15] ⊖	a	00 16			00 38		05 46	06 16				06 19	06 26	06 46		06 49	06 56	07 04		07 16			07 19	07 26	

Table T149-R

Saturdays
26 May to 6 October

Reading, Guildford, Ascot, Weybridge, Windsor, Kingston, Richmond and Hounslow - London

		SW ■	SW	SW	SW	SW		SW	SW ■	SW ■	SW	SW	SW	SW	SW	SW		SW	SW	SW ■	SW	SW ■	SW	SW	SW
Reading ■7	d	06 12							06 42											07 12					
Earley	d	06 17							06 47											07 17					
Winnersh Triangle	d	06 19							06 49											07 19					
Winnersh	d	06 21							06 51											07 21					
Wokingham	d	06 26							06 56											07 26					
Bracknell	d	06 32							07 02											07 32					
Martins Heron	d	06 35							07 05											07 35					
Guildford	d									06 30												07 00			
Wanborough	d									06 36												07 06			
Ash ■5	d									06 40												07 10			
Aldershot	a									06 47												07 17			
	d									07 00												07 30			
Ash Vale	d									07 04												07 34			
Frimley	d									07 10												07 40			
Camberley	a									07 14												07 44			
	d									07 18												07 48			
Bagshot	d									07 23												07 53			
Ascot ■8	d	06 40							07 10	07a30										07 40		08a00			
Sunningdale	d	06 43							07 13											07 43					
Longcross	d																								
Weybridge	d							07 03								07 33									
Addlestone	d							07 07								07 37									
Chertsey	d			←				07 10					←			07 40								←	
Virginia Water	a	06 49		06 45				07 15	07 19				07 15			07 45				07 49				07 45	
	d	06 49		06 54				07 24	07 19				07 24			07 54				07 49				07 54	
Egham	d	06 53		06 57				→	07 23				07 27			→				07 53				07 57	
Windsor & Eton Riverside	d				06 53									07 23											07 53
Datchet	d				06 56									07 26											07 56
Sunnymeads	d				06 59									07 29											07 59
Wraysbury	d				07 02									07 32											08 02
Staines	d	06 59		07 03	07 08				07 29				07 33	07 38						07 59				08 03	08 08
Ashford (Surrey)	d			07 06	07 11								07 36	07 41										08 06	08 11
Feltham	d	07 05		07 11	07 16				07 35				07 41	07 46						08 05				08 11	08 16
Whitton	d				07 20									07 50				07 50	07 53						08 20
Kingston	d		06 59									07 29											07 59		
Hampton Wick	d		07 01									07 31											08 01		
Teddington	d		07 05									07 35											08 05		
Fulwell	d																								
Strawberry Hill	d		07 08									07 38											08 08		
Twickenham	a	07 10	07 12		07 23				07 40			07 42		07 53					07 56	08 10			08 12		08 23
	d	07 11	07 13		07 23				07 41			07 43		07 53					07 58	08 11			08 13		08 23
St Margarets	d		07 15									07 45							08 00				08 15		
Richmond ⊖	d	07 15	07 19		07 28				07 45			07 49		07 58					08 04	08 15			08 19		08 28
North Sheen	d		07 21									07 51							08 06				08 21		
Mortlake	d		07 23									07 53							08 08				08 23		
Hounslow	d			07 16							07 31		07 46					08 01						08 16	
Isleworth	d			07 19							07 34		07 49					08 04						08 19	
Syon Lane	d			07 21							07 36		07 51					08 06						08 21	
Brentford	d			07 24							07 39		07 54					08 09						08 24	
Kew Bridge	d			07 26							07 41		07 56					08 11						08 26	
Chiswick	d			07 29							07 44		07 59					08 14						08 29	
Barnes Bridge	d			07 31							07 46		08 01					08 16			←			08 31	
Barnes	d		07 26	07 34		←					07 49	07 56	08 04		←			08 19	08 11		08 19		08 26	08 34	
Putney	d		07 29	07 37	07 34	07 37					07 52	07 59	08 07	08 04	08 07			→	08 14		08 22		08 29	08 37	08 34
Wandsworth Town	d		07 32	→		07 40					07 55	08 02	→		08 10				08 17		08 25		08 32	→	
Clapham Junction ■10	d	07 24	07 35		07 39	07 43			07 54		07 58	08 05		08 09	08 13				08 20	08 24	08 28		08 35		08 39
Queenstown Rd.(Battersea)	d		07 38			07 46					08 01	08 08			08 16				08 23		08 31		08 38		
Vauxhall ⊖	d		07 42		07 45	07 50					08 05	08 12		08 15	08 20				08 27		08 35		08 42		08 45
London Waterloo ■15 ⊖	a	07 34	07 46		07 49	07 56			08 04		08 11	08 16		08 19	08 26				08 32	08 34	08 41		08 46		08 49

Table T149-R

Saturdays
26 May to 6 October

Reading, Guildford, Ascot, Weybridge, Windsor, Kingston, Richmond and Hounslow - London

		SW		SW	SW	SW	SW ■	SW	SW ■	SW	SW	SW		SW	SW	SW	SW	SW ■	SW	SW ■	SW	SW		SW	SW
Reading ■7	d						07 42											08 12							
Earley	d						07 47											08 17							
Winnersh Triangle	d						07 49											08 19							
Winnersh	d						07 51											08 21							
Wokingham	d						07 56											08 26							
Bracknell	d						08 02											08 32							
Martins Heron	d						08 05											08 35							
Guildford	d								07 30											08 00					
Wanborough	d								07 36											08 06					
Ash ■5	d								07 40											08 10					
Aldershot	a								07 47											08 17					
	d								08 00											08 30					
Ash Vale	d								08 04											08 34					
Frimley	d								08 10											08 40					
Camberley	a								08 14											08 44					
	d								08 18											08 48					
Bagshot	d								08 23											08 53					
Ascot ■8	d						08 10		08a30									08 40		09a00					
Sunningdale	d						08 13											08 43							
Longcross	d																								
Weybridge	d			08 03											08 33										
Addlestone	d			08 07											08 37										
Chertsey	d			08 10							←				08 40							←			
Virginia Water	a			08 15			08 19				08 15				08 45			08 49				08 45			
	d			08 24			08 19				08 24				08 54			08 49				08 54			
Egham	d			→			08 23				08 27				→			08 53				08 57			
Windsor & Eton Riverside	d											08 23												08 53	
Datchet	d											08 26												08 56	
Sunnymeads	d											08 29												08 59	
Wraysbury	d											08 32												09 02	
Staines	d						08 29				08 33	08 38						08 59				09 03		09 08	
Ashford (Surrey)	d										08 36	08 41										09 06		09 11	
Feltham	d						08 35				08 41	08 46						09 05				09 11		09 16	
Whitton	d				08 20	08 23						08 50				08 50	08 53							09 20	
Kingston	d									08 29											08 59				
Hampton Wick	d									08 31											09 01				
Teddington	d									08 35											09 05				
Fulwell	d																								
Strawberry Hill	d									08 38											09 08				
Twickenham	a					08 26	08 40			08 42		08 53					08 56	09 10			09 12			09 23	
	d					08 28	08 41			08 43		08 53					08 58	09 11			09 13			09 23	
St Margarets	d					08 30				08 45							09 00				09 15				
Richmond ⊖	d					08 34	08 45			08 49		08 58					09 04	09 15			09 19			09 28	
North Sheen	d					08 36				08 51							09 06				09 21				
Mortlake	d					08 38				08 53							09 08				09 23				
Hounslow	d				08 31						08 46					09 01						09 16			
Isleworth	d				08 34						08 49					09 04						09 19			
Syon Lane	d				08 36						08 51					09 06						09 21			
Brentford	d				08 39						08 54					09 09						09 24			
Kew Bridge	d				08 41						08 56					09 11						09 26			
Chiswick	d				08 44						08 59					09 14						09 29			
Barnes Bridge	d				08 46			←			09 01					09 16			←			09 31			
Barnes	d	←			08 49	08 41		08 49		08 56	09 04			←		09 19	09 11		09 19		09 26	09 34			←
Putney	d	08 37			→	08 44		08 52		08 59	09 07	09 04		09 07		→	09 14		09 22		09 29	09 37		09 34	09 37
Wandsworth Town	d	08 40				08 47		08 55		09 02	→			09 10			09 17		09 25		09 32	→			09 40
Clapham Junction ■10	d	08 43				08 50	08 54	08 58		09 05		09 09		09 13			09 20	09 24	09 28		09 35			09 39	09 43
Queenstown Rd.(Battersea)	d	08 46				08 53		09 01		09 08				09 16			09 23		09 31		09 38				09 46
Vauxhall ⊖	d	08 50				08 57		09 05		09 12		09 15		09 20			09 27		09 35		09 42			09 45	09 50
London Waterloo ■15 ⊖	a	08 56				09 02	09 04	09 11		09 16		09 19		09 26			09 32	09 34	09 43		09 46			09 49	09 56

Table T149-R

Saturdays
26 May to 6 October

Reading, Guildford, Ascot, Weybridge, Windsor, Kingston, Richmond and Hounslow - London

		SW	SW	SW	SW ■	SW	SW ■	SW	SW	SW	SW	SW	SW	SW	SW ■	SW	SW ■	SW	SW	SW	SW	SW	SW
Reading ■	d				08 42										09 12								
Earley	d				08 47										09 17								
Winnersh Triangle	d				08 49										09 19								
Winnersh	d				08 51										09 21								
Wokingham	d				08 56										09 26								
Bracknell	d				09 02										09 32								
Martins Heron	d				09 05										09 35								
Guildford	d						08 30										09 00						
Wanborough	d						08 36										09 06						
Ash ■	d						08 40										09 10						
Aldershot	a						08 47										09 17						
	d						09 00										09 30						
Ash Vale	d						09 04										09 34						
Frimley	d						09 10										09 40						
Camberley	a						09 14										09 44						
	d						09 18										09 48						
Bagshot	d						09 23										09 53						
Ascot ■	d				09 10		09a30								09 40		10a00						
Sunningdale	d				09 13										09 43								
Longcross	d																						
Weybridge	d	09 03										09 33										10 03	
Addlestone	d	09 07										09 37										10 07	
Chertsey	d	09 10							←			09 40							←			10 10	
Virginia Water	a	09 15			09 19				09 15			09 45			09 49				09 45			10 15	
	d	09 24			09 19				09 24			09 54			09 49				09 54			10 24	
Egham	d	→			09 23				09 27			→			09 53				09 57			→	
Windsor & Eton Riverside	d									09 23										09 53			
Datchet	d									09 26										09 56			
Sunnymeads	d									09 29										09 59			
Wraysbury	d									09 32										10 02			
Staines	d				09 29				09 33	09 38					09 59				10 03	10 08			
Ashford (Surrey)	d								09 36	09 41									10 06	10 11			
Feltham	d				09 35				09 41	09 46					10 05				10 11	10 16			
Whitton	d		09 20	09 23						09 50			09 50	09 53						10 20			10 20
Kingston	d							09 29										09 59					
Hampton Wick	d							09 31										10 01					
Teddington	d							09 35										10 05					
Fulwell	d																						
Strawberry Hill	d							09 38										10 08					
Twickenham	a			09 26	09 40			09 42		09 53				09 56	10 10			10 12		10 23			
	d			09 28	09 41			09 43		09 53				09 58	10 11			10 13		10 23			
St Margarets	d			09 30				09 45						10 00				10 15					
Richmond ⊖	d			09 34	09 45			09 49		09 58				10 04	10 15			10 19		10 28			
North Sheen	d			09 36				09 51						10 06				10 21					
Mortlake	d			09 38				09 53						10 08				10 23					
Hounslow	d		09 31						09 46				10 01						10 16				10 31
Isleworth	d		09 34						09 49				10 04						10 19				10 34
Syon Lane	d		09 36						09 51				10 06						10 21				10 36
Brentford	d		09 39						09 54				10 09						10 24				10 39
Kew Bridge	d		09 41						09 56				10 11						10 26				10 41
Chiswick	d		09 44						09 59				10 14						10 29				10 44
Barnes Bridge	d		09 46			←			10 01				10 16			←			10 31				10 46
Barnes	d		09 49	09 41		09 49		09 56	10 04		←		10 19	10 11		10 19		10 26	10 34		←		10 49
Putney	d		→	09 44		09 52		09 59	10 07	10 04	10 07		→	10 14		10 22		10 29	10 37	10 34	10 37		→
Wandsworth Town	d			09 47		09 55		10 02	→		10 10			10 17		10 25		10 32	→		10 40		
Clapham Junction ■	d			09 50	09 54	09 58		10 05		10 09	10 13			10 20	10 24	10 28		10 35		10 39	10 43		
Queenstown Rd.(Battersea)	d			09 53		10 01		10 08			10 16			10 23		10 31		10 38			10 46		
Vauxhall ⊖	d			09 57		10 05		10 12		10 15	10 20			10 27		10 35		10 42		10 45	10 50		
London Waterloo ■ ⊖	a			10 02	10 04	10 11		10 16		10 19	10 26			10 32	10 34	10 41		10 46		10 49	10 56		

Table T149-R

Saturdays
26 May to 6 October

Reading, Guildford, Ascot, Weybridge, Windsor, Kingston, Richmond and Hounslow - London

		SW	SW ■	SW	SW ■	SW	SW	SW	SW	SW	SW	SW	SW ■	SW	SW ■	SW	SW	SW	SW	SW	SW	SW
Reading ■	d		09 42										10 12									
Earley	d		09 47										10 17									
Winnersh Triangle	d		09 49										10 19									
Winnersh	d		09 51										10 21									
Wokingham	d		09 56										10 26									
Bracknell	d		10 02										10 32									
Martins Heron	d		10 05										10 35									
Guildford	d				09 30										10 00							
Wanborough	d				09 36										10 06							
Ash ■	d				09 40										10 10							
Aldershot	a				09 47										10 17							
	d				10 00										10 30							
Ash Vale	d				10 04										10 34							
Frimley	d				10 10										10 40							
Camberley	a				10 14										10 44							
	d				10 18										10 48							
Bagshot	d				10 23										10 53							
Ascot ■	d		10 10		10a30								10 40		11a00							
Sunningdale	d		10 13										10 43									
Longcross	d																					
Weybridge	d									10 33										11 03		
Addlestone	d									10 37										11 07		
Chertsey	d						←			10 40							←			11 10		
Virginia Water	a		10 19				10 15			10 45			10 49				10 45			11 15		
	d		10 19				10 24			10 54			10 49				10 54			11 24		
Egham	d		10 23				10 27			→			10 53				10 57			→		
Windsor & Eton Riverside	d							10 23										10 53				
Datchet	d							10 26										10 56				
Sunnymeads	d							10 29										10 59				
Wraysbury	d							10 32										11 02				
Staines	d		10 29				10 33	10 38					10 59				11 03	11 08				
Ashford (Surrey)	d						10 36	10 41									11 06	11 11				
Feltham	d		10 35				10 41	10 46					11 05				11 11	11 16				
Whitton	d	10 23						10 50			10 50	10 53						11 20			11 20	11 23
Kingston	d					10 29										10 59						
Hampton Wick	d					10 31										11 01						
Teddington	d					10 35										11 05						
Fulwell	d																					
Strawberry Hill	d					10 38										11 08						
Twickenham	a	10 26	10 40			10 42		10 53				10 56	11 10			11 12		11 23				11 26
	d	10 28	10 41			10 43		10 53				10 58	11 11			11 13		11 23				11 28
St Margarets	d	10 30				10 45						11 00				11 15						11 30
Richmond ⊖	d	10 34	10 45			10 49		10 58				11 04	11 15			11 19		11 28				11 34
North Sheen	d	10 36				10 51						11 06				11 21						11 36
Mortlake	d	10 38				10 53						11 08				11 23						11 38
Hounslow	d						10 46				11 01						11 16				11 31	
Isleworth	d						10 49				11 04						11 19				11 34	
Syon Lane	d						10 51				11 06						11 21				11 36	
Brentford	d						10 54				11 09						11 24				11 39	
Kew Bridge	d						10 56				11 11						11 26				11 41	
Chiswick	d						10 59				11 14						11 29				11 44	
Barnes Bridge	d			←			11 01				11 16			←			11 31				11 46	
Barnes	d	10 41		10 49		10 56	11 04		←		11 19	11 11		11 19		11 26	11 34		←		11 49	11 41
Putney	d	10 44		10 52		10 59	11 07	11 04	11 07		→	11 14		11 22		11 29	11 37	11 34	11 37		→	11 44
Wandsworth Town	d	10 47		10 55		11 02	→		11 10			11 17		11 25		11 32	→		11 40			11 47
Clapham Junction ■	d	10 50	10 54	10 58		11 05		11 09	11 13			11 20	11 24	11 28		11 35		11 39	11 43			11 50
Queenstown Rd.(Battersea)	d	10 53		11 01		11 08			11 16			11 23		11 31		11 38			11 46			11 53
Vauxhall ⊖	d	10 57		11 05		11 12		11 15	11 20			11 27		11 35		11 42		11 45	11 50			11 57
London Waterloo ■ ⊖	a	11 02	11 04	11 11		11 16		11 19	11 26			11 32	11 34	11 41		11 46		11 49	11 56			12 02

Table T149-R

Saturdays

26 May to 6 October

Reading, Guildford, Ascot, Weybridge, Windsor, Kingston, Richmond and Hounslow - London

		SW ■	SW	SW ■	SW	SW	SW	SW	SW	SW		SW	SW ■	SW	SW ■	SW	SW	SW	SW	SW		SW	SW	SW ■	SW
Reading ■	d	10 42											11 12											11 42	
Earley	d	10 47											11 17											11 47	
Winnersh Triangle	d	10 49											11 19											11 49	
Winnersh	d	10 51											11 21											11 51	
Wokingham	d	10 56											11 26											11 56	
Bracknell	d	11 02											11 32											12 02	
Martins Heron	d	11 05											11 35											12 05	
Guildford	d			10 30											11 00										
Wanborough	d			10 36											11 06										
Ash ■	d			10 40											11 10										
Aldershot	a			10 47											11 17										
	d			11 00											11 30										
Ash Vale	d			11 04											11 34										
Frimley	d			11 10											11 40										
Camberley	a			11 14											11 44										
	d			11 18											11 48										
Bagshot	d			11 23											11 53										
Ascot ■	d	11 10		11a30									11 40		12a00									12 10	
Sunningdale	d	11 13											11 43											12 13	
Longcross	d																								
Weybridge	d								11 33											12 03					
Addlestone	d								11 37											12 07					
Chertsey	d					←			11 40								←			12 10					
Virginia Water	a	11 19				11 15			11 45				11 49				11 45			12 15				12 19	
	d	11 19				11 24			11 54				11 49				11 54			12 24				12 19	
Egham	d	11 23				11 27			→				11 53				11 57			→				12 23	
Windsor & Eton Riverside	d						11 23											11 53							
Datchet	d						11 26											11 56							
Sunnymeads	d						11 29											11 59							
Wraysbury	d						11 32											12 02							
Staines	d	11 29				11 33	11 38						11 59				12 03	12 08						12 29	
Ashford (Surrey)	d					11 36	11 41										12 06	12 11							
Feltham	d	11 35				11 41	11 46						12 05				12 11	12 16						12 35	
Whitton	d						11 50			11 50		11 53						12 20				12 20	12 23		
Kingston	d				11 29											11 59									
Hampton Wick	d				11 31											12 01									
Teddington	d				11 35											12 05									
Fulwell	d																								
Strawberry Hill	d				11 38											12 08									
Twickenham	a	11 40			11 42		11 53					11 56	12 10			12 12		12 23					12 26	12 40	
	d	11 41			11 43		11 53					11 58	12 11			12 13		12 23					12 28	12 41	
St Margarets	d				11 45							12 00				12 15							12 30		
Richmond ⊖	d	11 45			11 49		11 58					12 04	12 15			12 19		12 28					12 34	12 45	
North Sheen	d				11 51							12 06				12 21							12 36		
Mortlake	d				11 53							12 08				12 23							12 38		
Hounslow	d					11 46				12 01							12 16					12 31			
Isleworth	d					11 49				12 04							12 19					12 34			
Syon Lane	d					11 51				12 06							12 21					12 36			
Brentford	d					11 54				12 09							12 24					12 39			
Kew Bridge	d					11 56				12 11							12 26					12 41			
Chiswick	d					11 59				12 14							12 29					12 44			
Barnes Bridge	d		←			12 01				12 16				←			12 31					12 46			←
Barnes	d		11 49		11 56	12 04		←		12 19		12 11		12 19		12 26	12 34		←			12 49	12 41		12 49
Putney	d		11 52		11 59	12 07	12 04	12 07		→		12 14		12 22		12 29	12 37	12 34	12 37			→	12 44		12 52
Wandsworth Town	d		11 55		12 02	→		12 10				12 17		12 25		12 32	→		12 40				12 47		12 55
Clapham Junction ■	d	11 54	11 58		12 05		12 09	12 13				12 20	12 24	12 28		12 35		12 39	12 43				12 50	12 54	12 59
Queenstown Rd.(Battersea)	d		12 01		12 08			12 16				12 23		12 31		12 38			12 46				12 53		13 02
Vauxhall ⊖	d		12 05		12 12		12 15	12 20				12 27		12 35		12 42		12 45	12 50				12 57		13 05
London Waterloo ■ ⊖	a	12 04	12 11		12 16		12 19	12 26				12 32	12 34	12 41		12 46		12 49	12 56				13 02	13 04	13 11

Table T149-R

Saturdays

26 May to 6 October

Reading, Guildford, Ascot, Weybridge, Windsor, Kingston, Richmond and Hounslow - London

		SW ■	SW	SW	SW	SW		SW	SW	SW	SW ■	SW	SW ■	SW	SW	SW		SW	SW	SW	SW	SW ■	SW	SW ■	SW
Reading ■	d										12 12											12 42			
Earley	d										12 17											12 47			
Winnersh Triangle	d										12 19											12 49			
Winnersh	d										12 21											12 51			
Wokingham	d										12 26											12 56			
Bracknell	d										12 32											13 02			
Martins Heron	d										12 35											13 05			
Guildford	d	11 30											12 00											12 30	
Wanborough	d	11 36											12 06											12 36	
Ash ■	d	11 40											12 10											12 40	
Aldershot	a	11 47											12 17											12 47	
	d	12 00											12 30											13 00	
Ash Vale	d	12 04											12 34											13 04	
Frimley	d	12 10											12 40											13 10	
Camberley	a	12 14											12 44											13 14	
	d	12 18											12 48											13 18	
Bagshot	d	12 23											12 53											13 23	
Ascot ■	d	12a30									12 40		13a00									13 10		13a30	
Sunningdale	d										12 43											13 13			
Longcross	d																								
Weybridge	d							12 33											13 03						
Addlestone	d							12 37											13 07						
Chertsey	d			←				12 40							←				13 10						
Virginia Water	a			12 15				12 45			12 49				12 45				13 15			13 19			
	d			12 24				12 54			12 49				12 54				13 24			13 19			
Egham	d			12 27				→			12 53				12 57				→			13 23			
Windsor & Eton Riverside	d				12 23											12 53									
Datchet	d				12 26											12 56									
Sunnymeads	d				12 29											12 59									
Wraysbury	d				12 32											13 02									
Staines	d			12 33	12 38						12 59				13 03	13 08						13 29			
Ashford (Surrey)	d			12 36	12 41										13 06	13 11									
Feltham	d			12 41	12 46						13 05				13 11	13 16						13 35			
Whitton	d				12 50				12 50	12 53						13 20				13 20	13 23				
Kingston	d		12 29											12 59											13 29
Hampton Wick	d		12 31											13 01											13 31
Teddington	d		12 35											13 05											13 35
Fulwell	d																								
Strawberry Hill	d		12 38											13 08											13 38
Twickenham	a		12 42		12 53					12 56	13 10			13 12		13 23					13 26	13 40			13 42
	d		12 43		12 53					12 58	13 11			13 13		13 23					13 28	13 41			13 43
St Margarets	d		12 45							13 00				13 15							13 30				13 45
Richmond ⊖	d		12 49		12 58					13 04	13 15			13 19		13 28					13 34	13 45			13 49
North Sheen	d		12 51							13 06				13 21							13 36				13 51
Mortlake	d		12 53							13 08				13 23							13 38				13 53
Hounslow	d			12 46					13 01						13 16					13 31					
Isleworth	d			12 49					13 04						13 19					13 34					
Syon Lane	d			12 51					13 06						13 21					13 36					
Brentford	d			12 54					13 09						13 24					13 39					
Kew Bridge	d			12 56					13 11						13 26					13 41					
Chiswick	d			12 59					13 14						13 29					13 44					
Barnes Bridge	d			13 01					13 16			←			13 31					13 46			←		
Barnes	d		12 56	13 04		←			13 19	13 11		13 19		13 26	13 34			←		13 49	13 41		13 49		13 56
Putney	d		12 59	13 07	13 04	13 07			→	13 14		13 22		13 29	13 37	13 34		13 37		→	13 44		13 52		13 59
Wandsworth Town	d		13 02	→		13 10				13 17		13 25		13 32	→			13 40			13 47		13 55		14 02
Clapham Junction ■	d		13 05		13 09	13 13				13 20	13 24	13 28		13 35		13 39		13 43			13 50	13 54	13 58		14 05
Queenstown Rd.(Battersea)	d		13 08			13 16				13 23		13 31		13 38				13 46			13 53		14 01		14 08
Vauxhall ⊖	d		13 12		13 15	13 20				13 27		13 35		13 42		13 45		13 50			13 57		14 05		14 12
London Waterloo ■ ⊖	a		13 16		13 19	13 26				13 32	13 34	13 41		13 46		13 49		13 56			14 02	14 04	14 11		14 16

Table T149-R

Saturdays
26 May to 6 October

Reading, Guildford, Ascot, Weybridge, Windsor, Kingston, Richmond and Hounslow - London

		SW		SW	SW	SW	SW	SW	SW ■	SW	SW ■	SW		SW	SW	SW	SW	SW	SW	SW ■	SW	SW ■		SW	SW
Reading ■	d								13 12											13 42					
Earley	d								13 17											13 47					
Winnersh Triangle	d								13 19											13 49					
Winnersh	d								13 21											13 51					
Wokingham	d								13 26											13 56					
Bracknell	d								13 32											14 02					
Martins Heron	d								13 35											14 05					
Guildford	d										13 00											13 30			
Wanborough	d										13 06											13 36			
Ash ■	d										13 10											13 40			
Aldershot	a										13 17											13 47			
	d										13 30											14 00			
Ash Vale	d										13 34											14 04			
Frimley	d										13 40											14 10			
Camberley	a										13 44											14 14			
	d										13 48											14 18			
Bagshot	d										13 53											14 23			
Ascot ■	d								13 40		14a00									14 10		14a30			
Sunningdale	d								13 43											14 13					
Longcross	d																								
Weybridge	d				13 33												14 03								
Addlestone	d				13 37												14 07								
Chertsey	d	←			13 40									←			14 10								←
Virginia Water	a	13 15			13 45				13 49					13 45			14 15			14 19					14 15
	d	13 24			13 54				13 49					13 54			14 24			14 19					14 24
Egham	d	13 27			→				13 53					13 57			→			14 23					14 27
Windsor & Eton Riverside	d			13 23											13 53										
Datchet	d			13 26											13 56										
Sunnymeads	d			13 29											13 59										
Wraysbury	d			13 32											14 02										
Staines	d	13 33		13 38					13 59					14 03	14 08					14 29					14 33
Ashford (Surrey)	d	13 36		13 41										14 06	14 11										14 36
Feltham	d	13 41		13 46					14 05					14 11	14 16					14 35					14 41
Whitton	d			13 50			13 50	13 53							14 20			14 20	14 23						
Kingston	d											13 59												14 29	
Hampton Wick	d											14 01												14 31	
Teddington	d											14 05												14 35	
Fulwell	d																								
Strawberry Hill	d											14 08												14 38	
Twickenham	a			13 53				13 56	14 10			14 12			14 23				14 26	14 40				14 42	
	d			13 53				13 58	14 11			14 13			14 23				14 28	14 41				14 43	
St Margarets	d							14 00				14 15							14 30					14 45	
Richmond ⊖	d			13 58				14 04	14 15			14 19			14 28				14 34	14 45				14 49	
North Sheen	d							14 06				14 21							14 36					14 51	
Mortlake	d							14 08				14 23							14 38					14 53	
Hounslow	d	13 46					14 01							14 16				14 31							14 46
Isleworth	d	13 49					14 04							14 19				14 34							14 49
Syon Lane	d	13 51					14 06							14 21				14 36							14 51
Brentford	d	13 54					14 09							14 24				14 39							14 54
Kew Bridge	d	13 56					14 11							14 26				14 41							14 56
Chiswick	d	13 59					14 14							14 29				14 44							14 59
Barnes Bridge	d	14 01					14 16			←				14 31				14 46			←				15 01
Barnes	d	14 04			←		14 19	14 11		14 19		14 26		14 34		←		14 49	14 41		14 49			14 56	15 04
Putney	d	14 07		14 04	14 07		→	14 14		14 22		14 29		14 37	14 34	14 37		→	14 44		14 52			14 59	15 07
Wandsworth Town	d	→			14 10			14 17		14 25		14 32		→		14 40			14 47		14 55			15 02	→
Clapham Junction ■	d			14 09	14 13			14 20	14 24	14 28		14 35			14 39	14 43			14 50	14 54	14 58			15 05	
Queenstown Rd.(Battersea)	d				14 16			14 23		14 31		14 38				14 46			14 53		15 01			15 08	
Vauxhall ⊖	d			14 15	14 20			14 27		14 35		14 42			14 45	14 50			14 57		15 05			15 12	
London Waterloo ■ ⊖	a			14 19	14 26			14 32	14 34	14 41		14 46			14 49	14 56			15 02	15 04	15 11			15 16	

Table T149-R

Saturdays
26 May to 6 October

Reading, Guildford, Ascot, Weybridge, Windsor, Kingston, Richmond and Hounslow - London

		SW	SW	SW	SW	SW	SW ■	SW		SW ■	SW	SW	SW	SW	SW	SW	SW	SW ■		SW	SW ■	SW	SW	SW	SW
Reading ■	d						14 12											14 42							
Earley	d						14 17											14 47							
Winnersh Triangle	d						14 19											14 49							
Winnersh	d						14 21											14 51							
Wokingham	d						14 26											14 56							
Bracknell	d						14 32											15 02							
Martins Heron	d						14 35											15 05							
Guildford	d									14 00											14 30				
Wanborough	d									14 06											14 36				
Ash ■	d									14 10											14 40				
Aldershot	a									14 17											14 47				
	d									14 30											15 00				
Ash Vale	d									14 34											15 04				
Frimley	d									14 40											15 10				
Camberley	a									14 44											15 14				
	d									14 48											15 18				
Bagshot	d									14 53											15 23				
Ascot ■	d						14 40			15a00								15 10			15a30				
Sunningdale	d						14 43											15 13							
Longcross	d																								
Weybridge	d			14 33											15 03										
Addlestone	d			14 37											15 07										
Chertsey	d			14 40								←			15 10								←		
Virginia Water	a			14 45			14 49					14 45			15 15			15 19					15 15		
	d			14 54			14 49					14 54			15 24			15 19					15 24		
Egham	d			→			14 53					14 57			→			15 23					15 27		
Windsor & Eton Riverside	d	14 23											14 53											15 23	
Datchet	d	14 26											14 56											15 26	
Sunnymeads	d	14 29											14 59											15 29	
Wraysbury	d	14 32											15 02											15 32	
Staines	d	14 38					14 59					15 03	15 08					15 29					15 33	15 38	
Ashford (Surrey)	d	14 41										15 06	15 11										15 36	15 41	
Feltham	d	14 46					15 05					15 11	15 16					15 35					15 41	15 46	
Whitton	d	14 50			14 50	14 53							15 20			15 20	15 23							15 50	
Kingston	d										14 59											15 29			
Hampton Wick	d										15 01											15 31			
Teddington	d										15 05											15 35			
Fulwell	d																								
Strawberry Hill	d										15 08											15 38			
Twickenham	a	14 53				14 56	15 10				15 12		15 23				15 26	15 40				15 42		15 53	
	d	14 53				14 58	15 11				15 13		15 23				15 28	15 41				15 43		15 53	
St Margarets	d					15 00					15 15						15 30					15 45			
Richmond ⊖	d	14 58				15 04	15 15				15 19		15 28				15 34	15 45				15 49		15 58	
North Sheen	d					15 06					15 21						15 36					15 51			
Mortlake	d					15 08					15 23						15 38					15 53			
Hounslow	d				15 01							15 16				15 31							15 46		
Isleworth	d				15 04							15 19				15 34							15 49		
Syon Lane	d				15 06							15 21				15 36							15 51		
Brentford	d				15 09							15 24				15 39							15 54		
Kew Bridge	d				15 11							15 26				15 41							15 56		
Chiswick	d				15 14							15 29				15 44							15 59		
Barnes Bridge	d				15 16			←				15 31				15 46				←			16 01		
Barnes	d		←		15 19	15 11		15 19			15 26	15 34		←		15 49	15 41			15 49		15 56	16 04		←
Putney	d	15 04	15 07		→	15 14		15 22			15 29	15 37	15 34	15 37		→	15 44			15 52		15 59	16 07	16 04	16 07
Wandsworth Town	d		15 10			15 17		15 25			15 32	→		15 40			15 47			15 55		16 02	→		16 10
Clapham Junction ■	d	15 09	15 13			15 20	15 24	15 28			15 35		15 39	15 43			15 50	15 54		15 58		16 05		16 09	16 13
Queenstown Rd.(Battersea)	d		15 16			15 23		15 31			15 38			15 46			15 53			16 01		16 08			16 16
Vauxhall ⊖	d	15 15	15 20			15 27		15 35			15 42		15 45	15 50			15 57			16 05		16 12		16 15	16 20
London Waterloo ■ ⊖	a	15 19	15 26			15 32	15 34	15 41			15 46		15 49	15 56			16 02	16 04		16 11		16 16		16 19	16 26

Table T149-R

Saturdays
26 May to 6 October

Reading, Guildford, Ascot, Weybridge, Windsor, Kingston, Richmond and Hounslow - London

		SW	SW	SW	SW ■	SW	SW ■	SW	SW	SW	SW	SW	SW	SW	SW ■	SW	SW ■	SW	SW	SW	SW	SW
Reading ■	d				15 12										15 42							
Earley	d				15 17										15 47							
Winnersh Triangle	d				15 19										15 49							
Winnersh	d				15 21										15 51							
Wokingham	d				15 26										15 56							
Bracknell	d				15 32										16 02							
Martins Heron	d				15 35										16 05							
Guildford	d						15 00										15 30					
Wanborough	d						15 06										15 36					
Ash ■	d						15 10										15 40					
Aldershot	a						15 17										15 47					
	d						15 30										16 00					
Ash Vale	d						15 34										16 04					
Frimley	d						15 40										16 10					
Camberley	a						15 44										16 14					
	d						15 48										16 18					
Bagshot	d						15 53										16 23					
Ascot ■	d				15 40		16a00								16 10		16a30					
Sunningdale	d				15 43										16 13							
Longcross	d																					
Weybridge	d	15 33									16 03											16 33
Addlestone	d	15 37									16 07											16 37
Chertsey	d	15 40							←			16 10							←			16 40
Virginia Water	a	15 45			15 49				15 45			16 15			16 19				16 15			16 45
	d	15 54			15 49				15 54			16 24			16 19				16 24			16 54
Egham	d	→			15 53				15 57			→			16 23				16 27			→
Windsor & Eton Riverside	d									15 53										16 23		
Datchet	d									15 56										16 26		
Sunnymeads	d									15 59										16 29		
Wraysbury	d									16 02										16 32		
Staines	d				15 59				16 03	16 08					16 29				16 33	16 38		
Ashford (Surrey)	d								16 06	16 11									16 36	16 41		
Feltham	d				16 05				16 11	16 16					16 35				16 41	16 46		
Whitton	d		15 50	15 53						16 20			16 20	16 23						16 50		
Kingston	d							15 59										16 29				
Hampton Wick	d							16 01										16 31				
Teddington	d							16 05										16 35				
Fulwell	d																					
Strawberry Hill	d							16 08										16 38				
Twickenham	a			15 56	16 10			16 12		16 23				16 26	16 40			16 42		16 53		
	d			15 58	16 11			16 13		16 23				16 28	16 41			16 43		16 53		
St Margarets	d			16 00				16 15						16 30				16 45				
Richmond ⊖	d			16 04	16 15			16 19		16 28				16 34	16 45			16 49		16 58		
North Sheen	d			16 06				16 21						16 36				16 51				
Mortlake	d			16 08				16 23						16 38				16 53				
Hounslow	d		16 01						16 16				16 31						16 46			
Isleworth	d		16 04						16 19				16 34						16 49			
Syon Lane	d		16 06						16 21				16 36						16 51			
Brentford	d		16 09						16 24				16 39						16 54			
Kew Bridge	d		16 11						16 26				16 41						16 56			
Chiswick	d		16 14						16 29				16 44						16 59			
Barnes Bridge	d		16 16			←			16 31				16 46			←			17 01			
Barnes	d		16 19	16 11		16 19		16 26	16 34		←		16 49	16 41		16 49		16 56	17 04		←	
Putney	d		→	16 14		16 22		16 29	16 37	16 34	16 37		→	16 44		16 52		16 59	17 07	17 04	17 07	
Wandsworth Town	d			16 17		16 25		16 32	→		16 40			16 47		16 55		17 02	→		17 10	
Clapham Junction ■	d			16 20	16 24	16 28		16 35		16 39	16 43			16 50	16 54	16 58		17 05		17 09	17 13	
Queenstown Rd.(Battersea)	d			16 23		16 31		16 38			16 46			16 53		17 01		17 08			17 16	
Vauxhall ⊖	d			16 27		16 35		16 42		16 45	16 50			16 57		17 05		17 12		17 15	17 20	
London Waterloo ■ ⊖	a			16 32	16 34	16 41		16 46		16 49	16 56			17 02	17 04	17 11		17 16		17 19	17 26	

Table T149-R

Saturdays
26 May to 6 October

Reading, Guildford, Ascot, Weybridge, Windsor, Kingston, Richmond and Hounslow - London

		SW	SW	SW ■	SW	SW ■	SW	SW	SW	SW	SW	SW	SW	SW ■	SW	SW ■	SW	SW	SW	SW	SW	SW	SW
Reading ■	d			16 12										16 42									
Earley	d			16 17										16 47									
Winnersh Triangle	d			16 19										16 49									
Winnersh	d			16 21										16 51									
Wokingham	d			16 26										16 56									
Bracknell	d			16 32										17 02									
Martins Heron	d			16 35										17 05									
Guildford	d					16 00										16 30							
Wanborough	d					16 06										16 36							
Ash ■	d					16 10										16 40							
Aldershot	a					16 17										16 47							
	d					16 30										17 00							
Ash Vale	d					16 34										17 04							
Frimley	d					16 40										17 10							
Camberley	a					16 44										17 14							
	d					16 48										17 18							
Bagshot	d					16 53										17 23							
Ascot ■	d			16 40		17a00								17 10		17a30							
Sunningdale	d			16 43										17 13									
Longcross	d																						
Weybridge	d										17 03										17 33		
Addlestone	d										17 07										17 37		
Chertsey	d							←			17 10							←			17 40		
Virginia Water	a			16 49				16 45			17 15			17 19				17 15			17 45		
	d			16 49				16 54			17 24			17 19				17 24			17 54		
Egham	d			16 53				16 57			→			17 23				17 27			→		
Windsor & Eton Riverside	d								16 53										17 23				
Datchet	d								16 56										17 26				
Sunnymeads	d								16 59										17 29				
Wraysbury	d								17 02										17 32				
Staines	d			16 59				17 03	17 08					17 29				17 33	17 38				
Ashford (Surrey)	d							17 06	17 11									17 36	17 41				
Feltham	d			17 05				17 11	17 16					17 35				17 41	17 46				
Whitton	d	16 50	16 53						17 20			17 20	17 23						17 50			17 50	17 53
Kingston	d						16 59										17 29						
Hampton Wick	d						17 01										17 31						
Teddington	d						17 05										17 35						
Fulwell	d																						
Strawberry Hill	d						17 08										17 38						
Twickenham	a		16 56	17 10			17 12		17 23				17 26	17 40			17 42		17 53				17 56
	d		16 58	17 11			17 13		17 23				17 28	17 41			17 43		17 53				17 58
St Margarets	d		17 00				17 15						17 30				17 45						18 00
Richmond ⊖	d		17 04	17 15			17 19		17 28				17 34	17 45			17 49		17 58				18 04
North Sheen	d		17 06				17 21						17 36				17 51						18 06
Mortlake	d		17 08				17 23						17 38				17 53						18 08
Hounslow	d	17 01						17 16				17 31						17 46				18 01	
Isleworth	d	17 04						17 19				17 34						17 49				18 04	
Syon Lane	d	17 06						17 21				17 36						17 51				18 06	
Brentford	d	17 09						17 24				17 39						17 54				18 09	
Kew Bridge	d	17 11						17 26				17 41						17 56				18 11	
Chiswick	d	17 14						17 29				17 44						17 59				18 14	
Barnes Bridge	d	17 16			←			17 31				17 46			←			18 01				18 16	
Barnes	d	17 19	17 11		17 19		17 26	17 34		←		17 49	17 41		17 49		17 56	18 04		←		18 19	18 11
Putney	d	→	17 14		17 22		17 29	17 37	17 34	17 37		→	17 44		17 52		17 59	18 07	18 04	18 07		→	18 14
Wandsworth Town	d		17 17		17 25		17 32	→		17 40			17 47		17 55		18 02	→		18 10			18 17
Clapham Junction ■	d		17 20	17 24	17 28		17 35		17 39	17 43			17 50	17 54	17 58		18 05		18 09	18 13			18 20
Queenstown Rd.(Battersea)	d		17 23		17 31		17 38			17 46			17 53		18 01		18 08			18 16			18 23
Vauxhall ⊖	d		17 27		17 35		17 42		17 45	17 50			17 57		18 05		18 12		18 15	18 20			18 27
London Waterloo ■ ⊖	a		17 32	17 34	17 41		17 46		17 49	17 56			18 02	18 04	18 11		18 16		18 19	18 26			18 32

Reading, Guildford, Ascot, Weybridge, Windsor, Kingston, Richmond and Hounslow - London

		SW 1	SW	SW 1	SW	SW		SW	SW	SW	SW	SW	SW 1	SW	SW 1	SW		SW	SW	SW	SW	SW	SW	SW 1	SW
Reading 7	d	17 12											17 42											18 12	
Earley	d	17 17											17 47											18 17	
Winnersh Triangle	d	17 19											17 49											18 19	
Winnersh	d	17 21											17 51											18 21	
Wokingham	d	17 26											17 56											18 26	
Bracknell	d	17 32											18 02											18 32	
Martins Heron	d	17 35											18 05											18 35	
Guildford	d			17 00											17 30										
Wanborough	d			17 06											17 36										
Ash 5	d			17 10											17 40										
Aldershot	a			17 17											17 47										
	d			17 30											18 00										
Ash Vale	d			17 34											18 04										
Frimley	d			17 40											18 10										
Camberley	a			17 44											18 14										
	d			17 48											18 18										
Bagshot	d			17 53											18 23										
Ascot 3	d	17 40		18a00									18 10		18a30									18 40	
Sunningdale	d	17 43											18 13											18 43	
Longcross	d																								
Weybridge	d									18 03											18 33				
Addlestone	d									18 07											18 37				
Chertsey	d					←				18 10								←			18 40				
Virginia Water	a	17 49				17 45				18 15			18 19					18 15			18 45			18 49	
	d	17 49				17 54				18 24			18 19					18 24			18 54			18 49	
Egham	d	17 53				17 57				→			18 23					18 27			→			18 53	
Windsor & Eton Riverside	d							17 53											18 23						
Datchet	d							17 56											18 26						
Sunnymeads	d							17 59											18 29						
Wraysbury	d							18 02											18 32						
Staines	d	17 59				18 03		18 08					18 29					18 33	18 38					18 59	
Ashford (Surrey)	d					18 06		18 11										18 36	18 41						
Feltham	d	18 05				18 11		18 16					18 35					18 41	18 46					19 05	
Whitton	d							18 20			18 20	18 23							18 50			18 50	18 53		
Kingston	d				17 59											18 29									
Hampton Wick	d				18 01											18 31									
Teddington	d				18 05											18 35									
Fulwell	d																								
Strawberry Hill	d				18 08											18 38									
Twickenham	a	18 10			18 12			18 23				18 26	18 40			18 42			18 53				18 56	19 10	
	d	18 11			18 13			18 23				18 28	18 41			18 43			18 53				18 58	19 11	
St Margarets	d				18 15							18 30				18 45							19 00		
Richmond ⊖	d	18 15			18 19			18 28				18 34	18 45			18 49			18 58				19 04	19 15	
North Sheen	d				18 21							18 36				18 51							19 06		
Mortlake	d				18 23							18 38				18 53							19 08		
Hounslow	d					18 16					18 31							18 46				19 01			
Isleworth	d					18 19					18 34							18 49				19 04			
Syon Lane	d					18 21					18 36							18 51				19 06			
Brentford	d					18 24					18 39							18 54				19 09			
Kew Bridge	d					18 26					18 41							18 56				19 11			
Chiswick	d					18 29					18 44							18 59				19 14			
Barnes Bridge	d		←			18 31					18 46			←								19 16			←
Barnes	d		18 19		18 26	18 34			←		18 49	18 41		18 49		18 56		19 04		←		19 19	19 11		19 19
Putney	d		18 22		18 29	18 37		18 34	18 37		→	18 44		18 52		18 59		19 07	19 04	19 07		→	19 14		19 22
Wandsworth Town	d		18 25		18 32	→			18 40			18 47		18 55		19 02		→		19 10			19 17		19 25
Clapham Junction 10	d	18 24	18 28		18 35			18 39	18 43			18 50	18 54	18 58		19 05			19 09	19 13			19 20	19 24	19 29
Queenstown Rd.(Battersea)	d		18 31		18 38				18 46			18 53		19 01		19 08				19 16			19 23		19 32
Vauxhall ⊖	d		18 35		18 42			18 45	18 50			18 57		19 05		19 12			19 15	19 20			19 27		19 36
London Waterloo 15 ⊖	a	18 34	18 41		18 46			18 49	18 56			19 02	19 04	19 11		19 16			19 19	19 26			19 32	19 34	19 41

Reading, Guildford, Ascot, Weybridge, Windsor, Kingston, Richmond and Hounslow - London

		SW 1		SW	SW	SW	SW	SW	SW	SW	SW 1	SW		SW 1	SW	SW	SW	SW	SW	SW	SW	SW 1		SW	SW 1
Reading 7	d										18 42											19 12			
Earley	d										18 47											19 17			
Winnersh Triangle	d										18 49											19 19			
Winnersh	d										18 51											19 21			
Wokingham	d										18 56											19 26			
Bracknell	d										19 02											19 32			
Martins Heron	d										19 05											19 35			
Guildford	d	18 00												18 30											19 00
Wanborough	d	18 06												18 36											19 06
Ash 5	d	18 10												18 40											19 10
Aldershot	a	18 17												18 47											19 17
	d	18 30												19 00											19 30
Ash Vale	d	18 34												19 04											19 34
Frimley	d	18 40												19 10											19 40
Camberley	a	18 44												19 14											19 44
	d	18 48												19 18											19 48
Bagshot	d	18 53												19 23											19 53
Ascot 3	d	19a00									19 10			19a30								19 40			20a00
Sunningdale	d										19 13											19 43			
Longcross	d																								
Weybridge	d							19 03											19 33						
Addlestone	d							19 07											19 37						
Chertsey	d				←			19 10								←			19 40						
Virginia Water	a				18 45			19 15			19 19					19 15			19 45			19 49			
	d				18 54			19 24			19 19					19 24			19 54			19 49			
Egham	d				18 57			→			19 23					19 27			→			19 53			
Windsor & Eton Riverside	d					18 53											19 23								
Datchet	d					18 56											19 26								
Sunnymeads	d					18 59											19 29								
Wraysbury	d					19 02											19 32								
Staines	d				19 03	19 08					19 29					19 33	19 38					19 59			
Ashford (Surrey)	d				19 06	19 11										19 36	19 41								
Feltham	d				19 11	19 16					19 35					19 41	19 46					20 05			
Whitton	d					19 20			19 20	19 23							19 50			19 50	19 53				
Kingston	d			18 59											19 29										
Hampton Wick	d			19 01											19 31										
Teddington	d			19 05											19 35										
Fulwell	d																								
Strawberry Hill	d			19 08											19 38										
Twickenham	a			19 12		19 23				19 26	19 40				19 42		19 53				19 56	20 10			
	d			19 13		19 23				19 28	19 41				19 43		19 53				19 58	20 11			
St Margarets	d			19 15						19 30					19 45						20 00				
Richmond ⊖	d			19 19		19 28				19 34	19 45				19 49		19 58				20 04	20 15			
North Sheen	d			19 21						19 36					19 51						20 06				
Mortlake	d			19 23						19 38					19 53						20 08				
Hounslow	d				19 16				19 31							19 46				20 01					
Isleworth	d				19 19				19 34							19 49				20 04					
Syon Lane	d				19 21				19 36							19 51				20 06					
Brentford	d				19 24				19 39							19 54				20 09					
Kew Bridge	d				19 26				19 41							19 56				20 11					
Chiswick	d				19 29				19 44							19 59				20 14					
Barnes Bridge	d				19 31				19 46			←				20 01				20 16				←	
Barnes	d			19 26	19 34		←		19 49	19 41		19 49			19 56	20 04		←		20 19	20 11			20 19	
Putney	d			19 29	19 37	19 34	19 37		→	19 44		19 52			19 59	20 07	20 04	20 07		→	20 14			20 22	
Wandsworth Town	d			19 32	→		19 40			19 47		19 55			20 02	→		20 10			20 17			20 25	
Clapham Junction 10	d			19 35		19 39	19 43			19 50	19 54	19 58			20 05		20 09	20 13			20 20	20 24		20 28	
Queenstown Rd.(Battersea)	d			19 38			19 46			19 53		20 01			20 08			20 16			20 23			20 31	
Vauxhall ⊖	d			19 42		19 45	19 50			19 57		20 05			20 12		20 15	20 20			20 27			20 35	
London Waterloo 15 ⊖	a			19 46		19 49	19 56			20 02	20 04	20 11			20 16		20 19	20 26			20 32	20 34		20 41	

Table T149-R

Saturdays
26 May to 6 October

Reading, Guildford, Ascot, Weybridge, Windsor, Kingston, Richmond and Hounslow - London

		SW	SW	SW	SW	SW	SW	SW		SW ■	SW	SW ■	SW	SW	SW	SW	SW	SW		SW	SW ■	SW	SW ■	SW ■	SW
Reading ■	d									19 42											20 12				
Earley	d									19 47											20 17				
Winnersh Triangle	d									19 49											20 19				
Winnersh	d									19 51											20 21				
Wokingham	d									19 56											20 26				
Bracknell	d									20 02											20 32				
Martins Heron	d									20 05											20 35				
Guildford	d											19 30											20 00	20 30	
Wanborough	d											19 36											20 06	20 36	
Ash ■	d											19 40											20 10	20 40	
Aldershot	a											19 47											20 17	20 47	
	d											20 00											20 30		
Ash Vale	d											20 04											20 34		
Frimley	d											20 10											20 40		
Camberley	a											20 14											20 44		
	d											20 18											20 48		
Bagshot	d											20 23											20 53		
Ascot ■	d									20 10		20a30									20 40		21a00		
Sunningdale	d									20 13											20 43				
Longcross	d																								
Weybridge	d					20 03										20 33									
Addlestone	d					20 07										20 37									
Chertsey	d		←			20 10								←			20 40								
Virginia Water	a		19 45			20 15				20 19				20 15			20 45				20 49				
	d		19 54			20 24				20 19				20 24			20 54				20 49				
Egham	d		19 57			→				20 23				20 27			→				20 53				
Windsor & Eton Riverside	d			19 53											20 23										
Datchet	d			19 56											20 26										
Sunnymeads	d			19 59											20 29										
Wraysbury	d			20 02											20 32										
Staines	d		20 03	20 08						20 29				20 33	20 38						20 59				
Ashford (Surrey)	d		20 06	20 11										20 36	20 41										
Feltham	d		20 11	20 16						20 35				20 41	20 46						21 05				
Whitton	d			20 20			20 20	20 23							20 50			20 50		20 53					
Kingston	d	19 59											20 29												20 59
Hampton Wick	d	20 01											20 31												21 01
Teddington	d	20 05											20 35												21 05
Fulwell	d																								
Strawberry Hill	d	20 08											20 38												21 08
Twickenham	a	20 12		20 23				20 26		20 40			20 42		20 53					20 56	21 10				21 12
	d	20 13		20 23				20 28		20 41			20 43		20 53					20 58	21 11				21 13
St Margarets	d	20 15						20 30					20 45							21 00					21 15
Richmond ⊖	d	20 19		20 28				20 34		20 45			20 49		20 58					21 04	21 15				21 19
North Sheen	d	20 21						20 36					20 51							21 06					21 21
Mortlake	d	20 23						20 38					20 53							21 08					21 23
Hounslow	d		20 16				20 31							20 46				21 01							
Isleworth	d		20 19				20 34							20 49				21 04							
Syon Lane	d		20 21				20 36							20 51				21 06							
Brentford	d		20 24				20 39							20 54				21 09							
Kew Bridge	d		20 26				20 41							20 56				21 11							
Chiswick	d		20 29				20 44							20 59				21 14							
Barnes Bridge	d		20 31				20 46				←			21 01				21 16				←			
Barnes	d	20 26	20 34		←		20 49	20 41			20 49		20 56	21 04		←		21 19		21 11		21 19			21 26
Putney	d	20 29	20 37	20 34	20 37		→	20 44			20 52		20 59	21 07	21 04	21 07		→		21 14		21 22			21 29
Wandsworth Town	d	20 32	→		20 40			20 47			20 55		21 02	→		21 10				21 17		21 25			21 32
Clapham Junction ■	d	20 35		20 39	20 43			20 50		20 54	20 58		21 05		21 09	21 13				21 20	21 24	21 28			21 35
Queenstown Rd.(Battersea)	d	20 38			20 46			20 53			21 01		21 08			21 16				21 23		21 31			21 38
Vauxhall ⊖	d	20 42		20 45	20 50			20 57			21 05		21 12		21 15	21 20				21 27		21 35			21 42
London Waterloo ■ ⊖	a	20 46		20 49	20 56			21 02		21 04	21 11		21 16		21 19	21 26				21 32	21 34	21 41			21 46

Table T149-R

Saturdays
26 May to 6 October

Reading, Guildford, Ascot, Weybridge, Windsor, Kingston, Richmond and Hounslow - London

		SW	SW	SW		SW	SW	SW	SW ■	SW	SW	SW	SW	SW		SW	SW	SW	SW ■	SW	SW ■	SW ■	SW	SW	
Reading ■	d								20 42										21 12						
Earley	d								20 47										21 17						
Winnersh Triangle	d								20 49										21 19						
Winnersh	d								20 51										21 21						
Wokingham	d								20 56										21 26						
Bracknell	d								21 02										21 32						
Martins Heron	d								21 05										21 35						
Guildford	d																				21 00	21 30			
Wanborough	d																				21 06	21 36			
Ash ■	d																				21 10	21 40			
Aldershot	a																				21 17	21 47			
	d																				21 30				
Ash Vale	d																				21 34				
Frimley	d																				21 40				
Camberley	a																				21 44				
	d																				21 48				
Bagshot	d																				21 53				
Ascot ■	d								21 10										21 40		22a00				
Sunningdale	d								21 13										21 43						
Longcross	d																								
Weybridge	d					21 03										21 33									
Addlestone	d					21 07										21 37									
Chertsey	d	←				21 10						←				21 40								←	
Virginia Water	a	20 45				21 15			21 19			21 15				21 45			21 49					21 45	
	d	20 54				21 24			21 19			21 24				21 54			21 49					21 54	
Egham	d	20 57				→			21 23			21 27				→			21 53					21 57	
Windsor & Eton Riverside	d		20 53										21 23												
Datchet	d		20 56										21 26												
Sunnymeads	d		20 59										21 29												
Wraysbury	d		21 02										21 32												
Staines	d	21 03	21 08						21 29			21 33	21 38						21 59					22 03	
Ashford (Surrey)	d	21 06	21 11									21 36	21 41											22 06	
Feltham	d	21 11	21 16						21 35			21 41	21 46						22 05					22 11	
Whitton	d		21 20				21 20	21 23					21 50				21 50	21 53							
Kingston	d										21 29												21 59		
Hampton Wick	d										21 31												22 01		
Teddington	d										21 35												22 05		
Fulwell	d																								
Strawberry Hill	d										21 38												22 08		
Twickenham	a		21 23					21 26	21 40		21 42		21 53					21 56	22 10				22 12		
	d		21 23					21 28	21 41		21 43		21 53					21 58	22 11				22 13		
St Margarets	d							21 30			21 45							22 00					22 15		
Richmond ⊖	d		21 28					21 34	21 45		21 49		21 58					22 04	22 15				22 19		
North Sheen	d							21 36			21 51							22 06					22 21		
Mortlake	d							21 38			21 53							22 08					22 23		
Hounslow	d	21 16					21 31					21 46					22 01							22 16	
Isleworth	d	21 19					21 34					21 49					22 04							22 19	
Syon Lane	d	21 21					21 36					21 51					22 06							22 21	
Brentford	d	21 24					21 39					21 54					22 09							22 24	
Kew Bridge	d	21 26					21 41					21 56					22 11							22 26	
Chiswick	d	21 29					21 44					21 59					22 14							22 29	
Barnes Bridge	d	21 31					21 46			←		22 01					22 16			←				22 31	
Barnes	d	21 34		←			21 49	21 41		21 49	21 56	22 04		←			22 19	22 11		22 19			22 26	22 34	
Putney	d	21 37	21 34	21 37			→	21 44		21 52	21 59	22 07	22 04	22 07			→	22 14		22 22			22 29	22 37	
Wandsworth Town	d	→		21 40				21 47		21 55	22 02	→		22 10				22 17		22 25			22 32	→	
Clapham Junction ■	d		21 39	21 43				21 50	21 54	21 58	22 05		22 09	22 13				22 20	22 24	22 28			22 35		
Queenstown Rd.(Battersea)	d			21 46				21 53		22 01	22 08			22 16				22 23		22 31			22 38		
Vauxhall ⊖	d		21 45	21 50				21 57		22 05	22 12		22 15	22 20				22 27		22 35			22 42		
London Waterloo ■ ⊖	a		21 49	21 56				22 02	22 04	22 13	22 17		22 19	22 26				22 32	22 34	22 41			22 46		

Table T149-R

Saturdays
26 May to 6 October

Reading, Guildford, Ascot, Weybridge, Windsor, Kingston, Richmond and Hounslow - London

		SW	SW	SW	SW	SW	SW	SW	SW	SW	SW	SW	SW	SW	SW	SW	SW	SW	SW	SW	SW	SW	SW
						■						■	■	■						■			
Reading ■	d					21 42						22 12								22 42			
Earley	d					21 47						22 17								22 47			
Winnersh Triangle	d					21 49						22 19								22 49			
Winnersh	d					21 51						22 21								22 51			
Wokingham	d					21 56						22 26								22 56			
Bracknell	d					22 02						22 32								23 02			
Martins Heron	d					22 05						22 35								23 05			
Guildford	d												22 00	22 30									
Wanborough	d												22 06	22 36									
Ash ■	d												22 10	22 40									
Aldershot	a												22 17	22 47									
	d												22 30										
Ash Vale	d												22 34										
Frimley	d												22 40										
Camberley	a												22 44										
	d												22 48										
Bagshot	d												22 53										
Ascot ■	d					22 10						22 40	23a00							23 10			
Sunningdale	d					22 13						22 43								23 13			
Longcross	d																						
Weybridge	d				22 03						22 33								23 03				
Addlestone	d				22 07						22 37								23 07				
Chertsey	d				22 10			←			22 40					←			23 10		←		
Virginia Water	a				22 15	22 19		22 15			22 45	22 49				22 45			23 15	23 19	23 15		
	d				22 24	22 19		22 24			22 54	22 49				22 54			23 24	23 19	23 24		
Egham	d				→	22 23		22 27			→	22 53				22 57			→	23 23	23 27		
Windsor & Eton Riverside	d	21 53							22 23								22 53					23 28	
Datchet	d	21 56							22 26								22 56					23 31	
Sunnymeads	d	21 59							22 29								22 59					23 34	
Wraysbury	d	22 02							22 32								23 02					23 37	
Staines	d	22 08				22 29		22 33	22 38			22 59				23 03	23 08			23 29	23a32	23a42	
Ashford (Surrey)	d	22 11						22 36	22 41							23 06	23 11						
Feltham	d	22 16				22 35		22 41	22 46			23 05				23 11	23 16			23 35			
Whitton	d	22 20		22 23					22 50								23 20						
Kingston	d						22 29								22 59								23 29
Hampton Wick	d						22 31								23 01								23 31
Teddington	d						22 35								23 05								23 35
Fulwell	d																						
Strawberry Hill	d						22 38								23 08								23 38
Twickenham	a	22 23		22 26		22 40	22 42		22 53			23 10			23 12		23 23			23 40			23 42
	d	22 23		22 28		22 41	22 43		22 53			23 11			23 13		23 23			23 41			23 43
St Margarets	d			22 30			22 45								23 15								23 45
Richmond ⊖	d	22 28		22 34		22 45	22 49		22 58			23 15			23 19		23 28			23 45			23 49
North Sheen	d			22 36			22 51								23 21								23 51
Mortlake	d			22 38			22 53								23 23								23 53
Hounslow	d							22 46								23 16							
Isleworth	d							22 49								23 19							
Syon Lane	d							22 51								23 21							
Brentford	d							22 54								23 24							
Kew Bridge	d							22 56								23 26							
Chiswick	d							22 59								23 29							
Barnes Bridge	d							23 01								23 31							
Barnes	d		←	22 41			22 56	23 04		←					23 26	23 34		←					23 56
Putney	d	22 34	22 37	22 44			22 59	23 07	23 04	23 07					23 29	23 37	23 34	23 37					23 59
Wandsworth Town	d		22 40	22 47			23 02	→		23 10					23 32	→		23 40					00 02
Clapham Junction ■	d	22 39	22 43	22 50		22 54	23 05		23 09	23 13		23 24			23 35		23 39	23 43		23 54			00 05
Queenstown Rd.(Battersea)	d		22 46	22 53			23 08			23 16					23 38			23 46					00 08
Vauxhall ⊖	d	22 45	22 50	22 57			23 12		23 15	23 20					23 42		23 45	23 50					00 12
London Waterloo ■ ⊖	a	22 49	22 56	23 02		23 04	23 17		23 19	23 26		23 34			23 46		23 49	23 56		00 02			00 16

Table T149-R

Saturdays
26 May to 6 October

Reading, Guildford, Ascot, Weybridge, Windsor, Kingston, Richmond and Hounslow - London

		SW	SW	SW	SW	SW	SW
				■		■	■
Reading ■	d			23 12			
Earley	d			23 17			
Winnersh Triangle	d			23 19			
Winnersh	d			23 21			
Wokingham	d			23 26			
Bracknell	d			23 32			
Martins Heron	d			23 35			
Guildford	d					23 00	23 30
Wanborough	d					23 06	23 36
Ash ■	d					23 10	23 40
Aldershot	a					23 17	23 47
	d					23 30	
Ash Vale	d					23 34	
Frimley	d					23 40	
Camberley	a					23 44	
	d					23 48	
Bagshot	d					23 53	
Ascot ■	d			23 40		00a01	
Sunningdale	d			23 43			
Longcross	d						
Weybridge	d		23 33				
Addlestone	d		23 37				
Chertsey	d		23 40		←		
Virginia Water	a		23 45	23 49	23 45		
	d		23 54	23 49	23 54		
Egham	d		→	23 53	23 57		
Windsor & Eton Riverside	d						
Datchet	d						
Sunnymeads	d						
Wraysbury	d						
Staines	d			23 59	00a02		
Ashford (Surrey)	d						
Feltham	d			00 05			
Whitton	d						
Kingston	d	23 55					
Hampton Wick	d	23 57					
Teddington	d	23 59					
Fulwell	d						
Strawberry Hill	d	00 03					
Twickenham	a	00 06		00 10			
	d			00 11			
St Margarets	d						
Richmond ⊖	d			00 15			
North Sheen	d						
Mortlake	d						
Hounslow	d						
Isleworth	d						
Syon Lane	d						
Brentford	d						
Kew Bridge	d						
Chiswick	d						
Barnes Bridge	d						
Barnes	d						
Putney	d						
Wandsworth Town	d						
Clapham Junction ■	d			00 25			
Queenstown Rd.(Battersea)	d						
Vauxhall ⊖	d						
London Waterloo ■ ⊖	a			00 37			

Table T149-R

Saturdays

13 October to 8 December

Reading, Guildford, Ascot, Weybridge, Windsor, Kingston, Richmond and Hounslow - London

		SW	SW ■	SW	SW ■	SW	SW	SW	GW	SW		SW	SW	SW	SW	SW	SW	SW ■	SW ■	SW		SW	SW	SW	SW
Reading ■	d																	05 39							
Earley	d																	05 44							
Winnersh Triangle	d																	05 46							
Winnersh	d																	05 48							
Wokingham	d		00 02						05 45									05 53							
Bracknell	d		00 08															05 59							
Martins Heron	d		00 11															06 02							
Guildford	d								06a07																
Wanborough	d																								
Ash ■	d																								
Aldershot	a																								
	d																		06 00						
Ash Vale	d																		06 04						
Frimley	d																		06 10						
Camberley	a																		06 14						
	d																		06 18						
Bagshot	d																		06 23						
Ascot ■	d		00a17															06 07	06a30						
Sunningdale	d																	06 10							
Longcross	d																								
Weybridge	d																								06 33
Addlestone	d														05 39										06 37
Chertsey	d														05 42										06 40
Virginia Water	a														05 47			06 19							06 45
	d														05 54			06 19							06 54
Egham	d														05 57			06 23							→
Windsor & Eton Riverside	d															05 51							06 21		
Datchet	d															05 55							06 25		
Sunnymeads	d															05 58							06 28		
Wraysbury	d															06 02							06 32		
Staines	d						04 58					05 37			06 03	06 08		06 29				06 33	06 38		
Ashford (Surrey)	d						05 01					05 40			06 06	06 11						06 36	06 41		
Feltham	d				00 05		05 06					05 45			06 11	06 16		06 35				06 41	06 46		
Whitton	d						05 10			05 41		05 49				06 20							06 50		
Kingston	d					01 17								05 59						06 29					
Hampton Wick	d					01s19								06 01						06 31					
Teddington	d					01s22								06 05						06 35					
Fulwell	d																								
Strawberry Hill	d			00 03		01a28		05 38						06 08						06 38					
Twickenham	a			00 06	00 10		05 13	05 41				05 52		06 12		06 23		06 40		06 42			06 53		
	d				00 11		05 13	05 43				05 53		06 13		06 23		06 41		06 43			06 53		
St Margarets	d						05 15	05 45						06 15						06 45					
Richmond ⊖	d				00 15		05 19	05 49				05 58		06 19		06 28		06 45		06 49			06 58		
North Sheen	d						05 21	05 51						06 21						06 51					
Mortlake	d						05 23	05 53						06 23						06 53					
Hounslow	d									05 46					06 16							06 46			
Isleworth	d									05 49					06 19							06 49			
Syon Lane	d									05 51					06 21							06 51			
Brentford	d									05 54					06 24							06 54			
Kew Bridge	d									05 56					06 26							06 56			
Chiswick	d									05 59					06 29							06 59			
Barnes Bridge	d									06 01					06 31							07 01			
Barnes	d						05 26	05 56		06 04			←	06 26	06 34		←			06 56		07 04		←	
Putney	d						05 29	05 59		06 07		06 04	06 07	06 29	06 37	06 34	06 37			06 59		07 07	07 04	07 07	
Wandsworth Town	d	00 02					05 32	06 02		→			06 10	06 32	→		06 40			07 02		→		07 10	
Clapham Junction ■	d	00 05			00 24		05 35	06 05				06 09	06 13	06 35		06 39	06 43	06 54		07 05			07 09	07 13	
Queenstown Rd.(Battersea)	d	00 08					05 38	06 08					06 16	06 38			06 46			07 08				07 16	
Vauxhall ⊖	d	00 12					05 42	06 12				06 15	06 20	06 42		06 45	06 50			07 12			07 15	07 20	
London Waterloo ■ ⊖	a	00 16			00 38		05 46	06 16				06 19	06 26	06 46		06 49	06 56	07 04		07 16			07 19	07 26	

Table T149-R

Saturdays

13 October to 8 December

Reading, Guildford, Ascot, Weybridge, Windsor, Kingston, Richmond and Hounslow - London

		SW ■	SW	SW	SW	SW		SW	SW ■	SW ■	SW	SW	SW	SW	SW	SW		SW	SW	SW ■	SW	SW ■	SW	SW	SW
Reading ■	d	06 09							06 39											07 09					
Earley	d	06 14							06 44											07 14					
Winnersh Triangle	d	06 16							06 46											07 16					
Winnersh	d	06 18							06 48											07 18					
Wokingham	d	06 23							06 53											07 23					
Bracknell	d	06 29							06 59											07 29					
Martins Heron	d	06 32							07 02											07 32					
Guildford	d									06 30												07 00			
Wanborough	d									06 36												07 06			
Ash ■	d									06 40												07 10			
Aldershot	a									06 47												07 17			
	d									07 00												07 30			
Ash Vale	d									07 04												07 34			
Frimley	d									07 10												07 40			
Camberley	a									07 14												07 44			
	d									07 18												07 48			
Bagshot	d									07 23												07 53			
Ascot ■	d	06 37							07 07	07a30										07 37		08a00			
Sunningdale	d	06 40							07 10											07 40					
Longcross	d																								
Weybridge	d							07 03								07 33									
Addlestone	d							07 07								07 37									
Chertsey	d			←				07 10					←			07 40								←	
Virginia Water	a	06 49		06 45				07 15	07 19				07 15			07 45				07 49				07 45	
	d	06 49		06 54				07 24	07 19				07 24			07 54				07 49				07 54	
Egham	d	06 53		06 57				→	07 23				07 27			→				07 53				07 57	
Windsor & Eton Riverside	d				06 51									07 21											07 51
Datchet	d				06 55									07 25											07 55
Sunnymeads	d				06 58									07 28											07 58
Wraysbury	d				07 02									07 32											08 02
Staines	d	06 59		07 03	07 08				07 29				07 33	07 38						07 59				08 03	08 08
Ashford (Surrey)	d			07 06	07 11								07 36	07 41										08 06	08 11
Feltham	d	07 05		07 11	07 16				07 35				07 41	07 46						08 05				08 11	08 16
Whitton	d				07 20									07 50				07 50	07 53						08 20
Kingston	d		06 59									07 29											07 59		
Hampton Wick	d		07 01									07 31											08 01		
Teddington	d		07 05									07 35											08 05		
Fulwell	d																								
Strawberry Hill	d		07 08									07 38											08 08		
Twickenham	a	07 10	07 12		07 23				07 40			07 42		07 53					07 56	08 10			08 12		08 23
	d	07 11	07 13		07 23				07 41			07 43		07 53					07 58	08 11			08 13		08 23
St Margarets	d		07 15									07 45							08 00				08 15		
Richmond ⊖	d	07 15	07 19		07 28				07 45			07 49		07 58					08 04	08 15			08 19		08 28
North Sheen	d		07 21									07 51							08 06				08 21		
Mortlake	d		07 23									07 53							08 08				08 23		
Hounslow	d			07 16							07 31		07 46					08 01						08 16	
Isleworth	d			07 19							07 34		07 49					08 04						08 19	
Syon Lane	d			07 21							07 36		07 51					08 06						08 21	
Brentford	d			07 24							07 39		07 54					08 09						08 24	
Kew Bridge	d			07 26							07 41		07 56					08 11						08 26	
Chiswick	d			07 29							07 44		07 59					08 14						08 29	
Barnes Bridge	d			07 31							07 46		08 01					08 16			←			08 31	
Barnes	d		07 26	07 34		←					07 49	07 56	08 04		←			08 19	08 11		08 19		08 26	08 34	
Putney	d		07 29	07 37	07 34	07 37					07 52	07 59	08 07	08 04	08 07			→	08 14		08 22		08 29	08 37	08 34
Wandsworth Town	d		07 32	→		07 40					07 55	08 02	→		08 10				08 17		08 25		08 32	→	
Clapham Junction ■	d	07 24	07 35		07 39	07 43			07 54		07 58	08 05		08 09	08 13				08 20	08 24	08 28		08 35		08 39
Queenstown Rd.(Battersea)	d		07 38			07 46					08 01	08 08			08 16				08 23		08 31		08 38		
Vauxhall ⊖	d		07 42		07 45	07 50					08 05	08 12		08 15	08 20				08 27		08 35		08 42		08 45
London Waterloo ■ ⊖	a	07 34	07 46		07 49	07 56			08 04		08 11	08 16		08 19	08 26				08 32	08 34	08 41		08 46		08 49

Table T149-R

Saturdays

13 October to 8 December

Reading, Guildford, Ascot, Weybridge, Windsor, Kingston, Richmond and Hounslow - London

		SW		SW	SW	SW	SW ■	SW	SW ■	SW	SW	SW		SW	SW	SW	SW	SW ■	SW	SW ■	SW	SW		SW	SW
Reading ■	d						07 39											08 09							
Earley	d						07 44											08 14							
Winnersh Triangle	d						07 46											08 16							
Winnersh	d						07 48											08 18							
Wokingham	d						07 53											08 23							
Bracknell	d						07 59											08 29							
Martins Heron	d						08 02											08 32							
Guildford	d								07 30											08 00					
Wanborough	d								07 36											08 06					
Ash ■	d								07 40											08 10					
Aldershot	a								07 47											08 17					
	d								08 00											08 30					
Ash Vale	d								08 04											08 34					
Frimley	d								08 10											08 40					
Camberley	a								08 14											08 44					
	d								08 18											08 48					
Bagshot	d								08 23											08 53					
Ascot ■	d						08 07		08a30									08 37		09a00					
Sunningdale	d						08 10											08 40							
Longcross	d																								
Weybridge	d			08 03											08 33										
Addlestone	d			08 07											08 37										
Chertsey	d			08 10							←				08 40							←			
Virginia Water	a			08 15			08 19				08 15				08 45			08 49				08 45			
	d			08 24			08 19				08 24				08 54			08 49				08 54			
Egham	d			→			08 23				08 27				→			08 53				08 57			
Windsor & Eton Riverside	d											08 21												08 51	
Datchet	d											08 25												08 55	
Sunnymeads	d											08 28												08 58	
Wraysbury	d											08 32												09 02	
Staines	d						08 29				08 33	08 38						08 59				09 03		09 08	
Ashford (Surrey)	d										08 36	08 41										09 06		09 11	
Feltham	d						08 35				08 41	08 46						09 05				09 11		09 16	
Whitton	d				08 20	08 23						08 50				08 50	08 53							09 20	
Kingston	d									08 29											08 59				
Hampton Wick	d									08 31											09 01				
Teddington	d									08 35											09 05				
Fulwell	d																								
Strawberry Hill	d									08 38											09 08				
Twickenham	a					08 26	08 40			08 42		08 53					08 56	09 10			09 12			09 23	
	d					08 28	08 41			08 43		08 53					08 58	09 11			09 13			09 23	
St Margarets	d					08 30				08 45							09 00				09 15				
Richmond ⊖	d					08 34	08 45			08 49		08 58					09 04	09 15			09 19			09 28	
North Sheen	d					08 36				08 51							09 06				09 21				
Mortlake	d					08 38				08 53							09 08				09 23				
Hounslow	d				08 31						08 46					09 01						09 16			
Isleworth	d				08 34						08 49					09 04						09 19			
Syon Lane	d				08 36						08 51					09 06						09 21			
Brentford	d				08 39						08 54					09 09						09 24			
Kew Bridge	d				08 41						08 56					09 11						09 26			
Chiswick	d				08 44						08 59					09 14						09 29			
Barnes Bridge	d				08 46			←			09 01					09 16			←			09 31			
Barnes	d	←			08 49	08 41		08 49		08 56	09 04			←		09 19	09 11		09 19		09 26	09 34			←
Putney	d	08 37			→	08 44		08 52		08 59	09 07	09 04		09 07		→	09 14		09 22		09 29	09 37		09 34	09 37
Wandsworth Town	d	08 40				08 47		08 55		09 02	→			09 10			09 17		09 25		09 32	→			09 40
Clapham Junction ■	d	08 43				08 50	08 54	08 58		09 05		09 09		09 13			09 20	09 24	09 28		09 35			09 39	09 43
Queenstown Rd.(Battersea)	d	08 46				08 53		09 01		09 08				09 16			09 23		09 31		09 38				09 46
Vauxhall ⊖	d	08 50				08 57		09 05		09 12		09 15		09 20			09 27		09 35		09 42			09 45	09 50
London Waterloo ■ ⊖	a	08 56				09 02	09 04	09 11		09 16		09 19		09 26			09 32	09 34	09 43		09 46			09 49	09 56

Table T149-R

Saturdays

13 October to 8 December

Reading, Guildford, Ascot, Weybridge, Windsor, Kingston, Richmond and Hounslow - London

		SW	SW	SW	SW ■	SW	SW ■	SW		SW	SW	SW	SW	SW	SW	SW ■	SW	SW ■		SW	SW	SW	SW	SW	SW
Reading ■	d				08 39											09 09									
Earley	d				08 44											09 14									
Winnersh Triangle	d				08 46											09 16									
Winnersh	d				08 48											09 18									
Wokingham	d				08 53											09 23									
Bracknell	d				08 59											09 29									
Martins Heron	d				09 02											09 32									
Guildford	d						08 30											09 00							
Wanborough	d						08 36											09 06							
Ash ■	d						08 40											09 10							
Aldershot	a						08 47											09 17							
	d						09 00											09 30							
Ash Vale	d						09 04											09 34							
Frimley	d						09 10											09 40							
Camberley	a						09 14											09 44							
	d						09 18											09 48							
Bagshot	d						09 23											09 53							
Ascot ■	d				09 07		09a30									09 37		10a00							
Sunningdale	d				09 10											09 40									
Longcross	d																								
Weybridge	d	09 03											09 33											10 03	
Addlestone	d	09 07											09 37											10 07	
Chertsey	d	09 10								←			09 40								←			10 10	
Virginia Water	a	09 15			09 19					09 15			09 45			09 49					09 45			10 15	
	d	09 24			09 19					09 24			09 54			09 49					09 54			10 24	
Egham	d	→			09 23					09 27			→			09 53					09 57			→	
Windsor & Eton Riverside	d										09 21											09 51			
Datchet	d										09 25											09 55			
Sunnymeads	d										09 28											09 58			
Wraysbury	d										09 32											10 02			
Staines	d				09 29					09 33	09 38					09 59					10 03	10 08			
Ashford (Surrey)	d									09 36	09 41										10 06	10 11			
Feltham	d				09 35					09 41	09 46					10 05					10 11	10 16			
Whitton	d		09 20	09 23							09 50			09 50	09 53							10 20			10 20
Kingston	d							09 29												09 59					
Hampton Wick	d							09 31												10 01					
Teddington	d							09 35												10 05					
Fulwell	d																								
Strawberry Hill	d							09 38												10 08					
Twickenham	a			09 26	09 40			09 42			09 53				09 56	10 10				10 12		10 23			
	d			09 28	09 41			09 43			09 53				09 58	10 11				10 13		10 23			
St Margarets	d			09 30				09 45							10 00					10 15					
Richmond ⊖	d			09 34	09 45			09 49			09 58				10 04	10 15				10 19		10 28			
North Sheen	d			09 36				09 51							10 06					10 21					
Mortlake	d			09 38				09 53							10 08					10 23					
Hounslow	d		09 31							09 46				10 01							10 16				10 31
Isleworth	d		09 34							09 49				10 04							10 19				10 34
Syon Lane	d		09 36							09 51				10 06							10 21				10 36
Brentford	d		09 39							09 54				10 09							10 24				10 39
Kew Bridge	d		09 41							09 56				10 11							10 26				10 41
Chiswick	d		09 44							09 59				10 14							10 29				10 44
Barnes Bridge	d		09 46			←				10 01				10 16			←				10 31				10 46
Barnes	d		09 49	09 41		09 49		09 56		10 04		←		10 19	10 11		10 19			10 26	10 34		←		10 49
Putney	d		→	09 44		09 52		09 59		10 07	10 04	10 07		→	10 14		10 22			10 29	10 37	10 34	10 37		→
Wandsworth Town	d			09 47		09 55		10 02		→		10 10			10 17		10 25			10 32	→		10 40		
Clapham Junction ■	d			09 50	09 54	09 58		10 05			10 09	10 13			10 20	10 24	10 28			10 35		10 39	10 43		
Queenstown Rd.(Battersea)	d			09 53		10 01		10 08				10 16			10 23		10 31			10 38			10 46		
Vauxhall ⊖	d			09 57		10 05		10 12			10 15	10 20			10 27		10 35			10 42		10 45	10 50		
London Waterloo ■ ⊖	a			10 02	10 04	10 11		10 16			10 19	10 26			10 32	10 34	10 41			10 46		10 49	10 56		

Table T149-R

Saturdays

13 October to 8 December

Reading, Guildford, Ascot, Weybridge, Windsor, Kingston, Richmond and Hounslow - London

		SW	SW ■	SW	SW ■	SW	SW	SW	SW	SW	SW	SW	SW ■	SW	SW ■	SW	SW	SW	SW	SW	SW	SW
Reading ■	d		09 39										10 09									
Earley	d		09 44										10 14									
Winnersh Triangle	d		09 46										10 16									
Winnersh	d		09 48										10 18									
Wokingham	d		09 53										10 23									
Bracknell	d		09 59										10 29									
Martins Heron	d		10 02										10 32									
Guildford	d				09 30										10 00							
Wanborough	d				09 36										10 06							
Ash ■	d				09 40										10 10							
Aldershot	a				09 47										10 17							
	d				10 00										10 30							
Ash Vale	d				10 04										10 34							
Frimley	d				10 10										10 40							
Camberley	a				10 14										10 44							
	d				10 18										10 48							
Bagshot	d				10 23										10 53							
Ascot ■	d		10 07		10a30								10 37		11a00							
Sunningdale	d		10 10										10 40									
Longcross	d																					
Weybridge	d									10 33										11 03		
Addlestone	d									10 37										11 07		
Chertsey	d						←			10 40							←			11 10		
Virginia Water	a		10 19				10 15			10 45			10 49				10 45			11 15		
	d		10 19				10 24			10 54			10 49				10 54			11 24		
Egham	d		10 23				10 27			→			10 53				10 57			→		
Windsor & Eton Riverside	d							10 21										10 51				
Datchet	d							10 25										10 55				
Sunnymeads	d							10 28										10 58				
Wraysbury	d							10 32										11 02				
Staines	d		10 29				10 33	10 38					10 59				11 03	11 08				
Ashford (Surrey)	d						10 36	10 41									11 06	11 11				
Feltham	d		10 35				10 41	10 46					11 05				11 11	11 16				
Whitton	d	10 23						10 50			10 50	10 53						11 20			11 20	11 23
Kingston	d					10 29										10 59						
Hampton Wick	d					10 31										11 01						
Teddington	d					10 35										11 05						
Fulwell	d																					
Strawberry Hill	d					10 38										11 08						
Twickenham	a	10 26	10 40			10 42		10 53				10 56	11 10			11 12		11 23				11 26
	d	10 28	10 41			10 43		10 53				10 58	11 11			11 13		11 23				11 28
St Margarets	d	10 30				10 45						11 00				11 15						11 30
Richmond ⊖	d	10 34	10 45			10 49		10 58				11 04	11 15			11 19		11 28				11 34
North Sheen	d	10 36				10 51						11 06				11 21						11 36
Mortlake	d	10 38				10 53						11 08				11 23						11 38
Hounslow	d						10 46				11 01						11 16				11 31	
Isleworth	d						10 49				11 04						11 19				11 34	
Syon Lane	d						10 51				11 06						11 21				11 36	
Brentford	d						10 54				11 09						11 24				11 39	
Kew Bridge	d						10 56				11 11						11 26				11 41	
Chiswick	d						10 59				11 14						11 29				11 44	
Barnes Bridge	d			←			11 01				11 16			←			11 31				11 46	
Barnes	d	10 41		10 49		10 56	11 04		←		11 19	11 11		11 19		11 26	11 34		←		11 49	11 41
Putney	d	10 44		10 52		10 59	11 07	11 04	11 07		→	11 14		11 22		11 29	11 37	11 34	11 37		→	11 44
Wandsworth Town	d	10 47		10 55		11 02	→		11 10			11 17		11 25		11 32	→		11 40			11 47
Clapham Junction 10	d	10 50	10 54	10 58		11 05		11 09	11 13			11 20	11 24	11 28		11 35		11 39	11 43			11 50
Queenstown Rd.(Battersea)	d	10 53		11 01		11 08			11 16			11 23		11 31		11 38			11 46			11 53
Vauxhall ⊖	d	10 57		11 05		11 12		11 15	11 20			11 27		11 35		11 42		11 45	11 50			11 57
London Waterloo 15 ⊖	a	11 02	11 04	11 11		11 16		11 19	11 26			11 32	11 34	11 41		11 46		11 49	11 56			12 02

Table T149-R

Saturdays

13 October to 8 December

Reading, Guildford, Ascot, Weybridge, Windsor, Kingston, Richmond and Hounslow - London

		SW ■	SW	SW ■	SW	SW	SW	SW	SW	SW	SW	SW ■	SW	SW ■	SW	SW	SW	SW	SW	SW	SW	SW ■	SW
Reading ■	d	10 39										11 09										11 39	
Earley	d	10 44										11 14										11 44	
Winnersh Triangle	d	10 46										11 16										11 46	
Winnersh	d	10 48										11 18										11 48	
Wokingham	d	10 53										11 23										11 53	
Bracknell	d	10 59										11 29										11 59	
Martins Heron	d	11 02										11 32										12 02	
Guildford	d			10 30										11 00									
Wanborough	d			10 36										11 06									
Ash ■	d			10 40										11 10									
Aldershot	a			10 47										11 17									
	d			11 00										11 30									
Ash Vale	d			11 04										11 34									
Frimley	d			11 10										11 40									
Camberley	a			11 14										11 44									
	d			11 18										11 48									
Bagshot	d			11 23										11 53									
Ascot ■	d	11 07		11a30								11 37		12a00								12 07	
Sunningdale	d	11 10										11 40										12 10	
Longcross	d																						
Weybridge	d								11 33										12 03				
Addlestone	d								11 37										12 07				
Chertsey	d					←			11 40							←			12 10				
Virginia Water	a	11 19				11 15			11 45			11 49				11 45			12 15			12 19	
	d	11 19				11 24			11 54			11 49				11 54			12 24			12 19	
Egham	d	11 23				11 27			→			11 53				11 57			→			12 23	
Windsor & Eton Riverside	d						11 21										11 51						
Datchet	d						11 25										11 55						
Sunnymeads	d						11 28										11 58						
Wraysbury	d						11 32										12 02						
Staines	d	11 29				11 33	11 38					11 59				12 03	12 08					12 29	
Ashford (Surrey)	d					11 36	11 41									12 06	12 11						
Feltham	d	11 35				11 41	11 46					12 05				12 11	12 16					12 35	
Whitton	d						11 50			11 50	11 53						12 20			12 20	12 23		
Kingston	d				11 29										11 59								
Hampton Wick	d				11 31										12 01								
Teddington	d				11 35										12 05								
Fulwell	d																						
Strawberry Hill	d				11 38										12 08								
Twickenham	a	11 40			11 42		11 53				11 56	12 10			12 12		12 23				12 26	12 40	
	d	11 41			11 43		11 53				11 58	12 11			12 13		12 23				12 28	12 41	
St Margarets	d				11 45						12 00				12 15						12 30		
Richmond ⊖	d	11 45			11 49		11 58				12 04	12 15			12 19		12 28				12 34	12 45	
North Sheen	d				11 51						12 06				12 21						12 36		
Mortlake	d				11 53						12 08				12 23						12 38		
Hounslow	d					11 46				12 01						12 16				12 31			
Isleworth	d					11 49				12 04						12 19				12 34			
Syon Lane	d					11 51				12 06						12 21				12 36			
Brentford	d					11 54				12 09						12 24				12 39			
Kew Bridge	d					11 56				12 11						12 26				12 41			
Chiswick	d					11 59				12 14						12 29				12 44			
Barnes Bridge	d		←			12 01				12 16			←			12 31				12 46			←
Barnes	d		11 49		11 56	12 04		←		12 19	12 11		12 19		12 26	12 34		←		12 49	12 41		12 49
Putney	d		11 52		11 59	12 07	12 04	12 07		→	12 14		12 22		12 29	12 37	12 34	12 37		→	12 44		12 52
Wandsworth Town	d		11 55		12 02	→		12 10			12 17		12 25		12 32	→		12 40			12 47		12 55
Clapham Junction 10	d	11 54	11 58		12 05		12 09	12 13			12 20	12 24	12 28		12 35		12 39	12 43			12 50	12 54	12 59
Queenstown Rd.(Battersea)	d		12 01		12 08			12 16			12 23		12 31		12 38			12 46			12 53		13 02
Vauxhall ⊖	d		12 05		12 12		12 15	12 20			12 27		12 35		12 42		12 45	12 50			12 57		13 05
London Waterloo 15 ⊖	a	12 04	12 11		12 16		12 19	12 26			12 32	12 34	12 41		12 46		12 49	12 56			13 02	13 04	13 11

Table T149-R

Saturdays

13 October to 8 December

Reading, Guildford, Ascot, Weybridge, Windsor, Kingston, Richmond and Hounslow - London

		SW ■	SW	SW	SW	SW		SW	SW	SW	SW ■	SW	SW ■	SW	SW	SW		SW	SW	SW	SW	SW ■	SW	SW ■	SW
Reading [7]	d										12 09											12 39			
Earley	d										12 14											12 44			
Winnersh Triangle	d										12 16											12 46			
Winnersh	d										12 18											12 48			
Wokingham	d										12 23											12 53			
Bracknell	d										12 29											12 59			
Martins Heron	d										12 32											13 02			
Guildford	d	11 30											12 00											12 30	
Wanborough	d	11 36											12 06											12 36	
Ash [5]	d	11 40											12 10											12 40	
Aldershot	a	11 47											12 17											12 47	
	d	12 00											12 30											13 00	
Ash Vale	d	12 04											12 34											13 04	
Frimley	d	12 10											12 40											13 10	
Camberley	a	12 14											12 44											13 14	
	d	12 18											12 48											13 18	
Bagshot	d	12 23											12 53											13 23	
Ascot [3]	d	12a30									12 37		13a00									13 07		13a30	
Sunningdale	d										12 40											13 10			
Longcross	d																								
Weybridge	d							12 33											13 03						
Addlestone	d							12 37											13 07						
Chertsey	d			←				12 40							←				13 10						
Virginia Water	a			12 15				12 45			12 49				12 45				13 15			13 19			
	d			12 24				12 54			12 49				12 54				13 24			13 19			
Egham	d			12 27				→			12 53				12 57				→			13 23			
Windsor & Eton Riverside	d				12 21											12 51									
Datchet	d				12 25											12 55									
Sunnymeads	d				12 28											12 58									
Wraysbury	d				12 32											13 02									
Staines	d			12 33	12 38						12 59				13 03	13 08						13 29			
Ashford (Surrey)	d			12 36	12 41										13 06	13 11									
Feltham	d			12 41	12 46						13 05				13 11	13 16						13 35			
Whitton	d				12 50				12 50	12 53						13 20				13 20	13 23				
Kingston	d		12 29											12 59											13 29
Hampton Wick	d		12 31											13 01											13 31
Teddington	d		12 35											13 05											13 35
Fulwell	d																								
Strawberry Hill	d		12 38											13 08											13 38
Twickenham	a		12 42		12 53					12 56	13 10			13 12		13 23					13 26	13 40			13 42
	d		12 43		12 53					12 58	13 11			13 13		13 23					13 28	13 41			13 43
St Margarets	d		12 45							13 00				13 15							13 30				13 45
Richmond ⊖	d		12 49		12 58					13 04	13 15			13 19		13 28					13 34	13 45			13 49
North Sheen	d		12 51							13 06				13 21							13 36				13 51
Mortlake	d		12 53							13 08				13 23							13 38				13 53
Hounslow	d			12 46					13 01						13 16					13 31					
Isleworth	d			12 49					13 04						13 19					13 34					
Syon Lane	d			12 51					13 06						13 21					13 36					
Brentford	d			12 54					13 09						13 24					13 39					
Kew Bridge	d			12 56					13 11						13 26					13 41					
Chiswick	d			12 59					13 14						13 29					13 44					
Barnes Bridge	d			13 01					13 16			←			13 31					13 46			←		
Barnes	d		12 56	13 04		←			13 19	13 11		13 19		13 26	13 34			←		13 49	13 41		13 49		13 56
Putney	d		12 59	13 07	13 04	13 07			→	13 14		13 22		13 29	13 37	13 34		13 37		→	13 44		13 52		13 59
Wandsworth Town	d		13 02	→		13 10				13 17		13 25		13 32	→			13 40			13 47		13 55		14 02
Clapham Junction [10]	d		13 05		13 09	13 13				13 20	13 24	13 28		13 35		13 39		13 43			13 50	13 54	13 58		14 05
Queenstown Rd.(Battersea)	d		13 08			13 16				13 23		13 31		13 38				13 46			13 53		14 01		14 08
Vauxhall ⊖	d		13 12		13 15	13 20				13 27		13 35		13 42		13 45		13 50			13 57		14 05		14 12
London Waterloo [15] ⊖	a		13 16		13 19	13 26				13 32	13 34	13 41		13 46		13 49		13 56			14 02	14 04	14 11		14 16

Table T149-R

Saturdays

13 October to 8 December

Reading, Guildford, Ascot, Weybridge, Windsor, Kingston, Richmond and Hounslow - London

		SW		SW	SW	SW	SW	SW	SW ■	SW	SW ■	SW		SW	SW	SW	SW	SW	SW	SW ■	SW	SW ■		SW	SW
Reading [7]	d								13 09											13 39					
Earley	d								13 14											13 44					
Winnersh Triangle	d								13 16											13 46					
Winnersh	d								13 18											13 48					
Wokingham	d								13 23											13 53					
Bracknell	d								13 29											13 59					
Martins Heron	d								13 32											14 02					
Guildford	d										13 00											13 30			
Wanborough	d										13 06											13 36			
Ash [5]	d										13 10											13 40			
Aldershot	a										13 17											13 47			
	d										13 30											14 00			
Ash Vale	d										13 34											14 04			
Frimley	d										13 40											14 10			
Camberley	a										13 44											14 14			
	d										13 48											14 18			
Bagshot	d										13 53											14 23			
Ascot [3]	d								13 37		14a00									14 07		14a30			
Sunningdale	d								13 40											14 10					
Longcross	d																								
Weybridge	d					13 33											14 03								
Addlestone	d					13 37											14 07								
Chertsey	d	←				13 40								←			14 10								←
Virginia Water	a	13 15				13 45			13 49					13 45			14 15			14 19					14 15
	d	13 24				13 54			13 49					13 54			14 24			14 19					14 24
Egham	d	13 27				→			13 53					13 57			→			14 23					14 27
Windsor & Eton Riverside	d			13 21											13 51										
Datchet	d			13 25											13 55										
Sunnymeads	d			13 28											13 58										
Wraysbury	d			13 32											14 02										
Staines	d	13 33		13 38					13 59					14 03	14 08					14 29					14 33
Ashford (Surrey)	d	13 36		13 41										14 06	14 11										14 36
Feltham	d	13 41		13 46					14 05					14 11	14 16					14 35					14 41
Whitton	d			13 50			13 50	13 53							14 20			14 20	14 23						
Kingston	d											13 59												14 29	
Hampton Wick	d											14 01												14 31	
Teddington	d											14 05												14 35	
Fulwell	d																								
Strawberry Hill	d											14 08												14 38	
Twickenham	a			13 53				13 56	14 10			14 12			14 23				14 26	14 40				14 42	
	d			13 53				13 58	14 11			14 13			14 23				14 28	14 41				14 43	
St Margarets	d							14 00				14 15							14 30					14 45	
Richmond ⊖	d			13 58				14 04	14 15			14 19			14 28				14 34	14 45				14 49	
North Sheen	d							14 06				14 21							14 36					14 51	
Mortlake	d							14 08				14 23							14 38					14 53	
Hounslow	d	13 46					14 01							14 16				14 31							14 46
Isleworth	d	13 49					14 04							14 19				14 34							14 49
Syon Lane	d	13 51					14 06							14 21				14 36							14 51
Brentford	d	13 54					14 09							14 24				14 39							14 54
Kew Bridge	d	13 56					14 11							14 26				14 41							14 56
Chiswick	d	13 59					14 14							14 29				14 44							14 59
Barnes Bridge	d	14 01					14 16			←				14 31				14 46			←				15 01
Barnes	d	14 04			←		14 19	14 11		14 19		14 26		14 34		←		14 49	14 41		14 49			14 56	15 04
Putney	d	14 07		14 04	14 07		→	14 14		14 22		14 29		14 37	14 34	14 37		→	14 44		14 52			14 59	15 07
Wandsworth Town	d	→			14 10			14 17		14 25		14 32		→		14 40			14 47		14 55			15 02	→
Clapham Junction [10]	d			14 09	14 13			14 20	14 24	14 28		14 35			14 39	14 43			14 50	14 54	14 58			15 05	
Queenstown Rd.(Battersea)	d				14 16			14 23		14 31		14 38				14 46			14 53		15 01			15 08	
Vauxhall ⊖	d			14 15	14 20			14 27		14 35		14 42			14 45	14 50			14 57		15 05			15 12	
London Waterloo [15] ⊖	a			14 19	14 26			14 32	14 34	14 41		14 46			14 49	14 56			15 02	15 04	15 11			15 16	

Table T149-R

Saturdays

13 October to 8 December

Reading, Guildford, Ascot, Weybridge, Windsor, Kingston, Richmond and Hounslow - London

		SW	SW	SW	SW	SW	SW 1	SW		SW 1	SW	SW	SW	SW	SW	SW	SW	SW 1		SW	SW 1	SW	SW	SW	SW
Reading [7]	d						14 09											14 39							
Earley	d						14 14											14 44							
Winnersh Triangle	d						14 16											14 46							
Winnersh	d						14 18											14 48							
Wokingham	d						14 23											14 53							
Bracknell	d						14 29											14 59							
Martins Heron	d						14 32											15 02							
Guildford	d									14 00											14 30				
Wanborough	d									14 06											14 36				
Ash [5]	d									14 10											14 40				
Aldershot	a									14 17											14 47				
	d									14 30											15 00				
Ash Vale	d									14 34											15 04				
Frimley	d									14 40											15 10				
Camberley	a									14 44											15 14				
	d									14 48											15 18				
Bagshot	d									14 53											15 23				
Ascot [3]	d						14 37			15a00								15 07			15a30				
Sunningdale	d						14 40											15 10							
Longcross	d																								
Weybridge	d			14 33											15 03										
Addlestone	d			14 37											15 07										
Chertsey	d			14 40								←			15 10								←		
Virginia Water	a			14 45			14 49					14 45			15 15			15 19					15 15		
	d			14 54			14 49					14 54			15 24			15 19					15 24		
Egham	d			→			14 53					14 57			→			15 23					15 27		
Windsor & Eton Riverside	d	14 21											14 51											15 21	
Datchet	d	14 25											14 55											15 25	
Sunnymeads	d	14 28											14 58											15 28	
Wraysbury	d	14 32											15 02											15 32	
Staines	d	14 38					14 59					15 03	15 08					15 29					15 33	15 38	
Ashford (Surrey)	d	14 41										15 06	15 11										15 36	15 41	
Feltham	d	14 46					15 05					15 11	15 16					15 35					15 41	15 46	
Whitton	d	14 50			14 50	14 53							15 20			15 20	15 23							15 50	
Kingston	d										14 59											15 29			
Hampton Wick	d										15 01											15 31			
Teddington	d										15 05											15 35			
Fulwell	d																								
Strawberry Hill	d										15 08											15 38			
Twickenham	a	14 53				14 56	15 10				15 12		15 23				15 26	15 40				15 42		15 53	
	d	14 53				14 58	15 11				15 13		15 23				15 28	15 41				15 43		15 53	
St Margarets	d					15 00					15 15						15 30					15 45			
Richmond ⊖	d	14 58				15 04	15 15				15 19		15 28				15 34	15 45				15 49		15 58	
North Sheen	d					15 06					15 21						15 36					15 51			
Mortlake	d					15 08					15 23						15 38					15 53			
Hounslow	d				15 01							15 16				15 31							15 46		
Isleworth	d				15 04							15 19				15 34							15 49		
Syon Lane	d				15 06							15 21				15 36							15 51		
Brentford	d				15 09							15 24				15 39							15 54		
Kew Bridge	d				15 11							15 26				15 41							15 56		
Chiswick	d				15 14							15 29				15 44							15 59		
Barnes Bridge	d				15 16			←				15 31				15 46				←			16 01		
Barnes	d		←		15 19	15 11		15 19			15 26	15 34		←		15 49	15 41			15 49		15 56	16 04		←
Putney	d	15 04	15 07		→	15 14		15 22			15 29	15 37	15 34	15 37		→	15 44			15 52		15 59	16 07	16 04	16 07
Wandsworth Town	d		15 10			15 17		15 25			15 32	→		15 40			15 47			15 55		16 02	→		16 10
Clapham Junction [10]	d	15 09	15 13			15 20	15 24	15 28			15 35		15 39	15 43			15 50	15 54		15 58		16 05		16 09	16 13
Queenstown Rd.(Battersea)	d		15 16			15 23		15 31			15 38			15 46			15 53			16 01		16 08			16 16
Vauxhall ⊖	d	15 15	15 20			15 27		15 35			15 42		15 45	15 50			15 57			16 05		16 12		16 15	16 20
London Waterloo [15] ⊖	a	15 19	15 26			15 32	15 34	15 41			15 46		15 49	15 56			16 02	16 04		16 11		16 16		16 19	16 26

Table T149-R

Saturdays

13 October to 8 December

Reading, Guildford, Ascot, Weybridge, Windsor, Kingston, Richmond and Hounslow - London

		SW	SW	SW		SW 1	SW	SW 1	SW	SW	SW	SW	SW	SW		SW	SW 1	SW	SW 1	SW	SW	SW	SW	SW	
Reading [7]	d					15 09											15 39								
Earley	d					15 14											15 44								
Winnersh Triangle	d					15 16											15 46								
Winnersh	d					15 18											15 48								
Wokingham	d					15 23											15 53								
Bracknell	d					15 29											15 59								
Martins Heron	d					15 32											16 02								
Guildford	d							15 00											15 30						
Wanborough	d							15 06											15 36						
Ash [5]	d							15 10											15 40						
Aldershot	a							15 17											15 47						
	d							15 30											16 00						
Ash Vale	d							15 34											16 04						
Frimley	d							15 40											16 10						
Camberley	a							15 44											16 14						
	d							15 48											16 18						
Bagshot	d							15 53											16 23						
Ascot [3]	d					15 37		16a00									16 07		16a30						
Sunningdale	d					15 40											16 10								
Longcross	d																								
Weybridge	d	15 33											16 03											16 33	
Addlestone	d	15 37											16 07											16 37	
Chertsey	d	15 40								←			16 10								←			16 40	
Virginia Water	a	15 45				15 49				15 45			16 15				16 19				16 15			16 45	
	d	15 54				15 49				15 54			16 24				16 19				16 24			16 54	
Egham	d	→				15 53				15 57			→				16 23				16 27			→	
Windsor & Eton Riverside	d										15 51											16 21			
Datchet	d										15 55											16 25			
Sunnymeads	d										15 58											16 28			
Wraysbury	d										16 02											16 32			
Staines	d					15 59				16 03	16 08						16 29				16 33	16 38			
Ashford (Surrey)	d									16 06	16 11										16 36	16 41			
Feltham	d					16 05				16 11	16 16						16 35				16 41	16 46			
Whitton	d		15 50	15 53							16 20			16 20		16 23						16 50			
Kingston	d								15 59											16 29					
Hampton Wick	d								16 01											16 31					
Teddington	d								16 05											16 35					
Fulwell	d																								
Strawberry Hill	d								16 08											16 38					
Twickenham	a			15 56		16 10			16 12		16 23					16 26	16 40			16 42		16 53			
	d			15 58		16 11			16 13		16 23					16 28	16 41			16 43		16 53			
St Margarets	d			16 00					16 15							16 30				16 45					
Richmond ⊖	d			16 04		16 15			16 19		16 28					16 34	16 45			16 49		16 58			
North Sheen	d			16 06					16 21							16 36				16 51					
Mortlake	d			16 08					16 23							16 38				16 53					
Hounslow	d		16 01							16 16				16 31							16 46				
Isleworth	d		16 04							16 19				16 34							16 49				
Syon Lane	d		16 06							16 21				16 36							16 51				
Brentford	d		16 09							16 24				16 39							16 54				
Kew Bridge	d		16 11							16 26				16 41							16 56				
Chiswick	d		16 14							16 29				16 44							16 59				
Barnes Bridge	d		16 16				←			16 31				16 46				←			17 01				
Barnes	d		16 19	16 11			16 19		16 26	16 34		←		16 49		16 41		16 49		16 56	17 04		←		
Putney	d		→	16 14			16 22		16 29	16 37	16 34	16 37		→		16 44		16 52		16 59	17 07	17 04	17 07		
Wandsworth Town	d			16 17			16 25		16 32	→		16 40				16 47		16 55		17 02	→		17 10		
Clapham Junction [10]	d			16 20		16 24	16 28		16 35		16 39	16 43				16 50	16 54	16 58		17 05		17 09	17 13		
Queenstown Rd.(Battersea)	d			16 23			16 31		16 38			16 46				16 53		17 01		17 08			17 16		
Vauxhall ⊖	d			16 27			16 35		16 42		16 45	16 50				16 57		17 05		17 12		17 15	17 20		
London Waterloo [15] ⊖	a			16 32		16 34	16 41		16 46		16 49	16 56				17 02	17 04	17 11		17 16		17 19	17 26		

Table T149-R

Saturdays

13 October to 8 December

Reading, Guildford, Ascot, Weybridge, Windsor, Kingston, Richmond and Hounslow - London

		SW	SW	SW ■	SW	SW ■	SW	SW	SW	SW		SW	SW	SW	SW ■	SW	SW ■	SW	SW	SW		SW	SW	SW	SW
Reading ■	d			16 09											16 39										
Earley	d			16 14											16 44										
Winnersh Triangle	d			16 16											16 46										
Winnersh	d			16 18											16 48										
Wokingham	d			16 23											16 53										
Bracknell	d			16 29											16 59										
Martins Heron	d			16 32											17 02										
Guildford	d					16 00											16 30								
Wanborough	d					16 06											16 36								
Ash ■	d					16 10											16 40								
Aldershot	a					16 17											16 47								
	d					16 30											17 00								
Ash Vale	d					16 34											17 04								
Frimley	d					16 40											17 10								
Camberley	a					16 44											17 14								
	d					16 48											17 18								
Bagshot	d					16 53											17 23								
Ascot ■	d			16 37		17a00									17 07		17a30								
Sunningdale	d			16 40											17 10										
Longcross	d																								
Weybridge	d											17 03											17 33		
Addlestone	d											17 07											17 37		
Chertsey	d							←				17 10							←				17 40		
Virginia Water	a			16 49				16 45				17 15			17 19				17 15				17 45		
	d			16 49				16 54				17 24			17 19				17 24				17 54		
Egham	d			16 53				16 57				→			17 23				17 27				→		
Windsor & Eton Riverside	d								16 51											17 21					
Datchet	d								16 55											17 25					
Sunnymeads	d								16 58											17 28					
Wraysbury	d								17 02											17 32					
Staines	d			16 59				17 03	17 08						17 29				17 33	17 38					
Ashford (Surrey)	d							17 06	17 11										17 36	17 41					
Feltham	d			17 05				17 11	17 16						17 35				17 41	17 46					
Whitton	d	16 50	16 53						17 20				17 20	17 23						17 50				17 50	17 53
Kingston	d						16 59											17 29							
Hampton Wick	d						17 01											17 31							
Teddington	d						17 05											17 35							
Fulwell	d																								
Strawberry Hill	d						17 08											17 38							
Twickenham	a		16 56	17 10			17 12		17 23					17 26	17 40			17 42		17 53					17 56
	d		16 58	17 11			17 13		17 23					17 28	17 41			17 43		17 53					17 58
St Margarets	d		17 00				17 15							17 30				17 45							18 00
Richmond ⊖	d		17 04	17 15			17 19		17 28					17 34	17 45			17 49		17 58					18 04
North Sheen	d		17 06				17 21							17 36				17 51							18 06
Mortlake	d		17 08				17 23							17 38				17 53							18 08
Hounslow	d	17 01						17 16					17 31						17 46					18 01	
Isleworth	d	17 04						17 19					17 34						17 49					18 04	
Syon Lane	d	17 06						17 21					17 36						17 51					18 06	
Brentford	d	17 09						17 24					17 39						17 54					18 09	
Kew Bridge	d	17 11						17 26					17 41						17 56					18 11	
Chiswick	d	17 14						17 29					17 44						17 59					18 14	
Barnes Bridge	d	17 16			←			17 31					17 46			←			18 01					18 16	
Barnes	d	17 19	17 11		17 19		17 26	17 34		←			17 49	17 41		17 49		17 56	18 04			←		18 19	18 11
Putney	d	→	17 14		17 22		17 29	17 37	17 34	17 37			→	17 44		17 52		17 59	18 07	18 04		18 07		→	18 14
Wandsworth Town	d		17 17		17 25		17 32	→		17 40				17 47		17 55		18 02	→			18 10			18 17
Clapham Junction ■	d		17 20	17 24	17 28		17 35		17 39	17 43				17 50	17 54	17 58		18 05		18 09		18 13			18 20
Queenstown Rd.(Battersea)	d		17 23		17 31		17 38			17 46				17 53		18 01		18 08				18 16			18 23
Vauxhall ⊖	d		17 27		17 35		17 42		17 45	17 50				17 57		18 05		18 12		18 15		18 20			18 27
London Waterloo ■ ⊖	a		17 32	17 34	17 41		17 46		17 49	17 56				18 02	18 04	18 11		18 16		18 19		18 26			18 32

Table T149-R

Saturdays

13 October to 8 December

Reading, Guildford, Ascot, Weybridge, Windsor, Kingston, Richmond and Hounslow - London

		SW ■	SW	SW ■	SW	SW		SW	SW	SW	SW	SW	SW ■	SW	SW ■	SW		SW	SW	SW	SW	SW	SW	SW ■	SW
Reading ■	d	17 09											17 39											18 09	
Earley	d	17 14											17 44											18 14	
Winnersh Triangle	d	17 16											17 46											18 16	
Winnersh	d	17 18											17 48											18 18	
Wokingham	d	17 23											17 53											18 23	
Bracknell	d	17 29											17 59											18 29	
Martins Heron	d	17 32											18 02											18 32	
Guildford	d			17 00											17 30										
Wanborough	d			17 06											17 36										
Ash ■	d			17 10											17 40										
Aldershot	a			17 17											17 47										
	d			17 30											18 00										
Ash Vale	d			17 34											18 04										
Frimley	d			17 40											18 10										
Camberley	a			17 44											18 14										
	d			17 48											18 18										
Bagshot	d			17 53											18 23										
Ascot ■	d	17 37		18a00									18 07		18a30									18 37	
Sunningdale	d	17 40											18 10											18 40	
Longcross	d																								
Weybridge	d									18 03											18 33				
Addlestone	d									18 07											18 37				
Chertsey	d					←				18 10								←			18 40				
Virginia Water	a	17 49				17 45				18 15			18 19					18 15			18 45			18 49	
	d	17 49				17 54				18 24			18 19					18 24			18 54			18 49	
Egham	d	17 53				17 57				→			18 23					18 27			→			18 53	
Windsor & Eton Riverside	d							17 51											18 21						
Datchet	d							17 55											18 25						
Sunnymeads	d							17 58											18 28						
Wraysbury	d							18 02											18 32						
Staines	d	17 59				18 03		18 08					18 29					18 33	18 38					18 59	
Ashford (Surrey)	d					18 06		18 11										18 36	18 41						
Feltham	d	18 05				18 11		18 16					18 35					18 41	18 46					19 05	
Whitton	d							18 20			18 20	18 23							18 50			18 50	18 53		
Kingston	d				17 59											18 29									
Hampton Wick	d				18 01											18 31									
Teddington	d				18 05											18 35									
Fulwell	d																								
Strawberry Hill	d				18 08											18 38									
Twickenham	a	18 10			18 12			18 23				18 26	18 40			18 42			18 53				18 56	19 10	
	d	18 11			18 13			18 23				18 28	18 41			18 43			18 53				18 58	19 11	
St Margarets	d				18 15							18 30				18 45							19 00		
Richmond ⊖	d	18 15			18 19			18 28				18 34	18 45			18 49			18 58				19 04	19 15	
North Sheen	d				18 21							18 36				18 51							19 06		
Mortlake	d				18 23							18 38				18 53							19 08		
Hounslow	d					18 16					18 31							18 46				19 01			
Isleworth	d					18 19					18 34							18 49				19 04			
Syon Lane	d					18 21					18 36							18 51				19 06			
Brentford	d					18 24					18 39							18 54				19 09			
Kew Bridge	d					18 26					18 41							18 56				19 11			
Chiswick	d					18 29					18 44							18 59				19 14			
Barnes Bridge	d		←			18 31					18 46			←				19 01				19 16			←
Barnes	d		18 19		18 26	18 34			←		18 49	18 41		18 49		18 56		19 04		←		19 19	19 11		19 19
Putney	d		18 22		18 29	18 37		18 34	18 37		→	18 44		18 52		18 59		19 07	19 04	19 07		→	19 14		19 22
Wandsworth Town	d		18 25		18 32	→			18 40			18 47		18 55		19 02		→		19 10			19 17		19 25
Clapham Junction ■	d	18 24	18 28		18 35			18 39	18 43			18 50	18 54	18 58		19 05			19 09	19 13			19 20	19 24	19 29
Queenstown Rd.(Battersea)	d		18 31		18 38				18 46			18 53		19 01		19 08				19 16			19 23		19 32
Vauxhall ⊖	d		18 35		18 42			18 45	18 50			18 57		19 05		19 12			19 15	19 20			19 27		19 36
London Waterloo ■ ⊖	a	18 34	18 41		18 46			18 49	18 56			19 02	19 04	19 11		19 16			19 19	19 26			19 32	19 34	19 41

Table T149-R

Saturdays

13 October to 8 December

Reading, Guildford, Ascot, Weybridge, Windsor, Kingston, Richmond and Hounslow - London

		SW ■		SW	SW	SW	SW	SW	SW	SW	SW ■	SW		SW ■	SW	SW	SW	SW	SW	SW	SW	SW ■		SW	SW ■
Reading ■	d										18 39											19 09			
Earley	d										18 44											19 14			
Winnersh Triangle	d										18 46											19 16			
Winnersh	d										18 48											19 18			
Wokingham	d										18 53											19 23			
Bracknell	d										18 59											19 29			
Martins Heron	d										19 02											19 32			
Guildford	d	18 00												18 30											19 00
Wanborough	d	18 06												18 36											19 06
Ash ■	d	18 10												18 40											19 10
Aldershot	a	18 17												18 47											19 17
	d	18 30												19 00											19 30
Ash Vale	d	18 34												19 04											19 34
Frimley	d	18 40												19 10											19 40
Camberley	a	18 44												19 14											19 44
	d	18 48												19 18											19 48
Bagshot	d	18 53												19 23											19 53
Ascot ■	d	19a00									19 07			19a30								19 37			20a00
Sunningdale	d										19 10											19 40			
Longcross	d																								
Weybridge	d							19 03												19 33					
Addlestone	d							19 07												19 37					
Chertsey	d				←			19 10								←			19 40						
Virginia Water	a				18 45			19 15			19 19					19 15			19 45			19 49			
	d				18 54			19 24			19 19					19 24			19 54			19 49			
Egham	d				18 57			→			19 23					19 27			→			19 53			
Windsor & Eton Riverside	d					18 51											19 21								
Datchet	d					18 55											19 25								
Sunnymeads	d					18 58											19 28								
Wraysbury	d					19 02											19 32								
Staines	d				19 03	19 08					19 29					19 33	19 38					19 59			
Ashford (Surrey)	d				19 06	19 11										19 36	19 41								
Feltham	d				19 11	19 16					19 35					19 41	19 46					20 05			
Whitton	d					19 20			19 20	19 23							19 50			19 50	19 53				
Kingston	d			18 59											19 29										
Hampton Wick	d			19 01											19 31										
Teddington	d			19 05											19 35										
Fulwell	d																								
Strawberry Hill	d			19 08											19 38										
Twickenham	a			19 12		19 23				19 26	19 40				19 42		19 53				19 56	20 10			
	d			19 13		19 23				19 28	19 41				19 43		19 53				19 58	20 11			
St Margarets	d			19 15						19 30					19 45						20 00				
Richmond ⊖	d			19 19		19 28				19 34	19 45				19 49		19 58				20 04	20 15			
North Sheen	d			19 21						19 36					19 51						20 06				
Mortlake	d			19 23						19 38					19 53						20 08				
Hounslow	d				19 16				19 31							19 46				20 01					
Isleworth	d				19 19				19 34							19 49				20 04					
Syon Lane	d				19 21				19 36							19 51				20 06					
Brentford	d				19 24				19 39							19 54				20 09					
Kew Bridge	d				19 26				19 41							19 56				20 11					
Chiswick	d				19 29				19 44							19 59				20 14					
Barnes Bridge	d				19 31				19 46			←				20 01				20 16				←	
Barnes	d			19 26	19 34		←		19 49	19 41		19 49			19 56	20 04		←		20 19	20 11			20 19	
Putney	d			19 29	19 37	19 34	19 37		→	19 44		19 52			19 59	20 07	20 04	20 07		→	20 14			20 22	
Wandsworth Town	d			19 32	→		19 40			19 47		19 55			20 02	→		20 10			20 17			20 25	
Clapham Junction ■	d			19 35		19 39	19 43			19 50	19 54	19 58			20 05		20 09	20 13			20 20	20 24		20 28	
Queenstown Rd.(Battersea)	d			19 38			19 46			19 53		20 01			20 08			20 16			20 23			20 31	
Vauxhall ⊖	d			19 42		19 45	19 50			19 57		20 05			20 12		20 15	20 20			20 27			20 35	
London Waterloo ■ ⊖	a			19 46		19 49	19 56			20 02	20 04	20 11			20 16		20 19	20 26			20 32	20 34		20 41	

Table T149-R

Saturdays

13 October to 8 December

Reading, Guildford, Ascot, Weybridge, Windsor, Kingston, Richmond and Hounslow - London

		SW	SW	SW	SW	SW	SW	SW		SW ■	SW	SW ■	SW	SW	SW	SW	SW	SW		SW	SW ■	SW	SW ■	SW ■	SW
Reading ■	d									19 39											20 09				
Earley	d									19 44											20 14				
Winnersh Triangle	d									19 46											20 16				
Winnersh	d									19 48											20 18				
Wokingham	d									19 53											20 23				
Bracknell	d									19 59											20 29				
Martins Heron	d									20 02											20 32				
Guildford	d											19 30											20 00	20 30	
Wanborough	d											19 36											20 06	20 36	
Ash ■	d											19 40											20 10	20 40	
Aldershot	a											19 47											20 17	20 47	
	d											20 00											20 30		
Ash Vale	d											20 04											20 34		
Frimley	d											20 10											20 40		
Camberley	a											20 14											20 44		
	d											20 18											20 48		
Bagshot	d											20 23											20 53		
Ascot ■	d									20 07		20a30									20 37		21a00		
Sunningdale	d									20 10											20 40				
Longcross	d																								
Weybridge	d					20 03											20 33								
Addlestone	d					20 07											20 37								
Chertsey	d		←			20 10								←			20 40								
Virginia Water	a		19 45			20 15				20 19				20 15			20 45				20 49				
	d		19 54			20 24				20 19				20 24			20 54				20 49				
Egham	d		19 57			→				20 23				20 27			→				20 53				
Windsor & Eton Riverside	d			19 51											20 21										
Datchet	d			19 55											20 25										
Sunnymeads	d			19 58											20 28										
Wraysbury	d			20 02											20 32										
Staines	d		20 03	20 08						20 29				20 33	20 38						20 59				
Ashford (Surrey)	d		20 06	20 11										20 36	20 41										
Feltham	d		20 11	20 16						20 35				20 41	20 46						21 05				
Whitton	d			20 20			20 20	20 23							20 50			20 50		20 53					
Kingston	d	19 59											20 29												20 59
Hampton Wick	d	20 01											20 31												21 01
Teddington	d	20 05											20 35												21 05
Fulwell	d																								
Strawberry Hill	d	20 08											20 38												21 08
Twickenham	a	20 12		20 23				20 26		20 40			20 42		20 53					20 56	21 10				21 12
	d	20 13		20 23				20 28		20 41			20 43		20 53					20 58	21 11				21 13
St Margarets	d	20 15						20 30					20 45							21 00					21 15
Richmond ⊖	d	20 19		20 28				20 34		20 45			20 49		20 58					21 04	21 15				21 19
North Sheen	d	20 21						20 36					20 51							21 06					21 21
Mortlake	d	20 23						20 38					20 53							21 08					21 23
Hounslow	d		20 16				20 31							20 46				21 01							
Isleworth	d		20 19				20 34							20 49				21 04							
Syon Lane	d		20 21				20 36							20 51				21 06							
Brentford	d		20 24				20 39							20 54				21 09							
Kew Bridge	d		20 26				20 41							20 56				21 11							
Chiswick	d		20 29				20 44							20 59				21 14							
Barnes Bridge	d		20 31				20 46				←			21 01				21 16				←			
Barnes	d	20 26	20 34		←		20 49	20 41			20 49		20 56	21 04		←		21 19		21 11		21 19			21 26
Putney	d	20 29	20 37	20 34	20 37		→	20 44			20 52		20 59	21 07	21 04	21 07		→		21 14		21 22			21 29
Wandsworth Town	d	20 32	→		20 40			20 47			20 55		21 02	→		21 10				21 17		21 25			21 32
Clapham Junction ■	d	20 35		20 39	20 43			20 50		20 54	20 58		21 05		21 09	21 13				21 20	21 24	21 28			21 35
Queenstown Rd.(Battersea)	d	20 38			20 46			20 53			21 01		21 08			21 16				21 23		21 31			21 38
Vauxhall ⊖	d	20 42		20 45	20 50			20 57			21 05		21 12		21 15	21 20				21 27		21 35			21 42
London Waterloo ■ ⊖	a	20 46		20 49	20 56			21 02		21 04	21 11		21 16		21 19	21 26				21 32	21 34	21 41			21 46

Reading, Guildford, Ascot, Weybridge, Windsor, Kingston, Richmond and Hounslow - London

		SW	SW	SW	SW	SW	SW	SW 1	SW	SW	SW	SW	SW	SW	SW	SW	SW 1	SW	SW 1	SW 1	SW	SW
Reading 7	d							20 39									21 09					
Earley	d							20 44									21 14					
Winnersh Triangle	d							20 46									21 16					
Winnersh	d							20 48									21 18					
Wokingham	d							20 53									21 23					
Bracknell	d							20 59									21 29					
Martins Heron	d							21 02									21 32					
Guildford	d																		21 00	21 30		
Wanborough	d																		21 06	21 36		
Ash 5	d																		21 10	21 40		
Aldershot	a																		21 17	21 47		
	d																		21 30			
Ash Vale	d																		21 34			
Frimley	d																		21 40			
Camberley	a																		21 44			
	d																		21 48			
Bagshot	d																		21 53			
Ascot 3	d							21 07									21 37		22a00			
Sunningdale	d							21 10									21 40					
Longcross	d																					
Weybridge	d				21 03									21 33								
Addlestone	d				21 07									21 37								
Chertsey	d	←			21 10						←			21 40								←
Virginia Water	a	20 45			21 15			21 19			21 15			21 45			21 49					21 45
	d	20 54			21 24			21 19			21 24			21 54			21 49					21 54
Egham	d	20 57			→			21 23			21 27			→			21 53					21 57
Windsor & Eton Riverside	d		20 51									21 21										
Datchet	d		20 55									21 25										
Sunnymeads	d		20 58									21 28										
Wraysbury	d		21 02									21 32										
Staines	d	21 03	21 08					21 29			21 33	21 38					21 59					22 03
Ashford (Surrey)	d	21 06	21 11								21 36	21 41										22 06
Feltham	d	21 11	21 16					21 35			21 41	21 46					22 05					22 11
Whitton	d		21 20			21 20	21 23					21 50			21 50	21 53						
Kingston	d									21 29											21 59	
Hampton Wick	d									21 31											22 01	
Teddington	d									21 35											22 05	
Fulwell	d																					
Strawberry Hill	d									21 38											22 08	
Twickenham	a		21 23				21 26	21 40		21 42		21 53				21 56	22 10				22 12	
	d		21 23				21 28	21 41		21 43		21 53				21 58	22 11				22 13	
St Margarets	d						21 30			21 45						22 00					22 15	
Richmond ⊖	d		21 28				21 34	21 45		21 49		21 58				22 04	22 15				22 19	
North Sheen	d						21 36			21 51						22 06					22 21	
Mortlake	d						21 38			21 53						22 08					22 23	
Hounslow	d	21 16				21 31					21 46				22 01							22 16
Isleworth	d	21 19				21 34					21 49				22 04							22 19
Syon Lane	d	21 21				21 36					21 51				22 06							22 21
Brentford	d	21 24				21 39					21 54				22 09							22 24
Kew Bridge	d	21 26				21 41					21 56				22 11							22 26
Chiswick	d	21 29				21 44					21 59				22 14							22 29
Barnes Bridge	d	21 31				21 46			←		22 01				22 16			←				22 31
Barnes	d	21 34		←		21 49	21 41		21 49	21 56	22 04		←		22 19	22 11		22 19			22 26	22 34
Putney	d	21 37	21 34	21 37		→	21 44		21 52	21 59	22 07	22 04	22 07		→	22 14		22 22			22 29	22 37
Wandsworth Town	d	→		21 40			21 47		21 55	22 02	→		22 10			22 17		22 25			22 32	→
Clapham Junction 10	d		21 39	21 43			21 50	21 54	21 58	22 05		22 09	22 13			22 20	22 24	22 28			22 35	
Queenstown Rd.(Battersea)	d			21 46			21 53		22 01	22 08			22 16			22 23		22 31			22 38	
Vauxhall ⊖	d		21 45	21 50			21 57		22 05	22 12		22 15	22 20			22 27		22 35			22 42	
London Waterloo 15 ⊖	a		21 49	21 56			22 02	22 04	22 13	22 17		22 19	22 26			22 32	22 34	22 41			22 46	

Reading, Guildford, Ascot, Weybridge, Windsor, Kingston, Richmond and Hounslow - London

		SW	SW	SW	SW	SW 1	SW	SW	SW	SW	SW	SW 1	SW 1	SW 1	SW	SW	SW	SW	SW	SW 1	SW	SW	SW
Reading 7	d					21 39						22 09								22 39			
Earley	d					21 44						22 14								22 44			
Winnersh Triangle	d					21 46						22 16								22 46			
Winnersh	d					21 48						22 18								22 48			
Wokingham	d					21 53						22 23								22 53			
Bracknell	d					21 59						22 29								22 59			
Martins Heron	d					22 02						22 32								23 02			
Guildford	d												22 00	22 30									
Wanborough	d												22 06	22 36									
Ash 5	d												22 10	22 40									
Aldershot	a												22 17	22 47									
	d												22 30										
Ash Vale	d												22 34										
Frimley	d												22 40										
Camberley	a												22 44										
	d												22 48										
Bagshot	d												22 53										
Ascot 3	d					22 07						22 37	23a00							23 07			
Sunningdale	d					22 10						22 40								23 10			
Longcross	d																						
Weybridge	d				22 03						22 33								23 03				
Addlestone	d				22 07						22 37								23 07				
Chertsey	d				22 10			←			22 40					←			23 10		←		
Virginia Water	a				22 15	22 19		22 15			22 45	22 49				22 45			23 15	23 19	23 15		
	d				22 24	22 19		22 24			22 54	22 49				22 54			23 24	23 19	23 24		
Egham	d				→	22 23		22 27			→	22 53				22 57			→	23 23	23 27		
Windsor & Eton Riverside	d	21 51							22 21								22 53					23 28	
Datchet	d	21 55							22 25								22 56					23 31	
Sunnymeads	d	21 58							22 28								22 59					23 34	
Wraysbury	d	22 02							22 32								23 02					23 37	
Staines	d	22 08				22 29		22 33	22 38			22 59				23 03	23 08			23 29	23a32	23a42	
Ashford (Surrey)	d	22 11						22 36	22 41							23 06	23 11						
Feltham	d	22 16				22 35		22 41	22 46			23 05				23 11	23 16			23 35			
Whitton	d	22 20		22 23					22 50								23 20						
Kingston	d						22 29								22 59								23 29
Hampton Wick	d						22 31								23 01								23 31
Teddington	d						22 35								23 05								23 35
Fulwell	d																						
Strawberry Hill	d						22 38								23 08								23 38
Twickenham	a	22 23		22 26		22 40	22 42		22 53			23 10			23 12		23 23			23 40			23 42
	d	22 23		22 28		22 41	22 43		22 53			23 11			23 13		23 23			23 41			23 43
St Margarets	d			22 30			22 45								23 15								23 45
Richmond ⊖	d	22 28		22 34		22 45	22 49		22 58			23 15			23 19		23 28			23 45			23 49
North Sheen	d			22 36			22 51								23 21								23 51
Mortlake	d			22 38			22 53								23 23								23 53
Hounslow	d							22 46								23 16							
Isleworth	d							22 49								23 19							
Syon Lane	d							22 51								23 21							
Brentford	d							22 54								23 24							
Kew Bridge	d							22 56								23 26							
Chiswick	d							22 59								23 29							
Barnes Bridge	d							23 01								23 31							
Barnes	d		←	22 41			22 56	23 04		←					23 26	23 34		←					23 56
Putney	d	22 34	22 37	22 44			22 59	23 07	23 04	23 07					23 29	23 37	23 34	23 37					23 59
Wandsworth Town	d		22 40	22 47			23 02	→		23 10					23 32	→		23 40					00 02
Clapham Junction 10	d	22 39	22 43	22 50		22 54	23 05		23 09	23 13		23 24			23 35		23 39	23 43		23 54			00 05
Queenstown Rd.(Battersea)	d		22 46	22 53			23 08			23 16					23 38			23 46					00 08
Vauxhall ⊖	d	22 45	22 50	22 57			23 12		23 15	23 20					23 42		23 45	23 50					00 12
London Waterloo 15 ⊖	a	22 49	22 56	23 02		23 04	23 17		23 19	23 26		23 34			23 46		23 49	23 56		00 02			00 16

Table T149-R

Saturdays
13 October to 8 December

Reading, Guildford, Ascot, Weybridge, Windsor, Kingston, Richmond and Hounslow - London

		SW	SW	SW ■	SW	SW ■	SW ■
Reading ■	d			23 12			
Earley	d			23 17			
Winnersh Triangle	d			23 19			
Winnersh	d			23 21			
Wokingham	d			23 26			
Bracknell	d			23 32			
Martins Heron	d			23 35			
Guildford	d					23 00	23 30
Wanborough	d					23 06	23 36
Ash ■	d					23 10	23 40
Aldershot	a					23 17	23 47
	d					23 30	
Ash Vale	d					23 34	
Frimley	d					23 40	
Camberley	a					23 44	
	d					23 48	
Bagshot	d					23 53	
Ascot ■	d			23 40		00a01	
Sunningdale	d			23 43			
Longcross	d						
Weybridge	d		23 33				
Addlestone	d		23 37				
Chertsey	d		23 40		←		
Virginia Water	a		23 45	23 49	23 45		
	d		23 54	23 49	23 54		
Egham	d		→	23 53	23 57		
Windsor & Eton Riverside	d						
Datchet	d						
Sunnymeads	d						
Wraysbury	d						
Staines	d			23 59	00a02		
Ashford (Surrey)	d						
Feltham	d			00 05			
Whitton	d						
Kingston	d	23 55					
Hampton Wick	d	23 57					
Teddington	d	23 59					
Fulwell	d						
Strawberry Hill	d	00 03					
Twickenham	a	00 06		00 10			
	d			00 11			
St Margarets	d						
Richmond ⊖	d			00 15			
North Sheen	d						
Mortlake	d						
Hounslow	d						
Isleworth	d						
Syon Lane	d						
Brentford	d						
Kew Bridge	d						
Chiswick	d						
Barnes Bridge	d						
Barnes	d						
Putney	d						
Wandsworth Town	d						
Clapham Junction ■	d			00 25			
Queenstown Rd.(Battersea)	d						
Vauxhall ⊖	d						
London Waterloo ■ ⊖	a			00 37			

Table T149-R

Sundays
20 May to 30 September

Reading, Guildford, Ascot, Weybridge, Windsor, Kingston, Richmond and Hounslow - London

		SW A	SW A	SW ■ A	SW	SW	SW	SW	SW	SW ■		SW ■	SW
Reading ■	d												
Earley	d												
Winnersh Triangle	d												
Winnersh	d												
Wokingham	d												
Bracknell	d												
Martins Heron	d												
Guildford	d											07 17	
Wanborough	d											07 23	
Ash ■	d											07 27	
Aldershot	a											07 34	
	d											07 40	
Ash Vale	d											07 45	
Frimley	d											07 51	
Camberley	a											07 55	
	d											07 55	
Bagshot	d											08 01	
Ascot ■	d									07 22		08a07	
Sunningdale	d									07 25			
Longcross	d												
Weybridge	d								07 00				
Addlestone	d								07 04				
Chertsey	d								07 07				
Virginia Water	a								07 12	07 31			
	d								07 12	07 31			
Egham	d								07 16	07 36			
Windsor & Eton Riverside	d							07 01					
Datchet	d							07 04					
Sunnymeads	d							07 07					
Wraysbury	d							07 10					
Staines	d							07 16	07 21	07 41			
Ashford (Surrey)	d							07 19	07 24				
Feltham	d			00 05				07 24	07 29	07 47			
Whitton	d							07 28					
Kingston	d				01 17	02 11	06 49						07 49
Hampton Wick	d				01s22	02s13	06 51						07 51
Teddington	d				01s25	02s15	06 56						07 56
Fulwell	d												
Strawberry Hill	d		00 03		01a37	02s18	06 59						07 59
Twickenham	a		00 06	00 10		02 22	07 02	07 31		07 52			08 02
	d			00 11			07 03	07 32		07 53			08 03
St Margarets	d						07 05	07 34					08 05
Richmond ⊖	d			00 15			07 09	07 37		07 57			08 09
North Sheen	d						07 11	07 39					08 11
Mortlake	d						07 13	07 42					08 13
Hounslow	d								07 35				
Isleworth	d								07 38				
Syon Lane	d								07 40				
Brentford	d								07 42				
Kew Bridge	d								07 45				
Chiswick	d								07 47				
Barnes Bridge	d								07 50				
Barnes	d						07 16	07 45	07 53				08 16
Putney	d						07 19	07 48	07 56	08 04			08 19
Wandsworth Town	d	00 02					07 22	07 51	07 59				08 22
Clapham Junction ■	d	00 05		00 25			07 25	07 54	08 02	08 08			08 25
Queenstown Rd.(Battersea)	d	00 08					07 28	07 57	08 05				08 28
Vauxhall ⊖	d	00 12					07 32	08 00	08 08	08 14			08 32
London Waterloo ■ ⊖	a	00 16		00 37			07 36	08 06	08 13	08 23			08 36

		SW	SW	SW ■	SW	SW ■	SW ■	SW		SW	SW ■	SW	SW
Reading ■	d			07 54		08 24					08 54		
Earley	d			07 59		08 29					08 59		
Winnersh Triangle	d			08 01		08 31					09 01		
Winnersh	d			08 03		08 33					09 03		
Wokingham	d			08 08		08 38					09 08		
Bracknell	d			08 14		08 44					09 14		
Martins Heron	d			08 17		08 47					09 17		
Guildford	d						08 17						
Wanborough	d						08 23						
Ash ■	d						08 27						
Aldershot	a						08 34						
	d						08 40						
Ash Vale	d						08 45						
Frimley	d						08 51						
Camberley	a						08 55						
	d						08 55						
Bagshot	d						09 01						
Ascot ■	d			08 22		08 52	09a07				09 22		
Sunningdale	d			08 25		08 55					09 25		
Longcross	d												
Weybridge	d												
Addlestone	d		08 04							09 04			
Chertsey	d		08 07							09 07			
Virginia Water	a		08 12	08 31		09 01				09 12	09 31		
	d		08 12	08 31		09 01				09 12	09 31		
Egham	d		08 16	08 36		09 06				09 16	09 36		
Windsor & Eton Riverside	d	08 01						09 01				09 34	
Datchet	d	08 04						09 04				09 37	
Sunnymeads	d	08 07						09 07					
Wraysbury	d	08 10						09 10					
Staines	d	08 16	08 21	08 41		09 11		09 16		09 21	09 41	09 45	
Ashford (Surrey)	d	08 19	08 24					09 19		09 24		09 48	
Feltham	d	08 24	08 29	08 47		09 17		09 24		09 29	09 47	09 53	
Whitton	d	08 28						09 28				09 57	
Kingston	d				08 49								09 49
Hampton Wick	d				08 51								09 51
Teddington	d				08 56								09 56
Fulwell	d												
Strawberry Hill	d				08 59								09 59
Twickenham	a	08 31		08 52	09 02	09 22		09 31			09 52	10 00	10 02
	d	08 32		08 53	09 03	09 23		09 32			09 53	10 01	10 03
St Margarets	d	08 34			09 05			09 34					10 05
Richmond ⊖	d	08 37		08 57	09 09	09 27		09 37			09 57	10 05	10 09
North Sheen	d	08 39			09 11			09 39					10 11
Mortlake	d	08 42			09 13			09 42					10 13
Hounslow	d		08 35							09 35			
Isleworth	d		08 38							09 38			
Syon Lane	d		08 40							09 40			
Brentford	d		08 42							09 42			
Kew Bridge	d		08 45							09 45			
Chiswick	d		08 47							09 47			
Barnes Bridge	d		08 50							09 50			
Barnes	d	08 45	08 53		09 16			09 45		09 53			10 16
Putney	d	08 48	08 56	09 04	09 19	09 34		09 48		09 56	10 04	10 14	10 19
Wandsworth Town	d	08 51	08 59		09 22			09 51		09 59			10 22
Clapham Junction ■	d	08 54	09 02	09 08	09 25	09 38		09 54		10 02	10 08	10 18	10 25
Queenstown Rd.(Battersea)	d	08 57	09 05		09 28			09 57		10 05			10 28
Vauxhall ⊖	d	09 00	09 08	09 14	09 32	09 44		10 00		10 08	10 14	10 24	10 32
London Waterloo ■ ⊖	a	09 06	09 13	09 23	09 41	09 53		10 05		10 13	10 23	10 29	10 41

A not 20 May

20 May to 30 September

Reading, Guildford, Ascot, Weybridge, Windsor, Kingston, Richmond and Hounslow - London

		SW ■	SW ■	SW	SW	SW ■	SW	SW	SW ■	SW ■	SW	SW	SW ■	SW	SW	SW ■	SW ■	SW	SW	SW	SW ■	SW	SW
Reading 7	d	09 24				09 54			10 24				10 54			11 24					11 54		
Earley	d	09 29				09 59			10 29				10 59			11 29					11 59		
Winnersh Triangle	d	09 31				10 01			10 31				11 01			11 31					12 01		
Winnersh	d	09 33				10 03			10 33				11 03			11 33					12 03		
Wokingham	d	09 38				10 08			10 38				11 08			11 38					12 08		
Bracknell	d	09 44				10 14			10 44				11 14			11 44					12 14		
Martins Heron	d	09 47				10 17			10 47				11 17			11 47					12 17		
Guildford	d		09 17							10 17							11 17						
Wanborough	d		09 23							10 23							11 23						
Ash 5	d		09 27							10 27							11 27						
Aldershot	a		09 34							10 34							11 34						
	d		09 40							10 40							11 40						
Ash Vale	d		09 45							10 45							11 45						
Frimley	d		09 51							10 51							11 51						
Camberley	a		09 55							10 55							11 55						
	d		09 55							10 55							11 55						
Bagshot	d		10 01							11 01							12 01						
Ascot 3	d	09 52	10a07			10 22			10 52	11a07			11 22			11 52	12a07				12 22		
Sunningdale	d	09 55				10 25			10 55				11 25			11 55					12 25		
Longcross	d																						
Weybridge	d																						
Addlestone	d				10 04							11 04							12 04				
Chertsey	d				10 07							11 07							12 07				
Virginia Water	a	10 01			10 12	10 31			11 01			11 12	11 31			12 01			12 12		12 31		
	d	10 01			10 12	10 31			11 01			11 12	11 31			12 01			12 12		12 31		
Egham	d	10 05			10 16	10 35			11 05			11 16	11 35			12 05			12 16		12 35		
Windsor & Eton Riverside	d			10 01			10 34				11 01			11 34				12 01					12 34
Datchet	d			10 04			10 37				11 04			11 37				12 04					12 37
Sunnymeads	d			10 07							11 07							12 07					
Wraysbury	d			10 10							11 10							12 10					
Staines	d	10 11		10 16	10 21	10 41	10 45		11 11		11 16	11 21	11 41	11 45		12 11		12 16	12 21		12 41		12 45
Ashford (Surrey)	d			10 19	10 24		10 48				11 19	11 24		11 48				12 19	12 24				12 48
Feltham	d	10 17		10 24	10 29	10 47	10 53		11 17		11 24	11 29	11 47	11 53		12 17		12 24	12 29		12 47		12 53
Whitton	d			10 28			10 57				11 28			11 57				12 28					12 57
Kingston	d							10 49							11 49					12 35			
Hampton Wick	d							10 51							11 51					12 37			
Teddington	d							10 56							11 56					12 40			
Fulwell	d																						
Strawberry Hill	d							10 59							11 59					12 43		←	
Twickenham	a	10 22		10 31		10 52	11 00	11 02	11 22		11 31		11 52	12 00	12 02	12 22		12 31		12 46	12 52	12 46	13 00
	d	10 23		10 32		10 53	11 01	11 03	11 23		11 32		11 53	12 01	12 03	12 23		12 32		12 56	12 53	12 56	13 01
St Margarets	d			10 34				11 05			11 34				12 05			12 34		→			
Richmond ⊖	d	10 27		10 37		10 57	11 05	11 09	11 27		11 37		11 57	12 05	12 09	12 27		12 37			12 57		13 05
North Sheen	d			10 39				11 11			11 39				12 11			12 39					
Mortlake	d			10 42				11 13			11 42				12 13			12 42					
Hounslow	d				10 35							11 35							12 35			13 05	
Isleworth	d				10 38							11 38							12 38			13 08	
Syon Lane	d				10 40							11 40							12 40			13 10	
Brentford	d				10 42							11 42							12 42			13 12	
Kew Bridge	d				10 45							11 45							12 45			13 15	
Chiswick	d				10 47							11 47							12 47			13 17	
Barnes Bridge	d				10 50							11 50							12 50			13 20	
Barnes	d			10 45	10 53			11 16			11 45	11 53			12 16			12 45	12 53			13 23	
Putney	d	10 34		10 48	10 56	11 04	11 14	11 19	11 34		11 48	11 56	12 04	12 14	12 19	12 34		12 48	12 56		13 04	→	13 14
Wandsworth Town	d			10 51	10 59			11 22			11 51	11 59			12 22			12 51	12 59				
Clapham Junction 10	d	10 38		10 53	11 02	11 08	11 18	11 25	11 38		11 53	12 02	12 08	12 18	12 25	12 38		12 53	13 02		13 08		13 18
Queenstown Rd.(Battersea)	d			10 57	11 05			11 28			11 57	12 05			12 28			12 57	13 05				
Vauxhall ⊖	d	10 44		11 00	11 08	11 14	11 24	11 32	11 44		12 00	12 08	12 14	12 24	12 32	12 44		13 00	13 08		13 14		13 24
London Waterloo 15 ⊖	a	10 53		11 05	11 13	11 23	11 29	11 41	11 53		12 05	12 13	12 23	12 29	12 41	12 53		13 05	13 13		13 23		13 29

20 May to 30 September

Reading, Guildford, Ascot, Weybridge, Windsor, Kingston, Richmond and Hounslow - London

		SW	SW	SW ■	SW ■	SW	SW	SW	SW ■	SW	SW	SW	SW	SW ■	SW ■	SW	SW	SW	SW ■	SW	SW	SW
Reading 7	d			12 24					12 54					13 24					13 54			
Earley	d			12 29					12 59					13 29					13 59			
Winnersh Triangle	d			12 31					13 01					13 31					14 01			
Winnersh	d			12 33					13 03					13 33					14 03			
Wokingham	d			12 38					13 08					13 38					14 08			
Bracknell	d			12 44					13 14					13 44					14 14			
Martins Heron	d			12 47					13 17					13 47					14 17			
Guildford	d				12 17										13 17							
Wanborough	d				12 23										13 23							
Ash 5	d				12 27										13 27							
Aldershot	a				12 35										13 34							
	d				12 40										13 40							
Ash Vale	d				12 45										13 45							
Frimley	d				12 51										13 51							
Camberley	a				12 55										13 55							
	d				12 55										13 55							
Bagshot	d				13 01										14 01							
Ascot 3	d			12 52	13a07				13 22					13 52	14a07				14 22			
Sunningdale	d			12 55					13 25					13 55					14 25			
Longcross	d																					
Weybridge	d																					
Addlestone	d						13 04										14 04					
Chertsey	d						13 07										14 07					
Virginia Water	a			13 01			13 12		13 31					14 01			14 12		14 31			
	d			13 01			13 12		13 31					14 01			14 12		14 31			
Egham	d			13 05			13 16		13 35					14 05			14 16		14 35			
Windsor & Eton Riverside	d					13 01					13 34					14 01					14 34	
Datchet	d					13 04					13 37					14 04					14 37	
Sunnymeads	d					13 07										14 07						
Wraysbury	d					13 10										14 10						
Staines	d			13 11		13 16	13 21		13 41		13 45			14 11		14 16	14 21		14 41		14 45	
Ashford (Surrey)	d					13 19	13 24				13 48					14 19	14 24				14 48	
Feltham	d			13 17		13 24	13 29		13 47		13 53			14 17		14 24	14 29		14 47		14 53	
Whitton	d					13 28					13 57					14 28					14 57	
Kingston	d	12 49						13 35				13 49						14 35				14 49
Hampton Wick	d	12 51						13 37				13 51						14 37				14 51
Teddington	d	12 56						13 40				13 56						14 40				14 56
Fulwell	d																					
Strawberry Hill	d	12 59						13 43		←		13 59						14 43		←		14 59
Twickenham	a	13 02		13 22		13 31		13 46	13 52	13 46	14 00	14 02		14 22		14 31		14 46	14 52	14 46	15 00	15 02
	d	13 03		13 23		13 32		13 56	13 53	13 56	14 01	14 03		14 23		14 32		14 56	14 53	14 56	15 01	15 03
St Margarets	d	13 05				13 34		→				14 05				14 34		→				15 05
Richmond ⊖	d	13 09		13 27		13 37			13 57		14 05	14 08		14 27		14 37			14 57		15 05	15 09
North Sheen	d	13 11				13 39						14 10				14 39						15 11
Mortlake	d	13 13				13 42						14 13				14 42						15 13
Hounslow	d						13 35			14 05							14 35			15 05		
Isleworth	d						13 38			14 08							14 38			15 08		
Syon Lane	d						13 40			14 10							14 40			15 10		
Brentford	d						13 42			14 12							14 42			15 12		
Kew Bridge	d						13 45			14 15							14 45			15 15		
Chiswick	d						13 47			14 17							14 47			15 17		
Barnes Bridge	d		←				13 50			14 20			←				14 50			15 20		
Barnes	d	13 16	13 23			13 45	13 53			14 23		14 16	14 23			14 45	14 53			15 23		15 16
Putney	d	13 19	13 26	13 34		13 48	13 56		14 04	→	14 14	14 19	14 26	14 34		14 48	14 56		15 04	→	15 14	15 19
Wandsworth Town	d	13 22	13 29			13 51	13 59					14 22	14 29			14 51	14 59					15 22
Clapham Junction 10	d	13 25	13 32	13 38		13 54	14 02		14 08		14 18	14 25	14 32	14 38		14 54	15 02		15 08		15 18	15 25
Queenstown Rd.(Battersea)	d	13 28	13 35			13 57	14 05					14 28	14 35			14 57	15 05					15 28
Vauxhall ⊖	d	13 32	13 38	13 44		14 00	14 08		14 14		14 24	14 32	14 38	14 44		15 00	15 08		15 14		15 24	15 32
London Waterloo 15 ⊖	a	13 41	13 43	13 53		14 05	14 13		14 23		14 29	14 41	14 43	14 53		15 05	15 13		15 18		15 29	15 36

Table T149-R

Sundays

20 May to 30 September

Reading, Guildford, Ascot, Weybridge, Windsor, Kingston, Richmond and Hounslow - London

		SW	SW	SW ■	SW ■	SW	SW	SW		SW ■	SW	SW	SW	SW	SW	SW ■	SW ■	SW		SW	SW	SW ■	SW	SW	SW
Reading ■	d			14 24						14 54						15 24						15 54			
Earley	d			14 29						14 59						15 29						15 59			
Winnersh Triangle	d			14 31						15 01						15 31						16 01			
Winnersh	d			14 33						15 03						15 33						16 03			
Wokingham	d			14 38						15 08						15 38						16 08			
Bracknell	d			14 44						15 14						15 44						16 14			
Martins Heron	d			14 47						15 17						15 47						16 17			
Guildford	d				14 17												15 17								
Wanborough	d				14 23												15 23								
Ash ■	d				14 27												15 27								
Aldershot	a				14 34												15 34								
	d				14 40												15 40								
Ash Vale	d				14 45												15 45								
Frimley	d				14 51												15 51								
Camberley	a				14 55												15 55								
	d				14 55												15 55								
Bagshot	d				15 01												16 01								
Ascot ■	d			14 52	15a07					15 22						15 52	16a07					16 22			
Sunningdale	d			14 55						15 25						15 55						16 25			
Longcross	d																								
Weybridge	d																								
Addlestone	d						15 04													16 04					
Chertsey	d						15 07													16 07					
Virginia Water	a			15 01			15 12			15 31						16 01				16 12		16 31			
	d			15 01			15 12			15 31						16 01				16 12		16 31			
Egham	d			15 05			15 16			15 35						16 05				16 16		16 35			
Windsor & Eton Riverside	d					15 01						15 34						16 01						16 34	
Datchet	d					15 04						15 37						16 04						16 37	
Sunnymeads	d					15 07												16 07							
Wraysbury	d					15 10												16 10							
Staines	d			15 11		15 16	15 21			15 41		15 45				16 11		16 16		16 21		16 41		16 45	
Ashford (Surrey)	d					15 19	15 24					15 48						16 19		16 24				16 48	
Feltham	d			15 17		15 24	15 29			15 47		15 53				16 17		16 24		16 29		16 47		16 53	
Whitton	d		15 01			15 28						15 57			16 01			16 28						16 57	
Kingston	d							15 35					15 49								16 35				16 49
Hampton Wick	d							15 37					15 51								16 37				16 51
Teddington	d							15 40					15 56								16 40				16 56
Fulwell	d																								
Strawberry Hill	d							15 43			←		15 59								16 43		←		16 59
Twickenham	a		15 04	15 22		15 31		15 46		15 52	15 46	16 00	16 02		16 04	16 22		16 31			16 46	16 52	16 46	17 00	17 02
	d			15 23		15 32		15 56		15 53	15 56	16 01	16 03			16 23		16 32			16 56	16 53	16 56	17 01	17 03
St Margarets	d					15 34		→					16 05					16 34			→				17 05
Richmond ⊖	d			15 27		15 37				15 57		16 05	16 09			16 27		16 37				16 57		17 05	17 09
North Sheen	d					15 39							16 11					16 39							17 11
Mortlake	d					15 42							16 13					16 42							17 13
Hounslow	d						15 35				16 05									16 35			17 05		
Isleworth	d						15 38				16 08									16 38			17 08		
Syon Lane	d						15 40				16 10									16 40			17 10		
Brentford	d						15 42				16 12									16 42			17 12		
Kew Bridge	d						15 45				16 15									16 45			17 15		
Chiswick	d						15 47				16 17									16 47			17 17		
Barnes Bridge	d	←					15 50				16 20			←						16 50			17 20		
Barnes	d	15 23				15 45	15 53				16 23		16 16	16 23				16 45		16 53			17 23		17 16
Putney	d	15 26		15 34		15 48	15 56			16 04	→	16 14	16 19	16 26		16 34		16 48		16 56		17 04	→	17 14	17 19
Wandsworth Town	d	15 29				15 51	15 59						16 22	16 29				16 51		16 59					17 22
Clapham Junction ■	d	15 32		15 38		15 54	16 02			16 08		16 18	16 25	16 32		16 38		16 54		17 02		17 08		17 18	17 25
Queenstown Rd.(Battersea)	d	15 35				15 57	16 05						16 28	16 35				16 57		17 05					17 28
Vauxhall ⊖	d	15 38		15 44		16 00	16 08			16 14		16 24	16 32	16 38		16 44		17 00		17 08		17 14		17 24	17 32
London Waterloo ■ ⊖	a	15 43		15 48		16 05	16 13			16 18		16 29	16 36	16 43		16 48		17 05		17 13		17 18		17 29	17 36

Table T149-R

Sundays

20 May to 30 September

Reading, Guildford, Ascot, Weybridge, Windsor, Kingston, Richmond and Hounslow - London

		SW	SW	SW ■		SW ■	SW	SW	SW	SW ■	SW	SW	SW	SW	SW	SW ■	SW ■	SW	SW	SW	SW ■	
Reading ■	d			16 24						16 54						17 24					17 54	
Earley	d			16 29						16 59						17 29					17 59	
Winnersh Triangle	d			16 31						17 01						17 31					18 01	
Winnersh	d			16 33						17 03						17 33					18 03	
Wokingham	d			16 38						17 08						17 38					18 08	
Bracknell	d			16 44						17 14						17 44					18 14	
Martins Heron	d			16 47						17 17						17 47					18 17	
Guildford	d					16 17											17 17					
Wanborough	d					16 23											17 23					
Ash ■	d					16 27											17 27					
Aldershot	a					16 34											17 34					
	d					16 40											17 40					
Ash Vale	d					16 45											17 45					
Frimley	d					16 51											17 51					
Camberley	a					16 55											17 55					
	d					16 55											17 55					
Bagshot	d					17 01											18 01					
Ascot ■	d			16 52		17a07				17 22						17 52	18a07				18 22	
Sunningdale	d			16 55						17 25						17 55					18 25	
Longcross	d																					
Weybridge	d																					
Addlestone	d							17 04											18 04			
Chertsey	d							17 07											18 07			
Virginia Water	a			17 01				17 12		17 31						18 01			18 12		18 31	
	d			17 01				17 12		17 31						18 01			18 12		18 31	
Egham	d			17 05				17 16		17 36						18 05			18 16		18 35	and at the same minutes past each hour until
Windsor & Eton Riverside	d						17 01					17 34						18 01				
Datchet	d						17 04					17 37						18 04				
Sunnymeads	d						17 07											18 07				
Wraysbury	d						17 10											18 10				
Staines	d			17 11			17 16	17 21		17 41		17 45				18 11		18 16	18 21		18 41	
Ashford (Surrey)	d						17 19	17 24				17 48						18 19	18 24			
Feltham	d			17 17			17 24	17 29		17 47		17 53				18 17		18 24	18 29		18 47	
Whitton	d		17 01				17 28					17 57			18 01			18 28				
Kingston	d								17 35				17 49							18 35		
Hampton Wick	d								17 37				17 51							18 37		
Teddington	d								17 40				17 56							18 40		
Fulwell	d																					
Strawberry Hill	d								17 43		←		17 59							18 43		
Twickenham	a		17 04	17 22			17 31		17 46	17 52	17 46	18 00	18 02		18 04	18 22		18 31		18 46	18 52	
	d			17 23			17 32		17 56	17 53	17 56	18 01	18 03			18 23		18 32		18 56	18 53	
St Margarets	d						17 34		→				18 05					18 34		→		
Richmond ⊖	d			17 27			17 37			17 57		18 05	18 09			18 27		18 37			18 57	
North Sheen	d						17 39						18 11					18 39				
Mortlake	d						17 42						18 13					18 42				
Hounslow	d							17 35			18 05								18 35			
Isleworth	d							17 38			18 08								18 38			
Syon Lane	d							17 40			18 10								18 40			
Brentford	d							17 42			18 12								18 42			
Kew Bridge	d							17 45			18 15								18 45			
Chiswick	d							17 47			18 17								18 47			
Barnes Bridge	d	←						17 50			18 20			←					18 50			
Barnes	d	17 23					17 45	17 53			18 23		18 16	18 23				18 45	18 53			
Putney	d	17 26		17 34			17 48	17 56		18 04	→	18 14	18 19	18 26		18 34		18 48	18 56		19 04	
Wandsworth Town	d	17 29					17 51	17 59					18 22	18 29				18 51	18 59			
Clapham Junction ■	d	17 32		17 38			17 54	18 02		18 08		18 18	18 25	18 32		18 38		18 54	19 02		19 08	
Queenstown Rd.(Battersea)	d	17 35					17 57	18 05					18 28	18 35				18 57	19 05			
Vauxhall ⊖	d	17 38		17 44			18 00	18 08		18 14		18 24	18 32	18 38		18 44		19 00	19 08		19 14	
London Waterloo ■ ⊖	a	17 43		17 48			18 05	18 13		18 18		18 29	18 36	18 43		18 48		19 05	19 13		19 18	

Table T149-R

Sundays

20 May to 30 September

Reading, Guildford, Ascot, Weybridge, Windsor, Kingston, Richmond and Hounslow - London

		SW	SW	SW	SW	SW	SW ■	SW ■	SW	SW	SW	SW ■
Reading ■	d						20 24					20 54
Earley	d						20 29					20 59
Winnersh Triangle	d						20 31					21 01
Winnersh	d						20 33					21 03
Wokingham	d						20 38					21 08
Bracknell	d						20 44					21 14
Martins Heron	d						20 47					21 17
Guildford	d							20 17				
Wanborough	d							20 23				
Ash ■	d							20 27				
Aldershot	a							20 34				
	d							20 40				
Ash Vale	d							20 45				
Frimley	d							20 51				
Camberley	a							20 55				
	d							20 55				
Bagshot	d							21 01				
Ascot ■	d						20 52	21a07				21 22
Sunningdale	d						20 55					21 25
Longcross	d											
Weybridge	d											
Addlestone	d									21 04		
Chertsey	d									21 07		
Virginia Water	a						21 01			21 12		21 31
	d						21 01			21 12		21 31
Egham	d						21 05			21 16		21 35
Windsor & Eton Riverside	d		20 34						21 01			
Datchet	d		20 37						21 04			
Sunnymeads	d								21 07			
Wraysbury	d								21 10			
Staines	d		20 45				21 11		21 16	21 21		21 41
Ashford (Surrey)	d		20 48						21 19	21 24		
Feltham	d		20 53				21 17		21 24	21 29		21 47
Whitton	d		20 57			21 01			21 28			
Kingston	d			20 49							21 35	
Hampton Wick	d			20 51							21 37	
Teddington	d			20 56							21 40	
Fulwell	d											
Strawberry Hill	d	←		20 59							21 43	
Twickenham	a	20 46	21 00	21 02		21 04	21 22		21 31		21 46	21 52
	d	20 56	21 01	21 03			21 23		21 32		21 56	21 53
St Margarets	d			21 05					21 34		→	
Richmond ⊖	d		21 05	21 09			21 27		21 37			21 57
North Sheen	d			21 11					21 39			
Mortlake	d			21 13					21 42			
Hounslow	d	21 05								21 35		
Isleworth	d	21 08								21 38		
Syon Lane	d	21 10								21 40		
Brentford	d	21 12								21 42		
Kew Bridge	d	21 15								21 45		
Chiswick	d	21 17								21 47		
Barnes Bridge	d	21 20			←					21 50		
Barnes	d	21 23		21 16	21 23				21 45	21 53		
Putney	d	→	21 14	21 19	21 26		21 34		21 48	21 56		22 04
Wandsworth Town	d			21 22	21 29				21 51	21 59		
Clapham Junction ■	d		21 18	21 25	21 32		21 38		21 54	22 02		22 08
Queenstown Rd.(Battersea)	d			21 28	21 35				21 57	22 05		
Vauxhall ⊖	d		21 24	21 32	21 38		21 44		22 00	22 08		22 14
London Waterloo ■ ⊖	a		21 29	21 36	21 43		21 48		22 05	22 13		22 18

		SW	SW	SW	SW	SW	SW ■	SW ■	SW	SW	SW	SW ■
Reading ■	d						21 24					21 54
Earley	d						21 29					21 59
Winnersh Triangle	d						21 31					22 01
Winnersh	d						21 33					22 03
Wokingham	d						21 38					22 08
Bracknell	d						21 44					22 14
Martins Heron	d						21 47					22 17
Guildford	d							21 17				
Wanborough	d							21 23				
Ash ■	d							21 27				
Aldershot	a							21 34				
	d							21 40				
Ash Vale	d							21 45				
Frimley	d							21 51				
Camberley	a							21 55				
	d							21 55				
Bagshot	d							22 01				
Ascot ■	d						21 52	22a07				22 22
Sunningdale	d						21 55					22 25
Longcross	d											
Weybridge	d											
Addlestone	d									22 04		
Chertsey	d									22 07		
Virginia Water	a						22 01			22 12		22 31
	d						22 01			22 12		22 31
Egham	d						22 05			22 16		22 35
Windsor & Eton Riverside	d		21 34						22 01			
Datchet	d		21 37						22 04			
Sunnymeads	d								22 07			
Wraysbury	d								22 10			
Staines	d		21a45				22 11		22 16	22 21		22 41
Ashford (Surrey)	d								22 19	22 24		
Feltham	d						22 17		22 24	22 29		22 47
Whitton	d					22 01			22 28			
Kingston	d			21 49							22 35	
Hampton Wick	d			21 51							22 37	
Teddington	d			21 56							22 40	
Fulwell	d											
Strawberry Hill	d	←		21 59							22 43	
Twickenham	a	21 46		22 02		22 04	22 22		22 31		22 46	22 52
	d	21 56		22 03			22 23		22 32		22 56	22 53
St Margarets	d			22 05					22 34		→	
Richmond ⊖	d			22 09			22 27		22 37			22 57
North Sheen	d			22 11					22 39			
Mortlake	d			22 13					22 42			
Hounslow	d	22 05								22 35		
Isleworth	d	22 08								22 38		
Syon Lane	d	22 10								22 40		
Brentford	d	22 12								22 42		
Kew Bridge	d	22 15								22 45		
Chiswick	d	22 17								22 47		
Barnes Bridge	d	22 20			←					22 50		
Barnes	d	22 23		22 16	22 23				22 45	22 53		
Putney	d	→		22 19	22 26		22 34		22 48	22 56		23 04
Wandsworth Town	d			22 22	22 29				22 51	22 59		
Clapham Junction ■	d			22 25	22 32		22 38		22 54	23 02		23 08
Queenstown Rd.(Battersea)	d			22 28	22 35				22 57	23 05		
Vauxhall ⊖	d			22 32	22 38		22 44		23 00	23 08		23 14
London Waterloo ■ ⊖	a			22 36	22 43		22 48		23 05	23 13		23 18

Table T149-R

Sundays

20 May to 30 September

Reading, Guildford, Ascot, Weybridge, Windsor, Kingston, Richmond and Hounslow - London

		SW	SW	SW	SW	SW ■	SW ■	SW	SW	SW ■	SW	SW ■	SW
Reading ■	d					22 24						22 54	
Earley	d					22 29						22 59	
Winnersh Triangle	d					22 31						23 01	
Winnersh	d					22 33						23 03	
Wokingham	d					22 38						23 08	
Bracknell	d					22 44						23 14	
Martins Heron	d					22 47						23 17	
Guildford	d						22 17			23 17			
Wanborough	d						22 23			23 23			
Ash ■	d						22 27			23 27			
Aldershot	a						22 34			23 34			
	d						22 40						
Ash Vale	d						22 45						
Frimley	d						22 51						
Camberley	a						22 55						
	d						22 55						
Bagshot	d						23 01						
Ascot ■	d					22 52	23a07					23 22	
Sunningdale	d					22 55						23 25	
Longcross	d												
Weybridge	d												
Addlestone	d								23 04				
Chertsey	d								23 07				
Virginia Water	a					23 01			23 12			23 31	
	d					23 01			23 12			23 31	
Egham	d					23 05			23 16			23 35	
Windsor & Eton Riverside	d							23 01					
Datchet	d							23 04					
Sunnymeads	d							23 07					
Wraysbury	d							23 10					
Staines	d					23 11		23 16	23 21			23 41	
Ashford (Surrey)	d							23 19	23 24				
Feltham	d					23 17		23 24	23 29			23 47	
Whitton	d				23 01			23 28					
Kingston	d		22 49								23 35		23 47
Hampton Wick	d		22 51								23 37		23 49
Teddington	d		22 56								23 40		23 51
Fulwell	d												
Strawberry Hill	d	←	22 59								23 43		23a54
Twickenham	a	22 46	23 02		23 04	23 22		23 31			23 46	23 52	
	d	22 56	23 03			23 23		23 32				23 54	
St Margarets	d		23 05					23 34					
Richmond ⊖	d		23 09			23 27		23 37				23 58	
North Sheen	d		23 11					23 39					
Mortlake	d		23 13					23 42					
Hounslow	d	23 05							23 35				
Isleworth	d	23 08							23 38				
Syon Lane	d	23 10							23 40				
Brentford	d	23 12							23 42				
Kew Bridge	d	23 15							23 45				
Chiswick	d	23 17							23 47				
Barnes Bridge	d	23 20		←					23 50				
Barnes	d	23 23	23 16	23 23				23 45	23 53				
Putney	d	→	23 19	23 26		23 34		23 48	23 56			00 05	
Wandsworth Town	d		23 22	23 29				23 51	23 59				
Clapham Junction ■	d		23 25	23 32		23 38		23 54	00 02			00 09	
Queenstown Rd.(Battersea)	d		23 28	23 35				23 57	00 05				
Vauxhall ⊖	d		23 32	23 38		23 44		23 59	00 08			00 15	
London Waterloo ■ ⊖	a		23 36	23 43		23 48		00 05	00 13			00 19	

Table T149-R

Sundays

7 October to 2 December

Reading, Guildford, Ascot, Weybridge, Windsor, Kingston, Richmond and Hounslow - London

Station		SW	SW	SW ■	SW	SW	SW	SW	SW	SW ■	SW ■	SW
Reading ■7	d											
Earley	d											
Winnersh Triangle	d											
Winnersh	d											
Wokingham	d											
Bracknell	d											
Martins Heron	d											
Guildford	d										07 17	
Wanborough	d										07 23	
Ash ■5	d										07 27	
Aldershot	a										07 34	
	d										07 40	
Ash Vale	d										07 45	
Frimley	d										07 51	
Camberley	a										07 55	
	d										07 55	
Bagshot	d										08 01	
Ascot ■3	d									07 22	08a07	
Sunningdale	d									07 25		
Longcross	d											
Weybridge	d								07 00			
Addlestone	d								07 04			
Chertsey	d								07 07			
Virginia Water	a								07 12	07 31		
	d								07 12	07 31		
Egham	d								07 16	07 36		
Windsor & Eton Riverside	d							06 59				
Datchet	d							07 03				
Sunnymeads	d							07 06				
Wraysbury	d							07 10				
Staines	d							07 16	07 21	07 41		
Ashford (Surrey)	d							07 19	07 24			
Feltham	d			00 05				07 24	07 29	07 47		
Whitton	d							07 28				
Kingston	d				01 17	02 11	06 49					07 49
Hampton Wick	d				01s22	02s13	06 51					07 51
Teddington	d				01s25	02s15	06 56					07 56
Fulwell	d											
Strawberry Hill	d		00 03		01a37	02s18	06 59					07 59
Twickenham	a		00 06	00 10		02 22	07 02	07 31		07 52		08 02
	d			00 11			07 03	07 32		07 53		08 03
St Margarets	d						07 05	07 34				08 05
Richmond ⊖	d			00 15			07 09	07 37		07 57		08 09
North Sheen	d						07 11	07 39				08 11
Mortlake	d						07 13	07 42				08 13
Hounslow	d								07 35			
Isleworth	d								07 38			
Syon Lane	d								07 40			
Brentford	d								07 42			
Kew Bridge	d								07 45			
Chiswick	d								07 47			
Barnes Bridge	d								07 50			
Barnes	d						07 16	07 45	07 53			08 16
Putney	d						07 19	07 48	07 56	08 04		08 19
Wandsworth Town	d	00 02					07 22	07 51	07 59			08 22
Clapham Junction ■10	d	00 05		00 25			07 25	07 54	08 02	08 08		08 25
Queenstown Rd.(Battersea)	d	00 08					07 28	07 57	08 05			08 28
Vauxhall ⊖	d	00 12					07 32	08 00	08 08	08 14		08 32
London Waterloo ■15 ⊖	a	00 16		00 37			07 36	08 06	08 13	08 23		08 36

Station		SW	SW	SW ■	SW	SW ■	SW ■	SW	SW	SW ■	SW	SW
Reading ■7	d			07 51		08 21				08 51		
Earley	d			07 56		08 26				08 56		
Winnersh Triangle	d			07 58		08 28				08 58		
Winnersh	d			08 00		08 30				09 00		
Wokingham	d			08 05		08 35				09 05		
Bracknell	d			08 11		08 41				09 11		
Martins Heron	d			08 14		08 44				09 14		
Guildford	d						08 17					
Wanborough	d						08 23					
Ash ■5	d						08 27					
Aldershot	a						08 34					
	d						08 40					
Ash Vale	d						08 45					
Frimley	d						08 51					
Camberley	a						08 55					
	d						08 55					
Bagshot	d						09 01					
Ascot ■3	d			08 19		08 49	09a07			09 19		
Sunningdale	d			08 22		08 52				09 22		
Longcross	d											
Weybridge	d											
Addlestone	d		08 04						09 04			
Chertsey	d		08 07						09 07			
Virginia Water	a		08 12	08 31		09 01			09 12	09 31		
	d		08 12	08 31		09 01			09 12	09 31		
Egham	d		08 16	08 36		09 06			09 16	09 36		
Windsor & Eton Riverside	d	07 59						08 59			09 32	
Datchet	d	08 03						09 03			09 36	
Sunnymeads	d	08 06						09 06				
Wraysbury	d	08 10						09 10				
Staines	d	08 16	08 21	08 41		09 11		09 16	09 21	09 41	09 45	
Ashford (Surrey)	d	08 19	08 24					09 19	09 24		09 48	
Feltham	d	08 24	08 29	08 47		09 17		09 24	09 29	09 47	09 53	
Whitton	d	08 28						09 28			09 57	
Kingston	d				08 49							09 49
Hampton Wick	d				08 51							09 51
Teddington	d				08 56							09 56
Fulwell	d											
Strawberry Hill	d				08 59							09 59
Twickenham	a	08 31		08 52	09 02	09 22		09 31		09 52	10 00	10 02
	d	08 32		08 53	09 03	09 23		09 32		09 53	10 01	10 03
St Margarets	d	08 34			09 05			09 34				10 05
Richmond ⊖	d	08 37		08 57	09 09	09 27		09 37		09 57	10 05	10 09
North Sheen	d	08 39			09 11			09 39				10 11
Mortlake	d	08 42			09 13			09 42				10 13
Hounslow	d		08 35						09 35			
Isleworth	d		08 38						09 38			
Syon Lane	d		08 40						09 40			
Brentford	d		08 42						09 42			
Kew Bridge	d		08 45						09 45			
Chiswick	d		08 47						09 47			
Barnes Bridge	d		08 50						09 50			
Barnes	d	08 45	08 53		09 16			09 45	09 53			10 16
Putney	d	08 48	08 56	09 04	09 19	09 34		09 48	09 56	10 04	10 14	10 19
Wandsworth Town	d	08 51	08 59		09 22			09 51	09 59			10 22
Clapham Junction ■10	d	08 54	09 02	09 08	09 25	09 38		09 54	10 02	10 08	10 18	10 25
Queenstown Rd.(Battersea)	d	08 57	09 05		09 28			09 57	10 05			10 28
Vauxhall ⊖	d	09 00	09 08	09 14	09 32	09 44		10 00	10 08	10 14	10 24	10 32
London Waterloo ■15 ⊖	a	09 06	09 13	09 23	09 41	09 53		10 05	10 13	10 23	10 29	10 41

Table T149-R

Sundays

7 October to 2 December

Reading, Guildford, Ascot, Weybridge, Windsor, Kingston, Richmond and Hounslow - London

Station		SW ■	SW ■	SW	SW	SW ■	SW	SW	SW ■	SW ■	SW	SW
Reading ■7	d	09 21				09 51			10 21			
Earley	d	09 26				09 56			10 26			
Winnersh Triangle	d	09 28				09 58			10 28			
Winnersh	d	09 30				10 00			10 30			
Wokingham	d	09 35				10 05			10 35			
Bracknell	d	09 41				10 11			10 41			
Martins Heron	d	09 44				10 14			10 44			
Guildford	d		09 17							10 17		
Wanborough	d		09 23							10 23		
Ash ■5	d		09 27							10 27		
Aldershot	a		09 34							10 34		
	d		09 40							10 40		
Ash Vale	d		09 45							10 45		
Frimley	d		09 51							10 51		
Camberley	a		09 55							10 55		
	d		09 55							10 55		
Bagshot	d		10 01							11 01		
Ascot ■3	d	09 49	10a07			10 19			10 49	11a07		
Sunningdale	d	09 52				10 22			10 52			
Longcross	d											
Weybridge	d											
Addlestone	d				10 04							11 04
Chertsey	d				10 07							11 07
Virginia Water	a	10 01			10 12	10 31			11 01			11 12
	d	10 01			10 12	10 31			11 01			11 12
Egham	d	10 05			10 16	10 35			11 05			11 16
Windsor & Eton Riverside	d			09 59			10 32				10 59	
Datchet	d			10 03			10 36				11 03	
Sunnymeads	d			10 06							11 06	
Wraysbury	d			10 10							11 10	
Staines	d	10 11		10 16	10 21	10 41	10 45		11 11		11 16	11 21
Ashford (Surrey)	d			10 19	10 24		10 48				11 19	11 24
Feltham	d	10 17		10 24	10 29	10 47	10 53		11 17		11 24	11 29
Whitton	d			10 28			10 57				11 28	
Kingston	d							10 49				
Hampton Wick	d							10 51				
Teddington	d							10 56				
Fulwell	d											
Strawberry Hill	d							10 59				
Twickenham	a	10 22		10 31		10 52	11 00	11 02	11 22		11 31	
	d	10 23		10 32		10 53	11 01	11 03	11 23		11 32	
St Margarets	d			10 34				11 05			11 34	
Richmond ⊖	d	10 27		10 37		10 57	11 05	11 09	11 27		11 37	
North Sheen	d			10 39				11 11			11 39	
Mortlake	d			10 42				11 13			11 42	
Hounslow	d				10 35							11 35
Isleworth	d				10 38							11 38
Syon Lane	d				10 40							11 40
Brentford	d				10 42							11 42
Kew Bridge	d				10 45							11 45
Chiswick	d				10 47							11 47
Barnes Bridge	d				10 50							11 50
Barnes	d			10 45	10 53			11 16			11 45	11 53
Putney	d	10 34		10 48	10 56	11 04	11 14	11 19	11 34		11 48	11 56
Wandsworth Town	d			10 51	10 59			11 22			11 51	11 59
Clapham Junction ■10	d	10 38		10 53	11 02	11 08	11 18	11 25	11 38		11 53	12 02
Queenstown Rd.(Battersea)	d			10 57	11 05			11 28			11 57	12 05
Vauxhall ⊖	d	10 44		11 00	11 08	11 14	11 24	11 32	11 44		12 00	12 08
London Waterloo ■15 ⊖	a	10 53		11 05	11 13	11 23	11 29	11 41	11 53		12 05	12 13

Station		SW ■	SW	SW	SW ■	SW ■	SW	SW	SW	SW ■	SW	SW
Reading ■7	d	10 51			11 21					11 51		
Earley	d	10 56			11 26					11 56		
Winnersh Triangle	d	10 58			11 28					11 58		
Winnersh	d	11 00			11 30					12 00		
Wokingham	d	11 05			11 35					12 05		
Bracknell	d	11 11			11 41					12 11		
Martins Heron	d	11 14			11 44					12 14		
Guildford	d					11 17						
Wanborough	d					11 23						
Ash ■5	d					11 27						
Aldershot	a					11 34						
	d					11 40						
Ash Vale	d					11 45						
Frimley	d					11 51						
Camberley	a					11 55						
	d					11 55						
Bagshot	d					12 01						
Ascot ■3	d	11 19			11 49	12a07				12 19		
Sunningdale	d	11 22			11 52					12 22		
Longcross	d											
Weybridge	d											
Addlestone	d							12 04				
Chertsey	d							12 07				
Virginia Water	a	11 31			12 01			12 12		12 31		
	d	11 31			12 01			12 12		12 31		
Egham	d	11 35			12 05			12 16		12 35		
Windsor & Eton Riverside	d		11 32				11 59					12 32
Datchet	d		11 36				12 03					12 36
Sunnymeads	d						12 06					
Wraysbury	d						12 10					
Staines	d	11 41	11 45		12 11		12 16	12 21		12 41		12 45
Ashford (Surrey)	d		11 48				12 19	12 24				12 48
Feltham	d	11 47	11 53		12 17		12 24	12 29		12 47		12 53
Whitton	d		11 57				12 28					12 57
Kingston	d			11 49					12 35			
Hampton Wick	d			11 51					12 37			
Teddington	d			11 56					12 40			
Fulwell	d											
Strawberry Hill	d			11 59					12 43		←	
Twickenham	a	11 52	12 00	12 02	12 22		12 31		12 46	12 52	12 46	13 00
	d	11 53	12 01	12 03	12 23		12 32		12 56	12 53	12 56	13 01
St Margarets	d			12 05			12 34		→			
Richmond ⊖	d	11 57	12 05	12 09	12 27		12 37			12 57		13 05
North Sheen	d			12 11			12 39					
Mortlake	d			12 13			12 42					
Hounslow	d							12 35			13 05	
Isleworth	d							12 38			13 08	
Syon Lane	d							12 40			13 10	
Brentford	d							12 42			13 12	
Kew Bridge	d							12 45			13 15	
Chiswick	d							12 47			13 17	
Barnes Bridge	d							12 50			13 20	
Barnes	d			12 16			12 45	12 53			13 23	
Putney	d	12 04	12 14	12 19	12 34		12 48	12 56		13 04	→	13 14
Wandsworth Town	d			12 22			12 51	12 59				
Clapham Junction ■10	d	12 08	12 18	12 25	12 38		12 53	13 02		13 08		13 18
Queenstown Rd.(Battersea)	d			12 28			12 57	13 05				
Vauxhall ⊖	d	12 14	12 24	12 32	12 44		13 00	13 08		13 14		13 24
London Waterloo ■15 ⊖	a	12 23	12 29	12 41	12 53		13 05	13 13		13 23		13 29

Table T149-R

Sundays

7 October to 2 December

Reading, Guildford, Ascot, Weybridge, Windsor, Kingston, Richmond and Hounslow - London

		SW		SW	SW ■	SW ■	SW	SW	SW	SW ■	SW	SW		SW	SW	SW ■	SW ■	SW	SW	SW	SW ■	SW		SW	SW
Reading ■	d				12 21					12 51						13 21					13 51				
Earley	d				12 26					12 56						13 26					13 56				
Winnersh Triangle	d				12 28					12 58						13 28					13 58				
Winnersh	d				12 30					13 00						13 30					14 00				
Wokingham	d				12 35					13 05						13 35					14 05				
Bracknell	d				12 41					13 11						13 41					14 11				
Martins Heron	d				12 44					13 14						13 44					14 14				
Guildford	d					12 17											13 17								
Wanborough	d					12 23											13 23								
Ash ■	d					12 27											13 27								
Aldershot	a					12 35											13 34								
	d					12 40											13 40								
Ash Vale	d					12 45											13 45								
Frimley	d					12 51											13 51								
Camberley	a					12 55											13 55								
	d					12 55											13 55								
Bagshot	d					13 01											14 01								
Ascot ■	d				12 49	13a07				13 19						13 49	14a07				14 19				
Sunningdale	d				12 52					13 22						13 52					14 22				
Longcross	d																								
Weybridge	d																								
Addlestone	d							13 04											14 04						
Chertsey	d							13 07											14 07						
Virginia Water	a				13 01			13 12		13 31						14 01			14 12		14 31				
	d				13 01			13 12		13 31						14 01			14 12		14 31				
Egham	d				13 05			13 16		13 35						14 05			14 16		14 35				
Windsor & Eton Riverside	d						12 59					13 32						14 01						14 32	
Datchet	d						13 03					13 36						14 04						14 36	
Sunnymeads	d						13 06											14 07							
Wraysbury	d						13 10											14 10							
Staines	d				13 11		13 16	13 21		13 41		13 45				14 11		14 16	14 21		14 41			14 45	
Ashford (Surrey)	d						13 19	13 24				13 48						14 19	14 24					14 48	
Feltham	d				13 17		13 24	13 29		13 47		13 53				14 17		14 24	14 29		14 47			14 53	
Whitton	d						13 28					13 57						14 28						14 57	
Kingston	d	12 49							13 35					13 49						14 35					14 49
Hampton Wick	d	12 51							13 37					13 51						14 37					14 51
Teddington	d	12 56							13 40					13 56						14 40					14 56
Fulwell	d																								
Strawberry Hill	d	12 59							13 43		←			13 59						14 43		←			14 59
Twickenham	a	13 02			13 22		13 31		13 46	13 52	13 46	14 00		14 02		14 22		14 31		14 46	14 52	14 46		15 00	15 02
	d	13 03			13 23		13 32		13 56	13 53	13 56	14 01		14 03		14 23		14 32		14 56	14 53	14 56		15 01	15 03
St Margarets	d	13 05					13 34		→					14 05				14 34		→					15 05
Richmond ⊖	d	13 09			13 27		13 37			13 57		14 05		14 08		14 27		14 37			14 57			15 05	15 09
North Sheen	d	13 11					13 39							14 10				14 39							15 11
Mortlake	d	13 13					13 42							14 13				14 42							15 13
Hounslow	d							13 35			14 05								14 35			15 05			
Isleworth	d							13 38			14 08								14 38			15 08			
Syon Lane	d							13 40			14 10								14 40			15 10			
Brentford	d							13 42			14 12								14 42			15 12			
Kew Bridge	d							13 45			14 15								14 45			15 15			
Chiswick	d							13 47			14 17								14 47			15 17			
Barnes Bridge	d			←				13 50			14 20				←				14 50			15 20			
Barnes	d	13 16		13 23			13 45	13 53			14 23			14 16	14 23			14 45	14 53			15 23			15 16
Putney	d	13 19		13 26	13 34		13 48	13 56		14 04	→	14 14		14 19	14 26	14 34		14 48	14 56		15 04	→		15 14	15 19
Wandsworth Town	d	13 22		13 29			13 51	13 59						14 22	14 29			14 51	14 59						15 22
Clapham Junction ■	d	13 25		13 32	13 38		13 54	14 02		14 08		14 18		14 25	14 32	14 38		14 54	15 02		15 08			15 18	15 25
Queenstown Rd.(Battersea)	d	13 28		13 35			13 57	14 05						14 28	14 35			14 57	15 05						15 28
Vauxhall ⊖	d	13 32		13 38	13 44		14 00	14 08		14 14		14 24		14 32	14 38	14 44		15 00	15 08		15 14			15 24	15 32
London Waterloo ■ ⊖	a	13 41		13 43	13 53		14 05	14 13		14 23		14 29		14 41	14 43	14 53		15 05	15 13		15 18			15 29	15 36

Table T149-R

Sundays

7 October to 2 December

Reading, Guildford, Ascot, Weybridge, Windsor, Kingston, Richmond and Hounslow - London

		SW	SW	SW ■	SW ■	SW	SW	SW		SW ■	SW	SW	SW	SW	SW	SW ■	SW ■	SW		SW	SW	SW ■	SW	SW	SW
Reading ■	d			14 21						14 51						15 21						15 51			
Earley	d			14 26						14 56						15 26						15 56			
Winnersh Triangle	d			14 28						14 58						15 28						15 58			
Winnersh	d			14 30						15 00						15 30						16 00			
Wokingham	d			14 35						15 05						15 35						16 05			
Bracknell	d			14 41						15 11						15 41						16 11			
Martins Heron	d			14 44						15 14						15 44						16 14			
Guildford	d				14 17												15 17								
Wanborough	d				14 23												15 23								
Ash ■	d				14 27												15 27								
Aldershot	a				14 34												15 34								
	d				14 40												15 40								
Ash Vale	d				14 45												15 45								
Frimley	d				14 51												15 51								
Camberley	a				14 55												15 55								
	d				14 55												15 55								
Bagshot	d				15 01												16 01								
Ascot ■	d			14 49	15a07					15 19						15 49	16a07					16 19			
Sunningdale	d			14 52						15 22						15 52						16 22			
Longcross	d																								
Weybridge	d																								
Addlestone	d						15 04													16 04					
Chertsey	d						15 07													16 07					
Virginia Water	a			15 01			15 12			15 31						16 01				16 12		16 31			
	d			15 01			15 12			15 31						16 01				16 12		16 31			
Egham	d			15 05			15 16			15 35						16 05				16 16		16 35			
Windsor & Eton Riverside	d					14 59						15 32						15 59						16 32	
Datchet	d					15 03						15 36						16 03						16 36	
Sunnymeads	d					15 06												16 06							
Wraysbury	d					15 10												16 10							
Staines	d			15 11		15 16	15 21			15 41		15 45				16 11		16 16		16 21		16 41		16 45	
Ashford (Surrey)	d					15 19	15 24					15 48						16 19		16 24				16 48	
Feltham	d			15 17		15 24	15 29			15 47		15 53				16 17		16 24		16 29		16 47		16 53	
Whitton	d		15 01			15 28						15 57			16 01			16 28						16 57	
Kingston	d							15 35					15 49								16 35				16 49
Hampton Wick	d							15 37					15 51								16 37				16 51
Teddington	d							15 40					15 56								16 40				16 56
Fulwell	d																								
Strawberry Hill	d							15 43			←		15 59								16 43		←		16 59
Twickenham	a		15 04	15 22		15 31		15 46		15 52	15 46	16 00	16 02		16 04	16 22		16 31			16 46	16 52	16 46	17 00	17 02
	d			15 23		15 32		15 56		15 53	15 56	16 01	16 03			16 23		16 32			16 56	16 53	16 56	17 01	17 03
St Margarets	d					15 34		→					16 05					16 34			→				17 05
Richmond ⊖	d			15 27		15 37				15 57		16 05	16 09			16 27		16 37				16 57		17 05	17 09
North Sheen	d					15 39							16 11					16 39							17 11
Mortlake	d					15 42							16 13					16 42							17 13
Hounslow	d						15 35				16 05									16 35			17 05		
Isleworth	d						15 38				16 08									16 38			17 08		
Syon Lane	d						15 40				16 10									16 40			17 10		
Brentford	d						15 42				16 12									16 42			17 12		
Kew Bridge	d						15 45				16 15									16 45			17 15		
Chiswick	d						15 47				16 17									16 47			17 17		
Barnes Bridge	d	←					15 50				16 20			←						16 50			17 20		
Barnes	d	15 23				15 45	15 53				16 23		16 16	16 23				16 45		16 53			17 23		17 16
Putney	d	15 26		15 34		15 48	15 56			16 04	→	16 14	16 19	16 26		16 34		16 48		16 56		17 04	→	17 14	17 19
Wandsworth Town	d	15 29				15 51	15 59						16 22	16 29				16 51		16 59					17 22
Clapham Junction ■	d	15 32		15 38		15 54	16 02			16 08		16 18	16 25	16 32		16 38		16 54		17 02		17 08		17 18	17 25
Queenstown Rd.(Battersea)	d	15 35				15 57	16 05						16 28	16 35				16 57		17 05					17 28
Vauxhall ⊖	d	15 38		15 44		16 00	16 08			16 14		16 24	16 32	16 38		16 44		17 00		17 08		17 14		17 24	17 32
London Waterloo ■ ⊖	a	15 43		15 48		16 05	16 13			16 18		16 29	16 36	16 43		16 48		17 05		17 13		17 18		17 29	17 36

Table T149-R

Sundays

7 October to 2 December

Reading, Guildford, Ascot, Weybridge, Windsor, Kingston, Richmond and Hounslow - London

		SW	SW	SW ■	SW ■	SW	SW	SW	SW ■	SW	SW	SW	SW	SW	SW ■	SW ■	SW	SW	SW	SW ■	SW	SW
Reading ■	d			16 21					16 51						17 21					17 51		
Earley	d			16 26					16 56						17 26					17 56		
Winnersh Triangle	d			16 28					16 58						17 28					17 58		
Winnersh	d			16 30					17 00						17 30					18 00		
Wokingham	d			16 35					17 05						17 35					18 05		
Bracknell	d			16 41					17 11						17 41					18 11		
Martins Heron	d			16 44					17 14						17 44					18 14		
Guildford	d				16 17											17 17						
Wanborough	d				16 23											17 23						
Ash ■	d				16 27											17 27						
Aldershot	a				16 34											17 34						
	d				16 40											17 40						
Ash Vale	d				16 45											17 45						
Frimley	d				16 51											17 51						
Camberley	a				16 55											17 55						
	d				16 55											17 55						
Bagshot	d				17 01											18 01						
Ascot ■	d			16 49	17a07				17 19						17 49	18a07				18 19		
Sunningdale	d			16 52					17 22						17 52					18 22		
Longcross	d																					
Weybridge	d																					
Addlestone	d						17 04											18 04				
Chertsey	d						17 07											18 07				
Virginia Water	a			17 01			17 12		17 31						18 01			18 12		18 31		
	d			17 01			17 12		17 31						18 01			18 12		18 31		
Egham	d			17 05			17 16		17 36						18 05			18 16		18 35		
Windsor & Eton Riverside	d					16 59					17 32						17 59					18 32
Datchet	d					17 03					17 36						18 03					18 36
Sunnymeads	d					17 06											18 06					
Wraysbury	d					17 10											18 10					
Staines	d			17 11		17 16	17 21		17 41		17 45				18 11		18 16	18 21		18 41		18 45
Ashford (Surrey)	d					17 19	17 24				17 48						18 19	18 24				18 48
Feltham	d			17 17		17 24	17 29		17 47		17 53				18 17		18 24	18 29		18 47		18 53
Whitton	d		17 01			17 28					17 57			18 01			18 28					18 57
Kingston	d							17 35				17 49							18 35			
Hampton Wick	d							17 37				17 51							18 37			
Teddington	d							17 40				17 56							18 40			
Fulwell	d																					
Strawberry Hill	d							17 43		←		17 59							18 43		←	
Twickenham	a		17 04	17 22		17 31		17 46	17 52	17 46	18 00	18 02		18 04	18 22		18 31		18 46	18 52	18 46	19 00
	d			17 23		17 32		17 56	17 53	17 56	18 01	18 03			18 23		18 32		18 56	18 53	18 56	19 01
St Margarets	d					17 34		→				18 05					18 34		→			
Richmond	⊖ d			17 27		17 37			17 57		18 05	18 09			18 27		18 37			18 57		19 05
North Sheen	d					17 39						18 11					18 39					
Mortlake	d					17 42						18 13					18 42					
Hounslow	d						17 35			18 05								18 35			19 05	
Isleworth	d						17 38			18 08								18 38			19 08	
Syon Lane	d						17 40			18 10								18 40			19 10	
Brentford	d						17 42			18 12								18 42			19 12	
Kew Bridge	d						17 45			18 15								18 45			19 15	
Chiswick	d						17 47			18 17								18 47			19 17	
Barnes Bridge	d	←					17 50			18 20			←					18 50			19 20	
Barnes	d	17 23				17 45	17 53			18 23		18 16	18 23				18 45	18 53			19 23	
Putney	d	17 26		17 34		17 48	17 56		18 04	→	18 14	18 19	18 26		18 34		18 48	18 56		19 04	→	19 14
Wandsworth Town	d	17 29				17 51	17 59					18 22	18 29				18 51	18 59				
Clapham Junction ■	d	17 32		17 38		17 54	18 02		18 08		18 18	18 25	18 32		18 38		18 54	19 02		19 08		19 18
Queenstown Rd.(Battersea)	d	17 35				17 57	18 05					18 28	18 35				18 57	19 05				
Vauxhall	⊖ d	17 38		17 44		18 00	18 08		18 14		18 24	18 32	18 38		18 44		19 00	19 08		19 14		19 24
London Waterloo ■	⊖ a	17 43		17 48		18 05	18 13		18 18		18 29	18 36	18 43		18 48		19 05	19 13		19 18		19 29

Table T149-R

Sundays

7 October to 2 December

Reading, Guildford, Ascot, Weybridge, Windsor, Kingston, Richmond and Hounslow - London

		SW	SW	SW	SW ■	SW ■	SW	SW	SW	SW ■	SW	SW	SW	SW	SW	SW ■	SW ■	SW	SW	SW	SW ■	SW	SW
Reading ■	d				18 21					18 51						19 21					19 51		
Earley	d				18 26					18 56						19 26					19 56		
Winnersh Triangle	d				18 28					18 58						19 28					19 58		
Winnersh	d				18 30					19 00						19 30					20 00		
Wokingham	d				18 35					19 05						19 35					20 05		
Bracknell	d				18 41					19 11						19 41					20 11		
Martins Heron	d				18 44					19 14						19 44					20 14		
Guildford	d					18 17											19 17						
Wanborough	d					18 23											19 23						
Ash ■	d					18 27											19 27						
Aldershot	a					18 34											19 34						
	d					18 40											19 40						
Ash Vale	d					18 45											19 45						
Frimley	d					18 51											19 51						
Camberley	a					18 55											19 55						
	d					18 55											19 55						
Bagshot	d					19 01											20 01						
Ascot ■	d				18 49	19a07				19 19						19 49	20a07				20 19		
Sunningdale	d				18 52					19 22						19 52					20 22		
Longcross	d																						
Weybridge	d																						
Addlestone	d							19 04											20 04				
Chertsey	d							19 07											20 07				
Virginia Water	a				19 01			19 12		19 31						20 01			20 12		20 31		
	d				19 01			19 12		19 31						20 01			20 12		20 31		
Egham	d				19 05			19 16		19 35						20 05			20 16		20 35		
Windsor & Eton Riverside	d						18 59					19 32						19 59					20 32
Datchet	d						19 03					19 36						20 03					20 36
Sunnymeads	d						19 06											20 06					
Wraysbury	d						19 10											20 10					
Staines	d				19 11		19 16	19 21		19 41		19 45				20 11		20 16	20 21		20 41		20 45
Ashford (Surrey)	d						19 19	19 24				19 48						20 19	20 24				20 48
Feltham	d				19 17		19 24	19 29		19 47		19 53				20 17		20 24	20 29		20 47		20 53
Whitton	d			19 01			19 28					19 57			20 01			20 28					20 57
Kingston	d	18 49							19 35				19 49							20 35			
Hampton Wick	d	18 51							19 37				19 51							20 37			
Teddington	d	18 56							19 40				19 56							20 40			
Fulwell	d																						
Strawberry Hill	d	18 59							19 43		←		19 59							20 43		←	
Twickenham	a	19 02		19 04	19 22		19 31		19 46	19 52	19 46	20 00	20 02		20 04	20 22		20 31		20 46	20 52	20 46	21 00
	d	19 03			19 23		19 32		19 56	19 53	19 56	20 01	20 03			20 23		20 32		20 56	20 53	20 56	21 01
St Margarets	d	19 05					19 34		→				20 05					20 34		→			
Richmond	⊖ d	19 09			19 27		19 37			19 57		20 05	20 09			20 27		20 37			20 57		21 05
North Sheen	d	19 11					19 39						20 11					20 39					
Mortlake	d	19 13					19 42						20 13					20 42					
Hounslow	d							19 35			20 05								20 35			21 05	
Isleworth	d							19 38			20 08								20 38			21 08	
Syon Lane	d							19 40			20 10								20 40			21 10	
Brentford	d							19 42			20 12								20 42			21 12	
Kew Bridge	d							19 45			20 15								20 45			21 15	
Chiswick	d							19 47			20 17								20 47			21 17	
Barnes Bridge	d		←					19 50			20 20			←					20 50			21 20	
Barnes	d	19 16	19 23				19 45	19 53			20 23		20 16	20 23				20 45	20 53			21 23	
Putney	d	19 19	19 26		19 34		19 48	19 56		20 04	→	20 14	20 19	20 26		20 34		20 48	20 56		21 04	→	21 14
Wandsworth Town	d	19 22	19 29				19 51	19 59					20 22	20 29				20 51	20 59				
Clapham Junction ■	d	19 25	19 32		19 38		19 54	20 02		20 08		20 18	20 25	20 32		20 38		20 54	21 02		21 08		21 18
Queenstown Rd.(Battersea)	d	19 28	19 35				19 57	20 05					20 28	20 35				20 57	21 05				
Vauxhall	⊖ d	19 32	19 38		19 44		20 00	20 08		20 14		20 24	20 32	20 38		20 44		21 00	21 08		21 14		21 24
London Waterloo ■	⊖ a	19 36	19 43		19 48		20 05	20 13		20 18		20 29	20 36	20 43		20 48		21 05	21 13		21 18		21 29

Table T149-R

Sundays

7 October to 2 December

Reading, Guildford, Ascot, Weybridge, Windsor, Kingston, Richmond and Hounslow - London

		SW	SW	SW	SW ■	SW ■	SW	SW	SW	SW ■	SW	SW	SW	SW	SW	SW ■	SW ■	SW	SW	SW	SW ■	SW	SW
Reading ■	d				20 21					20 51						21 21					21 51		
Earley	d				20 26					20 56						21 26					21 56		
Winnersh Triangle	d				20 28					20 58						21 28					21 58		
Winnersh	d				20 30					21 00						21 30					22 00		
Wokingham	d				20 35					21 05						21 35					22 05		
Bracknell	d				20 41					21 11						21 41					22 11		
Martins Heron	d				20 44					21 14						21 44					22 14		
Guildford	d					20 17											21 17						
Wanborough	d					20 23											21 23						
Ash ■	d					20 27											21 27						
Aldershot	a					20 34											21 34						
	d					20 40											21 40						
Ash Vale	d					20 45											21 45						
Frimley	d					20 51											21 51						
Camberley	a					20 55											21 55						
	d					20 55											21 55						
Bagshot	d					21 01											22 01						
Ascot ■	d				20 49	21a07				21 19						21 49	22a07				22 19		
Sunningdale	d				20 52					21 22						21 52					22 22		
Longcross	d																						
Weybridge	d																						
Addlestone	d							21 04											22 04				
Chertsey	d							21 07											22 07				
Virginia Water	a				21 01			21 12		21 31						22 01			22 12		22 31		
	d				21 01			21 12		21 31						22 01			22 12		22 31		
Egham	d				21 05			21 16		21 35						22 05			22 16		22 35		
Windsor & Eton Riverside	d						21 01					21 32						22 01					
Datchet	d						21 04					21 36						22 04					
Sunnymeads	d						21 07											22 07					
Wraysbury	d						21 10											22 10					
Staines	d				21 11		21 16	21 21		21 41		21a45				22 11		22 16	22 21		22 41		
Ashford (Surrey)	d						21 19	21 24										22 19	22 24				
Feltham	d				21 17		21 24	21 29		21 47						22 17		22 24	22 29		22 47		
Whitton	d			21 01			21 28								22 01			22 28					
Kingston	d	20 49							21 35				21 49							22 35			22 49
Hampton Wick	d	20 51							21 37				21 51							22 37			22 51
Teddington	d	20 56							21 40				21 56							22 40			22 56
Fulwell	d																						
Strawberry Hill	d	20 59							21 43		←		21 59							22 43		←	22 59
Twickenham	a	21 02		21 04	21 22		21 31		21 46	21 52	21 46		22 02		22 04	22 22		22 31		22 46	22 52	22 46	23 02
	d	21 03			21 23		21 32		21 56	21 53	21 56		22 03			22 23		22 32		22 56	22 53	22 56	23 03
St Margarets	d	21 05					21 34		→				22 05					22 34		→			23 05
Richmond ⊖	d	21 09			21 27		21 37			21 57			22 09			22 27		22 37			22 57		23 09
North Sheen	d	21 11					21 39						22 11					22 39					23 11
Mortlake	d	21 13					21 42						22 13					22 42					23 13
Hounslow	d							21 35			22 05								22 35			23 05	
Isleworth	d							21 38			22 08								22 38			23 08	
Syon Lane	d							21 40			22 10								22 40			23 10	
Brentford	d							21 42			22 12								22 42			23 12	
Kew Bridge	d							21 45			22 15								22 45			23 15	
Chiswick	d							21 47			22 17								22 47			23 17	
Barnes Bridge	d		←					21 50			22 20			←					22 50			23 20	
Barnes	d	21 16	21 23				21 45	21 53			22 23		22 16	22 23				22 45	22 53			23 23	23 16
Putney	d	21 19	21 26		21 34		21 48	21 56		22 04	→		22 19	22 26		22 34		22 48	22 56		23 04	→	23 19
Wandsworth Town	d	21 22	21 29				21 51	21 59					22 22	22 29				22 51	22 59				23 22
Clapham Junction ■	d	21 25	21 32		21 38		21 54	22 02		22 08			22 25	22 32		22 38		22 54	23 02		23 08		23 25
Queenstown Rd.(Battersea)	d	21 28	21 35				21 57	22 05					22 28	22 35				22 57	23 05				23 28
Vauxhall ⊖	d	21 32	21 38		21 44		22 00	22 08		22 14			22 32	22 38		22 44		23 00	23 08		23 14		23 32
London Waterloo ■ ⊖	a	21 36	21 43		21 48		22 05	22 13		22 18			22 36	22 43		22 48		23 05	23 13		23 18		23 36

Table T149-R

Sundays

7 October to 2 December

Reading, Guildford, Ascot, Weybridge, Windsor, Kingston, Richmond and Hounslow - London

		SW	SW	SW ■	SW ■	SW	SW	SW ■	SW	SW ■	SW
Reading ■	d			22 21						22 54	
Earley	d			22 26						22 59	
Winnersh Triangle	d			22 28						23 01	
Winnersh	d			22 30						23 03	
Wokingham	d			22 35						23 08	
Bracknell	d			22 41						23 14	
Martins Heron	d			22 44						23 17	
Guildford	d				22 17			23 17			
Wanborough	d				22 23			23 23			
Ash ■	d				22 27			23 27			
Aldershot	a				22 34			23 34			
	d				22 40						
Ash Vale	d				22 45						
Frimley	d				22 51						
Camberley	a				22 55						
	d				22 55						
Bagshot	d				23 01						
Ascot ■	d			22 49	23a07					23 22	
Sunningdale	d			22 52						23 25	
Longcross	d										
Weybridge	d										
Addlestone	d						23 04				
Chertsey	d						23 07				
Virginia Water	a			23 01			23 12			23 31	
	d			23 01			23 12			23 31	
Egham	d			23 05			23 16			23 35	
Windsor & Eton Riverside	d					23 01					
Datchet	d					23 04					
Sunnymeads	d					23 07					
Wraysbury	d					23 10					
Staines	d			23 11		23 16	23 21			23 41	
Ashford (Surrey)	d					23 19	23 24				
Feltham	d			23 17		23 24	23 29			23 47	
Whitton	d		23 01			23 28					
Kingston	d								23 35		23 47
Hampton Wick	d								23 37		23 49
Teddington	d								23 40		23 51
Fulwell	d										
Strawberry Hill	d								23 43		23a54
Twickenham	a		23 04	23 22		23 31			23 46	23 52	
	d			23 23		23 32				23 54	
St Margarets	d					23 34					
Richmond ⊖	d			23 27		23 37				23 58	
North Sheen	d					23 39					
Mortlake	d					23 42					
Hounslow	d						23 35				
Isleworth	d						23 38				
Syon Lane	d						23 40				
Brentford	d						23 42				
Kew Bridge	d						23 45				
Chiswick	d						23 47				
Barnes Bridge	d	←					23 50				
Barnes	d	23 23				23 45	23 53				
Putney	d	23 26		23 34		23 48	23 56			00 05	
Wandsworth Town	d	23 29				23 51	23 59				
Clapham Junction ■	d	23 32		23 38		23 54	00 02			00 09	
Queenstown Rd.(Battersea)	d	23 35				23 57	00 05				
Vauxhall ⊖	d	23 38		23 44		23 59	00 08			00 15	
London Waterloo ■ ⊖	a	23 43		23 48		00 05	00 13			00 19	

Table T152-F

Mondays to Fridays

21 May to 5 October

London - Chessington South, Dorking, Guildford, Shepperton and Hampton Court

Miles	Miles	Miles	Miles	Miles	Station		TL MO	SW MO	SW MO	SW MX	SW MX	SW MX	SW MX	SW MO	SW MX	SW MX	SW MX	SW	SW ◇1	SW	SW ◇1	SW	SW	SW
							A	B	B	B	B	B	B				C		D		D			C
0	—	—	—	0	**London Waterloo** ⊖	d								00 01	00 09	00 15	00 27	00 42	05 00	05 12	05 20		05 47	05 50
1¼	—	—	—	1¼	Vauxhall ⊖	d							00 01	00 04	00 13	00 19	00 31	00 46	05 04	05 16	05 24		05 51	05 54
4	—	—	—	4	**Clapham Junction**	d							00 06	00 09	00 20	00 26	00 37	00 51	05 11	05 21	05 29		05 56	05 59
5½	—	—	—	5½	Earlsfield	d					00 02		00 09	00 12	00 24	00 29	00s41		05 14	05 24	05 32		05 59	06 02
7¼	—	—	—	7¼	**Wimbledon** ⊖ ⇌	d					00 06		00 13	00 16	00 28	00 33	00 45	01 05	05 18	05 28	05 36	05 49	06 03	06 06
8¾	—	0	0	8¾	Raynes Park	d						00 01	00 16	00 19		00 36	00 48	01 08		05 31			06 06	
—	—	1	1	—	Motspur Park	d						00 04				00 39							06 09	
—	—	—	2½	—	Malden Manor	d																		
—	—	—	3½	—	Tolworth	d																		
—	—	—	4½	—	Chessington North	d																		
—	—	—	5¼	—	**Chessington South**	a																		
—	—	2	—	—	Worcester Park	d						00 06				00 41							06 11	
—	—	3¼	—	—	Stoneleigh	d						00 09				00 44							06 14	
—	—	4¼	—	—	Ewell West	d			00 03			00 12				00 47							06 17	
—	—	5½	—	—	**Epsom** 182	a			00 06			00 16				00 50							06 20	
—	—	—	—	—		d						00 19											06 21	
—	—	7½	—	—	Ashtead 182	d						00 23											06 25	
—	0	9¼	—	—	Leatherhead 182	d	00 02					00 26											06 28	
—	—	12½	—	—	Box Hill & Westhumble 182	d	00 07																	
—	—	13¾	—	—	**Dorking** 182	a	00 09																	
9¾	—	—	—	9¾	New Malden	d							00 19	00 22			00 50	01 11		05 34				
—	—	—	—	11¼	Norbiton	d							00 22					01 14		05 37				
—	—	—	—	12	Kingston	a							00 25					01 17		05 40				
—	—	—	—	—		d							00 25					01 17		05 40				
—	—	—	—	12½	Hampton Wick	d							00 27					01s22		05 42				
—	—	—	—	13¾	Teddington	d							00 30					01s25		05 45				
—	—	—	—	—	Strawberry Hill	a												01 28						
—	—	—	—	14¾	Fulwell	d							00 34							05 49				
—	—	—	—	16½	Hampton	d							00 38							05 53				
—	—	—	—	18¼	Kempton Park	d							00 41											
—	—	—	—	18¾	Sunbury	d							00 43							05 57				
—	—	—	—	19¾	Upper Halliford	d							00 45							05 59				
—	—	—	—	20¾	**Shepperton**	a							00 50							06 04				
11	—	—	—	—	Berrylands	d								00 25			00s53							
12	—	—	0	—	**Surbiton**	d				00 05	00 14			00 31	00 35		00s56		05 26		05 44	05 57		06a13
—	—	—	2	—	Thames Ditton	d				00 09														
—	—	—	3	—	**Hampton Court**	a				00 12														
14	—	—	—	—	Hinchley Wood	d					00 18			00 35								06 01		
15½	—	—	—	—	Claygate	d					00 20			00 38								06 04		
17	—	—	—	—	Oxshott	d					00 24			00 41								06 07		
19	—	—	—	—	Cobham & Stoke D'abernon	d					00 27			00 45								06 13		
—	2½	—	—	—	Bookham	d						00 31											06 33	
21¼	4¾	—	—	—	Effingham Junction	d					00 32	00 36		00 49								06 19	06 37	
22¾	—	—	—	—	Horsley	d					00 34	00 39		00 52								06 22		
25½	—	—	—	—	Clandon	d					00 39	00 44		00 57								06 27		
28¾	—	—	—	—	London Road (Guildford)	d		00 03			00 44	00 49		01 02								06 32	06 46	
30	—	—	—	—	**Guildford**	a		00 07			00 50	00 53		01 06	01 08				06 00		06 24	06 37	06 50	

A From London Victoria
B From London Waterloo
C To Woking
D To Portsmouth Harbour

The xx27 and xx57 London Waterloo to Strawberry Hill services continue to London Waterloo via Richmond

Table T152-F

Mondays to Fridays

21 May to 5 October

London - Chessington South, Dorking, Guildford, Shepperton and Hampton Court

Station		SW	SW	SW	SW	SW	SW	SW	TL	SW	SW	SW	SW	SW	SW	SW	SW	SW	SW	SW	SW	SW
			A	A					B			A									A	
London Waterloo ⊖	d				06 03	06 06	06 12	06 16		06 20	06 24	06 27	06 33	06 36	06 39		06 42	06 47	06 50	06 54	06 57	07 03
Vauxhall ⊖	d				06 07	06 10	06 16	06 20		06 24	06 28	06 31	06 37	06 40	06 43		06 46	06 51	06 54	06 58	07 01	07 07
Clapham Junction	d				06 12	06 15	06 21	06 25		06 29	06 33	06 36	06 42	06 45	06 48		06 51	06 56	06 59	07 03	07 06	07 12
Earlsfield	d				06 15	06 18	06 24	06 28		06 32	06 36	06 39	06 45	06 48	06 51		06 54	06 59	07 02	07 06	07 09	07 15
Wimbledon ⊖ ⇌	d	06 10		06 13	06 19	06 22	06 28	06 33		06 36	06 40	06 43	06 49	06 52	06 55		06 58	07 03	07 06	07 10	07 13	07 19
Raynes Park	d	06 13		06 16		06 25	06 31	06 35			06 43	06 46		06 55	06 58		07 01	07 06		07 13	07 16	
Motspur Park	d	06 16						06 39			06 46							07 09		07 16		
Malden Manor	d	06 19						06 41										07 12				
Tolworth	d	06 22						06 45										07 15				
Chessington North	d	06 25						06 48										07 18				
Chessington South	a	06 28						06 52										07 23				
Worcester Park	d										06 48				07 02					07 18		
Stoneleigh	d										06 51				07 05					07 21		
Ewell West	d										06 54				07 08					07 24		
Epsom 182	a										06 57				07 11					07 27		
	d								06 39		06 58				07 12					07 28		
Ashtead 182	d										07 02				07 16					07 32		
Leatherhead 182	d								06 45		07 05				07 19					07 35		
Box Hill & Westhumble 182	d																					
Dorking 182	a										07 12									07 42		
New Malden	d			06 19		06 28	06 34					06 49		06 58			07 04				07 19	
Norbiton	d			06 22			06 37					06 52					07 07				07 22	
Kingston	a			06 25			06 40					06 55					07 10				07 25	
	d		05 59	06 29			06 40					06 59					07 10				07 29	
Hampton Wick	d		06 01	06 31			06 42					07 01					07 12				07 31	
Teddington	d		06 05	06 35			06 45					07 05					07 15				07 35	
Strawberry Hill	a		06 08	06 38								07 08									07 38	
Fulwell	d						06 49									07 07	07 19					
Hampton	d						06 53									07 10	07 23					
Kempton Park	d															07 14						
Sunbury	d						06 57									07 15	07 27					
Upper Halliford	d						06 59									07 17	07 29					
Shepperton	a						07 05									07 23	07 35					
Berrylands	d					06 30								07 00								
Surbiton	d				06 27	06 35				06 44			06 57	07 05					07 14			07 27
Thames Ditton	d					06 39								07 09								
Hampton Court	a					06 42								07 12								
Hinchley Wood	d				06 31								07 01									07 31
Claygate	d				06 34								07 04									07 34
Oxshott	d				06 37								07 07									07 37
Cobham & Stoke D'abernon	d				06 41								07 11									07 41
Bookham	d								06 50						07 24							
Effingham Junction	d				06 45				06 54				07 15		07a28							07 45
Horsley	d				06 48								07 18									07 48
Clandon	d				06 53								07 23									07 53
London Road (Guildford)	d				06 58								07 28									07 58
Guildford	a				07 04				07 06	07 19			07 34						07 47			08 04

A To London Waterloo
B From London Bridge

The xx27 and xx57 London Waterloo to Strawberry Hill services continue to London Waterloo via Richmond

Table T152-F

Mondays to Fridays

21 May to 5 October

London - Chessington South, Dorking, Guildford, Shepperton and Hampton Court

		SW	SW	SW A	SW	SW	SW B	SW	SW C	SW	SW	SW	SW	SW C	SW	SW	SW	SW C	SW	SW	SW	SW	SW
London Waterloo ⊖	d	07 06	07 09		07 12	07 17	07 20	07 24	07 27	07 33	07 36	07 39	07 42		07 47	07 50	07 54	07 57	08 03	08 06	08 09	08 12	08 17
Vauxhall ⊖	d	07 10	07 13		07 16	07 21	07 24	07 28	07 31	07 37	07 40	07 43	07 46		07 51	07 54	07 58	08 01	08 07	08 10	08 13	08 16	08 21
Clapham Junction	d	07 15	07 18		07 21	07 26	07 29	07 33	07 36	07 42	07 45	07 48	07 51	07 54	07 56	07 59	08 03	08 06	08 12	08 15	08 18	08 21	08 26
Earlsfield	d	07 18	07 21		07 24	07 29	07 32	07 36	07 39	07 45	07 48	07 51	07 54		07 59	08 02	08 06	08 09	08 15	08 18	08 21	08 24	08 29
Wimbledon ⊖	d	07 22	07 25		07 28	07 33	07 36	07 40	07 43	07 49	07 52	07 55	07 58		08 03	08 06	08 10	08 13	08 19	08 22	08 25	08 28	08 33
Raynes Park	d	07 25	07 28		07 31	07 36		07 43	07 46		07 55	07 58	08 01		08 06		08 13	08 16		08 25	08 28	08 31	08 36
Motspur Park	d		07 31			07 39		07 46				08 01			08 09		08 16				08 31		08 39
Malden Manor	d					07 42									08 12								08 42
Tolworth	d					07 45									08 15								08 45
Chessington North	d					07 48									08 18								08 48
Chessington South	a					07 53									08 24								08 53
Worcester Park	d		07 33					07 48				08 03					08 18				08 33		
Stoneleigh	d		07 36					07 51				08 06					08 21				08 36		
Ewell West	d		07 39					07 54				08 09					08 24				08 39		
Epsom 182	a		07 42					07 58				08 13					08 27				08 42		
	d							07 58				08 17					08 28				08 47		
Ashtead 182	d							08 02				08 21					08 32				08 51		
Leatherhead 182	d							08 05				08 24					08 35				08 54		
Box Hill & Westhumble 182	d																						
Dorking 182	a							08 12									08 42						
New Malden	d	07 28			07 34				07 49		07 58		08 04					08 19		08 28		08 34	
Norbiton	d				07 37				07 52				08 07					08 22				08 37	
Kingston	a				07 40				07 55				08 10	08 23				08 25				08 40	
	d				07 40				07 59				08 10					08 29				08 40	
Hampton Wick	d				07 42				08 01				08 12					08 31				08 42	
Teddington	d				07 45				08 05				08 15					08 35				08 45	
Strawberry Hill	a								08 08									08 38					
Fulwell	d			07 33	07 49								08 19									08 49	
Hampton	d			07 36	07 53								08 23									08 53	
Kempton Park	d			07 40	07 56								08 26									08 56	
Sunbury	d			07 41	07 58								08 28									08 58	
Upper Halliford	d			07 44	08 00								08 30									09 00	
Shepperton	a			07 49	08 05								08 35									09 05	
Berrylands	d	07 30									08 00									08 30			
Surbiton	d	07 35					07a43			07 57	08 05					08 14			08 27	08 35			
Thames Ditton	d	07 39									08 09									08 39			
Hampton Court	a	07 42									08 12									08 42			
Hinchley Wood	d									08 01									08 31				
Claygate	d									08 04									08 34				
Oxshott	d									08 07									08 37				
Cobham & Stoke D'abernon	d									08 11									08 41				
Bookham	d											08 29									08 59		
Effingham Junction	d									08 15		08 33							08 45		09 03		
Horsley	d									08 18		08 36							08 48		09 06		
Clandon	d									08 23		08 41							08 53		09 11		
London Road (Guildford)	d									08 28		08 46							08 58		09 16		
Guildford	a									08 34		08 50				08 50			09 04		09 20		

A From Twickenham **B** To Woking **C** To London Waterloo

The xx27 and xx57 London Waterloo to Strawberry Hill services continue to London Waterloo via Richmond

Table T152-F

Mondays to Fridays

21 May to 5 October

London - Chessington South, Dorking, Guildford, Shepperton and Hampton Court

		SW A	SW	SW B	SW	SW	SW	SW	SW	SW A	SW	SW B	SW	SW	SW	SW	SW	SW A	SW	SW B	SW	SW
London Waterloo ⊖	d	08 20	08 24	08 27	08 33	08 36	08 39	08 42	08 47	08 50	08 54	08 57	09 03	09 06	09 09	09 12	09 17	09 20	09 24	09 27	09 33	09 36
Vauxhall ⊖	d	08 24	08 28	08 31	08 37	08 40	08 43	08 46	08 51	08 54	08 58	09 01	09 07	09 10	09 13	09 16	09 21	09 24	09 28	09 31	09 37	09 40
Clapham Junction	d	08 29	08 33	08 36	08 42	08 45	08 48	08 51	08 56	08 59	09 03	09 06	09 12	09 15	09 18	09 21	09 26	09 29	09 33	09 36	09 42	09 45
Earlsfield	d	08 32	08 36	08 39	08 45	08 48	08 51	08 54	08 59	09 02	09 06	09 09	09 15	09 18	09 21	09 24	09 29	09 32	09 36	09 39	09 45	09 48
Wimbledon ⊖	d	08 36	08 40	08 43	08 49	08 52	08 55	08 58	09 03	09 06	09 10	09 13	09 19	09 22	09 25	09 28	09 33	09 36	09 40	09 43	09 49	09 52
Raynes Park	d		08 43	08 46		08 55	08 58	09 01	09 06		09 13	09 16		09 25	09 28	09 31	09 36		09 43	09 46		09 55
Motspur Park	d		08 46				09 01		09 09		09 16				09 31		09 39		09 46			
Malden Manor	d								09 12								09 42					
Tolworth	d								09 15								09 45					
Chessington North	d								09 18								09 48					
Chessington South	a								09 23								09 53					
Worcester Park	d		08 48				09 03				09 18				09 33				09 48			
Stoneleigh	d		08 51				09 06				09 21				09 36				09 51			
Ewell West	d		08 54				09 09				09 24				09 39				09 54			
Epsom 182	a		08 57				09 16				09 27				09 42				09 57			
	d		08 58				09 17				09 28				09 47				09 58			
Ashtead 182	d		09 02				09 21				09 32				09 51				10 02			
Leatherhead 182	d		09 05				09 24				09 35				09 54				10 05			
Box Hill & Westhumble 182	d																					
Dorking 182	a		09 12								09 42								10 12			
New Malden	d			08 49		08 58		09 04				09 19		09 28		09 34				09 49		09 58
Norbiton	d			08 52				09 07				09 22				09 37				09 52		
Kingston	a			08 55				09 10				09 25				09 40				09 55		
	d			08 59				09 10				09 29				09 40				09 59		
Hampton Wick	d			09 01				09 12				09 31				09 42				10 01		
Teddington	d			09 05				09 15				09 35				09 45				10 05		
Strawberry Hill	a			09 08								09 38								10 08		
Fulwell	d							09 19								09 49						
Hampton	d							09 23								09 53						
Kempton Park	d							09 26								09 56						
Sunbury	d							09 28								09 58						
Upper Halliford	d							09 30								10 00						
Shepperton	a							09 35								10 05						
Berrylands	d					09 00								09 30								10 00
Surbiton	d	08a43			08 57	09 05				09a13			09 27	09 35				09a43			09 57	10 05
Thames Ditton	d					09 09								09 39								10 09
Hampton Court	a					09 12								09 42								10 12
Hinchley Wood	d				09 01								09 31								10 01	
Claygate	d				09 04								09 34								10 04	
Oxshott	d				09 07								09 37								10 07	
Cobham & Stoke D'abernon	d				09 11								09 41								10 11	
Bookham	d						09 29								09 59							
Effingham Junction	d				09 15		09 33						09 45		10 03						10 15	
Horsley	d				09 18		09 36						09 48		10 06						10 18	
Clandon	d				09 23		09 41						09 53		10 11						10 23	
London Road (Guildford)	d				09 28		09 46						09 58		10 16						10 28	
Guildford	a				09 35		09 50						10 04		10 20						10 34	

A To Woking **B** To London Waterloo

The xx27 and xx57 London Waterloo to Strawberry Hill services continue to London Waterloo via Richmond

Table T152-F

Mondays to Fridays

21 May to 5 October

London - Chessington South, Dorking, Guildford, Shepperton and Hampton Court

		SW	SW	SW	SW A	SW	SW B	SW	SW	SW	SW	SW	SW A	SW	SW B	SW	SW	SW	SW	SW	SW A	SW	SW B
London Waterloo 15 ⊖	d	09 39	09 42	09 47	09 50	09 54	09 57	10 03	10 06	10 09	10 12	10 17	10 20	10 24	10 27	10 33	10 36	10 39	10 42	10 47	10 50	10 54	10 57
Vauxhall ⊖	d	09 43	09 46	09 51	09 54	09 58	10 01	10 07	10 10	10 13	10 16	10 21	10 24	10 28	10 31	10 37	10 40	10 43	10 46	10 51	10 54	10 58	11 01
Clapham Junction 10	d	09 48	09 51	09 56	09 59	10 03	10 06	10 12	10 15	10 18	10 21	10 26	10 29	10 33	10 36	10 42	10 45	10 48	10 51	10 56	10 59	11 03	11 06
Earlsfield	d	09 51	09 54	09 59	10 02	10 06	10 09	10 15	10 18	10 21	10 24	10 29	10 32	10 36	10 39	10 45	10 48	10 51	10 54	10 59	11 02	11 06	11 09
Wimbledon 6 ⊖	d	09 55	09 58	10 03	10 06	10 10	10 13	10 19	10 22	10 25	10 28	10 33	10 36	10 40	10 43	10 49	10 52	10 55	10 58	11 03	11 06	11 10	11 13
Raynes Park 6	d	09 58	10 01	10 06		10 13	10 16		10 25	10 28	10 31	10 36		10 43	10 46		10 55	10 58	11 01	11 06		11 13	11 16
Motspur Park	d	10 01		10 09		10 16				10 31		10 39		10 46				11 01		11 09		11 16	
Malden Manor	d			10 12								10 42								11 12			
Tolworth	d			10 15								10 45								11 15			
Chessington North	d			10 18								10 48								11 18			
Chessington South	a			10 21								10 53								11 23			
Worcester Park	d	10 03				10 18				10 33				10 48				11 03				11 18	
Stoneleigh	d	10 06				10 21				10 36				10 51				11 06				11 21	
Ewell West	d	10 09				10 24				10 39				10 54				11 09				11 24	
Epsom 3 182	a	10 17				10 27				10 46				10 57				11 17				11 27	
	d	10 18				10 28				10 47				10 58				11 17				11 28	
Ashtead 182	d	10 22				10 32				10 51				11 02				11 21				11 32	
Leatherhead 182	d	10 25				10 35				10 54				11 05				11 24				11 35	
Box Hill & Westhumble 182	d																						
Dorking 4 182	a					10 42								11 12								11 42	
New Malden 6	d		10 04				10 19		10 28		10 34				10 49		10 58		11 04				11 19
Norbiton	d		10 07				10 22				10 37				10 52				11 07				11 22
Kingston	a		10 10				10 25				10 40				10 55				11 10				11 25
	d		10 10				10 29				10 40				10 59				11 10				11 29
Hampton Wick	d		10 12				10 31				10 42				11 01				11 12				11 31
Teddington	d		10 15				10 35				10 45				11 05				11 15				11 35
Strawberry Hill	a						10 38								11 08								11 38
Fulwell	d		10 19								10 49								11 19				
Hampton	d		10 23								10 53								11 23				
Kempton Park	d		10 26								10 56								11 26				
Sunbury	d		10 28								10 58								11 28				
Upper Halliford	d		10 30								11 00								11 30				
Shepperton	a		10 35								11 05								11 35				
Berrylands	d								10 30								11 00						
Surbiton 6	d				10a13			10 27	10 35				10a43			10 57	11 05				11a13		
Thames Ditton	d								10 39								11 09						
Hampton Court	a								10 42								11 12						
Hinchley Wood	d							10 31								11 01							
Claygate	d							10 34								11 04							
Oxshott	d							10 37								11 07							
Cobham & Stoke D'abernon	d							10 41								11 11							
Bookham	d	10 30								10 59								11 29					
Effingham Junction 6	d	10 34						10 45		11 03						11 15		11 33					
Horsley	d	10 36						10 48		11 06						11 18		11 36					
Clandon	d	10 41						10 53		11 11						11 23		11 41					
London Road (Guildford)	d	10 46						10 58		11 16						11 28		11 46					
Guildford	a	10 50						11 05		11 20						11 34		11 50					

A To Woking B To London Waterloo

The xx27 and xx57 London Waterloo to Strawberry Hill services continue to London Waterloo via Richmond

Table T152-F

Mondays to Fridays

21 May to 5 October

London - Chessington South, Dorking, Guildford, Shepperton and Hampton Court

		SW	SW	SW	SW	SW	SW A	SW	SW B	SW	SW	SW	SW	SW	SW A	SW	SW B	SW	SW	SW	SW	SW	SW A
London Waterloo 15 ⊖	d	11 03	11 06	11 09	11 12	11 17	11 20	11 24	11 27	11 33	11 36	11 39	11 42	11 47	11 50	11 54	11 57	12 03	12 06	12 09	12 12	12 17	12 20
Vauxhall ⊖	d	11 07	11 10	11 13	11 16	11 21	11 24	11 28	11 31	11 37	11 40	11 43	11 46	11 51	11 54	11 58	12 01	12 07	12 10	12 13	12 16	12 21	12 24
Clapham Junction 10	d	11 12	11 15	11 18	11 21	11 26	11 29	11 33	11 36	11 42	11 45	11 48	11 51	11 56	11 59	12 03	12 06	12 12	12 15	12 18	12 21	12 26	12 29
Earlsfield	d	11 15	11 18	11 21	11 24	11 29	11 32	11 36	11 39	11 45	11 48	11 51	11 54	11 59	12 02	12 06	12 09	12 15	12 18	12 21	12 24	12 29	12 32
Wimbledon 6 ⊖	d	11 19	11 22	11 25	11 28	11 33	11 36	11 40	11 43	11 49	11 52	11 55	11 58	12 03	12 06	12 10	12 13	12 19	12 22	12 25	12 28	12 33	12 36
Raynes Park 6	d		11 25	11 28	11 31	11 36		11 43	11 46		11 55	11 58	12 01	12 06		12 13	12 16		12 25	12 28	12 31	12 36	
Motspur Park	d			11 31		11 39		11 46				12 01		12 09		12 16				12 31		12 39	
Malden Manor	d					11 42								12 12								12 42	
Tolworth	d					11 45								12 15								12 45	
Chessington North	d					11 48								12 18								12 48	
Chessington South	a					11 53								12 23								12 53	
Worcester Park	d			11 33				11 48				12 03				12 18				12 33			
Stoneleigh	d			11 36				11 51				12 06				12 21				12 36			
Ewell West	d			11 39				11 54				12 09				12 24				12 39			
Epsom 3 182	a			11 46				11 57				12 17				12 27				12 46			
	d			11 47				11 58				12 17				12 28				12 47			
Ashtead 182	d			11 51				12 02				12 21				12 32				12 51			
Leatherhead 182	d			11 54				12 05				12 24				12 35				12 54			
Box Hill & Westhumble 182	d																						
Dorking 4 182	a							12 12								12 42							
New Malden 6	d		11 28		11 34				11 49		11 58		12 04				12 19		12 28		12 34		
Norbiton	d				11 37				11 52				12 07				12 22				12 37		
Kingston	a				11 40				11 55				12 10				12 25				12 40		
	d				11 40				11 59				12 10				12 29				12 40		
Hampton Wick	d				11 42				12 01				12 12				12 31				12 42		
Teddington	d				11 45				12 05				12 15				12 35				12 45		
Strawberry Hill	a								12 08								12 38						
Fulwell	d				11 49								12 19								12 49		
Hampton	d				11 53								12 23								12 53		
Kempton Park	d				11 56								12 26								12 56		
Sunbury	d				11 58								12 28								12 58		
Upper Halliford	d				12 00								12 30								13 00		
Shepperton	a				12 05								12 35								13 05		
Berrylands	d		11 30								12 00								12 30				
Surbiton 6	d	11 27	11 35				11a43			11 57	12 05				12a13			12 27	12 35				12a43
Thames Ditton	d		11 39								12 09								12 39				
Hampton Court	a		11 42								12 12								12 42				
Hinchley Wood	d	11 31								12 01								12 31					
Claygate	d	11 34								12 04								12 34					
Oxshott	d	11 37								12 07								12 37					
Cobham & Stoke D'abernon	d	11 41								12 11								12 41					
Bookham	d			11 59								12 29								12 59			
Effingham Junction 6	d	11 45		12 03						12 15		12 33						12 45		13 03			
Horsley	d	11 48		12 06						12 18		12 36						12 48		13 06			
Clandon	d	11 53		12 11						12 23		12 41						12 53		13 11			
London Road (Guildford)	d	11 58		12 16						12 28		12 46						12 58		13 16			
Guildford	a	12 04		12 20						12 34		12 50						13 04		13 20			

A To Woking B To London Waterloo

The xx27 and xx57 London Waterloo to Strawberry Hill services continue to London Waterloo via Richmond

Table T152-F

Mondays to Fridays

21 May to 5 October

London - Chessington South, Dorking, Guildford, Shepperton and Hampton Court

	SW	SW A	SW	SW	SW	SW	SW	SW B	SW	SW A	SW	SW	SW	SW	SW	SW B	SW	SW A	SW	SW	SW
London Waterloo ⊖ d	12 24	12 27	12 33	12 36	12 39	12 42	12 47	12 50	12 54	12 57	13 03	13 06	13 09	13 12	13 17	13 20	13 24	13 27	13 33	13 36	13 39
Vauxhall ⊖ d	12 28	12 31	12 37	12 40	12 43	12 46	12 51	12 54	12 58	13 01	13 07	13 10	13 13	13 16	13 21	13 24	13 28	13 31	13 37	13 40	13 43
Clapham Junction d	12 33	12 36	12 42	12 45	12 48	12 51	12 56	12 59	13 03	13 06	13 12	13 15	13 18	13 21	13 26	13 29	13 33	13 36	13 42	13 45	13 48
Earlsfield d	12 36	12 39	12 45	12 48	12 51	12 54	12 59	13 02	13 06	13 09	13 15	13 18	13 21	13 24	13 29	13 32	13 36	13 39	13 45	13 48	13 51
Wimbledon ⊖ d	12 40	12 43	12 49	12 52	12 55	12 58	13 03	13 06	13 10	13 13	13 19	13 22	13 25	13 28	13 33	13 36	13 40	13 43	13 49	13 52	13 55
Raynes Park d	12 43	12 46		12 55	12 58	13 01	13 06		13 13	13 16		13 25	13 28	13 31	13 36		13 43	13 46		13 55	13 58
Motspur Park d	12 46				13 01		13 09		13 16				13 31		13 39		13 46				14 01
Malden Manor d							13 12								13 42						
Tolworth d							13 15								13 45						
Chessington North d							13 18								13 48						
Chessington South a							13 23								13 53						
Worcester Park d	12 48				13 03				13 18				13 33				13 48				14 03
Stoneleigh d	12 51				13 06				13 21				13 36				13 51				14 06
Ewell West d	12 54				13 09				13 24				13 39				13 54				14 09
Epsom 182 a	12 57				13 17				13 27				13 46				13 57				14 17
d	12 58				13 17				13 28				13 47				13 58				14 17
Ashtead 182 d	13 02				13 21				13 32				13 51				14 02				14 21
Leatherhead 182 d	13 05				13 24				13 35				13 54				14 05				14 24
Box Hill & Westhumble 182 d																					
Dorking 182 a	13 12								13 42								14 12				
New Malden d		12 49		12 58		13 04				13 19		13 28		13 34				13 49		13 58	
Norbiton d		12 52				13 07				13 22				13 37				13 52			
Kingston a		12 55				13 10				13 25				13 40				13 55			
d		12 59				13 10				13 29				13 40				13 59			
Hampton Wick d		13 01				13 12				13 31				13 42				14 01			
Teddington d		13 05				13 15				13 35				13 45				14 05			
Strawberry Hill a		13 08								13 38								14 08			
Fulwell d						13 19								13 49							
Hampton d						13 23								13 53							
Kempton Park d						13 26								13 56							
Sunbury d						13 28								13 58							
Upper Halliford d						13 30								14 00							
Shepperton a						13 35								14 05							
Berrylands d				13 00								13 30								14 00	
Surbiton d			12 57	13 05				13a13			13 27	13 35				13a43			13 57	14 05	
Thames Ditton d				13 09								13 39								14 09	
Hampton Court a				13 12								13 42								14 12	
Hinchley Wood d			13 01								13 31								14 01		
Claygate d			13 04								13 34								14 04		
Oxshott d			13 07								13 37								14 07		
Cobham & Stoke D'abernon d			13 11								13 41								14 11		
Bookham d					13 29								13 59								14 29
Effingham Junction d			13 15		13 33						13 45		14 03						14 15		14 33
Horsley d			13 18		13 36						13 48		14 06						14 18		14 36
Clandon d			13 23		13 41						13 53		14 11						14 23		14 41
London Road (Guildford) d			13 28		13 46						13 58		14 16						14 28		14 46
Guildford a			13 34		13 50						14 04		14 20						14 34		14 50

A To London Waterloo

B To Woking

The xx27 and xx57 London Waterloo to Strawberry Hill services continue to London Waterloo via Richmond

Table T152-F

Mondays to Fridays

21 May to 5 October

London - Chessington South, Dorking, Guildford, Shepperton and Hampton Court

	SW	SW	SW A	SW	SW B	SW	SW	SW	SW	SW	SW A	SW	SW B	SW	SW	SW	SW	SW	SW A	SW	SW B	SW
London Waterloo ⊖ d	13 42	13 47	13 50	13 54	13 57	14 03	14 06	14 09	14 12	14 17	14 20	14 24	14 27	14 33	14 36	14 39	14 42	14 47	14 50	14 54	14 57	15 03
Vauxhall ⊖ d	13 46	13 51	13 54	13 58	14 01	14 07	14 10	14 13	14 16	14 21	14 24	14 28	14 31	14 37	14 40	14 43	14 46	14 51	14 54	14 58	15 01	15 07
Clapham Junction d	13 51	13 56	13 59	14 03	14 06	14 12	14 15	14 18	14 21	14 26	14 29	14 33	14 36	14 42	14 45	14 48	14 51	14 56	14 59	15 03	15 06	15 12
Earlsfield d	13 54	13 59	14 02	14 06	14 09	14 15	14 18	14 21	14 24	14 29	14 32	14 36	14 39	14 45	14 48	14 51	14 54	14 59	15 02	15 06	15 09	15 15
Wimbledon ⊖ d	13 58	14 03	14 06	14 10	14 13	14 19	14 22	14 25	14 28	14 33	14 36	14 40	14 43	14 49	14 52	14 55	14 58	15 03	15 06	15 10	15 13	15 19
Raynes Park d	14 01	14 06		14 13	14 16		14 25	14 28	14 31	14 36		14 43	14 46		14 55	14 58	15 01	15 06		15 13	15 16	
Motspur Park d		14 09		14 16				14 31		14 39		14 46				15 01		15 09		15 16		
Malden Manor d		14 12								14 42								15 12				
Tolworth d		14 15								14 45								15 15				
Chessington North d		14 18								14 48								15 18				
Chessington South a		14 23								14 53								15 23				
Worcester Park d				14 18				14 33				14 48				15 03				15 18		
Stoneleigh d				14 21				14 36				14 51				15 06				15 21		
Ewell West d				14 24				14 39				14 54				15 09				15 24		
Epsom 182 a				14 27				14 46				14 57				15 16				15 27		
d				14 28				14 47				14 58				15 17				15 28		
Ashtead 182 d				14 32				14 51				15 02				15 21				15 32		
Leatherhead 182 d				14 35				14 54				15 05				15 24				15 35		
Box Hill & Westhumble 182 d																						
Dorking 182 a				14 42								15 12								15 42		
New Malden d	14 04				14 19		14 28		14 34				14 49		14 58		15 04				15 19	
Norbiton d	14 07				14 22				14 37				14 52				15 07				15 22	
Kingston a	14 10				14 25				14 40				14 55				15 10				15 25	
d	14 10				14 29				14 40				14 59				15 10				15 29	
Hampton Wick d	14 12				14 31				14 42				15 01				15 12				15 31	
Teddington d	14 15				14 35				14 45				15 05				15 15				15 35	
Strawberry Hill a					14 38								15 08								15 38	
Fulwell d	14 19								14 49								15 19					
Hampton d	14 23								14 53								15 23					
Kempton Park d	14 26								14 56								15 26					
Sunbury d	14 28								14 58								15 28					
Upper Halliford d	14 30								15 00								15 30					
Shepperton a	14 35								15 05								15 35					
Berrylands d							14 30								15 00							
Surbiton d			14a13			14 27	14 35				14a43			14 57	15 05				15a13			15 27
Thames Ditton d							14 39								15 09							
Hampton Court a							14 42								15 12							
Hinchley Wood d						14 31								15 01								15 31
Claygate d						14 34								15 04								15 34
Oxshott d						14 37								15 07								15 37
Cobham & Stoke D'abernon d						14 41								15 11								15 41
Bookham d								14 59								15 29						
Effingham Junction d						14 45		15 03						15 15		15 33						15 45
Horsley d						14 48		15 06						15 18		15 36						15 48
Clandon d						14 53		15 11						15 23		15 41						15 53
London Road (Guildford) d						14 58		15 16						15 28		15 46						15 58
Guildford a						15 04		15 20						15 34		15 50						16 04

A To Woking

B To London Waterloo

The xx27 and xx57 London Waterloo to Strawberry Hill services continue to London Waterloo via Richmond

Table T152-F

Mondays to Fridays
21 May to 5 October

London - Chessington South, Dorking, Guildford, Shepperton and Hampton Court

		SW	SW	SW	SW	SW	SW	SW	SW	SW	SW	SW
						A		B				
London Waterloo ⊖	d	15 06	15 09	15 12	15 17	15 20	15 24	15 27	15 33	15 36	15 39	15 42
Vauxhall ⊖	d	15 10	15 13	15 16	15 21	15 24	15 28	15 31	15 37	15 40	15 43	15 46
Clapham Junction	d	15 15	15 18	15 21	15 26	15 29	15 33	15 36	15 42	15 45	15 48	15 51
Earlsfield	d	15 18	15 21	15 24	15 29	15 32	15 36	15 39	15 45	15 48	15 51	15 54
Wimbledon ⊖	d	15 22	15 25	15 28	15 33	15 36	15 40	15 43	15 49	15 52	15 55	15 58
Raynes Park	d	15 25	15 28	15 31	15 36		15 43	15 46		15 55	15 58	16 01
Motspur Park	d		15 31		15 39		15 46				16 01	
Malden Manor	d				15 42							
Tolworth	d				15 45							
Chessington North	d				15 48							
Chessington South	a				15 53							
Worcester Park	d		15 33				15 48				16 03	
Stoneleigh	d		15 36				15 51				16 06	
Ewell West	d		15 39				15 54				16 09	
Epsom 182	a		15 46				15 57				16 15	
	d		15 47				15 58				16 17	
Ashtead 182	d		15 51				16 02				16 21	
Leatherhead 182	d		15 54				16 05				16 24	
Box Hill & Westhumble 182	d											
Dorking 182	a						16 12					
New Malden	d	15 28		15 34				15 49		15 58		16 04
Norbiton	d			15 37				15 52				16 07
Kingston	a			15 40				15 55				16 10
	d			15 40				15 59				16 10
Hampton Wick	d			15 42				16 01				16 12
Teddington	d			15 45				16 05				16 15
Strawberry Hill	a							16 08				
Fulwell	d			15 49								16 19
Hampton	d			15 53								16 23
Kempton Park	d			15 56								16 26
Sunbury	d			15 58								16 28
Upper Halliford	d			16 00								16 30
Shepperton	a			16 05								16 35
Berrylands	d	15 30								16 00		
Surbiton	d	15 35				15a43			15 57	16 05		
Thames Ditton	d	15 39								16 09		
Hampton Court	a	15 42								16 12		
Hinchley Wood	d								16 01			
Claygate	d								16 04			
Oxshott	d								16 07			
Cobham & Stoke D'abernon	d								16 11			
Bookham	d		15 59								16 29	
Effingham Junction	d		16 03						16 15		16 33	
Horsley	d		16 06						16 18		16 36	
Clandon	d		16 11						16 23		16 41	
London Road (Guildford)	d		16 16						16 28		16 46	
Guildford	a		16 20						16 34		16 50	

		SW	SW	SW	SW	SW	SW	SW	SW	SW	SW
			A		B						◇ A
London Waterloo ⊖	d	15 47	15 50	15 54	15 57	16 03	16 06	16 09	16 12	16 17	16 20
Vauxhall ⊖	d	15 51	15 54	15 58	16 01	16 07	16 10	16 13	16 16	16 21	16 24
Clapham Junction	d	15 56	15 59	16 03	16 06	16 12	16 15	16 18	16 21	16 26	16 29
Earlsfield	d	15 59	16 02	16 06	16 09	16 15	16 18	16 21	16 24	16 29	16 32
Wimbledon ⊖	d	16 03	16 06	16 10	16 13	16 19	16 22	16 25	16 28	16 33	16 36
Raynes Park	d	16 06		16 13	16 16		16 25	16 28	16 31	16 36	
Motspur Park	d	16 09		16 16				16 31		16 39	
Malden Manor	d	16 12								16 42	
Tolworth	d	16 15								16 45	
Chessington North	d	16 18								16 48	
Chessington South	a	16 23								16 53	
Worcester Park	d			16 18				16 33			
Stoneleigh	d			16 21				16 36			
Ewell West	d			16 24				16 39			
Epsom 182	a			16 27				16 46			
	d			16 28				16 47			
Ashtead 182	d			16 32				16 51			
Leatherhead 182	d			16 35				16 54			
Box Hill & Westhumble 182	d										
Dorking 182	a			16 42							
New Malden	d				16 19		16 28		16 34		
Norbiton	d				16 22				16 37		
Kingston	a				16 25				16 40		
	d				16 29				16 40		
Hampton Wick	d				16 31				16 42		
Teddington	d				16 35				16 45		
Strawberry Hill	a				16 38						
Fulwell	d								16 49		
Hampton	d								16 53		
Kempton Park	d								16 56		
Sunbury	d								16 58		
Upper Halliford	d								17 00		
Shepperton	a								17 05		
Berrylands	d						16 30				
Surbiton	d		16a13			16 27	16 35				16a43
Thames Ditton	d						16 39				
Hampton Court	a						16 44				
Hinchley Wood	d					16 31					
Claygate	d					16 34					
Oxshott	d					16 37					
Cobham & Stoke D'abernon	d					16 41					
Bookham	d							16 59			
Effingham Junction	d					16 45		17 03			
Horsley	d					16 48		17 06			
Clandon	d					16 53		17 11			
London Road (Guildford)	d					16 58		17 16			
Guildford	a					17 04		17 22			

A To Woking
B To London Waterloo

The xx27 and xx57 London Waterloo to Strawberry Hill services continue to London Waterloo via Richmond

Table T152-F

Mondays to Fridays
21 May to 5 October

London - Chessington South, Dorking, Guildford, Shepperton and Hampton Court

		SW	SW	SW	SW	SW	SW	SW	SW	SW	SW	SW
			A						◇ B		A	◇■
London Waterloo ⊖	d	16 24	16 27	16 33	16 36	16 39	16 42	16 47	16 50	16 54	16 57	17 02
Vauxhall ⊖	d	16 28	16 31	16 37	16 40	16 43	16 46	16 51	16 54	16 58	17 01	
Clapham Junction	d	16 33	16 36	16 42	16 45	16 48	16 51	16 56	16 59	17 03	17 06	
Earlsfield	d	16 36	16 39	16 45	16 48	16 51	16 54	16 59	17 02	17 06	17 09	
Wimbledon ⊖	d	16 40	16 43	16 49	16 52	16 55	16 58	17 03	17 06	17 10	17 13	
Raynes Park	d	16 43	16 46		16 55	16 58	17 01	17 06		17 13	17 16	
Motspur Park	d	16 46				17 01		17 09		17 16		
Malden Manor	d							17 12				
Tolworth	d							17 15				
Chessington North	d							17 18				
Chessington South	a							17 23				
Worcester Park	d	16 48				17 03				17 18		
Stoneleigh	d	16 51				17 06				17 21		
Ewell West	d	16 54				17 09				17 24		
Epsom 182	a	16 57				17 12				17 27		
	d	16 58				17 17				17 28		
Ashtead 182	d	17 02				17 21				17 32		
Leatherhead 182	d	17 05				17 24				17 35		
Box Hill & Westhumble 182	d	17 10								17 40		
Dorking 182	a	17 14								17 44		
New Malden	d		16 49		16 58		17 04				17 19	
Norbiton	d		16 52				17 07				17 22	
Kingston	a		16 55				17 10				17 25	
	d		16 59				17 10				17 29	
Hampton Wick	d		17 01				17 12				17 31	
Teddington	d		17 05				17 15				17 35	
Strawberry Hill	a		17 08								17 38	
Fulwell	d						17 19					
Hampton	d						17 23					
Kempton Park	d						17 26					
Sunbury	d						17 28					
Upper Halliford	d						17 30					
Shepperton	a						17 35					
Berrylands	d				17 00							
Surbiton	d			16 57	17 05				17a13			17 18
Thames Ditton	d				17 09							
Hampton Court	a				17 14							
Hinchley Wood	d			17 01								
Claygate	d			17 04								
Oxshott	d			17 07								
Cobham & Stoke D'abernon	d			17 11								
Bookham	d					17 29						
Effingham Junction	d			17 15		17 33						
Horsley	d			17 18		17 36						
Clandon	d			17 23		17 41						
London Road (Guildford)	d			17 28		17 46						
Guildford	a			17 34		17 52						17 56

		SW	SW	SW	SW	SW	SW	SW	SW	SW	SW	SW
							◇ B		A		◇■	
London Waterloo ⊖	d	17 03	17 06	17 09	17 12	17 17	17 20	17 24	17 27	17 31	17 32	17 33
Vauxhall ⊖	d	17 07	17 10	17 13	17 16	17 21	17 24	17 28	17 31	17 35		17 38
Clapham Junction	d	17 12	17 15	17 18	17 21	17 26	17 29	17 33	17 36	17 40		17 43
Earlsfield	d	17 15	17 18	17 21	17 24	17 29	17 32	17 36	17 39	17 43		17 46
Wimbledon ⊖	d	17 19	17 22	17 25	17 28	17 33	17 36	17 40	17 43	17 47		17 50
Raynes Park	d		17 25	17 28	17 31	17 36		17 43	17 46	17 50		
Motspur Park	d			17 31		17 39				17 53		
Malden Manor	d					17 42						
Tolworth	d					17 45						
Chessington North	d					17 48						
Chessington South	a					17 53						
Worcester Park	d			17 33				17 47		17 56		
Stoneleigh	d			17 36						18 00		
Ewell West	d			17 39						18 03		
Epsom 182	a			17 42				17 57		18 08		
	d			17 47				17 57				
Ashtead 182	d			17 51				18 01				
Leatherhead 182	d			17 54				18 04				
Box Hill & Westhumble 182	d							18 09				
Dorking 182	a							18 15				
New Malden	d		17 28		17 34				17 49			
Norbiton	d				17 37				17 52			
Kingston	a				17 40				17 55			
	d				17 40				17 59			
Hampton Wick	d				17 42				18 01			
Teddington	d				17 45				18 05			
Strawberry Hill	a								18 08			
Fulwell	d				17 49							
Hampton	d				17 53							
Kempton Park	d				17 56							
Sunbury	d				17 58							
Upper Halliford	d				18 00							
Shepperton	a				18 06							
Berrylands	d		17 30									
Surbiton	d	17 27	17 35				17a43				17 48	17 58
Thames Ditton	d		17 39									
Hampton Court	a		17 44									
Hinchley Wood	d	17 31										18 05
Claygate	d	17 34										18 08
Oxshott	d	17 37										18 11
Cobham & Stoke D'abernon	d	17 41										18 15
Bookham	d			17 59								
Effingham Junction	d	17 45		18a05								18 20
Horsley	d	17 48										18 22
Clandon	d	17 53										18 27
London Road (Guildford)	d	17 58										18 32
Guildford	a	18 04									18 30	18 40

A To London Waterloo
B To Woking

The xx27 and xx57 London Waterloo to Strawberry Hill services continue to London Waterloo via Richmond

London - Chessington South, Dorking, Guildford, Shepperton and Hampton Court

	SW	TL A	SW	SW	SW	SW	SW ◇ B	SW	SW C	SW	SW ◇■ B	SW	SW	SW	SW	SW	SW	SW ◇ B	SW	SW C	SW	SW
London Waterloo ⊖ d	17 36		17 39	17 43	17 42	17 47	17 50	17 54	17 57	18 01	18 02	18 03	18 06	18 09	18 13	18 12	18 17	18 20	18 24	18 27	18 31	18 33
Vauxhall ⊖ d	17 41		17 44	17 47	17 47	17 51	17 54	17 58	18 01	18 05		18 08	18 11	18 14	18 17	18 17	18 21	18 24	18 28	18 31	18 35	18 38
Clapham Junction d	17 46		17 49	17 53	17 52	17 56	17 59	18 03	18 06	18 10		18 13	18 16	18 19	18 23	18 22	18 26	18 29	18 33	18 36	18 40	18 43
Earlsfield d	17 49		17 52		17 55	17 59	18 02	18 06	18 09	18 13		18 16	18 19	18 22		18 25	18 29	18 32	18 36	18 39	18 43	18 46
Wimbledon ⊖ d	17 53		17 56		17 59	18 03	18 06	18 10	18 13	18 17		18 20	18 23	18 26		18 29	18 33	18 36	18 40	18 43	18 47	18 50
Raynes Park d	17 56		17 59		18 02	18 06		18 13	18 16	18 20			18 26	18 29		18 32	18 36		18 43	18 46	18 50	
Motspur Park d			18 02			18 09				18 23				18 32			18 39				18 53	
Malden Manor d						18 12											18 42					
Tolworth d						18 15											18 45					
Chessington North d						18 18											18 48					
Chessington South a						18 23											18 53					
Worcester Park d			18 04					18 17		18 25				18 34					18 47		18 56	
Stoneleigh d			18 07							18 28				18 37							18 59	
Ewell West d			18 10							18 31				18 40							19 02	
Epsom 182 a			18 17					18 27		18 38				18 49					18 57		19 07	
d		18 10	18 19					18 27						18 52					18 57			
Ashtead 182 d		18 15	18 23					18 31						18 56					19 01			
Leatherhead 182 d		18 19	18 26					18 34						18 59					19 04			
Box Hill & Westhumble 182 d								18 39											19 09			
Dorking 182 a								18 45											19 14			
New Malden d	17 59				18 05				18 19				18 29			18 35				18 49		
Norbiton d					18 08				18 22							18 38				18 52		
Kingston a					18 11				18 25							18 41				18 55		
d					18 11				18 29							18 41				18 59		
Hampton Wick d					18 13				18 31							18 43				19 01		
Teddington d					18 16				18 35							18 46				19 05		
Strawberry Hill a				18 11					18 38						18 41					19 08		
Fulwell d				18 13	18 20										18 43	18 50						
Hampton d				18 17	18 24										18 47	18 54						
Kempton Park d					18 27											18 57						
Sunbury d				18 21	18 29										18 51	18 59						
Upper Halliford d				18 23	18 31										18 53	19 01						
Shepperton a				18 28	18 40										18 58	19 10						
Berrylands d	18 01												18 31									
Surbiton d	18 06						18a13				18a17	18 28	18 36					18a43				18 58
Thames Ditton d	18 10												18 40									
Hampton Court a	18 15												18 45									
Hinchley Wood d												18 35										19 02
Claygate d												18 38										19 05
Oxshott d												18 41										19 08
Cobham & Stoke D'abernon d												18 45										19 12
Bookham d		18 24	18 31											19 05								
Effingham Junction d		18 28	18a42									18 50		19 09								19 16
Horsley d		18 30										18 52		19 11								19 19
Clandon d		18 35										18 57		19 16								19 24
London Road (Guildford) d		18 40										19 02		19 21								19 29
Guildford a		18 44										19 09		19 27								19 35

A From London Bridge B To Woking C To London Waterloo

The xx27 and xx57 London Waterloo to Strawberry Hill services continue to London Waterloo via Richmond

London - Chessington South, Dorking, Guildford, Shepperton and Hampton Court

	SW	SW	SW	SW	SW	SW ◇ A	SW	SW	SW B	SW	SW ■ A	SW	SW	TL C	SW	SW	SW	SW A	SW	SW	SW B
London Waterloo ⊖ d	18 36	18 39	18 43	18 42	18 47	18 50	18 52	18 54	18 57	19 01	19 02	19 03	19 06		19 09	19 12	19 17	19 20	19 23	19 24	19 27
Vauxhall ⊖ d	18 41	18 44	18 47	18 47	18 51	18 54		18 58	19 01	19 05		19 08	19 11		19 14	19 17	19 21	19 24		19 28	19 31
Clapham Junction d	18 46	18 49	18 53	18 52	18 56	18 59		19 03	19 06	19 10		19 13	19 16		19 19	19 22	19 26	19 29		19 33	19 36
Earlsfield d	18 49	18 52		18 55	18 59	19 02		19 06	19 09	19 13		19 16	19 19		19 22	19 25	19 29	19 32		19 36	19 39
Wimbledon ⊖ d	18 53	18 56		18 59	19 03	19 06		19 10	19 13	19 17		19 20	19 23		19 26	19 29	19 33	19 36		19 40	19 43
Raynes Park d	18 56	18 59		19 02	19 06			19 13	19 16	19 20			19 26		19 29	19 32	19 36			19 43	19 46
Motspur Park d		19 02			19 09					19 23					19 32		19 39			19 46	
Malden Manor d					19 12												19 42				
Tolworth d					19 15												19 45				
Chessington North d					19 18												19 48				
Chessington South a					19 23												19 53				
Worcester Park d		19 04						19 17		19 25					19 34					19 48	
Stoneleigh d		19 07								19 28					19 37					19 51	
Ewell West d		19 10								19 31					19 40					19 54	
Epsom 182 a		19 16						19 27		19 36					19 48					19 57	
d		19 18						19 27						19 40	19 52					19 58	
Ashtead 182 d		19 22						19 31						19 45	19 56					20 02	
Leatherhead 182 d		19 25						19 34						19 48	19 59					20 05	
Box Hill & Westhumble 182 d								19 39												20 10	
Dorking 182 a								19 44												20 14	
New Malden d	18 59			19 05					19 19				19 29			19 35					19 49
Norbiton d				19 08					19 22							19 38					19 52
Kingston a				19 11					19 25							19 41					19 55
d				19 11					19 29							19 41					19 59
Hampton Wick d				19 13					19 31							19 43					20 01
Teddington d				19 16					19 35							19 46					20 05
Strawberry Hill a			19 11						19 38												20 08
Fulwell d			19 13	19 20												19 50					
Hampton d			19 17	19 24												19 54					
Kempton Park d				19 27												19 57					
Sunbury d			19 21	19 29												19 59					
Upper Halliford d			19 23	19 31												20 01					
Shepperton a			19 28	19 39												20 05					
Berrylands d	19 01												19 31								
Surbiton d	19 06					19a13	19 08				19a17	19 28	19 36					19a43	19 40		
Thames Ditton d	19 10												19 40						19 45		
Hampton Court a	19 15												19 43						19 47		
Hinchley Wood d							19 12					19 32									
Claygate d							19 15					19 35									
Oxshott d							19 18					19 38									
Cobham & Stoke D'abernon d							19 22					19 42									
Bookham d		19 30												19 53	20 04						
Effingham Junction d		19 34					19 26					19 46		19 58	20 08						
Horsley d		19 37					19 29					19 48		20 00	20 10						
Clandon d		19 42					19 34					19 53		20 05	20 15						
London Road (Guildford) d		19 47					19 39					19 58		20 10	20 20						
Guildford a		19 53					19 46					20 03		20 15	20 24						

A To Woking B To London Waterloo C From London Bridge

The xx27 and xx57 London Waterloo to Strawberry Hill services continue to London Waterloo via Richmond

21 May to 5 October

London - Chessington South, Dorking, Guildford, Shepperton and Hampton Court

		SW	SW	SW	SW	SW	SW A	SW	SW B	SW	SW	SW	SW	SW	SW A	SW	SW B	SW	SW	SW	SW	SW	SW A
London Waterloo ⊖	d	19 33	19 36	19 39	19 42	19 47	19 50	19 54	19 57	20 03	20 06	20 09	20 12	20 17	20 20	20 24	20 27	20 33	20 36	20 39	20 42	20 47	20 50
Vauxhall ⊖	d	19 37	19 40	19 43	19 46	19 51	19 54	19 58	20 01	20 07	20 10	20 13	20 16	20 21	20 24	20 28	20 31	20 37	20 40	20 43	20 46	20 51	20 54
Clapham Junction	d	19 42	19 45	19 48	19 51	19 56	19 59	20 03	20 06	20 12	20 15	20 18	20 21	20 26	20 29	20 33	20 36	20 42	20 45	20 48	20 51	20 56	20 59
Earlsfield	d	19 45	19 48	19 51	19 54	19 59	20 02	20 06	20 09	20 15	20 18	20 21	20 24	20 29	20 32	20 36	20 39	20 45	20 48	20 51	20 54	20 59	21 02
Wimbledon ⊖ ⇌	d	19 49	19 52	19 55	19 58	20 03	20 06	20 10	20 13	20 19	20 22	20 25	20 28	20 33	20 36	20 40	20 43	20 49	20 52	20 55	20 58	21 03	21 06
Raynes Park	d		19 55	19 58	20 01	20 06		20 13	20 16		20 25	20 28	20 31	20 36		20 43	20 46		20 55	20 58	21 01	21 06	
Motspur Park	d			20 01		20 09		20 16				20 31		20 39		20 46				21 01		21 09	
Malden Manor	d					20 12								20 42								21 12	
Tolworth	d					20 15								20 45								21 15	
Chessington North	d					20 18								20 48								21 18	
Chessington South	a					20 23								20 53								21 23	
Worcester Park	d			20 03				20 18				20 33				20 48				21 03			
Stoneleigh	d			20 06				20 21				20 36				20 51				21 06			
Ewell West	d			20 09				20 24				20 39				20 54				21 09			
Epsom 182	a			20 16				20 27				20 42				20 57				21 12			
	d			20 17								20 43								21 13			
Ashtead 182	d			20 21								20 47								21 17			
Leatherhead 182	d			20 24								20 50								21 20			
Box Hill & Westhumble 182	d											20 55											
Dorking 182	a											20 57											
New Malden	d		19 58		20 04				20 19		20 28		20 34				20 49		20 58		21 04		
Norbiton	d				20 07				20 22				20 37				20 52				21 07		
Kingston	a				20 10				20 25				20 40				20 55				21 10		
	d				20 10				20 29				20 40				20 59				21 10		
Hampton Wick	d				20 12				20 31				20 42				21 01				21 12		
Teddington	d				20 15				20 35				20 45				21 05				21 15		
Strawberry Hill	a								20 38								21 08						
Fulwell	d				20 19								20 49								21 19		
Hampton	d				20 23								20 53								21 23		
Kempton Park	d				20 26								20 56								21 26		
Sunbury	d				20 28								20 58								21 28		
Upper Halliford	d				20 30								21 00								21 30		
Shepperton	a				20 35								21 05								21 35		
Berrylands	d		20 00								20 30								21 00				
Surbiton	d	19 57	20 05				20a13			20 27	20 35				20a43			20 57	21 05				21a13
Thames Ditton	d		20 09								20 39								21 09				
Hampton Court	a		20 12								20 42								21 12				
Hinchley Wood	d	20 01								20 31								21 01					
Claygate	d	20 04								20 34								21 04					
Oxshott	d	20 07								20 37								21 07					
Cobham & Stoke D'abernon	d	20 11								20 41								21 11					
Bookham	d			20 29																21 25			
Effingham Junction	d	20 15		20 33						20 45								21 15		21 29			
Horsley	d	20 18		20 36						20 48								21 18		21 32			
Clandon	d	20 23		20 41						20 53								21 23		21 37			
London Road (Guildford)	d	20 28		20 46						20 58								21 28		21 42			
Guildford	a	20 34		20 50						21 04								21 34		21 46			

A To Woking

B To London Waterloo

The xx27 and xx57 London Waterloo to Strawberry Hill services continue to London Waterloo via Richmond

21 May to 5 October

London - Chessington South, Dorking, Guildford, Shepperton and Hampton Court

		SW	SW A	SW	SW	SW	SW	SW	SW B	SW	SW A	SW	SW	SW	SW	SW	SW	SW	SW A	SW	SW	SW
London Waterloo ⊖	d	20 54	20 57	21 03	21 06	21 09	21 12	21 17	21 20	21 24	21 27	21 33	21 36	21 39	21 42	21 47	21 50	21 54	21 57	22 03		22 09
Vauxhall ⊖	d	20 58	21 01	21 07	21 10	21 13	21 16	21 21	21 24	21 28	21 31	21 37	21 40	21 43	21 46	21 51	21 54	21 58	22 01	22 07		22 13
Clapham Junction	d	21 03	21 06	21 12	21 15	21 18	21 21	21 26	21 29	21 33	21 36	21 42	21 45	21 48	21 51	21 56	21 59	22 03	22 06	22 12		22 18
Earlsfield	d	21 06	21 09	21 15	21 18	21 21	21 24	21 29	21 32	21 36	21 39	21 45	21 48	21 51	21 54	21 59	22 02	22 06	22 09	22 15		22 21
Wimbledon ⊖ ⇌	d	21 10	21 13	21 19	21 22	21 25	21 28	21 33	21 36	21 40	21 43	21 49	21 52	21 55	21 58	22 03	22 06	22 10	22 13	22 19		22 25
Raynes Park	d	21 13	21 16		21 25	21 28	21 31	21 36		21 43	21 46		21 55	21 58	22 01	22 06		22 13	22 16			22 28
Motspur Park	d	21 16				21 31		21 39		21 46				22 01		22 09		22 16				22 31
Malden Manor	d							21 42								22 12						
Tolworth	d							21 45								22 15						
Chessington North	d							21 48								22 18						
Chessington South	a							21 53								22 23						
Worcester Park	d	21 18				21 33				21 48				22 03				22 18				22 33
Stoneleigh	d	21 21				21 36				21 51				22 06				22 21				22 36
Ewell West	d	21 24				21 39				21 54				22 09				22 24				22 39
Epsom 182	a	21 27				21 42				21 57				22 12				22 27				22 42
	d					21 43								22 13								22 43
Ashtead 182	d					21 47								22 17								22 47
Leatherhead 182	d					21 50								22 20								22 50
Box Hill & Westhumble 182	d					21 55																22 55
Dorking 182	a					21 57																22 57
New Malden	d		21 19		21 28		21 34				21 49		21 58		22 04				22 19			
Norbiton	d		21 22				21 37				21 52				22 07				22 22			
Kingston	a		21 25				21 40				21 55				22 10				22 25			
	d		21 29				21 40				21 59				22 10				22 29			
Hampton Wick	d		21 31				21 42				22 01				22 12				22 31			
Teddington	d		21 35				21 45				22 05				22 15				22 35			
Strawberry Hill	a		21 38								22 08								22 38			
Fulwell	d						21 49								22 19							
Hampton	d						21 53								22 23							
Kempton Park	d						21 56								22 26							
Sunbury	d						21 58								22 28							
Upper Halliford	d						22 00								22 30							
Shepperton	a						22 05								22 35							
Berrylands	d				21 30								22 00									
Surbiton	d			21 27	21 35				21a43			21 57	22 05				22 14			22 27	22 39	
Thames Ditton	d				21 39								22 09								22 43	
Hampton Court	a				21 42								22 12								22 46	
Hinchley Wood	d			21 31								22 01								22 31		
Claygate	d			21 34								22 04								22 34		
Oxshott	d			21 37								22 07								22 37		
Cobham & Stoke D'abernon	d			21 41								22 11								22 41		
Bookham	d													22 25								
Effingham Junction	d			21 45								22 15		22 29						22 45		
Horsley	d			21 48								22 18		22 32						22 48		
Clandon	d			21 53								22 23		22 37						22 53		
London Road (Guildford)	d			21 58								22 28		22 42						22 58		
Guildford	a			22 04								22 34		22 46			22 47			23 04		

A To London Waterloo

B To Woking

The xx27 and xx57 London Waterloo to Strawberry Hill services continue to London Waterloo via Richmond

Table T152-F

Mondays to Fridays

21 May to 5 October

London - Chessington South, Dorking, Guildford, Shepperton and Hampton Court

		SW	SW A	SW B	SW	SW	SW	SW	SW A	SW B	SW	SW	SW	SW	SW	SW A	SW C	SW	SW	SW	SW
London Waterloo ⊖	d	22 12	22 20	22 27	22 33	22 36	22 39	22 42	22 50	22 57	23 00	23 03		23 09	23 12	23 20	23 27	23 36	23 42	23 50	23 57
Vauxhall ⊖	d	22 16	22 24	22 31	22 37	22 40	22 43	22 46	22 54	23 01	23 04	23 07		23 13	23 16	23 24	23 31	23 40	23 46	23 54	00 01
Clapham Junction	d	22 21	22 29	22 36	22 42	22 45	22 48	22 51	22 59	23 06	23 09	23 12		23 18	23 21	23 29	23 36	23 45	23 51	23 59	00 06
Earlsfield	d	22 24	22 32	22 39	22 45	22 48	22 51	22 54	23 02	23 09	23 12	23 15		23 21	23 24	23 32	23 39	23 48	23 54	00 02	00 09
Wimbledon ⊖	d	22 28	22 36	22 43	22 49	22 52	22 55	22 58	23 06	23 13	23 16	23 19		23 25	23 28	23 36	23 43	23 52	23 58	00 06	00 13
Raynes Park	d	22 31		22 46		22 55	22 58	23 01		23 16	23 19			23 28	23 31		23 46	23 55	00 01		00 16
Motspur Park	d						23 01				23 22			23 31					00 04		
Malden Manor	d										23 25										
Tolworth	d										23 28										
Chessington North	d										23 31										
Chessington South	a										23 36										
Worcester Park	d						23 03							23 33					00 06		
Stoneleigh	d						23 06							23 36					00 09		
Ewell West	d						23 09							23 39					00 12		
Epsom 182	a						23 12							23 42					00 16		
	d						23 13							23 43					00 19		
Ashtead 182	d						23 17							23 47					00 23		
Leatherhead 182	d						23 20							23 50					00 26		
Box Hill & Westhumble 182	d													23 55							
Dorking 182	a													23 57							
New Malden	d	22 34		22 49		22 58		23 04		23 19					23 34		23 49	23 58			00 19
Norbiton	d	22 37		22 52				23 07		23 22					23 37		23 52				00 22
Kingston	a	22 40		22 55				23 10		23 25					23 40		23 55				00 25
	d	22 40		22 59				23 10		23 29					23 40		23 55				00 25
Hampton Wick	d	22 42		23 01				23 12		23 31					23 42		23 57				00 27
Teddington	d	22 45		23 05				23 15		23 35					23 45		23 59				00 30
Strawberry Hill	a			23 08						23 38							00 03				
Fulwell	d	22 49						23 19							23 49						00 34
Hampton	d	22 53						23 23							23 53						00 38
Kempton Park	d	22 56						23 26							23 56						00 41
Sunbury	d	22 58						23 28							23 58						00 43
Upper Halliford	d	23 00						23 30							23 59						00 45
Shepperton	a	23 05						23 35							00 05						00 50
Berrylands	d					23 00												23 59			
Surbiton	d		22a43		22 57	23 05			23a13			23 27	23 43			23a44		00 05		00 14	
Thames Ditton	d					23 09							23 47					00 09			
Hampton Court	a					23 12							23 50					00 12			
Hinchley Wood	d				23 01							23 31								00 18	
Claygate	d				23 04							23 34								00 20	
Oxshott	d				23 07							23 37								00 24	
Cobham & Stoke D'abernon	d				23 11							23 41								00 27	
Bookham	d						23 25												00 31		
Effingham Junction	d				23 15		23 29					23 45							00 36	00 32	
Horsley	d				23 18		23 32					23 48							00 39	00 34	
Clandon	d				23 23		23 37					23 53							00 44	00 39	
London Road (Guildford)	d				23 28		23 42					23 58							00 49	00 44	
Guildford	a				23 34		23 46					00 04							00 53	00 50	

A To Woking B To London Waterloo C To Twickenham

The xx27 and xx57 London Waterloo to Strawberry Hill services continue to London Waterloo via Richmond

Table T152-F

Mondays to Fridays

8 October to 7 December

London - Chessington South, Dorking, Guildford, Shepperton and Hampton Court

		TL MO A	SW MO B	SW MO B	SW MX B	SW MX B	SW MX B	SW MX B	SW MO	SW MX	SW MX	SW MX C	SW	SW ◇ D	SW	SW ◇ D	SW	SW	SW C	SW	SW E	SW E	SW
London Waterloo ⊖	d								00 01	00 09	00 15	00 27	00 42	05 00	05 12	05 20		05 47	05 50				06 03
Vauxhall ⊖	d							00 01	00 04	00 13	00 19	00 31	00 46	05 04	05 16	05 24		05 51	05 54				06 07
Clapham Junction	d							00 06	00 09	00 20	00 26	00 37	00 51	05 11	05 21	05 29		05 56	05 59				06 12
Earlsfield	d					00 02		00 09	00 12	00 24	00 29	00s41		05 14	05 24	05 32		05 59	06 02				06 15
Wimbledon ⊖	d					00 06		00 13	00 16	00 28	00 33	00 45	01 05	05 18	05 28	05 36	05 49	06 03	06 06	06 10		06 13	06 19
Raynes Park	d						00 01	00 16	00 19		00 36	00 48	01 08		05 31			06 06		06 13		06 16	
Motspur Park	d						00 04				00 39							06 09		06 16			
Malden Manor	d																			06 19			
Tolworth	d																			06 22			
Chessington North	d																			06 25			
Chessington South	a																			06 28			
Worcester Park	d						00 06				00 41							06 11					
Stoneleigh	d						00 09				00 44							06 14					
Ewell West	d			00 03			00 12				00 47							06 17					
Epsom 182	a			00 06			00 16				00 50							06 20					
	d						00 19											06 21					
Ashtead 182	d						00 23											06 25					
Leatherhead 182	d	00 02					00 26											06 28					
Box Hill & Westhumble 182	d	00 07																					
Dorking 182	a	00 09																					
New Malden	d							00 19	00 22			00 50	01 11		05 34							06 19	
Norbiton	d							00 22					01 14		05 37							06 22	
Kingston	a							00 25					01 17		05 40							06 25	
	d							00 25					01 17		05 40						05 59	06 29	
Hampton Wick	d							00 27					01s22		05 42						06 01	06 31	
Teddington	d							00 30					01s25		05 45						06 05	06 35	
Strawberry Hill	a												01 28								06 08	06 38	
Fulwell	d							00 34							05 49								
Hampton	d							00 38							05 53								
Kempton Park	d							00 41															
Sunbury	d							00 43							05 57								
Upper Halliford	d							00 45							05 59								
Shepperton	a							00 52							06 06								
Berrylands	d								00 25			00s53											
Surbiton	d				00 05	00 14			00 31	00 35		00s56		05 26		05 44	05 57		06a13				06 27
Thames Ditton	d				00 09																		
Hampton Court	a				00 12																		
Hinchley Wood	d					00 18			00 35								06 01						06 31
Claygate	d					00 20			00 38								06 04						06 34
Oxshott	d					00 24			00 41								06 07						06 37
Cobham & Stoke D'abernon	d					00 27			00 45								06 13						06 41
Bookham	d						00 31											06 33					
Effingham Junction	d					00 32	00 36		00 49								06 19	06 37					06 45
Horsley	d					00 34	00 39		00 52								06 22						06 48
Clandon	d					00 39	00 44		00 57								06 27						06 53
London Road (Guildford)	d		00 03			00 44	00 49		01 02								06 32	06 46					06 58
Guildford	a		00 10			00 53	00 56		01 09	01 08				06 00		06 24	06 39	06 53					07 07

A From London Victoria B From London Waterloo C To Woking D To Portsmouth Harbour E To London Waterloo

The xx27 and xx57 London Waterloo to Strawberry Hill services continue to London Waterloo via Richmond

Table T152-F

Mondays to Fridays

8 October to 7 December

London - Chessington South, Dorking, Guildford, Shepperton and Hampton Court

		SW	SW	SW	TL A	SW	SW	SW B	SW	SW	SW	SW	SW	SW	SW	SW	SW B	SW	SW	SW	SW C	SW	SW
London Waterloo ⊖	d	06 06	06 12	06 16		06 20	06 24	06 27	06 33	06 36	06 39		06 42	06 47	06 50	06 54	06 57	07 03	07 06	07 09		07 12	07 17
Vauxhall ⊖	d	06 10	06 16	06 20		06 24	06 28	06 31	06 37	06 40	06 43		06 46	06 51	06 54	06 58	07 01	07 07	07 10	07 13		07 16	07 21
Clapham Junction	d	06 15	06 21	06 25		06 29	06 33	06 36	06 42	06 45	06 48		06 51	06 56	06 59	07 03	07 06	07 12	07 15	07 18		07 21	07 26
Earlsfield	d	06 18	06 24	06 28		06 32	06 36	06 39	06 45	06 48	06 51		06 54	06 59	07 02	07 06	07 09	07 15	07 18	07 21		07 24	07 29
Wimbledon ⊖	d	06 22	06 28	06 33		06 36	06 40	06 43	06 49	06 52	06 55		06 58	07 03	07 06	07 10	07 13	07 19	07 22	07 25		07 28	07 33
Raynes Park	d	06 25	06 31	06 35			06 43	06 46		06 55	06 58		07 01	07 06		07 13	07 16		07 25	07 28		07 31	07 36
Motspur Park	d			06 39			06 46							07 09		07 16				07 31			07 39
Malden Manor	d			06 41										07 12									07 42
Tolworth	d			06 45										07 15									07 45
Chessington North	d			06 48										07 18									07 48
Chessington South	a			06 52										07 23									07 53
Worcester Park	d						06 48				07 02					07 18				07 33			
Stoneleigh	d						06 51				07 05					07 21				07 36			
Ewell West	d						06 54				07 08					07 24				07 39			
Epsom 182	a						06 57				07 11					07 27				07 42			
	d				06 39		06 58				07 12					07 28							
Ashtead 182	d						07 02				07 16					07 32							
Leatherhead 182	d				06 45		07 05				07 19					07 35							
Box Hill & Westhumble 182	d																						
Dorking 182	a						07 14									07 44							
New Malden	d	06 28	06 34					06 49		06 58			07 04				07 19		07 28			07 34	
Norbiton	d		06 37					06 52					07 07				07 22					07 37	
Kingston	a		06 40					06 55					07 10				07 25					07 40	
	d		06 40					06 59					07 10				07 29					07 40	
Hampton Wick	d		06 42					07 01					07 12				07 31					07 42	
Teddington	d		06 45					07 05					07 15				07 35					07 45	
Strawberry Hill	a							07 08									07 38						
Fulwell	d		06 49									07 07	07 19								07 33	07 49	
Hampton	d		06 53									07 10	07 23								07 36	07 53	
Kempton Park	d											07 14									07 40	07 56	
Sunbury	d		06 57									07 15	07 27								07 41	07 58	
Upper Halliford	d		06 59									07 17	07 29								07 44	08 00	
Shepperton	a		07 07									07 25	07 37								07 51	08 07	
Berrylands	d	06 30								07 00									07 30				
Surbiton	d	06 35				06 44			06 57	07 05					07 14			07 27	07 35				
Thames Ditton	d	06 39								07 09									07 39				
Hampton Court	a	06 42								07 12									07 42				
Hinchley Wood	d								07 01									07 31					
Claygate	d								07 04									07 34					
Oxshott	d								07 07									07 37					
Cobham & Stoke D'abernon	d								07 11									07 41					
Bookham	d				06 50						07 24												
Effingham Junction	d				06 54				07 15		07a28							07 45					
Horsley	d								07 18									07 48					
Clandon	d								07 23									07 53					
London Road (Guildford)	d								07 28									07 58					
Guildford	a				07 06	07 19			07 37						07 47			08 07					

A From London Bridge B To London Waterloo C From Twickenham

The xx27 and xx57 London Waterloo to Strawberry Hill services continue to London Waterloo via Richmond

Table T152-F

Mondays to Fridays

8 October to 7 December

London - Chessington South, Dorking, Guildford, Shepperton and Hampton Court

		SW A	SW	SW B	SW	SW	SW	SW	SW B	SW	SW	SW	SW B	SW	SW	SW	SW	SW	SW A	SW	SW B	SW
London Waterloo ⊖	d	07 20	07 24	07 27	07 33	07 36	07 39	07 42		07 47	07 50	07 54	07 57	08 03	08 06	08 09	08 12	08 17	08 20	08 24	08 27	08 33
Vauxhall ⊖	d	07 24	07 28	07 31	07 37	07 40	07 43	07 46		07 51	07 54	07 58	08 01	08 07	08 10	08 13	08 16	08 21	08 24	08 28	08 31	08 37
Clapham Junction	d	07 29	07 33	07 36	07 42	07 45	07 48	07 51	07 54	07 56	07 59	08 03	08 06	08 12	08 15	08 18	08 21	08 26	08 29	08 33	08 36	08 42
Earlsfield	d	07 32	07 36	07 39	07 45	07 48	07 51	07 54		07 59	08 02	08 06	08 09	08 15	08 18	08 21	08 24	08 29	08 32	08 36	08 39	08 45
Wimbledon ⊖	d	07 36	07 40	07 43	07 49	07 52	07 55	07 58		08 03	08 06	08 10	08 13	08 19	08 22	08 25	08 28	08 33	08 36	08 40	08 43	08 49
Raynes Park	d		07 43	07 46		07 55	07 58	08 01		08 06		08 13	08 16		08 25	08 28	08 31	08 36		08 43	08 46	
Motspur Park	d		07 46				08 01			08 09		08 16				08 31		08 39		08 46		
Malden Manor	d									08 12								08 42				
Tolworth	d									08 15								08 45				
Chessington North	d									08 18								08 48				
Chessington South	a									08 24								08 53				
Worcester Park	d		07 48				08 03					08 18				08 33				08 48		
Stoneleigh	d		07 51				08 06					08 21				08 36				08 51		
Ewell West	d		07 54				08 09					08 24				08 39				08 54		
Epsom 182	a		07 58				08 13					08 27				08 42				08 57		
	d		07 58				08 17					08 28				08 47				08 58		
Ashtead 182	d		08 02				08 21					08 32				08 51				09 02		
Leatherhead 182	d		08 05				08 24					08 35				08 54				09 05		
Box Hill & Westhumble 182	d																					
Dorking 182	a		08 14									08 44								09 14		
New Malden	d			07 49		07 58		08 04					08 19		08 28		08 34				08 49	
Norbiton	d			07 52				08 07					08 22				08 37				08 52	
Kingston	a			07 55				08 10	08 23				08 25				08 40				08 55	
	d			07 59				08 10					08 29				08 40				08 59	
Hampton Wick	d			08 01				08 12					08 31				08 42				09 01	
Teddington	d			08 05				08 15					08 35				08 45				09 05	
Strawberry Hill	a			08 08									08 38								09 08	
Fulwell	d							08 19									08 49					
Hampton	d							08 23									08 53					
Kempton Park	d							08 26									08 56					
Sunbury	d							08 28									08 58					
Upper Halliford	d							08 30									09 00					
Shepperton	a							08 37									09 07					
Berrylands	d					08 00									08 30							
Surbiton	d	07a43			07 57	08 05					08 14			08 27	08 35				08a43			08 57
Thames Ditton	d					08 09									08 39							
Hampton Court	a					08 12									08 42							
Hinchley Wood	d				08 01									08 31								09 01
Claygate	d				08 04									08 34								09 04
Oxshott	d				08 07									08 37								09 07
Cobham & Stoke D'abernon	d				08 11									08 41								09 11
Bookham	d						08 29									08 59						
Effingham Junction	d				08 15		08 33							08 45		09 03						09 15
Horsley	d				08 18		08 36							08 48		09 06						09 18
Clandon	d				08 23		08 41							08 53		09 11						09 23
London Road (Guildford)	d				08 28		08 46							08 58		09 16						09 28
Guildford	a				08 37		08 53				08 50			09 07		09 23						09 38

A To Woking B To London Waterloo

The xx27 and xx57 London Waterloo to Strawberry Hill services continue to London Waterloo via Richmond

Table T152-F

Mondays to Fridays

8 October to 7 December

London - Chessington South, Dorking, Guildford, Shepperton and Hampton Court

		SW	SW	SW	SW	SW A	SW	SW B	SW	SW	SW	SW	SW	SW A	SW	SW B	SW	SW	SW	SW	SW	SW A	SW
London Waterloo	d	08 36	08 39	08 42	08 47	08 50	08 54	08 57	09 03	09 06	09 09	09 12	09 17	09 20	09 24	09 27	09 33	09 36	09 39	09 42	09 47	09 50	09 54
Vauxhall	d	08 40	08 43	08 46	08 51	08 54	08 58	09 01	09 07	09 10	09 13	09 16	09 21	09 24	09 28	09 31	09 37	09 40	09 43	09 46	09 51	09 54	09 58
Clapham Junction	d	08 45	08 48	08 51	08 56	08 59	09 03	09 06	09 12	09 15	09 18	09 21	09 26	09 29	09 33	09 36	09 42	09 45	09 48	09 51	09 56	09 59	10 03
Earlsfield	d	08 48	08 51	08 54	08 59	09 02	09 06	09 09	09 15	09 18	09 21	09 24	09 29	09 32	09 36	09 39	09 45	09 48	09 51	09 54	09 59	10 02	10 06
Wimbledon	d	08 52	08 55	08 58	09 03	09 06	09 10	09 13	09 19	09 22	09 25	09 28	09 33	09 36	09 40	09 43	09 49	09 52	09 55	09 58	10 03	10 06	10 10
Raynes Park	d	08 55	08 58	09 01	09 06		09 13	09 16		09 25	09 28	09 31	09 36		09 43	09 46		09 55	09 58	10 01	10 06		10 13
Motspur Park	d		09 01		09 09		09 16				09 31		09 39		09 46				10 01		10 09		10 16
Malden Manor	d				09 12								09 42								10 12		
Tolworth	d				09 15								09 45								10 15		
Chessington North	d				09 18								09 48								10 18		
Chessington South	a				09 23								09 53								10 21		
Worcester Park	d		09 03				09 18				09 33				09 48				10 03				10 18
Stoneleigh	d		09 06				09 21				09 36				09 51				10 06				10 21
Ewell West	d		09 09				09 24				09 39				09 54				10 09				10 24
Epsom 182	a		09 16				09 27				09 42				09 57				10 17				10 27
	d		09 17				09 28				09 47				09 58				10 18				10 28
Ashtead 182	d		09 21				09 32				09 51				10 02				10 22				10 32
Leatherhead 182	d		09 24				09 35				09 54				10 05				10 25				10 35
Box Hill & Westhumble 182	d																						
Dorking 182	a						09 44								10 14								10 44
New Malden	d	08 58		09 04				09 19		09 28		09 34				09 49		09 58		10 04			
Norbiton	d			09 07				09 22				09 37				09 52				10 07			
Kingston	a			09 10				09 25				09 40				09 55				10 10			
	d			09 10				09 29				09 40				09 59				10 10			
Hampton Wick	d			09 12				09 31				09 42				10 01				10 12			
Teddington	d			09 15				09 35				09 45				10 05				10 15			
Strawberry Hill	a							09 38								10 08							
Fulwell	d			09 19								09 49								10 19			
Hampton	d			09 23								09 53								10 23			
Kempton Park	d			09 26								09 56								10 26			
Sunbury	d			09 28								09 58								10 28			
Upper Halliford	d			09 30								10 00								10 30			
Shepperton	a			09 37								10 07								10 37			
Berrylands	d	09 00								09 30								10 00					
Surbiton	d	09 05				09a13			09 27	09 35				09a43			09 57	10 05				10a13	
Thames Ditton	d	09 09								09 39								10 09					
Hampton Court	a	09 12								09 42								10 12					
Hinchley Wood	d								09 31								10 01						
Claygate	d								09 34								10 04						
Oxshott	d								09 37								10 07						
Cobham & Stoke D'abernon	d								09 41								10 11						
Bookham	d		09 29								09 59								10 30				
Effingham Junction	d		09 33						09 45		10 03						10 15		10 34				
Horsley	d		09 36						09 48		10 06						10 18		10 36				
Clandon	d		09 41						09 53		10 11						10 23		10 41				
London Road (Guildford)	d		09 46						09 58		10 16						10 28		10 46				
Guildford	a		09 53						10 07		10 23						10 37		10 53				

A To Woking B To London Waterloo

The xx27 and xx57 London Waterloo to Strawberry Hill services continue to London Waterloo via Richmond

Table T152-F

Mondays to Fridays

8 October to 7 December

London - Chessington South, Dorking, Guildford, Shepperton and Hampton Court

		SW A	SW	SW	SW	SW	SW	SW B	SW	SW A	SW	SW	SW	SW	SW	SW B	SW	SW A	SW	SW	SW	SW
London Waterloo	d	09 57	10 03	10 06	10 09	10 12	10 17	10 20	10 24	10 27	10 33	10 36	10 39	10 42	10 47	10 50	10 54	10 57	11 03	11 06	11 09	11 12
Vauxhall	d	10 01	10 07	10 10	10 13	10 16	10 21	10 24	10 28	10 31	10 37	10 40	10 43	10 46	10 51	10 54	10 58	11 01	11 07	11 10	11 13	11 16
Clapham Junction	d	10 06	10 12	10 15	10 18	10 21	10 26	10 29	10 33	10 36	10 42	10 45	10 48	10 51	10 56	10 59	11 03	11 06	11 12	11 15	11 18	11 21
Earlsfield	d	10 09	10 15	10 18	10 21	10 24	10 29	10 32	10 36	10 39	10 45	10 48	10 51	10 54	10 59	11 02	11 06	11 09	11 15	11 18	11 21	11 24
Wimbledon	d	10 13	10 19	10 22	10 25	10 28	10 33	10 36	10 40	10 43	10 49	10 52	10 55	10 58	11 03	11 06	11 10	11 13	11 19	11 22	11 25	11 28
Raynes Park	d	10 16		10 25	10 28	10 31	10 36		10 43	10 46		10 55	10 58	11 01	11 06		11 13	11 16		11 25	11 28	11 31
Motspur Park	d				10 31		10 39		10 46				11 01		11 09		11 16				11 31	
Malden Manor	d						10 42								11 12							
Tolworth	d						10 45								11 15							
Chessington North	d						10 48								11 18							
Chessington South	a						10 53								11 23							
Worcester Park	d				10 33				10 48				11 03				11 18				11 33	
Stoneleigh	d				10 36				10 51				11 06				11 21				11 36	
Ewell West	d				10 39				10 54				11 09				11 24				11 39	
Epsom 182	a				10 46				10 57				11 17				11 27				11 46	
	d				10 47				10 58				11 17				11 28				11 47	
Ashtead 182	d				10 51				11 02				11 21				11 32				11 51	
Leatherhead 182	d				10 54				11 05				11 24				11 35				11 54	
Box Hill & Westhumble 182	d																					
Dorking 182	a								11 14								11 44					
New Malden	d	10 19		10 28		10 34				10 49		10 58		11 04				11 19		11 28		11 34
Norbiton	d	10 22				10 37				10 52				11 07				11 22				11 37
Kingston	a	10 25				10 40				10 55				11 10				11 25				11 40
	d	10 29				10 40				10 59				11 10				11 29				11 40
Hampton Wick	d	10 31				10 42				11 01				11 12				11 31				11 42
Teddington	d	10 35				10 45				11 05				11 15				11 35				11 45
Strawberry Hill	a	10 38								11 08								11 38				
Fulwell	d					10 49								11 19								11 49
Hampton	d					10 53								11 23								11 53
Kempton Park	d					10 56								11 26								11 56
Sunbury	d					10 58								11 28								11 58
Upper Halliford	d					11 00								11 30								12 00
Shepperton	a					11 07								11 37								12 07
Berrylands	d			10 30								11 00								11 30		
Surbiton	d		10 27	10 35				10a43			10 57	11 05				11a13			11 27	11 35		
Thames Ditton	d			10 39								11 09								11 39		
Hampton Court	a			10 42								11 12								11 42		
Hinchley Wood	d		10 31								11 01								11 31			
Claygate	d		10 34								11 04								11 34			
Oxshott	d		10 37								11 07								11 37			
Cobham & Stoke D'abernon	d		10 41								11 11								11 41			
Bookham	d				10 59								11 29								11 59	
Effingham Junction	d		10 45		11 03						11 15		11 33						11 45		12 03	
Horsley	d		10 48		11 06						11 18		11 36						11 48		12 06	
Clandon	d		10 53		11 11						11 23		11 41						11 53		12 11	
London Road (Guildford)	d		10 58		11 16						11 28		11 46						11 58		12 16	
Guildford	a		11 08		11 23						11 35		11 53						12 07		12 23	

A To London Waterloo B To Woking

The xx27 and xx57 London Waterloo to Strawberry Hill services continue to London Waterloo via Richmond

Table T152-F

Mondays to Fridays

8 October to 7 December

London - Chessington South, Dorking, Guildford, Shepperton and Hampton Court

		SW	SW	SW	SW	SW	SW	SW	SW	SW	SW	SW	SW	SW	SW	SW	SW	SW	SW	SW	SW	SW	SW
			A		B						A		B						A		B		
London Waterloo ⊖	d	11 17	11 20	11 24	11 27	11 33	11 36	11 39	11 42	11 47	11 50	11 54	11 57	12 03	12 06	12 09	12 12	12 17	12 20	12 24	12 27	12 33	12 36
Vauxhall ⊖	d	11 21	11 24	11 28	11 31	11 37	11 40	11 43	11 46	11 51	11 54	11 58	12 01	12 07	12 10	12 13	12 16	12 21	12 24	12 28	12 31	12 37	12 40
Clapham Junction	d	11 26	11 29	11 33	11 36	11 42	11 45	11 48	11 51	11 56	11 59	12 03	12 06	12 12	12 15	12 18	12 21	12 26	12 29	12 33	12 36	12 42	12 45
Earlsfield	d	11 29	11 32	11 36	11 39	11 45	11 48	11 51	11 54	11 59	12 02	12 06	12 09	12 15	12 18	12 21	12 24	12 29	12 32	12 36	12 39	12 45	12 48
Wimbledon ⊖	d	11 33	11 36	11 40	11 43	11 49	11 52	11 55	11 58	12 03	12 06	12 10	12 13	12 19	12 22	12 25	12 28	12 33	12 36	12 40	12 43	12 49	12 52
Raynes Park	d	11 36		11 43	11 46		11 55	11 58	12 01	12 06		12 13	12 16		12 25	12 28	12 31	12 36		12 43	12 46		12 55
Motspur Park	d	11 39		11 46				12 01		12 09		12 16				12 31		12 39		12 46			
Malden Manor	d	11 42								12 12								12 42					
Tolworth	d	11 45								12 15								12 45					
Chessington North	d	11 48								12 18								12 48					
Chessington South	a	11 53								12 23								12 53					
Worcester Park	d			11 48				12 03				12 18				12 33				12 48			
Stoneleigh	d			11 51				12 06				12 21				12 36				12 51			
Ewell West	d			11 54				12 09				12 24				12 39				12 54			
Epsom 182	a			11 57				12 17				12 27				12 46				12 57			
	d			11 58				12 17				12 28				12 47				12 58			
Ashtead 182	d			12 02				12 21				12 32				12 51				13 02			
Leatherhead 182	d			12 05				12 24				12 35				12 54				13 05			
Box Hill & Westhumble 182	d																						
Dorking 182	a			12 14								12 44								13 14			
New Malden	d				11 49		11 58		12 04				12 19		12 28		12 34				12 49		12 58
Norbiton	d				11 52				12 07				12 22				12 37				12 52		
Kingston	a				11 55				12 10				12 25				12 40				12 55		
	d				11 59				12 10				12 29				12 40				12 59		
Hampton Wick	d				12 01				12 12				12 31				12 42				13 01		
Teddington	d				12 05				12 15				12 35				12 45				13 05		
Strawberry Hill	a				12 08								12 38								13 08		
Fulwell	d								12 19								12 49						
Hampton	d								12 23								12 53						
Kempton Park	d								12 26								12 56						
Sunbury	d								12 28								12 58						
Upper Halliford	d								12 30								13 00						
Shepperton	a								12 37								13 07						
Berrylands	d						12 00								12 30								13 00
Surbiton	d		11a43			11 57	12 05				12a13			12 27	12 35				12a43			12 57	13 05
Thames Ditton	d						12 09								12 39								13 09
Hampton Court	a						12 12								12 42								13 12
Hinchley Wood	d					12 01								12 31								13 01	
Claygate	d					12 04								12 34								13 04	
Oxshott	d					12 07								12 37								13 07	
Cobham & Stoke D'abernon	d					12 11								12 41								13 11	
Bookham	d							12 29								12 59							
Effingham Junction	d					12 15		12 33						12 45		13 03						13 15	
Horsley	d					12 18		12 36						12 48		13 06						13 18	
Clandon	d					12 23		12 41						12 53		13 11						13 23	
London Road (Guildford)	d					12 28		12 46						12 58		13 16						13 28	
Guildford	a					12 37		12 53						13 07		13 23						13 37	

A To Woking B To London Waterloo

The xx27 and xx57 London Waterloo to Strawberry Hill services continue to London Waterloo via Richmond

Table T152-F

Mondays to Fridays

8 October to 7 December

London - Chessington South, Dorking, Guildford, Shepperton and Hampton Court

		SW	SW	SW	SW	SW	SW	SW	SW	SW	SW	SW	SW	SW	SW	SW	SW	SW	SW	SW	SW	SW	SW
					A		B						A		B						A		B
London Waterloo ⊖	d	12 39	12 42	12 47	12 50	12 54	12 57	13 03	13 06	13 09	13 12	13 17	13 20	13 24	13 27	13 33	13 36	13 39	13 42	13 47	13 50	13 54	13 57
Vauxhall ⊖	d	12 43	12 46	12 51	12 54	12 58	13 01	13 07	13 10	13 13	13 16	13 21	13 24	13 28	13 31	13 37	13 40	13 43	13 46	13 51	13 54	13 58	14 01
Clapham Junction	d	12 48	12 51	12 56	12 59	13 03	13 06	13 12	13 15	13 18	13 21	13 26	13 29	13 33	13 36	13 42	13 45	13 48	13 51	13 56	13 59	14 03	14 06
Earlsfield	d	12 51	12 54	12 59	13 02	13 06	13 09	13 15	13 18	13 21	13 24	13 29	13 32	13 36	13 39	13 45	13 48	13 51	13 54	13 59	14 02	14 06	14 09
Wimbledon ⊖	d	12 55	12 58	13 03	13 06	13 10	13 13	13 19	13 22	13 25	13 28	13 33	13 36	13 40	13 43	13 49	13 52	13 55	13 58	14 03	14 06	14 10	14 13
Raynes Park	d	12 58	13 01	13 06		13 13	13 16		13 25	13 28	13 31	13 36		13 43	13 46		13 55	13 58	14 01	14 06		14 13	14 16
Motspur Park	d	13 01		13 09		13 16				13 31		13 39		13 46				14 01		14 09		14 16	
Malden Manor	d			13 12								13 42								14 12			
Tolworth	d			13 15								13 45								14 15			
Chessington North	d			13 18								13 48								14 18			
Chessington South	a			13 23								13 53								14 23			
Worcester Park	d	13 03				13 18				13 33				13 48				14 03				14 18	
Stoneleigh	d	13 06				13 21				13 36				13 51				14 06				14 21	
Ewell West	d	13 09				13 24				13 39				13 54				14 09				14 24	
Epsom 182	a	13 17				13 27				13 46				13 57				14 17				14 27	
	d	13 17				13 28				13 47				13 58				14 17				14 28	
Ashtead 182	d	13 21				13 32				13 51				14 02				14 21				14 32	
Leatherhead 182	d	13 24				13 35				13 54				14 05				14 24				14 35	
Box Hill & Westhumble 182	d																						
Dorking 182	a					13 44								14 14								14 44	
New Malden	d		13 04				13 19		13 28		13 34				13 49		13 58		14 04				14 19
Norbiton	d		13 07				13 22				13 37				13 52				14 07				14 22
Kingston	a		13 10				13 25				13 40				13 55				14 10				14 25
	d		13 10				13 29				13 40				13 59				14 10				14 29
Hampton Wick	d		13 12				13 31				13 42				14 01				14 12				14 31
Teddington	d		13 15				13 35				13 45				14 05				14 15				14 35
Strawberry Hill	a						13 38								14 08								14 38
Fulwell	d		13 19								13 49								14 19				
Hampton	d		13 23								13 53								14 23				
Kempton Park	d		13 26								13 56								14 26				
Sunbury	d		13 28								13 58								14 28				
Upper Halliford	d		13 30								14 00								14 30				
Shepperton	a		13 37								14 07								14 37				
Berrylands	d								13 30								14 00						
Surbiton	d				13a13			13 27	13 35				13a43			13 57	14 05				14a13		
Thames Ditton	d								13 39								14 09						
Hampton Court	a								13 42								14 12						
Hinchley Wood	d							13 31								14 01							
Claygate	d							13 34								14 04							
Oxshott	d							13 37								14 07							
Cobham & Stoke D'abernon	d							13 41								14 11							
Bookham	d	13 29								13 59								14 29					
Effingham Junction	d	13 33						13 45		14 03						14 15		14 33					
Horsley	d	13 36						13 48		14 06						14 18		14 36					
Clandon	d	13 41						13 53		14 11						14 23		14 41					
London Road (Guildford)	d	13 46						13 58		14 16						14 28		14 46					
Guildford	a	13 53						14 07		14 23						14 37		14 53					

A To Woking B To London Waterloo

The xx27 and xx57 London Waterloo to Strawberry Hill services continue to London Waterloo via Richmond

London - Chessington South, Dorking, Guildford, Shepperton and Hampton Court

		SW	SW	SW	SW	SW	SW	SW	SW	SW	SW	SW	SW	SW	SW	SW	SW	SW	SW	SW	SW	SW
							A		B						A		B					
London Waterloo ⊖	d	14 03	14 06	14 09	14 12	14 17	14 20	14 24	14 27	14 33	14 36	14 39	14 42	14 47	14 50	14 54	14 57	15 03	15 06	15 09	15 12	15 17
Vauxhall ⊖	d	14 07	14 10	14 13	14 16	14 21	14 24	14 28	14 31	14 37	14 40	14 43	14 46	14 51	14 54	14 58	15 01	15 07	15 10	15 13	15 16	15 21
Clapham Junction	d	14 12	14 15	14 18	14 21	14 26	14 29	14 33	14 36	14 42	14 45	14 48	14 51	14 56	14 59	15 03	15 06	15 12	15 15	15 18	15 21	15 26
Earlsfield	d	14 15	14 18	14 21	14 24	14 29	14 32	14 36	14 39	14 45	14 48	14 51	14 54	14 59	15 02	15 06	15 09	15 15	15 18	15 21	15 24	15 29
Wimbledon ⊖	d	14 19	14 22	14 25	14 28	14 33	14 36	14 40	14 43	14 49	14 52	14 55	14 58	15 03	15 06	15 10	15 13	15 19	15 22	15 25	15 28	15 33
Raynes Park	d		14 25	14 28	14 31	14 36		14 43	14 46		14 55	14 58	15 01	15 06		15 13	15 16		15 25	15 28	15 31	15 36
Motspur Park	d			14 31		14 39		14 46				15 01		15 09		15 16				15 31		15 39
Malden Manor	d					14 42								15 12								15 42
Tolworth	d					14 45								15 15								15 45
Chessington North	d					14 48								15 18								15 48
Chessington South	a					14 53								15 23								15 53
Worcester Park	d			14 33				14 48				15 03				15 18				15 33		
Stoneleigh	d			14 36				14 51				15 06				15 21				15 36		
Ewell West	d			14 39				14 54				15 09				15 24				15 39		
Epsom 182	a			14 46				14 57				15 16				15 27				15 46		
	d			14 47				14 58				15 17				15 28				15 47		
Ashtead 182	d			14 51				15 02				15 21				15 32				15 51		
Leatherhead 182	d			14 54				15 05				15 24				15 35				15 54		
Box Hill & Westhumble 182	d																					
Dorking 182	a							15 14								15 44						
New Malden	d		14 28		14 34				14 49		14 58		15 04				15 19		15 28		15 34	
Norbiton	d				14 37				14 52				15 07				15 22				15 37	
Kingston	a				14 40				14 55				15 10				15 25				15 40	
	d				14 40				14 59				15 10				15 29				15 40	
Hampton Wick	d				14 42				15 01				15 12				15 31				15 42	
Teddington	d				14 45				15 05				15 15				15 35				15 45	
Strawberry Hill	a								15 08								15 38					
Fulwell	d				14 49								15 19								15 49	
Hampton	d				14 53								15 23								15 53	
Kempton Park	d				14 56								15 26								15 56	
Sunbury	d				14 58								15 28								15 58	
Upper Halliford	d				15 00								15 30								16 00	
Shepperton	a				15 07								15 37								16 07	
Berrylands	d		14 30								15 00								15 30			
Surbiton	d	14 27	14 35				14a43			14 57	15 05				15a13			15 27	15 35			
Thames Ditton	d		14 39								15 09								15 39			
Hampton Court	a		14 42								15 12								15 42			
Hinchley Wood	d	14 31								15 01								15 31				
Claygate	d	14 34								15 04								15 34				
Oxshott	d	14 37								15 07								15 37				
Cobham & Stoke D'abernon	d	14 41								15 11								15 41				
Bookham	d			14 59								15 29								15 59		
Effingham Junction	d	14 45		15 03						15 15		15 33						15 45		16 03		
Horsley	d	14 48		15 06						15 18		15 36						15 48		16 06		
Clandon	d	14 53		15 11						15 23		15 41						15 53		16 11		
London Road (Guildford)	d	14 58		15 16						15 28		15 46						15 58		16 16		
Guildford	a	15 07		15 23						15 37		15 53						16 07		16 23		

A To Woking

B To London Waterloo

The xx27 and xx57 London Waterloo to Strawberry Hill services continue to London Waterloo via Richmond

London - Chessington South, Dorking, Guildford, Shepperton and Hampton Court

		SW	SW	SW	SW	SW	SW	SW	SW	SW	SW	SW	SW	SW	SW	SW	SW	SW	SW	SW	SW	SW	SW
		A		B						A		B						◇ A		B			
London Waterloo ⊖	d	15 20	15 24	15 27	15 33	15 36	15 39	15 42	15 47	15 50	15 54	15 57	16 03	16 06	16 09	16 12	16 17	16 20	16 24	16 27	16 33	16 36	16 39
Vauxhall ⊖	d	15 24	15 28	15 31	15 37	15 40	15 43	15 46	15 51	15 54	15 58	16 01	16 07	16 10	16 13	16 16	16 21	16 24	16 28	16 31	16 37	16 40	16 43
Clapham Junction	d	15 29	15 33	15 36	15 42	15 45	15 48	15 51	15 56	15 59	16 03	16 06	16 12	16 15	16 18	16 21	16 26	16 29	16 33	16 36	16 42	16 45	16 48
Earlsfield	d	15 32	15 36	15 39	15 45	15 48	15 51	15 54	15 59	16 02	16 06	16 09	16 15	16 18	16 21	16 24	16 29	16 32	16 36	16 39	16 45	16 48	16 51
Wimbledon ⊖	d	15 36	15 40	15 43	15 49	15 52	15 55	15 58	16 03	16 06	16 10	16 13	16 19	16 22	16 25	16 28	16 33	16 36	16 40	16 43	16 49	16 52	16 55
Raynes Park	d		15 43	15 46		15 55	15 58	16 01	16 06		16 13	16 16		16 25	16 28	16 31	16 36		16 43	16 46		16 55	16 58
Motspur Park	d		15 46				16 01		16 09		16 16				16 31		16 39		16 46				17 01
Malden Manor	d								16 12								16 42						
Tolworth	d								16 15								16 45						
Chessington North	d								16 18								16 48						
Chessington South	a								16 23								16 53						
Worcester Park	d		15 48				16 03				16 18				16 33				16 48				17 03
Stoneleigh	d		15 51				16 06				16 21				16 36				16 51				17 06
Ewell West	d		15 54				16 09				16 24				16 39				16 54				17 09
Epsom 182	a		15 57				16 15				16 27				16 46				16 57				17 12
	d		15 58				16 17				16 28				16 47				16 58				17 17
Ashtead 182	d		16 02				16 21				16 32				16 51				17 02				17 21
Leatherhead 182	d		16 05				16 24				16 35				16 54				17 05				17 24
Box Hill & Westhumble 182	d																		17 10				
Dorking 182	a		16 14								16 44								17 16				
New Malden	d			15 49		15 58		16 04				16 19		16 28		16 34				16 49		16 58	
Norbiton	d			15 52				16 07				16 22				16 37				16 52			
Kingston	a			15 55				16 10				16 25				16 40				16 55			
	d			15 59				16 10				16 29				16 40				16 59			
Hampton Wick	d			16 01				16 12				16 31				16 42				17 01			
Teddington	d			16 05				16 15				16 35				16 45				17 05			
Strawberry Hill	a			16 08								16 38								17 08			
Fulwell	d							16 19								16 49							
Hampton	d							16 23								16 53							
Kempton Park	d							16 26								16 56							
Sunbury	d							16 28								16 58							
Upper Halliford	d							16 30								17 00							
Shepperton	a							16 37								17 07							
Berrylands	d					16 00								16 30								17 00	
Surbiton	d	15a43			15 57	16 05				16a13			16 27	16 35				16a43			16 57	17 05	
Thames Ditton	d					16 09								16 39								17 09	
Hampton Court	a					16 12								16 44								17 14	
Hinchley Wood	d				16 01								16 31								17 01		
Claygate	d				16 04								16 34								17 04		
Oxshott	d				16 07								16 37								17 07		
Cobham & Stoke D'abernon	d				16 11								16 41								17 11		
Bookham	d						16 29								16 59								17 29
Effingham Junction	d				16 15		16 33						16 45		17 03						17 15		17 33
Horsley	d				16 18		16 36						16 48		17 06						17 18		17 36
Clandon	d				16 23		16 41						16 53		17 11						17 23		17 41
London Road (Guildford)	d				16 28		16 46						16 58		17 16						17 28		17 46
Guildford	a				16 37		16 53						17 07		17 25						17 37		17 55

A To Woking

B To London Waterloo

The xx27 and xx57 London Waterloo to Strawberry Hill services continue to London Waterloo via Richmond

Table T152-F

Mondays to Fridays
8 October to 7 December

London - Chessington South, Dorking, Guildford, Shepperton and Hampton Court

		SW	SW	SW	SW	SW	SW	SW	SW	SW	SW	SW	SW	SW	SW	SW	SW	SW	SW	TL	SW	SW
				◇ A		B	◇1						◇ A		B		◇1			C		
London Waterloo 15 ⊖	d	16 42	16 47	16 50	16 54	16 57	17 02	17 03	17 06	17 09	17 12	17 17	17 20	17 24	17 27	17 31	17 32	17 33	17 36		17 39	17 43
Vauxhall ⊖	d	16 46	16 51	16 54	16 58	17 01		17 07	17 10	17 13	17 16	17 21	17 24	17 28	17 31	17 35		17 38	17 41		17 44	17 47
Clapham Junction 10	d	16 51	16 56	16 59	17 03	17 06		17 12	17 15	17 18	17 21	17 26	17 29	17 33	17 36	17 40		17 43	17 46		17 49	17 53
Earlsfield	d	16 54	16 59	17 02	17 06	17 09		17 15	17 18	17 21	17 24	17 29	17 32	17 36	17 39	17 43		17 46	17 49		17 52	
Wimbledon 8 ⊖ ⇌	d	16 58	17 03	17 06	17 10	17 13		17 19	17 22	17 25	17 28	17 33	17 36	17 40	17 43	17 47		17 50	17 53		17 56	
Raynes Park 8	d	17 01	17 06		17 13	17 16			17 25	17 28	17 31	17 36		17 43	17 46	17 50			17 56		17 59	
Motspur Park	d		17 09		17 16					17 31		17 39				17 53					18 02	
Malden Manor	d		17 12									17 42										
Tolworth	d		17 15									17 45										
Chessington North	d		17 18									17 48										
Chessington South	a		17 23									17 53										
Worcester Park	d				17 18					17 33				17 47		17 56					18 04	
Stoneleigh	d				17 21					17 36						18 00					18 07	
Ewell West	d				17 24					17 39						18 03					18 10	
Epsom 8 182	a				17 27					17 42				17 57		18 08					18 17	
	d				17 28					17 47				17 57						18 10	18 19	
Ashtead 182	d				17 32					17 51				18 01						18 15	18 23	
Leatherhead 182	d				17 35					17 54				18 04						18 19	18 26	
Box Hill & Westhumble 182	d				17 40									18 09								
Dorking 4 182	a				17 46									18 17								
New Malden 8	d	17 04				17 19			17 28		17 34				17 49				17 59			
Norbiton	d	17 07				17 22					17 37				17 52							
Kingston	a	17 10				17 25					17 40				17 55							
	d	17 10				17 29					17 40				17 59							
Hampton Wick	d	17 12				17 31					17 42				18 01							
Teddington	d	17 15				17 35					17 45				18 05							
Strawberry Hill	a					17 38									18 08							18 11
Fulwell	d	17 19									17 49											18 13
Hampton	d	17 23									17 53											18 17
Kempton Park	d	17 26									17 56											
Sunbury	d	17 28									17 58											18 21
Upper Halliford	d	17 30									18 00											18 23
Shepperton	a	17 37									18 06											18 30
Berrylands	d								17 30										18 01			
Surbiton 8	d			17a13			17 18	17 27	17 35				17a43				17 48	17 58	18 06			
Thames Ditton	d								17 39										18 10			
Hampton Court	a								17 44										18 15			
Hinchley Wood	d							17 31										18 05				
Claygate	d							17 34										18 08				
Oxshott	d							17 37										18 11				
Cobham & Stoke D'abernon	d							17 41										18 15				
Bookham	d									17 59										18 24	18 31	
Effingham Junction 8	d							17 45		18a05								18 20		18 28	18a42	
Horsley	d							17 48										18 22		18 30		
Clandon	d							17 53										18 27		18 35		
London Road (Guildford)	d							17 58										18 32		18 40		
Guildford	a						17 56	18 07									18 30	18 43		18 44		

A To Woking
B To London Waterloo
C From London Bridge

The xx27 and xx57 London Waterloo to Strawberry Hill services continue to London Waterloo via Richmond

Table T152-F

Mondays to Fridays
8 October to 7 December

London - Chessington South, Dorking, Guildford, Shepperton and Hampton Court

		SW	SW	SW	SW	SW	SW	SW	SW	SW	SW	SW	SW	SW	SW	SW	SW	SW	SW	SW	SW	SW	SW
				◇ A		B		◇1 A							◇ A		B						
London Waterloo 15 ⊖	d	17 42	17 47	17 50	17 54	17 57	18 01	18 02	18 03	18 06	18 09	18 13	18 12	18 17	18 20	18 24	18 27	18 31	18 33	18 36	18 39	18 43	18 42
Vauxhall ⊖	d	17 47	17 51	17 54	17 58	18 01	18 05		18 08	18 11	18 14	18 17	18 17	18 21	18 24	18 28	18 31	18 35	18 38	18 41	18 44	18 47	18 47
Clapham Junction 10	d	17 52	17 56	17 59	18 03	18 06	18 10		18 13	18 16	18 19	18 23	18 22	18 26	18 29	18 33	18 36	18 40	18 43	18 46	18 49	18 53	18 52
Earlsfield	d	17 55	17 59	18 02	18 06	18 09	18 13		18 16	18 19	18 22		18 25	18 29	18 32	18 36	18 39	18 43	18 46	18 49	18 52		18 55
Wimbledon 8 ⊖ ⇌	d	17 59	18 03	18 06	18 10	18 13	18 17		18 20	18 23	18 26		18 29	18 33	18 36	18 40	18 43	18 47	18 50	18 53	18 56		18 59
Raynes Park 8	d	18 02	18 06		18 13	18 16	18 20			18 26	18 29		18 32	18 36		18 43	18 46	18 50		18 56	18 59		19 02
Motspur Park	d		18 09				18 23				18 32			18 39				18 53			19 02		
Malden Manor	d		18 12											18 42									
Tolworth	d		18 15											18 45									
Chessington North	d		18 18											18 48									
Chessington South	a		18 23											18 53									
Worcester Park	d				18 17		18 25				18 34					18 47		18 56			19 04		
Stoneleigh	d						18 28				18 37							18 59			19 07		
Ewell West	d						18 31				18 40							19 02			19 10		
Epsom 8 182	a				18 27		18 38				18 49					18 57		19 07			19 16		
	d				18 27						18 52					18 57					19 18		
Ashtead 182	d				18 31						18 56					19 01					19 22		
Leatherhead 182	d				18 34						18 59					19 04					19 25		
Box Hill & Westhumble 182	d				18 39											19 09							
Dorking 4 182	a				18 47											19 16							
New Malden 8	d	18 05				18 19				18 29			18 35				18 49			18 59			19 05
Norbiton	d	18 08				18 22							18 38				18 52						19 08
Kingston	a	18 11				18 25							18 41				18 55						19 11
	d	18 11				18 29							18 41				18 59						19 11
Hampton Wick	d	18 13				18 31							18 43				19 01						19 13
Teddington	d	18 16				18 35							18 46				19 05						19 16
Strawberry Hill	a					18 38						18 41					19 08					19 11	
Fulwell	d	18 20										18 43	18 50									19 13	19 20
Hampton	d	18 24										18 47	18 54									19 17	19 24
Kempton Park	d	18 27											18 57										19 27
Sunbury	d	18 29										18 51	18 59									19 21	19 29
Upper Halliford	d	18 31										18 53	19 01									19 23	19 31
Shepperton	a	18 40										19 00	19 10									19 30	19 39
Berrylands	d									18 31										19 01			
Surbiton 8	d			18a13				18a17	18 28	18 36					18a43				18 58	19 06			
Thames Ditton	d									18 40										19 10			
Hampton Court	a									18 45										19 15			
Hinchley Wood	d								18 35										19 02				
Claygate	d								18 38										19 05				
Oxshott	d								18 41										19 08				
Cobham & Stoke D'abernon	d								18 45										19 12				
Bookham	d										19 05										19 30		
Effingham Junction 8	d								18 50		19 09								19 16		19 34		
Horsley	d								18 52		19 11								19 19		19 37		
Clandon	d								18 57		19 16								19 24		19 42		
London Road (Guildford)	d								19 02		19 21								19 29		19 47		
Guildford	a								19 12		19 30								19 38		19 56		

A To Woking
B To London Waterloo

The xx27 and xx57 London Waterloo to Strawberry Hill services continue to London Waterloo via Richmond

Table T152-F

Mondays to Fridays

8 October to 7 December

London - Chessington South, Dorking, Guildford, Shepperton and Hampton Court

		SW	SW	SW	SW	SW		SW	SW	SW	SW	TL	SW	SW	SW	SW		SW	SW	SW	SW	SW	SW	SW	SW
			◇ A			B			■ A			C				A				B					
London Waterloo ⊖	d	18 47	18 50	18 52	18 54	18 57		19 01	19 02	19 03	19 06		19 09	19 12	19 17	19 20		19 23	19 24	19 27	19 33	19 36	19 39	19 42	19 47
Vauxhall ⊖	d	18 51	18 54		18 58	19 01		19 05		19 08	19 11		19 14	19 17	19 21	19 24			19 28	19 31	19 37	19 40	19 43	19 46	19 51
Clapham Junction	d	18 56	18 59		19 03	19 06		19 10		19 13	19 16		19 19	19 22	19 26	19 29			19 33	19 36	19 42	19 45	19 48	19 51	19 56
Earlsfield	d	18 59	19 02		19 06	19 09		19 13		19 16	19 19		19 22	19 25	19 29	19 32			19 36	19 39	19 45	19 48	19 51	19 54	19 59
Wimbledon ⊖ ⇌	d	19 03	19 06		19 10	19 13		19 17		19 20	19 23		19 26	19 29	19 33	19 36			19 40	19 43	19 49	19 52	19 55	19 58	20 03
Raynes Park	d	19 06			19 13	19 16		19 20			19 26		19 29	19 32	19 36				19 43	19 46		19 55	19 58	20 01	20 06
Motspur Park	d	19 09						19 23					19 32		19 39				19 46				20 01		20 09
Malden Manor	d	19 12													19 42										20 12
Tolworth	d	19 15													19 45										20 15
Chessington North	d	19 18													19 48										20 18
Chessington South	a	19 23													19 53										20 23
Worcester Park	d				19 17			19 25					19 34						19 48				20 03		
Stoneleigh	d							19 28					19 37						19 51				20 06		
Ewell West	d							19 31					19 40						19 54				20 09		
Epsom 182	a				19 27			19 36					19 48						19 57				20 16		
	d				19 27							19 40	19 52						19 58				20 17		
Ashtead 182	d				19 31							19 45	19 56						20 02				20 21		
Leatherhead 182	d				19 34							19 48	19 59						20 05				20 24		
Box Hill & Westhumble 182	d				19 39														20 10						
Dorking 182	a				19 46														20 16						
New Malden	d					19 19					19 29			19 35						19 49		19 58		20 04	
Norbiton	d					19 22								19 38						19 52				20 07	
Kingston	a					19 25								19 41						19 55				20 10	
	d					19 29								19 41						19 59				20 10	
Hampton Wick	d					19 31								19 43						20 01				20 12	
Teddington	d					19 35								19 46						20 05				20 15	
Strawberry Hill	a					19 38														20 08					
Fulwell	d													19 50										20 19	
Hampton	d													19 54										20 23	
Kempton Park	d													19 57										20 26	
Sunbury	d													19 59										20 28	
Upper Halliford	d													20 01										20 30	
Shepperton	a													20 07										20 37	
Berrylands	d										19 31											20 00			
Surbiton	d		19a13	19 08					19a17	19 28	19 36					19a43		19 40			19 57	20 05			
Thames Ditton	d										19 40							19 45				20 09			
Hampton Court	a										19 43							19 47				20 12			
Hinchley Wood	d			19 12						19 32											20 01				
Claygate	d			19 15						19 35											20 04				
Oxshott	d			19 18						19 38											20 07				
Cobham & Stoke D'abernon	d			19 22						19 42											20 11				
Bookham	d											19 53	20 04										20 29		
Effingham Junction	d			19 26						19 46		19 58	20 08								20 15		20 33		
Horsley	d			19 29						19 48		20 00	20 10								20 18		20 36		
Clandon	d			19 34						19 53		20 05	20 15								20 23		20 41		
London Road (Guildford)	d			19 39						19 58		20 10	20 20								20 28		20 46		
Guildford	a			19 48						20 06		20 15	20 27								20 37		20 53		

A To Woking **B** To London Waterloo **C** From London Bridge

The xx27 and xx57 London Waterloo to Strawberry Hill services continue to London Waterloo via Richmond

Table T152-F

Mondays to Fridays

8 October to 7 December

London - Chessington South, Dorking, Guildford, Shepperton and Hampton Court

		SW		SW	SW	SW	SW	SW	SW	SW	SW	SW		SW	SW	SW	SW	SW	SW	SW	SW	SW		SW	SW
		A			B						A			B						A		B			
London Waterloo ⊖	d	19 50		19 54	19 57	20 03	20 06	20 09	20 12	20 17	20 20	20 24		20 27	20 33	20 36	20 39	20 42	20 47	20 50	20 54	20 57		21 03	21 06
Vauxhall ⊖	d	19 54		19 58	20 01	20 07	20 10	20 13	20 16	20 21	20 24	20 28		20 31	20 37	20 40	20 43	20 46	20 51	20 54	20 58	21 01		21 07	21 10
Clapham Junction	d	19 59		20 03	20 06	20 12	20 15	20 18	20 21	20 26	20 29	20 33		20 36	20 42	20 45	20 48	20 51	20 56	20 59	21 03	21 06		21 12	21 15
Earlsfield	d	20 02		20 06	20 09	20 15	20 18	20 21	20 24	20 29	20 32	20 36		20 39	20 45	20 48	20 51	20 54	20 59	21 02	21 06	21 09		21 15	21 18
Wimbledon ⊖ ⇌	d	20 06		20 10	20 13	20 19	20 22	20 25	20 28	20 33	20 36	20 40		20 43	20 49	20 52	20 55	20 58	21 03	21 06	21 10	21 13		21 19	21 22
Raynes Park	d			20 13	20 16		20 25	20 28	20 31	20 36		20 43		20 46		20 55	20 58	21 01	21 06		21 13	21 16			21 25
Motspur Park	d			20 16				20 31		20 39		20 46					21 01		21 09		21 16				
Malden Manor	d									20 42									21 12						
Tolworth	d									20 45									21 15						
Chessington North	d									20 48									21 18						
Chessington South	a									20 53									21 23						
Worcester Park	d			20 18				20 33				20 48					21 03				21 18				
Stoneleigh	d			20 21				20 36				20 51					21 06				21 21				
Ewell West	d			20 24				20 39				20 54					21 09				21 24				
Epsom 182	a			20 27				20 42				20 57					21 12				21 27				
	d							20 43									21 13								
Ashtead 182	d							20 47									21 17								
Leatherhead 182	d							20 50									21 20								
Box Hill & Westhumble 182	d							20 55																	
Dorking 182	a							20 59																	
New Malden	d				20 19		20 28		20 34					20 49		20 58		21 04				21 19			21 28
Norbiton	d				20 22				20 37					20 52				21 07				21 22			
Kingston	a				20 25				20 40					20 55				21 10				21 25			
	d				20 29				20 40					20 59				21 10				21 29			
Hampton Wick	d				20 31				20 42					21 01				21 12				21 31			
Teddington	d				20 35				20 45					21 05				21 15				21 35			
Strawberry Hill	a				20 38									21 08								21 38			
Fulwell	d								20 49									21 19							
Hampton	d								20 53									21 23							
Kempton Park	d								20 56									21 26							
Sunbury	d								20 58									21 28							
Upper Halliford	d								21 00									21 30							
Shepperton	a								21 07									21 37							
Berrylands	d						20 30									21 00									21 30
Surbiton	d	20a13				20 27	20 35				20a43				20 57	21 05				21a13				21 27	21 35
Thames Ditton	d						20 39									21 09									21 39
Hampton Court	a						20 42									21 12									21 42
Hinchley Wood	d					20 31									21 01									21 31	
Claygate	d					20 34									21 04									21 34	
Oxshott	d					20 37									21 07									21 37	
Cobham & Stoke D'abernon	d					20 41									21 11									21 41	
Bookham	d																21 25								
Effingham Junction	d					20 45									21 15		21 29							21 45	
Horsley	d					20 48									21 18		21 32							21 48	
Clandon	d					20 53									21 23		21 37							21 53	
London Road (Guildford)	d					20 58									21 28		21 42							21 58	
Guildford	a					21 07									21 37		21 49							22 07	

A To Woking **B** To London Waterloo

The xx27 and xx57 London Waterloo to Strawberry Hill services continue to London Waterloo via Richmond

Table T152-F

Mondays to Fridays
8 October to 7 December

London - Chessington South, Dorking, Guildford, Shepperton and Hampton Court

		SW	SW	SW	SW A	SW	SW B	SW	SW	SW	SW	SW	SW	SW	SW B	SW	SW	SW	SW	SW A	SW B	SW	SW
London Waterloo ⊖	d	21 09	21 12	21 17	21 20	21 24	21 27	21 33	21 36	21 39	21 42	21 47	21 50	21 54	21 57	22 03		22 09	22 12	22 20	22 27	22 33	22 36
Vauxhall ⊖	d	21 13	21 16	21 21	21 24	21 28	21 31	21 37	21 40	21 43	21 46	21 51	21 54	21 58	22 01	22 07		22 13	22 16	22 24	22 31	22 37	22 40
Clapham Junction	d	21 18	21 21	21 26	21 29	21 33	21 36	21 42	21 45	21 48	21 51	21 56	21 59	22 03	22 06	22 12		22 18	22 21	22 29	22 36	22 42	22 45
Earlsfield	d	21 21	21 24	21 29	21 32	21 36	21 39	21 45	21 48	21 51	21 54	21 59	22 02	22 06	22 09	22 15		22 21	22 24	22 32	22 39	22 45	22 48
Wimbledon ⊖	d	21 25	21 28	21 33	21 36	21 40	21 43	21 49	21 52	21 55	21 58	22 03	22 06	22 10	22 13	22 19		22 25	22 28	22 36	22 43	22 49	22 52
Raynes Park	d	21 28	21 31	21 36		21 43	21 46		21 55	21 58	22 01	22 06		22 13	22 16			22 28	22 31		22 46		22 55
Motspur Park	d	21 31		21 39		21 46				22 01		22 09		22 16				22 31					
Malden Manor	d			21 42								22 12											
Tolworth	d			21 45								22 15											
Chessington North	d			21 48								22 18											
Chessington South	a			21 53								22 23											
Worcester Park	d	21 33				21 48				22 03				22 18				22 33					
Stoneleigh	d	21 36				21 51				22 06				22 21				22 36					
Ewell West	d	21 39				21 54				22 09				22 24				22 39					
Epsom 182	a	21 42				21 57				22 12				22 27				22 42					
	d	21 43								22 13								22 43					
Ashtead 182	d	21 47								22 17								22 47					
Leatherhead 182	d	21 50								22 20								22 50					
Box Hill & Westhumble 182	d	21 55																22 55					
Dorking 182	a	21 59																22 59					
New Malden	d		21 34				21 49		21 58		22 04				22 19				22 34		22 49		22 58
Norbiton	d		21 37				21 52				22 07				22 22				22 37		22 52		
Kingston	a		21 40				21 55				22 10				22 25				22 40		22 55		
	d		21 40				21 59				22 10				22 29				22 40		22 59		
Hampton Wick	d		21 42				22 01				22 12				22 31				22 42		23 01		
Teddington	d		21 45				22 05				22 15				22 35				22 45		23 05		
Strawberry Hill	a						22 08								22 38						23 08		
Fulwell	d		21 49								22 19								22 49				
Hampton	d		21 53								22 23								22 53				
Kempton Park	d		21 56								22 26								22 56				
Sunbury	d		21 58								22 28								22 58				
Upper Halliford	d		22 00								22 30								23 00				
Shepperton	a		22 07								22 37								23 07				
Berrylands	d								22 00														23 00
Surbiton	d				21a43			21 57	22 05				22 14			22 27	22 39			22a43		22 57	23 05
Thames Ditton	d								22 09								22 43						23 09
Hampton Court	a								22 12								22 46						23 12
Hinchley Wood	d							22 01								22 31						23 01	
Claygate	d							22 04								22 34						23 04	
Oxshott	d							22 07								22 37						23 07	
Cobham & Stoke D'abernon	d							22 11								22 41						23 11	
Bookham	d									22 25													
Effingham Junction	d							22 15		22 29						22 45						23 15	
Horsley	d							22 18		22 32						22 48						23 18	
Clandon	d							22 23		22 37						22 53						23 23	
London Road (Guildford)	d							22 28		22 42						22 58						23 28	
Guildford	a							22 37		22 49			22 47			23 07						23 37	

A To Woking
B To London Waterloo

The xx27 and xx57 London Waterloo to Strawberry Hill services continue to London Waterloo via Richmond

Table T152-F

Mondays to Fridays
8 October to 7 December

London - Chessington South, Dorking, Guildford, Shepperton and Hampton Court

		SW	SW	SW A	SW B	SW	SW	SW	SW	SW	SW A	SW C	SW	SW	SW	SW
London Waterloo ⊖	d	22 39	22 42	22 50	22 57	23 00	23 03		23 09	23 12	23 20	23 27	23 36	23 42	23 50	23 57
Vauxhall ⊖	d	22 43	22 46	22 54	23 01	23 04	23 07		23 13	23 16	23 24	23 31	23 40	23 46	23 54	00 01
Clapham Junction	d	22 48	22 51	22 59	23 06	23 09	23 12		23 18	23 21	23 29	23 36	23 45	23 51	23 59	00 06
Earlsfield	d	22 51	22 54	23 02	23 09	23 12	23 15		23 21	23 24	23 32	23 39	23 48	23 54	00 02	00 09
Wimbledon ⊖	d	22 55	22 58	23 06	23 13	23 16	23 19		23 25	23 28	23 36	23 43	23 52	23 58	00 06	00 13
Raynes Park	d	22 58	23 01		23 16	23 19			23 28	23 31		23 46	23 55	00 01		00 16
Motspur Park	d	23 01				23 22			23 31					00 04		
Malden Manor	d					23 25										
Tolworth	d					23 28										
Chessington North	d					23 31										
Chessington South	a					23 36										
Worcester Park	d	23 03							23 33					00 06		
Stoneleigh	d	23 06							23 36					00 09		
Ewell West	d	23 09							23 39					00 12		
Epsom 182	a	23 12							23 42					00 16		
	d	23 13							23 43					00 19		
Ashtead 182	d	23 17							23 47					00 23		
Leatherhead 182	d	23 20							23 50					00 26		
Box Hill & Westhumble 182	d								23 55							
Dorking 182	a								23 59							
New Malden	d		23 04		23 19					23 34		23 49	23 58			00 19
Norbiton	d		23 07		23 22					23 37		23 52				00 22
Kingston	a		23 10		23 25					23 40		23 55				00 25
	d		23 10		23 29					23 40		23 55				00 25
Hampton Wick	d		23 12		23 31					23 42		23 57				00 27
Teddington	d		23 15		23 35					23 45		23 59				00 30
Strawberry Hill	a				23 38							00 03				
Fulwell	d		23 19							23 49						00 34
Hampton	d		23 23							23 53						00 38
Kempton Park	d		23 26							23 56						00 41
Sunbury	d		23 28							23 58						00 43
Upper Halliford	d		23 30							23 59						00 45
Shepperton	a		23 37							00 07						00 52
Berrylands	d												23 59			
Surbiton	d			23a13			23 27	23 43			23a44		00 05		00 14	
Thames Ditton	d							23 47					00 09			
Hampton Court	a							23 50					00 12			
Hinchley Wood	d						23 31								00 18	
Claygate	d						23 34								00 20	
Oxshott	d						23 37								00 24	
Cobham & Stoke D'abernon	d						23 41								00 27	
Bookham	d	23 25												00 31		
Effingham Junction	d	23 29					23 45							00 36	00 32	
Horsley	d	23 32					23 48							00 39	00 34	
Clandon	d	23 37					23 53							00 44	00 39	
London Road (Guildford)	d	23 42					23 58							00 49	00 44	
Guildford	a	23 49					00 07							00 56	00 53	

A To Woking
B To London Waterloo
C To Twickenham

The xx27 and xx57 London Waterloo to Strawberry Hill services continue to London Waterloo via Richmond

London - Chessington South, Dorking, Guildford, Shepperton and Hampton Court

Saturdays
26 May to 6 October

		SW A	SW A	SW A	SW A	SW	SW	SW B	SW	SW 1 C	SW	SW ◇1 D	SW B	SW E	SW E	SW	SW	SW	SW B	SW E	SW	SW	SW
London Waterloo ⊖	d					00 09	00 15	00 27	00 42	05 00	05 12	05 20	05 50			06 06	06 12	06 17	06 20	06 27	06 33	06 36	06 39
Vauxhall ⊖	d				00 01	00 13	00 19	00 31	00 46	05 04	05 16	05 24	05 54			06 10	06 16	06 21	06 24	06 31	06 37	06 40	06 43
Clapham Junction	d				00 06	00 20	00 26	00 37	00 51	05 11	05 21	05 29	05 59			06 15	06 21	06 26	06 29	06 36	06 42	06 45	06 48
Earlsfield	d		00 02		00 09	00 23	00 29	00s41		05 14	05 24	05 32	06 02			06 18	06 24	06 29	06 32	06 39	06 45	06 48	06 51
Wimbledon ⊖	d		00 06		00 13	00 27	00 33	00 45	01 05	05 18	05 28	05 36	06 06		06 13	06 22	06 28	06 33	06 36	06 43	06 49	06 52	06 55
Raynes Park	d			00 01	00 16		00 36	00 48	01 08		05 31				06 16	06 25	06 31	06 36		06 46		06 55	06 58
Motspur Park	d			00 04			00 39											06 39					07 01
Malden Manor	d																	06 42					
Tolworth	d																	06 45					
Chessington North	d																	06 48					
Chessington South	a																	06 51					
Worcester Park	d			00 06			00 41																07 03
Stoneleigh	d			00 09			00 44																07 06
Ewell West	d			00 12			00 47																07 09
Epsom 182	a			00 16			00 50																07 12
	d			00 19																			07 13
Ashtead 182	d			00 23																			07 17
Leatherhead 182	d			00 26																			07 20
Box Hill & Westhumble 182	d																						
Dorking 182	a																						
New Malden	d				00 19			00 50	01 11		05 34				06 19	06 28	06 34			06 49		06 58	
Norbiton	d				00 22				01 14		05 37				06 22		06 37			06 52			
Kingston	a				00 25				01 17		05 40				06 25		06 40			06 55			
	d				00 25				01 17		05 40			05 59	06 29		06 40			06 59			
Hampton Wick	d				00 27				01s19		05 42			06 01	06 31		06 42			07 01			
Teddington	d				00 30				01s22		05 45			06 05	06 35		06 45			07 05			
Strawberry Hill	a								01 28					06 08	06 38					07 08			
Fulwell	d				00 34						05 49						06 49						
Hampton	d				00 38						05 53						06 53						
Kempton Park	d				00 41						05 56						06 56						
Sunbury	d				00 43						05 58						06 58						
Upper Halliford	d				00 45						06 00						07 00						
Shepperton	a				00 50						06 03						07 03						
Berrylands	d							00s53								06 30						07 00	
Surbiton	d	00 05	00 14			00 35		00s56		05 26		05 44	06a13			06 35			06a43		06 57	07 05	
Thames Ditton	d	00 09														06 39						07 09	
Hampton Court	a	00 12														06 42						07 12	
Hinchley Wood	d		00 18																		07 01		
Claygate	d		00 20																		07 04		
Oxshott	d		00 24																		07 07		
Cobham & Stoke D'abernon	d		00 27																		07 11		
Bookham	d			00 31																			07 25
Effingham Junction	d		00 32	00 36																	07 15		07 29
Horsley	d		00 34	00 39																	07 18		07 32
Clandon	d		00 39	00 44																	07 23		07 37
London Road (Guildford)	d		00 44	00 49																	07 28		07 42
Guildford	a		00 50	00 53		01 07				06 00		06 23									07 32		07 46

A From London Waterloo
B To Woking
C To Haslemere
D To Portsmouth Harbour
E To London Waterloo

London - Chessington South, Dorking, Guildford, Shepperton and Hampton Court

Saturdays
26 May to 6 October

		SW	SW	SW A	SW B	SW	SW	SW	SW	SW	SW A	SW	SW B	SW	SW	SW	SW	SW	SW A	SW	SW B	SW	SW
London Waterloo ⊖	d	06 42	06 47	06 50	06 57	07 03	07 06	07 09	07 12	07 17	07 20	07 24	07 27	07 33	07 36	07 39	07 42	07 47	07 50	07 54	07 57	08 03	08 06
Vauxhall ⊖	d	06 46	06 51	06 54	07 01	07 07	07 10	07 13	07 16	07 21	07 24	07 28	07 31	07 37	07 40	07 43	07 46	07 51	07 54	07 58	08 01	08 07	08 10
Clapham Junction	d	06 51	06 56	06 59	07 06	07 12	07 15	07 18	07 21	07 26	07 29	07 33	07 36	07 42	07 45	07 48	07 51	07 56	07 59	08 03	08 06	08 12	08 15
Earlsfield	d	06 54	06 59	07 02	07 09	07 15	07 18	07 21	07 24	07 29	07 32	07 36	07 39	07 45	07 48	07 51	07 54	07 59	08 02	08 06	08 09	08 15	08 18
Wimbledon ⊖	d	06 58	07 03	07 06	07 13	07 19	07 22	07 25	07 28	07 33	07 36	07 40	07 43	07 49	07 52	07 55	07 58	08 03	08 06	08 10	08 13	08 19	08 22
Raynes Park	d	07 01	07 06		07 16		07 25	07 28	07 31	07 36		07 43	07 46		07 55	07 58	08 01	08 06		08 13	08 16		08 25
Motspur Park	d		07 09					07 31		07 39		07 46				08 01		08 09		08 16			
Malden Manor	d		07 12							07 42								08 12					
Tolworth	d		07 15							07 45								08 15					
Chessington North	d		07 18							07 48								08 18					
Chessington South	a		07 21							07 51								08 21					
Worcester Park	d							07 33				07 48				08 03				08 18			
Stoneleigh	d							07 36				07 51				08 06				08 21			
Ewell West	d							07 39				07 54				08 09				08 24			
Epsom 182	a							07 42				07 57				08 12				08 27			
	d							07 43				07 58				08 13				08 28			
Ashtead 182	d							07 47				08 02				08 17				08 32			
Leatherhead 182	d							07 50				08 05				08 20				08 35			
Box Hill & Westhumble 182	d																						
Dorking 182	a											08 11								08 41			
New Malden	d	07 04			07 19		07 28		07 34				07 49		07 58		08 04				08 19		08 28
Norbiton	d	07 07			07 22				07 37				07 52				08 07				08 22		
Kingston	a	07 10			07 25				07 40				07 55				08 10				08 25		
	d	07 10			07 29				07 40				07 59				08 10				08 29		
Hampton Wick	d	07 12			07 31				07 42				08 01				08 12				08 31		
Teddington	d	07 15			07 35				07 45				08 05				08 15				08 35		
Strawberry Hill	a				07 38								08 08								08 38		
Fulwell	d	07 19							07 49								08 19						
Hampton	d	07 23							07 53								08 23						
Kempton Park	d	07 26							07 56								08 26						
Sunbury	d	07 28							07 58								08 28						
Upper Halliford	d	07 30							08 00								08 30						
Shepperton	a	07 33							08 03								08 33						
Berrylands	d						07 30								08 00								08 30
Surbiton	d			07a13		07 27	07 35				07a43			07 57	08 05				08a13			08 27	08 35
Thames Ditton	d						07 39								08 09								08 39
Hampton Court	a						07 42								08 12								08 42
Hinchley Wood	d					07 31								08 01								08 31	
Claygate	d					07 34								08 04								08 34	
Oxshott	d					07 37								08 07								08 37	
Cobham & Stoke D'abernon	d					07 41								08 11								08 41	
Bookham	d							07 55								08 25							
Effingham Junction	d					07 45		07 59						08 15		08 29						08 45	
Horsley	d					07 48		08 02						08 18		08 32						08 48	
Clandon	d					07 53		08 07						08 23		08 37						08 53	
London Road (Guildford)	d					07 58		08 12						08 28		08 42						08 58	
Guildford	a					08 02		08 16						08 32		08 46						09 02	

A To Woking
B To London Waterloo

Table T152-F

Saturdays
26 May to 6 October

London - Chessington South, Dorking, Guildford, Shepperton and Hampton Court

		SW	SW	SW	SW A	SW	SW B	SW	SW	SW	SW	SW	SW A	SW	SW B	SW	SW	SW	SW	SW	SW A	SW
London Waterloo 15 ⊖	d	08 09	08 12	08 17	08 20	08 24	08 27	08 33	08 36	08 39	08 42	08 47	08 50	08 54	08 57	09 03	09 06	09 09	09 12	09 17	09 20	09 24
Vauxhall ⊖	d	08 13	08 16	08 21	08 24	08 28	08 31	08 37	08 40	08 43	08 46	08 51	08 54	08 58	09 01	09 07	09 10	09 13	09 16	09 21	09 24	09 28
Clapham Junction 10	d	08 18	08 21	08 26	08 29	08 33	08 36	08 42	08 45	08 48	08 51	08 56	08 59	09 03	09 06	09 12	09 15	09 18	09 21	09 26	09 29	09 33
Earlsfield	d	08 21	08 24	08 29	08 32	08 36	08 39	08 45	08 48	08 51	08 54	08 59	09 02	09 06	09 09	09 15	09 18	09 21	09 24	09 29	09 32	09 36
Wimbledon 6 ⊖	d	08 25	08 28	08 33	08 36	08 40	08 43	08 49	08 52	08 55	08 58	09 03	09 06	09 10	09 13	09 19	09 22	09 25	09 28	09 33	09 36	09 40
Raynes Park 6	d	08 28	08 31	08 36		08 43	08 46		08 55	08 58	09 01	09 06		09 13	09 16		09 25	09 28	09 31	09 36		09 43
Motspur Park	d	08 31		08 39		08 46				09 01		09 09		09 16				09 31		09 39		09 46
Malden Manor	d			08 42								09 12								09 42		
Tolworth	d			08 45								09 15								09 45		
Chessington North	d			08 48								09 18								09 48		
Chessington South	a			08 51								09 21								09 51		
Worcester Park	d	08 33				08 48				09 03				09 18				09 33				09 48
Stoneleigh	d	08 36				08 51				09 06				09 21				09 36				09 51
Ewell West	d	08 39				08 54				09 09				09 24				09 39				09 54
Epsom 3 182	a	08 42				08 57				09 12				09 27				09 42				09 57
	d	08 43				08 58				09 13				09 28				09 43				09 58
Ashtead 182	d	08 47				09 02				09 17				09 32				09 47				10 02
Leatherhead 182	d	08 50				09 05				09 20				09 35				09 50				10 05
Box Hill & Westhumble 182	d																					
Dorking 4 182	a					09 11								09 41								10 11
New Malden 6	d		08 34				08 49		08 58		09 04				09 19		09 28		09 34			
Norbiton	d		08 37				08 52				09 07				09 22				09 37			
Kingston	a		08 40				08 55				09 10				09 25				09 40			
	d		08 40				08 59				09 10				09 29				09 40			
Hampton Wick	d		08 42				09 01				09 12				09 31				09 42			
Teddington	d		08 45				09 05				09 15				09 35				09 45			
Strawberry Hill	a						09 08								09 38							
Fulwell	d		08 49								09 19								09 49			
Hampton	d		08 53								09 23								09 53			
Kempton Park	d		08 56								09 26								09 56			
Sunbury	d		08 58								09 28								09 58			
Upper Halliford	d		09 00								09 30								10 00			
Shepperton	a		09 03								09 33								10 03			
Berrylands	d								09 00								09 30					
Surbiton 6	d				08a43			08 57	09 05				09a13			09 27	09 35				09a43	
Thames Ditton	d								09 09								09 39					
Hampton Court	a								09 12								09 42					
Hinchley Wood	d							09 01								09 31						
Claygate	d							09 04								09 34						
Oxshott	d							09 07								09 37						
Cobham & Stoke D'abernon	d							09 11								09 41						
Bookham	d	08 55								09 25								09 55				
Effingham Junction 6	d	08 59						09 15		09 29						09 45		09 59				
Horsley	d	09 02						09 18		09 32						09 48		10 02				
Clandon	d	09 07						09 23		09 37						09 53		10 07				
London Road (Guildford)	d	09 12						09 28		09 42						09 58		10 12				
Guildford	a	09 16						09 32		09 46						10 02		10 16				

A To Woking
B To London Waterloo

Table T152-F

Saturdays
26 May to 6 October

London - Chessington South, Dorking, Guildford, Shepperton and Hampton Court

		SW A	SW	SW	SW	SW	SW	SW B	SW	SW A	SW	SW	SW	SW	SW	SW B	SW	SW A	SW	SW	SW	SW	SW
London Waterloo 15 ⊖	d	09 27	09 33	09 36	09 39	09 42	09 47	09 50	09 54	09 57	10 03	10 06	10 09	10 12	10 17	10 20	10 24	10 27	10 33	10 36	10 39	10 42	10 47
Vauxhall ⊖	d	09 31	09 37	09 40	09 43	09 46	09 51	09 54	09 58	10 01	10 07	10 10	10 13	10 16	10 21	10 24	10 28	10 31	10 37	10 40	10 43	10 46	10 51
Clapham Junction 10	d	09 36	09 42	09 45	09 48	09 51	09 56	09 59	10 03	10 06	10 12	10 15	10 18	10 21	10 26	10 29	10 33	10 36	10 42	10 45	10 48	10 51	10 56
Earlsfield	d	09 39	09 45	09 48	09 51	09 54	09 59	10 02	10 06	10 09	10 15	10 18	10 21	10 24	10 29	10 32	10 36	10 39	10 45	10 48	10 51	10 54	10 59
Wimbledon 6 ⊖	d	09 43	09 49	09 52	09 55	09 58	10 03	10 06	10 10	10 13	10 19	10 22	10 25	10 28	10 33	10 36	10 40	10 43	10 49	10 52	10 55	10 58	11 03
Raynes Park 6	d	09 46		09 55	09 58	10 01	10 06		10 13	10 16		10 25	10 28	10 31	10 36		10 43	10 46		10 55	10 58	11 01	11 06
Motspur Park	d				10 01		10 09		10 16				10 31		10 39		10 46				11 01		11 09
Malden Manor	d						10 12								10 42								11 12
Tolworth	d						10 15								10 45								11 15
Chessington North	d						10 18								10 48								11 18
Chessington South	a						10 21								10 51								11 21
Worcester Park	d				10 03				10 18				10 33				10 48				11 03		
Stoneleigh	d				10 06				10 21				10 36				10 51				11 06		
Ewell West	d				10 09				10 24				10 39				10 54				11 09		
Epsom 3 182	a				10 12				10 27				10 42				10 57				11 12		
	d				10 13				10 28				10 43				10 58				11 13		
Ashtead 182	d				10 17				10 32				10 47				11 02				11 17		
Leatherhead 182	d				10 20				10 35				10 50				11 05				11 20		
Box Hill & Westhumble 182	d																						
Dorking 4 182	a								10 41								11 11						
New Malden 6	d	09 49		09 58		10 04				10 19		10 28		10 34				10 49		10 58		11 04	
Norbiton	d	09 52				10 07				10 22				10 37				10 52				11 07	
Kingston	a	09 55				10 10				10 25				10 40				10 55				11 10	
	d	09 59				10 10				10 29				10 40				10 59				11 10	
Hampton Wick	d	10 01				10 12				10 31				10 42				11 01				11 12	
Teddington	d	10 05				10 15				10 35				10 45				11 05				11 15	
Strawberry Hill	a	10 08								10 38								11 08					
Fulwell	d					10 19								10 49								11 19	
Hampton	d					10 23								10 53								11 23	
Kempton Park	d					10 26								10 56								11 26	
Sunbury	d					10 28								10 58								11 28	
Upper Halliford	d					10 30								11 00								11 30	
Shepperton	a					10 33								11 03								11 33	
Berrylands	d			10 00								10 30								11 00			
Surbiton 6	d		09 57	10 05				10a13			10 27	10 35				10a43			10 57	11 05			
Thames Ditton	d			10 09								10 39								11 09			
Hampton Court	a			10 12								10 42								11 12			
Hinchley Wood	d		10 01								10 31								11 01				
Claygate	d		10 04								10 34								11 04				
Oxshott	d		10 07								10 37								11 07				
Cobham & Stoke D'abernon	d		10 11								10 41								11 11				
Bookham	d				10 25								10 55								11 25		
Effingham Junction 6	d		10 15		10 29						10 45		10 59						11 15		11 29		
Horsley	d		10 18		10 32						10 48		11 02						11 18		11 32		
Clandon	d		10 23		10 37						10 53		11 07						11 23		11 37		
London Road (Guildford)	d		10 28		10 42						10 58		11 12						11 28		11 42		
Guildford	a		10 32		10 46						11 02		11 16						11 32		11 46		

A To London Waterloo
B To Woking

Table T152-F

Saturdays

26 May to 6 October

London - Chessington South, Dorking, Guildford, Shepperton and Hampton Court

		SW A	SW	SW B	SW	SW	SW	SW	SW	SW A	SW	SW B	SW	SW	SW	SW	SW	SW A	SW	SW B	SW	SW
London Waterloo 15	⊖ d	10 50	10 54	10 57	11 03	11 06	11 09	11 12	11 17	11 20	11 24	11 27	11 33	11 36	11 39	11 42	11 47	11 50	11 54	11 57	12 03	12 06
Vauxhall	⊖ d	10 54	10 58	11 01	11 07	11 10	11 13	11 16	11 21	11 24	11 28	11 31	11 37	11 40	11 43	11 46	11 51	11 54	11 58	12 01	12 07	12 10
Clapham Junction 10	d	10 59	11 03	11 06	11 12	11 15	11 18	11 21	11 26	11 29	11 33	11 36	11 42	11 45	11 48	11 51	11 56	11 59	12 03	12 06	12 12	12 15
Earlsfield	d	11 02	11 06	11 09	11 15	11 18	11 21	11 24	11 29	11 32	11 36	11 39	11 45	11 48	11 51	11 54	11 59	12 02	12 06	12 09	12 15	12 18
Wimbledon 8	⊖ ⇌ d	11 06	11 10	11 13	11 19	11 22	11 25	11 28	11 33	11 36	11 40	11 43	11 49	11 52	11 55	11 58	12 03	12 06	12 10	12 13	12 19	12 22
Raynes Park 8	d		11 13	11 16		11 25	11 28	11 31	11 36		11 43	11 46		11 55	11 58	12 01	12 06		12 13	12 16		12 25
Motspur Park	d		11 16				11 31		11 39		11 46				12 01		12 09		12 16			
Malden Manor	d								11 42								12 12					
Tolworth	d								11 45								12 15					
Chessington North	d								11 48								12 18					
Chessington South	a								11 51								12 21					
Worcester Park	d		11 18				11 33				11 48				12 03				12 18			
Stoneleigh	d		11 21				11 36				11 51				12 06				12 21			
Ewell West	d		11 24				11 39				11 54				12 09				12 24			
Epsom 8	182 a		11 27				11 42				11 57				12 12				12 27			
	d		11 28				11 43				11 58				12 13				12 28			
Ashtead	182 d		11 32				11 47				12 02				12 17				12 32			
Leatherhead	182 d		11 35				11 50				12 05				12 20				12 35			
Box Hill & Westhumble	182 d																					
Dorking 4	182 a		11 41								12 11								12 41			
New Malden 8	d			11 19		11 28		11 34				11 49		11 58		12 04				12 19		12 28
Norbiton	d			11 22				11 37				11 52				12 07				12 22		
Kingston	a			11 25				11 40				11 55				12 10				12 25		
	d			11 29				11 40				11 59				12 10				12 29		
Hampton Wick	d			11 31				11 42				12 01				12 12				12 31		
Teddington	d			11 35				11 45				12 05				12 15				12 35		
Strawberry Hill	a			11 38								12 08								12 38		
Fulwell	d							11 49								12 19						
Hampton	d							11 53								12 23						
Kempton Park	d							11 56								12 26						
Sunbury	d							11 58								12 28						
Upper Halliford	d							12 00								12 30						
Shepperton	a							12 03								12 33						
Berrylands	d					11 30								12 00								12 30
Surbiton 8	d	11a13			11 27	11 35				11a43			11 57	12 05				12a13			12 27	12 35
Thames Ditton	d					11 39								12 09								12 39
Hampton Court	a					11 42								12 12								12 42
Hinchley Wood	d				11 31								12 01								12 31	
Claygate	d				11 34								12 04								12 34	
Oxshott	d				11 37								12 07								12 37	
Cobham & Stoke D'abernon	d				11 41								12 11								12 41	
Bookham	d						11 55								12 25							
Effingham Junction 6	d				11 45		11 59						12 15		12 29						12 45	
Horsley	d				11 48		12 02						12 18		12 32						12 48	
Clandon	d				11 53		12 07						12 23		12 37						12 53	
London Road (Guildford)	d				11 58		12 12						12 28		12 42						12 58	
Guildford	a				12 02		12 16						12 32		12 46						13 02	

A To Woking B To London Waterloo

Table T152-F

Saturdays

26 May to 6 October

London - Chessington South, Dorking, Guildford, Shepperton and Hampton Court

		SW	SW	SW	SW A	SW	SW B	SW	SW	SW	SW	SW	SW A	SW	SW B	SW	SW	SW	SW	SW	SW A	SW	SW B
London Waterloo 15	⊖ d	12 09	12 12	12 17	12 20	12 24	12 27	12 33	12 36	12 39	12 42	12 47	12 50	12 54	12 57	13 03	13 06	13 09	13 12	13 17	13 20	13 24	13 27
Vauxhall	⊖ d	12 13	12 16	12 21	12 24	12 28	12 31	12 37	12 40	12 43	12 46	12 51	12 54	12 58	13 01	13 07	13 10	13 13	13 16	13 21	13 24	13 28	13 31
Clapham Junction 10	d	12 18	12 21	12 26	12 29	12 33	12 36	12 42	12 45	12 48	12 51	12 56	12 59	13 03	13 06	13 12	13 15	13 18	13 21	13 26	13 29	13 33	13 36
Earlsfield	d	12 21	12 24	12 29	12 32	12 36	12 39	12 45	12 48	12 51	12 54	12 59	13 02	13 06	13 09	13 15	13 18	13 21	13 24	13 29	13 32	13 36	13 39
Wimbledon 8	⊖ ⇌ d	12 25	12 28	12 33	12 36	12 40	12 43	12 49	12 52	12 55	12 58	13 03	13 06	13 10	13 13	13 19	13 22	13 25	13 28	13 33	13 36	13 40	13 43
Raynes Park 8	d	12 28	12 31	12 36		12 43	12 46		12 55	12 58	13 01	13 06		13 13	13 16		13 25	13 28	13 31	13 36		13 43	13 46
Motspur Park	d	12 31		12 39		12 46				13 01		13 09		13 16				13 31		13 39		13 46	
Malden Manor	d			12 42								13 12								13 42			
Tolworth	d			12 45								13 15								13 45			
Chessington North	d			12 48								13 18								13 48			
Chessington South	a			12 51								13 21								13 51			
Worcester Park	d	12 33				12 48				13 03				13 18				13 33				13 48	
Stoneleigh	d	12 36				12 51				13 06				13 21				13 36				13 51	
Ewell West	d	12 39				12 54				13 09				13 24				13 39				13 54	
Epsom 8	182 a	12 42				12 57				13 12				13 27				13 42				13 57	
	d	12 43				12 58				13 13				13 28				13 43				13 58	
Ashtead	182 d	12 47				13 02				13 17				13 32				13 47				14 02	
Leatherhead	182 d	12 50				13 05				13 20				13 35				13 50				14 05	
Box Hill & Westhumble	182 d																						
Dorking 4	182 a					13 11								13 41								14 11	
New Malden 8	d		12 34				12 49		12 58		13 04				13 19		13 28		13 34				13 49
Norbiton	d		12 37				12 52				13 07				13 22				13 37				13 52
Kingston	a		12 40				12 55				13 10				13 25				13 40				13 55
	d		12 40				12 59				13 10				13 29				13 40				13 59
Hampton Wick	d		12 42				13 01				13 12				13 31				13 42				14 01
Teddington	d		12 45				13 05				13 15				13 35				13 45				14 05
Strawberry Hill	a						13 08								13 38								14 08
Fulwell	d		12 49								13 19								13 49				
Hampton	d		12 53								13 23								13 53				
Kempton Park	d		12 56								13 26								13 56				
Sunbury	d		12 58								13 28								13 58				
Upper Halliford	d		13 00								13 30								14 00				
Shepperton	a		13 03								13 33								14 03				
Berrylands	d								13 00								13 30						
Surbiton 8	d				12a43			12 57	13 05				13a13			13 27	13 35				13a43		
Thames Ditton	d								13 09								13 39						
Hampton Court	a								13 12								13 42						
Hinchley Wood	d							13 01								13 31							
Claygate	d							13 04								13 34							
Oxshott	d							13 07								13 37							
Cobham & Stoke D'abernon	d							13 11								13 41							
Bookham	d	12 55								13 25								13 55					
Effingham Junction 6	d	12 59						13 15		13 29						13 45		13 59					
Horsley	d	13 02						13 18		13 32						13 48		14 02					
Clandon	d	13 07						13 23		13 37						13 53		14 07					
London Road (Guildford)	d	13 12						13 28		13 42						13 58		14 12					
Guildford	a	13 16						13 32		13 46						14 02		14 17					

A To Woking B To London Waterloo

Table T152-F

Saturdays

26 May to 6 October

London - Chessington South, Dorking, Guildford, Shepperton and Hampton Court

Station		SW	SW	SW	SW	SW	SW A	SW	SW B	SW	SW	SW	SW	SW	SW A	SW	SW B	SW	SW	SW	SW	SW	SW A
London Waterloo ⊖	d	13 33	13 36	13 39	13 42	13 47	13 50	13 54	13 57	14 03	14 06	14 09	14 12	14 17	14 20	14 24	14 27	14 33	14 36	14 39	14 42	14 47	14 50
Vauxhall ⊖	d	13 37	13 40	13 43	13 46	13 51	13 54	13 58	14 01	14 07	14 10	14 13	14 16	14 21	14 24	14 28	14 31	14 37	14 40	14 43	14 46	14 51	14 54
Clapham Junction	d	13 42	13 45	13 48	13 51	13 56	13 59	14 03	14 06	14 12	14 15	14 18	14 21	14 26	14 29	14 33	14 36	14 42	14 45	14 48	14 51	14 56	14 59
Earlsfield	d	13 45	13 48	13 51	13 54	13 59	14 02	14 06	14 09	14 15	14 18	14 21	14 24	14 29	14 32	14 36	14 39	14 45	14 48	14 51	14 54	14 59	15 02
Wimbledon ⊖	d	13 49	13 52	13 55	13 58	14 03	14 06	14 10	14 13	14 19	14 22	14 25	14 28	14 33	14 36	14 40	14 43	14 49	14 52	14 55	14 58	15 03	15 06
Raynes Park	d		13 55	13 58	14 01	14 06		14 13	14 16		14 25	14 28	14 31	14 36		14 43	14 46		14 55	14 58	15 01	15 06	
Motspur Park	d			14 01		14 09		14 16				14 31		14 39		14 46				15 01		15 09	
Malden Manor	d					14 12								14 42								15 12	
Tolworth	d					14 15								14 45								15 15	
Chessington North	d					14 18								14 48								15 18	
Chessington South	a					14 21								14 51								15 21	
Worcester Park	d			14 03				14 18				14 33				14 48				15 03			
Stoneleigh	d			14 06				14 21				14 36				14 51				15 06			
Ewell West	d			14 09				14 24				14 39				14 54				15 09			
Epsom 182	a			14 12				14 27				14 42				14 57				15 12			
	d			14 13				14 28				14 43				14 58				15 13			
Ashtead 182	d			14 17				14 32				14 47				15 02				15 17			
Leatherhead 182	d			14 20				14 35				14 50				15 05				15 20			
Box Hill & Westhumble 182	d																						
Dorking 182	a							14 41								15 11							
New Malden	d		13 58		14 04				14 19		14 28		14 34				14 49		14 58		15 04		
Norbiton	d				14 07				14 22				14 37				14 52				15 07		
Kingston	a				14 10				14 25				14 40				14 55				15 10		
	d				14 10				14 29				14 40				14 59				15 10		
Hampton Wick	d				14 12				14 31				14 42				15 01				15 12		
Teddington	d				14 15				14 35				14 45				15 05				15 15		
Strawberry Hill	a								14 38								15 08						
Fulwell	d				14 19								14 49								15 19		
Hampton	d				14 23								14 53								15 23		
Kempton Park	d				14 26								14 56								15 26		
Sunbury	d				14 28								14 58								15 28		
Upper Halliford	d				14 30								15 00								15 30		
Shepperton	a				14 33								15 03								15 33		
Berrylands	d		14 00								14 30								15 00				
Surbiton	d	13 57	14 05				14a13			14 27	14 35				14a43			14 57	15 05				15a13
Thames Ditton	d		14 09								14 39								15 09				
Hampton Court	a		14 12								14 42								15 12				
Hinchley Wood	d	14 01								14 31								15 01					
Claygate	d	14 04								14 34								15 04					
Oxshott	d	14 07								14 37								15 07					
Cobham & Stoke D'abernon	d	14 11								14 41								15 11					
Bookham	d			14 25								14 55								15 25			
Effingham Junction	d	14 15		14 29						14 45		14 59						15 15		15 29			
Horsley	d	14 18		14 32						14 48		15 02						15 18		15 32			
Clandon	d	14 23		14 37						14 53		15 07						15 23		15 37			
London Road (Guildford)	d	14 28		14 42						14 58		15 12						15 28		15 42			
Guildford	a	14 32		14 46						15 02		15 16						15 32		15 46			

A To Woking B To London Waterloo

Table T152-F

Saturdays

26 May to 6 October

London - Chessington South, Dorking, Guildford, Shepperton and Hampton Court

Station		SW	SW A	SW	SW	SW	SW	SW	SW B	SW	SW A	SW	SW	SW	SW	SW	SW B	SW	SW A	SW	SW	SW
London Waterloo ⊖	d	14 54	14 57	15 03	15 06	15 09	15 12	15 17	15 20	15 24	15 27	15 33	15 36	15 39	15 42	15 47	15 50	15 54	15 57	16 03	16 06	16 09
Vauxhall ⊖	d	14 58	15 01	15 07	15 10	15 13	15 16	15 21	15 24	15 28	15 31	15 37	15 40	15 43	15 46	15 51	15 54	15 58	16 01	16 07	16 10	16 13
Clapham Junction	d	15 03	15 06	15 12	15 15	15 18	15 21	15 26	15 29	15 33	15 36	15 42	15 45	15 48	15 51	15 56	15 59	16 03	16 06	16 12	16 15	16 18
Earlsfield	d	15 06	15 09	15 15	15 18	15 21	15 24	15 29	15 32	15 36	15 39	15 45	15 48	15 51	15 54	15 59	16 02	16 06	16 09	16 15	16 18	16 21
Wimbledon ⊖	d	15 10	15 13	15 19	15 22	15 25	15 28	15 33	15 36	15 40	15 43	15 49	15 52	15 55	15 58	16 03	16 06	16 10	16 13	16 19	16 22	16 25
Raynes Park	d	15 13	15 16		15 25	15 28	15 31	15 36		15 43	15 46		15 55	15 58	16 01	16 06		16 13	16 16		16 25	16 28
Motspur Park	d	15 16				15 31		15 39		15 46				16 01		16 09		16 16				16 31
Malden Manor	d							15 42								16 12						
Tolworth	d							15 45								16 15						
Chessington North	d							15 48								16 18						
Chessington South	a							15 51								16 21						
Worcester Park	d	15 18				15 33				15 48				16 03				16 18				16 33
Stoneleigh	d	15 21				15 36				15 51				16 06				16 21				16 36
Ewell West	d	15 24				15 39				15 54				16 09				16 24				16 39
Epsom 182	a	15 27				15 42				15 57				16 12				16 27				16 42
	d	15 28				15 43				15 58				16 13				16 28				16 43
Ashtead 182	d	15 32				15 47				16 02				16 17				16 32				16 47
Leatherhead 182	d	15 35				15 50				16 05				16 20				16 35				16 50
Box Hill & Westhumble 182	d																					
Dorking 182	a	15 41								16 11								16 41				
New Malden	d		15 19		15 28		15 34				15 49		15 58		16 04				16 19		16 28	
Norbiton	d		15 22				15 37				15 52				16 07				16 22			
Kingston	a		15 25				15 40				15 55				16 10				16 25			
	d		15 29				15 40				15 59				16 10				16 29			
Hampton Wick	d		15 31				15 42				16 01				16 12				16 31			
Teddington	d		15 35				15 45				16 05				16 15				16 35			
Strawberry Hill	a		15 38								16 08								16 38			
Fulwell	d						15 49								16 19							
Hampton	d						15 53								16 23							
Kempton Park	d						15 56								16 26							
Sunbury	d						15 58								16 28							
Upper Halliford	d						16 00								16 30							
Shepperton	a						16 03								16 33							
Berrylands	d				15 30								16 00								16 30	
Surbiton	d			15 27	15 35				15a43			15 57	16 05				16a13			16 27	16 35	
Thames Ditton	d				15 39								16 09								16 39	
Hampton Court	a				15 42								16 12								16 42	
Hinchley Wood	d			15 31								16 01								16 31		
Claygate	d			15 34								16 04								16 34		
Oxshott	d			15 37								16 07								16 37		
Cobham & Stoke D'abernon	d			15 41								16 11								16 41		
Bookham	d					15 55								16 25								16 55
Effingham Junction	d			15 45		15 59						16 15		16 29						16 45		16 59
Horsley	d			15 48		16 02						16 18		16 32						16 48		17 02
Clandon	d			15 53		16 07						16 23		16 37						16 53		17 07
London Road (Guildford)	d			15 58		16 12						16 28		16 42						16 58		17 12
Guildford	a			16 02		16 16						16 32		16 46						17 02		17 16

A To London Waterloo B To Woking

Table T152-F

Saturdays

26 May to 6 October

London - Chessington South, Dorking, Guildford, Shepperton and Hampton Court

			SW	SW	SW A	SW	SW B	SW	SW	SW	SW	SW	SW A	SW	SW B	SW	SW	SW	SW	SW	SW A	SW	SW B	SW
London Waterloo 15	⊖	d	16 12	16 17	16 20	16 24	16 27	16 33	16 36	16 39	16 42	16 47	16 50	16 54	16 57	17 03	17 06	17 09	17 12	17 17	17 20	17 24	17 27	17 33
Vauxhall	⊖	d	16 16	16 21	16 24	16 28	16 31	16 37	16 40	16 43	16 46	16 51	16 54	16 58	17 01	17 07	17 10	17 13	17 16	17 21	17 24	17 28	17 31	17 37
Clapham Junction 10		d	16 21	16 26	16 29	16 33	16 36	16 42	16 45	16 48	16 51	16 56	16 59	17 03	17 06	17 12	17 15	17 18	17 21	17 26	17 29	17 33	17 36	17 42
Earlsfield		d	16 24	16 29	16 32	16 36	16 39	16 45	16 48	16 51	16 54	16 59	17 02	17 06	17 09	17 15	17 18	17 21	17 24	17 29	17 32	17 36	17 39	17 45
Wimbledon 6	⊖ ⇌	d	16 28	16 33	16 36	16 40	16 43	16 49	16 52	16 55	16 58	17 03	17 06	17 10	17 13	17 19	17 22	17 25	17 28	17 33	17 36	17 40	17 43	17 49
Raynes Park 6		d	16 31	16 36		16 43	16 46		16 55	16 58	17 01	17 06		17 13	17 16		17 25	17 28	17 31	17 36		17 43	17 46	
Motspur Park		d		16 39		16 46				17 01		17 09		17 16				17 31		17 39		17 46		
Malden Manor		d		16 42								17 12								17 42				
Tolworth		d		16 45								17 15								17 45				
Chessington North		d		16 48								17 18								17 48				
Chessington South		a		16 51								17 21								17 51				
Worcester Park		d				16 48				17 03				17 18				17 33				17 48		
Stoneleigh		d				16 51				17 06				17 21				17 36				17 51		
Ewell West		d				16 54				17 09				17 24				17 39				17 54		
Epsom 3	182	a				16 57				17 12				17 27				17 42				17 57		
		d				16 58				17 13				17 28				17 43				17 58		
Ashtead	182	d				17 02				17 17				17 32				17 47				18 02		
Leatherhead	182	d				17 05				17 20				17 35				17 50				18 05		
Box Hill & Westhumble	182	d																						
Dorking 4	182	a				17 11								17 41								18 11		
New Malden 6		d	16 34				16 49		16 58		17 04				17 19		17 28		17 34				17 49	
Norbiton		d	16 37				16 52				17 07				17 22				17 37				17 52	
Kingston		a	16 40				16 55				17 10				17 25				17 40				17 55	
		d	16 40				16 59				17 10				17 29				17 40				17 59	
Hampton Wick		d	16 42				17 01				17 12				17 31				17 42				18 01	
Teddington		d	16 45				17 05				17 15				17 35				17 45				18 05	
Strawberry Hill		a					17 08								17 38								18 08	
Fulwell		d	16 49								17 19								17 49					
Hampton		d	16 53								17 23								17 53					
Kempton Park		d	16 56								17 26								17 56					
Sunbury		d	16 58								17 28								17 58					
Upper Halliford		d	17 00								17 30								18 00					
Shepperton		a	17 03								17 33								18 03					
Berrylands		d							17 00								17 30							
Surbiton 6		d			16a43			16 57	17 05				17a13			17 27	17 35				17a43			17 57
Thames Ditton		d							17 09								17 39							
Hampton Court		a							17 12								17 42							
Hinchley Wood		d						17 01								17 31								18 01
Claygate		d						17 04								17 34								18 04
Oxshott		d						17 07								17 37								18 07
Cobham & Stoke D'abernon		d						17 11								17 41								18 11
Bookham		d								17 25								17 55						
Effingham Junction 6		d						17 15		17 29						17 45		17 59						18 15
Horsley		d						17 18		17 32						17 48		18 02						18 18
Clandon		d						17 23		17 37						17 53		18 07						18 23
London Road (Guildford)		d						17 28		17 42						17 58		18 12						18 28
Guildford		a						17 32		17 46						18 02		18 16						18 32

A To Woking B To London Waterloo

Table T152-F

Saturdays

26 May to 6 October

London - Chessington South, Dorking, Guildford, Shepperton and Hampton Court

			SW	SW	SW	SW	SW A	SW	SW B	SW	SW	SW	SW	SW	SW A	SW	SW B	SW	SW	SW	SW	SW	SW A
London Waterloo 15	⊖	d	17 36	17 39	17 42	17 47	17 50	17 54	17 57	18 03	18 06	18 09	18 12	18 17	18 20	18 24	18 27	18 33	18 36	18 39	18 42	18 47	18 50
Vauxhall	⊖	d	17 40	17 43	17 46	17 51	17 54	17 58	18 01	18 07	18 10	18 13	18 16	18 21	18 24	18 28	18 31	18 37	18 40	18 43	18 46	18 51	18 54
Clapham Junction 10		d	17 45	17 48	17 51	17 56	17 59	18 03	18 06	18 12	18 15	18 18	18 21	18 26	18 29	18 33	18 36	18 42	18 45	18 48	18 51	18 56	18 59
Earlsfield		d	17 48	17 51	17 54	17 59	18 02	18 06	18 09	18 15	18 18	18 21	18 24	18 29	18 32	18 36	18 39	18 45	18 48	18 51	18 54	18 59	19 02
Wimbledon 6	⊖ ⇌	d	17 52	17 55	17 58	18 03	18 06	18 10	18 13	18 19	18 22	18 25	18 28	18 33	18 36	18 40	18 43	18 49	18 52	18 55	18 58	19 03	19 06
Raynes Park 6		d	17 55	17 58	18 01	18 06		18 13	18 16		18 25	18 28	18 31	18 36		18 43	18 46		18 55	18 58	19 01	19 06	
Motspur Park		d		18 01		18 09		18 16				18 31		18 39		18 46				19 01		19 09	
Malden Manor		d				18 12								18 42								19 12	
Tolworth		d				18 15								18 45								19 15	
Chessington North		d				18 18								18 48								19 18	
Chessington South		a				18 21								18 51								19 21	
Worcester Park		d		18 03				18 18				18 33				18 48				19 03			
Stoneleigh		d		18 06				18 21				18 36				18 51				19 06			
Ewell West		d		18 09				18 24				18 39				18 54				19 09			
Epsom 3	182	a		18 12				18 27				18 42				18 57				19 12			
		d		18 13				18 28				18 43				18 58				19 13			
Ashtead	182	d		18 17				18 32				18 47				19 02				19 17			
Leatherhead	182	d		18 20				18 35				18 50				19 05				19 20			
Box Hill & Westhumble	182	d																					
Dorking 4	182	a						18 41								19 11							
New Malden 6		d	17 58		18 04				18 19		18 28		18 34				18 49		18 58		19 04		
Norbiton		d			18 07				18 22				18 37				18 52				19 07		
Kingston		a			18 10				18 25				18 40				18 55				19 10		
		d			18 10				18 29				18 40				18 59				19 10		
Hampton Wick		d			18 12				18 31				18 42				19 01				19 12		
Teddington		d			18 15				18 35				18 45				19 05				19 15		
Strawberry Hill		a							18 38								19 08						
Fulwell		d			18 19								18 49								19 19		
Hampton		d			18 23								18 53								19 23		
Kempton Park		d			18 26								18 56								19 26		
Sunbury		d			18 28								18 58								19 28		
Upper Halliford		d			18 30								19 00								19 30		
Shepperton		a			18 33								19 03								19 33		
Berrylands		d	18 00								18 30								19 00				
Surbiton 6		d	18 05				18a13			18 27	18 35				18a43			18 57	19 05				19a13
Thames Ditton		d	18 09								18 39								19 09				
Hampton Court		a	18 12								18 42								19 12				
Hinchley Wood		d								18 31								19 01					
Claygate		d								18 34								19 04					
Oxshott		d								18 37								19 07					
Cobham & Stoke D'abernon		d								18 41								19 11					
Bookham		d		18 25								18 55								19 25			
Effingham Junction 6		d		18 29						18 45		18 59						19 15		19 29			
Horsley		d		18 32						18 48		19 02						19 18		19 32			
Clandon		d		18 37						18 53		19 07						19 23		19 37			
London Road (Guildford)		d		18 42						18 58		19 12						19 28		19 42			
Guildford		a		18 46						19 02		19 16						19 32		19 46			

A To Woking B To London Waterloo

Table T152-F

Saturdays

26 May to 6 October

London - Chessington South, Dorking, Guildford, Shepperton and Hampton Court

		SW	SW A	SW	SW	SW	SW	SW	SW B	SW	SW A	SW	SW	SW	SW	SW	SW B	SW	SW A	SW	SW	SW	SW
London Waterloo 15 ⊖	d	18 54	18 57	19 03	19 06	19 09	19 12	19 17	19 20	19 24	19 27	19 33	19 36	19 39	19 42	19 47	19 50	19 54	19 57	20 03	20 06	20 09	20 12
Vauxhall ⊖	d	18 58	19 01	19 07	19 10	19 13	19 16	19 21	19 24	19 28	19 31	19 37	19 40	19 43	19 46	19 51	19 54	19 58	20 01	20 07	20 10	20 13	20 16
Clapham Junction 10	d	19 03	19 06	19 12	19 15	19 18	19 21	19 26	19 29	19 33	19 36	19 42	19 45	19 48	19 51	19 56	19 59	20 03	20 06	20 12	20 15	20 18	20 21
Earlsfield	d	19 06	19 09	19 15	19 18	19 21	19 24	19 29	19 32	19 36	19 39	19 45	19 48	19 51	19 54	19 59	20 02	20 06	20 09	20 15	20 18	20 21	20 24
Wimbledon 8 ⊖	d	19 10	19 13	19 19	19 22	19 25	19 28	19 33	19 36	19 40	19 43	19 49	19 52	19 55	19 58	20 03	20 06	20 10	20 13	20 19	20 22	20 25	20 28
Raynes Park 8	d	19 13	19 16		19 25	19 28	19 31	19 36		19 43	19 46		19 55	19 58	20 01	20 06		20 13	20 16		20 25	20 28	20 31
Motspur Park	d	19 16				19 31		19 39		19 46				20 01		20 09		20 16				20 31	
Malden Manor	d							19 42								20 12							
Tolworth	d							19 45								20 15							
Chessington North	d							19 48								20 18							
Chessington South	a							19 51								20 21							
Worcester Park	d	19 18				19 33				19 48				20 03				20 18				20 33	
Stoneleigh	d	19 21				19 36				19 51				20 06				20 21				20 36	
Ewell West	d	19 24				19 39				19 54				20 09				20 24				20 39	
Epsom 3	182 a	19 27				19 42				19 57				20 12				20 27				20 42	
	d	19 28				19 43				19 58				20 13								20 43	
Ashtead	182 d	19 32				19 47				20 02				20 17								20 47	
Leatherhead	182 d	19 35				19 50				20 05				20 20								20 50	
Box Hill & Westhumble	182 d																						
Dorking 4	182 a	19 41								20 11												20 57	
New Malden 8	d		19 19		19 28		19 34				19 49		19 58		20 04				20 19		20 28		20 34
Norbiton	d		19 22				19 37				19 52				20 07				20 22				20 37
Kingston	a		19 25				19 40				19 55				20 10				20 25				20 40
	d		19 29				19 40				19 59				20 10				20 29				20 40
Hampton Wick	d		19 31				19 42				20 01				20 12				20 31				20 42
Teddington	d		19 35				19 45				20 05				20 15				20 35				20 45
Strawberry Hill	a		19 38								20 08								20 38				
Fulwell	d						19 49								20 19								20 49
Hampton	d						19 53								20 23								20 53
Kempton Park	d						19 56								20 26								20 56
Sunbury	d						19 58								20 28								20 58
Upper Halliford	d						20 00								20 30								21 00
Shepperton	a						20 03								20 33								21 03
Berrylands	d				19 30								20 00								20 30		
Surbiton 6	d			19 27	19 35				19a43			19 57	20 05				20a13			20 27	20 35		
Thames Ditton	d				19 39								20 09								20 39		
Hampton Court	a				19 42								20 12								20 42		
Hinchley Wood	d			19 31								20 01								20 31			
Claygate	d			19 34								20 04								20 34			
Oxshott	d			19 37								20 07								20 37			
Cobham & Stoke D'abernon	d			19 41								20 11								20 41			
Bookham	d					19 55								20 25									
Effingham Junction 6	d			19 45		19 59						20 15		20 29						20 45			
Horsley	d			19 48		20 02						20 18		20 32						20 48			
Clandon	d			19 53		20 07						20 23		20 37						20 53			
London Road (Guildford)	d			19 58		20 12						20 28		20 42						20 58			
Guildford	a			20 02		20 16						20 32		20 49						21 02			

A To London Waterloo
B To Woking

Table T152-F

Saturdays

26 May to 6 October

London - Chessington South, Dorking, Guildford, Shepperton and Hampton Court

		SW	SW A	SW	SW B	SW	SW	SW	SW	SW	SW A	SW	SW B	SW	SW	SW	SW	SW A	SW	SW B	SW	SW	SW
London Waterloo 15 ⊖	d	20 17	20 20	20 24	20 27	20 33	20 36	20 39	20 42	20 47	20 50	20 54	20 57	21 03	21 06	21 09	21 12	21 20	21 24	21 27	21 33	21 36	21 39
Vauxhall ⊖	d	20 21	20 24	20 28	20 31	20 37	20 40	20 43	20 46	20 51	20 54	20 58	21 01	21 07	21 10	21 13	21 16	21 24	21 28	21 31	21 37	21 40	21 43
Clapham Junction 10	d	20 26	20 29	20 33	20 36	20 42	20 45	20 48	20 51	20 56	20 59	21 03	21 06	21 12	21 15	21 18	21 21	21 29	21 33	21 36	21 42	21 45	21 48
Earlsfield	d	20 29	20 32	20 36	20 39	20 45	20 48	20 51	20 54	20 59	21 02	21 06	21 09	21 15	21 18	21 21	21 24	21 32	21 36	21 39	21 45	21 48	21 51
Wimbledon 8 ⊖	d	20 33	20 36	20 40	20 43	20 49	20 52	20 55	20 58	21 03	21 06	21 10	21 13	21 19	21 22	21 25	21 28	21 36	21 40	21 43	21 49	21 52	21 55
Raynes Park 8	d	20 36		20 43	20 46		20 55	20 58	21 01	21 06		21 13	21 16		21 25	21 28	21 31		21 43	21 46		21 55	21 58
Motspur Park	d	20 39		20 46				21 01		21 09		21 16				21 31			21 46				22 01
Malden Manor	d	20 42								21 12													
Tolworth	d	20 45								21 15													
Chessington North	d	20 48								21 18													
Chessington South	a	20 51								21 21													
Worcester Park	d			20 48				21 03				21 18				21 33			21 48				22 03
Stoneleigh	d			20 51				21 06				21 21				21 36			21 51				22 06
Ewell West	d			20 54				21 09				21 24				21 39			21 54				22 09
Epsom 3	182 a			20 57				21 12				21 27				21 42			21 57				22 12
	d							21 13								21 43							22 13
Ashtead	182 d							21 17								21 47							22 17
Leatherhead	182 d							21 20								21 50							22 20
Box Hill & Westhumble	182 d																						
Dorking 4	182 a															21 57							
New Malden 8	d				20 49		20 58		21 04				21 19		21 28		21 34			21 49		21 58	
Norbiton	d				20 52				21 07				21 22				21 37			21 52			
Kingston	a				20 55				21 10				21 25				21 40			21 55			
	d				20 59				21 10				21 29				21 40			21 59			
Hampton Wick	d				21 01				21 12				21 31				21 42			22 01			
Teddington	d				21 05				21 15				21 35				21 45			22 05			
Strawberry Hill	a				21 08								21 38							22 08			
Fulwell	d								21 19								21 49						
Hampton	d								21 23								21 53						
Kempton Park	d								21 26								21 56						
Sunbury	d								21 28								21 58						
Upper Halliford	d								21 30								22 00						
Shepperton	a								21 33								22 03						
Berrylands	d						21 00								21 30							22 00	
Surbiton 6	d		20a43			20 57	21 05				21a13			21 27	21 35			21a43			21 57	22 05	
Thames Ditton	d						21 09								21 39							22 09	
Hampton Court	a						21 12								21 42							22 12	
Hinchley Wood	d					21 01								21 31							22 01		
Claygate	d					21 04								21 34							22 04		
Oxshott	d					21 07								21 37							22 07		
Cobham & Stoke D'abernon	d					21 11								21 41							22 11		
Bookham	d							21 25															22 25
Effingham Junction 6	d					21 15		21 29						21 45							22 15		22 29
Horsley	d					21 18		21 32						21 48							22 18		22 32
Clandon	d					21 23		21 37						21 53							22 23		22 37
London Road (Guildford)	d					21 28		21 42						21 58							22 28		22 42
Guildford	a					21 32		21 49						22 02							22 32		22 46

A To Woking
B To London Waterloo

Table T152-F

Saturdays

26 May to 6 October

London - Chessington South, Dorking, Guildford, Shepperton and Hampton Court

		SW		SW	SW	SW	SW A	SW	SW	SW	SW	SW B		SW A	SW	SW	SW	SW	SW B	SW A	SW	SW		SW	SW
London Waterloo 15 ⊖	d	21 42		21 47	21 50	21 54	21 57	22 03		22 09	22 12	22 20		22 27	22 33	22 36	22 39	22 42	22 50	22 57	23 00	23 03			23 09
Vauxhall ⊖	d	21 46		21 51	21 54	21 58	22 01	22 07		22 13	22 16	22 24		22 31	22 37	22 40	22 43	22 46	22 54	23 01	23 04	23 07			23 13
Clapham Junction 10	d	21 51		21 56	21 59	22 03	22 06	22 12		22 18	22 21	22 29		22 36	22 42	22 45	22 48	22 51	22 59	23 06	23 09	23 12			23 18
Earlsfield	d	21 54		21 59	22 02	22 06	22 09	22 15		22 21	22 24	22 32		22 39	22 45	22 48	22 51	22 54	23 02	23 09	23 12	23 15			23 21
Wimbledon 8 ⊖	d	21 58		22 03	22 06	22 10	22 13	22 19		22 25	22 28	22 36		22 43	22 49	22 52	22 55	22 58	23 06	23 13	23 16	23 19			23 25
Raynes Park 6	d	22 01		22 06		22 13	22 16			22 28	22 31			22 46		22 55	22 58	23 01		23 16	23 19				23 28
Motspur Park	d			22 09		22 16				22 31							23 01				23 22				23 31
Malden Manor	d			22 12																	23 25				
Tolworth	d			22 15																	23 28				
Chessington North	d			22 18																	23 31				
Chessington South	a			22 21																	23 33				
Worcester Park	d					22 18				22 33							23 03								23 33
Stoneleigh	d					22 21				22 36							23 06								23 36
Ewell West	d					22 24				22 39							23 09								23 39
Epsom 3 182	a					22 27				22 42							23 12								23 42
	d									22 43							23 13								23 43
Ashtead 182	d									22 47							23 17								23 47
Leatherhead 182	d									22 50							23 20								23 50
Box Hill & Westhumble 182	d																								
Dorking 4 182	a									22 57															23 57
New Malden 6	d	22 04					22 19				22 34			22 49		22 58		23 04		23 19					
Norbiton	d	22 07					22 22				22 37			22 52				23 07		23 22					
Kingston	a	22 10					22 25				22 40			22 55				23 10		23 25					
	d	22 10					22 29				22 40			22 59				23 10		23 29					
Hampton Wick	d	22 12					22 31				22 42			23 01				23 12		23 31					
Teddington	d	22 15					22 35				22 45			23 05				23 15		23 35					
Strawberry Hill	a						22 38							23 08						23 38					
Fulwell	d	22 19									22 49							23 19							
Hampton	d	22 23									22 53							23 23							
Kempton Park	d	22 26									22 56							23 26							
Sunbury	d	22 28									22 58							23 28							
Upper Halliford	d	22 30									23 00							23 30							
Shepperton	a	22 33									23 03							23 33							
Berrylands	d															23 00									
Surbiton 6	d				22 14			22 27	22 38			22a43			22 57	23 05			23a13			23 27		23 43	
Thames Ditton	d								22 42							23 09								23 47	
Hampton Court	a								22 45							23 12								23 50	
Hinchley Wood	d							22 31							23 01							23 31			
Claygate	d							22 34							23 04							23 34			
Oxshott	d							22 37							23 07							23 37			
Cobham & Stoke D'abernon	d							22 41							23 11							23 41			
Bookham	d																23 25								
Effingham Junction 6	d							22 45							23 15		23 29					23 45			
Horsley	d							22 48							23 18		23 32					23 48			
Clandon	d							22 53							23 23		23 37					23 53			
London Road (Guildford)	d							22 58							23 28		23 42					23 58			
Guildford	a				22 47			23 02							23 32		23 46					00 02			

A To London Waterloo

B To Woking

Table T152-F

Saturdays

26 May to 6 October

London - Chessington South, Dorking, Guildford, Shepperton and Hampton Court

		SW	SW A	SW B	SW	SW	SW	SW
London Waterloo 15 ⊖	d	23 12	23 20	23 27	23 36	23 42	23 50	23 57
Vauxhall ⊖	d	23 16	23 24	23 31	23 40	23 46	23 54	00 01
Clapham Junction 10	d	23 21	23 29	23 36	23 45	23 51	23 59	00 06
Earlsfield	d	23 24	23 32	23 39	23 48	23 54	00 02	00 09
Wimbledon 8 ⊖	d	23 28	23 36	23 43	23 52	23 58	00 06	00 13
Raynes Park 6	d	23 31		23 46	23 55	00 01		00 16
Motspur Park	d					00 04		
Malden Manor	d							
Tolworth	d							
Chessington North	d							
Chessington South	a							
Worcester Park	d					00 06		
Stoneleigh	d					00 09		
Ewell West	d					00 12		
Epsom 3 182	a					00 15		
	d					00 19		
Ashtead 182	d					00 23		
Leatherhead 182	d					00 26		
Box Hill & Westhumble 182	d							
Dorking 4 182	a							
New Malden 6	d	23 34		23 49	23 58			00 19
Norbiton	d	23 37		23 52				00 22
Kingston	a	23 40		23 55				00 25
	d	23 40		23 55				00 25
Hampton Wick	d	23 42		23 57				00 27
Teddington	d	23 45		23 59				00 30
Strawberry Hill	a			00 03				
Fulwell	d	23 49						00 34
Hampton	d	23 53						00 38
Kempton Park	d	23 56						00 41
Sunbury	d	23 58						00 43
Upper Halliford	d	23 59						00 45
Shepperton	a	00 03						00 48
Berrylands	d				23 59			
Surbiton 6	d		23a44		00 05		00 14	
Thames Ditton	d				00 09			
Hampton Court	a				00 12			
Hinchley Wood	d						00 18	
Claygate	d						00 20	
Oxshott	d						00 24	
Cobham & Stoke D'abernon	d						00 27	
Bookham	d					00 31		
Effingham Junction 6	d					00 36	00 32	
Horsley	d					00 39	00 34	
Clandon	d					00 44	00 39	
London Road (Guildford)	d					00 49	00 44	
Guildford	a					00 53	00 48	

A To Woking

B To Twickenham

Table T152-F

Saturdays

13 October to 8 December

London - Chessington South, Dorking, Guildford, Shepperton and Hampton Court

		SW A	SW A	SW A	SW A	SW	SW	SW B	SW	SW C	SW	SW ◇ D	SW B	SW E	SW E	SW	SW	SW	SW B	SW E	SW	SW	SW
London Waterloo ⊖	d					00 09	00 15	00 27	00 42	05 00	05 12	05 20	05 50			06 06	06 12	06 17	06 20	06 27	06 33	06 36	06 39
Vauxhall ⊖	d				00 01	00 13	00 19	00 31	00 46	05 04	05 16	05 24	05 54			06 10	06 16	06 21	06 24	06 31	06 37	06 40	06 43
Clapham Junction	d				00 06	00 20	00 26	00 37	00 51	05 11	05 21	05 29	05 59			06 15	06 21	06 26	06 29	06 36	06 42	06 45	06 48
Earlsfield	d		00 02		00 09	00 23	00 29	00s41		05 14	05 24	05 32	06 02			06 18	06 24	06 29	06 32	06 39	06 45	06 48	06 51
Wimbledon ⊖	d		00 06		00 13	00 27	00 33	00 45	01 05	05 18	05 28	05 36	06 06		06 13	06 22	06 28	06 33	06 36	06 43	06 49	06 52	06 55
Raynes Park	d			00 01	00 16		00 36	00 48	01 08		05 31				06 16	06 25	06 31	06 36		06 46		06 55	06 58
Motspur Park	d			00 04			00 39											06 39					07 01
Malden Manor	d																	06 42					
Tolworth	d																	06 45					
Chessington North	d																	06 48					
Chessington South	a																	06 51					
Worcester Park	d			00 06			00 41																07 03
Stoneleigh	d			00 09			00 44																07 06
Ewell West	d			00 12			00 47																07 09
Epsom 182	a			00 16			00 50																07 12
	d			00 19																			07 13
Ashtead 182	d			00 23																			07 17
Leatherhead 182	d			00 26																			07 20
Box Hill & Westhumble 182	d																						
Dorking 182	a																						
New Malden	d				00 19			00 50	01 11		05 34				06 19	06 28	06 34			06 49		06 58	
Norbiton	d				00 22				01 14		05 37				06 22		06 37			06 52			
Kingston	a				00 25				01 17		05 40				06 25		06 40			06 55			
	d				00 25				01 17		05 40			05 59	06 29		06 40			06 59			
Hampton Wick	d				00 27				01s19		05 42			06 01	06 31		06 42			07 01			
Teddington	d				00 30				01s22		05 45			06 05	06 35		06 45			07 05			
Strawberry Hill	a								01 28					06 08	06 38					07 08			
Fulwell	d				00 34						05 49						06 49						
Hampton	d				00 38						05 53						06 53						
Kempton Park	d				00 41						05 56						06 56						
Sunbury	d				00 43						05 58						06 58						
Upper Halliford	d				00 45						06 00						07 00						
Shepperton	a				00 52						06 05						07 05						
Berrylands	d							00s53								06 30						07 00	
Surbiton	d	00 05	00 14			00 35		00s56		05 26		05 44	06a13			06 35			06a43		06 57	07 05	
Thames Ditton	d	00 09														06 39						07 09	
Hampton Court	a	00 12														06 42						07 12	
Hinchley Wood	d		00 18																		07 01		
Claygate	d		00 20																		07 04		
Oxshott	d		00 24																		07 07		
Cobham & Stoke D'abernon	d		00 27																		07 11		
Bookham	d			00 31																			07 25
Effingham Junction	d		00 32	00 36																	07 15		07 29
Horsley	d		00 34	00 39																	07 18		07 32
Clandon	d		00 39	00 44																	07 23		07 37
London Road (Guildford)	d		00 44	00 49																	07 28		07 42
Guildford	a		00 53	00 56		01 07				06 00		06 23									07 35		07 49

A From London Waterloo
B To Woking
C To Haslemere
D To Portsmouth Harbour
E To London Waterloo

Table T152-F

Saturdays

13 October to 8 December

London - Chessington South, Dorking, Guildford, Shepperton and Hampton Court

		SW	SW	SW A	SW B	SW	SW	SW	SW	SW	SW A	SW	SW B	SW	SW	SW	SW	SW	SW A	SW	SW B	SW	SW
London Waterloo ⊖	d	06 42	06 47	06 50	06 57	07 03	07 06	07 09	07 12	07 17	07 20	07 24	07 27	07 33	07 36	07 39	07 42	07 47	07 50	07 54	07 57	08 03	08 06
Vauxhall ⊖	d	06 46	06 51	06 54	07 01	07 07	07 10	07 13	07 16	07 21	07 24	07 28	07 31	07 37	07 40	07 43	07 46	07 51	07 54	07 58	08 01	08 07	08 10
Clapham Junction	d	06 51	06 56	06 59	07 06	07 12	07 15	07 18	07 21	07 26	07 29	07 33	07 36	07 42	07 45	07 48	07 51	07 56	07 59	08 03	08 06	08 12	08 15
Earlsfield	d	06 54	06 59	07 02	07 09	07 15	07 18	07 21	07 24	07 29	07 32	07 36	07 39	07 45	07 48	07 51	07 54	07 59	08 02	08 06	08 09	08 15	08 18
Wimbledon ⊖	d	06 58	07 03	07 06	07 13	07 19	07 22	07 25	07 28	07 33	07 36	07 40	07 43	07 49	07 52	07 55	07 58	08 03	08 06	08 10	08 13	08 19	08 22
Raynes Park	d	07 01	07 06		07 16		07 25	07 28	07 31	07 36		07 43	07 46		07 55	07 58	08 01	08 06		08 13	08 16		08 25
Motspur Park	d		07 09					07 31		07 39		07 46				08 01		08 09		08 16			
Malden Manor	d		07 12							07 42								08 12					
Tolworth	d		07 15							07 45								08 15					
Chessington North	d		07 18							07 48								08 18					
Chessington South	a		07 21							07 51								08 21					
Worcester Park	d							07 33				07 48				08 03				08 18			
Stoneleigh	d							07 36				07 51				08 06				08 21			
Ewell West	d							07 39				07 54				08 09				08 24			
Epsom 182	a							07 42				07 57				08 12				08 27			
	d							07 43				07 58				08 13				08 28			
Ashtead 182	d							07 47				08 02				08 17				08 32			
Leatherhead 182	d							07 50				08 05				08 20				08 35			
Box Hill & Westhumble 182	d																						
Dorking 182	a											08 13								08 43			
New Malden	d	07 04			07 19		07 28		07 34				07 49		07 58		08 04				08 19		08 28
Norbiton	d	07 07			07 22				07 37				07 52				08 07				08 22		
Kingston	a	07 10			07 25				07 40				07 55				08 10				08 25		
	d	07 10			07 29				07 40				07 59				08 10				08 29		
Hampton Wick	d	07 12			07 31				07 42				08 01				08 12				08 31		
Teddington	d	07 15			07 35				07 45				08 05				08 15				08 35		
Strawberry Hill	a				07 38								08 08								08 38		
Fulwell	d	07 19							07 49								08 19						
Hampton	d	07 23							07 53								08 23						
Kempton Park	d	07 26							07 56								08 26						
Sunbury	d	07 28							07 58								08 28						
Upper Halliford	d	07 30							08 00								08 30						
Shepperton	a	07 35							08 05								08 35						
Berrylands	d						07 30								08 00								08 30
Surbiton	d			07a13		07 27	07 35				07a43			07 57	08 05				08a13			08 27	08 35
Thames Ditton	d						07 39								08 09								08 39
Hampton Court	a						07 42								08 12								08 42
Hinchley Wood	d					07 31								08 01								08 31	
Claygate	d					07 34								08 04								08 34	
Oxshott	d					07 37								08 07								08 37	
Cobham & Stoke D'abernon	d					07 41								08 11								08 41	
Bookham	d							07 55								08 25							
Effingham Junction	d					07 45		07 59						08 15		08 29						08 45	
Horsley	d					07 48		08 02						08 18		08 32						08 48	
Clandon	d					07 53		08 07						08 23		08 37						08 53	
London Road (Guildford)	d					07 58		08 12						08 28		08 42						08 58	
Guildford	a					08 05		08 19						08 35		08 49						09 05	

A To Woking
B To London Waterloo

Table T152-F

Saturdays

13 October to 8 December

London - Chessington South, Dorking, Guildford, Shepperton and Hampton Court

		SW	SW	SW	SW A	SW	SW B	SW	SW	SW	SW	SW	SW A	SW	SW B	SW	SW	SW	SW	SW	SW A	SW
London Waterloo ⊖	d	08 09	08 12	08 17	08 20	08 24	08 27	08 33	08 36	08 39	08 42	08 47	08 50	08 54	08 57	09 03	09 06	09 09	09 12	09 17	09 20	09 24
Vauxhall ⊖	d	08 13	08 16	08 21	08 24	08 28	08 31	08 37	08 40	08 43	08 46	08 51	08 54	08 58	09 01	09 07	09 10	09 13	09 16	09 21	09 24	09 28
Clapham Junction	d	08 18	08 21	08 26	08 29	08 33	08 36	08 42	08 45	08 48	08 51	08 56	08 59	09 03	09 06	09 12	09 15	09 18	09 21	09 26	09 29	09 33
Earlsfield	d	08 21	08 24	08 29	08 32	08 36	08 39	08 45	08 48	08 51	08 54	08 59	09 02	09 06	09 09	09 15	09 18	09 21	09 24	09 29	09 32	09 36
Wimbledon ⊖	d	08 25	08 28	08 33	08 36	08 40	08 43	08 49	08 52	08 55	08 58	09 03	09 06	09 10	09 13	09 19	09 22	09 25	09 28	09 33	09 36	09 40
Raynes Park	d	08 28	08 31	08 36		08 43	08 46		08 55	08 58	09 01	09 06		09 13	09 16		09 25	09 28	09 31	09 36		09 43
Motspur Park	d	08 31		08 39		08 46				09 01		09 09		09 16				09 31		09 39		09 46
Malden Manor	d			08 42								09 12								09 42		
Tolworth	d			08 45								09 15								09 45		
Chessington North	d			08 48								09 18								09 48		
Chessington South	a			08 51								09 21								09 51		
Worcester Park	d	08 33				08 48				09 03				09 18				09 33				09 48
Stoneleigh	d	08 36				08 51				09 06				09 21				09 36				09 51
Ewell West	d	08 39				08 54				09 09				09 24				09 39				09 54
Epsom 182	a	08 42				08 57				09 12				09 27				09 42				09 57
	d	08 43				08 58				09 13				09 28				09 43				09 58
Ashtead 182	d	08 47				09 02				09 17				09 32				09 47				10 02
Leatherhead 182	d	08 50				09 05				09 20				09 35				09 50				10 05
Box Hill & Westhumble 182	d																					
Dorking 182	a					09 13								09 43								10 13
New Malden	d		08 34				08 49		08 58		09 04				09 19		09 28		09 34			
Norbiton	d		08 37				08 52				09 07				09 22				09 37			
Kingston	a		08 40				08 55				09 10				09 25				09 40			
	d		08 40				08 59				09 10				09 29				09 40			
Hampton Wick	d		08 42				09 01				09 12				09 31				09 42			
Teddington	d		08 45				09 05				09 15				09 35				09 45			
Strawberry Hill	a						09 08								09 38							
Fulwell	d		08 49								09 19								09 49			
Hampton	d		08 53								09 23								09 53			
Kempton Park	d		08 56								09 26								09 56			
Sunbury	d		08 58								09 28								09 58			
Upper Halliford	d		09 00								09 30								10 00			
Shepperton	a		09 05								09 35								10 05			
Berrylands	d								09 00								09 30					
Surbiton	d				08a43			08 57	09 05				09a13			09 27	09 35				09a43	
Thames Ditton	d								09 09								09 39					
Hampton Court	a								09 12								09 42					
Hinchley Wood	d							09 01								09 31						
Claygate	d							09 04								09 34						
Oxshott	d							09 07								09 37						
Cobham & Stoke D'abernon	d							09 11								09 41						
Bookham	d	08 55								09 25								09 55				
Effingham Junction	d	08 59						09 15		09 29						09 45		09 59				
Horsley	d	09 02						09 18		09 32						09 48		10 02				
Clandon	d	09 07						09 23		09 37						09 53		10 07				
London Road (Guildford)	d	09 12						09 28		09 42						09 58		10 12				
Guildford	a	09 19						09 35		09 49						10 05		10 19				

A To Woking B To London Waterloo

Table T152-F

Saturdays

13 October to 8 December

London - Chessington South, Dorking, Guildford, Shepperton and Hampton Court

		SW A	SW	SW	SW	SW	SW	SW B	SW	SW A	SW	SW	SW	SW	SW	SW B	SW	SW A	SW	SW	SW	SW	SW
London Waterloo ⊖	d	09 27	09 33	09 36	09 39	09 42	09 47	09 50	09 54	09 57	10 03	10 06	10 09	10 12	10 17	10 20	10 24	10 27	10 33	10 36	10 39	10 42	10 47
Vauxhall ⊖	d	09 31	09 37	09 40	09 43	09 46	09 51	09 54	09 58	10 01	10 07	10 10	10 13	10 16	10 21	10 24	10 28	10 31	10 37	10 40	10 43	10 46	10 51
Clapham Junction	d	09 36	09 42	09 45	09 48	09 51	09 56	09 59	10 03	10 06	10 12	10 15	10 18	10 21	10 26	10 29	10 33	10 36	10 42	10 45	10 48	10 51	10 56
Earlsfield	d	09 39	09 45	09 48	09 51	09 54	09 59	10 02	10 06	10 09	10 15	10 18	10 21	10 24	10 29	10 32	10 36	10 39	10 45	10 48	10 51	10 54	10 59
Wimbledon ⊖	d	09 43	09 49	09 52	09 55	09 58	10 03	10 06	10 10	10 13	10 19	10 22	10 25	10 28	10 33	10 36	10 40	10 43	10 49	10 52	10 55	10 58	11 03
Raynes Park	d	09 46		09 55	09 58	10 01	10 06		10 13	10 16		10 25	10 28	10 31	10 36		10 43	10 46		10 55	10 58	11 01	11 06
Motspur Park	d				10 01		10 09		10 16				10 31		10 39		10 46				11 01		11 09
Malden Manor	d						10 12								10 42								11 12
Tolworth	d						10 15								10 45								11 15
Chessington North	d						10 18								10 48								11 18
Chessington South	a						10 21								10 51								11 21
Worcester Park	d				10 03				10 18				10 33				10 48				11 03		
Stoneleigh	d				10 06				10 21				10 36				10 51				11 06		
Ewell West	d				10 09				10 24				10 39				10 54				11 09		
Epsom 182	a				10 12				10 27				10 42				10 57				11 12		
	d				10 13				10 28				10 43				10 58				11 13		
Ashtead 182	d				10 17				10 32				10 47				11 02				11 17		
Leatherhead 182	d				10 20				10 35				10 50				11 05				11 20		
Box Hill & Westhumble 182	d																						
Dorking 182	a								10 43								11 13						
New Malden	d	09 49		09 58		10 04				10 19		10 28		10 34				10 49		10 58		11 04	
Norbiton	d	09 52				10 07				10 22				10 37				10 52				11 07	
Kingston	a	09 55				10 10				10 25				10 40				10 55				11 10	
	d	09 59				10 10				10 29				10 40				10 59				11 10	
Hampton Wick	d	10 01				10 12				10 31				10 42				11 01				11 12	
Teddington	d	10 05				10 15				10 35				10 45				11 05				11 15	
Strawberry Hill	a	10 08								10 38								11 08					
Fulwell	d					10 19								10 49								11 19	
Hampton	d					10 23								10 53								11 23	
Kempton Park	d					10 26								10 56								11 26	
Sunbury	d					10 28								10 58								11 28	
Upper Halliford	d					10 30								11 00								11 30	
Shepperton	a					10 35								11 05								11 35	
Berrylands	d			10 00								10 30								11 00			
Surbiton	d		09 57	10 05				10a13			10 27	10 35				10a43			10 57	11 05			
Thames Ditton	d			10 09								10 39								11 09			
Hampton Court	a			10 12								10 42								11 12			
Hinchley Wood	d		10 01								10 31								11 01				
Claygate	d		10 04								10 34								11 04				
Oxshott	d		10 07								10 37								11 07				
Cobham & Stoke D'abernon	d		10 11								10 41								11 11				
Bookham	d				10 25								10 55								11 25		
Effingham Junction	d		10 15		10 29						10 45		10 59						11 15		11 29		
Horsley	d		10 18		10 32						10 48		11 02						11 18		11 32		
Clandon	d		10 23		10 37						10 53		11 07						11 23		11 37		
London Road (Guildford)	d		10 28		10 42						10 58		11 12						11 28		11 42		
Guildford	a		10 35		10 49						11 05		11 19						11 35		11 49		

A To London Waterloo B To Woking

Table T152-F

Saturdays

13 October to 8 December

London - Chessington South, Dorking, Guildford, Shepperton and Hampton Court

Station			SW A	SW	SW B	SW	SW	SW	SW	SW	SW A	SW	SW B	SW	SW	SW	SW	SW	SW A	SW	SW B	SW	SW
London Waterloo	⊖	d	10 50	10 54	10 57	11 03	11 06	11 09	11 12	11 17	11 20	11 24	11 27	11 33	11 36	11 39	11 42	11 47	11 50	11 54	11 57	12 03	12 06
Vauxhall	⊖	d	10 54	10 58	11 01	11 07	11 10	11 13	11 16	11 21	11 24	11 28	11 31	11 37	11 40	11 43	11 46	11 51	11 54	11 58	12 01	12 07	12 10
Clapham Junction		d	10 59	11 03	11 06	11 12	11 15	11 18	11 21	11 26	11 29	11 33	11 36	11 42	11 45	11 48	11 51	11 56	11 59	12 03	12 06	12 12	12 15
Earlsfield		d	11 02	11 06	11 09	11 15	11 18	11 21	11 24	11 29	11 32	11 36	11 39	11 45	11 48	11 51	11 54	11 59	12 02	12 06	12 09	12 15	12 18
Wimbledon	⊖	d	11 06	11 10	11 13	11 19	11 22	11 25	11 28	11 33	11 36	11 40	11 43	11 49	11 52	11 55	11 58	12 03	12 06	12 10	12 13	12 19	12 22
Raynes Park		d		11 13	11 16		11 25	11 28	11 31	11 36		11 43	11 46		11 55	11 58	12 01	12 06		12 13	12 16		12 25
Motspur Park		d		11 16				11 31		11 39		11 46				12 01		12 09		12 16			
Maiden Manor		d								11 42								12 12					
Tolworth		d								11 45								12 15					
Chessington North		d								11 48								12 18					
Chessington South		a								11 51								12 21					
Worcester Park		d		11 18				11 33				11 48				12 03				12 18			
Stoneleigh		d		11 21				11 36				11 51				12 06				12 21			
Ewell West		d		11 24				11 39				11 54				12 09				12 24			
Epsom	182	a		11 27				11 42				11 57				12 12				12 27			
		d		11 28				11 43				11 58				12 13				12 28			
Ashtead	182	d		11 32				11 47				12 02				12 17				12 32			
Leatherhead	182	d		11 35				11 50				12 05				12 20				12 35			
Box Hill & Westhumble	182	d																					
Dorking	182	a		11 43								12 13								12 43			
New Malden		d			11 19		11 28		11 34				11 49		11 58		12 04				12 19		12 28
Norbiton		d			11 22				11 37				11 52				12 07				12 22		
Kingston		a			11 25				11 40				11 55				12 10				12 25		
		d			11 29				11 40				11 59				12 10				12 29		
Hampton Wick		d			11 31				11 42				12 01				12 12				12 31		
Teddington		d			11 35				11 45				12 05				12 15				12 35		
Strawberry Hill		a			11 38								12 08								12 38		
Fulwell		d							11 49								12 19						
Hampton		d							11 53								12 23						
Kempton Park		d							11 56								12 26						
Sunbury		d							11 58								12 28						
Upper Halliford		d							12 00								12 30						
Shepperton		a							12 05								12 35						
Berrylands		d					11 30								12 00								12 30
Surbiton		d	11a13			11 27	11 35				11a43			11 57	12 05				12a13			12 27	12 35
Thames Ditton		d					11 39								12 09								12 39
Hampton Court		a					11 42								12 12								12 42
Hinchley Wood		d				11 31								12 01								12 31	
Claygate		d				11 34								12 04								12 34	
Oxshott		d				11 37								12 07								12 37	
Cobham & Stoke D'abernon		d				11 41								12 11								12 41	
Bookham		d						11 55								12 25							
Effingham Junction		d				11 45		11 59						12 15		12 29						12 45	
Horsley		d				11 48		12 02						12 18		12 32						12 48	
Clandon		d				11 53		12 07						12 23		12 37						12 53	
London Road (Guildford)		d				11 58		12 12						12 28		12 42						12 58	
Guildford		a				12 05		12 19						12 35		12 49						13 05	

A To Woking
B To London Waterloo

Table T152-F

Saturdays

13 October to 8 December

London - Chessington South, Dorking, Guildford, Shepperton and Hampton Court

Station			SW	SW	SW	SW A	SW	SW B	SW	SW	SW	SW	SW	SW A	SW	SW B	SW	SW	SW	SW	SW	SW A	SW	SW B
London Waterloo	⊖	d	12 09	12 12	12 17	12 20	12 24	12 27	12 33	12 36	12 39	12 42	12 47	12 50	12 54	12 57	13 03	13 06	13 09	13 12	13 17	13 20	13 24	13 27
Vauxhall	⊖	d	12 13	12 16	12 21	12 24	12 28	12 31	12 37	12 40	12 43	12 46	12 51	12 54	12 58	13 01	13 07	13 10	13 13	13 16	13 21	13 24	13 28	13 31
Clapham Junction		d	12 18	12 21	12 26	12 29	12 33	12 36	12 42	12 45	12 48	12 51	12 56	12 59	13 03	13 06	13 12	13 15	13 18	13 21	13 26	13 29	13 33	13 36
Earlsfield		d	12 21	12 24	12 29	12 32	12 36	12 39	12 45	12 48	12 51	12 54	12 59	13 02	13 06	13 09	13 15	13 18	13 21	13 24	13 29	13 32	13 36	13 39
Wimbledon	⊖	d	12 25	12 28	12 33	12 36	12 40	12 43	12 49	12 52	12 55	12 58	13 03	13 06	13 10	13 13	13 19	13 22	13 25	13 28	13 33	13 36	13 40	13 43
Raynes Park		d	12 28	12 31	12 36		12 43	12 46		12 55	12 58	13 01	13 06		13 13	13 16		13 25	13 28	13 31	13 36		13 43	13 46
Motspur Park		d	12 31		12 39		12 46				13 01		13 09		13 16				13 31		13 39		13 46	
Maiden Manor		d			12 42								13 12								13 42			
Tolworth		d			12 45								13 15								13 45			
Chessington North		d			12 48								13 18								13 48			
Chessington South		a			12 51								13 21								13 51			
Worcester Park		d	12 33				12 48				13 03				13 18				13 33				13 48	
Stoneleigh		d	12 36				12 51				13 06				13 21				13 36				13 51	
Ewell West		d	12 39				12 54				13 09				13 24				13 39				13 54	
Epsom	182	a	12 42				12 57				13 12				13 27				13 42				13 57	
		d	12 43				12 58				13 13				13 28				13 43				13 58	
Ashtead	182	d	12 47				13 02				13 17				13 32				13 47				14 02	
Leatherhead	182	d	12 50				13 05				13 20				13 35				13 50				14 05	
Box Hill & Westhumble	182	d																						
Dorking	182	a					13 13								13 43								14 13	
New Malden		d		12 34				12 49		12 58		13 04				13 19		13 28		13 34				13 49
Norbiton		d		12 37				12 52				13 07				13 22				13 37				13 52
Kingston		a		12 40				12 55				13 10				13 25				13 40				13 55
		d		12 40				12 59				13 10				13 29				13 40				13 59
Hampton Wick		d		12 42				13 01				13 12				13 31				13 42				14 01
Teddington		d		12 45				13 05				13 15				13 35				13 45				14 05
Strawberry Hill		a						13 08								13 38								14 08
Fulwell		d		12 49								13 19								13 49				
Hampton		d		12 53								13 23								13 53				
Kempton Park		d		12 56								13 26								13 56				
Sunbury		d		12 58								13 28								13 58				
Upper Halliford		d		13 00								13 30								14 00				
Shepperton		a		13 05								13 35								14 05				
Berrylands		d								13 00								13 30						
Surbiton		d				12a43			12 57	13 05				13a13			13 27	13 35				13a43		
Thames Ditton		d								13 09								13 39						
Hampton Court		a								13 12								13 42						
Hinchley Wood		d							13 01								13 31							
Claygate		d							13 04								13 34							
Oxshott		d							13 07								13 37							
Cobham & Stoke D'abernon		d							13 11								13 41							
Bookham		d	12 55								13 25								13 55					
Effingham Junction		d	12 59						13 15		13 29						13 45		13 59					
Horsley		d	13 02						13 18		13 32						13 48		14 02					
Clandon		d	13 07						13 23		13 37						13 53		14 07					
London Road (Guildford)		d	13 12						13 28		13 42						13 58		14 12					
Guildford		a	13 19						13 35		13 49						14 05		14 20					

A To Woking
B To London Waterloo

Table T152-F

Saturdays

13 October to 8 December

London - Chessington South, Dorking, Guildford, Shepperton and Hampton Court

Station			SW	SW	SW	SW	SW	SW A	SW	SW B	SW	SW	SW	SW	SW	SW A	SW	SW B	SW	SW	SW	SW	SW	SW A
London Waterloo 15	⊖	d	13 33	13 36	13 39	13 42	13 47	13 50	13 54	13 57	14 03	14 06	14 09	14 12	14 17	14 20	14 24	14 27	14 33	14 36	14 39	14 42	14 47	14 50
Vauxhall	⊖	d	13 37	13 40	13 43	13 46	13 51	13 54	13 58	14 01	14 07	14 10	14 13	14 16	14 21	14 24	14 28	14 31	14 37	14 40	14 43	14 46	14 51	14 54
Clapham Junction 10		d	13 42	13 45	13 48	13 51	13 56	13 59	14 03	14 06	14 12	14 15	14 18	14 21	14 26	14 29	14 33	14 36	14 42	14 45	14 48	14 51	14 56	14 59
Earlsfield		d	13 45	13 48	13 51	13 54	13 59	14 02	14 06	14 09	14 15	14 18	14 21	14 24	14 29	14 32	14 36	14 39	14 45	14 48	14 51	14 54	14 59	15 02
Wimbledon 6	⊖ ⇌	d	13 49	13 52	13 55	13 58	14 03	14 06	14 10	14 13	14 19	14 22	14 25	14 28	14 33	14 36	14 40	14 43	14 49	14 52	14 55	14 58	15 03	15 06
Raynes Park 8		d		13 55	13 58	14 01	14 06		14 13	14 16		14 25	14 28	14 31	14 36		14 43	14 46		14 55	14 58	15 01	15 06	
Motspur Park		d			14 01		14 09		14 16				14 31		14 39		14 46				15 01		15 09	
Malden Manor		d					14 12								14 42								15 12	
Tolworth		d					14 15								14 45								15 15	
Chessington North		d					14 18								14 48								15 18	
Chessington South		a					14 21								14 51								15 21	
Worcester Park		d			14 03				14 18				14 33				14 48				15 03			
Stoneleigh		d			14 06				14 21				14 36				14 51				15 06			
Ewell West		d			14 09				14 24				14 39				14 54				15 09			
Epsom 3	182	a			14 12				14 27				14 42				14 57				15 12			
		d			14 13				14 28				14 43				14 58				15 13			
Ashtead	182	d			14 17				14 32				14 47				15 02				15 17			
Leatherhead	182	d			14 20				14 35				14 50				15 05				15 20			
Box Hill & Westhumble	182	d																						
Dorking 4	182	a							14 43								15 13							
New Malden 6		d		13 58		14 04				14 19		14 28		14 34				14 49		14 58		15 04		
Norbiton		d				14 07				14 22				14 37				14 52				15 07		
Kingston		a				14 10				14 25				14 40				14 55				15 10		
		d				14 10				14 29				14 40				14 59				15 10		
Hampton Wick		d				14 12				14 31				14 42				15 01				15 12		
Teddington		d				14 15				14 35				14 45				15 05				15 15		
Strawberry Hill		a								14 38								15 08						
Fulwell		d				14 19								14 49								15 19		
Hampton		d				14 23								14 53								15 23		
Kempton Park		d				14 26								14 56								15 26		
Sunbury		d				14 28								14 58								15 28		
Upper Halliford		d				14 30								15 00								15 30		
Shepperton		a				14 35								15 05								15 35		
Berrylands		d		14 00								14 30								15 00				
Surbiton 6		d	13 57	14 05				14a13			14 27	14 35				14a43			14 57	15 05				15a13
Thames Ditton		d		14 09								14 39								15 09				
Hampton Court		a		14 12								14 42								15 12				
Hinchley Wood		d	14 01								14 31								15 01					
Claygate		d	14 04								14 34								15 04					
Oxshott		d	14 07								14 37								15 07					
Cobham & Stoke D'abernon		d	14 11								14 41								15 11					
Bookham		d			14 25								14 55								15 25			
Effingham Junction 6		d	14 15		14 29						14 45		14 59						15 15		15 29			
Horsley		d	14 18		14 32						14 48		15 02						15 18		15 32			
Clandon		d	14 23		14 37						14 53		15 07						15 23		15 37			
London Road (Guildford)		d	14 28		14 42						14 58		15 12						15 28		15 42			
Guildford		a	14 35		14 49						15 05		15 19						15 35		15 49			

A To Woking
B To London Waterloo

Table T152-F

Saturdays

13 October to 8 December

London - Chessington South, Dorking, Guildford, Shepperton and Hampton Court

Station			SW	SW A	SW	SW	SW	SW	SW	SW B	SW	SW A	SW	SW	SW	SW	SW	SW B	SW	SW A	SW	SW	SW
London Waterloo 15	⊖	d	14 54	14 57	15 03	15 06	15 09	15 12	15 17	15 20	15 24	15 27	15 33	15 36	15 39	15 42	15 47	15 50	15 54	15 57	16 03	16 06	16 09
Vauxhall	⊖	d	14 58	15 01	15 07	15 10	15 13	15 16	15 21	15 24	15 28	15 31	15 37	15 40	15 43	15 46	15 51	15 54	15 58	16 01	16 07	16 10	16 13
Clapham Junction 10		d	15 03	15 06	15 12	15 15	15 18	15 21	15 26	15 29	15 33	15 36	15 42	15 45	15 48	15 51	15 56	15 59	16 03	16 06	16 12	16 15	16 18
Earlsfield		d	15 06	15 09	15 15	15 18	15 21	15 24	15 29	15 32	15 36	15 39	15 45	15 48	15 51	15 54	15 59	16 02	16 06	16 09	16 15	16 18	16 21
Wimbledon 6	⊖ ⇌	d	15 10	15 13	15 19	15 22	15 25	15 28	15 33	15 36	15 40	15 43	15 49	15 52	15 55	15 58	16 03	16 06	16 10	16 13	16 19	16 22	16 25
Raynes Park 8		d	15 13	15 16		15 25	15 28	15 31	15 36		15 43	15 46		15 55	15 58	16 01	16 06		16 13	16 16		16 25	16 28
Motspur Park		d	15 16				15 31		15 39		15 46				16 01		16 09		16 16				16 31
Malden Manor		d							15 42								16 12						
Tolworth		d							15 45								16 15						
Chessington North		d							15 48								16 18						
Chessington South		a							15 51								16 21						
Worcester Park		d	15 18				15 33				15 48				16 03				16 18				16 33
Stoneleigh		d	15 21				15 36				15 51				16 06				16 21				16 36
Ewell West		d	15 24				15 39				15 54				16 09				16 24				16 39
Epsom 3	182	a	15 27				15 42				15 57				16 12				16 27				16 42
		d	15 28				15 43				15 58				16 13				16 28				16 43
Ashtead	182	d	15 32				15 47				16 02				16 17				16 32				16 47
Leatherhead	182	d	15 35				15 50				16 05				16 20				16 35				16 50
Box Hill & Westhumble	182	d																					
Dorking 4	182	a	15 43								16 13								16 43				
New Malden 6		d		15 19		15 28		15 34				15 49		15 58		16 04				16 19		16 28	
Norbiton		d		15 22				15 37				15 52				16 07				16 22			
Kingston		a		15 25				15 40				15 55				16 10				16 25			
		d		15 29				15 40				15 59				16 10				16 29			
Hampton Wick		d		15 31				15 42				16 01				16 12				16 31			
Teddington		d		15 35				15 45				16 05				16 15				16 35			
Strawberry Hill		a		15 38								16 08								16 38			
Fulwell		d						15 49								16 19							
Hampton		d						15 53								16 23							
Kempton Park		d						15 56								16 26							
Sunbury		d						15 58								16 28							
Upper Halliford		d						16 00								16 30							
Shepperton		a						16 05								16 35							
Berrylands		d				15 30								16 00								16 30	
Surbiton 6		d			15 27	15 35				15a43			15 57	16 05				16a13			16 27	16 35	
Thames Ditton		d				15 39								16 09								16 39	
Hampton Court		a				15 42								16 12								16 42	
Hinchley Wood		d			15 31								16 01								16 31		
Claygate		d			15 34								16 04								16 34		
Oxshott		d			15 37								16 07								16 37		
Cobham & Stoke D'abernon		d			15 41								16 11								16 41		
Bookham		d					15 55								16 25								16 55
Effingham Junction 6		d			15 45		15 59						16 15		16 29						16 45		16 59
Horsley		d			15 48		16 02						16 18		16 32						16 48		17 02
Clandon		d			15 53		16 07						16 23		16 37						16 53		17 07
London Road (Guildford)		d			15 58		16 12						16 28		16 42						16 58		17 12
Guildford		a			16 05		16 19						16 35		16 49						17 05		17 19

A To London Waterloo
B To Woking

Table T152-F

Saturdays

13 October to 8 December

London - Chessington South, Dorking, Guildford, Shepperton and Hampton Court

		SW	SW	SW	SW	SW	SW	SW	SW	SW	SW	SW	SW	SW	SW	SW	SW	SW	SW	SW	SW	SW	SW
				A		B						A		B						A		B	
London Waterloo ⊖	d	16 12	16 17	16 20	16 24	16 27	16 33	16 36	16 39	16 42	16 47	16 50	16 54	16 57	17 03	17 06	17 09	17 12	17 17	17 20	17 24	17 27	17 33
Vauxhall ⊖	d	16 16	16 21	16 24	16 28	16 31	16 37	16 40	16 43	16 46	16 51	16 54	16 58	17 01	17 07	17 10	17 13	17 16	17 21	17 24	17 28	17 31	17 37
Clapham Junction	d	16 21	16 26	16 29	16 33	16 36	16 42	16 45	16 48	16 51	16 56	16 59	17 03	17 06	17 12	17 15	17 18	17 21	17 26	17 29	17 33	17 36	17 42
Earlsfield	d	16 24	16 29	16 32	16 36	16 39	16 45	16 48	16 51	16 54	16 59	17 02	17 06	17 09	17 15	17 18	17 21	17 24	17 29	17 32	17 36	17 39	17 45
Wimbledon ⊖	d	16 28	16 33	16 36	16 40	16 43	16 49	16 52	16 55	16 58	17 03	17 06	17 10	17 13	17 19	17 22	17 25	17 28	17 33	17 36	17 40	17 43	17 49
Raynes Park	d	16 31	16 36		16 43	16 46		16 55	16 58	17 01	17 06		17 13	17 16		17 25	17 28	17 31	17 36		17 43	17 46	
Motspur Park	d		16 39		16 46				17 01		17 09		17 16				17 31		17 39		17 46		
Malden Manor	d		16 42								17 12								17 42				
Tolworth	d		16 45								17 15								17 45				
Chessington North	d		16 48								17 18								17 48				
Chessington South	a		16 51								17 21								17 51				
Worcester Park	d				16 48				17 03				17 18				17 33				17 48		
Stoneleigh	d				16 51				17 06				17 21				17 36				17 51		
Ewell West	d				16 54				17 09				17 24				17 39				17 54		
Epsom	182 a				16 57				17 12				17 27				17 42				17 57		
	d				16 58				17 13				17 28				17 43				17 58		
Ashtead	182 d				17 02				17 17				17 32				17 47				18 02		
Leatherhead	182 d				17 05				17 20				17 35				17 50				18 05		
Box Hill & Westhumble	182 d																						
Dorking	182 a				17 13								17 43								18 13		
New Malden	d	16 34				16 49		16 58		17 04				17 19		17 28		17 34				17 49	
Norbiton	d	16 37				16 52				17 07				17 22				17 37				17 52	
Kingston	a	16 40				16 55				17 10				17 25				17 40				17 55	
	d	16 40				16 59				17 10				17 29				17 40				17 59	
Hampton Wick	d	16 42				17 01				17 12				17 31				17 42				18 01	
Teddington	d	16 45				17 05				17 15				17 35				17 45				18 05	
Strawberry Hill	a					17 08								17 38								18 08	
Fulwell	d	16 49								17 19								17 49					
Hampton	d	16 53								17 23								17 53					
Kempton Park	d	16 56								17 26								17 56					
Sunbury	d	16 58								17 28								17 58					
Upper Halliford	d	17 00								17 30								18 00					
Shepperton	a	17 05								17 35								18 05					
Berrylands	d							17 00								17 30							
Surbiton	d			16a43			16 57	17 05				17a13			17 27	17 35				17a43			17 57
Thames Ditton	d							17 09								17 39							
Hampton Court	a							17 12								17 42							
Hinchley Wood	d						17 01								17 31								18 01
Claygate	d						17 04								17 34								18 04
Oxshott	d						17 07								17 37								18 07
Cobham & Stoke D'abernon	d						17 11								17 41								18 11
Bookham	d								17 25								17 55						
Effingham Junction	d						17 15		17 29						17 45		17 59						18 15
Horsley	d						17 18		17 32						17 48		18 02						18 18
Clandon	d						17 23		17 37						17 53		18 07						18 23
London Road (Guildford)	d						17 28		17 42						17 58		18 12						18 28
Guildford	a						17 35		17 49						18 05		18 19						18 35

A To Woking

B To London Waterloo

Table T152-F

Saturdays

13 October to 8 December

London - Chessington South, Dorking, Guildford, Shepperton and Hampton Court

		SW	SW	SW	SW	SW	SW	SW	SW	SW	SW	SW	SW	SW	SW	SW	SW	SW	SW	SW	SW	SW
						A		B						A		B						A
London Waterloo ⊖	d	17 36	17 39	17 42	17 47	17 50	17 54	17 57	18 03	18 06	18 09	18 12	18 17	18 20	18 24	18 27	18 33	18 36	18 39	18 42	18 47	18 50
Vauxhall ⊖	d	17 40	17 43	17 46	17 51	17 54	17 58	18 01	18 07	18 10	18 13	18 16	18 21	18 24	18 28	18 31	18 37	18 40	18 43	18 46	18 51	18 54
Clapham Junction	d	17 45	17 48	17 51	17 56	17 59	18 03	18 06	18 12	18 15	18 18	18 21	18 26	18 29	18 33	18 36	18 42	18 45	18 48	18 51	18 56	18 59
Earlsfield	d	17 48	17 51	17 54	17 59	18 02	18 06	18 09	18 15	18 18	18 21	18 24	18 29	18 32	18 36	18 39	18 45	18 48	18 51	18 54	18 59	19 02
Wimbledon ⊖	d	17 52	17 55	17 58	18 03	18 06	18 10	18 13	18 19	18 22	18 25	18 28	18 33	18 36	18 40	18 43	18 49	18 52	18 55	18 58	19 03	19 06
Raynes Park	d	17 55	17 58	18 01	18 06		18 13	18 16		18 25	18 28	18 31	18 36		18 43	18 46		18 55	18 58	19 01	19 06	
Motspur Park	d		18 01		18 09		18 16				18 31		18 39		18 46				19 01		19 09	
Malden Manor	d				18 12								18 42								19 12	
Tolworth	d				18 15								18 45								19 15	
Chessington North	d				18 18								18 48								19 18	
Chessington South	a				18 21								18 51								19 21	
Worcester Park	d		18 03				18 18				18 33				18 48				19 03			
Stoneleigh	d		18 06				18 21				18 36				18 51				19 06			
Ewell West	d		18 09				18 24				18 39				18 54				19 09			
Epsom	182 a		18 12				18 27				18 42				18 57				19 12			
	d		18 13				18 28				18 43				18 58				19 13			
Ashtead	182 d		18 17				18 32				18 47				19 02				19 17			
Leatherhead	182 d		18 20				18 35				18 50				19 05				19 20			
Box Hill & Westhumble	182 d																					
Dorking	182 a						18 43								19 13							
New Malden	d	17 58		18 04				18 19		18 28		18 34				18 49		18 58		19 04		
Norbiton	d			18 07				18 22				18 37				18 52				19 07		
Kingston	a			18 10				18 25				18 40				18 55				19 10		
	d			18 10				18 29				18 40				18 59				19 10		
Hampton Wick	d			18 12				18 31				18 42				19 01				19 12		
Teddington	d			18 15				18 35				18 45				19 05				19 15		
Strawberry Hill	a							18 38								19 08						
Fulwell	d			18 19								18 49								19 19		
Hampton	d			18 23								18 53								19 23		
Kempton Park	d			18 26								18 56								19 26		
Sunbury	d			18 28								18 58								19 28		
Upper Halliford	d			18 30								19 00								19 30		
Shepperton	a			18 35								19 05								19 35		
Berrylands	d	18 00								18 30								19 00				
Surbiton	d	18 05				18a13			18 27	18 35				18a43			18 57	19 05				19a13
Thames Ditton	d	18 09								18 39								19 09				
Hampton Court	a	18 12								18 42								19 12				
Hinchley Wood	d								18 31								19 01					
Claygate	d								18 34								19 04					
Oxshott	d								18 37								19 07					
Cobham & Stoke D'abernon	d								18 41								19 11					
Bookham	d		18 25								18 55								19 25			
Effingham Junction	d		18 29						18 45		18 59						19 15		19 29			
Horsley	d		18 32						18 48		19 02						19 18		19 32			
Clandon	d		18 37						18 53		19 07						19 23		19 37			
London Road (Guildford)	d		18 42						18 58		19 12						19 28		19 42			
Guildford	a		18 49						19 05		19 19						19 35		19 49			

A To Woking

B To London Waterloo

Table T152-F

Saturdays

13 October to 8 December

London - Chessington South, Dorking, Guildford, Shepperton and Hampton Court

		SW	SW A	SW	SW	SW	SW	SW	SW B	SW	SW A	SW	SW	SW	SW	SW	SW B	SW	SW A	SW	SW	SW	SW
London Waterloo ⊖	d	18 54	18 57	19 03	19 06	19 09	19 12	19 17	19 20	19 24	19 27	19 33	19 36	19 39	19 42	19 47	19 50	19 54	19 57	20 03	20 06	20 09	20 12
Vauxhall ⊖	d	18 58	19 01	19 07	19 10	19 13	19 16	19 21	19 24	19 28	19 31	19 37	19 40	19 43	19 46	19 51	19 54	19 58	20 01	20 07	20 10	20 13	20 16
Clapham Junction	d	19 03	19 06	19 12	19 15	19 18	19 21	19 26	19 29	19 33	19 36	19 42	19 45	19 48	19 51	19 56	19 59	20 03	20 06	20 12	20 15	20 18	20 21
Earlsfield	d	19 06	19 09	19 15	19 18	19 21	19 24	19 29	19 32	19 36	19 39	19 45	19 48	19 51	19 54	19 59	20 02	20 06	20 09	20 15	20 18	20 21	20 24
Wimbledon ⊖	d	19 10	19 13	19 19	19 22	19 25	19 28	19 33	19 36	19 40	19 43	19 49	19 52	19 55	19 58	20 03	20 06	20 10	20 13	20 19	20 22	20 25	20 28
Raynes Park	d	19 13	19 16		19 25	19 28	19 31	19 36		19 43	19 46		19 55	19 58	20 01	20 06		20 13	20 16		20 25	20 28	20 31
Motspur Park	d	19 16				19 31		19 39		19 46				20 01		20 09		20 16				20 31	
Malden Manor	d							19 42								20 12							
Tolworth	d							19 45								20 15							
Chessington North	d							19 48								20 18							
Chessington South	a							19 51								20 21							
Worcester Park	d	19 18				19 33				19 48				20 03				20 18				20 33	
Stoneleigh	d	19 21				19 36				19 51				20 06				20 21				20 36	
Ewell West	d	19 24				19 39				19 54				20 09				20 24				20 39	
Epsom 182	a	19 27				19 42				19 57				20 12				20 27				20 42	
	d	19 28				19 43				19 58				20 13								20 43	
Ashtead 182	d	19 32				19 47				20 02				20 17								20 47	
Leatherhead 182	d	19 35				19 50				20 05				20 20								20 50	
Box Hill & Westhumble 182	d																						
Dorking 182	a	19 43								20 13												20 59	
New Malden	d		19 19		19 28		19 34				19 49		19 58		20 04				20 19		20 28		20 34
Norbiton	d		19 22				19 37				19 52				20 07				20 22				20 37
Kingston	a		19 25				19 40				19 55				20 10				20 25				20 40
	d		19 29				19 40				19 59				20 10				20 29				20 40
Hampton Wick	d		19 31				19 42				20 01				20 12				20 31				20 42
Teddington	d		19 35				19 45				20 05				20 15				20 35				20 45
Strawberry Hill	a		19 38								20 08								20 38				
Fulwell	d						19 49								20 19								20 49
Hampton	d						19 53								20 23								20 53
Kempton Park	d						19 56								20 26								20 56
Sunbury	d						19 58								20 28								20 58
Upper Halliford	d						20 00								20 30								21 00
Shepperton	a						20 05								20 36								21 05
Berrylands	d				19 30								20 00								20 30		
Surbiton	d			19 27	19 35				19a43			19 57	20 05				20a13			20 27	20 35		
Thames Ditton	d				19 39								20 09								20 39		
Hampton Court	a				19 42								20 12								20 42		
Hinchley Wood	d			19 31								20 01								20 31			
Claygate	d			19 34								20 04								20 34			
Oxshott	d			19 37								20 07								20 37			
Cobham & Stoke D'abernon	d			19 41								20 11								20 41			
Bookham	d					19 55								20 25									
Effingham Junction	d			19 45		19 59						20 15		20 29						20 45			
Horsley	d			19 48		20 02						20 18		20 32						20 48			
Clandon	d			19 53		20 07						20 23		20 37						20 53			
London Road (Guildford)	d			19 58		20 12						20 28		20 42						20 58			
Guildford	a			20 05		20 19						20 35		20 52						21 05			

A To London Waterloo
B To Woking

Table T152-F

Saturdays

13 October to 8 December

London - Chessington South, Dorking, Guildford, Shepperton and Hampton Court

		SW	SW A	SW	SW B	SW	SW	SW	SW	SW	SW A	SW	SW B	SW	SW	SW	SW	SW A	SW	SW B	SW	SW	SW
London Waterloo ⊖	d	20 17	20 20	20 24	20 27	20 33	20 36	20 39	20 42	20 47	20 50	20 54	20 57	21 03	21 06	21 09	21 12	21 20	21 24	21 27	21 33	21 36	21 39
Vauxhall ⊖	d	20 21	20 24	20 28	20 31	20 37	20 40	20 43	20 46	20 51	20 54	20 58	21 01	21 07	21 10	21 13	21 16	21 24	21 28	21 31	21 37	21 40	21 43
Clapham Junction	d	20 26	20 29	20 33	20 36	20 42	20 45	20 48	20 51	20 56	20 59	21 03	21 06	21 12	21 15	21 18	21 21	21 29	21 33	21 36	21 42	21 45	21 48
Earlsfield	d	20 29	20 32	20 36	20 39	20 45	20 48	20 51	20 54	20 59	21 02	21 06	21 09	21 15	21 18	21 21	21 24	21 32	21 36	21 39	21 45	21 48	21 51
Wimbledon ⊖	d	20 33	20 36	20 40	20 43	20 49	20 52	20 55	20 58	21 03	21 06	21 10	21 13	21 19	21 22	21 25	21 28	21 36	21 40	21 43	21 49	21 52	21 55
Raynes Park	d	20 36		20 43	20 46		20 55	20 58	21 01	21 06		21 13	21 16		21 25	21 28	21 31		21 43	21 46		21 55	21 58
Motspur Park	d	20 39		20 46				21 01		21 09		21 16				21 31			21 46				22 01
Malden Manor	d	20 42								21 12													
Tolworth	d	20 45								21 15													
Chessington North	d	20 48								21 18													
Chessington South	a	20 51								21 21													
Worcester Park	d			20 48				21 03				21 18				21 33			21 48				22 03
Stoneleigh	d			20 51				21 06				21 21				21 36			21 51				22 06
Ewell West	d			20 54				21 09				21 24				21 39			21 54				22 09
Epsom 182	a			20 57				21 12				21 27				21 42			21 57				22 12
	d							21 13								21 43							22 13
Ashtead 182	d							21 17								21 47							22 17
Leatherhead 182	d							21 20								21 50							22 20
Box Hill & Westhumble 182	d																						
Dorking 182	a															21 59							
New Malden	d				20 49		20 58		21 04				21 19		21 28		21 34			21 49		21 58	
Norbiton	d				20 52				21 07				21 22				21 37			21 52			
Kingston	a				20 55				21 10				21 25				21 40			21 55			
	d				20 59				21 10				21 29				21 40			21 59			
Hampton Wick	d				21 01				21 12				21 31				21 42			22 01			
Teddington	d				21 05				21 15				21 35				21 45			22 05			
Strawberry Hill	a				21 08								21 38							22 08			
Fulwell	d								21 19								21 49						
Hampton	d								21 23								21 53						
Kempton Park	d								21 26								21 56						
Sunbury	d								21 28								21 58						
Upper Halliford	d								21 30								22 00						
Shepperton	a								21 35								22 05						
Berrylands	d						21 00								21 30							22 00	
Surbiton	d		20a43			20 57	21 05				21a13			21 27	21 35			21a43			21 57	22 05	
Thames Ditton	d						21 09								21 39							22 09	
Hampton Court	a						21 12								21 42							22 12	
Hinchley Wood	d					21 01								21 31							22 01		
Claygate	d					21 04								21 34							22 04		
Oxshott	d					21 07								21 37							22 07		
Cobham & Stoke D'abernon	d					21 11								21 41							22 11		
Bookham	d							21 25															22 25
Effingham Junction	d					21 15		21 29						21 45							22 15		22 29
Horsley	d					21 18		21 32						21 48							22 18		22 32
Clandon	d					21 23		21 37						21 53							22 23		22 37
London Road (Guildford)	d					21 28		21 42						21 58							22 28		22 42
Guildford	a					21 35		21 52						22 05							22 35		22 49

A To Woking
B To London Waterloo

Table T152-F

Saturdays

13 October to 8 December

London - Chessington South, Dorking, Guildford, Shepperton and Hampton Court

		SW	SW	SW	SW	SW A	SW	SW	SW	SW	SW B
London Waterloo ⊖	d	21 42	21 47	21 50	21 54	21 57	22 03		22 09	22 12	22 20
Vauxhall ⊖	d	21 46	21 51	21 54	21 58	22 01	22 07		22 13	22 16	22 24
Clapham Junction	d	21 51	21 56	21 59	22 03	22 06	22 12		22 18	22 21	22 29
Earlsfield	d	21 54	21 59	22 02	22 06	22 09	22 15		22 21	22 24	22 32
Wimbledon ⊖	d	21 58	22 03	22 06	22 10	22 13	22 19		22 25	22 28	22 36
Raynes Park	d	22 01	22 06		22 13	22 16			22 28	22 31	
Motspur Park	d		22 09		22 16				22 31		
Malden Manor	d		22 12								
Tolworth	d		22 15								
Chessington North	d		22 18								
Chessington South	a		22 21								
Worcester Park	d				22 18				22 33		
Stoneleigh	d				22 21				22 36		
Ewell West	d				22 24				22 39		
Epsom 182	a				22 27				22 42		
	d								22 43		
Ashtead 182	d								22 47		
Leatherhead 182	d								22 50		
Box Hill & Westhumble 182	d										
Dorking 182	a								22 59		
New Malden	d	22 04				22 19				22 34	
Norbiton	d	22 07				22 22				22 37	
Kingston	a	22 10				22 25				22 40	
	d	22 10				22 29				22 40	
Hampton Wick	d	22 12				22 31				22 42	
Teddington	d	22 15				22 35				22 45	
Strawberry Hill	a					22 38					
Fulwell	d	22 19								22 49	
Hampton	d	22 23								22 53	
Kempton Park	d	22 26								22 56	
Sunbury	d	22 28								22 58	
Upper Halliford	d	22 30								23 00	
Shepperton	a	22 35								23 05	
Berrylands	d										
Surbiton	d			22 14			22 27	22 38			22a43
Thames Ditton	d							22 42			
Hampton Court	a							22 45			
Hinchley Wood	d						22 31				
Claygate	d						22 34				
Oxshott	d						22 37				
Cobham & Stoke D'abernon	d						22 41				
Bookham	d										
Effingham Junction	d						22 45				
Horsley	d						22 48				
Clandon	d						22 53				
London Road (Guildford)	d						22 58				
Guildford	a			22 47			23 05				

		SW A	SW	SW	SW	SW	SW B	SW A	SW	SW	SW	SW
London Waterloo ⊖	d	22 27	22 33	22 36	22 39	22 42	22 50	22 57	23 00	23 03		23 09
Vauxhall ⊖	d	22 31	22 37	22 40	22 43	22 46	22 54	23 01	23 04	23 07		23 13
Clapham Junction	d	22 36	22 42	22 45	22 48	22 51	22 59	23 06	23 09	23 12		23 18
Earlsfield	d	22 39	22 45	22 48	22 51	22 54	23 02	23 09	23 12	23 15		23 21
Wimbledon ⊖	d	22 43	22 49	22 52	22 55	22 58	23 06	23 13	23 16	23 19		23 25
Raynes Park	d	22 46		22 55	22 58	23 01		23 16	23 19			23 28
Motspur Park	d				23 01				23 22			23 31
Malden Manor	d								23 25			
Tolworth	d								23 28			
Chessington North	d								23 31			
Chessington South	a								23 33			
Worcester Park	d				23 03							23 33
Stoneleigh	d				23 06							23 36
Ewell West	d				23 09							23 39
Epsom 182	a				23 12							23 42
	d				23 13							23 43
Ashtead 182	d				23 17							23 47
Leatherhead 182	d				23 20							23 50
Box Hill & Westhumble 182	d											
Dorking 182	a											23 59
New Malden	d	22 49		22 58		23 04		23 19				
Norbiton	d	22 52				23 07		23 22				
Kingston	a	22 55				23 10		23 25				
	d	22 59				23 10		23 29				
Hampton Wick	d	23 01				23 12		23 31				
Teddington	d	23 05				23 15		23 35				
Strawberry Hill	a	23 08						23 38				
Fulwell	d					23 19						
Hampton	d					23 23						
Kempton Park	d					23 26						
Sunbury	d					23 28						
Upper Halliford	d					23 30						
Shepperton	a					23 35						
Berrylands	d			23 00								
Surbiton	d		22 57	23 05			23a13			23 27	23 43	
Thames Ditton	d			23 09							23 47	
Hampton Court	a			23 12							23 50	
Hinchley Wood	d		23 01							23 31		
Claygate	d		23 04							23 34		
Oxshott	d		23 07							23 37		
Cobham & Stoke D'abernon	d		23 11							23 41		
Bookham	d				23 25							
Effingham Junction	d		23 15		23 29					23 45		
Horsley	d		23 18		23 32					23 48		
Clandon	d		23 23		23 37					23 53		
London Road (Guildford)	d		23 28		23 42					23 58		
Guildford	a		23 35		23 49					00 05		

A To London Waterloo
B To Woking

Table T152-F

Saturdays

13 October to 8 December

London - Chessington South, Dorking, Guildford, Shepperton and Hampton Court

		SW	SW A	SW B	SW	SW	SW	SW
London Waterloo ⊖	d	23 12	23 20	23 27	23 36	23 42	23 50	23 57
Vauxhall ⊖	d	23 16	23 24	23 31	23 40	23 46	23 54	00 01
Clapham Junction	d	23 21	23 29	23 36	23 45	23 51	23 59	00 06
Earlsfield	d	23 24	23 32	23 39	23 48	23 54	00 02	00 09
Wimbledon ⊖	d	23 28	23 36	23 43	23 52	23 58	00 06	00 13
Raynes Park	d	23 31		23 46	23 55	00 01		00 16
Motspur Park	d					00 04		
Malden Manor	d							
Tolworth	d							
Chessington North	d							
Chessington South	a							
Worcester Park	d					00 06		
Stoneleigh	d					00 09		
Ewell West	d					00 12		
Epsom 182	a					00 15		
	d					00 19		
Ashtead 182	d					00 23		
Leatherhead 182	d					00 26		
Box Hill & Westhumble 182	d							
Dorking 182	a							
New Malden	d	23 34		23 49	23 58			00 19
Norbiton	d	23 37		23 52				00 22
Kingston	a	23 40		23 55				00 25
	d	23 40		23 55				00 25
Hampton Wick	d	23 42		23 57				00 27
Teddington	d	23 45		23 59				00 30
Strawberry Hill	a			00 03				
Fulwell	d	23 49						00 34
Hampton	d	23 53						00 38
Kempton Park	d	23 56						00 41
Sunbury	d	23 58						00 43
Upper Halliford	d	23 59						00 45
Shepperton	a	00 05						00 50
Berrylands	d				23 59			
Surbiton	d		23a44		00 05		00 14	
Thames Ditton	d				00 09			
Hampton Court	a				00 12			
Hinchley Wood	d						00 18	
Claygate	d						00 20	
Oxshott	d						00 24	
Cobham & Stoke D'abernon	d						00 27	
Bookham	d					00 31		
Effingham Junction	d					00 36	00 32	
Horsley	d					00 39	00 34	
Clandon	d					00 44	00 39	
London Road (Guildford)	d					00 49	00 44	
Guildford	a					00 56	00 51	

A To Woking
B To Twickenham

London - Chessington South, Dorking, Guildford, Shepperton and Hampton Court

		SW A	SW A	SW A	SW A	SW	SW	SW B	SW	SW C	SW D	SW	SW	SW	SW	SW	SW D	SW	SW	SW	SW	SW	SW
London Waterloo ⊖	d					00 09	00 15	00 27	00 42	01 42	06 18		06 57			07 10	07 18		07 27		07 40	07 48	07 57
Vauxhall ⊖	d				00 01	00 13	00 19	00 31	00 46	01 46	06 22		07 01			07 14	07 22		07 31		07 44	07 52	08 01
Clapham Junction	d				00 06	00 20	00 26	00 38	00 53	01 53	06 27		07 06			07 19	07 27		07 36		07 49	07 57	08 06
Earlsfield	d		00 02		00 09	00 23	00 29	00s41					07 09			07 22	07 30		07 39		07 52	08 00	08 09
Wimbledon ⊖	d		00 06		00 13	00 27	00 33	00 45	01 05	01 59	06 34	06 48	07 13	07 16	07 20	07 26	07 34	07 38	07 43	07 48	07 56	08 04	08 13
Raynes Park	d			00 01	00 16		00 36	00 48	01 08	02 02	06 37	06 52	07 17		07 23		07 38	07 40	07 47	07 52		08 07	08 17
Motspur Park	d			00 04			00 39					06 55			07 26			07 43		07 55			
Malden Manor	d																	07 46					
Tolworth	d																	07 49					
Chessington North	d																	07 52					
Chessington South	a																	07 56					
Worcester Park	d			00 06			00 41					06 57			07 28					07 57			
Stoneleigh	d			00 09			00 44					07 00			07 31					08 00			
Ewell West	d			00 12			00 47					07 03			07 34					08 03			
Epsom 182	a			00 15			00 50					07 06			07 37					08 06			
	d			00 19																08 08			
Ashtead 182	d			00 23																08 12			
Leatherhead 182	d			00 26																08 15			
Box Hill & Westhumble 182	d																						
Dorking 182	a																						
New Malden	d				00 19			00 51	01 11	02 04	06 40		07 19				07 40		07 49			08 11	08 19
Norbiton	d				00 22				01 14	02 08	06 43						07 44					08 13	
Kingston	a				00 25				01 17	02 10	06 46						07 46					08 16	
	d				00 25				01 17	02 11	06 49						07 49					08 16	
Hampton Wick	d				00 27				01s22	02s13	06 51						07 51					08 18	
Teddington	d				00 30				01s25	02s15	06 56						07 56					08 22	
Strawberry Hill	a								01 37	02s18	06 59						07 59						
Fulwell	d				00 34																	08 25	
Hampton	d				00 38																	08 30	
Kempton Park	d				00 41																	08 32	
Sunbury	d				00 43																	08 35	
Upper Halliford	d				00 45																	08 37	
Shepperton	a				00 48																	08 40	
Berrylands	d							00s53					07 22						07 52				08 22
Surbiton	d	00 05	00 14			00 35		00s57					07 26	07 32		07 35			07 56		08 05		08 26
Thames Ditton	d	00 09											07 30						08 00				08 30
Hampton Court	a	00 12											07 33						08 03				08 33
Hinchley Wood	d		00 18											07 36									
Claygate	d		00 20											07 39									
Oxshott	d		00 24											07 42									
Cobham & Stoke D'abernon	d		00 27											07 46									
Bookham	d			00 31																08 21			
Effingham Junction	d		00 32	00 36										07 50						08 25			
Horsley	d		00 34	00 39										07 53						08 27			
Clandon	d		00 39	00 44										07 58						08 32			
London Road (Guildford)	d		00 44	00 49										08 03						08 37			
Guildford	a		00 48	00 53		01 07								08 07		08 14				08 41	08 39		

A not 20 May. From London Waterloo
B To Woking
C To Twickenham
D To London Waterloo

London - Chessington South, Dorking, Guildford, Shepperton and Hampton Court

		SW	SW	SW	SW	SW A	SW	SW	SW	SW	SW	SW	SW	SW	SW	SW	SW A	SW	SW	SW	SW	SW	SW
London Waterloo ⊖	d			08 02	08 10	08 18	08 21	08 27	08 33	08 40	08 48	08 51	08 57	09 02		09 10	09 18	09 21	09 27	09 32	09 40	09 48	09 51
Vauxhall ⊖	d			08 06	08 14	08 22	08 25	08 31	08 37	08 44	08 52	08 55	09 01	09 06		09 14	09 22	09 25	09 31	09 36	09 44	09 52	09 55
Clapham Junction	d			08 11	08 19	08 27	08 30	08 36	08 41	08 49	08 57	09 00	09 06	09 11		09 19	09 27	09 30	09 36	09 41	09 49	09 57	10 00
Earlsfield	d			08 14	08 22	08 30	08 33	08 39	08 44	08 52	09 00	09 03	09 09	09 14		09 22	09 30	09 33	09 39	09 44	09 52	10 00	10 03
Wimbledon ⊖	d	08 02	08 08	08 18	08 26	08 34	08 37	08 43	08 48	08 56	09 04	09 07	09 13	09 18		09 26	09 34	09 37	09 43	09 48	09 56	10 04	10 07
Raynes Park	d	08 05	08 10	08 22		08 38	08 41	08 47	08 53		09 07	09 11	09 16	09 22			09 37	09 40	09 46	09 52		10 07	10 10
Motspur Park	d		08 13	08 25			08 43		08 55			09 13		09 25				09 43		09 55			10 13
Malden Manor	d		08 16				08 47					09 17						09 46					10 16
Tolworth	d		08 19				08 49					09 19						09 49					10 19
Chessington North	d		08 22				08 52					09 22						09 52					10 22
Chessington South	a		08 26				08 56					09 25						09 55					10 25
Worcester Park	d			08 27					08 58					09 27						09 57			
Stoneleigh	d			08 30					09 01					09 30						10 00			
Ewell West	d			08 33					09 03					09 33						10 03			
Epsom 182	a			08 36					09 07					09 36						10 06			
	d			08 38					09 08					09 38						10 08			
Ashtead 182	d			08 42					09 12					09 42						10 12			
Leatherhead 182	d			08 45					09 15					09 45						10 15			
Box Hill & Westhumble 182	d			08 50										09 50									
Dorking 182	a			08 52										09 55									
New Malden	d	08 08				08 40		08 49			09 10		09 19				09 40		09 49			10 10	
Norbiton	d					08 44					09 13						09 43					10 13	
Kingston	a					08 46					09 15						09 46					10 16	
	d					08 49					09 16						09 49					10 16	
Hampton Wick	d					08 51					09 18						09 51					10 18	
Teddington	d					08 56					09 21						09 56					10 21	
Strawberry Hill	a					08 59											09 59						
Fulwell	d										09 25											10 25	
Hampton	d										09 29											10 29	
Kempton Park	d										09 32											10 32	
Sunbury	d										09 34											10 34	
Upper Halliford	d										09 36											10 36	
Shepperton	a										09 40											10 39	
Berrylands	d	08 10						08 52					09 21						09 51				
Surbiton	d	08 32			08 35			08 56		09 05			09 25		09 32	09 36			09 55		10 05		
Thames Ditton	d							09 00					09 30						10 00				
Hampton Court	a							09 03					09 33						10 03				
Hinchley Wood	d	08 36													09 36								
Claygate	d	08 39													09 39								
Oxshott	d	08 42													09 42								
Cobham & Stoke D'abernon	d	08 46													09 46								
Bookham	d								09 21											10 21			
Effingham Junction	d	08 50							09 25						09 50					10 25			
Horsley	d	08 53							09 27						09 53					10 27			
Clandon	d	08 58							09 32						09 58					10 32			
London Road (Guildford)	d	09 03							09 37						10 03					10 37			
Guildford	a	09 07			09 09				09 41	09 39					10 07	10 09				10 41	10 44		

A To London Waterloo

Table T152-F

Sundays
20 May to 30 September

London - Chessington South, Dorking, Guildford, Shepperton and Hampton Court

Station		SW		SW	SW	SW	SW A	SW	SW	SW	SW	SW		SW	SW	SW	SW	SW	SW A	SW	SW	SW		SW	SW
London Waterloo	⊖ d	09 57			10 02	10 10	10 18	10 21	10 27	10 32	10 40	10 48		10 51	10 57		11 02	11 10	11 18	11 21	11 27	11 32		11 40	11 48
Vauxhall	⊖ d	10 01			10 06	10 14	10 22	10 25	10 31	10 36	10 44	10 52		10 55	11 01		11 06	11 14	11 22	11 25	11 31	11 36		11 44	11 52
Clapham Junction	d	10 06			10 11	10 19	10 27	10 30	10 36	10 41	10 49	10 57		11 00	11 06		11 12	11 19	11 27	11 30	11 36	11 42		11 49	11 57
Earlsfield	d	10 09			10 14	10 22	10 30	10 33	10 39	10 44	10 52	11 00		11 03	11 10		11 15	11 22	11 30	11 33	11 39	11 45		11 52	12 00
Wimbledon	⊖ d	10 13		10 17	10 18	10 26	10 34	10 37	10 43	10 48	10 56	11 04		11 07	11 14	11 14	11 19	11 26	11 34	11 37	11 43	11 49		11 56	12 04
Raynes Park	d	10 16			10 22		10 37	10 40	10 46	10 52		11 07		11 10	11 17		11 23		11 37	11 40	11 46	11 52			12 07
Motspur Park	d				10 25			10 43		10 55				11 13			11 25			11 43		11 55			
Malden Manor	d							10 46						11 16						11 46					
Tolworth	d							10 49						11 19						11 49					
Chessington North	d							10 52						11 22						11 52					
Chessington South	a							10 55						11 25						11 55					
Worcester Park	d				10 27					10 57							11 28					11 57			
Stoneleigh	d				10 30					11 00							11 31					12 00			
Ewell West	d				10 33					11 03							11 33					12 03			
Epsom	182 a				10 36					11 06							11 37					12 06			
	d				10 38					11 08							11 38					12 08			
Ashtead	182 d				10 42					11 12							11 42					12 12			
Leatherhead	182 d				10 45					11 15							11 45					12 15			
Box Hill & Westhumble	182 d				10 50												11 50								
Dorking	182 a				10 52												11 52								
New Malden	d	10 19					10 40		10 49			11 10			11 20				11 40		11 49				12 10
Norbiton	d						10 43					11 13							11 43						12 13
Kingston	a						10 46					11 16							11 46						12 16
	d						10 49					11 16							11 49						12 16
Hampton Wick	d						10 51					11 18							11 51						12 18
Teddington	d						10 56					11 21							11 56						12 21
Strawberry Hill	a						10 59												11 59						
Fulwell	d											11 25													12 25
Hampton	d											11 29													12 29
Kempton Park	d											11 32													12 32
Sunbury	d											11 34													12 34
Upper Halliford	d											11 36													12 36
Shepperton	a											11 39													12 39
Berrylands	d	10 21							10 51						11 23						11 51				
Surbiton	d	10 25		10 32		10 35			10 55		11 05				11 27	11 32		11 35			11 55			12 05	
Thames Ditton	d	10 30							11 00						11 31						12 00				
Hampton Court	a	10 33							11 03						11 34						12 03				
Hinchley Wood	d			10 36												11 36									
Claygate	d			10 39												11 39									
Oxshott	d			10 42												11 42									
Cobham & Stoke D'abernon	d			10 46												11 46									
Bookham	d									11 21												12 21			
Effingham Junction	d			10 50						11 25						11 50						12 25			
Horsley	d			10 53						11 27						11 53						12 27			
Clandon	d			10 58						11 32						11 58						12 32			
London Road (Guildford)	d			11 03						11 37						12 03						12 37			
Guildford	a			11 07		11 14				11 41	11 44					12 07		12 14				12 41		12 44	

A To London Waterloo

Table T152-F

Sundays
20 May to 30 September

London - Chessington South, Dorking, Guildford, Shepperton and Hampton Court

Station		SW	SW	SW	SW	SW	SW A	SW A		SW	SW	SW	SW	SW	SW	SW	SW	SW		SW	SW A	SW A	SW	SW	SW
London Waterloo	⊖ d	11 51	11 57	12 02		12 10		12 18		12 21	12 27	12 32	12 40	12 48	12 51	12 57	13 00	13 02		13 10		13 18	13 21	13 27	13 32
Vauxhall	⊖ d	11 55	12 01	12 06		12 14		12 22		12 25	12 31	12 36	12 44	12 52	12 55	13 01	13 04	13 06		13 14		13 22	13 25	13 31	13 36
Clapham Junction	d	12 00	12 06	12 11		12 19		12 27		12 30	12 36	12 42	12 49	12 57	13 00	13 06	13 09	13 11		13 19		13 27	13 30	13 36	13 41
Earlsfield	d	12 03	12 10	12 15		12 22		12 30		12 33	12 39	12 45	12 52	13 00	13 03	13 09	13 12	13 14		13 22		13 30	13 33	13 39	13 44
Wimbledon	⊖ d	12 07	12 14	12 19	12 19	12 26		12 34		12 37	12 43	12 49	12 56	13 04	13 07	13 13	13 16	13 18		13 26		13 34	13 37	13 43	13 48
Raynes Park	d	12 10	12 17	12 23				12 37		12 40	12 46	12 52		13 07	13 10	13 16		13 22				13 37	13 40	13 46	13 52
Motspur Park	d	12 13		12 25						12 43		12 55			13 13			13 25					13 43		13 55
Malden Manor	d	12 16								12 46					13 16								13 46		
Tolworth	d	12 19								12 49					13 19								13 49		
Chessington North	d	12 22								12 52					13 22								13 52		
Chessington South	a	12 25								12 55					13 25								13 55		
Worcester Park	d			12 28								12 57						13 27							13 57
Stoneleigh	d			12 31								13 00						13 30							14 00
Ewell West	d			12 33								13 03						13 33							14 03
Epsom	182 a			12 37								13 06						13 36							14 06
	d			12 38								13 08						13 38							14 08
Ashtead	182 d			12 42								13 12						13 42							14 12
Leatherhead	182 d			12 45								13 15						13 45							14 15
Box Hill & Westhumble	182 d			12 50														13 50							
Dorking	182 a			12 52														13 52							
New Malden	d		12 19					12 40			12 49			13 10		13 19						13 40		13 49	
Norbiton	d							12 43						13 13								13 43			
Kingston	a							12 46						13 16								13 46			
	d						12 35	12 49						13 16							13 35	13 49			
Hampton Wick	d						12 37	12 51						13 18							13 37	13 51			
Teddington	d						12 40	12 56						13 21							13 40	13 56			
Strawberry Hill	a						12 43	12 59													13 43	13 59			
Fulwell	d													13 25											
Hampton	d													13 29											
Kempton Park	d													13 32											
Sunbury	d													13 34											
Upper Halliford	d													13 36											
Shepperton	a													13 39											
Berrylands	d		12 22								12 51					13 21								13 51	
Surbiton	d		12 26		12 32	12 35					12 55		13 05			13 25	13 32			13 35				13 55	
Thames Ditton	d		12 30								13 00					13 30								14 00	
Hampton Court	a		12 33								13 03					13 33								14 03	
Hinchley Wood	d				12 36												13 36								
Claygate	d				12 39												13 39								
Oxshott	d				12 42												13 42								
Cobham & Stoke D'abernon	d				12 46												13 46								
Bookham	d											13 21													14 21
Effingham Junction	d				12 50							13 25					13 50								14 25
Horsley	d				12 53							13 27					13 53								14 27
Clandon	d				12 58							13 32					13 58								14 32
London Road (Guildford)	d				13 03							13 37					14 03								14 37
Guildford	a				13 07	13 14						13 41	13 44				14 07			14 14					14 41

A To London Waterloo

Table T152-F

Sundays

20 May to 30 September

London - Chessington South, Dorking, Guildford, Shepperton and Hampton Court

		SW	SW	SW		SW	SW	SW	SW	SW A	SW A	SW	SW	SW		SW	SW	SW	SW	SW	SW	SW	SW A	SW A
London Waterloo 15 ⊖	d	13 40	13 48	13 51		13 57	14 00	14 02	14 10		14 18	14 21	14 27	14 32		14 40	14 48	14 51	14 57	15 00	15 02	15 10		15 18
Vauxhall ⊖	d	13 44	13 52	13 55		14 01	14 04	14 06	14 14		14 22	14 25	14 31	14 36		14 44	14 52	14 55	15 01	15 04	15 06	15 14		15 22
Clapham Junction 10	d	13 49	13 57	14 00		14 06	14 09	14 11	14 19		14 27	14 30	14 36	14 41		14 49	14 57	15 00	15 06	15 09	15 11	15 19		15 27
Earlsfield	d	13 52	14 00	14 03		14 09	14 12	14 14	14 22		14 30	14 33	14 39	14 44		14 52	15 00	15 03	15 09	15 12	15 14	15 22		15 30
Wimbledon 3 ⊖	d	13 56	14 04	14 07		14 13	14 16	14 18	14 26		14 34	14 37	14 43	14 48		14 56	15 04	15 07	15 13	15 16	15 18	15 26		15 34
Raynes Park 3	d		14 07	14 10		14 16		14 22			14 37	14 40	14 46	14 52			15 07	15 10	15 16		15 22			15 37
Motspur Park	d			14 13				14 25				14 43		14 55				15 13			15 25			
Malden Manor	d			14 16								14 46						15 16						
Tolworth	d			14 19								14 49						15 19						
Chessington North	d			14 22								14 52						15 22						
Chessington South	a			14 25								14 55						15 25						
Worcester Park	d							14 27						14 57							15 27			
Stoneleigh	d							14 30						15 00							15 30			
Ewell West	d							14 33						15 03							15 33			
Epsom 3 182	a							14 36						15 06							15 36			
	d							14 38						15 08							15 38			
Ashtead 182	d							14 42						15 12							15 42			
Leatherhead 182	d							14 45						15 15							15 45			
Box Hill & Westhumble 182	d							14 50													15 50			
Dorking 4 182	a							14 52													15 52			
New Malden 3	d		14 10			14 19					14 40		14 49				15 10		15 19					15 40
Norbiton	d		14 13								14 43						15 13							15 43
Kingston	a		14 16								14 46						15 16							15 46
	d		14 16							14 35	14 49						15 16						15 35	15 49
Hampton Wick	d		14 18							14 37	14 51						15 18						15 37	15 51
Teddington	d		14 21							14 40	14 56						15 21						15 40	15 56
Strawberry Hill	a									14 43	14 59												15 43	15 59
Fulwell	d		14 25														15 25							
Hampton	d		14 29														15 29							
Kempton Park	d		14 32														15 32							
Sunbury	d		14 34														15 34							
Upper Halliford	d		14 36														15 36							
Shepperton	a		14 39														15 39							
Berrylands	d					14 21							14 51						15 21					
Surbiton 3	d	14 05				14 25	14 32		14 35				14 55			15 05			15 25	15 32		15 35		
Thames Ditton	d					14 30							15 00						15 30					
Hampton Court	a					14 33							15 03						15 33					
Hinchley Wood	d						14 36													15 36				
Claygate	d						14 39													15 39				
Oxshott	d						14 42													15 42				
Cobham & Stoke D'abernon	d						14 46													15 46				
Bookham	d													15 21										
Effingham Junction 3	d						14 50							15 25						15 50				
Horsley	d						14 53							15 27						15 53				
Clandon	d						14 58							15 32						15 58				
London Road (Guildford)	d						15 03							15 37						16 03				
Guildford	a	14 44					15 07		15 14					15 41		15 44				16 07		16 14		

A To London Waterloo

Table T152-F

Sundays

20 May to 30 September

London - Chessington South, Dorking, Guildford, Shepperton and Hampton Court

		SW	SW	SW	SW	SW	SW	SW	SW	SW		SW	SW A	SW A	SW	SW	SW	SW	SW	SW		SW	SW	SW	SW
London Waterloo 15 ⊖	d	15 21	15 27	15 32	15 40	15 48	15 51	15 57	16 00	16 02		16 10		16 18	16 21	16 27	16 32	16 40	16 48	16 51		16 57	17 00	17 02	17 10
Vauxhall ⊖	d	15 25	15 31	15 36	15 44	15 52	15 55	16 01	16 04	16 06		16 14		16 22	16 25	16 31	16 36	16 44	16 52	16 55		17 01	17 04	17 06	17 14
Clapham Junction 10	d	15 30	15 36	15 41	15 49	15 57	16 00	16 06	16 09	16 11		16 19		16 27	16 30	16 36	16 41	16 49	16 57	17 00		17 06	17 09	17 11	17 19
Earlsfield	d	15 33	15 39	15 44	15 52	16 00	16 03	16 09	16 12	16 14		16 22		16 30	16 33	16 39	16 44	16 52	17 00	17 03		17 09	17 12	17 14	17 22
Wimbledon 3 ⊖	d	15 37	15 43	15 48	15 56	16 04	16 07	16 13	16 16	16 18		16 26		16 34	16 37	16 43	16 48	16 56	17 04	17 07		17 13	17 16	17 18	17 26
Raynes Park 3	d	15 40	15 46	15 52		16 07	16 10	16 16		16 22				16 37	16 40	16 46	16 52		17 07	17 10		17 16		17 22	
Motspur Park	d	15 43		15 55			16 13			16 25					16 43		16 55			17 13				17 25	
Malden Manor	d	15 46					16 16								16 46					17 16					
Tolworth	d	15 49					16 19								16 49					17 19					
Chessington North	d	15 52					16 22								16 52					17 22					
Chessington South	a	15 55					16 25								16 55					17 25					
Worcester Park	d			15 57						16 27							16 57							17 27	
Stoneleigh	d			16 00						16 30							17 00							17 30	
Ewell West	d			16 03						16 33							17 03							17 33	
Epsom 3 182	a			16 06						16 36							17 06							17 36	
	d			16 08						16 38							17 08							17 38	
Ashtead 182	d			16 12						16 42							17 12							17 42	
Leatherhead 182	d			16 15						16 45							17 15							17 45	
Box Hill & Westhumble 182	d																								
Dorking 4 182	a									16 52														17 52	
New Malden 3	d		15 49			16 10		16 19						16 40		16 49			17 10			17 19			
Norbiton	d					16 13								16 43					17 13						
Kingston	a					16 16								16 46					17 16						
	d					16 16							16 35	16 49					17 16						
Hampton Wick	d					16 18							16 37	16 51					17 18						
Teddington	d					16 21							16 40	16 56					17 21						
Strawberry Hill	a												16 43	16 59											
Fulwell	d					16 25													17 25						
Hampton	d					16 29													17 29						
Kempton Park	d					16 32													17 32						
Sunbury	d					16 34													17 34						
Upper Halliford	d					16 36													17 36						
Shepperton	a					16 39													17 39						
Berrylands	d		15 51					16 21								16 51						17 21			
Surbiton 3	d		15 55		16 05			16 25	16 32			16 35				16 55		17 05				17 25	17 32		17 35
Thames Ditton	d		16 00					16 30								17 00						17 30			
Hampton Court	a		16 03					16 33								17 03						17 33			
Hinchley Wood	d								16 36														17 36		
Claygate	d								16 39														17 39		
Oxshott	d								16 42														17 42		
Cobham & Stoke D'abernon	d								16 46														17 46		
Bookham	d			16 21													17 21								
Effingham Junction 3	d			16 25					16 50								17 25						17 50		
Horsley	d			16 27					16 53								17 27						17 53		
Clandon	d			16 32					16 58								17 32						17 58		
London Road (Guildford)	d			16 37					17 03								17 37						18 03		
Guildford	a			16 41	16 44				17 07			17 14					17 41	17 44					18 07		18 14

A To London Waterloo

Table T152-F

Sundays

20 May to 30 September

London - Chessington South, Dorking, Guildford, Shepperton and Hampton Court

		SW A	SW A	SW	SW	SW	SW	SW	SW	SW	SW	SW	SW	SW A	SW A	SW	SW	SW	SW	SW	SW	SW	SW
London Waterloo ⊖	d		17 18	17 21	17 27	17 32	17 40	17 48	17 51	17 57	18 00	18 02	18 10		18 18	18 21	18 27	18 32	18 40	18 48	18 51	18 57	19 00
Vauxhall ⊖	d		17 22	17 25	17 31	17 36	17 44	17 52	17 55	18 01	18 04	18 06	18 14		18 22	18 25	18 31	18 36	18 44	18 52	18 55	19 01	19 04
Clapham Junction	d		17 27	17 30	17 36	17 41	17 49	17 57	18 00	18 06	18 09	18 11	18 19		18 27	18 30	18 36	18 41	18 49	18 57	19 00	19 06	19 09
Earlsfield	d		17 30	17 33	17 39	17 44	17 52	18 00	18 03	18 09	18 12	18 14	18 22		18 30	18 33	18 39	18 44	18 52	19 00	19 03	19 09	19 12
Wimbledon ⊖	d		17 34	17 37	17 43	17 48	17 56	18 04	18 07	18 13	18 16	18 18	18 26		18 34	18 37	18 43	18 48	18 56	19 04	19 07	19 13	19 16
Raynes Park	d		17 37	17 40	17 46	17 52		18 07	18 10	18 16		18 22			18 37	18 40	18 46	18 52		19 07	19 10	19 16	
Motspur Park	d			17 43		17 55			18 13			18 25				18 43		18 55			19 13		
Malden Manor	d			17 46					18 16							18 46					19 16		
Tolworth	d			17 49					18 19							18 49					19 19		
Chessington North	d			17 52					18 22							18 52					19 22		
Chessington South	a			17 55					18 25							18 55					19 25		
Worcester Park	d					17 57						18 27						18 57					
Stoneleigh	d					18 00						18 30						19 00					
Ewell West	d					18 03						18 33						19 03					
Epsom 182	a					18 06						18 36						19 06					
	d					18 08						18 38						19 08					
Ashtead 182	d					18 12						18 42						19 12					
Leatherhead 182	d					18 15						18 45						19 15					
Box Hill & Westhumble 182	d																						
Dorking 182	a											18 52											
New Malden	d		17 40		17 49			18 10		18 19					18 40		18 49			19 10		19 19	
Norbiton	d		17 43					18 13							18 43					19 13			
Kingston	a		17 46					18 16							18 46					19 16			
	d	17 35	17 49					18 16						18 35	18 49					19 16			
Hampton Wick	d	17 37	17 51					18 18						18 37	18 51					19 18			
Teddington	d	17 40	17 56					18 21						18 40	18 56					19 21			
Strawberry Hill	a	17 43	17 59											18 43	18 59								
Fulwell	d							18 25												19 25			
Hampton	d							18 29												19 29			
Kempton Park	d							18 32												19 32			
Sunbury	d							18 34												19 34			
Upper Halliford	d							18 36												19 36			
Shepperton	a							18 39												19 39			
Berrylands	d				17 51					18 21							18 51					19 21	
Surbiton	d				17 55		18 05			18 25	18 32		18 35				18 55		19 05			19 25	19 32
Thames Ditton	d				18 00					18 30							19 00					19 30	
Hampton Court	a				18 03					18 33							19 03					19 33	
Hinchley Wood	d										18 36												19 36
Claygate	d										18 39												19 39
Oxshott	d										18 42												19 42
Cobham & Stoke D'abernon	d										18 46												19 46
Bookham	d					18 21												19 21					
Effingham Junction	d					18 25					18 50							19 25					19 50
Horsley	d					18 27					18 53							19 27					19 53
Clandon	d					18 32					18 58							19 32					19 58
London Road (Guildford)	d					18 37					19 03							19 37					20 03
Guildford	a					18 41	18 44				19 07		19 14					19 41	19 44				20 07

A To London Waterloo

Table T152-F

Sundays

20 May to 30 September

London - Chessington South, Dorking, Guildford, Shepperton and Hampton Court

		SW	SW	SW A	SW A	SW	SW	SW	SW	SW	SW	SW	SW	SW	SW A	SW A	SW	SW	SW	SW	SW	SW
London Waterloo ⊖	d	19 02	19 10		19 18	19 21	19 27	19 32	19 40	19 48	19 57	20 00	20 02	20 10		20 18	20 21	20 27	20 32	20 40	20 48	20 57
Vauxhall ⊖	d	19 06	19 14		19 22	19 25	19 31	19 36	19 44	19 52	20 01	20 04	20 06	20 14		20 22	20 25	20 31	20 36	20 44	20 52	21 01
Clapham Junction	d	19 11	19 19		19 27	19 30	19 36	19 41	19 49	19 57	20 06	20 09	20 11	20 19		20 27	20 30	20 36	20 41	20 49	20 57	21 06
Earlsfield	d	19 14	19 22		19 30	19 33	19 39	19 44	19 52	20 00	20 09	20 12	20 14	20 22		20 30	20 33	20 39	20 44	20 52	21 00	21 09
Wimbledon ⊖	d	19 18	19 26		19 34	19 37	19 43	19 48	19 56	20 04	20 13	20 16	20 18	20 26		20 34	20 37	20 43	20 48	20 56	21 04	21 13
Raynes Park	d	19 22			19 37	19 40	19 46	19 52		20 07	20 16		20 22			20 37	20 40	20 46	20 52		21 07	21 16
Motspur Park	d	19 25				19 43		19 55					20 25				20 43		20 55			
Malden Manor	d					19 46											20 46					
Tolworth	d					19 49											20 49					
Chessington North	d					19 52											20 52					
Chessington South	a					19 55											20 55					
Worcester Park	d	19 27						19 57					20 27						20 57			
Stoneleigh	d	19 30						20 00					20 30						21 00			
Ewell West	d	19 33						20 03					20 33						21 03			
Epsom 182	a	19 36						20 06					20 36						21 06			
	d	19 38						20 08					20 38						21 08			
Ashtead 182	d	19 42						20 12					20 42						21 12			
Leatherhead 182	d	19 45						20 15					20 45						21 15			
Box Hill & Westhumble 182	d																					
Dorking 182	a	19 52											20 52									
New Malden	d				19 40		19 49			20 10	20 19					20 40		20 49			21 10	21 19
Norbiton	d				19 43					20 13						20 43					21 13	
Kingston	a				19 46					20 16						20 46					21 16	
	d			19 35	19 49					20 16					20 35	20 49					21 16	
Hampton Wick	d			19 37	19 51					20 18					20 37	20 51					21 18	
Teddington	d			19 40	19 56					20 21					20 40	20 56					21 21	
Strawberry Hill	a			19 43	19 59										20 43	20 59						
Fulwell	d									20 25											21 25	
Hampton	d									20 29											21 29	
Kempton Park	d									20 32											21 32	
Sunbury	d									20 34											21 34	
Upper Halliford	d									20 36											21 36	
Shepperton	a									20 39											21 39	
Berrylands	d						19 51				20 21							20 51				21 21
Surbiton	d		19 35				19 55		20 05		20 25	20 32		20 35				20 55		21 05		21 25
Thames Ditton	d						20 00				20 30							21 00				21 30
Hampton Court	a						20 03				20 33							21 03				21 33
Hinchley Wood	d											20 36										
Claygate	d											20 39										
Oxshott	d											20 42										
Cobham & Stoke D'abernon	d											20 46										
Bookham	d							20 21											21 21			
Effingham Junction	d							20 25				20 50							21 25			
Horsley	d							20 27				20 53							21 27			
Clandon	d							20 32				20 58							21 32			
London Road (Guildford)	d							20 37				21 03							21 37			
Guildford	a		20 14					20 41	20 44			21 07		21 14					21 41	21 44		

A To London Waterloo

Table T152-F

Sundays

20 May to 30 September

London - Chessington South, Dorking, Guildford, Shepperton and Hampton Court

		SW	SW	SW	SW A	SW A	SW	SW	SW	SW	SW	SW	SW	SW	SW A	SW A	SW	SW	SW	SW	SW	SW	SW
London Waterloo 15 ⊖	d	21 00	21 02	21 10		21 18	21 21	21 32	21 40	21 48	21 57	22 00	22 02	22 10		22 18	22 21	22 32	22 40	22 48	22 51	22 57	23 00
Vauxhall ⊖	d	21 04	21 06	21 14		21 22	21 25	21 36	21 44	21 52	22 01	22 04	22 06	22 14		22 22	22 25	22 36	22 44	22 52	22 55	23 01	23 04
Clapham Junction 10	d	21 09	21 11	21 19		21 27	21 30	21 41	21 49	21 57	22 06	22 09	22 11	22 19		22 27	22 30	22 41	22 49	22 57	23 00	23 06	23 09
Earlsfield	d	21 12	21 14	21 22		21 30	21 33	21 44	21 52	22 00	22 09	22 12	22 14	22 22		22 30	22 33	22 44	22 52	23 00	23 03	23 09	23 12
Wimbledon 5 ⊖ ⛴	d	21 16	21 18	21 26		21 34	21 37	21 48	21 56	22 04	22 13	22 16	22 18	22 26		22 34	22 37	22 48	22 56	23 04	23 07	23 13	23 16
Raynes Park 5	d		21 22			21 37	21 40	21 52		22 07	22 16		22 22			22 37	22 40	22 52		23 07	23 10	23 16	
Motspur Park	d		21 25				21 43	21 55					22 25				22 43	22 55			23 13		
Malden Manor	d						21 46										22 46				23 16		
Tolworth	d						21 49										22 49				23 19		
Chessington North	d						21 52										22 52				23 22		
Chessington South	a						21 55										22 55				23 25		
Worcester Park	d		21 27					21 57					22 27					22 57					
Stoneleigh	d		21 30					22 00					22 30					23 00					
Ewell West	d		21 33					22 03					22 33					23 03					
Epsom 5 182	a		21 36					22 06					22 36					23 06					
	d		21 38					22 08					22 38					23 08					
Ashtead 182	d		21 42					22 12					22 42					23 12					
Leatherhead 182	d		21 45					22 15					22 45					23 15					
Box Hill & Westhumble 182	d																						
Dorking 4 182	a		21 52										22 52										
New Malden 5	d					21 40				22 10	22 19					22 40				23 10		23 19	
Norbiton	d					21 43				22 13						22 43				23 13			
Kingston	a					21 46				22 16						22 46				23 16			
	d				21 35	21 49				22 16					22 35	22 49				23 16			
Hampton Wick	d				21 37	21 51				22 18					22 37	22 51				23 18			
Teddington	d				21 40	21 56				22 21					22 40	22 56				23 21			
Strawberry Hill	a				21 43	21 59									22 43	22 59							
Fulwell	d									22 25										23 25			
Hampton	d									22 29										23 29			
Kempton Park	d									22 32										23 32			
Sunbury	d									22 34										23 34			
Upper Halliford	d									22 36										23 36			
Shepperton	a									22 39										23 39			
Berrylands	d										22 21											23 21	
Surbiton 5	d	21 32		21 35					22 05		22 25	22 32		22 35					23 05			23 25	23 32
Thames Ditton	d										22 30											23 30	
Hampton Court	a										22 33											23 33	
Hinchley Wood	d	21 36										22 36											23 36
Claygate	d	21 39										22 39											23 39
Oxshott	d	21 42										22 42											23 42
Cobham & Stoke D'abernon	d	21 46										22 46											23 46
Bookham	d							22 21										23 21					
Effingham Junction 5	d	21 50						22 25				22 50						23 25					23 50
Horsley	d	21 53						22 27				22 53						23 27					23 53
Clandon	d	21 58						22 32				22 58						23 32					23 58
London Road (Guildford)	d	22 03						22 37				23 03						23 37					00 03
Guildford	a	22 07		22 14				22 41	22 44			23 07		23 13				23 41	23 45				00 07

A To London Waterloo

Table T152-F

Sundays

20 May to 30 September

London - Chessington South, Dorking, Guildford, Shepperton and Hampton Court

		SW	SW	SW A	SW	SW
London Waterloo 15 ⊖	d	23 02	23 10		23 18	23 32
Vauxhall ⊖	d	23 06	23 14		23 22	23 36
Clapham Junction 10	d	23 11	23 19		23 27	23 41
Earlsfield	d	23 14	23 22		23 30	23 44
Wimbledon 5 ⊖ ⛴	d	23 18	23 26		23 34	23 48
Raynes Park 5	d	23 22			23 37	23 52
Motspur Park	d	23 25				23 55
Malden Manor	d					
Tolworth	d					
Chessington North	d					
Chessington South	a					
Worcester Park	d	23 27				23 57
Stoneleigh	d	23 30				23 59
Ewell West	d	23 33				00 03
Epsom 5 182	a	23 36				00 06
	d					
Ashtead 182	d					
Leatherhead 182	d					
Box Hill & Westhumble 182	d					
Dorking 4 182	a					
New Malden 5	d				23 40	
Norbiton	d				23 43	
Kingston	a				23 46	
	d			23 35	23 47	
Hampton Wick	d			23 37	23 49	
Teddington	d			23 40	23 51	
Strawberry Hill	a			23 43	23 54	
Fulwell	d					
Hampton	d					
Kempton Park	d					
Sunbury	d					
Upper Halliford	d					
Shepperton	a					
Berrylands	d					
Surbiton 5	d		23 35			
Thames Ditton	d					
Hampton Court	a					
Hinchley Wood	d					
Claygate	d					
Oxshott	d					
Cobham & Stoke D'abernon	d					
Bookham	d					
Effingham Junction 5	d					
Horsley	d					
Clandon	d					
London Road (Guildford)	d					
Guildford	a		00 14			

A To Twickenham

Table T152-F

Sundays

7 October to 2 December

London - Chessington South, Dorking, Guildford, Shepperton and Hampton Court

		SW A	SW B	SW C	SW B	SW C	SW B	SW C	SW	SW	SW D	SW	SW E	SW F	SW	SW	SW	SW	SW	SW F	SW	SW	SW
London Waterloo ⊖	d								00 09	00 15	00 27	00 42	01 42	06 18		06 57			07 10	07 18		07 27	
Vauxhall ⊖	d						00 01	00 01	00 13	00 19	00 31	00 46	01 46	06 22		07 01			07 14	07 22		07 31	
Clapham Junction	d						00 06	00 06	00 20	00 26	00 38	00 53	01 53	06 27		07 06			07 19	07 27		07 36	
Earlsfield	d		00 02	00 02			00 09	00 09	00 23	00 29	00s41					07 09			07 22	07 30		07 39	
Wimbledon ⊖ ⛴	d		00 06	00 06			00 13	00 13	00 27	00 33	00 45	01 05	01 59	06 34	06 48	07 13	07 16	07 20	07 26	07 34	07 38	07 43	07 48
Raynes Park	d				00 01	00 01	00 16	00 16		00 36	00 48	01 08	02 02	06 37	06 52	07 17		07 23		07 38	07 40	07 47	07 52
Motspur Park	d				00 04	00 04				00 39					06 55			07 26			07 43		07 55
Malden Manor	d																				07 46		
Tolworth	d																				07 49		
Chessington North	d																				07 52		
Chessington South	a																				07 56		
Worcester Park	d				00 06	00 06				00 41					06 57			07 28					07 57
Stoneleigh	d				00 09	00 09				00 44					07 00			07 31					08 00
Ewell West	d				00 12	00 12				00 47					07 03			07 34					08 03
Epsom 182	a				00 15	00 15				00 50					07 06			07 37					08 06
	d				00 19	00 19																	08 08
Ashtead 182	d				00 23	00 23																	08 12
Leatherhead 182	d				00 26	00 26																	08 15
Box Hill & Westhumble 182	d																						
Dorking 182	a																						
New Malden	d						00 19	00 19			00 51	01 11	02 04	06 40		07 19				07 40		07 49	
Norbiton	d						00 22	00 22				01 14	02 08	06 43						07 44			
Kingston	a						00 25	00 25				01 17	02 10	06 46						07 46			
	d						00 25	00 25				01 17	02 11	06 49						07 49			
Hampton Wick	d						00 27	00 27				01s22	02s13	06 51						07 51			
Teddington	d						00 30	00 30				01s25	02s15	06 56						07 56			
Strawberry Hill	a											01 37	02s18	06 59						07 59			
Fulwell	d						00 34	00 34															
Hampton	d						00 38	00 38															
Kempton Park	d						00 41	00 41															
Sunbury	d						00 43	00 43															
Upper Halliford	d						00 45	00 45															
Shepperton	a						00 48	00 50															
Berrylands	d										00s53					07 22						07 52	
Surbiton	d	00 05	00 14	00 14					00 35		00s57					07 26	07 32		07 35			07 56	
Thames Ditton	d	00 09														07 30						08 00	
Hampton Court	a	00 12														07 33						08 03	
Hinchley Wood	d		00 18	00 18													07 36						
Claygate	d		00 20	00 20													07 39						
Oxshott	d		00 24	00 24													07 42						
Cobham & Stoke D'abernon	d		00 27	00 27													07 46						
Bookham	d				00 31	00 31																	08 21
Effingham Junction	d		00 32	00 32	00 36	00 36											07 50						08 25
Horsley	d		00 34	00 34	00 39	00 39											07 53						08 27
Clandon	d		00 39	00 39	00 44	00 44											07 58						08 32
London Road (Guildford)	d		00 44	00 44	00 49	00 49											08 03						08 37
Guildford	a		00 48	00 51	00 53	00 56			01 07								08 10		08 14				08 44

A From London Waterloo
B 7 October. From London Waterloo
C not 7 October. From London Waterloo
D To Woking
E To Twickenham
F To London Waterloo

Table T152-F

Sundays

7 October to 2 December

London - Chessington South, Dorking, Guildford, Shepperton and Hampton Court

		SW	SW	SW	SW	SW	SW	SW	SW A	SW	SW	SW	SW	SW	SW	SW	SW	SW	SW	SW A	SW	SW	SW
London Waterloo ⊖	d	07 40	07 48	07 57			08 02	08 10	08 18	08 21	08 27	08 33	08 40	08 48	08 51	08 57	09 02		09 10	09 18	09 21	09 27	09 32
Vauxhall ⊖	d	07 44	07 52	08 01			08 06	08 14	08 22	08 25	08 31	08 37	08 44	08 52	08 55	09 01	09 06		09 14	09 22	09 25	09 31	09 36
Clapham Junction	d	07 49	07 57	08 06			08 11	08 19	08 27	08 30	08 36	08 41	08 49	08 57	09 00	09 06	09 11		09 19	09 27	09 30	09 36	09 41
Earlsfield	d	07 52	08 00	08 09			08 14	08 22	08 30	08 33	08 39	08 44	08 52	09 00	09 03	09 09	09 14		09 22	09 30	09 33	09 39	09 44
Wimbledon ⊖ ⛴	d	07 56	08 04	08 13	08 02	08 08	08 18	08 26	08 34	08 37	08 43	08 48	08 56	09 04	09 07	09 13	09 18		09 26	09 34	09 37	09 43	09 48
Raynes Park	d		08 07	08 17	08 05	08 10	08 22		08 38	08 41	08 47	08 53		09 07	09 11	09 16	09 22			09 37	09 40	09 46	09 52
Motspur Park	d					08 13	08 25			08 43		08 55			09 13		09 25				09 43		09 55
Malden Manor	d					08 16				08 47					09 17						09 46		
Tolworth	d					08 19				08 49					09 19						09 49		
Chessington North	d					08 22				08 52					09 22						09 52		
Chessington South	a					08 26				08 56					09 25						09 55		
Worcester Park	d						08 27					08 58					09 27						09 57
Stoneleigh	d						08 30					09 01					09 30						10 00
Ewell West	d						08 33					09 03					09 33						10 03
Epsom 182	a						08 36					09 07					09 36						10 06
	d						08 38					09 08					09 38						10 08
Ashtead 182	d						08 42					09 12					09 42						10 12
Leatherhead 182	d						08 45					09 15					09 45						10 15
Box Hill & Westhumble 182	d						08 50										09 50						
Dorking 182	a						08 54										09 54						
New Malden	d		08 11	08 19	08 08				08 40		08 49			09 10		09 19				09 40		09 49	
Norbiton	d		08 13						08 44					09 13						09 43			
Kingston	a		08 16						08 46					09 15						09 46			
	d		08 16						08 49					09 16						09 49			
Hampton Wick	d		08 18						08 51					09 18						09 51			
Teddington	d		08 22						08 56					09 21						09 56			
Strawberry Hill	a								08 59											09 59			
Fulwell	d		08 25											09 25									
Hampton	d		08 30											09 29									
Kempton Park	d		08 32											09 32									
Sunbury	d		08 35											09 34									
Upper Halliford	d		08 37											09 36									
Shepperton	a		08 42											09 42									
Berrylands	d			08 22	08 10						08 52					09 21						09 51	
Surbiton	d	08 05		08 26	08 32			08 35			08 56		09 05			09 25		09 32	09 36			09 55	
Thames Ditton	d			08 30							09 00					09 30						10 00	
Hampton Court	a			08 33							09 03					09 33						10 03	
Hinchley Wood	d				08 36													09 36					
Claygate	d				08 39													09 39					
Oxshott	d				08 42													09 42					
Cobham & Stoke D'abernon	d				08 46													09 46					
Bookham	d											09 21											10 21
Effingham Junction	d				08 50							09 25						09 50					10 25
Horsley	d				08 53							09 27						09 53					10 27
Clandon	d				08 58							09 32						09 58					10 32
London Road (Guildford)	d				09 03							09 37						10 03					10 37
Guildford	a	08 39			09 10			09 09				09 44	09 39					10 10	10 09				10 44

A To London Waterloo

London - Chessington South, Dorking, Guildford, Shepperton and Hampton Court

			SW		SW	SW	SW	SW	SW	SW	SW A	SW	SW		SW	SW	SW	SW	SW	SW	SW	SW	SW A		SW	SW
London Waterloo	⊖	d	09 40		09 48	09 51	09 57		10 02	10 10	10 18	10 21	10 27		10 32	10 40	10 48	10 51	10 57		11 02	11 10	11 18		11 21	11 27
Vauxhall	⊖	d	09 44		09 52	09 55	10 01		10 06	10 14	10 22	10 25	10 31		10 36	10 44	10 52	10 55	11 01		11 06	11 14	11 22		11 25	11 31
Clapham Junction		d	09 49		09 57	10 00	10 06		10 11	10 19	10 27	10 30	10 36		10 41	10 49	10 57	11 00	11 06		11 12	11 19	11 27		11 30	11 36
Earlsfield		d	09 52		10 00	10 03	10 09		10 14	10 22	10 30	10 33	10 39		10 44	10 52	11 00	11 03	11 10		11 15	11 22	11 30		11 33	11 39
Wimbledon	⊖	d	09 56		10 04	10 07	10 13	10 17	10 18	10 26	10 34	10 37	10 43		10 48	10 56	11 04	11 07	11 14	11 14	11 19	11 26	11 34		11 37	11 43
Raynes Park		d			10 07	10 10	10 16		10 22		10 37	10 40	10 46		10 52		11 07	11 10	11 17		11 23		11 37		11 40	11 46
Motspur Park		d				10 13			10 25			10 43			10 55			11 13			11 25				11 43	
Malden Manor		d				10 16						10 46						11 16							11 46	
Tolworth		d				10 19						10 49						11 19							11 49	
Chessington North		d				10 22						10 52						11 22							11 52	
Chessington South		a				10 25						10 55						11 25							11 55	
Worcester Park		d							10 27						10 57						11 28					
Stoneleigh		d							10 30						11 00						11 31					
Ewell West		d							10 33						11 03						11 33					
Epsom	182	a							10 36						11 06						11 37					
		d							10 38						11 08						11 38					
Ashtead	182	d							10 42						11 12						11 42					
Leatherhead	182	d							10 45						11 15						11 45					
Box Hill & Westhumble	182	d							10 50												11 50					
Dorking	182	a							10 54												11 54					
New Malden		d			10 10		10 19				10 40		10 49				11 10		11 20				11 40			11 49
Norbiton		d			10 13						10 43						11 13						11 43			
Kingston		a			10 16						10 46						11 16						11 46			
		d			10 16						10 49						11 16						11 49			
Hampton Wick		d			10 18						10 51						11 18						11 51			
Teddington		d			10 21						10 56						11 21						11 56			
Strawberry Hill		a									10 59												11 59			
Fulwell		d			10 25												11 25									
Hampton		d			10 29												11 29									
Kempton Park		d			10 32												11 32									
Sunbury		d			10 34												11 34									
Upper Halliford		d			10 36												11 36									
Shepperton		a			10 41												11 41									
Berrylands		d					10 21						10 51						11 23							11 51
Surbiton		d	10 05				10 25	10 32		10 35			10 55			11 05			11 27	11 32		11 35				11 55
Thames Ditton		d					10 30						11 00						11 31							12 00
Hampton Court		a					10 33						11 03						11 34							12 03
Hinchley Wood		d						10 36												11 36						
Claygate		d						10 39												11 39						
Oxshott		d						10 42												11 42						
Cobham & Stoke D'abernon		d						10 46												11 46						
Bookham		d													11 21											
Effingham Junction		d						10 50							11 25					11 50						
Horsley		d						10 53							11 27					11 53						
Clandon		d						10 58							11 32					11 58						
London Road (Guildford)		d						11 03							11 37					12 03						
Guildford		a	10 44					11 10		11 14					11 44	11 44				12 10		12 14				

A To London Waterloo

Table T152-F

Sundays

7 October to 2 December

London - Chessington South, Dorking, Guildford, Shepperton and Hampton Court

			SW	SW	SW	SW	SW	SW	SW		SW	SW A	SW A	SW	SW	SW	SW	SW	SW		SW	SW	SW	SW	SW A	SW A
London Waterloo	⊖	d	11 32	11 40	11 48	11 51	11 57	12 02			12 10		12 18	12 21	12 27	12 32	12 40	12 48	12 51		12 57	13 00	13 02	13 10		13 18
Vauxhall	⊖	d	11 36	11 44	11 52	11 55	12 01	12 06			12 14		12 22	12 25	12 31	12 36	12 44	12 52	12 55		13 01	13 04	13 06	13 14		13 22
Clapham Junction		d	11 42	11 49	11 57	12 00	12 06	12 11			12 19		12 27	12 30	12 36	12 42	12 49	12 57	13 00		13 06	13 09	13 11	13 19		13 27
Earlsfield		d	11 45	11 52	12 00	12 03	12 10	12 15			12 22		12 30	12 33	12 39	12 45	12 52	13 00	13 03		13 09	13 12	13 14	13 22		13 30
Wimbledon	⊖	d	11 49	11 56	12 04	12 07	12 14	12 19	12 19		12 26		12 34	12 37	12 43	12 49	12 56	13 04	13 07		13 13	13 16	13 18	13 26		13 34
Raynes Park		d	11 52		12 07	12 10	12 17	12 23					12 37	12 40	12 46	12 52		13 07	13 10		13 16		13 22			13 37
Motspur Park		d	11 55			12 13		12 25						12 43		12 55			13 13				13 25			
Malden Manor		d				12 16								12 46					13 16							
Tolworth		d				12 19								12 49					13 19							
Chessington North		d				12 22								12 52					13 22							
Chessington South		a				12 25								12 55					13 25							
Worcester Park		d	11 57					12 28								12 57							13 27			
Stoneleigh		d	12 00					12 31								13 00							13 30			
Ewell West		d	12 03					12 33								13 03							13 33			
Epsom	182	a	12 06					12 37								13 06							13 36			
		d	12 08					12 38								13 08							13 38			
Ashtead	182	d	12 12					12 42								13 12							13 42			
Leatherhead	182	d	12 15					12 45								13 15							13 45			
Box Hill & Westhumble	182	d						12 50															13 50			
Dorking	182	a						12 54															13 54			
New Malden		d			12 10		12 19						12 40		12 49			13 10			13 19					13 40
Norbiton		d			12 13								12 43					13 13								13 43
Kingston		a			12 16								12 46					13 16								13 46
		d			12 16							12 35	12 49					13 16							13 35	13 49
Hampton Wick		d			12 18							12 37	12 51					13 18							13 37	13 51
Teddington		d			12 21							12 40	12 56					13 21							13 40	13 56
Strawberry Hill		a										12 43	12 59												13 43	13 59
Fulwell		d			12 25													13 25								
Hampton		d			12 29													13 29								
Kempton Park		d			12 32													13 32								
Sunbury		d			12 34													13 34								
Upper Halliford		d			12 36													13 36								
Shepperton		a			12 41													13 41								
Berrylands		d					12 22								12 51						13 21					
Surbiton		d		12 05			12 26		12 32		12 35				12 55		13 05				13 25	13 32		13 35		
Thames Ditton		d					12 30								13 00						13 30					
Hampton Court		a					12 33								13 03						13 33					
Hinchley Wood		d							12 36													13 36				
Claygate		d							12 39													13 39				
Oxshott		d							12 42													13 42				
Cobham & Stoke D'abernon		d							12 46													13 46				
Bookham		d	12 21													13 21										
Effingham Junction		d	12 25						12 50							13 25						13 50				
Horsley		d	12 27						12 53							13 27						13 53				
Clandon		d	12 32						12 58							13 32						13 58				
London Road (Guildford)		d	12 37						13 03							13 37						14 03				
Guildford		a	12 44	12 44					13 10		13 14					13 44	13 44					14 10		14 14		

A To London Waterloo

Table T152-F

Sundays

7 October to 2 December

London - Chessington South, Dorking, Guildford, Shepperton and Hampton Court

		SW	SW	SW	SW	SW	SW	SW	SW	SW	SW	SW A	SW A	SW	SW	SW	SW	SW	SW	SW	SW	SW
London Waterloo ⊖	d	13 21	13 27	13 32	13 40	13 48	13 51	13 57	14 00	14 02	14 10		14 18	14 21	14 27	14 32	14 40	14 48	14 51	14 57	15 00	15 02
Vauxhall ⊖	d	13 25	13 31	13 36	13 44	13 52	13 55	14 01	14 04	14 06	14 14		14 22	14 25	14 31	14 36	14 44	14 52	14 55	15 01	15 04	15 06
Clapham Junction	d	13 30	13 36	13 41	13 49	13 57	14 00	14 06	14 09	14 11	14 19		14 27	14 30	14 36	14 41	14 49	14 57	15 00	15 06	15 09	15 11
Earlsfield	d	13 33	13 39	13 44	13 52	14 00	14 03	14 09	14 12	14 14	14 22		14 30	14 33	14 39	14 44	14 52	15 00	15 03	15 09	15 12	15 14
Wimbledon ⊖	d	13 37	13 43	13 48	13 56	14 04	14 07	14 13	14 16	14 18	14 26		14 34	14 37	14 43	14 48	14 56	15 04	15 07	15 13	15 16	15 18
Raynes Park	d	13 40	13 46	13 52		14 07	14 10	14 16		14 22			14 37	14 40	14 46	14 52		15 07	15 10	15 16		15 22
Motspur Park	d	13 43		13 55			14 13			14 25				14 43		14 55			15 13			15 25
Malden Manor	d	13 46					14 16							14 46					15 16			
Tolworth	d	13 49					14 19							14 49					15 19			
Chessington North	d	13 52					14 22							14 52					15 22			
Chessington South	a	13 55					14 25							14 55					15 25			
Worcester Park	d			13 57						14 27						14 57						15 27
Stoneleigh	d			14 00						14 30						15 00						15 30
Ewell West	d			14 03						14 33						15 03						15 33
Epsom 182	a			14 06						14 36						15 06						15 36
	d			14 08						14 38						15 08						15 38
Ashtead 182	d			14 12						14 42						15 12						15 42
Leatherhead 182	d			14 15						14 45						15 15						15 45
Box Hill & Westhumble 182	d									14 50												15 50
Dorking 182	a									14 54												15 54
New Malden	d		13 49			14 10		14 19					14 40		14 49			15 10		15 19		
Norbiton	d					14 13							14 43					15 13				
Kingston	a					14 16							14 46					15 16				
	d					14 16						14 35	14 49					15 16				
Hampton Wick	d					14 18						14 37	14 51					15 18				
Teddington	d					14 21						14 40	14 56					15 21				
Strawberry Hill	a											14 43	14 59									
Fulwell	d					14 25												15 25				
Hampton	d					14 29												15 29				
Kempton Park	d					14 32												15 32				
Sunbury	d					14 34												15 34				
Upper Halliford	d					14 36												15 36				
Shepperton	a					14 41												15 41				
Berrylands	d		13 51					14 21							14 51					15 21		
Surbiton	d		13 55		14 05			14 25	14 32		14 35				14 55		15 05			15 25	15 32	
Thames Ditton	d		14 00					14 30							15 00					15 30		
Hampton Court	a		14 03					14 33							15 03					15 33		
Hinchley Wood	d								14 36												15 36	
Claygate	d								14 39												15 39	
Oxshott	d								14 42												15 42	
Cobham & Stoke D'abernon	d								14 46												15 46	
Bookham	d			14 21												15 21						
Effingham Junction	d			14 25					14 50							15 25					15 50	
Horsley	d			14 27					14 53							15 27					15 53	
Clandon	d			14 32					14 58							15 32					15 58	
London Road (Guildford)	d			14 37					15 03							15 37					16 03	
Guildford	a			14 44	14 44				15 10		15 14					15 44	15 44				16 10	

A To London Waterloo

Table T152-F

Sundays

7 October to 2 December

London - Chessington South, Dorking, Guildford, Shepperton and Hampton Court

		SW	SW A	SW A	SW	SW	SW	SW	SW	SW	SW	SW	SW	SW	SW A	SW A	SW	SW	SW	SW	SW	SW	SW
London Waterloo ⊖	d	15 10		15 18	15 21	15 27	15 32	15 40	15 48	15 51	15 57	16 00	16 02	16 10		16 18	16 21	16 27	16 32	16 40	16 48	16 51	16 57
Vauxhall ⊖	d	15 14		15 22	15 25	15 31	15 36	15 44	15 52	15 55	16 01	16 04	16 06	16 14		16 22	16 25	16 31	16 36	16 44	16 52	16 55	17 01
Clapham Junction	d	15 19		15 27	15 30	15 36	15 41	15 49	15 57	16 00	16 06	16 09	16 11	16 19		16 27	16 30	16 36	16 41	16 49	16 57	17 00	17 06
Earlsfield	d	15 22		15 30	15 33	15 39	15 44	15 52	16 00	16 03	16 09	16 12	16 14	16 22		16 30	16 33	16 39	16 44	16 52	17 00	17 03	17 09
Wimbledon ⊖	d	15 26		15 34	15 37	15 43	15 48	15 56	16 04	16 07	16 13	16 16	16 18	16 26		16 34	16 37	16 43	16 48	16 56	17 04	17 07	17 13
Raynes Park	d			15 37	15 40	15 46	15 52		16 07	16 10	16 16		16 22			16 37	16 40	16 46	16 52		17 07	17 10	17 16
Motspur Park	d				15 43		15 55			16 13			16 25				16 43		16 55			17 13	
Malden Manor	d				15 46					16 16							16 46					17 16	
Tolworth	d				15 49					16 19							16 49					17 19	
Chessington North	d				15 52					16 22							16 52					17 22	
Chessington South	a				15 55					16 25							16 55					17 25	
Worcester Park	d						15 57						16 27						16 57				
Stoneleigh	d						16 00						16 30						17 00				
Ewell West	d						16 03						16 33						17 03				
Epsom 182	a						16 06						16 36						17 06				
	d						16 08						16 38						17 08				
Ashtead 182	d						16 12						16 42						17 12				
Leatherhead 182	d						16 15						16 45						17 15				
Box Hill & Westhumble 182	d																						
Dorking 182	a												16 54										
New Malden	d			15 40		15 49			16 10		16 19					16 40		16 49			17 10		17 19
Norbiton	d			15 43					16 13							16 43					17 13		
Kingston	a			15 46					16 16							16 46					17 16		
	d		15 35	15 49					16 16						16 35	16 49					17 16		
Hampton Wick	d		15 37	15 51					16 18						16 37	16 51					17 18		
Teddington	d		15 40	15 56					16 21						16 40	16 56					17 21		
Strawberry Hill	a		15 43	15 59											16 43	16 59							
Fulwell	d								16 25												17 25		
Hampton	d								16 29												17 29		
Kempton Park	d								16 32												17 32		
Sunbury	d								16 34												17 34		
Upper Halliford	d								16 36												17 36		
Shepperton	a								16 41												17 41		
Berrylands	d					15 51					16 21							16 51					17 21
Surbiton	d	15 35				15 55		16 05			16 25	16 32		16 35				16 55		17 05			17 25
Thames Ditton	d					16 00					16 30							17 00					17 30
Hampton Court	a					16 03					16 33							17 03					17 33
Hinchley Wood	d											16 36											
Claygate	d											16 39											
Oxshott	d											16 42											
Cobham & Stoke D'abernon	d											16 46											
Bookham	d						16 21												17 21				
Effingham Junction	d						16 25					16 50							17 25				
Horsley	d						16 27					16 53							17 27				
Clandon	d						16 32					16 58							17 32				
London Road (Guildford)	d						16 37					17 03							17 37				
Guildford	a	16 14					16 44	16 44				17 10		17 14					17 44	17 44			

A To London Waterloo

Table T152-F

Sundays
7 October to 2 December

London - Chessington South, Dorking, Guildford, Shepperton and Hampton Court

		SW	SW	SW	SW	SW	SW	SW	SW	SW	SW	SW	SW	SW	SW	SW	SW	SW	SW	SW	SW	SW	SW
					A	A											A	A					
London Waterloo ⊖	d	17 00	17 02	17 10		17 18	17 21	17 27	17 32	17 40	17 48	17 51	17 57	18 00	18 02	18 10		18 18	18 21	18 27	18 32	18 40	18 48
Vauxhall ⊖	d	17 04	17 06	17 14		17 22	17 25	17 31	17 36	17 44	17 52	17 55	18 01	18 04	18 06	18 14		18 22	18 25	18 31	18 36	18 44	18 52
Clapham Junction	d	17 09	17 11	17 19		17 27	17 30	17 36	17 41	17 49	17 57	18 00	18 06	18 09	18 11	18 19		18 27	18 30	18 36	18 41	18 49	18 57
Earlsfield	d	17 12	17 14	17 22		17 30	17 33	17 39	17 44	17 52	18 00	18 03	18 09	18 12	18 14	18 22		18 30	18 33	18 39	18 44	18 52	19 00
Wimbledon ⊖	d	17 16	17 18	17 26		17 34	17 37	17 43	17 48	17 56	18 04	18 07	18 13	18 16	18 18	18 26		18 34	18 37	18 43	18 48	18 56	19 04
Raynes Park	d		17 22			17 37	17 40	17 46	17 52		18 07	18 10	18 16		18 22			18 37	18 40	18 46	18 52		19 07
Motspur Park	d		17 25				17 43		17 55			18 13			18 25				18 43		18 55		
Malden Manor	d						17 46					18 16							18 46				
Tolworth	d						17 49					18 19							18 49				
Chessington North	d						17 52					18 22							18 52				
Chessington South	a						17 55					18 25							18 55				
Worcester Park	d		17 27						17 57						18 27						18 57		
Stoneleigh	d		17 30						18 00						18 30						19 00		
Ewell West	d		17 33						18 03						18 33						19 03		
Epsom	182 a		17 36						18 06						18 36						19 06		
	d		17 38						18 08						18 38						19 08		
Ashtead	182 d		17 42						18 12						18 42						19 12		
Leatherhead	182 d		17 45						18 15						18 45						19 15		
Box Hill & Westhumble	182 d																						
Dorking	182 a		17 54												18 54								
New Malden	d					17 40		17 49			18 10		18 19					18 40		18 49			19 10
Norbiton	d					17 43					18 13							18 43					19 13
Kingston	a					17 46					18 16							18 46					19 16
	d				17 35	17 49					18 16						18 35	18 49					19 16
Hampton Wick	d				17 37	17 51					18 18						18 37	18 51					19 18
Teddington	d				17 40	17 56					18 21						18 40	18 56					19 21
Strawberry Hill	a				17 43	17 59											18 43	18 59					
Fulwell	d										18 25												19 25
Hampton	d										18 29												19 29
Kempton Park	d										18 32												19 32
Sunbury	d										18 34												19 34
Upper Halliford	d										18 36												19 36
Shepperton	a										18 41												19 41
Berrylands	d							17 51					18 21							18 51			
Surbiton	d	17 32		17 35				17 55		18 05			18 25	18 32		18 35				18 55		19 05	
Thames Ditton	d							18 00					18 30							19 00			
Hampton Court	a							18 03					18 33							19 03			
Hinchley Wood	d	17 36												18 36									
Claygate	d	17 39												18 39									
Oxshott	d	17 42												18 42									
Cobham & Stoke D'abernon	d	17 46												18 46									
Bookham	d								18 21												19 21		
Effingham Junction	d	17 50							18 25					18 50							19 25		
Horsley	d	17 53							18 27					18 53							19 27		
Clandon	d	17 58							18 32					18 58							19 32		
London Road (Guildford)	d	18 03							18 37					19 03							19 37		
Guildford	a	18 10		18 14					18 44	18 44				19 10		19 14					19 44	19 44	

A To London Waterloo

Table T152-F

Sundays
7 October to 2 December

London - Chessington South, Dorking, Guildford, Shepperton and Hampton Court

		SW	SW	SW	SW	SW	SW	SW	SW	SW	SW	SW	SW	SW	SW	SW	SW	SW	SW	SW	SW	SW
							A	A										A	A			
London Waterloo ⊖	d	18 51	18 57	19 00	19 02	19 10		19 18	19 21	19 27	19 32	19 40	19 48	19 57	20 00	20 02	20 10		20 18	20 21	20 27	20 32
Vauxhall ⊖	d	18 55	19 01	19 04	19 06	19 14		19 22	19 25	19 31	19 36	19 44	19 52	20 01	20 04	20 06	20 14		20 22	20 25	20 31	20 36
Clapham Junction	d	19 00	19 06	19 09	19 11	19 19		19 27	19 30	19 36	19 41	19 49	19 57	20 06	20 09	20 11	20 19		20 27	20 30	20 36	20 41
Earlsfield	d	19 03	19 09	19 12	19 14	19 22		19 30	19 33	19 39	19 44	19 52	20 00	20 09	20 12	20 14	20 22		20 30	20 33	20 39	20 44
Wimbledon ⊖	d	19 07	19 13	19 16	19 18	19 26		19 34	19 37	19 43	19 48	19 56	20 04	20 13	20 16	20 18	20 26		20 34	20 37	20 43	20 48
Raynes Park	d	19 10	19 16		19 22			19 37	19 40	19 46	19 52		20 07	20 16		20 22			20 37	20 40	20 46	20 52
Motspur Park	d	19 13			19 25				19 43		19 55					20 25				20 43		20 55
Malden Manor	d	19 16							19 46											20 46		
Tolworth	d	19 19							19 49											20 49		
Chessington North	d	19 22							19 52											20 52		
Chessington South	a	19 25							19 55											20 55		
Worcester Park	d				19 27						19 57					20 27						20 57
Stoneleigh	d				19 30						20 00					20 30						21 00
Ewell West	d				19 33						20 03					20 33						21 03
Epsom	182 a				19 36						20 06					20 36						21 06
	d				19 38						20 08					20 38						21 08
Ashtead	182 d				19 42						20 12					20 42						21 12
Leatherhead	182 d				19 45						20 15					20 45						21 15
Box Hill & Westhumble	182 d																					
Dorking	182 a				19 54											20 54						
New Malden	d		19 19					19 40		19 49			20 10	20 19					20 40		20 49	
Norbiton	d							19 43					20 13						20 43			
Kingston	a							19 46					20 16						20 46			
	d						19 35	19 49					20 16					20 35	20 49			
Hampton Wick	d						19 37	19 51					20 18					20 37	20 51			
Teddington	d						19 40	19 56					20 21					20 40	20 56			
Strawberry Hill	a						19 43	19 59										20 43	20 59			
Fulwell	d												20 25									
Hampton	d												20 29									
Kempton Park	d												20 32									
Sunbury	d												20 34									
Upper Halliford	d												20 36									
Shepperton	a												20 41									
Berrylands	d		19 21							19 51				20 21							20 51	
Surbiton	d		19 25	19 32		19 35				19 55		20 05		20 25	20 32		20 35				20 55	
Thames Ditton	d		19 30							20 00				20 30							21 00	
Hampton Court	a		19 33							20 03				20 33							21 03	
Hinchley Wood	d			19 36											20 36							
Claygate	d			19 39											20 39							
Oxshott	d			19 42											20 42							
Cobham & Stoke D'abernon	d			19 46											20 46							
Bookham	d										20 21											21 21
Effingham Junction	d			19 50							20 25				20 50							21 25
Horsley	d			19 53							20 27				20 53							21 27
Clandon	d			19 58							20 32				20 58							21 32
London Road (Guildford)	d			20 03							20 37				21 03							21 37
Guildford	a			20 10		20 14					20 44	20 44			21 10		21 14					21 44

A To London Waterloo

Table T152-F

Sundays
7 October to 2 December

London - Chessington South, Dorking, Guildford, Shepperton and Hampton Court

		SW	SW	SW	SW	SW	SW	SW A		SW A	SW	SW	SW	SW	SW	SW	SW	SW		SW A	SW A	SW	SW	SW	SW
London Waterloo ⊖	d	20 40	20 48	20 57	21 00	21 02	21 10			21 18	21 21	21 32	21 40	21 48	21 57	22 00	22 02	22 10			22 18	22 21	22 32	22 40	22 48
Vauxhall ⊖	d	20 44	20 52	21 01	21 04	21 06	21 14			21 22	21 25	21 36	21 44	21 52	22 01	22 04	22 06	22 14			22 22	22 25	22 36	22 44	22 52
Clapham Junction	d	20 49	20 57	21 06	21 09	21 11	21 19			21 27	21 30	21 41	21 49	21 57	22 06	22 09	22 11	22 19			22 27	22 30	22 41	22 49	22 57
Earlsfield	d	20 52	21 00	21 09	21 12	21 14	21 22			21 30	21 33	21 44	21 52	22 00	22 09	22 12	22 14	22 22			22 30	22 33	22 44	22 52	23 00
Wimbledon ⊖	d	20 56	21 04	21 13	21 16	21 18	21 26			21 34	21 37	21 48	21 56	22 04	22 13	22 16	22 18	22 26			22 34	22 37	22 48	22 56	23 04
Raynes Park	d		21 07	21 16		21 22				21 37	21 40	21 52		22 07	22 16		22 22				22 37	22 40	22 52		23 07
Motspur Park	d					21 25					21 43	21 55					22 25					22 43	22 55		
Malden Manor	d										21 46											22 46			
Tolworth	d										21 49											22 49			
Chessington North	d										21 52											22 52			
Chessington South	a										21 55											22 55			
Worcester Park	d					21 27						21 57					22 27						22 57		
Stoneleigh	d					21 30						22 00					22 30						23 00		
Ewell West	d					21 33						22 03					22 33						23 03		
Epsom 182	a					21 36						22 06					22 36						23 06		
	d					21 38						22 08					22 38						23 08		
Ashtead 182	d					21 42						22 12					22 42						23 12		
Leatherhead 182	d					21 45						22 15					22 45						23 15		
Box Hill & Westhumble 182	d																								
Dorking 182	a					21 54											22 54								
New Malden	d		21 10	21 19						21 40				22 10	22 19						22 40				23 10
Norbiton	d		21 13							21 43				22 13							22 43				23 13
Kingston	a		21 16							21 46				22 16							22 46				23 16
	d		21 16					21 35		21 49				22 16						22 35	22 49				23 16
Hampton Wick	d		21 18					21 37		21 51				22 18						22 37	22 51				23 18
Teddington	d		21 21					21 40		21 56				22 21						22 40	22 56				23 21
Strawberry Hill	a							21 43		21 59										22 43	22 59				
Fulwell	d		21 25											22 25											23 25
Hampton	d		21 29											22 29											23 29
Kempton Park	d		21 32											22 32											23 32
Sunbury	d		21 34											22 34											23 34
Upper Halliford	d		21 36											22 36											23 36
Shepperton	a		21 41											22 41											23 41
Berrylands	d			21 21											22 21										
Surbiton	d	21 05		21 25	21 32		21 35						22 05		22 25	22 32		22 35						23 05	
Thames Ditton	d			21 30											22 30										
Hampton Court	a			21 33											22 33										
Hinchley Wood	d				21 36											22 36									
Claygate	d				21 39											22 39									
Oxshott	d				21 42											22 42									
Cobham & Stoke D'abernon	d				21 46											22 46									
Bookham	d											22 21											23 21		
Effingham Junction	d				21 50							22 25				22 50							23 25		
Horsley	d				21 53							22 27				22 53							23 27		
Clandon	d				21 58							22 32				22 58							23 32		
London Road (Guildford)	d				22 03							22 37				23 03							23 37		
Guildford	a	21 44			22 10		22 14					22 44	22 44			23 10		23 13					23 44	23 45	

A To London Waterloo

Table T152-F

Sundays
7 October to 2 December

London - Chessington South, Dorking, Guildford, Shepperton and Hampton Court

		SW	SW	SW		SW	SW	SW A	SW	SW
London Waterloo ⊖	d	22 51	22 57	23 00		23 02	23 10		23 18	23 32
Vauxhall ⊖	d	22 55	23 01	23 04		23 06	23 14		23 22	23 36
Clapham Junction	d	23 00	23 06	23 09		23 11	23 19		23 27	23 41
Earlsfield	d	23 03	23 09	23 12		23 14	23 22		23 30	23 44
Wimbledon ⊖	d	23 07	23 13	23 16		23 18	23 26		23 34	23 48
Raynes Park	d	23 10	23 16			23 22			23 37	23 52
Motspur Park	d	23 13				23 25				23 55
Malden Manor	d	23 16								
Tolworth	d	23 19								
Chessington North	d	23 22								
Chessington South	a	23 25								
Worcester Park	d					23 27				23 57
Stoneleigh	d					23 30				23 59
Ewell West	d					23 33				00 03
Epsom 182	a					23 36				00 06
	d									
Ashtead 182	d									
Leatherhead 182	d									
Box Hill & Westhumble 182	d									
Dorking 182	a									
New Malden	d		23 19						23 40	
Norbiton	d								23 43	
Kingston	a								23 46	
	d							23 35	23 47	
Hampton Wick	d							23 37	23 49	
Teddington	d							23 40	23 51	
Strawberry Hill	a							23 43	23 54	
Fulwell	d									
Hampton	d									
Kempton Park	d									
Sunbury	d									
Upper Halliford	d									
Shepperton	a									
Berrylands	d		23 21							
Surbiton	d		23 25	23 32			23 35			
Thames Ditton	d		23 30							
Hampton Court	a		23 33							
Hinchley Wood	d			23 36						
Claygate	d			23 39						
Oxshott	d			23 42						
Cobham & Stoke D'abernon	d			23 46						
Bookham	d									
Effingham Junction	d			23 50						
Horsley	d			23 53						
Clandon	d			23 58						
London Road (Guildford)	d			00 03						
Guildford	a			00 10			00 14			

A To Twickenham

Table T152-R

Mondays to Fridays

21 May to 5 October

Hampton Court, Shepperton, Guildford, Dorking and Chessington South - London

Miles	Miles	Miles	Miles	Miles			SW MO A	SW MX B	SW MX C	SW MX D	SW MO D	SW MX D	SW MX ◇ E	SW MX A	SW	SW F	SW	SW	SW	SW ◇	SW	SW	SW	SW D
0	—	—	—	—	**Guildford**	d									04 20		04 58			05 14		05 37		
1¼	—	—	—	—	London Road (Guildford)	d											05 02					05 41		
4½	—	—	—	—	Clandon	d											05 07					05 46		
7¾	—	—	—	—	Horsley	d											05 11					05 50		
8¾	0	—	—	—	Effingham Junction	d											05 15					05 53		
—	1¾	—	—	—	Bookham	d											05 18							
11	—	—	—	—	Cobham & Stoke d'Abernon	d																05 57		
13	—	—	—	—	Oxshott	d																06 00		
14¾	—	—	—	—	Claygate	d																06 03		
16	—	—	—	—	Hinchley Wood	d																06 06		
—	—	—	0	—	**Hampton Court**	d															05 54			
—	—	—	1	—	Thames Ditton	d								00 02							05 56			
18	—	—	3	—	**Surbiton**	d							00 08	00 12	04 54					05 56	06 02	06 11		
19	—	—	—	—	Berrylands	d								00 14							06 04			
—	—	—	—	0	**Shepperton**	d												05 23						
—	—	—	—	1½	Upper Halliford	d												05 26						
—	—	—	—	2	Sunbury	d												05 28						
—	—	—	—	2½	Kempton Park	d																		
—	—	—	—	4¼	Hampton	d												05 33						
—	—	—	—	6	Fulwell	d												05 36						
—	—	—	0	—	Strawberry Hill	d				00 09	00 15					04 55		05 38						06 07
—	—	—	1¼	7	Teddington	d				00 12	00 18					04 59			05 44					06 11
—	—	—	—	8¼	Hampton Wick	d				00 14	00 21					05 01			05 46					06 14
—	—	—	—	8¾	Kingston	a				00 16	00 23					05 03			05 48					06 16
—	—	—	—	—		d										05 04			05 49					06 19
—	—	—	—	9½	Norbiton	d										05 06			05 51					06 21
20	—	—	—	11	New Malden	d								00 17		05 10			05 55		06 07			06 25
—	—	0	—	—	**Dorking** 182	d																	05 47	
—	—	0¾	—	—	Box Hill & Westhumble 182	d																	05 50	
—	4½	4	—	—	Leatherhead 182	d											05 23						05 56	
—	—	5¾	—	—	Ashtead 182	d											05 27						05 59	
—	—	7¾	—	—	**Epsom** 182	a											05 31						06 04	
—	—	—	—	—		d											05 33						06 04	
—	—	9	—	—	Ewell West	d											05 36						06 07	
—	—	10	—	—	Stoneleigh	d											05 39						06 10	
—	—	11¼	—	—	Worcester Park	d											05 41						06 12	
—	0	—	—	—	**Chessington South**	d																		
—	0¾	—	—	—	Chessington North	d																		
—	1¾	—	—	—	Tolworth	d																		
—	2¾	—	—	—	Malden Manor	d																		
—	3¾	12¼	—	—	Motspur Park	d											05 45						06 16	
21¼	5¼	13¼	—	12	Raynes Park	d	00 01							00 20		05 13	05 49		05 58		06 10		06 19	06 28
22¾	6¾	14¾	—	13½	**Wimbledon** ⊖	d	00a04						00 16	00a23	05 02	05 17	05 53		06 02	06 05	06 14	06 20	06 23	06 32
24½	8½	16½	—	15¼	Earlsfield	d										05 21	05 58		06 05	06 08	06 17	06 24	06 27	06 35
26	10	18	—	16¾	**Clapham Junction**	d						00 05	00 23		05 09	05 25	06 02	06 05	06 09	06 12	06 21	06 28	06 31	06 39
28¾	12¾	20¾	—	19½	Vauxhall ⊖	d		00 02	00 05			00 12				05 31	06 07	06 12	06 14	06 17	06 26	06 33	06 36	06 44
30	14	22	—	20¾	**London Waterloo** ⊖	a		00 08	00 13			00 16	00 33		05 18	05 35	06 11	06 16	06 20	06 22	06 31	06 37	06 40	06 49

A From Hampton Court
B From Shepperton
C From Guildford
D From London Waterloo
E From Portsmouth Harbour
F From Twickenham

Table T152-R

Mondays to Fridays

21 May to 5 October

Hampton Court, Shepperton, Guildford, Dorking and Chessington South - London

		SW ◇ A	SW	SW	SW	SW	SW	SW	SW B	SW ◇ A	SW	SW	SW	SW	SW	TL C	SW D	SW	SW B	SW	SW	SW
Guildford	d					05 58	06 04							06 28	06 34	06 39						
London Road (Guildford)	d					06 02	06 08							06 32	06 38	06 42						
Clandon	d					06 07	06 13							06 37	06 43	06 47						
Horsley	d					06 11	06 17							06 41	06 47	06 52						
Effingham Junction	d					06 15	06 21							06 46	06 51	06 55						
Bookham	d					06 18								06 49		06 59						
Cobham & Stoke d'Abernon	d						06 25								06 54							
Oxshott	d						06 28								06 58							
Claygate	d						06 31								07 01							
Hinchley Wood	d						06 34								07 04							
Hampton Court	d			06 23								06 53										
Thames Ditton	d			06 25								06 55										
Surbiton	d	06 28		06 31			06 41			06 57		07 01			07 11							
Berrylands	d			06 34								07 03										
Shepperton	d				06 10								06 40									
Upper Halliford	d				06 13								06 43									
Sunbury	d				06 15								06 45									
Kempton Park	d																					
Hampton	d				06 20								06 50									
Fulwell	d				06 23								06 53									
Strawberry Hill	d								06 37										07 07			
Teddington	d				06 28				06 41				06 58						07 11		07 19	
Hampton Wick	d				06 30				06 44				07 00						07 14		07 21	
Kingston	a				06 32				06 46				07 02						07 16		07 23	
	d				06 33				06 48				07 03						07 18		07 25	
Norbiton	d				06 35				06 50				07 05						07 20		07 27	
New Malden	d			06 37	06 40				06 55			07 06	07 09						07 25		07 31	
Dorking 182	d										06 30									07 01		
Box Hill & Westhumble 182	d										06 33									07 04		
Leatherhead 182	d					06 23					06 38			06 54		07 05				07 09		
Ashtead 182	d					06 27					06 42			06 57		07 09				07 13		
Epsom 182	a					06 31					06 46			07 02		07 13				07 17		
	d		06 18			06 33					06 47			07 03						07 18		07 22
Ewell West	d		06 21			06 36					06 50			07 06								07 25
Stoneleigh	d		06 24			06 39					06 52			07 09								07 27
Worcester Park	d		06 27			06 41					06 55			07 11						07 24		07 30
Chessington South	d							06 38										07 08				
Chessington North	d							06 40										07 10				
Tolworth	d							06 43										07 13				
Malden Manor	d							06 45										07 15				
Motspur Park	d		06 30			06 45		06 50			06 59			07 14				07 20				07 33
Raynes Park	d		06 34	06 40	06 43	06 49		06 54	06 58		07 04	07 09	07 12	07 18			07 21	07 24	07 28	07 31	07 34	07 37
Wimbledon ⊖	d	06 35	06 38	06 44	06 47	06 53	06 50	06 58	07 02	07 05	07 08	07 13	07 16	07 22	07 19		07 25	07 28	07 32	07 35	07 38	07 41
Earlsfield	d	06 39	06 42	06 48	06 51	06 57	06 54	07 02	07 06	07 09	07 12	07 17	07 20	07 26	07 23		07 29	07 32	07 36	07 39	07 42	07 45
Clapham Junction	d	06 43	06 46	06 52	06 55	07 01	06 58	07 06	07 10	07 13	07 16	07 21	07 24	07 30	07 27			07 36	07 40	07 43	07 46	07 49
Vauxhall ⊖	d	06 48	06 51	06 57	07 00	07 06	07 03	07 11	07 15	07 18	07 21	07 26	07 29	07 35	07 32			07 41	07 45	07 48	07 51	07 54
London Waterloo ⊖	a	06 53	06 56	07 03	07 06	07 12	07 09	07 18	07 22	07 24	07 27	07 33	07 35	07 41	07 39		07 43	07 48	07 51	07 56	07 58	08 00

A From Woking
B From London Waterloo
C To London Bridge
D From Esher

Table T152-R

Mondays to Fridays

21 May to 5 October

Hampton Court, Shepperton, Guildford, Dorking and Chessington South - London

		SW	SW	SW	SW	SW	TL A		SW	SW	SW B	SW	SW	SW C	SW	SW	SW		SW	SW	SW	SW B	SW	SW	SW D
Guildford	d				06 58	07 03	07 12		07 16											07 35					
London Road (Guildford)	d				07 02	07 07	07 15		07 20											07 39					
Clandon	d				07 07	07 12			07 25											07 44					
Horsley	d				07 11	07 17			07 29											07 48					
Effingham Junction	d				07 16	07 21	07 25		07 33										07 46	07 52					
Bookham	d				07 19		07 29												07 49						
Cobham & Stoke d'Abernon	d					07 24			07 36											07 55					
Oxshott	d					07 28			07 40											07 59					
Claygate	d					07 31			07 43											08 02					
Hinchley Wood	d					07 34			07 46											08 05					
Hampton Court	d		07 23													07 53									
Thames Ditton	d		07 25													07 55									
Surbiton	d		07 31			07 41			07 53							08 01				08 11					
Berrylands	d		07 33													08 03									
Shepperton	d	07 00		07 11									07 30				07 41							08 00	
Upper Halliford	d	07 03		07 14									07 33				07 44							08 03	
Sunbury	d	07 05		07 16									07 35				07 46							08 05	
Kempton Park	d																								
Hampton	d	07 09		07 20									07 39				07 50							08 09	
Fulwell	d	07 12		07 23									07 42				07 53							08 12	
Strawberry Hill	d	07 14									07 37		07 44	07 46								08 07		08 14	08 16
Teddington	d			07 28							07 41			07 49			07 58					08 11			08 19
Hampton Wick	d			07 30							07 44			07 51			08 00					08 14			08 21
Kingston	a			07 32							07 46			07 53			08 02					08 16			08 23
	d			07 33							07 48			07 55			08 03					08 18			08 25
Norbiton	d			07 35							07 50			07 57			08 05					08 20			08 27
New Malden	d		07 37	07 40		07 45					07 55			08 01		08 06	08 10			08 15		08 25			08 31
Dorking 182	d											07 32											08 00		
Box Hill & Westhumble 182	d											07 35											08 03		
Leatherhead 182	d				07 24		07 35					07 40							07 55				08 08		
Ashtead 182	d				07 27		07 39					07 43							07 58				08 12		
Epsom 182	a				07 32		07 44					07 48							08 03				08 16		
	d				07 34							07 48			07 52				08 04				08 17		
Ewell West	d				07 37										07 55				08 07						
Stoneleigh	d				07 40										07 57				08 09						
Worcester Park	d				07 43							07 54			08 00				08 12				08 24		
Chessington South	d									07 38											08 08				
Chessington North	d									07 40											08 10				
Tolworth	d									07 43											08 13				
Malden Manor	d									07 45											08 15				
Motspur Park	d				07 46					07 50					08 03				08 16		08 20				
Raynes Park	d		07 40	07 43	07 50					07 54	07 58	08 01		08 04	08 07	08 10	08 13		08 20		08 24	08 28	08 31		08 34
Wimbledon	d		07 44	07 47	07 54	07 50				07 58	08 02	08 05		08 08	08 11	08 14	08 17		08 24	08 20	08 28	08 32	08 35		08 38
Earlsfield	d		07 48	07 51	07 58	07 54				08 02	08 06	08 09		08 12	08 15	08 18	08 21		08 28	08 24	08 32	08 36	08 39		08 42
Clapham Junction	d	07 49	07 52	07 55	08 02	07 58				08 06	08 10	08 13	08 19	08 16	08 19	08 22	08 25		08 32	08 28	08 36	08 40	08 43	08 49	08 46
Vauxhall	d	07 56	07 57	08 00	08 07	08 03				08 11	08 15	08 18	08 26	08 21	08 24	08 27	08 30		08 37	08 33	08 41	08 45	08 48	08 56	08 51
London Waterloo	a	08 04	08 02	08 06	08 13	08 10			08 13	08 18	08 21	08 24	08 34	08 27	08 30	08 33	08 36		08 43	08 40	08 48	08 51	08 54	09 04	08 57

A To London Bridge
B From London Waterloo
C From Twickenham
D From Clapham Junction

Table T152-R

Mondays to Fridays

21 May to 5 October

Hampton Court, Shepperton, Guildford, Dorking and Chessington South - London

		SW	SW		SW	SW	SW	SW	SW A	SW ◇	SW	SW	SW		SW	SW	SW	SW	SW A	SW ◇	SW	SW	SW		SW
Guildford	d					07 58	08 07			08 22						08 34				08 46					08 58
London Road (Guildford)	d					08 02	08 11									08 38									09 02
Clandon	d					08 07	08 16									08 43									09 07
Horsley	d					08 11	08 20									08 47									09 11
Effingham Junction	d					08 16	08 24								08 46	08 51									09 15
Bookham	d					08 19									08 49										09 18
Cobham & Stoke d'Abernon	d						08 27									08 54									
Oxshott	d						08 31									08 58									
Claygate	d						08 34									09 01									
Hinchley Wood	d						08 37									09 04									
Hampton Court	d		08 23									08 53										09 23			
Thames Ditton	d		08 25									08 55										09 25			
Surbiton	d		08 31				08 42			08 57		09 01				09 11				09 27		09 31			
Berrylands	d		08 33									09 03										09 33			
Shepperton	d				08 11								08 41										09 11		
Upper Halliford	d				08 14								08 44										09 14		
Sunbury	d				08 16								08 46										09 16		
Kempton Park	d																						09 18		
Hampton	d				08 20								08 50										09 21		
Fulwell	d				08 23								08 53										09 24		
Strawberry Hill	d								08 38										09 08						
Teddington	d				08 28				08 41				08 58						09 12				09 29		
Hampton Wick	d				08 30				08 44				09 00						09 14				09 31		
Kingston	a				08 32				08 46				09 02						09 16				09 33		
	d				08 33				08 48				09 03						09 18				09 34		
Norbiton	d				08 35				08 50				09 05						09 20				09 36		
New Malden	d		08 36		08 40				08 55			09 06	09 10						09 25			09 36	09 40		
Dorking 182	d										08 30										09 00				
Box Hill & Westhumble 182	d										08 33										09 03				
Leatherhead 182	d					08 24					08 38				08 54						09 08				09 23
Ashtead 182	d					08 27					08 41				08 57						09 11				09 27
Epsom 182	a					08 32					08 46				09 02						09 16				09 31
	d	08 22				08 34					08 47				09 04						09 17				09 34
Ewell West	d	08 25				08 37					08 50				09 07						09 20				09 37
Stoneleigh	d	08 27				08 39					08 53				09 10						09 23				09 39
Worcester Park	d	08 30				08 42					08 56				09 12						09 26				09 42
Chessington South	d							08 38										09 08							
Chessington North	d							08 40										09 10							
Tolworth	d							08 43										09 13							
Malden Manor	d							08 45										09 15							
Motspur Park	d	08 33				08 45		08 50			08 59				09 15			09 20			09 29				09 45
Raynes Park	d	08 37	08 40		08 43	08 49		08 54	08 58		09 04	09 10	09 13		09 19		09 22	09 24	09 28		09 34	09 40	09 43		09 49
Wimbledon	d	08 41	08 44		08 47	08 53		08 58	09 02	09 05	09 08	09 14	09 17		09 23	09 20	09 26	09 29	09 32	09 35	09 38	09 44	09 47		09 53
Earlsfield	d	08 45	08 48		08 51	08 57		09 02	09 06	09 09	09 12	09 18	09 21		09 27	09 24	09 30	09 32	09 36	09 39	09 42	09 47	09 50		09 57
Clapham Junction	d	08 49	08 52		08 55	09 01		09 06	09 10	09 13	09 16	09 22	09 25		09 31	09 28		09 36	09 40	09 43	09 46	09 51	09 54		10 01
Vauxhall	d	08 54	08 57		09 00	09 06		09 11	09 15	09 18	09 21	09 27	09 30		09 36	09 33		09 41	09 45	09 48	09 51	09 56	09 59		10 06
London Waterloo	a	09 00	09 03		09 06	09 13	09 01	09 18	09 22	09 24	09 27	09 33	09 36		09 42	09 39	09 46	09 47	09 51	09 54	09 57	10 01	10 04		10 10

A From London Waterloo

Hampton Court, Shepperton, Guildford, Dorking and Chessington South - London

		SW	SW	SW A	SW B	SW	SW	SW	SW	SW	SW	SW A	SW B	SW	SW	SW	SW	SW	SW	SW A	SW B	SW	SW
Guildford	d	09 07							09 28	09 37							09 58	10 07					
London Road (Guildford)	d	09 11							09 32	09 41							10 02	10 11					
Clandon	d	09 16							09 37	09 46							10 07	10 16					
Horsley	d	09 20							09 41	09 50							10 11	10 20					
Effingham Junction	d	09 23							09 45	09 53							10 15	10 23					
Bookham	d								09 48								10 18						
Cobham & Stoke d'Abernon	d	09 27								09 57								10 27					
Oxshott	d	09 30								10 00								10 30					
Claygate	d	09 33								10 03								10 33					
Hinchley Wood	d	09 36								10 06								10 36					
Hampton Court	d						09 54								10 24								10 54
Thames Ditton	d						09 56								10 26								10 56
Surbiton	d	09 41			09 57		10 02			10 11			10 27		10 32			10 41			10 57		11 02
Berrylands	d						10 04								10 34								11 04
Shepperton	d							09 41								10 11							
Upper Halliford	d							09 44								10 14							
Sunbury	d							09 46								10 16							
Kempton Park	d							09 48								10 18							
Hampton	d							09 51								10 21							
Fulwell	d							09 54								10 24							
Strawberry Hill	d			09 37								10 07								10 37			
Teddington	d			09 41				09 59				10 11				10 29				10 41			
Hampton Wick	d			09 44				10 01				10 14				10 31				10 44			
Kingston	a			09 46				10 03				10 16				10 33				10 46			
	d			09 48				10 04				10 18				10 34				10 48			
Norbiton	d			09 50				10 06				10 20				10 36				10 50			
New Malden	d			09 55			10 07	10 10				10 25			10 37	10 40				10 55			11 07
Dorking 182	d					09 33								10 03								10 33	
Box Hill & Westhumble 182	d																						
Leatherhead 182	d					09 39			09 53					10 09			10 23					10 39	
Ashtead 182	d					09 43			09 57					10 13			10 27					10 43	
Epsom 182	a					09 47			10 01					10 17			10 31					10 47	
	d					09 49			10 04					10 19			10 34					10 49	
Ewell West	d					09 52			10 07					10 22			10 37					10 52	
Stoneleigh	d					09 54			10 09					10 24			10 39					10 54	
Worcester Park	d					09 57			10 12					10 27			10 42					10 57	
Chessington South	d		09 38								10 08								10 38				
Chessington North	d		09 40								10 10								10 40				
Tolworth	d		09 43								10 13								10 43				
Malden Manor	d		09 45								10 15								10 45				
Motspur Park	d		09 49			10 00			10 15		10 19			10 30			10 45		10 49			11 00	
Raynes Park	d		09 53	09 58		10 04	10 10	10 13	10 19		10 23	10 28		10 34	10 40	10 43	10 49		10 53	10 58		11 04	11 10
Wimbledon ⊖	d	09 50	09 57	10 02	10 05	10 08	10 14	10 17	10 23	10 20	10 27	10 32	10 35	10 38	10 44	10 47	10 53	10 50	10 57	11 02	11 05	11 08	11 14
Earlsfield	d	09 54	10 01	10 05	10 08	10 12	10 17	10 20	10 27	10 24	10 31	10 35	10 38	10 42	10 47	10 50	10 57	10 54	11 01	11 05	11 08	11 12	11 17
Clapham Junction	d	09 58	10 05	10 09	10 12	10 16	10 21	10 24	10 31	10 28	10 35	10 39	10 42	10 46	10 51	10 54	11 01	10 58	11 05	11 09	11 12	11 16	11 21
Vauxhall ⊖	d	10 03	10 10	10 14	10 17	10 21	10 26	10 29	10 36	10 33	10 40	10 44	10 47	10 51	10 56	10 59	11 06	11 03	11 10	11 14	11 17	11 21	11 26
London Waterloo ⊖	a	10 07	10 16	10 19	10 23	10 25	10 31	10 34	10 40	10 37	10 46	10 49	10 52	10 55	11 01	11 04	11 10	11 07	11 16	11 19	11 22	11 25	11 31

A From London Waterloo
B From Woking

Table T152-R

Mondays to Fridays

21 May to 5 October

Hampton Court, Shepperton, Guildford, Dorking and Chessington South - London

		SW	SW	SW	SW	SW A	SW B	SW	SW	SW	SW	SW	SW	SW A	SW B	SW	SW	SW	SW	SW	SW	SW A	SW B
Guildford	d		10 28	10 37							10 58	11 07							11 28	11 37			
London Road (Guildford)	d		10 32	10 41							11 02	11 11							11 32	11 41			
Clandon	d		10 37	10 46							11 07	11 16							11 37	11 46			
Horsley	d		10 41	10 50							11 11	11 20							11 41	11 50			
Effingham Junction	d		10 45	10 53							11 15	11 23							11 45	11 53			
Bookham	d		10 48								11 18								11 48				
Cobham & Stoke d'Abernon	d			10 57								11 27								11 57			
Oxshott	d			11 00								11 30								12 00			
Claygate	d			11 03								11 33								12 03			
Hinchley Wood	d			11 06								11 36								12 06			
Hampton Court	d								11 24								11 54						
Thames Ditton	d								11 26								11 56						
Surbiton	d			11 11			11 27		11 32			11 41			11 57		12 02			12 11			12 27
Berrylands	d								11 34								12 04						
Shepperton	d	10 41								11 11								11 41					
Upper Halliford	d	10 44								11 14								11 44					
Sunbury	d	10 46								11 16								11 46					
Kempton Park	d	10 48								11 18								11 48					
Hampton	d	10 51								11 21								11 51					
Fulwell	d	10 54								11 24								11 54					
Strawberry Hill	d					11 07								11 37								12 07	
Teddington	d	10 59				11 11				11 29				11 41				11 59				12 11	
Hampton Wick	d	11 01				11 14				11 31				11 44				12 01				12 14	
Kingston	a	11 03				11 16				11 33				11 46				12 03				12 16	
	d	11 04				11 18				11 34				11 48				12 04				12 18	
Norbiton	d	11 06				11 20				11 36				11 50				12 06				12 20	
New Malden	d	11 10				11 25			11 37	11 40				11 55			12 07	12 10				12 25	
Dorking 182	d							11 03								11 33							
Box Hill & Westhumble 182	d																						
Leatherhead 182	d		10 53					11 09			11 23					11 39			11 53				
Ashtead 182	d		10 57					11 13			11 27					11 43			11 57				
Epsom 182	a		11 01					11 17			11 31					11 47			12 01				
	d		11 04					11 19			11 34					11 49			12 04				
Ewell West	d		11 07					11 22			11 37					11 52			12 07				
Stoneleigh	d		11 09					11 24			11 39					11 54			12 09				
Worcester Park	d		11 12					11 27			11 42					11 57			12 12				
Chessington South	d				11 08								11 38								12 08		
Chessington North	d				11 10								11 40								12 10		
Tolworth	d				11 13								11 43								12 13		
Malden Manor	d				11 15								11 45								12 15		
Motspur Park	d		11 15		11 19			11 30			11 45		11 49			12 00			12 15		12 19		
Raynes Park	d	11 13	11 19		11 23	11 28		11 34	11 40	11 43	11 49		11 53	11 58		12 04	12 10	12 13	12 19		12 23	12 28	
Wimbledon ⊖	d	11 17	11 23	11 20	11 27	11 32	11 35	11 38	11 44	11 47	11 53	11 50	11 57	12 02	12 05	12 08	12 14	12 16	12 23	12 20	12 27	12 32	12 35
Earlsfield	d	11 20	11 27	11 24	11 31	11 35	11 38	11 42	11 47	11 50	11 57	11 54	12 01	12 05	12 08	12 12	12 17	12 20	12 27	12 24	12 31	12 35	12 38
Clapham Junction	d	11 24	11 31	11 28	11 35	11 39	11 42	11 46	11 51	11 54	12 01	11 58	12 05	12 09	12 12	12 16	12 21	12 24	12 31	12 28	12 35	12 39	12 42
Vauxhall ⊖	d	11 29	11 36	11 33	11 40	11 44	11 47	11 51	11 56	11 59	12 06	12 03	12 10	12 14	12 17	12 21	12 26	12 29	12 36	12 33	12 40	12 44	12 47
London Waterloo ⊖	a	11 34	11 40	11 37	11 46	11 49	11 52	11 55	12 01	12 04	12 10	12 07	12 16	12 19	12 22	12 25	12 31	12 34	12 40	12 37	12 46	12 49	12 52

A From London Waterloo
B From Woking

Table T152-R

Mondays to Fridays

21 May to 5 October

Hampton Court, Shepperton, Guildford, Dorking and Chessington South - London

		SW	SW	SW	SW	SW	SW	SW A	SW B	SW	SW	SW	SW	SW	SW	SW A	SW B	SW	SW	SW	SW	SW
Guildford	d				11 58	12 07							12 28	12 37							12 58	13 07
London Road (Guildford)	d				12 02	12 11							12 32	12 41							13 02	13 11
Clandon	d				12 07	12 16							12 37	12 46							13 07	13 16
Horsley	d				12 11	12 20							12 41	12 50							13 11	13 20
Effingham Junction 6	d				12 15	12 23							12 45	12 53							13 15	13 23
Bookham	d				12 18								12 48								13 18	
Cobham & Stoke d'Abernon	d					12 27								12 57								13 27
Oxshott	d					12 30								13 00								13 30
Claygate	d					12 33								13 03								13 33
Hinchley Wood	d					12 36								13 06								13 36
Hampton Court	d		12 24								12 54								13 24			
Thames Ditton	d		12 26								12 56								13 26			
Surbiton 6	d		12 32			12 41			12 57		13 02			13 11			13 27		13 32			13 41
Berrylands	d		12 34								13 04								13 34			
Shepperton	d			12 11								12 41								13 11		
Upper Halliford	d			12 14								12 44								13 14		
Sunbury	d			12 16								12 46								13 16		
Kempton Park	d			12 18								12 48								13 18		
Hampton	d			12 21								12 51								13 21		
Fulwell	d			12 24								12 54								13 24		
Strawberry Hill	d							12 37								13 07						
Teddington	d			12 29				12 41				12 59				13 11				13 29		
Hampton Wick	d			12 31				12 44				13 01				13 14				13 31		
Kingston	a			12 33				12 46				13 03				13 16				13 33		
	d			12 34				12 48				13 04				13 18				13 34		
Norbiton	d			12 36				12 50				13 06				13 20				13 36		
New Malden 6	d		12 37	12 40				12 55			13 07	13 10				13 25			13 37	13 40		
Dorking 4	182 d	12 03								12 33								13 03				
Box Hill & Westhumble	182 d																					
Leatherhead	182 d	12 09			12 23					12 39			12 53					13 09			13 23	
Ashtead	182 d	12 13			12 27					12 43			12 57					13 13			13 27	
Epsom 3	182 a	12 17			12 31					12 47			13 01					13 17			13 31	
	d	12 19			12 34					12 49			13 04					13 19			13 34	
Ewell West	d	12 22			12 37					12 52			13 07					13 22			13 37	
Stoneleigh	d	12 24			12 39					12 54			13 09					13 24			13 39	
Worcester Park	d	12 27			12 42					12 57			13 12					13 27			13 42	
Chessington South	d						12 38								13 08							
Chessington North	d						12 40								13 10							
Tolworth	d						12 43								13 13							
Malden Manor	d						12 45								13 15							
Motspur Park	d	12 30			12 45		12 49			13 00			13 15		13 19			13 30			13 45	
Raynes Park 6	d	12 34	12 40	12 43	12 49		12 53	12 58		13 04	13 10	13 13	13 19		13 23	13 28		13 34	13 40	13 43	13 49	
Wimbledon 6 ⊖ ⇌	d	12 38	12 44	12 47	12 53	12 50	12 57	13 02	13 05	13 08	13 14	13 17	13 23	13 20	13 27	13 32	13 35	13 38	13 44	13 47	13 53	13 50
Earlsfield	d	12 42	12 47	12 50	12 57	12 54	13 01	13 05	13 08	13 12	13 17	13 20	13 27	13 24	13 31	13 35	13 38	13 42	13 47	13 50	13 57	13 54
Clapham Junction 10	d	12 46	12 51	12 54	13 01	12 58	13 05	13 09	13 12	13 16	13 21	13 24	13 31	13 28	13 35	13 39	13 42	13 46	13 51	13 54	14 01	13 58
Vauxhall ⊖	d	12 51	12 56	12 59	13 06	13 03	13 10	13 14	13 17	13 21	13 26	13 29	13 36	13 33	13 40	13 44	13 47	13 51	13 56	13 59	14 06	14 03
London Waterloo 15 ⊖	a	12 55	13 01	13 04	13 10	13 07	13 16	13 19	13 22	13 25	13 31	13 34	13 40	13 37	13 46	13 49	13 52	13 55	14 01	14 04	14 10	14 07

A From London Waterloo
B From Woking

Table T152-R

Mondays to Fridays

21 May to 5 October

Hampton Court, Shepperton, Guildford, Dorking and Chessington South - London

		SW	SW A	SW B	SW	SW	SW	SW	SW	SW	SW A	SW B	SW	SW	SW	SW	SW	SW	SW A	SW B	SW	SW	SW
Guildford	d							13 28	13 37							13 58	14 07						
London Road (Guildford)	d							13 32	13 41							14 02	14 11						
Clandon	d							13 37	13 46							14 07	14 16						
Horsley	d							13 41	13 50							14 11	14 20						
Effingham Junction 6	d							13 45	13 53							14 15	14 23						
Bookham	d							13 48								14 18							
Cobham & Stoke d'Abernon	d								13 57								14 27						
Oxshott	d								14 00								14 30						
Claygate	d								14 03								14 33						
Hinchley Wood	d								14 06								14 36						
Hampton Court	d					13 54								14 24								14 54	
Thames Ditton	d					13 56								14 26								14 56	
Surbiton 6	d			13 57		14 02			14 11			14 27		14 32			14 41			14 57		15 02	
Berrylands	d					14 04								14 34								15 04	
Shepperton	d						13 41								14 11								14 41
Upper Halliford	d						13 44								14 14								14 44
Sunbury	d						13 46								14 16								14 46
Kempton Park	d						13 48								14 18								14 48
Hampton	d						13 51								14 21								14 51
Fulwell	d						13 54								14 24								14 54
Strawberry Hill	d		13 37								14 07								14 37				
Teddington	d		13 41				13 59				14 11				14 29				14 41				14 59
Hampton Wick	d		13 44				14 01				14 14				14 31				14 44				15 01
Kingston	a		13 46				14 03				14 16				14 33				14 46				15 03
	d		13 48				14 04				14 18				14 34				14 48				15 04
Norbiton	d		13 50				14 06				14 20				14 36				14 50				15 06
New Malden 6	d		13 55			14 07	14 10				14 25			14 37	14 40				14 55			15 07	15 10
Dorking 4	182 d				13 33								14 02								14 33		
Box Hill & Westhumble	182 d																						
Leatherhead	182 d				13 39			13 53					14 08			14 23					14 39		
Ashtead	182 d				13 43			13 57					14 12			14 27					14 43		
Epsom 3	182 a				13 47			14 01					14 16			14 31					14 47		
	d				13 49			14 04					14 19			14 34					14 49		
Ewell West	d				13 52			14 07					14 22			14 37					14 52		
Stoneleigh	d				13 54			14 09					14 24			14 39					14 54		
Worcester Park	d				13 57			14 12					14 27			14 42					14 57		
Chessington South	d	13 38								14 08								14 38					
Chessington North	d	13 40								14 10								14 40					
Tolworth	d	13 43								14 13								14 43					
Malden Manor	d	13 45								14 15								14 45					
Motspur Park	d	13 49			14 00			14 15		14 19			14 30			14 45		14 49			15 00		
Raynes Park 6	d	13 53	13 58		14 04	14 10	14 13	14 19		14 23	14 28		14 34	14 40	14 43	14 49		14 53	14 58		15 04	15 10	15 13
Wimbledon 6 ⊖ ⇌	d	13 57	14 02	14 05	14 08	14 14	14 17	14 23	14 20	14 27	14 32	14 35	14 38	14 44	14 47	14 53	14 50	14 57	15 02	15 05	15 08	15 14	15 17
Earlsfield	d	14 01	14 05	14 08	14 12	14 17	14 20	14 27	14 24	14 31	14 35	14 38	14 42	14 47	14 50	14 57	14 54	15 01	15 05	15 08	15 12	15 17	15 20
Clapham Junction 10	d	14 05	14 09	14 12	14 16	14 21	14 24	14 31	14 28	14 35	14 39	14 42	14 46	14 51	14 54	15 01	14 58	15 05	15 09	15 12	15 16	15 21	15 24
Vauxhall ⊖	d	14 10	14 14	14 17	14 21	14 26	14 29	14 36	14 33	14 40	14 44	14 47	14 51	14 56	14 59	15 06	15 03	15 10	15 14	15 17	15 21	15 26	15 29
London Waterloo 15 ⊖	a	14 16	14 19	14 22	14 25	14 31	14 34	14 40	14 37	14 46	14 49	14 52	14 55	15 01	15 04	15 10	15 07	15 16	15 19	15 22	15 25	15 31	15 34

A From London Waterloo
B From Woking

Table T152-R

Mondays to Fridays
21 May to 5 October

Hampton Court, Shepperton, Guildford, Dorking and Chessington South - London

Station		SW	SW		SW	SW A	SW B	SW	SW	SW	SW	SW	SW		SW A	SW B	SW	SW	SW	SW	SW	SW	SW A		SW B
Guildford	d	14 28	14 37								14 58	15 07								15 28	15 37				
London Road (Guildford)	d	14 32	14 41								15 02	15 11								15 32	15 41				
Clandon	d	14 37	14 46								15 07	15 16								15 37	15 46				
Horsley	d	14 41	14 50								15 11	15 20								15 41	15 50				
Effingham Junction	d	14 45	14 53								15 15	15 23								15 45	15 53				
Bookham	d	14 48									15 18									15 48					
Cobham & Stoke d'Abernon	d		14 57									15 27									15 57				
Oxshott	d		15 00									15 30									16 00				
Claygate	d		15 03									15 33									16 03				
Hinchley Wood	d		15 06									15 36									16 06				
Hampton Court	d								15 24									15 54							
Thames Ditton	d								15 26									15 56							
Surbiton	d		15 11				15 27		15 32			15 41				15 57		16 02			16 11				16 27
Berrylands	d								15 34									16 04							
Shepperton	d									15 11									15 41						
Upper Halliford	d									15 14									15 44						
Sunbury	d									15 16									15 46						
Kempton Park	d									15 18									15 48						
Hampton	d									15 21									15 51						
Fulwell	d									15 24									15 54						
Strawberry Hill	d					15 07									15 37								16 07		
Teddington	d					15 11				15 29					15 41				15 59				16 11		
Hampton Wick	d					15 14				15 31					15 44				16 01				16 14		
Kingston	a					15 16				15 33					15 46				16 03				16 16		
	d					15 18				15 34					15 48				16 04				16 18		
Norbiton	d					15 20				15 36					15 50				16 06				16 20		
New Malden	d					15 25			15 37	15 40					15 55			16 07	16 10				16 25		
Dorking	182 d							15 03									15 33								
Box Hill & Westhumble	182 d																								
Leatherhead	182 d	14 53						15 09			15 23						15 39			15 53					
Ashtead	182 d	14 57						15 13			15 27						15 43			15 57					
Epsom	182 a	15 01						15 17			15 31						15 47			16 01					
	d	15 04						15 19			15 34						15 49			16 04					
Ewell West	d	15 07						15 22			15 37						15 52			16 07					
Stoneleigh	d	15 09						15 24			15 39						15 54			16 09					
Worcester Park	d	15 12						15 27			15 42						15 57			16 12					
Chessington South	d				15 08								15 38									16 08			
Chessington North	d				15 10								15 40									16 10			
Tolworth	d				15 13								15 43									16 13			
Malden Manor	d				15 15								15 45									16 15			
Motspur Park	d	15 15			15 19			15 30			15 45		15 49				16 00			16 15		16 19			
Raynes Park	d	15 19			15 23	15 28		15 34	15 40	15 43	15 49		15 53		15 58		16 04	16 10	16 13	16 19		16 23	16 28		
Wimbledon ⊖	d	15 23	15 20		15 27	15 32	15 35	15 38	15 44	15 47	15 53	15 50	15 57		16 02	16 05	16 08	16 14	16 17	16 23	16 20	16 27	16 32		16 35
Earlsfield	d	15 27	15 24		15 31	15 35	15 38	15 42	15 47	15 50	15 57	15 54	16 01		16 05	16 08	16 12	16 17	16 20	16 27	16 24	16 31	16 35		16 38
Clapham Junction	d	15 31	15 28		15 35	15 39	15 42	15 46	15 51	15 54	16 01	15 58	16 05		16 09	16 12	16 16	16 21	16 24	16 31	16 28	16 35	16 39		16 42
Vauxhall ⊖	d	15 36	15 33		15 40	15 44	15 47	15 51	15 56	15 59	16 06	16 03	16 10		16 14	16 17	16 21	16 26	16 29	16 36	16 33	16 40	16 44		16 47
London Waterloo ⊖	a	15 40	15 37		15 46	15 49	15 52	15 55	16 01	16 04	16 10	16 07	16 16		16 19	16 22	16 25	16 31	16 34	16 40	16 37	16 46	16 49		16 52

A From London Waterloo
B From Woking

Table T152-R

Mondays to Fridays
21 May to 5 October

Hampton Court, Shepperton, Guildford, Dorking and Chessington South - London

Station		SW	SW	SW	SW	SW	SW	SW A	SW B		SW	SW	SW	SW	SW	SW	SW A	SW B	SW		SW	SW	SW	SW	SW
Guildford	d				15 58	16 07								16 28	16 37								16 58	17 07	
London Road (Guildford)	d				16 02	16 11								16 32	16 41								17 02	17 11	
Clandon	d				16 07	16 16								16 37	16 46								17 07	17 16	
Horsley	d				16 11	16 20								16 41	16 50								17 11	17 20	
Effingham Junction	d				16 15	16 23								16 45	16 53								17 15	17 23	
Bookham	d				16 18									16 48									17 18		
Cobham & Stoke d'Abernon	d					16 27									16 57									17 27	
Oxshott	d					16 30									17 00									17 30	
Claygate	d					16 33									17 03									17 33	
Hinchley Wood	d					16 36									17 06									17 36	
Hampton Court	d		16 24									16 54									17 24				
Thames Ditton	d		16 26									16 56									17 26				
Surbiton	d		16 32			16 41			16 56			17 01			17 11			17 27			17 31			17 41	
Berrylands	d		16 34									17 04									17 34				
Shepperton	d			16 11									16 41									17 11			
Upper Halliford	d			16 14									16 44									17 14			
Sunbury	d			16 16									16 46									17 16			
Kempton Park	d			16 18									16 48									17 18			
Hampton	d			16 21									16 51									17 21			
Fulwell	d			16 24									16 54									17 24			
Strawberry Hill	d							16 37									17 07								
Teddington	d			16 29				16 43					16 59				17 13					17 29			
Hampton Wick	d			16 31				16 46					17 01				17 16					17 31			
Kingston	a			16 33				16 48					17 03				17 18					17 33			
	d			16 34				16 48					17 04				17 18					17 34			
Norbiton	d			16 36				16 50					17 06				17 20					17 36			
New Malden	d		16 37	16 40				16 55				17 07	17 10				17 25				17 37	17 40			
Dorking	182 d	16 03									16 33								17 03						
Box Hill & Westhumble	182 d																								
Leatherhead	182 d	16 09			16 23						16 39			16 53					17 09				17 23		
Ashtead	182 d	16 13			16 27						16 43			16 57					17 13				17 27		
Epsom	182 a	16 17			16 31						16 47			17 01					17 17				17 31		
	d	16 19			16 34						16 49			17 04					17 19				17 34		
Ewell West	d	16 22			16 37						16 52			17 07					17 22				17 37		
Stoneleigh	d	16 24			16 39						16 54			17 09					17 24				17 39		
Worcester Park	d	16 27			16 42						16 57			17 12					17 27				17 42		
Chessington South	d						16 38									17 08									17 38
Chessington North	d						16 40									17 10									17 40
Tolworth	d						16 43									17 13									17 43
Malden Manor	d						16 45									17 15									17 45
Motspur Park	d	16 30			16 45		16 49				17 00			17 15		17 19			17 30				17 45		17 49
Raynes Park	d	16 34	16 40	16 43	16 49		16 53	16 58			17 04	17 09	17 13	17 19		17 23	17 28		17 34		17 39	17 43	17 49		17 53
Wimbledon ⊖	d	16 38	16 44	16 47	16 53	16 50	16 57	17 02	17 05		17 08	17 13	17 17	17 23	17 20	17 28	17 32	17 35	17 38		17 43	17 47	17 53	17 50	17 57
Earlsfield	d	16 42	16 47	16 50	16 57	16 54	17 01	17 05	17 08		17 12	17 17	17 20	17 27	17 24	17 31	17 35	17 38	17 42		17 47	17 50	17 57	17 54	18 01
Clapham Junction	d	16 46	16 51	16 54	17 01	16 58	17 05	17 09	17 12		17 16	17 21	17 24	17 31	17 28	17 35	17 39	17 42	17 46		17 51	17 54	18 01	17 58	18 05
Vauxhall ⊖	d	16 51	16 56	16 59	17 06	17 03	17 10	17 14	17 17		17 21	17 26	17 29	17 36	17 33	17 40	17 44	17 47	17 51		17 56	17 59	18 06	18 03	18 10
London Waterloo ⊖	a	16 55	17 01	17 04	17 10	17 07	17 16	17 19	17 22		17 25	17 30	17 35	17 40	17 37	17 46	17 49	17 52	17 55		18 00	18 04	18 10	18 07	18 16

A From London Waterloo
B From Woking

21 May to 5 October

Hampton Court, Shepperton, Guildford, Dorking and Chessington South - London

Station		SW A	SW B	SW	SW A	SW	SW	SW	SW	SW	SW A	SW B	SW	SW	SW	SW	SW	SW	SW A	SW B	SW	SW	SW
Guildford	d							17 28	17 37							17 58	18 07						
London Road (Guildford)	d							17 32	17 41							18 02	18 11						
Clandon	d							17 37	17 46							18 07	18 16						
Horsley	d							17 41	17 50							18 11	18 20						
Effingham Junction	d							17 45	17 53							18 15	18 23						
Bookham	d							17 48								18 18							
Cobham & Stoke d'Abernon	d								17 57								18 27						
Oxshott	d								18 00								18 30						
Claygate	d								18 03								18 33						
Hinchley Wood	d								18 06								18 36						
Hampton Court	d					17 54								18 24								18 54	
Thames Ditton	d					17 56								18 26								18 56	
Surbiton	d		17 56			18 01			18 11			18 26		18 31			18 41			18 56		19 02	
Berrylands	d					18 04								18 34								19 04	
Shepperton	d						17 41								18 11								18 36
Upper Halliford	d						17 44								18 14								18 39
Sunbury	d						17 46								18 16								18 41
Kempton Park	d						17 48								18 18								18 43
Hampton	d						17 51								18 21								18 51
Fulwell	d						17 54								18 24								18 54
Strawberry Hill	d	17 37			17 41						18 07								18 37				
Teddington	d	17 43			17 52		17 59				18 13				18 29				18 43				18 59
Hampton Wick	d	17 46			17 54		18 01				18 16				18 31				18 46				19 01
Kingston	a	17 48			17 56		18 03				18 18				18 33				18 48				19 03
	d	17 48			17 58		18 04				18 18				18 34				18 48				19 04
Norbiton	d	17 50			18 00		18 06				18 20				18 36				18 50				19 06
New Malden	d	17 55			18 04	18 07	18 10				18 25			18 37	18 40				18 55			19 07	19 10
Dorking	182 d			17 28									18 03								18 33		
Box Hill & Westhumble	182 d																						
Leatherhead	182 d			17 35				17 53					18 09			18 23					18 39		
Ashtead	182 d			17 38				17 57					18 13			18 27					18 43		
Epsom	182 a			17 43				18 01					18 17			18 31					18 47		
	d			17 49				18 04					18 19			18 34					18 49		
Ewell West	d			17 52				18 07					18 22			18 37					18 52		
Stoneleigh	d			17 54				18 09					18 24			18 39					18 54		
Worcester Park	d			17 57				18 12					18 27			18 42					18 57		
Chessington South	d									18 08								18 38					
Chessington North	d									18 10								18 40					
Tolworth	d									18 13								18 43					
Malden Manor	d									18 15								18 45					
Motspur Park	d			18 00				18 15		18 19			18 30			18 45		18 49			19 00		
Raynes Park	d	17 57		18 03	18 06	18 09	18 13	18 19		18 22	18 28		18 34	18 39	18 43	18 49		18 53	18 58		19 04	19 10	19 13
Wimbledon ⊖	d	18 01	18 04	18 07	18 10	18 13	18 17	18 23	18 20	18 26	18 32	18 35	18 38	18 43	18 47	18 53	18 50	18 57	19 02	19 05	19 09	19 14	19 17
Earlsfield	d	18 05	18 08	18 11	18 14	18 17	18 20	18 27	18 24	18 30	18 35	18 38	18 42	18 47	18 50	18 57	18 54	19 01	19 05	19 09	19 12	19 17	19 20
Clapham Junction	d	18 09	18 12	18 15	18 18	18 21	18 24	18 31	18 28	18 34	18 39	18 42	18 46	18 51	18 54	19 01	18 58	19 05	19 09	19 12	19 16	19 21	19 24
Vauxhall ⊖	d	18 14	18 17	18 20	18 23	18 26	18 29	18 36	18 33	18 39	18 44	18 47	18 51	18 56	18 59	19 06	19 03	19 10	19 14	19 17	19 21	19 26	19 29
London Waterloo ⊖	a	18 18	18 21	18 24	18 28	18 30	18 34	18 40	18 37	18 45	18 49	18 52	18 55	19 00	19 05	19 10	19 07	19 14	19 19	19 23	19 26	19 31	19 34

A From London Waterloo
B From Woking

Table T152-R

Mondays to Fridays

21 May to 5 October

Hampton Court, Shepperton, Guildford, Dorking and Chessington South - London

Station		SW	SW	SW	SW A	SW B	SW	SW	SW	SW	TL C	SW	SW	SW A	SW B	SW	SW	SW	SW	SW	SW	SW A
Guildford	d	18 35									19 03	19 07							19 28	19 37		
London Road (Guildford)	d	18 39									19 07	19 11							19 32	19 41		
Clandon	d	18 44									19 12	19 16							19 37	19 46		
Horsley	d	18 48									19 17	19 20							19 41	19 50		
Effingham Junction	d	18 51					18 59				19 20	19 23							19 45	19 53		
Bookham	d						19 02				19 24								19 48			
Cobham & Stoke d'Abernon	d	18 55										19 27								19 57		
Oxshott	d	18 58										19 30								20 00		
Claygate	d	19 01										19 33								20 03		
Hinchley Wood	d	19 04										19 36								20 06		
Hampton Court	d							19 24									19 54					
Thames Ditton	d							19 26									19 56					
Surbiton	d	19 11				19 27		19 32				19 41			19 57		20 02			20 11		
Berrylands	d							19 34									20 04					
Shepperton	d								19 06									19 36				
Upper Halliford	d								19 09									19 39				
Sunbury	d								19 11									19 41				
Kempton Park	d								19 13									19 43				
Hampton	d								19 21									19 51				
Fulwell	d								19 24									19 54				
Strawberry Hill	d				19 07									19 37								20 08
Teddington	d				19 13				19 29					19 43				19 59				20 12
Hampton Wick	d				19 16				19 31					19 46				20 01				20 14
Kingston	a				19 18				19 33					19 48				20 03				20 16
	d				19 18				19 34					19 48				20 04				20 18
Norbiton	d				19 20				19 36					19 50				20 06				20 20
New Malden	d				19 25			19 37	19 40					19 55			20 07	20 10				20 25
Dorking	182 d		18 50													19 33						
Box Hill & Westhumble	182 d																					
Leatherhead	182 d		18 56				19 08				19 29					19 39			19 53			
Ashtead	182 d		18 59				19 12				19 34					19 43			19 57			
Epsom	182 a		19 03				19 16				19 39					19 47			20 01			
	d		19 04				19 19			19 34						19 49			20 04			
Ewell West	d		19 07				19 22			19 37						19 52			20 07			
Stoneleigh	d		19 09				19 24			19 39						19 54			20 09			
Worcester Park	d		19 12				19 27			19 42						19 57			20 12			
Chessington South	d			19 08									19 38								20 08	
Chessington North	d			19 10									19 40								20 10	
Tolworth	d			19 13									19 43								20 13	
Malden Manor	d			19 15									19 45								20 15	
Motspur Park	d		19 15	19 20			19 30			19 45			19 49			20 00			20 15		20 19	
Raynes Park	d		19 19	19 23	19 28		19 34	19 40	19 43	19 49			19 53	19 58		20 04	20 10	20 13	20 19		20 23	20 28
Wimbledon ⊖	d	19 20	19 23	19 27	19 32	19 35	19 38	19 44	19 47	19 53		19 50	19 57	20 02	20 05	20 08	20 14	20 17	20 23	20 20	20 27	20 32
Earlsfield	d	19 24	19 27	19 31	19 35	19 39	19 42	19 47	19 50	19 57		19 54	20 01	20 05	20 08	20 12	20 17	20 20	20 27	20 24	20 31	20 35
Clapham Junction	d	19 28	19 31	19 35	19 39	19 42	19 46	19 51	19 54	20 01		19 58	20 05	20 09	20 12	20 16	20 21	20 24	20 31	20 28	20 35	20 39
Vauxhall ⊖	d	19 33	19 36	19 40	19 44	19 47	19 51	19 56	19 59	20 06		20 03	20 10	20 14	20 17	20 21	20 26	20 29	20 36	20 33	20 40	20 44
London Waterloo ⊖	a	19 37	19 41	19 46	19 49	19 52	19 55	20 01	20 04	20 10		20 07	20 16	20 19	20 22	20 25	20 31	20 34	20 40	20 37	20 46	20 49

A From London Waterloo
B From Woking
C To London Bridge

Table T152-R

Mondays to Fridays

21 May to 5 October

Hampton Court, Shepperton, Guildford, Dorking and Chessington South - London

		SW A	SW	SW	SW	SW	SW		SW	SW B	SW A	SW	SW	SW	SW	SW	SW		SW B	SW A	SW	SW	SW	SW	SW
Guildford	d					19 58	20 07								20 37						20 46			21 07	
London Road (Guildford)	d					20 02	20 11								20 41						20 50			21 11	
Clandon	d					20 07	20 16								20 46						20 55			21 16	
Horsley	d					20 11	20 20								20 50						20 59			21 20	
Effingham Junction 6	d					20 15	20 23								20 53						21 03			21 23	
Bookham	d					20 18															21 06				
Cobham & Stoke d'Abernon	d						20 27								20 57									21 27	
Oxshott	d						20 30								21 00									21 30	
Claygate	d						20 33								21 03									21 33	
Hinchley Wood	d						20 36								21 06									21 36	
Hampton Court	d			20 24									20 54									21 24			
Thames Ditton	d			20 26									20 56									21 26			
Surbiton 6	d	20 26		20 32			20 41				20 57		21 02		21 11					21 27		21 32		21 41	
Berrylands	d			20 34									21 04									21 34			
Shepperton	d				20 11									20 41									21 11		
Upper Halliford	d				20 14									20 44									21 14		
Sunbury	d				20 16									20 46									21 16		
Kempton Park	d				20 18									20 48									21 18		
Hampton	d				20 21									20 51									21 21		
Fulwell	d				20 24									20 54									21 24		
Strawberry Hill	d									20 37									21 07						
Teddington	d				20 29					20 41				20 59					21 11				21 29		
Hampton Wick	d				20 31					20 44				21 01					21 14				21 31		
Kingston	a				20 33					20 46				21 03					21 16				21 33		
	d				20 34					20 48				21 04					21 18				21 34		
Norbiton	d				20 36					20 50				21 06					21 20				21 36		
New Malden 6	d			20 37	20 40					20 55			21 07	21 10					21 25			21 37	21 40		
Dorking 4 182	d		20 03									20 33													
Box Hill & Westhumble 182	d																								
Leatherhead 182	d		20 09			20 23						20 39									21 11				
Ashtead 182	d		20 13			20 27						20 42									21 14				
Epsom 6 182	a		20 17			20 31						20 48									21 19				
	d		20 19			20 34						20 49				21 04					21 19				21 34
Ewell West	d		20 22			20 37						20 52				21 07					21 22				21 37
Stoneleigh	d		20 24			20 39						20 54				21 09					21 24				21 39
Worcester Park	d		20 27			20 42						20 57				21 12					21 27				21 42
Chessington South	d								20 38								21 08								
Chessington North	d								20 40								21 10								
Tolworth	d								20 43								21 13								
Malden Manor	d								20 45								21 15								
Motspur Park	d		20 30			20 45			20 49			21 00				21 16	21 19				21 30				21 45
Raynes Park 6	d		20 34	20 40	20 43	20 49			20 53	20 58		21 04	21 10	21 13		21 20	21 23		21 28		21 34	21 40	21 43		21 49
Wimbledon 6 ⊖ ⇌	d	20 35	20 38	20 44	20 47	20 53	20 50		20 57	21 02	21 05	21 08	21 14	21 17	21 21	21 24	21 27		21 32	21 35	21 38	21 44	21 47	21 50	21 53
Earlsfield	d	20 39	20 42	20 47	20 50	20 57	20 54		21 01	21 05	21 09	21 12	21 17	21 20	21 25	21 28	21 31		21 35	21 38	21 42	21 47	21 50	21 54	21 57
Clapham Junction 10	d	20 42	20 46	20 51	20 54	21 01	20 58		21 05	21 09	21 12	21 16	21 21	21 24	21 29	21 32	21 35		21 39	21 42	21 46	21 51	21 54	21 58	22 01
Vauxhall ⊖	d	20 47	20 51	20 56	20 59	21 06	21 03		21 10	21 14	21 17	21 21	21 26	21 29	21 34	21 37	21 40		21 44	21 47	21 51	21 56	21 59	22 03	22 06
London Waterloo 15 ⊖	a	20 52	20 55	21 01	21 04	21 10	21 07		21 16	21 19	21 22	21 25	21 31	21 34	21 38	21 41	21 46		21 49	21 52	21 55	22 01	22 04	22 07	22 10

A From Woking
B From London Waterloo

Table T152-R

Mondays to Fridays

21 May to 5 October

Hampton Court, Shepperton, Guildford, Dorking and Chessington South - London

		SW	SW A		SW B	SW	SW	SW	SW	SW A	SW B	SW	SW		SW	SW	SW	SW A	SW	SW	SW	SW	SW		SW A
Guildford	d								21 37			21 46				22 07			22 20				22 37		
London Road (Guildford)	d								21 41			21 50				22 11							22 41		
Clandon	d								21 46			21 55				22 16							22 46		
Horsley	d								21 50			21 59				22 20							22 50		
Effingham Junction 6	d								21 53			22 03				22 23							22 53		
Bookham	d											22 06													
Cobham & Stoke d'Abernon	d								21 57							22 27							22 57		
Oxshott	d								22 00							22 30							23 00		
Claygate	d								22 03							22 33							23 03		
Hinchley Wood	d								22 06							22 36							23 06		
Hampton Court	d						21 54								22 24						22 54				
Thames Ditton	d						21 56								22 26						22 56				
Surbiton 6	d				21 57		22 02		22 11		22 27				22a32	22 41			22 57		23 02		23 11		
Berrylands	d						22 04														23 04				
Shepperton	d							21 41					22 11									22 41			
Upper Halliford	d							21 44					22 14									22 44			
Sunbury	d							21 46					22 16									22 46			
Kempton Park	d							21 48					22 18									22 48			
Hampton	d							21 51					22 21									22 51			
Fulwell	d							21 54					22 24									22 54			
Strawberry Hill	d		21 37							22 07								22 37							23 07
Teddington	d		21 41					21 59		22 11			22 29					22 41				22 59			23 11
Hampton Wick	d		21 44					22 01		22 14			22 31					22 44				23 01			23 14
Kingston	a		21 46					22 03		22 16			22 33					22 46				23 03			23 16
	d		21 48					22 04		22 18			22 34					22 48				23 04			23 18
Norbiton	d		21 50					22 06		22 20			22 36					22 50				23 06			23 20
New Malden 6	d		21 55				22 07	22 10		22 25			22 40					22 55			23 07	23 10			23 25
Dorking 4 182	d					21 33														22 33					
Box Hill & Westhumble 182	d																								
Leatherhead 182	d					21 40						22 11								22 39					
Ashtead 182	d					21 43						22 14								22 43					
Epsom 6 182	a					21 48						22 19								22 48					
	d					21 49						22 19								22 49					
Ewell West	d					21 52						22 22								22 52					
Stoneleigh	d					21 54						22 24								22 54					
Worcester Park	d					21 57						22 27								22 57					
Chessington South	d	21 38															22 38								
Chessington North	d	21 40															22 40								
Tolworth	d	21 43															22 43								
Malden Manor	d	21 45															22 45								
Motspur Park	d	21 49				22 00						22 30					22 49			23 00					
Raynes Park 6	d	21 53	21 58			22 04	22 10	22 13		22 28		22 34	22 43				22 53	22 58		23 04	23 10	23 13			23 28
Wimbledon 6 ⊖ ⇌	d	21 57	22 02		22 05	22 08	22 14	22 17	22 20	22 32	22 35	22 38	22 47			22 50	22 57	23 02	23 05	23 09	23 14	23 17	23 20		23 32
Earlsfield	d	22 01	22 05		22 08	22 12	22 17	22 20	22 24	22 35	22 38	22 42	22 50			22 54	23 01	23 05	23 08	23 12	23 17	23 20	23 24		23 36
Clapham Junction 10	d	22 05	22 09		22 12	22 16	22 21	22 24	22 28	22 39	22 42	22 46	22 54			22 58	23 05	23 09	23 12	23 16	23 21	23 25	23 28		23 40
Vauxhall ⊖	d	22 10	22 14		22 17	22 21	22 26	22 29	22 33	22 44	22 47	22 51	22 59			23 03	23 10	23 14	23 17	23 21	23 26	23 30	23 33		23 45
London Waterloo 15 ⊖	a	22 16	22 19		22 22	22 25	22 31	22 34	22 42	22 49	22 52	22 55	23 04			23 09	23 16	23 19	23 26	23 28	23 31	23 34	23 40		23 49

A From London Waterloo
B From Woking

Table T152-R

Mondays to Fridays

21 May to 5 October

Hampton Court, Shepperton, Guildford, Dorking and Chessington South - London

		SW	SW	SW	SW	SW	SW	SW	SW	SW	SW	SW
								FO	FX	FO	FX	
										◇1	◇1	
								A	A	B	B	
Guildford	d	22 46	22 55			23 07				23 39	23 39	
London Road (Guildford)	d	22 50				23 11						
Clandon	d	22 55				23 16						
Horsley	d	22 59				23 20						
Effingham Junction	d	23 03				23 23						
Bookham	d	23 06										
Cobham & Stoke d'Abernon	d					23 27						
Oxshott	d					23 30						
Claygate	d					23 33						
Hinchley Wood	d					23 36						
Hampton Court	d				23 24							23 59
Thames Ditton	d				23 26							00 02
Surbiton	d		23 30		23a32	23 41				00 08	00 08	00 12
Berrylands	d					23 43						00 14
Shepperton	d			23 11								
Upper Halliford	d			23 14								
Sunbury	d			23 16								
Kempton Park	d			23 18								
Hampton	d			23 21								
Fulwell	d			23 24								
Strawberry Hill	d							23 37	23 37			
Teddington	d			23 29				23 41	23 41			
Hampton Wick	d			23 31				23 44	23 44			
Kingston	a			23 33				23 46	23 46			
	d			23 34				23 49	23 49			
Norbiton	d			23 36				23 51	23 51			
New Malden	d			23 41		23 46		23 55	23 55			00 17
Dorking 182	d											
Box Hill & Westhumble 182	d											
Leatherhead 182	d	23 11										
Ashtead 182	d	23 14										
Epsom 182	a	23 19										
	d	23 19										
Ewell West	d	23 22										
Stoneleigh	d	23 24										
Worcester Park	d	23 27										
Chessington South	d						23 40					
Chessington North	d						23 42					
Tolworth	d						23 44					
Malden Manor	d						23 47					
Motspur Park	d	23 30					23 50					
Raynes Park	d	23 37		23 43		23 49	23 54	23 58	23 58			00 20
Wimbledon ⊖	d	23 41	23 37	23 50		23 53	23a57	00 02	00 02	00 16	00 16	00a23
Earlsfield	d	23 44	23 41	23 53		23 56		00 05	00 05			
Clapham Junction	d	23 48	23 45	23 57		23 59		00 09	00 09	00 23	00 23	
Vauxhall ⊖	d	23 53	23 50	00 02		00 05		00 14	00 15			
London Waterloo ⊖	a	23 58	23 54	00 08		00 13		00 22	00 22	00 32	00 33	

A From London Waterloo
B From Portsmouth Harbour

Table T152-R

Mondays to Fridays

8 October to 7 December

Hampton Court, Shepperton, Guildford, Dorking and Chessington South - London

		SW	SW	SW	SW	SW	SW	SW	SW	SW	SW	SW	SW	SW	SW	SW	SW	SW	SW	SW	SW	SW	SW
		MO	MX	MX	MX	MO	MX	MX	MX														
								◇1							◇					◇			
		A	B	C	D	D	D	E	A		F								D	G			
Guildford	d									04 20		04 58			05 14		05 34						
London Road (Guildford)	d											05 02					05 38						
Clandon	d											05 07					05 43						
Horsley	d											05 11					05 47						
Effingham Junction	d											05 15					05 50						
Bookham	d											05 18											
Cobham & Stoke d'Abernon	d																05 54						
Oxshott	d																05 57						
Claygate	d																06 00						
Hinchley Wood	d																06 03						
Hampton Court	d															05 54						06 23	
Thames Ditton	d								00 02							05 56						06 25	
Surbiton	d							00 08	00 12	04 54					05 56	06 02	06 11			06 28		06 31	
Berrylands	d								00 14							06 04						06 34	
Shepperton	d												05 23										06 10
Upper Halliford	d												05 26										06 13
Sunbury	d												05 28										06 15
Kempton Park	d																						
Hampton	d												05 33										06 20
Fulwell	d												05 36										06 23
Strawberry Hill	d				00 09	00 15					04 55		05 38						06 07				
Teddington	d				00 12	00 18					04 59			05 44					06 11				06 28
Hampton Wick	d				00 14	00 21					05 01			05 46					06 14				06 30
Kingston	a				00 16	00 23					05 03			05 48					06 16				06 32
	d										05 04			05 49					06 19				06 33
Norbiton	d										05 06			05 51					06 21				06 35
New Malden	d								00 17		05 10			05 55		06 07			06 25			06 37	06 40
Dorking 182	d																	05 47					
Box Hill & Westhumble 182	d																	05 50					
Leatherhead 182	d											05 23						05 56					
Ashtead 182	d											05 27						05 59					
Epsom 182	a											05 31						06 04					
	d											05 33						06 04			06 18		
Ewell West	d											05 36						06 07			06 21		
Stoneleigh	d											05 39						06 10			06 24		
Worcester Park	d											05 41						06 12			06 27		
Chessington South	d																						
Chessington North	d																						
Tolworth	d																						
Malden Manor	d																						
Motspur Park	d											05 45						06 16			06 30		
Raynes Park	d	00 01							00 20		05 13	05 49		05 58		06 10		06 19	06 28		06 34	06 40	06 43
Wimbledon ⊖	d	00a04						00 16	00a23	05 02	05 17	05 53		06 02	06 05	06 14	06 20	06 23	06 32	06 35	06 38	06 44	06 47
Earlsfield	d										05 21	05 58		06 05	06 08	06 17	06 24	06 27	06 35	06 39	06 42	06 48	06 51
Clapham Junction	d						00 05	00 23		05 09	05 25	06 02	06 05	06 09	06 12	06 21	06 28	06 31	06 39	06 43	06 46	06 52	06 55
Vauxhall ⊖	d		00 02	00 05			00 12				05 31	06 07	06 12	06 14	06 17	06 26	06 33	06 36	06 44	06 48	06 51	06 57	07 00
London Waterloo ⊖	a		00 08	00 13			00 16	00 33		05 18	05 35	06 11	06 16	06 20	06 22	06 31	06 37	06 40	06 49	06 53	06 56	07 03	07 06

A From Hampton Court
B From Shepperton
C From Guildford
D From London Waterloo
E From Portsmouth Harbour
F From Twickenham
G From Woking

Table T152-R

Mondays to Fridays

8 October to 7 December

Hampton Court, Shepperton, Guildford, Dorking and Chessington South - London

		SW	SW	SW	SW	SW	SW	SW	SW	SW	SW	TL	SW	SW	SW	SW	SW	SW	SW	SW	SW	SW	SW
					A	◇ B						C	D		A								
Guildford	d	05 58	06 01							06 28	06 31	06 39										06 58	07 03
London Road (Guildford)	d	06 02	06 05							06 32	06 35	06 42										07 02	07 07
Clandon	d	06 07	06 10							06 37	06 40	06 47										07 07	07 12
Horsley	d	06 11	06 15							06 41	06 47	06 52										07 11	07 17
Effingham Junction	d	06 15	06 19							06 46	06 51	06 55										07 16	07 21
Bookham	d	06 18								06 49		06 59										07 19	
Cobham & Stoke d'Abernon	d		06 22								06 54												07 24
Oxshott	d		06 26								06 58												07 28
Claygate	d		06 29								07 01												07 31
Hinchley Wood	d		06 32								07 04												07 34
Hampton Court	d							06 53												07 23			
Thames Ditton	d							06 55												07 25			
Surbiton	d		06 41			06 57		07 01			07 11									07 31			07 41
Berrylands	d							07 03												07 33			
Shepperton	d								06 40										07 00		07 11		
Upper Halliford	d								06 43										07 03		07 14		
Sunbury	d								06 45										07 05		07 16		
Kempton Park	d																						
Hampton	d								06 50										07 09		07 20		
Fulwell	d								06 53										07 12		07 23		
Strawberry Hill	d				06 37										07 07				07 14				
Teddington	d				06 41				06 58						07 11		07 19				07 28		
Hampton Wick	d				06 44				07 00						07 14		07 21				07 30		
Kingston	a				06 46				07 02						07 16		07 23				07 32		
	d				06 48				07 03						07 18		07 25				07 33		
Norbiton	d				06 50				07 05						07 20		07 27				07 35		
New Malden	d				06 55			07 06	07 09						07 25		07 31			07 37	07 40		07 45
Dorking	182 d						06 30									07 01							
Box Hill & Westhumble	182 d						06 33									07 04							
Leatherhead	182 d	06 23					06 38			06 54		07 05				07 09						07 24	
Ashtead	182 d	06 27					06 42			06 57		07 09				07 13						07 27	
Epsom	182 a	06 31					06 46			07 02		07 13				07 17						07 32	
	d	06 33					06 47			07 03						07 18		07 22				07 34	
Ewell West	d	06 36					06 50			07 06								07 25				07 37	
Stoneleigh	d	06 39					06 52			07 09								07 27				07 40	
Worcester Park	d	06 41					06 55			07 11						07 24		07 30				07 43	
Chessington South	d			06 38										07 08									
Chessington North	d			06 40										07 10									
Tolworth	d			06 43										07 13									
Malden Manor	d			06 45										07 15									
Motspur Park	d	06 45		06 50			06 59			07 14				07 20				07 33				07 46	
Raynes Park	d	06 49		06 54	06 58		07 04	07 09	07 12	07 18			07 21	07 24	07 28	07 31	07 34	07 37		07 40	07 43	07 50	
Wimbledon ⊖	d	06 53	06 50	06 58	07 02	07 05	07 08	07 13	07 16	07 22	07 19		07 25	07 28	07 32	07 35	07 38	07 41		07 44	07 47	07 54	07 50
Earlsfield	d	06 57	06 54	07 02	07 06	07 09	07 12	07 17	07 20	07 26	07 23		07 29	07 32	07 36	07 39	07 42	07 45		07 48	07 51	07 58	07 54
Clapham Junction	d	07 01	06 58	07 06	07 10	07 13	07 16	07 21	07 24	07 30	07 27			07 36	07 40	07 43	07 46	07 49	07 49	07 52	07 55	08 02	07 58
Vauxhall ⊖	d	07 06	07 03	07 11	07 15	07 18	07 21	07 26	07 29	07 35	07 32			07 41	07 45	07 48	07 51	07 54	07 56	07 57	08 00	08 07	08 03
London Waterloo ⊖	a	07 12	07 09	07 18	07 22	07 24	07 27	07 33	07 35	07 41	07 39		07 43	07 48	07 51	07 56	07 58	08 00	08 04	08 02	08 06	08 13	08 10

A From London Waterloo
B From Woking
C To London Bridge
D From Esher

Table T152-R

Mondays to Fridays

8 October to 7 December

Hampton Court, Shepperton, Guildford, Dorking and Chessington South - London

		TL	SW	SW	SW	SW	SW	SW	SW	SW	SW	SW	SW	SW	SW	SW	SW	SW	SW	SW	SW	SW
		A			B			C							B			D				
Guildford	d	07 12	07 15										07 32									07 58
London Road (Guildford)	d	07 15	07 19										07 36									08 02
Clandon	d		07 24										07 41									08 07
Horsley	d		07 27										07 45									08 11
Effingham Junction	d	07 25	07 31									07 46	07 49									08 16
Bookham	d	07 29										07 49										08 19
Cobham & Stoke d'Abernon	d		07 34										07 52									
Oxshott	d		07 38										07 56									
Claygate	d		07 41										07 59									
Hinchley Wood	d		07 44										08 02									
Hampton Court	d									07 53										08 23		
Thames Ditton	d									07 55										08 25		
Surbiton	d		07 53							08 01			08 11							08 31		
Berrylands	d									08 03										08 33		
Shepperton	d						07 30				07 41						08 00				08 11	
Upper Halliford	d						07 33				07 44						08 03				08 14	
Sunbury	d						07 35				07 46						08 05				08 16	
Kempton Park	d																					
Hampton	d						07 39				07 50						08 09				08 20	
Fulwell	d						07 42				07 53						08 12				08 23	
Strawberry Hill	d				07 37		07 44	07 46							08 07		08 14	08 16				
Teddington	d				07 41			07 49			07 58				08 11			08 19			08 28	
Hampton Wick	d				07 44			07 51			08 00				08 14			08 21			08 30	
Kingston	a				07 46			07 53			08 02				08 16			08 23			08 32	
	d				07 48			07 55			08 03				08 18			08 25			08 33	
Norbiton	d				07 50			07 57			08 05				08 20			08 27			08 35	
New Malden	d				07 55			08 01		08 06	08 10		08 15		08 25			08 31		08 36	08 40	
Dorking	182 d					07 32										08 00						
Box Hill & Westhumble	182 d					07 35										08 03						
Leatherhead	182 d	07 35				07 40						07 55				08 08						08 24
Ashtead	182 d	07 39				07 43						07 58				08 12						08 27
Epsom	182 a	07 44				07 48						08 03				08 16						08 32
	d					07 48			07 52			08 04				08 17			08 22			08 34
Ewell West	d								07 55			08 07							08 25			08 37
Stoneleigh	d								07 57			08 09							08 27			08 39
Worcester Park	d					07 54			08 00			08 12				08 24			08 30			08 42
Chessington South	d			07 38										08 08								
Chessington North	d			07 40										08 10								
Tolworth	d			07 43										08 13								
Malden Manor	d			07 45										08 15								
Motspur Park	d			07 50					08 03			08 16		08 20					08 33			08 45
Raynes Park	d			07 54	07 58	08 01		08 04	08 07	08 10	08 13	08 20		08 24	08 28	08 31		08 34	08 37	08 40	08 43	08 49
Wimbledon ⊖	d			07 58	08 02	08 05		08 08	08 11	08 14	08 17	08 24	08 20	08 28	08 32	08 35		08 38	08 41	08 44	08 47	08 53
Earlsfield	d			08 02	08 06	08 09		08 12	08 15	08 18	08 21	08 28	08 24	08 32	08 36	08 39		08 42	08 45	08 48	08 51	08 57
Clapham Junction	d			08 06	08 10	08 13	08 19	08 16	08 19	08 22	08 25	08 32	08 28	08 36	08 40	08 43	08 49	08 46	08 49	08 52	08 55	09 01
Vauxhall ⊖	d			08 11	08 15	08 18	08 26	08 21	08 24	08 27	08 30	08 37	08 33	08 41	08 45	08 48	08 56	08 51	08 54	08 57	09 00	09 06
London Waterloo ⊖	a		08 13	08 18	08 21	08 24	08 34	08 27	08 30	08 33	08 36	08 43	08 40	08 48	08 51	08 54	09 04	08 57	09 00	09 03	09 06	09 13

A To London Bridge
B From London Waterloo
C From Twickenham
D From Clapham Junction

Table T152-R

Mondays to Fridays

8 October to 7 December

Hampton Court, Shepperton, Guildford, Dorking and Chessington South - London

		SW	SW	SW A	SW ◇	SW	SW	SW	SW	SW	SW	SW	SW A	SW ◇	SW	SW	SW	SW	SW	SW	SW A	SW B	SW
Guildford	d	08 03			08 22					08 31				08 46				08 58	09 04				
London Road (Guildford)	d	08 07								08 35								09 02	09 08				
Clandon	d	08 12								08 40								09 07	09 13				
Horsley	d	08 17								08 44								09 11	09 17				
Effingham Junction	d	08 21							08 46	08 51								09 15	09 23				
Bookham	d								08 49									09 18					
Cobham & Stoke d'Abernon	d	08 24								08 54									09 27				
Oxshott	d	08 28								08 58									09 30				
Claygate	d	08 31								09 01									09 33				
Hinchley Wood	d	08 34								09 04									09 36				
Hampton Court	d						08 53									09 23							
Thames Ditton	d						08 55									09 25							
Surbiton	d	08 42			08 57		09 01			09 11				09 27		09 31			09 41			09 57	
Berrylands	d						09 03									09 33							
Shepperton	d							08 41									09 11						
Upper Halliford	d							08 44									09 14						
Sunbury	d							08 46									09 16						
Kempton Park	d																09 18						
Hampton	d							08 50									09 21						
Fulwell	d							08 53									09 24						
Strawberry Hill	d			08 38									09 08								09 37		
Teddington	d			08 41				08 58					09 12				09 29				09 41		
Hampton Wick	d			08 44				09 00					09 14				09 31				09 44		
Kingston	a			08 46				09 02					09 16				09 33				09 46		
	d			08 48				09 03					09 18				09 34				09 48		
Norbiton	d			08 50				09 05					09 20				09 36				09 50		
New Malden	d			08 55			09 06	09 10					09 25			09 36	09 40				09 55		
Dorking 182	d					08 30									09 00								09 33
Box Hill & Westhumble 182	d					08 33									09 03								
Leatherhead 182	d					08 38			08 54						09 08			09 23					09 39
Ashtead 182	d					08 41			08 57						09 11			09 27					09 43
Epsom 182	a					08 46			09 02						09 16			09 31					09 47
	d					08 47			09 04						09 17			09 34					09 49
Ewell West	d					08 50			09 07						09 20			09 37					09 52
Stoneleigh	d					08 53			09 10						09 23			09 39					09 54
Worcester Park	d					08 56			09 12						09 26			09 42					09 57
Chessington South	d		08 38									09 08								09 38			
Chessington North	d		08 40									09 10								09 40			
Tolworth	d		08 43									09 13								09 43			
Malden Manor	d		08 45									09 15								09 45			
Motspur Park	d		08 50			08 59			09 15			09 20			09 29			09 45		09 49			10 00
Raynes Park	d		08 54	08 58		09 04	09 10	09 13	09 19		09 22	09 24	09 28		09 34	09 40	09 43	09 49		09 53	09 58		10 04
Wimbledon ⊖	d		08 58	09 02	09 05	09 08	09 14	09 17	09 23	09 20	09 26	09 29	09 32	09 35	09 38	09 44	09 47	09 53	09 50	09 57	10 02	10 05	10 08
Earlsfield	d		09 02	09 06	09 09	09 12	09 18	09 21	09 27	09 24	09 30	09 32	09 36	09 39	09 42	09 47	09 50	09 57	09 54	10 01	10 05	10 08	10 12
Clapham Junction	d		09 06	09 10	09 13	09 16	09 22	09 25	09 31	09 28		09 36	09 40	09 43	09 46	09 51	09 54	10 01	09 58	10 05	10 09	10 12	10 16
Vauxhall ⊖	d		09 11	09 15	09 18	09 21	09 27	09 30	09 36	09 33		09 41	09 45	09 48	09 51	09 56	09 59	10 06	10 03	10 10	10 14	10 17	10 21
London Waterloo ⊖	a	09 01	09 18	09 22	09 24	09 27	09 33	09 36	09 42	09 39	09 46	09 47	09 51	09 54	09 57	10 01	10 04	10 10	10 07	10 16	10 19	10 23	10 25

A From London Waterloo
B From Woking

Table T152-R

Mondays to Fridays

8 October to 7 December

Hampton Court, Shepperton, Guildford, Dorking and Chessington South - London

		SW	SW	SW	SW	SW	SW A	SW B	SW	SW	SW	SW	SW	SW	SW A	SW B	SW	SW	SW	SW	SW	SW
Guildford	d			09 28	09 34							09 58	10 04							10 28	10 34	
London Road (Guildford)	d			09 32	09 38							10 02	10 08							10 32	10 38	
Clandon	d			09 37	09 43							10 07	10 13							10 37	10 43	
Horsley	d			09 41	09 47							10 11	10 17							10 41	10 47	
Effingham Junction	d			09 45	09 50							10 15	10 20							10 45	10 52	
Bookham	d			09 48								10 18								10 48		
Cobham & Stoke d'Abernon	d				09 54								10 24								10 56	
Oxshott	d				09 57								10 27								10 59	
Claygate	d				10 00								10 30								11 02	
Hinchley Wood	d				10 03								10 33								11 05	
Hampton Court	d	09 54								10 24								10 54				
Thames Ditton	d	09 56								10 26								10 56				
Surbiton	d	10 02			10 11			10 27		10 32			10 41			10 57		11 02			11 11	
Berrylands	d	10 04								10 34								11 04				
Shepperton	d		09 41								10 11								10 41			
Upper Halliford	d		09 44								10 14								10 44			
Sunbury	d		09 46								10 16								10 46			
Kempton Park	d		09 48								10 18								10 48			
Hampton	d		09 51								10 21								10 51			
Fulwell	d		09 54								10 24								10 54			
Strawberry Hill	d						10 07								10 37							
Teddington	d		09 59				10 11				10 29				10 41				10 59			
Hampton Wick	d		10 01				10 14				10 31				10 44				11 01			
Kingston	a		10 03				10 16				10 33				10 46				11 03			
	d		10 04				10 18				10 34				10 48				11 04			
Norbiton	d		10 06				10 20				10 36				10 50				11 06			
New Malden	d	10 07	10 10				10 25			10 37	10 40				10 55			11 07	11 10			
Dorking 182	d								10 03								10 33					
Box Hill & Westhumble 182	d																					
Leatherhead 182	d			09 53					10 09			10 23					10 39			10 53		
Ashtead 182	d			09 57					10 13			10 27					10 43			10 57		
Epsom 182	a			10 01					10 17			10 31					10 47			11 01		
	d			10 04					10 19			10 34					10 49			11 04		
Ewell West	d			10 07					10 22			10 37					10 52			11 07		
Stoneleigh	d			10 09					10 24			10 39					10 54			11 09		
Worcester Park	d			10 12					10 27			10 42					10 57			11 12		
Chessington South	d					10 08								10 38								11 08
Chessington North	d					10 10								10 40								11 10
Tolworth	d					10 13								10 43								11 13
Malden Manor	d					10 15								10 45								11 15
Motspur Park	d			10 15		10 19			10 30			10 45		10 49			11 00			11 15		11 19
Raynes Park	d	10 10	10 13	10 19		10 23	10 28		10 34	10 40	10 43	10 49		10 53	10 58		11 04	11 10	11 13	11 19		11 23
Wimbledon ⊖	d	10 14	10 17	10 23	10 20	10 27	10 32	10 35	10 38	10 44	10 47	10 53	10 50	10 57	11 02	11 05	11 08	11 14	11 17	11 23	11 20	11 27
Earlsfield	d	10 17	10 20	10 27	10 24	10 31	10 35	10 38	10 42	10 47	10 50	10 57	10 54	11 01	11 05	11 08	11 12	11 17	11 20	11 27	11 24	11 31
Clapham Junction	d	10 21	10 24	10 31	10 28	10 35	10 39	10 42	10 46	10 51	10 54	11 01	10 58	11 05	11 09	11 12	11 16	11 21	11 24	11 31	11 28	11 35
Vauxhall ⊖	d	10 26	10 29	10 36	10 33	10 40	10 44	10 47	10 51	10 56	10 59	11 06	11 03	11 10	11 14	11 17	11 21	11 26	11 29	11 36	11 33	11 40
London Waterloo ⊖	a	10 31	10 34	10 40	10 37	10 46	10 49	10 52	10 55	11 01	11 04	11 10	11 07	11 16	11 19	11 22	11 25	11 31	11 34	11 40	11 37	11 46

A From London Waterloo
B From Woking

Table T152-R

Mondays to Fridays

8 October to 7 December

Hampton Court, Shepperton, Guildford, Dorking and Chessington South - London

		SW A	SW B	SW	SW	SW	SW	SW	SW	SW A	SW B	SW	SW	SW	SW	SW	SW	SW A	SW B	SW	SW	SW	SW
Guildford	d						10 58	11 04							11 28	11 34							11 58
London Road (Guildford)	d						11 02	11 08							11 32	11 38							12 02
Clandon	d						11 07	11 13							11 37	11 43							12 07
Horsley	d						11 11	11 17							11 41	11 47							12 11
Effingham Junction	d						11 15	11 20							11 45	11 50							12 15
Bookham	d						11 18								11 48								12 18
Cobham & Stoke d'Abernon	d							11 24								11 54							
Oxshott	d							11 27								11 57							
Claygate	d							11 30								12 00							
Hinchley Wood	d							11 33								12 03							
Hampton Court	d				11 24								11 54								12 24		
Thames Ditton	d				11 26								11 56								12 26		
Surbiton	d		11 27		11 32			11 41			11 57		12 02			12 11			12 27		12 32		
Berrylands	d				11 34								12 04								12 34		
Shepperton	d					11 11								11 41								12 11	
Upper Halliford	d					11 14								11 44								12 14	
Sunbury	d					11 16								11 46								12 16	
Kempton Park	d					11 18								11 48								12 18	
Hampton	d					11 21								11 51								12 21	
Fulwell	d					11 24								11 54								12 24	
Strawberry Hill	d	11 07								11 37								12 07					
Teddington	d	11 11				11 29				11 41				11 59				12 11				12 29	
Hampton Wick	d	11 14				11 31				11 44				12 01				12 14				12 31	
Kingston	a	11 16				11 33				11 46				12 03				12 16				12 33	
	d	11 18				11 34				11 48				12 04				12 18				12 34	
Norbiton	d	11 20				11 36				11 50				12 06				12 20				12 36	
New Malden	d	11 25			11 37	11 40				11 55			12 07	12 10				12 25			12 37	12 40	
Dorking 182	d			11 03								11 33								12 03			
Box Hill & Westhumble 182	d																						
Leatherhead 182	d			11 09			11 23					11 39			11 53					12 09			12 23
Ashtead 182	d			11 13			11 27					11 43			11 57					12 13			12 27
Epsom 182	a			11 17			11 31					11 47			12 01					12 17			12 31
	d			11 19			11 34					11 49			12 04					12 19			12 34
Ewell West	d			11 22			11 37					11 52			12 07					12 22			12 37
Stoneleigh	d			11 24			11 39					11 54			12 09					12 24			12 39
Worcester Park	d			11 27			11 42					11 57			12 12					12 27			12 42
Chessington South	d								11 38								12 08						
Chessington North	d								11 40								12 10						
Tolworth	d								11 43								12 13						
Malden Manor	d								11 45								12 15						
Motspur Park	d			11 30			11 45		11 49			12 00			12 15		12 19			12 30			12 45
Raynes Park	d	11 28		11 34	11 40	11 43	11 49		11 53	11 58		12 04	12 10	12 13	12 19		12 23	12 28		12 34	12 40	12 43	12 49
Wimbledon ⊖ ⛴	d	11 32	11 35	11 38	11 44	11 47	11 53	11 50	11 57	12 02	12 05	12 08	12 14	12 16	12 23	12 20	12 27	12 32	12 35	12 38	12 44	12 47	12 53
Earlsfield	d	11 35	11 38	11 42	11 47	11 50	11 57	11 54	12 01	12 05	12 08	12 12	12 17	12 20	12 27	12 24	12 31	12 35	12 38	12 42	12 47	12 50	12 57
Clapham Junction	d	11 39	11 42	11 46	11 51	11 54	12 01	11 58	12 05	12 09	12 12	12 16	12 21	12 24	12 31	12 28	12 35	12 39	12 42	12 46	12 51	12 54	13 01
Vauxhall ⊖	d	11 44	11 47	11 51	11 56	11 59	12 06	12 03	12 10	12 14	12 17	12 21	12 26	12 29	12 36	12 33	12 40	12 44	12 47	12 51	12 56	12 59	13 06
London Waterloo ⊖	a	11 49	11 52	11 55	12 01	12 04	12 10	12 07	12 16	12 19	12 22	12 25	12 31	12 34	12 40	12 37	12 46	12 49	12 52	12 55	13 01	13 04	13 10

A From London Waterloo   B From Woking

Table T152-R

Mondays to Fridays

8 October to 7 December

Hampton Court, Shepperton, Guildford, Dorking and Chessington South - London

		SW	SW	SW A	SW B	SW	SW	SW	SW	SW	SW	SW A	SW B	SW	SW	SW	SW	SW	SW	SW A	SW B	SW	SW
Guildford	d	12 04							12 28	12 34							12 58	13 04					
London Road (Guildford)	d	12 08							12 32	12 38							13 02	13 08					
Clandon	d	12 13							12 37	12 43							13 07	13 13					
Horsley	d	12 17							12 41	12 47							13 11	13 17					
Effingham Junction	d	12 20							12 45	12 50							13 15	13 23					
Bookham	d								12 48								13 18						
Cobham & Stoke d'Abernon	d	12 24								12 54								13 27					
Oxshott	d	12 27								12 57								13 30					
Claygate	d	12 30								13 00								13 33					
Hinchley Wood	d	12 33								13 03								13 36					
Hampton Court	d						12 54								13 24								13 54
Thames Ditton	d						12 56								13 26								13 56
Surbiton	d	12 41			12 57		13 02			13 11			13 27		13 32			13 41			13 57		14 02
Berrylands	d						13 04								13 34								14 04
Shepperton	d							12 41								13 11							
Upper Halliford	d							12 44								13 14							
Sunbury	d							12 46								13 16							
Kempton Park	d							12 48								13 18							
Hampton	d							12 51								13 21							
Fulwell	d							12 54								13 24							
Strawberry Hill	d			12 37								13 07								13 37			
Teddington	d			12 41				12 59				13 11				13 29				13 41			
Hampton Wick	d			12 44				13 01				13 14				13 31				13 44			
Kingston	a			12 46				13 03				13 16				13 33				13 46			
	d			12 48				13 04				13 18				13 34				13 48			
Norbiton	d			12 50				13 06				13 20				13 36				13 50			
New Malden	d			12 55			13 07	13 10				13 25			13 37	13 40				13 55			14 07
Dorking 182	d					12 33								13 03								13 33	
Box Hill & Westhumble 182	d																						
Leatherhead 182	d					12 39			12 53					13 09			13 23					13 39	
Ashtead 182	d					12 43			12 57					13 13			13 27					13 43	
Epsom 182	a					12 47			13 01					13 17			13 31					13 47	
	d					12 49			13 04					13 19			13 34					13 49	
Ewell West	d					12 52			13 07					13 22			13 37					13 52	
Stoneleigh	d					12 54			13 09					13 24			13 39					13 54	
Worcester Park	d					12 57			13 12					13 27			13 42					13 57	
Chessington South	d		12 38								13 08								13 38				
Chessington North	d		12 40								13 10								13 40				
Tolworth	d		12 43								13 13								13 43				
Malden Manor	d		12 45								13 15								13 45				
Motspur Park	d		12 49			13 00			13 15		13 19			13 30			13 45		13 49			14 00	
Raynes Park	d		12 53	12 58		13 04	13 10	13 13	13 19		13 23	13 28		13 34	13 40	13 43	13 49		13 53	13 58		14 04	14 10
Wimbledon ⊖ ⛴	d	12 50	12 57	13 02	13 05	13 08	13 14	13 17	13 23	13 20	13 27	13 32	13 35	13 38	13 44	13 47	13 53	13 50	13 57	14 02	14 05	14 08	14 14
Earlsfield	d	12 54	13 01	13 05	13 08	13 12	13 17	13 20	13 27	13 24	13 31	13 35	13 38	13 42	13 47	13 50	13 57	13 54	14 01	14 05	14 08	14 12	14 17
Clapham Junction	d	12 58	13 05	13 09	13 12	13 16	13 21	13 24	13 31	13 28	13 35	13 39	13 42	13 46	13 51	13 54	14 01	13 58	14 05	14 09	14 12	14 16	14 21
Vauxhall ⊖	d	13 03	13 10	13 14	13 17	13 21	13 26	13 29	13 36	13 33	13 40	13 44	13 47	13 51	13 56	13 59	14 06	14 03	14 10	14 14	14 17	14 21	14 26
London Waterloo ⊖	a	13 07	13 16	13 19	13 22	13 25	13 31	13 34	13 40	13 37	13 46	13 49	13 52	13 55	14 01	14 04	14 10	14 07	14 16	14 19	14 22	14 25	14 31

A From London Waterloo   B From Woking

Table T152-R

Mondays to Fridays

8 October to 7 December

Hampton Court, Shepperton, Guildford, Dorking and Chessington South - London

		SW		SW	SW	SW	SW	SW	SW	SW	SW	SW		SW	SW	SW	SW	SW	SW	SW	SW	SW		SW	SW
							A	B								A	B								A
Guildford	d			13 28	13 34							13 58		14 04							14 28	14 34			
London Road (Guildford)	d			13 32	13 38							14 02		14 08							14 32	14 38			
Clandon	d			13 37	13 43							14 07		14 13							14 37	14 43			
Horsley	d			13 41	13 47							14 11		14 17							14 41	14 47			
Effingham Junction	d			13 45	13 50							14 15		14 20							14 45	14 50			
Bookham	d			13 48								14 18									14 48				
Cobham & Stoke d'Abernon	d				13 54									14 24								14 54			
Oxshott	d				13 57									14 27								14 57			
Claygate	d				14 00									14 30								15 00			
Hinchley Wood	d				14 03									14 33								15 03			
Hampton Court	d									14 24									14 54						
Thames Ditton	d									14 26									14 56						
Surbiton	d				14 11			14 27		14 32				14 41			14 57		15 02			15 11			
Berrylands	d									14 34									15 04						
Shepperton	d	13 41									14 11									14 41					
Upper Halliford	d	13 44									14 14									14 44					
Sunbury	d	13 46									14 16									14 46					
Kempton Park	d	13 48									14 18									14 48					
Hampton	d	13 51									14 21									14 51					
Fulwell	d	13 54									14 24									14 54					
Strawberry Hill	d						14 07									14 37									15 07
Teddington	d	13 59					14 11				14 29					14 41				14 59					15 11
Hampton Wick	d	14 01					14 14				14 31					14 44				15 01					15 14
Kingston	a	14 03					14 16				14 33					14 46				15 03					15 16
	d	14 04					14 18				14 34					14 48				15 04					15 18
Norbiton	d	14 06					14 20				14 36					14 50				15 06					15 20
New Malden	d	14 10					14 25			14 37	14 40					14 55			15 07	15 10					15 25
Dorking	182 d								14 02									14 33							
Box Hill & Westhumble	182 d																								
Leatherhead	182 d			13 53					14 08			14 23						14 39			14 53				
Ashtead	182 d			13 57					14 12			14 27						14 43			14 57				
Epsom	182 a			14 01					14 16			14 31						14 47			15 01				
	d			14 04					14 19			14 34						14 49			15 04				
Ewell West	d			14 07					14 22			14 37						14 52			15 07				
Stoneleigh	d			14 09					14 24			14 39						14 54			15 09				
Worcester Park	d			14 12					14 27			14 42						14 57			15 12				
Chessington South	d					14 08									14 38									15 08	
Chessington North	d					14 10									14 40									15 10	
Tolworth	d					14 13									14 43									15 13	
Malden Manor	d					14 15									14 45									15 15	
Motspur Park	d			14 15		14 19			14 30			14 45			14 49			15 00			15 15			15 19	
Raynes Park	d	14 13		14 19		14 23	14 28		14 34	14 40	14 43	14 49			14 53	14 58		15 04	15 10	15 13	15 19			15 23	15 28
Wimbledon	d	14 17		14 23	14 20	14 27	14 32	14 35	14 38	14 44	14 47	14 53		14 50	14 57	15 02	15 05	15 08	15 14	15 17	15 23	15 20		15 27	15 32
Earlsfield	d	14 20		14 27	14 24	14 31	14 35	14 38	14 42	14 47	14 50	14 57		14 54	15 01	15 05	15 08	15 12	15 17	15 20	15 27	15 24		15 31	15 35
Clapham Junction	d	14 24		14 31	14 28	14 35	14 39	14 42	14 46	14 51	14 54	15 01		14 58	15 05	15 09	15 12	15 16	15 21	15 24	15 31	15 28		15 35	15 39
Vauxhall	d	14 29		14 36	14 33	14 40	14 44	14 47	14 51	14 56	14 59	15 06		15 03	15 10	15 14	15 17	15 21	15 26	15 29	15 36	15 33		15 40	15 44
London Waterloo	a	14 34		14 40	14 37	14 46	14 49	14 52	14 55	15 01	15 04	15 10		15 07	15 16	15 19	15 22	15 25	15 31	15 34	15 40	15 37		15 46	15 49

A From London Waterloo B From Woking

Table T152-R

Mondays to Fridays

8 October to 7 December

Hampton Court, Shepperton, Guildford, Dorking and Chessington South - London

		SW	SW	SW	SW	SW	SW	SW		SW	SW	SW	SW	SW	SW	SW	SW	SW		SW	SW	SW	SW	SW	SW
		A								B	A							B		A					
Guildford	d					14 58	15 04								15 28	15 34								15 58	16 04
London Road (Guildford)	d					15 02	15 08								15 32	15 38								16 02	16 08
Clandon	d					15 07	15 13								15 37	15 43								16 07	16 13
Horsley	d					15 11	15 17								15 41	15 47								16 11	16 17
Effingham Junction	d					15 15	15 20								15 45	15 50								16 15	16 20
Bookham	d					15 18									15 48									16 18	
Cobham & Stoke d'Abernon	d						15 24									15 54									16 24
Oxshott	d						15 27									15 57									16 27
Claygate	d						15 30									16 00									16 30
Hinchley Wood	d						15 33									16 03									16 33
Hampton Court	d			15 24									15 54									16 24			
Thames Ditton	d			15 26									15 56									16 26			
Surbiton	d	15 27		15 32			15 41				15 57		16 02			16 11				16 27		16 32			16 41
Berrylands	d			15 34									16 04									16 34			
Shepperton	d				15 11									15 41									16 11		
Upper Halliford	d				15 14									15 44									16 14		
Sunbury	d				15 16									15 46									16 16		
Kempton Park	d				15 18									15 48									16 18		
Hampton	d				15 21									15 51									16 21		
Fulwell	d				15 24									15 54									16 24		
Strawberry Hill	d									15 37								16 07							
Teddington	d				15 29					15 41				15 59				16 11					16 29		
Hampton Wick	d				15 31					15 44				16 01				16 14					16 31		
Kingston	a				15 33					15 46				16 03				16 16					16 33		
	d				15 34					15 48				16 04				16 18					16 34		
Norbiton	d				15 36					15 50				16 06				16 20					16 36		
New Malden	d			15 37	15 40					15 55			16 07	16 10				16 25				16 37	16 40		
Dorking	182 d		15 03									15 33									16 03				
Box Hill & Westhumble	182 d																								
Leatherhead	182 d		15 09			15 23						15 39			15 53						16 09			16 23	
Ashtead	182 d		15 13			15 27						15 43			15 57						16 13			16 27	
Epsom	182 a		15 17			15 31						15 47			16 01						16 17			16 31	
	d		15 19			15 34						15 49			16 04						16 19			16 34	
Ewell West	d		15 22			15 37						15 52			16 07						16 22			16 37	
Stoneleigh	d		15 24			15 39						15 54			16 09						16 24			16 39	
Worcester Park	d		15 27			15 42						15 57			16 12						16 27			16 42	
Chessington South	d							15 38									16 08								
Chessington North	d							15 40									16 10								
Tolworth	d							15 43									16 13								
Malden Manor	d							15 45									16 15								
Motspur Park	d		15 30			15 45		15 49				16 00			16 15		16 19				16 30			16 45	
Raynes Park	d		15 34	15 40	15 43	15 49		15 53		15 58		16 04	16 10	16 13	16 19		16 23	16 28			16 34	16 40	16 43	16 49	
Wimbledon	d	15 35	15 38	15 44	15 47	15 53	15 50	15 57		16 02	16 05	16 08	16 14	16 17	16 23	16 20	16 27	16 32		16 35	16 38	16 44	16 47	16 53	16 50
Earlsfield	d	15 38	15 42	15 47	15 50	15 57	15 54	16 01		16 05	16 08	16 12	16 17	16 20	16 27	16 24	16 31	16 35		16 38	16 42	16 47	16 50	16 57	16 54
Clapham Junction	d	15 42	15 46	15 51	15 54	16 01	15 58	16 05		16 09	16 12	16 16	16 21	16 24	16 31	16 28	16 35	16 39		16 42	16 46	16 51	16 54	17 01	16 58
Vauxhall	d	15 47	15 51	15 56	15 59	16 06	16 03	16 10		16 14	16 17	16 21	16 26	16 29	16 36	16 33	16 40	16 44		16 47	16 51	16 56	16 59	17 06	17 03
London Waterloo	a	15 52	15 55	16 01	16 04	16 10	16 07	16 16		16 19	16 22	16 25	16 31	16 34	16 40	16 37	16 46	16 49		16 52	16 55	17 01	17 04	17 10	17 07

A From Woking B From London Waterloo

Table T152-R

Mondays to Fridays

8 October to 7 December

Hampton Court, Shepperton, Guildford, Dorking and Chessington South - London

		SW	SW A	SW B	SW	SW	SW	SW	SW	SW	SW A	SW B	SW	SW	SW	SW	SW	SW	SW A	SW B	SW	SW A
Guildford	d							16 28	16 34							16 58	17 04					
London Road (Guildford)	d							16 32	16 38							17 02	17 08					
Clandon	d							16 37	16 43							17 07	17 13					
Horsley	d							16 41	16 47							17 11	17 17					
Effingham Junction	d							16 45	16 50							17 15	17 20					
Bookham	d							16 48								17 18						
Cobham & Stoke d'Abernon	d								16 54								17 24					
Oxshott	d								16 57								17 27					
Claygate	d								17 00								17 30					
Hinchley Wood	d								17 03								17 33					
Hampton Court	d					16 54								17 24								
Thames Ditton	d					16 56								17 26								
Surbiton	d			16 56		17 01			17 11			17 27		17 31			17 41			17 56		
Berrylands	d					17 04								17 34								
Shepperton	d						16 41								17 11							
Upper Halliford	d						16 44								17 14							
Sunbury	d						16 46								17 16							
Kempton Park	d						16 48								17 18							
Hampton	d						16 51								17 21							
Fulwell	d						16 54								17 24							
Strawberry Hill	d		16 37								17 07								17 37			17 41
Teddington	d		16 43				16 59				17 13				17 29				17 43			17 52
Hampton Wick	d		16 46				17 01				17 16				17 31				17 46			17 54
Kingston	a		16 48				17 03				17 18				17 33				17 48			17 56
	d		16 48				17 04				17 18				17 34				17 48			17 58
Norbiton	d		16 50				17 06				17 20				17 36				17 50			18 00
New Malden	d		16 55			17 07	17 10				17 25			17 37	17 40				17 55			18 04
Dorking 182	d				16 33								17 03								17 28	
Box Hill & Westhumble 182	d																					
Leatherhead 182	d				16 39			16 53					17 09			17 23					17 35	
Ashtead 182	d				16 43			16 57					17 13			17 27					17 38	
Epsom 182	a				16 47			17 01					17 17			17 31					17 43	
	d				16 49			17 04					17 19			17 34					17 49	
Ewell West	d				16 52			17 07					17 22			17 37					17 52	
Stoneleigh	d				16 54			17 09					17 24			17 39					17 54	
Worcester Park	d				16 57			17 12					17 27			17 42					17 57	
Chessington South	d	16 38								17 08								17 38				
Chessington North	d	16 40								17 10								17 40				
Tolworth	d	16 43								17 13								17 43				
Malden Manor	d	16 45								17 15								17 45				
Motspur Park	d	16 49			17 00			17 15		17 19			17 30			17 45		17 49			18 00	
Raynes Park	d	16 53	16 58		17 04	17 09	17 13	17 19		17 23	17 28		17 34	17 39	17 43	17 49		17 53	17 57		18 03	18 06
Wimbledon ⊖	d	16 57	17 02	17 05	17 08	17 13	17 17	17 23	17 20	17 28	17 32	17 35	17 38	17 43	17 47	17 53	17 50	17 57	18 01	18 04	18 07	18 10
Earlsfield	d	17 01	17 05	17 08	17 12	17 17	17 20	17 27	17 24	17 31	17 35	17 38	17 42	17 47	17 50	17 57	17 54	18 01	18 05	18 08	18 11	18 14
Clapham Junction	d	17 05	17 09	17 12	17 16	17 21	17 24	17 31	17 28	17 35	17 39	17 42	17 46	17 51	17 54	18 01	17 58	18 05	18 09	18 12	18 15	18 18
Vauxhall ⊖	d	17 10	17 14	17 17	17 21	17 26	17 29	17 36	17 33	17 40	17 44	17 47	17 51	17 56	17 59	18 06	18 03	18 10	18 14	18 17	18 20	18 23
London Waterloo ⊖	a	17 16	17 19	17 22	17 25	17 30	17 35	17 40	17 37	17 46	17 49	17 52	17 55	18 00	18 04	18 10	18 07	18 16	18 18	18 21	18 24	18 28

A From London Waterloo

B From Woking

Table T152-R

Mondays to Fridays

8 October to 7 December

Hampton Court, Shepperton, Guildford, Dorking and Chessington South - London

		SW	SW	SW	SW	SW	SW A	SW B	SW	SW	SW	SW	SW	SW	SW A	SW B	SW	SW	SW	SW	SW	SW	SW A
Guildford	d			17 28	17 34							17 58	18 04							18 32			
London Road (Guildford)	d			17 32	17 38							18 02	18 08							18 36			
Clandon	d			17 37	17 43							18 07	18 13							18 41			
Horsley	d			17 41	17 47							18 11	18 17							18 45			
Effingham Junction	d			17 45	17 50							18 15	18 20							18 48			
Bookham	d			17 48								18 18											
Cobham & Stoke d'Abernon	d				17 54								18 24							18 52			
Oxshott	d				17 57								18 27							18 55			
Claygate	d				18 00								18 30							18 58			
Hinchley Wood	d				18 03								18 33							19 01			
Hampton Court	d	17 54								18 24								18 54					
Thames Ditton	d	17 56								18 26								18 56					
Surbiton	d	18 01			18 11			18 26		18 31			18 41			18 56		19 02		19 11			
Berrylands	d	18 04								18 34								19 04					
Shepperton	d		17 41								18 11								18 36				
Upper Halliford	d		17 44								18 14								18 39				
Sunbury	d		17 46								18 16								18 41				
Kempton Park	d		17 48								18 18								18 43				
Hampton	d		17 51								18 21								18 51				
Fulwell	d		17 54								18 24								18 54				
Strawberry Hill	d						18 07								18 37								19 07
Teddington	d		17 59				18 13				18 29				18 43				18 59				19 13
Hampton Wick	d		18 01				18 16				18 31				18 46				19 01				19 16
Kingston	a		18 03				18 18				18 33				18 48				19 03				19 18
	d		18 04				18 18				18 34				18 48				19 04				19 18
Norbiton	d		18 06				18 20				18 36				18 50				19 06				19 20
New Malden	d	18 07	18 10				18 25			18 37	18 40				18 55			19 07	19 10				19 25
Dorking 182	d								18 03								18 33				18 50		
Box Hill & Westhumble 182	d																						
Leatherhead 182	d			17 53					18 09			18 23					18 39				18 56		
Ashtead 182	d			17 57					18 13			18 27					18 43				18 59		
Epsom 182	a			18 01					18 17			18 31					18 47				19 03		
	d			18 04					18 19			18 34					18 49				19 04		
Ewell West	d			18 07					18 22			18 37					18 52				19 07		
Stoneleigh	d			18 09					18 24			18 39					18 54				19 09		
Worcester Park	d			18 12					18 27			18 42					18 57				19 12		
Chessington South	d					18 08								18 38								19 08	
Chessington North	d					18 10								18 40								19 10	
Tolworth	d					18 13								18 43								19 13	
Malden Manor	d					18 15								18 45								19 15	
Motspur Park	d			18 15		18 19			18 30			18 45		18 49			19 00				19 15	19 20	
Raynes Park	d	18 09	18 13	18 19		18 22	18 28		18 34	18 39	18 43	18 49		18 53	18 58		19 04	19 10	19 13		19 19	19 23	19 28
Wimbledon ⊖	d	18 13	18 17	18 23	18 20	18 26	18 32	18 35	18 38	18 43	18 47	18 53	18 50	18 57	19 02	19 05	19 09	19 14	19 17	19 20	19 23	19 27	19 32
Earlsfield	d	18 17	18 20	18 27	18 24	18 30	18 35	18 38	18 42	18 47	18 50	18 57	18 54	19 01	19 05	19 09	19 12	19 17	19 20	19 24	19 27	19 31	19 35
Clapham Junction	d	18 21	18 24	18 31	18 28	18 34	18 39	18 42	18 46	18 51	18 54	19 01	18 58	19 05	19 09	19 12	19 16	19 21	19 24	19 28	19 31	19 35	19 39
Vauxhall ⊖	d	18 26	18 29	18 36	18 33	18 39	18 44	18 47	18 51	18 56	18 59	19 06	19 03	19 10	19 14	19 17	19 21	19 26	19 29	19 33	19 36	19 40	19 44
London Waterloo ⊖	a	18 30	18 34	18 40	18 37	18 45	18 49	18 52	18 55	19 00	19 05	19 10	19 07	19 14	19 19	19 23	19 26	19 31	19 34	19 37	19 41	19 46	19 49

A From London Waterloo

B From Woking

Table T152-R

Mondays to Fridays

8 October to 7 December

Hampton Court, Shepperton, Guildford, Dorking and Chessington South - London

		SW A	SW	SW	SW	SW	TL B	SW	SW	SW C	SW A	SW	SW	SW	SW	SW	SW	SW C	SW A	SW	SW	SW	SW
Guildford	d						19 03	19 07							19 28	19 34							19 58
London Road (Guildford)	d						19 07	19 11							19 32	19 38							20 02
Clandon	d						19 12	19 16							19 37	19 43							20 07
Horsley	d						19 17	19 20							19 41	19 47							20 11
Effingham Junction 6	d		18 59				19 20	19 23							19 45	19 53							20 15
Bookham	d		19 02				19 24								19 48								20 18
Cobham & Stoke d'Abernon	d							19 27								19 57							
Oxshott	d							19 30								20 00							
Claygate	d							19 33								20 03							
Hinchley Wood	d							19 36								20 06							
Hampton Court	d			19 24									19 54								20 24		
Thames Ditton	d			19 26									19 56								20 26		
Surbiton 6	d	19 27		19 32				19 41			19 57		20 02			20 11			20 26		20 32		
Berrylands	d			19 34									20 04								20 34		
Shepperton	d				19 06									19 36								20 11	
Upper Halliford	d				19 09									19 39								20 14	
Sunbury	d				19 11									19 41								20 16	
Kempton Park	d				19 13									19 43								20 18	
Hampton	d				19 21									19 51								20 21	
Fulwell	d				19 24									19 54								20 24	
Strawberry Hill	d									19 37								20 08					
Teddington	d				19 29					19 43				19 59				20 12				20 29	
Hampton Wick	d				19 31					19 46				20 01				20 14				20 31	
Kingston	a				19 33					19 48				20 03				20 16				20 33	
	d				19 34					19 48				20 04				20 18				20 34	
Norbiton	d				19 36					19 50				20 06				20 20				20 36	
New Malden 6	d			19 37	19 40					19 55			20 07	20 10				20 25			20 37	20 40	
Dorking 4	182 d											19 33								20 03			
Box Hill & Westhumble	182 d																						
Leatherhead	182 d		19 08				19 29					19 39			19 53					20 09			20 23
Ashtead	182 d		19 12				19 34					19 43			19 57					20 13			20 27
Epsom 5	182 a		19 16				19 39					19 47			20 01					20 17			20 31
	d		19 19			19 34						19 49			20 04					20 19			20 34
Ewell West	d		19 22			19 37						19 52			20 07					20 22			20 37
Stoneleigh	d		19 24			19 39						19 54			20 09					20 24			20 39
Worcester Park	d		19 27			19 42						19 57			20 12					20 27			20 42
Chessington South	d								19 38								20 08						
Chessington North	d								19 40								20 10						
Tolworth	d								19 43								20 13						
Malden Manor	d								19 45								20 15						
Motspur Park	d		19 30			19 45			19 49			20 00			20 15		20 19			20 30			20 45
Raynes Park 6	d		19 34	19 40	19 43	19 49			19 53	19 58		20 04	20 10	20 13	20 19		20 23	20 28		20 34	20 40	20 43	20 49
Wimbledon 6 ⊖ ⛴	d	19 35	19 38	19 44	19 47	19 53		19 50	19 57	20 02	20 05	20 08	20 14	20 17	20 23	20 20	20 27	20 32	20 35	20 38	20 44	20 47	20 53
Earlsfield	d	19 39	19 42	19 47	19 50	19 57		19 54	20 01	20 05	20 08	20 12	20 17	20 20	20 27	20 24	20 31	20 35	20 39	20 42	20 47	20 50	20 57
Clapham Junction 10	d	19 42	19 46	19 51	19 54	20 01		19 58	20 05	20 09	20 12	20 16	20 21	20 24	20 31	20 28	20 35	20 39	20 42	20 46	20 51	20 54	21 01
Vauxhall ⊖	d	19 47	19 51	19 56	19 59	20 06		20 03	20 10	20 14	20 17	20 21	20 26	20 29	20 36	20 33	20 40	20 44	20 47	20 51	20 56	20 59	21 06
London Waterloo 15 ⊖	a	19 52	19 55	20 01	20 04	20 10		20 07	20 16	20 19	20 22	20 25	20 31	20 34	20 40	20 37	20 46	20 49	20 52	20 55	21 01	21 04	21 10

A From Woking B To London Bridge C From London Waterloo

Table T152-R

Mondays to Fridays

8 October to 7 December

Hampton Court, Shepperton, Guildford, Dorking and Chessington South - London

		SW	SW	SW A	SW B	SW	SW	SW	SW	SW	SW	SW A	SW B	SW	SW	SW	SW	SW	SW	SW A	SW B	SW
Guildford	d	20 04							20 34					20 46			21 04					
London Road (Guildford)	d	20 08							20 38					20 50			21 08					
Clandon	d	20 13							20 43					20 55			21 13					
Horsley	d	20 17							20 47					20 59			21 17					
Effingham Junction 6	d	20 23							20 50					21 03			21 20					
Bookham	d													21 06								
Cobham & Stoke d'Abernon	d	20 27							20 54								21 24					
Oxshott	d	20 30							20 57								21 27					
Claygate	d	20 33							21 00								21 30					
Hinchley Wood	d	20 36							21 03								21 33					
Hampton Court	d						20 54								21 24							
Thames Ditton	d						20 56								21 26							
Surbiton 6	d	20 41			20 57		21 02		21 11				21 27		21 32		21 41				21 57	
Berrylands	d						21 04								21 34							
Shepperton	d							20 41								21 11						
Upper Halliford	d							20 44								21 14						
Sunbury	d							20 46								21 16						
Kempton Park	d							20 48								21 18						
Hampton	d							20 51								21 21						
Fulwell	d							20 54								21 24						
Strawberry Hill	d			20 37								21 07								21 37		
Teddington	d			20 41				20 59				21 11				21 29				21 41		
Hampton Wick	d			20 44				21 01				21 14				21 31				21 44		
Kingston	a			20 46				21 03				21 16				21 33				21 46		
	d			20 48				21 04				21 18				21 34				21 48		
Norbiton	d			20 50				21 06				21 20				21 36				21 50		
New Malden 6	d			20 55			21 07	21 10				21 25			21 37	21 40				21 55		
Dorking 4	182 d					20 33																21 33
Box Hill & Westhumble	182 d																					
Leatherhead	182 d					20 39								21 11								21 40
Ashtead	182 d					20 42								21 14								21 43
Epsom 5	182 a					20 48								21 19								21 48
	d					20 49				21 04				21 19				21 34				21 49
Ewell West	d					20 52				21 07				21 22				21 37				21 52
Stoneleigh	d					20 54				21 09				21 24				21 39				21 54
Worcester Park	d					20 57				21 12				21 27				21 42				21 57
Chessington South	d		20 38								21 08								21 38			
Chessington North	d		20 40								21 10								21 40			
Tolworth	d		20 43								21 13								21 43			
Malden Manor	d		20 45								21 15								21 45			
Motspur Park	d		20 49			21 00				21 16	21 19			21 30				21 45	21 49			22 00
Raynes Park 6	d		20 53	20 58		21 04	21 10	21 13		21 20	21 23	21 28		21 34	21 40	21 43		21 49	21 53	21 58		22 04
Wimbledon 6 ⊖ ⛴	d	20 50	20 57	21 02	21 05	21 08	21 14	21 17	21 21	21 24	21 27	21 32	21 35	21 38	21 44	21 47	21 50	21 53	21 57	22 02	22 05	22 08
Earlsfield	d	20 54	21 01	21 05	21 09	21 12	21 17	21 20	21 25	21 28	21 31	21 35	21 38	21 42	21 47	21 50	21 54	21 57	22 01	22 05	22 08	22 12
Clapham Junction 10	d	20 58	21 05	21 09	21 12	21 16	21 21	21 24	21 29	21 32	21 35	21 39	21 42	21 46	21 51	21 54	21 58	22 01	22 05	22 09	22 12	22 16
Vauxhall ⊖	d	21 03	21 10	21 14	21 17	21 21	21 26	21 29	21 34	21 37	21 40	21 44	21 47	21 51	21 56	21 59	22 03	22 06	22 10	22 14	22 17	22 21
London Waterloo 15 ⊖	a	21 07	21 16	21 19	21 22	21 25	21 31	21 34	21 38	21 41	21 46	21 49	21 52	21 55	22 01	22 04	22 07	22 10	22 16	22 19	22 22	22 25

A From London Waterloo B From Woking

Hampton Court, Shepperton, Guildford, Dorking and Chessington South - London

		SW	SW	SW	SW A	SW B	SW	SW		SW	SW	SW	SW A	SW	SW	SW	SW	SW		SW A	SW	SW	SW	SW	SW
Guildford	d			21 34			21 46				22 04			22 20				22 34			22 46	22 55			23 07
London Road (Guildford)	d			21 38			21 50				22 08							22 38			22 50				23 11
Clandon	d			21 43			21 55				22 13							22 43			22 55				23 16
Horsley	d			21 47			21 59				22 17							22 47			22 59				23 20
Effingham Junction	d			21 50			22 03				22 20							22 50			23 03				23 23
Bookham	d						22 06														23 06				
Cobham & Stoke d'Abernon	d			21 54							22 24							22 54							23 27
Oxshott	d			21 57							22 27							22 57							23 30
Claygate	d			22 00							22 30							23 00							23 33
Hinchley Wood	d			22 03							22 33							23 03							23 36
Hampton Court	d	21 54								22 24						22 54								23 24	
Thames Ditton	d	21 56								22 26						22 56								23 26	
Surbiton	d	22 02		22 11		22 27				22a32	22 41			22 57		23 02		23 11				23 30		23a32	23 41
Berrylands	d	22 04														23 04									23 43
Shepperton	d		21 41					22 11									22 41						23 11		
Upper Halliford	d		21 44					22 14									22 44						23 14		
Sunbury	d		21 46					22 16									22 46						23 16		
Kempton Park	d		21 48					22 18									22 48						23 18		
Hampton	d		21 51					22 21									22 51						23 21		
Fulwell	d		21 54					22 24									22 54						23 24		
Strawberry Hill	d				22 07								22 37							23 07					
Teddington	d		21 59		22 11			22 29					22 41				22 59			23 11			23 29		
Hampton Wick	d		22 01		22 14			22 31					22 44				23 01			23 14			23 31		
Kingston	a		22 03		22 16			22 33					22 46				23 03			23 16			23 33		
	d		22 04		22 18			22 34					22 48				23 04			23 18			23 34		
Norbiton	d		22 06		22 20			22 36					22 50				23 06			23 20			23 36		
New Malden	d	22 07	22 10		22 25			22 40					22 55			23 07	23 10			23 25			23 41		23 46
Dorking 182	d														22 33										
Box Hill & Westhumble 182	d																								
Leatherhead 182	d						22 11								22 39						23 11				
Ashtead 182	d						22 14								22 43						23 14				
Epsom 182	a						22 19								22 48						23 19				
	d						22 19								22 49						23 19				
Ewell West	d						22 22								22 52						23 22				
Stoneleigh	d						22 24								22 54						23 24				
Worcester Park	d						22 27								22 57						23 27				
Chessington South	d											22 38													
Chessington North	d											22 40													
Tolworth	d											22 43													
Malden Manor	d											22 45													
Motspur Park	d						22 30					22 49			23 00						23 30				
Raynes Park	d	22 10	22 13		22 28		22 34	22 43				22 53	22 58		23 04	23 10	23 13			23 28	23 37		23 43		23 49
Wimbledon ⊖	d	22 14	22 17	22 20	22 32	22 35	22 38	22 47			22 50	22 57	23 02	23 05	23 09	23 14	23 17	23 20		23 32	23 41	23 37	23 50		23 53
Earlsfield	d	22 17	22 20	22 24	22 35	22 38	22 42	22 50			22 54	23 01	23 05	23 08	23 12	23 17	23 20	23 24		23 36	23 44	23 41	23 53		23 56
Clapham Junction	d	22 21	22 24	22 28	22 39	22 42	22 46	22 54			22 58	23 05	23 09	23 12	23 16	23 21	23 25	23 28		23 40	23 48	23 45	23 57		23 59
Vauxhall ⊖	d	22 26	22 29	22 33	22 44	22 47	22 51	22 59			23 03	23 10	23 14	23 17	23 21	23 26	23 30	23 33		23 45	23 53	23 50	00 02		00 05
London Waterloo ⊖	a	22 31	22 34	22 42	22 49	22 52	22 55	23 04			23 09	23 16	23 19	23 26	23 28	23 31	23 34	23 40		23 49	23 58	23 54	00 08		00 13

A From London Waterloo   B From Woking

Table T152-R

Mondays to Fridays

8 October to 7 December

Hampton Court, Shepperton, Guildford, Dorking and Chessington South - London

		SW	SW FO A	SW FX A		SW FO ◇1 B	SW FX ◇1 B	SW
Guildford	d					23 39	23 39	
London Road (Guildford)	d							
Clandon	d							
Horsley	d							
Effingham Junction	d							
Bookham	d							
Cobham & Stoke d'Abernon	d							
Oxshott	d							
Claygate	d							
Hinchley Wood	d							
Hampton Court	d							23 59
Thames Ditton	d							00 02
Surbiton	d					00 08	00 08	00 12
Berrylands	d							00 14
Shepperton	d							
Upper Halliford	d							
Sunbury	d							
Kempton Park	d							
Hampton	d							
Fulwell	d							
Strawberry Hill	d		23 37	23 37				
Teddington	d		23 41	23 41				
Hampton Wick	d		23 44	23 44				
Kingston	a		23 46	23 46				
	d		23 49	23 49				
Norbiton	d		23 51	23 51				
New Malden	d		23 55	23 55				00 17
Dorking 182	d							
Box Hill & Westhumble 182	d							
Leatherhead 182	d							
Ashtead 182	d							
Epsom 182	a							
	d							
Ewell West	d							
Stoneleigh	d							
Worcester Park	d							
Chessington South	d	23 40						
Chessington North	d	23 42						
Tolworth	d	23 44						
Malden Manor	d	23 47						
Motspur Park	d	23 50						
Raynes Park	d	23 54	23 58	23 58				00 20
Wimbledon ⊖	d	23a57	00 02	00 02		00 16	00 16	00a23
Earlsfield	d		00 05	00 05				
Clapham Junction	d		00 09	00 09		00 23	00 23	
Vauxhall ⊖	d		00 14	00 15				
London Waterloo ⊖	a		00 22	00 22		00 32	00 33	

A From London Waterloo   B From Portsmouth Harbour

Table T152-R

Saturdays
26 May to 6 October

Hampton Court, Shepperton, Guildford, Dorking and Chessington South - London

		SW A	SW B	SW C	SW C	SW ◇1 D	SW E	SW	SW F	SW	SW	SW
Guildford	d							04 25				05 14
London Road (Guildford)	d											
Clandon	d											
Horsley	d											
Effingham Junction 8	d											
Bookham	d											
Cobham & Stoke d'Abernon	d											
Oxshott	d											
Claygate	d											
Hinchley Wood	d											
Hampton Court	d											
Thames Ditton	d						00 02					
Surbiton 8	d					00 08	00 12	04 54				05 56
Berrylands	d						00 14					
Shepperton	d											
Upper Halliford	d											
Sunbury	d											
Kempton Park	d											
Hampton	d											
Fulwell	d											
Strawberry Hill	d			00 09					04 55			
Teddington	d			00 12					04 59		05 44	
Hampton Wick	d			00 14					05 01		05 46	
Kingston	a			00 16					05 03		05 48	
	d								05 04		05 49	
Norbiton	d								05 06		05 51	
New Malden 6	d						00 17		05 10		05 55	
Dorking 4	182 d											
Box Hill & Westhumble	182 d											
Leatherhead	182 d											
Ashtead	182 d											
Epsom 3	182 a											
	d									05 34		
Ewell West	d									05 37		
Stoneleigh	d									05 39		
Worcester Park	d									05 42		
Chessington South	d											
Chessington North	d											
Tolworth	d											
Malden Manor	d											
Motspur Park	d									05 45		
Raynes Park 8	d						00 20		05 13	05 49	05 58	
Wimbledon 8 ⊖	d					00 16	00a23	05 02	05 17	05 53	06 02	06 05
Earlsfield	d								05 21	05 58	06 05	06 08
Clapham Junction 10	d				00 05	00 23		05 09	05 25	06 02	06 09	06 12
Vauxhall ⊖	d	00 02	00 05		00 12				05 30	06 07	06 14	06 17
London Waterloo 15 ⊖	a	00 08	00 13		00 16	00 32		05 18	05 35	06 11	06 19	06 22

		SW	SW	SW C	SW G	SW	SW	SW	SW	SW C	SW G	SW
Guildford	d											
London Road (Guildford)	d											
Clandon	d											
Horsley	d											
Effingham Junction 8	d											
Bookham	d											
Cobham & Stoke d'Abernon	d											
Oxshott	d											
Claygate	d											
Hinchley Wood	d											
Hampton Court	d	05 54				06 24						06 54
Thames Ditton	d	05 56				06 26						06 56
Surbiton 8	d	06 02			06 26	06 32					06 57	07 02
Berrylands	d	06 04				06 34						07 04
Shepperton	d						06 11					
Upper Halliford	d						06 14					
Sunbury	d						06 16					
Kempton Park	d						06 18					
Hampton	d						06 21					
Fulwell	d						06 24					
Strawberry Hill	d			06 07						06 37		
Teddington	d			06 11			06 29			06 41		
Hampton Wick	d			06 14			06 31			06 44		
Kingston	a			06 16			06 33			06 46		
	d			06 18			06 34			06 48		
Norbiton	d			06 20			06 36			06 50		
New Malden 6	d	06 07		06 25		06 37	06 40			06 55		07 07
Dorking 4	182 d											
Box Hill & Westhumble	182 d											
Leatherhead	182 d											
Ashtead	182 d											
Epsom 3	182 a											
	d		06 04					06 34				
Ewell West	d		06 07					06 37				
Stoneleigh	d		06 09					06 39				
Worcester Park	d		06 12					06 42				
Chessington South	d								06 38			
Chessington North	d								06 40			
Tolworth	d								06 43			
Malden Manor	d								06 45			
Motspur Park	d		06 15					06 45	06 49			
Raynes Park 8	d	06 10	06 19	06 28		06 40	06 43	06 49	06 53	06 58		07 10
Wimbledon 8 ⊖	d	06 14	06 23	06 32	06 35	06 44	06 47	06 53	06 57	07 02	07 05	07 14
Earlsfield	d	06 17	06 27	06 35	06 38	06 47	06 50	06 57	07 01	07 05	07 08	07 17
Clapham Junction 10	d	06 21	06 31	06 39	06 42	06 51	06 54	07 01	07 05	07 09	07 12	07 21
Vauxhall ⊖	d	06 26	06 36	06 44	06 47	06 56	06 59	07 06	07 10	07 14	07 17	07 26
London Waterloo 15 ⊖	a	06 31	06 40	06 49	06 52	07 01	07 05	07 10	07 16	07 19	07 22	07 31

A From Shepperton
B From Guildford
C From London Waterloo
D From Portsmouth Harbour
E From Hampton Court
F From Twickenham
G From Woking

Table T152-R

Saturdays
26 May to 6 October

Hampton Court, Shepperton, Guildford, Dorking and Chessington South - London

		SW	SW	SW	SW	SW A	SW B	SW	SW	SW	SW	SW
Guildford	d		06 28	06 37						06 58	07 07	
London Road (Guildford)	d		06 32	06 41						07 02	07 11	
Clandon	d		06 37	06 46						07 07	07 16	
Horsley	d		06 41	06 50						07 11	07 20	
Effingham Junction 8	d		06 45	06 53						07 15	07 23	
Bookham	d		06 48							07 18		
Cobham & Stoke d'Abernon	d			06 57							07 27	
Oxshott	d			07 00							07 30	
Claygate	d			07 03							07 33	
Hinchley Wood	d			07 06							07 36	
Hampton Court	d							07 24				
Thames Ditton	d							07 26				
Surbiton 8	d			07 11			07 27	07 32			07 41	
Berrylands	d							07 34				
Shepperton	d	06 41							07 11			
Upper Halliford	d	06 44							07 14			
Sunbury	d	06 46							07 16			
Kempton Park	d	06 48							07 18			
Hampton	d	06 51							07 21			
Fulwell	d	06 54							07 24			
Strawberry Hill	d					07 07						
Teddington	d	06 59				07 11			07 29			
Hampton Wick	d	07 01				07 14			07 31			
Kingston	a	07 03				07 16			07 33			
	d	07 04				07 18			07 34			
Norbiton	d	07 06				07 20			07 36			
New Malden 6	d	07 10				07 25		07 37	07 40			
Dorking 4	182 d											
Box Hill & Westhumble	182 d											
Leatherhead	182 d		06 55							07 23		
Ashtead	182 d		06 59							07 27		
Epsom 3	182 a		07 03							07 31		
	d		07 04							07 34		
Ewell West	d		07 07							07 37		
Stoneleigh	d		07 09							07 39		
Worcester Park	d		07 12							07 42		
Chessington South	d				07 08							07 38
Chessington North	d				07 10							07 40
Tolworth	d				07 13							07 43
Malden Manor	d				07 15							07 45
Motspur Park	d		07 15		07 19					07 45		07 49
Raynes Park 8	d	07 13	07 19		07 23	07 28		07 40	07 43	07 49		07 53
Wimbledon 8 ⊖	d	07 17	07 23	07 20	07 27	07 32	07 35	07 44	07 47	07 53	07 50	07 57
Earlsfield	d	07 20	07 27	07 24	07 31	07 35	07 38	07 47	07 50	07 57	07 54	08 01
Clapham Junction 10	d	07 24	07 31	07 28	07 35	07 39	07 42	07 51	07 54	08 01	07 58	08 05
Vauxhall ⊖	d	07 29	07 36	07 33	07 40	07 44	07 47	07 56	07 59	08 06	08 03	08 10
London Waterloo 15 ⊖	a	07 35	07 40	07 37	07 46	07 49	07 52	08 01	08 05	08 10	08 07	08 16

		SW A	SW B	SW	SW	SW	SW	SW	SW A	SW B	SW	SW
Guildford	d					07 28	07 37					
London Road (Guildford)	d					07 32	07 41					
Clandon	d					07 37	07 46					
Horsley	d					07 41	07 50					
Effingham Junction 8	d					07 45	07 53					
Bookham	d					07 48						
Cobham & Stoke d'Abernon	d						07 57					
Oxshott	d						08 00					
Claygate	d						08 03					
Hinchley Wood	d						08 06					
Hampton Court	d			07 54								08 24
Thames Ditton	d			07 56								08 26
Surbiton 8	d		07 57	08 02			08 11			08 27		08 32
Berrylands	d			08 04								08 34
Shepperton	d				07 41							
Upper Halliford	d				07 44							
Sunbury	d				07 46							
Kempton Park	d				07 48							
Hampton	d				07 51							
Fulwell	d				07 54							
Strawberry Hill	d	07 37							08 07			
Teddington	d	07 41			07 59				08 11			
Hampton Wick	d	07 44			08 01				08 14			
Kingston	a	07 46			08 03				08 16			
	d	07 48			08 04				08 18			
Norbiton	d	07 50			08 06				08 20			
New Malden 6	d	07 55		08 07	08 10				08 25			08 37
Dorking 4	182 d										08 03	
Box Hill & Westhumble	182 d											
Leatherhead	182 d					07 53					08 09	
Ashtead	182 d					07 57					08 13	
Epsom 3	182 a					08 01					08 17	
	d					08 04					08 19	
Ewell West	d					08 07					08 22	
Stoneleigh	d					08 09					08 24	
Worcester Park	d					08 12					08 27	
Chessington South	d							08 08				
Chessington North	d							08 10				
Tolworth	d							08 13				
Malden Manor	d							08 15				
Motspur Park	d					08 15		08 19			08 30	
Raynes Park 8	d	07 58		08 10	08 13	08 19		08 23	08 28		08 34	08 40
Wimbledon 8 ⊖	d	08 02	08 05	08 14	08 17	08 23	08 20	08 27	08 32	08 35	08 38	08 44
Earlsfield	d	08 05	08 08	08 17	08 20	08 27	08 24	08 31	08 35	08 38	08 42	08 47
Clapham Junction 10	d	08 09	08 12	08 21	08 24	08 31	08 28	08 35	08 39	08 42	08 46	08 51
Vauxhall ⊖	d	08 14	08 17	08 26	08 29	08 36	08 33	08 40	08 44	08 47	08 51	08 56
London Waterloo 15 ⊖	a	08 19	08 22	08 31	08 35	08 40	08 37	08 46	08 49	08 52	08 55	09 01

A From London Waterloo
B From Woking

Hampton Court, Shepperton, Guildford, Dorking and Chessington South - London

		SW		SW	SW	SW	SW A	SW B	SW	SW	SW	SW		SW	SW	SW A	SW B	SW	SW	SW	SW	SW		SW	SW A
Guildford	d			07 58	08 07							08 28		08 37							08 58	09 07			
London Road (Guildford)	d			08 02	08 11							08 32		08 41							09 02	09 11			
Clandon	d			08 07	08 16							08 37		08 46							09 07	09 16			
Horsley	d			08 11	08 20							08 41		08 50							09 11	09 20			
Effingham Junction	d			08 15	08 23							08 45		08 53							09 15	09 23			
Bookham	d			08 18								08 48									09 18				
Cobham & Stoke d'Abernon	d				08 27									08 57								09 27			
Oxshott	d				08 30									09 00								09 30			
Claygate	d				08 33									09 03								09 33			
Hinchley Wood	d				08 36									09 06								09 36			
Hampton Court	d									08 54									09 24						
Thames Ditton	d									08 56									09 26						
Surbiton	d				08 41			08 57		09 02				09 11			09 27		09 32			09 41			
Berrylands	d									09 04									09 34						
Shepperton	d	08 11									08 41									09 11					
Upper Halliford	d	08 14									08 44									09 14					
Sunbury	d	08 16									08 46									09 16					
Kempton Park	d	08 18									08 48									09 18					
Hampton	d	08 21									08 51									09 21					
Fulwell	d	08 24									08 54									09 24					
Strawberry Hill	d						08 37									09 07									09 37
Teddington	d	08 29					08 41				08 59					09 11				09 29					09 41
Hampton Wick	d	08 31					08 44				09 01					09 14				09 31					09 44
Kingston	a	08 33					08 46				09 03					09 16				09 33					09 46
	d	08 34					08 48				09 04					09 18				09 34					09 48
Norbiton	d	08 36					08 50				09 06					09 20				09 36					09 50
New Malden	d	08 40					08 55			09 07	09 10					09 25			09 37	09 40					09 55
Dorking 182	d								08 33									09 03							
Box Hill & Westhumble 182	d																								
Leatherhead 182	d			08 23					08 39			08 53						09 09			09 23				
Ashtead 182	d			08 27					08 43			08 57						09 13			09 27				
Epsom 182	a			08 31					08 47			09 01						09 17			09 31				
	d			08 34					08 49			09 04						09 19			09 34				
Ewell West	d			08 37					08 52			09 07						09 22			09 37				
Stoneleigh	d			08 39					08 54			09 09						09 24			09 39				
Worcester Park	d			08 42					08 57			09 12						09 27			09 42				
Chessington South	d					08 38									09 08									09 38	
Chessington North	d					08 40									09 10									09 40	
Tolworth	d					08 43									09 13									09 43	
Malden Manor	d					08 45									09 15									09 45	
Motspur Park	d			08 45		08 49			09 00			09 15			09 19			09 30			09 45			09 49	
Raynes Park	d	08 43		08 49		08 53	08 58		09 04	09 10	09 13	09 19			09 23	09 28		09 34	09 40	09 43	09 49			09 53	09 58
Wimbledon ⊖	d	08 47		08 53	08 50	08 57	09 02	09 05	09 08	09 14	09 17	09 23		09 20	09 27	09 32	09 35	09 38	09 44	09 47	09 53	09 50		09 57	10 02
Earlsfield	d	08 50		08 57	08 54	09 01	09 05	09 08	09 12	09 17	09 20	09 27		09 24	09 31	09 35	09 38	09 42	09 47	09 50	09 57	09 54		10 01	10 05
Clapham Junction	d	08 54		09 01	08 58	09 05	09 09	09 12	09 16	09 21	09 24	09 31		09 28	09 35	09 39	09 42	09 46	09 51	09 54	10 01	09 58		10 05	10 09
Vauxhall ⊖	d	08 59		09 06	09 03	09 10	09 14	09 17	09 21	09 26	09 29	09 36		09 33	09 40	09 44	09 47	09 51	09 56	09 59	10 06	10 03		10 10	10 14
London Waterloo ⊖	a	09 05		09 10	09 07	09 16	09 19	09 22	09 25	09 31	09 35	09 40		09 37	09 46	09 49	09 52	09 55	10 01	10 05	10 10	10 07		10 16	10 19

A From London Waterloo
B From Woking

Hampton Court, Shepperton, Guildford, Dorking and Chessington South - London

		SW A	SW	SW	SW	SW	SW	SW		SW B	SW A	SW	SW	SW	SW	SW	SW	SW B		SW A	SW	SW	SW	SW	SW
Guildford	d					09 28	09 37								09 58	10 07								10 28	10 37
London Road (Guildford)	d					09 32	09 41								10 02	10 11								10 32	10 41
Clandon	d					09 37	09 46								10 07	10 16								10 37	10 46
Horsley	d					09 41	09 50								10 11	10 20								10 41	10 50
Effingham Junction	d					09 45	09 53								10 15	10 23								10 45	10 53
Bookham	d					09 48									10 18									10 48	
Cobham & Stoke d'Abernon	d						09 57									10 27									10 57
Oxshott	d						10 00									10 30									11 00
Claygate	d						10 03									10 33									11 03
Hinchley Wood	d						10 06									10 36									11 06
Hampton Court	d			09 54									10 24									10 54			
Thames Ditton	d			09 56									10 26									10 56			
Surbiton	d	09 57		10 02			10 11				10 27		10 32			10 41				10 57		11 02			11 11
Berrylands	d			10 04									10 34									11 04			
Shepperton	d				09 41									10 11									10 41		
Upper Halliford	d				09 44									10 14									10 44		
Sunbury	d				09 46									10 16									10 46		
Kempton Park	d				09 48									10 18									10 48		
Hampton	d				09 51									10 21									10 51		
Fulwell	d				09 54									10 24									10 54		
Strawberry Hill	d									10 07								10 37							
Teddington	d				09 59					10 11				10 29				10 41					10 59		
Hampton Wick	d				10 01					10 14				10 31				10 44					11 01		
Kingston	a				10 03					10 16				10 33				10 46					11 03		
	d				10 04					10 18				10 34				10 48					11 04		
Norbiton	d				10 06					10 20				10 36				10 50					11 06		
New Malden	d			10 07	10 10					10 25			10 37	10 40				10 55				11 07	11 10		
Dorking 182	d		09 33									10 03									10 33				
Box Hill & Westhumble 182	d																								
Leatherhead 182	d		09 39			09 53						10 09			10 23						10 39			10 53	
Ashtead 182	d		09 43			09 57						10 13			10 27						10 43			10 57	
Epsom 182	a		09 47			10 01						10 17			10 31						10 47			11 01	
	d		09 49			10 04						10 19			10 34						10 49			11 04	
Ewell West	d		09 52			10 07						10 22			10 37						10 52			11 07	
Stoneleigh	d		09 54			10 09						10 24			10 39						10 54			11 09	
Worcester Park	d		09 57			10 12						10 27			10 42						10 57			11 12	
Chessington South	d							10 08									10 38								
Chessington North	d							10 10									10 40								
Tolworth	d							10 13									10 43								
Malden Manor	d							10 15									10 45								
Motspur Park	d		10 00			10 15		10 19				10 30			10 45		10 49				11 00			11 15	
Raynes Park	d		10 04	10 10	10 13	10 19		10 23		10 28		10 34	10 40	10 43	10 49		10 53	10 58			11 04	11 10	11 13	11 19	
Wimbledon ⊖	d	10 05	10 08	10 14	10 17	10 23	10 20	10 27		10 32	10 35	10 38	10 44	10 47	10 53	10 50	10 57	11 02		11 05	11 08	11 14	11 17	11 23	11 20
Earlsfield	d	10 08	10 12	10 17	10 20	10 27	10 24	10 31		10 35	10 38	10 42	10 47	10 50	10 57	10 54	11 01	11 05		11 08	11 12	11 17	11 20	11 27	11 24
Clapham Junction	d	10 12	10 16	10 21	10 24	10 31	10 28	10 35		10 39	10 42	10 46	10 51	10 54	11 01	10 58	11 05	11 09		11 12	11 16	11 21	11 24	11 31	11 28
Vauxhall ⊖	d	10 17	10 21	10 26	10 29	10 36	10 33	10 40		10 44	10 47	10 51	10 56	10 59	11 06	11 03	11 10	11 14		11 17	11 21	11 26	11 29	11 36	11 33
London Waterloo ⊖	a	10 22	10 25	10 31	10 35	10 40	10 37	10 46		10 49	10 52	10 55	11 01	11 05	11 10	11 07	11 16	11 19		11 22	11 25	11 31	11 35	11 40	11 37

A From Woking
B From London Waterloo

Table T152-R

Saturdays
26 May to 6 October

Hampton Court, Shepperton, Guildford, Dorking and Chessington South - London

		SW	SW A	SW B	SW	SW	SW	SW	SW	SW	SW A	SW B	SW	SW	SW	SW	SW	SW	SW A	SW B	SW	SW
Guildford	d							10 58	11 07							11 28	11 37					
London Road (Guildford)	d							11 02	11 11							11 32	11 41					
Clandon	d							11 07	11 16							11 37	11 46					
Horsley	d							11 11	11 20							11 41	11 50					
Effingham Junction	d							11 15	11 23							11 45	11 53					
Bookham	d							11 18								11 48						
Cobham & Stoke d'Abernon	d								11 27								11 57					
Oxshott	d								11 30								12 00					
Claygate	d								11 33								12 03					
Hinchley Wood	d								11 36								12 06					
Hampton Court	d					11 24								11 54								12 24
Thames Ditton	d					11 26								11 56								12 26
Surbiton	d			11 27		11 32			11 41			11 57		12 02			12 11			12 27		12 32
Berrylands	d					11 34								12 04								12 34
Shepperton	d						11 11								11 41							
Upper Halliford	d						11 14								11 44							
Sunbury	d						11 16								11 46							
Kempton Park	d						11 18								11 48							
Hampton	d						11 21								11 51							
Fulwell	d						11 24								11 54							
Strawberry Hill	d		11 07								11 37								12 07			
Teddington	d		11 11				11 29				11 41				11 59				12 11			
Hampton Wick	d		11 14				11 31				11 44				12 01				12 14			
Kingston	a		11 16				11 33				11 46				12 03				12 16			
	d		11 18				11 34				11 48				12 04				12 18			
Norbiton	d		11 20				11 36				11 50				12 06				12 20			
New Malden	d		11 25			11 37	11 40				11 55			12 07	12 10				12 25			12 37
Dorking 182	d				11 03								11 33								12 03	
Box Hill & Westhumble 182	d																					
Leatherhead 182	d				11 09			11 23					11 39			11 53					12 09	
Ashtead 182	d				11 13			11 27					11 43			11 57					12 13	
Epsom 182	a				11 17			11 31					11 47			12 01					12 17	
	d				11 19			11 34					11 49			12 04					12 19	
Ewell West	d				11 22			11 37					11 52			12 07					12 22	
Stoneleigh	d				11 24			11 39					11 54			12 09					12 24	
Worcester Park	d				11 27			11 42					11 57			12 12					12 27	
Chessington South	d	11 08								11 38								12 08				
Chessington North	d	11 10								11 40								12 10				
Tolworth	d	11 13								11 43								12 13				
Malden Manor	d	11 15								11 45								12 15				
Motspur Park	d	11 19			11 30			11 45		11 49			12 00			12 15		12 19			12 30	
Raynes Park	d	11 23	11 28		11 34	11 40	11 43	11 49		11 53	11 58		12 04	12 10	12 13	12 19		12 23	12 28		12 34	12 40
Wimbledon ⊖ ⛴	d	11 27	11 32	11 35	11 38	11 44	11 47	11 53	11 50	11 57	12 02	12 05	12 08	12 14	12 17	12 23	12 20	12 27	12 32	12 35	12 38	12 44
Earlsfield	d	11 31	11 35	11 38	11 42	11 47	11 50	11 57	11 54	12 01	12 05	12 08	12 12	12 17	12 20	12 27	12 24	12 31	12 35	12 38	12 42	12 47
Clapham Junction 10	d	11 35	11 39	11 42	11 46	11 51	11 54	12 01	11 58	12 05	12 09	12 12	12 16	12 21	12 24	12 31	12 28	12 35	12 39	12 42	12 46	12 51
Vauxhall ⊖	d	11 40	11 44	11 47	11 51	11 56	11 59	12 06	12 03	12 10	12 14	12 17	12 21	12 26	12 29	12 36	12 33	12 40	12 44	12 47	12 51	12 56
London Waterloo 15 ⊖	a	11 46	11 49	11 52	11 55	12 01	12 05	12 10	12 07	12 16	12 19	12 22	12 25	12 31	12 35	12 40	12 37	12 46	12 49	12 52	12 55	13 01

A From London Waterloo
B From Woking

Table T152-R

Saturdays
26 May to 6 October

Hampton Court, Shepperton, Guildford, Dorking and Chessington South - London

		SW	SW	SW	SW	SW A	SW B	SW	SW	SW	SW	SW	SW	SW A	SW B	SW	SW	SW	SW	SW	SW	SW A	SW B
Guildford	d		11 58	12 07							12 28	12 37							12 58	13 07			
London Road (Guildford)	d		12 02	12 11							12 32	12 41							13 02	13 11			
Clandon	d		12 07	12 16							12 37	12 46							13 07	13 16			
Horsley	d		12 11	12 20							12 41	12 50							13 11	13 20			
Effingham Junction	d		12 15	12 23							12 45	12 53							13 15	13 23			
Bookham	d		12 18								12 48								13 18				
Cobham & Stoke d'Abernon	d			12 27								12 57								13 27			
Oxshott	d			12 30								13 00								13 30			
Claygate	d			12 33								13 03								13 33			
Hinchley Wood	d			12 36								13 06								13 36			
Hampton Court	d								12 54								13 24						
Thames Ditton	d								12 56								13 26						
Surbiton	d			12 41			12 57		13 02			13 11			13 27		13 32			13 41			13 57
Berrylands	d								13 04								13 34						
Shepperton	d	12 11								12 41								13 11					
Upper Halliford	d	12 14								12 44								13 14					
Sunbury	d	12 16								12 46								13 16					
Kempton Park	d	12 18								12 48								13 18					
Hampton	d	12 21								12 51								13 21					
Fulwell	d	12 24								12 54								13 24					
Strawberry Hill	d					12 37								13 07								13 37	
Teddington	d	12 29				12 41				12 59				13 11				13 29				13 41	
Hampton Wick	d	12 31				12 44				13 01				13 14				13 31				13 44	
Kingston	a	12 33				12 46				13 03				13 16				13 33				13 46	
	d	12 34				12 48				13 04				13 18				13 34				13 48	
Norbiton	d	12 36				12 50				13 06				13 20				13 36				13 50	
New Malden	d	12 40				12 55			13 07	13 10				13 25			13 37	13 40				13 55	
Dorking 182	d							12 33								13 03							
Box Hill & Westhumble 182	d																						
Leatherhead 182	d		12 23					12 39			12 53					13 09			13 23				
Ashtead 182	d		12 27					12 43			12 57					13 13			13 27				
Epsom 182	a		12 31					12 47			13 01					13 17			13 31				
	d		12 34					12 49			13 04					13 19			13 34				
Ewell West	d		12 37					12 52			13 07					13 22			13 37				
Stoneleigh	d		12 39					12 54			13 09					13 24			13 39				
Worcester Park	d		12 42					12 57			13 12					13 27			13 42				
Chessington South	d				12 38								13 08								13 38		
Chessington North	d				12 40								13 10								13 40		
Tolworth	d				12 43								13 13								13 43		
Malden Manor	d				12 45								13 15								13 45		
Motspur Park	d		12 45		12 49			13 00			13 15		13 19			13 30			13 45		13 49		
Raynes Park	d	12 43	12 49		12 53	12 58		13 04	13 10	13 13	13 19		13 23	13 28		13 34	13 40	13 43	13 49		13 53	13 58	
Wimbledon ⊖ ⛴	d	12 47	12 53	12 50	12 57	13 02	13 05	13 08	13 14	13 17	13 23	13 20	13 27	13 32	13 35	13 38	13 44	13 47	13 53	13 50	13 57	14 02	14 05
Earlsfield	d	12 50	12 57	12 54	13 01	13 05	13 08	13 12	13 17	13 20	13 27	13 24	13 31	13 35	13 38	13 42	13 47	13 50	13 57	13 54	14 01	14 05	14 08
Clapham Junction 10	d	12 54	13 01	12 58	13 05	13 09	13 12	13 16	13 21	13 24	13 31	13 28	13 35	13 39	13 42	13 46	13 51	13 54	14 01	13 58	14 05	14 09	14 12
Vauxhall ⊖	d	12 59	13 06	13 03	13 10	13 14	13 17	13 21	13 26	13 29	13 36	13 33	13 40	13 44	13 47	13 51	13 56	13 59	14 06	14 03	14 10	14 14	14 17
London Waterloo 15 ⊖	a	13 05	13 10	13 07	13 16	13 19	13 22	13 25	13 31	13 35	13 40	13 37	13 46	13 49	13 52	13 55	14 01	14 05	14 10	14 07	14 16	14 19	14 22

A From London Waterloo
B From Woking

Table T152-R

Saturdays
26 May to 6 October

Hampton Court, Shepperton, Guildford, Dorking and Chessington South - London

		SW	SW	SW	SW	SW		SW	SW A	SW B	SW	SW	SW	SW	SW	SW		SW A	SW B	SW	SW	SW	SW	SW	SW
Guildford	d				13 28	13 37								13 58	14 07								14 28	14 37	
London Road (Guildford)	d				13 32	13 41								14 02	14 11								14 32	14 41	
Clandon	d				13 37	13 46								14 07	14 16								14 37	14 46	
Horsley	d				13 41	13 50								14 11	14 20								14 41	14 50	
Effingham Junction	d				13 45	13 53								14 15	14 23								14 45	14 53	
Bookham	d				13 48									14 18									14 48		
Cobham & Stoke d'Abernon	d					13 57									14 27									14 57	
Oxshott	d					14 00									14 30									15 00	
Claygate	d					14 03									14 33									15 03	
Hinchley Wood	d					14 06									14 36									15 06	
Hampton Court	d		13 54									14 24									14 54				
Thames Ditton	d		13 56									14 26									14 56				
Surbiton	d		14 02			14 11				14 27		14 32			14 41				14 57		15 02			15 11	
Berrylands	d		14 04									14 34									15 04				
Shepperton	d			13 41									14 11									14 41			
Upper Halliford	d			13 44									14 14									14 44			
Sunbury	d			13 46									14 16									14 46			
Kempton Park	d			13 48									14 18									14 48			
Hampton	d			13 51									14 21									14 51			
Fulwell	d			13 54									14 24									14 54			
Strawberry Hill	d								14 07									14 37							
Teddington	d			13 59					14 11				14 29					14 41				14 59			
Hampton Wick	d			14 01					14 14				14 31					14 44				15 01			
Kingston	a			14 03					14 16				14 33					14 46				15 03			
	d			14 04					14 18				14 34					14 48				15 04			
Norbiton	d			14 06					14 20				14 36					14 50				15 06			
New Malden	d		14 07	14 10					14 25			14 37	14 40					14 55			15 07	15 10			
Dorking	182 d	13 33									14 03									14 33					
Box Hill & Westhumble	182 d																								
Leatherhead	182 d	13 39			13 53						14 09			14 23						14 39			14 53		
Ashtead	182 d	13 43			13 57						14 13			14 27						14 43			14 57		
Epsom	182 a	13 47			14 01						14 17			14 31						14 47			15 01		
	d	13 49			14 04						14 19			14 34						14 49			15 04		
Ewell West	d	13 52			14 07						14 22			14 37						14 52			15 07		
Stoneleigh	d	13 54			14 09						14 24			14 39						14 54			15 09		
Worcester Park	d	13 57			14 12						14 27			14 42						14 57			15 12		
Chessington South	d							14 08								14 38									15 08
Chessington North	d							14 10								14 40									15 10
Tolworth	d							14 13								14 43									15 13
Malden Manor	d							14 15								14 45									15 15
Motspur Park	d	14 00			14 15			14 19			14 30			14 45		14 49				15 00			15 15		15 19
Raynes Park	d	14 04	14 10	14 13	14 19			14 23	14 28		14 34	14 40	14 43	14 49		14 53		14 58		15 04	15 10	15 13	15 19		15 23
Wimbledon ⊖	d	14 08	14 14	14 17	14 23	14 20		14 27	14 32	14 35	14 38	14 44	14 47	14 53	14 50	14 57		15 02	15 05	15 08	15 14	15 17	15 23	15 20	15 27
Earlsfield	d	14 12	14 17	14 20	14 27	14 24		14 31	14 35	14 38	14 42	14 47	14 50	14 57	14 54	15 01		15 05	15 08	15 12	15 17	15 20	15 27	15 24	15 31
Clapham Junction	d	14 16	14 21	14 24	14 31	14 28		14 35	14 39	14 42	14 46	14 51	14 54	15 01	14 58	15 05		15 09	15 12	15 16	15 21	15 24	15 31	15 28	15 35
Vauxhall ⊖	d	14 21	14 26	14 29	14 36	14 33		14 40	14 44	14 47	14 51	14 56	14 59	15 06	15 03	15 10		15 14	15 17	15 21	15 26	15 29	15 36	15 33	15 40
London Waterloo ⊖	a	14 25	14 31	14 35	14 40	14 37		14 46	14 49	14 52	14 55	15 01	15 05	15 10	15 07	15 16		15 19	15 22	15 25	15 31	15 35	15 40	15 37	15 46

A From London Waterloo
B From Woking

Table T152-R

Saturdays
26 May to 6 October

Hampton Court, Shepperton, Guildford, Dorking and Chessington South - London

		SW A		SW B	SW	SW	SW	SW	SW	SW	SW A	SW B		SW	SW	SW	SW	SW	SW	SW A	SW B	SW		SW	SW
Guildford	d							14 58	15 07								15 28	15 37							
London Road (Guildford)	d							15 02	15 11								15 32	15 41							
Clandon	d							15 07	15 16								15 37	15 46							
Horsley	d							15 11	15 20								15 41	15 50							
Effingham Junction	d							15 15	15 23								15 45	15 53							
Bookham	d							15 18									15 48								
Cobham & Stoke d'Abernon	d								15 27									15 57							
Oxshott	d								15 30									16 00							
Claygate	d								15 33									16 03							
Hinchley Wood	d								15 36									16 06							
Hampton Court	d					15 24									15 54									16 24	
Thames Ditton	d					15 26									15 56									16 26	
Surbiton	d			15 27		15 32			15 41			15 57			16 02			16 11			16 27			16 32	
Berrylands	d					15 34									16 04									16 34	
Shepperton	d						15 11									15 41									16 11
Upper Halliford	d						15 14									15 44									16 14
Sunbury	d						15 16									15 46									16 16
Kempton Park	d						15 18									15 48									16 18
Hampton	d						15 21									15 51									16 21
Fulwell	d						15 24									15 54									16 24
Strawberry Hill	d	15 07									15 37									16 07					
Teddington	d	15 11					15 29				15 41					15 59				16 11					16 29
Hampton Wick	d	15 14					15 31				15 44					16 01				16 14					16 31
Kingston	a	15 16					15 33				15 46					16 03				16 16					16 33
	d	15 18					15 34				15 48					16 04				16 18					16 34
Norbiton	d	15 20					15 36				15 50					16 06				16 20					16 36
New Malden	d	15 25				15 37	15 40				15 55				16 07	16 10				16 25				16 37	16 40
Dorking	182 d				15 03									15 33								16 03			
Box Hill & Westhumble	182 d																								
Leatherhead	182 d				15 09			15 23						15 39			15 53					16 09			
Ashtead	182 d				15 13			15 27						15 43			15 57					16 13			
Epsom	182 a				15 17			15 31						15 47			16 01					16 17			
	d				15 19			15 34						15 49			16 04					16 19			
Ewell West	d				15 22			15 37						15 52			16 07					16 22			
Stoneleigh	d				15 24			15 39						15 54			16 09					16 24			
Worcester Park	d				15 27			15 42						15 57			16 12					16 27			
Chessington South	d									15 38									16 08						
Chessington North	d									15 40									16 10						
Tolworth	d									15 43									16 13						
Malden Manor	d									15 45									16 15						
Motspur Park	d				15 30			15 45		15 49				16 00			16 15		16 19			16 30			
Raynes Park	d	15 28			15 34	15 40	15 43	15 49		15 53	15 58			16 04	16 10	16 13	16 19		16 23	16 28		16 34		16 40	16 43
Wimbledon ⊖	d	15 32		15 35	15 38	15 44	15 47	15 53	15 50	15 57	16 02	16 05		16 08	16 14	16 17	16 23	16 20	16 27	16 32	16 35	16 38		16 44	16 47
Earlsfield	d	15 35		15 38	15 42	15 47	15 50	15 57	15 54	16 01	16 05	16 08		16 12	16 17	16 20	16 27	16 24	16 31	16 35	16 38	16 42		16 47	16 50
Clapham Junction	d	15 39		15 42	15 46	15 51	15 54	16 01	15 58	16 05	16 09	16 12		16 16	16 21	16 24	16 31	16 28	16 35	16 39	16 42	16 46		16 51	16 54
Vauxhall ⊖	d	15 44		15 47	15 51	15 56	15 59	16 06	16 03	16 10	16 14	16 17		16 21	16 26	16 29	16 36	16 33	16 40	16 44	16 47	16 51		16 56	16 59
London Waterloo ⊖	a	15 49		15 52	15 55	16 01	16 05	16 10	16 07	16 16	16 19	16 22		16 25	16 31	16 35	16 40	16 37	16 46	16 49	16 52	16 55		17 01	17 05

A From London Waterloo
B From Woking

Table T152-R

Saturdays
26 May to 6 October

Hampton Court, Shepperton, Guildford, Dorking and Chessington South - London

		SW	SW	SW	SW A	SW B	SW	SW	SW	SW	SW	SW
Guildford	d	15 58	16 07							16 28	16 37	
London Road (Guildford)	d	16 02	16 11							16 32	16 41	
Clandon	d	16 07	16 16							16 37	16 46	
Horsley	d	16 11	16 20							16 41	16 50	
Effingham Junction	d	16 15	16 23							16 45	16 53	
Bookham	d	16 18								16 48		
Cobham & Stoke d'Abernon	d		16 27								16 57	
Oxshott	d		16 30								17 00	
Claygate	d		16 33								17 03	
Hinchley Wood	d		16 36								17 06	
Hampton Court	d							16 54				
Thames Ditton	d							16 56				
Surbiton	d		16 41			16 57		17 02			17 11	
Berrylands	d							17 04				
Shepperton	d								16 41			
Upper Halliford	d								16 44			
Sunbury	d								16 46			
Kempton Park	d								16 48			
Hampton	d								16 51			
Fulwell	d								16 54			
Strawberry Hill	d				16 37							
Teddington	d				16 41				16 59			
Hampton Wick	d				16 44				17 01			
Kingston	a				16 46				17 03			
	d				16 48				17 04			
Norbiton	d				16 50				17 06			
New Malden	d				16 55			17 07	17 10			
Dorking 182	d						16 33					
Box Hill & Westhumble 182	d											
Leatherhead 182	d	16 23					16 39			16 53		
Ashtead 182	d	16 27					16 43			16 57		
Epsom 182	a	16 31					16 47			17 01		
	d	16 34					16 49			17 04		
Ewell West	d	16 37					16 52			17 07		
Stoneleigh	d	16 39					16 54			17 09		
Worcester Park	d	16 42					16 57			17 12		
Chessington South	d			16 38								17 08
Chessington North	d			16 40								17 10
Tolworth	d			16 43								17 13
Malden Manor	d			16 45								17 15
Motspur Park	d	16 45		16 49			17 00			17 15		17 19
Raynes Park	d	16 49		16 53	16 58		17 04	17 10	17 13	17 19		17 23
Wimbledon ⊖	d	16 53	16 50	16 57	17 02	17 05	17 08	17 14	17 17	17 23	17 20	17 27
Earlsfield	d	16 57	16 54	17 01	17 05	17 08	17 12	17 17	17 20	17 27	17 24	17 31
Clapham Junction	d	17 01	16 58	17 05	17 09	17 12	17 16	17 21	17 24	17 31	17 28	17 35
Vauxhall ⊖	d	17 06	17 03	17 10	17 14	17 17	17 21	17 26	17 29	17 36	17 33	17 40
London Waterloo ⊖	a	17 10	17 07	17 16	17 19	17 22	17 25	17 31	17 35	17 40	17 37	17 46

		SW A	SW B	SW	SW	SW	SW	SW	SW	SW A	SW B	SW
Guildford	d						16 58	17 07				
London Road (Guildford)	d						17 02	17 11				
Clandon	d						17 07	17 16				
Horsley	d						17 11	17 20				
Effingham Junction	d						17 15	17 23				
Bookham	d						17 18					
Cobham & Stoke d'Abernon	d							17 27				
Oxshott	d							17 30				
Claygate	d							17 33				
Hinchley Wood	d							17 36				
Hampton Court	d				17 24							
Thames Ditton	d				17 26							
Surbiton	d		17 27		17 32			17 41			17 57	
Berrylands	d				17 34							
Shepperton	d					17 11						
Upper Halliford	d					17 14						
Sunbury	d					17 16						
Kempton Park	d					17 18						
Hampton	d					17 21						
Fulwell	d					17 24						
Strawberry Hill	d	17 07								17 37		
Teddington	d	17 11				17 29				17 41		
Hampton Wick	d	17 14				17 31				17 44		
Kingston	a	17 16				17 33				17 46		
	d	17 18				17 34				17 48		
Norbiton	d	17 20				17 36				17 50		
New Malden	d	17 25			17 37	17 40				17 55		
Dorking 182	d			17 03								17 33
Box Hill & Westhumble 182	d											
Leatherhead 182	d			17 09			17 23					17 39
Ashtead 182	d			17 13			17 27					17 43
Epsom 182	a			17 17			17 31					17 47
	d			17 19			17 34					17 49
Ewell West	d			17 22			17 37					17 52
Stoneleigh	d			17 24			17 39					17 54
Worcester Park	d			17 27			17 42					17 57
Chessington South	d								17 38			
Chessington North	d								17 40			
Tolworth	d								17 43			
Malden Manor	d								17 45			
Motspur Park	d			17 30			17 45		17 49			18 00
Raynes Park	d	17 28		17 34	17 40	17 43	17 49		17 53	17 58		18 04
Wimbledon ⊖	d	17 32	17 35	17 38	17 44	17 47	17 53	17 50	17 57	18 02	18 05	18 08
Earlsfield	d	17 35	17 38	17 42	17 47	17 50	17 57	17 54	18 01	18 05	18 08	18 12
Clapham Junction	d	17 39	17 42	17 46	17 51	17 54	18 01	17 58	18 05	18 09	18 12	18 16
Vauxhall ⊖	d	17 44	17 47	17 51	17 56	17 59	18 06	18 03	18 10	18 14	18 17	18 21
London Waterloo ⊖	a	17 49	17 52	17 55	18 01	18 05	18 10	18 07	18 16	18 19	18 22	18 25

A From London Waterloo
B From Woking

Table T152-R

Saturdays
26 May to 6 October

Hampton Court, Shepperton, Guildford, Dorking and Chessington South - London

		SW	SW	SW	SW	SW	SW A	SW B	SW	SW	SW
Guildford	d			17 28	17 37						
London Road (Guildford)	d			17 32	17 41						
Clandon	d			17 37	17 46						
Horsley	d			17 41	17 50						
Effingham Junction	d			17 45	17 53						
Bookham	d			17 48							
Cobham & Stoke d'Abernon	d				17 57						
Oxshott	d				18 00						
Claygate	d				18 03						
Hinchley Wood	d				18 06						
Hampton Court	d	17 54								18 24	
Thames Ditton	d	17 56								18 26	
Surbiton	d	18 02			18 11			18 27		18 32	
Berrylands	d	18 04								18 34	
Shepperton	d		17 41								18 11
Upper Halliford	d		17 44								18 14
Sunbury	d		17 46								18 16
Kempton Park	d		17 48								18 18
Hampton	d		17 51								18 21
Fulwell	d		17 54								18 24
Strawberry Hill	d						18 07				
Teddington	d		17 59				18 11				18 29
Hampton Wick	d		18 01				18 14				18 31
Kingston	a		18 03				18 16				18 33
	d		18 04				18 18				18 34
Norbiton	d		18 06				18 20				18 36
New Malden	d	18 07	18 10				18 25			18 37	18 40
Dorking 182	d								18 03		
Box Hill & Westhumble 182	d										
Leatherhead 182	d			17 53					18 09		
Ashtead 182	d			17 57					18 13		
Epsom 182	a			18 01					18 17		
	d			18 04					18 19		
Ewell West	d			18 07					18 22		
Stoneleigh	d			18 09					18 24		
Worcester Park	d			18 12					18 27		
Chessington South	d					18 08					
Chessington North	d					18 10					
Tolworth	d					18 13					
Malden Manor	d					18 15					
Motspur Park	d			18 15		18 19			18 30		
Raynes Park	d	18 10	18 13	18 19		18 23	18 28		18 34	18 40	18 43
Wimbledon ⊖	d	18 14	18 17	18 23	18 20	18 27	18 32	18 35	18 38	18 44	18 47
Earlsfield	d	18 17	18 20	18 27	18 24	18 31	18 35	18 38	18 42	18 47	18 50
Clapham Junction	d	18 21	18 24	18 31	18 28	18 35	18 39	18 42	18 46	18 51	18 54
Vauxhall ⊖	d	18 26	18 29	18 36	18 33	18 40	18 44	18 47	18 51	18 56	18 59
London Waterloo ⊖	a	18 31	18 35	18 40	18 37	18 46	18 49	18 52	18 55	19 01	19 05

		SW	SW	SW	SW A	SW B	SW	SW	SW	SW	SW	SW
Guildford	d	17 58	18 07							18 28	18 37	
London Road (Guildford)	d	18 02	18 11							18 32	18 41	
Clandon	d	18 07	18 16							18 37	18 46	
Horsley	d	18 11	18 20							18 41	18 50	
Effingham Junction	d	18 15	18 23							18 45	18 53	
Bookham	d	18 18								18 48		
Cobham & Stoke d'Abernon	d		18 27								18 57	
Oxshott	d		18 30								19 00	
Claygate	d		18 33								19 03	
Hinchley Wood	d		18 36								19 06	
Hampton Court	d							18 54				
Thames Ditton	d							18 56				
Surbiton	d		18 41			18 57		19 02			19 11	
Berrylands	d							19 04				
Shepperton	d								18 41			
Upper Halliford	d								18 44			
Sunbury	d								18 46			
Kempton Park	d								18 48			
Hampton	d								18 51			
Fulwell	d								18 54			
Strawberry Hill	d				18 37							
Teddington	d				18 41				18 59			
Hampton Wick	d				18 44				19 01			
Kingston	a				18 46				19 03			
	d				18 48				19 04			
Norbiton	d				18 50				19 06			
New Malden	d				18 55			19 07	19 10			
Dorking 182	d						18 33					
Box Hill & Westhumble 182	d											
Leatherhead 182	d	18 23					18 39			18 53		
Ashtead 182	d	18 27					18 43			18 57		
Epsom 182	a	18 31					18 47			19 01		
	d	18 34					18 49			19 04		
Ewell West	d	18 37					18 52			19 07		
Stoneleigh	d	18 39					18 54			19 09		
Worcester Park	d	18 42					18 57			19 12		
Chessington South	d			18 38								19 08
Chessington North	d			18 40								19 10
Tolworth	d			18 43								19 13
Malden Manor	d			18 45								19 15
Motspur Park	d	18 45		18 49			19 00			19 15		19 19
Raynes Park	d	18 49		18 53	18 58		19 04	19 10	19 13	19 19		19 23
Wimbledon ⊖	d	18 53	18 50	18 57	19 02	19 05	19 08	19 14	19 17	19 23	19 20	19 27
Earlsfield	d	18 57	18 54	19 01	19 05	19 08	19 12	19 17	19 20	19 27	19 24	19 31
Clapham Junction	d	19 01	18 58	19 05	19 09	19 12	19 16	19 21	19 24	19 31	19 28	19 35
Vauxhall ⊖	d	19 06	19 03	19 10	19 14	19 17	19 21	19 26	19 29	19 36	19 33	19 40
London Waterloo ⊖	a	19 10	19 07	19 16	19 19	19 22	19 25	19 31	19 35	19 40	19 37	19 46

A From London Waterloo
B From Woking

Table T152-R

Saturdays

26 May to 6 October

Hampton Court, Shepperton, Guildford, Dorking and Chessington South - London

Station		SW A	SW B	SW	SW	SW	SW	SW	SW	SW A		SW B	SW	SW	SW	SW	SW	SW	SW A	SW B		SW	SW	SW	SW
Guildford	d						18 58	19 07								19 28	19 37								19 58
London Road (Guildford)	d						19 02	19 11								19 32	19 41								20 02
Clandon	d						19 07	19 16								19 37	19 46								20 07
Horsley	d						19 11	19 20								19 41	19 50								20 11
Effingham Junction 6	d						19 15	19 23								19 45	19 53								20 15
Bookham	d						19 18									19 48									20 18
Cobham & Stoke d'Abernon	d							19 27									19 57								
Oxshott	d							19 30									20 00								
Claygate	d							19 33									20 03								
Hinchley Wood	d							19 36									20 06								
Hampton Court	d				19 24									19 54									20 24		
Thames Ditton	d				19 26									19 56									20 26		
Surbiton 6	d		19 27		19 32			19 41				19 57		20 02			20 11			20 27			20 32		
Berrylands	d				19 34									20 04									20 34		
Shepperton	d					19 11									19 41									20 11	
Upper Halliford	d					19 14									19 44									20 14	
Sunbury	d					19 16									19 46									20 16	
Kempton Park	d					19 18									19 48									20 18	
Hampton	d					19 21									19 51									20 21	
Fulwell	d					19 24									19 54									20 24	
Strawberry Hill	d	19 07								19 37									20 07						
Teddington	d	19 11				19 29				19 41					19 59				20 11					20 29	
Hampton Wick	d	19 14				19 31				19 44					20 01				20 14					20 31	
Kingston	a	19 16				19 33				19 46					20 03				20 16					20 33	
	d	19 18				19 34				19 48					20 04				20 18					20 34	
Norbiton	d	19 20				19 36				19 50					20 06				20 20					20 36	
New Malden 6	d	19 25			19 37	19 40				19 55				20 07	20 10				20 25				20 37	20 40	
Dorking 4 182	d			19 03									19 33									20 03			
Box Hill & Westhumble 182	d																								
Leatherhead 182	d			19 10			19 23						19 40			19 53						20 10			20 23
Ashtead 182	d			19 13			19 27						19 43			19 57						20 13			20 27
Epsom 8 182	a			19 18			19 31						19 48			20 01						20 18			20 31
	d			19 19			19 34						19 49			20 04						20 19			20 34
Ewell West	d			19 22			19 37						19 52			20 07						20 22			20 37
Stoneleigh	d			19 24			19 39						19 54			20 09						20 24			20 39
Worcester Park	d			19 27			19 42						19 57			20 12						20 27			20 42
Chessington South	d								19 38									20 08							
Chessington North	d								19 40									20 10							
Tolworth	d								19 43									20 13							
Malden Manor	d								19 45									20 15							
Motspur Park	d			19 30			19 45		19 49				20 00			20 15		20 19				20 30			20 45
Raynes Park 6	d	19 28		19 34	19 40	19 43	19 49		19 53	19 58			20 04	20 10	20 13	20 19		20 23	20 28			20 34	20 40	20 43	20 49
Wimbledon 6 ⊖ ⇌	d	19 32	19 35	19 38	19 44	19 47	19 53	19 50	19 57	20 02		20 05	20 08	20 14	20 17	20 23	20 20	20 27	20 32	20 35		20 38	20 44	20 47	20 53
Earlsfield	d	19 35	19 38	19 42	19 47	19 50	19 57	19 54	20 01	20 05		20 08	20 12	20 17	20 20	20 27	20 24	20 31	20 35	20 38		20 42	20 47	20 50	20 57
Clapham Junction 10	d	19 39	19 42	19 46	19 51	19 54	20 01	19 58	20 05	20 09		20 12	20 16	20 21	20 24	20 31	20 28	20 35	20 39	20 42		20 46	20 51	20 54	21 01
Vauxhall ⊖	d	19 44	19 47	19 51	19 56	19 59	20 06	20 03	20 10	20 14		20 17	20 21	20 26	20 29	20 36	20 33	20 40	20 44	20 47		20 51	20 56	20 59	21 06
London Waterloo 15 ⊖	a	19 49	19 52	19 55	20 01	20 05	20 10	20 07	20 16	20 19		20 22	20 25	20 31	20 35	20 40	20 37	20 46	20 49	20 52		20 55	21 01	21 05	21 11

A From London Waterloo B From Woking

Table T152-R

Saturdays

26 May to 6 October

Hampton Court, Shepperton, Guildford, Dorking and Chessington South - London

Station		SW	SW	SW A	SW B	SW		SW	SW	SW	SW	SW	SW A	SW B	SW	SW		SW	SW	SW	SW	SW A	SW B	SW	SW
Guildford	d	20 07								20 37					20 46				21 07						
London Road (Guildford)	d	20 11								20 41					20 50				21 11						
Clandon	d	20 16								20 46					20 55				21 16						
Horsley	d	20 20								20 50					20 59				21 20						
Effingham Junction 6	d	20 23								20 53					21 03				21 23						
Bookham	d														21 06										
Cobham & Stoke d'Abernon	d	20 27								20 57									21 27						
Oxshott	d	20 30								21 00									21 30						
Claygate	d	20 33								21 03									21 33						
Hinchley Wood	d	20 36								21 06									21 36						
Hampton Court	d							20 54								21 24									21 54
Thames Ditton	d							20 56								21 26									21 56
Surbiton 6	d	20 41			20 57			21 02		21 11				21 27		21 32			21 41				21 57		22 02
Berrylands	d							21 04								21 34									22 04
Shepperton	d								20 41									21 11							
Upper Halliford	d								20 44									21 14							
Sunbury	d								20 46									21 16							
Kempton Park	d								20 48									21 18							
Hampton	d								20 51									21 21							
Fulwell	d								20 54									21 24							
Strawberry Hill	d			20 37									21 07									21 37			
Teddington	d			20 41					20 59				21 11					21 29				21 41			
Hampton Wick	d			20 44					21 01				21 14					21 31				21 44			
Kingston	a			20 46					21 03				21 16					21 33				21 46			
	d			20 48					21 04				21 18					21 34				21 48			
Norbiton	d			20 50					21 06				21 20					21 36				21 50			
New Malden 6	d			20 55				21 07	21 10				21 25			21 37		21 40				21 55			22 07
Dorking 4 182	d					20 33																		21 33	
Box Hill & Westhumble 182	d																								
Leatherhead 182	d					20 40									21 11									21 39	
Ashtead 182	d					20 43									21 14									21 43	
Epsom 8 182	a					20 48									21 19									21 47	
	d					20 49					21 04				21 19					21 34				21 49	
Ewell West	d					20 52					21 07				21 22					21 37				21 52	
Stoneleigh	d					20 54					21 09				21 24					21 39				21 54	
Worcester Park	d					20 57					21 12				21 27					21 42				21 57	
Chessington South	d		20 38									21 08									21 38				
Chessington North	d		20 40									21 10									21 40				
Tolworth	d		20 43									21 13									21 43				
Malden Manor	d		20 45									21 15									21 45				
Motspur Park	d		20 49			21 00					21 15	21 19			21 30					21 45	21 49			22 00	
Raynes Park 6	d		20 53	20 58		21 04		21 10	21 13		21 19	21 23	21 28		21 34	21 40		21 43		21 49	21 53	21 58		22 04	22 10
Wimbledon 6 ⊖ ⇌	d	20 50	20 57	21 02	21 05	21 08		21 14	21 17	21 20	21 23	21 27	21 32	21 35	21 38	21 44		21 47	21 50	21 53	21 57	22 02	22 05	22 08	22 14
Earlsfield	d	20 54	21 01	21 06	21 08	21 12		21 17	21 20	21 24	21 27	21 31	21 35	21 38	21 42	21 47		21 50	21 54	21 57	22 01	22 05	22 08	22 12	22 17
Clapham Junction 10	d	20 58	21 05	21 09	21 12	21 16		21 21	21 24	21 28	21 31	21 35	21 39	21 42	21 46	21 51		21 54	21 58	22 01	22 05	22 09	22 12	22 16	22 21
Vauxhall ⊖	d	21 03	21 10	21 14	21 17	21 21		21 26	21 29	21 33	21 36	21 40	21 44	21 47	21 51	21 56		21 59	22 03	22 06	22 10	22 14	22 17	22 21	22 26
London Waterloo 15 ⊖	a	21 09	21 16	21 19	21 23	21 25		21 31	21 35	21 37	21 40	21 46	21 49	21 52	21 55	22 01		22 05	22 07	22 10	22 16	22 19	22 22	22 25	22 31

A From London Waterloo B From Woking

Saturdays

26 May to 6 October

Hampton Court, Shepperton, Guildford, Dorking and Chessington South - London

		SW		SW	SW A	SW B	SW	SW	SW	SW	SW	SW A		SW	SW	SW	SW	SW	SW A	SW	SW	SW		SW	SW
Guildford	d			21 37			21 46			22 07				22 20				22 37		22 46	22 55				23 07
London Road (Guildford)	d			21 41			21 50			22 11								22 41		22 50					23 11
Clandon	d			21 46			21 55			22 16								22 46		22 55					23 16
Horsley	d			21 50			21 59			22 20								22 50		22 59					23 20
Effingham Junction	d			21 53			22 03			22 23								22 53		23 03					23 23
Bookham	d						22 06													23 06					
Cobham & Stoke d'Abernon	d			21 57						22 27								22 57							23 27
Oxshott	d			22 00						22 30								23 00							23 30
Claygate	d			22 03						22 33								23 03							23 33
Hinchley Wood	d			22 06						22 36								23 06							23 36
Hampton Court	d								22 24							22 54								23 24	
Thames Ditton	d								22 26							22 56								23 26	
Surbiton	d			22 11		22 27			22a32	22 41				22 57		23 02		23 11			23 30			23a32	23 41
Berrylands	d															23 04									23 43
Shepperton	d	21 41						22 11									22 41					23 11			
Upper Halliford	d	21 44						22 14									22 44					23 14			
Sunbury	d	21 46						22 16									22 46					23 16			
Kempton Park	d	21 48						22 18									22 48					23 18			
Hampton	d	21 51						22 21									22 51					23 21			
Fulwell	d	21 54						22 24									22 54					23 24			
Strawberry Hill	d				22 07							22 37							23 07						
Teddington	d	21 59			22 11			22 29				22 41					22 59		23 11			23 29			
Hampton Wick	d	22 01			22 14			22 31				22 44					23 01		23 14			23 31			
Kingston	a	22 03			22 16			22 33				22 46					23 03		23 16			23 33			
	d	22 04			22 18			22 34				22 48					23 04		23 18			23 34			
Norbiton	d	22 06			22 20			22 36				22 50					23 06		23 20			23 36			
New Malden	d	22 10			22 25			22 40				22 55				23 07	23 10		23 25			23 40			23 46
Dorking	182 d														22 33										
Box Hill & Westhumble	182 d																								
Leatherhead	182 d						22 11								22 39					23 11					
Ashtead	182 d						22 14								22 43					23 14					
Epsom	182 a						22 19								22 48					23 19					
	d						22 19								22 49					23 19					
Ewell West	d						22 22								22 52					23 22					
Stoneleigh	d						22 24								22 54					23 24					
Worcester Park	d						22 27								22 57					23 27					
Chessington South	d										22 38														
Chessington North	d										22 40														
Tolworth	d										22 43														
Malden Manor	d										22 45														
Motspur Park	d						22 30				22 49				23 00					23 30					
Raynes Park	d	22 13			22 28		22 34	22 43			22 53	22 58			23 04	23 10	23 13		23 28	23 37		23 43			23 49
Wimbledon ⊖	d	22 17		22 20	22 32	22 35	22 38	22 47		22 50	22 57	23 02		23 05	23 08	23 14	23 17	23 20	23 32	23 41	23 37	23 47			23 53
Earlsfield	d	22 20		22 24	22 35	22 38	22 42	22 50		22 54	23 01	23 05		23 08	23 12	23 17	23 20	23 24	23 35	23 44	23 41	23 50			23 56
Clapham Junction	d	22 24		22 28	22 39	22 42	22 46	22 54		22 58	23 05	23 09		23 12	23 16	23 21	23 24	23 28	23 39	23 48	23 45	23 54			23 59
Vauxhall ⊖	d	22 29		22 33	22 44	22 47	22 51	22 59		23 03	23 10	23 14		23 17	23 21	23 26	23 29	23 33	23 44	23 53	23 50	23 59			00 05
London Waterloo ⊖	a	22 35		22 40	22 49	22 52	22 55	23 04		23 07	23 16	23 19		23 22	23 25	23 31	23 35	23 37	23 49	23 58	23 54	00 05			00 14

A From London Waterloo
B From Woking

Table T152-R

Saturdays

26 May to 6 October

Hampton Court, Shepperton, Guildford, Dorking and Chessington South - London

		SW	SW A	SW ◇ B	SW
Guildford	d			23 39	
London Road (Guildford)	d				
Clandon	d				
Horsley	d				
Effingham Junction	d				
Bookham	d				
Cobham & Stoke d'Abernon	d				
Oxshott	d				
Claygate	d				
Hinchley Wood	d				
Hampton Court	d				23 59
Thames Ditton	d				00 02
Surbiton	d			00 08	00 12
Berrylands	d				00 14
Shepperton	d				
Upper Halliford	d				
Sunbury	d				
Kempton Park	d				
Hampton	d				
Fulwell	d				
Strawberry Hill	d		23 37		
Teddington	d		23 41		
Hampton Wick	d		23 44		
Kingston	a		23 46		
	d		23 48		
Norbiton	d		23 50		
New Malden	d		23 55		00 17
Dorking	182 d				
Box Hill & Westhumble	182 d				
Leatherhead	182 d				
Ashtead	182 d				
Epsom	182 a				
	d				
Ewell West	d				
Stoneleigh	d				
Worcester Park	d				
Chessington South	d	23 40			
Chessington North	d	23 42			
Tolworth	d	23 44			
Malden Manor	d	23 47			
Motspur Park	d	23 50			
Raynes Park	d	23 54	23 58		00 20
Wimbledon ⊖	d	23a57	00 02	00 16	00a23
Earlsfield	d		00 05		
Clapham Junction	d		00 09	00 23	
Vauxhall ⊖	d		00 15		
London Waterloo ⊖	a		00 22	00 32	

A From London Waterloo
B From Portsmouth Harbour

Table T152-R

Saturdays

13 October to 8 December

Hampton Court, Shepperton, Guildford, Dorking and Chessington South - London

		SW A	SW B	SW C	SW C	SW ◇1 D	SW E	SW	SW F	SW	SW	SW	SW	SW	SW C	SW G	SW	SW	SW	SW	SW C	SW G	SW
Guildford	d							04 25				05 14											
London Road (Guildford)	d																						
Clandon	d																						
Horsley	d																						
Effingham Junction	d																						
Bookham	d																						
Cobham & Stoke d'Abernon	d																						
Oxshott	d																						
Claygate	d																						
Hinchley Wood	d																						
Hampton Court	d												05 54				06 24						06 54
Thames Ditton	d						00 02						05 56				06 26						06 56
Surbiton	d					00 08	00 12	04 54				05 56	06 02			06 26	06 32					06 57	07 02
Berrylands	d						00 14						06 04				06 34						07 04
Shepperton	d																	06 11					
Upper Halliford	d																	06 14					
Sunbury	d																	06 16					
Kempton Park	d																	06 18					
Hampton	d																	06 21					
Fulwell	d																	06 24					
Strawberry Hill	d			00 09					04 55						06 07						06 37		
Teddington	d			00 12					04 59		05 44				06 11			06 29			06 41		
Hampton Wick	d			00 14					05 01		05 46				06 14			06 31			06 44		
Kingston	a			00 16					05 03		05 48				06 16			06 33			06 46		
	d								05 04		05 49				06 18			06 34			06 48		
Norbiton	d								05 06		05 51				06 20			06 36			06 50		
New Malden	d						00 17		05 10		05 55			06 07	06 25		06 37	06 40			06 55		07 07
Dorking 182	d																						
Box Hill & Westhumble 182	d																						
Leatherhead 182	d																						
Ashtead 182	d																						
Epsom 182	a																						
	d									05 34				06 04					06 34				
Ewell West	d									05 37				06 07					06 37				
Stoneleigh	d									05 39				06 09					06 39				
Worcester Park	d									05 42				06 12					06 42				
Chessington South	d																			06 38			
Chessington North	d																			06 40			
Tolworth	d																			06 43			
Malden Manor	d																			06 45			
Motspur Park	d									05 45				06 15					06 45	06 49			
Raynes Park	d						00 20		05 13	05 49	05 58		06 10	06 19	06 28		06 40	06 43	06 49	06 53	06 58		07 10
Wimbledon ⊖	d					00 16	00a23	05 02	05 17	05 53	06 02	06 05	06 14	06 23	06 32	06 35	06 44	06 47	06 53	06 57	07 02	07 05	07 14
Earlsfield	d								05 21	05 58	06 05	06 08	06 17	06 27	06 35	06 38	06 47	06 50	06 57	07 01	07 05	07 08	07 17
Clapham Junction	d				00 05	00 23		05 09	05 25	06 02	06 09	06 12	06 21	06 31	06 39	06 42	06 51	06 54	07 01	07 05	07 09	07 12	07 21
Vauxhall ⊖	d	00 02	00 05		00 12				05 30	06 07	06 14	06 17	06 26	06 36	06 44	06 47	06 56	06 59	07 06	07 10	07 14	07 17	07 26
London Waterloo ⊖	a	00 08	00 13		00 16	00 32		05 18	05 35	06 11	06 19	06 22	06 31	06 40	06 49	06 52	07 01	07 05	07 10	07 16	07 19	07 22	07 31

A From Shepperton
B From Guildford
C From London Waterloo
D From Portsmouth Harbour
E From Hampton Court
F From Twickenham
G From Woking

Table T152-R

Saturdays

13 October to 8 December

Hampton Court, Shepperton, Guildford, Dorking and Chessington South - London

		SW	SW	SW	SW	SW A	SW B	SW	SW	SW	SW	SW	SW A	SW B	SW	SW	SW	SW	SW	SW A	SW B	SW	SW
Guildford	d		06 28	06 34						06 58	07 04						07 28	07 34					
London Road (Guildford)	d		06 32	06 38						07 02	07 08						07 32	07 38					
Clandon	d		06 37	06 43						07 07	07 13						07 37	07 43					
Horsley	d		06 41	06 47						07 11	07 17						07 41	07 47					
Effingham Junction	d		06 45	06 50						07 15	07 20						07 45	07 50					
Bookham	d		06 48							07 18							07 48						
Cobham & Stoke d'Abernon	d			06 54							07 24							07 54					
Oxshott	d			06 57							07 27							07 57					
Claygate	d			07 00							07 30							08 00					
Hinchley Wood	d			07 03							07 33							08 03					
Hampton Court	d							07 24							07 54								08 24
Thames Ditton	d							07 26							07 56								08 26
Surbiton	d			07 11			07 27	07 32			07 41			07 57	08 02			08 11			08 27		08 32
Berrylands	d							07 34							08 04								08 34
Shepperton	d	06 41							07 11							07 41							
Upper Halliford	d	06 44							07 14							07 44							
Sunbury	d	06 46							07 16							07 46							
Kempton Park	d	06 48							07 18							07 48							
Hampton	d	06 51							07 21							07 51							
Fulwell	d	06 54							07 24							07 54							
Strawberry Hill	d					07 07							07 37							08 07			
Teddington	d	06 59				07 11			07 29				07 41			07 59				08 11			
Hampton Wick	d	07 01				07 14			07 31				07 44			08 01				08 14			
Kingston	a	07 03				07 16			07 33				07 46			08 03				08 16			
	d	07 04				07 18			07 34				07 48			08 04				08 18			
Norbiton	d	07 06				07 20			07 36				07 50			08 06				08 20			
New Malden	d	07 10				07 25		07 37	07 40				07 55		08 07	08 10				08 25			08 37
Dorking 182	d																					08 03	
Box Hill & Westhumble 182	d																						
Leatherhead 182	d		06 55							07 23							07 53					08 09	
Ashtead 182	d		06 59							07 27							07 57					08 13	
Epsom 182	a		07 03							07 31							08 01					08 17	
	d		07 04							07 34							08 04					08 19	
Ewell West	d		07 07							07 37							08 07					08 22	
Stoneleigh	d		07 09							07 39							08 09					08 24	
Worcester Park	d		07 12							07 42							08 12					08 27	
Chessington South	d				07 08							07 38							08 08				
Chessington North	d				07 10							07 40							08 10				
Tolworth	d				07 13							07 43							08 13				
Malden Manor	d				07 15							07 45							08 15				
Motspur Park	d		07 15		07 19					07 45		07 49					08 15		08 19			08 30	
Raynes Park	d	07 13	07 19		07 23	07 28		07 40	07 43	07 49		07 53	07 58		08 10	08 13	08 19		08 23	08 28		08 34	08 40
Wimbledon ⊖	d	07 17	07 23	07 20	07 27	07 32	07 35	07 44	07 47	07 53	07 50	07 57	08 02	08 05	08 14	08 17	08 23	08 20	08 27	08 32	08 35	08 38	08 44
Earlsfield	d	07 20	07 27	07 24	07 31	07 35	07 38	07 47	07 50	07 57	07 54	08 01	08 05	08 08	08 17	08 20	08 27	08 24	08 31	08 35	08 38	08 42	08 47
Clapham Junction	d	07 24	07 31	07 28	07 35	07 39	07 42	07 51	07 54	08 01	07 58	08 05	08 09	08 12	08 21	08 24	08 31	08 28	08 35	08 39	08 42	08 46	08 51
Vauxhall ⊖	d	07 29	07 36	07 33	07 40	07 44	07 47	07 56	07 59	08 06	08 03	08 10	08 14	08 17	08 26	08 29	08 36	08 33	08 40	08 44	08 47	08 51	08 56
London Waterloo ⊖	a	07 35	07 40	07 37	07 46	07 49	07 52	08 01	08 05	08 10	08 07	08 16	08 19	08 22	08 31	08 35	08 40	08 40	08 46	08 49	08 52	08 55	09 01

A From London Waterloo
B From Woking

Table T152-R

Saturdays

13 October to 8 December

Hampton Court, Shepperton, Guildford, Dorking and Chessington South - London

		SW		SW	SW	SW	SW A	SW B	SW	SW	SW	SW		SW	SW	SW A	SW B	SW	SW	SW	SW	SW		SW	SW A
Guildford	d			07 58	08 04							08 28		08 34							08 58	09 04			
London Road (Guildford)	d			08 02	08 08							08 32		08 38							09 02	09 08			
Clandon	d			08 07	08 13							08 37		08 43							09 07	09 13			
Horsley	d			08 11	08 17							08 41		08 47							09 11	09 17			
Effingham Junction	d			08 15	08 20							08 45		08 50							09 15	09 20			
Bookham	d			08 18								08 48									09 18				
Cobham & Stoke d'Abernon	d				08 24									08 54								09 24			
Oxshott	d				08 27									08 57								09 27			
Claygate	d				08 30									09 00								09 30			
Hinchley Wood	d				08 33									09 03								09 33			
Hampton Court	d									08 54									09 24						
Thames Ditton	d									08 56									09 26						
Surbiton	d				08 41			08 57		09 02				09 11			09 27		09 32			09 41			
Berrylands	d									09 04									09 34						
Shepperton	d	08 11									08 41									09 11					
Upper Halliford	d	08 14									08 44									09 14					
Sunbury	d	08 16									08 46									09 16					
Kempton Park	d	08 18									08 48									09 18					
Hampton	d	08 21									08 51									09 21					
Fulwell	d	08 24									08 54									09 24					
Strawberry Hill	d						08 37									09 07									09 37
Teddington	d	08 29					08 41				08 59					09 11				09 29					09 41
Hampton Wick	d	08 31					08 44				09 01					09 14				09 31					09 44
Kingston	a	08 33					08 46				09 03					09 16				09 33					09 46
	d	08 34					08 48				09 04					09 18				09 34					09 48
Norbiton	d	08 36					08 50				09 06					09 20				09 36					09 50
New Malden	d	08 40					08 55			09 07	09 10					09 25			09 37	09 40					09 55
Dorking	182 d								08 33									09 03							
Box Hill & Westhumble	182 d																								
Leatherhead	182 d			08 23					08 39			08 53						09 09			09 23				
Ashtead	182 d			08 27					08 43			08 57						09 13			09 27				
Epsom	182 a			08 31					08 47			09 01						09 17			09 31				
	d			08 34					08 49			09 04						09 19			09 34				
Ewell West	d			08 37					08 52			09 07						09 22			09 37				
Stoneleigh	d			08 39					08 54			09 09						09 24			09 39				
Worcester Park	d			08 42					08 57			09 12						09 27			09 42				
Chessington South	d					08 38									09 08									09 38	
Chessington North	d					08 40									09 10									09 40	
Tolworth	d					08 43									09 13									09 43	
Malden Manor	d					08 45									09 15									09 45	
Motspur Park	d			08 45		08 49			09 00			09 15			09 19			09 30			09 45			09 49	
Raynes Park	d	08 43		08 49		08 53	08 58		09 04	09 10	09 13	09 19			09 23	09 28		09 34	09 40	09 43	09 49			09 53	09 58
Wimbledon ⊖	d	08 47		08 53	08 50	08 57	09 02	09 05	09 08	09 14	09 17	09 23		09 20	09 27	09 32	09 35	09 38	09 44	09 47	09 53	09 50		09 57	10 02
Earlsfield	d	08 50		08 57	08 54	09 01	09 05	09 08	09 12	09 17	09 20	09 27		09 24	09 31	09 35	09 38	09 42	09 47	09 50	09 57	09 54		10 01	10 05
Clapham Junction	d	08 54		09 01	08 58	09 05	09 09	09 12	09 16	09 21	09 24	09 31		09 28	09 35	09 39	09 42	09 46	09 51	09 54	10 01	09 58		10 05	10 09
Vauxhall ⊖	d	08 59		09 06	09 03	09 10	09 14	09 17	09 21	09 26	09 29	09 36		09 33	09 40	09 44	09 47	09 51	09 56	09 59	10 06	10 03		10 10	10 14
London Waterloo ⊖	a	09 05		09 10	09 07	09 16	09 19	09 22	09 25	09 31	09 35	09 40		09 37	09 46	09 49	09 52	09 55	10 01	10 05	10 10	10 07		10 16	10 19

A From London Waterloo
B From Woking

Table T152-R

Saturdays

13 October to 8 December

Hampton Court, Shepperton, Guildford, Dorking and Chessington South - London

		SW A	SW	SW	SW	SW	SW	SW		SW B	SW A	SW	SW	SW	SW	SW	SW	SW B		SW A	SW	SW	SW	SW	SW
Guildford	d					09 28	09 34								09 58	10 04								10 28	10 34
London Road (Guildford)	d					09 32	09 38								10 02	10 08								10 32	10 38
Clandon	d					09 37	09 43								10 07	10 13								10 37	10 43
Horsley	d					09 41	09 47								10 11	10 17								10 41	10 47
Effingham Junction	d					09 45	09 50								10 15	10 20								10 45	10 50
Bookham	d					09 48									10 18									10 48	
Cobham & Stoke d'Abernon	d						09 54									10 24									10 54
Oxshott	d						09 57									10 27									10 57
Claygate	d						10 00									10 30									11 00
Hinchley Wood	d						10 03									10 33									11 03
Hampton Court	d			09 54									10 24									10 54			
Thames Ditton	d			09 56									10 26									10 56			
Surbiton	d	09 57		10 02			10 11				10 27		10 32			10 41				10 57		11 02			11 11
Berrylands	d			10 04									10 34									11 04			
Shepperton	d				09 41									10 11									10 41		
Upper Halliford	d				09 44									10 14									10 44		
Sunbury	d				09 46									10 16									10 46		
Kempton Park	d				09 48									10 18									10 48		
Hampton	d				09 51									10 21									10 51		
Fulwell	d				09 54									10 24									10 54		
Strawberry Hill	d									10 07								10 37							
Teddington	d				09 59					10 11				10 29				10 41					10 59		
Hampton Wick	d				10 01					10 14				10 31				10 44					11 01		
Kingston	a				10 03					10 16				10 33				10 46					11 03		
	d				10 04					10 18				10 34				10 48					11 04		
Norbiton	d				10 06					10 20				10 36				10 50					11 06		
New Malden	d			10 07	10 10					10 25			10 37	10 40				10 55				11 07	11 10		
Dorking	182 d		09 33									10 03									10 33				
Box Hill & Westhumble	182 d																								
Leatherhead	182 d		09 39			09 53						10 09			10 23						10 39			10 53	
Ashtead	182 d		09 43			09 57						10 13			10 27						10 43			10 57	
Epsom	182 a		09 47			10 01						10 17			10 31						10 47			11 01	
	d		09 49			10 04						10 19			10 34						10 49			11 04	
Ewell West	d		09 52			10 07						10 22			10 37						10 52			11 07	
Stoneleigh	d		09 54			10 09						10 24			10 39						10 54			11 09	
Worcester Park	d		09 57			10 12						10 27			10 42						10 57			11 12	
Chessington South	d							10 08									10 38								
Chessington North	d							10 10									10 40								
Tolworth	d							10 13									10 43								
Malden Manor	d							10 15									10 45								
Motspur Park	d		10 00			10 15		10 19				10 30			10 45		10 49				11 00			11 15	
Raynes Park	d		10 04	10 10	10 13	10 19		10 23		10 28		10 34	10 40	10 43	10 49		10 53	10 58			11 04	11 10	11 13	11 19	
Wimbledon ⊖	d	10 05	10 08	10 14	10 17	10 23	10 20	10 27		10 32	10 35	10 38	10 44	10 47	10 53	10 50	10 57	11 02		11 05	11 08	11 14	11 17	11 23	11 20
Earlsfield	d	10 08	10 12	10 17	10 20	10 27	10 24	10 31		10 35	10 38	10 42	10 47	10 50	10 57	10 54	11 01	11 05		11 08	11 12	11 17	11 20	11 27	11 24
Clapham Junction	d	10 12	10 16	10 21	10 24	10 31	10 28	10 35		10 39	10 42	10 46	10 51	10 54	11 01	10 58	11 05	11 09		11 12	11 16	11 21	11 24	11 31	11 28
Vauxhall ⊖	d	10 17	10 21	10 26	10 29	10 36	10 33	10 40		10 44	10 47	10 51	10 56	10 59	11 06	11 03	11 10	11 14		11 17	11 21	11 26	11 29	11 36	11 33
London Waterloo ⊖	a	10 22	10 25	10 31	10 35	10 40	10 37	10 46		10 49	10 52	10 55	11 01	11 05	11 10	11 07	11 16	11 19		11 22	11 25	11 31	11 35	11 40	11 37

A From Woking
B From London Waterloo

Table T152-R

Saturdays

13 October to 8 December

Hampton Court, Shepperton, Guildford, Dorking and Chessington South - London

Station		SW	SW A	SW B	SW	SW	SW	SW	SW	SW	SW A	SW B	SW	SW	SW	SW	SW	SW	SW A	SW B	SW	SW
Guildford	d							10 58	11 04							11 28	11 34					
London Road (Guildford)	d							11 02	11 08							11 32	11 38					
Clandon	d							11 07	11 13							11 37	11 43					
Horsley	d							11 11	11 17							11 41	11 47					
Effingham Junction	d							11 15	11 20							11 45	11 50					
Bookham	d							11 18								11 48						
Cobham & Stoke d'Abernon	d								11 24								11 54					
Oxshott	d								11 27								11 57					
Claygate	d								11 30								12 00					
Hinchley Wood	d								11 33								12 03					
Hampton Court	d					11 24								11 54								12 24
Thames Ditton	d					11 26								11 56								12 26
Surbiton	d			11 27		11 32			11 41			11 57		12 02			12 11			12 27		12 32
Berrylands	d					11 34								12 04								12 34
Shepperton	d						11 11								11 41							
Upper Halliford	d						11 14								11 44							
Sunbury	d						11 16								11 46							
Kempton Park	d						11 18								11 48							
Hampton	d						11 21								11 51							
Fulwell	d						11 24								11 54							
Strawberry Hill	d		11 07								11 37								12 07			
Teddington	d		11 11				11 29				11 41				11 59				12 11			
Hampton Wick	d		11 14				11 31				11 44				12 01				12 14			
Kingston	a		11 16				11 33				11 46				12 03				12 16			
	d		11 18				11 34				11 48				12 04				12 18			
Norbiton	d		11 20				11 36				11 50				12 06				12 20			
New Malden	d		11 25			11 37	11 40				11 55			12 07	12 10				12 25			12 37
Dorking	182 d				11 03								11 33								12 03	
Box Hill & Westhumble	182 d																					
Leatherhead	182 d				11 09			11 23					11 39			11 53					12 09	
Ashtead	182 d				11 13			11 27					11 43			11 57					12 13	
Epsom	182 a				11 17			11 31					11 47			12 01					12 17	
	d				11 19			11 34					11 49			12 04					12 19	
Ewell West	d				11 22			11 37					11 52			12 07					12 22	
Stoneleigh	d				11 24			11 39					11 54			12 09					12 24	
Worcester Park	d				11 27			11 42					11 57			12 12					12 27	
Chessington South	d	11 08								11 38								12 08				
Chessington North	d	11 10								11 40								12 10				
Tolworth	d	11 13								11 43								12 13				
Malden Manor	d	11 15								11 45								12 15				
Motspur Park	d	11 19			11 30			11 45		11 49			12 00			12 15		12 19			12 30	
Raynes Park	d	11 23	11 28		11 34	11 40	11 43	11 49		11 53	11 58		12 04	12 10	12 13	12 19		12 23	12 28		12 34	12 40
Wimbledon ⊖	d	11 27	11 32	11 35	11 38	11 44	11 47	11 53	11 50	11 57	12 02	12 05	12 08	12 14	12 17	12 23	12 20	12 27	12 32	12 35	12 38	12 44
Earlsfield	d	11 31	11 35	11 38	11 42	11 47	11 50	11 57	11 54	12 01	12 05	12 08	12 12	12 17	12 20	12 27	12 24	12 31	12 35	12 38	12 42	12 47
Clapham Junction	d	11 35	11 39	11 42	11 46	11 51	11 54	12 01	11 58	12 05	12 09	12 12	12 16	12 21	12 24	12 31	12 28	12 35	12 39	12 42	12 46	12 51
Vauxhall ⊖	d	11 40	11 44	11 47	11 51	11 56	11 59	12 06	12 03	12 10	12 14	12 17	12 21	12 26	12 29	12 36	12 33	12 40	12 44	12 47	12 51	12 56
London Waterloo ⊖	a	11 46	11 49	11 52	11 55	12 01	12 05	12 10	12 07	12 16	12 19	12 22	12 25	12 31	12 35	12 40	12 37	12 46	12 49	12 52	12 55	13 01

A From London Waterloo

B From Woking

Table T152-R

Saturdays

13 October to 8 December

Hampton Court, Shepperton, Guildford, Dorking and Chessington South - London

Station		SW	SW	SW	SW	SW A	SW B	SW	SW	SW	SW	SW	SW	SW A	SW B	SW	SW	SW	SW	SW	SW	SW A	SW B
Guildford	d		11 58	12 04							12 28	12 34							12 58	13 04			
London Road (Guildford)	d		12 02	12 08							12 32	12 38							13 02	13 08			
Clandon	d		12 07	12 13							12 37	12 43							13 07	13 13			
Horsley	d		12 11	12 17							12 41	12 47							13 11	13 17			
Effingham Junction	d		12 15	12 20							12 45	12 50							13 15	13 20			
Bookham	d		12 18								12 48								13 18				
Cobham & Stoke d'Abernon	d			12 24								12 54								13 24			
Oxshott	d			12 27								12 57								13 27			
Claygate	d			12 30								13 00								13 30			
Hinchley Wood	d			12 33								13 03								13 33			
Hampton Court	d								12 54								13 24						
Thames Ditton	d								12 56								13 26						
Surbiton	d			12 41			12 57		13 02			13 11			13 27		13 32			13 41			13 57
Berrylands	d								13 04								13 34						
Shepperton	d	12 11								12 41								13 11					
Upper Halliford	d	12 14								12 44								13 14					
Sunbury	d	12 16								12 46								13 16					
Kempton Park	d	12 18								12 48								13 18					
Hampton	d	12 21								12 51								13 21					
Fulwell	d	12 24								12 54								13 24					
Strawberry Hill	d					12 37								13 07								13 37	
Teddington	d	12 29				12 41				12 59				13 11				13 29				13 41	
Hampton Wick	d	12 31				12 44				13 01				13 14				13 31				13 44	
Kingston	a	12 33				12 46				13 03				13 16				13 33				13 46	
	d	12 34				12 48				13 04				13 18				13 34				13 48	
Norbiton	d	12 36				12 50				13 06				13 20				13 36				13 50	
New Malden	d	12 40				12 55			13 07	13 10				13 25			13 37	13 40				13 55	
Dorking	182 d							12 33								13 03							
Box Hill & Westhumble	182 d																						
Leatherhead	182 d		12 23					12 39			12 53					13 09			13 23				
Ashtead	182 d		12 27					12 43			12 57					13 13			13 27				
Epsom	182 a		12 31					12 47			13 01					13 17			13 31				
	d		12 34					12 49			13 04					13 19			13 34				
Ewell West	d		12 37					12 52			13 07					13 22			13 37				
Stoneleigh	d		12 39					12 54			13 09					13 24			13 39				
Worcester Park	d		12 42					12 57			13 12					13 27			13 42				
Chessington South	d				12 38								13 08								13 38		
Chessington North	d				12 40								13 10								13 40		
Tolworth	d				12 43								13 13								13 43		
Malden Manor	d				12 45								13 15								13 45		
Motspur Park	d		12 45		12 49			13 00			13 15		13 19			13 30			13 45		13 49		
Raynes Park	d	12 43	12 49		12 53	12 58		13 04	13 10	13 13	13 19		13 23	13 28		13 34	13 40	13 43	13 49		13 53	13 58	
Wimbledon ⊖	d	12 47	12 53	12 50	12 57	13 02	13 05	13 08	13 14	13 17	13 23	13 20	13 27	13 32	13 35	13 38	13 44	13 47	13 53	13 50	13 57	14 02	14 05
Earlsfield	d	12 50	12 57	12 54	13 01	13 05	13 08	13 12	13 17	13 20	13 27	13 24	13 31	13 35	13 38	13 42	13 47	13 50	13 57	13 54	14 01	14 05	14 08
Clapham Junction	d	12 54	13 01	12 58	13 05	13 09	13 12	13 16	13 21	13 24	13 31	13 28	13 35	13 39	13 42	13 46	13 51	13 54	14 01	13 58	14 05	14 09	14 12
Vauxhall ⊖	d	12 59	13 06	13 03	13 10	13 14	13 17	13 21	13 26	13 29	13 36	13 33	13 40	13 44	13 47	13 51	13 56	13 59	14 06	14 03	14 10	14 14	14 17
London Waterloo ⊖	a	13 05	13 10	13 07	13 16	13 19	13 22	13 25	13 31	13 35	13 40	13 37	13 46	13 49	13 52	13 55	14 01	14 05	14 10	14 07	14 16	14 19	14 22

A From London Waterloo

B From Woking

Table T152-R

Saturdays

13 October to 8 December

Hampton Court, Shepperton, Guildford, Dorking and Chessington South - London

		SW	SW	SW	SW	SW		SW	SW A	SW B	SW	SW	SW	SW	SW	SW		SW A	SW B	SW	SW	SW	SW	SW	SW
Guildford	d				13 28	13 34								13 58	14 04								14 28	14 34	
London Road (Guildford)	d				13 32	13 38								14 02	14 08								14 32	14 38	
Clandon	d				13 37	13 43								14 07	14 13								14 37	14 43	
Horsley	d				13 41	13 47								14 11	14 17								14 41	14 47	
Effingham Junction ■	d				13 45	13 50								14 15	14 20								14 45	14 50	
Bookham	d				13 48									14 18									14 48		
Cobham & Stoke d'Abernon	d					13 54									14 24									14 54	
Oxshott	d					13 57									14 27									14 57	
Claygate	d					14 00									14 30									15 00	
Hinchley Wood	d					14 03									14 33									15 03	
Hampton Court	d		13 54									14 24									14 54				
Thames Ditton	d		13 56									14 26									14 56				
Surbiton ■	d		14 02			14 11				14 27		14 32			14 41				14 57		15 02			15 11	
Berrylands	d		14 04									14 34									15 04				
Shepperton	d			13 41									14 11									14 41			
Upper Halliford	d			13 44									14 14									14 44			
Sunbury	d			13 46									14 16									14 46			
Kempton Park	d			13 48									14 18									14 48			
Hampton	d			13 51									14 21									14 51			
Fulwell	d			13 54									14 24									14 54			
Strawberry Hill	d								14 07									14 37							
Teddington	d			13 59					14 11				14 29					14 41				14 59			
Hampton Wick	d			14 01					14 14				14 31					14 44				15 01			
Kingston	a			14 03					14 16				14 33					14 46				15 03			
	d			14 04					14 18				14 34					14 48				15 04			
Norbiton	d			14 06					14 20				14 36					14 50				15 06			
New Malden ■	d		14 07	14 10					14 25			14 37	14 40					14 55			15 07	15 10			
Dorking ■ 182	d	13 33									14 03									14 33					
Box Hill & Westhumble 182	d																								
Leatherhead 182	d	13 39			13 53						14 09			14 23						14 39			14 53		
Ashtead 182	d	13 43			13 57						14 13			14 27						14 43			14 57		
Epsom ■ 182	a	13 47			14 01						14 17			14 31						14 47			15 01		
	d	13 49			14 04						14 19			14 34						14 49			15 04		
Ewell West	d	13 52			14 07						14 22			14 37						14 52			15 07		
Stoneleigh	d	13 54			14 09						14 24			14 39						14 54			15 09		
Worcester Park	d	13 57			14 12						14 27			14 42						14 57			15 12		
Chessington South	d							14 08								14 38									15 08
Chessington North	d							14 10								14 40									15 10
Tolworth	d							14 13								14 43									15 13
Malden Manor	d							14 15								14 45									15 15
Motspur Park	d	14 00			14 15			14 19			14 30			14 45		14 49				15 00			15 15		15 19
Raynes Park ■	d	14 04	14 10	14 13	14 19			14 23	14 28		14 34	14 40	14 43	14 49		14 53		14 58		15 04	15 10	15 13	15 19		15 23
Wimbledon ■ ⊖ ⇌	d	14 08	14 14	14 17	14 23	14 20		14 27	14 32	14 35	14 38	14 44	14 47	14 53	14 50	14 57		15 02	15 05	15 08	15 14	15 17	15 23	15 20	15 27
Earlsfield	d	14 12	14 17	14 20	14 27	14 24		14 31	14 35	14 38	14 42	14 47	14 50	14 57	14 54	15 01		15 05	15 08	15 12	15 17	15 20	15 27	15 24	15 31
Clapham Junction ■	d	14 16	14 21	14 24	14 31	14 28		14 35	14 39	14 42	14 46	14 51	14 54	15 01	14 58	15 05		15 09	15 12	15 16	15 21	15 24	15 31	15 28	15 35
Vauxhall ⊖	d	14 21	14 26	14 29	14 36	14 33		14 40	14 44	14 47	14 51	14 56	14 59	15 06	15 03	15 10		15 14	15 17	15 21	15 26	15 29	15 36	15 33	15 40
London Waterloo ■ ⊖	a	14 25	14 31	14 35	14 40	14 37		14 46	14 49	14 52	14 55	15 01	15 05	15 10	15 07	15 16		15 19	15 22	15 25	15 31	15 35	15 40	15 37	15 46

A From London Waterloo
B From Woking

Table T152-R

Saturdays

13 October to 8 December

Hampton Court, Shepperton, Guildford, Dorking and Chessington South - London

		SW A		SW B	SW	SW	SW	SW	SW	SW	SW A	SW B		SW	SW	SW	SW	SW	SW	SW A	SW B	SW		SW	SW
Guildford	d							14 58	15 04								15 28	15 34							
London Road (Guildford)	d							15 02	15 08								15 32	15 38							
Clandon	d							15 07	15 13								15 37	15 43							
Horsley	d							15 11	15 17								15 41	15 47							
Effingham Junction ■	d							15 15	15 20								15 45	15 50							
Bookham	d							15 18									15 48								
Cobham & Stoke d'Abernon	d								15 24									15 54							
Oxshott	d								15 27									15 57							
Claygate	d								15 30									16 00							
Hinchley Wood	d								15 33									16 03							
Hampton Court	d					15 24									15 54									16 24	
Thames Ditton	d					15 26									15 56									16 26	
Surbiton ■	d			15 27		15 32			15 41			15 57			16 02			16 11			16 27			16 32	
Berrylands	d					15 34									16 04									16 34	
Shepperton	d						15 11									15 41									16 11
Upper Halliford	d						15 14									15 44									16 14
Sunbury	d						15 16									15 46									16 16
Kempton Park	d						15 18									15 48									16 18
Hampton	d						15 21									15 51									16 21
Fulwell	d						15 24									15 54									16 24
Strawberry Hill	d	15 07									15 37									16 07					
Teddington	d	15 11					15 29				15 41					15 59				16 11					16 29
Hampton Wick	d	15 14					15 31				15 44					16 01				16 14					16 31
Kingston	a	15 16					15 33				15 46					16 03				16 16					16 33
	d	15 18					15 34				15 48					16 04				16 18					16 34
Norbiton	d	15 20					15 36				15 50					16 06				16 20					16 36
New Malden ■	d	15 25				15 37	15 40				15 55				16 07	16 10				16 25				16 37	16 40
Dorking ■ 182	d				15 03									15 33								16 03			
Box Hill & Westhumble 182	d																								
Leatherhead 182	d				15 09			15 23						15 39			15 53					16 09			
Ashtead 182	d				15 13			15 27						15 43			15 57					16 13			
Epsom ■ 182	a				15 17			15 31						15 47			16 01					16 17			
	d				15 19			15 34						15 49			16 04					16 19			
Ewell West	d				15 22			15 37						15 52			16 07					16 22			
Stoneleigh	d				15 24			15 39						15 54			16 09					16 24			
Worcester Park	d				15 27			15 42						15 57			16 12					16 27			
Chessington South	d									15 38									16 08						
Chessington North	d									15 40									16 10						
Tolworth	d									15 43									16 13						
Malden Manor	d									15 45									16 15						
Motspur Park	d				15 30			15 45		15 49				16 00			16 15		16 19			16 30			
Raynes Park ■	d	15 28			15 34	15 40	15 43	15 49		15 53	15 58			16 04	16 10	16 13	16 19		16 23	16 28		16 34		16 40	16 43
Wimbledon ■ ⊖ ⇌	d	15 32		15 35	15 38	15 44	15 47	15 53	15 50	15 57	16 02	16 05		16 08	16 14	16 17	16 23	16 20	16 27	16 32	16 35	16 38		16 44	16 47
Earlsfield	d	15 35		15 38	15 42	15 47	15 50	15 57	15 54	16 01	16 05	16 08		16 12	16 17	16 20	16 27	16 24	16 31	16 35	16 38	16 42		16 47	16 50
Clapham Junction ■	d	15 39		15 42	15 46	15 51	15 54	16 01	15 58	16 05	16 09	16 12		16 16	16 21	16 24	16 31	16 28	16 35	16 39	16 42	16 46		16 51	16 54
Vauxhall ⊖	d	15 44		15 47	15 51	15 56	15 59	16 06	16 03	16 10	16 14	16 17		16 21	16 26	16 29	16 36	16 33	16 40	16 44	16 47	16 51		16 56	16 59
London Waterloo ■ ⊖	a	15 49		15 52	15 55	16 01	16 05	16 10	16 07	16 16	16 19	16 22		16 25	16 31	16 35	16 40	16 37	16 46	16 49	16 52	16 55		17 01	17 05

A From London Waterloo
B From Woking

Table T152-R

Saturdays

13 October to 8 December

Hampton Court, Shepperton, Guildford, Dorking and Chessington South - London

		SW	SW	SW	SW A	SW B	SW	SW	SW	SW	SW	SW	SW A	SW B	SW	SW	SW	SW	SW	SW	SW A	SW B	SW
Guildford	d	15 58	16 04							16 28	16 34							16 58	17 04				
London Road (Guildford)	d	16 02	16 08							16 32	16 38							17 02	17 08				
Clandon	d	16 07	16 13							16 37	16 43							17 07	17 13				
Horsley	d	16 11	16 17							16 41	16 47							17 11	17 17				
Effingham Junction	d	16 15	16 20							16 45	16 50							17 15	17 20				
Bookham	d	16 18								16 48								17 18					
Cobham & Stoke d'Abernon	d		16 24								16 54								17 24				
Oxshott	d		16 27								16 57								17 27				
Claygate	d		16 30								17 00								17 30				
Hinchley Wood	d		16 33								17 03								17 33				
Hampton Court	d							16 54								17 24							
Thames Ditton	d							16 56								17 26							
Surbiton	d		16 41			16 57		17 02			17 11			17 27		17 32			17 41			17 57	
Berrylands	d							17 04								17 34							
Shepperton	d								16 41								17 11						
Upper Halliford	d								16 44								17 14						
Sunbury	d								16 46								17 16						
Kempton Park	d								16 48								17 18						
Hampton	d								16 51								17 21						
Fulwell	d								16 54								17 24						
Strawberry Hill	d				16 37								17 07								17 37		
Teddington	d				16 41				16 59				17 11				17 29				17 41		
Hampton Wick	d				16 44				17 01				17 14				17 31				17 44		
Kingston	a				16 46				17 03				17 16				17 33				17 46		
	d				16 48				17 04				17 18				17 34				17 48		
Norbiton	d				16 50				17 06				17 20				17 36				17 50		
New Malden	d				16 55			17 07	17 10				17 25			17 37	17 40				17 55		
Dorking 182	d						16 33								17 03								17 33
Box Hill & Westhumble 182	d																						
Leatherhead 182	d	16 23					16 39			16 53					17 09			17 23					17 39
Ashtead 182	d	16 27					16 43			16 57					17 13			17 27					17 43
Epsom 182	a	16 31					16 47			17 01					17 17			17 31					17 47
	d	16 34					16 49			17 04					17 19			17 34					17 49
Ewell West	d	16 37					16 52			17 07					17 22			17 37					17 52
Stoneleigh	d	16 39					16 54			17 09					17 24			17 39					17 54
Worcester Park	d	16 42					16 57			17 12					17 27			17 42					17 57
Chessington South	d			16 38								17 08								17 38			
Chessington North	d			16 40								17 10								17 40			
Tolworth	d			16 43								17 13								17 43			
Malden Manor	d			16 45								17 15								17 45			
Motspur Park	d	16 45		16 49			17 00			17 15		17 19			17 30			17 45		17 49			18 00
Raynes Park	d	16 49		16 53	16 58		17 04	17 10	17 13	17 19		17 23	17 28		17 34	17 40	17 43	17 49		17 53	17 58		18 04
Wimbledon ⊖	d	16 53	16 50	16 57	17 02	17 05	17 08	17 14	17 17	17 23	17 20	17 27	17 32	17 35	17 38	17 44	17 47	17 53	17 50	17 57	18 02	18 05	18 08
Earlsfield	d	16 57	16 54	17 01	17 05	17 08	17 12	17 17	17 20	17 27	17 24	17 31	17 35	17 38	17 42	17 47	17 50	17 57	17 54	18 01	18 05	18 08	18 12
Clapham Junction	d	17 01	16 58	17 05	17 09	17 12	17 16	17 21	17 24	17 31	17 28	17 35	17 39	17 42	17 46	17 51	17 54	18 01	17 58	18 05	18 09	18 12	18 16
Vauxhall ⊖	d	17 06	17 03	17 10	17 14	17 17	17 21	17 26	17 29	17 36	17 33	17 40	17 44	17 47	17 51	17 56	17 59	18 06	18 03	18 10	18 14	18 17	18 21
London Waterloo ⊖	a	17 10	17 07	17 16	17 19	17 22	17 25	17 31	17 35	17 40	17 37	17 46	17 49	17 52	17 55	18 01	18 05	18 10	18 07	18 16	18 19	18 22	18 25

A From London Waterloo   B From Woking

Table T152-R

Saturdays

13 October to 8 December

Hampton Court, Shepperton, Guildford, Dorking and Chessington South - London

		SW	SW	SW	SW	SW	SW A	SW B	SW	SW	SW	SW	SW	SW	SW A	SW B	SW	SW	SW	SW	SW	SW
Guildford	d			17 28	17 34							17 58	18 04							18 28	18 34	
London Road (Guildford)	d			17 32	17 38							18 02	18 08							18 32	18 38	
Clandon	d			17 37	17 43							18 07	18 13							18 37	18 43	
Horsley	d			17 41	17 47							18 11	18 17							18 41	18 47	
Effingham Junction	d			17 45	17 50							18 15	18 20							18 45	18 50	
Bookham	d			17 48								18 18								18 48		
Cobham & Stoke d'Abernon	d				17 54								18 24								18 54	
Oxshott	d				17 57								18 27								18 57	
Claygate	d				18 00								18 30								19 00	
Hinchley Wood	d				18 03								18 33								19 03	
Hampton Court	d	17 54								18 24								18 54				
Thames Ditton	d	17 56								18 26								18 56				
Surbiton	d	18 02			18 11			18 27		18 32			18 41			18 57		19 02			19 11	
Berrylands	d	18 04								18 34								19 04				
Shepperton	d		17 41								18 11								18 41			
Upper Halliford	d		17 44								18 14								18 44			
Sunbury	d		17 46								18 16								18 46			
Kempton Park	d		17 48								18 18								18 48			
Hampton	d		17 51								18 21								18 51			
Fulwell	d		17 54								18 24								18 54			
Strawberry Hill	d						18 07								18 37							
Teddington	d		17 59				18 11				18 29				18 41				18 59			
Hampton Wick	d		18 01				18 14				18 31				18 44				19 01			
Kingston	a		18 03				18 16				18 33				18 46				19 03			
	d		18 04				18 18				18 34				18 48				19 04			
Norbiton	d		18 06				18 20				18 36				18 50				19 06			
New Malden	d	18 07	18 10				18 25			18 37	18 40				18 55			19 07	19 10			
Dorking 182	d								18 03								18 33					
Box Hill & Westhumble 182	d																					
Leatherhead 182	d			17 53					18 09			18 23					18 39			18 53		
Ashtead 182	d			17 57					18 13			18 27					18 43			18 57		
Epsom 182	a			18 01					18 17			18 31					18 47			19 01		
	d			18 04					18 19			18 34					18 49			19 04		
Ewell West	d			18 07					18 22			18 37					18 52			19 07		
Stoneleigh	d			18 09					18 24			18 39					18 54			19 09		
Worcester Park	d			18 12					18 27			18 42					18 57			19 12		
Chessington South	d					18 08								18 38								19 08
Chessington North	d					18 10								18 40								19 10
Tolworth	d					18 13								18 43								19 13
Malden Manor	d					18 15								18 45								19 15
Motspur Park	d			18 15		18 19			18 30			18 45		18 49			19 00			19 15		19 19
Raynes Park	d	18 10	18 13	18 19		18 23	18 28		18 34	18 40	18 43	18 49		18 53	18 58		19 04	19 10	19 13	19 19		19 23
Wimbledon ⊖	d	18 14	18 17	18 23	18 20	18 27	18 32	18 35	18 38	18 44	18 47	18 53	18 50	18 57	19 02	19 05	19 08	19 14	19 17	19 23	19 20	19 27
Earlsfield	d	18 17	18 20	18 27	18 24	18 31	18 35	18 38	18 42	18 47	18 50	18 57	18 54	19 01	19 05	19 08	19 12	19 17	19 20	19 27	19 24	19 31
Clapham Junction	d	18 21	18 24	18 31	18 28	18 35	18 39	18 42	18 46	18 51	18 54	19 01	18 58	19 05	19 09	19 12	19 16	19 21	19 24	19 31	19 28	19 35
Vauxhall ⊖	d	18 26	18 29	18 36	18 33	18 40	18 44	18 47	18 51	18 56	18 59	19 06	19 03	19 10	19 14	19 17	19 21	19 26	19 29	19 36	19 33	19 40
London Waterloo ⊖	a	18 31	18 35	18 40	18 37	18 46	18 49	18 52	18 55	19 01	19 05	19 10	19 07	19 16	19 19	19 22	19 25	19 31	19 35	19 40	19 37	19 46

A From London Waterloo   B From Woking

Table T152-R

Saturdays
13 October to 8 December

Hampton Court, Shepperton, Guildford, Dorking and Chessington South - London

		SW A	SW B	SW	SW	SW	SW	SW	SW	SW A		SW B	SW	SW	SW	SW	SW	SW	SW A	SW B		SW	SW	SW	SW
Guildford	d						18 58	19 04								19 28	19 34								19 58
London Road (Guildford)	d						19 02	19 08								19 32	19 38								20 02
Clandon	d						19 07	19 13								19 37	19 43								20 07
Horsley	d						19 11	19 17								19 41	19 47								20 11
Effingham Junction	d						19 15	19 20								19 45	19 50								20 15
Bookham	d						19 18									19 48									20 18
Cobham & Stoke d'Abernon	d							19 24									19 54								
Oxshott	d							19 27									19 57								
Claygate	d							19 30									20 00								
Hinchley Wood	d							19 33									20 03								
Hampton Court	d				19 24									19 54									20 24		
Thames Ditton	d				19 26									19 56									20 26		
Surbiton	d		19 27		19 32			19 41				19 57		20 02			20 11			20 27			20 32		
Berrylands	d				19 34									20 04									20 34		
Shepperton	d					19 11									19 41									20 11	
Upper Halliford	d					19 14									19 44									20 14	
Sunbury	d					19 16									19 46									20 16	
Kempton Park	d					19 18									19 48									20 18	
Hampton	d					19 21									19 51									20 21	
Fulwell	d					19 24									19 54									20 24	
Strawberry Hill	d	19 07								19 37									20 07						
Teddington	d	19 11				19 29				19 41					19 59				20 11					20 29	
Hampton Wick	d	19 14				19 31				19 44					20 01				20 14					20 31	
Kingston	a	19 16				19 33				19 46					20 03				20 16					20 33	
	d	19 18				19 34				19 48					20 04				20 18					20 34	
Norbiton	d	19 20				19 36				19 50					20 06				20 20					20 36	
New Malden	d	19 25			19 37	19 40				19 55				20 07	20 10				20 25				20 37	20 40	
Dorking	182 d			19 03									19 33									20 03			
Box Hill & Westhumble	182 d																								
Leatherhead	182 d			19 10			19 23						19 40			19 53						20 10			20 23
Ashtead	182 d			19 13			19 27						19 43			19 57						20 13			20 27
Epsom	182 a			19 18			19 31						19 48			20 01						20 18			20 31
	d			19 19			19 34						19 49			20 04						20 19			20 34
Ewell West	d			19 22			19 37						19 52			20 07						20 22			20 37
Stoneleigh	d			19 24			19 39						19 54			20 09						20 24			20 39
Worcester Park	d			19 27			19 42						19 57			20 12						20 27			20 42
Chessington South	d								19 38									20 08							
Chessington North	d								19 40									20 10							
Tolworth	d								19 43									20 13							
Malden Manor	d								19 45									20 15							
Motspur Park	d			19 30			19 45		19 49				20 00			20 15		20 19				20 30			20 45
Raynes Park	d	19 28		19 34	19 40	19 43	19 49		19 53	19 58			20 04	20 10	20 13	20 19		20 23	20 28			20 34	20 40	20 43	20 49
Wimbledon ⊖	d	19 32	19 35	19 38	19 44	19 47	19 53	19 50	19 57	20 02		20 05	20 08	20 14	20 17	20 23	20 20	20 27	20 32	20 35		20 38	20 44	20 47	20 53
Earlsfield	d	19 35	19 38	19 42	19 47	19 50	19 57	19 54	20 01	20 05		20 08	20 12	20 17	20 20	20 27	20 24	20 31	20 35	20 38		20 42	20 47	20 50	20 57
Clapham Junction	d	19 39	19 42	19 46	19 51	19 54	20 01	19 58	20 05	20 09		20 12	20 16	20 21	20 24	20 31	20 28	20 35	20 39	20 42		20 46	20 51	20 54	21 01
Vauxhall ⊖	d	19 44	19 47	19 51	19 56	19 59	20 06	20 03	20 10	20 14		20 17	20 21	20 26	20 29	20 36	20 33	20 40	20 44	20 47		20 51	20 56	20 59	21 06
London Waterloo ⊖	a	19 49	19 52	19 55	20 01	20 05	20 10	20 07	20 16	20 19		20 22	20 25	20 31	20 35	20 40	20 37	20 46	20 49	20 52		20 55	21 01	21 05	21 11

A From London Waterloo
B From Woking

Table T152-R

Saturdays
13 October to 8 December

Hampton Court, Shepperton, Guildford, Dorking and Chessington South - London

		SW	SW	SW A	SW B	SW		SW	SW	SW	SW	SW	SW A	SW B	SW	SW		SW	SW	SW	SW	SW A	SW B	SW	SW
Guildford	d	20 04								20 34					20 46				21 04						
London Road (Guildford)	d	20 08								20 38					20 50				21 08						
Clandon	d	20 13								20 43					20 55				21 13						
Horsley	d	20 17								20 47					20 59				21 17						
Effingham Junction	d	20 20								20 50					21 03				21 20						
Bookham	d														21 06										
Cobham & Stoke d'Abernon	d	20 24								20 54									21 24						
Oxshott	d	20 27								20 57									21 27						
Claygate	d	20 30								21 00									21 30						
Hinchley Wood	d	20 33								21 03									21 33						
Hampton Court	d							20 54								21 24									21 54
Thames Ditton	d							20 56								21 26									21 56
Surbiton	d	20 41			20 57			21 02		21 11				21 27		21 32			21 41				21 57		22 02
Berrylands	d							21 04								21 34									22 04
Shepperton	d								20 41									21 11							
Upper Halliford	d								20 44									21 14							
Sunbury	d								20 46									21 16							
Kempton Park	d								20 48									21 18							
Hampton	d								20 51									21 21							
Fulwell	d								20 54									21 24							
Strawberry Hill	d			20 37									21 07									21 37			
Teddington	d			20 41					20 59				21 11					21 29				21 41			
Hampton Wick	d			20 44					21 01				21 14					21 31				21 44			
Kingston	a			20 46					21 03				21 16					21 33				21 46			
	d			20 48					21 04				21 18					21 34				21 48			
Norbiton	d			20 50					21 06				21 20					21 36				21 50			
New Malden	d			20 55				21 07	21 10				21 25			21 37		21 40				21 55			22 07
Dorking	182 d					20 33																		21 33	
Box Hill & Westhumble	182 d																								
Leatherhead	182 d					20 40									21 11									21 39	
Ashtead	182 d					20 43									21 14									21 43	
Epsom	182 a					20 48									21 19									21 47	
	d					20 49					21 04				21 19					21 34				21 49	
Ewell West	d					20 52					21 07				21 22					21 37				21 52	
Stoneleigh	d					20 54					21 09				21 24					21 39				21 54	
Worcester Park	d					20 57					21 12				21 27					21 42				21 57	
Chessington South	d		20 38									21 08									21 38				
Chessington North	d		20 40									21 10									21 40				
Tolworth	d		20 43									21 13									21 43				
Malden Manor	d		20 45									21 15									21 45				
Motspur Park	d		20 49			21 00					21 15	21 19			21 30					21 45	21 49			22 00	
Raynes Park	d		20 53	20 58		21 04		21 10	21 13		21 19	21 23	21 28		21 34	21 40		21 43		21 49	21 53	21 58		22 04	22 10
Wimbledon ⊖	d	20 50	20 57	21 02	21 05	21 08		21 14	21 17	21 20	21 23	21 27	21 32	21 35	21 38	21 44		21 47	21 50	21 53	21 57	22 02	22 05	22 08	22 14
Earlsfield	d	20 54	21 01	21 06	21 08	21 12		21 17	21 20	21 24	21 27	21 31	21 35	21 38	21 42	21 47		21 50	21 54	21 57	22 01	22 05	22 08	22 12	22 17
Clapham Junction	d	20 58	21 05	21 09	21 12	21 16		21 21	21 24	21 28	21 31	21 35	21 39	21 42	21 46	21 51		21 54	21 58	22 01	22 05	22 09	22 12	22 16	22 21
Vauxhall ⊖	d	21 03	21 10	21 14	21 17	21 21		21 26	21 29	21 33	21 36	21 40	21 44	21 47	21 51	21 56		21 59	22 03	22 06	22 10	22 14	22 17	22 21	22 26
London Waterloo ⊖	a	21 09	21 16	21 19	21 23	21 25		21 31	21 35	21 37	21 40	21 46	21 49	21 52	21 55	22 01		22 05	22 07	22 10	22 16	22 19	22 22	22 25	22 31

A From London Waterloo
B From Woking

Table T152-R

Saturdays
13 October to 8 December

Hampton Court, Shepperton, Guildford, Dorking and Chessington South - London

		SW		SW	SW	SW	SW	SW	SW	SW	SW	SW		SW	SW	SW	SW	SW	SW	SW	SW	SW		SW	SW
					A	B						A							A						
Guildford	d			21 34			21 46			22 04				22 20				22 34		22 46	22 55				23 07
London Road (Guildford)	d			21 38			21 50			22 08								22 38		22 50					23 11
Clandon	d			21 43			21 55			22 13								22 43		22 55					23 16
Horsley	d			21 47			21 59			22 17								22 47		22 59					23 20
Effingham Junction 6	d			21 50			22 03			22 20								22 50		23 03					23 23
Bookham	d						22 06													23 06					
Cobham & Stoke d'Abernon	d			21 54						22 24								22 54							23 27
Oxshott	d			21 57						22 27								22 57							23 30
Claygate	d			22 00						22 30								23 00							23 33
Hinchley Wood	d			22 03						22 33								23 03							23 36
Hampton Court	d								22 24							22 54								23 24	
Thames Ditton	d								22 26							22 56								23 26	
Surbiton 6	d			22 11		22 27			22a32	22 41				22 57		23 02		23 11			23 30			23a32	23 41
Berrylands	d															23 04									23 43
Shepperton	d	21 41						22 11									22 41					23 11			
Upper Halliford	d	21 44						22 14									22 44					23 14			
Sunbury	d	21 46						22 16									22 46					23 16			
Kempton Park	d	21 48						22 18									22 48					23 18			
Hampton	d	21 51						22 21									22 51					23 21			
Fulwell	d	21 54						22 24									22 54					23 24			
Strawberry Hill	d				22 07							22 37							23 07						
Teddington	d	21 59			22 11			22 29				22 41					22 59		23 11			23 29			
Hampton Wick	d	22 01			22 14			22 31				22 44					23 01		23 14			23 31			
Kingston	a	22 03			22 16			22 33				22 46					23 03		23 16			23 33			
	d	22 04			22 18			22 34				22 48					23 04		23 18			23 34			
Norbiton	d	22 06			22 20			22 36				22 50					23 06		23 20			23 36			
New Malden 6	d	22 10			22 25			22 40				22 55				23 07	23 10		23 25			23 40			23 46
Dorking 4 182	d														22 33										
Box Hill & Westhumble 182	d																								
Leatherhead 182	d						22 11								22 39					23 11					
Ashtead 182	d						22 14								22 43					23 14					
Epsom 3 182	a						22 19								22 48					23 19					
	d						22 19								22 49					23 19					
Ewell West	d						22 22								22 52					23 22					
Stoneleigh	d						22 24								22 54					23 24					
Worcester Park	d						22 27								22 57					23 27					
Chessington South	d										22 38														
Chessington North	d										22 40														
Tolworth	d										22 43														
Malden Manor	d										22 45														
Motspur Park	d						22 30				22 49				23 00					23 30					
Raynes Park 6	d	22 13			22 28		22 34	22 43			22 53	22 58			23 04	23 10	23 13		23 28	23 37		23 43			23 49
Wimbledon 6 ⊖ ⛴	d	22 17		22 20	22 32	22 35	22 38	22 47		22 50	22 57	23 02		23 05	23 08	23 14	23 17	23 20	23 32	23 41	23 37	23 47			23 53
Earlsfield	d	22 20		22 24	22 35	22 38	22 42	22 50		22 54	23 01	23 05		23 08	23 12	23 17	23 20	23 24	23 35	23 44	23 41	23 50			23 56
Clapham Junction 10	d	22 24		22 28	22 39	22 42	22 46	22 54		22 58	23 05	23 09		23 12	23 16	23 21	23 24	23 28	23 39	23 48	23 45	23 54			23 59
Vauxhall ⊖	d	22 29		22 33	22 44	22 47	22 51	22 59		23 03	23 10	23 14		23 17	23 21	23 26	23 29	23 33	23 44	23 53	23 50	23 59			00 05
London Waterloo 15 ⊖	a	22 35		22 40	22 49	22 52	22 55	23 04		23 07	23 16	23 19		23 22	23 25	23 31	23 35	23 37	23 49	23 58	23 54	00 05			00 14

A From London Waterloo
B From Woking

Table T152-R

Saturdays
13 October to 8 December

Hampton Court, Shepperton, Guildford, Dorking and Chessington South - London

		SW	SW	SW	SW
				◇1	
			A	B	
Guildford	d			23 39	
London Road (Guildford)	d				
Clandon	d				
Horsley	d				
Effingham Junction 6	d				
Bookham	d				
Cobham & Stoke d'Abernon	d				
Oxshott	d				
Claygate	d				
Hinchley Wood	d				
Hampton Court	d				23 59
Thames Ditton	d				00 02
Surbiton 6	d			00 08	00 12
Berrylands	d				00 14
Shepperton	d				
Upper Halliford	d				
Sunbury	d				
Kempton Park	d				
Hampton	d				
Fulwell	d				
Strawberry Hill	d		23 37		
Teddington	d		23 41		
Hampton Wick	d		23 44		
Kingston	a		23 46		
	d		23 48		
Norbiton	d		23 50		
New Malden 6	d		23 55		00 17
Dorking 4 182	d				
Box Hill & Westhumble 182	d				
Leatherhead 182	d				
Ashtead 182	d				
Epsom 3 182	a				
	d				
Ewell West	d				
Stoneleigh	d				
Worcester Park	d				
Chessington South	d	23 40			
Chessington North	d	23 42			
Tolworth	d	23 44			
Malden Manor	d	23 47			
Motspur Park	d	23 50			
Raynes Park 6	d	23 54	23 58		00 20
Wimbledon 6 ⊖ ⛴	d	23a57	00 02	00 16	00a23
Earlsfield	d		00 05		
Clapham Junction 10	d		00 09	00 23	
Vauxhall ⊖	d		00 15		
London Waterloo 15 ⊖	a		00 22	00 32	

A From London Waterloo
B From Portsmouth Harbour

Table T152-R

Sundays

20 May to 30 September

Hampton Court, Shepperton, Guildford, Dorking and Chessington South - London

		SW	SW	SW	SW	SW	SW	SW	SW	SW	SW	SW	SW	SW	SW	SW	SW	SW	SW	SW	SW	SW	SW
					◇[1]											[1]							
		A	B	B	C	D	E	F							F	G							
Guildford	d								06 57				07 27					07 50		07 57			
London Road (Guildford)	d																	07 54					
Clandon	d																	07 59					
Horsley	d																	08 03					
Effingham Junction [6]	d																	08 06					
Bookham	d																						
Cobham & Stoke d'Abernon	d																	08 10					
Oxshott	d																	08 13					
Claygate	d																	08 16					
Hinchley Wood	d																	08 19					
Hampton Court	d											07 35					08 05						08 35
Thames Ditton	d					00 02						07 37					08 07						08 37
Surbiton [6]	d				00 08	00 12	07 00		07 30			07 43	08 00			08 10	08 13	08a23		08 30			08 43
Berrylands	d					00 14						07 45					08 15						08 45
Shepperton	d										07 11											08 11	
Upper Halliford	d										07 14											08 14	
Sunbury	d										07 16											08 16	
Kempton Park	d										07 18											08 18	
Hampton	d										07 21											08 21	
Fulwell	d										07 24											08 24	
Strawberry Hill	d		00 09					06 49							07 49								
Teddington	d		00 12					06 55			07 29				07 55							08 29	
Hampton Wick	d		00 14					06 57			07 31				07 57							08 31	
Kingston	a		00 16					06 59			07 33				07 59							08 33	
	d							07 04			07 34				08 04							08 34	
Norbiton	d							07 06			07 36				08 06							08 36	
New Malden [6]	d					00 17		07 10			07 40	07 48			08 10		08 18					08 40	08 48
Dorking [4] 182	d																						
Box Hill & Westhumble 182	d																						
Leatherhead 182	d																						
Ashtead 182	d																						
Epsom [3] 182	a																						
	d									07 24				07 54							08 24		
Ewell West	d									07 27				07 57							08 27		
Stoneleigh	d									07 29				07 59							08 29		
Worcester Park	d									07 32				08 02							08 32		
Chessington South	d																		08 10				
Chessington North	d																		08 12				
Tolworth	d																		08 14				
Malden Manor	d																		08 17				
Motspur Park	d									07 35				08 05					08 20		08 35		
Raynes Park [6]	d					00 20		07 13		07 38	07 43	07 51		08 08	08 13		08 21		08 24		08 38	08 43	08 51
Wimbledon [6] ⊖	d				00 16	00a23	07 08	07 20	07 38	07 42	07 47	07 55	08 08	08 12	08 17	08 20	08 26		08 29	08 37	08 42	08 47	08 55
Earlsfield	d						07 12	07 24	07 42	07 46	07 51	07 59	08 12	08 17	08 21		08 30		08 33	08 41	08 46	08 51	08 59
Clapham Junction [10]	d			00 05	00 23		07 16	07 28	07 46	07 50	07 57	08 03	08 16	08 22	08 27	08 29	08 36		08 39	08 45	08 50	08 57	09 03
Vauxhall ⊖	d	00 05		00 12			07 21	07 33	07 51	07 55	08 02	08 08	08 21	08 27	08 32		08 41		08 44	08 50	08 55	09 02	09 08
London Waterloo [15] ⊖	a	00 14		00 16	00 32		07 25	07 37	07 55	08 04	08 11	08 17	08 25	08 39	08 36	08 39	08 49		08 52	08 55	09 05	09 09	09 17

A not 20 May. From Guildford
B not 20 May. From London Waterloo
C not 20 May. From Portsmouth Harbour
D not 20 May. From Hampton Court
E From Woking
F From London Waterloo
G From Farnham

Table T152-R

Sundays

20 May to 30 September

Hampton Court, Shepperton, Guildford, Dorking and Chessington South - London

		SW	SW	SW	SW	SW	SW	SW	SW	SW	SW	SW	SW	SW	SW	SW	SW	SW	SW	SW	SW	SW	SW
					A											A							
Guildford	d		08 20	08 27				08 50	08 57					09 20	09 27				09 50	09 57			
London Road (Guildford)	d		08 24					08 54						09 24					09 54				
Clandon	d		08 29					08 59						09 29					09 59				
Horsley	d		08 33					09 03						09 33					10 03				
Effingham Junction [6]	d		08 36					09 06						09 36					10 06				
Bookham	d		08 39											09 39									
Cobham & Stoke d'Abernon	d							09 10											10 10				
Oxshott	d							09 13											10 13				
Claygate	d							09 16											10 16				
Hinchley Wood	d							09 19											10 19				
Hampton Court	d					09 05						09 35					10 05						10 35
Thames Ditton	d					09 07						09 37					10 07						10 37
Surbiton [6]	d			09 00		09 13		09 24	09 30			09 43			10 00		10 13		10 24	10 30			10 43
Berrylands	d					09 15						09 45					10 15						10 45
Shepperton	d										09 11											10 11	
Upper Halliford	d										09 14											10 14	
Sunbury	d										09 16											10 16	
Kempton Park	d										09 18											10 18	
Hampton	d										09 21											10 21	
Fulwell	d										09 24											10 24	
Strawberry Hill	d				08 49											09 49							
Teddington	d				08 55						09 29					09 55						10 29	
Hampton Wick	d				08 57						09 31					09 57						10 31	
Kingston	a				08 59						09 33					09 59						10 33	
	d				09 04						09 34					10 04						10 34	
Norbiton	d				09 06						09 36					10 06						10 36	
New Malden [6]	d				09 10	09 18					09 40	09 48				10 10	10 18					10 40	10 48
Dorking [4] 182	d									09 07											10 07		
Box Hill & Westhumble 182	d																						
Leatherhead 182	d		08 45							09 15				09 45							10 15		
Ashtead 182	d		08 48							09 18				09 48							10 18		
Epsom [3] 182	a		08 53							09 23				09 53							10 23		
	d		08 54							09 24				09 54							10 24		
Ewell West	d		08 57							09 27				09 57							10 27		
Stoneleigh	d		08 59							09 29				09 59							10 29		
Worcester Park	d		09 02							09 32				10 02							10 32		
Chessington South	d	08 40					09 10						09 40					10 10					
Chessington North	d	08 42					09 12						09 42					10 12					
Tolworth	d	08 44					09 14						09 44					10 14					
Malden Manor	d	08 47					09 17						09 47					10 17					
Motspur Park	d	08 50	09 05				09 20			09 35			09 50	10 05				10 20			10 35		
Raynes Park [6]	d	08 54	09 08		09 13	09 21	09 24			09 38	09 43	09 51	09 54	10 08		10 13	10 21	10 24			10 38	10 43	10 51
Wimbledon [6] ⊖	d	08 58	09 12	09 07	09 17	09 25	09 28	09a33	09 38	09 42	09 47	09 55	09 58	10 12	10 08	10 17	10 25	10 28	10a33	10 38	10 42	10 47	10 55
Earlsfield	d	09 02	09 16	09 11	09 21	09 29	09 32		09 41	09 46	09 50	09 58	10 01	10 16	10 11	10 20	10 28	10 31		10 41	10 46	10 50	10 58
Clapham Junction [10]	d	09 09	09 20	09 15	09 25	09 33	09 36		09 45	09 50	09 54	10 06	10 09	10 20	10 15	10 24	10 32	10 36		10 45	10 50	10 54	11 02
Vauxhall ⊖	d	09 14	09 25	09 20	09 30	09 38	09 41		09 50	09 55	09 59	10 11	10 14	10 25	10 20	10 32	10 37	10 41		10 50	10 55	10 59	11 07
London Waterloo [15] ⊖	a	09 24	09 35	09 28	09 34	09 47	09 50		09 55	10 04	10 09	10 20	10 23	10 29	10 25	10 36	10 47	10 50		10 55	11 04	11 09	11 17

A From London Waterloo

Table T152-R

Sundays

20 May to 30 September

Hampton Court, Shepperton, Guildford, Dorking and Chessington South - London

		SW		SW	SW	SW A	SW	SW	SW	SW	SW	SW		SW	SW	SW	SW	SW A	SW	SW	SW	SW		SW	SW
Guildford	d			10 20	10 27				10 50	10 57						11 20	11 27				11 50	11 57			
London Road (Guildford)	d			10 24					10 54							11 24					11 54				
Clandon	d			10 29					10 59							11 29					11 59				
Horsley	d			10 33					11 03							11 33					12 03				
Effingham Junction	d			10 36					11 06							11 36					12 06				
Bookham	d			10 39												11 39									
Cobham & Stoke d'Abernon	d								11 10												12 10				
Oxshott	d								11 13												12 13				
Claygate	d								11 16												12 16				
Hinchley Wood	d								11 19												12 19				
Hampton Court	d						11 05							11 35					12 05						
Thames Ditton	d						11 07							11 37					12 07						
Surbiton	d				11 00		11 13		11 24	11 30				11 43			12 00		12 13		12 24	12 30			
Berrylands	d						11 15							11 45					12 15						
Shepperton	d											11 11													12 11
Upper Halliford	d											11 14													12 14
Sunbury	d											11 16													12 16
Kempton Park	d											11 18													12 18
Hampton	d											11 21													12 21
Fulwell	d											11 24													12 24
Strawberry Hill	d					10 49												11 50							
Teddington	d					10 55						11 29						11 55							12 29
Hampton Wick	d					10 57						11 31						11 57							12 31
Kingston	a					10 59						11 33						11 59							12 33
	d					11 04						11 34						12 04							12 34
Norbiton	d					11 06						11 36						12 06							12 36
New Malden	d					11 10	11 18					11 40		11 48				12 10	12 18						12 40
Dorking	182 d										11 07													12 07	
Box Hill & Westhumble	182 d																							12 10	
Leatherhead	182 d			10 45							11 15					11 45								12 15	
Ashtead	182 d			10 48							11 18					11 48								12 18	
Epsom	182 a			10 53							11 23					11 53								12 23	
	d			10 54							11 24					11 54								12 24	
Ewell West	d			10 57							11 27					11 57								12 27	
Stoneleigh	d			10 59							11 29					11 59								12 29	
Worcester Park	d			11 02							11 32					12 02								12 32	
Chessington South	d	10 40						11 10							11 40					12 10					
Chessington North	d	10 42						11 12							11 42					12 12					
Tolworth	d	10 44						11 14							11 44					12 14					
Malden Manor	d	10 47						11 17							11 47					12 17					
Motspur Park	d	10 50		11 05				11 20			11 35				11 50	12 05				12 20				12 35	
Raynes Park	d	10 54		11 08		11 13	11 21	11 24			11 38	11 43		11 51	11 54	12 08		12 13	12 21	12 24				12 38	12 43
Wimbledon ⊖	d	10 58		11 12	11 08	11 17	11 25	11 28	11a33	11 38	11 42	11 47		11 55	11 58	12 12	12 08	12 17	12 25	12 28	12 31	12 38		12 42	12 47
Earlsfield	d	11 01		11 16	11 11	11 20	11 28	11 31		11 41	11 46	11 50		11 58	12 01	12 16	12 11	12 20	12 28	12 31	12 35	12 41		12 46	12 50
Clapham Junction	d	11 05		11 20	11 15	11 24	11 32	11 35		11 45	11 50	11 54		12 02	12 05	12 20	12 15	12 24	12 32	12 35	12 39	12 45		12 50	12 54
Vauxhall ⊖	d	11 13		11 25	11 20	11 32	11 37	11 40		11 50	11 55	11 59		12 07	12 13	12 25	12 20	12 29	12 37	12 40	12 44	12 50		12 55	12 59
London Waterloo ⊖	a	11 22		11 29	11 25	11 36	11 47	11 50		11 55	12 04	12 09		12 17	12 22	12 29	12 25	12 34	12 47	12 50	12 48	12 55		12 59	13 06

A From London Waterloo

Table T152-R

Sundays

20 May to 30 September

Hampton Court, Shepperton, Guildford, Dorking and Chessington South - London

		SW	SW	SW	SW	SW A	SW	SW		SW	SW	SW	SW	SW	SW	SW	SW	SW A		SW	SW	SW	SW	SW	SW
Guildford	d			12 20	12 27					12 50	12 57					13 20	13 27					13 50	13 57		
London Road (Guildford)	d			12 24						12 54						13 24						13 54			
Clandon	d			12 29						12 59						13 29						13 59			
Horsley	d			12 33						13 03						13 33						14 03			
Effingham Junction	d			12 36						13 06						13 36						14 06			
Bookham	d			12 39												13 39									
Cobham & Stoke d'Abernon	d									13 10												14 10			
Oxshott	d									13 13												14 13			
Claygate	d									13 16												14 16			
Hinchley Wood	d									13 19												14 19			
Hampton Court	d	12 35					13 05							13 35						14 05					
Thames Ditton	d	12 37					13 07							13 37						14 07					
Surbiton	d	12 43			13 00		13 13			13 24	13 30			13 43			14 00			14 13		14 24	14 30		
Berrylands	d	12 45					13 15							13 45						14 15					
Shepperton	d												13 11												14 11
Upper Halliford	d												13 14												14 14
Sunbury	d												13 16												14 16
Kempton Park	d												13 18												14 18
Hampton	d												13 21												14 21
Fulwell	d												13 24												14 24
Strawberry Hill	d					12 50												13 49							
Teddington	d					12 55							13 29					13 55							14 29
Hampton Wick	d					12 57							13 31					13 57							14 31
Kingston	a					12 59							13 33					13 59							14 33
	d					13 04							13 34					14 04							14 34
Norbiton	d					13 06							13 36					14 06							14 36
New Malden	d	12 48				13 10	13 18						13 40	13 48				14 10		14 18					14 40
Dorking	182 d											13 07												14 07	
Box Hill & Westhumble	182 d											13 10												14 10	
Leatherhead	182 d			12 45								13 15				13 45								14 15	
Ashtead	182 d			12 48								13 18				13 48								14 18	
Epsom	182 a			12 53								13 23				13 53								14 23	
	d			12 54								13 24				13 54								14 24	
Ewell West	d			12 57								13 27				13 57								14 27	
Stoneleigh	d			12 59								13 29				13 59								14 29	
Worcester Park	d			13 02								13 32				14 02								14 32	
Chessington South	d		12 40					13 10							13 40						14 10				
Chessington North	d		12 42					13 12							13 42						14 12				
Tolworth	d		12 44					13 14							13 44						14 14				
Malden Manor	d		12 47					13 17							13 47						14 17				
Motspur Park	d		12 50	13 05				13 20				13 35			13 50	14 05					14 20			14 35	
Raynes Park	d	12 51	12 54	13 08		13 13	13 21	13 24				13 38	13 43	13 51	13 54	14 08		14 13		14 21	14 24			14 38	14 43
Wimbledon ⊖	d	12 55	12 58	13 12	13 08	13 17	13 25	13 28		13 31	13 38	13 42	13 47	13 55	13 58	14 12	14 08	14 17		14 25	14 28	14 31	14 38	14 42	14 47
Earlsfield	d	12 58	13 01	13 16	13 11	13 20	13 28	13 31		13 35	13 41	13 46	13 50	13 58	14 01	14 16	14 11	14 20		14 28	14 31	14 35	14 41	14 46	14 50
Clapham Junction	d	13 02	13 05	13 20	13 15	13 24	13 32	13 35		13 39	13 45	13 50	13 54	14 02	14 05	14 20	14 15	14 24		14 32	14 35	14 39	14 45	14 50	14 54
Vauxhall ⊖	d	13 07	13 10	13 25	13 20	13 29	13 37	13 40		13 44	13 50	13 55	13 59	14 07	14 10	14 25	14 20	14 29		14 37	14 40	14 44	14 50	14 55	14 59
London Waterloo ⊖	a	13 12	13 15	13 29	13 25	13 34	13 42	13 45		13 48	13 55	13 59	14 04	14 12	14 15	14 29	14 25	14 34		14 42	14 45	14 48	14 55	14 59	15 04

A From London Waterloo

Table T152-R

Sundays

20 May to 30 September

Hampton Court, Shepperton, Guildford, Dorking and Chessington South - London

		SW	SW	SW	SW	SW A	SW	SW	SW	SW	SW	SW A
Guildford	d			14 20	14 27				14 50	14 57		
London Road (Guildford)	d			14 24					14 54			
Clandon	d			14 29					14 59			
Horsley	d			14 33					15 03			
Effingham Junction	d			14 36					15 06			
Bookham	d			14 39								
Cobham & Stoke d'Abernon	d								15 10			
Oxshott	d								15 13			
Claygate	d								15 16			
Hinchley Wood	d								15 19			
Hampton Court	d	14 35					15 05					
Thames Ditton	d	14 37					15 07					
Surbiton	d	14 43			15 00		15 13		15 24	15 30		
Berrylands	d	14 45					15 15					
Shepperton	d											
Upper Halliford	d											
Sunbury	d											
Kempton Park	d											
Hampton	d											
Fulwell	d											
Strawberry Hill	d					14 49						15 14
Teddington	d					14 55						15 17
Hampton Wick	d					14 57						15 20
Kingston	a					14 59						15 22
	d					15 04						
Norbiton	d					15 06						
New Malden	d	14 48				15 10	15 18					
Dorking 182	d										15 07	
Box Hill & Westhumble 182	d										15 10	
Leatherhead 182	d			14 45							15 15	
Ashtead 182	d			14 48							15 18	
Epsom 182	a			14 53							15 23	
	d			14 54							15 24	
Ewell West	d			14 57							15 27	
Stoneleigh	d			14 59							15 29	
Worcester Park	d			15 02							15 32	
Chessington South	d		14 40					15 10				
Chessington North	d		14 42					15 12				
Tolworth	d		14 44					15 14				
Malden Manor	d		14 47					15 17				
Motspur Park	d		14 50	15 05				15 20			15 35	
Raynes Park	d	14 51	14 54	15 08		15 13	15 21	15 24			15 38	
Wimbledon ⊖	d	14 55	14 58	15 12	15 08	15 17	15 25	15 28	15 31	15 38	15 42	
Earlsfield	d	14 58	15 01	15 16	15 11	15 20	15 28	15 31	15 35	15 41	15 46	
Clapham Junction	d	15 02	15 05	15 20	15 15	15 24	15 32	15 35	15 39	15 45	15 50	
Vauxhall ⊖	d	15 07	15 10	15 25	15 20	15 29	15 37	15 40	15 44	15 50	15 55	
London Waterloo ⊖	a	15 12	15 15	15 29	15 25	15 34	15 42	15 45	15 48	15 55	15 59	

		SW	SW	SW	SW	SW	SW A	SW	SW	SW	SW
Guildford	d				15 20	15 27				15 50	15 57
London Road (Guildford)	d				15 24					15 54	
Clandon	d				15 29					15 59	
Horsley	d				15 33					16 03	
Effingham Junction	d				15 36					16 06	
Bookham	d				15 39						
Cobham & Stoke d'Abernon	d									16 10	
Oxshott	d									16 13	
Claygate	d									16 16	
Hinchley Wood	d									16 19	
Hampton Court	d		15 35					16 05			
Thames Ditton	d		15 37					16 07			
Surbiton	d		15 43			16 00		16 13		16 24	16 30
Berrylands	d		15 45					16 15			
Shepperton	d	15 11									
Upper Halliford	d	15 14									
Sunbury	d	15 16									
Kempton Park	d	15 18									
Hampton	d	15 21									
Fulwell	d	15 24									
Strawberry Hill	d						15 49				
Teddington	d	15 29					15 55				
Hampton Wick	d	15 31					15 57				
Kingston	a	15 33					15 59				
	d	15 34					16 04				
Norbiton	d	15 36					16 06				
New Malden	d	15 40	15 48				16 10	16 18			
Dorking 182	d										
Box Hill & Westhumble 182	d										
Leatherhead 182	d				15 45						
Ashtead 182	d				15 48						
Epsom 182	a				15 53						
	d				15 54						
Ewell West	d				15 57						
Stoneleigh	d				15 59						
Worcester Park	d				16 02						
Chessington South	d			15 40					16 10		
Chessington North	d			15 42					16 12		
Tolworth	d			15 44					16 14		
Malden Manor	d			15 47					16 17		
Motspur Park	d			15 50	16 05				16 20		
Raynes Park	d	15 43	15 51	15 54	16 08		16 13	16 21	16 24		
Wimbledon ⊖	d	15 47	15 55	15 58	16 12	16 08	16 17	16 25	16 28	16 31	16 38
Earlsfield	d	15 50	15 58	16 01	16 16	16 11	16 20	16 28	16 31	16 35	16 41
Clapham Junction	d	15 54	16 02	16 05	16 20	16 15	16 24	16 32	16 35	16 39	16 45
Vauxhall ⊖	d	15 59	16 07	16 10	16 25	16 20	16 29	16 37	16 40	16 44	16 50
London Waterloo ⊖	a	16 04	16 12	16 15	16 29	16 25	16 34	16 42	16 45	16 48	16 55

A From London Waterloo

Table T152-R

Sundays

20 May to 30 September

Hampton Court, Shepperton, Guildford, Dorking and Chessington South - London

		SW	SW A	SW	SW	SW	SW	SW	SW A	SW	SW	SW
Guildford	d						16 20	16 27				16 50
London Road (Guildford)	d						16 24					16 54
Clandon	d						16 29					16 59
Horsley	d						16 33					17 03
Effingham Junction	d						16 36					17 06
Bookham	d						16 39					
Cobham & Stoke d'Abernon	d											17 10
Oxshott	d											17 13
Claygate	d											17 16
Hinchley Wood	d											17 19
Hampton Court	d				16 35					17 05		
Thames Ditton	d				16 37					17 07		
Surbiton	d				16 43			17 00		17 13		17 24
Berrylands	d				16 45					17 15		
Shepperton	d			16 11								
Upper Halliford	d			16 14								
Sunbury	d			16 16								
Kempton Park	d			16 18								
Hampton	d			16 21								
Fulwell	d			16 24								
Strawberry Hill	d		16 14						16 49			
Teddington	d		16 17	16 29					16 55			
Hampton Wick	d		16 20	16 31					16 57			
Kingston	a		16 22	16 33					16 59			
	d			16 34					17 04			
Norbiton	d			16 36					17 06			
New Malden	d			16 40	16 48				17 10	17 18		
Dorking 182	d	16 07										
Box Hill & Westhumble 182	d	16 10										
Leatherhead 182	d	16 15					16 45					
Ashtead 182	d	16 18					16 48					
Epsom 182	a	16 23					16 53					
	d	16 24					16 54					
Ewell West	d	16 27					16 57					
Stoneleigh	d	16 29					16 59					
Worcester Park	d	16 32					17 02					
Chessington South	d					16 40					17 10	
Chessington North	d					16 42					17 12	
Tolworth	d					16 44					17 14	
Malden Manor	d					16 47					17 17	
Motspur Park	d	16 35				16 50	17 05				17 20	
Raynes Park	d	16 38		16 43	16 51	16 54	17 08		17 13	17 21	17 24	
Wimbledon ⊖	d	16 42		16 47	16 55	16 58	17 12	17 08	17 17	17 25	17 28	17 31
Earlsfield	d	16 46		16 50	16 58	17 01	17 16	17 11	17 20	17 28	17 31	17 35
Clapham Junction	d	16 50		16 54	17 02	17 05	17 20	17 15	17 24	17 32	17 35	17 39
Vauxhall ⊖	d	16 55		16 59	17 07	17 10	17 25	17 20	17 29	17 37	17 40	17 44
London Waterloo ⊖	a	16 59		17 04	17 12	17 15	17 29	17 25	17 34	17 42	17 45	17 48

		SW	SW	SW A	SW	SW	SW	SW	SW	SW A	SW	SW
Guildford	d	16 57						17 20	17 27			
London Road (Guildford)	d							17 24				
Clandon	d							17 29				
Horsley	d							17 33				
Effingham Junction	d							17 36				
Bookham	d							17 39				
Cobham & Stoke d'Abernon	d											
Oxshott	d											
Claygate	d											
Hinchley Wood	d											
Hampton Court	d					17 35					18 05	
Thames Ditton	d					17 37					18 07	
Surbiton	d	17 30				17 43			18 00		18 13	
Berrylands	d					17 45					18 15	
Shepperton	d				17 11							
Upper Halliford	d				17 14							
Sunbury	d				17 16							
Kempton Park	d				17 18							
Hampton	d				17 21							
Fulwell	d				17 24							
Strawberry Hill	d			17 14						17 49		
Teddington	d			17 17	17 29					17 55		
Hampton Wick	d			17 20	17 31					17 57		
Kingston	a			17 22	17 33					17 59		
	d				17 34					18 04		
Norbiton	d				17 36					18 06		
New Malden	d				17 40	17 48				18 10	18 18	
Dorking 182	d		17 07									
Box Hill & Westhumble 182	d		17 10									
Leatherhead 182	d		17 15					17 45				
Ashtead 182	d		17 18					17 48				
Epsom 182	a		17 23					17 53				
	d		17 24					17 54				
Ewell West	d		17 27					17 57				
Stoneleigh	d		17 29					17 59				
Worcester Park	d		17 32					18 02				
Chessington South	d						17 40					18 10
Chessington North	d						17 42					18 12
Tolworth	d						17 44					18 14
Malden Manor	d						17 47					18 17
Motspur Park	d		17 35				17 50	18 05				18 20
Raynes Park	d		17 38		17 43	17 51	17 54	18 08		18 13	18 21	18 24
Wimbledon ⊖	d	17 38	17 42		17 47	17 55	17 58	18 12	18 08	18 17	18 25	18 28
Earlsfield	d	17 41	17 46		17 50	17 58	18 01	18 16	18 11	18 20	18 28	18 31
Clapham Junction	d	17 45	17 50		17 54	18 02	18 05	18 20	18 15	18 24	18 32	18 35
Vauxhall ⊖	d	17 50	17 55		17 59	18 07	18 10	18 25	18 20	18 29	18 37	18 40
London Waterloo ⊖	a	17 55	17 59		18 04	18 12	18 15	18 29	18 25	18 34	18 42	18 45

A From London Waterloo

Table T152-R

Sundays

20 May to 30 September

Hampton Court, Shepperton, Guildford, Dorking and Chessington South - London

		SW	SW	SW	SW A	SW	SW	SW	SW	SW	SW A	SW	SW	SW	SW	SW	SW A	SW	SW	SW	SW	SW	SW A
Guildford	d	17 50	17 57						18 20	18 27				18 50	18 57						19 20	19 27	
London Road (Guildford)	d	17 54							18 24					18 54							19 24		
Clandon	d	17 59							18 29					18 59							19 29		
Horsley	d	18 03							18 33					19 03							19 33		
Effingham Junction	d	18 06							18 36					19 06							19 36		
Bookham	d								18 39												19 39		
Cobham & Stoke d'Abernon	d	18 10												19 10									
Oxshott	d	18 13												19 13									
Claygate	d	18 16												19 16									
Hinchley Wood	d	18 19												19 19									
Hampton Court	d						18 35					19 05							19 35				
Thames Ditton	d						18 37					19 07							19 37				
Surbiton	d	18 24	18 30				18 43			19 00		19 13		19 24	19 30				19 43			20 00	
Berrylands	d						18 45					19 15							19 45				
Shepperton	d					18 11												19 11					
Upper Halliford	d					18 14												19 14					
Sunbury	d					18 16												19 16					
Kempton Park	d					18 18												19 18					
Hampton	d					18 21												19 21					
Fulwell	d					18 24												19 24					
Strawberry Hill	d				18 14						18 49						19 14						19 49
Teddington	d				18 17	18 29					18 55						19 17	19 29					19 55
Hampton Wick	d				18 20	18 31					18 57						19 20	19 31					19 57
Kingston	a				18 22	18 33					18 59						19 22	19 33					19 59
	d					18 34					19 04							19 34					20 04
Norbiton	d					18 36					19 06							19 36					20 06
New Malden	d					18 40	18 48				19 10	19 18						19 40	19 48				20 10
Dorking	182 d			18 07												19 07							
Box Hill & Westhumble	182 d			18 10												19 10							
Leatherhead	182 d			18 15					18 45							19 15					19 45		
Ashtead	182 d			18 18					18 48							19 18					19 48		
Epsom	182 a			18 23					18 53							19 23					19 53		
	d			18 24					18 54							19 24					19 54		
Ewell West	d			18 27					18 57							19 27					19 57		
Stoneleigh	d			18 29					18 59							19 29					19 59		
Worcester Park	d			18 32					19 02							19 32					20 02		
Chessington South	d							18 40					19 10							19 40			
Chessington North	d							18 42					19 12							19 42			
Tolworth	d							18 44					19 14							19 44			
Malden Manor	d							18 47					19 17							19 47			
Motspur Park	d			18 35				18 50	19 05				19 20			19 35				19 50	20 05		
Raynes Park	d			18 38		18 43	18 51	18 54	19 08		19 13	19 21	19 24			19 38		19 43	19 51	19 54	20 08		20 13
Wimbledon	d	18 31	18 38	18 42		18 47	18 55	18 58	19 12	19 08	19 17	19 25	19 28	19 31	19 38	19 42		19 47	19 55	19 58	20 12	20 08	20 17
Earlsfield	d	18 35	18 41	18 46		18 50	18 58	19 01	19 16	19 11	19 20	19 28	19 31	19 35	19 41	19 46		19 50	19 58	20 01	20 16	20 11	20 20
Clapham Junction	d	18 39	18 45	18 50		18 54	19 02	19 05	19 20	19 15	19 24	19 32	19 35	19 39	19 45	19 50		19 54	20 02	20 05	20 20	20 15	20 24
Vauxhall	d	18 44	18 50	18 55		18 59	19 07	19 10	19 25	19 20	19 29	19 37	19 40	19 44	19 50	19 55		19 59	20 07	20 10	20 25	20 20	20 29
London Waterloo	a	18 48	18 55	18 59		19 04	19 12	19 15	19 29	19 25	19 34	19 42	19 45	19 48	19 55	19 59		20 04	20 12	20 15	20 29	20 25	20 34

A From London Waterloo

Table T152-R

Sundays

20 May to 30 September

Hampton Court, Shepperton, Guildford, Dorking and Chessington South - London

		SW	SW	SW	SW	SW	SW A	SW	SW	SW	SW	SW A	SW	SW	SW	SW	SW	SW A	SW	SW	SW	SW
Guildford	d			19 50	19 57					20 20	20 27				20 50	20 57					21 20	21 27
London Road (Guildford)	d			19 54						20 24					20 54						21 24	
Clandon	d			19 59						20 29					20 59						21 29	
Horsley	d			20 03						20 33					21 03						21 33	
Effingham Junction	d			20 06						20 36					21 06						21 36	
Bookham	d									20 39											21 39	
Cobham & Stoke d'Abernon	d			20 10											21 10							
Oxshott	d			20 13											21 13							
Claygate	d			20 16											21 16							
Hinchley Wood	d			20 19											21 19							
Hampton Court	d	20 05							20 35				21 05							21 35		
Thames Ditton	d	20 07							20 37				21 07							21 37		
Surbiton	d	20 13		20 24	20 30				20 43		21 00		21 13		21 24	21 30				21 43		22 00
Berrylands	d	20 15							20 45				21 15							21 45		
Shepperton	d							20 11											21 11			
Upper Halliford	d							20 14											21 14			
Sunbury	d							20 16											21 16			
Kempton Park	d							20 18											21 18			
Hampton	d							20 21											21 21			
Fulwell	d							20 24											21 24			
Strawberry Hill	d						20 14					20 49						21 14				
Teddington	d						20 17	20 29				20 55						21 17	21 29			
Hampton Wick	d						20 20	20 31				20 57						21 20	21 31			
Kingston	a						20 22	20 33				20 59						21 22	21 33			
	d							20 34				21 04							21 34			
Norbiton	d							20 36				21 06							21 36			
New Malden	d	20 18						20 40	20 48			21 10	21 18						21 40	21 48		
Dorking	182 d					20 07											21 07					
Box Hill & Westhumble	182 d																					
Leatherhead	182 d					20 15				20 45							21 15				21 45	
Ashtead	182 d					20 18				20 48							21 18				21 48	
Epsom	182 a					20 23				20 53							21 23				21 53	
	d					20 24				20 54							21 24				21 54	
Ewell West	d					20 27				20 57							21 27				21 57	
Stoneleigh	d					20 29				20 59							21 29				21 59	
Worcester Park	d					20 32				21 02							21 32				22 02	
Chessington South	d		20 10											21 10								
Chessington North	d		20 12											21 12								
Tolworth	d		20 14											21 14								
Malden Manor	d		20 17											21 17								
Motspur Park	d		20 20			20 35				21 05				21 20			21 35				22 05	
Raynes Park	d	20 21	20 24			20 38		20 43	20 51	21 08		21 13	21 21	21 24			21 38		21 43	21 51	22 08	
Wimbledon	d	20 25	20 28	20 31	20 38	20 42		20 47	20 55	21 12	21 08	21 17	21 25	21 28	21 31	21 38	21 42		21 47	21 55	22 12	22 08
Earlsfield	d	20 28	20 31	20 35	20 41	20 46		20 50	20 58	21 16	21 11	21 20	21 28	21 31	21 35	21 41	21 46		21 50	21 58	22 16	22 11
Clapham Junction	d	20 32	20 35	20 39	20 45	20 50		20 54	21 02	21 20	21 15	21 24	21 32	21 35	21 39	21 45	21 50		21 54	22 02	22 20	22 15
Vauxhall	d	20 37	20 40	20 44	20 50	20 55		20 59	21 07	21 25	21 20	21 29	21 37	21 40	21 44	21 50	21 55		21 59	22 07	22 25	22 20
London Waterloo	a	20 42	20 45	20 48	20 55	21 01		21 04	21 13	21 29	21 25	21 36	21 42	21 45	21 48	21 55	22 00		22 04	22 12	22 29	22 25

A From London Waterloo

Table T152-R

Sundays

20 May to 30 September

Hampton Court, Shepperton, Guildford, Dorking and Chessington South - London

		SW A	SW	SW	SW	SW	SW	SW A	SW	SW	SW	SW A	SW	SW	SW	SW	SW	SW A	SW	SW	SW	SW A
Guildford	d				21 50	21 57				22 20	22 27				22 50	22 57						
London Road (Guildford)	d				21 54					22 24					22 54							
Clandon	d				21 59					22 29					22 59							
Horsley	d				22 03					22 33					23 03							
Effingham Junction ■	d				22 06					22 36					23 06							
Bookham	d									22 39												
Cobham & Stoke d'Abernon	d				22 10										23 10							
Oxshott	d				22 13										23 13							
Claygate	d				22 16										23 16							
Hinchley Wood	d				22 19										23 19							
Hampton Court	d		22 05										23 05								23 45	
Thames Ditton	d		22 07										23 07								23 47	
Surbiton ■	d		22 13		22 24	22 30					23 00		23 13		23 24	23 30					23 53	
Berrylands	d		22 15										23 15								23 55	
Shepperton	d								22 11										23 11			
Upper Halliford	d								22 14										23 14			
Sunbury	d								22 16										23 16			
Kempton Park	d								22 18										23 18			
Hampton	d								22 21										23 21			
Fulwell	d								22 24										23 24			
Strawberry Hill	d	21 49						22 14				22 49						23 14				23 48
Teddington	d	21 55						22 17	22 29			22 55						23 17	23 29			23 51
Hampton Wick	d	21 57						22 20	22 31			22 57						23 20	23 31			23 54
Kingston	a	21 59						22 22	22 33			22 59						23 22	23 33			23 56
	d	22 04							22 34			23 04							23 34			
Norbiton	d	22 06							22 36			23 06							23 36			
New Malden ■	d	22 10	22 18						22 40			23 10	23 18						23 40		23 58	
Dorking ■ 182	d						22 07										23 07					
Box Hill & Westhumble 182	d																					
Leatherhead 182	d						22 15			22 45							23 15					
Ashtead 182	d						22 18			22 48							23 18					
Epsom ■ 182	a						22 23			22 53							23 23					
	d						22 24			22 54							23 24					
Ewell West	d						22 27			22 57							23 27					
Stoneleigh	d						22 29			22 59							23 29					
Worcester Park	d						22 32			23 02							23 32					
Chessington South	d			22 10										23 10						23 40		
Chessington North	d			22 12										23 12						23 42		
Tolworth	d			22 14										23 14						23 44		
Malden Manor	d			22 17										23 17						23 47		
Motspur Park	d			22 20			22 35			23 05				23 20			23 35			23 50		
Raynes Park ■	d	22 13	22 21	22 24			22 38		22 43	23 08		23 13	23 21	23 24			23 38		23 43	23 54	00 01	
Wimbledon ■ ⊖ ⇌	d	22 17	22 25	22 28	22 31	22 38	22 42		22 47	23 12	23 08	23 17	23 25	23 28	23 31	23 38	23 42		23 47	23a59	00a04	
Earlsfield	d	22 20	22 28	22 31	22 35	22 41	22 46		22 50	23 16	23 11	23 20	23 28	23 31	23 35	23 41	23 46		23 50			
Clapham Junction ■	d	22 24	22 32	22 35	22 39	22 45	22 50		22 54	23 20	23 15	23 24	23 32	23 35	23 39	23 45	23 50		23 54			
Vauxhall ⊖	d	22 29	22 37	22 40	22 44	22 50	22 55		22 59	23 25	23 20	23 29	23 37	23 40	23 44	23 50	23 55		23 59			
London Waterloo ■ ⊖	a	22 36	22 42	22 45	22 48	22 55	23 00		23 04	23 29	23 25	23 35	23 42	23 45	23 48	23 55	00 01		00 04			

A From London Waterloo

Table T152-R

Sundays

7 October to 2 December

Hampton Court, Shepperton, Guildford, Dorking and Chessington South - London

		SW A	SW B	SW B	SW ◇■ C	SW D	SW E	SW B	SW	SW	SW	SW	SW	SW	SW B	SW	SW	SW	SW	SW	SW	SW	SW
Guildford	d								06 57				07 27				07 48		07 57				
London Road (Guildford)	d																07 52						
Clandon	d																07 57						
Horsley	d																08 01						
Effingham Junction ■	d																08 04						
Bookham	d																						
Cobham & Stoke d'Abernon	d																08 08						
Oxshott	d																08 11						
Claygate	d																08 14						
Hinchley Wood	d																08 17						
Hampton Court	d											07 35				08 05						08 35	
Thames Ditton	d					00 02						07 37				08 07						08 37	
Surbiton ■	d				00 08	00 12	07 00		07 30			07 43	08 00			08 13	08a23		08 30			08 43	
Berrylands	d					00 14						07 45				08 15						08 45	
Shepperton	d										07 11										08 11		
Upper Halliford	d										07 14										08 14		
Sunbury	d										07 16										08 16		
Kempton Park	d										07 18										08 18		
Hampton	d										07 21										08 21		
Fulwell	d										07 24										08 24		
Strawberry Hill	d		00 09					06 49							07 49								
Teddington	d		00 12					06 55			07 29				07 55						08 29		
Hampton Wick	d		00 14					06 57			07 31				07 57						08 31		
Kingston	a		00 16					06 59			07 33				07 59						08 33		
	d							07 04			07 34				08 04						08 34		
Norbiton	d							07 06			07 36				08 06						08 36		
New Malden ■	d					00 17		07 10			07 40	07 48			08 10	08 18					08 40	08 48	
Dorking ■ 182	d																						
Box Hill & Westhumble 182	d																						
Leatherhead 182	d																						
Ashtead 182	d																						
Epsom ■ 182	a																						
	d									07 24				07 54						08 24			
Ewell West	d									07 27				07 57						08 27			
Stoneleigh	d									07 29				07 59						08 29			
Worcester Park	d									07 32				08 02						08 32			
Chessington South	d																	08 10					08 40
Chessington North	d																	08 12					08 42
Tolworth	d																	08 14					08 44
Malden Manor	d																	08 17					08 47
Motspur Park	d									07 35				08 05				08 20		08 35			08 50
Raynes Park ■	d					00 20		07 13		07 38	07 43	07 51		08 08	08 13	08 21		08 24		08 38	08 43	08 51	08 54
Wimbledon ■ ⊖ ⇌	d				00 16	00a23	07 08	07 20	07 38	07 42	07 47	07 55	08 08	08 12	08 17	08 26		08 29	08 37	08 42	08 47	08 55	08 58
Earlsfield	d						07 12	07 24	07 42	07 46	07 51	07 59	08 12	08 17	08 21	08 30		08 33	08 41	08 46	08 51	08 59	09 02
Clapham Junction ■	d			00 05	00 23		07 16	07 28	07 46	07 50	07 57	08 03	08 16	08 22	08 27	08 36		08 39	08 45	08 50	08 57	09 03	09 09
Vauxhall ⊖	d	00 05		00 12			07 21	07 33	07 51	07 55	08 02	08 08	08 21	08 27	08 32	08 41		08 44	08 50	08 55	09 02	09 08	09 14
London Waterloo ■ ⊖	a	00 14		00 16	00 32		07 25	07 37	07 55	08 04	08 11	08 17	08 25	08 39	08 36	08 49		08 52	08 55	09 05	09 09	09 17	09 24

A From Guildford
B From London Waterloo
C From Portsmouth Harbour
D From Hampton Court
E From Woking

Table T152-R

Sundays

7 October to 2 December

Hampton Court, Shepperton, Guildford, Dorking and Chessington South - London

		SW	SW	SW A	SW	SW		SW	SW	SW	SW	SW	SW	SW	SW	SW A		SW	SW	SW	SW	SW	SW	SW	SW
Guildford	d	08 18	08 27					08 48	08 57					09 18	09 27					09 48	09 57				
London Road (Guildford)	d	08 22						08 52						09 22						09 52					
Clandon	d	08 27						08 57						09 27						09 57					
Horsley	d	08 31						09 01						09 31						10 01					
Effingham Junction	d	08 34						09 04						09 34						10 04					
Bookham	d	08 37												09 37											
Cobham & Stoke d'Abernon	d							09 08												10 08					
Oxshott	d							09 11												10 11					
Claygate	d							09 14												10 14					
Hinchley Wood	d							09 17												10 17					
Hampton Court	d				09 05							09 35						10 05						10 35	
Thames Ditton	d				09 07							09 37						10 07						10 37	
Surbiton	d		09 00		09 13			09 24	09 30			09 43			10 00			10 13		10 24	10 30			10 43	
Berrylands	d				09 15							09 45						10 15						10 45	
Shepperton	d										09 11												10 11		
Upper Halliford	d										09 14												10 14		
Sunbury	d										09 16												10 16		
Kempton Park	d										09 18												10 18		
Hampton	d										09 21												10 21		
Fulwell	d										09 24												10 24		
Strawberry Hill	d			08 49												09 49									
Teddington	d			08 55							09 29					09 55							10 29		
Hampton Wick	d			08 57							09 31					09 57							10 31		
Kingston	a			08 59							09 33					09 59							10 33		
	d			09 04							09 34					10 04							10 34		
Norbiton	d			09 06							09 36					10 06							10 36		
New Malden	d			09 10	09 18						09 40	09 48				10 10		10 18					10 40	10 48	
Dorking	182 d									09 07												10 07			
Box Hill & Westhumble	182 d																								
Leatherhead	182 d	08 45								09 15				09 45								10 15			
Ashtead	182 d	08 48								09 18				09 48								10 18			
Epsom	182 a	08 53								09 23				09 53								10 23			
	d	08 54								09 24				09 54								10 24			
Ewell West	d	08 57								09 27				09 57								10 27			
Stoneleigh	d	08 59								09 29				09 59								10 29			
Worcester Park	d	09 02								09 32				10 02								10 32			
Chessington South	d					09 10							09 40						10 10						10 40
Chessington North	d					09 12							09 42						10 12						10 42
Tolworth	d					09 14							09 44						10 14						10 44
Malden Manor	d					09 17							09 47						10 17						10 47
Motspur Park	d	09 05				09 20				09 35			09 50	10 05					10 20			10 35			10 50
Raynes Park	d	09 08		09 13	09 21	09 24				09 38	09 43	09 51	09 54	10 08		10 13		10 21	10 24			10 38	10 43	10 51	10 54
Wimbledon ⊖	d	09 12	09 07	09 17	09 25	09 28		09a33	09 38	09 42	09 47	09 55	09 58	10 12	10 08	10 17		10 25	10 28	10a33	10 38	10 42	10 47	10 55	10 58
Earlsfield	d	09 16	09 11	09 21	09 29	09 32			09 41	09 46	09 50	09 58	10 01	10 16	10 11	10 20		10 28	10 31		10 41	10 46	10 50	10 58	11 01
Clapham Junction	d	09 20	09 15	09 25	09 33	09 36			09 45	09 50	09 54	10 06	10 09	10 20	10 15	10 24		10 32	10 36		10 45	10 50	10 54	11 02	11 05
Vauxhall ⊖	d	09 25	09 20	09 30	09 38	09 41			09 50	09 55	09 59	10 11	10 14	10 25	10 20	10 32		10 37	10 41		10 50	10 55	10 59	11 07	11 13
London Waterloo ⊖	a	09 35	09 28	09 34	09 47	09 50			09 55	10 04	10 09	10 20	10 23	10 29	10 25	10 36		10 47	10 50		10 55	11 04	11 09	11 17	11 22

A From London Waterloo

Table T152-R

Sundays

7 October to 2 December

Hampton Court, Shepperton, Guildford, Dorking and Chessington South - London

		SW		SW	SW A	SW	SW	SW	SW	SW	SW	SW		SW	SW	SW	SW A	SW	SW	SW	SW	SW		SW	SW
Guildford	d	10 18		10 27				10 48	10 57						11 18	11 27				11 48	11 57				
London Road (Guildford)	d	10 22						10 52							11 22					11 52					
Clandon	d	10 27						10 57							11 27					11 57					
Horsley	d	10 31						11 01							11 31					12 01					
Effingham Junction	d	10 34						11 04							11 34					12 04					
Bookham	d	10 37													11 37										
Cobham & Stoke d'Abernon	d							11 08												12 08					
Oxshott	d							11 11												12 11					
Claygate	d							11 14												12 14					
Hinchley Wood	d							11 17												12 17					
Hampton Court	d					11 05						11 35						12 05							12 35
Thames Ditton	d					11 07						11 37						12 07							12 37
Surbiton	d			11 00		11 13		11 24	11 30			11 43				12 00		12 13		12 24	12 30				12 43
Berrylands	d					11 15						11 45						12 15							12 45
Shepperton	d										11 11													12 11	
Upper Halliford	d										11 14													12 14	
Sunbury	d										11 16													12 16	
Kempton Park	d										11 18													12 18	
Hampton	d										11 21													12 21	
Fulwell	d										11 24													12 24	
Strawberry Hill	d				10 49												11 50								
Teddington	d				10 55						11 29						11 55							12 29	
Hampton Wick	d				10 57						11 31						11 57							12 31	
Kingston	a				10 59						11 33						11 59							12 33	
	d				11 04						11 34						12 04							12 34	
Norbiton	d				11 06						11 36						12 06							12 36	
New Malden	d				11 10	11 18					11 40	11 48					12 10	12 18						12 40	12 48
Dorking	182 d									11 07												12 07			
Box Hill & Westhumble	182 d																					12 10			
Leatherhead	182 d	10 45								11 15					11 45							12 15			
Ashtead	182 d	10 48								11 18					11 48							12 18			
Epsom	182 a	10 53								11 23					11 53							12 23			
	d	10 54								11 24					11 54							12 24			
Ewell West	d	10 57								11 27					11 57							12 27			
Stoneleigh	d	10 59								11 29					11 59							12 29			
Worcester Park	d	11 02								11 32					12 02							12 32			
Chessington South	d						11 10							11 40					12 10						
Chessington North	d						11 12							11 42					12 12						
Tolworth	d						11 14							11 44					12 14						
Malden Manor	d						11 17							11 47					12 17						
Motspur Park	d	11 05					11 20			11 35				11 50	12 05				12 20			12 35			
Raynes Park	d	11 08			11 13	11 21	11 24			11 38	11 43	11 51		11 54	12 08		12 13	12 21	12 24			12 38		12 43	12 51
Wimbledon ⊖	d	11 12		11 08	11 17	11 25	11 28	11a33	11 38	11 42	11 47	11 55		11 58	12 12	12 08	12 17	12 25	12 28	12 31	12 38	12 42		12 47	12 55
Earlsfield	d	11 16		11 11	11 20	11 28	11 31		11 41	11 46	11 50	11 58		12 01	12 16	12 11	12 20	12 28	12 31	12 35	12 41	12 46		12 50	12 58
Clapham Junction	d	11 20		11 15	11 24	11 32	11 35		11 45	11 50	11 54	12 02		12 05	12 20	12 15	12 24	12 32	12 35	12 39	12 45	12 50		12 54	13 02
Vauxhall ⊖	d	11 25		11 20	11 32	11 37	11 40		11 50	11 55	11 59	12 07		12 13	12 25	12 20	12 29	12 37	12 40	12 44	12 50	12 55		12 59	13 07
London Waterloo ⊖	a	11 29		11 25	11 36	11 47	11 50		11 55	12 04	12 09	12 17		12 22	12 29	12 25	12 34	12 47	12 50	12 48	12 55	12 59		13 06	13 12

A From London Waterloo

Table T152-R

Sundays

7 October to 2 December

Hampton Court, Shepperton, Guildford, Dorking and Chessington South - London

		SW	SW	SW	SW A	SW	SW	SW		SW	SW	SW	SW	SW	SW	SW	SW A	SW		SW	SW	SW	SW	SW	SW
Guildford	d		12 18	12 27				12 48		12 57					13 18	13 27					13 48	13 57			
London Road (Guildford)	d		12 22					12 52							13 22						13 52				
Clandon	d		12 27					12 57							13 27						13 57				
Horsley	d		12 31					13 01							13 31						14 01				
Effingham Junction 6	d		12 34					13 04							13 34						14 04				
Bookham	d		12 37												13 37										
Cobham & Stoke d'Abernon	d							13 08													14 08				
Oxshott	d							13 11													14 11				
Claygate	d							13 14													14 14				
Hinchley Wood	d							13 17													14 17				
Hampton Court	d					13 05							13 35					14 05							14 35
Thames Ditton	d					13 07							13 37					14 07							14 37
Surbiton 6	d			13 00		13 13		13 24		13 30			13 43			14 00		14 13			14 24	14 30			14 43
Berrylands	d					13 15							13 45					14 15							14 45
Shepperton	d											13 11												14 11	
Upper Halliford	d											13 14												14 14	
Sunbury	d											13 16												14 16	
Kempton Park	d											13 18												14 18	
Hampton	d											13 21												14 21	
Fulwell	d											13 24												14 24	
Strawberry Hill	d				12 50												13 49								
Teddington	d				12 55							13 29					13 55							14 29	
Hampton Wick	d				12 57							13 31					13 57							14 31	
Kingston	a				12 59							13 33					13 59							14 33	
	d				13 04							13 34					14 04							14 34	
Norbiton	d				13 06							13 36					14 06							14 36	
New Malden 6	d				13 10	13 18						13 40	13 48				14 10	14 18						14 40	14 48
Dorking 4 182	d										13 07												14 07		
Box Hill & Westhumble 182	d										13 10												14 10		
Leatherhead 182	d		12 45								13 15				13 45								14 15		
Ashtead 182	d		12 48								13 18				13 48								14 18		
Epsom 8 182	a		12 53								13 23				13 53								14 23		
	d		12 54								13 24				13 54								14 24		
Ewell West	d		12 57								13 27				13 57								14 27		
Stoneleigh	d		12 59								13 29				13 59								14 29		
Worcester Park	d		13 02								13 32				14 02								14 32		
Chessington South	d	12 40					13 10							13 40						14 10					
Chessington North	d	12 42					13 12							13 42						14 12					
Tolworth	d	12 44					13 14							13 44						14 14					
Malden Manor	d	12 47					13 17							13 47						14 17					
Motspur Park	d	12 50	13 05				13 20				13 35			13 50	14 05					14 20			14 35		
Raynes Park 6	d	12 54	13 08		13 13	13 21	13 24				13 38	13 43	13 51	13 54	14 08		14 13	14 21		14 24			14 38	14 43	14 51
Wimbledon 6 ⊖	d	12 58	13 12	13 08	13 17	13 25	13 28	13 31		13 38	13 42	13 47	13 55	13 58	14 12	14 08	14 17	14 25		14 28	14 31	14 38	14 42	14 47	14 55
Earlsfield	d	13 01	13 16	13 11	13 20	13 28	13 31	13 35		13 41	13 46	13 50	13 58	14 01	14 16	14 11	14 20	14 28		14 31	14 35	14 41	14 46	14 50	14 58
Clapham Junction 10	d	13 05	13 20	13 15	13 24	13 32	13 35	13 39		13 45	13 50	13 54	14 02	14 05	14 20	14 15	14 24	14 32		14 35	14 39	14 45	14 50	14 54	15 02
Vauxhall ⊖	d	13 10	13 25	13 20	13 29	13 37	13 40	13 44		13 50	13 55	13 59	14 07	14 10	14 25	14 20	14 29	14 37		14 40	14 44	14 50	14 55	14 59	15 07
London Waterloo 15 ⊖	a	13 15	13 29	13 25	13 34	13 42	13 45	13 48		13 55	13 59	14 04	14 12	14 15	14 29	14 25	14 34	14 42		14 45	14 48	14 55	14 59	15 04	15 12

A From London Waterloo

Table T152-R

Sundays

7 October to 2 December

Hampton Court, Shepperton, Guildford, Dorking and Chessington South - London

		SW	SW	SW		SW A	SW	SW	SW	SW	SW	SW A	SW	SW		SW	SW	SW	SW A	SW	SW	SW	SW	SW	
Guildford	d		14 18	14 27					14 48	14 57							15 18	15 27				15 48	15 57		
London Road (Guildford)	d		14 22						14 52								15 22					15 52			
Clandon	d		14 27						14 57								15 27					15 57			
Horsley	d		14 31						15 01								15 31					16 01			
Effingham Junction 6	d		14 34						15 04								15 34					16 04			
Bookham	d		14 37														15 37								
Cobham & Stoke d'Abernon	d								15 08													16 08			
Oxshott	d								15 11													16 11			
Claygate	d								15 14													16 14			
Hinchley Wood	d								15 17													16 17			
Hampton Court	d						15 05							15 35						16 05					
Thames Ditton	d						15 07							15 37						16 07					
Surbiton 6	d			15 00			15 13		15 24	15 30				15 43				16 00		16 13		16 24	16 30		
Berrylands	d						15 15							15 45						16 15					
Shepperton	d												15 11												
Upper Halliford	d												15 14												
Sunbury	d												15 16												
Kempton Park	d												15 18												
Hampton	d												15 21												
Fulwell	d												15 24												
Strawberry Hill	d					14 49						15 14							15 49						
Teddington	d					14 55						15 17	15 29						15 55						
Hampton Wick	d					14 57						15 20	15 31						15 57						
Kingston	a					14 59						15 22	15 33						15 59						
	d					15 04							15 34						16 04						
Norbiton	d					15 06							15 36						16 06						
New Malden 6	d					15 10	15 18						15 40	15 48					16 10	16 18					
Dorking 4 182	d										15 07													16 07	
Box Hill & Westhumble 182	d										15 10													16 10	
Leatherhead 182	d		14 45								15 15						15 45							16 15	
Ashtead 182	d		14 48								15 18						15 48							16 18	
Epsom 8 182	a		14 53								15 23						15 53							16 23	
	d		14 54								15 24						15 54							16 24	
Ewell West	d		14 57								15 27						15 57							16 27	
Stoneleigh	d		14 59								15 29						15 59							16 29	
Worcester Park	d		15 02								15 32						16 02							16 32	
Chessington South	d	14 40						15 10								15 40					16 10				
Chessington North	d	14 42						15 12								15 42					16 12				
Tolworth	d	14 44						15 14								15 44					16 14				
Malden Manor	d	14 47						15 17								15 47					16 17				
Motspur Park	d	14 50	15 05					15 20			15 35					15 50	16 05				16 20			16 35	
Raynes Park 6	d	14 54	15 08			15 13	15 21	15 24			15 38		15 43	15 51		15 54	16 08		16 13	16 21	16 24			16 38	
Wimbledon 6 ⊖	d	14 58	15 12	15 08		15 17	15 25	15 28	15 31	15 38	15 42		15 47	15 55		15 58	16 12	16 08	16 17	16 25	16 28	16 31	16 38	16 42	
Earlsfield	d	15 01	15 16	15 11		15 20	15 28	15 31	15 35	15 41	15 46		15 50	15 58		16 01	16 16	16 11	16 20	16 28	16 31	16 35	16 41	16 46	
Clapham Junction 10	d	15 05	15 20	15 15		15 24	15 32	15 35	15 39	15 45	15 50		15 54	16 02		16 05	16 20	16 15	16 24	16 32	16 35	16 39	16 45	16 50	
Vauxhall ⊖	d	15 10	15 25	15 20		15 29	15 37	15 40	15 44	15 50	15 55		15 59	16 07		16 10	16 25	16 20	16 29	16 37	16 40	16 44	16 50	16 55	
London Waterloo 15 ⊖	a	15 15	15 29	15 25		15 34	15 42	15 45	15 48	15 55	15 59		16 04	16 12		16 15	16 29	16 25	16 34	16 42	16 45	16 48	16 55	16 59	

A From London Waterloo

Hampton Court, Shepperton, Guildford, Dorking and Chessington South - London

		SW A	SW	SW	SW	SW	SW	SW A	SW	SW	SW	SW	SW	SW A	SW	SW	SW	SW	SW	SW A	SW	SW	SW
Guildford	d					16 18	16 27				16 48	16 57						17 18	17 27				17 48
London Road (Guildford)	d					16 22					16 52							17 22					17 52
Clandon	d					16 27					16 57							17 27					17 57
Horsley	d					16 31					17 01							17 31					18 01
Effingham Junction ■	d					16 34					17 04							17 34					18 04
Bookham	d					16 37												17 37					
Cobham & Stoke d'Abernon	d										17 08												18 08
Oxshott	d										17 11												18 11
Claygate	d										17 14												18 14
Hinchley Wood	d										17 17												18 17
Hampton Court	d			16 35					17 05							17 35					18 05		
Thames Ditton	d			16 37					17 07							17 37					18 07		
Surbiton ■	d			16 43			17 00		17 13		17 24	17 30				17 43			18 00		18 13		18 24
Berrylands	d			16 45					17 15							17 45					18 15		
Shepperton	d		16 11												17 11								
Upper Halliford	d		16 14												17 14								
Sunbury	d		16 16												17 16								
Kempton Park	d		16 18												17 18								
Hampton	d		16 21												17 21								
Fulwell	d		16 24												17 24								
Strawberry Hill	d	16 14						16 49						17 14						17 49			
Teddington	d	16 17	16 29					16 55						17 17	17 29					17 55			
Hampton Wick	d	16 20	16 31					16 57						17 20	17 31					17 57			
Kingston	a	16 22	16 33					16 59						17 22	17 33					17 59			
	d		16 34					17 04							17 34					18 04			
Norbiton	d		16 36					17 06							17 36					18 06			
New Malden ■	d		16 40	16 48				17 10	17 18						17 40	17 48				18 10	18 18		
Dorking ■	182 d												17 07										
Box Hill & Westhumble	182 d												17 10										
Leatherhead	182 d					16 45							17 15					17 45					
Ashtead	182 d					16 48							17 18					17 48					
Epsom ■	182 a					16 53							17 23					17 53					
	d					16 54							17 24					17 54					
Ewell West	d					16 57							17 27					17 57					
Stoneleigh	d					16 59							17 29					17 59					
Worcester Park	d					17 02							17 32					18 02					
Chessington South	d				16 40					17 10							17 40					18 10	
Chessington North	d				16 42					17 12							17 42					18 12	
Tolworth	d				16 44					17 14							17 44					18 14	
Malden Manor	d				16 47					17 17							17 47					18 17	
Motspur Park	d				16 50	17 05				17 20			17 35				17 50	18 05				18 20	
Raynes Park ■	d		16 43	16 51	16 54	17 08		17 13	17 21	17 24			17 38		17 43	17 51	17 54	18 08		18 13	18 21	18 24	
Wimbledon ■ ⊖	d		16 47	16 55	16 58	17 12	17 08	17 17	17 25	17 28	17 31	17 38	17 42		17 47	17 55	17 58	18 12	18 08	18 17	18 25	18 28	18 31
Earlsfield	d		16 50	16 58	17 01	17 16	17 11	17 20	17 28	17 31	17 35	17 41	17 46		17 50	17 58	18 01	18 16	18 11	18 20	18 28	18 31	18 35
Clapham Junction ■	d		16 54	17 02	17 05	17 20	17 15	17 24	17 32	17 35	17 39	17 45	17 50		17 54	18 02	18 05	18 20	18 15	18 24	18 32	18 35	18 39
Vauxhall ⊖	d		16 59	17 07	17 10	17 25	17 20	17 29	17 37	17 40	17 44	17 50	17 55		17 59	18 07	18 10	18 25	18 20	18 29	18 37	18 40	18 44
London Waterloo ■ ⊖	a		17 04	17 12	17 15	17 29	17 25	17 34	17 42	17 45	17 48	17 55	17 59		18 04	18 12	18 15	18 29	18 25	18 34	18 42	18 45	18 48

A From London Waterloo

Hampton Court, Shepperton, Guildford, Dorking and Chessington South - London

		SW	SW	SW A	SW	SW	SW	SW	SW	SW A	SW	SW	SW	SW	SW	SW A	SW	SW	SW	SW	SW	SW A	SW
Guildford	d	17 57						18 18	18 27				18 48	18 57						19 18	19 27		
London Road (Guildford)	d							18 22					18 52							19 22			
Clandon	d							18 27					18 57							19 27			
Horsley	d							18 31					19 01							19 31			
Effingham Junction ■	d							18 34					19 04							19 34			
Bookham	d							18 37												19 37			
Cobham & Stoke d'Abernon	d												19 08										
Oxshott	d												19 11										
Claygate	d												19 14										
Hinchley Wood	d												19 17										
Hampton Court	d					18 35					19 05							19 35					20 05
Thames Ditton	d					18 37					19 07							19 37					20 07
Surbiton ■	d	18 30				18 43			19 00		19 13		19 24	19 30				19 43			20 00		20 13
Berrylands	d					18 45					19 15							19 45					20 15
Shepperton	d				18 11												19 11						
Upper Halliford	d				18 14												19 14						
Sunbury	d				18 16												19 16						
Kempton Park	d				18 18												19 18						
Hampton	d				18 21												19 21						
Fulwell	d				18 24												19 24						
Strawberry Hill	d			18 14						18 49						19 14						19 49	
Teddington	d			18 17	18 29					18 55						19 17	19 29					19 55	
Hampton Wick	d			18 20	18 31					18 57						19 20	19 31					19 57	
Kingston	a			18 22	18 33					18 59						19 22	19 33					19 59	
	d				18 34					19 04							19 34					20 04	
Norbiton	d				18 36					19 06							19 36					20 06	
New Malden ■	d				18 40	18 48				19 10	19 18						19 40	19 48				20 10	20 18
Dorking ■	182 d		18 07												19 07								
Box Hill & Westhumble	182 d		18 10												19 10								
Leatherhead	182 d		18 15					18 45							19 15					19 45			
Ashtead	182 d		18 18					18 48							19 18					19 48			
Epsom ■	182 a		18 23					18 53							19 23					19 53			
	d		18 24					18 54							19 24					19 54			
Ewell West	d		18 27					18 57							19 27					19 57			
Stoneleigh	d		18 29					18 59							19 29					19 59			
Worcester Park	d		18 32					19 02							19 32					20 02			
Chessington South	d						18 40					19 10							19 40				
Chessington North	d						18 42					19 12							19 42				
Tolworth	d						18 44					19 14							19 44				
Malden Manor	d						18 47					19 17							19 47				
Motspur Park	d		18 35				18 50	19 05				19 20			19 35				19 50	20 05			
Raynes Park ■	d		18 38		18 43	18 51	18 54	19 08		19 13	19 21	19 24			19 38		19 43	19 51	19 54	20 08		20 13	20 21
Wimbledon ■ ⊖	d	18 38	18 42		18 47	18 55	18 58	19 12	19 08	19 17	19 25	19 28	19 31	19 38	19 42		19 47	19 55	19 58	20 12	20 08	20 17	20 25
Earlsfield	d	18 41	18 46		18 50	18 58	19 01	19 16	19 11	19 20	19 28	19 31	19 35	19 41	19 46		19 50	19 58	20 01	20 16	20 11	20 20	20 28
Clapham Junction ■	d	18 45	18 50		18 54	19 02	19 05	19 20	19 15	19 24	19 32	19 35	19 39	19 45	19 50		19 54	20 02	20 05	20 20	20 15	20 24	20 32
Vauxhall ⊖	d	18 50	18 55		18 59	19 07	19 10	19 25	19 20	19 29	19 37	19 40	19 44	19 50	19 55		19 59	20 07	20 10	20 25	20 20	20 29	20 37
London Waterloo ■ ⊖	a	18 55	18 59		19 04	19 12	19 15	19 29	19 25	19 34	19 42	19 45	19 48	19 55	19 59		20 04	20 12	20 15	20 29	20 25	20 34	20 42

A From London Waterloo

Table T152-R

Sundays

7 October to 2 December

Hampton Court, Shepperton, Guildford, Dorking and Chessington South - London

		SW		SW	SW	SW	SW A	SW	SW	SW	SW	SW A		SW	SW	SW	SW	SW	SW A	SW	SW	SW		SW	SW A
Guildford	d			19 48	19 57					20 18	20 27					20 48	20 57					21 18		21 27	
London Road (Guildford)	d			19 52						20 22						20 52						21 22			
Clandon	d			19 57						20 27						20 57						21 27			
Horsley	d			20 01						20 31						21 01						21 31			
Effingham Junction	d			20 04						20 34						21 04						21 34			
Bookham	d									20 37												21 37			
Cobham & Stoke d'Abernon	d			20 08												21 08									
Oxshott	d			20 11												21 11									
Claygate	d			20 14												21 14									
Hinchley Wood	d			20 17												21 17									
Hampton Court	d								20 35					21 05							21 35				
Thames Ditton	d								20 37					21 07							21 37				
Surbiton	d			20 24	20 30				20 43		21 00			21 13		21 24	21 30				21 43			22 00	
Berrylands	d								20 45					21 15							21 45				
Shepperton	d							20 11												21 11					
Upper Halliford	d							20 14												21 14					
Sunbury	d							20 16												21 16					
Kempton Park	d							20 18												21 18					
Hampton	d							20 21												21 21					
Fulwell	d							20 24												21 24					
Strawberry Hill	d						20 14					20 49							21 14						21 49
Teddington	d						20 17	20 29				20 55							21 17	21 29					21 55
Hampton Wick	d						20 20	20 31				20 57							21 20	21 31					21 57
Kingston	a						20 22	20 33				20 59							21 22	21 33					21 59
	d							20 34				21 04								21 34					22 04
Norbiton	d							20 36				21 06								21 36					22 06
New Malden	d							20 40	20 48			21 10		21 18						21 40	21 48				22 10
Dorking 182	d					20 07												21 07							
Box Hill & Westhumble 182	d																								
Leatherhead 182	d					20 15				20 45								21 15				21 45			
Ashtead 182	d					20 18				20 48								21 18				21 48			
Epsom 182	a					20 23				20 53								21 23				21 53			
	d					20 24				20 54								21 24				21 54			
Ewell West	d					20 27				20 57								21 27				21 57			
Stoneleigh	d					20 29				20 59								21 29				21 59			
Worcester Park	d					20 32				21 02								21 32				22 02			
Chessington South	d	20 10													21 10										
Chessington North	d	20 12													21 12										
Tolworth	d	20 14													21 14										
Malden Manor	d	20 17													21 17										
Motspur Park	d	20 20				20 35				21 05					21 20			21 35				22 05			
Raynes Park	d	20 24				20 38		20 43	20 51	21 08		21 13		21 21	21 24			21 38		21 43	21 51	22 08			22 13
Wimbledon ⊖ ⇌	d	20 28		20 31	20 38	20 42		20 47	20 55	21 12	21 08	21 17		21 25	21 28	21 31	21 38	21 42		21 47	21 55	22 12		22 08	22 17
Earlsfield	d	20 31		20 35	20 41	20 46		20 50	20 58	21 16	21 11	21 20		21 28	21 31	21 35	21 41	21 46		21 50	21 58	22 16		22 11	22 20
Clapham Junction	d	20 35		20 39	20 45	20 50		20 54	21 02	21 20	21 15	21 24		21 32	21 35	21 39	21 45	21 50		21 54	22 02	22 20		22 15	22 24
Vauxhall ⊖	d	20 40		20 44	20 50	20 55		20 59	21 07	21 25	21 20	21 29		21 37	21 40	21 44	21 50	21 55		21 59	22 07	22 25		22 20	22 29
London Waterloo ⊖	a	20 45		20 48	20 55	21 01		21 04	21 13	21 29	21 25	21 36		21 42	21 45	21 48	21 55	22 00		22 04	22 12	22 29		22 25	22 36

A From London Waterloo

Table T152-R

Sundays

7 October to 2 December

Hampton Court, Shepperton, Guildford, Dorking and Chessington South - London

		SW	SW	SW	SW	SW	SW A	SW		SW	SW	SW A	SW	SW	SW	SW	SW	SW A		SW	SW	SW	SW A		
Guildford	d			21 48	21 57					22 20	22 27				22 50	22 57									
London Road (Guildford)	d			21 52						22 24					22 54										
Clandon	d			21 57						22 29					22 59										
Horsley	d			22 01						22 33					23 03										
Effingham Junction	d			22 04						22 36					23 06										
Bookham	d									22 39															
Cobham & Stoke d'Abernon	d			22 08											23 10										
Oxshott	d			22 11											23 13										
Claygate	d			22 14											23 16										
Hinchley Wood	d			22 17											23 19										
Hampton Court	d	22 05											23 05									23 45			
Thames Ditton	d	22 07											23 07									23 47			
Surbiton	d	22 13		22 24	22 30						23 00		23 13		23 24	23 30						23 53			
Berrylands	d	22 15											23 15									23 55			
Shepperton	d							22 11												23 11					
Upper Halliford	d							22 14												23 14					
Sunbury	d							22 16												23 16					
Kempton Park	d							22 18												23 18					
Hampton	d							22 21												23 21					
Fulwell	d							22 24												23 24					
Strawberry Hill	d						22 14					22 49						23 14					23 48		
Teddington	d						22 17	22 29				22 55						23 17		23 29			23 51		
Hampton Wick	d						22 20	22 31				22 57						23 20		23 31			23 54		
Kingston	a						22 22	22 33				22 59						23 22		23 33			23 56		
	d							22 34				23 04								23 34					
Norbiton	d							22 36				23 06								23 36					
New Malden	d	22 18						22 40				23 10	23 18							23 40		23 58			
Dorking 182	d					22 07											23 07								
Box Hill & Westhumble 182	d																								
Leatherhead 182	d					22 15				22 45							23 15								
Ashtead 182	d					22 18				22 48							23 18								
Epsom 182	a					22 23				22 53							23 23								
	d					22 24				22 54							23 24								
Ewell West	d					22 27				22 57							23 27								
Stoneleigh	d					22 29				22 59							23 29								
Worcester Park	d					22 32				23 02							23 32								
Chessington South	d		22 10											23 10							23 40				
Chessington North	d		22 12											23 12							23 42				
Tolworth	d		22 14											23 14							23 44				
Malden Manor	d		22 17											23 17							23 47				
Motspur Park	d		22 20			22 35				23 05				23 20			23 35				23 50				
Raynes Park	d	22 21	22 24			22 38		22 43		23 08		23 13	23 21	23 24			23 38			23 43	23 54	00 01			
Wimbledon ⊖ ⇌	d	22 25	22 28	22 31	22 38	22 42		22 47		23 12	23 08	23 17	23 25	23 28	23 31	23 38	23 42			23 47	23a59	00a04			
Earlsfield	d	22 28	22 31	22 35	22 41	22 46		22 50		23 16	23 11	23 20	23 28	23 31	23 35	23 41	23 46			23 50					
Clapham Junction	d	22 32	22 35	22 39	22 45	22 50		22 54		23 20	23 15	23 24	23 32	23 35	23 39	23 45	23 50			23 54					
Vauxhall ⊖	d	22 37	22 40	22 44	22 50	22 55		22 59		23 25	23 20	23 29	23 37	23 40	23 44	23 50	23 55			23 59					
London Waterloo ⊖	a	22 42	22 45	22 48	22 55	23 00		23 04		23 29	23 25	23 35	23 42	23 45	23 48	23 55	00 01			00 04					

A From London Waterloo

London - Woking, Guildford, Alton and Basingstoke

Miles	Miles	Miles			SW MX ■	SW MO ■	SW MO ■	SW MX ■	SW MX ■	SW MO ◇■	SW MX ■	SW MO	SW MX		SW MX ■	SW MO ■	SW MO	SW MX ◇■	SW MX	SW MO ■	SW MX ■	SW MO ■	SW MX ◇■		SW MX ■
0	—	—	London Waterloo 15 ⊖	d																		00 05		
1¼	—	—	Vauxhall ⊖	d																				
4	—	—	Clapham Junction 10	d																		00u12		
5½	—	—	Earlsfield	d																				
7¼	—	—	Wimbledon 6 ⊖	d																		00u18		
12	—	—	Surbiton 5	d															00 05	00 09				
14½	—	—	Esher	d															00 09					
16	—	—	Hersham	d															00 12					
17	—	—	Walton-on-Thames	d															00 15	00 16				
19	—	—	Weybridge	d															00 18	00 20				
20½	—	—	Byfleet & New Haw	d												00 02		00 06	00 21					
21¾	—	—	West Byfleet	d									00 03				00 05		00 09	00 24		←			
24½	0	—	Woking	a									00 08				00 11		00 15	00 30	00 26	00 30	00 35		
—	—	—		d					00 01	00 03	00 03	00 05			00 08	00 08		00 13		00 33	00 28	00 33	00 37		00 40
—	2½	—	Worplesdon	d														00 18		→					
—	6	—	Guildford	a						00 10		00 14						00 24							
28	—	0	Brookwood	d				00 03	00 07												00 34	00 39			00 45
—	—	4½	Ash Vale	d		00 03			00 15													00 47			00 53
—	—	7	Aldershot	a		00 07			00 19													00 51			00 58
—	—	—		d		00 08			00 20													00 52			00 58
—	—	10	Farnham	a		00 13			00 25													00 57			01 04
—	—	—		d		00 14			00 26																01 04
—	—	14	Bentley	d	00 03	00 24			00 33																01s10
—	—	18¾	Alton	a	00 10	00 31			00 40																01 18
33¼	—	—	Farnborough (Main)	d				00 10			00 14					00 19					00 41				
36½	—	—	Fleet	d			00 04	00 16			00 20					00 25					00 47				
40	—	—	Winchfield	d			00 10	00 21													00s52				
42¼	—	—	Hook	d			00 14	00 26													00s57				
47¾	—	—	Basingstoke	a			00 21	00 33			00 33				00 27	00 39					01 06		00 55		

		SW MX	SW MX	SW MO ◇■	SW ■	SW ◇■	SW ◇■	SW ◇■	SW ■		SW ◇■	SW ■	SW ■	SW	SW ◇■	SW ◇■	SW ◇■	SW	SW ◇■		SW ■	SW	SW ■	SW ◇■ A	SW ◇■ B
London Waterloo 15 ⊖	d	00 09	00 27	00 50	01 05	05 00	05 20	05 30						05 50	06 12	06 15		06 20	06 30				06 42	06 45	06 45
Vauxhall ⊖	d	00 13	00 31		01 09	05 04	05 24							05 54				06 24							
Clapham Junction 10	d	00 20	00 37	00 57	01 15	05 11	05 29	05u37						05 59	06u19	06u22		06 29	06u37				06u49	06u52	06u52
Earlsfield	d	00 24	00s41			05 14	05 32							06 02				06 32							
Wimbledon 6 ⊖	d	00 28	00 45		01s27	05 18	05 36	05 43						06 06				06 36							
Surbiton 5	d	00 35	00s56		01s35	05 26	05 44							06 14	06 30			06 44					07 00		
Esher	d	00s39				05 30	05 48							06 18				06 48							
Hersham	d	00s42				05 33	05 51							06 21				06 51							
Walton-on-Thames	d	00s45				05 37	05 54							06 24	06 37			06 54					07 07		
Weybridge	d	00s48				05 41	05 57							06 27	06 41			06 57					07 11		
Byfleet & New Haw	d	00s51				05 44	06 00							06 30				07 00							
West Byfleet	d	00s54	01s07			05 47	06 03				←			06 33			←	07 03				←			
Woking	a	00 59	01 12	01 16	01 48	05 51	06 08	05 59			06 08			06 38	06 48	06 42	06 48	07 07	06 56			07 07	07 18	07 12	07 12
	d	01 00		01 18	01 49	05 53	06 11	06 01	06 02		06 11	06 19	06 30		06 50	06 43	06 50	07 10	06 57		06 58	07 10	07 19	07 13	07 16
Worplesdon	d						→				06 16				→	06 48		→					→	07 18	07 21
Guildford	a	01 08		01s26		06 00					06 24					06 54						07 19		07 24	07 26
Brookwood	d								06 08			06 25	06 36				06 56				07 06				
Ash Vale	d								06 16				06 44								07 14				
Aldershot	a								06 20				06 49								07 19				
	d								06 21				06 50								07 20				
Farnham	a								06 26				06 55								07 25				
	d								06 27				06 56								07 26				
Bentley	d								06 33				07 02								07 32				
Alton	a								06 40				07 10								07 40				
Farnborough (Main)	d				01s58							06 33					07 04								
Fleet	d				02s04							06 38					07 09								
Winchfield	d											06 44					07 15								
Hook	d											06 48					07 19								
Basingstoke	a				02s16			06 20				06 58					07 28		07 16						

A until 5 October

B from 8 October

London - Woking, Guildford, Alton and Basingstoke

			SW ■	SW ■	SW	SW ■	SW ◇■	SW ◇■ ✠	SW	SW ■	SW ◇■		SW ■	SW	SW ■	SW ■	SW ◇■ ✠	SW ■	SW ◇■ ✠	SW ■	SW		SW ◇■ ✠	SW ■	SW ◇■
London Waterloo 15 ⊖	d		06 50		06 50	06 53	07 03	07 10		07 12	07 15			07 20	07 23	07 25	07 30	07 34	07 35				07 39	07 42	07 45
Vauxhall ⊖	d				06 54									07 24				07 39							
Clapham Junction 10	d				06 59	07u00	07u10	07u17		07u20	07u23			07 29	07u31			07 46					07u45		07u52
Earlsfield	d				07 02									07 32											
Wimbledon 6 ⊖	d				07 06				←					07 36							←				
Surbiton 5	d				07 14	07 11			07 14	07 31				07 44	07 41						07 44			08 00	
Esher	d				→				07 18					→							07 48				
Hersham	d								07 21												07 51				
Walton-on-Thames	d								07 24	07 38											07 54			08 07	
Weybridge	d								07 27	07 42											07 57			08 11	
Byfleet & New Haw	d								07 30												08 00				
West Byfleet	d			←		07 21			07 33				←		07 51					←	08 03				
Woking	a		07 14	07 18		07 26	07 29	07 35	07 37	07 48	07 43		07 48		08 00	07 53	07 56		07 58	08 00	08 08			08 18	08 11
	d			07 19		07 30	07 30	07 36	07 39	07 50	07 44		07 50		08 02		07 56		08 00	08 02				08 19	08 13
Worplesdon	d									→	07 49				→									→	08 18
Guildford	a								07 47		07 55						08 05	09 25							08 24
Brookwood	d			07 25		07 36							07 56							08 08					
Ash Vale	d					07 44														08 16					
Aldershot	a					07 49														08 20					
	d					07 50														08 21					
Farnham	a					07 55														08 26					
	d					07 56														08 27					
Bentley	d					08 02														08 33					
Alton	a					08 10														08 40					
Farnborough (Main)	d			07 33									08 03										08 13		
Fleet	d			07 38									08 09										08 19		
Winchfield	d			07 44									08 14												
Hook	d			07 48									08 19												
Basingstoke	a			07 56			07 48	07 55					08 26						08 19				08 32		

		SW ◇■ ✠	SW ■	SW	SW ■	SW ◇■ ✠	SW ■		SW ◇■ ✠	SW ■	SW	SW ■	SW ■	SW ◇■ ✠	SW ■	SW	SW ■		SW ◇■ ✠	SW ◇■ ✠	SW ■	SW	SW ◇■	SW ■	SW ◇■
London Waterloo 15 ⊖	d	07 50		07 50	07 53	08 00			08 05	08 09		08 12	08 15	08 20		08 20	08 24		08 30	08 35			08 39	08 42	08 45
Vauxhall ⊖	d			07 54												08 24									
Clapham Junction 10	d	07u57		07 59	08u00				08u12			08u19	08u22	08u27		08 29							08u46		08u52
Earlsfield	d			08 02												08 32									
Wimbledon 6 ⊖	d			08 06							←					08 36						←			
Surbiton 5	d			08 14	08 11						08 14	08 30				08 44	08 41					08 44		09 00	
Esher	d			→							08 18					→						08 48			
Hersham	d										08 21											08 51			
Walton-on-Thames	d										08 24	08 37										08 54		09 07	
Weybridge	d										08 27	08 41										08 57		09 11	
Byfleet & New Haw	d										08 30											09 00			
West Byfleet	d		←		08 21		←				08 33				←		08 51				←	09 03			
Woking	a	08 16	08 18		08 30	08 25	08 30			08 33	08 37	08 49	08 43	08 46	08 49		09 00		08 55	08 58	09 00	09 08		09 18	09 12
	d	08 17	08 19		08 31	08 25	08 31			08 35	08 39	08 49	08 44	08 46	08 49		09 00		08 55		09 00			09 19	09 13
Worplesdon	d				→							→	08 49				→							→	09 18
Guildford	a					08 34					08 50		08 54						09 05						09 24
Brookwood	d		08 25				08 37								08 55						09 06				
Ash Vale	d						08 45														09 14				
Aldershot	a						08 49														09 19				
	d						08 50														09 20				
Farnham	a						08 55														09 25				
	d						08 56														09 26				
Bentley	d						09 02																		
Alton	a						09 10														09 38				
Farnborough (Main)	d		08 33							08 45					09 03								09 13		
Fleet	d		08 38												09 08								09 19		
Winchfield	d		08 44												09 14										
Hook	d		08 48												09 18										
Basingstoke	a	08 36	08 58						08 47	08 58				09 05	09 28								09 32		

		SW ◇■ ✠	SW ■		SW	SW ■	SW ◇■ ✠	SW ■	SW ◇■ ✠	SW ■	SW	SW ■	SW ■		SW ◇■ ✠	SW ■	SW	SW ■	SW ◇■ ✠	SW ◇■ ✠	SW ■	SW	SW ◇■		SW ■
London Waterloo 15 ⊖	d	08 50			08 50	08 53	09 00		09 05	09 09		09 12	09 15		09 20		09 20	09 24	09 30	09 35			09 39		09 42
Vauxhall ⊖	d				08 54												09 24								
Clapham Junction 10	d				08 59	09u00			09u12			09u19	09u22		09u27		09 29						09u46		
Earlsfield	d				09 02												09 32								
Wimbledon 6 ⊖	d				09 06						←						09 36					←			
Surbiton 5	d				09 14	09 11					09 14	09 30					09 44	09 41				09 44			10 00
Esher	d				→						09 18						→					09 48			
Hersham	d										09 21											09 51			
Walton-on-Thames	d										09 24	09 37										09 54			10 07
Weybridge	d										09 27	09 41										09 57			10 11
Byfleet & New Haw	d										09 30											10 00			
West Byfleet	d		←			09 21		←			09 33					←		09 51			←	10 03			
Woking	a	09 15	09 18			09 29	09 24	09 29		09 33	09 38	09 48	09 42		09 45	09 48		09 59	09 54	09 58	09 59	10 08			10 18
	d	09 16	09 19			09 30	09 25	09 30		09 35		09 49	09 43		09 46	09 49		10 00	09 55		10 00				10 19
Worplesdon	d					→						→						→							→
Guildford	a						09 33						09 51						10 03						
Brookwood	d		09 25					09 36								09 55					10 06				
Ash Vale	d							09 44													10 14				
Aldershot	a							09 49													10 19				
	d							09 50													10 20				
Farnham	a							09 55													10 25				
	d							09 56													10 26				
Bentley	d							10 02																	
Alton	a							10 10													10 37				
Farnborough (Main)	d		09 33							09 45						10 03							10 13		
Fleet	d		09 38													10 08							10 19		
Winchfield	d		09 44													10 14									
Hook	d		09 48													10 18									
Basingstoke	a	09 36	09 58						09 47	09 58					10 05	10 28							10 31		

London - Woking, Guildford, Alton and Basingstoke

		SW ◇1	SW ◇1 ⚒	SW 1	SW	SW 1	SW ◇1 ⚒	SW 1	SW ◇1 A ⚒	SW 1	SW	SW 1	SW 1	SW ◇1 ⚒	SW 1	SW	SW 1	SW ◇1 ⚒	SW ◇1 ⚒	SW 1	SW	SW ◇1	SW 1
London Waterloo 15 ⊖	d	09 45	09 50		09 50	09 53	10 00		10 05	10 09		10 12	10 15	10 20		10 20	10 23	10 30	10 35			10 39	10 42
Vauxhall ⊖	d				09 54											10 24							
Clapham Junction 10	d	09u52			09 59	10u00			10u12			10u19	10u22	10u27		10 29						10u46	
Earlsfield	d				10 02											10 32							
Wimbledon ⊖	d				10 06						←					10 36					←		
Surbiton	d				10 14	10 11					10 14	10 30				10 44	10 41				10 44		11 00
Esher	d				→						10 18					→					10 48		
Hersham	d										10 21										10 51		
Walton-on-Thames	d										10 24	10 37									10 54		11 07
Weybridge	d										10 27	10 41									10 57		11 11
Byfleet & New Haw	d										10 30										11 00		
West Byfleet	d			←		10 21		←							←		10 51			←	11 03		
Woking	a	10 12	10 14	10 18		10 29	10 24	10 29		10 33	10 38	10 49	10 41	10 45	10 49		10 59	10 54	10 58	10 59	11 08		11 19
	d	10 13	10 16	10 19		10 30	10 25	10 30		10 35		10 49	10 43	10 46	10 49		11 00	10 55		11 00			11 20
Worplesdon	d	10 18				→						→					→						→
Guildford	a	10 24					10 33						10 50					11 03					
Brookwood	d			10 25				10 36							10 56					11 06			
Ash Vale	d							10 44												11 14			
Aldershot	a							10 49												11 19			
	d							10 50												11 20			
Farnham	a							10 55												11 25			
	d							10 56															
Bentley	d							11 02															
Alton	a							11 10															
Farnborough (Main)	d			10 33						10 45					11 04							11 13	
Fleet	d			10 38											11 09							11 19	
Winchfield	d			10 44											11 15								
Hook	d			10 48											11 18								
Basingstoke	a		10 36	10 58					10 47	10 58				11 05	11 28							11 31	

		SW ◇1	SW ◇1 ⚒	SW 1	SW	SW 1	SW ◇1 ⚒	SW 1	SW ◇1 ⚒	SW 1	SW	SW 1	SW 1	SW ◇1 ⚒	SW 1	SW	SW 1	SW ◇1 ⚒	SW ◇1 ⚒	SW 1	SW	SW ◇1	SW 1
London Waterloo 15 ⊖	d	10 45	10 50		10 50	10 53	11 00		11 05	11 09		11 12	11 15	11 20		11 20	11 23	11 30	11 35			11 39	11 42
Vauxhall ⊖	d				10 54											11 24							
Clapham Junction 10	d	10u52			10 59	11u00			11u12			11u19	11u22	11u27		11 29						11u46	
Earlsfield	d				11 02											11 32							
Wimbledon ⊖	d				11 06						←					11 36					←		
Surbiton	d				11 14	11 11					11 14	11 30				11 44	11 41				11 44		12 00
Esher	d				→						11 18					→					11 48		
Hersham	d										11 21										11 51		
Walton-on-Thames	d										11 24	11 37									11 54		12 07
Weybridge	d										11 27	11 41									11 57		12 11
Byfleet & New Haw	d										11 30										12 00		
West Byfleet	d			←		11 21		←							←		11 51			←	12 03		
Woking	a	11 12	11 14	11 19		11 29	11 24	11 29		11 33	11 38	11 48	11 41	11 45	11 48		11 59	11 54	11 58	11 59	12 08		12 18
	d	11 13	11 16	11 20		11 30	11 25	11 30		11 35		11 49	11 43	11 46	11 49		12 00	11 55		12 00			12 19
Worplesdon	d	11 18				→						→					→						→
Guildford	a	11 24					11 33						11 50					12 03					
Brookwood	d			11 26				11 36							11 55					12 06			
Ash Vale	d							11 44												12 14			
Aldershot	a							11 49												12 19			
	d							11 50												12 20			
Farnham	a							11 55												12 25			
	d							11 56												12 26			
Bentley	d							12 02															
Alton	a							12 10												12 37			
Farnborough (Main)	d			11 34						11 45					12 03							12 13	
Fleet	d			11 39											12 08							12 19	
Winchfield	d			11 45											12 14								
Hook	d			11 49											12 18								
Basingstoke	a		11 36	11 58					11 47	11 58				12 05	12 28							12 31	

A not 21 May

London - Woking, Guildford, Alton and Basingstoke

		SW ◇1	SW ◇1 ⚒	SW 1	SW	SW 1	SW ◇1 ⚒	SW 1	SW ◇1 ⚒	SW 1	SW	SW 1	SW 1	SW ◇1 ⚒	SW 1	SW	SW 1	SW ◇1 ⚒	SW ◇1 ⚒	SW 1	SW	SW ◇1	SW 1
London Waterloo 15 ⊖	d	11 45	11 50		11 50	11 53	12 00		12 05	12 09		12 12	12 15	12 20		12 20	12 23	12 30	12 35			12 39	12 42
Vauxhall ⊖	d				11 54											12 24							
Clapham Junction 10	d	11u52			11 59	12u00			12u12			12u19	12u22	12u27		12 29						12u46	
Earlsfield	d				12 02											12 32							
Wimbledon ⊖	d				12 06						←					12 36					←		
Surbiton	d				12 14	12 11					12 14	12 30				12 44	12 41				12 44		13 00
Esher	d				→						12 18					→					12 48		
Hersham	d										12 21										12 51		
Walton-on-Thames	d										12 24	12 37									12 54		13 07
Weybridge	d										12 27	12 41									12 57		13 11
Byfleet & New Haw	d										12 30										13 00		
West Byfleet	d			←		12 21		←							←		12 51			←	13 03		
Woking	a	12 12	12 14	12 18		12 29	12 24	12 29		12 33	12 38	12 48	12 41	12 45	12 48		12 59	12 54	12 58	12 59	13 08		13 18
	d	12 13	12 16	12 19		12 30	12 25	12 30		12 35		12 49	12 43	12 46	12 49		13 00	12 55		13 00			13 19
Worplesdon	d	12 18				→						→					→						→
Guildford	a	12 24					12 33						12 50					13 03					
Brookwood	d			12 25				12 36							12 55					13 06			
Ash Vale	d							12 44												13 14			
Aldershot	a							12 49												13 19			
	d							12 50												13 20			
Farnham	a							12 55												13 25			
	d							12 56												13 26			
Bentley	d							13 02															
Alton	a							13 10												13 37			
Farnborough (Main)	d			12 33						12 45					13 03							13 13	
Fleet	d			12 38											13 08							13 19	
Winchfield	d			12 44											13 14								
Hook	d			12 48											13 18								
Basingstoke	a		12 36	12 58					12 47	12 58				13 05	13 28							13 31	

		SW ◇1	SW ◇1 ⚒	SW 1	SW	SW 1	SW ◇1 ⚒	SW 1	SW ◇1 ⚒	SW 1	SW	SW 1	SW 1	SW ◇1 ⚒	SW 1	SW	SW 1	SW ◇1 ⚒	SW ◇1 ⚒	SW 1	SW	SW ◇1
London Waterloo 15 ⊖	d	12 45	12 50		12 50	12 53	13 00		13 05	13 09		13 12	13 15	13 20		13 20	13 23	13 30	13 35			13 39
Vauxhall ⊖	d				12 54											13 24						
Clapham Junction 10	d	12u52	12u57		12 59	13u01			13u12			13u19	13u22	13u27		13 29						13u46
Earlsfield	d				13 02											13 32						
Wimbledon ⊖	d				13 06						←					13 36					←	
Surbiton	d				13 14	13 11					13 14	13 30				13 44	13 41				13 44	
Esher	d				→						13 18					→					13 48	
Hersham	d										13 21										13 51	
Walton-on-Thames	d										13 24	13 37									13 54	
Weybridge	d										13 27	13 41									13 57	
Byfleet & New Haw	d										13 30										14 00	
West Byfleet	d			←		13 21		←							←		13 51			←	14 03	
Woking	a	13 12	13 15	13 18		13 29	13 24	13 29		13 33	13 38	13 48	13 41	13 45	13 48		13 59	13 54	13 58	13 59	14 08	
	d	13 13	13 16	13 19		13 30	13 25	13 30		13 35		13 49	13 43	13 46	13 49		14 00	13 55		14 00		
Worplesdon	d	13 18				→						→					→					
Guildford	a	13 24					13 33						13 50					14 03				
Brookwood	d			13 25				13 36							13 55					14 06		
Ash Vale	d							13 44												14 14		
Aldershot	a							13 49												14 19		
	d							13 50												14 20		
Farnham	a							13 55												14 25		
	d							13 56												14 26		
Bentley	d							14 02														
Alton	a							14 11												14 37		
Farnborough (Main)	d			13 33						13 45					14 03							14 13
Fleet	d			13 38											14 08							14 19
Winchfield	d			13 44											14 14							
Hook	d			13 48											14 18							
Basingstoke	a		13 36	13 58					13 47	13 58				14 05	14 28							14 31

		SW 1	SW ◇1	SW ◇1 ⚒	SW 1	SW	SW 1	SW ◇1 ⚒	SW 1	SW ◇1 ⚒	SW 1	SW	SW 1	SW 1	SW ◇1 ⚒	SW 1	SW	SW 1	SW ◇1 ⚒	SW ◇1 ⚒	SW 1	SW	SW ◇1
London Waterloo 15 ⊖	d	13 42	13 45	13 50		13 50	13 53	14 00		14 05	14 09		14 12	14 15	14 20		14 20	14 23	14 30	14 35			14 39
Vauxhall ⊖	d					13 54											14 24						
Clapham Junction 10	d		13u52			13 59	14u00			14u12			14u19	14u22	14u27		14 29						14u46
Earlsfield	d					14 02											14 32						
Wimbledon ⊖	d					14 06						←					14 36					←	
Surbiton	d	14 00				14 14	14 11					14 14	14 30				14 44	14 41				14 44	
Esher	d					→						14 18					→					14 48	
Hersham	d											14 21										14 51	
Walton-on-Thames	d	14 07										14 24	14 37									14 54	
Weybridge	d	14 11										14 27	14 41									14 57	
Byfleet & New Haw	d											14 30										15 00	
West Byfleet	d				←		14 21		←							←		14 51			←	15 03	
Woking	a	14 19	14 12	14 14	14 19		14 29	14 24	14 29		14 33	14 38	14 48	14 42	14 45	14 48		14 59	14 54	14 58	14 59	15 08	
	d	14 20	14 13	14 16	14 20		14 30	14 25	14 30		14 35		14 49	14 43	14 46	14 49		15 00	14 55		15 00		
Worplesdon	d	→	14 18				→						→					→					
Guildford	a		14 24					14 33						14 51					15 03				
Brookwood	d				14 26				14 36							14 55					15 06		
Ash Vale	d								14 44												15 14		
Aldershot	a								14 49												15 19		
	d								14 50												15 20		
Farnham	a								14 55												15 25		
	d								14 56												15 26		
Bentley	d								15 02														
Alton	a								15 10												15 37		
Farnborough (Main)	d				14 34						14 45					15 03							15 13
Fleet	d				14 39											15 08							15 19
Winchfield	d				14 45											15 14							
Hook	d				14 49											15 18							
Basingstoke	a			14 36	14 58					14 47	14 58				15 05	15 28							15 31

London - Woking, Guildford, Alton and Basingstoke

Station		SW ■	SW ◇■	SW ◇■ ⊼	SW ■	SW	SW ■	SW ◇■ ⊼	SW ■	SW ◇■ ⊼	SW ■	SW	SW ■	SW ◇■	SW ◇■ ⊼	SW ■	SW	SW ■	SW ◇■ ⊼	SW ◇■ ⊼	SW ■	SW	SW ◇■
London Waterloo ■ ⊖	d	14 42	14 45	14 50		14 50	14 53	15 00		15 05	15 09		15 12	15 15	15 20		15 20	15 25	15 30	15 35			15 39
Vauxhall ⊖	d					14 54											15 24						
Clapham Junction ■	d		14u52			14 59	15u00			15u12			15u19	15u22	15u27		15 29						15u46
Earlsfield	d					15 02											15 32						
Wimbledon ■ ⊖	d					15 06						←					15 36					←	
Surbiton ■	d	15 00				15 14	15 11					15 14	15 30				15 44	15 41				15 44	
Esher	d					→						15 18					→					15 48	
Hersham	d											15 21										15 51	
Walton-on-Thames	d	15 07										15 24	15 37									15 54	
Weybridge	d	15 11										15 27	15 41									15 57	
Byfleet & New Haw	d											15 30										16 00	
West Byfleet	d				←		15 21		←			15 33				←		15 51			←	16 03	
Woking	a	15 18	15 12	15 14	15 18		15 29	15 24	15 29		15 33	15 38	15 48	15 42	15 45	15 48		15 59	15 54	15 58	15 59	16 08	
	d	15 19	15 13	15 16	15 19		15 30	15 25	15 30		15 35		15 49	15 43	15 46	15 49		16 00	15 55		16 00		
Worplesdon	d	→	15 18				→						→	15 48				→					
Guildford	a		15 24					15 33						15 54					16 03				
Brookwood	d				15 25				15 36							15 55					16 06		
Ash Vale	d								15 44												16 14		
Aldershot	a								15 49												16 19		
	d								15 50												16 20		
Farnham	a								15 55												16 25		
	d								15 56												16 26		
Bentley	d								16 02														
Alton	a								16 10												16 37		
Farnborough (Main)	d				15 33						15 45					16 03							16 13
Fleet	d				15 38											16 08							16 19
Winchfield	d				15 44											16 14							
Hook	d				15 48											16 18							
Basingstoke	a			15 36	15 58					15 47	15 58				16 05	16 28							16 31

Station		SW ■	SW ◇■	SW ◇■ ⊼	SW ■	SW	SW ■	SW ◇■ ⊼	SW ■	SW ◇■ ⊼	SW ◇■	SW	SW ◇■	SW ◇■	SW ◇■ ⊼	SW ◇■	SW ◇	SW ◇■	SW ◇■ ⊼	SW ◇■	SW ◇	SW ◇■
London Waterloo ■ ⊖	d	15 42	15 45	15 50		15 50	15 53	16 00		16 05	16 09		16 12	16 15	16 20		16 20	16 25	16 30			16 39
Vauxhall ⊖	d					15 54											16 24					
Clapham Junction ■	d		15u52	15u57		15 59	16u00			16u12			16u19	16u22	16u27		16 29					16u46
Earlsfield	d					16 02											16 32					
Wimbledon ■ ⊖	d					16 06						←					16 36				←	
Surbiton ■	d	16 00				16 14	16 11					16 14	16 30				16 44	16 41			16 44	
Esher	d					→						16 18					→				16 48	
Hersham	d											16 21									16 51	
Walton-on-Thames	d	16 07										16 24	16 37								16 54	
Weybridge	d	16 11										16 27	16 41								16 57	
Byfleet & New Haw	d											16 30									17 00	
West Byfleet	d				←		16 21		←			16 33				←		16 51		←	17 03	
Woking	a	16 18	16 12	16 15	16 18		16 29	16 24	16 29		16 33	16 38	16 48	16 42	16 45	16 48		16 59	16 54	16 59	17 10	
	d	16 19	16 13	16 16	16 19		16 30	16 25	16 30		16 35		16 49	16 43	16 46	16 49		17 01	16 56	17 01		
Worplesdon	d	→					→						→	16 48				→				
Guildford	a		16 21					16 33						16 54					17 03			
Brookwood	d				16 25				16 36							16 55				17 07		
Ash Vale	d								16 44											17 15		
Aldershot	a								16 49											17 19		
	d								16 50											17 20		
Farnham	a								16 55											17 25		
	d								16 56											17 26		
Bentley	d								17 02											17 32		
Alton	a								17 10											17 39		
Farnborough (Main)	d				16 33						16 45					17 03						17 13
Fleet	d				16 38											17 08						17 19
Winchfield	d				16 44											17 14						
Hook	d				16 48											17 18						
Basingstoke	a			16 36	16 58					16 47	16 58				17 05	17 30						17 31

Station		SW ◇■	SW ◇■	SW ◇■ ⊼	SW ◇■	SW ◇	SW ◇■	SW ◇■ ⊼	SW ◇■	SW ◇■	SW ◇■	SW ◇■	SW ◇■	SW ◇■	SW ◇■ ⊼	SW ◇	SW ◇■	SW ◇■	SW ◇■	SW ◇■ ⊼	SW ◇	SW ◇■	SW ◇■
London Waterloo ■ ⊖	d	16 42	16 45	16 50		16 50	16 55	17 00		17 02	17 09	17 11	17 15		17 20	17 20	17 23	17 25		17 30		17 32	17 39
Vauxhall ⊖	d					16 54										17 24							
Clapham Junction ■	d		16u52	16u57		16 59	17u02									17 29							
Earlsfield	d					17 02										17 32							
Wimbledon ■ ⊖	d					17 06										17 36					←		
Surbiton ■	d	17 00				17 14				17 18						17 44	17 39				17 44	17 48	
Esher	d					17 18				17 22						→					17 48	17 52	
Hersham	d					17 21				17 25											17 51	17 55	
Walton-on-Thames	d	17 07				17 24				17 29											17 54	17 59	
Weybridge	d	17 11				17 27				17 33											17 57	18 03	
Byfleet & New Haw	d					17 30				17 36											18 00	18 06	
West Byfleet	d				←	17 33	17 21		←	17 39				←					←		18 03	18 09	
Woking	a	17 19	17 12		17 19	17 43	17 29	17 24	17 29	17 44	17 32	17 35	17 38	17 44			17 51	17 50	17 51	17 54	18 10	18 14	18 02
	d	17 20	17 13	17u16	17 20		17 30	17 25	17 30	17 46	17 34	17 37	17 40	17 46	17u46		17 52	17 51	17 52	17 56		18 16	18 04
Worplesdon	d	→					→	17 30		→			17 45				→			18 00		→	
Guildford	a		17 21					17 36					17 50	17 56						18 06			
Brookwood	d				17 26				17 36			17 43							18 00				
Ash Vale	d								17 44									18 03					
Aldershot	a								17 49									18 08					
	d								17 50									18 09					
Farnham	a								17 55									18 14					
	d								17 56									18 15					
Bentley	d								18 02									18 24					
Alton	a								18 09									18 31					
Farnborough (Main)	d				17 34							17 51							18 08				
Fleet	d				17 39							17 56							18 13				
Winchfield	d				17 45							18 02							18 19				
Hook	d				17 49							18 06							18 23				
Basingstoke	a			17 36	18 00						17 52	18 16			18 05				18 32				18 22

Station		SW ◇■	SW ■	SW ◇■	SW ◇■	SW ◇■ ⊼	SW ◇	SW ◇■	SW ◇■	SW ◇■	SW ◇	SW ◇■ ⊼	SW ◇■	SW ◇■	SW ◇■	SW ◇■	SW ◇■	SW ◇■ ⊼	SW ◇	SW ◇■	SW ◇■	SW ◇■
London Waterloo ■ ⊖	d	17 41	17 45	17 48		17 50	17 50	17 53	17 55			18 00	18 02	18 09	18 12	18 15	18 17	18 20	18 20	18 23	18 25	
Vauxhall ⊖	d						17 54												18 24			
Clapham Junction ■	d						17 59										18u24	18u27	18 29		18u33	
Earlsfield	d						18 02												18 32			
Wimbledon ■ ⊖	d						18 06				←								18 36			
Surbiton ■	d						18 14	18 09			18 14		18 18						18 44	18 40		
Esher	d						→				18 18		18 22						→			
Hersham	d										18 21		18 25									
Walton-on-Thames	d										18 24		18 29									
Weybridge	d										18 27		18 33									
Byfleet & New Haw	d										18 30		18 36									
West Byfleet	d				←			18 19		←	18 33		18 39									←
Woking	a			18 11	18 14			18 23	18 20	18 23	18 41		18 49	18 33			18 43	18 45		18 52	18 52	18 52
	d			18 13	18 16			18 25	18 21	18 25				18 35			18 44	18 46		18 54	18 53	18 54
Worplesdon	d				18 21			→									18 49			→		
Guildford	a		18 21		18 30							18 32				18 50	18 55					
Brookwood	d	18 11							18 27						18 41							19 02
Ash Vale	d								18 35												19 05	
Aldershot	a								18 40												19 10	
	d								18 41												19 11	
Farnham	a								18 46												19 16	
	d								18 48												19 18	
Bentley	d								18 54												19 24	
Alton	a								19 01												19 31	
Farnborough (Main)	d	18 19								18 39					18 48							19 10
Fleet	d	18 24								18 44					18 54							19 15
Winchfield	d	18 30								18 50					18 59							19 21
Hook	d	18 34								18 54					19 04							19 25
Basingstoke	a	18 45		18 31		18 37				19 03				18 53	19 16			19 05				19 34

Station		SW ◇■ ⊼	SW ◇	SW ◇■	SW ◇■	SW ◇■	SW ◇■	SW ◇■ ⊼	SW ◇■	SW ◇	SW ◇■	SW ◇■ ⊼	SW ■	SW ◇■ ⊼	SW ■	SW ■	SW ◇■	SW ◇■ ⊼	SW	SW ■	SW ◇■ ⊼	SW ◇■ ⊼	SW ■
London Waterloo ■ ⊖	d	18 30		18 32	18 39	18 41	18 45	18 50		18 50	18 55	19 00	19 02	19 05	19 09	19 12	19 15	19 20	19 20	19 25	19 30	19 35	
Vauxhall ⊖	d									18 54									19 24				
Clapham Junction ■	d				18u46					18 59	19u02			19u12		19u19	19u22	19u27	19 29	19u33			
Earlsfield	d									19 02									19 32				
Wimbledon ■ ⊖	d		←							19 06									19 36				
Surbiton ■	d		18 44	18 48						19 14			19 18						19 44				
Esher	d		18 48	18 52						19 18			19 22						19 48				
Hersham	d		18 51	18 55						19 21			19 25						19 51				
Walton-on-Thames	d		18 54	18 59						19 24			19 29						19 54				
Weybridge	d		18 57	19 03						19 27			19 33						19 57				
Byfleet & New Haw	d		19 00	19 06						19 30			19 36						20 00				
West Byfleet	d		19 03	19 09			19 08		←	19 33			19 39						20 03	19 51			←
Woking	a	18 57	19 12	19 18	19 05		19 13	19 16	19 18	19 42	19 21	19 24	19 48		19 33	19 38	19 43	19 45	20 08	19 59	19 54	19 58	19 59
	d	18 58		19 20	19 06		19 14	19 18	19 20		19 23	19 25			19 35	19 39	19 44	19 46		20 00	19 55		20 00
Worplesdon	d			→													19 49			→			
Guildford	a	19 06					19 22					19 33					19 55				20 03		
Brookwood	d					19 13					19 29					19 46							20 06
Ash Vale	d										19 37												20 14
Aldershot	a										19 41												20 19
	d										19 43												20 20
Farnham	a										19 48												20 25
	d										19 49												20 26
Bentley	d										19 55												20 32
Alton	a										20 02												20 39
Farnborough (Main)	d					19 20			19 31						19 45	19 53							
Fleet	d					19 26			19 37							19 59							
Winchfield	d					19 31			19 42							20 04							
Hook	d					19 36			19 47							20 09							
Basingstoke	a				19 28	19 45		19 37	20 00					19 47	19 58	20 16		20 06					

Station		SW ◇■	SW ■	SW ◇■	SW ◇■ ⊼	SW ■	SW	SW ■	SW ◇■ ⊼	SW ■	SW ◇■ ⊼	SW ■	SW	SW ■	SW ■	SW ◇■ ⊼	SW ■	SW	SW ■	SW ◇■ ⊼	SW ◇■ ⊼	SW ■	SW
London Waterloo ■ ⊖	d	19 39	19 42	19 45	19 50		19 50	19 53	20 00		20 05	20 09		20 12	20 15	20 20		20 20	20 25	20 30	20 35		
Vauxhall ⊖	d						19 54											20 24					
Clapham Junction ■	d	19u46		19u52			19 59	20u00			20u12			20u19	20u22	20u27		20 29					
Earlsfield	d						20 02											20 32					
Wimbledon ■ ⊖	d						20 06						←					20 36					←
Surbiton ■	d		20 00				20 14	20 11					20 14	20 30				20 44	20 41				20 44
Esher	d						→						20 18					→					20 48
Hersham	d												20 21										20 51
Walton-on-Thames	d		20 07										20 24	20 37									20 54
Weybridge	d		20 11										20 27	20 41									20 57
Byfleet & New Haw	d												20 30										21 00
West Byfleet	d					←		20 21		←			20 33				←		20 51			←	21 03
Woking	a		20 18	20 12	20 14	20 18		20 29	20 24	20 29		20 33	20 38	20 48	20 42	20 45	20 48		20 59	20 55	20 58	20 59	21 08
	d		20 19	20 13	20 16	20 19		20 30	20 25	20 30		20 35		20 49	20 43	20 46	20 49		21 00	20 56		21 00	
Worplesdon	d		→	20 18				→						→					→				
Guildford	a			20 24					20 33						20 51					21 04			
Brookwood	d					20 25				20 36							20 55					21 06	
Ash Vale	d									20 44												21 14	
Aldershot	a									20 49												21 19	
	d									20 50												21 20	
Farnham	a									20 55												21 25	
	d									20 56												21 26	
Bentley	d									21 02												21 32	
Alton	a									21 10												21 39	
Farnborough (Main)	d	20 13				20 33						20 45					21 03						
Fleet	d	20 19				20 38											21 08						
Winchfield	d					20 44											21 14						
Hook	d					20 48											21 18						
Basingstoke	a	20 30			20 35	20 58					20 47	20 58				21 05	21 28						

Table T155-F

London - Woking, Guildford, Alton and Basingstoke

Mondays to Fridays
21 May to 7 December

			SW ◇1	SW 1	SW ◇1	SW 1	SW	SW 1	SW ◇1 ⊼	SW 1	SW ◇1 ⊼		SW	SW 1	SW ◇1 ⊼	SW 1	SW	SW 1	SW ◇1	SW ◇1 ⊼	SW 1		SW	SW ◇1	SW 1
London Waterloo ⊖	d		20 39	20 42	20 45		20 50	20 53	21 00		21 05			21 12	21 20		21 20	21 23	21 30	21 35				21 39	21 42
Vauxhall ⊖	d						20 54										21 24								
Clapham Junction	d		20u46		20u52		20 59	21u00			21u12			21u19	21u27		21 29							21u46	
Earlsfield	d						21 02										21 32								
Wimbledon ⊖	d						21 06						←				21 36						←		
Surbiton	d			21 00			21 14	21 11					21 14	21 30			21 44	21 41					21 44		22 00
Esher	d						→						21 18				→						21 48		
Hersham	d												21 21										21 51		
Walton-on-Thames	d			21 07									21 24	21 37									21 54		22 07
Weybridge	d			21 11									21 27	21 41									21 57		22 11
Byfleet & New Haw	d												21 30										22 00		
West Byfleet	d					←		21 21		←			21 33			←		21 51			←		22 03		
Woking	a			21 18	21 12	21 18		21 29	21 24	21 29	21 31		21 38	21 48	21 45	21 48		21 59	21 54	21 58	21 59		22 08		22 18
	d			21 19	21 13	21 19		21 30	21 25	21 30	21 32			21 49	21 49	21 49		22 00	21 55		22 00				22 19
Worplesdon	d			→	21 18			→						→				→							→
Guildford	a				21 24				21 33										22 03						
Brookwood	d					21 25				21 36						21 55					22 06				
Ash Vale	d									21 44											22 14				
Aldershot	a									21 49											22 19				
	d									21 50											22 20				
Farnham	a									21 55											22 25				
	d									21 56											22 26				
Bentley	d									22 02											22 32				
Alton	a									22 10											22 39				
Farnborough (Main)	d		21 13			21 33										22 03								22 13	
Fleet	d		21 19			21 38										22 08								22 19	
Winchfield	d					21 44										22 14									
Hook	d					21 48										22 18									
Basingstoke	a		21 31			21 58					21 50				22 12	22 28								22 31	

		SW ◇1	SW 1	SW	SW 1	SW ◇1	SW 1		SW ◇1 ⊼	SW	SW 1	SW 1 ⊼	SW 1	SW	SW 1	SW ◇1	SW ◇1 ⊼		SW 1	SW	SW ◇1	SW 1	SW ◇1	SW 1	SW
London Waterloo ⊖	d	21 45		21 50	21 53	22 00			22 05		22 12	22 20		22 20	22 23	22 30	22 35				22 39	22 42	22 45		22 50
Vauxhall ⊖	d			21 54										22 24											22 54
Clapham Junction	d	21u52		21 59	22u00				22u12		22u19	22u27		22 29	22u30						22u46	22u49	22u52		22 59
Earlsfield	d			22 02										22 32											23 02
Wimbledon ⊖	d			22 06						←				22 36						←					23 06
Surbiton	d			22 14	22 11					22 14	22 30			22 44	22 41					22 44		23 00			23 14
Esher	d			→						22 18				→						22 48					→
Hersham	d									22 21										22 51					
Walton-on-Thames	d									22 24	22 37									22 54		23 07			
Weybridge	d									22 27	22 41									22 57		23 11			
Byfleet & New Haw	d									22 30										23 00					
West Byfleet	d		←		22 21		←			22 33			←		22 51				←	23 03				←	
Woking	a	22 12	22 18		22 29	22 24	22 29		22 31	22 37	22 48	22 45	22 48		22 59	22 54	22 58		22 59	23 08		23 18	23 12	23 18	
	d	22 13	22 19		22 30	22 25	22 30		22 32	22 39	22 49	22 49	22 49		23 00	22 56			23 00			23 19	23 13	23 19	
Worplesdon	d	22 18			→						→				→							→	23 18		
Guildford	a	22 24				22 33				22 47						23 03							23 24		
Brookwood	d		22 25				22 36						22 55						23 06					23 25	
Ash Vale	d						22 44												23 14						
Aldershot	a						22 49												23 19						
	d						22 50												23 20						
Farnham	a						22 55												23 25						
	d						22 56												23 26						
Bentley	d						23 02												23 33						
Alton	a						23 09												23 41						
Farnborough (Main)	d		22 33										23 03								23 16			23 33	
Fleet	d		22 38										23 08								23 21			23 38	
Winchfield	d		22 44										23 14											23 44	
Hook	d		22 48										23 18											23 48	
Basingstoke	a		22 58						22 50			23 09	23 28								23 33			23 57	

		SW	SW 1		SW ◇1	SW	SW 1	SW ◇1	SW 1	SW	SW 1	SW 1	SW 1		SW	SW ◇1	SW	SW 1
London Waterloo ⊖	d	22 52	22 53		23 05		23 12	23 15		23 20	23 23	23 35	23 40			23 45		23 48
Vauxhall ⊖	d	22 56								23 24								
Clapham Junction	d	23 02	23u00		23u12		23u19	23u22		23 29	23u30	23u42	23u47			23u52		23u55
Earlsfield	d									23 32								
Wimbledon ⊖	d					←				23 36					←			
Surbiton	d		23 11			23 14	23 38			23 44	23 41				23 44			00 09
Esher	d					23 18				→					23 48			
Hersham	d					23 21									23 51			
Walton-on-Thames	d					23 24	23 45								23 54			00 16
Weybridge	d					23 27	23 49								23 57		←	00 20
Byfleet & New Haw	d	00 06				23 30									23 59		00 06	
West Byfleet	d	→	23 21			23 33			←		23 55				00 03		00 09	
Woking	a		23 29		23 31	23 37	23 55	23 41	23 55		23 59	00 01	00 06		00 08	00 11	00 15	00 26
	d		23 30		23 32		23 57	23 43	23 57		00 01	00 03	00 08			00 13		00 28
Worplesdon	d						→									00 18		
Guildford	a							23 50								00 24		
Brookwood	d		23 36						00 03		00 07							00 34
Ash Vale	d		23 44								00 15							
Aldershot	a		23 49								00 19							
	d		23 50								00 20							
Farnham	a		23 55								00 25							
	d		23 56								00 26							
Bentley	d		00 03								00 33							
Alton	a		00 10								00 40							
Farnborough (Main)	d								00 10			00 14						00 41
Fleet	d								00 16			00 20						00 47
Winchfield	d								00 21									00s52
Hook	d								00 26									00s57
Basingstoke	a				23 51				00 33			00 33	00 27					01 06

Table T155-F

London - Woking, Guildford, Alton and Basingstoke

Saturdays
26 May to 8 December

		SW 1	SW 1	SW 1	SW 1	SW	SW 1	SW ◇1	SW	SW 1		SW ◇1	SW 1	SW	SW	SW 1	SW 1	SW ◇1	SW ◇1	SW 1		SW ◇1	SW 1	SW 1	SW
London Waterloo ⊖	d											00 05		00 09	00 27	01 05	05 00	05 20	05 30						05 50
Vauxhall ⊖	d													00 13	00 31	01 09	05 04	05 24							05 54
Clapham Junction	d											00u12		00 20	00 37	01 15	05 11	05 29	05u37						05 59
Earlsfield	d													00 23	00s41		05 14	05 32							06 02
Wimbledon ⊖	d											00u18		00 27	00 45	01s20	05 18	05 36	05 43						06 06
Surbiton	d									00 09				00 35	00s56	01s28	05 26	05 44							06 14
Esher	d													00s39			05 30	05 48							06 18
Hersham	d													00s42			05 33	05 51							06 21
Walton-on-Thames	d									00 16				00s44			05 37	05 54							06 24
Weybridge	d									00 20				00s48			05 41	05 57							06 27
Byfleet & New Haw	d								00 06					00s51			05 44	06 00							06 30
West Byfleet	d					00 03			00 09					00s54	01s07		05 47	06 03				←			06 33
Woking	a					00 08			00 15	00 26		00 35		00 58	01 12	01 41	05 51	06 08	05 59			06 08			06 38
	d			00 01	00 03		00 08	00 13		00 28		00 37	00 40	01 00		01 42	05 53	06 13	06 01	06 02		06 13	06 19	06 30	
Worplesdon	d							00 18										→				06 18			
Guildford	a							00 24						01 07			06 00					06 23			
Brookwood	d		00 03	00 07						00 34			00 45							06 08			06 25	06 36	
Ash Vale	d			00 15									00 53							06 16				06 44	
Aldershot	a			00 19									00 58							06 20				06 49	
	d			00 20									00 58							06 21				06 50	
Farnham	a			00 25									01 04							06 26				06 55	
	d			00 26									01 04							06 27				06 56	
Bentley	d	00 03		00 33									01s10							06 33				07 02	
Alton	a	00 10		00 40									01 18							06 41				07 10	
Farnborough (Main)	d		00 10		00 14					00 41						01s51							06 33		
Fleet	d		00 16		00 20					00 47						01s57							06 38		
Winchfield	d		00 21							00s52													06 43		
Hook	d		00 26							00s57													06 48		
Basingstoke	a		00 33		00 33		00 27			01 06		00 55				02s09			06 20				06 58		

		SW 1	SW 1	SW 1	SW 1	SW		SW ◇1	SW 1	SW 1	SW ◇1	SW 1	SW	SW 1	SW ◇1 ⊼	SW		SW 1	SW 1	SW 1	SW	SW 1	SW ◇1	SW ◇1	SW 1
London Waterloo ⊖	d	06 12	06 15			06 20		06 30		06 42	06 45		06 50	06 53	07 10			07 12	07 15		07 20	07 23	07 30	07 35	
Vauxhall ⊖	d					06 24							06 54								07 24				
Clapham Junction	d	06u19	06u22			06 29		06u37		06u49	06u52		06 59	07u00	07u17			07u20	07u23		07 29	07u30			
Earlsfield	d					06 32							07 02								07 32				
Wimbledon ⊖	d					06 36							07 06			←					07 36				
Surbiton	d	06 30				06 44				07 00			07 14	07 11		07 14		07 31			07 44	07 41			
Esher	d					06 48							→			07 18					→				
Hersham	d					06 51										07 21									
Walton-on-Thames	d	06 37				06 54				07 07						07 24		07 38							
Weybridge	d	06 41				06 57				07 11						07 27		07 42							
Byfleet & New Haw	d					07 00										07 30									
West Byfleet	d			←		07 03			←			←		07 21		07 33				←		07 51			←
Woking	a	06 48	06 42	06 48		07 08		06 56		07 18	07 12	07 18		07 26	07 35	07 38		07 48	07 43	07 48		07 59	07 54	07 58	07 59
	d	06 49	06 43	06 49	07 00			06 57	07 00	07 19	07 13	07 19		07 30	07 36			07 50	07 44	07 50		08 00	07 55	08 00	08 00
Worplesdon	d	→			→					→	07 18							→				→			
Guildford	a		06 51								07 23								07 52				08 03		
Brookwood	d			06 55					07 06			07 25		07 36						07 56					08 06
Ash Vale	d								07 14					07 44											08 14
Aldershot	a								07 19					07 49											08 19
	d								07 20					07 50											08 20
Farnham	a								07 25					07 55											08 25
	d								07 26					07 56											08 26
Bentley	d								07 32					08 02											08 32
Alton	a								07 40					08 10											08 39
Farnborough (Main)	d			07 03								07 33								08 03					
Fleet	d			07 08								07 38								08 09					
Winchfield	d			07 14								07 44								08 14					
Hook	d			07 18								07 48								08 19					
Basingstoke	a			07 28				07 16				07 58			07 57					08 28				08 20	

		SW		SW ◇1	SW 1	SW ◇1	SW ◇1 ⊼	SW 1	SW	SW 1	SW ◇1	SW 1		SW ◇1	SW 1	SW	SW 1	SW 1	SW ◇1 ⊼	SW 1	SW	SW 1		SW ◇1	SW ◇1 ⊼
London Waterloo ⊖	d			07 39	07 42	07 45	07 50		07 50	07 53	08 00			08 05	08 09		08 12	08 15	08 20		08 20	08 23		08 30	08 35
Vauxhall ⊖	d								07 54												08 24				
Clapham Junction	d			07u46		07u52	07u57		07 59	08u00				08u12			08u19	08u22	08u27		08 29				
Earlsfield	d								08 02												08 32				
Wimbledon ⊖	d	←							08 06							←					08 36				
Surbiton	d	07 44			08 00				08 14	08 11						08 14	08 30				08 44	08 41			
Esher	d	07 48							→							08 18					→				
Hersham	d	07 51														08 21									
Walton-on-Thames	d	07 54			08 07											08 24	08 37								
Weybridge	d	07 57			08 11											08 27	08 41								
Byfleet & New Haw	d	08 00														08 30									
West Byfleet	d	08 03						←		08 21		←				08 33				←		08 51			
Woking	a	08 08			08 18	08 12	08 15	08 18		08 29	08 24	08 29			08 33	08 38	08 48	08 42	08 45	08 48		08 59		08 54	08 58
	d				08 19	08 13	08 16	08 19		08 30	08 25	08 30			08 35		08 49	08 43	08 46	08 49		09 00		08 55	
Worplesdon	d				→	08 18				→							→					→			
Guildford	a					08 24					08 33							08 51						09 03	
Brookwood	d							08 25				08 36								08 55					
Ash Vale	d											08 44													
Aldershot	a											08 49													
	d											08 50													
Farnham	a											08 55													
	d											08 56													
Bentley	d											09 02													
Alton	a											09 10													
Farnborough (Main)	d			08 13				08 33							08 45					09 03					
Fleet	d			08 19				08 38												09 08					
Winchfield	d							08 44												09 14					
Hook	d							08 48												09 18					
Basingstoke	a			08 31			08 36	08 58						08 47	08 58				09 05	09 28					

London - Woking, Guildford, Alton and Basingstoke

		SW ■	SW	SW ◇■	SW ■	SW ◇■	SW ◇■ ✕	SW ■		SW	SW ■	SW ◇■ ✕	SW ■	SW ◇■	SW ■	SW	SW ■	SW ■		SW ◇■ ✕	SW ■	SW	SW ■	SW ◇■ ✕	SW ◇■ ✕
London Waterloo ⊖	d			08 39	08 42	08 45	08 50			08 50	08 53	09 00		09 05	09 09		09 12	09 15		09 20		09 20	09 23	09 30	09 35
Vauxhall ⊖	d									08 54												09 24			
Clapham Junction	d			08u46		08u52	08u57			08 59	09u00			09u12			09u19	09u22		09u27		09 29			
Earlsfield	d									09 02												09 32			
Wimbledon ⊖	d		←							09 06						←						09 36			
Surbiton	d		08 44		09 00					09 14	09 11					09 14	09 30					09 44	09 41		
Esher	d		08 48							→						09 18						→			
Hersham	d		08 51													09 21									
Walton-on-Thames	d		08 54		09 07											09 24	09 37								
Weybridge	d		08 57		09 11											09 27	09 41								
Byfleet & New Haw	d		09 00													09 30									
West Byfleet	d	←	09 03					←			09 21		←			09 33					←		09 51		
Woking	a	08 59	09 08		09 18	09 12	09 15	09 18			09 29	09 24	09 29		09 33	09 38	09 48	09 42		09 45	09 48		09 59	09 54	09 58
	d	09 00			09 19	09 13	09 16	09 19			09 30	09 25	09 30		09 35		09 49	09 43		09 46	09 49		10 00	09 55	
Worplesdon	d				→	09 18					→						→						→		
Guildford	a					09 24						09 33						09 51						10 03	
Brookwood	d	09 06						09 25					09 36								09 55				
Ash Vale	d	09 14											09 44												
Aldershot	a	09 19											09 49												
	d	09 20											09 50												
Farnham	a	09 25											09 55												
	d	09 26											09 56												
Bentley	d												10 02												
Alton	a	09 37											10 10												
Farnborough (Main)	d			09 13				09 33							09 45						10 03				
Fleet	d			09 19				09 38													10 08				
Winchfield	d							09 44													10 14				
Hook	d							09 48													10 18				
Basingstoke	a			09 32			09 36	09 58						09 47	09 58					10 05	10 28				

		SW ■	SW	SW ◇■		SW ■	SW ◇■	SW ◇■ ✕	SW ■	SW	SW ■	SW ◇■ ✕	SW ■	SW ◇■		SW ■	SW	SW ■	SW ■	SW ◇■ ✕	SW ■	SW	SW ■	SW ◇■ ✕	
London Waterloo ⊖	d			09 39		09 42	09 45	09 50		09 50	09 53	10 00		10 05		10 09		10 12	10 15	10 20		10 20	10 23	10 30	
Vauxhall ⊖	d									09 54												10 24			
Clapham Junction	d			09u46			09u52	09u57		09 59	10u00			10u12				10u19	10u22	10u27		10 29			
Earlsfield	d									10 02												10 32			
Wimbledon ⊖	d		←							10 06							←					10 36			
Surbiton	d		09 44			10 00				10 14	10 11						10 14	10 30				10 44	10 41		
Esher	d		09 48							→							10 18					→			
Hersham	d		09 51														10 21								
Walton-on-Thames	d		09 54			10 07											10 24	10 37							
Weybridge	d		09 57			10 11											10 27	10 41							
Byfleet & New Haw	d		10 00														10 30								
West Byfleet	d	←	10 03						←		10 21		←				10 33				←		10 51		
Woking	a	09 59	10 08			10 18	10 12	10 15	10 18		10 29	10 24	10 29			10 33	10 38	10 48	10 42	10 45	10 48		10 59	10 54	
	d	10 00				10 19	10 13	10 16	10 19		10 30	10 25	10 30			10 35		10 49	10 43	10 46	10 49		11 00	10 55	
Worplesdon	d					→	10 18				→							→					→		
Guildford	a						10 24					10 33							10 51					11 03	
Brookwood	d	10 06							10 25				10 36								10 55				
Ash Vale	d	10 14											10 44												
Aldershot	a	10 19											10 49												
	d	10 20											10 50												
Farnham	a	10 25											10 55												
	d	10 26											10 56												
Bentley	d												11 02												
Alton	a	10 37											11 10												
Farnborough (Main)	d			10 13					10 33							10 45					11 03				
Fleet	d			10 19					10 38												11 08				
Winchfield	d								10 44												11 14				
Hook	d								10 48												11 18				
Basingstoke	a			10 31				10 36	10 58					10 47		10 58				11 05	11 28				

		SW ◇■ ✕	SW ■	SW	SW ◇■	SW ■	SW ◇■	SW ◇■ ✕	SW ■	SW		SW ■	SW ◇■ ✕	SW ■	SW ◇■ ✕	SW ■	SW	SW ■	SW ■	SW ◇■ ✕		SW ■	SW	SW ■	SW ◇■ ✕
London Waterloo ⊖	d	10 35			10 39	10 42	10 45	10 50		10 50		10 53	11 00		11 05	11 09		11 12	11 15	11 20			11 20	11 23	11 30
Vauxhall ⊖	d									10 54													11 24		
Clapham Junction	d				10u46		10u52	10u57		10 59		11u00			11u12			11u19	11u22	11u27			11 29		
Earlsfield	d									11 02													11 32		
Wimbledon ⊖	d			←						11 06							←						11 36		
Surbiton	d			10 44		11 00				11 14		11 11					11 14	11 30					11 44	11 41	
Esher	d			10 48						→							11 18						→		
Hersham	d			10 51													11 21								
Walton-on-Thames	d			10 54		11 07											11 24	11 37							
Weybridge	d			10 57		11 11											11 27	11 41							
Byfleet & New Haw	d			11 00													11 30								
West Byfleet	d		←	11 03					←			11 21		←			11 33					←		11 51	
Woking	a	10 58	10 59	11 08		11 18	11 12	11 15	11 18			11 29	11 24	11 29		11 33	11 38	11 48	11 42	11 45		11 48		11 59	11 54
	d		11 00			11 19	11 13	11 16	11 19			11 30	11 25	11 30		11 35		11 49	11 43	11 46		11 49		12 00	11 55
Worplesdon	d					→	11 18					→						→						→	
Guildford	a						11 24						11 33						11 51						12 03
Brookwood	d		11 06						11 25					11 36								11 55			
Ash Vale	d		11 14											11 44											
Aldershot	a		11 19											11 49											
	d		11 20											11 50											
Farnham	a		11 25											11 55											
	d		11 26											11 56											
Bentley	d													12 02											
Alton	a		11 37											12 10											
Farnborough (Main)	d				11 13				11 33							11 45						12 03			
Fleet	d				11 19				11 38													12 08			
Winchfield	d								11 44													12 14			
Hook	d								11 48													12 18			
Basingstoke	a				11 31			11 36	11 58						11 47	11 58				12 05		12 28			

Please check the 'Additional Notes to Individual Tables' section for any other general notes that apply to this Table

Table T155-F

Saturdays

26 May to 8 December

London - Woking, Guildford, Alton and Basingstoke

		SW ◇■ ✕	SW ■	SW	SW ◇■	SW ■		SW ◇■	SW ◇■ ✕	SW ■	SW	SW ■	SW ◇■ ✕	SW ■	SW ◇■ ✕	SW ■		SW	SW ■	SW ■	SW ◇■ ✕	SW ■	SW	SW ■	SW ◇■ ✕
London Waterloo ⊖	d	11 35			11 39	11 42		11 45	11 50		11 50	11 53	12 00		12 05	12 09			12 12	12 15	12 20		12 20	12 23	12 30
Vauxhall ⊖	d										11 54												12 24		
Clapham Junction	d				11u46			11u52	11u57		11 59	12u00			12u12				12u19	12u22	12u27		12 29		
Earlsfield	d										12 02												12 32		
Wimbledon ⊖	d			←							12 06							←					12 36		
Surbiton	d			11 44		12 00					12 14	12 11						12 14	12 30				12 44	12 41	
Esher	d			11 48							→							12 18					→		
Hersham	d			11 51														12 21							
Walton-on-Thames	d			11 54		12 07												12 24	12 37						
Weybridge	d			11 57		12 11												12 27	12 41						
Byfleet & New Haw	d			12 00														12 30							
West Byfleet	d		←	12 03						←		12 21		←				12 33				←		12 51	
Woking	a	11 58	11 59	12 08		12 18		12 12	12 15	12 18		12 29	12 24	12 29		12 33		12 38	12 48	12 42	12 45	12 48		12 59	12 54
	d		12 00			12 19		12 13	12 16	12 19		12 30	12 25	12 30		12 35			12 49	12 43	12 46	12 49		13 00	12 55
Worplesdon	d					→		12 18				→							→					→	
Guildford	a							12 24					12 33							12 51					13 03
Brookwood	d		12 06							12 25				12 36								12 55			
Ash Vale	d		12 14											12 44											
Aldershot	a		12 19											12 49											
	d		12 20											12 50											
Farnham	a		12 25											12 55											
	d		12 26											12 56											
Bentley	d													13 02											
Alton	a		12 37											13 10											
Farnborough (Main)	d				12 13					12 33						12 45						13 03			
Fleet	d				12 19					12 38												13 08			
Winchfield	d									12 44												13 14			
Hook	d									12 48												13 18			
Basingstoke	a				12 31				12 36	12 58					12 47	12 58					13 05	13 28			

		SW ◇■ ✕		SW ■	SW	SW ◇■	SW ■	SW ◇■	SW ◇■ ✕	SW ■	SW	SW ■		SW ◇■ ✕	SW ■	SW ◇■ ✕	SW ■	SW	SW ■	SW ■	SW ◇■ ✕	SW ■		SW	SW ■
London Waterloo ⊖	d	12 35				12 39	12 42	12 45	12 50		12 50	12 53		13 00		13 05	13 09		13 12	13 15	13 20			13 20	13 23
Vauxhall ⊖	d										12 54													13 24	
Clapham Junction	d					12u46		12u52	12u57		12 59	13u00				13u12			13u19	13u22	13u27			13 29	
Earlsfield	d										13 02													13 32	
Wimbledon ⊖	d				←						13 06							←						13 36	
Surbiton	d				12 44		13 00				13 14	13 11						13 14	13 30					13 44	13 41
Esher	d				12 48						→							13 18						→	
Hersham	d				12 51													13 21							
Walton-on-Thames	d				12 54		13 07											13 24	13 37						
Weybridge	d				12 57		13 11											13 27	13 41						
Byfleet & New Haw	d				13 00													13 30							
West Byfleet	d			←	13 03					←		13 21			←			13 33				←			13 51
Woking	a	12 58		12 59	13 08		13 18	13 12	13 15	13 18		13 29		13 24	13 29		13 33	13 38	13 49	13 42	13 45	13 49			13 59
	d			13 00			13 19	13 13	13 16	13 19		13 30		13 25	13 30		13 35		13 50	13 43	13 46	13 50			14 00
Worplesdon	d						→	13 18				→							→						→
Guildford	a							13 24						13 33						13 51					
Brookwood	d			13 06						13 25					13 36							13 56			
Ash Vale	d			13 14											13 44										
Aldershot	a			13 19											13 49										
	d			13 20											13 50										
Farnham	a			13 25											13 55										
	d			13 26											13 56										
Bentley	d														14 02										
Alton	a			13 37											14 10										
Farnborough (Main)	d					13 13				13 33							13 45					14 04			
Fleet	d					13 19				13 38												14 09			
Winchfield	d									13 44												14 15			
Hook	d									13 48												14 19			
Basingstoke	a					13 31			13 36	13 58						13 47	13 58				14 05	14 28			

		SW ◇■ ✕	SW ◇■ ✕	SW ■	SW	SW ◇■	SW ■	SW ◇■		SW ◇■ ✕	SW ■	SW	SW ■	SW ◇■ ✕	SW ■	SW ◇■ ✕	SW ■	SW		SW ■	SW ■	SW ◇■ ✕	SW ■	SW	SW ■
London Waterloo ⊖	d	13 30	13 35			13 39	13 42	13 45		13 50		13 50	13 53	14 00		14 05	14 09			14 12	14 15	14 20		14 20	14 23
Vauxhall ⊖	d											13 54												14 24	
Clapham Junction	d					13u46		13u52		13u57		13 59	14u00			14u12				14u19	14u22	14u27		14 29	
Earlsfield	d											14 02												14 32	
Wimbledon ⊖	d				←							14 06						←						14 36	
Surbiton	d				13 44		14 00					14 14	14 11					14 14		14 30				14 44	14 41
Esher	d				13 48							→						14 18						→	
Hersham	d				13 51													14 21							
Walton-on-Thames	d				13 54		14 07											14 24		14 37					
Weybridge	d				13 57		14 11											14 27		14 41					
Byfleet & New Haw	d				14 00													14 30							
West Byfleet	d			←	14 03						←		14 21		←			14 33					←		14 51
Woking	a	13 54	13 58	13 59	14 08		14 18	14 12		14 15	14 18		14 29	14 24	14 29		14 33	14 38		14 48	14 42	14 45	14 48		14 59
	d	13 55		14 00			14 19	14 13		14 16	14 19		14 30	14 25	14 30		14 35			14 49	14 43	14 46	14 49		15 00
Worplesdon	d						→	14 18					→							→					→
Guildford	a	14 03						14 24						14 33							14 51				
Brookwood	d			14 06							14 25				14 36								14 55		
Ash Vale	d			14 14											14 44										
Aldershot	a			14 19											14 49										
	d			14 20											14 50										
Farnham	a			14 25											14 55										
	d			14 26											14 56										
Bentley	d														15 02										
Alton	a			14 37											15 10										
Farnborough (Main)	d					14 13					14 33						14 45						15 03		
Fleet	d					14 19					14 38												15 08		
Winchfield	d										14 44												15 14		
Hook	d										14 48												15 18		
Basingstoke	a					14 31				14 36	14 58					14 47	14 58					15 05	15 28		

Table T155-F

Saturdays

26 May to 8 December

London - Woking, Guildford, Alton and Basingstoke

	SW ◇1 ⊼	SW ◇1 ⊼	SW 1		SW	SW ◇1	SW 1	SW ◇1	SW ◇1 ⊼	SW 1	SW	SW 1	SW ◇1 ⊼		SW 1	SW ◇1 ⊼	SW 1	SW	SW 1	SW 1	SW ◇1 ⊼	SW 1	SW
London Waterloo ⊖ d	14 30	14 35				14 39	14 42	14 45	14 50		14 50	14 53	15 00			15 05	15 09		15 12	15 15	15 20		15 20
Vauxhall ⊖ d											14 54												15 24
Clapham Junction d						14u46		14u52	14u57		14 59	15u00				15u12			15u19	15u22	15u27		15 29
Earlsfield d											15 02												15 32
Wimbledon ⊖ d					←						15 06							←					15 36
Surbiton d					14 44		15 00				15 14	15 11						15 14	15 30				15 44
Esher d					14 48						→							15 18					→
Hersham d					14 51													15 21					
Walton-on-Thames d					14 54		15 07											15 24	15 37				
Weybridge d					14 57		15 11											15 27	15 41				
Byfleet & New Haw d					15 00													15 30					
West Byfleet d			←		15 03					←		15 21			←			15 33				←	
Woking a	14 54	14 58	14 59		15 08		15 18	15 12	15 15	15 18		15 29	15 24		15 29		15 33	15 38	15 48	15 42	15 45	15 48	
Woking d	14 55		15 00				15 19	15 13	15 16	15 19		15 30	15 25		15 30		15 35		15 49	15 43	15 46	15 49	
Worplesdon d							→	15 18				→							→				
Guildford a	15 03							15 24					15 33							15 51			
Brookwood d			15 06							15 25					15 36							15 55	
Ash Vale d			15 14												15 44								
Aldershot a			15 19												15 49								
Aldershot d			15 20												15 50								
Farnham a			15 25												15 55								
Farnham d			15 26												15 56								
Bentley d															16 02								
Alton a			15 37												16 10								
Farnborough (Main) d						15 13				15 33							15 45					16 03	
Fleet d						15 19				15 38												16 08	
Winchfield d										15 44												16 14	
Hook d										15 48												16 18	
Basingstoke a						15 31			15 36	15 58						15 47	15 58				16 05	16 28	

	SW 1	SW ◇1 ⊼	SW ◇1 ⊼	SW 1	SW	SW ◇1	SW 1	SW ◇1	SW ◇1 ⊼		SW 1	SW	SW 1	SW ◇1 ⊼	SW 1	SW ◇1 ⊼	SW 1	SW	SW 1		SW 1	SW ◇1 ⊼	SW 1	SW
London Waterloo ⊖ d	15 23	15 30	15 35			15 39	15 42	15 45	15 50			15 50	15 53	16 00		16 05	16 09		16 12		16 15	16 20		16 20
Vauxhall ⊖ d												15 54												16 24
Clapham Junction d						15u46		15u52	15u57			15 59	16u00			16u12			16u19		16u22	16u27		16 29
Earlsfield d												16 02												16 32
Wimbledon ⊖ d					←							16 06						←						16 36
Surbiton d	15 41				15 44		16 00					16 14	16 11					16 14	16 30					16 44
Esher d					15 48							→						16 18						→
Hersham d					15 51													16 21						
Walton-on-Thames d					15 54		16 07											16 24	16 37					
Weybridge d					15 57		16 11											16 27	16 41					
Byfleet & New Haw d					16 00													16 30						
West Byfleet d	15 51			←	16 03						←		16 21		←			16 33					←	
Woking a	15 59	15 54	15 58	15 59	16 08		16 19	16 12	16 15		16 19		16 29	16 24	16 29		16 33	16 38	16 48		16 42	16 45	16 48	
Woking d	16 00	15 55		16 00			16 20	16 13	16 16		16 20		16 30	16 25	16 30		16 35		16 49		16 43	16 46	16 49	
Worplesdon d	→						→	16 18					→						→					
Guildford a		16 03						16 24						16 33							16 51			
Brookwood d				16 06							16 26				16 36								16 55	
Ash Vale d				16 14											16 44									
Aldershot a				16 19											16 49									
Aldershot d				16 20											16 50									
Farnham a				16 25											16 55									
Farnham d				16 26											16 56									
Bentley d															17 02									
Alton a				16 37											17 10									
Farnborough (Main) d						16 13					16 34						16 45						17 03	
Fleet d						16 19					16 39												17 08	
Winchfield d											16 45												17 14	
Hook d											16 49												17 18	
Basingstoke a						16 31			16 36		16 58					16 47	16 58					17 05	17 28	

	SW 1	SW ◇1 ⊼	SW ◇1 ⊼	SW 1	SW		SW ◇1	SW 1	SW ◇1	SW ◇1 ⊼	SW 1	SW	SW 1	SW ◇1 ⊼	SW 1		SW ◇1 ⊡	SW 1	SW	SW 1	SW 1	SW ◇1 ⊼	SW 1	SW
London Waterloo ⊖ d	16 23	16 30	16 35				16 39	16 42	16 45	16 50		16 50	16 53	17 00			17 05	17 09		17 12	17 15	17 20		17 20
Vauxhall ⊖ d												16 54												17 24
Clapham Junction d							16u46		16u52	16u57		16 59	17u00				17u12			17u19	17u22	17u27		17 29
Earlsfield d												17 02												17 32
Wimbledon ⊖ d					←							17 06							←					17 36
Surbiton d	16 41				16 44			17 00				17 14	17 11						17 14	17 30				17 44
Esher d					16 48							→							17 18					→
Hersham d					16 51														17 21					
Walton-on-Thames d					16 54			17 07											17 24	17 37				
Weybridge d					16 57			17 11											17 27	17 41				
Byfleet & New Haw d					17 00														17 30					
West Byfleet d	16 51			←	17 03						←		17 21		←				17 33				←	
Woking a	16 59	16 54	16 58	16 59	17 08			17 18	17 12	17 15	17 18		17 29	17 24	17 29			17 33	17 38	17 48	17 42	17 45	17 48	
Woking d	17 00	16 55		17 00				17 19	17 13	17 16	17 19		17 30	17 25	17 30			17 35		17 49	17 43	17 46	17 49	
Worplesdon d	→							→	17 18				→							→				
Guildford a		17 03							17 24					17 33							17 51			
Brookwood d				17 06							17 25				17 36								17 55	
Ash Vale d				17 14											17 44									
Aldershot a				17 19											17 49									
Aldershot d				17 20											17 50									
Farnham a				17 25											17 55									
Farnham d				17 26											17 56									
Bentley d				17 32											18 02									
Alton a				17 39											18 10									
Farnborough (Main) d							17 13				17 33							17 45					18 03	
Fleet d							17 19				17 38												18 08	
Winchfield d											17 44												18 14	
Hook d											17 48												18 18	
Basingstoke a							17 31			17 36	17 58						17 47	17 58				18 05	18 28	

Please check the 'Additional Notes to Individual Tables' section for any other general notes that apply to this Table

Table T155-F

Saturdays

26 May to 8 December

London - Woking, Guildford, Alton and Basingstoke

	SW 1		SW ◇1 ⊼	SW ◇1 ⊼	SW 1	SW	SW ◇1	SW 1	SW ◇1	SW ◇1 ⊼	SW 1		SW	SW 1	SW ◇1 ⊼	SW 1	SW ◇1 ⊼	SW 1	SW	SW 1	SW 1		SW ◇1 ⊼	SW 1
London Waterloo ⊖ d	17 23		17 30	17 35			17 39	17 42	17 45	17 50			17 50	17 53	18 00		18 05	18 09		18 12	18 15		18 20	
Vauxhall ⊖ d													17 54											
Clapham Junction d							17u46		17u52	17u57			17 59	18u00			18u12			18u19	18u22		18u27	
Earlsfield d													18 02											
Wimbledon ⊖ d						←							18 06						←					
Surbiton d	17 41					17 44		18 00					18 14	18 11					18 14	18 30				
Esher d						17 48							→						18 18					
Hersham d						17 51													18 21					
Walton-on-Thames d						17 54		18 07											18 24	18 37				
Weybridge d						17 57		18 11											18 27	18 41				
Byfleet & New Haw d						18 00													18 30					
West Byfleet d	17 51				←	18 03					←			18 21		←			18 33					←
Woking a	17 59		17 54	17 58	17 59	18 08		18 18	18 12	18 15	18 18			18 29	18 24	18 29		18 33	18 38	18 48	18 42		18 45	18 48
Woking d	18 00		17 55		18 00			18 19	18 13	18 16	18 19			18 30	18 25	18 30		18 35		18 49	18 43		18 46	18 49
Worplesdon d	→							→	18 18					→						→				
Guildford a			18 03						18 24						18 33						18 51			
Brookwood d					18 06						18 25					18 36								18 55
Ash Vale d					18 14											18 44								
Aldershot a					18 19											18 49								
Aldershot d					18 20											18 50								
Farnham a					18 25											18 55								
Farnham d					18 26											18 56								
Bentley d					18 32											19 02								
Alton a					18 39											19 10								
Farnborough (Main) d							18 13				18 33							18 45						19 03
Fleet d							18 19				18 38													19 08
Winchfield d											18 44													19 14
Hook d											18 48													19 18
Basingstoke a							18 31			18 36	18 58						18 47	18 58					19 05	19 28

	SW	SW 1	SW ◇1 ⊼	SW ◇1 ⊼	SW 1	SW	SW ◇1		SW 1	SW ◇1	SW ◇1 ⊼	SW 1	SW	SW 1	SW ◇1 ⊼	SW 1	SW ◇1 ⊼		SW 1	SW	SW 1	SW 1	SW ◇1 ⊼	SW 1
London Waterloo ⊖ d	18 20	18 23	18 30	18 35			18 39		18 42	18 45	18 50		18 50	18 53	19 00		19 05		19 09		19 12	19 15	19 20	
Vauxhall ⊖ d	18 24												18 54											
Clapham Junction d	18 29						18u46			18u52	18u57		18 59	19u00			19u12				19u19	19u22	19u27	
Earlsfield d	18 32												19 02											
Wimbledon ⊖ d	18 36					←							19 06							←				
Surbiton d	18 44	18 41				18 44			19 00				19 14	19 11						19 14	19 30			
Esher d	→					18 48							→							19 18				
Hersham d						18 51														19 21				
Walton-on-Thames d						18 54			19 07											19 24	19 37			
Weybridge d						18 57			19 11											19 27	19 41			
Byfleet & New Haw d						19 00														19 30				
West Byfleet d		18 51			←	19 03						←		19 21		←				19 33				←
Woking a		18 59	18 54	18 58	18 59	19 08			19 18	19 12	19 15	19 18		19 29	19 24	19 29			19 33	19 38	19 48	19 42	19 45	19 48
Woking d		19 00	18 55		19 00				19 19	19 13	19 16	19 19		19 30	19 25	19 30			19 35		19 49	19 43	19 46	19 49
Worplesdon d		→							→	19 18				→							→			
Guildford a			19 03							19 24					19 33							19 51		
Brookwood d					19 06							19 25				19 36								19 55
Ash Vale d					19 14											19 44								
Aldershot a					19 19											19 49								
Aldershot d					19 20											19 50								
Farnham a					19 25											19 55								
Farnham d					19 26											19 56								
Bentley d					19 32											20 02								
Alton a					19 39											20 10								
Farnborough (Main) d							19 13					19 33							19 45					20 03
Fleet d							19 19					19 38												20 08
Winchfield d												19 44												20 14
Hook d												19 48												20 18
Basingstoke a							19 31				19 36	19 58					19 47		19 58				20 05	20 28

	SW	SW 1	SW ◇1 ⊼		SW ◇1 ⊼	SW 1	SW	SW ◇1	SW 1	SW ◇1	SW ◇1 ⊼	SW 1	SW		SW 1	SW ◇1	SW 1	SW ◇1 ⊼	SW 1	SW	SW 1	SW 1	SW ◇1 ⊼
London Waterloo ⊖ d	19 20	19 23	19 30		19 35			19 39	19 42	19 45	19 50		19 50		19 53	20 00		20 05	20 09		20 12	20 15	20 20
Vauxhall ⊖ d	19 24												19 54										
Clapham Junction d	19 29							19u46		19u52	19u57		19 59		20u00			20u12			20u19	20u22	20u27
Earlsfield d	19 32												20 02										
Wimbledon ⊖ d	19 36						←						20 06							←			
Surbiton d	19 44	19 41					19 44		20 00				20 14		20 11					20 14	20 30		
Esher d	→						19 48						→							20 18			
Hersham d							19 51													20 21			
Walton-on-Thames d							19 54		20 07											20 24	20 37		
Weybridge d							19 57		20 11											20 27	20 41		
Byfleet & New Haw d							20 00													20 30			
West Byfleet d		19 51				←	20 03					←			20 21		←			20 33			
Woking a		19 59	19 54		19 58	19 59	20 08		20 18	20 12	20 15	20 18			20 29	20 24	20 29		20 33	20 38	20 48	20 41	20 45
Woking d		20 00	19 55			20 00			20 19	20 13	20 16	20 19			20 30	20 25	20 30		20 35		20 49	20 43	20 46
Worplesdon d		→							→	20 18					→						→		
Guildford a			20 03							20 24						20 33						20 50	
Brookwood d						20 06						20 25					20 36						
Ash Vale d						20 14											20 44						
Aldershot a						20 19											20 49						
Aldershot d						20 20											20 50						
Farnham a						20 25											20 55						
Farnham d						20 26											20 56						
Bentley d						20 32											21 02						
Alton a						20 39											21 10						
Farnborough (Main) d								20 13				20 33							20 45				
Fleet d								20 19				20 38											
Winchfield d												20 44											
Hook d												20 48											
Basingstoke a								20 31			20 36	20 58						20 47	20 58				21 05

Table T155-F

Saturdays
26 May to 8 December

London - Woking, Guildford, Alton and Basingstoke

	SW ■	SW	SW ■	SW ◇■	SW ◇■ 🛒	SW ■	SW	SW ◇■	SW ■	SW ◇■	SW ■	SW	SW ■	SW ◇■	SW ■	SW ◇■ 🛒	SW	SW ■	SW ◇■ 🛒	SW ■	SW	SW ■
London Waterloo ⊖ d		20 20	20 23	20 30	20 35			20 39	20 42	20 45		20 50	20 53	21 00		21 05		21 12	21 20		21 20	21 23
Vauxhall ⊖ d		20 24										20 54									21 24	
Clapham Junction d		20 29						20u46		20u52		20 59	21u00			21u12		21u19	21u27		21 29	
Earlsfield d		20 32										21 02									21 32	
Wimbledon ⊖ d		20 36					←					21 06					←				21 36	
Surbiton d		20 44	20 41				20 44		21 00			21 14	21 11				21 14	21 30			21 44	21 41
Esher d		→					20 48					→					21 18				→	
Hersham d							20 51										21 21					
Walton-on-Thames d							20 54		21 07								21 24	21 37				
Weybridge d							20 57		21 11								21 27	21 41				
Byfleet & New Haw d							21 00										21 30					
West Byfleet d	←		20 51			←	21 03				←		21 21		←		21 33			←		21 51
Woking a	20 48		20 59	20 54	20 58	20 59	21 08		21 18	21 12	21 18		21 29	21 24	21 29	21 31	21 38	21 48	21 45	21 48		21 59
d	20 49		21 00	20 55		21 00			21 19	21 13	21 19		21 30	21 25	21 30	21 32		21 49	21 49	21 49		22 00
Worplesdon d			→						→	21 18			→					→				→
Guildford a				21 03						21 24				21 33								
Brookwood d	20 55					21 06					21 25				21 36					21 55		
Ash Vale d						21 14									21 44							
Aldershot a						21 19									21 49							
d						21 20									21 50							
Farnham a						21 25									21 55							
d						21 26									21 56							
Bentley d						21 32									22 02							
Alton a						21 39									22 10							
Farnborough (Main) d	21 03							21 13			21 33									22 03		
Fleet d	21 08							21 19			21 38									22 08		
Winchfield d	21 14										21 44									22 14		
Hook d	21 18										21 48									22 18		
Basingstoke a	21 28							21 31			21 58					21 50			22 12	22 25		

	SW ◇■	SW ◇■ 🛒	SW ■	SW	SW ◇■	SW ■	SW ◇■	SW ■	SW	SW ■	SW ◇■	SW ■	SW ◇■ 🛒	SW	SW ■	SW ■ 🛒	SW ■	SW	SW ■	SW ◇■	SW ◇■ 🛒	SW ■
London Waterloo ⊖ d	21 30	21 35			21 39	21 42	21 45		21 50	21 53	22 00		22 05		22 12	22 20		22 20	22 23	22 30	22 35	
Vauxhall ⊖ d									21 54									22 24				
Clapham Junction d					21u46		21u52		21 59	22u00			22u12		22u19	22u27		22 29	22u30			
Earlsfield d									22 02									22 32				
Wimbledon ⊖ d				←					22 06					←				22 36				
Surbiton d				21 44		22 00			22 14	22 11				22 14	22 30			22 44	22 41			
Esher d				21 48					→					22 18				→				
Hersham d				21 51										22 21								
Walton-on-Thames d				21 54		22 07								22 24	22 37							
Weybridge d				21 57		22 11								22 27	22 41							
Byfleet & New Haw d				22 00										22 30								
West Byfleet d			←	22 03				←		22 21		←		22 33			←		22 51			←
Woking a	21 54	21 58	21 59	22 08		22 18	22 12	22 18		22 29	22 24	22 29	22 31	22 37	22 48	22 45	22 48		22 59	22 54	22 58	22 59
d	21 55		22 00			22 19	22 13	22 19		22 30	22 25	22 30	22 32	22 39	22 49	22 49	22 49		23 00	22 55		23 00
Worplesdon d						→	22 18			→					→				→			
Guildford a	22 03						22 24				22 33			22 47						23 03		
Brookwood d			22 06					22 25				22 36					22 55					23 06
Ash Vale d			22 14									22 44										23 14
Aldershot a			22 19									22 49										23 19
d			22 20									22 50										23 20
Farnham a			22 25									22 55										23 25
d			22 26									22 56										23 26
Bentley d			22 32									23 02										23 33
Alton a			22 39									23 10										23 40
Farnborough (Main) d					22 13			22 33									23 03					
Fleet d					22 19			22 38									23 08					
Winchfield d								22 44									23 14					
Hook d								22 48									23 18					
Basingstoke a					22 31			22 58					22 50			23 10	23 25					

	SW	SW ◇■	SW ■	SW ◇■	SW ■	SW	SW	SW ■	SW ◇■	SW	SW ■	SW ◇■	SW ■	SW	SW ■	SW ■	SW ■	SW	SW ◇■	SW	SW ■
London Waterloo ⊖ d		22 39	22 42	22 45		22 50	22 52	22 53	23 05		23 12	23 15		23 20	23 23	23 35	23 40		23 45		23 48
Vauxhall ⊖ d						22 54	22 56							23 24							
Clapham Junction d		22u46	22u49	22u52		22 59	23 02	23u00	23u12		23u19	23u22		23 29	23u30	23u42	23u47		23u52		23u54
Earlsfield d						23 02								23 32							
Wimbledon ⊖ d	←					23 06				←				23 36				←			
Surbiton d	22 44		23 00			23 14		23 11		23 14	23 38			23 44	23 41			23 44			00 09
Esher d	22 48					→				23 18				→				23 48			
Hersham d	22 51									23 21								23 51			
Walton-on-Thames d	22 54		23 07							23 24	23 45							23 54			00 16
Weybridge d	22 57		23 11							23 27	23 49							23 57		←	00 20
Byfleet & New Haw d	23 00						00 06			23 30								23 59		00 06	
West Byfleet d	23 03				←		→	23 21		23 33			←		23 55			00 03		00 09	
Woking a	23 08		23 18	23 12	23 18			23 29	23 31	23 38	23 55	23 41	23 55		23 59	00 01	00 06	00 08	00 11	00 15	00 27
d			23 19	23 13	23 19			23 30	23 32		23 57	23 43	23 57		00 01	00 03	00 08		00 13		00 28
Worplesdon d			→	23 18							→								00 18		
Guildford a				23 23								23 50							00 24		
Brookwood d					23 25			23 35					00 03		00 07						00 34
Ash Vale d								23 44							00 15						
Aldershot a								23 49							00 19						
d								23 50							00 20						
Farnham a								23 55							00 25						
d								23 58							00 26						
Bentley d								00 04							00 33						
Alton a								00 11							00 40						
Farnborough (Main) d		23 16			23 33								00 10			00 14					00 41
Fleet d		23 21			23 38								00 16			00 20					00 47
Winchfield d					23 44								00 21								00s52
Hook d					23 48								00 26								00s57
Basingstoke a		23 34			23 55				23 50				00 33			00 33	00 27				01 06

Table T155-F

Sundays
20 May to 2 December

London - Woking, Guildford, Alton and Basingstoke

	SW ■ A	SW ■ A	SW ■ A	SW ■ A	SW A	SW ■ A	SW ◇■ A	SW A	SW ■ A	SW ■	SW ■	SW	SW	SW ■	SW ■	SW ■	SW ■	SW	SW	SW	SW	SW ◇■
London Waterloo ⊖ d										00 05		00 09	00 27	01 05				07 10		07 40	07 50	07 54
Vauxhall ⊖ d												00 13	00 31	01 09				07 14		07 44	07 54	
Clapham Junction d										00u12		00 20	00 38	01 15				07 19		07 49	08 00	08u03
Earlsfield d												00 23	00s41					07 22		07 52		
Wimbledon ⊖ d										00u18		00 27	00 45	01s27				07 26		07 56		
Surbiton d									00 09			00 35	00s57	01s35				07 35		08 05		
Esher d												00s39						07 39		08 09		
Hersham d												00s42						07 42		08 12		
Walton-on-Thames d									00 16			00s44						07 45		08 15		
Weybridge d									00 20			00s48						07 49		08 19		
Byfleet & New Haw d								00 06				00s51						07 51	08 02	08 21	09 02	
West Byfleet d					00 03			00 09				00s54	01s07					07 54	08 05	08 24	→	
Woking a					00 08			00 15	00 27	00 35		00 58	01 12	01 48				07 59	08 11	08 29		08 27
d			00 01	00 03		00 08	00 13		00 28	00 37	00 40	01 00		01 49	07 32	07 46	07 49	08 05		08 31		08 28
Worplesdon d							00 18													→		
Guildford a							00 24					01 07			07 39			08 14				
Brookwood d	00 03		00 07						00 34		00 45					07 51	07 55					
Ash Vale d			00 15								00 53						08 03					
Aldershot a			00 19								00 58						08 07					
d			00 20								00 58						08 08					
Farnham a			00 25								01 04						08 13					
d			00 26								01 04						08 14					
Bentley d		00 04	00 33								01s10						08 24					
Alton a		00 11	00 40								01 18						08 31					
Farnborough (Main) d	00 10			00 14					00 41					01s58		07 59						
Fleet d	00 16			00 20					00 47					02s04		08 04						
Winchfield d	00 21								00s52							08 10						
Hook d	00 26								00s57							08 14						
Basingstoke a	00 33			00 33		00 27			01 06	00 55				02s16		08 21						08 46

	SW	SW ◇■	SW ■		SW	SW ◇■ B 🛒	SW ■	SW ■	SW	SW ◇■	SW ◇■	SW	SW	SW	SW ◇■	SW	SW ◇■	SW ■		SW	SW ◇■ 🛒	SW ■
London Waterloo ⊖ d		08 00	08 07		08 10	08 15				08 30	08 35		08 40	08 50	08 54		09 00	09 07		09 10	09 15	
Vauxhall ⊖ d					08 14								08 44	08 54						09 14		
Clapham Junction d		08u09	08 15		08 19	08u23				08u39	08u45		08 49	09 00	09u03		09u09	09 15		09 19	09u22	
Earlsfield d					08 22								08 52							09 22		
Wimbledon ⊖ d			08 22		08 26								08 56					09 22		09 26		
Surbiton d			08 30		08 35								09 05					09 30		09 36		
Esher d					08 39								09 09							09 40		
Hersham d					08 42								09 12							09 43		
Walton-on-Thames d					08 45								09 15							09 46		
Weybridge d					08 49							←	09 19							09 50		
Byfleet & New Haw d					08 51							09 02	09 21	10 02						09 52		
West Byfleet d	←				08 54		←		←			09 05	09 24	→		←				09 55		←
Woking a	08 29	08 34	08 42		08 59	08 46	08 42		08 59	09 03	09 08	09 11	09 29		09 27	09 29	09 34	09 42		10 00	09 47	09 42
d	08 31	08 35	08 46	08 49	09 01	08 47	08 49	08 49	09 01	09 04	09 09		09 31		09 28	09 31	09 35	09 46	09 49	10 01	09 48	09 49
Worplesdon d				→	→								→						→	→		
Guildford a	08 39	08 43							09 09	09 12						09 39	09 43					
Brookwood d			08 51				08 55	08 55										09 51				09 55
Ash Vale d							09 03	09 03														10 03
Aldershot a							09 07	09 07														10 07
d							09 08	09 08														10 08
Farnham a							09 13	09 13														10 13
d							09 14	09 14														10 14
Bentley d							09 24	09 24														10 24
Alton a							09 31	09 31														10 31
Farnborough (Main) d			08 59															09 59				
Fleet d			09 04															10 04				
Winchfield d			09 10															10 10				
Hook d			09 14															10 14				
Basingstoke a			09 21			09 06					09 28				09 46			10 24			10 07	

A not 20 May

B 🛒 from Woking

Table T155-F

Sundays

20 May to 2 December

London - Woking, Guildford, Alton and Basingstoke

		SW	SW	SW	SW	SW	SW	SW		SW	SW	SW	SW		SW	SW	SW	SW		SW	SW	SW	SW	SW	SW
		1		◇1	◇1 ✠					◇1	◇1		1			◇1 ✠	1	1		◇1		◇1 ✠			
London Waterloo 15 ⊖	d			09 30	09 35		09 40	09 50		09 54	10 00		10 07		10 10	10 15				10 30		10 35		10 40	10 50
Vauxhall ⊖	d						09 44	09 54							10 14									10 44	10 54
Clapham Junction 10	d			09u39	09u45		09 49	10 00		10u03	10u09		10 15		10 19	10u22				10u39		10u45		10 49	11 00
Earlsfield	d						09 52								10 22									10 52	
Wimbledon 8 ⊖	d						09 56						10 22		10 26									10 56	
Surbiton 8	d						10 05						10 30		10 35									11 05	
Esher	d						10 09								10 39									11 09	
Hersham	d						10 12								10 42									11 12	
Walton-on-Thames	d						10 15								10 45									11 15	
Weybridge	d					←	10 19								10 49								←	11 19	
Byfleet & New Haw	d					10 02	10 21	11 02							10 51								11 02	11 21	12 02
West Byfleet	d		←			10 05	10 24	→				←			10 54		←				←		11 05	11 24	→
Woking	a		10 00	10 03	10 08	10 11	10 29			10 26	10 31	10 29	10 42		10 59	10 45	10 42			11 01	10 59	11 07	11 11	11 29	
	d	09 49	10 01	10 04	10 09		10 35			10 28	10 32	10 35	10 46	10 49	11 05	10 46	10 49	10 49		11 02	11 05	11 08		11 35	
Worplesdon	d						→							→	→									→	
Guildford	a		10 09	10 12							10 40	10 44								11 10	11 14				
Brookwood	d	09 55											10 51				10 55	10 55							
Ash Vale	d	10 03															11 03	11 03							
Aldershot	a	10 07															11 07	11 07							
	d	10 08															11 08	11 08							
Farnham	a	10 13															11 13	11 13							
	d	10 14															11 14	11 14							
Bentley	d	10 24															11 24	11 24							
Alton	a	10 31															11 31	11 31							
Farnborough (Main)	d												10 59												
Fleet	d												11 04												
Winchfield	d												11 10												
Hook	d												11 14												
Basingstoke	a				10 28					10 46			11 21			11 05						11 26			

		SW	SW	SW		SW		SW	SW	SW	SW	SW	SW	SW		SW	SW	SW	SW	SW	SW	SW		SW	
		◇1	◇1			1			◇1 ✠	1	1	◇1 ✠		◇1 ✠					◇1 ✠	◇1		1			
London Waterloo 15 ⊖	d	10 54	11 00			11 07		11 10	11 15			11 30		11 35			11 40	11 50	11 54	12 00		12 07		12 10	
Vauxhall ⊖	d							11 14									11 44	11 54						12 14	
Clapham Junction 10	d	11u03	11u09			11 16		11 19	11u22			11u39		11u45			11 49	12 00	12u03	12u09		12 16		12 19	
Earlsfield	d							11 22									11 52							12 22	
Wimbledon 8 ⊖	d					11 23		11 26									11 56					12 23		12 26	
Surbiton 8	d					11 30		11 35									12 05					12 30		12 35	
Esher	d							11 39									12 09							12 39	
Hersham	d							11 42									12 12							12 42	
Walton-on-Thames	d							11 45									12 15							12 45	
Weybridge	d							11 49								←	12 19							12 49	
Byfleet & New Haw	d							11 51								12 02	12 21	13 02						12 51	
West Byfleet	d			←				11 54		←			←			12 05	12 24	→			←			12 54	
Woking	a	11 26	11 32	11 29		11 42		11 59	11 45	11 42		12 01	11 59	12 07		12 11	12 29		12 26	12 32	12 29	12 42		12 59	
	d	11 28	11 33	11 35		11 46	11 49	12 05	11 46	11 49	11 49	12 02	12 05	12 08			12 35		12 28	12 33	12 35	12 46	12 49	13 05	
Worplesdon	d						→	→									→						→	→	
Guildford	a		11 41	11 44								12 10	12 14							12 41	12 44				
Brookwood	d					11 51				11 55	11 55											12 51			
Ash Vale	d									12 03	12 03														
Aldershot	a									12 07	12 07														
	d									12 08	12 08														
Farnham	a									12 13	12 13														
	d									12 14	12 14														
Bentley	d									12 24	12 24														
Alton	a									12 31	12 31														
Farnborough (Main)	d					11 59																12 59			
Fleet	d					12 04																13 04			
Winchfield	d					12 10																13 10			
Hook	d					12 14																13 14			
Basingstoke	a	11 46				12 21			12 05					12 26					12 46			13 21			

Table T155-F

Sundays

20 May to 2 December

London - Woking, Guildford, Alton and Basingstoke

		SW	SW	SW	SW	SW		SW	SW	SW	SW	SW	SW	SW	SW			SW	SW	SW	SW	SW	SW	SW	SW
		◇1 ✠	1	1	◇1 ✠			◇1 ✠				◇1 ✠	◇1		1				◇1 ✠	1	1	◇1 ✠		◇1 ✠	
London Waterloo 15 ⊖	d	12 15			12 30			12 35		12 40	12 50	12 54	13 00		13 07			13 10	13 15			13 30		13 35	
Vauxhall ⊖	d									12 44	12 54							13 14							
Clapham Junction 10	d	12u22			12u39			12u45		12 49	13 00	13u03	13u09		13 15			13 19	13u22			13u39		13u42	
Earlsfield	d									12 52								13 22							
Wimbledon 8 ⊖	d									12 56					13 22			13 26							
Surbiton 8	d									13 05					13 30			13 35							
Esher	d									13 09								13 39							
Hersham	d									13 12								13 42							
Walton-on-Thames	d									13 15								13 45							
Weybridge	d								←	13 19								13 49							←
Byfleet & New Haw	d								13 02	13 21	14 02							13 51							14 02
West Byfleet	d		←			←			13 05	13 24	→			←				13 54		←			←		14 05
Woking	a	12 45	12 42		13 01	12 59		13 07	13 11	13 29		13 26	13 31	13 29	13 42			13 59	13 45	13 42		14 01	13 59	14 06	14 11
	d	12 46	12 49	12 49	13 02	13 05		13 08		13 35		13 28	13 32	13 35	13 46	13 49		14 05	13 46	13 49	13 49	14 02	14 05	14 07	
Worplesdon	d									→						→		→							
Guildford	a				13 10	13 14							13 40	13 44								14 10	14 14		
Brookwood	d		12 55	12 55											13 51					13 55	13 55				
Ash Vale	d		13 03	13 03																14 03	14 03				
Aldershot	a		13 07	13 07																14 07	14 07				
	d		13 08	13 08																14 08	14 08				
Farnham	a		13 13	13 13																14 13	14 13				
	d		13 14	13 14																14 14	14 14				
Bentley	d		13 24	13 24																14 24	14 24				
Alton	a		13 31	13 31																14 31	14 31				
Farnborough (Main)	d														13 59										
Fleet	d														14 04										
Winchfield	d														14 10										
Hook	d														14 14										
Basingstoke	a	13 05						13 26				13 46			14 21				14 05					14 26	

		SW		SW	SW	SW	SW	SW		SW	SW	SW		SW	SW	SW	SW	SW	SW	SW	SW	SW		SW	
					◇1 ✠	◇1		1			◇1 ✠	1		1	◇1 ✠		◇1 ✠				◇1 ✠	◇1			
London Waterloo 15 ⊖	d	13 40		13 50	13 54	14 00		14 07		14 10	14 15				14 30		14 35		14 40	14 50	14 54	15 00			
Vauxhall ⊖	d	13 44		13 54						14 14									14 44	14 54					
Clapham Junction 10	d	13 49		14 00	14u03	14u09		14 15		14 19	14u22				14u39		14u42		14 49	15 00	15u03	15u09			
Earlsfield	d	13 52								14 22									14 52						
Wimbledon 8 ⊖	d	13 56						14 22		14 26									14 56						
Surbiton 8	d	14 05						14 30		14 35									15 05						
Esher	d	14 09								14 39									15 09						
Hersham	d	14 12								14 42									15 12						
Walton-on-Thames	d	14 15								14 45									15 15						
Weybridge	d	14 19								14 49								←	15 19						
Byfleet & New Haw	d	14 21		15 02						14 51								15 02	15 21	16 02					
West Byfleet	d	14 24		→			←			14 54		←				←		15 05	15 24	→				←	
Woking	a	14 29			14 26	14 31	14 29	14 42		14 59	14 45	14 42			15 01	14 59	15 06	15 11	15 29		15 26	15 31		15 29	
	d	14 35			14 28	14 32	14 35	14 46	14 49	15 05	14 46	14 49		14 49	15 02	15 05	15 07		15 35		15 28	15 32		15 35	
Worplesdon	d	→							→	→									→						
Guildford	a					14 40	14 44								15 10	15 14						15 40		15 44	
Brookwood	d							14 51				14 55		14 55											
Ash Vale	d											15 03		15 03											
Aldershot	a											15 07		15 07											
	d											15 08		15 08											
Farnham	a											15 13		15 13											
	d											15 14		15 14											
Bentley	d											15 24		15 24											
Alton	a											15 31		15 31											
Farnborough (Main)	d							14 59																	
Fleet	d							15 04																	
Winchfield	d							15 10																	
Hook	d							15 14																	
Basingstoke	a				14 46			15 21			15 05						15 26				15 46				

Table T155-F

Sundays

20 May to 2 December

London - Woking, Guildford, Alton and Basingstoke

		SW ■		SW	SW ◇■ ⚲		SW ■	SW ■	SW ◇■ ⚲	SW	SW ◇■ ⚲	SW	SW ■		SW		SW ◇■	SW ■	SW ■	SW	SW ◇■	SW	SW ◇■ ⚲	SW ■	SW
London Waterloo ■ ⊖	d	15 07		15 10	15 15				15 30		15 35		15 37		15 40		15 50			15 50	16 00		16 05	16 07	16 10
Vauxhall ⊖	d			15 14											15 44					15 54					16 14
Clapham Junction ■	d	15 15		15 19	15u22				15u39		15u42		15 46		15 49		15u58			16 00	16u09		16u12	16 16	16 19
Earlsfield	d			15 22											15 52										16 22
Wimbledon ■ ⊖	d	15 22		15 26									15 53		15 56									16 22	16 26
Surbiton ■	d	15 30		15 35									16 02		16 05									16 30	16 35
Esher	d			15 39											16 09										16 39
Hersham	d			15 42											16 12										16 42
Walton-on-Thames	d			15 45									16 09		16 15										16 45
Weybridge	d			15 49								←	16 13		16 19										16 49
Byfleet & New Haw	d			15 51								16 02			16 21					17 02					16 51
West Byfleet	d			15 54			←			←		16 05			16 24			←	←	→		←			16 54
Woking	a	15 42		15 59	15 45		15 42		16 01	15 59	16 06	16 11	16 19		16 29		16 19	16 19	16 19		16 31	16 29	16 35	16 42	16 59
	d	15 46	15 49	16 05	15 46		15 49	15 49	16 02	16 05	16 07		16 23	16 26	16 35		16 21	16 23	16 26		16 32	16 35	16 37	16 46	17 05
Worplesdon	d		→	→									→	→	→										→
Guildford	a								16 10	16 14											16 40	16 44			
Brookwood	d	15 51					15 55	15 55										16 28	16 32					16 51	
Ash Vale	d						16 03	16 03											16 41						
Aldershot	a						16 07	16 07											16 45						
	d						16 08	16 08											16 46						
Farnham	a						16 13	16 13											16 51						
	d						16 14	16 14											16 55						
Bentley	d						16 24	16 24																	
Alton	a						16 31	16 31											17 06						
Farnborough (Main)	d	15 59															16 32	16 36						16 59	
Fleet	d	16 04																16 42						17 04	
Winchfield	d	16 10																						17 10	
Hook	d	16 14																						17 14	
Basingstoke	a	16 21			16 05						16 26						16 46	16 54					16 56	17 21	

			SW ◇■ ⚲	SW ■	SW ◇■ ⚲	SW	SW ◇■ ⚲	SW	SW ■		SW		SW ◇■	SW ■	SW ■	SW	SW ◇■	SW	SW ◇■ ⚲	SW ■			SW	SW ◇■ ⚲	SW ■
London Waterloo ■ ⊖	d		16 15		16 30		16 35		16 37		16 40		16 50			16 50	17 00		17 05	17 07			17 10	17 15	
Vauxhall ⊖	d										16 44					16 54							17 14		
Clapham Junction ■	d		16u22		16u39		16u42		16 46		16 49		16u58			17 00	17u09		17u12	17 16			17 19	17u22	
Earlsfield	d										16 52												17 22		
Wimbledon ■ ⊖	d								16 53		16 56									17 22			17 26		
Surbiton ■	d								17 02		17 05									17 30			17 35		
Esher	d										17 09												17 39		
Hersham	d										17 12												17 42		
Walton-on-Thames	d								17 09		17 15												17 45		
Weybridge	d							←	17 13		17 19												17 49		
Byfleet & New Haw	d							17 02			17 21					18 02							17 51		
West Byfleet	d					←		17 05			17 24			←	←	→		←					17 54		←
Woking	a		16 45		17 01	16 59	17 06	17 11	17 19		17 29		17 19	17 19	17 19		17 31	17 29	17 35	17 42			17 59	17 45	17 42
	d		16 46	16 49	17 02	17 05	17 07		17 23	17 26	17 35		17 21	17 23	17 26		17 32	17 35	17 37	17 46	17 49		18 05	17 46	17 49
Worplesdon	d								→	→	→										→		→		
Guildford	a				17 10	17 14											17 40	17 44							
Brookwood	d			16 55										17 28	17 32					17 51					17 55
Ash Vale	d			17 03											17 41										18 03
Aldershot	a			17 07											17 45										18 07
	d			17 08											17 46										18 08
Farnham	a			17 13											17 51										18 13
	d			17 14											17 55										18 14
Bentley	d			17 24																					18 24
Alton	a			17 31											18 06										18 31
Farnborough (Main)	d												17 32	17 36						17 59					
Fleet	d													17 42						18 04					
Winchfield	d																			18 10					
Hook	d																			18 14					
Basingstoke	a		17 05				17 26						17 46	17 54					17 56	18 21				18 05	

Table T155-F

Sundays

20 May to 2 December

London - Woking, Guildford, Alton and Basingstoke

		SW ■	SW ◇■ ⚲	SW	SW ◇■ ⚲		SW	SW ■		SW	SW ◇■	SW ■	SW ■	SW	SW ◇■		SW	SW ◇■ ⚲	SW ■		SW	SW ◇■ ⚲	SW ■	SW ■	SW ◇■ ⚲
London Waterloo ■ ⊖	d		17 30		17 35			17 37		17 40	17 50			17 50	18 00			18 05	18 07		18 10	18 15			18 30
Vauxhall ⊖	d									17 44				17 54							18 14				
Clapham Junction ■	d		17u39		17u42			17 46		17 49	17u58			18 00	18u09			18u12	18 16		18 19	18u22			18u39
Earlsfield	d									17 52											18 22				
Wimbledon ■ ⊖	d							17 53		17 56									18 22		18 26				
Surbiton ■	d							18 02		18 05									18 30		18 35				
Esher	d									18 09											18 39				
Hersham	d									18 12											18 42				
Walton-on-Thames	d							18 09		18 15											18 45				
Weybridge	d						←	18 13		18 19											18 49				
Byfleet & New Haw	d						18 02			18 21				19 02							18 51				
West Byfleet	d			←			18 05			18 24		←	←	→			←				18 54		←		
Woking	a		18 01	17 59	18 06		18 11	18 19		18 29	18 19	18 19	18 19		18 31		18 29	18 35	18 42		18 59	18 45	18 42		19 01
	d	17 49	18 02	18 05	18 07			18 23	18 26	18 35	18 21	18 23	18 26		18 32		18 35	18 37	18 46	18 49	19 05	18 46	18 49	18 49	19 02
Worplesdon	d							→	→	→										→	→				
Guildford	a		18 10	18 14											18 40		18 44								19 10
Brookwood	d	17 55										18 28	18 32						18 51				18 55	18 55	
Ash Vale	d	18 03											18 41										19 03	19 03	
Aldershot	a	18 07											18 45										19 07	19 07	
	d	18 08											18 46										19 08	19 08	
Farnham	a	18 13											18 51										19 13	19 13	
	d	18 14											18 55										19 14	19 14	
Bentley	d	18 24																					19 24	19 24	
Alton	a	18 31											19 06										19 31	19 31	
Farnborough (Main)	d										18 32	18 36							18 59						
Fleet	d											18 42							19 04						
Winchfield	d																		19 10						
Hook	d																		19 14						
Basingstoke	a				18 26						18 46	18 54						18 56	19 21			19 05			

			SW	SW ◇■ ⚲	SW	SW ■		SW	SW ◇■	SW ■	SW ■		SW	SW ◇■	SW	SW ◇■ ⚲	SW ■		SW	SW ◇■ ⚲	SW ■		SW ■	SW ◇■ ⚲	SW
London Waterloo ■ ⊖	d			18 35		18 37		18 40	18 50				18 50	19 00		19 05	19 07		19 10	19 15				19 30	
Vauxhall ⊖	d							18 44					18 54						19 14						
Clapham Junction ■	d			18u42		18 46		18 49	18u58				19 00	19u09		19u12	19 16		19 19	19u22				19u39	
Earlsfield	d							18 52											19 22						
Wimbledon ■ ⊖	d					18 53		18 56									19 22		19 26						
Surbiton ■	d					19 02		19 05									19 30		19 35						
Esher	d							19 09											19 39						
Hersham	d							19 12											19 42						
Walton-on-Thames	d					19 09		19 15											19 45						
Weybridge	d				←	19 13		19 19											19 49						
Byfleet & New Haw	d				19 02			19 21					20 02						19 51						
West Byfleet	d		←		19 05			19 24		←	←		→		←				19 54		←				←
Woking	a		18 59	19 06	19 11	19 19		19 29	19 19	19 19	19 19			19 31	19 29	19 35	19 42		19 59	19 45	19 42			20 01	19 59
	d		19 05	19 07		19 23	19 26	19 35	19 21	19 23	19 26			19 32	19 35	19 37	19 46	19 49	20 05	19 46	19 49		19 49	20 02	20 05
Worplesdon	d					→	→	→										→	→						
Guildford	a		19 14											19 40	19 44									20 10	20 14
Brookwood	d									19 28	19 32						19 51				19 55		19 55		
Ash Vale	d										19 41										20 03		20 03		
Aldershot	a										19 45										20 07		20 07		
	d										19 46										20 08		20 08		
Farnham	a										19 51										20 13		20 13		
	d										19 55										20 14		20 14		
Bentley	d																				20 24		20 24		
Alton	a										20 06										20 31		20 31		
Farnborough (Main)	d								19 32	19 36							19 59								
Fleet	d									19 42							20 04								
Winchfield	d																20 10								
Hook	d																20 14								
Basingstoke	a			19 26					19 46	19 54						19 56	20 21			20 05					

Table T155-F

Sundays

20 May to 2 December

London - Woking, Guildford, Alton and Basingstoke

		SW ◇1 ✠	SW	SW 1		SW	SW ◇1	SW 1	SW 1	SW	SW ◇1	SW	SW ◇1 ✠	SW 1		SW	SW ◇1 ✠	SW 1	SW 1	SW ◇1 ✠	SW	SW ◇1 ✠
London Waterloo 15 ⊖	d	19 35		19 37		19 40	19 50			19 50	20 00		20 05	20 07		20 10	20 15			20 30		20 35
Vauxhall ⊖	d					19 44				19 54						20 14						
Clapham Junction 10	d	19u42		19 46		19 49	19u58			20 00	20u09		20u12	20 16		20 19	20u22			20u39		20u42
Earlsfield	d					19 52										20 22						
Wimbledon 8 ⊖	d			19 53		19 56								20 22		20 26						
Surbiton 6	d			20 02		20 05								20 30		20 35						
Esher	d					20 09										20 39						
Hersham	d					20 12										20 42						
Walton-on-Thames	d			20 09		20 15										20 45						
Weybridge	d		←	20 13		20 19										20 49						
Byfleet & New Haw	d		20 02			20 21				21 02						20 51						
West Byfleet	d		20 05			20 24		←	←	→		←				20 54		←			←	
Woking	a	20 06	20 11	20 19		20 29	20 19	20 19	20 19		20 31	20 29	20 35	20 42		20 59	20 45	20 42		21 01	20 59	21 06
	d	20 07		20 23	20 26	20 35	20 21	20 23	20 26		20 32	20 35	20 37	20 46	20 49	21 05	20 46	20 49	20 49	21 02	21 05	21 07
Worplesdon	d			→	→	→									→	→						
Guildford	a										20 40	20 44								21 10	21 14	
Brookwood	d							20 28	20 32					20 51				20 55	20 55			
Ash Vale	d								20 41									21 03	21 03			
Aldershot	a								20 45									21 07	21 07			
	d								20 46									21 08	21 08			
Farnham	a								20 51									21 13	21 13			
	d								20 55									21 14	21 14			
Bentley	d																	21 24	21 24			
Alton	a								21 06									21 31	21 31			
Farnborough (Main)	d						20 32	20 36						20 59								
Fleet	d							20 42						21 04								
Winchfield	d													21 10								
Hook	d													21 14								
Basingstoke	a	20 26					20 46	20 54					20 56	21 21			21 05					21 26

		SW	SW 1	SW	SW ◇1	SW 1	SW 1	SW	SW ◇1	SW	SW ◇1	SW 1	SW	SW ◇1 ✠	SW 1	SW ◇1	SW	SW ◇1 ✠	SW	SW 1		SW	SW ◇1 ✠
London Waterloo 15 ⊖	d		20 37	20 40	20 50			20 50	21 00		21 05	21 07	21 10	21 15		21 30		21 35		21 37		21 40	21 50
Vauxhall ⊖	d			20 44				20 54					21 14									21 44	
Clapham Junction 10	d		20 46	20 49	20u58			21 00	21u09		21u12	21 16	21 19	21u22		21u39		21u42		21 46		21 49	21u58
Earlsfield	d			20 52									21 22									21 52	
Wimbledon 8 ⊖	d		20 53	20 56								21 22	21 26							21 53		21 56	
Surbiton 6	d		21 02	21 05								21 30	21 35							22 02		22 05	
Esher	d			21 09									21 39									22 09	
Hersham	d			21 12									21 42									22 12	
Walton-on-Thames	d		21 09	21 15									21 45							22 09		22 15	
Weybridge	d	←	21 13	21 19									21 49						←	22 13		22 19	
Byfleet & New Haw	d	21 02		21 21				22 02					21 51						22 02			22 21	
West Byfleet	d	21 05		21 24		←		→		←			21 54				←		22 05			22 24	
Woking	a	21 11	21 19	21 29	21 19	21 19			21 31	21 29	21 35	21 42	21 59	21 45		22 01	21 59	22 06	22 11	22 19		22 29	22 19
	d		21 23	21 35	21 21	21 23	21 26		21 32	21 35	21 37	21 46	22 05	21 46	21 49	22 02	22 05	22 07		22 23	22 26	22 35	22 21
Worplesdon	d		→	→									→							→	→	→	
Guildford	a								21 40	21 44						22 10	22 14						
Brookwood	d					21 28	21 32					21 51			21 55								
Ash Vale	d						21 41								22 03								
Aldershot	a						21 45								22 07								
	d						21 46								22 08								
Farnham	a						21 51								22 13								
	d						21 55								22 14								
Bentley	d														22 24								
Alton	a						22 06								22 31								
Farnborough (Main)	d				21 32	21 36						21 59											22 32
Fleet	d					21 42						22 04											
Winchfield	d											22 10											
Hook	d											22 14											
Basingstoke	a				21 46	21 54					21 56	22 21		22 05				22 26					22 46

Table T155-F

Sundays

20 May to 2 December

London - Woking, Guildford, Alton and Basingstoke

		SW 1	SW 1	SW	SW ◇1	SW	SW ◇1	SW 1		SW	SW 1 ✠	SW 1	SW 1	SW ◇1	SW	SW	SW 1		SW	SW ◇1 ✠	SW 1	SW 1
London Waterloo 15 ⊖	d			21 50	22 00		22 05	22 07		22 10	22 15			22 30			22 37		22 40	22 50		
Vauxhall ⊖	d			21 54						22 14									22 44			
Clapham Junction 10	d			22 00	22u09		22u12	22 16		22 19	22u22			22u39			22 46		22 49	22u58		
Earlsfield	d									22 22									22 52			
Wimbledon 8 ⊖	d							22 22		22 26							22 53		22 56			
Surbiton 6	d							22 30		22 35							23 02		23 05			
Esher	d									22 39									23 09			
Hersham	d									22 42									23 12			
Walton-on-Thames	d									22 45							23 09		23 15			
Weybridge	d									22 49					←		23 13		23 19			
Byfleet & New Haw	d			23 02						22 51					23 02				23 21			
West Byfleet	d	←	←	→		←				22 54		←			23 05	←			23 24		←	←
Woking	a	22 19	22 19		22 31	22 29	22 35	22 42		22 59	22 45	22 42		23 01	23 11	22 59	23 19		23 29	23 19	23 19	23 19
	d	22 23	22 26		22 32	22 35	22 37	22 46	22 49	23 05	22 46	22 49	22 49	23 02		23 05	23 26	23 23	23 35	23 21	23 23	23 26
Worplesdon	d								→	→							→	→	→			
Guildford	a				22 40	22 44								23 10		23 13						
Brookwood	d	22 28	22 32					22 51				22 55	22 55								23 28	23 32
Ash Vale	d		22 41									23 03	23 03									23 41
Aldershot	a		22 45									23 07	23 07									23 45
	d		22 46									23 08	23 08									23 49
Farnham	a		22 51									23 13	23 13									23 54
	d		22 55									23 14	23 14									23 55
Bentley	d											23 24	23 24									
Alton	a		23 06									23 31	23 31									00 06
Farnborough (Main)	d	22 36						22 59												23 32	23 36	
Fleet	d	22 42						23 04													23 42	
Winchfield	d							23 10														
Hook	d							23 14														
Basingstoke	a	22 54					22 56	23 22			23 05									23 46	23 54	

		SW 1	SW	SW ◇1	SW	SW ◇1	SW 1		SW	SW ◇1	SW	SW 1	SW	SW 1
London Waterloo 15 ⊖	d		22 50	23 00		23 05	23 07		23 10	23 30		23 35		23 40
Vauxhall ⊖	d		22 54						23 14					23 44
Clapham Junction 10	d		23 00	23u09		23u12	23 16		23 19	23u39		23u44		23 49
Earlsfield	d								23 22					23 52
Wimbledon 8 ⊖	d						23 22		23 26					23 56
Surbiton 6	d						23 30		23 35					00 05
Esher	d								23 39					00 09
Hersham	d								23 42					00 12
Walton-on-Thames	d								23 45					00 15
Weybridge	d								23 49				←	00 18
Byfleet & New Haw	d		00 02						23 51				00 02	00 21
West Byfleet	d		→		←				23 54		←		00 05	00 24
Woking	a			23 31	23 29	23 35	23 42		23 59	00 01	23 59	00 07	00 11	00 30
	d	23 26		23 32	23 35	23 37	23 46	23 49	00 05	00 03	00 05	00 08		00 33
Worplesdon	d								→					
Guildford	a			23 40	23 45					00 10	00 14			
Brookwood	d	23 32					23 51	23 55						00 39
Ash Vale	d	23 41						00 03						00 47
Aldershot	a	23 45						00 07						00 51
	d	23 49						00 08						00 52
Farnham	a	23 54						00 13						00 57
	d	23 55						00 14						
Bentley	d							00 24						
Alton	a	00 06						00 31						
Farnborough (Main)	d						23 59					00 19		
Fleet	d						00 04					00 25		
Winchfield	d						00 10							
Hook	d						00 14							
Basingstoke	a					23 56	00 21					00 39		

Table T155-R

Mondays to Fridays

21 May to 7 December

Basingstoke, Alton, Guildford and Woking - Waterloo

Miles	Miles	Miles			SW MO ◇1	SW MX 1	SW MO 1	SW MX 1	SW	SW ◇	SW ◇	SW ◇1 A	SW ◇1 B	SW ◇	SW	SW ◇1	SW ◇	SW ◇1	SW ◇1	SW ◇1 ⊥	SW ◇	SW ◇	SW ◇1 A
0	—	—	**Basingstoke**	d								04 54	04 54					05 39	05 54	05 59			
5½	—	—	Hook	d								05 01	05 01						06 01				
7¾	—	—	Winchfield	d								05 05	05 05						06 05				
11¼	—	—	Fleet	d				00 01				05 10	05 10					05 50	06 10				
14½	—	—	Farnborough (Main)	d				00 06				05 16	05 16					05 56	06 16				
—	0	—	**Alton**	d																			05 42
—	4¾	—	Bentley	d		00 04																	05 49
—	8¾	—	Farnham	a		00 09																	05 54
—	—	—		d																			05 56
—	11¾	—	**Aldershot**	d																			06 02
—	14¾	—	Ash Vale	d																			06 07
19¾	18¾	—	Brookwood	d				00 13				05 23	05 23						06 23				06 14
—	—	0	**Guildford**	d			00 05		04 20		05 14					05 49							
—	—	3½	Worplesdon	d							05 19			←		05 54							
23½	—	6	**Woking**	a			00 13	00 18	04 28		05 24	05 28	05 28	05 24		06 00		06 05	06 28	06 18			06 19
—	—	—		d	00 04			00 20	04 30	05 27	05 32	05 29	05 29	05 32	05 43	06 01	06 04	06 06	06 29	06 19			06 20
26	—	—	West Byfleet	d				00 25		05 32	→			05 36	05 47		06 08		→				06 25
27¼	—	—	Byfleet & New Haw	d						05 35				05 39			06 11						
28¾	—	—	Weybridge	d				00 29						05 42	05 51		06 14						
30¾	—	—	Walton-on-Thames	d				00 33						05 46	05 55		06 18						
31¾	—	—	Hersham	d										05 48			06 20						
33¼	—	—	Esher	d										05 51			06 23				←		
35¾	—	—	**Surbiton** 8	a				00 39	04 54			05 40	05 40	05 55	06 01		06 27				06 27		06 35
40½	—	—	Wimbledon 8 ⊖	a				00 47	05 01			05 48	05 48	06 04			→				06 35		
42¼	—	—	Earlsfield	a										06 08							06 39	←	
43¾	—	—	Clapham Junction 10	a	00 23			00 53	05 08	06 43		06 00	06 00	06 12		06 20		06 25		06 38	06 42	06 43	06 46
46½	—	—	Vauxhall ⊖	a						→		06 07	06 07	06 17							06 47	06 49	
47¾	—	—	**London Waterloo** 15 ⊖	a	00 33			01 04	05 18			06 12	06 15	06 22	06 20	06 29		06 34		06 49	06 53	06 56	06 55

		SW ◇1 B	SW ◇1	SW ◇1	SW ◇	SW ◇1	SW	SW ◇1 ⊥	SW ◇1	SW ◇1 ⊥	SW ◇1	SW ◇	SW ◇1 ⊥	SW ◇1	SW 1	SW ◇1	SW ◇1	SW 1	SW ◇1 ⊥	SW ◇1	SW ◇1	SW ◇1 ⊥	SW ◇1
Basingstoke	d		06 03						06 23	06 27			06 35					06 42	06 51				06 54
Hook	d								06 31														07 01
Winchfield	d								06 35														07 05
Fleet	d								06 40									06 54					07 10
Farnborough (Main)	d								06 46									07 00					07 16
Alton	d	05 42									06 12										06 44		
Bentley	d	05 49									06 19										06 51		
Farnham	a	05 54									06 24										06 56		
	d	05 56									06 26										06 58		
Aldershot	d	06 02									06 32										07 04		
Ash Vale	d	06 07									06 37										07 09		
Brookwood	d	06 14							06 53		06 44										07 16		07 23
Guildford	d					06 24		06 33								06 53				07 07		07 18	
Worplesdon	d			←		06 30								←		06 59							
Woking	a	06 19	06 22	06 28		06 35		06 41	06 58	06 46	06 49		06 53	06 58		07 03		07 10		07 15	07 21	07 25	07 28
	d	06 20	06 23	06 29	06 32	06 37	06 41	06 43	06 59	06 47	06 50		06 55	06 59	07 02	07 05	07 07	07 11		07 16	07 22	07 27	07 29
West Byfleet	d	06 25			06 36		06 46		→						07 07		07 16						
Byfleet & New Haw	d				06 39		06 49										07 19						
Weybridge	d				06 43		06 52								07 11		07 22						
Walton-on-Thames	d				06 47		06 56								07 16		07 27						
Hersham	d				06 49		06 59								07 19		07 30						
Esher	d				06 52		07 02					←			07 22		07 33						
Surbiton 8	a	06 35		06 40	06 56		07 06					06 56			07 26		07 37						
Wimbledon 8 ⊖	a			06 47	→							07 04											
Earlsfield	a											07 08											
Clapham Junction 10	a	06 46		06 54		06 58		07 02			07 10	07 12	07 14	07 20		07 24			07 28				
Vauxhall ⊖	a											07 17											
London Waterloo 15 ⊖	a	06 57	06 53	07 04		07 08	07 26	07 12		07 16	07 20	07 24	07 25	07 31	07 49	07 36	07 56	07 41	07 39	07 45	07 51	07 54	07 59

A until 5 October

B from 8 October

Table T155-R

Mondays to Fridays

21 May to 7 December

Basingstoke, Alton, Guildford and Woking - Waterloo

		SW ◇1	SW 1	SW ◇1	SW ◇1	SW ◇1	SW ◇1	SW ◇1	SW ◇1	SW ◇1	SW ◇1	SW ◇1 ⊥	SW ◇1 ⊥	SW ◇1	SW 1	SW ◇1	SW ◇1	SW ◇1	SW ◇1	SW ◇	SW ◇1	SW ◇1 ⊥	SW ◇1
Basingstoke	d	07 06	07 17								07 24	07 29				07 36	07 47				07 52	07 59	
Hook	d	07 13									07 31					07 43					07 59		
Winchfield	d	07 17									07 35					07 47					08 04		
Fleet	d	07 22									07 40					07 52					08 09		
Farnborough (Main)	d	07 28									07 46					07 58					08 16		
Alton	d								07 14														07 44
Bentley	d								07 21														07 51
Farnham	a								07 26														07 56
	d								07 28						07 39								07 58
Aldershot	d								07 34						07 46								08 04
Ash Vale	d								07 39						07 50								08 09
Brookwood	d								07 46		07 53				07 57						08 23		08 16
Guildford	d					07 34				07 45			07 54						08 02				
Worplesdon	d					07 40				07 50								←	08 08				
Woking	a								07 51	07 55	07 58				08 03	08 08	08 05	08 08	08 13		08 28	08 18	08 21
	d			07 32	07 40			07 47	07 52	07 57	07 59			08 02	08 05	08 09	08 06	08 09	08 14	08 17	08 30	08 19	08 24
West Byfleet	d			07 37			07 46	07 54						08 06	08 16	→				08 26	→		
Byfleet & New Haw	d						07 49	07 57							08 19					08 29			
Weybridge	d			07 41			07 52	08 01						08 11	08 22					08 32			
Walton-on-Thames	d			07 46			07 57	08 06						08 15	08 27					08 36			
Hersham	d			07 49			08 00	08 09						08 17	08 30					08 39			
Esher	d			07 52			08 03	08 13						08 21	08 33					08 43			
Surbiton 8	a			07 56			08 07	08 18						08 25	08 37					08 47			
Wimbledon 8 ⊖	a																						
Earlsfield	a																						
Clapham Junction 10	a																						
Vauxhall ⊖	a																						
London Waterloo 15 ⊖	a	08 06	08 01	08 20	08 08	08 10	08 26	08 36	08 20	08 24	08 29	08 14	08 32	08 46	08 59		08 34	08 39	08 41	09 06		08 46	08 52

		SW ◇1 ⊥	SW ◇1	SW ◇	SW ◇1	SW ◇1	SW ◇1	SW ◇1	SW ◇1	SW ◇1	SW ◇1 ⊥	SW ◇1	SW ◇	SW ◇1 ⊥	SW ◇1	SW ◇1 ⊥	SW ◇1	SW ◇1	SW ◇	SW ◇1	SW 1	SW ◇1 ⊥	SW ◇
Basingstoke	d				08 05	08 16				08 24	08 29			08 35			08 43				08 54	08 59	
Hook	d				08 12					08 31											09 01		
Winchfield	d				08 16					08 35											09 05		
Fleet	d				08 22					08 40							08 54				09 10		
Farnborough (Main)	d				08 28					08 46							09 00				09 16		
Alton	d											08 14											
Bentley	d											08 21											
Farnham	a											08 26											
	d											08 28											
Aldershot	d											08 34											
Ash Vale	d											08 39											
Brookwood	d									08 53		08 46									09 23		
Guildford	d	08 18		08 22				08 30								08 53			08 46	09 03			
Worplesdon	d		←				←	08 36							←				08 51				
Woking	a	08 26	08 28	08 30	08 38	08 34	08 38	08 41		08 58	08 48	08 51		08 53	08 58				08 59	09 11	09 28	09 18	
	d	08 28	08 30	08 32	08 39	08 36	08 39	08 43	08 47	08 59	08 49	08 52		08 55	08 59				09 02	09 13	09 29	09 19	
West Byfleet	d			08 36	→				08 54	→									09 06		→		
Byfleet & New Haw	d			08 39					08 57										09 09				
Weybridge	d			08 43					09 02										09 13				
Walton-on-Thames	d			08 47					09 07										09 17				
Hersham	d			08 49					09 10										09 19				
Esher	d			08 52					09 13				←					←	09 22				←
Surbiton 8	a			08 56					09 18				08 56		09 10			09 18	09 26				09 26
Wimbledon 8 ⊖	a			→					→				09 04						→				09 34
Earlsfield	a												09 08										09 38
Clapham Junction 10	a							09 03					09 12	09 14			09 26			09 32		09 38	09 42
Vauxhall ⊖	a												09 17										09 47
London Waterloo 15 ⊖	a	08 54	09 00			09 03	09 10	09 13			09 17	09 21	09 24	09 25	09 29	09 31	09 38	09 40		09 43		09 51	09 54

		SW 1	SW ◇1 ⊥	SW ◇1 ⊥	SW 1	SW 1	SW	SW 1	SW ◇1	SW 1	SW ◇1 ⊥	SW	SW 1	SW ◇1 ⊥	SW 1	SW ◇1 ⊥	SW	SW ◇1 ⊥	SW 1	SW 1	SW ◇1 ⊥	SW ◇1 ⊥
Basingstoke	d							09 16		09 24	09 30			09 36				09 43		09 54	09 57	
Hook	d									09 31										10 01		
Winchfield	d									09 35										10 05		
Fleet	d							09 27		09 40								09 54		10 10		
Farnborough (Main)	d							09 32		09 46								10 00		10 16		
Alton	d	08 44											09 14									
Bentley	d	08 51											09 21									
Farnham	a	08 56											09 26									
	d	08 58											09 28									
Aldershot	d	09 04											09 34									
Ash Vale	d	09 09											09 39									
Brookwood	d	09 16								09 53			09 46							10 23		
Guildford	d			09 19					09 34							09 47			10 02			
Worplesdon	d					←			09 40						←							
Woking	a	09 21		09 27		09 28		09 41	09 44	09 58	09 49		09 51	09 54	09 58	09 59			10 11	10 28	10 15	
	d	09 22	09 24	09 28		09 29	09 33	09 43	09 46	09 59	09 50		09 52	09 56	09 59	10 00	10 03		10 12	10 29	10 17	10 21
West Byfleet	d	09 27					09 37			→			09 57				10 07			→		
Byfleet & New Haw	d						09 40										10 10					
Weybridge	d					09 36	09 43								10 06		10 13					
Walton-on-Thames	d					09 40	09 47								10 10		10 17					
Hersham	d						09 49										10 19					
Esher	d				←		09 52					←					10 22					
Surbiton 8	a	09 37			09 37	09 46	09 56					09 56	10 07		10 16		10 26					
Wimbledon 8 ⊖	a	→					→					10 04					→					
Earlsfield	a											10 08										
Clapham Junction 10	a		09 43		09 50	09 57			10 05		10 09	10 12		10 15				10 25	10 31		10 36	
Vauxhall ⊖	a											10 17										
London Waterloo 15 ⊖	a		09 53	09 55	09 59	10 08		10 08	10 13		10 19	10 23	10 29	10 23	10 36	10 29		10 34	10 40		10 49	10 49

Basingstoke, Alton, Guildford and Woking - Waterloo

		SW	SW 1	SW ◇1 🛒	SW 1	SW	SW 1	SW ◇1		SW 1	SW ◇1 🛒	SW ◇1 🛒	SW	SW 1	SW ◇1 🛒	SW ◇1	SW 1	SW		SW 1	SW 1	SW ◇1 🛒	SW ◇1 🛒	SW	SW 1
Basingstoke	d						10 17			10 24	10 30	10 35				10 43					10 54	10 57			
Hook	d									10 31											11 01				
Winchfield	d									10 35											11 05				
Fleet	d									10 40						10 54					11 10				
Farnborough (Main)	d						10 30			10 46						11 00					11 16				
Alton	d		09 44											10 14											10 44
Bentley	d		09 51											10 21											10 51
Farnham	a		09 56											10 26											10 56
	d		09 58											10 28											10 58
Aldershot	d		10 04											10 34											11 04
Ash Vale	d		10 09											10 39											11 09
Brookwood	d		10 16							10 53				10 46							11 23				11 16
Guildford	d			10 17				10 34							10 47					11 02					
Worplesdon	d				←			10 40									←								
Woking	a		10 21	10 25	10 28		10 39	10 44		10 58	10 49			10 51	10 57		10 58			11 11	11 28	11 15			11 21
	d		10 22	10 26	10 29	10 33	10 41	10 46		10 59	10 50			10 52	10 59		10 59	11 03		11 12	11 29	11 17	11 21		11 22
West Byfleet	d		10 27			10 37				→				10 57				11 07			→				11 27
Byfleet & New Haw	d					10 40												11 10							
Weybridge	d				10 36	10 43											11 06	11 13							
Walton-on-Thames	d				10 40	10 47											11 10	11 17							
Hersham	d					10 49												11 19							
Esher	d	←				10 52							←					11 22						←	
Surbiton 5	a	10 26	10 37		10 46	10 56							10 56	11 07			11 16	11 26						11 26	11 37
Wimbledon 5 ⊖	a	10 34				→							11 04					→						11 34	
Earlsfield	a	10 38											11 08											11 38	
Clapham Junction 10	a	10 42	10 48		10 57			11 05				11 11	11 12			11 25				11 31		11 36		11 42	11 48
Vauxhall ⊖	a	10 47											11 17											11 47	
London Waterloo 15 ⊖	a	10 52	10 57	10 54	11 05		11 08	11 13			11 19	11 20	11 22	11 27	11 23	11 34	11 36			11 40		11 49	11 49	11 52	11 57

		SW ◇1 🛒	SW 1	SW		SW 1	SW ◇1	SW 1	SW ◇1 🛒	SW ◇1 🛒	SW	SW 1	SW ◇1 🛒	SW ◇1		SW 1	SW	SW 1	SW 1	SW ◇1 🛒	SW ◇1 🛒	SW	SW 1	SW ◇1 🛒	
Basingstoke	d					11 17		11 24	11 30	11 35				11 43					11 54	11 57					
Hook	d							11 31											12 01						
Winchfield	d							11 35											12 05						
Fleet	d							11 40						11 54					12 10						
Farnborough (Main)	d					11 30		11 46						12 00					12 16						
Alton	d											11 15											11 44		
Bentley	d																						11 51		
Farnham	a											11 25											11 56		
	d											11 28											11 58		
Aldershot	d											11 34											12 04		
Ash Vale	d											11 39											12 09		
Brookwood	d							11 53				11 46							12 23				12 16		
Guildford	d	11 17					11 34						11 47					12 02						12 17	
Worplesdon	d		←				11 40									←									
Woking	a	11 25	11 28			11 39	11 44	11 58	11 49			11 51	11 57			11 58		12 11	12 28	12 15			12 21	12 25	
	d	11 26	11 29	11 33		11 41	11 46	11 59	11 50			11 52	11 59			11 59	12 03	12 12	12 29	12 17	12 21		12 22	12 26	
West Byfleet	d			11 37				→				11 57					12 07		→				12 27		
Byfleet & New Haw	d			11 40													12 10								
Weybridge	d		11 36	11 43												12 06	12 13								
Walton-on-Thames	d		11 40	11 47												12 10	12 17								
Hersham	d			11 49													12 19								
Esher	d			11 52							←						12 22					←			
Surbiton 5	a		11 46	11 56							11 56	12 07				12 16	12 26					12 26	12 37		
Wimbledon 5 ⊖	a			→							12 04						→					12 34			
Earlsfield	a										12 08											12 38			
Clapham Junction 10	a		11 57				12 05			12 11	12 12			12 25				12 31		12 36		12 42	12 48		
Vauxhall ⊖	a										12 17											12 47			
London Waterloo 15 ⊖	a	11 51	12 08			12 08	12 13		12 19	12 20	12 22	12 27	12 23	12 34		12 36		12 40		12 49	12 49	12 52	12 57	12 51	

		SW 1	SW	SW 1	SW ◇1	SW 1	SW ◇1 🛒	SW ◇1 🛒	SW	SW 1		SW ◇1 🛒	SW ◇1	SW 1	SW	SW 1	SW 1	SW ◇1 🛒	SW ◇1 🛒	SW		SW 1	SW ◇1 🛒	SW 1	SW
Basingstoke	d			12 17		12 24	12 30	12 35					12 43				12 54	12 57							
Hook	d					12 31											13 01								
Winchfield	d					12 35											13 05								
Fleet	d					12 40							12 54				13 10								
Farnborough (Main)	d			12 31		12 46							13 00				13 16								
Alton	d																					12 44			
Bentley	d																					12 51			
Farnham	a																					12 56			
	d									12 28												12 58			
Aldershot	d									12 34												13 04			
Ash Vale	d									12 39												13 09			
Brookwood	d					12 53				12 46							13 23					13 16			
Guildford	d				12 34							12 47				13 02							13 17		
Worplesdon	d	←			12 40									←										←	
Woking	a	12 28		12 40	12 44	12 58	12 49			12 51		12 57		12 58		13 11	13 28	13 15				13 21	13 25	13 28	
	d	12 29	12 33	12 41	12 46	12 59	12 50			12 52		12 59		12 59	13 03	13 12	13 29	13 17	13 21			13 22	13 26	13 29	13 33
West Byfleet	d		12 37			→				12 57					13 07		→					13 27			13 37
Byfleet & New Haw	d		12 40												13 10										13 40
Weybridge	d	12 36	12 43											13 06	13 13									13 36	13 43
Walton-on-Thames	d	12 40	12 47											13 10	13 17									13 40	13 47
Hersham	d		12 49												13 19										13 49
Esher	d		12 52						←						13 22					←					13 52
Surbiton 5	a	12 46	12 56						12 56	13 07				13 16	13 26					13 26		13 37		13 46	13 56
Wimbledon 5 ⊖	a		→						13 04						→					13 34					→
Earlsfield	a								13 08											13 38					
Clapham Junction 10	a	12 57			13 05			13 11	13 12				13 25			13 31		13 36		13 42		13 48		13 57	
Vauxhall ⊖	a								13 17											13 47					
London Waterloo 15 ⊖	a	13 05		13 08	13 13		13 19	13 20	13 22	13 27		13 23	13 34	13 36		13 40		13 49	13 49	13 52		13 59	13 51	14 06	

Table T155-R

Mondays to Fridays
21 May to 7 December

Basingstoke, Alton, Guildford and Woking - Waterloo

		SW 1	SW ◇1	SW 1	SW ◇1 🛒	SW ◇1 🛒		SW	SW 1	SW ◇1 🛒	SW ◇1	SW 1	SW	SW 1	SW 1	SW ◇1 🛒		SW ◇1 🛒	SW	SW 1	SW ◇1 🛒	SW 1	SW	SW 1	SW ◇1
Basingstoke	d	13 17		13 24	13 30	13 35					13 43				13 54	13 57								14 17	
Hook	d			13 31											14 01										
Winchfield	d			13 35											14 05										
Fleet	d			13 40							13 54				14 10										
Farnborough (Main)	d	13 30		13 46							14 00				14 16									14 30	
Alton	d								13 15											13 44					
Bentley	d																			13 51					
Farnham	a								13 25											13 56					
	d								13 28											13 58					
Aldershot	d								13 34											14 04					
Ash Vale	d								13 39											14 09					
Brookwood	d			13 53					13 46						14 23					14 16					
Guildford	d		13 34							13 47				14 02							14 17				14 34
Worplesdon	d		13 40									←										←			14 40
Woking	a	13 39	13 44	13 58	13 49				13 51	13 57		13 58		14 11	14 28	14 15				14 21	14 25	14 28		14 39	14 44
	d	13 41	13 46	13 59	13 50				13 52	13 59		13 59	14 03	14 12	14 29	14 17		14 22		14 22	14 26	14 29	14 33	14 41	14 46
West Byfleet	d			→					13 57				14 07		→					14 27			14 37		
Byfleet & New Haw	d												14 10										14 40		
Weybridge	d											14 06	14 13									14 36	14 43		
Walton-on-Thames	d											14 10	14 17									14 40	14 47		
Hersham	d												14 19										14 49		
Esher	d							←					14 22						←				14 52		
Surbiton 5	a							13 56	14 07			14 16	14 26						14 26	14 37		14 46	14 56		
Wimbledon 5 ⊖	a							14 04					→						14 34				→		
Earlsfield	a							14 08											14 38						
Clapham Junction 10	a		14 05			14 11		14 12			14 25			14 31		14 36			14 42	14 49		14 57			15 05
Vauxhall ⊖	a							14 17											14 47						
London Waterloo 15 ⊖	a	14 08	14 13		14 19	14 20		14 22	14 29	14 23	14 34	14 36		14 43		14 49		14 49	14 52	14 59	14 53	15 08		15 08	15 13

		SW 1		SW ◇1 🛒	SW ◇1 🛒	SW	SW 1	SW ◇1 🛒	SW ◇1	SW 1	SW	SW 1		SW 1	SW ◇1 🛒	SW ◇1 🛒	SW	SW 1	SW ◇1 🛒	SW 1	SW	SW 1		SW ◇1	SW 1
Basingstoke	d	14 24		14 30	14 35				14 43					14 54	14 57							15 17			15 24
Hook	d	14 31												15 01											15 31
Winchfield	d	14 35												15 05											15 35
Fleet	d	14 40							14 54					15 10											15 40
Farnborough (Main)	d	14 46							15 00					15 16								15 30			15 46
Alton	d						14 15											14 44							
Bentley	d																	14 51							
Farnham	a						14 25											14 56							
	d						14 28											14 58							
Aldershot	d						14 34											15 04							
Ash Vale	d						14 39											15 09							
Brookwood	d	14 53					14 46							15 23				15 16							15 53
Guildford	d							14 47				15 02							15 17					15 34	
Worplesdon	d									←										←				15 40	
Woking	a	14 58		14 49			14 51	14 57		14 58		15 11		15 28	15 15			15 21	15 25	15 28		15 39		15 44	15 58
	d	14 59		14 50			14 52	14 59		14 59	15 03	15 12		15 29	15 17	15 21		15 22	15 26	15 29	15 33	15 41		15 46	15 59
West Byfleet	d	→					14 57				15 07			→				15 27			15 37				→
Byfleet & New Haw	d										15 10										15 40				
Weybridge	d									15 06	15 13									15 36	15 43				
Walton-on-Thames	d									15 10	15 17									15 40	15 47				
Hersham	d										15 19										15 49				
Esher	d					←					15 22						←				15 52				
Surbiton 5	a					14 56	15 07			15 16	15 26						15 26	15 37		15 46	15 56				
Wimbledon 5 ⊖	a					15 04					→						15 34				→				
Earlsfield	a					15 08											15 38								
Clapham Junction 10	a				15 11	15 12			15 25			15 32			15 36		15 42	15 48		15 57				16 05	
Vauxhall ⊖	a					15 17											15 47								
London Waterloo 15 ⊖	a			15 19	15 20	15 22	15 29	15 23	15 34	15 37		15 43			15 49	15 49	15 52	15 57	15 51	16 05		16 07		16 15	

		SW ◇1 🛒	SW ◇1 🛒	SW	SW 1	SW ◇1 🛒	SW ◇1	SW 1		SW	SW 1	SW 1	SW ◇1 🛒	SW ◇1 🛒	SW	SW 1	SW ◇1 🛒	SW 1		SW	SW 1	SW ◇1	SW 1	SW ◇1 🛒	SW ◇1 🛒
Basingstoke	d	15 30	15 35				15 43					15 54	15 57								16 17		16 24	16 30	16 36
Hook	d											16 01											16 31		
Winchfield	d											16 05											16 35		
Fleet	d						15 54					16 10											16 40		
Farnborough (Main)	d						16 00					16 16									16 30		16 46		
Alton	d				15 15											15 44									
Bentley	d															15 51									
Farnham	a				15 25											15 56									
	d				15 28											15 58									
Aldershot	d				15 34											16 04									
Ash Vale	d				15 39											16 09									
Brookwood	d				15 46							16 23				16 16							16 53		
Guildford	d					15 47					16 00						16 17					16 34			
Worplesdon	d							←			16 06							←				16 40			
Woking	a	15 49			15 51	15 57		15 58			16 11	16 28	16 15			16 21	16 25	16 28			16 39	16 44	16 58	16 49	
	d	15 50			15 52	15 59		15 59		16 03	16 12	16 29	16 17	16 21		16 22	16 26	16 29		16 32	16 41	16 46	16 59	16 50	
West Byfleet	d				15 57					16 07		→				16 27				16 36			→		
Byfleet & New Haw	d									16 10										16 39					
Weybridge	d							16 06		16 13								16 36		16 42					
Walton-on-Thames	d							16 10		16 17								16 40		16 46					
Hersham	d									16 19										16 48					
Esher	d			←						16 22					←					16 51					
Surbiton 5	a			15 56	16 07			16 16		16 26					16 26	16 37		16 46		16 55					
Wimbledon 5 ⊖	a			16 04						→					16 34					→					
Earlsfield	a			16 08											16 38										
Clapham Junction 10	a		16 11	16 12			16 25				16 31		16 36		16 42	16 48		16 57				17 05			17 11
Vauxhall ⊖	a			16 17											16 47										
London Waterloo 15 ⊖	a	16 19	16 20	16 22	16 29	16 24	16 34	16 36			16 40		16 47	16 49	16 52	16 59	16 53	17 08			17 08	17 14		17 19	17 21

Table T155-R

Mondays to Fridays

21 May to 7 December

Basingstoke, Alton, Guildford and Woking - Waterloo

	SW	SW ■	SW ■		SW ■	SW ◇■	SW	SW ◇■ 🛒	SW ■	SW ◇■ 🛒	SW	SW ◇■ 🛒	SW ■		SW ◇■ 🛒	SW ■	SW	SW ■	SW ◇■	SW ■	SW ◇■ 🛒	SW	SW ◇■ 🛒
Basingstoke d						16 43			16 54	16 57								17 17		17 24	17 30		17 35
Hook d									17 01											17 31			
Winchfield d									17 05											17 35			
Fleet d						16 54			17 10											17 40			
Farnborough (Main) d						17 00			17 16									17 30		17 46			
Alton d		16 15											16 44										
Bentley d													16 51										
Farnham a		16 25											16 56										
d		16 28											16 58										
Aldershot d		16 34											17 04										
Ash Vale d		16 39											17 09										
Brookwood d		16 46							17 23				17 16							17 53			
Guildford d			16 47					17 00							17 17				17 34				
Worplesdon d					←			17 06								←			17 40				
Woking a		16 51	16 57		16 58			17 11	17 28	17 15			17 21		17 25	17 28		17 39	17 44	17 58	17 49		
d		16 52	16 59		16 59		17 03	17 12	17 29	17 17		17 21	17 22		17 26	17 29	17 32	17 41	17 46	17 59	17 50		
West Byfleet d		16 57					17 07		→				17 27				17 36			→			
Byfleet & New Haw d							17 10										17 39						
Weybridge d					17 06		17 13									17 36	17 42						
Walton-on-Thames d					17 10		17 17									17 40	17 46						
Hersham d							17 19										17 48						
Esher d	←						17 22				←						17 51					←	
Surbiton ■ a	16 55	17 07			17 16		17 26				17 26		17 37			17 46	17 55					17 55	
Wimbledon ■ ⊖ a	17 05						→				17 34						→					18 04	
Earlsfield a	17 08										17 38											18 08	
Clapham Junction ■ a	17 12					17 25		17 31		17 36	17 42		17 48			17 57			18 05			18 11	18 11
Vauxhall ⊖ a	17 17										17 47											18 16	
London Waterloo ■ ⊖ a	17 22	17 29	17 27		17 36	17 38		17 43		17 49	17 52	17 52	17 59		17 54	18 09		18 09	18 14		18 16	18 21	18 23

	SW ■	SW ■	SW ◇■	SW ■	SW	SW ◇■ 🛒	SW ■	SW ◇■ 🛒	SW ◇■ 🛒		SW	SW ■	SW ◇■ 🛒	SW ■	SW	SW ■	SW ◇■	SW ■	SW ◇■ 🛒		SW ◇■ 🛒	SW	SW ■	SW ◇■
Basingstoke d			17 43				17 54	17 57								18 17		18 24	18 30		18 36			18 43
Hook d							18 01											18 31						
Winchfield d							18 05											18 35						
Fleet d			17 54				18 10											18 40						18 54
Farnborough (Main) d			18 00				18 16									18 31		18 46						19 00
Alton d	17 14											17 44											18 14	
Bentley d	17 21											17 51											18 23	
Farnham a	17 26											17 56											18 27	
d	17 28											17 58											18 28	
Aldershot d	17 34											18 04											18 34	
Ash Vale d	17 39											18 09											18 39	
Brookwood d	17 46						18 23					18 16						18 53					18 46	
Guildford d		17 47				18 00							18 17				18 34							
Worplesdon d				←		18 06								←			18 40							
Woking a	17 51	17 58		17 58		18 11	18 28	18 15				18 21		18 28		18 40	18 44	18 58	18 49				18 52	
d	17 52	17 59		17 59	18 02	18 12	18 29	18 17	18 21			18 22		18 29	18 32	18 41	18 46	18 59	18 50				18 52	
West Byfleet d	17 57				18 06		→					18 27			18 36			→					18 57	
Byfleet & New Haw d					18 09										18 39									
Weybridge d				18 06	18 12									18 36	18 42									
Walton-on-Thames d				18 10	18 16									18 40	18 46									
Hersham d					18 18										18 48									
Esher d					18 21						←				18 51							←		
Surbiton ■ a	18 07			18 16	18 25						18 25	18 37		18 47	18 55							18 55	19 07	
Wimbledon ■ ⊖ a					→						18 34				→							19 05		
Earlsfield a											18 38											19 09		
Clapham Junction ■ a			18 25			18 32		18 36			18 42	18 48		18 58			19 05				19 11	19 11		19 26
Vauxhall ⊖ a											18 47											19 16		
London Waterloo ■ ⊖ a	18 29	18 27	18 34	18 36		18 43		18 49	18 50		18 52	18 57	18 59	19 07		19 09	19 13		19 19		19 20	19 23	19 26	19 34

	SW ■	SW	SW ◇■ 🛒	SW ■	SW ■		SW ◇■ 🛒	SW ◇■ 🛒	SW ■	SW ■	SW ◇■ 🛒	SW	SW ■	SW ◇■	SW ■		SW ◇■ 🛒	SW ◇■ 🛒	SW	SW ■	SW ◇■ 🛒	SW ◇■	SW ■	SW
Basingstoke d					18 54		19 02						19 17		19 24		19 30	19 35				19 43		
Hook d					19 01										19 31									
Winchfield d					19 05										19 35									
Fleet d					19 10										19 40							19 54		
Farnborough (Main) d					19 16								19 32		19 46							20 00		
Alton d				18 35																19 08				
Bentley d				18 42																				
Farnham a				18 47																19 18				
d				18 58																19 28				
Aldershot d				19 04																19 34				
Ash Vale d				19 09																19 39				
Brookwood d				19 16	19 23										19 53					19 46				
Guildford d			18 55								19 21			19 34							19 49			
Worplesdon d	←									←				19 40									←	
Woking a	18 58		19 03	19 21	19 28		19 21			19 28	19 29		19 41	19 45	19 58		19 49			19 51	19 57		19 58	
d	18 59	19 03	19 05	19 22	19 29		19 22	19 26		19 29	19 30	19 33	19 42	19 46	19 59		19 50			19 52	19 59		19 59	20 02
West Byfleet d		19 07		19 27	→							19 37			→					19 57				20 06
Byfleet & New Haw d		19 10										19 40												20 09
Weybridge d	19 06	19 13								19 36		19 43											20 06	20 12
Walton-on-Thames d	19 10	19 17								19 40		19 47											20 10	20 16
Hersham d		19 19										19 49												20 18
Esher d		19 22							←			19 52							←					20 21
Surbiton ■ a	19 16	19 26		19 37					19 37	19 46		19 56							19 56	20 07			20 16	20 25
Wimbledon ■ ⊖ a		19 35		→								→							20 04					→
Earlsfield a		19 39																	20 08					
Clapham Junction ■ a		19 41					19 41		19 48	19 57				20 05				20 11	20 12			20 25		
Vauxhall ⊖ a		19 46																	20 17					
London Waterloo ■ ⊖ a	19 39	19 52	19 29				19 50	19 52	19 57	20 05	19 59		20 08	20 14			20 19	20 20	20 22	20 26	20 24	20 34	20 36	

Table T155-R

Mondays to Fridays

21 May to 7 December

Basingstoke, Alton, Guildford and Woking - Waterloo

	SW ■		SW ◇■ 🛒	SW	SW ■	SW ◇■	SW ■	SW ◇■ 🛒	SW ■	SW	SW ■		SW ■	SW ◇■	SW ■	SW ◇■ 🛒	SW ◇■	SW	SW ◇■	SW ◇■ 🛒	SW		SW ■	SW ◇■
Basingstoke d							19 54	20 09			20 17				20 24	20 36			20 43					
Hook d							20 01								20 31									
Winchfield d							20 05								20 35									
Fleet d							20 10								20 40				20 54					
Farnborough (Main) d							20 16				20 30				20 46				21 00					
Alton d					19 35								20 15										20 44	
Bentley d					19 42																		20 51	
Farnham a					19 47								20 25										20 56	
d					19 58								20 28										20 58	
Aldershot d					20 04								20 34										21 04	
Ash Vale d					20 09								20 39										21 09	
Brookwood d					20 16		20 23						20 46		20 53								21 16	
Guildford d	20 02					20 17								20 39			20 49							21 17
Worplesdon d														20 45										
Woking a	20 11				20 21	20 25	20 28	20 29			20 39		20 51	20 52	20 58		20 59		21 09				21 21	21 25
d	20 12		20 21		20 22	20 26	20 29	20 30		20 33	20 41		20 52	20 53	20 59		21 01	21 03	21 10	21 21			21 22	21 26
West Byfleet d					20 27					20 37			20 57					21 07					21 27	
Byfleet & New Haw d										20 40								21 10						
Weybridge d							20 36			20 43					21 06			21 13						
Walton-on-Thames d							20 40			20 47					21 10			21 17						
Hersham d										20 49								21 19						
Esher d				←					←	20 52								21 22			←			
Surbiton ■ a				20 25	20 37		20 46		20 46	20 56			21 07		21 16			21 26			21 26		21 37	
Wimbledon ■ ⊖ a				20 35			→			21 05								→			21 34			
Earlsfield a				20 39						21 09											21 38			
Clapham Junction ■ a	20 32			20 41	20 48			20 52	20 59	21 11				21 12		21 16			21 29		21 42		21 48	
Vauxhall ⊖ a				20 46						21 16											21 47			
London Waterloo ■ ⊖ a	20 40		20 49	20 52	20 57	20 51		21 00	21 08	21 22	21 09		21 29	21 21	21 34	21 25	21 29		21 38	21 49	21 52		21 57	21 51

	SW ■	SW ◇■ 🛒	SW ■	SW	SW ◇■	SW	SW ■		SW ◇■	SW ■	SW	SW ◇■	SW ◇■	SW ◇■	SW	SW ■	SW ■		SW ◇■	SW ■	SW ■	SW	SW ◇■	SW
Basingstoke d	20 54	21 09								21 24		21 35	21 43				21 54		22 09					
Hook d	21 01									21 31							22 01							
Winchfield d	21 05									21 35							22 05							
Fleet d	21 10									21 40			21 54				22 10							
Farnborough (Main) d	21 16									21 46			22 00				22 16							
Alton d							21 15									21 44								
Bentley d																21 51								
Farnham a							21 25									21 56								
d							21 28									21 58								
Aldershot d							21 34									22 04								
Ash Vale d							21 39									22 09								
Brookwood d	21 23						21 46			21 53						22 16	22 23							
Guildford d					21 39				21 49													22 20	22 39	
Worplesdon d					21 44																		22 44	
Woking a	21 28	21 29			21 49		21 51		21 57	21 58			22 09			22 21	22 28		22 28			22 32	22 49	
d	21 29	21 30		21 33	21 50		21 52		21 59	21 59	22 03		22 10	22 21		22 22	22 29		22 29			22 33	22 50	
West Byfleet d				21 37			21 57				22 07					22 27						22 37		
Byfleet & New Haw d				21 40							22 10											22 40		
Weybridge d	21 36			21 43						22 06	22 13						22 36					22 43		
Walton-on-Thames d	21 40			21 47						22 10	22 17						22 40					22 47		
Hersham d				21 49							22 19											22 49		
Esher d			←	21 52		←					22 22				←					←	←	22 52		←
Surbiton ■ a	21 46		21 46	21 56		21 56	22 07			22 16	22 26				22 26	22 37	22 46			22 37	22 46	22 56		22 56
Wimbledon ■ ⊖ a	→			→		22 04					→				22 34	→	→					→		23 04
Earlsfield a						22 08									22 38									23 08
Clapham Junction ■ a		21 52	21 57		22 09	22 12						22 13	22 29		22 42				22 48	22 52	22 57		23 09	23 12
Vauxhall ⊖ a						22 17									22 47									23 17
London Waterloo ■ ⊖ a		22 04	22 06		22 18	22 22	22 27		22 27	22 34		22 22	22 38	22 49	22 52				22 58	23 01	23 08		23 19	23 26

	SW ■	SW ■	SW ◇■		SW ■	SW	SW ◇■	SW	SW FO ■	SW FX ■	SW FX ■	SW FO ■	SW ◇■		SW FX ■	SW FO ■	SW FO ◇■	SW FX ◇■	SW ■	SW ■	SW ■
Basingstoke d		22 24	22 36				22 43				22 54	22 54	23 13							23 44	
Hook d		22 31									23 01	23 01								23 51	
Winchfield d		22 35									23 05	23 05								23 55	
Fleet d		22 40					22 54				23 10	23 10								00 01	
Farnborough (Main) d		22 46					23 00				23 16	23 16								00 06	
Alton d	22 15								22 44	22 44									23 15		23 48
Bentley d									22 51	22 51											00 04
Farnham a	22 25								22 56	22 56									23 26		00 09
d	22 28								22 58	22 58									23 28		
Aldershot d	22 34								23 04	23 04									23 34		
Ash Vale d	22 39								23 09	23 09									23 39		
Brookwood d	22 46	22 53							23 16	23 16	23 23	23 23							23 46	00 13	
Guildford d						22 55											23 39	23 39			
Worplesdon d					←										←	←	23 44	23 44			
Woking a	22 51	22 58	22 54		22 58	23 05	23 09		23 21	23 21	23 28	23 28	23 31		23 28	23 28	23 49	23 49	23 51	00 18	
d	22 52	22 59	22 55		22 59	23 06	23 10		23 22	23 22	23 33	23 33	23 32		23 33	23 33	23 56	23 56		00 20	
West Byfleet d	22 57	→				23 10			23 27	23 27	→	→			23 37	23 37				00 25	
Byfleet & New Haw d						23 13									23 40	23 40					
Weybridge d					23 06	23 16									23 43	23 43				00 29	
Walton-on-Thames d					23 10	23 20									23 47	23 47				00 33	
Hersham d						23 22									23 49	23 49					
Esher d						23 25		←							23 52	23 52					
Surbiton ■ a	23 07				23 16	23 29		23 29	23 37	23 37					23 57	23 57	00 08	00 08		00 39	
Wimbledon ■ ⊖ a						→		23 37							00 06	00 06	00 16	00 16		00 47	
Earlsfield a								23 41													
Clapham Junction ■ a			23 14				23 29	23 44	23 51	23 51			23 55		00 21	00 21	00 22	00 22		00 53	
Vauxhall ⊖ a								23 49							00 30	00 31					
London Waterloo ■ ⊖ a	23 27		23 23		23 32		23 39	23 54	00 02	00 04			00 08		00 36	00 36	00 32	00 33		01 04	

Table T155-R

Saturdays
26 May to 8 December

Basingstoke, Alton, Guildford and Woking - Waterloo

	SW 1	SW 1	SW	SW	SW	SW 1	SW	SW	SW ◇1		SW 1	SW ◇1 🛒	SW	SW	SW 1	SW	SW ◇1	SW 1	SW ◇1 🛒		SW	SW 1 A	SW 1 B	SW 1
Basingstoke d						04 54					05 54	05 59						06 24	06 30					
Hook d						05 01					06 01							06 31						
Winchfield d						05 05					06 05							06 35						
Fleet d	00 01					05 10					06 10							06 40						
Farnborough (Main) d	00 06					05 16					06 16							06 46						
Alton d																						06 14	06 14	
Bentley d		00 04																				06 21	06 21	
Farnham a		00 09																				06 26	06 26	
d																						06 28	06 28	
Aldershot d																						06 34	06 34	
Ash Vale d																						06 39	06 39	
Brookwood d	00 13					05 23					06 23							06 53				06 46	06 46	
Guildford d			04 25		05 14				06 02								06 34							
Worplesdon d					05 19		←								←		06 40							←
Woking a	00 18		04 33		05 24	05 28	05 24		06 11		06 28	06 18			06 28		06 44	06 58	06 49			06 51	06 51	06 58
d	00 20		04 35	05 27	05 32	05 29	05 32	06 02	06 13		06 29	06 19			06 29	06 33	06 46	06 59	06 50			06 52	06 52	06 59
West Byfleet d	00 25			05 32	→		05 36	06 06			→					06 37		→				06 57	06 57	
Byfleet & New Haw d				05 35			05 39	06 09								06 40								
Weybridge d	00 29						05 42	06 12							06 36	06 43								07 06
Walton-on-Thames d	00 33						05 46	06 16							06 40	06 47								07 10
Hersham d							05 48	06 18								06 49								
Esher d							05 51	06 21					←			06 52					←			
Surbiton 5 a	00 39		04 54			05 40	05 55	06 25					06 25		06 46	06 56					06 56	07 07	07 07	07 16
Wimbledon 5 ⊖ a	00 47		05 01			05 48	06 04	→					06 34			→					07 04			
Earlsfield a							06 08						06 38	←							07 08			
Clapham Junction 10 a	00 53		05 08	06 43		06 00	06 12		06 32			06 38	06 42	06 43	06 57		07 05				07 12	07 18	07 18	
Vauxhall ⊖ a				→		06 07	06 17						06 47	06 49							07 17			
London Waterloo 15 ⊖ a	01 04		05 18			06 12	06 22		06 40			06 49	06 52	06 56	07 05		07 13		07 19		07 22	07 27	07 30	07 35

	SW 1	SW	SW 1	SW 1	SW ◇1 🛒		SW	SW 1	SW ◇1 🛒	SW 1	SW	SW ◇1	SW 1	SW ◇1 🛒	SW		SW 1	SW ◇1 🛒	SW 1	SW	SW 1	SW 1	SW 1	SW ◇1 🛒
Basingstoke d	06 40			06 54	06 57				07 09				07 24	07 30							07 43		07 54	07 57
Hook d				07 01									07 31										08 01	
Winchfield d				07 05									07 35										08 05	
Fleet d				07 10									07 40								07 54		08 10	
Farnborough (Main) d				07 16									07 46								08 00		08 16	
Alton d								06 44									07 14							
Bentley d								06 51									07 21							
Farnham a								06 56									07 26							
d								06 58									07 28							
Aldershot d								07 04									07 34							
Ash Vale d								07 09									07 39							
Brookwood d				07 23				07 16					07 53				07 46						08 23	
Guildford d			07 02									07 34						07 47				08 02		
Worplesdon d										←		07 40							←					
Woking a	06 58		07 11	07 28	07 15			07 21	07 27	07 28		07 44	07 58	07 49			07 51	07 57	07 58		08 09	08 10	08 28	08 17
d	07 00	07 03	07 12	07 29	07 17			07 22	07 29	07 29	07 33	07 46	07 59	07 50			07 52	07 59	07 59	08 03	08 11	08 13	08 29	08 18
West Byfleet d		07 07		→				07 27			07 37		→				07 57			08 07			→	
Byfleet & New Haw d		07 10									07 40									08 10				
Weybridge d		07 13								07 36	07 43								08 06	08 13				
Walton-on-Thames d		07 17								07 40	07 47								08 10	08 17				
Hersham d		07 19									07 49									08 19				
Esher d		07 22					←				07 52				←					08 22				
Surbiton 5 a		07 26					07 26	07 37		07 46	07 56				07 56		08 07		08 16	08 26				
Wimbledon 5 ⊖ a		→					07 34				→				08 04					→				
Earlsfield a							07 38								08 08									
Clapham Junction 10 a			07 31		07 38		07 42	07 50		07 57		08 05			08 12						08 30	08 33		08 37
Vauxhall ⊖ a							07 47								08 17									
London Waterloo 15 ⊖ a	07 29		07 40		07 49		07 52	07 58	07 53	08 05		08 13		08 19	08 22		08 27	08 23	08 34		08 39	08 42		08 49

A until 6 October

B from 13 October

Table T155-R

Saturdays
26 May to 8 December

Basingstoke, Alton, Guildford and Woking - Waterloo

	SW	SW 1	SW ◇1 🛒	SW ◇1 🛒	SW 1	SW	SW 1		SW ◇1	SW ◇1	SW ◇1 🛒	SW 1	SW	SW 1	SW ◇1 🛒	SW ◇1	SW ◇1		SW	SW 1	SW 1	SW ◇1 🛒	SW ◇1 🛒	SW
Basingstoke d							08 17			08 24	08 30	08 36				08 43					08 54	08 57		
Hook d										08 31											09 01			
Winchfield d										08 35											09 05			
Fleet d										08 40						08 54					09 10			
Farnborough (Main) d							08 30			08 46						09 00					09 16			
Alton d		07 44												08 14										
Bentley d		07 51												08 21										
Farnham a		07 56												08 26										
d		07 58												08 28										
Aldershot d		08 04												08 34										
Ash Vale d		08 09												08 39										
Brookwood d		08 16								08 53				08 46							09 23			
Guildford d				08 17					08 34						08 47					09 02				
Worplesdon d					←				08 40								←							
Woking a		08 21		08 26	08 28		08 39		08 44	08 58	08 49			08 51	08 57		08 58			09 11	09 28	09 15		
d		08 22	08 23	08 27	08 29	08 33	08 41		08 46	08 59	08 50			08 52	08 59		08 59		09 03	09 12	09 29	09 17	09 21	
West Byfleet d		08 27				08 37				→				08 57					09 07		→			
Byfleet & New Haw d						08 40													09 10					
Weybridge d					08 36	08 43											09 06		09 13					
Walton-on-Thames d					08 40	08 47											09 10		09 17					
Hersham d						08 49													09 19					
Esher d	←					08 52							←						09 22					←
Surbiton 5 a	08 26	08 37			08 46	08 56							08 56	09 07			09 16		09 26					09 26
Wimbledon 5 ⊖ a	08 34					→							09 04						→					09 34
Earlsfield a	08 38												09 08											09 38
Clapham Junction 10 a	08 42	08 49			08 57				09 05			09 11	09 12			09 25				09 31		09 36		09 42
Vauxhall ⊖ a	08 47												09 17											09 47
London Waterloo 15 ⊖ a	08 52	08 57	08 49	08 51	09 05		09 08		09 13		09 19	09 20	09 22	09 27	09 23	09 34	09 36			09 41		09 49	09 49	09 52

	SW 1	SW ◇1 🛒	SW 1		SW	SW 1	SW ◇1	SW 1	SW ◇1 🛒	SW ◇1 🛒	SW	SW 1	SW ◇1 🛒		SW ◇1	SW 1	SW	SW 1	SW 1	SW ◇1 🛒	SW ◇1 🛒	SW	SW 1	
Basingstoke d						09 17		09 24	09 30	09 35					09 43				09 54	09 57				
Hook d								09 31											10 01					
Winchfield d								09 35											10 05					
Fleet d								09 40							09 54				10 10					
Farnborough (Main) d						09 30		09 46							10 00				10 16					
Alton d	08 44											09 14											09 44	
Bentley d	08 51											09 21											09 51	
Farnham a	08 56											09 26											09 56	
d	08 58											09 28											09 58	
Aldershot d	09 04											09 34											10 04	
Ash Vale d	09 09											09 39											10 09	
Brookwood d	09 16							09 53				09 46							10 23				10 16	
Guildford d		09 17					09 34						09 47					10 02						
Worplesdon d			←				09 40									←								
Woking a	09 21	09 25	09 28			09 39	09 44	09 58	09 49			09 51	09 57			09 58		10 11	10 28	10 15			10 21	
d	09 22	09 26	09 29		09 33	09 41	09 46	09 59	09 50			09 52	09 59			09 59	10 03	10 12	10 29	10 17	10 21		10 22	
West Byfleet d	09 27				09 37			→				09 57					10 07		→				10 27	
Byfleet & New Haw d					09 40												10 10							
Weybridge d			09 36		09 43											10 06	10 13							
Walton-on-Thames d			09 40		09 47											10 10	10 17							
Hersham d					09 49												10 19							
Esher d					09 52						←						10 22					←		
Surbiton 5 a	09 37		09 46		09 56						09 56	10 07				10 16	10 26					10 26	10 37	
Wimbledon 5 ⊖ a					→						10 04						→					10 34		
Earlsfield a											10 08											10 38		
Clapham Junction 10 a	09 48		09 57				10 05			10 11	10 12				10 25			10 31		10 36		10 42	10 48	
Vauxhall ⊖ a											10 17											10 47		
London Waterloo 15 ⊖ a	09 57	09 51	10 05			10 08	10 13		10 19	10 21	10 22	10 29	10 23		10 34	10 36		10 40		10 49	10 49	10 52	10 57	

	SW ◇1 🛒	SW 1	SW	SW 1	SW ◇1	SW 1	SW ◇1 🛒	SW ◇1 🛒	SW		SW 1	SW ◇1 🛒	SW ◇1	SW 1	SW	SW 1	SW 1	SW ◇1 🛒	SW ◇1 🛒		SW	SW 1	SW ◇1 🛒	SW 1
Basingstoke d				10 17		10 24	10 30	10 35					10 43				10 54	10 57						
Hook d						10 31											11 01							
Winchfield d						10 35											11 05							
Fleet d						10 40							10 54				11 10							
Farnborough (Main) d				10 30		10 46							11 00				11 16							
Alton d											10 14											10 44		
Bentley d											10 21											10 51		
Farnham a											10 26											10 56		
d											10 28											10 58		
Aldershot d											10 34											11 04		
Ash Vale d											10 39											11 09		
Brookwood d						10 53					10 46						11 23					11 16		
Guildford d	10 17				10 34							10 47				11 02							11 17	
Worplesdon d		←			10 40									←										←
Woking a	10 25	10 28		10 39	10 44	10 58	10 49				10 51	10 57		10 58		11 11	11 28	11 15				11 21	11 25	11 28
d	10 26	10 29	10 33	10 41	10 46	10 59	10 50				10 52	10 59		10 59	11 03	11 12	11 29	11 17	11 21			11 22	11 26	11 29
West Byfleet d			10 37			→					10 57				11 07		→					11 27		
Byfleet & New Haw d			10 40												11 10									
Weybridge d		10 36	10 43											11 06	11 13									11 36
Walton-on-Thames d		10 40	10 47											11 10	11 17									11 40
Hersham d			10 49												11 19									
Esher d			10 52						←						11 22						←			
Surbiton 5 a		10 46	10 56						10 56		11 07			11 16	11 26						11 26	11 37		11 46
Wimbledon 5 ⊖ a			→						11 04						→						11 34			
Earlsfield a									11 08												11 38			
Clapham Junction 10 a		10 57			11 05			11 11	11 12				11 25			11 31		11 36			11 42	11 48		11 57
Vauxhall ⊖ a									11 17												11 47			
London Waterloo 15 ⊖ a	10 51	11 05		11 08	11 13		11 19	11 20	11 22		11 27	11 23	11 34	11 36		11 40		11 49	11 49		11 52	11 58	11 51	12 09

Table T155-R

Saturdays

26 May to 8 December

Basingstoke, Alton, Guildford and Woking - Waterloo

		SW	SW ■	SW ◇■	SW ■	SW ◇■ 🛒		SW ◇■ 🛒	SW	SW ■	SW ◇■ 🛒	SW ◇■	SW ■	SW	SW ■	SW ■		SW ◇■ 🛒	SW ◇■ 🛒	SW	SW ■	SW ◇■ 🛒	SW ■	SW	SW ■
Basingstoke	d		11 17		11 24	11 30		11 35				11 43				11 54		11 57							12 17
Hook	d				11 31											12 01									
Winchfield	d				11 35											12 05									
Fleet	d				11 40							11 54				12 10									
Farnborough (Main)	d		11 31		11 46							12 00				12 16									12 30
Alton	d									11 15											11 44				
Bentley	d																				11 51				
Farnham	a									11 25											11 56				
Farnham	d									11 28											11 58				
Aldershot	d									11 34											12 04				
Ash Vale	d									11 39											12 09				
Brookwood	d				11 53					11 46						12 23					12 16				
Guildford	d			11 34							11 47				12 02							12 17			
Worplesdon	d			11 40									←										←		
Woking	a		11 40	11 44	11 58	11 49				11 51	11 57		11 58		12 11	12 28		12 15			12 21	12 26	12 28		12 39
Woking	d	11 33	11 41	11 46	11 59	11 50				11 52	11 59		11 59	12 03	12 12	12 29		12 17	12 21		12 22	12 27	12 29	12 33	12 41
West Byfleet	d	11 37			→					11 57				12 07		→					12 27			12 37	
Byfleet & New Haw	d	11 40												12 10										12 40	
Weybridge	d	11 43											12 06	12 13									12 36	12 43	
Walton-on-Thames	d	11 47											12 10	12 17									12 40	12 47	
Hersham	d	11 49												12 19										12 49	
Esher	d	11 52							←					12 22						←				12 52	
Surbiton ■	a	11 56							11 56	12 07			12 16	12 26						12 26	12 37		12 46	12 56	
Wimbledon ■ ⊖	a	→							12 04					→						12 34				→	
Earlsfield	a								12 08											12 38					
Clapham Junction ■	a			12 05				12 11	12 12			12 25			12 31			12 36		12 42	12 49		12 57		
Vauxhall ⊖	a								12 17											12 47					
London Waterloo ■ ⊖	a		12 11	12 13		12 19		12 21	12 22	12 29	12 27	12 34	12 38		12 43			12 49	12 51	12 52	12 59	12 57	13 09		13 11

		SW ◇■		SW ■	SW ◇■ 🛒	SW ◇■ 🛒	SW	SW ■	SW ◇■ 🛒	SW ◇■	SW ■	SW		SW ■	SW ■	SW ◇■ 🛒	SW ◇■ 🛒	SW	SW ■	SW ◇■ 🛒	SW ■	SW		SW ■	SW ◇■
Basingstoke	d			12 24	12 30	12 35				12 43					12 54	12 57								13 17	
Hook	d			12 31											13 01										
Winchfield	d			12 35											13 05										
Fleet	d			12 40						12 54					13 10										
Farnborough (Main)	d			12 46						13 00					13 16									13 30	
Alton	d							12 15											12 44						
Bentley	d																		12 51						
Farnham	a							12 25											12 56						
Farnham	d							12 28											12 58						
Aldershot	d							12 34											13 04						
Ash Vale	d							12 39											13 09						
Brookwood	d			12 53				12 46							13 23				13 16						
Guildford	d	12 34							12 47					13 02						13 17					13 34
Worplesdon	d	12 40									←										←				13 40
Woking	a	12 44		12 58	12 49			12 51	12 57		12 58			13 11	13 28	13 15			13 21	13 25	13 28			13 39	13 44
Woking	d	12 46		12 59	12 50			12 52	12 59		12 59	13 03		13 12	13 29	13 17	13 21		13 22	13 26	13 29	13 33		13 41	13 46
West Byfleet	d			→				12 57				13 07			→				13 27			13 37			
Byfleet & New Haw	d											13 10										13 40			
Weybridge	d										13 06	13 13									13 36	13 43			
Walton-on-Thames	d										13 10	13 17									13 40	13 47			
Hersham	d											13 19										13 49			
Esher	d						←					13 22						←				13 52			
Surbiton ■	a						12 56	13 07			13 16	13 26						13 26	13 37		13 46	13 56			
Wimbledon ■ ⊖	a						13 04					→						13 34				→			
Earlsfield	a						13 08											13 38							
Clapham Junction ■	a	13 05				13 11	13 12			13 25				13 31		13 36		13 42	13 48		13 57				14 05
Vauxhall ⊖	a						13 17											13 47							
London Waterloo ■ ⊖	a	13 13			13 19	13 21	13 22	13 29	13 27	13 34	13 38			13 43		13 49	13 51	13 52	13 59	13 57	14 08			14 11	14 14

		SW ■	SW ◇■ 🛒	SW ◇■ 🛒	SW	SW ■	SW ◇■ 🛒	SW ◇■		SW ■	SW	SW ■	SW ■	SW ◇■ 🛒	SW ◇■ 🛒	SW	SW ■	SW ◇■ 🛒		SW ■	SW	SW ■	SW ◇■	SW ■	SW ◇■ 🛒
Basingstoke	d	13 24	13 30	13 35				13 43					13 54	13 57								14 17		14 24	14 30
Hook	d	13 31											14 01											14 31	
Winchfield	d	13 35											14 05											14 35	
Fleet	d	13 40						13 54					14 10											14 40	
Farnborough (Main)	d	13 46						14 00					14 16									14 30		14 46	
Alton	d					13 15											13 44								
Bentley	d																13 51								
Farnham	a					13 25											13 56								
Farnham	d					13 28											13 58								
Aldershot	d					13 34											14 04								
Ash Vale	d					13 39											14 09								
Brookwood	d	13 53				13 46							14 23				14 16							14 53	
Guildford	d						13 47					14 02						14 17					14 34		
Worplesdon	d									←										←			14 40		
Woking	a	13 58	13 49			13 51	13 57			13 58		14 11	14 28	14 15			14 21	14 25		14 28		14 39	14 44	14 58	14 49
Woking	d	13 59	13 50			13 52	13 59			13 59	14 03	14 12	14 29	14 17	14 21		14 22	14 26		14 29	14 33	14 41	14 46	14 59	14 50
West Byfleet	d	→				13 57					14 07		→				14 27				14 37			→	
Byfleet & New Haw	d										14 10										14 40				
Weybridge	d									14 06	14 13									14 36	14 43				
Walton-on-Thames	d									14 10	14 17									14 40	14 47				
Hersham	d										14 19										14 49				
Esher	d				←						14 22					←					14 52				
Surbiton ■	a				13 56	14 07				14 16	14 26					14 26	14 37			14 46	14 56				
Wimbledon ■ ⊖	a				14 04						→					14 34					→				
Earlsfield	a				14 08											14 38									
Clapham Junction ■	a			14 11	14 12			14 25				14 31		14 36		14 42	14 48			14 57			15 05		
Vauxhall ⊖	a				14 17											14 47									
London Waterloo ■ ⊖	a		14 19	14 24	14 22	14 29	14 27	14 34		14 38		14 41		14 49	14 51	14 52	14 59	14 57		15 08		15 11	15 14		15 19

Table T155-R

Saturdays

26 May to 8 December

Basingstoke, Alton, Guildford and Woking - Waterloo

		SW ◇■ 🛒	SW	SW ■		SW ◇■ 🛒	SW ◇■	SW ■	SW	SW ■	SW ■	SW ◇■ 🛒	SW ◇■ 🛒	SW		SW ■	SW ◇■ 🛒	SW ■	SW	SW ■	SW ◇■	SW ■	SW ◇■ 🛒	SW ◇■ 🛒	
Basingstoke	d	14 35					14 43				14 54	14 57								15 17		15 24	15 30	15 35	
Hook	d										15 01											15 31			
Winchfield	d										15 05											15 35			
Fleet	d						14 54				15 10											15 40			
Farnborough (Main)	d						15 00				15 16									15 30		15 46			
Alton	d			14 15												14 44									
Bentley	d															14 51									
Farnham	a			14 25												14 56									
Farnham	d			14 28												14 58									
Aldershot	d			14 34												15 04									
Ash Vale	d			14 39												15 09									
Brookwood	d			14 46							15 23					15 16						15 53			
Guildford	d					14 47				15 02							15 17				15 34				
Worplesdon	d							←										←			15 40				
Woking	a			14 51		14 57		14 58		15 11	15 28	15 15				15 21	15 25	15 28		15 39	15 44	15 58	15 49		
Woking	d			14 52		14 59		14 59	15 03	15 12	15 29	15 17	15 21			15 22	15 26	15 29	15 33	15 41	15 46	15 59	15 50		
West Byfleet	d			14 57					15 07		→					15 27			15 37			→			
Byfleet & New Haw	d								15 10										15 40						
Weybridge	d							15 06	15 13									15 36	15 43						
Walton-on-Thames	d							15 10	15 17									15 40	15 47						
Hersham	d								15 19										15 49						
Esher	d		←						15 22					←					15 52						
Surbiton ■	a		14 56	15 07				15 16	15 26					15 26		15 37		15 46	15 56						
Wimbledon ■ ⊖	a		15 04						→					15 34					→						
Earlsfield	a		15 08											15 38											
Clapham Junction ■	a	15 11	15 12				15 25			15 31		15 36		15 42		15 48		15 57			16 05			16 11	
Vauxhall ⊖	a		15 17											15 47											
London Waterloo ■ ⊖	a	15 21	15 22	15 29		15 27	15 34	15 38		15 41		15 49	15 51	15 52		15 59	15 57	16 05		16 07	16 13		16 19	16 20	

		SW	SW ■	SW ◇■ 🛒	SW ◇■	SW ■	SW	SW ■	SW ■	SW ◇■ 🛒		SW ◇■ 🛒	SW	SW ■	SW ◇■ 🛒	SW ■	SW	SW ■	SW ◇■	SW ■		SW ◇■ 🛒	SW ◇■ 🛒	SW	SW ■
Basingstoke	d				15 43				15 54	15 57								16 17		16 24		16 30	16 35		
Hook	d								16 01											16 31					
Winchfield	d								16 05											16 35					
Fleet	d				15 54				16 10											16 40					
Farnborough (Main)	d				16 00				16 16									16 30		16 46					
Alton	d		15 15											15 44											16 15
Bentley	d													15 51											
Farnham	a		15 25											15 56											16 25
Farnham	d		15 28											15 58											16 28
Aldershot	d		15 34											16 04											16 34
Ash Vale	d		15 39											16 09											16 39
Brookwood	d		15 46						16 23					16 16						16 53					16 46
Guildford	d			15 47				16 02							16 17				16 34						
Worplesdon	d					←										←			16 40						
Woking	a		15 51	15 57		15 58		16 11	16 28	16 15				16 21	16 25	16 28		16 39	16 44	16 58		16 49			16 51
Woking	d		15 52	15 59		15 59	16 03	16 12	16 29	16 17		16 21		16 22	16 26	16 29	16 33	16 41	16 46	16 59		16 50			16 52
West Byfleet	d		15 57				16 07		→					16 27			16 37			→					16 57
Byfleet & New Haw	d						16 10										16 40								
Weybridge	d					16 06	16 13									16 36	16 43								
Walton-on-Thames	d					16 10	16 17									16 40	16 47								
Hersham	d						16 19										16 49								
Esher	d	←					16 22						←				16 52							←	
Surbiton ■	a	15 56	16 07			16 16	16 26						16 26	16 37		16 46	16 56							16 56	17 07
Wimbledon ■ ⊖	a	16 04					→						16 34				→							17 04	
Earlsfield	a	16 08											16 38											17 08	
Clapham Junction ■	a	16 12			16 25			16 31		16 36			16 42	16 48		16 57			17 05				17 11	17 12	
Vauxhall ⊖	a	16 17											16 47											17 17	
London Waterloo ■ ⊖	a	16 22	16 29	16 23	16 34	16 36		16 40		16 49		16 49	16 52	16 57	16 51	17 05		17 07	17 13			17 19	17 20	17 22	17 27

		SW ◇■ 🛒	SW ◇■	SW ■	SW	SW ■		SW ■	SW ◇■ 🛒	SW ◇■ 🛒	SW	SW ■	SW ◇■ 🛒	SW ■	SW	SW ■		SW ◇■	SW ■	SW ◇■ 🛒	SW ◇■ 🛒	SW	SW ■	SW ◇■ 🛒	SW ◇■
Basingstoke	d		16 43					16 54	16 57							17 17			17 24	17 30	17 35				17 43
Hook	d							17 01											17 31						
Winchfield	d							17 05											17 35						
Fleet	d		16 54					17 10											17 40						17 54
Farnborough (Main)	d		17 00					17 16								17 30			17 46						18 00
Alton	d											16 44											17 15		
Bentley	d											16 51													
Farnham	a											16 56											17 25		
Farnham	d											16 58											17 28		
Aldershot	d											17 04											17 34		
Ash Vale	d											17 09											17 39		
Brookwood	d							17 23				17 16							17 53				17 46		
Guildford	d	16 47				17 02							17 17					17 34						17 47	
Worplesdon	d			←										←				17 40							
Woking	a	16 57		16 58		17 11		17 28	17 15			17 21	17 25	17 28		17 39		17 44	17 58	17 49			17 51	17 57	
Woking	d	16 59		16 59	17 03	17 12		17 29	17 17	17 21		17 22	17 26	17 29	17 33	17 41		17 46	17 59	17 50			17 52	17 59	
West Byfleet	d				17 07			→				17 27			17 37				→				17 57		
Byfleet & New Haw	d				17 10										17 40										
Weybridge	d			17 06	17 13									17 36	17 43										
Walton-on-Thames	d			17 10	17 17									17 40	17 47										
Hersham	d				17 19										17 49										
Esher	d				17 22						←				17 52							←			
Surbiton ■	a			17 16	17 26						17 26	17 37		17 46	17 56							17 56	18 07		
Wimbledon ■ ⊖	a				→						17 34				→							18 04			
Earlsfield	a										17 38											18 08			
Clapham Junction ■	a		17 25			17 31			17 36		17 42	17 48		17 57				18 05			18 11	18 12			18 25
Vauxhall ⊖	a										17 47											18 17			
London Waterloo ■ ⊖	a	17 23	17 34	17 36		17 40			17 49	17 49	17 52	17 57	17 51	18 05		18 07		18 13		18 19	18 21	18 22	18 28	18 23	18 34

Table T155-R

Saturdays

26 May to 8 December

Basingstoke, Alton, Guildford and Woking - Waterloo

		SW 1		SW	SW 1	SW 1	SW ◇1 ⌶	SW ◇1 ⌶	SW	SW 1	SW ◇1	SW 1		SW	SW 1	SW ◇1	SW 1	SW ◇1 ⌶	SW ◇1 ⌶	SW	SW 1	SW ◇1 ⌶		SW ◇1	SW 1
Basingstoke	d					17 54	17 57								18 17		18 24	18 30	18 35					18 43	
Hook	d					18 01											18 31								
Winchfield	d					18 05											18 35								
Fleet	d					18 10											18 40							18 54	
Farnborough (Main)	d					18 16									18 30		18 46							19 00	
Alton	d									17 44											18 15				
Bentley	d									17 51															
Farnham	a									17 56											18 25				
	d									17 58											18 28				
Aldershot	d									18 04											18 34				
Ash Vale	d									18 09											18 39				
Brookwood	d					18 23				18 16							18 53				18 46				
Guildford	d				18 02						18 17					18 34						18 49			
Worplesdon	d	←										←				18 40									←
Woking	a	17 58			18 11	18 28	18 15			18 21	18 25	18 28			18 39	18 44	18 58	18 49			18 51	18 57			18 58
	d	17 59		18 03	18 12	18 29	18 17	18 21		18 22	18 26	18 29		18 33	18 41	18 46	18 59	18 50			18 52	18 59			18 59
West Byfleet	d			18 07		→				18 27				18 37			→				18 57				
Byfleet & New Haw	d			18 10										18 40											
Weybridge	d	18 06		18 13								18 36		18 43											19 06
Walton-on-Thames	d	18 10		18 17								18 40		18 47											19 10
Hersham	d			18 19										18 49											
Esher	d			18 22					←					18 52						←					
Surbiton	a	18 16		18 26					18 26	18 37		18 46		18 56						18 56	19 07				19 16
Wimbledon ⊖	a			→					18 34					→						19 04					
Earlsfield	a								18 38											19 08					
Clapham Junction	a				18 31		18 36		18 42	18 48		18 57				19 05			19 11	19 12				19 25	
Vauxhall ⊖	a								18 47											19 17					
London Waterloo ⊖	a	18 36			18 40		18 49	18 49	18 52	18 57	18 51	19 05			19 07	19 13		19 19	19 20	19 22	19 27	19 23		19 34	19 36

		SW	SW 1	SW 1	SW ◇1 ⌶	SW ◇1 ⌶	SW	SW 1		SW ◇1	SW 1	SW	SW 1	SW ◇1	SW 1	SW ◇1	SW ◇1	SW		SW 1	SW ◇1	SW ◇1	SW 1	SW	SW 1
Basingstoke	d			18 54	18 57								19 17		19 24	19 30	19 35					19 43			
Hook	d			19 01											19 31										
Winchfield	d			19 05											19 35										
Fleet	d			19 10											19 40							19 54			
Farnborough (Main)	d			19 16									19 30		19 46							20 00			
Alton	d							18 44												19 15					
Bentley	d							18 51																	
Farnham	a							18 56												19 25					
	d							18 58												19 28					
Aldershot	d							19 04												19 34					
Ash Vale	d							19 09												19 39					
Brookwood	d			19 23				19 16							19 53					19 46					
Guildford	d		19 02							19 17				19 34							19 47				20 02
Worplesdon	d										←			19 40									←		
Woking	a		19 11	19 28	19 15			19 21		19 25	19 28		19 39	19 44	19 58	19 49				19 51	19 57		19 58		20 11
	d	19 03	19 12	19 29	19 17	19 21		19 22		19 26	19 29	19 33	19 41	19 46	19 59	19 50				19 52	19 59		19 59	20 03	20 12
West Byfleet	d	19 07		→				19 27				19 37			→					19 57				20 07	
Byfleet & New Haw	d	19 10										19 40												20 10	
Weybridge	d	19 13									19 36	19 43											20 06	20 13	
Walton-on-Thames	d	19 17									19 40	19 47											20 10	20 17	
Hersham	d	19 19										19 49												20 19	
Esher	d	19 22					←					19 52						←						20 22	
Surbiton	a	19 26					19 26	19 37			19 46	19 56						19 56		20 07			20 16	20 26	
Wimbledon ⊖	a	→					19 34					→						20 04						→	
Earlsfield	a						19 38											20 08							
Clapham Junction	a		19 31		19 36		19 42	19 48			19 57			20 05			20 11	20 12				20 25			20 31
Vauxhall ⊖	a						19 47											20 17							
London Waterloo ⊖	a		19 40		19 49	19 49	19 52	19 57		19 51	20 05		20 07	20 13		20 19	20 20	20 22		20 28	20 23	20 34	20 38		20 40

		SW ◇1 ⌶	SW	SW 1		SW ◇1	SW 1	SW ◇1 ⌶	SW 1	SW	SW 1	SW 1	SW ◇1	SW 1		SW ◇1 ⌶	SW ◇1	SW	SW ◇1	SW ◇1 ⌶	SW	SW 1	SW ◇1	SW 1
Basingstoke	d						19 54	20 09			20 17			20 24		20 35			20 43					20 54
Hook	d						20 01							20 31										21 01
Winchfield	d						20 05							20 35										21 05
Fleet	d						20 10							20 40					20 54					21 10
Farnborough (Main)	d						20 16				20 30			20 46					21 00					21 16
Alton	d			19 44								20 15										20 44		
Bentley	d			19 51																		20 51		
Farnham	a			19 56								20 25										20 56		
	d			19 58								20 28										20 58		
Aldershot	d			20 04								20 34										21 04		
Ash Vale	d			20 09								20 39										21 09		
Brookwood	d			20 16			20 23					20 46		20 53								21 16		21 23
Guildford	d					20 17							20 39				20 49						21 17	
Worplesdon	d												20 44											
Woking	a			20 21		20 25	20 28	20 29			20 39	20 51	20 52	20 58			20 59		21 09			21 21	21 25	21 28
	d	20 21		20 22		20 26	20 29	20 30		20 33	20 41	20 52	20 53	20 59			21 01	21 03	21 10	21 21		21 22	21 26	21 29
West Byfleet	d			20 27						20 37		20 57						21 07				21 27		
Byfleet & New Haw	d									20 40								21 10						
Weybridge	d						20 36			20 43				21 06				21 13						21 36
Walton-on-Thames	d						20 40			20 47				21 10				21 17						21 40
Hersham	d									20 49								21 19						
Esher	d		←						←	20 52								21 22			←			
Surbiton	a		20 26	20 37			20 46		20 46	20 56		21 07		21 16				21 26			21 26	21 37		21 46
Wimbledon ⊖	a		20 34				→			21 05								→			21 34			→
Earlsfield	a		20 38							21 08											21 38			
Clapham Junction	a		20 42	20 48				20 52	20 57	21 12			21 12			21 16			21 29		21 42	21 48		
Vauxhall ⊖	a		20 47							21 17											21 47			
London Waterloo ⊖	a	20 45	20 52	20 57		20 50		21 04	21 06	21 23	21 08	21 29	21 21	21 34		21 24	21 27		21 38	21 49	21 52	21 57	21 51	

Table T155-R

Saturdays

26 May to 8 December

Basingstoke, Alton, Guildford and Woking - Waterloo

		SW ◇1 ⌶	SW 1	SW	SW ◇1	SW	SW 1	SW ◇1	SW 1	SW		SW ◇1 ⌶	SW ◇1	SW 1	SW	SW 1	SW 1	SW ◇1	SW 1	SW 1		SW	SW ◇1	SW	SW 1
Basingstoke	d	21 09							21 24			21 35	21 43				21 54	22 09							
Hook	d								21 31								22 01								
Winchfield	d								21 35								22 05								
Fleet	d								21 40				21 54				22 10								
Farnborough (Main)	d								21 46				22 00				22 16								
Alton	d						21 15									21 44									22 15
Bentley	d															21 51									
Farnham	a						21 25									21 56									22 25
	d						21 28									21 58									22 28
Aldershot	d						21 34									22 04									22 34
Ash Vale	d						21 39									22 09									22 39
Brookwood	d						21 46		21 53							22 16	22 23								22 46
Guildford	d				21 39			21 49														22 20	22 39		
Worplesdon	d				21 44																		22 44		
Woking	a	21 29			21 49		21 51	21 57	21 58				22 09			22 21	22 28	22 28				22 32	22 49		22 51
	d	21 30		21 33	21 50		21 52	21 59	21 59	22 03			22 10	22 21		22 22	22 29	22 29				22 33	22 50		22 52
West Byfleet	d			21 37			21 57			22 07						22 27						22 37			22 57
Byfleet & New Haw	d			21 40						22 10												22 40			
Weybridge	d			21 43					22 06	22 13							22 36					22 43			
Walton-on-Thames	d			21 47					22 10	22 17							22 40					22 47			
Hersham	d			21 49						22 19												22 49			
Esher	d		←	21 52		←				22 22					←				←	←		22 52		←	
Surbiton	a		21 46	21 56		21 56	22 07		22 16	22 27					22 27	22 37	22 46		22 37	22 46		22 56		22 56	23 07
Wimbledon ⊖	a			→		22 04				→					22 34	→	→					→		23 04	
Earlsfield	a					22 08									22 38									23 08	
Clapham Junction	a	21 52	21 57		22 09	22 12						22 14	22 29		22 42			22 48	22 52	22 57			23 09	23 12	
Vauxhall ⊖	a					22 17									22 47									23 17	
London Waterloo ⊖	a	22 04	22 07		22 18	22 22	22 27	22 27	22 34			22 22	22 38	22 49	22 52			22 57	23 01	23 05			23 19	23 22	23 28

		SW 1	SW ◇1	SW 1	SW	SW 1		SW	SW 1	SW 1	SW 1	SW 1	SW ◇1	SW 1	SW 1	SW 1
Basingstoke	d	22 24	22 35			22 43				22 54	23 14				23 44	
Hook	d	22 31								23 01					23 51	
Winchfield	d	22 35								23 05					23 55	
Fleet	d	22 40				22 54				23 10					00 01	
Farnborough (Main)	d	22 46				23 00				23 16					00 06	
Alton	d								22 44					23 15		23 46
Bentley	d								22 51							23 53
Farnham	a								22 56					23 25		23 58
	d								22 58					23 28		
Aldershot	d								23 04					23 34		
Ash Vale	d								23 09					23 39		
Brookwood	d	22 53							23 16	23 23				23 46	00 13	
Guildford	d				22 55								23 39			
Worplesdon	d			←									23 44			
Woking	a	22 58	22 53	22 58	23 05	23 09			23 21	23 28	23 32		23 49	23 51	00 18	
	d	22 59	22 55	22 59	23 06	23 10			23 22	23 33	23 33		23 56		00 20	
West Byfleet	d	→			23 10				23 27	23 37					00 25	
Byfleet & New Haw	d				23 13					23 40						
Weybridge	d			23 06	23 16					23 43					00 29	
Walton-on-Thames	d			23 10	23 20					23 47					00 33	
Hersham	d				23 22					23 49						
Esher	d				23 25			←		23 52		←				
Surbiton	a			23 16	23 29			23 29	23 37	23 57		23 57	00 07		00 39	
Wimbledon ⊖	a				→			23 37		→		00 06	00 16		00 47	
Earlsfield	a							23 41								
Clapham Junction	a		23 14			23 29		23 44	23 48		23 52	00 21	00 22		00 53	
Vauxhall ⊖	a							23 49				00 30				
London Waterloo ⊖	a		23 22	23 32		23 39		23 54	00 01		00 03	00 35	00 32		01 04	

Basingstoke, Alton, Guildford and Woking - Waterloo

		SW ■ A	SW	SW	SW	SW ■ B		SW ■ C	SW ■ C	SW ◇■ 🛒	SW	SW	SW ■ C	SW ■ B	SW ■	SW		SW ◇■	SW	SW ◇■ 🛒	SW	SW	SW ◇■	SW	SW
Basingstoke	d					07 16		07 16		07 20					07 44					08 10					
Hook	d					07 23		07 23																	
Winchfield	d					07 27		07 27																	
Fleet	d	00 01				07 32		07 32																	
Farnborough (Main)	d	00 06				07 38		07 38																	
Alton	d																								
Bentley	d																								
Farnham	a																								
	d								07 30																
Aldershot	d								07 36																
Ash Vale	d								07 41																
Brookwood	d	00 13				07 45		07 45	07 48																
Guildford	d			06 57	07 27											07 57		08 05				08 27	08 35		
Worplesdon	d												←	←											
Woking	a	00 18		07 05	07 35	07 50		07 50	07 54	07 39			07 50	07 50	08 02	08 05		08 13		08 28		08 35	08 42		
	d	00 20	06 36	07 06	07 36	07 58		07 58		07 40		07 52	07 58	07 58	08 04	08 06		08 15		08 30		08 36	08 45		08 52
West Byfleet	d	00 25	06 40	07 10	07 40	→		→				07 56				08 10						08 40			08 56
Byfleet & New Haw	d		06 43	07 13	07 43							08 00				08 13						08 43			09 00
Weybridge	d	00 29	06 46	07 16	07 46											08 16						08 46			
Walton-on-Thames	d	00 33	06 50	07 20	07 50											08 20						08 50			
Hersham	d		06 52	07 22	07 52											08 22						08 52			
Esher	d		06 55	07 25	07 55						←					08 25			←			08 55		←	
Surbiton ■	a	00 39	06 59	07 29	07 59						07 59		08 09	08 09		08 30			08 30			08 59		08 59	
Wimbledon ■ ⊖	a	00 47	07 07	07 37	→						08 07		08 20	08 20		→			08 36			→		09 06	
Earlsfield	a		07 12	07 42							08 12								08 41		←			09 11	
Clapham Junction ■	a	00 53	07 15	07 45						08 05	08 15	09 01	08 27	08 27	08 31			08 39	08 44	08 57	09 01		09 06	09 14	10 01
Vauxhall ⊖	a		07 20	07 50							08 20	→							08 50		09 08			09 20	→
London Waterloo ■ ⊖	a	01 04	07 25	07 55						08 20	08 25		08 39	08 42	08 46			08 50	08 55	09 12	09 13		09 16	09 28	

		SW ■ B		SW ■	SW ■ C	SW ■ C	SW ■	SW	SW ◇■	SW	SW ◇■ 🛒	SW		SW	SW ◇■	SW	SW	SW ■	SW ■	SW ■	SW	SW ◇■		SW ◇■ 🛒	SW
Basingstoke	d	08 16			08 16		08 44				09 10							09 16		09 44				10 00	
Hook	d	08 23			08 23													09 23							
Winchfield	d	08 27			08 27													09 27							
Fleet	d	08 32			08 32													09 32							
Farnborough (Main)	d	08 38			08 38													09 38							
Alton	d			08 15		08 15													09 15						
Bentley	d			08 23		08 23													09 23						
Farnham	a			08 28		08 28													09 28						
	d			08 30		08 30													09 30						
Aldershot	d			08 36		08 36													09 36						
Ash Vale	d			08 41		08 41													09 41						
Brookwood	d	08 45		08 48	08 45	08 48												09 45	09 48						
Guildford	d							08 57	09 05					09 27	09 35						09 57	0 07			
Worplesdon	d																								
Woking	a	08 50		08 54	08 50	08 54	09 02	09 05	09 15		09 28			09 35	09 42			09 50	09 54	10 02	10 05	10 15		10 19	
	d	08 58			08 58		09 04	09 06	09 15		09 30			09 36	09 45		09 52	09 58		10 04	10 06	10 16		10 20	
West Byfleet	d							09 10						09 40			09 56				10 10				
Byfleet & New Haw	d							09 13						09 43			10 00				10 13				
Weybridge	d							09 16						09 46							10 16				
Walton-on-Thames	d							09 20						09 50							10 20				
Hersham	d							09 22						09 52							10 22				
Esher	d							09 25		←				09 55		←					10 25				←
Surbiton ■	a	09 09			09 09			09 30		09 30				09 59		09 59		10 09			10 29				10 29
Wimbledon ■ ⊖	a	09 19			09 19			→		09 37				→		10 07		10 17			→				10 37
Earlsfield	a									09 41		←				10 11									10 41
Clapham Junction ■	a	09 26			09 26		09 30		09 38	09 45	09 57	10 01			10 04	10 15	11 01	10 23		10 27		10 36		10 39	10 45
Vauxhall ⊖	a									09 50		10 08				10 20	→								10 50
London Waterloo ■ ⊖	a	09 42			09 39		09 41		09 48	09 55	10 11	10 13			10 14	10 25		10 34		10 39		10 46		10 50	10 55

A not 20 May **B** from 7 October **C** until 30 September

Table T155-R

Sundays
20 May to 2 December

Basingstoke, Alton, Guildford and Woking - Waterloo

		SW ◇■ 🛒	SW	SW	SW ◇■ 🛒		SW	SW	SW ■	SW ■	SW ■ 🛒	SW	SW ◇■	SW ◇■ 🛒	SW		SW ◇■ 🛒	SW	SW	SW ◇■ 🛒	SW	SW	SW ■	SW ■	SW ■ 🛒
Basingstoke	d	10 10							10 16		10 44			11 00			11 10						11 16		11 44
Hook	d								10 23														11 23		
Winchfield	d								10 27														11 27		
Fleet	d								10 32														11 32		
Farnborough (Main)	d								10 38														11 38		
Alton	d									10 15														11 15	
Bentley	d									10 23														11 23	
Farnham	a									10 28														11 28	
	d									10 30														11 30	
Aldershot	d									10 36														11 36	
Ash Vale	d									10 41														11 41	
Brookwood	d								10 45	10 48													11 45	11 48	
Guildford	d			10 27	10 35							10 57	11 06						11 27	11 35					
Worplesdon	d																								
Woking	a	10 28		10 35	10 42				10 50	10 54	11 02	11 05	11 13	11 18			11 28		11 35	11 42			11 50	11 54	12 02
	d	10 30		10 36	10 45			10 52	10 58		11 04	11 06	11 15	11 20			11 30		11 36	11 45		11 52	11 58		12 04
West Byfleet	d			10 40				10 56				11 10							11 40			11 56			
Byfleet & New Haw	d			10 43				11 00				11 13							11 43			12 00			
Weybridge	d			10 46								11 16							11 46						
Walton-on-Thames	d			10 50								11 20							11 50						
Hersham	d			10 52								11 22							11 52						
Esher	d			10 55			←					11 25			←				11 55		←				
Surbiton ■	a			10 59			10 59		11 09			11 29			11 29				11 59		11 59		12 09		
Wimbledon ■ ⊖	a			→			11 07		11 17			→			11 37				→		12 07		12 17		
Earlsfield	a		←				11 11								11 41			←			12 11				
Clapham Junction ■	a	10 49	11 01		11 04		11 15	12 01	11 23		11 27		11 34	11 39	11 45		11 49	12 01		12 04	12 15	13 01	12 23		12 27
Vauxhall ⊖	a		11 08				11 20	→							11 50			12 08			12 20	→			
London Waterloo ■ ⊖	a	11 04	11 13		11 14		11 25		11 34		11 39		11 49	11 50	11 55		12 04	12 13		12 14	12 25		12 34		12 37

			SW	SW ◇■	SW ◇■ 🛒	SW	SW ◇■ 🛒	SW	SW	SW ◇■ 🛒	SW		SW	SW ■	SW ■	SW ■ 🛒	SW	SW ◇■	SW ◇■ 🛒	SW	SW ◇■ 🛒		SW	SW	SW ◇■ 🛒
Basingstoke	d				12 00		12 10							12 16		12 44			13 00		13 10				
Hook	d													12 23											
Winchfield	d													12 27											
Fleet	d													12 32											
Farnborough (Main)	d													12 38											
Alton	d														12 15										
Bentley	d														12 23										
Farnham	a														12 28										
	d														12 30										
Aldershot	d														12 36										
Ash Vale	d														12 41										
Brookwood	d													12 45	12 48										
Guildford	d		11 57	12 06					12 27	12 35							12 57	13 05						13 27	13 35
Worplesdon	d																								
Woking	a		12 05	12 13	12 18		12 28		12 35	12 42				12 50	12 54	13 02	13 05	13 13	13 18		13 28			13 35	13 42
	d		12 06	12 15	12 20		12 30		12 36	12 45			12 52	12 58		13 04	13 06	13 15	13 20		13 30			13 36	13 45
West Byfleet	d		12 10						12 40				12 56				13 10							13 40	
Byfleet & New Haw	d		12 13						12 43				13 00				13 13							13 43	
Weybridge	d		12 16						12 46								13 16							13 46	
Walton-on-Thames	d		12 20						12 50								13 20							13 50	
Hersham	d		12 22						12 52								13 22							13 52	
Esher	d		12 25			←			12 55		←						13 25			←				13 55	
Surbiton ■	a		12 29			12 29			12 59		12 59			13 09			13 29			13 29				13 59	
Wimbledon ■ ⊖	a		→			12 37			→		13 07			13 17			→			13 37				→	
Earlsfield	a					12 41		←			13 11									13 41			←		
Clapham Junction ■	a			12 34	12 39	12 45	12 49	13 01		13 05	13 15		14 01	13 23		13 27		13 34	13 39	13 45	13 49		14 01		14 04
Vauxhall ⊖	a					12 50		13 08			13 20		→							13 50			14 08		
London Waterloo ■ ⊖	a			12 48	12 49	12 55	13 04	13 13		13 14	13 25			13 34		13 37		13 44	13 49	13 55	13 59		14 13		14 14

		SW	SW	SW ■	SW ■	SW ■ 🛒	SW		SW ◇■	SW ■	SW ◇■ 🛒	SW	SW ■	SW ■	SW ◇■ 🛒	SW ■	SW		SW	SW ◇■ 🛒	SW	SW	SW ■	SW ■	SW ■ 🛒
Basingstoke	d			13 16		13 44				13 50	14 00				14 10								14 16		14 44
Hook	d			13 23																			14 23		
Winchfield	d			13 27																			14 27		
Fleet	d			13 32						14 02													14 32		
Farnborough (Main)	d			13 38						14 08													14 38		
Alton	d				13 15									13 45										14 15	
Bentley	d				13 23																			14 23	
Farnham	a				13 28									13 55										14 28	
	d				13 30									14 00										14 30	
Aldershot	d				13 36									14 06										14 36	
Ash Vale	d				13 41									14 11										14 41	
Brookwood	d			13 45	13 48					14 15				14 18									14 45	14 48	
Guildford	d						13 57		14 05										14 27	14 35					
Worplesdon	d												←												
Woking	a			13 50	13 54	14 02	14 05		14 13	14 20	14 18		14 20	14 24	14 28				14 35	14 42			14 50	14 54	15 02
	d		13 52	13 58		14 04	14 06		14 15	14 28	14 20		14 28		14 30				14 36	14 45		14 52	14 58		15 04
West Byfleet	d		13 56				14 10			→									14 40			14 56			
Byfleet & New Haw	d		14 00				14 13												14 43			15 00			
Weybridge	d						14 16						14 34						14 46						
Walton-on-Thames	d						14 20						14 38						14 50						
Hersham	d						14 22												14 52						
Esher	d	←					14 25					←				←			14 55		←				
Surbiton ■	a	13 59		14 09			14 29					14 29	14 45			14 45			14 59		14 59		15 09		
Wimbledon ■ ⊖	a	14 07		14 17			→					14 37	→			14 53			→		15 07		15 17		
Earlsfield	a	14 11										14 41					←				15 11				
Clapham Junction ■	a	14 15	15 01	14 23		14 27			14 34		14 39	14 45			14 49	14 59	15 01			15 04	15 15	16 01	15 23		15 27
Vauxhall ⊖	a	14 20	→									14 50					15 08				15 20	→			
London Waterloo ■ ⊖	a	14 25		14 34		14 37			14 44		14 49	14 55			14 59	15 10	15 13			15 14	15 25		15 34		15 37

Table T155-R

Sundays
20 May to 2 December

Basingstoke, Alton, Guildford and Woking - Waterloo

		SW	SW ◇1	SW 1	SW 1	SW ◇1 ⚒	SW	SW 1	SW ◇1 ⚒	SW 1	SW 1	SW	SW	SW ◇1 ⚒	SW	SW	SW 1	SW 1	SW 1 ⚒	SW	SW ◇1
Basingstoke	d			14 50		15 00			15 10								15 16		15 44		
Hook	d																15 23				
Winchfield	d																15 27				
Fleet	d			15 02													15 32				
Farnborough (Main)	d			15 08													15 38				
Alton	d				14 45													15 15			
Bentley	d																	15 23			
Farnham	a				14 55													15 28			
	d				15 00													15 30			
Aldershot	d				15 06													15 36			
Ash Vale	d				15 11													15 41			
Brookwood	d			15 15	15 18												15 45	15 48			
Guildford	d	14 57	15 05										15 27	15 35						15 57	16 05
Worplesdon	d							←													
Woking	a	15 05	15 13	15 20	15 24	15 18		15 20	15 28				15 35	15 42			15 50	15 54	16 02	16 05	16 13
	d	15 06	15 15	15 28		15 20		15 28	15 30				15 36	15 45		15 52	15 58		16 04	16 06	16 15
West Byfleet	d	15 10		→									15 40			15 56				16 10	
Byfleet & New Haw	d	15 13											15 43			16 00				16 13	
Weybridge	d	15 16						15 34					15 46							16 16	
Walton-on-Thames	d	15 20						15 38					15 50							16 20	
Hersham	d	15 22											15 52							16 22	
Esher	d	15 25					←			←	←		15 55		←					16 25	
Surbiton	a	15 29					15 29	15 45		15 45	15 45		15 59		15 59		16 09			16 29	
Wimbledon ⊖	a	→					15 37	→		15 53	15 53		→		16 07		16 17			→	
Earlsfield	a						15 41					←			16 11						
Clapham Junction	a		15 34			15 39	15 45		15 49	15 59	15 59	16 01		16 04	16 15	17 01	16 23		16 27		16 34
Vauxhall ⊖	a						15 50					16 08			16 20	→					
London Waterloo ⊖	a		15 44			15 49	15 55		15 59	16 11	16 11	16 13		16 14	16 25		16 34		16 37		16 44

		SW 1	SW 1	SW ◇1 ⚒	SW	SW 1	SW ◇1 ⚒	SW 1	SW 1	SW	SW	SW ◇1 ⚒	SW	SW 1	SW 1	SW ◇1	SW	SW 1	SW	SW 1 ⚒	SW ◇1	SW 1	SW 1
Basingstoke	d	15 50		16 00			16 10							16 16		16 35				16 44		16 50	
Hook	d													16 23									
Winchfield	d													16 27									
Fleet	d	16 02												16 32								17 02	
Farnborough (Main)	d	16 08												16 38						16 58		17 08	
Alton	d		15 45												16 15								16 45
Bentley	d														16 23								
Farnham	a		15 55												16 28								16 55
	d		16 00												16 30								17 00
Aldershot	d		16 06												16 36								17 06
Ash Vale	d		16 11												16 41								17 11
Brookwood	d	16 15	16 18											16 45	16 48							17 15	17 18
Guildford	d										16 27	16 35							16 57		17 05		
Worplesdon	d					←												←					
Woking	a	16 20	16 24	16 18		16 20	16 28				16 35	16 42		16 50	16 54	16 53		16 50	17 05	17 07	17 13	17 20	17 24
	d	16 28		16 20		16 28	16 30				16 36	16 45	16 52	16 58		16 55		16 58	17 06	17 09	17 15	17 28	
West Byfleet	d	→									16 40		16 56	→					17 10			→	
Byfleet & New Haw	d										16 43		17 00						17 13				
Weybridge	d					16 34					16 46								17 16				
Walton-on-Thames	d					16 38					16 50								17 20				
Hersham	d										16 52								17 22				
Esher	d				←			←	←		16 55								17 25				
Surbiton	a				16 29	16 45		16 45	16 45		16 59							17 09	17 29				
Wimbledon ⊖	a				16 37	→		16 53	16 53		17 07							17 17	→				
Earlsfield	a				16 41					←	17 11						←						
Clapham Junction	a			16 39	16 45		16 49	16 59	16 59	17 01	17 15	17 04	18 01			17 14	17 15	17 23		17 28	17 34		
Vauxhall ⊖	a				16 50					17 08	→		→				17 20						
London Waterloo ⊖	a			16 49	16 55		16 59	17 10	17 10	17 13		17 14				17 24	17 25	17 34		17 39	17 44		

		SW ◇1 ⚒	SW	SW 1	SW ◇1 ⚒	SW 1	SW 1	SW	SW	SW ◇1 ⚒	SW 1	SW 1	SW ◇1	SW	SW ◇1 ⚒	SW	SW 1	SW	SW 1 ⚒	SW ◇1	SW 1	SW 1	SW ◇1 ⚒
Basingstoke	d	17 00			17 10						17 16		17 27		17 35				17 44		17 50		18 00
Hook	d										17 23												
Winchfield	d										17 27												
Fleet	d										17 32										18 02		
Farnborough (Main)	d										17 38								17 58		18 08		
Alton	d											17 15										17 45	
Bentley	d											17 23											
Farnham	a											17 28										17 55	
	d											17 30										18 00	
Aldershot	d											17 36										18 06	
Ash Vale	d											17 41										18 11	
Brookwood	d										17 45	17 48									18 15	18 18	
Guildford	d								17 27	17 35								17 57		18 05			
Worplesdon	d			←													←						
Woking	a	17 18		17 20	17 28				17 35	17 42	17 50	17 54	17 48		17 53		17 50	18 05	18 07	18 13	18 20	18 24	18 18
	d	17 20		17 28	17 30				17 36	17 45	17 58		17 49	17 52	17 55		17 58	18 06	18 09	18 15	18 28		18 20
West Byfleet	d								17 40		→			17 56				18 10			→		
Byfleet & New Haw	d								17 43					18 00				18 13					
Weybridge	d			17 34					17 46									18 16					
Walton-on-Thames	d			17 38					17 50									18 20					
Hersham	d								17 52									18 22					
Esher	d		←			←	←		17 55									18 25					
Surbiton	a		17 29	17 45		17 45	17 45		17 59								18 09	18 29					
Wimbledon ⊖	a		17 37	→		17 53	17 53		18 07								18 17	→					
Earlsfield	a		17 41					←	18 11							←							
Clapham Junction	a	17 39	17 45		17 49	17 59	17 59	18 01	18 15	18 04			18 08	19 01	18 14	18 15	18 23		18 28	18 34			18 39
Vauxhall ⊖	a		17 50					18 08	→					→		18 20							
London Waterloo ⊖	a	17 49	17 55		17 59	18 10	18 10	18 13		18 14			18 19		18 24	18 25	18 34		18 39	18 44			18 49

Please check the 'Additional Notes to Individual Tables' section for any other general notes that apply to this Table

Table T155-R

Sundays
20 May to 2 December

Basingstoke, Alton, Guildford and Woking - Waterloo

		SW	SW 1	SW ◇1 ⚒	SW 1	SW 1	SW	SW	SW ◇1 ⚒	SW 1	SW 1	SW ◇1	SW	SW ◇1	SW	SW 1	SW	SW 1	SW ◇1	SW 1	SW 1	SW ◇1 ⚒
Basingstoke	d			18 10						18 16		18 27		18 35				18 44		18 50		19 00
Hook	d									18 23												
Winchfield	d									18 27												
Fleet	d									18 32										19 02		
Farnborough (Main)	d									18 38								18 58		19 08		
Alton	d										18 15										18 45	
Bentley	d										18 23											
Farnham	a										18 28										18 55	
	d										18 30										19 00	
Aldershot	d										18 36										19 06	
Ash Vale	d										18 41										19 11	
Brookwood	d									18 45	18 48									19 15	19 18	
Guildford	d							18 27	18 35								18 57		19 05			
Worplesdon	d		←													←						
Woking	a		18 20	18 28				18 35	18 42	18 50	18 54	18 48		18 53		18 50	19 05	19 07	19 13	19 20	19 24	19 18
	d		18 28	18 30				18 36	18 45	18 58		18 49	18 52	18 55		18 58	19 06	19 09	19 15	19 28		19 20
West Byfleet	d							18 40		→			18 56				19 10			→		
Byfleet & New Haw	d							18 43					19 00				19 13					
Weybridge	d		18 34					18 46									19 16					
Walton-on-Thames	d		18 38					18 50									19 20					
Hersham	d							18 52									19 22					
Esher	d	←			←	←		18 55									19 25					
Surbiton	a	18 29	18 45		18 45	18 45		18 59								19 09	19 29					
Wimbledon ⊖	a	18 37	→		18 53	18 53		19 07								19 17	→					
Earlsfield	a	18 41					←	19 11							←							
Clapham Junction	a	18 45		18 49	18 59	18 59	19 01	19 15	19 04			19 08	20 01	19 14	19 15	19 23		19 28	19 34			19 39
Vauxhall ⊖	a	18 50					19 08	→					→		19 20							
London Waterloo ⊖	a	18 55		18 59	19 10	19 10	19 13		19 14			19 19		19 24	19 25	19 34		19 39	19 44			19 49

		SW	SW 1	SW ◇1 ⚒	SW 1	SW 1	SW	SW	SW ◇1 ⚒	SW 1	SW 1	SW ◇1	SW	SW ◇1	SW	SW 1	SW	SW 1	SW ◇1	SW 1	SW 1	SW ◇1 ⚒	SW
Basingstoke	d			19 10						19 16		19 27		19 35				19 44		19 50		20 00	
Hook	d									19 23													
Winchfield	d									19 27													
Fleet	d									19 32										20 02			
Farnborough (Main)	d									19 38								19 58		20 08			
Alton	d										19 15										19 45		
Bentley	d										19 23												
Farnham	a										19 28										19 55		
	d										19 30										20 00		
Aldershot	d										19 36										20 06		
Ash Vale	d										19 41										20 11		
Brookwood	d									19 45	19 48									20 15	20 18		
Guildford	d							19 27	19 35								19 57		20 05				
Worplesdon	d		←													←							
Woking	a		19 20	19 28				19 35	19 42	19 50	19 54	19 48		19 53		19 50	20 05	20 07	20 13	20 20	20 24	20 18	
	d		19 28	19 30				19 36	19 45	19 58		19 49	19 52	19 55		19 58	20 06	20 09	20 15	20 28		20 20	
West Byfleet	d							19 40		→			19 56				20 10			→			
Byfleet & New Haw	d							19 43					20 00				20 13						
Weybridge	d		19 34					19 46									20 16						
Walton-on-Thames	d		19 38					19 50									20 20						
Hersham	d							19 52									20 22						
Esher	d	←			←	←		19 55									20 25						←
Surbiton	a	19 29	19 45		19 45	19 45		19 59								20 09	20 29						20 29
Wimbledon ⊖	a	19 37	→		19 53	19 53		20 07								20 17	→						20 37
Earlsfield	a	19 41					←	20 11							←								20 41
Clapham Junction	a	19 45		19 49	19 59	19 59	20 01	20 15	20 04			20 08	21 01	20 14	20 15	20 23		20 28	20 34			20 39	20 45
Vauxhall ⊖	a	19 50					20 08	→					→		20 20								20 50
London Waterloo ⊖	a	19 55		19 59	20 10	20 10	20 13		20 14			20 19		20 24	20 25	20 34		20 39	20 44			20 49	20 55

Table T155-R

Sundays

20 May to 2 December

Basingstoke, Alton, Guildford and Woking - Waterloo

			SW ■	SW ◇■ A ⚒	SW ■	SW ■	SW	SW	SW ◇■	SW	SW ■	SW ■		SW ◇■	SW	SW ■	SW	SW ■	SW ◇■	SW ■	SW ■	SW ◇■ ⚒		SW	SW ■
Basingstoke	d			20 10							20 16			20 35				20 44		20 50		21 00			
Hook	d										20 23														
Winchfield	d										20 27														
Fleet	d										20 32									21 02					
Farnborough (Main)	d										20 38							20 58		21 08					
Alton	d											20 15									20 45				
Bentley	d											20 23													
Farnham	a											20 28									20 55				
	d											20 30									21 00				
Aldershot	d											20 36									21 06				
Ash Vale	d											20 41									21 11				
Brookwood	d										20 45	20 48								21 15	21 18				
Guildford	d							20 27	20 35								20 57		21 05						
Worplesdon	d		←													←									←
Woking	a		20 20	20 28				20 35	20 42		20 50	20 54		20 53		20 50	21 05	21 07	21 13	21 20	21 24	21 18			21 20
	d		20 28	20 30				20 36	20 45	20 52	20 58			20 55		20 58	21 06	21 09	21 15	21 28		21 20			21 28
West Byfleet	d							20 40		20 56	→						21 10			→					
Byfleet & New Haw	d							20 43		21 00							21 13								
Weybridge	d		20 34					20 46									21 16								21 34
Walton-on-Thames	d		20 38					20 50									21 20								21 38
Hersham	d							20 52									21 22								
Esher	d				←	←		20 55									21 25							←	
Surbiton ■	a		20 45		20 45	20 45		20 59								21 09	21 29							21 29	21 45
Wimbledon ■	⊖ a		→		20 53	20 53		21 07								21 17	→							21 37	→
Earlsfield	a						←	21 11							←									21 41	
Clapham Junction ■	a			20 49	20 59	20 59	21 01	21 15	21 04	22 01				21 14	21 15	21 23		21 28	21 34			21 39		21 45	
Vauxhall	⊖ a						21 08	→		→					21 20									21 50	
London Waterloo ■	⊖ a			20 59	21 11	21 11	21 13		21 14					21 24	21 25	21 34		21 39	21 44			21 49		21 55	

		SW ◇■ ⚒	SW ■	SW ■	SW	SW	SW ◇■	SW		SW ■	SW ■	SW ◇■	SW	SW ■	SW	SW ■	SW ◇■	SW		SW ■	SW ■	SW ◇■	SW ■	SW ■	SW
Basingstoke	d	21 10								21 16		21 35				21 44				21 50		22 10			
Hook	d									21 23															
Winchfield	d									21 27															
Fleet	d									21 32										22 02					
Farnborough (Main)	d									21 38						21 58				22 08					
Alton	d										21 15										21 45				
Bentley	d										21 23														
Farnham	a										21 28										21 55				
	d										21 30										22 00				
Aldershot	d										21 36										22 06				
Ash Vale	d										21 41										22 11				
Brookwood	d									21 45	21 48									22 15	22 18				
Guildford	d					21 27	21 35								21 57		22 05								
Worplesdon	d													←											
Woking	a	21 28				21 35	21 42			21 50	21 54	21 53		21 50	22 05	22 07	22 13			22 21	22 24	22 28			
	d	21 30				21 36	21 45	21 52		21 58		21 55		21 58	22 06	22 09	22 15			22 28		22 30			
West Byfleet	d					21 40		21 56		→					22 10										
Byfleet & New Haw	d					21 43		22 00							22 13										
Weybridge	d					21 46									22 16					22 34					
Walton-on-Thames	d					21 50									22 20					22 38					
Hersham	d					21 52									22 22										
Esher	d		←	←		21 55									22 25			←					←	←	
Surbiton ■	a		21 45	21 45		21 59								22 09	22 29			22 29		22 45			22 45	22 45	
Wimbledon ■	⊖ a		21 53	21 53		22 07								22 17	→			22 37		→			22 53	22 53	
Earlsfield	a				←	22 11							←					22 41							←
Clapham Junction ■	a	21 49	21 59	21 59	22 01	22 15	22 04	23 01				22 14	22 15	22 23		22 28	22 34	22 45				22 49	22 59	22 59	23 01
Vauxhall	⊖ a				22 08	→		→					22 20					22 50							23 08
London Waterloo ■	⊖ a	21 59	22 10	22 10	22 13		22 14					22 24	22 25	22 34		22 39	22 44	22 55				22 59	23 10	23 10	23 13

		SW	SW ◇■	SW		SW ■	SW ■	SW	SW ◇■	SW ■	SW	SW ■	SW ◇■	SW		SW ■	SW	SW ◇■	SW ■	SW ■	SW ◇■				
Basingstoke	d					22 16			22 36			22 44							23 16		23 44				
Hook	d					22 23													23 23						
Winchfield	d					22 27													23 27						
Fleet	d					22 32													23 32						
Farnborough (Main)	d					22 38						22 58							23 38						
Alton	d						22 15									22 45				23 15					
Bentley	d						22 23													23 23					
Farnham	a						22 28									22 55				23 28					
	d						22 30									23 00				23 30					
Aldershot	d						22 36									23 06				23 36					
Ash Vale	d						22 41									23 11				23 41					
Brookwood	d					22 45	22 48									23 18			23 45	23 48					
Guildford	d	22 27	22 35								22 57		23 05					23 35							
Worplesdon	d									←															
Woking	a	22 35	22 42			22 50	22 54		22 54	22 50	23 05	23 07	23 13			23 24		23 42	23 50	23 54	00 02				
	d	22 36	22 45			22 58		22 52	22 56	22 58	23 06	23 09	23 15			23 28		23 45			00 04				
West Byfleet	d	22 40				→		22 56			23 10														
Byfleet & New Haw	d	22 43						23 00			23 13														
Weybridge	d	22 46									23 16					23 34									
Walton-on-Thames	d	22 50									23 20					23 38									
Hersham	d	22 52									23 22														
Esher	d	22 55		←							23 25			←											
Surbiton ■	a	22 59		22 59						23 09	23 29			23 29		23 45									
Wimbledon ■	⊖ a	→		23 07						23 17	→			23 37		23 53									
Earlsfield	a			23 11										23 41			←								
Clapham Junction ■	a		23 04	23 15				00 01	23 15	23 23		23 28	23 34	23 45		23 59	00 01	00 04			00 23				
Vauxhall	⊖ a			23 20				→						23 50			00 08								
London Waterloo ■	⊖ a		23 14	23 25					23 25	23 33		23 39	23 44	23 55		00 10	00 13	00 14			00 33				

A ⚒ to Woking

Table T156-F

Mondays to Fridays

21 May to 7 December

London - Guildford, Haslemere and Portsmouth

Miles			SW MX ◇■	SW MO ◇■	SW MX ◇■	SW MO ◇■	SW MX ◇■	SW MO ◇■	SW ■	SW ◇■	SW ◇■		SW ◇■	SW ◇■ A	SW ◇■ B	SW ◇■	SW ◇■ ⚒	SW ◇■	SW ◇■	SW ◇■ ⚒	SW ◇■		SW ■	SW ◇■ ⚒	SW ◇■
0	**London Waterloo** ■	⊖ d						00 50		05 00	05 20		06 15	06 45	06 45	07 15	07 30		07 45	08 00			08 15	08 30	08 45
—	Clapham Junction	d						00 57		05 11	05 29		06u22	06u52	06u52	07u23			07u52				08u22		08u52
24½	**Woking**	a						01 16		05 51	06 08		06 42	07 12	07 12	07 43	07 56		08 11	08 25			08 43	08 55	09 12
—		d				00 03	00 13	01 18		05 53	06 11		06 43	07 13	07 16	07 44	07 56		08 13	08 25			08 44	08 55	09 13
26¾	Worplesdon	d					00 18				06 16		06 48	07 18	07 21	07 49			08 18				08 49		09 18
30¼	**Guildford**	a				00 10	00 24	01s26		06 00	06 24		06 54	07 24	07 26	07 55	08 05		08 24	08 34			08 54	09 05	09 24
—		d				00 12	00 25		05 09	06 04	06 30		06 55	07 25	07 28	07 56	08 05		08 25	08 38			08 56	09 10	09 25
33½	Farncombe	d					00 31			06 10	06 36		07 01	07 31	07 34	08 02			08 31				09 02		09 31
34½	Godalming	d			00 01	00 18	00 34			06 13	06 39		07 04	07 34	07 37	08 05	08 13		08 34				09 05		09 34
36½	Milford (Surrey)	d					00s38			06 17	06 43		07 08	07 38	07 41	08 09			08 38				09 09		
38½	Witley	d					00s43			06 21	06 47		07 13	07 43	07 45	08 14		←	08 43		←		09 13		
43	**Haslemere** ■	a			00 12	00 29	00 49		05 23	06 28	06 54		07 19	07 49	07 52	08 20	08 24	08 20	08 50	08 53	08 50		09 20	09 25	09 45
—		d		00 07	00 12	00 29	00 50		05 24	06 28	06 55		07 20	07 53	07 53	08 30	08 25	08 30	08 57	08 54	08 57			09 26	09 55
46¾	Liphook	d		00 12			00s55		05 29	06 33	07 00		07 25	07 58	07 58	→		08 35	→		09 02				→
51½	Liss	d	00 01	00 18			01s01		05 35	06 39	07 06		07 31	08 05	08 05			08 41			09 08				
55	Petersfield	d	00 06	00 23	00 23	00 40	01 06		05 45	06 45	07 11		07 37	08 10	08 10		08 36	08 46		09 05	09 14			09 37	
63¼	Rowlands Castle	d	00 15	00 33			01s16		05 55	06 54	07 21		07 46	08 20	08 20			08 56			09 23				
66½	**Havant**	a	00 20	00 38	00 36	00 53	01 21	02s00	06 00	06 59	07 26		07 52	08 25	08 25		08 50	09 01		09 18	09 28			09 51	
—		d	00 21	00 39	00 36	00 53	01 21		06 00	07 00	07 27		07 53	08 26	08 26		08 50	09 01		09 19	09 29			09 51	
67¼	Bedhampton	a	00 24	00 41			01s24		06 03	07 02	07 30		07 55	08 29	08 29			09 04			09 31				
70½	Hilsea	a	00 29				01s29		06 08	07 08	07 37		08 01	08 34	08 34			09 09			09 37				
72¾	Fratton	a	00 33	00 49	00 45	01 02	01s33	02s10	06 12	07 12	07 42		08 05	08 38	08 38		08 59	09 13		09 27	09 41			10 00	
73¾	**Portsmouth & Southsea**	a	00 38	00 53	00 50	01 05	01 38	02s14	06 16	07 16	07 46		08 08	08 42	08 42		09 03	09 17		09 31	09 45			10 03	
74½	**Portsmouth Harbour**	⛴ a		00 58	00 55	01 09		02 19	06 20	07 21	07 51		08 13	08 48	08 48		09 08	09 22		09 36				10 08	

		SW ◇■ ⚒	SW ◇■	SW ■	SW ◇■ ⚒	SW ◇■	SW ◇■ ⚒		SW ◇■	SW ■	SW ◇■ ⚒	SW ◇■	SW ◇■ ⚒	SW ◇■	SW ■	SW ◇■ ⚒	SW ◇■		SW ◇■ ⚒	SW ◇■	SW ■	SW ◇■ ⚒	SW ◇■	SW ◇■ ⚒	SW ◇■
London Waterloo ■	⊖ d	09 00		09 15	09 30	09 45	10 00			10 15	10 30	10 45	11 00		11 15	11 30	11 45		12 00		12 15	12 30	12 45	13 00	
Clapham Junction	d			09u22		09u52				10u22		10u52			11u22		11u52				12u22		12u52		
Woking	a	09 24		09 42	09 54	10 12	10 24			10 41	10 54	11 12	11 24		11 41	11 54	12 12		12 24		12 41	12 54	13 12	13 24	
	d	09 25		09 43	09 55	10 13	10 25			10 43	10 55	11 13	11 25		11 43	11 55	12 13		12 25		12 43	12 55	13 13	13 25	
Worplesdon	d					10 18						11 18					12 18						13 18		
Guildford	a	09 33		09 51	10 03	10 24	10 33			10 50	11 03	11 24	11 33		11 50	12 03	12 24		12 33		12 50	13 03	13 24	13 33	
	d	09 34		09 54	10 04	10 25	10 34			10 52	11 04	11 25	11 34		11 52	12 04	12 25		12 34		12 52	13 04	13 25	13 34	
Farncombe	d			10 00		10 31				10 58		11 31			11 58		12 31				12 58		13 31		
Godalming	d			10 03	10 11	10 34				11 01		11 34			12 01		12 34				13 01		13 34		
Milford (Surrey)	d			10 07						11 05					12 05						13 05				
Witley	d		←	10 11					←	11 09				←	12 09					←	13 09				←
Haslemere ■	a	09 49	09 45	10 19	10 22	10 45	10 49		10 45	11 17	11 20	11 45	11 49	11 45	12 17	12 20	12 45		12 49	12 45	13 17	13 20	13 45	13 49	13 45
	d	09 50	09 55		10 23	10 55	10 50		10 55		11 21	11 55	11 50	11 55		12 21	12 55		12 50	12 55		13 21	13 55	13 50	13 55
Liphook	d		10 00			→			11 00			→		12 00			→			13 00			→		14 00
Liss	d		10 06						11 06					12 06						13 06					14 06
Petersfield	d	10 01	10 11		10 34		11 01		11 11		11 32		12 01	12 11		12 32			13 01	13 11		13 32		14 01	14 11
Rowlands Castle	d		10 21						11 21					12 21						13 21					14 21
Havant	a	10 13	10 26		10 51		11 13		11 26		11 44		12 13	12 26		12 44			13 13	13 26		13 44		14 13	14 26
	d	10 14	10 27		10 51		11 14		11 27		11 45		12 14	12 27		12 45			13 14	13 27		13 45		14 14	14 27
Bedhampton	a		10 29						11 29					12 29						13 29					14 29
Hilsea	a		10 36						11 36					12 36						13 36					14 36
Fratton	a	10 23	10 40		11 00		11 24		11 40		11 53		12 23	12 40		12 53			13 23	13 40		13 53		14 23	14 40
Portsmouth & Southsea	a	10 27	10 45		11 03		11 27		11 45		11 57		12 27	12 45		12 57			13 27	13 45		13 57		14 27	14 45
Portsmouth Harbour	⛴ a	10 32			11 08		11 32				12 02		12 32			13 02			13 32			14 02		14 32	

		SW ■	SW ◇■ ⚒		SW ◇■	SW ◇■ ⚒	SW ◇■	SW ■	SW ◇■ ⚒	SW ◇■	SW ◇■ ⚒	SW ◇■	SW ◇■		SW ◇■ ⚒	SW ◇■	SW ◇■	SW ◇■ ⚒	SW ◇■	SW ◇■	SW ◇■ ⚒	SW ◇■	SW ◇■		SW ◇■ ⚒
London Waterloo ■	⊖ d	13 15	13 30		13 45	14 00		14 15	14 30	14 45	15 00		15 15		15 30		15 45	16 00		16 15	16 30		16 45		17 00
Clapham Junction	d	13u22			13u52			14u22		14u52			15u22				15u52			16u22			16u52		
Woking	a	13 41	13 54		14 12	14 24		14 42	14 54	15 12	15 24		15 42		15 54		16 12	16 24		16 42	16 54		17 12		17 24
	d	13 43	13 55		14 13	14 25		14 43	14 55	15 13	15 25		15 43		15 55		16 13	16 25		16 43	16 56		17 13		17 25
Worplesdon	d				14 18					15 18			15 48							16 48					17 30
Guildford	a	13 50	14 03		14 24	14 33		14 51	15 03	15 24	15 33		15 54		16 03		16 21	16 33		16 54	17 03		17 21		17 36
	d	13 52	14 04		14 25	14 34		14 52	15 04	15 25	15 34		15 55		16 04		16 22	16 34		16 55	17 05		17 22		17 40
Farncombe	d	13 58			14 31			14 58		15 31			16 01				16 28			17 01			17 28		
Godalming	d	14 01			14 34			15 01	15 11	15 34			16 04		16 11		16 31	16 41		17 04	17 11		17 31		
Milford (Surrey)	d	14 05						15 05					16 08				16 35			17 08			17 35		
Witley	d	14 09					←	15 10				←	16 13			←	16 40		←	17 13		←	17 40		
Haslemere ■	a	14 17	14 20		14 45	14 49	14 45	15 18	15 21	15 45	15 49	15 45	16 20		16 23	16 20	16 47	16 52	16 47	17 20	17 23	17 20	17 47		17 54
	d		14 21		14 55	14 50	14 55		15 22	15 55	15 50	15 55	16 29		16 24	16 29	16 56	16 53	16 56	17 29	17 24	17 29	17 58		17 55
Liphook	d				→		15 00			→		16 00	→			16 34	→		17 01	→		17 34	→		
Liss	d						15 06					16 06				16 40			17 07			17 40			
Petersfield	d		14 32			15 01	15 11		15 33		16 01	16 11			16 35	16 45		17 04	17 12		17 35	17 45			18 06
Rowlands Castle	d						15 21					16 21				16 55			17 22			17 55			
Havant	a		14 44			15 15	15 26		15 51		16 13	16 26			16 51	17 00		17 17	17 27		17 49	18 01			18 18
	d		14 45			15 16	15 27		15 51		16 14	16 27			16 51	17 01		17 17	17 28		17 50	18 02			18 19
Bedhampton	a						15 29					16 29				17 03			17 30			18 04			
Hilsea	a						15 36					16 36				17 08			17 36			18 10			
Fratton	a		14 53			15 24	15 40		16 00		16 22	16 40			17 00	17 12		17 26	17 40		17 59	18 14			18 27
Portsmouth & Southsea	a		14 57			15 28	15 45		16 03		16 26	16 44			17 03	17 16		17 30	17 43		18 02	18 17			18 31
Portsmouth Harbour	⛴ a		15 02			15 33			16 08		16 31	16 50			17 08	17 23		17 38	17 50		18 09	18 24			18 38

A until 5 October

B from 8 October

Table T156-F

London - Guildford, Haslemere and Portsmouth

Mondays to Fridays
21 May to 7 December

		SW	SW	SW	SW	SW	SW	SW	SW	SW	SW	SW	SW	SW	SW	SW	SW	SW	SW	SW	SW	SW	SW
		◇1	◇1	◇1 ⊥	◇1	1	◇1 ⊥	1	◇1	◇1	◇1 ⊥	◇1	◇1 ⊥	◇1	◇1	◇1 ⊥	◇1	◇1	◇1 ⊥	◇1	1	◇1 ⊥	◇1
London Waterloo 15 ⊖	d		17 15	17 30		17 45	18 00		18 15	18 17	18 30	18 45	19 00		19 15	19 30		19 45	20 00		20 15	20 30	20 45
Clapham Junction	d									18u24					19u22			19u52			20u22		20u52
Woking	a		17 38	17 54						18 43	18 57	19 13	19 24		19 43	19 54		20 12	20 24		20 42	20 55	21 12
	d		17 40	17 56						18 44	18 58	19 14	19 25		19 44	19 55		20 13	20 25		20 43	20 56	21 13
Worplesdon	d		17 45	18 00						18 49					19 49			20 18					21 18
Guildford	a		17 50	18 06		18 21	18 32		18 50	18 55	19 06	19 22	19 33		19 55	20 03		20 24	20 33		20 51	21 04	21 24
	d		17 54	18 08		18 23	18 34		18 51	18 57	19 09	19 24	19 34		19 56	20 04		20 25	20 34		20 52	21 05	21 25
Farncombe	d		18 00			18 29				19 03		19 30			20 02			20 31	20 40		20 58		21 31
Godalming	d		18 03	18 15		18 32	18 41		18 58	19 06	19 16	19 33	19 41		20 05	20 11		20 34	20 43		21 01	21 12	21 34
Milford (Surrey)	d		18 07			18 36				19 10		19 37			20 09			20 38			21 05		21 38
Witley	d	←	18 11		←	18 40		←		19 14		19 41		←	20 14		←	20 43		←	21 10		21 43
Haslemere 4	a	17 47	18 18	18 25	18 18	18 49	18 51	18 49	19 08	19 23	19 27	19 48	19 52	19 48	20 21	20 24	20 21	20 50	20 54	20 50	21 18	21 22	21 50
	d	17 58	18 30	18 26	18 30	18 55	18 52	18 55	19 09		19 28	19 56	19 53	19 56	20 29	20 25	20 29	20 58	20 55	20 58		21 23	21 58
Liphook	d	18 03	→		18 35	→		19 00	19 14			→		20 01	→		20 34	→		21 03			→
Liss	d	18 09			18 41			19 06	19 20					20 07			20 40			21 09			
Petersfield	d	18 15		18 37	18 46		19 03	19 12	19 26		19 39		20 04	20 13		20 36	20 45		21 06	21 15		21 34	
Rowlands Castle	d	18 24			18 56			19 21	19 35					20 22			20 55			21 24			
Havant	a	18 29		18 52	19 01		19 17	19 28	19 43		19 52		20 17	20 27		20 51	21 00		21 18	21 29		21 46	
	d	18 30		18 52	19 02		19 17		19 43		19 52		20 17	20 28		20 51			21 19	21 30		21 47	
Bedhampton	a	18 33			19 04				19 46					20 31						21 32			
Hilsea	a	18 39			19 10				19 51					20 36						21 38			
Fratton	a	18 43		19 01	19 14		19 26		19 55		20 01		20 26	20 40		21 00			21 27	21 42		21 55	
Portsmouth & Southsea	a	18 47		19 04			19 29		20 03		20 04		20 29	20 44		21 03			21 31	21 47		21 59	
Portsmouth Harbour ⛴	a	18 52		19 11			19 36				20 11		20 34	20 53		21 08			21 36			22 03	

		SW	SW	SW	SW	SW	SW	SW	SW	SW	SW
		◇1 ⊥	◇1	◇1	◇1	◇1	◇1	◇1	◇1	◇1	◇1
London Waterloo 15 ⊖	d	21 00		21 30	21 45	22 00		22 30	22 45	23 15	23 45
Clapham Junction	d				21u52				22u52	23u22	23u52
Woking	a	21 24		21 54	22 12	22 24		22 54	23 12	23 41	00 11
	d	21 25		21 55	22 13	22 25		22 56	23 13	23 43	00 13
Worplesdon	d				22 18				23 18		00 18
Guildford	a	21 33		22 03	22 24	22 33		23 03	23 24	23 50	00 24
	d	21 34		22 04	22 25	22 34		23 05	23 25	23 52	00 25
Farncombe	d	21 40		22 10	22 31	22 40		23 11	23 31	23 58	00 31
Godalming	d	21 43		22 13	22 34	22 43		23 14	23 34	00 01	00 34
Milford (Surrey)	d				22 38				23 38		00s38
Witley	d		←		22 43		←		23 43		00s43
Haslemere 4	a	21 54	21 50	22 24	22 50	22 54	22 50	23 24	23 49	00 12	00 49
	d	21 55	21 58	22 25	22 58	22 55	22 58	23 25	23 50	00 12	00 50
Liphook	d		22 03		→		23 03		23 55		00s55
Liss	d		22 09				23 09		00 01		01s01
Petersfield	d	22 06	22 15	22 36		23 06	23 15	23 36	00 06	00 23	01 06
Rowlands Castle	d		22 24				23 24		00 15		01s16
Havant	a	22 18	22 31	22 48		23 18	23 29	23 49	00 20	00 36	01 21
	d	22 19	22 31	22 49		23 19	23 30	23 50	00 21	00 36	01 21
Bedhampton	a		22 34				23 33		00 24		01s24
Hilsea	a		22 39				23 38		00 29		01s29
Fratton	a	22 27	22 43	22 58		23 27	23 42	23 58	00 33	00 45	01s33
Portsmouth & Southsea	a	22 31	22 49	23 02		23 31	23 47	00 02	00 38	00 50	01 38
Portsmouth Harbour ⛴	a	22 36		23 07		23 36		00 07		00 55	

Saturdays
26 May to 8 December

		SW	SW	SW	SW	SW	SW	SW	SW	SW	SW	SW	SW	SW	SW	SW	SW	SW	SW	SW	SW	SW
		◇1	◇1	◇1	1	1	◇1	1	◇1	1	◇1	◇1	◇1	◇1	1	◇1	◇1	◇1 ⊥	◇1	1	◇1 ⊥	◇1
London Waterloo 15 ⊖	d					05 00	05 20	06 15	06 45	07 15	07 30	07 45	08 00		08 15	08 30	08 45	09 00		09 15	09 30	09 45
Clapham Junction	d					05 11	05 29	06u22	06u52	07u23		07u52			08u22		08u52			09u22		09u52
Woking	a					05 51	06 08	06 42	07 12	07 43	07 54	08 12	08 24		08 42	08 54	09 12	09 24		09 42	09 54	10 12
	d			00 13		05 53	06 13	06 43	07 13	07 44	07 55	08 13	08 25		08 43	08 55	09 13	09 25		09 43	09 55	10 13
Worplesdon	d			00 18			06 18		07 18			08 18					09 18					10 18
Guildford	a			00 24		06 00	06 23	06 51	07 23	07 52	08 03	08 24	08 33		08 51	09 03	09 24	09 33		09 51	10 03	10 24
	d			00 25	05 15	06 02	06 25	06 53	07 25	07 53	08 04	08 25	08 34		08 52	09 04	09 25	09 35		09 52	10 04	10 25
Farncombe	d			00 31		06 08	06 31	06 59	07 31	07 59		08 31			08 58		09 31			09 58		10 31
Godalming	d		00 01	00 34		06 11	06 34	07 02	07 34	08 02		08 34			09 01		09 34			10 01		10 34
Milford (Surrey)	d			00s38		06 15		07 06		08 06					09 05					10 05		
Witley	d			00s43		06 19		07 10		08 11				←	09 10				←	10 10		
Haslemere 4	a		00 12	00 49	05 29	06 26	06 44	07 17	07 44	08 18	08 22	08 45	08 49	08 45	09 17	09 21	09 45	09 49	09 45	10 17	10 21	10 45
	d		00 12	00 50	05 30		06 45		07 45		08 22	08 55	08 50	08 55		09 22	09 55	09 50	09 55		10 22	10 55
Liphook	d			00s55	05 35		06 50		07 50			→		09 00			→		10 00			→
Liss	d	00 01		01s01	05 41		06 56		07 56					09 06					10 06			
Petersfield	d	00 06	00 23	01 06	05 46		07 02		08 01		08 33		09 01	09 11		09 33		10 01	10 11		10 33	
Rowlands Castle	d	00 15		01s16	05 56		07 11		08 11					09 21					10 21			
Havant	a	00 20	00 36	01 21	06 01		07 23		08 17		08 50		09 17	09 26		09 51		10 17	10 26		10 51	
	d	00 21	00 36	01 21	06 02		07 23		08 17		08 51		09 17	09 27		09 51		10 17	10 27		10 51	
Bedhampton	a	00 24		01s24	06 04		07 26		08 20					09 29					10 29			
Hilsea	a	00 29		01s29	06 10		07 31		08 25					09 36					10 36			
Fratton	a	00 33	00 45	01s33	06 14		07 35		08 29		09 00		09 26	09 40		10 00		10 26	10 40		11 00	
Portsmouth & Southsea	a	00 38	00 50	01 38	06 17		07 38		08 33		09 03		09 29	09 44		10 03		10 29	10 44		11 03	
Portsmouth Harbour ⛴	a		00 55		06 22		07 43		08 38		09 08		09 34			10 08		10 34			11 08	

Table T156-F

London - Guildford, Haslemere and Portsmouth

Saturdays
26 May to 8 December

		SW	and at the same minutes past each hour until	SW	SW	SW	SW	SW	SW	SW	SW	SW	SW	SW	SW	SW	SW	SW	and at the same minutes past each hour until
		◇1 ⊥		◇1	1	◇1 ⊥	◇1	◇1 ⊥	◇1	1	◇1 ⊥	◇1	◇1 ⊥	◇1	1	◇1 ⊥	◇1	◇1 ⊥	
London Waterloo 15 ⊖	d	10 00			12 15	12 30	12 45	13 00		13 15	13 30	13 45	14 00		14 15	14 30	14 45	15 00	
Clapham Junction	d				12u22		12u52			13u22		13u52			14u22		14u52		
Woking	a	10 24			12 42	12 54	13 12	13 24		13 42	13 54	14 12	14 24		14 42	14 54	15 12	15 24	
	d	10 25			12 43	12 55	13 13	13 25		13 43	13 55	14 13	14 25		14 43	14 55	15 13	15 25	
Worplesdon	d						13 18					14 18					15 18		
Guildford	a	10 33			12 51	13 03	13 24	13 33		13 51	14 03	14 24	14 33		14 51	15 03	15 24	15 33	
	d	10 34			12 52	13 04	13 25	13 34		13 52	14 04	14 25	14 34		14 52	15 04	15 25	15 34	
Farncombe	d				12 58		13 31			13 58		14 31			14 58		15 31		
Godalming	d				13 01		13 34			14 01		14 34			15 01		15 34		
Milford (Surrey)	d				13 05					14 05					15 05				
Witley	d			←	13 10				←	14 10				←	15 10				
Haslemere 4	a	10 49		12 45	13 17	13 21	13 45	13 49	13 45	14 17	14 21	14 45	14 49	14 45	15 17	15 21	15 45	15 49	
	d	10 50		12 55		13 22	13 55	13 50	13 55		14 22	14 55	14 50	14 55		15 22	15 55	15 50	
Liphook	d			13 00			→		14 00			→		15 00			→		
Liss	d			13 06					14 06					15 06					
Petersfield	d	11 01		13 11		13 33		14 01	14 11		14 33		15 01	15 11		15 33		16 01	
Rowlands Castle	d			13 21					14 21					15 21					
Havant	a	11 17		13 26		13 51		14 17	14 26		14 51		15 16	15 26		15 51		16 17	
	d	11 17		13 27		13 51		14 17	14 27		14 51		15 17	15 27		15 51		16 17	
Bedhampton	a			13 29					14 29					15 29					
Hilsea	a			13 36					14 36					15 36					
Fratton	a	11 26		13 40		14 00		14 26	14 40		15 00		15 25	15 40		16 00		16 26	
Portsmouth & Southsea	a	11 29		13 44		14 03		14 29	14 44		15 03		15 29	15 44		16 03		16 29	
Portsmouth Harbour ⛴	a	11 34				14 08		14 34			15 08		15 33			16 08		16 34	

		SW	SW	SW	SW	SW	SW	SW	SW	SW	SW	SW	SW	SW	SW	SW	SW	SW	SW	SW	SW	SW	SW
		◇1	1	◇1 ⊥	◇1	◇1 ⊥	◇1	1	◇1 ⊥	◇1	◇1	◇1	1	◇1	◇1	◇1	◇1	◇1	◇1	◇1	◇1	◇1	◇1
London Waterloo 15 ⊖	d		18 15	18 30	18 45	19 00		19 15	19 30	19 45	20 00		20 15	20 30	20 45	21 00		21 30	21 45	22 00		22 30	22 45
Clapham Junction	d		18u22		18u52			19u22		19u52			20u22		20u52				21u52				22u52
Woking	a		18 42	18 54	19 12	19 24		19 42	19 54	20 12	20 24		20 41	20 54	21 12	21 24		21 54	22 12	22 24		22 54	23 12
	d		18 43	18 55	19 13	19 25		19 43	19 55	20 13	20 25		20 43	20 55	21 13	21 25		21 55	22 13	22 25		22 55	23 13
Worplesdon	d				19 18					20 18					21 18				22 18				23 18
Guildford	a		18 51	19 03	19 24	19 33		19 51	20 03	20 24	20 33		20 50	21 03	21 24	21 33		22 03	22 24	22 33		23 03	23 23
	d		18 52	19 04	19 25	19 34		19 52	20 04	20 25	20 34		20 52	21 04	21 25	21 34		22 04	22 25	22 34		23 04	23 25
Farncombe	d		18 58		19 31			19 58		20 31			20 58		21 31	21 40		22 10	22 31	22 40		23 10	23 31
Godalming	d		19 01		19 34			20 01		20 34			21 01		21 34	21 43		22 13	22 34	22 43		23 13	23 34
Milford (Surrey)	d		19 05					20 05					21 05		21 38				22 38				23 38
Witley	d	←	19 10				←	20 10				←	21 09		21 43		←		22 43		←		23 42
Haslemere 4	a	18 45	19 17	19 21	19 45	19 49	19 45	20 17	20 21	20 45	20 49	20 45	21 16	21 20	21 50	21 54	21 50	22 24	22 50	22 54	22 50	23 24	23 49
	d	18 55		19 22	19 55	19 50	19 55		20 22	20 55	20 50	20 55		21 21	21 58	21 55	21 58	22 25	22 58	22 55	22 58	23 25	23 50
Liphook	d	19 00			→		20 00			→		21 00			→		22 03		→		23 03		23 55
Liss	d	19 06					20 06					21 06					22 09				23 09		00 01
Petersfield	d	19 11		19 33		20 01	20 11		20 33		21 01	21 11		21 32		22 06	22 15	22 36		23 06	23 15	23 36	00 06
Rowlands Castle	d	19 21					20 21					21 21					22 24				23 24		00 15
Havant	a	19 26		19 51		20 17	20 26		20 51		21 17	21 26		21 44		22 18	22 31	22 48		23 18	23 29	23 48	00 20
	d	19 27		19 51		20 17	20 30		20 51		21 17	21 27		21 45		22 19	22 31	22 49		23 19	23 30	23 49	00 21
Bedhampton	a	19 29					20 32					21 29					22 34				23 33		00 24
Hilsea	a	19 36					20 40					21 36					22 40				23 41		00 29
Fratton	a	19 40		20 00		20 26	20 44		21 00		21 26	21 40		21 54		22 28	22 44	22 58		23 28	23 45	23 58	00 33
Portsmouth & Southsea	a	19 44		20 03		20 29	20 48		21 03		21 29	21 43		21 58		22 32	22 49	23 02		23 31	23 49	00 02	00 37
Portsmouth Harbour ⛴	a			20 08		20 34			21 08		21 34			22 03		22 36	22 53	23 08		23 36	23 54	00 07	

		SW	SW
		◇1	◇1
London Waterloo 15 ⊖	d	23 15	23 45
Clapham Junction	d	23u22	23u52
Woking	a	23 41	00 11
	d	23 43	00 13
Worplesdon	d		00 18
Guildford	a	23 50	00 24
	d	23 52	00 25
Farncombe	d	23 58	00 31
Godalming	d	00 01	00 34
Milford (Surrey)	d		00s38
Witley	d		00s43
Haslemere 4	a	00 12	00 49
	d	00 12	00 50
Liphook	d		00s55
Liss	d		01s01
Petersfield	d	00 23	01 06
Rowlands Castle	d		01s16
Havant	a	00 36	01 21
	d	00 36	01 21
Bedhampton	a		01s24
Hilsea	a		01s29
Fratton	a	00 45	01s33
Portsmouth & Southsea	a	00 49	01 37
Portsmouth Harbour ⛴	a	00 54	

Table T156-F

Sundays
20 May to 2 December

London - Guildford, Haslemere and Portsmouth

Station		SW ◇■ A	SW ◇■ A	SW ◇■ A	SW ■	SW ◇■	SW ◇■	SW ◇■	SW ◇■	SW ◇■	SW ◇■	SW ◇■
London Waterloo ⊖	d					08 00	08 30	09 00	09 30	10 00	10 30	11 00
Clapham Junction	d					08u09	08u39	09u09	09u39	10u09	10u39	11u09
Woking	a					08 34	09 03	09 34	10 03	10 31	11 01	11 32
	d			00 13	07 32	08 35	09 04	09 35	10 04	10 32	11 02	11 33
Worplesdon	d			00 18								
Guildford	a			00 24	07 39	08 43	09 12	09 43	10 12	10 40	11 10	11 41
	d			00 25	07 41	08 45	09 14	09 45	10 14	10 42	11 12	11 43
Farncombe	d			00 31	07 48	08 53		09 53		10 48		11 49
Godalming	d		00 01	00 34	07 51	08 56	09 21	09 56	10 21	10 51	11 18	11 52
Milford (Surrey)	d			00s38	07 55	09 00		10 00		10 55		11 56
Witley	d			00s43	07 59	09 04		10 04		10 59		12 00
Haslemere ■	a		00 12	00 49	08 06	09 11	09 32	10 11	10 32	11 06	11 29	12 07
	d		00 12	00 50	08 07	09 12	09 32	10 12	10 32	11 07	11 30	12 08
Liphook	d			00s55	08 12	09 17		10 17		11 12		12 13
Liss	d	00 01		01s01	08 18	09 23		10 23		11 18		12 19
Petersfield	d	00 06	00 23	01 06	08 23	09 28	09 43	10 28	10 43	11 23	11 41	12 24
Rowlands Castle	d	00 15		01s16	08 33	09 38		10 38		11 33		12 34
Havant	a	00 20	00 36	01 21	08 38	09 43	09 56	10 43	10 56	11 40	11 53	12 40
	d	00 21	00 36	01 21	08 39	09 44	09 56	10 44	10 56	11 41	11 54	12 41
Bedhampton	a	00 24		01s24	08 41	09 46		10 46		11 43		12 43
Hilsea	a	00 29		01s29								
Fratton	a	00 33	00 45	01s33	08 49	09 54	10 05	10 54	11 05	11 51	12 02	12 51
Portsmouth & Southsea	a	00 37	00 49	01 37	08 53	09 58	10 08	10 58	11 08	11 55	12 07	12 56
Portsmouth Harbour ⛴	a		00 54		08 57	10 04	10 13	11 04	11 13	12 00	12 11	13 00

Station		SW ◇■ 🛒	SW ◇■	SW ◇■ 🛒	SW ◇■	SW ◇■ 🛒	SW ◇■	SW ◇■ 🛒	SW ◇■	SW ◇■ 🛒	SW ◇■	SW ◇■ 🛒
London Waterloo ⊖	d	11 30	12 00	12 30	13 00	13 30	14 00	14 30	15 00	15 30	16 00	16 30
Clapham Junction	d	11u39	12u09	12u39	13u09	13u39	14u09	14u39	15u09	15u39	16u09	16u39
Woking	a	12 01	12 32	13 01	13 31	14 01	14 31	15 01	15 31	16 01	16 31	17 01
	d	12 02	12 33	13 02	13 32	14 02	14 32	15 02	15 32	16 02	16 32	17 02
Worplesdon	d											
Guildford	a	12 10	12 41	13 10	13 40	14 10	14 40	15 10	15 40	16 10	16 40	17 10
	d	12 12	12 43	13 12	13 42	14 12	14 42	15 12	15 42	16 12	16 42	17 12
Farncombe	d		12 49		13 48		14 48		15 48		16 48	
Godalming	d	12 18	12 52	13 18	13 51	14 18	14 51	15 18	15 51	16 18	16 51	17 18
Milford (Surrey)	d		12 56		13 55		14 55		15 55		16 55	
Witley	d		13 00		13 59		14 59		15 59		16 59	
Haslemere ■	a	12 29	13 07	13 29	14 06	14 29	15 06	15 29	16 06	16 29	17 06	17 29
	d	12 30	13 08	13 30	14 07	14 30	15 07	15 30	16 07	16 30	17 07	17 30
Liphook	d		13 13		14 12		15 12		16 12		17 12	
Liss	d		13 19		14 18		15 18		16 18		17 18	
Petersfield	d	12 41	13 24	13 41	14 23	14 41	15 23	15 41	16 23	16 41	17 23	17 41
Rowlands Castle	d		13 34		14 33		15 33		16 33		17 33	
Havant	a	12 53	13 40	13 53	14 40	14 53	15 40	15 53	16 40	16 53	17 40	17 53
	d	12 54	13 40	13 54	14 41	14 54	15 41	15 54	16 41	16 54	17 41	17 54
Bedhampton	a		13 43		14 43		15 43		16 43		17 43	
Hilsea	a											
Fratton	a	13 02	13 50	14 03	14 51	15 02	15 51	16 02	16 51	17 02	17 51	18 02
Portsmouth & Southsea	a	13 07	13 54	14 07	14 55	15 08	15 55	16 07	16 55	17 07	17 55	18 07
Portsmouth Harbour ⛴	a	13 11	14 04	14 11	15 00	15 11	15 59	16 13	17 04	17 11	18 04	18 11

Station		SW ◇■	SW ◇■ 🛒	SW ◇■	SW ◇■ 🛒	SW ◇■	SW ◇■ 🛒	SW ◇■	SW ◇■ 🛒	SW ◇■	SW ◇■	SW ◇■	SW ◇■	SW ◇■	SW ◇■
London Waterloo ⊖	d	17 00	17 30	18 00	18 30	19 00	19 30	20 00	20 30	21 00	21 30	22 00	22 30	23 00	23 30
Clapham Junction	d	17u09	17u39	18u09	18u39	19u09	19u39	20u09	20u39	21u09	21u39	22u09	22u39	23u09	23u39
Woking	a	17 31	18 01	18 31	19 01	19 31	20 01	20 31	21 01	21 31	22 01	22 31	23 01	23 31	00 01
	d	17 32	18 02	18 32	19 02	19 32	20 02	20 32	21 02	21 32	22 02	22 32	23 02	23 32	00 03
Worplesdon	d														
Guildford	a	17 40	18 10	18 40	19 10	19 40	20 10	20 40	21 10	21 40	22 10	22 40	23 10	23 40	00 10
	d	17 42	18 12	18 42	19 12	19 42	20 12	20 42	21 12	21 42	22 12	22 42	23 12	23 42	00 12
Farncombe	d	17 48		18 48		19 48		20 48		21 48		22 48		23 48	
Godalming	d	17 51	18 18	18 51	19 18	19 51	20 18	20 51	21 18	21 51	22 18	22 51	23 18	23 51	00 18
Milford (Surrey)	d	17 55		18 55		19 55		20 55		21 55		22 55		23 55	
Witley	d	17 59		18 59		19 59		20 59		21 59		22 59		23 59	
Haslemere ■	a	18 06	18 29	19 06	19 29	20 06	20 29	21 06	21 29	22 06	22 29	23 06	23 29	00 06	00 29
	d	18 07	18 30	19 07	19 30	20 07	20 30	21 07	21 30	22 07	22 30	23 07	23 30	00 07	00 29
Liphook	d	18 12		19 12		20 12		21 12		22 12		23 12		00 12	
Liss	d	18 18		19 18		20 18		21 18		22 18		23 18		00 18	
Petersfield	d	18 23	18 41	19 23	19 41	20 23	20 41	21 23	21 41	22 23	22 41	23 23	23 41	00 23	00 40
Rowlands Castle	d	18 33		19 33		20 33		21 33		22 33		23 33		00 33	
Havant	a	18 40	18 53	19 40	19 53	20 40	20 53	21 40	21 53	22 40	22 53	23 42	23 53	00 38	00 53
	d	18 40	18 54	19 41	19 54	20 41	20 54	21 41	21 54	22 41	22 54	23 43	23 54	00 39	00 53
Bedhampton	a	18 43		19 43		20 43		21 43		22 43		23 45		00 41	
Hilsea	a														
Fratton	a	18 51	19 02	19 51	20 02	20 51	21 02	21 51	22 03	22 51	23 02	23 53	00 02	00 49	01 02
Portsmouth & Southsea	a	18 55	19 07	19 55	20 07	20 55	21 07	21 55	22 07	22 56	23 07	23 57	00 06	00 53	01 05
Portsmouth Harbour ⛴	a	18 59	19 11	20 04	20 11	21 00	21 11	22 00	22 11	23 00	23 11	00 01	00 10	00 58	01 09

A not 20 May

Table T156-R

Mondays to Fridays
21 May to 7 December

Portsmouth, Haslemere and Guildford - London

Miles	Station		SW MO ■	SW MX ■	SW ◇■ A	SW ◇■ B	SW ◇■ A	SW ◇■ B	SW ◇■ A 🛒	SW ◇■ B 🛒	SW ◇■ A	SW ◇■ B	SW ◇■	SW ◇■ 🛒
0	Portsmouth Harbour ⛴	d			04 25	04 25			05 14	05 19			05 50	06 15
0¾	Portsmouth & Southsea	d			04 29	04 30			05 19	05 24			05 55	06 20
1¾	Fratton	d			04 33	04 34			05 23	05 28			05 59	06 24
4	Hilsea	d			04 37	04 38			05 27	05 32			06 03	
7¼	Bedhampton	d			04 42	04 43			05 32	05 37			06 08	
8	Havant	a			04 44	04 45			05 35	05 39			06 10	06 34
—		d			04 45	04 46			05 35	05 40			06 11	06 35
11¼	Rowlands Castle	d			04 50	04 52			05 41	05 46			06 16	
19½	Petersfield	d			05 01	05 03			05 52	05 57	06 09	06 12	06 29	06 49
23	Liss	d		00 02	05 06	05 08			05 57	06 02	06 14	06 17	06 34	
27¾	Liphook	d		00 09	05 13	05 15			06 04	06 09	06 21	06 24	06 41	
31½	Haslemere ■	a		00 15	05 19	05 25			06 12	06 14	06 26	06 29	06 46	07 02
—		d		00 15	05 20	05 26	05 57	06 00	06 14	06 16	06 27	06 30	06 47	07 03
36	Witley	d		00 21	05 26	05 32	06 03	06 06			06 33	06 36		
38¼	Milford (Surrey)	d		00 25	05 30	05 36	06 08	06 11			06 37	06 40		
40	Godalming	d		00 29	05 34	05 40	06 12	06 15	06 24	06 26	06 41	06 44	06 57	
41	Farncombe	d		00 32	05 37	05 43	06 15	06 18			06 44	06 47	07 00	
44¼	Guildford	a		00 37	05 48	05 48	06 23	06 23	06 32	06 32	06 52	06 52	07 06	07 16
—		d	00 05		05 49	05 49	06 24	06 24	06 33	06 33	06 53	06 53	07 07	07 18
47¾	Worplesdon	d			05 54	05 54	06 30	06 30			06 59	06 59		
50½	Woking	a	00 13		06 00	06 00	06 35	06 35	06 41	06 41	07 03	07 03	07 15	07 25
—		d			06 01	06 01	06 37	06 37	06 43	06 43	07 05	07 05	07 16	07 27
—	Clapham Junction	a			06 20	06 20	06 58	06 58	07 02	07 02	07 24	07 24		
74½	London Waterloo ⊖	a			06 29	06 29	07 08	07 08	07 12	07 12	07 36	07 36	07 45	07 54

Miles	Station		SW ◇■	SW ◇■	SW ◇■ 🛒	SW ◇■	SW ◇■	SW ◇■ 🛒	SW ◇■	SW ◇■	SW ◇■ 🛒
0	Portsmouth Harbour ⛴	d			06 42		06 54	07 12		07 30	07 45
0¾	Portsmouth & Southsea	d			06 47		06 58	07 17		07 35	07 50
1¾	Fratton	d			06 51		07 03	07 21		07 39	07 54
4	Hilsea	d		06 40			07 07			07 43	
7¼	Bedhampton	d		06 45			07 12			07 49	
8	Havant	a		06 47	06 59		07 14	07 30		07 51	08 03
—		d		06 48	07 00	07 10	07 15	07 32		07 52	08 04
11¼	Rowlands Castle	d		06 54			07 21			07 57	
19½	Petersfield	d		07 05	07 14	07 24	07 33	07 46		08 09	08 18
23	Liss	d		07 10	07 20		07 38			08 14	
27¾	Liphook	d		07 17	07 27		07 46		←	08 21	
31½	Haslemere ■	a		07 23	07 33	07 37	07 52	07 59	07 52	08 27	08 30
—		d	07 10	07 26	07 35	07 39	08 04	08 00	08 04	08 39	08 32
36	Witley	d	07 16			07 45	→		08 10	→	
38¼	Milford (Surrey)	d	07 21			07 49			08 15		
40	Godalming	d	07 25	07 35	07 45	07 53		08 10	08 19		08 41
41	Farncombe	d	07 28	07 38		07 56			08 23		
44¼	Guildford	a	07 33	07 43	07 51	08 01		08 16	08 28		08 48
—		d	07 34	07 45	07 54	08 02		08 18	08 30		08 53
47¾	Worplesdon	d	07 40	07 50		08 08			08 36		
50½	Woking	a		07 55		08 13		08 26	08 41		
—		d		07 57		08 14		08 28	08 43		
—	Clapham Junction	a							09 03		
74½	London Waterloo ⊖	a	08 10	08 24	08 32	08 41		08 54	09 13		09 31

Station		SW ◇■	SW ◇■ 🛒	SW ◇■	SW ◇■ 🛒	SW ■	SW ◇■ 🛒	SW ◇■	SW ◇■ 🛒	SW ■	SW ◇■ 🛒	SW ◇■
Portsmouth Harbour ⛴	d		08 15		08 45		09 15	09 19	09 45		10 15	
Portsmouth & Southsea	d		08 20	08 24	08 50		09 20	09 24	09 50		10 20	10 24
Fratton	d		08 24	08 28	08 54		09 24	09 28	09 54		10 24	10 28
Hilsea	d			08 32				09 32				10 32
Bedhampton	d			08 37				09 37				10 37
Havant	a		08 32	08 39	09 02		09 33	09 39	10 03		10 32	10 39
	d		08 34	08 40	09 04		09 34	09 40	10 04		10 34	10 40
Rowlands Castle	d			08 46				09 46				10 46
Petersfield	d		08 48	08 57	09 18		09 48	09 57	10 18		10 48	10 57
Liss	d			09 02				10 02				11 02
Liphook	d	←		09 09				10 09				11 09
Haslemere ■	a	08 27	09 01	09 15	09 31		10 00	10 15	10 31		11 00	11 15
	d	08 39	09 02	09 15	09 32	09 39	10 02	10 15	10 32	10 39	11 02	11 15
Witley	d	08 45				09 45				10 45		
Milford (Surrey)	d	08 49				09 49				10 49		
Godalming	d	08 53	09 11	09 25		09 53		10 25		10 53		11 25
Farncombe	d	08 57		09 28		09 56		10 28		10 56		11 28
Guildford	a	09 02	09 17	09 33	09 45	10 01	10 15	10 33	10 46	11 01	11 15	11 33
	d	09 03	09 19	09 34	09 47	10 02	10 17	10 34	10 47	11 02	11 17	11 34
Worplesdon	d			09 40				10 40				11 40
Woking	a	09 11	09 27	09 44	09 59	10 11	10 25	10 44	10 57	11 11	11 25	11 44
	d	09 13	09 28	09 46	10 00	10 12	10 26	10 46	10 59	11 12	11 26	11 46
Clapham Junction	a	09 32		10 05		10 31		11 05		11 31		12 05
London Waterloo ⊖	a	09 43	09 55	10 13	10 29	10 40	10 54	11 13	11 23	11 40	11 51	12 13

Station		SW ◇■ 🛒	SW ■	SW ◇■ 🛒	SW ◇■	SW ◇■ 🛒	SW ■	SW ◇■ 🛒	SW ◇■	SW ◇■ 🛒	SW ■
Portsmouth Harbour ⛴	d	10 45		11 15		11 45		12 15		12 45	
Portsmouth & Southsea	d	10 50		11 20	11 24	11 50		12 20	12 24	12 50	
Fratton	d	10 54		11 24	11 28	11 54		12 24	12 28	12 54	
Hilsea	d				11 32				12 32		
Bedhampton	d				11 37				12 37		
Havant	a	11 03		11 33	11 39	12 03		12 32	12 39	13 03	
	d	11 04		11 34	11 40	12 04		12 34	12 40	13 04	
Rowlands Castle	d				11 46				12 46		
Petersfield	d	11 18		11 48	11 57	12 18		12 48	12 57	13 18	
Liss	d				12 02				13 02		
Liphook	d				12 09				13 09		
Haslemere ■	a	11 31		12 00	12 15	12 31		13 00	13 15	13 31	
	d	11 32	11 39	12 02	12 15	12 32	12 39	13 02	13 15	13 32	13 39
Witley	d		11 45				12 45				13 45
Milford (Surrey)	d		11 49				12 49				13 49
Godalming	d		11 53		12 25		12 53		13 25		13 53
Farncombe	d		11 56		12 28		12 56		13 28		13 56
Guildford	a	11 45	12 01	12 15	12 33	12 45	13 01	13 15	13 33	13 45	14 01
	d	11 47	12 02	12 17	12 34	12 47	13 02	13 17	13 34	13 47	14 02
Worplesdon	d				12 40				13 40		
Woking	a	11 57	12 11	12 25	12 44	12 57	13 11	13 25	13 44	13 57	14 11
	d	11 59	12 12	12 26	12 46	12 59	13 12	13 26	13 46	13 59	14 12
Clapham Junction	a		12 31		13 05		13 31		14 05		14 31
London Waterloo ⊖	a	12 23	12 40	12 51	13 13	13 23	13 40	13 51	14 13	14 23	14 43

Station		SW ◇■ 🛒	SW ◇■	SW ◇■ 🛒	SW ■	SW ◇■ 🛒	SW ◇■	SW ◇■ 🛒	SW ■	SW ◇■ 🛒	SW ◇■	SW ■
Portsmouth Harbour ⛴	d	13 15		13 45		14 15		14 45		15 15		
Portsmouth & Southsea	d	13 20	13 24	13 50		14 20	14 24	14 50		15 20	15 24	
Fratton	d	13 24	13 28	13 54		14 24	14 28	14 54		15 24	15 28	
Hilsea	d		13 32				14 32				15 32	
Bedhampton	d		13 37				14 37				15 37	
Havant	a	13 32	13 39	14 03		14 33	14 39	15 03		15 32	15 39	
	d	13 34	13 40	14 04		14 34	14 40	15 04		15 34	15 40	15 52
Rowlands Castle	d		13 46				14 46				15 46	
Petersfield	d	13 48	13 57	14 18		14 48	14 57	15 18		15 48	15 57	16 06
Liss	d		14 02				15 02				16 02	
Liphook	d		14 09				15 09				16 09	
Haslemere ■	a	14 00	14 15	14 31		15 00	15 15	15 31		16 00	16 15	16 19
	d	14 02	14 15	14 32	14 39	15 02	15 15	15 32	15 37	16 02	16 15	16 24
Witley	d				14 45				15 43			16 30
Milford (Surrey)	d				14 49				15 47			16 34
Godalming	d		14 25		14 53		15 25		15 51		16 25	16 38
Farncombe	d		14 28		14 56		15 28		15 54		16 28	16 41
Guildford	a	14 15	14 33	14 45	15 01	15 15	15 33	15 45	15 59	16 15	16 33	16 46
	d	14 17	14 34	14 47	15 02	15 17	15 34	15 47	16 00	16 17	16 34	16 47
Worplesdon	d		14 40				15 40		16 06		16 40	
Woking	a	14 25	14 44	14 57	15 11	15 25	15 44	15 57	16 11	16 25	16 44	16 57
	d	14 26	14 46	14 59	15 12	15 26	15 46	15 59	16 12	16 26	16 46	16 59
Clapham Junction	a		15 05		15 32		16 05		16 31		17 05	
London Waterloo ⊖	a	14 53	15 13	15 23	15 43	15 51	16 15	16 24	16 40	16 53	17 14	17 27

Station		SW ◇■ 🛒	SW ◇■ 🛒	SW ◇■	SW ■	SW ◇■ 🛒	SW ◇■ 🛒	SW ◇■	SW ◇■ 🛒	SW ◇■ 🛒	SW ◇■	SW ◇■ 🛒
Portsmouth Harbour ⛴	d	15 45	16 15			16 45	17 15	17 19	17 45	18 15	18 19	18 45
Portsmouth & Southsea	d	15 50	16 20	16 24		16 50	17 20	17 24	17 50	18 20	18 24	18 50
Fratton	d	15 54	16 24	16 28		16 54	17 24	17 28	17 54	18 24	18 28	18 54
Hilsea	d			16 32				17 32			18 32	
Bedhampton	d			16 37				17 37			18 37	
Havant	a	16 03	16 32	16 39		17 03	17 33	17 39	18 03	18 33	18 39	19 03
	d	16 04	16 34	16 40	16 59	17 04	17 34	17 40	18 04	18 34	18 40	19 04
Rowlands Castle	d			16 46				17 46			18 46	
Petersfield	d	16 18	16 48	16 57	17 13	17 18	17 48	17 57	18 18	18 48	18 57	19 18
Liss	d	16 23		17 02		17 23		18 02			19 02	
Liphook	d	16 30		17 09		17 30		18 09			19 09	
Haslemere ■	a	16 35	17 00	17 15	17 26	17 35	18 01	18 15	18 31	19 00	19 14	19 31
	d	16 37	17 02	17 15	17 30	17 37	18 02	18 15	18 32	19 02	19 15	19 32
Witley	d	16 43				17 43			18 38			
Milford (Surrey)	d	16 47				17 47			18 42			
Godalming	d	16 51		17 25	17 40	17 51		18 25	18 46	19 11	19 25	19 41
Farncombe	d	16 54		17 28		17 54		18 28	18 49	19 14	19 28	
Guildford	a	16 59	17 15	17 33	17 46	17 59	18 15	18 33	18 54	19 19	19 33	19 47
	d	17 00	17 17	17 34	17 47	18 00	18 17	18 34	18 55	19 21	19 34	19 49
Worplesdon	d	17 06		17 40		18 06		18 40			19 40	
Woking	a	17 11	17 25	17 44	17 58	18 11		18 44	19 03	19 29	19 45	19 57
	d	17 12	17 26	17 46	17 59	18 12		18 46	19 05	19 30	19 46	19 59
Clapham Junction	a	17 31		18 05		18 32		19 05			20 05	
London Waterloo ⊖	a	17 43	17 54	18 14	18 27	18 43	18 59	19 13	19 29	19 59	20 14	20 24

A from 8 October
B until 5 October

Table T156-R

Portsmouth, Haslemere and Guildford - London

Mondays to Fridays
21 May to 7 December

		SW	SW	SW	SW	SW	SW	SW	SW	SW FO	SW FX	SW
		1	◇1	◇1	◇1	◇1	◇1	◇1	◇1	◇1	◇1	1
Portsmouth Harbour ⛴	d		19 15	19 19	19 45	20 15	20 19	20 45	21 19	22 19	22 19	23 19
Portsmouth & Southsea	d		19 20	19 24	19 50	20 20	20 24	20 50	21 24	22 24	22 24	23 24
Fratton	d		19 24	19 28	19 54	20 24	20 28	20 54	21 28	22 28	22 28	23 28
Hilsea	d			19 32			20 32		21 32	22 32	22 32	23 32
Bedhampton	d			19 37			20 37		21 37	22 38	22 38	23 37
Havant	a		19 33	19 39	20 03	20 32	20 39	21 02	21 39	22 40	22 40	23 39
	d		19 34	19 40	20 04	20 34	20 40	21 04	21 40	22 41	22 41	23 40
Rowlands Castle	d			19 46			20 46		21 46	22 46	22 46	23 46
Petersfield	d		19 48	19 57	20 18	20 48	20 57	21 18	21 57	22 57	22 57	23 57
Liss	d			20 02			21 02		22 02	23 02	23 02	00 02
Liphook	d			20 09			21 09		22 09	23 09	23 09	00 09
Haslemere 4	a		20 01	20 15	20 31	21 01	21 15	21 31	22 14	23 14	23 14	00 15
	d	19 39	20 02	20 15	20 32	21 02	21 15	21 32	22 15	23 15	23 15	00 15
Witley	d	19 45		20 21			21 21		22 21	23 21	23 21	00 21
Milford (Surrey)	d	19 49		20 25			21 25		22 25	23 25	23 25	00 25
Godalming	d	19 53		20 29	20 41		21 29	21 41	22 29	23 29	23 29	00 29
Farncombe	d	19 56		20 32			21 32		22 32	23 32	23 32	00 32
Guildford	a	20 01	20 15	20 38	20 47	21 16	21 37	21 47	22 37	23 37	23 37	00 37
	d	20 02	20 17	20 39	20 49	21 17	21 39	21 49	22 39	23 39	23 39	
Worplesdon	d			20 45			21 44		22 44	23 44	23 44	
Woking	a	20 11	20 25	20 52	20 59	21 25	21 49	21 57	22 49	23 49	23 49	
	d	20 12	20 26	20 53	21 01	21 26	21 50	21 59	22 50	23 56	23 56	
Clapham Junction	a	20 32		21 12			22 09		23 09	00 22	00 22	
London Waterloo 15 ⊖	a	20 40	20 51	21 21	21 29	21 51	22 18	22 27	23 19	00 32	00 33	

Saturdays
26 May to 8 December

		SW	SW	SW	SW	SW	SW	SW	SW	SW	SW	SW	SW	SW	SW	SW	SW	SW	SW	SW	SW	SW	SW
		1	◇1	◇1	◇1	◇1	1	1	◇1	◇1	1	◇1	◇1	◇1	1	◇1	◇1	◇1	1	◇1	◇1	◇1	1
			A	B	A	B																	
										⊤		⊤		⊤		⊤		⊤		⊤		⊤	
Portsmouth Harbour ⛴	d		04 38	04 43	05 14	05 19		05 40	06 19	06 45		07 15		07 45		08 15		08 45		09 15		09 45	
Portsmouth & Southsea	d		04 43	04 48	05 19	05 24		05 44	06 24	06 50		07 20	07 24	07 50		08 20	08 24	08 50		09 20	09 24	09 50	
Fratton	d		04 47	04 52	05 23	05 28		05a47	06 28	06 54		07 24	07 28	07 54		08 24	08 28	08 54		09 24	09 28	09 54	
Hilsea	d		04 51	04 56	05 27	05 32			06 32				07 32				08 32				09 32		
Bedhampton	d		04 56	05 01	05 32	05 37			06 37				07 37				08 37				09 37		
Havant	a		04 58	05 03	05 35	05 39			06 40	07 03		07 32	07 40	08 03		08 32	08 39	09 03		09 33	09 39	10 03	
	d		04 59	05 04	05 35	05 40			06 40	07 04		07 34	07 40	08 04		08 34	08 40	09 04		09 34	09 40	10 04	
Rowlands Castle	d		05 04	05 09	05 41	05 46			06 46				07 46				08 46				09 46		
Petersfield	d		05 15	05 20	05 52	05 57			06 57	07 18		07 48	07 57	08 18		08 48	08 57	09 18		09 48	09 57	10 18	
Liss	d	00 02	05 20	05 25	05 57	06 02			07 02				08 02				09 02				10 02		
Liphook	d	00 09	05 27	05 32	06 04	06 09			07 09				08 09				09 09				10 09		
Haslemere 4	a	00 15	05 33	05 38	06 12	06 14			07 14	07 31		08 00	08 15	08 31		09 00	09 15	09 31		10 00	10 15	10 31	
	d	00 15	05 34	05 39	06 13	06 15	06 39		07 15	07 32	07 39	08 02	08 15	08 32	08 39	09 02	09 15	09 32	09 39	10 02	10 15	10 32	10 39
Witley	d	00 21	05 40	05 45			06 45				07 45				08 45				09 45				10 45
Milford (Surrey)	d	00 25	05 44	05 49			06 49				07 49				08 49				09 49				10 49
Godalming	d	00 29	05 48	05 53	06 23	06 25	06 53		07 25		07 53		08 25		08 53		09 25		09 53		10 25		10 53
Farncombe	d	00 32	05 51	05 56	06 26	06 28	06 56		07 28		07 56		08 28		08 56		09 28		09 56		10 28		10 56
Guildford	a	00 37	06 01	06 01	06 33	06 33	07 01		07 33	07 45	08 01	08 15	08 33	08 45	09 01	09 15	09 33	09 45	10 01	10 15	10 33	10 45	11 01
	d		06 02	06 02	06 34	06 34	07 02		07 34	07 47	08 02	08 17	08 34	08 47	09 02	09 17	09 34	09 47	10 02	10 17	10 34	10 47	11 02
Worplesdon	d				06 40	06 40			07 40				08 40				09 40				10 40		
Woking	a		06 11	06 11	06 44	06 44	07 11		07 44	07 57	08 10	08 26	08 44	08 57	09 11	09 25	09 44	09 57	10 11	10 25	10 44	10 57	11 11
	d		06 13	06 13	06 46	06 46	07 12		07 46	07 59	08 13	08 27	08 46	08 59	09 12	09 26	09 46	09 59	10 12	10 26	10 46	10 59	11 12
Clapham Junction	a		06 32	06 32	07 05	07 05	07 31		08 05		08 33		09 05		09 31		10 05		10 31		11 05		11 31
London Waterloo 15 ⊖	a		06 40	06 40	07 13	07 13	07 40		08 13	08 23	08 42	08 51	09 13	09 23	09 41	09 51	10 13	10 23	10 40	10 51	11 13	11 23	11 40

		SW	SW	SW	SW	SW	SW	SW	SW	SW	SW	SW	SW	SW	SW	SW	SW	SW	SW	SW	SW	SW	SW
		◇1	◇1	◇1	1	◇1	◇1	◇1	1	◇1	◇1	◇1	1	◇1	◇1	◇1	1	◇1	◇1	◇1	1	◇1	◇1
		⊤		⊤		⊤		⊤		⊤		⊤		⊤		⊤		⊤		⊤		⊤	
Portsmouth Harbour ⛴	d	10 15		10 45		11 15		11 45		12 15		12 45		13 15		13 45		14 15		14 45		15 15	
Portsmouth & Southsea	d	10 20	10 24	10 50		11 20	11 24	11 50		12 20	12 24	12 50		13 20	13 24	13 50		14 20	14 24	14 50		15 20	15 24
Fratton	d	10 24	10 28	10 54		11 24	11 28	11 54		12 24	12 28	12 54		13 24	13 28	13 54		14 24	14 28	14 54		15 24	15 28
Hilsea	d		10 32				11 32				12 32				13 32				14 32				15 32
Bedhampton	d		10 37				11 37				12 37				13 37				14 37				15 37
Havant	a	10 32	10 39	11 03		11 33	11 39	12 03		12 32	12 39	13 03		13 32	13 39	14 03		14 32	14 39	15 03		15 32	15 39
	d	10 34	10 40	11 04		11 34	11 40	12 04		12 34	12 40	13 04		13 34	13 40	14 04		14 34	14 40	15 04		15 34	15 40
Rowlands Castle	d		10 46				11 46				12 46				13 46				14 46				15 46
Petersfield	d	10 48	10 57	11 18		11 48	11 57	12 18		12 48	12 57	13 18		13 48	13 57	14 18		14 48	14 57	15 18		15 48	15 57
Liss	d		11 02				12 02				13 02				14 02				15 02				16 02
Liphook	d		11 09				12 09				13 09				14 09				15 09				16 09
Haslemere 4	a	11 00	11 15	11 31		12 00	12 15	12 31		13 00	13 15	13 31		14 00	14 15	14 31		15 00	15 15	15 31		16 00	16 15
	d	11 02	11 15	11 32	11 39	12 02	12 15	12 32	12 39	13 02	13 15	13 32	13 39	14 02	14 15	14 32	14 39	15 02	15 15	15 32	15 39	16 02	16 15
Witley	d				11 45				12 45				13 45				14 45				15 45		
Milford (Surrey)	d				11 49				12 49				13 49				14 49				15 49		
Godalming	d		11 25		11 53		12 25		12 53		13 25		13 53		14 25		14 53		15 25		15 53		16 25
Farncombe	d		11 28		11 56		12 28		12 56		13 28		13 56		14 28		14 56		15 28		15 56		16 28
Guildford	a	11 15	11 33	11 45	12 01	12 15	12 33	12 45	13 01	13 15	13 33	13 45	14 01	14 15	14 33	14 45	15 01	15 15	15 33	15 45	16 01	16 15	16 33
	d	11 17	11 34	11 47	12 02	12 17	12 34	12 47	13 02	13 17	13 34	13 47	14 02	14 17	14 34	14 47	15 02	15 17	15 34	15 47	16 02	16 17	16 34
Worplesdon	d		11 40				12 40				13 40				14 40				15 40				16 40
Woking	a	11 25	11 44	11 57	12 11	12 26	12 44	12 57	13 11	13 25	13 44	13 57	14 11	14 25	14 44	14 57	15 11	15 25	15 44	15 57	16 11	16 25	16 44
	d	11 26	11 46	11 59	12 12	12 27	12 46	12 59	13 12	13 26	13 46	13 59	14 12	14 26	14 46	14 59	15 12	15 26	15 46	15 59	16 12	16 26	16 46
Clapham Junction	a		12 05		12 31		13 05		13 31		14 05		14 31		15 05		15 31		16 05		16 31		17 05
London Waterloo 15 ⊖	a	11 51	12 13	12 27	12 43	12 57	13 13	13 27	13 43	13 57	14 14	14 27	14 41	14 57	15 14	15 27	15 41	15 57	16 13	16 23	16 40	16 51	17 13

A from 13 October
B until 6 October

Table T156-R

Portsmouth, Haslemere and Guildford - London

Saturdays
26 May to 8 December

		SW	SW	SW	SW	SW	SW	SW	SW	SW	SW	SW	SW	SW	SW	SW	SW	SW	SW	SW	SW	SW
		◇1	1	◇1	◇1	◇1	1	◇1	◇1	◇1	1	◇1	◇1	◇1	1	◇1	◇1	◇1	◇1	◇1	◇1	◇1
		⊤		⊤		⊤				⊤												
Portsmouth Harbour ⛴	d	15 45		16 15		16 45			17 19	17 45		18 15		18 45		19 15		19 45	20 15		20 45	21 19
Portsmouth & Southsea	d	15 50		16 20	16 24	16 50		17 08	17 24	17 50		18 20	18 24	18 50		19 20	19 24	19 50	20 20	20 24	20 50	21 24
Fratton	d	15 54		16 24	16 28	16 54		17 12	17 28	17 54		18 24	18 28	18 54		19 24	19 28	19 54	20 24	20 28	20 54	21 28
Hilsea	d				16 32			17 16	17 32				18 32				19 32			20 32		21 32
Bedhampton	d				16 37			17 21	17 37				18 37				19 37			20 37		21 37
Havant	a	16 03		16 32	16 39	17 03		17 23	17 39	18 05		18 32	18 39	19 03		19 32	19 39	20 03	20 32	20 39	21 03	21 39
	d	16 04		16 34	16 40	17 04		17 24	17 40	18 06		18 34	18 40	19 04		19 34	19 40	20 04	20 34	20 40	21 04	21 40
Rowlands Castle	d				16 46			17 30	17 46				18 46				19 46			20 46		21 46
Petersfield	d	16 18		16 48	16 57	17 18		17 41	17 57	18 20		18 48	18 57	19 18		19 48	19 57	20 18	20 48	20 57	21 18	21 57
Liss	d				17 02			17 46	18 02				19 02				20 02			21 02		22 02
Liphook	d				17 09			17 53	18 09				19 09				20 09			21 09		22 09
Haslemere 4	a	16 31		17 00	17 15	17 31		17 59	18 15	18 33		19 00	19 15	19 31		20 00	20 15	20 31	21 00	21 15	21 31	22 14
	d	16 32	16 39	17 02	17 15	17 32	17 39	18 02	18 15	18 34	18 39	19 02	19 15	19 32	19 39	20 02	20 15	20 32	21 02	21 15	21 32	22 15
Witley	d		16 45				17 45				18 45				19 45		20 21			21 21		22 21
Milford (Surrey)	d		16 49				17 49				18 49				19 49		20 25			21 25		22 25
Godalming	d		16 53		17 25		17 53		18 25		18 53		19 25		19 53		20 29	20 41		21 29	21 41	22 29
Farncombe	d		16 56		17 28		17 56		18 28		18 56		19 28		19 56		20 32			21 32		22 32
Guildford	a	16 45	17 01	17 15	17 33	17 45	18 01	18 15	18 33	18 47	19 01	19 15	19 33	19 45	20 01	20 15	20 37	20 47	21 15	21 37	21 47	22 37
	d	16 47	17 02	17 17	17 34	17 47	18 02	18 17	18 34	18 49	19 02	19 17	19 34	19 47	20 02	20 17	20 39	20 49	21 17	21 39	21 49	22 39
Worplesdon	d				17 40				18 40				19 40				20 44			21 44		22 44
Woking	a	16 57	17 11	17 25	17 44	17 57	18 11	18 25	18 44	18 57	19 11	19 25	19 44	19 57	20 11	20 25	20 52	20 59	21 25	21 49	21 57	22 49
	d	16 59	17 12	17 26	17 46	17 59	18 12	18 26	18 46	18 59	19 12	19 26	19 46	19 59	20 12	20 26	20 53	21 01	21 26	21 50	21 59	22 50
Clapham Junction	a		17 31		18 05		18 31		19 05		19 31		20 05		20 31		21 12			22 09		23 09
London Waterloo 15 ⊖	a	17 23	17 40	17 51	18 13	18 23	18 40	18 51	19 13	19 23	19 40	19 51	20 13	20 23	20 40	20 50	21 21	21 27	21 51	22 18	22 27	23 19

		SW	SW
		◇1	1
Portsmouth Harbour ⛴	d	22 19	23 19
Portsmouth & Southsea	d	22 24	23 24
Fratton	d	22 28	23 28
Hilsea	d	22 32	23 32
Bedhampton	d	22 38	23 37
Havant	a	22 40	23 39
	d	22 41	23 40
Rowlands Castle	d	22 46	23 46
Petersfield	d	22 57	23 57
Liss	d	23 02	00 02
Liphook	d	23 09	00 09
Haslemere 4	a	23 15	00 14
	d	23 15	00 15
Witley	d	23 21	00 21
Milford (Surrey)	d	23 25	00 25
Godalming	d	23 29	00 29
Farncombe	d	23 32	00 32
Guildford	a	23 37	00 37
	d	23 39	
Worplesdon	d	23 44	
Woking	a	23 49	
	d	23 56	
Clapham Junction	a	00 22	
London Waterloo 15 ⊖	a	00 32	

Sundays
20 May to 2 December

		SW	SW	SW	SW	SW	SW	SW	SW	SW	SW	SW	SW	SW	SW	SW	SW	SW	SW		SW	SW
		1	◇1	◇1	◇1	◇1	◇1	◇1	◇1	◇1	◇1	◇1	◇1	◇1	◇1	◇1	◇1	◇1	◇1		◇1	◇1
		A	B	C	B	C		B	C													
											⊤		⊤		⊤		⊤		⊤			⊤
Portsmouth Harbour ⛴	d		06 43	06 48	07 28	07 32	07 48	08 28	08 32	08 48	09 32	09 48	10 32	10 48	11 32	11 48	12 32	12 48	13 32		15 48	16 32
Portsmouth & Southsea	d		06 48	06 53	07 33	07 37	07 53	08 33	08 37	08 53	09 37	09 53	10 37	10 53	11 37	11 53	12 37	12 53	13 37		15 53	16 37
Fratton	d		06 52	06 57	07 37	07 41	07 57	08 38	08 41	08 57	09 42	09 57	10 41	10 57	11 41	11 57	12 41	12 57	13 41		15 57	16 41
Hilsea	d																					
Bedhampton	d		06 59	07 04			08 04			09 06		10 04		11 04		12 04		13 04			16 04	
Havant	a		07 02	07 07	07 45	07 49	08 07	08 46	08 49	09 09	09 50	10 07	10 49	11 07	11 49	12 07	12 50	13 07	13 49		16 07	16 49
	d		07 02	07 07	07 46	07 50	08 07	08 47	08 50	09 09	09 50	10 07	10 50	11 07	11 50	12 07	12 50	13 07	13 50	and at the same minutes past each hour until	16 07	16 50
Rowlands Castle	d		07 08	07 13			08 13			09 15		10 13		11 13		12 13		13 13			16 13	
Petersfield	d		07 19	07 24	08 00	08 04	08 24	09 01	09 04	09 26	10 04	10 24	11 04	11 24	12 04	12 24	13 04	13 24	14 04		16 24	17 04
Liss	d	00 02	07 24	07 29			08 29			09 31		10 29		11 29		12 29		13 29			16 29	
Liphook	d	00 09	07 31	07 36			08 36			09 38		10 36		11 36		12 36		13 36			16 36	
Haslemere 4	a	00 14	07 36	07 41	08 12	08 16	08 41	09 13	09 16	09 43	10 17	10 41	11 16	11 41	12 16	12 41	13 17	13 41	14 16		16 41	17 16
	d	00 15	07 37	07 42	08 13	08 17	08 42	09 14	09 17	09 44	10 17	10 42	11 17	11 42	12 17	12 42	13 17	13 42	14 17		16 42	17 17
Witley	d	00 21	07 43	07 48			08 48			09 50		10 48		11 48		12 48		13 48			16 48	
Milford (Surrey)	d	00 25	07 47	07 52			08 52			09 54		10 52		11 52		12 52		13 52			16 52	
Godalming	d	00 29	07 51	07 56	08 23	08 27	08 56	09 24	09 27	09 58	10 27	10 56	11 27	11 56	12 27	12 56	13 27	13 56	14 27		16 56	17 27
Farncombe	d	00 32	07 54	07 59			08 59			10 01		10 59		11 59		12 59		13 59			16 59	
Guildford	a	00 37	08 04	08 04	08 33	08 33	09 04	09 33	09 33	10 06	10 33	11 04	11 33	12 04	12 33	13 04	13 33	14 04	14 33		17 04	17 33
	d		08 05	08 05	08 35	08 35	09 05	09 35	09 35	10 07	10 35	11 06	11 35	12 06	12 35	13 05	13 35	14 05	14 35		17 05	17 35
Worplesdon	d																					
Woking	a		08 13	08 13	08 42	08 42	09 15	09 42	09 42	10 15	10 42	11 13	11 42	12 13	12 42	13 13	13 42	14 13	14 42		17 13	17 42
	d		08 15	08 15	08 45	08 45	09 15	09 45	09 45	10 16	10 45	11 15	11 45	12 15	12 45	13 15	13 45	14 15	14 45		17 15	17 45
Clapham Junction	a		08 39	08 39	09 06	09 06	09 38	10 04	10 04	10 36	11 04	11 34	12 04	12 34	13 05	13 34	14 04	14 34	15 04		17 34	18 04
London Waterloo 15 ⊖	a		08 50	08 50	09 16	09 16	09 48	10 14	10 14	10 46	11 14	11 49	12 14	12 48	13 14	13 44	14 14	14 44	15 14		17 44	18 14

A not 20 May
B from 7 October
C until 30 September

Table T156-R

Sundays

20 May to 2 December

Portsmouth, Haslemere and Guildford - London

		SW ◇[1]	SW ◇[1] 🛒	SW ◇[1]	SW ◇[1] 🛒	SW ◇[1]	SW ◇[1]	SW ◇[1]	SW ◇[1]	SW ◇[1]		SW ◇[1]	SW ◇[1]	SW ◇[1]	SW [1]
Portsmouth Harbour ⛴	d	16 48	17 32	17 48	18 32	18 48	19 32	19 48	20 32	20 48		21 32	21 48	22 32	22 48
Portsmouth & Southsea	d	16 52	17 37	17 53	18 37	18 53	19 37	19 53	20 37	20 53		21 37	21 53	22 37	22 52
Fratton	d	16 56	17 41	17 57	18 41	18 57	19 41	19 57	20 41	20 57		21 41	21 57	22 41	22 56
Hilsea	d														
Bedhampton	d	17 04		18 04		19 04		20 05		21 04			22 04		23 03
Havant	a	17 06	17 49	18 07	18 49	19 07	19 49	20 07	20 49	21 07		21 49	22 07	22 49	23 06
	d	17 07	17 50	18 07	18 50	19 07	19 50	20 08	20 50	21 07		21 50	22 07	22 50	23 07
Rowlands Castle	d	17 13		18 13		19 13		20 13		21 13			22 13		23 13
Petersfield	d	17 24	18 04	18 24	19 04	19 24	20 04	20 24	21 04	21 24		22 04	22 24	23 04	23 24
Liss	d	17 29		18 29		19 29		20 29		21 29			22 29		23 29
Liphook	d	17 36		18 36		19 36		20 36		21 36			22 36		23 36
Haslemere [4]	a	17 41	18 16	18 41	19 16	19 41	20 16	20 41	21 16	21 41		22 16	22 41	23 16	23 41
	d	17 42	18 17	18 42	19 17	19 42	20 17	20 42	21 17	21 42		22 17	22 42	23 17	23 42
Witley	d	17 48		18 48		19 48		20 48		21 48			22 48		23 48
Milford (Surrey)	d	17 52		18 52		19 52		20 52		21 52			22 52		23 52
Godalming	d	17 56	18 27	18 56	19 27	19 56	20 27	20 56	21 27	21 56		22 27	22 56	23 27	23 56
Farncombe	d	17 59		18 59		19 59		20 59		21 59			22 59		23 59
Guildford	a	18 04	18 33	19 04	19 33	20 04	20 33	21 04	21 33	22 04		22 33	23 04	23 33	00 04
	d	18 05	18 35	19 05	19 35	20 05	20 35	21 05	21 35	22 05		22 35	23 05	23 35	00 05
Worplesdon	d														
Woking	a	18 13	18 42	19 13	19 42	20 13	20 42	21 13	21 42	22 13		22 42	23 13	23 42	00 13
	d	18 15	18 45	19 15	19 45	20 15	20 45	21 15	21 45	22 15		22 45	23 15	23 45	
Clapham Junction	a	18 34	19 04	19 34	20 04	20 34	21 04	21 34	22 04	22 34		23 04	23 34	00 04	
London Waterloo [15] ⊖	a	18 44	19 14	19 44	20 14	20 44	21 14	21 44	22 14	22 44		23 14	23 44	00 14	

Table T157-F

Mondays to Fridays

21 May to 7 December

Havant - Portsmouth Harbour

(Complete service)

		SW MX ◇[1]	SW MO ◇[1]	SW MO ◇[1] 🛒	SW MX [1]	SW MX ◇[1]	SW MX ◇[1]	SW MO ◇[1]	SW MO ◇[1]	SW MX ◇[1]		SW [1]	SN	SN	SW [1]	SN	SW [1]	SN	SW [1]	SW ◇[1]		SW [1]	SN	GW	SW [1]
Havant	d					00 21	00 36	00 39	00 53	01 21		04 40	05 21	05 40	06 00	06 07		06 35		07 00			07 11		
Bedhampton	d					00 24		00 41		01s24		04 43			06 03			06 37		07 03					
Hilsea	d			00 01	00 03	00 29				01s29		04 48			06 08		06 34	06 43	07 05	07 08		07 13			07 35
Fratton	d		00 03	00 07	00 08	00 34	00 46	00 50	01 02	01s33		04 52	05 30	05 49	06 13	06 16	06 41	06 48	07 09	07 12		07 18	07 21	07 35	07 39
Portsmouth & Southsea	a		00 06	00 10	00 11	00 38	00 50	00 53	01 05	01 38		04 55	05 33	05 52	06 16	06 20	06 44	06 51	07 12	07 16		07 21	07 25	07 38	07 42
	d	00 03	00 07	00 11	00 13		00 51	00 54	01 06			04 56	05 34	05 52	06 17	06 20	06 45	06 52	07 13	07 17				07 39	07 43
Portsmouth Harbour ⛴	a	00 07	00 10	00 14	00 16		00 55	00 58	01 09			04 59	05 37	05 56	06 20	06 24	06 49	06 57	07 17	07 21				07 42	07 48

		SW ◇[1]	SN	SN	SW ◇[1]	SW [1]		SW [1]	SN	GW ◇	SW ◇[1]	SN	SW [1]	SN	SW ◇[1] 🛒	SW [1]		SW ◇[1]	SN	SW ◇[1] 🛒	SW [1]	SW ◇[1]	GW ◇ 🛒	SN	SN [1]
Havant	d	07 27	07 32	07 49	07 53				08 06		08 26	08 34		08 47	08 50			09 01	09 10	09 19		09 29		09 34	09 48
Bedhampton	d	07 30	07 35	07 52	07 56						08 29	08 36						09 04				09 32		09 36	
Hilsea	d	07 37	07 40	07 57	08 01	08 03		08 06			08 34	08 41	08 45			09 05		09 09			09 33	09 37		09 42	
Fratton	d	07 43	07 45	08 01	08 05	08 08		08 11	08 16	08 21	08 39	08 46	08 50	08 56	09 00	09 09		09 14	09 19	09 28	09 37	09 41	09 44	09 47	09 57
Portsmouth & Southsea	a	07 46	07 48	08 05	08 08	08 13		08 18	08 19	08 24	08 42	08 49	08 53	08 59	09 03	09 12		09 17	09 23	09 31	09 44	09 45	09 47	09 50	10 00
	d	07 47			08 10	08 14			08 20	08 24	08 44		08 55	09 00	09 05	09 14		09 18		09 33			09 48		10 00
Portsmouth Harbour ⛴	a	07 51			08 13	08 17			08 23	08 28	08 48		08 58	09 04	09 08	09 18		09 22		09 36			09 51		10 04

		SW ◇[1] 🛒		SW [1]	SN	SW ◇[1] 🛒	SW [1]	GW ▣ 🛒	SW ◇[1]	SN	SN [1]	SW ◇[1] 🛒		SW [1]	SN	SW ◇[1] 🛒	SW [1]	SW ◇[1]	GW ◇ 🛒	SN	SW ◇[1] 🛒	SN [1]		SW [1]	SN
Havant	d	09 51			10 10	10 14			10 27	10 34	10 48	10 51			11 06	11 14		11 27		11 34	11 45	11 48			12 06
Bedhampton	d								10 30	10 36								11 30		11 36					
Hilsea	d			10 03			10 33		10 36	10 42				11 03			11 33	11 36		11 42				12 03	
Fratton	d	10 00		10 08	10 19	10 24	10 37	10 39	10 40	10 47	10 57	11 00		11 09	11 15	11 24	11 37	11 40	11 42	11 47	11 54	11 57		12 08	12 15
Portsmouth & Southsea	a	10 03		10 11	10 23	10 27	10 44	10 44	10 45	10 50	11 00	11 03		11 12	11 18	11 27	11 44	11 45	11 46	11 50	11 57	12 01		12 11	12 18
	d	10 05		10 12		10 28		10 44			11 00	11 05		11 13	11 18	11 29			11 46		11 58	12 01		12 12	12 18
Portsmouth Harbour ⛴	a	10 08		10 20		10 32		10 50			11 04	11 08		11 20	11 22	11 32			11 52		12 02	12 05		12 20	12 22

		SW ◇[1] 🛒	SW [1]	SW ◇[1]	GW ◇ 🛒	SN	SW ◇[1] 🛒	SN [1]		SW [1]	SN	SW ◇[1] 🛒	SW [1]	SW ◇[1]	GW ◇ 🛒	SN	SW ◇[1] 🛒	SN [1]		SW [1]	SN	SW ◇[1] 🛒	SW [1]	SW ◇[1]	GW ◇ 🛒
Havant	d	12 14		12 27		12 34	12 45	12 48			13 06	13 14		13 27		13 34	13 45	13 48			14 06	14 14		14 27	
Bedhampton	d			12 30		12 36								13 30		13 36								14 30	
Hilsea	d		12 33	12 36		12 42				13 03			13 33	13 36		13 42				14 03			14 33	14 36	
Fratton	d	12 24	12 37	12 40	12 42	12 47	12 54	12 57		13 08	13 15	13 24	13 37	13 40	13 42	13 47	13 54	13 57		14 08	14 15	14 24	14 37	14 40	14 42
Portsmouth & Southsea	a	12 27	12 44	12 45	12 46	12 50	12 57	13 01		13 11	13 18	13 27	13 44	13 45	13 46	13 50	13 57	14 01		14 11	14 18	14 27	14 44	14 45	14 46
	d	12 28			12 46		12 58	13 01		13 12	13 18	13 28			13 46		13 58	14 01		14 12	14 18	14 28			14 46
Portsmouth Harbour ⛴	a	12 32			12 52		13 02	13 05		13 18	13 22	13 32			13 52		14 02	14 05		14 20	14 22	14 32			14 52

		SN	SW ◇[1] 🛒	SN [1]		SW [1]	SN	SW ◇[1] 🛒	SW [1]	SW ◇[1]	GW ◇ 🛒	SN	SN [1]	SW ◇[1] 🛒		SW [1]	SN	SW ◇[1] 🛒	SW [1]	SW ◇[1]	GW ◇ 🛒	SN	SN [1]	SW ◇[1] 🛒	
Havant	d	14 34	14 45	14 48			15 06	15 16		15 27		15 34	15 48	15 51			16 09	16 14		16 27		16 34	16 48	16 51	
Bedhampton	d	14 36								15 30		15 36								16 30		16 36			
Hilsea	d	14 42				15 03			15 33	15 36		15 42				16 03			16 33	16 36		16 42			
Fratton	d	14 47	14 54	14 57		15 08	15 15	15 25	15 37	15 40	15 42	15 47	15 57	16 00		16 08	16 19	16 23	16 37	16 40	16 42	16 47	16 57	17 00	
Portsmouth & Southsea	a	14 50	14 57	15 01		15 11	15 18	15 28	15 43	15 45	15 46	15 50	16 00	16 03		16 11	16 23	16 26	16 40	16 44	16 46	16 50	17 00	17 03	
	d		14 58	15 01		15 12	15 18	15 30	15 44		15 46		16 00	16 05		16 12		16 28	16 41	16 45	16 46		17 00	17 05	
Portsmouth Harbour ⛴	a		15 02	15 05		15 20	15 22	15 33	15 48		15 52		16 04	16 08		16 20		16 31	16 44	16 50	16 52		17 04	17 08	

		SW [1]	SW ◇[1]	SN	SW ◇[1] 🛒	SW	SW ◇[1]	SW [1]	GW ◇ 🛒	SN		SW ◇[1] 🛒	SN [1]	SW ◇[1]	SW ◇[1]	SN	SW ◇[1] 🛒	SW ◇[1]	SW [1]	SW ◇[1]		GW ◇ 🛒	SN	SN [1]	SW ◇[1] 🛒
Havant	d		17 01	17 09	17 17		17 28			17 34		17 50	17 54		18 02	18 14	18 19			18 30			18 34	18 49	18 52
Bedhampton	d		17 03				17 31			17 36					18 05					18 33			18 36		
Hilsea	d	17 03	17 08				17 36	17 33		17 42				18 03	18 10				18 33	18 39			18 44		
Fratton	d	17 08	17 13	17 19	17 27	17 31	17 40	17 37	17 42	17 47		17 59	18 03	18 08	18 14	18 23	18 28	18 40	18 37	18 43		18 45	18 48	18 58	19 01
Portsmouth & Southsea	a	17 11	17 16	17 23	17 30	17 34	17 43	17 44	17 46	17 50		18 02	18 08	18 11	18 17	18 26	18 31	18 43	18 44	18 47		18 52	18 52	19 01	19 04
	d	17 12	17 18		17 31	17 36	17 45		17 46			18 04		18 13	18 19		18 33	18 45		18 49		18 52		19 01	19 06
Portsmouth Harbour ⛴	a	17 20	17 23		17 38	17 39	17 50		17 52			18 09		18 20	18 24		18 38	18 50		18 52		18 58		19 05	19 11

		SW ◇[1]	SN	SW ◇[1] 🛒	SW ◇[1]	SW [1]		GW ▣ 🛒	SN	SN [1]	SW ◇[1]	SW ◇[1] 🛒	SW ◇[1]	SN	SW ◇[1] 🛒	SW [1]		SW ◇[1]	GW ▣ 🛒	SN	SN [1]	SW ◇[1] 🛒	SW [1]	SN	SW ◇[1] 🛒
Havant	d		19 11	19 17					19 34	19 49	19 43	19 52		20 10	20 17			20 28		20 35	20 48	20 51		21 11	21 19
Bedhampton	d								19 36		19 46							20 31		20 38					
Hilsea	d	19 05			19 28	19 33			19 42		19 51		20 03			20 33		20 36		20 44			21 03		
Fratton	d	19 09	19 20	19 26	19 33	19 37		19 44	19 47	19 58	19 57	20 01	20 08	20 19	20 26	20 37		20 41	20 45	20 48	20 57	21 00	21 08	21 20	21 28
Portsmouth & Southsea	a	19 12	19 23	19 29	19 36	19 44		19 47	19 50	20 01	20 03	20 04	20 12	20 23	20 29	20 44		20 44	20 49	20 53	21 00	21 03	21 11	21 23	21 31
	d	19 14		19 31	19 38			19 48		20 01		20 06	20 14		20 31			20 45	20 50		21 00	21 05	21 13		21 32
Portsmouth Harbour ⛴	a	19 20		19 36	19 43			19 51		20 05		20 11	20 20		20 34			20 53	20 54		21 04	21 08	21 18		21 36

Table T157-F

Havant - Portsmouth Harbour

(Complete service)

Mondays to Fridays

21 May to 7 December

	SW	SW	GW	SW	SN	SW	SN	SW	SW	SW	GW	SW	SN	SN	SW	SW	SW	SW	GW	SN	SW
	■	◇■	◇ 🍴	◇■ 🍴	■	■		◇■ 🍴	■	◇■	◇	◇■	■		◇■	■	■	◇■	◇	■	◇■
Havant d		21 30		21 47	21 50		22 11	22 19		22 31		22 49	22 53	23 11	23 19			23 30		23 37	23 50
Bedhampton d		21 33								22 34								23 33			
Hilsea d	21 33	21 38				22 04			22 33	22 39						23 24	23 33	23 38			
Fratton d	21 37	21 43	21 48	21 56	22 00	22 08	22 20	22 28	22 37	22 44	22 54	22 59	23 04	23 20	23 28	23 33	23 37	23 43	23 44	23 49	23 59
Portsmouth & Southsea a	21 41	21 47	21 51	21 59	22 03	22 11	22 23	22 31	22 45	22 49	22 57	23 02	23 07	23 23	23 31	23 36	23 44	23 47	23 48	23 54	00 02
d	21 42		21 52	22 00	22 03	22 13	22 23	22 33			22 58	23 03	23 08	23 24	23 33	23 37			23 48		00 03
Portsmouth Harbour ⛴ a	21 46		21 55	22 03	22 07	22 18	22 27	22 36			23 02	23 07	23 11	23 28	23 36	23 40			23 52		00 07

Saturdays

26 May to 8 December

	SW	SW	SW	SW	SW	SW	SN	SN	SW	SN	SW	SN	SN	SW	SN	SW	SW	GW	SN	SN	SW	SN
	◇■	■	◇■	◇■	◇■	■		■	■		■		■	■		◇■	■			■	■	
Havant d			00 21	00 36	01 21	04 40	05 34	05 48	06 02	06 06		06 34	06 48		07 06	07 23			07 34	07 48		08 06
Bedhampton d			00 24		01s24	04 43	05 36		06 05			06 36				07 26			07 36			
Hilsea d		00 03	00 29		01s29	04 48	05 42		06 10		06 38	06 42		07 03		07 31	07 33		07 42		08 03	
Fratton d		00 08	00 34	00 46	01s33	04 52	05 47	05 57	06 14	06 18	06 43	06 47	06 57	07 08	07 15	07 35	07 38	07 43	07 47	07 57	08 08	08 17
Portsmouth & Southsea a		00 11	00 38	00 50	01 38	04 55	05 50	06 00	06 17	06 21	06 46	06 50	07 00	07 11	07 18	07 38	07 42	07 46	07 50	08 00	08 11	08 20
d	00 03	00 13		00 51		04 57		06 00	06 18	06 22			07 00	07 12	07 18	07 40		07 46		08 00	08 13	08 20
Portsmouth Harbour ⛴ a	00 07	00 16		00 55		05 00		06 04	06 22	06 25			07 04	07 16	07 22	07 43		07 52		08 04	08 18	08 24

	SW	SW	GW	SN	SN	SW	SW	SN	SW	SW	SW	GW	SN	SN	SW	SW	SN	SW	SW	SW	GW	SN
	◇■	■	◇		■	◇■	■		◇■	■	◇■	◇		■	◇■	■		◇■ 🍴	■	◇■	◇	
Havant d	08 17			08 34	08 48	08 51		09 06	09 17		09 27		09 34	09 48	09 51		10 09	10 17		10 27		10 34
Bedhampton d	08 20			08 36							09 30		09 36							10 30		10 36
Hilsea d	08 25	08 33		08 42			09 04			09 33	09 36		09 42			10 03			10 33	10 36		10 42
Fratton d	08 30	08 37	08 40	08 47	08 57	09 00	09 09	09 15	09 26	09 37	09 40	09 43	09 47	09 57	10 00	10 08	10 18	10 26	10 37	10 40	10 43	10 47
Portsmouth & Southsea a	08 33	08 42	08 45	08 50	09 00	09 03	09 12	09 18	09 29	09 42	09 44	09 46	09 50	10 00	10 03	10 11	10 21	10 29	10 42	10 44	10 46	10 50
d	08 34		08 46		09 00	09 05	09 13	09 18	09 31			09 47		10 00	10 05	10 12	10 22	10 31			10 47	
Portsmouth Harbour ⛴ a	08 38		08 51		09 04	09 08	09 18	09 22	09 34			09 52		10 04	10 08	10 18	10 26	10 34			10 52	

	SN	SW	SW	SN	SW	SW	SW	GW	SN	SN	SW	SW	SN	SW	SW	SW	GW	SN	SN	SW	SW
	■	◇■ 🍴	■		◇■ 🍴	■	◇■	◇		■	◇■ 🍴	■		◇■ 🍴	■	◇■	◇ 🍴		■	◇■ 🍴	■
Havant d	10 48	10 51		11 06	11 17		11 27		11 34	11 48	11 51		12 06	12 17		12 27		12 34	12 48	12 51	
Bedhampton d							11 30		11 36							12 30		12 36			
Hilsea d			11 03			11 33	11 36		11 42			12 03			12 33	12 36		12 42			13 03
Fratton d	10 57	11 00	11 08	11 15	11 26	11 37	11 40	11 43	11 47	11 57	12 00	12 08	12 15	12 26	12 37	12 40	12 43	12 47	12 57	13 00	13 08
Portsmouth & Southsea a	11 00	11 03	11 11	11 18	11 29	11 42	11 44	11 46	11 50	12 00	12 03	12 11	12 18	12 29	12 42	12 44	12 46	12 50	13 00	13 03	13 11
d	11 00	11 05	11 12	11 18	11 31			11 47		12 00	12 05	12 12	12 18	12 31			12 47		13 00	13 05	13 12
Portsmouth Harbour ⛴ a	11 04	11 08	11 18	11 22	11 34			11 52		12 04	12 08	12 18	12 22	12 34			12 52		13 04	13 08	13 18

	SN	SW	SW	SW	GW	SN	SN	SW	SW	SN	SW	SW	SW	GW	SN	SN	SW	SW	SN	SW	SW	SW
		◇■ 🍴	■	◇■	◇ 🍴		■	◇■ 🍴	■		◇■ 🍴	■	◇■	◇ 🍴		■	◇■ 🍴	■		◇■ 🍴	■	◇■
Havant d	13 06	13 17		13 27		13 34	13 48	13 51		14 06	14 17		14 27		14 34	14 48	14 51		15 06	15 17		15 27
Bedhampton d				13 30		13 36							14 30		14 36							15 30
Hilsea d			13 33	13 36		13 42			14 03			14 33	14 36		14 42			15 03			15 33	15 36
Fratton d	13 15	13 26	13 37	13 40	13 43	13 47	13 57	14 00	14 08	14 15	14 26	14 37	14 40	14 43	14 47	14 57	15 00	15 08	15 15	15 26	15 37	15 40
Portsmouth & Southsea a	13 18	13 29	13 42	13 44	13 46	13 50	14 00	14 03	14 11	14 18	14 29	14 42	14 44	14 46	14 50	15 00	15 03	15 11	15 18	15 29	15 42	15 44
d	13 18	13 31			13 47		14 00	14 05	14 12	14 18	14 31			14 47		15 00	15 05	15 12	15 18	15 30		
Portsmouth Harbour ⛴ a	13 22	13 34			13 52		14 04	14 08	14 18	14 22	14 34			14 52		15 04	15 08	15 18	15 22	15 33		

	GW	SN	SN	SW	SW	SN	SW	SW	SW	GW	SN	SN	SW	SW	SN	SW	SW	SW	GW	SN	SN
	◇ 🍴		■	◇■ 🍴	■		◇■ 🍴	■	◇■	◇		■	◇■ 🍴	■		◇■ 🍴	■	◇■	◇		■
Havant d		15 34	15 48	15 51		16 06	16 17		16 27		16 34	16 48	16 51		17 06	17 17		17 27		17 34	17 48
Bedhampton d		15 36							16 30		16 36							17 30		17 36	
Hilsea d		15 42			16 03			16 33	16 36		16 42			17 03			17 33	17 36		17 42	
Fratton d	15 43	15 47	15 57	16 00	16 08	16 15	16 26	16 37	16 40	16 43	16 47	16 57	17 00	17 08	17 15	17 26	17 37	17 40	17 43	17 47	17 57
Portsmouth & Southsea a	15 46	15 50	16 00	16 03	16 11	16 18	16 29	16 40	16 44	16 46	16 50	17 00	17 03	17 11	17 18	17 29	17 42	17 44	17 46	17 50	18 00
d	15 47		16 00	16 05	16 12	16 18	16 31	16 41		16 47		17 00	17 05	17 12	17 18	17 31			17 47		18 00
Portsmouth Harbour ⛴ a	15 52		16 04	16 08	16 18	16 22	16 34	16 44		16 52		17 04	17 08	17 16	17 22	17 34			17 52		18 04

	SW	SW	SN	SW	SW	SW	GW	SN	SN	SW	SW	SN	SW	SW	SW	GW	SN	SN	SW	SW	SN	SW
	◇■ 🍴	■		◇■ 🍴	■	◇■	◇		■	◇■ 🍴	■		◇■ 🍴	■	◇■	■		■	◇■ 🍴	■		◇■ 🍴
Havant d	17 51		18 09	18 17		18 27		18 34	18 48	18 51		19 06	19 17		19 27		19 34	19 48	19 51		20 06	20 17
Bedhampton d						18 30		18 36							19 30		19 36					
Hilsea d		18 03			18 33	18 36		18 42			19 03			19 33	19 36		19 42			20 03		
Fratton d	18 00	18 08	18 18	18 26	18 37	18 40	18 43	18 47	18 57	19 00	19 08	19 15	19 26	19 37	19 40	19 43	19 47	19 57	20 00	20 08	20 15	20 26
Portsmouth & Southsea a	18 03	18 11	18 21	18 29	18 42	18 44	18 46	18 50	19 00	19 03	19 11	19 18	19 29	19 42	19 44	19 46	19 50	20 00	20 03	20 11	20 18	20 29
d	18 05	18 12	18 22	18 31			18 47		19 00	19 05	19 12	19 18	19 31			19 47		20 00	20 05	20 12	20 18	20 31
Portsmouth Harbour ⛴ a	18 08	18 18	18 26	18 34			18 52		19 04	19 08	19 18	19 22	19 34			19 52		20 04	20 08	20 18	20 22	20 34

Table T157-F

Havant - Portsmouth Harbour

(Complete service)

Saturdays

26 May to 8 December

	SW	GW	SW	SN	SN	SW	SW	SN	SW	SW	SW	GW	SW	SN	SW	SN	SW	SW	GW	SW	SN
	■	◇	◇■		■	◇■ 🍴	■		◇■	■	◇■	◇	◇■	■	■		◇■	■	◇	◇■	
Havant d			20 30	20 34	20 48	20 51		21 06	21 17		21 27		21 45	21 49		22 06	22 19			22 31	22 39
Bedhampton d			20 33	20 36							21 30									22 34	
Hilsea d	20 33		20 40	20 42			21 03			21 33	21 36				22 03			22 33		22 40	
Fratton d	20 37	20 41	20 44	20 47	20 57	21 00	21 08	21 15	21 26	21 37	21 40	21 43	21 55	21 58	22 08	22 15	22 29	22 37	22 42	22 45	22 49
Portsmouth & Southsea a	20 42	20 44	20 48	20 50	21 00	21 03	21 11	21 18	21 29	21 40	21 43	21 46	21 58	22 03	22 11	22 18	22 32	22 40	22 45	22 49	22 52
d		20 44			21 00	21 05	21 12	21 18	21 31	21 41		21 47	21 59	22 03	22 12	22 18	22 33	22 41	22 46	22 50	22 53
Portsmouth Harbour ⛴ a		20 50			21 04	21 08	21 16	21 22	21 34	21 45		21 52	22 03	22 07	22 18	22 22	22 36	22 47	22 52	22 53	22 56

	SW	SW	SN	SW	SW	GW	SW	SN	SW
	◇■	■		◇■	■	◇	◇■	■	◇■
Havant d	22 49		23 06	23 19			23 30	23 37	23 49
Bedhampton d							23 33		
Hilsea d		23 03			23 33		23 41		
Fratton d	22 59	23 08	23 15	23 28	23 37	23 42	23 46	23 49	23 59
Portsmouth & Southsea a	23 02	23 11	23 18	23 31	23 40	23 45	23 49	23 55	00 02
d	23 03	23 12	23 18	23 33		23 46	23 50		00 03
Portsmouth Harbour ⛴ a	23 08	23 18	23 22	23 36		23 52	23 54		00 07

Sundays

20 May to 2 December

	SW	SW	SW	SW	SW	SN	SW	SW	SN	SW	SW	SW	SN	SW	SN	SW	SW	SN	SW	SW	SW	SN
	◇■ A	■ A	◇■ A	◇■ A	◇■ A		■	■		■ B	■ C	■		■		■	◇■		◇■	■	■	
Havant d			00 21	00 36	01 21	07 15			08 16			08 39	08 50		09 19		09 44	09 51	09 56			10 37
Bedhampton d			00 24		01s24							08 41	08 52				09 46	09 53				
Hilsea d		00 03	00 29		01s29		07 24	08 00		08 26	08 26			09 00		09 30				10 00	10 24	
Fratton d		00 07	00 34	00 46	01s33	07 24	07 29	08 04	08 25	08 31	08 31	08 50	09 00	09 05	09 28	09 34	09 55	10 01	10 05	10 09	10 29	10 47
Portsmouth & Southsea a		00 11	00 37	00 49	01 37	07 27	07 32	08 08	08 28	08 35	08 37	08 53	09 03	09 08	09 31	09 37	09 58	10 04	10 08	10 12	10 32	10 52
d	00 03	00 12		00 50		07 27		08 09	08 29			08 54	09 04	09 09	09 32		09 59	10 05	10 09	10 13		10 53
Portsmouth Harbour ⛴ a	00 07	00 16		00 54		07 31		08 13	08 32			08 57	09 07	09 13	09 35		10 04	10 08	10 13	10 16		10 56

	SW	SN	SW	SW	SW	GW	SN	SW	SN	SW	SW	SW	GW	SN	SW	SN	SW	SW	SW	SN	SW	SN
	◇■		◇■	■	■	◇		◇■		◇■	■	■	◇		◇■		◇■ 🍴	■	■		◇■	
Havant d	10 44	10 50	10 56				11 37	11 41	11 50	11 54				12 37	12 41	12 50	12 54			13 37	13 40	13 50
Bedhampton d	10 46	10 52						11 43	11 52						12 43	12 52					13 43	13 52
Hilsea d				11 00	11 24						12 00	12 28						13 00	13 26			
Fratton d	10 55	11 00	11 05	11 09	11 29	11 42	11 47	11 52	12 00	12 03	12 09	12 33	12 42	12 48	12 52	13 00	13 03	13 09	13 30	13 46	13 51	14 00
Portsmouth & Southsea a	10 58	11 03	11 08	11 12	11 32	11 46	11 50	11 55	12 03	12 07	12 12	12 36	12 46	12 52	12 56	13 03	13 07	13 12	13 33	13 49	13 54	14 03
d	10 59	11 04	11 09	11 13		11 47	11 52	11 56	12 04	12 08	12 13		12 47	12 53	12 57	13 04	13 08	13 13		13 50	13 56	14 04
Portsmouth Harbour ⛴ a	11 04	11 07	11 13	11 16		11 51	11 55	12 00	12 07	12 11	12 16		12 53	12 56	13 00	13 07	13 11	13 16		13 53	14 04	14 07

	SW	SW	SW	GW	SN	SW	SN	SW	SW	SW	SN	SW	SN	SW	SW	SW	GW	SN	SW	SW	SW
	◇■ 🍴	■	■	◇		◇■		◇■ 🍴	■	■		◇■		◇■ 🍴	■	■	◇		◇■	◇■ 🍴	■
Havant d	13 54				14 37	14 41	14 50	14 54			15 37	15 41	15 50	15 54				16 37	16 41	16 54	
Bedhampton d						14 43	14 52					15 43	15 52						16 43		
Hilsea d		14 00	14 26						15 00	15 26					16 00	16 26					17 00
Fratton d	14 04	14 09	14 30	14 42	14 48	14 52	15 00	15 03	15 09	15 30	15 46	15 52	16 00	16 03	16 09	16 30	16 42	16 48	16 52	17 03	17 09
Portsmouth & Southsea a	14 07	14 12	14 33	14 46	14 51	14 55	15 03	15 08	15 12	15 33	15 49	15 55	16 03	16 07	16 12	16 33	16 46	16 51	16 55	17 07	17 12
d	14 08	14 13		14 47	14 52	14 56	15 04	15 08	15 13		15 50	15 56	16 04	16 08	16 13		16 47	16 52	16 56	17 08	17 13
Portsmouth Harbour ⛴ a	14 11	14 16		14 53	14 56	15 00	15 07	15 11	15 20		15 53	15 59	16 07	16 13	16 17		16 52	16 55	17 04	17 11	17 16

	SW	GW	SN	SW	SN	SW	SW	SW	GW	SN	SW	SW	SW	SW	GW	SN	SW	SN	SW	SW	SW	GW
	■	◇		◇■		◇■ 🍴	◇■	■	◇		◇■	◇■ 🍴	◇■	■	◇		◇■		◇■ 🍴	◇■	■	◇
Havant d			17 37	17 41	17 50	17 54				18 37	18 40	18 54				19 37	19 41	19 50	19 54			
Bedhampton d				17 43	17 52						18 43						19 43	19 52				
Hilsea d	17 26						18 00	18 26					19 00	19 26						20 05	20 25	
Fratton d	17 30	17 42	17 47	17 52	18 00	18 03	18 09	18 30	18 42	18 48	18 52	19 03	19 09	19 30	19 42	19 48	19 52	20 00	20 03	20 09	20 30	20 42
Portsmouth & Southsea a	17 33	17 46	17 50	17 55	18 03	18 07	18 12	18 33	18 46	18 51	18 55	19 07	19 12	19 33	19 46	19 51	19 55	20 03	20 07	20 12	20 33	20 47
d		17 47	17 51	17 56	18 04	18 08	18 13		18 47	18 52	18 56	19 08	19 14		19 47	19 52	19 56	20 04	20 08	20 14		20 48
Portsmouth Harbour ⛴ a		17 51	17 54	18 04	18 07	18 11	18 16		18 52	18 55	18 59	19 11	19 17		19 52	19 55	20 04	20 07	20 11	20 17		20 52

	SN	SW	SN	SW	SW	GW	SW	GW	SN	SW	SN	SW	SW	SW	GW	SN	SW	GW	SW	SW	SN
		◇■		◇■ 🍴	◇■	◇	■	◇		◇■		◇■ 🍴	◇■	■	◇		◇■		◇■	◇■	
Havant d	20 37	20 41	20 50	20 54					21 37	21 41	21 50	21 54				22 37	22 41	22 44	22 54		22 58
Bedhampton d		20 43	20 52							21 43	21 52						22 43				23 01
Hilsea d					21 00		21 25						22 00	22 26						23 00	
Fratton d	20 48	20 52	21 00	21 03	21 09	21 13	21 30	21 41	21 46	21 52	22 00	22 04	22 09	22 30	22 43	22 48	22 52	22 59	23 03	23 08	23 12
Portsmouth & Southsea a	20 51	20 55	21 03	21 07	21 12	21 17	21 33	21 43	21 49	21 55	22 03	22 07	22 12	22 33	22 46	22 52	22 56	23 02	23 07	23 11	23 15
d	20 52	20 56	21 04	21 08	21 14	21 18		21 44	21 50	21 56	22 04	22 08	22 13		22 47	22 53	22 56	23 03	23 08	23 12	23 16
Portsmouth Harbour ⛴ a	20 55	21 00	21 07	21 11	21 17	21 21		21 51	21 54	22 00	22 07	22 11	22 16		22 52	22 56	23 00	23 07	23 11	23 16	23 20

A not 20 May

B until 30 September

C from 7 October

Table T157-F

Sundays
20 May to 2 December

Havant - Portsmouth Harbour
(Complete service)

		SW	SN	GW	SW		SW
		■		◇	◇■		◇■
Havant	d		23 26		23 43		23 54
Bedhampton	d				23 45		
Hilsea	d	23 28					
Fratton	d	23 33	23 35	23 43	23 54		00 03
Portsmouth & Southsea	a	23 36	23 38	23 46	23 57		00 06
	d		23 39	23 47	23 58		00 07
Portsmouth Harbour	a		23 42	23 50	00 01		00 10

AVAILABLE FROM MP Middleton Press

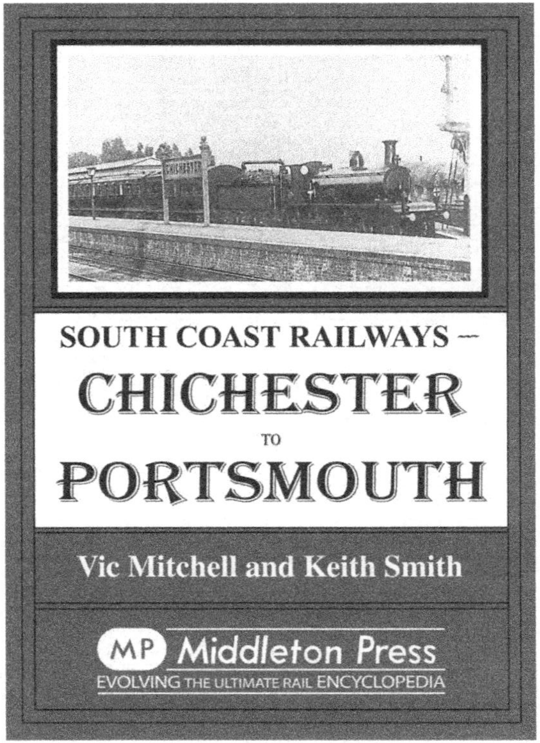

Table T157-R

Mondays to Fridays
21 May to 7 December

Portsmouth Harbour - Havant
(Complete service)

Network Diagram - see first page of Table 155

		SW	SW	SW	SW	SW		SW	SW	SN	SW	SW	SN	GW	SN	SW		SW	SW	SN	SW	SW	SW	GW	GW
		◇■ A	◇■ B	■ A	■ B	■		◇■ A ⊥	◇■ B ⊥	■	■	◇■	■	▪ ⊥		◇■ ⊥		■	◇■		◇■ ⊥	◇■	◇■	◇ ⊥	
Portsmouth Harbour	d	04 25	04 25	04 55	05 00			05 14	05 19	05 28	05 43	05 50	05 57	06 00	06 12	06 15			06 23	06 32	06 42	06 50	06 54	07 05	07 09
Portsmouth & Southsea	a	04 28	04 28	04 58	05 03			05 17	05 22	05 31	05 46	05 53	06 00	06 03	06 15	06 18			06 26	06 35	06 45	06 53	06 57	07 08	07 12
	d	04 29	04 30	05 00	05 05	05 16		05 19	05 24	05 32	05 48	05 55	06 01	06 04	06 16	06 20		06 23	06 28	06 36	06 47	06 55	06 58	07 09	07 13
Fratton	d	04 33	04 34	05 04	05 09	05 20		05 23	05 28	05 36	05 52	05 59	06 05	06a07	06 20	06 24		06 27	06 32	06 40	06 51	06 59	07 03	07a13	07 17
Hilsea	d	04 37	04 38	05a08	05a13	05a24		05 27	05 32	05 40	05a56	06 03			06 24			06a31	06a36			07a03	07 07		
Bedhampton	d	04 42	04 43					05 32	05 37	05 45		06 08			06 29								07 12		
Havant	a	04 44	04 45					05 35	05 39	05 47		06 10	06 13		06 31	06 34				06 50	06 59		07 14		07 25

		SW		SN	SW	SN	SW	SW	SW	SN	SW	SW		SN	SW	SW	GW	SN	SW	SW	SN	SW		SN	SW
		◇■ ⊥			◇■		◇■	■	◇■ ⊥		■			■	◇■ ⊥	◇■	◇ ⊥		■	◇■ ⊥		■		■	◇■ ⊥
Portsmouth Harbour	d	07 12		07 18	07 23		07 30		07 45		07 55	08 05			08 15		08 23	08 29	08 33	08 45		08 59		09 11	09 15
Portsmouth & Southsea	a	07 15		07 22	07 26		07 33		07 48		07 58	08 08			08 18		08 26	08 32	08 36	08 48		09 02		09 14	09 18
	d	07 17		07 22	07 28	07 32	07 35	07 39	07 50	07 57	08 00	08 10		08 14	08 20	08 24	08 27	08 33	08 38	08 50	08 57	09 04		09 15	09 20
Fratton	d	07 21		07 26	07 32	07 36	07 39	07 43	07 54	08 01	08 04	08 14		08 18	08 24	08 28	08a31	08 37	08 42	08 54	09 01	09 08		09 19	09 24
Hilsea	d			07 30	07a36		07 43	07a47		08 05	08a08	08a18				08 32			08a46		09 05	09a12			
Bedhampton	d			07 35			07 49							08 25		08 37					09 12				
Havant	a	07 30		07 38		07 45	07 51		08 03	08 15				08 28	08 32	08 39		08 45		09 02	09 14			09 27	09 33

		SW	GW	SN	SW	SW	SN	SW		SN	SW	SW	GW	SN	SW	SW	SN	SW		SN	SW	SW	GW	SN	SW
		◇■	◇ ⊥		■	◇■ ⊥		■		■	◇■ ⊥	◇■	◇ ⊥		■	◇■ ⊥		■		■	◇■ ⊥	◇■	◇ ⊥		■
Portsmouth Harbour	d	09 19	09 23		09 33	09 45		09 59		10 11	10 15		10 23		10 33	10 45		10 59		11 11	11 15		11 23	11 29	
Portsmouth & Southsea	a	09 22	09 26		09 36	09 48		10 02		10 14	10 18		10 26		10 36	10 48		11 02		11 14	11 18		11 26	11 32	
	d	09 24	09 27	09 33	09 38	09 50	09 57	10 04		10 15	10 20	10 24	10 27	10 33	10 38	10 50	10 57	11 04		11 15	11 20	11 24	11 27	11 33	11 38
Fratton	d	09 28	09a31	09 37	09 42	09 54	10 01	10 08		10 19	10 24	10 28	10a31	10 37	10 42	10 54	11 01	11 08		11 19	11 24	11 28	11a31	11 37	11 42
Hilsea	d	09 32			09a46		10 05	10a12				10 32			10a46		11 05	11a12				11 32			11a46
Bedhampton	d	09 37					10 10					10 37					11 10					11 37			
Havant	a	09 39		09 45		10 03	10 13			10 27	10 32	10 39		10 45		11 03	11 13			11 27	11 33	11 39		11 45	

		SW	SN	SW		SN	SW	SW	GW	SN	SW	SW	SN	SW		SN	SW	SW	GW	SN	SW	SW	SN	SW	
		◇■ ⊥		■		■	◇■ ⊥	◇■	◇ ⊥		■	◇■ ⊥		■		■	◇■ ⊥	◇■	◇ ⊥		■	◇■ ⊥		■	
Portsmouth Harbour	d	11 45		11 59		12 11	12 15		12 23	12 29		12 45		12 59		13 11	13 15		13 23	13 29		13 45		13 59	
Portsmouth & Southsea	a	11 48		12 02		12 14	12 18		12 26	12 32		12 48		13 02		13 14	13 18		13 26	13 32		13 48		14 02	
	d	11 50	11 57	12 04		12 15	12 20	12 24	12 27	12 33	12 38	12 50	12 57	13 04		13 15	13 20	13 24	13 27	13 33	13 38	13 50	13 57	14 04	
Fratton	d	11 54	12 01	12 08		12 19	12 24	12 28	12a31	12 37	12 42	12 54	13 01	13 08		13 19	13 24	13 28	13a31	13 37	13 42	13 54	14 01	14 08	
Hilsea	d		12 05	12a12				12 32			12a46		13 05	13a12				13 32			13a46		14 05	14a12	
Bedhampton	d		12 10					12 37					13 10					13 37					14 10		
Havant	a	12 03	12 13			12 27	12 32	12 39		12 45		13 03	13 13			13 27	13 32	13 39		13 45		14 03	14 13		

		SN	SW	SW	GW	SN	SW	SW	SN	SW		SN	SW	SW	GW	SN	SW	SW	SN	SW		SN	SW	SW	GW
		■	◇■ ⊥	◇■	▪ ⊥		■	◇■ ⊥		■		■	◇■ ⊥	◇■	▪ ⊥		■	◇■ ⊥		■		■	◇■ ⊥	◇■	▪ ⊥
Portsmouth Harbour	d	14 11	14 15		14 23	14 29		14 45		14 59		15 11	15 15		15 23	15 29		15 45		15 59		16 11	16 15		16 23
Portsmouth & Southsea	a	14 14	14 18		14 26	14 32		14 48		15 02		15 14	15 18		15 26	15 32		15 48		16 02		16 14	16 18		16 26
	d	14 15	14 20	14 24	14 27	14 33	14 38	14 50	14 57	15 04		15 15	15 20	15 24	15 27	15 33	15 38	15 50	15 57	16 04		16 15	16 20	16 24	16 27
Fratton	d	14 19	14 24	14 28	14a31	14 37	14 42	14 54	15 01	15 08		15 19	15 24	15 28	15a31	15 37	15 42	15 54	16 01	16 08		16 19	16 24	16 28	16a31
Hilsea	d			14 32			14a46		15 05	15a12				15 32			15a46		16 05	16a12				16 32	
Bedhampton	d			14 37					15 13					15 37					16 10					16 37	
Havant	a	14 27	14 33	14 39		14 45		15 03	15 16			15 27	15 32	15 39		15 45		16 03	16 13			16 27	16 32	16 39	

		SN	SW	SW	SN	SW		SN	SW	SW	GW	SN	SW	SW	SW	SN		SW	SN	SW	SW	GW	SN	SW	SW
			■	◇■ ⊥		■		■	◇■ ⊥	◇■	◇ ⊥		■	◇■ ⊥	■			■	■	◇■ ⊥	◇■	◇ ⊥		■	◇■ ⊥
Portsmouth Harbour	d		16 33	16 45		16 59		17 11	17 15	17 19	17 23		17 33	17 45	17 49			17 59		18 15	18 19	18 23			18 45
Portsmouth & Southsea	a		16 36	16 48		17 02		17 14	17 18	17 22	17 26		17 36	17 48	17 53			18 02		18 18	18 22	18 26			18 48
	d	16 33	16 38	16 50	16 57	17 04		17 15	17 20	17 24	17 27	17 33	17 38	17 50	17 54	17 57		18 04	18 15	18 20	18 24	18 27	18 33	18 38	18 50
Fratton	d	16 37	16 42	16 54	17 01	17 08		17 19	17 24	17 28	17a31	17 37	17 42	17 54	17 58	18 02		18 08	18 19	18 24	18 28	18a31	18 37	18 42	18 54
Hilsea	d		16a46		17 05	17a12				17 32			17a46		18a02	18 06		18a12			18 32			18a46	
Bedhampton	d				17 10					17 37						18 11					18 37				
Havant	a	16 45		17 03	17 13			17 27	17 33	17 39		17 45		18 03		18 13			18 27	18 33	18 39		18 46		19 03

		SN		SW	SN	SW	SW	GW	SN	SW	SW	SN		SW	SN	SW	SW	GW	SN	SW	SW	SN		SW	SN
				■	■	◇■	◇■	◇		■	◇■			■	■	◇■	◇■	◇		■	◇■			■	■
Portsmouth Harbour	d			18 59	19 11	19 15	19 19	19 23			19 45			19 59	20 11	20 15	20 19	20 23			20 45			20 59	21 11
Portsmouth & Southsea	a			19 02	19 14	19 18	19 23	19 26			19 48			20 02	20 14	20 18	20 22	20 26			20 48			21 02	21 14
	d	18 57		19 04	19 15	19 20	19 24	19 27	19 33	19 38	19 50	19 57		20 04	20 15	20 20	20 24	20 27	20 33	20 38	20 50	20 57		21 04	21 15
Fratton	d	19 01		19 08	19 19	19 24	19 28	19a31	19 37	19 42	19 54	20 01		20 08	20 19	20 24	20 28	20a31	20 37	20 42	20 54	21 01		21 08	21 19
Hilsea	d	19 05		19a12			19 32			19a46		20 05		20a12			20 32			20a46		21 05		21a12	
Bedhampton	d	19 10					19 37					20 10					20 37					21 10			
Havant	a	19 13			19 27	19 33	19 39		19 45		20 03	20 13			20 27	20 32	20 39		20 45		21 02	21 13			21 29

A from 8 October

B until 5 October

Table T157-R

Portsmouth Harbour - Havant

(Complete service)

Network Diagram - see first page of Table 155

Mondays to Fridays

21 May to 7 December

	SW ◇■	GW	SN	SW ■	SW ■	SN	SW ◇■	SW ■	SN	SN	SW ■	SW ■
Portsmouth Harbour ⛴ d	21 19	21 23			21 54	22 15	22 19	22 33	22 40	23 16	23 19	23 24
Portsmouth & Southsea a	21 22	21 26			21 57	22 18	22 22	22 37	22 43	23 19	23 22	23 28
d	21 24	21 27	21 33	21 38	21 59	22 19	22 24	22 38	22 44	23 20	23 24	23 29
Fratton d	21 28	21a31	21 37	21 42	22 03	22 23	22 28	22 42	22 48	23 24	23 28	23 33
Hilsea d	21 32			21a46	22a07	22 27	22 32	22a46	22 52	23 28	23 32	23a37
Bedhampton d	21 37					22 32	22 38		22 57	23 33	23 37	
Havant a	21 39		21 46			22 34	22 40		22 59	23 35	23 39	

Saturdays

26 May to 8 December

	SW ◇■ A	SW ◇■ B	SN ■	SW ■	SW ◇■ A	SW ◇■ B	SW ■	SW ■	SN	GW ◇	SN ■	SW ◇■	SN	SW ■	SW ◇■ ⊼	GW	SN	SW ■	SN ■	SW ◇■ ⊼	SW ◇■	GW ◇ ⊼
Portsmouth Harbour ⛴ d	04 38	04 43			05 14	05 19	05 40	05 48		06 08	06 11	06 19	06 29		06 45	06 50		06 59	07 11	07 15		07 23
Portsmouth & Southsea a	04 41	04 46			05 17	05 22	05 43	05 51		06 11	06 14	06 22	06 32		06 48	06 53		07 02	07 14	07 18		07 26
d	04 43	04 48	04 55	05 16	05 19	05 24	05 44	05 53	05 57	06 12	06 15	06 24	06 33	06 38	06 50	06 54	06 57	07 04	07 15	07 20	07 24	07 27
Fratton d	04 47	04 52	04 59	05 20	05 23	05 28	05a47	05 57	06 01	06a15	06 19	06 28	06 37	06 42	06 54	06 58	07 01	07 08	07 19	07 24	07 28	07a31
Hilsea d	04 51	04 56		05a24	05 27	05 32		06a01	06 05			06 32		06a46			07 05	07a12			07 32	
Bedhampton d	04 56	05 01			05 32	05 37			06 10			06 37					07 11				07 37	
Havant a	04 58	05 03	05 07		05 35	05 39			06 13		06 27	06 40	06 45		07 03	07 07	07 14		07 27	07 32	07 40	

	SN	SW ■	SW ◇■ ⊼	SN	SW ■	SN ■	SW ◇■ ⊼	SW ◇■	GW ■ ⊼	SN	SW ■	SW ◇■ ⊼	SN	SW ■	SN ■	SW ◇■ ⊼	SW ◇■	GW ◇ ⊼	SN	SW ■	SW ◇■ ⊼	SN
Portsmouth Harbour ⛴ d	07 29		07 45		07 59	08 11	08 15		08 23	08 29		08 45		08 59	09 11	09 15		09 23	09 29		09 45	
Portsmouth & Southsea a	07 32		07 48		08 02	08 14	08 18		08 26	08 32		08 48		09 02	09 14	09 18		09 26	09 32		09 48	
d	07 33	07 38	07 50	07 57	08 04	08 15	08 20	08 24	08 27	08 33	08 38	08 50	08 57	09 04	09 15	09 20	09 24	09 27	09 33	09 38	09 50	09 57
Fratton d	07 37	07 42	07 54	08 01	08 08	08 19	08 24	08 28	08a31	08 37	08 42	08 54	09 01	09 08	09 19	09 24	09 28	09a31	09 37	09 42	09 54	10 01
Hilsea d		07a46		08 05	08a12			08 32			08a46		09 05	09a12			09 32			09a46		10 05
Bedhampton d				08 10				08 37					09 10				09 37					10 10
Havant a	07 45		08 03	08 13		08 27	08 32	08 39		08 45		09 03	09 13		09 27	09 33	09 39		09 45		10 03	10 13

	SW ■	SN ■	SW ◇■ ⊼	SW ◇■	GW ◇ ⊼	SN	SW ■	SW ◇■ ⊼	SN	SW ■	SN ■	SW ◇■ ⊼	SW ◇■	GW ◇	SN	SW ■	SW ◇■ ⊼	SN	SW ■	SN ■	SW ◇■ ⊼
Portsmouth Harbour ⛴ d	09 59	10 11	10 15		10 23	10 29		10 45		10 59	11 11	11 15		11 23	11 29		11 45		11 59	12 11	12 15
Portsmouth & Southsea a	10 02	10 14	10 18		10 26	10 32		10 48		11 02	11 14	11 18		11 26	11 32		11 48		12 02	12 14	12 18
d	10 04	10 15	10 20	10 24	10 27	10 33	10 38	10 50	10 57	11 04	11 15	11 20	11 24	11 27	11 33	11 38	11 50	11 57	12 04	12 15	12 20
Fratton d	10 08	10 19	10 24	10 28	10a31	10 37	10 42	10 54	11 01	11 08	11 19	11 24	11 28	11a31	11 37	11 42	11 54	12 01	12 08	12 19	12 24
Hilsea d	10a12			10 32			10a46		11 05	11a12			11 32			11a46		12 05	12a12		
Bedhampton d				10 37					11 10				11 37					12 10			
Havant a		10 27	10 32	10 39		10 45		11 03	11 13		11 27	11 33	11 39		11 45		12 03	12 13		12 27	12 32

	SW ◇■	GW ◇	SN	SW ■	SW ◇■ ⊼	SN	SW ■	SN ■	SW ◇■ ⊼	SW ◇■	GW ◇	SN	SW ■	SW ◇■ ⊼	SN	SW ■	SN ■	SW ◇■ ⊼	SW ◇■	GW ◇	SN	SW ■
Portsmouth Harbour ⛴ d		12 23	12 29		12 45		12 59	13 11	13 15		13 23	13 29		13 45		13 59	14 11	14 15		14 23	14 29	
Portsmouth & Southsea a		12 26	12 32		12 48		13 02	13 14	13 18		13 26	13 32		13 48		14 02	14 14	14 18		14 26	14 32	
d	12 24	12 27	12 33	12 38	12 50	12 57	13 04	13 15	13 20	13 24	13 27	13 33	13 38	13 50	13 57	14 04	14 15	14 20	14 24	14 27	14 33	14 38
Fratton d	12 28	12a31	12 37	12 42	12 54	13 01	13 08	13 19	13 24	13 28	13a31	13 37	13 42	13 54	14 01	14 08	14 19	14 24	14 28	14a31	14 37	14 42
Hilsea d	12 32			12a46		13 05	13a12			13 32			13a46		14 05	14a12			14 32			14a46
Bedhampton d	12 37					13 10				13 37					14 10				14 37			
Havant a	12 39		12 45		13 03	13 13		13 27	13 32	13 39		13 45		14 03	14 13		14 27	14 32	14 39		14 45	

	SW ◇■ ⊼	SN	SW ■	SN ■	SW ◇■ ⊼	SW ◇■	GW ◇	SN	SW ■	SW ◇■ ⊼	SN	SW ■	SN ■	SW ◇■ ⊼	SW ◇■	GW ■	SN	SW ■	SW ◇■ ⊼	SN	SW ■
Portsmouth Harbour ⛴ d	14 45		14 59	15 11	15 15		15 23	15 29		15 45		15 59	16 11	16 15		16 23	16 29		16 45		16 59
Portsmouth & Southsea a	14 48		15 02	15 14	15 18		15 26	15 32		15 48		16 02	16 14	16 18		16 26	16 32		16 48		17 02
d	14 50	14 57	15 04	15 15	15 20	15 24	15 27	15 33	15 38	15 50	15 57	16 04	16 15	16 20	16 24	16 27	16 33	16 38	16 50	16 57	17 04
Fratton d	14 54	15 01	15 08	15 19	15 24	15 28	15a31	15 37	15 42	15 54	16 01	16 08	16 19	16 24	16 28	16a31	16 37	16 42	16 54	17 01	17 08
Hilsea d		15 08	15a12			15 32			15a46		16 05	16a12			16 32			16a46		17 05	17a12
Bedhampton d		15 14				15 37					16 10				16 37					17 10	
Havant a	15 03	15 16		15 27	15 32	15 39		15 45		16 03	16 13		16 27	16 32	16 39		16 45		17 03	17 13	

	SW ◇■	SN ■	SW ◇■	GW ◇	SN	SW ■	SW ◇■ ⊼	SN	SW ■	SN ■	SW ◇■	SW ◇■	GW ◇	SN	SW ■	SW ◇■	SN	SW ■	SN ■	SW ◇■	SW ◇■	GW ◇
Portsmouth Harbour ⛴ d		17 11	17 19	17 23	17 29	17 33	17 45		17 59	18 11	18 15		18 23	18 29		18 45		18 59	19 11	19 15		19 23
Portsmouth & Southsea a		17 14	17 22	17 26	17 32	17 36	17 48		18 02	18 14	18 18		18 26	18 32		18 48		19 02	19 14	19 18		19 26
d	17 08	17 15	17 24	17 27	17 33	17 38	17 50	17 57	18 04	18 15	18 20	18 24	18 27	18 33	18 38	18 50	18 57	19 04	19 15	19 20	19 24	19 27
Fratton d	17 12	17 19	17 28	17a31	17 37	17 42	17 54	18 01	18 08	18 19	18 24	18 28	18a31	18 37	18 42	18 54	19 01	19 08	19 19	19 24	19 28	19a31
Hilsea d	17 16		17 32			17a46		18 05	18a12			18 32			18a46		19 05	19a12			19 32	
Bedhampton d	17 21		17 37					18 10				18 37					19 10				19 37	
Havant a	17 23	17 27	17 39		17 45		18 05	18 13		18 27	18 32	18 39		18 45		19 03	19 13		19 27	19 32	19 39	

A from 13 October B until 6 October

Table T157-R

Portsmouth Harbour - Havant

(Complete service)

Network Diagram - see first page of Table 155

Saturdays

26 May to 8 December

	SN	SW ■	SW ◇■	SN	SW ■	SN ■	SW ◇■	SW ◇■	GW ◇	SN	SW ■	SW ◇■	SN	SW ■	SN ■	SW ◇■	SW ■	SN	SW ■	SN	SW ◇■
Portsmouth Harbour ⛴ d	19 29		19 45		19 59	20 11	20 15		20 23	20 29		20 45		20 59	21 11	21 19		21 40	21 54	22 15	22 19
Portsmouth & Southsea a	19 32		19 48		20 02	20 14	20 18		20 26	20 32		20 48		21 02	21 14	21 22		21 43	21 57	22 18	22 22
d	19 33	19 38	19 50	19 57	20 04	20 15	20 20	20 24	20 27	20 33	20 38	20 50	20 57	21 04	21 15	21 24	21 38	21 44	21 59	22 19	22 24
Fratton d	19 37	19 42	19 54	20 01	20 08	20 19	20 24	20 28	20a31	20 37	20 42	20 54	21 01	21 08	21 19	21 28	21 42	21 48	22 03	22 23	22 28
Hilsea d		19a46		20 05	20a12			20 32			20a46		21 05	21a12		21 32	21a46	21 52	22a07	22 27	22 32
Bedhampton d				20 10				20 37					21 10			21 37		21 57		22 32	22 38
Havant a	19 45		20 03	20 13		20 27	20 32	20 39		20 45		21 03	21 13		21 27	21 39		21 59		22 35	22 40

	SW ■	SN	SN	SW ■	SW ■
Portsmouth Harbour ⛴ d	22 33	22 40	23 15	23 19	23 24
Portsmouth & Southsea a	22 36	22 43	23 18	23 22	23 27
d	22 38	22 44	23 19	23 24	23 29
Fratton d	22 42	22 48	23 23	23 28	23 33
Hilsea d	22a46	22 52	23 27	23 32	23a37
Bedhampton d		22 57	23 32	23 37	
Havant a		22 59	23 34	23 39	

Sundays

20 May to 2 December

	SW ■	SW ◇■ A	SW ◇■ B	SN	SW ■	SW ◇■ A	SW ◇■ B	SW ■	SW ◇■	SN	SN	SW ■	SW ◇■ A	SW ◇■ B	SW ■	SW ◇■	SN	GW ■	SN	SW ■ ⊼	SW ◇■ ⊼	SW ■
Portsmouth Harbour ⛴ d	06 37	06 43	06 48	07 14	07 17	07 28	07 32		07 48	08 01	08 14	08 17	08 28	08 32		08 48	09 01	09 08	09 14	09 17	09 32	
Portsmouth & Southsea a	06 40	06 46	06 51	07 17	07 20	07 31	07 35		07 51	08 04	08 17	08 21	08 31	08 36		08 51	09 04	09 11	09 17	09 21	09 35	
d	06 42	06 48	06 53	07 18	07 22	07 33	07 37	07 42	07 53	08 05	08 18	08 22	08 33	08 37	08 42	08 53	09 05	09 12	09 18	09 22	09 37	09 42
Fratton d	06 46	06 52	06 57	07 22	07 26	07 37	07 41	07 46	07 57	08 09	08 22	08 26	08 38	08 41	08 46	08 57	09 09	09a14	09 22	09 26	09 42	09 46
Hilsea d	06a50				07a30			07a50				08a30			08a50					09a30		09a50
Bedhampton d		06 59	07 04	07 30					08 04		08 30					09 06			09 30			
Havant a		07 02	07 07	07 33		07 45	07 49		08 07	08 17	08 33		08 46	08 49		09 09	09 17		09 33		09 50	

	SW ◇■	SN	SN	SW ■ ⊼	SW ◇■ ⊼	SW ■	SW ◇■	SN	GW ◇	SN	SW ■ ⊼	SW ◇■ ⊼	SW ■	SW ◇■	SN	SN	SW ■ ⊼	SW ◇■ ⊼	SW ■	SW ◇■	SN	GW ◇
Portsmouth Harbour ⛴ d	09 48	10 01	10 14	10 17	10 32		10 48	11 01	11 08	11 14	11 17	11 32		11 48	12 01	12 13	12 17	12 32		12 48	13 01	13 08
Portsmouth & Southsea a	09 51	10 04	10 17	10 21	10 35		10 51	11 04	11 11	11 17	11 21	11 35		11 51	12 04	12 16	12 20	12 35		12 51	13 04	13 11
d	09 53	10 05	10 18	10 22	10 37	10 42	10 53	11 05	11 12	11 18	11 22	11 37	11 42	11 53	12 05	12 17	12 22	12 37	12 42	12 53	13 05	13 12
Fratton d	09 57	10 09	10 22	10 26	10 41	10 46	10 57	11 09	11a15	11 22	11 26	11 41	11 46	11 57	12 09	12 21	12 26	12 41	12 46	12 57	13 09	13a15
Hilsea d				10a30		10a50					11a30		11a50				12a30		12a50			
Bedhampton d	10 04		10 30				11 04			11 30				12 04		12 29				13 04		
Havant a	10 07	10 17	10 33		10 49		11 07	11 17		11 33		11 49		12 07	12 17	12 32		12 50		13 07	13 17	

	SN	SW ■ ⊼	SW ◇■ ⊼	SW ■	SW ◇■	SN	GW ◇	SN	SW ■ ⊼	SW ◇■ ⊼	SW ■	SW ◇■	SN	GW ■	SN	SW ■ ⊼	SW ◇■ ⊼	SW ■	SW ◇■	SN	GW ◇
Portsmouth Harbour ⛴ d	13 14	13 17	13 32		13 48	14 01	14 08	14 14	14 17	14 32		14 48	15 01	15 08	15 14	15 17	15 32		15 48	16 01	16 10
Portsmouth & Southsea a	13 17	13 21	13 35		13 51	14 04	14 11	14 17	14 21	14 35		14 51	15 04	15 11	15 17	15 21	15 35		15 51	16 04	16 13
d	13 18	13 22	13 37	13 42	13 53	14 05	14 12	14 18	14 22	14 37	14 42	14 53	15 05	15 12	15 18	15 22	15 37	15 42	15 53	16 05	16 14
Fratton d	13 22	13 26	13 41	13 46	13 57	14 09	14a15	14 22	14 26	14 41	14 46	14 57	15 09	15a15	15 22	15 26	15 41	15 46	15 57	16 09	16a17
Hilsea d		13a30		13a50					14a30		14a50					15a30		15a50			
Bedhampton d	13 30				14 04			14 30				15 04			15 30				16 04		
Havant a	13 33		13 49		14 07	14 17		14 33		14 49		15 07	15 17		15 33		15 49		16 07	16 17	

	SN	SW ■ ⊼	SW ◇■ ⊼	SW ■	SW ◇■	SN	GW ◇	SW ■	SW ◇■ ⊼	SW ■	SW ◇■	SN	GW ◇	SN	SW ■	SW ◇■ ⊼	SW ■	SW ◇■	SN	GW ◇	SW ■	SW ◇■
Portsmouth Harbour ⛴ d	16 14	16 17	16 32		16 48	17 01	17 08	17 17	17 32		17 48	18 01	18 08	18 14	18 17	18 32		18 48	19 01	19 08	19 17	19 32
Portsmouth & Southsea a	16 17	16 21	16 35		16 51	17 04	17 11	17 20	17 35		17 51	18 04	18 11	18 17	18 21	18 35		18 51	19 04	19 11	19 20	19 35
d	16 18	16 22	16 37	16 42	16 52	17 05	17 12	17 22	17 37	17 42	17 53	18 05	18 12	18 18	18 22	18 37	18 42	18 53	19 05	19 12	19 22	19 37
Fratton d	16 22	16 26	16 41	16 46	16 56	17 09	17a15	17 26	17 41	17 46	17 57	18 09	18a15	18 22	18 26	18 41	18 46	18 57	19 09	19a15	19 26	19 41
Hilsea d		16a30		16a50				17a30		17a50					18a30		18a50				19a30	
Bedhampton d	16 30				17 04						18 04			18 30				19 04				
Havant a	16 33		16 49		17 06	17 17			17 49		18 07	18 17		18 33		18 49		19 07	19 17			19 49

	SW ■	SW ◇■	SN	GW ◇	SN	SW ■	SW ◇■	SW ■	SW ◇■	SN	SN	SW ■	SW ◇■	SW ■	SW ◇■	SN	GW	SN	SW ■	SW ◇■	SW ■
Portsmouth Harbour ⛴ d		19 48	20 01	20 08	20 14	20 18	20 32		20 48	21 01	21 14	21 18	21 32		21 48	22 01	22 08	22 14	22 17	22 32	
Portsmouth & Southsea a		19 51	20 04	20 11	20 17	20 20	20 35		20 51	21 04	21 17	21 20	21 35		21 51	22 04	22 11	22 17	22 21	22 35	
d	19 42	19 53	20 05	20 12	20 18	20 22	20 37	20 42	20 53	21 05	21 18	21 22	21 37	21 42	21 53	22 05	22 12	22 18	22 22	22 37	22 42
Fratton d	19 46	19 57	20 09	20a15	20 22	20 26	20 41	20 46	20 57	21 09	21 22	21 26	21 41	21 46	21 57	22 09	22a14	22 22	22 26	22 41	22 46
Hilsea d	19a50					20a30		20a50				21a30		21a50					22a30		22a50
Bedhampton d		20 05			20 30				21 04		21 30				22 04						
Havant a		20 07	20 17		20 33		20 49		21 07	21 17	21 33		21 49		22 07	22 17		22 31		22 49	

A from 7 October B until 30 September

Table T157-R

Sundays
20 May to 2 December

Portsmouth Harbour - Havant
(Complete service)

Network Diagram - see first page of Table 155

		SW 1	SN	SW 1
Portsmouth Harbour ⛴	d	22 48	23 01	23 17
Portsmouth & Southsea	a	22 51	23 04	23 20
	d	22 52	23 05	23 22
Fratton	d	22 56	23 09	23 26
Hilsea	d			23a30
Bedhampton	d	23 03		
Havant	a	23 06	23 18	

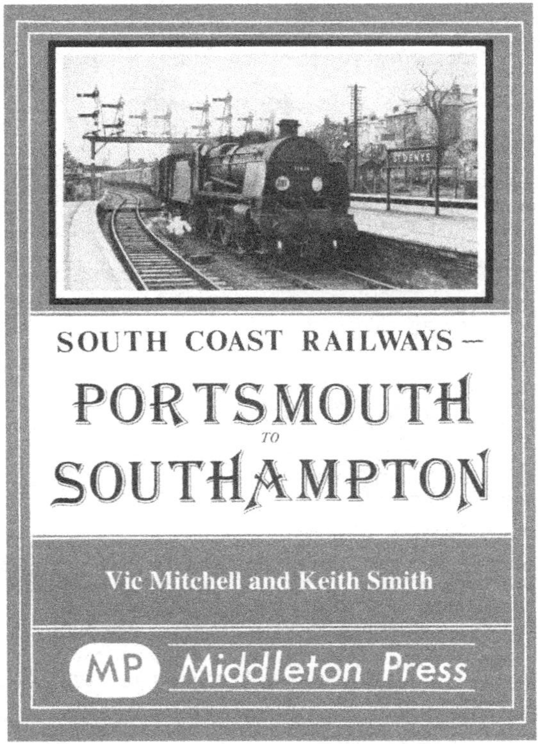

Table T158-F

Mondays to Fridays
21 May to 5 October

London - Basingstoke, Southampton, Romsey, Bournemouth and Weymouth

Miles	Miles	Miles			SW MX 1	SW MX ◇1 🚌	SW MX ◇1	SW MO ◇1	SW MX ◇1 🚌	SW MO 1	SW MX ◇1	SW MO ◇1	SW MX 1	SW MO ◇1 🚌	SW MX ◇1	SW MO ◇1	SW MO ◇1 🚌	SW MX 1	SW MX 1	SW MX 1	SW MX ◇1	SW 1	SW MO ◇1
0	—	—	**London Waterloo 15** ⊖	d																	00 05		00 50
4	—	—	**Clapham Junction 10**	d																	00u12		00 57
24¼	—	—	**Woking**	d															00 03	00 28	00 37		01 18
33¼	—	—	Farnborough (Main)	d									00 10						00 14	00 41			
36½	—	—	Fleet	d						00 04			00 16						00 20	00 47			
—	—	—	Reading 7	d																			
47¾	—	—	**Basingstoke**	a						00 21			00 33						00 33	01 06	00 55		
—	—	—		d															00 35		00 56		
58	—	—	Micheldever	d											00 03								
66½	—	—	**Winchester**	d										00 07	00 12	00 14			00 51		01 13		
69¾	—	—	Shawford	d										00 12									
—	0	0	**Romsey**	d																			
—	—	5¼	Chandlers Ford	d													←						
73½	0	7¼	Eastleigh 8	a										00 17	00 22	00 23	00 17		00 59		01 21		
—	—	—		d			00 02							00 30	00 23	00 24	00 30	00 30	01 00		01 22		
—	4½	—	Hedge End	d										→			00s36	00s36					
—	5½	—	Botley	d													00s39	00s39					
—	11	—	Fareham	d													00s47	00s47					
—	14¼	—	Portchester	d													00s53	00s53					
—	16¾	—	Cosham	d													00s57	00s57					
—	18¼	—	Hilsea	a																			
—	20½	—	Fratton	a													01s05	01s05					02s10
—	21½	—	**Portsmouth & Southsea**	a													01s08	01s08					02s14
—	22¼	—	**Portsmouth Harbour** ⛴	a													01 12	01 12					02 19
75	—	—	**Southampton Airport Pkwy** ✈	d			00 06								00 28	00 28			01 05		01 26		
75¾	—	—	Swaythling	d																			
77¼	—	—	St Denys	d											00s32	00s32							
79¼	—	—	**Southampton Central** ⛴	a			00 13								00 37	00 38			01 12		01 35		
—	—	—		d											00 38	00 42					01 37		
80¼	—	—	Millbrook (Hants)	d																			
82	0	—	Redbridge	d																			
—	6	—	**Romsey**	d																			
—	9¾	—	Mottisfont & Dunbridge	d	00 01																		
—	13½	—	Dean	d	00 07																		
—	22½	—	**Salisbury**	a	00 19																		
82½	—	—	Totton	d											00s43	00s47					01s42		
85½	—	—	Ashurst New Forest	d																			
88	—	—	Beaulieu Road	d																			
92¾	—	—	**Brockenhurst 3**	a											00s54	00s58					01s53		
—	—	—		d					00 05														
95½	—	—	Sway	d																			
98½	—	—	New Milton	d				00 04							01s02	01s06					02s00		
101	—	—	Hinton Admiral	d		00 02		00 08															
104¼	—	—	Christchurch	d		00 07		00 13							01s09	01s13					02s07		
106½	—	—	Pokesdown	d		00 11		00 17							01s13	01s17					02s11		
108	—	—	**Bournemouth**	a		00 15		00 21	00 21						01 17	01 21					02 15		
—	—	—		d		00 16		00 22	00 22						01 18	01 22						06 11	
110¾	—	—	Branksome	d		00 21		00 27	00 27						01s23	01s27						06 16	
112	—	—	Parkstone (Dorset)	d		00 24		00 30	00 30						01s26	01s30						06 19	
113¾	—	—	**Poole 4**	a		00 28		00 34	00 35						01 30	01 34						06 23	
—	—	—		d																		06 24	
116	—	—	Hamworthy	d																		06 29	
118¾	—	—	Holton Heath	d																		06 33	
120¾	—	—	Wareham	d								00 03										06 38	
125¾	—	—	Wool	d								00 10										06 44	
130¼	—	—	Moreton (Dorset)	d							00 05	00 17										06 50	
135¾	—	—	**Dorchester South**	d							00 13	00 25										06 58	
—	—	—	Dorchester West	d																			
140½	—	—	Upwey	d							00 19	00 32										07 05	
142¾	—	—	**Weymouth**	a							00 24	00 36										07 09	

For services from Brockenhurst - Lymington refer to Table T159

Table T158-F

Mondays to Fridays

21 May to 5 October

London - Basingstoke, Southampton, Romsey, Bournemouth and Weymouth

		SW MO ■	SW MX ■	SW ■	SW ■	SW ■	SW ■	SW ■	GW		SW ◇■	SW ■	SW ■	SW ■	SW ■	SW ■	XC ◇■ ⚒	SW ◇■	SW ◇■		SW ■	SW ◇■	SW ■	SW ◇■	SW
London Waterloo ⊖	d	01 05	01 05								05 30							06 12	06 30				06 42	07 03	
Clapham Junction	d	01 15	01 15								05u37							06u19	06u37				06u49	07u10	
Woking	d	01 49	01 49								06 01					06 19		06 50	06 57				07 19	07 30	
Farnborough (Main)	d	01s58	01s58													06 33		07 04					07 33		
Fleet	d	02s04	02s04													06 38		07 09					07 38		
Reading	d																					←			
Basingstoke	a	02s16	02s16								06 20					06 58		07 28	07 16			07 28	07 56	07 48	
	d					05 40					06 21			06 45		07 00		07 30	07 18			07 30	08 00	07 50	
Micheldever	d					05 50										07 10		→				07 41	→		
Winchester	d	02s33	02s33			05 59		06 18			06 38			07 01		07 19			07 34			07 50		08 06	
Shawford	d							06 23						07 06								07 55			
Romsey	d						05 58								07 07						07 13				08 07
Chandlers Ford	d						06 06								07 14										08 14
Eastleigh	a	02s42	02s42			06 07	06 11	06 28			06 47			07 12	07 20	07 27			07 43		07 49	08 00			08 20
	d			06 01		06 08	06 12	06 29			06 48		07 02	07 14	07 21	07 28			07 44		07 50	08 02			08 21
Hedge End	d			06 07				06 35					07 08			07 34									
Botley	d			06 11				06 39					07 12			07 38									
Fareham	d			06 19				06 50					07 21			07 47									
Portchester	d			06 24				06 55					07 26			07 52									
Cosham	d			06 29				07 00					07 30			07 57									
Hilsea	a			06 34				07 05					07 35			08 03									
Fratton	a			06 40				07 09					07 39			08 07									
Portsmouth & Southsea	a			06 44				07 12					07 42			08 13									
Portsmouth Harbour ⛴	a			06 49				07 17					07 48			08 17									
Southampton Airport Pkwy ✈	d	02s46	02s46			06 13	06 17				06 53			07 18	07 26				07 49			08 06		08 16	08 25
Swaythling	d					06 15	06 20							07 21	07 29							08 09			08 27
St Denys	d	02s51	02s51			06 18	06 24							07 24	07 32							08 12			08 30
Southampton Central ⛴	a	02 56	02 57			06 23	06 29				07 00			07 29	07 37				07 57			08 17		08 25	08 35
	d					06 25	06 30				07 01	07 19			07 38		07 56		07 59			08 18		08 27	08 37
Millbrook (Hants)	d						06 33					07 21			07 41							08 21			08 40
Redbridge	d						06 36					07 25			07 45							08 24			08 43
Romsey	d						06 44								07 53						08a03				08 51
Mottisfont & Dunbridge	d						06 49								07 58										08 56
Dean	d						06 55								08 03										09 02
Salisbury	a						07 07								08 16										09 15
Totton	d					06 30					07 07	07 28							08 04			08 27		08 33	
Ashurst New Forest	d					06 35						07 32							08 09			08 32			
Beaulieu Road	d											07 37							08 13						
Brockenhurst	a					06 43					07 17	07 43					08 09		08 19			08 40		08 45	
	d				06 15	06 44					07 18	07 44					08 10		08 20			08 41		08 46	
Sway	d				06 20	06 48					07 23	07 48							08 25					08 51	
New Milton	d				06 25	06 53					07 28	07 53							08 30					08 56	
Hinton Admiral	d				06 29	06 57					07 32	07 57							08 34					09 00	
Christchurch	d				06 34	07 02					07 37	08 02							08 39					09 05	
Pokesdown	d				06 37	07 06					07 40	08 06							08 42					09 08	
Bournemouth	a				06 41	07 10					07 44	08 10					08 23		08 46			08 55		09 12	
	d				06 44	07 11					07 46	08 11							08 48			08 57		09 14	
Branksome	d				06 49	07 16					07 51	08 16							08 53			09a02		09 19	
Parkstone (Dorset)	d				06 52	07 19					07 54	08 19							08 56					09 22	
Poole	a				06 55	07 23					07 57	08 23							08 59					09 25	
	d				06 57	07 24					07 58	08 24							09 00					09 26	
Hamworthy	d				07 02	07 29					08 03	08 29							09 05					09 31	
Holton Heath	d				07 06	07 33					08 07	08 33												09 35	
Wareham	d				07 11	07 38					08 12	08 38							09 12					09 40	
Wool	d				07 17	07 44					08 19	08 44							09 19					09 47	
Moreton (Dorset)	d				07 23	07 50					08 25	08 50							09 25					09 53	
Dorchester South	d				07 31	07 58					08 33	08 58							09 33					10 01	
Dorchester West	d								08 09																
Upwey	d				07 38	08 05			08 17		08 39	09 05							09 39					10 07	
Weymouth	a				07 42	08 09			08 23		08 44	09 09							09 44					10 12	

For services from Brockenhurst - Lymington refer to Table T159

Table T158-F

Mondays to Fridays

21 May to 5 October

London - Basingstoke, Southampton, Romsey, Bournemouth and Weymouth

		SW ■	XC ◇■ ⚒	SW ◇■ A ⚒	SW		GW ◇	SW ◇■ ⚒	XC ◇■ ⚒	SW ◇■ A ⚒	SW ◇■ ⚒	SW ■	SW ■	XC ◇■ ⚒	SW ◇■ A ⚒		SW ◇■ ⚒	SN	SW ■	SW ◇■	SW ◇■ A ⚒	SW ◇■	SW ■	SW ■	XC ◇■ ⚒
London Waterloo ⊖	d			07 35				07 39		08 05			08 09		08 35					08 39	09 05			09 09	
Clapham Junction	d							07u45		08u12										08u46	09u12				
Woking	d			08 00									08 35		09 00									09 35	
Farnborough (Main)	d							08 13					08 45							09 13				09 45	
Fleet	d							08 19												09 19					
Reading	d	←	07 52						08 20					08 49											09 47
Basingstoke	a	07 56	08 08	08 19				08 32	08 41	08 47			08 58	09 10						09 32	09 47			09 58	10 09
	d	08 00	08 10	08 20				08 33	08 42	08 49			09 00	09 11						09 33	09 49			10 00	10 10
Micheldever	d	08 10											09 10											10 10	
Winchester	d	08 19	08 25	08 37				08 50	08 57	09 05			09 19	09 26	09 33					09 49	10 05			10 19	10 25
Shawford	d	08 24						08 54												09 54					
Romsey	d				08 13							09 07							09 14				10 07		
Chandlers Ford	d											09 14											10 14		
Eastleigh	a	08 30		08 47	08 49			09 00				09 20	09 27						09 49	09 59			10 20	10 27	
	d	08 31		08 48	08 50			09 01				09 21	09 28					09 42	09 50	10 04			10 21	10 28	
Hedge End	d	08 37											09 34											10 34	
Botley	d	08 42											09 38											10 38	
Fareham	d	08 50											09 48											10 48	
Portchester	d	08 55											09 53											10 53	
Cosham	d	09 00											09 58					10a02						10 58	
Hilsea	a	09 05											10 03											11 03	
Fratton	a	09 09											10 07											11 07	
Portsmouth & Southsea	a	09 12											10 11											11 12	
Portsmouth Harbour ⛴	a	09 18											10 20											11 20	
Southampton Airport Pkwy ✈	d		08 34	08 52				09 05	09 09	09 14		09 25		09 35	09 43					10 08	10 14		10 25		10 34
Swaythling	d											09 27											10 27		
St Denys	d										←	09 30										←	10 30		
Southampton Central ⛴	a		08 44	08 59				09 12	09 18	09 22	09 12	09 35		09 43	09 50					10 17	10 22	10 17	10 36		10 43
	d		08 46	09 01				09 30		09 24	09 30	09 37		09 45	09 51					10 30	10 24	10 30	10 45		10 45
Millbrook (Hants)	d							→				09 40								→			10 48		
Redbridge	d											09 43											10 51		
Romsey	d				09a03							09 51							10a03				10 59		
Mottisfont & Dunbridge	d											09 56											11 04		
Dean	d											10 02											11 10		
Salisbury	a											10 17											11 22		
Totton	d			09 06							09 35											10 35			
Ashurst New Forest	d										09 40											10 40			
Beaulieu Road	d																←					10 44			
Brockenhurst	a		08 59	09 17						09 37	09 49			09 58	10 05		09 49				10 37	10 51			10 58
	d		09 00	09 18						09 38	10 16			09 59	10 05		10 16				10 38	11 16			10 59
Sway	d			09 22							→						10 20					→			
New Milton	d			09 27						09 45							10 25				10 45				
Hinton Admiral	d			09 31													10 29								
Christchurch	d			09 36						09 52							10 34				10 52				
Pokesdown	d			09 40						09 56							10 38				10 56				
Bournemouth	a		09 15	09 44						10 00				10 13	10 20		10 42				11 00				11 13
	d			09 45						10 04					10 24		10 43				11 04				
Branksome	d			09 50											10 29		10 48								
Parkstone (Dorset)	d			09 53											10 32		10 51								
Poole	a			09 57						10 13					10 36		10 55				11 13				
	d			09 58						10 14					10 37						11 14				
Hamworthy	d			10 03						10 19					10 42						11 19				
Holton Heath	d									10 23											11 23				
Wareham	d			10 10						10 28					10 49						11 28				
Wool	d									10 35											11 35				
Moreton (Dorset)	d									10 41											11 41				
Dorchester South	d			10 26						10 54					11 05						11 49				
Dorchester West	d						10 48																		
Upwey	d						10 55			11 01											11 55				
Weymouth	a			10 35			11 03			11 06					11 14						12 02				

A ⚒ to Bournemouth

For services from Brockenhurst - Lymington refer to Table T159

Table T158-F

Mondays to Fridays
21 May to 5 October

London - Basingstoke, Southampton, Romsey, Bournemouth and Weymouth

		SW	GW	SW	SW	SW	XC	SW	SW	SW	SW	XC	SW	SW	SN	SW	SW	SW	SW	SW	SW	XC
		■	◇	◇■ A ✕	◇■	◇■	◇■ ✕	◇■ B ✕	◇■	■	■	■ ✕	◇■ A ✕	◇■		■	◇■	◇■ A ✕	◇■	■	■	◇■ ✕
London Waterloo ■ ⊖	d			09 35		09 39		10 05			10 09		10 35				10 39	11 05			11 09	
Clapham Junction ■	d					09u46		10u12									10u46	11u12				
Woking	d			10 00							10 35		11 00								11 35	
Farnborough (Main)	d					10 13					10 45						11 13				11 45	
Fleet	d					10 19											11 19					
Reading ■	d						10 20					10 52										11 52
Basingstoke	a					10 31	10 39	10 47			10 58	11 09					11 31	11 47			11 58	12 09
	d					10 33	10 40	10 49			11 00	11 10					11 33	11 49			12 00	12 10
Micheldever	d										11 10										12 10	
Winchester	d			10 33		10 49	10 55	11 05			11 19	11 25	11 33				11 49	12 05			12 19	12 25
Shawford	d					10 54											11 54					
Romsey	d	10 20								11 07						11 20				12 07		
Chandlers Ford	d									11 14										12 14		
Eastleigh ■	a	10 49				10 59				11 20	11 27					11 49	11 59			12 20	12 27	
	d	10 50				11 00				11 21	11 28				11 41	11 50	12 00			12 21	12 28	
Hedge End	d										11 34										12 34	
Botley	d										11 38										12 38	
Fareham	d										11 48										12 48	
Portchester	d										11 53										12 53	
Cosham	d										11 58				12a01						12 58	
Hilsea	a										12 03										13 03	
Fratton	a										12 07										13 07	
Portsmouth & Southsea	a										12 11										13 11	
Portsmouth Harbour ⛴	a										12 20										13 18	
Southampton Airport Pkwy ✈	d			10 42		11 05	11 09	11 14		11 25		11 34	11 42				12 05	12 14		12 25		12 34
Swaythling	d									11 27										12 27		
St Denys	d								←	11 30									←	12 30		
Southampton Central ⛴	a			10 49		11 12	11 17	11 22	11 12	11 36		11 43	11 49				12 12	12 21	12 12	12 36		12 41
	d			10 51		11 30		11 24	11 30	11 37		11 45	11 51				12 30	12 24	12 30	12 37		12 43
Millbrook (Hants)	d					→				11 40							→			12 40		
Redbridge	d									11 43										12 43		
Romsey	d	11a03								11 51						12a03				12 51		
Mottisfont & Dunbridge	d									11 56										12 56		
Dean	d									12 02										13 02		
Salisbury	a									12 15										13 15		
Totton	d								11 35										12 35			
Ashurst New Forest	d								11 40										12 40			
Beaulieu Road	d				←				11 44					←								
Brockenhurst ■	a			11 04	10 51			11 37	11 51			11 58	12 04	11 51				12 37	12 51			12 57
	d			11 05	11 16			11 38	12 16			11 59	12 05	12 16				12 38	13 16			12 58
Sway	d				11 21				→					12 21					→			
New Milton	d				11 26			11 45						12 26				12 45				
Hinton Admiral	d				11 30									12 30								
Christchurch	d				11 35			11 52						12 35				12 52				
Pokesdown	d				11 38			11 56						12 38				12 56				
Bournemouth	a			11 20	11 42			12 00				12 13	12 20	12 42				13 00				13 12
	d			11 24	11 44			12 04					12 24	12 44				13 04				
Branksome	d			11 29	11 49								12 29	12 49								
Parkstone (Dorset)	d			11 32	11 52								12 32	12 52								
Poole ■	a			11 36	11 55			12 13					12 36	12 55				13 13				
	d			11 37				12 14					12 37					13 14				
Hamworthy	d			11 42				12 19					12 42					13 19				
Holton Heath	d							12 23										13 23				
Wareham	d			11 49				12 28					12 49					13 28				
Wool	d							12 35										13 35				
Moreton (Dorset)	d							12 41										13 41				
Dorchester South	d			12 05				12 49					13 05					13 49				
Dorchester West	d		11 49																			
Upwey	d		12 02					12 55										13 55				
Weymouth	a		12 09	12 15				13 02					13 15					14 02				

A ✕ to Bournemouth

B not 21 May. ✕ to Bournemouth

For services from Brockenhurst - Lymington refer to Table T159

Table T158-F

Mondays to Fridays
21 May to 5 October

London - Basingstoke, Southampton, Romsey, Bournemouth and Weymouth

		SW	GW	SW	SW	SW	XC	SW	SW	SW	SW	XC	SW	SW	SW	SW	SW	SW	SW	SW	XC	SW	SW
		■	◇	◇■ A ✕	◇■	◇■	◇■ ✕	◇■ A ✕	◇■	■	■	◇■ ✕	◇■ A ✕	◇■	■	◇■	◇■ A ✕	◇■	■	■	◇■ ✕	◇■ A ✕	◇■
London Waterloo ■ ⊖	d			11 35		11 39		12 05			12 09		12 35			12 39	13 05			13 09		13 35	
Clapham Junction ■	d					11u46		12u12								12u46	13u12						
Woking	d			12 00							12 35		13 00							13 35		14 00	
Farnborough (Main)	d					12 13					12 45					13 13				13 45			
Fleet	d					12 19										13 19							
Reading ■	d						12 20					12 50									13 49		
Basingstoke	a					12 31	12 39	12 47			12 58	13 09				13 31	13 47			13 58	14 09		
	d					12 33	12 40	12 49			13 00	13 10				13 33	13 49			14 00	14 10		
Micheldever	d										13 10									14 10			
Winchester	d			12 33		12 49	12 55	13 05			13 19	13 25	13 33			13 49	14 05			14 19	14 26	14 33	
Shawford	d					12 54										13 54							
Romsey	d	12 20								13 07					13 20				14 07				
Chandlers Ford	d									13 14									14 14				
Eastleigh ■	a	12 49				12 59				13 20	13 27				13 49	13 59			14 20	14 27			
	d	12 50				13 00				13 21	13 28				13 50	14 00			14 21	14 28			
Hedge End	d										13 34									14 34			
Botley	d										13 38									14 38			
Fareham	d										13 48									14 48			
Portchester	d										13 53									14 53			
Cosham	d										13 58									14 58			
Hilsea	a										14 03									15 03			
Fratton	a										14 07									15 07			
Portsmouth & Southsea	a										14 11									15 11			
Portsmouth Harbour ⛴	a										14 20									15 20			
Southampton Airport Pkwy ✈	d			12 42		13 05	13 09	13 14		13 25		13 34	13 42			14 05	14 14		14 25		14 35	14 42	
Swaythling	d									13 27									14 27				
St Denys	d								←	13 30								←	14 30				
Southampton Central ⛴	a			12 49		13 12	13 17	13 22	13 12	13 36		13 41	13 49			14 12	14 22	14 12	14 35		14 41	14 49	
	d			12 51		13 30		13 24	13 30	13 37		13 43	13 51			14 30	14 24	14 30	14 37		14 43	14 51	
Millbrook (Hants)	d					→				13 40						→			14 40				
Redbridge	d									13 43									14 43				
Romsey	d	13a03								13 51					14a03				14 51				
Mottisfont & Dunbridge	d									13 56									14 56				
Dean	d									14 02									15 02				
Salisbury	a									14 15									15 15				
Totton	d								13 35									14 35					
Ashurst New Forest	d								13 40									14 40					
Beaulieu Road	d				←				13 44					←									←
Brockenhurst ■	a			13 04	12 51			13 37	13 51			13 56	14 04	13 51			14 37	14 51			14 56	15 04	14 51
	d			13 05	13 16			13 38	14 16			13 57	14 05	14 16			14 38	15 16			14 57	15 05	15 16
Sway	d				13 21				→					14 21				→					15 21
New Milton	d				13 26			13 45						14 26			14 45						15 26
Hinton Admiral	d				13 30									14 30									15 30
Christchurch	d				13 35			13 52						14 35			14 52						15 35
Pokesdown	d				13 38			13 56						14 38			14 56						15 38
Bournemouth	a			13 20	13 42			14 00				14 11	14 20	14 42			15 00				15 11	15 20	15 42
	d			13 24	13 44			14 04					14 24	14 44			15 04					15 24	15 44
Branksome	d			13 29	13 49								14 29	14 49								15 29	15 49
Parkstone (Dorset)	d			13 32	13 52								14 32	14 52								15 32	15 52
Poole ■	a			13 36	13 55			14 13					14 36	14 55			15 13					15 36	15 55
	d			13 37				14 14					14 37				15 14					15 37	
Hamworthy	d			13 42				14 19					14 42				15 19					15 42	
Holton Heath	d							14 23									15 23						
Wareham	d			13 49				14 28					14 49				15 28					15 49	
Wool	d							14 35									15 35						
Moreton (Dorset)	d							14 41									15 41						
Dorchester South	d			14 05				14 49					15 05				15 49					16 05	
Dorchester West	d		13 56																				
Upwey	d		14 03					14 55									15 55						
Weymouth	a		14 10	14 15				15 02					15 15				16 02					16 15	

A ✕ to Bournemouth

For services from Brockenhurst - Lymington refer to Table T159

Table T158-F

Mondays to Fridays

21 May to 5 October

London - Basingstoke, Southampton, Romsey, Bournemouth and Weymouth

		SW ■	SW ◇■	XC ◇■ 🛒	SW ◇■ A 🛒	SW ◇■	SW ■	SW ■	XC ◇■ 🛒	SW ■	GW ◇	SW ◇■ A 🛒	SW ◇■	SW ◇■	SW ◇■ A 🛒	SW ◇■	SW ■	SW ■	XC ◇■ 🛒	SW ◇■ A 🛒	SW ◇■	SW
London Waterloo ⊖	d		13 39		14 05			14 09				14 35		14 39	15 05			15 09		15 35		
Clapham Junction	d		13u46		14u12									14u46	15u12							
Woking	d							14 35				15 00						15 35		16 00		
Farnborough (Main)	d		14 13					14 45						15 13				15 45				
Fleet	d		14 19											15 19								
Reading	d			14 18					14 52										15 52			
Basingstoke	a		14 31	14 40	14 47			14 58	15 09					15 31	15 47			15 58	16 09			
	d		14 33	14 42	14 49			15 00	15 10					15 33	15 49			16 00	16 10			
Micheldever	d							15 10										16 10				
Winchester	d		14 49	14 57	15 04			15 19	15 25			15 33		15 49	16 05			16 19	16 25	16 33		16 38
Shawford	d		14 54											15 54								16 43
Romsey	d	14 13					15 07			15 20							16 07					
Chandlers Ford	d						15 14										16 14					
Eastleigh	a	14 49	14 59				15 20	15 27		15 49				15 59			16 20	16 27				16 48
	d	14 50	15 00				15 21	15 28		15 50				16 00			16 21	16 28				16 49
Hedge End	d							15 34										16 34				
Botley	d							15 38										16 38				
Fareham	d							15 48										16 48				
Portchester	d							15 53										16 53				
Cosham	d							15 58										16 58				
Hilsea	a							16 03										17 03				
Fratton	a							16 07										17 07				
Portsmouth & Southsea	a							16 11										17 11				
Portsmouth Harbour ⛴	a							16 20										17 20				
Southampton Airport Pkwy ✈	d		15 05	15 10	15 13		15 25		15 34			15 42		16 05	16 14		16 25		16 34	16 42		16 54
Swaythling	d						15 27										16 27					16 56
St Denys	d					←	15 30									←	16 30					16 59
Southampton Central ⛴	a		15 12	15 17	15 22	15 12	15 36		15 41			15 49		16 15	16 21	16 15	16 36		16 41	16 49		17 04
	d		15 30		15 24	15 30	15 37		15 43			15 51		16 30	16 23	16 30	16 37		16 43	16 54	16 56	17 06
Millbrook (Hants)	d		→				15 40							→			16 40					
Redbridge	d						15 43										16 43					17 10
Romsey	d	15a03					15 51			16a03							16 51					
Mottisfont & Dunbridge	d						15 56										16 56					
Dean	d						16 02										17 02					
Salisbury	a						16 15										17 15					
Totton	d					15 35										16 35					17 02	17a14
Ashurst New Forest	d					15 40										16 40					17 07	
Beaulieu Road	d					15 44							←			16 44						
Brockenhurst	a				15 38	15 51			15 57			16 04	15 51		16 37	16 51			16 57	17 08	17 15	
	d				15 38	16 28			15 58			16 05	16 28		16 38				16 58	17 09	17 16	
Sway	d					→							16 33		16 43						17 20	
New Milton	d				15 45								16 38		16 48						17 25	
Hinton Admiral	d												16 42		16 52						17 29	
Christchurch	d				15 52								16 47		16 57						17 34	
Pokesdown	d				15 56								16 50		17 00						17 38	
Bournemouth	a				16 00				16 12			16 20	16 54		17 04				17 12	17 24	17 42	
	d				16 04							16 24	16 56		17 09					17 25	17 43	
Branksome	d											16 29	17 01							17 30	17 48	
Parkstone (Dorset)	d											16 32	17 04							17 33	17 51	
Poole	a				16 13							16 36	17 07		17 18					17 37	17 55	
	d				16 14							16 37			17 19					17 38		
Hamworthy	d				16 19							16 42			17 24					17 43		
Holton Heath	d				16 23										17 28							
Wareham	d				16 28							16 49			17 33					17 50		
Wool	d				16 35							16 55			17 39					17 56		
Moreton (Dorset)	d				16 41										17 45							
Dorchester South	d				16 49							17 06			17 53					18 09		
Dorchester West	d										16 58											
Upwey	d				16 55						17 05				18 00							
Weymouth	a				17 02						17 10	17 15			18 06					18 18		

A 🛒 to Bournemouth

For services from Brockenhurst - Lymington refer to Table T159

Table T158-F

Mondays to Fridays

21 May to 5 October

London - Basingstoke, Southampton, Romsey, Bournemouth and Weymouth

		SW ■	SW	SW ◇■	XC ◇■ 🛒	SW ◇■ A 🛒	SW ◇■	SW	SW ◇■	XC ◇■ 🛒	SW	GW ◇	SW ◇■ A 🛒	SW ◇■	SW	SW ◇■	SW ◇■ A 🛒	SW ◇■ 🛒	SW ■	SW ◇■	XC ◇■ 🛒	SW ■	GW ◇
London Waterloo ⊖	d			15 39		16 05			16 09				16 35			16 39	17 05			17 09			
Clapham Junction	d			15u46		16u12										16u46							
Woking	d								16 35				17u00							17 34			
Farnborough (Main)	d			16 13					16 45							17 13							
Fleet	d			16 19												17 19							
Reading	d				16 20					16 52											17 52		
Basingstoke	a			16 31	16 40	16 47			16 58	17 09						17 31				17 52	18 09		
	d		16 26	16 33	16 42	16 49			17 00	17 10					17 24	17 32				17 54	18 11		
Micheldever	d								17 10						17 34					18 04			
Winchester	d		16 45	16 49	16 58	17 05			17 19	17 25			17 33		17 44	17 49	18 00			18 14	18 26		
Shawford	d			16 54											17 49	17 54				18 18			
Romsey	d	16 20						17 07			17 20								18 07			18 20	
Chandlers Ford	d							17 14											18 14				
Eastleigh	a	16 49	16 53	16 59				17 20	17 27		17 49				17 54	17 59			18 20	18 24		18 49	
	d	16 50	16 54	17 00				17 21	17 28		17 50				17 55	18 01			18 21	18 25		18 50	
Hedge End	d		17 00						17 34							18 07				18 31			
Botley	d		17 04						17 39							18 11				18 36			
Fareham	d		17 12						17 48							18 23				18 45			
Portchester	d		17 17						17 53							18 28				18 50			
Cosham	d		17 22						17 58							18 33				18 55			
Hilsea	a								18 03											19 05			
Fratton	a		17 30						18 07							18 40				19 09			
Portsmouth & Southsea	a		17 34						18 11							18 43				19 12			
Portsmouth Harbour ⛴	a		17 39						18 20							18 50				19 20			
Southampton Airport Pkwy ✈	d			17 05	17 09	17 14		17 25		17 34			17 42		18 00		18 09		18 25		18 34		
Swaythling	d							17 27							18 02				18 27				
St Denys	d						←	17 30							18 05				18 30				
Southampton Central ⛴	a			17 13	17 17	17 22	17 13	17 36		17 41			17 49		18 10		18 17		18 36		18 43		
	d			17 30		17 24	17 30	17 37		17 43			17 53	17 56			18 21	18 24	18 40		18 45		
Millbrook (Hants)	d			→				17 40											18 48				
Redbridge	d							17 43											18 52				
Romsey	d	17a03						17 51			18a03								19 01			19a04	
Mottisfont & Dunbridge	d							17 56											19 06				
Dean	d							18 02											19 11				
Salisbury	a							18 15											19 24				
Totton	d						17 35							18 02				18 29					
Ashurst New Forest	d						17 40							18 06				18 34					
Beaulieu Road	d						17 44																
Brockenhurst	a					17 37	17 51			17 57			18 07	18 14				18 42			18 58		
	d					17 38				17 58			18 08	18 15				18 43			18 59		
Sway	d					17 43								18 20				18 47					
New Milton	d					17 48								18 25				18 52					
Hinton Admiral	d					17 52								18 29				18 56					
Christchurch	d					17 57								18 34				19 01					
Pokesdown	d					18 00								18 37				19 05					
Bournemouth	a					18 04				18 15			18 24	18 41			18 48	19 09			19 12		
	d					18 09							18 25				18 50	19 10					
Branksome	d												18 30				18 55	19 15					
Parkstone (Dorset)	d												18 33				18 58	19 18					
Poole	a					18 18							18 37				19 02	19 24					
	d					18 19							18 38				19 03						
Hamworthy	d					18 24							18 43				19 08						
Holton Heath	d					18 28											19 12						
Wareham	d					18 33							18 50				19 17						
Wool	d					18 39							18 56				19 23						
Moreton (Dorset)	d					18 49											19 29						
Dorchester South	d					18 57							19 09				19 37						
Dorchester West	d											19 02											19 54
Upwey	d					19 03						19 10					19 44						20 02
Weymouth	a					19 08						19 16	19 23				19 50						20 10

A 🛒 to Bournemouth

For services from Brockenhurst - Lymington refer to Table T159

Table T158-F

Mondays to Fridays

21 May to 5 October

London - Basingstoke, Southampton, Romsey, Bournemouth and Weymouth

		SW	SW	SW	SW		SW	SW	SW	SW	XC	SW	SW	SW	SW		SW	SW	SW	SW	SW	XC	SW	SW	SW
		◇1	◇1	◇1	◇1		◇1	1	1	◇1	◇1	◇1	◇1	1	◇1		1	◇1	◇1	1	1	◇1	◇1	◇1	◇1
		A ⚯	⚯				A ⚯				⚯	A ⚯	⚯					A ⚯				⚯		A ⚯	
London Waterloo ⊖	d	17 35		17 39	17 48		18 05			18 09		18 35			18 39			19 05			19 09		19 15	19 35	
Clapham Junction	d														18u46			19u12					19u22		
Woking	d			18 04	18 13					18 35					19 06						19 35		19 44	20 00	
Farnborough (Main)	d																				19 45				
Fleet	d																								
Reading	d										18 52											19 52			
Basingstoke	a			18 22	18 31					18 53	19 09				19 28			19 47			19 58	20 09			
	d			18 24	18 33					18 55	19 10				19 30			19 49			20 00	20 10			
Micheldever	d			18 34						19 05					19 40						20 10				
Winchester	d	18 30		18 44	18 50		19 00	19 05		19 14	19 25	19 30			19 49			20 05			20 19	20 26		20 33	
Shawford	d			18 49				19 09		19 19					19 54						20 24				
Romsey	d								19 07					19 20						20 07					
Chandlers Ford	d								19 14											20 14					
Eastleigh	a			18 54	18 58			19 15	19 20	19 25				19 49	19 59					20 20	20 29				
	d			18 55	18 59			19 16	19 21	19 29				19 50	20 04		20 08			20 21	20 30				
Hedge End	d			19 01						19 35							20 14				20 36				
Botley	d			19 05						19 38							20 18				20 40				
Fareham	d			19 14						19 48							20a30				20 49		21 18		
Portchester	d			19 19						19 53											20 54				
Cosham	d			19 24						19 58											20 59				
Hilsea	a			19 28						20 03											21 03				
Fratton	a			19 32						20 07											21 07				
Portsmouth & Southsea	a			19 36						20 12											21 11				
Portsmouth Harbour ⛴	a			19 43						20 20											21 18				
Southampton Airport Pkwy ✈	d	18 39			19 03		19 09	19 20	19 25		19 34	19 39			20 08			20 14		20 25		20 35		20 42	
Swaythling	d				19 06			19 23	19 27											20 27					
St Denys	d				19 09			19 26	19 30										←	20 30					
Southampton Central ⛴	a	18 46			19 18		19 18	19 33	19 35		19 42	19 46			20 16			20 21	20 16	20 36		20 42	21 43	20 49	
	d	18 51	18 54				19 19		19 37		19 43	19 51	19 54		20 30			20 24	20 30	20 37		20 43		20 51	
Millbrook (Hants)	d								19 40						→					20 40					
Redbridge	d								19 43											20 43					
Romsey	d								19 51					20a03						20 51					
Mottisfont & Dunbridge	d								19 56											20 56					
Dean	d								20 02											21 02					
Salisbury	a								20 15											21 15					
Totton	d		18 59				19 25						19 59						20 35					20 56	
Ashurst New Forest	d		19 04										20 04						20 40						
Beaulieu Road	d																		20 44						←
Brockenhurst	a		19 12				19 35				19 56		20 12					20 37	20 51			20 58		21 07	20 51
	d		19 13				19 36				19 57		20 13					20 38	21 16			20 59		21 08	21 16
Sway	d		19 17				19 41						20 17						→						21 20
New Milton	d		19 22				19 46						20 22					20 45							21 25
Hinton Admiral	d		19 26				19 50						20 26												21 29
Christchurch	d		19 31				19 55						20 31					20 52							21 34
Pokesdown	d		19 35				19 58						20 35					20 56							21 38
Bournemouth	a	19 20	19 39				20 03				20 11	20 21	20 39					21 00				21 15		21 22	21 42
	d	19 21	19 40				20 07					20 22	20 40					21 04						21 27	21 44
Branksome	d	19 26	19 45				20 12					20 27	20 45											21 32	21 49
Parkstone (Dorset)	d	19 29	19 48				20 15					20 30	20 48											21 35	21 52
Poole	a	19 33	19 54				20 19					20 34	20 54					21 13						21 38	21 58
	d	19 34					20 20					20 35						21 15						21 39	
Hamworthy	d	19 39					20 25					20 40						21 20						21 44	
Holton Heath	d						20 29																		
Wareham	d	19 46					20 34					20 47						21 27						21 51	
Wool	d	19 52					20 40					20 53						21 33						21 58	
Moreton (Dorset)	d						20 46											21 39						22 04	
Dorchester South	d	20 03					20 54					21 04						21 47						22 12	
Dorchester West	d																								
Upwey	d						21 01											21 54						22 18	
Weymouth	a	20 15					21 07					21 15						22 00						22 23	

A ⚯ to Bournemouth

For services from Brockenhurst - Lymington refer to Table T159

Table T158-F

Mondays to Fridays

21 May to 5 October

London - Basingstoke, Southampton, Romsey, Bournemouth and Weymouth

			SW	SW	SW	SW	SW	XC	SW	GW	SW		SW	GW	SW	SW	XC	SW	SW	SW	SW		XC	SW	SW
			1	◇1	◇1	1	1	◇1	1		◇1		◇1		◇1	1	◇1	◇1	1	1	◇1		◇1	1	◇1
					⚯						A ⚯				⚯			A ⚯							⚯
London Waterloo ⊖	d			19 39	20 05		20 09				20 35		20 39		21 05			21 35			21 39			21 42	22 05
Clapham Junction	d			19u46	20u12								20u46		21u12						21u46				22u12
Woking	d						20 35				21 00				21 32			22 00						22 19	22 32
Farnborough (Main)	d			20 13			20 45						21 13								22 13			22 33	
Fleet	d			20 19									21 19								22 19			22 38	
Reading	d							20 52									21 52						22 22		
Basingstoke	a			20 30	20 47		20 58	21 09					21 31		21 50		22 09				22 31		22 39	22 58	22 50
	d			20 33	20 49		21 00	21 10					21 33		21 52		22 10			22 21	22 33		22 40	23 00	22 52
Micheldever	d			20 43			21 10						21 43							22 31	22 43			→	
Winchester	d			20 52	21 05		21 19	21 25			21 33		21 52		22 08		22 25	22 33		22 40	22 52		22 57		23 08
Shawford	d			20 57			21 24						21 57							22 45	22 57				
Romsey	d		20 20			21 07			21 20							22 07			22 20						
Chandlers Ford	d					21 14										22 14									
Eastleigh	a		20 49	21 02		21 20	21 30		21 49				22 02		22 17	22 21			22 49	22 50	23 02				23 16
	d		20 50	21 03		21 21	21 31		21 50				22 03	22 09	22 18	22 22			22 50	22 51	23 03				23 17
Hedge End	d						21 37													22 57					
Botley	d						21 41													23 01					
Fareham	d						21 49													23 10					
Portchester	d						21 54													23 15					
Cosham	d						21 59													23 20					
Hilsea	a						22 04													23 24					
Fratton	a						22 08													23 32					
Portsmouth & Southsea	a						22 11													23 36					
Portsmouth Harbour ⛴	a						22 18													23 40					
Southampton Airport Pkwy ✈	d			21 08	21 15	21 25		21 34			21 42		22 08	22 13	22 22	22 26	22 34	22 42			23 08		23 13		23 22
Swaythling	d					21 27										22 28									
St Denys	d					21 30										22 31									
Southampton Central ⛴	a			21 17	21 24	21 35		21 40			21 49		22 17	22 21	22 29	22 36	22 42	22 50			23 17		23 20		23 29
	d				21 25	21 37		21 42			21 51			22 23	22 31	22 38	22 43	22 51							23 30
Millbrook (Hants)	d					21 40										22 40									
Redbridge	d					21 43										22 44									
Romsey	d		21a03			21 51			22a03					22 34		22a51			23a04						
Mottisfont & Dunbridge	d					21 56																			
Dean	d					22 02																			
Salisbury	a					22 15								22 58											
Totton	d				21 31										22 36										23 36
Ashurst New Forest	d				21 35										22 41										23 40
Beaulieu Road	d																								
Brockenhurst	a				21 43			21 56			22 04				22 49		22 56	23 05							23 48
	d				21 44			21 57			22 05				22 50		22 59	23 06							23 49
Sway	d				21 49										22 54										23 54
New Milton	d				21 54										22 59										23 58
Hinton Admiral	d				21 58										23 03										00 02
Christchurch	d				22 03										23 08										00 07
Pokesdown	d				22 06										23 12										00 11
Bournemouth	a				22 10			22 15			22 20				23 16		23 19	23 25							00 15
	d				22 12						22 24				23 17			23 28							00 16
Branksome	d				22 17						22 29				23 22			23 33							00 21
Parkstone (Dorset)	d				22 20						22 32				23 25			23 36							00 24
Poole	a				22 23						22 36				23 29			23 40							00 28
	d										22 37							23 41							
Hamworthy	d										22 42							23 46							
Holton Heath	d																								
Wareham	d										22 49							23 52							
Wool	d										22 55							23 59							
Moreton (Dorset)	d										23 01							00 05							
Dorchester South	d										23 09							00 13							
Dorchester West	d									22 58															
Upwey	d									23 06	23 16							00 19							
Weymouth	a									23 13	23 20							00 24							

A ⚯ to Bournemouth

For services from Brockenhurst - Lymington refer to Table T159

Table T158-F

Mondays to Fridays

21 May to 5 October

London - Basingstoke, Southampton, Romsey, Bournemouth and Weymouth

		SW 1	SW 1	XC ◇1	SW ◇1 🛒	SW 1	SW ◇1	SW ◇1	SW 1
London Waterloo 15 ⊖	d				22 35		22 39	23 05	23 35
Clapham Junction 10	d						22u46	23u12	23u42
Woking	d				23 00			23 32	00 03
Farnborough (Main)	d						23 16		00 14
Fleet	d						23 21		00 20
Reading 7	d		←	22 48					
Basingstoke	a		22 58	23 06			23 33	23 51	00 33
	d		23 00	23 09			23 34	23 53	00 35
Micheldever	d		23 10					00 03	
Winchester	d		23 19	23 25	23 33		23 51	00 12	00 51
Shawford	d		23 24				23 55		
Romsey	d	23 07				22 58			
Chandlers Ford	d	23 14							
Eastleigh 5	a	23 21	23 29			23 34	00 01	00 22	00 59
	d	23 22	23 30			23 36	00 02	00 23	01 00
Hedge End	d		23 36						
Botley	d		23 40						
Fareham	d		23 49						
Portchester	d		23 54						
Cosham	d		23 59						
Hilsea	a		00 03						
Fratton	a		00 07						
Portsmouth & Southsea	a		00 11						
Portsmouth Harbour ⛴	a		00 16						
Southampton Airport Pkwy ✈	d	23 26		23 37	23 42		00 06	00 28	01 05
Swaythling	d	23 28							
St Denys	d	23 31						00s32	
Southampton Central ⛴	a	23 37		23 43	23 49		00 13	00 37	01 12
	d	23 38			23 51			00 38	
Millbrook (Hants)	d	23 40							
Redbridge	d	23 44							
Romsey	d	23 56				23a48			
Mottisfont & Dunbridge	d	00 01							
Dean	d	00 07							
Salisbury	a	00 19							
Totton	d							00s43	
Ashurst New Forest	d								
Beaulieu Road	d								
Brockenhurst 5	a				00 04			00s54	
	d				00 05				
Sway	d								
New Milton	d							01s02	
Hinton Admiral	d								
Christchurch	d							01s09	
Pokesdown	d							01s13	
Bournemouth	a				00 21			01 17	
	d				00 22			01 18	
Branksome	d				00 27			01s23	
Parkstone (Dorset)	d				00 30			01s26	
Poole 4	a				00 35			01 30	
	d								
Hamworthy	d								
Holton Heath	d								
Wareham	d								
Wool	d								
Moreton (Dorset)	d								
Dorchester South	d								
Dorchester West	d								
Upwey	d								
Weymouth	a								

For services from Brockenhurst - Lymington refer to Table T159

Table T158-F

Mondays to Fridays

8 October to 7 December

London - Basingstoke, Southampton, Romsey, Bournemouth and Weymouth

		SW MX 1	SW MX ◇1 🛒	SW MX ◇1	SW MO ◇1	SW MX ◇1 🛒	SW MO 1	SW MX ◇1	SW MO ◇1	SW MX 1	SW MO ◇1 🛒	SW MX ◇1	SW MO ◇1	SW MO ◇1 🛒	SW MX 1	SW MX 1	SW MX 1	SW MX ◇1	SW 1	SW MO ◇1	SW MO 1	SW MX 1	SW 1
London Waterloo 15 ⊖	d																	00 05		00 50	01 05	01 05	
Clapham Junction 10	d																	00u12		00 57	01 15	01 15	
Woking	d															00 03	00 28	00 37		01 18	01 49	01 49	
Farnborough (Main)	d									00 10						00 14	00 41				01s58	01s58	
Fleet	d						00 04			00 16						00 20	00 47				02s04	02s04	
Reading 7	d																						
Basingstoke	a						00 21			00 33						00 33	01 06	00 55			02s16	02s16	
	d															00 35		00 56					
Micheldever	d											00 03											
Winchester	d										00 07	00 12	00 14			00 51		01 13			02s33	02s33	
Shawford	d										00 12												
Romsey	d																						
Chandlers Ford	d													←									
Eastleigh 5	a										00 17	00 22	00 23	00 17		00 59		01 21			02s42	02s42	
	d			00 02							00 30	00 23	00 24	00 30	00 30	01 00		01 22					06 01
Hedge End	d										→			00s36	00s36								06 07
Botley	d													00s39	00s39								06 11
Fareham	d													00s47	00s47								06 19
Portchester	d													00s53	00s53								06 24
Cosham	d													00s57	00s57								06 29
Hilsea	a																						06 34
Fratton	a													01s05	01s05					02s10			06 40
Portsmouth & Southsea	a													01s08	01s08					02s14			06 44
Portsmouth Harbour ⛴	a													01 12	01 12					02 19			06 49
Southampton Airport Pkwy ✈	d			00 06								00 28	00 28			01 05		01 26			02s46	02s46	
Swaythling	d																						
St Denys	d											00s32	00s32								02s51	02s51	
Southampton Central ⛴	a			00 13								00 37	00 38			01 12		01 35			02 56	02 57	
	d											00 38	00 42					01 37					
Millbrook (Hants)	d																						
Redbridge	d																						
Romsey	d																						
Mottisfont & Dunbridge	d	00 01																					
Dean	d	00 07																					
Salisbury	a	00 19																					
Totton	d											00s43	00s47					01s42					
Ashurst New Forest	d																						
Beaulieu Road	d																						
Brockenhurst 5	a											00s54	00s58					01s53					
	d					00 05																	
Sway	d																						
New Milton	d				00 04							01s02	01s06					02s00					
Hinton Admiral	d		00 02		00 08																		
Christchurch	d		00 07		00 13							01s09	01s13					02s07					
Pokesdown	d		00 11		00 17							01s13	01s17					02s11					
Bournemouth	a		00 15		00 21	00 21						01 17	01 21					02 15					
	d		00 16		00 22	00 22						01 18	01 22						06 11				
Branksome	d		00 21		00 27	00 27						01s23	01s27						06 16				
Parkstone (Dorset)	d		00 24		00 30	00 30						01s26	01s30						06 19				
Poole 4	a		00 28		00 34	00 35						01 30	01 34						06 23				
	d																		06 24				
Hamworthy	d																		06 29				
Holton Heath	d																		06 33				
Wareham	d								00 03										06 38				
Wool	d								00 10										06 44				
Moreton (Dorset)	d							00 05	00 17										06 50				
Dorchester South	d							00 13	00 25										06 58				
Dorchester West	d																						
Upwey	d							00 19	00 32										07 05				
Weymouth	a							00 24	00 36										07 14				

For services from Brockenhurst - Lymington refer to Table T159

Table T158-F

Mondays to Fridays

8 October to 7 December

London - Basingstoke, Southampton, Romsey, Bournemouth and Weymouth

		SW	SW	SW	SW	GW	SW	SW	SW	SW	SW	SW	XC	SW	SW	SW	SW	SW	SW	SW	SW	XC	SW
		1	1	1	1		◇1	1	1	1	1	1	◇1 ✠	◇1	◇1	1	◇1	1	◇1		1	◇1 ✠	◇1 A ✠
London Waterloo 15 ⊖	d						05 30							06 12	06 30			06 42	07 03				07 35
Clapham Junction 10	d						05u37							06u19	06u37			06u49	07u10				
Woking	d						06 01					06 19		06 50	06 57			07 19	07 30				08 00
Farnborough (Main)	d											06 33		07 04				07 33					
Fleet	d											06 38		07 09				07 38					
Reading 7	d																←				←	07 52	
Basingstoke	a						06 20					06 58		07 28	07 16		07 28	07 56	07 48		07 56	08 08	08 19
	d		05 40				06 21			06 45		07 00		07 30	07 18		07 30	08 00	07 50		08 00	08 10	08 20
Micheldever	d		05 50									07 10		→			07 41	→			08 10		
Winchester	d		05 59		06 18		06 38			07 01		07 19			07 34		07 50		08 06		08 19	08 25	08 37
Shawford	d				06 23					07 06							07 55				08 24		
Romsey	d			05 58							07 07					07 13				08 07			
Chandlers Ford	d			06 06							07 14									08 14			
Eastleigh 5	a		06 07	06 11	06 28		06 47			07 12	07 20	07 27			07 43	07 49	08 00			08 20	08 30		08 47
	d		06 08	06 12	06 29		06 48		07 02	07 14	07 21	07 28			07 44	07 50	08 02			08 21	08 31		08 48
Hedge End	d				06 35				07 08			07 34									08 37		
Botley	d				06 39				07 12			07 38									08 42		
Fareham	d				06 50				07 21			07 47									08 50		
Portchester	d				06 55				07 26			07 52									08 55		
Cosham	d				07 00				07 30			07 57									09 00		
Hilsea	a				07 05				07 35			08 03									09 05		
Fratton	a				07 09				07 39			08 07									09 09		
Portsmouth & Southsea	a				07 12				07 42			08 13									09 12		
Portsmouth Harbour ⛴	a				07 17				07 48			08 17									09 18		
Southampton Airport Pkwy ✈	d		06 13	06 17			06 53			07 18	07 26				07 49		08 06		08 16	08 25		08 34	08 52
Swaythling	d		06 15	06 20						07 21	07 29						08 09			08 27			
St Denys	d		06 18	06 24						07 24	07 32						08 12			08 30			
Southampton Central ⛴	a		06 23	06 29			07 00			07 29	07 37				07 57		08 17		08 25	08 35		08 44	08 59
	d		06 25	06 30			07 01	07 19			07 38		07 56		07 59		08 18		08 27	08 37		08 46	09 01
Millbrook (Hants)	d			06 33				07 21			07 41						08 21			08 40			
Redbridge	d			06 36				07 25			07 45						08 24			08 43			
Romsey	d			06 44							07 53					08a03				08 51			
Mottisfont & Dunbridge	d			06 49							07 58									08 56			
Dean	d			06 55							08 03									09 02			
Salisbury	a			07 07							08 16									09 15			
Totton	d		06 30				07 07	07 28							08 04		08 27		08 33				09 06
Ashurst New Forest	d		06 35					07 32							08 09		08 32						
Beaulieu Road	d							07 37							08 13								
Brockenhurst 5	a		06 43				07 17	07 43					08 09		08 19		08 40		08 45			08 59	09 17
	d	06 15	06 44				07 18	07 44					08 10		08 20		08 41		08 46			09 00	09 18
Sway	d	06 20	06 48				07 23	07 48							08 25				08 51				09 22
New Milton	d	06 25	06 53				07 28	07 53							08 30				08 56				09 27
Hinton Admiral	d	06 29	06 57				07 32	07 57							08 34				09 00				09 31
Christchurch	d	06 34	07 02				07 37	08 02							08 39				09 05				09 36
Pokesdown	d	06 37	07 06				07 40	08 06							08 42				09 08				09 40
Bournemouth	a	06 41	07 10				07 44	08 10					08 23		08 46		08 55		09 12			09 15	09 44
	d	06 44	07 11				07 46	08 11							08 48		08 57		09 14				09 45
Branksome	d	06 49	07 16				07 51	08 16							08 53		09a02		09 19				09 50
Parkstone (Dorset)	d	06 52	07 19				07 54	08 19							08 56				09 22				09 53
Poole 4	a	06 55	07 23				07 57	08 23							08 59				09 25				09 57
	d	06 57	07 24				07 58	08 24							09 00				09 26				09 58
Hamworthy	d	07 02	07 29				08 03	08 29							09 05				09 31				10 03
Holton Heath	d	07 06	07 33				08 07	08 33											09 35				
Wareham	d	07 11	07 38				08 12	08 38							09 12				09 40				10 10
Wool	d	07 17	07 44				08 19	08 44							09 19				09 47				
Moreton (Dorset)	d	07 23	07 50				08 25	08 50							09 25				09 53				
Dorchester South	d	07 31	07 58				08 33	08 58							09 33				10 01				10 26
Dorchester West	d					08 09																	
Upwey	d	07 38	08 05			08 17	08 39	09 05							09 39				10 07				
Weymouth	a	07 47	08 14			08 23	08 44	09 09							09 44				10 12				10 35

A ✠ to Bournemouth

For services from Brockenhurst - Lymington refer to Table T159

Table T158-F

Mondays to Fridays

8 October to 7 December

London - Basingstoke, Southampton, Romsey, Bournemouth and Weymouth

		SW	GW	SW	XC	SW	SW	SW	SW	XC	SW	SW	SN	SW	SW	SW	SW	SW	SW	XC	SW	GW
			◇	◇1 ✠	◇1 ✠	◇1 A ✠	◇1 ✠	1	1	◇1 ✠	◇1 A ✠	◇1 ✠		1	◇1	◇1 A ✠	◇1	1	1	◇1 ✠	1	◇
London Waterloo 15 ⊖	d			07 39		08 05			08 09		08 35				08 39	09 05			09 09			
Clapham Junction 10	d			07u45		08u12									08u46	09u12						
Woking	d								08 35		09 00								09 35			
Farnborough (Main)	d			08 13					08 45						09 13				09 45			
Fleet	d			08 19											09 19							
Reading 7	d				08 20					08 49										09 47		
Basingstoke	a			08 32	08 41	08 47			08 58	09 10					09 32	09 47			09 58	10 09		
	d			08 33	08 42	08 49			09 00	09 11					09 33	09 49			10 00	10 10		
Micheldever	d								09 10										10 10			
Winchester	d			08 50	08 57	09 05			09 19	09 26	09 33				09 49	10 05			10 19	10 25		
Shawford	d			08 54											09 54							
Romsey	d	08 13						09 07						09 14				10 07			10 20	
Chandlers Ford	d							09 14										10 14				
Eastleigh 5	a	08 49		09 00				09 20	09 27					09 49	09 59			10 20	10 27		10 49	
	d	08 50		09 01				09 21	09 28				09 42	09 50	10 04			10 21	10 28		10 50	
Hedge End	d								09 34										10 34			
Botley	d								09 38										10 38			
Fareham	d								09 48										10 48			
Portchester	d								09 53										10 53			
Cosham	d								09 58				10a02						10 58			
Hilsea	a								10 03										11 03			
Fratton	a								10 07										11 07			
Portsmouth & Southsea	a								10 11										11 12			
Portsmouth Harbour ⛴	a								10 20										11 20			
Southampton Airport Pkwy ✈	d			09 05	09 09	09 14		09 25		09 35	09 43				10 08	10 14		10 25		10 34		
Swaythling	d							09 27										10 27				
St Denys	d						←	09 30									←	10 30				
Southampton Central ⛴	a			09 12	09 18	09 22	09 12	09 35		09 43	09 50				10 17	10 22	10 17	10 36		10 43		
	d			09 30		09 24	09 30	09 37		09 45	09 51				10 30	10 24	10 30	10 45		10 45		
Millbrook (Hants)	d			→				09 40							→			10 48				
Redbridge	d							09 43										10 51				
Romsey	d	09a03						09 51						10a03				10 59			11a03	
Mottisfont & Dunbridge	d							09 56										11 04				
Dean	d							10 02										11 10				
Salisbury	a							10 17										11 22				
Totton	d						09 35										10 35					
Ashurst New Forest	d						09 40										10 40					
Beaulieu Road	d											←					10 44					
Brockenhurst 5	a					09 37	09 49			09 58	10 05	09 49				10 37	10 51			10 58		
	d					09 38	10 16			09 59	10 05	10 16				10 38	11 16			10 59		
Sway	d						→					10 20					→					
New Milton	d					09 45						10 25				10 45						
Hinton Admiral	d											10 29										
Christchurch	d					09 52						10 34				10 52						
Pokesdown	d					09 56						10 38				10 56						
Bournemouth	a					10 00				10 13	10 20	10 42				11 00				11 13		
	d					10 04					10 24	10 43				11 04						
Branksome	d										10 29	10 48										
Parkstone (Dorset)	d										10 32	10 51										
Poole 4	a					10 13					10 36	10 55				11 13						
	d					10 14					10 37					11 14						
Hamworthy	d					10 19					10 42					11 19						
Holton Heath	d					10 23										11 23						
Wareham	d					10 28					10 49					11 28						
Wool	d					10 35										11 35						
Moreton (Dorset)	d					10 41										11 41						
Dorchester South	d					10 54					11 05					11 49						
Dorchester West	d		10 48																			11 49
Upwey	d		10 55			11 01										11 55						12 02
Weymouth	a		11 03			11 06					11 14					12 02						12 09

A ✠ to Bournemouth

For services from Brockenhurst - Lymington refer to Table T159

Table T158-F

Mondays to Fridays

8 October to 7 December

London - Basingstoke, Southampton, Romsey, Bournemouth and Weymouth

		SW	SW	SW	XC	SW	SW	SW	SW	XC	SW	SW	SN	SW	SW	SW	SW	SW	SW	XC	SW	GW	SW
		◇1 A ⊼	◇1	◇1	◇1 ⊼	◇1 A ⊼	◇1	1	1	1 ⊼	◇1 A ⊼	◇1		1	◇1	◇1 A ⊼	◇1	1	1	◇1 ⊼	1	◇	◇1 A ⊼
London Waterloo 15 ⊖	d	09 35		09 39		10 05			10 09		10 35				10 39	11 05			11 09				11 35
Clapham Junction 10	d			09u46		10u12									10u46	11u12							
Woking	d	10 00							10 35		11 00								11 35				12 00
Farnborough (Main)	d			10 13					10 45						11 13				11 45				
Fleet	d			10 19											11 19								
Reading 7	d				10 20					10 52										11 52			
Basingstoke	a			10 31	10 39	10 47			10 58	11 09					11 31	11 47			11 58	12 09			
	d			10 33	10 40	10 49			11 00	11 10					11 33	11 49			12 00	12 10			
Micheldever	d								11 10										12 10				
Winchester	d	10 33		10 49	10 55	11 05			11 19	11 25	11 33				11 49	12 05			12 19	12 25			12 33
Shawford	d			10 54											11 54								
Romsey	d							11 07						11 20				12 07			12 20		
Chandlers Ford	d							11 14										12 14					
Eastleigh 8	a			10 59				11 20	11 27					11 49	11 59			12 20	12 27		12 49		
	d			11 00				11 21	11 28				11 41	11 50	12 00			12 21	12 28		12 50		
Hedge End	d								11 34										12 34				
Botley	d								11 38										12 38				
Fareham	d								11 48										12 48				
Portchester	d								11 53										12 53				
Cosham	d								11 58				12a01						12 58				
Hilsea	a								12 03										13 03				
Fratton	a								12 07										13 07				
Portsmouth & Southsea	a								12 11										13 11				
Portsmouth Harbour ⛴	a								12 20										13 18				
Southampton Airport Pkwy ✈	d	10 42		11 05	11 09	11 14		11 25		11 34	11 42				12 05	12 14		12 25		12 34			12 42
Swaythling	d							11 27										12 27					
St Denys	d						←	11 30									←	12 30					
Southampton Central ⛴	a	10 49		11 12	11 17	11 22	11 12	11 36		11 43	11 49				12 12	12 21	12 12	12 36		12 41			12 49
	d	10 51		11 30		11 24	11 30	11 37		11 45	11 51				12 30	12 24	12 30	12 37		12 43			12 51
Millbrook (Hants)	d			→				11 40							→			12 40					
Redbridge	d							11 43										12 43					
Romsey	d							11 51						12a03				12 51			13a03		
Mottisfont & Dunbridge	d							11 56										12 56					
Dean	d							12 02										13 02					
Salisbury	a							12 15										13 15					
Totton	d						11 35										12 35						
Ashurst New Forest	d						11 40										12 40						
Beaulieu Road	d		←				11 44					←											
Brockenhurst 3	a	11 04	10 51			11 37	11 51			11 58	12 04	11 51				12 37	12 51			12 57			13 04
	d	11 05	11 16			11 38	12 16			11 59	12 05	12 16				12 38	13 16			12 58			13 05
Sway	d		11 21				→					12 21					→						
New Milton	d		11 26			11 45						12 26				12 45							
Hinton Admiral	d		11 30									12 30											
Christchurch	d		11 35			11 52						12 35				12 52							
Pokesdown	d		11 38			11 56						12 38				12 56							
Bournemouth	a	11 20	11 42			12 00				12 13	12 20	12 42				13 00				13 12			13 20
	d	11 24	11 44			12 04					12 24	12 44				13 04							13 24
Branksome	d	11 29	11 49								12 29	12 49											13 29
Parkstone (Dorset)	d	11 32	11 52								12 32	12 52											13 32
Poole 4	a	11 36	11 55			12 13					12 36	12 55				13 13							13 36
	d	11 37				12 14					12 37					13 14							13 37
Hamworthy	d	11 42				12 19					12 42					13 19							13 42
Holton Heath	d					12 23										13 23							
Wareham	d	11 49				12 28					12 49					13 28							13 49
Wool	d					12 35										13 35							
Moreton (Dorset)	d					12 41										13 41							
Dorchester South	d	12 05				12 49					13 05					13 49							14 05
Dorchester West	d																					13 56	
Upwey	d					12 55										13 55						14 03	
Weymouth	a	12 15				13 02					13 15					14 02						14 10	14 15

A ⊼ to Bournemouth

For services from Brockenhurst - Lymington refer to Table T159

Table T158-F

Mondays to Fridays

8 October to 7 December

London - Basingstoke, Southampton, Romsey, Bournemouth and Weymouth

		SW	SW	XC	SW	SW	SW	SW	XC	SW	SW	SW	SW	SW	SW	SW	SW	XC	SW	SW	SW	SW
		◇1	◇1	◇1 ⊼	◇1 A ⊼	◇1	1	1	◇1 ⊼	◇1 A ⊼	◇1	1	◇1	◇1 A ⊼	◇1	1	1	◇1 ⊼	◇1 A ⊼	◇1	1	◇1
London Waterloo 15 ⊖	d		11 39		12 05			12 09		12 35			12 39	13 05			13 09		13 35			13 39
Clapham Junction 10	d		11u46		12u12								12u46	13u12								13u46
Woking	d							12 35		13 00							13 35		14 00			
Farnborough (Main)	d		12 13					12 45					13 13				13 45					14 13
Fleet	d		12 19										13 19									14 19
Reading 7	d			12 20					12 50									13 49				
Basingstoke	a		12 31	12 39	12 47			12 58	13 09				13 31	13 47			13 58	14 09				14 31
	d		12 33	12 40	12 49			13 00	13 10				13 33	13 49			14 00	14 10				14 33
Micheldever	d							13 10									14 10					
Winchester	d		12 49	12 55	13 05			13 19	13 25	13 33			13 49	14 05			14 19	14 26	14 33			14 49
Shawford	d		12 54										13 54									14 54
Romsey	d						13 07					13 20				14 07					14 13	
Chandlers Ford	d						13 14									14 14						
Eastleigh 8	a		12 59				13 20	13 27				13 49	13 59			14 20	14 27				14 49	14 59
	d		13 00				13 21	13 28				13 50	14 00			14 21	14 28				14 50	15 00
Hedge End	d							13 34									14 34					
Botley	d							13 38									14 38					
Fareham	d							13 48									14 48					
Portchester	d							13 53									14 53					
Cosham	d							13 58									14 58					
Hilsea	a							14 03									15 03					
Fratton	a							14 07									15 07					
Portsmouth & Southsea	a							14 11									15 11					
Portsmouth Harbour ⛴	a							14 20									15 20					
Southampton Airport Pkwy ✈	d		13 05	13 09	13 14		13 25		13 34	13 42			14 05	14 14		14 25		14 35	14 42			15 05
Swaythling	d						13 27									14 27						
St Denys	d					←	13 30								←	14 30						
Southampton Central ⛴	a		13 12	13 17	13 22	13 12	13 36		13 41	13 49			14 12	14 22	14 12	14 35		14 41	14 49			15 12
	d		13 30		13 24	13 30	13 37		13 43	13 51			14 30	14 24	14 30	14 37		14 43	14 51			15 30
Millbrook (Hants)	d		→				13 40						→			14 40						→
Redbridge	d						13 43									14 43						
Romsey	d						13 51					14a03				14 51					15a03	
Mottisfont & Dunbridge	d						13 56									14 56						
Dean	d						14 02									15 02						
Salisbury	a						14 15									15 15						
Totton	d					13 35									14 35							
Ashurst New Forest	d					13 40									14 40							
Beaulieu Road	d	←				13 44					←									←		
Brockenhurst 3	a	12 51			13 37	13 51			13 56	14 04	13 51			14 37	14 51			14 56	15 04	14 51		
	d	13 16			13 38	14 16			13 57	14 05	14 16			14 38	15 16			14 57	15 05	15 16		
Sway	d	13 21				→					14 21				→					15 21		
New Milton	d	13 26			13 45						14 26			14 45						15 26		
Hinton Admiral	d	13 30									14 30									15 30		
Christchurch	d	13 35			13 52						14 35			14 52						15 35		
Pokesdown	d	13 38			13 56						14 38			14 56						15 38		
Bournemouth	a	13 42			14 00				14 11	14 20	14 42			15 00				15 11	15 20	15 42		
	d	13 44			14 04					14 24	14 44			15 04					15 24	15 44		
Branksome	d	13 49								14 29	14 49								15 29	15 49		
Parkstone (Dorset)	d	13 52								14 32	14 52								15 32	15 52		
Poole 4	a	13 55			14 13					14 36	14 55			15 13					15 36	15 55		
	d				14 14					14 37				15 14					15 37			
Hamworthy	d				14 19					14 42				15 19					15 42			
Holton Heath	d				14 23									15 23								
Wareham	d				14 28					14 49				15 28					15 49			
Wool	d				14 35									15 35								
Moreton (Dorset)	d				14 41									15 41								
Dorchester South	d				14 49					15 05				15 49					16 05			
Dorchester West	d																					
Upwey	d				14 55									15 55								
Weymouth	a				15 02					15 15				16 02					16 15			

A ⊼ to Bournemouth

For services from Brockenhurst - Lymington refer to Table T159

Table T158-F

8 October to 7 December

London - Basingstoke, Southampton, Romsey, Bournemouth and Weymouth

Station		XC	SW	SW	SW	SW	XC	SW	GW	SW		SW	SW	SW	SW	SW	SW	XC	SW	SW		SW	SW	SW	SW
		◇1	◇1	◇1	1	1	◇1	1	◇	◇1		◇1	◇1	◇1	◇1	1	1	◇1	◇1	◇1			1		◇1
			A							A				A					A						
		[trolley]	[trolley]				[trolley]			[trolley]				[trolley]				[trolley]	[trolley]						
London Waterloo 15 ⊖	d		14 05			14 09				14 35			14 39	15 05			15 09		15 35						15 39
Clapham Junction 10	d		14u12										14u46	15u12											15u46
Woking	d					14 35				15 00							15 35		16 00						
Farnborough (Main)	d					14 45							15 13				15 45								16 13
Fleet	d												15 19												16 19
Reading 7	d	14 18					14 52											15 52							
Basingstoke	a	14 40	14 47			14 58	15 09						15 31	15 47			15 58	16 09							16 31
	d	14 42	14 49			15 00	15 10						15 33	15 49			16 00	16 10						16 26	16 33
Micheldever	d					15 10											16 10								
Winchester	d	14 57	15 04			15 19	15 25			15 33			15 49	16 05			16 19	16 25	16 33			16 38		16 45	16 49
Shawford	d												15 54									16 43			16 54
Romsey	d				15 07			15 20								16 07							16 20		
Chandlers Ford	d				15 14											16 14									
Eastleigh 8	a				15 20	15 27		15 49					15 59			16 20	16 27					16 48	16 49	16 53	16 59
	d				15 21	15 28		15 50					16 00			16 21	16 28					16 49	16 50	16 54	17 00
Hedge End	d					15 34											16 34							17 00	
Botley	d					15 38											16 38							17 04	
Fareham	d					15 48											16 48							17 12	
Portchester	d					15 53											16 53							17 17	
Cosham	d					15 58											16 58							17 22	
Hilsea	a					16 03											17 03								
Fratton	a					16 07											17 07							17 30	
Portsmouth & Southsea	a					16 11											17 11							17 34	
Portsmouth Harbour ⛴	a					16 20											17 20							17 39	
Southampton Airport Pkwy ✈	d	15 10	15 13		15 25		15 34			15 42			16 05	16 14		16 25		16 34	16 42			16 54			17 05
Swaythling	d				15 27											16 27						16 56			
St Denys	d			←	15 30										←	16 30						16 59			
Southampton Central ⛴	a	15 17	15 22	15 12	15 36		15 41			15 49			16 15	16 21	16 15	16 36		16 41	16 49			17 04			17 13
	d		15 24	15 30	15 37		15 43			15 51			16 30	16 23	16 30	16 37		16 43	16 54	16 56		17 06			17 30
Millbrook (Hants)	d				15 40								→			16 40									→
Redbridge	d				15 43											16 43						17 10			
Romsey	d				15 51			16a03								16 51							17a03		
Mottisfont & Dunbridge	d				15 56											16 56									
Dean	d				16 02											17 02									
Salisbury	a				16 15											17 15									
Totton	d			15 35											16 35					17 02		17a14			
Ashurst New Forest	d			15 40											16 40					17 07					
Beaulieu Road	d			15 44								←			16 44										
Brockenhurst 3	a		15 38	15 51			15 57			16 04		15 51		16 37	16 51			16 57	17 08	17 15					
	d		15 38	16 28			15 58			16 05		16 28		16 38				16 58	17 09	17 16					
Sway	d			→								16 33		16 43						17 20					
New Milton	d		15 45									16 38		16 48						17 25					
Hinton Admiral	d											16 42		16 52						17 29					
Christchurch	d		15 52									16 47		16 57						17 34					
Pokesdown	d		15 56									16 50		17 00						17 38					
Bournemouth	a		16 00				16 12			16 20		16 54		17 04				17 12	17 24	17 42					
	d		16 04							16 24		16 56		17 09					17 25	17 43					
Branksome	d									16 29		17 01							17 30	17 48					
Parkstone (Dorset)	d									16 32		17 04							17 33	17 51					
Poole 4	a		16 13							16 36		17 07		17 18					17 37	17 55					
	d		16 14							16 37				17 19					17 38						
Hamworthy	d		16 19							16 42				17 24					17 43						
Holton Heath	d		16 23											17 28											
Wareham	d		16 28							16 49				17 33					17 50						
Wool	d		16 35							16 55				17 39					17 56						
Moreton (Dorset)	d		16 41											17 45											
Dorchester South	d		16 49							17 06				17 53					18 09						
Dorchester West	d								16 58																
Upwey	d		16 55						17 05					18 00											
Weymouth	a		17 02						17 10	17 15				18 06					18 18						

A [trolley] to Bournemouth

For services from Brockenhurst - Lymington refer to Table T159

Table T158-F

8 October to 7 December

London - Basingstoke, Southampton, Romsey, Bournemouth and Weymouth

Station		XC	SW	SW	SW	SW		XC	SW	GW	SW	SW	SW	SW	SW	SW		SW	SW	XC	SW	GW	SW	SW	SW
		◇1	◇1	◇1		◇1		◇1		◇	◇1	◇1		◇1	◇1	◇1		1	◇1	◇1	1	◇	◇1	◇1	◇1
			A								A				A								A		
		[trolley]	[trolley]					[trolley]			[trolley]				[trolley]	[trolley]				[trolley]			[trolley]	[trolley]	
London Waterloo 15 ⊖	d		16 05			16 09					16 35			16 39	17 05				17 09				17 35		17 39
Clapham Junction 10	d		16u12											16u46											
Woking	d					16 35					17u00								17 34						18 04
Farnborough (Main)	d					16 45								17 13											
Fleet	d													17 19											
Reading 7	d	16 20						16 52												17 52					
Basingstoke	a	16 40	16 47			16 58		17 09						17 31					17 52	18 09					18 22
	d	16 42	16 49			17 00		17 10					17 24	17 32					17 54	18 11					18 24
Micheldever	d					17 10							17 34						18 04						18 34
Winchester	d	16 58	17 05			17 19		17 25			17 33		17 44	17 49	18 00				18 14	18 26			18 30		18 44
Shawford	d												17 49	17 54					18 18						18 49
Romsey	d				17 07				17 20									18 07			18 20				
Chandlers Ford	d				17 14													18 14							
Eastleigh 8	a				17 20	17 27			17 49				17 54	17 59				18 20	18 24		18 49				18 54
	d				17 21	17 28			17 50				17 55	18 01				18 21	18 25		18 50				18 55
Hedge End	d					17 34								18 07					18 31						19 01
Botley	d					17 39								18 11					18 36						19 05
Fareham	d					17 48								18 23					18 45						19 14
Portchester	d					17 53								18 28					18 50						19 19
Cosham	d					17 58								18 33					18 55						19 24
Hilsea	a					18 03													19 05						19 28
Fratton	a					18 07								18 40					19 09						19 32
Portsmouth & Southsea	a					18 11								18 43					19 12						19 36
Portsmouth Harbour ⛴	a					18 20								18 50					19 20						19 43
Southampton Airport Pkwy ✈	d	17 09	17 14		17 25			17 34			17 42		18 00		18 09			18 25		18 34			18 39		
Swaythling	d				17 27								18 02					18 27							
St Denys	d			←	17 30								18 05					18 30							
Southampton Central ⛴	a	17 17	17 22	17 13	17 36			17 41			17 49		18 10		18 17			18 36		18 43			18 46		
	d		17 24	17 30	17 37			17 43			17 53	17 56			18 21	18 24		18 40		18 45			18 51	18 54	
Millbrook (Hants)	d				17 40													18 48							
Redbridge	d				17 43													18 52							
Romsey	d				17 51				18a03									19 01			19a04				
Mottisfont & Dunbridge	d				17 56													19 06							
Dean	d				18 02													19 11							
Salisbury	a				18 15													19 24							
Totton	d			17 35								18 02				18 29								18 59	
Ashurst New Forest	d			17 40								18 06				18 34								19 04	
Beaulieu Road	d			17 44																					
Brockenhurst 3	a		17 37	17 51				17 57			18 07	18 14				18 42				18 58				19 12	
	d		17 38					17 58			18 08	18 15				18 43				18 59				19 13	
Sway	d		17 43									18 20				18 47								19 17	
New Milton	d		17 48									18 25				18 52								19 22	
Hinton Admiral	d		17 52									18 29				18 56								19 26	
Christchurch	d		17 57									18 34				19 01								19 31	
Pokesdown	d		18 00									18 37				19 05								19 35	
Bournemouth	a		18 04					18 15			18 24	18 41			18 48	19 09				19 12			19 20	19 39	
	d		18 09								18 25				18 50	19 10							19 21	19 40	
Branksome	d										18 30				18 55	19 15							19 26	19 45	
Parkstone (Dorset)	d										18 33				18 58	19 18							19 29	19 48	
Poole 4	a		18 18								18 37				19 02	19 24							19 33	19 54	
	d		18 19								18 38				19 03								19 34		
Hamworthy	d		18 24								18 43				19 08								19 39		
Holton Heath	d		18 28												19 12										
Wareham	d		18 33								18 50				19 17								19 46		
Wool	d		18 39								18 56				19 23								19 52		
Moreton (Dorset)	d		18 49												19 29										
Dorchester South	d		18 57								19 09				19 37								20 03		
Dorchester West	d									19 02												19 54			
Upwey	d		19 03							19 10					19 44							20 02			
Weymouth	a		19 08							19 16	19 23				19 50							20 10	20 15		

A [trolley] to Bournemouth

For services from Brockenhurst - Lymington refer to Table T159

Table T158-F

London - Basingstoke, Southampton, Romsey, Bournemouth and Weymouth

Mondays to Fridays
8 October to 7 December

		SW ◇1	SW ◇1 A ⚒	SW 1	SW 1	SW ◇1	XC ◇1 ⚒	SW ◇1 A ⚒	SW ◇1 ⚒	SW 1	SW ◇1	SW 1	SW ◇1 A ⚒	SW ◇1	SW 1	SW 1	XC ◇1 ⚒	SW ◇1	SW ◇1 A ⚒	SW ◇1	SW 1	SW ◇1
London Waterloo 15 ⊖	d	17 48	18 05			18 09		18 35			18 39		19 05			19 09		19 15	19 35			19 39
Clapham Junction 10	d										18u46		19u12					19u22				19u46
Woking	d	18 13				18 35					19 06					19 35		19 44	20 00			
Farnborough (Main)	d															19 45						20 13
Fleet	d																					20 19
Reading 7	d						18 52										19 52					
Basingstoke	a	18 31				18 53	19 09				19 28		19 47			19 58	20 09					20 30
	d	18 33				18 55	19 10				19 30		19 49			20 00	20 10					20 33
Micheldever	d					19 05					19 40					20 10						20 43
Winchester	d	18 50	19 00	19 05		19 14	19 25	19 30			19 49		20 05			20 19	20 26		20 33			20 52
Shawford	d			19 09		19 19					19 54					20 24						20 57
Romsey	d				19 07					19 20					20 07						20 20	
Chandlers Ford	d				19 14										20 14							
Eastleigh 8	a	18 58		19 15	19 20	19 25				19 49	19 59				20 20	20 29					20 49	21 02
	d	18 59		19 16	19 21	19 29				19 50	20 04	20 08			20 21	20 30					20 50	21 03
Hedge End	d					19 35						20 14				20 36						
Botley	d					19 38						20 18				20 40						
Fareham	d					19 48						20a30				20 49		21 18				
Portchester	d					19 53										20 54						
Cosham	d					19 58										20 59						
Hilsea	a					20 03										21 03						
Fratton	a					20 07										21 07						
Portsmouth & Southsea	a					20 12										21 11						
Portsmouth Harbour ⛴	a					20 20										21 18						
Southampton Airport Pkwy ✈	d	19 03	19 09	19 20	19 25		19 34	19 39			20 08		20 14		20 25		20 35		20 42			21 08
Swaythling	d	19 06		19 23	19 27										20 27							
St Denys	d	19 09		19 26	19 30									←	20 30							
Southampton Central ⛴	a	19 18	19 18	19 33	19 35		19 42	19 46			20 16		20 21	20 16	20 36		20 42	21 43	20 49			21 17
	d		19 19		19 37		19 43	19 51	19 54		20 30		20 24	20 30	20 37		20 43		20 51			
Millbrook (Hants)	d				19 40						→				20 40							
Redbridge	d				19 43										20 43							
Romsey	d				19 51					20a03					20 51						21a03	
Mottisfont & Dunbridge	d				19 56										20 56							
Dean	d				20 02										21 02							
Salisbury	a				20 15										21 15							
Totton	d		19 25						19 59					20 35					20 56			
Ashurst New Forest	d								20 04					20 40								
Beaulieu Road	d													20 44						←		
Brockenhurst 3	a		19 35				19 56		20 12				20 37	20 51			20 58		21 07	20 51		
	d		19 36				19 57		20 13				20 38	21 16			20 59		21 08	21 16		
Sway	d		19 41						20 17					→						21 20		
New Milton	d		19 46						20 22				20 45							21 25		
Hinton Admiral	d		19 50						20 26											21 29		
Christchurch	d		19 55						20 31				20 52							21 34		
Pokesdown	d		19 58						20 35				20 56							21 38		
Bournemouth	a		20 03				20 11	20 21	20 39				21 00				21 15		21 22	21 42		
	d		20 07					20 22	20 40				21 04						21 27	21 44		
Branksome	d		20 12					20 27	20 45										21 32	21 49		
Parkstone (Dorset)	d		20 15					20 30	20 48										21 35	21 52		
Poole 4	a		20 19					20 34	20 54				21 13						21 38	21 58		
	d		20 20					20 35					21 15						21 39			
Hamworthy	d		20 25					20 40					21 20						21 44			
Holton Heath	d		20 29																			
Wareham	d		20 34					20 47					21 27						21 51			
Wool	d		20 40					20 53					21 33						21 58			
Moreton (Dorset)	d		20 46										21 39						22 04			
Dorchester South	d		20 54					21 04					21 47						22 12			
Dorchester West	d																					
Upwey	d		21 01										21 54						22 18			
Weymouth	a		21 07					21 15					22 00						22 23			

A ⚒ to Bournemouth

For services from Brockenhurst - Lymington refer to Table T159

Table T158-F

London - Basingstoke, Southampton, Romsey, Bournemouth and Weymouth

Mondays to Fridays
8 October to 7 December

		SW ◇1 ⚒	SW 1 A	SW 1	XC ◇1	SW 1	GW	SW ◇1 B ⚒	SW ◇1	GW	SW ◇1 ⚒	SW 1	XC ◇1	SW ◇1 B ⚒	SW 1	SW 1	SW ◇1	XC ◇1	SW 1	SW ◇1 ⚒	SW 1	SW 1	XC ◇1
London Waterloo 15 ⊖	d	20 05		20 09				20 35	20 39		21 05			21 35			21 39		21 42	22 05			
Clapham Junction 10	d	20u12							20u46		21u12						21u46			22u12			
Woking	d			20 35				21 00			21 32			22 00					22 19	22 32			
Farnborough (Main)	d			20 45					21 13								22 13		22 33				
Fleet	d								21 19								22 19		22 38				
Reading 7	d				20 52								21 52					22 22				←	22 48
Basingstoke	a	20 47		20 58	21 09				21 31		21 50		22 09				22 31	22 39	22 58	22 50		22 58	23 06
	d	20 49		21 00	21 10				21 33		21 52		22 10			22 21	22 33	22 40	23 00	22 52		23 00	23 09
Micheldever	d			21 10					21 43							22 31	22 43		→			23 10	
Winchester	d	21 05		21 19	21 25			21 33	21 52		22 08		22 25	22 33		22 40	22 52	22 57		23 08		23 19	23 25
Shawford	d			21 24					21 57							22 45	22 57					23 24	
Romsey	d		21 07			21 20						22 07			22 20						23 07		
Chandlers Ford	d		21 14									22 14									23 14		
Eastleigh 8	a		21 20	21 30		21 49			22 02		22 17	22 21			22 49	22 50	23 02			23 16	23 21	23 29	
	d		21 21	21 31		21 50			22 03	22 09	22 18	22 22			22 50	22 51	23 03			23 17	23 22	23 30	
Hedge End	d			21 37												22 57						23 36	
Botley	d			21 41												23 01						23 40	
Fareham	d			21 49												23 10						23 49	
Portchester	d			21 54												23 15						23 54	
Cosham	d			21 59												23 20						23 59	
Hilsea	a			22 04												23 24						00 03	
Fratton	a			22 08												23 32						00 07	
Portsmouth & Southsea	a			22 11												23 36						00 11	
Portsmouth Harbour ⛴	a			22 18												23 40						00 16	
Southampton Airport Pkwy ✈	d	21 15	21 25		21 34			21 42	22 08	22 13	22 22	22 26	22 34	22 42			23 08	23 13		23 22	23 26		23 37
Swaythling	d		21 27									22 28									23 28		
St Denys	d		21 30									22 31									23 31		
Southampton Central ⛴	a	21 24	21 35		21 40			21 49	22 17	22 21	22 29	22 36	22 42	22 50			23 17	23 20		23 29	23 37		23 43
	d	21 25	21 37		21 42			21 51		22 23	22 31	22 38	22 43	22 51						23 30	23 38		
Millbrook (Hants)	d		21 40									22 40									23 40		
Redbridge	d		21 43									22 44									23 44		
Romsey	d		21 51			22a03				22 34		22a51			23a04						23 56		
Mottisfont & Dunbridge	d		21 56																		00 01		
Dean	d		22 02																		00 07		
Salisbury	a		22 15							22 58											00 19		
Totton	d	21 31									22 36									23 36			
Ashurst New Forest	d	21 35									22 41									23 40			
Beaulieu Road	d																						
Brockenhurst 3	a	21 43			21 56			22 04			22 49		22 56	23 05						23 48			
	d	21 44			21 57			22 05			22 50		22 59	23 06						23 49			
Sway	d	21 49									22 54									23 54			
New Milton	d	21 54									22 59									23 58			
Hinton Admiral	d	21 58									23 03									00 02			
Christchurch	d	22 03									23 08									00 07			
Pokesdown	d	22 06									23 12									00 11			
Bournemouth	a	22 10			22 15			22 20			23 16		23 19	23 25						00 15			
	d	22 12						22 24			23 17			23 28						00 16			
Branksome	d	22 17						22 29			23 22			23 33						00 21			
Parkstone (Dorset)	d	22 20						22 32			23 25			23 36						00 24			
Poole 4	a	22 23						22 36			23 29			23 40						00 28			
	d							22 37						23 41									
Hamworthy	d							22 42						23 46									
Holton Heath	d																						
Wareham	d							22 49						23 52									
Wool	d							22 55						23 59									
Moreton (Dorset)	d							23 01						00 05									
Dorchester South	d							23 09						00 13									
Dorchester West	d						22 58																
Upwey	d						23 06	23 16						00 19									
Weymouth	a						23 13	23 20						00 24									

A not 7 December
B ⚒ to Bournemouth

For services from Brockenhurst - Lymington refer to Table T159

Table T158-F

Mondays to Fridays

8 October to 7 December

London - Basingstoke, Southampton, Romsey, Bournemouth and Weymouth

		SW ◇1	SW 1	SW ◇1	SW ◇1	SW 1
London Waterloo 15 ⊖	d	22 35		22 39	23 05	23 35
Clapham Junction 10	d			22u46	23u12	23u42
Woking	d	23 00			23 32	00 03
Farnborough (Main)	d			23 16		00 14
Fleet	d			23 21		00 20
Reading 7	d					
Basingstoke	a			23 33	23 51	00 33
	d			23 34	23 53	00 35
Micheldever	d				00 03	
Winchester	d	23 33		23 51	00 12	00 51
Shawford	d			23 55		
Romsey	d		22 58			
Chandlers Ford	d					
Eastleigh 8	a		23 34	00 01	00 22	00 59
	d		23 36	00 02	00 23	01 00
Hedge End	d					
Botley	d					
Fareham	d					
Portchester	d					
Cosham	d					
Hilsea	a					
Fratton	a					
Portsmouth & Southsea	a					
Portsmouth Harbour	a					
Southampton Airport Pkwy ✈	d	23 42		00 06	00 28	01 05
Swaythling	d					
St Denys	d				00s32	
Southampton Central	a	23 49		00 13	00 37	01 12
	d	23 51			00 38	
Millbrook (Hants)	d					
Redbridge	d					
Romsey	d		23a48			
Mottisfont & Dunbridge	d					
Dean	d					
Salisbury	a					
Totton	d				00s43	
Ashurst New Forest	d					
Beaulieu Road	d					
Brockenhurst 3	a	00 04			00s54	
	d	00 05				
Sway	d					
New Milton	d				01s02	
Hinton Admiral	d					
Christchurch	d				01s09	
Pokesdown	d				01s13	
Bournemouth	a	00 21			01 17	
	d	00 22			01 18	
Branksome	d	00 27			01s23	
Parkstone (Dorset)	d	00 30			01s26	
Poole 4	a	00 35			01 30	
	d					
Hamworthy	d					
Holton Heath	d					
Wareham	d					
Wool	d					
Moreton (Dorset)	d					
Dorchester South	d					
Dorchester West	d					
Upwey	d					
Weymouth	a					

For services from Brockenhurst - Lymington refer to Table T159

Table T158-F

Saturdays

26 May to 8 December

London - Basingstoke, Southampton, Romsey, Bournemouth and Weymouth

		SW 1	SW ◇1	SW ◇1	SW ◇1	SW ◇1	SW ◇1	SW 1	SW 1	SW 1	SW 1	SW ◇1	SW 1	SW 1	SW 1	SW 1	SW 1	SW 1	SW 1	SW 1	GW	SW ◇1	SW 1
London Waterloo 15 ⊖	d											00 05		01 05								05 30	
Clapham Junction 10	d											00u12		01 15								05u37	
Woking	d									00 03	00 28	00 37		01 42								06 01	
Farnborough (Main)	d								00 10	00 14	00 41			01s51									
Fleet	d								00 16	00 20	00 47			01s57									
Reading 7	d																						
Basingstoke	a								00 33	00 33	01 06	00 55		02s09								06 20	
	d									00 35		00 56			05 10							06 21	
Micheldever	d						00 03															06 31	
Winchester	d						00 12			00 51		01 13		02s26	05 26							06 41	
Shawford	d																						
Romsey	d																	05 58					
Chandlers Ford	d																	06 06					
Eastleigh 8	a						00 22			00 59		01 21		02s35	05 34			06 12				06 50	
	d			00 02			00 23	00 30		01 00		01 22			05 35			06 13	06 24	06 28		06 51	
Hedge End	d							00s36												06 34			
Botley	d							00s39												06 38			
Fareham	d							00s47												06 46			
Portchester	d							00s53												06 51			
Cosham	d							00s57												06 56			
Hilsea	a																			07 03			
Fratton	a							01s05												07 07			
Portsmouth & Southsea	a							01s08												07 11			
Portsmouth Harbour	a							01 12												07 16			
Southampton Airport Pkwy ✈	d			00 06			00 28			01 05		01 26		02s39	05 40			06 18	06 28			06 56	
Swaythling	d																	06 20					
St Denys	d						00s32							02s44	05 44			06 23					
Southampton Central	a			00 13			00 37			01 12		01 35		02 49	05 49			06 28	06 35			07 03	
	d						00 38					01 37					06 21	06 30				07 05	07 21
Millbrook (Hants)	d																	06 32					
Redbridge	d																	06 36					
Romsey	d																	06 44					
Mottisfont & Dunbridge	d	00 01																06 49					
Dean	d	00 07																06 54					
Salisbury	a	00 19																07 07					
Totton	d						00s43					01s42					06 26					07 10	07 26
Ashurst New Forest	d																06 31						07 31
Beaulieu Road	d																						
Brockenhurst 3	a						00s54					01s53					06 39					07 21	07 39
	d					00 05										06 15	06 40					07 22	07 40
Sway	d															06 20	06 44					07 26	07 44
New Milton	d						01s02					02s00				06 25	06 49					07 31	07 49
Hinton Admiral	d		00 02													06 29	06 53					07 35	07 53
Christchurch	d		00 07				01s09					02s07				06 34	06 58					07 40	07 58
Pokesdown	d		00 11				01s13					02s11				06 37	07 02					07 44	08 02
Bournemouth	a		00 15			00 21	01 17					02 15				06 41	07 06					07 48	08 06
	d		00 16			00 22	01 18						06 11			06 44	07 11					07 49	08 11
Branksome	d		00 21			00 27	01s23						06 16			06 49	07 16					07 54	08 16
Parkstone (Dorset)	d		00 24			00 30	01s26						06 19			06 52	07 19					07 57	08 19
Poole 4	a		00 28			00 35	01 30						06 23			06 55	07 23					08 01	08 23
	d												06 24			06 57	07 24					08 02	08 24
Hamworthy	d												06 29			07 02	07 29					08 07	08 29
Holton Heath	d												06 33			07 06	07 33						08 33
Wareham	d												06 38			07 11	07 38					08 14	08 38
Wool	d												06 44			07 17	07 44					08 20	08 44
Moreton (Dorset)	d				00 05								06 50			07 23	07 50					08 26	08 50
Dorchester South	d				00 13								06 58			07 31	07 58					08 34	08 58
Dorchester West	d																				08 13		
Upwey	d				00 19								07 05			07 38	08 05				08 21	08 41	09 05
Weymouth	a				00 24								07 09			07 42	08 09				08 26	08 45	09 09

For services from Brockenhurst - Lymington refer to Table T159

Table T158-F

Saturdays

26 May to 8 December

London - Basingstoke, Southampton, Romsey, Bournemouth and Weymouth

		SW	SW	SW	SW	SW	SW	SW	XC	SW	SW	SW	SW	XC	SW	SW	SW	SW	XC	SW	GW	SW	SW
		■	■	◇■	■	■	■	■	◇■	◇■	◇■	■	◇■	◇■	◇■	◇■	■	■	◇■	■	◇	◇■	◇■
									⚲	A	B			⚲					⚲			C ⚲	
London Waterloo ⊖	d			06 30				06 42		07 35	07 35		07 39		08 05			08 09				08 35	
Clapham Junction	d			06u37				06u49					07u46		08u12								
Woking	d		06 19	06 57				07 19		08 00	08 00							08 35				09 00	
Farnborough (Main)	d		06 33					07 33					08 13					08 45					
Fleet	d		06 38					07 38					08 19										
Reading	d								07 52					08 20					08 52				
Basingstoke	a		06 58	07 16				07 58	08 08	08 20	08 20		08 31	08 39	08 47			08 58	09 09				
	d		07 00	07 18				08 00	08 10	08 21	08 21		08 33	08 40	08 49			09 00	09 11				
Micheldever	d		07 10					08 10										09 10					
Winchester	d		07 19	07 34				08 19	08 25	08 38	08 38		08 49	08 59	09 05			09 19	09 26			09 33	
Shawford	d		07 24					08 24					08 54										
Romsey	d	07 07			07 13		08 07					08 13					09 07			09 20			
Chandlers Ford	d	07 14					08 14										09 14						
Eastleigh	a	07 20	07 29	07 42	07 49		08 20	08 30		08 46	08 46	08 49	08 59				09 20	09 27		09 49			
	d	07 21	07 30	07 43	07 50		08 21	08 31		08 47	08 47	08 50	09 00				09 21	09 28		09 50			
Hedge End	d		07 36					08 37										09 34					
Botley	d		07 40					08 41										09 38					
Fareham	d		07 49					08 49										09 48					
Portchester	d		07 54					08 54										09 53					
Cosham	d		07 59					08 59										09 58					
Hilsea	a		08 03					09 04										10 03					
Fratton	a		08 07					09 08										10 07					
Portsmouth & Southsea	a		08 11					09 12										10 11					
Portsmouth Harbour ⛴	a		08 18					09 18										10 18					
Southampton Airport Pkwy ✈	d	07 25		07 48			08 25		08 33	08 51	08 51		09 05	09 09	09 14		09 25		09 34			09 42	
Swaythling	d	07 27					08 27										09 27						
St Denys	d	07 30					08 30									←	09 30						
Southampton Central ⛴	a	07 35		07 56			08 36		08 41	08 58	08 58		09 12	09 17	09 22	09 12	09 36		09 41			09 49	
	d	07 37		08 00		08 19	08 37		08 43	09 00	09 00		09 30		09 24	09 30	09 37		09 43			09 51	
Millbrook (Hants)	d	07 40					08 40						→				09 40						
Redbridge	d	07 43					08 43										09 43						
Romsey	d	07 51			08a03		08 51					09a03					09 51			10a03			
Mottisfont & Dunbridge	d	07 56					08 56										09 56						
Dean	d	08 02					09 02										10 02						
Salisbury	a	08 15					09 15										10 15						
Totton	d			08 05		08 24				09 05	09 05					09 35							
Ashurst New Forest	d					08 29										09 40							
Beaulieu Road	d					08 33										09 44							←
Brockenhurst	a			08 16		08 39			08 56	09 16	09 16				09 37	09 51			09 57			10 04	09 51
	d			08 17		08 40			08 58	09 17	09 17				09 38	10 16			09 58			10 05	10 16
Sway	d			08 21		08 45				09 21	09 21					→							10 21
New Milton	d			08 26		08 50				09 26	09 26				09 45								10 26
Hinton Admiral	d			08 30		08 54				09 30	09 30												10 30
Christchurch	d			08 35		08 59				09 35	09 35				09 52								10 35
Pokesdown	d			08 39		09 02				09 39	09 39				09 56								10 38
Bournemouth	a			08 43		09 08			09 14	09 43	09 43				10 00				10 11			10 20	10 42
	d			08 44		09 12				09 44	09 44				10 04							10 24	10 44
Branksome	d			08 49		09 18				09 49	09 49											10 29	10 49
Parkstone (Dorset)	d			08 52		09 21				09 52	09 52											10 32	10 52
Poole	a			08 56		09 24				09 56	09 56				10 13							10 36	10 55
	d			08 57		09 25				09 57	09 57				10 14							10 37	
Hamworthy	d			09 02		09 30				10 02	10 02				10 19							10 42	
Holton Heath	d					09 34									10 23								
Wareham	d			09 09		09 39				10 09	10 09				10 28							10 49	
Wool	d			09 15		09 46									10 35								
Moreton (Dorset)	d			09 21		09 52									10 41								
Dorchester South	d			09 29		10 00				10 27	10 27				10 49							11 05	
Dorchester West	d																				10 54		
Upwey	d			09 36		10 06									10 55						11 01		
Weymouth	a			09 40		10 11				10 35	10 36				11 00						11 09	11 13	

A from 15 September
B until 8 September
C ⚲ to Bournemouth

For services from Brockenhurst - Lymington refer to Table T159

Table T158-F

Saturdays

26 May to 8 December

London - Basingstoke, Southampton, Romsey, Bournemouth and Weymouth

		GW	SW	SW	SW	SW	SW	XC	XC	SW	GW	SW	SW	SW	XC	SW	SW	SW	SW	XC	SW	SW
			◇■	◇■	◇■	■	■	◇■	◇■	■	◇	◇■	◇■	◇■	◇■	◇■	◇■	■	■	◇■	◇■	◇■
		A						B ⚲	C			D ⚲			⚲					⚲	D ⚲	
London Waterloo ⊖	d		08 39	09 05			09 09					09 35		09 39		10 05			10 09		10 35	
Clapham Junction	d		08u46	09u12										09u46		10u12						
Woking	d						09 35					10 00							10 35		11 00	
Farnborough (Main)	d		09 13				09 45							10 13					10 45			
Fleet	d		09 19											10 19								
Reading	d							09 52	09 52						10 20					10 48		
Basingstoke	a		09 32	09 47			09 58	10 09	10 09					10 31	10 40	10 47			10 58	11 09		
	d		09 33	09 49			10 00	10 10	10 10					10 33	10 42	10 49			11 00	11 11		
Micheldever	d						10 10												11 10			
Winchester	d		09 49	10 05			10 19	10 25	10 25			10 33		10 49	10 57	11 05			11 19	11 26	11 33	
Shawford	d		09 54											10 54								
Romsey	d					10 07				10 20								11 07				
Chandlers Ford	d					10 14												11 14				
Eastleigh	a		09 59			10 20	10 27			10 49				10 59				11 20	11 27			
	d		10 00			10 21	10 28			10 50				11 00				11 21	11 28			
Hedge End	d						10 34												11 34			
Botley	d						10 38												11 38			
Fareham	d						10 48												11 48			
Portchester	d						10 53												11 53			
Cosham	d						10 58												11 58			
Hilsea	a						11 03												12 03			
Fratton	a						11 07												12 07			
Portsmouth & Southsea	a						11 11												12 11			
Portsmouth Harbour ⛴	a						11 18												12 18			
Southampton Airport Pkwy ✈	d		10 05	10 14		10 25		10 34	10 34			10 42		11 05	11 09	11 14		11 25		11 34	11 42	
Swaythling	d					10 27												11 27				
St Denys	d				←	10 30											←	11 30				
Southampton Central ⛴	a		10 12	10 22	10 12	10 36		10 41	10 41			10 49		11 12	11 17	11 22	11 12	11 36		11 41	11 49	
	d		10 30	10 24	10 30	10 37		10 43	10 43			10 51		11 30		11 24	11 30	11 37		11 43	11 51	
Millbrook (Hants)	d		→			10 40								→				11 40				
Redbridge	d					10 43												11 43				
Romsey	d					10 59				11a03								11 51				
Mottisfont & Dunbridge	d					11 04												11 56				
Dean	d					11 10												12 02				
Salisbury	a					11 22												12 15				
Totton	d				10 35												11 35					
Ashurst New Forest	d				10 40												11 40					
Beaulieu Road	d												←				11 44					←
Brockenhurst	a			10 37	10 51			10 57	10 57			11 04	10 51			11 37	11 51			11 57	12 04	11 51
	d			10 38	11 16			10 58	10 58			11 05	11 16			11 38	12 16			11 58	12 05	12 16
Sway	d				→								11 21				→					12 21
New Milton	d			10 45									11 26			11 45						12 26
Hinton Admiral	d												11 30									12 30
Christchurch	d			10 52									11 35			11 52						12 35
Pokesdown	d			10 56									11 38			11 56						12 38
Bournemouth	a			11 00				11 13	11 13			11 20	11 42			12 00				12 12	12 20	12 42
	d			11 04								11 24	11 44			12 04					12 24	12 44
Branksome	d											11 29	11 49								12 29	12 49
Parkstone (Dorset)	d											11 32	11 52								12 32	12 52
Poole	a			11 13								11 36	11 55			12 13					12 36	12 55
	d			11 14								11 37				12 14					12 37	
Hamworthy	d			11 19								11 42				12 19					12 42	
Holton Heath	d			11 23												12 23						
Wareham	d			11 28								11 49				12 28					12 49	
Wool	d			11 35												12 35						
Moreton (Dorset)	d			11 41												12 41						
Dorchester South	d			11 49								12 05				12 49					13 05	
Dorchester West	d	11 13									11 54											
Upwey	d			11 55							12 02					12 55						
Weymouth	a	11 25		12 00							12 09	12 13				13 00					13 13	

A until 8 September
B until 21 July, from 8 September
C from 28 July until 1 September
D ⚲ to Bournemouth

For services from Brockenhurst - Lymington refer to Table T159

Table T158-F

Saturdays
26 May to 8 December

London - Basingstoke, Southampton, Romsey, Bournemouth and Weymouth

		SW ■	SW ◇■	SW ◇■ A ✠	SW ◇■	SW ■	SW ■	XC ◇■ ✠	SW ■	GW ◇	SW ◇■ A ✠	SW ◇■	SW ◇■	XC ◇■ ✠	SW ◇■ A ✠	SW ◇■	SW ■	SW ■	XC ◇■ ✠	SW ■	SW ◇■ B	SW ◇■ A ✠	SW ◇■
London Waterloo ⊖	d		10 39	11 05			11 09				11 35		11 39		12 05			12 09				12 35	
Clapham Junction	d		10u46	11u12									11u46		12u12								
Woking	d						11 35				12 00							12 35				13 00	
Farnborough (Main)	d		11 13				11 45						12 13					12 45					
Fleet	d		11 19										12 19										
Reading	d							11 52						12 20					12 52				
Basingstoke	a		11 31	11 47			11 58	12 09					12 31	12 40	12 47			12 58	13 09				
	d		11 33	11 49			12 00	12 10					12 33	12 41	12 49			13 00	13 10				
Micheldever	d						12 10											13 10					
Winchester	d		11 49	12 05			12 19	12 25			12 33		12 49	12 56	13 05			13 19	13 25			13 33	
Shawford	d		11 54										12 54										
Romsey	d	11 20				12 07			12 20								13 07			13 20			
Chandlers Ford	d					12 14											13 14						
Eastleigh	a	11 49	11 59			12 20	12 27		12 49				12 59				13 20	13 27		13 49			
	d	11 50	12 00			12 21	12 28		12 50				13 00				13 21	13 28		13 50			
Hedge End	d						12 34											13 34					
Botley	d						12 38											13 38					
Fareham	d						12 48											13 48					
Portchester	d						12 53											13 53					
Cosham	d						12 58											13 58					
Hilsea	a						13 03											14 03					
Fratton	a						13 07											14 07					
Portsmouth & Southsea	a						13 11											14 11					
Portsmouth Harbour	a						13 18											14 18					
Southampton Airport Pkwy	d		12 05	12 14		12 25		12 34			12 42		13 05	13 09	13 14		13 25		13 34			13 42	
Swaythling	d					12 27											13 27						
St Denys	d				←	12 30										←	13 30						
Southampton Central	a		12 12	12 22	12 12	12 36		12 41			12 49		13 12	13 17	13 22	13 12	13 36		13 41			13 49	
	d		12 30	12 24	12 30	12 37		12 43			12 51		13 30		13 24	13 30	13 37		13 43			13 51	
Millbrook (Hants)	d		→			12 40							→				13 40						
Redbridge	d					12 43											13 43						
Romsey	d	12a03				12 51			13a03								13 51			14a03			
Mottisfont & Dunbridge	d					12 56											13 56						
Dean	d					13 02											14 02						
Salisbury	a					13 15											14 15						
Totton	d				12 35											13 35							
Ashurst New Forest	d				12 40											13 40							
Beaulieu Road	d											←				13 44							←
Brockenhurst	a			12 37	12 51			12 57			13 04	12 51			13 37	13 51			13 57			14 04	13 51
	d			12 38	13 16			12 58			13 05	13 16			13 38	14 16			13 58			14 05	14 16
Sway	d				→							13 21				→							14 21
New Milton	d			12 45								13 26			13 45								14 26
Hinton Admiral	d											13 30											14 30
Christchurch	d			12 52								13 35			13 52								14 35
Pokesdown	d			12 56								13 38			13 56								14 38
Bournemouth	a			13 00				13 12			13 20	13 42			14 00				14 12			14 20	14 42
	d			13 04							13 24	13 44			14 04							14 24	14 44
Branksome	d										13 29	13 49										14 29	14 49
Parkstone (Dorset)	d										13 32	13 52										14 32	14 52
Poole	a			13 13							13 36	13 55			14 13							14 36	14 55
	d			13 14							13 37				14 14							14 37	
Hamworthy	d			13 19							13 42				14 19							14 42	
Holton Heath	d			13 23											14 23								
Wareham	d			13 28							13 49				14 28							14 49	
Wool	d			13 35											14 35								
Moreton (Dorset)	d			13 41											14 41								
Dorchester South	d			13 49							14 05				14 49							15 05	
Dorchester West	d									13 56											14 54		
Upwey	d			13 55						14 03					14 55						15 01		
Weymouth	a			14 00						14 10	14 14				15 00						15 06	15 13	

A ✠ to Bournemouth
B until 8 September

For services from Brockenhurst - Lymington refer to Table T159

Table T158-F

Saturdays
26 May to 8 December

London - Basingstoke, Southampton, Romsey, Bournemouth and Weymouth

		SW ◇■	SW ◇■ A ✠	SW ◇■	SW ■	SW ■	XC ◇■ ✠	SW ◇■ A ✠	SW ◇■	SN ■	SW ■	SW ◇■	XC ◇■ ✠	SW ◇■ ✠	SW ◇■	SW ■	SW ■	XC ◇■ ✠	SW ■	GW ◇ B	GW ◇ C	SW ◇■ A ✠
London Waterloo ⊖	d	12 39	13 05			13 09		13 35				13 39		14 05			14 09					14 35
Clapham Junction	d	12u46	13u12									13u46		14u12								
Woking	d					13 35		14 00									14 35					15 00
Farnborough (Main)	d	13 13				13 45						14 13					14 45					
Fleet	d	13 19										14 19										
Reading	d						13 46						14 20					14 52				
Basingstoke	a	13 31	13 47			13 58	14 09					14 31	14 40	14 47			14 58	15 09				
	d	13 33	13 49			14 00	14 10					14 33	14 42	14 49			15 00	15 10				
Micheldever	d					14 10											15 10					
Winchester	d	13 49	14 05			14 19	14 25	14 33				14 49	14 57	15 05			15 19	15 25				15 33
Shawford	d	13 54										14 54										
Romsey	d				14 07						14 13					15 07			15 20			
Chandlers Ford	d				14 14											15 14						
Eastleigh	a	13 59			14 20	14 27					14 49	14 59				15 20	15 27		15 49			
	d	14 00			14 21	14 28				14 41	14 50	15 00				15 21	15 28		15 50			
Hedge End	d					14 34											15 34					
Botley	d					14 38											15 38					
Fareham	d					14 47				14a59							15 48					
Portchester	d					14 52											15 53					
Cosham	d					14 57											15 58					
Hilsea	a					15 03											16 03					
Fratton	a					15 07											16 07					
Portsmouth & Southsea	a					15 11											16 11					
Portsmouth Harbour	a					15 18											16 18					
Southampton Airport Pkwy	d	14 05	14 14		14 25		14 33	14 42				15 05	15 08	15 14		15 25		15 34				15 42
Swaythling	d				14 27											15 27						
St Denys	d			←	14 30										←	15 30						
Southampton Central	a	14 12	14 22	14 12	14 35		14 41	14 49				15 12	15 17	15 22	15 12	15 36		15 41				15 49
	d	14 30	14 24	14 30	14 37		14 43	14 51				15 30		15 24	15 30	15 37		15 43				15 51
Millbrook (Hants)	d	→			14 40							→				15 40						
Redbridge	d				14 43											15 43						
Romsey	d				14 51						15a03					15 51			16a03			
Mottisfont & Dunbridge	d				14 56											15 56						
Dean	d				15 02											16 02						
Salisbury	a				15 15											16 15						
Totton	d			14 35											15 35							
Ashurst New Forest	d			14 40											15 40							
Beaulieu Road	d								←						15 44							
Brockenhurst	a		14 37	14 51			14 57	15 04	14 51					15 37	15 51			15 57				16 04
	d		14 38	15 16			14 58	15 05	15 16					15 38	16 16			15 58				16 05
Sway	d			→					15 21						→							
New Milton	d		14 45						15 26					15 45								
Hinton Admiral	d								15 30													
Christchurch	d		14 52						15 35					15 52								
Pokesdown	d		14 56						15 38					15 56								
Bournemouth	a		15 00				15 12	15 20	15 42					16 00				16 12				16 20
	d		15 04					15 24	15 44					16 04								16 24
Branksome	d							15 29	15 49													16 29
Parkstone (Dorset)	d							15 32	15 52													16 32
Poole	a		15 13					15 36	15 55					16 13								16 36
	d		15 14					15 37						16 14								16 37
Hamworthy	d		15 19					15 42						16 19								16 42
Holton Heath	d		15 23											16 23								
Wareham	d		15 28					15 49						16 28								16 49
Wool	d		15 35											16 35								
Moreton (Dorset)	d		15 41											16 41								
Dorchester South	d		15 49					16 05						16 49								17 06
Dorchester West	d																			16 55	16 58	
Upwey	d		15 55											16 55						17 03	17 05	
Weymouth	a		16 00					16 13						17 00						17 08	17 10	17 16

A ✠ to Bournemouth
B until 8 September
C from 15 September

For services from Brockenhurst - Lymington refer to Table T159

Table T158-F

Saturdays
26 May to 8 December

London - Basingstoke, Southampton, Romsey, Bournemouth and Weymouth

		SW	SW	SW	SW	SW	SW	XC	SW	SW	SW	SW	XC	SW	SW	SW	SW	XC	SW	GW	SW	SW	GW
		◇■	◇■	◇■	◇■	■	■	◇■	◇■	◇■	■	◇■	◇■	◇■	◇■	■	■	◇■	■	◇	◇■	◇■	◇
				A ✠				✠	A ✠				✠	A ✠				✠		B	A ✠		C
London Waterloo ⊖	d		14 39	15 05			15 09		15 35			15 39		16 05			16 09				16 35		
Clapham Junction	d		14u46	15u12								15u46		16u12									
Woking	d						15 35		16 00								16 35				17 00		
Farnborough (Main)	d		15 13				15 45					16 13					16 45						
Fleet	d		15 19									16 19											
Reading	d							15 52					16 20					16 52					
Basingstoke	a		15 31	15 47			15 58	16 09				16 31	16 40	16 47			16 58	17 09					
	d		15 33	15 49			16 00	16 10				16 33	16 41	16 49			17 00	17 10					
Micheldever	d						16 10										17 10						
Winchester	d		15 49	16 05			16 19	16 25	16 33			16 49	16 56	17 05			17 19	17 25			17 33		
Shawford	d		15 54									16 54											
Romsey	d					16 07					16 20					17 07			17 20				
Chandlers Ford	d					16 14										17 14							
Eastleigh	a		15 59			16 20	16 27				16 49	16 59				17 20	17 27		17 49				
	d		16 00			16 21	16 28				16 50	17 00				17 21	17 28		17 50				
Hedge End	d						16 34										17 34						
Botley	d						16 38										17 38						
Fareham	d						16 48										17 48						
Portchester	d						16 53										17 53						
Cosham	d						16 58										17 58						
Hilsea	a						17 03										18 03						
Fratton	a						17 07										18 07						
Portsmouth & Southsea	a						17 11										18 11						
Portsmouth Harbour ⛴	a						17 16										18 18						
Southampton Airport Pkwy ✈	d		16 05	16 14		16 25		16 34	16 42			17 05	17 09	17 14		17 25		17 34			17 42		
Swaythling	d					16 27										17 27							
St Denys	d				←	16 30									←	17 30							
Southampton Central ⛴	a		16 12	16 22	16 12	16 36		16 41	16 49			17 12	17 17	17 22	17 12	17 36		17 41			17 49		
	d		16 30	16 24	16 30	16 37		16 43	16 51			17 30		17 24	17 30	17 37		17 43			17 51		
Millbrook (Hants)	d		→			16 40						→				17 40							
Redbridge	d					16 43										17 43							
Romsey	d					16 51					17a03					17 51			18a03				
Mottisfont & Dunbridge	d					16 56										17 56							
Dean	d					17 02										18 02							
Salisbury	a					17 15										18 15							
Totton	d				16 35										17 35								
Ashurst New Forest	d				16 40										17 40								
Beaulieu Road	d	←								←					17 44							←	
Brockenhurst	a	15 51		16 37	16 51			16 57	17 04	16 51				17 37	17 51			17 57			18 04	17 51	
	d	16 16		16 38	17 16			16 58	17 05	17 16				17 38	18 16			17 58			18 05	18 16	
Sway	d	16 21			→					17 21					→							18 21	
New Milton	d	16 26		16 45						17 26				17 45								18 26	
Hinton Admiral	d	16 30								17 30												18 30	
Christchurch	d	16 35		16 52						17 35				17 52								18 35	
Pokesdown	d	16 38		16 56						17 38				17 56								18 38	
Bournemouth	a	16 42		17 00				17 12	17 20	17 42				18 00				18 12			18 20	18 42	
	d	16 44		17 04					17 24	17 44				18 04							18 24	18 44	
Branksome	d	16 49							17 29	17 49											18 29	18 49	
Parkstone (Dorset)	d	16 52							17 32	17 52											18 32	18 52	
Poole	a	16 55		17 13					17 36	17 55				18 13							18 36	18 55	
	d			17 14					17 37					18 14							18 37		
Hamworthy	d			17 19					17 42					18 19							18 42		
Holton Heath	d			17 23										18 23									
Wareham	d			17 28					17 49					18 28							18 49		
Wool	d			17 35										18 35									
Moreton (Dorset)	d			17 41										18 41									
Dorchester South	d			17 49					18 05					18 49							19 05		
Dorchester West	d																			18 55			19 13
Upwey	d			17 55										18 55						19 02			19 21
Weymouth	a			18 00					18 13					19 00						19 10	19 13		19 27

A ✠ to Bournemouth
B from 15 September
C until 8 September

For services from Brockenhurst - Lymington refer to Table T159

Table T158-F

Saturdays
26 May to 8 December

London - Basingstoke, Southampton, Romsey, Bournemouth and Weymouth

		SW	SW	SW	SW	SW	XC	SW	GW	SW	SW	SW	SW	SW	SW	SW	XC	SW	SW	SW	SW	SW	SW
		◇■	◇■	◇■	■	■	◇■	■	◇	◇■	◇■	◇■	◇■	◇■	■	■	◇■	◇■	◇■	■	◇■	◇■	◇■
			A 🝖				✠			B ✠			B ✠				✠	B ✠				B ✠	
London Waterloo ⊖	d	16 39	17 05			17 09				17 35		17 39	18 05			18 09		18 35			18 39	19 05	
Clapham Junction	d	16u46	17u12									17u46	18u12								18u46	19u12	
Woking	d					17 35				18 00						18 35		19 00					
Farnborough (Main)	d	17 13				17 45						18 13				18 45					19 13		
Fleet	d	17 19										18 19									19 19		
Reading	d						17 52										18 52						
Basingstoke	a	17 31	17 47			17 58	18 09					18 31	18 47			18 58	19 09				19 31	19 47	
	d	17 33	17 49			18 00	18 10					18 33	18 49			19 00	19 10				19 33	19 49	
Micheldever	d					18 10										19 10							
Winchester	d	17 49	18 05			18 19	18 25			18 33		18 49	19 05			19 19	19 25	19 33			19 49	20 05	
Shawford	d	17 54										18 54									19 54		
Romsey	d				18 07			18 20							19 07					19 20			
Chandlers Ford	d				18 14										19 14								
Eastleigh	a	17 59			18 20	18 27		18 49				18 59			19 20	19 27				19 49	19 59		
	d	18 00			18 21	18 28		18 50				19 00			19 21	19 28				19 50	20 00		
Hedge End	d					18 34										19 34							
Botley	d					18 38										19 38							
Fareham	d					18 48										19 48							
Portchester	d					18 53										19 53							
Cosham	d					18 58										19 58							
Hilsea	a					19 03										20 03							
Fratton	a					19 07										20 07							
Portsmouth & Southsea	a					19 11										20 11							
Portsmouth Harbour ⛴	a					19 18										20 18							
Southampton Airport Pkwy ✈	d	18 05	18 14		18 25		18 34			18 42		19 05	19 14		19 25		19 34	19 42			20 05	20 14	
Swaythling	d				18 27										19 27								
St Denys	d			←	18 30									←	19 30								←
Southampton Central ⛴	a	18 12	18 22	18 12	18 36		18 41			18 50		19 12	19 21	19 12	19 36		19 41	19 49			20 14	20 21	20 14
	d	18 30	18 24	18 30	18 37		18 43			18 51		19 30	19 24	19 30	19 37		19 43	19 51			20 30	20 24	20 30
Millbrook (Hants)	d	→			18 40							→			19 40						→		
Redbridge	d				18 43										19 43								
Romsey	d				19 01			19a04							19 51					20a03			
Mottisfont & Dunbridge	d				19 06										19 56								
Dean	d				19 11										20 02								
Salisbury	a				19 24										20 15								
Totton	d			18 35										19 35									20 35
Ashurst New Forest	d			18 40										19 40									20 40
Beaulieu Road	d										←			19 44					←				
Brockenhurst	a		18 37	18 51			18 57			19 05	18 51		19 37	19 51			19 57	20 04	19 51			20 37	20 51
	d		18 38	19 16			18 58			19 06	19 16		19 38	20 16			19 58	20 05	20 16			20 38	21 16
Sway	d			→							19 21			→					20 21				→
New Milton	d		18 45								19 26		19 45						20 26			20 45	
Hinton Admiral	d										19 30								20 30				
Christchurch	d		18 52								19 35		19 52						20 35			20 52	
Pokesdown	d		18 56								19 38		19 56						20 38			20 56	
Bournemouth	a		19 00				19 12			19 21	19 42		20 00				20 12	20 20	20 42			21 00	
	d		19 04							19 25	19 44		20 04					20 24	20 44			21 04	
Branksome	d									19 30	19 49							20 29	20 49				
Parkstone (Dorset)	d									19 33	19 52							20 32	20 52				
Poole	a		19 13							19 36	19 55		20 13					20 36	20 55			21 13	
	d		19 14							19 37			20 14					20 37				21 14	
Hamworthy	d		19 19							19 42			20 19					20 42				21 19	
Holton Heath	d		19 23										20 23										
Wareham	d		19 28							19 49			20 28					20 49				21 26	
Wool	d		19 35										20 35									21 33	
Moreton (Dorset)	d		19 41										20 41									21 39	
Dorchester South	d		19 49							20 05			20 49					21 05				21 47	
Dorchester West	d								19 54														
Upwey	d		19 55						20 02				20 55									21 54	
Weymouth	a		20 00						20 10	20 14			21 00					21 13				21 58	

A 🝖 to Bournemouth
B ✠ to Bournemouth

For services from Brockenhurst - Lymington refer to Table T159

Table T158-F

Saturdays

26 May to 8 December

London - Basingstoke, Southampton, Romsey, Bournemouth and Weymouth

	SW		SW	XC	SW	SW	SW	SW	SW	SW	SW		XC	SW	GW	SW	SW	SW	SW	SW	SW		XC	SW
	1		1	◇1	◇1	◇1	1	◇1	◇1	1	1		◇1	1		◇1	◇1	1	◇1	1	1		◇1	◇1
				☕	A ☕				☕							A ☕			☕					A ☕
London Waterloo 15 ⊖ d			19 09		19 35			19 39	20 05		20 09					20 35	20 39	20 42	21 05					21 35
Clapham Junction 10 d								19u46	20u12								20u46		21u12					
Woking d			19 35		20 00						20 35					21 00		21 19	21 32					22 00
Farnborough (Main) d			19 45					20 13			20 45						21 13	21 33						
Fleet d								20 19									21 19	21 38						
Reading 7 d				19 52									20 52								←		21 52	
Basingstoke a			19 58	20 09				20 31	20 47		20 58		21 09				21 31	21 58	21 50		21 58		22 08	
d			20 00	20 11				20 33	20 49		21 00		21 10				21 33	22 00	21 52		22 00		22 10	
Micheldever d			20 10								21 10						21 43	→			22 10			
Winchester d			20 19	20 26	20 33			20 49	21 05		21 19		21 25			21 33	21 52		22 08		22 19		22 27	22 33
Shawford d								20 54									21 57							
Romsey d	20 07						20 20			21 07				21 20						22 07				
Chandlers Ford d	20 14									21 14										22 14				
Eastleigh 8 a	20 20		20 27				20 49	20 59		21 20	21 27			21 49			22 02		22 16	22 20	22 27			
d	20 21		20 28				20 50	21 00		21 21	21 28			21 50			22 03		22 17	22 22	22 28			
Hedge End d			20 34								21 34										22 34			
Botley d			20 38								21 38										22 38			
Fareham d			20 48								21 48										22 48			
Portchester d			20 53								21 53										22 53			
Cosham d			20 58								21 58										22 58			
Hilsea a			21 03								22 03										23 03			
Fratton a			21 07								22 07										23 07			
Portsmouth & Southsea a			21 11								22 11										23 11			
Portsmouth Harbour ⛴ a			21 16								22 18										23 18			
Southampton Airport Pkwy ✈ d	20 25			20 34	20 42			21 05	21 14	21 25			21 33			21 42	22 08		22 22	22 26			22 35	22 42
Swaythling d	20 27									21 27										22 28				
St Denys d	20 30									21 30										22 31				
Southampton Central ⛴ a	20 36			20 41	20 49			21 12	21 22	21 35			21 40			21 49	22 17		22 29	22 36			22 42	22 49
d	20 37			20 43	20 51				21 24	21 37			21 43			21 51			22 30	22 38			22 44	22 51
Millbrook (Hants) d	20 40									21 40										22 40				
Redbridge d	20 43									21 43										22 44				
Romsey d	20 51						21a03			21 51				22a03						22a51				
Mottisfont & Dunbridge d	20 56									21 56														
Dean d	21 02									22 02														
Salisbury a	21 15									22 15														
Totton d									21 29										22 36					
Ashurst New Forest d									21 34										22 40					
Beaulieu Road d						←																		
Brockenhurst 3 a				20 57	21 04	20 51			21 42				21 56			22 04			22 48				22 59	23 04
d				20 58	21 05	21 16			21 43				21 57			22 05			22 49				23 00	23 05
Sway d						21 20			21 47										22 54					
New Milton d						21 25			21 52										22 59					
Hinton Admiral d						21 29			21 56										23 03					
Christchurch d						21 34			22 01										23 08					
Pokesdown d						21 38			22 05										23 11					
Bournemouth a				21 12	21 20	21 42			22 09				22 15			22 20			23 15				23 19	23 24
d					21 24	21 43			22 10							22 24			23 17					23 27
Branksome d					21 29	21 48			22 15							22 29			23 22					23 32
Parkstone (Dorset) d					21 32	21 51			22 18							22 32			23 25					23 35
Poole 4 a					21 36	21 55			22 23							22 36			23 29					23 39
d					21 37											22 37								23 40
Hamworthy d					21 42											22 42								23 45
Holton Heath d																								
Wareham d					21 49											22 49								23 51
Wool d					21 55											22 55								23 58
Moreton (Dorset) d					22 01											23 01								00 04
Dorchester South d					22 09											23 09								00 12
Dorchester West d															22 58									
Upwey d					22 16										23 06	23 16								00 18
Weymouth a					22 20										23 14	23 20								00 23

A ☕ to Bournemouth

For services from Brockenhurst - Lymington refer to Table T159

Table T158-F

Saturdays

26 May to 8 December

London - Basingstoke, Southampton, Romsey, Bournemouth and Weymouth

	SW	SW	XC	SW	SW	SW	SW		XC	SW	SW	SW	SW	SW
	1	◇1	◇1	1	◇1	1	1		◇1	◇1	1	◇1	◇1	1
					☕					☕				
London Waterloo 15 ⊖ d		21 39		21 42	22 05					22 35		22 39	23 05	23 35
Clapham Junction 10 d		21u46			22u12							22u46	23u12	23u42
Woking d				22 19	22 32					23 00			23 32	00 03
Farnborough (Main) d		22 13		22 33								23 16		00 14
Fleet d		22 19		22 38								23 21		00 20
Reading 7 d			22 22				←		22 50					
Basingstoke a		22 31	22 39	22 58	22 50		22 58		23 07			23 34	23 50	00 33
d		22 33	22 40	23 00	22 52		23 00		23 10			23 36	23 52	00 35
Micheldever d		22 43		→			23 10						00 02	
Winchester d		22 53	22 57		23 08		23 19		23 25	23 33		23 52	00 11	00 51
Shawford d		22 57										23 57		
Romsey d	22 20					23 09					23 00			
Chandlers Ford d						23 16								
Eastleigh 8 a	22 49	23 03			23 16	23 22	23 27				23 35	00 02	00 19	00 59
d	22 50	23 04			23 17	23 23	23 28				23 37	00 03	00 20	01 00
Hedge End d							23 34							
Botley d							23 38							
Fareham d							23 48							
Portchester d							23 53							
Cosham d							23 58							
Hilsea a							00 03							
Fratton a							00 07							
Portsmouth & Southsea a							00 11							
Portsmouth Harbour ⛴ a							00 16							
Southampton Airport Pkwy ✈ d		23 08	23 13		23 22	23 27			23 33	23 42		00 08	00 25	01 05
Swaythling d						23 29								
St Denys d						23 32							00s29	
Southampton Central ⛴ a		23 17	23 20		23 29	23 38			23 41	23 49		00 18	00 34	01 12
d					23 30	23 40				23 51			00 35	
Millbrook (Hants) d						23 42								
Redbridge d						23 46								
Romsey d	23a03					23 57					23a49			
Mottisfont & Dunbridge d						00 02								
Dean d						00 08								
Salisbury a						00 21								
Totton d					23 36								00s40	
Ashurst New Forest d					23 40									
Beaulieu Road d														
Brockenhurst 3 a					23 48					00 04			00s51	
d					23 49					00 05				
Sway d					23 54									
New Milton d					23 58								00s59	
Hinton Admiral d					00 02									
Christchurch d					00 07								01s06	
Pokesdown d					00 11								01s10	
Bournemouth a					00 15					00 21			01 14	
d					00 16					00 22			01 15	
Branksome d					00 21					00 27			01s20	
Parkstone (Dorset) d					00 24					00 30			01s23	
Poole 4 a					00 30					00 35			01 27	
d														
Hamworthy d														
Holton Heath d														
Wareham d														
Wool d														
Moreton (Dorset) d														
Dorchester South d														
Dorchester West d														
Upwey d														
Weymouth a														

For services from Brockenhurst - Lymington refer to Table T159

Table T158-F

Sundays
20 May to 2 December

London - Basingstoke, Southampton, Romsey, Bournemouth and Weymouth

		SW	SW	SW	SW	SW	SW	SW	SW	SW	SW	SW	SW	SW	SW	SW	SW	SW	SW	SW	SW	SW	GW
		◇[1]	[1]	◇[1]	◇[1]	◇[1]	◇[1]	[1]	[1]	[1]	[1]	[1]	[1]	[1]	[1]	[1]	[1]	[1]	[1]	[1]	◇[1]	[1]	
		A	A	A	A	A	A		A	A	A												
		⌶				⌶																	
London Waterloo [15] ⊖	d											00 05		01 05							07 54		
Clapham Junction [10]	d											00u12		01 15							08u03		
Woking	d									00 03	00 28	00 37		01 49							08 28		
Farnborough (Main)	d								00 10	00 14	00 41			01s58									
Fleet	d								00 16	00 20	00 47			02s04									
Reading [7]	d																					
Basingstoke	a								00 33	00 33	01 06	00 55		02s16							08 46		
	d									00 35		00 56			07 48						08 48		
Micheldever	d						00 02								07 58						08 58		
Winchester	d						00 11			00 51		01 13		02s33	08 07						09 08		
Shawford	d														08 12						09 12		
Romsey	d																		08 35	08 39			
Chandlers Ford	d																		08 42				
Eastleigh [8]	a						00 19			00 59		01 21		02s42	08 17				08 47	09 13	09 18		
	d			00 03			00 20	00 30		01 00		01 22			08 21		08 24		08 54	09 15	09 22	09 26	
Hedge End	d							00s36									08 30					09 32	
Botley	d							00s39									08 34					09 36	
Fareham	d							00s47								07 44	08 42					09 45	
Portchester	d							00s53								07 49	08 47					09 50	
Cosham	d							00s57								07 54	08 52					09 55	
Hilsea	a															08 00	09 00					10 00	
Fratton	a							01s05								08 04	09 04					10 09	
Portsmouth & Southsea	a							01s08								08 08	09 08					10 12	
Portsmouth Harbour ⛴	a							01 12								08 13	09 13					10 16	
Southampton Airport Pkwy ✈	d			00 08			00 25			01 05		01 26		02s46	08 25				08 58		09 27		
Swaythling	d																		09 01				
St Denys	d						00s29							02s51					09 04				
Southampton Central ⛴	a			00 18			00 34			01 12		01 35		02 56	08 32				09 09		09 34		
	d						00 35					01 37			08 34			09 03	09 10		09 35		
Millbrook (Hants)	d																		09 13				
Redbridge	d																		09 16				
Romsey	d																		09 24	09a28			
Mottisfont & Dunbridge	d		00 02																09 29				
Dean	d		00 08																09 35				
Salisbury	a		00 21																09 49				
Totton	d						00s40					01s42			08 39						09 41		
Ashurst New Forest	d														08 44						09 45		
Beaulieu Road	d														08 48						09 50		
Brockenhurst [3]	a						00s51					01s53			08 54			09 16			09 56		
	d					00 05									08 55			09 17			09 57		
Sway	d														09 00						10 01		
New Milton	d						00s59					02s00			09 05			09 24			10 06		
Hinton Admiral	d	00 02													09 09						10 10		
Christchurch	d	00 07					01s06					02s07			09 14						10 15		
Pokesdown	d	00 11					01s10					02s11			09 17						10 19		
Bournemouth	a	00 15				00 21	01 14					02 15			09 21			09 34			10 23		
	d	00 16				00 22	01 15						08 39		09 25			09 39			10 24		
Branksome	d	00 21				00 27	01s20						08 44					09 44					
Parkstone (Dorset)	d	00 24				00 30	01s23						08 47					09 47					
Poole [4]	a	00 30				00 35	01 27						08 50		09 34			09 50			10 33		
	d												08 51					09 51					
Hamworthy	d												08 56					09 56					
Holton Heath	d																					
Wareham	d												09 03					10 03					
Wool	d												09 10					10 10					
Moreton (Dorset)	d				00 04								09 16					10 16					
Dorchester South	d				00 12								09 24					10 24					
Dorchester West	d																						10 29
Upwey	d				00 18								09 31					10 31					10 37
Weymouth	a				00 23								09 35					10 35					10 42

A not 20 May

For services from Brockenhurst - Lymington refer to Table T159

Table T158-F

Sundays
20 May to 2 December

London - Basingstoke, Southampton, Romsey, Bournemouth and Weymouth

		SW	SW	SW	SW	SW	XC	GW	GW	SW	SW	SW	SW	SW	XC	SW	SW	SW	SW	SW	XC	SW	SW
		◇[1]	[1]	[1]	◇[1]	[1]	◇[1]			◇[1]	[1]	[1]	◇[1]	[1]	◇[1]	◇[1]	[1]	[1]	◇[1]	[1]	◇[1]	◇[1]	[1]
								A	B	C						C						C	
							⌶			⌶					⌶	⌶					⌶	⌶	
London Waterloo [15] ⊖	d	08 35			08 54					09 35			09 54			10 35			10 54			11 35	
Clapham Junction [10]	d	08u45			09u03					09u45			10u03			10u45			11u03			11u45	
Woking	d	09 09			09 28					10 09			10 28			11 08			11 28			12 08	
Farnborough (Main)	d																					
Fleet	d																					
Reading [7]	d						09 52								10 52						11 52		
Basingstoke	a	09 28			09 46		10 11			10 28			10 46		11 09	11 26			11 46		12 09	12 26	
	d	09 29			09 48		10 12			10 29			10 48		11 10	11 28			11 48		12 11	12 28	
Micheldever	d				09 58								10 58						11 58				
Winchester	d	09 46			10 08		10 27			10 46			11 08		11 25	11 44			12 08		12 26	12 44	
Shawford	d				10 12								11 12						12 12				
Romsey	d		09 35	09 32							10 35	10 32					11 35	11 32					12 35
Chandlers Ford	d		09 42								10 42						11 42						12 42
Eastleigh [8]	a		09 48	10 13	10 18						10 48	11 13	11 18				11 48	12 13	12 18				12 48
	d		09 54	10 15	10 22	10 26					10 54	11 15	11 22	11 26			11 54	12 15	12 22	12 26			12 54
Hedge End	d					10 32								11 32						12 32			
Botley	d					10 36								11 36						12 36			
Fareham	d					10 45								11 45						12 45			
Portchester	d					10 50								11 50						12 50			
Cosham	d					10 55								11 55						12 55			
Hilsea	a					11 00								12 00						13 00			
Fratton	a					11 09								12 09						13 09			
Portsmouth & Southsea	a					11 12								12 12						13 12			
Portsmouth Harbour ⛴	a					11 16								12 16						13 16			
Southampton Airport Pkwy ✈	d	09 55	09 58		10 27		10 36			10 55	10 58		11 27		11 34	11 53	11 58		12 27		12 35	12 53	12 58
Swaythling	d		10 01								11 01						12 01						13 01
St Denys	d		10 04								11 04						12 04						13 04
Southampton Central ⛴	a	10 02	10 09		10 34		10 42			11 02	11 09		11 34		11 42	12 00	12 09		12 34		12 43	13 00	13 09
	d	10 03	10 10		10 35		10 49			11 03	11 10		11 35		11 49	12 03	12 10		12 35		12 50	13 03	13 10
Millbrook (Hants)	d		10 13								11 13						12 13						13 13
Redbridge	d		10 16								11 16						12 16						13 16
Romsey	d		10 24	10a28							11 24	11a28					12 24	12a28					13 24
Mottisfont & Dunbridge	d										11 29												13 29
Dean	d										11 35												13 35
Salisbury	a		10 42								11 48						12 42						13 48
Totton	d				10 41								11 41						12 41				
Ashurst New Forest	d				10 45								11 45						12 45				
Beaulieu Road	d				10 50								11 50						12 50				
Brockenhurst [3]	a	10 17			10 56		11 06			11 17			11 56		12 06	12 16			12 56		13 07	13 16	
	d	10 18			10 57		11 11			11 18			11 57		12 11	12 17			12 57		13 12	13 17	
Sway	d				11 01								12 01						13 01				
New Milton	d	10 25			11 06					11 25			12 06			12 24			13 06			13 24	
Hinton Admiral	d				11 10								12 10						13 10				
Christchurch	d				11 15								12 15						13 15				
Pokesdown	d				11 19								12 19						13 19				
Bournemouth	a	10 35			11 23		11 26			11 35			12 23		12 26	12 34			13 23		13 26	13 34	
	d	10 39			11 24					11 39			12 24			12 39			13 24			13 39	
Branksome	d	10 44								11 44						12 44						13 44	
Parkstone (Dorset)	d	10 47								11 47						12 47						13 47	
Poole [4]	a	10 50			11 33					11 50			12 33			12 50			13 33			13 50	
	d	10 51								11 51						12 51						13 51	
Hamworthy	d	10 56								11 56						12 56						13 56	
Holton Heath	d																					
Wareham	d	11 03								12 03						13 03						14 03	
Wool	d	11 10								12 10						13 10						14 10	
Moreton (Dorset)	d	11 16								12 16						13 16						14 16	
Dorchester South	d	11 24								12 24						13 24						14 24	
Dorchester West	d							11 34	11 41														
Upwey	d	11 31						11 41	11 49	12 31						13 31						14 31	
Weymouth	a	11 35						11 45	11 54	12 35						13 35						14 35	

A until 9 September
B from 16 September
C ⌶ to Bournemouth

For services from Brockenhurst - Lymington refer to Table T159

Sundays

20 May to 2 December

London - Basingstoke, Southampton, Romsey, Bournemouth and Weymouth

		SW		SW	SW	XC	SW	SW	SW	SW	SW	XC		GW	SW	SW	SW	SW	SW	XC	SW	SW		SW	SW
		■		◇■	■	◇■	◇■	■	■	◇■	■	◇■			◇■	■	■	◇■	■	◇■	◇■	■		■	◇■
							A								A						A				
				🍴		🍴	🍴			🍴		🍴			🍴			🍴		🍴	🍴				🍴
London Waterloo ■ ⊖	d			11 54			12 35			12 54					13 35			13 54			14 35				14 54
Clapham Junction ■	d			12u03			12u45			13u03					13u42			14u03			14u42				15u03
Woking	d			12 28			13 08			13 28					14 07			14 28			15 07				15 28
Farnborough (Main)	d																								
Fleet	d																								
Reading ■	d					12 52						13 52								14 52					
Basingstoke	a			12 46		13 09	13 26			13 46		14 09			14 26			14 46		15 09	15 26				15 46
	d			12 48		13 10	13 28			13 48		14 10			14 28			14 48		15 10	15 28				15 48
Micheldever	d			12 58						13 58								14 58							15 58
Winchester	d			13 08		13 25	13 44			14 08		14 25			14 44			15 08		15 25	15 44				16 08
Shawford	d			13 12						14 12								15 12							16 12
Romsey	d	12 32						13 35	13 32							14 35	14 32					15 35		15 32	
Chandlers Ford	d							13 42								14 42						15 42			
Eastleigh ■	a	13 13		13 18				13 48	14 13	14 18						14 48	15 13	15 18				15 48		16 13	16 18
	d	13 15		13 22	13 26			13 54	14 15	14 22	14 26					14 54	15 15	15 22	15 26			15 54		16 15	16 22
Hedge End	d				13 32						14 32								15 32						
Botley	d				13 36						14 36								15 36						
Fareham	d				13 45						14 45								15 45						
Portchester	d				13 50						14 50								15 50						
Cosham	d				13 55						14 55								15 55						
Hilsea	a				14 00						15 00								16 00						
Fratton	a				14 09						15 09								16 09						
Portsmouth & Southsea	a				14 12						15 12								16 12						
Portsmouth Harbour ⛴	a				14 16						15 20								16 17						
Southampton Airport Pkwy ✈	d			13 27		13 34	13 53	13 58		14 27		14 34			14 53	14 58		15 27		15 34	15 53	15 58			16 27
Swaythling	d							14 01								15 01						16 01			
St Denys	d							14 04								15 04						16 04			
Southampton Central ⛴	a			13 34		13 42	14 00	14 09		14 34		14 42			15 00	15 09		15 34		15 43	16 00	16 09			16 34
	d			13 35		13 49	14 03	14 10		14 35		14 49			15 03	15 10		15 35		15 48	16 03	16 10			16 35
Millbrook (Hants)	d							14 13								15 13						16 13			
Redbridge	d							14 16								15 16						16 16			
Romsey	d	13a28						14 24	14a28							15 24	15a28					16 24		16a28	
Mottisfont & Dunbridge	d															15 29									
Dean	d															15 35									
Salisbury	a							14 42								15 48						16 42			
Totton	d			13 41						14 41								15 41							16 41
Ashurst New Forest	d			13 45						14 45								15 45							16 45
Beaulieu Road	d			13 50						14 50								15 50							16 50
Brockenhurst ■	a			13 56		14 06	14 16			14 56		15 06			15 16			15 56		16 03	16 16				16 56
	d			13 57		14 11	14 17			14 57		15 11			15 17			15 57		16 11	16 17				16 57
Sway	d			14 01						15 01								16 01							17 01
New Milton	d			14 06			14 24			15 06					15 24			16 06			16 24				17 06
Hinton Admiral	d			14 10						15 10								16 10							17 10
Christchurch	d			14 15						15 15								16 15							17 15
Pokesdown	d			14 19						15 19								16 19							17 19
Bournemouth	a			14 23		14 26	14 34			15 23		15 26			15 34			16 23		16 26	16 34				17 23
	d			14 24			14 39			15 24					15 39			16 24			16 39				17 24
Branksome	d						14 44								15 44						16 44				
Parkstone (Dorset)	d						14 47								15 47						16 47				
Poole ■	a			14 33			14 50			15 33					15 50			16 33			16 50				17 33
	d						14 51								15 51						16 51				
Hamworthy	d						14 56								15 56						16 56				
Holton Heath	d																								
Wareham	d						15 03								16 03						17 03				
Wool	d						15 10								16 10						17 10				
Moreton (Dorset)	d						15 16								16 16						17 16				
Dorchester South	d						15 24								16 24						17 24				
Dorchester West	d													15 40											
Upwey	d						15 31							15 49	16 31						17 31				
Weymouth	a						15 35							15 54	16 35						17 35				

A 🍴 to Bournemouth

For services from Brockenhurst - Lymington refer to Table T159

Sundays

20 May to 2 December

London - Basingstoke, Southampton, Romsey, Bournemouth and Weymouth

		SW	XC	SW	SW	SW	SW	SW		SW	XC	SW	SW	SW	GW	SW	SW	SW		XC	SW	SW	SW	SW	SW
		■	◇■	◇■	■	■	◇■	◇■		◇■	◇■	◇■	■	■	◇	◇■	◇■	◇■		◇■	◇■	■	■	◇■	◇■
				A								A									A				
			🍴	🍴				🍴			🍴	🍴					🍴			🍴	🍴				🍴
London Waterloo ■ ⊖	d			15 35			15 50	16 05				16 35				16 50	17 05				17 35			17 50	18 05
Clapham Junction ■	d			15u42			15u58	16u12				16u42				16u58	17u12				17u42			17u58	18u12
Woking	d			16 07			16 21	16 37				17 07				17 21	17 37				18 07			18 21	18 37
Farnborough (Main)	d						16 32									17 32								18 32	
Fleet	d																								
Reading ■	d		15 52								16 52									17 52					
Basingstoke	a		16 09	16 26			16 46	16 56			17 09	17 26				17 46	17 56			18 09	18 26			18 46	18 56
	d		16 10	16 28			16 47	16 57			17 10	17 28				17 47	17 57			18 10	18 28			18 47	18 57
Micheldever	d						16 57									17 57								18 57	
Winchester	d		16 25	16 44			17 07	17 14			17 25	17 44				18 07	18 14			18 25	18 44			19 07	19 14
Shawford	d						17 12									18 12								19 12	
Romsey	d				16 35	16 32							17 35	17 32								18 35	18 32		
Chandlers Ford	d				16 42					←			17 42					←				18 42			
Eastleigh ■	a				16 48	17 13	17 17	17 22		17 17			17 48	18 13		18 17	18 22	18 17				18 48	19 13	19 17	19 22
	d	16 26			16 54	17 15	17 26	17 23		17 26			17 54	18 15		18 26	18 23	18 26				18 54	19 15	19 26	19 23
Hedge End	d	16 32					→			17 32						→		18 32						→	
Botley	d	16 36								17 36								18 36							
Fareham	d	16 45								17 45								18 45							
Portchester	d	16 50								17 50								18 50							
Cosham	d	16 55								17 55								18 55							
Hilsea	a	17 00								18 00								19 00							
Fratton	a	17 09								18 09								19 09							
Portsmouth & Southsea	a	17 12								18 12								19 12							
Portsmouth Harbour ⛴	a	17 16								18 16								19 17							
Southampton Airport Pkwy ✈	d		16 34	16 53	16 58			17 27			17 34	17 53	17 58				18 27			18 34	18 53	18 58			19 27
Swaythling	d				17 01								18 01									19 01			
St Denys	d				17 04								18 04									19 04			
Southampton Central ⛴	a		16 42	17 00	17 09			17 34			17 42	18 00	18 09				18 34			18 44	19 00	19 09			19 34
	d		16 49	17 03	17 10			17 36			17 49	18 03	18 10				18 36			18 49	19 03	19 10			19 36
Millbrook (Hants)	d				17 13								18 13									19 13			
Redbridge	d				17 16								18 16									19 16			
Romsey	d				17 24	17a28							18 24	18a28								19 24	19a28		
Mottisfont & Dunbridge	d				17 29																	19 29			
Dean	d				17 35																	19 35			
Salisbury	a				17 48								18 42									19 48			
Totton	d							17 41									18 41								19 41
Ashurst New Forest	d							17 46									18 46								19 46
Beaulieu Road	d							17 50									18 50								19 50
Brockenhurst ■	a		17 06	17 16				17 56			18 06	18 16					18 56			19 03	19 16				19 56
	d		17 11	17 17				17 57			18 11	18 17					18 57			19 11	19 17				19 57
Sway	d							18 02									19 02								20 02
New Milton	d			17 24				18 07				18 24					19 07				19 24				20 07
Hinton Admiral	d							18 11									19 11								20 11
Christchurch	d							18 16									19 16								20 16
Pokesdown	d							18 19									19 19								20 19
Bournemouth	a		17 26	17 34				18 23			18 26	18 34					19 23			19 26	19 34				20 23
	d			17 39				18 25				18 39					19 25				19 39				20 25
Branksome	d			17 44								18 44									19 44				
Parkstone (Dorset)	d			17 47								18 47									19 47				
Poole ■	a			17 50				18 34				18 50					19 34				19 50				20 34
	d			17 51								18 51									19 51				
Hamworthy	d			17 56								18 56									19 56				
Holton Heath	d																								
Wareham	d			18 03								19 03									20 03				
Wool	d			18 10								19 10									20 10				
Moreton (Dorset)	d			18 16								19 16									20 17				
Dorchester South	d			18 24								19 24									20 25				
Dorchester West	d														19 47										
Upwey	d			18 31								19 31			19 55						20 32				
Weymouth	a			18 35								19 35			20 01						20 36				

A 🍴 to Bournemouth

For services from Brockenhurst - Lymington refer to Table T159

Table T158-F

Sundays

20 May to 2 December

London - Basingstoke, Southampton, Romsey, Bournemouth and Weymouth

	SW	XC	SW	SW	SW	SW	SW	SW	XC	SW	SW	SW	GW	SW	SW	SW	XC	SW	SW	SW	SW
	◇1	◇1	◇1	1	1	◇1	◇1	◇1	◇1	◇1	1	1		◇1	◇1	◇1	◇1	◇1	◇1	1	1
			A							A								A			
		trolley	trolley				trolley		trolley	trolley					trolley			trolley			
London Waterloo ⊖ d			18 35			18 50	19 05			19 35				19 50	20 05			20 35	20 45		
Clapham Junction d			18u42			18u58	19u12			19u42				19u58	20u12			20u42	20u53		
Woking d			19 07			19 21	19 37			20 07				20 21	20 37			21 07			
Farnborough (Main) d						19 32								20 32							
Fleet d																					
Reading d		18 51							19 52								20 52				
Basingstoke a		19 09	19 26			19 46	19 56		20 09	20 26				20 46	20 56		21 08	21 26			
d		19 10	19 28			19 47	19 57		20 10	20 28				20 47	20 57		21 10	21 28			
Micheldever d						19 57								20 57							
Winchester d		19 25	19 44			20 07	20 14		20 25	20 44				21 07	21 14		21 25	21 44			
Shawford d						20 12								21 12							
Romsey d				19 35	19 32						20 35	20 32								21 35	21 32
Chandlers Ford d	←			19 42				←			20 42					←				21 42	
Eastleigh a	19 17			19 48	20 13	20 17	20 22	20 17			20 48	21 13		21 17	21 22	21 17				21 48	22 13
d	19 26			19 54	20 15	20 26	20 23	20 26			20 54	21 15		21 26	21 23	21 26				21 54	22 15
Hedge End d	19 32					→		20 32						→		21 32					
Botley d	19 36							20 36								21 36					
Fareham d	19 44							20 45								21 45					
Portchester d	19 49							20 50								21 50					
Cosham d	19 54							20 55								21 55					
Hilsea a	20 05							21 00								22 00					
Fratton a	20 09							21 09								22 09					
Portsmouth & Southsea a	20 12							21 12								22 12					
Portsmouth Harbour ⛴ a	20 17							21 17								22 16					
Southampton Airport Pkwy ✈ d		19 34	19 54	19 58			20 27		20 34	20 53	20 58				21 27		21 34	21 53		21 58	
Swaythling d				20 01							21 01									22 01	
St Denys d				20 04							21 04									22 04	
Southampton Central ⛴ a		19 42	20 01	20 09			20 34		20 43	21 00	21 09				21 34		21 42	22 00		22 09	
d		19 49	20 03	20 10			20 36		20 49	21 03	21 10				21 36		21 51	22 03		22 10	
Millbrook (Hants) d				20 13							21 13									22 13	
Redbridge d				20 16							21 16									22 16	
Romsey d				20 24	20a28						21 24	21a28								22a24	22a31
Mottisfont & Dunbridge d											21 29										
Dean d											21 35										
Salisbury a				20 42							21 48								22 05		
Totton d							20 41								21 41						
Ashurst New Forest d							20 46								21 46						
Beaulieu Road d							20 50								21 50						
Brockenhurst a		20 06	20 16				20 56		21 06	21 16					21 56		22 06	22 16			
d		20 11	20 17				20 57		21 11	21 17					21 57		22 11	22 17			
Sway d							21 02								22 02						
New Milton d			20 24				21 07			21 24					22 07			22 24			
Hinton Admiral d							21 11								22 11						
Christchurch d							21 16								22 16						
Pokesdown d							21 19								22 19						
Bournemouth a		20 26	20 34				21 23		21 26	21 34					22 23		22 26	22 34			
d			20 39				21 25			21 39					22 25			22 39			
Branksome d			20 44							21 44								22 44			
Parkstone (Dorset) d			20 47							21 47								22 47			
Poole a			20 50				21 34			21 50					22 34			22 50			
d			20 51							21 51								22 51			
Hamworthy d			20 56							21 56								22 56			
Holton Heath d																					
Wareham d			21 03							22 03								23 03			
Wool d			21 10							22 10								23 10			
Moreton (Dorset) d			21 17							22 17								23 17			
Dorchester South d			21 25							22 25								23 25			
Dorchester West d													22 55								
Upwey d			21 32							22 32			23 02					23 32			
Weymouth a			21 36							22 36			23 07					23 36			

A trolley to Bournemouth

For services from Brockenhurst - Lymington refer to Table T159

Table T158-F

Sundays

20 May to 2 December

London - Basingstoke, Southampton, Romsey, Bournemouth and Weymouth

	SW	SW	SW	XC	SW	SW	SW	SW	SW	SW	SW	SW	SW
	◇1	◇1	◇1	◇1	◇1	1	◇1	1	◇1	◇1	◇1	◇1	◇1
					A								
					trolley		trolley			trolley	trolley		trolley
London Waterloo ⊖ d	20 50	21 05			21 35		21 50		22 05		22 50	23 05	
Clapham Junction d	20u58	21u12			21u42		21u58		22u12		22u58	23u12	
Woking d	21 21	21 37			22 07		22 21		22 37		23 21	23 37	
Farnborough (Main) d	21 32						22 32				23 32		
Fleet d													
Reading d				21 52									
Basingstoke a	21 46	21 56		22 09	22 26		22 46		22 56		23 46	23 56	
d	21 47	21 57		22 10	22 28		22 47		22 57		23 47	23 57	
Micheldever d	21 57						22 57				23 57		
Winchester d	22 07	22 14		22 24	22 44		23 07		23 14		00 07	00 14	
Shawford d	22 12						23 12				00 12		
Romsey d						22 35		22 28					
Chandlers Ford d			←			22 42				←			←
Eastleigh a	22 17	22 22	22 17			22 48	23 17	23 19	23 22	23 17	00 17	00 23	00 17
d	22 26	22 23	22 26			22 54	23 26	23 22	23 23	23 26	00 30	00 24	00 30
Hedge End d	→		22 32				→			23 32	→		00s36
Botley d			22 36							23 36			00s39
Fareham d			22 45							23 45			00s47
Portchester d			22 50							23 50			00s53
Cosham d			22 55							23 55			00s57
Hilsea a			23 00							00 01			
Fratton a			23 08							00 07			01s05
Portsmouth & Southsea a			23 11							00 10			01s08
Portsmouth Harbour ⛴ a			23 16							00 14			01 12
Southampton Airport Pkwy ✈ d		22 27		22 34	22 53	22 58			23 27			00 28	
Swaythling d						23 01							
St Denys d						23 04						00s32	
Southampton Central ⛴ a		22 34		22 42	23 00	23 08			23 34			00 38	
d		22 36			23 03	23 10			23 36			00 42	
Millbrook (Hants) d						23 13							
Redbridge d						23 16							
Romsey d						23 24		23a35					
Mottisfont & Dunbridge d						23 29							
Dean d						23 35							
Salisbury a						23 51							
Totton d		22 41							23 41			00s47	
Ashurst New Forest d		22 46							23 46				
Beaulieu Road d		22 50											
Brockenhurst a		22 56			23 16				23 54			00s58	
d		22 57			23 17				23 55				
Sway d		23 02							23 59				
New Milton d		23 07			23 24				00 04			01s06	
Hinton Admiral d		23 11							00 08				
Christchurch d		23 16							00 13			01s13	
Pokesdown d		23 19							00 17			01s17	
Bournemouth a		23 23			23 34				00 21			01 21	
d		23 25			23 39				00 22			01 22	
Branksome d					23 44				00 27			01s27	
Parkstone (Dorset) d					23 47				00 30			01s30	
Poole a		23 34			23 50				00 34			01 34	
d					23 51								
Hamworthy d					23 56								
Holton Heath d													
Wareham d					00 03								
Wool d					00 10								
Moreton (Dorset) d					00 17								
Dorchester South d					00 25								
Dorchester West d													
Upwey d					00 32								
Weymouth a					00 36								

A trolley to Bournemouth

For services from Brockenhurst - Lymington refer to Table T159

Table T158-R

Mondays to Fridays

21 May to 5 October

Weymouth, Bournemouth, Romsey, Southampton and Basingstoke - London

Miles	Miles	Miles			SW MX	SW MX	SW MX	SW	XC	SW	SW	GW	SW	SW	SW	SW	XC	SW	SW	SW	SW	SW	SW
					1	1	◇1	◇1	◇1	◇1	1	◇	1	1	◇1 ✠	1	◇1	1	◇1 ✠	1	1	◇1	◇1
0	—	—	**Weymouth**	d								05 33											
2¼	—	—	Upwey	d								05 38											
—	—	—	Dorchester West	a								05 45											
7	—	—	**Dorchester South**	d																			
12½	—	—	Moreton (Dorset)	d																			
17	—	—	Wool	d																			
22	—	—	Wareham	d																			
24	—	—	Holton Heath	d																			
26¾	—	—	Hamworthy	d																			
29	—	—	**Poole** 4	a																			
—	—	—		d											05 00			05 26	05 45				
30¾	—	—	Parkstone (Dorset)	d											05 04			05 30					
32	—	—	Branksome	d											05 07			05 33					
34¾	—	—	**Bournemouth**	a											05 12			05 38	05 54				
—	—	—		d											05 15			05 40	05 57				
36½	—	—	Pokesdown	d											05 19			05 44					
38½	—	—	Christchurch	d											05 23			05 48					
41¾	—	—	Hinton Admiral	d														05 53					
44¼	—	—	New Milton	d											05 30			05 57					
47¼	—	—	Sway	d														06 02					
50	—	—	**Brockenhurst** 3	a											05 37			06 07	06 12				
—	—	—		d											05 38				06 14				
54¾	—	—	Beaulieu Road	d																			
57¼	—	—	Ashurst New Forest	d																			
60¼	—	—	Totton	d											05 49	06 14							
—	0	—	**Salisbury**	d									05 35										
—	9	—	Dean	d									05 47										
—	12¾	—	Mottisfont & Dunbridge	d									05 53										
—	16½	—	**Romsey**	d									05 58										
60¾	22½	—	Redbridge	d												06 16							
62½	—	—	Millbrook (Hants)	d												06 20					←		
63½	—	—	**Southampton Central** ⛴	a											05 54	06 25			06 27		06 25		
—	—	—		d				04 52	05 15	05 20				05 40	05 55	06 33	06 15		06 30		06 33		06 43
65½	—	—	St Denys	d			00 04	04 57						05 45		→					06 39		06 48
67	—	—	Swaythling	d			00 07	05 00						05 48							06 42		06 51
67¾	—	—	**Southampton Airport Pkwy** ✈	d			00 10	05 03	05 22	05 28				05 51	06 03		06 22		06 38		06 45	06 51	06 55
—	0	—	**Portsmouth Harbour** ⛴	d							05 00									05 43			
—	0¾	—	**Portsmouth & Southsea**	d							05 05									05 48			
—	1¾	—	Fratton	d							05 09									05 52			
—	4	—	Hilsea	d							05 13									05 56			
—	5½	—	Cosham	d							05 19									06 03			
—	8	—	Portchester	d							05 23									06 08			
—	11¼	—	Fareham	d							05 29									06 19			
—	16¾	—	Botley	d							05 37									06 26			
—	17¾	—	Hedge End	d		00 05					05 41									06 31			
69¾	22¼	0	Eastleigh 3	a		00 11	00 14	05 06		05 31	05 49			05 55	06 07					06 38	06 48	06 54	06 58
—	—	—		d		00 19		05 07		05 32	05 50				06 08					06 43	06 50	06 55	06 59
—	24¼	2	Chandlers Ford	d									06 06								06 55		
—	29½	7¼	**Romsey**	a									06 44								07 03		
73	—	—	Shawford	d				05 13			05 56									06 49			07 05
76¼	—	—	**Winchester**	d		00a28		05 19	05 31	05 42	06 02				06 18		06 31		06 48	06 55		07 05	07 11
84¾	—	—	Micheldever	d				05 27		05 51	06 10									07 04			
95	—	—	**Basingstoke**	a				05 38	05 46	06 01	06 20				06 34		06 46			07 14			07 27
—	—	—		d				05 39	05 47	06 03					06 35		06 47			07 17			07 36
—	—	—	Reading 7	a					06 05								07 05						
106¾	—	—	Fleet	d	00 01			05 50															07 52
109½	—	—	Farnborough (Main)	d	00 06			05 56															07 58
118½	—	—	**Woking**	a	00 18			06 05		06 22					06 53							07 38	08 08
138¾	—	—	**Clapham Junction** 10	a	00 53			06 25							07 14								
142¾	—	—	**London Waterloo** 15 ⊖	a	01 04			06 34		06 53					07 25				07 48	08 01		08 08	08 39

For services from Brockenhurst - Lymington refer to Table T159

Table T158-R

Mondays to Fridays

21 May to 5 October

Weymouth, Bournemouth, Romsey, Southampton and Basingstoke - London

		SW	SW	SW	SW	SW	XC	SW	SW	SW	SW	SW	SW	XC	XC	SW	SW	GW	SW	XC	SW	SW	SW
		◇1 ✠	◇1 ✠	◇1	1	◇1	◇1 ✠	◇1	◇1 ✠	◇1 A ✠	◇1	1	◇1	◇1 B	◇1 C ✠	◇1 ✠	◇1 A ✠	◇	◇1	◇1 ✠		◇1 ✠	
Weymouth	d									05 55							06 25	06 44					
Upwey	d									05 59							06 29	06 49					
Dorchester West	a																	06 56					
Dorchester South	d									06 07							06 37						
Moreton (Dorset)	d									06 14							06 44						
Wool	d									06 20							06 50						
Wareham	d									06 27							06 57						
Holton Heath	d									06 31													
Hamworthy	d									06 36							07 04						
Poole 4	a									06 40							07 08						
	d		06 11							06 41							07 11					07 20	
Parkstone (Dorset)	d		06 15							06 45							07 15					07 24	
Branksome	d		06 18							06 49							07 19					07 27	
Bournemouth	a		06 23							06 54							07 24					07 32	
	d	06 04	06 25				06 30		06 34	06 56						07 04	07 26			07 30		07 34	
Pokesdown	d	06 08							06 38							07 08						07 38	
Christchurch	d	06 12							06 42							07 12						07 42	
Hinton Admiral	d	06 17							06 47							07 17						07 47	
New Milton	d	06 21							06 51							07 21						07 51	
Sway	d	06 26							06 56							07 26						07 56	
Brockenhurst 3	a	06 31					06 44		07 01							07 31				07 44		08 01	
	d	06 33					06 45		07 03							07 33				07 50		08 03	
Beaulieu Road	d																					08 08	
Ashurst New Forest	d	06 41							07 11							07 41						08 12	
Totton	d	06 46							07 16							07 46						08 17	
Salisbury	d											06 50											07 50
Dean	d											07 02											08 02
Mottisfont & Dunbridge	d											07 08											08 08
Romsey	d				07 07							07 13									08 07		08 13
Redbridge	d											07 23											08 21
Millbrook (Hants)	d											07 26											08 25
Southampton Central ⛴	a	06 51	06 55				06 59		07 21	07 25		07 30				07 51	07 55			08 03		08 23	08 27
	d	07 00				07 10	07 15		07 30			07 35	07 38			08 00				08 15		08 48	08 35
St Denys	d											07 40	07 43									→	→
Swaythling	d											07 43	07 46										
Southampton Airport Pkwy ✈	d	07 08				07 18	07 22		07 38			07 46	07 49			08 08				08 22			
Portsmouth Harbour ⛴	d			06 23							06 50								07 23				
Portsmouth & Southsea	d			06 28							06 55								07 28				
Fratton	d			06 32							06 59								07 32				
Hilsea	d			06 36							07 03								07 36				
Cosham	d			06 42							07 08								07 41				
Portchester	d			06 46							07 13								07 46				
Fareham	d			06 53							07 20								07 52				
Botley	d			07 01							07 28								08 00				
Hedge End	d			07 05							07 32								08 05				
Eastleigh 3	a			07 11	07 20	07 21					07 38	07 49	07 53						08 11		08 20		
	d			07 13	07 21	07 30					07 43	07 50	07 54						08 13		08 21		
Chandlers Ford	d											07 55											
Romsey	a				07 52							08 03									08 51		
Shawford	d					07 36		←			07 49		08 00						08 20				
Winchester	d	07 18		07 22		07 42	07 31	07 42	07 48		07 55		08 06	08 12	08 12	08 18			08 26	08 31			
Micheldever	d			07 31		→					08 03												
Basingstoke	a			07 41			07 46	07 58			08 14		08 22	08 26	08 26	08 34			08 42	08 46			
	d			07 47			07 47	08 05			08 16		08 24	08 28	08 28	08 35			08 43	08 47			
Reading 7	a						08 04							08 44	08 44					09 04			
Fleet	d							08 22					08 40						08 54				
Farnborough (Main)	d							08 28					08 46						09 00				
Woking	a			08 05				08 38			08 34		08 58			08 53							
Clapham Junction 10	a															09 14			09 26				
London Waterloo 15 ⊖	a	08 16		08 34				09 10	08 50		09 03		09 29			09 25			09 38				

A ✠ from Bournemouth
B until 20 July
C from 23 July

For services from Brockenhurst - Lymington refer to Table T159

Table T158-R

Mondays to Fridays

21 May to 5 October

Weymouth, Bournemouth, Romsey, Southampton and Basingstoke - London

		SW	SW	SW	SW	SW	SW	SW	SW	XC	SW	SN	SW	SW	SW	XC	SW	SW	SW	GW	XC	SW	SW
		◇1 A ⚒	1			◇1 ⚒	◇1 ⚒	◇1 ⚒	1	■ 1 ⚒	1		◇1 A ⚒	1	1	◇1 ⚒	◇1	◇1 A ⚒	◇1	◇	◇1 ⚒	◇1 A ⚒	1
Weymouth	d	06 55							07 25				07 55					08 20		08 53		09 03	
Upwey	d	06 59							07 29				07 59					08 24		08 58			
Dorchester West	a																			09 05			
Dorchester South	d	07 07							07 37				08 07					08 33				09 13	
Moreton (Dorset)	d	07 14							07 44				08 14					08 39					
Wool	d	07 20							07 50				08 20					08 45					
Wareham	d	07 27							07 57				08 27					08 53				09 28	
Holton Heath	d	07 31							08 01				08 31					08 56					
Hamworthy	d	07 36							08 06				08 36					09 01				09 35	
Poole 4	a	07 40							08 10				08 40					09 06				09 39	
	d	07 41					07 55		08 11				08 41				08 50	09 07				09 40	
Parkstone (Dorset)	d	07 45					07 59		08 15				08 45				08 54					09 44	
Branksome	d	07 49					08 02		08 19				08 49				08 57					09 48	
Bournemouth	a	07 54					08 07		08 24				08 54				09 02	09 16				09 53	
	d	07 59					08 10		08 25	08 45			08 59				09 05	09 18			09 45	09 55	
Pokesdown	d						08 14		08 29								09 09	09 22					
Christchurch	d						08 18		08 33								09 13	09 26					
Hinton Admiral	d						08 24		08 38								09 18						
New Milton	d						08 29		08 42								09 22	09 33					
Sway	d						08 34		08 47								09 27						
Brockenhurst 3	a	08 14					08 39		08 52	08 58			09 14				09 32	09 40			09 58	10 11	
	d	08 15					08 41			09 00			09 15				09 33	09 41			10 00	10 12	
Beaulieu Road	d																						
Ashurst New Forest	d						08 48										09 40						
Totton	d						08 53										09 45						
Salisbury	d														08 50								
Dean	d														09 02								
Mottisfont & Dunbridge	d														09 08								
Romsey	d										09 07				09 14								10 07
Redbridge	d														09 21								
Millbrook (Hants)	d			←		←									09 25								
Southampton Central	a	08 28		08 27		08 23	08 58			09 12			09 28		09 28		09 53	09 56			10 13	10 26	
	d	08 30		08 35		08 48	09 00			09 16		09 26	09 30		09 35	09 46	09 55	10 00			10 17	10 30	
St Denys	d			08 40		08 53									09 40								
Swaythling	d			08 43		08 56									09 43								
Southampton Airport Pkwy	d	08 38		08 46		08 59	09 08			09 23		09 34	09 38		09 46	09 55	10 03	10 08			10 24	10 38	
Portsmouth Harbour	d		07 55		08 05									08 59									
Portsmouth & Southsea	d		08 00		08 10									09 04									
Fratton	d		08 04		08 14									09 08									
Hilsea	d		08 08		08 18									09 12									
Cosham	d		08 13		08 24									09 17									
Portchester	d		08 18		08 28									09 22									
Fareham	d		08 24		08 33									09 28									
Botley	d		08 31		08 41									09 35									
Hedge End	d		08 36		08 45									09 40									
Eastleigh 3	a		08 42	08 49	08 51	09 03					09 20	09 38		09 47	09 49		10 06						10 20
	d		08 43	08 50	08 54	09 14					09 21			09 47	09 50		10 14						10 21
Chandlers Ford	d			08 55											09 55								
Romsey	a			09 03							09 51				10 03								10 59
Shawford	d		08 49			09 19		←									10 20		←				
Winchester	d	08 48	08 55		09 02	09 25	09 18	09 25		09 32			09 48	09 57		10 03	10 25	10 18	10 25		10 33	10 48	
Micheldever	d		09 03			→								10 05			→						
Basingstoke	a		09 14		09 19		09 35	09 41		09 46				10 15		10 18		10 34	10 42		10 47		
	d		09 16				09 36	09 43		09 49				10 17		10 19		10 35	10 43		10 49		
Reading 7	a									10 07						10 37					11 06		
Fleet	d		09 27					09 54											10 54				
Farnborough (Main)	d		09 32					10 00						10 30					11 00				
Woking	a	09 22	09 41				09 54						10 20	10 39								11 19	
Clapham Junction 10	a	09 43					10 15	10 25										11 11	11 25				
London Waterloo 15 ⊖	a	09 53	10 08				10 23	10 34					10 49	11 08				11 20	11 34			11 49	

A ⚒ from Bournemouth

For services from Brockenhurst - Lymington refer to Table T159

Table T158-R

Mondays to Fridays

21 May to 5 October

Weymouth, Bournemouth, Romsey, Southampton and Basingstoke - London

		SW	SW	SW	SW	SW	XC	SW	SN	SW	SW	SW	XC	XC	SW	SW	SW	XC	SW	GW	SW	SW
		1	1	◇1	◇1 A ⚒	◇1	◇1 ⚒	1		◇1 A ⚒	1	1	■ 1 B ⚒	◇1 C ⚒	◇1	◇1 A ⚒	◇1	◇1 ⚒	◇1 A ⚒	◇	1	1
Weymouth	d				09 20					10 03						10 20			11 02	11 10		
Upwey	d				09 24											10 24				11 15		
Dorchester West	a																			11 22		
Dorchester South	d				09 33					10 13						10 33			11 13			
Moreton (Dorset)	d				09 39											10 39						
Wool	d				09 45											10 45						
Wareham	d				09 53					10 28						10 53			11 28			
Holton Heath	d				09 56											10 56						
Hamworthy	d				10 01					10 35						11 01			11 35			
Poole 4	a				10 06					10 39						11 06			11 39			
	d			09 50	10 07					10 40					10 50	11 07			11 40			
Parkstone (Dorset)	d			09 54						10 44					10 54				11 44			
Branksome	d			09 57						10 48					10 57				11 48			
Bournemouth	a			10 02	10 17					10 54					11 02	11 17			11 54			
	d			10 05	10 22		10 45			10 59					11 05	11 22		11 45	11 59			
Pokesdown	d			10 09	10 26										11 09	11 26						
Christchurch	d			10 13	10 30										11 13	11 30						
Hinton Admiral	d			10 18											11 18							
New Milton	d			10 22	10 37										11 22	11 37						
Sway	d			10 27											11 27							
Brockenhurst 3	a			10 32	10 44		10 58			11 14					11 32	11 44		11 58	12 14			
	d			10 33	10 45		11 00			11 15					11 33	11 45		12 00	12 15			
Beaulieu Road	d														11 38							
Ashurst New Forest	d			10 40											11 42							
Totton	d			10 45											11 47							
Salisbury	d		09 56									10 56										
Dean	d		10 08									11 08										
Mottisfont & Dunbridge	d		10 14									11 14										
Romsey	d		10 20					11 07				11 20									12 07	
Redbridge	d		10 27									11 27										
Millbrook (Hants)	d		10 31									11 31										
Southampton Central	a		10 34	10 53	10 58		11 13			11 28		11 34			11 53	11 58		12 14	12 28			
	d		10 35	10 55	11 00		11 17		11 26	11 30		11 35	11 46	11 46	11 55	12 00		12 17	12 30			
St Denys	d		10 40									11 40										
Swaythling	d		10 43									11 43										
Southampton Airport Pkwy	d		10 46	11 03	11 08		11 24		11 34	11 38		11 46	11 53	11 53	12 03	12 08		12 24	12 38			
Portsmouth Harbour	d	09 59									10 59											11 59
Portsmouth & Southsea	d	10 04									11 04											12 04
Fratton	d	10 08									11 08											12 08
Hilsea	d	10 12									11 12											12 12
Cosham	d	10 17									11 17											12 17
Portchester	d	10 22									11 22											12 22
Fareham	d	10 28									11 28											12 28
Botley	d	10 35									11 35											12 35
Hedge End	d	10 40									11 40											12 40
Eastleigh 3	a	10 46	10 49	11 06				11 20	11 37		11 46	11 49			12 06						12 20	12 46
	d	10 47	10 50	11 14				11 21			11 47	11 50			12 14						12 21	12 47
Chandlers Ford	d		10 55									11 55										
Romsey	a		11 03					11 51				12 03									12 51	
Shawford	d			11 19		←									12 19		←					
Winchester	d	10 56		11 25	11 18	11 25	11 33			11 48	11 56		12 02	12 02	12 25	12 18	12 25	12 33	12 48			12 56
Micheldever	d	11 05		→							12 05				→							13 05
Basingstoke	a	11 15			11 34	11 41	11 47				12 15		12 17	12 17		12 34	12 41	12 47				13 15
	d	11 17			11 35	11 43	11 49				12 17		12 18	12 18		12 35	12 43	12 49				13 17
Reading 7	a						12 05						12 37	12 37				13 06				
Fleet	d					11 54											12 54					
Farnborough (Main)	d	11 30				12 00					12 31						13 00					13 30
Woking	a	11 39								12 19	12 40								13 19			13 39
Clapham Junction 10	a				12 11	12 25										13 11	13 25					
London Waterloo 15 ⊖	a	12 08			12 20	12 34				12 49	13 08					13 20	13 34		13 49			14 08

A ⚒ from Bournemouth
B until 20 July
C from 23 July

For services from Brockenhurst - Lymington refer to Table T159

Table T158-R

Mondays to Fridays

21 May to 5 October

Weymouth, Bournemouth, Romsey, Southampton and Basingstoke - London

		SW	SW	SW	SW	XC	SW	SW	SW	SW	XC	SW	SW	SW	XC	SW	GW	SW	SW	SW	SW	SW	SW
		1	◇1	◇1	◇1	◇1	◇1	1	1	1	◇1	◇1	◇1	◇1	◇1	◇1	◇	1	1	1	◇1	◇1	◇1
				A 🛒		🛒	A 🛒				🛒		A 🛒		🛒	A 🛒						A 🛒	
Weymouth	d			11 20			12 03						12 20			13 03	13 10					13 20	
Upwey	d			11 24									12 24				13 15					13 24	
Dorchester West	a																13 22						
Dorchester South	d			11 33			12 13						12 33			13 13						13 33	
Moreton (Dorset)	d			11 39									12 39									13 39	
Wool	d			11 45									12 45									13 45	
Wareham	d			11 53			12 28						12 53			13 28						13 53	
Holton Heath	d			11 56									12 56									13 56	
Hamworthy	d			12 01			12 35						13 01			13 35						14 01	
Poole 4	a			12 06			12 39						13 06			13 39						14 06	
	d		11 50	12 07			12 40					12 50	13 07			13 40					13 50	14 07	
Parkstone (Dorset)	d		11 54				12 44					12 54				13 44					13 54		
Branksome	d		11 57				12 48					12 57				13 48					13 57		
Bournemouth	a		12 02	12 17			12 54					13 02	13 17			13 54					14 02	14 17	
	d		12 05	12 22		12 45	12 59					13 05	13 22		13 45	13 59					14 05	14 22	
Pokesdown	d		12 09	12 26								13 09	13 26								14 09	14 26	
Christchurch	d		12 13	12 30								13 13	13 30								14 13	14 30	
Hinton Admiral	d		12 18									13 18									14 18		
New Milton	d		12 22	12 37								13 22	13 37								14 22	14 37	
Sway	d		12 27									13 27									14 27		
Brockenhurst 3	a		12 32	12 44		12 58	13 14					13 32	13 44		13 58	14 14					14 32	14 44	
	d		12 33	12 45		13 00	13 15					13 33	13 45		14 00	14 15					14 33	14 45	
Beaulieu Road	d											13 38											
Ashurst New Forest	d		12 40									13 42									14 40		
Totton	d		12 45									13 47									14 45		
Salisbury	d	11 56								12 56										13 50			
Dean	d	12 08								13 08										14 02			
Mottisfont & Dunbridge	d	12 14								13 14										14 08			
Romsey	d	12 20						13 07		13 20								14 07		14 13			
Redbridge	d	12 27								13 27										14 21			
Millbrook (Hants)	d	12 31								13 31										14 24			
Southampton Central ⛴	a	12 34	12 52	12 58		13 13	13 28			13 34		13 53	13 58		14 13	14 28				14 28	14 53	14 58	
	d	12 35	12 55	13 00		13 16	13 30			13 35	13 46	13 55	14 00		14 17	14 30				14 36	14 55	15 00	
St Denys	d	12 40								13 40										14 40			
Swaythling	d	12 43								13 43										14 43			
Southampton Airport Pkwy ✈	d	12 46	13 03	13 08		13 23	13 38			13 46	13 54	14 03	14 08		14 24	14 38				14 46	15 03	15 08	
Portsmouth Harbour ⛴	d								12 59										13 59				
Portsmouth & Southsea	d								13 04										14 04				
Fratton	d								13 08										14 08				
Hilsea	d								13 12										14 12				
Cosham	d								13 17										14 17				
Portchester	d								13 22										14 22				
Fareham	d								13 28										14 28				
Botley	d								13 35										14 35				
Hedge End	d								13 40										14 40				
Eastleigh 3	a	12 49	13 06					13 20	13 46	13 49		14 06						14 20	14 46	14 49	15 06		
	d	12 50	13 14					13 21	13 47	13 50		14 14						14 21	14 47	14 50	15 14		
Chandlers Ford	d	12 55								13 55										14 55			
Romsey	a	13 03						13 51		14 03								14 51		15 03			
Shawford	d		13 19		←							14 19		←							15 19		←
Winchester	d		13 25	13 18	13 25	13 32	13 48		13 56		14 03	14 25	14 18	14 25	14 33	14 48			14 56		15 25	15 18	15 25
Micheldever	d		→						14 05			→							15 05		→		
Basingstoke	a			13 34	13 41	13 46			14 15		14 18		14 34	14 41	14 47				15 15			15 34	15 41
	d			13 35	13 43	13 49			14 17		14 19		14 35	14 43	14 49				15 17			15 35	15 43
Reading 7	a					14 05					14 36				15 05								
Fleet	d				13 54									14 54									15 54
Farnborough (Main)	d				14 00				14 30					15 00					15 30				16 00
Woking	a						14 20		14 39							15 19			15 39				
Clapham Junction 10	a			14 11	14 25								15 11	15 25								16 11	16 25
London Waterloo 15 ⊖	a			14 20	14 34		14 49		15 08				15 20	15 34		15 49			16 07			16 20	16 34

A 🛒 from Bournemouth

For services from Brockenhurst - Lymington refer to Table T159

Table T158-R

Mondays to Fridays

21 May to 5 October

Weymouth, Bournemouth, Romsey, Southampton and Basingstoke - London

		XC	SW	SW	SW	SW	XC	SW	SW	SW	XC	SW	GW	SW	SW	SW	SW	SW	SW	XC	SW	SW
		◇1	◇1	1	1	1	◇1	◇1	◇1	◇1	◇1	◇1	◇	1	1	1	◇1	◇1	◇1	◇1	◇1	
		🛒	A 🛒				🛒		A 🛒		🛒	A 🛒						A 🛒		🛒	A 🛒	
Weymouth	d		14 03						14 20			15 03	15 08					15 20			16 03	
Upwey	d								14 24				15 13					15 24				
Dorchester West	a												15 20									
Dorchester South	d		14 13						14 33			15 13						15 33			16 13	
Moreton (Dorset)	d								14 39									15 39				
Wool	d								14 45									15 45				
Wareham	d		14 28						14 53			15 28						15 53			16 28	
Holton Heath	d								14 56									15 56				
Hamworthy	d		14 35						15 01			15 35						16 01			16 35	
Poole 4	a		14 39						15 06			15 39						16 06			16 39	
	d		14 40					14 50	15 07			15 40					15 50	16 07			16 40	
Parkstone (Dorset)	d		14 44					14 54				15 44					15 54				16 44	
Branksome	d		14 48					14 57				15 48					15 57				16 48	
Bournemouth	a		14 54					15 02	15 17			15 54					16 02	16 17			16 54	
	d	14 45	14 59					15 05	15 22		15 45	15 59					16 05	16 22		16 45	16 59	
Pokesdown	d							15 09	15 26								16 09	16 26				
Christchurch	d							15 13	15 30								16 13	16 30				
Hinton Admiral	d							15 18									16 18					
New Milton	d							15 22	15 37								16 22	16 37				
Sway	d							15 27									16 27					
Brockenhurst 3	a	14 58	15 14					15 32	15 44		15 58	16 14					16 32	16 44		16 58	17 14	
	d	15 00	15 15					15 33	15 45		16 00	16 15					16 33	16 45		17 00	17 15	
Beaulieu Road	d																					
Ashurst New Forest	d							15 40									16 40					
Totton	d							15 45									16 45					
Salisbury	d					14 56										15 56						
Dean	d					15 08										16 08						
Mottisfont & Dunbridge	d					15 14										16 14						
Romsey	d			15 07		15 20								16 07		16 20						17 07
Redbridge	d					15 27										16 27						
Millbrook (Hants)	d					15 31										16 31						
Southampton Central ⛴	a	15 13	15 28			15 34		15 53	15 58		16 13	16 28				16 34	16 51	16 58		17 13	17 28	
	d	15 16	15 30			15 35	15 46	15 55	16 00		16 17	16 30				16 35	16 52	17 00		17 17	17 30	
St Denys	d					15 40										16 40	16 57					
Swaythling	d					15 43										16 43	17 00					
Southampton Airport Pkwy ✈	d	15 23	15 38			15 46	15 53	16 03	16 08		16 24	16 38				16 46	17 04	17 08		17 24	17 38	
Portsmouth Harbour ⛴	d				14 59										15 59							
Portsmouth & Southsea	d				15 04										16 04							
Fratton	d				15 08										16 08							
Hilsea	d				15 12										16 12							
Cosham	d				15 17										16 17							
Portchester	d				15 22										16 22							
Fareham	d				15 28										16 28							
Botley	d				15 35										16 35							
Hedge End	d				15 40										16 40							
Eastleigh 3	a			15 20	15 46	15 49		16 08						16 20	16 46	16 49	17 07					17 20
	d			15 21	15 47	15 50		16 14						16 21	16 47	16 50	17 14					17 21
Chandlers Ford	d					15 55										16 55						
Romsey	a			15 51		16 03								16 51		17 03						17 51
Shawford	d							16 19		←							17 19		←			
Winchester	d	15 32	15 48		15 56		16 02	16 25	16 18	16 25	16 33	16 48			16 56		17 25	17 18	17 25	17 33	17 48	
Micheldever	d				16 05			→							17 05		→					
Basingstoke	a	15 46			16 15		16 17		16 34	16 41	16 47				17 15			17 33	17 42	17 47		
	d	15 48			16 17		16 18		16 36	16 43	16 49				17 17			17 35	17 43	17 49		
Reading 7	a	16 04					16 34				17 08									18 04		
Fleet	d									16 54									17 54			
Farnborough (Main)	d				16 30					17 00					17 30				18 00			
Woking	a		16 19		16 39							17 20			17 39						18 19	
Clapham Junction 10	a								17 11	17 25								18 11	18 25			
London Waterloo 15 ⊖	a		16 49		17 08				17 21	17 38		17 52			18 09			18 23	18 34		18 50	

A 🛒 from Bournemouth

For services from Brockenhurst - Lymington refer to Table T159

Table T158-R

Mondays to Fridays

21 May to 5 October

Weymouth, Bournemouth, Romsey, Southampton and Basingstoke - London

		SW ■	SW	SW ■	XC ◇■ ⚒	SW ◇■	SW ◇■ A ⚒	SW ◇■	XC ◇■ ⚒	SW ■	SW ■	SW ◇■ A ⚒	SW ■	SW ■	SW ■	SW ◇■	SW ◇■ A ⚒	SW ◇■	GW ◇	XC ◇■ ⚒	SW ◇■ A ⚒	SW ■	SW ■
Weymouth	d						16 20					17 03					17 20		17 30		18 03		
Upwey	d						16 24										17 24		17 35				
Dorchester West	a																		17 42				
Dorchester South	d						16 33					17 13					17 33				18 13		
Moreton (Dorset)	d						16 39										17 39						
Wool	d						16 45										17 45						
Wareham	d						16 53					17 28					17 53				18 28		
Holton Heath	d						16 56										17 56						
Hamworthy	d						17 01					17 35					18 01				18 35		
Poole ■	a						17 06					17 39					18 06				18 39		
	d					16 50	17 07					17 40				17 50	18 07				18 40		
Parkstone (Dorset)	d					16 54						17 44				17 54					18 44		
Branksome	d					16 57						17 48				17 57					18 48		
Bournemouth	a					17 03	17 18					17 54				18 02	18 17				18 55		
	d					17 05	17 22		17 45			17 59				18 05	18 22			18 45	18 59		
Pokesdown	d					17 09	17 26									18 09	18 26						
Christchurch	d					17 13	17 30									18 13	18 30						
Hinton Admiral	d					17 18										18 18							
New Milton	d					17 22	17 37									18 22	18 37						
Sway	d					17 27										18 27							
Brockenhurst ■	a					17 32	17 44		17 58			18 14				18 32	18 44			18 58	19 14		
	d			17 20		17 33	17 45		18 00			18 15				18 33	18 45			19 00	19 15		
Beaulieu Road	d					17 38										18 38							
Ashurst New Forest	d			17 28		17 42										18 42							
Totton	d			17 33		17 47										18 47							
Salisbury	d		16 56												17 56								
Dean	d		17 08												18 08								
Mottisfont & Dunbridge	d		17 14												18 14								
Romsey	d		17 20							18 07					18 20							19 07	
Redbridge	d		17 27												18 27								
Millbrook (Hants)	d		17 31												18 31								
Southampton Central ⛴	a		17 34	17 40		17 52	17 58		18 13			18 28			18 34	18 53	18 58			19 13	19 28		
	d		17 35		17 46	17 55	18 00		18 15		18 17	18 30			18 35	18 55	19 00			19 16	19 30		
St Denys	d		17 40								18 22				18 40								
Swaythling	d		17 43								18 25				18 43								
Southampton Airport Pkwy ✈	d		17 46		17 53	18 03	18 08		18 22		18 28	18 38			18 46	19 03	19 08			19 23	19 38		
Portsmouth Harbour ⛴	d	16 59											17 49	17 59									18 59
Portsmouth & Southsea	d	17 04											17 54	18 04									19 04
Fratton	d	17 08											17 58	18 08									19 08
Hilsea	d	17 12											18 02	18 12									19 12
Cosham	d	17 17											18 09	18 17									19 17
Portchester	d	17 22											18 13	18 22									19 22
Fareham	d	17 28											18 19	18 28									19 28
Botley	d	17 35											18 27	18 35									19 35
Hedge End	d	17 40											18 31	18 40									19 40
Eastleigh ■	a	17 46	17 49			18 06				18 20	18 32		18 37	18 46	18 49	19 06						19 20	19 46
	d	17 47	17 50			18 14				18 21	18 33			18 47	18 50	19 14						19 21	19 47
Chandlers Ford	d		17 55												18 55								
Romsey	a		18 03							19 00					19 04							19 51	
Shawford	d					18 19		←								19 19		←					
Winchester	d	17 57			18 02	18 25	18 18	18 25	18 31		18a41	18 48		18 57		19 25	19 18	19 25		19 32	19 48		19 56
Micheldever	d	18 05				→								19 05		→							20 05
Basingstoke	a	18 15			18 17		18 34	18 41	18 45					19 15			19 34	19 41		19 46			20 15
	d	18 17			18 18		18 36	18 43	18 47					19 17			19 35	19 43		19 49			20 17
Reading ■	a				18 35				19 04											20 05			
Fleet	d							18 54										19 54					
Farnborough (Main)	d	18 31						19 00						19 32				20 00					20 30
Woking	a	18 40										19 25		19 41							20 19		20 39
Clapham Junction ■	a						19 11	19 26									20 11	20 25					
London Waterloo ■ ⊖	a	19 09					19 20	19 34				19 52		20 08			20 20	20 34			20 49		21 09

A ⚒ from Bournemouth

For services from Brockenhurst - Lymington refer to Table T159

Table T158-R

Mondays to Fridays

21 May to 5 October

Weymouth, Bournemouth, Romsey, Southampton and Basingstoke - London

		SW ■	SW ◇■	SW ◇■ A ⚒	SW ◇■	XC ◇■	SW ◇■ A ⚒	SW ■	SW ■	SW ■	SW ◇■	SW ◇■	SW ◇■	SW ■	SW ◇■	SW ■	SW ■	SW ◇■	SW ◇■	SW ◇■	GW	GW ◇	SW ■
Weymouth	d			18 20			19 03					19 20							20 10		20 21		
Upwey	d			18 24								19 24							20 14		20 26		
Dorchester West	a																				20 33		
Dorchester South	d			18 33			19 13					19 37							20 22				
Moreton (Dorset)	d			18 39								19 43							20 28				
Wool	d			18 45								19 49							20 34				
Wareham	d			18 53			19 28					19 57							20 42				
Holton Heath	d			18 56																			
Hamworthy	d			19 01			19 35					20 03							20 48				
Poole ■	a			19 06			19 39					20 08							20 53				
	d		18 50	19 07			19 40				19 50	20 09							20 54				
Parkstone (Dorset)	d		18 54				19 44				19 54								20 58				
Branksome	d		18 57				19 48				19 57								21 01				
Bournemouth	a		19 02	19 17			19 54				20 02	20 19							21 07				
	d		19 05	19 22		19 45	19 59				20 05	20 22							21 12				
Pokesdown	d		19 09	19 26							20 09	20 26							21 16				
Christchurch	d		19 13	19 30							20 13	20 30							21 20				
Hinton Admiral	d		19 18								20 18								21 25				
New Milton	d		19 22	19 37							20 22	20 37							21 29				
Sway	d		19 27								20 27								21 34				
Brockenhurst ■	a		19 32	19 44		19 58	20 14				20 32	20 44							21 39				
	d		19 33	19 45		20 00	20 15				20 33	20 45							21 40				
Beaulieu Road	d										20 38												
Ashurst New Forest	d		19 41								20 42								21 47				
Totton	d		19 46								20 47								21 52				
Salisbury	d	18 56								19 56							20 56					21 32	
Dean	d	19 08								20 08							21 08						
Mottisfont & Dunbridge	d	19 14								20 14							21 14						
Romsey	d	19 20						20 07		20 20				21 07			21 20					21 50	22 07
Redbridge	d	19 27								20 27							21 27						
Millbrook (Hants)	d	19 31								20 31							21 31						
Southampton Central ⛴	a	19 34	19 51	19 58		20 13	20 28			20 34	20 53	20 58					21 34		21 57			22 02	
	d	19 35	19 55	20 00		20 17	20 30			20 35	20 55	21 00			21 30		21 35	21 55	22 00			22 04	
St Denys	d	19 40								20 40							21 40						
Swaythling	d	19 43								20 43							21 43						
Southampton Airport Pkwy ✈	d	19 46	20 03	20 08		20 24	20 38			20 46	21 03	21 08			21 38		21 46	22 03	22 08			22 12	
Portsmouth Harbour ⛴	d								19 59							20 59							
Portsmouth & Southsea	d								20 04							21 04							
Fratton	d								20 08							21 08							
Hilsea	d								20 12							21 12							
Cosham	d								20 17							21 17							
Portchester	d								20 22							21 22							
Fareham	d								20 28							21 28							
Botley	d								20 35							21 35							
Hedge End	d								20 40							21 40							
Eastleigh ■	a	19 49	20 06					20 20	20 46	20 49	21 06			21 20		21 46	21 49	22 06				22 15	22 21
	d	19 50	20 14					20 21	20 47	20 50	21 14			21 21		21 47	21 50	22 14					22 22
Chandlers Ford	d	19 55								20 55							21 55						
Romsey	a	20 03						20 51		21 03				21 51			22 03						22 51
Shawford	d		20 19		←				20 53		21 20		←					22 20		←			
Winchester	d		20 25	20 18	20 25	20 33	20 48		20 59		21 26	21 18	21 26		21 48	21 56		22 26	22 18	22 26			
Micheldever	d		→						21 07		→					22 05		→					
Basingstoke	a			20 34	20 41	20 47			21 21			21 34	21 42			22 15			22 34	22 42			
	d			20 36	20 43	20 49			21 24			21 35	21 43			22 24			22 36	22 43			
Reading ■	a					21 06																	
Fleet	d				20 54				21 40				21 54			22 40				22 54			
Farnborough (Main)	d				21 00				21 46				22 00			22 46				23 00			
Woking	a				21 09		21 19		21 58				22 09		22 19	22 58			22 54	23 09			
Clapham Junction ■	a			21 16	21 29							22 13	22 29						23 14	23 29			
London Waterloo ■ ⊖	a			21 25	21 38		21 49		22 34			22 22	22 38		22 49	23 32			23 23	23 39			

A ⚒ from Bournemouth

For services from Brockenhurst - Lymington refer to Table T159

Table T158-R

Mondays to Fridays

21 May to 5 October

Weymouth, Bournemouth, Romsey, Southampton and Basingstoke - London

		SW	SW	SW	SW	SW	SW	SW	SW	SW
		1	◇1	1	1	1	1	1	◇1	1
Weymouth	d				21 10				22 10	23 10
Upwey	d				21 14				22 14	23 14
Dorchester West	a									
Dorchester South	d				21 22				22 22	23 22
Moreton (Dorset)	d				21 28				22 28	23 28
Wool	d				21 34				22 34	23 34
Wareham	d				21 42				22 42	23 42
Holton Heath	d									
Hamworthy	d				21 48				22 48	23 48
Poole 4	a				21 53				22 53	23 53
	d				21 54				22 54	23 54
Parkstone (Dorset)	d				21 58				22 58	
Branksome	d				22 01				23 01	
Bournemouth	a				22 07				23 07	00 03
	d				22 12				23 12	
Pokesdown	d				22 16				23 16	
Christchurch	d				22 20				23 20	
Hinton Admiral	d				22 25				23 25	
New Milton	d				22 29				23 29	
Sway	d				22 34				23 34	
Brockenhurst 3	a				22 39				23 39	
	d				22 40				23 40	
Beaulieu Road	d									
Ashurst New Forest	d				22 47				23 47	
Totton	d				22 52				23 52	
Salisbury	d			21 56						
Dean	d			22 08						
Mottisfont & Dunbridge	d			22 14						
Romsey	d			22 20		23 07	22 58			
Redbridge	d			22 27			23 05			
Millbrook (Hants)	d			22 31			23 09			
Southampton Central ⛴	a			22 34	22 57		23 11		23 57	
	d		22 30	22 35	23 00		23 20		23 59	
St Denys	d			22 40			23 25		00 04	
Swaythling	d			22 43			23 28		00 07	
Southampton Airport Pkwy ✈	d		22 38	22 46	23 08		23 31		00 10	
Portsmouth Harbour ⛴	d	21 54						23 24		
Portsmouth & Southsea	d	21 59						23 29		
Fratton	d	22 03						23 33		
Hilsea	d	22 07						23 37		
Cosham	d	22 12						23 42		
Portchester	d	22 17						23 47		
Fareham	d	22 20						23 53		
Botley	d	22 28						23 59		
Hedge End	d	22 33						00 05		
Eastleigh 8	a	22 41	22 41	22 49	23 11	23 21	23 34	00 11	00 14	
	d		22 46	22 50	23 12	23 22	23 36	00 19		
Chandlers Ford	d			22 55			23 41			
Romsey	a			23 04		23 55	23 48			
Shawford	d				23 18					
Winchester	d		22 55		23 24			00a28		
Micheldever	d				23 33					
Basingstoke	a		23 11		23 43					
	d		23 13		23 44					
Reading 7	a									
Fleet	d				00 01					
Farnborough (Main)	d				00 06					
Woking	a		23 31		00 18					
Clapham Junction 10	a		23 55		00 53					
London Waterloo 15 ⊖	a		00 08		01 04					

For services from Brockenhurst - Lymington refer to Table T159

Table T158-R

Mondays to Fridays

8 October to 7 December

Weymouth, Bournemouth, Romsey, Southampton and Basingstoke - London

		SW MX	SW MX	SW MX	SW	XC	SW	SW	GW	SW
		1	1	◇1	◇1	◇1	◇1	1	◇	1
Weymouth	d								05 33	
Upwey	d								05 38	
Dorchester West	a								05 45	
Dorchester South	d									
Moreton (Dorset)	d									
Wool	d									
Wareham	d									
Holton Heath	d									
Hamworthy	d									
Poole 4	a									
	d									
Parkstone (Dorset)	d									
Branksome	d									
Bournemouth	a									
	d									
Pokesdown	d									
Christchurch	d									
Hinton Admiral	d									
New Milton	d									
Sway	d									
Brockenhurst 3	a									
	d									
Beaulieu Road	d									
Ashurst New Forest	d									
Totton	d									
Salisbury	d									05 35
Dean	d									05 47
Mottisfont & Dunbridge	d									05 53
Romsey	d									05 58
Redbridge	d									
Millbrook (Hants)	d									
Southampton Central ⛴	a									
	d				04 52	05 15	05 20			
St Denys	d			00 04	04 57					
Swaythling	d			00 07	05 00					
Southampton Airport Pkwy ✈	d			00 10	05 03	05 22	05 28			
Portsmouth Harbour ⛴	d							04 55		
Portsmouth & Southsea	d							05 00		
Fratton	d							05 04		
Hilsea	d							05 08		
Cosham	d							05 16		
Portchester	d							05 20		
Fareham	d							05 26		
Botley	d							05 34		
Hedge End	d		00 05					05 38		
Eastleigh 8	a		00 11	00 14	05 06		05 31	05 46		
	d		00 19		05 07		05 32	05 47		
Chandlers Ford	d									06 06
Romsey	a									06 44
Shawford	d				05 13			05 53		
Winchester	d		00a28		05 19	05 31	05 42	05 59		
Micheldever	d				05 27		05 51	06 07		
Basingstoke	a				05 38	05 46	06 01	06 20		
	d				05 39	05 47	06 03			
Reading 7	a					06 05				
Fleet	d	00 01			05 50					
Farnborough (Main)	d	00 06			05 56					
Woking	a	00 18			06 05		06 22			
Clapham Junction 10	a	00 53			06 25					
London Waterloo 15 ⊖	a	01 04			06 34		06 53			

		SW	SW	SW	XC	SW	SW	SW	SW	SW	SW	SW	SW	SW
		1	◇1 🚲	1	◇1	1	◇1 🚲	1	1	◇1	◇1	◇1 🚲	◇1 🚲	◇1
Weymouth	d													
Upwey	d													
Dorchester West	a													
Dorchester South	d													
Moreton (Dorset)	d													
Wool	d													
Wareham	d													
Holton Heath	d													
Hamworthy	d													
Poole 4	a													
	d		04 57			05 23	05 42						06 08	
Parkstone (Dorset)	d		05 01			05 27							06 12	
Branksome	d		05 04			05 30							06 15	
Bournemouth	a		05 09			05 36	05 52						06 23	
	d		05 12			05 38	05 54					06 04	06 25	
Pokesdown	d		05 16			05 42						06 08		
Christchurch	d		05 20			05 46						06 12		
Hinton Admiral	d					05 51						06 17		
New Milton	d		05 27			05 55						06 21		
Sway	d					06 00						06 26		
Brockenhurst 3	a		05 37			06 07	06 12					06 31		
	d		05 38				06 14					06 33		
Beaulieu Road	d													
Ashurst New Forest	d											06 41		
Totton	d		05 49	06 14								06 46		
Salisbury	d													
Dean	d													
Mottisfont & Dunbridge	d													
Romsey	d													
Redbridge	d			06 16										
Millbrook (Hants)	d			06 20					←					
Southampton Central ⛴	a		05 54	06 25			06 27		06 25			06 51	06 55	
	d	05 40	05 55	06 33	06 15		06 30		06 33		06 43	07 00		
St Denys	d	05 45		→					06 39		06 48			
Swaythling	d	05 48							06 42		06 51			
Southampton Airport Pkwy ✈	d	05 51	06 03		06 22		06 38		06 45	06 51	06 55	07 08		
Portsmouth Harbour ⛴	d							05 43						06 23
Portsmouth & Southsea	d							05 48						06 28
Fratton	d							05 52						06 32
Hilsea	d							05 56						06 36
Cosham	d							06 03						06 42
Portchester	d							06 08						06 46
Fareham	d							06 19						06 53
Botley	d							06 26						07 01
Hedge End	d							06 31						07 05
Eastleigh 8	a	05 55	06 07					06 38	06 48	06 54	06 58			07 11
	d		06 08					06 43	06 50	06 55	06 59			07 13
Chandlers Ford	d								06 55					
Romsey	a								07 03					
Shawford	d							06 49			07 05			
Winchester	d		06 18		06 31		06 48	06 55		07 05	07 11	07 18		07 22
Micheldever	d							07 04						07 31
Basingstoke	a		06 34		06 46			07 14			07 27			07 41
	d		06 35		06 47			07 17			07 36			07 47
Reading 7	a				07 05									
Fleet	d										07 52			
Farnborough (Main)	d										07 58			
Woking	a		06 53							07 38	08 08			08 05
Clapham Junction 10	a		07 14											
London Waterloo 15 ⊖	a		07 25				07 47	08 01		08 08	08 39	08 16		08 34

For services from Brockenhurst - Lymington refer to Table T159

Table T158-R

Mondays to Fridays
8 October to 7 December

Weymouth, Bournemouth, Romsey, Southampton and Basingstoke - London

		SW ■	SW ◇■	XC ◇■ ✠	SW ◇■	SW ◇■ ✠	SW ◇■ A ✠	SW ◇■	SW ■	SW ◇■	XC ◇■	SW ◇■ ✠	SW ◇■ A ✠	GW ◇	SW ◇■	XC ◇■ ✠	SW	SW ◇■ ✠	SW	SW ◇■ A ✠	SW ■	SW	SW
Weymouth	d						05 50						06 20	06 44						06 50			
Upwey	d						05 54						06 24	06 49						06 54			
Dorchester West	a													06 56									
Dorchester South	d						06 02						06 32							07 02			
Moreton (Dorset)	d						06 09						06 39							07 09			
Wool	d						06 15						06 45							07 15			
Wareham	d						06 22						06 52							07 22			
Holton Heath	d						06 26													07 26			
Hamworthy	d						06 31						06 59							07 31			
Poole ■	a						06 38						07 06							07 38			
	d						06 39						07 09					07 20		07 39			
Parkstone (Dorset)	d						06 43						07 13					07 24		07 43			
Branksome	d						06 47						07 17					07 27		07 47			
Bournemouth	a						06 54						07 24					07 32		07 54			
	d			06 30		06 34	06 56					07 04	07 26			07 30		07 34		07 59			
Pokesdown	d					06 38						07 08						07 38					
Christchurch	d					06 42						07 12						07 42					
Hinton Admiral	d					06 47						07 17						07 47					
New Milton	d					06 51						07 21						07 51					
Sway	d					06 56						07 26						07 56					
Brockenhurst ■	a			06 44		07 01						07 31				07 44		08 01		08 14			
	d			06 45		07 03						07 33				07 50		08 03		08 15			
Beaulieu Road	d																	08 08					
Ashurst New Forest	d					07 11						07 41						08 12					
Totton	d					07 16						07 46						08 17					
Salisbury	d								06 50										07 50				
Dean	d								07 02										08 02				
Mottisfont & Dunbridge	d								07 08										08 08				
Romsey	d	07 07							07 13								08 07		08 13				
Redbridge	d								07 23										08 21				
Millbrook (Hants)	d								07 26										08 25			←	
Southampton Central	a			06 59		07 21	07 25		07 30			07 51	07 55			08 03		08 23	08 27	08 28		08 27	
	d		07 10	07 15		07 30			07 35	07 38		08 00				08 15		08 48	08 35	08 30		08 35	
St Denys	d								07 40	07 43								→	→			08 40	
Swaythling	d								07 43	07 46												08 43	
Southampton Airport Pkwy	d		07 18	07 22		07 38			07 46	07 49		08 08				08 22				08 38		08 46	
Portsmouth Harbour	d							06 50							07 23						07 55		08 05
Portsmouth & Southsea	d							06 55							07 28						08 00		08 10
Fratton	d							06 59							07 32						08 04		08 14
Hilsea	d							07 03							07 36						08 08		08 18
Cosham	d							07 08							07 41						08 13		08 24
Portchester	d							07 13							07 46						08 18		08 28
Fareham	d							07 20							07 52						08 24		08 33
Botley	d							07 28							08 00						08 31		08 41
Hedge End	d							07 32							08 05						08 36		08 45
Eastleigh ■	a	07 20	07 21					07 38	07 49	07 53					08 11		08 20				08 42	08 49	08 51
	d	07 21	07 30					07 43	07 50	07 54					08 13		08 21				08 43	08 50	08 54
Chandlers Ford	d								07 55													08 55	
Romsey	a	07 52							08 03								08 51					09 03	
Shawford	d		07 36		←			07 49		08 00					08 20						08 49		
Winchester	d		07 42	07 31	07 42	07 48		07 55		08 06	08 12	08 18			08 26	08 31				08 48	08 55		09 02
Micheldever	d		→					08 03													09 03		
Basingstoke	a			07 46	07 58			08 14		08 22	08 26	08 34			08 42	08 46					09 14		09 19
	d			07 47	08 05			08 16		08 24	08 28	08 35			08 43	08 47					09 16		
Reading ■	a			08 04							08 44					09 04							
Fleet	d				08 22					08 40					08 54						09 27		
Farnborough (Main)	d				08 28					08 46					09 00						09 32		
Woking	a				08 38			08 34		08 58		08 53								09 22	09 41		
Clapham Junction ■	a											09 14			09 26					09 43			
London Waterloo ■ ⊖	a				09 10	08 50		09 03		09 29		09 25			09 38					09 53	10 08		

A ✠ from Bournemouth

For services from Brockenhurst - Lymington refer to Table T159

Table T158-R

Mondays to Fridays
8 October to 7 December

Weymouth, Bournemouth, Romsey, Southampton and Basingstoke - London

		SW ◇■ ✠	SW ◇■ ✠	SW ◇■ ✠	SW ■	XC ■ ■ ✠	SW ■	SN	SW ◇■ A ✠	SW ■	SW ■	XC ◇■ ✠	SW ◇■	SW ◇■ A ✠	SW ◇■	GW ◇	XC ◇■ ✠	SW ◇■ A ✠	SW ■	SW ■	SW ■	SW ◇■
Weymouth	d				07 25				07 55					08 20		08 53		09 03				
Upwey	d				07 29				07 59					08 24		08 58						
Dorchester West	a															09 05						
Dorchester South	d				07 37				08 07					08 33				09 13				
Moreton (Dorset)	d				07 44				08 14					08 39								
Wool	d				07 50				08 20					08 45								
Wareham	d				07 57				08 27					08 53				09 28				
Holton Heath	d				08 01				08 31					08 56								
Hamworthy	d				08 06				08 36					09 01				09 35				
Poole ■	a				08 10				08 40					09 06				09 39				
	d		07 55		08 11				08 41				08 50	09 07				09 40				09 50
Parkstone (Dorset)	d		07 59		08 15				08 45				08 54					09 44				09 54
Branksome	d		08 02		08 19				08 49				08 57					09 48				09 57
Bournemouth	a		08 07		08 24				08 54				09 02	09 16				09 53				10 02
	d		08 10		08 25	08 45			08 59				09 05	09 18			09 45	09 55				10 05
Pokesdown	d		08 14		08 29								09 09	09 22								10 09
Christchurch	d		08 18		08 33								09 13	09 26								10 13
Hinton Admiral	d		08 24		08 38								09 18									10 18
New Milton	d		08 29		08 42								09 22	09 33								10 22
Sway	d		08 34		08 47								09 27									10 27
Brockenhurst ■	a		08 39		08 52	08 58			09 14				09 32	09 40			09 58	10 11				10 32
	d		08 41			09 00			09 15				09 33	09 41			10 00	10 12				10 33
Beaulieu Road	d																					
Ashurst New Forest	d		08 48										09 40									10 40
Totton	d		08 53										09 45									10 45
Salisbury	d										08 50										09 56	
Dean	d										09 02										10 08	
Mottisfont & Dunbridge	d										09 08										10 14	
Romsey	d						09 07				09 14								10 07		10 20	
Redbridge	d										09 21										10 27	
Millbrook (Hants)	d	←									09 25										10 31	
Southampton Central	a	08 23	08 58			09 12			09 28		09 28		09 53	09 56			10 13	10 26			10 34	10 53
	d	08 48	09 00			09 16		09 26	09 30		09 35	09 46	09 55	10 00			10 17	10 30			10 35	10 55
St Denys	d	08 53									09 40										10 40	
Swaythling	d	08 56									09 43										10 43	
Southampton Airport Pkwy	d	08 59	09 08			09 23		09 34	09 38		09 46	09 55	10 03	10 08			10 24	10 38			10 46	11 03
Portsmouth Harbour	d									08 59										09 59		
Portsmouth & Southsea	d									09 04										10 04		
Fratton	d									09 08										10 08		
Hilsea	d									09 12										10 12		
Cosham	d									09 17										10 17		
Portchester	d									09 22										10 22		
Fareham	d									09 28										10 28		
Botley	d									09 35										10 35		
Hedge End	d									09 40										10 40		
Eastleigh ■	a	09 03					09 20	09 38		09 47	09 49		10 06						10 20	10 46	10 49	11 06
	d	09 14					09 21			09 47	09 50		10 14						10 21	10 47	10 50	11 14
Chandlers Ford	d										09 55										10 55	
Romsey	a						09 51				10 03								10 59		11 03	
Shawford	d	09 19		←									10 20		←							11 19
Winchester	d	09 25	09 18	09 25		09 32			09 48	09 57		10 03	10 25	10 18	10 25		10 33	10 48		10 56		11 25
Micheldever	d	→								10 05			→							11 05		→
Basingstoke	a		09 35	09 41		09 46				10 15		10 18		10 34	10 42		10 47			11 15		
	d		09 36	09 43		09 49				10 17		10 19		10 35	10 43		10 49			11 17		
Reading ■	a					10 07						10 37					11 06					
Fleet	d			09 54											10 54							
Farnborough (Main)	d			10 00						10 30					11 00					11 30		
Woking	a		09 54						10 20	10 39								11 19		11 39		
Clapham Junction ■	a		10 15	10 25										11 11	11 25							
London Waterloo ■ ⊖	a		10 23	10 34					10 49	11 08				11 20	11 34			11 49		12 08		

A ✠ from Bournemouth

For services from Brockenhurst - Lymington refer to Table T159

Table T158-R

Mondays to Fridays
8 October to 7 December

Weymouth, Bournemouth, Romsey, Southampton and Basingstoke - London

		SW	SW	XC	SW	SN	SW	SW	SW	XC	SW	SW	SW	XC	SW	GW	SW	SW	SW	SW	SW	SW	XC
		◇■ A 🍴	◇■	◇■ 🍴	■		◇■ A 🍴	■	■	■ ■ 🍴	◇■	◇■ A 🍴	◇■	◇■ 🍴	◇■ A 🍴	◇	■	■	■	◇■	◇■ A 🍴	◇■	◇■ 🍴
Weymouth	d	09 20					10 03					10 20			11 02	11 10					11 20		
Upwey	d	09 24										10 24				11 15					11 24		
Dorchester West	a															11 22							
Dorchester South	d	09 33					10 13					10 33			11 13						11 33		
Moreton (Dorset)	d	09 39										10 39									11 39		
Wool	d	09 45										10 45									11 45		
Wareham	d	09 53					10 28					10 53			11 28						11 53		
Holton Heath	d	09 56										10 56									11 56		
Hamworthy	d	10 01					10 35					11 01			11 35						12 01		
Poole	a	10 06					10 39					11 06			11 39						12 06		
	d	10 07					10 40				10 50	11 07			11 40					11 50	12 07		
Parkstone (Dorset)	d						10 44				10 54				11 44					11 54			
Branksome	d						10 48				10 57				11 48					11 57			
Bournemouth	a	10 17					10 54				11 02	11 17			11 54					12 02	12 17		
	d	10 22		10 45			10 59				11 05	11 22		11 45	11 59					12 05	12 22		12 45
Pokesdown	d	10 26									11 09	11 26								12 09	12 26		
Christchurch	d	10 30									11 13	11 30								12 13	12 30		
Hinton Admiral	d										11 18									12 18			
New Milton	d	10 37									11 22	11 37								12 22	12 37		
Sway	d										11 27									12 27			
Brockenhurst	a	10 44		10 58			11 14				11 32	11 44		11 58	12 14					12 32	12 44		12 58
	d	10 45		11 00			11 15				11 33	11 45		12 00	12 15					12 33	12 45		13 00
Beaulieu Road	d										11 38												
Ashurst New Forest	d										11 42									12 40			
Totton	d										11 47									12 45			
Salisbury	d								10 56										11 56				
Dean	d								11 08										12 08				
Mottisfont & Dunbridge	d								11 14										12 14				
Romsey	d				11 07				11 20								12 07		12 20				
Redbridge	d								11 27										12 27				
Millbrook (Hants)	d								11 31										12 31				
Southampton Central	a	10 58		11 13			11 28		11 34		11 53	11 58		12 14	12 28				12 34	12 52	12 58		13 13
	d	11 00		11 17		11 26	11 30		11 35	11 46	11 55	12 00		12 17	12 30				12 35	12 55	13 00		13 16
St Denys	d								11 40										12 40				
Swaythling	d								11 43										12 43				
Southampton Airport Pkwy	d	11 08		11 24		11 34	11 38		11 46	11 53	12 03	12 08		12 24	12 38				12 46	13 03	13 08		13 23
Portsmouth Harbour	d							10 59										11 59					
Portsmouth & Southsea	d							11 04										12 04					
Fratton	d							11 08										12 08					
Hilsea	d							11 12										12 12					
Cosham	d							11 17										12 17					
Portchester	d							11 22										12 22					
Fareham	d							11 28										12 28					
Botley	d							11 35										12 35					
Hedge End	d							11 40										12 40					
Eastleigh	a				11 20	11 37		11 46	11 49		12 06						12 20	12 46	12 49	13 06			
	d				11 21			11 47	11 50		12 14						12 21	12 47	12 50	13 14			
Chandlers Ford	d								11 55										12 55				
Romsey	a				11 51				12 03								12 51		13 03				
Shawford	d		←								12 19		←							13 19		←	
Winchester	d	11 18	11 25	11 33			11 48	11 56		12 02	12 25	12 18	12 25	12 33	12 48			12 56		13 25	13 18	13 25	13 32
Micheldever	d							12 05			→							13 05		→			
Basingstoke	a	11 34	11 41	11 47				12 15		12 17		12 34	12 41	12 47				13 15			13 34	13 41	13 46
	d	11 35	11 43	11 49				12 17		12 18		12 35	12 43	12 49				13 17			13 35	13 43	13 49
Reading	a			12 05						12 37				13 06									14 05
Fleet	d		11 54										12 54									13 54	
Farnborough (Main)	d		12 00					12 31					13 00					13 30				14 00	
Woking	a						12 19	12 40							13 19			13 39					
Clapham Junction	a	12 11	12 25									13 11	13 25								14 11	14 25	
London Waterloo ⊖	a	12 20	12 34				12 49	13 08				13 20	13 34		13 49			14 08			14 20	14 34	

A 🍴 from Bournemouth

For services from Brockenhurst - Lymington refer to Table T159

Table T158-R

Mondays to Fridays
8 October to 7 December

Weymouth, Bournemouth, Romsey, Southampton and Basingstoke - London

		SW	SW	SW	SW	XC	SW	SW	SW	XC	SW	GW	SW	SW	SW	SW	SW	SW	XC	SW	SW	SW
		◇■ A 🍴	■	■	■	◇■ 🍴	◇■	◇■ A 🍴	◇■	◇■ 🍴	◇■ A 🍴	◇	■	■	■	◇■	◇■ A 🍴	◇■	◇■ 🍴	◇■ A 🍴	■	■
Weymouth	d	12 03						12 20			13 03	13 10					13 20			14 03		
Upwey	d							12 24				13 15					13 24					
Dorchester West	a											13 22										
Dorchester South	d	12 13						12 33			13 13						13 33			14 13		
Moreton (Dorset)	d							12 39									13 39					
Wool	d							12 45									13 45					
Wareham	d	12 28						12 53			13 28						13 53			14 28		
Holton Heath	d							12 56									13 56					
Hamworthy	d	12 35						13 01			13 35						14 01			14 35		
Poole	a	12 39						13 06			13 39						14 06			14 39		
	d	12 40					12 50	13 07			13 40					13 50	14 07			14 40		
Parkstone (Dorset)	d	12 44					12 54				13 44					13 54				14 44		
Branksome	d	12 48					12 57				13 48					13 57				14 48		
Bournemouth	a	12 54					13 02	13 17			13 54					14 02	14 17			14 54		
	d	12 59					13 05	13 22		13 45	13 59					14 05	14 22		14 45	14 59		
Pokesdown	d						13 09	13 26								14 09	14 26					
Christchurch	d						13 13	13 30								14 13	14 30					
Hinton Admiral	d						13 18									14 18						
New Milton	d						13 22	13 37								14 22	14 37					
Sway	d						13 27									14 27						
Brockenhurst	a	13 14					13 32	13 44		13 58	14 14					14 32	14 44		14 58	15 14		
	d	13 15					13 33	13 45		14 00	14 15					14 33	14 45		15 00	15 15		
Beaulieu Road	d						13 38															
Ashurst New Forest	d						13 42									14 40						
Totton	d						13 47									14 45						
Salisbury	d				12 56										13 50							
Dean	d				13 08										14 02							
Mottisfont & Dunbridge	d				13 14										14 08							
Romsey	d		13 07		13 20								14 07		14 13						15 07	
Redbridge	d				13 27										14 21							
Millbrook (Hants)	d				13 31										14 24							
Southampton Central	a	13 28			13 34		13 53	13 58		14 13	14 28				14 28	14 53	14 58		15 13	15 28		
	d	13 30			13 35	13 46	13 55	14 00		14 17	14 30				14 36	14 55	15 00		15 16	15 30		
St Denys	d				13 40										14 40							
Swaythling	d				13 43										14 43							
Southampton Airport Pkwy	d	13 38			13 46	13 54	14 03	14 08		14 24	14 38				14 46	15 03	15 08		15 23	15 38		
Portsmouth Harbour	d			12 59										13 59								14 59
Portsmouth & Southsea	d			13 04										14 04								15 04
Fratton	d			13 08										14 08								15 08
Hilsea	d			13 12										14 12								15 12
Cosham	d			13 17										14 17								15 17
Portchester	d			13 22										14 22								15 22
Fareham	d			13 28										14 28								15 28
Botley	d			13 35										14 35								15 35
Hedge End	d			13 40										14 40								15 40
Eastleigh	a		13 20	13 46	13 49		14 06						14 20	14 46	14 49	15 06					15 20	15 46
	d		13 21	13 47	13 50		14 14						14 21	14 47	14 50	15 14					15 21	15 47
Chandlers Ford	d				13 55										14 55							
Romsey	a		13 51		14 03								14 51		15 03						15 51	
Shawford	d						14 19		←							15 19		←				
Winchester	d	13 48		13 56		14 03	14 25	14 18	14 25	14 33	14 48			14 56		15 25	15 18	15 25	15 32	15 48		15 56
Micheldever	d			14 05			→							15 05		→						16 05
Basingstoke	a			14 15		14 18		14 34	14 41	14 47				15 15			15 34	15 41	15 46			16 15
	d			14 17		14 19		14 35	14 43	14 49				15 17			15 35	15 43	15 48			16 17
Reading	a					14 36				15 05									16 04			
Fleet	d								14 54									15 54				
Farnborough (Main)	d			14 30					15 00					15 30				16 00				16 30
Woking	a	14 20		14 39							15 19			15 39						16 19		16 39
Clapham Junction	a							15 11	15 25								16 11	16 25				
London Waterloo ⊖	a	14 49		15 08				15 20	15 34		15 49			16 07			16 20	16 34		16 49		17 08

A 🍴 from Bournemouth

For services from Brockenhurst - Lymington refer to Table T159

Table T158-R

Mondays to Fridays

8 October to 7 December

Weymouth, Bournemouth, Romsey, Southampton and Basingstoke - London

		SW	XC	SW	SW	SW	XC	SW	GW	SW	SW	SW	SW	SW	SW	XC	SW	SW	SW	SW	SW	XC	SW
		1	◇1 [trolley]	◇1	◇1 A [trolley]	◇1	◇1 [trolley]	◇1 A [trolley]	◇	1	1	1	◇1	◇1 A [trolley]	◇1	◇1 [trolley]	◇1 A [trolley]		1		1	◇1 [trolley]	◇1
Weymouth	d				14 20			15 03	15 08					15 20			16 03						
Upwey	d				14 24				15 13					15 24									
Dorchester West	a								15 20														
Dorchester South	d				14 33			15 13						15 33			16 13						
Moreton (Dorset)	d				14 39									15 39									
Wool	d				14 45									15 45									
Wareham	d				14 53			15 28						15 53			16 28						
Holton Heath	d				14 56									15 56									
Hamworthy	d				15 01			15 35						16 01			16 35						
Poole 4	a				15 06			15 39						16 06			16 39						
	d			14 50	15 07			15 40					15 50	16 07			16 40						16 50
Parkstone (Dorset)	d			14 54				15 44					15 54				16 44						16 54
Branksome	d			14 57				15 48					15 57				16 48						16 57
Bournemouth	a			15 02	15 17			15 54					16 02	16 17			16 54						17 03
	d			15 05	15 22		15 45	15 59					16 05	16 22		16 45	16 59						17 05
Pokesdown	d			15 09	15 26								16 09	16 26									17 09
Christchurch	d			15 13	15 30								16 13	16 30									17 13
Hinton Admiral	d			15 18									16 18										17 18
New Milton	d			15 22	15 37								16 22	16 37									17 22
Sway	d			15 27									16 27										17 27
Brockenhurst 3	a			15 32	15 44		15 58	16 14					16 32	16 44		16 58	17 14						17 32
	d			15 33	15 45		16 00	16 15					16 33	16 45		17 00	17 15				17 20		17 33
Beaulieu Road	d																						17 38
Ashurst New Forest	d			15 40									16 40								17 28		17 42
Totton	d			15 45									16 45								17 33		17 47
Salisbury	d	14 56										15 56								16 56			
Dean	d	15 08										16 08								17 08			
Mottisfont & Dunbridge	d	15 14										16 14								17 14			
Romsey	d	15 20								16 07		16 20						17 07		17 20			
Redbridge	d	15 27										16 27								17 27			
Millbrook (Hants)	d	15 31										16 31								17 31			
Southampton Central ⛴	a	15 34		15 53	15 58		16 13	16 28				16 34	16 51	16 58		17 13	17 28			17 34	17 40		17 52
	d	15 35	15 46	15 55	16 00		16 17	16 30				16 35	16 52	17 00		17 17	17 30			17 35		17 46	17 55
St Denys	d	15 40										16 40	16 57							17 40			
Swaythling	d	15 43										16 43	17 00							17 43			
Southampton Airport Pkwy ✈	d	15 46	15 53	16 03	16 08		16 24	16 38				16 46	17 04	17 08		17 24	17 38			17 46		17 53	18 03
Portsmouth Harbour ⛴	d										15 59								16 59				
Portsmouth & Southsea	d										16 04								17 04				
Fratton	d										16 08								17 08				
Hilsea	d										16 12								17 12				
Cosham	d										16 17								17 17				
Portchester	d										16 22								17 22				
Fareham	d										16 28								17 28				
Botley	d										16 35								17 35				
Hedge End	d										16 40								17 40				
Eastleigh 8	a	15 49		16 08						16 20	16 46	16 49	17 07					17 20	17 46	17 49			18 06
	d	15 50		16 14						16 21	16 47	16 50	17 14					17 21	17 47	17 50			18 14
Chandlers Ford	d	15 55										16 55								17 55			
Romsey	a	16 03								16 51		17 03						17 51		18 03			
Shawford	d			16 19		←							17 19		←								18 19
Winchester	d		16 02	16 25	16 18	16 25	16 33	16 48			16 56		17 25	17 18	17 25	17 33	17 48		17 57			18 02	18 25
Micheldever	d			→							17 05		→						18 05				→
Basingstoke	a		16 17		16 34	16 41	16 47				17 15			17 33	17 42	17 47			18 15			18 17	
	d		16 18		16 36	16 43	16 49				17 17			17 35	17 43	17 49			18 17			18 18	
Reading 7	a		16 34				17 08									18 04						18 35	
Fleet	d					16 54									17 54								
Farnborough (Main)	d					17 00					17 30				18 00				18 31				
Woking	a							17 20			17 39						18 19		18 40				
Clapham Junction 10	a				17 11	17 25								18 11	18 25								
London Waterloo 15 ⊖	a				17 21	17 38		17 52			18 09			18 23	18 34		18 50		19 09				

A [trolley] from Bournemouth

For services from Brockenhurst - Lymington refer to Table T159

Table T158-R

Mondays to Fridays

8 October to 7 December

Weymouth, Bournemouth, Romsey, Southampton and Basingstoke - London

		SW	SW	XC	SW	SW	SW	SW	SW	SW	SW	SW	SW	GW	XC	SW	SW	SW	SW	SW	SW	SW	XC
		◇1 A [trolley]	◇1	◇1 [trolley]	1	1	◇1 A [trolley]	1	1	1	◇1	◇1 A [trolley]	◇1	◇	◇1 [trolley]	◇1 A [trolley]	1	1	1	◇1	◇1 A [trolley]	◇1	◇1
Weymouth	d	16 20					17 03					17 20		17 30		18 03					18 20		
Upwey	d	16 24										17 24		17 35							18 24		
Dorchester West	a													17 42									
Dorchester South	d	16 33					17 13					17 33				18 13					18 33		
Moreton (Dorset)	d	16 39										17 39									18 39		
Wool	d	16 45										17 45									18 45		
Wareham	d	16 53					17 28					17 53				18 28					18 53		
Holton Heath	d	16 56										17 56									18 56		
Hamworthy	d	17 01					17 35					18 01				18 35					19 01		
Poole 4	a	17 06					17 39					18 06				18 39					19 06		
	d	17 07					17 40				17 50	18 07				18 40				18 50	19 07		
Parkstone (Dorset)	d						17 44				17 54					18 44				18 54			
Branksome	d						17 48				17 57					18 48				18 57			
Bournemouth	a	17 18					17 54				18 02	18 17				18 55				19 02	19 17		
	d	17 22		17 45			17 59				18 05	18 22			18 45	18 59				19 05	19 22		19 45
Pokesdown	d	17 26									18 09	18 26								19 09	19 26		
Christchurch	d	17 30									18 13	18 30								19 13	19 30		
Hinton Admiral	d										18 18									19 18			
New Milton	d	17 37									18 22	18 37								19 22	19 37		
Sway	d										18 27									19 27			
Brockenhurst 3	a	17 44		17 58			18 14				18 32	18 44			18 58	19 14				19 32	19 44		19 58
	d	17 45		18 00			18 15				18 33	18 45			19 00	19 15				19 33	19 45		20 00
Beaulieu Road	d										18 38												
Ashurst New Forest	d										18 42									19 41			
Totton	d										18 47									19 46			
Salisbury	d									17 56									18 56				
Dean	d									18 08									19 08				
Mottisfont & Dunbridge	d									18 14									19 14				
Romsey	d				18 07					18 20							19 07		19 20				
Redbridge	d									18 27									19 27				
Millbrook (Hants)	d									18 31									19 31				
Southampton Central ⛴	a	17 58		18 13			18 28			18 34	18 53	18 58			19 13	19 28			19 34	19 51	19 58		20 13
	d	18 00		18 15		18 17	18 30			18 35	18 55	19 00			19 16	19 30			19 35	19 55	20 00		20 17
St Denys	d					18 22				18 40									19 40				
Swaythling	d					18 25				18 43									19 43				
Southampton Airport Pkwy ✈	d	18 08		18 22		18 28	18 38			18 46	19 03	19 08			19 23	19 38			19 46	20 03	20 08		20 24
Portsmouth Harbour ⛴	d							17 49	17 59									18 59					
Portsmouth & Southsea	d							17 54	18 04									19 04					
Fratton	d							17 58	18 08									19 08					
Hilsea	d							18 02	18 12									19 12					
Cosham	d							18 09	18 17									19 17					
Portchester	d							18 13	18 22									19 22					
Fareham	d							18 19	18 28									19 28					
Botley	d							18 27	18 35									19 35					
Hedge End	d							18 31	18 40									19 40					
Eastleigh 8	a				18 20	18 32		18 37	18 46	18 49	19 06						19 20	19 46	19 49	20 06			
	d				18 21	18 33			18 47	18 50	19 14						19 21	19 47	19 50	20 14			
Chandlers Ford	d									18 55									19 55				
Romsey	a				19 00					19 04							19 51		20 03				
Shawford	d		←								19 19		←							20 19		←	
Winchester	d	18 18	18 25	18 31		18a41	18 48		18 57		19 25	19 18	19 25		19 32	19 48		19 56		20 25	20 18	20 25	20 33
Micheldever	d								19 05		→							20 05		→			
Basingstoke	a	18 34	18 41	18 45					19 15			19 34	19 41		19 46			20 15			20 34	20 41	20 47
	d	18 36	18 43	18 47					19 17			19 35	19 43		19 49			20 17			20 36	20 43	20 49
Reading 7	a			19 04											20 05								21 06
Fleet	d		18 54										19 54									20 54	
Farnborough (Main)	d		19 00						19 32				20 00					20 30				21 00	
Woking	a						19 25		19 41							20 19		20 39				21 09	
Clapham Junction 10	a	19 11	19 26									20 11	20 25								21 16	21 29	
London Waterloo 15 ⊖	a	19 20	19 34				19 52		20 08			20 20	20 34			20 49		21 09			21 25	21 38	

A [trolley] from Bournemouth

For services from Brockenhurst - Lymington refer to Table T159

Weymouth, Bournemouth, Romsey, Southampton and Basingstoke - London

		SW	SW	SW	SW	SW	SW	SW	SW	SW	SW
		◇1	1	1	1	◇1	◇1	◇1	1	◇1	1
		A 🚌							B		
Weymouth	d	19 03					19 20				
Upwey	d						19 24				
Dorchester West	a										
Dorchester South	d	19 13					19 37				
Moreton (Dorset)	d						19 43				
Wool	d						19 49				
Wareham	d	19 28					19 57				
Holton Heath	d										
Hamworthy	d	19 35					20 03				
Poole 4	a	19 39					20 08				
	d	19 40				19 50	20 09				
Parkstone (Dorset)	d	19 44				19 54					
Branksome	d	19 48				19 57					
Bournemouth	a	19 54				20 02	20 19				
	d	19 59				20 05	20 22				
Pokesdown	d					20 09	20 26				
Christchurch	d					20 13	20 30				
Hinton Admiral	d					20 18					
New Milton	d					20 22	20 37				
Sway	d					20 27					
Brockenhurst 3	a	20 14				20 32	20 44				
	d	20 15				20 33	20 45				
Beaulieu Road	d					20 38					
Ashurst New Forest	d					20 42					
Totton	d					20 47					
Salisbury	d				19 56						
Dean	d				20 08						
Mottisfont & Dunbridge	d				20 14						
Romsey	d		20 07		20 20				21 07		
Redbridge	d				20 27						
Millbrook (Hants)	d				20 31						
Southampton Central ⛴	a	20 28			20 34	20 53	20 58				
	d	20 30			20 35	20 55	21 00			21 30	
St Denys	d				20 40						
Swaythling	d				20 43						
Southampton Airport Pkwy ✈	d	20 38			20 46	21 03	21 08			21 38	
Portsmouth Harbour ⛴	d			19 59							20 59
Portsmouth & Southsea	d			20 04							21 04
Fratton	d			20 08							21 08
Hilsea	d			20 12							21 12
Cosham	d			20 17							21 17
Portchester	d			20 22							21 22
Fareham	d			20 28							21 28
Botley	d			20 35							21 35
Hedge End	d			20 40							21 40
Eastleigh 8	a		20 20	20 46	20 49	21 06			21 20		21 46
	d		20 21	20 47	20 50	21 14			21 21		21 47
Chandlers Ford	d				20 55						
Romsey	a		20 51		21 03				21 51		
Shawford	d			20 53		21 20		←			
Winchester	d	20 48		20 59		21 26	21 18	21 26		21 48	21 56
Micheldever	d			21 07		→					22 05
Basingstoke	a			21 21			21 34	21 42			22 15
	d			21 24			21 35	21 43			22 24
Reading 7	a										
Fleet	d			21 40				21 54			22 40
Farnborough (Main)	d			21 46				22 00			22 46
Woking	a	21 19		21 58				22 09		22 19	22 58
Clapham Junction 10	a						22 13	22 29			
London Waterloo 15 ⊖	a	21 49		22 34			22 22	22 38		22 49	23 32

		SW	SW	SW	SW	GW	GW	SW	SW	SW	SW	SW
		1	◇1	◇1	◇1		◇	1	1	◇1	1	1
Weymouth	d			20 10		20 21						21 10
Upwey	d			20 14		20 26						21 14
Dorchester West	a					20 33						
Dorchester South	d			20 22								21 22
Moreton (Dorset)	d			20 28								21 28
Wool	d			20 34								21 34
Wareham	d			20 42								21 42
Holton Heath	d											
Hamworthy	d			20 48								21 48
Poole 4	a			20 53								21 53
	d			20 54								21 54
Parkstone (Dorset)	d			20 58								21 58
Branksome	d			21 01								22 01
Bournemouth	a			21 07								22 07
	d			21 12								22 12
Pokesdown	d			21 16								22 16
Christchurch	d			21 20								22 20
Hinton Admiral	d			21 25								22 25
New Milton	d			21 29								22 29
Sway	d			21 34								22 34
Brockenhurst 3	a			21 39								22 39
	d			21 40								22 40
Beaulieu Road	d											
Ashurst New Forest	d			21 47								22 47
Totton	d			21 52								22 52
Salisbury	d	20 56					21 32				21 56	
Dean	d	21 08									22 08	
Mottisfont & Dunbridge	d	21 14									22 14	
Romsey	d	21 20					21 50	22 07			22 20	
Redbridge	d	21 27									22 27	
Millbrook (Hants)	d	21 31									22 31	
Southampton Central ⛴	a	21 34		21 57			22 02				22 34	22 57
	d	21 35	21 55	22 00			22 04			22 30	22 35	23 00
St Denys	d	21 40									22 40	
Swaythling	d	21 43									22 43	
Southampton Airport Pkwy ✈	d	21 46	22 03	22 08			22 12			22 38	22 46	23 08
Portsmouth Harbour ⛴	d								21 54			
Portsmouth & Southsea	d								21 59			
Fratton	d								22 03			
Hilsea	d								22 07			
Cosham	d								22 12			
Portchester	d								22 17			
Fareham	d								22 20			
Botley	d								22 28			
Hedge End	d								22 33			
Eastleigh 8	a	21 49	22 06				22 15	22 21	22 41	22 41	22 49	23 11
	d	21 50	22 14					22 22		22 46	22 50	23 12
Chandlers Ford	d	21 55									22 55	
Romsey	a	22 03						22 51			23 04	
Shawford	d		22 20		←							23 18
Winchester	d		22 26	22 18	22 26					22 55		23 24
Micheldever	d		→									23 33
Basingstoke	a			22 34	22 42					23 11		23 43
	d			22 36	22 43					23 13		23 44
Reading 7	a											
Fleet	d				22 54							00 01
Farnborough (Main)	d				23 00							00 06
Woking	a			22 54	23 09					23 31		00 18
Clapham Junction 10	a			23 14	23 29					23 55		00 53
London Waterloo 15 ⊖	a			23 23	23 39					00 08		01 04

A 🚌 from Bournemouth
B not 7 December

For services from Brockenhurst - Lymington refer to Table T159

Table T158-R

Mondays to Fridays
8 October to 7 December

Weymouth, Bournemouth, Romsey, Southampton and Basingstoke - London

		SW	SW	SW	SW	SW
		1	1	1	◇1	1
Weymouth	d				22 10	23 10
Upwey	d				22 14	23 14
Dorchester West	a					
Dorchester South	d				22 22	23 22
Moreton (Dorset)	d				22 28	23 28
Wool	d				22 34	23 34
Wareham	d				22 42	23 42
Holton Heath	d					
Hamworthy	d				22 48	23 48
Poole 4	a				22 53	23 53
	d				22 54	23 54
Parkstone (Dorset)	d				22 58	
Branksome	d				23 01	
Bournemouth	a				23 07	00 03
	d				23 12	
Pokesdown	d				23 16	
Christchurch	d				23 20	
Hinton Admiral	d				23 25	
New Milton	d				23 29	
Sway	d				23 34	
Brockenhurst 3	a				23 39	
	d				23 40	
Beaulieu Road	d					
Ashurst New Forest	d				23 47	
Totton	d				23 52	
Salisbury	d					
Dean	d					
Mottisfont & Dunbridge	d					
Romsey	d	23 07	22 58			
Redbridge	d		23 05			
Millbrook (Hants)	d		23 09			
Southampton Central ⛴	a		23 11		23 57	
	d		23 20		23 59	
St Denys	d		23 25		00 04	
Swaythling	d		23 28		00 07	
Southampton Airport Pkwy ✈	d		23 31		00 10	
Portsmouth Harbour ⛴	d			23 24		
Portsmouth & Southsea	d			23 29		
Fratton	d			23 33		
Hilsea	d			23 37		
Cosham	d			23 42		
Portchester	d			23 47		
Fareham	d			23 53		
Botley	d			23 59		
Hedge End	d			00 05		
Eastleigh 8	a	23 21	23 34	00 11	00 14	
	d	23 22	23 36	00 19		
Chandlers Ford	d		23 41			
Romsey	a	23 55	23 48			
Shawford	d					
Winchester	d			00a28		
Micheldever	d					
Basingstoke	a					
	d					
Reading 7	a					
Fleet	d					
Farnborough (Main)	d					
Woking	a					
Clapham Junction 10	a					
London Waterloo 15 ⊖	a					

For services from Brockenhurst - Lymington refer to Table T159

Table T158-R

Saturdays
26 May to 8 December

Weymouth, Bournemouth, Romsey, Southampton and Basingstoke - London

		SW ■	SW ■	SW ◇■	XC ◇■	SW ■	SW ■	SW ■	SW ■	SW ■	SW ■	XC ◇■ ✠	SW ■	SW ■	SW ◇■ ✠	SW ■	SW ■	XC ◇■ A	XC ◇■ B ✠	SW ■	XC ◇■ ✠	SW ◇■ C ✠	SW ◇■ D ✠
Weymouth	d																					05 37	05 42
Upwey	d																						
Dorchester West	a																						
Dorchester South	d																					05 47	05 52
Moreton (Dorset)	d																						
Wool	d																					05 57	06 02
Wareham	d																					06 05	06 10
Holton Heath	d																					06 08	06 13
Hamworthy	d																					06 13	06 18
Poole ■	a																					06 21	06 23
	d														05 28							06 22	06 24
Parkstone (Dorset)	d														05 32							06 26	06 28
Branksome	d														05 35							06 29	06 31
Bournemouth	a														05 40							06 37	06 37
	d														05 42			06 25	06 25		06 37	06 42	06 42
Pokesdown	d														05 46							06 46	06 46
Christchurch	d														05 50							06 50	06 50
Hinton Admiral	d														05 55							06 55	06 55
New Milton	d														05 59							06 59	06 59
Sway	d														06 04							07 04	07 04
Brockenhurst ■	a														06 09			06 38	06 38		06 52	07 09	07 09
	d														06 10			06 39	06 39		06 55	07 10	07 10
Beaulieu Road	d																						
Ashurst New Forest	d														06 17							07 17	07 17
Totton	d													06 14	06 22							07 22	07 22
Salisbury	d								05 35														
Dean	d								05 47														
Mottisfont & Dunbridge	d								05 53														
Romsey	d								05 58														
Redbridge	d													06 16									
Millbrook (Hants)	d													06 20			←						
Southampton Central ⛴	a													06 22	06 27		06 22	06 52	06 52		07 08	07 27	07 27
	d				05 09	05 12		05 30		06 00		06 20		06 35	06 30		06 35	06 53	06 53	07 00	07 20	07 30	07 30
St Denys	d			00 04				05 35						→			06 40						
Swaythling	d			00 07				05 38									06 43						
Southampton Airport Pkwy ✈	d			00 10	05 16	05 20		05 41		06 08		06 27			06 38		06 46	07 01	07 01	07 08	07 27	07 38	07 38
Portsmouth Harbour ⛴	d										05 40		05 48										
Portsmouth & Southsea	d										05 44		05 53										
Fratton	d										05 48		05 57										
Hilsea	d												06 01										
Cosham	d						05 09				05 56		06 06										
Portchester	d						05 14						06 11										
Fareham	d						05 20				06 04		06 17										
Botley	d						05 27						06 24										
Hedge End	d		00 05				05 32						06 29										
Eastleigh ■	a		00 11	00 14		05 23	05 39	05 45		06 11	06 17		06 37		06 42		06 49			07 11			
	d		00 19			05 24		05 46		06 13			06 47		06 42		06 50			07 14			
Chandlers Ford	d								06 06								06 55						
Romsey	a								06 43								07 03						
Shawford	d							05 52					06 53			←				07 19			
Winchester	d		00a28		05 25	05 34		06 00		06 23		06 36	07 00		06 52	07 00		07 09	07 09	07 25	07 36	07 48	07 48
Micheldever	d							06 08					→			07 08							
Basingstoke	a				05 40	05 50		06 19		06 39		06 51			07 08	07 19		07 24	07 24	07 41	07 51		
	d				05 41	05 54		06 24		06 40		06 52			07 09	07 24		07 25	07 25	07 43	07 52		
Reading ■	a				06 00							07 08						07 42	07 42		08 08		
Fleet	d	00 01				06 10		06 40								07 40				07 54			
Farnborough (Main)	d	00 06				06 16		06 46								07 46				08 00			
Woking	a	00 18				06 28		06 58		06 58					07 27	07 58				08 09		08 21	08 21
Clapham Junction ■	a	00 53				06 57														08 30			
London Waterloo ■ ⊖	a	01 04				07 05		07 35		07 29					07 53	08 34				08 39		08 49	08 49

A until 21 July, from 13 October
B from 28 July until 6 October
C from 13 October. ✠ from Bournemouth
D until 6 October. ✠ from Bournemouth

For services from Brockenhurst - Lymington refer to Table T159

Table T158-R

Saturdays
26 May to 8 December

Weymouth, Bournemouth, Romsey, Southampton and Basingstoke - London

		SW ■	SW ■	SW ■	XC ◇■ A	XC ◇■ B ✠	SW ◇■	SW ■ C	SW ■ D	SW ◇■	GW ◇	XC ◇■ ✠	SW ◇■ E ✠	SW ■	SW ■	SW ■	SW ◇■	SW ◇■ E ✠	SW ◇■	XC ◇■ ✠	SW ◇■ E ✠	SW ■	SW ■
Weymouth	d							06 15	06 20		06 44		06 55					07 20			08 03		
Upwey	d							06 19	06 24		06 49		06 59					07 24					
Dorchester West	a										06 56												
Dorchester South	d							06 28	06 33				07 07					07 33			08 13		
Moreton (Dorset)	d							06 34	06 39				07 14					07 39					
Wool	d							06 40	06 45				07 20					07 45					
Wareham	d							06 48	06 53				07 27					07 53			08 28		
Holton Heath	d							06 51	06 56				07 31					07 56					
Hamworthy	d							06 56	07 01				07 36					08 01			08 35		
Poole ■	a							07 04	07 06				07 40					08 06			08 39		
	d						06 50	07 05	07 07				07 41				07 50	08 07			08 40		
Parkstone (Dorset)	d						06 54						07 45				07 54				08 44		
Branksome	d						06 57						07 49				07 57				08 48		
Bournemouth	a						07 02	07 17	07 17				07 54				08 02	08 17			08 54		
	d						07 05	07 22	07 22			07 47	07 59				08 05	08 22		08 47	08 59		
Pokesdown	d						07 09	07 26	07 26								08 09	08 26					
Christchurch	d						07 13	07 30	07 30								08 13	08 30					
Hinton Admiral	d						07 18										08 18						
New Milton	d						07 22	07 37	07 37								08 22	08 37					
Sway	d						07 27										08 27						
Brockenhurst ■	a						07 32	07 44	07 44			08 00	08 14				08 32	08 44		09 00	09 14		
	d						07 33	07 45	07 45			08 02	08 15				08 33	08 45		09 02	09 15		
Beaulieu Road	d																						
Ashurst New Forest	d						07 40										08 40						
Totton	d						07 45										08 45						
Salisbury	d			06 50												07 50							
Dean	d			07 02												08 02							
Mottisfont & Dunbridge	d			07 08												08 08							
Romsey	d	07 07		07 13										08 07		08 13						09 07	
Redbridge	d			07 21												08 21							
Millbrook (Hants)	d			07 24												08 24							
Southampton Central ⛴	a			07 27			07 52	07 59	07 59			08 15	08 28			08 28	08 52	08 58		09 15	09 28		
	d			07 35	07 47	07 47	07 55	08 00	08 00			08 20	08 30			08 35	08 55	09 00		09 18	09 30		
St Denys	d			07 40												08 40							
Swaythling	d			07 43												08 43							
Southampton Airport Pkwy ✈	d			07 46	07 54	07 54	08 03	08 08	08 08			08 27	08 38			08 46	09 03	09 08		09 25	09 38		
Portsmouth Harbour ⛴	d		06 59												07 59								08 59
Portsmouth & Southsea	d		07 04												08 04								09 04
Fratton	d		07 08												08 08								09 08
Hilsea	d		07 12												08 12								09 12
Cosham	d		07 17												08 17								09 17
Portchester	d		07 22												08 22								09 22
Fareham	d		07 28												08 28								09 28
Botley	d		07 35												08 35								09 35
Hedge End	d		07 40												08 40								09 40
Eastleigh ■	a	07 20	07 46	07 49			08 06							08 20	08 46	08 49	09 06					09 20	09 46
	d	07 21	07 47	07 50			08 14							08 21	08 47	08 50	09 14					09 21	09 47
Chandlers Ford	d			07 55												08 55							
Romsey	a	07 51		08 03										08 51		09 03						09 51	
Shawford	d						08 19			←							09 19		←				
Winchester	d		07 56		08 03	08 03	08 25	08 18	08 18	08 25		08 36	08 48		08 57		09 25	09 18	09 25	09 34	09 48		09 56
Micheldever	d		08 05				→								09 05		→						10 05
Basingstoke	a		08 15		08 17	08 17		08 34	08 34	08 41		08 50			09 15			09 34	09 41	09 48			10 15
	d		08 17		08 19	08 19		08 36	08 36	08 43		08 52			09 17			09 35	09 43	09 52			10 17
Reading ■	a				08 35	08 35						09 08								10 08			
Fleet	d									08 54									09 54				
Farnborough (Main)	d		08 30							09 00					09 30				10 00				10 30
Woking	a		08 39										09 19		09 39						10 19		10 39
Clapham Junction ■	a							09 11	09 11	09 25								10 11	10 25				
London Waterloo ■ ⊖	a		09 08					09 20	09 20	09 34			09 49		10 08			10 21	10 34		10 49		11 08

A until 21 July, from 13 October
B from 28 July until 6 October
C from 13 October
D until 6 October
E ✠ from Bournemouth

For services from Brockenhurst - Lymington refer to Table T159

Table T158-R

Saturdays

26 May to 8 December

Weymouth, Bournemouth, Romsey, Southampton and Basingstoke - London

		SW	XC	SW	SW	SW	GW	XC	SW	SW	SW	SW	SW	SW	SW	XC	SW	SW	SW	SW	XC	SW
		■	◇■	◇■	◇■	◇■	◇	◇■	◇■	■	■	■	◇■	◇■	◇■	◇■	◇■	■	■	■	◇■	◇■
					A				A					A			A					
			✠		✠			✠	✠					✠		✠	✠				✠	
Weymouth	d				08 20		08 53		09 03					09 20			10 03					
Upwey	d				08 24		08 58							09 24								
Dorchester West	a						09 05															
Dorchester South	d				08 33				09 13					09 33			10 13					
Moreton (Dorset)	d				08 39									09 39								
Wool	d				08 45									09 45								
Wareham	d				08 53				09 28					09 53			10 28					
Holton Heath	d				08 56									09 56								
Hamworthy	d				09 01				09 35					10 01			10 35					
Poole ■	a				09 07				09 39					10 06			10 39					
	d			08 50	09 07				09 40				09 50	10 07			10 40					10 50
Parkstone (Dorset)	d			08 54					09 44				09 54				10 44					10 54
Branksome	d			08 57					09 48				09 57				10 48					10 57
Bournemouth	a			09 02	09 18				09 54				10 02	10 17			10 54					11 02
	d			09 05	09 22			09 47	09 59				10 05	10 22		10 47	10 59					11 05
Pokesdown	d			09 09	09 26								10 09	10 26								11 09
Christchurch	d			09 13	09 30								10 13	10 30								11 13
Hinton Admiral	d			09 18									10 18									11 18
New Milton	d			09 22	09 37								10 22	10 37								11 22
Sway	d			09 27									10 27									11 27
Brockenhurst ■	a			09 32	09 44			10 00	10 14				10 32	10 44		11 00	11 14					11 32
	d			09 33	09 45			10 02	10 15				10 33	10 45		11 02	11 15					11 33
Beaulieu Road	d			09 38																		11 38
Ashurst New Forest	d			09 42									10 40									11 42
Totton	d			09 47									10 45									11 47
Salisbury	d	08 56										09 56								10 56		
Dean	d	09 08										10 08								11 08		
Mottisfont & Dunbridge	d	09 14										10 14								11 14		
Romsey	d	09 20								10 07		10 20						11 07		11 20		
Redbridge	d	09 27										10 27								11 27		
Millbrook (Hants)	d	09 31										10 31								11 31		
Southampton Central ⛴	a	09 34		09 53	09 58			10 14	10 28			10 34	10 53	10 58		11 15	11 28			11 34		11 53
	d	09 35	09 47	09 55	10 00			10 17	10 30			10 35	10 55	11 00		11 20	11 30			11 35	11 47	11 55
St Denys	d	09 40										10 40								11 40		
Swaythling	d	09 43										10 43								11 43		
Southampton Airport Pkwy ✈	d	09 46	09 54	10 03	10 08			10 24	10 38			10 46	11 03	11 08		11 27	11 38			11 46	11 54	12 03
Portsmouth Harbour ⛴	d										09 59								10 59			
Portsmouth & Southsea	d										10 04								11 04			
Fratton	d										10 08								11 08			
Hilsea	d										10 12								11 12			
Cosham	d										10 17								11 17			
Portchester	d										10 22								11 22			
Fareham	d										10 28								11 28			
Botley	d										10 35								11 35			
Hedge End	d										10 40								11 40			
Eastleigh ■	a	09 49		10 06						10 20	10 46	10 49	11 06					11 20	11 46	11 49		12 06
	d	09 50		10 14						10 21	10 47	10 50	11 14					11 21	11 47	11 50		12 14
Chandlers Ford	d	09 55										10 55								11 55		
Romsey	a	10 03								10 59		11 03						11 51		12 03		
Shawford	d			10 19		←							11 19		←							12 19
Winchester	d		10 03	10 25	10 18	10 25		10 33	10 48		10 56		11 25	11 18	11 25	11 36	11 48		11 56		12 03	12 25
Micheldever	d			→							11 05		→						12 05			→
Basingstoke	a		10 17		10 34	10 41		10 50			11 15			11 34	11 41	11 50			12 15		12 17	
	d		10 19		10 35	10 43		10 52			11 17			11 35	11 43	11 52			12 17		12 19	
Reading ■	a		10 35					11 07								12 08					12 35	
Fleet	d					10 54									11 54							
Farnborough (Main)	d					11 00					11 31				12 00				12 30			
Woking	a								11 19		11 40						12 19		12 39			
Clapham Junction ■	a				11 11	11 25								12 11	12 25							
London Waterloo ■ ⊖	a				11 20	11 34			11 49		12 11			12 21	12 34		12 51		13 11			

A ✠ from Bournemouth

For services from Brockenhurst - Lymington refer to Table T159

Table T158-R

Saturdays

26 May to 8 December

Weymouth, Bournemouth, Romsey, Southampton and Basingstoke - London

		SW	SW	XC	SW	GW	SW	SW	SW	SW	SW	SW	XC	SW	SW	SW	SW	SW	XC	SW	SW	SW	XC
		◇■	◇■	◇■	◇■	◇	■	■	■	◇■	◇■	◇■	◇■	◇■	◇■	■	■	■	◇■	◇■	◇■	◇■	◇■
		A			A						A			A	B						A		
		✠		✠	✠						✠		✠	✠					✠		✠		✠
Weymouth	d	10 20			11 03	11 14					11 20			12 03	12 10						12 20		
Upwey	d	10 24				11 19					11 24				12 15						12 24		
Dorchester West	a					11 27									12 22								
Dorchester South	d	10 33			11 13						11 33			12 13							12 33		
Moreton (Dorset)	d	10 39									11 39										12 39		
Wool	d	10 45									11 45										12 45		
Wareham	d	10 53			11 28						11 53			12 28							12 53		
Holton Heath	d	10 56									11 56										12 56		
Hamworthy	d	11 01			11 35						12 01			12 35							13 01		
Poole ■	a	11 06			11 39						12 06			12 39							13 06		
	d	11 07			11 40					11 50	12 07			12 40						12 50	13 07		
Parkstone (Dorset)	d				11 44					11 54				12 44						12 54			
Branksome	d				11 48					11 57				12 48						12 57			
Bournemouth	a	11 17			11 54					12 02	12 17			12 54						13 02	13 17		
	d	11 22		11 47	11 59					12 05	12 22		12 47	12 59						13 05	13 22		13 47
Pokesdown	d	11 26								12 09	12 26									13 09	13 26		
Christchurch	d	11 30								12 13	12 30									13 13	13 30		
Hinton Admiral	d									12 18										13 18			
New Milton	d	11 37								12 22	12 37									13 22	13 37		
Sway	d									12 27										13 27			
Brockenhurst ■	a	11 44		12 00	12 14					12 32	12 44		13 00	13 14						13 32	13 44		14 00
	d	11 45		12 02	12 15					12 33	12 45		13 02	13 15						13 33	13 45		14 02
Beaulieu Road	d																			13 38			
Ashurst New Forest	d									12 40										13 42			
Totton	d									12 45										13 47			
Salisbury	d								11 56									12 56					
Dean	d								12 08									13 08					
Mottisfont & Dunbridge	d								12 14									13 14					
Romsey	d						12 07		12 20							13 07		13 20					
Redbridge	d								12 27									13 27					
Millbrook (Hants)	d								12 31									13 31					
Southampton Central ⛴	a	11 58		12 15	12 28				12 34	12 51	12 58		13 15	13 28				13 34		13 53	13 58		14 15
	d	12 00		12 20	12 30				12 35	12 55	13 00		13 18	13 30				13 35	13 47	13 55	14 00		14 20
St Denys	d								12 40									13 40					
Swaythling	d								12 43									13 43					
Southampton Airport Pkwy ✈	d	12 08		12 27	12 38				12 46	13 03	13 08		13 25	13 38				13 46	13 54	14 03	14 08		14 27
Portsmouth Harbour ⛴	d							11 59									12 59						
Portsmouth & Southsea	d							12 04									13 04						
Fratton	d							12 08									13 08						
Hilsea	d							12 12									13 12						
Cosham	d							12 17									13 17						
Portchester	d							12 22									13 22						
Fareham	d							12 28									13 28						
Botley	d							12 35									13 35						
Hedge End	d							12 40									13 40						
Eastleigh ■	a						12 20	12 46	12 49	13 06						13 20	13 46	13 49		14 06			
	d						12 21	12 47	12 50	13 14						13 21	13 47	13 50		14 14			
Chandlers Ford	d								12 55									13 55					
Romsey	a						12 51		13 03							13 51		14 03					
Shawford	d		←							13 19		←								14 19		←	
Winchester	d	12 18	12 25	12 36	12 48			12 56		13 25	13 18	13 25	13 34	13 48			13 56		14 03	14 25	14 18	14 25	14 36
Micheldever	d							13 05		→							14 05			→			
Basingstoke	a	12 34	12 41	12 50				13 15			13 34	13 41	13 48				14 15		14 17		14 34	14 41	14 50
	d	12 35	12 43	12 52				13 17			13 35	13 43	13 52				14 17		14 19		14 35	14 43	14 52
Reading ■	a			13 08									14 08						14 35				15 07
Fleet	d		12 54									13 54										14 54	
Farnborough (Main)	d		13 00					13 30				14 00					14 30					15 00	
Woking	a				13 19			13 39						14 19			14 39						
Clapham Junction ■	a	13 11	13 25								14 11	14 25									15 11	15 25	
London Waterloo ■ ⊖	a	13 21	13 34		13 51			14 11			14 24	14 34		14 51			15 11				15 21	15 34	

A ✠ from Bournemouth

B until 8 September

For services from Brockenhurst - Lymington refer to Table T159

Table T158-R

Saturdays
26 May to 8 December

Weymouth, Bournemouth, Romsey, Southampton and Basingstoke - London

		SW ■	SN ■	SW ◇■ A 🍴	GW ◇	SW ■	SW ■	SW ◇■	SW ◇■ A 🍴	SW ◇■	XC ◇■ 🍴	SW ◇■ A 🍴	SW ■	SW ■	SW ■	XC ◇■ 🍴	SW ◇■	SW ◇■ A 🍴	SW ◇■	XC ◇■ 🍴	SW ◇■ A 🍴	GW ◇ B
Weymouth	d			13 03	13 10				13 20			14 03						14 20			15 03	15 08
Upwey	d				13 15				13 24									14 24				15 13
Dorchester West	a				13 22																	15 20
Dorchester South	d			13 13					13 33			14 13						14 33			15 13	
Moreton (Dorset)	d								13 39									14 39				
Wool	d								13 45									14 45				
Wareham	d			13 28					13 53			14 28						14 53			15 28	
Holton Heath	d								13 56									14 56				
Hamworthy	d			13 35					14 01			14 35						15 01			15 35	
Poole	a			13 39					14 06			14 39						15 06			15 39	
	d			13 40				13 50	14 07			14 40					14 50	15 07			15 40	
Parkstone (Dorset)	d			13 44				13 54				14 44					14 54				15 44	
Branksome	d			13 48				13 57				14 48					14 57				15 48	
Bournemouth	a			13 54				14 02	14 17			14 54					15 02	15 17			15 54	
	d			13 59				14 05	14 22		14 47	14 59					15 05	15 22		15 47	15 59	
Pokesdown	d							14 09	14 26								15 09	15 26				
Christchurch	d							14 13	14 30								15 13	15 30				
Hinton Admiral	d							14 18									15 18					
New Milton	d							14 22	14 37								15 22	15 37				
Sway	d							14 27									15 27					
Brockenhurst	a			14 14				14 32	14 44		15 00	15 14					15 32	15 44		16 00	16 14	
	d			14 15				14 33	14 45		15 02	15 15					15 33	15 45		16 02	16 15	
Beaulieu Road	d																15 38					
Ashurst New Forest	d							14 40									15 42					
Totton	d							14 45									15 47					
Salisbury	d						13 50								14 56							
Dean	d						14 02								15 08							
Mottisfont & Dunbridge	d						14 08								15 14							
Romsey	d	14 07					14 13						15 07		15 20							
Redbridge	d						14 21								15 27							
Millbrook (Hants)	d						14 24								15 31							
Southampton Central	a			14 28			14 28	14 51	14 58		15 15	15 28			15 34		15 53	15 58		16 15	16 28	
	d		14 26	14 30			14 35	14 55	15 00		15 18	15 30			15 35	15 47	15 55	16 00		16 20	16 30	
St Denys	d						14 40								15 40							
Swaythling	d						14 43								15 43							
Southampton Airport Pkwy	d		14 34	14 38			14 46	15 03	15 08		15 25	15 38			15 46	15 54	16 03	16 08		16 27	16 38	
Portsmouth Harbour	d					13 59								14 59								
Portsmouth & Southsea	d					14 04								15 04								
Fratton	d					14 08								15 08								
Hilsea	d					14 12								15 12								
Cosham	d					14 17								15 17								
Portchester	d					14 22								15 22								
Fareham	d					14 28								15 28								
Botley	d					14 35								15 35								
Hedge End	d					14 40								15 40								
Eastleigh	a	14 20	14 37			14 46	14 49	15 06					15 20	15 46	15 49		16 06					
	d	14 21				14 47	14 50	15 14					15 21	15 47	15 50		16 14					
Chandlers Ford	d						14 55								15 55							
Romsey	a	14 51					15 03						15 51		16 03							
Shawford	d							15 19		←							16 19		←			
Winchester	d			14 48		14 56		15 25	15 18	15 25	15 34	15 48		15 56		16 03	16 25	16 18	16 25	16 36	16 48	
Micheldever	d					15 05		→						16 05			→					
Basingstoke	a					15 15			15 34	15 41	15 49			16 15		16 17		16 34	16 41	16 50		
	d					15 17			15 35	15 43	15 52			16 17		16 18		16 35	16 43	16 52		
Reading	a										16 07					16 35				17 08		
Fleet	d									15 54									16 54			
Farnborough (Main)	d					15 30				16 00				16 30					17 00			
Woking	a			15 19		15 39						16 19		16 39							17 19	
Clapham Junction	a								16 11	16 25								17 11	17 25			
London Waterloo ⊖	a			15 51		16 07			16 20	16 34		16 49		17 07				17 20	17 34		17 49	

A 🍴 from Bournemouth
B from 15 September

For services from Brockenhurst - Lymington refer to Table T159

Table T158-R

Saturdays
26 May to 8 December

Weymouth, Bournemouth, Romsey, Southampton and Basingstoke - London

		SW ■	SW ■	SW ■	SW ◇■	SW ◇■ A 🍴	SW ◇■	XC ◇■ 🍴	SW ◇■ A 🍴	GW B	SW ■	SW ■	SW ■	SW ■	XC ◇■ 🍴	SW ■	SW ◇■	SW ◇■ A 🍴	SW ◇■	XC ◇■ 🍴	SW ◇■ A 🍴	SW ■	SW ■
Weymouth	d					15 20			16 03	16 08								16 20			17 03		
Upwey	d					15 24				16 13								16 24					
Dorchester West	a									16 21													
Dorchester South	d					15 33			16 13									16 33			17 13		
Moreton (Dorset)	d					15 39												16 39					
Wool	d					15 45												16 45					
Wareham	d					15 53			16 28									16 53			17 28		
Holton Heath	d					15 56												16 56					
Hamworthy	d					16 01			16 35									17 01			17 35		
Poole	a					16 06			16 39									17 06			17 39		
	d				15 50	16 07			16 40								16 50	17 07			17 40		
Parkstone (Dorset)	d				15 54				16 44								16 54				17 44		
Branksome	d				15 57				16 48								16 57				17 48		
Bournemouth	a				16 02	16 17			16 54								17 02	17 17			17 54		
	d				16 05	16 22		16 47	16 59								17 05	17 22		17 47	17 59		
Pokesdown	d				16 09	16 26											17 09	17 26					
Christchurch	d				16 13	16 30											17 13	17 30					
Hinton Admiral	d				16 18												17 18						
New Milton	d				16 22	16 37											17 22	17 37					
Sway	d				16 27												17 27						
Brockenhurst	a				16 32	16 44		17 00	17 14								17 32	17 44		18 00	18 14		
	d				16 33	16 45		17 02	17 15								17 33	17 45		18 02	18 15		
Beaulieu Road	d																17 38						
Ashurst New Forest	d				16 40												17 42						
Totton	d				16 45												17 47						
Salisbury	d			15 56									16 56										
Dean	d			16 08									17 08										
Mottisfont & Dunbridge	d			16 14									17 14										
Romsey	d	16 07		16 20							17 07		17 20									18 07	
Redbridge	d			16 27									17 27										
Millbrook (Hants)	d			16 31									17 31										
Southampton Central	a			16 34	16 51	16 58		17 15	17 28				17 34				17 53	17 58		18 15	18 28		
	d			16 35	16 55	17 00		17 20	17 30				17 35	17 39	17 47		17 55	18 00		18 20	18 30		
St Denys	d			16 40									17 40	17 44									
Swaythling	d			16 43									17 43	17 47									
Southampton Airport Pkwy	d			16 46	17 03	17 08		17 27	17 38				17 46	17 50	17 54		18 03	18 08		18 27	18 38		
Portsmouth Harbour	d		15 59									16 59											17 59
Portsmouth & Southsea	d		16 04									17 04											18 04
Fratton	d		16 08									17 08											18 08
Hilsea	d		16 12									17 12											18 12
Cosham	d		16 17									17 17											18 17
Portchester	d		16 22									17 22											18 22
Fareham	d		16 28									17 28											18 28
Botley	d		16 35									17 35											18 35
Hedge End	d		16 40									17 40											18 40
Eastleigh	a	16 20	16 46	16 49	17 06						17 20	17 46	17 49	17 54			18 06					18 20	18 46
	d	16 21	16 47	16 50	17 14						17 21	17 47	17 50	17 55			18 14					18 21	18 47
Chandlers Ford	d			16 55									17 55										
Romsey	a	16 51		17 03							17 51		18 03									19 00	
Shawford	d				17 19		←							18 03		←	18 19		←				
Winchester	d		16 56		17 25	17 18	17 25	17 36	17 48			17 56		18 09	18 03	18 09	18 25	18 18	18 25	18 36	18 48		18 56
Micheldever	d		17 05		→							18 05		→		18 18	→						19 05
Basingstoke	a		17 15			17 34	17 41	17 50				18 15			18 17	18 28		18 34	18 41	18 50			19 15
	d		17 17			17 35	17 43	17 52				18 17			18 18			18 35	18 43	18 52			19 17
Reading	a							18 07							18 35					19 08			
Fleet	d						17 54												18 54				
Farnborough (Main)	d		17 30				18 00					18 30							19 00				19 30
Woking	a		17 39						18 19			18 39									19 19		19 39
Clapham Junction	a					18 11	18 25											19 11	19 25				
London Waterloo ⊖	a		18 07			18 21	18 34		18 49			19 07						19 20	19 34		19 49		20 07

A 🍴 from Bournemouth
B until 8 September

For services from Brockenhurst - Lymington refer to Table T159

Table T158-R

Saturdays

26 May to 8 December

Weymouth, Bournemouth, Romsey, Southampton and Basingstoke - London

		SW ■	SW ◇■	SW ◇■	SW ◇■	GW ◇	XC ◇■ ⚒	SW ◇■ A ⚒	SW ■	SW ■	SW ■	SW ◇■	SW ◇■ A ⚒	SW ◇■	GW B	XC ◇■	SW ◇■ A ⚒	SW ■	SW ■	SW ■	SW ◇■	SW ◇■ A ⚒	SW ◇■
Weymouth	d			17 20		17 30		18 03					18 20		18 30		19 03					19 20	
Upwey	d			17 24		17 35							18 24		18 35							19 24	
Dorchester West	a					17 42									18 42								
Dorchester South	d			17 33				18 13					18 33				19 13					19 33	
Moreton (Dorset)	d			17 39									18 39									19 39	
Wool	d			17 45									18 45									19 45	
Wareham	d			17 53				18 28					18 53				19 28					19 53	
Holton Heath	d			17 56									18 56									19 56	
Hamworthy	d			18 01				18 35					19 01				19 35					20 01	
Poole ■	a			18 06				18 39					19 06				19 39					20 06	
	d		17 50	18 07				18 40				18 50	19 07				19 40				19 50	20 07	
Parkstone (Dorset)	d		17 54					18 44				18 54					19 44				19 54		
Branksome	d		17 57					18 48				18 57					19 48				19 57		
Bournemouth	a		18 02	18 17				18 54				19 02	19 17				19 54				20 02	20 17	
	d		18 05	18 22			18 47	18 59				19 05	19 22			19 47	19 59				20 05	20 22	
Pokesdown	d		18 09	18 26								19 09	19 26								20 09	20 26	
Christchurch	d		18 13	18 30								19 13	19 30								20 13	20 30	
Hinton Admiral	d		18 18									19 18									20 18		
New Milton	d		18 22	18 37								19 22	19 37								20 22	20 37	
Sway	d		18 27									19 27									20 27		
Brockenhurst ■	a		18 32	18 44			19 00	19 14				19 32	19 44			20 00	20 14				20 32	20 44	
	d		18 33	18 45			19 02	19 15				19 33	19 45			20 02	20 15				20 33	20 45	
Beaulieu Road	d																				20 38		
Ashurst New Forest	d		18 40									19 40									20 42		
Totton	d		18 45									19 45									20 47		
Salisbury	d	17 56									18 56									19 56			
Dean	d	18 08									19 08									20 08			
Mottisfont & Dunbridge	d	18 14									19 14									20 14			
Romsey	d	18 20							19 07		19 20							20 07		20 20			
Redbridge	d	18 27									19 27									20 27			
Millbrook (Hants)	d	18 31									19 31									20 31			
Southampton Central ⛴	a	18 34	18 51	18 58			19 15	19 28			19 34	19 51	19 58			20 15	20 28			20 34	20 53	20 58	
	d	18 35	18 55	19 00			19 20	19 30			19 35	19 55	20 00			20 19	20 30			20 35	20 55	21 00	
St Denys	d	18 40									19 40									20 40			
Swaythling	d	18 43									19 43									20 43			
Southampton Airport Pkwy ✈	d	18 46	19 03	19 08			19 27	19 38			19 46	20 03	20 08			20 26	20 38			20 46	21 03	21 08	
Portsmouth Harbour ⛴	d									18 59									19 59				
Portsmouth & Southsea	d									19 04									20 04				
Fratton	d									19 08									20 08				
Hilsea	d									19 12									20 12				
Cosham	d									19 17									20 17				
Portchester	d									19 22									20 22				
Fareham	d									19 28									20 28				
Botley	d									19 35									20 35				
Hedge End	d									19 40									20 40				
Eastleigh ■	a	18 49	19 06						19 20	19 46	19 49	20 06						20 20	20 46	20 49	21 06		
	d	18 50	19 14						19 21	19 47	19 50	20 14						20 21	20 47	20 50	21 14		
Chandlers Ford	d	18 55									19 55									20 55			
Romsey	a	19 04							19 51		20 03							20 51		21 03			
Shawford	d		19 19		←							20 19		←							21 19		←
Winchester	d		19 25	19 18	19 25		19 36	19 48		19 56		20 25	20 18	20 25		20 36	20 48		20 57		21 25	21 18	21 25
Micheldever	d		→							20 05		→							21 05		→		
Basingstoke	a			19 34	19 41		19 50			20 15			20 34	20 41		20 50			21 17			21 34	21 41
	d			19 35	19 43		19 52			20 17			20 35	20 43		20 52			21 24			21 35	21 43
Reading ■	a						20 09									21 08							
Fleet	d				19 54									20 54					21 40				21 54
Farnborough (Main)	d				20 00					20 30				21 00					21 46				22 00
Woking	a							20 19		20 39				21 09			21 20		21 58				22 09
Clapham Junction ■	a			20 11	20 25								21 16	21 29								22 14	22 29
London Waterloo ■ ⊖	a			20 20	20 34			20 45		21 08			21 24	21 38			21 49		22 34			22 22	22 38

A ⚒ from Bournemouth

B until 8 September

For services from Brockenhurst - Lymington refer to Table T159

Table T158-R

Saturdays

26 May to 8 December

Weymouth, Bournemouth, Romsey, Southampton and Basingstoke - London

		SW ■	SW ■	SW ■	SW ■	SW ■	SW ◇■	SW ■	GW	SW ■	SW ■	SW ■	SW ■	SW ■	SW ■	SW ■	SW ■	SW ■	SW ■
Weymouth	d						20 10		20 23					21 10				22 10	23 10
Upwey	d						20 14		20 28					21 14				22 14	23 14
Dorchester West	a								20 36										
Dorchester South	d						20 22							21 22				22 22	23 22
Moreton (Dorset)	d						20 28							21 28				22 28	23 28
Wool	d						20 34							21 34				22 34	23 34
Wareham	d						20 42							21 42				22 42	23 42
Holton Heath	d																		
Hamworthy	d						20 48							21 48				22 48	23 48
Poole ■	a						20 53							21 53				22 53	23 53
	d						20 54							21 54				22 54	23 54
Parkstone (Dorset)	d						20 58							21 58				22 58	
Branksome	d						21 01							22 01				23 01	
Bournemouth	a						21 07							22 07				23 07	00 03
	d						21 12							22 12				23 12	
Pokesdown	d						21 16							22 16				23 16	
Christchurch	d						21 20							22 20				23 20	
Hinton Admiral	d						21 25							22 25				23 25	
New Milton	d						21 29							22 29				23 29	
Sway	d						21 34							22 34				23 34	
Brockenhurst ■	a						21 39							22 39				23 39	
	d						21 40							22 40				23 40	
Beaulieu Road	d																		
Ashurst New Forest	d						21 47							22 47				23 47	
Totton	d						21 52							22 52				23 52	
Salisbury	d				20 56								21 56						
Dean	d				21 08								22 08						
Mottisfont & Dunbridge	d				21 14								22 14						
Romsey	d	21 07			21 20					22 07			22 20		23 09	23 00			
Redbridge	d				21 27								22 27			23 08			
Millbrook (Hants)	d				21 31								22 31			23 12			
Southampton Central ⛴	a				21 34		21 57						22 34	22 57		23 15		23 57	
	d		21 30		21 35	21 55	22 00					22 30	22 35	23 00		23 21		23 59	
St Denys	d				21 40								22 40			23 26		00 04	
Swaythling	d				21 43								22 43			23 29		00 07	
Southampton Airport Pkwy ✈	d		21 38		21 46	22 03	22 08					22 38	22 46	23 08		23 32		00 10	
Portsmouth Harbour ⛴	d			20 59							21 54						23 24		
Portsmouth & Southsea	d			21 04							21 59						23 29		
Fratton	d			21 08							22 03						23 33		
Hilsea	d			21 12							22 07						23 37		
Cosham	d			21 17							22 12						23 42		
Portchester	d			21 22							22 17						23 47		
Fareham	d			21 28							22 23						23 53		
Botley	d			21 35							22 30						23 59		
Hedge End	d			21 40							22 35						00 05		
Eastleigh ■	a	21 20		21 46	21 49	22 06				22 20	22 41	22 42	22 49	23 11	23 22	23 35	00 11	00 14	
	d	21 21		21 47	21 50	22 14				22 22		22 46	22 50	23 12	23 23	23 37	00 21		
Chandlers Ford	d				21 55								22 55			23 42			
Romsey	a	21 51			22 03					22 51			23 03		23 57	23 49			
Shawford	d					22 20		←						23 18					
Winchester	d		21 48	21 56		22 26	22 18	22 26				22 55		23 24			00a31		
Micheldever	d			22 05		→								23 33					
Basingstoke	a			22 15			22 34	22 42				23 11		23 43					
	d			22 24			22 35	22 43				23 14		23 44					
Reading ■	a																		
Fleet	d			22 40				22 54						00 01					
Farnborough (Main)	d			22 46				23 00						00 06					
Woking	a		22 19	22 58			22 53	23 09				23 32		00 18					
Clapham Junction ■	a						23 14	23 29				23 52		00 53					
London Waterloo ■ ⊖	a		22 49	23 32			23 22	23 39				00 03		01 04					

For services from Brockenhurst - Lymington refer to Table T159

Table T158-R

Sundays

20 May to 2 December

Weymouth, Bournemouth, Romsey, Southampton and Basingstoke - London

		SW 1 A	SW 1 A	SW 1 A	SW 1	SW 1	SW ◇1 B 🛒	SW 1	SW 1	SW 1	SW ◇1	SW 1	XC ◇1 🛒	SW ◇1 C 🛒	SW ◇1 D 🛒	SW 1	SW 1	SW 1 🛒	SW ◇1	SW 1	XC ◇1 🛒	SW ◇1 C 🛒	SW ◇1 D 🛒
Weymouth	d													07 43	07 48							08 43	08 48
Upwey	d													07 47	07 52							08 47	08 52
Dorchester West	a																						
Dorchester South	d													07 57	08 00							08 55	09 00
Moreton (Dorset)	d													08 04	08 07							09 02	09 07
Wool	d													08 10	08 13							09 08	09 13
Wareham	d													08 17	08 20							09 15	09 20
Holton Heath	d																						
Hamworthy	d													08 24	08 27							09 22	09 27
Poole	a													08 29	08 31							09 29	09 31
	d						06 50				07 50			08 30	08 32				08 55			09 30	09 32
Parkstone (Dorset)	d						06 54				07 54			08 34	08 36							09 34	09 36
Branksome	d						06 57				07 57			08 38	08 40							09 38	09 40
Bournemouth	a						07 02				08 02			08 46	08 46				09 04			09 46	09 46
	d						07 06				08 06			08 50	08 50				09 06		09 40	09 50	09 50
Pokesdown	d						07 10				08 10								09 10				
Christchurch	d						07 14				08 14								09 14				
Hinton Admiral	d						07 19				08 19								09 19				
New Milton	d						07 23				08 23			09 01	09 01				09 23			10 01	10 01
Sway	d						07 28				08 28								09 28				
Brockenhurst	a						07 33				08 33			09 08	09 08				09 33		09 53	10 08	10 08
	d						07 34				08 34			09 09	09 09				09 34		09 57	10 09	10 09
Beaulieu Road	d										08 39								09 39				
Ashurst New Forest	d						07 43				08 43								09 43				
Totton	d						07 48				08 48								09 48				
Salisbury	d							08 08		08 20						09 08							
Dean	d							08 20								09 20							
Mottisfont & Dunbridge	d							08 26								09 26							
Romsey	d							08 35		08 39						09 32	09 35						
Redbridge	d									08 46						09 39							
Millbrook (Hants)	d									08 50		←				09 43				←			
Southampton Central ⛴	a						07 53			08 52	08 53	08 52		09 23	09 23	09 45			09 53	09 45	10 10	10 23	10 23
	d				06 55		07 55			08 59	08 55	08 59	09 15	09 25	09 25	09 59			09 55	09 59	10 15	10 25	10 25
St Denys	d			00 04						→		09 04				→				10 04			
Swaythling	d			00 07								09 07								10 07			
Southampton Airport Pkwy ✈	d			00 10	07 03		08 03				09 03	09 10	09 22	09 33	09 33				10 03	10 10	10 22	10 33	10 33
Portsmouth Harbour ⛴	d					07 17			08 17									09 17					
Portsmouth & Southsea	d					07 22			08 22									09 22					
Fratton	d					07 26			08 26									09 26					
Hilsea	d					07 30			08 30									09 30					
Cosham	d					07 35			08 35									09 35					
Portchester	d					07 40			08 40									09 40					
Fareham	d					07 46			08 46									09 46					
Botley	d					07 54			08 54									09 54					
Hedge End	d		00 05			07 58			08 58									09 58					
Eastleigh	a		00 11	00 14	07 07	08 04	08 07		09 04		09 07	09 13					09 48	10 04	10 07	10 13			
	d		00 21		07 11	08 11			09 11			09 15					09 54	10 11		10 15			
Chandlers Ford	d							08 42				09 20								10 20			
Romsey	a							09 24				09 28					10 24			10 28			
Shawford	d				07 17	08 17			09 17									10 17					
Winchester	d		00a31		07 23	08 23			09 23				09 31	09 42	09 42			10 23			10 31	10 42	10 42
Micheldever	d				07 32	08 32			09 32									10 32					
Basingstoke	a				07 42	08 42			09 42				09 46	09 58	09 58			10 42			10 46	10 58	10 58
	d				07 44	08 44			09 44				09 47	10 00	10 00			10 44			10 47	11 00	11 00
Reading	a												10 04								11 03		
Fleet	d	00 01																					
Farnborough (Main)	d	00 06																					
Woking	a	00 18			08 02	09 02			10 02					10 19	10 19			11 02				11 18	11 18
Clapham Junction	a	00 53			08 31	09 30			10 27					10 39	10 39			11 27				11 39	11 39
London Waterloo ⊖	a	01 04			08 46	09 41			10 39					10 50	10 50			11 39				11 50	11 50

A not 20 May

B 🛒 ◇ to Eastleigh

C from 7 October. 🛒 from Bournemouth

D until 30 September. 🛒 from Bournemouth

For services from Brockenhurst - Lymington refer to Table T159

Table T158-R

Sundays

20 May to 2 December

Weymouth, Bournemouth, Romsey, Southampton and Basingstoke - London

		SW 1	SW 1	SW 1 🛒	SW ◇1 A 🛒	SW 1	XC ◇1 🛒	SW ◇1 A 🛒	SW 1	SW 1	SW 1 🛒	SW ◇1	SW 1	XC ◇1 🛒	SW ◇1 A 🛒	GW ◇ B	GW ◇ C	SW 1	SW 1	SW 1 🛒	SW ◇1 A 🛒	SW 1	XC ◇1 🛒
Weymouth	d							09 48							10 48	11 00	11 05						
Upwey	d							09 52							10 52	11 05	11 10						
Dorchester West	a															11 12	11 17						
Dorchester South	d							10 00							11 00								
Moreton (Dorset)	d							10 07							11 07								
Wool	d							10 13							11 13								
Wareham	d							10 20							11 20								
Holton Heath	d																						
Hamworthy	d							10 27							11 27								
Poole	a							10 31							11 31								
	d				09 55			10 32				10 55			11 32						11 55		
Parkstone (Dorset)	d							10 36							11 36								
Branksome	d							10 40							11 40								
Bournemouth	a				10 04			10 46				11 04			11 46						12 04		
	d				10 06		10 40	10 50				11 06		11 40	11 50						12 06		12 40
Pokesdown	d				10 10							11 10									12 10		
Christchurch	d				10 14							11 14									12 14		
Hinton Admiral	d				10 19							11 19									12 19		
New Milton	d				10 23			11 01				11 23			12 01						12 23		
Sway	d				10 28							11 28									12 28		
Brockenhurst	a				10 33		10 53	11 08				11 33		11 53	12 08						12 33		12 53
	d				10 34		10 57	11 09				11 34		11 57	12 09						12 34		12 57
Beaulieu Road	d				10 39							11 39									12 39		
Ashurst New Forest	d				10 43							11 43									12 43		
Totton	d				10 48							11 48									12 48		
Salisbury	d	10 13							11 08									12 13					
Dean	d								11 20														
Mottisfont & Dunbridge	d								11 26														
Romsey	d	10 32	10 35						11 32	11 35								12 32	12 35				
Redbridge	d	10 39							11 39									12 39					
Millbrook (Hants)	d	10 43				←			11 43				←					12 43				←	
Southampton Central ⛴	a	10 45			10 53	10 45	11 10	11 23	11 45			11 53	11 45	12 10	12 23			12 45			12 53	12 45	13 10
	d	10 59			10 55	10 59	11 15	11 25	11 59			11 55	11 59	12 15	12 25			12 59			12 55	12 59	13 15
St Denys	d	→				11 04			→				12 04					→				13 04	
Swaythling	d					11 07							12 07									13 07	
Southampton Airport Pkwy ✈	d				11 03	11 10	11 22	11 33				12 03	12 10	12 22	12 33						13 03	13 10	13 22
Portsmouth Harbour ⛴	d			10 17							11 17									12 17			
Portsmouth & Southsea	d			10 22							11 22									12 22			
Fratton	d			10 26							11 26									12 26			
Hilsea	d			10 30							11 30									12 30			
Cosham	d			10 35							11 35									12 35			
Portchester	d			10 40							11 40									12 40			
Fareham	d			10 46							11 46									12 46			
Botley	d			10 54							11 54									12 54			
Hedge End	d			10 58							11 58									12 58			
Eastleigh	a		10 48	11 04	11 07	11 13				11 48	12 04	12 07	12 13						12 48	13 04	13 07	13 13	
	d		10 54	11 11		11 15				11 54	12 11		12 15						12 54	13 11		13 15	
Chandlers Ford	d					11 20							12 20									13 20	
Romsey	a		11 24			11 28				12 24			12 28						13 24			13 28	
Shawford	d			11 17							12 17									13 17			
Winchester	d			11 23			11 31	11 42			12 23			12 31	12 42					13 23			13 31
Micheldever	d			11 32							12 32									13 32			
Basingstoke	a			11 42			11 46	11 58			12 42			12 46	12 58					13 42			13 46
	d			11 44			11 47	12 00			12 44			12 47	13 00					13 44			13 47
Reading	a						12 03							13 04									14 03
Fleet	d																						
Farnborough (Main)	d																						
Woking	a			12 02				12 18			13 02				13 18					14 02			
Clapham Junction	a			12 27				12 39			13 27				13 39					14 27			
London Waterloo ⊖	a			12 37				12 49			13 37				13 49					14 37			

A 🛒 from Bournemouth

B until 9 September

C from 16 September

For services from Brockenhurst - Lymington refer to Table T159

Table T158-R

Sundays
20 May to 2 December

Weymouth, Bournemouth, Romsey, Southampton and Basingstoke - London

		SW ◇1 A 🍴	SW 1	SW 1	SW 1 🍴	SW ◇1	SW 1	XC ◇1 🍴	SW ◇1 A 🍴	SW 1	SW 1	SW 1 🍴	SW ◇1	SW 1	XC ◇1 🍴	SW ◇1 A 🍴	GW ◇	SW 1	SW 1	SW 1 🍴	SW ◇1	SW 1
Weymouth	d	11 48							12 48							13 48	14 14					
Upwey	d	11 52							12 52							13 52	14 19					
Dorchester West	a																14 26					
Dorchester South	d	12 00							13 00							14 00						
Moreton (Dorset)	d	12 07							13 07							14 07						
Wool	d	12 13							13 13							14 13						
Wareham	d	12 20							13 20							14 20						
Holton Heath	d																					
Hamworthy	d	12 27							13 27							14 27						
Poole 4	a	12 31							13 31							14 31						
	d	12 32				12 55			13 32				13 55			14 32					14 55	
Parkstone (Dorset)	d	12 36							13 36							14 36						
Branksome	d	12 40							13 40							14 40						
Bournemouth	a	12 46				13 04			13 46				14 04			14 46					15 04	
	d	12 50				13 06		13 40	13 50				14 06		14 40	14 50					15 06	
Pokesdown	d					13 10							14 10								15 10	
Christchurch	d					13 14							14 14								15 14	
Hinton Admiral	d					13 19							14 19								15 19	
New Milton	d	13 01				13 23			14 01				14 23			15 01					15 23	
Sway	d					13 28							14 28								15 28	
Brockenhurst 3	a	13 08				13 33		13 53	14 08				14 33		14 53	15 08					15 33	
	d	13 09				13 34		13 57	14 09				14 34		14 57	15 09					15 34	
Beaulieu Road	d					13 39							14 39								15 39	
Ashurst New Forest	d					13 43							14 43								15 43	
Totton	d					13 48							14 48								15 48	
Salisbury	d		13 08							14 13								15 08				
Dean	d		13 20															15 20				
Mottisfont & Dunbridge	d		13 26															15 26				
Romsey	d		13 32	13 35						14 32	14 35							15 32	15 35			
Redbridge	d		13 39							14 39								15 39				
Millbrook (Hants)	d		13 43				←			14 43				←				15 43				←
Southampton Central ⛴	a	13 23	13 45			13 53	13 45	14 10	14 23	14 45			14 53	14 45	15 10	15 23		15 45			15 53	15 45
	d	13 25	13 59			13 55	13 59	14 15	14 25	14 59			14 55	14 59	15 15	15 25		15 59			15 55	15 59
St Denys	d		→				14 04			→				15 04				→				16 04
Swaythling	d						14 07							15 07								16 07
Southampton Airport Pkwy ✈	d	13 33				14 03	14 10	14 22	14 33				15 03	15 10	15 22	15 33					16 03	16 10
Portsmouth Harbour ⛴	d				13 17							14 17								15 17		
Portsmouth & Southsea	d				13 22							14 22								15 22		
Fratton	d				13 26							14 26								15 26		
Hilsea	d				13 30							14 30								15 30		
Cosham	d				13 35							14 35								15 35		
Portchester	d				13 40							14 40								15 40		
Fareham	d				13 46							14 46								15 46		
Botley	d				13 54							14 54								15 54		
Hedge End	d				13 58							14 58								15 58		
Eastleigh 3	a			13 48	14 04	14 07	14 13				14 48	15 04	15 07	15 13					15 48	16 04	16 06	16 13
	d			13 54	14 11		14 15				14 54	15 11		15 15					15 54	16 11	16 07	16 15
Chandlers Ford	d						14 20							15 20								16 20
Romsey	a			14 24			14 28				15 24			15 28					16 24			16 28
Shawford	d				14 17							15 17								16 17		
Winchester	d	13 42			14 23			14 31	14 42			15 23			15 31	15 42				16 23	16 17	
Micheldever	d				14 32							15 32								→		
Basingstoke	a	13 58			14 42			14 46	14 58			15 42			15 46	15 58					16 33	
	d	14 00			14 44			14 47	15 00			15 44			15 47	16 00					16 35	
Reading 7	a							15 05							16 03							
Fleet	d																					
Farnborough (Main)	d																					
Woking	a	14 18			15 02				15 18			16 02				16 18					16 53	
Clapham Junction 10	a	14 39			15 27				15 39			16 27				16 39					17 14	
London Waterloo 15 ⊖	a	14 49			15 37				15 49			16 37				16 49					17 24	

A 🍴 from Bournemouth

For services from Brockenhurst - Lymington refer to Table T159

Table T158-R

Sundays
20 May to 2 December

Weymouth, Bournemouth, Romsey, Southampton and Basingstoke - London

		SW 1 🍴	XC ◇1 🍴	SW ◇1 A 🍴	SW 1	SW 1	SW 1 🍴	SW ◇1 🍴	SW 1	SW 1 🍴	XC ◇1 🍴	SW ◇1 A 🍴	GW ◇	SW 1	SW 1	SW 1	SW ◇1	SW 1	SW 1	XC ◇1 🍴	SW ◇1 A 🍴	SW 1	SW 1
Weymouth	d			14 48								15 48	16 10								16 48		
Upwey	d			14 52								15 52	16 15								16 52		
Dorchester West	a												16 22										
Dorchester South	d			15 00								16 00									17 00		
Moreton (Dorset)	d			15 07								16 07									17 07		
Wool	d			15 13								16 13									17 13		
Wareham	d			15 20								16 20									17 20		
Holton Heath	d																						
Hamworthy	d			15 27								16 27									17 27		
Poole 4	a			15 31								16 31									17 31		
	d			15 32				15 55				16 32					16 55				17 32		
Parkstone (Dorset)	d			15 36								16 36									17 36		
Branksome	d			15 40								16 40									17 40		
Bournemouth	a			15 46				16 04				16 46					17 04				17 46		
	d		15 40	15 50				16 06			16 40	16 50					17 06			17 40	17 50		
Pokesdown	d							16 10									17 10						
Christchurch	d							16 14									17 14						
Hinton Admiral	d							16 19									17 19						
New Milton	d			16 01				16 23				17 01					17 23				18 01		
Sway	d							16 28									17 28						
Brockenhurst 3	a		15 53	16 08				16 33			16 53	17 08					17 33			17 53	18 08		
	d		15 57	16 09				16 34			16 57	17 09					17 34			17 57	18 09		
Beaulieu Road	d							16 39									17 39						
Ashurst New Forest	d							16 43									17 43						
Totton	d							16 48									17 48						
Salisbury	d				16 13									17 08								18 13	
Dean	d													17 20									
Mottisfont & Dunbridge	d													17 26									
Romsey	d				16 32	16 35								17 32	17 35							18 32	18 35
Redbridge	d				16 39									17 39								18 39	
Millbrook (Hants)	d				16 43				←					17 43				←				18 43	
Southampton Central ⛴	a		16 10	16 23	16 45			16 53	16 45		17 10	17 23		17 45			17 53	17 45		18 10	18 23	18 45	
	d		16 15	16 25	16 59			16 55	16 59		17 15	17 25		17 59			17 55	17 59		18 15	18 25	18 59	
St Denys	d				→				17 04					→				18 04				→	
Swaythling	d								17 07									18 07					
Southampton Airport Pkwy ✈	d		16 22	16 33				17 03	17 10		17 22	17 33					18 03	18 10		18 22	18 33		
Portsmouth Harbour ⛴	d						16 17									17 17							
Portsmouth & Southsea	d						16 22									17 22							
Fratton	d						16 26									17 26							
Hilsea	d						16 30									17 30							
Cosham	d						16 35									17 35							
Portchester	d						16 40									17 40							
Fareham	d						16 46									17 46							
Botley	d						16 54									17 54							
Hedge End	d						16 58									17 58							
Eastleigh 3	a					16 48	17 04	17 06	17 13						17 48	18 04	18 06	18 13					18 48
	d					16 54	17 11	17 07	17 15						17 54	18 11	18 07	18 15					18 54
Chandlers Ford	d								17 20									18 20					
Romsey	a					17 24			17 28						18 24			18 28					19 24
Shawford	d	←					17 17			←						18 17			←				
Winchester	d	16 23	16 31	16 42			17 23	17 17		17 23	17 31	17 42				18 23	18 17		18 23	18 31	18 42		
Micheldever	d	16 32					→			17 32						→			18 32				
Basingstoke	a	16 42	16 46	16 58				17 33		17 42	17 46	17 58					18 33		18 42	18 46	18 58		
	d	16 44	16 47	17 00				17 35		17 44	17 47	18 00					18 35		18 44	18 47	19 00		
Reading 7	a		17 03								18 03									19 03			
Fleet	d																						
Farnborough (Main)	d	16 58								17 58									18 58				
Woking	a	17 07		17 18				17 53		18 07		18 18					18 53		19 07		19 18		
Clapham Junction 10	a	17 28		17 39				18 14		18 28		18 39					19 14		19 28		19 39		
London Waterloo 15 ⊖	a	17 39		17 49				18 24		18 39		18 49					19 24		19 39		19 49		

A 🍴 from Bournemouth

For services from Brockenhurst - Lymington refer to Table T159

Table T158-R

Sundays

20 May to 2 December

Weymouth, Bournemouth, Romsey, Southampton and Basingstoke - London

		SW	SW	SW	SW	XC	SW	GW	SW	SW	SW	SW	SW	SW	XC	SW	SW	SW	SW	SW	SW	SW
		■	◇■	■	■	◇■ 🍴	◇■ A 🍴	◇	■	■	■	◇■	■	■	◇■	◇■ A 🍴	■	■	■	◇■	■	■
Weymouth	d						17 48	17 56								18 48						
Upwey	d						17 52	18 01								18 52						
Dorchester West	a							18 08														
Dorchester South	d						18 00									19 00						
Moreton (Dorset)	d						18 07									19 07						
Wool	d						18 13									19 13						
Wareham	d						18 20									19 20						
Holton Heath	d																					
Hamworthy	d						18 27									19 27						
Poole ■	a						18 31									19 31						
	d		17 55				18 32					18 55				19 32				19 55		
Parkstone (Dorset)	d						18 36									19 36						
Branksome	d						18 40									19 40						
Bournemouth	a		18 04				18 46					19 04				19 46				20 04		
	d		18 06			18 40	18 50					19 06			19 40	19 50				20 06		
Pokesdown	d		18 10									19 10								20 10		
Christchurch	d		18 14									19 14								20 14		
Hinton Admiral	d		18 19									19 19								20 19		
New Milton	d		18 23				19 01					19 23				20 01				20 23		
Sway	d		18 28									19 28								20 28		
Brockenhurst ■	a		18 33			18 53	19 08					19 33			19 53	20 08				20 33		
	d		18 34			18 57	19 09					19 34			19 57	20 09				20 34		
Beaulieu Road	d		18 39									19 39								20 39		
Ashurst New Forest	d		18 43									19 43								20 43		
Totton	d		18 48									19 48								20 48		
Salisbury	d								19 08								20 13					
Dean	d								19 20													
Mottisfont & Dunbridge	d								19 26													
Romsey	d								19 32	19 35							20 32	20 35				
Redbridge	d								19 39								20 39					
Millbrook (Hants)	d			←					19 43				←				20 43				←	
Southampton Central ⛴	a		18 53	18 45		19 10	19 23		19 45			19 53	19 45		20 10	20 23	20 45			20 53	20 45	
	d		18 55	18 59		19 15	19 25		19 59			19 55	19 59		20 15	20 25	20 59			20 55	20 59	
St Denys	d			19 04					→				20 04				→				21 04	
Swaythling	d			19 07									20 07								21 07	
Southampton Airport Pkwy ✈	d		19 03	19 10		19 22	19 33					20 03	20 10		20 22	20 33				21 03	21 10	
Portsmouth Harbour ⛴	d	18 17									19 17								20 18			
Portsmouth & Southsea	d	18 22									19 22								20 22			
Fratton	d	18 26									19 26								20 26			
Hilsea	d	18 30									19 30								20 30			
Cosham	d	18 35									19 35								20 35			
Portchester	d	18 40									19 40								20 40			
Fareham	d	18 46									19 46								20 46			
Botley	d	18 54									19 54								20 54			
Hedge End	d	18 58									19 58								20 58			
Eastleigh ■	a	19 04	19 06	19 13						19 48	20 04	20 06	20 13					20 48	21 04	21 06	21 13	
	d	19 11	19 07	19 15						19 54	20 11	20 07	20 15					20 54	21 11	21 07	21 15	
Chandlers Ford	d			19 20									20 20								21 20	
Romsey	a			19 28						20 24			20 28					21 24			21 28	
Shawford	d	19 17			←						20 17			←					21 17			←
Winchester	d	19 23	19 17		19 23	19 31	19 42				20 23	20 17		20 23	20 31	20 42			21 23	21 17		21 23
Micheldever	d	→			19 32						→			20 32					→			21 32
Basingstoke	a		19 33		19 42	19 46	19 58					20 33		20 42	20 46	20 58				21 33		21 42
	d		19 35		19 44	19 47	20 00					20 35		20 44	20 47	21 00				21 35		21 44
Reading ■	a					20 03									21 03							
Fleet	d																					
Farnborough (Main)	d				19 58									20 58								21 58
Woking	a		19 53		20 07		20 18					20 53		21 07		21 18				21 53		22 07
Clapham Junction ■	a		20 14		20 28		20 39					21 14		21 28		21 39				22 14		22 28
London Waterloo ■ ⊖	a		20 24		20 39		20 49					21 24		21 39		21 49				22 24		22 39

A 🍴 from Bournemouth

For services from Brockenhurst - Lymington refer to Table T159

Table T158-R

Sundays

20 May to 2 December

Weymouth, Bournemouth, Romsey, Southampton and Basingstoke - London

		SW	SW	SW	SW	SW	SW	GW	SW	SW	SW	SW	SW	SW	SW	SW
		■	■	■	◇■	■	■		■	■	■	◇■	■	■	■	■
Weymouth	d				19 58			20 09				20 58		21 58	22 58	
Upwey	d				20 02			20 14				21 02		22 02	23 02	
Dorchester West	a							20 21								
Dorchester South	d				20 10							21 10		22 10	23 10	
Moreton (Dorset)	d				20 17							21 17		22 17	23 17	
Wool	d				20 23							21 23		22 23	23 23	
Wareham	d				20 30							21 30		22 30	23 30	
Holton Heath	d															
Hamworthy	d				20 37							21 37		22 37	23 37	
Poole ■	a				20 42							21 42		22 42	23 41	
	d				20 50							21 50		22 50	23 50	
Parkstone (Dorset)	d				20 54							21 54		22 54	23 54	
Branksome	d				20 57							21 57		22 57	23 57	
Bournemouth	a				21 03							22 03		23 03	00 03	
	d				21 06							22 06		23 08		
Pokesdown	d				21 10							22 10		23 12		
Christchurch	d				21 14							22 14		23 16		
Hinton Admiral	d				21 19							22 19		23 21		
New Milton	d				21 23							22 23		23 25		
Sway	d				21 28							22 28		23 30		
Brockenhurst ■	a				21 33							22 33		23 35		
	d				21 34							22 34		23 36		
Beaulieu Road	d				21 39							22 39				
Ashurst New Forest	d				21 43							22 43		23 43		
Totton	d				21 48							22 48		23 48		
Salisbury	d	21 08														
Dean	d	21 20														
Mottisfont & Dunbridge	d	21 26														
Romsey	d	21 32	21 35						22 28	22 35						
Redbridge	d	21 39							22 35							
Millbrook (Hants)	d	21 43				←			22 39				←			
Southampton Central ⛴	a	21 45			21 53	21 45			22 41			22 53	22 41	23 54		
	d	21 59			21 55	21 59			23 05			22 55	23 05			
St Denys	d	→				22 04			→				23 10			
Swaythling	d					22 07							23 13			
Southampton Airport Pkwy ✈	d				22 03	22 10						23 03	23 16			
Portsmouth Harbour ⛴	d			21 18							22 17					23 17
Portsmouth & Southsea	d			21 22							22 22					23 22
Fratton	d			21 26							22 26					23 26
Hilsea	d			21 30							22 30					23 30
Cosham	d			21 35							22 35					23 35
Portchester	d			21 40							22 40					23 40
Fareham	d			21 46							22 46					23 46
Botley	d			21 54							22 54					23 54
Hedge End	d			21 58							22 58					23 58
Eastleigh ■	a		21 48	22 04	22 07	22 13				22 48	23 04	23 09	23 19			00 04
	d		21 54	22 11	22 08	22 15				22 54		23 11	23 22			
Chandlers Ford	d					22 20							23 27			
Romsey	a		22 24			22 31				23 23			23 35			
Shawford	d			22 17			←					23 17				
Winchester	d			22 23	22 18		22 23					23 23				
Micheldever	d			→			22 32					23 32				
Basingstoke	a				22 35		22 42					23 42				
	d				22 36		22 44					23 44				
Reading ■	a															
Fleet	d															
Farnborough (Main)	d						22 58									
Woking	a				22 54		23 07					00 02				
Clapham Junction ■	a				23 15		23 28					00 23				
London Waterloo ■ ⊖	a				23 25		23 39					00 33				

For services from Brockenhurst - Lymington refer to Table T159

Table T159-F

Mondays to Fridays
21 May to 7 December

Brockenhurst - Lymington - Yarmouth (Isle of Wight)

		SW 1		SW 1	SW 1		SW 1	SW 1		SW 1
Brockenhurst 3	d	05 59	and every 30 minutes until	09 29	10 12	and every 30 minutes until	18 12	18 48	and every 30 minutes until	22 18
Lymington Town	d	06 07		09 37	10 20		18 20	18 56		22 26
Lymington Pier ⛴	a	06 10		09 40	10 23		18 23	18 59		22 29
	d									
Yarmouth (I.O.W.) ⛴	a									

Saturdays
26 May to 8 December

		SW 1		SW 1	SW 1	SW 1
Brockenhurst 3	d	06 12	and every 30 minutes until	21 12	21 48	22 18
Lymington Town	d	06 20		21 20	21 56	22 26
Lymington Pier ⛴	a	06 22		21 22	21 58	22 28
	d					
Yarmouth (I.O.W.) ⛴	a					

Sundays
20 May to 2 December

		SW 1		SW 1
Brockenhurst 3	d	08 59	and every 30 minutes until	21 59
Lymington Town	d	09 07		22 07
Lymington Pier ⛴	a	09 09		22 09
	d			
Yarmouth (I.O.W.) ⛴	a			

For connections from Brockenhurst refer to Table T158

Table T159-R

Mondays to Fridays
21 May to 7 December

Yarmouth (Isle of Wight) - Lymington - Brockenhurst

		SW 1		SW 1	SW 1		SW 1	SW 1		SW 1	SW 1
Yarmouth (I.O.W.) ⛴	d		and every 30 minutes until			and every 30 minutes until			and every 30 minutes until		
Lymington Pier ⛴	a										
	d	06 14		09 44	10 27		18 27	19 03		22 03	22 36
Lymington Town	d	06 16		09 46	10 29		18 29	19 05		22 05	22 38
Brockenhurst 3	a	06 25		09 55	10 38		18 38	19 14		22 14	22 47

Saturdays
26 May to 8 December

		SW 1		SW 1	SW 1	SW 1
Yarmouth (I.O.W.) ⛴	d		and every 30 minutes until			
Lymington Pier ⛴	a					
	d	06 27		21 27	22 03	22 36
Lymington Town	d	06 29		21 29	22 05	22 38
Brockenhurst 3	a	06 37		21 37	22 13	22 46

Sundays
20 May to 2 December

		SW 1		SW 1
Yarmouth (I.O.W.) ⛴	d		and every 30 minutes until	
Lymington Pier ⛴	a			
	d	09 14		22 14
Lymington Town	d	09 16		22 16
Brockenhurst 3	a	09 24		22 24

For connections from Brockenhurst refer to Table T158

Table T160-F

Mondays to Fridays
21 May to 7 December

London - Salisbury - Yeovil and Exeter

Miles			SW MO ◇1 A	SW MX 1 A	SW MO 1 A	SW 1	SW 1	SW 1	GW B	SW 1	SW ◇1	SW ◇1	SW ◇1 C 🛒	SW ◇1 🛒	SW ◇1 C 🛒	SW ◇1 🛒	SW ◇1 C 🛒	SW ◇1	SW ◇1 🛒	SW ◇1 C 🛒	SW ◇1 🛒	SW ◇1 C 🛒	SW ◇1 🛒
0	**London Waterloo** 15 ⊖	d											07 10	07 50	08 20	08 50	09 20		09 50	10 20	10 50	11 20	11 50
4	Clapham Junction 10	d											07u17	07u57	08u27		09u27			10u27		11u27	
24½	Woking	d		00 08	00 08								07 36	08 17	08 46	09 16	09 46		10 16	10 46	11 16	11 46	12 16
47¾	**Basingstoke**	d		00 28	00 41							07 22	07 57	08 38	09 07	09 38	10 07		10 38	11 07	11 38	12 07	12 38
55½	Overton	d		00s37	00s49							07 30	08 05	08 46		09 46			10 46		11 46		12 46
59¼	Whitchurch (Hants)	d		00s42	00s54							07 35	08 10	08 51		09 51			10 51		11 51		12 51
66½	Andover	d		00 50	01 03							07 44	08 19	09 00	09 24	10 00	10 24		11 00	11 24	12 00	12 24	13 00
72¾	Grateley	d		00s58	01s10							07 51	08 26	09 07		10 07			11 07		12 07		13 07
83¾	**Salisbury** 123	a		01 10	01 22							08 03	08 39	09 20	09 43	10 20	10 42		11 20	11 42	12 20	12 42	13 20
—		d						06 07	06 10	06 40	07 40	08 08	08 47		09 47		10 47	10 52		11 47		12 47	
—	Warminster 123	d							06 30	07 00								11 12					
—	Westbury 123	d							06 41	07 09								11 23					
—	Trowbridge 123	d							06 47	07 15								11 29					
—	Bradford-on-Avon 123	d							06 53	07 21								11 35					
—	Bath Spa 7 123	a							07 09	07 33								11 47					
—	Bristol Temple Meads 10 123	a							07 29	07 52								12 06					
—	Frome	d																					
—	Bruton	d																					
—	Castle Cary	d																					
—	Yeovil Pen Mill	a																					
—		d																					
96¼	Tisbury	d						06 29			07 59	08 27	09 06		10 06		11 06			12 06		13 06	
105¼	Gillingham (Dorset)	a						06 39			08 09	08 37	09 16		10 16		11 16			12 16		13 16	
—		d					05 51	06 42			08 11		09 17		10 17		11 17			12 17		13 17	
112¼	Templecombe	d					05 58	06 50			08 19		09 25		10 25		11 25			12 25		13 25	
118¼	Sherborne	d					06 06	06 57			08 26		09 32		10 32		11 32			12 32		13 32	
122¾	Yeovil Junction	a					06 11	07 03			08 32		09 38		10 38		11 38			12 38		13 38	
—		d					06 15	07 07			08 39		09 39		10 39		11 39			12 39		13 39	
—	Yeovil Pen Mill	a																					
—		d																					
131¾	Crewkerne	d					06 24	07 16			08 49		09 49		10 49		11 49			12 49		13 49	
144¾	Axminster	a					06 43	07 36			09 02		10 02		11 02		12 02			13 02		14 02	
—		d	00 08			05 52	06 56	07 37			09 03		10 03		11 03		12 03			13 03		14 03	
155	Honiton	a	00 19			06 03	07 07	07 48			09 15		10 15		11 15		12 15			13 15		14 15	
—		d	00 20			06 07	07 12	07 53			09 16		10 16		11 16		12 16			13 16		14 16	
159½	Feniton	d	00 25			06 12	07 18	07 59			09 21		10 21				12 21					14 21	
163¼	Whimple	d	00 30			06 17	07 23	08 04			09 26				11 24					13 24			
—	Cranbrook	d	00 35			06 22	07 28	08 08			09 31		10 29		11 28		12 29			13 28		14 29	
169	Pinhoe	d	00 39			06 26	07 32	08 12			09 35		10 33		11 32		12 33			13 32		14 33	
171¾	**Exeter Central**	a				06 30	07 37	08 17			09 39		10 37		11 37		12 37			13 37		14 37	
172¾	**Exeter St Davids** 6	a	00 46			06 35	07 42	08 21			09 44		10 42		11 43		12 43			13 43		14 43	

		SW ◇1 C 🛒		SW ◇1 🛒	SW ◇1 C 🛒	SW ◇1 D 🛒	SW ◇1 🛒	SW ◇1 C 🛒	SW ◇1 🛒	SW ◇1 C 🛒	SW ◇1 D 🛒	SW ◇1 C 🛒	SW ◇1 E 🛒	SW ◇1 C 🛒	SW ◇1 D 🛒	SW ◇1 D 🛒	SW ◇1 F 🛒	SW ◇1 D 🛒		SW ◇1 🛒	SW ◇1 D 🛒	SW ◇1 D 🛒	SW 1 🛒
London Waterloo 15 ⊖	d	12 20		12 50	13 20	13 50		14 20	14 50	15 20	15 50	16 20	16 50	17 20	17 50	18 20	18 50	19 20		19 50	20 20	21 20	22 20
Clapham Junction 10	d	12u27		12u57	13u27			14u27		15u27	15u57	16u27	16u57			18u27		19u27			20u27	21u27	22u27
Woking	d	12 46		13 16	13 46	14 16		14 46	15 16	15 46	16 16	16 46	17u16	17u46		18 46	19 18	19 46		20 16	20 46	21 49	22 49
Basingstoke	d	13 07		13 38	14 07	14 38		15 07	15 38	16 07	16 38	17 07	17 38	18 07	18 38	19 07	19 39	20 07		20 37	21 07	22 14	23 11
Overton	d			13 46		14 46			15 46		16 46	17 15	17 46	18 15	18 47	19 15	19 47	20 15		20 46	21 15	22 22	23 20
Whitchurch (Hants)	d			13 51		14 51			15 51		16 51	17 20	17 51	18 20	18 52	19 20	19 52	20 20		20 51	21 20	22 27	23 25
Andover	d	13 24		14 00	14 24	15 00		15 24	16 00	16 24	17 00	17 29	18 00	18 29	19 00	19 29	20 01	20 29		21 00	21 29	22 36	23 33
Grateley	d			14 07		15 07			16 07		17 07	17 36	18 07	18 36	19 08	19 36	20 08	20 36		21 07	21 36	22 43	23 41
Salisbury 123	a	13 43		14 19	14 42	15 20		15 42	16 20	16 44	17 20	17 48	18 20	18 50	19 20	19 48	20 20	20 49		21 20	21 48	22 55	23 53
	d	13 47	13 52	14 24	14 47	15 23		15 47		16 47	17 23	17 53	18 23	18 54	19 23	19 53	20 25	20 53	20 57		22 06	23 03	
Warminster 123	d		14 12	14 44															21 17				
Westbury 123	d		14 21	14 57															21 25				
Trowbridge 123	d		14 27																21 31				
Bradford-on-Avon 123	d		14 33																21 37				
Bath Spa 7 123	a		14 46																21 50				
Bristol Temple Meads 10 123	a		15 05																22 06				
Frome	d			15 07																			
Bruton	d			15 18																			
Castle Cary	d			15 24																			
Yeovil Pen Mill	a			15 35																			
	d																						
Tisbury	d	14 06			15 06	15 37		16 06		17 06	17 37	18 09	18 37	19 08	19 37	20 11	20 39	21 08			22 24	23s16	
Gillingham (Dorset)	a	14 16			15 16	15 47		16 16		17 16	17 47	18 18	18 47	19 18	19 48	20 21	20 48	21 18			22 34	23s27	
	d	14 17			15 17	15 52		16 17		17 17	17 53	18 19	18 52	19 19	19 54	20 22	20 52	21 19			22 35		
Templecombe	d	14 25			15 25	16 00		16 25		17 25	18 00	18 27	18 59	19 26	20 02	20 30	21 00	21 27			22 42	23s35	
Sherborne	d	14 32			15 32	16 07		16 32		17 32	18 08	18 34	19 07	19 34	20 09	20 37	21 07	21 34			22 50	23s42	
Yeovil Junction	a	14 38			15 38	16 13		16 38		17 38	18 13	18 40	19 12	19 39	20 15	20 43	21 13	21 40			22 55	23 48	
	d	14 39			15 39	16 20		16 39		17 39		18 43	19 17	19 41	20 20	20 44	21 17	21 41			22 57		
Yeovil Pen Mill	a					16 27							19 25		20 25		21 23						
	d																						
Crewkerne	d	14 49			15 49			16 49		17 49		18 53		19 50		20 54		21 51			23 06		
Axminster	a	15 02			16 02			17 02		18 02		19 06		20 03		21 07		22 04			23 19		
	d	15 03			16 03			17 03		18 03		19 07		20 04		21 08		22 05			23 20		
Honiton	a	15 15			16 15			17 15		18 14		19 18		20 16		21 19		22 18			23 31		
	d	15 16			16 16		17 07	17 16		18 18		19 19		20 17		21 20		22 19			23 32		
Feniton	d	15 21			16 21					18 23				20 22				22 25			23 38		
Whimple	d	15 26						17 24				19 27				21 28		22 30			23 43		
Cranbrook	d	15 31			16 29			17 29		18 31		19 32		20 30		21 33		22 34			23 47		
Pinhoe	d	15 35						17 33				19 36				21 37		22 38			23 51		
Exeter Central	a	15 39			16 35		17 28	17 37		18 37		19 40		20 37		21 43		22 43			23 56		
Exeter St Davids 6	a	15 44			16 43		17 33	17 42		18 43		19 46		20 43		21 47		22 47			00 01		

A From London Waterloo
B To Gloucester
C 🛒 to Axminster
D 🛒 to Salisbury
E To Westbury. 🛒 to Salisbury
F To Westbury

For alternative services from London Waterloo to Woking and Basingstoke, refer to Table T155

For services between Salisbury and Bristol Temple Meads, refer to Table T123

Table T160-F

Mondays to Fridays

21 May to 7 December

London - Salisbury - Yeovil and Exeter

Station		SW FX ■	SW FO ■
London Waterloo ⊖	d	23 40	23 40
Clapham Junction	d	23u47	23u47
Woking	d	00 08	00 08
Basingstoke	d	00 28	00 28
Overton	d	00s37	00s37
Whitchurch (Hants)	d	00s42	00s42
Andover	d	00 50	00 50
Grateley	d	00s58	00s58
Salisbury	123 a	01 10	01s10
	d		
Warminster	123 d		
Westbury	123 d		
Trowbridge	123 d		
Bradford-on-Avon	123 d		
Bath Spa	123 a		
Bristol Temple Meads	123 a		
Frome	d		
Bruton	d		
Castle Cary	d		
Yeovil Pen Mill	a		
	d		
Tisbury	d		01s25
Gillingham (Dorset)	a		01s36
	d		
Templecombe	d		01s44
Sherborne	d		01s51
Yeovil Junction	a		01 57
	d		
Yeovil Pen Mill	a		
	d		
Crewkerne	d		
Axminster	a		
	d		
Honiton	a		
	d		
Feniton	d		
Whimple	d		
Cranbrook	d		
Pinhoe	d		
Exeter Central	a		
Exeter St Davids	a		

For alternative services from London Waterloo to Woking and Basingstoke, refer to Table T155

For services between Salisbury and Bristol Temple Meads, refer to Table T123

Table T160-F

Saturdays

26 May to 8 December

London - Salisbury - Yeovil and Exeter

Station		SW ■ A	GW B	SW ■	SW ■	SW ■	SW ■	SW ◇■	SW ◇■ C	SW ◇■ D
London Waterloo ⊖	d									
Clapham Junction	d									
Woking	d	00 08								
Basingstoke	d	00 28							07 22	07 22
Overton	d	00s37							07 30	07 30
Whitchurch (Hants)	d	00s42							07 35	07 35
Andover	d	00 50							07 44	07 44
Grateley	d	00s58							07 51	07 51
Salisbury	123 a	01s10							08 04	08 05
	d		06 07			06 15	06 40	07 45	08 08	
Warminster	123 d		06 28				07 00			
Westbury	123 d		06 38				07 09			
Trowbridge	123 d		06 44				07 15			
Bradford-on-Avon	123 d		06 50				07 21			
Bath Spa	123 a		07 06				07 33			
Bristol Temple Meads	123 a		07 28				07 52			
Frome	d									
Bruton	d									
Castle Cary	d									
Yeovil Pen Mill	a									
	d									
Tisbury	d	01s25				06 29		07 59	08 27	
Gillingham (Dorset)	a	01s36				06 39		08 09	08 36	
	d					06 42		08 11	08 52	
Templecombe	d	01s44				06 50		08 19	08 59	
Sherborne	d	01s51				06 57		08 26	09 07	
Yeovil Junction	a	01 57				07 03		08 32	09 12	
	d				06 15	07 07		08 39	09 23	
Yeovil Pen Mill	a								09 45	
	d									
Crewkerne	d				06 24	07 16		08 49		
Axminster	a				06 43	07 36		09 02		
	d			05 52	06 56	07 38		09 03		
Honiton	a			06 03	07 07	07 49		09 15		
	d			06 07	07 12	07 54		09 16		
Feniton	d			06 12	07 18	08 00		09 21		
Whimple	d			06 17	07 23	08 05		09 26		
Cranbrook	d			06 22	07 28	08 09		09 31		
Pinhoe	d			06 26	07 32	08 13		09 35		
Exeter Central	a			06 30	07 37	08 18		09 39		
Exeter St Davids	a			06 35	07 42	08 22		09 44		

Station		SW ◇■ E ✠	SW ◇■ ✠	SW ◇■ E ✠	SW ◇■ ✠	SW ◇■ E ✠		SW ◇■ ✠	SW ◇■ E ✠	SW ◇■ ✠	SW ◇■ E ✠	SW ◇■ ✠	SW ◇■ E ✠	
London Waterloo ⊖	d	07 10	07 50	08 20	08 50	09 20		09 50	10 20	10 50	11 20	11 50	12 20	
Clapham Junction	d	07u17	07u57	08u27	08u57	09u27		09u57	10u27	10u57	11u27	11u57	12u27	
Woking	d	07 36	08 16	08 46	09 16	09 46		10 16	10 46	11 16	11 46	12 16	12 46	
Basingstoke	d	07 59	08 38	09 07	09 38	10 07		10 38	11 07	11 38	12 07	12 38	13 07	
Overton	d	08 07	08 46		09 46			10 46		11 46		12 46		
Whitchurch (Hants)	d	08 12	08 51		09 51			10 51		11 51		12 51		
Andover	d	08 21	09 00	09 24	10 00	10 24		11 00	11 24	12 00	12 24	13 00	13 24	
Grateley	d	08 28	09 07		10 07			11 07		12 07		13 07		
Salisbury	123 a	08 42	09 20	09 42	10 20	10 42		11 20	11 42	12 20	12 42	13 20	13 42	
	d	08 47		09 47		10 47	10 52		11 47		12 47		13 47	13 52
Warminster	123 d						11 12							14 12
Westbury	123 d						11 21							14 21
Trowbridge	123 d						11 27							14 27
Bradford-on-Avon	123 d						11 33							14 33
Bath Spa	123 a						11 46							14 46
Bristol Temple Meads	123 a						12 05							15 05
Frome	d													
Bruton	d													
Castle Cary	d													
Yeovil Pen Mill	a													
	d													
Tisbury	d	09 06		10 06		11 06			12 06		13 06		14 06	
Gillingham (Dorset)	a	09 16		10 16		11 16			12 16		13 16		14 16	
	d	09 17		10 17		11 17			12 17		13 17		14 17	
Templecombe	d	09 25		10 25		11 25			12 25		13 25		14 25	
Sherborne	d	09 32		10 32		11 32			12 32		13 32		14 32	
Yeovil Junction	a	09 38		10 38		11 38			12 38		13 38		14 38	
	d	09 39		10 39		11 39			12 39		13 39		14 39	
Yeovil Pen Mill	a													
	d													
Crewkerne	d	09 49		10 49		11 49			12 49		13 49		14 49	
Axminster	a	10 02		11 02		12 02			13 02		14 02		15 02	
	d	10 03		11 03		12 03			13 03		14 03		15 03	
Honiton	a	10 15		11 15		12 15			13 15		14 15		15 15	
	d	10 16		11 16		12 16			13 16		14 16		15 16	
Feniton	d	10 21				12 21					14 21			
Whimple	d			11 24					13 24				15 24	
Cranbrook	d	10 29		11 28		12 29			13 28		14 29		15 28	
Pinhoe	d	10 33		11 32		12 33			13 32		14 33		15 32	
Exeter Central	a	10 37		11 37		12 37			13 37		14 37		15 37	
Exeter St Davids	a	10 42		11 42		12 42			13 42		14 42		15 42	

A From London Waterloo
B To Gloucester
C until 8 September. To Weymouth
D from 15 September
E ✠ to Axminster

For alternative services from London Waterloo to Woking and Basingstoke, refer to Table T155

For services between Salisbury and Bristol Temple Meads, refer to Table T123

Table T160-F

Saturdays
26 May to 8 December

London - Salisbury - Yeovil and Exeter

Station		SW ◇1 ⚒	SW ◇1 A ⚒	SW ◇1 ⚒	SW ◇1 A ⚒	SW ◇1 ⚒	SW ◇1 B ⚒	SW ◇1 C ⚒	SW ◇1 ⚒	SW ◇1 A ⚒	SW ◇1 ⚒
London Waterloo 15 ⊖	d	12 50	13 20	13 50	14 20	14 50	15 20	15 20	15 50	16 20	16 50
Clapham Junction 10	d	12u57	13u27	13u57	14u27	14u57	15u27	15u27	15u57	16u27	16u57
Woking	d	13 16	13 46	14 16	14 46	15 16	15 46	15 46	16 16	16 46	17 16
Basingstoke	d	13 38	14 07	14 38	15 07	15 38	16 07	16 07	16 38	17 07	17 38
Overton	d	13 46		14 46		15 46			16 46		17 46
Whitchurch (Hants)	d	13 51		14 51		15 51			16 51		17 51
Andover	d	14 00	14 24	15 00	15 24	16 00	16 24	16 24	17 00	17 24	18 00
Grateley	d	14 07		15 07		16 07			17 07		18 07
Salisbury 123	a	14 20	14 42	15 20	15 42	16 20	16 42	16 42	17 20	17 42	18 20
	d		14 47		15 47		16 47	16 47		17 47	
Warminster 123	d										
Westbury 123	d										
Trowbridge 123	d										
Bradford-on-Avon 123	d										
Bath Spa 7 123	a										
Bristol Temple Meads 10 123	a										
Frome	d										
Bruton	d										
Castle Cary	d										
Yeovil Pen Mill	a										
	d										
Tisbury	d		15 06		16 06		17 06	17 06		18 06	
Gillingham (Dorset)	a		15 16		16 16		17 16	17 16		18 16	
	d		15 17		16 17		17 17	17 17		18 17	
Templecombe	d		15 25		16 25		17 25	17 25		18 25	
Sherborne	d		15 32		16 32		17 32	17 32		18 32	
Yeovil Junction	a		15 38		16 38		17 38	17 38		18 38	
	d		15 39		16 39		17 39	17 39		18 39	
Yeovil Pen Mill	a										
	d										
Crewkerne	d		15 49		16 49		17 49	17 49		18 49	
Axminster	a		16 02		17 02		18 02	18 02		19 02	
	d		16 03		17 03		18 03	18 03		19 03	
Honiton	a		16 15		17 15		18 16	18 16		19 15	
	d		16 16		17 16		18 17	18 17		19 16	
Feniton	d		16 21				18 23	18 23			
Whimple	d				17 24					19 24	
Cranbrook	d		16 29		17 28		18 30	18 30		19 28	
Pinhoe	d		16 33		17 32					19 32	
Exeter Central	a		16 37		17 37		18 37	18 37		19 37	
Exeter St Davids 6	a		16 42		17 42		18 42	18 47		19 42	

Station		SW ◇1 A ⚒	SW ◇1 ⚒	SW ◇1 D ⚒	SW ◇1 ⚒	SW ◇1 D ⚒		SW ◇1 ⚒	SW ◇1 D ⚒	SW ◇1 D ⚒	SW 1 ⚒	SW 1
London Waterloo 15 ⊖	d	17 20	17 50	18 20	18 50	19 20		19 50	20 20	21 20	22 20	23 40
Clapham Junction 10	d	17u27	17u57	18u27	18u57	19u27		19u57	20u27	21u27	22u27	23u47
Woking	d	17 46	18 16	18 46	19 16	19 46		20 16	20 46	21 49	22 49	00 08
Basingstoke	d	18 07	18 38	19 07	19 38	20 07		20 38	21 07	22 14	23 12	00 28
Overton	d		18 46		19 46			20 46	21 15	22 22	23 20	00s37
Whitchurch (Hants)	d		18 51		19 51			20 51	21 20	22 27	23 25	00s42
Andover	d	18 24	19 00	19 24	20 00	20 24		21 00	21 29	22 36	23 34	00 51
Grateley	d		19 07		20 07			21 07	21 36	22 43	23 41	00s58
Salisbury 123	a	18 43	19 20	19 43	20 20	20 42		21 20	21 48	22 55	23 53	01 10
	d	18 47		19 47		20 47	20 57		21 53	23 03		
Warminster 123	d						21 17					
Westbury 123	d						21 25					
Trowbridge 123	d						21 31					
Bradford-on-Avon 123	d						21 37					
Bath Spa 7 123	a						21 50					
Bristol Temple Meads 10 123	a						22 06					
Frome	d											
Bruton	d											
Castle Cary	d											
Yeovil Pen Mill	a											
	d											
Tisbury	d	19 08		20 06		21 06			22 09	23s16		
Gillingham (Dorset)	a	19 18		20 16		21 16			22 19	23s27		
	d	19 19		20 17		21 17			22 20			
Templecombe	d	19 26		20 25		21 25			22 28	23s35		
Sherborne	d	19 34		20 32		21 32			22 35	23s42		
Yeovil Junction	a	19 39		20 38		21 38			22 41	23 49		
	d	19 41		20 39		21 39			22 42			
Yeovil Pen Mill	a											
	d											
Crewkerne	d	19 50		20 49		21 49			22 52			
Axminster	a	20 03		21 02		22 02			23 05			
	d	20 05		21 03		22 03						
Honiton	a	20 16		21 16		22 16						
	d	20 17		21 17		22 17						
Feniton	d	20 23				22 23						
Whimple	d			21 25		22 28						
Cranbrook	d	20 30		21 29		22 32						
Pinhoe	d			21 33		22 36						
Exeter Central	a	20 41		21 38		22 41						
Exeter St Davids 6	a	20 45		21 42		22 45						

A ⚒ to Axminster
B from 15 September. ⚒ to Axminster
C until 8 September. ⚒ to Axminster
D ⚒ to Salisbury

For alternative services from London Waterloo to Woking and Basingstoke, refer to Table T155

For services between Salisbury and Bristol Temple Meads, refer to Table T123

NRT MAY 2018 EDITION

Table T160-F

Sundays
20 May to 2 December

London - Salisbury - Yeovil and Exeter

Station		SW 1 A	SW 1	SW ◇1	SW ◇1 B ⚒	SW ◇1 C ⚒	SW ◇1 C ⚒	SW ◇1 C ⚒	SW ◇1 C ⚒	
London Waterloo 15 ⊖	d				08 15	09 15	10 15	11 15	12 15	
Clapham Junction 10	d				08u23	09u22	10u22	11u22	12u22	
Woking	d	00 08			08 47	09 48	10 46	11 46	12 46	
Basingstoke	d	00 28		08 05	09 08	10 09	11 07	12 07	13 07	
Overton	d	00s37		08 13	09 16		11 15		13 15	
Whitchurch (Hants)	d	00s42		08 18	09 21	10 20	11 20	12 18	13 20	
Andover	d	00 51		08 27	09 30	10 28	11 29	12 26	13 29	
Grateley	d	00s58		08 34		10 36		12 34		
Salisbury 123	a	01 10		08 46	09 46	10 48	11 45	12 46	13 45	
	d		07 06	08 51	09 51	10 51	11 51	12 51	13 51	13 55
Warminster 123	d									14 15
Westbury 123	d									14 25
Trowbridge 123	d									14 31
Bradford-on-Avon 123	d									14 37
Bath Spa 7 123	a									14 50
Bristol Temple Meads 10 123	a									15 06
Frome	d									
Bruton	d									
Castle Cary	d									
Yeovil Pen Mill	a									
	d									
Tisbury	d		07 20	09 10	10 10	11 10	12 10	13 10	14 10	
Gillingham (Dorset)	a		07 30	09 20	10 20	11 20	12 20	13 20	14 20	
	d		07 31	09 21	10 21	11 21	12 21	13 21	14 21	
Templecombe	d		07 38	09 28	10 28	11 28	12 28	13 28	14 28	
Sherborne	d		07 46	09 36	10 36	11 36	12 36	13 36	14 36	
Yeovil Junction	a		07 51	09 41	10 41	11 41	12 41	13 41	14 41	
	d		07 53	09 43	10 43	11 43	12 43	13 43	14 43	
Yeovil Pen Mill	a									
	d									
Crewkerne	d		08 02	09 52	10 52	11 52	12 52	13 52	14 52	
Axminster	a		08 15	10 05	11 05	12 05	13 05	14 05	15 05	
	d		08 16	10 06	11 06	12 06	13 06	14 06	15 06	
Honiton	a		08 27	10 17	11 17	12 17	13 17	14 17	15 17	
	d		08 31	10 18	11 18	12 18	13 18	14 18	15 18	
Feniton	d		08 36	10 24		12 24		14 24		
Whimple	d		08 41		11 26		13 26		15 26	
Cranbrook	d		08 46	10 31	11 31	12 31	13 31	14 31	15 31	
Pinhoe	d		08 50	10 35	11 35	12 35	13 35	14 35	15 35	
Exeter Central	a		08 54	10 40	11 40	12 40	13 40	14 40	15 39	
Exeter St Davids 6	a		08 59	10 45	11 45	12 45	13 45	14 45	15 44	

Station		SW ◇1 C ⚒	SW ◇1 C ⚒	SW ◇1 C ⚒	SW ◇1	SW ◇1 C ⚒	SW ◇1 C ⚒	SW ◇1	SW ◇1 C ⚒	SW ◇1 D	SW ◇1 E	SW ◇1	SW ◇1 F ⚒	SW ◇1
London Waterloo 15 ⊖	d	13 15	14 15	15 15		16 15	17 15	17 45	18 15			18 45	19 15	19 45
Clapham Junction 10	d	13u22	14u22	15u22		16u22	17u22	17u53	18u22			18u53	19u22	19u53
Woking	d	13 46	14 46	15 46		16 46	17 46		18 46				19 46	
Basingstoke	d	14 07	15 07	16 07		17 07	18 07		19 07				20 07	
Overton	d		15 15			17 15			19 15					
Whitchurch (Hants)	d	14 18	15 20	16 18		17 20	18 18		19 20				20 18	
Andover	d	14 26	15 29	16 26		17 29	18 26	18 49	19 29			19 49	20 26	20 49
Grateley	d	14 34		16 34			18 34						20 34	
Salisbury 123	a	14 46	15 45	16 46		17 45	18 46	19 05	19 45			20 05	20 46	21 05
	d	14 51	15 51	16 51	17 10	17 51	18 51		19 51	19 55	19 55		20 51	
Warminster 123	d				17 36					20 15	20 15			
Westbury 123	d				17 48					20 23	20 23			
Trowbridge 123	d									20 29	20 29			
Bradford-on-Avon 123	d									20 35	20 35			
Bath Spa 7 123	a									20 49	20 50			
Bristol Temple Meads 10 123	a									21 05	21 07			
Frome	d				17a57									
Bruton	d													
Castle Cary	d													
Yeovil Pen Mill	a													
	d													
Tisbury	d	15 10	16 10	17 10		18 10	19 10		20 10				21 10	
Gillingham (Dorset)	a	15 20	16 20	17 20		18 20	19 20		20 20				21 20	
	d	15 21	16 21	17 21		18 21	19 21		20 21				21 21	
Templecombe	d	15 28	16 28	17 28		18 28	19 28		20 28				21 28	
Sherborne	d	15 36	16 36	17 36		18 36	19 36		20 36				21 36	
Yeovil Junction	a	15 41	16 41	17 41		18 41	19 41		20 41				21 41	
	d	15 43	16 43	17 43		18 43	19 43		20 43				21 43	
Yeovil Pen Mill	a													
	d													
Crewkerne	d	15 52	16 52	17 52		18 52	19 52		20 52				21 52	
Axminster	a	16 05	17 05	18 05		19 05	20 05		21 05				22 05	
	d	16 06	17 06	18 06		19 06	20 06		21 06				22 06	
Honiton	a	16 17	17 17	18 17		19 17	20 17		21 17				22 19	
	d	16 18	17 18	18 18		19 18	20 18		21 18				22 20	
Feniton	d	16 24		18 24			20 24		21 24				22 25	
Whimple	d		17 26			19 26			21 29				22 30	
Cranbrook	d	16 31	17 31	18 31		19 31	20 31		21 33				22 35	
Pinhoe	d	16 35	17 35	18 35		19 35	20 35		21 37				22 39	
Exeter Central	a	16 40	17 40	18 40		19 40	20 40		21 42				22 43	
Exeter St Davids 6	a	16 45	17 45	18 45		19 45	20 45		21 46				22 48	

Station		SW ◇1 F ⚒	SW ◇1	SW ◇1 F ⚒	SW 1 ⚒	SW 1
London Waterloo 15 ⊖	d	20 15	20 45	21 15	22 15	23 35
Clapham Junction 10	d	20u22	20u53	21u22	22u22	23u44
Woking	d	20 46		21 46	22 46	00 08
Basingstoke	d	21 07		22 07	23 07	00 41
Overton	d	21 15			23 15	00s49
Whitchurch (Hants)	d	21 20		22 20	23 20	00s54
Andover	d	21 29		22 28	23 29	01 03
Grateley	d			22 36	23 36	01s10
Salisbury 123	a	21 45	22 05	22 48	23 48	01 22
	d	21 51		22 52		
Warminster 123	d					
Westbury 123	d					
Trowbridge 123	d					
Bradford-on-Avon 123	d					
Bath Spa 7 123	a					
Bristol Temple Meads 10 123	a					
Frome	d					
Bruton	d					
Castle Cary	d					
Yeovil Pen Mill	a					
	d					
Tisbury	d	22 10		23 11		
Gillingham (Dorset)	a	22 20		23 21		
	d	22 21		23 22		
Templecombe	d	22 28		23 30		
Sherborne	d	22 36		23 37		
Yeovil Junction	a	22 42		23 43		
	d			23 44		
Yeovil Pen Mill	a					
	d					
Crewkerne	d			23 54		
Axminster	a			00 07		
	d			00 08		
Honiton	a			00 19		
	d			00 20		
Feniton	d			00 25		
Whimple	d			00 30		
Cranbrook	d			00 35		
Pinhoe	d			00 39		
Exeter Central	a					
Exeter St Davids 6	a			00 46		

A not 20 May. From London Waterloo
B ⚒ from Woking to Axminster
C ⚒ to Axminster
D from 16 September
E until 9 September
F ⚒ to Salisbury

For alternative services from London Waterloo to Woking and Basingstoke, refer to Table T155

For services between Salisbury and Bristol Temple Meads, refer to Table T123

Table T160-R

Mondays to Fridays

21 May to 7 December

Yeovil and Exeter - Salisbury - London

Miles			SW	SW	SW	SW	SW	GW	SW	SW	SW	SW	SW	SW	SW	SW	SW	SW	SW	SW	SW	SW	SW
			MX 1	◇1	◇1	◇1	◇1		◇1	◇1	◇1	◇1	◇1	◇1	◇1	◇1	◇1	◇1	◇1	◇1	◇1	◇1	◇1
			A	B	C	B	C		D	E	F	F	G	F	G	G	F		G		G		G
				🛒	🛒	🛒	🛒		🛒	🛒	🛒	🛒	🛒	🛒	🛒	🛒	🛒		🛒	🛒	🛒	🛒	🛒
0	**Exeter St Davids 6**	d										05 10			06 41	07 25			08 23		09 25		10 25
0¾	**Exeter Central**	d										05 14			06 45	07 30			08 27		09 30		10 30
3½	Pinhoe	d										05 19			06 50	07 34			08 32		09 34		10 34
—	Cranbrook	d										05 23			06 54	07 39			08 36		09 40		10 39
9¼	Whimple	d										05 28			06 59				08 41		09 45		
13	Feniton	d										05 34			07 05				08 47				10 47
17½	Honiton	a										05 40			07 11	07 51			08 53		09 54		10 53
—		d										05 41	06 19		07 12	07 52			08 55		09 55		10 55
27¾	Axminster	a										05 51	06 29		07 22	08 02			09 05		10 05		11 05
—		d										05 52	06 30		07 23	08 03			09 06		10 06		11 06
40¾	Crewkerne	d										06 05	06 43		07 36	08 16			09 19		10 19		11 19
—	Yeovil Pen Mill	a																					
—		d									05 41												
49¾	Yeovil Junction	a									05 46	06 14	06 52		07 45	08 25			09 27		10 27		11 27
—		d	00 06						05 11	05 14	05 50	06 20	06 53	07 22	07 50	08 29			09 29		10 29		11 29
54¼	Sherborne	d							05 17	05 20	05 56	06 26	07 00	07 28	07 56	08 35			09 35		10 35		11 35
60¼	Templecombe	d							05 25	05 28	06 04	06 34	07 07	07 36	08 04	08 43			09 43		10 43		11 43
67¾	Gillingham (Dorset)	a							05 32	05 35	06 11	06 41	07 14	07 43	08 11	08 50			09 50		10 50		11 50
—		d							05 33	05 36	06 12	06 42	07 15	07 44	08 12	08 51	09 18		09 51		10 51		11 51
76¼	Tisbury	d							05 43	05 46	06 24	06 52	07 26	07 54	08 22	09 01	09 28		10 01		11 01		12 01
—	Yeovil Pen Mill	a																					
—		d																					
—	Castle Cary	d																					
—	Bruton	d																					
—	Frome	d																					
—	Bristol Temple Meads 10	123 d																08 51					
—	Bath Spa 7	123 d																09 07					
—	Bradford-on-Avon	123 d																09 22					
—	Trowbridge	123 d																09 29					
—	Westbury	123 d						05 24										09 39					
—	Warminster	123 d						05 32										09 46					
88¾	**Salisbury**	123 a	00 43					05 53	05 58	06 01	06 39	07 07	07 40	08 09	08 37	09 16	09 42	10 09	10 16		11 16		12 16
—		d		05 12	05 15	05 40	05 43		06 03	06 06	06 45	07 15	07 45	08 15	08 47	09 21	09 47		10 21	10 47	11 21	11 47	12 21
99¾	Grateley	d		05 24	05 27	05 52	05 55		06 16	06 19	06 57	07 27	07 57	08 27	08 59		09 59			10 59		11 59	
106	Andover	d		05 32	05 35	06 00	06 03		06 23	06 26	07 05	07 35	08 05	08 35	09 06	09 38	10 06		10 38	11 06	11 38	12 06	12 38
113¼	Whitchurch (Hants)	d		05 40	05 43	06 08	06 11		06 32	06 35	07 13	07 43	08 13	08 43	09 14		10 14			11 14		12 14	
117	Overton	d		05 46	05 49	06 14	06 17		06 38	06 41	07 19	07 49	08 19	08 49	09 20		10 20			11 20		12 20	
124¾	**Basingstoke**	a		05 58	05 58	06 26	06 26		06 49	06 49	07 28	07 58	08 28	08 58	09 28	09 55	10 28		10 55	11 28	11 55	12 28	12 55
148¼	Woking	a		06 18	06 18	06 46	06 46					08 18	08 48	09 18	09 49	10 15	10 49		11 15	11 49	12 15	12 49	13 15
168¼	Clapham Junction 10	a		06 38	06 38				07 28	07 28				09 38	10 09	10 36			11 36		12 36		13 36
172½	**London Waterloo 15**	⊖ a		06 49	06 49	07 16	07 16		07 39	07 39	08 14	08 46	09 17	09 51	10 19	10 49	11 19		11 49	12 19	12 49	13 19	13 49

A From Exeter St Davids
B from 8 October
C until 5 October
D from 8 October. 🛒 from Salisbury
E until 5 October. 🛒 from Salisbury
F 🛒 from Salisbury
G 🛒 from Axminster

For alternative services from Woking and Basingstoke to London Waterloo, refer to Table T155

For services between Bristol Temple Meads and Salisbury, refer to Table T123

Table T160-R

Mondays to Fridays

21 May to 7 December

Yeovil and Exeter - Salisbury - London

		SW	SW	SW	SW	SW	SW	SW	SW	SW	SW	SW	SW	SW	SW	SW	SW	SW	SW	SW	SW	SW
		◇1	◇1	◇1	◇1	◇1	◇1	◇1	◇1	◇1	◇1	◇1	◇1	◇1	◇1	◇1	◇1	◇1	1	◇1	◇1	◇1
			A			A		A		A	B		A			A		A		A		
		🛒	🛒	🛒	🛒	🛒	🛒	🛒	🛒	🛒	🛒		🛒	🛒		🛒	🛒	🛒		🛒		
Exeter St Davids 6	d		11 25			12 25		13 25		14 25			15 25			16 24		17 25	17 46	18 25		19 25
Exeter Central	d		11 30			12 30		13 30		14 30			15 30			16 28		17 30	17 50	18 30		19 30
Pinhoe	d		11 34			12 34		13 34		14 34			15 34			16 33		17 34	17 56	18 36		19 36
Cranbrook	d		11 39			12 39		13 39		14 39			15 39			16 37		17 39	18 00	18 40		19 40
Whimple	d		11 44					13 44					15 44						18 05	18 45		19 45
Feniton	d					12 47				14 47								17 47	18 10	18 50		
Honiton	a		11 54			12 53		13 54		14 53			15 54			16 49		17 54	18 17	18 56		19 54
	d		11 55			12 55		13 55		14 55			15 55			16 56		17 55	18 19	18 59		19 55
Axminster	a		12 05			13 05		14 05		15 05			16 05			17 06		18 05	18 29	19 09		20 05
	d		12 06			13 06		14 06		15 06			16 06			17 07		18 06		19 10		20 06
Crewkerne	d		12 19			13 19		14 19		15 19			16 19			17 20		18 19		19 23		20 19
Yeovil Pen Mill	a																					
	d										15 44											
Yeovil Junction	a		12 27			13 27		14 27		15 27	15 49		16 27			17 28		18 27		19 31		20 28
	d		12 29			13 29		14 29		15 29	15 53		16 29		16 46	17 30		18 29		19 33		20 29
Sherborne	d		12 35			13 35		14 35		15 35	15 59		16 35			17 36		18 35		19 39		20 36
Templecombe	d		12 43			13 43		14 43		15 43	16 07		16 43			17 44		18 43		19 47		20 43
Gillingham (Dorset)	a		12 50			13 50		14 50		15 50	16 14		16 50			17 51		18 50		19 54		20 50
	d		12 51			13 51		14 51		15 51	16 17		16 51			17 52		18 51		19 55		20 51
Tisbury	d		13 01			14 01		15 01		16 01	16 28		17 01			18 02		19 01		20 07		21 02
Yeovil Pen Mill	a														16 51							
	d														16 53							
Castle Cary	d														17 07							
Bruton	d														17 12							
Frome	d														17 24							
Bristol Temple Meads 10	123 d				12 49							15 51										
Bath Spa 7	123 d				13 07							16 08										
Bradford-on-Avon	123 d				13 19							16 24										
Trowbridge	123 d				13 28							16 30										
Westbury	123 d				13 39							16 39			17 45						20 15	
Warminster	123 d				13 46							16 47			17 52						20 23	
Salisbury	123 a		13 16		14 12	14 16		15 16		16 16	16 43	17 09	17 16		18 17	18 22		19 23		20 22	20 44	21 22
	d	12 47	13 21	13 47		14 21	14 47	15 21	15 47	16 21	16 47		17 21	17 47		18 27	18 47	19 26		20 26		21 26
Grateley	d	12 59		13 59			14 59		15 59		16 59			17 59			18 59	19 38		20 38		21 38
Andover	d	13 06	13 38	14 06		14 38	15 06	15 38	16 06	16 38	17 06		17 38	18 06		18 44	19 06	19 45		20 45		21 45
Whitchurch (Hants)	d	13 14		14 14			15 14		16 14		17 14			18 14			19 14	19 53		20 53		21 53
Overton	d	13 20		14 20			15 20		16 20		17 20			18 20			19 20	19 59		20 59		21 59
Basingstoke	a	13 28	13 55	14 28		14 55	15 28	15 55	16 28	16 55	17 29		17 55	18 28		19 01	19 28	20 08		21 08		22 07
Woking	a	13 49	14 15	14 49		15 15	15 49	16 15	16 49	17 15	17 49		18 15	18 49		19 21	19 49	20 29		21 29		22 28
Clapham Junction 10	a		14 36			15 36		16 36		17 36			18 36			19 41		20 52		21 52		22 48
London Waterloo 15	⊖ a	14 19	14 49	15 19		15 49	16 19	16 47	17 19	17 49	18 16		18 49	19 19		19 50	20 19	21 00		22 04		22 58

		SW	SW	SW	SW	SW
		◇	1	1	1	1
Exeter St Davids 6	d	20 25		21 25		22 57
Exeter Central	d	20 30		21 30		23 01
Pinhoe	d	20 35		21 37		23 06
Cranbrook	d	20 39		21 41		23 10
Whimple	d	20 44		21 46		23 15
Feniton	d	20 50		21 52		23 21
Honiton	a	20 56		21 58		23 27
	d	20 57		21 59		23 32
Axminster	a	21 07		22 09		23 42
	d	21 08		22 10		23 43
Crewkerne	d	21 21		22 23		23 56
Yeovil Pen Mill	a					
	d					
Yeovil Junction	a	21 29		22 31		00 04
	d	21 31		22 33		00 06
Sherborne	d	21 37		22 39		
Templecombe	d	21 45		22 47		
Gillingham (Dorset)	a	21 52		22 54		
	d	21 53		22 55		
Tisbury	d	22 03		23 05		
Yeovil Pen Mill	a					
	d					
Castle Cary	d					
Bruton	d					
Frome	d					
Bristol Temple Meads 10	123 d				22 23	
Bath Spa 7	123 d				22 36	
Bradford-on-Avon	123 d				22 47	
Trowbridge	123 d				22 53	
Westbury	123 d		22 18		23 05	
Warminster	123 d		22 26		23 12	
Salisbury	123 a	22 18	22 48	23 29	23 38	00 43
	d	22 26				
Grateley	d	22 38				
Andover	d	22 45				
Whitchurch (Hants)	d	22 53				
Overton	d	22 59				
Basingstoke	a	23 07				
Woking	a					
Clapham Junction 10	a					
London Waterloo 15	⊖ a					

A 🛒 from Axminster
B 🛒 from Salisbury

For alternative services from Woking and Basingstoke to London Waterloo, refer to Table T155

For services between Bristol Temple Meads and Salisbury, refer to Table T123

Table T160-R

Saturdays

26 May to 8 December

Yeovil and Exeter - Salisbury - London

		SW	SW	SW	SW	SW	GW	SW	SW	SW	SW	SW	SW	SW	SW	SW	SW	SW	SW	SW	SW	SW	SW
		1	◇1	◇1	◇1	◇1		◇1	◇1	◇1	◇1	◇1	◇1	◇1	◇1	◇1	◇1	◇1	◇1	◇1	◇1	◇1	◇1
		A	B	C	B	C				D	E		E	E		D	E		E		E		E
			🛒	🛒	🛒	🛒		🛒	🛒	🛒	🛒	🛒	🛒	🛒	🛒	🛒	🛒	🛒	🛒	🛒	🛒	🛒	🛒
Exeter St Davids 6	d									05 10			06 41	07 25			08 24		09 25		10 25		11 25
Exeter Central	d									05 14			06 45	07 30			08 28		09 30		10 30		11 30
Pinhoe	d									05 19			06 50	07 34			08 33		09 34		10 34		11 34
Cranbrook	d									05 23			06 54	07 39			08 37		09 40		10 39		11 39
Whimple	d									05 28			06 59	07 44			08 42		09 45				11 44
Feniton	d									05 34			07 05				08 47				10 47		
Honiton	a									05 40			07 11	07 53			08 54		09 54		10 53		11 54
	d									05 41	06 19		07 13	07 55			08 55		09 55		10 55		11 55
Axminster	a									05 51	06 29		07 23	08 05			09 05		10 05		11 05		12 05
	d									05 52	06 30		07 24	08 06			09 06		10 06		11 06		12 06
Crewkerne	d									06 05	06 43		07 37	08 19			09 19		10 19		11 19		12 19
Yeovil Pen Mill	a																						
	d																						
Yeovil Junction	a									06 14	06 52		07 45	08 27			09 27		10 27		11 27		12 27
	d	00 06								06 20	06 53		07 50	08 29			09 29		10 29		11 29		12 29
Sherborne	d									06 26	07 00		07 56	08 35			09 35		10 35		11 35		12 35
Templecombe	d									06 34	07 07		08 04	08 43			09 43		10 43		11 43		12 43
Gillingham (Dorset)	a									06 41	07 14		08 11	08 50			09 50		10 50		11 50		12 50
	d									06 42	07 15		08 12	08 51			09 51		10 51		11 51		12 51
Tisbury	d									06 52	07 26		08 22	09 01			10 01		11 01		12 01		13 01
Yeovil Pen Mill	a																						
	d																						
Castle Cary	d																						
Bruton	d																						
Frome	d																						
Bristol Temple Meads 10 123	d															08 51							
Bath Spa 7 123	d															09 07							
Bradford-on-Avon 123	d															09 21							
Trowbridge 123	d															09 27							
Westbury 123	d						05 24									09 39							
Warminster 123	d						05 32									09 46							
Salisbury 123	a	00 43					05 55			07 07	07 40		08 37	09 16		10 09	10 16		11 16		12 16		13 16
	d		05 12	05 15	05 44	05 47		06 21	06 47	07 21	07 47	08 21	08 47	09 21	09 47		10 21	10 47	11 21	11 47	12 21	12 47	13 21
Grateley	d		05 24	05 27	05 56	05 59			06 59		07 59		08 59		09 59			10 59		11 59		12 59	
Andover	d		05 32	05 35	06 03	06 06		06 38	07 06	07 38	08 06	08 38	09 06	09 38	10 06		10 38	11 06	11 38	12 06	12 38	13 06	13 38
Whitchurch (Hants)	d		05 40	05 43	06 11	06 14			07 14		08 14		09 14		10 14			11 14		12 14		13 14	
Overton	d		05 46	05 49	06 17	06 20			07 20		08 20		09 20		10 20			11 20		12 20		13 20	
Basingstoke	a		05 58	05 58	06 28	06 28		06 55	07 28	07 55	08 28	08 55	09 28	09 55	10 28		10 55	11 28	11 55	12 28	12 55	13 28	13 55
Woking	a		06 18	06 18	06 49	06 49		07 15	07 49	08 17	08 49	09 15	09 49	10 15	10 49		11 15	11 49	12 15	12 49	13 15	13 49	14 15
Clapham Junction 10	a		06 38	06 38				07 38		08 37		09 36		10 36			11 36		12 36		13 36		14 36
London Waterloo 15 ⊖	a		06 49	06 49	07 19	07 19		07 49	08 19	08 49	09 19	09 49	10 19	10 49	11 19		11 49	12 19	12 49	13 19	13 49	14 19	14 49

A From Exeter St Davids
B from 13 October
C until 6 October
D 🛒 from Salisbury
E 🛒 from Axminster

For alternative services from Woking and Basingstoke to London Waterloo, refer to Table T155

For services between Bristol Temple Meads and Salisbury, refer to Table T123

Table T160-R

Saturdays

26 May to 8 December

Yeovil and Exeter - Salisbury - London

		SW	SW	SW	SW	SW	SW	SW	SW	SW	SW	SW	SW	SW	SW	SW	SW	SW	SW	SW	SW	SW
		◇1	◇1	◇1	◇1	◇1	◇1	◇1	◇1	◇1	◇1	◇1	◇1	◇1	◇1	◇1	◇1	◇1	◇1	1	1	1
				A		A		A		B	A		A	C	D	A	A					
		🛒	🛒	🛒	🛒	🛒	🛒	🛒	🛒	🛒	🛒	🛒	🛒	🛒	🛒	🛒	🛒					
Exeter St Davids 6	d			12 25		13 25		14 25			15 25		16 25			17 25	18 25	19 25	20 25	21 25		22 57
Exeter Central	d			12 30		13 30		14 30			15 30		16 30			17 30	18 30	19 30	20 30	21 30		23 01
Pinhoe	d			12 34		13 34		14 35			15 34		16 35			17 34	18 34	19 34	20 34	21 34		23 06
Cranbrook	d			12 39		13 39		14 39			15 39		16 39			17 39	18 40	19 39	20 39	21 39		23 10
Whimple	d					13 44					15 44					17 44		19 44	20 44	21 44		23 15
Feniton	d			12 47				14 47					16 47			17 50	18 48		20 49	21 50		23 21
Honiton	a			12 54		13 54		14 53			15 54		16 53			17 56	18 54	19 54	20 55	21 56		23 27
	d			12 55		13 55		14 55			15 55		16 55			17 57	18 55	19 55	20 56	21 57		23 32
Axminster	a			13 05		14 05		15 05			16 05		17 05			18 07	19 05	20 05	21 06	22 07		23 42
	d			13 06		14 06		15 06			16 06		17 06			18 08	19 06	20 06	21 07	22 08		23 43
Crewkerne	d			13 19		14 19		15 19			16 19		17 19			18 21	19 19	20 19	21 20	22 21		23 56
Yeovil Pen Mill	a																					
	d														17 38							
Yeovil Junction	a			13 27		14 27		15 27			16 27		17 27		17 44	18 29	19 27	20 27	21 29	22 29		00 07
	d			13 29		14 29		15 29			16 29		17 29		17 52	18 31	19 29	20 29	21 30	22 31		00 09
Sherborne	d			13 35		14 35		15 35			16 35		17 35		17 59	18 37	19 35	20 35	21 37	22 37		
Templecombe	d			13 43		14 43		15 43			16 43		17 43		18 06	18 45	19 43	20 43	21 44	22 45		
Gillingham (Dorset)	a			13 50		14 50		15 50			16 50		17 50		18 13	18 52	19 50	20 50	21 51	22 52		
	d			13 51		14 51		15 51			16 51		17 51		18 17	18 53	19 51	20 51	21 52	22 53		
Tisbury	d			14 01		15 01		16 01			17 01		18 01		18 28	19 03	20 01	21 01	22 03	23 03		
Yeovil Pen Mill	a																					
	d																					
Castle Cary	d																					
Bruton	d																					
Frome	d																					
Bristol Temple Meads 10 123	d		12 51							15 51											22 23	
Bath Spa 7 123	d		13 07							16 07											22 36	
Bradford-on-Avon 123	d		13 20							16 24											22 47	
Trowbridge 123	d		13 27							16 30											22 53	
Westbury 123	d		13 39							16 39											23 05	
Warminster 123	d		13 46							16 47											23 12	
Salisbury 123	a		14 10	14 16		15 16		16 16		17 09	17 16		18 16		18 42	19 18	20 16	21 19	22 23	23 29	23 35	00 44
	d	13 47		14 21	14 47	15 21	15 47	16 21	16 47		17 21	17 47	18 21	18 47	18 47	19 26	20 26	21 26	22 27			
Grateley	d	13 59			14 59		15 59		16 59			17 59		18 59	18 59	19 38	20 38	21 38	22 39			
Andover	d	14 06		14 38	15 06	15 38	16 06	16 38	17 06		17 38	18 06	18 38	19 06	19 06	19 45	20 45	21 45	22 47			
Whitchurch (Hants)	d	14 14			15 14		16 14		17 14			18 14		19 14	19 14	19 53	20 53	21 53	22 55			
Overton	d	14 20			15 20		16 20		17 20			18 20		19 20	19 20	19 59	20 59	21 59	23 00			
Basingstoke	a	14 28		14 55	15 28	15 55	16 28	16 55	17 28		17 55	18 28	18 55	19 28	19 28	20 08	21 08	22 07	23 09			
Woking	a	14 49		15 15	15 49	16 15	16 49	17 15	17 49		18 15	18 49	19 15	19 49	19 49	20 29	21 29	22 28				
Clapham Junction 10	a			15 36		16 36		17 36			18 36		19 36			20 52	21 52	22 48				
London Waterloo 15 ⊖	a	15 19		15 49	16 19	16 49	17 19	17 49	18 19		18 49	19 19	19 49	20 19	20 19	21 04	22 04	22 57				

A 🛒 from Axminster
B 🛒 from Salisbury
C from 15 September. 🛒 to Basingstoke
D until 8 September. From Weymouth. 🛒 to Basingstoke

For alternative services from Woking and Basingstoke to London Waterloo, refer to Table T155

For services between Bristol Temple Meads and Salisbury, refer to Table T123

Table T160-R

Sundays

20 May to 2 December

Yeovil and Exeter - Salisbury - London

	SW	SW	SW	SW	SW	SW	SW	SW	SW	SW	SW
	1	◇1	◇1	◇1	◇1	◇1	◇1	◇1	◇1	◇1	◇1
	A	B	C	B	C	D	D	D	E	F	F
Exeter St Davids d									09 25	10 25	11 25
Exeter Central d									09 30	10 30	11 30
Pinhoe d									09 35	10 37	11 37
Cranbrook d									09 39	10 42	11 42
Whimple d									09 44		11 47
Feniton d									09 49	10 50	
Honiton a									09 56	10 56	11 56
d								08 58	09 57	10 57	11 57
Axminster a								09 08	10 07	11 07	12 07
d								09 09	10 09	11 09	12 09
Crewkerne d								09 22	10 22	11 22	12 22
Yeovil Pen Mill a											
d											
Yeovil Junction a								09 30	10 30	11 30	12 30
d	00 09					07 32		09 32	10 32	11 32	12 32
Sherborne d						07 38		09 38	10 38	11 38	12 38
Templecombe d						07 46		09 46	10 46	11 46	12 46
Gillingham (Dorset) a						07 53		09 53	10 53	11 53	12 53
d						07 54	08 54	09 54	10 54	11 54	12 54
Tisbury d						08 05	09 05	10 05	11 05	12 05	13 05
Yeovil Pen Mill a											
d											
Castle Cary d											
Bruton d											
Frome d											
Bristol Temple Meads 10 123 d											
Bath Spa 7 123 d											
Bradford-on-Avon 123 d											
Trowbridge 123 d											
Westbury 123 d											
Warminster 123 d											
Salisbury 123 a	00 44					08 20	09 20	10 20	11 20	12 20	13 20
d		06 42	06 45	07 24	07 27	08 27	09 27	10 27	11 29	12 27	13 27
Grateley d				07 36	07 39	08 39	09 39		11 39		13 39
Andover d		06 59	07 02	07 43	07 46	08 46	09 46	10 44	11 46	12 44	13 46
Whitchurch (Hants) d				07 51	07 54	08 54	09 54	10 52	11 55	12 52	13 54
Overton d				07 57	08 00	09 00		10 58		12 58	
Basingstoke a		07 19	07 19	08 08	08 08	09 08	10 05	11 06	12 07	13 06	14 05
Woking a		07 39	07 39	08 28	08 28	09 28	10 28	11 28	12 28	13 28	14 28
Clapham Junction 10 a		08 05	08 05	08 57	08 57	09 57	10 49	11 49	12 49	13 49	14 49
London Waterloo 15 ⊖ a		08 20	08 20	09 12	09 12	10 11	11 04	12 04	13 04	13 59	14 59

	SW	SW	SW	SW	SW	SW	SW	SW	SW	SW	SW
	◇1	◇1	◇1	◇1	◇1	◇1	◇1	◇1	◇1	◇1	◇1
	F	F	F		D	F		F		G	F
Exeter St Davids d	12 25	13 25	14 25			15 25		16 25		17 25	18 25
Exeter Central d	12 30	13 30	14 30			15 30		16 30		17 30	18 30
Pinhoe d	12 37	13 37	14 37			15 37		16 37		17 37	18 37
Cranbrook d	12 42	13 42	14 41			15 42		16 42		17 42	18 42
Whimple d		13 47				15 47				17 47	
Feniton d	12 50		14 49					16 50			18 50
Honiton a	12 56	13 56	14 55			15 56		16 56		17 56	18 56
d	12 57	13 57	14 57			15 57		16 57		17 57	18 57
Axminster a	13 07	14 07	15 07			16 07		17 07		18 07	19 07
d	13 09	14 09	15 09			16 09		17 09		18 09	19 09
Crewkerne d	13 22	14 22	15 22			16 22		17 22		18 22	19 22
Yeovil Pen Mill a											
d											
Yeovil Junction a	13 30	14 30	15 30			16 30		17 30		18 30	19 30
d	13 32	14 32	15 32			16 32		17 32		18 32	19 32
Sherborne d	13 38	14 38	15 38			16 38		17 38		18 38	19 38
Templecombe d	13 46	14 46	15 46			16 46		17 46		18 46	19 46
Gillingham (Dorset) a	13 53	14 53	15 53			16 53		17 53		18 53	19 53
d	13 54	14 54	15 54	16 21		16 54	17 21	17 54		18 54	19 54
Tisbury d	14 05	15 05	16 05	16 32		17 05	17 32	18 05		19 05	20 05
Yeovil Pen Mill a											
d											
Castle Cary d											
Bruton d											
Frome d									18 04		
Bristol Temple Meads 10 123 d					16 04						
Bath Spa 7 123 d					16 20						
Bradford-on-Avon 123 d					16 31						
Trowbridge 123 d					16 37						
Westbury 123 d					16 46				18 16		
Warminster 123 d					16 53				18 23		
Salisbury 123 a	14 20	15 20	16 20	16 47	17 16	17 20	17 47	18 20	18 43	19 20	20 20
d	14 27	15 27	16 27	16 52		17 27	17 52	18 27	18 52	19 27	20 27
Grateley d		15 39				17 39				19 39	
Andover d	14 44	15 46	16 44	17 09		17 46	18 09	18 44	19 09	19 46	20 44
Whitchurch (Hants) d	14 52	15 54	16 52			17 54		18 52		19 54	20 52
Overton d	14 58		16 58					18 58			20 58
Basingstoke a	15 06	16 05	17 06	17 26		18 05	18 26	19 06	19 26	20 05	21 06
Woking a	15 28	16 28	17 28	17 48		18 28	18 48	19 28	19 48	20 28	21 28
Clapham Junction 10 a	15 49	16 49	17 49	18 08		18 49	19 08	19 49	20 08	20 49	21 49
London Waterloo 15 ⊖ a	15 59	16 59	17 59	18 19		18 59	19 19	19 59	20 19	20 59	21 59

	SW	SW	SW	SW	SW
	◇1	◇1	1	1	1
Exeter St Davids d	19 25	20 25		21 25	23 15
Exeter Central d	19 30	20 30		21 30	23 19
Pinhoe d	19 37			21 37	23s24
Cranbrook d	19 42	20 41		21 42	23s28
Whimple d	19 47	20 46		21 47	
Feniton d		20 51		21 52	
Honiton a	19 56	20 56		21 58	23s40
d	19 57	20 57		21 59	
Axminster a	20 07	21 08		22 09	23s51
d	20 09	21 09		22 10	
Crewkerne d	20 22	21 22		22 23	00s12
Yeovil Pen Mill a					
d					
Yeovil Junction a	20 30	21 31		22 32	00s21
d	20 32	21 32		22 33	
Sherborne d	20 38	21 38		22 40	
Templecombe d	20 46	21 46		22 47	
Gillingham (Dorset) a	20 53	21 53		22 54	
d	20 54	21 54		22 56	
Tisbury d	21 05	22 05		23 07	
Yeovil Pen Mill a					
d					
Castle Cary d					
Bruton d					
Frome d					
Bristol Temple Meads 10 123 d			21 35		
Bath Spa 7 123 d			21 49		
Bradford-on-Avon 123 d			22 00		
Trowbridge 123 d			22 06		
Westbury 123 d			22 15		
Warminster 123 d			22 22		
Salisbury 123 a	21 20	22 20	22 45	23 21	00 57
d	21 27	22 27			
Grateley d	21 39	22 39			
Andover d	21 46	22 46			
Whitchurch (Hants) d	21 54	22 54			
Overton d		23 00			
Basingstoke a	22 06	23 08			
Woking a	22 28				
Clapham Junction 10 a	22 49				
London Waterloo 15 ⊖ a	22 59				

A not 20 May. From Exeter St Davids
B from 7 October
C until 30 September
D from Salisbury
E from Yeovil Junction
F from Axminster
G from Axminster to Woking

For alternative services from Woking and Basingstoke to London Waterloo, refer to Table T155

For services between Bristol Temple Meads and Salisbury, refer to Table T123

Table T165-F

Mondays to Fridays

21 May to 7 December

Portsmouth and Chichester - Fareham and Southampton

Miles	Miles		SW	SW	SN	SW	SN	SW	GW	SN	SW
			1	1	1	1	1	1		1	1
			A	B	C		D	E	F	C	
0	—	Portsmouth Harbour d	04 55	05 00				05 43	06 00		
0¾	—	Portsmouth & Southsea d	05 00	05 05		05 16		05 48	06 04		06 23
1¾	—	Fratton d	05 04	05 09		05 20		05 52	06 08		06 27
4	—	Hilsea d	05 08	05 13		05 24		05 56			06 31
—	0	Chichester 4 d			05 07		05 23			06 11	
—	8¾	Havant d			05 17		05 34			06 22	
5½	12¾	**Cosham** d	05 16	05 19	05 24	05 29	05 42	06 03	06 15	06 30	06 36
8	—	**Portchester** d	05 20	05 23	05 28	05 34	05 46	06 08			06 41
11¼	—	**Fareham** a	05 25	05 28	05 33	05 39	05 51	06 13	06 23	06 38	06 46
—	—	d			05 34	05 40	05 52		06 24	06 38	06 47
15	—	**Swanwick** d			05 40	05 46	05 58			06 44	06 53
17	—	**Bursledon** d				05 50					06 57
18¼	—	**Hamble** d				05 53					07 00
19	—	**Netley** d			05 46	05 55	06 04				07 02
20¾	—	**Sholing** d				05 59					07 06
21½	—	**Woolston** d			05 50	06 01	06 08				07 08
23¼	—	**Bitterne** d				06 05					07 12
—	—	St Denys d				06 08					07 15
25¾	—	Southampton Central a			06 00	06 13	06 18		06 45	07 02	07 21

Miles	Miles		SW	SN	SW	GW	SN	SW	SN	SW	SN	SW	SW
			◇1	1	◇1	◇	1	◇1	1	1	1	1	
			E	G	E	F	H	E	G		I	E	J
0	—	Portsmouth Harbour d	06 23		06 50	07 05		07 23				07 55	08 05
0¾	—	Portsmouth & Southsea d	06 28		06 55	07 09		07 28		07 39		08 00	08 10
1¾	—	Fratton d	06 32		06 59	07 13		07 32		07 43		08 04	08 14
4	—	Hilsea d	06 36		07 03			07 36		07 47		08 08	08 18
—	0	Chichester 4 d		06 27			07 06		07 27		07 44		
—	8¾	Havant d		06 42			07 20		07 39		08 00		
5½	12¾	**Cosham** d	06 42	06 50	07 08	07 21	07 27	07 41	07 46	07 52	08 09	08 13	08 24
8	—	**Portchester** d	06 46	06 54	07 13		07 31	07 46		07 57	08 13	08 18	08 28
11¼	—	**Fareham** a	06 51	06 59	07 18	07 28	07 36	07 51	07 55	08 02	08 18	08 23	08 33
—	—	d		07 00		07 29	07 37		07 56	08 03	08 19		
15	—	**Swanwick** d		07 06			07 43		08 02	08 09	08 25		
17	—	**Bursledon** d								08 13	08 29		
18¼	—	**Hamble** d								08 16	08 32		
19	—	**Netley** d					07 49			08 18	08 34		
20¾	—	**Sholing** d								08 22	08 37		
21½	—	**Woolston** d					07 54			08 24	08 39		
23¼	—	**Bitterne** d								08 28	08 43		
—	—	St Denys d								08 31	08 46		
25¾	—	Southampton Central a		07 25		07 50	08 03		08 19	08 38	08 52		

	GW	SN	SW	SW	SN	GW	SN	SW	GW	SW	SN
	◇	1	1	1	1	◇	1	1	◇	1	1
	F	G		E	I	F	G		K	E	I
Portsmouth Harbour d	08 23		08 33	08 59		09 23		09 33		09 59	
Portsmouth & Southsea d	08 27		08 38	09 04		09 27		09 38		10 04	
Fratton d	08 31		08 42	09 08		09 31		09 42		10 08	
Hilsea d			08 46	09 12				09 46		10 12	
Chichester 4 d		08 27			09 07		09 27		09 46		10 07
Havant d		08 39			09 23		09 40		09 58		10 21
Cosham d	08 39	08 46	08 51	09 17	09 30	09 39	09 47	09 51	10 05	10 17	10 29
Portchester d			08 56	09 22	09 34			09 56		10 22	10 33
Fareham a	08 46	08 54	09 01	09 27	09 39	09 46	09 55	10 01	10 12	10 27	10 38
d	08 47	08 54	09 03		09 40	09 47	09 55	10 03	10 13		10 39
Swanwick d		09 00	09 09		09 46		10 01	10 09			10 45
Bursledon d			09 13					10 13			
Hamble d			09 16					10 16			
Netley d			09 18					10 18			
Sholing d			09 22					10 22			
Woolston d			09 24					10 24			
Bitterne d			09 28					10 28			
St Denys d			09 31					10 31			
Southampton Central a	09 08	09 20	09 38		10 05	10 08	10 19	10 38	10 40		11 03

	GW	SN	SW	SW	SN	GW	SN	SW	SW	SN	GW
	◇	1	1	1	1	◇	1	1	1	1	◇
	F	G		E	I	F	G		E	I	F
Portsmouth Harbour d	10 23		10 33	10 59		11 23			11 59		12 23
Portsmouth & Southsea d	10 27		10 38	11 04		11 27		11 38	12 04		12 27
Fratton d	10 31		10 42	11 08		11 31		11 42	12 08		12 31
Hilsea d			10 46	11 12				11 46	12 12		
Chichester 4 d		10 27			11 07		11 27			12 07	
Havant d		10 39			11 21		11 39			12 21	
Cosham d	10 39	10 46	10 51	11 17	11 29	11 39	11 46	11 51	12 17	12 29	12 39
Portchester d			10 56	11 22	11 33			11 56	12 22	12 33	
Fareham a	10 46	10 54	11 01	11 27	11 38	11 46	11 54	12 01	12 27	12 38	12 46
d	10 47	10 55	11 03		11 39	11 47	11 55	12 03		12 39	12 47
Swanwick d		11 01	11 09		11 45		12 01	12 09		12 45	
Bursledon d			11 13					12 13			
Hamble d			11 16					12 16			
Netley d			11 18					12 18			
Sholing d			11 22					12 22			
Woolston d			11 24					12 24			
Bitterne d			11 28					12 28			
St Denys d			11 31					12 31			
Southampton Central a	11 08	11 19	11 38		12 03	12 08	12 19	12 38		13 03	13 08

	SN	SW	SW	SN	GW	SN	SW	SW	SN	GW	SN
	1	1	1	1	◇	1	1	1	1		1
	G		E	I	F	G		E	I	F	G
Portsmouth Harbour d			12 59		13 23			13 59		14 23	
Portsmouth & Southsea d		12 38	13 04		13 27		13 38	14 04		14 27	
Fratton d		12 42	13 08		13 31		13 42	14 08		14 31	
Hilsea d		12 46	13 12				13 46	14 12			
Chichester 4 d	12 27			13 07		13 27			14 07		14 27
Havant d	12 39			13 21		13 39			14 21		14 39
Cosham d	12 46	12 51	13 17	13 29	13 39	13 46	13 51	14 17	14 29	14 39	14 46
Portchester d		12 56	13 22	13 33			13 56	14 22	14 33		
Fareham a	12 54	13 01	13 27	13 38	13 46	13 54	14 01	14 27	14 38	14 46	14 54
d	12 55	13 03		13 39	13 47	13 55	14 03		14 39	14 47	14 55
Swanwick d	13 01	13 09		13 45		14 01	14 09		14 45		15 01
Bursledon d		13 13					14 13				
Hamble d		13 16					14 16				
Netley d		13 18					14 18				
Sholing d		13 22					14 22				
Woolston d		13 24					14 24				
Bitterne d		13 28					14 28				
St Denys d		13 31					14 31				
Southampton Central a	13 19	13 38		14 03	14 08	14 19	14 39		15 03	15 08	15 19

	SW	SW	SN	GW	SN	SW	SW	SN	GW	SN
	1	1	1		1	1	1	1		1
		E	I	F	G		E	I	F	G
Portsmouth Harbour d		14 59		15 23			15 59		16 23	
Portsmouth & Southsea d	14 38	15 04		15 27		15 38	16 04		16 27	
Fratton d	14 42	15 08		15 31		15 42	16 08		16 31	
Hilsea d	14 46	15 12				15 46	16 12			
Chichester 4 d			15 07		15 27			16 07		16 27
Havant d			15 21		15 39			16 21		16 39
Cosham d	14 51	15 17	15 29	15 39	15 46	15 51	16 17	16 29	16 39	16 46
Portchester d	14 56	15 22	15 33			15 56	16 22	16 33		
Fareham a	15 01	15 27	15 38	15 46	15 54	16 01	16 27	16 38	16 46	16 54
d	15 03		15 39	15 47	15 55	16 03		16 39	16 47	16 55
Swanwick d	15 09		15 45		16 01	16 09		16 45		17 01
Bursledon d	15 13					16 13				
Hamble d	15 16					16 16				
Netley d	15 18					16 18				
Sholing d	15 22					16 22				
Woolston d	15 24					16 24				
Bitterne d	15 28					16 28				
St Denys d	15 31					16 31				
Southampton Central a	15 38		16 03	16 08	16 20	16 38		17 02	17 08	17 19

A from 8 October. To Basingstoke
B until 5 October. To Basingstoke
C From Barnham
D From Littlehampton
E To London Waterloo
F To Cardiff Central
G From Brighton
H From Gatwick Airport
I From London Victoria
J To Basingstoke
K From Brighton to Great Malvern

Please note, Network Rail have stated that further updates to this timetable are possible during the validity period.

Please note, Network Rail have stated that further updates to this timetable are possible during the validity period.

Portsmouth and Chichester - Fareham and Southampton

Mondays to Fridays
21 May to 7 December

		SW	SW	SN	GW	SN	SW	GW	SW	SW	SN	GW	SN	SW	SW	SN	GW	SN	SW	SW	SN	GW	SN
		■	■ A	■ B	◇ C	■ D	■	◇ E	■ F	■ A	■ B	◇ C	■ D	■	■ A	■ B	◇ C	■ D	■	■ A	■ B	◇ C	■ D
Portsmouth Harbour	d	16 33	16 59		17 23		17 33		17 49	17 59		18 23			18 59		19 23			19 59		20 23	
Portsmouth & Southsea	d	16 38	17 04		17 27		17 38		17 54	18 04		18 27		18 38	19 04		19 27		19 38	20 04		20 27	
Fratton	d	16 42	17 08		17 31		17 42		17 58	18 08		18 31		18 42	19 08		19 31		19 42	20 08		20 31	
Hilsea	d	16 46	17 12				17 46		18 02	18 12				18 46	19 12				19 46	20 12			
Chichester	d			17 07		17 27		17 46			18 07		18 27			19 07		19 28			20 07		20 28
Havant	d			17 21		17 39		17 58			18 22		18 40			19 21		19 40			20 21		20 40
Cosham	d	16 51	17 17	17 29	17 39	17 46	17 51	18 05	18 09	18 17	18 30	18 39	18 47	18 51	19 17	19 29	19 38	19 47	19 51	20 17	20 29		20 47
Portchester	d	16 56	17 22	17 33			17 56		18 13	18 22	18 34			18 56	19 22	19 33			19 56	20 22	20 33		
Fareham	a	17 01	17 27	17 38	17 46	17 54	18 01	18 12	18 18	18 27	18 39	18 46	18 54	19 01	19 27	19 38	19 46	19 54	20 01	20 27	20 38	20 45	20 54
	d	17 03		17 39	17 47	17 55	18 03	18 14			18 40	18 47	18 55	19 03		19 39	19 47	19 55	20 03		20 39	20 46	20 55
Swanwick	d	17 09		17 45		18 01	18 09				18 46		19 01	19 09		19 45		20 01	20 09		20 45		21 01
Bursledon	d	17 13					18 13							19 13					20 13				
Hamble	d	17 16					18 16							19 16					20 16				
Netley	d	17 18		17 51			18 18							19 18					20 18				
Sholing	d	17 22					18 22							19 22					20 22				
Woolston	d	17 24		17 55			18 24							19 24					20 24				
Bitterne	d	17 28					18 28							19 28					20 28				
St Denys	d	17 31		18 00			18 31							19 31					20 31				
Southampton Central	a	17 38		18 05	18 08	18 19	18 38	18 39			19 03	19 08	19 20	19 38		20 03	20 08	20 19	20 38		21 03	21 08	21 19

		SW	SW	SW	GW	SN	SN	SW	SW	SN	SW	SW
		■	◇■ G	■ A	H	■ B	■ D	■	■ F	■ B	■	■ I
Portsmouth Harbour	d			20 59	21 23				21 54		22 33	23 24
Portsmouth & Southsea	d	20 38		21 04	21 27			21 38	21 59		22 38	23 29
Fratton	d	20 42		21 08	21 31			21 42	22 03		22 42	23 33
Hilsea	d	20 46		21 12				21 46	22 07		22 46	23 37
Chichester	d					21 11	21 27			22 07		
Havant	d		21 00			21 34	21 39			22 28		
Cosham	d	20 51	21 07	21 17		21 41	21 46	21 51	22 12	22 35	22 51	23 42
Portchester	d	20 56	21 12	21 22		21 45		21 56	22 17	22 39	22 56	23 47
Fareham	a	21 01	21 17	21 27	21 43	21 50	21 55	22 01	22 19	22 44	23 01	23 52
	d	21 03	21 18		21 44	21 51	21 56	22 03		22 44	23 02	
Swanwick	d	21 09				21 57	22 02	22 09		22 50	23 09	
Bursledon	d	21 13						22 13			23 12	
Hamble	d	21 16						22 16			23 16	
Netley	d	21 18						22 18			23 18	
Sholing	d	21 22						22 22			23 22	
Woolston	d	21 24				22 05		22 24			23 24	
Bitterne	d	21 28						22 28			23 27	
St Denys	d	21 31				22 10		22 31			23 30	
Southampton Central	a	21 38	21 43		22 21	22 15	22 23	22 38		23 08	23 39	

Saturdays
26 May to 8 December

		SW	SN	SW	SN	SW	SW	GW	SN	SN	SW	SW	SN	GW	SN	SW	SW	SN	GW	SN	SW	SW	SN
		■ F	■ J	■	■ J	■	■ A	◇ C	■ D	■ D	■	■ A	■ K	◇ C	■ D	■	■ A	■ B	■ C	■ D	■	■ A	■ B
Portsmouth Harbour	d					05 40	05 48	06 08				06 59		07 23			07 59		08 23			08 59	
Portsmouth & Southsea	d			05 16		05 44	05 53	06 12			06 38	07 04		07 27		07 38	08 04		08 27		08 38	09 04	
Fratton	d			05 20		05 48	05 57	06 16			06 42	07 08		07 31		07 42	08 08		08 31		08 42	09 08	
Hilsea	d			05 24			06 01				06 46	07 12				07 46	08 12				08 46	09 12	
Chichester	d		05 08		05 27				06 09	06 27			07 06		07 27			08 07		08 27			09 07
Havant	d		05 20		05 39				06 21	06 39			07 20		07 39			08 21		08 39			09 21
Cosham	d	05 09	05 27	05 31	05 46	05 56	06 06	06 23	06 28	06 46	06 51	07 17	07 27	07 39	07 46	07 51	08 17	08 29	08 39	08 46	08 51	09 17	09 29
Portchester	d	05 14		05 35			06 11				06 56	07 22	07 31			07 56	08 22	08 33			08 56	09 22	09 33
Fareham	a	05 19	05 35	05 40	05 54	06 03	06 16	06 31	06 36	06 54	07 01	07 27	07 36	07 46	07 54	08 01	08 27	08 38	08 46	08 54	09 01	09 27	09 38
	d		05 36	05 41	05 55	06 04		06 32	06 37	06 55	07 03		07 37	07 47	07 55	08 03		08 39	08 47	08 55	09 03		09 39
Swanwick	d		05 42	05 48	06 01				06 43	07 01	07 09		07 43		08 01	08 09		08 45		09 01	09 09		09 45
Bursledon	d			05 51							07 13					08 13					09 13		
Hamble	d			05 55							07 16					08 16					09 16		
Netley	d			05 57							07 18		07 49			08 18					09 18		
Sholing	d			06 01							07 22					08 22					09 22		
Woolston	d			06 03							07 24		07 54			08 24					09 24		
Bitterne	d			06 06							07 28					08 28					09 28		
St Denys	d			06 09							07 31					08 31					09 31		
Southampton Central	a		06 01	06 14	06 19	06 35		06 53	07 01	07 19	07 38		08 03	08 08	08 19	08 38		09 03	09 08	09 19	09 38		10 03

A To London Waterloo
B From London Victoria
C To Cardiff Central
D From Brighton
E From Brighton to Bristol Temple Meads
F To Eastleigh
G From London Waterloo
H To Westbury
I To Winchester
J From Barnham
K From Gatwick Airport

Portsmouth and Chichester - Fareham and Southampton

Saturdays
26 May to 8 December

		GW	SN	SW	GW	SW	SN	GW	SN	SW	SW	SN	GW	SN	SW	SW	SN	GW	SN	SW	SW	SN
		◇ A	■ B	■	◇ C	■ D	■ E	◇ A	■ B	■	■ D	■ E	◇ A	■ B	■	■ D	■ E	◇ A	■ B	■	■ D	■ E
Portsmouth Harbour	d	09 23				09 59		10 23			10 59		11 23			11 59		12 23			12 59	
Portsmouth & Southsea	d	09 27		09 38		10 04		10 27		10 38	11 04		11 27		11 38	12 04		12 27		12 38	13 04	
Fratton	d	09 31		09 42		10 08		10 31		10 42	11 08		11 31		11 42	12 08		12 31		12 42	13 08	
Hilsea	d			09 46		10 12				10 46	11 12				11 46	12 12				12 46	13 12	
Chichester	d		09 27		09 51		10 07		10 27			11 07		11 27			12 07		12 27			13 07
Havant	d		09 39		10 02		10 21		10 39			11 21		11 39			12 21		12 39			13 21
Cosham	d	09 39	09 46	09 51	10 08	10 17	10 29	10 39	10 46	10 51	11 17	11 29	11 39	11 46	11 51	12 17	12 29	12 39	12 46	12 51	13 17	13 29
Portchester	d			09 56		10 22	10 33			10 56	11 22	11 33			11 56	12 22	12 33			12 56	13 22	13 33
Fareham	a	09 46	09 54	10 01	10 16	10 27	10 38	10 46	10 54	11 01	11 27	11 38	11 46	11 54	12 01	12 27	12 38	12 46	12 54	13 01	13 27	13 38
	d	09 47	09 55	10 03	10 17		10 39	10 47	10 55	11 03		11 39	11 47	11 55	12 03		12 39	12 47	12 55	13 03		13 39
Swanwick	d		10 01	10 09			10 45		11 01	11 09		11 45		12 01	12 09		12 45		13 01	13 09		13 45
Bursledon	d			10 13						11 13					12 13					13 13		
Hamble	d			10 16						11 16					12 16					13 16		
Netley	d			10 18						11 18					12 18					13 18		
Sholing	d			10 22						11 22					12 22					13 22		
Woolston	d			10 24						11 24					12 24					13 24		
Bitterne	d			10 28						11 28					12 28					13 28		
St Denys	d			10 31						11 31					12 31					13 31		
Southampton Central	a	10 08	10 19	10 38	10 40		11 03	11 08	11 19	11 38		12 03	12 08	12 19	12 38		13 03	13 08	13 19	13 38		14 03

		GW	SN	SW	SW	SN	GW	SN	SW	SW	SN	GW	SN	SW	SW	SN	GW	SN	SW	SW	SN	GW	SN
		◇ A	■ B	■	■ D	■ E	◇ A	■ B	■	■ D	■ E	◇ A	■ B	■	■ D	■ E	■ A	■ B	■	■ D	■ E	◇ A	■ B
Portsmouth Harbour	d	13 23			13 59		14 23			14 59		15 23			15 59		16 23			16 59		17 23	
Portsmouth & Southsea	d	13 27		13 38	14 04		14 27		14 38	15 04		15 27		15 38	16 04		16 27		16 38	17 04		17 27	
Fratton	d	13 31		13 42	14 08		14 31		14 42	15 08		15 31		15 42	16 08		16 31		16 42	17 08		17 31	
Hilsea	d			13 46	14 12				14 46	15 12				15 46	16 12				16 46	17 12			
Chichester	d		13 27			14 07		14 27			15 07		15 27			16 07		16 27			17 07		17 27
Havant	d		13 39			14 21		14 39			15 21		15 39			16 21		16 39			17 21		17 39
Cosham	d	13 39	13 46	13 51	14 17	14 29	14 39	14 46	14 51	15 17	15 29	15 39	15 46	15 51	16 17	16 29	16 39	16 46	16 51	17 17	17 29	17 39	17 46
Portchester	d			13 56	14 22	14 33			14 56	15 22	15 33			15 56	16 22	16 33			16 56	17 22	17 33		
Fareham	a	13 46	13 54	14 01	14 27	14 38	14 46	14 54	15 01	15 27	15 38	15 46	15 54	16 01	16 27	16 38	16 46	16 54	17 01	17 27	17 38	17 46	17 54
	d	13 47	13 55	14 03		14 39	14 47	14 55	15 03		15 39	15 47	15 55	16 03		16 39	16 47	16 55	17 03		17 39	17 47	17 55
Swanwick	d		14 01	14 09		14 45		15 01	15 09		15 45		16 01	16 09		16 45		17 01	17 09		17 45		18 01
Bursledon	d			14 13					15 13					16 13					17 13				
Hamble	d			14 16					15 16					16 16					17 16				
Netley	d			14 18					15 18					16 18					17 18				
Sholing	d			14 22					15 22					16 22					17 22				
Woolston	d			14 24					15 24					16 24					17 24				
Bitterne	d			14 28					15 28					16 28					17 28				
St Denys	d			14 31					15 31					16 31					17 31				
Southampton Central	a	14 08	14 19	14 38		15 03	15 08	15 19	15 38		16 03	16 08	16 19	16 38		17 03	17 08	17 19	17 38		18 03	18 08	18 20

		SW	GW	SW	SN	GW	SN	SW	SW	SN	GW	SN	SW	SW	SN	GW	SN	SW	SW	SN	SN	SW
		■	◇ F	■ D	■ E	◇ A	■ B	■	■ D	■ E	◇ A	■ B	■	■ D	■ E	◇ A	■ B	■	■ D	■ E	■ B	■
Portsmouth Harbour	d	17 33		17 59		18 23			18 59		19 23			19 59		20 23			20 59			
Portsmouth & Southsea	d	17 38		18 04		18 27		18 38	19 04		19 27		19 38	20 04		20 27		20 38	21 04			21 38
Fratton	d	17 42		18 08		18 31		18 42	19 08		19 31		19 42	20 08		20 31		20 42	21 08			21 42
Hilsea	d	17 46		18 12				18 46	19 12				19 46	20 12				20 46	21 12			21 46
Chichester	d		17 50		18 07		18 27			19 07		19 27			20 07		20 27			21 11	21 27	
Havant	d		18 02		18 21		18 39			19 21		19 39			20 21		20 39			21 32	21 39	
Cosham	d	17 51	18 08	18 17	18 29	18 39	18 46	18 51	19 17	19 29	19 39	19 46	19 51	20 17	20 29		20 46	20 51	21 17	21 40	21 46	21 51
Portchester	d	17 56		18 22	18 33			18 56	19 22	19 33			19 56	20 22	20 33			20 56	21 22	21 44		21 56
Fareham	a	18 01	18 16	18 27	18 38	18 46	18 54	19 01	19 27	19 38	19 46	19 54	20 01	20 27	20 38	20 45	20 54	21 01	21 27	21 49	21 54	22 01
	d	18 03	18 17		18 39	18 47	18 55	19 03		19 39	19 47	19 55	20 03		20 39	20 47	20 55	21 03		21 50	21 56	22 03
Swanwick	d	18 09			18 45		19 01	19 09		19 45		20 01	20 09		20 45		21 01	21 09		21 56	22 02	22 09
Bursledon	d	18 13						19 13					20 13					21 13				22 13
Hamble	d	18 16						19 16					20 16					21 16				22 16
Netley	d	18 18						19 18					20 18					21 18				22 18
Sholing	d	18 22						19 22					20 22					21 22				22 22
Woolston	d	18 24						19 24					20 24					21 24		22 05		22 24
Bitterne	d	18 28						19 28					20 28					21 28				22 28
St Denys	d	18 31						19 31					20 31					21 31		22 09		22 31
Southampton Central	a	18 38	18 43		19 03	19 08	19 19	19 38		20 03	20 08	20 19	20 38		21 03	21 10	21 19	21 38		22 15	22 19	22 38

		SW	SN	SW	SW
		■ G	■ E	■	■ H
Portsmouth Harbour	d	21 54		22 33	23 24
Portsmouth & Southsea	d	21 59		22 38	23 29
Fratton	d	22 03		22 42	23 33
Hilsea	d	22 07		22 46	23 37
Chichester	d		22 07		
Havant	d		22 28		
Cosham	d	22 12	22 35	22 51	23 42
Portchester	d	22 17	22 39	22 56	23 47
Fareham	a	22 22	22 44	23 01	23 52
	d		22 45	23 03	
Swanwick	d		22 51	23 09	
Bursledon	d			23 13	
Hamble	d			23 16	
Netley	d			23 18	
Sholing	d			23 22	
Woolston	d			23 24	
Bitterne	d			23 28	
St Denys	d			23 31	
Southampton Central	a		23 08	23 36	

A To Cardiff Central
B From Brighton
C From Brighton to Great Malvern
D To London Waterloo
E From London Victoria
F From Brighton to Bristol Temple Meads
G To Eastleigh
H To Winchester

Table T165-F

Sundays

20 May to 2 December

Portsmouth and Chichester - Fareham and Southampton

	SW	SW	SW	SN	SW	SW	SN	GW	SW	SW	SN	SW	SW	SN	GW	SW	SW	SN	GW	SW	SW	SN
	■	■ A	■	B	■ A	■	C	▪ D	■ A 🍴	■	C	■ A 🍴	■	C	◇ D	■ A 🍴	■	C	◇ E	■ A 🍴	■	C
Portsmouth Harbour ⛴ d	06 37	07 17			08 17			09 08	09 17			10 17			11 08	11 17				12 17		
Portsmouth & Southsea d	06 42	07 22	07 42		08 22	08 42		09 12	09 22	09 42		10 22	10 42		11 12	11 22	11 42			12 22	12 42	
Fratton d	06 46	07 26	07 46		08 26	08 46		09 15	09 26	09 46		10 26	10 46		11 15	11 26	11 46			12 26	12 46	
Hilsea d	06 50	07 30	07 50		08 30	08 50			09 30	09 50		10 30	10 50			11 30	11 50			12 30	12 50	
Chichester ■ d				07 57			08 59				09 59			10 59				11 59	12 04			12 59
Havant d				08 10			09 11				10 11			11 11				12 11	12 15			13 11
Cosham d	06 55	07 35	07 55	08 17	08 35	08 55	09 18	09 23	09 35	09 55	10 18	10 35	10 55	11 18	11 23	11 35	11 55	12 18	12 25	12 35	12 55	13 18
Portchester d	07 00	07 40	08 00		08 40	09 00			09 40	10 00		10 40	11 00			11 40	12 00			12 40	13 00	
Fareham a	07 05	07 45	08 05	08 25	08 45	09 05	09 25	09 31	09 45	10 05	10 25	10 45	11 05	11 25	11 31	11 45	12 05	12 25	12 33	12 45	13 05	13 25
d	07 06		08 06	08 26		09 06	09 26	09 33		10 06	10 26		11 06	11 26	11 33		12 06	12 26	12 34		13 06	13 26
Swanwick d	07 12		08 12	08 32		09 12	09 33			10 12	10 33		11 12	11 33			12 12	12 33			13 12	13 33
Bursledon d	07 16		08 16			09 16				10 16			11 16				12 16				13 16	
Hamble d	07 19		08 19			09 19				10 19			11 19				12 19				13 19	
Netley d	07 21		08 21			09 21				10 21			11 21				12 21				13 21	
Sholing d	07 25		08 25			09 25				10 25			11 25				12 25				13 25	
Woolston d	07 27		08 27			09 27				10 27			11 27				12 27				13 27	
Bitterne d	07 31		08 31			09 31				10 31			11 31				12 31				13 31	
St Denys d	07 34		08 34			09 34				10 34			11 34				12 34				13 34	
Southampton Central ⛴ a	07 40		08 40	08 50		09 40	09 50	09 54		10 40	10 50		11 40	11 50	11 55		12 40	12 50	12 55		13 40	13 50

	GW	SW	SW	SN	GW	SW	SW	SN	GW	SW	SW	SN	GW	SW	GW	GW	GW	SW	SN	GW	SW	SW
	◇ D	■ A 🍴	■	C	◇ D	■ A 🍴	■	C	▪ D	■ A 🍴	■	C	◇ D	■ A 🍴	◇ F	◇ G	◇ F	■	C	◇ D	■ A	■
Portsmouth Harbour ⛴ d	13 08	13 17			14 08	14 17			15 08	15 17			16 10	16 17						17 08	17 17	
Portsmouth & Southsea d	13 12	13 22	13 42		14 12	14 22	14 42		15 12	15 22	15 42		16 14	16 22				16 42		17 12	17 22	17 42
Fratton d	13 16	13 26	13 46		14 16	14 26	14 46		15 16	15 26	15 46		16 18	16 26				16 46		17 16	17 26	17 46
Hilsea d		13 30	13 50			14 30	14 50			15 30	15 50			16 30				16 50			17 30	17 50
Chichester ■ d				13 59				14 59				15 59			16 35	16 35			16 59			
Havant d				14 11				15 11				16 11			16 45	16 46			17 11			
Cosham d	13 24	13 35	13 55	14 18	14 23	14 35	14 55	15 18	15 23	15 35	15 55	16 18	16 25	16 35	16 52	16 53		17 00	17 18	17 23	17 35	17 55
Portchester d		13 40	14 00			14 40	15 00			15 40	16 00			16 40			←	17 04			17 40	18 00
Fareham a	13 31	13 45	14 05	14 25	14 31	14 45	15 05	15 25	15 31	15 45	16 05	16 25	16 33	16 45	16 59	16 59	16 59	17 09	17 25	17 31	17 45	18 05
d	13 32		14 06	14 26	14 34		15 06	15 26	15 34		16 06	16 26	16 34		17 00	16 59	17 00	17 10	17 26	17 34		18 06
Swanwick d			14 12	14 33			15 12	15 33			16 12	16 33			→			17 17	17 33			18 12
Bursledon d			14 16				15 16				16 16							17 20				18 16
Hamble d			14 19				15 19				16 19							17 24				18 19
Netley d			14 21				15 21				16 21							17 26				18 21
Sholing d			14 25				15 25				16 25							17 30				18 25
Woolston d			14 27				15 27				16 27							17 32				18 27
Bitterne d			14 31				15 31				16 31							17 35				18 31
St Denys d			14 34				15 34				16 34							17 38				18 34
Southampton Central ⛴ a	13 53		14 40	14 50	14 55		15 40	15 50	15 55		16 40	16 50	16 55			17 20	17 20	17 44	17 50	17 55		18 41

	SN	GW	SW	GW	SW	SN	GW	SW	SW	SN	GW	SW	SW	SN	SW	SW	SN	GW	SW	SW	SW
	C	◇ D	■ A	◇ H	■	C	◇ D	■ A	■	C	◇ D	■ A	■	C	■ A	■	C	I	■ J	■	■ J
Portsmouth Harbour ⛴ d		18 08	18 17				19 08	19 17			20 08	20 18			21 18			22 08	22 17		23 17
Portsmouth & Southsea d		18 12	18 22		18 42		19 12	19 22	19 42		20 12	20 22	20 42		21 22	21 42		22 12	22 22	22 42	23 22
Fratton d		18 16	18 26		18 46		19 16	19 26	19 46		20 16	20 26	20 46		21 26	21 46		22 15	22 26	22 46	23 26
Hilsea d			18 30		18 50			19 30	19 50			20 30	20 50		21 30	21 50			22 30	22 50	23 30
Chichester ■ d	17 59			18 35		18 59				19 59				20 59			21 59				
Havant d	18 11			18 50		19 11				20 11				21 11			22 11				
Cosham d	18 18	18 23	18 35	18 57	19 00	19 18	19 23	19 35	19 55	20 18		20 35	20 55	21 18	21 35	21 55	22 18		22 35	22 55	23 35
Portchester d			18 40		19 05			19 40	20 00			20 40	21 00		21 40	22 00			22 40	23 00	23 40
Fareham a	18 25	18 31	18 45	19 04	19 10	19 25	19 31	19 45	20 05	20 25	20 31	20 45	21 05	21 25	21 45	22 05	22 25	22 31	22 45	23 05	23 45
d	18 26	18 34		19 05	19 11	19 26	19 33		20 06	20 26	20 34		21 06	21 26		22 06	22 26	22 32		23 06	
Swanwick d	18 33				19 17	19 33			20 12	20 33			21 12	21 33		22 12	22 33			23 12	
Bursledon d					19 21				20 16				21 16			22 16				23 16	
Hamble d					19 24				20 19				21 19			22 19				23 19	
Netley d					19 26				20 21				21 21			22 21				23 21	
Sholing d					19 30				20 25				21 25			22 25				23 25	
Woolston d					19 32				20 27				21 27			22 27				23 27	
Bitterne d					19 36				20 31				21 31			22 31				23 31	
St Denys d					19 39				20 34				21 34			22 34				23 34	
Southampton Central ⛴ a	18 50	18 55		19 26	19 44	19 50	19 54		20 40	20 50	20 55		21 40	21 50		22 40	22 50	22 55		23 40	

A To London Waterloo
B From Littlehampton
C From Brighton
D To Cardiff Central
E From Brighton to Cardiff Central
F until 9 September. From Brighton to Bristol Temple Meads
G from 16 September. From Brighton to Bristol Temple Meads
H From Brighton to Bristol Temple Meads
I To Westbury
J To Eastleigh

Table T165-R

Mondays to Fridays

21 May to 7 December

Southampton and Fareham - Chichester and Portsmouth

Miles	Miles		SN	SW	SN	SW	SW	SN	GW	SW	SN	SW	SW	SN	GW	SW	SN	SW	SN	SW	GW	SN
			■ A	■ B	■ C	■ D	■	■ E	F	■ B	■ E	■ G	■	■ A	◇ H	■	■ E	■ I	■ A	■	◇ J 🍴	■ E
0	—	Southampton Central ⛴ d	05 46		06 10		06 23	06 36	06 53		07 12		07 17	07 33	07 42	07 52	08 10		08 26	08 44	09 06	09 13
2	—	St Denys d					06 29						07 23			07 58	08 15			08 49		
2½	—	**Bitterne** d					06 31						07 25			08 00				08 52		
4¼	—	**Woolston** d	05 55		06 20		06 35	06 46					07 29			08 04				08 55		
5	—	**Sholing** d					06 37						07 31			08 06				08 58		
6¾	—	**Netley** d					06 41						07 35			08 11				09 02		
7½	—	**Hamble** d					06 43						07 37			08 13				09 04		
8¾	—	**Bursledon** d					06 46						07 40			08 16				09 07		
10¾	—	**Swanwick** d	06 04		06 28		06 50	06 56			07 31		07 44	07 51		08 20	08 28		08 48	09 11		09 32
14½	—	**Fareham** a	06 10		06 34		06 57	07 02	07 15		07 37		07 51	07 57	08 05	08 27	08 34		08 55	09 17	09 27	09 38
—	—	d	06 11	06 19	06 36	06 50	06 58	07 03	07 16	07 21	07 38	07 47	07 52	07 57	08 06	08 28	08 35	08 50	08 56	09 18	09 28	09 39
17¾	—	**Portchester** d	06 16	06 24	06 41	06 55	07 03	07 08		07 26	07 43	07 52	07 57			08 33	08 40	08 55		09 23		09 44
20¼	0	**Cosham** d	06 20	06 29	06 46	07 00	07 08	07 12	07 25	07 30	07 47	07 57	08 02	08 06	08 14	08 38	08 44	09 00	09 04	09 28	09 36	09 48
—	4	Havant a	06 27		06 53			07 18			07 54			08 12			08 51		09 10			09 54
—	12¾	Chichester ■ a	06 43		07 08			07 36			08 08			08 23			09 06		09 22			10 08
21¾	—	Hilsea a		06 34		07 05	07 13			07 35		08 03	08 06			08 45		09 05		09 33		
24	—	Fratton a		06 40		07 09	07 17		07 34	07 39		08 07	08 10		08 20	08 49		09 09		09 37	09 43	
25	—	Portsmouth & Southsea a		06 44		07 12	07 21		07 38	07 42		08 13	08 18		08 24	08 53		09 12		09 44	09 47	
25¾	—	Portsmouth Harbour ⛴ a		06 49		07 17			07 42	07 48		08 17			08 28	08 58		09 18			09 51	

	SW	SN	SW	GW	SN	SW	SN	SW	GW	SN	SW	SN	SW	GW	SN	SW	SN	SW	GW	SN	SW	SN
	■ I	A	■	▪ J 🍴	■ E	■ I	■ A	■	◇ J 🍴	■ E	■ I	A	■	◇ J 🍴	■ E	■ I	■ A	■	◇ J 🍴	■ E	■ I	■ A
Southampton Central ⛴ d		09 26	09 44	10 02	10 13		10 26	10 44	11 04	11 13		11 26	11 44	12 05	12 13		12 29	12 44	13 05	13 13		13 26
St Denys d			09 49					10 49					11 49					12 49				
Bitterne d			09 52					10 52					11 52					12 52				
Woolston d			09 55					10 55					11 55					12 55				
Sholing d			09 58					10 58					11 58					12 58				
Netley d			10 02					11 02					12 02					13 02				
Hamble d			10 04					11 04					12 04					13 04				
Bursledon d			10 07					11 07					12 07					13 07				
Swanwick d			10 11		10 32		10 46	11 11		11 32			12 11		12 32		12 46	13 11		13 32		13 46
Fareham a			10 17	10 25	10 38		10 52	11 17	11 27	11 38			12 17	12 28	12 38		12 52	13 17	13 27	13 38		13 52
d	09 48		10 18	10 25	10 39	10 48	10 53	11 18	11 27	11 39	11 48		12 18	12 28	12 39	12 48	12 53	13 18	13 27	13 39	13 48	13 53
Portchester d	09 53		10 23		10 44	10 53		11 23		11 44	11 53		12 23		12 44	12 53		13 23		13 44	13 53	
Cosham d	09 58	10 02	10 28	10 33	10 48	10 58	11 02	11 28	11 35	11 48	11 58	12 01	12 28	12 36	12 48	12 58	13 02	13 28	13 35	13 48	13 58	14 02
Havant a		10 09			10 54		11 09			11 54		12 09			12 54		13 09			13 54		14 09
Chichester ■ a		10 21			11 08		11 21			12 08		12 21			13 08		13 21			14 08		14 21
Hilsea a	10 03		10 33			11 03		11 33			12 03		12 33			13 03		13 33			14 03	
Fratton a	10 07		10 37	10 39		11 07		11 37	11 42		12 07		12 37	12 42		13 07		13 37	13 42		14 07	
Portsmouth & Southsea a	10 11		10 44	10 44		11 12		11 44	11 46		12 11		12 44	12 46		13 11		13 44	13 46		14 11	
Portsmouth Harbour ⛴ a	10 20			10 50		11 20			11 52		12 20			12 52		13 18			13 52		14 20	

	SW	GW	SN	SW	SN	GW	SW	GW	SN	SW	SN	SW	GW	SN	SW	SW	SN	SW	SW	GW	SN
	■	◇ J 🍴	■ E	■ I	■ A	▪ K 🍴	■	◇ J 🍴	■ E	■ I	■ A	■	◇ J 🍴	■ E	■ L	■ I	■ A	M	■	◇ J 🍴	■ E
Southampton Central ⛴ d	13 44	14 04	14 13		14 26	14 34	14 44	15 05	15 13		15 26	15 44	16 05	16 12			16 26		16 44	17 04	17 14
St Denys d	13 49						14 49					15 49							16 49		
Bitterne d	13 52						14 52					15 52							16 52		
Woolston d	13 55						14 55					15 55							16 55		
Sholing d	13 58						14 58					15 58							16 58		
Netley d	14 02						15 02					16 02							17 02		
Hamble d	14 04						15 04					16 04							17 04		
Bursledon d	14 07						15 07					16 07							17 07		
Swanwick d	14 11		14 32		14 46		15 11		15 32		15 46	16 11		16 32			16 46		17 11		17 32
Fareham a	14 17	14 27	14 38		14 52	14 55	15 17	15 26	15 38		15 52	16 17	16 27	16 38			16 52		17 17	17 26	17 38
d	14 18	14 27	14 39	14 48	14 53	14 56	15 18	15 26	15 39	15 48	15 53	16 18	16 27	16 39	16 44	16 48	16 53	17 12	17 18	17 27	17 39
Portchester d	14 23		14 44	14 53			15 23		15 44	15 53		16 23		16 44		16 53		17 17	17 23		17 44
Cosham d	14 28	14 35	14 48	14 58	15 01	15 04	15 28	15 35	15 49	15 58	16 02	16 28	16 35	16 48		16 58	17 02	17 22	17 28	17 35	17 48
Havant a			14 54		15 08	15 10			15 55		16 09			16 54	16 58		17 09				17 54
Chichester ■ a			15 08		15 19	15 23			16 09		16 21			17 08			17 21				18 08
Hilsea a	14 33			15 03			15 33			16 03		16 33				17 03			17 33		
Fratton a	14 37	14 42		15 07			15 37	15 42		16 07		16 37	16 42			17 07		17 30	17 37	17 42	
Portsmouth & Southsea a	14 44	14 46		15 11			15 43	15 46		16 11		16 40	16 46			17 11		17 34	17 44	17 46	
Portsmouth Harbour ⛴ a		14 52		15 20			15 48	15 52		16 20		16 44	16 52			17 20		17 39		17 52	

A To Brighton
B From Eastleigh
C To London Bridge
D From Winchester
E To London Victoria
F From Westbury
G From Woking
H From Bristol Temple Meads
I From London Waterloo
J From Cardiff Central
K From Great Malvern to Brighton
L To London Waterloo
M From Basingstoke

Table T165-R

Mondays to Fridays
21 May to 7 December

Southampton and Fareham - Chichester and Portsmouth

	SW	SN	SW	SW	GW	SN	SW	SN	SW	SW	GW	SN	SW	SN	SW	GW	SN	SW	SN	SW	GW
	◇■ A	■ B	■	◇■ A	◇ C	■ D	◇■ A	■ B	◇■ A	■	■ C	■ D	◇■ A	■ B	■	■ C	■ D	■ A	■ B	■	◇ C
Southampton Central d		17 26	17 44		18 05	18 13		18 26		18 44	19 07	19 12		19 26	19 44	20 06	20 13		20 26	20 44	21 09
St Denys d			17 49							18 49					19 49					20 49	
Bitterne d			17 52							18 52					19 52					20 52	
Woolston d			17 55							18 55					19 55					20 55	
Sholing d			17 58							18 58					19 58					20 58	
Netley d			18 02							19 02					20 02					21 02	
Hamble d			18 04							19 04					20 04					21 04	
Bursledon d			18 07							19 07					20 07					21 07	
Swanwick d		17 46	18 11			18 32		18 46		19 11		19 32		19 46	20 11		20 32		20 46	21 11	
Fareham a		17 52	18 17		18 27	18 38		18 52		19 17	19 27	19 38		19 52	20 17	20 28	20 38		20 53	21 17	21 31
d	17 48	17 53	18 18	18 23	18 27	18 39	18 45	18 53	19 14	19 18	19 28	19 39	19 48	19 53	20 18	20 29	20 39	20 49	20 54	21 18	21 32
Portchester d	17 53		18 23	18 28		18 44	18 50		19 19	19 23		19 44	19 53		20 23		20 44	20 54		21 23	
Cosham d	17 58	18 02	18 28	18 33	18 35	18 48	18 55	19 02	19 24	19 28	19 36	19 48	19 58	20 02	20 28		20 48	20 59	21 02	21 28	
Havant a		18 09				18 54		19 09				19 54		20 09			20 54		21 09		
Chichester a		18 21				19 08		19 21				20 08		20 21			21 08		21 21		
Hilsea a	18 03		18 33				19 05		19 28	19 33			20 03		20 33			21 03		21 33	
Fratton a	18 07		18 37	18 40	18 45		19 09		19 32	19 37	19 43		20 07		20 37	20 44		21 07		21 37	21 48
Portsmouth & Southsea a	18 11		18 44	18 43	18 52		19 12		19 36	19 44	19 47		20 12		20 44	20 49		21 11		21 41	21 51
Portsmouth Harbour a	18 20			18 50	18 58		19 20		19 43		19 51		20 20			20 54		21 18		21 46	21 55

	SN	SW	SN	SW	GW	SN	SN	SW	SW	GW	SN	SW
	B	■ A	■ E	■	◇ C	F	■ F	■ G	■	◇ C	H	■ A
Southampton Central d	21 13		21 32	21 44	22 04	22 21	22 33		22 44	23 05	23 12	
St Denys d				21 49					22 49		23 22	
Bitterne d				21 52					22 52			
Woolston d				21 55					22 55			
Sholing d				21 58					22 58			
Netley d				22 02					23 02			
Hamble d				22 04					23 04			
Bursledon d				22 07					23 07			
Swanwick d	21 33		21 50	22 11		22 40	22 51		23 11			
Fareham a	21 39		21 56	22 17	22 41	22 46	22 57		23 17	23 27	23 38	
d	21 40	21 49	21 57	22 18	22 41	22 47	22 57	23 10	23 18	23 27	23 38	23 49
Portchester d	21 45	21 54	22 02	22 23		22 52		23 15	23 23			23 54
Cosham d	21 49	21 59	22 06	22 28		22 56	23 06	23 20	23 28		23 47	23 59
Havant a	21 55		22 13			23 02	23 12				23 53	
Chichester a	22 06		22 33			23 17	23 22				00 05	
Hilsea a		22 04		22 33				23 24	23 33			00 03
Fratton a		22 08		22 37	22 54			23 32	23 37	23 44		00 07
Portsmouth & Southsea a		22 11		22 45	22 57			23 36	23 44	23 48		00 11
Portsmouth Harbour a		22 18			23 02			23 40		23 52		00 16

Saturdays
26 May to 8 December

	SW	SN	SW	SN	SW	GW	SN	SW	SN	SW	GW	SN	SW	SN	SW	GW	SN	SW	SN	SW	GW	SN
	■	■ D	■ I	■ B	■	J	■ D	■ K	■ B	■	◇ L	■ D	■ A	■ B	■	◇ M	■ D	■ A	■ B	■	◇ C	■ D
Southampton Central d	05 44	06 13		06 26	06 44	07 06	07 13		07 26	07 44	07 57	08 13		08 27	08 44	09 05	09 13		09 26	09 44	10 05	10 13
St Denys d	05 49				06 49					07 49					08 49					09 49		
Bitterne d	05 52				06 52					07 52					08 52					09 52		
Woolston d	05 55				06 55					07 55					08 55					09 55		
Sholing d	05 58				06 58					07 58					08 58					09 58		
Netley d	06 02				07 02					08 02					09 02					10 02		
Hamble d	06 04				07 04					08 04					09 04					10 04		
Bursledon d	06 07				07 07					08 07					09 07					10 07		
Swanwick d	06 11	06 32		06 43	07 11		07 32		07 46	08 11		08 32		08 46	09 11		09 32		09 46	10 11		10 32
Fareham a	06 20	06 38		06 50	07 17	07 27	07 38		07 52	08 17	08 23	08 38		08 52	09 17	09 27	09 38		09 52	10 17	10 27	10 38
d	06 21	06 39	06 46	06 51	07 18	07 28	07 39	07 49	07 53	08 18	08 24	08 39	08 49	08 53	09 18	09 28	09 39	09 48	09 53	10 18	10 28	10 39
Portchester d	06 26	06 44	06 51		07 23		07 44	07 54		08 23		08 44	08 54		09 23		09 44	09 53		10 23		10 44
Cosham d	06 31	06 48	06 56	07 00	07 28	07 36	07 48	07 59	08 02	08 28	08 33	08 48	08 59	09 02	09 28	09 36	09 48	09 58	10 02	10 28	10 36	10 48
Havant a		06 54		07 10			07 54		08 09			08 54		09 09			09 54		10 09			10 54
Chichester a		07 08		07 23			08 08		08 21			09 08		09 21			10 08		10 21			11 08
Hilsea a	06 38		07 03		07 33			08 03		08 33			09 04		09 33			10 03		10 33		
Fratton a	06 42		07 07		07 37	07 42		08 07		08 37	08 39		09 08		09 37	09 43		10 07		10 37	10 42	
Portsmouth & Southsea a	06 46		07 11		07 42	07 46		08 11		08 42	08 45		09 12		09 42	09 46		10 11		10 42	10 46	
Portsmouth Harbour a			07 16			07 52		08 18			08 51		09 18			09 52		10 18			10 52	

A From London Waterloo
B To Brighton
C From Cardiff Central
D To London Victoria
E To Three Bridges
F To Littlehampton
G From Basingstoke
H To Barnham
I From Eastleigh
J From Westbury
K From Woking
L From Bristol Temple Meads
M From Cardiff Canton Sidings

Table T165-R

Saturdays
26 May to 8 December

Southampton and Fareham - Chichester and Portsmouth

	SW	SN	SW	GW	SN	SW	SN	SW	GW	SN	SW	SN	SW	GW	SN	SW	SN	SW	GW	SN	SW
	■ A	■ B	■	◇ C	■ D	■ A	■ B	■	◇ C	■ D	■ A	■ B	■	◇ C	■ D	■ A	■ B	■	◇ C	■ D	■ A
Southampton Central d		10 26	10 44	11 05	11 13		11 26	11 44	12 05	12 13		12 26	12 44	13 05	13 13		13 26	13 44	14 05	14 13	
St Denys d			10 49					11 49					12 49					13 49			
Bitterne d			10 52					11 52					12 52					13 52			
Woolston d			10 55					11 55					12 55					13 55			
Sholing d			10 58					11 58					12 58					13 58			
Netley d			11 02					12 02					13 02					14 02			
Hamble d			11 04					12 04					13 04					14 04			
Bursledon d			11 07					12 07					13 07					14 07			
Swanwick d		10 46	11 11		11 32		11 46	12 11		12 32		12 46	13 11		13 32		13 46	14 11		14 32	
Fareham a		10 52	11 17	11 27	11 38		11 52	12 17	12 27	12 38		12 52	13 17	13 27	13 38		13 52	14 17	14 27	14 38	
d	10 48	10 53	11 18	11 28	11 39	11 48	11 53	12 18	12 28	12 39	12 48	12 53	13 18	13 28	13 39	13 48	13 53	14 18	14 28	14 39	14 47
Portchester d	10 53		11 23		11 44	11 53		12 23		12 44	12 53		13 23		13 44	13 53		14 23		14 44	14 52
Cosham d	10 58	11 02	11 28	11 36	11 48	11 58	12 02	12 28	12 36	12 48	12 58	13 02	13 28	13 36	13 48	13 58	14 02	14 28	14 36	14 48	14 57
Havant a		11 09			11 54		12 09			12 54		13 09			13 54		14 09			14 54	
Chichester a		11 21			12 08		12 21			13 08		13 21			14 08		14 21			15 08	
Hilsea a	11 03		11 33			12 03		12 33			13 03		13 33			14 03		14 33			15 03
Fratton a	11 07		11 37	11 42		12 07		12 37	12 42		13 07		13 37	13 42		14 07		14 37	14 42		15 07
Portsmouth & Southsea a	11 11		11 42	11 46		12 11		12 42	12 46		13 11		13 42	13 46		14 11		14 42	14 46		15 11
Portsmouth Harbour a	11 18			11 52		12 18			12 52		13 18			13 52		14 18			14 52		15 18

	SN	GW	SN	SW	GW	SN	SW	SN	SW	GW	SN	SW	SN	SW	GW	SN	SW	SN	SW	GW	SN	SW
	■ B	■ E	■ F	■	◇ C	■ D	■ A	■ B	■	◇ C	■ D	■ A	■ B	■	◇ C	■ D	■ A	■ B	■	◇ C	■ D	■ A
Southampton Central d	14 26	14 34		14 44	15 05	15 13		15 26	15 44	16 05	16 13		16 26	16 44	17 05	17 13		17 26	17 44	18 05	18 13	
St Denys d				14 49					15 49					16 49					17 49			
Bitterne d				14 52					15 52					16 52					17 52			
Woolston d				14 55					15 55					16 55					17 55			
Sholing d				14 58					15 58					16 58					17 58			
Netley d				15 02					16 02					17 02					18 02			
Hamble d				15 04					16 04					17 04					18 04			
Bursledon d				15 07					16 07					17 07					18 07			
Swanwick d			←	15 11		15 32		15 46	16 11		16 32		16 46	17 11		17 32		17 46	18 11		18 32	
Fareham a	14 59	14 55	14 59	15 17	15 27	15 38		15 52	16 17	16 27	16 38		16 52	17 17	17 27	17 38		17 52	18 17	18 27	18 38	
d	15 00	14 56	15 00	15 18	15 28	15 39	15 48	15 53	16 18	16 28	16 39	16 48	16 53	17 18	17 28	17 39	17 48	17 53	18 18	18 28	18 39	18 48
Portchester d	→			15 23		15 44	15 53		16 23		16 44	16 53		17 23		17 44	17 53		18 23		18 44	18 53
Cosham d		15 04		15 28	15 36	15 48	15 58	16 02	16 28	16 36	16 48	16 58	17 02	17 28	17 36	17 48	17 58	18 02	18 28	18 36	18 48	18 58
Havant a		15 10	15 13			15 54		16 09			16 54		17 09			17 54		18 09			18 54	
Chichester a		15 21	15 24			16 08		16 21			17 08		17 21			18 08		18 21			19 08	
Hilsea a				15 33			16 03		16 33			17 03		17 33			18 03		18 33			19 03
Fratton a				15 37	15 42		16 07		16 37	16 42		17 07		17 37	17 42		18 07		18 37	18 42		19 07
Portsmouth & Southsea a				15 42	15 46		16 11		16 40	16 46		17 11		17 42	17 46		18 11		18 42	18 46		19 11
Portsmouth Harbour a					15 52		16 18		16 44	16 52		17 16			17 52		18 18			18 52		19 18

	SN	SW	GW	SN	SW	SN	SW	GW	SN	SW	SN	SW	GW	SN	SW	SN	SW	GW	SN	SW	SN
	■ B	■	■ C	■ D	■ A	■ B	■	◇ C	■ D	■ A	■ B	■	◇ C	B	■ A	■ G	■	◇ C	H	■ A	■ H
Southampton Central d	18 26	18 44	19 05	19 13		19 26	19 44	20 05	20 13		20 26	20 44	21 05	21 13		21 32	21 44	22 05	22 21		22 26
St Denys d		18 49					19 49					20 49					21 49				
Bitterne d		18 52					19 52					20 52					21 52				
Woolston d		18 55					19 55					20 55					21 55				
Sholing d		18 58					19 58					20 58					21 58				
Netley d		19 02					20 02					21 02					22 02				
Hamble d		19 04					20 04					21 04					22 04				
Bursledon d		19 07					20 07					21 07					22 07				
Swanwick d	18 46	19 11		19 32		19 46	20 11		20 32		20 46	21 11		21 33		21 51	22 11		22 40		22 46
Fareham a	18 52	19 17	19 27	19 38		19 52	20 17	20 27	20 38		20 52	21 17	21 27	21 39		21 57	22 17	22 26	22 46		22 52
d	18 53	19 18	19 28	19 39	19 48	19 53	20 18	20 28	20 39	20 48	20 53	21 18	21 28	21 40	21 48	21 58	22 18	22 27	22 47	22 48	22 53
Portchester d		19 23		19 44	19 53		20 23		20 44	20 53		21 23		21 45	21 53	22 03	22 23		22 52	22 53	
Cosham d	19 02	19 28	19 36	19 48	19 58	20 02	20 28		20 48	20 58	21 02	21 28		21 49	21 58	22 07	22 28		22 56	22 58	23 02
Havant a	19 09			19 54		20 09			20 54		21 09			21 55		22 13			23 02		23 09
Chichester a	19 21			20 08		20 21			21 08		21 21			22 06		22 33			23 17		23 21
Hilsea a		19 33			20 03		20 33			21 03		21 33			22 03		22 33			23 03	
Fratton a		19 37	19 42		20 07		20 37	20 40		21 07		21 37	21 42		22 07		22 37	22 41		23 07	
Portsmouth & Southsea a		19 42	19 46		20 11		20 42	20 44		21 11		21 40	21 46		22 11		22 40	22 45		23 11	
Portsmouth Harbour a			19 52		20 18			20 50		21 16		21 45	21 52		22 18		22 47	22 52		23 18	

A From London Waterloo
B To Brighton
C From Cardiff Central
D To London Victoria
E From Great Malvern to Brighton
F From Southampton Central to Brighton
G To Three Bridges
H To Littlehampton

Please note, Network Rail have stated that further updates to this timetable are possible during the validity period.

Table T165-R

Saturdays
26 May to 8 December

Southampton and Fareham - Chichester and Portsmouth

		SW 1	GW ◇ A	SN B	SW 1 C
Southampton Central ⛴	d	22 44	23 06	23 16	
St Denys	d	22 49		23 22	
Bitterne	d	22 52			
Woolston	d	22 55			
Sholing	d	22 58			
Netley	d	23 02			
Hamble	d	23 04			
Bursledon	d	23 07			
Swanwick	d	23 11			
Fareham	a	23 17	23 27	23 38	
	d	23 18	23 28	23 38	23 48
Portchester	d	23 23			23 53
Cosham	d	23 28		23 47	23 58
Havant	a			23 53	
Chichester 4	a			00 05	
Hilsea	a	23 33			00 03
Fratton	a	23 37	23 41		00 07
Portsmouth & Southsea	a	23 40	23 45		00 11
Portsmouth Harbour ⛴	a		23 52		00 16

Sundays
20 May to 2 December

		SW 1	SW 1	SN D	SW 1 E	SW 1 F	SW 1 G	SN D	GW H	SW 1	SW 1 G	SN D	SW 1	SW 1 G	SN D	SW 1	GW ◇ A	SW 1 G	SN D	SW 1	GW ◇ A	SW 1 G	SN D
Southampton Central ⛴	d	06 35		07 30	07 35	07 35		08 21	08 31	08 35		09 30	09 35		10 30	10 35	11 04		11 30	11 35	12 04		12 30
St Denys	d	06 41			07 41	07 41				08 41			09 41			10 41				11 41			
Bitterne	d	06 43			07 43	07 43				08 43			09 43			10 43				11 43			
Woolston	d	06 47			07 47	07 47				08 47			09 47			10 47				11 47			
Sholing	d	06 49			07 49	07 49				08 49			09 49			10 49				11 49			
Netley	d	06 53			07 53	07 53				08 53			09 53			10 53				11 53			
Hamble	d	06 55			07 55	07 55				08 55			09 55			10 55				11 55			
Bursledon	d	06 58			07 58	07 58				08 58			09 58			10 58				11 58			
Swanwick	d	07 02		07 47	08 02	08 02		08 40		09 02		09 47	10 02		10 47	11 02			11 47	12 02			12 47
Fareham	a	07 09		07 53	08 09	08 09		08 46	08 53	09 09		09 53	10 09		10 53	11 09	11 26		11 53	12 09	12 26		12 53
	d	07 10	07 44	07 54	08 10	08 10	08 42	08 47	08 54	09 10	09 45	09 54	10 10	10 45	10 54	11 10	11 26	11 45	11 54	12 10	12 26	12 45	12 54
Portchester	d	07 15	07 49		08 15	08 15	08 47			09 15	09 50		10 15	10 50		11 15		11 50		12 15		12 50	
Cosham	d	07 20	07 54	08 03	08 20	08 20	08 52	08 56	09 02	09 20	09 55	10 03	10 20	10 55	11 03	11 20	11 34	11 55	12 03	12 21	12 34	12 55	13 03
Havant	a			08 10				09 02	09 13			10 10			11 10				12 10				13 10
Chichester 4	a			08 22				09 14	09 24			10 22			11 22				12 22				13 22
Hilsea	a	07 24	08 00		08 26	08 26	09 00			09 30	10 00		10 24	11 00		11 24		12 00		12 28		13 00	
Fratton	a	07 28	08 04		08 31	08 31	09 04			09 34	10 09		10 28	11 09		11 28	11 42	12 09		12 32	12 42	13 09	
Portsmouth & Southsea	a	07 32	08 08		08 35	08 37	09 08			09 37	10 12		10 32	11 12		11 32	11 46	12 12		12 36	12 46	13 12	
Portsmouth Harbour ⛴	a		08 13				09 13				10 16			11 16			11 51	12 16			12 53	13 16	

		SW 1	GW ◇ I	SW 1 G	SN D	SW 1	GW ◇ A	SW 1 G	SN D	SW 1	GW ◇ I	SW 1 G	SN D	SW 1	GW ◇ A	SW 1 G	SN D	SW 1	GW ◇ A	SW ◇1 C	SN D	SW 1	GW ◇ A
Southampton Central ⛴	d	12 35	13 04		13 30	13 35	14 04		14 30	14 35	15 06		15 30	15 35	16 04		16 30	16 35	17 04		17 30	17 35	18 04
St Denys	d	12 41				13 41				14 41				15 41				16 41				17 41	
Bitterne	d	12 43				13 43				14 43				15 43				16 43				17 43	
Woolston	d	12 47				13 47				14 47				15 47				16 47				17 47	
Sholing	d	12 49				13 49				14 49				15 49				16 49				17 49	
Netley	d	12 53				13 53				14 53				15 53				16 53				17 53	
Hamble	d	12 55				13 55				14 55				15 55				16 55				17 55	
Bursledon	d	12 58				13 58				14 58				15 58				16 58				17 58	
Swanwick	d	13 02			13 47	14 02			14 47	15 02			15 47	16 02			16 47	17 02			17 47	18 02	
Fareham	a	13 09	13 29		13 53	14 09	14 26		14 53	15 09	15 27		15 53	16 09	16 26		16 53	17 09	17 26		17 53	18 09	18 26
	d	13 10	13 30	13 45	13 54	14 10	14 26	14 45	14 54	15 10	15 28	15 45	15 54	16 10	16 26	16 45	16 54	17 10	17 26	17 45	17 54	18 10	18 26
Portchester	d	13 15		13 50		14 15		14 50		15 15		15 50		16 15		16 50		17 15		17 50		18 15	
Cosham	d	13 20	13 38	13 55	14 03	14 20	14 34	14 55	15 03	15 20	15 36	15 55	16 03	16 20	16 34	16 55	17 03	17 20	17 34	17 55	18 03	18 20	18 34
Havant	a		13 45		14 10				15 10		15 42		16 10				17 10				18 10		
Chichester 4	a		13 57		14 22				15 22		15 53		16 22				17 22				18 22		
Hilsea	a	13 26		14 00		14 26		15 00		15 26		16 00		16 26		17 00		17 26		18 00		18 26	
Fratton	a	13 30		14 09		14 30	14 42	15 09		15 30		16 09		16 30	16 42	17 09		17 30	17 42	18 09		18 30	18 42
Portsmouth & Southsea	a	13 33		14 12		14 33	14 46	15 12		15 33		16 12		16 33	16 46	17 12		17 33	17 46	18 12		18 33	18 46
Portsmouth Harbour ⛴	a			14 16			14 53	15 20				16 17			16 52	17 16			17 51	18 16			18 52

A From Cardiff Central
B To Littlehampton
C From London Waterloo
D To Brighton
E until 30 September
F from 7 October
G From Eastleigh
H From Romsey to Brighton
I From Cardiff Central to Brighton

Table T165-R

Sundays
20 May to 2 December

Southampton and Fareham - Chichester and Portsmouth

		SW ◇1 A	SN B	SW 1	GW ◇ C	SW ◇1 A	SN B	GW ◇ D	SW 1	GW ◇ C	SW ◇1 A	SN B	GW ◇ C	SW 1	GW ◇ C	SW ◇1 A	SN B
Southampton Central ⛴	d		18 30	18 35	19 04		19 21	19 28	19 35	20 04		20 28	20 33	20 35	21 04		21 30
St Denys	d			18 41					19 41					20 40			
Bitterne	d			18 43					19 43					20 42			
Woolston	d			18 47					19 47					20 46			
Sholing	d			18 49					19 49					20 48			
Netley	d			18 53					19 53					20 52			
Hamble	d			18 55					19 55					20 54			
Bursledon	d			18 58					19 58					20 57			
Swanwick	d		18 47	19 02			19 41		20 02			20 46		21 01			21 47
Fareham	a		18 53	19 09	19 26		19 48	19 53	20 09	20 26		20 52	20 58	21 09	21 26		21 53
	d	18 45	18 54	19 10	19 26	19 44	19 49	19 54	20 10	20 26	20 45	20 53	20 59	21 10	21 26	21 45	21 54
Portchester	d	18 50		19 15		19 49			20 15		20 50			21 15		21 50	
Cosham	d	18 55	19 03	19 20	19 34	19 54	19 57	20 02	20 20		20 55	21 03		21 20		21 55	22 03
Havant	a		19 10				20 03	20 10				21 10					22 10
Chichester 4	a		19 22				20 15	20 21				21 22					22 22
Hilsea	a	19 00		19 26		20 05			20 25		21 00			21 25		22 00	
Fratton	a	19 09		19 30	19 42	20 09			20 29	20 40	21 09		21 13	21 29	21 40	22 09	
Portsmouth & Southsea	a	19 12		19 33	19 46	20 12			20 33	20 47	21 12		21 17	21 33	21 43	22 12	
Portsmouth Harbour ⛴	a	19 17			19 52	20 17				20 52	21 17		21 21		21 51	22 16	

		SW 1	GW ◇ C	SW ◇1 A	SN E	SW 1	SN E
Southampton Central ⛴	d	21 35	22 04		22 30	22 35	22 58
St Denys	d	21 41				22 41	
Bitterne	d	21 43				22 43	
Woolston	d	21 47				22 47	
Sholing	d	21 49				22 49	
Netley	d	21 53				22 53	
Hamble	d	21 55				22 55	
Bursledon	d	21 58				22 58	
Swanwick	d	22 02			22 47	23 02	23 15
Fareham	a	22 09	22 26		22 53	23 09	23 21
	d	22 10	22 26	22 45	22 54	23 10	23 22
Portchester	d	22 15		22 50		23 15	
Cosham	d	22 20		22 55	23 04	23 20	23 31
Havant	a				23 11		23 38
Chichester 4	a				23 22		23 50
Hilsea	a	22 26		23 00		23 28	
Fratton	a	22 30	22 42	23 08		23 32	
Portsmouth & Southsea	a	22 33	22 46	23 11		23 36	
Portsmouth Harbour ⛴	a		22 52	23 16			

		GW ◇ C	SW ◇1 A ⚯
Southampton Central ⛴	d	23 08	
St Denys	d		
Bitterne	d		
Woolston	d		
Sholing	d		
Netley	d		
Hamble	d		
Bursledon	d		
Swanwick	d		
Fareham	a	23 29	
	d	23 30	23 45
Portchester	d		23 50
Cosham	d		23 55
Havant	a		
Chichester 4	a		
Hilsea	a		00 01
Fratton	a	23 43	00 07
Portsmouth & Southsea	a	23 46	00 10
Portsmouth Harbour ⛴	a	23 50	00 14

A From London Waterloo
B To Brighton
C From Cardiff Central
D From Cardiff Central to Brighton
E To Littlehampton

Please note, Network Rail have stated that further updates to this timetable are possible during the validity period.

Table T167-F

Ryde - Shanklin (Isle of Wight)

Mondays to Fridays
21 May to 7 December

Miles			IL	IL	IL	IL	IL	IL	IL	IL	IL	IL	IL	IL	IL	IL	IL	IL	IL	IL	IL	IL	IL
0	**Ryde Pier Head**	d	05 49	06 07	06 49	07 07	07 49	08 07	08 49	09 07	09 49	10 07	10 49	11 07	11 49	12 07	12 49	13 07	13 49	14 07	14 49	15 07	15 49
0½	**Ryde Esplanade**	d	05 51	06 09	06 52	07 09	07 52	08 09	08 52	09 09	09 52	10 09	10 52	11 09	11 52	12 09	12 52	13 09	13 52	14 09	14 52	15 09	15 52
1¼	Ryde St Johns Road	d	05 55	06 13	06 55	07 13	07 55	08 13	08 55	09 13	09 55	10 13	10 55	11 13	11 55	12 13	12 55	13 13	13 55	14 13	14 55	15 13	15 55
2¼	Smallbrook Junction §	d											10 58		11 58	12 15	12 58	13 15			14 58	15 15	15 58
4¾	Brading	d	06 02	06 20	07 03	07 20	08 03	08 20	09 03	09 20	10 03	10 20	11 03	11 20	12 03	12 20	13 03	13 20	14 03	14 20	15 03	15 20	16 03
6½	Sandown	d	06 07	06 25	07 07	07 25	08 07	08 25	09 07	09 25	10 07	10 25	11 07	11 25	12 07	12 25	13 07	13 25	14 07	14 25	15 07	15 25	16 07
7¾	Lake	d	06 09	06 27	07 10	07 27	08 10	08 27	09 10	09 27	10 10	10 27	11 10	11 27	12 10	12 27	13 10	13 27	14 10	14 27	15 10	15 27	16 10
8½	**Shanklin**	a	06 12	06 30	07 13	07 30	08 13	08 30	09 13	09 30	10 13	10 30	11 13	11 30	12 13	12 30	13 13	13 30	14 13	14 30	15 13	15 30	16 13

		IL	IL	IL	IL	IL	IL	IL	IL	IL	IL	IL	IL
Ryde Pier Head	d	16 07	16 49	17 07	17 49	18 07	18 49	19 07	19 49	20 07	20 49	21 49	23 15
Ryde Esplanade	d	16 09	16 52	17 09	17 52	18 09	18 52	19 09	19 52	20 09	20 51	21 51	23 17
Ryde St Johns Road	d	16 13	16 55	17 13	17 55	18 13	18 55	19 13	19 55	20 13	20 55	21 55	23a20
Smallbrook Junction §	d	16 15											
Brading	d	16 20	17 03	17 20	18 03	18 20	19 03	19 20	20 03	20 20	21 01	22 01	
Sandown	d	16 25	17 07	17 25	18 07	18 25	19 07	19 25	20 07	20 25	21 05	22 05	
Lake	d	16 27	17 10	17 27	18 10	18 27	19 10	19 27	20 10	20 27	21 08	22 08	
Shanklin	a	16 30	17 13	17 30	18 13	18 30	19 13	19 30	20 13	20 30	21 11	22 11	

Saturdays
26 May to 8 December

		IL	IL	IL	IL	IL	IL	IL	IL	IL	IL	IL	IL	IL	IL	IL	IL	IL	IL	IL	IL	IL	IL
Ryde Pier Head	d	05 49	06 07	06 49	07 07	07 49	08 07	08 49	09 07	09 49	10 07	10 49	11 07	11 49	12 07	12 49	13 07	13 49	14 07	14 49	15 07	15 49	16 07
Ryde Esplanade	d	05 51	06 09	06 52	07 09	07 52	08 09	08 52	09 09	09 52	10 09	10 52	11 09	11 52	12 09	12 52	13 09	13 52	14 09	14 52	15 09	15 52	16 09
Ryde St Johns Road	d	05 55	06 13	06 55	07 13	07 55	08 13	08 55	09 13	09 55	10 13	10 55	11 13	11 55	12 13	12 55	13 13	13 55	14 13	14 55	15 13	15 55	16 13
Smallbrook Junction §	d											10 58		11 58	12 15	12 58	13 15			14 58	15 15	15 58	16 15
Brading	d	06 02	06 20	07 03	07 20	08 03	08 20	09 03	09 20	10 03	10 20	11 03	11 20	12 03	12 20	13 03	13 20	14 03	14 20	15 03	15 20	16 03	16 20
Sandown	d	06 07	06 25	07 07	07 25	08 07	08 25	09 07	09 25	10 07	10 25	11 07	11 25	12 07	12 25	13 07	13 25	14 07	14 25	15 07	15 25	16 07	16 25
Lake	d	06 09	06 27	07 10	07 27	08 10	08 27	09 10	09 27	10 10	10 27	11 10	11 27	12 10	12 27	13 10	13 27	14 10	14 27	15 10	15 27	16 10	16 27
Shanklin	a	06 12	06 30	07 13	07 30	08 13	08 30	09 13	09 30	10 13	10 30	11 13	11 30	12 13	12 30	13 13	13 30	14 13	14 30	15 13	15 30	16 13	16 30

		IL	IL	IL	IL	IL	IL	IL	IL	IL	IL	IL
Ryde Pier Head	d	16 49	17 07	17 49	18 07	18 49	19 07	19 49	20 07	20 49	21 49	23 15
Ryde Esplanade	d	16 52	17 09	17 52	18 09	18 52	19 09	19 52	20 09	20 51	21 51	23 17
Ryde St Johns Road	d	16 55	17 13	17 55	18 13	18 55	19 13	19 55	20 13	20 55	21 55	23a20
Smallbrook Junction §	d											
Brading	d	17 03	17 20	18 03	18 20	19 03	19 20	20 03	20 20	21 01	22 01	
Sandown	d	17 07	17 25	18 07	18 25	19 07	19 25	20 07	20 25	21 05	22 05	
Lake	d	17 10	17 27	18 10	18 27	19 10	19 27	20 10	20 27	21 08	22 08	
Shanklin	a	17 13	17 30	18 13	18 30	19 13	19 30	20 13	20 30	21 11	22 11	

Sundays
20 May to 2 December

		IL	IL	IL A	IL	IL A	IL	IL A	IL	IL A	IL	IL A	IL	IL	IL	IL	IL	IL	IL	IL	IL	IL	IL
Ryde Pier Head	d	06 49	07 49		08 49	09 07	09 49	10 07	10 49	11 07	11 49	12 07	12 49	13 07	13 49	14 07	14 49	15 07	15 49	16 07	16 49	17 07	17 49
Ryde Esplanade	d	06 52	07 52		08 52	09 09	09 52	10 09	10 52	11 09	11 52	12 09	12 52	13 09	13 52	14 09	14 52	15 09	15 52	16 09	16 52	17 09	17 52
Ryde St Johns Road	d	06 55	07 55	08 13	08 55	09 13	09 55	10 13	10 55	11 13	11 55	12 13	12 55	13 13	13 55	14 13	14 55	15 13	15 55	16 13	16 55	17 13	17 55
Smallbrook Junction §	d								10 58		11 58	12 15	12 58	13 15			14 58	15 15	15 58	16 15			
Brading	d	07 03	08 03	08 20	09 03	09 20	10 03	10 20	11 03	11 20	12 03	12 20	13 03	13 20	14 03	14 20	15 03	15 20	16 03	16 20	17 03	17 20	18 03
Sandown	d	07 07	08 07	08 25	09 07	09 25	10 07	10 25	11 07	11 25	12 07	12 25	13 07	13 25	14 07	14 25	15 07	15 25	16 07	16 25	17 07	17 25	18 07
Lake	d	07 10	08 10	08 27	09 10	09 27	10 10	10 27	11 10	11 27	12 10	12 27	13 10	13 27	14 10	14 27	15 10	15 27	16 10	16 27	17 10	17 27	18 10
Shanklin	a	07 13	08 13	08 30	09 13	09 30	10 13	10 30	11 13	11 30	12 13	12 30	13 13	13 30	14 13	14 30	15 13	15 30	16 13	16 30	17 13	17 30	18 13

		IL	IL	IL A	IL	IL A	IL	IL	IL
Ryde Pier Head	d	18 07	18 49	19 07	19 49	20 07	20 49	21 49	23 15
Ryde Esplanade	d	18 09	18 52	19 09	19 52	20 09	20 51	21 51	23 17
Ryde St Johns Road	d	18 13	18 55	19 13	19 55	20a13	20 55	21 55	23a20
Smallbrook Junction §	d								
Brading	d	18 20	19 03	19 20	20 03		21 01	22 01	
Sandown	d	18 25	19 07	19 25	20 07		21 05	22 05	
Lake	d	18 27	19 10	19 27	20 10		21 08	22 08	
Shanklin	a	18 30	19 13	19 30	20 13		21 11	22 11	

§ Smallbrook Jn. is only open for access to the I.O.W Steam Railway. For days of operation please enquire locally.

A until 30 September

Table T167-R

Shanklin - Ryde (Isle of Wight)

Mondays to Fridays
21 May to 7 December

Miles			IL	IL	IL	IL	IL	IL	IL	IL	IL	IL	IL	IL	IL	IL	IL	IL	IL	IL	IL	IL	IL
0	**Shanklin**	d			06 18	06 38	07 18	07 38	08 18	08 38	09 18	09 38	10 18	10 38	11 18	11 38	12 18	12 38	13 18	13 38	14 18	14 38	15 18
1¾	Lake	d			06 21	06 41	07 21	07 41	08 21	08 41	09 21	09 41	10 21	10 41	11 21	11 41	12 21	12 41	13 21	13 41	14 21	14 41	15 21
2	Sandown	d			06 24	06 44	07 24	07 44	08 24	08 44	09 24	09 44	10 24	10 44	11 24	11 44	12 24	12 44	13 24	13 44	14 24	14 44	15 24
3¾	Brading	d			06 28	06 48	07 28	07 48	08 28	08 48	09 28	09 48	10 28	10 48	11 28	11 48	12 28	12 48	13 28	13 48	14 28	14 48	15 28
6¼	Smallbrook Junction §	d												10 53		11 53	12 33	12 53	13 33			14 53	15 33
7¼	Ryde St Johns Road	d	05 35	05 56	06 35	06 55	07 35	07 55	08 35	08 55	09 35	09 55	10 35	10 55	11 35	11 55	12 35	12 55	13 35	13 55	14 35	14 55	15 35
8¼	**Ryde Esplanade**	d	05 40	06 00	06 40	07 00	07 40	08 00	08 40	09 00	09 40	10 00	10 40	11 00	11 40	12 00	12 40	13 00	13 40	14 00	14 40	15 00	15 40
8½	**Ryde Pier Head**	a	05 42	06 02	06 42	07 02	07 42	08 02	08 42	09 02	09 42	10 02	10 42	11 02	11 42	12 02	12 42	13 02	13 42	14 02	14 42	15 02	15 42

		IL	IL	IL	IL	IL	IL	IL	IL	IL	IL	IL	IL	IL
Shanklin	d	15 38	16 18	16 38	17 18	17 38	18 18	18 38	19 18	19 38	20 18	20 38	21 18	22 38
Lake	d	15 41	16 21	16 41	17 21	17 41	18 21	18 41	19 21	19 41	20 21	20 41	21 21	22 41
Sandown	d	15 44	16 24	16 44	17 24	17 44	18 24	18 44	19 24	19 44	20 24	20 44	21 24	22 44
Brading	d	15 48	16 28	16 48	17 28	17 48	18 28	18 48	19 28	19 48	20 28	20 48	21 28	22 48
Smallbrook Junction §	d	15 53	16 33											
Ryde St Johns Road	d	15 55	16 35	16 55	17 35	17 55	18 35	18 55	19 35	19 55	20 34	20a54	21 34	22 54
Ryde Esplanade	d	16 00	16 40	17 00	17 40	18 00	18 40	19 00	19 40	20 00	20 38		21 38	22 58
Ryde Pier Head	a	16 02	16 42	17 02	17 42	18 02	18 42	19 02	19 42	20 02	20 41		21 41	23 00

Saturdays
26 May to 8 December

		IL	IL	IL	IL	IL	IL	IL	IL	IL	IL	IL	IL	IL	IL	IL	IL	IL	IL	IL	IL	IL	IL
Shanklin	d			06 18	06 38	07 18	07 38	08 18	08 38	09 18	09 38	10 18	10 38	11 18	11 38	12 18	12 38	13 18	13 38	14 18	14 38	15 18	15 38
Lake	d			06 21	06 41	07 21	07 41	08 21	08 41	09 21	09 41	10 21	10 41	11 21	11 41	12 21	12 41	13 21	13 41	14 21	14 41	15 21	15 41
Sandown	d			06 24	06 44	07 24	07 44	08 24	08 44	09 24	09 44	10 24	10 44	11 24	11 44	12 24	12 44	13 24	13 44	14 24	14 44	15 24	15 44
Brading	d			06 28	06 48	07 28	07 48	08 28	08 48	09 28	09 48	10 28	10 48	11 28	11 48	12 28	12 48	13 28	13 48	14 28	14 48	15 28	15 48
Smallbrook Junction §	d												10 53		11 53	12 33	12 53	13 33			14 53	15 33	15 53
Ryde St Johns Road	d	05 35	05 56	06 35	06 55	07 35	07 55	08 35	08 55	09 35	09 55	10 35	10 55	11 35	11 55	12 35	12 55	13 35	13 55	14 35	14 55	15 35	15 55
Ryde Esplanade	d	05 40	06 00	06 40	07 00	07 40	08 00	08 40	09 00	09 40	10 00	10 40	11 00	11 40	12 00	12 40	13 00	13 40	14 00	14 40	15 00	15 40	16 00
Ryde Pier Head	a	05 42	06 02	06 42	07 02	07 42	08 02	08 42	09 02	09 42	10 02	10 42	11 02	11 42	12 02	12 42	13 02	13 42	14 02	14 42	15 02	15 42	16 02

		IL	IL	IL	IL	IL	IL	IL	IL	IL	IL	IL	IL
Shanklin	d	16 18	16 38	17 18	17 38	18 18	18 38	19 18	19 38	20 18	20 38	21 18	22 38
Lake	d	16 21	16 41	17 21	17 41	18 21	18 41	19 21	19 41	20 21	20 41	21 21	22 41
Sandown	d	16 24	16 44	17 24	17 44	18 24	18 44	19 24	19 44	20 24	20 44	21 24	22 44
Brading	d	16 28	16 48	17 28	17 48	18 28	18 48	19 28	19 48	20 28	20 48	21 28	22 48
Smallbrook Junction §	d	16 33											
Ryde St Johns Road	d	16 35	16 55	17 35	17 55	18 35	18 55	19 35	19 55	20 34	20a54	21 34	22 54
Ryde Esplanade	d	16 40	17 00	17 40	18 00	18 40	19 00	19 40	20 00	20 38		21 38	22 58
Ryde Pier Head	a	16 42	17 02	17 42	18 02	18 42	19 02	19 42	20 02	20 41		21 41	23 00

Sundays
20 May to 2 December

		IL	IL	IL	IL A	IL	IL A	IL	IL A	IL	IL A	IL	IL A	IL B	IL	IL	IL	IL	IL	IL	IL	IL	IL
Shanklin	d		07 18	08 18	08 38	09 18	09 38	10 18	10 38	11 18	11 38	12 18	12 38		13 18	13 38	14 18	14 38	15 18	15 38	16 18	16 38	17 18
Lake	d		07 21	08 21	08 41	09 21	09 41	10 21	10 41	11 21	11 41	12 21	12 41		13 21	13 41	14 21	14 41	15 21	15 41	16 21	16 41	17 21
Sandown	d		07 24	08 24	08 44	09 24	09 44	10 24	10 44	11 24	11 44	12 24	12 44		13 24	13 44	14 24	14 44	15 24	15 44	16 24	16 44	17 24
Brading	d		07 28	08 28	08 48	09 28	09 48	10 28	10 48	11 28	11 48	12 28	12 48		13 28	13 48	14 28	14 48	15 28	15 48	16 28	16 48	17 28
Smallbrook Junction §	d								10 53		11 53	12 33	12 53		13 33			14 53	15 33	15 53	16 33		
Ryde St Johns Road	d	06 35	07 35	08 35	08 55	09 35	09 55	10 35	10 55	11 35	11 55	12 35	12 55	12 55	13 35	13 55	14 35	14 55	15 35	15 55	16 35	16 55	17 35
Ryde Esplanade	d	06 40	07 40	08 40	09 00	09 40	10 00	10 40	11 00	11 40	12 00	12 40	13 00	13 00	13 40	14 00	14 40	15 00	15 40	16 00	16 40	17 00	17 40
Ryde Pier Head	a	06 42	07 42	08 42	09 02	09 42	10 02	10 42	11 02	11 42	12 02	12 42	13 02	13 02	13 42	14 02	14 42	15 02	15 42	16 02	16 42	17 02	17 42

		IL	IL	IL B	IL A	IL	IL A	IL	IL	IL
Shanklin	d	17 38	18 18	18 38	18 38	19 18	19 38	20 18	21 18	22 38
Lake	d	17 41	18 21	18 41	18 41	19 21	19 41	20 21	21 21	22 41
Sandown	d	17 44	18 24	18 44	18 44	19 24	19 44	20 24	21 24	22 44
Brading	d	17 48	18 28	18 48	18 48	19 28	19 48	20 28	21 28	22 48
Smallbrook Junction §	d									
Ryde St Johns Road	d	17 55	18 35	18a54	18 55	19 35	19 55	20 34	21 34	22 54
Ryde Esplanade	d	18 00	18 40		19 00	19 40	20 00	20 38	21 38	22 58
Ryde Pier Head	a	18 02	18 42		19 02	19 42	20 02	20 41	21 41	23 00

§ Smallbrook Jn. is only open for access to the I.O.W Steam Railway. For days of operation please enquire locally.

A until 30 September
B from 7 October

Table T167-A

Provided by *European Rail Timetable Ltd*

PORTSMOUTH - RYDE - SHANKLIN

2nd class Island Line

Through fares including ferry travel are available. Allow 10 minutes for connections between trains and ferries. Operator: Wightlink ✆ 0333 999 7333. www.wightlink.co.uk

Portsmouth Harbour - Ryde Pierhead:
0515Ⓐ, 0615⚒, 0715 and hourly until 1815, 1920, 2020, 2120, 2245.

Ryde Pierhead - Portsmouth Harbour — Journey time: ± 20 minutes
0547Ⓐ, 0647⚒, 0747 and hourly until 2147, 2310.

Additional services operate on Ⓐ and on public holidays.

Ryde Pierhead - Shanklin: Trains call at **Sandown** 18 minutes later — *14 km*

⚒: 0549, 0607, 0649, 0707, 0749, 0807, 0849, 0907, 0949, 1007, 1049*, 1107, 1149*, 1207*, 1249*, 1307*, 1349, 1407, 1449*, 1507*, 1549*, 1607*, 1649, 1707, 1749, 1807, 1849, 1907, 1949, 2007, 2049, 2149.

⑦: 0649, 0749, 0849, 0907 **a**, 0949, 1007 **a**, 1049*, 1107 **a**, 1149*, 1207* **a**, 1249*, 1307*, 1349, 1407, 1449*, 1507*, 1549*, 1607*, 1649, 1707, 1749, 1807, 1849, 1907 **a** 1949, 2049, 2149.

Shanklin - Ryde Pierhead: Trains call at **Sandown** 6 minutes later. Journey time: ± 24 minutes

⚒: 0618, 0638, 0718, 0738, 0818, 0838, 0918, 0938, 1018, 1038*, 1118, 1138*, 1218*, 1238*, 1318*, 1338, 1418, 1438*, 1518*, 1538*, 1618*, 1638, 1718, 1738, 1818, 1838, 1918, 1938, 2018, 2118, 2238.

⑦: 0718, 0818, 0838 **a** 0918, 0938 **a**, 1018, 1038* **a**, 1118, 1138* **a**, 1218*, 1238* **a**, 1318*, 1338, 1418, 1438*, 1518*, 1538*, 1618*, 1638, 1718, 1738, 1818, 1838 **a** 1918, 1938 **a**, 2018, 2118, 2238.

a – Until Sept. 30.

* – Also calls at Smallbrook Junction (connection with **Isle of Wight Steam Railway**, see note △) 9 minutes from Ryde / 15 minutes from Shanklin, when Steam Railway is operating.

△ – **Isle of Wight Steam Railway** (Smallbrook Junction - Wootton: *9 km*). ✆ 01983 882204. www.iwsteamrailway.co.uk

Table T170-F

Mondays to Fridays

21 May to 7 December

London Victoria - Battersea Park, Wandsworth Common, Balham, Streatham Common, Norbury, Thornton Heath & Selhurst-Croydon

Miles	Miles	Miles	Miles		SN MX A	SN MO A	SN MX A	SN MO B	SN MX C	SN	SN ■ D	SN E	SN F		SN F	SN	SN E	SN	SN	SN	SN ■ G	SN F	SN	
0	0	—	—	London Victoria ⊖ d						00 12	04 35	05 41			06 00	06 06	06 11	06 16		06 20		06 30	06 36	
1½	1½	—	—	Battersea Park d				00 01		00 16					06 04	06 10		06 20		06 24		06 34	06 40	
—	—	—	0	Shepherd's Bush ⊖ d																	06 21			
—	—	—	0¾	Kensington (Olympia) ⊖ d																	06 24			
—	—	—	1½	West Brompton ⊖ d																	06 27			
—	—	—	2¼	Imperial Wharf d																	06 29			
2¾	2¾	—	4	Clapham Junction a				00 05		00 20	04 42	05 48			06 08	06 14	06 18	06 24		06 28	06 34	06 38	06 44	
—	—	—	—	Clapham Junction d			00 04	00 06		00 20	04 42	05 48			06 09	06 14	06 18	06 24		06 28	06 35	06 39	06 44	
4	4	—	5¼	Wandsworth Common d			00 07	00 09		00 23					06 12	06 17		06 27		06 31		06 42	06 47	
4½	4½	—	6	Balham ⊖ d		00 02	00 10	00a11		00 26		05 53			06 15	06 20	06 23	06 30		06 34	06 41	06 45	06 50	
—	—	0	—	London Bridge d			00a47												06 14	07a18				
6¾	6¾	8¾	7¼	Streatham Common d		00 06			00 26	00 31					06 20			06 35	06 42		06 46	06 50		
7½	7½	9	8¼	Norbury d	00 01	00 09			00 28	00 33					06 22			06 37	06 44		06 48	06 52		
8¾	8¾	10¼	10	Thornton Heath d	00 04	00 12			00 31	00 36					06 25			06 40	06 47		06 51	06 55		
9½	9½	11	10¾	Selhurst d	00 07	00a14			00a34	00 39	04 53		05 58		06 29			06 44	06a50		06 55	06 58		
—	10½	—	11¾	East Croydon a						00 43	04 57										06 59			
—	13½	—	—	Purley a							05 02													
10½	—	12¼	—	West Croydon a	00 12								06 03		06 33	06 52		06 49				07 03	07 22	
15	—	—	—	Sutton a	00 25							06 13	06 19		06 46		06 43	07 03				07 16		

	SN E	SN	SN	SN	SN F	SN	SN E	SN	SN		SN	SN ■ G	SN F	SN	SN E	SN	SN	SN	SN ■ G		SN F	SN	SN E	SN
London Victoria ⊖ d	06 41	06 46		06 50	07 00	07 06	07 11	07 16			07 20		07 30	07 36	07 41	07 46		07 50			08 00	08 06	08 11	08 16
Battersea Park d		06 50		06 54	07 04	07 10		07 20			07 24		07 34	07 40		07 50		07 54			08 04	08 10		08 20
Shepherd's Bush ⊖ d												07 22							07 50					
Kensington (Olympia) ⊖ d												07 25							07 52					
West Brompton ⊖ d												07 28							07 55					
Imperial Wharf d												07 30							07 57					
Clapham Junction a	06 48	06 54		06 58	07 08	07 14	07 18	07 24			07 28	07 35	07 38	07 44	07 48	07 54		07 58	08 02		08 08	08 14	08 18	08 24
Clapham Junction d	06 48	06 54		06 58	07 09	07 14	07 18	07 24			07 28	07 35	07 39	07 44	07 48	07 54		07 58	08 05		08 09	08 14	08 18	08 24
Wandsworth Common d		06 57		07 01	07 12	07 17		07 27			07 31	07 39	07 42	07 47		07 57		08 01			08 12	08 17		08 27
Balham ⊖ d	06 53	07 00		07 04	07 15	07 20	07 23	07 30			07 35	07 42	07 45	07 50	07 53	08 00		08 04	08 11		08 15	08 20	08 23	08 30
London Bridge d			06 44	07a48					07 14		08a18						07 44	08a48						
Streatham Common d		07 05	07 12		07 20			07 35	07 42			07 46	07 50			08 05	08 12		08 16		08 20			08 35
Norbury d		07 07	07 14		07 22			07 37	07 44			07 49	07 53			08 07	08 14		08 18		08 22			08 37
Thornton Heath d		07 10	07 17		07 25			07 40	07 47			07 52	07 56			08 10	08 17		08 21		08 25			08 40
Selhurst d		07 14	07a20		07 28			07 44	07a50			07 56	07 59			08 14	08a20		08 26		08 29			08 44
East Croydon a												08 01							08 31					
Purley a																								
West Croydon a		07 19			07 33	07 52		07 49					08 04	08 22		08 19					08 33	08 52		08 48
Sutton a	07 13	07 33			07 46		07 43	08 03					08 17		08 13	08 33					08 46		08 43	09 03

	SN	SN ■ H	SN	SN ■ I	SN F		SN	SN E	SN	SN	SN	SN J	SN F	SN	SN E		SN	SN	SN	SN ■ I	SN F	SN	SN E	SN
London Victoria ⊖ d			08 20		08 30		08 36	08 41	08 46		08 50	08 57	09 00	09 07	09 11		09 16		09 20		09 30	09 36	09 41	09 46
Battersea Park d			08 24		08 34		08 40		08 50		08 54		09 04	09 12			09 20		09 24		09 34	09 40		09 50
Shepherd's Bush ⊖ d		08 11																		09 22				
Kensington (Olympia) ⊖ d		08 14																		09 25				
West Brompton ⊖ d		08 17																		09 28				
Imperial Wharf d		08 19		←																09 30				
Clapham Junction a		08 24	08 28	08 24	08 38		08 44	08 48	08 54		08 58	09 05	09 08	09 15	09 18		09 24		09 28	09 35	09 38	09 44	09 48	09 54
Clapham Junction d		08 35	08 28	08 35	08 39		08 44	08 48	08 54		08 58	09 06	09 09	09 16	09 19		09 24		09 28	09 35	09 39	09 45	09 48	09 54
Wandsworth Common d		→	08 31		08 42		08 47		08 57		09 01		09 12	09 19			09 27		09 31		09 42	09 48		09 57
Balham ⊖ d			08 34	08 41	08 45		08 50	08 53	09 00		09 04	09 11	09 15	09 21	09 24		09 30		09 34	09 41	09 45	09 50	09 53	10 00
London Bridge d	08 14		09a18							08 44	09a48							09 14	10a17					
Streatham Common d	08 42			08 46	08 50				09 05	09 12		09 16	09 20				09 35	09 42		09 46	09 49			10 05
Norbury d	08 44			08 48	08 52				09 07	09 14		09 18	09 22				09 37	09 44		09 48	09 52			10 07
Thornton Heath d	08 47			08 51	08 55				09 10	09 17		09 21	09 25				09 40	09 47		09 51	09 55			10 10
Selhurst d	08a50			08 55	08 58				09 14	09a20		09 25	09 28				09 44	09a50		09 55	09 58			10 14
East Croydon a				09 01								09 30								10 00				
Purley a																								
West Croydon a					09 03		09 22		09 18				09 33	09 52			09 48				10 03	10 22		10 18
Sutton a					09 16			09 13	09 33				09 46		09 43		10 03				10 16		10 13	10 33

A From London Victoria
B From London Victoria to Norwood Junction
C From London Bridge
D To Gatwick Airport
E To Epsom
F To Epsom Downs
G From Watford Junction
H From Milton Keynes Central to East Croydon
I From Milton Keynes Central
J until 30 November

For faster services between London Victoria, Clapham Junction and East Croydon, refer to Table T175

For other Shepherd's Bush connecting trains, refer to Table T176

Table T170-F

Mondays to Fridays

21 May to 7 December

London Victoria - Battersea Park, Wandsworth Common, Balham, Streatham Common, Norbury, Thornton Heath & Selhurst-Croydon

	SN A	SN	SN B	SN	SN C	SN	SN A		SN	SN ■ D	SN B	SN	SN C	SN	SN A	SN	SN B		SN	SN C	SN	SN A	SN	SN ■ D
London Victoria ⊖ d		09 50	10 00	10 06	10 11	10 16			10 20		10 30	10 36	10 41	10 46		10 50	11 00		11 06	11 11	11 16		11 20	
Battersea Park d		09 54	10 04	10 10		10 20			10 24		10 34	10 40		10 50		10 54	11 04		11 10		11 20		11 24	
Shepherd's Bush ⊖ d										10 22														11 22
Kensington (Olympia) ⊖ d										10 25														11 25
West Brompton ⊖ d										10 28														11 28
Imperial Wharf d										10 30														11 30
Clapham Junction a		09 58	10 08	10 14	10 18	10 24			10 28	10 35	10 38	10 44	10 48	10 54		10 58	11 08		11 14	11 18	11 24		11 28	11 35
Clapham Junction d		09 58	10 09	10 14	10 18	10 24			10 28	10 35	10 39	10 44	10 48	10 54		10 58	11 09		11 14	11 18	11 24		11 28	11 35
Wandsworth Common d		10 01	10 12	10 17		10 27			10 31		10 42	10 47		10 57		11 01	11 12		11 17		11 27		11 31	
Balham ⊖ d		10 04	10 15	10 20	10 23	10 30			10 34	10 41	10 45	10 50	10 53	11 00		11 04	11 15		11 20	11 23	11 30		11 34	11 41
London Bridge d	09 44	10a47					10 14		11a17						10 44	11a47						11 14	12a17	
Streatham Common d	10 12		10 20			10 35	10 42			10 46	10 50			11 05	11 12		11 20				11 35	11 42		11 46
Norbury d	10 14		10 22			10 37	10 44			10 48	10 52			11 07	11 14		11 22				11 37	11 44		11 48
Thornton Heath d	10 17		10 25			10 40	10 47			10 51	10 55			11 10	11 17		11 25				11 40	11 47		11 51
Selhurst d	10 21		10 28			10 45	10 51			10 55	10 58			11 13	11 21		11 28				11 45	11 51		11 55
East Croydon a	10 24						10 54			10 59					11 24							11 54		11 59
Purley a	10 31						11 01								11 31							12 01		
West Croydon a			10 33	10 57		10 50					11 03	11 21		11 18			11 33		11 57		11 50			
Sutton a			10 46		10 43	11 03					11 16		11 13	11 33			11 46			11 43	12 03			

	SN B	SN	SN C		SN	SN A	SN	SN B	SN	SN C	SN	SN A	SN		SN MW FO ■ D	SN MW FO B	SN TThO B	SN MW FO	SN TThO	SN C	SN MW FO	SN TThO	SN A	
London Victoria ⊖ d	11 30	11 36	11 41		11 46		11 50	12 00	12 06	12 11	12 16		12 20			12 30	12 30	12 36	12 36	12 41	12 46	12 46		
Battersea Park d	11 34	11 40			11 50		11 54	12 04	12 10		12 20		12 24			12 34	12 34	12 40	12 40		12 50	12 50		
Shepherd's Bush ⊖ d															12 22									
Kensington (Olympia) ⊖ d															12 25									
West Brompton ⊖ d															12 28									
Imperial Wharf d															12 30									
Clapham Junction a	11 38	11 44	11 48		11 54		11 58	12 08	12 14	12 18	12 24		12 28		12 35	12 38	12 42	12 44	12 45	12 48	12 54	12 54		
Clapham Junction d	11 39	11 45	11 48		11 54		11 58	12 09	12 14	12 18	12 24		12 28		12 35	12 39	12 42	12 44	12 45	12 48	12 54	12 54		
Wandsworth Common d	11 42	11 48			11 57		12 01	12 12	12 17		12 27		12 31			12 42	12 45	12 47	12 48		12 57	12 57		
Balham ⊖ d	11 45	11 50	11 53		12 00		12 04	12 15	12 20	12 23	12 30		12 34		12 41	12 45	12 48	12 50	12 51	12 54	13 00	13 00		
London Bridge d						11 44	12a47					12 14	13a17										12 44	
Streatham Common d	11 50				12 05	12 12		12 20			12 35	12 42			12 46	12 50	12 53				13 05	13 05	13 12	
Norbury d	11 52				12 07	12 14		12 22			12 37	12 44			12 48	12 52	12 55				13 07	13 07	13 14	
Thornton Heath d	11 55				12 10	12 17		12 25			12 40	12 47			12 51	12 55	12 58				13 10	13 10	13 17	
Selhurst d	11 58				12 13	12 21		12 28			12 45	12 51			12 55	12 58	13 04				13 13	13 15	13 21	
East Croydon a						12 24						12 54			12 59								13 24	
Purley a						12 31						13 01											13 31	
West Croydon a	12 03	12 21			12 18			12 33	12 57		12 50					13 03	13 11	13 21	13 27		13 18	13 19		
Sutton a	12 16		12 13		12 33			12 46		12 43	13 03					13 16	13 24			13 13	13 33	13 33		

	SN	SN B	SN	SN C	SN	SN A	SN	SN ■ D	SN B		SN	SN C	SN	SN A	SN	SN	SN	SN C	SN E		SN F	SN A	SN	SN ■ D
London Victoria ⊖ d	12 50	13 00	13 06	13 11	13 16		13 20		13 30		13 36	13 41	13 46		13 50	14 00	14 06	14 11	14 16		14 16		14 20	
Battersea Park d	12 54	13 04	13 10		13 20		13 24		13 34		13 40		13 50		13 54	14 04	14 10		14 20		14 20		14 24	
Shepherd's Bush ⊖ d								13 22																14 22
Kensington (Olympia) ⊖ d								13 25																14 25
West Brompton ⊖ d								13 28																14 28
Imperial Wharf d								13 30																14 30
Clapham Junction a	12 58	13 08	13 14	13 18	13 24		13 28	13 35	13 38		13 44	13 48	13 54		13 58	14 08	14 14	14 18	14 24		14 24		14 28	14 35
Clapham Junction d	12 58	13 09	13 14	13 18	13 24		13 28	13 35	13 39		13 44	13 48	13 54		13 58	14 09	14 14	14 18	14 24		14 24		14 28	14 35
Wandsworth Common d	13 01	13 12	13 17		13 27		13 31		13 42		13 47		13 57		14 01	14 12	14 17		14 27		14 27		14 31	
Balham ⊖ d	13 04	13 15	13 20	13 23	13 30		13 34	13 41	13 45		13 50	13 53	14 00		14 04	14 15	14 20	14 23	14 30		14 30		14 34	14 41
London Bridge d	13a47					13 14	14a17							13 44	14a47							14 14	15a17	
Streatham Common d		13 20			13 35	13 42		13 46	13 50				14 05	14 12		14 20			14 35		14 35	14 42		14 46
Norbury d		13 22			13 37	13 44		13 48	13 52				14 07	14 14		14 22			14 37		14 37	14 44		14 48
Thornton Heath d		13 25			13 40	13 47		13 51	13 55				14 10	14 17		14 25			14 40		14 40	14 47		14 51
Selhurst d		13 28			13 45	13 51		13 55	13 58				14 13	14 21		14 28			14 45		14 45	14 51		14 55
East Croydon a						13 54		13 59						14 24								14 54		14 59
Purley a						14 01								14 31								15 01		
West Croydon a		13 33	13 57		13 50				14 03		14 21		14 18			14 33	14 57		14 50		14 50			
Sutton a		13 46		13 43	14 03				14 16			14 13	14 33			14 46		14 43	15 03		15 06			

A To Caterham
B To Epsom Downs
C To Epsom
D From Milton Keynes Central
E until 21 September
F from 24 September

For faster services between London Victoria, Clapham Junction and East Croydon, refer to Table T175

For other Shepherd's Bush connecting trains, refer to Table T176

London Victoria - Battersea Park, Wandsworth Common, Balham, Streatham Common, Norbury, Thornton Heath & Selhurst-Croydon

		SN		SN	SN	SN	SN	SN	SN	SN	SN	SN		SN	SN	SN	SN	SN	SN	SN	SN	SN		SN	SN
		A			B		C		A		B			C		1 D	A		B		C			1	A
London Victoria 15 ⊖	d	14 30		14 36	14 41	14 46		14 50	15 00	15 06	15 11	15 16			15 20		15 30	15 36	15 41	15 46		15 50			16 00
Battersea Park	d	14 34		14 40		14 50		14 54	15 04	15 10		15 20			15 24		15 34	15 40		15 50		15 54			16 04
Shepherd's Bush ⊖	d															15 22								15 49	
Kensington (Olympia) ⊖	d															15 25								15 52	
West Brompton ⊖	d															15 28								15 55	
Imperial Wharf	d															15 30								15 57	
Clapham Junction 10	a	14 38		14 44	14 48	14 54		14 58	15 08	15 14	15 18	15 24			15 28	15 35	15 38	15 44	15 48	15 54		15 58		16 02	16 08
Clapham Junction	d	14 39		14 44	14 48	14 54		14 58	15 09	15 14	15 18	15 24			15 28	15 35	15 39	15 44	15 48	15 54		15 58		16 05	16 09
Wandsworth Common	d	14 42		14 47		14 57		15 01	15 12	15 17		15 27			15 31		15 42	15 47		15 57		16 01			16 12
Balham 4 ⊖	d	14 45		14 50	14 53	15 00		15 04	15 15	15 20	15 23	15 30			15 34	15 41	15 45	15 50	15 53	16 00		16 04		16 11	16 15
London Bridge	d						14 44	15a47						15 14	16a18						15 44	16a48			
Streatham Common 4	d	14 50				15 05	15 12		15 20			15 35		15 42		15 46	15 50			16 05	16 12			16 16	16 20
Norbury	d	14 52				15 07	15 14		15 22			15 37		15 44		15 48	15 52			16 07	16 14			16 18	16 22
Thornton Heath	d	14 55				15 10	15 17		15 25			15 40		15 47		15 51	15 55			16 10	16 17			16 21	16 25
Selhurst 4	d	14 58				15 13	15 21		15 28			15 45		15 51		15 55	15 58			16 13	16 21			16 25	16 28
East Croydon	a						15 24							15 54		16 00					16 24			16 30	
Purley	a						15 31							16 01							16 31				
West Croydon 4	a	15 03		15 21		15 18			15 33	15 57		15 50					16 03	16 21		16 18					16 33
Sutton 4	a	15 16			15 13	15 33			15 46		15 43	16 03					16 16		16 13	16 33					16 46

		SN	SN	SN	SN	SN	SN	SN		SN	SN	SN	SN	SN	SN	SN	SN	SN		SN	SN	SN	SN	SN	SN
			E	F				1 D		A		B				1 G	A			B				1 D	A
London Victoria 15 ⊖	d	16 06	16 11	16 12	16 16		16 20			16 30	16 36	16 41	16 46		16 50		17 00	17 06		17 11	17 16		17 20		17 30
Battersea Park	d	16 10			16 20		16 24			16 34	16 40		16 50		16 54		17 04	17 10			17 20		17 24		17 34
Shepherd's Bush ⊖	d							16 22								16 46								17 22	
Kensington (Olympia) ⊖	d							16 25								16 49								17 25	
West Brompton ⊖	d							16 28								16 52								17 28	
Imperial Wharf	d							16 30								16 55								17 30	
Clapham Junction 10	a	16 14	16 18	16 19	16 24		16 28	16 35		16 38	16 44	16 48	16 54		16 58	16 59	17 08	17 14		17 18	17 24		17 28	17 35	17 38
Clapham Junction	d	16 14	16 18	16 19	16 24		16 28	16 35		16 39	16 44	16 48	16 54		16 58	17 05	17 09	17 14		17 18	17 24		17 28	17 35	17 39
Wandsworth Common	d	16 17			16 27		16 31			16 42	16 47		16 57		17 01		17 12	17 17			17 27		17 31		17 42
Balham 4 ⊖	d	16 20	16 23	16 24	16 30		16 34	16 41		16 45	16 50	16 53	17 00		17 04	17 11	17 15	17 20		17 23	17 30		17 34	17 41	17 45
London Bridge	d					16 14	17a18							16 44	17a48							17 14	18a18		
Streatham Common 4	d				16 35	16 42		16 46		16 50			17 05	17 12		17 16	17 20				17 35	17 42		17 46	17 50
Norbury	d				16 37	16 44		16 48		16 52			17 07	17 14		17 18	17 22				17 37	17 44		17 48	17 52
Thornton Heath	d				16 40	16 47		16 51		16 55			17 10	17 17		17 21	17 25				17 40	17 47		17 51	17 55
Selhurst 4	d				16 44	16a50		16 55		16 58			17 14	17a20		17 25	17 28				17 44	17a50		17 55	17 58
East Croydon	a							17 00								17 30								18 00	
Purley	a																								
West Croydon 4	a	16 52			16 49					17 03	17 22		17 19				17 33	17 52			17 49				18 03
Sutton 4	a		16 43	16 43	17 03					17 16		17 13	17 33				17 46			17 43	18 03				18 16

		SN	SN	SN		SN	SN	SN	SN	SN	SN	SN	SN	SN		SN	SN	SN	SN	SN	SN	SN	SN	SN	
			B					1	A		B					1 D	A		B				A		
London Victoria 15 ⊖	d	17 36	17 41	17 46			17 50		18 00	18 06	18 11	18 16		18 20			18 30	18 36	18 41	18 46		18 50	19 00	19 06	
Battersea Park	d	17 40		17 50			17 54		18 04	18 10		18 20		18 24			18 34	18 40		18 50		18 54	19 04	19 10	
Shepherd's Bush ⊖	d							17 49								18 22									
Kensington (Olympia) ⊖	d							17 52								18 25									
West Brompton ⊖	d							17 55								18 28									
Imperial Wharf	d							17 57								18 30									
Clapham Junction 10	a	17 44	17 48	17 54			17 58	18 02	18 08	18 14	18 18	18 24		18 28		18 35	18 38	18 44	18 48	18 54		18 58	19 08	19 14	
Clapham Junction	d	17 44	17 48	17 54			17 58	18 05	18 09	18 14	18 18	18 24		18 28		18 35	18 39	18 44	18 48	18 54		18 58	19 09	19 14	
Wandsworth Common	d	17 47		17 57			18 01		18 12	18 17		18 27		18 31			18 42	18 47		18 57		19 01	19 12	19 17	
Balham 4 ⊖	d	17 50	17 53	18 00			18 04	18 11	18 15	18 20	18 23	18 30		18 34		18 41	18 45	18 50	18 53	19 00		19 04	19 15	19 20	
London Bridge	d					17 44	18a48						18 14	19a18							18 44	19a48			
Streatham Common 4	d			18 05		18 12		18 16	18 20			18 35	18 42			18 46	18 50			19 05	19 12		19 20		
Norbury	d			18 07		18 14		18 18	18 22			18 37	18 44			18 48	18 52			19 07	19 14		19 22		
Thornton Heath	d			18 10		18 17		18 21	18 25			18 40	18 47			18 51	18 55			19 10	19 17		19 25		
Selhurst 4	d			18 14		18a20		18 26	18 28			18 44	18a50			18 55	18 58			19 13	19a20		19 28		
East Croydon	a							18 31								19 00									
Purley	a																								
West Croydon 4	a	18 22		18 19					18 33	18 52		18 49					19 03	19 21		19 18			19 33	19 51	
Sutton 4	a		18 13	18 33					18 46		18 43	19 03					19 16		19 13	19 33			19 46		

A To Epsom Downs
B To Epsom
C To Caterham
D From Milton Keynes Central
E until 21 September. To Epsom
F from 24 September. To Epsom
G From Watford Junction

For faster services between London Victoria, Clapham Junction and East Croydon, refer to Table T175

For other Shepherd's Bush connecting trains, refer to Table T176

Table T170-F
Mondays to Fridays
21 May to 7 December

London Victoria - Battersea Park, Wandsworth Common, Balham, Streatham Common, Norbury, Thornton Heath & Selhurst-Croydon

		SN	SN	SN	SN	SN		SN	SN	SN	SN	SN	SN	SN	SN	SN		SN	SN	SN	SN	SN	SN	SN	SN
		A		B		1 C		D		A		B		D		A			B		1 C	D		A	
London Victoria 15 ⊖	d	19 11	19 16		19 20			19 30	19 36	19 41	19 46		19 50	20 00	20 06	20 11		20 16		20 20		20 30	20 36	20 41	20 46
Battersea Park	d		19 20		19 24			19 34	19 40		19 50		19 54	20 04	20 10			20 20		20 24		20 34	20 40		20 50
Shepherd's Bush ⊖	d					19 22															20 22				
Kensington (Olympia) ⊖	d					19 25															20 25				
West Brompton ⊖	d					19 28															20 28				
Imperial Wharf	d					19 30															20 30				
Clapham Junction 10	a	19 18	19 24		19 28	19 35		19 38	19 44	19 48	19 54		19 58	20 08	20 14	20 18		20 24		20 28	20 35	20 38	20 44	20 48	20 54
Clapham Junction	d	19 18	19 24		19 28	19 35		19 39	19 44	19 48	19 54		19 58	20 09	20 14	20 18		20 24		20 28	20 35	20 39	20 45	20 48	20 54
Wandsworth Common	d		19 27		19 31			19 42	19 47		19 57		20 01	20 12	20 17			20 27		20 31		20 42	20 48		20 57
Balham 4 ⊖	d	19 23	19 30		19 34	19 41		19 45	19 50	19 53	20 00		20 04	20 15	20 20	20 23		20 30		20 34	20 41	20 45	20 51	20 53	21 00
London Bridge	d			19 14	20a18							19 44	20a47						20 14	21a17					
Streatham Common 4	d		19 35	19 42		19 46		19 50			20 05	20 12		20 20				20 35	20 42		20 46	20 50			21 05
Norbury	d		19 37	19 44		19 48		19 52			20 07	20 14		20 22				20 37	20 44		20 48	20 52			21 07
Thornton Heath	d		19 40	19 47		19 51		19 55			20 10	20 17		20 25				20 40	20 47		20 51	20 55			21 10
Selhurst 4	d		19 43	19 51		19 55		19 58			20 13	20 21		20 28				20 45	20 50		20 55	20 58			21 13
East Croydon	a			19 54		19 59						20 24							20 53		21 00				
Purley	a			20 01								20 31							21 01						
West Croydon 4	a		19 48					20 03	20 21		20 18			20 33	20 57			20 50				21 03	21 21		21 18
Sutton 4	a	19 43	20 03					20 16		20 13	20 33			20 46		20 43		21 03				21 16		21 13	21 33

		SN		SN	SN	SN	SN	SN	SN	SN	SN	SN		SN	SN	SN	SN	SN	SN	SN	SN	SN		SN	SN
		B			D		A		B		D			A		B		D		A		B			1 C
London Victoria 15 ⊖	d			20 50	21 00	21 06	21 11	21 16		21 20	21 30	21 36		21 41	21 46		21 50	22 00	22 06	22 11	22 16			22 20	
Battersea Park	d			20 54	21 04	21 10		21 20		21 24	21 34	21 40			21 50		21 54	22 04	22 10		22 20			22 24	
Shepherd's Bush ⊖	d																								22 19
Kensington (Olympia) ⊖	d																								22 21
West Brompton ⊖	d																								22 24
Imperial Wharf	d																								22 27
Clapham Junction 10	a			20 58	21 08	21 14	21 18	21 24		21 28	21 42	21 45		21 48	21 56		21 59	22 08	22 14	22 18	22 24			22 28	22 31
Clapham Junction	d			20 58	21 09	21 14	21 18	21 24		21 28	21 42	21 45		21 48	21 57		22 00	22 09	22 14	22 18	22 24			22 28	22 35
Wandsworth Common	d			21 01	21 12	21 17		21 27		21 31	21 45	21 48			22 00		22 03	22 12	22 17		22 27			22 31	
Balham 4 ⊖	d			21 04	21 15	21 20	21 23	21 30		21 34	21 48	21 51		21 54	22 02		22 06	22 15	22 20	22 23	22 30			22 34	22 41
London Bridge	d	20 44		21a47					21 14	22a17						21 44	22a47					22 14		23a17	
Streatham Common 4	d	21 12			21 20			21 35	21 42		21 53				22 06	22 12		22 20			22 35	22 42			22 46
Norbury	d	21 14			21 22			21 37	21 44		21 55				22 09	22 14		22 22			22 37	22 44			22 48
Thornton Heath	d	21 17			21 25			21 40	21 47		21 58				22 12	22 17		22 25			22 40	22 47			22 51
Selhurst 4	d	21 21			21 28			21 43	21 51		22 04				22 15	22 21		22 28			22 43	22 51			22 55
East Croydon	a	21 24							21 54							22 24						22 54			22 59
Purley	a	21 32							22 01							22 31						23 01			
West Croydon 4	a				21 33	21 51		21 48			22 11	22 27			22 19			22 33	22 51		22 48				
Sutton 4	a				21 46		21 43	22 03			22 24			22 13	22 33			22 46		22 43	23 03				

		SN	SN	SN	SN	SN	SN	SN		SN	SN	SN	SN	SN	TL	SN	SN	SN		SN					
		D		A				D			A				E										
London Victoria 15 ⊖	d	22 30	22 36	22 41	22 46		22 50	23 00		23 06	23 11	23 16		23 20	23 25	23 32	23 40			23 56					
Battersea Park	d	22 34	22 40		22 50		22 54	23 04		23 10		23 20		23 24			23 44								
Shepherd's Bush ⊖	d																								
Kensington (Olympia) ⊖	d																								
West Brompton ⊖	d																								
Imperial Wharf	d																								
Clapham Junction 10	a	22 38	22 44	22 48	22 54		22 58	23 08		23 14	23 18	23 24		23 28	23 32	23 38	23 48			00 03					
Clapham Junction	d	22 39	22 45	22 48	22 54		22 58	23 09		23 14	23 18	23 24		23 28	23 32	23 39	23 48			00 04					
Wandsworth Common	d	22 42	22 48		22 57		23 01	23 12		23 17		23 27		23 31			23 51			00 07					
Balham 4 ⊖	d	22 45	22 50	22 53	23 00		23 04	23 15		23 20	23 23	23 30		23 34	23 37	23 44	23 54			00 10					
London Bridge	d					22 44	23a47						23 14	00a15				23 54		00a47					
Streatham Common 4	d	22 50			23 05	23 12		23 20				23 35	23 42				23 59	00 26							
Norbury	d	22 52			23 07	23 14		23 22				23 37	23 44				00 01	00 28							
Thornton Heath	d	22 55			23 10	23 17		23 25				23 40	23 47				00 04	00 31							
Selhurst 4	d	22 58			23 13	23a20		23 28				23 43	23a50				00 07	00a34							
East Croydon	a																								
Purley	a																								
West Croydon 4	a	23 03	23 21		23 18			23 33		23 52		23 48				00 16	00 12								
Sutton 4	a	23 16		23 13	23 33			23 46			23 43	00 03			23 58		00 25								

A To Epsom
B To Caterham
C From Milton Keynes Central
D To Epsom Downs
E To Horsham

For faster services between London Victoria, Clapham Junction and East Croydon, refer to Table T175

For other Shepherd's Bush connecting trains, refer to Table T176

26 May to 8 December

London Victoria - Battersea Park, Wandsworth Common, Balham, Streatham Common, Norbury, Thornton Heath & Selhurst-Croydon

	SN A	SN A	SN B	SN C	SN		SN D	SN B	SN	SN	SN 1 E	SN 1 E	SN 1 F	SN G	SN H		SN	SN 1 I	SN G	SN	SN D	SN	SN H	SN
London Victoria ⊖ d			00 10		00 12		00 20	00 25	00 30		01 10	05 08	05 21	06 00			06 20		06 30	06 36	06 41	06 46		06 50
Battersea Park d			00 14		00 16			00 29	00 34					06 04			06 24		06 34	06 40		06 50		06 54
Shepherd's Bush ⊖ d																		06 19						
Kensington (Olympia) ⊖ d																		06 22						
West Brompton ⊖ d																		06 25						
Imperial Wharf d																		06 28						
Clapham Junction a			00 18		00 20		00 27	00 33	00 38		01 17	05 15	05 28	06 08			06 28	06 32	06 38	06 44	06 48	06 54		06 58
Clapham Junction d		00 04	00 18		00 20		00 27	00 33	00 39		01 17	05 16	05 28	06 09			06 28	06 35	06 39	06 44	06 48	06 54		06 58
Wandsworth Common d		00 07	00 21		00 23			00 36	00 42					06 12			06 31		06 42	06 47		06 57		07 01
Balham ⊖ d		00 10	00a24		00 26		00 33	00a39	00 45					06 15			06 34	06 41	06 45	06 50	06 53	07 00		07 04
London Bridge d		00a47								00 25					06 14		07a14						06 44	07a44
Streatham Common d				00 26	00 31				00 52	00 55				06 20	06 42			06 46	06 50			07 05	07 12	
Norbury d	00 01			00 28	00 33				00 54	00 57				06 22	06 44			06 48	06 52			07 07	07 14	
Thornton Heath d	00 04			00 31	00 36				00 57	01 00				06 25	06 47			06 51	06 55			07 10	07 17	
Selhurst d	00 07			00a34	00 39				01 00	01a03	01 29	05 27	05 40	06 28	06 51			06 55	06 58			07 13	07 21	
East Croydon a					00 43						01 32	05 31	05 44		06 54			06 59					07 24	
Purley a											01 38	05 37			07 01								07 31	
West Croydon a	00 12								01 05					06 35					07 03	07 21		07 18		
Sutton a	00 25						00 53		01 18					06 48					07 16		07 13	07 33		

	SN G		SN	SN D	SN	SN H	SN	SN 1 I	SN G	SN	SN D	SN	SN H	SN	SN G	SN	SN D	SN	SN H	SN	SN 1 J	and at the same minutes past each hour until	
London Victoria ⊖ d	07 00		07 06	07 11	07 16		07 20		07 30	07 36	07 41	07 46		07 50	08 00	08 06	08 11	08 16		08 20			
Battersea Park d	07 04		07 10		07 20		07 24		07 34	07 40		07 50		07 54	08 04	08 10		08 20		08 24			
Shepherd's Bush ⊖ d								07 21													08 19		
Kensington (Olympia) ⊖ d								07 24													08 22		
West Brompton ⊖ d								07 27													08 25		
Imperial Wharf d								07 29													08 28		
Clapham Junction a	07 08		07 14	07 18	07 24		07 28	07 34	07 38	07 44	07 48	07 54		07 58	08 08	08 14	08 18	08 24		08 28	08 32		
Clapham Junction d	07 09		07 14	07 18	07 24		07 28	07 35	07 39	07 44	07 48	07 54		07 58	08 09	08 14	08 18	08 24		08 28	08 35		
Wandsworth Common d	07 12		07 17		07 27		07 31		07 42	07 47		07 57		08 01	08 12	08 17		08 27		08 31			
Balham ⊖ d	07 15		07 20	07 23	07 30		07 34	07 41	07 45	07 50	07 53	08 00		08 04	08 15	08 20	08 23	08 30		08 34	08 41		
London Bridge d						07 14	08a14						07 44	08a44					08 14	09a14			
Streatham Common d	07 21				07 35	07 42		07 46	07 50			08 05	08 12		08 21			08 35	08 42		08 46		
Norbury d	07 23				07 37	07 44		07 48	07 52			08 07	08 14		08 23			08 37	08 44		08 48		
Thornton Heath d	07 26				07 40	07 47		07 51	07 55			08 10	08 17		08 26			08 40	08 47		08 51		
Selhurst d	07 29				07 45	07 51		07 55	07 58			08 13	08 21		08 29			08 45	08 51		08 55		
East Croydon a						07 54		07 59					08 24						08 54		08 59		
Purley a						08 01							08 31						09 01				
West Croydon a	07 34		07 57		07 50				08 03	08 21		08 18			08 34	08 57		08 50					
Sutton a	07 46			07 43	08 03				08 16		08 13	08 33			08 46		08 43	09 03					

	SN G	SN	SN D	SN	SN H	SN	SN G	SN	SN D	SN	SN H	SN	SN 1 J		SN G	SN	SN D	SN	SN H	SN	SN K	SN L	SN	
London Victoria ⊖ d	12 30	12 36	12 41	12 46		12 50	13 00	13 06	13 11	13 16		13 20			13 30	13 36	13 41	13 46		13 50	14 00	14 00	14 06	
Battersea Park d	12 34	12 40		12 50		12 54	13 04	13 10		13 20		13 24			13 34	13 40		13 50		13 54	14 04	14 04	14 10	
Shepherd's Bush ⊖ d													13 19											
Kensington (Olympia) ⊖ d													13 22											
West Brompton ⊖ d													13 25											
Imperial Wharf d													13 28											
Clapham Junction a	12 38	12 44	12 48	12 54		12 58	13 08	13 14	13 18	13 24		13 28	13 32		13 38	13 44	13 48	13 54		13 58	14 08	14 08	14 14	
Clapham Junction d	12 39	12 44	12 48	12 54		12 58	13 09	13 14	13 18	13 24		13 28	13 35		13 39	13 44	13 48	13 54		13 58	14 09	14 09	14 14	
Wandsworth Common d	12 42	12 47		12 57		13 01	13 12	13 17		13 27		13 31			13 42	13 47		13 57		14 01	14 12	14 12	14 17	
Balham ⊖ d	12 45	12 50	12 53	13 00		13 04	13 15	13 20	13 23	13 30		13 34	13 41		13 45	13 50	13 53	14 00		14 04	14 15	14 15	14 20	
London Bridge d					12 44	13a44					13 14	14a14							13 44	14a44				
Streatham Common d	12 50			13 05	13 12		13 21			13 35	13 42		13 46		13 50			14 05	14 12		14 21	14 21		
Norbury d	12 52			13 07	13 14		13 23			13 37	13 44		13 48		13 52			14 07	14 14		14 23	14 23		
Thornton Heath d	12 55			13 10	13 17		13 26			13 40	13 47		13 51		13 55			14 10	14 17		14 26	14 26		
Selhurst d	12 58			13 13	13 21		13 29			13 45	13 51		13 55		13 58			14 13	14 21		14 29	14 29		
East Croydon a					13 24						13 54		13 59						14 24					
Purley a					13 31						14 01								14 31					
West Croydon a	13 03	13 21		13 18			13 34	13 57		13 50					14 03	14 21		14 18			14 34	14 34	14 57	
Sutton a	13 16		13 13	13 33			13 46		13 43	14 03					14 16		14 13	14 33			14 46	14 47		

A From London Victoria
B To Norwood Junction
C From London Bridge
D To Epsom
E To Brighton
F To East Grinstead
G To Epsom Downs
H To Caterham
I From Watford Junction
J From Milton Keynes Central
K from 29 September
L until 22 September. To Epsom Downs

For faster services between London Victoria, Clapham Junction and East Croydon, refer to Table T175

For other Shepherd's Bush connecting trains, refer to Table T176

Table T170-F

Saturdays

26 May to 8 December

London Victoria - Battersea Park, Wandsworth Common, Balham, Streatham Common, Norbury, Thornton Heath & Selhurst-Croydon

		SN A	SN B	SN C	SN D	SN	SN 1 E	SN F	SN	SN A	SN	SN D	SN	SN F	SN	SN A	SN	and at the same minutes past each hour until	SN D	SN	SN 1 E	SN F	SN
London Victoria ⊖ d		14 11	14 16	14 16		14 20		14 30	14 36	14 41	14 46		14 50	15 00	15 06	15 11	15 16			18 20		18 30	18 36
Battersea Park d			14 20	14 20		14 24		14 34	14 40		14 50		14 54	15 04	15 10		15 20			18 24		18 34	18 40
Shepherd's Bush ⊖ d							14 19														18 19		
Kensington (Olympia) ⊖ d							14 22														18 22		
West Brompton ⊖ d							14 25														18 25		
Imperial Wharf d							14 28														18 28		
Clapham Junction a		14 18	14 24	14 24		14 28	14 32	14 38	14 44	14 48	14 54		14 58	15 08	15 14	15 18	15 24			18 28	18 32	18 38	18 44
Clapham Junction d		14 18	14 24	14 24		14 28	14 35	14 39	14 44	14 48	14 54		14 58	15 09	15 14	15 18	15 24			18 28	18 35	18 39	18 44
Wandsworth Common d			14 27	14 27		14 31		14 42	14 47		14 57		15 01	15 12	15 17		15 27			18 31		18 42	18 47
Balham ⊖ d		14 23	14 30	14 30		14 34	14 41	14 45	14 50	14 53	15 00		15 04	15 15	15 20	15 23	15 30			18 34	18 41	18 45	18 50
London Bridge d					14 14	15a14						14 44	15a44						18 14	19a14			
Streatham Common d			14 35	14 35	14 42		14 46	14 50			15 05	15 12		15 21			15 35		18 42		18 46	18 50	
Norbury d			14 37	14 37	14 44		14 48	14 52			15 07	15 14		15 23			15 37		18 44		18 48	18 52	
Thornton Heath d			14 40	14 40	14 47		14 51	14 55			15 10	15 17		15 26			15 40		18 47		18 51	18 55	
Selhurst d			14 45	14 45	14 51		14 55	14 58			15 13	15 21		15 29			15 45		18 51		18 55	18 58	
East Croydon a					14 54		14 59					15 24							18 54		18 59		
Purley a					15 01							15 31							19 01				
West Croydon a			14 50	14 50				15 03	15 21		15 18			15 34	15 57		15 50					19 03	19 21
Sutton a		14 43	15 03	15 06				15 16		15 13	15 33			15 46		15 43	16 03					19 16	

	SN A	SN	SN D	SN	SN F	SN	SN A	SN		SN D	SN	SN 1 E	SN F	SN	SN A	SN	SN D	SN		SN F	SN	SN A	SN	SN D
London Victoria ⊖ d	18 41	18 46		18 50	19 00	19 06	19 11	19 16			19 20		19 30	19 36	19 41	19 46		19 50		20 00	20 06	20 11	20 16	
Battersea Park d		18 50		18 54	19 04	19 10		19 20			19 24		19 34	19 40		19 50		19 54		20 04	20 10		20 20	
Shepherd's Bush ⊖ d												19 19												
Kensington (Olympia) ⊖ d												19 22												
West Brompton ⊖ d												19 25												
Imperial Wharf d												19 28												
Clapham Junction a	18 48	18 54		18 58	19 08	19 14	19 18	19 24			19 28	19 32	19 38	19 44	19 48	19 54		19 58		20 08	20 14	20 17	20 24	
Clapham Junction d	18 48	18 54		18 58	19 09	19 14	19 18	19 24			19 28	19 35	19 39	19 44	19 48	19 54		19 58		20 09	20 14	20 18	20 24	
Wandsworth Common d		18 57		19 01	19 12	19 17		19 27			19 31		19 42	19 47		19 57		20 01		20 12	20 17		20 27	
Balham ⊖ d	18 53	19 00		19 04	19 15	19 20	19 23	19 30			19 34	19 41	19 45	19 50	19 53	20 00		20 04		20 15	20 20	20 23	20 30	
London Bridge d			18 44	19a44						19 14	20a14						19 44	20a44						20 14
Streatham Common d		19 05	19 12		19 21			19 35		19 42		19 46	19 50			20 05	20 12			20 21			20 35	20 42
Norbury d		19 07	19 14		19 23			19 37		19 44		19 48	19 52			20 07	20 14			20 23			20 37	20 44
Thornton Heath d		19 10	19 17		19 26			19 40		19 47		19 51	19 55			20 10	20 17			20 26			20 40	20 47
Selhurst d		19 13	19 21		19 29			19 45		19 51		19 55	19 58			20 13	20 21			20 29			20 45	20 51
East Croydon a			19 24							19 54		19 59					20 24							20 54
Purley a			19 31							20 01							20 31							21 01
West Croydon a		19 18			19 34	19 57		19 50					20 03	20 21		20 18				20 34	20 57		20 50	
Sutton a	19 13	19 33			19 46		19 43	20 03					20 16		20 13	20 33				20 46		20 43	21 03	

	SN	SN 1 E	SN F	SN		SN A	SN	SN D	SN	SN F	SN	SN A	SN	SN D		SN	SN 1 G	SN F	SN	SN A	SN	SN D	SN	SN F
London Victoria ⊖ d	20 20		20 30	20 36		20 41	20 46		20 50	21 00	21 06	21 11	21 16			21 20		21 30	21 36	21 41	21 46		21 50	22 00
Battersea Park d	20 24		20 34	20 40			20 50		20 54	21 04	21 10		21 20			21 24		21 34	21 40		21 50		21 54	22 04
Shepherd's Bush ⊖ d		20 20															21 16							
Kensington (Olympia) ⊖ d		20 22															21 18							
West Brompton ⊖ d		20 25															21 21							
Imperial Wharf d		20 28															21 24							
Clapham Junction a	20 28	20 33	20 38	20 44		20 48	20 54		20 58	21 08	21 14	21 18	21 24			21 28	21 28	21 38	21 44	21 48	21 54		21 58	22 08
Clapham Junction d	20 28	20 35	20 39	20 44		20 48	20 54		20 58	21 09	21 14	21 18	21 24			21 28	21 35	21 39	21 44	21 48	21 54		21 58	22 09
Wandsworth Common d	20 31		20 42	20 47			20 57		21 01	21 12	21 17		21 27			21 31		21 42	21 47		21 57		22 01	22 12
Balham ⊖ d	20 34	20 41	20 45	20 50		20 53	21 00		21 04	21 15	21 20	21 23	21 30			21 34	21 41	21 45	21 50	21 53	22 00		22 04	22 15
London Bridge d	21a14							20 44	21a44					21 14		22a14						21 44	22a44	
Streatham Common d		20 46	20 50				21 05	21 12		21 21			21 35	21 42			21 46	21 50			22 05	22 12		22 21
Norbury d		20 48	20 52				21 07	21 14		21 23			21 37	21 44			21 48	21 52			22 07	22 14		22 23
Thornton Heath d		20 51	20 55				21 10	21 17		21 26			21 40	21 47			21 51	21 55			22 10	22 17		22 26
Selhurst d		20 55	20 58				21 13	21 21		21 29			21 45	21 51			21 55	21 58			22 13	22 21		22 29
East Croydon a		20 59						21 24						21 54			21 59					22 24		
Purley a								21 31						22 01								22 31		
West Croydon a			21 03	21 21			21 18			21 34	21 57		21 50					22 03	22 21		22 18			22 34
Sutton a			21 16			21 13	21 33			21 46		21 43	22 03					22 16		22 13	22 33			22 46

A To Epsom
B until 22 September
C from 29 September
D To Caterham
E From Milton Keynes Central
F To Epsom Downs
G From Watford Junction

For faster services between London Victoria, Clapham Junction and East Croydon, refer to Table T175

For other Shepherd's Bush connecting trains, refer to Table T176

Table T170-F

Saturdays
26 May to 8 December

London Victoria - Battersea Park, Wandsworth Common, Balham, Streatham Common, Norbury, Thornton Heath & Selhurst-Croydon

		SN	SN A	SN	SN B	SN	SN C	SN D	SN	SN A	SN	SN	SN	SN D	SN	SN A	SN	SN	SN	SN	SN	SN A	SN
London Victoria	d	22 06	22 11	22 16		22 20		22 30	22 36	22 41	22 46		22 50	23 00	23 06	23 11	23 16		23 20	23 32	23 40	23 45	
Battersea Park	d	22 10		22 20		22 24		22 34	22 40		22 50		22 54	23 04	23 10		23 20		23 24		23 44		
Shepherd's Bush	d						22 15																
Kensington (Olympia)	d						22 23																
West Brompton	d						22 26																
Imperial Wharf	d						22 29																
Clapham Junction	a	22 14	22 18	22 24		22 28	22 33	22 38	22 44	22 48	22 54		22 58	23 08	23 14	23 18	23 24		23 28	23 39	23 48	23 52	
Clapham Junction	d	22 14	22 18	22 24		22 28	22 35	22 39	22 44	22 49	22 54		22 58	23 09	23 14	23 18	23 24		23 28	23 39	23 48	23 53	
Wandsworth Common	d	22 17		22 27		22 31		22 42	22 47		22 57		23 01	23 12	23 17		23 27		23 31		23 51		
Balham	d	22 20	22 23	22 30		22 34	22 41	22 45	22 50	22 53	23 00		23 04	23 15	23 20	23 23	23 30		23 34	23 44	23 54	23 57	
London Bridge	d				22 14	23a14						22 44	23a44					23 14	00a17				23 55
Streatham Common	d			22 35	22 42		22 46	22 50			23 05	23 17		23 20			23 35	23 42			23 59		00 27
Norbury	d			22 37	22 44		22 48	22 52			23 07	23 19		23 23			23 37	23 44			00 01		00 29
Thornton Heath	d			22 40	22 47		22 51	22 55			23 10	23 22		23 26			23 40	23 47			00 04		00 32
Selhurst	d			22 45	22 51		22 55	22 58			23 13	23a25		23 29			23 43	23a50			00 07		00a35
East Croydon	a				22 54		22 59																
Purley	a				23 01																		
West Croydon	a	22 57		22 50				23 03	23 21		23 18			23 34	23 51		23 48			00 18	00 14		
Sutton	a		22 43	23 03				23 16		23 13	23 33			23 46		23 43	00 03				00 27	00 17	

		SN
London Victoria	d	23 56
Battersea Park	d	
Shepherd's Bush	d	
Kensington (Olympia)	d	
West Brompton	d	
Imperial Wharf	d	
Clapham Junction	a	00 03
Clapham Junction	d	00 04
Wandsworth Common	d	00 07
Balham	d	00 10
London Bridge	d	00a47
Streatham Common	d	
Norbury	d	
Thornton Heath	d	
Selhurst	d	
East Croydon	a	
Purley	a	
West Croydon	a	
Sutton	a	

Sundays
20 May to 2 December

		SN E	SN E	SN F	SN G	SN	SN F	SN	SN F	SN H	TL I	SN	SN H	TL I	SN	SN	SN J	SN	SN D	TL I	SN	SN	SN H
London Victoria	d			00 10		00 15	00 25		00 40	01 10	06 40	06 45	07 02	07 10	07 16	07 21	07 32		07 34	07 40	07 46	07 51	08 02
Battersea Park	d			00 14		00 19	00 29		00 44			06 49			07 20	07 25			07 38		07 50	07 55	
Shepherd's Bush	d																						
Kensington (Olympia)	d																						
West Brompton	d																						
Imperial Wharf	d																						
Clapham Junction	a			00 18		00 23	00 33		00 48	01 17	06 47	06 53	07 10	07 17	07 24	07 29	07 39		07 42	07 47	07 54	07 59	08 09
Clapham Junction	d		00 04	00 18		00 23	00 33		00 48	01 17	06 47	06 53	07 10	07 17	07 24	07 30	07 40		07 43	07 47	07 54	08 00	08 10
Wandsworth Common	d		00 07	00 21		00 26	00 36		00 51			06 56			07 27	07 33			07 46		07 57	08 03	
Balham	d		00 10	00a24		00 29	00a39		00a54		06 53	07 00		07 23	07 31	07 36			07 49	07 53	08 01	08 06	
London Bridge	d		00a47					00 25										07 16					
Streatham Common	d				00 27	00 34		00 56				07 04			07 35			07 49	07 54		08 05		
Norbury	d	00 01			00 29	00 37		00 58				07 07			07 37			07 51	07 56		08 07		
Thornton Heath	d	00 04			00 32	00 40		01 01				07 10			07 40			07 54	07 59		08 10		
Selhurst	d	00 07			00a35	00 43		01a04		01 29		07 13	07 22		07 43		07 51	07 57	08 02		08 13		08 21
East Croydon	a					00 46				01 32			07 26				07 56	08 00					08 26
Purley	a									01 38			07 32										08 32
West Croydon	a	00 14										07 19			07 48	08 10			08 07		08 19	08 40	
Sutton	a	00 27									07 12	07 32		07 42	08 01				08 20	08 12	08 32		

A To Epsom
B To Caterham
C From Watford Junction
D To Epsom Downs
E not 20 May. From London Victoria
F To Norwood Junction
G not 20 May. From London Bridge
H To Brighton
I To Dorking
J To Bognor Regis

For faster services between London Victoria, Clapham Junction and East Croydon, refer to Table T175

For other Shepherd's Bush connecting trains, refer to Table T176

Table T170-F

Sundays
20 May to 2 December

London Victoria - Battersea Park, Wandsworth Common, Balham, Streatham Common, Norbury, Thornton Heath & Selhurst-Croydon

		SN	SN A	TL B	SN	SN	SN	SN A	SN	SN	SN C	SN	SN A	SN	SN	SN C	SN	SN A	SN	SN	SN C	SN	SN A
London Victoria	d		08 04	08 10	08 16		08 21	08 34	08 46		08 52	08 56	09 02	09 16		09 22	09 26	09 32	09 46		09 52	09 56	10 02
Battersea Park	d		08 08		08 20		08 25	08 38	08 50			09 00	09 06	09 20			09 30	09 36	09 50			10 00	10 06
Shepherd's Bush	d																						
Kensington (Olympia)	d																						
West Brompton	d																						
Imperial Wharf	d																						
Clapham Junction	a		08 13	08 17	08 24		08 29	08 42	08 54		08 58	09 04	09 10	09 24		09 28	09 34	09 40	09 54		09 58	10 04	10 10
Clapham Junction	d		08 14	08 17	08 24		08 30	08 43	08 54		08 58	09 04	09 10	09 24		09 28	09 34	09 40	09 54		09 58	10 04	10 10
Wandsworth Common	d		08 17		08 27		08 33	08 46	08 57			09 07	09 13	09 27			09 37	09 43	09 57			10 07	10 13
Balham	d		08 20	08 23	08 31		08 36	08 49	09 00		09 03	09 10	09 16	09 30		09 33	09 40	09 46	10 00		10 03	10 10	10 16
London Bridge	d	07 46				08 16				08 47					09 19					09 49			
Streatham Common	d	08 19	08 24		08 35	08 46		08 54	09 05	09 16			09 21	09 35	09 46			09 51	10 05	10 17			10 21
Norbury	d	08 21	08 26		08 37	08 49		08 56	09 07	09 19			09 23	09 37	09 49			09 53	10 07	10 20			10 23
Thornton Heath	d	08 24	08 29		08 40	08 52		08 59	09 10	09 22			09 26	09 40	09 52			09 56	10 10	10 23			10 26
Selhurst	d	08 27	08 32		08 43	08 56		09 02	09 13	09 26			09 30	09 43	09 56			10 00	10 13	10 26			10 30
East Croydon	a	08 30				08 59				09 29					09 59					10 29			
Purley	a																						
West Croydon	a		08 37		08 49		09 05	09 09	09 19			09 38	09 34	09 49			10 08	10 04	10 19			10 38	10 34
Sutton	a		08 49	08 42	09 02			09 21	09 32		09 23		09 47	10 02		09 53		10 17	10 32		10 23		10 47

		SN	SN		SN C	SN	SN A	SN	SN	SN C	SN	SN A	SN	SN	SN C	SN	SN A	SN	SN	SN C	SN	SN A	SN
London Victoria	d	10 16		and at the same minutes past each hour until	17 22	17 26	17 32	17 46		17 52	17 56	18 02	18 16		18 22	18 26	18 32	18 46		18 52	18 56	19 02	19 16
Battersea Park	d	10 20				17 30	17 36	17 50			18 00	18 06	18 20			18 30	18 36	18 50			19 00	19 06	19 20
Shepherd's Bush	d																						
Kensington (Olympia)	d																						
West Brompton	d																						
Imperial Wharf	d																						
Clapham Junction	a	10 24			17 28	17 34	17 40	17 54		17 58	18 04	18 10	18 24		18 28	18 34	18 40	18 54		18 58	19 04	19 10	19 24
Clapham Junction	d	10 24			17 28	17 34	17 40	17 54		17 58	18 04	18 10	18 24		18 28	18 34	18 40	18 54		18 58	19 04	19 10	19 24
Wandsworth Common	d	10 27				17 37	17 43	17 57			18 07	18 13	18 27			18 37	18 43	18 57			19 07	19 13	19 27
Balham	d	10 30			17 33	17 40	17 46	18 00		18 03	18 10	18 16	18 30		18 33	18 40	18 46	19 00		19 03	19 10	19 16	19 30
London Bridge	d		10 19						17 49					18 19					18 49				
Streatham Common	d	10 35	10 47				17 51	18 05	18 17			18 21	18 35	18 47			18 51	19 05	19 17			19 21	19 35
Norbury	d	10 37	10 50				17 53	18 07	18 20			18 23	18 37	18 50			18 53	19 07	19 20			19 23	19 37
Thornton Heath	d	10 40	10 53				17 56	18 10	18 23			18 26	18 40	18 53			18 56	19 10	19 23			19 26	19 40
Selhurst	d	10 43	10 56				18 00	18 13	18 26			18 30	18 43	18 56			19 00	19 13	19 26			19 30	19 43
East Croydon	a		10 59						18 29					18 59					19 29				
Purley	a																						
West Croydon	a	10 49				18 08	18 04	18 19			18 38	18 34	18 49			19 08	19 04	19 19			19 38	19 34	19 49
Sutton	a	11 02			17 53		18 17	18 32		18 23		18 47	19 02		18 53		19 17	19 32		19 23		19 47	20 03

		SN	SN C	SN	SN A	SN	SN	SN C	SN	SN A	SN	SN	SN C	SN	SN A	SN	SN	SN C	SN	SN A	SN	SN
London Victoria	d		19 22	19 26	19 32	19 46		19 52	19 56	20 02	20 16		20 22	20 26	20 32	20 46		20 52	20 56	21 02	21 16	
Battersea Park	d			19 30	19 36	19 50			20 00	20 06	20 20			20 30	20 36	20 50			21 00	21 06	21 20	
Shepherd's Bush	d																					
Kensington (Olympia)	d																					
West Brompton	d																					
Imperial Wharf	d																					
Clapham Junction	a		19 28	19 34	19 40	19 54		19 58	20 04	20 10	20 24		20 28	20 34	20 40	20 54		20 58	21 04	21 10	21 24	
Clapham Junction	d		19 28	19 34	19 40	19 54		19 58	20 04	20 10	20 24		20 28	20 34	20 40	20 54		20 58	21 04	21 10	21 24	
Wandsworth Common	d			19 37	19 43	19 57			20 07	20 13	20 27			20 37	20 43	20 57			21 07	21 13	21 27	
Balham	d		19 33	19 40	19 46	20 00		20 03	20 10	20 16	20 30		20 33	20 40	20 46	21 00		21 03	21 10	21 16	21 30	
London Bridge	d	19 19					19 49					20 19					20 49					21 19
Streatham Common	d	19 47			19 51	20 05	20 17			20 21	20 35	20 47			20 51	21 05	21 17			21 21	21 35	21 47
Norbury	d	19 50			19 53	20 07	20 20			20 23	20 37	20 50			20 53	21 07	21 20			21 23	21 37	21 50
Thornton Heath	d	19 53			19 56	20 10	20 23			20 26	20 40	20 53			20 56	21 10	21 23			21 26	21 40	21 53
Selhurst	d	19 56			20 00	20 13	20 26			20 30	20 43	20 56			21 00	21 13	21 26			21 30	21 43	21 56
East Croydon	a	19 59					20 29					20 59					21 29					21 59
Purley	a																					
West Croydon	a			20 08	20 04	20 19			20 38	20 34	20 49			21 08	21 04	21 19			21 38	21 34	21 49	
Sutton	a		19 53		20 17	20 32		20 23		20 47	21 02		20 53		21 17	21 32		21 23		21 47	22 02	

		SN C	SN	SN A	SN	SN	SN C	SN	SN	SN	SN	SN C	SN	SN	SN	SN	SN C	SN	SN	SN	SN C	SN	SN D
London Victoria	d	21 22	21 26	21 32	21 46		21 52	21 56	22 02	22 16		22 22	22 26	22 32	22 46		22 52	22 56	23 02	23 16	23 22	23 26	23 32
Battersea Park	d		21 30	21 36	21 50			22 00	22 06	22 20			22 30	22 36	22 50			23 00	23 06	23 20		23 30	
Shepherd's Bush	d																						
Kensington (Olympia)	d																						
West Brompton	d																						
Imperial Wharf	d																						
Clapham Junction	a	21 28	21 34	21 40	21 54		21 58	22 04	22 10	22 24		22 28	22 34	22 40	22 54		22 58	23 04	23 10	23 24	23 29	23 34	23 39
Clapham Junction	d	21 28	21 34	21 40	21 54		21 58	22 04	22 10	22 24		22 28	22 34	22 40	22 54		22 58	23 04	23 10	23 24	23 29	23 34	23 40
Wandsworth Common	d		21 37	21 43	21 57			22 07	22 13	22 27			22 37	22 43	22 57			23 07	23 13	23 27		23 37	
Balham	d	21 33	21 40	21 46	22 00		22 03	22 10	22 16	22 30		22 33	22 40	22 46	23 00		23 03	23 10	23 16	23 31	23 35	23 40	
London Bridge	d					21 49					22 19					22 49							
Streatham Common	d			21 51	22 05	22 17			22 24	22 35	22 47			22 51	23 07	23 17			23 21	23 36			
Norbury	d			21 53	22 07	22 20			22 27	22 37	22 50			22 53	23 09	23 20			23 23	23 38			
Thornton Heath	d			21 56	22 10	22 23			22 30	22 40	22 53			22 56	23 12	23 23			23 26	23 41			
Selhurst	d			22 00	22 13	22 26			22 33	22 43	22 56			23 00	23 15	23 26			23a29	23 44			23 51
East Croydon	a					22 29					22 59					23 29							23 56
Purley	a																						00 02
West Croydon	a		22 08	22 04	22 19			22 36	22 39	22 49			23 08	23 04	23 21			23 38		23 49		00 08	
Sutton	a	21 53		22 17	22 33		22 23		22 52	23 02		22 53		23 17	23 35		23 23			00 02	23 54		

A To Epsom Downs
B To Dorking
C To Epsom
D To Brighton

For faster services between London Victoria, Clapham Junction and East Croydon, refer to Table T175

For other Shepherd's Bush connecting trains, refer to Table T176

Table T170-F

Sundays
20 May to 2 December

London Victoria - Battersea Park, Wandsworth Common, Balham, Streatham Common, Norbury, Thornton Heath & Selhurst-Croydon

		SN	SN		SN	SN A
London Victoria ⊖	d		23 34		23 46	23 56
Battersea Park	d		23 39		23 50	00 01
Shepherd's Bush ⊖	d					
Kensington (Olympia) ⊖	d					
West Brompton ⊖	d					
Imperial Wharf	d					
Clapham Junction	a		23 42		23 54	00 05
Clapham Junction	d		23 43		23 55	00 06
Wandsworth Common	d		23 46		23 58	00 09
Balham ⊖	d		23 49		00 02	00a11
London Bridge	d	23 17				
Streatham Common	d	23 49	23 53		00 06	
Norbury	d	23 51	23 56		00 09	
Thornton Heath	d	23 54	23 59		00 12	
Selhurst	d	23 59	00a01		00a14	
East Croydon	a	00 02				
Purley	a					
West Croydon	a					
Sutton	a					

A To Norwood Junction

For faster services between London Victoria, Clapham Junction and East Croydon, refer to Table T175

For other Shepherd's Bush connecting trains, refer to Table T176

Table T170-R

Mondays to Fridays
21 May to 7 December

Croydon-Selhurst, Thornton Heath, Norbury, Streatham Common, Balham, Wandsworth Common & Battersea Park - London Victoria

Miles	Miles	Miles	Miles			SN MO A	TL MO B	SN MO C	SN	SN D	SN	SN E	SN	SN		SN E	SN F	SN	SN D	SN G	SN H	SN	SN E	SN	
0	—	—	—	Sutton	d													05 51		06 12					
4½	—	—	0	West Croydon	d													06 06							
—	0	—	—	Purley	d																				
3	—	0	—	East Croydon	d												06 08								
5½	4¼	1	1¼	**Selhurst**	d						05 28		05 40	06 01			06 11	06 11	06 16			06 25		06 31	
—	5	1	2	**Thornton Heath**	d						05 30		05 43	06 03				06 13	06 19			06 28		06 33	
2¼	6	3	3¼	**Norbury**	d						05 33		05 46	06 06				06 16	06 22			06 31		06 36	
8½	7	4	4	**Streatham Common**	d						05 35		05 49	06 09				06 19	06 25			06 36		06 39	
—	—	—	10½	London Bridge	a						06 01			06 36								07 06			
10½	9	6	—	**Balham** ⊖	d		00 06		05 03	05 27		05 40	05 55			06 10		06 25	06 29	06 33			06 40	06 44	
11	9½	6½	—	**Wandsworth Common**	d	00 01	00 08		05 05			05 42	05 57			06 12		06 27			←		06 42	06 46	
12½	10¾	8	—	Clapham Junction	a	00 05	00 12		05 08	05 31		05 46	06 01			06 16	06 19	06 31	06 35	06 37	06 35		06 46	06 50	
—	—	—	—	Clapham Junction	d	00 05	00 13	00 16	05 09	05 32		05 46	06 01			06 16	06 20	06 31	06 40	06 38	06 40		06 46	06 50	
—	—	9¾	—	Imperial Wharf	a					05 37									→		06 44				
—	—	10¾	—	West Brompton ⊖	a					05 40											06 47				
—	—	11¼	—	Kensington (Olympia) ⊖	a					05 43											06 50				
—	—	11¾	—	Shepherd's Bush ⊖	a					05 46											06 53				
13¾	12¼	—	—	**Battersea Park**	d	00 09	00 16		05 12			05 50	06 05			06 20		06 35					06 50	06 54	
15	13½	—	—	London Victoria ⊖	a	00 13	00 21	00 23	05 17			05 54	06 09			06 24	06 27	06 40		06 45			06 54	06 58	

		SN	SN	SN G	SN I	SN	SN J	SN	SN A	SN K		SN D	SN G	SN L	SN	SN	SN I	SN J	SN	SN A		SN K	SN M	SN G	SN
Sutton	d		06 16	06 42				06 41		06 51			07 12			07 00			07 11			07 21		07 42	
West Croydon	d	06 21	06 34				06 52	06 56		07 04						07 18		07 22	07 26			07 34			
Purley	d																								
East Croydon	d											07 10											07 40		
Selhurst	d		06 40			06 56		07 01		07 10		07 16			07 20	07 26			07 31			07 40	07 46		07 50
Thornton Heath	d		06 43			06 58		07 03		07 13		07 19			07 23	07 28			07 33			07 43	07 49		07 53
Norbury	d		06 46			07 01		07 06		07 16		07 22			07 27	07 31			07 36			07 46	07 52		07 57
Streatham Common	d		06 49			07 06		07 09		07 19		07 25			07 31	07 36			07 39			07 49	07 55		08 01
London Bridge	a					07 36			←							08 06				←					
Balham ⊖	d	06 51	06 55	07 03	07 10		07 21	07 14	07 21	07 25		07 29	07 32		07 36		07 40	07 51	07 44	07 51		07 55	07 59	08 02	08 05
Wandsworth Common	d	06 53	06 57		07 12		→	07 16	07 23	07 27				←	07 38		07 42	→	07 46	07 53		07 57			08 07
Clapham Junction	a	06 57	07 01	07 07	07 16			07 20	07 27	07 31		07 35	07 37	07 35	07 41		07 46		07 50	07 57		08 01	08 05	08 07	08 11
Clapham Junction	d	06 57	07 01	07 08	07 16			07 20	07 27	07 31		07 40	07 38	07 40	07 42		07 46		07 50	07 57		08 01	08 18	08 08	08 11
Imperial Wharf	a											→		07 44									→		
West Brompton ⊖	a													07 47											
Kensington (Olympia) ⊖	a													07 50											
Shepherd's Bush ⊖	a													07 53											
Battersea Park	d	07 01	07 05		07 20			07 24	07 31	07 35					07 45		07 50		07 54	08 01		08 05			08 15
London Victoria ⊖	a	07 05	07 09	07 15	07 24			07 28	07 35	07 39			07 46		07 50		07 54		07 59	08 05		08 09		08 16	08 19

		SN	SN I	SN N	SN J	SN		SN A	SN K	SN D	SN G	SN L	SN	SN	SN I	SN J		SN	SN A	SN K	SN	SN	SN G	SN I	SN J
Sutton	d	07 30				07 41			07 51		08 12			08 00				08 11		08 21		08 30	08 42		
West Croydon	d	07 48			07 52	07 56			08 04					08 18		08 22		08 25		08 34		08 48			08 52
Purley	d																								
East Croydon	d									08 11											08 40				
Selhurst	d	07 56				08 01			08 10	08 16			08 20	08 26				08 31		08 40	08 46	08 56			
Thornton Heath	d	07 58				08 03			08 13	08 19			08 23	08 28				08 34		08 43	08 49	08 58			
Norbury	d	08 01				08 06			08 16	08 22			08 27	08 31				08 37		08 46	08 52	09 01			
Streatham Common	d	08 06				08 09			08 19	08 25			08 31	08 36				08 40		08 49	08 55	09 06			
London Bridge	a	08 36						←						09 06					←			09 36			
Balham ⊖	d		08 10		08 21	08 14		08 21	08 25	08 29	08 32		08 35		08 40	08 51		08 45	08 51	08 55	08 59		09 03	09 10	09 21
Wandsworth Common	d		08 12	←	→	08 16		08 23	08 27			←	08 37		08 42	→		08 47	08 54	08 57				09 12	→
Clapham Junction	a		08 16	08 05		08 20		08 27	08 31	08 35	08 37	08 35	08 41		08 46			08 51	08 57	09 01	09 05		09 07	09 16	
Clapham Junction	d		08 16	08 18		08 20		08 27	08 31	08 40	08 38	08 40	08 41		08 46			08 53	08 58	09 01	09 06		09 09	09 16	
Imperial Wharf	a			08 22						→		08 44									09 10				
West Brompton ⊖	a			08 25								08 47									09 13				
Kensington (Olympia) ⊖	a			08 29								08 50									09 16				
Shepherd's Bush ⊖	a			08 32								08 53									09 19				
Battersea Park	d		08 20			08 24		08 31	08 35				08 45		08 50			08 57	09 02	09 05				09 20	
London Victoria ⊖	a		08 24			08 30		08 35	08 40		08 45		08 50		08 54			09 04	09 08	09 10			09 19	09 24	

A From West Croydon
B From Dorking
C From East Grinstead
D To Milton Keynes Central
E From Norwood Junction
F From Eastbourne
G From Epsom
H From Selhurst to Milton Keynes Central
I From London Bridge
J To London Victoria
K From Epsom Downs
L From East Croydon to Milton Keynes Central
M To Watford Junction
N From East Croydon to Watford Junction

For faster services between London Victoria, Clapham Junction and East Croydon, refer to Table T175

For other Shepherd's Bush connecting trains, refer to Table T176

Croydon-Selhurst, Thornton Heath, Norbury, Streatham Common, Balham, Wandsworth Common & Battersea Park - London Victoria

Station		SN	SN A	SN B	SN 1 C	SN D	SN 1 E	SN F	SN G	SN H	SN	SN A	SN B	SN D	SN G	SN F	SN H	SN	SN A	SN B	SN 1 C	SN D	SN 1 E
Sutton 4	d	08 41		08 51		09 12					09 11		09 21	09 42				09 41		09 51		10 12	
West Croydon 4	d	08 56		09 04						09 21	09 26		09 34				09 51	09 56		10 04			
Purley	d							09 15								09 45							
East Croydon	d				09 10			09 21								09 51					10 10		
Selhurst 4	d	09 01		09 10	09 16			09 27			09 31		09 40			09 56		10 01		10 10	10 16		
Thornton Heath	d	09 03		09 13	09 19			09 29			09 33		09 43			09 58		10 03		10 13	10 19		
Norbury	d	09 06		09 16	09 22			09 32			09 36		09 46			10 01		10 06		10 16	10 22		
Streatham Common 4	d	09 09		09 19	09 25			09 36			09 39		09 49			10 06		10 09		10 19	10 25		
London Bridge	a		←					10 06				←				10 36			←				
Balham 4 ⊖	d	09 14	09 21	09 25	09 29	09 33			09 40	09 51	09 44	09 51	09 55	10 03	10 10		10 21	10 14	10 21	10 25	10 29	10 33	
Wandsworth Common	d	09 16	09 23	09 27			←		09 42	→	09 46	09 53	09 57		10 12		→	10 16	10 23	10 27			←
Clapham Junction	a	09 20	09 27	09 31	09 35	09 37	09 35		09 46		09 50	09 57	10 01	10 07	10 16			10 20	10 27	10 31	10 35	10 37	10 35
Clapham Junction 10	d	09 20	09 27	09 31	09 39	09 38	09 39		09 46		09 50	09 57	10 01	10 08	10 16			10 20	10 27	10 31	10 41	10 38	10 41
Imperial Wharf	a				→		09 43														→		10 45
West Brompton ⊖	a						09 46																10 48
Kensington (Olympia) ⊖	a						09 50																10 51
Shepherd's Bush ⊖	a						09 53																10 54
Battersea Park	d	09 24	09 31	09 35					09 50		09 54	10 01	10 05		10 20			10 24	10 31	10 35			
London Victoria 15 ⊖	a	09 30	09 35	09 40		09 45			09 54		09 58	10 05	10 09	10 15	10 24			10 28	10 35	10 39		10 45	

Station		SN F	SN G	SN H	SN	SN A	SN B	SN D	SN G	SN F	SN H	SN	SN A	SN B	SN 1 C	SN D	SN 1 E	SN F	SN G	SN H	SN	SN A
Sutton 4	d				10 11		10 21	10 42				10 41		10 51		11 12					11 11	
West Croydon 4	d			10 21	10 26		10 34				10 51	10 56		11 04						11 21	11 26	
Purley	d	10 15								10 45								11 15				
East Croydon	d	10 22								10 52					11 10			11 22				
Selhurst 4	d	10 26			10 31		10 40			10 56		11 01		11 10	11 16			11 26			11 31	
Thornton Heath	d	10 28			10 33		10 43			10 58		11 03		11 13	11 19			11 28			11 33	
Norbury	d	10 31			10 36		10 46			11 01		11 06		11 16	11 22			11 31			11 36	
Streatham Common 4	d	10 36			10 39		10 49			11 06		11 09		11 19	11 25			11 36			11 39	
London Bridge	a	11 06				←				11 36			←					12 06				←
Balham 4 ⊖	d		10 40	10 51	10 44	10 51	10 55	11 03	11 10		11 21	11 14	11 21	11 25	11 29	11 33			11 40	11 51	11 44	11 51
Wandsworth Common	d		10 42	→	10 46	10 53	10 57		11 12		→	11 16	11 23	11 27			←		11 42	→	11 46	11 53
Clapham Junction	a		10 46		10 50	10 57	11 01	11 07	11 16			11 20	11 27	11 31	11 35	11 37	11 35		11 46		11 50	11 57
Clapham Junction 10	d		10 46		10 50	10 57	11 01	11 08	11 16			11 20	11 27	11 31	11 39	11 38	11 39		11 46		11 50	11 57
Imperial Wharf	a														→		11 43					
West Brompton ⊖	a																11 46					
Kensington (Olympia) ⊖	a																11 50					
Shepherd's Bush ⊖	a																11 53					
Battersea Park	d		10 50		10 54	11 01	11 05		11 20			11 24	11 31	11 35					11 50		11 54	12 01
London Victoria 15 ⊖	a		10 54		10 58	11 05	11 09	11 15	11 24			11 28	11 35	11 39		11 45			11 54		11 58	12 05

Station		SN B	SN D	SN G	SN F	SN H	SN	SN A	SN B	SN 1 C	SN D	SN 1 E	SN F	SN G	SN H	SN	SN A	SN B	SN D	SN G	SN F	SN H	SN
Sutton 4	d	11 21	11 42				11 41		11 51		12 12					12 11		12 21	12 42				12 41
West Croydon 4	d	11 34				11 51	11 56		12 04						12 21	12 26		12 34				12 51	12 56
Purley	d				11 45								12 15								12 45		
East Croydon	d				11 52					12 10			12 22								12 52		
Selhurst 4	d	11 40			11 56		12 01		12 10	12 16			12 26			12 31		12 40			12 56		13 01
Thornton Heath	d	11 43			11 58		12 03		12 13	12 19			12 28			12 33		12 43			12 58		13 03
Norbury	d	11 46			12 01		12 06		12 16	12 22			12 31			12 36		12 46			13 01		13 06
Streatham Common 4	d	11 49			12 06		12 09		12 19	12 25			12 36			12 39		12 49			13 06		13 09
London Bridge	a				12 36			←					13 06				←				13 36		
Balham 4 ⊖	d	11 55	12 03	12 10		12 21	12 14	12 21	12 25	12 29	12 33			12 40	12 51	12 44	12 51	12 55	13 03	13 10		13 21	13 14
Wandsworth Common	d	11 57		12 12		→	12 16	12 23	12 27			←		12 42	→	12 46	12 53	12 57		13 12		→	13 16
Clapham Junction	a	12 01	12 07	12 16			12 20	12 27	12 31	12 35	12 37	12 35		12 46		12 50	12 57	13 01	13 07	13 16			13 20
Clapham Junction 10	d	12 01	12 08	12 16			12 20	12 27	12 31	12 39	12 38	12 39		12 46		12 50	12 57	13 01	13 08	13 16			13 20
Imperial Wharf	a									→		12 43											
West Brompton ⊖	a											12 46											
Kensington (Olympia) ⊖	a											12 50											
Shepherd's Bush ⊖	a											12 53											
Battersea Park	d	12 05		12 20			12 24	12 31	12 35					12 50		12 54	13 01	13 05		13 20			13 24
London Victoria 15 ⊖	a	12 09	12 15	12 24			12 28	12 35	12 39		12 45			12 54		12 58	13 05	13 09	13 15	13 24			13 28

A From West Croydon
B From Epsom Downs
C To Milton Keynes Central
D From Epsom
E From East Croydon to Milton Keynes Central
F From Caterham
G From London Bridge
H To London Victoria

For faster services between London Victoria, Clapham Junction and East Croydon, refer to Table T175

For other Shepherd's Bush connecting trains, refer to Table T176

Table T170-R

Mondays to Fridays

21 May to 7 December

Croydon-Selhurst, Thornton Heath, Norbury, Streatham Common, Balham, Wandsworth Common & Battersea Park - London Victoria

Station		SN A	SN TThO B	SN MWFO B	SN MWFO 1 C	SN TThO 1 C	SN D	SN MWFO 1 E	SN TThO 1 F	SN G	SN H	SN I	SN	SN A	SN B	SN D	SN H	SN G	SN I	SN	SN A	SN B
Sutton 4	d		12 50	12 51			13 12						13 11		13 21	13 42				13 41		13 51
West Croydon 4	d		13 04	13 04								13 21	13 26		13 34				13 51	13 56		14 04
Purley	d									13 15								13 45				
East Croydon	d				13 10					13 22								13 52				
Selhurst 4	d		13 09	13 10	13 16	13 18				13 26			13 31		13 40			13 56		14 01		14 10
Thornton Heath	d		13 13	13 13	13 19	13 20				13 28			13 33		13 43			13 58		14 03		14 13
Norbury	d		13 16	13 16	13 22	13 23				13 31			13 36		13 46			14 01		14 06		14 16
Streatham Common 4	d		13 19	13 19	13 25	13 26				13 36			13 39		13 49			14 06		14 09		14 19
London Bridge	a	←								14 06				←				14 36			←	
Balham 4 ⊖	d	13 21	13 25	13 25	13 29	13 30	13 33				13 40	13 51	13 44	13 51	13 55	14 03	14 10		14 21	14 14	14 21	14 25
Wandsworth Common	d	13 23	13 27	13 27				←	←		13 42	→	13 46	13 53	13 57		14 12		→	14 16	14 23	14 27
Clapham Junction	a	13 27	13 31	13 31	13 35	13 35	13 37	13 35	13 35		13 46		13 50	13 57	14 01	14 07	14 16			14 20	14 27	14 31
Clapham Junction 10	d	13 27	13 31	13 31	13 39	13 39	13 38	13 39	13 39		13 46		13 50	13 57	14 01	14 08	14 16			14 20	14 27	14 31
Imperial Wharf	a				→	→		13 43	13 43													
West Brompton ⊖	a							13 46	13 46													
Kensington (Olympia) ⊖	a							13 50	13 50													
Shepherd's Bush ⊖	a							13 53	13 53													
Battersea Park	d	13 31	13 35	13 35							13 50		13 54	14 01	14 05		14 20			14 24	14 31	14 35
London Victoria 15 ⊖	a	13 35	13 39	13 39			13 45				13 54		13 58	14 05	14 09	14 15	14 24			14 28	14 35	14 39

Station		SN 1 C	SN D	SN 1 E	SN G	SN H	SN I	SN	SN A	SN B	SN 1 J	SN D	SN 1 K	SN G	SN H	SN I	SN	SN A	SN B	SN 1 C	SN D	SN 1 E	SN G
Sutton 4	d		14 12					14 11		14 21		14 42					14 41		14 51		15 12		
West Croydon 4	d						14 21	14 26		14 34						14 51	14 56		15 04				
Purley	d				14 15									14 45									15 15
East Croydon	d	14 10			14 22									14 52						15 10			15 22
Selhurst 4	d	14 16			14 26			14 31		14 40	14 46			14 56			15 01		15 10	15 16			15 26
Thornton Heath	d	14 19			14 28			14 33		14 43	14 49			14 58			15 03		15 13	15 19			15 28
Norbury	d	14 22			14 31			14 36		14 46	14 52			15 01			15 06		15 16	15 22			15 31
Streatham Common 4	d	14 25			14 36			14 39		14 49	14 55			15 06			15 09		15 19	15 25			15 36
London Bridge	a				15 06				←					15 36				←					16 06
Balham 4 ⊖	d	14 29	14 33			14 40	14 51	14 44	14 51	14 55	14 59	15 03			15 10	15 21	15 14	15 21	15 25	15 29	15 33		
Wandsworth Common	d			←		14 42	→	14 46	14 53	14 57			←		15 12	→	15 16	15 23	15 27			←	
Clapham Junction	a	14 35	14 37	14 35		14 46		14 50	14 57	15 01	15 05	15 07	15 05		15 16		15 20	15 27	15 31	15 35	15 37	15 35	
Clapham Junction 10	d	14 40	14 38	14 40		14 46		14 50	14 57	15 01	15 10	15 08	15 10		15 16		15 20	15 27	15 31	15 39	15 38	15 39	
Imperial Wharf	a	→		14 44							→		15 14							→		15 44	
West Brompton ⊖	a			14 47									15 17									15 47	
Kensington (Olympia) ⊖	a			14 51									15 21									15 50	
Shepherd's Bush ⊖	a			14 54									15 24									15 53	
Battersea Park	d					14 50		14 54	15 01	15 05					15 20		15 24	15 31	15 35				
London Victoria 15 ⊖	a		14 45			14 54		14 58	15 05	15 09		15 15			15 24		15 28	15 35	15 39		15 45		

Station		SN H	SN I	SN L	SN M	SN A	SN N	SN M	SN 1 O	SN 1 P	SN D	SN H	SN G	SN I	SN	SN A	SN B	SN 1 C	SN D	SN 1 E	SN G	SN H
Sutton 4	d			15 11	15 12		15 21	15 21			15 42				15 41		15 51		16 12			
West Croydon 4	d		15 21	15 26	15 26		15 34	15 34						15 51	15 56		16 04					
Purley	d												15 45								16 15	
East Croydon	d								15 43	15 43			15 51					16 10			16 21	
Selhurst 4	d			15 31	15 31		15 40	15 40	15 46	15 46			15 56		16 01		16 10	16 16			16 26	
Thornton Heath	d			15 33	15 33		15 43	15 43	15 49	15 49			15 58		16 03		16 13	16 19			16 28	
Norbury	d			15 36	15 36		15 46	15 46	15 52	15 52			16 01		16 06		16 16	16 22			16 31	
Streatham Common 4	d			15 39	15 39		15 49	15 49	15 55	15 55			16 06		16 09		16 19	16 25			16 36	
London Bridge	a					←							16 36			←					17 06	
Balham 4 ⊖	d	15 40	15 51	15 44	15 44	15 51	15 55	15 55	16 00	16 00	16 03	16 10		16 21	16 14	16 21	16 25	16 29	16 33			16 40
Wandsworth Common	d	15 42	→	15 46	15 46	15 53	15 57	15 57				16 12		→	16 16	16 23	16 27			←		16 42
Clapham Junction	a	15 46		15 50	15 50	15 57	16 01	16 01	16 04	16 04	16 07	16 16			16 20	16 27	16 31	16 35	16 37	16 35		16 46
Clapham Junction 10	d	15 46		15 50	15 50	15 57	16 01	16 01	16 04	16 04	16 08	16 16			16 20	16 27	16 31	16 39	16 38	16 39		16 46
Imperial Wharf	a																	→		16 44		
West Brompton ⊖	a																			16 47		
Kensington (Olympia) ⊖	a																			16 50		
Shepherd's Bush ⊖	a																			16 53		
Battersea Park	d	15 50		15 54	15 54	16 01	16 05	16 05				16 20			16 24	16 31	16 35					16 50
London Victoria 15 ⊖	a	15 54		15 58	15 58	16 05	16 09	16 11	16 12	16 13	16 15	16 24			16 28	16 35	16 39		16 45			16 54

A From West Croydon
B From Epsom Downs
C To Milton Keynes Central
D From Epsom
E From East Croydon to Milton Keynes Central
F From Selhurst to Milton Keynes Central
G From Caterham
H From London Bridge
I To London Victoria
J To Shepherd's Bush
K From Selhurst
L until 21 September
M from 24 September
N until 21 September. From Epsom Downs
O until 21 September. From South Croydon
P from 24 September. From South Croydon

For faster services between London Victoria, Clapham Junction and East Croydon, refer to Table T175

For other Shepherd's Bush connecting trains, refer to Table T176

Croydon-Selhurst, Thornton Heath, Norbury, Streatham Common, Balham, Wandsworth Common & Battersea Park - London Victoria

		SN A	SN	SN B	SN C	SN ■ D		SN E	SN ■ F	SN G	SN H	SN A	SN	SN B	SN C	SN ■ I		SN E	SN ■ J	SN G	SN H	SN A	SN	SN B	SN C
Sutton	d		16 11		16 21			16 42					16 41		16 51			17 12					17 11		17 21
West Croydon	d	16 21	16 26		16 34							16 51	16 56		17 04							17 22	17 26		17 34
Purley	d									16 45										17 15					
East Croydon	d					16 40				16 51						17 10				17 21					
Selhurst	d		16 31		16 40	16 46				16 56			17 01		17 10	17 16				17 26			17 31		17 40
Thornton Heath	d		16 33		16 43	16 49				16 58			17 03		17 13	17 19				17 28			17 33		17 43
Norbury	d		16 36		16 46	16 52				17 01			17 06		17 16	17 22				17 31			17 36		17 46
Streatham Common	d		16 39		16 49	16 55				17 06			17 09		17 19	17 25				17 36			17 39		17 49
London Bridge	a			←						17 36				←						18 06				←	
Balham ⊖	d	16 51	16 44	16 51	16 55	16 59		17 03			17 10	17 21	17 14	17 21	17 25	17 30		17 33			17 40	17 51	17 44	17 51	17 55
Wandsworth Common	d	→	16 46	16 53	16 57				←		17 12	→	17 16	17 23	17 27				←		17 42	→	17 46	17 53	17 57
Clapham Junction	a		16 50	16 57	17 01	17 05		17 07	17 05		17 16		17 20	17 27	17 31	17 35		17 37	17 35		17 46		17 50	17 57	18 01
Clapham Junction	d		16 50	16 57	17 01	17 09		17 08	17 09		17 16		17 20	17 27	17 31	17 39		17 38	17 39		17 46		17 50	17 57	18 01
Imperial Wharf	a					→			17 13							→			17 44						
West Brompton ⊖	a								17 16										17 47						
Kensington (Olympia) ⊖	a								17 19										17 50						
Shepherd's Bush ⊖	a								17 22										17 53						
Battersea Park	d		16 54	17 01	17 05						17 20		17 24	17 31	17 35						17 50		17 54	18 01	18 05
London Victoria ⊖	a		16 58	17 05	17 09			17 15			17 24		17 28	17 35	17 39			17 45			17 54		17 58	18 05	18 09

		SN ■		SN E	SN H	SN G	SN A	SN	SN B	SN C	SN ■ I	SN		SN E	SN ■ J	SN H	SN A	SN	SN B	SN C	SN	SN E		SN H	SN A
Sutton	d			17 42				17 41		17 51		18 00		18 12				18 11		18 21	18 30	18 42			
West Croydon	d						17 52	17 56		18 04		18 18					18 22	18 26		18 34	18 48				18 52
Purley	d					17 45																			
East Croydon	d	17 40				17 51					18 10														
Selhurst	d	17 46				17 56		18 01		18 10	18 16	18 26						18 31		18 40	18 56				
Thornton Heath	d	17 49				17 58		18 03		18 13	18 19	18 28						18 33		18 43	18 58				
Norbury	d	17 52				18 01		18 06		18 16	18 22	18 31						18 36		18 46	19 01				
Streatham Common	d	17 55				18 06		18 09		18 19	18 25	18 36						18 39		18 49	19 06				
London Bridge	a					18 36			←			19 06							←		19 36				
Balham ⊖	d	17 59		18 03	18 10		18 21	18 14	18 21	18 25	18 29			18 33		18 40	18 51	18 44	18 51	18 55		19 03		19 10	19 21
Wandsworth Common	d				18 12		→	18 16	18 23	18 27					←	18 42	→	18 46	18 53	18 57				19 12	→
Clapham Junction	a	18 04		18 07	18 16			18 20	18 27	18 31	18 35			18 37	18 35	18 46		18 50	18 57	19 01		19 07		19 16	
Clapham Junction	d	18 05		18 08	18 16			18 20	18 27	18 31	18 39			18 38	18 39	18 46		18 50	18 57	19 01		19 08		19 16	
Imperial Wharf	a										→				18 44										
West Brompton ⊖	a														18 47										
Kensington (Olympia) ⊖	a														18 50										
Shepherd's Bush ⊖	a														18 53										
Battersea Park	d				18 20			18 24	18 31	18 35						18 50		18 54	19 01	19 05				19 20	
London Victoria ⊖	a	18 14		18 19	18 24			18 30	18 36	18 39				18 45		18 54		19 00	19 05	19 09		19 15		19 24	

		SN	SN B	SN C	SN ■ I	SN	SN E	SN ■ J		SN H	SN A	SN	SN B	SN C	SN E	SN H	SN	SN A		SN	SN B	SN C	SN ■ I	SN E	SN H
Sutton	d	18 41		18 51		19 00	19 12					19 11		19 21	19 42					19 41		19 51		20 12	
West Croydon	d	18 56		19 04		19 18					19 22	19 26		19 34				19 51		19 56		20 04			
Purley	d																								
East Croydon	d				19 10																		20 10		
Selhurst	d	19 01		19 10	19 16	19 26						19 31		19 40			19 56			20 01		20 10	20 16		
Thornton Heath	d	19 03		19 13	19 19	19 28						19 33		19 43			19 58			20 03		20 13	20 19		
Norbury	d	19 06		19 16	19 22	19 31						19 36		19 46			20 01			20 06		20 16	20 22		
Streatham Common	d	19 09		19 19	19 25	19 36						19 39		19 49			20 06			20 09		20 19	20 25		
London Bridge	a		←			20 06							←				20 36				←				
Balham ⊖	d	19 14	19 21	19 25	19 29		19 33			19 40	19 51	19 44	19 51	19 55	20 03	20 10		20 21		20 14	20 21	20 25	20 29	20 33	20 40
Wandsworth Common	d	19 16	19 23	19 27				←		19 42	→	19 46	19 53	19 57		20 12		→		20 16	20 23	20 27			20 42
Clapham Junction	a	19 20	19 27	19 31	19 35		19 37	19 35		19 46		19 50	19 57	20 01	20 07	20 16				20 20	20 27	20 31	20 35	20 37	20 46
Clapham Junction	d	19 20	19 27	19 31	19 40		19 38	19 40		19 46		19 50	19 57	20 01	20 08	20 16				20 20	20 27	20 31	20 36	20 38	20 46
Imperial Wharf	a				→			19 44															20 40		
West Brompton ⊖	a							19 47															20 43		
Kensington (Olympia) ⊖	a							19 51															20 47		
Shepherd's Bush ⊖	a							19 54															20 50		
Battersea Park	d	19 24	19 31	19 35						19 50		19 54	20 01	20 05		20 20				20 24	20 31	20 35			20 50
London Victoria ⊖	a	19 28	19 35	19 39			19 45			19 54		19 58	20 05	20 09	20 17	20 24				20 30	20 35	20 39		20 45	20 54

A To London Victoria
B From West Croydon
C From Epsom Downs
D To Shepherd's Bush
E From Epsom
F From East Croydon
G From Caterham
H From London Bridge
I To Milton Keynes Central
J From East Croydon to Milton Keynes Central

For faster services between London Victoria, Clapham Junction and East Croydon, refer to Table T175

For other Shepherd's Bush connecting trains, refer to Table T176

Croydon-Selhurst, Thornton Heath, Norbury, Streatham Common, Balham, Wandsworth Common & Battersea Park - London Victoria

		SN	SN A	SN	SN B	SN C	SN D	SN E	SN F	SN A		SN	SN B	SN C	SN ■ G	SN D	SN E	SN F	SN A	SN		SN B	SN C	SN D	SN E
Sutton	d			20 11		20 21	20 42					20 41		20 51		21 12				21 11			21 21	21 42	
West Croydon	d		20 21	20 26		20 34				20 51		20 56		21 04					21 22	21 26			21 34		
Purley	d								20 45									21 15							
East Croydon	d								20 54						21 10			21 22							
Selhurst	d	20 26		20 31		20 40			20 58			21 01		21 10	21 16			21 26		21 31			21 40		
Thornton Heath	d	20 28		20 33		20 43			21 00			21 03		21 13	21 19			21 28		21 33			21 43		
Norbury	d	20 31		20 36		20 46			21 03			21 06		21 16	21 22			21 31		21 36			21 46		
Streatham Common	d	20 36		20 39		20 49			21 06			21 09		21 19	21 25			21 36		21 39			21 49		
London Bridge	a	21 06			←				21 36				←					22 06				←			
Balham ⊖	d		20 51	20 44	20 51	20 55	21 03	21 10		21 21		21 14	21 21	21 25	21 29	21 33	21 40		21 51	21 44		21 51	21 55	22 03	22 10
Wandsworth Common	d		→	20 46	20 53	20 57		21 12		→		21 16	21 23	21 27			21 42		→	21 46		21 53	21 57		22 12
Clapham Junction	a			20 50	20 57	21 01	21 07	21 16				21 20	21 27	21 31	21 35	21 37	21 46			21 50		21 57	22 01	22 07	22 16
Clapham Junction	d			20 50	20 57	21 01	21 08	21 16				21 20	21 27	21 31	21 36	21 38	21 46			21 50		21 57	22 01	22 08	22 16
Imperial Wharf	a														21 40										
West Brompton ⊖	a														21 43										
Kensington (Olympia) ⊖	a														21 47										
Shepherd's Bush ⊖	a														21 50										
Battersea Park	d			20 54	21 01	21 05		21 20				21 24	21 31	21 35			21 50			21 54		22 01	22 05		22 20
London Victoria ⊖	a			20 58	21 05	21 09	21 15	21 24				21 28	21 35	21 39		21 45	21 54			21 58		22 05	22 09	22 16	22 24

		SN F	SN A	SN	SN B	SN C		SN ■ G	SN D	SN E	SN F	SN A	SN	SN B	SN C	SN D		SN E	SN F	SN A	SN	SN B	SN C	SN D	SN E
Sutton	d			21 41		21 50			22 12				22 11		22 21	22 42					22 41		22 51	23 12	
West Croydon	d		21 51	21 56		22 04						22 21	22 26		22 34					22 51	22 56		23 04		
Purley	d	21 45									22 15								22 45						
East Croydon	d	21 52									22 22								22 52						
Selhurst	d	21 56		22 01		22 09		22 17			22 26		22 31		22 40				22 56		23 01		23 10		
Thornton Heath	d	21 58		22 03		22 13		22 19			22 28		22 33		22 43				22 58		23 03		23 13		
Norbury	d	22 01		22 06		22 16		22 22			22 31		22 36		22 46				23 01		23 06		23 16		
Streatham Common	d	22 06		22 09		22 19		22 25			22 36		22 39		22 49				23 06		23 09		23 19		
London Bridge	a	22 36			←						23 06			←					23 36			←			
Balham ⊖	d		22 21	22 14	22 21	22 25		22 30	22 33	22 40		22 51	22 44	22 51	22 55	23 03		23 10		23 21	23 14	23 21	23 25	23 33	23 37
Wandsworth Common	d		→	22 16	22 23	22 27				22 42		→	22 46	22 53	22 57			23 12		→	23 16	23 23	23 27		
Clapham Junction	a			22 20	22 27	22 31		22 35	22 37	22 46			22 50	22 57	23 01	23 07		23 16			23 20	23 27	23 31	23 37	23 41
Clapham Junction	d			22 20	22 27	22 31		22 36	22 38	22 46			22 50	22 57	23 01	23 08		23 16			23 20	23 27	23 31	23 38	23 42
Imperial Wharf	a							22 40																	
West Brompton ⊖	a							22 43																	
Kensington (Olympia) ⊖	a							22 47																	
Shepherd's Bush ⊖	a							22 50																	
Battersea Park	d			22 24	22 31	22 35				22 50			22 54	23 01	23 05			23 20			23 24	23 31	23 35		
London Victoria ⊖	a			22 28	22 37	22 39			22 45	22 55			23 00	23 05	23 09	23 15		23 24			23 28	23 37	23 39	23 47	23 50

		SN C
Sutton	d	23 15
West Croydon	d	23 28
Purley	d	
East Croydon	d	
Selhurst	d	23 35
Thornton Heath	d	23 38
Norbury	d	23 41
Streatham Common	d	23 44
London Bridge	a	
Balham ⊖	d	23 48
Wandsworth Common	d	23 50
Clapham Junction	a	23 54
Clapham Junction	d	23 54
Imperial Wharf	a	
West Brompton ⊖	a	
Kensington (Olympia) ⊖	a	
Shepherd's Bush ⊖	a	
Battersea Park	d	23 58
London Victoria ⊖	a	00 02

A To London Victoria
B From West Croydon
C From Epsom Downs
D From Epsom
E From London Bridge
F From Caterham
G To Watford Junction

For faster services between London Victoria, Clapham Junction and East Croydon, refer to Table T175

For other Shepherd's Bush connecting trains, refer to Table T176

Croydon-Selhurst, Thornton Heath, Norbury, Streatham Common, Balham, Wandsworth Common & Battersea Park - London Victoria

		SN	SN 1 A	SN 1 B	SN C	SN		SN 1 A	SN C	SN	SN	SN	SN	SN D	SN E	SN		SN F	SN	SN G	SN	SN 1 A	SN H	SN 1 I	SN J
Sutton 4	d												06 21	06 42					06 41		06 51		07 12		
West Croydon 4	d											06 21	06 34					06 51	06 56		07 04				
Purley	d			05 24																					07 15
East Croydon	d			05 30				06 10														07 10			07 23
Selhurst 4	d			05 33		06 10		06 16		06 26	06 32		06 40			06 56			07 01		07 10	07 16			07 27
Thornton Heath	d			05 36		06 13		06 19		06 28	06 34		06 43			06 58			07 03		07 13	07 19			07 29
Norbury	d			05 39		06 16		06 22		06 31	06 37		06 46			07 01			07 06		07 16	07 22			07 32
Streatham Common 4	d			05 41		06 19		06 25		06 36	06 40		06 49			07 06			07 09		07 19	07 25			07 36
London Bridge	a									07 06						07 36				←					08 06
Balham 4 ⊖	d		05 33	05 46	06 10	06 25		06 29	06 40		06 44	06 51	06 55	07 03	07 10			07 21	07 14	07 21	07 25	07 29	07 33		
Wandsworth Common	d				06 12	06 27			06 42		06 46	06 53	06 57		07 12			→	07 16	07 23	07 27			←	
Clapham Junction	a		05 37	05 50	06 16	06 31		06 35	06 46		06 50	06 57	07 01	07 07	07 16				07 20	07 27	07 31	07 35	07 37	07 35	
Clapham Junction 10	d	05 02	05 39	05 51	06 16	06 31		06 40	06 46		06 50	06 57	07 01	07 08	07 16				07 20	07 27	07 31	07 40	07 38	07 40	
Imperial Wharf	a		05 43					06 44														→		07 44	
West Brompton ⊖	a		05 46					06 47																07 47	
Kensington (Olympia) ⊖	a		05 49					06 51																07 51	
Shepherd's Bush ⊖	a		05 52					06 54																07 54	
Battersea Park	d	05 06		05 54	06 20	06 35			06 50		06 54	07 01	07 05		07 20				07 24	07 31	07 35				
London Victoria 15 ⊖	a	05 11		05 59	06 24	06 39			06 54		06 58	07 05	07 09	07 15	07 24				07 28	07 35	07 39		07 45		

		SN E		SN F	SN	SN G	SN K	SN D	SN E	SN J	SN F	SN		SN G	SN K	SN 1 A	SN D	SN 1 I	SN J	SN E	SN F	SN	SN G	SN K	SN D
Sutton 4	d				07 11		07 21	07 42				07 41			07 51		08 12					08 11		08 21	08 42
West Croydon 4	d			07 21	07 26		07 34				07 51	07 56			08 04						08 21	08 26		08 34	
Purley	d									07 45									08 15						
East Croydon	d									07 53						08 10			08 23						
Selhurst 4	d				07 31		07 40			07 57		08 01			08 10	08 16			08 27			08 31		08 40	
Thornton Heath	d				07 33		07 43			07 59		08 03			08 13	08 19			08 29			08 33		08 43	
Norbury	d				07 36		07 46			08 02		08 06			08 16	08 22			08 32			08 36		08 46	
Streatham Common 4	d				07 39		07 49			08 06		08 09			08 19	08 25			08 36			08 39		08 49	
London Bridge	a					←				08 36				←					09 06				←		
Balham 4 ⊖	d	07 40		07 51	07 44	07 51	07 55	08 03	08 10		08 21	08 14		08 21	08 25	08 29	08 33			08 40	08 51	08 44	08 51	08 55	09 03
Wandsworth Common	d	07 42		→	07 46	07 53	07 57		08 12		→	08 16		08 23	08 27			←		08 42	→	08 46	08 53	08 57	
Clapham Junction	a	07 46			07 50	07 57	08 01	08 07	08 16			08 20		08 27	08 31	08 35	08 37	08 35		08 46		08 50	08 57	09 01	09 07
Clapham Junction 10	d	07 46			07 50	07 57	08 01	08 08	08 16			08 20		08 27	08 31	08 40	08 38	08 40		08 46		08 50	08 57	09 01	09 08
Imperial Wharf	a															→		08 45							
West Brompton ⊖	a																	08 47							
Kensington (Olympia) ⊖	a																	08 51							
Shepherd's Bush ⊖	a																	08 54							
Battersea Park	d	07 50			07 54	08 01	08 05		08 20			08 24		08 31	08 35					08 50		08 54	09 01	09 05	
London Victoria 15 ⊖	a	07 54			07 58	08 05	08 09	08 15	08 24			08 28		08 35	08 39		08 45			08 54		08 58	09 05	09 09	09 15

		SN E	SN J	SN F	SN	SN G	SN K	SN 1 A	SN D	SN 1 I		SN J	SN E	SN F	SN	SN G	SN K	SN D	SN E	SN J	SN F	SN	SN G	SN K
Sutton 4	d				08 41		08 51		09 12						14 11		14 21	14 42				14 41		14 51
West Croydon 4	d			08 51	08 56		09 04							14 21	14 26		14 34				14 51	14 56		15 04
Purley	d		08 45									14 15								14 45				
East Croydon	d		08 53					09 10				14 23								14 53				
Selhurst 4	d		08 57		09 01		09 10	09 16			and at	14 27			14 31		14 40			14 57		15 01		15 10
Thornton Heath	d		08 59		09 03		09 13	09 19			the same	14 29			14 33		14 43			14 59		15 03		15 13
Norbury	d		09 02		09 06		09 16	09 22			minutes	14 32			14 36		14 46			15 02		15 06		15 16
Streatham Common 4	d		09 06		09 09		09 19	09 25			past	14 36			14 39		14 49			15 06		15 09		15 19
London Bridge	a		09 36			←					each	15 06				←				15 36			←	
Balham 4 ⊖	d	09 10		09 21	09 14	09 21	09 25	09 29	09 33		hour until		14 40	14 51	14 44	14 51	14 55	15 03	15 10		15 21	15 14	15 21	15 25
Wandsworth Common	d	09 12		→	09 16	09 23	09 27			←			14 42	→	14 46	14 53	14 57		15 12		→	15 16	15 23	15 27
Clapham Junction	a	09 16			09 20	09 27	09 31	09 35	09 37	09 35			14 46		14 50	14 57	15 01	15 07	15 16			15 20	15 27	15 31
Clapham Junction 10	d	09 16			09 20	09 27	09 31	09 40	09 38	09 40			14 46		14 50	14 57	15 01	15 08	15 16			15 20	15 27	15 31
Imperial Wharf	a							→		09 44														
West Brompton ⊖	a									09 47														
Kensington (Olympia) ⊖	a									09 51														
Shepherd's Bush ⊖	a									09 54														
Battersea Park	d	09 20			09 24	09 31	09 35						14 50		14 54	15 01	15 05		15 20			15 24	15 31	15 35
London Victoria 15 ⊖	a	09 24			09 28	09 35	09 39		09 45				14 54		14 58	15 05	15 09	15 15	15 24			15 28	15 35	15 39

A To Milton Keynes Central
B From Brighton
C From Norwood Junction
D From Epsom
E From London Bridge
F To London Victoria
G From West Croydon
H From Dorking
I From East Croydon to Milton Keynes Central
J From Caterham
K From Epsom Downs

For faster services between London Victoria, Clapham Junction and East Croydon, refer to Table T175

For other Shepherd's Bush connecting trains, refer to Table T176

Table T170-R

Saturdays
26 May to 8 December

Croydon-Selhurst, Thornton Heath, Norbury, Streatham Common, Balham, Wandsworth Common & Battersea Park - London Victoria

		SN 1 A	SN B	SN 1 C	SN D	SN E	SN F	SN G	SN H	SN I		SN J	SN B	SN E	SN D	SN F	SN	SN I	SN J	SN 1 A		SN B	SN 1 C	SN D	SN E
Sutton 4	d		15 12					15 11	15 12			15 21	15 42				15 41		15 51			16 12			
West Croydon 4	d						15 21	15 26	15 26			15 34				15 51	15 56		16 04						
Purley	d				15 15										15 45									16 15	
East Croydon	d	15 10			15 23										15 53					16 10				16 23	
Selhurst 4	d	15 16			15 27			15 31	15 31			15 40			15 57		16 01		16 10	16 16				16 27	
Thornton Heath	d	15 19			15 29			15 33	15 33			15 43			15 59		16 03		16 13	16 19				16 29	
Norbury	d	15 22			15 32			15 36	15 36			15 46			16 02		16 06		16 16	16 22				16 32	
Streatham Common 4	d	15 25			15 36			15 39	15 39			15 49			16 06		16 09		16 19	16 25				16 36	
London Bridge	a				16 06					←					16 36			←						17 06	
Balham 4 ⊖	d	15 29	15 33			15 40	15 51	15 44	15 44	15 51		15 55	16 03	16 10		16 21	16 14	16 21	16 25	16 29		16 33			16 40
Wandsworth Common	d			←		15 42	→	15 46	15 46	15 53		15 57		16 12		→	16 16	16 23	16 27				←		16 42
Clapham Junction	a	15 35	15 37	15 35		15 46		15 50	15 50	15 57		16 01	16 07	16 16			16 20	16 27	16 31	16 35		16 37	16 35		16 46
Clapham Junction 10	d	15 40	15 38	15 40		15 46		15 50	15 50	15 57		16 01	16 08	16 16			16 20	16 27	16 31	16 40		16 38	16 40		16 46
Imperial Wharf	a	→		15 44																→			16 44		
West Brompton ⊖	a			15 47																			16 47		
Kensington (Olympia) ⊖	a			15 51																			16 51		
Shepherd's Bush ⊖	a			15 54																			16 54		
Battersea Park	d					15 50		15 54	15 54	16 01		16 05		16 20			16 24	16 31	16 35						16 50
London Victoria 15 ⊖	a		15 45			15 54		15 58	15 58	16 05		16 09	16 15	16 24			16 28	16 35	16 39			16 45			16 54

		SN F	SN	SN I	SN J	SN B		SN E	SN D	SN F	SN	SN I	SN J	SN 1 A	SN B	SN 1 C		SN D	SN E	SN F	SN	SN I	SN J	SN B	SN E
Sutton 4	d		16 11		16 21	16 42					16 41		16 51		17 12						17 11		17 21	17 42	
West Croydon 4	d	16 21	16 26		16 34					16 52	16 56		17 04							17 21	17 26		17 34		
Purley	d								16 45									17 15							
East Croydon	d								16 53					17 10				17 23							
Selhurst 4	d		16 31		16 40				16 57		17 01		17 10	17 16				17 27			17 31		17 40		
Thornton Heath	d		16 33		16 43				16 59		17 03		17 13	17 19				17 29			17 33		17 43		
Norbury	d		16 36		16 46				17 02		17 06		17 16	17 22				17 32			17 36		17 46		
Streatham Common 4	d		16 39		16 49				17 06		17 09		17 19	17 25				17 36			17 39		17 49		
London Bridge	a			←					17 36			←						18 06				←			
Balham 4 ⊖	d	16 51	16 44	16 51	16 55	17 03		17 10		17 21	17 14	17 21	17 25	17 29	17 33				17 40	17 51	17 44	17 51	17 55	18 03	18 10
Wandsworth Common	d	→	16 46	16 53	16 57			17 12		→	17 16	17 23	17 27			←			17 42	→	17 46	17 53	17 57		18 12
Clapham Junction	a		16 50	16 57	17 01	17 07		17 16			17 20	17 27	17 31	17 35	17 37	17 35			17 46		17 50	17 57	18 01	18 07	18 16
Clapham Junction 10	d		16 50	16 57	17 01	17 08		17 16			17 20	17 27	17 31	17 40	17 38	17 40			17 46		17 50	17 57	18 01	18 08	18 16
Imperial Wharf	a													→		17 44									
West Brompton ⊖	a															17 47									
Kensington (Olympia) ⊖	a															17 51									
Shepherd's Bush ⊖	a															17 54									
Battersea Park	d		16 54	17 01	17 05			17 20			17 24	17 31	17 35						17 50		17 54	18 01	18 05		18 20
London Victoria 15 ⊖	a		16 58	17 05	17 09	17 15		17 24			17 28	17 35	17 39		17 45				17 54		17 58	18 05	18 09	18 15	18 24

		SN D		SN F	SN	SN I	SN J	SN 1 K	SN B	SN 1 L	SN D	SN E		SN F	SN	SN I	SN J	SN B	SN E	SN D	SN F	SN		SN I	SN J
Sutton 4	d				17 41		17 51		18 12						18 11		18 21	18 42				18 41			18 51
West Croydon 4	d			17 51	17 56		18 04							18 21	18 26		18 34				18 51	18 56			19 04
Purley	d	17 45									18 15									18 45					
East Croydon	d	17 53						18 10			18 23									18 53					
Selhurst 4	d	17 57			18 01		18 10	18 16			18 27				18 31		18 40			18 57		19 01			19 10
Thornton Heath	d	17 59			18 03		18 13	18 19			18 29				18 33		18 43			18 59		19 03			19 13
Norbury	d	18 02			18 06		18 16	18 22			18 32				18 36		18 46			19 02		19 06			19 16
Streatham Common 4	d	18 06			18 09		18 19	18 25			18 36				18 39		18 49			19 06		19 09			19 19
London Bridge	a	18 36				←					19 06					←				19 36				←	
Balham 4 ⊖	d			18 21	18 14	18 21	18 25	18 29	18 33			18 40		18 51	18 44	18 51	18 55	19 03	19 10		19 21	19 14		19 21	19 25
Wandsworth Common	d			→	18 16	18 23	18 27			←		18 42		→	18 46	18 53	18 57		19 12		→	19 16		19 23	19 27
Clapham Junction	a				18 20	18 27	18 31	18 35	18 37	18 35		18 46			18 50	18 57	19 01	19 07	19 16			19 20		19 27	19 31
Clapham Junction 10	d				18 20	18 27	18 31	18 40	18 38	18 40		18 46			18 50	18 57	19 01	19 08	19 16			19 20		19 27	19 31
Imperial Wharf	a							→		18 44															
West Brompton ⊖	a									18 47															
Kensington (Olympia) ⊖	a									18 51															
Shepherd's Bush ⊖	a									18 54															
Battersea Park	d				18 24	18 31	18 35					18 50			18 54	19 01	19 05		19 20			19 24		19 31	19 35
London Victoria 15 ⊖	a				18 28	18 35	18 39		18 45			18 54			18 58	19 05	19 09	19 15	19 24			19 28		19 35	19 39

A To Milton Keynes Central
B From Epsom
C From East Croydon to Milton Keynes Central
D From Caterham
E From London Bridge
F To London Victoria
G until 22 September
H from 29 September
I From West Croydon
J From Epsom Downs
K To Watford Junction
L From East Croydon to Watford Junction

For faster services between London Victoria, Clapham Junction and East Croydon, refer to Table T175

For other Shepherd's Bush connecting trains, refer to Table T176

Table T170-R

Saturdays
26 May to 8 December

Croydon-Selhurst, Thornton Heath, Norbury, Streatham Common, Balham, Wandsworth Common & Battersea Park - London Victoria

	SN A	SN B	SN C	SN D	SN E	SN	SN F	SN G	SN B	SN C	SN D	SN E	SN	SN F	SN G	SN A	SN B	SN C	SN D	SN E	SN
Sutton d		19 12				19 11		19 21	19 42				19 41		19 51		20 12				20 11
West Croydon d					19 21	19 26		19 34				19 51	19 56		20 04					20 21	20 26
Purley d				19 15							19 45								20 15		
East Croydon d	19 10			19 23							19 53					20 10			20 23		
Selhurst d	19 16			19 27		19 31		19 40			19 57		20 01		20 10	20 16			20 27		20 31
Thornton Heath d	19 19			19 29		19 33		19 43			19 59		20 03		20 13	20 19			20 29		20 33
Norbury d	19 22			19 32		19 36		19 46			20 02		20 06		20 16	20 22			20 32		20 36
Streatham Common d	19 25			19 36		19 39		19 49			20 06		20 09		20 19	20 25			20 36		20 39
London Bridge a				20 06			←				20 36			←					21 06		
Balham d	19 29	19 33	19 40		19 51	19 44	19 51	19 55	20 03	20 10		20 21	20 14	20 21	20 25	20 29	20 33	20 40		20 51	20 44
Wandsworth Common d			19 42		→	19 46	19 53	19 57		20 12		→	20 16	20 23	20 27			20 42		→	20 46
Clapham Junction a	19 35	19 37	19 46			19 50	19 57	20 01	20 07	20 16			20 20	20 27	20 31	20 35	20 37	20 46			20 50
Clapham Junction d	19 36	19 38	19 46			19 50	19 57	20 01	20 08	20 16			20 20	20 27	20 31	20 51	20 38	20 46			20 50
Imperial Wharf a	19 40															→					
West Brompton a	19 43																				
Kensington (Olympia) a	19 47																				
Shepherd's Bush a	19 50																				
Battersea Park d			19 50			19 54	20 01	20 05		20 20			20 24	20 31	20 35			20 50			20 54
London Victoria a		19 45	19 54			19 58	20 05	20 09	20 15	20 24			20 28	20 35	20 39		20 45	20 54			20 58

	SN H	SN F	SN G	SN B	SN C	SN D	SN E	SN	SN F	SN G	SN A	SN B	SN H	SN D	SN C	SN E	SN	SN F	SN G	SN B	SN C	SN D
Sutton d			20 21	20 42				20 41		20 51		21 12					21 11		21 21	21 42		
West Croydon d			20 34				20 51	20 56		21 04						21 21	21 26		21 34			
Purley d						20 45								21 15								21 45
East Croydon d						20 53					21 10			21 23								21 53
Selhurst d			20 40			20 57		21 01		21 10	21 16			21 27			21 31		21 40			21 57
Thornton Heath d			20 43			20 59		21 03		21 13	21 19			21 29			21 33		21 43			21 59
Norbury d			20 46			21 02		21 06		21 16	21 22			21 32			21 36		21 46			22 02
Streatham Common d			20 49			21 06		21 09		21 19	21 25			21 36			21 39		21 49			22 06
London Bridge a		←				21 36			←					22 06				←				22 36
Balham d		20 51	20 55	21 03	21 10		21 21	21 14	21 21	21 25	21 29	21 33			21 40	21 51	21 44	21 51	21 55	22 03	22 10	
Wandsworth Common d	←	20 53	20 57		21 12		→	21 16	21 23	21 27			←		21 42	→	21 46	21 53	21 57		22 12	
Clapham Junction a	20 35	20 57	21 01	21 07	21 16			21 20	21 27	21 31	21 35	21 37	21 35		21 46		21 50	21 57	22 01	22 07	22 16	
Clapham Junction d	20 51	20 57	21 01	21 08	21 16			21 20	21 27	21 31	21 39	21 38	21 39		21 46		21 50	21 57	22 01	22 08	22 16	
Imperial Wharf a	20 56										→		21 43									
West Brompton a	20 59												21 46									
Kensington (Olympia) a	21 02												21 50									
Shepherd's Bush a	21 05												21 53									
Battersea Park d		21 01	21 05		21 20			21 24	21 31	21 35					21 50		21 54	22 01	22 05		22 20	
London Victoria a		21 05	21 09	21 15	21 24			21 28	21 35	21 39		21 45			21 54		21 58	22 05	22 09	22 15	22 24	

	SN E	SN	SN F	SN G	SN A	SN B	SN H	SN D	SN C	SN E	SN	SN F	SN G	SN B	SN C	SN D	SN E	SN	SN F	SN G	SN B	SN C
Sutton d		21 41		21 51		22 12					22 11		22 21	22 42				22 41		22 51	23 12	
West Croydon d	21 51	21 56		22 04						22 21	22 26		22 34				22 51	22 56		23 04		
Purley d								22 15								22 45						
East Croydon d					22 10			22 23								22 53						
Selhurst d		22 01		22 10	22 16			22 27			22 31		22 40			22 57		23 01		23 10		
Thornton Heath d		22 03		22 13	22 19			22 29			22 33		22 43			22 59		23 03		23 13		
Norbury d		22 06		22 16	22 22			22 32			22 36		22 46			23 02		23 06		23 16		
Streatham Common d		22 09		22 19	22 25			22 36			22 39		22 49			23 06		23 09		23 19		
London Bridge a			←					23 06				←				23 36			←			
Balham d	22 21	22 14	22 21	22 25	22 29	22 33			22 40	22 51	22 44	22 51	22 55	23 03	23 10		23 21	23 14	23 21	23 25	23 33	23 40
Wandsworth Common d	→	22 16	22 23	22 27			←		22 42	→	22 46	22 53	22 57		23 12		→	23 16	23 23	23 27		23 42
Clapham Junction a		22 20	22 27	22 31	22 35	22 37	22 35		22 46		22 50	22 57	23 01	23 07	23 16			23 20	23 27	23 31	23 37	23 46
Clapham Junction d		22 20	22 27	22 31	22 39	22 38	22 39		22 46		22 50	22 57	23 01	23 08	23 16			23 20	23 27	23 31	23 39	23 46
Imperial Wharf a					→		22 43															
West Brompton a							22 46															
Kensington (Olympia) a							22 50															
Shepherd's Bush a							22 53															
Battersea Park d		22 24	22 31	22 35					22 50		22 54	23 01	23 05		23 20			23 24	23 31	23 35		23 50
London Victoria a		22 30	22 35	22 39		22 45			22 54		23 00	23 05	23 09	23 15	23 24			23 30	23 35	23 39	23 46	23 54

A To Watford Junction
B From Epsom
C From London Bridge
D From Caterham
E To London Victoria
F From West Croydon
G From Epsom Downs
H From East Croydon to Watford Junction

For faster services between London Victoria, Clapham Junction and East Croydon, refer to Table T175

For other Shepherd's Bush connecting trains, refer to Table T176

Table T170-R

Saturdays
26 May to 8 December

Croydon-Selhurst, Thornton Heath, Norbury, Streatham Common, Balham, Wandsworth Common & Battersea Park - London Victoria

	SN A	SN	SN B
Sutton d			23 21
West Croydon d		23 21	23 34
Purley d	23 15		
East Croydon d	23 23		
Selhurst d	23 27		23 42
Thornton Heath d	23 29		23 44
Norbury d	23 32		23 47
Streatham Common d	23 36		23 50
London Bridge a	00 06		
Balham d		23 51	23 56
Wandsworth Common d		23 53	23 58
Clapham Junction a		23 57	00 01
Clapham Junction d		23 57	00 02
Imperial Wharf a			
West Brompton a			
Kensington (Olympia) a			
Shepherd's Bush a			
Battersea Park d		00 01	00 05
London Victoria a		00 05	00 09

Sundays
20 May to 2 December

	SN C	SN D	SN E	SN F	SN	SN	SN G	SN H	SN I	SN H	SN	SN	SN	SN	TL J	SN	SN	SN	SN	TL J	SN	SN
Sutton d								06 53		07 14		07 09			07 44		07 39			08 14		08 09
West Croydon d							06 59	07 07				07 23		07 31			07 53		08 03			08 22
Purley d				05 23																		
East Croydon d				05 30		06 44					07 14					07 44					08 14	
Selhurst d				05 33	06 27	06 47		07 12			07 17	07 28	07 41			07 47	07 58	08 11			08 17	08 28
Thornton Heath d				05 36	06 30	06 49		07 14			07 19	07 30	07 43			07 49	08 00	08 13			08 19	08 30
Norbury d				05 39	06 33	06 52		07 17			07 22	07 33	07 46			07 52	08 03	08 16			08 22	08 33
Streatham Common d				05 42	06 36	06 55		07 20			07 25	07 36	07 49			07 55	08 06	08 19			08 25	08 36
London Bridge a						07 22			←		07 52					08 22					08 53	
Balham d			00 10	05 47	06 41		07 28	07 25	07 28	07 35		07 41	07 54	07 59	08 05		08 11	08 24	08 29	08 35		08 41
Wandsworth Common d			00 12		06 43		→	07 27	07 30			07 43	07 56	08 01			08 13	08 26	08 31			08 43
Clapham Junction a			00 16	05 51	06 47			07 30	07 34	07 40		07 46	08 00	08 04	08 10		08 16	08 30	08 35	08 41		08 46
Clapham Junction d		00 02	00 16	05 51	06 47			07 31	07 34	07 41		07 47	08 01	08 05	08 11		08 17	08 32	08 35	08 42		08 47
Imperial Wharf a																						
West Brompton a																						
Kensington (Olympia) a																						
Shepherd's Bush a																						
Battersea Park d	00 01	00 05	00 20	05 55	06 51			07 34	07 38			07 50	08 05	08 08			08 20	08 36	08 39			08 50
London Victoria a	00 05	00 09	00 24	05 59	06 55			07 39	07 42	07 48		07 55	08 09	08 13	08 19		08 25	08 40	08 43	08 49		08 55

	SN H	SN	SN	SN	SN	SN H	SN G	SN B	SN I	SN	SN	SN H	SN G	SN B	SN I	and at the same minutes past each hour until	SN	SN	SN H	SN G	SN B	SN I	SN
Sutton d	08 26				08 39	08 56		08 51			09 09	09 26		09 21				11 39	11 56		11 51		
West Croydon d			08 33		08 52		09 01	09 04			09 22		09 31	09 34				11 52		12 01	12 04		
Purley d																							
East Croydon d				08 44						09 14							11 44						12 14
Selhurst d		08 41		08 47	08 57			09 11		09 17	09 27			09 41			11 47	11 57			12 11		12 17
Thornton Heath d		08 43		08 49	08 59			09 13		09 19	09 29			09 43			11 49	11 59			12 13		12 19
Norbury d		08 46		08 52	09 02			09 16		09 22	09 32			09 46			11 52	12 02			12 16		12 22
Streatham Common d		08 49		08 55	09 05			09 19		09 25	09 35			09 49			11 55	12 05			12 19		12 25
London Bridge a				09 22					←	09 52					←		12 22					←	12 52
Balham d	08 49	08 54	08 58		09 10	09 17	09 28	09 24	09 28		09 40	09 47	09 58	09 54	09 58			12 10	12 17	12 28	12 24	12 28	
Wandsworth Common d		08 56	09 00		09 12		→	09 26	09 30		09 42		→	09 56	10 00			12 12		→	12 26	12 30	
Clapham Junction a	08 53	09 00	09 03		09 16	09 21		09 30	09 33		09 46	09 51		10 00	10 03			12 16	12 21		12 30	12 33	
Clapham Junction d	08 53	09 01	09 04		09 17	09 22		09 31	09 34		09 47	09 52		10 01	10 04			12 17	12 22		12 31	12 34	
Imperial Wharf a																							
West Brompton a																							
Kensington (Olympia) a																							
Shepherd's Bush a																							
Battersea Park d		09 04	09 07		09 20			09 34	09 37		09 50			10 04	10 07			12 20			12 34	12 37	
London Victoria a	09 00	09 09	09 12		09 25	09 29		09 39	09 42		09 55	09 59		10 09	10 12			12 25	12 29		12 39	12 42	

A From Caterham
B From Epsom Downs
C not 20 May. From West Croydon
D not 20 May. From Epsom Downs
E not 20 May. From London Bridge
F From Brighton
G To London Victoria
H From Epsom
I From West Croydon
J From Dorking

For faster services between London Victoria, Clapham Junction and East Croydon, refer to Table T175

For other Shepherd's Bush connecting trains, refer to Table T176

Table T170-R

Sundays

20 May to 2 December

Croydon-Selhurst, Thornton Heath, Norbury, Streatham Common, Balham, Wandsworth Common & Battersea Park - London Victoria

		SN	SN A	SN B	SN C	SN D	SN	SN	SN A	SN B	SN C	SN D	SN	SN	SN A	SN B	SN C	SN D	SN	SN	SN A	SN B	SN C
Sutton	d	12 09	12 26		12 21			12 39	12 56		12 51			13 09	13 26		13 21			13 39	13 56		13 51
West Croydon	d	12 22		12 31	12 34			12 52		13 01	13 04			13 22		13 31	13 34			13 52		14 01	14 04
Purley	d																						
East Croydon	d						12 44						13 14						13 44				
Selhurst	d	12 27			12 41		12 47	12 57			13 11		13 17	13 27			13 41		13 47	13 57			14 11
Thornton Heath	d	12 29			12 43		12 49	12 59			13 14		13 19	13 29			13 43		13 49	13 59			14 13
Norbury	d	12 32			12 46		12 52	13 02			13 17		13 22	13 32			13 46		13 52	14 02			14 16
Streatham Common	d	12 35			12 49		12 55	13 05			13 19		13 25	13 35			13 49		13 55	14 05			14 19
London Bridge	a					←	13 22					←	13 52					←	14 22				
Balham	d	12 40	12 47	12 58	12 54	12 58		13 10	13 17	13 28	13 24	13 28		13 40	13 47	13 58	13 54	13 58		14 10	14 17	14 28	14 24
Wandsworth Common	d	12 42		→	12 56	13 00		13 12		→	13 26	13 30		13 42		→	13 56	14 00		14 12		→	14 26
Clapham Junction	a	12 46	12 51		13 00	13 03		13 16	13 21		13 30	13 33		13 46	13 51		14 00	14 03		14 16	14 21		14 30
Clapham Junction	d	12 47	12 52		13 01	13 04		13 17	13 22		13 31	13 34		13 47	13 52		14 01	14 04		14 17	14 22		14 31
Imperial Wharf	a																						
West Brompton	a																						
Kensington (Olympia)	a																						
Shepherd's Bush	a																						
Battersea Park	d	12 50			13 04	13 07		13 20			13 34	13 37		13 50			14 04	14 07		14 20			14 34
London Victoria	a	12 55	12 59		13 09	13 12		13 25	13 29		13 39	13 42		13 55	13 59		14 09	14 12		14 25	14 29		14 39

		SN D	SN	SN	SN A	SN B	SN C	SN D	SN	SN	SN A	SN B	SN C	SN D	SN	SN	SN A	SN B	SN C	SN D	SN	SN
Sutton	d			14 09	14 26		14 21			14 39	14 56		14 51			15 09	15 26		15 21			15 39
West Croydon	d			14 22		14 31	14 34			14 52		15 01	15 04			15 22		15 31	15 34			15 52
Purley	d																					
East Croydon	d		14 14						14 44						15 14						15 44	
Selhurst	d		14 17	14 27			14 41		14 47	14 57			15 11		15 17	15 27			15 41		15 47	15 57
Thornton Heath	d		14 19	14 29			14 43		14 49	14 59			15 13		15 19	15 29			15 43		15 49	15 59
Norbury	d		14 22	14 32			14 46		14 52	15 02			15 16		15 22	15 32			15 46		15 52	16 02
Streatham Common	d		14 25	14 35			14 49		14 55	15 05			15 19		15 25	15 35			15 49		15 55	16 05
London Bridge	a	←	14 52					←	15 22					←	15 52					←	16 22	
Balham	d	14 28		14 40	14 47	14 58	14 54	14 58		15 10	15 17	15 28	15 24	15 28		15 40	15 47	15 58	15 54	15 58		16 10
Wandsworth Common	d	14 30		14 42		→	14 56	15 00		15 12		→	15 26	15 30		15 42		→	15 56	16 00		16 12
Clapham Junction	a	14 33		14 46	14 51		15 00	15 03		15 16	15 21		15 30	15 33		15 46	15 51		16 00	16 03		16 16
Clapham Junction	d	14 34		14 47	14 52		15 01	15 04		15 17	15 22		15 31	15 34		15 47	15 52		16 01	16 04		16 17
Imperial Wharf	a																					
West Brompton	a																					
Kensington (Olympia)	a																					
Shepherd's Bush	a																					
Battersea Park	d	14 37		14 50			15 04	15 07		15 20			15 34	15 37		15 50			16 04	16 07		16 20
London Victoria	a	14 42		14 55	14 59		15 09	15 12		15 25	15 29		15 39	15 42		15 55	15 59		16 09	16 12		16 25

		SN A	SN B	SN C	SN D	SN	SN	SN A	SN B	SN C	SN D	SN	SN	SN A	SN B	SN C	SN D	SN	SN	SN A	SN B	SN C	SN D
Sutton	d	15 56		15 51			16 09	16 26		16 21			16 39	16 56		16 51			17 09	17 26		17 21	
West Croydon	d		16 01	16 04			16 22		16 31	16 34			16 52		17 01	17 04			17 22		17 31	17 34	
Purley	d																						
East Croydon	d					16 14						16 44						17 14					
Selhurst	d			16 11		16 17	16 27			16 41		16 47	16 57			17 11		17 17	17 27			17 41	
Thornton Heath	d			16 14		16 19	16 29			16 43		16 49	16 59			17 14		17 19	17 29			17 43	
Norbury	d			16 17		16 22	16 32			16 46		16 52	17 02			17 17		17 22	17 32			17 46	
Streatham Common	d			16 19		16 25	16 35			16 49		16 55	17 05			17 19		17 25	17 35			17 49	
London Bridge	a				←	16 52					←	17 22					←	17 52					←
Balham	d	16 17	16 28	16 24	16 28		16 40	16 47	16 58	16 54	16 58		17 10	17 17	17 28	17 24	17 28		17 40	17 47	17 58	17 54	17 58
Wandsworth Common	d		→	16 26	16 30		16 42		→	16 56	17 00		17 12		→	17 26	17 30		17 42		→	17 56	18 00
Clapham Junction	a	16 21		16 30	16 33		16 46	16 51		17 00	17 03		17 16	17 21		17 30	17 33		17 46	17 51		18 00	18 03
Clapham Junction	d	16 22		16 31	16 34		16 47	16 52		17 01	17 04		17 17	17 22		17 31	17 34		17 47	17 52		18 01	18 04
Imperial Wharf	a																						
West Brompton	a																						
Kensington (Olympia)	a																						
Shepherd's Bush	a																						
Battersea Park	d			16 34	16 37		16 50			17 04	17 07		17 20			17 34	17 37		17 50			18 04	18 07
London Victoria	a	16 29		16 39	16 42		16 55	16 59		17 09	17 12		17 25	17 29		17 39	17 42		17 55	17 59		18 09	18 12

		SN	SN	SN A	SN B	SN C	SN D	SN	SN	SN A	SN B	SN C	SN D	SN	SN	SN A	SN B	SN C	SN D	SN	SN	SN A
Sutton	d		17 39	17 56		17 51			18 09	18 28		18 21			18 39	18 56		18 51			19 09	19 26
West Croydon	d		17 52		18 01	18 04			18 22		18 31	18 34			18 52		19 01	19 04			19 22	
Purley	d																					
East Croydon	d	17 44						18 14						18 44						19 14		
Selhurst	d	17 47	17 57			18 11		18 17	18 27			18 41		18 47	18 57			19 11		19 17	19 27	
Thornton Heath	d	17 49	17 59			18 13		18 19	18 29			18 43		18 49	18 59			19 13		19 19	19 29	
Norbury	d	17 52	18 02			18 16		18 22	18 32			18 46		18 52	19 02			19 16		19 22	19 32	
Streatham Common	d	17 55	18 05			18 19		18 25	18 35			18 49		18 55	19 05			19 19		19 25	19 35	
London Bridge	a	18 22					←	18 52					←	19 22					←	19 52		
Balham	d		18 10	18 17	18 28	18 24	18 28		18 40	18 47	18 58	18 54	18 58		19 10	19 17	19 28	19 24	19 28		19 40	19 47
Wandsworth Common	d		18 12		→	18 26	18 30		18 42		→	18 56	19 00		19 12		→	19 26	19 30		19 42	
Clapham Junction	a		18 16	18 21		18 30	18 33		18 46	18 51		19 00	19 03		19 16	19 21		19 30	19 33		19 46	19 51
Clapham Junction	d		18 17	18 22		18 31	18 34		18 47	18 52		19 01	19 04		19 17	19 22		19 31	19 34		19 47	19 52
Imperial Wharf	a																					
West Brompton	a																					
Kensington (Olympia)	a																					
Shepherd's Bush	a																					
Battersea Park	d		18 20			18 34	18 37		18 50			19 04	19 07		19 20			19 34	19 37		19 50	
London Victoria	a		18 25	18 29		18 39	18 42		18 55	18 59		19 09	19 12		19 25	19 29		19 39	19 42		19 55	19 59

and at the same minutes past each hour until

A From Epsom
B To London Victoria
C From Epsom Downs
D From West Croydon

For faster services between London Victoria, Clapham Junction and East Croydon, refer to Table T175

For other Shepherd's Bush connecting trains, refer to Table T176

Table T170-R

Sundays

20 May to 2 December

Croydon-Selhurst, Thornton Heath, Norbury, Streatham Common, Balham, Wandsworth Common & Battersea Park - London Victoria

		SN A	SN B	SN C	SN	SN	SN D	SN A	SN B	SN C	SN	SN	SN D	SN A	SN B	SN C	SN	SN	SN D	SN A	SN B	SN C	SN
Sutton	d		21 21			21 39	21 56		21 51			22 09	22 26		22 21			22 39	22 56		22 51		23 09
West Croydon	d	21 31	21 34			21 52		22 01	22 04			22 22		22 31	22 34			22 52		23 01	23 04		23 22
Purley	d																						
East Croydon	d				21 44						22 14						22 42						
Selhurst	d		21 41		21 47	21 57			22 11		22 17	22 27			22 41		22 47	22 57			23 11		23 27
Thornton Heath	d		21 43		21 49	21 59			22 13		22 19	22 29			22 43		22 49	22 59			23 13		23 29
Norbury	d		21 46		21 52	22 02			22 16		22 22	22 32			22 46		22 52	23 02			23 16		23 32
Streatham Common	d		21 49		21 55	22 05			22 19		22 25	22 35			22 50		22 56	23 05			23 19		23 35
London Bridge	a			←	22 22					←	22 52					←	23 22					←	
Balham	d	21 58	21 54	21 58		22 10	22 17	22 28	22 24	22 28		22 40	22 47	22 58	22 55	22 58		23 10	23 17	23 28	23 24	23 28	23 40
Wandsworth Common	d	→	21 56	22 00		22 12		→	22 26	22 30		22 42		→	22 57	23 00		23 12		→	23 26	23 30	23 42
Clapham Junction	a		22 00	22 03		22 16	22 21		22 30	22 33		22 46	22 51		23 00	23 03		23 16	23 21		23 30	23 33	23 46
Clapham Junction	d		22 01	22 04		22 17	22 22		22 31	22 34		22 47	22 52		23 01	23 04		23 17	23 22		23 31	23 34	23 47
Imperial Wharf	a																						
West Brompton	a																						
Kensington (Olympia)	a																						
Shepherd's Bush	a																						
Battersea Park	d		22 04	22 07		22 20			22 34	22 37		22 50			23 04	23 07		23 20			23 34	23 37	23 50
London Victoria	a		22 09	22 12		22 25	22 29		22 39	22 42		22 55	22 59		23 09	23 12		23 25	23 29		23 39	23 43	23 55

		SN	TL E	SN F
Sutton	d		23 46	
West Croydon	d	23 31		
Purley	d			
East Croydon	d			23 55
Selhurst	d			23 59
Thornton Heath	d			
Norbury	d			
Streatham Common	d			
London Bridge	a			
Balham	d	23 58	00 06	
Wandsworth Common	d	00 01	00 08	
Clapham Junction	a	00 05	00 12	00 15
Clapham Junction	d	00 05	00 13	00 16
Imperial Wharf	a			
West Brompton	a			
Kensington (Olympia)	a			
Shepherd's Bush	a			
Battersea Park	d	00 09	00 16	
London Victoria	a	00 13	00 21	00 23

A To London Victoria
B From Epsom Downs
C From West Croydon
D From Epsom
E From Dorking
F From East Grinstead

For faster services between London Victoria, Clapham Junction and East Croydon, refer to Table T175

For other Shepherd's Bush connecting trains, refer to Table T176

Table T171-F

Mondays to Fridays

21 May to 7 December

London Victoria - Streatham Hill, West Norwood, Gipsy Hill and Crystal Palace - Norwood Junction & Croydon

Miles	Miles			SN MO	SN MX	SN MX	SN MO	SN MX	SN	SN	SN	SN	SN	SN	SN	SN	SN	SN	SN	SN	SN	SN	SN
0	—	London Victoria 15 ⊖	d									06 06	06 20		06 36	06 50		07 06	07 20		07 36	07 50	
1¾	—	Battersea Park 4	d				00 01					06 10	06 24		06 40	06 54		07 10	07 24		07 40	07 54	
—	—	Clapham Junction 10	d		00 04		00 06					06 14	06 28		06 44	06 58		07 14	07 28		07 44	07 58	
4	—	Wandsworth Common	d		00 07		00 09					06 17	06 31		06 47	07 01		07 17	07 31		07 47	08 01	
5	—	Balham 4 ⊖	d		00 10		00 12					06 20	06 34		06 50	07 04		07 20	07 35		07 50	08 04	
6	—	**Streatham Hill**	d		00 15		00 16		05 39	06 09		06 25	06 39		06 55	07 09		07 25	07 39		07 55	08 09	
—	0	London Bridge	d					00 01			06 01			06 31			07 01			07 31			08 01
7¼	6¾	**West Norwood 4**	d		00 18		00 19	00 24	05 42	06 12	06 24	06 28	06 42	06 54	06 58	07 12	07 24	07 28	07 42	07 54	07 58	08 12	08 24
8¼	7¾	**Gipsy Hill**	d		00 21		00 22	00 27	05 45	06 15	06 27	06 31	06 45	06 57	07 01	07 15	07 27	07 31	07 45	07 57	08 01	08 15	08 27
9	8½	**Crystal Palace 4**	a		00 25		00 26	00 31	05 49	06 19	06 31	06 35	06 49	07 01	07 05	07 19	07 31	07 35	07 49	08 01	08 05	08 19	08 31
—	—	Crystal Palace	d		00 25		00 26		05 52	06 22		06 38	06 52		07 08	07 22		07 38	07 52		08 08	08 22	
—	—	Sydenham	a		00 29				05 56	06 26			06 56			07 26			07 56			08 26	
—	—	Forest Hill	a		00 32				05 58	06 28			06 58			07 28			07 58			08 28	
—	—	Honor Oak Park	a		00 35				06 01	06 31			07 01			07 31			08 01			08 31	
—	—	Brockley	a		00 37				06 03	06 33			07 03			07 33			08 03			08 33	
—	—	New Cross Gate	a		00 39				06 05	06 35			07 05			07 35			08 05			08 35	
—	—	London Bridge	a		00 47				06 18	06 48			07 18			07 48			08 18			08 48	
—	—	Norwood Junction 2	a				00 31					06 42			07 12			07 42			08 12		
—	—		d	00 01		00 10						06 46			07 16			07 46			08 16		
12¼	—	West Croydon	a	00 08		00 16						06 52			07 22			07 52			08 22		
16¾	—	Sutton	a																				

		SN	SN	SN	SN	SN	SN	SN	SN	SN	SN	SN	SN	SN	SN	SN	SN	SN	SN	SN	SN	SN	SN
London Victoria 15 ⊖	d	08 06	08 20		08 36	08 50		09 07	09 20		09 36	09 50		10 06	10 20		10 36	10 50		11 06	11 20		11 36
Battersea Park 4	d	08 10	08 24		08 40	08 54		09 12	09 24		09 40	09 54		10 10	10 24		10 40	10 54		11 10	11 24		11 40
Clapham Junction 10	d	08 14	08 28		08 44	08 58		09 16	09 28		09 45	09 58		10 14	10 28		10 44	10 58		11 14	11 28		11 45
Wandsworth Common	d	08 17	08 31		08 47	09 01		09 19	09 31		09 48	10 01		10 17	10 31		10 47	11 01		11 17	11 31		11 48
Balham 4 ⊖	d	08 20	08 34		08 50	09 04		09 21	09 34		09 50	10 04		10 20	10 34		10 50	11 04		11 20	11 34		11 50
Streatham Hill	d	08 25	08 39		08 55	09 09		09 25	09 39		09 55	10 09		10 25	10 39		10 55	11 09		11 25	11 39		11 55
London Bridge	d			08 31			09 01			09 31			10 01			10 31			11 01			11 31	
West Norwood 4	d	08 28	08 42	08 54	08 58	09 12	09 24	09 29	09 42	09 54	09 58	10 12	10 24	10 28	10 42	10 54	10 58	11 12	11 24	11 28	11 42	11 54	11 58
Gipsy Hill	d	08 31	08 45	08 57	09 01	09 15	09 27	09 32	09 45	09 57	10 01	10 15	10 27	10 31	10 45	10 57	11 01	11 15	11 27	11 31	11 45	11 57	12 01
Crystal Palace 4	a	08 35	08 49	09 01	09 05	09 19	09 31	09 35	09 49	10 01	10 05	10 19	10 31	10 35	10 49	11 01	11 05	11 19	11 31	11 35	11 49	12 01	12 05
Crystal Palace	d	08 38	08 52		09 08	09 22		09 38	09 52		10 08	10 22		10 38	10 52		11 08	11 22		11 38	11 52		12 08
Sydenham	a		08 56			09 26			09 56			10 26			10 56			11 26			11 56		
Forest Hill	a		08 58			09 28			09 58			10 28			10 58			11 28			11 58		
Honor Oak Park	a		09 01			09 31			10 01			10 31			11 01			11 31			12 01		
Brockley	a		09 03			09 33			10 03			10 33			11 03			11 33			12 03		
New Cross Gate	a		09 05			09 35			10 05			10 35			11 05			11 35			12 05		
London Bridge	a		09 18			09 48			10 17			10 47			11 17			11 47			12 17		
Norwood Junction 2	a	08 42			09 12			09 42			10 12			10 42			11 12			11 42			12 12
	d	08 46			09 16			09 46			10 16			10 51			11 15			11 51			12 15
West Croydon	a	08 52			09 22			09 52			10 22			10 57			11 21			11 57			12 21
Sutton	a																						

		SN	SN	SN	SN	SN	SN MWFO	SN TThO	SN	SN	SN	SN	SN	SN	SN	SN	SN	SN	SN	SN	SN	SN
London Victoria 15 ⊖	d	11 50		12 06	12 20		12 36	12 36	12 50		13 06	13 20		13 36	13 50		14 06	14 20		14 36	14 50	
Battersea Park 4	d	11 54		12 10	12 24		12 40	12 40	12 54		13 10	13 24		13 40	13 54		14 10	14 24		14 40	14 54	
Clapham Junction 10	d	11 58		12 14	12 28		12 44	12 45	12 58		13 14	13 28		13 44	13 58		14 14	14 28		14 44	14 58	
Wandsworth Common	d	12 01		12 17	12 31		12 47	12 48	13 01		13 17	13 31		13 47	14 01		14 17	14 31		14 47	15 01	
Balham 4 ⊖	d	12 04		12 20	12 34		12 50	12 51	13 04		13 20	13 34		13 50	14 04		14 20	14 34		14 50	15 04	
Streatham Hill	d	12 09		12 25	12 39		12 55	12 56	13 09		13 25	13 39		13 55	14 09		14 25	14 39		14 55	15 09	
London Bridge	d		12 01			12 31				13 01			13 31			14 01			14 31			15 01
West Norwood 4	d	12 12	12 24	12 28	12 42	12 54	12 58	12 59	13 12	13 24	13 28	13 42	13 54	13 58	14 12	14 24	14 28	14 42	14 54	14 58	15 12	15 24
Gipsy Hill	d	12 15	12 27	12 31	12 45	12 57	13 01	13 02	13 15	13 27	13 31	13 45	13 57	14 01	14 15	14 27	14 31	14 45	14 57	15 01	15 15	15 27
Crystal Palace 4	a	12 19	12 31	12 35	12 49	13 01	13 05	13 06	13 19	13 31	13 35	13 49	14 01	14 05	14 19	14 31	14 35	14 49	15 01	15 05	15 19	15 31
Crystal Palace	d	12 22		12 38	12 52		13 08	13 09	13 22		13 38	13 52		14 08	14 22		14 38	14 52		15 08	15 22	
Sydenham	a	12 26			12 56				13 26			13 56			14 26			14 56			15 26	
Forest Hill	a	12 28			12 58				13 28			13 58			14 28			14 58			15 28	
Honor Oak Park	a	12 31			13 01				13 31			14 01			14 31			15 01			15 31	
Brockley	a	12 33			13 03				13 33			14 03			14 33			15 03			15 33	
New Cross Gate	a	12 35			13 05				13 35			14 05			14 35			15 05			15 35	
London Bridge	a	12 47			13 17				13 47			14 17			14 47			15 17			15 47	
Norwood Junction 2	a			12 42			13 12	13 13			13 42			14 12			14 42			15 12		
	d			12 51			13 15	13 22			13 51			14 15			14 51			15 15		
West Croydon	a			12 57			13 21	13 27			13 57			14 21			14 57			15 21		
Sutton	a																					

For complete service between London Victoria and Balham, refer to Table T170

For faster services between London Victoria, Clapham Junction and East Croydon, refer to Table T175

For Shepherd's Bush connecting trains, refer to Table T176

Table T171-F

Mondays to Fridays

21 May to 7 December

London Victoria - Streatham Hill, West Norwood, Gipsy Hill and Crystal Palace - Norwood Junction & Croydon

		SN	SN	SN	SN	SN	SN	SN	SN	SN	SN	SN	SN	SN	SN	SN	SN	SN	SN	SN	SN	SN	SN
London Victoria 15 ⊖	d	15 06	15 20		15 36	15 50			16 06	16 20		16 36	16 50		17 06	17 20		17 36	17 50		18 06	18 20	
Battersea Park 4	d	15 10	15 24		15 40	15 54			16 10	16 24		16 40	16 54		17 10	17 24		17 40	17 54		18 10	18 24	
Clapham Junction 10	d	15 14	15 28		15 44	15 58			16 14	16 28		16 44	16 58		17 14	17 28		17 44	17 58		18 14	18 28	
Wandsworth Common	d	15 17	15 31		15 47	16 01			16 17	16 31		16 47	17 01		17 17	17 31		17 47	18 01		18 17	18 31	
Balham 4 ⊖	d	15 20	15 34		15 50	16 04			16 20	16 34		16 50	17 04		17 20	17 34		17 50	18 04		18 20	18 34	
Streatham Hill	d	15 25	15 39		15 55	16 09		16 17	16 25	16 39		16 55	17 09		17 25	17 39		17 55	18 09		18 25	18 39	
London Bridge	d			15 31			16 01	16a45			16 31			17 01			17 31			18 01			18 31
West Norwood 4	d	15 28	15 42	15 54	15 58	16 12	16 24		16 28	16 42	16 54	16 58	17 12	17 24	17 28	17 42	17 54	17 58	18 12	18 24	18 28	18 42	18 54
Gipsy Hill	d	15 31	15 45	15 57	16 01	16 15	16 27		16 31	16 45	16 57	17 01	17 15	17 27	17 31	17 45	17 57	18 01	18 15	18 27	18 31	18 45	18 57
Crystal Palace 4	a	15 35	15 49	16 01	16 05	16 19	16 31		16 35	16 49	17 01	17 05	17 19	17 31	17 35	17 49	18 01	18 05	18 19	18 31	18 35	18 49	19 01
Crystal Palace	d	15 38	15 52		16 08	16 22			16 38	16 52		17 08	17 22		17 38	17 52		18 08	18 22		18 38	18 52	
Sydenham	a		15 56			16 26				16 56			17 26			17 56			18 26			18 56	
Forest Hill	a		15 58			16 28				16 58			17 28			17 58			18 28			18 58	
Honor Oak Park	a		16 01			16 31				17 01			17 31			18 01			18 31			19 01	
Brockley	a		16 03			16 33				17 03			17 33			18 03			18 33			19 03	
New Cross Gate	a		16 05			16 35				17 05			17 35			18 05			18 35			19 05	
London Bridge	a		16 18			16 48				17 18			17 48			18 18			18 48			19 18	
Norwood Junction 2	a	15 42			16 12				16 42			17 12			17 42			18 12			18 42		
	d	15 51			16 15				16 46			17 16			17 46			18 16			18 46		
West Croydon	a	15 57			16 21				16 52			17 22			17 52			18 22			18 52		
Sutton	a																						

		SN	SN	SN	SN	SN	SN	SN	SN	SN	SN	SN	SN	SN	SN	SN	SN	SN	SN	SN	SN	SN
London Victoria 15 ⊖	d	18 36	18 50		19 06	19 20		19 36	19 50		20 06	20 20		20 36	20 50		21 06	21 20		21 36	21 50	
Battersea Park 4	d	18 40	18 54		19 10	19 24		19 40	19 54		20 10	20 24		20 40	20 54		21 10	21 24		21 40	21 54	
Clapham Junction 10	d	18 44	18 58		19 14	19 28		19 44	19 58		20 14	20 28		20 45	20 58		21 14	21 28		21 45	22 00	
Wandsworth Common	d	18 47	19 01		19 17	19 31		19 47	20 01		20 17	20 31		20 48	21 01		21 17	21 31		21 48	22 03	
Balham 4 ⊖	d	18 50	19 04		19 20	19 34		19 50	20 04		20 20	20 34		20 51	21 04		21 20	21 34		21 51	22 06	
Streatham Hill	d	18 55	19 09		19 25	19 39		19 55	20 09		20 25	20 39		20 55	21 09		21 25	21 39		21 56	22 10	
London Bridge	d			19 01			19 31			20 01			20 31			21 01			21 31			22 01
West Norwood 4	d	18 58	19 12	19 24	19 28	19 42	19 54	19 58	20 12	20 24	20 28	20 42	20 54	20 58	21 12	21 24	21 28	21 42	21 54	21 59	22 14	22 24
Gipsy Hill	d	19 01	19 15	19 27	19 31	19 45	19 57	20 01	20 15	20 27	20 31	20 45	20 57	21 01	21 15	21 27	21 31	21 45	21 57	22 02	22 17	22 27
Crystal Palace 4	a	19 05	19 19	19 31	19 35	19 49	20 01	20 05	20 19	20 31	20 35	20 49	21 01	21 05	21 19	21 31	21 35	21 49	22 01	22 06	22 19	22 31
Crystal Palace	d	19 08	19 22		19 38	19 52		20 08	20 22		20 38	20 52		21 08	21 22		21 38	21 52		22 09	22 22	
Sydenham	a		19 26			19 56			20 26			20 56			21 26			21 56			22 26	
Forest Hill	a		19 28			19 58			20 28			20 58			21 28			21 58			22 28	
Honor Oak Park	a		19 31			20 01			20 31			21 01			21 31			22 01			22 31	
Brockley	a		19 33			20 03			20 33			21 03			21 33			22 03			22 33	
New Cross Gate	a		19 35			20 05			20 35			21 05			21 35			22 05			22 35	
London Bridge	a		19 48			20 18			20 47			21 17			21 47			22 17			22 47	
Norwood Junction 2	a	19 12			19 42			20 12			20 42			21 12			21 42			22 13		
	d	19 15			19 45			20 15			20 51			21 15			21 45			22 22		
West Croydon	a	19 21			19 51			20 21			20 57			21 21			21 51			22 27		
Sutton	a																					

		SN	SN	SN	SN	SN	SN	SN	SN	SN	SN	SN
London Victoria 15 ⊖	d	22 06	22 20		22 36	22 50		23 06	23 20	23 32		23 56
Battersea Park 4	d	22 10	22 24		22 40	22 54		23 10	23 24			
Clapham Junction 10	d	22 14	22 28		22 45	22 58		23 14	23 28	23 39		00 04
Wandsworth Common	d	22 17	22 31		22 48	23 01		23 17	23 31			00 07
Balham 4 ⊖	d	22 20	22 34		22 50	23 04		23 20	23 34	23 44		00 10
Streatham Hill	d	22 25	22 39		22 55	23 09		23 25	23 39	23 48		00 15
London Bridge	d			22 31			23 01				23 31	
West Norwood 4	d	22 28	22 42	22 54	22 58	23 12	23 24	23 28	23 42	23 51	23 54	00 18
Gipsy Hill	d	22 31	22 45	22 57	23 01	23 15	23 27	23 31	23 45	23 54	23 57	00 21
Crystal Palace 4	a	22 35	22 49	23 01	23 05	23 19	23 31	23 36	23 49	23 58	00 01	00 25
Crystal Palace	d	22 38	22 52		23 08	23 22		23 38	23 53	23 58		00 25
Sydenham	a		22 56			23 26			23 57			00 29
Forest Hill	a		22 58			23 28			23 59			00 32
Honor Oak Park	a		23 01			23 31			00 03			00 35
Brockley	a		23 03			23 33			00 05			00 37
New Cross Gate	a		23 05			23 35			00 07			00 39
London Bridge	a		23 17			23 47			00 15			00 47
Norwood Junction 2	a	22 42			23 12			23 42		00 03		
	d	22 45			23 15			23 46		00 10		
West Croydon	a	22 51			23 21			23 52		00 16		
Sutton	a											

For complete service between London Victoria and Balham, refer to Table T170

For faster services between London Victoria, Clapham Junction and East Croydon, refer to Table T175

For Shepherd's Bush connecting trains, refer to Table T176

Table T171-F

Saturdays
26 May to 8 December

London Victoria - Streatham Hill, West Norwood, Gipsy Hill and Crystal Palace - Norwood Junction & Croydon

		SN	SN	SN	SN	SN	SN	SN	SN	SN	SN	SN	SN	SN	SN	SN		SN	SN	SN	SN	SN	SN
London Victoria 15 ⊖	d				00 10	00 25				06 20	06 36	06 50		07 06	07 20			12 36	12 50		13 06	13 20	
Battersea Park 4	d				00 14	00 29				06 24	06 40	06 54		07 10	07 24			12 40	12 54		13 10	13 24	
Clapham Junction 10	d	00 04			00 18	00 33				06 28	06 44	06 58		07 14	07 28			12 44	12 58		13 14	13 28	
Wandsworth Common	d	00 07			00 21	00 36				06 31	06 47	07 01		07 17	07 31			12 47	13 01		13 17	13 31	
Balham 4 ⊖	d	00 10			00 24	00 39				06 34	06 50	07 04		07 20	07 34			12 50	13 04		13 20	13 34	
Streatham Hill	d	00 15			00 29	00 44		05 39	06 09	06 39	06 55	07 09		07 25	07 39			12 55	13 09		13 25	13 39	
London Bridge	d		00 01				00 31						07 01			07 31	and at the same minutes past each hour until			13 01			13 31
West Norwood 4	d	00 18	00 24		00 32	00 47	00 54	05 42	06 12	06 42	06 58	07 12	07 24	07 28	07 42	07 54		12 58	13 12	13 24	13 28	13 42	13 54
Gipsy Hill	d	00 21	00 27		00 35	00 50	00 57	05 45	06 15	06 45	07 01	07 15	07 27	07 31	07 45	07 57		13 01	13 15	13 27	13 31	13 45	13 57
Crystal Palace 4	a	00 25	00 31		00 39	00 54	01 01	05 49	06 19	06 49	07 05	07 19	07 31	07 35	07 49	08 01		13 05	13 19	13 31	13 35	13 49	14 01
Crystal Palace	d	00 25			00 40	00 55	01 04	05 52	06 22	06 52	07 08	07 22		07 38	07 52			13 08	13 22		13 38	13 52	
Sydenham	a	00 29						05 56	06 26	06 56		07 26			07 56				13 26			13 56	
Forest Hill	a	00 32						05 58	06 28	06 58		07 28			07 58				13 28			13 58	
Honor Oak Park	a	00 35						06 01	06 31	07 01		07 31			08 01				13 31			14 01	
Brockley	a	00 37						06 03	06 33	07 03		07 33			08 03				13 33			14 03	
New Cross Gate	a	00 39						06 05	06 35	07 05		07 35			08 05				13 35			14 05	
London Bridge	a	00 47						06 13	06 44	07 14		07 44			08 14				13 44			14 14	
Norwood Junction 2	a				00 46	01 02	01 10				07 12			07 42				13 12			13 42		
	d			00 10							07 15			07 51				13 15			13 51		
West Croydon	a			00 16							07 21			07 57				13 21			13 57		
Sutton	a																						

		SN	SN	SN	SN A	SN B	SN	SN	SN	SN	SN	SN		SN	SN	SN	SN	SN	SN	SN	SN	SN	SN
London Victoria 15 ⊖	d	13 36	13 50		14 06	14 06	14 20		14 36	14 50		15 06		21 20		21 36	21 50		22 06	22 20		22 36	22 50
Battersea Park 4	d	13 40	13 54		14 10	14 10	14 24		14 40	14 54		15 10		21 24		21 40	21 54		22 10	22 24		22 40	22 54
Clapham Junction 10	d	13 44	13 58		14 14	14 14	14 28		14 44	14 58		15 14		21 28		21 44	21 58		22 14	22 28		22 44	22 58
Wandsworth Common	d	13 47	14 01		14 17	14 17	14 31		14 47	15 01		15 17		21 31		21 47	22 01		22 17	22 31		22 47	23 01
Balham 4 ⊖	d	13 50	14 04		14 20	14 20	14 34		14 50	15 04		15 20		21 34		21 50	22 04		22 20	22 34		22 50	23 04
Streatham Hill	d	13 55	14 09		14 25	14 25	14 39		14 55	15 09		15 25		21 39		21 55	22 09		22 25	22 39		22 55	23 09
London Bridge	d			14 01				14 31			15 01		and at the same minutes past each hour until		21 31			22 01			22 31		
West Norwood 4	d	13 58	14 12	14 24	14 28	14 28	14 42	14 54	14 58	15 12	15 24	15 28		21 42	21 54	21 58	22 12	22 24	22 28	22 42	22 54	22 58	23 12
Gipsy Hill	d	14 01	14 15	14 27	14 31	14 31	14 45	14 57	15 01	15 15	15 27	15 31		21 45	21 57	22 01	22 15	22 27	22 31	22 45	22 57	23 01	23 15
Crystal Palace 4	a	14 05	14 19	14 31	14 35	14 35	14 49	15 01	15 05	15 19	15 31	15 35		21 49	22 01	22 05	22 19	22 31	22 35	22 49	23 01	23 05	23 19
Crystal Palace	d	14 08	14 22		14 38	14 38	14 52		15 08	15 22		15 38		21 52		22 08	22 22		22 38	22 52		23 08	23 22
Sydenham	a		14 26				14 56			15 26				21 56			22 26			22 56			23 26
Forest Hill	a		14 28				14 58			15 28				21 58			22 28			22 58			23 28
Honor Oak Park	a		14 31				15 01			15 31				22 01			22 31			23 01			23 31
Brockley	a		14 33				15 03			15 33				22 03			22 33			23 03			23 33
New Cross Gate	a		14 35				15 05			15 35				22 05			22 35			23 05			23 35
London Bridge	a		14 44				15 14			15 44				22 14			22 44			23 14			23 44
Norwood Junction 2	a	14 12			14 42	14 45			15 12			15 42				22 12			22 42			23 12	
	d	14 15			14 51	14 51			15 15			15 51				22 15			22 51			23 15	
West Croydon	a	14 21			14 57	14 57			15 21			15 57				22 21			22 57			23 21	
Sutton	a																						

		SN	SN	SN	SN	SN	SN
London Victoria 15 ⊖	d		23 06	23 20	23 32		23 56
Battersea Park 4	d		23 10	23 24			
Clapham Junction 10	d		23 14	23 28	23 39		00 04
Wandsworth Common	d		23 17	23 31			00 07
Balham 4 ⊖	d		23 20	23 34	23 44		00 10
Streatham Hill	d		23 25	23 39	23 48		00 15
London Bridge	d	23 01				23 31	
West Norwood 4	d	23 24	23 28	23 42	23 52	23 54	00 18
Gipsy Hill	d	23 27	23 31	23 45	23 55	23 57	00 21
Crystal Palace 4	a	23 31	23 35	23 49	23 58	00 01	00 25
Crystal Palace	d	23 34	23 38	23 53	23 59	00 04	00 25
Sydenham	a			23 59			00 30
Forest Hill	a			00 01			00 33
Honor Oak Park	a			00 05			00 36
Brockley	a			00 07			00 38
New Cross Gate	a			00 09			00 40
London Bridge	a			00 17			00 47
Norwood Junction 2	a	23 39	23 43		00 04	00 09	
	d		23 45		00 06		
West Croydon	a		23 51		00 18		
Sutton	a						

A until 22 September

B from 29 September

For complete service between London Victoria and Balham, refer to Table T170

For faster services between London Victoria, Clapham Junction and East Croydon, refer to Table T175

For Shepherd's Bush connecting trains, refer to Table T176

Table T171-F

Sundays
20 May to 2 December

London Victoria - Streatham Hill, West Norwood, Gipsy Hill and Crystal Palace - Norwood Junction & Croydon

		SN A	SN A	SN A	SN	SN	SN	SN	SN	SN	SN	SN	SN	SN	SN	SN	SN	SN	
London Victoria 15 ⊖	d					00 10	00 25		00 40	07 21		07 51		08 21		08 56		09 26	
Battersea Park 4	d					00 14	00 29		00 44	07 25		07 55		08 25		09 00		09 30	
Clapham Junction 10	d			00 04		00 18	00 33		00 48	07 30		08 00		08 30		09 04		09 34	
Wandsworth Common	d			00 07		00 21	00 36		00 51	07 33		08 03		08 33		09 07		09 37	
Balham 4 ⊖	d			00 10		00 24	00 39		00 54	07 36		08 06		08 36		09 10		09 40	
Streatham Hill	d			00 15		00 29	00 44		00 59	07 43		08 13		08 43		09 14		09 44	
London Bridge	d				00 01			00 31			07 35		08 03		08 35		09 05		and at the same minutes past each hour until
West Norwood 4	d			00 18	00 24	00 32	00 47	00 54	01 02	07 48	07 58	08 18	08 28	08 47	08 58	09 18	09 28	09 48	
Gipsy Hill	d			00 21	00 27	00 35	00 50	00 57	01 05	07 51	08 01	08 21	08 31	08 50	09 01	09 21	09 31	09 51	
Crystal Palace 4	a			00 25	00 31	00 39	00 54	01 01	01 09	07 54	08 05	08 24	08 35	08 53	09 05	09 24	09 35	09 54	
Crystal Palace	d		00 04	00 25	00 34	00 40	00 55	01 04	01 10	07 55		08 25		08 54		09 25		09 55	
Sydenham	a			00 30															
Forest Hill	a			00 33															
Honor Oak Park	a			00 36															
Brockley	a			00 38															
New Cross Gate	a			00 40															
London Bridge	a			00 47															
Norwood Junction 2	a		00 09		00 39	00 47	01 02	01 10	01 15	07 59		08 29		08 58		09 29		09 59	
	d	00 06								08 04		08 34		08 59		09 31		10 01	
West Croydon	a	00 18								08 10		08 40		09 05		09 38		10 08	
Sutton	a																		

		SN	SN	SN	SN	SN	SN	SN	SN	SN	SN	SN	SN	SN
London Victoria 15 ⊖	d		20 56		21 26		21 56		22 26		22 56		23 26	23 56
Battersea Park 4	d		21 00		21 30		22 00		22 30		23 00		23 30	00 01
Clapham Junction 10	d		21 04		21 34		22 04		22 34		23 04		23 34	00 06
Wandsworth Common	d		21 07		21 37		22 07		22 37		23 07		23 37	00 09
Balham 4 ⊖	d		21 10		21 40		22 10		22 40		23 10		23 40	00 12
Streatham Hill	d		21 14		21 44		22 14		22 44		23 14		23 44	00 16
London Bridge	d	20 35		21 05		21 35		22 05		22 35		23 05		
West Norwood 4	d	20 58	21 18	21 28	21 48	21 58	22 18	22 28	22 48	22 58	23 18	23 28	23 48	00 19
Gipsy Hill	d	21 01	21 21	21 31	21 51	22 01	22 21	22 31	22 51	23 01	23 21	23 31	23 51	00 22
Crystal Palace 4	a	21 05	21 24	21 35	21 54	22 05	22 24	22 35	22 54	23 05	23 24	23 35	23 54	00 26
Crystal Palace	d		21 25		21 55		22 25		22 55	23 06	23 25	23 36	23 55	00 26
Sydenham	a													
Forest Hill	a													
Honor Oak Park	a													
Brockley	a													
New Cross Gate	a													
London Bridge	a													
Norwood Junction 2	a		21 29		21 59		22 29		22 59	23 11	23 29	23 40	23 59	00 31
	d		21 31		22 01		22 30		23 01		23 31		00 01	
West Croydon	a		21 38		22 08		22 36		23 08		23 38		00 08	
Sutton	a													

A not 20 May

For complete service between London Victoria and Balham, refer to Table T170

For faster services between London Victoria, Clapham Junction and East Croydon, refer to Table T175

For Shepherd's Bush connecting trains, refer to Table T176

21 May to 7 December

Croydon & Norwood Junction- Crystal Palace, Gipsy Hill, West Norwood and Streatham Hill - London Victoria

Miles	Miles	Station		SN MX	SN	SN	SN	SN	SN	SN	SN	SN	SN	SN	SN	SN	SN	SN	SN	SN	SN	SN	SN
0	—	Sutton	d																				
4½	—	West Croydon	d							06 21			06 52			07 22			07 52			08 22	
—	—	Norwood Junction	a							06 27			06 58			07 28			07 58			08 28	
—	—		d		05 21		05 51		06 21	06 28			06 59			07 28			07 58			08 28	
—	—	London Bridge	d									06 28			06 58			07 28			07 58		
—	—	New Cross Gate	d	00 04								06 34			07 04			07 34			08 04		
—	—	Brockley	d	00 07								06 37			07 07			07 37			08 07		
—	—	Honor Oak Park	d	00 09								06 39			07 09			07 39			08 09		
—	—	Forest Hill	d	00 12								06 42			07 12			07 42			08 12		
—	—	Sydenham	d	00 15								06 45			07 15			07 45			08 15		
7¾	0	Crystal Palace	a	00 20	05 25		05 55		06 25	06 33		06 50	07 04		07 20	07 33		07 50	08 03		08 20	08 33	
—	—	**Crystal Palace**	d	00 20	05 26	05 53	05 56	06 23	06 26	06 37	06 53	06 56	07 07	07 23	07 26	07 37	07 53	07 56	08 07	08 23	08 26	08 37	08 53
8½	0¾	**Gipsy Hill**	a	00 23	05 29	05 55	05 59	06 25	06 29	06 39	06 55	06 59	07 09	07 25	07 29	07 39	07 55	07 59	08 09	08 25	08 29	08 39	08 55
9½	1¾	**West Norwood**	a	00 26	05 32	05 58	06 02	06 28	06 32	06 42	06 58	07 02	07 12	07 28	07 32	07 42	07 58	08 02	08 12	08 28	08 32	08 42	08 58
—	8½	London Bridge	a			06 21		06 51			07 21			07 51			08 21			08 51			09 21
10¾	—	**Streatham Hill**	a	00 30	05 36		06 06		06 36	06 46		07 06	07 16		07 36	07 46		08 06	08 16		08 36	08 46	
11¾	—	Balham ⊖	a		05 40		06 10		06 40	06 51		07 10	07 21		07 40	07 51		08 10	08 21		08 40	08 51	
12¾	—	Wandsworth Common	a		05 42		06 12		06 42	06 53		07 12	07 23		07 42	07 53		08 12	08 23		08 42	08 53	
14	—	Clapham Junction	a		05 46		06 16		06 46	06 57		07 16	07 27		07 46	07 57		08 16	08 27		08 46	08 57	
15½	—	Battersea Park	a		05 50		06 20		06 50	07 01		07 20	07 31		07 50	08 01		08 20	08 31		08 50	09 01	
16¾	—	London Victoria ⊖	a		05 54		06 24		06 54	07 05		07 24	07 35		07 54	08 05		08 24	08 35		08 54	09 08	

Station		SN	SN	SN	SN	SN	SN	SN	SN		SN	SN	SN	SN	SN	SN	SN	SN	SN	SN	SN	SN	SN
Sutton	d																						
West Croydon	d		08 52			09 21			09 51				16 21			16 51			17 22			17 52	
Norwood Junction	a		08 58			09 27			09 57				16 27			16 57			17 28			17 58	
	d		08 58			09 28			09 58				16 28			16 58			17 29			17 59	
London Bridge	d	08 28			08 58			09 28				15 58			16 28			16 58			17 28		
New Cross Gate	d	08 34			09 04			09 34				16 04			16 34			17 04			17 34		
Brockley	d	08 37			09 07			09 37		and at		16 07			16 37			17 07			17 37		
Honor Oak Park	d	08 39			09 09			09 39		the same		16 09			16 39			17 09			17 39		
Forest Hill	d	08 42			09 12			09 42		minutes		16 12			16 42			17 12			17 42		
Sydenham	d	08 45			09 15			09 45		past		16 15			16 45			17 15			17 45		
Crystal Palace	a	08 50	09 03		09 20	09 33		09 50	10 03	each		16 20	16 33		16 50	17 03		17 20	17 34		17 50	18 04	
Crystal Palace	d	08 56	09 07	09 23	09 26	09 37	09 53	09 56	10 07	hour until	16 23	16 26	16 37	16 53	16 56	17 07	17 23	17 26	17 37	17 53	17 56	18 07	18 23
Gipsy Hill	a	08 59	09 09	09 25	09 29	09 39	09 55	09 59	10 09		16 25	16 29	16 39	16 55	16 59	17 09	17 25	17 29	17 39	17 55	17 59	18 09	18 25
West Norwood	a	09 02	09 12	09 28	09 32	09 42	09 58	10 02	10 12		16 28	16 32	16 42	16 58	17 02	17 12	17 28	17 32	17 42	17 58	18 02	18 12	18 28
London Bridge	a			09 51			10 21				16 51			17 21			17 51			18 21			18 51
Streatham Hill	a	09 06	09 16		09 36	09 46		10 06	10 16			16 36	16 46		17 06	17 16		17 36	17 46		18 06	18 16	
Balham ⊖	a	09 10	09 21		09 40	09 51		10 10	10 21			16 40	16 51		17 10	17 21		17 40	17 51		18 10	18 21	
Wandsworth Common	a	09 12	09 23		09 42	09 53		10 12	10 23			16 42	16 53		17 12	17 23		17 42	17 53		18 12	18 23	
Clapham Junction	a	09 16	09 27		09 46	09 57		10 16	10 27			16 46	16 57		17 16	17 27		17 46	17 57		18 16	18 27	
Battersea Park	a	09 20	09 31		09 50	10 01		10 20	10 31			16 50	17 01		17 20	17 31		17 50	18 01		18 20	18 31	
London Victoria ⊖	a	09 24	09 35		09 54	10 05		10 24	10 35			16 54	17 05		17 24	17 35		17 54	18 05		18 24	18 36	

Station		SN	SN	SN	SN	SN	SN	SN	SN	SN	SN	SN	SN	SN	SN	SN	SN	SN	SN	SN	SN	SN
Sutton	d																					
West Croydon	d		18 22			18 52			19 22			19 51			20 21			20 51			21 22	
Norwood Junction	a		18 28			18 58			19 28			19 58			20 27			20 58			21 27	
	d		18 28			18 58			19 28			19 58			20 28			20 59			21 28	
London Bridge	d	17 58			18 28			18 58			19 28			19 58			20 28			20 58		
New Cross Gate	d	18 04			18 34			19 04			19 34			20 04			20 34			21 04		
Brockley	d	18 07			18 37			19 07			19 37			20 07			20 37			21 07		
Honor Oak Park	d	18 09			18 39			19 09			19 39			20 09			20 39			21 09		
Forest Hill	d	18 12			18 42			19 12			19 42			20 12			20 42			21 12		
Sydenham	d	18 15			18 45			19 15			19 45			20 15			20 45			21 15		
Crystal Palace	a	18 20	18 33		18 50	19 03		19 20	19 33		19 50	20 03		20 20	20 33		20 50	21 03		21 20	21 33	
Crystal Palace	d	18 26	18 37	18 53	18 56	19 07	19 23	19 26	19 37	19 53	19 56	20 07	20 23	20 26	20 37	20 53	20 56	21 07	21 23	21 26	21 37	21 53
Gipsy Hill	a	18 29	18 39	18 55	18 59	19 09	19 25	19 29	19 39	19 55	19 59	20 09	20 25	20 29	20 39	20 55	20 59	21 09	21 25	21 29	21 39	21 55
West Norwood	a	18 32	18 42	18 58	19 02	19 12	19 28	19 32	19 42	19 58	20 02	20 12	20 28	20 32	20 42	20 58	21 02	21 12	21 28	21 32	21 42	21 58
London Bridge	a			19 21			19 51			20 21			20 51			21 21			21 51			22 21
Streatham Hill	a	18 36	18 46		19 06	19 16		19 36	19 46		20 06	20 16		20 36	20 46		21 06	21 16		21 36	21 46	
Balham ⊖	a	18 40	18 51		19 10	19 21		19 40	19 51		20 10	20 21		20 40	20 51		21 10	21 21		21 40	21 51	
Wandsworth Common	a	18 42	18 53		19 12	19 23		19 42	19 53		20 12	20 23		20 42	20 53		21 12	21 23		21 42	21 53	
Clapham Junction	a	18 46	18 57		19 16	19 27		19 46	19 57		20 16	20 27		20 46	20 57		21 16	21 27		21 46	21 57	
Battersea Park	a	18 50	19 01		19 20	19 31		19 50	20 01		20 20	20 31		20 50	21 01		21 20	21 31		21 50	22 01	
London Victoria ⊖	a	18 54	19 05		19 24	19 35		19 54	20 05		20 24	20 35		20 54	21 05		21 24	21 35		21 54	22 05	

For complete service between London Victoria and Balham, refer to Table T170

For faster services between London Victoria, Clapham Junction and East Croydon, refer to Table T175

For Shepherd's Bush connecting trains, refer to Table T176

Table T171-R

Mondays to Fridays

21 May to 7 December

Croydon & Norwood Junction- Crystal Palace, Gipsy Hill, West Norwood and Streatham Hill - London Victoria

Station		SN	SN	SN	SN	SN	SN	SN	SN	SN	SN	SN	SN
Sutton	d												
West Croydon	d		21 51			22 21			22 51				
Norwood Junction	a		21 57			22 27			22 57				
	d		21 58			22 28			22 58				
London Bridge	d	21 28			21 58			22 28		22 58		23 28	23 58
New Cross Gate	d	21 34			22 04			22 34		23 04		23 34	00 04
Brockley	d	21 37			22 07			22 37		23 07		23 37	00 07
Honor Oak Park	d	21 39			22 09			22 39		23 09		23 39	00 09
Forest Hill	d	21 42			22 12			22 42		23 12		23 42	00 12
Sydenham	d	21 45			22 15			22 45		23 15		23 45	00 15
Crystal Palace	a	21 50	22 03		22 20	22 33		22 50	23 03	23 20		23 50	00 20
Crystal Palace	d	21 56	22 07	22 23	22 26	22 37	22 53	22 56	23 07	23 20	23 24	23 50	00 20
Gipsy Hill	a	21 59	22 09	22 25	22 29	22 39	22 55	22 59	23 09	23 23	23 26	23 53	00 23
West Norwood	a	22 02	22 12	22 28	22 32	22 42	22 58	23 02	23 12	23 26	23 29	23 56	00 26
London Bridge	a			22 51			23 21				23 52		
Streatham Hill	a	22 06	22 16		22 36	22 46		23 06	23 16	23 30		00 01	00 30
Balham ⊖	a	22 10	22 21		22 40	22 51		23 10	23 21	23 37			
Wandsworth Common	a	22 12	22 23		22 42	22 53		23 12	23 23				
Clapham Junction	a	22 16	22 27		22 46	22 57		23 16	23 27	23 41			
Battersea Park	a	22 20	22 31		22 50	23 01		23 20	23 31				
London Victoria ⊖	a	22 24	22 37		22 55	23 05		23 24	23 37	23 50			

Saturdays

26 May to 8 December

Station		SN	SN	SN	SN	SN	SN	SN	SN	SN	SN	SN	SN	SN	SN	SN	SN	SN	SN	SN	SN	SN	SN
Sutton	d																						
West Croydon	d				06 21			06 51			07 21			07 51			08 21			08 51			09 21
Norwood Junction	a				06 27			06 57			07 27			07 57			08 27			08 57			09 27
	d		05 51	06 21	06 28	06 48		06 58	07 18		07 28			07 58			08 28			08 58			09 28
London Bridge	d						06 28			06 58			07 28			07 58			08 28			08 58	
New Cross Gate	d	00 04					06 35			07 05			07 35			08 05			08 35			09 05	
Brockley	d	00 07					06 37			07 07			07 37			08 07			08 37			09 07	
Honor Oak Park	d	00 09					06 40			07 10			07 40			08 10			08 40			09 10	
Forest Hill	d	00 12					06 42			07 12			07 42			08 12			08 42			09 12	
Sydenham	d	00 15					06 46			07 16			07 46			08 16			08 46			09 16	
Crystal Palace	a	00 20	05 55	06 25	06 33	06 52	06 50	07 03	07 22	07 20	07 33		07 50	08 03		08 20	08 33		08 50	09 03		09 20	09 33
Crystal Palace	d	00 20	05 56	06 26	06 37	06 53	06 56	07 07	07 23	07 26	07 37	07 53	07 56	08 07	08 23	08 26	08 37	08 53	08 56	09 07	09 23	09 26	09 37
Gipsy Hill	a	00 23	05 58	06 28	06 39	06 55	06 59	07 09	07 25	07 29	07 39	07 55	07 59	08 09	08 25	08 29	08 39	08 55	08 59	09 09	09 25	09 29	09 39
West Norwood	a	00 26	06 01	06 31	06 42	06 58	07 02	07 12	07 28	07 32	07 42	07 58	08 02	08 12	08 28	08 32	08 42	08 58	09 02	09 12	09 28	09 32	09 42
London Bridge	a					07 21			07 51			08 21			08 51			09 21			09 51		
Streatham Hill	a	00 30	06 05	06 35	06 46		07 06	07 16		07 36	07 46		08 06	08 16		08 36	08 46		09 06	09 16		09 36	09 46
Balham ⊖	a		06 10	06 40	06 51		07 10	07 21		07 40	07 51		08 10	08 21		08 40	08 51		09 10	09 21		09 40	09 51
Wandsworth Common	a		06 12	06 42	06 53		07 12	07 23		07 42	07 53		08 12	08 23		08 42	08 53		09 12	09 23		09 42	09 53
Clapham Junction	a		06 16	06 46	06 57		07 16	07 27		07 46	07 57		08 16	08 27		08 46	08 57		09 16	09 27		09 46	09 57
Battersea Park	a		06 20	06 50	07 01		07 20	07 31		07 50	08 01		08 20	08 31		08 50	09 01		09 20	09 31		09 50	10 01
London Victoria ⊖	a		06 24	06 54	07 05		07 24	07 35		07 54	08 05		08 24	08 35		08 54	09 05		09 24	09 35		09 54	10 05

Station		SN	SN	SN	SN	SN	SN	SN	SN	SN	SN	SN	SN	SN	SN		SN	SN	SN	SN	SN	SN
Sutton	d																					
West Croydon	d			09 51			10 21			10 51			11 21				15 51			16 21		
Norwood Junction	a			09 57			10 27			10 57			11 27				15 57			16 27		
	d			09 58			10 28			10 58			11 28				15 58			16 28		
London Bridge	d		09 28			09 58			10 28			10 58			11 28				15 58			16 28
New Cross Gate	d		09 35			10 05			10 34			11 05			11 35				16 05			16 35
Brockley	d		09 37			10 07			10 36			11 07			11 37	and at			16 07			16 37
Honor Oak Park	d		09 40			10 10			10 39			11 10			11 40	the same			16 10			16 40
Forest Hill	d		09 42			10 12			10 41			11 12			11 42	minutes			16 12			16 42
Sydenham	d		09 46			10 16			10 45			11 16			11 46	past			16 16			16 46
Crystal Palace	a		09 50	10 03		10 20	10 33		10 49	11 03		11 20	11 33		11 50	each	16 03		16 20	16 33		16 50
Crystal Palace	d	09 53	09 56	10 07	10 23	10 26	10 37	10 53	10 56	11 07	11 23	11 26	11 37	11 53	11 56	hour until	16 07	16 23	16 26	16 37	16 53	16 56
Gipsy Hill	a	09 55	09 59	10 09	10 25	10 29	10 39	10 55	10 59	11 09	11 25	11 29	11 39	11 55	11 59		16 09	16 25	16 29	16 39	16 55	16 59
West Norwood	a	09 58	10 02	10 12	10 28	10 32	10 42	10 58	11 02	11 12	11 28	11 32	11 42	11 58	12 02		16 12	16 28	16 32	16 42	16 58	17 02
London Bridge	a	10 21			10 51			11 21			11 51			12 21				16 51			17 21	
Streatham Hill	a		10 06	10 16		10 36	10 46		11 06	11 16		11 36	11 46		12 06		16 16		16 36	16 46		17 06
Balham ⊖	a		10 10	10 21		10 40	10 51		11 10	11 21		11 40	11 51		12 10		16 21		16 40	16 51		17 10
Wandsworth Common	a		10 12	10 23		10 42	10 53		11 12	11 23		11 42	11 53		12 12		16 23		16 42	16 53		17 12
Clapham Junction	a		10 16	10 27		10 46	10 57		11 16	11 27		11 46	11 57		12 16		16 27		16 46	16 57		17 16
Battersea Park	a		10 20	10 31		10 50	11 01		11 20	11 31		11 50	12 01		12 20		16 31		16 50	17 01		17 20
London Victoria ⊖	a		10 24	10 35		10 54	11 05		11 24	11 35		11 54	12 05		12 24		16 35		16 54	17 05		17 24

For complete service between London Victoria and Balham, refer to Table T170

For faster services between London Victoria, Clapham Junction and East Croydon, refer to Table T175

For Shepherd's Bush connecting trains, refer to Table T176

Table T171-R

Saturdays

26 May to 8 December

Croydon & Norwood Junction- Crystal Palace, Gipsy Hill, West Norwood and Streatham Hill - London Victoria

		SN	SN	SN	SN	SN	SN	SN		SN	SN	SN	SN	SN	SN	SN	SN	SN	SN	SN
Sutton	d																			
West Croydon	d	16 52			17 21			17 51				22 21			22 51			23 21		
Norwood Junction	a	16 58			17 27			17 57				22 27			22 57			23 27		
	d	16 59			17 28			17 58				22 28			22 58			23 28		
London Bridge	d			16 58			17 28				21 58			22 28			22 58		23 28	23 58
New Cross Gate	d			17 05			17 35				22 05			22 35			23 05		23 35	00 05
Brockley	d			17 07			17 37				22 07			22 37			23 07		23 37	00 07
Honor Oak Park	d			17 10			17 40				22 10			22 40			23 10		23 40	00 10
Forest Hill	d			17 12			17 42				22 12			22 42			23 12		23 42	00 12
Sydenham	d			17 16			17 46				22 16			22 46			23 16		23 46	00 16
Crystal Palace	a	17 04		17 20	17 33		17 50	18 03			22 20	22 33		22 50	23 03		23 20	23 33	23 50	00 20
Crystal Palace	d	17 07	17 23	17 26	17 37	17 53	17 56	18 07	and at the same minutes past each hour until	22 23	22 26	22 37	22 53	22 56	23 07	23 23	23 26	23 37	23 56	00 21
Gipsy Hill	a	17 09	17 25	17 29	17 39	17 55	17 59	18 09		22 25	22 29	22 39	22 55	22 59	23 09	23 25	23 29	23 39	23 59	00 23
West Norwood	a	17 12	17 28	17 32	17 42	17 58	18 02	18 12		22 28	22 32	22 42	22 58	23 02	23 12	23 28	23 32	23 42	00 02	00 26
London Bridge	a		17 51			18 21				22 51			23 21			23 51				
Streatham Hill	a	17 16		17 36	17 46		18 06	18 16			22 36	22 46		23 06	23 16		23 36	23 46	00 06	00 30
Balham	a	17 21		17 40	17 51		18 10	18 21			22 40	22 51		23 10	23 21		23 40	23 51	00 10	
Wandsworth Common	a	17 23		17 42	17 53		18 12	18 23			22 42	22 53		23 12	23 23		23 42	23 53	00 12	
Clapham Junction	a	17 27		17 46	17 57		18 16	18 27			22 46	22 57		23 16	23 27		23 46	23 57	00 16	
Battersea Park	a	17 31		17 50	18 01		18 20	18 31			22 50	23 01		23 20	23 31		23 50	00 01	00 20	
London Victoria	a	17 35		17 54	18 05		18 24	18 35			22 54	23 05		23 24	23 35		23 54	00 05	00 24	

Sundays

20 May to 2 December

		SN A	SN	SN	SN	SN	SN	SN	SN	SN	SN	SN	SN	SN		SN	SN	SN	SN	SN	SN	SN	SN
Sutton	d																						
West Croydon	d			06 59		07 31		08 03		08 33		09 01		09 31			22 01		22 31		23 01		23 31
Norwood Junction	a			07 07		07 38		08 09		08 39		09 08		09 38			22 08		22 38		23 08		23 38
	d			07 09		07 38		08 09		08 39		09 09		09 39			22 09		22 39		23 09		23 39
London Bridge	d																						
New Cross Gate	d	00 05																					
Brockley	d	00 07																					
Honor Oak Park	d	00 10																					
Forest Hill	d	00 12																					
Sydenham	d	00 16																					
Crystal Palace	a	00 20		07 14		07 43		08 14		08 44		09 14		09 44			22 14		22 44		23 14		23 44
Crystal Palace	d	00 21	07 11	07 14	07 41	07 43	08 11	08 14	08 41	08 44	09 11	09 14	09 41	09 44	and at the same minutes past each hour until	22 11	22 14	22 41	22 44	23 11	23 14	23 41	23 44
Gipsy Hill	a	00 23	07 13	07 17	07 43	07 46	08 13	08 17	08 43	08 47	09 13	09 17	09 43	09 47		22 13	22 17	22 43	22 47	23 13	23 17	23 43	23 47
West Norwood	a	00 26	07 16	07 20	07 46	07 49	08 16	08 20	08 46	08 50	09 16	09 20	09 46	09 50		22 16	22 20	22 46	22 50	23 16	23 20	23 46	23 50
London Bridge	a		07 39		08 09		08 43		09 09		09 39		10 09			22 39		23 09		23 39		00 09	
Streatham Hill	a	00 30		07 24		07 53		08 24		08 54		09 24		09 54			22 24		22 54		23 24		23 54
Balham	a			07 28		07 58		08 29		08 57		09 27		09 57			22 27		22 57		23 27		23 58
Wandsworth Common	a			07 30		08 01		08 31		09 00		09 30		10 00			22 30		23 00		23 30		00 01
Clapham Junction	a			07 34		08 04		08 35		09 03		09 33		10 03			22 33		23 03		23 33		00 05
Battersea Park	a			07 38		08 08		08 39		09 07		09 37		10 07			22 37		23 07		23 37		00 09
London Victoria	a			07 42		08 13		08 43		09 12		09 42		10 12			22 42		23 12		23 43		00 13

A not 20 May

For complete service between London Victoria and Balham, refer to Table T170

For faster services between London Victoria, Clapham Junction and East Croydon, refer to Table T175

For Shepherd's Bush connecting trains, refer to Table T176

Table T172-F

Mondays to Fridays

21 May to 7 December

London via Wallington - Epsom Downs

Miles	Miles			SN MX	SN	SN	TL	SN	SN	SN	SN	SN	TL	SN	SN	SN	SN	SN	SN	TL	SN	SN	TL
0	0	London Victoria	d					06 00		06 16	06 30			06 46	07 00		07 16	07 30			07 46	08 00	
2¾	2¾	Clapham Junction	d					06 09		06 24	06 39			06 54	07 09		07 24	07 39			07 54	08 09	
4¾	4¾	Balham	d					06 15		06 30	06 45			07 00	07 15		07 30	07 45			08 00	08 15	
—	—	London Bridge	d				05 55		06 10			06 40	06 55			07 10			07 40	07 55			08 25
—	—	Norwood Junction	d				06 09		06 36			07 06	07 09			07 36			08 06	08 09			08 39
—	—	West Croydon	d	00 13	05 53	06 04	06 15	06 34	06 42	06 49	07 04	07 12	07 16	07 19	07 34	07 42	07 49	08 05	08 12	08 16	08 19	08 34	08 45
11¾	13	Waddon	d	00 15	05 55	06 07	06 18	06 36		06 52	07 06		07 18	07 22	07 36		07 52	08 07		08 18	08 22	08 36	08 48
13¼	14½	Wallington	d	00 19	05 59	06 11	06 22	06 40	06 47	06 56	07 10	07 17	07 22	07 26	07 40	07 47	07 56	08 11	08 17	08 22	08 26	08 40	08 52
14¼	15½	Carshalton Beeches	d	00 21	06 02	06 13	06 24	06 43		06 58	07 13		07 24	07 28	07 43		07 58	08 14		08 24	08 28	08 43	08 54
15¼	16½	Sutton	a	00 25	06 05	06 19	06 28	06 46	06 52	07 03	07 16	07 22	07 28	07 33	07 46	07 52	08 03	08 17	08 22	08 28	08 33	08 46	08 58
—	—	Sutton	d			06 20		06 49			07 19				07 49			08 19				08 49	
—	—	Belmont	d			06 23		06 52			07 22				07 52			08 22				08 52	
—	—	Banstead	d			06 27		06 56			07 26				07 56			08 26				08 56	
—	—	Epsom Downs	a			06 30		06 59			07 29				07 59			08 29				08 59	

		SN	SN	TL	SN	SN	TL	SN	SN	TL	SN	SN	TL	SN	SN	TL	SN	SN	TL	SN	SN	TL	SN
London Victoria	d	08 16	08 30		08 46	09 00		09 16	09 30		09 46	10 00		10 16	10 30		10 46	11 00		11 16	11 30		11 46
Clapham Junction	d	08 24	08 39		08 54	09 09		09 24	09 39		09 54	10 09		10 24	10 39		10 54	11 09		11 24	11 39		11 54
Balham	d	08 30	08 45		09 00	09 15		09 30	09 45		10 00	10 15		10 30	10 45		11 00	11 15		11 30	11 45		12 00
London Bridge	d			08 55			09 25			09 55			10 25			10 55			11 25			11 55	
Norwood Junction	d			09 09			09 39			10 09			10 39			11 09			11 39			12 09	
West Croydon	d	08 49	09 04	09 15	09 19	09 34	09 45	09 49	10 04	10 15	10 19	10 34	10 45	10 50	11 04	11 15	11 19	11 34	11 45	11 50	12 04	12 15	12 18
Waddon	d	08 52	09 06	09 18	09 22	09 36	09 48	09 52	10 06	10 18	10 22	10 36	10 48	10 53	11 06	11 18	11 21	11 36	11 48	11 53	12 06	12 18	12 21
Wallington	d	08 56	09 10	09 22	09 26	09 40	09 52	09 56	10 10	10 22	10 26	10 40	10 52	10 57	11 10	11 22	11 25	11 40	11 52	11 57	12 10	12 22	12 25
Carshalton Beeches	d	08 58	09 13	09 24	09 28	09 43	09 54	09 58	10 13	10 24	10 28	10 43	10 54	11 00	11 13	11 24	11 28	11 43	11 54	12 00	12 13	12 24	12 28
Sutton	a	09 03	09 16	09 28	09 33	09 46	09 58	10 03	10 16	10 28	10 33	10 46	10 58	11 03	11 16	11 28	11 33	11 46	11 58	12 03	12 16	12 28	12 33
Sutton	d		09 19			09 49			10 19			10 49			11 19			11 49			12 19		
Belmont	d		09 22			09 52			10 22			10 52			11 22			11 52			12 22		
Banstead	d		09 26			09 56			10 26			10 56			11 26			11 56			12 26		
Epsom Downs	a		09 29			09 59			10 29			10 59			11 29			11 59			12 29		

		SN	TL	SN	SN MWFO	SN TThO	TL	SN MWFO	SN TThO	SN	TL	SN	SN	TL	SN	SN A	SN B	TL	SN B	SN A	SN B	SN A
London Victoria	d	12 00		12 16	12 30	12 30		12 46	12 46	13 00		13 16	13 30		13 46	14 00	14 00		14 16	14 16	14 30	14 30
Clapham Junction	d	12 09		12 24	12 39	12 42		12 54	12 54	13 09		13 24	13 39		13 54	14 09	14 09		14 24	14 24	14 39	14 39
Balham	d	12 15		12 30	12 45	12 48		13 00	13 00	13 15		13 30	13 45		14 00	14 15	14 15		14 30	14 30	14 45	14 45
London Bridge	d		12 25				12 55				13 25			13 55				14 25				
Norwood Junction	d		12 39				13 09				13 39			14 09				14 39				
West Croydon	d	12 34	12 45	12 50	13 04	13 12	13 15	13 18	13 20	13 34	13 45	13 50	14 04	14 15	14 18	14 34	14 34	14 45	14 50	14 50	15 04	15 04
Waddon	d	12 36	12 48	12 53	13 06	13 14	13 18	13 21	13 23	13 36	13 48	13 53	14 06	14 18	14 21	14 36	14 36	14 48	14 53	14 53	15 06	15 06
Wallington	d	12 40	12 52	12 57	13 10	13 18	13 22	13 25	13 27	13 40	13 52	13 57	14 10	14 22	14 25	14 40	14 40	14 52	14 57	14 57	15 10	15 10
Carshalton Beeches	d	12 43	12 54	13 00	13 13	13 21	13 24	13 28	13 29	13 43	13 54	14 00	14 13	14 24	14 28	14 43	14 43	14 54	15 00	15 00	15 13	15 13
Sutton	a	12 46	12 58	13 03	13 16	13 24	13 28	13 33	13 33	13 46	13 58	14 03	14 16	14 28	14 33	14 46	14 46	14 58	15 03	15 06	15 16	15 16
Sutton	d	12 49			13 19	13 25				13 49			14 19				14 49				15 19	15 24
Belmont	d	12 52			13 22	13 28				13 52			14 22				14 52				15 22	15 27
Banstead	d	12 56			13 26	13 32				13 56			14 26				14 56				15 26	15 31
Epsom Downs	a	12 59			13 29	13 35				13 59			14 29				14 59				15 29	15 34

		TL	SN	SN	TL	SN	SN	TL	SN	SN	SN	TL	SN	SN	SN	TL	SN	SN	SN	TL	SN	SN	SN
London Victoria	d		14 46	15 00		15 16	15 30		15 46	16 00			16 16	16 30			16 46	17 00			17 16	17 30	
Clapham Junction	d		14 54	15 09		15 24	15 39		15 54	16 09			16 24	16 39			16 54	17 09			17 24	17 39	
Balham	d		15 00	15 15		15 30	15 45		16 00	16 15			16 30	16 45			17 00	17 15			17 30	17 45	
London Bridge	d	14 55			15 25			15 55			16 10	16 25			16 40	16 55			17 10	17 25			17 40
Norwood Junction	d	15 09			15 39			16 09			16 36	16 39			17 06	17 09			17 36	17 39			18 06
West Croydon	d	15 15	15 18	15 34	15 45	15 50	16 04	16 15	16 18	16 34	16 42	16 46	16 49	17 04	17 12	17 16	17 19	17 34	17 42	17 46	17 49	18 04	18 12
Waddon	d	15 18	15 21	15 36	15 48	15 53	16 06	16 18	16 21	16 36		16 48	16 52	17 06		17 18	17 22	17 36		17 48	17 52	18 06	
Wallington	d	15 22	15 25	15 40	15 52	15 57	16 10	16 22	16 25	16 40	16 47	16 52	16 56	17 10	17 17	17 22	17 26	17 40	17 47	17 52	17 56	18 10	18 17
Carshalton Beeches	d	15 24	15 28	15 43	15 54	16 00	16 13	16 24	16 28	16 43		16 54	16 58	17 13		17 24	17 28	17 43		17 54	17 58	18 13	
Sutton	a	15 28	15 33	15 46	15 58	16 03	16 16	16 28	16 33	16 46	16 52	16 58	17 03	17 16	17 22	17 28	17 33	17 46	17 52	17 59	18 03	18 16	18 22
Sutton	d			15 49			16 19			16 49				17 19				17 49				18 19	
Belmont	d			15 52			16 22			16 52				17 22				17 52				18 22	
Banstead	d			15 56			16 26			16 56				17 26				17 56				18 26	
Epsom Downs	a			15 59			16 29			16 59				17 29				17 59				18 29	

		TL	SN	SN	SN	TL	SN	SN	TL	SN	SN	TL	SN	SN	TL	SN	SN	TL	SN	SN	TL	SN	SN
London Victoria	d		17 46	18 00			18 16	18 30		18 46	19 00		19 16	19 30		19 46	20 00		20 16	20 30		20 46	21 00
Clapham Junction	d		17 54	18 09			18 24	18 39		18 54	19 09		19 24	19 39		19 54	20 09		20 24	20 39		20 54	21 09
Balham	d		18 00	18 15			18 30	18 45		19 00	19 15		19 30	19 45		20 00	20 15		20 30	20 45		21 00	21 15
London Bridge	d	17 55			18 10	18 25			18 55			19 25			19 55			20 25			20 55		
Norwood Junction	d	18 09			18 36	18 39			19 09			19 39			20 09			20 39			21 09		
West Croydon	d	18 16	18 19	18 34	18 42	18 46	18 49	19 04	19 15	19 18	19 34	19 45	19 48	20 04	20 15	20 18	20 34	20 45	20 50	21 04	21 15	21 18	21 34
Waddon	d	18 18	18 22	18 36		18 48	18 52	19 06	19 18	19 21	19 36	19 48	19 51	20 06	20 18	20 21	20 36	20 48	20 53	21 06	21 18	21 21	21 36
Wallington	d	18 22	18 26	18 40	18 47	18 52	18 56	19 10	19 22	19 25	19 40	19 52	19 55	20 10	20 22	20 25	20 40	20 52	20 57	21 10	21 22	21 25	21 40
Carshalton Beeches	d	18 24	18 28	18 43		18 54	18 58	19 13	19 24	19 28	19 43	19 54	19 58	20 13	20 24	20 28	20 43	20 54	21 00	21 13	21 24	21 28	21 43
Sutton	a	18 29	18 33	18 46	18 52	18 59	19 03	19 16	19 28	19 33	19 46	19 58	20 03	20 16	20 28	20 33	20 46	20 58	21 03	21 16	21 28	21 33	21 46
Sutton	d			18 49				19 19			19 49			20 19			20 49			21 19			21 49
Belmont	d			18 52				19 22			19 52			20 22			20 52			21 22			21 52
Banstead	d			18 56				19 26			19 56			20 26			20 56			21 26			21 56
Epsom Downs	a			18 59				19 29			19 59			20 29			20 59			21 29			21 59

A from 24 September

B until 21 September

Please note, Network Rail have stated that further updates to this timetable are possible during the validity period.

Table T172-F

Mondays to Fridays

21 May to 7 December

London via Wallington - Epsom Downs

		TL	SN	SN	TL	SN	SN	TL	SN	SN	TL	SN	SN	SN	SN
London Victoria ⊖	d		21 16	21 30		21 46	22 00		22 16	22 30		22 46	23 00	23 16	23 40
Clapham Junction	d		21 24	21 42		21 57	22 09		22 24	22 39		22 54	23 09	23 24	23 48
Balham ⊖	d		21 30	21 48		22 02	22 15		22 30	22 45		23 00	23 15	23 30	23 54
London Bridge	d	21 25			21 55			22 25			22 55				
Norwood Junction	d	21 39			22 09			22 39			23 09				
West Croydon	d	21 45	21 48	22 12	22 15	22 20	22 34	22 45	22 48	23 04	23 15	23 18	23 34	23 49	00 13
Waddon	d	21 48	21 51	22 14	22 18	22 23	22 36	22 48	22 51	23 06	23 18	23 21	23 36	23 52	00 15
Wallington	d	21 52	21 55	22 18	22 22	22 27	22 40	22 52	22 55	23 10	23 22	23 25	23 40	23 56	00 19
Carshalton Beeches	d	21 54	21 58	22 21	22 24	22 29	22 43	22 54	22 58	23 13	23 24	23 28	23 43	23 58	00 21
Sutton	a	21 58	22 03	22 24	22 28	22 33	22 46	22 58	23 03	23 16	23 28	23 33	23 46	00 03	00 25
Sutton	d			22 25			22 49			23 19			23 49		
Belmont	d			22 28			22 52			23 22			23 52		
Banstead	d			22 32			22 56			23 26			23 56		
Epsom Downs	a			22 35			22 59			23 29			23 59		

Saturdays

26 May to 8 December

		SN	SN	SN	SN	TL	SN	SN	TL	SN		SN	TL	SN	SN	TL	SN	SN	TL	SN	SN A	SN B	TL
London Victoria ⊖	d		00 30	06 00	06 30		06 46	07 00		07 16	and at the same minutes past each hour until	12 30		12 46	13 00		13 16	13 30		13 46	14 00	14 00	
Clapham Junction	d		00 39	06 09	06 39		06 54	07 09		07 24		12 39		12 54	13 09		13 24	13 39		13 54	14 09	14 09	
Balham ⊖	d		00 45	06 15	06 45		07 00	07 15		07 30		12 45		13 00	13 15		13 30	13 45		14 00	14 15	14 15	
London Bridge	d					06 55			07 25				12 55			13 25			13 55				14 25
Norwood Junction	d					07 09			07 39				13 09			13 39			14 09				14 39
West Croydon	d	00 13	01 06	06 35	07 04	07 15	07 18	07 34	07 45	07 50		13 04	13 15	13 18	13 34	13 45	13 50	14 04	14 15	14 18	14 34	14 34	14 45
Waddon	d	00 15	01 08	06 38	07 06	07 18	07 21	07 37	07 48	07 53		13 06	13 18	13 21	13 37	13 48	13 53	14 06	14 18	14 21	14 37	14 37	14 48
Wallington	d	00 19	01 12	06 42	07 10	07 22	07 25	07 40	07 52	07 57		13 10	13 22	13 25	13 40	13 52	13 57	14 10	14 22	14 25	14 40	14 40	14 52
Carshalton Beeches	d	00 21	01 15	06 44	07 13	07 24	07 28	07 43	07 54	08 00		13 13	13 24	13 28	13 43	13 54	14 00	14 13	14 24	14 28	14 43	14 43	14 54
Sutton	a	00 25	01 18	06 48	07 16	07 28	07 33	07 46	07 58	08 03		13 16	13 28	13 33	13 46	13 58	14 03	14 16	14 28	14 33	14 46	14 47	14 58
Sutton	d			06 49	07 19			07 49				13 19			13 49			14 19				14 49	
Belmont	d			06 52	07 22			07 52				13 22			13 52			14 22				14 53	
Banstead	d			06 56	07 26			07 56				13 26			13 56			14 26				14 56	
Epsom Downs	a			06 59	07 29			07 59				13 29			13 59			14 29				15 00	

		SN B	SN A	SN B	SN A	TL	SN	SN	TL	SN	SN		TL	SN	SN	TL	SN	SN	TL	SN	SN	SN
London Victoria ⊖	d	14 16	14 16	14 30	14 30		14 46	15 00		15 16	15 30	and at the same minutes past each hour until		21 46	22 00		22 16	22 30		22 46	23 00	23 16
Clapham Junction	d	14 24	14 24	14 39	14 39		14 54	15 09		15 24	15 39			21 54	22 09		22 24	22 39		22 54	23 09	23 24
Balham ⊖	d	14 30	14 30	14 45	14 45		15 00	15 15		15 30	15 45			22 00	22 15		22 30	22 45		23 00	23 15	23 30
London Bridge	d					14 55			15 25				21 55			22 25			22 55			
Norwood Junction	d					15 09			15 39				22 09			22 39			23 09			
West Croydon	d	14 50	14 50	15 04	15 04	15 15	15 18	15 34	15 45	15 50	16 04		22 15	22 18	22 34	22 45	22 50	23 04	23 15	23 18	23 34	23 48
Waddon	d	14 53	14 53	15 06	15 06	15 18	15 21	15 37	15 48	15 53	16 06		22 18	22 21	22 37	22 48	22 53	23 06	23 18	23 21	23 37	23 51
Wallington	d	14 57	14 57	15 10	15 10	15 22	15 25	15 40	15 52	15 57	16 10		22 22	22 25	22 40	22 52	22 57	23 10	23 22	23 25	23 40	23 55
Carshalton Beeches	d	15 00	15 00	15 13	15 13	15 24	15 28	15 43	15 54	16 00	16 13		22 24	22 28	22 43	22 54	23 00	23 13	23 24	23 28	23 43	23 58
Sutton	a	15 03	15 06	15 16	15 16	15 28	15 33	15 46	15 58	16 03	16 16		22 28	22 33	22 46	22 58	23 03	23 16	23 28	23 33	23 46	00 03
Sutton	d			15 19	15 24			15 49			16 19				22 49			23 19			23 49	
Belmont	d			15 22	15 27			15 52			16 22				22 52			23 22			23 52	
Banstead	d			15 26	15 31			15 56			16 26				22 56			23 26			23 56	
Epsom Downs	a			15 29	15 34			15 59			16 29				22 59			23 29			23 59	

		SN
London Victoria ⊖	d	23 40
Clapham Junction	d	23 48
Balham ⊖	d	23 54
London Bridge	d	
Norwood Junction	d	
West Croydon	d	00 14
Waddon	d	00 17
Wallington	d	00 21
Carshalton Beeches	d	00 23
Sutton	a	00 27
Sutton	d	
Belmont	d	
Banstead	d	
Epsom Downs	a	

Sundays

20 May to 2 December

		SN C	SN	SN	SN	SN	SN	SN	SN	SN	SN	SN	SN		SN	SN	SN	SN	SN	SN	SN	SN D	SN E
London Victoria ⊖	d		06 45	07 16	07 34	07 46	08 04	08 16	08 34	08 46	09 02	09 16	09 32	and at the same minutes past each hour until	12 46	13 02	13 16	13 32	13 46	14 02	14 16	14 32	14 32
Clapham Junction	d		06 53	07 24	07 43	07 54	08 14	08 24	08 43	08 54	09 10	09 24	09 40		12 54	13 10	13 24	13 40	13 54	14 10	14 24	14 40	14 40
Balham ⊖	d		07 00	07 31	07 49	08 01	08 20	08 31	08 49	09 00	09 16	09 30	09 46		13 00	13 16	13 30	13 46	14 00	14 16	14 30	14 46	14 46
London Bridge	d																						
Norwood Junction	d																						
West Croydon	d	00 14	07 20	07 49	08 07	08 19	08 37	08 49	09 09	09 20	09 35	09 50	10 05		13 20	13 35	13 50	14 05	14 20	14 35	14 50	15 05	15 05
Waddon	d	00 17	07 22	07 51	08 10	08 22	08 40	08 52	09 12	09 22	09 37	09 52	10 07		13 22	13 37	13 52	14 07	14 22	14 37	14 52	15 07	15 07
Wallington	d	00 21	07 26	07 55	08 14	08 26	08 43	08 56	09 15	09 26	09 41	09 56	10 11		13 26	13 41	13 56	14 11	14 26	14 41	14 56	15 11	15 11
Carshalton Beeches	d	00 23	07 29	07 58	08 16	08 28	08 46	08 58	09 18	09 29	09 44	09 59	10 14		13 29	13 44	13 59	14 14	14 29	14 44	14 59	15 14	15 14
Sutton	a	00 27	07 32	08 01	08 20	08 32	08 49	09 02	09 21	09 32	09 47	10 02	10 17		13 32	13 47	14 02	14 17	14 32	14 47	15 02	15 17	15 17
Sutton	d				08 21		08 50		09 22		09 50		10 20			13 50		14 20		14 50			15 20
Belmont	d				08 24		08 53		09 25		09 53		10 23			13 53		14 23		14 53			15 23
Banstead	d				08 28		08 57		09 29		09 57		10 27			13 57		14 27		14 57			15 27
Epsom Downs	a				08 31		09 00		09 32		10 00		10 30			14 00		14 30		15 00			15 30

A from 29 September
B until 22 September
C not 20 May
D from 23 September
E until 16 September

Table T172-F

Sundays

20 May to 2 December

London via Wallington - Epsom Downs

		SN	SN A	SN B	SN	SN	SN	SN		SN	SN	SN	SN	SN	SN	SN	SN	SN	SN	SN	SN	SN
London Victoria ⊖	d	14 46	15 02	15 02	15 16	15 32	15 46	16 02	and at the same minutes past each hour until	18 16	18 32	18 46	19 02	19 16	19 32	19 46	20 02	20 16	20 32	20 46	21 02	21 16
Clapham Junction	d	14 54	15 10	15 10	15 24	15 40	15 54	16 10		18 24	18 40	18 54	19 10	19 24	19 40	19 54	20 10	20 24	20 40	20 54	21 10	21 24
Balham ⊖	d	15 00	15 16	15 16	15 30	15 46	16 00	16 16		18 30	18 46	19 00	19 16	19 30	19 46	20 00	20 16	20 30	20 46	21 00	21 16	21 30
London Bridge	d																					
Norwood Junction	d																					
West Croydon	d	15 20	15 35	15 35	15 50	16 05	16 20	16 35		18 50	19 05	19 20	19 35	19 50	20 05	20 20	20 35	20 50	21 05	21 20	21 35	21 50
Waddon	d	15 22	15 37	15 37	15 52	16 07	16 22	16 37		18 52	19 07	19 22	19 37	19 52	20 07	20 22	20 37	20 52	21 07	21 22	21 37	21 52
Wallington	d	15 26	15 41	15 41	15 56	16 11	16 26	16 41		18 56	19 11	19 26	19 41	19 56	20 11	20 26	20 41	20 56	21 11	21 26	21 41	21 56
Carshalton Beeches	d	15 29	15 44	15 44	15 59	16 14	16 29	16 44		18 59	19 14	19 29	19 44	19 59	20 14	20 29	20 44	20 59	21 14	21 29	21 44	21 59
Sutton	a	15 32	15 47	15 47	16 02	16 17	16 32	16 47		19 02	19 17	19 32	19 47	20 03	20 17	20 32	20 47	21 02	21 17	21 32	21 47	22 02
Sutton	d		15 50	15 54		16 20		16 50			19 20		19 50		20 20		20 50		21 20		21 50	
Belmont	d		15 53	15 57		16 23		16 53			19 23		19 53		20 23		20 53		21 23		21 53	
Banstead	d		15 57	16 01		16 27		16 57			19 27		19 57		20 27		20 57		21 27		21 57	
Epsom Downs	a		16 00	16 04		16 30		17 00			19 30		20 00		20 30		21 00		21 30		22 00	

		SN	SN	SN	SN	SN	SN	SN
London Victoria ⊖	d	21 32	21 46	22 02	22 16	22 32	22 46	23 16
Clapham Junction	d	21 40	21 54	22 10	22 24	22 40	22 54	23 24
Balham ⊖	d	21 46	22 00	22 16	22 30	22 46	23 00	23 31
London Bridge	d							
Norwood Junction	d							
West Croydon	d	22 05	22 20	22 40	22 49	23 05	23 22	23 49
Waddon	d	22 07	22 22	22 42	22 52	23 07	23 24	23 52
Wallington	d	22 11	22 26	22 46	22 56	23 11	23 28	23 56
Carshalton Beeches	d	22 14	22 29	22 49	22 58	23 14	23 31	23 58
Sutton	a	22 17	22 33	22 52	23 02	23 17	23 35	00 02
Sutton	d	22 20						
Belmont	d	22 23						
Banstead	d	22 27						
Epsom Downs	a	22 30						

A until 23 September
B from 30 September

Table T172-R

Sundays

20 May to 2 December

Epsom Downs via Wallington - London

		SN	SN	SN	SN		SN	SN	SN	SN	SN	SN	SN	SN	SN	SN	SN
Epsom Downs	d		16 39		17 09	and at the same minutes past each hour until		20 39		21 09		21 39		22 09		22 39	
Banstead	d		16 42		17 12			20 42		21 12		21 42		22 12		22 42	
Belmont	d		16 45		17 15			20 45		21 15		21 45		22 15		22 45	
Sutton	a		16 48		17 18			20 48		21 18		21 48		22 18		22 48	
Sutton	d	16 39	16 51	17 09	17 21		20 39	20 51	21 09	21 21	21 39	21 51	22 09	22 21	22 39	22 51	23 09
Carshalton Beeches	d	16 42	16 54	17 12	17 24		20 42	20 54	21 12	21 24	21 42	21 54	22 12	22 24	22 42	22 54	23 12
Wallington	d	16 45	16 57	17 15	17 27		20 45	20 57	21 15	21 27	21 45	21 57	22 15	22 27	22 45	22 57	23 15
Waddon	d	16 48	17 00	17 18	17 30		20 48	21 00	21 18	21 30	21 48	22 00	22 18	22 30	22 48	23 00	23 18
West Croydon	a	16 51	17 04	17 21	17 34		20 51	21 04	21 21	21 34	21 51	22 04	22 21	22 34	22 51	23 04	23 21
Norwood Junction	a																
London Bridge	a																
Balham	d	17 10	17 24	17 40	17 54		21 10	21 24	21 40	21 54	22 10	22 24	22 40	22 55	23 10	23 24	23 40
Clapham Junction	d	17 17	17 31	17 47	18 01		21 17	21 31	21 47	22 01	22 17	22 31	22 47	23 01	23 17	23 31	23 47
London Victoria ⊖	a	17 25	17 39	17 55	18 09		21 25	21 39	21 55	22 09	22 25	22 39	22 55	23 09	23 25	23 39	23 55

Please note, Network Rail have stated that further updates to this timetable are possible during the validity period.

Table T172-R

Epsom Downs via Wallington - London

Mondays to Fridays
21 May to 7 December

Miles	Miles		TL	SN	TL	SN	TL	SN	SN		TL	SN	SN	SN	TL	SN	SN	SN	TL		SN	SN	SN	TL
—	—	Epsom Downs d							06 39					07 09				07 39					08 09	
—	—	Banstead d							06 42					07 12				07 42					08 12	
—	—	Belmont d							06 45					07 15				07 45					08 15	
—	—	Sutton a							06 48					07 18				07 48					08 18	
0	0	Sutton d	05 42	05 51	05 56	06 16	06 26	06 41	06 51		06 56	07 00	07 11	07 21	07 26	07 30	07 41	07 51	07 56		08 00	08 11	08 21	08 26
1	1	Carshalton Beeches d	05 45	05 54	05 59	06 19	06 29	06 44	06 54		06 59		07 14	07 24	07 29		07 44	07 54	07 59		08 04	08 14	08 24	08 29
2	2	Wallington d	05 48	05 57	06 02	06 22	06 32	06 47	06 57		07 02	07 07	07 17	07 27	07 32	07 37	07 47	07 57	08 02		08 07	08 17	08 27	08 32
3½	3½	Waddon d	05 51	06 00	06 05	06 25	06 35	06 50	07 00		07 05		07 20	07 30	07 35		07 50	08 00	08 05		08 10	08 21	08 30	08 35
4½	4½	West Croydon a	05 55	06 05	06 09	06 32	06 39	06 55	07 04		07 09	07 12	07 25	07 34	07 39	07 42	07 55	08 04	08 09		08 15	08 24	08 34	08 39
—	—	Norwood Junction a	06 02		06 15		06 45				07 15				07 45				08 15					08 45
—	—	London Bridge a	06 31		06 28		06 58				07 28	08 06			07 58	08 36			08 28		09 06			08 58
10½	11¾	Balham d		06 25		06 55		07 14	07 25				07 44	07 55			08 14	08 25				08 45	08 55	
12½	13¾	Clapham Junction d		06 31		07 01		07 20	07 31				07 50	08 01			08 20	08 31				08 53	09 01	
15¼	16½	London Victoria ⊖ a		06 40		07 09		07 28	07 39				07 59	08 09			08 30	08 40				09 04	09 10	

	SN	SN	SN	TL	SN		SN	TL	SN	SN	TL	SN	SN	TL	SN		SN	TL	SN	SN	TL	SN	SN	TL
Epsom Downs d			08 39				09 09			09 39			10 09				10 39			11 09			11 39	
Banstead d			08 42				09 12			09 42			10 12				10 42			11 12			11 42	
Belmont d			08 45				09 15			09 45			10 15				10 45			11 15			11 45	
Sutton a			08 48				09 18			09 48			10 18				10 48			11 18			11 48	
Sutton d	08 30	08 41	08 51	08 56	09 11		09 21	09 26	09 41	09 51	09 56	10 11	10 21	10 26	10 41		10 51	10 56	11 11	11 21	11 26	11 41	11 51	11 56
Carshalton Beeches d		08 44	08 54	08 59	09 14		09 24	09 29	09 44	09 54	09 59	10 14	10 24	10 29	10 44		10 54	10 59	11 14	11 24	11 29	11 44	11 54	11 59
Wallington d	08 37	08 47	08 57	09 02	09 17		09 27	09 32	09 47	09 57	10 02	10 17	10 27	10 32	10 47		10 57	11 02	11 17	11 27	11 32	11 47	11 57	12 02
Waddon d		08 50	09 00	09 05	09 20		09 30	09 35	09 50	10 00	10 05	10 20	10 30	10 35	10 50		11 00	11 05	11 20	11 30	11 35	11 50	12 00	12 05
West Croydon a	08 42	08 55	09 04	09 09	09 25		09 34	09 39	09 55	10 04	10 09	10 25	10 34	10 39	10 55		11 04	11 09	11 25	11 34	11 39	11 55	12 04	12 09
Norwood Junction a				09 15				09 45			10 15			10 45				11 15			11 45			12 15
London Bridge a	09 36			09 28				09 58			10 28			10 58				11 28			11 58			12 28
Balham d		09 14	09 25		09 44		09 55		10 14	10 25		10 44	10 55		11 14		11 25		11 44	11 55		12 14	12 25	
Clapham Junction d		09 20	09 31		09 50		10 01		10 20	10 31		10 50	11 01		11 20		11 31		11 50	12 01		12 20	12 31	
London Victoria ⊖ a		09 30	09 40		09 58		10 09		10 28	10 39		10 58	11 09		11 28		11 39		11 58	12 09		12 28	12 39	

	SN		SN	TL	SN	SN TThO	SN MWFO	TL	SN	SN	TL		SN	SN MWFO	SN TThO	TL	SN	SN	TL	SN	SN		TL	SN A
Epsom Downs d			12 09			12 39	12 39			13 09				13 39	13 41			14 09			14 39			
Banstead d			12 12			12 42	12 42			13 12				13 42	13 44			14 12			14 42			
Belmont d			12 15			12 45	12 45			13 15				13 45	13 47			14 15			14 45			
Sutton a			12 18			12 48	12 48			13 18				13 48	13 50			14 18			14 48			
Sutton d	12 11		12 21	12 26	12 41	12 50	12 51	12 56	13 11	13 21	13 26		13 41	13 51	13 51	13 56	14 11	14 21	14 26	14 41	14 51		14 56	15 11
Carshalton Beeches d	12 14		12 24	12 29	12 44	12 53	12 54	12 59	13 14	13 24	13 29		13 44	13 54	13 54	13 59	14 14	14 24	14 29	14 44	14 54		14 59	15 14
Wallington d	12 17		12 27	12 32	12 47	12 56	12 57	13 02	13 17	13 27	13 32		13 47	13 57	13 57	14 02	14 17	14 27	14 32	14 47	14 57		15 02	15 17
Waddon d	12 20		12 30	12 35	12 50	12 59	13 00	13 05	13 20	13 30	13 35		13 50	14 00	14 00	14 05	14 20	14 30	14 35	14 50	15 00		15 05	15 20
West Croydon a	12 25		12 34	12 39	12 55	13 03	13 04	13 09	13 25	13 34	13 39		13 55	14 04	14 04	14 09	14 25	14 34	14 39	14 55	15 04		15 09	15 25
Norwood Junction a				12 45				13 15			13 45					14 15			14 45				15 15	
London Bridge a				12 58				13 28			13 58					14 28			14 58				15 28	
Balham d	12 44		12 55		13 14	13 25	13 25		13 44	13 55			14 14	14 25	14 25		14 44	14 55		15 14	15 25			15 44
Clapham Junction d	12 50		13 01		13 20	13 31	13 31		13 50	14 01			14 20	14 31	14 31		14 50	15 01		15 20	15 31			15 50
London Victoria ⊖ a	12 58		13 09		13 28	13 39	13 39		13 58	14 09			14 28	14 39	14 39		14 58	15 09		15 28	15 39			15 58

	SN B	SN A	SN B	TL	SN	SN A	SN B		TL	SN	SN	TL	SN	SN	TL	SN	SN		TL	SN	SN	SN	SN	SN
Epsom Downs d		15 09				15 39	15 41				16 09			16 39			17 09				17 39			18 09
Banstead d		15 12				15 42	15 44				16 12			16 42			17 12				17 42			18 12
Belmont d		15 15				15 45	15 47				16 15			16 45			17 15				17 45			18 15
Sutton a		15 18				15 48	15 50				16 18			16 48			17 18				17 48			18 18
Sutton d	15 12	15 21	15 21	15 26	15 41	15 51	15 51		15 56	16 11	16 21	16 26	16 41	16 51	16 56	17 11	17 21		17 26	17 41	17 51	18 00	18 11	18 21
Carshalton Beeches d	15 15	15 24	15 24	15 29	15 44	15 54	15 54		15 59	16 14	16 24	16 29	16 44	16 54	16 59	17 14	17 24		17 29	17 44	17 54		18 14	18 24
Wallington d	15 18	15 27	15 27	15 32	15 47	15 57	15 57		16 02	16 17	16 27	16 32	16 47	16 57	17 02	17 17	17 27		17 32	17 47	17 57	18 07	18 17	18 27
Waddon d	15 21	15 30	15 30	15 35	15 50	16 00	16 00		16 05	16 20	16 30	16 35	16 50	17 00	17 05	17 20	17 30		17 35	17 50	18 00		18 20	18 30
West Croydon a	15 25	15 34	15 34	15 39	15 55	16 04	16 04		16 09	16 25	16 34	16 39	16 55	17 04	17 09	17 25	17 34		17 39	17 55	18 04	18 12	18 25	18 34
Norwood Junction a				15 45					16 15			16 45			17 15				17 45					
London Bridge a				15 58					16 28			16 58			17 28				17 58			19 06		
Balham d	15 44	15 55	15 55		16 14	16 25	16 25			16 44	16 55		17 14	17 25		17 44	17 55			18 14	18 25		18 44	18 55
Clapham Junction d	15 50	16 01	16 01		16 20	16 31	16 31			16 50	17 01		17 20	17 31		17 50	18 01			18 20	18 31		18 50	19 01
London Victoria ⊖ a	15 58	16 09	16 11		16 28	16 39	16 39			16 58	17 09		17 28	17 39		17 58	18 09			18 30	18 39		19 00	19 09

	TL	SN	SN		SN	SN	SN	SN	TL	SN	SN	TL	SN		SN	TL	SN	SN	TL	SN	SN	TL	SN	
Epsom Downs d					18 39			19 09			19 39				20 09			20 39			21 09			
Banstead d					18 42			19 12			19 42				20 12			20 42			21 12			
Belmont d					18 45			19 15			19 45				20 15			20 45			21 15			
Sutton a					18 48			19 18			19 48				20 18			20 48			21 18			
Sutton d	18 26	18 30	18 41		18 51	19 00	19 11	19 21	19 26	19 41	19 51	19 56	20 11		20 21	20 26	20 41	20 51	20 56	21 11	21 21	21 26	21 41	
Carshalton Beeches d	18 29		18 44		18 54		19 14	19 24	19 29	19 44	19 54	19 59	20 14		20 24	20 29	20 44	20 54	20 59	21 14	21 24	21 29	21 44	
Wallington d	18 32	18 37	18 47		18 57	19 07	19 17	19 27	19 32	19 47	19 57	20 02	20 17		20 27	20 32	20 47	20 57	21 02	21 17	21 27	21 32	21 47	
Waddon d	18 35		18 50		19 00		19 20	19 30	19 35	19 50	20 00	20 05	20 20		20 30	20 35	20 50	21 00	21 05	21 20	21 30	21 35	21 50	
West Croydon a	18 39	18 42	18 55		19 04	19 12	19 25	19 34	19 39	19 55	20 04	20 09	20 25		20 34	20 39	20 55	21 04	21 09	21 25	21 34	21 39	21 55	
Norwood Junction a	18 45								19 45			20 15				20 45			21 15			21 45		
London Bridge a	18 58	19 36				20 06			19 58			20 28				20 58			21 28			21 58		
Balham d			19 14		19 25		19 44	19 55		20 14	20 25		20 44		20 55		21 14	21 25		21 44	21 55		22 14	
Clapham Junction d			19 20		19 31		19 50	20 01		20 20	20 31		20 50		21 01		21 20	21 31		21 50	22 01		22 20	
London Victoria ⊖ a			19 28		19 39		19 58	20 09		20 30	20 39		20 58		21 09		21 28	21 39		21 58	22 09		22 28	

A until 21 September
B from 24 September

Table T172-R

Epsom Downs via Wallington - London

Mondays to Fridays
21 May to 7 December

	SN	TL	SN	SN	TL	SN	SN		TL	SN	TL	SN
Epsom Downs d	21 39			22 09			22 41			23 05		23 37
Banstead d	21 42			22 12			22 44			23 08		23 40
Belmont d	21 45			22 15			22 47			23 11		23 43
Sutton a	21 48			22 18			22 50			23 14		23 46
Sutton d	21 50	21 56	22 11	22 21	22 26	22 41	22 51		22 56	23 15	23 26	23 49
Carshalton Beeches d	21 53	21 59	22 14	22 24	22 29	22 44	22 54		22 59	23 18	23 29	23 52
Wallington d	21 56	22 02	22 17	22 27	22 32	22 47	22 57		23 02	23 21	23 32	23 55
Waddon d	22 00	22 05	22 20	22 30	22 35	22 50	23 00		23 05	23 24	23 35	23 58
West Croydon a	22 03	22 09	22 25	22 34	22 39	22 55	23 04		23 09	23 27	23 39	00 02
Norwood Junction a		22 15			22 45				23 15			
London Bridge a		22 28			22 58				23 28			
Balham d	22 25		22 44	22 55		23 14	23 25			23 48		
Clapham Junction d	22 31		22 50	23 01		23 20	23 31			23 54		
London Victoria ⊖ a	22 39		23 00	23 09		23 28	23 39			00 02		

Saturdays
26 May to 8 December

	SN	SN	SN	TL	SN	SN	TL	SN	SN		TL	SN	SN	TL	SN	SN		TL	SN A	SN B	SN A	SN B	TL
Epsom Downs d						07 09			07 39				14 09			14 39					15 09		
Banstead d						07 12			07 42				14 12			14 42					15 12		
Belmont d						07 15			07 45				14 15			14 45					15 15		
Sutton a						07 18			07 48				14 18			14 48					15 18		
Sutton d	06 21	06 41	06 51	06 56	07 11	07 21	07 26	07 41	07 51	and at the same minutes past each hour until	13 56	14 11	14 21	14 26	14 41	14 51		14 56	15 11	15 12	15 21	15 21	15 26
Carshalton Beeches d	06 24	06 44	06 54	06 59	07 14	07 24	07 29	07 44	07 54		13 59	14 14	14 24	14 29	14 44	14 54		14 59	15 14	15 15	15 24	15 24	15 29
Wallington d	06 27	06 47	06 57	07 02	07 17	07 27	07 32	07 47	07 57		14 02	14 17	14 27	14 32	14 47	14 57		15 02	15 17	15 18	15 27	15 27	15 32
Waddon d	06 30	06 50	07 00	07 05	07 20	07 30	07 35	07 50	08 00		14 05	14 20	14 30	14 35	14 50	15 00		15 05	15 20	15 21	15 30	15 30	15 35
West Croydon a	06 34	06 55	07 04	07 09	07 25	07 34	07 39	07 55	08 04		14 09	14 25	14 34	14 39	14 55	15 04		15 09	15 25	15 25	15 34	15 34	15 39
Norwood Junction a				07 15			07 45				14 15			14 45				15 15					15 45
London Bridge a				07 28			07 58				14 28			14 58				15 28					15 58
Balham d	06 55	07 14	07 25		07 44	07 55		08 14	08 25			14 44	14 55		15 14	15 25			15 44	15 44	15 55	15 55	
Clapham Junction d	07 01	07 20	07 31		07 50	08 01		08 20	08 31			14 50	15 01		15 20	15 31			15 50	15 50	16 01	16 01	
London Victoria ⊖ a	07 09	07 28	07 39		07 58	08 09		08 28	08 39			14 58	15 09		15 28	15 39			15 58	15 58	16 09	16 09	

	SN	SN A	SN B	TL	SN	SN	TL	SN	SN		TL	SN	SN	TL	SN	SN		TL	SN	SN	TL	SN	SN
Epsom Downs d		15 39	15 41			16 09			16 39				20 09			20 39				21 09			21 39
Banstead d		15 42	15 44			16 12			16 42				20 12			20 42				21 12			21 42
Belmont d		15 45	15 47			16 15			16 45				20 15			20 45				21 15			21 45
Sutton a		15 48	15 50			16 18			16 48				20 18			20 48				21 18			21 48
Sutton d	15 41	15 51	15 51	15 56	16 11	16 21	16 26	16 41	16 51	and at the same minutes past each hour until	19 56	20 11	20 21	20 26	20 41	20 51		20 56	21 11	21 21	21 26	21 41	21 51
Carshalton Beeches d	15 44	15 54	15 54	15 59	16 14	16 24	16 29	16 44	16 54		19 59	20 14	20 24	20 29	20 44	20 54		20 59	21 14	21 24	21 29	21 44	21 54
Wallington d	15 47	15 57	15 57	16 02	16 17	16 27	16 32	16 47	16 57		20 02	20 17	20 27	20 32	20 47	20 57		21 02	21 17	21 27	21 32	21 47	21 57
Waddon d	15 50	16 00	16 00	16 05	16 20	16 30	16 35	16 50	17 00		20 05	20 20	20 30	20 35	20 50	21 00		21 05	21 20	21 30	21 35	21 50	22 00
West Croydon a	15 55	16 04	16 04	16 09	16 25	16 34	16 39	16 55	17 04		20 09	20 25	20 34	20 39	20 55	21 04		21 09	21 25	21 34	21 39	21 55	22 04
Norwood Junction a				16 15			16 45				20 15			20 45				21 15			21 45		
London Bridge a				16 28			16 58				20 28			20 58				21 28			21 58		
Balham d	16 14	16 25	16 25		16 44	16 55		17 14	17 25			20 44	20 55		21 14	21 25			21 44	21 55		22 14	22 25
Clapham Junction d	16 20	16 31	16 31		16 50	17 01		17 20	17 31			20 50	21 01		21 20	21 31			21 50	22 01		22 20	22 31
London Victoria ⊖ a	16 28	16 39	16 39		16 58	17 09		17 28	17 39			20 58	21 09		21 28	21 39			21 58	22 09		22 30	22 39

	TL	SN	SN		TL	SN	SN	TL	SN	TL	SN
Epsom Downs d			22 09				22 39		23 09		23 39
Banstead d			22 12				22 42		23 12		23 42
Belmont d			22 15				22 45		23 15		23 45
Sutton a			22 18				22 48		23 18		23 48
Sutton d	21 56	22 11	22 21		22 26	22 41	22 51	22 56	23 21	23 32	23 51
Carshalton Beeches d	21 59	22 14	22 24		22 29	22 44	22 54	22 59	23 24	23 35	23 54
Wallington d	22 02	22 17	22 27		22 32	22 47	22 57	23 02	23 27	23 37	23 57
Waddon d	22 05	22 20	22 30		22 35	22 50	23 00	23 05	23 30	23 40	00 01
West Croydon a	22 09	22 25	22 34		22 39	22 55	23 04	23 09	23 34	23 45	00 05
Norwood Junction a	22 15				22 45			23 15			
London Bridge a	22 28				22 58			23 28			
Balham d		22 44	22 55			23 14	23 25		23 56		
Clapham Junction d		22 50	23 01			23 20	23 31		00 02		
London Victoria ⊖ a		23 00	23 09			23 30	23 39		00 09		

Sundays
20 May to 2 December

	SN C	SN C	TL C	SN	SN	SN	SN	SN	SN	SN	SN		SN	SN	SN	SN		SN	SN D	SN E	SN	SN D	SN E
Epsom Downs d									08 39		09 09			14 39		15 09			15 39			16 09	16 11
Banstead d									08 42		09 12			14 42		15 12			15 42			16 12	16 14
Belmont d									08 45		09 15			14 45		15 15			15 45			16 15	16 17
Sutton a									08 48		09 18			14 48		15 18			15 48			16 18	16 20
Sutton d			00 03	06 53	07 09	07 39	08 09	08 39	08 51	09 09	09 21	and at the same minutes past each hour until	14 39	14 51	15 09	15 21		15 39	15 51	15 51	16 09	16 21	16 21
Carshalton Beeches d			00 06	06 56	07 12	07 42	08 12	08 42	08 54	09 12	09 24		14 42	14 54	15 12	15 24		15 42	15 54	15 54	16 12	16 24	16 24
Wallington d			00 08	06 59	07 15	07 45	08 15	08 45	08 57	09 15	09 27		14 45	14 57	15 15	15 27		15 45	15 57	15 57	16 15	16 27	16 27
Waddon d	00 01		00 11	07 02	07 18	07 48	08 18	08 48	09 00	09 18	09 30		14 48	15 00	15 18	15 30		15 48	16 00	16 00	16 18	16 30	16 30
West Croydon a	00 05		00 15	07 06	07 21	07 51	08 21	08 51	09 04	09 21	09 34		14 51	15 04	15 21	15 34		15 51	16 04	16 04	16 21	16 34	16 34
Norwood Junction a																							
London Bridge a																							
Balham d				07 25	07 41	08 11	08 41	09 10	09 24	09 40	09 54		15 10	15 24	15 40	15 54		16 10	16 24	16 24	16 40	16 54	16 54
Clapham Junction d		00 02		07 31	07 47	08 17	08 47	09 17	09 31	09 47	10 01		15 17	15 31	15 47	16 01		16 17	16 31	16 31	16 47	17 01	17 01
London Victoria ⊖ a		00 09		07 39	07 55	08 25	08 55	09 25	09 39	09 55	10 09		15 25	15 39	15 55	16 09		16 25	16 39	16 39	16 55	17 09	17 09

A until 22 September
B from 29 September
C not 20 May
D until 23 September
E from 30 September

Table T173-F

Mondays to Fridays

21 May to 7 December

London Bridge - South Bermondsey, Queens Road Peckham, Peckham Rye, East Dulwich, North Dulwich, Tulse Hill and Streatham

Miles	Miles	Miles	Miles			TL MX A	SN MX B	SN MX	TL C	TL D	SN	TL C	SN	TL E	SN	SN	TL C	SN	TL C	SN	SN	TL A	SN
0	0	—	—	London Bridge ⊖	d			00 01			05 38		06 01		06 08	06 14		06 31		06 38	06 44		07 01
1¾	1¾	—	—	**South Bermondsey**	d			00 05			05 44		06 05		06 14	06 19		06 35		06 44	06 49		07 05
2¾	2¾	—	—	Queens Rd Peckham	d		00 02	00 08			05 47		06 08		06 17	06 22		06 38		06 47	06 52		07 08
3½	3½	—	—	Peckham Rye	d		00 06	00 11			05 50		06 11		06 20	06 25		06 41		06 50	06 55		07 11
4¼	4¼	—	—	**East Dulwich**	d		00 09	00 14			05 53		06 14		06 23	06 28		06 44		06 53	06 58		07 14
4¾	4¾	—	—	**North Dulwich**	d		00 11	00 17			05 55		06 17		06 25	06 30		06 47		06 55	07 00		07 17
—	—	0	0	St Pancras International	d				05 12	05 27		05 42		05 57			06 12		06 27			06 42	
—	—	1¼	1¼	Farringdon	d				05 17	05 32		05 47		06 02			06 17		06 32			06 47	
—	—	1½	1½	City Thameslink	d				05 19	05 34		05 49		06 04			06 19		06 34			06 49	
—	—	2	2	London Blackfriars	d				05 21	05 36		05 51		06 06			06 21		06 36			06 51	
—	—	3¼	3¼	Elephant & Castle	d				05 25	05 40		05 55		06 10			06 25		06 40			06 55	
—	—	5	5	Loughborough Jn	d	00 02			05 30	05 45		06 00		06 15			06 30		06 45			07 00	
—	—	6	6	Herne Hill	d	00 06			05 35	05 50		06 05		06 20			06 35		06 50			07 05	
6	6	7	7	**Tulse Hill**	d	00 11	00 18	00 21	05 40	05 56	05 59	06 10	06 21	06 26	06 29	06 34	06 40	06 51	06 56	06 59	07 04	07 10	07 21
—	6¾	—	—	West Norwood	a			00 24					06 24					06 54					07 24
—	7¾	—	—	Gipsy Hill	a			00 27					06 27					06 57					07 27
—	8½	—	—	Crystal Palace	a			00 31					06 31					07 01					07 31
—	10	—	—	**Birkbeck**	a								06 35					07 05					07 35
—	11½	—	—	Beckenham Junction	a								06 39					07 09					07 39
7½	—	8½	8½	**Streatham**	d	00 14	00 22		05 44	06 00	06 04	06 14		06 30	06 34	06 38	06 44		07 00	07 04	07 08	07 14	
8	—	—	—	Streatham Common	a		00 25									06 41					07 11		
9	—	—	—	Norbury	a		00 28									06 44					07 14		
10¼	—	—	—	Thornton Heath	a		00 31									06 47					07 17		
11	—	—	—	Selhurst	a		00 34									06 50					07 20		
12	—	—	—	East Croydon	a																		
—	—	10	—	Tooting	a	00 18			05 48		06 08	06 18			06 38		06 48			07 08		07 18	
—	—	11½	—	Haydons Road	a	00 22			05 52		06 12	06 22			06 42		06 52			07 12		07 22	
—	—	12¼	—	Wimbledon	a	00 24			05 54		06 14	06 24			06 44		06 54			07 14		07 24	
—	—	—	10¼	Mitcham Eastfields	a					06 04				06 34					07 04				
—	—	—	11¼	Mitcham Junction	a					06 07				06 37					07 07				
—	—	—	12½	Hackbridge	a					06 10				06 40					07 10				
—	—	—	13¼	Carshalton	a					06 13				06 43					07 13				
—	—	—	14½	Sutton	a	00 44			06 14	06 17	06 34	06 44		06 47	07 04		07 14		07 17	07 34		07 44	

		TL A	SN	SN	TL A	SN	TL A	SN	SN	TL A	SN	TL A	SN	TL A	SN	TL A	SN	TL A	SN	TL A	SN
London Bridge ⊖	d		07 07	07 14		07 31		07 37	07 44		08 01		08 14		08 31		08 44		09 01		09 14
South Bermondsey	d		07 14	07 19		07 35		07 44	07 49		08 05		08 19		08 35		08 49		09 05		09 19
Queens Rd Peckham	d		07 17	07 22		07 38		07 47	07 52		08 08		08 22		08 38		08 52		09 08		09 22
Peckham Rye	d		07 20	07 25		07 41		07 50	07 55		08 11		08 25		08 41		08 55		09 11		09 25
East Dulwich	d		07 23	07 28		07 44		07 53	07 58		08 14		08 28		08 44		08 58		09 14		09 28
North Dulwich	d		07 25	07 30		07 47		07 55	08 00		08 17		08 30		08 47		09 00		09 17		09 30
St Pancras International	d	06 57			07 12		07 27			07 42		07 57		08 12		08 27		08 42		08 57	
Farringdon	d	07 02			07 17		07 32			07 47		08 02		08 17		08 32		08 47		09 02	
City Thameslink	d	07 04			07 19		07 34			07 49		08 04		08 19		08 34		08 49		09 04	
London Blackfriars	d	07 06			07 21		07 36			07 51		08 06		08 21		08 36		08 51		09 06	
Elephant & Castle	d	07 10			07 25		07 40			07 55		08 10		08 25		08 40		08 55		09 10	
Loughborough Jn	d	07 15			07 30		07 45			08 00		08 15		08 30		08 45		09 00		09 15	
Herne Hill	d	07 20			07 35		07 50			08 05		08 20		08 35		08 50		09 05		09 20	
Tulse Hill	d	07 26	07 29	07 34	07 40	07 51	07 56	07 59	08 04	08 10	08 21	08 27	08 34	08 40	08 51	08 57	09 04	09 10	09 21	09 27	09 34
West Norwood	a					07 54					08 24				08 54				09 24		
Gipsy Hill	a					07 57					08 27				08 57				09 27		
Crystal Palace	a					08 01					08 31				09 01				09 31		
Birkbeck	a					08 05					08 35				09 05				09 35		
Beckenham Junction	a					08 09					08 39				09 09				09 39		
Streatham	d	07 30	07 34	07 38	07 44		08 00	08 04	08 08	08 14		08 30	08 38	08 44		09 00	09 08	09 14		09 30	09 38
Streatham Common	a			07 41					08 11				08 41				09 11				09 41
Norbury	a			07 44					08 14				08 44				09 14				09 44
Thornton Heath	a			07 47					08 17				08 47				09 17				09 47
Selhurst	a			07 50					08 20				08 50				09 20				09 50
East Croydon	a																				
Tooting	a		07 38		07 48			08 08		08 18				08 48				09 18			
Haydons Road	a		07 42		07 52			08 12		08 22				08 52				09 22			
Wimbledon	a		07 44		07 54			08 14		08 24				08 54				09 24			
Mitcham Eastfields	a	07 34					08 04					08 34				09 04				09 34	
Mitcham Junction	a	07 37					08 07					08 37				09 07				09 37	
Hackbridge	a	07 40					08 10					08 40				09 10				09 40	
Carshalton	a	07 43					08 13					08 43				09 13				09 43	
Sutton	a	07 47	08 04		08 14		08 17	08 34		08 44		08 47		09 14		09 17		09 44		09 47	

A From St Albans City
B From London Bridge
C From Luton
D From West Hampstead Thameslink
E From Kentish Town

Table T173-F

Mondays to Fridays

21 May to 7 December

London Bridge - South Bermondsey, Queens Road Peckham, Peckham Rye, East Dulwich, North Dulwich, Tulse Hill and Streatham

		TL A	SN	TL A	SN B	TL A	SN	TL A	SN B		TL A	SN	TL A	SN B	TL A	SN	TL A	SN B	TL A	SN	TL A	SN B	TL A
London Bridge ⊖	d		09 31		09 44		10 01		10 14			13 31		13 44		14 01		14 14		14 31		14 44	
South Bermondsey	d		09 35		09 49		10 05		10 19			13 35		13 49		14 05		14 19		14 35		14 49	
Queens Rd Peckham	d		09 38		09 52		10 08		10 22			13 38		13 52		14 08		14 22		14 38		14 52	
Peckham Rye	d		09 41		09 55		10 11		10 25			13 41		13 55		14 11		14 25		14 41		14 55	
East Dulwich	d		09 44		09 58		10 14		10 28			13 44		13 58		14 14		14 28		14 44		14 58	
North Dulwich	d		09 47		10 00		10 17		10 30			13 47		14 00		14 17		14 30		14 47		15 00	
St Pancras International	d	09 12		09 27		09 42		09 57			13 12		13 27		13 42		13 57		14 12		14 27		14 42
Farringdon	d	09 17		09 32		09 47		10 02			13 17		13 32		13 47		14 02		14 17		14 32		14 47
City Thameslink	d	09 19		09 34		09 49		10 04			13 19		13 34		13 49		14 04		14 19		14 34		14 49
London Blackfriars	d	09 21		09 36		09 51		10 06			13 21		13 36		13 51		14 06		14 21		14 36		14 51
Elephant & Castle	d	09 25		09 40		09 55		10 10			13 25		13 40		13 55		14 10		14 25		14 40		14 55
Loughborough Jn	d	09 30		09 45		10 00		10 15			13 30		13 45		14 00		14 15		14 30		14 45		15 00
Herne Hill	d	09 35		09 50		10 05		10 20		and at	13 35		13 50		14 05		14 20		14 35		14 50		15 05
Tulse Hill	d	09 40	09 51	09 56	10 04	10 10	10 21	10 26	10 34	the same	13 40	13 51	13 56	14 04	14 10	14 21	14 26	14 34	14 39	14 51	14 56	15 04	15 10
West Norwood	a		09 54				10 24			minutes		13 54				14 24				14 54			
Gipsy Hill	a		09 57				10 27			past		13 57				14 27				14 57			
Crystal Palace	a		10 01				10 31			each		14 01				14 31				15 01			
Birkbeck	a		10 05				10 35			hour until		14 05				14 35				15 05			
Beckenham Junction	a		10 09				10 39					14 09				14 39				15 09			
Streatham	d	09 44		10 00	10 08	10 14		10 30	10 38		13 44		14 00	14 08	14 14		14 30	14 38	14 42		15 00	15 08	15 14
Streatham Common	a				10 11				10 41					14 11				14 41				15 11	
Norbury	a				10 14				10 44					14 14				14 44				15 14	
Thornton Heath	a				10 17				10 47					14 17				14 47				15 17	
Selhurst	a				10 20				10 50					14 20				14 50				15 20	
East Croydon	a				10 24				10 54					14 24				14 54				15 24	
Tooting	a	09 48				10 18					13 48				14 18				14 46				15 18
Haydons Road	a	09 52				10 22					13 52				14 22				14 50				15 22
Wimbledon	a	09 54				10 24					13 54				14 24				14 52				15 24
Mitcham Eastfields	a			10 04				10 34					14 04				14 34				15 04		
Mitcham Junction	a			10 07				10 37					14 07				14 37				15 07		
Hackbridge	a			10 10				10 40					14 10				14 40				15 10		
Carshalton	a			10 13				10 43					14 13				14 43				15 13		
Sutton	a	10 14		10 17		10 44		10 47			14 14		14 17		14 44		14 47		15 14		15 17		15 44

		SN	TL A	SN B	TL A	SN	TL A	SN B	TL A	SN	TL A	SN	TL A	SN	TL A	SN	TL A	SN	SN	TL A	SN	TL A	SN
London Bridge ⊖	d	15 01		15 14		15 31		15 44		16 01		16 14		16 31		16 44		16 52	17 01		17 14		17 22
South Bermondsey	d	15 05		15 19		15 35		15 49		16 05		16 19		16 35		16 49		16 59	17 05		17 19		17 29
Queens Rd Peckham	d	15 08		15 22		15 38		15 52		16 08		16 22		16 38		16 52		17 02	17 08		17 22		17 32
Peckham Rye	d	15 11		15 25		15 41		15 55		16 11		16 25		16 41		16 55		17 05	17 11		17 25		17 35
East Dulwich	d	15 14		15 28		15 44		15 58		16 14		16 28		16 44		16 58		17 08	17 14		17 28		17 38
North Dulwich	d	15 17		15 30		15 47		16 00		16 17		16 30		16 47		17 00		17 10	17 17		17 30		17 40
St Pancras International	d		14 57		15 12		15 27		15 42		15 57		16 12		16 27		16 42			16 57		17 12	
Farringdon	d		15 02		15 17		15 32		15 47		16 02		16 17		16 32		16 47			17 02		17 17	
City Thameslink	d		15 04		15 19		15 34		15 49		16 04		16 19		16 34		16 49			17 04		17 19	
London Blackfriars	d		15 06		15 21		15 36		15 51		16 06		16 21		16 36		16 51			17 06		17 21	
Elephant & Castle	d		15 10		15 25		15 40		15 55		16 10		16 25		16 40		16 55			17 10		17 25	
Loughborough Jn	d		15 15		15 30		15 45		16 00		16 15		16 30		16 45		17 00			17 15		17 30	
Herne Hill	d		15 20		15 35		15 50		16 05		16 20		16 35		16 50		17 05			17 20		17 35	
Tulse Hill	d	15 21	15 26	15 34	15 40	15 51	15 56	16 04	16 10	16 21	16 26	16 34	16 40	16 51	16 56	17 04	17 10	17 16	17 21	17 26	17 34	17 40	17 46
West Norwood	a	15 24				15 54				16 24				16 54					17 24				
Gipsy Hill	a	15 27				15 57				16 27				16 57					17 27				
Crystal Palace	a	15 31				16 01				16 31				17 01					17 31				
Birkbeck	a	15 35				16 05				16 35				17 05					17 35				
Beckenham Junction	a	15 39				16 09				16 39				17 09					17 39				
Streatham	d		15 30	15 38	15 44		16 00	16 08	16 14		16 30	16 38	16 44		17 00	17 08	17 14	17 20		17 30	17 38	17 44	17 50
Streatham Common	a			15 41				16 11				16 41				17 11					17 41		
Norbury	a			15 44				16 14				16 44				17 14					17 44		
Thornton Heath	a			15 47				16 17				16 47				17 17					17 47		
Selhurst	a			15 50				16 20				16 50				17 20					17 50		
East Croydon	a			15 54				16 24															
Tooting	a				15 48				16 18				16 48				17 18					17 48	
Haydons Road	a				15 52				16 22				16 52				17 22					17 52	
Wimbledon	a				15 54				16 24				16 54				17 24					17 54	
Mitcham Eastfields	a		15 34				16 04				16 34				17 04			17 24		17 34			17 54
Mitcham Junction	a		15 37				16 07				16 37				17 07			17 27		17 37			17 57
Hackbridge	a		15 40				16 10				16 40				17 10			17 30		17 40			18 00
Carshalton	a		15 43				16 13				16 43				17 13			17 33		17 43			18 03
Sutton	a		15 47		16 14		16 17		16 44		16 47		17 14		17 17		17 44	17 37		17 47		18 14	18 07

A From St Albans City
B To Caterham

21 May to 7 December

London Bridge - South Bermondsey, Queens Road Peckham, Peckham Rye, East Dulwich, North Dulwich, Tulse Hill and Streatham

			SN	TL A	SN	TL A	SN	SN	TL A	SN	TL A		SN	SN	TL A	SN	TL A	SN	TL A	SN B	TL A		SN	TL A	SN B
London Bridge ⊖	d		17 31		17 44		17 52	18 01		18 14			18 22	18 31		18 44		19 01		19 14			19 31		19 44
South Bermondsey	d		17 35		17 49		17 59	18 05		18 19			18 29	18 35		18 49		19 05		19 19			19 35		19 49
Queens Rd Peckham	d		17 38		17 52		18 02	18 08		18 22			18 32	18 38		18 52		19 08		19 22			19 38		19 52
Peckham Rye	d		17 41		17 55		18 05	18 11		18 25			18 35	18 41		18 55		19 11		19 25			19 41		19 55
East Dulwich	d		17 44		17 58		18 08	18 14		18 28			18 38	18 44		18 58		19 14		19 28			19 44		19 58
North Dulwich	d		17 47		18 00		18 10	18 17		18 30			18 40	18 47		19 00		19 17		19 30			19 47		20 00
St Pancras International	d			17 27		17 42			17 57		18 12				18 27		18 42		18 57		19 12			19 27	
Farringdon	d			17 32		17 47			18 02		18 17				18 32		18 47		19 02		19 17			19 32	
City Thameslink	d			17 34		17 49			18 04		18 19				18 34		18 49		19 04		19 19			19 34	
London Blackfriars	d			17 36		17 51			18 06		18 21				18 36		18 51		19 06		19 21			19 36	
Elephant & Castle	d			17 40		17 55			18 10		18 25				18 40		18 55		19 10		19 25			19 40	
Loughborough Jn	d			17 45		18 00			18 15		18 30				18 45		19 00		19 15		19 30			19 45	
Herne Hill	d			17 50		18 05			18 20		18 35				18 50		19 05		19 20		19 35			19 50	
Tulse Hill	d		17 51	17 56	18 04	18 10	18 16	18 21	18 26	18 34	18 40		18 46	18 51	18 56	19 04	19 10	19 21	19 26	19 34	19 40		19 51	19 56	20 04
West Norwood	a		17 54					18 24						18 54				19 24					19 54		
Gipsy Hill	a		17 57					18 27						18 57				19 27					19 57		
Crystal Palace	a		18 01					18 31						19 01				19 31					20 01		
Birkbeck	a		18 05					18 35						19 05				19 35					20 05		
Beckenham Junction	a		18 09					18 39						19 09				19 39					20 09		
Streatham	d			18 00	18 08	18 14	18 20		18 30	18 38	18 44		18 50		19 00	19 08	19 14		19 30	19 38	19 44			20 00	20 08
Streatham Common	a				18 11					18 41						19 11				19 41					20 11
Norbury	a				18 14					18 44						19 14				19 44					20 14
Thornton Heath	a				18 17					18 47						19 17				19 47					20 17
Selhurst	a				18 20					18 50						19 20				19 50					20 20
East Croydon	a																			19 54					20 24
Tooting	a					18 18					18 48						19 18				19 48				
Haydons Road	a					18 22					18 52						19 22				19 52				
Wimbledon	a					18 24					18 54						19 24				19 54				
Mitcham Eastfields	a			18 04			18 24		18 34				18 54		19 04				19 34					20 04	
Mitcham Junction	a			18 07			18 27		18 37				18 57		19 07				19 37					20 07	
Hackbridge	a			18 10			18 30		18 40				19 00		19 10				19 40					20 10	
Carshalton	a			18 13			18 33		18 43				19 03		19 13				19 43					20 13	
Sutton	a			18 17		18 44	18 37		18 47		19 14		19 07		19 17		19 44		19 47		20 14			20 17	

		TL A	SN	TL A	SN B	TL A	SN		TL A	SN B	TL A	SN	TL A	SN B	TL A	SN	TL A		SN B	TL A	SN	TL A	SN B	TL A	SN
London Bridge ⊖	d		20 01		20 14		20 31			20 44		21 01		21 14		21 31			21 44		22 01		22 14		22 31
South Bermondsey	d		20 05		20 19		20 35			20 49		21 05		21 19		21 35			21 49		22 05		22 19		22 35
Queens Rd Peckham	d		20 08		20 22		20 38			20 52		21 08		21 22		21 38			21 52		22 08		22 22		22 38
Peckham Rye	d		20 11		20 25		20 41			20 55		21 11		21 25		21 41			21 55		22 11		22 25		22 41
East Dulwich	d		20 14		20 28		20 44			20 58		21 14		21 28		21 44			21 58		22 14		22 28		22 44
North Dulwich	d		20 17		20 30		20 47			21 00		21 17		21 30		21 47			22 00		22 17		22 30		22 47
St Pancras International	d	19 42		19 57		20 12			20 27		20 42		20 57		21 12		21 27			21 42		21 57		22 12	
Farringdon	d	19 47		20 02		20 17			20 32		20 47		21 02		21 17		21 32			21 47		22 02		22 17	
City Thameslink	d	19 49		20 04		20 19			20 34		20 49		21 04		21 19		21 34			21 49		22 04		22 19	
London Blackfriars	d	19 51		20 06		20 21			20 36		20 51		21 06		21 21		21 36			21 51		22 06		22 21	
Elephant & Castle	d	19 55		20 10		20 25			20 40		20 55		21 10		21 25		21 40			21 55		22 10		22 25	
Loughborough Jn	d	20 00		20 15		20 30			20 45		21 00		21 15		21 30		21 45			22 00		22 15		22 30	
Herne Hill	d	20 05		20 20		20 35			20 50		21 05		21 20		21 35		21 50			22 05		22 20		22 35	
Tulse Hill	d	20 10	20 21	20 26	20 34	20 40	20 51		20 56	21 04	21 10	21 21	21 26	21 34	21 40	21 51	21 56		22 04	22 10	22 21	22 26	22 34	22 40	22 51
West Norwood	a		20 24				20 54					21 24				21 54					22 24				22 54
Gipsy Hill	a		20 27				20 57					21 27				21 57					22 27				22 57
Crystal Palace	a		20 31				21 01					21 31				22 01					22 31				23 01
Birkbeck	a		20 35				21 05					21 35				22 05					22 35				23 05
Beckenham Junction	a		20 39				21 09					21 39				22 09					22 39				23 09
Streatham	d	20 14		20 30	20 38	20 44			21 00	21 08	21 14		21 30	21 38	21 44		22 00		22 08	22 14		22 30	22 38	22 44	
Streatham Common	a				20 41					21 11				21 41					22 11				22 41		
Norbury	a				20 44					21 14				21 44					22 14				22 44		
Thornton Heath	a				20 47					21 17				21 47					22 17				22 47		
Selhurst	a				20 50					21 20				21 50					22 20				22 50		
East Croydon	a				20 53					21 24				21 54					22 24				22 54		
Tooting	a	20 18				20 48					21 18				21 48					22 18				22 48	
Haydons Road	a	20 22				20 52					21 22				21 52					22 22				22 52	
Wimbledon	a	20 24				20 54					21 24				21 54					22 24				22 54	
Mitcham Eastfields	a			20 34					21 04				21 34				22 04					22 34			
Mitcham Junction	a			20 37					21 07				21 37				22 07					22 37			
Hackbridge	a			20 40					21 10				21 40				22 10					22 40			
Carshalton	a			20 43					21 13				21 43				22 13					22 43			
Sutton	a	20 44		20 47		21 14			21 17		21 44		21 47		22 14		22 17			22 44		22 47		23 14	

A From St Albans City
B To Caterham

Table T173-F

Mondays to Fridays

21 May to 7 December

London Bridge - South Bermondsey, Queens Road Peckham, Peckham Rye, East Dulwich, North Dulwich, Tulse Hill and Streatham

		TL A	SN		TL A	SN	TL A	SN	TL A	SN	TL A	SN
London Bridge ⊖	d		22 44			23 01		23 14		23 31		23 54
South Bermondsey	d		22 49			23 05		23 19		23 35		23 59
Queens Rd Peckham	d		22 52			23 08		23 22		23 38		00 02
Peckham Rye	d		22 55			23 11		23 25		23 41		00 06
East Dulwich	d		22 58			23 14		23 28		23 44		00 09
North Dulwich	d		23 00			23 17		23 30		23 47		00 11
St Pancras International	d	22 27			22 42		22 57		23 12		23 44	
Farringdon	d	22 32			22 47		23 02		23 17		23 49	
City Thameslink	d	22 34			22 49							
London Blackfriars	d	22 36			22 51		23 06		23 21		23 53	
Elephant & Castle	d	22 40			22 55		23 10		23 25		23 57	
Loughborough Jn	d	22 45			23 00		23 15		23 30		00 02	
Herne Hill	d	22 50			23 05		23 20		23 35		00 06	
Tulse Hill	d	22 56	23 04		23 10	23 21	23 26	23 34	23 40	23 51	00 11	00 18
West Norwood	a					23 24				23 54		
Gipsy Hill	a					23 27				23 57		
Crystal Palace	a					23 31				00 01		
Birkbeck	a											
Beckenham Junction	a											
Streatham	d	23 00	23 08		23 14		23 30	23 38	23 44		00 14	00 22
Streatham Common	a		23 11					23 41				00 25
Norbury	a		23 14					23 44				00 28
Thornton Heath	a		23 17					23 47				00 31
Selhurst	a		23 20					23 50				00 34
East Croydon	a											
Tooting	a				23 18				23 48		00 18	
Haydons Road	a				23 22				23 52		00 22	
Wimbledon	a				23 24				23 54		00 24	
Mitcham Eastfields	a	23 04					23 34					
Mitcham Junction	a	23 07					23 37					
Hackbridge	a	23 10					23 40					
Carshalton	a	23 13					23 43					
Sutton	a	23 17			23 44		23 47		00 14		00 44	

Saturdays

26 May to 8 December

		TL A	SN B	SN	SN	SN C	TL D	TL E	TL D	TL E		SN F	TL D	TL D	SN F	TL A	SN	TL A	SN F	TL A		SN	TL A	SN F	TL A
London Bridge ⊖	d			00 01	00 25	00 31						06 14			06 44		07 01		07 14			07 31		07 44	
South Bermondsey	d			00 05	00 29	00 35						06 19			06 49		07 05		07 19			07 35		07 49	
Queens Rd Peckham	d		00 02	00 08	00 33	00 38						06 22			06 52		07 08		07 22			07 38		07 52	
Peckham Rye	d		00 06	00 11	00 37	00 41						06 25			06 55		07 11		07 25			07 41		07 55	
East Dulwich	d		00 09	00 14	00 41	00 44						06 28			06 58		07 14		07 28			07 44		07 58	
North Dulwich	d		00 11	00 17	00 43	00 47						06 30			07 00		07 17		07 30			07 47		08 00	
St Pancras International	d						05 12	05 27	05 42	05 57			06 12	06 27		06 42		06 57		07 12			07 27		07 42
Farringdon	d						05 17	05 32	05 47	06 02			06 17	06 32		06 47		07 02		07 17			07 32		07 47
City Thameslink	d																								
London Blackfriars	d						05 21	05 36	05 51	06 06			06 21	06 36		06 51		07 06		07 21			07 36		07 51
Elephant & Castle	d						05 25	05 40	05 55	06 10			06 25	06 40		06 55		07 10		07 25			07 40		07 55
Loughborough Jn	d	00 02					05 30	05 45	06 00	06 15			06 30	06 45		07 00		07 15		07 30			07 45		08 00
Herne Hill	d	00 06					05 35	05 50	06 05	06 20			06 35	06 50		07 05		07 20		07 35			07 50		08 05
Tulse Hill	d	00 11	00 18	00 21	00 47	00 51	05 40	05 56	06 10	06 26		06 34	06 40	06 56	07 04	07 10	07 21	07 26	07 34	07 40		07 51	07 56	08 04	08 10
West Norwood	a			00 24		00 54											07 24					07 54			
Gipsy Hill	a			00 27		00 57											07 27					07 57			
Crystal Palace	a			00 31		01 01											07 31					08 01			
Birkbeck	a																07 35					08 05			
Beckenham Junction	a																07 39					08 09			
Streatham	d	00 14	00 22		00 51		05 44	06 00	06 14	06 30		06 38	06 44	07 00	07 08	07 14		07 30	07 38	07 44			08 00	08 08	08 14
Streatham Common	a		00 25		00 54							06 41			07 11				07 41					08 11	
Norbury	a		00 28		00 57							06 44			07 14				07 44					08 14	
Thornton Heath	a		00 31		01 00							06 47			07 17				07 47					08 17	
Selhurst	a		00 34		01 03							06 50			07 20				07 50					08 20	
East Croydon	a											06 54			07 24				07 54					08 24	
Tooting	a	00 18					05 48		06 18				06 48			07 18				07 48					08 18
Haydons Road	a	00 22					05 52		06 22				06 52			07 22				07 52					08 22
Wimbledon	a	00 24					05 54		06 24				06 54			07 24				07 54					08 24
Mitcham Eastfields	a							06 04		06 34				07 04				07 34					08 04		
Mitcham Junction	a							06 07		06 37				07 07				07 37					08 07		
Hackbridge	a							06 10		06 40				07 10				07 40					08 10		
Carshalton	a							06 13		06 43				07 13				07 43					08 13		
Sutton	a	00 44					06 14	06 17	06 44	06 47			07 14	07 17		07 44		07 47		08 14			08 17		08 44

A From St Albans City
B From London Bridge
C To Norwood Junction
D From Luton
E From West Hampstead Thameslink
F To Caterham

T173 UPDATE: Monday – Friday 'Sutton-London Bridge' service stops at West Croydon (not East Croydon) at 07:18, 07:48, 08:18, 8:48, 18:18, 18:48 and 19:18.

London Bridge - South Bermondsey, Queens Road Peckham, Peckham Rye, East Dulwich, North Dulwich, Tulse Hill and Streatham

Saturdays
26 May to 8 December

		SN	TL A	SN B	TL A	SN		TL A	SN B	TL A	SN	TL A	SN B	TL A	SN	TL A	SN B	TL A		SN	TL A	SN B	TL A	SN
London Bridge ⊖	d	08 01		08 14		08 31			08 44		09 01		09 14		09 31		09 44			20 01		20 14		20 31
South Bermondsey	d	08 05		08 19		08 35			08 49		09 05		09 19		09 35		09 49			20 05		20 19		20 35
Queens Rd Peckham	d	08 08		08 22		08 38			08 52		09 08		09 22		09 38		09 52			20 08		20 22		20 38
Peckham Rye	d	08 11		08 25		08 41			08 55		09 11		09 25		09 41		09 55			20 11		20 25		20 41
East Dulwich	d	08 14		08 28		08 44			08 58		09 14		09 28		09 44		09 58			20 14		20 28		20 44
North Dulwich	d	08 17		08 30		08 47			09 00		09 17		09 30		09 47		10 00			20 17		20 30		20 47
St Pancras International	d		07 57		08 12			08 27		08 42		08 57		09 12		09 27		09 42			19 57		20 12	
Farringdon	d		08 02		08 17			08 32		08 47		09 02		09 17		09 32		09 47			20 02		20 17	
City Thameslink	d											09 04		09 19		09 34		09 49			20 04		20 19	
London Blackfriars	d		08 06		08 21			08 36		08 51		09 06		09 21		09 36		09 51			20 06		20 21	
Elephant & Castle	d		08 10		08 25			08 40		08 55		09 10		09 25		09 40		09 55			20 10		20 25	
Loughborough Jn	d		08 15		08 30			08 45		09 00		09 15		09 30		09 45		10 00			20 15		20 30	
Herne Hill	d		08 20		08 35			08 50		09 05		09 20		09 35		09 50		10 05			20 20		20 35	
Tulse Hill	d	08 21	08 26	08 34	08 40	08 51		08 56	09 04	09 10	09 21	09 26	09 34	09 40	09 51	09 56	10 04	10 10	and at the same minutes past each hour until	20 21	20 26	20 34	20 40	20 51
West Norwood	a	08 24				08 54					09 24				09 54					20 24				20 54
Gipsy Hill	a	08 27				08 57					09 27				09 57					20 27				20 57
Crystal Palace	a	08 31				09 01					09 31				10 01					20 31				21 01
Birkbeck	a	08 35				09 05					09 35				10 05					20 35				21 05
Beckenham Junction	a	08 39				09 09					09 39				10 09					20 39				21 09
Streatham	d		08 30	08 38	08 44			09 00	09 08	09 14		09 30	09 38	09 44		10 00	10 08	10 14			20 30	20 38	20 44	
Streatham Common	a			08 41					09 11				09 41				10 11					20 41		
Norbury	a			08 44					09 14				09 44				10 14					20 44		
Thornton Heath	a			08 47					09 17				09 47				10 17					20 47		
Selhurst	a			08 50					09 20				09 50				10 20					20 50		
East Croydon	a			08 54					09 24				09 54				10 24					20 54		
Tooting	a				08 48					09 18				09 48				10 18					20 48	
Haydons Road	a				08 52					09 22				09 52				10 22					20 52	
Wimbledon	a				08 54					09 24				09 54				10 24					20 54	
Mitcham Eastfields	a		08 34					09 04				09 34				10 04					20 34			
Mitcham Junction	a		08 37					09 07				09 37				10 07					20 37			
Hackbridge	a		08 40					09 10				09 40				10 10					20 40			
Carshalton	a		08 43					09 13				09 43				10 13					20 43			
Sutton	a		08 47		09 14			09 17		09 44		09 47		10 14		10 17		10 44			20 47		21 14	

		TL A	SN B	TL A		SN	TL A	SN B	TL A	SN	TL A	SN B	TL A	SN		TL A	SN B	TL A	SN	TL A	SN	TL A	SN C	TL A
London Bridge ⊖	d		20 44			21 01		21 14		21 31		21 44		22 01			22 14		22 31		22 44		23 01	
South Bermondsey	d		20 49			21 05		21 19		21 35		21 49		22 05			22 19		22 35		22 49		23 05	
Queens Rd Peckham	d		20 52			21 08		21 22		21 38		21 52		22 08			22 22		22 38		22 52		23 08	
Peckham Rye	d		20 55			21 11		21 25		21 41		21 55		22 11			22 25		22 41		22 55		23 11	
East Dulwich	d		20 58			21 14		21 28		21 44		21 58		22 14			22 28		22 44		22 58		23 14	
North Dulwich	d		21 00			21 17		21 30		21 47		22 00		22 17			22 30		22 47		23 00		23 17	
St Pancras International	d	20 27		20 42			20 57		21 12		21 27		21 42			21 57		22 12		22 27		22 42		22 57
Farringdon	d	20 32		20 47			21 02		21 17		21 32		21 47			22 02		22 17		22 32		22 47		23 02
City Thameslink	d	20 34		20 49																				
London Blackfriars	d	20 36		20 51			21 06		21 21		21 36		21 51			22 06		22 21		22 36		22 51		23 06
Elephant & Castle	d	20 40		20 55			21 10		21 25		21 40		21 55			22 10		22 25		22 40		22 55		23 10
Loughborough Jn	d	20 45		21 00			21 15		21 30		21 45		22 00			22 15		22 30		22 45		23 00		23 15
Herne Hill	d	20 50		21 05			21 20		21 35		21 50		22 05			22 20		22 35		22 50		23 05		23 20
Tulse Hill	d	20 56	21 04	21 10		21 21	21 26	21 34	21 40	21 51	21 56	22 04	22 10	22 21		22 26	22 34	22 40	22 51	22 56	23 04	23 10	23 21	23 26
West Norwood	a					21 24				21 54				22 24					22 54				23 24	
Gipsy Hill	a					21 27				21 57				22 27					22 57				23 27	
Crystal Palace	a					21 31				22 01				22 31					23 01				23 31	
Birkbeck	a					21 35				22 05				22 35					23 05					
Beckenham Junction	a					21 39				22 09				22 39					23 09					
Streatham	d	21 00	21 08	21 14			21 30	21 38	21 44		22 00	22 08	22 14			22 30	22 38	22 44		23 00	23 13	23 14		23 30
Streatham Common	a		21 11					21 41				22 11					22 41				23 16			
Norbury	a		21 14					21 44				22 14					22 44				23 19			
Thornton Heath	a		21 17					21 47				22 17					22 47				23 22			
Selhurst	a		21 20					21 50				22 20					22 50				23 25			
East Croydon	a		21 24					21 54				22 24					22 54							
Tooting	a			21 18					21 48				22 18					22 48				23 18		
Haydons Road	a			21 22					21 52				22 22					22 52				23 22		
Wimbledon	a			21 24					21 54				22 24					22 54				23 24		
Mitcham Eastfields	a	21 04					21 34				22 04					22 34				23 04				23 34
Mitcham Junction	a	21 07					21 37				22 07					22 37				23 07				23 37
Hackbridge	a	21 10					21 40				22 10					22 40				23 10				23 40
Carshalton	a	21 13					21 43				22 13					22 43				23 13				23 43
Sutton	a	21 17		21 44			21 47		22 14		22 17		22 44			22 47		23 14		23 17		23 44		23 47

A From St Albans City
B To Caterham
C To Norwood Junction

Table T173-F

London Bridge - South Bermondsey, Queens Road Peckham, Peckham Rye, East Dulwich, North Dulwich, Tulse Hill and Streatham

Saturdays
26 May to 8 December

		SN	TL A	SN B	TL A	SN
London Bridge ⊖	d	23 14		23 31		23 55
South Bermondsey	d	23 19		23 35		23 59
Queens Rd Peckham	d	23 22		23 38		00 02
Peckham Rye	d	23 25		23 41		00 05
East Dulwich	d	23 28		23 44		00 08
North Dulwich	d	23 30		23 47		00 10
St Pancras International	d		23 12		23 44	
Farringdon	d		23 17		23 49	
City Thameslink	d					
London Blackfriars	d		23 21		23 53	
Elephant & Castle	d		23 25		23 57	
Loughborough Jn	d		23 30		00 02	
Herne Hill	d		23 35		00 06	
Tulse Hill	d	23 34	23 40	23 51	00 11	00 19
West Norwood	a			23 54		
Gipsy Hill	a			23 57		
Crystal Palace	a			00 01		
Birkbeck	a					
Beckenham Junction	a					
Streatham	d	23 38	23 44		00 14	00 23
Streatham Common	a	23 41				00 26
Norbury	a	23 44				00 29
Thornton Heath	a	23 47				00 32
Selhurst	a	23 50				00 35
East Croydon	a					
Tooting	a		23 48		00 18	
Haydons Road	a		23 52		00 22	
Wimbledon	a		23 54		00 24	
Mitcham Eastfields	a					
Mitcham Junction	a					
Hackbridge	a					
Carshalton	a					
Sutton	a		00 14		00 44	

Sundays
20 May to 2 December

		TL C	SN D	SN B	SN	SN B	SN	SN	SN	SN		SN	TL	SN	SN	TL	SN	SN	TL	SN		TL E	SN	TL	SN
London Bridge ⊖	d			00 01	00 25	00 31	07 16	07 35	07 46	08 03		08 16	08 30	08 35	08 47	09 00	09 05	09 19		09 35			09 49		10 05
South Bermondsey	d			00 05	00 29	00 35	07 24	07 39	07 54	08 09		08 24		08 39	08 54		09 09	09 24		09 39			09 55		10 09
Queens Rd Peckham	d		00 02	00 08	00 33	00 38	07 27	07 42	07 57	08 12		08 27		08 42	08 57		09 12	09 27		09 42			09 58		10 12
Peckham Rye	d		00 05	00 11	00 38	00 41	07 31	07 45	08 01	08 15		08 30		08 45	09 00		09 15	09 30		09 45			10 01		10 15
East Dulwich	d		00 08	00 14	00 42	00 44	07 34	07 48	08 04	08 18		08 33		08 48	09 03		09 18	09 33		09 48			10 04		10 18
North Dulwich	d		00 10	00 17	00 44	00 47	07 37	07 51	08 07	08 21		08 35		08 51	09 05		09 21	09 35		09 51			10 06		10 21
St Pancras International	d																					09 38			
Farringdon	d																					09 42			
City Thameslink	d																								
London Blackfriars	d																		09 30			09 47		10 00	
Elephant & Castle	d																		09 34			09 51		10 04	
Loughborough Jn	d	00 02																	09 39			09 56		10 09	
Herne Hill	d	00 06																	09 44			10 00		10 14	
Tulse Hill	d	00 11	00 19	00 21	00 48	00 51	07 42	07 55	08 12	08 25		08 39	08 46	08 55	09 09	09 16	09 25	09 39	09 48	09 55		10 04	10 10	10 18	10 25
West Norwood	a			00 24		00 54		07 58		08 28				08 58			09 28			09 58					10 28
Gipsy Hill	a			00 27		00 57		08 01		08 31				09 01			09 31			10 01					10 31
Crystal Palace	a			00 31		01 01		08 05		08 35				09 05			09 35			10 05					10 35
Birkbeck	a																								
Beckenham Junction	a																								
Streatham	d	00 14	00 23		00 52		07 46		08 16			08 43	08 50		09 13	09 20		09 43	09 52			10 08	10 14	10 22	
Streatham Common	a		00 26		00 55		07 49		08 19			08 46			09 16			09 46					10 17		
Norbury	a		00 29		00 58		07 51		08 21			08 49			09 19			09 49					10 20		
Thornton Heath	a		00 32		01 01		07 54		08 24			08 52			09 22			09 52					10 23		
Selhurst	a		00 35		01 04		07 57		08 27			08 54			09 24			09 54					10 25		
East Croydon	a						08 00		08 30			08 59			09 29			09 59					10 29		
Tooting	a	00 18																				10 12			
Haydons Road	a	00 22																				10 16			
Wimbledon	a	00 24																				10 18			
Mitcham Eastfields	a												08 53			09 23			09 55					10 25	
Mitcham Junction	a												08 56			09 26			09 58					10 28	
Hackbridge	a												08 59			09 29			10 01					10 31	
Carshalton	a												09 02			09 32			10 04					10 34	
Sutton	a	00 44											09 05			09 35			10 07			10 38		10 37	

A From St Albans City
B To Norwood Junction
C not 20 May. From St Albans City
D not 20 May. From London Bridge
E From Luton

London Bridge - South Bermondsey, Queens Road Peckham, Peckham Rye, East Dulwich, North Dulwich, Tulse Hill and Streatham

		TL A	SN	TL	SN	TL A		SN	TL	SN	TL A	SN	TL	SN	TL A	SN		TL	SN	TL A	SN	TL	SN	TL A	SN
London Bridge ⊖	d		10 19		10 35			10 49		11 05		11 19		11 35		11 49			12 05		12 19		12 35		12 49
South Bermondsey	d		10 25		10 39			10 55		11 09		11 25		11 39		11 55			12 09		12 25		12 39		12 55
Queens Rd Peckham	d		10 28		10 42			10 58		11 12		11 28		11 42		11 58			12 12		12 28		12 42		12 58
Peckham Rye	d		10 31		10 45			11 01		11 15		11 31		11 45		12 01			12 15		12 31		12 45		13 01
East Dulwich	d		10 34		10 48			11 04		11 18		11 34		11 48		12 04			12 18		12 34		12 48		13 04
North Dulwich	d		10 36		10 51			11 06		11 21		11 36		11 51		12 06			12 21		12 36		12 51		13 06
St Pancras International	d	10 08				10 38					11 08				11 38					12 08		12 21		12 38	
Farringdon	d	10 12				10 42					11 12				11 42					12 12		12 25		12 42	
City Thameslink	d																								
London Blackfriars	d	10 17		10 30		10 47			11 00		11 17		11 30		11 47			12 00		12 17		12 30		12 47	
Elephant & Castle	d	10 21		10 34		10 51			11 04		11 21		11 34		11 51			12 04		12 21		12 34		12 51	
Loughborough Jn	d	10 26		10 39		10 56			11 09		11 26		11 39		11 56			12 09		12 26		12 39		12 56	
Herne Hill	d	10 30		10 44		11 00			11 14		11 30		11 44		12 00			12 14		12 30		12 44		13 00	
Tulse Hill	d	10 34	10 40	10 48	10 55	11 04		11 10	11 18	11 25	11 34	11 40	11 48	11 55	12 04	12 10		12 18	12 25	12 34	12 40	12 48	12 55	13 04	13 10
West Norwood	a				10 58					11 28				11 58					12 28				12 58		
Gipsy Hill	a				11 01					11 31				12 01					12 31				13 01		
Crystal Palace	a				11 05					11 35				12 05					12 35				13 05		
Birkbeck	a																								
Beckenham Junction	a																								
Streatham	d	10 38	10 44	10 52		11 08		11 14	11 22		11 38	11 44	11 52		12 08	12 14		12 22		12 38	12 44	12 52		13 08	13 14
Streatham Common	a		10 47					11 17				11 47				12 17					12 47				13 17
Norbury	a		10 50					11 20				11 50				12 20					12 50				13 20
Thornton Heath	a		10 53					11 23				11 53				12 23					12 53				13 23
Selhurst	a		10 55					11 25				11 55				12 25					12 55				13 25
East Croydon	a		10 59					11 29				11 59				12 29					12 59				13 29
Tooting	a	10 42				11 12					11 42				12 12					12 42				13 12	
Haydons Road	a	10 46				11 16					11 46				12 16					12 46				13 16	
Wimbledon	a	10 48				11 18					11 48				12 18					12 48				13 18	
Mitcham Eastfields	a			10 55					11 25				11 55					12 25				12 55			
Mitcham Junction	a			10 58					11 28				11 58					12 28				12 58			
Hackbridge	a			11 01					11 31				12 01					12 31				13 01			
Carshalton	a			11 04					11 34				12 04					12 34				13 04			
Sutton	a	11 08		11 07		11 38			11 37		12 08		12 07		12 38			12 37		13 08		13 07		13 38	

		TL A		SN	TL A	SN	TL B	SN	TL A	SN	TL B		SN	TL A	SN	TL B	SN	TL A	SN	SN	SN		SN C	SN
London Bridge ⊖	d			20 05		20 19		20 35		20 49			21 05		21 19		21 35		21 49	22 05	22 19		22 35	22 49
South Bermondsey	d			20 09		20 25		20 39		20 55			21 09		21 25		21 39		21 55	22 09	22 25		22 39	22 55
Queens Rd Peckham	d			20 12		20 28		20 42		20 58			21 12		21 28		21 42		21 58	22 12	22 28		22 42	22 58
Peckham Rye	d			20 15		20 31		20 45		21 01			21 15		21 31		21 45		22 01	22 15	22 31		22 45	23 01
East Dulwich	d			20 18		20 34		20 48		21 04			21 18		21 34		21 48		22 04	22 18	22 34		22 48	23 04
North Dulwich	d			20 21		20 36		20 51		21 06			21 21		21 36		21 51		22 06	22 21	22 36		22 51	23 06
St Pancras International	d	12 51			20 08		20 21		20 38		20 51			21 08		21 21		21 38						
Farringdon	d	12 55			20 12		20 25		20 42		20 55			21 12		21 25		21 42						
City Thameslink	d																							
London Blackfriars	d	13 00			20 17		20 30		20 47		21 00			21 17		21 30		21 47						
Elephant & Castle	d	13 04			20 21		20 34		20 51		21 04			21 21		21 34		21 51						
Loughborough Jn	d	13 09			20 26		20 39		20 56		21 09			21 26		21 39		21 56						
Herne Hill	d	13 14	and at		20 30		20 44		21 00		21 14			21 30		21 44		22 00						
Tulse Hill	d	13 18	the same	20 25	20 34	20 40	20 48	20 55	21 04	21 10	21 18		21 25	21 34	21 40	21 48	21 55	22 04	22 10	22 25	22 40		22 55	23 10
West Norwood	a		minutes	20 28				20 58					21 28				21 58			22 28			22 58	
Gipsy Hill	a		past	20 31				21 01					21 31				22 01			22 31			23 01	
Crystal Palace	a		each	20 35				21 05					21 35				22 05			22 35			23 05	
Birkbeck	a		hour until																					
Beckenham Junction	a																							
Streatham	d	13 22			20 38	20 44	20 52		21 08	21 14	21 22			21 38	21 44	21 52		22 08	22 14		22 44			23 14
Streatham Common	a					20 47				21 17					21 47				22 17		22 47			23 17
Norbury	a					20 50				21 20					21 50				22 20		22 50			23 20
Thornton Heath	a					20 53				21 23					21 53				22 23		22 53			23 23
Selhurst	a					20 55				21 25					21 55				22 25		22 55			23 25
East Croydon	a					20 59				21 29					21 59				22 29		22 59			23 29
Tooting	a				20 42				21 12					21 42				22 12						
Haydons Road	a				20 46				21 16					21 46				22 16						
Wimbledon	a				20 48				21 18					21 48				22 18						
Mitcham Eastfields	a	13 25					20 55				21 25					21 55								
Mitcham Junction	a	13 28					20 58				21 28					21 58								
Hackbridge	a	13 31					21 01				21 31					22 01								
Carshalton	a	13 34					21 04				21 34					22 04								
Sutton	a	13 37			21 08		21 07		21 38		21 37			22 08		22 07		22 38						

A From Luton B From St Albans City C To Norwood Junction

London Bridge - South Bermondsey, Queens Road Peckham, Peckham Rye, East Dulwich, North Dulwich, Tulse Hill and Streatham

		SN A	SN
London Bridge ⊖	d	23 05	23 17
South Bermondsey	d	23 09	23 24
Queens Rd Peckham	d	23 12	23 27
Peckham Rye	d	23 15	23 31
East Dulwich	d	23 18	23 34
North Dulwich	d	23 21	23 37
St Pancras International	d		
Farringdon	d		
City Thameslink	d		
London Blackfriars	d		
Elephant & Castle	d		
Loughborough Jn	d		
Herne Hill	d		
Tulse Hill	d	23 25	23 42
West Norwood	a	23 28	
Gipsy Hill	a	23 31	
Crystal Palace	a	23 35	
Birkbeck	a		
Beckenham Junction	a		
Streatham	d		23 46
Streatham Common	a		23 49
Norbury	a		23 51
Thornton Heath	a		23 54
Selhurst	a		23 57
East Croydon	a		00 02
Tooting	a		
Haydons Road	a		
Wimbledon	a		
Mitcham Eastfields	a		
Mitcham Junction	a		
Hackbridge	a		
Carshalton	a		
Sutton	a		

A To Norwood Junction

<u>T173 UPDATE:</u> Monday – Friday 'Sutton-London Bridge' service stops at West Croydon (not East Croydon) at 07:18, 07:48, 08:18, 8:48, 18:18, 18:48 and 19:18.

Table T173-R

Mondays to Fridays

21 May to 7 December

Tulse Hill, Streatham, North Dulwich, East Dulwich, Peckham Rye, Queens Road Peckham and South Bermondsey - London Bridge

Miles	Miles	Miles	Miles			SN MO A	SN	SN	TL B	SN	TL B	SN	TL B	SN		TL B	SN	SN	TL B	SN	TL B	SN	SN	TL B	
—	—	—	0	Sutton	d				05 46		05 49		06 16			06 19	06 36		06 46		06 49	07 06		07 16	
—	—	—	1¼	Carshalton	d				05 49				06 19				06 39		06 49			07 09		07 19	
—	—	—	2¼	Hackbridge	d				05 52				06 22				06 42		06 52			07 12		07 22	
—	—	—	3¼	Mitcham Junction	d				05 55				06 25				06 45		06 55			07 15		07 25	
—	—	—	4½	Mitcham Eastfields	d				05 58				06 28				06 48		06 58			07 18		07 28	
—	—	0	—	Wimbledon	d						06 07					06 37					07 07				
—	—	0¾	—	Haydons Road	d						06 10					06 40					07 10				
—	—	2	—	Tooting	d						06 13					06 43					07 13				
0	—	—	—	East Croydon	d																				
1	—	—	—	Selhurst	d		05 28			06 01				06 25						06 56					
2	—	—	—	Thornton Heath	d		05 30			06 03				06 28						06 58					
3	—	—	—	Norbury	d		05 33			06 06				06 31						07 01					
4	—	—	—	Streatham Common	d		05 35			06 09				06 36						07 06					
4½	—	3½	6¼	**Streatham**	d		05 39		06 03	06 13	06 18		06 33	06 43		06 48	06 53		07 03	07 13	07 18	07 23		07 33	
—	0	—	—	Beckenham Junction	d													06 45					07 15		
—	1½	—	—	**Birkbeck**	d													06 48					07 18		
—	3	—	—	Crystal Palace	d			05 53				06 23						06 53					07 23		
—	3¾	—	—	Gipsy Hill	d			05 55				06 25						06 55					07 25		
—	4¾	—	—	West Norwood	d			05 58				06 28						06 58					07 28		
6	5½	5	7¾	**Tulse Hill**	d		05 43	06 02	06 08	06 17	06 23	06 32	06 38	06 47		06 53	06 57	07 02	07 08	07 17	07 23	07 27	07 32	07 38	
—	—	6	8¾	Herne Hill	a				06 11		06 26		06 41			06 56			07 11		07 26			07 41	
—	—	7	9¾	Loughborough Jn	a				06 15		06 30		06 45			07 00			07 15		07 30			07 45	
—	—	9	11¾	Elephant & Castle	a				06 19		06 34		06 49			07 04			07 19		07 34			07 49	
—	—	10¾	13	London Blackfriars ⊖	a				06 24		06 39		06 54			07 09			07 24		07 39			07 54	
—	—	10¾	13½	City Thameslink	a				06 26		06 41		06 56			07 11			07 26		07 41			07 56	
—	—	11¾	14	Farringdon	a				06 28		06 43		06 58			07 13			07 28		07 43			07 58	
—	—	12½	15¾	St Pancras International	a				06 33		06 48		07 03			07 18			07 33		07 48			08 03	
7½	6¾	—	—	**North Dulwich**	d		05 46	06 06		06 21		06 36		06 51			07 00	07 06		07 21		07 30	07 36		
8	7¼	—	—	**East Dulwich**	d		05 49	06 08		06 23		06 38		06 53			07 02	07 08		07 23		07 32	07 38		
8¾	8	—	—	Peckham Rye	d		05 52	06 11		06 26		06 41		06 56			07 06	07 11		07 26		07 36	07 41		
9½	8¾	—	—	Queens Rd Peckham	d	00 01	05 54	06 13		06 28		06 43		06 58			07 08	07 13		07 28		07 38	07 43		
10½	9¾	—	—	**South Bermondsey**	d	00 04	05 56	06 16		06 31		06 46		07 01			07 10	07 16		07 31		07 40	07 46		
12¼	11½	—	—	London Bridge ⊖	a	00 09	06 01	06 21		06 36		06 51		07 06			07 15	07 21		07 36		07 45	07 51		

		SN	TL B	SN	SN	TL B	SN	TL B	SN	SN		TL B	SN	TL B	SN	SN	TL B	SN	TL B	SN		TL B	SN C	TL B	SN
Sutton	d	07 00	07 19	07 36		07 46	07 30	07 49	08 06			08 16	08 00	08 19	08 36		08 46	08 30	08 49			09 16		09 19	
Carshalton	d			07 39		07 49			08 09			08 19			08 39		08 49					09 19			
Hackbridge	d			07 42		07 52			08 12			08 22			08 42		08 52					09 22			
Mitcham Junction	d			07 45		07 55			08 15			08 25			08 45		08 55					09 25			
Mitcham Eastfields	d			07 49		07 58			08 19			08 28			08 49		08 58					09 28			
Wimbledon	d		07 37					08 07						08 37					09 07					09 37	
Haydons Road	d		07 40					08 10						08 40					09 10					09 40	
Tooting	d		07 43					08 13						08 43					09 13					09 43	
East Croydon	d																						09 21		
Selhurst	d	07 26					07 56						08 26					08 56					09 27		
Thornton Heath	d	07 28					07 58						08 28					08 58					09 29		
Norbury	d	07 31					08 01						08 31					09 01					09 32		
Streatham Common	d	07 36					08 06						08 36					09 06					09 36		
Streatham	d	07 43	07 48	07 53		08 03	08 13	08 18	08 23			08 33	08 43	08 48	08 53		09 03	09 13	09 18			09 33	09 43	09 48	
Beckenham Junction	d				07 45					08 15						08 45				09 15					09 45
Birkbeck	d				07 48					08 18						08 48				09 18					09 48
Crystal Palace	d				07 53					08 23						08 53				09 23					09 53
Gipsy Hill	d				07 55					08 25						08 55				09 25					09 55
West Norwood	d				07 58					08 28						08 58				09 28					09 58
Tulse Hill	d	07 47	07 53	07 57	08 02	08 08	08 17	08 23	08 27	08 32		08 38	08 47	08 53	08 57	09 02	09 08	09 17	09 23	09 32		09 38	09 47	09 53	10 02
Herne Hill	a		07 56			08 11		08 26				08 41		08 56			09 11		09 26			09 41		09 56	
Loughborough Jn	a		08 00			08 15		08 30				08 45		09 00			09 15		09 30			09 45		10 00	
Elephant & Castle	a		08 04			08 19		08 34				08 49		09 04			09 19		09 34			09 49		10 04	
London Blackfriars ⊖	a		08 09			08 24		08 39				08 54		09 09			09 24		09 39			09 54		10 09	
City Thameslink	a		08 11			08 26		08 41				08 56		09 11			09 26		09 41			09 56		10 11	
Farringdon	a		08 13			08 28		08 43				08 58		09 13			09 28		09 43			09 58		10 13	
St Pancras International	a		08 18			08 33		08 48				09 03		09 18			09 33		09 48			10 03		10 18	
North Dulwich	d	07 51		08 00	08 06		08 21		08 30	08 36			08 51		09 00	09 06		09 21		09 36			09 51		10 06
East Dulwich	d	07 53		08 02	08 08		08 23		08 32	08 38			08 53		09 02	09 08		09 23		09 38			09 53		10 08
Peckham Rye	d	07 56		08 06	08 11		08 26		08 36	08 41			08 56		09 06	09 11		09 26		09 41			09 56		10 11
Queens Rd Peckham	d	07 58		08 08	08 13		08 28		08 38	08 43			08 58		09 08	09 13		09 28		09 43			09 58		10 13
South Bermondsey	d	08 01		08 10	08 16		08 31		08 40	08 46			09 01		09 10	09 16		09 31		09 46			10 01		10 16
London Bridge ⊖	a	08 06		08 15	08 21		08 36		08 47	08 51			09 06		09 17	09 21		09 36		09 51			10 06		10 21

A From Crystal Palace B To St Albans City C From Caterham

Table T173-R

Mondays to Fridays

21 May to 7 December

Tulse Hill, Streatham, North Dulwich, East Dulwich, Peckham Rye, Queens Road Peckham and South Bermondsey - London Bridge

		TL A	SN B	TL A	SN	TL A	SN B	TL A	SN	TL A	SN B		TL A	SN	TL A	SN B	TL A	SN	TL A	SN B		TL A	SN	TL A
Sutton	d	09 46		09 49		10 16		10 19		10 46			12 49		13 16		13 19		13 46			13 49		14 16
Carshalton	d	09 49				10 19				10 49					13 19				13 49					14 19
Hackbridge	d	09 52				10 22				10 52					13 22				13 52					14 22
Mitcham Junction	d	09 55				10 25				10 55					13 25				13 55					14 25
Mitcham Eastfields	d	09 58				10 28				10 58					13 28				13 58					14 28
Wimbledon	d			10 07				10 37					13 07				13 37					14 07		
Haydons Road	d			10 10				10 40					13 10				13 40					14 10		
Tooting	d			10 13				10 43					13 13				13 43					14 13		
East Croydon	d		09 51				10 22				10 52					13 22				13 52				
Selhurst	d		09 56				10 26				10 56					13 26				13 56				
Thornton Heath	d		09 58				10 28				10 58					13 28				13 58				
Norbury	d		10 01				10 31				11 01					13 31				14 01				
Streatham Common	d		10 06				10 36				11 06	and at				13 36				14 06				
Streatham	d	10 03	10 13	10 18		10 33	10 43	10 48		11 03	11 13	the same	13 18		13 33	13 43	13 48		14 03	14 13		14 18		14 33
Beckenham Junction	d				10 15				10 45			minutes		13 15				13 45					14 15	
Birkbeck	d				10 18				10 48			past		13 18				13 48					14 18	
Crystal Palace	d				10 23				10 53			each		13 23				13 53					14 23	
Gipsy Hill	d				10 25				10 55			hour until		13 25				13 55					14 25	
West Norwood	d				10 28				10 58					13 28				13 58					14 28	
Tulse Hill	d	10 08	10 17	10 23	10 32	10 38	10 47	10 53	11 02	11 08	11 17		13 23	13 32	13 38	13 47	13 53	14 02	14 08	14 17		14 23	14 32	14 38
Herne Hill	a	10 11		10 26		10 41		10 56		11 11			13 26		13 41		13 56		14 11			14 26		14 41
Loughborough Jn	a	10 15		10 30		10 45		11 00		11 15			13 30		13 45		14 00		14 15			14 30		14 45
Elephant & Castle	a	10 19		10 34		10 49		11 04		11 19			13 34		13 49		14 04		14 19			14 34		14 49
London Blackfriars ⊖	a	10 24		10 39		10 54		11 09		11 24			13 39		13 54		14 09		14 24			14 39		14 54
City Thameslink	a	10 26		10 41		10 56		11 11		11 26			13 41		13 56		14 11		14 26			14 41		14 56
Farringdon	a	10 28		10 43		10 58		11 13		11 28			13 43		13 58		14 13		14 28			14 43		14 58
St Pancras International	a	10 33		10 48		11 03		11 18		11 33			13 48		14 03		14 18		14 33			14 48		15 03
North Dulwich	d		10 21		10 36		10 51		11 06		11 21			13 36		13 51		14 06		14 21			14 36	
East Dulwich	d		10 23		10 38		10 53		11 08		11 23			13 38		13 53		14 08		14 23			14 38	
Peckham Rye	d		10 26		10 41		10 56		11 11		11 26			13 41		13 56		14 11		14 26			14 41	
Queens Rd Peckham	d		10 28		10 43		10 58		11 13		11 28			13 43		13 58		14 13		14 28			14 43	
South Bermondsey	d		10 31		10 46		11 01		11 16		11 31			13 46		14 01		14 16		14 31			14 46	
London Bridge ⊖	a		10 36		10 51		11 06		11 21		11 36			13 51		14 06		14 21		14 36			14 51	

		SN B	TL A	SN	TL A	SN B	TL A		SN	TL A	SN B	TL A	SN	TL A	SN B	TL A	SN C		SN	TL A	SN B	TL A	SN	TL A	SN B
Sutton	d		14 18		14 46		14 49			15 16		15 19		15 46		15 49				16 16		16 19		16 46	
Carshalton	d				14 49					15 19				15 49						16 19				16 49	
Hackbridge	d				14 52					15 22				15 52						16 22				16 52	
Mitcham Junction	d				14 55					15 25				15 55						16 25				16 55	
Mitcham Eastfields	d				14 58					15 28				15 58						16 28				16 58	
Wimbledon	d		14 36				15 07					15 37				16 07						16 37			
Haydons Road	d		14 38				15 10					15 40				16 10						16 40			
Tooting	d		14 41				15 13					15 43				16 13						16 43			
East Croydon	d	14 22				14 52					15 22				15 51						16 21				16 51
Selhurst	d	14 26				14 56					15 26				15 56						16 26				16 56
Thornton Heath	d	14 28				14 58					15 28				15 58						16 28				16 58
Norbury	d	14 31				15 01					15 31				16 01						16 31				17 01
Streatham Common	d	14 36				15 06					15 36				16 06						16 36				17 06
Streatham	d	14 43	14 46		15 03	15 13	15 18			15 33	15 43	15 48		16 03	16 13	16 18				16 33	16 43	16 48		17 03	17 13
Beckenham Junction	d			14 45					15 15				15 45						16 15				16 45		
Birkbeck	d			14 48					15 18				15 48						16 18				16 48		
Crystal Palace	d			14 53					15 23				15 53						16 23				16 53		
Gipsy Hill	d			14 55					15 25				15 55						16 25				16 55		
West Norwood	d			14 58					15 28				15 58						16 28				16 58		
Tulse Hill	d	14 47	14 53	15 02	15 08	15 17	15 23		15 32	15 38	15 47	15 53	16 02	16 08	16 17	16 23	16 25		16 32	16 38	16 47	16 53	17 02	17 08	17 17
Herne Hill	a		14 56		15 11		15 26			15 41		15 56		16 11		16 26				16 41		16 56		17 11	
Loughborough Jn	a		15 00		15 15		15 30			15 45		16 00		16 15		16 30				16 45		17 00		17 15	
Elephant & Castle	a		15 04		15 19		15 34			15 49		16 04		16 19		16 34				16 49		17 04		17 19	
London Blackfriars ⊖	a		15 09		15 24		15 39			15 54		16 09		16 24		16 39				16 54		17 09		17 24	
City Thameslink	a		15 11		15 26		15 41			15 56		16 11		16 26		16 41				16 56		17 11		17 26	
Farringdon	a		15 13		15 28		15 43			15 58		16 13		16 28		16 43				16 58		17 13		17 28	
St Pancras International	a		15 18		15 33		15 48			16 03		16 18		16 33		16 48				17 03		17 18		17 33	
North Dulwich	d	14 51		15 06		15 21			15 36		15 51		16 06		16 21		16 28		16 36		16 51		17 06		17 21
East Dulwich	d	14 53		15 08		15 23			15 38		15 53		16 08		16 23		16 30		16 38		16 53		17 08		17 23
Peckham Rye	d	14 56		15 11		15 26			15 41		15 56		16 11		16 26		16 35		16 41		16 56		17 11		17 26
Queens Rd Peckham	d	14 58		15 13		15 28			15 43		15 58		16 13		16 28		16 37		16 43		16 58		17 13		17 28
South Bermondsey	d	15 01		15 16		15 31			15 46		16 01		16 16		16 31		16 40		16 46		17 01		17 16		17 31
London Bridge ⊖	a	15 06		15 21		15 36			15 51		16 06		16 21		16 36		16 45		16 51		17 06		17 21		17 36

A To St Albans City B From Caterham C From Streatham Hill

Table T173-R

Mondays to Fridays
21 May to 7 December

Tulse Hill, Streatham, North Dulwich, East Dulwich, Peckham Rye, Queens Road Peckham and South Bermondsey - London Bridge

		TL A	SN	TL A	SN B	TL A	SN	TL A	SN	SN B	TL A	SN
Sutton	d	16 49		17 16		17 19		17 46	17 38		17 49	
Carshalton	d			17 19				17 49				
Hackbridge	d			17 22				17 52				
Mitcham Junction	d			17 25				17 55				
Mitcham Eastfields	d			17 28				17 58				
Wimbledon	d	17 07				17 37			17 59		18 07	
Haydons Road	d	17 10				17 40			18 01		18 10	
Tooting	d	17 13				17 43			18 05		18 13	
East Croydon	d				17 21					17 51		
Selhurst	d				17 26					17 56		
Thornton Heath	d				17 28					17 58		
Norbury	d				17 31					18 01		
Streatham Common	d				17 36					18 06		
Streatham	d	17 18		17 33	17 43	17 48		18 03	18 10	18 13	18 18	
Beckenham Junction	d		17 15				17 45					18 15
Birkbeck	d		17 18				17 48					18 18
Crystal Palace	d		17 23				17 53					18 23
Gipsy Hill	d		17 25				17 55					18 25
West Norwood	d		17 28				17 58					18 28
Tulse Hill	d	17 23	17 32	17 38	17 47	17 53	18 02	18 08	18 14	18 17	18 23	18 32
Herne Hill	a	17 26		17 41		17 56		18 11			18 26	
Loughborough Jn	a	17 30		17 45		18 00		18 15			18 30	
Elephant & Castle	a	17 34		17 49		18 04		18 19			18 34	
London Blackfriars ⊖	a	17 39		17 54		18 09		18 24			18 39	
City Thameslink	a	17 41		17 56		18 11		18 26			18 41	
Farringdon	a	17 43		17 58		18 13		18 28			18 43	
St Pancras International	a	17 48		18 03		18 18		18 33			18 48	
North Dulwich	d		17 36		17 51		18 06		18 18	18 21		18 36
East Dulwich	d		17 38		17 53		18 08		18 20	18 23		18 38
Peckham Rye	d		17 41		17 56		18 11		18 23	18 26		18 41
Queens Rd Peckham	d		17 43		17 58		18 13		18 25	18 28		18 43
South Bermondsey	d		17 46		18 01		18 16		18 28	18 31		18 46
London Bridge ⊖	a		17 51		18 06		18 21		18 33	18 36		18 51

		TL A	SN	SN	TL A	SN	TL A	SN	SN	TL A	SN
Sutton	d	18 16	18 08	18 00	18 19		18 46	18 38	18 30	18 49	
Carshalton	d	18 19					18 49				
Hackbridge	d	18 22					18 52				
Mitcham Junction	d	18 25					18 55				
Mitcham Eastfields	d	18 28					18 58				
Wimbledon	d		18 29		18 37			18 59		19 07	
Haydons Road	d		18 31		18 40			19 01		19 10	
Tooting	d		18 35		18 43			19 05		19 13	
East Croydon	d										
Selhurst	d			18 26					18 56		
Thornton Heath	d			18 28					18 58		
Norbury	d			18 31					19 01		
Streatham Common	d			18 36					19 06		
Streatham	d	18 33	18 40	18 43	18 48		19 03	19 10	19 13	19 18	
Beckenham Junction	d					18 45					19 15
Birkbeck	d					18 48					19 18
Crystal Palace	d					18 53					19 23
Gipsy Hill	d					18 55					19 25
West Norwood	d					18 58					19 28
Tulse Hill	d	18 38	18 44	18 47	18 53	19 02	19 08	19 14	19 17	19 23	19 32
Herne Hill	a	18 41			18 56		19 11			19 26	
Loughborough Jn	a	18 45			19 00		19 15			19 30	
Elephant & Castle	a	18 49			19 04		19 19			19 34	
London Blackfriars ⊖	a	18 54			19 09		19 24			19 39	
City Thameslink	a	18 56			19 11		19 26			19 41	
Farringdon	a	18 58			19 13		19 28			19 43	
St Pancras International	a	19 03			19 18		19 33			19 48	
North Dulwich	d		18 47	18 51		19 06		19 17	19 21		19 36
East Dulwich	d		18 49	18 53		19 08		19 19	19 23		19 38
Peckham Rye	d		18 53	18 56		19 11		19 23	19 26		19 41
Queens Rd Peckham	d		18 55	18 58		19 13		19 25	19 28		19 43
South Bermondsey	d		18 58	19 01		19 16		19 28	19 31		19 46
London Bridge ⊖	a		19 03	19 06		19 21		19 33	19 36		19 51

		TL A	SN	SN	TL A	SN	TL A	SN	TL A	SN	TL A	SN	TL A
Sutton	d	19 16	19 08	19 00	19 19		19 46		19 49		20 16		20 21
Carshalton	d	19 19					19 49				20 19		
Hackbridge	d	19 22					19 52				20 22		
Mitcham Junction	d	19 25					19 55				20 25		
Mitcham Eastfields	d	19 28					19 58				20 28		
Wimbledon	d		19 29		19 37				20 07				20 43
Haydons Road	d		19 31		19 40				20 10				20 46
Tooting	d		19 35		19 43				20 13				20 49
East Croydon	d												
Selhurst	d			19 26				19 56				20 26	
Thornton Heath	d			19 28				19 58				20 28	
Norbury	d			19 31				20 01				20 31	
Streatham Common	d			19 36				20 06				20 36	
Streatham	d	19 33	19 40	19 43	19 48		20 03	20 13	20 18		20 33	20 43	20 54
Beckenham Junction	d					19 45				20 15			
Birkbeck	d					19 48				20 18			
Crystal Palace	d					19 53				20 23			
Gipsy Hill	d					19 55				20 25			
West Norwood	d					19 58				20 28			
Tulse Hill	d	19 38	19 44	19 47	19 53	20 02	20 08	20 17	20 23	20 32	20 38	20 47	20 59
Herne Hill	a	19 41			19 56		20 11		20 26		20 41		21 02
Loughborough Jn	a	19 45			20 00		20 15		20 30		20 45		21 07
Elephant & Castle	a	19 49			20 04		20 19		20 34		20 49		21 11
London Blackfriars ⊖	a	19 54			20 09		20 24		20 39		20 54		21 16
City Thameslink	a	19 56			20 11		20 26		20 41		20 56		21 18
Farringdon	a	19 58			20 13		20 28		20 43		20 58		21 21
St Pancras International	a	20 03			20 18		20 33		20 48		21 03		21 25
North Dulwich	d		19 47	19 51		20 06		20 21		20 36		20 51	
East Dulwich	d		19 49	19 53		20 08		20 23		20 38		20 53	
Peckham Rye	d		19 53	19 56		20 11		20 26		20 41		20 56	
Queens Rd Peckham	d		19 55	19 58		20 13		20 28		20 43		20 58	
South Bermondsey	d		19 58	20 01		20 16		20 31		20 46		21 01	
London Bridge ⊖	a		20 03	20 06		20 21		20 36		20 51		21 06	

		SN	TL A	SN B	TL A	SN	TL A	SN B	TL A	SN	TL C
Sutton	d		20 46		20 49		21 16		21 19		21 46
Carshalton	d		20 49				21 19				21 49
Hackbridge	d		20 52				21 22				21 52
Mitcham Junction	d		20 55				21 25				21 55
Mitcham Eastfields	d		20 58				21 28				21 58
Wimbledon	d				21 07				21 37		
Haydons Road	d				21 10				21 40		
Tooting	d				21 13				21 43		
East Croydon	d			20 54				21 22			
Selhurst	d			20 58				21 26			
Thornton Heath	d			21 00				21 28			
Norbury	d			21 03				21 31			
Streatham Common	d			21 06				21 36			
Streatham	d		21 03	21 13	21 18		21 33	21 43	21 48		22 03
Beckenham Junction	d	20 45				21 15				21 45	
Birkbeck	d	20 48				21 18				21 48	
Crystal Palace	d	20 53				21 23				21 53	
Gipsy Hill	d	20 55				21 25				21 55	
West Norwood	d	20 58				21 28				21 58	
Tulse Hill	d	21 02	21 08	21 17	21 23	21 32	21 38	21 47	21 53	22 02	22 08
Herne Hill	a		21 11		21 26		21 41		21 56		22 11
Loughborough Jn	a		21 15		21 30		21 45		22 00		22 15
Elephant & Castle	a		21 19		21 34		21 49		22 04		22 19
London Blackfriars ⊖	a		21 24		21 39		21 54		22 09		22 24
City Thameslink	a		21 26		21 41		21 56		22 11		22 26
Farringdon	a		21 28		21 43		21 58		22 13		22 28
St Pancras International	a		21 33		21 48		22 03		22 18		22 33
North Dulwich	d	21 06		21 21		21 36		21 51		22 06	
East Dulwich	d	21 08		21 23		21 38		21 53		22 08	
Peckham Rye	d	21 11		21 26		21 41		21 56		22 11	
Queens Rd Peckham	d	21 13		21 28		21 43		21 58		22 13	
South Bermondsey	d	21 16		21 31		21 46		22 01		22 16	
London Bridge ⊖	a	21 21		21 36		21 51		22 06		22 21	

A To St Albans City
B From Caterham
C To Bedford

Table T173-R

Mondays to Fridays
21 May to 7 December

Tulse Hill, Streatham, North Dulwich, East Dulwich, Peckham Rye, Queens Road Peckham and South Bermondsey - London Bridge

		SN A	TL B	SN	TL B	SN A	TL B	SN	TL B	SN A	TL B	SN	TL B	TL B
Sutton	d		21 49		22 18		22 19		22 48		22 49		23 18	23 19
Carshalton	d				22 21				22 51				23 21	
Hackbridge	d				22 24				22 54				23 24	
Mitcham Junction	d				22 27				22 57				23 27	
Mitcham Eastfields	d				22 30				23 00				23 30	
Wimbledon	d		22 07				22 41				23 11			23 37
Haydons Road	d		22 10				22 44				23 14			23 40
Tooting	d		22 13				22 47				23 17			23 43
East Croydon	d	21 52				22 22				22 52				
Selhurst	d	21 56				22 26				22 56				
Thornton Heath	d	21 58				22 28				22 58				
Norbury	d	22 01				22 31				23 01				
Streatham Common	d	22 06				22 36				23 06				
Streatham	d	22 13	22 18		22 35	22 43	22 52		23 05	23 13	23 22		23 35	23 48
Beckenham Junction	d			22 15				22 45				23 15		
Birkbeck	d			22 18				22 48				23 18		
Crystal Palace	d			22 23				22 53				23 24		
Gipsy Hill	d			22 25				22 55				23 26		
West Norwood	d			22 28				22 58				23 29		
Tulse Hill	d	22 17	22 23	22 32	22 40	22 47	22 57	23 02	23 10	23 17	23 27	23 33	23 40	23 53
Herne Hill	a		22 26		22 43		23 00		23 13		23 30		23 43	23 56
Loughborough Jn	a		22 30		22 47		23 07		23 17		23 37		23 47	
Elephant & Castle	a		22 34		22 51		23 11		23 21		23 41		23 51	00 03
London Blackfriars ⊖	a		22 39		22 56		23 16		23 26		23 46		00 01	00 08
City Thameslink	a		22 41											
Farringdon	a		22 43		23 03		23 21		23 31		23 53		00 06	00 13
St Pancras International	a		22 48		23 08		23 25		23 35		23 57		00 10	00 17
North Dulwich	d	22 21		22 36		22 51		23 06		23 21		23 37		
East Dulwich	d	22 23		22 38		22 53		23 08		23 23		23 39		
Peckham Rye	d	22 26		22 41		22 56		23 11		23 26		23 42		
Queens Rd Peckham	d	22 28		22 43		22 58		23 13		23 28		23 44		
South Bermondsey	d	22 31		22 46		23 01		23 16		23 31		23 47		
London Bridge ⊖	a	22 36		22 51		23 06		23 21		23 36		23 52		

Saturdays
26 May to 8 December

		TL C	TL C	TL C	SN	TL C	SN D	TL C	SN	TL C
Sutton	d	05 46	05 49	06 16		06 19		06 46		06 49
Carshalton	d	05 49		06 19				06 49		
Hackbridge	d	05 52		06 22				06 52		
Mitcham Junction	d	05 55		06 25				06 55		
Mitcham Eastfields	d	05 58		06 28				06 58		
Wimbledon	d		06 07			06 37				07 07
Haydons Road	d		06 10			06 40				07 10
Tooting	d		06 13			06 43				07 13
East Croydon	d									
Selhurst	d				06 26				06 56	
Thornton Heath	d				06 28				06 58	
Norbury	d				06 31				07 01	
Streatham Common	d				06 36				07 06	
Streatham	d	06 03	06 18	06 33	06 43	06 48		07 03	07 13	07 18
Beckenham Junction	d									
Birkbeck	d									
Crystal Palace	d						06 53			
Gipsy Hill	d						06 55			
West Norwood	d						06 58			
Tulse Hill	d	06 08	06 23	06 38	06 47	06 53	07 02	07 08	07 17	07 23
Herne Hill	a	06 11	06 26	06 41		06 56		07 11		07 26
Loughborough Jn	a	06 15	06 30	06 45		07 00		07 15		07 30
Elephant & Castle	a	06 19	06 34	06 49		07 04		07 19		07 34
London Blackfriars ⊖	a	06 24	06 39	06 54		07 09		07 24		07 39
City Thameslink	a									
Farringdon	a	06 28	06 43	06 58		07 13		07 28		07 43
St Pancras International	a	06 33	06 48	07 03		07 18		07 33		07 48
North Dulwich	d				06 51		07 06		07 21	
East Dulwich	d				06 53		07 08		07 23	
Peckham Rye	d				06 56		07 11		07 26	
Queens Rd Peckham	d				06 58		07 13		07 28	
South Bermondsey	d				07 01		07 16		07 31	
London Bridge ⊖	a				07 06		07 21		07 36	

		SN D	TL C	SN A	TL C	SN	TL C	SN A	TL C	SN	TL C
Sutton	d		07 16		07 19		07 46		07 49		08 16
Carshalton	d		07 19				07 49				08 19
Hackbridge	d		07 22				07 52				08 22
Mitcham Junction	d		07 25				07 55				08 25
Mitcham Eastfields	d		07 28				07 58				08 28
Wimbledon	d				07 37				08 07		
Haydons Road	d				07 40				08 10		
Tooting	d				07 43				08 13		
East Croydon	d			07 23				07 53			
Selhurst	d			07 27				07 57			
Thornton Heath	d			07 29				07 59			
Norbury	d			07 32				08 02			
Streatham Common	d			07 36				08 06			
Streatham	d		07 33	07 43	07 48		08 03	08 13	08 18		08 33
Beckenham Junction	d					07 45				08 15	
Birkbeck	d					07 48				08 18	
Crystal Palace	d	07 23				07 53				08 23	
Gipsy Hill	d	07 25				07 55				08 25	
West Norwood	d	07 28				07 58				08 28	
Tulse Hill	d	07 32	07 38	07 47	07 53	08 02	08 08	08 17	08 23	08 32	08 38
Herne Hill	a		07 41		07 56		08 11		08 26		08 41
Loughborough Jn	a		07 45		08 00		08 15		08 30		08 45
Elephant & Castle	a		07 49		08 04		08 19		08 34		08 49
London Blackfriars ⊖	a		07 54		08 09		08 24		08 39		08 54
City Thameslink	a										
Farringdon	a		07 58		08 13		08 28		08 43		08 58
St Pancras International	a		08 03		08 18		08 33		08 48		09 03
North Dulwich	d	07 36		07 51		08 06		08 21		08 36	
East Dulwich	d	07 38		07 53		08 08		08 23		08 38	
Peckham Rye	d	07 41		07 56		08 11		08 26		08 41	
Queens Rd Peckham	d	07 43		07 58		08 13		08 28		08 43	
South Bermondsey	d	07 46		08 01		08 16		08 31		08 46	
London Bridge ⊖	a	07 51		08 06		08 21		08 36		08 51	

A From Caterham
B To Bedford
C To St Albans City
D From Norwood Junction

T173 UPDATE: Monday – Friday 'Sutton-London Bridge' service stops at West Croydon (not East Croydon) at 07:18, 07:48, 08:18, 8:48, 18:18, 18:48 and 19:18.

Table T173-R

Saturdays

26 May to 8 December

Tulse Hill, Streatham, North Dulwich, East Dulwich, Peckham Rye, Queens Road Peckham and South Bermondsey - London Bridge

		SN A	TL B	SN	TL B	SN A	TL B	SN	TL B		SN A	TL B	SN	TL B	SN A	TL B	SN	TL B	SN A	TL B	SN	TL B	SN A
Sutton	d		08 19		08 46		08 49		09 16			19 19		19 46		19 49		20 16		20 19		20 46	
Carshalton	d				08 49				09 19					19 49				20 19				20 49	
Hackbridge	d				08 52				09 22					19 52				20 22				20 52	
Mitcham Junction	d				08 55				09 25					19 55				20 25				20 55	
Mitcham Eastfields	d				08 58				09 28					19 58				20 28				20 58	
Wimbledon	d		08 37				09 07					19 37				20 07				20 37			
Haydons Road	d		08 40				09 10					19 40				20 10				20 40			
Tooting	d		08 43				09 13					19 43				20 13				20 43			
East Croydon	d	08 23				08 53					19 23				19 53				20 23				20 53
Selhurst	d	08 27				08 57					19 27				19 57				20 27				20 57
Thornton Heath	d	08 29				08 59					19 29				19 59				20 29				20 59
Norbury	d	08 32				09 02					19 32				20 02				20 32				21 02
Streatham Common	d	08 36				09 06					19 36				20 06				20 36				21 06
Streatham	d	08 43	08 48		09 03	09 13	09 18		09 33	and at the same minutes past each hour until	19 43	19 48		20 03	20 13	20 18		20 33	20 43	20 48		21 03	21 13
Beckenham Junction	d			08 45				09 15					19 45				20 15				20 45		
Birkbeck	d			08 48				09 18					19 48				20 18				20 48		
Crystal Palace	d			08 53				09 23					19 53				20 23				20 53		
Gipsy Hill	d			08 55				09 25					19 55				20 25				20 55		
West Norwood	d			08 58				09 28					19 58				20 28				20 58		
Tulse Hill	d	08 47	08 53	09 02	09 08	09 17	09 23	09 32	09 38		19 47	19 53	20 02	20 08	20 17	20 23	20 32	20 38	20 47	20 53	21 02	21 08	21 17
Herne Hill	a		08 56		09 11		09 26		09 41			19 56		20 11		20 26		20 41		20 56		21 11	
Loughborough Jn	a		09 00		09 15		09 30		09 45			20 00		20 15		20 30		20 45		21 00		21 15	
Elephant & Castle	a		09 04		09 19		09 34		09 49			20 04		20 19		20 34		20 49		21 04		21 19	
London Blackfriars ⊖	a		09 09		09 24		09 39		09 54			20 09		20 24		20 39		20 54		21 09		21 24	
City Thameslink	a		09 11		09 26		09 41		09 56			20 11		20 26		20 41		20 56					
Farringdon	a		09 13		09 28		09 43		09 58			20 13		20 28		20 43		20 58		21 13		21 28	
St Pancras International	a		09 18		09 33		09 48		10 03			20 18		20 33		20 48		21 03		21 18		21 33	
North Dulwich	d	08 51		09 06		09 21		09 36			19 51		20 06		20 21		20 36		20 51		21 06		21 21
East Dulwich	d	08 53		09 08		09 23		09 38			19 53		20 08		20 23		20 38		20 53		21 08		21 23
Peckham Rye	d	08 56		09 11		09 26		09 41			19 56		20 11		20 26		20 41		20 56		21 11		21 26
Queens Rd Peckham	d	08 58		09 13		09 28		09 43			19 58		20 13		20 28		20 43		20 58		21 13		21 28
South Bermondsey	d	09 01		09 16		09 31		09 46			20 01		20 16		20 31		20 46		21 01		21 16		21 31
London Bridge ⊖	a	09 06		09 21		09 36		09 51			20 06		20 21		20 36		20 51		21 06		21 21		21 36

		TL B	SN	TL B	SN A	TL B	SN	TL C	SN A	TL C	SN	TL C	SN A	TL C	SN	TL C	SN A	TL C	SN	TL C	SN A	TL C
Sutton	d	20 49		21 16		21 19		21 46		21 49		22 18		22 19		22 48		22 49		23 18		23 19
Carshalton	d			21 19				21 49				22 21				22 51				23 21		
Hackbridge	d			21 22				21 52				22 24				22 54				23 24		
Mitcham Junction	d			21 25				21 55				22 27				22 57				23 27		
Mitcham Eastfields	d			21 28				21 58				22 30				23 00				23 30		
Wimbledon	d	21 07				21 37				22 07				22 41				23 11				23 37
Haydons Road	d	21 10				21 40				22 10				22 44				23 14				23 40
Tooting	d	21 13				21 43				22 13				22 47				23 17				23 43
East Croydon	d				21 23				21 53				22 23				22 53				23 23	
Selhurst	d				21 27				21 57				22 27				22 57				23 27	
Thornton Heath	d				21 29				21 59				22 29				22 59				23 29	
Norbury	d				21 32				22 02				22 32				23 02				23 32	
Streatham Common	d				21 36				22 06				22 36				23 06				23 36	
Streatham	d	21 18		21 33	21 43	21 48		22 03	22 13	22 18		22 35	22 43	22 52		23 05	23 12	23 22		23 35	23 43	23 48
Beckenham Junction	d		21 15				21 45				22 15				22 45				23 15			
Birkbeck	d		21 18				21 48				22 18				22 48				23 18			
Crystal Palace	d		21 23				21 53				22 23				22 53				23 23			
Gipsy Hill	d		21 25				21 55				22 25				22 55				23 25			
West Norwood	d		21 28				21 58				22 28				22 58				23 28			
Tulse Hill	d	21 23	21 32	21 38	21 47	21 53	22 02	22 08	22 17	22 23	22 32	22 40	22 47	22 57	23 02	23 10	23 17	23 27	23 32	23 40	23 47	23 53
Herne Hill	a	21 26		21 41		21 56		22 11		22 26		22 43		23 00		23 13		23 30		23 43		23 56
Loughborough Jn	a	21 30		21 45		22 00		22 15		22 30		22 47		23 07		23 17		23 37		23 47		
Elephant & Castle	a	21 34		21 49		22 04		22 19		22 34		22 51		23 11		23 21		23 41		23 51		00 03
London Blackfriars ⊖	a	21 39		21 54		22 09		22 24		22 39		22 59		23 16		23 26		23 46		00 01		00 08
City Thameslink	a																					
Farringdon	a	21 43		21 58		22 13		22 28		22 43		23 03		23 21		23 31		23 53		00 06		00 13
St Pancras International	a	21 48		22 03		22 18		22 33		22 48		23 08		23 25		23 35		23 57		00 10		00 17
North Dulwich	d		21 36		21 51		22 06		22 21		22 36		22 51		23 06		23 21		23 36		23 51	
East Dulwich	d		21 38		21 53		22 08		22 23		22 38		22 53		23 08		23 23		23 38		23 53	
Peckham Rye	d		21 41		21 56		22 11		22 26		22 41		22 56		23 11		23 26		23 41		23 56	
Queens Rd Peckham	d		21 43		21 58		22 13		22 28		22 43		22 58		23 13		23 28		23 43		23 58	
South Bermondsey	d		21 46		22 01		22 16		22 31		22 46		23 01		23 16		23 31		23 46		00 02	
London Bridge ⊖	a		21 51		22 06		22 21		22 36		22 51		23 06		23 21		23 36		23 51		00 06	

A From Caterham
B To St Albans City
C To Bedford

Table T173-R

Sundays

20 May to 2 December

Tulse Hill, Streatham, North Dulwich, East Dulwich, Peckham Rye, Queens Road Peckham and South Bermondsey - London Bridge

		SN A	SN	SN	SN	SN	SN	SN	SN	SN	SN	SN	SN	TL B	SN	SN	TL B	SN	SN	TL B	SN	TL	SN
Sutton	d													09 09			09 39			10 09		10 40	
Carshalton	d																					10 43	
Hackbridge	d																					10 45	
Mitcham Junction	d																					10 48	
Mitcham Eastfields	d																					10 51	
Wimbledon	d													09 27			09 57			10 27			
Haydons Road	d													09 29			09 59			10 29			
Tooting	d													09 32			10 02			10 32			
East Croydon	d		06 44		07 14		07 44		08 14		08 44		09 14			09 44			10 14				10 44
Selhurst	d		06 47		07 17		07 47		08 17		08 47		09 17			09 47			10 17				10 47
Thornton Heath	d		06 49		07 19		07 49		08 19		08 49		09 19			09 49			10 19				10 49
Norbury	d		06 52		07 22		07 52		08 22		08 52		09 22			09 52			10 22				10 52
Streatham Common	d		06 55		07 25		07 55		08 25		08 55		09 25			09 55			10 25				10 55
Streatham	d		06 59		07 29		07 59		08 29		08 59		09 29	09 37		09 59	10 07		10 29	10 37		10 55	10 59
Beckenham Junction	d																						
Birkbeck	d																						
Crystal Palace	d			07 11		07 41		08 11		08 41		09 11			09 41			10 11			10 41		
Gipsy Hill	d			07 13		07 43		08 13		08 43		09 13			09 43			10 13			10 43		
West Norwood	d			07 16		07 46		08 16		08 46		09 16			09 46			10 16			10 46		
Tulse Hill	d		07 03	07 20	07 33	07 50	08 03	08 20	08 33	08 50	09 03	09 20	09 33	09 41	09 50	10 03	10 11	10 20	10 33	10 41	10 50	10 59	11 03
Herne Hill	a													09 45			10 15			10 45		11 03	
Loughborough Jn	a													09 48			10 18			10 48		11 06	
Elephant & Castle	a													09 52			10 22			10 52		11 10	
London Blackfriars ⊖	a													09 57			10 27			10 57		11 15	
City Thameslink	a																						
Farringdon	a													10 02			10 32			11 02			
St Pancras International	a													10 06			10 36			11 06			
North Dulwich	d		07 06	07 23	07 36	07 53	08 06	08 23	08 36	08 53	09 06	09 23	09 36		09 53	10 06		10 23	10 36		10 53		11 06
East Dulwich	d		07 08	07 25	07 38	07 55	08 08	08 25	08 38	08 55	09 08	09 25	09 38		09 55	10 08		10 25	10 38		10 55		11 08
Peckham Rye	d		07 11	07 29	07 42	07 59	08 11	08 29	08 41	08 59	09 11	09 29	09 41		09 59	10 11		10 29	10 41		10 59		11 11
Queens Rd Peckham	d		07 13	07 31	07 44	08 01	08 13	08 31	08 43	09 01	09 13	09 31	09 43		10 01	10 13		10 31	10 43		11 01		11 13
South Bermondsey	d	00 02	07 17	07 33	07 47	08 03	08 17	08 33	08 47	09 03	09 17	09 33	09 47		10 03	10 17		10 33	10 47		11 03		11 17
London Bridge ⊖	a	00 06	07 22	07 39	07 52	08 09	08 22	08 43	08 53	09 09	09 22	09 39	09 52		10 09	10 22		10 39	10 52		11 09		11 22

		TL B	SN	TL	SN	TL C	SN	TL B	SN	TL C	SN	TL B		SN	TL C	SN	TL B	SN	TL C	SN	TL B	SN	TL D
Sutton	d	10 39		11 10		11 09		11 40		11 39		12 10			20 09		20 40		20 39		21 10		21 09
Carshalton	d			11 13				11 43				12 13					20 43				21 13		
Hackbridge	d			11 15				11 45				12 15					20 45				21 15		
Mitcham Junction	d			11 18				11 48				12 18					20 48				21 18		
Mitcham Eastfields	d			11 21				11 51				12 21					20 51				21 21		
Wimbledon	d	10 57				11 27				11 57					20 27				20 57				21 27
Haydons Road	d	10 59				11 29				11 59					20 29				20 59				21 29
Tooting	d	11 02				11 32				12 02					20 32				21 02				21 32
East Croydon	d				11 14				11 44					20 14				20 44				21 14	
Selhurst	d				11 17				11 47					20 17				20 47				21 17	
Thornton Heath	d				11 19				11 49					20 19				20 49				21 19	
Norbury	d				11 22				11 52					20 22				20 52				21 22	
Streatham Common	d				11 25				11 55					20 25				20 55				21 25	
Streatham	d	11 07		11 25	11 29	11 37		11 55	11 59	12 07		12 25	and at the same minutes past each hour until	20 29	20 37		20 55	20 59	21 07		21 25	21 29	21 37
Beckenham Junction	d																						
Birkbeck	d																						
Crystal Palace	d		11 11				11 41				12 11					20 41				21 11			
Gipsy Hill	d		11 13				11 43				12 13					20 43				21 13			
West Norwood	d		11 16				11 46				12 16					20 46				21 16			
Tulse Hill	d	11 11	11 20	11 29	11 33	11 41	11 50	11 59	12 03	12 11	12 20	12 29		20 33	20 41	20 50	20 59	21 03	21 11	21 20	21 29	21 33	21 41
Herne Hill	a	11 15		11 33		11 45		12 03		12 15		12 33			20 45		21 03		21 15		21 33		21 45
Loughborough Jn	a	11 18		11 36		11 48		12 06		12 18		12 36			20 48		21 06		21 18		21 36		21 48
Elephant & Castle	a	11 22		11 40		11 52		12 10		12 22		12 40			20 52		21 10		21 22		21 40		21 52
London Blackfriars ⊖	a	11 27		11 45		11 57		12 15		12 27		12 45			20 57		21 15		21 27		21 45		21 57
City Thameslink	a																						
Farringdon	a	11 32				12 02		12 20		12 32		12 50			21 02		21 20		21 32		21 50		22 02
St Pancras International	a	11 36				12 06		12 24		12 36		12 54			21 06		21 24		21 36		21 54		22 06
North Dulwich	d		11 23		11 36		11 53		12 06		12 23			20 36		20 53		21 06		21 23		21 36	
East Dulwich	d		11 25		11 38		11 55		12 08		12 25			20 38		20 55		21 08		21 25		21 38	
Peckham Rye	d		11 29		11 41		11 59		12 11		12 29			20 41		20 59		21 11		21 29		21 41	
Queens Rd Peckham	d		11 31		11 43		12 01		12 13		12 31			20 43		21 01		21 13		21 31		21 43	
South Bermondsey	d		11 33		11 47		12 03		12 17		12 33			20 47		21 03		21 17		21 33		21 47	
London Bridge ⊖	a		11 39		11 52		12 09		12 22		12 39			20 52		21 09		21 22		21 39		21 52	

A not 20 May. From Caterham
B To Luton
C To St Albans City
D To Bedford

Please note, Network Rail have stated that further updates to this timetable are possible during the validity period.

Table T173-R

Sundays
20 May to 2 December

Tulse Hill, Streatham, North Dulwich, East Dulwich, Peckham Rye, Queens Road Peckham and South Bermondsey - London Bridge

	SN	TL A	SN	SN	TL	SN	TL B	SN	TL B	SN	SN	SN
Sutton d		21 40			22 10		22 09		22 40			
Carshalton d		21 43			22 13				22 43			
Hackbridge d		21 45			22 15				22 45			
Mitcham Junction d		21 48			22 18				22 48			
Mitcham Eastfields d		21 51			22 21				22 51			
Wimbledon d							22 27					
Haydons Road d							22 29					
Tooting d							22 32					
East Croydon d			21 44			22 14				22 42		
Selhurst d			21 47			22 17				22 47		
Thornton Heath d			21 49			22 19				22 49		
Norbury d			21 52			22 22				22 52		
Streatham Common d			21 55			22 25				22 56		
Streatham d		21 55	21 59		22 25	22 29	22 37		22 55	22 59		
Beckenham Junction d												
Birkbeck d												
Crystal Palace d	21 41			22 11				22 41			23 11	23 41
Gipsy Hill d	21 43			22 13				22 43			23 13	23 43
West Norwood d	21 46			22 16				22 46			23 16	23 46
Tulse Hill d	21 50	21 59	22 03	22 20	22 29	22 33	22 41	22 50	22 59	23 03	23 20	23 50
Herne Hill a		22 03			22 33		22 45		23 03			
Loughborough Jn a		22 06			22 36		22 48		23 06			
Elephant & Castle a		22 10			22 40		22 52		23 10			
London Blackfriars 3 ⊖ a		22 15			22 45		22 57		23 15			
City Thameslink a												
Farringdon a		22 20					23 02		23 20			
St Pancras International a		22 24					23 06		23 24			
North Dulwich d	21 53		22 06	22 23		22 36		22 53		23 06	23 23	23 53
East Dulwich d	21 55		22 08	22 25		22 38		22 55		23 08	23 25	23 55
Peckham Rye 4 d	21 59		22 11	22 29		22 41		22 59		23 12	23 29	23 59
Queens Rd Peckham d	22 01		22 13	22 31		22 43		23 01		23 14	23 31	00 01
South Bermondsey d	22 03		22 17	22 33		22 47		23 03		23 17	23 33	00 04
London Bridge 4 ⊖ a	22 09		22 22	22 39		22 52		23 09		23 22	23 39	00 09

A To West Hampstead Thameslink B To Bedford

<u>T173 UPDATE:</u> Monday – Friday 'Sutton-London Bridge' service stops at West Croydon (not East Croydon) at 07:18, 07:48, 08:18, 8:48, 18:18, 18:48 and 19:18.

Table T175-F

Mondays to Fridays
21 May to 7 December

London - Norwood Junction and East Croydon - Summary of Fast Trains

Summary of Fast Trains

	SN MX	TL	SN	SN MX	SN MX	SN	TL	SN MX	TL MO	TL MX	TL	TL		TL	SN	TL	TL	SN	TL	SN	TL
London Victoria 15 ⊖ d	00 02		00 08			00 12							and		04 35			05 21		05 32	
Clapham Junction 10 d	00 09		00 15			00 20							every 30		04 42			05 28		05 39	
St Pancras International d							00 21		00 51	00 52	01 32	02 32	minutes	04 02		04 32	04 51		05 20		
Farringdon 3 ⊖ d							00 26						until				04 56		05 24		
City Thameslink 3 d																	04 58		05 26		
London Blackfriars 3 ⊖ d		00 01					00 31		01 01	01 02	01 40	02 40		04 10		04 40	05 01		05 29		
London Bridge 4 ⊖ d				00 17	00 10			00 35											05 35		05 37
Norwood Junction 2 a				00 30	00 34			00 59													05 50
East Croydon a	00 23	00 27	00 30	00 34	00 38	00 43	00 57	01 13	01 27	01 28	02 06	03 06		04 36	04 57	05 06	05 27	05 41	05 48	05 51	05 54

	SN	SN	SN	SN	TL	TL	SN	SN	TL	SN	TL	SN	SN	TL	TL	SN	SN	SN	TL	SN	SN	SN
London Victoria 15 ⊖ d	05 39		05 51	05 54			06 02			06 09			06 21			06 32		06 36		06 39		
Clapham Junction 10 d	05 46		05 58	06 01			06 09			06 16			06 28			06 39		06 43		06 46	06 35	
St Pancras International d					05 45	05 50			05 55		06 00			06 15	06 20				06 25			
Farringdon 3 ⊖ d					05 49	05 54			05 59		06 04			06 19	06 24				06 29			
City Thameslink 3 d					05 51	05 56			06 01		06 06			06 21	06 26				06 31			
London Blackfriars 3 ⊖ d					05 54	05 59			06 04		06 09			06 24	06 29				06 34			
London Bridge 4 ⊖ d		05 34			06 00	06 05		06 07	06 11		06 15	06 17		06 30	06 35		06 37		06 41			06 47
Norwood Junction 2 a		05 58			06 12									06 42								
East Croydon a	05 55	06 02	06 09	06 10	06 16	06 18	06 19	06 21	06 24	06 26	06 28	06 31	06 39	06 46	06 48	06 49	06 51	06 52	06 54	06 56	06 59	07 01

	SN	TL	SN	TL	TL	SN	SN	SN	TL	SN	TL	SN	SN	TL	SN	TL	TL	SN	SN	TL	SN
London Victoria 15 ⊖ d	06 46		06 51			07 02		07 06		07 09		07 16			07 21			07 32	07 36		07 39
Clapham Junction 10 d	06 53		06 58			07 09		07 13		07 16		07 23			07 28			07 39	07 43		07 46
St Pancras International d		06 35		06 45	06 50				06 55		07 00			07 10		07 15	07 20			07 25	
Farringdon 3 ⊖ d		06 39		06 49	06 54				06 59		07 04			07 14		07 19	07 24			07 29	
City Thameslink 3 d		06 41		06 51	06 56				07 01		07 06			07 16		07 21	07 26			07 31	
London Blackfriars 3 ⊖ d		06 44		06 54	06 59				07 04		07 09			07 19		07 24	07 29			07 34	
London Bridge 4 ⊖ d		06 51		07 00	07 05		07 07		07 11		07 15		07 17	07 25		07 30	07 35			07 41	
Norwood Junction 2 a		07 02		07 12												07 42					
East Croydon a	07 02	07 06	07 09	07 16	07 18	07 19	07 21	07 22	07 24	07 27	07 29	07 32	07 32	07 38	07 39	07 46	07 48	07 49	07 52	07 54	07 57

	SN	SN	SN	TL	SN	SN	TL	TL	SN	SN	SN	TL	SN	TL	SN	SN	SN	TL	SN	SN	SN	TL
London Victoria 15 ⊖ d		07 46			07 51	07 55			08 01		08 06		08 09			08 16			08 21	08 25		
Clapham Junction 10 d	07 35	07 53			07 58	08 02			08 08		08 13		08 16		08 05	08 23			08 28	08 32		
St Pancras International d				07 40			07 45	07 50				07 55		08 00				08 10				08 15
Farringdon 3 ⊖ d				07 44			07 49	07 54				07 59		08 04				08 14				08 19
City Thameslink 3 d				07 46			07 51	07 56				08 01		08 06				08 16				08 21
London Blackfriars 3 ⊖ d				07 49			07 54	07 59				08 04		08 09				08 19				08 24
London Bridge 4 ⊖ d			07 47	07 55			08 00	08 05		08 07		08 11		08 15			08 17	08 25			08 10	08 30
Norwood Junction 2 a							08 12														08 36	08 42
East Croydon a	08 01	08 03	08 03	08 08	08 09	08 11	08 16	08 18	08 19	08 21	08 22	08 24	08 27	08 30	08 31	08 33	08 33	08 38	08 39	08 41	08 42	08 46

	TL	SN	SN	TL	SN	SN	SN	SN	TL	TL	SN	SN	SN	TL	TL	SN	SN A	SN	TL	SN	TL	SN
London Victoria 15 ⊖ d			08 36		08 39		08 46				08 51	08 55					08 57	09 06		09 09		09 16
Clapham Junction 10 d			08 43		08 46	08 35	08 53				08 58	09 02					09 06	09 13		09 16		09 23
St Pancras International d	08 20			08 25					08 35	08 40				08 45	08 50				08 55		09 00	
Farringdon 3 ⊖ d	08 24			08 29					08 39	08 44				08 49	08 54				08 59		09 04	
City Thameslink 3 d	08 26			08 31					08 41	08 46				08 51	08 56				09 01		09 06	
London Blackfriars 3 ⊖ d	08 29			08 34					08 44	08 49				08 54	08 59				09 04		09 09	
London Bridge 4 ⊖ d	08 35	08 37		08 41				08 47	08 51	08 55			08 40	09 00	09 05	09 07			09 11		09 15	
Norwood Junction 2 a									09 02				09 06									
East Croydon a	08 48	08 51	08 52	08 54	08 57	09 01	09 02	09 03	09 06	09 08	09 09	09 11	09 12	09 14	09 18	09 21	09 30	09 22	09 24	09 26	09 28	09 32

	SN	TL	TL	SN	SN	SN	TL	TL	SN	SN	SN	SN	SN	TL	TL	SN	SN	SN	TL	TL	SN
London Victoria 15 ⊖ d				09 21	09 25				09 36	09 39		09 46				09 51	09 55				
Clapham Junction 10 d				09 28	09 32				09 43	09 46	09 35	09 53				09 58	10 02				
St Pancras International d		09 05	09 10				09 15	09 20						09 35	09 40				09 45	09 50	
Farringdon 3 ⊖ d		09 09	09 14				09 19	09 24						09 39	09 44				09 49	09 54	
City Thameslink 3 d		09 11	09 16				09 21	09 26						09 41	09 46				09 51	09 56	
London Blackfriars 3 ⊖ d		09 14	09 19				09 24	09 29						09 44	09 49				09 54	09 59	
London Bridge 4 ⊖ d	09 17	09 21	09 25			09 10	09 30	09 35					09 47	09 51	09 55			09 40	10 00	10 05	10 07
Norwood Junction 2 a		09 32				09 36								10 02				10 06			
East Croydon a	09 32	09 36	09 38	09 39	09 41	09 42	09 44	09 48	09 52	09 56	10 00	10 02	10 02	10 06	10 08	10 09	10 11	10 13	10 14	10 18	10 21

	SN	SN	SN	TL	SN	SN	TL	TL	SN	SN	SN	TL	TL	SN	SN	SN	SN	SN	SN	TL	SN	SN
London Victoria 15 ⊖ d	10 06		10 09			10 16			10 21	10 25				10 36		10 39			10 46		10 51	10 55
Clapham Junction 10 d	10 13		10 16			10 23			10 28	10 32				10 43		10 46	10 35		10 53		10 58	11 02
St Pancras International d				10 00			10 05					10 15	10 20							10 35		
Farringdon 3 ⊖ d				10 04			10 09					10 19	10 24							10 39		
City Thameslink 3 d				10 06			10 11					10 21	10 26							10 41		
London Blackfriars 3 ⊖ d				10 09			10 14					10 24	10 29							10 44		
London Bridge 4 ⊖ d		09 44		10 15	10 17		10 21	10 22			10 10	10 30	10 35		10 14			10 47		10 51		
Norwood Junction 2 a							10 32				10 36									11 02		
East Croydon a	10 22	10 24	10 26	10 28	10 31	10 32	10 36	10 38	10 39	10 41	10 43	10 44	10 48	10 52	10 54	10 56	10 59	11 01	11 02	11 06	11 09	11 11

A until 30 November

London - Norwood Junction and East Croydon - Summary of Fast Trains

Summary of Fast Trains

	SN	TL	TL	SN	SN	SN	SN	TL		SN	SN	TL	SN	SN	SN	TL	TL	SN		SN	SN	SN	SN	SN
London Victoria ⊖ d					11 06		11 09				11 16		11 21	11 25				11 36			11 39			11 46
Clapham Junction d					11 13		11 16				11 23		11 28	11 32				11 43			11 46	11 35		11 53
St Pancras International d		10 45	10 50					11 00				11 05				11 15	11 20							
Farringdon ⊖ d		10 49	10 54					11 04				11 09				11 19	11 24							
City Thameslink d		10 51	10 56					11 06				11 11				11 21	11 26							
London Blackfriars ⊖ d		10 54	10 59					11 09				11 14				11 24	11 29							
London Bridge ⊖ d	10 40	11 00	11 05	11 07		10 44		11 15		11 17		11 21			11 10	11 30	11 35			11 14			11 47	
Norwood Junction a	11 06											11 32			11 36									
East Croydon a	11 13	11 14	11 18	11 21	11 22	11 24	11 26	11 28		11 31	11 32	11 36	11 39	11 41	11 43	11 44	11 48	11 52		11 54	11 56	11 59	12 01	12 02

	TL	SN	SN	SN		TL	TL	TL	SN	SN	SN	SN	TL	SN		SN	TL	SN	SN	SN	TL	TL	SN	SN
							A	B																
London Victoria ⊖ d		11 51	11 55							12 06		12 09				12 16		12 21	12 25				12 36	
Clapham Junction d		11 58	12 02							12 13		12 16				12 23		12 28	12 32				12 43	
St Pancras International d	11 35					11 45	11 50	11 51					12 00				12 05				12 15	12 20		
Farringdon ⊖ d	11 39					11 49	11 54	11 55					12 04				12 09				12 19	12 24		
City Thameslink d	11 41					11 51	11 56	11 57					12 06				12 11				12 21	12 26		
London Blackfriars ⊖ d	11 44					11 54	11 59	12 00					12 09				12 14				12 24	12 29		
London Bridge ⊖ d	11 51			11 40		12 00	12 05	12 06	12 07		11 44		12 15	12 17			12 21			12 10	12 30	12 35		12 14
Norwood Junction a	12 02			12 06													12 32			12 36				
East Croydon a	12 06	12 09	12 11	12 13		12 14	12 18	12 19	12 21	12 22	12 24	12 26	12 28	12 31		12 32	12 36	12 39	12 41	12 43	12 44	12 48	12 52	12 54

		SN	SN	SN	SN	TL	SN	SN	SN	TL		TL	SN	SN	SN	SN	TL	SN	SN	TL		SN	SN	SN
			MW FO																					
London Victoria ⊖ d		12 39			12 46		12 51	12 55						13 06		13 09			13 16			13 21	13 25	
Clapham Junction d		12 46	12 35		12 53		12 58	13 02						13 13		13 16			13 23			13 28	13 32	
St Pancras International d						12 35				12 45		12 50					13 00			13 05				
Farringdon ⊖ d						12 39				12 49		12 54					13 04			13 09				
City Thameslink d						12 41				12 51		12 56					13 06			13 11				
London Blackfriars ⊖ d						12 44				12 54		12 59					13 09			13 14				
London Bridge ⊖ d				12 47		12 51			12 40	13 00		13 05	13 07		12 44		13 15	13 17		13 21				13 10
Norwood Junction a						13 02			13 06											13 32				13 36
East Croydon a		12 56	12 59	13 01	13 02	13 06	13 09	13 11	13 13	13 14		13 18	13 21	13 22	13 24	13 26	13 28	13 31	13 32	13 36		13 39	13 41	13 43

	TL	TL	SN	SN	SN	SN		SN	SN	TL	SN	SN	SN	TL	TL	TL		SN	SN	SN	SN	TL	SN	SN
															A	B								
London Victoria ⊖ d			13 36		13 39				13 46		13 51	13 55							14 06		14 09			14 16
Clapham Junction d			13 43		13 46	13 35			13 53		13 58	14 02							14 13		14 16			14 23
St Pancras International d	13 15	13 20								13 35				13 45	13 50	13 51						14 00		
Farringdon ⊖ d	13 19	13 24								13 39				13 49	13 54	13 55						14 04		
City Thameslink d	13 21	13 26								13 41				13 51	13 56	13 57						14 06		
London Blackfriars ⊖ d	13 24	13 29								13 44				13 54	13 59	14 00						14 09		
London Bridge ⊖ d	13 30	13 35		13 14				13 47		13 51			13 40	14 00	14 05	14 06		14 07		13 44		14 15	14 17	
Norwood Junction a										14 02			14 06											
East Croydon a	13 44	13 48	13 52	13 54	13 56	13 59		14 01	14 02	14 06	14 09	14 11	14 13	14 14	14 18	14 19		14 21	14 22	14 24	14 26	14 28	14 31	14 32

	TL	SN		SN	SN	TL	TL	SN	SN	SN	SN	SN		SN	TL	SN	SN	SN	TL	TL	TL	SN		SN
																				C	D			
London Victoria ⊖ d		14 21		14 25				14 36		14 39				14 46		14 51	14 55							15 06
Clapham Junction d		14 28		14 32				14 43		14 46	14 35			14 53		14 58	15 02							15 13
St Pancras International d	14 05					14 15	14 20								14 35				14 45	14 50	14 51			
Farringdon ⊖ d	14 09					14 19	14 24								14 39				14 49	14 54	14 55			
City Thameslink d	14 11					14 21	14 26								14 41				14 51	14 56	14 57			
London Blackfriars ⊖ d	14 14					14 24	14 29								14 44				14 54	14 59	15 00			
London Bridge ⊖ d	14 21				14 10	14 30	14 35		14 14			14 47			14 51			14 40	15 00	15 05	15 06	15 07		
Norwood Junction a	14 32				14 36										15 02			15 06						
East Croydon a	14 36	14 39		14 41	14 43	14 44	14 48	14 53	14 54	14 56	14 59	15 01		15 02	15 06	15 09	15 11	15 13	15 14	15 18	15 19	15 21		15 22

	SN	SN	TL	SN	SN	TL	SN	SN		SN	TL	TL	SN	SN	SN	SN	SN	SN		TL	SN	SN	SN	TL
London Victoria ⊖ d		15 09			15 16		15 21	15 25					15 36		15 39		15 46				15 51	15 55		
Clapham Junction d		15 16			15 23		15 28	15 32					15 43		15 46	15 35	15 53				15 58	16 02		
St Pancras International d			15 00			15 05					15 15	15 20								15 35				15 45
Farringdon ⊖ d			15 04			15 09					15 19	15 24								15 39				15 49
City Thameslink d			15 06			15 11					15 21	15 26								15 41				15 51
London Blackfriars ⊖ d			15 09			15 14					15 24	15 29								15 44				15 54
London Bridge ⊖ d	14 44		15 15	15 17		15 21				15 10	15 30	15 35		15 14				15 47		15 51			15 40	16 00
Norwood Junction a						15 32				15 36										16 02			16 06	
East Croydon a	15 24	15 26	15 28	15 31	15 32	15 36	15 39	15 41		15 43	15 44	15 48	15 52	15 54	15 56	16 00	16 02	16 02		16 06	16 09	16 11	16 13	16 14

	TL	SN	SN	SN		SN	TL	SN	SN	SN	TL	SN	SN	TL		SN	TL	SN	SN	TL	SN	SN	SN	SN
London Victoria ⊖ d			16 06			16 09			16 16			16 21	16 25			16 31			16 36		16 39		16 45	
Clapham Junction d			16 13			16 16		16 05	16 23			16 28	16 32			16 38			16 43		16 46	16 35	16 52	
St Pancras International d	15 50						16 00				16 05			16 15			16 20			16 25				
Farringdon ⊖ d	15 54						16 04				16 09			16 19			16 24			16 29				
City Thameslink d	15 56						16 06				16 11			16 21			16 26			16 31				
London Blackfriars ⊖ d	15 59						16 09				16 14			16 24			16 29			16 34				
London Bridge ⊖ d	16 05	16 07		15 44			16 15			16 17	16 21			16 30			16 35	16 37		16 41				16 47
Norwood Junction a											16 32													
East Croydon a	16 19	16 21	16 23	16 24		16 26	16 29	16 30	16 32	16 32	16 36	16 39	16 41	16 44		16 49	16 49	16 51	16 52	16 54	16 56	17 00	17 01	17 02

A from 23 July until 5 October
B until 20 July, from 8 October
C from 30 July
D until 27 July

Please check the 'Additional Notes to Individual Tables' section for any other general notes that apply to this Table

London - Norwood Junction and East Croydon - Summary of Fast Trains

Summary of Fast Trains

	TL	TL	SN	SN	TL	SN		SN	TL	SN	SN	TL	SN	TL	SN	SN		SN	TL	SN	SN	TL	SN	SN
London Victoria ⊖ d			16 51	16 54				17 02			17 06		17 09			17 15				17 21	17 24			17 32
Clapham Junction d			16 58	17 02				17 09			17 13		17 16		17 05	17 22				17 28	17 32			17 39
St Pancras International d	16 35	16 40			16 45				16 50			16 55		17 00					17 05			17 15		
Farringdon ⊖ d	16 39	16 44			16 49				16 54			16 59		17 04					17 09			17 19		
City Thameslink d	16 41	16 46			16 51				16 56			17 01		17 06					17 11			17 21		
London Blackfriars ⊖ d	16 44	16 49			16 54				16 59			17 04		17 09					17 14			17 24		
London Bridge ⊖ d	16 51	16 55			17 00	17 03			17 05	17 07		17 11		17 15				17 17	17 21			17 30	17 33	
Norwood Junction a	17 02																		17 32					
East Croydon a	17 06	17 08	17 09	17 11	17 14	17 16		17 19	17 19	17 21	17 22	17 24	17 26	17 29	17 30	17 31		17 32	17 36	17 39	17 41	17 44	17 47	17 49

	TL	SN		SN	TL	SN	SN	SN	SN	TL	TL	SN		SN	TL	SN	SN	TL	SN	SN	TL	SN		TL
London Victoria ⊖ d				17 36		17 39		17 45				17 51		17 54			18 02			18 06		18 09		
Clapham Junction d				17 43		17 46	17 35	17 52				17 58		18 02			18 09			18 13		18 16		
St Pancras International d	17 20				17 25					17 35	17 40				17 45			17 50			17 55			18 00
Farringdon ⊖ d	17 24				17 29					17 39	17 44				17 49			17 54			17 59			18 04
City Thameslink d	17 26				17 31					17 41	17 46				17 51			17 56			18 01			18 06
London Blackfriars ⊖ d	17 29				17 34					17 44	17 49				17 54			17 59			18 04			18 09
London Bridge ⊖ d	17 35	17 37			17 41				17 47	17 51	17 55				18 00	18 03		18 05	18 07		18 11			18 15
Norwood Junction a										18 02														
East Croydon a	17 49	17 51		17 52	17 54	17 56	18 00	18 01	18 02	18 06	18 08	18 09		18 11	18 14	18 16	18 19	18 19	18 21	18 22	18 24	18 27		18 29

	SN	SN	SN	TL	SN	SN	TL	SN		SN	TL	SN	TL	SN	SN	SN	SN	TL		SN	SN	SN	TL	TL
London Victoria ⊖ d		18 15			18 21	18 24				18 32		18 36		18 39		18 45				18 51	18 54			
Clapham Junction d	18 05	18 22			18 28	18 32				18 39		18 43		18 46	18 35	18 52				18 58	19 02			
St Pancras International d				18 05			18 15				18 20		18 25					18 35					18 45	18 50
Farringdon ⊖ d				18 09			18 19				18 24		18 29					18 39					18 49	18 54
City Thameslink d				18 11			18 21				18 26		18 31					18 41					18 51	18 56
London Blackfriars ⊖ d				18 14			18 24				18 29		18 34					18 44					18 54	18 59
London Bridge ⊖ d			18 17	18 21			18 30	18 33			18 35		18 41				18 47	18 51				18 40	19 00	19 05
Norwood Junction a				18 32														19 02				19 06		
East Croydon a	18 31	18 31	18 33	18 36	18 39	18 41	18 44	18 47		18 49	18 49	18 52	18 54	18 57	19 00	19 01	19 03	19 06		19 09	19 11	19 13	19 14	19 19

	SN	SN	TL	SN		TL	SN	SN	TL	SN	SN	SN	TL	TL		SN	SN	SN	SN	SN	SN	TL	SN	SN
London Victoria ⊖ d		19 06		19 09			19 16			19 21	19 25					19 36		19 39		19 46			19 51	19 55
Clapham Junction d		19 13		19 16			19 23			19 28	19 32					19 43		19 46	19 35	19 53			19 58	20 02
St Pancras International d			18 55			19 00			19 05				19 15	19 20								19 35		
Farringdon ⊖ d			18 59			19 04			19 09				19 19	19 24								19 39		
City Thameslink d			19 01			19 06			19 11				19 21	19 26								19 41		
London Blackfriars ⊖ d			19 04			19 09			19 14				19 24	19 29								19 44		
London Bridge ⊖ d	19 07		19 11			19 15		19 17	19 21			19 10	19 30	19 35			19 14				19 47	19 51		
Norwood Junction a									19 32			19 36										20 02		
East Croydon a	19 21	19 22	19 24	19 27		19 29	19 32	19 32	19 36	19 39	19 41	19 42	19 44	19 48		19 52	19 54	19 57	19 59	20 02	20 02	20 06	20 09	20 11

		SN	TL	TL	TL	SN	SN	SN	SN	TL		SN	SN	TL	TL	SN	SN	SN	TL	TL		SN	SN	SN
				A	B																			
London Victoria ⊖ d							20 06		20 09				20 16			20 21	20 25					20 36		20 39
Clapham Junction d							20 13		20 16				20 23			20 28	20 32					20 43		20 46
St Pancras International d			19 45	19 50	19 51					20 00				20 05					20 15	20 20				
Farringdon ⊖ d			19 49	19 54	19 55					20 04				20 09					20 19	20 24				
City Thameslink d			19 51	19 56	19 57					20 06				20 11					20 21	20 26				
London Blackfriars ⊖ d			19 54	19 59	20 00					20 09				20 14					20 24	20 29				
London Bridge ⊖ d		19 40	20 00	20 05	20 06	20 07		19 44		20 15		20 17		20 21	20 22			20 10	20 30	20 35			20 14	
Norwood Junction a		20 06												20 32				20 36						
East Croydon a		20 13	20 14	20 18	20 19	20 21	20 22	20 24	20 26	20 28		20 31	20 32	20 36	20 38	20 39	20 41	20 43	20 44	20 48		20 52	20 53	20 57

	SN	SN	SN	TL	TL	SN		SN	SN	TL	TL	SN	SN	SN	SN	TL		SN	SN	TL	TL	SN	SN	SN
London Victoria ⊖ d		20 46				20 51		20 55					21 06		21 09				21 16			21 21	21 25	
Clapham Junction d	20 35	20 53				20 58		21 02					21 13		21 16				21 23			21 28	21 32	
St Pancras International d				20 35						20 45	20 50					21 00				21 05				
Farringdon ⊖ d				20 39						20 49	20 54					21 04				21 09				
City Thameslink d				20 41						20 51	20 56					21 06				21 11				
London Blackfriars ⊖ d				20 44						20 54	20 59					21 09				21 14				
London Bridge ⊖ d			20 47	20 51	20 52				20 40	21 00	21 05	21 07		20 44		21 15		21 17		21 21	21 22			21 10
Norwood Junction a				21 02					21 06											21 32				21 36
East Croydon a	21 00	21 02	21 02	21 06	21 08	21 09		21 11	21 13	21 14	21 18	21 21	21 22	21 24	21 26	21 28		21 31	21 32	21 36	21 38	21 39	21 41	21 43

	TL	TL		SN	SN	SN	SN	SN	TL	SN	SN	SN		TL	TL	SN	SN	SN	SN	TL	SN	SN		TL
																						C		
London Victoria ⊖ d				21 36		21 39		21 46		21 51	21 55						22 06		22 09			22 16		
Clapham Junction d				21 43		21 46		21 53		21 58	22 02						22 13		22 16			22 23		
St Pancras International d	21 15	21 20							21 35					21 45	21 51					22 00				22 05
Farringdon ⊖ d	21 19	21 24							21 39					21 49	21 55					22 04				22 09
City Thameslink d	21 21	21 26							21 41					21 51	21 57					22 06				22 11
London Blackfriars ⊖ d	21 24	21 29							21 44					21 54	22 00					22 09				22 14
London Bridge ⊖ d	21 30	21 35			21 14		21 47		21 51			21 40		22 00	22 06	22 07		21 44		22 15	22 17			22 21
Norwood Junction a									22 02			22 06												22 32
East Croydon a	21 44	21 48		21 52	21 54	21 56	22 01	22 02	22 06	22 09	22 11	22 13		22 14	22 19	22 21	22 22	22 24	22 26	22 28	22 31	22 32		22 36

A from 30 July
B until 27 July
C not 7 December

Mondays to Fridays
21 May to 7 December

London - Norwood Junction and East Croydon - Summary of Fast Trains

Summary of Fast Trains

	SN	SN	SN	TL		TL	SN	SN	SN	SN	SN	SN	TL	SN		SN	SN	SN	TL	TL	SN	SN	SN	TL
																FX	FO							
	■	■		■		■	■		■	■		■	■	■		■	■		■	■	■	■	■	■
London Victoria ⊖ d	22 21	22 25					22 36		22 39			22 46		22 52		22 55	22 55					23 06	23 09	
Clapham Junction d	22 28	22 32					22 43		22 46	22 35		22 53		22 59		23 02	23 02					23 13	23 16	
St Pancras International d				22 15		22 20							22 35						22 45	22 50				23 00
Farringdon ⊖ d				22 19		22 24							22 39						22 49	22 54				23 04
City Thameslink d				22 21		22 26							22 41						22 51	22 56				
London Blackfriars ⊖ d				22 24		22 29							22 44						22 54	22 59				23 09
London Bridge ⊖ d			22 10	22 30		22 35		22 14			22 47		22 51					22 40	23 00	23 05	23 07			23 15
Norwood Junction a			22 36										23 02					23 06						
East Croydon a	22 39	22 41	22 43	22 44		22 48	22 52	22 54	22 56	22 59	23 01	23 02	23 06	23 09		23 11	23 11	23 13	23 14	23 18	23 21	23 22	23 26	23 28

		SN	SN	TL	SN	SN	TL	SN	TL	SN		SN	SN	SN	TL
			■	■	■	■	■		■	■				■	■
London Victoria ⊖ d			23 16		23 21	23 25				23 36				23 53	
Clapham Junction d			23 23		23 28	23 32				23 43				23 59	
St Pancras International d				23 05			23 15		23 22						23 51
Farringdon ⊖ d				23 09			23 19		23 27						23 56
City Thameslink d															
London Blackfriars ⊖ d				23 14			23 24		23 31						00 01
London Bridge ⊖ d		23 17		23 21			23 30	23 10	23 37			23 47	23 40		
Norwood Junction a				23 32				23 36					00 06		
East Croydon a		23 31	23 32	23 36	23 39	23 41	23 44	23 47	23 50	23 58		00 01	00 10	00 14	00 27

Saturdays
26 May to 8 December

	SN	TL	SN	SN	SN	SN	TL	SN	TL		SN	TL	SN	TL	SN	TL	TL	SN	TL		TL	TL	SN	SN
	■	■	■				■		■		■	■	■	■	■	■	■	■	■		■	■	■	■
London Victoria ⊖ d	00 02		00 08			00 12					01 10		02 10		03 10			04 10					05 08	05 21
Clapham Junction d	00 09		00 15			00 20					01 17		02 17		03 17			04 17					05 16	05 28
St Pancras International d							00 21		00 52			01 32		02 32		03 02	03 32		04 02		04 32	04 51		
Farringdon ⊖ d							00 26															04 56		
City Thameslink d																								
London Blackfriars ⊖ d		00 01					00 31		01 02			01 40		02 40		03 10	03 40		04 10		04 40	05 01		
London Bridge ⊖ d				00 17	00 10			00 35																
Norwood Junction a				00 30	00 34			00 59																
East Croydon a	00 23	00 27	00 30	00 34	00 38	00 43	00 57	01 13	01 28		01 32	02 06	02 32	03 06	03 32	03 36	04 06	04 31	04 36		05 06	05 27	05 31	05 44

	TL	SN	TL	TL	SN		SN	SN	TL	SN	SN	SN	TL	TL	SN		SN	SN	SN	SN	SN	SN	SN	TL
	■	■	■	■	■		■	■	■		■		■	■	■			■	■		■	■		■
London Victoria ⊖ d		05 39					06 06	06 09			06 21				06 36			06 39			06 51	06 55		
Clapham Junction d		05 46					06 13	06 16			06 28				06 43			06 46	06 35		06 58	07 02		
St Pancras International d	05 20		05 45	05 50					06 00				06 15	06 20										06 45
Farringdon ⊖ d	05 24		05 49	05 54					06 04				06 19	06 24										06 49
City Thameslink d																								
London Blackfriars ⊖ d	05 29		05 54	05 59					06 09				06 24	06 29										06 54
London Bridge ⊖ d	05 35		06 00	06 05	06 07				06 15	06 17		06 11	06 30	06 35			06 14			06 47			06 40	07 00
Norwood Junction a												06 37											07 06	
East Croydon a	05 48	05 56	06 14	06 18	06 21		06 22	06 26	06 28	06 31	06 39	06 43	06 44	06 48	06 52		06 54	06 56	06 59	07 01	07 09	07 11	07 13	07 14

	TL		SN	SN	SN	SN	TL	SN	TL	SN	SN		SN	TL	TL	SN	SN	SN	SN	SN	SN		TL	SN
	■		■	■		■	■		■	■	■			■	■	■		■	■		■		■	■
London Victoria ⊖ d				07 06		07 09				07 21	07 25					07 36		07 39			07 46			07 51
Clapham Junction d				07 13		07 16				07 28	07 32					07 43		07 46	07 35		07 53			07 58
St Pancras International d	06 50						07 00		07 05					07 15	07 20								07 35	
Farringdon ⊖ d	06 54						07 04		07 09					07 19	07 24								07 39	
City Thameslink d																								
London Blackfriars ⊖ d	06 59						07 09		07 14					07 24	07 29								07 44	
London Bridge ⊖ d	07 05		07 07		06 44		07 15	07 17	07 22				07 10	07 30	07 35		07 14			07 47			07 52	
Norwood Junction a									07 32				07 36										08 02	
East Croydon a	07 18		07 21	07 22	07 24	07 26	07 28	07 31	07 36	07 39	07 41		07 43	07 44	07 48	07 52	07 54	07 56	07 59	08 01	08 02		08 06	08 09

	SN	SN	TL	TL	SN	SN	SN		SN	TL	SN	SN	TL	SN	SN	SN	TL		TL	SN	SN	SN	SN	SN
	■		■	■	■	■			■	■		■	■	■	■		■		■	■		■	■	
London Victoria ⊖ d	07 55					08 06			08 09			08 16		08 21	08 25					08 36		08 39		
Clapham Junction d	08 02					08 13			08 16			08 23		08 28	08 32					08 43		08 46	08 35	
St Pancras International d			07 45	07 50						08 00			08 05				08 15		08 20					
Farringdon ⊖ d			07 49	07 54						08 04			08 09				08 19		08 24					
City Thameslink d																								
London Blackfriars ⊖ d			07 54	07 59						08 09			08 14				08 24		08 29					
London Bridge ⊖ d		07 40	08 00	08 05	08 07		07 44			08 15	08 17		08 22			08 10	08 30		08 35		08 14			08 47
Norwood Junction a		08 06											08 32			08 36								
East Croydon a	08 11	08 13	08 14	08 18	08 21	08 22	08 24		08 26	08 28	08 31	08 32	08 36	08 39	08 41	08 43	08 44		08 48	08 52	08 54	08 56	08 59	09 01

	SN	TL	SN		SN	SN	TL	TL	SN	SN	SN	SN	TL	SN	SN	TL	SN	SN	SN	TL	TL	SN	SN	SN
	■	■	■		■		■	■	■	■		■	■		■	■	■	■		■	■	■		■
London Victoria ⊖ d	08 46		08 51		08 55					09 06		09 09			09 16		09 21	09 25				09 36		09 39
Clapham Junction d	08 53		08 58		09 02					09 13		09 16			09 23		09 28	09 32				09 43		09 46
St Pancras International d		08 35					08 45	08 50					09 00			09 05				09 15	09 20			
Farringdon ⊖ d		08 39					08 49	08 54					09 04			09 09				09 19	09 24			
City Thameslink d													09 06			09 11				09 21	09 26			
London Blackfriars ⊖ d		08 44					08 54	08 59					09 09			09 14				09 24	09 29			
London Bridge ⊖ d		08 52				08 40	09 00	09 05	09 07		08 44		09 15	09 17		09 22			09 10	09 30	09 35		09 14	
Norwood Junction a		09 02				09 06										09 32			09 36					
East Croydon a	09 02	09 06	09 09		09 11	09 13	09 14	09 18	09 21	09 22	09 24	09 26	09 28	09 31	09 32	09 36	09 39	09 41	09 43	09 44	09 48	09 52	09 54	09 56

Saturdays
26 May to 8 December

London - Norwood Junction and East Croydon - Summary of Fast Trains

Summary of Fast Trains

	SN	SN	SN	TL	SN	SN	SN	TL	TL		SN	SN	SN	SN	TL	SN	SN	TL	SN	SN	SN	TL	TL
	■		■	■	■	■		■	■		■	■		■	■		■	■	■	■		■	■
London Victoria ⊖ d			09 46		09 51	09 55				and at the same minutes past each hour until		20 06		20 09			20 16		20 21	20 25			
Clapham Junction d	09 35		09 53		09 58	10 02						20 13		20 16			20 23		20 28	20 32			
St Pancras International d				09 35				09 45	09 50						20 00			20 05				20 15	20 20
Farringdon ⊖ d				09 39				09 49	09 54						20 04			20 09				20 19	20 24
City Thameslink d				09 41				09 51	09 56						20 06			20 11				20 21	20 26
London Blackfriars ⊖ d				09 44				09 54	09 59						20 09			20 14				20 24	20 29
London Bridge ⊖ d		09 47		09 52			09 40	10 00	10 05		20 07		19 44		20 15	20 17		20 22			20 10	20 30	20 35
Norwood Junction a				10 02			10 06											20 32			20 36		
East Croydon a	09 59	10 01	10 02	10 06	10 09	10 11	10 13	10 14	10 18		20 21	20 22	20 24	20 26	20 28	20 31	20 32	20 36	20 39	20 41	20 43	20 44	20 48

	SN	SN	SN	SN	SN	SN	TL	SN	SN	SN	TL	TL		SN	SN	SN	SN	TL	SN	SN	TL	SN		SN
	■		■	■		■	■	■	■		■	■		■	■		■	■		■	■	■		■
London Victoria ⊖ d	20 36		20 39			20 46		20 51	20 55						21 06		21 09			21 16		21 21		21 25
Clapham Junction d	20 43		20 46	20 35		20 53		20 58	21 02						21 13		21 16			21 23		21 28		21 32
St Pancras International d							20 35				20 45	20 50						21 00			21 05			
Farringdon ⊖ d							20 39				20 49	20 54						21 04			21 09			
City Thameslink d							20 41				20 51	20 56												
London Blackfriars ⊖ d							20 44				20 54	20 59						21 09			21 14			
London Bridge ⊖ d		20 14			20 47		20 52			20 40	21 00	21 05		21 07		20 44		21 15	21 17		21 22			
Norwood Junction a							21 02			21 06											21 32			
East Croydon a	20 52	20 54	20 56	20 59	21 01	21 02	21 06	21 09	21 11	21 13	21 14	21 18		21 21	21 22	21 24	21 26	21 28	21 31	21 32	21 36	21 39		21 41

	SN	TL	TL	SN	SN	SN	SN	SN		SN	TL	SN	SN	SN	TL	TL	SN	SN		SN	SN	TL	SN	SN
		■	■	■		■	■			■	■	■	■		■	■	■	■			■	■		■
London Victoria ⊖ d				21 36		21 39				21 46		21 51	21 55					22 06			22 09			22 16
Clapham Junction d				21 43		21 46	21 35			21 53		21 58	22 02					22 13			22 16			22 23
St Pancras International d		21 15	21 20								21 35				21 45	21 50						22 00		
Farringdon ⊖ d		21 19	21 24								21 39				21 49	21 54						22 04		
City Thameslink d																								
London Blackfriars ⊖ d		21 24	21 29								21 44				21 54	21 59						22 09		
London Bridge ⊖ d	21 10	21 30	21 35		21 14			21 47			21 52			21 40	22 00	22 05	22 07			21 44		22 15	22 17	
Norwood Junction a	21 36										22 02			22 06										
East Croydon a	21 43	21 44	21 48	21 52	21 54	21 56	21 59	22 01		22 02	22 06	22 09	22 11	22 13	22 14	22 18	22 21	22 22		22 24	22 26	22 28	22 31	22 32

	TL	SN	SN	SN		TL	TL	SN	SN	SN	TL	SN	SN	SN		TL	SN	SN	SN	TL	TL	SN	SN	SN
	■	■	■			■	■	■		■	■	■		■		■	■	■		■	■	■	■	■
London Victoria ⊖ d		22 21	22 25					22 36		22 39				22 46			22 51	22 55					23 06	23 09
Clapham Junction d		22 28	22 32					22 43		22 46		22 35		22 53			22 58	23 02					23 13	23 16
St Pancras International d	22 05					22 15	22 20				22 30					22 35				22 45	22 50			
Farringdon ⊖ d	22 09					22 19	22 24				22 34					22 39				22 49	22 54			
City Thameslink d																								
London Blackfriars ⊖ d	22 14					22 24	22 29				22 39					22 44				22 54	22 59			
London Bridge ⊖ d	22 22			22 10		22 30	22 35		22 14		22 45		22 47			22 52			22 40	23 00	23 05	23 07		
Norwood Junction a	22 32			22 36												23 02			23 06					
East Croydon a	22 36	22 39	22 41	22 43		22 44	22 48	22 52	22 54	22 56	22 58	22 59	23 01	23 02		23 06	23 09	23 11	23 13	23 14	23 18	23 21	23 22	23 26

		TL	SN	SN	TL	SN	SN	TL	SN	TL		SN	SN	SN	SN	TL
		■		■	■	■	■	■		■		■		■		■
London Victoria ⊖ d				23 16		23 21	23 25					23 36		23 53		
Clapham Junction d				23 23		23 28	23 32					23 43		23 59		
St Pancras International d		23 00			23 05			23 15		23 22						23 51
Farringdon ⊖ d		23 04			23 09			23 19		23 27						23 56
City Thameslink d																
London Blackfriars ⊖ d		23 09			23 14			23 24		23 31						00 01
London Bridge ⊖ d		23 15	23 17		23 21			23 30	23 10	23 37			23 47		23 40	
Norwood Junction a					23 32				23 36						00 08	
East Croydon a		23 28	23 31	23 32	23 36	23 39	23 41	23 44	23 47	23 50		23 58	00 01	00 15	00 17	00 27

Sundays
20 May to 2 December

	SN	TL	SN	SN	TL	SN	TL	SN	SN		SN	SN	SN	SN	SN	TL	SN	SN	TL		SN	SN	SN	SN
	■	■	■		■		■	■	■		■	■	■			■		■	■					
		A			A		A																	
London Victoria ⊖ d	00 02		00 08	00 15				01 10	02 08		03 08	04 10	05 02	05 45	06 32		07 02				07 32			07 43
Clapham Junction d	00 09		00 15	00 23				01 17	02 17		03 17	04 17	05 10	05 53	06 40		07 10				07 40			07 51
St Pancras International d					00 21		00 51																	
Farringdon ⊖ d					00 26																			
City Thameslink d																								
London Blackfriars ⊖ d		00 01			00 31		01 01																	
London Bridge ⊖ d						00 35										07 11		07 19	07 41			07 16	07 31	
Norwood Junction a						00 59												07 31					07 56	
East Croydon a	00 23	00 27	00 31	00 46	00 57	01 13	01 27	01 32	02 32		03 31	04 31	05 23	06 08	06 53	07 24	07 26	07 35	07 54		07 56	08 00	08 02	08 08

	TL	SN	SN	SN	SN		SN	SN	TL	SN	SN	SN	SN	SN	SN		TL	SN	SN	SN	SN	SN	SN	TL
	■				■				■								■				■			■
London Victoria ⊖ d		08 02					08 14	08 32				08 46	08 51	08 55	09 05					09 16		09 21	09 25	
Clapham Junction d		08 10					08 21	08 40				08 53	08 58	09 02	09 12					09 23		09 28	09 32	
St Pancras International d																								
Farringdon ⊖ d																								
City Thameslink d																								
London Blackfriars ⊖ d																								
London Bridge ⊖ d	08 11		07 46	08 01	08 19				08 41	08 24	08 16						09 11	08 54	08 47		09 19			09 27
Norwood Junction a				08 26	08 31					08 49								09 19			09 31			
East Croydon a	08 24	08 26	08 30	08 32	08 35		08 39	08 51	08 54	08 55	08 59	09 02	09 08	09 11	09 23		09 24	09 25	09 29	09 32	09 37	09 38	09 41	09 41

A not 20 May

London - Norwood Junction and East Croydon - Summary of Fast Trains

Summary of Fast Trains

		SN	TL	SN	SN	SN	TL	SN		TL	SN	SN	TL	SN	SN	SN	TL	SN		TL	SN	SN	TL	SN	SN
London Victoria	⊖ d	09 33				09 46		09 51			09 55	10 05				10 16		10 21			10 25	10 33			
Clapham Junction	d	09 40				09 53		09 58			10 02	10 12				10 23		10 28			10 32	10 40			
St Pancras International	d		09 26				09 35			09 41			09 56				10 05			10 11			10 26		
Farringdon	⊖ d		09 30				09 39			09 45			10 00				10 09			10 15			10 30		
City Thameslink	d																								
London Blackfriars	⊖ d		09 35				09 44			09 50			10 05				10 14			10 20			10 35		
London Bridge	⊖ d		09 41	09 24	09 19		09 51			09 56			10 11	09 54	09 49		10 21			10 26			10 41	10 24	10 19
Norwood Junction	a			09 49			10 03							10 19			10 33							10 49	
East Croydon	a	09 49	09 54	09 55	09 59	10 02	10 07	10 08		10 10	10 11	10 23	10 24	10 25	10 29	10 32	10 37	10 38		10 40	10 41	10 49	10 54	10 55	10 59

		SN	TL	SN		TL	SN	SN	TL	SN	SN	SN	TL	SN		TL	SN	SN	TL	SN	SN	SN	TL	SN	
London Victoria	⊖ d	10 46		10 51			10 55	11 05				11 16		11 21			11 25	11 33				11 46		11 51	
Clapham Junction	d	10 53		10 58			11 02	11 12				11 23		11 28			11 32	11 40				11 53		11 58	
St Pancras International	d		10 35			10 41			10 56				11 05			11 11			11 26				11 35		
Farringdon	⊖ d		10 39			10 45			11 00				11 09			11 15			11 30				11 39		
City Thameslink	d																								
London Blackfriars	⊖ d		10 44			10 50			11 05				11 14			11 20			11 35				11 44		
London Bridge	⊖ d		10 51			10 56			11 11	10 54	10 49		11 21			11 26			11 41	11 24	11 19		11 51		
Norwood Junction	a		11 03							11 19			11 33							11 49			12 03		
East Croydon	a	11 02	11 07	11 08		11 10	11 11	11 23	11 24	11 25	11 29	11 32	11 37	11 38		11 40	11 41	11 49	11 54	11 55	11 59	12 02	12 07	12 08	

		TL	SN	SN	TL	SN	SN	SN	TL	SN		TL	SN	SN	TL	SN	SN	SN	TL	TL		SN	SN	SN	TL
London Victoria	⊖ d		11 55	12 05				12 16		12 21			12 25	12 33				12 46				12 51	12 55	13 05	
Clapham Junction	d		12 02	12 12				12 23		12 28			12 32	12 40				12 53				12 58	13 02	13 12	
St Pancras International	d	11 41			11 56				12 05			12 11			12 26				12 35	12 41					12 56
Farringdon	⊖ d	11 45			12 00				12 09			12 15			12 30				12 39	12 45					13 00
City Thameslink	d																								
London Blackfriars	⊖ d	11 50			12 05				12 14			12 20			12 35				12 44	12 50					13 05
London Bridge	⊖ d	11 56			12 11	11 54	11 49		12 21			12 26			12 41	12 24	12 19		12 51	12 56					13 11
Norwood Junction	a					12 20			12 33							12 50			13 03						
East Croydon	a	12 10	12 11	12 23	12 24	12 25	12 29	12 32	12 37	12 38		12 40	12 41	12 49	12 54	12 55	12 59	13 02	13 07	13 10		13 11	13 12	13 23	13 24

		SN	SN	SN	TL	SN		TL	SN	SN	TL	SN	SN	SN	TL	SN		TL	SN	SN	TL	SN	SN	SN	TL
London Victoria	⊖ d			13 16		13 21			13 25	13 33				13 46		13 51			13 55	14 05				14 16	
Clapham Junction	d			13 23		13 28			13 32	13 40				13 53		13 58			14 02	14 12				14 23	
St Pancras International	d				13 05			13 11			13 26				13 35			13 41			13 56				14 05
Farringdon	⊖ d				13 09			13 15			13 30				13 39			13 45			14 00				14 09
City Thameslink	d																								
London Blackfriars	⊖ d				13 14			13 20			13 35				13 44			13 50			14 05				14 14
London Bridge	⊖ d	12 54	12 49		13 21			13 26			13 41	13 24	13 19		13 51			13 56			14 11	13 54	13 49		14 21
Norwood Junction	a	13 20			13 33							13 50			14 03							14 20			14 33
East Croydon	a	13 25	13 29	13 32	13 37	13 38		13 40	13 41	13 49	13 54	13 55	13 59	14 02	14 07	14 08		14 10	14 11	14 23	14 24	14 25	14 29	14 32	14 37

		SN		TL	SN	SN	TL	SN	SN	SN	TL	SN		TL	SN	SN	TL	SN	SN	SN	TL	SN		TL	SN
London Victoria	⊖ d	14 21			14 25	14 33				14 46		14 51			14 55	15 05				15 16		15 21			15 25
Clapham Junction	d	14 28			14 32	14 40				14 53		14 58			15 02	15 12				15 23		15 28			15 32
St Pancras International	d			14 11			14 26				14 35			14 41			14 56				15 05			15 11	
Farringdon	⊖ d			14 15			14 30				14 39			14 45			15 00				15 09			15 15	
City Thameslink	d																								
London Blackfriars	⊖ d			14 20			14 35				14 44			14 50			15 05				15 14			15 20	
London Bridge	⊖ d			14 26			14 41	14 24	14 19		14 51			14 56			15 11	14 54	14 49		15 21			15 26	
Norwood Junction	a							14 50			15 03							15 20			15 33				
East Croydon	a	14 38		14 40	14 41	14 49	14 54	14 55	14 59	15 02	15 07	15 08		15 10	15 11	15 23	15 24	15 25	15 29	15 32	15 37	15 38		15 40	15 41

		SN	TL	SN	SN	SN	TL	TL		SN	SN	SN	TL	SN	SN	SN	TL	SN		TL	SN	SN	TL	SN	SN
London Victoria	⊖ d	15 33				15 46				15 51	15 55	16 05				16 16		16 21			16 25	16 33			
Clapham Junction	d	15 40				15 53				15 58	16 02	16 12				16 23		16 28			16 32	16 40			
St Pancras International	d		15 26				15 35	15 41					15 56				16 05			16 11			16 26		
Farringdon	⊖ d		15 30				15 39	15 45					16 00				16 09			16 15			16 30		
City Thameslink	d																								
London Blackfriars	⊖ d		15 35				15 44	15 50					16 05				16 14			16 20			16 35		
London Bridge	⊖ d		15 41	15 24	15 19		15 51	15 56					16 11	15 54	15 49		16 21			16 26			16 41	16 24	16 19
Norwood Junction	a			15 50			16 03							16 20			16 33							16 50	
East Croydon	a	15 49	15 54	15 55	15 59	16 02	16 07	16 10		16 11	16 12	16 23	16 24	16 25	16 29	16 32	16 37	16 38		16 40	16 41	16 49	16 54	16 55	16 59

		SN	TL	TL		SN	SN	SN	TL	SN	SN	SN	TL	SN	TL	SN	SN	TL	SN	SN	SN	TL	SN	TL	
London Victoria	⊖ d	16 46				16 51	16 55	17 05				17 16		17 21		17 25	17 33				17 46		17 51		
Clapham Junction	d	16 53				16 58	17 02	17 12				17 23		17 28		17 32	17 40				17 53		17 58		
St Pancras International	d		16 35	16 41					16 56				17 05		17 11			17 26				17 35		17 41	
Farringdon	⊖ d		16 39	16 45					17 00				17 09		17 15			17 30				17 39		17 45	
City Thameslink	d																								
London Blackfriars	⊖ d		16 44	16 50					17 05				17 14		17 20			17 35				17 44		17 50	
London Bridge	⊖ d		16 51	16 56					17 11	16 54	16 49		17 21		17 26			17 41	17 24	17 19		17 51		17 56	
Norwood Junction	a		17 03							17 20			17 33						17 50			18 03			
East Croydon	a	17 02	17 07	17 10		17 11	17 12	17 23	17 24	17 25	17 29	17 32	17 37	17 38	17 40	17 41	17 49	17 54	17 55	17 59	18 02	18 07	18 08	18 10	

London - Norwood Junction and East Croydon - Summary of Fast Trains

Summary of Fast Trains

		SN		SN	TL	SN	SN	SN	TL	SN	TL	SN	SN	TL	SN	SN	SN	TL	SN	TL	SN		SN	TL
London Victoria	⊖ d	17 55	and at the same minutes past each hour until	21 05				21 16		21 21		21 25	21 33				21 46		21 51		21 55		22 05	
Clapham Junction	d	18 02		21 12				21 23		21 28		21 32	21 40				21 53		21 58		22 02		22 12	
St Pancras International	d				20 56				21 05		21 11			21 26				21 35		21 41				21 56
Farringdon	⊖ d				21 00				21 09		21 15			21 30				21 39		21 45				22 00
City Thameslink	d																							
London Blackfriars	⊖ d				21 05				21 14		21 20			21 35				21 44		21 50				22 05
London Bridge	⊖ d				21 11	20 54	20 49		21 21		21 26			21 41	21 24	21 19		21 51		21 56				22 11
Norwood Junction	a					21 20			21 33						21 50			22 03						
East Croydon	a	18 11		21 23	21 24	21 25	21 29	21 32	21 37	21 38	21 40	21 41	21 49	21 54	21 55	21 59	22 02	22 07	22 08	22 10	22 11		22 22	22 24

		SN	SN	SN	TL	SN	TL	SN		SN	TL	SN	SN	SN	TL	SN	SN	TL		SN	SN	SN	TL	SN	TL
London Victoria	⊖ d			22 16		22 21		22 25		22 35				22 46		22 51	23 05					23 16		23 32	
Clapham Junction	d			22 23		22 28		22 32		22 42				22 53		22 58	23 12					23 23		23 40	
St Pancras International	d				22 05		22 11				22 26				22 35			22 56					23 26		
Farringdon	⊖ d				22 09		22 15				22 30				22 39			23 00					23 30		
City Thameslink	d																								
London Blackfriars	⊖ d				22 14		22 20				22 35				22 44			23 05					23 35		
London Bridge	⊖ d	21 54	21 49		22 21		22 26				22 41	22 24	22 19		22 51			23 11		22 54	22 49		23 41		23 45
Norwood Junction	a	22 20			22 33							22 50			23 03					23 20					
East Croydon	a	22 25	22 29	22 32	22 37	22 38	22 40	22 41		22 51	22 54	22 55	22 59	23 02	23 07	23 08	23 22	23 24		23 25	23 29	23 32	23 54	23 56	23 59

		SN	SN	SN		TL
London Victoria	⊖ d					
Clapham Junction	d					
St Pancras International	d					23 51
Farringdon	⊖ d					23 56
City Thameslink	d					
London Blackfriars	⊖ d					00 01
London Bridge	⊖ d	23 17	23 31	23 50		
Norwood Junction	a		23 57	00 15		
East Croydon	a	00 02	00 02	00 19		00 27

Please note, Network Rail have stated that further updates to this timetable are possible during the validity period.

Please note, Network Rail have stated that further updates to this timetable are possible during the validity period.

East Croydon and Norwood Junction - London - Summary of Fast Trains

	SN MO	TL MO ■	TL MX ■	SN MX ■	TL MX ■	TL MO ■	TL MX ■	TL ■	TL ■		TL ■		TL ■	TL ■	SN	TL	TL ■	SN ■	SN ■	SN	TL ■		TL ■
East Croydon d	00 06	00 10	00 10	00 16	00 23	00 40	00 40	01 10	02 10	and every 30 minutes until	04 10		04 40	05 10		05 20	05 40	05 53	06 00		06 01		06 03
Norwood Junction d															05 21	05 25				05 51			06 08
London Bridge ⊖ a														05 24		05 50	05 54				06 15		06 20
London Blackfriars ⊖ a		00 36	00 36		00 49	01 06	01 07	01 36	02 36		04 36		05 06	05 31			06 01				06 21		06 26
City Thameslink a													05 08	05 33			06 03				06 23		06 28
Farringdon ⊖ a			00 41										05 10	05 35			06 05				06 26		06 31
St Pancras International a		00 45	00 45		00 59	01 15	01 15	01 43	02 43		04 43		05 15	05 40			06 10				06 30		06 35
Clapham Junction a	00 18			00 33											05 46			06 02	06 11	06 16			
London Victoria ⊖ a	00 27			00 41											05 54			06 10	06 18	06 24			

	SN ■	SN	SN ■	TL ■	SN	TL ■	SN ■	TL ■		SN	TL ■	SN ■	SN	SN ■	TL ■	SN ■	SN	TL ■		SN	SN ■	TL ■	SN ■	SN ■
East Croydon d	06 08	06 08	06 15	06 16	06 18	06 21	06 24	06 25		06 28	06 31	06 34		06 38	06 40	06 45		06 46		06 48	06 49	06 51	06 53	06 57
Norwood Junction d											06 37		06 21				06 28							
London Bridge ⊖ a		06 23		06 30	06 34	06 34		06 40			06 50			06 53	06 53			07 00		07 04		07 05		07 13
London Blackfriars ⊖ a				06 36		06 41		06 46			06 56				07 01			07 06				07 11		
City Thameslink a				06 38		06 43		06 48			06 58				07 03			07 08				07 13		
Farringdon ⊖ a				06 41		06 46		06 51			07 01				07 06			07 11				07 16		
St Pancras International a				06 45		06 50		06 55			07 05				07 10			07 15				07 20		
Clapham Junction a	06 19		06 25				06 33			06 39		06 44	06 46			06 55	06 57				06 58		07 02	
London Victoria ⊖ a	06 27		06 32				06 42			06 49		06 52	06 54			07 03	07 05				07 05		07 12	

	SN	TL ■	TL ■	SN ■		TL ■	SN ■	SN ■	SN	TL ■	SN	SN ■	SN ■	SN ■		TL ■	SN ■	SN	TL ■	SN ■	SN ■	SN	SN ■	TL ■
East Croydon d	06 58	07 01	07 01	07 04		07 10	07 10	07 15		07 16	07 18	07 19	07 21	07 24		07 25	07 27	07 28	07 31	07 34	07 38		07 38	07 40
Norwood Junction d			07 07						06 59										07 37			07 28		
London Bridge ⊖ a		07 15	07 20			07 23				07 30	07 34		07 34			07 40	07 43		07 50				07 53	07 53
London Blackfriars ⊖ a		07 21	07 26			07 31				07 36			07 41			07 46			07 56					08 01
City Thameslink a		07 23	07 28			07 33				07 38			07 43			07 48			07 58					08 03
Farringdon ⊖ a		07 26	07 31			07 36				07 41			07 46			07 51			08 01					08 06
St Pancras International a		07 30	07 35			07 40				07 45			07 50			07 55			08 05					08 10
Clapham Junction a	07 10			07 14			07 35	07 25	07 27			07 28		07 33				07 40		07 44	07 47	07 57		
London Victoria ⊖ a	07 19			07 22				07 32	07 35			07 35		07 40				07 49		07 52	07 54	08 05		

		SN ■	SN ■	TL ■	SN	SN ■	SN ■	TL ■	SN ■	SN		TL ■	TL ■	SN ■	SN	SN	SN ■	TL ■	SN ■	SN ■		TL ■	SN	SN ■
East Croydon d		07 40	07 45	07 46	07 48	07 50	07 54	07 55	07 57	07 58		08 01	08 01	08 04	08 08		08 08	08 10	08 11	08 15		08 16	08 18	08 20
Norwood Junction d													08 07			07 58								
London Bridge ⊖ a				08 00	08 04			08 10	08 13			08 15	08 20				08 23	08 23				08 30	08 34	
London Blackfriars ⊖ a				08 06				08 16				08 21	08 26					08 31				08 36		
City Thameslink a				08 08				08 18				08 23	08 28					08 33				08 38		
Farringdon ⊖ a				08 11				08 21				08 26	08 31					08 36				08 41		
St Pancras International a				08 15				08 25				08 30	08 35					08 40				08 45		
Clapham Junction a		08 05	07 57			08 00	08 03			08 10				08 14	08 17	08 27			08 35	08 27				08 30
London Victoria ⊖ a			08 06			08 08	08 12			08 19				08 22	08 24	08 35				08 35				08 37

	SN ■	SN ■	TL ■	SN ■	SN	TL ■		SN ■	SN ■	SN ■	SN ■	SN ■	SN	TL ■	SN	SN ■		TL ■	SN ■	TL ■	SN	TL ■	TL ■	SN ■
East Croydon d	08 21	08 24	08 25	08 27	08 28	08 31		08 34	08 38	08 38	08 40	08 45		08 46	08 48	08 50		08 51	08 54	08 55	08 58	09 01	09 01	09 04
Norwood Junction d						08 37							08 28										09 07	
London Bridge ⊖ a	08 34		08 40	08 43		08 50				08 53				09 00	09 04			09 04		09 10		09 15	09 20	
London Blackfriars ⊖ a	08 41		08 46			08 56								09 06				09 11		09 16		09 21	09 26	
City Thameslink a	08 43		08 48			08 58								09 08				09 13		09 18		09 23	09 28	
Farringdon ⊖ a	08 46		08 51			09 01								09 11				09 16		09 21		09 26	09 31	
St Pancras International a	08 50		08 55			09 05								09 15				09 20		09 25		09 30	09 35	
Clapham Junction a		08 33			08 40			08 44	08 47		09 05	08 57	08 57			09 00			09 03		09 10			09 14
London Victoria ⊖ a		08 40			08 49			08 52	08 54			09 05	09 08			09 08			09 10		09 19			09 24

	SN ■	SN ■		SN ■	SN ■	SN	TL ■	SN	SN ■	TL ■	SN	SN ■		TL ■	TL ■	SN ■	SN ■	SN ■	TL ■	SN ■	SN	SN		TL ■
East Croydon d	09 08	09 09		09 10	09 15		09 16	09 18	09 19	09 21	09 21	09 24		09 25	09 31	09 34	09 38	09 43	09 45	09 45		09 48		09 51
Norwood Junction d						08 58									09 37						09 28			
London Bridge ⊖ a	09 23						09 30	09 34		09 34	10 06			09 40	09 50		09 53		10 00			10 04		10 04
London Blackfriars ⊖ a							09 36			09 41				09 46	09 56				10 06					10 11
City Thameslink a							09 38			09 43				09 48	09 58				10 08					10 13
Farringdon ⊖ a							09 41			09 46				09 51	10 01				10 11					10 16
St Pancras International a							09 45			09 50				09 55	10 05				10 15					10 20
Clapham Junction a		09 18		09 35	09 25	09 27			09 28			09 33				09 44		09 52		09 55	09 57			
London Victoria ⊖ a		09 26			09 32	09 35			09 35			09 40				09 52		09 59		10 02	10 05			

	SN	SN ■	TL ■	SN ■	TL ■	TL ■	SN ■	SN ■		TL ■	SN ■	SN	SN	SN ■	TL ■	SN	SN ■	SN ■		TL ■	SN ■	SN ■	TL ■	SN ■
East Croydon d	09 51	09 54	09 54	10 00	10 01	10 03	10 10	10 12		10 15	10 15		10 18	10 19	10 21	10 22	10 24	10 30		10 33	10 38	10 42	10 45	10 45
Norwood Junction d						10 08						09 58								10 38				
London Bridge ⊖ a	10 36		10 11		10 15	10 20				10 30			10 34		10 34	11 06				10 50	10 53		11 00	
London Blackfriars ⊖ a					10 21	10 26				10 36					10 41					10 56			11 06	
City Thameslink a					10 23	10 28				10 38					10 43					10 58			11 08	
Farringdon ⊖ a					10 26	10 31				10 41					10 46					11 01			11 11	
St Pancras International a					10 30	10 35				10 45					10 50					11 05			11 15	
Clapham Junction a		10 03		10 10			10 35	10 21			10 25	10 27		10 28			10 33	10 40				10 51		10 55
London Victoria ⊖ a		10 11		10 18				10 29			10 32	10 35		10 35			10 41	10 48				10 59		11 02

East Croydon and Norwood Junction - London - Summary of Fast Trains

		SN	SN	SN ■	TL ■	SN	SN ■	SN	SN ■	TL ■		TL ■	SN ■	SN ■	TL ■	SN ■	SN	SN	SN ■	TL ■		SN	SN ■	SN
East Croydon d			10 48	10 49	10 51	10 52	10 54	10 57	11 00	11 01		11 03	11 10	11 12	11 15	11 15		11 18	11 19	11 21		11 22	11 24	11 27
Norwood Junction d		10 28						11 03				11 08					10 58							11 33
London Bridge ⊖ a			11 04		11 04	11 36		11 31		11 15		11 20			11 30			11 34		11 34		12 06		12 01
London Blackfriars ⊖ a					11 11					11 21		11 26			11 36					11 41				
City Thameslink a					11 13					11 23		11 28			11 38					11 43				
Farringdon ⊖ a					11 16					11 26		11 31			11 41					11 46				
St Pancras International a					11 20					11 30		11 35			11 45					11 50				
Clapham Junction a		10 57		10 58			11 03		11 10				11 35	11 21		11 25	11 27		11 28				11 33	
London Victoria ⊖ a		11 05		11 05			11 11		11 18					11 29		11 32	11 35		11 35				11 41	

	SN ■	TL ■	SN ■	SN ■	TL ■	SN ■		SN	SN	SN ■	TL ■	SN	SN ■	SN	SN ■	TL ■		TL ■	SN ■	SN ■	TL ■	SN ■	SN	SN
East Croydon d	11 30	11 33	11 38	11 42	11 45	11 45			11 48	11 49	11 51	11 52	11 54	11 57	12 00	12 01		12 03	12 10	12 12	12 15	12 15		12 18
Norwood Junction d		11 38						11 28						12 03				12 08					11 58	
London Bridge ⊖ a		11 50	11 53		12 00				12 04		12 04	12 36		12 31		12 15		12 20			12 30			12 34
London Blackfriars ⊖ a		11 56			12 06						12 11					12 21		12 26			12 36			
City Thameslink a		11 58			12 08						12 13					12 23		12 28			12 38			
Farringdon ⊖ a		12 01			12 11						12 16					12 26		12 31			12 41			
St Pancras International a		12 05			12 15						12 20					12 30		12 35			12 45			
Clapham Junction a	11 40			11 51		11 55		11 57		11 58			12 03		12 10				12 35	12 22		12 25	12 27	
London Victoria ⊖ a	11 48			11 59		12 02		12 05		12 05			12 11		12 18					12 29		12 32	12 35	

	SN ■	TL ■		SN	SN ■	SN	SN ■	TL ■	SN ■	SN ■	TL ■	SN ■		SN	SN	SN ■	TL ■	SN	SN ■	SN	SN ■	TL ■		TL ■
East Croydon d	12 19	12 21		12 22	12 24	12 27	12 30	12 33	12 38	12 42	12 45	12 45			12 48	12 49	12 51	12 52	12 54	12 57	13 00	13 01		13 03
Norwood Junction d						12 33		12 38						12 28						13 03				13 08
London Bridge ⊖ a		12 34		13 06		13 01		12 50	12 53		13 00				13 04		13 04	13 36		13 31		13 15		13 20
London Blackfriars ⊖ a		12 41						12 56			13 06						13 11					13 21		13 26
City Thameslink a		12 43						12 58			13 08						13 13					13 23		13 28
Farringdon ⊖ a		12 46						13 01			13 11						13 16					13 26		13 31
St Pancras International a		12 50						13 05			13 15						13 20					13 30		13 35
Clapham Junction a	12 28				12 33		12 40			12 51		12 55		12 57		12 58			13 03		13 10			
London Victoria ⊖ a	12 35				12 41		12 48			12 59		13 02		13 05		13 05			13 11		13 18			

	SN MW FO ■	SN ■	TL ■	SN ■	SN	SN	SN ■	TL ■		SN	SN ■	SN	SN ■	TL ■	SN ■	SN ■	TL ■	SN ■		SN	SN	SN ■	TL ■	SN
East Croydon d	13 10	13 12	13 15	13 15		13 18	13 19	13 21		13 22	13 24	13 27	13 30	13 33	13 38	13 42	13 45	13 45			13 48	13 49	13 51	13 52
Norwood Junction d					12 58							13 33		13 38						13 28				
London Bridge ⊖ a			13 30			13 34		13 34		14 06		14 01		13 50	13 53		14 00				14 04		14 04	14 36
London Blackfriars ⊖ a			13 36					13 41						13 56			14 06						14 11	
City Thameslink a			13 38					13 43						13 58			14 08						14 13	
Farringdon ⊖ a			13 41					13 46						14 01			14 11						14 16	
St Pancras International a			13 45					13 50						14 05			14 15						14 20	
Clapham Junction a	13 35	13 21		13 25	13 27		13 28				13 33		13 40			13 51		13 55		13 57		13 58		
London Victoria ⊖ a		13 29		13 32	13 35		13 35				13 41		13 48			13 59		14 02		14 05		14 05		

	SN ■	SN	SN ■	TL ■		TL ■	SN ■	SN ■	TL ■	SN ■	SN	SN	SN ■	TL ■		SN	SN ■	SN	SN ■	TL ■	SN ■	SN ■	TL ■	SN ■
East Croydon d	13 54	13 57	14 00	14 01		14 03	14 10	14 12	14 15	14 15		14 18	14 19	14 21		14 22	14 24	14 27	14 30	14 33	14 38	14 42	14 45	14 45
Norwood Junction d		14 03				14 08					13 58							14 33		14 38				
London Bridge ⊖ a		14 31		14 15		14 20			14 30			14 34		14 34		15 06		15 01		14 50	14 53		15 00	
London Blackfriars ⊖ a				14 21		14 26			14 36					14 41						14 56			15 06	
City Thameslink a				14 23		14 28			14 38					14 43						14 58			15 08	
Farringdon ⊖ a				14 26		14 31			14 41					14 46						15 01			15 11	
St Pancras International a				14 30		14 35			14 45					14 50						15 05			15 15	
Clapham Junction a	14 03		14 10				14 35	14 21		14 25	14 27		14 28				14 33		14 40			14 51		14 55
London Victoria ⊖ a	14 11		14 18					14 29		14 32	14 35		14 35				14 41		14 48			14 59		15 02

		SN	SN	SN ■	TL ■	SN	SN ■	SN	SN ■	TL ■		TL ■	SN ■	SN ■	TL ■	SN ■	SN	SN	SN ■	TL ■		SN	SN ■	SN
East Croydon d			14 48	14 49	14 52	14 52	14 54	14 57	15 00	15 01		15 03	15 10	15 12	15 15	15 15		15 18	15 19	15 21		15 22	15 24	15 27
Norwood Junction d		14 28						15 03				15 08					14 58							15 33
London Bridge ⊖ a			15 04		15 05	15 36		15 31		15 15		15 20			15 30			15 34		15 34		16 06		16 01
London Blackfriars ⊖ a					15 11					15 21		15 26			15 36					15 41				
City Thameslink a					15 13					15 23		15 28			15 38					15 43				
Farringdon ⊖ a					15 16					15 26		15 31			15 41					15 46				
St Pancras International a					15 20					15 30		15 35			15 45					15 50				
Clapham Junction a		14 57		14 58			15 03		15 10				15 35	15 21		15 25	15 27		15 28				15 33	
London Victoria ⊖ a		15 05		15 05			15 11		15 18					15 29		15 32	15 35		15 35				15 41	

	SN ■	TL ■	SN ■	SN ■	SN ■ A	SN ■ B		TL ■	SN ■	SN	SN	SN ■	TL ■	SN	SN ■	TL ■		SN	SN ■	TL ■	TL ■	SN ■	SN ■	TL ■
East Croydon d	15 30	15 33	15 38	15 42	15 43	15 43		15 45	15 46		15 48	15 49	15 51	15 51	15 54	15 54		15 57	16 00	16 01	16 03	16 10	16 12	16 15
Norwood Junction d		15 38								15 28								16 03			16 08			
London Bridge ⊖ a		15 50	15 53					16 00			16 04		16 04	16 36		16 10		16 31		16 15	16 20			16 30
London Blackfriars ⊖ a		15 56						16 06					16 11			16 16				16 21	16 26			16 36
City Thameslink a		15 58						16 08					16 13			16 18				16 23	16 28			16 38
Farringdon ⊖ a		16 01						16 11					16 16			16 21				16 26	16 31			16 41
St Pancras International a		16 05						16 15					16 20			16 25				16 30	16 35			16 45
Clapham Junction a	15 40			15 51	16 04	16 04			15 56	15 57		15 59			16 03				16 10			16 35	16 21	
London Victoria ⊖ a	15 49			16 00	16 12	16 13			16 03	16 05		16 09			16 11				16 18				16 29	

A until 21 September

B from 24 September

Table T175-R

Mondays to Fridays
21 May to 7 December

East Croydon and Norwood Junction - London - Summary of Fast Trains

		SN ■	SN	SN	SN ■	TL ■	SN	SN ■	TL ■		SN	SN ■	TL ■	SN ■	SN ■	SN ■	TL ■	SN ■	SN		SN	SN ■	TL ■	SN	TL ■
East Croydon	d	16 15		16 18	16 19	16 21	16 21	16 24	16 24		16 27	16 30	16 33	16 38	16 40	16 42	16 45	16 45			16 48	16 49	16 51	16 51	16 54
Norwood Junction ■	d		15 58								16 33		16 38						16 28						
London Bridge ■ ⊖	a			16 34		16 34	17 06		16 40		17 01		16 50	16 54			17 00				17 04		17 04	17 36	17 10
London Blackfriars ■ ⊖	a					16 41			16 46				16 56				17 06						17 11		17 16
City Thameslink ■	a					16 43			16 48				16 58				17 08						17 13		17 18
Farringdon ■ ⊖	a					16 46			16 51				17 01				17 11						17 16		17 21
St Pancras International	a					16 50			16 55				17 05				17 15						17 20		17 25
Clapham Junction ■	a	16 25	16 27		16 28			16 33				16 40			17 05	16 51		16 55	16 57			16 58			
London Victoria ■ ⊖	a	16 32	16 35		16 35			16 41				16 48				16 59		17 02	17 05			17 05			

		SN ■	SN	SN ■	TL ■		TL ■	TL ■	SN ■	SN ■	TL ■	SN ■	SN	SN ■	SN		TL ■	SN	SN ■	TL ■	SN ■	TL ■	SN ■	TL ■	SN ■
East Croydon	d	16 56	16 57	17 00	17 01		17 03	17 10	17 10	17 12	17 15	17 15		17 18	17 18		17 21	17 21	17 24	17 25	17 30	17 33	17 38	17 40	17 40
Norwood Junction ■	d		17 03				17 08						16 58									17 38			
London Bridge ■ ⊖	a		17 31		17 15		17 20	17 23			17 30				17 34		17 34	18 06		17 40		17 50	17 54	17 53	
London Blackfriars ■ ⊖	a				17 21		17 26	17 31			17 36						17 41			17 46		17 56		18 01	
City Thameslink ■	a				17 23		17 28	17 33			17 38						17 43			17 48		17 58		18 03	
Farringdon ■ ⊖	a				17 26		17 31	17 36			17 41						17 46			17 51		18 01		18 06	
St Pancras International	a				17 30		17 35	17 40			17 45						17 50			17 55		18 05		18 10	
Clapham Junction ■	a	17 05		17 10					17 35	17 21		17 25	17 27	17 28					17 33		17 40				18 04
London Victoria ■ ⊖	a	17 12		17 18						17 29		17 33	17 35	17 35					17 41		17 50				18 14

			SN ■	TL ■	SN ■	SN	SN ■	SN	TL ■	SN	SN ■		TL ■	SN ■	TL ■	TL ■	SN ■	SN ■	TL ■	SN ■	SN ■		SN	SN	TL ■
East Croydon	d		17 42	17 45	17 45		17 48	17 48	17 51	17 51	17 54		17 54	18 00	18 01	18 03	18 10	18 12	18 15	18 15	18 18			18 18	18 21
Norwood Junction ■	d					17 29										18 08							17 59		
London Bridge ■ ⊖	a			18 00				18 04	18 04	18 36			18 10		18 15	18 20			18 30					18 34	18 34
London Blackfriars ■ ⊖	a			18 06					18 11				18 16		18 21	18 26			18 36						18 41
City Thameslink ■	a			18 08					18 13				18 18		18 23	18 28			18 38						18 43
Farringdon ■ ⊖	a			18 11					18 16				18 21		18 26	18 31			18 41						18 46
St Pancras International	a			18 15					18 20				18 25		18 30	18 35			18 45						18 50
Clapham Junction ■	a		17 51		17 55	17 57	17 58				18 03			18 10			18 35	18 21		18 25	18 28		18 27		
London Victoria ■ ⊖	a		17 59		18 02	18 05	18 05				18 11			18 18				18 29		18 32	18 35		18 36		

		SN ■	TL ■	SN ■	TL ■	SN ■	SN ■		TL ■	SN ■	SN	SN ■	SN	TL ■	SN ■	TL ■	SN ■		TL ■	TL ■	SN ■	SN ■	SN ■	TL ■	SN ■
East Croydon	d	18 24	18 25	18 30	18 33	18 38	18 42		18 45	18 45		18 48	18 48	18 51	18 54	18 55	19 00		19 01	19 03	19 08	19 10	19 12	19 15	19 15
Norwood Junction ■	d				18 38						18 28									19 08					
London Bridge ■ ⊖	a		18 40		18 50	18 53			19 00				19 04	19 04		19 10			19 15	19 20	19 23			19 30	
London Blackfriars ■ ⊖	a		18 46		18 56				19 06					19 11		19 16			19 21	19 26				19 36	
City Thameslink ■	a		18 48		18 58				19 08					19 13		19 18			19 23	19 28				19 38	
Farringdon ■ ⊖	a		18 51		19 01				19 11					19 16		19 21			19 26	19 31				19 41	
St Pancras International	a		18 55		19 05				19 15					19 20		19 25			19 30	19 35				19 45	
Clapham Junction ■	a	18 34		18 40			18 51			18 55	18 57	18 58			19 03		19 10					19 35	19 21		19 25
London Victoria ■ ⊖	a	18 42		18 48			18 59			19 03	19 05	19 05			19 11		19 18						19 29		19 32

		SN	SN ■		SN	TL ■	TL ■	SN ■	SN ■	TL ■	SN ■	SN ■	TL ■		SN ■	SN	SN	SN ■	TL ■	TL ■	SN ■	SN	SN ■		TL ■
East Croydon	d		19 18		19 18	19 21	19 24	19 26	19 30	19 33	19 38	19 42	19 45		19 45		19 48	19 49	19 51	19 52	19 54	19 57	20 00		20 01
Norwood Junction ■	d	18 58								19 38						19 28						20 03			
London Bridge ■ ⊖	a				19 34	19 34	19 40			19 50	19 53		20 00				20 04		20 04	20 11		20 31			20 15
London Blackfriars ■ ⊖	a					19 41	19 46			19 56			20 06						20 11						20 21
City Thameslink ■	a					19 43	19 48			19 58			20 08						20 13						20 23
Farringdon ■ ⊖	a					19 46	19 51			20 01			20 11						20 16						20 26
St Pancras International	a					19 50	19 55			20 05			20 15						20 20						20 30
Clapham Junction ■	a	19 27	19 28					19 35	19 40			19 51			19 55	19 57		19 58			20 04		20 10		
London Victoria ■ ⊖	a	19 35	19 35					19 42	19 49			19 59			20 02	20 05		20 05			20 11		20 18		

		TL ■	SN ■	SN ■	SN ■	TL ■	SN ■	SN	SN		SN ■	TL ■	TL ■	SN ■	SN	SN ■	TL ■	SN ■	SN ■		SN	SN ■	TL ■	SN	SN ■
East Croydon	d	20 03	20 08	20 10	20 12	20 15	20 15		20 18		20 19	20 21	20 24	20 26	20 27	20 30	20 33	20 38	20 43			20 45	20 46	20 48	20 49
Norwood Junction ■	d	20 08						19 58							20 33		20 38				20 28				
London Bridge ■ ⊖	a	20 20	20 23			20 30			20 34			20 34	20 41		21 01		20 50	20 53					21 00	21 04	
London Blackfriars ■ ⊖	a	20 26				20 36						20 41					20 56						21 06		
City Thameslink ■	a	20 28				20 38						20 43					20 58						21 08		
Farringdon ■ ⊖	a	20 31				20 41						20 46					21 01						21 11		
St Pancras International	a	20 35				20 45						20 50					21 05						21 15		
Clapham Junction ■	a			20 35	20 21		20 25	20 27			20 28			20 35		20 40			20 52		20 57	20 58			21 01
London Victoria ■ ⊖	a				20 30		20 32	20 35			20 35			20 42		20 48			20 59		21 05	21 05			21 08

		TL ■	TL ■	SN ■	SN		SN	SN ■	TL ■	TL ■	SN ■	SN ■	TL ■	SN ■	SN		SN	SN ■	TL ■	SN	SN ■	SN	SN ■	TL ■	SN ■
East Croydon	d	20 51	20 52	20 54	20 54		20 57	21 00	21 01	21 03	21 10	21 12	21 15	21 15			21 18	21 19	21 21	21 22	21 24	21 27	21 30	21 33	21 38
Norwood Junction ■	d						21 03			21 08					20 59							21 33		21 38	
London Bridge ■ ⊖	a	21 04	21 11		21 36		21 31		21 15	21 20			21 30				21 34		21 34	22 06		22 01		21 50	21 53
London Blackfriars ■ ⊖	a	21 11							21 21	21 26			21 36						21 41					21 56	
City Thameslink ■	a	21 13							21 23	21 28			21 38						21 43					21 58	
Farringdon ■ ⊖	a	21 16							21 26	21 31			21 41						21 46					22 01	
St Pancras International	a	21 20							21 30	21 35			21 45						21 50					22 05	
Clapham Junction ■	a			21 06				21 12			21 35	21 21		21 25	21 27			21 28			21 33		21 40		
London Victoria ■ ⊖	a			21 13				21 19				21 29		21 32	21 35			21 35			21 41		21 48		

Table T175-R

Mondays to Fridays
21 May to 7 December

East Croydon and Norwood Junction - London - Summary of Fast Trains

		SN ■	TL ■	SN ■	SN	SN	SN ■		TL ■	SN	SN ■	SN	SN ■	TL ■	TL ■	SN ■	TL ■		SN ■	SN	SN ■	SN	TL ■	SN	SN ■
East Croydon	d	21 42	21 45	21 45		21 48	21 49		21 51	21 52	21 54	21 57	22 00	22 01	22 03	22 12	22 15		22 15	22 18	22 19		22 21	22 22	22 24
Norwood Junction ■	d				21 28							22 03			22 08							21 58			
London Bridge ■ ⊖	a		22 00			22 04			22 04	22 36		22 31		22 15	22 20		22 30			22 34			22 34	23 06	
London Blackfriars ■ ⊖	a		22 06						22 11					22 21	22 26		22 36						22 41		
City Thameslink ■	a		22 08						22 13					22 23	22 28		22 38						22 43		
Farringdon ■ ⊖	a		22 11						22 16					22 26	22 31		22 41						22 46		
St Pancras International	a		22 15						22 20					22 30	22 35		22 45						22 50		
Clapham Junction ■	a	21 51		21 55	21 57		21 58				22 03		22 10			22 21			22 25		22 28	22 27			22 33
London Victoria ■ ⊖	a	21 59		22 02	22 05		22 05				22 11		22 18			22 29			22 32		22 35	22 37			22 42

		SN	SN ■		SN ■	SN ■	TL ■	SN ■	SN	SN	SN ■	TL ■	SN		SN ■	SN	SN ■ A	TL ■	SN ■	TL ■	SN ■	SN	SN ■		SN
East Croydon	d	22 27	22 30		22 38	22 43	22 45	22 45		22 48	22 49	22 51	22 52		22 54	22 57	23 00	23 01	23 12	23 15	23 15	23 18	23 19		
Norwood Junction ■	d	22 33							22 28							23 03									22 58
London Bridge ■ ⊖	a	23 01			22 53		23 00			23 04		23 04	23 36			23 31		23 15		23 30		23 34			
London Blackfriars ■ ⊖	a						23 06					23 11						23 21		23 36					
City Thameslink ■	a																								
Farringdon ■ ⊖	a						23 11					23 16						23 26		23 41					
St Pancras International	a						23 15					23 20						23 30		23 45					
Clapham Junction ■	a		22 40			22 52		22 55	22 57		22 58				23 03		23 10		23 21		23 25		23 28		23 27
London Victoria ■ ⊖	a		22 49			23 00		23 02	23 05		23 05				23 11		23 20		23 30		23 32		23 35		23 37

		TL ■	SN ■	SN ■	SN ■	SN ■	TL ■
East Croydon	d	23 21	23 30	23 38	23 42	23 45	23 53
Norwood Junction ■	d						
London Bridge ■ ⊖	a	23 34		23 53			
London Blackfriars ■ ⊖	a	23 41					00 18
City Thameslink ■	a						
Farringdon ■ ⊖	a	23 46					00 25
St Pancras International	a	23 50					00 29
Clapham Junction ■	a		23 44		23 57	23 59	
London Victoria ■ ⊖	a		23 52		00 05	00 08	

Saturdays
26 May to 8 December

		TL ■	SN ■	TL ■	TL ■	TL ■	TL ■	SN ■	TL ■	TL ■		SN ■	TL ■	TL ■	SN ■	TL ■	TL ■	SN ■	TL ■	SN ■		SN	TL ■	TL ■	SN ■
East Croydon	d	00 10	00 16	00 23	00 40	01 10	02 10	02 36	02 40	03 10		03 36	03 40	04 10	04 36	04 40	05 10	05 30	05 39	06 00			06 01	06 03	06 10
Norwood Junction ■	d																					05 51		06 08	
London Bridge ■ ⊖	a																05 25		05 54				06 15	06 20	
London Blackfriars ■ ⊖	a	00 36		00 49	01 07	01 36	02 36		03 06	03 36			04 06	04 36		05 06	05 31		06 01				06 21	06 26	
City Thameslink ■	a																								
Farringdon ■ ⊖	a	00 41														05 10	05 36		06 06				06 26	06 31	
St Pancras International	a	00 45		00 59	01 15	01 43	02 43		03 13	03 43			04 13	04 43		05 15	05 40		06 10				06 30	06 35	
Clapham Junction ■	a		00 33					02 50				03 50			04 50			05 50		06 10		06 16			06 35
London Victoria ■ ⊖	a		00 41					02 58				03 58			04 58			05 59		06 18		06 24			

		TL ■	SN ■	TL ■	SN ■	SN		TL ■	SN ■	SN	TL ■	SN	SN ■	TL ■	SN ■	SN ■		TL ■	TL ■	SN ■	SN ■	TL ■	SN ■	SN	SN
East Croydon	d	06 15	06 19	06 21	06 24			06 33	06 42		06 45	06 48	06 49	06 51	06 54	07 00		07 01	07 03	07 10	07 12	07 15	07 15		07 18
Norwood Junction ■	d					06 21		06 38		06 28									07 08					06 58	
London Bridge ■ ⊖	a	06 30		06 34				06 50			07 00	07 04		07 04				07 15	07 20			07 30			07 34
London Blackfriars ■ ⊖	a	06 36		06 41				06 56			07 06			07 11				07 21	07 26			07 36			
City Thameslink ■	a																								
Farringdon ■ ⊖	a	06 41		06 46				07 01			07 11			07 16				07 26	07 31			07 41			
St Pancras International	a	06 45		06 50				07 05			07 15			07 20				07 30	07 35			07 45			
Clapham Junction ■	a		06 28		06 33	06 46			06 51	06 57			06 58		07 03	07 10				07 35	07 21		07 25	07 27	
London Victoria ■ ⊖	a		06 35		06 41	06 54			06 59	07 05			07 05		07 11	07 18					07 29		07 32	07 35	

		SN ■		TL ■	SN	SN ■	SN	SN ■	TL ■	SN ■	SN ■	TL ■		SN ■	SN	SN	SN ■	TL ■	SN	SN ■	SN	SN ■		TL ■	TL ■
East Croydon	d	07 19		07 21	07 23	07 24	07 27	07 30	07 33	07 37	07 42	07 45		07 45		07 48	07 49	07 51	07 53	07 54	07 57	08 00		08 01	08 03
Norwood Junction ■	d						07 33		07 38						07 28						08 03				08 08
London Bridge ■ ⊖	a			07 34	08 06		08 01		07 50	07 53		08 00				08 04		08 04	08 36		08 31			08 15	08 20
London Blackfriars ■ ⊖	a			07 41					07 56			08 06						08 11						08 21	08 26
City Thameslink ■	a																								
Farringdon ■ ⊖	a			07 46					08 01			08 11						08 16						08 26	08 31
St Pancras International	a			07 50					08 05			08 15						08 20						08 30	08 35
Clapham Junction ■	a	07 28				07 33		07 40			07 51			07 55	07 57		07 58			08 03		08 10			
London Victoria ■ ⊖	a	07 35				07 41		07 48			07 59			08 02	08 05		08 05			08 11		08 18			

		SN ■	SN ■	TL ■	SN ■	SN	SN	SN ■		TL ■	SN	SN ■	SN	SN ■	TL ■	SN ■	SN ■	TL ■	SN ■	SN	SN	SN ■	TL ■	SN	SN ■
East Croydon	d	08 10	08 12	08 15	08 15		08 18	08 19		08 21	08 23	08 24	08 27	08 30	08 33	08 37	08 42	08 45	08 45		08 48	08 49	08 51	08 53	08 54
Norwood Junction ■	d					07 58							08 33		08 38					08 28					
London Bridge ■ ⊖	a			08 30			08 34			08 34	09 06		09 01		08 50	08 53		09 00			09 04		09 04	09 36	
London Blackfriars ■ ⊖	a			08 36						08 41					08 56			09 06					09 11		
City Thameslink ■	a																	09 08					09 13		
Farringdon ■ ⊖	a			08 41						08 46					09 01			09 11					09 16		
St Pancras International	a			08 45						08 50					09 05			09 15					09 20		
Clapham Junction ■	a	08 35	08 21		08 25	08 27		08 28				08 33		08 40			08 51		08 55	08 57		08 58			09 03
London Victoria ■ ⊖	a		08 29		08 32	08 35		08 35				08 41		08 48			08 59		09 02	09 05		09 05			09 11

A not 7 December

Please note, Network Rail have stated that further updates to this timetable are possible during the validity period.

East Croydon and Norwood Junction - London - Summary of Fast Trains

Saturdays 26 May to 8 December

	SN	SN 1	TL 1	TL 1	SN 1	SN 1	TL 1	SN 1	SN	SN	SN 1	TL 1	SN	SN 1	SN	SN 1	TL 1		SN 1	SN 1	TL 1	SN 1	SN
East Croydon d	08 57	09 00	09 01	09 03	09 10	09 12	09 15	09 15		09 18	09 19	09 21	09 23	09 24	09 27	09 30	09 33	and at the same minutes past each hour until	15 37	15 42	15 45	15 45	
Norwood Junction [2] d	09 03			09 08					08 58						09 33		09 38						15 28
London Bridge [4] a	09 31		09 15	09 20			09 30			09 34		09 34	10 06		10 01		09 50		15 53		16 00		
London Blackfriars [3] a			09 21	09 26			09 36					09 41					09 56				16 06		
City Thameslink [3] a			09 23	09 28			09 38					09 43					09 58				16 08		
Farringdon [3] a			09 26	09 31			09 41					09 46					10 01				16 11		
St Pancras International a			09 30	09 35			09 45					09 50					10 05				16 15		
Clapham Junction [10] a		09 10			09 35	09 21		09 25	09 27		09 28			09 33		09 40				15 51		15 55	15 57
London Victoria [15] a		09 18				09 29		09 32	09 35		09 35			09 41		09 48				15 59		16 02	16 05

	SN	SN 1	TL 1	SN	SN 1	SN	SN 1	TL 1	TL 1	SN 1	SN 1	TL 1	SN 1	SN	SN	SN 1	TL 1	SN	SN 1	SN	SN 1	TL 1		SN 1
East Croydon d	15 48	15 49	15 51	15 53	15 54	15 57	16 00	16 01	16 03	16 10	16 12	16 15	16 15		16 18	16 19	16 21	16 23	16 24	16 27	16 30	16 33		16 37
Norwood Junction [2] d						16 03			16 08					15 58						16 33		16 38		
London Bridge [4] a	16 04		16 04	16 36		16 31		16 15	16 20			16 30			16 34		16 34	17 06		17 01		16 50		16 53
London Blackfriars [3] a			16 11					16 21	16 26			16 36					16 41					16 56		
City Thameslink [3] a			16 13					16 23	16 28			16 38					16 43					16 58		
Farringdon [3] a			16 16					16 26	16 31			16 41					16 46					17 01		
St Pancras International a			16 20					16 30	16 35			16 45					16 50					17 05		
Clapham Junction [10] a		15 58			16 03		16 10			16 35	16 21		16 25	16 27		16 28			16 33		16 40			
London Victoria [15] a		16 05			16 11		16 18				16 29		16 32	16 35		16 35			16 41		16 48			

	SN 1	TL 1	SN 1	SN	SN	SN 1	TL 1	SN		SN 1	SN	SN 1	TL 1	TL 1	SN 1	SN 1	TL 1	SN 1		SN	SN	SN 1	TL 1	SN
East Croydon d	16 42	16 45	16 45		16 48	16 49	16 51	16 53		16 56	16 57	17 00	17 01	17 03	17 10	17 12	17 15	17 15			17 18	17 19	17 21	17 23
Norwood Junction [2] d				16 28							17 03			17 08						16 59				
London Bridge [4] a		17 00			17 04		17 04	17 36			17 31		17 15	17 20			17 30				17 34		17 34	18 06
London Blackfriars [3] a		17 06					17 11						17 21	17 26			17 36						17 41	
City Thameslink [3] a		17 08					17 13						17 23	17 28			17 38						17 43	
Farringdon [3] a		17 11					17 16						17 26	17 31			17 41						17 46	
St Pancras International a		17 15					17 20						17 30	17 35			17 45						17 50	
Clapham Junction [10] a	16 51		16 55	16 57		16 58				17 05		17 10			17 35	17 21		17 25		17 27		17 28		
London Victoria [15] a	16 59		17 02	17 05		17 05				17 12		17 18				17 29		17 32		17 35		17 35		

	SN 1	SN	SN 1	TL 1		SN 1	SN 1	TL 1	SN 1	SN	SN	SN 1	TL 1	SN		SN 1	SN	SN 1	TL 1	TL 1	SN 1	SN 1	TL 1	SN 1
East Croydon d	17 24	17 27	17 30	17 33		17 37	17 42	17 45	17 45		17 48	17 49	17 51	17 53		17 54	17 57	18 00	18 01	18 03	18 10	18 12	18 15	18 15
Norwood Junction [2] d		17 33		17 38						17 28							18 03			18 08				
London Bridge [4] a		18 01		17 50		17 53		18 00			18 04		18 04	18 36			18 31		18 15	18 20			18 30	
London Blackfriars [3] a				17 56				18 06					18 11						18 21	18 26			18 36	
City Thameslink [3] a				17 58				18 08					18 13						18 23	18 28			18 38	
Farringdon [3] a				18 01				18 11					18 16						18 26	18 31			18 41	
St Pancras International a				18 05				18 15					18 20						18 30	18 35			18 45	
Clapham Junction [10] a	17 33		17 40				17 51		17 55	17 57		17 58				18 03		18 10			18 35	18 21		18 25
London Victoria [15] a	17 41		17 48				17 59		18 02	18 05		18 05				18 11		18 18				18 29		18 32

		SN	SN	SN 1	TL 1	SN	SN 1	SN	SN 1	TL 1		SN 1	SN 1	TL 1	SN 1	SN	SN	SN 1	TL 1	SN		SN 1	SN	SN 1
East Croydon d			18 18	18 19	18 21	18 23	18 24	18 27	18 30	18 33		18 37	18 42	18 45	18 45		18 48	18 49	18 51	18 53		18 54	18 57	19 00
Norwood Junction [2] d		17 58						18 33		18 38						18 28							19 03	
London Bridge [4] a			18 34		18 34	19 06		19 01		18 50		18 53		19 00			19 04		19 04	19 36			19 31	
London Blackfriars [3] a					18 41					18 56				19 06					19 11					
City Thameslink [3] a					18 43					18 58				19 08					19 13					
Farringdon [3] a					18 46					19 01				19 11					19 16					
St Pancras International a					18 50					19 05				19 15					19 20					
Clapham Junction [10] a		18 27		18 28			18 33		18 40				18 51		18 55	18 57		18 58				19 03		19 10
London Victoria [15] a		18 35		18 35			18 41		18 48				18 59		19 02	19 05		19 05				19 11		19 18

	TL 1	TL 1	SN 1	SN 1	TL 1	SN 1		SN	SN	SN 1	TL 1	SN	SN 1	SN	SN 1	TL 1		SN 1	SN 1	TL 1	SN 1	SN	SN	SN 1
East Croydon d	19 01	19 03	19 10	19 12	19 15	19 15			19 18	19 19	19 21	19 23	19 24	19 27	19 30	19 33		19 37	19 42	19 45	19 45		19 48	19 49
Norwood Junction [2] d		19 08						18 58						19 33		19 38						19 28		
London Bridge [4] a	19 15	19 20			19 30				19 34		19 34	20 06		20 01		19 50		19 53		20 00			20 04	
London Blackfriars [3] a	19 21	19 26			19 36						19 41					19 56				20 06				
City Thameslink [3] a	19 23	19 28			19 38						19 43					19 58				20 08				
Farringdon [3] a	19 26	19 31			19 41						19 46					20 01				20 11				
St Pancras International a	19 30	19 35			19 45						19 50					20 05				20 15				
Clapham Junction [10] a			19 35	19 21		19 25		19 27		19 28			19 33		19 40				19 51		19 55	19 57		19 58
London Victoria [15] a				19 29		19 32		19 35		19 35			19 41		19 48				19 59		20 02	20 05		20 05

	TL 1	SN		SN 1	SN	SN 1	TL 1	TL 1	SN 1	SN 1	TL 1	SN 1		SN	SN	SN 1	TL 1	SN	SN 1	SN	SN 1	TL 1		SN 1
East Croydon d	19 51	19 53		19 54	19 57	20 00	20 01	20 03	20 10	20 12	20 15	20 15			20 18	20 19	20 21	20 23	20 24	20 27	20 30	20 33		20 37
Norwood Junction [2] d					20 03			20 08						19 58						20 33		20 38		
London Bridge [4] a	20 04	20 36			20 31		20 15	20 20			20 30				20 34		20 34	21 06		21 01		20 50		20 53
London Blackfriars [3] a	20 11						20 21	20 26			20 36						20 41					20 56		
City Thameslink [3] a	20 13						20 23	20 28			20 38						20 43					20 58		
Farringdon [3] a	20 16						20 26	20 31			20 41						20 46					21 01		
St Pancras International a	20 20						20 30	20 35			20 45						20 50					21 05		
Clapham Junction [10] a				20 03		20 10			20 35	20 21		20 25		20 27		20 28			20 33		20 40			
London Victoria [15] a				20 11		20 18				20 29		20 32		20 35		20 35			20 41		20 48			

East Croydon and Norwood Junction - London - Summary of Fast Trains

Saturdays 26 May to 8 December

	SN 1	TL 1	SN 1	SN		SN	SN 1	TL 1	SN	SN 1	SN	SN 1	TL 1	TL 1		SN 1	SN 1	TL 1	SN 1	SN	SN	SN 1	TL 1	SN
East Croydon d	20 42	20 45	20 45			20 48	20 49	20 51	20 53	20 54	20 57	21 00	21 01	21 03		21 10	21 12	21 15	21 15		21 18	21 19	21 21	21 23
Norwood Junction [2] d				20 28							21 03			21 08						20 58				
London Bridge [4] a		21 00				21 04		21 04	21 36		21 31		21 15	21 20				21 30			21 34		21 34	22 06
London Blackfriars [3] a		21 06						21 11					21 21	21 26				21 36					21 41	
City Thameslink [3] a																								
Farringdon [3] a		21 11						21 16					21 26	21 31				21 41					21 46	
St Pancras International a		21 15						21 20					21 30	21 35				21 45					21 50	
Clapham Junction [10] a	20 51		20 55	20 57			20 58			21 03		21 10				21 35	21 21		21 25	21 27		21 28		
London Victoria [15] a	20 59		21 02	21 05			21 05			21 11		21 18					21 29		21 32	21 35		21 35		

		SN 1	SN	SN 1	TL 1	SN 1	SN 1	TL 1	SN 1	SN		SN	SN 1	TL 1	SN	SN 1	SN	SN 1	TL 1	TL 1		SN 1	SN 1	TL 1
East Croydon d		21 24	21 27	21 30	21 33	21 37	21 42	21 45	21 45			21 48	21 49	21 51	21 53	21 54	21 57	22 00	22 01	22 03		22 10	22 12	22 15
Norwood Junction [2] d			21 33		21 38					21 28							22 03			22 08				
London Bridge [4] a			22 01		21 50	21 53		22 00				22 04		22 04	22 36		22 31		22 15	22 20				22 30
London Blackfriars [3] a					21 56			22 06						22 11					22 21	22 26				22 36
City Thameslink [3] a																								
Farringdon [3] a					22 01			22 11						22 16					22 26	22 31				22 41
St Pancras International a					22 05			22 15						22 20					22 30	22 35				22 45
Clapham Junction [10] a		21 33		21 40			21 51		21 55	21 57			21 58			22 03		22 10				22 35	22 21	
London Victoria [15] a		21 41		21 48			21 59		22 02	22 05			22 05			22 11		22 18					22 29	

	SN 1	SN	SN	SN 1	TL 1	SN		SN 1	SN	SN 1	SN 1	SN 1	TL 1	SN 1	SN	SN		SN 1	TL 1	SN	SN 1	SN	SN 1	TL 1
East Croydon d	22 15		22 18	22 19	22 21	22 23		22 24	22 27	22 30	22 37	22 42	22 45	22 45		22 48		22 49	22 51	22 53	22 54	22 57	23 00	23 01
Norwood Junction [2] d		21 58							22 33						22 28							23 03		
London Bridge [4] a			22 34		22 34	23 06			23 01		22 53		23 00			23 04			23 04	23 36		23 31		23 15
London Blackfriars [3] a					22 41								23 06						23 11					23 21
City Thameslink [3] a																								
Farringdon [3] a					22 46								23 11						23 16					23 26
St Pancras International a					22 50								23 15						23 20					23 30
Clapham Junction [10] a	22 25	22 27		22 28				22 33		22 40		22 51		22 55	22 57			22 58			23 04		23 10	
London Victoria [15] a	22 32	22 35		22 35				22 41		22 48		22 59		23 02	23 05			23 05			23 11		23 18	

	SN 1	TL 1		SN 1	SN	SN	SN 1	TL 1	SN	SN 1	SN	SN 1		SN 1	SN	TL 1
East Croydon d	23 12	23 15		23 15		23 18	23 19	23 21	23 23	23 30		23 38		23 45	23 48	23 54
Norwood Junction [2] d					22 58						23 28				23 53	
London Bridge [4] a		23 30				23 34		23 34	00 06			23 53			00 06	
London Blackfriars [3] a		23 36						23 41								00 19
City Thameslink [3] a																
Farringdon [3] a		23 41						23 46								00 26
St Pancras International a		23 45						23 50								00 30
Clapham Junction [10] a	23 21			23 25	23 27		23 28			23 41	23 57			00 04		
London Victoria [15] a	23 29			23 32	23 35		23 35			23 50	00 05			00 12		

Sundays 20 May to 2 December

	TL 1 A	SN 1 A	TL 1 A	TL 1 A	TL 1	SN 1	SN 1	SN 1	TL 1		TL 1	SN	SN	SN	TL 1	SN	SN	SN	TL 1		SN	TL 1	SN	SN
East Croydon d	00 10	00 16	00 23	00 40	01 10	03 37	04 36	05 30	06 32		06 40	06 44	06 51		07 10	07 14	07 23	07 29	07 32			07 40	07 44	07 51
Norwood Junction [2] d									06 36					07 09				07 35	07 36		07 38			
London Bridge [4] a									06 50		06 55	07 22			07 25	07 52		08 05	07 50			07 58	08 22	
London Blackfriars [3] a	00 36		00 49	01 06	01 36																			
City Thameslink [3] a																								
Farringdon [3] a	00 41																							
St Pancras International a	00 45		00 59	01 15	01 45																			
Clapham Junction [10] a		00 33				03 50	04 49	05 51					07 05	07 34			07 37				08 04			08 07
London Victoria [15] a		00 41				03 58	04 58	05 59					07 15	07 42			07 46				08 13			08 15

	SN	SN	TL 1	SN	SN		SN	TL 1	TL 1	SN	SN	SN	SN	SN	SN		TL 1	TL 1	SN	SN	SN	TL 1	SN	SN
East Croydon d	07 59		08 10	08 14	08 23		08 29	08 32	08 40	08 44	08 46	08 51		08 59	08 59		09 02	09 07	09 11	09 14	09 15	09 18	09 21	
Norwood Junction [2] d	08 06	08 09					08 35	08 36					08 39		09 05			09 12						09 09
London Bridge [4] a	08 36		08 25	08 53			09 02	08 50	08 55	09 22					09 32		09 17	09 24		09 52		09 32		
London Blackfriars [3] a																		09 30				09 38		
City Thameslink [3] a																								
Farringdon [3] a																		09 35				09 43		
St Pancras International a																		09 39				09 47		
Clapham Junction [10] a		08 35			08 38						08 55	09 02	09 03	09 08					09 20		09 24		09 32	09 33
London Victoria [15] a		08 43			08 46						09 02	09 09	09 12	09 15					09 28		09 32		09 39	09 42

	SN		SN	TL 1	TL 1	SN	SN	SN	TL 1	SN	SN		SN	SN	TL 1	TL 1	SN	SN	SN	TL 1	SN		SN	SN
East Croydon d	09 30		09 31	09 34	09 37	09 41	09 44	09 45	09 48	09 51			10 01	10 04	10 04	10 07	10 11	10 14	10 15	10 18	10 21			10 30
Norwood Junction [2] d			09 35		09 42						09 39		10 05			10 12							10 09	
London Bridge [4] a			10 02	09 48	09 54		10 22		10 02				10 32		10 18	10 24		10 52		10 32				
London Blackfriars [3] a				09 54	10 00				10 08						10 24	10 30				10 38				
City Thameslink [3] a																								
Farringdon [3] a				09 59	10 05				10 13						10 29	10 35				10 43				
St Pancras International a				10 03	10 09				10 17						10 33	10 39				10 47				
Clapham Junction [10] a	09 39					09 50		09 54		10 02	10 03			10 14			10 20		10 24		10 32		10 33	10 39
London Victoria [15] a	09 47					09 58		10 02		10 09	10 12			10 21			10 28		10 32		10 39		10 42	10 47

A not 20 May

Please note, Network Rail have stated that further updates to this timetable are possible during the validity period.

Table T175-R

Sundays

20 May to 2 December

East Croydon and Norwood Junction - London - Summary of Fast Trains

	SN	TL ■	TL ■		SN	SN	SN	TL ■	SN	SN	SN	SN	TL ■		TL ■	SN	SN	SN	TL ■	SN	SN	SN	SN	
East Croydon d	10 31	10 34	10 37		10 41	10 44	10 45	10 48	10 51		11 01	11 04	11 04		11 07	11 11	11 14	11 15	11 18	11 21		11 30	11 31	
Norwood Junction d	10 35		10 42							10 39	11 05				11 12						11 09		11 35	
London Bridge a	11 02	10 48	10 54			11 22		11 02			11 32		11 18		11 24		11 52		11 32				12 02	
London Blackfriars a		10 54	11 00					11 08					11 24		11 30				11 38					
City Thameslink a																								
Farringdon a		10 59	11 05					11 13					11 29		11 35				11 43					
St Pancras International a		11 03	11 09					11 17					11 33		11 39				11 47					
Clapham Junction a					10 50		10 54		11 02	11 03		11 14				11 20		11 24		11 32	11 33	11 39		
London Victoria a					10 58		11 02		11 09	11 12		11 21				11 28		11 32		11 39	11 42	11 47		

	TL ■	TL ■	SN	SN	SN	TL ■	SN	SN	SN		SN	TL ■	TL ■	SN	SN	SN	TL ■	SN	SN		SN	SN	TL ■	TL ■
East Croydon d	11 34	11 37	11 40	11 44	11 45	11 48	11 51		12 01		12 04	12 04	12 07	12 11	12 14	12 15	12 18	12 21			12 30	12 31	12 34	12 37
Norwood Junction d		11 42						11 39	12 05				12 12						12 09			12 35		12 42
London Bridge a	11 48	11 54		12 22		12 02			12 32			12 18	12 24		12 52		12 32					13 02	12 48	12 54
London Blackfriars a	11 54	12 00				12 08						12 24	12 30				12 38						12 54	13 00
City Thameslink a																								
Farringdon a	11 59	12 05				12 13						12 29	12 35				12 45						12 59	13 05
St Pancras International a	12 03	12 09				12 17						12 33	12 39				12 49						13 03	13 09
Clapham Junction a			11 50		11 54		12 02	12 03			12 14			12 20		12 24		12 32	12 33		12 39			
London Victoria a			11 58		12 02		12 09	12 12			12 21			12 28		12 32		12 39	12 42		12 47			

	SN	SN	SN	TL ■	SN		SN	SN	TL ■	SN	TL ■	SN	SN	SN	TL ■		SN	SN	SN	SN	TL ■	TL ■	SN	SN
East Croydon d	12 41	12 44	12 45	12 48	12 51			13 01	13 04	13 06	13 07	13 11	13 14	13 15	13 18		13 21		13 30	13 31	13 34	13 37	13 41	13 44
Norwood Junction d							12 39	13 05			13 12							13 09		13 35		13 42		
London Bridge a		13 22		13 02				13 32	13 18		13 24		13 52		13 32					14 02	13 48	13 54		14 22
London Blackfriars a				13 08					13 24		13 30				13 38						13 54	14 00		
City Thameslink a																								
Farringdon a				13 13					13 29		13 35				13 43						13 59	14 05		
St Pancras International a				13 17					13 33		13 39				13 47						14 03	14 09		
Clapham Junction a	12 50		12 54		13 02		13 03			13 16		13 22		13 25			13 32	13 33	13 39				13 50	
London Victoria a	12 58		13 02		13 09		13 12			13 23		13 30		13 32			13 39	13 42	13 47				13 58	

	SN		TL ■	SN	SN	SN	SN	TL ■	TL ■	SN	SN		SN	TL ■	SN	SN	SN	SN	TL ■	TL ■	SN		SN	SN
East Croydon d	13 45		13 48	13 51		14 01	14 04	14 04	14 07	14 11	14 14		14 15	14 18	14 21		14 30	14 31	14 34	14 37	14 41		14 44	14 45
Norwood Junction d					13 39	14 05			14 12							14 09		14 35		14 42				
London Bridge a			14 02			14 32		14 18	14 24		14 52			14 32				15 02	14 48	14 54			15 22	
London Blackfriars a			14 08					14 24	14 30					14 38					14 54	15 00				
City Thameslink a																								
Farringdon a			14 13					14 29	14 35					14 43					14 59	15 05				
St Pancras International a			14 17					14 33	14 39					14 47					15 03	15 09				
Clapham Junction a	13 54			14 02	14 03		14 14			14 20			14 24		14 32	14 33	14 39				14 50			14 54
London Victoria a	14 02			14 09	14 12		14 21			14 28			14 32		14 39	14 42	14 47				14 58			15 02

	TL ■	SN	SN	SN	SN	TL ■	TL ■		SN	SN	SN	TL ■	SN	SN	SN	SN	TL ■		TL ■	SN	SN	SN	TL ■	SN
East Croydon d	14 48	14 51		15 01	15 04	15 04	15 07		15 11	15 14	15 15	15 18	15 21		15 30	15 31	15 34		15 37	15 41	15 44	15 45	15 48	15 51
Norwood Junction d			14 39	15 05			15 12							15 09		15 35			15 42					
London Bridge a	15 02			15 32		15 18	15 24			15 52		15 32				16 02	15 48		15 54		16 22		16 02	
London Blackfriars a	15 08					15 24	15 30					15 38					15 54		16 00				16 08	
City Thameslink a																								
Farringdon a	15 13					15 29	15 35					15 43					15 59		16 05				16 13	
St Pancras International a	15 17					15 33	15 39					15 47					16 03		16 09				16 17	
Clapham Junction a		15 02	15 03		15 14				15 20		15 24		15 32	15 33	15 39					15 50		15 54		16 02
London Victoria a		15 09	15 12		15 21				15 28		15 32		15 39	15 42	15 47					15 58		16 02		16 09

	SN	SN	TL ■		SN	TL ■	SN	SN	SN	TL ■	SN	SN	SN		SN	TL ■	TL ■	SN	SN	SN	TL ■	SN	SN	
East Croydon d		16 01	16 04		16 06	16 07	16 11	16 14	16 15	16 18	16 21		16 30		16 31	16 34	16 37	16 41	16 44	16 45	16 48	16 51		
Norwood Junction d	15 39	16 05				16 12						16 09			16 35		16 42						16 39	
London Bridge a		16 32	16 18			16 24		16 52		16 32					17 02	16 48	16 54		17 22		17 02			
London Blackfriars a			16 24			16 30				16 38						16 54	17 00				17 08			
City Thameslink a																								
Farringdon a			16 29			16 35				16 43						16 59	17 05				17 13			
St Pancras International a			16 33			16 39				16 47						17 03	17 09				17 17			
Clapham Junction a	16 03				16 16		16 22		16 24		16 32	16 33	16 39					16 50		16 54		17 02	17 03	
London Victoria a	16 12				16 23		16 30		16 32		16 39	16 42	16 47					16 58		17 02		17 09	17 12	

	SN	TL ■	SN	TL ■	SN	SN	SN	TL ■	SN	SN	SN	SN	TL ■	TL ■	SN	SN	SN	TL ■	SN	SN	SN	SN	TL ■	TL ■
East Croydon d	17 01	17 04	17 06	17 07	17 11	17 14	17 15	17 18	17 21		17 30	17 31	17 34	17 37	17 41	17 44	17 45	17 48	17 51		18 01	18 04	18 04	18 07
Norwood Junction d	17 05			17 12						17 09		17 35		17 42						17 39	18 05			18 12
London Bridge a	17 32	17 18		17 24		17 52		17 32				18 02	17 48	17 54		18 22		18 02			18 32		18 18	18 24
London Blackfriars a		17 24		17 30				17 38					17 54	18 00				18 08					18 24	18 30
City Thameslink a																								
Farringdon a		17 29		17 35				17 43					17 59	18 05				18 13					18 29	18 35
St Pancras International a		17 33		17 39				17 47					18 03	18 09				18 17					18 33	18 39
Clapham Junction a			17 16		17 22		17 25		17 32	17 33	17 39				17 50		17 54		18 02	18 03		18 14		
London Victoria a			17 23		17 30		17 32		17 39	17 42	17 47				17 58		18 02		18 09	18 12		18 21		

Table T175-R

Sundays

20 May to 2 December

East Croydon and Norwood Junction - London - Summary of Fast Trains

	SN	SN	SN		TL ■	SN	SN	SN	SN	TL ■	TL ■	SN	SN	SN	TL ■	SN	SN	SN	SN	TL ■	TL ■	SN	SN
East Croydon d	18 11	18 14	18 15	and at the same minutes past each hour until	20 18	20 21		20 30	20 31	20 34	20 37	20 41	20 44	20 45	20 48	20 51		21 01	21 04	21 04	21 07	21 11	21 14
Norwood Junction d							20 09		20 35		20 42						20 39	21 05			21 12		
London Bridge a		18 52			20 32				21 02	20 48	20 54		21 22		21 02			21 32		21 18	21 24		21 52
London Blackfriars a					20 38					20 54	21 00				21 08					21 24	21 30		
City Thameslink a																							
Farringdon a					20 43					20 59	21 05				21 13					21 29	21 35		
St Pancras International a					20 47					21 03	21 09				21 17					21 33	21 39		
Clapham Junction a	18 20		18 24			20 32	20 33	20 39				20 50		20 54		21 02	21 03		21 14			21 20	
London Victoria a	18 28		18 32			20 39	20 42	20 47				20 58		21 02		21 09	21 12		21 21			21 28	

	SN		TL ■	SN	SN	SN	SN	TL ■	TL ■	SN	SN		SN	TL ■	SN	SN	SN	SN	TL ■	TL ■	SN		SN	SN
East Croydon d	21 15		21 18	21 21		21 30	21 31	21 34	21 37	21 40	21 44		21 45	21 48	21 51		22 01	22 04	22 04	22 07	22 11		22 14	22 15
Norwood Junction d					21 09		21 35		21 42							21 39	22 05			22 12				
London Bridge a			21 32				22 02	21 48	21 54		22 22			22 02			22 32		22 18	22 24			22 52	
London Blackfriars a			21 38					21 54	22 00					22 08					22 24	22 30				
City Thameslink a																								
Farringdon a			21 43					21 59	22 05					22 13					22 29	22 35				
St Pancras International a			21 47					22 03	22 09					22 17					22 33	22 39				
Clapham Junction a	21 24			21 32	21 33	21 39				21 49			21 54		22 02	22 03		22 14			22 20			22 24
London Victoria a	21 32			21 39	21 42	21 47				21 58			22 02		22 09	22 12		22 21			22 28			22 32

	SN	SN	SN	SN	TL ■	SN	SN		TL ■	SN	SN	SN	SN	TL ■	TL ■	SN	SN		SN	SN	SN	TL ■	SN	SN
East Croydon d	22 21		22 30	22 31	22 34	22 42	22 45		22 47	22 51		23 01	23 04	23 04	23 12	23 15	23 21			23 31		23 40	23 52	23 55
Norwood Junction d		22 09		22 35					22 52		22 39	23 05			23 17				23 09	23 35	23 39			
London Bridge a				23 02	22 48	23 22			23 04			23 34		23 18	23 30					00 03				
London Blackfriars a					22 54				23 10					23 24								00 06		
City Thameslink a																								
Farringdon a					22 59				23 16					23 31								00 10		
St Pancras International a					23 03				23 20					23 35								00 15		
Clapham Junction a	22 32	22 33	22 39				22 54			23 02	23 03		23 14			23 24	23 32		23 33		00 05		00 08	00 15
London Victoria a	22 39	22 42	22 47				23 02			23 09	23 12		23 21			23 32	23 39		23 43		00 13		00 17	00 23

East Croydon, Balham and Clapham Junction-Imperial Wharf, West Brompton, Kensington Olympia and Shepherd's Bush - Willesden Junction, Stratford/Watford Junction, Milton Keynes

Miles	Miles			SN ■	SN ■	SN ■	LO	LO	SN ■	LO	LO	SN ■		LO	LO	LO	LO	SN ■	LO	LO	SN ■	LO		LO	SN ■
0	—	East Croydon	d															07 10			07 40				08 11
1	—	Selhurst ■	d									06 16						07 16			07 46				08 16
1¾	—	Thornton Heath	d									06 19						07 19			07 49				08 19
3	—	Norbury	d									06 22						07 22			07 52				08 22
4	—	Streatham Common ■	d									06 25						07 25			07 55				08 25
5¾	—	Balham ■ ⊖	d		05 27							06 29						07 29			07 59				08 29
6½	—	Wandsworth Common	d																						
7¾	—	Clapham Junction ■	a		05 31							06 35						07 35			08 05				08 35
—	—		d	05 03	05 32	05 53	06 00	06 12	06 20	06 25	06 36	06 40		07 01	07 13	07 25	07 36	07 40	08 01	08 13	08 18	08 25		08 36	08 40
8¾	—	**Imperial Wharf**	d	05 07	05 37	05 58	06 04	06 16	06 24	06 29	06 40	06 44		07 05	07 17	07 29	07 40	07 44	08 05	08 17	08 23	08 29		08 40	08 44
9½	—	**West Brompton** ⊖	d	05 10	05 40	06 01	06 07	06 19	06 27	06 32	06 43	06 47		07 08	07 20	07 32	07 43	07 47	08 08	08 20	08 26	08 32		08 43	08 47
11½	—	**Kensington (Olympia)** ⊖	d	05 14	05 44	06 05	06 10	06 22	06 31	06 35	06 46	06 51		07 11	07 23	07 35	07 46	07 51	08 11	08 23	08 29	08 35		08 46	08 51
12¾	0	**Shepherd's Bush** ⊖	d	05 17	05 47	06 08	06 12	06 24	06 34	06 37	06 49	06 54		07 13	07 25	07 37	07 48	07 53	08 13	08 25	08 32	08 37		08 48	08 53
—	1½	Willesden Jn. High Level ⊖	a				06 21	06 34		06 45	06 57			07 21	07 34	07 45	07 55		08 21	08 33		08 44		08 55	
—	4	West Hampstead ⊖	a				06 30	06 43		06 54	07 06			07 32	07 42	07 54	08 06		08 30	08 42		08 53		09 06	
—	6	Gospel Oak	a				06 37	06 49		07 00	07 13			07 39	07 48	08 00	08 13		08 36	08 49		08 59		09 13	
—	8¾	Highbury & Islington ⊖	a				06 47	07 01		07 14	07 23			07 49	07 59	08 13	08 24		08 48	09 02		09 10		09 23	
—	13½	Stratford ⊖	a				07 04	07 21		07 32	07 41			08 05	08 17	08 31	08 41		09 06	09 18		09 30		09 41	
17	—	Wembley Central ⊖	a		06 00	06 24			06 47			07 07						08 08			08 47				09 08
20½	—	Harrow & Wealdstone ⊖	a	05 33	06 07	06 29						07 12						08 13			08 52				09 13
25	—	Watford Junction	a	05 40	06 14	06 36			06 57			07 19						08 20			09 01				09 20
32	—	Hemel Hempstead	a		06 22							07 27						08 28							09 28
35½	—	Berkhamsted	a		06 26							07 32						08 32							09 32
39¼	—	Tring	a		06 33							07 39						08 38							09 39
47¾	—	Leighton Buzzard	a		06 42							07 50						08 46							09 47
54¼	—	Bletchley	a		06 49							07 57						08 53							09 55
57¼	—	Milton Keynes Central ■	a		06 55							08 03						09 00							10 01

		LO	SN ■	LO	LO	SN ■	LO	LO		LO	LO	SN ■	LO	LO	LO	LO	SN ■	LO		LO	LO	LO	SN ■	LO	LO
East Croydon	d		08 40			09 10						10 10					11 10						12 10		
Selhurst ■	d		08 46			09 16						10 16					11 16						12 16		
Thornton Heath	d		08 49			09 19						10 19					11 19						12 19		
Norbury	d		08 52			09 22						10 22					11 22						12 22		
Streatham Common ■	d		08 55			09 25						10 25					11 25						12 25		
Balham ■ ⊖	d		08 59			09 29						10 29					11 29						12 29		
Wandsworth Common	d																								
Clapham Junction ■	a		09 05			09 35						10 35					11 35						12 35		
	d	09 01	09 06	09 14	09 29	09 39	09 46	10 01		10 17	10 30	10 41	10 48	11 02	11 17	11 32	11 39	11 47		12 02	12 17	12 32	12 39	12 47	13 02
Imperial Wharf	d	09 05	09 10	09 18	09 33	09 44	09 50	10 05		10 21	10 34	10 45	10 52	11 06	11 21	11 36	11 44	11 51		12 06	12 21	12 36	12 44	12 51	13 06
West Brompton ⊖	d	09 08	09 13	09 21	09 36	09 47	09 53	10 08		10 24	10 37	10 48	10 55	11 09	11 24	11 39	11 47	11 54		12 09	12 24	12 39	12 47	12 54	13 09
Kensington (Olympia) ⊖	d	09 11	09 17	09 24	09 39	09 50	09 56	10 11		10 27	10 42	10 51	10 58	11 12	11 27	11 42	11 50	11 57		12 12	12 27	12 42	12 50	12 57	13 12
Shepherd's Bush ⊖	d	09 13	09a19	09 26	09 41	09 53	09 58	10 13		10 29	10 44	10 54	11 00	11 14	11 29	11 44	11 53	11 59		12 14	12 29	12 44	12 53	12 59	13 14
Willesden Jn. High Level ⊖	a	09 21		09 34	09 49		10 07	10 21		10 36	10 52		11 08	11 21	11 39	11 52		12 07		12 22	12 36	12 52		13 07	13 21
West Hampstead ⊖	a	09 32		09 43	09 58		10 16	10 30		10 45	11 01		11 17	11 31	11 48	12 01		12 16		12 31	12 45	13 01		13 16	13 30
Gospel Oak	a	09 39		09 49	10 04		10 22	10 38		10 51	11 07		11 23	11 37	11 57	12 07		12 22		12 38	12 51	13 08		13 22	13 36
Highbury & Islington ⊖	a	09 49		10 00	10 16		10 33	10 48		11 03	11 19		11 35	11 49	12 06	12 19		12 34		12 49	13 03	13 19		13 34	13 48
Stratford ⊖	a	10 07		10 18	10 33		10 51	11 05		11 21	11 36		11 52	12 06	12 21	12 36		12 51		13 06	13 21	13 37		13 51	14 06
Wembley Central ⊖	a					10 08						11 09					12 09						13 09		
Harrow & Wealdstone ⊖	a					10 13						11 14					12 14						13 14		
Watford Junction	a					10 20						11 21					12 21						13 21		
Hemel Hempstead	a					10 28						11 29					12 29						13 29		
Berkhamsted	a					10 32						11 33					12 33						13 33		
Tring	a					10 39						11 39					12 39						13 39		
Leighton Buzzard	a					10 47						11 47					12 47						13 47		
Bletchley	a					10 57						11 54					12 54						13 54		
Milton Keynes Central ■	a					11 02						12 00					13 00						14 00		

For other Norbury line connections, refer to Table T170

For other Stratford line connecting trains, refer to Table T59

Table T176-F

Mondays to Fridays

21 May to 7 December

East Croydon, Balham and Clapham Junction-Imperial Wharf, West Brompton, Kensington Olympia and Shepherd's Bush - Willesden Junction, Stratford/Watford Junction, Milton Keynes

		LO	LO	SN MWFO ■	SN TThO ■	LO	LO	LO	LO	SN ■		LO	LO	SN ■	LO	SN ■	LO	SN ■	LO	LO		LO	LO	SN ■	LO
East Croydon	d			13 10						14 10								15 10						16 10	
Selhurst ■	d			13 16	13 18					14 16				14 46				15 16						16 16	
Thornton Heath	d			13 19	13 20					14 19				14 49				15 19						16 19	
Norbury	d			13 22	13 23					14 22				14 52				15 22						16 22	
Streatham Common ■	d			13 25	13 26					14 25				14 55				15 25						16 25	
Balham ■ ⊖	d			13 29	13 30					14 29				14 59				15 29						16 29	
Wandsworth Common	d																								
Clapham Junction ■	a			13 35	13 35					14 35				15 05				15 35						16 35	
	d	13 17	13 32	13 39	13 39	13 47	14 02	14 14	14 36	14 40		14 49	15 01	15 10	15 14	15 19	15 36	15 39	15 49	16 01		16 13	16 36	16 39	16 49
Imperial Wharf	d	13 21	13 36	13 44	13 44	13 51	14 06	14 18	14 40	14 45		14 53	15 05	15 15	15 18	15 24	15 40	15 44	15 53	16 05		16 17	16 40	16 44	16 53
West Brompton ⊖	d	13 24	13 39	13 47	13 47	13 54	14 09	14 21	14 43	14 48		14 56	15 08	15 18	15 21	15 27	15 43	15 47	15 56	16 08		16 20	16 43	16 47	16 56
Kensington (Olympia) ⊖	d	13 27	13 42	13 50	13 50	13 57	14 12	14 24	14 46	14 51		14 59	15 11	15 21	15 24	15 30	15 46	15 51	15 59	16 11		16 23	16 46	16 51	16 59
Shepherd's Bush ⊖	d	13 29	13 44	13 53	13 53	13 59	14 14	14 27	14 48	14 54		15 01	15 13	15a24	15 26	15 33	15 48	15 53	16 01	16 13		16 25	16 48	16 53	17 01
Willesden Jn. High Level ⊖	a	13 37	13 52			14 06	14 21	14 35	14 55			15 08	15 21		15 33		15 54		16 08	16 22		16 33	16 54		17 09
West Hampstead ⊖	a	13 46	14 01			14 15	14 30	14 44	15 06			15 18	15 30		15 42		16 03		16 18	16 31		16 43	17 03		17 18
Gospel Oak	a	13 52	14 07			14 22	14 37	14 50	15 12			15 24	15 36		15 48		16 10		16 24	16 37		16 49	17 10		17 24
Highbury & Islington ⊖	a	14 04	14 19			14 32	14 47	15 00	15 23			15 36	15 48		16 01		16 22		16 36	16 49		17 00	17 23		17 35
Stratford ⊖	a	14 21	14 36			14 51	15 06	15 18	15 40			15 56	16 05		16 18		16 40		16 56	17 07		17 17	17 40		17 57
Wembley Central ⊖	a			14 09	14 09					15 09						15 51		16 08						17 07	
Harrow & Wealdstone ⊖	a			14 14	14 14					15 14						15 57		16 13						17 12	
Watford Junction	a			14 21	14 21					15 21						16 05		16 20						17 19	
Hemel Hempstead	a			14 29	14 29					15 29								16 28						17 27	
Berkhamsted	a			14 33	14 33					15 33								16 32						17 32	
Tring	a			14 39	14 39					15 39								16 38						17 39	
Leighton Buzzard	a			14 47	14 47					15 47								16 47						17 47	
Bletchley	a			14 54	14 54					15 54								16 54						17 54	
Milton Keynes Central ■	a			15 00	15 00					16 00								17 00						18 00	

		LO	SN ■	LO	LO	SN ■		LO	LO	LO	LO	SN ■	LO	LO	LO	LO		SN ■	LO	LO	LO	LO	SN ■	LO	LO
East Croydon	d		16 40			17 10						18 10						19 10					20 10		
Selhurst ■	d		16 46			17 16						18 16						19 16					20 16		
Thornton Heath	d		16 49			17 19						18 19						19 19					20 19		
Norbury	d		16 52			17 22						18 22						19 22					20 22		
Streatham Common ■	d		16 55			17 25						18 25						19 25					20 25		
Balham ■ ⊖	d		16 59			17 30						18 29						19 29					20 29		
Wandsworth Common	d																								
Clapham Junction ■	a		17 05			17 35						18 35						19 35					20 35		
	d	17 02	17 09	17 13	17 36	17 39		17 49	18 01	18 13	18 36	18 39	18 49	19 01	19 13	19 36		19 40	19 49	20 01	20 13	20 28	20 36	20 44	21 00
Imperial Wharf	d	17 06	17 13	17 17	17 40	17 44		17 53	18 05	18 17	18 40	18 44	18 53	19 05	19 17	19 40		19 45	19 53	20 05	20 17	20 32	20 41	20 48	21 04
West Brompton ⊖	d	17 10	17 16	17 20	17 43	17 47		17 56	18 08	18 20	18 43	18 47	18 56	19 08	19 20	19 43		19 48	19 56	20 08	20 20	20 35	20 44	20 51	21 07
Kensington (Olympia) ⊖	d	17 13	17 20	17 23	17 46	17 51		17 59	18 11	18 23	18 46	18 51	18 59	19 11	19 23	19 46		19 51	19 59	20 11	20 23	20 38	20 47	20 54	21 10
Shepherd's Bush ⊖	d	17 16	17a22	17 26	17 48	17 53		18 01	18 13	18 25	18 48	18 53	19 01	19 13	19 25	19 48		19 54	20 01	20 13	20 25	20 40	20 50	20 56	21 12
Willesden Jn. High Level ⊖	a	17 23		17 33	17 55			18 09	18 21	18 33	18 56		19 09	19 20	19 33	19 56			20 09	20 22	20 33	20 48		21 04	21 19
West Hampstead ⊖	a	17 32		17 42	18 05			18 18	18 30	18 42	19 05		19 18	19 29	19 43	20 05			20 18	20 31	20 43	20 57		21 13	21 28
Gospel Oak	a	17 39		17 48	18 11			18 24	18 36	18 48	19 11		19 24	19 35	19 49	20 12			20 25	20 38	20 50	21 03		21 19	21 34
Highbury & Islington ⊖	a	17 50		18 00	18 23			18 36	18 48	19 00	19 22		19 36	19 46	20 00	20 22			20 35	20 50	21 02	21 15		21 31	21 46
Stratford ⊖	a	18 12		18 18	18 41			18 56	19 06	19 18	19 41		19 56	20 06	20 17	20 40			20 53	21 08	21 17	21 32		21 48	22 04
Wembley Central ⊖	a					18 09						19 09						20 08					21 08		
Harrow & Wealdstone ⊖	a					18 14						19 14						20 13					21 13		
Watford Junction	a					18 21						19 21						20 20					21 20		
Hemel Hempstead	a					18 29						19 29						20 28					21 28		
Berkhamsted	a					18 33						19 33						20 32					21 32		
Tring	a					18 39						19 39						20 39					21 39		
Leighton Buzzard	a					18 47						19 47						20 47					21 50		
Bletchley	a					18 54						19 54						20 54					21 58		
Milton Keynes Central ■	a					19 00						20 00						21 00					22 05		

For other Norbury line connections, refer to Table T170

For other Stratford line connecting trains, refer to Table T59

Please note, Network Rail have stated that further updates to this timetable are possible during the validity period.

Table T176-F

Mondays to Fridays

21 May to 7 December

East Croydon, Balham and Clapham Junction-Imperial Wharf, West Brompton, Kensington Olympia and Shepherd's Bush - Willesden Junction, Stratford/Watford Junction, Milton Keynes

	LO	LO	SN 1	LO	LO	LO		LO	SN 1	LO	LO	LO	LO	LO
East Croydon d			21 10											
Selhurst 4 d			21 16						22 17					
Thornton Heath d			21 19						22 19					
Norbury d			21 22						22 22					
Streatham Common 4 d			21 25						22 25					
Balham 4 ⊖ d			21 29						22 30					
Wandsworth Common d														
Clapham Junction 10 a			21 35						22 35					
d	21 17	21 30	21 36	21 44	21 59	22 14		22 29	22 36	22 44	23 00	23 15	23 30	23 45
Imperial Wharf d	21 22	21 35	21 41	21 48	22 03	22 18		22 33	22 41	22 48	23 04	23 19	23 34	23 51
West Brompton ⊖ d	21 26	21 38	21 44	21 51	22 06	22 21		22 36	22 44	22 51	23 07	23 22	23 37	23 54
Kensington (Olympia) ⊖ d	21 29	21 42	21 47	21 54	22 09	22 24		22 39	22 47	22 54	23 10	23 25	23 40	23 57
Shepherd's Bush ⊖ d	21a34	21 44	21 50	21 56	22 11	22 26		22 41	22 50	22 56	23 12	23 27	23 42	23 59
Willesden Jn. High Level ⊖ a		21 51		22 05	22 19	22 34		22 49		23 03	23 21	23 36	23 51	00 06
West Hampstead ⊖ a		22 00			22 29	22 43		22 58		23 12				
Gospel Oak a		22 07			22 36	22 49		23 04		23 18				
Highbury & Islington ⊖ a		22 18			22 49	23 01		23 16		23 34				
Stratford ⊖ a		22 34			23 04	23 18		23 33		23 50				
Wembley Central ⊖ a														
Harrow & Wealdstone ⊖ a			22 16						23 24					
Watford Junction a			22 23						23 32					
Hemel Hempstead a														
Berkhamsted a														
Tring a														
Leighton Buzzard a														
Bletchley a														
Milton Keynes Central 10 a														

Saturdays

26 May to 8 December

	SN 1	SN 1	LO	LO	SN 1	LO	LO	SN 1	LO		LO	LO	LO	SN 1	LO	LO	LO	LO	SN 1		LO	LO	LO	LO
East Croydon d								06 10						07 10					08 10					
Selhurst 4 d								06 16						07 16					08 16					
Thornton Heath d								06 19						07 19					08 19					
Norbury d								06 22						07 22					08 22					
Streatham Common 4 d								06 25						07 25					08 25					
Balham 4 ⊖ d		05 33						06 29						07 29					08 29					
Wandsworth Common d																								
Clapham Junction 10 a		05 37						06 35						07 35					08 35					
d	05 07	05 39	05 50	06 02	06 09	06 17	06 32	06 40	06 47		07 02	07 17	07 32	07 40	07 47	08 02	08 17	08 32	08 40		08 47	09 02	09 17	09 32
Imperial Wharf d	05 12	05 43	05 54	06 06	06 14	06 21	06 36	06 45	06 51		07 06	07 21	07 36	07 45	07 51	08 06	08 21	08 36	08 45		08 51	09 06	09 21	09 36
West Brompton ⊖ d	05 15	05 46	05 57	06 09	06 17	06 24	06 39	06 48	06 54		07 09	07 24	07 39	07 48	07 54	08 09	08 24	08 39	08 48		08 54	09 09	09 24	09 39
Kensington (Olympia) ⊖ d	05 18	05 50	06 00	06 12	06 20	06 27	06 42	06 51	06 57		07 12	07 27	07 42	07 51	07 57	08 12	08 27	08 42	08 51		08 57	09 12	09 27	09 42
Shepherd's Bush ⊖ d	05 21	05 53	06 02	06 14	06 23	06 29	06 44	06 54	06 59		07 14	07 29	07 44	07 54	07 59	08 14	08 29	08 44	08 54		08 59	09 14	09 29	09 44
Willesden Jn. High Level ⊖ a			06 11	06 22		06 37	06 52		07 07		07 22	07 37	07 52		08 07	08 22	08 37	08 52			09 07	09 22	09 37	09 52
West Hampstead ⊖ a				06 31		06 46	07 01		07 16		07 31	07 46	08 01		08 16	08 31	08 46	09 01			09 16	09 31	09 46	10 01
Gospel Oak a				06 37		06 52	07 07		07 22		07 37	07 52	08 07		08 22	08 37	08 52	09 07			09 22	09 37	09 52	10 07
Highbury & Islington ⊖ a				06 49		07 04	07 18		07 34		07 49	08 05	08 19		08 34	08 48	09 04	09 19			09 34	09 50	10 04	10 19
Stratford ⊖ a				07 06		07 21	07 36		07 51		08 06	08 22	08 37		08 52	09 07	09 22	09 37			09 52	10 07	10 22	10 37
Wembley Central ⊖ a		06 07			06 38			07 09						08 09					09 09					
Harrow & Wealdstone ⊖ a	05 40	06 12						07 14						08 14					09 14					
Watford Junction a	05 47	06 19			06 49			07 21						08 21					09 21					
Hemel Hempstead a		06 27						07 29						08 29					09 29					
Berkhamsted a		06 32						07 33						08 33					09 33					
Tring a		06 38						07 39						08 39					09 39					
Leighton Buzzard a		06 46						07 47						08 47					09 49					
Bletchley a		06 54						07 54						08 54					09 56					
Milton Keynes Central 10 a		07 00						08 00						09 00					10 02					

For other Norbury line connections, refer to Table T170

For other Stratford line connecting trains, refer to Table T59

Table T176-F

Saturdays

26 May to 8 December

East Croydon, Balham and Clapham Junction-Imperial Wharf, West Brompton, Kensington Olympia and Shepherd's Bush - Willesden Junction, Stratford/Watford Junction, Milton Keynes

	SN 1		LO	LO	LO	LO	SN 1	LO	LO	LO	LO		SN 1	LO	LO	LO	LO	SN 1	LO	LO	LO		LO	SN 1
East Croydon d	09 10						10 10						11 10					12 10						13 10
Selhurst 4 d	09 16						10 16						11 16					12 16						13 16
Thornton Heath d	09 19						10 19						11 19					12 19						13 19
Norbury d	09 22						10 22						11 22					12 22						13 22
Streatham Common 4 d	09 25						10 25						11 25					12 25						13 25
Balham 4 ⊖ d	09 29						10 29						11 29					12 29						13 29
Wandsworth Common d																								
Clapham Junction 10 a	09 35						10 35						11 35					12 35						13 35
d	09 40		09 47	10 02	10 17	10 32	10 40	10 47	11 02	11 17	11 32		11 40	11 47	12 02	12 17	12 32	12 40	12 47	13 02	13 17		13 32	13 40
Imperial Wharf d	09 45		09 51	10 06	10 21	10 36	10 45	10 51	11 06	11 21	11 36		11 45	11 51	12 06	12 21	12 36	12 45	12 51	13 06	13 21		13 36	13 45
West Brompton ⊖ d	09 48		09 54	10 09	10 24	10 39	10 48	10 54	11 09	11 24	11 39		11 48	11 54	12 09	12 24	12 39	12 48	12 54	13 09	13 24		13 39	13 48
Kensington (Olympia) ⊖ d	09 51		09 57	10 12	10 27	10 42	10 51	10 57	11 12	11 27	11 42		11 51	11 57	12 12	12 27	12 42	12 51	12 57	13 12	13 27		13 42	13 51
Shepherd's Bush ⊖ d	09 54		09 59	10 14	10 29	10 44	10 54	10 59	11 14	11 29	11 44		11 54	11 59	12 14	12 29	12 44	12 54	12 59	13 14	13 29		13 44	13 54
Willesden Jn. High Level ⊖ a			10 07	10 22	10 37	10 52		11 07	11 22	11 36	11 53			12 07	12 22	12 37	12 52		13 06	13 22	13 37		13 51	
West Hampstead ⊖ a			10 16	10 31	10 46	11 01		11 16	11 31	11 45	12 02			12 16	12 31	12 46	13 01		13 15	13 31	13 46		14 01	
Gospel Oak a			10 22	10 37	10 52	11 07		11 23	11 37	11 51	12 08			12 22	12 37	12 52	13 07		13 21	13 37	13 52		14 07	
Highbury & Islington ⊖ a			10 34	10 49	11 04	11 19		11 35	11 49	12 04	12 19			12 34	12 49	13 04	13 19		13 34	13 49	14 02		14 19	
Stratford ⊖ a			10 51	11 06	11 21	11 36		11 51	12 06	12 21	12 36			12 51	13 06	13 21	13 36		13 51	14 06	14 21		14 36	
Wembley Central ⊖ a	10 09						11 09						12 09					13 09						14 09
Harrow & Wealdstone ⊖ a	10 14						11 14						12 14					13 14						14 14
Watford Junction a	10 21						11 21						12 21					13 21						14 21
Hemel Hempstead a	10 29						11 29						12 29					13 29						14 29
Berkhamsted a	10 33						11 33						12 33					13 33						14 33
Tring a	10 39						11 39						12 39					13 39						14 39
Leighton Buzzard a	10 47						11 47						12 47					13 48						14 47
Bletchley a	10 55						11 54						12 55					13 55						14 55
Milton Keynes Central 10 a	11 00						12 00						13 00					14 00						15 00

	LO	LO	LO	LO	SN 1	LO	LO		LO	LO	SN 1	LO	LO	LO	LO	SN 1	LO		LO	LO	LO	SN 1	LO	LO
East Croydon d					14 10						15 10					16 10						17 10		
Selhurst 4 d					14 16						15 16					16 16						17 16		
Thornton Heath d					14 19						15 19					16 19						17 19		
Norbury d					14 22						15 22					16 22						17 22		
Streatham Common 4 d					14 25						15 25					16 25						17 25		
Balham 4 ⊖ d					14 29						15 29					16 29						17 29		
Wandsworth Common d																								
Clapham Junction 10 a					14 35						15 35					16 35						17 35		
d	13 47	14 02	14 17	14 32	14 40	14 47	15 02		15 17	15 32	15 40	15 47	16 02	16 17	16 32	16 40	16 47		17 02	17 17	17 32	17 40	17 47	18 02
Imperial Wharf d	13 51	14 06	14 21	14 36	14 45	14 51	15 06		15 21	15 36	15 45	15 51	16 06	16 21	16 36	16 45	16 51		17 06	17 21	17 36	17 45	17 51	18 06
West Brompton ⊖ d	13 54	14 09	14 24	14 39	14 48	14 54	15 09		15 24	15 39	15 48	15 54	16 09	16 24	16 39	16 48	16 54		17 09	17 24	17 39	17 48	17 54	18 09
Kensington (Olympia) ⊖ d	13 57	14 12	14 27	14 42	14 51	14 57	15 12		15 27	15 42	15 51	15 57	16 12	16 27	16 42	16 51	16 57		17 12	17 27	17 42	17 51	17 57	18 12
Shepherd's Bush ⊖ d	13 59	14 14	14 29	14 44	14 54	14 59	15 14		15 29	15 44	15 54	15 59	16 14	16 29	16 44	16 54	16 59		17 14	17 29	17 44	17 54	17 59	18 14
Willesden Jn. High Level ⊖ a	14 06	14 22	14 37	14 52		15 07	15 22		15 37	15 52		16 07	16 22	16 37	16 52		17 07		17 22	17 37	17 51		18 06	18 22
West Hampstead ⊖ a	14 15	14 31	14 46	15 01		15 16	15 31		15 46	16 01		16 16	16 31	16 46	17 01		17 16		17 31	17 46	18 00		18 15	18 31
Gospel Oak a	14 21	14 37	14 52	15 07		15 22	15 37		15 52	16 07		16 22	16 37	16 52	17 07		17 22		17 37	17 52	18 06		18 21	18 37
Highbury & Islington ⊖ a	14 31	14 49	15 04	15 19		15 34	15 49		16 04	16 19		16 32	16 49	17 02	17 19		17 34		17 49	18 04	18 16		18 31	18 49
Stratford ⊖ a	14 51	15 06	15 21	15 36		15 51	16 06		16 21	16 36		16 51	17 07	17 22	17 37		17 52		18 07	18 22	18 37		18 52	19 07
Wembley Central ⊖ a					15 09						16 09					17 09						18 09		
Harrow & Wealdstone ⊖ a					15 14						16 14					17 14						18 14		
Watford Junction a					15 21						16 21					17 21						18 21		
Hemel Hempstead a					15 29						16 29					17 29						18 29		
Berkhamsted a					15 33						16 33					17 33						18 33		
Tring a					15 39						16 39					17 39						18 39		
Leighton Buzzard a					15 47						16 47					17 47						18 47		
Bletchley a					15 55						16 55					17 55						18 56		
Milton Keynes Central 10 a					16 00						17 01					18 00						19 02		

For other Norbury line connections, refer to Table T170

For other Stratford line connecting trains, refer to Table T59

Please note, Network Rail have stated that further updates to this timetable are possible during the validity period.

Table T176-F

Saturdays
26 May to 8 December

East Croydon, Balham and Clapham Junction-Imperial Wharf, West Brompton, Kensington Olympia and Shepherd's Bush - Willesden Junction, Stratford/Watford Junction, Milton Keynes

Station		LO	LO	SN 1	LO	LO	LO	LO	SN 1	LO
East Croydon	d			18 10					19 10	
Selhurst	d			18 16					19 16	
Thornton Heath	d			18 19					19 19	
Norbury	d			18 22					19 22	
Streatham Common	d			18 25					19 25	
Balham	d			18 29					19 29	
Wandsworth Common	d									
Clapham Junction	a			18 35					19 35	
	d	18 17	18 32	18 40	18 47	19 02	19 17	19 32	19 36	19 47
Imperial Wharf	d	18 21	18 36	18 45	18 51	19 06	19 21	19 36	19 41	19 51
West Brompton	d	18 24	18 39	18 48	18 54	19 09	19 24	19 39	19 44	19 54
Kensington (Olympia)	d	18 27	18 42	18 51	18 57	19 12	19 27	19 42	19 47	19 57
Shepherd's Bush	d	18 29	18 44	18 54	18 59	19 14	19 29	19 44	19 50	19 59
Willesden Jn. High Level	a	18 37	18 52		19 07	19 22	19 37	19 52		20 07
West Hampstead	a	18 46	19 01		19 16	19 31	19 46	20 01		20 16
Gospel Oak	a	18 52	19 07		19 22	19 39	19 52	20 07		20 22
Highbury & Islington	a	19 04	19 19		19 34	19 49	20 04	20 19		20 34
Stratford	a	19 22	19 37		19 51	20 06	20 21	20 36		20 51
Wembley Central	a			19 08						
Harrow & Wealdstone	a			19 13					20 07	
Watford Junction	a			19 20					20 14	
Hemel Hempstead	a									
Berkhamsted	a									
Tring	a									
Leighton Buzzard	a									
Bletchley	a									
Milton Keynes Central	a									

Station		LO	LO	LO	LO	SN 1	LO	LO	LO	SN 1	LO	LO	LO	LO
East Croydon	d					20 10				21 10				
Selhurst	d					20 16				21 16				
Thornton Heath	d					20 19				21 19				
Norbury	d					20 22				21 22				
Streatham Common	d					20 25				21 25				
Balham	d					20 29				21 29				
Wandsworth Common	d													
Clapham Junction	a					20 35				21 35				
	d	20 02	20 17	20 32	20 47	20 51	21 02	21 17	21 32	21 39	21 47	22 02	22 17	22 32
Imperial Wharf	d	20 06	20 21	20 36	20 51	20 56	21 06	21 21	21 36	21 44	21 51	22 06	22 21	22 36
West Brompton	d	20 09	20 24	20 39	20 54	20 59	21 09	21 24	21 39	21 47	21 54	22 09	22 24	22 39
Kensington (Olympia)	d	20 12	20 27	20 42	20 57	21 03	21 12	21 27	21 42	21 50	21 57	22 12	22 27	22 42
Shepherd's Bush	d	20 14	20 29	20 44	20 59	21 06	21 14	21 29	21 44	21 53	21 59	22 14	22 29	22 44
Willesden Jn. High Level	a	20 22	20 37	20 52	21 07		21 22	21 37	21 52		22 07	22 22	22 39	22 52
West Hampstead	a	20 31	20 46	21 01	21 16		21 31	21 46	22 01		22 16	22 31		23 01
Gospel Oak	a	20 37	20 52	21 07	21 22		21 37	21 52	22 07		22 22	22 37		23 07
Highbury & Islington	a	20 49	21 04	21 19	21 34		21 49	22 04	22 19		22 34	22 49		23 19
Stratford	a	21 06	21 21	21 36	21 51		22 06	22 21	22 36		22 51	23 06		23 36
Wembley Central	a					21 20				22 08				
Harrow & Wealdstone	a					21 25				22 13				
Watford Junction	a					21 33				22 26				
Hemel Hempstead	a													
Berkhamsted	a													
Tring	a													
Leighton Buzzard	a													
Bletchley	a													
Milton Keynes Central	a													

Station		SN 1	LO	LO	LO	LO	LO
East Croydon	d	22 10					
Selhurst	d	22 16					
Thornton Heath	d	22 19					
Norbury	d	22 22					
Streatham Common	d	22 25					
Balham	d	22 29					
Wandsworth Common	d						
Clapham Junction	a	22 35					
	d	22 39	22 47	23 02	23 17	23 32	23 47
Imperial Wharf	d	22 44	22 51	23 06	23 21	23 36	23 51
West Brompton	d	22 47	22 54	23 09	23 24	23 39	23 54
Kensington (Olympia)	d	22 50	22 57	23 12	23 27	23 42	23 57
Shepherd's Bush	d	22 53	22 59	23 14	23 29	23 44	23 59
Willesden Jn. High Level	a		23 08	23 21	23 38	23 55	00 09
West Hampstead	a			23 30			
Gospel Oak	a			23 36			
Highbury & Islington	a			23 48			
Stratford	a			00 06			
Wembley Central	a	23 07					
Harrow & Wealdstone	a	23 12					
Watford Junction	a	23 19					
Hemel Hempstead	a						
Berkhamsted	a						
Tring	a						
Leighton Buzzard	a						
Bletchley	a						
Milton Keynes Central	a						

For other Norbury line connections, refer to Table T170

For other Stratford line connecting trains, refer to Table T59

Table T176-F

Sundays
20 May to 2 December

East Croydon, Balham and Clapham Junction-Imperial Wharf, West Brompton, Kensington Olympia and Shepherd's Bush - Willesden Junction, Stratford/Watford Junction, Milton Keynes

Station		SN	SN	SN	LO	LO	LO	SN	LO	LO	LO	LO	LO	SN	LO
East Croydon	d														
Selhurst	d														
Thornton Heath	d														
Norbury	d														
Streatham Common	d														
Balham	d														
Wandsworth Common	d														
Clapham Junction	a														
	d	07 31	08 15	08 20	08 31	08 51	09 01	09 13	09 21	09 31	09 50	10 01	10 13	10 17	10 29
Imperial Wharf	d	07 35	08 19	08 24	08 35	08 55	09 05	09 17	09 25	09 35	09 54	10 05	10 17	10 21	10 33
West Brompton	d	07 38	08 22	08 27	08 38	08 58	09 08	09 20	09 28	09 38	09 57	10 08	10 20	10 24	10 36
Kensington (Olympia)	d	07 42	08 26	08 31	08 41	09 01	09 11	09 24	09 31	09 41	10 00	10 11	10 23	10 28	10 39
Shepherd's Bush	d	07a44	08 29	08a33	08 43	09 03	09 13	09 27	09 33	09 43	10 02	10 13	10 25	10 31	10 41
Willesden Jn. High Level	a				08 52	09 10	09 22		09 41	09 51	10 10	10 21	10 33		10 50
West Hampstead	a					09 19			09 50	10 00	10 19	10 30	10 42		10 59
Gospel Oak	a					09 25			09 57	10 07	10 25	10 36	10 48		11 05
Highbury & Islington	a					09 37			10 06	10 17	10 36	10 48	11 00		11 17
Stratford	a					09 55			10 25	10 35	10 54	11 05	11 17		11 34
Wembley Central	a														
Harrow & Wealdstone	a		08 47					09 45						10 47	
Watford Junction	a		08 55					09 55						10 55	
Hemel Hempstead	a														
Berkhamsted	a														
Tring	a														
Leighton Buzzard	a														
Bletchley	a														
Milton Keynes Central	a														

Station		LO	LO	LO	SN	LO	LO	LO	SN
East Croydon	d								
Selhurst	d								
Thornton Heath	d								
Norbury	d								
Streatham Common	d								
Balham	d								
Wandsworth Common	d								
Clapham Junction	a								
	d	10 44	10 59	11 12	11 16	11 29	11 44	11 59	12 05
Imperial Wharf	d	10 48	11 03	11 16	11 20	11 33	11 48	12 03	12 09
West Brompton	d	10 51	11 06	11 19	11 23	11 36	11 51	12 06	12 12
Kensington (Olympia)	d	10 54	11 09	11 22	11 27	11 39	11 54	12 09	12 16
Shepherd's Bush	d	10 56	11 11	11 24	11 30	11 41	11 56	12 11	12 19
Willesden Jn. High Level	a	11 05	11 20	11 33		11 50	12 05	12 20	
West Hampstead	a	11 14	11 29	11 42		11 59	12 14	12 29	
Gospel Oak	a	11 20	11 35	11 48		12 05	12 20	12 35	
Highbury & Islington	a	11 32	11 47	12 00		12 17	12 32	12 47	
Stratford	a	11 49	12 04	12 17		12 33	12 48	13 03	
Wembley Central	a								
Harrow & Wealdstone	a				11 48				12 35
Watford Junction	a				11 56				12 43
Hemel Hempstead	a								
Berkhamsted	a								
Tring	a								
Leighton Buzzard	a								
Bletchley	a								
Milton Keynes Central	a								

Station		LO	LO	LO	LO	SN	LO	LO	LO	LO	SN
East Croydon	d										
Selhurst	d										
Thornton Heath	d										
Norbury	d										
Streatham Common	d										
Balham	d										
Wandsworth Common	d										
Clapham Junction	a										
	d	12 14	12 29	12 44	12 59	13 05	13 14	13 29	13 43	13 59	14 05
Imperial Wharf	d	12 18	12 33	12 48	13 03	13 09	13 18	13 33	13 47	14 03	14 09
West Brompton	d	12 21	12 36	12 51	13 06	13 12	13 21	13 36	13 50	14 06	14 12
Kensington (Olympia)	d	12 24	12 39	12 54	13 09	13 16	13 24	13 39	13 53	14 09	14 16
Shepherd's Bush	d	12 26	12 41	12 56	13 11	13 19	13 26	13 41	13 55	14 11	14 19
Willesden Jn. High Level	a	12 35	12 50	13 05	13 20		13 35	13 50	14 03	14 20	
West Hampstead	a	12 44	12 59	13 14	13 29		13 44	13 59	14 13	14 29	
Gospel Oak	a	12 50	13 05	13 20	13 35		13 50	14 05	14 19	14 35	
Highbury & Islington	a	13 02	13 17	13 32	13 47		14 02	14 17	14 31	14 47	
Stratford	a	13 18	13 33	13 48	14 03		14 18	14 33	14 47	15 03	
Wembley Central	a										
Harrow & Wealdstone	a					13 35					14 35
Watford Junction	a					13 43					14 43
Hemel Hempstead	a										
Berkhamsted	a										
Tring	a										
Leighton Buzzard	a										
Bletchley	a										
Milton Keynes Central	a										

Station		LO	LO	LO	LO	SN	LO	LO	LO	LO	SN	LO
East Croydon	d											
Selhurst	d											
Thornton Heath	d											
Norbury	d											
Streatham Common	d											
Balham	d											
Wandsworth Common	d											
Clapham Junction	a											
	d	14 14	14 29	14 44	14 59	15 05	15 14	15 29	15 44	15 59	16 05	16 14
Imperial Wharf	d	14 18	14 33	14 49	15 03	15 09	15 18	15 33	15 48	16 03	16 09	16 19
West Brompton	d	14 21	14 36	14 52	15 06	15 12	15 21	15 36	15 51	16 06	16 12	16 22
Kensington (Olympia)	d	14 24	14 39	14 55	15 09	15 16	15 24	15 39	15 54	16 09	16 16	16 25
Shepherd's Bush	d	14 26	14 41	14 58	15 11	15 19	15 26	15 41	15 56	16 11	16 19	16 28
Willesden Jn. High Level	a	14 35	14 50	15 07	15 20		15 35	15 50	16 05	16 20		16 37
West Hampstead	a	14 44	14 59	15 16	15 29		15 44	15 59	16 14	16 29		16 46
Gospel Oak	a	14 50	15 05	15 22	15 35		15 50	16 05	16 20	16 35		16 52
Highbury & Islington	a	15 02	15 17	15 33	15 47		16 02	16 17	16 32	16 47		17 03
Stratford	a	15 18	15 33	15 48	16 03		16 18	16 33	16 48	17 03		17 18
Wembley Central	a											
Harrow & Wealdstone	a					15 35					16 35	
Watford Junction	a					15 43					16 43	
Hemel Hempstead	a											
Berkhamsted	a											
Tring	a											
Leighton Buzzard	a											
Bletchley	a											
Milton Keynes Central	a											

Station		LO	LO	LO	SN	LO	LO	LO	LO	SN	LO	LO	LO
East Croydon	d												
Selhurst	d												
Thornton Heath	d												
Norbury	d												
Streatham Common	d												
Balham	d												
Wandsworth Common	d												
Clapham Junction	a												
	d	16 29	16 44	16 59	17 05	17 14	17 29	17 44	17 59	18 05	18 14	18 29	18 44
Imperial Wharf	d	16 33	16 48	17 03	17 09	17 18	17 33	17 48	18 03	18 09	18 18	18 33	18 48
West Brompton	d	16 36	16 51	17 06	17 12	17 21	17 36	17 51	18 06	18 12	18 21	18 36	18 51
Kensington (Olympia)	d	16 39	16 54	17 09	17 16	17 24	17 39	17 54	18 09	18 16	18 24	18 39	18 54
Shepherd's Bush	d	16 41	16 56	17 11	17 19	17 26	17 41	17 56	18 11	18 19	18 26	18 41	18 56
Willesden Jn. High Level	a	16 50	17 05	17 20		17 35	17 50	18 05	18 20		18 35	18 50	19 05
West Hampstead	a	16 59	17 14	17 29		17 44	17 59	18 14	18 29		18 44	18 59	19 14
Gospel Oak	a	17 05	17 20	17 35		17 50	18 05	18 20	18 35		18 50	19 05	19 20
Highbury & Islington	a	17 17	17 32	17 47		18 02	18 17	18 32	18 47		19 02	19 17	19 32
Stratford	a	17 33	17 48	18 03		18 18	18 33	18 48	19 03		19 18	19 33	19 48
Wembley Central	a												
Harrow & Wealdstone	a				17 35					18 35			
Watford Junction	a				17 43					18 43			
Hemel Hempstead	a												
Berkhamsted	a												
Tring	a												
Leighton Buzzard	a												
Bletchley	a												
Milton Keynes Central	a												

Station		LO	SN	LO	LO	LO	LO	SN	LO	LO	LO
East Croydon	d										
Selhurst	d										
Thornton Heath	d										
Norbury	d										
Streatham Common	d										
Balham	d										
Wandsworth Common	d										
Clapham Junction	a										
	d	18 59	19 05	19 14	19 29	19 44	19 59	20 05	20 14	20 29	20 44
Imperial Wharf	d	19 03	19 09	19 18	19 33	19 48	20 03	20 09	20 18	20 33	20 48
West Brompton	d	19 06	19 12	19 21	19 36	19 51	20 06	20 12	20 21	20 36	20 51
Kensington (Olympia)	d	19 09	19 16	19 24	19 39	19 54	20 09	20 16	20 24	20 39	20 54
Shepherd's Bush	d	19 11	19 19	19 26	19 41	19 56	20 11	20 19	20 26	20 41	20 56
Willesden Jn. High Level	a	19 20		19 35	19 50	20 05	20 20		20 35	20 50	21 05
West Hampstead	a	19 29		19 44	19 59	20 14	20 29			20 59	
Gospel Oak	a	19 35		19 50	20 05	20 20	20 35			21 05	
Highbury & Islington	a	19 47		20 02	20 17	20 32	20 47			21 17	
Stratford	a	20 03		20 18	20 33	20 48	21 03			21 33	
Wembley Central	a										
Harrow & Wealdstone	a		19 35					20 35			
Watford Junction	a		19 43					20 43			
Hemel Hempstead	a										
Berkhamsted	a										
Tring	a										
Leighton Buzzard	a										
Bletchley	a										
Milton Keynes Central	a										

For other Norbury line connections, refer to Table T170

For other Stratford line connecting trains, refer to Table T59

Table T176-F

Sundays
20 May to 2 December

East Croydon, Balham and Clapham Junction-Imperial Wharf, West Brompton, Kensington Olympia and Shepherd's Bush - Willesden Junction, Stratford/Watford Junction, Milton Keynes

		LO	LO	SN	LO	LO	LO	LO	SN	LO	LO	LO	LO	LO	LO
East Croydon	d														
Selhurst	d														
Thornton Heath	d														
Norbury	d														
Streatham Common	d														
Balham ⊖	d														
Wandsworth Common	d														
Clapham Junction	a														
	d	20 59	21 14	21 19	21 29	21 44	22 00	22 15	22 19	22 31	22 46	23 01	23 16	23 31	23 46
Imperial Wharf	d	21 03	21 18	21 23	21 33	21 48	22 04	22 19	22 23	22 35	22 50	23 05	23 20	23 35	23 50
West Brompton ⊖	d	21 06	21 21	21 26	21 36	21 51	22 07	22 22	22 26	22 38	22 53	23 08	23 23	23 38	23 53
Kensington (Olympia) ⊖	d	21 09	21 24	21 30	21 39	21 54	22 10	22 25	22 30	22 41	22 56	23 11	23 26	23 41	23 56
Shepherd's Bush ⊖	d	21 11	21 26	21 33	21 41	21 56	22 12	22 27	22 33	22 43	22 58	23 13	23 28	23 43	23 58
Willesden Jn. High Level ⊖	a	21 20	21 35		21 50	22 05	22 21	22 37		22 52	23 07	23 22	23 37	23 52	00 05
West Hampstead ⊖	a	21 29			21 59		22 30								
Gospel Oak	a	21 37			22 05		22 36								
Highbury & Islington ⊖	a	21 47			22 17		22 48								
Stratford ⊖	a	22 03			22 33		23 04								
Wembley Central ⊖	a														
Harrow & Wealdstone ⊖	a			21 50					22 49						
Watford Junction	a			21 59					22 57						
Hemel Hempstead	a														
Berkhamsted	a														
Tring	a														
Leighton Buzzard	a														
Bletchley	a														
Milton Keynes Central	a														

For other Norbury line connections, refer to Table T170

For other Stratford line connecting trains, refer to Table T59

Table T176-R

Mondays to Fridays
21 May to 7 December

Milton Keynes, Watford Junction/Stratford, Willesden Junction-Shepherd's Bush, Kensington Olympia, West Brompton and Imperial Wharf-Clapham Junction, Balham and East Croydon

Miles	Miles			LO MO	SN MX	LO MO	LO MX	LO	LO	SN	LO	LO	LO	LO	SN	LO	SN	LO	LO	SN	LO	LO	LO
0	—	Milton Keynes Central	d																	07 01			
3	—	Bletchley	d																	07 06			
9½	—	Leighton Buzzard	d																	07 13			
18	—	Tring	d																	07 22			
21¾	—	Berkhamsted	d																	07 26			
25¼	—	Hemel Hempstead	d																	07 30			
32¼	—	Watford Junction	d							05 54					06 53		07 24			07 38			
36¾	—	Harrow & Wealdstone ⊖	d							06 00					07 00		07 31			07 45			
40¼	—	Wembley Central ⊖	d							06 05					07 05		07 36			07 50			
—	0	Stratford ⊖	d									06 07	06 17	06 27		06 53		07 05	07 18		07 29	07 54	08 06
—	4¾	Highbury & Islington ⊖	d									06 21	06 31	06 42		07 09		07 20	07 33		07 44	08 09	08 21
—	7½	Gospel Oak	d									06 31	06 43	06 52		07 20		07 31	07 43		07 55	08 19	08 31
—	9½	West Hampstead ⊖	d									06 37	06 49	06 58		07 26		07 37	07 49		08 01	08 25	08 37
—	12	Willesden Jn. High Level ⊖	d				00 01	05 58	06 10		06 35	06 47	06 59	07 08		07 35		07 47	07 59		08 11	08 35	08 47
44½	13½	**Shepherd's Bush** ⊖	d		00 05	00 05	00 09	06 05	06 16	06 21	06 41	06 53	07 05	07 17	07 22	07 42	07 50	07 54	08 06	08 11	08 17	08 41	08 54
45¾	—	**Kensington (Olympia)** ⊖	d		00 07	00 07	00 11	06 07	06 18	06 24	06 43	06 55	07 07	07 19	07 25	07 44	07 52	07 56	08 08	08 14	08 19	08 43	08 56
47¼	—	**West Brompton** ⊖	d		00 10	00 10	00 14	06 10	06 21	06 27	06 46	06 58	07 10	07 22	07 28	07 46	07 55	07 59	08 10	08 17	08 22	08 46	08 58
48½	—	**Imperial Wharf**	d	00 01	00 12	00 13	00 17	06 13	06 24	06 29	06 49	07 01	07 13	07 25	07 30	07 49	07 57	08 02	08 13	08 19	08 25	08 49	09 01
49½	—	Clapham Junction	a	00 08	00 17	00 20	00 22	06 19	06 31	06 34	06 56	07 09	07 22	07 32	07 35	07 55	08 02	08 07	08 23	08 24	08 31	08 56	09 11
—	—		d							06 35					07 35		08 05			08 35			
50¾	—	Wandsworth Common	a												07 38								
51½	—	Balham ⊖	a							06 40					07 41		08 10			08 40			
53¼	—	Streatham Common	a							06 45					07 46		08 15			08 45			
54¼	—	Norbury	a							06 48					07 49		08 18			08 48			
55½	—	Thornton Heath	a							06 51					07 52		08 21			08 51			
56¼	—	Selhurst	a							06 54					07 54		08 24			08 54			
57¼	—	East Croydon	a							06 59					08 01		08 31			09 01			

		LO	LO	SN	LO	SN	LO	SN	LO	LO	SN	LO	LO	LO	SN	LO	LO	LO	LO	SN TThO	SN MWFO	LO	LO
Milton Keynes Central	d			08 12							09 12				10 12					11 12	11 12		
Bletchley	d			08 17							09 17				10 17					11 17	11 17		
Leighton Buzzard	d			08 24							09 24				10 24					11 24	11 24		
Tring	d			08 34							09 34				10 34					11 34	11 34		
Berkhamsted	d			08 39							09 39				10 39					11 39	11 39		
Hemel Hempstead	d			08 43							09 43				10 43					11 43	11 43		
Watford Junction	d			08 52		09 16					09 52				10 52					11 52	11 52		
Harrow & Wealdstone ⊖	d			08 59		09 23					09 59				10 59					11 59	11 59		
Wembley Central ⊖	d			09 04		09 28					10 04				11 04					12 03	12 03		
Stratford ⊖	d	08 17	08 29		08 53		09 06		09 15	09 28		09 53	10 08	10 23		10 38	10 53	11 08	11 23			11 38	11 53
Highbury & Islington ⊖	d	08 32	08 43		09 07		09 19		09 31	09 44		10 07	10 24	10 37		10 53	11 07	11 22	11 37			11 52	12 07
Gospel Oak	d	08 43	08 53		09 20		09 32		09 41	09 54		10 17	10 35	10 49		11 03	11 19	11 34	11 49			12 02	12 17
West Hampstead ⊖	d	08 49	08 59		09 26		09 38		09 47	10 01		10 23	10 41	10 56		11 09	11 26	11 40	11 55			12 08	12 23
Willesden Jn. High Level ⊖	d	08 59	09 09		09 35		09 47		09 56	10 10		10 33	10 50	11 05		11 19	11 35	11 50	12 05			12 17	12 32
Shepherd's Bush ⊖	d	09 06	09 17	09 22	09 41	09 46	09 56	10 00	10 05	10 17	10 22	10 41	10 56	11 11	11 22	11 26	11 41	11 56	12 11	12 22	12 22	12 27	12 41
Kensington (Olympia) ⊖	d	09 08	09 19	09 25	09 43	09 49	09 58	10 02	10 07	10 19	10 25	10 43	10 58	11 13	11 25	11 29	11 43	11 58	12 13	12 25	12 25	12 29	12 43
West Brompton ⊖	d	09 10	09 22	09 28	09 46	09 52	10 01	10 05	10 10	10 22	10 28	10 46	11 01	11 16	11 28	11 32	11 46	12 01	12 16	12 28	12 28	12 32	12 46
Imperial Wharf	d	09 13	09 25	09 30	09 49	09 54	10 04	10 08	10 13	10 25	10 30	10 49	11 04	11 19	11 30	11 35	11 49	12 04	12 19	12 30	12 30	12 35	12 49
Clapham Junction	a	09 22	09 34	09 35	09 55	09 59	10 11	10 12	10 20	10 33	10 35	10 55	11 10	11 25	11 35	11 40	11 55	12 10	12 25	12 35	12 35	12 40	12 55
	d			09 35							10 35				11 35						12 35		
Wandsworth Common	a																						
Balham ⊖	a			09 40							10 40				11 40						12 40		
Streatham Common	a			09 45							10 45				11 45						12 45		
Norbury	a			09 48							10 48				11 48						12 48		
Thornton Heath	a			09 51							10 51				11 51						12 51		
Selhurst	a			09 54							10 54				11 54						12 54		
East Croydon	a			10 00							10 59				11 59						12 59		

For other Norbury line connections, refer to Table T170

For other Stratford line connecting trains, refer to Table T59

Table T176-R

Mondays to Fridays
21 May to 7 December

Milton Keynes, Watford Junction/Stratford, Willesden Junction-Shepherd's Bush, Kensington Olympia, West Brompton and Imperial Wharf-Clapham Junction, Balham and East Croydon

		LO	LO	SN 1	LO	LO	LO	LO		SN 1	LO	LO	LO	LO	SN 1	LO	LO	SN 1		LO	LO	SN 1	LO	LO	SN 1
Milton Keynes Central 10	d			12 12						13 12					14 12							15 12			
Bletchley	d			12 17						13 17					14 17							15 17			
Leighton Buzzard	d			12 24						13 24					14 24							15 24			
Tring	d			12 34						13 34					14 34							15 34			
Berkhamsted	d			12 39						13 39					14 39							15 39			
Hemel Hempstead	d			12 43						13 43					14 43							15 43			
Watford Junction	d			12 52						13 52					14 52							15 52			16 12
Harrow & Wealdstone ⊖	d			12 59						13 59					14 59							15 59			16 20
Wembley Central ⊖	d			13 04						14 04					15 04							16 04			16 25
Stratford 7 ⊖	d	12 08	12 23		12 38	12 53	13 08	13 23			13 39	13 53	14 07	14 23		14 38	14 53			15 05	15 29		15 42	15 53	
Highbury & Islington ⊖	d	12 22	12 37		12 52	13 07	13 22	13 37			13 55	14 07	14 21	14 37		14 52	15 07			15 19	15 43		15 56	16 07	
Gospel Oak	d	12 34	12 49		13 03	13 19	13 34	13 49			14 05	14 19	14 33	14 50		15 04	15 20			15 31	15 53		16 07	16 17	
West Hampstead ⊖	d	12 40	12 55		13 09	13 25	13 40	13 55			14 11	14 26	14 39	14 56		15 11	15 26			15 38	15 59		16 13	16 23	
Willesden Jn. High Level ⊖	d	12 49	13 05		13 19	13 34	13 50	14 04			14 21	14 35	14 49	15 05		15 21	15 35			15 48	16 08		16 23	16 35	
Shepherd's Bush ⊖	d	12 55	13 11	13 22	13 27	13 41	13 56	14 11		14 22	14 28	14 41	14 56	15 11	15 22	15 27	15 41	15 49		15 54	16 15	16 22	16 29	16 41	16 46
Kensington (Olympia) ⊖	d	12 57	13 13	13 25	13 29	13 43	13 58	14 13		14 25	14 30	14 43	14 58	15 13	15 25	15 30	15 43	15 52		15 56	16 17	16 25	16 31	16 43	16 49
West Brompton ⊖	d	13 00	13 16	13 28	13 32	13 46	14 01	14 16		14 28	14 32	14 46	15 01	15 16	15 28	15 33	15 46	15 55		15 59	16 20	16 28	16 34	16 46	16 52
Imperial Wharf	d	13 03	13 19	13 30	13 35	13 49	14 04	14 19		14 30	14 35	14 49	15 04	15 19	15 30	15 36	15 49	15 57		16 02	16 24	16 30	16 37	16 49	16 55
Clapham Junction 10	a	13 10	13 25	13 35	13 40	13 55	14 10	14 25		14 35	14 41	14 55	15 09	15 28	15 35	15 43	15 55	16 02		16 07	16 31	16 35	16 44	16 58	16 59
	d			13 35						14 35					15 35			16 05				16 35			17 05
Wandsworth Common	a																								
Balham 4 ⊖	a			13 40						14 40					15 40			16 10				16 40			17 10
Streatham Common 4	a			13 45						14 45					15 45			16 15				16 45			17 15
Norbury	a			13 48						14 48					15 48			16 18				16 48			17 18
Thornton Heath	a			13 51						14 51					15 51			16 21				16 51			17 21
Selhurst 4	a			13 54						14 54					15 54			16 24				16 54			17 24
East Croydon	a			13 59						14 59					16 00			16 30				17 00			17 30

		LO	LO	SN 1		LO	LO	SN 1	LO	LO	SN 1	LO	LO	LO		LO	SN 1	LO	LO	LO	LO	LO	SN 1	LO	
Milton Keynes Central 10	d			16 12							17 12						18 12						19 15		
Bletchley	d			16 17							17 17						18 17						19 20		
Leighton Buzzard	d			16 24							17 24						18 24						19 27		
Tring	d			16 34							17 34						18 34						19 36		
Berkhamsted	d			16 39							17 39						18 39						19 41		
Hemel Hempstead	d			16 43							17 43						18 43						19 45		
Watford Junction	d			16 52							17 52						18 51						19 54		
Harrow & Wealdstone ⊖	d			16 59							17 59						18 59						20 02		
Wembley Central ⊖	d			17 04							18 04						19 05						20 06		
Stratford 7 ⊖	d	16 05	16 29			16 41	16 53		17 06	17 31		17 41	17 54	18 06		18 29		18 41	18 53	19 05	19 17	19 29		19 53	
Highbury & Islington ⊖	d	16 19	16 44			16 56	17 08		17 21	17 46		17 56	18 09	18 21		18 44		18 56	19 07	19 19	19 31	19 43		20 07	
Gospel Oak	d	16 30	16 55			17 07	17 19		17 31	17 55		18 07	18 18	18 31		18 55		19 07	19 17	19 30	19 43	19 55		20 19	
West Hampstead ⊖	d	16 36	17 01			17 13	17 25		17 37	18 01		18 13	18 24	18 37		19 01		19 13	19 23	19 36	19 50	20 01		20 26	
Willesden Jn. High Level ⊖	d	16 47	17 11			17 23	17 35		17 47	18 11		18 23	18 33	18 47		19 11		19 23	19 32	19 47	19 59	20 11		20 35	
Shepherd's Bush ⊖	d	16 54	17 17	17 22		17 30	17 42	17 49	17 54	18 17	18 22	18 30	18 41	18 54		19 17	19 22	19 30	19 40	19 53	20 05	20 17	20 22	20 41	
Kensington (Olympia) ⊖	d	16 56	17 19	17 25		17 32	17 44	17 52	17 56	18 19	18 25	18 32	18 43	18 56		19 19	19 25	19 32	19 42	19 55	20 07	20 19	20 25	20 43	
West Brompton ⊖	d	16 59	17 22	17 28		17 34	17 46	17 55	17 58	18 22	18 28	18 34	18 45	18 58		19 22	19 28	19 34	19 45	19 58	20 10	20 22	20 28	20 46	
Imperial Wharf	d	17 02	17 25	17 30		17 37	17 49	17 57	18 01	18 25	18 30	18 37	18 48	19 01		19 25	19 30	19 37	19 49	20 01	20 13	20 25	20 30	20 49	
Clapham Junction 10	a	17 10	17 31	17 35		17 43	17 58	18 02	18 08	18 36	18 35	18 46	18 59	19 11		19 34	19 35	19 46	19 58	20 07	20 19	20 31	20 35	20 55	
	d			17 35				18 05			18 35						19 35						20 35		
Wandsworth Common	a																								
Balham 4 ⊖	a			17 40				18 10			18 40						19 40						20 40		
Streatham Common 4	a			17 45				18 15			18 45						19 45						20 45		
Norbury	a			17 48				18 18			18 48						19 48						20 48		
Thornton Heath	a			17 51				18 21			18 51						19 51						20 51		
Selhurst 4	a			17 54				18 24			18 54						19 54						20 54		
East Croydon	a			18 00				18 31			19 00						19 59						21 00		

For other Norbury line connections, refer to Table T170

For other Stratford line connecting trains, refer to Table T59

Table T176-R

Mondays to Fridays
21 May to 7 December

Milton Keynes, Watford Junction/Stratford, Willesden Junction-Shepherd's Bush, Kensington Olympia, West Brompton and Imperial Wharf-Clapham Junction, Balham and East Croydon

			LO	LO	SN 1	LO	LO	LO	LO	SN 1	LO		LO	LO	SN 1	LO	SN 1	LO	LO	LO	SN 1				
Milton Keynes Central 10	d				20 12					21 12							22 10								
Bletchley	d				20 19					21 17							22 15								
Leighton Buzzard	d				20 26					21 24							22 22								
Tring	d				20 36					21 34							22 34								
Berkhamsted	d				20 40					21 39							22 39								
Hemel Hempstead	d				20 44					21 43							22 43								
Watford Junction	d				20 52					21 51					22 27		22 53				23 36				
Harrow & Wealdstone ⊖	d				20 59					21 59					22 33		23 00				23 42				
Wembley Central ⊖	d				21 04																				
Stratford 7 ⊖	d		20 05	20 20		20 35	20 46	21 07	21 19		21 34		21 49	22 04		22 14		22 36							
Highbury & Islington ⊖	d		20 19	20 35		20 50	21 00	21 21	21 33		21 48		22 03	22 18		22 28		22 50							
Gospel Oak	d		20 30	20 45		21 00	21 12	21 31	21 43		22 00		22 15	22 30		22 40		23 02							
West Hampstead ⊖	d		20 36	20 51		21 06	21 19	21 38	21 51		22 06		22 21	22 36		22 47		23 10							
Willesden Jn. High Level ⊖	d		20 45	21 01		21 16	21 28	21 48	22 01		22 16		22 31	22 46		22 59		23 19	23 30	23 44					
Shepherd's Bush ⊖	d		20 53	21 07	21 19	21 23	21 36	21 55	22 07	22 19	22 23		22 37	22 52	22 57	23 07	23 22	23 26	23 36	23 50	00 05				
Kensington (Olympia) ⊖	d		20 55	21 09	21 21	21 26	21 38	21 57	22 09	22 21	22 25		22 39	22 54	23 00	23 09	23 24	23 28	23 38	23 52	00 07				
West Brompton ⊖	d		20 57	21 12	21 24	21 29	21 41	21 59	22 12	22 24	22 28		22 42	22 57	23 03	23 12	23 27	23 31	23 41	23 55	00 10				
Imperial Wharf	d		21 01	21 15	21 27	21 32	21 45	22 02	22 15	22 27	22 31		22 45	23 00	23 05	23 15	23 29	23 34	23 44	23 58	00 12				
Clapham Junction 10	a		21 07	21 22	21 32	21 37	21 51	22 09	22 21	22 31	22 36		22 51	23 06	23 10	23 21	23 34	23 42	23 51	00 05	00 17				
	d									22 35															
Wandsworth Common	a																								
Balham 4 ⊖	a									22 40															
Streatham Common 4	a									22 45															
Norbury	a									22 48															
Thornton Heath	a									22 51															
Selhurst 4	a									22 54															
East Croydon	a									22 59															

Saturdays
26 May to 8 December

		SN 1	LO	LO	SN 1	LO	LO	LO	LO	SN 1		LO	LO	LO	LO	SN 1	LO	LO	LO	LO		SN 1	LO	LO	LO
Milton Keynes Central 10	d															07 13						08 13			
Bletchley	d															07 18						08 18			
Leighton Buzzard	d															07 25						08 25			
Tring	d															07 34						08 34			
Berkhamsted	d															07 39						08 39			
Hemel Hempstead	d															07 43						08 43			
Watford Junction	d				05 52					06 55						07 52						08 52			
Harrow & Wealdstone ⊖	d				05 58					07 01						07 59						08 59			
Wembley Central ⊖	d				06 03					07 06						08 04						09 04			
Stratford 7 ⊖	d						05 55	06 08	06 23			06 38	06 53	07 08	07 23		07 38	07 53	08 08	08 23			08 38	08 53	09 08
Highbury & Islington ⊖	d						06 09	06 22	06 38			06 53	07 07	07 22	07 37		07 53	08 07	08 22	08 38			08 52	09 07	09 22
Gospel Oak	d						06 21	06 34	06 49			07 04	07 19	07 34	07 49		08 03	08 19	08 34	08 49			09 04	09 19	09 34
West Hampstead ⊖	d						06 27	06 40	06 55			07 10	07 25	07 40	07 55		08 09	08 25	08 40	08 55			09 10	09 25	09 40
Willesden Jn. High Level ⊖	d		00 01	06 05		06 20	06 37	06 50	07 05			07 20	07 35	07 50	08 05		08 20	08 35	08 50	09 05			09 20	09 35	09 50
Shepherd's Bush ⊖	d	00 05	00 09	06 11	06 19	06 26	06 43	06 56	07 11	07 21		07 26	07 41	07 56	08 11	08 19	08 27	08 41	08 56	09 11		09 19	09 26	09 41	09 56
Kensington (Olympia) ⊖	d	00 07	00 11	06 13	06 22	06 28	06 45	06 58	07 13	07 24		07 28	07 43	07 58	08 13	08 22	08 29	08 43	08 58	09 13		09 22	09 28	09 43	09 58
West Brompton ⊖	d	00 10	00 14	06 16	06 25	06 31	06 48	07 01	07 16	07 27		07 31	07 46	08 01	08 16	08 25	08 31	08 46	09 01	09 16		09 25	09 31	09 46	10 01
Imperial Wharf	d	00 12	00 17	06 19	06 28	06 34	06 51	07 04	07 19	07 29		07 34	07 49	08 04	08 19	08 28	08 34	08 49	09 04	09 19		09 28	09 34	09 49	10 04
Clapham Junction 10	a	00 17	00 22	06 26	06 32	06 41	06 57	07 10	07 25	07 34		07 40	07 55	08 10	08 25	08 32	08 40	08 55	09 10	09 25		09 32	09 40	09 55	10 10
	d				06 35					07 35						08 35						09 35			
Wandsworth Common	a																								
Balham 4 ⊖	a				06 40					07 40						08 40						09 40			
Streatham Common 4	a				06 45					07 45						08 45						09 45			
Norbury	a				06 48					07 48						08 48						09 48			
Thornton Heath	a				06 51					07 51						08 51						09 51			
Selhurst 4	a				06 54					07 54						08 54						09 54			
East Croydon	a				06 59					07 59						08 59						09 59			

For other Norbury line connections, refer to Table T170

For other Stratford line connecting trains, refer to Table T59

Table T176-R

Saturdays
26 May to 8 December

Milton Keynes, Watford Junction/Stratford, Willesden Junction-Shepherd's Bush, Kensington Olympia, West Brompton and Imperial Wharf-Clapham Junction, Balham and East Croydon

		LO	SN 1	LO	LO	LO	LO	SN 1	LO	LO	LO	LO	SN 1	LO	LO	LO	LO	SN 1	LO	LO	LO	LO
Milton Keynes Central 10	d		09 12					10 12					11 12					12 12				
Bletchley	d		09 17					10 17					11 17					12 17				
Leighton Buzzard	d		09 24					10 24					11 24					12 24				
Tring	d		09 34					10 34					11 34					12 34				
Berkhamsted	d		09 39					10 39					11 39					12 39				
Hemel Hempstead	d		09 43					10 43					11 43					12 43				
Watford Junction	d		09 52					10 52					11 52					12 52				
Harrow & Wealdstone	⊖ d		09 59					10 59					11 59					12 59				
Wembley Central	⊖ d		10 04					11 04					12 04					13 04				
Stratford 7	⊖ d	09 23		09 38	09 53	10 08	10 23		10 38	10 53	11 08	11 23		11 38	11 53	12 08	12 23		12 38	12 53	13 07	13 23
Highbury & Islington	⊖ d	09 37		09 52	10 08	10 22	10 37		10 53	11 07	11 22	11 37		11 52	12 07	12 23	12 37		12 53	13 07	13 21	13 37
Gospel Oak	d	09 49		10 04	10 21	10 34	10 49		11 04	11 19	11 34	11 49		12 04	12 19	12 35	12 49		13 04	13 19	13 33	13 49
West Hampstead	⊖ d	09 55		10 10	10 27	10 40	10 55		11 10	11 26	11 40	11 55		12 10	12 25	12 41	12 55		13 10	13 25	13 39	13 55
Willesden Jn. High Level	⊖ d	10 04		10 20	10 36	10 50	11 05		11 20	11 35	11 50	12 05		12 20	12 35	12 51	13 05		13 20	13 35	13 49	14 05
Shepherd's Bush	⊖ d	10 11	10 19	10 26	10 42	10 56	11 11	11 19	11 26	11 41	11 56	12 11	12 19	12 26	12 41	12 57	13 11	13 19	13 26	13 41	13 56	14 11
Kensington (Olympia)	⊖ d	10 13	10 22	10 28	10 44	10 58	11 13	11 22	11 28	11 43	11 58	12 13	12 22	12 28	12 43	12 59	13 13	13 22	13 28	13 43	13 58	14 13
West Brompton	⊖ d	10 16	10 25	10 31	10 47	11 01	11 16	11 25	11 31	11 46	12 01	12 16	12 25	12 31	12 46	13 02	13 16	13 25	13 31	13 46	14 01	14 16
Imperial Wharf	d	10 19	10 28	10 34	10 50	11 04	11 19	11 28	11 34	11 49	12 04	12 19	12 28	12 34	12 49	13 05	13 19	13 28	13 34	13 49	14 04	14 19
Clapham Junction 10	a	10 25	10 32	10 40	10 55	11 10	11 25	11 32	11 40	11 55	12 10	12 25	12 32	12 40	12 55	13 13	13 25	13 32	13 40	13 55	14 12	14 25
	d		10 35					11 35					12 35					13 35				
Wandsworth Common	a																					
Balham 4	⊖ a		10 40					11 40					12 40					13 40				
Streatham Common 4	a		10 45					11 45					12 45					13 45				
Norbury	a		10 48					11 48					12 48					13 48				
Thornton Heath	a		10 51					11 51					12 51					13 51				
Selhurst 4	a		10 54					11 54					12 54					13 54				
East Croydon	a		10 59					11 59					12 59					13 59				

		SN 1	LO		LO	SN 1	LO		LO	SN 1	LO		LO	SN 1	LO	LO	LO	LO	SN 1	LO
Milton Keynes Central 10	d	13 12				14 12				15 12				16 12					17 12	
Bletchley	d	13 17				14 17				15 17				16 17					17 17	
Leighton Buzzard	d	13 24				14 24				15 24				16 24					17 24	
Tring	d	13 34				14 34				15 34				16 34					17 34	
Berkhamsted	d	13 39				14 39				15 39				16 39					17 39	
Hemel Hempstead	d	13 43				14 43				15 43				16 43					17 43	
Watford Junction	d	13 52				14 52				15 52				16 52					17 52	
Harrow & Wealdstone	⊖ d	13 59				14 59				15 59				16 59					17 59	
Wembley Central	⊖ d	14 04				15 04				16 04				17 04					18 04	
Stratford 7	⊖ d		13 38	and every 15 minutes until	14 23		14 38	and every 15 minutes until	15 23		15 38	and every 15 minutes until	16 23		16 38	16 53	17 08	17 23		17 38
Highbury & Islington	⊖ d		13 52		14 37		14 52		15 37		15 52		16 37		16 52	17 07	17 22	17 37		17 52
Gospel Oak	d		14 04		14 49		15 04		15 49		16 04		16 49		17 04	17 19	17 34	17 49		18 04
West Hampstead	⊖ d		14 10		14 55		15 10		15 55		16 10		16 55		17 10	17 25	17 40	17 55		18 10
Willesden Jn. High Level	⊖ d		14 20		15 05		15 20		16 05		16 20		17 05		17 20	17 35	17 50	18 05		18 20
Shepherd's Bush	⊖ d	14 19	14 26		15 11	15 19	15 26		16 11	16 19	16 26		17 11	17 19	17 26	17 41	17 56	18 11	18 19	18 26
Kensington (Olympia)	⊖ d	14 22	14 28		15 13	15 22	15 28		16 13	16 22	16 28		17 13	17 22	17 28	17 43	17 58	18 13	18 22	18 28
West Brompton	⊖ d	14 25	14 31		15 16	15 25	15 31		16 16	16 25	16 31		17 16	17 25	17 31	17 46	18 01	18 16	18 25	18 31
Imperial Wharf	d	14 28	14 34		15 19	15 28	15 34		16 19	16 28	16 34		17 19	17 28	17 34	17 49	18 04	18 19	18 28	18 34
Clapham Junction 10	a	14 32	14 40		15 25	15 32	15 40		16 25	16 32	16 40		17 25	17 32	17 40	17 55	18 13	18 28	18 32	18 43
	d	14 35				15 35				16 35				17 35					18 35	
Wandsworth Common	a																			
Balham 4	⊖ a	14 40				15 40				16 40				17 40					18 40	
Streatham Common 4	a	14 45				15 45				16 45				17 45					18 45	
Norbury	a	14 48				15 48				16 48				17 48					18 48	
Thornton Heath	a	14 51				15 51				16 51				17 51					18 51	
Selhurst 4	a	14 54				15 54				16 54				17 54					18 54	
East Croydon	a	14 59				15 59				16 59				17 59					18 59	

For other Norbury line connections, refer to Table T170

For other Stratford line connecting trains, refer to Table T59

Table T176-R

Saturdays
26 May to 8 December

Milton Keynes, Watford Junction/Stratford, Willesden Junction-Shepherd's Bush, Kensington Olympia, West Brompton and Imperial Wharf-Clapham Junction, Balham and East Croydon

		LO	LO	LO	SN 1	LO	LO	LO	SN 1	LO	SN 1	LO		LO	SN 1	LO	LO	LO	LO	SN 1	LO	LO
Milton Keynes Central 10	d				18 12						19 13											
Bletchley	d				18 17						19 18											
Leighton Buzzard	d				18 24						19 25											
Tring	d				18 34						19 34											
Berkhamsted	d				18 39						19 39											
Hemel Hempstead	d				18 43						19 43											
Watford Junction	d				18 51				19 31		19 51				20 43					21 44		
Harrow & Wealdstone	⊖ d				18 59				19 37		19 59				20 49					21 50		
Wembley Central	⊖ d				19 03				19 42		20 04				20 54					21 55		
Stratford 7	⊖ d	17 53	18 08	18 23		18 38	18 53	19 08		19 23		19 38	and every 15 minutes until	20 23		20 38	20 53	21 08	21 23		21 38	21 53
Highbury & Islington	⊖ d	18 07	18 22	18 37		18 52	19 07	19 22		19 37		19 52		20 37		20 52	21 07	21 22	21 37		21 52	22 07
Gospel Oak	d	18 19	18 34	18 49		19 04	19 19	19 32		19 49		20 04		20 49		21 04	21 18	21 34	21 49		22 04	22 19
West Hampstead	⊖ d	18 25	18 40	18 55		19 10	19 25	19 38		19 55		20 10		20 55		21 10	21 24	21 40	21 55		22 10	22 25
Willesden Jn. High Level	⊖ d	18 35	18 50	19 05		19 20	19 35	19 50		20 05		20 20		21 05		21 20	21 35	21 50	22 05		22 20	22 35
Shepherd's Bush	⊖ d	18 41	18 56	19 11	19 19	19 26	19 41	19 56	20 01	20 11	20 20	20 26		21 11	21 16	21 26	21 41	21 57	22 11	22 15	22 26	22 41
Kensington (Olympia)	⊖ d	18 43	18 58	19 13	19 22	19 28	19 43	19 58	20 03	20 13	20 22	20 28		21 13	21 18	21 28	21 43	21 59	22 13	22 23	22 28	22 43
West Brompton	⊖ d	18 46	19 01	19 16	19 25	19 31	19 46	20 01	20 06	20 16	20 25	20 31		21 16	21 21	21 31	21 46	22 01	22 16	22 26	22 31	22 46
Imperial Wharf	d	18 49	19 04	19 19	19 28	19 34	19 49	20 04	20 09	20 19	20 28	20 34		21 19	21 24	21 34	21 49	22 04	22 19	22 29	22 34	22 49
Clapham Junction 10	a	18 58	19 10	19 25	19 32	19 40	19 55	20 10	20 13	20 25	20 33	20 40		21 25	21 28	21 40	21 55	22 10	22 25	22 33	22 40	22 55
	d				19 35						20 35				21 35					22 35		
Wandsworth Common	a																					
Balham 4	⊖ a				19 40						20 40				21 40					22 40		
Streatham Common 4	a				19 45						20 45				21 45					22 45		
Norbury	a				19 48						20 48				21 48					22 48		
Thornton Heath	a				19 51						20 51				21 51					22 51		
Selhurst 4	a				19 54						20 54				21 54					22 54		
East Croydon	a				19 59						20 59				21 59					22 59		

		LO	LO	SN 1	LO	LO	SN 1	LO
Milton Keynes Central 10	d							
Bletchley	d							
Leighton Buzzard	d							
Tring	d							
Berkhamsted	d							
Hemel Hempstead	d							
Watford Junction	d			22 53			23 26	
Harrow & Wealdstone	⊖ d			22 59			23 32	
Wembley Central	⊖ d			23 04			23 37	
Stratford 7	⊖ d	22 08			22 38			23 08
Highbury & Islington	⊖ d	22 22			22 52			23 22
Gospel Oak	d	22 34			23 04			23 34
West Hampstead	⊖ d	22 40			23 11			23 40
Willesden Jn. High Level	⊖ d	22 50	23 05		23 20	23 35		23 50
Shepherd's Bush	⊖ d	22 56	23 11	23 22	23 26	23 41	23 52	23 56
Kensington (Olympia)	⊖ d	22 58	23 13	23 24	23 28	23 43	23 54	23 58
West Brompton	⊖ d	23 01	23 16	23 27	23 31	23 46	23 57	00 02
Imperial Wharf	d	23 04	23 19	23 29	23 34	23 49	00 01	00 05
Clapham Junction 10	a	23 10	23 26	23 34	23 40	23 56	00 06	00 10
	d							
Wandsworth Common	a							
Balham 4	⊖ a							
Streatham Common 4	a							
Norbury	a							
Thornton Heath	a							
Selhurst 4	a							
East Croydon	a							

For other Norbury line connections, refer to Table T170

For other Stratford line connecting trains, refer to Table T59

Please note, Network Rail have stated that further updates to this timetable are possible during the validity period.

Milton Keynes, Watford Junction/Stratford, Willesden Junction-Shepherd's Bush, Kensington Olympia, West Brompton and Imperial Wharf-Clapham Junction, Balham and East Croydon

		SN	LO	LO	SN	LO	SN	LO	LO	LO	LO	SN	LO	LO	LO	LO	SN	LO		LO	SN
		A	A																		
Milton Keynes Central	d																				
Bletchley	d																				
Leighton Buzzard	d																				
Tring	d																				
Berkhamsted	d																				
Hemel Hempstead	d																				
Watford Junction	d											09 17					10 17				11 22
Harrow & Wealdstone ⊖	d											09 23					10 23				11 28
Wembley Central ⊖	d																				
Stratford ⊖	d												09 05		09 35	09 50		10 05	and every 15 minutes until	10 50	
Highbury & Islington ⊖	d												09 19		09 49	10 04		10 19		11 04	
Gospel Oak	d												09 31		10 01	10 16		10 31		11 16	
West Hampstead ⊖	d												09 37		10 07	10 22		10 37		11 22	
Willesden Jn. High Level ⊖	d			00 05		08 35		08 47	09 05	09 20	09 32		09 48	10 02	10 17	10 32		10 47		11 32	
Shepherd's Bush ⊖	d			00 11	07 57	08 41	08 47	08 53	09 11	09 26	09 38	09 44	09 54	10 08	10 23	10 38	10 44	10 53		11 38	11 47
Kensington (Olympia) ⊖	d			00 13	08 00	08 43	08 50	08 55	09 13	09 28	09 40	09 47	09 56	10 10	10 25	10 40	10 47	10 55		11 40	11 50
West Brompton ⊖	d		00 02	00 16	08 02	08 46	08 53	08 58	09 16	09 31	09 43	09 50	09 59	10 13	10 28	10 43	10 50	10 58		11 43	11 53
Imperial Wharf	d	00 01	00 05	00 19	08 05	08 49	08 55	09 01	09 19	09 34	09 46	09 52	10 02	10 16	10 31	10 46	10 52	11 01		11 46	11 55
Clapham Junction	a	00 06	00 10	00 26	08 09	08 56	09 00	09 08	09 26	09 41	09 53	09 57	10 08	10 24	10 37	10 52	10 57	11 07		11 52	12 00
	d																				
Wandsworth Common	a																				
Balham ⊖	a																				
Streatham Common	a																				
Norbury	a																				
Thornton Heath	a																				
Selhurst	a																				
East Croydon	a																				

		LO	LO	LO	LO	SN		LO	LO	LO	LO	SN	LO		LO	SN	LO	LO	LO	LO
Milton Keynes Central	d																			
Bletchley	d																			
Leighton Buzzard	d																			
Tring	d																			
Berkhamsted	d																			
Hemel Hempstead	d																			
Watford Junction	d					12 23						16 23				17 23				
Harrow & Wealdstone ⊖	d					12 29						16 29				17 29				
Wembley Central ⊖	d																			
Stratford ⊖	d	11 05	11 20	11 35	11 50		and at the same minutes past each hour until	15 05	15 20	15 35	15 50		16 05	and every 15 minutes until	16 50		17 05	17 20	17 35	17 50
Highbury & Islington ⊖	d	11 19	11 34	11 49	12 04			15 19	15 34	15 49	16 04		16 19		17 04		17 19	17 34	17 49	18 04
Gospel Oak	d	11 31	11 46	12 01	12 16			15 31	15 46	16 01	16 16		16 31		17 16		17 31	17 46	18 01	18 16
West Hampstead ⊖	d	11 37	11 52	12 07	12 22			15 37	15 52	16 07	16 22		16 37		17 22		17 37	17 52	18 07	18 22
Willesden Jn. High Level ⊖	d	11 47	12 02	12 17	12 32			15 47	16 02	16 17	16 32		16 47		17 32		17 47	18 02	18 17	18 32
Shepherd's Bush ⊖	d	11 53	12 08	12 23	12 38	12 48		15 53	16 08	16 23	16 38	16 48	16 53		17 38	17 48	17 53	18 08	18 23	18 38
Kensington (Olympia) ⊖	d	11 55	12 10	12 25	12 40	12 50		15 55	16 10	16 25	16 40	16 50	16 55		17 40	17 50	17 55	18 10	18 25	18 40
West Brompton ⊖	d	11 58	12 13	12 28	12 43	12 53		15 58	16 13	16 28	16 43	16 53	16 58		17 43	17 53	17 58	18 13	18 28	18 43
Imperial Wharf	d	12 01	12 16	12 31	12 46	12 56		16 01	16 16	16 31	16 46	16 56	17 01		17 46	17 56	18 01	18 16	18 31	18 46
Clapham Junction	a	12 07	12 22	12 37	12 52	13 00		16 07	16 22	16 37	16 52	17 00	17 10		17 55	18 00	18 10	18 22	18 37	18 52
	d																			
Wandsworth Common	a																			
Balham ⊖	a																			
Streatham Common	a																			
Norbury	a																			
Thornton Heath	a																			
Selhurst	a																			
East Croydon	a																			

A not 20 May

For other Norbury line connections, refer to Table T170

For other Stratford line connecting trains, refer to Table T59

Milton Keynes, Watford Junction/Stratford, Willesden Junction-Shepherd's Bush, Kensington Olympia, West Brompton and Imperial Wharf-Clapham Junction, Balham and East Croydon

		SN	LO		LO	SN	LO	LO	LO	LO	SN	LO		LO	SN	LO	LO	LO	LO	SN	LO
Milton Keynes Central	d																				
Bletchley	d																				
Leighton Buzzard	d																				
Tring	d																				
Berkhamsted	d																				
Hemel Hempstead	d																				
Watford Junction	d	18 23				19 23					20 23				21 17					22 18	
Harrow & Wealdstone ⊖	d	18 29				19 29					20 29				21 24					22 24	
Wembley Central ⊖	d																				
Stratford ⊖	d		18 05	and every 15 minutes until	18 50		19 05	19 20	19 35	19 50		20 05	and every 15 minutes until	20 50		21 05		21 35			22 05
Highbury & Islington ⊖	d		18 19		19 04		19 19	19 34	19 49	20 04		20 19		21 04		21 19		21 49			22 19
Gospel Oak	d		18 31		19 16		19 31	19 45	20 01	20 16		20 31		21 16		21 30		22 01			22 31
West Hampstead ⊖	d		18 37		19 22		19 37	19 51	20 07	20 22		20 37		21 22		21 36		22 07			22 37
Willesden Jn. High Level ⊖	d		18 47		19 32		19 47	20 01	20 17	20 32		20 47		21 32		21 46	22 02	22 17	22 32		22 47
Shepherd's Bush ⊖	d	18 48	18 53		19 38	19 48	19 53	20 08	20 23	20 38	20 48	20 53		21 38	21 43	21 53	22 08	22 23	22 38	22 45	22 53
Kensington (Olympia) ⊖	d	18 50	18 55		19 40	19 50	19 55	20 10	20 25	20 40	20 50	20 55		21 40	21 45	21 55	22 10	22 25	22 40	22 47	22 55
West Brompton ⊖	d	18 53	18 58		19 43	19 53	19 58	20 13	20 28	20 43	20 53	20 58		21 43	21 47	21 58	22 13	22 28	22 43	22 50	22 58
Imperial Wharf	d	18 56	19 01		19 46	19 56	20 01	20 16	20 31	20 46	20 56	21 01		21 46	21 50	22 01	22 16	22 31	22 46	22 53	23 01
Clapham Junction	a	19 00	19 07		19 52	20 00	20 07	20 22	20 37	20 52	21 00	21 07		21 52	21 54	22 07	22 23	22 37	22 53	22 57	23 07
	d																				
Wandsworth Common	a																				
Balham ⊖	a																				
Streatham Common	a																				
Norbury	a																				
Thornton Heath	a																				
Selhurst	a																				
East Croydon	a																				

		LO	LO	LO	SN	LO	LO
Milton Keynes Central	d						
Bletchley	d						
Leighton Buzzard	d						
Tring	d						
Berkhamsted	d						
Hemel Hempstead	d						
Watford Junction	d				23 17		
Harrow & Wealdstone ⊖	d				23 23		
Wembley Central ⊖	d						
Stratford ⊖	d						
Highbury & Islington ⊖	d						
Gospel Oak	d						
West Hampstead ⊖	d						
Willesden Jn. High Level ⊖	d	23 02	23 17	23 32		23 47	23 59
Shepherd's Bush ⊖	d	23 08	23 23	23 38	23 45	23 53	00 05
Kensington (Olympia) ⊖	d	23 10	23 25	23 40	23 47	23 55	00 07
West Brompton ⊖	d	23 13	23 28	23 43	23 50	23 58	00 10
Imperial Wharf	d	23 16	23 31	23 46	23 53	00 01	00 13
Clapham Junction	a	23 23	23 38	23 53	23 57	00 08	00 20
	d						
Wandsworth Common	a						
Balham ⊖	a						
Streatham Common	a						
Norbury	a						
Thornton Heath	a						
Selhurst	a						
East Croydon	a						

For other Norbury line connections, refer to Table T170

For other Stratford line connecting trains, refer to Table T59

Table T177-F

London Bridge-New Cross Gate,Brockley, Honor Oak Park, Forest Hill, Sydenham, Crystal Palace, Penge West, Anerley-Norwood Junction and Croydon

Miles	Miles	Miles	Miles			LO MX A	SN MX B	LO MO A	LO MX A	SN MO C	LO MX A	SN MX D	LO MX A	SN MX	SN MX	SN E	LO	LO	LO	LO	LO	SN F	LO
0	—	—	0	London Bridge ■ ⊖	d									00 10	00 35	05 34						06 10	
—	—	0	—	Highbury & Islington	d														05 32	05 40	05 47		05 55
—	—	0½	—	Canonbury	d														05 34	05 42	05 49		05 57
—	0	1½	—	Dalston Junction	d														05 37	05 45	05 52		06 00
—	0½	2	—	Haggerston	d														05 39	05 47	05 54		06 02
—	1	2½	—	Hoxton	d														05 41	05 49	05 56		06 04
—	1¾	3¼	—	Shoreditch High Street	d														05 43	05 52	05 58		06 07
—	2¼	3¾	—	Whitechapel	d														05 46	05 54	06 01		06 09
—	3	4½	—	Shadwell	d														05 48	05 56	06 03		06 11
—	3½	5	—	Wapping	d														05 50	05 58	06 05		06 13
—	4	5½	—	Rotherhithe	d														05 51	06 00	06 06		06 15
—	4¼	5¾	—	Canada Water	d								00 02						05 53	06 02	06 08		06 17
—	4½	6	—	Surrey Quays	d								00 04						05 55	06 04	06 10		06 19
2¾	5¾	7¼	2¾	New Cross Gate ■	d						00 01	00 04	00 08	00 16	00 41	05 40	05 45	05 53	06 00	06 08	06 15	06 18	06 23
3¾	6½	8	3¾	**Brockley**	d						00 03	00 07	00 11	00 19	00 44	05 43	05 47	05 55	06 02	06 11	06 17	06 20	06 26
4¾	7½	9	4¾	**Honor Oak Park**	d					00 02	00 06	00 09	00 13	00 21	00 46	05 45	05 50	05 58	06 05	06 13	06 20	06 23	06 28
5½	8½	10	5½	**Forest Hill ■**	d				00 01	00 04	00 08	00 12	00 16	00 24	00 49	05 48	05 52	06 00	06 07	06 16	06 22	06 25	06 31
6¼	9¼	10¼	6¼	**Sydenham**	d			00 01	00 04	00 08	00 11	00 15	00 19	00 27	00 52	05 51	05 56	06 04	06 11	06 19	06 26	06 29	06 34
—	—	12	7½	**Crystal Palace ■**	a				00 09			00 20	00 24					06 11		06 24			06 39
7	10	—	—	**Penge West**	d		00 01	00 03		00 10	00 13			00 29	00 54	05 53	05 58		06 13		06 28	06 31	
7½	10½	—	—	**Anerley**	d	00 01	00 03	00 05		00 12	00 15			00 31	00 56	05 55	06 00		06 15		06 30	06 33	
8¾	11½	—	—	Norwood Junction ■	a	00 03	00 06	00 08		00 15	00 18			00 34	00 59	05 58	06 03		06 18		06 33	06 36	
—	—	—	—	Norwood Junction	d	00 03		00 08			00 19						06 03		06 19		06 33	06 36	
—	13¼	—	—	West Croydon ■	a	00 10		00 16			00 31						06 09		06 28		06 39	06 42	
—	—	—	—	Norwood Junction	d		00 06			00 16				00 35	01 08	05 58							
10¼	—	—	—	East Croydon	a		00 10			00 19				00 38	01 13	06 02							
13¼	—	—	—	Purley	a					00 28						06 11							

		LO	SN G	LO	LO	SN F	LO	LO	SN G	LO	LO	SN F	LO	LO	SN G	LO	LO	SN F	LO	LO	SN G	LO	LO
London Bridge ■ ⊖	d		06 28			06 40			06 58			07 10			07 28			07 40			07 58		
Highbury & Islington	d	06 02		06 10	06 17		06 25	06 32		06 40	06 47		06 55	07 02		07 10	07 17		07 25	07 32		07 40	07 47
Canonbury	d	06 04		06 12	06 19		06 27	06 34		06 42	06 49		06 57	07 04		07 12	07 19		07 27	07 34		07 42	07 49
Dalston Junction	d	06 07		06 15	06 22		06 30	06 37		06 45	06 52		07 00	07 07		07 15	07 22		07 30	07 37		07 45	07 52
Haggerston	d	06 09		06 17	06 24		06 32	06 39		06 47	06 54		07 02	07 09		07 17	07 24		07 32	07 39		07 47	07 54
Hoxton	d	06 11		06 19	06 26		06 34	06 41		06 49	06 56		07 04	07 11		07 19	07 26		07 34	07 41		07 49	07 56
Shoreditch High Street	d	06 13		06 22	06 28		06 37	06 43		06 52	06 58		07 07	07 13		07 22	07 28		07 37	07 43		07 52	07 58
Whitechapel	d	06 16		06 24	06 31		06 39	06 46		06 54	07 01		07 09	07 16		07 24	07 31		07 39	07 46		07 54	08 01
Shadwell	d	06 18		06 26	06 33		06 41	06 48		06 56	07 03		07 11	07 18		07 26	07 33		07 41	07 48		07 56	08 03
Wapping	d	06 20		06 28	06 35		06 43	06 50		06 58	07 05		07 13	07 20		07 28	07 35		07 43	07 50		07 58	08 05
Rotherhithe	d	06 21		06 30	06 36		06 45	06 51		07 00	07 06		07 15	07 21		07 30	07 36		07 45	07 51		08 00	08 06
Canada Water	d	06 23		06 32	06 38		06 47	06 53		07 02	07 08		07 17	07 23		07 32	07 38		07 47	07 53		08 02	08 08
Surrey Quays	d	06 25		06 34	06 40		06 49	06 55		07 04	07 10		07 19	07 25		07 34	07 40		07 49	07 55		08 04	08 10
New Cross Gate ■	d	06 30	06 34	06 38	06 45	06 48	06 53	07 00	07 04	07 08	07 15	07 18	07 23	07 30	07 34	07 38	07 45	07 48	07 53	08 00	08 04	08 08	08 15
Brockley	d	06 32	06 37	06 41	06 47	06 50	06 56	07 02	07 07	07 11	07 17	07 20	07 26	07 32	07 37	07 41	07 47	07 50	07 56	08 02	08 07	08 11	08 17
Honor Oak Park	d	06 35	06 39	06 43	06 50	06 53	06 58	07 05	07 09	07 13	07 20	07 23	07 28	07 35	07 39	07 43	07 50	07 53	07 58	08 05	08 09	08 13	08 20
Forest Hill ■	d	06 37	06 42	06 46	06 52	06 55	07 01	07 07	07 12	07 16	07 22	07 25	07 31	07 37	07 42	07 46	07 52	07 55	08 01	08 07	08 12	08 16	08 22
Sydenham	d	06 41	06 45	06 49	06 56	06 59	07 04	07 11	07 15	07 19	07 26	07 29	07 34	07 41	07 45	07 49	07 56	07 59	08 04	08 11	08 15	08 19	08 26
Crystal Palace ■	a		06 50	06 54			07 09		07 20	07 24			07 39		07 50	07 54			08 09		08 20	08 24	
Penge West	d	06 43			06 58	07 01		07 13			07 28	07 31		07 43			07 58	08 01		08 13			08 28
Anerley	d	06 45			07 00	07 03		07 15			07 30	07 33		07 45			08 00	08 03		08 15			08 30
Norwood Junction ■	a	06 48			07 03	07 06		07 18			07 33	07 36		07 48			08 03	08 06		08 18			08 33
Norwood Junction	d	06 49			07 03	07 06		07 19			07 33	07 36		07 49			08 03	08 06		08 19			08 33
West Croydon ■	a	06 58			07 09	07 12		07 28			07 39	07 42		07 58			08 09	08 12		08 29			08 39
Norwood Junction	d																						
East Croydon	a																						
Purley	a																						

A From Highbury and Islington Ell
B From London Bridge
C From London Bridge to Caterham
D From London Bridge to Streatham Hill
E To Caterham
F To Sutton (Surrey)
G To London Victoria

For full service between Highbury & Islington and Surrey Quays, refer to Table T178

For Sutton connections at West Croydon, refer to Table T172

Table T177-F

London Bridge-New Cross Gate,Brockley, Honor Oak Park, Forest Hill, Sydenham, Crystal Palace, Penge West, Anerley-Norwood Junction and Croydon

		SN A	LO	LO	SN B	LO	LO	LO	LO	SN B	LO	LO	SN A	LO	LO	SN B	LO	LO	SN C	LO	LO	SN B
London Bridge ■ ⊖	d	08 10			08 28					08 58			09 10			09 28			09 40			09 58
Highbury & Islington	d		07 55	08 02		08 10	08 17	08 25	08 32		08 40	08 47		08 55	09 02		09 10	09 17		09 25	09 32	
Canonbury	d		07 57	08 04		08 12	08 19	08 27	08 34		08 42	08 49		08 57	09 04		09 12	09 19		09 27	09 34	
Dalston Junction	d		08 00	08 07		08 15	08 22	08 30	08 37		08 46	08 52		09 00	09 08		09 16	09 22		09 30	09 37	
Haggerston	d		08 02	08 09		08 17	08 24	08 32	08 39		08 48	08 54		09 02	09 10		09 18	09 24		09 32	09 39	
Hoxton	d		08 04	08 11		08 19	08 26	08 34	08 41		08 50	08 56		09 04	09 12		09 20	09 26		09 34	09 41	
Shoreditch High Street	d		08 07	08 13		08 22	08 28	08 37	08 43		08 52	08 58		09 07	09 14		09 22	09 28		09 37	09 43	
Whitechapel	d		08 09	08 16		08 24	08 31	08 39	08 46		08 55	09 01		09 09	09 17		09 25	09 31		09 39	09 46	
Shadwell	d		08 11	08 18		08 26	08 33	08 41	08 48		08 57	09 03		09 11	09 19		09 27	09 33		09 41	09 48	
Wapping	d		08 13	08 20		08 28	08 35	08 43	08 50		08 59	09 05		09 13	09 21		09 29	09 35		09 43	09 50	
Rotherhithe	d		08 15	08 21		08 30	08 36	08 45	08 51		09 00	09 06		09 15	09 22		09 30	09 36		09 45	09 51	
Canada Water	d		08 17	08 23		08 32	08 38	08 47	08 53		09 02	09 08		09 17	09 24		09 32	09 38		09 47	09 53	
Surrey Quays	d		08 19	08 25		08 34	08 40	08 49	08 55		09 04	09 10		09 19	09 26		09 34	09 40		09 49	09 55	
New Cross Gate ■	d	08 18	08 23	08 30	08 34	08 38	08 45	08 53	09 00	09 04	09 09	09 15	09 18	09 23	09 31	09 34	09 39	09 45	09 48	09 53	10 00	10 04
Brockley	d	08 20	08 26	08 32	08 37	08 41	08 47	08 56	09 02	09 07	09 11	09 17	09 20	09 26	09 33	09 37	09 41	09 47	09 50	09 56	10 02	10 07
Honor Oak Park	d	08 23	08 28	08 35	08 39	08 43	08 50	08 58	09 05	09 09	09 14	09 20	09 23	09 28	09 36	09 39	09 44	09 50	09 53	09 58	10 05	10 09
Forest Hill ■	d	08 25	08 31	08 37	08 42	08 46	08 52	09 01	09 07	09 12	09 16	09 22	09 25	09 31	09 38	09 42	09 46	09 52	09 55	10 01	10 07	10 12
Sydenham	d	08 29	08 34	08 41	08 45	08 49	08 56	09 04	09 11	09 15	09 20	09 26	09 29	09 34	09 42	09 45	09 50	09 56	09 59	10 04	10 11	10 15
Crystal Palace ■	a		08 39		08 50	08 54		09 09		09 20	09 24			09 39		09 50	09 54			10 09		10 20
Penge West	d	08 31		08 43			08 58		09 13			09 28	09 31		09 44			09 58	10 01		10 13	
Anerley	d	08 33		08 45			09 00		09 15			09 30	09 33		09 46			10 00	10 03		10 15	
Norwood Junction ■	a	08 36		08 48			09 03		09 18			09 33	09 36		09 49			10 03	10 06		10 18	
Norwood Junction	d			08 49			09 03		09 19			09 33			09 49			10 03			10 19	
West Croydon ■	a			08 58			09 09		09 28			09 43			09 58			10 13			10 28	
Norwood Junction	d	08 39											09 39						10 09			
East Croydon	a	08 42											09 42						10 13			
Purley	a	08 50											09 54						10 24			

		LO	LO	SN C	LO	LO	SN B	LO	LO	SN C	LO	LO	SN B	LO	LO	SN C	LO	LO	SN B	LO	LO	SN C	LO
London Bridge ■ ⊖	d			10 10			10 28			10 40			10 58			11 10			11 28			11 40	
Highbury & Islington	d	09 40	09 47		09 55	10 02		10 10	10 17		10 25	10 32		10 40	10 47		10 55	11 02		11 10	11 17		11 25
Canonbury	d	09 42	09 49		09 57	10 04		10 12	10 19		10 27	10 34		10 42	10 49		10 57	11 04		11 12	11 19		11 27
Dalston Junction	d	09 45	09 52		10 00	10 07		10 15	10 22		10 30	10 37		10 45	10 52		11 00	11 07		11 15	11 22		11 30
Haggerston	d	09 47	09 54		10 02	10 09		10 17	10 24		10 32	10 39		10 47	10 54		11 02	11 09		11 17	11 24		11 32
Hoxton	d	09 49	09 56		10 04	10 11		10 19	10 26		10 34	10 41		10 49	10 56		11 04	11 11		11 19	11 26		11 34
Shoreditch High Street	d	09 52	09 58		10 07	10 13		10 22	10 28		10 37	10 43		10 52	10 58		11 07	11 13		11 22	11 28		11 37
Whitechapel	d	09 54	10 01		10 09	10 16		10 24	10 31		10 39	10 46		10 54	11 01		11 09	11 16		11 24	11 31		11 39
Shadwell	d	09 56	10 03		10 11	10 18		10 26	10 33		10 41	10 48		10 56	11 03		11 11	11 18		11 26	11 33		11 41
Wapping	d	09 58	10 05		10 13	10 20		10 28	10 35		10 43	10 50		10 58	11 05		11 13	11 20		11 28	11 35		11 43
Rotherhithe	d	10 00	10 06		10 15	10 21		10 30	10 36		10 45	10 51		11 00	11 06		11 15	11 21		11 30	11 36		11 45
Canada Water	d	10 02	10 08		10 17	10 23		10 32	10 38		10 47	10 53		11 02	11 08		11 17	11 23		11 32	11 38		11 47
Surrey Quays	d	10 04	10 10		10 19	10 25		10 34	10 40		10 49	10 55		11 04	11 10		11 19	11 25		11 34	11 40		11 49
New Cross Gate ■	d	10 08	10 15	10 18	10 23	10 30	10 34	10 38	10 45	10 48	10 53	11 00	11 04	11 08	11 15	11 18	11 23	11 30	11 34	11 38	11 45	11 48	11 53
Brockley	d	10 11	10 17	10 20	10 26	10 32	10 37	10 41	10 47	10 50	10 56	11 02	11 07	11 11	11 17	11 20	11 26	11 32	11 37	11 41	11 47	11 50	11 56
Honor Oak Park	d	10 13	10 20	10 23	10 28	10 35	10 39	10 43	10 50	10 53	10 58	11 05	11 09	11 13	11 20	11 23	11 28	11 35	11 39	11 43	11 50	11 53	11 58
Forest Hill ■	d	10 16	10 22	10 25	10 31	10 37	10 42	10 46	10 52	10 55	11 01	11 07	11 12	11 16	11 22	11 25	11 31	11 37	11 42	11 46	11 52	11 55	12 01
Sydenham	d	10 19	10 26	10 29	10 34	10 41	10 45	10 49	10 56	10 59	11 04	11 11	11 15	11 19	11 26	11 29	11 34	11 41	11 45	11 49	11 56	11 59	12 04
Crystal Palace ■	a	10 24			10 39		10 50	10 54			11 09		11 20	11 24			11 39		11 50	11 54			12 09
Penge West	d		10 28	10 31		10 43			10 58	11 01		11 13			11 28	11 31		11 43			11 58	12 01	
Anerley	d		10 30	10 33		10 45			11 00	11 03		11 15			11 30	11 33		11 45			12 00	12 03	
Norwood Junction ■	a		10 33	10 36		10 48			11 03	11 06		11 18			11 33	11 36		11 48			12 03	12 06	
Norwood Junction	d		10 33			10 48			11 03			11 18			11 33			11 48			12 03		
West Croydon ■	a		10 43			10 58			11 09			11 28			11 39			11 54			12 09		
Norwood Junction	d			10 39						11 09						11 39						12 09	
East Croydon	a			10 43						11 13						11 43						12 13	
Purley	a			10 54						11 24						11 54						12 24	

A To Caterham
B To London Victoria
C To Coulsdon Town

For full service between Highbury & Islington and Surrey Quays, refer to Table T178

For Sutton connections at West Croydon, refer to Table T172

Table T177-F

Mondays to Fridays
21 May to 7 December

London Bridge-New Cross Gate,Brockley, Honor Oak Park, Forest Hill, Sydenham, Crystal Palace, Penge West, Anerley-Norwood Junction and Croydon

	LO	and at the same minutes past each hour until	SN A	LO	LO	SN B	LO	LO	SN A	LO	LO	SN B	LO	LO	SN A	LO	LO	SN B	LO	LO	SN A	LO
London Bridge ⊖ d			13 58			14 10			14 28			14 40			14 58			15 10			15 28	
Highbury & Islington d	11 32			13 40	13 47		13 55	14 02		14 10	14 17		14 25	14 32		14 40	14 47		14 55	15 02		15 10
Canonbury d	11 34			13 42	13 49		13 57	14 04		14 12	14 19		14 27	14 34		14 42	14 49		14 57	15 04		15 12
Dalston Junction d	11 37			13 45	13 52		14 00	14 07		14 15	14 22		14 30	14 37		14 45	14 52		15 00	15 07		15 15
Haggerston d	11 39			13 47	13 54		14 02	14 09		14 17	14 24		14 32	14 39		14 47	14 54		15 02	15 09		15 17
Hoxton d	11 41			13 49	13 56		14 04	14 11		14 19	14 26		14 34	14 41		14 49	14 56		15 04	15 11		15 19
Shoreditch High Street d	11 43			13 52	13 58		14 07	14 13		14 22	14 28		14 37	14 43		14 52	14 58		15 07	15 13		15 22
Whitechapel d	11 46			13 54	14 01		14 09	14 16		14 24	14 31		14 39	14 46		14 54	15 01		15 09	15 16		15 24
Shadwell d	11 48			13 56	14 03		14 11	14 18		14 26	14 33		14 41	14 48		14 56	15 03		15 11	15 18		15 26
Wapping d	11 50			13 58	14 05		14 13	14 20		14 28	14 35		14 43	14 50		14 58	15 05		15 13	15 20		15 28
Rotherhithe d	11 51			14 00	14 06		14 15	14 21		14 30	14 36		14 45	14 51		15 00	15 06		15 15	15 21		15 30
Canada Water d	11 53			14 02	14 08		14 17	14 23		14 32	14 38		14 47	14 53		15 02	15 08		15 17	15 23		15 32
Surrey Quays d	11 55			14 04	14 10		14 19	14 25		14 34	14 40		14 49	14 55		15 04	15 10		15 19	15 25		15 34
New Cross Gate d	12 00		14 04	14 08	14 15	14 18	14 23	14 30	14 34	14 38	14 45	14 48	14 53	15 00	15 04	15 08	15 15	15 18	15 23	15 30	15 34	15 38
Brockley d	12 02		14 07	14 11	14 17	14 20	14 26	14 32	14 37	14 41	14 47	14 50	14 56	15 02	15 07	15 11	15 17	15 20	15 26	15 32	15 37	15 41
Honor Oak Park d	12 05		14 09	14 13	14 20	14 23	14 28	14 35	14 39	14 43	14 50	14 53	14 58	15 05	15 09	15 13	15 20	15 23	15 28	15 35	15 39	15 43
Forest Hill d	12 07		14 12	14 16	14 22	14 25	14 31	14 37	14 42	14 46	14 52	14 55	15 01	15 07	15 12	15 16	15 22	15 25	15 31	15 37	15 42	15 46
Sydenham d	12 11		14 15	14 19	14 26	14 29	14 34	14 41	14 45	14 49	14 56	14 59	15 04	15 11	15 15	15 19	15 26	15 29	15 34	15 41	15 45	15 49
Crystal Palace a			14 20	14 24			14 39		14 50	14 54			15 09		15 20	15 24			15 39		15 50	15 54
Penge West d	12 13				14 28	14 31		14 43			14 58	15 01		15 13			15 28	15 31		15 43		
Anerley d	12 15				14 30	14 33		14 45			15 00	15 03		15 15			15 30	15 33		15 45		
Norwood Junction a	12 18				14 33	14 36		14 48			15 03	15 06		15 18			15 33	15 36		15 48		
Norwood Junction d	12 18				14 33			14 48			15 03			15 18			15 33			15 48		
West Croydon a	12 24				14 39			14 54			15 09			15 24			15 39			15 54		
Norwood Junction d						14 39						15 09						15 39				
East Croydon a						14 43						15 13						15 43				
Purley a						14 54						15 24						15 54				

	LO	SN B	LO	LO	SN A	LO	LO	SN C	LO	LO	SN A	LO	LO	SN C	LO	LO	SN A	LO	LO	SN C	LO
London Bridge ⊖ d		15 40			15 58			16 10			16 28			16 40			16 58			17 10	
Highbury & Islington d	15 17		15 25	15 32		15 40	15 47		15 55	16 02		16 10	16 17		16 25	16 32		16 40	16 47		16 55
Canonbury d	15 19		15 27	15 34		15 42	15 49		15 57	16 04		16 12	16 19		16 27	16 34		16 42	16 49		16 57
Dalston Junction d	15 22		15 30	15 37		15 45	15 52		16 00	16 07		16 15	16 22		16 30	16 37		16 45	16 52		17 00
Haggerston d	15 24		15 32	15 39		15 47	15 54		16 02	16 09		16 17	16 24		16 32	16 39		16 47	16 54		17 02
Hoxton d	15 26		15 34	15 41		15 49	15 56		16 04	16 11		16 19	16 26		16 34	16 41		16 49	16 56		17 04
Shoreditch High Street d	15 28		15 37	15 43		15 52	15 58		16 07	16 13		16 22	16 28		16 37	16 43		16 52	16 58		17 07
Whitechapel d	15 31		15 39	15 46		15 54	16 01		16 09	16 16		16 24	16 31		16 39	16 46		16 54	17 01		17 09
Shadwell d	15 33		15 41	15 48		15 56	16 03		16 11	16 18		16 26	16 33		16 41	16 48		16 56	17 03		17 11
Wapping d	15 35		15 43	15 50		15 58	16 05		16 13	16 20		16 28	16 35		16 43	16 50		16 58	17 05		17 13
Rotherhithe d	15 36		15 45	15 51		16 00	16 06		16 15	16 21		16 30	16 36		16 45	16 51		17 00	17 06		17 15
Canada Water d	15 38		15 47	15 53		16 02	16 08		16 17	16 23		16 32	16 38		16 47	16 53		17 02	17 08		17 17
Surrey Quays d	15 40		15 49	15 55		16 04	16 10		16 19	16 25		16 34	16 40		16 49	16 55		17 04	17 10		17 19
New Cross Gate d	15 45	15 48	15 53	16 00	16 04	16 08	16 15	16 18	16 23	16 30	16 34	16 38	16 45	16 48	16 53	17 00	17 04	17 08	17 15	17 18	17 23
Brockley d	15 47	15 50	15 56	16 02	16 07	16 11	16 17	16 20	16 26	16 32	16 37	16 41	16 47	16 50	16 56	17 02	17 07	17 11	17 17	17 20	17 26
Honor Oak Park d	15 50	15 53	15 58	16 05	16 09	16 13	16 20	16 23	16 28	16 35	16 39	16 43	16 50	16 53	16 58	17 05	17 09	17 13	17 20	17 23	17 28
Forest Hill d	15 52	15 55	16 01	16 07	16 12	16 16	16 22	16 25	16 31	16 37	16 42	16 46	16 52	16 55	17 01	17 07	17 12	17 16	17 22	17 25	17 31
Sydenham d	15 56	15 59	16 04	16 11	16 15	16 19	16 26	16 29	16 34	16 41	16 45	16 49	16 56	16 59	17 04	17 11	17 15	17 19	17 26	17 29	17 34
Crystal Palace a			16 09		16 20	16 24			16 39		16 50	16 54			17 09		17 20	17 24			17 39
Penge West d	15 58	16 01		16 13			16 28	16 31		16 43			16 58	17 01		17 13			17 28	17 31	
Anerley d	16 00	16 03		16 15			16 30	16 33		16 45			17 00	17 03		17 15			17 30	17 33	
Norwood Junction a	16 03	16 06		16 18			16 33	16 36		16 48			17 03	17 06		17 18			17 33	17 36	
Norwood Junction d	16 03			16 18			16 33	16 36		16 48			17 03	17 06		17 18			17 33	17 36	
West Croydon a	16 09			16 28			16 43	16 42		16 58			17 13	17 12		17 28			17 43	17 42	
Norwood Junction d		16 09																			
East Croydon a		16 13																			
Purley a		16 24																			

A To London Victoria
B To Coulsdon Town
C To Sutton (Surrey)

For full service between Highbury & Islington and Surrey Quays, refer to Table T178

For Sutton connections at West Croydon, refer to Table T172

Table T177-F

Mondays to Fridays
21 May to 7 December

London Bridge-New Cross Gate,Brockley, Honor Oak Park, Forest Hill, Sydenham, Crystal Palace, Penge West, Anerley-Norwood Junction and Croydon

	LO	SN A	LO	LO	SN B	LO	LO	SN A	LO	LO	SN B	LO	LO	SN A	LO	LO	SN C	LO	LO	SN A	LO
London Bridge ⊖ d		17 28			17 40			17 58			18 10			18 28			18 40			18 58	
Highbury & Islington d	17 02		17 10	17 17		17 25	17 32		17 40	17 47		17 55	18 02		18 10	18 17		18 25	18 32		18 40
Canonbury d	17 04		17 12	17 19		17 27	17 34		17 42	17 49		17 57	18 04		18 12	18 19		18 27	18 34		18 42
Dalston Junction d	17 07		17 15	17 22		17 30	17 37		17 45	17 52		18 00	18 07		18 15	18 22		18 30	18 37		18 45
Haggerston d	17 09		17 17	17 24		17 32	17 39		17 47	17 54		18 02	18 09		18 17	18 24		18 32	18 39		18 47
Hoxton d	17 11		17 19	17 26		17 34	17 41		17 49	17 56		18 04	18 11		18 19	18 26		18 34	18 41		18 49
Shoreditch High Street d	17 13		17 22	17 28		17 37	17 43		17 52	17 58		18 07	18 13		18 22	18 28		18 37	18 43		18 52
Whitechapel d	17 16		17 24	17 31		17 39	17 46		17 54	18 01		18 09	18 16		18 24	18 31		18 39	18 46		18 54
Shadwell d	17 18		17 26	17 33		17 41	17 48		17 56	18 03		18 11	18 18		18 26	18 33		18 41	18 48		18 56
Wapping d	17 20		17 28	17 35		17 43	17 50		17 58	18 05		18 13	18 20		18 28	18 35		18 43	18 50		18 58
Rotherhithe d	17 21		17 30	17 36		17 45	17 51		18 00	18 06		18 15	18 21		18 30	18 36		18 45	18 51		19 00
Canada Water d	17 23		17 32	17 38		17 47	17 53		18 02	18 08		18 17	18 23		18 32	18 38		18 47	18 53		19 02
Surrey Quays d	17 25		17 34	17 40		17 49	17 55		18 04	18 10		18 19	18 25		18 34	18 40		18 49	18 55		19 04
New Cross Gate d	17 30	17 34	17 38	17 45	17 48	17 53	18 00	18 04	18 08	18 15	18 18	18 23	18 30	18 34	18 38	18 45	18 48	18 53	19 00	19 04	19 08
Brockley d	17 32	17 37	17 41	17 47	17 50	17 56	18 02	18 07	18 11	18 17	18 20	18 26	18 32	18 37	18 41	18 47	18 50	18 56	19 02	19 07	19 11
Honor Oak Park d	17 35	17 39	17 43	17 50	17 53	17 58	18 05	18 09	18 13	18 20	18 23	18 28	18 35	18 39	18 43	18 50	18 53	18 58	19 05	19 09	19 13
Forest Hill d	17 37	17 42	17 46	17 52	17 55	18 01	18 07	18 12	18 16	18 22	18 25	18 31	18 37	18 42	18 46	18 52	18 55	19 01	19 07	19 12	19 16
Sydenham d	17 41	17 45	17 49	17 56	17 59	18 04	18 11	18 15	18 19	18 26	18 29	18 34	18 41	18 45	18 49	18 56	18 59	19 04	19 11	19 15	19 19
Crystal Palace a		17 50	17 54			18 09		18 20	18 24			18 39		18 50	18 54			19 09		19 20	19 24
Penge West d	17 43			17 58	18 01		18 13			18 28	18 31		18 43			18 58	19 01		19 13		
Anerley d	17 45			18 00	18 03		18 15			18 30	18 33		18 45			19 00	19 03		19 15		
Norwood Junction a	17 48			18 03	18 06		18 18			18 33	18 36		18 48			19 03	19 06		19 18		
Norwood Junction d	17 48			18 03	18 06		18 18			18 33	18 36		18 48			19 03			19 18		
West Croydon a	17 58			18 13	18 12		18 28			18 43	18 42		18 58			19 13			19 28		
Norwood Junction d																	19 09				
East Croydon a																	19 13				
Purley a																	19 22				

	LO	SN C	LO	LO	SN A	LO	LO	SN C	LO	LO	SN A	LO	LO	SN C	LO	LO	SN A	LO	LO	SN C	LO	LO
London Bridge ⊖ d		19 10			19 28			19 40			19 58			20 10			20 28			20 40		
Highbury & Islington d	18 47		18 55	19 02		19 10	19 17		19 25	19 32		19 40	19 47		19 55	20 02		20 10	20 17		20 25	20 32
Canonbury d	18 49		18 57	19 04		19 12	19 19		19 27	19 34		19 42	19 49		19 57	20 04		20 12	20 19		20 27	20 34
Dalston Junction d	18 52		19 00	19 07		19 15	19 22		19 30	19 37		19 45	19 52		20 00	20 07		20 15	20 22		20 30	20 37
Haggerston d	18 54		19 02	19 09		19 17	19 24		19 32	19 39		19 47	19 54		20 02	20 09		20 17	20 24		20 32	20 39
Hoxton d	18 56		19 04	19 11		19 19	19 26		19 34	19 41		19 49	19 56		20 04	20 11		20 19	20 26		20 34	20 41
Shoreditch High Street d	18 58		19 07	19 13		19 22	19 28		19 37	19 43		19 52	19 58		20 07	20 13		20 22	20 28		20 37	20 43
Whitechapel d	19 01		19 09	19 16		19 24	19 31		19 39	19 46		19 54	20 01		20 09	20 16		20 24	20 31		20 39	20 46
Shadwell d	19 03		19 11	19 18		19 26	19 33		19 41	19 48		19 56	20 03		20 11	20 18		20 26	20 33		20 41	20 48
Wapping d	19 05		19 13	19 20		19 28	19 35		19 43	19 50		19 58	20 05		20 13	20 20		20 28	20 35		20 43	20 50
Rotherhithe d	19 06		19 15	19 21		19 30	19 36		19 45	19 51		20 00	20 06		20 15	20 21		20 30	20 36		20 45	20 51
Canada Water d	19 08		19 17	19 23		19 32	19 38		19 47	19 53		20 02	20 08		20 17	20 23		20 32	20 38		20 47	20 53
Surrey Quays d	19 10		19 19	19 25		19 34	19 40		19 49	19 55		20 04	20 10		20 19	20 25		20 34	20 40		20 49	20 55
New Cross Gate d	19 15	19 18	19 23	19 30	19 34	19 38	19 45	19 48	19 53	20 00	20 04	20 08	20 15	20 18	20 23	20 30	20 34	20 38	20 45	20 48	20 53	21 00
Brockley d	19 17	19 20	19 26	19 32	19 37	19 41	19 47	19 50	19 56	20 02	20 07	20 11	20 17	20 20	20 26	20 32	20 37	20 41	20 47	20 50	20 56	21 02
Honor Oak Park d	19 20	19 23	19 28	19 35	19 39	19 43	19 50	19 53	19 58	20 05	20 09	20 13	20 20	20 23	20 28	20 35	20 39	20 43	20 50	20 53	20 58	21 05
Forest Hill d	19 22	19 25	19 31	19 37	19 42	19 46	19 52	19 55	20 01	20 07	20 12	20 16	20 22	20 25	20 31	20 37	20 42	20 46	20 52	20 55	21 01	21 07
Sydenham d	19 26	19 29	19 34	19 41	19 45	19 49	19 56	19 59	20 04	20 11	20 15	20 19	20 26	20 29	20 34	20 41	20 45	20 49	20 56	20 59	21 04	21 11
Crystal Palace a			19 39		19 50	19 54			20 09		20 20	20 24			20 39		20 50	20 54			21 09	
Penge West d	19 28	19 31		19 43			19 58	20 01		20 13			20 28	20 31		20 43			20 58	21 01		21 13
Anerley d	19 30	19 33		19 45			20 00	20 03		20 15			20 30	20 33		20 45			21 00	21 03		21 15
Norwood Junction a	19 33	19 36		19 48			20 03	20 06		20 18			20 33	20 36		20 48			21 03	21 06		21 18
Norwood Junction d	19 33			19 48			20 03			20 18			20 33			20 48			21 03			21 18
West Croydon a	19 43			19 58			20 13			20 28			20 43			20 58			21 13			21 24
Norwood Junction d		19 39						20 09						20 39						21 09		
East Croydon a		19 42						20 13						20 43						21 13		
Purley a		19 54						20 24						20 54						21 24		

A To London Victoria
B To Sutton (Surrey)
C To Coulsdon Town

For full service between Highbury & Islington and Surrey Quays, refer to Table T178

For Sutton connections at West Croydon, refer to Table T172

Table T177-F

Mondays to Fridays

21 May to 7 December

London Bridge-New Cross Gate,Brockley, Honor Oak Park, Forest Hill, Sydenham, Crystal Palace, Penge West, Anerley-Norwood Junction and Croydon

		SN		LO	LO	SN	LO	LO	SN	LO	LO	SN		LO	LO	SN	LO	LO	SN	LO	LO	SN		LO	LO
		A				B			A			B				A			B			A			
London Bridge ■ ⊖	d	20 58				21 10			21 28			21 40				21 58			22 10			22 28			
Highbury & Islington	d			20 40	20 47		20 55	21 02		21 10	21 17			21 25	21 32		21 40	21 47		21 55	22 02			22 10	22 17
Canonbury	d			20 42	20 49		20 57	21 04		21 12	21 19			21 27	21 34		21 42	21 49		21 57	22 04			22 12	22 19
Dalston Junction	d			20 45	20 52		21 00	21 07		21 15	21 22			21 30	21 37		21 45	21 52		22 00	22 07			22 15	22 22
Haggerston	d			20 47	20 54		21 02	21 09		21 17	21 24			21 32	21 39		21 47	21 54		22 02	22 09			22 17	22 24
Hoxton	d			20 49	20 56		21 04	21 11		21 19	21 26			21 34	21 41		21 49	21 56		22 04	22 11			22 19	22 26
Shoreditch High Street	d			20 52	20 58		21 07	21 13		21 22	21 28			21 37	21 43		21 52	21 58		22 07	22 13			22 22	22 28
Whitechapel	d			20 54	21 01		21 09	21 16		21 24	21 31			21 39	21 46		21 54	22 01		22 09	22 16			22 24	22 31
Shadwell	d			20 56	21 03		21 11	21 18		21 26	21 33			21 41	21 48		21 56	22 03		22 11	22 18			22 26	22 33
Wapping	d			20 58	21 05		21 13	21 20		21 28	21 35			21 43	21 50		21 58	22 05		22 13	22 20			22 28	22 35
Rotherhithe	d			21 00	21 06		21 15	21 21		21 30	21 36			21 45	21 51		22 00	22 06		22 15	22 21			22 30	22 36
Canada Water	d			21 02	21 08		21 17	21 23		21 32	21 38			21 47	21 53		22 02	22 08		22 17	22 23			22 32	22 38
Surrey Quays	d			21 04	21 10		21 19	21 25		21 34	21 40			21 49	21 55		22 04	22 10		22 19	22 25			22 34	22 40
New Cross Gate ■	d	21 04		21 08	21 15	21 18	21 23	21 30	21 34	21 38	21 45	21 48		21 53	22 00	22 04	22 08	22 15	22 18	22 23	22 30	22 34		22 38	22 45
Brockley	d	21 07		21 11	21 17	21 20	21 26	21 32	21 37	21 41	21 47	21 50		21 56	22 02	22 07	22 11	22 17	22 20	22 26	22 32	22 37		22 41	22 47
Honor Oak Park	d	21 09		21 13	21 20	21 23	21 28	21 35	21 39	21 43	21 50	21 53		21 58	22 05	22 09	22 13	22 20	22 23	22 28	22 35	22 39		22 43	22 50
Forest Hill ■	d	21 12		21 16	21 22	21 25	21 31	21 37	21 42	21 46	21 52	21 55		22 01	22 07	22 12	22 16	22 22	22 25	22 31	22 37	22 42		22 46	22 52
Sydenham	d	21 15		21 19	21 26	21 29	21 34	21 41	21 45	21 49	21 56	21 59		22 04	22 11	22 15	22 19	22 26	22 29	22 34	22 41	22 45		22 49	22 56
Crystal Palace ■	a	21 20		21 24			21 39		21 50	21 54				22 09		22 20	22 24			22 39		22 50		22 54	
Penge West	d				21 28	21 31		21 43			21 58	22 01			22 13			22 28	22 31		22 43				22 58
Anerley	d				21 30	21 33		21 45			22 00	22 03			22 15			22 30	22 33		22 45				23 00
Norwood Junction ■	a				21 33	21 36		21 48			22 03	22 06			22 18			22 33	22 36		22 48				23 03
Norwood Junction	d				21 33			21 48			22 03				22 18			22 33			22 48				23 03
West Croydon ■ ⇌	a				21 39			21 54			22 09				22 24			22 39			22 54				23 09
Norwood Junction	d					21 39						22 09							22 39						
East Croydon ⇌	a					21 43						22 13							22 43						
Purley	a					21 54						22 24							22 54						

		SN	LO	LO	SN	LO	LO	SN		LO	LO	SN	LO	LO	SN	LO	LO	SN		LO
		B			A							C						C		
London Bridge ■ ⊖	d	22 40			22 58			23 10				23 28			23 40			23 58		
Highbury & Islington	d		22 25	22 32		22 40	22 47			22 55	23 02		23 10	23 17		23 25	23 32			23 40
Canonbury	d		22 27	22 34		22 42	22 49			22 57	23 04		23 12	23 19		23 27	23 34			23 42
Dalston Junction	d		22 30	22 37		22 45	22 52			23 00	23 07		23 15	23 22		23 30	23 37			23 45
Haggerston	d		22 32	22 39		22 47	22 54			23 02	23 09		23 17	23 24		23 32	23 39			23 47
Hoxton	d		22 34	22 41		22 49	22 56			23 04	23 11		23 19	23 26		23 34	23 41			23 49
Shoreditch High Street	d		22 37	22 43		22 52	22 58			23 07	23 13		23 22	23 28		23 37	23 43			23 52
Whitechapel	d		22 39	22 46		22 54	23 01			23 09	23 16		23 24	23 31		23 39	23 46			23 54
Shadwell	d		22 41	22 48		22 56	23 03			23 11	23 18		23 26	23 33		23 41	23 48			23 56
Wapping	d		22 43	22 50		22 58	23 05			23 13	23 20		23 28	23 35		23 43	23 50			23 58
Rotherhithe	d		22 45	22 51		23 00	23 06			23 15	23 21		23 30	23 36		23 45	23 51			23 59
Canada Water	d		22 47	22 53		23 02	23 08			23 17	23 23		23 32	23 38		23 47	23 53			00 02
Surrey Quays	d		22 49	22 55		23 04	23 10			23 19	23 25		23 34	23 40		23 49	23 55			00 04
New Cross Gate ■	d	22 48	22 53	23 00	23 04	23 08	23 15	23 18		23 23	23 30	23 34	23 38	23 45	23 48	23 53	00 01	00 04		00 08
Brockley	d	22 50	22 56	23 02	23 07	23 11	23 17	23 20		23 26	23 32	23 37	23 41	23 47	23 50	23 56	00 03	00 07		00 11
Honor Oak Park	d	22 53	22 58	23 05	23 09	23 13	23 20	23 23		23 28	23 35	23 39	23 43	23 50	23 53	23 58	00 06	00 09		00 13
Forest Hill ■	d	22 55	23 01	23 07	23 12	23 16	23 22	23 25		23 31	23 37	23 42	23 46	23 52	23 55	00 01	00 08	00 12		00 16
Sydenham	d	22 59	23 04	23 11	23 15	23 19	23 26	23 29		23 34	23 41	23 45	23 49	23 56	23 59	00 04	00 11	00 15		00 19
Crystal Palace ■	a		23 09		23 20	23 24				23 39		23 50	23 54			00 09		00 20		00 24
Penge West	d	23 01		23 13			23 28	23 31			23 43			23 58	00 01		00 13			
Anerley	d	23 03		23 15			23 30	23 33			23 45			00 01	00 03		00 15			
Norwood Junction ■	a	23 06		23 18			23 33	23 36			23 48			00 03	00 06		00 18			
Norwood Junction	d			23 18			23 33				23 48			00 03			00 19			
West Croydon ■ ⇌	a			23 24			23 39				23 55			00 10			00 31			
Norwood Junction	d	23 09						23 39							00 06					
East Croydon ⇌	a	23 13						23 47							00 10					
Purley	a	23 24																		

A To London Victoria — B To Coulsdon Town — C To Streatham Hill

For full service between Highbury & Islington and Surrey Quays, refer to Table T178

For Sutton connections at West Croydon, refer to Table T172

Table T177-F

Saturdays

26 May to 8 December

London Bridge-New Cross Gate,Brockley, Honor Oak Park, Forest Hill, Sydenham, Crystal Palace, Penge West, Anerley-Norwood Junction and Croydon

		LO	LO	SN	LO	SN		LO	SN	SN	LO	LO	LO	LO	SN	LO		LO	SN	LO	LO	SN	LO	LO	SN
		A	A	B	A	C		A							D				E			D			E
London Bridge ■ ⊖	d								00 10	00 35					06 11				06 28			06 40			06 58
Highbury & Islington	d										05 25		05 40	05 47		05 55		06 02		06 10	06 17		06 25	06 32	
Canonbury	d										05 27		05 42	05 49		05 57		06 04		06 12	06 19		06 27	06 34	
Dalston Junction	d										05 30	05 37	05 45	05 52		06 00		06 07		06 15	06 22		06 30	06 37	
Haggerston	d										05 32	05 39	05 47	05 54		06 02		06 09		06 17	06 24		06 32	06 39	
Hoxton	d										05 34	05 41	05 49	05 56		06 04		06 11		06 19	06 26		06 34	06 41	
Shoreditch High Street	d										05 37	05 43	05 52	05 58		06 07		06 13		06 22	06 28		06 37	06 43	
Whitechapel	d										05 39	05 46	05 54	06 01		06 09		06 16		06 24	06 31		06 39	06 46	
Shadwell	d										05 41	05 48	05 56	06 03		06 11		06 18		06 26	06 33		06 41	06 48	
Wapping	d										05 43	05 50	05 58	06 05		06 13		06 20		06 28	06 35		06 43	06 50	
Rotherhithe	d										05 45	05 51	06 00	06 06		06 15		06 21		06 30	06 36		06 45	06 51	
Canada Water	d							00 02			05 47	05 53	06 02	06 08		06 17		06 23		06 32	06 38		06 47	06 53	
Surrey Quays	d							00 04			05 49	05 55	06 04	06 10		06 19		06 25		06 34	06 40		06 49	06 55	
New Cross Gate ■	d				00 01	00 04		00 08	00 16	00 41	05 53	06 00	06 08	06 15	06 18	06 23		06 30	06 35	06 38	06 45	06 48	06 53	07 00	07 05
Brockley	d				00 03	00 07		00 11	00 19	00 44	05 56	06 02	06 11	06 17	06 21	06 26		06 32	06 37	06 41	06 47	06 50	06 56	07 02	07 07
Honor Oak Park	d				00 06	00 09		00 13	00 21	00 46	05 58	06 05	06 13	06 20	06 23	06 28		06 35	06 40	06 43	06 50	06 53	06 58	07 05	07 10
Forest Hill ■	d		00 01		00 08	00 12		00 16	00 24	00 49	06 01	06 07	06 16	06 22	06 26	06 31		06 37	06 42	06 46	06 52	06 55	07 01	07 07	07 12
Sydenham	d		00 04		00 11	00 15		00 19	00 27	00 52	06 04	06 11	06 19	06 26	06 29	06 34		06 41	06 46	06 49	06 56	06 59	07 04	07 11	07 16
Crystal Palace ■	a		00 09			00 20		00 24			06 08		06 23			06 38			06 50	06 53			07 08		07 20
Penge West	d			00 01	00 13				00 29	00 54		06 13		06 28	06 31			06 43			06 58	07 01		07 13	
Anerley	d	00 01		00 03	00 15				00 31	00 56		06 15		06 30	06 33			06 45			07 00	07 03		07 15	
Norwood Junction ■	a	00 03		00 06	00 18				00 34	00 59		06 18		06 33	06 37			06 48			07 03	07 06		07 18	
Norwood Junction	d	00 03			00 19							06 18		06 33				06 48			07 03			07 18	
West Croydon ■ ⇌	a	00 10			00 31							06 24		06 39				06 54			07 09			07 24	
Norwood Junction	d			00 06					00 35	01 08					06 39							07 09			
East Croydon ⇌	a			00 10					00 38	01 13					06 43							07 13			
Purley	a														06 54							07 24			

		LO		LO	SN	LO	LO	SN	LO	LO	SN	LO		LO	SN	LO	LO	SN	LO	LO	SN	LO		LO	SN
					D			E			D				E			D			E				D
London Bridge ■ ⊖	d				07 10			07 28			07 40				07 58			08 10			08 28				08 40
Highbury & Islington	d	06 40		06 47		06 55	07 02		07 10	07 17		07 25		07 32		07 40	07 47		07 55	08 02		08 10		08 17	
Canonbury	d	06 42		06 49		06 57	07 04		07 12	07 19		07 27		07 34		07 42	07 49		07 57	08 04		08 12		08 19	
Dalston Junction	d	06 45		06 52		07 00	07 07		07 15	07 22		07 30		07 37		07 45	07 52		08 00	08 07		08 15		08 22	
Haggerston	d	06 47		06 54		07 02	07 09		07 17	07 24		07 32		07 39		07 47	07 54		08 02	08 09		08 17		08 24	
Hoxton	d	06 49		06 56		07 04	07 11		07 19	07 26		07 34		07 41		07 49	07 56		08 04	08 11		08 19		08 26	
Shoreditch High Street	d	06 52		06 58		07 07	07 13		07 22	07 28		07 37		07 43		07 52	07 58		08 07	08 13		08 22		08 28	
Whitechapel	d	06 54		07 01		07 09	07 16		07 24	07 31		07 39		07 46		07 54	08 01		08 09	08 16		08 24		08 31	
Shadwell	d	06 56		07 03		07 11	07 18		07 26	07 33		07 41		07 48		07 56	08 03		08 11	08 18		08 26		08 33	
Wapping	d	06 58		07 05		07 13	07 20		07 28	07 35		07 43		07 50		07 58	08 05		08 13	08 20		08 28		08 35	
Rotherhithe	d	07 00		07 06		07 15	07 21		07 30	07 36		07 45		07 51		08 00	08 06		08 15	08 21		08 30		08 36	
Canada Water	d	07 02		07 08		07 17	07 23		07 32	07 38		07 47		07 53		08 02	08 08		08 17	08 23		08 32		08 38	
Surrey Quays	d	07 04		07 10		07 19	07 25		07 34	07 40		07 49		07 55		08 04	08 10		08 19	08 25		08 34		08 40	
New Cross Gate ■	d	07 08		07 15	07 18	07 23	07 30	07 35	07 38	07 45	07 48	07 53		08 00	08 05	08 08	08 15	08 18	08 23	08 30	08 35	08 38		08 45	08 48
Brockley	d	07 11		07 17	07 21	07 26	07 32	07 37	07 41	07 47	07 51	07 56		08 02	08 07	08 11	08 17	08 21	08 26	08 32	08 37	08 41		08 47	08 51
Honor Oak Park	d	07 13		07 20	07 23	07 28	07 35	07 40	07 43	07 50	07 53	07 58		08 05	08 10	08 13	08 20	08 23	08 28	08 35	08 40	08 43		08 50	08 53
Forest Hill ■	d	07 16		07 22	07 26	07 31	07 37	07 42	07 46	07 52	07 56	08 01		08 07	08 12	08 16	08 22	08 26	08 31	08 37	08 42	08 46		08 52	08 56
Sydenham	d	07 19		07 26	07 29	07 34	07 41	07 46	07 49	07 56	07 59	08 04		08 11	08 16	08 19	08 26	08 29	08 34	08 41	08 46	08 49		08 56	08 59
Crystal Palace ■	a	07 23				07 38		07 50	07 53			08 08			08 20	08 23			08 39		08 50	08 54			
Penge West	d			07 28	07 31		07 43			07 58	08 01			08 13			08 28	08 31		08 43				08 58	09 01
Anerley	d			07 30	07 33		07 45			08 00	08 03			08 15			08 30	08 33		08 45				09 00	09 03
Norwood Junction ■	a			07 33	07 36		07 48			08 03	08 06			08 18			08 33	08 36		08 48				09 03	09 06
Norwood Junction	d			07 33			07 48			08 03				08 18			08 33			08 48				09 03	
West Croydon ■ ⇌	a			07 39			07 54			08 09				08 24			08 39			08 58				09 13	
Norwood Junction	d				07 39						08 09							08 39							09 09
East Croydon ⇌	a				07 43						08 13							08 43							09 13
Purley	a				07 54						08 24							08 54							09 24

A From Highbury and Islington Ell — B From London Bridge — C From London Bridge to Streatham Hill — D To Coulsdon Town — E To London Victoria

For full service between Highbury & Islington and Surrey Quays, refer to Table T178

For Sutton connections at West Croydon, refer to Table T172

London Bridge-New Cross Gate,Brockley, Honor Oak Park, Forest Hill, Sydenham, Crystal Palace, Penge West, Anerley-Norwood Junction and Croydon

		LO	LO	SN A	LO	LO	SN B	LO	LO	SN A	LO	LO	SN B	LO	LO	SN A	LO	LO	SN B	LO	LO	SN A
London Bridge ⊖	d			08 58			09 10			09 28			09 40			09 58			10 10			10 28
Highbury & Islington	d	08 25	08 32		08 40	08 47		08 55	09 02		09 10	09 17		09 25	09 32		09 40	09 47		09 55	10 02	
Canonbury	d	08 27	08 34		08 42	08 49		08 57	09 04		09 12	09 19		09 27	09 34		09 42	09 49		09 57	10 04	
Dalston Junction	d	08 30	08 37		08 45	08 52		09 00	09 07		09 15	09 22		09 30	09 37		09 45	09 52		10 00	10 07	
Haggerston	d	08 32	08 39		08 47	08 54		09 02	09 09		09 17	09 24		09 32	09 39		09 47	09 54		10 02	10 09	
Hoxton	d	08 34	08 41		08 49	08 56		09 04	09 11		09 19	09 26		09 34	09 41		09 49	09 56		10 04	10 11	
Shoreditch High Street	d	08 37	08 43		08 52	08 58		09 07	09 13		09 22	09 28		09 37	09 43		09 52	09 58		10 07	10 13	
Whitechapel	d	08 39	08 46		08 54	09 01		09 09	09 16		09 24	09 31		09 39	09 46		09 54	10 01		10 09	10 16	
Shadwell	d	08 41	08 48		08 56	09 03		09 11	09 18		09 26	09 33		09 41	09 48		09 56	10 03		10 11	10 18	
Wapping	d	08 43	08 50		08 58	09 05		09 13	09 20		09 28	09 35		09 43	09 50		09 58	10 05		10 13	10 20	
Rotherhithe	d	08 45	08 51		09 00	09 06		09 15	09 21		09 30	09 36		09 45	09 51		10 00	10 06		10 15	10 21	
Canada Water	d	08 47	08 53		09 02	09 08		09 17	09 23		09 32	09 38		09 47	09 53		10 02	10 08		10 17	10 23	
Surrey Quays	d	08 49	08 55		09 04	09 10		09 19	09 25		09 34	09 40		09 49	09 55		10 04	10 10		10 19	10 25	
New Cross Gate	d	08 53	09 00	09 05	09 08	09 15	09 18	09 23	09 30	09 35	09 38	09 45	09 48	09 53	10 00	10 05	10 08	10 15	10 18	10 23	10 30	10 34
Brockley	d	08 56	09 02	09 07	09 11	09 17	09 21	09 26	09 32	09 37	09 41	09 47	09 51	09 56	10 02	10 07	10 11	10 17	10 21	10 26	10 32	10 36
Honor Oak Park	d	08 58	09 05	09 10	09 13	09 20	09 23	09 28	09 35	09 40	09 43	09 50	09 53	09 58	10 05	10 10	10 13	10 20	10 23	10 28	10 35	10 39
Forest Hill	d	09 01	09 07	09 12	09 16	09 22	09 26	09 31	09 37	09 42	09 46	09 52	09 56	10 01	10 07	10 12	10 16	10 22	10 26	10 31	10 37	10 41
Sydenham	d	09 04	09 11	09 16	09 19	09 26	09 29	09 34	09 41	09 46	09 49	09 56	09 59	10 04	10 11	10 16	10 19	10 26	10 29	10 34	10 41	10 45
Crystal Palace	a	09 09		09 20	09 24			09 38		09 50	09 53			10 08		10 20	10 23			10 38		10 49
Penge West	d		09 13			09 28	09 31		09 43			09 58	10 01		10 13			10 28	10 31		10 43	
Anerley	d		09 15			09 30	09 33		09 45			10 00	10 03		10 15			10 30	10 33		10 45	
Norwood Junction	a		09 18			09 33	09 36		09 48			10 03	10 06		10 18			10 33	10 36		10 48	
Norwood Junction	d		09 18			09 33			09 48			10 03			10 18			10 33			10 48	
West Croydon	a		09 28			09 43			09 58			10 13			10 28			10 43			10 54	
Norwood Junction	d						09 39						10 09						10 39			
East Croydon	a						09 43						10 13						10 43			
Purley	a						09 54						10 24						10 54			

		LO	LO	SN B	LO	LO	SN A	LO	LO	SN B	LO	LO	SN A		LO	LO	SN B	LO	LO	SN A	LO	LO	SN B	LO
London Bridge ⊖	d			10 40			10 58			11 10			11 28				13 40			13 58			14 10	
Highbury & Islington	d	10 10	10 17		10 25	10 32		10 40	10 47		10 55	11 02			13 10	13 17		13 25	13 32		13 40	13 47		13 55
Canonbury	d	10 12	10 19		10 27	10 34		10 42	10 49		10 57	11 04			13 12	13 19		13 27	13 34		13 42	13 49		13 57
Dalston Junction	d	10 15	10 22		10 30	10 37		10 45	10 52		11 00	11 07			13 15	13 22		13 30	13 37		13 45	13 52		14 00
Haggerston	d	10 17	10 24		10 32	10 39		10 47	10 54		11 02	11 09			13 17	13 24		13 32	13 39		13 47	13 54		14 02
Hoxton	d	10 19	10 26		10 34	10 41		10 49	10 56		11 04	11 11			13 19	13 26		13 34	13 41		13 49	13 56		14 04
Shoreditch High Street	d	10 22	10 28		10 37	10 43		10 52	10 58		11 07	11 13			13 22	13 28		13 37	13 43		13 52	13 58		14 07
Whitechapel	d	10 24	10 31		10 39	10 46		10 54	11 01		11 09	11 16			13 24	13 31		13 39	13 46		13 54	14 01		14 09
Shadwell	d	10 26	10 33		10 41	10 48		10 56	11 03		11 11	11 18			13 26	13 33		13 41	13 48		13 56	14 03		14 11
Wapping	d	10 28	10 35		10 43	10 50		10 58	11 05		11 13	11 20		and at the same minutes past each hour until	13 28	13 35		13 43	13 50		13 58	14 05		14 13
Rotherhithe	d	10 30	10 36		10 45	10 51		11 00	11 06		11 15	11 21			13 30	13 36		13 45	13 51		14 00	14 06		14 15
Canada Water	d	10 32	10 38		10 47	10 53		11 02	11 08		11 17	11 23			13 32	13 38		13 47	13 53		14 02	14 08		14 17
Surrey Quays	d	10 34	10 40		10 49	10 55		11 04	11 10		11 19	11 25			13 34	13 40		13 49	13 55		14 04	14 10		14 19
New Cross Gate	d	10 38	10 45	10 48	10 53	11 00	11 05	11 08	11 15	11 18	11 23	11 30	11 35		13 38	13 45	13 48	13 53	14 00	14 05	14 08	14 15	14 18	14 23
Brockley	d	10 41	10 47	10 51	10 56	11 02	11 07	11 11	11 17	11 21	11 26	11 32	11 37		13 41	13 47	13 51	13 56	14 02	14 07	14 11	14 17	14 21	14 26
Honor Oak Park	d	10 43	10 50	10 53	10 58	11 05	11 10	11 13	11 20	11 23	11 28	11 35	11 40		13 43	13 50	13 53	13 58	14 05	14 10	14 13	14 20	14 23	14 28
Forest Hill	d	10 46	10 52	10 56	11 01	11 07	11 12	11 16	11 22	11 26	11 31	11 37	11 42		13 46	13 52	13 56	14 01	14 07	14 12	14 16	14 22	14 26	14 31
Sydenham	d	10 49	10 56	10 59	11 04	11 11	11 16	11 19	11 26	11 29	11 34	11 41	11 46		13 49	13 56	13 59	14 04	14 11	14 16	14 19	14 26	14 29	14 34
Crystal Palace	a	10 53			11 08		11 20	11 23			11 38		11 50		13 53			14 08		14 20	14 23			14 38
Penge West	d		10 58	11 01		11 13			11 28	11 31		11 43				13 58	14 01		14 13			14 28	14 31	
Anerley	d		11 00	11 03		11 15			11 30	11 33		11 45				14 00	14 03		14 15			14 30	14 33	
Norwood Junction	a		11 03	11 06		11 18			11 33	11 36		11 48				14 03	14 06		14 18			14 33	14 36	
Norwood Junction	d		11 03			11 18			11 33			11 48				14 03			14 18			14 33		
West Croydon	a		11 09			11 24			11 39			11 54				14 09			14 24			14 39		
Norwood Junction	d			11 09						11 39							14 09						14 39	
East Croydon	a			11 13						11 43							14 13						14 43	
Purley	a			11 24						11 54							14 24						14 54	

A To London Victoria

B To Coulsdon Town

For full service between Highbury & Islington and Surrey Quays, refer to Table T178

For Sutton connections at West Croydon, refer to Table T172

London Bridge-New Cross Gate,Brockley, Honor Oak Park, Forest Hill, Sydenham, Crystal Palace, Penge West, Anerley-Norwood Junction and Croydon

		LO	SN A	LO	LO	SN B	LO	LO	SN A	LO	LO	SN B	LO	LO	SN A	LO	LO	SN B	LO	LO	SN A	LO
London Bridge ⊖	d		14 28			14 40			14 58			15 10			15 28			15 40			15 58	
Highbury & Islington	d	14 02		14 10	14 17		14 25	14 32		14 40	14 47		14 55	15 02		15 10	15 17		15 25	15 32		15 40
Canonbury	d	14 04		14 12	14 19		14 27	14 34		14 42	14 49		14 57	15 04		15 12	15 19		15 27	15 34		15 42
Dalston Junction	d	14 07		14 15	14 22		14 30	14 37		14 45	14 52		15 00	15 07		15 15	15 22		15 30	15 37		15 45
Haggerston	d	14 09		14 17	14 24		14 32	14 39		14 47	14 54		15 02	15 09		15 17	15 24		15 32	15 39		15 47
Hoxton	d	14 11		14 19	14 26		14 34	14 41		14 49	14 56		15 04	15 11		15 19	15 26		15 34	15 41		15 49
Shoreditch High Street	d	14 13		14 22	14 28		14 37	14 43		14 52	14 58		15 07	15 13		15 22	15 28		15 37	15 43		15 52
Whitechapel	d	14 16		14 24	14 31		14 39	14 46		14 54	15 01		15 09	15 16		15 24	15 31		15 39	15 46		15 54
Shadwell	d	14 18		14 26	14 33		14 41	14 48		14 56	15 03		15 11	15 18		15 26	15 33		15 41	15 48		15 56
Wapping	d	14 20		14 28	14 35		14 43	14 50		14 58	15 05		15 13	15 20		15 28	15 35		15 43	15 50		15 58
Rotherhithe	d	14 21		14 30	14 36		14 45	14 51		15 00	15 06		15 15	15 21		15 30	15 36		15 45	15 51		16 00
Canada Water	d	14 23		14 32	14 38		14 47	14 53		15 02	15 08		15 17	15 23		15 32	15 38		15 47	15 53		16 02
Surrey Quays	d	14 25		14 34	14 40		14 49	14 55		15 04	15 10		15 19	15 25		15 34	15 40		15 49	15 55		16 04
New Cross Gate	d	14 30	14 35	14 38	14 45	14 48	14 53	15 00	15 05	15 08	15 15	15 18	15 23	15 30	15 35	15 38	15 45	15 48	15 53	16 00	16 05	16 08
Brockley	d	14 32	14 37	14 41	14 47	14 51	14 56	15 02	15 07	15 11	15 17	15 21	15 26	15 32	15 37	15 41	15 47	15 51	15 56	16 02	16 07	16 11
Honor Oak Park	d	14 35	14 40	14 43	14 50	14 53	14 58	15 05	15 10	15 13	15 20	15 23	15 28	15 35	15 40	15 43	15 50	15 53	15 58	16 05	16 10	16 13
Forest Hill	d	14 37	14 42	14 46	14 52	14 56	15 01	15 07	15 12	15 16	15 22	15 26	15 31	15 37	15 42	15 46	15 52	15 56	16 01	16 07	16 12	16 16
Sydenham	d	14 41	14 46	14 49	14 56	14 59	15 04	15 11	15 16	15 19	15 26	15 29	15 34	15 41	15 46	15 49	15 56	15 59	16 04	16 11	16 16	16 19
Crystal Palace	a		14 50	14 53			15 08		15 20	15 23			15 38		15 50	15 53			16 08		16 20	16 23
Penge West	d	14 43			14 58	15 01		15 13			15 28	15 31		15 43			15 58	16 01		16 13		
Anerley	d	14 45			15 00	15 03		15 15			15 30	15 33		15 45			16 00	16 03		16 15		
Norwood Junction	a	14 48			15 03	15 06		15 18			15 33	15 36		15 48			16 03	16 06		16 18		
Norwood Junction	d	14 48			15 03			15 18			15 33			15 48			16 03			16 18		
West Croydon	a	14 54			15 09			15 24			15 39			15 58			16 13			16 28		
Norwood Junction	d					15 09						15 39						16 09				
East Croydon	a					15 13						15 43						16 13				
Purley	a					15 24						15 54						16 24				

		LO		SN B	LO	LO	SN A	LO	LO	SN B	LO	LO	SN A	LO	LO	SN B	LO	LO	SN A	LO	LO	SN B	LO
London Bridge ⊖	d			19 10			19 28			19 40			19 58			20 10			20 28			20 40	
Highbury & Islington	d	15 47			18 55	19 02		19 10	19 17		19 25	19 32		19 40	19 47		19 55	20 02		20 10	20 17		20 25
Canonbury	d	15 49			18 57	19 04		19 12	19 19		19 27	19 34		19 42	19 49		19 57	20 04		20 12	20 19		20 27
Dalston Junction	d	15 52			19 00	19 07		19 15	19 22		19 30	19 37		19 45	19 52		20 00	20 07		20 15	20 22		20 30
Haggerston	d	15 54			19 02	19 09		19 17	19 24		19 32	19 39		19 47	19 54		20 02	20 09		20 17	20 24		20 32
Hoxton	d	15 56			19 04	19 11		19 19	19 26		19 34	19 41		19 49	19 56		20 04	20 11		20 19	20 26		20 34
Shoreditch High Street	d	15 58			19 07	19 13		19 22	19 28		19 37	19 43		19 52	19 58		20 07	20 13		20 22	20 28		20 37
Whitechapel	d	16 01			19 09	19 16		19 24	19 31		19 39	19 46		19 54	20 01		20 09	20 16		20 24	20 31		20 39
Shadwell	d	16 03			19 11	19 18		19 26	19 33		19 41	19 48		19 56	20 03		20 11	20 18		20 26	20 33		20 41
Wapping	d	16 05	and at the same minutes past each hour until		19 13	19 20		19 28	19 35		19 43	19 50		19 58	20 05		20 13	20 20		20 28	20 35		20 43
Rotherhithe	d	16 06			19 15	19 21		19 30	19 36		19 45	19 51		20 00	20 06		20 15	20 21		20 30	20 36		20 45
Canada Water	d	16 08			19 17	19 23		19 32	19 38		19 47	19 53		20 02	20 08		20 17	20 23		20 32	20 38		20 47
Surrey Quays	d	16 10			19 19	19 25		19 34	19 40		19 49	19 55		20 04	20 10		20 19	20 25		20 34	20 40		20 49
New Cross Gate	d	16 15		19 18	19 23	19 30	19 35	19 38	19 45	19 48	19 53	20 00	20 05	20 08	20 15	20 18	20 23	20 30	20 35	20 38	20 45	20 48	20 53
Brockley	d	16 17		19 21	19 26	19 32	19 37	19 41	19 47	19 51	19 56	20 02	20 07	20 11	20 17	20 21	20 26	20 32	20 37	20 41	20 47	20 51	20 56
Honor Oak Park	d	16 20		19 23	19 28	19 35	19 40	19 43	19 50	19 53	19 58	20 05	20 10	20 13	20 20	20 23	20 28	20 35	20 40	20 43	20 50	20 53	20 58
Forest Hill	d	16 22		19 26	19 31	19 37	19 42	19 46	19 52	19 56	20 01	20 07	20 12	20 16	20 22	20 26	20 31	20 37	20 42	20 46	20 52	20 56	21 01
Sydenham	d	16 26		19 29	19 34	19 41	19 46	19 49	19 56	19 59	20 04	20 11	20 16	20 19	20 26	20 29	20 34	20 41	20 46	20 49	20 56	20 59	21 04
Crystal Palace	a				19 38		19 50	19 53			20 08		20 20	20 23			20 38		20 50	20 53			21 08
Penge West	d	16 28		19 31		19 43			19 58	20 01		20 13			20 28	20 31		20 43			20 58	21 01	
Anerley	d	16 30		19 33		19 45			20 00	20 03		20 15			20 30	20 33		20 45			21 00	21 03	
Norwood Junction	a	16 33		19 36		19 48			20 03	20 06		20 18			20 33	20 36		20 48			21 03	21 06	
Norwood Junction	d	16 33				19 48			20 03			20 18			20 33			20 48			21 03		
West Croydon	a	16 43				19 58			20 13			20 28			20 43			20 58			21 13		
Norwood Junction	d			19 39						20 09						20 39						21 09	
East Croydon	a			19 43						20 13						20 43						21 13	
Purley	a			19 54						20 24						20 54						21 24	

A To London Victoria

B To Coulsdon Town

For full service between Highbury & Islington and Surrey Quays, refer to Table T178

For Sutton connections at West Croydon, refer to Table T172

Table T177-F

Saturdays
26 May to 8 December

London Bridge-New Cross Gate,Brockley, Honor Oak Park, Forest Hill, Sydenham, Crystal Palace, Penge West, Anerley-Norwood Junction and Croydon

		LO	SN A	LO	LO	SN B	LO	LO	SN A	LO	LO	SN B	LO	LO	SN A	LO	LO	SN B	LO	LO	SN A	LO	LO
London Bridge ⊖	d		20 58			21 10			21 28			21 40			21 58			22 10			22 28		
Highbury & Islington	d	20 32		20 40	20 47		20 55	21 02		21 10	21 17		21 25	21 32		21 40	21 47		21 55	22 02		22 10	22 17
Canonbury	d	20 34		20 42	20 49		20 57	21 04		21 12	21 19		21 27	21 34		21 42	21 49		21 57	22 04		22 12	22 19
Dalston Junction	d	20 37		20 45	20 52		21 00	21 07		21 15	21 22		21 30	21 37		21 45	21 52		22 00	22 07		22 15	22 22
Haggerston	d	20 39		20 47	20 54		21 02	21 09		21 17	21 24		21 32	21 39		21 47	21 54		22 02	22 09		22 17	22 24
Hoxton	d	20 41		20 49	20 56		21 04	21 11		21 19	21 26		21 34	21 41		21 49	21 56		22 04	22 11		22 19	22 26
Shoreditch High Street	d	20 43		20 52	20 58		21 07	21 13		21 22	21 28		21 37	21 43		21 52	21 58		22 07	22 13		22 22	22 28
Whitechapel	d	20 46		20 54	21 01		21 09	21 16		21 24	21 31		21 39	21 46		21 54	22 01		22 09	22 16		22 24	22 31
Shadwell	d	20 48		20 56	21 03		21 11	21 18		21 26	21 33		21 41	21 48		21 56	22 03		22 11	22 18		22 26	22 33
Wapping	d	20 50		20 58	21 05		21 13	21 20		21 28	21 35		21 43	21 50		21 58	22 05		22 13	22 20		22 28	22 35
Rotherhithe	d	20 51		21 00	21 06		21 15	21 21		21 30	21 36		21 45	21 51		22 00	22 06		22 15	22 21		22 30	22 36
Canada Water	d	20 53		21 02	21 08		21 17	21 23		21 32	21 38		21 47	21 53		22 02	22 08		22 17	22 23		22 32	22 38
Surrey Quays	d	20 55		21 04	21 10		21 19	21 25		21 34	21 40		21 49	21 55		22 04	22 10		22 19	22 25		22 34	22 40
New Cross Gate	d	21 00	21 05	21 08	21 15	21 18	21 23	21 30	21 35	21 38	21 45	21 48	21 53	22 00	22 05	22 08	22 15	22 18	22 23	22 30	22 35	22 38	22 45
Brockley	d	21 02	21 07	21 11	21 17	21 21	21 26	21 32	21 37	21 41	21 47	21 51	21 56	22 02	22 07	22 11	22 17	22 21	22 26	22 32	22 37	22 41	22 47
Honor Oak Park	d	21 05	21 10	21 13	21 20	21 23	21 28	21 35	21 40	21 43	21 50	21 53	21 58	22 05	22 10	22 13	22 20	22 23	22 28	22 35	22 40	22 43	22 50
Forest Hill	d	21 07	21 12	21 16	21 22	21 26	21 31	21 37	21 42	21 46	21 52	21 56	22 01	22 07	22 12	22 16	22 22	22 26	22 31	22 37	22 42	22 46	22 52
Sydenham	d	21 11	21 16	21 19	21 26	21 29	21 34	21 41	21 46	21 49	21 56	21 59	22 04	22 11	22 16	22 19	22 26	22 29	22 34	22 41	22 46	22 49	22 56
Crystal Palace	a		21 20	21 23			21 38		21 50	21 53			22 08		22 20	22 23			22 38		22 50	22 53	
Penge West	d	21 13			21 28	21 31		21 43			21 58	22 01		22 13			22 28	22 31		22 43			22 58
Anerley	d	21 15			21 30	21 33		21 45			22 00	22 03		22 15			22 30	22 33		22 45			23 00
Norwood Junction	a	21 18			21 33	21 36		21 48			22 03	22 06		22 18			22 33	22 36		22 48			23 03
Norwood Junction	d	21 18			21 33			21 48			22 03			22 18			22 33			22 48			23 03
West Croydon	a	21 24			21 39			21 54			22 09			22 24			22 39			22 54			23 13
Norwood Junction	d					21 39						22 09						22 39					
East Croydon	a					21 43						22 13						22 43					
Purley	a					21 54						22 24						22 54					

		SN B	LO	LO	SN A	LO	LO	SN	LO	LO	SN A	LO	LO	SN	LO	LO	SN C	LO
London Bridge ⊖	d	22 40			22 58			23 10			23 28			23 40			23 58	
Highbury & Islington	d		22 25	22 32		22 40	22 47		22 55	23 02		23 10	23 17		23 25	23 32		23 40
Canonbury	d		22 27	22 34		22 42	22 49		22 57	23 04		23 12	23 19		23 27	23 34		23 42
Dalston Junction	d		22 30	22 37		22 45	22 52		23 00	23 07		23 15	23 22		23 30	23 37		23 45
Haggerston	d		22 32	22 39		22 47	22 54		23 02	23 09		23 17	23 24		23 32	23 39		23 47
Hoxton	d		22 34	22 41		22 49	22 56		23 04	23 11		23 19	23 26		23 34	23 41		23 49
Shoreditch High Street	d		22 37	22 43		22 52	22 58		23 07	23 13		23 22	23 28		23 37	23 43		23 52
Whitechapel	d		22 39	22 46		22 54	23 01		23 09	23 16		23 24	23 31		23 39	23 46		23 54
Shadwell	d		22 41	22 48		22 56	23 03		23 11	23 18		23 26	23 33		23 41	23 48		23 56
Wapping	d		22 43	22 50		22 58	23 05		23 13	23 20		23 28	23 35		23 43	23 50		23 58
Rotherhithe	d		22 45	22 51		23 00	23 06		23 15	23 21		23 30	23 36		23 45	23 51		23 59
Canada Water	d		22 47	22 53		23 02	23 08		23 17	23 23		23 32	23 38		23 47	23 53		00 02
Surrey Quays	d		22 49	22 55		23 04	23 10		23 19	23 25		23 34	23 40		23 49	23 55		00 04
New Cross Gate	d	22 48	22 53	23 00	23 05	23 08	23 15	23 18	23 23	23 30	23 35	23 38	23 45	23 48	23 53	00 01	00 05	00 08
Brockley	d	22 51	22 56	23 02	23 07	23 11	23 17	23 20	23 26	23 32	23 37	23 41	23 47	23 50	23 56	00 03	00 07	00 11
Honor Oak Park	d	22 53	22 58	23 05	23 10	23 13	23 20	23 23	23 28	23 35	23 40	23 43	23 50	23 53	23 58	00 06	00 10	00 13
Forest Hill	d	22 56	23 01	23 07	23 12	23 16	23 22	23 25	23 31	23 37	23 42	23 46	23 52	23 55	00 01	00 08	00 12	00 16
Sydenham	d	22 59	23 04	23 11	23 16	23 19	23 26	23 29	23 34	23 41	23 46	23 49	23 56	23 59	00 04	00 11	00 16	00 19
Crystal Palace	a		23 08		23 20	23 23			23 38		23 50	23 53			00 08		00 20	00 23
Penge West	d	23 01		23 13			23 28	23 31		23 43			23 58	00 01		00 13		
Anerley	d	23 03		23 15			23 30	23 33		23 45			00 01	00 05		00 15		
Norwood Junction	a	23 06		23 18			23 33	23 36		23 48			00 03	00 08		00 18		
Norwood Junction	d			23 18			23 33			23 48			00 03			00 19		
West Croydon	a			23 28			23 43			23 58			00 13			00 28		
Norwood Junction	d	23 09						23 39						00 09				
East Croydon	a	23 13						23 47						00 17				
Purley	a	23 24																

A To London Victoria B To Coulsdon Town C To Streatham Hill

For full service between Highbury & Islington and Surrey Quays, refer to Table T178

For Sutton connections at West Croydon, refer to Table T172

Table T177-F

Sundays
20 May to 2 December

London Bridge-New Cross Gate,Brockley, Honor Oak Park, Forest Hill, Sydenham, Crystal Palace, Penge West, Anerley-Norwood Junction and Croydon

		LO A	LO A	SN B	LO A	SN C	LO A	SN	LO	LO	LO	SN D	SN	LO	LO	SN D	SN	LO	SN D	LO	SN	LO	SN D
London Bridge ⊖	d							00 35				07 31	07 38			08 01	08 08		08 24		08 38		08 54
Highbury & Islington	d								06 35	06 51				07 21				07 51		08 07		08 21	
Canonbury	d								06 37	06 53				07 23				07 53		08 09		08 23	
Dalston Junction	d								06 40	06 56	07 12			07 26	07 42			07 56		08 12		08 26	
Haggerston	d								06 42	06 57	07 13			07 27	07 43			07 57		08 13		08 27	
Hoxton	d								06 44	06 59	07 15			07 29	07 45			07 59		08 15		08 29	
Shoreditch High Street	d								06 46	07 02	07 18			07 32	07 48			08 02		08 18		08 32	
Whitechapel	d								06 49	07 04	07 20			07 34	07 50			08 04		08 20		08 34	
Shadwell	d								06 51	07 06	07 22			07 36	07 52			08 06		08 22		08 36	
Wapping	d								06 53	07 08	07 24			07 38	07 54			08 08		08 24		08 38	
Rotherhithe	d								06 54	07 10	07 26			07 40	07 56			08 10		08 26		08 40	
Canada Water	d						00 02		06 56	07 12	07 28			07 42	07 58			08 12		08 28		08 42	
Surrey Quays	d						00 04		06 58	07 14	07 30			07 44	08 00			08 14		08 30		08 44	
New Cross Gate	d				00 01	00 05	00 08	00 41	07 04	07 18	07 34	07 38	07 44	07 48	08 04	08 08	08 14	08 18	08 30	08 34	08 44	08 48	09 00
Brockley	d				00 03	00 07	00 11	00 44	07 07	07 21	07 37	07 40	07 47	07 51	08 07	08 10	08 17	08 21	08 33	08 37	08 47	08 51	09 03
Honor Oak Park	d				00 06	00 10	00 13	00 46	07 09	07 23	07 39	07 43	07 49	07 53	08 09	08 13	08 19	08 23	08 35	08 39	08 49	08 53	09 05
Forest Hill	d		00 01		00 08	00 12	00 16	00 49	07 12	07 26	07 42	07 45	07 52	07 56	08 12	08 15	08 22	08 26	08 38	08 42	08 52	08 56	09 08
Sydenham	d		00 04		00 11	00 16	00 19	00 52	07 15	07 29	07 45	07 49	07 55	07 59	08 15	08 19	08 25	08 29	08 41	08 45	08 55	08 59	09 11
Crystal Palace	a		00 08			00 20	00 23			07 34			08 00	08 04			08 30	08 34			09 00	09 04	
Penge West	d			00 01	00 13			00 54	07 17		07 47	07 51			08 17	08 21			08 43	08 47			09 13
Anerley	d	00 01		00 05	00 15			00 56	07 19		07 49	07 53			08 19	08 23			08 45	08 49			09 15
Norwood Junction	a	00 03		00 08	00 18			00 59	07 22		07 52	07 56			08 22	08 26			08 49	08 52			09 19
Norwood Junction	d	00 03			00 19				07 22		07 52				08 22					08 52			
West Croydon	a	00 13			00 28				07 27		07 58				08 28					08 59			
Norwood Junction	d			00 09				01 08				07 56				08 26			08 52				09 22
East Croydon	a			00 17				01 13				08 02				08 32			08 55				09 25
Purley	a											08 11				08 41			09 04				09 34

		LO	SN	LO	SN D	LO	SN	LO	SN D	LO	SN	LO	SN D	LO	SN	LO	SN D	LO	SN	LO	SN D	LO
London Bridge ⊖	d		09 08		09 24		09 38		09 54		10 08		10 24		10 38		10 54		11 08		11 24	
Highbury & Islington	d	08 37		08 51		09 07		09 21		09 37		09 51		10 07		10 21		10 37		10 51		11 07
Canonbury	d	08 39		08 53		09 09		09 23		09 39		09 53		10 09		10 23		10 39		10 53		11 09
Dalston Junction	d	08 42		08 56		09 12		09 26		09 42		09 56		10 12		10 26		10 42		10 56		11 12
Haggerston	d	08 43		08 57		09 13		09 27		09 43		09 57		10 13		10 27		10 43		10 57		11 13
Hoxton	d	08 45		08 59		09 15		09 29		09 45		09 59		10 15		10 29		10 45		10 59		11 15
Shoreditch High Street	d	08 48		09 02		09 18		09 32		09 48		10 02		10 18		10 32		10 48		11 02		11 18
Whitechapel	d	08 50		09 04		09 20		09 34		09 50		10 04		10 20		10 34		10 50		11 04		11 20
Shadwell	d	08 52		09 06		09 22		09 36		09 52		10 06		10 22		10 36		10 52		11 06		11 22
Wapping	d	08 54		09 08		09 24		09 38		09 54		10 08		10 24		10 38		10 54		11 08		11 24
Rotherhithe	d	08 56		09 10		09 26		09 40		09 56		10 10		10 26		10 40		10 56		11 10		11 26
Canada Water	d	08 58		09 12		09 28		09 42		09 58		10 12		10 28		10 42		10 58		11 12		11 28
Surrey Quays	d	09 00		09 14		09 30		09 44		10 00		10 14		10 30		10 44		11 00		11 14		11 30
New Cross Gate	d	09 04	09 14	09 18	09 30	09 34	09 44	09 48	10 00	10 04	10 14	10 18	10 30	10 34	10 44	10 48	11 00	11 04	11 14	11 18	11 30	11 34
Brockley	d	09 07	09 17	09 21	09 33	09 37	09 47	09 51	10 03	10 07	10 17	10 21	10 33	10 37	10 47	10 51	11 03	11 07	11 17	11 21	11 33	11 37
Honor Oak Park	d	09 09	09 19	09 23	09 35	09 39	09 49	09 53	10 05	10 09	10 19	10 23	10 35	10 39	10 49	10 53	11 05	11 09	11 19	11 23	11 35	11 39
Forest Hill	d	09 12	09 22	09 26	09 38	09 42	09 52	09 56	10 08	10 12	10 22	10 26	10 38	10 42	10 52	10 56	11 08	11 12	11 22	11 26	11 38	11 42
Sydenham	d	09 15	09 25	09 29	09 41	09 45	09 55	09 59	10 11	10 15	10 25	10 29	10 41	10 45	10 55	10 59	11 11	11 15	11 25	11 29	11 41	11 45
Crystal Palace	a		09 30	09 34			10 00	10 04			10 30	10 34			11 00	11 04			11 30	11 34		
Penge West	d	09 17			09 43	09 47			10 13	10 17			10 43	10 47			11 13	11 17			11 43	11 47
Anerley	d	09 19			09 45	09 49			10 15	10 19			10 45	10 49			11 15	11 19			11 45	11 49
Norwood Junction	a	09 22			09 49	09 52			10 19	10 22			10 49	10 52			11 19	11 22			11 49	11 52
Norwood Junction	d	09 22				09 52				10 22				10 52				11 22				11 52
West Croydon	a	09 29				09 59				10 29				10 59				11 29				11 59
Norwood Junction	d				09 52				10 22				10 52				11 22				11 52	
East Croydon	a				09 55				10 25				10 55				11 25				11 55	
Purley	a				10 04				10 34				11 04				11 34				12 04	

A not 20 May. From Highbury and Islington Ell
B not 20 May. From London Bridge
C not 20 May. From London Bridge to Streatham Hill
D To Caterham

For full service between Highbury & Islington and Surrey Quays, refer to Table T178

For Sutton connections at West Croydon, refer to Table T172

Table T177-F

Sundays
20 May to 2 December

London Bridge-New Cross Gate,Brockley, Honor Oak Park, Forest Hill, Sydenham, Crystal Palace, Penge West, Anerley-Norwood Junction and Croydon

		SN	LO	SN A	LO	LO	SN	LO	LO	SN A	LO	LO	SN	LO	LO	SN A	LO	LO	SN	LO	LO	SN A
London Bridge ⊖	d	11 38		11 54			12 08			12 24			12 38			12 54			13 08			13 24
Highbury & Islington	d		11 21		11 37			11 53			12 08				12 28			12 43			12 58	
Canonbury	d		11 23		11 39			11 55			12 10				12 30			12 45			13 00	
Dalston Junction	d		11 26		11 42	11 48		11 58	12 03		12 13	12 18		12 28	12 33		12 43	12 48		12 58	13 03	
Haggerston	d		11 27		11 43	11 49		11 59	12 04		12 14	12 19		12 29	12 34		12 44	12 49		12 59	13 04	
Hoxton	d		11 29		11 45	11 51		12 01	12 06		12 16	12 21		12 31	12 36		12 46	12 51		13 01	13 06	
Shoreditch High Street	d		11 32		11 48	11 54		12 04	12 09		12 19	12 24		12 34	12 39		12 49	12 54		13 04	13 09	
Whitechapel	d		11 34		11 50	11 56		12 06	12 11		12 21	12 26		12 36	12 41		12 51	12 56		13 06	13 11	
Shadwell	d		11 36		11 52	11 58		12 08	12 13		12 23	12 28		12 38	12 43		12 53	12 58		13 08	13 13	
Wapping	d		11 38		11 54	12 00		12 10	12 15		12 25	12 30		12 40	12 45		12 55	13 00		13 10	13 15	
Rotherhithe	d		11 40		11 56	12 02		12 12	12 17		12 27	12 32		12 42	12 47		12 57	13 02		13 12	13 17	
Canada Water	d		11 42		11 58	12 04		12 14	12 19		12 29	12 34		12 44	12 49		12 59	13 04		13 14	13 19	
Surrey Quays	d		11 44		12 00	12 06		12 16	12 21		12 31	12 36		12 46	12 51		13 01	13 06		13 16	13 21	
New Cross Gate	d	11 44	11 48	12 00	12 04	12 10	12 14	12 20	12 25	12 30	12 35	12 40	12 44	12 50	12 55	13 00	13 05	13 10	13 14	13 20	13 25	13 30
Brockley	d	11 47	11 51	12 03	12 07	12 13	12 17	12 23	12 28	12 33	12 38	12 43	12 47	12 53	12 58	13 03	13 08	13 13	13 17	13 23	13 28	13 33
Honor Oak Park	d	11 49	11 53	12 05	12 09	12 15	12 19	12 25	12 30	12 35	12 40	12 45	12 49	12 55	13 00	13 05	13 10	13 15	13 19	13 25	13 30	13 35
Forest Hill	d	11 52	11 56	12 08	12 12	12 18	12 22	12 28	12 33	12 38	12 43	12 48	12 52	12 58	13 03	13 08	13 13	13 18	13 22	13 28	13 33	13 38
Sydenham	d	11 55	11 59	12 11	12 15	12 21	12 25	12 31	12 36	12 41	12 46	12 51	12 55	13 01	13 06	13 11	13 16	13 21	13 25	13 31	13 36	13 41
Crystal Palace	a	12 00	12 04			12 25	12 30		12 40			12 55	13 00		13 11			13 26	13 30		13 41	
Penge West	d			12 14	12 17			12 33		12 44	12 48			13 03		13 14	13 18			13 33		13 44
Anerley	d			12 16	12 19			12 35		12 46	12 50			13 05		13 16	13 20			13 35		13 46
Norwood Junction	a			12 20	12 22			12 38		12 50	12 53			13 08		13 20	13 23			13 38		13 50
Norwood Junction	d				12 22			12 38			12 53			13 08			13 23			13 38		
West Croydon	a				12 29			12 45			13 00			13 14			13 30			13 44		
Norwood Junction	d			12 22						12 52						13 22						13 52
East Croydon	a			12 25						12 55						13 25						13 55
Purley	a			12 34						13 04						13 34						14 04

		LO	LO	SN	LO	LO	SN A	LO	LO	SN	LO	LO	SN A	LO	LO	SN	LO	LO	SN A	LO	LO	SN	LO
London Bridge ⊖	d			13 38			13 54			14 08			14 24			14 38			14 54			15 08	
Highbury & Islington	d		13 13			13 28			13 43			13 58			14 13			14 28			14 43		
Canonbury	d		13 15			13 30			13 45			14 00			14 15			14 30			14 45		
Dalston Junction	d	13 13	13 18		13 28	13 33		13 43	13 48		13 58	14 03		14 13	14 18		14 28	14 33		14 43	14 48		14 58
Haggerston	d	13 14	13 19		13 29	13 34		13 44	13 49		13 59	14 04		14 14	14 19		14 29	14 34		14 44	14 49		14 59
Hoxton	d	13 16	13 21		13 31	13 36		13 46	13 51		14 01	14 06		14 16	14 21		14 31	14 36		14 46	14 51		15 01
Shoreditch High Street	d	13 19	13 24		13 34	13 39		13 49	13 54		14 04	14 09		14 19	14 24		14 34	14 39		14 49	14 54		15 04
Whitechapel	d	13 21	13 26		13 36	13 41		13 51	13 56		14 06	14 11		14 21	14 26		14 36	14 41		14 51	14 56		15 06
Shadwell	d	13 23	13 28		13 38	13 43		13 53	13 58		14 08	14 13		14 23	14 28		14 38	14 43		14 53	14 58		15 08
Wapping	d	13 25	13 30		13 40	13 45		13 55	14 00		14 10	14 15		14 25	14 30		14 40	14 45		14 55	15 00		15 10
Rotherhithe	d	13 27	13 32		13 42	13 47		13 57	14 02		14 12	14 17		14 27	14 32		14 42	14 47		14 57	15 02		15 12
Canada Water	d	13 29	13 34		13 44	13 49		13 59	14 04		14 14	14 19		14 29	14 34		14 44	14 49		14 59	15 04		15 14
Surrey Quays	d	13 31	13 36		13 46	13 51		14 01	14 06		14 16	14 21		14 31	14 36		14 46	14 51		15 01	15 06		15 16
New Cross Gate	d	13 35	13 40	13 44	13 50	13 55	14 00	14 05	14 10	14 14	14 20	14 25	14 30	14 35	14 40	14 44	14 50	14 55	15 00	15 05	15 10	15 14	15 20
Brockley	d	13 38	13 43	13 47	13 53	13 58	14 03	14 08	14 13	14 17	14 23	14 28	14 33	14 38	14 43	14 47	14 53	14 58	15 03	15 08	15 13	15 17	15 23
Honor Oak Park	d	13 40	13 45	13 49	13 55	14 00	14 05	14 10	14 15	14 19	14 25	14 30	14 35	14 40	14 45	14 49	14 55	15 00	15 05	15 10	15 15	15 19	15 25
Forest Hill	d	13 43	13 48	13 52	13 58	14 03	14 08	14 13	14 18	14 22	14 28	14 33	14 38	14 43	14 48	14 52	14 58	15 03	15 08	15 13	15 18	15 22	15 28
Sydenham	d	13 46	13 51	13 55	14 01	14 06	14 11	14 16	14 21	14 25	14 31	14 36	14 41	14 46	14 51	14 55	15 01	15 06	15 11	15 16	15 21	15 25	15 31
Crystal Palace	a		13 56	14 00		14 11			14 26	14 30		14 41			14 56	15 00		15 11			15 26	15 30	
Penge West	d	13 48			14 03		14 14	14 18			14 33		14 44	14 48			15 03		15 14	15 18			15 33
Anerley	d	13 50			14 05		14 16	14 20			14 35		14 46	14 50			15 05		15 16	15 20			15 35
Norwood Junction	a	13 53			14 08		14 20	14 23			14 38		14 50	14 53			15 08		15 20	15 23			15 38
Norwood Junction	d	13 53			14 08			14 23			14 38			14 53			15 08			15 23			15 38
West Croydon	a	13 59			14 14			14 29			14 44			14 59			15 14			15 29			15 44
Norwood Junction	d						14 22						14 52						15 22				
East Croydon	a						14 25						14 55						15 25				
Purley	a						14 34						15 04						15 34				

A To Caterham

For full service between Highbury & Islington and Surrey Quays, refer to Table T178

For Sutton connections at West Croydon, refer to Table T172

Table T177-F

Sundays
20 May to 2 December

London Bridge-New Cross Gate,Brockley, Honor Oak Park, Forest Hill, Sydenham, Crystal Palace, Penge West, Anerley-Norwood Junction and Croydon

		LO	SN A	LO	LO	SN	LO	LO	SN A	LO	LO	SN	LO	LO	SN A	LO	LO	SN	LO	LO	SN A	LO
London Bridge ⊖	d		15 24			15 38			15 54			16 08			16 24			16 38			16 54	
Highbury & Islington	d	14 58			15 13			15 28			15 43			15 58			16 13			16 28		
Canonbury	d	15 00			15 15			15 30			15 45			16 00			16 15			16 30		
Dalston Junction	d	15 03		15 13	15 18		15 28	15 33		15 43	15 48		15 58	16 03		16 13	16 18		16 28	16 33		16 43
Haggerston	d	15 04		15 14	15 19		15 29	15 34		15 44	15 49		15 59	16 04		16 14	16 19		16 29	16 34		16 44
Hoxton	d	15 06		15 16	15 21		15 31	15 36		15 46	15 51		16 01	16 06		16 16	16 21		16 31	16 36		16 46
Shoreditch High Street	d	15 09		15 19	15 24		15 34	15 39		15 49	15 54		16 04	16 09		16 19	16 24		16 34	16 39		16 49
Whitechapel	d	15 11		15 21	15 26		15 36	15 41		15 51	15 56		16 06	16 11		16 21	16 26		16 36	16 41		16 51
Shadwell	d	15 13		15 23	15 28		15 38	15 43		15 53	15 58		16 08	16 13		16 23	16 28		16 38	16 43		16 53
Wapping	d	15 15		15 25	15 30		15 40	15 45		15 55	16 00		16 10	16 15		16 25	16 30		16 40	16 45		16 55
Rotherhithe	d	15 17		15 27	15 32		15 42	15 47		15 57	16 02		16 12	16 17		16 27	16 32		16 42	16 47		16 57
Canada Water	d	15 19		15 29	15 34		15 44	15 49		15 59	16 04		16 14	16 19		16 29	16 34		16 44	16 49		16 59
Surrey Quays	d	15 21		15 31	15 36		15 46	15 51		16 01	16 06		16 16	16 21		16 31	16 36		16 46	16 51		17 01
New Cross Gate	d	15 25	15 30	15 35	15 40	15 44	15 50	15 55	16 00	16 05	16 10	16 14	16 20	16 25	16 30	16 35	16 40	16 44	16 50	16 55	17 00	17 05
Brockley	d	15 28	15 33	15 38	15 43	15 47	15 53	15 58	16 03	16 08	16 13	16 17	16 23	16 28	16 33	16 38	16 43	16 47	16 53	16 58	17 03	17 08
Honor Oak Park	d	15 30	15 35	15 40	15 45	15 49	15 55	16 00	16 05	16 10	16 15	16 19	16 25	16 30	16 35	16 40	16 45	16 49	16 55	17 00	17 05	17 10
Forest Hill	d	15 33	15 38	15 43	15 48	15 52	15 58	16 03	16 08	16 13	16 18	16 22	16 28	16 33	16 38	16 43	16 48	16 52	16 58	17 03	17 08	17 13
Sydenham	d	15 36	15 41	15 46	15 51	15 55	16 01	16 06	16 11	16 16	16 21	16 25	16 31	16 36	16 41	16 46	16 51	16 55	17 01	17 06	17 11	17 16
Crystal Palace	a	15 41			15 56	16 00		16 11			16 26	16 30		16 41			16 56	17 00		17 11		
Penge West	d		15 44	15 48			16 03		16 14	16 18			16 33		16 44	16 48			17 03		17 14	17 18
Anerley	d		15 46	15 50			16 05		16 16	16 20			16 35		16 46	16 50			17 05		17 16	17 20
Norwood Junction	a		15 50	15 53			16 08		16 20	16 23			16 38		16 50	16 53			17 08		17 20	17 23
Norwood Junction	d			15 53			16 08			16 23			16 38			16 53			17 08			17 23
West Croydon	a			15 59			16 14			16 29			16 44			16 59			17 15			17 30
Norwood Junction	d		15 52						16 22						16 52						17 22	
East Croydon	a		15 55						16 25						16 55						17 25	
Purley	a		16 04						16 34						17 04						17 34	

		LO	SN	LO	LO	SN A	LO	LO	SN	LO	LO	SN A	LO	LO	SN	LO	LO	SN A	LO	LO	SN	LO
London Bridge ⊖	d		17 08			17 24			17 38			17 54			18 08			18 24			18 38	
Highbury & Islington	d	16 43			16 58			17 13			17 28			17 43			17 58			18 13		
Canonbury	d	16 45			17 00			17 15			17 30			17 45			18 00			18 15		
Dalston Junction	d	16 48		16 58	17 03		17 13	17 18		17 28	17 33		17 43	17 48		17 58	18 03		18 13	18 18		18 28
Haggerston	d	16 49		16 59	17 04		17 14	17 19		17 29	17 34		17 44	17 49		17 59	18 04		18 14	18 19		18 29
Hoxton	d	16 51		17 01	17 06		17 16	17 21		17 31	17 36		17 46	17 51		18 01	18 06		18 16	18 21		18 31
Shoreditch High Street	d	16 54		17 04	17 09		17 19	17 24		17 34	17 39		17 49	17 54		18 04	18 09		18 19	18 24		18 34
Whitechapel	d	16 56		17 06	17 11		17 21	17 26		17 36	17 41		17 51	17 56		18 06	18 11		18 21	18 26		18 36
Shadwell	d	16 58		17 08	17 13		17 23	17 28		17 38	17 43		17 53	17 58		18 08	18 13		18 23	18 28		18 38
Wapping	d	17 00		17 10	17 15		17 25	17 30		17 40	17 45		17 55	18 00		18 10	18 15		18 25	18 30		18 40
Rotherhithe	d	17 02		17 12	17 17		17 27	17 32		17 42	17 47		17 57	18 02		18 12	18 17		18 27	18 32		18 42
Canada Water	d	17 04		17 14	17 19		17 29	17 34		17 44	17 49		17 59	18 04		18 14	18 19		18 29	18 34		18 44
Surrey Quays	d	17 06		17 16	17 21		17 31	17 36		17 46	17 51		18 01	18 06		18 16	18 21		18 31	18 36		18 46
New Cross Gate	d	17 10	17 14	17 20	17 25	17 30	17 35	17 40	17 44	17 50	17 55	18 00	18 05	18 10	18 14	18 20	18 25	18 30	18 35	18 40	18 44	18 50
Brockley	d	17 13	17 17	17 23	17 28	17 33	17 38	17 43	17 47	17 53	17 58	18 03	18 08	18 13	18 17	18 23	18 28	18 33	18 38	18 43	18 47	18 53
Honor Oak Park	d	17 15	17 19	17 25	17 30	17 35	17 40	17 45	17 49	17 55	18 00	18 05	18 10	18 15	18 19	18 25	18 30	18 35	18 40	18 45	18 49	18 55
Forest Hill	d	17 18	17 22	17 28	17 33	17 38	17 43	17 48	17 52	17 58	18 03	18 08	18 13	18 18	18 22	18 28	18 33	18 38	18 43	18 48	18 52	18 58
Sydenham	d	17 21	17 25	17 31	17 36	17 41	17 46	17 51	17 55	18 01	18 06	18 11	18 16	18 21	18 25	18 31	18 36	18 41	18 46	18 51	18 55	19 01
Crystal Palace	a	17 26	17 30		17 41			17 56	18 00		18 11			18 26	18 30		18 41			18 56	19 00	
Penge West	d			17 33		17 44	17 48			18 03		18 14	18 18			18 33		18 44	18 48			19 03
Anerley	d			17 35		17 46	17 50			18 05		18 16	18 20			18 35		18 46	18 50			19 05
Norwood Junction	a			17 38		17 50	17 53			18 08		18 20	18 23			18 38		18 50	18 53			19 08
Norwood Junction	d			17 38			17 53			18 08			18 23			18 38			18 53			19 08
West Croydon	a			17 45			18 00			18 15			18 30			18 45			19 00			19 15
Norwood Junction	d					17 52						18 22						18 52				
East Croydon	a					17 55						18 25						18 55				
Purley	a					18 04						18 34						19 04				

A To Caterham

For full service between Highbury & Islington and Surrey Quays, refer to Table T178

For Sutton connections at West Croydon, refer to Table T172

Table T177-F

Sundays

20 May to 2 December

London Bridge-New Cross Gate,Brockley, Honor Oak Park, Forest Hill, Sydenham, Crystal Palace, Penge West, Anerley-Norwood Junction and Croydon

		LO	SN A	LO	LO	SN	LO	LO	SN A	LO	LO	SN	LO
London Bridge ■ ⊖	d		18 54			19 08			19 24			19 38	
Highbury & Islington	d	18 28			18 43			18 58			19 13		
Canonbury	d	18 30			18 45			19 00			19 15		
Dalston Junction	d	18 33		18 43	18 48		18 58	19 03		19 13	19 18		19 28
Haggerston	d	18 34		18 44	18 49		18 59	19 04		19 14	19 19		19 29
Hoxton	d	18 36		18 46	18 51		19 01	19 06		19 16	19 21		19 31
Shoreditch High Street	d	18 39		18 49	18 54		19 04	19 09		19 19	19 24		19 34
Whitechapel	d	18 41		18 51	18 56		19 06	19 11		19 21	19 26		19 36
Shadwell	d	18 43		18 53	18 58		19 08	19 13		19 23	19 28		19 38
Wapping	d	18 45		18 55	19 00		19 10	19 15		19 25	19 30		19 40
Rotherhithe	d	18 47		18 57	19 02		19 12	19 17		19 27	19 32		19 42
Canada Water	d	18 49		18 59	19 04		19 14	19 19		19 29	19 34		19 44
Surrey Quays	d	18 51		19 01	19 06		19 16	19 21		19 31	19 36		19 46
New Cross Gate ■	d	18 55	19 00	19 05	19 10	19 14	19 20	19 25	19 30	19 35	19 40	19 44	19 50
Brockley	d	18 58	19 03	19 08	19 13	19 17	19 23	19 28	19 33	19 38	19 43	19 47	19 53
Honor Oak Park	d	19 00	19 05	19 10	19 15	19 19	19 25	19 30	19 35	19 40	19 45	19 49	19 55
Forest Hill ■	d	19 03	19 08	19 13	19 18	19 22	19 28	19 33	19 38	19 43	19 48	19 52	19 58
Sydenham	d	19 06	19 11	19 16	19 21	19 25	19 31	19 36	19 41	19 46	19 51	19 55	20 01
Crystal Palace ■	a	19 11			19 26	19 30		19 41			19 56	20 00	
Penge West	d		19 14	19 18			19 33		19 44	19 48			20 03
Anerley	d		19 16	19 20			19 35		19 46	19 50			20 05
Norwood Junction ■	a		19 20	19 23			19 38		19 50	19 53			20 08
Norwood Junction	d			19 23			19 38			19 53			20 08
West Croydon ■ ⇌	a			19 29			19 44			19 59			20 14
Norwood Junction	d		19 22						19 52				
East Croydon ⇌	a		19 25						19 55				
Purley	a		19 34						20 04				

and at the same minutes past each hour until

		LO	SN A	LO	LO	SN	LO	LO	SN A	LO	LO
London Bridge ■ ⊖	d		21 54			22 08			22 24		
Highbury & Islington	d	21 28			21 43			21 58			22 13
Canonbury	d	21 30			21 45			22 00			22 15
Dalston Junction	d	21 33		21 43	21 48		21 58	22 03		22 13	22 18
Haggerston	d	21 34		21 44	21 49		21 59	22 04		22 14	22 19
Hoxton	d	21 36		21 46	21 51		22 01	22 06		22 16	22 21
Shoreditch High Street	d	21 39		21 49	21 54		22 04	22 09		22 19	22 24
Whitechapel	d	21 41		21 51	21 56		22 06	22 11		22 21	22 26
Shadwell	d	21 43		21 53	21 58		22 08	22 13		22 23	22 28
Wapping	d	21 45		21 55	22 00		22 10	22 15		22 25	22 30
Rotherhithe	d	21 47		21 57	22 02		22 12	22 17		22 27	22 32
Canada Water	d	21 49		21 59	22 04		22 14	22 19		22 29	22 34
Surrey Quays	d	21 51		22 01	22 06		22 16	22 21		22 31	22 36
New Cross Gate ■	d	21 55	22 00	22 05	22 10	22 14	22 20	22 25	22 30	22 35	22 40
Brockley	d	21 58	22 03	22 08	22 13	22 17	22 23	22 28	22 33	22 38	22 43
Honor Oak Park	d	22 00	22 05	22 10	22 15	22 19	22 25	22 30	22 35	22 40	22 45
Forest Hill ■	d	22 03	22 08	22 13	22 18	22 22	22 28	22 33	22 38	22 43	22 48
Sydenham	d	22 06	22 11	22 16	22 21	22 25	22 31	22 36	22 41	22 46	22 51
Crystal Palace ■	a	22 11			22 26	22 30		22 41			22 56
Penge West	d		22 14	22 18			22 33		22 44	22 48	
Anerley	d		22 16	22 20			22 35		22 46	22 50	
Norwood Junction ■	a		22 20	22 23			22 38		22 50	22 53	
Norwood Junction	d			22 23			22 38			22 53	
West Croydon ■ ⇌	a			22 29			22 44			22 59	
Norwood Junction	d		22 22						22 52		
East Croydon ⇌	a		22 25						22 55		
Purley	a		22 34						23 04		

		SN	LO	SN B	LO	LO	SN	LO	LO	SN A	LO	LO	SN A
London Bridge ■ ⊖	d	22 38		22 54			23 11			23 31			23 50
Highbury & Islington	d					22 43					23 13	23 23	
Canonbury	d					22 45					23 15	23 25	
Dalston Junction	d		22 28		22 43	22 48		22 58	23 13		23 18	23 28	
Haggerston	d		22 29		22 44	22 49		22 59	23 14		23 19	23 29	
Hoxton	d		22 31		22 46	22 51		23 01	23 16		23 21	23 31	
Shoreditch High Street	d		22 34		22 49	22 54		23 04	23 19		23 24	23 34	
Whitechapel	d		22 36		22 51	22 56		23 06	23 21		23 26	23 36	
Shadwell	d		22 38		22 53	22 58		23 08	23 23		23 28	23 38	
Wapping	d		22 40		22 55	23 00		23 10	23 25		23 30	23 40	
Rotherhithe	d		22 42		22 57	23 02		23 12	23 27		23 32	23 42	
Canada Water	d		22 44		22 59	23 04		23 14	23 29		23 34	23 44	
Surrey Quays	d		22 46		23 01	23 06		23 16	23 31		23 36	23 46	
New Cross Gate ■	d	22 44	22 50	23 00	23 05	23 10	23 17	23 20	23 35	23 39	23 42	23 50	23 57
Brockley	d	22 47	22 53	23 03	23 08	23 13	23 19	23 23	23 38	23 41	23 45	23 53	23 59
Honor Oak Park	d	22 49	22 55	23 05	23 10	23 15	23 22	23 25	23 40	23 44	23 47	23 55	00 02
Forest Hill ■	d	22 52	22 58	23 08	23 13	23 18	23 24	23 28	23 43	23 46	23 50	23 58	00 04
Sydenham	d	22 55	23 01	23 11	23 16	23 21	23 28	23 31	23 46	23 50	23 53	00 01	00 08
Crystal Palace ■	a	23 00				23 26	23 33				23 57		
Penge West	d		23 03	23 14	23 18			23 33	23 48	23 52		00 03	00 10
Anerley	d		23 05	23 16	23 20			23 35	23 50	23 54		00 05	00 12
Norwood Junction ■	a		23 08	23 20	23 23			23 38	23 53	23 57		00 08	00 15
Norwood Junction	d		23 08		23 23			23 38	23 53			00 08	
West Croydon ■ ⇌	a		23 14		23 29			23 45	23 59			00 16	
Norwood Junction	d			23 22						23 58			00 16
East Croydon ⇌	a			23 25						00 02			00 19
Purley	a			23 34						00 11			00 28

A To Caterham

B To Tattenham Corner

For full service between Highbury & Islington and Surrey Quays, refer to Table T178

For Sutton connections at West Croydon, refer to Table T172

Table T177-R

Mondays to Fridays

21 May to 7 December

Croydon and Norwood Junction-Anerley, Penge West, Crystal Palace, Sydenham, Forest Hill, Honor Oak Park, Brockley, New Cross Gate-London Bridge

Miles	Miles	Miles	Miles			LO MX A	LO MX B	LO MX A	SN MX C	SN MX C	TL	LO	LO	LO	SN D	LO	LO	TL E	LO	LO	SN D	LO	LO
0	—	—	—	Purley	d						05 11												
3	—	—	—	East Croydon ⇌	d						05 20												
4¾	—	—	—	Norwood Junction ■	a						05 24												
—	0	—	—	West Croydon ■ ⇌	d								05 31			05 46		05 57	06 01			06 16	
—	1¾	—	—	Norwood Junction	a								05 36			05 51		06 02	06 06			06 21	
—	—	—	—	Norwood Junction	d						05 25		05 37			05 52		06 03	06 07			06 22	
6	3	—	—	**Anerley**	d						05 28		05 40			05 55		06 06	06 10			06 25	
6¼	3¼	—	—	**Penge West**	d						05 29		05 41			05 56		06 08	06 11			06 26	
—	—	0	0	**Crystal Palace** ■	d					00 25		05 32		05 47	05 52		06 02			06 17	06 22		06 32
7	4	1¼	1¼	**Sydenham**	d					00 30	05 32	05 36	05 44	05 51	05 56	05 59	06 06	06 11	06 14	06 21	06 26	06 29	06 36
7¾	4¾	2	2	**Forest Hill** ■	d					00 32	05 35	05 39	05 47	05 54	05 58	06 02	06 09	06 13	06 17	06 24	06 28	06 32	06 39
8¾	5¾	3	3	**Honor Oak Park**	d				00 03	00 35	05 37	05 41	05 49	05 56	06 01	06 04	06 11	06 16	06 19	06 26	06 31	06 34	06 41
9¾	6¾	4	4	**Brockley**	d			00 01	00 05	00 37	05 40	05 44	05 52	05 59	06 03	06 07	06 14	06 18	06 22	06 29	06 33	06 37	06 44
—	7½	4¾	4¾	New Cross Gate	d			00 03	00 08	00 40	05 42	05 46	05 54	06 01	06 06	06 09	06 16	06 21	06 24	06 31	06 36	06 39	06 46
—	8¾	6	—	Surrey Quays	d			00 09				05 50	05 57	06 05		06 12	06 20		06 27	06 35		06 42	06 50
—	9¼	6½	—	Canada Water	d			00 11				05 52	05 59	06 07		06 14	06 22		06 29	06 37		06 44	06 52
—	9½	6¾	—	Rotherhithe	d		00 01	00 12				05 54	06 01	06 08		06 16	06 23		06 31	06 38		06 46	06 53
—	9¾	7	—	Wapping	d		00 02	00 14				05 55	06 02	06 10		06 17	06 25		06 32	06 40		06 47	06 55
—	10¼	7½	—	Shadwell	d		00 04	00 16				05 57	06 04	06 12		06 19	06 27		06 34	06 42		06 49	06 57
—	11	8	—	Whitechapel	d		00 07	00 18				06 00	06 07	06 14		06 22	06 29		06 37	06 44		06 52	06 59
—	11¾	8¾	—	Shoreditch High Street	d	00 02	00 09	00 21				06 02	06 09	06 17		06 24	06 32		06 39	06 47		06 54	07 02
—	12½	9½	—	Hoxton	d	00 04	00 11	00 23				06 04	06 11	06 19		06 26	06 34		06 41	06 49		06 56	07 04
—	13	10	—	Haggerston	d	00 06	00 13	00 25				06 06	06 13	06 21		06 28	06 36		06 43	06 51		06 58	07 06
—	13½	10½	—	Dalston Junction	a	00 08	00 15	00 27				06 08	06 15	06 23		06 30	06 38		06 45	06 53		07 00	07 08
—	—	11½	—	Canonbury	a	00 11	00 18	00 30				06 11	06 18	06 26		06 33	06 41		06 48	06 56		07 03	07 11
—	—	12	—	Highbury & Islington	a	00 15	00 25	00 33				06 15	06 23	06 30		06 38	06 45		06 53	07 00		07 08	07 15
12½	—	—	7½	London Bridge ■ ⊖	a				00 15	00 47	05 50				06 18			06 31			06 48		

		SN	LO	LO	SN C	LO	LO	SN	LO	LO	SN C	LO	LO	SN	LO	LO	SN C	LO	SN	LO	SN	LO	LO
Purley	d																						
East Croydon ⇌	d																						
Norwood Junction ■	a																						
West Croydon ■ ⇌	d		06 31			06 46			07 01			07 15			07 31			07 45				08 01	
Norwood Junction	a		06 36			06 51			07 06			07 20			07 37			07 50				08 07	
Norwood Junction	d	06 34	06 37			06 52		07 04	07 07			07 22		07 34	07 37			07 52			08 04	08 07	
Anerley	d	06 37	06 40			06 55		07 07	07 10			07 25		07 37	07 40			07 55			08 07	08 10	
Penge West	d	06 38	06 41			06 56		07 08	07 11			07 26		07 38	07 42			07 56			08 08	08 12	
Crystal Palace ■	d			06 47	06 52		07 02			07 17	07 22		07 32			07 47	07 52		07 59	08 03			08 17
Sydenham	d	06 41	06 44	06 51	06 56	06 59	07 06	07 11	07 14	07 21	07 26	07 29	07 36	07 41	07 44	07 51	07 56	07 59	08 03	08 07	08 11	08 14	08 21
Forest Hill ■	d	06 43	06 47	06 54	06 58	07 02	07 09	07 13	07 17	07 24	07 28	07 32	07 39	07 43	07 47	07 54	07 58	08 02	08 06	08 10	08 13	08 17	08 24
Honor Oak Park	d	06 46	06 49	06 56	07 01	07 04	07 11	07 16	07 19	07 26	07 31	07 34	07 41	07 46	07 49	07 56	08 01	08 04	08 08	08 12	08 16	08 19	08 26
Brockley	d	06 48	06 52	06 59	07 03	07 07	07 14	07 18	07 22	07 29	07 33	07 37	07 44	07 48	07 52	07 59	08 03	08 07	08 11	08 15	08 18	08 22	08 29
New Cross Gate	d	06 51	06 54	07 01	07 06	07 09	07 16	07 21	07 24	07 31	07 36	07 39	07 46	07 51	07 54	08 01	08 06	08 09	08 14	08 17	08 21	08 24	08 31
Surrey Quays	d		06 57	07 05		07 12	07 20		07 28	07 35		07 43	07 50		07 58	08 05		08 13		08 21		08 28	08 35
Canada Water	d		06 59	07 07		07 14	07 22		07 30	07 37		07 45	07 52		08 00	08 07		08 15		08 23		08 30	08 37
Rotherhithe	d		07 01	07 08		07 16	07 23		07 31	07 38		07 46	07 53		08 01	08 08		08 16		08 24		08 31	08 38
Wapping	d		07 02	07 10		07 17	07 25		07 33	07 40		07 48	07 55		08 03	08 10		08 18		08 26		08 33	08 40
Shadwell	d		07 04	07 12		07 19	07 27		07 35	07 42		07 50	07 57		08 05	08 12		08 20		08 28		08 35	08 42
Whitechapel	d		07 07	07 14		07 22	07 29		07 37	07 44		07 52	07 59		08 07	08 14		08 22		08 30		08 37	08 44
Shoreditch High Street	d		07 09	07 17		07 24	07 32		07 40	07 47		07 55	08 02		08 10	08 17		08 25		08 33		08 40	08 47
Hoxton	d		07 11	07 19		07 26	07 34		07 42	07 49		07 57	08 04		08 12	08 19		08 27		08 35		08 42	08 49
Haggerston	d		07 13	07 21		07 28	07 36		07 44	07 51		07 59	08 06		08 14	08 21		08 29		08 37		08 44	08 51
Dalston Junction	a		07 15	07 23		07 30	07 38		07 46	07 53		08 01	08 08		08 16	08 23		08 31		08 39		08 46	08 53
Canonbury	a		07 18	07 26		07 33	07 41		07 49	07 56		08 04	08 11		08 19	08 26		08 34		08 42		08 49	08 56
Highbury & Islington	a		07 25	07 30		07 40	07 45		07 55	08 00		08 09	08 17		08 23	08 32		08 39		08 48		08 55	09 02
London Bridge ■ ⊖	a	07 01			07 18			07 31			07 48			08 01			08 18		08 25		08 31		

A From Crystal Palace

B From West Croydon

C From London Victoria

D From Streatham Hill

E From Epsom

For full service between Highbury & Islington and Surrey Quays, refer to Table T178

For Sutton connections at West Croydon, refer to Table T172

Table T177-R

Mondays to Fridays

21 May to 7 December

Croydon and Norwood Junction-Anerley, Penge West, Crystal Palace, Sydenham, Forest Hill, Honor Oak Park, Brockley, New Cross Gate-London Bridge

		SN A		LO	SN	LO	SN	LO	LO	SN A	LO	LO		SN	LO	LO	SN A	LO	LO	SN	LO	LO		SN A	LO
Purley	d																								
East Croydon	d																								
Norwood Junction	a																								
West Croydon	d			08 15				08 31			08 45				09 01			09 16			09 31				09 46
Norwood Junction	a			08 21				08 37			08 50				09 06			09 21			09 36				09 51
Norwood Junction	d			08 22			08 34	08 37			08 52			09 04	09 07			09 22		09 34	09 37				09 52
Anerley	d			08 25			08 37	08 40			08 55			09 07	09 10			09 25		09 37	09 40				09 55
Penge West	d			08 26			08 38	08 42			08 56			09 08	09 11			09 26		09 39	09 41				09 56
Crystal Palace	d	08 22			08 29	08 33			08 47	08 52		09 02				09 17	09 22		09 32			09 47		09 52	
Sydenham	d	08 26		08 29	08 33	08 37	08 41	08 44	08 51	08 56	08 59	09 06		09 11	09 14	09 21	09 26	09 29	09 36	09 41	09 44	09 51		09 56	09 59
Forest Hill	d	08 28		08 32	08 36	08 40	08 43	08 47	08 54	08 58	09 02	09 09		09 13	09 17	09 24	09 28	09 32	09 39	09 44	09 47	09 54		09 58	10 02
Honor Oak Park	d	08 31		08 34	08 38	08 42	08 46	08 49	08 56	09 01	09 04	09 11		09 16	09 19	09 26	09 31	09 34	09 41	09 46	09 49	09 56		10 01	10 04
Brockley	d	08 33		08 37	08 41	08 45	08 48	08 52	08 59	09 03	09 07	09 14		09 18	09 22	09 29	09 33	09 37	09 44	09 49	09 52	09 59		10 03	10 07
New Cross Gate	d	08 36		08 39	08 44	08 47	08 51	08 54	09 01	09 06	09 09	09 16		09 21	09 24	09 31	09 36	09 39	09 46	09 52	09 54	10 01		10 06	10 09
Surrey Quays	d			08 43		08 51		08 58	09 05		09 13	09 20			09 27	09 35		09 42	09 50		09 57	10 05			10 12
Canada Water	d			08 45		08 53		09 00	09 07		09 15	09 22			09 29	09 37		09 44	09 52		09 59	10 07			10 14
Rotherhithe	d			08 46		08 54		09 01	09 08		09 16	09 23			09 31	09 38		09 46	09 53		10 01	10 08			10 16
Wapping	d			08 48		08 56		09 03	09 10		09 18	09 25			09 32	09 40		09 47	09 55		10 02	10 10			10 17
Shadwell	d			08 50		08 58		09 05	09 12		09 20	09 27			09 34	09 42		09 49	09 57		10 04	10 12			10 19
Whitechapel	d			08 52		09 00		09 07	09 14		09 22	09 29			09 37	09 44		09 52	09 59		10 07	10 14			10 22
Shoreditch High Street	d			08 55		09 03		09 10	09 17		09 25	09 32			09 39	09 47		09 54	10 02		10 09	10 17			10 24
Hoxton	d			08 57		09 05		09 12	09 19		09 27	09 34			09 41	09 49		09 56	10 04		10 11	10 19			10 26
Haggerston	d			08 59		09 07		09 14	09 21		09 29	09 36			09 43	09 51		09 58	10 06		10 13	10 21			10 28
Dalston Junction	a			09 01		09 09		09 16	09 23		09 31	09 38			09 45	09 53		10 00	10 08		10 15	10 23			10 30
Canonbury	a			09 04		09 12		09 19	09 26		09 34	09 41			09 48	09 56		10 03	10 11		10 18	10 26			10 33
Highbury & Islington	a			09 09		09 18		09 25	09 32		09 39	09 47			09 55	10 00		10 10	10 15		10 25	10 30			10 40
London Bridge	a	08 48			08 56		09 01			09 18				09 31			09 48			10 01				10 17	

		LO	SN	LO	LO	SN A	LO	LO		SN	LO	LO	SN A	LO	LO	SN B	LO	LO		SN A	LO	LO	SN B	LO	LO
Purley	d															10 48							11 18		
East Croydon	d															10 57							11 27		
Norwood Junction	a															11 02							11 32		
West Croydon	d			10 01			10 15				10 31			10 46			11 01				11 16			11 31	
Norwood Junction	a			10 06			10 20				10 36			10 52			11 06				11 21			11 36	
Norwood Junction	d		10 03	10 07			10 21			10 33	10 37			10 52		11 03	11 07				11 22		11 33	11 37	
Anerley	d		10 06	10 10			10 24			10 36	10 40			10 55		11 06	11 10				11 25		11 36	11 40	
Penge West	d		10 07	10 11			10 25			10 37	10 41			10 57		11 08	11 11				11 26		11 38	11 41	
Crystal Palace	d	10 02			10 17	10 22		10 32				10 47	10 52		11 02			11 17		11 22		11 32			11 47
Sydenham	d	10 06	10 10	10 14	10 21	10 26	10 28	10 36		10 40	10 44	10 51	10 56	10 59	11 06	11 11	11 14	11 21		11 26	11 29	11 36	11 41	11 44	11 51
Forest Hill	d	10 09	10 13	10 17	10 24	10 28	10 32	10 39		10 43	10 47	10 54	10 58	11 02	11 09	11 13	11 17	11 24		11 28	11 32	11 39	11 43	11 47	11 54
Honor Oak Park	d	10 11	10 15	10 19	10 26	10 31	10 34	10 41		10 45	10 49	10 56	11 01	11 04	11 11	11 16	11 19	11 26		11 31	11 34	11 41	11 46	11 49	11 56
Brockley	d	10 14	10 18	10 22	10 29	10 33	10 37	10 44		10 48	10 52	10 59	11 03	11 07	11 14	11 18	11 22	11 29		11 33	11 37	11 44	11 48	11 52	11 59
New Cross Gate	d	10 16	10 20	10 24	10 31	10 36	10 39	10 46		10 50	10 54	11 01	11 06	11 09	11 16	11 21	11 24	11 31		11 36	11 39	11 46	11 51	11 54	12 01
Surrey Quays	d	10 20		10 27	10 35		10 42	10 50			10 57	11 05		11 12	11 20		11 27	11 35			11 42	11 50		11 57	12 05
Canada Water	d	10 22		10 29	10 37		10 44	10 52			10 59	11 07		11 14	11 22		11 29	11 37			11 44	11 52		11 59	12 07
Rotherhithe	d	10 23		10 31	10 38		10 46	10 53			11 01	11 08		11 16	11 23		11 31	11 38			11 46	11 53		12 01	12 08
Wapping	d	10 25		10 32	10 40		10 47	10 55			11 02	11 10		11 17	11 25		11 32	11 40			11 47	11 55		12 02	12 10
Shadwell	d	10 27		10 34	10 42		10 49	10 57			11 04	11 12		11 19	11 27		11 34	11 42			11 49	11 57		12 04	12 12
Whitechapel	d	10 29		10 37	10 44		10 52	10 59			11 07	11 14		11 22	11 29		11 37	11 44			11 52	11 59		12 07	12 14
Shoreditch High Street	d	10 32		10 39	10 47		10 54	11 02			11 09	11 17		11 24	11 32		11 39	11 47			11 54	12 02		12 09	12 17
Hoxton	d	10 34		10 41	10 49		10 56	11 04			11 11	11 19		11 26	11 34		11 41	11 49			11 56	12 04		12 11	12 19
Haggerston	d	10 36		10 43	10 51		10 58	11 06			11 13	11 21		11 28	11 36		11 43	11 51			11 58	12 06		12 13	12 21
Dalston Junction	a	10 38		10 45	10 53		11 00	11 08			11 15	11 23		11 30	11 38		11 45	11 53			12 00	12 08		12 15	12 23
Canonbury	a	10 41		10 48	10 56		11 03	11 11			11 18	11 26		11 33	11 41		11 48	11 56			12 03	12 11		12 18	12 26
Highbury & Islington	a	10 45		10 55	11 00		11 07	11 15			11 23	11 30		11 38	11 45		11 53	12 00			12 08	12 15		12 23	12 30
London Bridge	a		10 31			10 47				11 01			11 17			11 31				11 47			12 01		

A From London Victoria

B From Coulsdon Town

For full service between Highbury & Islington and Surrey Quays, refer to Table T178

For Sutton connections at West Croydon, refer to Table T172

Table T177-R

Mondays to Fridays

21 May to 7 December

Croydon and Norwood Junction-Anerley, Penge West, Crystal Palace, Sydenham, Forest Hill, Honor Oak Park, Brockley, New Cross Gate-London Bridge

		SN A	LO	LO	SN B	LO	LO	SN A	LO	LO		SN B	LO	LO	SN A	LO	LO	SN B	LO	LO		SN A	LO	LO	SN B
Purley	d				11 48							12 18						12 48							13 18
East Croydon	d				11 57							12 27						12 57							13 27
Norwood Junction	a				12 02							12 32						13 02							13 32
West Croydon	d		11 46			12 01			12 16				12 31			12 46			13 01				13 16		
Norwood Junction	a		11 52			12 06			12 21				12 36			12 52			13 06				13 21		
Norwood Junction	d		11 52		12 03	12 07			12 22			12 33	12 37			12 52		13 03	13 07				13 22		13 33
Anerley	d		11 55		12 06	12 10			12 25			12 36	12 40			12 55		13 06	13 10				13 25		13 36
Penge West	d		11 57		12 08	12 11			12 26			12 38	12 41			12 57		13 08	13 11				13 26		13 38
Crystal Palace	d	11 52		12 02			12 17	12 22		12 32				12 47	12 52		13 02			13 17		13 22		13 32	
Sydenham	d	11 56	11 59	12 06	12 11	12 14	12 21	12 26	12 29	12 36		12 41	12 44	12 51	12 56	12 59	13 06	13 11	13 14	13 21		13 26	13 29	13 36	13 41
Forest Hill	d	11 58	12 02	12 09	12 13	12 17	12 24	12 28	12 32	12 39		12 43	12 47	12 54	12 58	13 02	13 09	13 13	13 17	13 24		13 28	13 32	13 39	13 43
Honor Oak Park	d	12 01	12 04	12 11	12 16	12 19	12 26	12 31	12 34	12 41		12 46	12 49	12 56	13 01	13 04	13 11	13 16	13 19	13 26		13 31	13 34	13 41	13 46
Brockley	d	12 03	12 07	12 14	12 18	12 22	12 29	12 33	12 37	12 44		12 48	12 52	12 59	13 03	13 07	13 14	13 18	13 22	13 29		13 33	13 37	13 44	13 48
New Cross Gate	d	12 06	12 09	12 16	12 21	12 24	12 31	12 36	12 39	12 46		12 51	12 54	13 01	13 06	13 09	13 16	13 21	13 24	13 31		13 36	13 39	13 46	13 51
Surrey Quays	d		12 12	12 20		12 27	12 35		12 42	12 50			12 57	13 05		13 12	13 20		13 27	13 35			13 42	13 50	
Canada Water	d		12 14	12 22		12 29	12 37		12 44	12 52			12 59	13 07		13 14	13 22		13 29	13 37			13 44	13 52	
Rotherhithe	d		12 16	12 23		12 31	12 38		12 46	12 53			13 01	13 08		13 16	13 23		13 31	13 38			13 46	13 53	
Wapping	d		12 17	12 25		12 32	12 40		12 47	12 55			13 02	13 10		13 17	13 25		13 32	13 40			13 47	13 55	
Shadwell	d		12 19	12 27		12 34	12 42		12 49	12 57			13 04	13 12		13 19	13 27		13 34	13 42			13 49	13 57	
Whitechapel	d		12 22	12 29		12 37	12 44		12 52	12 59			13 07	13 14		13 22	13 29		13 37	13 44			13 52	13 59	
Shoreditch High Street	d		12 24	12 32		12 39	12 47		12 54	13 02			13 09	13 17		13 24	13 32		13 39	13 47			13 54	14 02	
Hoxton	d		12 26	12 34		12 41	12 49		12 56	13 04			13 11	13 19		13 26	13 34		13 41	13 49			13 56	14 04	
Haggerston	d		12 28	12 36		12 43	12 51		12 58	13 06			13 13	13 21		13 28	13 36		13 43	13 51			13 58	14 06	
Dalston Junction	a		12 30	12 38		12 45	12 53		13 00	13 08			13 15	13 23		13 30	13 38		13 45	13 53			14 00	14 08	
Canonbury	a		12 33	12 41		12 48	12 56		13 03	13 11			13 18	13 26		13 33	13 41		13 48	13 56			14 03	14 11	
Highbury & Islington	a		12 38	12 45		12 53	13 00		13 08	13 15			13 23	13 30		13 38	13 45		13 53	14 00			14 08	14 15	
London Bridge	a	12 17			12 31			12 47				13 01			13 17			13 31				13 47			14 01

		LO	LO	SN A	LO	LO		SN B	LO	LO	SN A	LO	LO	SN B	LO	LO		SN A	LO	LO	SN B	LO	LO	SN A	LO
Purley	d							13 48						14 18							14 48				
East Croydon	d							13 57						14 27							14 57				
Norwood Junction	a							14 02						14 32							15 02				
West Croydon	d	13 31			13 46				14 01			14 16			14 31				14 46			15 01			15 16
Norwood Junction	a	13 36			13 52				14 06			14 21			14 36				14 52			15 06			15 21
Norwood Junction	d	13 37			13 52			14 03	14 07			14 22		14 33	14 37				14 52		15 03	15 07			15 22
Anerley	d	13 40			13 55			14 06	14 10			14 25		14 36	14 40				14 55		15 06	15 10			15 25
Penge West	d	13 41			13 57			14 08	14 11			14 26		14 38	14 41				14 57		15 08	15 11			15 26
Crystal Palace	d		13 47	13 52		14 02				14 17	14 22		14 32			14 47		14 52		15 02			15 17	15 22	
Sydenham	d	13 44	13 51	13 56	13 59	14 06		14 11	14 14	14 21	14 26	14 29	14 36	14 41	14 44	14 51		14 56	14 59	15 06	15 11	15 14	15 21	15 26	15 29
Forest Hill	d	13 47	13 54	13 58	14 02	14 09		14 13	14 17	14 24	14 28	14 32	14 39	14 43	14 47	14 54		14 58	15 02	15 09	15 13	15 17	15 24	15 28	15 32
Honor Oak Park	d	13 49	13 56	14 01	14 04	14 11		14 16	14 19	14 26	14 31	14 34	14 41	14 46	14 49	14 56		15 01	15 04	15 11	15 16	15 19	15 26	15 31	15 34
Brockley	d	13 52	13 59	14 03	14 07	14 14		14 18	14 22	14 29	14 33	14 37	14 44	14 48	14 52	14 59		15 03	15 07	15 14	15 18	15 22	15 29	15 33	15 37
New Cross Gate	d	13 54	14 01	14 06	14 09	14 16		14 21	14 24	14 31	14 36	14 39	14 46	14 51	14 54	15 01		15 06	15 09	15 16	15 21	15 24	15 31	15 36	15 39
Surrey Quays	d	13 57	14 05		14 12	14 20			14 27	14 35		14 42	14 50		14 57	15 05			15 12	15 20		15 27	15 35		15 42
Canada Water	d	13 59	14 07		14 14	14 22			14 29	14 37		14 44	14 52		14 59	15 07			15 14	15 22		15 29	15 37		15 44
Rotherhithe	d	14 01	14 08		14 16	14 23			14 31	14 38		14 46	14 53		15 01	15 08			15 16	15 23		15 31	15 38		15 46
Wapping	d	14 02	14 10		14 17	14 25			14 32	14 40		14 47	14 55		15 02	15 10			15 17	15 25		15 32	15 40		15 47
Shadwell	d	14 04	14 12		14 19	14 27			14 34	14 42		14 49	14 57		15 04	15 12			15 19	15 27		15 34	15 42		15 49
Whitechapel	d	14 07	14 14		14 22	14 29			14 37	14 44		14 52	14 59		15 07	15 14			15 22	15 29		15 37	15 44		15 52
Shoreditch High Street	d	14 09	14 17		14 24	14 32			14 39	14 47		14 54	15 02		15 09	15 17			15 24	15 32		15 39	15 47		15 54
Hoxton	d	14 11	14 19		14 26	14 34			14 41	14 49		14 56	15 04		15 11	15 19			15 26	15 34		15 41	15 49		15 56
Haggerston	d	14 13	14 21		14 28	14 36			14 43	14 51		14 58	15 06		15 13	15 21			15 28	15 36		15 43	15 51		15 58
Dalston Junction	a	14 15	14 23		14 30	14 38			14 45	14 53		15 00	15 08		15 15	15 23			15 30	15 38		15 45	15 53		16 00
Canonbury	a	14 18	14 26		14 33	14 41			14 48	14 56		15 03	15 11		15 18	15 26			15 33	15 41		15 48	15 56		16 03
Highbury & Islington	a	14 23	14 30		14 38	14 45			14 53	15 00		15 08	15 15		15 23	15 30			15 38	15 45		15 53	16 00		16 08
London Bridge	a			14 17				14 31			14 47			15 01				15 17			15 31			15 47	

A From London Victoria

B From Coulsdon Town

For full service between Highbury & Islington and Surrey Quays, refer to Table T178

For Sutton connections at West Croydon, refer to Table T172

Table T177-R

Mondays to Fridays

21 May to 7 December

Croydon and Norwood Junction-Anerley, Penge West, Crystal Palace, Sydenham, Forest Hill, Honor Oak Park, Brockley, New Cross Gate-London Bridge

		LO	SN	LO	LO	SN	LO	LO		SN	LO	LO	SN	LO	LO	SN	LO	LO		SN	LO	LO	SN	LO	LO
			A			B				A			B			A				B			A		
Purley	d		15 18							15 50						16 20							16 50		
East Croydon	d		15 27							15 57						16 27							16 57		
Norwood Junction	a		15 32							16 02						16 32							17 03		
West Croydon	d			15 31			15 46				16 01			16 16			16 31				16 46			17 01	
Norwood Junction	a			15 36			15 52				16 06			16 21			16 36				16 51			17 06	
Norwood Junction	d		15 33	15 37			15 52			16 03	16 07			16 22		16 33	16 37				16 52		17 03	17 07	
Anerley	d		15 36	15 40			15 55			16 06	16 10			16 25		16 36	16 40				16 55		17 06	17 10	
Penge West	d		15 38	15 41			15 57			16 08	16 11			16 26		16 38	16 41				16 56		17 08	17 11	
Crystal Palace	d	15 32			15 47	15 52		16 02				16 17	16 22		16 32			16 47		16 52		17 02			17 17
Sydenham	d	15 36	15 41	15 44	15 51	15 56	15 59	16 06		16 11	16 14	16 21	16 26	16 29	16 36	16 41	16 44	16 51		16 56	16 59	17 06	17 11	17 14	17 21
Forest Hill	d	15 39	15 43	15 47	15 54	15 58	16 02	16 09		16 13	16 17	16 24	16 28	16 32	16 39	16 43	16 47	16 54		16 58	17 02	17 09	17 13	17 17	17 24
Honor Oak Park	d	15 41	15 46	15 49	15 56	16 01	16 04	16 11		16 16	16 19	16 26	16 31	16 34	16 41	16 46	16 49	16 56		17 01	17 04	17 11	17 16	17 19	17 26
Brockley	d	15 44	15 48	15 52	15 59	16 03	16 07	16 14		16 18	16 22	16 29	16 33	16 37	16 44	16 48	16 52	16 59		17 03	17 07	17 14	17 18	17 22	17 29
New Cross Gate	d	15 46	15 51	15 54	16 01	16 06	16 09	16 16		16 21	16 24	16 31	16 36	16 39	16 46	16 51	16 54	17 01		17 06	17 09	17 16	17 21	17 24	17 31
Surrey Quays	d	15 50		15 57	16 05		16 12	16 20			16 27	16 35		16 42	16 50		16 57	17 05			17 12	17 20		17 27	17 35
Canada Water	d	15 52		15 59	16 07		16 14	16 22			16 29	16 37		16 44	16 52		16 59	17 07			17 14	17 22		17 29	17 37
Rotherhithe	d	15 53		16 01	16 08		16 16	16 23			16 31	16 38		16 46	16 53		17 01	17 08			17 16	17 23		17 31	17 38
Wapping	d	15 55		16 02	16 10		16 17	16 25			16 32	16 40		16 47	16 55		17 02	17 10			17 17	17 25		17 32	17 40
Shadwell	d	15 57		16 04	16 12		16 19	16 27			16 34	16 42		16 49	16 57		17 04	17 12			17 19	17 27		17 34	17 42
Whitechapel	d	15 59		16 07	16 14		16 22	16 29			16 37	16 44		16 52	16 59		17 07	17 14			17 22	17 29		17 37	17 44
Shoreditch High Street	d	16 02		16 09	16 17		16 24	16 32			16 39	16 47		16 54	17 02		17 09	17 17			17 24	17 32		17 39	17 47
Hoxton	d	16 04		16 11	16 19		16 26	16 34			16 41	16 49		16 56	17 04		17 11	17 19			17 26	17 34		17 41	17 49
Haggerston	d	16 06		16 13	16 21		16 28	16 36			16 43	16 51		16 58	17 06		17 13	17 21			17 28	17 36		17 43	17 51
Dalston Junction	a	16 08		16 15	16 23		16 30	16 38			16 45	16 53		17 00	17 08		17 15	17 23			17 30	17 38		17 45	17 53
Canonbury	a	16 11		16 18	16 26		16 33	16 41			16 48	16 56		17 03	17 11		17 18	17 26			17 33	17 41		17 48	17 56
Highbury & Islington	a	16 15		16 25	16 30		16 40	16 45			16 55	17 00		17 10	17 15		17 25	17 30			17 40	17 45		17 55	18 00
London Bridge	a		16 01			16 18				16 31			16 48			17 01				17 18			17 31		

		SN	LO	LO		SN	LO	LO	SN	LO	LO	SN	LO	LO		SN	LO	LO	SN	LO	LO	SN	LO	LO	
		B							B							B						B			
Purley	d																								
East Croydon	d																								
Norwood Junction	a																								
West Croydon	d		17 16				17 31			17 46			18 01				18 16			18 31			18 46		
Norwood Junction	a		17 21				17 36			17 51			18 06				18 21			18 36			18 51		
Norwood Junction	d		17 22			17 34	17 37			17 52		18 04	18 07				18 22		18 34	18 37			18 52		
Anerley	d		17 25			17 37	17 40			17 55		18 07	18 10				18 25		18 37	18 40			18 55		
Penge West	d		17 26			17 38	17 41			17 56		18 08	18 11				18 26		18 38	18 41			18 56		
Crystal Palace	d	17 22		17 32				17 47	17 52		18 02			18 17		18 22		18 32			18 47	18 52		19 02	
Sydenham	d	17 26	17 29	17 36		17 41	17 44	17 51	17 56	17 59	18 06	18 11	18 14	18 21		18 26	18 29	18 36	18 41	18 44	18 51	18 56	18 59	19 06	
Forest Hill	d	17 28	17 32	17 39		17 43	17 47	17 54	17 58	18 02	18 09	18 13	18 17	18 24		18 28	18 32	18 39	18 43	18 47	18 54	18 58	19 02	19 09	
Honor Oak Park	d	17 31	17 34	17 41		17 46	17 49	17 56	18 01	18 04	18 11	18 16	18 19	18 26		18 31	18 34	18 41	18 46	18 49	18 56	19 01	19 04	19 11	
Brockley	d	17 33	17 37	17 44		17 48	17 52	17 59	18 03	18 07	18 14	18 18	18 22	18 29		18 33	18 37	18 44	18 48	18 52	18 59	19 03	19 07	19 14	
New Cross Gate	d	17 36	17 39	17 46		17 51	17 54	18 01	18 06	18 09	18 16	18 21	18 24	18 31		18 36	18 39	18 46	18 51	18 54	19 01	19 06	19 09	19 16	
Surrey Quays	d		17 42	17 50			17 57	18 05		18 12	18 20		18 27	18 35			18 42	18 50		18 57	19 05		19 12	19 20	
Canada Water	d		17 44	17 52			17 59	18 07		18 14	18 22		18 29	18 37			18 44	18 52		18 59	19 07		19 14	19 22	
Rotherhithe	d		17 46	17 53			18 01	18 08		18 16	18 23		18 31	18 38			18 46	18 53		19 01	19 08		19 16	19 23	
Wapping	d		17 47	17 55			18 02	18 10		18 17	18 25		18 32	18 40			18 47	18 55		19 02	19 10		19 17	19 25	
Shadwell	d		17 49	17 57			18 04	18 12		18 19	18 27		18 34	18 42			18 49	18 57		19 04	19 12		19 19	19 27	
Whitechapel	d		17 52	17 59			18 07	18 14		18 22	18 29		18 37	18 44			18 52	18 59		19 07	19 14		19 22	19 29	
Shoreditch High Street	d		17 54	18 02			18 09	18 17		18 24	18 32		18 39	18 47			18 54	19 02		19 09	19 17		19 24	19 32	
Hoxton	d		17 56	18 04			18 11	18 19		18 26	18 34		18 41	18 49			18 56	19 04		19 11	19 19		19 26	19 34	
Haggerston	d		17 58	18 06			18 13	18 21		18 28	18 36		18 43	18 51			18 58	19 06		19 13	19 21		19 28	19 36	
Dalston Junction	a		18 00	18 08			18 15	18 23		18 30	18 38		18 45	18 53			19 00	19 08		19 15	19 23		19 30	19 38	
Canonbury	a		18 03	18 11			18 18	18 26		18 33	18 41		18 48	18 56			19 03	19 11		19 18	19 26		19 33	19 41	
Highbury & Islington	a		18 10	18 15			18 25	18 30		18 40	18 45		18 55	19 00			19 10	19 15		19 25	19 30		19 40	19 45	
London Bridge	a	17 48				18 01			18 18			18 31				18 48			19 01			19 18			

A From Coulsdon Town

B From London Victoria

For full service between Highbury & Islington and Surrey Quays, refer to Table T178

For Sutton connections at West Croydon, refer to Table T172

Table T177-R

Mondays to Fridays

21 May to 7 December

Croydon and Norwood Junction-Anerley, Penge West, Crystal Palace, Sydenham, Forest Hill, Honor Oak Park, Brockley, New Cross Gate-London Bridge

		SN	LO	LO	SN	LO		LO	SN	LO	LO	SN	LO	LO	SN	LO		LO	SN	LO	LO	SN	LO	LO	SN
					A							A			B				A			B			A
Purley	d														19 48							20 18			
East Croydon	d														19 57							20 27			
Norwood Junction	a														20 02							20 32			
West Croydon	d		19 01			19 16				19 31			19 46			20 01				20 16			20 31		
Norwood Junction	a		19 06			19 21				19 36			19 51			20 06				20 21			20 36		
Norwood Junction	d	19 04	19 07			19 22			19 34	19 37			19 52		20 03	20 07				20 22		20 33	20 37		
Anerley	d	19 07	19 10			19 25			19 37	19 40			19 55		20 06	20 10				20 25		20 36	20 40		
Penge West	d	19 08	19 11			19 26			19 38	19 41			19 56		20 08	20 11				20 26		20 38	20 41		
Crystal Palace	d			19 17	19 22			19 32			19 47	19 52		20 02				20 17	20 22		20 32			20 47	20 52
Sydenham	d	19 11	19 14	19 21	19 26	19 29		19 36	19 41	19 44	19 51	19 56	19 59	20 06	20 11	20 14		20 21	20 26	20 29	20 36	20 41	20 44	20 51	20 56
Forest Hill	d	19 13	19 17	19 24	19 28	19 32		19 39	19 43	19 47	19 54	19 58	20 02	20 09	20 13	20 17		20 24	20 28	20 32	20 39	20 43	20 47	20 54	20 58
Honor Oak Park	d	19 16	19 19	19 26	19 31	19 34		19 41	19 46	19 49	19 56	20 01	20 04	20 11	20 16	20 19		20 26	20 31	20 34	20 41	20 46	20 49	20 56	21 01
Brockley	d	19 18	19 22	19 29	19 33	19 37		19 44	19 48	19 52	19 59	20 03	20 07	20 14	20 18	20 22		20 29	20 33	20 37	20 44	20 48	20 52	20 59	21 03
New Cross Gate	d	19 21	19 24	19 31	19 36	19 39		19 46	19 51	19 54	20 01	20 06	20 09	20 16	20 21	20 24		20 31	20 36	20 39	20 46	20 51	20 54	21 01	21 06
Surrey Quays	d		19 27	19 35		19 42		19 50		19 57	20 05		20 12	20 20		20 27		20 35		20 42	20 50		20 57	21 05	
Canada Water	d		19 29	19 37		19 44		19 52		19 59	20 07		20 14	20 22		20 29		20 37		20 44	20 52		20 59	21 07	
Rotherhithe	d		19 31	19 38		19 46		19 53		20 01	20 08		20 16	20 23		20 31		20 38		20 46	20 53		21 01	21 08	
Wapping	d		19 32	19 40		19 47		19 55		20 02	20 10		20 17	20 25		20 32		20 40		20 47	20 55		21 02	21 10	
Shadwell	d		19 34	19 42		19 49		19 57		20 04	20 12		20 19	20 27		20 34		20 42		20 49	20 57		21 04	21 12	
Whitechapel	d		19 37	19 44		19 52		19 59		20 07	20 14		20 22	20 29		20 37		20 44		20 52	20 59		21 07	21 14	
Shoreditch High Street	d		19 39	19 47		19 54		20 02		20 09	20 17		20 24	20 32		20 39		20 47		20 54	21 02		21 09	21 17	
Hoxton	d		19 41	19 49		19 56		20 04		20 11	20 19		20 26	20 34		20 41		20 49		20 56	21 04		21 11	21 19	
Haggerston	d		19 43	19 51		19 58		20 06		20 13	20 21		20 28	20 36		20 43		20 51		20 58	21 06		21 13	21 21	
Dalston Junction	a		19 45	19 53		20 00		20 08		20 15	20 23		20 30	20 38		20 45		20 53		21 00	21 08		21 15	21 23	
Canonbury	a		19 48	19 56		20 03		20 11		20 18	20 26		20 33	20 40		20 48		20 56		21 03	21 11		21 18	21 26	
Highbury & Islington	a		19 55	20 00		20 10		20 15		20 25	20 30		20 40	20 45		20 53		21 00		21 08	21 15		21 23	21 30	
London Bridge	a	19 31			19 48				20 01			20 18			20 31				20 47			21 01			21 17

		LO		LO	SN	LO	LO	SN	LO	LO	SN	LO		LO	SN	LO	LO	SN	LO	LO	SN	LO		LO	SN
					B			A			B				A			B			A				B
Purley	d				20 48						21 18							21 48							22 18
East Croydon	d				20 57						21 27							21 57							22 27
Norwood Junction	a				21 02						21 32							22 02							22 32
West Croydon	d	20 46				21 01			21 16			21 31				21 46			22 01			22 16			
Norwood Junction	a	20 52				21 06			21 21			21 36				21 51			22 06			22 21			
Norwood Junction	d	20 52			21 03	21 07			21 22		21 33	21 37				21 52		22 03	22 07			22 22			22 33
Anerley	d	20 55			21 06	21 10			21 25		21 36	21 40				21 55		22 06	22 10			22 25			22 36
Penge West	d	20 57			21 08	21 11			21 26		21 38	21 41				21 56		22 08	22 11			22 26			22 38
Crystal Palace	d			21 02			21 17	21 22		21 32				21 47	21 52		22 02			22 17	22 22			22 32	
Sydenham	d	20 59		21 06	21 11	21 14	21 21	21 26	21 29	21 36	21 41	21 44		21 51	21 56	21 59	22 06	22 11	22 14	22 21	22 26	22 29		22 36	22 41
Forest Hill	d	21 02		21 09	21 13	21 17	21 24	21 28	21 32	21 39	21 43	21 47		21 54	21 58	22 02	22 09	22 13	22 17	22 24	22 28	22 32		22 39	22 43
Honor Oak Park	d	21 04		21 11	21 16	21 19	21 26	21 31	21 34	21 41	21 46	21 49		21 56	22 01	22 04	22 11	22 16	22 19	22 26	22 31	22 34		22 41	22 46
Brockley	d	21 07		21 14	21 18	21 22	21 29	21 33	21 37	21 44	21 48	21 52		21 59	22 03	22 07	22 14	22 18	22 22	22 29	22 33	22 37		22 44	22 48
New Cross Gate	d	21 09		21 16	21 21	21 24	21 31	21 36	21 39	21 46	21 51	21 54		22 01	22 06	22 09	22 16	22 21	22 24	22 31	22 36	22 39		22 46	22 51
Surrey Quays	d	21 12		21 20		21 27	21 35		21 42	21 50		21 57		22 05		22 12	22 20		22 27	22 35		22 42		22 50	
Canada Water	d	21 14		21 22		21 29	21 37		21 44	21 52		21 59		22 07		22 14	22 22		22 29	22 37		22 44		22 52	
Rotherhithe	d	21 16		21 23		21 31	21 38		21 46	21 53		22 01		22 08		22 16	22 23		22 31	22 38		22 46		22 53	
Wapping	d	21 17		21 25		21 32	21 40		21 47	21 55		22 02		22 10		22 17	22 25		22 32	22 40		22 47		22 55	
Shadwell	d	21 19		21 27		21 34	21 42		21 49	21 57		22 04		22 12		22 19	22 27		22 34	22 42		22 49		22 57	
Whitechapel	d	21 22		21 29		21 37	21 44		21 52	21 59		22 07		22 14		22 22	22 29		22 37	22 44		22 52		22 59	
Shoreditch High Street	d	21 24		21 32		21 39	21 47		21 54	22 02		22 09		22 17		22 24	22 32		22 39	22 47		22 54		23 02	
Hoxton	d	21 26		21 34		21 41	21 49		21 56	22 04		22 11		22 19		22 26	22 34		22 41	22 49		22 56		23 04	
Haggerston	d	21 28		21 36		21 43	21 51		21 58	22 06		22 13		22 21		22 28	22 36		22 43	22 51		22 58		23 06	
Dalston Junction	a	21 30		21 38		21 45	21 53		22 00	22 08		22 15		22 23		22 30	22 38		22 45	22 53		23 00		23 08	
Canonbury	a	21 33		21 41		21 48	21 56		22 03	22 11		22 18		22 26		22 33	22 41		22 48	22 56		23 03		23 11	
Highbury & Islington	a	21 38		21 45		21 53	22 00		22 08	22 15		22 23		22 30		22 38	22 45		22 53	23 00		23 08		23 15	
London Bridge	a				21 31			21 47			22 01				22 17			22 31			22 47				23 01

A From London Victoria

B From Coulsdon Town

For full service between Highbury & Islington and Surrey Quays, refer to Table T178

For Sutton connections at West Croydon, refer to Table T172

Table T177-R

Mondays to Fridays

21 May to 7 December

Croydon and Norwood Junction-Anerley, Penge West, Crystal Palace, Sydenham, Forest Hill, Honor Oak Park, Brockley, New Cross Gate-London Bridge

		LO	LO	SN A	LO	LO	SN B	LO	LO	SN A	LO	LO	LO	LO	SN A
Purley	d						22 48								
East Croydon	d						22 57								
Norwood Junction	a						23 02								
West Croydon	d	22 31			22 46			23 01			23 16		23 31		
Norwood Junction	a	22 36			22 51			23 06			23 21		23 36		
Norwood Junction	d	22 37			22 52		23 03	23 07			23 22		23 37		
Anerley	d	22 40			22 55		23 06	23 10			23 25		23 40		
Penge West	d	22 41			22 56		23 08	23 11			23 26		23 41		
Crystal Palace	d		22 47	22 52		23 02			23 17	23 22		23 32		23 50	23 53
Sydenham	d	22 44	22 51	22 56	22 59	23 06	23 11	23 14	23 21	23 26	23 29	23 36	23 44	23 54	23 58
Forest Hill	d	22 47	22 54	22 58	23 02	23 09	23 13	23 17	23 24	23 28	23 32	23 39	23 47	23 56	23 59
Honor Oak Park	d	22 49	22 56	23 01	23 04	23 11	23 16	23 19	23 26	23 31	23 34	23 41	23 49	23 59	00 03
Brockley	d	22 52	22 59	23 03	23 07	23 14	23 18	23 22	23 29	23 33	23 37	23 44	23 52	00 01	00 05
New Cross Gate	d	22 54	23 01	23 06	23 09	23 16	23 21	23 24	23 31	23 36	23 39	23 46	23 54	00 03	00 08
Surrey Quays	d	22 57	23 05		23 12	23 20		23 27	23 35		23 42	23 50	23 57	00 09	
Canada Water	d	22 59	23 07		23 14	23 22		23 29	23 37		23 44	23 52	23 59	00 11	
Rotherhithe	d	23 01	23 08		23 16	23 23		23 31	23 38		23 46	23 53	00 01	00 12	
Wapping	d	23 02	23 10		23 17	23 25		23 32	23 40		23 47	23 55	00 02	00 14	
Shadwell	d	23 04	23 12		23 19	23 27		23 34	23 42		23 49	23 57	00 04	00 16	
Whitechapel	d	23 07	23 14		23 22	23 29		23 37	23 44		23 52	23 59	00 07	00 18	
Shoreditch High Street	d	23 09	23 17		23 24	23 32		23 39	23 47		23 54	00 02	00 09	00 21	
Hoxton	d	23 11	23 19		23 26	23 34		23 41	23 49		23 56	00 04	00 11	00 23	
Haggerston	d	23 13	23 21		23 28	23 36		23 43	23 51		23 58	00 06	00 13	00 25	
Dalston Junction	a	23 15	23 23		23 32	23 38		23 45	23 53		00 01	00 08	00 15	00 27	
Canonbury	a	23 18	23 26			23 41		23 50	23 56		00 03	00 11	00 18	00 30	
Highbury & Islington	a	23 23	23 30			23 45		23 55	23 59		00 10	00 15	00 25	00 33	
London Bridge	a			23 17			23 31			23 47					00 15

Saturdays

26 May to 8 December

		LO C	LO D	LO C	SN A	LO	SN A	LO	LO	LO	SN E	LO	LO	LO	LO	SN E	LO	LO	SN	LO	LO	SN A	LO
Purley	d																						
East Croydon	d																						
Norwood Junction	a																						
West Croydon	d								05 31			05 46		06 01			06 16			06 31			06 46
Norwood Junction	a								05 36			05 51		06 06			06 21			06 36			06 51
Norwood Junction	d								05 37			05 52		06 07			06 22		06 33	06 37			06 52
Anerley	d								05 40			05 55		06 10			06 25		06 36	06 40			06 55
Penge West	d								05 41			05 56		06 11			06 26		06 38	06 41			06 56
Crystal Palace	d					00 04	00 25	05 32		05 47	05 52		06 02		06 17	06 22		06 32			06 47	06 52	
Sydenham	d					00 08	00 30	05 36	05 44	05 51	05 56	05 59	06 06	06 14	06 21	06 26	06 29	06 36	06 41	06 44	06 51	06 56	06 59
Forest Hill	d					00 11	00 32	05 39	05 47	05 54	05 58	06 02	06 09	06 17	06 24	06 28	06 32	06 39	06 43	06 47	06 54	06 58	07 02
Honor Oak Park	d				00 03	00 13	00 35	05 41	05 49	05 56	06 01	06 04	06 11	06 19	06 26	06 31	06 34	06 41	06 46	06 49	06 56	07 01	07 04
Brockley	d			00 01	00 05	00 16	00 37	05 44	05 52	05 59	06 03	06 07	06 14	06 22	06 29	06 33	06 37	06 44	06 48	06 52	06 59	07 03	07 07
New Cross Gate	d			00 03	00 08	00 18	00 40	05 46	05 54	06 01	06 06	06 09	06 16	06 24	06 31	06 36	06 39	06 46	06 51	06 54	07 01	07 06	07 09
Surrey Quays	d			00 09		00 22		05 50	05 57	06 05		06 12	06 20	06 27	06 35		06 42	06 50		06 57	07 05		07 12
Canada Water	d			00 11		00 24		05 52	05 59	06 07		06 14	06 22	06 29	06 37		06 44	06 52		06 59	07 07		07 14
Rotherhithe	d		00 01	00 12		00 25		05 53	06 01	06 08		06 16	06 23	06 31	06 38		06 46	06 53		07 01	07 08		07 16
Wapping	d		00 02	00 14		00 27		05 55	06 02	06 10		06 17	06 25	06 32	06 40		06 47	06 55		07 02	07 10		07 17
Shadwell	d		00 04	00 16		00 29		05 57	06 04	06 12		06 19	06 27	06 34	06 42		06 49	06 57		07 04	07 12		07 19
Whitechapel	d		00 07	00 18		00 31		05 59	06 07	06 14		06 22	06 29	06 37	06 44		06 52	06 59		07 07	07 14		07 22
Shoreditch High Street	d	00 02	00 09	00 21		00 34		06 02	06 09	06 17		06 24	06 32	06 39	06 47		06 54	07 02		07 09	07 17		07 24
Hoxton	d	00 04	00 11	00 23		00 36		06 04	06 11	06 19		06 26	06 34	06 41	06 49		06 56	07 04		07 11	07 19		07 26
Haggerston	d	00 06	00 13	00 25		00 38		06 06	06 13	06 21		06 28	06 36	06 43	06 51		06 58	07 06		07 13	07 21		07 28
Dalston Junction	a	00 08	00 15	00 27		00 40		06 08	06 15	06 23		06 30	06 38	06 45	06 53		07 00	07 08		07 15	07 23		07 30
Canonbury	a	00 11	00 18	00 30		00 43		06 11	06 18	06 26		06 33	06 41	06 48	06 56		07 03	07 11		07 18	07 26		07 33
Highbury & Islington	a	00 15	00 25	00 33		00 47		06 15	06 23	06 30		06 38	06 45	06 53	07 00		07 10	07 15		07 25	07 30		07 40
London Bridge	a				00 15		00 47				06 13					06 44			07 01			07 14	

A From London Victoria
B From Coulsdon Town
C From Crystal Palace
D From West Croydon
E From Streatham Hill

For full service between Highbury & Islington and Surrey Quays, refer to Table T178

For Sutton connections at West Croydon, refer to Table T172

Table T177-R

Saturdays

26 May to 8 December

Croydon and Norwood Junction-Anerley, Penge West, Crystal Palace, Sydenham, Forest Hill, Honor Oak Park, Brockley, New Cross Gate-London Bridge

		LO	SN	LO	LO	SN A	LO	LO	SN B	LO	LO	SN A	LO	LO	SN B	LO	LO	SN A	LO	LO	SN B	LO
Purley	d								07 18						07 48						08 18	
East Croydon	d								07 27						07 57						08 27	
Norwood Junction	a								07 32						08 02						08 32	
West Croydon	d			07 01			07 16			07 31			07 46			08 01			08 16			08 31
Norwood Junction	a			07 06			07 21			07 36			07 52			08 06			08 21			08 36
Norwood Junction	d		07 03	07 07			07 22		07 33	07 37			07 52		08 03	08 07			08 22		08 33	08 37
Anerley	d		07 06	07 10			07 25		07 36	07 40			07 55		08 06	08 10			08 25		08 36	08 40
Penge West	d		07 08	07 11			07 26		07 38	07 41			07 57		08 08	08 11			08 26		08 38	08 41
Crystal Palace	d	07 02			07 17	07 22		07 32			07 47	07 52		08 02			08 17	08 22		08 32		
Sydenham	d	07 06	07 11	07 14	07 21	07 26	07 29	07 36	07 41	07 44	07 51	07 56	07 59	08 06	08 11	08 14	08 21	08 26	08 29	08 36	08 41	08 44
Forest Hill	d	07 09	07 13	07 17	07 24	07 28	07 32	07 39	07 43	07 47	07 54	07 58	08 02	08 09	08 13	08 17	08 24	08 28	08 32	08 39	08 43	08 47
Honor Oak Park	d	07 11	07 16	07 19	07 26	07 31	07 34	07 41	07 46	07 49	07 56	08 01	08 04	08 11	08 16	08 19	08 26	08 31	08 34	08 41	08 46	08 49
Brockley	d	07 14	07 18	07 22	07 29	07 33	07 37	07 44	07 48	07 52	07 59	08 03	08 07	08 14	08 18	08 22	08 29	08 33	08 37	08 44	08 48	08 52
New Cross Gate	d	07 16	07 21	07 24	07 31	07 36	07 39	07 46	07 51	07 54	08 01	08 06	08 09	08 16	08 21	08 24	08 31	08 36	08 39	08 46	08 51	08 54
Surrey Quays	d	07 20		07 27	07 35		07 42	07 50		07 57	08 05		08 12	08 20		08 27	08 35		08 42	08 50		08 57
Canada Water	d	07 22		07 29	07 37		07 44	07 52		07 59	08 07		08 14	08 22		08 29	08 37		08 44	08 52		08 59
Rotherhithe	d	07 23		07 31	07 38		07 46	07 53		08 01	08 08		08 16	08 23		08 31	08 38		08 46	08 53		09 01
Wapping	d	07 25		07 32	07 40		07 47	07 55		08 02	08 10		08 17	08 25		08 32	08 40		08 47	08 55		09 02
Shadwell	d	07 27		07 34	07 42		07 49	07 57		08 04	08 12		08 19	08 27		08 34	08 42		08 49	08 57		09 04
Whitechapel	d	07 29		07 37	07 44		07 52	07 59		08 07	08 14		08 22	08 29		08 37	08 44		08 52	08 59		09 07
Shoreditch High Street	d	07 32		07 39	07 47		07 54	08 02		08 09	08 17		08 24	08 32		08 39	08 47		08 54	09 02		09 09
Hoxton	d	07 34		07 41	07 49		07 56	08 04		08 11	08 19		08 26	08 34		08 41	08 49		08 56	09 04		09 11
Haggerston	d	07 36		07 43	07 51		07 58	08 06		08 13	08 21		08 28	08 36		08 43	08 51		08 58	09 06		09 13
Dalston Junction	a	07 38		07 45	07 53		08 00	08 08		08 15	08 23		08 30	08 38		08 45	08 53		09 00	09 08		09 15
Canonbury	a	07 41		07 48	07 56		08 03	08 11		08 18	08 26		08 33	08 41		08 48	08 56		09 03	09 11		09 18
Highbury & Islington	a	07 45		07 55	08 00		08 10	08 15		08 25	08 30		08 40	08 45		08 55	09 00		09 10	09 15		09 25
London Bridge	a		07 31			07 44			08 01			08 14			08 31			08 44			09 01	

		LO	SN A	LO	LO	SN B	LO	LO	SN A	LO	LO	SN B	LO	LO	SN A	LO	LO	SN B	LO	LO	SN A	LO	LO
Purley	d					08 48						09 18						09 48					
East Croydon	d					08 57						09 27						09 57					
Norwood Junction	a					09 02						09 32						10 02					
West Croydon	d			08 46			09 01			09 16			09 31			09 46			10 01			10 16	
Norwood Junction	a			08 52			09 06			09 21			09 36			09 52			10 06			10 21	
Norwood Junction	d			08 52		09 03	09 07			09 22		09 33	09 37			09 52		10 03	10 07			10 22	
Anerley	d			08 55		09 06	09 10			09 25		09 36	09 40			09 55		10 06	10 10			10 25	
Penge West	d			08 57		09 08	09 11			09 26		09 38	09 41			09 57		10 08	10 11			10 26	
Crystal Palace	d	08 47	08 52		09 02			09 17	09 22		09 32			09 47	09 52		10 02			10 17	10 22		10 32
Sydenham	d	08 51	08 56	08 59	09 06	09 11	09 14	09 21	09 26	09 29	09 36	09 41	09 44	09 51	09 56	09 59	10 06	10 11	10 14	10 21	10 26	10 29	10 36
Forest Hill	d	08 54	08 58	09 02	09 09	09 13	09 17	09 24	09 28	09 32	09 39	09 43	09 47	09 54	09 58	10 02	10 09	10 13	10 17	10 24	10 28	10 32	10 39
Honor Oak Park	d	08 56	09 01	09 04	09 11	09 16	09 19	09 26	09 31	09 34	09 41	09 46	09 49	09 56	10 01	10 04	10 11	10 16	10 19	10 26	10 31	10 34	10 41
Brockley	d	08 59	09 03	09 07	09 14	09 18	09 22	09 29	09 33	09 37	09 44	09 48	09 52	09 59	10 03	10 07	10 14	10 18	10 22	10 29	10 33	10 37	10 44
New Cross Gate	d	09 01	09 06	09 09	09 16	09 21	09 24	09 31	09 36	09 39	09 46	09 51	09 54	10 01	10 06	10 09	10 16	10 21	10 24	10 31	10 36	10 39	10 46
Surrey Quays	d	09 05		09 12	09 20		09 27	09 35		09 42	09 50		09 57	10 05		10 12	10 20		10 27	10 35		10 42	10 50
Canada Water	d	09 07		09 14	09 22		09 29	09 37		09 44	09 52		09 59	10 07		10 14	10 22		10 29	10 37		10 44	10 52
Rotherhithe	d	09 08		09 16	09 23		09 31	09 38		09 46	09 53		10 01	10 08		10 16	10 23		10 31	10 38		10 46	10 53
Wapping	d	09 10		09 17	09 25		09 32	09 40		09 47	09 55		10 02	10 10		10 17	10 25		10 32	10 40		10 47	10 55
Shadwell	d	09 12		09 19	09 27		09 34	09 42		09 49	09 57		10 04	10 12		10 19	10 27		10 34	10 42		10 49	10 57
Whitechapel	d	09 14		09 22	09 29		09 37	09 44		09 52	09 59		10 07	10 14		10 22	10 29		10 37	10 44		10 52	10 59
Shoreditch High Street	d	09 17		09 24	09 32		09 39	09 47		09 54	10 02		10 09	10 17		10 24	10 32		10 39	10 47		10 54	11 02
Hoxton	d	09 19		09 26	09 34		09 41	09 49		09 56	10 04		10 11	10 19		10 26	10 34		10 41	10 49		10 56	11 04
Haggerston	d	09 21		09 28	09 36		09 43	09 51		09 58	10 06		10 13	10 21		10 28	10 36		10 43	10 51		10 58	11 06
Dalston Junction	a	09 23		09 30	09 38		09 45	09 53		10 00	10 08		10 15	10 23		10 30	10 38		10 45	10 53		11 00	11 08
Canonbury	a	09 26		09 33	09 41		09 48	09 56		10 03	10 11		10 18	10 26		10 33	10 41		10 48	10 56		11 03	11 11
Highbury & Islington	a	09 30		09 40	09 45		09 55	10 00		10 10	10 15		10 25	10 30		10 40	10 45		10 55	11 00		11 08	11 15
London Bridge	a		09 14			09 31			09 44			10 01			10 14			10 31			10 44		

A From London Victoria
B From Coulsdon Town

For full service between Highbury & Islington and Surrey Quays, refer to Table T178

For Sutton connections at West Croydon, refer to Table T172

Table T177-R

Croydon and Norwood Junction-Anerley, Penge West, Crystal Palace, Sydenham, Forest Hill, Honor Oak Park, Brockley, New Cross Gate-London Bridge

	SN A	LO	LO	SN B	LO	LO	SN A	LO	LO		SN B	LO	LO	SN A	LO	LO	SN B	LO	LO		SN A	LO	LO	SN B
Purley d	10 18						10 48							11 18							11 48			
East Croydon d	10 27						10 57							11 27							11 57			
Norwood Junction a	10 32						11 02							11 32							12 02			
West Croydon d		10 31			10 46			11 01				11 16			11 31			11 46				12 01		
Norwood Junction a		10 36			10 52			11 06				11 21			11 36			11 52				12 06		
Norwood Junction d	10 33	10 37			10 52		11 03	11 07				11 22		11 33	11 37			11 52			12 03	12 07		
Anerley d	10 36	10 40			10 55		11 06	11 10				11 25		11 36	11 40			11 55			12 06	12 10		
Penge West d	10 38	10 41			10 57		11 08	11 11				11 26		11 38	11 41			11 57			12 08	12 11		
Crystal Palace d			10 47	10 52		11 02			11 17		11 22		11 32			11 47	11 52		12 02				12 17	12 22
Sydenham d	10 41	10 44	10 51	10 56	10 59	11 06	11 11	11 14	11 21		11 26	11 29	11 36	11 41	11 44	11 51	11 56	11 59	12 06		12 11	12 14	12 21	12 26
Forest Hill d	10 43	10 47	10 54	10 58	11 02	11 09	11 13	11 17	11 24		11 28	11 32	11 39	11 43	11 47	11 54	11 58	12 02	12 09		12 13	12 17	12 24	12 28
Honor Oak Park d	10 46	10 49	10 56	11 01	11 04	11 11	11 16	11 19	11 26		11 31	11 34	11 41	11 46	11 49	11 56	12 01	12 04	12 11		12 16	12 19	12 26	12 31
Brockley d	10 48	10 52	10 59	11 03	11 07	11 14	11 18	11 22	11 29		11 33	11 37	11 44	11 48	11 52	11 59	12 03	12 07	12 14		12 18	12 22	12 29	12 33
New Cross Gate d	10 51	10 54	11 01	11 06	11 09	11 16	11 21	11 24	11 31		11 36	11 39	11 46	11 51	11 54	12 01	12 06	12 09	12 16		12 21	12 24	12 31	12 36
Surrey Quays d		10 57	11 05		11 12	11 20		11 27	11 35			11 42	11 50		11 57	12 05		12 12	12 20			12 27	12 35	
Canada Water d		10 59	11 07		11 14	11 22		11 29	11 37			11 44	11 52		11 59	12 07		12 14	12 22			12 29	12 37	
Rotherhithe d		11 01	11 08		11 16	11 23		11 31	11 38			11 46	11 53		12 01	12 08		12 16	12 23			12 31	12 38	
Wapping d		11 02	11 10		11 17	11 25		11 32	11 40			11 47	11 55		12 02	12 10		12 17	12 25			12 32	12 40	
Shadwell d		11 04	11 12		11 19	11 27		11 34	11 42			11 49	11 57		12 04	12 12		12 19	12 27			12 34	12 42	
Whitechapel d		11 07	11 14		11 22	11 29		11 37	11 44			11 52	11 59		12 07	12 14		12 22	12 29			12 37	12 44	
Shoreditch High Street d		11 09	11 17		11 24	11 32		11 39	11 47			11 54	12 02		12 09	12 17		12 24	12 32			12 39	12 47	
Hoxton d		11 11	11 19		11 26	11 34		11 41	11 49			11 56	12 04		12 11	12 19		12 26	12 34			12 41	12 49	
Haggerston d		11 13	11 21		11 28	11 36		11 43	11 51			11 58	12 06		12 13	12 21		12 28	12 36			12 43	12 51	
Dalston Junction a		11 15	11 23		11 30	11 38		11 45	11 53			12 00	12 08		12 15	12 23		12 30	12 38			12 45	12 53	
Canonbury a		11 18	11 26		11 33	11 41		11 48	11 56			12 03	12 11		12 18	12 26		12 33	12 41			12 48	12 56	
Highbury & Islington a		11 23	11 30		11 38	11 45		11 53	12 00			12 08	12 15		12 23	12 30		12 38	12 45			12 53	13 00	
London Bridge a	11 01			11 14			11 31				11 44			12 01			12 14				12 31			12 44

	LO	LO	SN A	LO	LO		SN B	LO	LO	SN A	LO	LO	SN B	LO	LO		SN A	LO	LO	SN B	LO	LO	SN A	LO
Purley d			12 18							12 48							13 18						13 48	
East Croydon d			12 27							12 57							13 27						13 57	
Norwood Junction a			12 32							13 02							13 32						14 02	
West Croydon d	12 16			12 31				12 46			13 01			13 16				13 31			13 46			14 01
Norwood Junction a	12 21			12 36				12 52			13 06			13 21				13 36			13 52			14 06
Norwood Junction d	12 22		12 33	12 37				12 52		13 03	13 07			13 22			13 33	13 37			13 52		14 03	14 07
Anerley d	12 25		12 36	12 40				12 55		13 06	13 10			13 25			13 36	13 40			13 55		14 06	14 10
Penge West d	12 26		12 38	12 41				12 57		13 08	13 11			13 26			13 38	13 41			13 57		14 08	14 11
Crystal Palace d		12 32			12 47		12 52		13 02			13 17	13 22		13 32				13 47	13 52		14 02		
Sydenham d	12 29	12 36	12 41	12 44	12 51		12 56	12 59	13 06	13 11	13 14	13 21	13 26	13 29	13 36		13 41	13 44	13 51	13 56	13 59	14 06	14 11	14 14
Forest Hill d	12 32	12 39	12 43	12 47	12 54		12 58	13 02	13 09	13 13	13 17	13 24	13 28	13 32	13 39		13 43	13 47	13 54	13 58	14 02	14 09	14 13	14 17
Honor Oak Park d	12 34	12 41	12 46	12 49	12 56		13 01	13 04	13 11	13 16	13 19	13 26	13 31	13 34	13 41		13 46	13 49	13 56	14 01	14 04	14 11	14 16	14 19
Brockley d	12 37	12 44	12 48	12 52	12 59		13 03	13 07	13 14	13 18	13 22	13 29	13 33	13 37	13 44		13 48	13 52	13 59	14 03	14 07	14 14	14 18	14 22
New Cross Gate d	12 39	12 46	12 51	12 54	13 01		13 06	13 09	13 16	13 21	13 24	13 31	13 36	13 39	13 46		13 51	13 54	14 01	14 06	14 09	14 16	14 21	14 24
Surrey Quays d	12 42	12 50		12 57	13 05			13 12	13 20		13 27	13 35		13 42	13 50			13 57	14 05		14 12	14 20		14 27
Canada Water d	12 44	12 52		12 59	13 07			13 14	13 22		13 29	13 37		13 44	13 52			13 59	14 07		14 14	14 22		14 29
Rotherhithe d	12 46	12 53		13 01	13 08			13 16	13 23		13 31	13 38		13 46	13 53			14 01	14 08		14 16	14 23		14 31
Wapping d	12 47	12 55		13 02	13 10			13 17	13 25		13 32	13 40		13 47	13 55			14 02	14 10		14 17	14 25		14 32
Shadwell d	12 49	12 57		13 04	13 12			13 19	13 27		13 34	13 42		13 49	13 57			14 04	14 12		14 19	14 27		14 34
Whitechapel d	12 52	12 59		13 07	13 14			13 22	13 29		13 37	13 44		13 52	13 59			14 07	14 14		14 22	14 29		14 37
Shoreditch High Street d	12 54	13 02		13 09	13 17			13 24	13 32		13 39	13 47		13 54	14 02			14 09	14 17		14 24	14 32		14 39
Hoxton d	12 56	13 04		13 11	13 19			13 26	13 34		13 41	13 49		13 56	14 04			14 11	14 19		14 26	14 34		14 41
Haggerston d	12 58	13 06		13 13	13 21			13 28	13 36		13 43	13 51		13 58	14 06			14 13	14 21		14 28	14 36		14 43
Dalston Junction a	13 00	13 08		13 15	13 23			13 30	13 38		13 45	13 53		14 00	14 08			14 15	14 23		14 30	14 38		14 45
Canonbury a	13 03	13 11		13 18	13 26			13 33	13 41		13 48	13 56		14 03	14 11			14 18	14 26		14 33	14 41		14 48
Highbury & Islington a	13 08	13 15		13 23	13 30			13 38	13 45		13 53	14 00		14 08	14 15			14 23	14 30		14 38	14 45		14 53
London Bridge a			13 01				13 14			13 31			13 44				14 01			14 14			14 31	

A From Coulsdon Town

B From London Victoria

For full service between Highbury & Islington and Surrey Quays, refer to Table T178

For Sutton connections at West Croydon, refer to Table T172

Table T177-R

Croydon and Norwood Junction-Anerley, Penge West, Crystal Palace, Sydenham, Forest Hill, Honor Oak Park, Brockley, New Cross Gate-London Bridge

	LO	SN A	LO	LO	SN B	LO	LO		SN A	LO	LO	SN B	LO	LO	SN A	LO	LO		SN B	LO	LO	SN A	LO	LO
Purley d					14 18							14 48							15 18					
East Croydon d					14 27							14 57							15 27					
Norwood Junction a					14 32							15 02							15 32					
West Croydon d			14 16			14 31				14 46			15 01			15 16				15 31			15 46	
Norwood Junction a			14 21			14 36				14 52			15 06			15 21				15 36			15 52	
Norwood Junction d			14 22		14 33	14 37				14 52		15 03	15 07			15 22			15 33	15 37			15 52	
Anerley d			14 25		14 36	14 40				14 55		15 06	15 10			15 25			15 36	15 40			15 55	
Penge West d			14 26		14 38	14 41				14 57		15 08	15 11			15 26			15 38	15 41			15 57	
Crystal Palace d	14 17	14 22		14 32			14 47		14 52		15 02			15 17	15 22		15 32				15 47	15 52		16 02
Sydenham d	14 21	14 26	14 29	14 36	14 41	14 44	14 51		14 56	14 59	15 06	15 11	15 14	15 21	15 26	15 29	15 36		15 41	15 44	15 51	15 56	15 59	16 06
Forest Hill d	14 24	14 28	14 32	14 39	14 43	14 47	14 54		14 58	15 02	15 09	15 13	15 17	15 24	15 28	15 32	15 39		15 43	15 47	15 54	15 58	16 02	16 09
Honor Oak Park d	14 26	14 31	14 34	14 41	14 46	14 49	14 56		15 01	15 04	15 11	15 16	15 19	15 26	15 31	15 34	15 41		15 46	15 49	15 56	16 01	16 04	16 11
Brockley d	14 29	14 33	14 37	14 44	14 48	14 52	14 59		15 03	15 07	15 14	15 18	15 22	15 29	15 33	15 37	15 44		15 48	15 52	15 59	16 03	16 07	16 14
New Cross Gate d	14 31	14 36	14 39	14 46	14 51	14 54	15 01		15 06	15 09	15 16	15 21	15 24	15 31	15 36	15 39	15 46		15 51	15 54	16 01	16 06	16 09	16 16
Surrey Quays d	14 35		14 42	14 50		14 57	15 05			15 12	15 20		15 27	15 35		15 42	15 50			15 57	16 05		16 12	16 20
Canada Water d	14 37		14 44	14 52		14 59	15 07			15 14	15 22		15 29	15 37		15 44	15 52			15 59	16 07		16 14	16 22
Rotherhithe d	14 38		14 46	14 53		15 01	15 08			15 16	15 23		15 31	15 38		15 46	15 53			16 01	16 08		16 16	16 23
Wapping d	14 40		14 47	14 55		15 02	15 10			15 17	15 25		15 32	15 40		15 47	15 55			16 02	16 10		16 17	16 25
Shadwell d	14 42		14 49	14 57		15 04	15 12			15 19	15 27		15 34	15 42		15 49	15 57			16 04	16 12		16 19	16 27
Whitechapel d	14 44		14 52	14 59		15 07	15 14			15 22	15 29		15 37	15 44		15 52	15 59			16 07	16 14		16 22	16 29
Shoreditch High Street d	14 47		14 54	15 02		15 09	15 17			15 24	15 32		15 39	15 47		15 54	16 02			16 09	16 17		16 24	16 32
Hoxton d	14 49		14 56	15 04		15 11	15 19			15 26	15 34		15 41	15 49		15 56	16 04			16 11	16 19		16 26	16 34
Haggerston d	14 51		14 58	15 06		15 13	15 21			15 28	15 36		15 43	15 51		15 58	16 06			16 13	16 21		16 28	16 36
Dalston Junction a	14 53		15 00	15 08		15 15	15 23			15 30	15 38		15 45	15 53		16 00	16 08			16 15	16 23		16 30	16 38
Canonbury a	14 56		15 03	15 11		15 18	15 26			15 33	15 41		15 48	15 56		16 03	16 11			16 18	16 26		16 33	16 41
Highbury & Islington a	15 00		15 08	15 15		15 23	15 30			15 38	15 45		15 53	16 00		16 10	16 15			16 25	16 30		16 40	16 45
London Bridge a		14 44			15 01				15 14			15 31			15 44				16 01			16 14		

	SN B	LO	LO		SN A	LO	LO	SN B	LO	LO	SN A	LO	LO		SN B	LO	LO	SN A	LO	LO	SN B	LO	LO	
Purley d	15 48							16 18							16 48						17 18			
East Croydon d	15 57							16 27							16 57						17 27			
Norwood Junction a	16 02							16 32							17 02						17 32			
West Croydon d		16 01				16 16			16 31			16 46				17 01			17 16			17 31		
Norwood Junction a		16 06				16 21			16 36			16 52				17 06			17 21			17 36		
Norwood Junction d	16 03	16 07				16 22		16 33	16 37			16 52			17 03	17 07			17 22		17 33	17 37		
Anerley d	16 06	16 10				16 25		16 36	16 40			16 55			17 06	17 10			17 25		17 36	17 40		
Penge West d	16 08	16 11				16 26		16 38	16 41			16 57			17 08	17 11			17 26		17 38	17 41		
Crystal Palace d			16 17		16 22		16 32			16 47	16 52		17 02				17 17	17 22		17 32			17 47	
Sydenham d	16 11	16 14	16 21		16 26	16 29	16 36	16 41	16 44	16 51	16 56	16 59	17 06		17 11	17 14	17 21	17 26	17 29	17 36	17 41	17 44	17 51	
Forest Hill d	16 13	16 17	16 24		16 28	16 32	16 39	16 43	16 47	16 54	16 58	17 02	17 09		17 13	17 17	17 24	17 28	17 32	17 39	17 43	17 47	17 54	
Honor Oak Park d	16 16	16 19	16 26		16 31	16 34	16 41	16 46	16 49	16 56	17 01	17 04	17 11		17 16	17 19	17 26	17 31	17 34	17 41	17 46	17 49	17 56	
Brockley d	16 18	16 22	16 29		16 33	16 37	16 44	16 48	16 52	16 59	17 03	17 07	17 14		17 18	17 22	17 29	17 33	17 37	17 44	17 48	17 52	17 59	
New Cross Gate d	16 21	16 24	16 31		16 36	16 39	16 46	16 51	16 54	17 01	17 06	17 09	17 16		17 21	17 24	17 31	17 36	17 39	17 46	17 51	17 54	18 01	
Surrey Quays d		16 27	16 35			16 42	16 50		16 57	17 05		17 12	17 20			17 27	17 35		17 42	17 50		17 57	18 05	
Canada Water d		16 29	16 37			16 44	16 52		16 59	17 07		17 14	17 22			17 29	17 37		17 44	17 52		17 59	18 07	
Rotherhithe d		16 31	16 38			16 46	16 53		17 01	17 08		17 16	17 23			17 31	17 38		17 46	17 53		18 01	18 08	
Wapping d		16 32	16 40			16 47	16 55		17 02	17 10		17 17	17 25			17 32	17 40		17 47	17 55		18 02	18 10	
Shadwell d		16 34	16 42			16 49	16 57		17 04	17 12		17 19	17 27			17 34	17 42		17 49	17 57		18 04	18 12	
Whitechapel d		16 37	16 44			16 52	16 59		17 07	17 14		17 22	17 29			17 37	17 44		17 52	17 59		18 07	18 14	
Shoreditch High Street d		16 39	16 47			16 54	17 02		17 09	17 17		17 24	17 32			17 39	17 47		17 54	18 02		18 09	18 17	
Hoxton d		16 41	16 49			16 56	17 04		17 11	17 19		17 26	17 34			17 41	17 49		17 56	18 04		18 11	18 19	
Haggerston d		16 43	16 51			16 58	17 06		17 13	17 21		17 28	17 36			17 43	17 51		17 58	18 06		18 13	18 21	
Dalston Junction a		16 45	16 53			17 00	17 08		17 15	17 23		17 30	17 38			17 45	17 53		18 00	18 08		18 15	18 23	
Canonbury a		16 48	16 56			17 03	17 11		17 18	17 26		17 33	17 41			17 48	17 56		18 03	18 11		18 18	18 26	
Highbury & Islington a		16 55	17 00			17 10	17 15		17 25	17 30		17 40	17 45			17 55	18 00		18 10	18 15		18 25	18 30	
London Bridge a	16 31				16 44			17 01			17 14				17 31			17 44			18 01			

A From London Victoria

B From Coulsdon Town

For full service between Highbury & Islington and Surrey Quays, refer to Table T178

For Sutton connections at West Croydon, refer to Table T172

Table T177-R

Saturdays
26 May to 8 December

Croydon and Norwood Junction-Anerley, Penge West, Crystal Palace, Sydenham, Forest Hill, Honor Oak Park, Brockley, New Cross Gate-London Bridge

		SN A	LO	LO	SN B	LO		LO	SN A	LO	LO	SN B	LO	LO	SN A	LO		LO	SN B	LO	LO	SN A	LO	LO	SN B
Purley	d				17 48							18 18							18 48						19 18
East Croydon	d				17 57							18 27							18 57						19 27
Norwood Junction	a				18 02							18 32							19 02						19 32
West Croydon	d		17 46			18 01				18 16			18 31			18 46				19 01			19 16		
Norwood Junction	a		17 52			18 06				18 21			18 36			18 52				19 06			19 21		
Norwood Junction	d		17 52		18 03	18 07				18 22		18 33	18 37			18 52			19 03	19 07			19 22		19 33
Anerley	d		17 55		18 06	18 10				18 25		18 36	18 40			18 55			19 06	19 10			19 25		19 36
Penge West	d		17 57		18 08	18 11				18 26		18 38	18 41			18 57			19 08	19 11			19 26		19 38
Crystal Palace	d	17 52		18 02				18 17	18 22		18 32			18 47	18 52			19 02			19 17	19 22		19 32	
Sydenham	d	17 56	17 59	18 06	18 11	18 14		18 21	18 26	18 29	18 36	18 41	18 44	18 51	18 56	18 59		19 06	19 11	19 14	19 21	19 26	19 29	19 36	19 41
Forest Hill	d	17 58	18 02	18 09	18 13	18 17		18 24	18 28	18 32	18 39	18 43	18 47	18 54	18 58	19 02		19 09	19 13	19 17	19 24	19 28	19 32	19 39	19 43
Honor Oak Park	d	18 01	18 04	18 11	18 16	18 19		18 26	18 31	18 34	18 41	18 46	18 49	18 56	19 01	19 04		19 11	19 16	19 19	19 26	19 31	19 34	19 41	19 46
Brockley	d	18 03	18 07	18 14	18 18	18 22		18 29	18 33	18 37	18 44	18 48	18 52	18 59	19 03	19 07		19 14	19 18	19 22	19 29	19 33	19 37	19 44	19 48
New Cross Gate	d	18 06	18 09	18 16	18 21	18 24		18 31	18 36	18 39	18 46	18 51	18 54	19 01	19 06	19 09		19 16	19 21	19 24	19 31	19 36	19 39	19 46	19 51
Surrey Quays	d		18 12	18 20		18 27		18 35		18 42	18 50		18 57	19 05		19 12		19 20		19 27	19 35		19 42	19 50	
Canada Water	d		18 14	18 22		18 29		18 37		18 44	18 52		18 59	19 07		19 14		19 22		19 29	19 37		19 44	19 52	
Rotherhithe	d		18 16	18 23		18 31		18 38		18 46	18 53		19 01	19 08		19 16		19 23		19 31	19 38		19 46	19 53	
Wapping	d		18 17	18 25		18 32		18 40		18 47	18 55		19 02	19 10		19 17		19 25		19 32	19 40		19 47	19 55	
Shadwell	d		18 19	18 27		18 34		18 42		18 49	18 57		19 04	19 12		19 19		19 27		19 34	19 42		19 49	19 57	
Whitechapel	d		18 22	18 29		18 37		18 44		18 52	18 59		19 07	19 14		19 22		19 29		19 37	19 44		19 52	19 59	
Shoreditch High Street	d		18 24	18 32		18 39		18 47		18 54	19 02		19 09	19 17		19 24		19 32		19 39	19 47		19 54	20 02	
Hoxton	d		18 26	18 34		18 41		18 49		18 56	19 04		19 11	19 19		19 26		19 34		19 41	19 49		19 56	20 04	
Haggerston	d		18 28	18 36		18 43		18 51		18 58	19 06		19 13	19 21		19 28		19 36		19 43	19 51		19 58	20 06	
Dalston Junction	a		18 30	18 38		18 45		18 53		19 00	19 08		19 15	19 23		19 30		19 38		19 45	19 53		20 00	20 08	
Canonbury	a		18 33	18 41		18 48		18 56		19 03	19 11		19 18	19 26		19 33		19 41		19 48	19 56		20 03	20 11	
Highbury & Islington	a		18 40	18 45		18 55		19 00		19 10	19 15		19 25	19 30		19 40		19 45		19 53	20 00		20 08	20 15	
London Bridge ⊖	a	18 14			18 31				18 44			19 01			19 14				19 31			19 44			20 01

		LO		LO	SN A	LO	LO	SN B	LO	LO	SN A	LO		LO	SN B	LO	LO	SN A	LO	LO	SN B	LO		LO	SN A
Purley	d							19 48							20 18						20 48				
East Croydon	d							19 57							20 27						20 57				
Norwood Junction	a							20 02							20 32						21 02				
West Croydon	d	19 31				19 46			20 01			20 16				20 31			20 46			21 01			
Norwood Junction	a	19 36				19 52			20 06			20 21				20 36			20 52			21 06			
Norwood Junction	d	19 37				19 52		20 03	20 07			20 22			20 33	20 37			20 52		21 03	21 07			
Anerley	d	19 40				19 55		20 06	20 10			20 25			20 36	20 40			20 55		21 06	21 10			
Penge West	d	19 41				19 57		20 08	20 11			20 26			20 38	20 41			20 57		21 08	21 11			
Crystal Palace	d			19 47	19 52		20 02			20 17	20 22			20 32			20 47	20 52		21 02				21 17	21 22
Sydenham	d	19 44		19 51	19 56	19 59	20 06	20 11	20 14	20 21	20 26	20 29		20 36	20 41	20 44	20 51	20 56	20 59	21 06	21 11	21 14		21 21	21 26
Forest Hill	d	19 47		19 54	19 58	20 02	20 09	20 13	20 17	20 24	20 28	20 32		20 39	20 43	20 47	20 54	20 58	21 02	21 09	21 13	21 17		21 24	21 28
Honor Oak Park	d	19 49		19 56	20 01	20 04	20 11	20 16	20 19	20 26	20 31	20 34		20 41	20 46	20 49	20 56	21 01	21 04	21 11	21 16	21 19		21 26	21 31
Brockley	d	19 52		19 59	20 03	20 07	20 14	20 18	20 22	20 29	20 33	20 37		20 44	20 48	20 52	20 59	21 03	21 07	21 14	21 18	21 22		21 29	21 33
New Cross Gate	d	19 54		20 01	20 06	20 09	20 16	20 21	20 24	20 31	20 36	20 39		20 46	20 51	20 54	21 01	21 06	21 09	21 16	21 21	21 24		21 31	21 36
Surrey Quays	d	19 57		20 05		20 12	20 20		20 27	20 35		20 42		20 50		20 57	21 05		21 12	21 20		21 27		21 35	
Canada Water	d	19 59		20 07		20 14	20 22		20 29	20 37		20 44		20 52		20 59	21 07		21 14	21 22		21 29		21 37	
Rotherhithe	d	20 01		20 08		20 16	20 23		20 31	20 38		20 46		20 53		21 01	21 08		21 16	21 23		21 31		21 38	
Wapping	d	20 02		20 10		20 17	20 25		20 32	20 40		20 47		20 55		21 02	21 10		21 17	21 25		21 32		21 40	
Shadwell	d	20 04		20 12		20 19	20 27		20 34	20 42		20 49		20 57		21 04	21 12		21 19	21 27		21 34		21 42	
Whitechapel	d	20 07		20 14		20 22	20 29		20 37	20 44		20 52		20 59		21 07	21 14		21 22	21 29		21 37		21 44	
Shoreditch High Street	d	20 09		20 17		20 24	20 32		20 39	20 47		20 54		21 02		21 09	21 17		21 24	21 32		21 39		21 47	
Hoxton	d	20 11		20 19		20 26	20 34		20 41	20 49		20 56		21 04		21 11	21 19		21 26	21 34		21 41		21 49	
Haggerston	d	20 13		20 21		20 28	20 36		20 43	20 51		20 58		21 06		21 13	21 21		21 28	21 36		21 43		21 51	
Dalston Junction	a	20 15		20 23		20 30	20 38		20 45	20 53		21 00		21 08		21 15	21 23		21 30	21 38		21 45		21 53	
Canonbury	a	20 18		20 26		20 33	20 41		20 48	20 56		21 03		21 11		21 18	21 26		21 33	21 41		21 48		21 56	
Highbury & Islington	a	20 23		20 30		20 38	20 45		20 53	21 00		21 08		21 15		21 23	21 30		21 38	21 45		21 53		22 00	
London Bridge ⊖	a				20 14			20 31			20 44				21 01			21 14			21 31				21 44

A From London Victoria

B From Coulsdon Town

For full service between Highbury & Islington and Surrey Quays, refer to Table T178

For Sutton connections at West Croydon, refer to Table T172

Table T177-R

Saturdays
26 May to 8 December

Croydon and Norwood Junction-Anerley, Penge West, Crystal Palace, Sydenham, Forest Hill, Honor Oak Park, Brockley, New Cross Gate-London Bridge

		LO	LO	SN A		LO	LO	SN B	LO	LO	SN A	LO	LO	SN B		LO	LO	SN A	LO	LO	SN B	LO	LO	SN A
Purley	d			21 18							21 48							22 18						22 48
East Croydon	d			21 27							21 57							22 27						22 57
Norwood Junction	a			21 32							22 02							22 32						23 02
West Croydon	d	21 16				21 31			21 46			22 01				22 16			22 31			22 46		
Norwood Junction	a	21 21				21 36			21 52			22 06				22 21			22 36			22 52		
Norwood Junction	d	21 22		21 33		21 37			21 52		22 03	22 07				22 22		22 33	22 37			22 52		23 03
Anerley	d	21 25		21 36		21 40			21 55		22 06	22 10				22 25		22 36	22 40			22 55		23 06
Penge West	d	21 26		21 38		21 41			21 57		22 08	22 11				22 26		22 38	22 41			22 57		23 08
Crystal Palace	d		21 32				21 47	21 52		22 02			22 17	22 22			22 32			22 47	22 52		23 02	
Sydenham	d	21 29	21 36	21 41		21 44	21 51	21 56	21 59	22 06	22 11	22 14	22 21	22 26		22 29	22 36	22 41	22 44	22 51	22 56	22 59	23 06	23 11
Forest Hill	d	21 32	21 39	21 43		21 47	21 54	21 58	22 02	22 09	22 13	22 17	22 24	22 28		22 32	22 39	22 43	22 47	22 54	22 58	23 02	23 09	23 13
Honor Oak Park	d	21 34	21 41	21 46		21 49	21 56	22 01	22 04	22 11	22 16	22 19	22 26	22 31		22 34	22 41	22 46	22 49	22 56	23 01	23 04	23 11	23 16
Brockley	d	21 37	21 44	21 48		21 52	21 59	22 03	22 07	22 14	22 18	22 22	22 29	22 33		22 37	22 44	22 48	22 52	22 59	23 03	23 07	23 14	23 18
New Cross Gate	d	21 39	21 46	21 51		21 54	22 01	22 06	22 09	22 16	22 21	22 24	22 31	22 36		22 39	22 46	22 51	22 54	23 01	23 06	23 09	23 16	23 21
Surrey Quays	d	21 42	21 50			21 57	22 05		22 12	22 20		22 27	22 35			22 42	22 50		22 57	23 05		23 12	23 20	
Canada Water	d	21 44	21 52			21 59	22 07		22 14	22 22		22 29	22 37			22 44	22 52		22 59	23 07		23 14	23 22	
Rotherhithe	d	21 46	21 53			22 01	22 08		22 16	22 23		22 31	22 38			22 46	22 53		23 01	23 08		23 16	23 23	
Wapping	d	21 47	21 55			22 02	22 10		22 17	22 25		22 32	22 40			22 47	22 55		23 02	23 10		23 17	23 25	
Shadwell	d	21 49	21 57			22 04	22 12		22 19	22 27		22 34	22 42			22 49	22 57		23 04	23 12		23 19	23 27	
Whitechapel	d	21 52	21 59			22 07	22 14		22 22	22 29		22 37	22 44			22 52	22 59		23 07	23 14		23 22	23 29	
Shoreditch High Street	d	21 54	22 02			22 09	22 17		22 24	22 32		22 39	22 47			22 54	23 02		23 09	23 17		23 24	23 32	
Hoxton	d	21 56	22 04			22 11	22 19		22 26	22 34		22 41	22 49			22 56	23 04		23 11	23 19		23 26	23 34	
Haggerston	d	21 58	22 06			22 13	22 21		22 28	22 36		22 43	22 51			22 58	23 06		23 13	23 21		23 28	23 36	
Dalston Junction	a	22 00	22 08			22 15	22 23		22 30	22 38		22 45	22 53			23 00	23 08		23 15	23 23		23 34	23 38	
Canonbury	a	22 03	22 11			22 18	22 26		22 33	22 41		22 48	22 56			23 03	23 11		23 18	23 26			23 41	
Highbury & Islington	a	22 08	22 15			22 23	22 30		22 38	22 45		22 53	23 00			23 10	23 15		23 25	23 30			23 45	
London Bridge ⊖	a			22 01				22 14			22 31			22 44				23 01			23 14			23 31

		LO	LO	SN B	LO	LO	LO	LO	SN B
Purley	d								
East Croydon	d								
Norwood Junction	a								
West Croydon	d	23 01			23 16		23 31		
Norwood Junction	a	23 06			23 21		23 36		
Norwood Junction	d	23 07			23 22		23 37		
Anerley	d	23 10			23 25		23 40		
Penge West	d	23 11			23 26		23 41		
Crystal Palace	d		23 17	23 22		23 32		23 50	23 53
Sydenham	d	23 14	23 21	23 26	23 29	23 36	23 44	23 54	23 59
Forest Hill	d	23 17	23 24	23 28	23 32	23 39	23 47	23 56	00 01
Honor Oak Park	d	23 19	23 26	23 31	23 34	23 41	23 49	23 59	00 05
Brockley	d	23 22	23 29	23 33	23 37	23 44	23 52	00 01	00 07
New Cross Gate	d	23 24	23 31	23 36	23 39	23 46	23 54	00 03	00 10
Surrey Quays	d	23 27	23 35		23 42	23 50	23 57	00 09	
Canada Water	d	23 29	23 37		23 44	23 52	23 59	00 11	
Rotherhithe	d	23 31	23 38		23 46	23 53	00 01	00 12	
Wapping	d	23 32	23 40		23 47	23 55	00 02	00 14	
Shadwell	d	23 34	23 42		23 49	23 57	00 04	00 16	
Whitechapel	d	23 37	23 44		23 52	23 59	00 07	00 18	
Shoreditch High Street	d	23 39	23 47		23 54	00 02	00 09	00 21	
Hoxton	d	23 41	23 49		23 56	00 04	00 11	00 23	
Haggerston	d	23 43	23 51		23 58	00 06	00 13	00 25	
Dalston Junction	a	23 45	23 53		00 01	00 08	00 15	00 27	
Canonbury	a	23 50	23 56		00 03	00 11	00 18	00 30	
Highbury & Islington	a	23 58	23 59		00 10	00 15	00 25	00 33	
London Bridge ⊖	a			23 44					00 17

A From Coulsdon Town

B From London Victoria

For full service between Highbury & Islington and Surrey Quays, refer to Table T178

For Sutton connections at West Croydon, refer to Table T172

Sundays

20 May to 2 December

Croydon and Norwood Junction-Anerley, Penge West, Crystal Palace, Sydenham, Forest Hill, Honor Oak Park, Brockley, New Cross Gate-London Bridge

		LO A	LO B	LO A	SN C	LO		SN C	LO	LO	LO	LO	LO	SN D	LO	SN		LO	SN D	LO	SN	LO	SN E	LO	SN
Purley	d													07 20					07 50				08 20		
East Croydon	d													07 29					07 59				08 29		
Norwood Junction	a													07 33					08 05				08 33		
West Croydon	d									06 43		07 12			07 47					08 12				08 42	
Norwood Junction	a									06 48		07 18			07 52					08 18				08 48	
Norwood Junction	d									06 48		07 18		07 35	07 52				08 06	08 18			08 35	08 48	
Anerley	d									06 51		07 21		07 39	07 55				08 09	08 21			08 39	08 51	
Penge West	d									06 53		07 23		07 41	07 57				08 11	08 23			08 41	08 53	
Crystal Palace	d					00 04		00 25	06 36		07 07		07 37			07 58		08 07			08 24	08 37			08 54
Sydenham	d					00 08		00 31	06 40	06 55	07 11	07 25	07 41	07 45	07 59	08 03		08 11	08 15	08 25	08 29	08 41	08 45	08 55	08 59
Forest Hill	d				00 01	00 11		00 33	06 42	06 58	07 13	07 28	07 43	07 48	08 02	08 05		08 13	08 18	08 28	08 31	08 43	08 48	08 58	09 01
Honor Oak Park	d				00 05	00 13		00 36	06 45	07 00	07 16	07 30	07 46	07 50	08 04	08 08		08 16	08 20	08 30	08 34	08 46	08 50	09 00	09 04
Brockley	d			00 01	00 07	00 16		00 38	06 47	07 03	07 18	07 33	07 48	07 53	08 07	08 10		08 18	08 23	08 33	08 36	08 48	08 53	09 03	09 06
New Cross Gate	d			00 03	00 10	00 18		00 40	06 49	07 05	07 20	07 35	07 50	07 55	08 09	08 13		08 20	08 25	08 35	08 39	08 50	08 55	09 05	09 09
Surrey Quays	d			00 09		00 22			06 53	07 08	07 24	07 38	07 54		08 12			08 24		08 38		08 54		09 08	
Canada Water	d			00 11		00 24			06 55	07 10	07 26	07 40	07 56		08 14			08 26		08 40		08 56		09 10	
Rotherhithe	d		00 01	00 12		00 25			06 56	07 12	07 27	07 42	07 57		08 16			08 27		08 42		08 57		09 12	
Wapping	d		00 02	00 14		00 27			06 58	07 13	07 29	07 43	07 59		08 17			08 29		08 43		08 59		09 13	
Shadwell	d		00 04	00 16		00 29			07 00	07 15	07 31	07 45	08 01		08 19			08 31		08 45		09 01		09 15	
Whitechapel	d		00 07	00 18		00 31			07 02	07 18	07 33	07 48	08 03		08 22			08 33		08 48		09 03		09 18	
Shoreditch High Street	d	00 02	00 09	00 21		00 34			07 04	07 20	07 35	07 50	08 05		08 24			08 35		08 50		09 05		09 20	
Hoxton	d	00 04	00 11	00 23		00 36			07 06	07 22	07 37	07 52	08 07		08 26			08 37		08 52		09 07		09 22	
Haggerston	d	00 06	00 13	00 25		00 38			07 08	07 24	07 39	07 54	08 09		08 28			08 39		08 54		09 09		09 24	
Dalston Junction	a	00 08	00 15	00 27		00 40			07 10	07 26	07 41	07 56	08 11		08 30			08 41		08 56		09 11		09 26	
Canonbury	a	00 11	00 18	00 30		00 43			07 13	07 29	07 44	07 59	08 14		08 33			08 44		08 59		09 14		09 29	
Highbury & Islington	a	00 15	00 25	00 33		00 45			07 19	07 34	07 50	08 03	08 20		08 38			08 50		09 03		09 20		09 33	
London Bridge ⊖	a				00 17			00 47						08 05		08 20			08 36		08 46		09 02		09 16

		LO		SN E	LO	SN	LO	SN E	LO	SN	LO	SN E		LO	SN	LO	SN E	LO	SN	LO	SN E	LO		SN	LO
Purley	d			08 50				09 20				09 50					10 20				10 50				
East Croydon	d			08 59				09 31				10 01					10 31				11 01				
Norwood Junction	a			09 03				09 35				10 05					10 35				11 05				
West Croydon	d				09 13				09 42					10 12				10 42				11 12			
Norwood Junction	a				09 18				09 48					10 18				10 48				11 18			
Norwood Junction	d			09 05	09 18			09 35	09 48			10 05		10 18			10 35	10 48			11 05	11 18			
Anerley	d			09 09	09 21			09 39	09 51			10 09		10 21			10 39	10 51			11 09	11 21			
Penge West	d			09 11	09 23			09 41	09 53			10 11		10 23			10 41	10 53			11 11	11 23			
Crystal Palace	d	09 07				09 24	09 37			09 54	10 07				10 24	10 37			10 54	11 07				11 24	11 37
Sydenham	d	09 11		09 15	09 25	09 29	09 41	09 45	09 55	09 59	10 11	10 15		10 25	10 29	10 41	10 45	10 55	10 59	11 11	11 15	11 25		11 29	11 41
Forest Hill	d	09 13		09 18	09 28	09 31	09 43	09 48	09 58	10 01	10 13	10 18		10 28	10 31	10 43	10 48	10 58	11 01	11 13	11 18	11 28		11 31	11 43
Honor Oak Park	d	09 16		09 20	09 30	09 34	09 46	09 50	10 00	10 04	10 16	10 20		10 30	10 34	10 46	10 50	11 00	11 04	11 16	11 20	11 30		11 34	11 46
Brockley	d	09 18		09 23	09 33	09 36	09 48	09 53	10 03	10 06	10 18	10 23		10 33	10 36	10 48	10 53	11 03	11 06	11 18	11 23	11 33		11 36	11 48
New Cross Gate	d	09 20		09 25	09 35	09 39	09 50	09 55	10 05	10 09	10 20	10 25		10 35	10 39	10 50	10 55	11 05	11 09	11 20	11 25	11 35		11 39	11 50
Surrey Quays	d	09 24			09 38		09 54		10 08		10 24			10 38		10 54		11 08		11 24		11 38			11 54
Canada Water	d	09 26			09 40		09 56		10 10		10 26			10 40		10 56		11 10		11 26		11 40			11 56
Rotherhithe	d	09 27			09 42		09 57		10 12		10 27			10 42		10 57		11 12		11 27		11 42			11 57
Wapping	d	09 29			09 43		09 59		10 13		10 29			10 43		10 59		11 13		11 29		11 43			11 59
Shadwell	d	09 31			09 45		10 01		10 15		10 31			10 45		11 01		11 15		11 31		11 45			12 01
Whitechapel	d	09 33			09 48		10 03		10 18		10 33			10 48		11 03		11 18		11 33		11 48			12 03
Shoreditch High Street	d	09 35			09 50		10 05		10 20		10 35			10 50		11 05		11 20		11 35		11 50			12 05
Hoxton	d	09 37			09 52		10 07		10 22		10 37			10 52		11 07		11 22		11 37		11 52			12 07
Haggerston	d	09 39			09 54		10 09		10 24		10 39			10 54		11 09		11 24		11 39		11 54			12 09
Dalston Junction	a	09 41			09 56		10 11		10 26		10 41			10 56		11 11		11 26		11 41		11 57			12 11
Canonbury	a	09 44			09 59		10 14		10 29		10 44			10 59		11 14		11 29		11 44					12 14
Highbury & Islington	a	09 50			10 04		10 20		10 33		10 50			11 03		11 20		11 33		11 50					12 22
London Bridge ⊖	a			09 32		09 46		10 02		10 16		10 32			10 46		11 02		11 16		11 32			11 46	

A not 20 May. From Crystal Palace
B not 20 May. From West Croydon
C not 20 May. From London Victoria
D From Caterham
E From Tattenham Corner

For full service between Highbury & Islington and Surrey Quays, refer to Table T178

For Sutton connections at West Croydon, refer to Table T172

Sundays

20 May to 2 December

Croydon and Norwood Junction-Anerley, Penge West, Crystal Palace, Sydenham, Forest Hill, Honor Oak Park, Brockley, New Cross Gate-London Bridge

		SN A	LO	SN		LO	SN A	LO	LO	SN	LO	SN A	LO	LO		SN	LO	LO	SN A	LO	LO	SN	LO	LO
Purley	d	11 20					11 50					12 20							12 50					
East Croydon	d	11 31					12 01					12 31							13 01					
Norwood Junction	a	11 35					12 05					12 35							13 05					
West Croydon	d		11 42						12 12					12 42				12 57			13 12			13 27
Norwood Junction	a		11 47						12 17					12 47				13 02			13 17			13 32
Norwood Junction	d	11 35	11 47				12 05		12 17			12 35		12 47				13 02	13 05		13 17			13 32
Anerley	d	11 39	11 50				12 09		12 20			12 39		12 50				13 05	13 09		13 20			13 35
Penge West	d	11 41	11 52				12 11		12 22			12 41		12 52				13 07	13 11		13 22			13 37
Crystal Palace	d			11 54		12 07		12 16		12 24	12 31		12 46			12 54	13 01			13 16		13 24	13 31	
Sydenham	d	11 45	11 54	11 59		12 11	12 15	12 20	12 24	12 29	12 35	12 44	12 50	12 54		12 59	13 05	13 09	13 14	13 20	13 24	13 29	13 35	13 39
Forest Hill	d	11 48	11 57	12 01		12 13	12 18	12 22	12 27	12 31	12 37	12 46	12 52	12 57		13 01	13 07	13 12	13 16	13 22	13 27	13 31	13 37	13 42
Honor Oak Park	d	11 50	11 59	12 04		12 16	12 20	12 25	12 29	12 34	12 40	12 49	12 55	12 59		13 04	13 10	13 14	13 19	13 25	13 29	13 34	13 40	13 44
Brockley	d	11 53	12 02	12 06		12 18	12 23	12 27	12 32	12 36	12 42	12 51	12 57	13 02		13 06	13 12	13 17	13 21	13 27	13 32	13 36	13 42	13 47
New Cross Gate	d	11 55	12 04	12 09		12 20	12 25	12 29	12 34	12 39	12 44	12 54	12 59	13 04		13 09	13 14	13 19	13 24	13 29	13 34	13 39	13 44	13 49
Surrey Quays	d		12 07			12 24		12 35	12 37		12 48		13 03	13 07			13 18	13 22		13 33	13 37		13 48	13 52
Canada Water	d		12 09			12 26		12 37	12 39		12 50		13 05	13 09			13 20	13 24		13 35	13 39		13 50	13 54
Rotherhithe	d		12 11			12 27		12 39	12 41		12 51		13 06	13 11			13 21	13 26		13 36	13 41		13 51	13 56
Wapping	d		12 12			12 29		12 40	12 42		12 53		13 08	13 12			13 23	13 27		13 38	13 42		13 53	13 57
Shadwell	d		12 14			12 31		12 42	12 44		12 55		13 10	13 14			13 25	13 29		13 40	13 44		13 55	13 59
Whitechapel	d		12 17			12 33		12 45	12 47		12 57		13 12	13 17			13 27	13 32		13 42	13 47		13 57	14 02
Shoreditch High Street	d		12 19			12 35		12 47	12 49		12 59		13 14	13 19			13 29	13 34		13 44	13 49		13 59	14 04
Hoxton	d		12 21			12 37		12 49	12 51		13 01		13 16	13 21			13 31	13 36		13 46	13 51		14 01	14 06
Haggerston	d		12 23			12 39		12 51	12 53		13 03		13 18	13 23			13 33	13 38		13 48	13 53		14 03	14 08
Dalston Junction	a		12 25			12 41		12 55	12 58		13 05		13 20	13 27			13 35	13 42		13 50	13 57		14 05	14 12
Canonbury	a		12 28			12 44					13 08		13 23				13 38			13 53			14 08	
Highbury & Islington	a		12 33			12 50					13 16		13 29				13 44			13 59			14 14	
London Bridge ⊖	a	12 02		12 16			12 32			12 46		13 02				13 16			13 32			13 46		

		SN A	LO	LO	SN	LO	LO	SN A	LO	LO		SN	LO	LO	SN A	LO	LO	SN	LO	LO		SN A	LO	LO	SN
Purley	d	13 20						13 50							14 20							14 50			
East Croydon	d	13 31						14 01							14 31							15 01			
Norwood Junction	a	13 35						14 05							14 35							15 05			
West Croydon	d			13 42			13 57			14 12				14 27			14 42			14 57				15 12	
Norwood Junction	a			13 47			14 02			14 17				14 32			14 47			15 02				15 17	
Norwood Junction	d	13 35		13 47			14 02	14 05		14 17				14 32	14 35		14 47			15 02		15 05		15 17	
Anerley	d	13 39		13 50			14 05	14 09		14 20				14 35	14 39		14 50			15 05		15 09		15 20	
Penge West	d	13 41		13 52			14 07	14 11		14 22				14 37	14 41		14 52			15 07		15 11		15 22	
Crystal Palace	d		13 46		13 54	14 01			14 16			14 24	14 31			14 46		14 54	15 01				15 16		15 24
Sydenham	d	13 44	13 50	13 54	13 59	14 05	14 09	14 14	14 20	14 24		14 29	14 35	14 39	14 44	14 50	14 54	14 59	15 05	15 09		15 14	15 20	15 24	15 29
Forest Hill	d	13 46	13 52	13 57	14 01	14 07	14 12	14 16	14 22	14 27		14 31	14 37	14 42	14 46	14 52	14 57	15 01	15 07	15 12		15 16	15 22	15 27	15 31
Honor Oak Park	d	13 49	13 55	13 59	14 04	14 10	14 14	14 19	14 25	14 29		14 34	14 40	14 44	14 49	14 55	14 59	15 04	15 10	15 14		15 19	15 25	15 29	15 34
Brockley	d	13 51	13 57	14 02	14 06	14 12	14 17	14 21	14 27	14 32		14 36	14 42	14 47	14 51	14 57	15 02	15 06	15 12	15 17		15 21	15 27	15 32	15 36
New Cross Gate	d	13 54	13 59	14 04	14 09	14 14	14 19	14 24	14 29	14 34		14 39	14 44	14 49	14 54	14 59	15 04	15 09	15 14	15 19		15 24	15 29	15 34	15 39
Surrey Quays	d		14 03	14 07		14 18	14 22		14 33	14 37			14 48	14 52		15 03	15 07		15 18	15 22			15 33	15 37	
Canada Water	d		14 05	14 09		14 20	14 24		14 35	14 39			14 50	14 54		15 05	15 09		15 20	15 24			15 35	15 39	
Rotherhithe	d		14 06	14 11		14 21	14 26		14 36	14 41			14 51	14 56		15 06	15 11		15 21	15 26			15 36	15 41	
Wapping	d		14 08	14 12		14 23	14 27		14 38	14 42			14 53	14 57		15 08	15 12		15 23	15 27			15 38	15 42	
Shadwell	d		14 10	14 14		14 25	14 29		14 40	14 44			14 55	14 59		15 10	15 14		15 25	15 29			15 40	15 44	
Whitechapel	d		14 12	14 17		14 27	14 32		14 42	14 47			14 57	15 02		15 12	15 17		15 27	15 32			15 42	15 47	
Shoreditch High Street	d		14 14	14 19		14 29	14 34		14 44	14 49			14 59	15 04		15 14	15 19		15 29	15 34			15 44	15 49	
Hoxton	d		14 16	14 21		14 31	14 36		14 46	14 51			15 01	15 06		15 16	15 21		15 31	15 36			15 46	15 51	
Haggerston	d		14 18	14 23		14 33	14 38		14 48	14 53			15 03	15 08		15 18	15 23		15 33	15 38			15 48	15 53	
Dalston Junction	a		14 20	14 27		14 35	14 42		14 50	14 57			15 05	15 12		15 20	15 27		15 35	15 42			15 50	15 57	
Canonbury	a		14 23			14 38			14 53				15 08			15 23			15 38				15 53		
Highbury & Islington	a		14 29			14 44			14 59				15 14			15 29			15 44				15 59		
London Bridge ⊖	a	14 02			14 16			14 32				14 46			15 02			15 16				15 32			15 46

A From Tattenham Corner

For full service between Highbury & Islington and Surrey Quays, refer to Table T178

For Sutton connections at West Croydon, refer to Table T172

Table T177-R

Sundays
20 May to 2 December

Croydon and Norwood Junction-Anerley, Penge West, Crystal Palace, Sydenham, Forest Hill, Honor Oak Park, Brockley, New Cross Gate-London Bridge

		LO		LO	SN A	LO	LO	SN	LO	LO	SN A	LO		LO	SN	LO	LO	SN A	LO	LO	SN	LO		LO	SN A
Purley	d				15 20						15 50							16 20							16 50
East Croydon	d				15 31						16 01							16 31							17 01
Norwood Junction	a				15 35						16 05							16 35							17 05
West Croydon	d			15 27			15 42			15 57				16 12			16 27			16 42				16 57	
Norwood Junction	a			15 32			15 47			16 02				16 17			16 32			16 47				17 02	
Norwood Junction	d			15 32	15 35		15 47			16 02	16 05			16 17			16 32	16 35		16 47				17 02	17 05
Anerley	d			15 35	15 39		15 50			16 05	16 09			16 20			16 35	16 39		16 50				17 05	17 09
Penge West	d			15 37	15 41		15 52			16 07	16 11			16 22			16 37	16 41		16 52				17 07	17 11
Crystal Palace	d	15 31				15 46		15 54	16 01			16 16			16 24	16 31			16 46		16 54	17 01			
Sydenham	d	15 35		15 39	15 44	15 50	15 54	15 59	16 05	16 09	16 14	16 20		16 24	16 29	16 35	16 39	16 44	16 50	16 54	16 59	17 05		17 09	17 14
Forest Hill	d	15 37		15 42	15 46	15 52	15 57	16 01	16 07	16 12	16 16	16 22		16 27	16 31	16 37	16 42	16 46	16 52	16 57	17 01	17 07		17 12	17 16
Honor Oak Park	d	15 40		15 44	15 49	15 55	15 59	16 04	16 10	16 14	16 19	16 25		16 29	16 34	16 40	16 44	16 49	16 55	16 59	17 04	17 10		17 14	17 19
Brockley	d	15 42		15 47	15 51	15 57	16 02	16 06	16 12	16 17	16 21	16 27		16 32	16 36	16 42	16 47	16 51	16 57	17 02	17 06	17 12		17 17	17 21
New Cross Gate	d	15 44		15 49	15 54	15 59	16 04	16 09	16 14	16 19	16 24	16 29		16 34	16 39	16 44	16 49	16 54	16 59	17 04	17 09	17 14		17 19	17 24
Surrey Quays	d	15 48		15 52		16 03	16 07		16 18	16 22		16 33		16 37		16 48	16 52		17 03	17 07		17 18		17 22	
Canada Water	d	15 50		15 54		16 05	16 09		16 20	16 24		16 35		16 39		16 50	16 54		17 05	17 09		17 20		17 24	
Rotherhithe	d	15 51		15 56		16 06	16 11		16 21	16 26		16 36		16 41		16 51	16 56		17 06	17 11		17 21		17 26	
Wapping	d	15 53		15 57		16 08	16 12		16 23	16 27		16 38		16 42		16 53	16 57		17 08	17 12		17 23		17 27	
Shadwell	d	15 55		15 59		16 10	16 14		16 25	16 29		16 40		16 44		16 55	16 59		17 10	17 14		17 25		17 29	
Whitechapel	d	15 57		16 02		16 12	16 17		16 27	16 32		16 42		16 47		16 57	17 02		17 12	17 17		17 27		17 32	
Shoreditch High Street	d	15 59		16 04		16 14	16 19		16 29	16 34		16 44		16 49		16 59	17 04		17 14	17 19		17 29		17 34	
Hoxton	d	16 01		16 06		16 16	16 21		16 31	16 36		16 46		16 51		17 01	17 06		17 16	17 21		17 31		17 36	
Haggerston	d	16 03		16 08		16 18	16 23		16 33	16 38		16 48		16 53		17 03	17 08		17 18	17 23		17 33		17 38	
Dalston Junction	a	16 05		16 12		16 20	16 27		16 35	16 42		16 50		16 57		17 05	17 12		17 20	17 27		17 35		17 42	
Canonbury	a	16 08				16 23			16 38			16 53				17 08			17 23			17 38			
Highbury & Islington	a	16 14				16 29			16 44			16 59				17 14			17 29			17 44			
London Bridge	a				16 02			16 16			16 32				16 46			17 02			17 16				17 32

		LO	LO	SN	LO	LO	SN A	LO		LO	SN	LO	LO	SN A	LO	LO	SN	LO		LO	SN A	LO	LO	SN	LO
Purley	d						17 20							17 50							18 20				
East Croydon	d						17 31							18 01							18 31				
Norwood Junction	a						17 35							18 05							18 35				
West Croydon	d		17 12			17 27				17 42			17 57			18 12				18 27			18 42		
Norwood Junction	a		17 17			17 32				17 47			18 02			18 17				18 32			18 47		
Norwood Junction	d		17 17			17 32	17 35			17 47			18 02	18 05		18 17				18 32	18 35		18 47		
Anerley	d		17 20			17 35	17 39			17 50			18 05	18 09		18 20				18 35	18 39		18 50		
Penge West	d		17 22			17 37	17 41			17 52			18 07	18 11		18 22				18 37	18 41		18 52		
Crystal Palace	d	17 16		17 24	17 31			17 46			17 54	18 01			18 16		18 24	18 31				18 46		18 54	19 01
Sydenham	d	17 20	17 24	17 29	17 35	17 39	17 44	17 50		17 54	17 59	18 05	18 09	18 14	18 20	18 24	18 29	18 35		18 39	18 44	18 50	18 54	18 59	19 05
Forest Hill	d	17 22	17 27	17 31	17 37	17 42	17 46	17 52		17 57	18 01	18 07	18 12	18 16	18 22	18 27	18 31	18 37		18 42	18 46	18 52	18 57	19 01	19 07
Honor Oak Park	d	17 25	17 29	17 34	17 40	17 44	17 49	17 55		17 59	18 04	18 10	18 14	18 19	18 25	18 29	18 34	18 40		18 44	18 49	18 55	18 59	19 04	19 10
Brockley	d	17 27	17 32	17 36	17 42	17 47	17 51	17 57		18 02	18 06	18 12	18 17	18 21	18 27	18 32	18 36	18 42		18 47	18 51	18 57	19 02	19 06	19 12
New Cross Gate	d	17 29	17 34	17 39	17 44	17 49	17 54	17 59		18 04	18 09	18 14	18 19	18 24	18 29	18 34	18 39	18 44		18 49	18 54	18 59	19 04	19 09	19 14
Surrey Quays	d	17 33	17 37		17 48	17 52		18 03		18 07		18 18	18 22		18 33	18 37		18 48		18 52		19 03	19 07		19 18
Canada Water	d	17 35	17 39		17 50	17 54		18 05		18 09		18 20	18 24		18 35	18 39		18 50		18 54		19 05	19 09		19 20
Rotherhithe	d	17 36	17 41		17 51	17 56		18 06		18 11		18 21	18 26		18 36	18 41		18 51		18 56		19 06	19 11		19 21
Wapping	d	17 38	17 42		17 53	17 57		18 08		18 12		18 23	18 27		18 38	18 42		18 53		18 57		19 08	19 12		19 23
Shadwell	d	17 40	17 44		17 55	17 59		18 10		18 14		18 25	18 29		18 40	18 44		18 55		18 59		19 10	19 14		19 25
Whitechapel	d	17 42	17 47		17 57	18 02		18 12		18 17		18 27	18 32		18 42	18 47		18 57		19 02		19 12	19 17		19 27
Shoreditch High Street	d	17 44	17 49		17 59	18 04		18 14		18 19		18 29	18 34		18 44	18 49		18 59		19 04		19 14	19 19		19 29
Hoxton	d	17 46	17 51		18 01	18 06		18 16		18 21		18 31	18 36		18 46	18 51		19 01		19 06		19 16	19 21		19 31
Haggerston	d	17 48	17 53		18 03	18 08		18 18		18 23		18 33	18 38		18 48	18 53		19 03		19 08		19 18	19 23		19 33
Dalston Junction	a	17 50	17 57		18 05	18 12		18 20		18 27		18 35	18 42		18 50	18 57		19 05		19 12		19 20	19 27		19 35
Canonbury	a	17 53			18 08			18 23				18 38			18 53			19 08				19 23			19 38
Highbury & Islington	a	17 59			18 14			18 29				18 44			18 59			19 14				19 29			19 44
London Bridge	a			17 46			18 02				18 16			18 32			18 46				19 02			19 16	

A From Tattenham Corner

For full service between Highbury & Islington and Surrey Quays, refer to Table T178

For Sutton connections at West Croydon, refer to Table T172

Table T177-R

Sundays
20 May to 2 December

Croydon and Norwood Junction-Anerley, Penge West, Crystal Palace, Sydenham, Forest Hill, Honor Oak Park, Brockley, New Cross Gate-London Bridge

		LO	SN A	LO	LO	SN	LO	LO	SN A	LO		LO	SN	LO	LO	SN A	LO	LO	SN	LO		LO	SN A	LO	LO
Purley	d		18 50						19 20							19 50							20 20		
East Croydon	d		19 01						19 31							20 01							20 31		
Norwood Junction	a		19 05						19 35							20 05							20 35		
West Croydon	d	18 57			19 12			19 27				19 42			19 57			20 12				20 27			20 42
Norwood Junction	a	19 02			19 17			19 32				19 47			20 02			20 17				20 32			20 47
Norwood Junction	d	19 02	19 05		19 17			19 32	19 35			19 47			20 02	20 05		20 17				20 32	20 35		20 47
Anerley	d	19 05	19 09		19 20			19 35	19 39			19 50			20 05	20 09		20 20				20 35	20 39		20 50
Penge West	d	19 07	19 11		19 22			19 37	19 41			19 52			20 07	20 11		20 22				20 37	20 41		20 52
Crystal Palace	d			19 16		19 24	19 31			19 46			19 54	20 01			20 16		20 24	20 31				20 46	
Sydenham	d	19 09	19 14	19 20	19 24	19 29	19 35	19 39	19 44	19 50		19 54	19 59	20 05	20 09	20 14	20 20	20 24	20 29	20 35		20 39	20 44	20 50	20 54
Forest Hill	d	19 12	19 16	19 22	19 27	19 31	19 37	19 42	19 46	19 52		19 57	20 01	20 07	20 12	20 16	20 22	20 27	20 31	20 37		20 42	20 46	20 52	20 57
Honor Oak Park	d	19 14	19 19	19 25	19 29	19 34	19 40	19 44	19 49	19 55		19 59	20 04	20 10	20 14	20 19	20 25	20 29	20 34	20 40		20 44	20 49	20 55	20 59
Brockley	d	19 17	19 21	19 27	19 32	19 36	19 42	19 47	19 51	19 57		20 02	20 06	20 12	20 17	20 21	20 27	20 32	20 36	20 42		20 47	20 51	20 57	21 02
New Cross Gate	d	19 19	19 24	19 29	19 34	19 39	19 44	19 49	19 54	19 59		20 04	20 09	20 14	20 19	20 24	20 29	20 34	20 39	20 44		20 49	20 54	20 59	21 04
Surrey Quays	d	19 22		19 33	19 37		19 48	19 52		20 03		20 07		20 18	20 22		20 33	20 37		20 48		20 52		21 03	21 07
Canada Water	d	19 24		19 35	19 39		19 50	19 54		20 05		20 09		20 20	20 24		20 35	20 39		20 50		20 54		21 05	21 09
Rotherhithe	d	19 26		19 36	19 41		19 51	19 56		20 06		20 11		20 21	20 26		20 36	20 41		20 51		20 56		21 06	21 11
Wapping	d	19 27		19 38	19 42		19 53	19 57		20 08		20 12		20 23	20 27		20 38	20 42		20 53		20 57		21 08	21 12
Shadwell	d	19 29		19 40	19 44		19 55	19 59		20 10		20 14		20 25	20 29		20 40	20 44		20 55		20 59		21 10	21 14
Whitechapel	d	19 32		19 42	19 47		19 57	20 02		20 12		20 17		20 27	20 32		20 42	20 47		20 57		21 02		21 12	21 17
Shoreditch High Street	d	19 34		19 44	19 49		19 59	20 04		20 14		20 19		20 29	20 34		20 44	20 49		20 59		21 04		21 14	21 19
Hoxton	d	19 36		19 46	19 51		20 01	20 06		20 16		20 21		20 31	20 36		20 46	20 51		21 01		21 06		21 16	21 21
Haggerston	d	19 38		19 48	19 53		20 03	20 08		20 18		20 23		20 33	20 38		20 48	20 53		21 03		21 08		21 18	21 23
Dalston Junction	a	19 42		19 50	19 57		20 05	20 12		20 20		20 27		20 35	20 42		20 50	20 57		21 05		21 12		21 20	21 27
Canonbury	a			19 53			20 08			20 23				20 38			20 53			21 08				21 23	
Highbury & Islington	a			19 59			20 14			20 29				20 44			20 59			21 14				21 29	
London Bridge	a		19 32			19 46			20 02				20 16			20 32			20 46				21 02		

		SN	LO	LO	SN A	LO		LO	SN	LO	LO	SN A	LO	LO	SN	LO		LO	SN A	LO	LO	SN	LO	SN A	LO
Purley	d				20 50							21 20							21 50					22 20	
East Croydon	d				21 01							21 31							22 01					22 31	
Norwood Junction	a				21 05							21 35							22 05					22 35	
West Croydon	d			20 57				21 12			21 27			21 42				21 57			22 12		22 27		
Norwood Junction	a			21 02				21 17			21 32			21 47				22 02			22 17		22 32		
Norwood Junction	d			21 02	21 05			21 17			21 32	21 35		21 47				22 02	22 05		22 17		22 32	22 35	
Anerley	d			21 05	21 09			21 20			21 35	21 39		21 50				22 05	22 09		22 20		22 35	22 39	
Penge West	d			21 07	21 11			21 22			21 37	21 41		21 52				22 07	22 11		22 22		22 37	22 41	
Crystal Palace	d	20 54	21 01			21 16			21 24	21 31			21 46		21 54	22 01				22 16		22 24			22 46
Sydenham	d	20 59	21 05	21 09	21 14	21 20		21 24	21 29	21 35	21 39	21 44	21 50	21 54	21 59	22 05		22 09	22 14	22 20	22 24	22 29	22 39	22 44	22 50
Forest Hill	d	21 01	21 07	21 12	21 16	21 22		21 27	21 31	21 37	21 42	21 46	21 52	21 57	22 01	22 07		22 12	22 16	22 22	22 27	22 31	22 42	22 46	22 52
Honor Oak Park	d	21 04	21 10	21 14	21 19	21 25		21 29	21 34	21 40	21 44	21 49	21 55	21 59	22 04	22 10		22 14	22 19	22 25	22 29	22 34	22 44	22 49	22 55
Brockley	d	21 06	21 12	21 17	21 21	21 27		21 32	21 36	21 42	21 47	21 51	21 57	22 02	22 06	22 12		22 17	22 21	22 27	22 32	22 36	22 47	22 51	22 57
New Cross Gate	d	21 09	21 14	21 19	21 24	21 29		21 34	21 39	21 44	21 49	21 54	21 59	22 04	22 09	22 14		22 19	22 24	22 29	22 34	22 39	22 49	22 54	22 59
Surrey Quays	d		21 18	21 22		21 33		21 37		21 48	21 52		22 03	22 07		22 18		22 22		22 33	22 37		22 52		23 03
Canada Water	d		21 20	21 24		21 35		21 39		21 50	21 54		22 05	22 09		22 20		22 24		22 35	22 39		22 54		23 05
Rotherhithe	d		21 21	21 26		21 36		21 41		21 51	21 56		22 06	22 11		22 21		22 26		22 36	22 41		22 56		23 06
Wapping	d		21 23	21 27		21 38		21 42		21 53	21 57		22 08	22 12		22 23		22 27		22 38	22 42		22 57		23 08
Shadwell	d		21 25	21 29		21 40		21 44		21 55	21 59		22 10	22 14		22 25		22 29		22 40	22 44		22 59		23 10
Whitechapel	d		21 27	21 32		21 42		21 47		21 57	22 02		22 12	22 17		22 27		22 32		22 42	22 47		23 02		23 12
Shoreditch High Street	d		21 29	21 34		21 44		21 49		21 59	22 04		22 14	22 19		22 29		22 34		22 44	22 49		23 04		23 14
Hoxton	d		21 31	21 36		21 46		21 51		22 01	22 06		22 16	22 21		22 31		22 36		22 46	22 51		23 06		23 16
Haggerston	d		21 33	21 38		21 48		21 53		22 03	22 08		22 18	22 23		22 33		22 38		22 48	22 53		23 08		23 18
Dalston Junction	a		21 35	21 42		21 50		21 57		22 05	22 12		22 20	22 27		22 35		22 42		22 50	22 57		23 12		23 20
Canonbury	a		21 38			21 53				22 08			22 23			22 38				22 53					23 23
Highbury & Islington	a		21 44			21 59				22 14			22 29			22 44				22 59					23 29
London Bridge	a	21 16			21 32				21 46			22 02			22 16				22 32			22 46		23 02	

A From Tattenham Corner

For full service between Highbury & Islington and Surrey Quays, refer to Table T178

For Sutton connections at West Croydon, refer to Table T172

Table T177-R

Sundays
20 May to 2 December

Croydon and Norwood Junction-Anerley, Penge West, Crystal Palace, Sydenham, Forest Hill, Honor Oak Park, Brockley, New Cross Gate-London Bridge

		LO	SN	LO	SN A	LO	SN A
Purley	d				22 50		23 20
East Croydon	d				23 01		23 31
Norwood Junction 2	a				23 05		23 35
West Croydon 4	d	22 42		22 57			
Norwood Junction	a	22 47		23 02			
Norwood Junction	d	22 47		23 02	23 05		23 35
Anerley	d	22 50		23 05	23 09		23 39
Penge West	d	22 52		23 07	23 11		23 41
Crystal Palace 4	d		22 54			23 16	
Sydenham	d	22 54	22 59	23 09	23 14	23 20	23 44
Forest Hill 4	d	22 57	23 01	23 12	23 16	23 22	23 46
Honor Oak Park	d	22 59	23 04	23 14	23 19	23 25	23 49
Brockley	d	23 02	23 06	23 17	23 21	23 27	23 51
New Cross Gate	d	23 04	23 09	23 19	23 25	23 29	23 54
Surrey Quays	d	23 07		23 22		23 33	
Canada Water	d	23 09		23 24		23 35	
Rotherhithe	d	23 11		23 26		23 36	
Wapping	d	23 12		23 27		23 38	
Shadwell	d	23 14		23 29		23 40	
Whitechapel	d	23 17		23 32		23 42	
Shoreditch High Street	d	23 19		23 34		23 44	
Hoxton	d	23 21		23 36		23 46	
Haggerston	d	23 23		23 38		23 48	
Dalston Junction	a	23 27		23 42		23 50	
Canonbury	a					23 53	
Highbury & Islington	a					23 59	
London Bridge 4 ⊖	a		23 16		23 34		00 03

A From Tattenham Corner

For full service between Highbury & Islington and Surrey Quays, refer to Table T178

For Sutton connections at West Croydon, refer to Table T172

Table T178-F

Mondays to Fridays
21 May to 7 December

Highbury & Islington - New Cross, Crystal Palace, West Croydon and Clapham Junction

Miles	Miles	Miles	Miles			LO MX A	LO MO A	LO MX A	LO MX A	LO MX B	LO MX B	LO MX A	LO MX B	LO MX A	LO MX	LO MX	LO	LO	LO	LO	LO	LO	LO
0	0	—	—	Highbury & Islington	d										00 01	00 10	05 32		05 40		05 47	05 55	06 02
0½	0½	—	—	Canonbury	d										00 03	00 12	05 34		05 42		05 49	05 57	06 04
1½	1½	0	0	**Dalston Junction**	d										00 06	00 15	05 37	05 42	05 45	05 49	05 52	06 00	06 07
2	2	0½	0½	**Haggerston**	d										00 08	00 17	05 39	05 44	05 47	05 51	05 54	06 02	06 09
2½	2½	1	1	**Hoxton**	d										00 10	00 19	05 41	05 46	05 49	05 53	05 56	06 04	06 11
3¼	3¼	1¾	1¾	**Shoreditch High Street**	d									00 01	00 13	00 21	05 43	05 48	05 52	05 55	05 58	06 07	06 13
3¾	3¾	2¼	2¼	**Whitechapel**	d									00 04	00 15	00 24	05 46	05 51	05 54	05 58	06 01	06 09	06 16
4½	4½	3	3	**Shadwell**	d									00 06	00 17	00 26	05 48	05 53	05 56	06 00	06 03	06 11	06 18
5	5	3½	3½	**Wapping**	d								00 02	00 08	00 19	00 28	05 50	05 55	05 58	06 02	06 05	06 13	06 20
5½	5½	4	4	**Rotherhithe**	d								00 03	00 09	00 21	00 29	05 51	05 56	06 00	06 03	06 06	06 15	06 21
5¾	5¾	4¼	4¼	**Canada Water**	d							00 02	00 05	00 11	00 23	00 31	05 53	05 58	06 02	06 05	06 08	06 17	06 23
6	6	4½	4½	**Surrey Quays**	d						00 02	00 04	00 07	00 13	00 25	00 33	05 55	06 00	06 04	06 07	06 10	06 19	06 25
—	—	—	5¼	New Cross	a						00 04							06 04					
—	7¼	5¾	—	New Cross Gate 4	d				00 01			00 08		00a20		00a37	06 00		06 08		06 15	06 23	06 30
—	8	6½	—	Brockley	d				00 03			00 11					06 02		06 11		06 17	06 26	06 32
—	9	7½	—	Honor Oak Park	d				00 06			00 13					06 05		06 13		06 20	06 28	06 35
—	10	8½	—	Forest Hill 4	d			00 01	00 08			00 16					06 07		06 16		06 22	06 31	06 37
—	11¾	9	—	Sydenham	d		00 01	00 04	00 11			00 19					06 11		06 19		06 26	06 34	06 41
—	12	—	—	Crystal Palace 4	a			00 09				00 24							06 24			06 39	
—	—	10	—	Penge West	d		00 03		00 13								06 13				06 28		06 43
—	—	10½	—	Anerley	d	00 01	00 05		00 15								06 15				06 30		06 45
—	—	11½	—	Norwood Junction 2	d	00 03	00 08		00 19								06 19				06 33		06 49
—	—	13¼	—	West Croydon 4	a	00 10	00 16		00 31								06 28				06 39		06 58
7½	—	—	—	Queens Rd Peckham	d								00 14		00 31					06 14			
8	—	—	—	Peckham Rye 4	d					00 01			00 18		00 34					06 16			
9	—	—	—	Denmark Hill 4	d					00 05			00 22		00 38					06 20			
11	—	—	—	**Clapham High Street** ⊖	d					00 09			00 26		00 42					06 24			
11¾	—	—	—	**Wandsworth Road**	d					00 11			00 28		00 44					06 26			
12¾	—	—	—	Clapham Junction	a					00 19			00 35		00 52					06 34			

		LO	LO	LO	LO	LO	LO	LO	LO	LO	LO	LO	LO	LO	LO	LO	LO	LO	LO	LO	LO	LO	LO
Highbury & Islington	d		06 10		06 17		06 25		06 32		06 40		06 47		06 55		07 02		07 10		07 17		07 25
Canonbury	d		06 12		06 19		06 27		06 34		06 42		06 49		06 57		07 04		07 12		07 19		07 27
Dalston Junction	d	06 12	06 15	06 19	06 22	06 27	06 30	06 34	06 37	06 42	06 45	06 49	06 52	06 57	07 00	07 04	07 07	07 12	07 15	07 19	07 22	07 27	07 30
Haggerston	d	06 14	06 17	06 21	06 24	06 29	06 32	06 36	06 39	06 44	06 47	06 51	06 54	06 59	07 02	07 06	07 09	07 14	07 17	07 21	07 24	07 29	07 32
Hoxton	d	06 16	06 19	06 23	06 26	06 31	06 34	06 38	06 41	06 46	06 49	06 53	06 56	07 01	07 04	07 08	07 11	07 16	07 19	07 23	07 26	07 31	07 34
Shoreditch High Street	d	06 18	06 22	06 25	06 28	06 33	06 37	06 40	06 43	06 48	06 52	06 55	06 58	07 03	07 07	07 10	07 13	07 18	07 22	07 25	07 28	07 33	07 37
Whitechapel	d	06 21	06 24	06 28	06 31	06 36	06 39	06 43	06 46	06 51	06 54	06 58	07 01	07 06	07 09	07 13	07 16	07 21	07 24	07 28	07 31	07 36	07 39
Shadwell	d	06 23	06 26	06 30	06 33	06 38	06 41	06 45	06 48	06 53	06 56	07 00	07 03	07 08	07 11	07 15	07 18	07 23	07 26	07 30	07 33	07 38	07 41
Wapping	d	06 25	06 28	06 32	06 35	06 40	06 43	06 47	06 50	06 55	06 58	07 02	07 05	07 10	07 13	07 17	07 20	07 25	07 28	07 32	07 35	07 40	07 43
Rotherhithe	d	06 26	06 30	06 33	06 36	06 41	06 45	06 48	06 51	06 56	07 00	07 03	07 06	07 11	07 15	07 18	07 21	07 26	07 30	07 33	07 36	07 41	07 45
Canada Water	d	06 28	06 32	06 35	06 38	06 43	06 47	06 50	06 53	06 58	07 02	07 05	07 08	07 13	07 17	07 20	07 23	07 28	07 32	07 35	07 38	07 43	07 47
Surrey Quays	d	06 30	06 34	06 37	06 40	06 45	06 49	06 52	06 55	07 00	07 04	07 07	07 10	07 15	07 19	07 22	07 25	07 30	07 34	07 37	07 40	07 45	07 49
New Cross	a	06 34				06 49				07 04				07 19				07 34				07 49	
New Cross Gate 4	d		06 38		06 45		06 53		07 00		07 08		07 15		07 23		07 30		07 38		07 45		07 53
Brockley	d		06 41		06 47		06 56		07 02		07 11		07 17		07 26		07 32		07 41		07 47		07 56
Honor Oak Park	d		06 43		06 50		06 58		07 05		07 13		07 20		07 28		07 35		07 43		07 50		07 58
Forest Hill 4	d		06 46		06 52		07 01		07 07		07 16		07 22		07 31		07 37		07 46		07 52		08 01
Sydenham	d		06 49		06 56		07 04		07 11		07 19		07 26		07 34		07 41		07 49		07 56		08 04
Crystal Palace 4	a		06 54				07 09				07 24				07 39				07 54				08 09
Penge West	d				06 58				07 13				07 28				07 43				07 58		
Anerley	d				07 00				07 15				07 30				07 45				08 00		
Norwood Junction 2	d				07 03				07 19				07 33				07 49				08 03		
West Croydon 4	a				07 09				07 28				07 39				07 58				08 09		
Queens Rd Peckham	d			06 44				06 59				07 12				07 29				07 44			
Peckham Rye 4	d			06 46				07 04				07 15				07 34				07 46			
Denmark Hill 4	d			06 50				07 07				07 18				07 37				07 50			
Clapham High Street ⊖	d			06 54				07 11				07 23				07 41				07 54			
Wandsworth Road	d			06 56				07 13				07 24				07 43				07 56			
Clapham Junction	a			07 04				07 19				07 34				07 49				08 04			

		LO	LO	LO	LO	LO	LO	LO	LO	LO	LO	LO	LO	LO	LO	LO	LO	LO	LO	LO	LO	LO	LO
Highbury & Islington	d		07 32		07 40		07 47		07 55		08 02		08 10		08 17		08 25		08 32		08 40		08 47
Canonbury	d		07 34		07 42		07 49		07 57		08 04		08 12		08 19		08 27		08 34		08 42		08 49
Dalston Junction	d	07 34	07 37	07 42	07 45	07 49	07 52	07 57	08 00	08 04	08 07	08 12	08 15	08 19	08 22	08 27	08 30	08 34	08 37	08 43	08 46	08 49	08 52
Haggerston	d	07 36	07 39	07 44	07 47	07 51	07 54	07 59	08 02	08 06	08 09	08 14	08 17	08 21	08 24	08 29	08 32	08 36	08 39	08 44	08 48	08 51	08 54
Hoxton	d	07 38	07 41	07 46	07 49	07 53	07 56	08 01	08 04	08 08	08 11	08 16	08 19	08 23	08 26	08 31	08 34	08 38	08 41	08 46	08 50	08 53	08 56
Shoreditch High Street	d	07 40	07 43	07 48	07 52	07 55	07 58	08 03	08 07	08 10	08 13	08 18	08 22	08 25	08 28	08 33	08 37	08 40	08 43	08 49	08 52	08 55	08 58
Whitechapel	d	07 43	07 46	07 51	07 54	07 58	08 01	08 06	08 09	08 13	08 16	08 21	08 24	08 28	08 31	08 36	08 39	08 43	08 46	08 51	08 55	08 58	09 01
Shadwell	d	07 45	07 48	07 53	07 56	08 00	08 03	08 08	08 11	08 15	08 18	08 23	08 26	08 30	08 33	08 38	08 41	08 45	08 48	08 53	08 57	09 00	09 03
Wapping	d	07 47	07 50	07 55	07 58	08 02	08 05	08 10	08 13	08 17	08 20	08 25	08 28	08 32	08 35	08 40	08 43	08 47	08 50	08 55	08 59	09 02	09 05
Rotherhithe	d	07 48	07 51	07 56	08 00	08 03	08 06	08 11	08 15	08 18	08 21	08 26	08 30	08 33	08 36	08 41	08 45	08 48	08 51	08 57	09 00	09 03	09 06
Canada Water	d	07 50	07 53	07 58	08 02	08 05	08 08	08 13	08 17	08 20	08 23	08 28	08 32	08 35	08 38	08 43	08 47	08 50	08 53	08 59	09 02	09 05	09 08
Surrey Quays	d	07 52	07 55	08 00	08 04	08 07	08 10	08 15	08 19	08 22	08 25	08 30	08 34	08 37	08 40	08 45	08 49	08 52	08 55	09 01	09 04	09 07	09 10
New Cross	a			08 04				08 19				08 34				08 49				09 05			
New Cross Gate 4	d		08 00		08 08		08 15		08 23		08 30		08 38		08 45		08 53		09 00		09 09		09 15
Brockley	d		08 02		08 11		08 17		08 26		08 32		08 41		08 47		08 56		09 02		09 11		09 17
Honor Oak Park	d		08 05		08 13		08 20		08 28		08 35		08 43		08 50		08 58		09 05		09 14		09 20
Forest Hill 4	d		08 07		08 16		08 22		08 31		08 37		08 46		08 52		09 01		09 07		09 16		09 22
Sydenham	d		08 11		08 19		08 26		08 34		08 41		08 49		08 56		09 04		09 11		09 20		09 26
Crystal Palace 4	a				08 24				08 39				08 54				09 09				09 24		
Penge West	d		08 13				08 28				08 43				08 58				09 13				09 28
Anerley	d		08 15				08 30				08 45				09 00				09 15				09 30
Norwood Junction 2	d		08 19				08 33				08 49				09 03				09 19				09 33
West Croydon 4	a		08 29				08 39				08 58				09 09				09 28				09 43
Queens Rd Peckham	d	07 59				08 14				08 29				08 44				08 59				09 12	
Peckham Rye 4	d	08 04				08 16				08 34				08 48				09 04				09 15	
Denmark Hill 4	d	08 07				08 20				08 37				08 52				09 07				09 18	
Clapham High Street ⊖	d	08 11				08 24				08 41				08 56				09 11				09 23	
Wandsworth Road	d	08 13				08 26				08 43				08 58				09 13				09 24	
Clapham Junction	a	08 19				08 34				08 49				09 06				09 19				09 35	

A From Highbury and Islington Ell
B From Dalston Junction Stn Ell

Highbury & Islington - New Cross, Crystal Palace, West Croydon and Clapham Junction

		LO		LO	LO	LO	LO	LO	LO	LO	LO	LO		LO	LO	LO	LO	LO	LO	LO	LO	LO		LO	LO
Highbury & Islington	d			08 55		09 02		09 10		09 17		09 25			09 32		09 40		09 47		09 55			10 02	
Canonbury	d			08 57		09 04		09 12		09 19		09 27			09 34		09 42		09 49		09 57			10 04	
Dalston Junction	d	08 57		09 00	09 04	09 08	09 13	09 16	09 19	09 22	09 27	09 30		09 34	09 37	09 42	09 45	09 49	09 52	09 57	10 00	10 04		10 07	10 12
Haggerston	d	08 59		09 02	09 06	09 10	09 14	09 18	09 21	09 24	09 29	09 32		09 36	09 39	09 44	09 47	09 51	09 54	09 59	10 02	10 06		10 09	10 14
Hoxton	d	09 01		09 04	09 08	09 12	09 16	09 20	09 23	09 26	09 31	09 34		09 38	09 41	09 46	09 49	09 53	09 56	10 01	10 04	10 08		10 11	10 16
Shoreditch High Street	d	09 03		09 07	09 10	09 14	09 19	09 22	09 25	09 28	09 33	09 37		09 40	09 43	09 48	09 52	09 55	09 58	10 03	10 07	10 10		10 13	10 18
Whitechapel	d	09 06		09 09	09 13	09 17	09 21	09 25	09 28	09 31	09 36	09 39		09 43	09 46	09 51	09 54	09 58	10 01	10 06	10 09	10 13		10 16	10 21
Shadwell	d	09 08		09 11	09 15	09 19	09 23	09 27	09 30	09 33	09 38	09 41		09 45	09 48	09 53	09 56	10 00	10 03	10 08	10 11	10 15		10 18	10 23
Wapping	d	09 10		09 13	09 17	09 21	09 25	09 29	09 32	09 35	09 40	09 43		09 47	09 50	09 55	09 58	10 02	10 05	10 10	10 13	10 17		10 20	10 25
Rotherhithe	d	09 11		09 15	09 18	09 22	09 27	09 30	09 33	09 36	09 41	09 45		09 48	09 51	09 56	10 00	10 03	10 06	10 11	10 15	10 18		10 21	10 26
Canada Water	d	09 13		09 17	09 20	09 24	09 29	09 32	09 35	09 38	09 43	09 47		09 50	09 53	09 58	10 02	10 05	10 08	10 13	10 17	10 20		10 23	10 28
Surrey Quays	d	09 15		09 19	09 22	09 26	09 31	09 34	09 37	09 40	09 45	09 49		09 52	09 55	10 00	10 04	10 07	10 10	10 15	10 19	10 22		10 25	10 30
New Cross	a	09 19					09 35				09 49					10 04				10 19					10 34
New Cross Gate	d			09 23		09 31		09 39		09 45		09 53			10 00		10 08		10 15		10 23			10 30	
Brockley	d			09 26		09 33		09 41		09 47		09 56			10 02		10 11		10 17		10 26			10 32	
Honor Oak Park	d			09 28		09 36		09 44		09 50		09 58			10 05		10 13		10 20		10 28			10 35	
Forest Hill	d			09 31		09 38		09 46		09 52		10 01			10 07		10 16		10 22		10 31			10 37	
Sydenham	d			09 34		09 42		09 50		09 56		10 04			10 11		10 19		10 26		10 34			10 41	
Crystal Palace	a			09 39				09 54				10 09					10 24				10 39				
Penge West	d					09 44				09 58					10 13				10 28					10 43	
Anerley	d					09 46				10 00					10 15				10 30					10 45	
Norwood Junction	d					09 49				10 03					10 19				10 33					10 48	
West Croydon	a					09 58				10 13					10 28				10 43					10 58	
Queens Rd Peckham	d				09 29				09 44					09 59				10 14				10 29			
Peckham Rye	d				09 33				09 48					10 04				10 18				10 33			
Denmark Hill	d				09 37				09 52					10 07				10 22				10 37			
Clapham High Street	d				09 41				09 56					10 11				10 26				10 41			
Wandsworth Road	d				09 43				09 58					10 13				10 28				10 43			
Clapham Junction	a				09 50				10 05					10 19				10 35				10 50			

		LO	LO	LO	LO	LO	LO	LO		LO	LO	LO	LO	LO	LO	LO	LO	LO	LO	LO	LO	LO	LO
Highbury & Islington	d	10 10		10 17		10 25		10 32			10 40		10 47		10 55		11 02			11 10		11 17		11 25	
Canonbury	d	10 12		10 19		10 27		10 34			10 42		10 49		10 57		11 04			11 12		11 19		11 27	
Dalston Junction	d	10 15	10 19	10 22	10 27	10 30	10 34	10 37		10 42	10 45	10 49	10 52	10 57	11 00	11 04	11 07	11 12		11 15	11 19	11 22	11 27	11 30	11 34
Haggerston	d	10 17	10 21	10 24	10 29	10 32	10 36	10 39		10 44	10 47	10 51	10 54	10 59	11 02	11 06	11 09	11 14		11 17	11 21	11 24	11 29	11 32	11 36
Hoxton	d	10 19	10 23	10 26	10 31	10 34	10 38	10 41		10 46	10 49	10 53	10 56	11 01	11 04	11 08	11 11	11 16		11 19	11 23	11 26	11 31	11 34	11 38
Shoreditch High Street	d	10 22	10 25	10 28	10 33	10 37	10 40	10 43		10 48	10 52	10 55	10 58	11 03	11 07	11 10	11 13	11 18		11 22	11 25	11 28	11 33	11 37	11 40
Whitechapel	d	10 24	10 28	10 31	10 36	10 39	10 43	10 46		10 51	10 54	10 58	11 01	11 06	11 09	11 13	11 16	11 21		11 24	11 28	11 31	11 36	11 39	11 43
Shadwell	d	10 26	10 30	10 33	10 38	10 41	10 45	10 48		10 53	10 56	11 00	11 03	11 08	11 11	11 15	11 18	11 23		11 26	11 30	11 33	11 38	11 41	11 45
Wapping	d	10 28	10 32	10 35	10 40	10 43	10 47	10 50		10 55	10 58	11 02	11 05	11 10	11 13	11 17	11 20	11 25		11 28	11 32	11 35	11 40	11 43	11 47
Rotherhithe	d	10 30	10 33	10 36	10 41	10 45	10 48	10 51		10 56	11 00	11 03	11 06	11 11	11 15	11 18	11 21	11 26		11 30	11 33	11 36	11 41	11 45	11 48
Canada Water	d	10 32	10 35	10 38	10 43	10 47	10 50	10 53		10 58	11 02	11 05	11 08	11 13	11 17	11 20	11 23	11 28		11 32	11 35	11 38	11 43	11 47	11 50
Surrey Quays	d	10 34	10 37	10 40	10 45	10 49	10 52	10 55		11 00	11 04	11 07	11 10	11 15	11 19	11 22	11 25	11 30		11 34	11 37	11 40	11 45	11 49	11 52
New Cross	a				10 49					11 04				11 19				11 34					11 49		
New Cross Gate	d	10 38		10 45		10 53		11 00			11 08		11 15		11 23		11 30			11 38		11 45		11 53	
Brockley	d	10 41		10 47		10 56		11 02			11 11		11 17		11 26		11 32			11 41		11 47		11 56	
Honor Oak Park	d	10 43		10 50		10 58		11 05			11 13		11 20		11 28		11 35			11 43		11 50		11 58	
Forest Hill	d	10 46		10 52		11 01		11 07			11 16		11 22		11 31		11 37			11 46		11 52		12 01	
Sydenham	d	10 49		10 56		11 04		11 11			11 19		11 26		11 34		11 41			11 49		11 56		12 04	
Crystal Palace	a	10 54				11 09					11 24				11 39					11 54				12 09	
Penge West	d			10 58				11 13					11 28				11 43					11 58			
Anerley	d			11 00				11 15					11 30				11 45					12 00			
Norwood Junction	d			11 03				11 18					11 33				11 48					12 03			
West Croydon	a			11 09				11 28					11 39				11 54					12 09			
Queens Rd Peckham	d		10 44				10 59					11 14				11 29					11 44				11 59
Peckham Rye	d		10 48				11 04					11 18				11 34					11 48				12 04
Denmark Hill	d		10 52				11 07					11 22				11 37					11 52				12 07
Clapham High Street	d		10 56				11 11					11 26				11 41					11 56				12 11
Wandsworth Road	d		10 58				11 13					11 28				11 43					11 58				12 13
Clapham Junction	a		11 05				11 19					11 35				11 49					12 05				12 19

		LO	LO	LO		LO	LO	LO	LO	LO	LO	LO	LO	LO	LO	LO	LO	LO	LO	LO	LO	LO	LO	LO	
Highbury & Islington	d	11 32		11 40			11 47		11 55		12 02		12 10			12 17		12 25		12 32		12 40		12 47	
Canonbury	d	11 34		11 42			11 49		11 57		12 04		12 12			12 19		12 27		12 34		12 42		12 49	
Dalston Junction	d	11 37	11 42	11 45		11 49	11 52	11 57	12 00	12 04	12 07	12 12	12 15	12 19		12 22	12 27	12 30	12 34	12 37	12 42	12 45	12 49	12 52	
Haggerston	d	11 39	11 44	11 47		11 51	11 54	11 59	12 02	12 06	12 09	12 14	12 17	12 21		12 24	12 29	12 32	12 36	12 39	12 44	12 47	12 51	12 54	
Hoxton	d	11 41	11 46	11 49		11 53	11 56	12 01	12 04	12 08	12 11	12 16	12 19	12 23		12 26	12 31	12 34	12 38	12 41	12 46	12 49	12 53	12 56	
Shoreditch High Street	d	11 43	11 48	11 52		11 55	11 58	12 03	12 07	12 10	12 13	12 18	12 22	12 25		12 28	12 33	12 37	12 40	12 43	12 48	12 52	12 55	12 58	
Whitechapel	d	11 46	11 51	11 54		11 58	12 01	12 06	12 09	12 13	12 16	12 21	12 24	12 28		12 31	12 36	12 39	12 43	12 46	12 51	12 54	12 58	13 01	
Shadwell	d	11 48	11 53	11 56		12 00	12 03	12 08	12 11	12 15	12 18	12 23	12 26	12 30		12 33	12 38	12 41	12 45	12 48	12 53	12 56	13 00	13 03	
Wapping	d	11 50	11 55	11 58		12 02	12 05	12 10	12 13	12 17	12 20	12 25	12 28	12 32		12 35	12 40	12 43	12 47	12 50	12 55	12 58	13 02	13 05	
Rotherhithe	d	11 51	11 56	12 00		12 03	12 06	12 11	12 15	12 18	12 21	12 26	12 30	12 33		12 36	12 41	12 45	12 48	12 51	12 56	13 00	13 03	13 06	
Canada Water	d	11 53	11 58	12 02		12 05	12 08	12 13	12 17	12 20	12 23	12 28	12 32	12 35		12 38	12 43	12 47	12 50	12 53	12 58	13 02	13 05	13 08	
Surrey Quays	d	11 55	12 00	12 04		12 07	12 10	12 15	12 19	12 22	12 25	12 30	12 34	12 37		12 40	12 45	12 49	12 52	12 55	13 00	13 04	13 07	13 10	
New Cross	a		12 04					12 19				12 34					12 49				13 04				
New Cross Gate	d	12 00		12 08			12 15		12 23		12 30		12 38			12 45		12 53		13 00		13 08		13 15	
Brockley	d	12 02		12 11			12 17		12 26		12 32		12 41			12 47		12 56		13 02		13 11		13 17	
Honor Oak Park	d	12 05		12 13			12 20		12 28		12 35		12 43			12 50		12 58		13 05		13 13		13 20	
Forest Hill	d	12 07		12 16			12 22		12 31		12 37		12 46			12 52		13 01		13 07		13 16		13 22	
Sydenham	d	12 11		12 19			12 26		12 34		12 41		12 49			12 56		13 04		13 11		13 19		13 26	
Crystal Palace	a			12 24					12 39				12 54					13 09				13 24			
Penge West	d	12 13					12 28				12 43					12 58				13 13				13 28	
Anerley	d	12 15					12 30				12 45					13 00				13 15				13 30	
Norwood Junction	d	12 18					12 33				12 48					13 03				13 18				13 33	
West Croydon	a	12 24					12 39				12 54					13 09				13 24				13 39	
Queens Rd Peckham	d					12 14				12 29				12 44					12 59				13 14		
Peckham Rye	d					12 18				12 34				12 48					13 03				13 18		
Denmark Hill	d					12 22				12 37				12 52					13 07				13 22		
Clapham High Street	d					12 26				12 41				12 56					13 11				13 26		
Wandsworth Road	d					12 28				12 43				12 58					13 13				13 28		
Clapham Junction	a					12 35				12 50				13 05					13 20				13 35		

Highbury & Islington - New Cross, Crystal Palace, West Croydon and Clapham Junction

		LO	LO	LO	LO	LO	LO	LO	LO	LO		LO	LO	LO	LO	LO	LO	LO	LO	LO		LO	LO	LO	LO
Highbury & Islington	d		12 55		13 02		13 10		13 17			13 25		13 32		13 40		13 47		13 55			14 02		14 10
Canonbury	d		12 57		13 04		13 12		13 19			13 27		13 34		13 42		13 49		13 57			14 04		14 12
Dalston Junction	d	12 57	13 00	13 04	13 07	13 12	13 15	13 19	13 22	13 27		13 30	13 34	13 37	13 42	13 45	13 49	13 52	13 57	14 00		14 04	14 07	14 12	14 15
Haggerston	d	12 59	13 02	13 06	13 09	13 14	13 17	13 21	13 24	13 29		13 32	13 36	13 39	13 44	13 47	13 51	13 54	13 59	14 02		14 06	14 09	14 14	14 17
Hoxton	d	13 01	13 04	13 08	13 11	13 16	13 19	13 23	13 26	13 31		13 34	13 38	13 41	13 46	13 49	13 53	13 56	14 01	14 04		14 08	14 11	14 16	14 19
Shoreditch High Street	d	13 03	13 07	13 10	13 13	13 18	13 22	13 25	13 28	13 33		13 37	13 40	13 43	13 48	13 52	13 55	13 58	14 03	14 07		14 10	14 13	14 18	14 22
Whitechapel	d	13 06	13 09	13 13	13 16	13 21	13 24	13 28	13 31	13 36		13 39	13 43	13 46	13 51	13 54	13 58	14 01	14 06	14 09		14 13	14 16	14 21	14 24
Shadwell	d	13 08	13 11	13 15	13 18	13 23	13 26	13 30	13 33	13 38		13 41	13 45	13 48	13 53	13 56	14 00	14 03	14 08	14 11		14 15	14 18	14 23	14 26
Wapping	d	13 10	13 13	13 17	13 20	13 25	13 28	13 32	13 35	13 40		13 43	13 47	13 50	13 55	13 58	14 02	14 05	14 10	14 13		14 17	14 20	14 25	14 28
Rotherhithe	d	13 11	13 15	13 18	13 21	13 26	13 30	13 33	13 36	13 41		13 45	13 48	13 51	13 56	14 00	14 03	14 06	14 11	14 15		14 18	14 21	14 26	14 30
Canada Water	d	13 13	13 17	13 20	13 23	13 28	13 32	13 35	13 38	13 43		13 47	13 50	13 53	13 58	14 02	14 05	14 08	14 13	14 17		14 20	14 23	14 28	14 32
Surrey Quays	d	13 15	13 19	13 22	13 25	13 30	13 34	13 37	13 40	13 45		13 49	13 52	13 55	14 00	14 04	14 07	14 10	14 15	14 19		14 22	14 25	14 30	14 34
New Cross	a	13 19				13 34				13 49					14 04				14 19					14 34	
New Cross Gate	d		13 23		13 30		13 38		13 45			13 53		14 00		14 08		14 15		14 23			14 30		14 38
Brockley	d		13 26		13 32		13 41		13 47			13 56		14 02		14 11		14 17		14 26			14 32		14 41
Honor Oak Park	d		13 28		13 35		13 43		13 50			13 58		14 05		14 13		14 20		14 28			14 35		14 43
Forest Hill	d		13 31		13 37		13 46		13 52			14 01		14 07		14 16		14 22		14 31			14 37		14 46
Sydenham	d		13 34		13 41		13 49		13 56			14 04		14 11		14 19		14 26		14 34			14 41		14 49
Crystal Palace	a		13 39				13 54					14 09				14 24				14 39					14 54
Penge West	d				13 43				13 58					14 13				14 28					14 43		
Anerley	d				13 45				14 00					14 15				14 30					14 45		
Norwood Junction	d				13 48				14 03					14 18				14 33					14 48		
West Croydon	a				13 54				14 09					14 24				14 39					14 54		
Queens Rd Peckham	d			13 29				13 44					13 59				14 14					14 29			
Peckham Rye	d			13 34				13 48					14 04				14 18					14 34			
Denmark Hill	d			13 37				13 52					14 07				14 21					14 37			
Clapham High Street	d			13 41				13 56					14 11				14 25					14 41			
Wandsworth Road	d			13 43				13 58					14 13				14 27					14 43			
Clapham Junction	a			13 49				14 05					14 19				14 35					14 49			

		LO	LO	LO	LO	LO		LO	LO	LO	LO	LO	LO	LO	LO	LO		LO	LO	LO	LO	LO	LO	LO	LO
Highbury & Islington	d		14 17		14 25			14 32		14 40		14 47		14 55		15 02			15 10		15 17		15 25		15 32
Canonbury	d		14 19		14 27			14 34		14 42		14 49		14 57		15 04			15 12		15 19		15 27		15 34
Dalston Junction	d	14 19	14 22	14 27	14 30	14 34		14 37	14 42	14 45	14 49	14 52	14 57	15 00	15 04	15 07		15 12	15 15	15 19	15 22	15 27	15 30	15 34	15 37
Haggerston	d	14 21	14 24	14 29	14 32	14 36		14 39	14 44	14 47	14 51	14 54	14 59	15 02	15 06	15 09		15 14	15 17	15 21	15 24	15 29	15 32	15 36	15 39
Hoxton	d	14 23	14 26	14 31	14 34	14 38		14 41	14 46	14 49	14 53	14 56	15 01	15 04	15 08	15 11		15 16	15 19	15 23	15 26	15 31	15 34	15 38	15 41
Shoreditch High Street	d	14 25	14 28	14 33	14 37	14 40		14 43	14 48	14 52	14 55	14 58	15 03	15 07	15 10	15 13		15 18	15 22	15 25	15 28	15 33	15 37	15 40	15 43
Whitechapel	d	14 28	14 31	14 36	14 39	14 43		14 46	14 51	14 54	14 58	15 01	15 06	15 09	15 13	15 16		15 21	15 24	15 28	15 31	15 36	15 39	15 43	15 46
Shadwell	d	14 30	14 33	14 38	14 41	14 45		14 48	14 53	14 56	15 00	15 03	15 08	15 11	15 15	15 18		15 23	15 26	15 30	15 33	15 38	15 41	15 45	15 48
Wapping	d	14 32	14 35	14 40	14 43	14 47		14 50	14 55	14 58	15 02	15 05	15 10	15 13	15 17	15 20		15 25	15 28	15 32	15 35	15 40	15 43	15 47	15 50
Rotherhithe	d	14 33	14 36	14 41	14 45	14 48		14 51	14 56	15 00	15 03	15 06	15 11	15 15	15 18	15 21		15 26	15 30	15 33	15 36	15 41	15 45	15 48	15 51
Canada Water	d	14 35	14 38	14 43	14 47	14 50		14 53	14 58	15 02	15 05	15 08	15 13	15 17	15 20	15 23		15 28	15 32	15 35	15 38	15 43	15 47	15 50	15 53
Surrey Quays	d	14 37	14 40	14 45	14 49	14 52		14 55	15 00	15 04	15 07	15 10	15 15	15 19	15 22	15 25		15 30	15 34	15 37	15 40	15 45	15 49	15 52	15 55
New Cross	a			14 49					15 04				15 19					15 34				15 49			
New Cross Gate	d		14 45		14 53			15 00		15 08		15 15		15 23		15 30			15 38		15 45		15 53		16 00
Brockley	d		14 47		14 56			15 02		15 11		15 17		15 26		15 32			15 41		15 47		15 56		16 02
Honor Oak Park	d		14 50		14 58			15 05		15 13		15 20		15 28		15 35			15 43		15 50		15 58		16 05
Forest Hill	d		14 52		15 01			15 07		15 16		15 22		15 31		15 37			15 46		15 52		16 01		16 07
Sydenham	d		14 56		15 04			15 11		15 19		15 26		15 34		15 41			15 49		15 56		16 04		16 11
Crystal Palace	a				15 09					15 24				15 39					15 54				16 09		
Penge West	d		14 58					15 13				15 28				15 43					15 58				16 13
Anerley	d		15 00					15 15				15 30				15 45					16 00				16 15
Norwood Junction	d		15 03					15 18				15 33				15 48					16 03				16 18
West Croydon	a		15 09					15 24				15 39				15 54					16 09				16 28
Queens Rd Peckham	d	14 44				14 59					15 14				15 29					15 44				15 59	
Peckham Rye	d	14 48				15 04					15 18				15 34					15 48				16 04	
Denmark Hill	d	14 52				15 07					15 22				15 37					15 52				16 07	
Clapham High Street	d	14 56				15 11					15 26				15 41					15 56				16 11	
Wandsworth Road	d	14 58				15 13					15 28				15 43					15 58				16 13	
Clapham Junction	a	15 05				15 19					15 35				15 49					16 05				16 19	

		LO	LO	LO	LO	LO	LO	LO	LO	LO	LO	LO	LO		LO	LO	LO	LO	LO	LO	LO	LO	LO	LO
Highbury & Islington	d		15 40		15 47		15 55		16 02		16 10		16 17			19 25		19 32		19 40		19 47		19 55
Canonbury	d		15 42		15 49		15 57		16 04		16 12		16 19			19 27		19 34		19 42		19 49		19 57
Dalston Junction	d	15 42	15 45	15 49	15 52	15 57	16 00	16 04	16 07	16 12	16 15	16 19	16 22		19 27	19 30	19 34	19 37	19 42	19 45	19 49	19 52	19 57	20 00
Haggerston	d	15 44	15 47	15 51	15 54	15 59	16 02	16 06	16 09	16 14	16 17	16 21	16 24		19 29	19 32	19 36	19 39	19 44	19 47	19 51	19 54	19 59	20 02
Hoxton	d	15 46	15 49	15 53	15 56	16 01	16 04	16 08	16 11	16 16	16 19	16 23	16 26		19 31	19 34	19 38	19 41	19 46	19 49	19 53	19 56	20 01	20 04
Shoreditch High Street	d	15 48	15 52	15 55	15 58	16 03	16 07	16 10	16 13	16 18	16 22	16 25	16 28		19 33	19 37	19 40	19 43	19 48	19 52	19 55	19 58	20 03	20 07
Whitechapel	d	15 51	15 54	15 58	16 01	16 06	16 09	16 13	16 16	16 21	16 24	16 28	16 31		19 36	19 39	19 43	19 46	19 51	19 54	19 58	20 01	20 06	20 09
Shadwell	d	15 53	15 56	16 00	16 03	16 08	16 11	16 15	16 18	16 23	16 26	16 30	16 33		19 38	19 41	19 45	19 48	19 53	19 56	20 00	20 03	20 08	20 11
Wapping	d	15 55	15 58	16 02	16 05	16 10	16 13	16 17	16 20	16 25	16 28	16 32	16 35		19 40	19 43	19 47	19 50	19 55	19 58	20 02	20 05	20 10	20 13
Rotherhithe	d	15 56	16 00	16 03	16 06	16 11	16 15	16 18	16 21	16 26	16 30	16 33	16 36		19 41	19 45	19 48	19 51	19 56	20 00	20 03	20 06	20 11	20 15
Canada Water	d	15 58	16 02	16 05	16 08	16 13	16 17	16 20	16 23	16 28	16 32	16 35	16 38	and at	19 43	19 47	19 50	19 53	19 58	20 02	20 05	20 08	20 13	20 17
Surrey Quays	d	16 00	16 04	16 07	16 10	16 15	16 19	16 22	16 25	16 30	16 34	16 37	16 40	the same	19 45	19 49	19 52	19 55	20 00	20 04	20 07	20 10	20 15	20 19
New Cross	a	16 04				16 19				16 34				minutes	19 49				20 04				20 19	
New Cross Gate	d		16 08		16 15		16 23		16 30		16 38		16 45	past		19 53		20 00		20 08		20 15		20 23
Brockley	d		16 11		16 17		16 26		16 32		16 41		16 47	each		19 56		20 02		20 11		20 17		20 26
Honor Oak Park	d		16 13		16 20		16 28		16 35		16 43		16 50	hour until		19 58		20 05		20 13		20 20		20 28
Forest Hill	d		16 16		16 22		16 31		16 37		16 46		16 52			20 01		20 07		20 16		20 22		20 31
Sydenham	d		16 19		16 26		16 34		16 41		16 49		16 56			20 04		20 11		20 19		20 26		20 34
Crystal Palace	a		16 24				16 39				16 54					20 09				20 24				20 39
Penge West	d				16 28				16 43				16 58					20 13				20 28		
Anerley	d				16 30				16 45				17 00					20 15				20 30		
Norwood Junction	d				16 33				16 48				17 03					20 18				20 33		
West Croydon	a				16 43				16 58				17 13					20 28				20 43		
Queens Rd Peckham	d			16 14				16 29				16 44					19 59				20 14			
Peckham Rye	d			16 18				16 34				16 48					20 04				20 18			
Denmark Hill	d			16 22				16 37				16 52					20 07				20 22			
Clapham High Street	d			16 26				16 41				16 56					20 11				20 26			
Wandsworth Road	d			16 28				16 43				16 58					20 13				20 28			
Clapham Junction	a			16 35				16 49				17 05					20 19				20 35			

Highbury & Islington - New Cross, Crystal Palace, West Croydon and Clapham Junction

Mondays to Fridays

21 May to 7 December

		LO	LO	LO	LO	LO	LO	LO	LO	LO	LO	LO	LO	LO	LO	LO	LO	LO	LO	LO	LO	LO	LO
Highbury & Islington	d		20 02		20 10		20 17		20 25		20 32		20 40		20 47		20 55		21 02		21 10		21 17
Canonbury	d		20 04		20 12		20 19		20 27		20 34		20 42		20 49		20 57		21 04		21 12		21 19
Dalston Junction	d	20 04	20 07	20 12	20 15	20 19	20 22	20 27	20 30	20 34	20 37	20 42	20 45	20 49	20 52	20 57	21 00	21 04	21 07	21 12	21 15	21 19	21 22
Haggerston	d	20 06	20 09	20 14	20 17	20 21	20 24	20 29	20 32	20 36	20 39	20 44	20 47	20 51	20 54	20 59	21 02	21 06	21 09	21 14	21 17	21 21	21 24
Hoxton	d	20 08	20 11	20 16	20 19	20 23	20 26	20 31	20 34	20 38	20 41	20 46	20 49	20 53	20 56	21 01	21 04	21 08	21 11	21 16	21 19	21 23	21 26
Shoreditch High Street	d	20 10	20 13	20 18	20 22	20 25	20 28	20 33	20 37	20 40	20 43	20 48	20 52	20 55	20 58	21 03	21 07	21 10	21 13	21 18	21 22	21 25	21 28
Whitechapel	d	20 13	20 16	20 21	20 24	20 28	20 31	20 36	20 39	20 43	20 46	20 51	20 54	20 58	21 01	21 06	21 09	21 13	21 16	21 21	21 24	21 28	21 31
Shadwell	d	20 15	20 18	20 23	20 26	20 30	20 33	20 38	20 41	20 45	20 48	20 53	20 56	21 00	21 03	21 08	21 11	21 15	21 18	21 23	21 26	21 30	21 33
Wapping	d	20 17	20 20	20 25	20 28	20 32	20 35	20 40	20 43	20 47	20 50	20 55	20 58	21 02	21 05	21 10	21 13	21 17	21 20	21 25	21 28	21 32	21 35
Rotherhithe	d	20 18	20 21	20 26	20 30	20 33	20 36	20 41	20 45	20 48	20 51	20 56	21 00	21 03	21 06	21 11	21 15	21 18	21 21	21 26	21 30	21 33	21 36
Canada Water	d	20 20	20 23	20 28	20 32	20 35	20 38	20 43	20 47	20 50	20 53	20 58	21 02	21 05	21 08	21 13	21 17	21 20	21 23	21 28	21 32	21 35	21 38
Surrey Quays	d	20 22	20 25	20 30	20 34	20 37	20 40	20 45	20 49	20 52	20 55	21 00	21 04	21 07	21 10	21 15	21 19	21 22	21 25	21 30	21 34	21 37	21 40
New Cross	a			20 34				20 49				21 04				21 19				21 34			
New Cross Gate	d		20 30		20 38		20 45		20 53		21 00		21 08		21 15		21 23		21 30		21 38		21 45
Brockley	d		20 32		20 41		20 47		20 56		21 02		21 11		21 17		21 26		21 32		21 41		21 47
Honor Oak Park	d		20 35		20 43		20 50		20 58		21 05		21 13		21 20		21 28		21 35		21 43		21 50
Forest Hill	d		20 37		20 46		20 52		21 01		21 07		21 16		21 22		21 31		21 37		21 46		21 52
Sydenham	d		20 41		20 49		20 56		21 04		21 11		21 19		21 26		21 34		21 41		21 49		21 56
Crystal Palace	a				20 54				21 09				21 24				21 39				21 54		
Penge West	d		20 43				20 58				21 13				21 28				21 43				21 58
Anerley	d		20 45				21 00				21 15				21 30				21 45				22 00
Norwood Junction	d		20 48				21 03				21 18				21 33				21 48				22 03
West Croydon	a		20 58				21 13				21 24				21 39				21 54				22 09
Queens Rd Peckham	d	20 29				20 44				20 59				21 14				21 29				21 44	
Peckham Rye	d	20 34				20 48				21 04				21 18				21 34				21 48	
Denmark Hill	d	20 37				20 52				21 07				21 22				21 37				21 52	
Clapham High Street ⊖	d	20 41				20 56				21 11				21 26				21 41				21 56	
Wandsworth Road	d	20 43				20 58				21 13				21 28				21 43				21 58	
Clapham Junction	a	20 49				21 05				21 19				21 35				21 49				22 05	

		LO	LO	LO	LO	LO	LO	LO	LO	LO	LO	LO A	LO	LO	LO	LO	LO	LO	LO	LO	LO	LO
Highbury & Islington	d		21 25		21 32		21 40		21 47		21 55		22 02		22 10		22 17		22 25		22 32	
Canonbury	d		21 27		21 34		21 42		21 49		21 57		22 04		22 12		22 19		22 27		22 34	
Dalston Junction	d	21 27	21 30	21 34	21 37	21 42	21 45	21 49	21 52	21 57	22 00	22 04	22 07	22 12	22 15	22 19	22 22	22 27	22 30	22 34	22 37	22 42
Haggerston	d	21 29	21 32	21 36	21 39	21 44	21 47	21 51	21 54	21 59	22 02	22 06	22 09	22 14	22 17	22 21	22 24	22 29	22 32	22 36	22 39	22 44
Hoxton	d	21 31	21 34	21 38	21 41	21 46	21 49	21 53	21 56	22 01	22 04	22 08	22 11	22 16	22 19	22 23	22 26	22 31	22 34	22 38	22 41	22 46
Shoreditch High Street	d	21 33	21 37	21 40	21 43	21 48	21 52	21 55	21 58	22 03	22 07	22 10	22 13	22 18	22 22	22 25	22 28	22 33	22 37	22 40	22 43	22 48
Whitechapel	d	21 36	21 39	21 43	21 46	21 51	21 54	21 58	22 01	22 06	22 09	22 13	22 16	22 21	22 24	22 28	22 31	22 36	22 39	22 43	22 46	22 51
Shadwell	d	21 38	21 41	21 45	21 48	21 53	21 56	22 00	22 03	22 08	22 11	22 15	22 18	22 23	22 26	22 30	22 33	22 38	22 41	22 45	22 48	22 53
Wapping	d	21 40	21 43	21 47	21 50	21 55	21 58	22 02	22 05	22 10	22 13	22 17	22 20	22 25	22 28	22 32	22 35	22 40	22 43	22 47	22 50	22 55
Rotherhithe	d	21 41	21 45	21 48	21 51	21 56	22 00	22 03	22 06	22 11	22 15	22 18	22 21	22 26	22 30	22 33	22 36	22 41	22 45	22 48	22 51	22 56
Canada Water	d	21 43	21 47	21 50	21 53	21 58	22 02	22 05	22 08	22 13	22 17	22 20	22 23	22 28	22 32	22 35	22 38	22 43	22 47	22 50	22 53	22 58
Surrey Quays	d	21 45	21 49	21 52	21 55	22 00	22 04	22 07	22 10	22 15	22 19	22 22	22 25	22 30	22 34	22 37	22 40	22 45	22 49	22 52	22 55	23 00
New Cross	a	21 49				22 04				22 19				22 34				22 49				23 04
New Cross Gate	d		21 53		22 00		22 08		22 15		22 23		22 30		22 38		22 45		22 53		23 00	
Brockley	d		21 56		22 02		22 11		22 17		22 26		22 32		22 41		22 47		22 56		23 02	
Honor Oak Park	d		21 58		22 05		22 13		22 20		22 28		22 35		22 43		22 50		22 58		23 05	
Forest Hill	d		22 01		22 07		22 16		22 22		22 31		22 37		22 46		22 52		23 01		23 07	
Sydenham	d		22 04		22 11		22 19		22 26		22 34		22 41		22 49		22 56		23 04		23 11	
Crystal Palace	a		22 09				22 24				22 39				22 54				23 09			
Penge West	d				22 13				22 28				22 43				22 58				23 13	
Anerley	d				22 15				22 30				22 45				23 00				23 15	
Norwood Junction	d				22 18				22 33				22 48				23 03				23 18	
West Croydon	a				22 24				22 39				22 54				23 09				23 24	
Queens Rd Peckham	d			21 59				22 14				22 29				22 44				22 59		
Peckham Rye	d			22 04				22 18				22 32				22 48				23 04		
Denmark Hill	d			22 07				22 22				22 36				22 52				23 07		
Clapham High Street ⊖	d			22 11				22 26				22 40				22 56				23 11		
Wandsworth Road	d			22 13				22 28				22a42				22 58				23 13		
Clapham Junction	a			22 19				22 35								23 05				23 19		

		LO	LO	LO	LO	LO	LO	LO	LO	LO	LO	LO	LO	LO	LO	LO	LO	LO	LO	LO
Highbury & Islington	d	22 40		22 47		22 55		23 02		23 10		23 17		23 25		23 32		23 40		23 50
Canonbury	d	22 42		22 49		22 57		23 04		23 12		23 19		23 27		23 34		23 42		23 52
Dalston Junction	d	22 45	22 49	22 52	22 57	23 00	23 04	23 07	23 12	23 15	23 19	23 22	23 27	23 30	23 34	23 37	23 42	23 45	23 49	23 55
Haggerston	d	22 47	22 51	22 54	22 59	23 02	23 06	23 09	23 14	23 17	23 21	23 24	23 29	23 32	23 36	23 39	23 44	23 47	23 51	23 57
Hoxton	d	22 49	22 53	22 56	23 01	23 04	23 08	23 11	23 16	23 19	23 23	23 26	23 31	23 34	23 38	23 41	23 46	23 49	23 53	23 59
Shoreditch High Street	d	22 52	22 55	22 58	23 03	23 07	23 10	23 13	23 18	23 22	23 25	23 28	23 33	23 37	23 40	23 43	23 48	23 52	23 55	00 01
Whitechapel	d	22 54	22 58	23 01	23 06	23 09	23 13	23 16	23 21	23 24	23 28	23 31	23 36	23 39	23 43	23 46	23 51	23 54	23 58	00 04
Shadwell	d	22 56	23 00	23 03	23 08	23 11	23 15	23 18	23 23	23 26	23 30	23 33	23 38	23 41	23 45	23 48	23 53	23 56	23 59	00 06
Wapping	d	22 58	23 02	23 05	23 10	23 13	23 17	23 20	23 25	23 28	23 32	23 35	23 40	23 43	23 47	23 50	23 55	23 58	00 02	00 08
Rotherhithe	d	23 00	23 03	23 06	23 11	23 15	23 18	23 21	23 26	23 30	23 33	23 36	23 41	23 45	23 48	23 51	23 56	23 59	00 03	00 09
Canada Water	d	23 02	23 05	23 08	23 13	23 17	23 20	23 23	23 28	23 32	23 35	23 38	23 43	23 47	23 50	23 53	23 58	00 02	00 05	00 11
Surrey Quays	d	23 04	23 07	23 10	23 15	23 19	23 22	23 25	23 30	23 34	23 37	23 40	23 45	23 49	23 52	23 55	00 02	00 04	00 07	00 13
New Cross	a				23 19				23 34				23 49				00 04			
New Cross Gate	d	23 08		23 15		23 23		23 30		23 38		23 45		23 53		00 01		00 08		00a20
Brockley	d	23 11		23 17		23 26		23 32		23 41		23 47		23 56		00 03		00 11		
Honor Oak Park	d	23 13		23 20		23 28		23 35		23 43		23 50		23 58		00 06		00 13		
Forest Hill	d	23 16		23 22		23 31		23 37		23 46		23 52		00 01		00 08		00 16		
Sydenham	d	23 19		23 26		23 34		23 41		23 49		23 56		00 04		00 11		00 19		
Crystal Palace	a	23 24				23 39				23 54				00 09				00 24		
Penge West	d			23 28				23 43				23 58				00 13				
Anerley	d			23 30				23 45				00 01				00 15				
Norwood Junction	d			23 33				23 48				00 03				00 19				
West Croydon	a			23 39				23 55				00 10				00 31				
Queens Rd Peckham	d		23 16				23 29				23 44				23 59				00 14	
Peckham Rye	d		23 20				23 34				23 48				00 01				00 18	
Denmark Hill	d		23 24				23 37				23 52				00 05				00 22	
Clapham High Street ⊖	d		23 28				23 41				23 56				00 09				00 26	
Wandsworth Road	d		23 30				23 43				23 58				00 11				00 28	
Clapham Junction	a		23 38				23 50				00 06				00 19				00 35	

A To Battersea Park

Table T178-F

Highbury & Islington - New Cross, Crystal Palace, West Croydon and Clapham Junction

Saturdays

26 May to 8 December

		LO A	LO A	LO A	LO B	LO B	LO A	LO B	LO A	LO	LO	LO	LO		LO	LO	LO	LO	LO	LO	LO	LO
Highbury & Islington	d									00 01	00 10	00 26	00 40		04 10	04 26	04 41	04 56	05 10	05 25		
Canonbury	d									00 03	00 12	00 28	00 42		04 12	04 28	04 43	04 58	05 12	05 27		
Dalston Junction	d									00 06	00 15	00 31	00 45		04 15	04 31	04 46	05 01	05 15	05 30	05 37	05 42
Haggerston	d									00 08	00 17	00 33	00 47		04 17	04 33	04 48	05 03	05 17	05 32	05 39	05 44
Hoxton	d									00 10	00 19	00 35	00 49		04 19	04 35	04 50	05 05	05 19	05 34	05 41	05 46
Shoreditch High Street	d								00 01	00 13	00 21	00 37	00 51		04 21	04 37	04 52	05 07	05 21	05 37	05 43	05 48
Whitechapel	d								00 04	00 15	00 24	00 40	00 54		04 24	04 40	04 55	05 10	05 24	05 39	05 46	05 51
Shadwell	d								00 06	00 17	00 26	00 42	00 56		04 26	04 42	04 57	05 12	05 26	05 41	05 48	05 53
Wapping	d							00 02	00 08	00 19	00 28	00 44	00 58		04 28	04 44	04 59	05 14	05 28	05 43	05 50	05 55
Rotherhithe	d							00 03	00 09	00 21	00 29	00 45	00 59		04 29	04 45	05 00	05 15	05 29	05 45	05 51	05 56
Canada Water	d						00 02	00 05	00 11	00 23	00 31	00 47	01 01		04 31	04 47	05 02	05 17	05 31	05 47	05 53	05 58
Surrey Quays	d					00 02	00 04	00 07	00 13	00 25	00 33	00 49	01 03	and every 15 minutes until	04 33	04 49	05 04	05 19	05 33	05 49	05 55	06 00
New Cross	a					00 04																06 04
New Cross Gate	d			00 01			00 08		00a20		00a40	00a56	01a10		04a40	04a54	05a12	05a27	05a40	05 53	06 00	
Brockley	d			00 03			00 11													05 56	06 02	
Honor Oak Park	d			00 06			00 13													05 58	06 05	
Forest Hill	d		00 01	00 08			00 16													06 01	06 07	
Sydenham	d		00 04	00 11			00 19													06 04	06 11	
Crystal Palace	a		00 09				00 24													06 08		
Penge West	d			00 13																	06 13	
Anerley	d	00 01		00 15																	06 15	
Norwood Junction	d	00 03		00 19																	06 18	
West Croydon	a	00 10		00 31																	06 24	
Queens Rd Peckham	d							00 14		00 31												
Peckham Rye	d				00 01			00 18		00 34												
Denmark Hill	d				00 05			00 22		00 38												
Clapham High Street ⊖	d				00 09			00 26		00 42												
Wandsworth Road	d				00 11			00 28		00 44												
Clapham Junction	a				00 19			00 35		00 52												

		LO	LO	LO	LO	LO	LO	LO	LO	LO	LO	LO	LO	LO	LO	LO	LO	LO	LO	LO	LO	LO	LO
Highbury & Islington	d	05 40		05 47	05 55		06 02		06 10		06 17		06 25		06 32		06 40		06 47		06 55		07 02
Canonbury	d	05 42		05 49	05 57		06 04		06 12		06 19		06 27		06 34		06 42		06 49		06 57		07 04
Dalston Junction	d	05 45	05 49	05 52	06 00	06 04	06 07	06 12	06 15	06 19	06 22	06 27	06 30	06 34	06 37	06 42	06 45	06 49	06 52	06 57	07 00	07 04	07 07
Haggerston	d	05 47	05 51	05 54	06 02	06 06	06 09	06 14	06 17	06 21	06 24	06 29	06 32	06 36	06 39	06 44	06 47	06 51	06 54	06 59	07 02	07 06	07 09
Hoxton	d	05 49	05 53	05 56	06 04	06 08	06 11	06 16	06 19	06 23	06 26	06 31	06 34	06 38	06 41	06 46	06 49	06 53	06 56	07 01	07 04	07 08	07 11
Shoreditch High Street	d	05 52	05 55	05 58	06 07	06 10	06 13	06 18	06 22	06 25	06 28	06 33	06 37	06 40	06 43	06 48	06 52	06 55	06 58	07 03	07 07	07 10	07 13
Whitechapel	d	05 54	05 58	06 01	06 09	06 13	06 16	06 21	06 24	06 28	06 31	06 36	06 39	06 43	06 46	06 51	06 54	06 58	07 01	07 06	07 09	07 13	07 16
Shadwell	d	05 56	06 00	06 03	06 11	06 15	06 18	06 23	06 26	06 30	06 33	06 38	06 41	06 45	06 48	06 53	06 56	07 00	07 03	07 08	07 11	07 15	07 18
Wapping	d	05 58	06 02	06 05	06 13	06 17	06 20	06 25	06 28	06 32	06 35	06 40	06 43	06 47	06 50	06 55	06 58	07 02	07 05	07 10	07 13	07 17	07 20
Rotherhithe	d	06 00	06 03	06 06	06 15	06 18	06 21	06 26	06 30	06 33	06 36	06 41	06 45	06 48	06 51	06 56	07 00	07 03	07 06	07 11	07 15	07 18	07 21
Canada Water	d	06 02	06 05	06 08	06 17	06 20	06 23	06 28	06 32	06 35	06 38	06 43	06 47	06 50	06 53	06 58	07 02	07 05	07 08	07 13	07 17	07 20	07 23
Surrey Quays	d	06 04	06 07	06 10	06 19	06 22	06 25	06 30	06 34	06 37	06 40	06 45	06 49	06 52	06 55	07 00	07 04	07 07	07 10	07 15	07 19	07 22	07 25
New Cross	a							06 34				06 49				07 04				07 19			
New Cross Gate	d	06 08		06 15	06 23		06 30		06 38		06 45		06 53		07 00		07 08		07 15		07 23		07 30
Brockley	d	06 11		06 17	06 26		06 32		06 41		06 47		06 56		07 02		07 11		07 17		07 26		07 32
Honor Oak Park	d	06 13		06 20	06 28		06 35		06 43		06 50		06 58		07 05		07 13		07 20		07 28		07 35
Forest Hill	d	06 16		06 22	06 31		06 37		06 46		06 52		07 01		07 07		07 16		07 22		07 31		07 37
Sydenham	d	06 19		06 26	06 34		06 41		06 49		06 56		07 04		07 11		07 19		07 26		07 34		07 41
Crystal Palace	a	06 23			06 38				06 53				07 08				07 23				07 38		
Penge West	d			06 28			06 43				06 58				07 13				07 28				07 43
Anerley	d			06 30			06 45				07 00				07 15				07 30				07 45
Norwood Junction	d			06 33			06 48				07 03				07 18				07 33				07 48
West Croydon	a			06 39			06 54				07 09				07 24				07 39				07 54
Queens Rd Peckham	d		06 14			06 29				06 44				06 59				07 14				07 29	
Peckham Rye	d		06 18			06 34				06 48				07 04				07 18				07 34	
Denmark Hill	d		06 22			06 37				06 52				07 07				07 22				07 37	
Clapham High Street ⊖	d		06 26			06 41				06 56				07 11				07 26				07 41	
Wandsworth Road	d		06 28			06 43				06 58				07 13				07 28				07 43	
Clapham Junction	a		06 35			06 49				07 05				07 19				07 35				07 49	

		LO	LO	LO	LO	LO	LO	LO	LO	LO	LO	LO	LO	LO	LO	LO	LO	LO	LO	LO	LO	LO
Highbury & Islington	d		07 10		07 17		07 25		07 32		07 40		07 47		07 55		08 02		08 10		08 17	
Canonbury	d		07 12		07 19		07 27		07 34		07 42		07 49		07 57		08 04		08 12		08 19	
Dalston Junction	d	07 12	07 15	07 19	07 22	07 27	07 30	07 34	07 37	07 42	07 45	07 49	07 52	07 57	08 00	08 04	08 07	08 12	08 15	08 19	08 22	08 27
Haggerston	d	07 14	07 17	07 21	07 24	07 29	07 32	07 36	07 39	07 44	07 47	07 51	07 54	07 59	08 02	08 06	08 09	08 14	08 17	08 21	08 24	08 29
Hoxton	d	07 16	07 19	07 23	07 26	07 31	07 34	07 38	07 41	07 46	07 49	07 53	07 56	08 01	08 04	08 08	08 11	08 16	08 19	08 23	08 26	08 31
Shoreditch High Street	d	07 18	07 22	07 25	07 28	07 33	07 37	07 40	07 43	07 48	07 52	07 55	07 58	08 03	08 07	08 10	08 13	08 18	08 22	08 25	08 28	08 33
Whitechapel	d	07 21	07 24	07 28	07 31	07 36	07 39	07 43	07 46	07 51	07 54	07 58	08 01	08 06	08 09	08 13	08 16	08 21	08 24	08 28	08 31	08 36
Shadwell	d	07 23	07 26	07 30	07 33	07 38	07 41	07 45	07 48	07 53	07 56	08 00	08 03	08 08	08 11	08 15	08 18	08 23	08 26	08 30	08 33	08 38
Wapping	d	07 25	07 28	07 32	07 35	07 40	07 43	07 47	07 50	07 55	07 58	08 02	08 05	08 10	08 13	08 17	08 20	08 25	08 28	08 32	08 35	08 40
Rotherhithe	d	07 26	07 30	07 33	07 36	07 41	07 45	07 48	07 51	07 56	08 00	08 03	08 06	08 11	08 15	08 18	08 21	08 26	08 30	08 33	08 36	08 41
Canada Water	d	07 28	07 32	07 35	07 38	07 43	07 47	07 50	07 53	07 58	08 02	08 05	08 08	08 13	08 17	08 20	08 23	08 28	08 32	08 35	08 38	08 43
Surrey Quays	d	07 30	07 34	07 37	07 40	07 45	07 49	07 52	07 55	08 00	08 04	08 07	08 10	08 15	08 19	08 22	08 25	08 30	08 34	08 37	08 40	08 45
New Cross	a	07 34				07 49				08 04				08 19				08 34				08 49
New Cross Gate	d		07 38		07 45		07 53		08 00		08 08		08 15		08 23		08 30		08 38		08 45	
Brockley	d		07 41		07 47		07 56		08 02		08 11		08 17		08 26		08 32		08 41		08 47	
Honor Oak Park	d		07 43		07 50		07 58		08 05		08 13		08 20		08 28		08 35		08 43		08 50	
Forest Hill	d		07 46		07 52		08 01		08 07		08 16		08 22		08 31		08 37		08 46		08 52	
Sydenham	d		07 49		07 56		08 04		08 11		08 19		08 26		08 34		08 41		08 49		08 56	
Crystal Palace	a		07 53				08 08				08 23				08 39				08 54			
Penge West	d				07 58				08 13				08 28				08 43				08 58	
Anerley	d				08 00				08 15				08 30				08 45				09 00	
Norwood Junction	d				08 03				08 18				08 33				08 48				09 03	
West Croydon	a				08 09				08 24				08 39				08 58				09 13	
Queens Rd Peckham	d			07 44				07 59				08 14				08 29				08 44		
Peckham Rye	d			07 48				08 03				08 18				08 34				08 48		
Denmark Hill	d			07 52				08 07				08 22				08 37				08 52		
Clapham High Street ⊖	d			07 56				08 11				08 26				08 41				08 56		
Wandsworth Road	d			07 58				08 13				08 28				08 43				08 58		
Clapham Junction	a			08 05				08 20				08 35				08 49				09 05		

A From Highbury and Islington Ell

B From Dalston Junction Stn Ell

Highbury & Islington - New Cross, Crystal Palace, West Croydon and Clapham Junction

		LO	LO	LO	LO	LO	LO	LO	LO	LO	LO	LO	LO	LO	LO	LO	LO	LO	LO	LO	LO	LO	LO
Highbury & Islington	d	08 25		08 32		08 40		08 47		08 55		09 02		09 10		09 17		09 25		09 32		09 40	
Canonbury	d	08 27		08 34		08 42		08 49		08 57		09 04		09 12		09 19		09 27		09 34		09 42	
Dalston Junction	d	08 30	08 34	08 37	08 42	08 45	08 49	08 52	08 57	09 00	09 04	09 07	09 12	09 15	09 19	09 22	09 27	09 30	09 34	09 37	09 42	09 45	09 49
Haggerston	d	08 32	08 36	08 39	08 44	08 47	08 51	08 54	08 59	09 02	09 06	09 09	09 14	09 17	09 21	09 24	09 29	09 32	09 36	09 39	09 44	09 47	09 51
Hoxton	d	08 34	08 38	08 41	08 46	08 49	08 53	08 56	09 01	09 04	09 08	09 11	09 16	09 19	09 23	09 26	09 31	09 34	09 38	09 41	09 46	09 49	09 53
Shoreditch High Street	d	08 37	08 40	08 43	08 48	08 52	08 55	08 58	09 03	09 07	09 10	09 13	09 18	09 22	09 25	09 28	09 33	09 37	09 40	09 43	09 48	09 52	09 55
Whitechapel	d	08 39	08 43	08 46	08 51	08 54	08 58	09 01	09 06	09 09	09 13	09 16	09 21	09 24	09 28	09 31	09 36	09 39	09 43	09 46	09 51	09 54	09 58
Shadwell	d	08 41	08 45	08 48	08 53	08 56	09 00	09 03	09 08	09 11	09 15	09 18	09 23	09 26	09 30	09 33	09 38	09 41	09 45	09 48	09 53	09 56	10 00
Wapping	d	08 43	08 47	08 50	08 55	08 58	09 02	09 05	09 10	09 13	09 17	09 20	09 25	09 28	09 32	09 35	09 40	09 43	09 47	09 50	09 55	09 58	10 02
Rotherhithe	d	08 45	08 48	08 51	08 56	09 00	09 03	09 06	09 11	09 15	09 18	09 21	09 26	09 30	09 33	09 36	09 41	09 45	09 48	09 51	09 56	10 00	10 03
Canada Water	d	08 47	08 50	08 53	08 58	09 02	09 05	09 08	09 13	09 17	09 20	09 23	09 28	09 32	09 35	09 38	09 43	09 47	09 50	09 53	09 58	10 02	10 05
Surrey Quays	d	08 49	08 52	08 55	09 00	09 04	09 07	09 10	09 15	09 19	09 22	09 25	09 30	09 34	09 37	09 40	09 45	09 49	09 52	09 55	10 00	10 04	10 07
New Cross	a				09 04				09 19				09 34				09 49				10 04		
New Cross Gate ■4	d	08 53		09 00		09 08		09 15		09 23		09 30		09 38		09 45		09 53		10 00		10 08	
Brockley	d	08 56		09 02		09 11		09 17		09 26		09 32		09 41		09 47		09 56		10 02		10 11	
Honor Oak Park	d	08 58		09 05		09 13		09 20		09 28		09 35		09 43		09 50		09 58		10 05		10 13	
Forest Hill ■4	d	09 01		09 07		09 16		09 22		09 31		09 37		09 46		09 52		10 01		10 07		10 16	
Sydenham	d	09 04		09 11		09 19		09 26		09 34		09 41		09 49		09 56		10 04		10 11		10 19	
Crystal Palace ■4	a	09 09				09 24				09 38				09 53				10 08				10 23	
Penge West	d			09 13				09 28				09 43				09 58				10 13			
Anerley	d			09 15				09 30				09 45				10 00				10 15			
Norwood Junction ■2	d			09 18				09 33				09 48				10 03				10 18			
West Croydon ■4	a			09 28				09 43				09 58				10 13				10 28			
Queens Rd Peckham	d		08 59				09 14				09 29				09 44				09 59				10 14
Peckham Rye ■4	d		09 04				09 18				09 34				09 48				10 04				10 18
Denmark Hill ■4	d		09 07				09 22				09 37				09 52				10 07				10 22
Clapham High Street ⊖	d		09 11				09 26				09 41				09 56				10 11				10 26
Wandsworth Road	d		09 13				09 28				09 43				09 58				10 13				10 28
Clapham Junction	a		09 19				09 35				09 49				10 05				10 19				10 35

		LO	LO	LO	LO	LO	LO	LO	LO	LO	LO	LO	LO	LO	LO	LO	LO	LO	LO	LO	LO	LO	LO
Highbury & Islington	d	09 47		09 55		10 02		10 10		10 17		10 25		10 32		10 40		10 47		10 55		11 02	
Canonbury	d	09 49		09 57		10 04		10 12		10 19		10 27		10 34		10 42		10 49		10 57		11 04	
Dalston Junction	d	09 52	09 57	10 00	10 04	10 07	10 12	10 15	10 19	10 22	10 27	10 30	10 34	10 37	10 42	10 45	10 49	10 52	10 57	11 00	11 04	11 07	11 12
Haggerston	d	09 54	09 59	10 02	10 06	10 09	10 14	10 17	10 21	10 24	10 29	10 32	10 36	10 39	10 44	10 47	10 51	10 54	10 59	11 02	11 06	11 09	11 14
Hoxton	d	09 56	10 01	10 04	10 08	10 11	10 16	10 19	10 23	10 26	10 31	10 34	10 38	10 41	10 46	10 49	10 53	10 56	11 01	11 04	11 08	11 11	11 16
Shoreditch High Street	d	09 58	10 03	10 07	10 10	10 13	10 18	10 22	10 25	10 28	10 33	10 37	10 40	10 43	10 48	10 52	10 55	10 58	11 03	11 07	11 10	11 13	11 18
Whitechapel	d	10 01	10 06	10 09	10 13	10 16	10 21	10 24	10 28	10 31	10 36	10 39	10 43	10 46	10 51	10 54	10 58	11 01	11 06	11 09	11 13	11 16	11 21
Shadwell	d	10 03	10 08	10 11	10 15	10 18	10 23	10 26	10 30	10 33	10 38	10 41	10 45	10 48	10 53	10 56	11 00	11 03	11 08	11 11	11 15	11 18	11 23
Wapping	d	10 05	10 10	10 13	10 17	10 20	10 25	10 28	10 32	10 35	10 40	10 43	10 47	10 50	10 55	10 58	11 02	11 05	11 10	11 13	11 17	11 20	11 25
Rotherhithe	d	10 06	10 11	10 15	10 18	10 21	10 26	10 30	10 33	10 36	10 41	10 45	10 48	10 51	10 56	11 00	11 03	11 06	11 11	11 15	11 18	11 21	11 26
Canada Water	d	10 08	10 13	10 17	10 20	10 23	10 28	10 32	10 35	10 38	10 43	10 47	10 50	10 53	10 58	11 02	11 05	11 08	11 13	11 17	11 20	11 23	11 28
Surrey Quays	d	10 10	10 15	10 19	10 22	10 25	10 30	10 34	10 37	10 40	10 45	10 49	10 52	10 55	11 00	11 04	11 07	11 10	11 15	11 19	11 22	11 25	11 30
New Cross	a		10 19				10 34				10 49				11 04				11 19				11 34
New Cross Gate ■4	d	10 15		10 23		10 30		10 38		10 45		10 53		11 00		11 08		11 15		11 23		11 30	
Brockley	d	10 17		10 26		10 32		10 41		10 47		10 56		11 02		11 11		11 17		11 26		11 32	
Honor Oak Park	d	10 20		10 28		10 35		10 43		10 50		10 58		11 05		11 13		11 20		11 28		11 35	
Forest Hill ■4	d	10 22		10 31		10 37		10 46		10 52		11 01		11 07		11 16		11 22		11 31		11 37	
Sydenham	d	10 26		10 34		10 41		10 49		10 56		11 04		11 11		11 19		11 26		11 34		11 41	
Crystal Palace ■4	a			10 38				10 53				11 08				11 23				11 38			
Penge West	d	10 28				10 43				10 58				11 13				11 28				11 43	
Anerley	d	10 30				10 45				11 00				11 15				11 30				11 45	
Norwood Junction ■2	d	10 33				10 48				11 03				11 18				11 33				11 48	
West Croydon ■4	a	10 43				10 54				11 09				11 24				11 39				11 54	
Queens Rd Peckham	d				10 29				10 44				10 59				11 14				11 29		
Peckham Rye ■4	d				10 34				10 48				11 04				11 18				11 34		
Denmark Hill ■4	d				10 37				10 52				11 07				11 22				11 37		
Clapham High Street ⊖	d				10 41				10 56				11 11				11 26				11 41		
Wandsworth Road	d				10 43				10 58				11 13				11 28				11 43		
Clapham Junction	a				10 49				11 05				11 19				11 35				11 49		

		LO	LO	LO	LO	LO	LO	LO	LO	LO	LO	LO	LO	LO	LO	LO	LO	LO	LO	LO	LO	LO
Highbury & Islington	d	11 10		11 17		11 25		11 32		11 40		11 47		11 55		12 02		12 10		12 17		12 25
Canonbury	d	11 12		11 19		11 27		11 34		11 42		11 49		11 57		12 04		12 12		12 19		12 27
Dalston Junction	d	11 15	11 19	11 22	11 27	11 30	11 34	11 37	11 42	11 45	11 49	11 52	11 57	12 00	12 04	12 07	12 12	12 15	12 19	12 22	12 27	12 30
Haggerston	d	11 17	11 21	11 24	11 29	11 32	11 36	11 39	11 44	11 47	11 51	11 54	11 59	12 02	12 06	12 09	12 14	12 17	12 21	12 24	12 29	12 32
Hoxton	d	11 19	11 23	11 26	11 31	11 34	11 38	11 41	11 46	11 49	11 53	11 56	12 01	12 04	12 08	12 11	12 16	12 19	12 23	12 26	12 31	12 34
Shoreditch High Street	d	11 22	11 25	11 28	11 33	11 37	11 40	11 43	11 48	11 52	11 55	11 58	12 03	12 07	12 10	12 13	12 18	12 22	12 25	12 28	12 33	12 37
Whitechapel	d	11 24	11 28	11 31	11 36	11 39	11 43	11 46	11 51	11 54	11 58	12 01	12 06	12 09	12 13	12 16	12 21	12 24	12 28	12 31	12 36	12 39
Shadwell	d	11 26	11 30	11 33	11 38	11 41	11 45	11 48	11 53	11 56	12 00	12 03	12 08	12 11	12 15	12 18	12 23	12 26	12 30	12 33	12 38	12 41
Wapping	d	11 28	11 32	11 35	11 40	11 43	11 47	11 50	11 55	11 58	12 02	12 05	12 10	12 13	12 17	12 20	12 25	12 28	12 32	12 35	12 40	12 43
Rotherhithe	d	11 30	11 33	11 36	11 41	11 45	11 48	11 51	11 56	12 00	12 03	12 06	12 11	12 15	12 18	12 21	12 26	12 30	12 33	12 36	12 41	12 45
Canada Water	d	11 32	11 35	11 38	11 43	11 47	11 50	11 53	11 58	12 02	12 05	12 08	12 13	12 17	12 20	12 23	12 28	12 32	12 35	12 38	12 43	12 47
Surrey Quays	d	11 34	11 37	11 40	11 45	11 49	11 52	11 55	12 00	12 04	12 07	12 10	12 15	12 19	12 22	12 25	12 30	12 34	12 37	12 40	12 45	12 49
New Cross	a				11 49				12 04				12 19				12 34				12 49	
New Cross Gate ■4	d	11 38		11 45		11 53		12 00		12 08		12 15		12 23		12 30		12 38		12 45		12 53
Brockley	d	11 41		11 47		11 56		12 02		12 11		12 17		12 26		12 32		12 41		12 47		12 56
Honor Oak Park	d	11 43		11 50		11 58		12 05		12 13		12 20		12 28		12 35		12 43		12 50		12 58
Forest Hill ■4	d	11 46		11 52		12 01		12 07		12 16		12 22		12 31		12 37		12 46		12 52		13 01
Sydenham	d	11 49		11 56		12 04		12 11		12 19		12 26		12 34		12 41		12 49		12 56		13 04
Crystal Palace ■4	a	11 53				12 08				12 23				12 38				12 53				13 08
Penge West	d			11 58				12 13				12 28				12 43				12 58		
Anerley	d			12 00				12 15				12 30				12 45				13 00		
Norwood Junction ■2	d			12 03				12 18				12 33				12 48				13 03		
West Croydon ■4	a			12 09				12 24				12 39				12 54				13 09		
Queens Rd Peckham	d		11 44				11 59				12 14				12 29				12 44			
Peckham Rye ■4	d		11 48				12 04				12 18				12 34				12 48			
Denmark Hill ■4	d		11 52				12 07				12 22				12 37				12 52			
Clapham High Street ⊖	d		11 56				12 11				12 26				12 41				12 56			
Wandsworth Road	d		11 58				12 13				12 28				12 43				12 58			
Clapham Junction	a		12 05				12 19				12 35				12 49				13 05			

Table T178-F

Saturdays

26 May to 8 December

Highbury & Islington - New Cross, Crystal Palace, West Croydon and Clapham Junction

		LO	LO	LO	LO	LO	LO	LO	LO	LO	LO	LO	LO	LO	LO	LO	LO	LO	LO	LO	LO	LO	LO
Highbury & Islington	d		12 32		12 40		12 47		12 55		13 02		13 10		13 17		13 25		13 32		13 40		13 47
Canonbury	d		12 34		12 42		12 49		12 57		13 04		13 12		13 19		13 27		13 34		13 42		13 49
Dalston Junction	d	12 34	12 37	12 42	12 45	12 49	12 52	12 57	13 00	13 04	13 07	13 12	13 15	13 19	13 22	13 27	13 30	13 34	13 37	13 42	13 45	13 49	13 52
Haggerston	d	12 36	12 39	12 44	12 47	12 51	12 54	12 59	13 02	13 06	13 09	13 14	13 17	13 21	13 24	13 29	13 32	13 36	13 39	13 44	13 47	13 51	13 54
Hoxton	d	12 38	12 41	12 46	12 49	12 53	12 56	13 01	13 04	13 08	13 11	13 16	13 19	13 23	13 26	13 31	13 34	13 38	13 41	13 46	13 49	13 53	13 56
Shoreditch High Street	d	12 40	12 43	12 48	12 52	12 55	12 58	13 03	13 07	13 10	13 13	13 18	13 22	13 25	13 28	13 33	13 37	13 40	13 43	13 48	13 52	13 55	13 58
Whitechapel	d	12 43	12 46	12 51	12 54	12 58	13 01	13 06	13 09	13 13	13 16	13 21	13 24	13 28	13 31	13 36	13 39	13 43	13 46	13 51	13 54	13 58	14 01
Shadwell	d	12 45	12 48	12 53	12 56	13 00	13 03	13 08	13 11	13 15	13 18	13 23	13 26	13 30	13 33	13 38	13 41	13 45	13 48	13 53	13 56	14 00	14 03
Wapping	d	12 47	12 50	12 55	12 58	13 02	13 05	13 10	13 13	13 17	13 20	13 25	13 28	13 32	13 35	13 40	13 43	13 47	13 50	13 55	13 58	14 02	14 05
Rotherhithe	d	12 48	12 51	12 56	13 00	13 03	13 06	13 11	13 15	13 18	13 21	13 26	13 30	13 33	13 36	13 41	13 45	13 48	13 51	13 56	14 00	14 03	14 06
Canada Water	d	12 50	12 53	12 58	13 02	13 05	13 08	13 13	13 17	13 20	13 23	13 28	13 32	13 35	13 38	13 43	13 47	13 50	13 53	13 58	14 02	14 05	14 08
Surrey Quays	d	12 52	12 55	13 00	13 04	13 07	13 10	13 15	13 19	13 22	13 25	13 30	13 34	13 37	13 40	13 45	13 49	13 52	13 55	14 00	14 04	14 07	14 10
New Cross	a			13 04				13 19				13 34				13 49				14 04			
New Cross Gate ■4	d		13 00		13 08		13 15		13 23		13 30		13 38		13 45		13 53		14 00		14 08		14 15
Brockley	d		13 02		13 11		13 17		13 26		13 32		13 41		13 47		13 56		14 02		14 11		14 17
Honor Oak Park	d		13 05		13 13		13 20		13 28		13 35		13 43		13 50		13 58		14 05		14 13		14 20
Forest Hill ■4	d		13 07		13 16		13 22		13 31		13 37		13 46		13 52		14 01		14 07		14 16		14 22
Sydenham	d		13 11		13 19		13 26		13 34		13 41		13 49		13 56		14 04		14 11		14 19		14 26
Crystal Palace ■4	a				13 23				13 38				13 53				14 08				14 23		
Penge West	d		13 13				13 28				13 43				13 58				14 13				14 28
Anerley	d		13 15				13 30				13 45				14 00				14 15				14 30
Norwood Junction ■2	d		13 18				13 33				13 48				14 03				14 18				14 33
West Croydon ■4	a		13 24				13 39				13 54				14 09				14 24				14 39
Queens Rd Peckham	d	12 59				13 14				13 29				13 44				13 59				14 14	
Peckham Rye ■4	d	13 04				13 16				13 34				13 48				14 04				14 18	
Denmark Hill ■4	d	13 07				13 22				13 37				13 52				14 07				14 22	
Clapham High Street ⊖	d	13 11				13 26				13 41				13 56				14 11				14 26	
Wandsworth Road	d	13 13				13 28				13 43				13 58				14 13				14 28	
Clapham Junction	a	13 19				13 35				13 49				14 05				14 19				14 35	

		LO	LO	LO	LO	LO	LO	LO	LO	LO	LO	LO	LO	LO	LO	LO	LO	LO	LO	LO	LO	LO	LO
Highbury & Islington	d		13 55		14 02		14 10		14 17		14 25		14 32		14 40		14 47		14 55		15 02		15 10
Canonbury	d		13 57		14 04		14 12		14 19		14 27		14 34		14 42		14 49		14 57		15 04		15 12
Dalston Junction	d	13 57	14 00	14 04	14 07	14 12	14 15	14 19	14 22	14 27	14 30	14 34	14 37	14 42	14 45	14 49	14 52	14 57	15 00	15 04	15 07	15 12	15 15
Haggerston	d	13 59	14 02	14 06	14 09	14 14	14 17	14 21	14 24	14 29	14 32	14 36	14 39	14 44	14 47	14 51	14 54	14 59	15 02	15 06	15 09	15 14	15 17
Hoxton	d	14 01	14 04	14 08	14 11	14 16	14 19	14 23	14 26	14 31	14 34	14 38	14 41	14 46	14 49	14 53	14 56	15 01	15 04	15 08	15 11	15 16	15 19
Shoreditch High Street	d	14 03	14 07	14 10	14 13	14 18	14 22	14 25	14 28	14 33	14 37	14 40	14 43	14 48	14 52	14 55	14 58	15 03	15 07	15 10	15 13	15 18	15 22
Whitechapel	d	14 06	14 09	14 13	14 16	14 21	14 24	14 28	14 31	14 36	14 39	14 43	14 46	14 51	14 54	14 58	15 01	15 06	15 09	15 13	15 16	15 21	15 24
Shadwell	d	14 08	14 11	14 15	14 18	14 23	14 26	14 30	14 33	14 38	14 41	14 45	14 48	14 53	14 56	15 00	15 03	15 08	15 11	15 15	15 18	15 23	15 26
Wapping	d	14 10	14 13	14 17	14 20	14 25	14 28	14 32	14 35	14 40	14 43	14 47	14 50	14 55	14 58	15 02	15 05	15 10	15 13	15 17	15 20	15 25	15 28
Rotherhithe	d	14 11	14 15	14 18	14 21	14 26	14 30	14 33	14 36	14 41	14 45	14 48	14 51	14 56	15 00	15 03	15 06	15 11	15 15	15 18	15 21	15 26	15 30
Canada Water	d	14 13	14 17	14 20	14 23	14 28	14 32	14 35	14 38	14 43	14 47	14 50	14 53	14 58	15 02	15 05	15 08	15 13	15 17	15 20	15 23	15 28	15 32
Surrey Quays	d	14 15	14 19	14 22	14 25	14 30	14 34	14 37	14 40	14 45	14 49	14 52	14 55	15 00	15 04	15 07	15 10	15 15	15 19	15 22	15 25	15 30	15 34
New Cross	a	14 19				14 34				14 49				15 04				15 19				15 34	
New Cross Gate ■4	d		14 23		14 30		14 38		14 45		14 53		15 00		15 08		15 15		15 23		15 30		15 38
Brockley	d		14 26		14 32		14 41		14 47		14 56		15 02		15 11		15 17		15 26		15 32		15 41
Honor Oak Park	d		14 28		14 35		14 43		14 50		14 58		15 05		15 13		15 20		15 28		15 35		15 43
Forest Hill ■4	d		14 31		14 37		14 46		14 52		15 01		15 07		15 16		15 22		15 31		15 37		15 46
Sydenham	d		14 34		14 41		14 49		14 56		15 04		15 11		15 19		15 26		15 34		15 41		15 49
Crystal Palace ■4	a		14 38				14 53				15 08				15 23				15 38				15 53
Penge West	d				14 43				14 58				15 13				15 28				15 43		
Anerley	d				14 45				15 00				15 15				15 30				15 45		
Norwood Junction ■2	d				14 48				15 03				15 18				15 33				15 48		
West Croydon ■4	a				14 54				15 09				15 24				15 39				15 58		
Queens Rd Peckham	d			14 29				14 44				14 59				15 14				15 29			
Peckham Rye ■4	d			14 34				14 48				15 04				15 18				15 34			
Denmark Hill ■4	d			14 37				14 52				15 07				15 22				15 37			
Clapham High Street ⊖	d			14 41				14 56				15 11				15 26				15 41			
Wandsworth Road	d			14 43				14 58				15 13				15 28				15 43			
Clapham Junction	a			14 49				15 05				15 19				15 35				15 49			

		LO	LO	LO	LO	LO	LO	LO	LO	LO	LO		LO	LO	LO	LO	LO	LO	LO	LO	LO	LO	LO	LO
Highbury & Islington	d		15 17		15 25		15 32		15 40		15 47			18 55		19 02		19 10		19 17		19 25		19 32
Canonbury	d		15 19		15 27		15 34		15 42		15 49			18 57		19 04		19 12		19 19		19 27		19 34
Dalston Junction	d	15 19	15 22	15 27	15 30	15 34	15 37	15 42	15 45	15 49	15 52		18 57	19 00	19 04	19 07	19 12	19 15	19 19	19 22	19 27	19 30	19 34	19 37
Haggerston	d	15 21	15 24	15 29	15 32	15 36	15 39	15 44	15 47	15 51	15 54		18 59	19 02	19 06	19 09	19 14	19 17	19 21	19 24	19 29	19 32	19 36	19 39
Hoxton	d	15 23	15 26	15 31	15 34	15 38	15 41	15 46	15 49	15 53	15 56		19 01	19 04	19 08	19 11	19 16	19 19	19 23	19 26	19 31	19 34	19 38	19 41
Shoreditch High Street	d	15 25	15 28	15 33	15 37	15 40	15 43	15 48	15 52	15 55	15 58		19 03	19 07	19 10	19 13	19 18	19 22	19 25	19 28	19 33	19 37	19 40	19 43
Whitechapel	d	15 28	15 31	15 36	15 39	15 43	15 46	15 51	15 54	15 58	16 01		19 06	19 09	19 13	19 16	19 21	19 24	19 28	19 31	19 36	19 39	19 43	19 46
Shadwell	d	15 30	15 33	15 38	15 41	15 45	15 48	15 53	15 56	16 00	16 03		19 08	19 11	19 15	19 18	19 23	19 26	19 30	19 33	19 38	19 41	19 45	19 48
Wapping	d	15 32	15 35	15 40	15 43	15 47	15 50	15 55	15 58	16 02	16 05		19 10	19 13	19 17	19 20	19 25	19 28	19 32	19 35	19 40	19 43	19 47	19 50
Rotherhithe	d	15 33	15 36	15 41	15 45	15 48	15 51	15 56	16 00	16 03	16 06		19 11	19 15	19 18	19 21	19 26	19 30	19 33	19 36	19 41	19 45	19 48	19 51
Canada Water	d	15 35	15 38	15 43	15 47	15 50	15 53	15 58	16 02	16 05	16 08	and at the same minutes past each hour until	19 13	19 17	19 20	19 23	19 28	19 32	19 35	19 38	19 43	19 47	19 50	19 53
Surrey Quays	d	15 37	15 40	15 45	15 49	15 52	15 55	16 00	16 04	16 07	16 10		19 15	19 19	19 22	19 25	19 30	19 34	19 37	19 40	19 45	19 49	19 52	19 55
New Cross	a			15 49				16 04					19 19				19 34				19 49			
New Cross Gate ■4	d		15 45		15 53		16 00		16 08		16 15			19 23		19 30		19 38		19 45		19 53		20 00
Brockley	d		15 47		15 56		16 02		16 11		16 17			19 26		19 32		19 41		19 47		19 56		20 02
Honor Oak Park	d		15 50		15 58		16 05		16 13		16 20			19 28		19 35		19 43		19 50		19 58		20 05
Forest Hill ■4	d		15 52		16 01		16 07		16 16		16 22			19 31		19 37		19 46		19 52		20 01		20 07
Sydenham	d		15 56		16 04		16 11		16 19		16 26			19 34		19 41		19 49		19 56		20 04		20 11
Crystal Palace ■4	a				16 08				16 23					19 38				19 53				20 08		
Penge West	d		15 58				16 13				16 28					19 43				19 58				20 13
Anerley	d		16 00				16 15				16 30					19 45				20 00				20 15
Norwood Junction ■2	d		16 03				16 18				16 33					19 48				20 03				20 18
West Croydon ■4	a		16 13				16 28				16 43					19 58				20 13				20 28
Queens Rd Peckham	d	15 44				15 59				16 14					19 29				19 44				19 59	
Peckham Rye ■4	d	15 48				16 04				16 18					19 34				19 48				20 04	
Denmark Hill ■4	d	15 52				16 07				16 22					19 37				19 52				20 07	
Clapham High Street ⊖	d	15 56				16 11				16 26					19 41				19 56				20 11	
Wandsworth Road	d	15 58				16 13				16 28					19 43				19 58				20 13	
Clapham Junction	a	16 05				16 19				16 35					19 49				20 05				20 19	

Table T178-F

Saturdays
26 May to 8 December

Highbury & Islington - New Cross, Crystal Palace, West Croydon and Clapham Junction

		LO	LO	LO	LO	LO	LO	LO	LO	LO	LO	LO	LO	LO	LO	LO	LO	LO	LO	LO	LO	LO	LO
Highbury & Islington	d		19 40		19 47		19 55		20 02		20 10		20 17		20 25		20 32		20 40		20 47		20 55
Canonbury	d		19 42		19 49		19 57		20 04		20 12		20 19		20 27		20 34		20 42		20 49		20 57
Dalston Junction	d	19 42	19 45	19 49	19 52	19 57	20 00	20 04	20 07	20 12	20 15	20 19	20 22	20 27	20 30	20 34	20 37	20 42	20 45	20 49	20 52	20 57	21 00
Haggerston	d	19 44	19 47	19 51	19 54	19 59	20 02	20 06	20 09	20 14	20 17	20 21	20 24	20 29	20 32	20 36	20 39	20 44	20 47	20 51	20 54	20 59	21 02
Hoxton	d	19 46	19 49	19 53	19 56	20 01	20 04	20 08	20 11	20 16	20 19	20 23	20 26	20 31	20 34	20 38	20 41	20 46	20 49	20 53	20 56	21 01	21 04
Shoreditch High Street	d	19 48	19 52	19 55	19 58	20 03	20 07	20 10	20 13	20 18	20 22	20 25	20 28	20 33	20 37	20 40	20 43	20 48	20 52	20 55	20 58	21 03	21 07
Whitechapel	d	19 51	19 54	19 58	20 01	20 06	20 09	20 13	20 16	20 21	20 24	20 28	20 31	20 36	20 39	20 43	20 46	20 51	20 54	20 58	21 01	21 06	21 09
Shadwell	d	19 53	19 56	20 00	20 03	20 08	20 11	20 15	20 18	20 23	20 26	20 30	20 33	20 38	20 41	20 45	20 48	20 53	20 56	21 00	21 03	21 08	21 11
Wapping	d	19 55	19 58	20 02	20 05	20 10	20 13	20 17	20 20	20 25	20 28	20 32	20 35	20 40	20 43	20 47	20 50	20 55	20 58	21 02	21 05	21 10	21 13
Rotherhithe	d	19 56	20 00	20 03	20 06	20 11	20 15	20 18	20 21	20 26	20 30	20 33	20 36	20 41	20 45	20 48	20 51	20 56	21 00	21 03	21 06	21 11	21 15
Canada Water	d	19 58	20 02	20 05	20 08	20 13	20 17	20 20	20 23	20 28	20 32	20 35	20 38	20 43	20 47	20 50	20 53	20 58	21 02	21 05	21 08	21 13	21 17
Surrey Quays	d	20 00	20 04	20 07	20 10	20 15	20 19	20 22	20 25	20 30	20 34	20 37	20 40	20 45	20 49	20 52	20 55	21 00	21 04	21 07	21 10	21 15	21 19
New Cross	a	20 04				20 19				20 34				20 49				21 04				21 19	
New Cross Gate ❹	d		20 08		20 15		20 23		20 30		20 38		20 45		20 53		21 00		21 08		21 15		21 23
Brockley	d		20 11		20 17		20 26		20 32		20 41		20 47		20 56		21 02		21 11		21 17		21 26
Honor Oak Park	d		20 13		20 20		20 28		20 35		20 43		20 50		20 58		21 05		21 13		21 20		21 28
Forest Hill ❹	d		20 16		20 22		20 31		20 37		20 46		20 52		21 01		21 07		21 16		21 22		21 31
Sydenham	d		20 19		20 26		20 34		20 41		20 49		20 56		21 04		21 11		21 19		21 26		21 34
Crystal Palace ❹	a		20 23				20 38				20 53				21 08				21 23				21 38
Penge West	d				20 28				20 43				20 58				21 13				21 28		
Anerley	d				20 30				20 45				21 00				21 15				21 30		
Norwood Junction ❷	d				20 33				20 48				21 03				21 18				21 33		
West Croydon ❹ ⇌	a				20 43				20 58				21 13				21 24				21 39		
Queens Rd Peckham	d			20 14				20 29				20 44				20 59				21 14			
Peckham Rye ❹	d			20 18				20 33				20 48				21 04				21 18			
Denmark Hill ❹	d			20 22				20 37				20 52				21 07				21 22			
Clapham High Street ⊖	d			20 26				20 41				20 56				21 11				21 26			
Wandsworth Road	d			20 28				20 43				20 58				21 13				21 28			
Clapham Junction	a			20 35				20 50				21 05				21 19				21 35			

		LO	LO	LO	LO	LO	LO	LO	LO	LO	LO	LO	LO	LO	LO	LO	LO	LO	LO	LO	LO	LO
Highbury & Islington	d		21 02		21 10		21 17		21 25		21 32		21 40		21 47		21 55		22 02		22 10	
Canonbury	d		21 04		21 12		21 19		21 27		21 34		21 42		21 49		21 57		22 04		22 12	
Dalston Junction	d	21 04	21 07	21 12	21 15	21 19	21 22	21 27	21 30	21 34	21 37	21 42	21 45	21 49	21 52	21 57	22 00	22 04	22 07	22 12	22 15	22 19
Haggerston	d	21 06	21 09	21 14	21 17	21 21	21 24	21 29	21 32	21 36	21 39	21 44	21 47	21 51	21 54	21 59	22 02	22 06	22 09	22 14	22 17	22 21
Hoxton	d	21 08	21 11	21 16	21 19	21 23	21 26	21 31	21 34	21 38	21 41	21 46	21 49	21 53	21 56	22 01	22 04	22 08	22 11	22 16	22 19	22 23
Shoreditch High Street	d	21 10	21 13	21 18	21 22	21 25	21 28	21 33	21 37	21 40	21 43	21 48	21 52	21 55	21 58	22 03	22 07	22 10	22 13	22 18	22 22	22 25
Whitechapel	d	21 13	21 16	21 21	21 24	21 28	21 31	21 36	21 39	21 43	21 46	21 51	21 54	21 58	22 01	22 06	22 09	22 13	22 16	22 21	22 24	22 28
Shadwell	d	21 15	21 18	21 23	21 26	21 30	21 33	21 38	21 41	21 45	21 48	21 53	21 56	22 00	22 03	22 08	22 11	22 15	22 18	22 23	22 26	22 30
Wapping	d	21 17	21 20	21 25	21 28	21 32	21 35	21 40	21 43	21 47	21 50	21 55	21 58	22 02	22 05	22 10	22 13	22 17	22 20	22 25	22 28	22 32
Rotherhithe	d	21 18	21 21	21 26	21 30	21 33	21 36	21 41	21 45	21 48	21 51	21 56	22 00	22 03	22 06	22 11	22 15	22 18	22 21	22 26	22 30	22 33
Canada Water	d	21 20	21 23	21 28	21 32	21 35	21 38	21 43	21 47	21 50	21 53	21 58	22 02	22 05	22 08	22 13	22 17	22 20	22 23	22 28	22 32	22 35
Surrey Quays	d	21 22	21 25	21 30	21 34	21 37	21 40	21 45	21 49	21 52	21 55	22 00	22 04	22 07	22 10	22 15	22 19	22 22	22 25	22 30	22 34	22 37
New Cross	a			21 34				21 49				22 04				22 19				22 34		
New Cross Gate ❹	d		21 30		21 38		21 45		21 53		22 00		22 08		22 15		22 23		22 30		22 38	
Brockley	d		21 32		21 41		21 47		21 56		22 02		22 11		22 17		22 26		22 32		22 41	
Honor Oak Park	d		21 35		21 43		21 50		21 58		22 05		22 13		22 20		22 28		22 35		22 43	
Forest Hill ❹	d		21 37		21 46		21 52		22 01		22 07		22 16		22 22		22 31		22 37		22 46	
Sydenham	d		21 41		21 49		21 56		22 04		22 11		22 19		22 26		22 34		22 41		22 49	
Crystal Palace ❹	a				21 53				22 08				22 23				22 38				22 53	
Penge West	d		21 43				21 58				22 13				22 28				22 43			
Anerley	d		21 45				22 00				22 15				22 30				22 45			
Norwood Junction ❷	d		21 48				22 03				22 18				22 33				22 48			
West Croydon ❹ ⇌	a		21 54				22 09				22 24				22 39				22 54			
Queens Rd Peckham	d	21 29				21 44				21 59				22 14				22 29				22 44
Peckham Rye ❹	d	21 34				21 48				22 04				22 18				22 34				22 48
Denmark Hill ❹	d	21 37				21 52				22 07				22 22				22 37				22 52
Clapham High Street ⊖	d	21 41				21 56				22 11				22 26				22 41				22 56
Wandsworth Road	d	21 43				21 58				22 13				22 28				22 43				22 58
Clapham Junction	a	21 49				22 05				22 19				22 35				22 49				23 05

		LO	LO	LO	LO	LO	LO	LO	LO	LO	LO	LO	LO	LO	LO	LO	LO	LO	LO	LO	LO	LO	LO
Highbury & Islington	d	22 17		22 25		22 32		22 40		22 47		22 55		23 02		23 10		23 17		23 25		23 32	
Canonbury	d	22 19		22 27		22 34		22 42		22 49		22 57		23 04		23 12		23 19		23 27		23 34	
Dalston Junction	d	22 22	22 27	22 30	22 34	22 37	22 42	22 45	22 49	22 52	22 57	23 00	23 04	23 07	23 12	23 15	23 19	23 22	23 27	23 30	23 34	23 37	23 42
Haggerston	d	22 24	22 29	22 32	22 36	22 39	22 44	22 47	22 51	22 54	22 59	23 02	23 06	23 09	23 14	23 17	23 21	23 24	23 29	23 32	23 36	23 39	23 44
Hoxton	d	22 26	22 31	22 34	22 38	22 41	22 46	22 49	22 53	22 56	23 01	23 04	23 08	23 11	23 16	23 19	23 23	23 26	23 31	23 34	23 38	23 41	23 46
Shoreditch High Street	d	22 28	22 33	22 37	22 40	22 43	22 48	22 52	22 55	22 58	23 03	23 07	23 10	23 13	23 18	23 22	23 25	23 28	23 33	23 37	23 40	23 43	23 48
Whitechapel	d	22 31	22 36	22 39	22 43	22 46	22 51	22 54	22 58	23 01	23 06	23 09	23 13	23 16	23 21	23 24	23 28	23 31	23 36	23 39	23 43	23 46	23 51
Shadwell	d	22 33	22 38	22 41	22 45	22 48	22 53	22 56	23 00	23 03	23 08	23 11	23 15	23 18	23 23	23 26	23 30	23 33	23 38	23 41	23 45	23 48	23 53
Wapping	d	22 35	22 40	22 43	22 47	22 50	22 55	22 58	23 02	23 05	23 10	23 13	23 17	23 20	23 25	23 28	23 32	23 35	23 40	23 43	23 47	23 50	23 55
Rotherhithe	d	22 36	22 41	22 45	22 48	22 51	22 56	23 00	23 03	23 06	23 11	23 15	23 18	23 21	23 26	23 30	23 33	23 36	23 41	23 45	23 48	23 51	23 56
Canada Water	d	22 38	22 43	22 47	22 50	22 53	22 58	23 02	23 05	23 08	23 13	23 17	23 20	23 23	23 28	23 32	23 35	23 38	23 43	23 47	23 50	23 53	23 58
Surrey Quays	d	22 40	22 45	22 49	22 52	22 55	23 00	23 04	23 07	23 10	23 15	23 19	23 22	23 25	23 30	23 34	23 37	23 40	23 45	23 49	23 52	23 55	00 02
New Cross	a		22 49				23 04				23 19				23 34				23 49				00 04
New Cross Gate ❹	d	22 45		22 53		23 00		23 08		23 15		23 23		23 30		23 38		23 45		23 53		00 01	
Brockley	d	22 47		22 56		23 02		23 11		23 17		23 26		23 32		23 41		23 47		23 56		00 03	
Honor Oak Park	d	22 50		22 58		23 05		23 13		23 20		23 28		23 35		23 43		23 50		23 58		00 06	
Forest Hill ❹	d	22 52		23 01		23 07		23 16		23 22		23 31		23 37		23 46		23 52		00 01		00 08	
Sydenham	d	22 56		23 04		23 11		23 19		23 26		23 34		23 41		23 49		23 56		00 04		00 11	
Crystal Palace ❹	a			23 08				23 23				23 38				23 53				00 08			
Penge West	d	22 58				23 13				23 28				23 43				23 58				00 13	
Anerley	d	23 00				23 15				23 30				23 45				00 01				00 15	
Norwood Junction ❷	d	23 03				23 18				23 33				23 48				00 03				00 19	
West Croydon ❹ ⇌	a	23 13				23 28				23 43				23 58				00 13				00 28	
Queens Rd Peckham	d				22 57				23 14				23 29				23 44				23 59		
Peckham Rye ❹	d				23 02				23 18				23 34				23 48				00 04		
Denmark Hill ❹	d				23 05				23 22				23 37				23 52				00 07		
Clapham High Street ⊖	d				23 10				23 26				23 41				23 56				00 11		
Wandsworth Road	d				23 11				23 28				23 43				23 58				00 13		
Clapham Junction	a				23 19				23 35				23 49				00 06				00 19		

Table T178-F

Highbury & Islington - New Cross, Crystal Palace, West Croydon and Clapham Junction

Saturdays
26 May to 8 December

		LO	LO	LO
Highbury & Islington	d	23 40		23 50
Canonbury	d	23 42		23 52
Dalston Junction	d	23 45	23 49	23 55
Haggerston	d	23 47	23 51	23 57
Hoxton	d	23 49	23 53	23 59
Shoreditch High Street	d	23 52	23 55	00 01
Whitechapel	d	23 54	23 58	00 04
Shadwell	d	23 56	23 59	00 06
Wapping	d	23 58	00 02	00 08
Rotherhithe	d	23 59	00 03	00 09
Canada Water	d	00 02	00 05	00 11
Surrey Quays	d	00 04	00 07	00 13
New Cross	a			
New Cross Gate ❹	d	00 08		00a20
Brockley	d	00 11		
Honor Oak Park	d	00 13		
Forest Hill ❹	d	00 16		
Sydenham	d	00 19		
Crystal Palace ❹	a	00 23		
Penge West	d			
Anerley	d			
Norwood Junction ❷	d			
West Croydon ❹ ⇌	a			
Queens Rd Peckham	d		00 14	
Peckham Rye ❹	d		00 18	
Denmark Hill ❹	d		00 22	
Clapham High Street ⊖	d		00 26	
Wandsworth Road	d		00 28	
Clapham Junction	a		00 35	

Sundays
20 May to 2 December

		LO A	LO A	LO A	LO B	LO A	LO B	LO B	LO A	LO	LO		LO	LO	LO	LO	LO	LO	LO	LO	LO	LO
Highbury & Islington	d									00 01	00 10		05 55	06 08	06 20	06 35	06 51		07 11	07 21	07 26	
Canonbury	d									00 03	00 12		05 57	06 10	06 22	06 37	06 53		07 13	07 23	07 28	
Dalston Junction	d									00 06	00 15		06 00	06 13	06 25	06 40	06 56	07 12	07 16	07 26	07 31	07 42
Haggerston	d									00 08	00 17		06 02	06 14	06 27	06 42	06 57	07 13	07 17	07 27	07 32	07 43
Hoxton	d									00 10	00 19		06 04	06 16	06 29	06 44	06 59	07 15	07 19	07 29	07 34	07 45
Shoreditch High Street	d								00 01	00 13	00 21		06 06	06 19	06 31	06 46	07 02	07 18	07 22	07 32	07 37	07 48
Whitechapel	d								00 04	00 15	00 24		06 09	06 21	06 34	06 49	07 04	07 20	07 24	07 34	07 39	07 50
Shadwell	d								00 06	00 17	00 26		06 11	06 23	06 36	06 51	07 06	07 22	07 26	07 36	07 41	07 52
Wapping	d							00 02	00 08	00 19	00 28		06 13	06 25	06 38	06 53	07 08	07 24	07 28	07 38	07 43	07 54
Rotherhithe	d							00 03	00 09	00 21	00 29		06 14	06 27	06 39	06 54	07 10	07 26	07 30	07 40	07 45	07 56
Canada Water	d					00 02		00 05	00 11	00 23	00 31		06 16	06 29	06 41	06 56	07 12	07 28	07 32	07 42	07 47	07 58
Surrey Quays	d				00 02	00 04		00 07	00 13	00 25	00 33	and every 15 minutes until	06 18	06 31	06 43	06 58	07 14	07 30	07 34	07 44	07 49	08 00
New Cross	a				00 04																	
New Cross Gate ❹	d			00 01		00 08			00a20		00a40		06a25	06a38	06a50	07 04	07 18	07 34		07 48		08 04
Brockley	d			00 03		00 11										07 07	07 21	07 37		07 51		08 07
Honor Oak Park	d			00 06		00 13										07 09	07 23	07 39		07 53		08 09
Forest Hill ❹	d		00 01	00 08		00 16										07 12	07 26	07 42		07 56		08 12
Sydenham	d		00 04	00 11		00 19										07 15	07 29	07 45		07 59		08 15
Crystal Palace ❹	a		00 08			00 23											07 34			08 04		
Penge West	d			00 13												07 17		07 47				08 17
Anerley	d	00 01		00 15												07 19		07 49				08 19
Norwood Junction ❷	d	00 03		00 19												07 22		07 52				08 22
West Croydon ❹ ⇌	a	00 13		00 28												07 27		07 58				08 28
Queens Rd Peckham	d							00 14		00 31									07 38		07 53	
Peckham Rye ❹	d						00 04	00 18		00 34									07 42		07 57	
Denmark Hill ❹	d						00 07	00 22		00 38									07 44		07 59	
Clapham High Street ⊖	d						00 11	00 26		00 42									07 49		08 04	
Wandsworth Road	d						00 13	00 28		00 44									07 50		08 05	
Clapham Junction	a						00 19	00 35		00 52									08 02		08 17	

		LO	LO	LO	LO	LO	LO	LO	LO	LO	LO	LO	LO	LO	LO	LO	LO	LO	LO	LO	LO	LO	LO
Highbury & Islington	d	07 41	07 51	07 56	08 07	08 11		08 21	08 26		08 37	08 41		08 51	08 56		09 07	09 11		09 21	09 26		09 37
Canonbury	d	07 43	07 53	07 58	08 09	08 13		08 23	08 28		08 39	08 43		08 53	08 58		09 09	09 13		09 23	09 28		09 39
Dalston Junction	d	07 46	07 56	08 01	08 12	08 16	08 23	08 26	08 31	08 38	08 42	08 46	08 53	08 56	09 01	09 08	09 12	09 16	09 23	09 26	09 31	09 38	09 42
Haggerston	d	07 47	07 57	08 02	08 13	08 17	08 24	08 27	08 32	08 39	08 43	08 47	08 54	08 57	09 02	09 09	09 13	09 17	09 24	09 27	09 32	09 39	09 43
Hoxton	d	07 49	07 59	08 04	08 15	08 19	08 26	08 29	08 34	08 41	08 45	08 49	08 56	08 59	09 04	09 11	09 15	09 19	09 26	09 29	09 34	09 41	09 45
Shoreditch High Street	d	07 52	08 02	08 07	08 18	08 22	08 29	08 32	08 37	08 44	08 48	08 52	08 59	09 02	09 07	09 14	09 18	09 22	09 29	09 32	09 37	09 44	09 48
Whitechapel	d	07 54	08 04	08 09	08 20	08 24	08 31	08 34	08 39	08 46	08 50	08 54	09 01	09 04	09 09	09 16	09 20	09 24	09 31	09 34	09 39	09 46	09 50
Shadwell	d	07 56	08 06	08 11	08 22	08 26	08 33	08 36	08 41	08 48	08 52	08 56	09 03	09 06	09 11	09 18	09 22	09 26	09 33	09 36	09 41	09 48	09 52
Wapping	d	07 58	08 08	08 13	08 24	08 28	08 35	08 38	08 43	08 50	08 54	08 58	09 05	09 08	09 13	09 20	09 24	09 28	09 35	09 38	09 43	09 50	09 54
Rotherhithe	d	08 00	08 10	08 15	08 26	08 30	08 37	08 40	08 45	08 52	08 56	09 00	09 07	09 10	09 15	09 22	09 26	09 30	09 37	09 40	09 45	09 52	09 56
Canada Water	d	08 02	08 12	08 17	08 28	08 32	08 39	08 42	08 47	08 54	08 58	09 02	09 09	09 12	09 17	09 24	09 28	09 32	09 39	09 42	09 47	09 54	09 58
Surrey Quays	d	08 04	08 14	08 19	08 30	08 34	08 41	08 44	08 49	08 56	09 00	09 04	09 11	09 14	09 19	09 26	09 30	09 34	09 41	09 44	09 49	09 56	10 00
New Cross	a						08 45			09 00			09 15			09 30			09 45			10 00	
New Cross Gate ❹	d		08 18		08 34			08 48			09 04			09 18			09 34			09 48			10 04
Brockley	d		08 21		08 37			08 51			09 07			09 21			09 37			09 51			10 07
Honor Oak Park	d		08 23		08 39			08 53			09 09			09 23			09 39			09 53			10 09
Forest Hill ❹	d		08 26		08 42			08 56			09 12			09 26			09 42			09 56			10 12
Sydenham	d		08 29		08 45			08 59			09 15			09 29			09 45			09 59			10 15
Crystal Palace ❹	a		08 34					09 04						09 34						10 04			
Penge West	d				08 47						09 17						09 47						10 17
Anerley	d				08 49						09 19						09 49						10 19
Norwood Junction ❷	d				08 52						09 22						09 52						10 22
West Croydon ❹ ⇌	a				08 59						09 29						09 59						10 29
Queens Rd Peckham	d	08 08		08 23		08 38			08 53			09 08			09 23			09 38			09 53		
Peckham Rye ❹	d	08 12		08 27		08 42			08 57			09 12			09 27			09 42			09 57		
Denmark Hill ❹	d	08 14		08 29		08 44			08 59			09 14			09 29			09 44			09 59		
Clapham High Street ⊖	d	08 19		08 34		08 49			09 04			09 19			09 34			09 49			10 04		
Wandsworth Road	d	08 20		08 35		08 50			09 05			09 20			09 35			09 50			10 05		
Clapham Junction	a	08 32		08 47		09 02			09 17			09 32			09 47			10 02			10 17		

A not 20 May. From Highbury and Islington Ell
B not 20 May. From Dalston Junction Stn Ell

Table T178-F

Sundays

20 May to 2 December

Highbury & Islington - New Cross, Crystal Palace, West Croydon and Clapham Junction

		LO	LO	LO	LO	LO		LO	LO	LO	LO	LO	LO	LO	LO	LO		LO	LO	LO	LO	LO	LO	LO	LO
Highbury & Islington	d	09 41		09 51	09 56			10 07	10 11		10 21	10 26		10 37	10 41			10 51	10 56		11 07	11 11		11 21	11 26
Canonbury	d	09 43		09 53	09 58			10 09	10 13		10 23	10 28		10 39	10 43			10 53	10 58		11 09	11 13		11 23	11 28
Dalston Junction	d	09 46	09 53	09 56	10 01	10 08		10 12	10 16	10 23	10 26	10 31	10 38	10 42	10 46	10 53		10 56	11 01	11 08	11 12	11 16	11 23	11 26	11 31
Haggerston	d	09 47	09 54	09 57	10 02	10 09		10 13	10 17	10 24	10 27	10 32	10 39	10 43	10 47	10 54		10 57	11 02	11 09	11 13	11 17	11 24	11 27	11 32
Hoxton	d	09 49	09 56	09 59	10 04	10 11		10 15	10 19	10 26	10 29	10 34	10 41	10 45	10 49	10 56		10 59	11 04	11 11	11 15	11 19	11 26	11 29	11 34
Shoreditch High Street	d	09 52	09 59	10 02	10 07	10 14		10 18	10 22	10 29	10 32	10 37	10 44	10 48	10 52	10 59		11 02	11 07	11 14	11 18	11 22	11 29	11 32	11 37
Whitechapel	d	09 54	10 01	10 04	10 09	10 16		10 20	10 24	10 31	10 34	10 39	10 46	10 50	10 54	11 01		11 04	11 09	11 16	11 20	11 24	11 31	11 34	11 39
Shadwell	d	09 56	10 03	10 06	10 11	10 18		10 22	10 26	10 33	10 36	10 41	10 48	10 52	10 56	11 03		11 06	11 11	11 18	11 22	11 26	11 33	11 36	11 41
Wapping	d	09 58	10 05	10 08	10 13	10 20		10 24	10 28	10 35	10 38	10 43	10 50	10 54	10 58	11 05		11 08	11 13	11 20	11 24	11 28	11 35	11 38	11 43
Rotherhithe	d	10 00	10 07	10 10	10 15	10 22		10 26	10 30	10 37	10 40	10 45	10 52	10 56	11 00	11 07		11 10	11 15	11 22	11 26	11 30	11 37	11 40	11 45
Canada Water	d	10 02	10 09	10 12	10 17	10 24		10 28	10 32	10 39	10 42	10 47	10 54	10 58	11 02	11 09		11 12	11 17	11 24	11 28	11 32	11 39	11 42	11 47
Surrey Quays	d	10 04	10 11	10 14	10 19	10 26		10 30	10 34	10 41	10 44	10 49	10 56	11 00	11 04	11 11		11 14	11 19	11 26	11 30	11 34	11 41	11 44	11 49
New Cross	a		10 15			10 30				10 45			11 00			11 15				11 30			11 45		
New Cross Gate	d			10 18				10 34			10 48			11 04				11 18			11 34			11 48	
Brockley	d			10 21				10 37			10 51			11 07				11 21			11 37			11 51	
Honor Oak Park	d			10 23				10 39			10 53			11 09				11 23			11 39			11 53	
Forest Hill	d			10 26				10 42			10 56			11 12				11 26			11 42			11 56	
Sydenham	d			10 29				10 45			10 59			11 15				11 29			11 45			11 59	
Crystal Palace	a			10 34							11 04							11 34						12 04	
Penge West	d							10 47						11 17							11 47				
Anerley	d							10 49						11 19							11 49				
Norwood Junction	d							10 52						11 22							11 52				
West Croydon	a							10 59						11 29							11 59				
Queens Rd Peckham	d	10 08			10 23				10 38			10 53			11 08				11 23			11 38			11 53
Peckham Rye	d	10 12			10 27				10 42			10 57			11 12				11 27			11 42			11 57
Denmark Hill	d	10 14			10 29				10 44			10 59			11 14				11 29			11 44			11 59
Clapham High Street ⊖	d	10 19			10 34				10 49			11 04			11 19				11 34			11 49			12 04
Wandsworth Road	d	10 20			10 35				10 50			11 05			11 20				11 35			11 50			12 05
Clapham Junction	a	10 32			10 47				11 02			11 17			11 32				11 47			12 02			12 17

		LO		LO	LO	LO	LO	LO	LO	LO	LO	LO		LO	LO	LO	LO	LO	LO	LO	LO	LO		LO	LO
Highbury & Islington	d			11 35	11 37			11 50	11 53			12 05		12 08			12 20		12 28		12 35			12 43	
Canonbury	d			11 37	11 39			11 52	11 55			12 07		12 10			12 22		12 30		12 37			12 45	
Dalston Junction	d	11 38		11 40	11 42	11 48	11 53	11 55	11 58	12 03	12 08	12 10		12 13	12 18	12 23	12 25	12 28	12 33	12 38	12 40	12 43		12 48	12 53
Haggerston	d	11 39		11 41	11 43	11 49	11 54	11 56	11 59	12 04	12 09	12 11		12 14	12 19	12 24	12 26	12 29	12 34	12 39	12 41	12 44		12 49	12 54
Hoxton	d	11 41		11 43	11 45	11 51	11 56	11 58	12 01	12 06	12 11	12 13		12 16	12 21	12 26	12 28	12 31	12 36	12 41	12 43	12 46		12 51	12 56
Shoreditch High Street	d	11 44		11 46	11 48	11 54	11 59	12 01	12 04	12 09	12 14	12 16		12 19	12 24	12 29	12 31	12 34	12 39	12 44	12 46	12 49		12 54	12 59
Whitechapel	d	11 46		11 48	11 50	11 56	12 01	12 03	12 06	12 11	12 16	12 18		12 21	12 26	12 31	12 33	12 36	12 41	12 46	12 48	12 51		12 56	13 01
Shadwell	d	11 48		11 50	11 52	11 58	12 03	12 05	12 08	12 13	12 18	12 20		12 23	12 28	12 33	12 35	12 38	12 43	12 48	12 50	12 53		12 58	13 03
Wapping	d	11 50		11 52	11 54	12 00	12 05	12 07	12 10	12 15	12 20	12 22		12 25	12 30	12 35	12 37	12 40	12 45	12 50	12 52	12 55		13 00	13 05
Rotherhithe	d	11 52		11 54	11 56	12 02	12 07	12 09	12 12	12 17	12 22	12 24		12 27	12 32	12 37	12 39	12 42	12 47	12 52	12 54	12 57		13 02	13 07
Canada Water	d	11 54		11 56	11 58	12 04	12 09	12 11	12 14	12 19	12 24	12 26		12 29	12 34	12 39	12 41	12 44	12 49	12 54	12 56	12 59		13 04	13 09
Surrey Quays	d	11 56		11 58	12 00	12 06	12 11	12 13	12 16	12 21	12 26	12 28		12 31	12 36	12 41	12 43	12 46	12 51	12 56	12 58	13 01		13 06	13 11
New Cross	a	12 00					12 15				12 30					12 45				13 00					13 15
New Cross Gate	d				12 04	12 10			12 20	12 25				12 35	12 40			12 50	12 55			13 05		13 10	
Brockley	d				12 07	12 13			12 23	12 28				12 38	12 43			12 53	12 58			13 08		13 13	
Honor Oak Park	d				12 09	12 15			12 25	12 30				12 40	12 45			12 55	13 00			13 10		13 15	
Forest Hill	d				12 12	12 18			12 28	12 33				12 43	12 48			12 58	13 03			13 13		13 18	
Sydenham	d				12 15	12 21			12 31	12 36				12 46	12 51			13 01	13 06			13 16		13 21	
Crystal Palace	a					12 25				12 40					12 55				13 11					13 26	
Penge West	d				12 17				12 33					12 48				13 03				13 18			
Anerley	d				12 19				12 35					12 50				13 05				13 20			
Norwood Junction	d				12 22				12 38					12 53				13 08				13 23			
West Croydon	a				12 29				12 45					13 00				13 14				13 30			
Queens Rd Peckham	d			12 02				12 17				12 32					12 47				13 02				
Peckham Rye	d			12 06				12 20				12 36					12 50				13 06				
Denmark Hill	d			12 08				12 22				12 38					12 53				13 08				
Clapham High Street ⊖	d			12 13				12 27				12 43					12 57				13 13				
Wandsworth Road	d			12 14				12 28				12 44					12 59				13 14				
Clapham Junction	a			12 26				12 41				12 56					13 11				13 26				

		LO	LO	LO	LO	LO	LO	LO		LO	LO	LO	LO	LO	LO	LO	LO	LO		LO	LO	LO	LO	LO	LO
Highbury & Islington	d	12 50		12 58		13 05		13 13			13 20		13 28		13 35		13 43			13 50		13 58		14 05	
Canonbury	d	12 52		13 00		13 07		13 15			13 22		13 30		13 37		13 45			13 52		14 00		14 07	
Dalston Junction	d	12 55	12 58	13 03	13 07	13 10	13 13	13 18		13 22	13 25	13 28	13 33	13 37	13 40	13 43	13 48	13 52		13 55	13 58	14 03	14 07	14 10	14 13
Haggerston	d	12 56	12 59	13 04	13 08	13 11	13 14	13 19		13 23	13 26	13 29	13 34	13 38	13 41	13 44	13 49	13 53		13 56	13 59	14 04	14 08	14 11	14 14
Hoxton	d	12 58	13 01	13 06	13 10	13 13	13 16	13 21		13 25	13 28	13 31	13 36	13 40	13 43	13 46	13 51	13 55		13 58	14 01	14 06	14 10	14 13	14 16
Shoreditch High Street	d	13 01	13 04	13 09	13 13	13 16	13 19	13 24		13 28	13 31	13 34	13 39	13 43	13 46	13 49	13 54	13 58		14 01	14 04	14 09	14 13	14 16	14 19
Whitechapel	d	13 03	13 06	13 11	13 15	13 18	13 21	13 26		13 30	13 33	13 36	13 41	13 45	13 48	13 51	13 56	14 00		14 03	14 06	14 11	14 15	14 18	14 21
Shadwell	d	13 05	13 08	13 13	13 17	13 20	13 23	13 28		13 32	13 35	13 38	13 43	13 47	13 50	13 53	13 58	14 02		14 05	14 08	14 13	14 17	14 20	14 23
Wapping	d	13 07	13 10	13 15	13 19	13 22	13 25	13 30		13 34	13 37	13 40	13 45	13 49	13 52	13 55	14 00	14 04		14 07	14 10	14 15	14 19	14 22	14 25
Rotherhithe	d	13 09	13 12	13 17	13 21	13 24	13 27	13 32		13 36	13 39	13 42	13 47	13 51	13 54	13 57	14 02	14 06		14 09	14 12	14 17	14 21	14 24	14 27
Canada Water	d	13 11	13 14	13 19	13 23	13 26	13 29	13 34		13 38	13 41	13 44	13 49	13 53	13 56	13 59	14 04	14 08		14 11	14 14	14 19	14 23	14 26	14 29
Surrey Quays	d	13 13	13 16	13 21	13 25	13 28	13 31	13 36		13 40	13 43	13 46	13 51	13 55	13 58	14 01	14 06	14 10		14 13	14 16	14 21	14 25	14 28	14 31
New Cross	a				13 29					13 44				13 59				14 14					14 29		
New Cross Gate	d		13 20	13 25			13 35	13 40				13 50	13 55			14 05	14 10				14 20	14 25			14 35
Brockley	d		13 23	13 28			13 38	13 43				13 53	13 58			14 08	14 13				14 23	14 28			14 38
Honor Oak Park	d		13 25	13 30			13 40	13 45				13 55	14 00			14 10	14 15				14 25	14 30			14 40
Forest Hill	d		13 28	13 33			13 43	13 48				13 58	14 03			14 13	14 18				14 28	14 33			14 43
Sydenham	d		13 31	13 36			13 46	13 51				14 01	14 06			14 16	14 21				14 31	14 36			14 46
Crystal Palace	a			13 41				13 56					14 11				14 26					14 41			
Penge West	d		13 33				13 48					14 03				14 18					14 33				14 48
Anerley	d		13 35				13 50					14 05				14 20					14 35				14 50
Norwood Junction	d		13 38				13 53					14 08				14 23					14 38				14 53
West Croydon	a		13 44				13 59					14 14				14 29					14 44				14 59
Queens Rd Peckham	d	13 17				13 32					13 47				14 02					14 17				14 32	
Peckham Rye	d	13 21				13 36					13 50				14 06					14 20				14 36	
Denmark Hill	d	13 23				13 38					13 53				14 08					14 23				14 38	
Clapham High Street ⊖	d	13 28				13 43					13 57				14 13					14 27				14 43	
Wandsworth Road	d	13 29				13 44					13 59				14 14					14 29				14 44	
Clapham Junction	a	13 41				13 56					14 11				14 26					14 41				14 56	

Table T178-F

Sundays

20 May to 2 December

Highbury & Islington - New Cross, Crystal Palace, West Croydon and Clapham Junction

		LO	LO	LO		LO	LO	LO	LO	LO	LO	LO	LO	LO		LO	LO	LO	LO	LO	LO	LO	LO	LO	
Highbury & Islington	d	14 13		14 20			14 28		14 35		14 43		14 50			14 58		15 05		15 13		15 20		15 28	
Canonbury	d	14 15		14 22			14 30		14 37		14 45		14 52			15 00		15 07		15 15		15 22		15 30	
Dalston Junction	d	14 18	14 22	14 25		14 28	14 33	14 37	14 40	14 43	14 48	14 52	14 55	14 58		15 03	15 07	15 10	15 13	15 18	15 22	15 25	15 28	15 33	
Haggerston	d	14 19	14 23	14 26		14 29	14 34	14 38	14 41	14 44	14 49	14 53	14 56	14 59		15 04	15 08	15 11	15 14	15 19	15 23	15 26	15 29	15 34	
Hoxton	d	14 21	14 25	14 28		14 31	14 36	14 40	14 43	14 46	14 51	14 55	14 58	15 01		15 06	15 10	15 13	15 16	15 21	15 25	15 28	15 31	15 36	
Shoreditch High Street	d	14 24	14 28	14 31		14 34	14 39	14 43	14 46	14 49	14 54	14 58	15 01	15 04		15 09	15 13	15 16	15 19	15 24	15 28	15 31	15 34	15 39	
Whitechapel	d	14 26	14 30	14 33		14 36	14 41	14 45	14 48	14 51	14 56	15 00	15 03	15 06		15 11	15 15	15 18	15 21	15 26	15 30	15 33	15 36	15 41	
Shadwell	d	14 28	14 32	14 35		14 38	14 43	14 47	14 50	14 53	14 58	15 02	15 05	15 08		15 13	15 17	15 20	15 23	15 28	15 32	15 35	15 38	15 43	
Wapping	d	14 30	14 34	14 37		14 40	14 45	14 49	14 52	14 55	15 00	15 04	15 07	15 10		15 15	15 19	15 22	15 25	15 30	15 34	15 37	15 40	15 45	
Rotherhithe	d	14 32	14 36	14 39		14 42	14 47	14 51	14 54	14 57	15 02	15 06	15 09	15 12		15 17	15 21	15 24	15 27	15 32	15 36	15 39	15 42	15 47	
Canada Water	d	14 34	14 38	14 41		14 44	14 49	14 53	14 56	14 59	15 04	15 08	15 11	15 14		15 19	15 23	15 26	15 29	15 34	15 38	15 41	15 44	15 49	
Surrey Quays	d	14 36	14 40	14 43		14 46	14 51	14 55	14 58	15 01	15 06	15 10	15 13	15 16		15 21	15 25	15 28	15 31	15 36	15 40	15 43	15 46	15 51	
New Cross	a		14 44					14 59				15 14					15 29				15 44				
New Cross Gate	d	14 40				14 50	14 55			15 05	15 10			15 20		15 25			15 35	15 40			15 50	15 55	
Brockley	d	14 43				14 53	14 58			15 08	15 13			15 23		15 28			15 38	15 43			15 53	15 58	
Honor Oak Park	d	14 45				14 55	15 00			15 10	15 15			15 25		15 30			15 40	15 45			15 55	16 00	
Forest Hill	d	14 48				14 58	15 03			15 13	15 18			15 28		15 33			15 43	15 48			15 58	16 03	
Sydenham	d	14 51				15 01	15 06			15 16	15 21			15 31		15 36			15 46	15 51			16 01	16 06	
Crystal Palace	a	14 56					15 11				15 26					15 41				15 56				16 11	
Penge West	d					15 03				15 18				15 33					15 48				16 03		
Anerley	d					15 05				15 20				15 35					15 50				16 05		
Norwood Junction	d					15 08				15 23				15 38					15 53				16 08		
West Croydon	a					15 14				15 29				15 44					15 59				16 14		
Queens Rd Peckham	d			14 47					15 02				15 17					15 32				15 47			
Peckham Rye	d			14 50					15 06				15 20					15 36				15 50			
Denmark Hill	d			14 53					15 08				15 23					15 38				15 53			
Clapham High Street ⊖	d			14 57					15 13				15 27					15 43				15 57			
Wandsworth Road	d			14 59					15 14				15 29					15 44				15 59			
Clapham Junction	a			15 11					15 26				15 41					15 56				16 11			

		LO	LO	LO	LO	LO	LO	LO	LO	LO		LO	LO	LO	LO	LO	LO	LO	LO	LO		LO	LO	LO	LO
Highbury & Islington	d		15 35		15 43		15 50		15 58			16 05		16 13		16 20		16 28		16 35			16 43		16 50
Canonbury	d		15 37		15 45		15 52		16 00			16 07		16 15		16 22		16 30		16 37			16 45		16 52
Dalston Junction	d	15 37	15 40	15 43	15 48	15 52	15 55	15 58	16 03	16 07		16 10	16 13	16 18	16 22	16 25	16 28	16 33	16 37	16 40		16 43	16 48	16 52	16 55
Haggerston	d	15 38	15 41	15 44	15 49	15 53	15 56	15 59	16 04	16 08		16 11	16 14	16 19	16 23	16 26	16 29	16 34	16 38	16 41		16 44	16 49	16 53	16 56
Hoxton	d	15 40	15 43	15 46	15 51	15 55	15 58	16 01	16 06	16 10		16 13	16 16	16 21	16 25	16 28	16 31	16 36	16 40	16 43		16 46	16 51	16 55	16 58
Shoreditch High Street	d	15 43	15 46	15 49	15 54	15 58	16 01	16 04	16 09	16 13		16 16	16 19	16 24	16 28	16 31	16 34	16 39	16 43	16 46		16 49	16 54	16 58	17 01
Whitechapel	d	15 45	15 48	15 51	15 56	16 00	16 03	16 06	16 11	16 15		16 18	16 21	16 26	16 30	16 33	16 36	16 41	16 45	16 48		16 51	16 56	17 00	17 03
Shadwell	d	15 47	15 50	15 53	15 58	16 02	16 05	16 08	16 13	16 17		16 20	16 23	16 28	16 32	16 35	16 38	16 43	16 47	16 50		16 53	16 58	17 02	17 05
Wapping	d	15 49	15 52	15 55	16 00	16 04	16 07	16 10	16 15	16 19		16 22	16 25	16 30	16 34	16 37	16 40	16 45	16 49	16 52		16 55	17 00	17 04	17 07
Rotherhithe	d	15 51	15 54	15 57	16 02	16 06	16 09	16 12	16 17	16 21		16 24	16 27	16 32	16 36	16 39	16 42	16 47	16 51	16 54		16 57	17 02	17 06	17 09
Canada Water	d	15 53	15 56	15 59	16 04	16 08	16 11	16 14	16 19	16 23		16 26	16 29	16 34	16 38	16 41	16 44	16 49	16 53	16 56		16 59	17 04	17 08	17 11
Surrey Quays	d	15 55	15 58	16 01	16 06	16 10	16 13	16 16	16 21	16 25		16 28	16 31	16 36	16 40	16 43	16 46	16 51	16 55	16 58		17 01	17 06	17 10	17 13
New Cross	a	15 59				16 14				16 29					16 44				16 59					17 14	
New Cross Gate	d			16 05	16 10			16 20	16 25				16 35	16 40			16 50	16 55				17 05	17 10		
Brockley	d			16 08	16 13			16 23	16 28				16 38	16 43			16 53	16 58				17 08	17 13		
Honor Oak Park	d			16 10	16 15			16 25	16 30				16 40	16 45			16 55	17 00				17 10	17 15		
Forest Hill	d			16 13	16 18			16 28	16 33				16 43	16 48			16 58	17 03				17 13	17 18		
Sydenham	d			16 16	16 21			16 31	16 36				16 46	16 51			17 01	17 06				17 16	17 21		
Crystal Palace	a				16 26				16 41					16 56				17 11					17 26		
Penge West	d			16 18				16 33					16 48				17 03					17 18			
Anerley	d			16 20				16 35					16 50				17 05					17 20			
Norwood Junction	d			16 23				16 38					16 53				17 08					17 23			
West Croydon	a			16 29				16 44					16 59				17 15					17 30			
Queens Rd Peckham	d		16 02				16 17					16 32				16 47				17 02					17 17
Peckham Rye	d		16 06				16 20					16 36				16 50				17 06					17 20
Denmark Hill	d		16 08				16 23					16 38				16 53				17 08					17 23
Clapham High Street ⊖	d		16 13				16 27					16 43				16 57				17 13					17 27
Wandsworth Road	d		16 14				16 29					16 44				16 59				17 14					17 29
Clapham Junction	a		16 26				16 41					16 56				17 11				17 26					17 41

		LO	LO	LO	LO	LO		LO	LO	LO	LO	LO	LO	LO	LO	LO		LO	LO	LO	LO	LO	LO	LO	LO
Highbury & Islington	d		16 58		17 05			17 13		17 20		17 28		17 35		17 43			17 50		17 58		18 05		18 13
Canonbury	d		17 00		17 07			17 15		17 22		17 30		17 37		17 45			17 52		18 00		18 07		18 15
Dalston Junction	d	16 58	17 03	17 07	17 10	17 13		17 18	17 22	17 25	17 28	17 33	17 37	17 40	17 43	17 48		17 52	17 55	17 58	18 03	18 07	18 10	18 13	18 18
Haggerston	d	16 59	17 04	17 08	17 11	17 14		17 19	17 23	17 26	17 29	17 34	17 38	17 41	17 44	17 49		17 53	17 56	17 59	18 04	18 08	18 11	18 14	18 19
Hoxton	d	17 01	17 06	17 10	17 13	17 16		17 21	17 25	17 28	17 31	17 36	17 40	17 43	17 46	17 51		17 55	17 58	18 01	18 06	18 10	18 13	18 16	18 21
Shoreditch High Street	d	17 04	17 09	17 13	17 16	17 19		17 24	17 28	17 31	17 34	17 39	17 43	17 46	17 49	17 54		17 58	18 01	18 04	18 09	18 13	18 16	18 19	18 24
Whitechapel	d	17 06	17 11	17 15	17 18	17 21		17 26	17 30	17 33	17 36	17 41	17 45	17 48	17 51	17 56		18 00	18 03	18 06	18 11	18 15	18 18	18 21	18 26
Shadwell	d	17 08	17 13	17 17	17 20	17 23		17 28	17 32	17 35	17 38	17 43	17 47	17 50	17 53	17 58		18 02	18 05	18 08	18 13	18 17	18 20	18 23	18 28
Wapping	d	17 10	17 15	17 19	17 22	17 25		17 30	17 34	17 37	17 40	17 45	17 49	17 52	17 55	18 00		18 04	18 07	18 10	18 15	18 19	18 22	18 25	18 30
Rotherhithe	d	17 12	17 17	17 21	17 24	17 27		17 32	17 36	17 39	17 42	17 47	17 51	17 54	17 57	18 02		18 06	18 09	18 12	18 17	18 21	18 24	18 27	18 32
Canada Water	d	17 14	17 19	17 23	17 26	17 29		17 34	17 38	17 41	17 44	17 49	17 53	17 56	17 59	18 04		18 08	18 11	18 14	18 19	18 23	18 26	18 29	18 34
Surrey Quays	d	17 16	17 21	17 25	17 28	17 31		17 36	17 40	17 43	17 46	17 51	17 55	17 58	18 01	18 06		18 10	18 13	18 16	18 21	18 25	18 28	18 31	18 36
New Cross	a			17 29					17 44				17 59					18 14				18 29			
New Cross Gate	d	17 20	17 25			17 35		17 40			17 50	17 55			18 05	18 10				18 20	18 25			18 35	18 40
Brockley	d	17 23	17 28			17 38		17 43			17 53	17 58			18 08	18 13				18 23	18 28			18 38	18 43
Honor Oak Park	d	17 25	17 30			17 40		17 45			17 55	18 00			18 10	18 15				18 25	18 30			18 40	18 45
Forest Hill	d	17 28	17 33			17 43		17 48			17 58	18 03			18 13	18 18				18 28	18 33			18 43	18 48
Sydenham	d	17 31	17 36			17 46		17 51			18 01	18 06			18 16	18 21				18 31	18 36			18 46	18 51
Crystal Palace	a		17 41					17 56				18 11				18 26					18 41				18 56
Penge West	d	17 33				17 48					18 03				18 18					18 33				18 48	
Anerley	d	17 35				17 50					18 05				18 20					18 35				18 50	
Norwood Junction	d	17 38				17 53					18 08				18 23					18 38				18 53	
West Croydon	a	17 45				18 00					18 15				18 30					18 45				19 00	
Queens Rd Peckham	d				17 32					17 47				18 02					18 17				18 32		
Peckham Rye	d				17 36					17 50				18 06					18 20				18 36		
Denmark Hill	d				17 38					17 53				18 08					18 23				18 38		
Clapham High Street ⊖	d				17 43					17 57				18 13					18 27				18 43		
Wandsworth Road	d				17 44					17 59				18 14					18 29				18 44		
Clapham Junction	a				17 56					18 11				18 26					18 41				18 56		

Table T178-F

Sundays

20 May to 2 December

Highbury & Islington - New Cross, Crystal Palace, West Croydon and Clapham Junction

		LO	LO	LO	LO	LO	LO	LO	LO	LO	LO	LO	LO	LO	LO	LO	LO	LO	LO	LO	LO	LO
Highbury & Islington	d		18 20		18 28		18 35		18 43		18 50		18 58		19 05		19 13		19 20		19 28	
Canonbury	d		18 22		18 30		18 37		18 45		18 52		19 00		19 07		19 15		19 22		19 30	
Dalston Junction	d	18 22	18 25	18 28	18 33	18 37	18 40	18 43	18 48	18 52	18 55	18 58	19 03	19 07	19 10	19 13	19 18	19 22	19 25	19 28	19 33	19 37
Haggerston	d	18 23	18 26	18 29	18 34	18 38	18 41	18 44	18 49	18 53	18 56	18 59	19 04	19 08	19 11	19 14	19 19	19 23	19 26	19 29	19 34	19 38
Hoxton	d	18 25	18 28	18 31	18 36	18 40	18 43	18 46	18 51	18 55	18 58	19 01	19 06	19 10	19 13	19 16	19 21	19 25	19 28	19 31	19 36	19 40
Shoreditch High Street	d	18 28	18 31	18 34	18 39	18 43	18 46	18 49	18 54	18 58	19 01	19 04	19 09	19 13	19 16	19 19	19 24	19 28	19 31	19 34	19 39	19 43
Whitechapel	d	18 30	18 33	18 36	18 41	18 45	18 48	18 51	18 56	19 00	19 03	19 06	19 11	19 15	19 18	19 21	19 26	19 30	19 33	19 36	19 41	19 45
Shadwell	d	18 32	18 35	18 38	18 43	18 47	18 50	18 53	18 58	19 02	19 05	19 08	19 13	19 17	19 20	19 23	19 28	19 32	19 35	19 38	19 43	19 47
Wapping	d	18 34	18 37	18 40	18 45	18 49	18 52	18 55	19 00	19 04	19 07	19 10	19 15	19 19	19 22	19 25	19 30	19 34	19 37	19 40	19 45	19 49
Rotherhithe	d	18 36	18 39	18 42	18 47	18 51	18 54	18 57	19 02	19 06	19 09	19 12	19 17	19 21	19 24	19 27	19 32	19 36	19 39	19 42	19 47	19 51
Canada Water	d	18 38	18 41	18 44	18 49	18 53	18 56	18 59	19 04	19 08	19 11	19 14	19 19	19 23	19 26	19 29	19 34	19 38	19 41	19 44	19 49	19 53
Surrey Quays	d	18 40	18 43	18 46	18 51	18 55	18 58	19 01	19 06	19 10	19 13	19 16	19 21	19 25	19 28	19 31	19 36	19 40	19 43	19 46	19 51	19 55
New Cross	a	18 44				18 59				19 14				19 29				19 44				19 59
New Cross Gate	d			18 50	18 55			19 05	19 10			19 20	19 25			19 35	19 40			19 50	19 55	
Brockley	d			18 53	18 58			19 08	19 13			19 23	19 28			19 38	19 43			19 53	19 58	
Honor Oak Park	d			18 55	19 00			19 10	19 15			19 25	19 30			19 40	19 45			19 55	20 00	
Forest Hill	d			18 58	19 03			19 13	19 18			19 28	19 33			19 43	19 48			19 58	20 03	
Sydenham	d			19 01	19 06			19 16	19 21			19 31	19 36			19 46	19 51			20 01	20 06	
Crystal Palace	a				19 11				19 26				19 41				19 56				20 11	
Penge West	d			19 03				19 18				19 33				19 48				20 03		
Anerley	d			19 05				19 20				19 35				19 50				20 05		
Norwood Junction	d			19 08				19 23				19 38				19 53				20 08		
West Croydon	a			19 15				19 29				19 44				19 59				20 14		
Queens Rd Peckham	d		18 47				19 02				19 17				19 32				19 47			
Peckham Rye	d		18 50				19 06				19 20				19 36				19 50			
Denmark Hill	d		18 53				19 08				19 23				19 38				19 53			
Clapham High Street ⊖	d		18 57				19 13				19 27				19 43				19 57			
Wandsworth Road	d		18 59				19 14				19 29				19 44				19 59			
Clapham Junction	a		19 11				19 26				19 41				19 56				20 11			

		LO	LO	LO	LO	LO	LO	LO	LO	LO	LO	LO	LO	LO	LO	LO	LO	LO	LO	LO	LO	LO	LO
Highbury & Islington	d	19 35		19 43		19 50		19 58		20 05		20 13		20 20		20 28		20 35		20 43		20 50	
Canonbury	d	19 37		19 45		19 52		20 00		20 07		20 15		20 22		20 30		20 37		20 45		20 52	
Dalston Junction	d	19 40	19 43	19 48	19 52	19 55	19 58	20 03	20 07	20 10	20 13	20 18	20 22	20 25	20 28	20 33	20 37	20 40	20 43	20 48	20 52	20 55	20 58
Haggerston	d	19 41	19 44	19 49	19 53	19 56	19 59	20 04	20 08	20 11	20 14	20 19	20 23	20 26	20 29	20 34	20 38	20 41	20 44	20 49	20 53	20 56	20 59
Hoxton	d	19 43	19 46	19 51	19 55	19 58	20 01	20 06	20 10	20 13	20 16	20 21	20 25	20 28	20 31	20 36	20 40	20 43	20 46	20 51	20 55	20 58	21 01
Shoreditch High Street	d	19 46	19 49	19 54	19 58	20 01	20 04	20 09	20 13	20 16	20 19	20 24	20 28	20 31	20 34	20 39	20 43	20 46	20 49	20 54	20 58	21 01	21 04
Whitechapel	d	19 48	19 51	19 56	20 00	20 03	20 06	20 11	20 15	20 18	20 21	20 26	20 30	20 33	20 36	20 41	20 45	20 48	20 51	20 56	21 00	21 03	21 06
Shadwell	d	19 50	19 53	19 58	20 02	20 05	20 08	20 13	20 17	20 20	20 23	20 28	20 32	20 35	20 38	20 43	20 47	20 50	20 53	20 58	21 02	21 05	21 08
Wapping	d	19 52	19 55	20 00	20 04	20 07	20 10	20 15	20 19	20 22	20 25	20 30	20 34	20 37	20 40	20 45	20 49	20 52	20 55	21 00	21 04	21 07	21 10
Rotherhithe	d	19 54	19 57	20 02	20 06	20 09	20 12	20 17	20 21	20 24	20 27	20 32	20 36	20 39	20 42	20 47	20 51	20 54	20 57	21 02	21 06	21 09	21 12
Canada Water	d	19 56	19 59	20 04	20 08	20 11	20 14	20 19	20 23	20 26	20 29	20 34	20 38	20 41	20 44	20 49	20 53	20 56	20 59	21 04	21 08	21 11	21 14
Surrey Quays	d	19 58	20 01	20 06	20 10	20 13	20 16	20 21	20 25	20 28	20 31	20 36	20 40	20 43	20 46	20 51	20 55	20 58	21 01	21 06	21 10	21 13	21 16
New Cross	a				20 14				20 29				20 44				20 59				21 14		
New Cross Gate	d		20 05	20 10			20 20	20 25			20 35	20 40			20 50	20 55			21 05	21 10			21 20
Brockley	d		20 08	20 13			20 23	20 28			20 38	20 43			20 53	20 58			21 08	21 13			21 23
Honor Oak Park	d		20 10	20 15			20 25	20 30			20 40	20 45			20 55	21 00			21 10	21 15			21 25
Forest Hill	d		20 13	20 18			20 28	20 33			20 43	20 48			20 58	21 03			21 13	21 18			21 28
Sydenham	d		20 16	20 21			20 31	20 36			20 46	20 51			21 01	21 06			21 16	21 21			21 31
Crystal Palace	a			20 26				20 41				20 56				21 11				21 26			
Penge West	d		20 18				20 33				20 48				21 03				21 18				21 33
Anerley	d		20 20				20 35				20 50				21 05				21 20				21 35
Norwood Junction	d		20 23				20 38				20 53				21 08				21 23				21 38
West Croydon	a		20 29				20 44				20 59				21 14				21 29				21 44
Queens Rd Peckham	d	20 02				20 17				20 32				20 47				21 02				21 17	
Peckham Rye	d	20 06				20 20				20 36				20 50				21 06				21 20	
Denmark Hill	d	20 08				20 23				20 38				20 53				21 08				21 23	
Clapham High Street ⊖	d	20 13				20 27				20 43				20 57				21 13				21 27	
Wandsworth Road	d	20 14				20 29				20 44				20 59				21 14				21 29	
Clapham Junction	a	20 26				20 41				20 56				21 11				21 26				21 40	

		LO	LO	LO	LO	LO	LO	LO	LO	LO	LO	LO	LO	LO	LO	LO	LO	LO	LO	LO	LO	LO
Highbury & Islington	d	20 58		21 05		21 13		21 20		21 28		21 35		21 43		21 50		21 58		22 05		22 13
Canonbury	d	21 00		21 07		21 15		21 22		21 30		21 37		21 45		21 52		22 00		22 07		22 15
Dalston Junction	d	21 03	21 07	21 10	21 13	21 18	21 22	21 25	21 28	21 33	21 37	21 40	21 43	21 48	21 52	21 55	21 58	22 03	22 07	22 10	22 13	22 18
Haggerston	d	21 04	21 08	21 11	21 14	21 19	21 23	21 26	21 29	21 34	21 38	21 41	21 44	21 49	21 53	21 56	21 59	22 04	22 08	22 11	22 14	22 19
Hoxton	d	21 06	21 10	21 13	21 16	21 21	21 25	21 28	21 31	21 36	21 40	21 43	21 46	21 51	21 55	21 58	22 01	22 06	22 10	22 13	22 16	22 21
Shoreditch High Street	d	21 09	21 13	21 16	21 19	21 24	21 28	21 31	21 34	21 39	21 43	21 46	21 49	21 54	21 58	22 01	22 04	22 09	22 13	22 16	22 19	22 24
Whitechapel	d	21 11	21 15	21 18	21 21	21 26	21 30	21 33	21 36	21 41	21 45	21 48	21 51	21 56	22 00	22 03	22 06	22 11	22 15	22 18	22 21	22 26
Shadwell	d	21 13	21 17	21 20	21 23	21 28	21 32	21 35	21 38	21 43	21 47	21 50	21 53	21 58	22 02	22 05	22 08	22 13	22 17	22 20	22 23	22 28
Wapping	d	21 15	21 19	21 22	21 25	21 30	21 34	21 37	21 40	21 45	21 49	21 52	21 55	22 00	22 04	22 07	22 10	22 15	22 19	22 22	22 25	22 30
Rotherhithe	d	21 17	21 21	21 24	21 27	21 32	21 36	21 39	21 42	21 47	21 51	21 54	21 57	22 02	22 06	22 09	22 12	22 17	22 21	22 24	22 27	22 32
Canada Water	d	21 19	21 23	21 26	21 29	21 34	21 38	21 41	21 44	21 49	21 53	21 56	21 59	22 04	22 08	22 11	22 14	22 19	22 23	22 26	22 29	22 34
Surrey Quays	d	21 21	21 25	21 28	21 31	21 36	21 40	21 43	21 46	21 51	21 55	21 58	22 01	22 06	22 10	22 13	22 16	22 21	22 25	22 28	22 31	22 36
New Cross	a		21 29				21 44				21 59				22 14				22 29			
New Cross Gate	d	21 25			21 35	21 40			21 50	21 55			22 05	22 10			22 20	22 25			22 35	22 40
Brockley	d	21 28			21 38	21 43			21 53	21 58			22 08	22 13			22 23	22 28			22 38	22 43
Honor Oak Park	d	21 30			21 40	21 45			21 55	22 00			22 10	22 15			22 25	22 30			22 40	22 45
Forest Hill	d	21 33			21 43	21 48			21 58	22 03			22 13	22 18			22 28	22 33			22 43	22 48
Sydenham	d	21 36			21 46	21 51			22 01	22 06			22 16	22 21			22 31	22 36			22 46	22 51
Crystal Palace	a	21 41				21 56				22 11				22 26				22 41				22 56
Penge West	d				21 48				22 03				22 18				22 33				22 48	
Anerley	d				21 50				22 05				22 20				22 35				22 50	
Norwood Junction	d				21 53				22 08				22 23				22 38				22 53	
West Croydon	a				21 59				22 14				22 29				22 44				22 59	
Queens Rd Peckham	d			21 32				21 47				22 02				22 17				22 32		
Peckham Rye	d			21 36				21 50				22 06				22 20				22 36		
Denmark Hill	d			21 38				21 53				22 08				22 23				22 38		
Clapham High Street ⊖	d			21 43				21 57				22 13				22 27				22 43		
Wandsworth Road	d			21 44				21 59				22 14				22 29				22 44		
Clapham Junction	a			21 56				22 11				22 26				22 41				22 56		

Table T178-F

Sundays

20 May to 2 December

Highbury & Islington - New Cross, Crystal Palace, West Croydon and Clapham Junction

		LO	LO	LO	LO	LO	LO	LO	LO	LO	LO	LO	LO	LO	LO	LO
Highbury & Islington	d		22 20			22 35		22 43		22 50			23 05		23 13	23 23
Canonbury	d		22 22			22 37		22 45		22 52			23 07		23 15	23 25
Dalston Junction	d	22 22	22 25	22 28	22 37	22 40	22 43	22 48	22 52	22 55	22 58	23 07	23 10	23 13	23 18	23 28
Haggerston	d	22 23	22 26	22 29	22 38	22 41	22 44	22 49	22 53	22 56	22 59	23 08	23 11	23 14	23 19	23 29
Hoxton	d	22 25	22 28	22 31	22 40	22 43	22 46	22 51	22 55	22 58	23 01	23 10	23 13	23 16	23 21	23 31
Shoreditch High Street	d	22 28	22 31	22 34	22 43	22 46	22 49	22 54	22 58	23 01	23 04	23 13	23 16	23 19	23 24	23 34
Whitechapel	d	22 30	22 33	22 36	22 45	22 48	22 51	22 56	23 00	23 03	23 06	23 15	23 18	23 21	23 26	23 36
Shadwell	d	22 32	22 35	22 38	22 47	22 50	22 53	22 58	23 02	23 05	23 08	23 17	23 20	23 23	23 28	23 38
Wapping	d	22 34	22 37	22 40	22 49	22 52	22 55	23 00	23 04	23 07	23 10	23 19	23 22	23 25	23 30	23 40
Rotherhithe	d	22 36	22 39	22 42	22 51	22 54	22 57	23 02	23 06	23 09	23 12	23 21	23 24	23 27	23 32	23 42
Canada Water	d	22 38	22 41	22 44	22 53	22 56	22 59	23 04	23 08	23 11	23 14	23 23	23 26	23 29	23 34	23 44
Surrey Quays	d	22 40	22 43	22 46	22 55	22 58	23 01	23 06	23 10	23 13	23 16	23 25	23 28	23 31	23 36	23 46
New Cross	a	22 44			22 59				23 14			23 29				
New Cross Gate	d			22 50			23 05	23 10			23 20			23 35	23 42	23 50
Brockley	d			22 53			23 08	23 13			23 23			23 38	23 45	23 53
Honor Oak Park	d			22 55			23 10	23 15			23 25			23 40	23 47	23 55
Forest Hill	d			22 58			23 13	23 18			23 28			23 43	23 50	23 58
Sydenham	d			23 01			23 16	23 21			23 31			23 46	23 53	00 01
Crystal Palace	a							23 26							23 57	
Penge West	d			23 03			23 18				23 33			23 48		00 03
Anerley	d			23 05			23 20				23 35			23 50		00 05
Norwood Junction	d			23 08			23 23				23 38			23 53		00 08
West Croydon	a			23 14			23 29				23 45			23 59		00 16
Queens Rd Peckham	d		22 47			23 02				23 17			23 32			
Peckham Rye	d		22 50			23 06				23 20			23 36			
Denmark Hill	d		22 53			23 08				23 23			23 38			
Clapham High Street ⊖	d		22 57			23 13				23 27			23 43			
Wandsworth Road	d		22 59			23 14				23 29			23 44			
Clapham Junction	a		23 11			23 26				23 41			23 56			

Clapham Junction and West Croydon, Crystal Palace, New Cross - Highbury & Islington

Miles	Miles	Miles	Miles			LO MX A	LO MX B	LO MX C	LO MX D	LO MX C	LO MX B	LO	LO	LO	LO	LO	LO	LO	LO	LO	LO	LO	LO
0	—	—	—	Clapham Junction	d														06 00				06 15
1½	—	—	—	**Wandsworth Road**	d														06 06				06 21
1¾	—	—	—	**Clapham High Street** ⊖	d														06 08				06 23
3¾	—	—	—	Denmark Hill	d														06 13				06 28
4¾	—	—	—	Peckham Rye	d														06 15				06 30
5¼	—	—	—	Queens Rd Peckham	d					00 01									06 17				06 32
—	—	0	—	West Croydon	d								05 31			05 46				06 01			
—	—	1¾	—	Norwood Junction	d								05 37			05 52				06 07			
—	—	2¾	—	Anerley	d								05 40			05 55				06 10			
—	—	3¼	—	Penge West	d								05 41			05 56				06 11			
—	0	—	—	Crystal Palace	d							05 32			05 47			06 02				06 17	
—	1¼	4	—	Sydenham	d							05 36	05 44		05 51	05 59		06 06		06 14		06 21	
—	2	4¾	—	Forest Hill	d							05 39	05 47		05 54	06 02		06 09		06 17		06 24	
—	3	5¾	—	Honor Oak Park	d							05 41	05 49		05 56	06 04		06 11		06 19		06 26	
—	4	6¾	—	Brockley	d						00 01	05 44	05 52		05 59	06 07		06 14		06 22		06 29	
—	4¾	7½	—	New Cross Gate	d						00 03	05 46	05 54		06 01	06 09		06 16		06 24		06 31	
—	—	—	0	New Cross	d									05 57			06 12				06 27		
6¾	6	8¾	1½	**Surrey Quays**	d					00 05	00 09	05 50	05 57	06 01	06 05	06 12	06 16	06 20	06 23	06 27	06 31	06 35	06 38
7	6¼	9¼	1¾	**Canada Water**	d					00 07	00 11	05 52	05 59	06 03	06 07	06 14	06 18	06 22	06 25	06 29	06 33	06 37	06 40
7¼	6½	9½	2	**Rotherhithe**	d				00 01	00 09	00 12	05 54	06 01	06 05	06 08	06 16	06 20	06 23	06 27	06 31	06 35	06 38	06 42
7¾	6¾	9¾	2¼	**Wapping**	d				00 02	00 10	00 14	05 55	06 02	06 06	06 10	06 17	06 21	06 25	06 28	06 32	06 36	06 40	06 43
8¼	7¼	10¼	2¾	**Shadwell**	d			00 01	00 04	00 12	00 16	05 57	06 04	06 08	06 12	06 19	06 23	06 27	06 30	06 34	06 38	06 42	06 45
9	8	11	3½	**Whitechapel**	d			00 03	00 07	00 15	00 18	06 00	06 07	06 11	06 14	06 22	06 26	06 29	06 33	06 37	06 41	06 44	06 48
9¾	8¾	11¾	4¼	**Shoreditch High Street**	d		00 02	00 05	00 09	00 17	00 21	06 02	06 09	06 13	06 17	06 24	06 28	06 32	06 35	06 39	06 43	06 47	06 50
10¼	9½	12¼	5	**Hoxton**	d	00 01	00 04	00 07	00 11	00 19	00 23	06 04	06 11	06 15	06 19	06 26	06 30	06 34	06 37	06 41	06 45	06 49	06 52
10¾	10	12¾	5½	**Haggerston**	d	00 02	00 06	00 09	00 13	00 21	00 25	06 06	06 13	06 17	06 21	06 28	06 32	06 36	06 39	06 43	06 47	06 51	06 54
11¼	10½	13¼	5¾	**Dalston Junction**	a	00 04	00 08	00 14	00 15	00 28	00 27	06 08	06 15	06 19	06 23	06 30	06 34	06 38	06 44	06 45	06 49	06 53	06 59
12¼	11½	—	—	Canonbury	a		00 11		00 18		00 30	06 11	06 18		06 26	06 33		06 41		06 48		06 56	
12¾	12	—	—	Highbury & Islington	a		00 15		00 25		00 33	06 15	06 23		06 30	06 38		06 45		06 53		07 00	

		LO	LO	LO	LO E	LO	LO	LO	LO	LO	LO	LO	LO	LO	LO	LO	LO	LO	LO	LO	LO	LO	LO
Clapham Junction	d								06 45				07 00				07 15				07 30		
Wandsworth Road	d				06 36				06 51				07 06				07 21				07 36		
Clapham High Street ⊖	d				06 38				06 53				07 08				07 23				07 38		
Denmark Hill	d				06 43				06 58				07 13				07 28				07 43		
Peckham Rye	d				06 45				07 00				07 15				07 30				07 45		
Queens Rd Peckham	d				06 47				07 02				07 17				07 32				07 47		
West Croydon	d	06 16				06 31				06 46				07 01				07 15				07 31	
Norwood Junction	d	06 22				06 37				06 52				07 07				07 22				07 37	
Anerley	d	06 25				06 40				06 55				07 10				07 25				07 40	
Penge West	d	06 26				06 41				06 56				07 11				07 26				07 42	
Crystal Palace	d			06 32				06 47				07 02				07 17				07 32			
Sydenham	d	06 29		06 36		06 44		06 51		06 59		07 06		07 14		07 21		07 29		07 36		07 44	
Forest Hill	d	06 32		06 39		06 47		06 54		07 02		07 09		07 17		07 24		07 32		07 39		07 47	
Honor Oak Park	d	06 34		06 41		06 49		06 56		07 04		07 11		07 19		07 26		07 34		07 41		07 49	
Brockley	d	06 37		06 44		06 52		06 59		07 07		07 14		07 22		07 29		07 37		07 44		07 52	
New Cross Gate	d	06 39		06 46		06 54		07 01		07 09		07 16		07 24		07 31		07 39		07 46		07 54	
New Cross	d		06 42				06 57				07 12				07 27				07 42				07 57
Surrey Quays	d	06 42	06 46	06 50	06 53	06 57	07 01	07 05	07 08	07 12	07 16	07 20	07 23	07 28	07 31	07 35	07 38	07 43	07 46	07 50	07 53	07 58	08 01
Canada Water	d	06 44	06 48	06 52	06 55	06 59	07 03	07 07	07 10	07 14	07 18	07 22	07 25	07 30	07 33	07 37	07 40	07 45	07 48	07 52	07 55	08 00	08 03
Rotherhithe	d	06 46	06 50	06 53	06 57	07 01	07 05	07 08	07 12	07 16	07 20	07 23	07 27	07 31	07 35	07 38	07 42	07 46	07 50	07 53	07 57	08 01	08 05
Wapping	d	06 47	06 51	06 55	06 58	07 02	07 06	07 10	07 13	07 17	07 21	07 25	07 28	07 33	07 36	07 40	07 43	07 48	07 51	07 55	07 58	08 03	08 06
Shadwell	d	06 49	06 53	06 57	07 00	07 04	07 08	07 12	07 15	07 19	07 23	07 27	07 30	07 35	07 38	07 42	07 45	07 50	07 53	07 57	08 00	08 05	08 08
Whitechapel	d	06 52	06 56	06 59	07 03	07 07	07 11	07 14	07 18	07 22	07 26	07 29	07 33	07 37	07 41	07 44	07 48	07 52	07 56	07 59	08 03	08 07	08 11
Shoreditch High Street	d	06 54	06 58	07 02	07 05	07 09	07 13	07 17	07 20	07 24	07 28	07 32	07 35	07 40	07 43	07 47	07 50	07 55	07 58	08 02	08 05	08 10	08 13
Hoxton	d	06 56	07 00	07 04	07 07	07 11	07 15	07 19	07 22	07 26	07 30	07 34	07 37	07 42	07 45	07 49	07 52	07 57	08 00	08 04	08 07	08 12	08 15
Haggerston	d	06 58	07 02	07 06	07 09	07 13	07 17	07 21	07 24	07 28	07 32	07 36	07 39	07 44	07 47	07 51	07 54	07 59	08 02	08 06	08 09	08 14	08 17
Dalston Junction	a	07 00	07 04	07 08	07 14	07 15	07 19	07 23	07 29	07 30	07 34	07 38	07 44	07 46	07 49	07 53	07 59	08 01	08 04	08 08	08 14	08 16	08 19
Canonbury	a	07 03		07 11		07 18		07 26		07 33		07 41		07 49		07 56		08 04		08 11		08 19	
Highbury & Islington	a	07 08		07 15		07 25		07 30		07 40		07 45		07 55		08 00		08 09		08 17		08 23	

		LO	LO	LO	LO	LO	LO	LO	LO	LO	LO	LO	LO	LO	LO	LO	LO	LO	LO	LO	LO	LO	LO
Clapham Junction	d		07 45				08 00				08 15				08 30				08 45				09 00
Wandsworth Road	d		07 51				08 06				08 21				08 36				08 51				09 06
Clapham High Street ⊖	d		07 53				08 08				08 23				08 38				08 53				09 08
Denmark Hill	d		07 58				08 13				08 28				08 43				08 58				09 13
Peckham Rye	d		08 00				08 15				08 30				08 45				09 00				09 15
Queens Rd Peckham	d		08 02				08 17				08 32				08 47				09 02				09 17
West Croydon	d			07 45				08 01				08 15				08 31				08 45			
Norwood Junction	d			07 52				08 07				08 22				08 37				08 52			
Anerley	d			07 55				08 10				08 25				08 40				08 55			
Penge West	d			07 56				08 12				08 26				08 42				08 56			
Crystal Palace	d	07 47				08 03				08 17				08 33				08 47				09 02	
Sydenham	d	07 51		07 59		08 07		08 14		08 21		08 29		08 37		08 44		08 51		08 59		09 06	
Forest Hill	d	07 54		08 02		08 10		08 17		08 24		08 32		08 40		08 47		08 54		09 02		09 09	
Honor Oak Park	d	07 56		08 04		08 12		08 19		08 26		08 34		08 42		08 49		08 56		09 04		09 11	
Brockley	d	07 59		08 07		08 15		08 22		08 29		08 37		08 45		08 52		08 59		09 07		09 14	
New Cross Gate	d	08 01		08 09		08 17		08 24		08 31		08 39		08 47		08 54		09 01		09 09		09 16	
New Cross	d				08 12				08 27				08 42				08 57				09 12		
Surrey Quays	d	08 05	08 08	08 13	08 16	08 21	08 24	08 28	08 31	08 35	08 38	08 43	08 46	08 51	08 54	08 58	09 01	09 05	09 09	09 13	09 16	09 20	09 23
Canada Water	d	08 07	08 10	08 15	08 18	08 23	08 26	08 30	08 33	08 37	08 40	08 45	08 48	08 53	08 56	09 00	09 03	09 07	09 11	09 15	09 18	09 22	09 25
Rotherhithe	d	08 08	08 12	08 16	08 20	08 24	08 27	08 31	08 35	08 38	08 42	08 46	08 50	08 54	08 57	09 01	09 05	09 08	09 12	09 16	09 20	09 23	09 27
Wapping	d	08 10	08 13	08 18	08 21	08 26	08 29	08 33	08 36	08 40	08 43	08 48	08 51	08 56	08 59	09 03	09 06	09 10	09 14	09 18	09 21	09 25	09 28
Shadwell	d	08 12	08 15	08 20	08 23	08 28	08 31	08 35	08 38	08 42	08 45	08 50	08 53	08 58	09 01	09 05	09 08	09 12	09 16	09 20	09 23	09 27	09 30
Whitechapel	d	08 14	08 18	08 22	08 26	08 30	08 33	08 37	08 41	08 44	08 48	08 52	08 56	09 00	09 03	09 07	09 11	09 14	09 18	09 22	09 26	09 29	09 33
Shoreditch High Street	d	08 17	08 20	08 25	08 28	08 33	08 36	08 40	08 43	08 47	08 50	08 55	08 58	09 03	09 06	09 10	09 13	09 17	09 21	09 25	09 28	09 32	09 35
Hoxton	d	08 19	08 22	08 27	08 30	08 35	08 38	08 42	08 45	08 49	08 52	08 57	09 00	09 05	09 08	09 12	09 15	09 19	09 23	09 27	09 30	09 34	09 37
Haggerston	d	08 21	08 24	08 29	08 32	08 37	08 40	08 44	08 47	08 51	08 54	08 59	09 02	09 07	09 10	09 14	09 17	09 21	09 25	09 29	09 32	09 36	09 39
Dalston Junction	a	08 23	08 29	08 31	08 35	08 39	08 45	08 46	08 50	08 53	09 00	09 01	09 05	09 09	09 15	09 16	09 19	09 23	09 29	09 31	09 34	09 38	09 44
Canonbury	a	08 26		08 34		08 42		08 49		08 56		09 04		09 12		09 19		09 26		09 34		09 41	
Highbury & Islington	a	08 32		08 39		08 48		08 55		09 02		09 09		09 18		09 25		09 32		09 39		09 47	

A From New Cross ELL
B From Crystal Palace
C From Clapham Junction Plats 0-2
D From West Croydon
E From Battersea Park

Table T178-R

Mondays to Fridays
21 May to 7 December

Clapham Junction and West Croydon, Crystal Palace, New Cross - Highbury & Islington

		LO	LO	LO	LO	LO	LO	LO	LO	LO	LO	LO	LO	LO	LO	LO	LO	LO	LO	LO	LO	LO
Clapham Junction	d				09 15				09 30				09 45				10 00				10 15	
Wandsworth Road	d				09 21				09 36				09 51				10 06				10 21	
Clapham High Street ⊖	d				09 23				09 38				09 53				10 08				10 23	
Denmark Hill	d				09 28				09 43				09 58				10 13				10 28	
Peckham Rye	d				09 30				09 45				10 00				10 15				10 30	
Queens Rd Peckham	d				09 32				09 47				10 02				10 17				10 32	
West Croydon	d	09 01				09 16				09 31				09 46				10 01				10 15
Norwood Junction	d	09 07				09 22				09 37				09 52				10 07				10 21
Anerley	d	09 10				09 25				09 40				09 55				10 10				10 24
Penge West	d	09 11				09 26				09 41				09 56				10 11				10 25
Crystal Palace	d			09 17				09 32				09 47				10 02				10 17		
Sydenham	d	09 14		09 21		09 29		09 36		09 44		09 51		09 59		10 06		10 14		10 21		10 28
Forest Hill	d	09 17		09 24		09 32		09 39		09 47		09 54		10 02		10 09		10 17		10 24		10 32
Honor Oak Park	d	09 19		09 26		09 34		09 41		09 49		09 56		10 04		10 11		10 19		10 26		10 34
Brockley	d	09 22		09 29		09 37		09 44		09 52		09 59		10 07		10 14		10 22		10 29		10 37
New Cross Gate	d	09 24		09 31		09 39		09 46		09 54		10 01		10 09		10 16		10 24		10 31		10 39
New Cross	d		09 27				09 42				09 57				10 12				10 27			
Surrey Quays	d	09 27	09 31	09 35	09 38	09 42	09 46	09 50	09 53	09 57	10 01	10 05	10 08	10 12	10 16	10 20	10 23	10 27	10 31	10 35	10 38	10 42
Canada Water	d	09 29	09 33	09 37	09 40	09 44	09 48	09 52	09 55	09 59	10 03	10 07	10 10	10 14	10 18	10 22	10 25	10 29	10 33	10 37	10 40	10 44
Rotherhithe	d	09 31	09 35	09 38	09 42	09 46	09 50	09 53	09 57	10 01	10 05	10 08	10 12	10 16	10 20	10 23	10 27	10 31	10 35	10 38	10 42	10 46
Wapping	d	09 32	09 36	09 40	09 43	09 47	09 51	09 55	09 58	10 02	10 06	10 10	10 13	10 17	10 21	10 25	10 28	10 32	10 36	10 40	10 43	10 47
Shadwell	d	09 34	09 38	09 42	09 45	09 49	09 53	09 57	10 00	10 04	10 08	10 12	10 15	10 19	10 23	10 27	10 30	10 34	10 38	10 42	10 45	10 49
Whitechapel	d	09 37	09 41	09 44	09 48	09 52	09 56	09 59	10 03	10 07	10 11	10 14	10 18	10 22	10 26	10 29	10 33	10 37	10 41	10 44	10 48	10 52
Shoreditch High Street	d	09 39	09 43	09 47	09 50	09 54	09 58	10 02	10 05	10 09	10 13	10 17	10 20	10 24	10 28	10 32	10 35	10 39	10 43	10 47	10 50	10 54
Hoxton	d	09 41	09 45	09 49	09 52	09 56	10 00	10 04	10 07	10 11	10 15	10 19	10 22	10 26	10 30	10 34	10 37	10 41	10 45	10 49	10 52	10 56
Haggerston	d	09 43	09 47	09 51	09 54	09 58	10 02	10 06	10 09	10 13	10 17	10 21	10 24	10 28	10 32	10 36	10 39	10 43	10 47	10 51	10 54	10 58
Dalston Junction	a	09 45	09 49	09 53	09 59	10 00	10 04	10 08	10 14	10 15	10 19	10 23	10 29	10 30	10 34	10 38	10 44	10 45	10 49	10 53	10 59	11 00
Canonbury	a	09 48		09 56		10 03		10 11		10 18		10 26		10 33		10 41		10 48		10 56		11 03
Highbury & Islington	a	09 55		10 00		10 10		10 15		10 25		10 30		10 40		10 45		10 55		11 00		11 07

		LO	LO	LO	LO	LO	LO	LO	LO	LO	LO	LO	LO	LO	LO	LO	LO	LO	LO	LO	LO	LO	LO
Clapham Junction	d			10 30				10 45				11 00				11 15				11 30			
Wandsworth Road	d			10 36				10 51				11 06				11 21				11 36			
Clapham High Street ⊖	d			10 38				10 53				11 08				11 23				11 38			
Denmark Hill	d			10 43				10 58				11 13				11 28				11 43			
Peckham Rye	d			10 45				11 00				11 15				11 30				11 45			
Queens Rd Peckham	d			10 47				11 02				11 17				11 32				11 47			
West Croydon	d				10 31				10 46				11 01				11 16				11 31		
Norwood Junction	d				10 37				10 52				11 07				11 22				11 37		
Anerley	d				10 40				10 55				11 10				11 25				11 40		
Penge West	d				10 41				10 57				11 11				11 26				11 41		
Crystal Palace	d		10 32				10 47				11 02				11 17				11 32				11 47
Sydenham	d		10 36		10 44		10 51		10 59		11 06		11 14		11 21		11 29		11 36		11 44		11 51
Forest Hill	d		10 39		10 47		10 54		11 02		11 09		11 17		11 24		11 32		11 39		11 47		11 54
Honor Oak Park	d		10 41		10 49		10 56		11 04		11 11		11 19		11 26		11 34		11 41		11 49		11 56
Brockley	d		10 44		10 52		10 59		11 07		11 14		11 22		11 29		11 37		11 44		11 52		11 59
New Cross Gate	d		10 46		10 54		11 01		11 09		11 16		11 24		11 31		11 39		11 46		11 54		12 01
New Cross	d	10 42				10 57				11 12				11 27				11 42				11 57	
Surrey Quays	d	10 46	10 50	10 53	10 57	11 01	11 05	11 08	11 12	11 16	11 20	11 23	11 27	11 31	11 35	11 38	11 42	11 46	11 50	11 53	11 57	12 01	12 05
Canada Water	d	10 48	10 52	10 55	10 59	11 03	11 07	11 10	11 14	11 18	11 22	11 25	11 29	11 33	11 37	11 40	11 44	11 48	11 52	11 55	11 59	12 03	12 07
Rotherhithe	d	10 50	10 53	10 57	11 01	11 05	11 08	11 12	11 16	11 20	11 23	11 27	11 31	11 35	11 38	11 42	11 46	11 50	11 53	11 57	12 01	12 05	12 08
Wapping	d	10 51	10 55	10 58	11 02	11 06	11 10	11 13	11 17	11 21	11 25	11 28	11 32	11 36	11 40	11 43	11 47	11 51	11 55	11 58	12 02	12 06	12 10
Shadwell	d	10 53	10 57	11 00	11 04	11 08	11 12	11 15	11 19	11 23	11 27	11 30	11 34	11 38	11 42	11 45	11 49	11 53	11 57	12 00	12 04	12 08	12 12
Whitechapel	d	10 56	10 59	11 03	11 07	11 11	11 14	11 18	11 22	11 26	11 29	11 33	11 37	11 41	11 44	11 48	11 52	11 56	11 59	12 03	12 07	12 11	12 14
Shoreditch High Street	d	10 58	11 02	11 05	11 09	11 13	11 17	11 20	11 24	11 28	11 32	11 35	11 39	11 43	11 47	11 50	11 54	11 58	12 02	12 05	12 09	12 13	12 17
Hoxton	d	11 00	11 04	11 07	11 11	11 15	11 19	11 22	11 26	11 30	11 34	11 37	11 41	11 45	11 49	11 52	11 56	12 00	12 04	12 07	12 11	12 15	12 19
Haggerston	d	11 02	11 06	11 09	11 13	11 17	11 21	11 24	11 28	11 32	11 36	11 39	11 43	11 47	11 51	11 54	11 58	12 02	12 06	12 09	12 13	12 17	12 21
Dalston Junction	a	11 04	11 08	11 14	11 15	11 19	11 23	11 29	11 30	11 34	11 38	11 44	11 45	11 49	11 53	11 59	12 00	12 04	12 08	12 14	12 15	12 19	12 23
Canonbury	a		11 11		11 18		11 26		11 33		11 41		11 48		11 56		12 03		12 11		12 18		12 26
Highbury & Islington	a		11 15		11 23		11 30		11 38		11 45		11 53		12 00		12 08		12 15		12 23		12 30

		LO	LO	LO	LO	LO	LO	LO	LO	LO	LO	LO	LO	LO	LO	LO	LO	LO	LO	LO	LO	LO
Clapham Junction	d	11 45				12 00				12 15				12 30				12 45				13 00
Wandsworth Road	d	11 51				12 06				12 21				12 36				12 51				13 06
Clapham High Street ⊖	d	11 53				12 08				12 23				12 38				12 53				13 08
Denmark Hill	d	11 58				12 13				12 28				12 43				12 58				13 13
Peckham Rye	d	12 00				12 15				12 30				12 45				13 00				13 15
Queens Rd Peckham	d	12 02				12 17				12 32				12 47				13 02				13 17
West Croydon	d		11 46				12 01				12 16				12 31				12 46			
Norwood Junction	d		11 52				12 07				12 22				12 37				12 52			
Anerley	d		11 55				12 10				12 25				12 40				12 55			
Penge West	d		11 57				12 11				12 26				12 41				12 57			
Crystal Palace	d				12 02				12 17				12 32				12 47				13 02	
Sydenham	d		11 59		12 06		12 14		12 21		12 29		12 36		12 44		12 51		12 59		13 06	
Forest Hill	d		12 02		12 09		12 17		12 24		12 32		12 39		12 47		12 54		13 02		13 09	
Honor Oak Park	d		12 04		12 11		12 19		12 26		12 34		12 41		12 49		12 56		13 04		13 11	
Brockley	d		12 07		12 14		12 22		12 29		12 37		12 44		12 52		12 59		13 07		13 14	
New Cross Gate	d		12 09		12 16		12 24		12 31		12 39		12 46		12 54		13 01		13 09		13 16	
New Cross	d			12 12				12 27				12 42				12 57				13 12		
Surrey Quays	d	12 08	12 12	12 16	12 20	12 23	12 27	12 31	12 35	12 38	12 42	12 46	12 50	12 53	12 57	13 01	13 05	13 08	13 12	13 16	13 20	13 23
Canada Water	d	12 10	12 14	12 18	12 22	12 25	12 29	12 33	12 37	12 40	12 44	12 48	12 52	12 55	12 59	13 03	13 07	13 10	13 14	13 18	13 22	13 25
Rotherhithe	d	12 12	12 16	12 20	12 23	12 27	12 31	12 35	12 38	12 42	12 46	12 50	12 53	12 57	13 01	13 05	13 08	13 12	13 16	13 20	13 23	13 27
Wapping	d	12 13	12 17	12 21	12 25	12 28	12 32	12 36	12 40	12 43	12 47	12 51	12 55	12 58	13 02	13 06	13 10	13 13	13 17	13 21	13 25	13 28
Shadwell	d	12 15	12 19	12 23	12 27	12 30	12 34	12 38	12 42	12 45	12 49	12 53	12 57	13 00	13 04	13 08	13 12	13 15	13 19	13 23	13 27	13 30
Whitechapel	d	12 18	12 22	12 26	12 29	12 33	12 37	12 41	12 44	12 48	12 52	12 56	12 59	13 03	13 07	13 11	13 14	13 18	13 22	13 26	13 29	13 33
Shoreditch High Street	d	12 20	12 24	12 28	12 32	12 35	12 39	12 43	12 47	12 50	12 54	12 58	13 02	13 05	13 09	13 13	13 17	13 20	13 24	13 28	13 32	13 35
Hoxton	d	12 22	12 26	12 30	12 34	12 37	12 41	12 45	12 49	12 52	12 56	13 00	13 04	13 07	13 11	13 15	13 19	13 22	13 26	13 30	13 34	13 37
Haggerston	d	12 24	12 28	12 32	12 36	12 39	12 43	12 47	12 51	12 54	12 58	13 02	13 06	13 09	13 13	13 17	13 21	13 24	13 28	13 32	13 36	13 39
Dalston Junction	a	12 29	12 30	12 34	12 38	12 44	12 45	12 49	12 53	12 59	13 00	13 04	13 08	13 14	13 15	13 19	13 23	13 29	13 30	13 34	13 38	13 44
Canonbury	a		12 33		12 41		12 48		12 56		13 03		13 11		13 18		13 26		13 33		13 41	
Highbury & Islington	a		12 38		12 45		12 53		13 00		13 08		13 15		13 23		13 30		13 38		13 45	

Table T178-R

Mondays to Fridays

21 May to 7 December

Clapham Junction and West Croydon, Crystal Palace, New Cross - Highbury & Islington

		LO	LO	LO	LO	LO	LO	LO	LO	LO		LO	LO	LO	LO	LO	LO	LO	LO	LO		LO	LO	LO	LO
Clapham Junction	d				13 15				13 30					13 45				14 00					14 15		
Wandsworth Road	d				13 21				13 36					13 51				14 06					14 21		
Clapham High Street ⊖	d				13 23				13 38					13 53				14 08					14 23		
Denmark Hill	d				13 28				13 43					13 58				14 13					14 28		
Peckham Rye	d				13 30				13 45					14 00				14 15					14 30		
Queens Rd Peckham	d				13 32				13 47					14 02				14 17					14 32		
West Croydon	d	13 01				13 16				13 31					13 46				14 01					14 16	
Norwood Junction	d	13 07				13 22				13 37					13 52				14 07					14 22	
Anerley	d	13 10				13 25				13 40					13 55				14 10					14 25	
Penge West	d	13 11				13 26				13 41					13 57				14 11					14 26	
Crystal Palace	d			13 17				13 32					13 47				14 02					14 17			
Sydenham	d	13 14		13 21		13 29		13 36		13 44			13 51		13 59		14 06		14 14			14 21		14 29	
Forest Hill	d	13 17		13 24		13 32		13 39		13 47			13 54		14 02		14 09		14 17			14 24		14 32	
Honor Oak Park	d	13 19		13 26		13 34		13 41		13 49			13 56		14 04		14 11		14 19			14 26		14 34	
Brockley	d	13 22		13 29		13 37		13 44		13 52			13 59		14 07		14 14		14 22			14 29		14 37	
New Cross Gate	d	13 24		13 31		13 39		13 46		13 54			14 01		14 09		14 16		14 24			14 31		14 39	
New Cross	d		13 27				13 42					13 57				14 12				14 27					14 42
Surrey Quays	d	13 27	13 31	13 35	13 38	13 42	13 46	13 50	13 53	13 57		14 01	14 05	14 08	14 12	14 16	14 20	14 23	14 27	14 31		14 35	14 38	14 42	14 46
Canada Water	d	13 29	13 33	13 37	13 40	13 44	13 48	13 52	13 55	13 59		14 03	14 07	14 10	14 14	14 18	14 22	14 25	14 29	14 33		14 37	14 40	14 44	14 48
Rotherhithe	d	13 31	13 35	13 38	13 42	13 46	13 50	13 53	13 57	14 01		14 05	14 08	14 12	14 16	14 20	14 23	14 27	14 31	14 35		14 38	14 42	14 46	14 50
Wapping	d	13 32	13 36	13 40	13 43	13 47	13 51	13 55	13 58	14 02		14 06	14 10	14 13	14 17	14 21	14 25	14 28	14 32	14 36		14 40	14 43	14 47	14 51
Shadwell	d	13 34	13 38	13 42	13 45	13 49	13 53	13 57	14 00	14 04		14 08	14 12	14 15	14 19	14 23	14 27	14 30	14 34	14 38		14 42	14 45	14 49	14 53
Whitechapel	d	13 37	13 41	13 44	13 48	13 52	13 56	13 59	14 03	14 07		14 11	14 14	14 18	14 22	14 26	14 29	14 33	14 37	14 41		14 44	14 48	14 52	14 56
Shoreditch High Street	d	13 39	13 43	13 47	13 50	13 54	13 58	14 02	14 05	14 09		14 13	14 17	14 20	14 24	14 28	14 32	14 35	14 39	14 43		14 47	14 50	14 54	14 58
Hoxton	d	13 41	13 45	13 49	13 52	13 56	14 00	14 04	14 07	14 11		14 15	14 19	14 22	14 26	14 30	14 34	14 37	14 41	14 45		14 49	14 52	14 56	15 00
Haggerston	d	13 43	13 47	13 51	13 54	13 58	14 02	14 06	14 09	14 13		14 17	14 21	14 24	14 28	14 32	14 36	14 39	14 43	14 47		14 51	14 54	14 58	15 02
Dalston Junction	a	13 45	13 49	13 53	13 59	14 00	14 04	14 08	14 14	14 15		14 19	14 23	14 29	14 30	14 34	14 38	14 44	14 45	14 49		14 53	14 59	15 00	15 04
Canonbury	a	13 48		13 56		14 03		14 11		14 18			14 26		14 33		14 41		14 48			14 56		15 03	
Highbury & Islington	a	13 53		14 00		14 08		14 15		14 23			14 30		14 38		14 45		14 53			15 00		15 08	

		LO	LO	LO	LO	LO		LO	LO	LO	LO	LO	LO	LO	LO	LO		LO	LO	LO	LO	LO	LO	LO	LO
Clapham Junction	d		14 30					14 45				15 00				15 15					15 30				15 45
Wandsworth Road	d		14 36					14 51				15 06				15 21					15 36				15 51
Clapham High Street ⊖	d		14 38					14 53				15 08				15 23					15 38				15 53
Denmark Hill	d		14 43					14 58				15 13				15 28					15 43				15 58
Peckham Rye	d		14 45					15 00				15 15				15 30					15 45				16 00
Queens Rd Peckham	d		14 47					15 02				15 17				15 32					15 47				16 02
West Croydon	d			14 31					14 46				15 01					15 16				15 31			
Norwood Junction	d			14 37					14 52				15 07					15 22				15 37			
Anerley	d			14 40					14 55				15 10					15 25				15 40			
Penge West	d			14 41					14 57				15 11					15 26				15 41			
Crystal Palace	d	14 32				14 47					15 02				15 17					15 32				15 47	
Sydenham	d	14 36		14 44		14 51			14 59		15 06		15 14		15 21			15 29		15 36		15 44		15 51	
Forest Hill	d	14 39		14 47		14 54			15 02		15 09		15 17		15 24			15 32		15 39		15 47		15 54	
Honor Oak Park	d	14 41		14 49		14 56			15 04		15 11		15 19		15 26			15 34		15 41		15 49		15 56	
Brockley	d	14 44		14 52		14 59			15 07		15 14		15 22		15 29			15 37		15 44		15 52		15 59	
New Cross Gate	d	14 46		14 54		15 01			15 09		15 16		15 24		15 31			15 39		15 46		15 54		16 01	
New Cross	d				14 57					15 12				15 27					15 42				15 57		
Surrey Quays	d	14 50	14 53	14 57	15 01	15 05		15 08	15 12	15 16	15 20	15 23	15 27	15 31	15 35	15 38		15 42	15 46	15 50	15 53	15 57	16 01	16 05	16 08
Canada Water	d	14 52	14 55	14 59	15 03	15 07		15 10	15 14	15 18	15 22	15 25	15 29	15 33	15 37	15 40		15 44	15 48	15 52	15 55	15 59	16 03	16 07	16 10
Rotherhithe	d	14 53	14 57	15 01	15 05	15 08		15 12	15 16	15 20	15 23	15 27	15 31	15 35	15 38	15 42		15 46	15 50	15 53	15 57	16 01	16 05	16 08	16 12
Wapping	d	14 55	14 58	15 02	15 06	15 10		15 13	15 17	15 21	15 25	15 28	15 32	15 36	15 40	15 43		15 47	15 51	15 55	15 58	16 02	16 06	16 10	16 13
Shadwell	d	14 57	15 00	15 04	15 08	15 12		15 15	15 19	15 23	15 27	15 30	15 34	15 38	15 42	15 45		15 49	15 53	15 57	16 00	16 04	16 08	16 12	16 15
Whitechapel	d	14 59	15 03	15 07	15 11	15 14		15 18	15 22	15 26	15 29	15 33	15 37	15 41	15 44	15 48		15 52	15 56	15 59	16 03	16 07	16 11	16 14	16 18
Shoreditch High Street	d	15 02	15 05	15 09	15 13	15 17		15 20	15 24	15 28	15 32	15 35	15 39	15 43	15 47	15 50		15 54	15 58	16 02	16 05	16 09	16 13	16 17	16 20
Hoxton	d	15 04	15 07	15 11	15 15	15 19		15 22	15 26	15 30	15 34	15 37	15 41	15 45	15 49	15 52		15 56	16 00	16 04	16 07	16 11	16 15	16 19	16 22
Haggerston	d	15 06	15 09	15 13	15 17	15 21		15 24	15 28	15 32	15 36	15 39	15 43	15 47	15 51	15 54		15 58	16 02	16 06	16 09	16 13	16 17	16 21	16 24
Dalston Junction	a	15 08	15 14	15 15	15 19	15 23		15 29	15 30	15 34	15 38	15 44	15 45	15 49	15 53	15 59		16 00	16 04	16 08	16 14	16 15	16 19	16 23	16 29
Canonbury	a	15 11		15 18		15 26			15 33		15 41		15 48		15 56			16 03		16 11		16 18		16 26	
Highbury & Islington	a	15 15		15 23		15 30			15 38		15 45		15 53		16 00			16 08		16 15		16 25		16 30	

		LO		LO	LO	LO	LO	LO	LO	LO	LO	LO		LO	LO	LO	LO	LO	LO	LO	LO	LO		LO	LO
Clapham Junction	d					16 00				16 15					16 30				16 45					17 00	
Wandsworth Road	d					16 06				16 21					16 36				16 51					17 06	
Clapham High Street ⊖	d					16 08				16 23					16 38				16 53					17 08	
Denmark Hill	d					16 13				16 28					16 43				16 58					17 13	
Peckham Rye	d					16 15				16 30					16 45				17 00					17 15	
Queens Rd Peckham	d					16 17				16 32					16 47				17 02					17 17	
West Croydon	d	15 46					16 01				16 16					16 31				16 46					17 01
Norwood Junction	d	15 52					16 07				16 22					16 37				16 52					17 07
Anerley	d	15 55					16 10				16 25					16 40				16 55					17 10
Penge West	d	15 57					16 11				16 26					16 41				16 56					17 11
Crystal Palace	d				16 02				16 17					16 32				16 47				17 02			
Sydenham	d	15 59			16 06		16 14		16 21		16 29			16 36		16 44		16 51		16 59		17 06			17 14
Forest Hill	d	16 02			16 09		16 17		16 24		16 32			16 39		16 47		16 54		17 02		17 09			17 17
Honor Oak Park	d	16 04			16 11		16 19		16 26		16 34			16 41		16 49		16 56		17 04		17 11			17 19
Brockley	d	16 07			16 14		16 22		16 29		16 37			16 44		16 52		16 59		17 07		17 14			17 22
New Cross Gate	d	16 09			16 16		16 24		16 31		16 39			16 46		16 54		17 01		17 09		17 16			17 24
New Cross	d			16 12				16 27				16 42					16 57				17 12				
Surrey Quays	d	16 12		16 16	16 20	16 23	16 27	16 31	16 35	16 38	16 42	16 46		16 50	16 53	16 57	17 01	17 05	17 08	17 12	17 16	17 20		17 23	17 27
Canada Water	d	16 14		16 18	16 22	16 25	16 29	16 33	16 37	16 40	16 44	16 48		16 52	16 55	16 59	17 03	17 07	17 10	17 14	17 18	17 22		17 25	17 29
Rotherhithe	d	16 16		16 20	16 23	16 27	16 31	16 35	16 38	16 42	16 46	16 50		16 53	16 57	17 01	17 05	17 08	17 12	17 16	17 20	17 23		17 27	17 31
Wapping	d	16 17		16 21	16 25	16 28	16 32	16 36	16 40	16 43	16 47	16 51		16 55	16 58	17 02	17 06	17 10	17 13	17 17	17 21	17 25		17 28	17 32
Shadwell	d	16 19		16 23	16 27	16 30	16 34	16 38	16 42	16 45	16 49	16 53		16 57	17 00	17 04	17 08	17 12	17 15	17 19	17 23	17 27		17 30	17 34
Whitechapel	d	16 22		16 26	16 29	16 33	16 37	16 41	16 44	16 48	16 52	16 56		16 59	17 03	17 07	17 11	17 14	17 18	17 22	17 26	17 29		17 33	17 37
Shoreditch High Street	d	16 24		16 28	16 32	16 35	16 39	16 43	16 47	16 50	16 54	16 58		17 02	17 05	17 09	17 13	17 17	17 20	17 24	17 28	17 32		17 35	17 39
Hoxton	d	16 26		16 30	16 34	16 37	16 41	16 45	16 49	16 52	16 56	17 00		17 04	17 07	17 11	17 15	17 19	17 22	17 26	17 30	17 34		17 37	17 41
Haggerston	d	16 28		16 32	16 36	16 39	16 43	16 47	16 51	16 54	16 58	17 02		17 06	17 09	17 13	17 17	17 21	17 24	17 28	17 32	17 36		17 39	17 43
Dalston Junction	a	16 30		16 34	16 38	16 44	16 45	16 49	16 53	16 59	17 00	17 04		17 08	17 14	17 15	17 19	17 23	17 29	17 30	17 34	17 38		17 44	17 45
Canonbury	a	16 33			16 41		16 48		16 56		17 03			17 11		17 18		17 26		17 33		17 41			17 48
Highbury & Islington	a	16 40			16 45		16 55		17 00		17 10			17 15		17 25		17 30		17 40		17 45			17 55

Table T178-R

Mondays to Fridays

21 May to 7 December

Clapham Junction and West Croydon, Crystal Palace, New Cross - Highbury & Islington

		LO	LO	LO	LO	LO	LO	LO		LO	LO	LO	LO	LO	LO	LO	LO	LO		LO	LO	LO	LO	LO	LO
Clapham Junction	d			17 15				17 30					17 45				18 00					18 15			
Wandsworth Road	d			17 21				17 36					17 51				18 06					18 21			
Clapham High Street ⊖	d			17 23				17 38					17 53				18 08					18 23			
Denmark Hill	d			17 28				17 43					17 58				18 13					18 28			
Peckham Rye	d			17 30				17 45					18 00				18 15					18 30			
Queens Rd Peckham	d			17 32				17 47					18 02				18 17					18 32			
West Croydon	d				17 16					17 31				17 46				18 01					18 16		
Norwood Junction	d				17 22					17 37				17 52				18 07					18 22		
Anerley	d				17 25					17 40				17 55				18 10					18 25		
Penge West	d				17 26					17 41				17 56				18 11					18 26		
Crystal Palace	d		17 17				17 32					17 47				18 02					18 17				18 32
Sydenham	d		17 21		17 29		17 36			17 44		17 51		17 59		18 06		18 14			18 21		18 29		18 36
Forest Hill	d		17 24		17 32		17 39			17 47		17 54		18 02		18 09		18 17			18 24		18 32		18 39
Honor Oak Park	d		17 26		17 34		17 41			17 49		17 56		18 04		18 11		18 19			18 26		18 34		18 41
Brockley	d		17 29		17 37		17 44			17 52		17 59		18 07		18 14		18 22			18 29		18 37		18 44
New Cross Gate	d		17 31		17 39		17 46			17 54		18 01		18 09		18 16		18 24			18 31		18 39		18 46
New Cross	d	17 27				17 42					17 57				18 12					18 27				18 42	
Surrey Quays	d	17 31	17 35	17 38	17 42	17 46	17 50	17 53		17 57	18 01	18 05	18 08	18 12	18 16	18 20	18 23	18 27		18 31	18 35	18 38	18 42	18 46	18 50
Canada Water	d	17 33	17 37	17 40	17 44	17 48	17 52	17 55		17 59	18 03	18 07	18 10	18 14	18 18	18 22	18 25	18 29		18 33	18 37	18 40	18 44	18 48	18 52
Rotherhithe	d	17 35	17 38	17 42	17 46	17 50	17 53	17 57		18 01	18 05	18 08	18 12	18 16	18 20	18 23	18 27	18 31		18 35	18 38	18 42	18 46	18 50	18 53
Wapping	d	17 36	17 40	17 43	17 47	17 51	17 55	17 58		18 02	18 06	18 10	18 13	18 17	18 21	18 25	18 28	18 32		18 36	18 40	18 43	18 47	18 51	18 55
Shadwell	d	17 38	17 42	17 45	17 49	17 53	17 57	18 00		18 04	18 08	18 12	18 15	18 19	18 23	18 27	18 30	18 34		18 38	18 42	18 45	18 49	18 53	18 57
Whitechapel	d	17 41	17 44	17 48	17 52	17 56	17 59	18 03		18 07	18 11	18 14	18 18	18 22	18 26	18 29	18 33	18 37		18 41	18 44	18 48	18 52	18 56	18 59
Shoreditch High Street	d	17 43	17 47	17 50	17 54	17 58	18 02	18 05		18 09	18 13	18 17	18 20	18 24	18 28	18 32	18 35	18 39		18 43	18 47	18 50	18 54	18 58	19 02
Hoxton	d	17 45	17 49	17 52	17 56	18 00	18 04	18 07		18 11	18 15	18 19	18 22	18 26	18 30	18 34	18 37	18 41		18 45	18 49	18 52	18 56	19 00	19 04
Haggerston	d	17 47	17 51	17 54	17 58	18 02	18 06	18 09		18 13	18 17	18 21	18 24	18 28	18 32	18 36	18 39	18 43		18 47	18 51	18 54	18 58	19 02	19 06
Dalston Junction	a	17 49	17 53	17 59	18 00	18 04	18 08	18 14		18 15	18 19	18 23	18 29	18 30	18 34	18 38	18 44	18 45		18 49	18 53	18 59	19 00	19 04	19 08
Canonbury	a		17 56		18 03		18 11			18 18		18 26		18 33		18 41		18 48			18 56		19 03		19 11
Highbury & Islington	a		18 00		18 10		18 15			18 25		18 30		18 40		18 45		18 55			19 00		19 10		19 15

		LO	LO	LO		LO	LO	LO	LO	LO	LO	LO	LO	LO		LO	LO	LO	LO	LO	LO	LO	LO	LO	
Clapham Junction	d	18 30					18 45				19 00					19 15				19 30				19 45	
Wandsworth Road	d	18 36					18 51				19 06					19 21				19 36				19 51	
Clapham High Street ⊖	d	18 38					18 53				19 08					19 23				19 38				19 53	
Denmark Hill	d	18 43					18 58				19 13					19 28				19 43				19 58	
Peckham Rye	d	18 45					19 00				19 15					19 30				19 45				20 00	
Queens Rd Peckham	d	18 47					19 02				19 17					19 32				19 47				20 02	
West Croydon	d		18 31					18 46				19 01					19 16				19 31				
Norwood Junction	d		18 37					18 52				19 07					19 22				19 37				
Anerley	d		18 40					18 55				19 10					19 25				19 40				
Penge West	d		18 41					18 56				19 11					19 26				19 41				
Crystal Palace	d					18 47				19 02				19 17					19 32				19 47		
Sydenham	d		18 44			18 51		18 59		19 06		19 14		19 21			19 29		19 36		19 44		19 51		
Forest Hill	d		18 47			18 54		19 02		19 09		19 17		19 24			19 32		19 39		19 47		19 54		
Honor Oak Park	d		18 49			18 56		19 04		19 11		19 19		19 26			19 34		19 41		19 49		19 56		
Brockley	d		18 52			18 59		19 07		19 14		19 22		19 29			19 37		19 44		19 52		19 59		
New Cross Gate	d		18 54			19 01		19 09		19 16		19 24		19 31			19 39		19 46		19 54		20 01		
New Cross	d			18 57					19 12				19 27					19 42				19 57			
Surrey Quays	d	18 53	18 57	19 01		19 05	19 08	19 12	19 16	19 20	19 23	19 27	19 31	19 35		19 38	19 42	19 46	19 50	19 53	19 57	20 01	20 05	20 08	
Canada Water	d	18 55	18 59	19 03		19 07	19 10	19 14	19 18	19 22	19 25	19 29	19 33	19 37		19 40	19 44	19 48	19 52	19 55	19 59	20 03	20 07	20 10	
Rotherhithe	d	18 57	19 01	19 05		19 08	19 12	19 16	19 20	19 23	19 27	19 31	19 35	19 38		19 42	19 46	19 50	19 53	19 57	20 01	20 05	20 08	20 12	
Wapping	d	18 58	19 02	19 06		19 10	19 13	19 17	19 21	19 25	19 28	19 32	19 36	19 40		19 43	19 47	19 51	19 55	19 58	20 02	20 06	20 10	20 13	
Shadwell	d	19 00	19 04	19 08		19 12	19 15	19 19	19 23	19 27	19 30	19 34	19 38	19 42		19 45	19 49	19 53	19 57	20 00	20 04	20 08	20 12	20 15	
Whitechapel	d	19 03	19 07	19 11		19 14	19 18	19 22	19 26	19 29	19 33	19 37	19 41	19 44		19 48	19 52	19 56	19 59	20 03	20 07	20 11	20 14	20 18	
Shoreditch High Street	d	19 05	19 09	19 13		19 17	19 20	19 24	19 28	19 32	19 35	19 39	19 43	19 47		19 50	19 54	19 58	20 02	20 05	20 09	20 13	20 17	20 20	
Hoxton	d	19 07	19 11	19 15		19 19	19 22	19 26	19 30	19 34	19 37	19 41	19 45	19 49		19 52	19 56	20 00	20 04	20 07	20 11	20 15	20 19	20 22	
Haggerston	d	19 09	19 13	19 17		19 21	19 24	19 28	19 32	19 36	19 39	19 43	19 47	19 51		19 54	19 58	20 02	20 06	20 09	20 13	20 17	20 21	20 24	
Dalston Junction	a	19 14	19 15	19 19		19 23	19 29	19 30	19 34	19 38	19 44	19 45	19 49	19 53		19 59	20 00	20 04	20 08	20 14	20 15	20 19	20 23	20 29	
Canonbury	a		19 18			19 26		19 33		19 41		19 48		19 56			20 03		20 11		20 18		20 26		
Highbury & Islington	a		19 25			19 30		19 40		19 45		19 55		20 00			20 10		20 15		20 25		20 30		

		LO	LO	LO	LO	LO	LO	LO	LO	LO		LO	LO	LO	LO	LO	LO	LO	LO	LO		LO	LO	LO	LO
Clapham Junction	d				20 00				20 15					20 30				20 45					21 00		
Wandsworth Road	d				20 06				20 21					20 36				20 51					21 06		
Clapham High Street ⊖	d				20 08				20 23					20 38				20 53					21 08		
Denmark Hill	d				20 13				20 28					20 43				20 58					21 13		
Peckham Rye	d				20 15				20 30					20 45				21 00					21 15		
Queens Rd Peckham	d				20 17				20 32					20 47				21 02					21 17		
West Croydon	d	19 46				20 01				20 16					20 31				20 46					21 01	
Norwood Junction	d	19 52				20 07				20 22					20 37				20 52					21 07	
Anerley	d	19 55				20 10				20 25					20 40				20 55					21 10	
Penge West	d	19 56				20 11				20 26					20 41				20 57					21 11	
Crystal Palace	d			20 02				20 17					20 32				20 47					21 02			
Sydenham	d	19 59		20 06		20 14		20 21		20 29			20 36		20 44		20 51		20 59			21 06		21 14	
Forest Hill	d	20 02		20 09		20 17		20 24		20 32			20 39		20 47		20 54		21 02			21 09		21 17	
Honor Oak Park	d	20 04		20 11		20 19		20 26		20 34			20 41		20 49		20 56		21 04			21 11		21 19	
Brockley	d	20 07		20 14		20 22		20 29		20 37			20 44		20 52		20 59		21 07			21 14		21 22	
New Cross Gate	d	20 09		20 16		20 24		20 31		20 39			20 46		20 54		21 01		21 09			21 16		21 24	
New Cross	d		20 12				20 27					20 42				20 57				21 12					21 27
Surrey Quays	d	20 12	20 16	20 20	20 23	20 27	20 31	20 35	20 38	20 42		20 46	20 50	20 53	20 57	21 01	21 05	21 08	21 12	21 16		21 20	21 23	21 27	21 31
Canada Water	d	20 14	20 18	20 22	20 25	20 29	20 33	20 37	20 40	20 44		20 48	20 52	20 55	20 59	21 03	21 07	21 10	21 14	21 18		21 22	21 25	21 29	21 33
Rotherhithe	d	20 16	20 20	20 23	20 27	20 31	20 35	20 38	20 42	20 46		20 50	20 53	20 57	21 01	21 05	21 08	21 12	21 16	21 20		21 23	21 27	21 31	21 35
Wapping	d	20 17	20 21	20 25	20 28	20 32	20 36	20 40	20 43	20 47		20 51	20 55	20 58	21 02	21 06	21 10	21 13	21 17	21 21		21 25	21 28	21 32	21 36
Shadwell	d	20 19	20 23	20 27	20 30	20 34	20 38	20 42	20 45	20 49		20 53	20 57	21 00	21 04	21 08	21 12	21 15	21 19	21 23		21 27	21 30	21 34	21 38
Whitechapel	d	20 22	20 26	20 29	20 33	20 37	20 41	20 44	20 48	20 52		20 56	20 59	21 03	21 07	21 11	21 14	21 18	21 22	21 26		21 29	21 33	21 37	21 41
Shoreditch High Street	d	20 24	20 28	20 32	20 35	20 39	20 43	20 47	20 50	20 54		20 58	21 02	21 05	21 09	21 13	21 17	21 20	21 24	21 28		21 32	21 35	21 39	21 43
Hoxton	d	20 26	20 30	20 34	20 37	20 41	20 45	20 49	20 52	20 56		21 00	21 04	21 07	21 11	21 15	21 19	21 22	21 26	21 30		21 34	21 37	21 41	21 45
Haggerston	d	20 28	20 32	20 36	20 39	20 43	20 47	20 51	20 54	20 58		21 02	21 06	21 09	21 13	21 17	21 21	21 24	21 28	21 32		21 36	21 39	21 43	21 47
Dalston Junction	a	20 30	20 34	20 38	20 44	20 45	20 49	20 53	20 59	21 00		21 04	21 08	21 14	21 15	21 19	21 23	21 29	21 30	21 34		21 38	21 44	21 45	21 49
Canonbury	a	20 33		20 40		20 48		20 56		21 03			21 11		21 18		21 26		21 33			21 41		21 48	
Highbury & Islington	a	20 40		20 45		20 53		21 00		21 08			21 15		21 23		21 30		21 38			21 45		21 53	

21 May to 7 December

Clapham Junction and West Croydon, Crystal Palace, New Cross - Highbury & Islington

		LO	LO	LO	LO	LO		LO	LO	LO	LO	LO	LO	LO	LO	LO		LO	LO	LO	LO	LO	LO	LO	LO
Clapham Junction	d		21 15					21 30				21 45				22 00					22 15				22 30
Wandsworth Road	d		21 21					21 36				21 51				22 06					22 21				22 36
Clapham High Street ⊖	d		21 23					21 38				21 53				22 08					22 23				22 38
Denmark Hill	d		21 28					21 43				21 58				22 13					22 28				22 43
Peckham Rye	d		21 30					21 45				22 00				22 15					22 30				22 45
Queens Rd Peckham	d		21 32					21 47				22 02				22 17					22 32				22 47
West Croydon	d			21 16					21 31				21 46					22 01				22 16			
Norwood Junction	d			21 22					21 37				21 52					22 07				22 22			
Anerley	d			21 25					21 40				21 55					22 10				22 25			
Penge West	d			21 26					21 41				21 56					22 11				22 26			
Crystal Palace	d	21 17				21 32					21 47				22 02					22 17				22 32	
Sydenham	d	21 21		21 29		21 36			21 44		21 51		21 59		22 06			22 14		22 21		22 29		22 36	
Forest Hill	d	21 24		21 32		21 39			21 47		21 54		22 02		22 09			22 17		22 24		22 32		22 39	
Honor Oak Park	d	21 26		21 34		21 41			21 49		21 56		22 04		22 11			22 19		22 26		22 34		22 41	
Brockley	d	21 29		21 37		21 44			21 52		21 59		22 07		22 14			22 22		22 29		22 37		22 44	
New Cross Gate	d	21 31		21 39		21 46			21 54		22 01		22 09		22 16			22 24		22 31		22 39		22 46	
New Cross	d				21 42					21 57				22 12					22 27				22 42		
Surrey Quays	d	21 35	21 38	21 42	21 46	21 50		21 53	21 57	22 01	22 05	22 08	22 12	22 16	22 20	22 23		22 27	22 31	22 35	22 38	22 42	22 46	22 50	22 53
Canada Water	d	21 37	21 40	21 44	21 48	21 52		21 55	21 59	22 03	22 07	22 10	22 14	22 18	22 22	22 25		22 29	22 33	22 37	22 40	22 44	22 48	22 52	22 55
Rotherhithe	d	21 38	21 42	21 46	21 50	21 53		21 57	22 01	22 05	22 08	22 12	22 16	22 20	22 23	22 27		22 31	22 35	22 38	22 42	22 46	22 50	22 53	22 57
Wapping	d	21 40	21 43	21 47	21 51	21 55		21 58	22 02	22 06	22 10	22 13	22 17	22 21	22 25	22 28		22 32	22 36	22 40	22 43	22 47	22 51	22 55	22 58
Shadwell	d	21 42	21 45	21 49	21 53	21 57		22 00	22 04	22 08	22 12	22 15	22 19	22 23	22 27	22 30		22 34	22 38	22 42	22 45	22 49	22 53	22 57	23 00
Whitechapel	d	21 44	21 48	21 52	21 56	21 59		22 03	22 07	22 11	22 14	22 18	22 22	22 26	22 29	22 33		22 37	22 41	22 44	22 48	22 52	22 56	22 59	23 03
Shoreditch High Street	d	21 47	21 50	21 54	21 58	22 02		22 05	22 09	22 13	22 17	22 20	22 24	22 28	22 32	22 35		22 39	22 43	22 47	22 50	22 54	22 58	23 02	23 05
Hoxton	d	21 49	21 52	21 56	22 00	22 04		22 07	22 11	22 15	22 19	22 22	22 26	22 30	22 34	22 37		22 41	22 45	22 49	22 52	22 56	23 00	23 04	23 07
Haggerston	d	21 51	21 54	21 58	22 02	22 06		22 09	22 13	22 17	22 21	22 24	22 28	22 32	22 36	22 39		22 43	22 47	22 51	22 54	22 58	23 02	23 06	23 09
Dalston Junction	a	21 53	21 59	22 00	22 04	22 08		22 14	22 15	22 19	22 23	22 29	22 30	22 34	22 38	22 44		22 45	22 49	22 53	22 59	23 00	23 04	23 08	23 14
Canonbury	a	21 56		22 03		22 11			22 18		22 26		22 33		22 41			22 48		22 56		23 03		23 11	
Highbury & Islington	a	22 00		22 08		22 15			22 23		22 30		22 38		22 45			22 53		23 00		23 08		23 15	

		LO		LO	LO	LO	LO	LO	LO	LO A	LO	LO		LO	LO	LO	LO	LO	LO	LO	LO	LO			
Clapham Junction	d					22 45									23 15				23 30		23 44				
Wandsworth Road	d					22 51				23 06					23 21				23 36		23 50				
Clapham High Street ⊖	d					22 53				23 08					23 23				23 38		23 52				
Denmark Hill	d					22 58				23 13					23 28				23 43		23 57				
Peckham Rye	d					23 00				23 15					23 30				23 45		23 59				
Queens Rd Peckham	d					23 02				23 17					23 32				23 47		00 01				
West Croydon	d	22 31					22 46				23 01					23 16				23 31					
Norwood Junction	d	22 37					22 52				23 07					23 22				23 37					
Anerley	d	22 40					22 55				23 10					23 25				23 40					
Penge West	d	22 41					22 56				23 11					23 26				23 41					
Crystal Palace	d				22 47				23 02					23 17				23 32				23 50			
Sydenham	d	22 44			22 51		22 59		23 06		23 14			23 21		23 29		23 36		23 44		23 54			
Forest Hill	d	22 47			22 54		23 02		23 09		23 17			23 24		23 32		23 39		23 47		23 56			
Honor Oak Park	d	22 49			22 56		23 04		23 11		23 19			23 26		23 34		23 41		23 49		23 59			
Brockley	d	22 52			22 59		23 07		23 14		23 22			23 29		23 37		23 44		23 52		00 01			
New Cross Gate	d	22 54			23 01		23 09		23 16		23 24			23 31		23 39		23 46		23 54		00 03			
New Cross	d			22 57				23 12				23 27					23 42								
Surrey Quays	d	22 57		23 01	23 05	23 08	23 12	23 16	23 20	23 23	23 27	23 31		23 35	23 38	23 42	23 46	23 50	23 53	23 57	00 05	00 09			
Canada Water	d	22 59		23 03	23 07	23 10	23 14	23 18	23 22	23 25	23 29	23 33		23 37	23 40	23 44	23 48	23 52	23 55	23 59	00 07	00 11			
Rotherhithe	d	23 01		23 05	23 08	23 12	23 16	23 20	23 23	23 27	23 31	23 35		23 38	23 42	23 46	23 50	23 53	23 57	00 01	00 09	00 12			
Wapping	d	23 02		23 06	23 10	23 13	23 17	23 21	23 25	23 28	23 32	23 36		23 40	23 43	23 47	23 51	23 55	23 58	00 02	00 10	00 14			
Shadwell	d	23 04		23 08	23 12	23 15	23 19	23 23	23 27	23 30	23 34	23 38		23 42	23 45	23 49	23 53	23 57	00 01	00 04	00 12	00 16			
Whitechapel	d	23 07		23 11	23 14	23 18	23 22	23 26	23 29	23 33	23 37	23 41		23 44	23 48	23 52	23 56	23 59	00 03	00 07	00 15	00 18			
Shoreditch High Street	d	23 09		23 13	23 17	23 20	23 24	23 28	23 32	23 35	23 39	23 43		23 47	23 50	23 54	23 58	00 02	00 05	00 09	00 17	00 21			
Hoxton	d	23 11		23 15	23 19	23 22	23 26	23 30	23 34	23 37	23 41	23 45		23 49	23 52	23 56	00 01	00 04	00 07	00 11	00 19	00 23			
Haggerston	d	23 13		23 17	23 21	23 24	23 28	23 32	23 36	23 39	23 43	23 47		23 51	23 54	23 58	00 02	00 06	00 09	00 13	00 21	00 25			
Dalston Junction	a	23 15		23 19	23 23	23 29	23 32	23 34	23 38	23 44	23 45	23 49		23 53	23 59	00 01	00 04	00 08	00 14	00 15	00 28	00 27			
Canonbury	a	23 18			23 26			23 37	23 41		23 50			23 56		00 03		00 11		00 18		00 30			
Highbury & Islington	a	23 23			23 30			23 40	23 45		23 55			23 59		00 10		00 15		00 25		00 33			

Saturdays

26 May to 8 December

		LO B	LO C	LO D	LO E	LO D	LO C	LO	LO	and every 15 minutes until	LO		LO	LO	LO	LO	LO	LO	LO	LO	LO		LO	LO
Clapham Junction	d																				06 00			
Wandsworth Road	d																				06 06			
Clapham High Street ⊖	d																				06 08			
Denmark Hill	d																				06 13			
Peckham Rye	d																				06 15			
Queens Rd Peckham	d					00 01															06 17			
West Croydon	d														05 31			05 46					06 01	
Norwood Junction	d														05 37			05 52					06 07	
Anerley	d														05 40			05 55					06 10	
Penge West	d														05 41			05 56					06 11	
Crystal Palace	d							00 04						05 32			05 47			06 02				
Sydenham	d							00 08						05 36	05 44		05 51	05 59		06 06			06 14	
Forest Hill	d							00 11						05 39	05 47		05 54	06 02		06 09			06 17	
Honor Oak Park	d							00 13						05 41	05 49		05 56	06 04		06 11			06 19	
Brockley	d						00 01	00 16						05 44	05 52		05 59	06 07		06 14			06 22	
New Cross Gate	d						00 03	00 18	00 33		05 18		05 33	05 46	05 54		06 01	06 09		06 16			06 24	
New Cross	d															05 57			06 12					06 27
Surrey Quays	d					00 05	00 09	00 22	00 37		05 22		05 37	05 50	05 57	06 01	06 05	06 12	06 16	06 20	06 23		06 27	06 31
Canada Water	d					00 07	00 11	00 24	00 39		05 24		05 39	05 52	05 59	06 03	06 07	06 14	06 18	06 22	06 25		06 29	06 33
Rotherhithe	d				00 01	00 09	00 12	00 25	00 40		05 25		05 40	05 53	06 01	06 05	06 08	06 16	06 20	06 23	06 27		06 31	06 35
Wapping	d				00 02	00 10	00 14	00 27	00 42		05 27		05 42	05 55	06 02	06 06	06 10	06 17	06 21	06 25	06 28		06 32	06 36
Shadwell	d			00 01	00 04	00 12	00 16	00 29	00 44		05 29		05 44	05 57	06 04	06 08	06 12	06 19	06 23	06 27	06 30		06 34	06 38
Whitechapel	d			00 03	00 07	00 15	00 18	00 31	00 46		05 31		05 46	05 59	06 07	06 11	06 14	06 22	06 26	06 29	06 33		06 37	06 41
Shoreditch High Street	d		00 02	00 05	00 09	00 17	00 21	00 34	00 49		05 34		05 49	06 02	06 09	06 13	06 17	06 24	06 28	06 32	06 35		06 39	06 43
Hoxton	d	00 01	00 04	00 07	00 11	00 19	00 23	00 36	00 51		05 36		05 51	06 04	06 11	06 15	06 19	06 26	06 30	06 34	06 37		06 41	06 45
Haggerston	d	00 02	00 06	00 09	00 13	00 21	00 25	00 38	00 53		05 38		05 53	06 06	06 13	06 17	06 21	06 28	06 32	06 36	06 39		06 43	06 47
Dalston Junction	a	00 04	00 08	00 14	00 15	00 28	00 27	00 40	00 55		05 40		05 55	06 08	06 15	06 19	06 23	06 30	06 34	06 38	06 44		06 45	06 49
Canonbury	a		00 11		00 18		00 30	00 43	00 58		05 43		05 58	06 11	06 18		06 26	06 33		06 41			06 48	
Highbury & Islington	a		00 15		00 25		00 33	00 47	01 03		05 48		06 04	06 15	06 23		06 30	06 38		06 45			06 53	

A From Battersea Park
B From New Cross Ell
C From Crystal Palace
D From Clapham Junction Plats 0-2
E From West Croydon

26 May to 8 December

Clapham Junction and West Croydon, Crystal Palace, New Cross - Highbury & Islington

		LO	LO	LO	LO	LO	LO	LO		LO	LO	LO	LO	LO	LO	LO	LO	LO		LO	LO	LO	LO	LO	LO
Clapham Junction	d		06 15				06 30					06 45				07 00					07 15				07 30
Wandsworth Road	d		06 21				06 36					06 51				07 06					07 21				07 36
Clapham High Street ⊖	d		06 23				06 38					06 53				07 08					07 23				07 38
Denmark Hill	d		06 28				06 43					06 58				07 13					07 28				07 43
Peckham Rye	d		06 30				06 45					07 00				07 15					07 30				07 45
Queens Rd Peckham	d		06 32				06 47					07 02				07 17					07 32				07 47
West Croydon	d			06 16				06 31					06 46				07 01					07 16			
Norwood Junction	d			06 22				06 37					06 52				07 07					07 22			
Anerley	d			06 25				06 40					06 55				07 10					07 25			
Penge West	d			06 26				06 41					06 56				07 11					07 26			
Crystal Palace	d	06 17				06 32					06 47				07 02					07 17				07 32	
Sydenham	d	06 21		06 29		06 36		06 44			06 51		06 59		07 06		07 14			07 21		07 29		07 36	
Forest Hill	d	06 24		06 32		06 39		06 47			06 54		07 02		07 09		07 17			07 24		07 32		07 39	
Honor Oak Park	d	06 26		06 34		06 41		06 49			06 56		07 04		07 11		07 19			07 26		07 34		07 41	
Brockley	d	06 29		06 37		06 44		06 52			06 59		07 07		07 14		07 22			07 29		07 37		07 44	
New Cross Gate	d	06 31		06 39		06 46		06 54			07 01		07 09		07 16		07 24			07 31		07 39		07 46	
New Cross	d				06 42					06 57				07 12				07 27					07 42		
Surrey Quays	d	06 35	06 38	06 42	06 46	06 50	06 53	06 57		07 01	07 05	07 08	07 12	07 16	07 20	07 23	07 27	07 31		07 35	07 38	07 42	07 46	07 50	07 53
Canada Water	d	06 37	06 40	06 44	06 48	06 52	06 55	06 59		07 03	07 07	07 10	07 14	07 18	07 22	07 25	07 29	07 33		07 37	07 40	07 44	07 48	07 52	07 55
Rotherhithe	d	06 38	06 42	06 46	06 50	06 53	06 57	07 01		07 05	07 08	07 12	07 16	07 20	07 23	07 27	07 31	07 35		07 38	07 42	07 46	07 50	07 53	07 57
Wapping	d	06 40	06 43	06 47	06 51	06 55	06 58	07 02		07 06	07 10	07 13	07 17	07 21	07 25	07 28	07 32	07 36		07 40	07 43	07 47	07 51	07 55	07 58
Shadwell	d	06 42	06 45	06 49	06 53	06 57	07 00	07 04		07 08	07 12	07 15	07 19	07 23	07 27	07 30	07 34	07 38		07 42	07 45	07 49	07 53	07 57	08 00
Whitechapel	d	06 44	06 48	06 52	06 56	06 59	07 03	07 07		07 11	07 14	07 18	07 22	07 26	07 29	07 33	07 37	07 41		07 44	07 48	07 52	07 56	07 59	08 03
Shoreditch High Street	d	06 47	06 50	06 54	06 58	07 02	07 05	07 09		07 13	07 17	07 20	07 24	07 28	07 32	07 35	07 39	07 43		07 47	07 50	07 54	07 58	08 02	08 05
Hoxton	d	06 49	06 52	06 56	07 00	07 04	07 07	07 11		07 15	07 19	07 22	07 26	07 30	07 34	07 37	07 41	07 45		07 49	07 52	07 56	08 00	08 04	08 07
Haggerston	d	06 51	06 54	06 58	07 02	07 06	07 09	07 13		07 17	07 21	07 24	07 28	07 32	07 36	07 39	07 43	07 47		07 51	07 54	07 58	08 02	08 06	08 09
Dalston Junction	a	06 53	06 59	07 00	07 04	07 08	07 14	07 15		07 19	07 23	07 29	07 30	07 34	07 38	07 44	07 45	07 49		07 53	07 59	08 00	08 04	08 08	08 14
Canonbury	a	06 56		07 03		07 11		07 18			07 26		07 33		07 41		07 48			07 56		08 03		08 11	
Highbury & Islington	a	07 00		07 10		07 15		07 25			07 30		07 40		07 45		07 55			08 00		08 10		08 15	

		LO	LO	LO		LO	LO	LO	LO	LO	LO	LO	LO	LO		LO	LO	LO	LO	LO	LO	LO	LO	LO	
Clapham Junction	d					07 45				08 00				08 15					08 30				08 45		
Wandsworth Road	d					07 51				08 06				08 21					08 36				08 51		
Clapham High Street ⊖	d					07 53				08 08				08 23					08 38				08 53		
Denmark Hill	d					07 58				08 13				08 28					08 43				08 58		
Peckham Rye	d					08 00				08 15				08 30					08 45				09 00		
Queens Rd Peckham	d					08 02				08 17				08 32					08 47				09 02		
West Croydon	d	07 31					07 46				08 01					08 16				08 31				08 46	
Norwood Junction	d	07 37					07 52				08 07					08 22				08 37				08 52	
Anerley	d	07 40					07 55				08 10					08 25				08 40				08 55	
Penge West	d	07 41					07 57				08 11					08 26				08 41				08 57	
Crystal Palace	d			07 47					08 02				08 17					08 32				08 47			
Sydenham	d	07 44		07 51			07 59		08 06		08 14		08 21			08 29		08 36		08 44		08 51		08 59	
Forest Hill	d	07 47		07 54			08 02		08 09		08 17		08 24			08 32		08 39		08 47		08 54		09 02	
Honor Oak Park	d	07 49		07 56			08 04		08 11		08 19		08 26			08 34		08 41		08 49		08 56		09 04	
Brockley	d	07 52		07 59			08 07		08 14		08 22		08 29			08 37		08 44		08 52		08 59		09 07	
New Cross Gate	d	07 54		08 01			08 09		08 16		08 24		08 31			08 39		08 46		08 54		09 01		09 09	
New Cross	d		07 57					08 12				08 27					08 42				08 57				
Surrey Quays	d	07 57	08 01	08 05		08 08	08 12	08 16	08 20	08 23	08 27	08 31	08 35	08 38		08 42	08 46	08 50	08 53	08 57	09 01	09 05	09 08	09 12	
Canada Water	d	07 59	08 03	08 07		08 10	08 14	08 18	08 22	08 25	08 29	08 33	08 37	08 40		08 44	08 48	08 52	08 55	08 59	09 03	09 07	09 10	09 14	
Rotherhithe	d	08 01	08 05	08 08		08 12	08 16	08 20	08 23	08 27	08 31	08 35	08 38	08 42		08 46	08 50	08 53	08 57	09 01	09 05	09 08	09 12	09 16	
Wapping	d	08 02	08 06	08 10		08 13	08 17	08 21	08 25	08 28	08 32	08 36	08 40	08 43		08 47	08 51	08 55	08 58	09 02	09 06	09 10	09 13	09 17	
Shadwell	d	08 04	08 08	08 12		08 15	08 19	08 23	08 27	08 30	08 34	08 38	08 42	08 45		08 49	08 53	08 57	09 00	09 04	09 08	09 12	09 15	09 19	
Whitechapel	d	08 07	08 11	08 14		08 18	08 22	08 26	08 29	08 33	08 37	08 41	08 44	08 48		08 52	08 56	08 59	09 03	09 07	09 11	09 14	09 18	09 22	
Shoreditch High Street	d	08 09	08 13	08 17		08 20	08 24	08 28	08 32	08 35	08 39	08 43	08 47	08 50		08 54	08 58	09 02	09 05	09 09	09 13	09 17	09 20	09 24	
Hoxton	d	08 11	08 15	08 19		08 22	08 26	08 30	08 34	08 37	08 41	08 45	08 49	08 52		08 56	09 00	09 04	09 07	09 11	09 15	09 19	09 22	09 26	
Haggerston	d	08 13	08 17	08 21		08 24	08 28	08 32	08 36	08 39	08 43	08 47	08 51	08 54		08 58	09 02	09 06	09 09	09 13	09 17	09 21	09 24	09 28	
Dalston Junction	a	08 15	08 19	08 23		08 29	08 30	08 35	08 38	08 44	08 45	08 50	08 53	09 00		09 00	09 05	09 08	09 15	09 15	09 19	09 23	09 30	09 30	
Canonbury	a	08 18		08 26			08 33		08 41		08 48		08 56			09 03		09 11		09 18		09 26		09 33	
Highbury & Islington	a	08 25		08 30			08 40		08 45		08 55		09 00			09 10		09 15		09 25		09 30		09 40	

		LO	LO	LO	LO	LO	LO	LO	LO	LO		LO	LO	LO	LO	LO	LO	LO	LO	LO		LO	LO	LO	LO
Clapham Junction	d			09 00				09 15					09 30				09 45					10 00			
Wandsworth Road	d			09 06				09 21					09 36				09 51					10 06			
Clapham High Street ⊖	d			09 08				09 23					09 38				09 53					10 08			
Denmark Hill	d			09 13				09 28					09 43				09 58					10 13			
Peckham Rye	d			09 15				09 30					09 45				10 00					10 15			
Queens Rd Peckham	d			09 17				09 32					09 47				10 02					10 17			
West Croydon	d				09 01				09 16					09 31				09 46					10 01		
Norwood Junction	d				09 07				09 22					09 37				09 52					10 07		
Anerley	d				09 10				09 25					09 40				09 55					10 10		
Penge West	d				09 11				09 26					09 41				09 57					10 11		
Crystal Palace	d		09 02				09 17					09 32				09 47				10 02					10 17
Sydenham	d		09 06		09 14		09 21		09 29			09 36		09 44		09 51		09 59		10 06			10 14		10 21
Forest Hill	d		09 09		09 17		09 24		09 32			09 39		09 47		09 54		10 02		10 09			10 17		10 24
Honor Oak Park	d		09 11		09 19		09 26		09 34			09 41		09 49		09 56		10 04		10 11			10 19		10 26
Brockley	d		09 14		09 22		09 29		09 37			09 44		09 52		09 59		10 07		10 14			10 22		10 29
New Cross Gate	d		09 16		09 24		09 31		09 39			09 46		09 54		10 01		10 09		10 16			10 24		10 31
New Cross	d	09 12				09 27				09 42					09 57				10 12					10 27	
Surrey Quays	d	09 16	09 20	09 23	09 27	09 31	09 35	09 38	09 42	09 46		09 50	09 53	09 57	10 01	10 05	10 08	10 12	10 16	10 20		10 23	10 27	10 31	10 35
Canada Water	d	09 18	09 22	09 25	09 29	09 33	09 37	09 40	09 44	09 48		09 52	09 55	09 59	10 03	10 07	10 10	10 14	10 18	10 22		10 25	10 29	10 33	10 37
Rotherhithe	d	09 20	09 23	09 27	09 31	09 35	09 38	09 42	09 46	09 50		09 53	09 57	10 01	10 05	10 08	10 12	10 16	10 20	10 23		10 27	10 31	10 35	10 38
Wapping	d	09 21	09 25	09 28	09 32	09 36	09 40	09 43	09 47	09 51		09 55	09 58	10 02	10 06	10 10	10 13	10 17	10 21	10 25		10 28	10 32	10 36	10 40
Shadwell	d	09 23	09 27	09 30	09 34	09 38	09 42	09 45	09 49	09 53		09 57	10 00	10 04	10 08	10 12	10 15	10 19	10 23	10 27		10 30	10 34	10 38	10 42
Whitechapel	d	09 26	09 29	09 33	09 37	09 41	09 44	09 48	09 52	09 56		09 59	10 03	10 07	10 11	10 14	10 18	10 22	10 26	10 29		10 33	10 37	10 41	10 44
Shoreditch High Street	d	09 28	09 32	09 35	09 39	09 43	09 47	09 50	09 54	09 58		10 02	10 05	10 09	10 13	10 17	10 20	10 24	10 28	10 32		10 35	10 39	10 43	10 47
Hoxton	d	09 30	09 34	09 37	09 41	09 45	09 49	09 52	09 56	10 00		10 04	10 07	10 11	10 15	10 19	10 22	10 26	10 30	10 34		10 37	10 41	10 45	10 49
Haggerston	d	09 32	09 36	09 39	09 43	09 47	09 51	09 54	09 58	10 02		10 06	10 09	10 13	10 17	10 21	10 24	10 28	10 32	10 36		10 39	10 43	10 47	10 51
Dalston Junction	a	09 34	09 38	09 44	09 45	09 49	09 53	09 59	10 00	10 04		10 08	10 14	10 15	10 19	10 23	10 29	10 30	10 34	10 38		10 44	10 45	10 49	10 53
Canonbury	a		09 41		09 48		09 56		10 03			10 11		10 18		10 26		10 33		10 41			10 48		10 56
Highbury & Islington	a		09 45		09 55		10 00		10 10			10 15		10 25		10 30		10 40		10 45			10 55		11 00

Clapham Junction and West Croydon, Crystal Palace, New Cross - Highbury & Islington

		LO	LO	LO	LO	LO		LO	LO	LO	LO	LO	LO	LO	LO	LO		LO	LO	LO	LO	LO	LO	LO	LO
Clapham Junction	d	10 15				10 30					10 45				11 00					11 15				11 30	
Wandsworth Road	d	10 21				10 36					10 51				11 06					11 21				11 36	
Clapham High Street ⊖	d	10 23				10 38					10 53				11 08					11 23				11 38	
Denmark Hill	d	10 28				10 43					10 58				11 13					11 28				11 43	
Peckham Rye	d	10 30				10 45					11 00				11 15					11 30				11 45	
Queens Rd Peckham	d	10 32				10 47					11 02				11 17					11 32				11 47	
West Croydon	d		10 16					10 31				10 46				11 01					11 16				11 31
Norwood Junction	d		10 22					10 37				10 52				11 07					11 22				11 37
Anerley	d		10 25					10 40				10 55				11 10					11 25				11 40
Penge West	d		10 26					10 41				10 57				11 11					11 26				11 41
Crystal Palace	d				10 32					10 47				11 02					11 17				11 32		
Sydenham	d		10 29		10 36			10 44		10 51		10 59		11 06		11 14			11 21		11 29		11 36		11 44
Forest Hill	d		10 32		10 39			10 47		10 54		11 02		11 09		11 17			11 24		11 32		11 39		11 47
Honor Oak Park	d		10 34		10 41			10 49		10 56		11 04		11 11		11 19			11 26		11 34		11 41		11 49
Brockley	d		10 37		10 44			10 52		10 59		11 07		11 14		11 22			11 29		11 37		11 44		11 52
New Cross Gate	d		10 39		10 46			10 54		11 01		11 09		11 16		11 24			11 31		11 39		11 46		11 54
New Cross	d			10 42					10 57				11 12					11 27				11 42			
Surrey Quays	d	10 38	10 42	10 46	10 50	10 53		10 57	11 01	11 05	11 08	11 12	11 16	11 20	11 23	11 27		11 31	11 35	11 38	11 42	11 46	11 50	11 53	11 57
Canada Water	d	10 40	10 44	10 48	10 52	10 55		10 59	11 03	11 07	11 10	11 14	11 18	11 22	11 25	11 29		11 33	11 37	11 40	11 44	11 48	11 52	11 55	11 59
Rotherhithe	d	10 42	10 46	10 50	10 53	10 57		11 01	11 05	11 08	11 12	11 16	11 20	11 23	11 27	11 31		11 35	11 38	11 42	11 46	11 50	11 53	11 57	12 01
Wapping	d	10 43	10 47	10 51	10 55	10 58		11 02	11 06	11 10	11 13	11 17	11 21	11 25	11 28	11 32		11 36	11 40	11 43	11 47	11 51	11 55	11 58	12 02
Shadwell	d	10 45	10 49	10 53	10 57	11 00		11 04	11 08	11 12	11 15	11 19	11 23	11 27	11 30	11 34		11 38	11 42	11 45	11 49	11 53	11 57	12 00	12 04
Whitechapel	d	10 48	10 52	10 56	10 59	11 03		11 07	11 11	11 14	11 18	11 22	11 26	11 29	11 33	11 37		11 41	11 44	11 48	11 52	11 56	11 59	12 03	12 07
Shoreditch High Street	d	10 50	10 54	10 58	11 02	11 05		11 09	11 13	11 17	11 20	11 24	11 28	11 32	11 35	11 39		11 43	11 47	11 50	11 54	11 58	12 02	12 05	12 09
Hoxton	d	10 52	10 56	11 00	11 04	11 07		11 11	11 15	11 19	11 22	11 26	11 30	11 34	11 37	11 41		11 45	11 49	11 52	11 56	12 00	12 04	12 07	12 11
Haggerston	d	10 54	10 58	11 02	11 06	11 09		11 13	11 17	11 21	11 24	11 28	11 32	11 36	11 39	11 43		11 47	11 51	11 54	11 58	12 02	12 06	12 09	12 13
Dalston Junction	a	10 59	11 00	11 04	11 08	11 14		11 15	11 19	11 23	11 29	11 30	11 34	11 38	11 44	11 45		11 49	11 53	11 59	12 00	12 04	12 08	12 14	12 15
Canonbury	a		11 03		11 11			11 18		11 26		11 33		11 41		11 48			11 56		12 03		12 11		12 18
Highbury & Islington	a		11 08		11 15			11 23		11 30		11 38		11 45		11 53			12 00		12 08		12 15		12 23

		LO		LO	LO	LO	LO	LO	LO	LO	LO	LO		LO	LO	LO	LO	LO	LO	LO	LO	LO		LO	LO
Clapham Junction	d				11 45				12 00					12 15				12 30				12 45			
Wandsworth Road	d				11 51				12 06					12 21				12 36				12 51			
Clapham High Street ⊖	d				11 53				12 08					12 23				12 38				12 53			
Denmark Hill	d				11 58				12 13					12 28				12 43				12 58			
Peckham Rye	d				12 00				12 15					12 30				12 45				13 00			
Queens Rd Peckham	d				12 02				12 17					12 32				12 47				13 02			
West Croydon	d					11 46				12 01					12 16				12 31					12 46	
Norwood Junction	d					11 52				12 07					12 22				12 37					12 52	
Anerley	d					11 55				12 10					12 25				12 40					12 55	
Penge West	d					11 57				12 11					12 26				12 41					12 57	
Crystal Palace	d			11 47				12 02				12 17					12 32				12 47				
Sydenham	d			11 51		11 59		12 06		12 14		12 21			12 29		12 36		12 44		12 51			12 59	
Forest Hill	d			11 54		12 02		12 09		12 17		12 24			12 32		12 39		12 47		12 54			13 02	
Honor Oak Park	d			11 56		12 04		12 11		12 19		12 26			12 34		12 41		12 49		12 56			13 04	
Brockley	d			11 59		12 07		12 14		12 22		12 29			12 37		12 44		12 52		12 59			13 07	
New Cross Gate	d			12 01		12 09		12 16		12 24		12 31			12 39		12 46		12 54		13 01			13 09	
New Cross	d	11 57					12 12				12 27					12 42				12 57					13 12
Surrey Quays	d	12 01		12 05	12 08	12 12	12 16	12 20	12 23	12 27	12 31	12 35		12 38	12 42	12 46	12 50	12 53	12 57	13 01	13 05	13 08		13 12	13 16
Canada Water	d	12 03		12 07	12 10	12 14	12 18	12 22	12 25	12 29	12 33	12 37		12 40	12 44	12 48	12 52	12 55	12 59	13 03	13 07	13 10		13 14	13 18
Rotherhithe	d	12 05		12 08	12 12	12 16	12 20	12 23	12 27	12 31	12 35	12 38		12 42	12 46	12 50	12 53	12 57	13 01	13 05	13 08	13 12		13 16	13 20
Wapping	d	12 06		12 10	12 13	12 17	12 21	12 25	12 28	12 32	12 36	12 40		12 43	12 47	12 51	12 55	12 58	13 02	13 06	13 10	13 13		13 17	13 21
Shadwell	d	12 08		12 12	12 15	12 19	12 23	12 27	12 30	12 34	12 38	12 42		12 45	12 49	12 53	12 57	13 00	13 04	13 08	13 12	13 15		13 19	13 23
Whitechapel	d	12 11		12 14	12 18	12 22	12 26	12 29	12 33	12 37	12 41	12 44		12 48	12 52	12 56	12 59	13 03	13 07	13 11	13 14	13 18		13 22	13 26
Shoreditch High Street	d	12 13		12 17	12 20	12 24	12 28	12 32	12 35	12 39	12 43	12 47		12 50	12 54	12 58	13 02	13 05	13 09	13 13	13 17	13 20		13 24	13 28
Hoxton	d	12 15		12 19	12 22	12 26	12 30	12 34	12 37	12 41	12 45	12 49		12 52	12 56	13 00	13 04	13 07	13 11	13 15	13 19	13 22		13 26	13 30
Haggerston	d	12 17		12 21	12 24	12 28	12 32	12 36	12 39	12 43	12 47	12 51		12 54	12 58	13 02	13 06	13 09	13 13	13 17	13 21	13 24		13 28	13 32
Dalston Junction	a	12 19		12 23	12 29	12 30	12 34	12 38	12 44	12 45	12 49	12 53		12 59	13 00	13 04	13 08	13 14	13 15	13 19	13 23	13 29		13 30	13 34
Canonbury	a			12 26		12 33		12 41		12 48		12 56			13 03		13 11		13 18		13 26			13 33	
Highbury & Islington	a			12 30		12 38		12 45		12 53		13 00			13 08		13 15		13 23		13 30			13 38	

		LO	LO	LO	LO	LO	LO	LO		LO	LO	LO	LO	LO	LO	LO	LO	LO		LO	LO	LO	LO	LO	LO
Clapham Junction	d		13 00				13 15					13 30				13 45					14 00				14 15
Wandsworth Road	d		13 06				13 21					13 36				13 51					14 06				14 21
Clapham High Street ⊖	d		13 08				13 23					13 38				13 53					14 08				14 23
Denmark Hill	d		13 13				13 28					13 43				13 58					14 13				14 28
Peckham Rye	d		13 15				13 30					13 45				14 00					14 15				14 30
Queens Rd Peckham	d		13 17				13 32					13 47				14 02					14 17				14 32
West Croydon	d			13 01				13 16					13 31				13 46					14 01			
Norwood Junction	d			13 07				13 22					13 37				13 52					14 07			
Anerley	d			13 10				13 25					13 40				13 55					14 10			
Penge West	d			13 11				13 26					13 41				13 57					14 11			
Crystal Palace	d	13 02				13 17					13 32				13 47					14 02				14 17	
Sydenham	d	13 06		13 14		13 21		13 29			13 36		13 44		13 51		13 59			14 06		14 14		14 21	
Forest Hill	d	13 09		13 17		13 24		13 32			13 39		13 47		13 54		14 02			14 09		14 17		14 24	
Honor Oak Park	d	13 11		13 19		13 26		13 34			13 41		13 49		13 56		14 04			14 11		14 19		14 26	
Brockley	d	13 14		13 22		13 29		13 37			13 44		13 52		13 59		14 07			14 14		14 22		14 29	
New Cross Gate	d	13 16		13 24		13 31		13 39			13 46		13 54		14 01		14 09			14 16		14 24		14 31	
New Cross	d				13 27					13 42				13 57				14 12					14 27		
Surrey Quays	d	13 20	13 23	13 27	13 31	13 35	13 38	13 42		13 46	13 50	13 53	13 57	14 01	14 05	14 08	14 12	14 16		14 20	14 23	14 27	14 31	14 35	14 38
Canada Water	d	13 22	13 25	13 29	13 33	13 37	13 40	13 44		13 48	13 52	13 55	13 59	14 03	14 07	14 10	14 14	14 18		14 22	14 25	14 29	14 33	14 37	14 40
Rotherhithe	d	13 23	13 27	13 31	13 35	13 38	13 42	13 46		13 50	13 53	13 57	14 01	14 05	14 08	14 12	14 16	14 20		14 23	14 27	14 31	14 35	14 38	14 42
Wapping	d	13 25	13 28	13 32	13 36	13 40	13 43	13 47		13 51	13 55	13 58	14 02	14 06	14 10	14 13	14 17	14 21		14 25	14 28	14 32	14 36	14 40	14 43
Shadwell	d	13 27	13 30	13 34	13 38	13 42	13 45	13 49		13 53	13 57	14 00	14 04	14 08	14 12	14 15	14 19	14 23		14 27	14 30	14 34	14 38	14 42	14 45
Whitechapel	d	13 29	13 33	13 37	13 41	13 44	13 48	13 52		13 56	13 59	14 03	14 07	14 11	14 14	14 18	14 22	14 26		14 29	14 33	14 37	14 41	14 44	14 48
Shoreditch High Street	d	13 32	13 35	13 39	13 43	13 47	13 50	13 54		13 58	14 02	14 05	14 09	14 13	14 17	14 20	14 24	14 28		14 32	14 35	14 39	14 43	14 47	14 50
Hoxton	d	13 34	13 37	13 41	13 45	13 49	13 52	13 56		14 00	14 04	14 07	14 11	14 15	14 19	14 22	14 26	14 30		14 34	14 37	14 41	14 45	14 49	14 52
Haggerston	d	13 36	13 39	13 43	13 47	13 51	13 54	13 58		14 02	14 06	14 09	14 13	14 17	14 21	14 24	14 28	14 32		14 36	14 39	14 43	14 47	14 51	14 54
Dalston Junction	a	13 38	13 44	13 45	13 49	13 53	13 59	14 00		14 04	14 08	14 14	14 15	14 19	14 23	14 29	14 30	14 34		14 38	14 44	14 45	14 49	14 53	14 59
Canonbury	a	13 41		13 48		13 56		14 03			14 11		14 18		14 26		14 33			14 41		14 48		14 56	
Highbury & Islington	a	13 45		13 53		14 00		14 08			14 15		14 23		14 30		14 38			14 45		14 53		15 00	

Table T178-R

Saturdays

26 May to 8 December

Clapham Junction and West Croydon, Crystal Palace, New Cross - Highbury & Islington

		LO	LO	LO		LO	LO	LO	LO	LO	LO	LO	LO	LO		LO	LO	LO	LO	LO	LO	LO	LO	LO	
Clapham Junction	d					14 30				14 45				15 00					15 15				15 30		
Wandsworth Road	d					14 36				14 51				15 06					15 21				15 36		
Clapham High Street ⊖	d					14 38				14 53				15 08					15 23				15 38		
Denmark Hill	d					14 43				14 58				15 13					15 28				15 43		
Peckham Rye	d					14 45				15 00				15 15					15 30				15 45		
Queens Rd Peckham	d					14 47				15 02				15 17					15 32				15 47		
West Croydon	d	14 16					14 31				14 46					15 01				15 16				15 31	
Norwood Junction	d	14 22					14 37				14 52					15 07				15 22				15 37	
Anerley	d	14 25					14 40				14 55					15 10				15 25				15 40	
Penge West	d	14 26					14 41				14 57					15 11				15 26				15 41	
Crystal Palace	d			14 32					14 47				15 02					15 17				15 32			
Sydenham	d	14 29		14 36			14 44		14 51		14 59		15 06			15 14		15 21		15 29		15 36		15 44	
Forest Hill	d	14 32		14 39			14 47		14 54		15 02		15 09			15 17		15 24		15 32		15 39		15 47	
Honor Oak Park	d	14 34		14 41			14 49		14 56		15 04		15 11			15 19		15 26		15 34		15 41		15 49	
Brockley	d	14 37		14 44			14 52		14 59		15 07		15 14			15 22		15 29		15 37		15 44		15 52	
New Cross Gate	d	14 39		14 46			14 54		15 01		15 09		15 16			15 24		15 31		15 39		15 46		15 54	
New Cross	d		14 42					14 57				15 12					15 27				15 42				
Surrey Quays	d	14 42	14 46	14 50		14 53	14 57	15 01	15 05	15 08	15 12	15 16	15 20	15 23		15 27	15 31	15 35	15 38	15 42	15 46	15 50	15 53	15 57	
Canada Water	d	14 44	14 48	14 52		14 55	14 59	15 03	15 07	15 10	15 14	15 18	15 22	15 25		15 29	15 33	15 37	15 40	15 44	15 48	15 52	15 55	15 59	
Rotherhithe	d	14 46	14 50	14 53		14 57	15 01	15 05	15 08	15 12	15 16	15 20	15 23	15 27		15 31	15 35	15 38	15 42	15 46	15 50	15 53	15 57	16 01	
Wapping	d	14 47	14 51	14 55		14 58	15 02	15 06	15 10	15 13	15 17	15 21	15 25	15 28		15 32	15 36	15 40	15 43	15 47	15 51	15 55	15 58	16 02	
Shadwell	d	14 49	14 53	14 57		15 00	15 04	15 08	15 12	15 15	15 19	15 23	15 27	15 30		15 34	15 38	15 42	15 45	15 49	15 53	15 57	16 00	16 04	
Whitechapel	d	14 52	14 56	14 59		15 03	15 07	15 11	15 14	15 18	15 22	15 26	15 29	15 33		15 37	15 41	15 44	15 48	15 52	15 56	15 59	16 03	16 07	
Shoreditch High Street	d	14 54	14 58	15 02		15 05	15 09	15 13	15 17	15 20	15 24	15 28	15 32	15 35		15 39	15 43	15 47	15 50	15 54	15 58	16 02	16 05	16 09	
Hoxton	d	14 56	15 00	15 04		15 07	15 11	15 15	15 19	15 22	15 26	15 30	15 34	15 37		15 41	15 45	15 49	15 52	15 56	16 00	16 04	16 07	16 11	
Haggerston	d	14 58	15 02	15 06		15 09	15 13	15 17	15 21	15 24	15 28	15 32	15 36	15 39		15 43	15 47	15 51	15 54	15 58	16 02	16 06	16 09	16 13	
Dalston Junction	a	15 00	15 04	15 08		15 14	15 15	15 19	15 23	15 29	15 30	15 34	15 38	15 44		15 45	15 49	15 53	15 59	16 00	16 04	16 08	16 14	16 15	
Canonbury	a	15 03		15 11			15 18		15 26		15 33		15 41			15 48		15 56		16 03		16 11		16 18	
Highbury & Islington	a	15 08		15 15			15 23		15 30		15 38		15 45			15 53		16 00		16 10		16 15		16 25	

		LO	LO	LO	LO	LO	LO	LO	LO	LO		LO	LO	LO	LO	LO	LO	LO	LO	LO		LO	LO	LO	LO
Clapham Junction	d			15 45				16 00					16 15				16 30					16 45			
Wandsworth Road	d			15 51				16 06					16 21				16 36					16 51			
Clapham High Street ⊖	d			15 53				16 08					16 23				16 38					16 53			
Denmark Hill	d			15 58				16 13					16 28				16 43					16 58			
Peckham Rye	d			16 00				16 15					16 30				16 45					17 00			
Queens Rd Peckham	d			16 02				16 17					16 32				16 47					17 02			
West Croydon	d				15 46				16 01					16 16				16 31					16 46		
Norwood Junction	d				15 52				16 07					16 22				16 37					16 52		
Anerley	d				15 55				16 10					16 25				16 40					16 55		
Penge West	d				15 57				16 11					16 26				16 41					16 57		
Crystal Palace	d		15 47				16 02					16 17				16 32				16 47					17 02
Sydenham	d		15 51		15 59		16 06		16 14			16 21		16 29		16 36		16 44		16 51			16 59		17 06
Forest Hill	d		15 54		16 02		16 09		16 17			16 24		16 32		16 39		16 47		16 54			17 02		17 09
Honor Oak Park	d		15 56		16 04		16 11		16 19			16 26		16 34		16 41		16 49		16 56			17 04		17 11
Brockley	d		15 59		16 07		16 14		16 22			16 29		16 37		16 44		16 52		16 59			17 07		17 14
New Cross Gate	d		16 01		16 09		16 16		16 24			16 31		16 39		16 46		16 54		17 01			17 09		17 16
New Cross	d	15 57				16 12				16 27					16 42				16 57					17 12	
Surrey Quays	d	16 01	16 05	16 08	16 12	16 16	16 20	16 23	16 27	16 31		16 35	16 38	16 42	16 46	16 50	16 53	16 57	17 01	17 05		17 08	17 12	17 16	17 20
Canada Water	d	16 03	16 07	16 10	16 14	16 18	16 22	16 25	16 29	16 33		16 37	16 40	16 44	16 48	16 52	16 55	16 59	17 03	17 07		17 10	17 14	17 18	17 22
Rotherhithe	d	16 05	16 08	16 12	16 16	16 20	16 23	16 27	16 31	16 35		16 38	16 42	16 46	16 50	16 53	16 57	17 01	17 05	17 08		17 12	17 16	17 20	17 23
Wapping	d	16 06	16 10	16 13	16 17	16 21	16 25	16 28	16 32	16 36		16 40	16 43	16 47	16 51	16 55	16 58	17 02	17 06	17 10		17 13	17 17	17 21	17 25
Shadwell	d	16 08	16 12	16 15	16 19	16 23	16 27	16 30	16 34	16 38		16 42	16 45	16 49	16 53	16 57	17 00	17 04	17 08	17 12		17 15	17 19	17 23	17 27
Whitechapel	d	16 11	16 14	16 18	16 22	16 26	16 29	16 33	16 37	16 41		16 44	16 48	16 52	16 56	16 59	17 03	17 07	17 11	17 14		17 18	17 22	17 26	17 29
Shoreditch High Street	d	16 13	16 17	16 20	16 24	16 28	16 32	16 35	16 39	16 43		16 47	16 50	16 54	16 58	17 02	17 05	17 09	17 13	17 17		17 20	17 24	17 28	17 32
Hoxton	d	16 15	16 19	16 22	16 26	16 30	16 34	16 37	16 41	16 45		16 49	16 52	16 56	17 00	17 04	17 07	17 11	17 15	17 19		17 22	17 26	17 30	17 34
Haggerston	d	16 17	16 21	16 24	16 28	16 32	16 36	16 39	16 43	16 47		16 51	16 54	16 58	17 02	17 06	17 09	17 13	17 17	17 21		17 24	17 28	17 32	17 36
Dalston Junction	a	16 19	16 23	16 29	16 30	16 34	16 38	16 44	16 45	16 49		16 53	16 59	17 00	17 04	17 08	17 14	17 15	17 19	17 23		17 29	17 30	17 34	17 38
Canonbury	a		16 26		16 33		16 41		16 48			16 56		17 03		17 11		17 18		17 26			17 33		17 41
Highbury & Islington	a		16 30		16 40		16 45		16 55			17 00		17 10		17 15		17 25		17 30			17 40		17 45

		LO	LO	LO	LO	LO		LO	LO	LO	LO	LO	LO	LO	LO	LO		LO	LO	LO	LO	LO	LO	LO	LO
Clapham Junction	d	17 00				17 15					17 30				17 45					18 00				18 15	
Wandsworth Road	d	17 06				17 21					17 36				17 51					18 06				18 21	
Clapham High Street ⊖	d	17 08				17 23					17 38				17 53					18 08				18 23	
Denmark Hill	d	17 13				17 28					17 43				17 58					18 13				18 28	
Peckham Rye	d	17 15				17 30					17 45				18 00					18 15				18 30	
Queens Rd Peckham	d	17 17				17 32					17 47				18 02					18 17				18 32	
West Croydon	d		17 01					17 16				17 31				17 46					18 01				18 16
Norwood Junction	d		17 07					17 22				17 37				17 52					18 07				18 22
Anerley	d		17 10					17 25				17 40				17 55					18 10				18 25
Penge West	d		17 11					17 26				17 41				17 57					18 11				18 26
Crystal Palace	d				17 17					17 32				17 47					18 02				18 17		
Sydenham	d		17 14		17 21			17 29		17 36		17 44		17 51		17 59			18 06		18 14		18 21		18 29
Forest Hill	d		17 17		17 24			17 32		17 39		17 47		17 54		18 02			18 09		18 17		18 24		18 32
Honor Oak Park	d		17 19		17 26			17 34		17 41		17 49		17 56		18 04			18 11		18 19		18 26		18 34
Brockley	d		17 22		17 29			17 37		17 44		17 52		17 59		18 07			18 14		18 22		18 29		18 37
New Cross Gate	d		17 24		17 31			17 39		17 46		17 54		18 01		18 09			18 16		18 24		18 31		18 39
New Cross	d			17 27					17 42				17 57					18 12				18 27			
Surrey Quays	d	17 23	17 27	17 31	17 35	17 38		17 42	17 46	17 50	17 53	17 57	18 01	18 05	18 08	18 12		18 16	18 20	18 23	18 27	18 31	18 35	18 38	18 42
Canada Water	d	17 25	17 29	17 33	17 37	17 40		17 44	17 48	17 52	17 55	17 59	18 03	18 07	18 10	18 14		18 18	18 22	18 25	18 29	18 33	18 37	18 40	18 44
Rotherhithe	d	17 27	17 31	17 35	17 38	17 42		17 46	17 50	17 53	17 57	18 01	18 05	18 08	18 12	18 16		18 20	18 23	18 27	18 31	18 35	18 38	18 42	18 46
Wapping	d	17 28	17 32	17 36	17 40	17 43		17 47	17 51	17 55	17 58	18 02	18 06	18 10	18 13	18 17		18 21	18 25	18 28	18 32	18 36	18 40	18 43	18 47
Shadwell	d	17 30	17 34	17 38	17 42	17 45		17 49	17 53	17 57	18 00	18 04	18 08	18 12	18 15	18 19		18 23	18 27	18 30	18 34	18 38	18 42	18 45	18 49
Whitechapel	d	17 33	17 37	17 41	17 44	17 48		17 52	17 56	17 59	18 03	18 07	18 11	18 14	18 18	18 22		18 26	18 29	18 33	18 37	18 41	18 44	18 48	18 52
Shoreditch High Street	d	17 35	17 39	17 43	17 47	17 50		17 54	17 58	18 02	18 05	18 09	18 13	18 17	18 20	18 24		18 28	18 32	18 35	18 39	18 43	18 47	18 50	18 54
Hoxton	d	17 37	17 41	17 45	17 49	17 52		17 56	18 00	18 04	18 07	18 11	18 15	18 19	18 22	18 26		18 30	18 34	18 37	18 41	18 45	18 49	18 52	18 56
Haggerston	d	17 39	17 43	17 47	17 51	17 54		17 58	18 02	18 06	18 09	18 13	18 17	18 21	18 24	18 28		18 32	18 36	18 39	18 43	18 47	18 51	18 54	18 58
Dalston Junction	a	17 44	17 45	17 49	17 53	17 59		18 00	18 04	18 08	18 14	18 15	18 19	18 23	18 29	18 30		18 34	18 38	18 44	18 45	18 49	18 53	18 59	19 00
Canonbury	a		17 48		17 56			18 03		18 11		18 18		18 26		18 33			18 41		18 48		18 56		19 03
Highbury & Islington	a		17 55		18 00			18 10		18 15		18 25		18 30		18 40			18 45		18 55		19 00		19 10

Clapham Junction and West Croydon, Crystal Palace, New Cross - Highbury & Islington

		LO		LO	LO	LO	LO	LO	LO	LO	LO	LO		LO	LO	LO	LO	LO	LO	LO	LO	LO		LO	LO
Clapham Junction	d				18 30				18 45					19 00				19 15				19 30			
Wandsworth Road	d				18 36				18 51					19 06				19 21				19 36			
Clapham High Street ⊖	d				18 38				18 53					19 08				19 23				19 38			
Denmark Hill 4	d				18 43				18 58					19 13				19 28				19 43			
Peckham Rye 4	d				18 45				19 00					19 15				19 30				19 45			
Queens Rd Peckham	d				18 47				19 02					19 17				19 32				19 47			
West Croydon 4	d					18 31				18 46					19 01				19 16					19 31	
Norwood Junction 2	d					18 37				18 52					19 07				19 22					19 37	
Anerley	d					18 40				18 55					19 10				19 25					19 40	
Penge West	d					18 41				18 57					19 11				19 26					19 41	
Crystal Palace 4	d			18 32				18 47				19 02					19 17				19 32				
Sydenham	d			18 36		18 44		18 51		18 59		19 06			19 14		19 21		19 29		19 36			19 44	
Forest Hill 4	d			18 39		18 47		18 54		19 02		19 09			19 17		19 24		19 32		19 39			19 47	
Honor Oak Park	d			18 41		18 49		18 56		19 04		19 11			19 19		19 26		19 34		19 41			19 49	
Brockley	d			18 44		18 52		18 59		19 07		19 14			19 22		19 29		19 37		19 44			19 52	
New Cross Gate	d			18 46		18 54		19 01		19 09		19 16			19 24		19 31		19 39		19 46			19 54	
New Cross 4	d	18 42					18 57				19 12					19 27				19 42					19 57
Surrey Quays	d	18 46		18 50	18 53	18 57	19 01	19 05	19 08	19 12	19 16	19 20		19 23	19 27	19 31	19 35	19 38	19 42	19 46	19 50	19 53		19 57	20 01
Canada Water	d	18 48		18 52	18 55	18 59	19 03	19 07	19 10	19 14	19 18	19 22		19 25	19 29	19 33	19 37	19 40	19 44	19 48	19 52	19 55		19 59	20 03
Rotherhithe	d	18 50		18 53	18 57	19 01	19 05	19 08	19 12	19 16	19 20	19 23		19 27	19 31	19 35	19 38	19 42	19 46	19 50	19 53	19 57		20 01	20 05
Wapping	d	18 51		18 55	18 58	19 02	19 06	19 10	19 13	19 17	19 21	19 25		19 28	19 32	19 36	19 40	19 43	19 47	19 51	19 55	19 58		20 02	20 06
Shadwell	d	18 53		18 57	19 00	19 04	19 08	19 12	19 15	19 19	19 23	19 27		19 30	19 34	19 38	19 42	19 45	19 49	19 53	19 57	20 00		20 04	20 08
Whitechapel	d	18 56		18 59	19 03	19 07	19 11	19 14	19 18	19 22	19 26	19 29		19 33	19 37	19 41	19 44	19 48	19 52	19 56	19 59	20 03		20 07	20 11
Shoreditch High Street	d	18 58		19 02	19 05	19 09	19 13	19 17	19 20	19 24	19 28	19 32		19 35	19 39	19 43	19 47	19 50	19 54	19 58	20 02	20 05		20 09	20 13
Hoxton	d	19 00		19 04	19 07	19 11	19 15	19 19	19 22	19 26	19 30	19 34		19 37	19 41	19 45	19 49	19 52	19 56	20 00	20 04	20 07		20 11	20 15
Haggerston	d	19 02		19 06	19 09	19 13	19 17	19 21	19 24	19 28	19 32	19 36		19 39	19 43	19 47	19 51	19 54	19 58	20 02	20 06	20 09		20 13	20 17
Dalston Junction	a	19 04		19 08	19 14	19 15	19 19	19 23	19 29	19 30	19 34	19 38		19 44	19 45	19 49	19 53	19 59	20 00	20 04	20 08	20 14		20 15	20 19
Canonbury	a			19 11		19 18		19 26		19 33		19 41			19 48		19 56		20 03		20 11			20 18	
Highbury & Islington	a			19 15		19 25		19 30		19 40		19 45			19 53		20 00		20 08		20 15			20 23	

		LO	LO	LO	LO	LO	LO	LO		LO	LO	LO	LO	LO	LO	LO	LO	LO		LO	LO	LO	LO	LO	LO
Clapham Junction	d		19 45				20 00					20 15				20 30					20 45				21 00
Wandsworth Road	d		19 51				20 06					20 21				20 36					20 51				21 06
Clapham High Street ⊖	d		19 53				20 08					20 23				20 38					20 53				21 08
Denmark Hill 4	d		19 58				20 13					20 28				20 43					20 58				21 13
Peckham Rye 4	d		20 00				20 15					20 30				20 45					21 00				21 15
Queens Rd Peckham	d		20 02				20 17					20 32				20 47					21 02				21 17
West Croydon 4	d			19 46				20 01					20 16				20 31					20 46			
Norwood Junction 2	d			19 52				20 07					20 22				20 37					20 52			
Anerley	d			19 55				20 10					20 25				20 40					20 55			
Penge West	d			19 57				20 11					20 26				20 41					20 57			
Crystal Palace 4	d	19 47				20 02					20 17				20 32					20 47				21 02	
Sydenham	d	19 51		19 59		20 06		20 14			20 21		20 29		20 36		20 44			20 51		20 59		21 06	
Forest Hill 4	d	19 54		20 02		20 09		20 17			20 24		20 32		20 39		20 47			20 54		21 02		21 09	
Honor Oak Park	d	19 56		20 04		20 11		20 19			20 26		20 34		20 41		20 49			20 56		21 04		21 11	
Brockley	d	19 59		20 07		20 14		20 22			20 29		20 37		20 44		20 52			20 59		21 07		21 14	
New Cross Gate	d	20 01		20 09		20 16		20 24			20 31		20 39		20 46		20 54			21 01		21 09		21 16	
New Cross 4	d				20 12					20 27				20 42				20 57					21 12		
Surrey Quays	d	20 05	20 08	20 12	20 16	20 20	20 23	20 27		20 31	20 35	20 38	20 42	20 46	20 50	20 53	20 57	21 01		21 05	21 08	21 12	21 16	21 20	21 23
Canada Water	d	20 07	20 10	20 14	20 18	20 22	20 25	20 29		20 33	20 37	20 40	20 44	20 48	20 52	20 55	20 59	21 03		21 07	21 10	21 14	21 18	21 22	21 25
Rotherhithe	d	20 08	20 12	20 16	20 20	20 23	20 27	20 31		20 35	20 38	20 42	20 46	20 50	20 53	20 57	21 01	21 05		21 08	21 12	21 16	21 20	21 23	21 27
Wapping	d	20 10	20 13	20 17	20 21	20 25	20 28	20 32		20 36	20 40	20 43	20 47	20 51	20 55	20 58	21 02	21 06		21 10	21 13	21 17	21 21	21 25	21 28
Shadwell	d	20 12	20 15	20 19	20 23	20 27	20 30	20 34		20 38	20 42	20 45	20 49	20 53	20 57	21 00	21 04	21 08		21 12	21 15	21 19	21 23	21 27	21 30
Whitechapel	d	20 14	20 18	20 22	20 26	20 29	20 33	20 37		20 41	20 44	20 48	20 52	20 56	20 59	21 03	21 07	21 11		21 14	21 18	21 22	21 26	21 29	21 33
Shoreditch High Street	d	20 17	20 20	20 24	20 28	20 32	20 35	20 39		20 43	20 47	20 50	20 54	20 58	21 02	21 05	21 09	21 13		21 17	21 20	21 24	21 28	21 32	21 35
Hoxton	d	20 19	20 22	20 26	20 30	20 34	20 37	20 41		20 45	20 49	20 52	20 56	21 00	21 04	21 07	21 11	21 15		21 19	21 22	21 26	21 30	21 34	21 37
Haggerston	d	20 21	20 24	20 28	20 32	20 36	20 39	20 43		20 47	20 51	20 54	20 58	21 02	21 06	21 09	21 13	21 17		21 21	21 24	21 28	21 32	21 36	21 39
Dalston Junction	a	20 23	20 29	20 30	20 34	20 38	20 44	20 45		20 49	20 53	20 59	21 00	21 04	21 08	21 14	21 15	21 19		21 23	21 29	21 30	21 34	21 38	21 44
Canonbury	a	20 26		20 33		20 41		20 48			20 56		21 03		21 11		21 18			21 26		21 33		21 41	
Highbury & Islington	a	20 30		20 38		20 45		20 53			21 00		21 08		21 15		21 23			21 30		21 38		21 45	

		LO	LO	LO		LO	LO	LO	LO	LO	LO	LO	LO	LO		LO	LO	LO	LO	LO	LO	LO	LO	LO	
Clapham Junction	d					21 15				21 30				21 45					22 00				22 15		
Wandsworth Road	d					21 21				21 36				21 51					22 06				22 21		
Clapham High Street ⊖	d					21 23				21 38				21 53					22 08				22 23		
Denmark Hill 4	d					21 28				21 43				21 58					22 13				22 28		
Peckham Rye 4	d					21 30				21 45				22 00					22 15				22 30		
Queens Rd Peckham	d					21 32				21 47				22 02					22 17				22 32		
West Croydon 4	d	21 01					21 16				21 31					21 46				22 01				22 16	
Norwood Junction 2	d	21 07					21 22				21 37					21 52				22 07				22 22	
Anerley	d	21 10					21 25				21 40					21 55				22 10				22 25	
Penge West	d	21 11					21 26				21 41					21 57				22 11				22 26	
Crystal Palace 4	d			21 17					21 32				21 47					22 02				22 17			
Sydenham	d	21 14		21 21			21 29		21 36		21 44		21 51			21 59		22 06		22 14		22 21		22 29	
Forest Hill 4	d	21 17		21 24			21 32		21 39		21 47		21 54			22 02		22 09		22 17		22 24		22 32	
Honor Oak Park	d	21 19		21 26			21 34		21 41		21 49		21 56			22 04		22 11		22 19		22 26		22 34	
Brockley	d	21 22		21 29			21 37		21 44		21 52		21 59			22 07		22 14		22 22		22 29		22 37	
New Cross Gate	d	21 24		21 31			21 39		21 46		21 54		22 01			22 09		22 16		22 24		22 31		22 39	
New Cross 4	d		21 27					21 42				21 57					22 12				22 27				
Surrey Quays	d	21 27	21 31	21 35		21 38	21 42	21 46	21 50	21 53	21 57	22 01	22 05	22 08		22 12	22 16	22 20	22 23	22 27	22 31	22 35	22 38	22 42	
Canada Water	d	21 29	21 33	21 37		21 40	21 44	21 48	21 52	21 55	21 59	22 03	22 07	22 10		22 14	22 18	22 22	22 25	22 29	22 33	22 37	22 40	22 44	
Rotherhithe	d	21 31	21 35	21 38		21 42	21 46	21 50	21 53	21 57	22 01	22 05	22 08	22 12		22 16	22 20	22 23	22 27	22 31	22 35	22 38	22 42	22 46	
Wapping	d	21 32	21 36	21 40		21 43	21 47	21 51	21 55	21 58	22 02	22 06	22 10	22 13		22 17	22 21	22 25	22 28	22 32	22 36	22 40	22 43	22 47	
Shadwell	d	21 34	21 38	21 42		21 45	21 49	21 53	21 57	22 00	22 04	22 08	22 12	22 15		22 19	22 23	22 27	22 30	22 34	22 38	22 42	22 45	22 49	
Whitechapel	d	21 37	21 41	21 44		21 48	21 52	21 56	21 59	22 03	22 07	22 11	22 14	22 18		22 22	22 26	22 29	22 33	22 37	22 41	22 44	22 48	22 52	
Shoreditch High Street	d	21 39	21 43	21 47		21 50	21 54	21 58	22 02	22 05	22 09	22 13	22 17	22 20		22 24	22 28	22 32	22 35	22 39	22 43	22 47	22 50	22 54	
Hoxton	d	21 41	21 45	21 49		21 52	21 56	22 00	22 04	22 07	22 11	22 15	22 19	22 22		22 26	22 30	22 34	22 37	22 41	22 45	22 49	22 52	22 56	
Haggerston	d	21 43	21 47	21 51		21 54	21 58	22 02	22 06	22 09	22 13	22 17	22 21	22 24		22 28	22 32	22 36	22 39	22 43	22 47	22 51	22 54	22 58	
Dalston Junction	a	21 45	21 49	21 53		21 59	22 00	22 04	22 08	22 14	22 15	22 19	22 23	22 29		22 30	22 34	22 38	22 44	22 45	22 49	22 53	22 59	23 00	
Canonbury	a	21 48		21 56			22 03		22 11		22 18		22 26			22 33		22 41		22 48		22 56		23 03	
Highbury & Islington	a	21 53		22 00			22 08		22 15		22 23		22 30			22 38		22 45		22 53		23 00		23 10	

Clapham Junction and West Croydon, Crystal Palace, New Cross - Highbury & Islington

		LO	LO	LO	LO	LO	LO	LO	LO	LO		LO	LO	LO	LO	LO	LO	LO	LO	LO		LO	LO	LO	LO
Clapham Junction	d			22 30				22 45					23 00				23 15					23 30		23 44	
Wandsworth Road	d			22 36				22 51					23 06				23 21					23 36		23 50	
Clapham High Street ⊖	d			22 38				22 53					23 08				23 23					23 38		23 52	
Denmark Hill 4	d			22 43				22 58					23 13				23 28					23 43		23 57	
Peckham Rye 4	d			22 45				23 00					23 15				23 30					23 45		23 59	
Queens Rd Peckham	d			22 47				23 02					23 17				23 32					23 47		00 01	
West Croydon 4	d				22 31				22 46					23 01				23 16					23 31		
Norwood Junction 2	d				22 37				22 52					23 07				23 22					23 37		
Anerley	d				22 40				22 55					23 10				23 25					23 40		
Penge West	d				22 41				22 57					23 11				23 26					23 41		
Crystal Palace 4	d		22 32				22 47					23 02				23 17				23 32					23 50
Sydenham	d		22 36		22 44		22 51		22 59			23 06		23 14		23 21		23 29		23 36			23 44		23 54
Forest Hill 4	d		22 39		22 47		22 54		23 02			23 09		23 17		23 24		23 32		23 39			23 47		23 56
Honor Oak Park	d		22 41		22 49		22 56		23 04			23 11		23 19		23 26		23 34		23 41			23 49		23 59
Brockley	d		22 44		22 52		22 59		23 07			23 14		23 22		23 29		23 37		23 44			23 52		00 01
New Cross Gate	d		22 46		22 54		23 01		23 09			23 16		23 24		23 31		23 39		23 46			23 54		00 03
New Cross 4	d	22 42				22 57				23 12					23 27				23 42						
Surrey Quays	d	22 46	22 50	22 53	22 57	23 01	23 05	23 08	23 12	23 16		23 20	23 23	23 27	23 31	23 35	23 38	23 42	23 46	23 50		23 53	23 57	00 05	00 09
Canada Water	d	22 48	22 52	22 55	22 59	23 03	23 07	23 10	23 14	23 18		23 22	23 25	23 29	23 33	23 37	23 40	23 44	23 48	23 52		23 55	23 59	00 07	00 11
Rotherhithe	d	22 50	22 53	22 57	23 01	23 05	23 08	23 12	23 16	23 20		23 23	23 27	23 31	23 35	23 38	23 42	23 46	23 50	23 53		23 57	00 01	00 09	00 12
Wapping	d	22 51	22 55	22 58	23 02	23 06	23 10	23 13	23 17	23 21		23 25	23 28	23 32	23 36	23 40	23 43	23 47	23 51	23 55		23 58	00 02	00 10	00 14
Shadwell	d	22 53	22 57	23 00	23 04	23 08	23 12	23 15	23 19	23 23		23 27	23 30	23 34	23 38	23 42	23 45	23 49	23 53	23 57		00 01	00 04	00 12	00 16
Whitechapel	d	22 56	22 59	23 03	23 07	23 11	23 14	23 18	23 22	23 26		23 29	23 33	23 37	23 41	23 44	23 48	23 52	23 56	23 59		00 03	00 07	00 15	00 18
Shoreditch High Street	d	22 58	23 02	23 05	23 09	23 13	23 17	23 20	23 24	23 28		23 32	23 35	23 39	23 43	23 47	23 50	23 54	23 58	00 02		00 05	00 09	00 17	00 21
Hoxton	d	23 00	23 04	23 07	23 11	23 15	23 19	23 22	23 26	23 30		23 34	23 37	23 41	23 45	23 49	23 52	23 56	00 01	00 04		00 07	00 11	00 19	00 23
Haggerston	d	23 02	23 06	23 09	23 13	23 17	23 21	23 24	23 28	23 32		23 36	23 39	23 43	23 47	23 51	23 54	23 58	00 02	00 06		00 09	00 13	00 21	00 25
Dalston Junction	a	23 04	23 08	23 14	23 15	23 19	23 23	23 29	23 34	23 34		23 38	23 44	23 45	23 49	23 53	23 59	00 01	00 04	00 08		00 14	00 15	00 28	00 27
Canonbury	a		23 11		23 18		23 26			23 37		23 41		23 50		23 56		00 03		00 11			00 18		00 30
Highbury & Islington	a		23 15		23 25		23 30			23 40		23 45		23 58		23 59		00 10		00 15			00 25		00 33

Sundays

20 May to 2 December

		LO A	LO B	LO C	LO D	LO C	LO B	LO	LO		LO		LO	LO		LO	LO	LO	LO	LO	LO		LO
Clapham Junction	d																						
Wandsworth Road	d																						
Clapham High Street ⊖	d																						
Denmark Hill 4	d																						
Peckham Rye 4	d																						
Queens Rd Peckham	d					00 01																	
West Croydon 4	d																			06 43			07 12
Norwood Junction 2	d																			06 48			07 18
Anerley	d																			06 51			07 21
Penge West	d																			06 53			07 23
Crystal Palace 4	d							00 04											06 36		07 07		
Sydenham	d							00 08		and every 15 minutes until					and every 15 minutes until				06 40	06 55	07 11		07 25
Forest Hill 4	d							00 11											06 42	06 58	07 13		07 28
Honor Oak Park	d							00 13											06 45	07 00	07 16		07 30
Brockley	d						00 01	00 16											06 47	07 03	07 18		07 33
New Cross Gate	d						00 03	00 18	00 33		03 03		03 18	03 33		06 03	06 15	06 32	06 49	07 05	07 20		07 35
New Cross 4	d																						
Surrey Quays	d					00 05	00 09	00 22	00 37		03 07		03 22	03 37		06 07	06 19	06 36	06 53	07 08	07 24		07 38
Canada Water	d					00 07	00 11	00 24	00 39		03 09		03 24	03 39		06 09	06 21	06 38	06 55	07 10	07 26		07 40
Rotherhithe	d				00 01	00 09	00 12	00 25	00 40		03 10		03 25	03 40		06 10	06 22	06 39	06 56	07 12	07 27		07 42
Wapping	d				00 02	00 10	00 14	00 27	00 42		03 12		03 27	03 42		06 12	06 24	06 41	06 58	07 13	07 29		07 43
Shadwell	d			00 01	00 04	00 12	00 16	00 29	00 44		03 14		03 29	03 44		06 14	06 26	06 43	07 00	07 15	07 31		07 45
Whitechapel	d			00 03	00 07	00 15	00 18	00 31	00 46		03 16		03 31	03 46		06 16	06 28	06 45	07 02	07 18	07 33		07 48
Shoreditch High Street	d		00 02	00 05	00 09	00 17	00 21	00 34	00 49		03 19		03 34	03 49		06 19	06 31	06 48	07 04	07 20	07 35		07 50
Hoxton	d	00 01	00 04	00 07	00 11	00 19	00 23	00 36	00 51		03 21		03 36	03 51		06 21	06 33	06 50	07 06	07 22	07 37		07 52
Haggerston	d	00 02	00 06	00 09	00 13	00 21	00 25	00 38	00 53		03 23		03 38	03 53		06 23	06 35	06 52	07 08	07 24	07 39		07 54
Dalston Junction	a	00 04	00 08	00 14	00 15	00 28	00 27	00 40	00 55		03 25		03 40	03 55		06 25	06 37	06 54	07 10	07 26	07 41		07 56
Canonbury	a		00 11		00 18		00 30	00 43	00 58		03 28		03 43	03 58		06 28	06 40	06 57	07 13	07 29	07 44		07 59
Highbury & Islington	a		00 15		00 25		00 33	00 45	01 03		03 33		03 45	04 03		06 33	06 45	07 02	07 19	07 34	07 50		08 03

		LO E	LO	LO	LO	LO	LO	LO	LO		LO	LO	LO	LO	LO	LO	LO	LO	LO		LO	LO	LO	LO	LO
Clapham Junction	d			07 35		07 55		08 05			08 20			08 35			08 50				09 05			09 20	
Wandsworth Road	d	07 29		07 41		08 01		08 11			08 26			08 41			08 56				09 11			09 26	
Clapham High Street ⊖	d	07 30		07 43		08 03		08 13			08 28			08 43			08 58				09 13			09 28	
Denmark Hill 4	d	07 37		07 48		08 11		08 18			08 33			08 48			09 03				09 18			09 33	
Peckham Rye 4	d	07 39		07 50		08 14		08 20			08 35			08 50			09 05				09 20			09 35	
Queens Rd Peckham	d	07 41		07 52		08 16		08 22			08 37			08 52			09 07				09 22			09 37	
West Croydon 4	d				07 47				08 12						08 42							09 13			
Norwood Junction 2	d				07 52				08 18						08 48							09 18			
Anerley	d				07 55				08 21						08 51							09 21			
Penge West	d				07 57				08 23						08 53							09 23			
Crystal Palace 4	d		07 37				08 07					08 37						09 07							09 37
Sydenham	d		07 41		07 59		08 11		08 25			08 41			08 55			09 11				09 25			09 41
Forest Hill 4	d		07 43		08 02		08 13		08 28			08 43			08 58			09 13				09 28			09 43
Honor Oak Park	d		07 46		08 04		08 16		08 30			08 46			09 00			09 16				09 30			09 46
Brockley	d		07 48		08 07		08 18		08 33			08 48			09 03			09 18				09 33			09 48
New Cross Gate	d		07 50		08 09		08 20		08 35			08 50			09 05			09 20				09 35			09 50
New Cross 4	d												08 55			09 10			09 25				09 40		
Surrey Quays	d	07 48	07 54	08 00	08 12	08 19	08 24	08 33	08 38		08 48	08 54	08 59	09 03	09 08	09 14	09 18	09 24	09 29		09 33	09 38	09 44	09 48	09 54
Canada Water	d	07 50	07 56	08 02	08 14	08 21	08 26	08 35	08 40		08 50	08 56	09 01	09 05	09 10	09 16	09 20	09 26	09 31		09 35	09 40	09 46	09 50	09 56
Rotherhithe	d	07 51	07 57	08 04	08 16	08 23	08 27	08 36	08 42		08 51	08 57	09 03	09 06	09 12	09 18	09 21	09 27	09 33		09 36	09 42	09 48	09 51	09 57
Wapping	d	07 53	07 59	08 05	08 17	08 24	08 29	08 38	08 43		08 53	08 59	09 04	09 08	09 13	09 19	09 23	09 29	09 34		09 38	09 43	09 49	09 53	09 59
Shadwell	d	07 55	08 01	08 07	08 19	08 26	08 31	08 40	08 45		08 55	09 01	09 06	09 10	09 15	09 21	09 25	09 31	09 36		09 40	09 45	09 51	09 55	10 01
Whitechapel	d	07 57	08 03	08 10	08 22	08 29	08 33	08 42	08 48		08 57	09 03	09 09	09 12	09 18	09 24	09 27	09 33	09 39		09 42	09 48	09 54	09 57	10 03
Shoreditch High Street	d	07 59	08 05	08 12	08 24	08 31	08 35	08 44	08 50		08 59	09 05	09 11	09 14	09 20	09 26	09 29	09 35	09 41		09 44	09 50	09 56	09 59	10 05
Hoxton	d	08 01	08 07	08 14	08 26	08 33	08 37	08 46	08 52		09 01	09 07	09 13	09 16	09 22	09 28	09 31	09 37	09 43		09 46	09 52	09 58	10 01	10 07
Haggerston	d	08 03	08 09	08 16	08 28	08 35	08 39	08 48	08 54		09 03	09 09	09 15	09 18	09 24	09 30	09 33	09 39	09 45		09 48	09 54	10 00	10 03	10 09
Dalston Junction	a	08 05	08 11	08 18	08 30	08 37	08 41	08 50	08 56		09 05	09 11	09 17	09 20	09 26	09 32	09 35	09 41	09 47		09 50	09 56	10 02	10 05	10 11
Canonbury	a	08 08	08 14		08 33	08 40	08 44	08 53	08 59		09 08	09 14		09 23	09 29		09 38	09 44			09 53	09 59		10 08	10 14
Highbury & Islington	a	08 14	08 20		08 38	08 45	08 50	08 56	09 03		09 14	09 20		09 26	09 33		09 44	09 50			09 59	10 04		10 14	10 20

A not 20 May. From New Cross ELL
B not 20 May. From Crystal Palace
C not 20 May. From Clapham Junction Plats 0-2
D not 20 May. From West Croydon
E From Battersea Park

Table T178-R

Sundays

20 May to 2 December

Clapham Junction and West Croydon, Crystal Palace, New Cross - Highbury & Islington

		LO	LO	LO	LO		LO	LO	LO	LO	LO	LO	LO	LO	LO		LO	LO	LO	LO	LO	LO	LO	LO	LO
Clapham Junction	d		09 35				09 50			10 05			10 20				10 35			10 50				11 05	
Wandsworth Road	d		09 41				09 56			10 11			10 26				10 41			10 56				11 11	
Clapham High Street ⊖	d		09 43				09 58			10 13			10 28				10 43			10 58				11 13	
Denmark Hill	d		09 48				10 03			10 18			10 33				10 48			11 03				11 18	
Peckham Rye	d		09 50				10 05			10 20			10 35				10 50			11 05				11 20	
Queens Rd Peckham	d		09 52				10 07			10 22			10 37				10 52			11 07				11 22	
West Croydon	d			09 42							10 12							10 42							
Norwood Junction	d			09 48							10 18							10 48							
Anerley	d			09 51							10 21							10 51							
Penge West	d			09 53							10 23							10 53							
Crystal Palace	d							10 07						10 37								11 07			
Sydenham	d			09 55				10 11			10 25			10 41				10 55				11 11			
Forest Hill	d			09 58				10 13			10 28			10 43				10 58				11 13			
Honor Oak Park	d			10 00				10 16			10 30			10 46				11 00				11 16			
Brockley	d			10 03				10 18			10 33			10 48				11 03				11 18			
New Cross Gate	d			10 05				10 20			10 35			10 50				11 05				11 20			
New Cross	d	09 55			10 10				10 25			10 40			10 55				11 10				11 25		
Surrey Quays	d	09 59	10 03	10 08	10 14		10 18	10 24	10 29	10 33	10 38	10 44	10 48	10 54	10 59		11 03	11 08	11 14	11 18	11 21	11 24	11 29	11 32	11 35
Canada Water	d	10 01	10 05	10 10	10 16		10 20	10 26	10 31	10 35	10 40	10 46	10 50	10 56	11 01		11 05	11 10	11 16	11 20	11 23	11 26	11 31	11 34	11 37
Rotherhithe	d	10 03	10 06	10 12	10 18		10 21	10 27	10 33	10 36	10 42	10 48	10 51	10 57	11 03		11 06	11 12	11 18	11 21	11 24	11 27	11 33	11 36	11 38
Wapping	d	10 04	10 08	10 13	10 19		10 23	10 29	10 34	10 38	10 43	10 49	10 53	10 59	11 04		11 08	11 13	11 19	11 23	11 26	11 29	11 34	11 37	11 40
Shadwell	d	10 06	10 10	10 15	10 21		10 25	10 31	10 36	10 40	10 45	10 51	10 55	11 01	11 06		11 10	11 15	11 21	11 25	11 28	11 31	11 36	11 39	11 42
Whitechapel	d	10 09	10 12	10 18	10 24		10 27	10 33	10 39	10 42	10 48	10 54	10 57	11 03	11 09		11 12	11 18	11 24	11 27	11 30	11 33	11 39	11 42	11 44
Shoreditch High Street	d	10 11	10 14	10 20	10 26		10 29	10 35	10 41	10 44	10 50	10 56	10 59	11 05	11 11		11 14	11 20	11 26	11 29	11 32	11 35	11 41	11 44	11 46
Hoxton	d	10 13	10 16	10 22	10 28		10 31	10 37	10 43	10 46	10 52	10 58	11 01	11 07	11 13		11 16	11 22	11 28	11 31	11 34	11 37	11 43	11 46	11 48
Haggerston	d	10 15	10 18	10 24	10 30		10 33	10 39	10 45	10 48	10 54	11 00	11 03	11 09	11 15		11 18	11 24	11 30	11 33	11 36	11 39	11 45	11 48	11 50
Dalston Junction	a	10 17	10 20	10 26	10 32		10 35	10 41	10 47	10 50	10 56	11 02	11 05	11 11	11 17		11 20	11 26	11 32	11 35	11 41	11 41	11 47	11 50	11 52
Canonbury	a		10 23	10 29			10 38	10 44		10 53	10 59		11 08	11 14			11 23	11 29		11 38		11 44		11 53	11 55
Highbury & Islington	a		10 29	10 33			10 41	10 50		10 56	11 03		11 14	11 20			11 29	11 33		11 44		11 50		11 58	12 01

			LO	LO	LO	LO	LO	LO	LO	LO	LO		LO	LO	LO	LO	LO	LO	LO	LO	LO		LO	LO	LO
Clapham Junction	d				11 20				11 35					11 50				12 05			12 17				
Wandsworth Road	d				11 26				11 41					11 56				12 11			12 23				
Clapham High Street ⊖	d				11 28				11 43					11 58				12 13			12 25				
Denmark Hill	d				11 33				11 48					12 03				12 18			12 30				
Peckham Rye	d				11 35				11 50					12 05				12 20			12 32				
Queens Rd Peckham	d				11 37				11 52					12 07				12 22			12 34				
West Croydon	d		11 12								11 42									12 12					
Norwood Junction	d		11 18								11 47									12 17					
Anerley	d		11 21								11 50									12 20					
Penge West	d		11 23								11 52									12 22					
Crystal Palace	d						11 37									12 07			12 16					12 31	
Sydenham	d		11 25				11 41				11 54					12 11			12 20	12 24				12 35	
Forest Hill	d		11 28				11 43				11 57					12 13			12 22	12 27				12 37	
Honor Oak Park	d		11 30				11 46				11 59					12 16			12 25	12 29				12 40	
Brockley	d		11 33				11 48				12 02					12 18			12 27	12 32				12 42	
New Cross Gate	d		11 35				11 50				12 04					12 20			12 29	12 34				12 44	
New Cross	d			11 40				11 55					12 10				12 25						12 40		
Surrey Quays	d		11 38	11 44	11 48	11 51	11 54	11 59	12 02	12 05	12 07		12 14	12 17	12 21	12 24	12 29	12 32	12 35	12 37	12 41		12 44	12 48	12 53
Canada Water	d		11 40	11 46	11 50	11 53	11 56	12 01	12 04	12 07	12 09		12 16	12 19	12 23	12 26	12 31	12 34	12 37	12 39	12 43		12 46	12 50	12 55
Rotherhithe	d		11 42	11 48	11 51	11 54	11 57	12 03	12 06	12 08	12 11		12 18	12 21	12 24	12 27	12 33	12 36	12 39	12 41	12 45		12 48	12 51	12 56
Wapping	d		11 43	11 49	11 53	11 56	11 59	12 04	12 07	12 10	12 12		12 19	12 22	12 26	12 29	12 34	12 37	12 40	12 42	12 46		12 49	12 53	12 58
Shadwell	d		11 45	11 51	11 55	11 58	12 01	12 06	12 09	12 12	12 14		12 21	12 24	12 28	12 31	12 36	12 39	12 42	12 44	12 48		12 51	12 55	13 00
Whitechapel	d		11 48	11 54	11 57	12 00	12 03	12 09	12 12	12 14	12 17		12 24	12 27	12 30	12 33	12 39	12 42	12 45	12 47	12 51		12 54	12 57	13 02
Shoreditch High Street	d		11 50	11 56	11 59	12 02	12 05	12 11	12 14	12 16	12 19		12 26	12 29	12 32	12 35	12 41	12 44	12 47	12 49	12 53		12 56	12 59	13 04
Hoxton	d		11 52	11 58	12 01	12 04	12 07	12 13	12 16	12 18	12 21		12 28	12 31	12 34	12 37	12 43	12 46	12 49	12 51	12 55		12 58	13 01	13 06
Haggerston	d		11 54	12 00	12 03	12 06	12 09	12 15	12 18	12 20	12 23		12 30	12 33	12 36	12 39	12 45	12 48	12 51	12 53	12 57		13 00	13 03	13 08
Dalston Junction	a		11 57	12 02	12 05	12 11	12 11	12 17	12 20	12 25	12 25		12 32	12 35	12 41	12 41	12 47	12 50	12 55	12 58	12 59		13 02	13 05	13 13
Canonbury	a				12 08		12 14		12 23		12 28			12 38		12 44		12 53			13 02			13 08	
Highbury & Islington	a				12 14		12 22		12 28		12 33			12 43		12 50		12 58			13 07			13 16	

		LO	LO	LO	LO	LO	LO		LO	LO	LO	LO	LO	LO	LO	LO	LO		LO	LO	LO	LO	LO	LO	LO
Clapham Junction	d	12 32				12 47					13 02				13 17					13 32				13 47	
Wandsworth Road	d	12 38				12 53					13 08				13 23					13 38				13 53	
Clapham High Street ⊖	d	12 40				12 55					13 10				13 25					13 40				13 55	
Denmark Hill	d	12 45				13 00					13 15				13 30					13 45				14 00	
Peckham Rye	d	12 47				13 02					13 17				13 32					13 47				14 02	
Queens Rd Peckham	d	12 49				13 04					13 19				13 34					13 49				14 04	
West Croydon	d				12 42					12 57				13 12					13 27				13 42		
Norwood Junction	d				12 47					13 02				13 17					13 32				13 47		
Anerley	d				12 50					13 05				13 20					13 35				13 50		
Penge West	d				12 52					13 07				13 22					13 37				13 52		
Crystal Palace	d			12 46					13 01				13 16				13 31					13 46			
Sydenham	d			12 50	12 54				13 05	13 09			13 20	13 24			13 35		13 39			13 50	13 54		
Forest Hill	d			12 52	12 57				13 07	13 12			13 22	13 27			13 37		13 42			13 52	13 57		
Honor Oak Park	d			12 55	12 59				13 10	13 14			13 25	13 29			13 40		13 44			13 55	13 59		
Brockley	d			12 57	13 02				13 12	13 17			13 27	13 32			13 42		13 47			13 57	14 02		
New Cross Gate	d			12 59	13 04				13 14	13 19			13 29	13 34			13 44		13 49			13 59	14 04		
New Cross	d		12 55				13 10					13 25				13 40					13 55				14 10
Surrey Quays	d	12 56	12 59	13 03	13 07	13 11	13 14		13 18	13 22	13 26	13 29	13 33	13 37	13 41	13 44	13 48		13 52	13 56	13 59	14 03	14 07	14 11	14 14
Canada Water	d	12 58	13 01	13 05	13 09	13 13	13 16		13 20	13 24	13 28	13 31	13 35	13 39	13 43	13 46	13 50		13 54	13 58	14 01	14 05	14 09	14 13	14 16
Rotherhithe	d	12 59	13 03	13 06	13 11	13 14	13 18		13 21	13 26	13 29	13 33	13 36	13 41	13 44	13 48	13 51		13 56	13 59	14 03	14 06	14 11	14 14	14 18
Wapping	d	13 01	13 04	13 08	13 12	13 16	13 19		13 23	13 27	13 31	13 34	13 38	13 42	13 46	13 49	13 53		13 57	14 01	14 04	14 08	14 12	14 16	14 19
Shadwell	d	13 03	13 06	13 10	13 14	13 18	13 21		13 25	13 29	13 33	13 36	13 40	13 44	13 48	13 51	13 55		13 59	14 03	14 06	14 10	14 14	14 18	14 21
Whitechapel	d	13 05	13 09	13 12	13 17	13 20	13 24		13 27	13 32	13 35	13 39	13 42	13 47	13 50	13 54	13 57		14 02	14 05	14 09	14 12	14 17	14 20	14 24
Shoreditch High Street	d	13 07	13 11	13 14	13 19	13 22	13 26		13 29	13 34	13 37	13 41	13 44	13 49	13 52	13 56	13 59		14 04	14 07	14 11	14 14	14 19	14 22	14 26
Hoxton	d	13 09	13 13	13 16	13 21	13 24	13 28		13 31	13 36	13 39	13 43	13 46	13 51	13 54	13 58	14 01		14 06	14 09	14 13	14 16	14 21	14 24	14 28
Haggerston	d	13 11	13 15	13 18	13 23	13 26	13 30		13 33	13 38	13 41	13 45	13 48	13 53	13 56	14 00	14 03		14 08	14 11	14 15	14 18	14 23	14 26	14 30
Dalston Junction	a	13 13	13 17	13 20	13 27	13 28	13 32		13 35	13 42	13 43	13 47	13 50	13 57	13 58	14 02	14 05		14 12	14 13	14 17	14 20	14 27	14 28	14 32
Canonbury	a	13 16		13 23		13 31			13 38		13 46		13 53		14 01		14 08			14 16		14 23		14 31	
Highbury & Islington	a	13 22		13 29		13 37			13 44		13 52		13 59		14 07		14 14			14 21		14 29		14 37	

		LO	LO		LO	LO	LO	LO	LO	LO	LO	LO	LO		LO	LO	LO	LO	LO	LO	LO	LO	LO		LO
Clapham Junction	d				14 02				14 17				14 32					14 47				15 02			
Wandsworth Road	d				14 08				14 23				14 38					14 53				15 08			
Clapham High Street ⊖	d				14 10				14 25				14 40					14 55				15 10			
Denmark Hill	d				14 15				14 30				14 45					15 00				15 15			
Peckham Rye	d				14 17				14 32				14 47					15 02				15 17			
Queens Rd Peckham	d				14 19				14 34				14 49					15 04				15 19			
West Croydon	d		13 57					14 12				14 27					14 42				14 57				
Norwood Junction	d		14 02					14 17				14 32					14 47				15 02				
Anerley	d		14 05					14 20				14 35					14 50				15 05				
Penge West	d		14 07					14 22				14 37					14 52				15 07				
Crystal Palace	d	14 01					14 16				14 31					14 46				15 01					15 16
Sydenham	d	14 05	14 09				14 20	14 24			14 35	14 39				14 50	14 54			15 05	15 09				15 20
Forest Hill	d	14 07	14 12				14 22	14 27			14 37	14 42				14 52	14 57			15 07	15 12				15 22
Honor Oak Park	d	14 10	14 14				14 25	14 29			14 40	14 44				14 55	14 59			15 10	15 14				15 25
Brockley	d	14 12	14 17				14 27	14 32			14 42	14 47				14 57	15 02			15 12	15 17				15 27
New Cross Gate	d	14 14	14 19				14 29	14 34			14 44	14 49				14 59	15 04			15 14	15 19				15 29
New Cross	d					14 25				14 40					14 55				15 10				15 25		
Surrey Quays	d	14 18	14 22		14 26	14 29	14 33	14 37	14 41	14 44	14 48	14 52	14 56		14 59	15 03	15 07	15 11	15 14	15 18	15 22	15 26	15 29		15 33
Canada Water	d	14 20	14 24		14 28	14 31	14 35	14 39	14 43	14 46	14 50	14 54	14 58		15 01	15 05	15 09	15 13	15 16	15 20	15 24	15 28	15 31		15 35
Rotherhithe	d	14 21	14 26		14 29	14 33	14 36	14 41	14 44	14 48	14 51	14 56	14 59		15 03	15 06	15 11	15 14	15 18	15 21	15 26	15 29	15 33		15 36
Wapping	d	14 23	14 27		14 31	14 34	14 38	14 42	14 46	14 49	14 53	14 57	15 01		15 04	15 08	15 12	15 16	15 19	15 23	15 27	15 31	15 34		15 38
Shadwell	d	14 25	14 29		14 33	14 36	14 40	14 44	14 48	14 51	14 55	14 59	15 03		15 06	15 10	15 14	15 18	15 21	15 25	15 29	15 33	15 36		15 40
Whitechapel	d	14 27	14 32		14 35	14 39	14 42	14 47	14 50	14 54	14 57	15 02	15 05		15 09	15 12	15 17	15 20	15 24	15 27	15 32	15 35	15 39		15 42
Shoreditch High Street	d	14 29	14 34		14 37	14 41	14 44	14 49	14 52	14 56	14 59	15 04	15 07		15 11	15 14	15 19	15 22	15 26	15 29	15 34	15 37	15 41		15 44
Hoxton	d	14 31	14 36		14 39	14 43	14 46	14 51	14 54	14 58	15 01	15 06	15 09		15 13	15 16	15 21	15 24	15 28	15 31	15 36	15 39	15 43		15 46
Haggerston	d	14 33	14 38		14 41	14 45	14 48	14 53	14 56	15 00	15 03	15 08	15 11		15 15	15 18	15 23	15 26	15 30	15 33	15 38	15 41	15 45		15 48
Dalston Junction	a	14 35	14 42		14 43	14 47	14 50	14 57	14 58	15 02	15 05	15 12	15 13		15 17	15 20	15 27	15 28	15 32	15 35	15 42	15 43	15 47		15 50
Canonbury	a	14 38			14 46		14 53		15 01		15 08		15 16			15 23		15 31		15 38		15 46			15 53
Highbury & Islington	a	14 44			14 52		14 59		15 07		15 14		15 22			15 29		15 37		15 44		15 52			15 59

		LO	LO	LO	LO	LO	LO	LO	LO		LO	LO	LO	LO	LO	LO	LO	LO	LO		LO	LO	LO	LO	LO
Clapham Junction	d		15 17				15 32					15 47				16 02					16 17				16 32
Wandsworth Road	d		15 23				15 38					15 53				16 08					16 23				16 38
Clapham High Street ⊖	d		15 25				15 40					15 55				16 10					16 25				16 40
Denmark Hill	d		15 30				15 45					16 00				16 15					16 30				16 45
Peckham Rye	d		15 32				15 47					16 02				16 17					16 32				16 47
Queens Rd Peckham	d		15 34				15 49					16 04				16 19					16 34				16 49
West Croydon	d	15 12				15 27					15 42				15 57				16 12					16 27	
Norwood Junction	d	15 17				15 32					15 47				16 02				16 17					16 32	
Anerley	d	15 20				15 35					15 50				16 05				16 20					16 35	
Penge West	d	15 22				15 37					15 52				16 07				16 22					16 37	
Crystal Palace	d				15 31				15 46					16 01				16 16					16 31		
Sydenham	d	15 24			15 35	15 39			15 50		15 54			16 05	16 09			16 20	16 24				16 35	16 39	
Forest Hill	d	15 27			15 37	15 42			15 52		15 57			16 07	16 12			16 22	16 27				16 37	16 42	
Honor Oak Park	d	15 29			15 40	15 44			15 55		15 59			16 10	16 14			16 25	16 29				16 40	16 44	
Brockley	d	15 32			15 42	15 47			15 57		16 02			16 12	16 17			16 27	16 32				16 42	16 47	
New Cross Gate	d	15 34			15 44	15 49			15 59		16 04			16 14	16 19			16 29	16 34				16 44	16 49	
New Cross	d			15 40				15 55					16 10				16 25					16 40			
Surrey Quays	d	15 37	15 41	15 44	15 48	15 52	15 56	15 59	16 03		16 07	16 11	16 14	16 18	16 22	16 26	16 29	16 33	16 37		16 41	16 44	16 48	16 52	16 56
Canada Water	d	15 39	15 43	15 46	15 50	15 54	15 58	16 01	16 05		16 09	16 13	16 16	16 20	16 24	16 28	16 31	16 35	16 39		16 43	16 46	16 50	16 54	16 58
Rotherhithe	d	15 41	15 44	15 48	15 51	15 56	15 59	16 03	16 06		16 11	16 14	16 18	16 21	16 26	16 29	16 33	16 36	16 41		16 44	16 48	16 51	16 56	16 59
Wapping	d	15 42	15 46	15 49	15 53	15 57	16 01	16 04	16 08		16 12	16 16	16 19	16 23	16 27	16 31	16 34	16 38	16 42		16 46	16 49	16 53	16 57	17 01
Shadwell	d	15 44	15 48	15 51	15 55	15 59	16 03	16 06	16 10		16 14	16 18	16 21	16 25	16 29	16 33	16 36	16 40	16 44		16 48	16 51	16 55	16 59	17 03
Whitechapel	d	15 47	15 50	15 54	15 57	16 02	16 05	16 09	16 12		16 17	16 20	16 24	16 27	16 32	16 35	16 39	16 42	16 47		16 50	16 54	16 57	17 02	17 05
Shoreditch High Street	d	15 49	15 52	15 56	15 59	16 04	16 07	16 11	16 14		16 19	16 22	16 26	16 29	16 34	16 37	16 41	16 44	16 49		16 52	16 56	16 59	17 04	17 07
Hoxton	d	15 51	15 54	15 58	16 01	16 06	16 09	16 13	16 16		16 21	16 24	16 28	16 31	16 36	16 39	16 43	16 46	16 51		16 54	16 58	17 01	17 06	17 09
Haggerston	d	15 53	15 56	16 00	16 03	16 08	16 11	16 15	16 18		16 23	16 26	16 30	16 33	16 38	16 41	16 45	16 48	16 53		16 56	17 00	17 03	17 08	17 11
Dalston Junction	a	15 57	15 58	16 02	16 05	16 12	16 13	16 17	16 20		16 27	16 28	16 32	16 35	16 42	16 43	16 47	16 50	16 57		16 58	17 02	17 05	17 12	17 13
Canonbury	a		16 01		16 08		16 16		16 23			16 31		16 38		16 46		16 53			17 01		17 08		17 16
Highbury & Islington	a		16 07		16 14		16 22		16 29			16 37		16 44		16 52		16 59			17 07		17 14		17 22

		LO	LO	LO	LO		LO	LO	LO	LO	LO	LO	LO	LO	LO		LO	LO	LO	LO	LO	LO	LO	LO	LO
Clapham Junction	d				16 47					17 02				17 17					17 32				17 47		
Wandsworth Road	d				16 53					17 08				17 23					17 38				17 53		
Clapham High Street ⊖	d				16 55					17 10				17 25					17 40				17 55		
Denmark Hill	d				17 00					17 15				17 30					17 45				18 00		
Peckham Rye	d				17 02					17 17				17 32					17 47				18 02		
Queens Rd Peckham	d				17 04					17 19				17 34					17 49				18 04		
West Croydon	d			16 42					16 57				17 12					17 27				17 42			
Norwood Junction	d			16 47					17 02				17 17					17 32				17 47			
Anerley	d			16 50					17 05				17 20					17 35				17 50			
Penge West	d			16 52					17 07				17 22					17 37				17 52			
Crystal Palace	d		16 46					17 01				17 16					17 31				17 46				18 01
Sydenham	d		16 50	16 54				17 05	17 09			17 20	17 24				17 35	17 39			17 50	17 54			18 05
Forest Hill	d		16 52	16 57				17 07	17 12			17 22	17 27				17 37	17 42			17 52	17 57			18 07
Honor Oak Park	d		16 55	16 59				17 10	17 14			17 25	17 29				17 40	17 44			17 55	17 59			18 10
Brockley	d		16 57	17 02				17 12	17 17			17 27	17 32				17 42	17 47			17 57	18 02			18 12
New Cross Gate	d		16 59	17 04				17 14	17 19			17 29	17 34				17 44	17 49			17 59	18 04			18 14
New Cross	d	16 55					17 10				17 25				17 40					17 55				18 10	
Surrey Quays	d	16 59	17 03	17 07	17 11		17 14	17 18	17 22	17 26	17 29	17 33	17 37	17 41	17 44		17 48	17 52	17 56	17 59	18 03	18 07	18 11	18 14	18 18
Canada Water	d	17 01	17 05	17 09	17 13		17 16	17 20	17 24	17 28	17 31	17 35	17 39	17 43	17 46		17 50	17 54	17 58	18 01	18 05	18 09	18 13	18 16	18 20
Rotherhithe	d	17 03	17 06	17 11	17 14		17 18	17 21	17 26	17 29	17 33	17 36	17 41	17 44	17 48		17 51	17 56	17 59	18 03	18 06	18 11	18 14	18 18	18 21
Wapping	d	17 04	17 08	17 12	17 16		17 19	17 23	17 27	17 31	17 34	17 38	17 42	17 46	17 49		17 53	17 57	18 01	18 04	18 08	18 12	18 16	18 19	18 23
Shadwell	d	17 06	17 10	17 14	17 18		17 21	17 25	17 29	17 33	17 36	17 40	17 44	17 48	17 51		17 55	17 59	18 03	18 06	18 10	18 14	18 18	18 21	18 25
Whitechapel	d	17 09	17 12	17 17	17 20		17 24	17 27	17 32	17 35	17 39	17 42	17 47	17 50	17 54		17 57	18 02	18 05	18 09	18 12	18 17	18 20	18 24	18 27
Shoreditch High Street	d	17 11	17 14	17 19	17 22		17 26	17 29	17 34	17 37	17 41	17 44	17 49	17 52	17 56		17 59	18 04	18 07	18 11	18 14	18 19	18 22	18 26	18 29
Hoxton	d	17 13	17 16	17 21	17 24		17 28	17 31	17 36	17 39	17 43	17 46	17 51	17 54	17 58		18 01	18 06	18 09	18 13	18 16	18 21	18 24	18 28	18 31
Haggerston	d	17 15	17 18	17 23	17 26		17 30	17 33	17 38	17 41	17 45	17 48	17 53	17 56	18 00		18 03	18 08	18 11	18 15	18 18	18 23	18 26	18 30	18 33
Dalston Junction	a	17 17	17 20	17 27	17 28		17 32	17 35	17 42	17 43	17 47	17 50	17 57	17 58	18 02		18 05	18 12	18 13	18 17	18 20	18 27	18 28	18 32	18 35
Canonbury	a		17 23		17 31			17 38		17 46		17 53		18 01			18 08		18 16		18 23		18 31		18 38
Highbury & Islington	a		17 29		17 37			17 44		17 52		17 59		18 07			18 14		18 22		18 29		18 37		18 44

Clapham Junction and West Croydon, Crystal Palace, New Cross - Highbury & Islington

		LO	LO	LO	LO	LO	LO	LO	LO	LO	LO	LO	LO	LO	LO	LO	LO	LO	LO	LO	LO	LO
Clapham Junction	d		18 02				18 17				18 32				18 47				19 02			
Wandsworth Road	d		18 08				18 23				18 38				18 53				19 08			
Clapham High Street ⊖	d		18 10				18 25				18 40				18 55				19 10			
Denmark Hill	d		18 15				18 30				18 45				19 00				19 15			
Peckham Rye	d		18 17				18 32				18 47				19 02				19 17			
Queens Rd Peckham	d		18 19				18 34				18 49				19 04				19 19			
West Croydon	d	17 57				18 12				18 27				18 42				18 57				19 12
Norwood Junction	d	18 02				18 17				18 32				18 47				19 02				19 17
Anerley	d	18 05				18 20				18 35				18 50				19 05				19 20
Penge West	d	18 07				18 22				18 37				18 52				19 07				19 22
Crystal Palace	d				18 16				18 31				18 46				19 01				19 16	
Sydenham	d	18 09			18 20	18 24			18 35	18 39			18 50	18 54			19 05	19 09			19 20	19 24
Forest Hill	d	18 12			18 22	18 27			18 37	18 42			18 52	18 57			19 07	19 12			19 22	19 27
Honor Oak Park	d	18 14			18 25	18 29			18 40	18 44			18 55	18 59			19 10	19 14			19 25	19 29
Brockley	d	18 17			18 27	18 32			18 42	18 47			18 57	19 02			19 12	19 17			19 27	19 32
New Cross Gate	d	18 19			18 29	18 34			18 44	18 49			18 59	19 04			19 14	19 19			19 29	19 34
New Cross	d			18 25				18 40				18 55				19 10				19 25		
Surrey Quays	d	18 22	18 26	18 29	18 33	18 37	18 41	18 44	18 48	18 52	18 56	18 59	19 03	19 07	19 11	19 14	19 18	19 22	19 26	19 29	19 33	19 37
Canada Water	d	18 24	18 28	18 31	18 35	18 39	18 43	18 46	18 50	18 54	18 58	19 01	19 05	19 09	19 13	19 16	19 20	19 24	19 28	19 31	19 35	19 39
Rotherhithe	d	18 26	18 29	18 33	18 36	18 41	18 44	18 48	18 51	18 56	18 59	19 03	19 06	19 11	19 14	19 18	19 21	19 26	19 29	19 33	19 36	19 41
Wapping	d	18 27	18 31	18 34	18 38	18 42	18 46	18 49	18 53	18 57	19 01	19 04	19 08	19 12	19 16	19 19	19 23	19 27	19 31	19 34	19 38	19 42
Shadwell	d	18 29	18 33	18 36	18 40	18 44	18 48	18 51	18 55	18 59	19 03	19 06	19 10	19 14	19 18	19 21	19 25	19 29	19 33	19 36	19 40	19 44
Whitechapel	d	18 32	18 35	18 39	18 42	18 47	18 50	18 54	18 57	19 02	19 05	19 09	19 12	19 17	19 20	19 24	19 27	19 32	19 35	19 39	19 42	19 47
Shoreditch High Street	d	18 34	18 37	18 41	18 44	18 49	18 52	18 56	18 59	19 04	19 07	19 11	19 14	19 19	19 22	19 26	19 29	19 34	19 37	19 41	19 44	19 49
Hoxton	d	18 36	18 39	18 43	18 46	18 51	18 54	18 58	19 01	19 06	19 09	19 13	19 16	19 21	19 24	19 28	19 31	19 36	19 39	19 43	19 46	19 51
Haggerston	d	18 38	18 41	18 45	18 48	18 53	18 56	19 00	19 03	19 08	19 11	19 15	19 18	19 23	19 26	19 30	19 33	19 38	19 41	19 45	19 48	19 53
Dalston Junction	a	18 42	18 43	18 48	18 50	18 57	18 58	19 02	19 05	19 12	19 13	19 17	19 20	19 27	19 28	19 32	19 35	19 42	19 43	19 47	19 50	19 57
Canonbury	a		18 46		18 53		19 01		19 08		19 16		19 23		19 31		19 38		19 46		19 53	
Highbury & Islington	a		18 52		18 59		19 07		19 14		19 22		19 29		19 37		19 44		19 52		19 59	

		LO	LO	LO	LO	LO	LO	LO	LO	LO	LO	LO	LO	LO	LO	LO	LO	LO	LO	LO	LO	LO	LO
Clapham Junction	d	19 17				19 32				19 47				20 02				20 17				20 32	
Wandsworth Road	d	19 23				19 38				19 53				20 08				20 23				20 38	
Clapham High Street ⊖	d	19 25				19 40				19 55				20 10				20 25				20 40	
Denmark Hill	d	19 30				19 45				20 00				20 15				20 30				20 45	
Peckham Rye	d	19 32				19 47				20 02				20 17				20 32				20 47	
Queens Rd Peckham	d	19 34				19 49				20 04				20 19				20 34				20 49	
West Croydon	d				19 27				19 42				19 57				20 12				20 27		
Norwood Junction	d				19 32				19 47				20 02				20 17				20 32		
Anerley	d				19 35				19 50				20 05				20 20				20 35		
Penge West	d				19 37				19 52				20 07				20 22				20 37		
Crystal Palace	d			19 31				19 46				20 01				20 16				20 31			
Sydenham	d			19 35	19 39			19 50	19 54			20 05	20 09			20 20	20 24			20 35	20 39		
Forest Hill	d			19 37	19 42			19 52	19 57			20 07	20 12			20 22	20 27			20 37	20 42		
Honor Oak Park	d			19 40	19 44			19 55	19 59			20 10	20 14			20 25	20 29			20 40	20 44		
Brockley	d			19 42	19 47			19 57	20 02			20 12	20 17			20 27	20 32			20 42	20 47		
New Cross Gate	d			19 44	19 49			19 59	20 04			20 14	20 19			20 29	20 34			20 44	20 49		
New Cross	d		19 40				19 55				20 10				20 25				20 40				20 55
Surrey Quays	d	19 41	19 44	19 48	19 52	19 55	19 59	20 03	20 07	20 11	20 14	20 18	20 22	20 26	20 29	20 33	20 37	20 41	20 44	20 48	20 52	20 56	20 59
Canada Water	d	19 43	19 46	19 50	19 54	19 57	20 01	20 05	20 09	20 13	20 16	20 20	20 24	20 28	20 31	20 35	20 39	20 43	20 46	20 50	20 54	20 58	21 01
Rotherhithe	d	19 44	19 48	19 51	19 56	19 58	20 03	20 06	20 11	20 14	20 18	20 21	20 26	20 29	20 33	20 36	20 41	20 44	20 48	20 51	20 56	20 59	21 03
Wapping	d	19 46	19 49	19 53	19 57	20 00	20 04	20 08	20 12	20 16	20 19	20 23	20 27	20 31	20 34	20 38	20 42	20 46	20 49	20 53	20 57	21 01	21 04
Shadwell	d	19 48	19 51	19 55	19 59	20 02	20 06	20 10	20 14	20 18	20 21	20 25	20 29	20 33	20 36	20 40	20 44	20 48	20 51	20 55	20 59	21 03	21 06
Whitechapel	d	19 50	19 54	19 57	20 02	20 04	20 09	20 12	20 17	20 20	20 24	20 27	20 32	20 35	20 39	20 42	20 47	20 50	20 54	20 57	21 02	21 05	21 09
Shoreditch High Street	d	19 52	19 56	19 59	20 04	20 06	20 11	20 14	20 19	20 22	20 26	20 29	20 34	20 37	20 41	20 44	20 49	20 52	20 56	20 59	21 04	21 07	21 11
Hoxton	d	19 54	19 58	20 01	20 06	20 08	20 13	20 16	20 21	20 24	20 28	20 31	20 36	20 39	20 43	20 46	20 51	20 54	20 58	21 01	21 06	21 09	21 13
Haggerston	d	19 56	20 00	20 03	20 08	20 10	20 15	20 18	20 23	20 26	20 30	20 33	20 38	20 41	20 45	20 48	20 53	20 56	21 00	21 03	21 08	21 11	21 15
Dalston Junction	a	19 58	20 02	20 05	20 12	20 12	20 17	20 20	20 27	20 28	20 32	20 35	20 42	20 43	20 47	20 50	20 57	20 58	21 02	21 05	21 12	21 13	21 17
Canonbury	a	20 01		20 08		20 15		20 23		20 31		20 38		20 46		20 53		21 01		21 08		21 16	
Highbury & Islington	a	20 07		20 14		20 22		20 29		20 37		20 44		20 52		20 59		21 07		21 14		21 22	

		LO	LO	LO	LO	LO	LO	LO	LO	LO	LO	LO	LO	LO	LO	LO	LO	LO	LO	LO	LO	LO
Clapham Junction	d			20 47				21 02				21 17				21 32				21 47		
Wandsworth Road	d			20 53				21 08				21 23				21 38				21 53		
Clapham High Street ⊖	d			20 55				21 10				21 25				21 40				21 55		
Denmark Hill	d			21 00				21 15				21 30				21 45				22 00		
Peckham Rye	d			21 02				21 17				21 32				21 47				22 02		
Queens Rd Peckham	d			21 04				21 19				21 34				21 49				22 04		
West Croydon	d		20 42				20 57				21 12				21 27				21 42			
Norwood Junction	d		20 47				21 02				21 17				21 32				21 47			
Anerley	d		20 50				21 05				21 20				21 35				21 50			
Penge West	d		20 52				21 07				21 22				21 37				21 52			
Crystal Palace	d	20 46				21 01				21 16				21 31				21 46				22 01
Sydenham	d	20 50	20 54			21 05	21 09			21 20	21 24			21 35	21 39			21 50	21 54			22 05
Forest Hill	d	20 52	20 57			21 07	21 12			21 22	21 27			21 37	21 42			21 52	21 57			22 07
Honor Oak Park	d	20 55	20 59			21 10	21 14			21 25	21 29			21 40	21 44			21 55	21 59			22 10
Brockley	d	20 57	21 02			21 12	21 17			21 27	21 32			21 42	21 47			21 57	22 02			22 12
New Cross Gate	d	20 59	21 04			21 14	21 19			21 29	21 34			21 44	21 49			21 59	22 04			22 14
New Cross	d				21 10				21 25				21 40				21 55				22 10	
Surrey Quays	d	21 03	21 07	21 11	21 14	21 18	21 22	21 26	21 29	21 33	21 37	21 41	21 44	21 48	21 52	21 56	21 59	22 03	22 07	22 11	22 14	22 18
Canada Water	d	21 05	21 09	21 13	21 16	21 20	21 24	21 28	21 31	21 35	21 39	21 43	21 46	21 50	21 54	21 58	22 01	22 05	22 09	22 13	22 16	22 20
Rotherhithe	d	21 06	21 11	21 14	21 18	21 21	21 26	21 29	21 33	21 36	21 41	21 44	21 48	21 51	21 56	21 59	22 03	22 06	22 11	22 14	22 18	22 21
Wapping	d	21 08	21 12	21 16	21 19	21 23	21 27	21 31	21 34	21 38	21 42	21 46	21 49	21 53	21 57	22 01	22 04	22 08	22 12	22 16	22 19	22 23
Shadwell	d	21 10	21 14	21 18	21 21	21 25	21 29	21 33	21 36	21 40	21 44	21 48	21 51	21 55	21 59	22 03	22 06	22 10	22 14	22 18	22 21	22 25
Whitechapel	d	21 12	21 17	21 20	21 24	21 27	21 32	21 35	21 39	21 42	21 47	21 50	21 54	21 57	22 02	22 05	22 09	22 12	22 17	22 20	22 24	22 27
Shoreditch High Street	d	21 14	21 19	21 22	21 26	21 29	21 34	21 37	21 41	21 44	21 49	21 52	21 56	21 59	22 04	22 07	22 11	22 14	22 19	22 22	22 26	22 29
Hoxton	d	21 16	21 21	21 24	21 28	21 31	21 36	21 39	21 43	21 46	21 51	21 54	21 58	22 01	22 06	22 09	22 13	22 16	22 21	22 24	22 28	22 31
Haggerston	d	21 18	21 23	21 26	21 30	21 33	21 38	21 41	21 45	21 48	21 53	21 56	22 00	22 03	22 08	22 11	22 15	22 18	22 23	22 26	22 30	22 33
Dalston Junction	a	21 20	21 27	21 28	21 32	21 35	21 42	21 43	21 47	21 50	21 57	21 58	22 02	22 05	22 12	22 13	22 17	22 20	22 27	22 28	22 32	22 35
Canonbury	a	21 23		21 31		21 38		21 46		21 53		22 01		22 08		22 16		22 23		22 31		22 38
Highbury & Islington	a	21 29		21 37		21 44		21 52		21 59		22 07		22 14		22 22		22 29		22 37		22 44

Table T178-R

Sundays

20 May to 2 December

Clapham Junction and West Croydon, Crystal Palace, New Cross - Highbury & Islington

		LO	LO	LO	LO	LO	LO	LO	LO	LO	LO	LO	LO	LO	LO	LO	LO	LO	LO
Clapham Junction	d		22 02				22 17			22 32				22 47			23 02		23 17
Wandsworth Road	d		22 08				22 23			22 38				22 53			23 08		23 23
Clapham High Street ⊖	d		22 10				22 25			22 40				22 55			23 10		23 25
Denmark Hill	d		22 15				22 30			22 45				23 00			23 15		23 30
Peckham Rye	d		22 17				22 32			22 47				23 02			23 17		23 32
Queens Rd Peckham	d		22 19				22 34			22 49				23 04			23 19		23 34
West Croydon	d	21 57				22 12			22 27				22 42			22 57			
Norwood Junction	d	22 02				22 17			22 32				22 47			23 02			
Anerley	d	22 05				22 20			22 35				22 50			23 05			
Penge West	d	22 07				22 22			22 37				22 52			23 07			
Crystal Palace	d				22 16							22 46						23 16	
Sydenham	d	22 09			22 20	22 24			22 39			22 50	22 54			23 09		23 20	
Forest Hill	d	22 12			22 22	22 27			22 42			22 52	22 57			23 12		23 22	
Honor Oak Park	d	22 14			22 25	22 29			22 44			22 55	22 59			23 14		23 25	
Brockley	d	22 17			22 27	22 32			22 47			22 57	23 02			23 17		23 27	
New Cross Gate	d	22 19			22 29	22 34			22 49			22 59	23 04			23 19		23 29	
New Cross	d			22 25				22 40			22 55				23 10				
Surrey Quays	d	22 22	22 26	22 29	22 33	22 37	22 41	22 44	22 52	22 56	22 59	23 03	23 07	23 11	23 14	23 22	23 26	23 33	23 41
Canada Water	d	22 24	22 28	22 31	22 35	22 39	22 43	22 46	22 54	22 58	23 01	23 05	23 09	23 13	23 16	23 24	23 28	23 35	23 43
Rotherhithe	d	22 26	22 29	22 33	22 36	22 41	22 44	22 48	22 56	22 59	23 03	23 06	23 11	23 14	23 18	23 26	23 29	23 36	23 44
Wapping	d	22 27	22 31	22 34	22 38	22 42	22 46	22 49	22 57	23 01	23 04	23 08	23 12	23 16	23 19	23 27	23 31	23 38	23 46
Shadwell	d	22 29	22 33	22 36	22 40	22 44	22 48	22 51	22 59	23 03	23 06	23 10	23 14	23 18	23 21	23 29	23 33	23 40	23 48
Whitechapel	d	22 32	22 35	22 39	22 42	22 47	22 50	22 54	23 02	23 05	23 09	23 12	23 17	23 20	23 24	23 32	23 35	23 42	23 50
Shoreditch High Street	d	22 34	22 37	22 41	22 44	22 49	22 52	22 56	23 04	23 07	23 11	23 14	23 19	23 22	23 26	23 34	23 37	23 44	23 52
Hoxton	d	22 36	22 39	22 43	22 46	22 51	22 54	22 58	23 06	23 09	23 13	23 16	23 21	23 24	23 28	23 36	23 39	23 46	23 54
Haggerston	d	22 38	22 41	22 45	22 48	22 53	22 56	23 00	23 08	23 11	23 15	23 18	23 23	23 26	23 30	23 38	23 41	23 48	23 56
Dalston Junction	a	22 42	22 43	22 47	22 50	22 57	22 58	23 02	23 12	23 13	23 17	23 20	23 27	23 28	23 34	23 42	23 43	23 50	23 58
Canonbury	a		22 46		22 53		23 06			23 16		23 23		23 31			23 46	23 53	00 01
Highbury & Islington	a		22 52		22 59		23 09			23 22		23 29		23 37			23 52	23 59	00 07

Table T179-F

Thameslink - Wimbledon and Sutton

Mondays to Fridays

21 May to 20 July

Miles	Miles			TL MX A	TL MX A	TL B	TL	SN	TL B	TL C	SN	TL B	TL B	SN	TL	TL	SN	TL	TL	SN	TL	TL	TL
10¼	0	St Albans City	d			04 35			05 05			05 35	05 51		06 07	06 21		06 34	06 52		07 07	07 22	07 36
26¼	16	West Hampstead Thameslink	d			04 59	05 16		05 31			05 59	06 17		06 32	06 47		07 02	07 17		07 32	07 47	08 02
30¼	20	St Pancras International	d			05 12	05 27		05 42	05 57		06 12	06 27		06 42	06 57		07 12	07 27		07 42	07 57	08 12
31½	21¼	Farringdon	d			05 17	05 32		05 47	06 02		06 17	06 32		06 47	07 02		07 17	07 32		07 47	08 02	08 17
31¾	21½	City Thameslink	d			05 19	05 34		05 49	06 04		06 19	06 34		06 49	07 04		07 19	07 34		07 49	08 04	08 19
32¼	22	London Blackfriars	d			05 21	05 36		05 51	06 06		06 21	06 36		06 51	07 06		07 21	07 36		07 51	08 06	08 21
33½	23¼	Elephant & Castle	d			05 25	05 40		05 55	06 10		06 25	06 40		06 55	07 10		07 25	07 40		07 55	08 10	08 25
35¼	25	Loughborough Jn	d		00 02	05 30	05 45		06 00	06 15		06 30	06 45		07 00	07 15		07 30	07 45		08 00	08 15	08 30
36¼	26	Herne Hill	d		00 06	05 35	05 50		06 05	06 20		06 35	06 50		07 05	07 20		07 35	07 50		08 05	08 20	08 35
—	—	London Bridge	d					05 38			06 08			06 38			07 07			07 37			
37¼	27	Tulse Hill	a		00 10	05 39	05 54	05 59	06 09	06 24	06 29	06 39	06 54	06 59	07 09	07 24	07 29	07 39	07 54	07 59	08 09	08 24	08 39
—	—		d		00 11	05 40	05 56	05 59	06 10	06 26	06 29	06 40	06 56	06 59	07 10	07 26	07 29	07 40	07 56	07 59	08 10	08 27	08 40
39	28¾	Streatham	d		00 14	05 44	06 00	06 04	06 14	06 30	06 34	06 44	07 00	07 04	07 14	07 30	07 34	07 44	08 00	08 04	08 14	08 30	08 44
40½	—	**Tooting**	d		00 19	05 49		06 09	06 19		06 39	06 49		07 09	07 19		07 39	07 49		08 09	08 19		08 49
41¾	—	**Haydons Road**	d		00 22	05 52		06 12	06 22		06 42	06 52		07 12	07 22		07 42	07 52		08 12	08 22		08 52
42½	—	Wimbledon	a		00 24	05 54		06 14	06 24		06 44	06 54		07 14	07 24		07 44	07 54		08 14	08 24		08 54
—	—		d		00 25	05 55		06 15	06 25		06 45	06 55		07 15	07 25		07 45	07 55		08 15	08 25		08 55
43½	—	**Wimbledon Chase**	d		00 28	05 58		06 18	06 28		06 48	06 58		07 18	07 28		07 48	07 58		08 18	08 28		08 58
44¼	—	**South Merton**	d	00 01	00 30	06 00		06 20	06 30		06 50	07 00		07 20	07 30		07 50	08 00		08 20	08 30		09 00
44¾	—	**Morden South**	d	00 03	00 33	06 03		06 23	06 33		06 53	07 03		07 23	07 33		07 53	08 03		08 23	08 33		09 03
45¼	—	**St Helier**	d	00 05	00 35	06 05		06 25	06 35		06 55	07 05		07 25	07 35		07 55	08 05		08 25	08 35		09 05
46¼	—	**Sutton Common**	d	00 07	00 37	06 07		06 27	06 37		06 57	07 07		07 27	07 37		07 57	08 07		08 27	08 37		09 07
47	—	**West Sutton**	d	00 10	00 40	06 10		06 30	06 40		07 00	07 10		07 30	07 40		08 00	08 10		08 30	08 40		09 10
—	30¼	Mitcham Eastfields	d				06 04			06 34			07 04			07 34			08 04			08 34	
—	31½	Mitcham Junction	d				06 07			06 37			07 07			07 37			08 07			08 37	
—	32½	Hackbridge	d				06 10			06 40			07 10			07 40			08 10			08 40	
—	33½	Carshalton	d				06 13			06 43			07 13			07 43			08 13			08 43	
48	34¾	Sutton	a	00 14	00 44	06 14	06 17	06 34	06 44	06 47	07 04	07 14	07 17	07 34	07 44	07 47	08 04	08 14	08 17	08 34	08 44	08 47	09 14

		TL	TL	TL	TL	TL	TL	TL	TL	TL	TL	TL	TL	TL	TL	TL	TL	TL	TL	TL	TL	TL	TL
St Albans City	d	07 52	08 07	08 22	08 37	08 52	09 07	09 22	09 37	09 51	10 07	10 22	10 37	10 52	11 07	11 22	11 37	11 51	12 07	12 22	12 37	12 52	13 07
West Hampstead Thameslink	d	08 17	08 32	08 47	09 02	09 17	09 32	09 47	10 01	10 16	10 31	10 46	11 01	11 16	11 32	11 46	12 01	12 16	12 31	12 47	13 01	13 16	13 31
St Pancras International	d	08 27	08 42	08 57	09 12	09 27	09 42	09 57	10 12	10 27	10 42	10 57	11 12	11 27	11 42	11 57	12 12	12 27	12 42	12 57	13 12	13 27	13 42
Farringdon	d	08 32	08 47	09 02	09 17	09 32	09 47	10 02	10 17	10 32	10 47	11 02	11 17	11 32	11 47	12 02	12 17	12 32	12 47	13 02	13 17	13 32	13 47
City Thameslink	d	08 34	08 49	09 04	09 19	09 34	09 49	10 04	10 19	10 34	10 49	11 04	11 19	11 34	11 49	12 04	12 19	12 34	12 49	13 04	13 19	13 34	13 49
London Blackfriars	d	08 36	08 51	09 06	09 21	09 36	09 51	10 06	10 21	10 36	10 51	11 06	11 21	11 36	11 51	12 06	12 21	12 36	12 51	13 06	13 21	13 36	13 51
Elephant & Castle	d	08 40	08 55	09 10	09 25	09 40	09 55	10 10	10 25	10 40	10 55	11 10	11 25	11 40	11 55	12 10	12 25	12 40	12 55	13 10	13 25	13 40	13 55
Loughborough Jn	d	08 45	09 00	09 15	09 30	09 45	10 00	10 15	10 30	10 45	11 00	11 15	11 30	11 45	12 00	12 15	12 30	12 45	13 00	13 15	13 30	13 45	14 00
Herne Hill	d	08 50	09 05	09 20	09 35	09 50	10 05	10 20	10 35	10 50	11 05	11 20	11 35	11 50	12 05	12 20	12 35	12 50	13 05	13 20	13 35	13 50	14 05
London Bridge	d																						
Tulse Hill	a	08 54	09 09	09 24	09 39	09 54	10 09	10 24	10 39	10 54	11 09	11 24	11 39	11 54	12 09	12 24	12 39	12 54	13 09	13 24	13 39	13 54	14 09
	d	08 57	09 10	09 27	09 40	09 56	10 10	10 26	10 40	10 56	11 10	11 26	11 40	11 56	12 10	12 26	12 40	12 56	13 10	13 26	13 40	13 56	14 10
Streatham	d	09 00	09 14	09 30	09 44	10 00	10 14	10 30	10 44	11 00	11 14	11 30	11 44	12 00	12 14	12 30	12 44	13 00	13 14	13 30	13 44	14 00	14 14
Tooting	d		09 19		09 49		10 19		10 49		11 19		11 49		12 19		12 49		13 19		13 49		14 19
Haydons Road	d		09 22		09 52		10 22		10 52		11 22		11 52		12 22		12 52		13 22		13 52		14 22
Wimbledon	a		09 24		09 54		10 24		10 54		11 24		11 54		12 24		12 54		13 24		13 54		14 24
	d		09 25		09 55		10 25		10 55		11 25		11 55		12 25		12 55		13 25		13 55		14 25
Wimbledon Chase	d		09 28		09 58		10 28		10 58		11 28		11 58		12 28		12 58		13 28		13 58		14 28
South Merton	d		09 30		10 00		10 30		11 00		11 30		12 00		12 30		13 00		13 30		14 00		14 30
Morden South	d		09 33		10 03		10 33		11 03		11 33		12 03		12 33		13 03		13 33		14 03		14 33
St Helier	d		09 35		10 05		10 35		11 05		11 35		12 05		12 35		13 05		13 35		14 05		14 35
Sutton Common	d		09 37		10 07		10 37		11 07		11 37		12 07		12 37		13 07		13 37		14 07		14 37
West Sutton	d		09 40		10 10		10 40		11 10		11 40		12 10		12 40		13 10		13 40		14 10		14 40
Mitcham Eastfields	d	09 04		09 34		10 04		10 34		11 04		11 34		12 04		12 34		13 04		13 34		14 04	
Mitcham Junction	d	09 07		09 37		10 07		10 37		11 07		11 37		12 07		12 37		13 07		13 37		14 07	
Hackbridge	d	09 10		09 40		10 10		10 40		11 10		11 40		12 10		12 40		13 10		13 40		14 10	
Carshalton	d	09 13		09 43		10 13		10 43		11 13		11 43		12 13		12 43		13 13		13 43		14 13	
Sutton	a	09 17	09 44	09 47	10 14	10 17	10 44	10 47	11 14	11 17	11 44	11 47	12 14	12 17	12 44	12 47	13 14	13 17	13 44	13 47	14 14	14 17	14 44

		TL	TL	TL	TL	TL	TL	TL	TL	TL	TL	TL	TL	SN	TL	TL	SN	TL	TL	SN	TL	TL
St Albans City	d	13 22	13 37	13 51	14 07	14 22	14 37	14 51	15 07	15 22	15 37	15 52	16 07		16 22	16 37		16 52	17 07		17 22	17 37
West Hampstead Thameslink	d	13 46	14 01	14 16	14 31	14 46	15 01	15 16	15 31	15 47	16 01	16 17	16 32		16 47	17 02		17 17	17 32		17 47	18 01
St Pancras International	d	13 57	14 12	14 27	14 42	14 57	15 12	15 27	15 42	15 57	16 12	16 27	16 42		16 57	17 12		17 27	17 42		17 57	18 12
Farringdon	d	14 02	14 17	14 32	14 47	15 02	15 17	15 32	15 47	16 02	16 17	16 32	16 47		17 02	17 17		17 32	17 47		18 02	18 17
City Thameslink	d	14 04	14 19	14 34	14 49	15 04	15 19	15 34	15 49	16 04	16 19	16 34	16 49		17 04	17 19		17 34	17 49		18 04	18 19
London Blackfriars	d	14 06	14 21	14 36	14 51	15 06	15 21	15 36	15 51	16 06	16 21	16 36	16 51		17 06	17 21		17 36	17 51		18 06	18 21
Elephant & Castle	d	14 10	14 25	14 40	14 55	15 10	15 25	15 40	15 55	16 10	16 25	16 40	16 55		17 10	17 25		17 40	17 55		18 10	18 25
Loughborough Jn	d	14 15	14 30	14 45	15 00	15 15	15 30	15 45	16 00	16 15	16 30	16 45	17 00		17 15	17 30		17 45	18 00		18 15	18 30
Herne Hill	d	14 20	14 35	14 50	15 05	15 20	15 35	15 50	16 05	16 20	16 35	16 50	17 05		17 20	17 35		17 50	18 05		18 20	18 35
London Bridge	d													16 52			17 22			17 52		
Tulse Hill	a	14 24	14 39	14 54	15 09	15 24	15 39	15 54	16 09	16 24	16 39	16 54	17 09	17 14	17 24	17 39	17 44	17 54	18 09	18 14	18 24	18 39
	d	14 26	14 39	14 56	15 10	15 26	15 40	15 56	16 10	16 26	16 40	16 56	17 10	17 16	17 26	17 40	17 46	17 56	18 10	18 16	18 26	18 40
Streatham	d	14 30	14 42	15 00	15 14	15 30	15 44	16 00	16 14	16 30	16 44	17 00	17 14	17 20	17 30	17 44	17 50	18 00	18 14	18 20	18 30	18 44
Tooting	d		14 47		15 19		15 49		16 19		16 49		17 19			17 49			18 19			18 49
Haydons Road	d		14 50		15 22		15 52		16 22		16 52		17 22			17 52			18 22			18 52
Wimbledon	a		14 52		15 24		15 54		16 24		16 54		17 24			17 54			18 24			18 54
	d		14 55		15 25		15 55		16 25		16 55		17 25			17 55			18 25			18 55
Wimbledon Chase	d		14 58		15 28		15 58		16 28		16 58		17 28			17 58			18 28			18 58
South Merton	d		15 00		15 30		16 00		16 30		17 00		17 30			18 00			18 30			19 00
Morden South	d		15 03		15 33		16 03		16 33		17 03		17 33			18 03			18 33			19 03
St Helier	d		15 05		15 35		16 05		16 35		17 05		17 35			18 05			18 35			19 05
Sutton Common	d		15 07		15 37		16 07		16 37		17 07		17 37			18 07			18 37			19 07
West Sutton	d		15 10		15 40		16 10		16 40		17 10		17 40			18 10			18 40			19 10
Mitcham Eastfields	d	14 34		15 04		15 34		16 04		16 34		17 04		17 24	17 34		17 54	18 04		18 24	18 34	
Mitcham Junction	d	14 37		15 07		15 37		16 07		16 37		17 07		17 27	17 37		17 57	18 07		18 27	18 37	
Hackbridge	d	14 40		15 10		15 40		16 10		16 40		17 10		17 30	17 40		18 00	18 10		18 30	18 40	
Carshalton	d	14 43		15 13		15 43		16 13		16 43		17 13		17 33	17 43		18 03	18 13		18 33	18 43	
Sutton	a	14 47	15 14	15 17	15 44	15 47	16 14	16 17	16 44	16 47	17 14	17 17	17 44	17 37	17 47	18 14	18 07	18 17	18 44	18 37	18 47	19 14

A From St Albans City B From Luton C From Kentish Town

For more London Bridge connections, refer to Table T173

Most Thameslink services from Blackfriars via Wimbledon and Hackbridge continue back towards Blackfriars.

Table T179-F

Thameslink - Wimbledon and Sutton

Mondays to Fridays

21 May to 20 July

		SN	TL	TL	TL	TL	TL	TL	TL	TL	TL	TL	TL	TL	TL	TL	TL	TL	TL	TL	TL	TL	TL
St Albans City	d		17 52	18 07	18 22	18 37	18 52	19 07	19 22	19 37	19 51	20 07	20 22	20 37	20 52	21 07	21 22	21 37	21 52	22 08	22 22	22 37	23 09
West Hampstead Thameslink	d		18 17	18 31	18 47	19 00	19 16	19 31	19 46	20 01	20 16	20 31	20 46	21 01	21 16	21 31	21 46	22 01	22 16	22 31	22 46	23 01	23 33
St Pancras International	d		18 27	18 42	18 57	19 12	19 27	19 42	19 57	20 12	20 27	20 42	20 57	21 12	21 27	21 42	21 57	22 12	22 27	22 42	22 57	23 12	23 44
Farringdon	d		18 32	18 47	19 02	19 17	19 32	19 47	20 02	20 17	20 32	20 47	21 02	21 17	21 32	21 47	22 02	22 17	22 32	22 47	23 02	23 17	23 49
City Thameslink	d		18 34	18 49	19 04	19 19	19 34	19 49	20 04	20 19	20 34	20 49	21 04	21 19	21 34	21 49	22 04	22 19	22 34	22 49			
London Blackfriars	d		18 36	18 51	19 06	19 21	19 36	19 51	20 06	20 21	20 36	20 51	21 06	21 21	21 36	21 51	22 06	22 21	22 36	22 51	23 06	23 21	23 53
Elephant & Castle	d		18 40	18 55	19 10	19 25	19 40	19 55	20 10	20 25	20 40	20 55	21 10	21 25	21 40	21 55	22 10	22 25	22 40	22 55	23 10	23 25	23 57
Loughborough Jn	d		18 45	19 00	19 15	19 30	19 45	20 00	20 15	20 30	20 45	21 00	21 15	21 30	21 45	22 00	22 15	22 30	22 45	23 00	23 15	23 30	00 02
Herne Hill	d		18 50	19 05	19 20	19 35	19 50	20 05	20 20	20 35	20 50	21 05	21 20	21 35	21 50	22 05	22 20	22 35	22 50	23 05	23 20	23 35	00 06
London Bridge	d	18 22																					
Tulse Hill	a	18 44	18 54	19 09	19 24	19 39	19 54	20 09	20 24	20 39	20 54	21 09	21 24	21 39	21 54	22 09	22 24	22 39	22 54	23 09	23 24	23 39	00 10
	d	18 46	18 56	19 10	19 26	19 40	19 56	20 10	20 26	20 40	20 56	21 10	21 26	21 40	21 56	22 10	22 26	22 40	22 56	23 10	23 26	23 40	00 11
Streatham	d	18 50	19 00	19 14	19 30	19 44	20 00	20 14	20 30	20 44	21 00	21 14	21 30	21 44	22 00	22 14	22 30	22 44	23 00	23 14	23 30	23 44	00 14
Tooting	d			19 19		19 49		20 19		20 49		21 19		21 49		22 19		22 49		23 19		23 49	00 19
Haydons Road	d			19 22		19 52		20 22		20 52		21 22		21 52		22 22		22 52		23 22		23 52	00 22
Wimbledon	a			19 24		19 54		20 24		20 54		21 24		21 54		22 24		22 54		23 24		23 54	00 24
	d			19 25		19 55		20 25		20 55		21 25		21 55		22 25		22 55		23 25		23 55	00 25
Wimbledon Chase	d			19 28		19 58		20 28		20 58		21 28		21 58		22 28		22 58		23 28		23 58	00 28
South Merton	d			19 30		20 00		20 30		21 00		21 30		22 00		22 30		23 00		23 30		00 01	00 30
Morden South	d			19 33		20 03		20 33		21 03		21 33		22 03		22 33		23 03		23 33		00 03	00 33
St Helier	d			19 35		20 05		20 35		21 05		21 35		22 05		22 35		23 05		23 35		00 05	00 35
Sutton Common	d			19 37		20 07		20 37		21 07		21 37		22 07		22 37		23 07		23 37		00 07	00 37
West Sutton	d			19 40		20 10		20 40		21 10		21 40		22 10		22 40		23 10		23 40		00 10	00 40
Mitcham Eastfields	d	18 54	19 04		19 34		20 04		20 34		21 04		21 34		22 04		22 34		23 04		23 34		
Mitcham Junction	d	18 57	19 07		19 37		20 07		20 37		21 07		21 37		22 07		22 37		23 07		23 37		
Hackbridge	d	19 00	19 10		19 40		20 10		20 40		21 10		21 40		22 10		22 40		23 10		23 40		
Carshalton	d	19 03	19 13		19 43		20 13		20 43		21 13		21 43		22 13		22 43		23 13		23 43		
Sutton	a	19 07	19 17	19 44	19 47	20 14	20 17	20 44	20 47	21 14	21 17	21 44	21 47	22 14	22 17	22 44	22 47	23 14	23 17	23 44	23 47	00 14	00 44

Mondays to Fridays

23 July to 5 October

		TL MX A	TL MX A	TL B	TL	SN	TL B	TL C	SN	TL B	TL B	SN	TL	TL	SN	TL	TL	SN	TL	TL	TL	TL	TL
St Albans City	d			04 35			05 05			05 35	05 51		06 07	06 21		06 34	06 52		07 07	07 22	07 36	07 52	08 07
West Hampstead Thameslink	d			04 59	05 16		05 31			05 59	06 17		06 32	06 47		07 02	07 17		07 32	07 47	08 02	08 17	08 32
St Pancras International	d			05 12	05 27		05 42	05 57		06 12	06 27		06 42	06 57		07 12	07 27		07 42	07 57	08 12	08 27	08 42
Farringdon	d			05 17	05 32		05 47	06 02		06 17	06 32		06 47	07 02		07 17	07 32		07 47	08 02	08 17	08 32	08 47
City Thameslink	d			05 19	05 34		05 49	06 04		06 19	06 34		06 49	07 04		07 19	07 34		07 49	08 04	08 19	08 34	08 49
London Blackfriars	d			05 21	05 36		05 51	06 06		06 21	06 36		06 51	07 06		07 21	07 36		07 51	08 06	08 21	08 36	08 51
Elephant & Castle	d			05 25	05 40		05 55	06 10		06 25	06 40		06 55	07 10		07 25	07 40		07 55	08 10	08 25	08 40	08 55
Loughborough Jn	d		00 02	05 30	05 45		06 00	06 15		06 30	06 45		07 00	07 15		07 30	07 45		08 00	08 15	08 30	08 45	09 00
Herne Hill	d		00 06	05 35	05 50		06 05	06 20		06 35	06 50		07 05	07 20		07 35	07 50		08 05	08 20	08 35	08 50	09 05
London Bridge	d					05 38			06 08			06 38			07 07			07 37					
Tulse Hill	a		00 10	05 39	05 54	05 59	06 09	06 24	06 29	06 39	06 54	06 59	07 09	07 24	07 29	07 39	07 54	07 59	08 09	08 24	08 39	08 54	09 09
	d		00 11	05 40	05 56	05 59	06 10	06 26	06 29	06 40	06 56	06 59	07 10	07 26	07 29	07 40	07 56	07 59	08 10	08 27	08 40	08 57	09 10
Streatham	d		00 14	05 44	06 00	06 04	06 14	06 30	06 34	06 44	07 00	07 04	07 14	07 30	07 34	07 44	08 00	08 04	08 14	08 30	08 44	09 00	09 14
Tooting	d		00 19	05 49		06 09	06 19		06 39	06 49		07 09	07 19		07 39	07 49		08 09	08 19		08 49		09 19
Haydons Road	d		00 22	05 52		06 12	06 22		06 42	06 52		07 12	07 22		07 42	07 52		08 12	08 22		08 52		09 22
Wimbledon	a		00 24	05 54		06 14	06 24		06 44	06 54		07 14	07 24		07 44	07 54		08 14	08 24		08 54		09 24
	d		00 25	05 55		06 15	06 25		06 45	06 55		07 15	07 25		07 45	07 55		08 15	08 25		08 55		09 25
Wimbledon Chase	d		00 28	05 58		06 18	06 28		06 48	06 58		07 18	07 28		07 48	07 58		08 18	08 28		08 58		09 28
South Merton	d	00 01	00 30	06 00		06 20	06 30		06 50	07 00		07 20	07 30		07 50	08 00		08 20	08 30		09 00		09 30
Morden South	d	00 03	00 33	06 03		06 23	06 33		06 53	07 03		07 23	07 33		07 53	08 03		08 23	08 33		09 03		09 33
St Helier	d	00 05	00 35	06 05		06 25	06 35		06 55	07 05		07 25	07 35		07 55	08 05		08 25	08 35		09 05		09 35
Sutton Common	d	00 07	00 37	06 07		06 27	06 37		06 57	07 07		07 27	07 37		07 57	08 07		08 27	08 37		09 07		09 37
West Sutton	d	00 10	00 40	06 10		06 30	06 40		07 00	07 10		07 30	07 40		08 00	08 10		08 30	08 40		09 10		09 40
Mitcham Eastfields	d				06 04			06 34			07 04			07 34			08 04			08 34		09 04	
Mitcham Junction	d				06 07			06 37			07 07			07 37			08 07			08 37		09 07	
Hackbridge	d				06 10			06 40			07 10			07 40			08 10			08 40		09 10	
Carshalton	d				06 13			06 43			07 13			07 43			08 13			08 43		09 13	
Sutton	a	00 14	00 44	06 14	06 17	06 34	06 44	06 47	07 04	07 14	07 17	07 34	07 44	07 47	08 04	08 14	08 17	08 34	08 44	08 47	09 14	09 17	09 44

A From St Albans City B From Luton C From Kentish Town

For more London Bridge connections, refer to Table T173

Most Thameslink services from Blackfriars via Wimbledon and Hackbridge continue back towards Blackfriars.

Please note, Network Rail have stated that further updates to this timetable are possible during the validity period.

Please note, Network Rail have stated that further updates to this timetable are possible during the validity period.

Table T179-F

Mondays to Fridays

23 July to 5 October

Thameslink - Wimbledon and Sutton

		TL		TL	TL	TL	TL	TL	TL	TL	TL	TL		TL	TL	TL	TL	TL	TL	TL	TL	TL		TL	TL
St Albans City	d	08 22		08 37	08 52	09 07	09 22	09 37	09 51	10 07	10 22	10 37		10 52	11 07	11 22	11 37	11 52	12 07	12 22	12 37	12 52		13 07	13 22
West Hampstead Thameslink	d	08 47		09 02	09 17	09 32	09 47	10 01	10 16	10 31	10 46	11 01		11 16	11 32	11 46	12 01	12 16	12 31	12 47	13 01	13 16		13 31	13 46
St Pancras International ⊖	d	08 57		09 12	09 27	09 42	09 57	10 12	10 27	10 42	10 57	11 12		11 27	11 42	11 57	12 12	12 27	12 42	12 57	13 12	13 27		13 42	13 57
Farringdon ⊖	d	09 02		09 17	09 32	09 47	10 02	10 17	10 32	10 47	11 02	11 17		11 32	11 47	12 02	12 17	12 32	12 47	13 02	13 17	13 32		13 47	14 02
City Thameslink	d	09 04		09 19	09 34	09 49	10 04	10 19	10 34	10 49	11 04	11 19		11 34	11 49	12 04	12 19	12 34	12 49	13 04	13 19	13 34		13 49	14 04
London Blackfriars ⊖	d	09 06		09 21	09 36	09 51	10 06	10 21	10 36	10 51	11 06	11 21		11 36	11 51	12 06	12 21	12 36	12 51	13 06	13 21	13 36		13 51	14 06
Elephant & Castle ⊖	d	09 10		09 25	09 40	09 55	10 10	10 25	10 40	10 55	11 10	11 25		11 40	11 55	12 10	12 25	12 40	12 55	13 10	13 25	13 40		13 55	14 10
Loughborough Jn	d	09 15		09 30	09 45	10 00	10 15	10 30	10 45	11 00	11 15	11 30		11 45	12 00	12 15	12 30	12 45	13 00	13 15	13 30	13 45		14 00	14 15
Herne Hill	d	09 20		09 35	09 50	10 05	10 20	10 35	10 50	11 05	11 20	11 35		11 50	12 05	12 20	12 35	12 50	13 05	13 20	13 35	13 50		14 05	14 20
London Bridge ⊖	d																								
Tulse Hill	a	09 24		09 39	09 54	10 09	10 24	10 39	10 54	11 09	11 24	11 39		11 54	12 09	12 24	12 39	12 54	13 09	13 24	13 39	13 54		14 09	14 24
	d	09 27		09 40	09 56	10 10	10 26	10 40	10 56	11 10	11 26	11 40		11 56	12 10	12 26	12 40	12 56	13 10	13 26	13 40	13 56		14 10	14 26
Streatham	d	09 30		09 44	10 00	10 14	10 30	10 44	11 00	11 14	11 30	11 44		12 00	12 14	12 30	12 44	13 00	13 14	13 30	13 44	14 00		14 14	14 30
Tooting	d			09 49		10 19		10 49		11 19		11 49			12 19		12 49		13 19		13 49			14 19	
Haydons Road	d			09 52		10 22		10 52		11 22		11 52			12 22		12 52		13 22		13 52			14 22	
Wimbledon ⊖	a			09 54		10 24		10 54		11 24		11 54			12 24		12 54		13 24		13 54			14 24	
	d			09 55		10 25		10 55		11 25		11 55			12 25		12 55		13 25		13 55			14 25	
Wimbledon Chase	d			09 58		10 28		10 58		11 28		11 58			12 28		12 58		13 28		13 58			14 28	
South Merton	d			10 00		10 30		11 00		11 30		12 00			12 30		13 00		13 30		14 00			14 30	
Morden South	d			10 03		10 33		11 03		11 33		12 03			12 33		13 03		13 33		14 03			14 33	
St Helier	d			10 05		10 35		11 05		11 35		12 05			12 35		13 05		13 35		14 05			14 35	
Sutton Common	d			10 07		10 37		11 07		11 37		12 07			12 37		13 07		13 37		14 07			14 37	
West Sutton	d			10 10		10 40		11 10		11 40		12 10			12 40		13 10		13 40		14 10			14 40	
Mitcham Eastfields	d	09 34			10 04		10 34		11 04		11 34			12 04		12 34		13 04		13 34		14 04			14 34
Mitcham Junction	d	09 37			10 07		10 37		11 07		11 37			12 07		12 37		13 07		13 37		14 07			14 37
Hackbridge	d	09 40			10 10		10 40		11 10		11 40			12 10		12 40		13 10		13 40		14 10			14 40
Carshalton	d	09 43			10 13		10 43		11 13		11 43			12 13		12 43		13 13		13 43		14 13			14 43
Sutton	a	09 47		10 14	10 17	10 44	10 47	11 14	11 17	11 44	11 47	12 14		12 17	12 44	12 47	13 14	13 17	13 44	13 47	14 14	14 17		14 44	14 47

		TL	TL	TL	TL	TL	TL	TL		TL	TL	TL	TL	SN	TL	TL	SN	TL		TL	SN	TL	TL	SN	TL
St Albans City	d	13 37	13 52	14 07	14 22	14 37	14 52	15 07		15 22	15 37	15 52	16 07		16 22	16 37		16 52		17 07		17 22	17 37		17 52
West Hampstead Thameslink	d	14 01	14 16	14 31	14 46	15 01	15 16	15 31		15 47	16 01	16 17	16 32		16 47	17 02		17 17		17 32		17 47	18 01		18 17
St Pancras International ⊖	d	14 12	14 27	14 42	14 57	15 12	15 27	15 42		15 57	16 12	16 27	16 42		16 57	17 12		17 27		17 42		17 57	18 12		18 27
Farringdon ⊖	d	14 17	14 32	14 47	15 02	15 17	15 32	15 47		16 02	16 17	16 32	16 47		17 02	17 17		17 32		17 47		18 02	18 17		18 32
City Thameslink	d	14 19	14 34	14 49	15 04	15 19	15 34	15 49		16 04	16 19	16 34	16 49		17 04	17 19		17 34		17 49		18 04	18 19		18 34
London Blackfriars ⊖	d	14 21	14 36	14 51	15 06	15 21	15 36	15 51		16 06	16 21	16 36	16 51		17 06	17 21		17 36		17 51		18 06	18 21		18 36
Elephant & Castle ⊖	d	14 25	14 40	14 55	15 10	15 25	15 40	15 55		16 10	16 25	16 40	16 55		17 10	17 25		17 40		17 55		18 10	18 25		18 40
Loughborough Jn	d	14 30	14 45	15 00	15 15	15 30	15 45	16 00		16 15	16 30	16 45	17 00		17 15	17 30		17 45		18 00		18 15	18 30		18 45
Herne Hill	d	14 35	14 50	15 05	15 20	15 35	15 50	16 05		16 20	16 35	16 50	17 05		17 20	17 35		17 50		18 05		18 20	18 35		18 50
London Bridge ⊖	d													16 52			17 22				17 52			18 22	
Tulse Hill	a	14 39	14 54	15 09	15 24	15 39	15 54	16 09		16 24	16 39	16 54	17 09	17 14	17 24	17 39	17 44	17 54		18 09	18 14	18 24	18 39	18 44	18 54
	d	14 39	14 56	15 10	15 26	15 40	15 56	16 10		16 26	16 40	16 56	17 10	17 16	17 26	17 40	17 46	17 56		18 10	18 16	18 26	18 40	18 46	18 56
Streatham	d	14 42	15 00	15 14	15 30	15 44	16 00	16 14		16 30	16 44	17 00	17 14	17 20	17 30	17 44	17 50	18 00		18 14	18 20	18 30	18 44	18 50	19 00
Tooting	d	14 47		15 19		15 49		16 19			16 49		17 19			17 49				18 19			18 49		
Haydons Road	d	14 50		15 22		15 52		16 22			16 52		17 22			17 52				18 22			18 52		
Wimbledon ⊖	a	14 52		15 24		15 54		16 24			16 54		17 24			17 54				18 24			18 54		
	d	14 55		15 25		15 55		16 25			16 55		17 25			17 55				18 25			18 55		
Wimbledon Chase	d	14 58		15 28		15 58		16 28			16 58		17 28			17 58				18 28			18 58		
South Merton	d	15 00		15 30		16 00		16 30			17 00		17 30			18 00				18 30			19 00		
Morden South	d	15 03		15 33		16 03		16 33			17 03		17 33			18 03				18 33			19 03		
St Helier	d	15 05		15 35		16 05		16 35			17 05		17 35			18 05				18 35			19 05		
Sutton Common	d	15 07		15 37		16 07		16 37			17 07		17 37			18 07				18 37			19 07		
West Sutton	d	15 10		15 40		16 10		16 40			17 10		17 40			18 10				18 40			19 10		
Mitcham Eastfields	d		15 04		15 34		16 04			16 34		17 04		17 24	17 34		17 54	18 04			18 24	18 34		18 54	19 04
Mitcham Junction	d		15 07		15 37		16 07			16 37		17 07		17 27	17 37		17 57	18 07			18 27	18 37		18 57	19 07
Hackbridge	d		15 10		15 40		16 10			16 40		17 10		17 30	17 40		18 00	18 10			18 30	18 40		19 00	19 10
Carshalton	d		15 13		15 43		16 13			16 43		17 13		17 33	17 43		18 03	18 13			18 33	18 43		19 03	19 13
Sutton	a	15 14	15 17	15 44	15 47	16 14	16 17	16 44		16 47	17 14	17 17	17 44	17 37	17 47	18 14	18 07	18 17		18 44	18 37	18 47	19 14	19 07	19 17

		TL	TL	TL		TL	TL	TL	TL	TL	TL	TL	TL	TL		TL	TL	TL	TL	TL	TL	TL	TL		
St Albans City	d	18 07	18 22	18 37		18 52	19 07	19 22	19 37	19 52	20 07	20 22	20 37	20 52		21 07	21 22	21 37	21 52	22 08	22 22	22 37	23 09		
West Hampstead Thameslink	d	18 31	18 47	19 00		19 16	19 31	19 46	20 01	20 16	20 31	20 46	21 01	21 16		21 31	21 46	22 01	22 16	22 31	22 46	23 01	23 33		
St Pancras International ⊖	d	18 42	18 57	19 12		19 27	19 42	19 57	20 12	20 27	20 42	20 57	21 12	21 27		21 42	21 57	22 12	22 27	22 42	22 57	23 12	23 44		
Farringdon ⊖	d	18 47	19 02	19 17		19 32	19 47	20 02	20 17	20 32	20 47	21 02	21 17	21 32		21 47	22 02	22 17	22 32	22 47	23 02	23 17	23 49		
City Thameslink	d	18 49	19 04	19 19		19 34	19 49	20 04	20 19	20 34	20 49	21 04	21 19	21 34		21 49	22 04	22 19	22 34	22 49					
London Blackfriars ⊖	d	18 51	19 06	19 21		19 36	19 51	20 06	20 21	20 36	20 51	21 06	21 21	21 36		21 51	22 06	22 21	22 36	22 51	23 06	23 21	23 53		
Elephant & Castle ⊖	d	18 55	19 10	19 25		19 40	19 55	20 10	20 25	20 40	20 55	21 10	21 25	21 40		21 55	22 10	22 25	22 40	22 55	23 10	23 25	23 57		
Loughborough Jn	d	19 00	19 15	19 30		19 45	20 00	20 15	20 30	20 45	21 00	21 15	21 30	21 45		22 00	22 15	22 30	22 45	23 00	23 15	23 30	00 02		
Herne Hill	d	19 05	19 20	19 35		19 50	20 05	20 20	20 35	20 50	21 05	21 20	21 35	21 50		22 05	22 20	22 35	22 50	23 05	23 20	23 35	00 06		
London Bridge ⊖	d																								
Tulse Hill	a	19 09	19 24	19 39		19 54	20 09	20 24	20 39	20 54	21 09	21 24	21 39	21 54		22 09	22 24	22 39	22 54	23 09	23 24	23 39	00 10		
	d	19 10	19 26	19 40		19 56	20 10	20 26	20 40	20 56	21 10	21 26	21 40	21 56		22 10	22 26	22 40	22 56	23 10	23 26	23 40	00 11		
Streatham	d	19 14	19 30	19 44		20 00	20 14	20 30	20 44	21 00	21 14	21 30	21 44	22 00		22 14	22 30	22 44	23 00	23 14	23 30	23 44	00 14		
Tooting	d	19 19		19 49			20 19		20 49		21 19		21 49			22 19		22 49		23 19		23 49	00 19		
Haydons Road	d	19 22		19 52			20 22		20 52		21 22		21 52			22 22		22 52		23 22		23 52	00 22		
Wimbledon ⊖	a	19 24		19 54			20 24		20 54		21 24		21 54			22 24		22 54		23 24		23 54	00 24		
	d	19 25		19 55			20 25		20 55		21 25		21 55			22 25		22 55		23 25		23 55	00 25		
Wimbledon Chase	d	19 28		19 58			20 28		20 58		21 28		21 58			22 28		22 58		23 28		23 58	00 28		
South Merton	d	19 30		20 00			20 30		21 00		21 30		22 00			22 30		23 00		23 30		00 01	00 30		
Morden South	d	19 33		20 03			20 33		21 03		21 33		22 03			22 33		23 03		23 33		00 03	00 33		
St Helier	d	19 35		20 05			20 35		21 05		21 35		22 05			22 35		23 05		23 35		00 05	00 35		
Sutton Common	d	19 37		20 07			20 37		21 07		21 37		22 07			22 37		23 07		23 37		00 07	00 37		
West Sutton	d	19 40		20 10			20 40		21 10		21 40		22 10			22 40		23 10		23 40		00 10	00 40		
Mitcham Eastfields	d		19 34			20 04		20 34		21 04		21 34		22 04			22 34		23 04		23 34				
Mitcham Junction	d		19 37			20 07		20 37		21 07		21 37		22 07			22 37		23 07		23 37				
Hackbridge	d		19 40			20 10		20 40		21 10		21 40		22 10			22 40		23 10		23 40				
Carshalton	d		19 43			20 13		20 43		21 13		21 43		22 13			22 43		23 13		23 43				
Sutton	a	19 44	19 47	20 14		20 17	20 44	20 47	21 14	21 17	21 44	21 47	22 14	22 17		22 44	22 47	23 14	23 17	23 44	23 47	00 14	00 44		

For more London Bridge connections, refer to Table T173

Most Thameslink services from Blackfriars via Wimbledon and Hackbridge continue back towards Blackfriars.

Table T179-F

Mondays to Fridays

8 October to 7 December

Thameslink - Wimbledon and Sutton

		TL MX A	TL MX A	TL B	TL	SN	TL B	TL C	SN	TL B		TL B	SN	TL	TL	SN	TL	TL	SN	TL		TL	TL	TL	TL
St Albans City	d			04 35			05 05			05 35		05 51		06 07	06 21		06 34	06 52		07 07		07 22	07 36	07 52	08 07
West Hampstead Thameslink	d			04 59	05 16		05 31			05 59		06 17		06 32	06 47		07 02	07 17		07 32		07 47	08 02	08 17	08 32
St Pancras International ⊖	d			05 12	05 27		05 42	05 57		06 12		06 27		06 42	06 57		07 12	07 27		07 42		07 57	08 12	08 27	08 42
Farringdon ⊖	d			05 17	05 32		05 47	06 02		06 17		06 32		06 47	07 02		07 17	07 32		07 47		08 02	08 17	08 32	08 47
City Thameslink	d			05 19	05 34		05 49	06 04		06 19		06 34		06 49	07 04		07 19	07 34		07 49		08 04	08 19	08 34	08 49
London Blackfriars ⊖	d			05 21	05 36		05 51	06 06		06 21		06 36		06 51	07 06		07 21	07 36		07 51		08 06	08 21	08 36	08 51
Elephant & Castle ⊖	d			05 25	05 40		05 55	06 10		06 25		06 40		06 55	07 10		07 25	07 40		07 55		08 10	08 25	08 40	08 55
Loughborough Jn	d		00 02	05 30	05 45		06 00	06 15		06 30		06 45		07 00	07 15		07 30	07 45		08 00		08 15	08 30	08 45	09 00
Herne Hill	d		00 06	05 35	05 50		06 05	06 20		06 35		06 50		07 05	07 20		07 35	07 50		08 05		08 20	08 35	08 50	09 05
London Bridge ⊖	d					05 38			06 08				06 38			07 07			07 37						
Tulse Hill	a		00 10	05 39	05 54	05 59	06 09	06 24	06 29	06 39		06 54	06 59	07 09	07 24	07 29	07 39	07 54	07 59	08 09		08 24	08 39	08 54	09 09
	d		00 11	05 40	05 56	05 59	06 10	06 26	06 29	06 40		06 56	06 59	07 10	07 26	07 29	07 40	07 56	07 59	08 10		08 27	08 40	08 57	09 10
Streatham	d		00 14	05 44	06 00	06 04	06 14	06 30	06 34	06 44		07 00	07 04	07 14	07 30	07 34	07 44	08 00	08 04	08 14		08 30	08 44	09 00	09 14
Tooting	d		00 19	05 49		06 09	06 19		06 39	06 49			07 09	07 19		07 39	07 49		08 09	08 19			08 49		09 19
Haydons Road	d		00 22	05 52		06 12	06 22		06 42	06 52			07 12	07 22		07 42	07 52		08 12	08 22			08 52		09 22
Wimbledon ⊖	a		00 24	05 54		06 14	06 24		06 44	06 54			07 14	07 24		07 44	07 54		08 14	08 24			08 54		09 24
	d		00 25	05 55		06 15	06 25		06 45	06 55			07 15	07 25		07 45	07 55		08 15	08 25			08 55		09 25
Wimbledon Chase	d		00 28	05 58		06 18	06 28		06 48	06 58			07 18	07 28		07 48	07 58		08 18	08 28			08 58		09 28
South Merton	d	00 01	00 30	06 00		06 20	06 30		06 50	07 00			07 20	07 30		07 50	08 00		08 20	08 30			09 00		09 30
Morden South	d	00 03	00 33	06 03		06 23	06 33		06 53	07 03			07 23	07 33		07 53	08 03		08 23	08 33			09 03		09 33
St Helier	d	00 05	00 35	06 05		06 25	06 35		06 55	07 05			07 25	07 35		07 55	08 05		08 25	08 35			09 05		09 35
Sutton Common	d	00 07	00 37	06 07		06 27	06 37		06 57	07 07			07 27	07 37		07 57	08 07		08 27	08 37			09 07		09 37
West Sutton	d	00 10	00 40	06 10		06 30	06 40		07 00	07 10			07 30	07 40		08 00	08 10		08 30	08 40			09 10		09 40
Mitcham Eastfields	d				06 04			06 34				07 04			07 34			08 04				08 34		09 04	
Mitcham Junction	d				06 07			06 37				07 07			07 37			08 07				08 37		09 07	
Hackbridge	d				06 10			06 40				07 10			07 40			08 10				08 40		09 10	
Carshalton	d				06 13			06 43				07 13			07 43			08 13				08 43		09 13	
Sutton	a	00 14	00 44	06 14	06 17	06 34	06 44	06 47	07 04	07 14		07 17	07 34	07 44	07 47	08 04	08 14	08 17	08 34	08 44		08 47	09 14	09 17	09 44

		TL	TL	TL	TL	TL		TL	TL	TL	TL	TL	TL	TL	TL	TL		TL	TL	TL	TL	TL	TL	TL	TL
St Albans City	d	08 22	08 37	08 52	09 07	09 22		09 37	09 51	10 07	10 22	10 37	10 52	11 07	11 22	11 37		11 51	12 07	12 22	12 37	12 52	13 07	13 22	13 37
West Hampstead Thameslink	d	08 47	09 02	09 17	09 32	09 47		10 01	10 16	10 31	10 46	11 01	11 16	11 32	11 46	12 01		12 16	12 31	12 47	13 01	13 16	13 31	13 46	14 01
St Pancras International ⊖	d	08 57	09 12	09 27	09 42	09 57		10 12	10 27	10 42	10 57	11 12	11 27	11 42	11 57	12 12		12 27	12 42	12 57	13 12	13 27	13 42	13 57	14 12
Farringdon ⊖	d	09 02	09 17	09 32	09 47	10 02		10 17	10 32	10 47	11 02	11 17	11 32	11 47	12 02	12 17		12 32	12 47	13 02	13 17	13 32	13 47	14 02	14 17
City Thameslink	d	09 04	09 19	09 34	09 49	10 04		10 19	10 34	10 49	11 04	11 19	11 34	11 49	12 04	12 19		12 34	12 49	13 04	13 19	13 34	13 49	14 04	14 19
London Blackfriars ⊖	d	09 06	09 21	09 36	09 51	10 06		10 21	10 36	10 51	11 06	11 21	11 36	11 51	12 06	12 21		12 36	12 51	13 06	13 21	13 36	13 51	14 06	14 21
Elephant & Castle ⊖	d	09 10	09 25	09 40	09 55	10 10		10 25	10 40	10 55	11 10	11 25	11 40	11 55	12 10	12 25		12 40	12 55	13 10	13 25	13 40	13 55	14 10	14 25
Loughborough Jn	d	09 15	09 30	09 45	10 00	10 15		10 30	10 45	11 00	11 15	11 30	11 45	12 00	12 15	12 30		12 45	13 00	13 15	13 30	13 45	14 00	14 15	14 30
Herne Hill	d	09 20	09 35	09 50	10 05	10 20		10 35	10 50	11 05	11 20	11 35	11 50	12 05	12 20	12 35		12 50	13 05	13 20	13 35	13 50	14 05	14 20	14 35
London Bridge ⊖	d																								
Tulse Hill	a	09 24	09 39	09 54	10 09	10 24		10 39	10 54	11 09	11 24	11 39	11 54	12 09	12 24	12 39		12 54	13 09	13 24	13 39	13 54	14 09	14 24	14 39
	d	09 27	09 40	09 56	10 10	10 26		10 40	10 56	11 10	11 26	11 40	11 56	12 10	12 26	12 40		12 56	13 10	13 26	13 40	13 56	14 10	14 26	14 39
Streatham	d	09 30	09 44	10 00	10 14	10 30		10 44	11 00	11 14	11 30	11 44	12 00	12 14	12 30	12 44		13 00	13 14	13 30	13 44	14 00	14 14	14 30	14 42
Tooting	d		09 49		10 19			10 49		11 19		11 49		12 19		12 49			13 19		13 49		14 19		14 47
Haydons Road	d		09 52		10 22			10 52		11 22		11 52		12 22		12 52			13 22		13 52		14 22		14 50
Wimbledon ⊖	a		09 54		10 24			10 54		11 24		11 54		12 24		12 54			13 24		13 54		14 24		14 52
	d		09 55		10 25			10 55		11 25		11 55		12 25		12 55			13 25		13 55		14 25		14 55
Wimbledon Chase	d		09 58		10 28			10 58		11 28		11 58		12 28		12 58			13 28		13 58		14 28		14 58
South Merton	d		10 00		10 30			11 00		11 30		12 00		12 30		13 00			13 30		14 00		14 30		15 00
Morden South	d		10 03		10 33			11 03		11 33		12 03		12 33		13 03			13 33		14 03		14 33		15 03
St Helier	d		10 05		10 35			11 05		11 35		12 05		12 35		13 05			13 35		14 05		14 35		15 05
Sutton Common	d		10 07		10 37			11 07		11 37		12 07		12 37		13 07			13 37		14 07		14 37		15 07
West Sutton	d		10 10		10 40			11 10		11 40		12 10		12 40		13 10			13 40		14 10		14 40		15 10
Mitcham Eastfields	d	09 34		10 04		10 34			11 04		11 34		12 04		12 34			13 04		13 34		14 04		14 34	
Mitcham Junction	d	09 37		10 07		10 37			11 07		11 37		12 07		12 37			13 07		13 37		14 07		14 37	
Hackbridge	d	09 40		10 10		10 40			11 10		11 40		12 10		12 40			13 10		13 40		14 10		14 40	
Carshalton	d	09 43		10 13		10 43			11 13		11 43		12 13		12 43			13 13		13 43		14 13		14 43	
Sutton	a	09 47	10 14	10 17	10 44	10 47		11 14	11 17	11 44	11 47	12 14	12 17	12 44	12 47	13 14		13 17	13 44	13 47	14 14	14 17	14 44	14 47	15 14

		TL		TL	TL	TL	TL	TL	TL	TL	TL	TL		SN	TL	TL	SN	TL	TL	SN	TL	TL		SN	TL
St Albans City	d	13 51		14 07	14 22	14 37	14 51	15 07	15 22	15 37	15 52	16 07			16 22	16 37		16 52	17 07		17 22	17 37			17 52
West Hampstead Thameslink	d	14 16		14 31	14 46	15 01	15 16	15 31	15 47	16 01	16 17	16 32			16 47	17 02		17 17	17 32		17 47	18 01			18 17
St Pancras International ⊖	d	14 27		14 42	14 57	15 12	15 27	15 42	15 57	16 12	16 27	16 42			16 57	17 12		17 27	17 42		17 57	18 12			18 27
Farringdon ⊖	d	14 32		14 47	15 02	15 17	15 32	15 47	16 02	16 17	16 32	16 47			17 02	17 17		17 32	17 47		18 02	18 17			18 32
City Thameslink	d	14 34		14 49	15 04	15 19	15 34	15 49	16 04	16 19	16 34	16 49			17 04	17 19		17 34	17 49		18 04	18 19			18 34
London Blackfriars ⊖	d	14 36		14 51	15 06	15 21	15 36	15 51	16 06	16 21	16 36	16 51			17 06	17 21		17 36	17 51		18 06	18 21			18 36
Elephant & Castle ⊖	d	14 40		14 55	15 10	15 25	15 40	15 55	16 10	16 25	16 40	16 55			17 10	17 25		17 40	17 55		18 10	18 25			18 40
Loughborough Jn	d	14 45		15 00	15 15	15 30	15 45	16 00	16 15	16 30	16 45	17 00			17 15	17 30		17 45	18 00		18 15	18 30			18 45
Herne Hill	d	14 50		15 05	15 20	15 35	15 50	16 05	16 20	16 35	16 50	17 05			17 20	17 35		17 50	18 05		18 20	18 35			18 50
London Bridge ⊖	d													16 52			17 22			17 52				18 22	
Tulse Hill	a	14 54		15 09	15 24	15 39	15 54	16 09	16 24	16 39	16 54	17 09		17 14	17 24	17 39	17 44	17 54	18 09	18 14	18 24	18 39		18 44	18 54
	d	14 56		15 10	15 26	15 40	15 56	16 10	16 26	16 40	16 56	17 10		17 16	17 26	17 40	17 46	17 56	18 10	18 16	18 26	18 40		18 46	18 56
Streatham	d	15 00		15 14	15 30	15 44	16 00	16 14	16 30	16 44	17 00	17 14		17 20	17 30	17 44	17 50	18 00	18 14	18 20	18 30	18 44		18 50	19 00
Tooting	d			15 19		15 49		16 19		16 49		17 19				17 49			18 19			18 49			
Haydons Road	d			15 22		15 52		16 22		16 52		17 22				17 52			18 22			18 52			
Wimbledon ⊖	a			15 24		15 54		16 24		16 54		17 24				17 54			18 24			18 54			
	d			15 25		15 55		16 25		16 55		17 25				17 55			18 25			18 55			
Wimbledon Chase	d			15 28		15 58		16 28		16 58		17 28				17 58			18 28			18 58			
South Merton	d			15 30		16 00		16 30		17 00		17 30				18 00			18 30			19 00			
Morden South	d			15 33		16 03		16 33		17 03		17 33				18 03			18 33			19 03			
St Helier	d			15 35		16 05		16 35		17 05		17 35				18 05			18 35			19 05			
Sutton Common	d			15 37		16 07		16 37		17 07		17 37				18 07			18 37			19 07			
West Sutton	d			15 40		16 10		16 40		17 10		17 40				18 10			18 40			19 10			
Mitcham Eastfields	d	15 04			15 34		16 04		16 34		17 04			17 24	17 34		17 54	18 04		18 24	18 34			18 54	19 04
Mitcham Junction	d	15 07			15 37		16 07		16 37		17 07			17 27	17 37		17 57	18 07		18 27	18 37			18 57	19 07
Hackbridge	d	15 10			15 40		16 10		16 40		17 10			17 30	17 40		18 00	18 10		18 30	18 40			19 00	19 10
Carshalton	d	15 13			15 43		16 13		16 43		17 13			17 33	17 43		18 03	18 13		18 33	18 43			19 03	19 13
Sutton	a	15 17		15 44	15 47	16 14	16 17	16 44	16 47	17 14	17 17	17 44		17 37	17 47	18 14	18 07	18 17	18 44	18 37	18 47	19 14		19 07	19 17

A From St Albans City
B From Luton
C From Kentish Town

For more London Bridge connections, refer to Table T173

Most Thameslink services from Blackfriars via Wimbledon and Hackbridge continue back towards Blackfriars.

Table T179-F

Thameslink - Wimbledon and Sutton

Mondays to Fridays
8 October to 7 December

		TL	TL	TL	TL	TL	TL	TL	TL	TL	TL	TL	TL	TL	TL	TL	TL	TL	TL	TL	TL
St Albans City	d	18 07	18 22	18 37	18 52	19 07	19 22	19 37	19 51	20 07	20 22	20 37	20 52	21 07	21 22	21 37	21 52	22 08	22 22	22 37	23 09
West Hampstead Thameslink	d	18 31	18 47	19 00	19 16	19 31	19 46	20 01	20 16	20 31	20 46	21 01	21 16	21 31	21 46	22 01	22 16	22 31	22 46	23 01	23 33
St Pancras International 15 ⊖	d	18 42	18 57	19 12	19 27	19 42	19 57	20 12	20 27	20 42	20 57	21 12	21 27	21 42	21 57	22 12	22 27	22 42	22 57	23 12	23 44
Farringdon 3 ⊖	d	18 47	19 02	19 17	19 32	19 47	20 02	20 17	20 32	20 47	21 02	21 17	21 32	21 47	22 02	22 17	22 32	22 47	23 02	23 17	23 49
City Thameslink 3	d	18 49	19 04	19 19	19 34	19 49	20 04	20 19	20 34	20 49	21 04	21 19	21 34	21 49	22 04	22 19	22 34	22 49			
London Blackfriars 3 ⊖	d	18 51	19 06	19 21	19 36	19 51	20 06	20 21	20 36	20 51	21 06	21 21	21 36	21 51	22 06	22 21	22 36	22 51	23 06	23 21	23 53
Elephant & Castle ⊖	d	18 55	19 10	19 25	19 40	19 55	20 10	20 25	20 40	20 55	21 10	21 25	21 40	21 55	22 10	22 25	22 40	22 55	23 10	23 25	23 57
Loughborough Jn	d	19 00	19 15	19 30	19 45	20 00	20 15	20 30	20 45	21 00	21 15	21 30	21 45	22 00	22 15	22 30	22 45	23 00	23 15	23 30	00 02
Herne Hill 4	d	19 05	19 20	19 35	19 50	20 05	20 20	20 35	20 50	21 05	21 20	21 35	21 50	22 05	22 20	22 35	22 50	23 05	23 20	23 35	00 06
London Bridge 4 ⊖	d																				
Tulse Hill 3	a	19 09	19 24	19 39	19 54	20 09	20 24	20 39	20 54	21 09	21 24	21 39	21 54	22 09	22 24	22 39	22 54	23 09	23 24	23 39	00 10
	d	19 10	19 26	19 40	19 56	20 10	20 26	20 40	20 56	21 10	21 26	21 40	21 56	22 10	22 26	22 40	22 56	23 10	23 26	23 40	00 11
Streatham 4	d	19 14	19 30	19 44	20 00	20 14	20 30	20 44	21 00	21 14	21 30	21 44	22 00	22 14	22 30	22 44	23 00	23 14	23 30	23 44	00 14
Tooting	d	19 19		19 49		20 19		20 49		21 19		21 49		22 19		22 49		23 19		23 49	00 19
Haydons Road	d	19 22		19 52		20 22		20 52		21 22		21 52		22 22		22 52		23 22		23 52	00 22
Wimbledon 6 ⊖	a	19 24		19 54		20 24		20 54		21 24		21 54		22 24		22 54		23 24		23 54	00 24
	d	19 25		19 55		20 25		20 55		21 25		21 55		22 25		22 55		23 25		23 55	00 25
Wimbledon Chase	d	19 28		19 58		20 28		20 58		21 28		21 58		22 28		22 58		23 28		23 58	00 28
South Merton	d	19 30		20 00		20 30		21 00		21 30		22 00		22 30		23 00		23 30		00 01	00 30
Morden South	d	19 33		20 03		20 33		21 03		21 33		22 03		22 33		23 03		23 33		00 03	00 33
St Helier	d	19 35		20 05		20 35		21 05		21 35		22 05		22 35		23 05		23 35		00 05	00 35
Sutton Common	d	19 37		20 07		20 37		21 07		21 37		22 07		22 37		23 07		23 37		00 07	00 37
West Sutton	d	19 40		20 10		20 40		21 10		21 40		22 10		22 40		23 10		23 40		00 10	00 40
Mitcham Eastfields	d		19 34		20 04		20 34		21 04		21 34		22 04		22 34		23 04		23 34		
Mitcham Junction	d		19 37		20 07		20 37		21 07		21 37		22 07		22 37		23 07		23 37		
Hackbridge	d		19 40		20 10		20 40		21 10		21 40		22 10		22 40		23 10		23 40		
Carshalton	d		19 43		20 13		20 43		21 13		21 43		22 13		22 43		23 13		23 43		
Sutton 4	a	19 44	19 47	20 14	20 17	20 44	20 47	21 14	21 17	21 44	21 47	22 14	22 17	22 44	22 47	23 14	23 17	23 44	23 47	00 14	00 44

Saturdays
26 May to 8 December

		TL A	TL A	TL B	TL	TL B	TL	TL B	TL B	TL	TL	TL	TL	TL	TL	TL	TL	TL	TL	TL	TL	TL	
St Albans City	d			04 35		05 05		05 35	05 51	06 07	06 22	06 37	06 52	07 07	07 22	07 37	07 52	08 07	08 22	08 37	08 52	09 07	
West Hampstead Thameslink	d			04 59	05 16	05 29	05 46	05 59	06 17	06 31	06 46	07 01	07 16	07 31	07 46	08 01	08 16	08 31	08 46	09 01	09 16	09 31	
St Pancras International 15 ⊖	d			05 12	05 27	05 42	05 57	06 12	06 27	06 42	06 57	07 12	07 27	07 42	07 57	08 12	08 27	08 42	08 57	09 12	09 27	09 42	
Farringdon 3 ⊖	d			05 17	05 32	05 47	06 02	06 17	06 32	06 47	07 02	07 17	07 32	07 47	08 02	08 17	08 32	08 47	09 02	09 17	09 32	09 47	
City Thameslink 3	d																		09 04	09 19	09 34	09 49	
London Blackfriars 3 ⊖	d			05 21	05 36	05 51	06 06	06 21	06 36	06 51	07 06	07 21	07 36	07 51	08 06	08 21	08 36	08 51	09 06	09 21	09 36	09 51	
Elephant & Castle ⊖	d			05 25	05 40	05 55	06 10	06 25	06 40	06 55	07 10	07 25	07 40	07 55	08 10	08 25	08 40	08 55	09 10	09 25	09 40	09 55	
Loughborough Jn	d		00 02	05 30	05 45	06 00	06 15	06 30	06 45	07 00	07 15	07 30	07 45	08 00	08 15	08 30	08 45	09 00	09 15	09 30	09 45	10 00	
Herne Hill 4	d		00 06	05 35	05 50	06 05	06 20	06 35	06 50	07 05	07 20	07 35	07 50	08 05	08 20	08 35	08 50	09 05	09 20	09 35	09 50	10 05	
London Bridge 4 ⊖	d																						and at
Tulse Hill 3	a		00 10	05 39	05 54	06 09	06 24	06 39	06 54	07 09	07 24	07 39	07 54	08 09	08 24	08 39	08 54	09 09	09 24	09 39	09 54	10 09	the same
	d		00 11	05 40	05 56	06 10	06 26	06 40	06 56	07 10	07 26	07 40	07 56	08 10	08 26	08 40	08 56	09 10	09 26	09 40	09 56	10 10	minutes
Streatham 4	d		00 14	05 44	06 00	06 14	06 30	06 44	07 00	07 14	07 30	07 44	08 00	08 14	08 30	08 44	09 00	09 14	09 30	09 44	10 00	10 14	past
Tooting	d		00 19	05 49		06 19		06 49		07 19		07 49		08 19		08 49		09 19		09 49		10 19	each
Haydons Road	d		00 22	05 52		06 22		06 52		07 22		07 52		08 22		08 52		09 22		09 52		10 22	hour until
Wimbledon 6 ⊖	a		00 24	05 54		06 24		06 54		07 24		07 54		08 24		08 54		09 24		09 54		10 24	
	d		00 25	05 55		06 25		06 55		07 25		07 55		08 25		08 55		09 25		09 55		10 25	
Wimbledon Chase	d		00 28	05 58		06 28		06 58		07 28		07 58		08 28		08 58		09 28		09 58		10 28	
South Merton	d	00 01	00 30	06 00		06 30		07 00		07 30		08 00		08 30		09 00		09 30		10 00		10 30	
Morden South	d	00 03	00 33	06 03		06 33		07 03		07 33		08 03		08 33		09 03		09 33		10 03		10 33	
St Helier	d	00 05	00 35	06 05		06 35		07 05		07 35		08 05		08 35		09 05		09 35		10 05		10 35	
Sutton Common	d	00 07	00 37	06 07		06 37		07 07		07 37		08 07		08 37		09 07		09 37		10 07		10 37	
West Sutton	d	00 10	00 40	06 10		06 40		07 10		07 40		08 10		08 40		09 10		09 40		10 10		10 40	
Mitcham Eastfields	d				06 04		06 34		07 04		07 34		08 04		08 34		09 04		09 34		10 04		
Mitcham Junction	d				06 07		06 37		07 07		07 37		08 07		08 37		09 07		09 37		10 07		
Hackbridge	d				06 10		06 40		07 10		07 40		08 10		08 40		09 10		09 40		10 10		
Carshalton	d				06 13		06 43		07 13		07 43		08 13		08 43		09 13		09 43		10 13		
Sutton 4	a	00 14	00 44	06 14	06 17	06 44	06 47	07 14	07 17	07 44	07 47	08 14	08 17	08 44	08 47	09 14	09 17	09 44	09 47	10 14	10 17	10 44	

		TL	TL	TL	TL	TL	TL	TL	TL	TL	TL	TL	TL	TL	TL	TL
St Albans City	d	19 22	19 37	19 52	20 07	20 22	20 37	20 52	21 07	21 22	21 37	21 52	22 07	22 22	22 37	23 09
West Hampstead Thameslink	d	19 46	20 01	20 16	20 31	20 46	21 01	21 16	21 31	21 46	22 01	22 16	22 31	22 46	23 01	23 33
St Pancras International 15 ⊖	d	19 57	20 12	20 27	20 42	20 57	21 12	21 27	21 42	21 57	22 12	22 27	22 42	22 57	23 12	23 44
Farringdon 3 ⊖	d	20 02	20 17	20 32	20 47	21 02	21 17	21 32	21 47	22 02	22 17	22 32	22 47	23 02	23 17	23 49
City Thameslink 3	d	20 04	20 19	20 34	20 49											
London Blackfriars 3 ⊖	d	20 06	20 21	20 36	20 51	21 06	21 21	21 36	21 51	22 06	22 21	22 36	22 51	23 06	23 21	23 53
Elephant & Castle ⊖	d	20 10	20 25	20 40	20 55	21 10	21 25	21 40	21 55	22 10	22 25	22 40	22 55	23 10	23 25	23 57
Loughborough Jn	d	20 15	20 30	20 45	21 00	21 15	21 30	21 45	22 00	22 15	22 30	22 45	23 00	23 15	23 30	00 02
Herne Hill 4	d	20 20	20 35	20 50	21 05	21 20	21 35	21 50	22 05	22 20	22 35	22 50	23 05	23 20	23 35	00 06
London Bridge 4 ⊖	d															
Tulse Hill 3	a	20 24	20 39	20 54	21 09	21 24	21 39	21 54	22 09	22 24	22 39	22 54	23 09	23 24	23 39	00 10
	d	20 26	20 40	20 56	21 10	21 26	21 40	21 56	22 10	22 26	22 40	22 56	23 10	23 26	23 40	00 11
Streatham 4	d	20 30	20 44	21 00	21 14	21 30	21 44	22 00	22 14	22 30	22 44	23 00	23 14	23 30	23 44	00 14
Tooting	d		20 49		21 19		21 49		22 19		22 49		23 19		23 49	00 19
Haydons Road	d		20 52		21 22		21 52		22 22		22 52		23 22		23 52	00 22
Wimbledon 6 ⊖	a		20 54		21 24		21 54		22 24		22 54		23 24		23 54	00 24
	d		20 55		21 25		21 55		22 25		22 55		23 25		23 55	00 25
Wimbledon Chase	d		20 58		21 28		21 58		22 28		22 58		23 28		23 58	00 28
South Merton	d		21 00		21 30		22 00		22 30		23 00		23 30		00 01	00 30
Morden South	d		21 03		21 33		22 03		22 33		23 03		23 33		00 03	00 33
St Helier	d		21 05		21 35		22 05		22 35		23 05		23 35		00 05	00 35
Sutton Common	d		21 07		21 37		22 07		22 37		23 07		23 37		00 07	00 37
West Sutton	d		21 10		21 40		22 10		22 40		23 10		23 40		00 10	00 40
Mitcham Eastfields	d	20 34		21 04		21 34		22 04		22 34		23 04		23 34		
Mitcham Junction	d	20 37		21 07		21 37		22 07		22 37		23 07		23 37		
Hackbridge	d	20 40		21 10		21 40		22 10		22 40		23 10		23 40		
Carshalton	d	20 43		21 13		21 43		22 13		22 43		23 13		23 43		
Sutton 4	a	20 47	21 14	21 17	21 44	21 47	22 14	22 17	22 44	22 47	23 14	23 17	23 44	23 47	00 14	00 44

A From St Albans City
B From Luton

For more London Bridge connections, refer to Table T173

Most Thameslink services from Blackfriars via Wimbledon and Hackbridge continue back towards Blackfriars.

Table T179-F

Thameslink - Wimbledon and Sutton

Sundays
20 May to 2 December

		TL A	TL A	TL	TL	TL	TL B	TL	TL B	TL	TL B	TL	TL B	TL	TL B	TL	TL B	TL	TL B	TL B	TL B	TL
St Albans City	d						09 03		09 33		10 03		10 33		11 03		11 33		12 03	12 16	12 37	12 46
West Hampstead Thameslink	d						09 26		09 56		10 26		10 56		11 26		11 56		12 26	12 39	12 56	13 09
St Pancras International 15 ⊖	d						09 38		10 08		10 38		11 08		11 38		12 08	12 21	12 38	12 51	13 08	13 21
Farringdon 3 ⊖	d						09 42		10 12		10 42		11 12		11 42		12 12	12 25	12 42	12 55	13 12	13 25
City Thameslink 3	d																					
London Blackfriars 3 ⊖	d					09 30	09 47	10 00	10 17	10 30	10 47	11 00	11 17	11 30	11 47	12 00	12 17	12 30	12 47	13 00	13 17	13 30
Elephant & Castle ⊖	d					09 34	09 51	10 04	10 21	10 34	10 51	11 04	11 21	11 34	11 51	12 04	12 21	12 34	12 51	13 04	13 21	13 34
Loughborough Jn	d		00 02			09 39	09 56	10 09	10 26	10 39	10 56	11 09	11 26	11 39	11 56	12 09	12 26	12 39	12 56	13 09	13 26	13 39
Herne Hill 4	d		00 06			09 44	10 00	10 14	10 30	10 44	11 00	11 14	11 30	11 44	12 00	12 14	12 30	12 44	13 00	13 14	13 30	13 44
London Bridge 4 ⊖	d			08 30	09 00																	
Tulse Hill 3	a		00 10	08 43	09 13	09 48	10 04	10 18	10 34	10 48	11 04	11 18	11 34	11 48	12 04	12 18	12 34	12 48	13 04	13 18	13 34	13 48
	d		00 11	08 46	09 16	09 48	10 04	10 18	10 34	10 48	11 04	11 18	11 34	11 48	12 04	12 18	12 34	12 48	13 04	13 18	13 34	13 48
Streatham 4	d		00 14	08 50	09 20	09 52	10 08	10 22	10 38	10 52	11 08	11 22	11 38	11 52	12 08	12 22	12 38	12 52	13 08	13 22	13 38	13 52
Tooting	d		00 19				10 13		10 43		11 13		11 43		12 13		12 43		13 13		13 43	
Haydons Road	d		00 22				10 16		10 46		11 16		11 46		12 16		12 46		13 16		13 46	
Wimbledon 6 ⊖	a		00 24				10 18		10 48		11 18		11 48		12 18		12 48		13 18		13 48	
	d		00 25				10 19		10 49		11 19		11 49		12 19		12 49		13 19		13 49	
Wimbledon Chase	d		00 28				10 22		10 52		11 22		11 52		12 22		12 52		13 22		13 52	
South Merton	d	00 01	00 30				10 24		10 54		11 24		11 54		12 24		12 54		13 24		13 54	
Morden South	d	00 03	00 33				10 27		10 57		11 27		11 57		12 27		12 57		13 27		13 57	
St Helier	d	00 05	00 35				10 29		10 59		11 29		11 59		12 29		12 59		13 29		13 59	
Sutton Common	d	00 07	00 37				10 31		11 01		11 31		12 01		12 31		13 01		13 31		14 01	
West Sutton	d	00 10	00 40				10 34		11 04		11 34		12 04		12 34		13 04		13 34		14 04	
Mitcham Eastfields	d			08 53	09 23	09 55		10 25		10 55		11 25		11 55		12 25		12 55		13 25		13 55
Mitcham Junction	d			08 56	09 26	09 58		10 28		10 58		11 28		11 58		12 28		12 58		13 28		13 58
Hackbridge	d			08 59	09 29	10 01		10 31		11 01		11 31		12 01		12 31		13 01		13 31		14 01
Carshalton	d			09 02	09 32	10 04		10 34		11 04		11 34		12 04		12 34		13 04		13 34		14 04
Sutton 4	a	00 14	00 44	09 05	09 35	10 07	10 38	10 37	11 08	11 07	11 38	11 37	12 08	12 07	12 38	12 37	13 08	13 07	13 38	13 37	14 08	14 07

		TL B	TL	TL B	TL		TL B	TL	TL B	TL	TL B	TL	TL B	TL	TL B	TL	TL B	TL	TL B	TL	TL B	TL
St Albans City	d	13 07	13 16	13 37	13 47		17 07	17 16	17 37	17 47	18 07	18 16	18 37	18 46	19 07	19 16	19 37	19 47	20 07	20 17	20 37	20 46
West Hampstead Thameslink	d	13 26	13 39	13 56	14 09		17 26	17 39	17 56	18 09	18 26	18 39	18 57	19 09	19 26	19 39	19 56	20 09	20 26	20 39	20 57	21 09
St Pancras International 15 ⊖	d	13 38	13 51	14 08	14 21		17 38	17 51	18 08	18 21	18 38	18 51	19 08	19 21	19 38	19 51	20 08	20 21	20 38	20 51	21 08	21 21
Farringdon 3 ⊖	d	13 42	13 55	14 12	14 25		17 42	17 55	18 12	18 25	18 42	18 55	19 12	19 25	19 42	19 55	20 12	20 25	20 42	20 55	21 12	21 25
City Thameslink 3	d																					
London Blackfriars 3 ⊖	d	13 47	14 00	14 17	14 30		17 47	18 00	18 17	18 30	18 47	19 00	19 17	19 30	19 47	20 00	20 17	20 30	20 47	21 00	21 17	21 30
Elephant & Castle ⊖	d	13 51	14 04	14 21	14 34		17 51	18 04	18 21	18 34	18 51	19 04	19 21	19 34	19 51	20 04	20 21	20 34	20 51	21 04	21 21	21 34
Loughborough Jn	d	13 56	14 09	14 26	14 39		17 56	18 09	18 26	18 39	18 56	19 09	19 26	19 39	19 56	20 09	20 26	20 39	20 56	21 09	21 26	21 39
Herne Hill 4	d	14 00	14 14	14 30	14 44		18 00	18 14	18 30	18 44	19 00	19 14	19 30	19 44	20 00	20 14	20 30	20 44	21 00	21 14	21 30	21 44
London Bridge 4 ⊖	d					and at																
Tulse Hill 3	a	14 04	14 18	14 34	14 48	the same	18 04	18 18	18 34	18 48	19 04	19 18	19 34	19 48	20 04	20 18	20 34	20 48	21 04	21 18	21 34	21 48
	d	14 04	14 18	14 34	14 48	minutes	18 04	18 18	18 34	18 48	19 04	19 18	19 34	19 48	20 04	20 18	20 34	20 48	21 04	21 18	21 34	21 48
Streatham 4	d	14 08	14 22	14 38	14 52	past	18 08	18 22	18 38	18 52	19 08	19 22	19 38	19 52	20 08	20 22	20 38	20 52	21 08	21 22	21 38	21 52
Tooting	d	14 13		14 43		each	18 13		18 43		19 13		19 43		20 13		20 43		21 13		21 43	
Haydons Road	d	14 16		14 46		hour until	18 16		18 46		19 16		19 46		20 16		20 46		21 16		21 46	
Wimbledon 6 ⊖	a	14 18		14 48			18 18		18 48		19 18		19 48		20 18		20 48		21 18		21 48	
	d	14 19		14 49			18 19		18 49		19 19		19 49		20 19		20 49		21 19		21 49	
Wimbledon Chase	d	14 22		14 52			18 22		18 52		19 22		19 52		20 22		20 52		21 22		21 52	
South Merton	d	14 24		14 54			18 24		18 54		19 24		19 54		20 24		20 54		21 24		21 54	
Morden South	d	14 27		14 57			18 27		18 57		19 27		19 57		20 27		20 57		21 27		21 57	
St Helier	d	14 29		14 59			18 29		18 59		19 29		19 59		20 29		20 59		21 29		21 59	
Sutton Common	d	14 31		15 01			18 31		19 01		19 31		20 01		20 31		21 01		21 31		22 01	
West Sutton	d	14 34		15 04			18 34		19 04		19 34		20 04		20 34		21 04		21 34		22 04	
Mitcham Eastfields	d		14 25		14 55			18 25		18 55		19 25		19 55		20 25		20 55		21 25		21 55
Mitcham Junction	d		14 28		14 58			18 28		18 58		19 28		19 58		20 28		20 58		21 28		21 58
Hackbridge	d		14 31		15 01			18 31		19 01		19 31		20 01		20 31		21 01		21 31		22 01
Carshalton	d		14 34		15 04			18 34		19 04		19 34		20 04		20 34		21 04		21 34		22 04
Sutton 4	a	14 38	14 37	15 08	15 07		18 38	18 37	19 08	19 07	19 38	19 37	20 08	20 07	20 38	20 37	21 08	21 07	21 38	21 37	22 08	22 07

		TL B
St Albans City	d	21 07
West Hampstead Thameslink	d	21 26
St Pancras International 15 ⊖	d	21 38
Farringdon 3 ⊖	d	21 42
City Thameslink 3	d	
London Blackfriars 3 ⊖	d	21 47
Elephant & Castle ⊖	d	21 51
Loughborough Jn	d	21 56
Herne Hill 4	d	22 00
London Bridge 4 ⊖	d	
Tulse Hill 3	a	22 04
	d	22 04
Streatham 4	d	22 08
Tooting	d	22 13
Haydons Road	d	22 16
Wimbledon 6 ⊖	a	22 18
	d	22 19
Wimbledon Chase	d	22 22
South Merton	d	22 24
Morden South	d	22 27
St Helier	d	22 29
Sutton Common	d	22 31
West Sutton	d	22 34
Mitcham Eastfields	d	
Mitcham Junction	d	
Hackbridge	d	
Carshalton	d	
Sutton 4	a	22 38

A not 20 May. From St Albans City
B From Luton

For more London Bridge connections, refer to Table T173

Most Thameslink services from Blackfriars via Wimbledon and Hackbridge continue back towards Blackfriars.

Table T179-R

Mondays to Fridays

21 May to 20 July

Wimbledon and Sutton - Thameslink

Miles	Miles			TL MX A	TL MX A	TL MX A	TL	TL	TL	TL	SN	TL	TL	SN	TL	TL	SN	TL	TL	SN	TL	TL	SN
0	4½	Sutton	d				05 46	05 49	06 16	06 19	06 36	06 46	06 49	07 06	07 16	07 19	07 36	07 46	07 49	08 06	08 16	08 19	08 36
—	5¾	Carshalton	d				05 49		06 19		06 39	06 49		07 09	07 19		07 39	07 49		08 09	08 19		08 39
—	6¾	Hackbridge	d				05 52		06 22		06 42	06 52		07 12	07 22		07 42	07 52		08 12	08 22		08 42
—	7¾	Mitcham Junction	d				05 55		06 25		06 45	06 55		07 15	07 25		07 45	07 55		08 15	08 25		08 45
—	9	Mitcham Eastfields	d				05 58		06 28		06 48	06 58		07 18	07 28		07 49	07 58		08 19	08 28		08 49
1	—	**West Sutton**	d					05 52		06 22			06 52			07 22			07 52			08 22	
2	—	**Sutton Common**	d					05 54		06 24			06 54			07 24			07 54			08 24	
2¾	—	**St Helier**	d					05 57		06 27			06 57			07 27			07 57			08 27	
3¼	—	**Morden South**	d					05 59		06 29			06 59			07 29			07 59			08 29	
4	—	**South Merton**	d					06 01		06 31			07 01			07 31			08 01			08 31	
4½	—	**Wimbledon Chase**	d					06 03		06 33			07 03			07 33			08 03			08 33	
5½	—	Wimbledon	a					06 06		06 36			07 06			07 36			08 06			08 36	
—	—		d					06 07		06 37			07 07			07 37			08 07			08 37	
6¼	—	**Haydons Road**	d					06 10		06 40			07 10			07 40			08 10			08 40	
7½	—	**Tooting**	d					06 13		06 43			07 13			07 43			08 13			08 43	
9	10½	Streatham	d				06 03	06 18	06 33	06 48	06 53	07 03	07 18	07 23	07 33	07 48	07 53	08 03	08 18	08 23	08 33	08 48	08 53
10½	12	Tulse Hill	a				06 07	06 22	06 37	06 52	06 56	07 07	07 22	07 26	07 37	07 52	07 56	08 07	08 22	08 26	08 37	08 52	08 56
—	—		d				06 08	06 23	06 38	06 53	06 57	07 08	07 23	07 27	07 38	07 53	07 57	08 08	08 23	08 27	08 38	08 53	08 57
—	—	London Bridge	a								07 15			07 45			08 15			08 47			09 17
11¾	13¼	Herne Hill	d				06 12	06 27	06 42	06 57		07 12	07 27		07 42	07 57		08 12	08 27		08 42	08 57	
12¾	14¼	Loughborough Jn	d				06 15	06 30	06 45	07 00		07 15	07 30		07 45	08 00		08 15	08 30		08 45	09 00	
14½	16	Elephant & Castle	d			00 04	06 19	06 34	06 49	07 04		07 19	07 34		07 49	08 04		08 19	08 34		08 49	09 04	
15¾	17¼	London Blackfriars	d		00 02	00 09	06 24	06 39	06 54	07 09		07 24	07 39		07 54	08 09		08 24	08 39		08 54	09 09	
16	17¾	City Thameslink	d				06 26	06 41	06 56	07 11		07 26	07 41		07 56	08 11		08 26	08 41		08 56	09 11	
16½	18	Farringdon	d		00 06	00 13	06 29	06 44	06 59	07 14		07 29	07 44		07 59	08 14		08 29	08 44		08 59	09 14	
17¾	19¼	St Pancras International	d		00 11	00 18	06 33	06 48	07 03	07 18		07 33	07 48		08 03	08 18		08 33	08 48		09 03	09 18	
21¾	23¾	West Hampstead Thameslink	d	00 06	00 19	00 26	06 44	06 58	07 14	07 28		07 43	07 58		08 13	08 29		08 43	08 58		09 14	09 28	
37¾	39¼	St Albans City	a	00 31	00 35	00 51	07 08	07 22	07 38	07 51		08 06	08 21		08 36	08 51		09 06	09 21		09 36	09 51	

		TL	TL	TL	TL	TL	TL	TL	TL	TL	TL	TL	TL	TL	TL	TL	TL	TL	TL	TL	TL	TL	TL
Sutton	d	08 46	08 49	09 16	09 19	09 46	09 49	10 16	10 19	10 46	10 49	11 16	11 19	11 46	11 49	12 16	12 19	12 46	12 49	13 16	13 19	13 46	13 49
Carshalton	d	08 49		09 19		09 49		10 19		10 49		11 19		11 49		12 19		12 49		13 19		13 49	
Hackbridge	d	08 52		09 22		09 52		10 22		10 52		11 22		11 52		12 22		12 52		13 22		13 52	
Mitcham Junction	d	08 55		09 25		09 55		10 25		10 55		11 25		11 55		12 25		12 55		13 25		13 55	
Mitcham Eastfields	d	08 58		09 28		09 58		10 28		10 58		11 28		11 58		12 28		12 58		13 28		13 58	
West Sutton	d		08 52		09 22		09 52		10 22		10 52		11 22		11 52		12 22		12 52		13 22		13 52
Sutton Common	d		08 54		09 24		09 54		10 24		10 54		11 24		11 54		12 24		12 54		13 24		13 54
St Helier	d		08 57		09 27		09 57		10 27		10 57		11 27		11 57		12 27		12 57		13 27		13 57
Morden South	d		08 59		09 29		09 59		10 29		10 59		11 29		11 59		12 29		12 59		13 29		13 59
South Merton	d		09 01		09 31		10 01		10 31		11 01		11 31		12 01		12 31		13 01		13 31		14 01
Wimbledon Chase	d		09 03		09 33		10 03		10 33		11 03		11 33		12 03		12 33		13 03		13 33		14 03
Wimbledon	a		09 06		09 36		10 06		10 36		11 06		11 36		12 06		12 36		13 06		13 36		14 06
	d		09 07		09 37		10 07		10 37		11 07		11 37		12 07		12 37		13 07		13 37		14 07
Haydons Road	d		09 10		09 40		10 10		10 40		11 10		11 40		12 10		12 40		13 10		13 40		14 10
Tooting	d		09 13		09 43		10 13		10 43		11 13		11 43		12 13		12 43		13 13		13 43		14 13
Streatham	d	09 03	09 18	09 33	09 48	10 03	10 18	10 33	10 48	11 03	11 18	11 33	11 48	12 03	12 18	12 33	12 48	13 03	13 18	13 33	13 48	14 03	14 18
Tulse Hill	a	09 07	09 22	09 37	09 52	10 07	10 22	10 37	10 52	11 07	11 22	11 37	11 52	12 07	12 22	12 37	12 52	13 07	13 22	13 37	13 52	14 07	14 22
	d	09 08	09 23	09 38	09 53	10 08	10 23	10 38	10 53	11 08	11 23	11 38	11 53	12 08	12 23	12 38	12 53	13 08	13 23	13 38	13 53	14 08	14 23
London Bridge	a																						
Herne Hill	d	09 12	09 27	09 42	09 57	10 12	10 27	10 42	10 57	11 12	11 27	11 42	11 57	12 12	12 27	12 42	12 57	13 12	13 27	13 42	13 57	14 12	14 27
Loughborough Jn	d	09 15	09 30	09 45	10 00	10 15	10 30	10 45	11 00	11 15	11 30	11 45	12 00	12 15	12 30	12 45	13 00	13 15	13 30	13 45	14 00	14 15	14 30
Elephant & Castle	d	09 19	09 34	09 49	10 04	10 19	10 34	10 49	11 04	11 19	11 34	11 49	12 04	12 19	12 34	12 49	13 04	13 19	13 34	13 49	14 04	14 19	14 34
London Blackfriars	d	09 24	09 39	09 54	10 09	10 24	10 39	10 54	11 09	11 24	11 39	11 54	12 09	12 24	12 39	12 54	13 09	13 24	13 39	13 54	14 09	14 24	14 39
City Thameslink	d	09 26	09 41	09 56	10 11	10 26	10 41	10 56	11 11	11 26	11 41	11 56	12 11	12 26	12 41	12 56	13 11	13 26	13 41	13 56	14 11	14 26	14 41
Farringdon	d	09 29	09 44	09 59	10 14	10 29	10 44	10 59	11 14	11 29	11 44	11 59	12 14	12 29	12 44	12 59	13 14	13 29	13 44	13 59	14 14	14 29	14 44
St Pancras International	d	09 33	09 48	10 03	10 18	10 33	10 48	11 03	11 18	11 33	11 48	12 03	12 18	12 33	12 48	13 03	13 18	13 33	13 48	14 03	14 18	14 33	14 48
West Hampstead Thameslink	d	09 44	09 59	10 14	10 29	10 44	10 59	11 14	11 29	11 42	11 59	12 14	12 29	12 44	12 59	13 14	13 29	13 42	13 59	14 14	14 29	14 42	14 59
St Albans City	a	10 06	10 23	10 38	10 53	11 08	11 23	11 37	11 53	12 05	12 23	12 38	12 53	13 08	13 23	13 37	13 53	14 05	14 23	14 37	14 53	15 05	15 23

		TL	TL	TL	TL	TL	TL	TL	TL	TL	TL	TL	TL	TL	TL	TL	SN	TL	TL	SN	TL	TL
Sutton	d	14 16	14 18	14 46	14 49	15 16	15 19	15 46	15 49	16 16	16 19	16 46	16 49	17 16	17 19	17 46	17 38	17 49	18 16	18 08	18 19	18 46
Carshalton	d	14 19		14 49		15 19		15 49		16 19		16 49		17 19		17 49			18 19			18 49
Hackbridge	d	14 22		14 52		15 22		15 52		16 22		16 52		17 22		17 52			18 22			18 52
Mitcham Junction	d	14 25		14 55		15 25		15 55		16 25		16 55		17 25		17 55			18 25			18 55
Mitcham Eastfields	d	14 28		14 58		15 28		15 58		16 28		16 58		17 28		17 58			18 28			18 58
West Sutton	d		14 21		14 52		15 22		15 52		16 22		16 52		17 22		17 42	17 52		18 12	18 22	
Sutton Common	d		14 23		14 54		15 24		15 54		16 24		16 54		17 24		17 44	17 54		18 14	18 24	
St Helier	d		14 26		14 57		15 27		15 57		16 27		16 57		17 27		17 47	17 57		18 17	18 27	
Morden South	d		14 28		14 59		15 29		15 59		16 29		16 59		17 29		17 49	17 59		18 19	18 29	
South Merton	d		14 30		15 01		15 31		16 01		16 31		17 01		17 31		17 51	18 01		18 21	18 31	
Wimbledon Chase	d		14 32		15 03		15 33		16 03		16 33		17 03		17 33		17 53	18 03		18 23	18 33	
Wimbledon	a		14 35		15 06		15 36		16 06		16 36		17 06		17 36		17 58	18 06		18 28	18 36	
	d		14 36		15 07		15 37		16 07		16 37		17 07		17 37		17 59	18 07		18 29	18 37	
Haydons Road	d		14 38		15 10		15 40		16 10		16 40		17 10		17 40		18 01	18 10		18 31	18 40	
Tooting	d		14 41		15 13		15 43		16 13		16 43		17 13		17 43		18 05	18 13		18 35	18 43	
Streatham	d	14 33	14 46	15 03	15 18	15 33	15 48	16 03	16 18	16 33	16 48	17 03	17 18	17 33	17 48	18 03	18 10	18 18	18 33	18 40	18 48	19 03
Tulse Hill	a	14 37	14 50	15 07	15 22	15 37	15 52	16 07	16 22	16 37	16 52	17 07	17 22	17 37	17 52	18 07	18 14	18 22	18 37	18 43	18 52	19 07
	d	14 38	14 53	15 08	15 23	15 38	15 53	16 08	16 23	16 38	16 53	17 08	17 23	17 38	17 53	18 08	18 14	18 23	18 38	18 44	18 53	19 08
London Bridge	a																18 33			19 03		
Herne Hill	d	14 42	14 57	15 12	15 27	15 42	15 57	16 12	16 27	16 42	16 57	17 12	17 27	17 42	17 57	18 12		18 27	18 42		18 57	19 12
Loughborough Jn	d	14 45	15 00	15 15	15 30	15 45	16 00	16 15	16 30	16 45	17 00	17 15	17 30	17 45	18 00	18 15		18 30	18 45		19 00	19 15
Elephant & Castle	d	14 49	15 04	15 19	15 34	15 49	16 04	16 19	16 34	16 49	17 04	17 19	17 34	17 49	18 04	18 19		18 34	18 49		19 04	19 19
London Blackfriars	d	14 54	15 09	15 24	15 39	15 54	16 09	16 24	16 39	16 54	17 09	17 24	17 39	17 54	18 09	18 24		18 39	18 54		19 09	19 24
City Thameslink	d	14 56	15 11	15 26	15 41	15 56	16 11	16 26	16 41	16 56	17 11	17 26	17 41	17 56	18 11	18 26		18 41	18 56		19 11	19 26
Farringdon	d	14 59	15 14	15 29	15 44	15 59	16 14	16 29	16 44	16 59	17 14	17 29	17 44	17 59	18 14	18 29		18 44	18 59		19 14	19 29
St Pancras International	d	15 03	15 18	15 33	15 48	16 03	16 18	16 33	16 48	17 03	17 18	17 33	17 48	18 03	18 18	18 33		18 48	19 03		19 18	19 33
West Hampstead Thameslink	d	15 14	15 29	15 44	15 59	16 14	16 29	16 44	16 59	17 14	17 29	17 44	17 59	18 14	18 29	18 44		18 59	19 14		19 29	19 42
St Albans City	a	15 38	15 53	16 08	16 23	16 38	16 52	17 07	17 22	17 37	17 52	18 07	18 23	18 37	18 52	19 07		19 22	19 36		19 53	20 05

A From Sutton (Surrey) to Bedford

For more London Bridge connections, refer to Table T173

Most Thameslink services from Blackfriars via Wimbledon and Hackbridge continue back towards Blackfriars.

Table T179-R

Mondays to Fridays

21 May to 20 July

Wimbledon and Sutton - Thameslink

		SN	TL	TL	SN	TL	TL	TL	TL	TL	TL	TL	TL	TL	TL A	TL A	TL A	TL A	TL A	TL A	TL A	TL A
Sutton	d	18 38	18 49	19 16	19 08	19 19	19 46	19 49	20 16	20 21	20 46	20 49	21 16	21 19	21 46	21 49	22 18	22 19	22 48	22 49	23 18	23 19
Carshalton	d			19 19			19 49		20 19		20 49		21 19		21 49		22 21		22 51		23 21	
Hackbridge	d			19 22			19 52		20 22		20 52		21 22		21 52		22 24		22 54		23 24	
Mitcham Junction	d			19 25			19 55		20 25		20 55		21 25		21 55		22 27		22 57		23 27	
Mitcham Eastfields	d			19 28			19 58		20 28		20 58		21 28		21 58		22 30		23 00		23 30	
West Sutton	d	18 42	18 52		19 12	19 22		19 52		20 24		20 52		21 22		21 52		22 22		22 52		23 22
Sutton Common	d	18 44	18 54		19 14	19 24		19 54		20 26		20 54		21 24		21 54		22 24		22 54		23 24
St Helier	d	18 47	18 57		19 17	19 27		19 57		20 29		20 57		21 27		21 57		22 27		22 57		23 27
Morden South	d	18 49	18 59		19 19	19 29		19 59		20 31		20 59		21 29		21 59		22 29		22 59		23 29
South Merton	d	18 51	19 01		19 21	19 31		20 01		20 33		21 01		21 31		22 01		22 31		23 01		23 31
Wimbledon Chase	d	18 53	19 03		19 23	19 33		20 03		20 35		21 03		21 33		22 03		22 33		23 03		23 33
Wimbledon	a	18 58	19 06		19 28	19 36		20 06		20 41		21 06		21 36		22 06		22 36		23 06		23 36
	d	18 59	19 07		19 29	19 37		20 07		20 43		21 07		21 37		22 07		22 41		23 11		23 37
Haydons Road	d	19 01	19 10		19 31	19 40		20 10		20 46		21 10		21 40		22 10		22 44		23 14		23 40
Tooting	d	19 05	19 13		19 35	19 43		20 13		20 49		21 13		21 43		22 13		22 47		23 17		23 43
Streatham	d	19 10	19 18	19 33	19 40	19 48	20 03	20 18	20 33	20 54	21 03	21 18	21 33	21 48	22 03	22 18	22 35	22 52	23 05	23 22	23 35	23 48
Tulse Hill	a	19 13	19 22	19 37	19 43	19 52	20 07	20 22	20 37	20 58	21 07	21 22	21 37	21 52	22 07	22 22	22 39	22 56	23 09	23 26	23 39	23 52
	d	19 14	19 23	19 38	19 44	19 53	20 08	20 23	20 38	20 59	21 08	21 23	21 38	21 53	22 08	22 23	22 40	22 57	23 10	23 27	23 40	23 53
London Bridge	a	19 33			20 03																	
Herne Hill	d		19 27	19 42		19 57	20 12	20 27	20 42	21 04	21 12	21 27	21 42	21 57	22 12	22 27	22 44	23 04	23 14	23 34	23 44	23 57
Loughborough Jn	d		19 30	19 45		20 00	20 15	20 30	20 45	21 07	21 15	21 30	21 45	22 00	22 15	22 30	22 47	23 07	23 17	23 37	23 47	
Elephant & Castle	d		19 34	19 49		20 04	20 19	20 34	20 49	21 11	21 19	21 34	21 49	22 04	22 19	22 34	22 51	23 11	23 21	23 41	23 54	00 04
London Blackfriars	d		19 39	19 54		20 09	20 24	20 39	20 54	21 17	21 24	21 39	21 54	22 09	22 24	22 39	22 59	23 17	23 27	23 49	00 02	00 09
City Thameslink	d		19 41	19 56		20 11	20 26	20 41	20 56	21 19	21 26	21 41	21 56	22 11	22 26	22 41						
Farringdon	d		19 44	19 59		20 14	20 29	20 44	20 59	21 21	21 29	21 44	21 59	22 14	22 29	22 44	23 04	23 21	23 31	23 53	00 06	00 13
St Pancras International	d		19 48	20 03		20 18	20 33	20 48	21 03	21 26	21 33	21 48	22 03	22 18	22 33	22 48	23 08	23 26	23 36	23 58	00 11	00 18
West Hampstead Thameslink	d		19 59	20 14		20 29	20 44	20 59	21 14	21 34	21 44	21 59	22 14	22 29	22 44	23 02	23 17	23 34	23 44	00 06	00 19	00 26
St Albans City	a		20 23	20 38		20 53	21 08	21 23	21 38	21 54	22 08	22 23	22 38	22 53	23 08	23 26	23 41	23 58	00 09	00 31	00 35	00 51

Mondays to Fridays

23 July to 5 October

		TL MX B	TL MX B	TL MX B	TL	TL	TL	TL	SN	TL	TL	SN	TL	TL	SN	TL	TL	SN	TL	TL	SN	TL
Sutton	d				05 46	05 49	06 16	06 19	06 36	06 46	06 49	07 06	07 16	07 19	07 36	07 46	07 49	08 06	08 16	08 19	08 36	08 46
Carshalton	d				05 49		06 19		06 39	06 49		07 09	07 19		07 39	07 49		08 09	08 19		08 39	08 49
Hackbridge	d				05 52		06 22		06 42	06 52		07 12	07 22		07 42	07 52		08 12	08 22		08 42	08 52
Mitcham Junction	d				05 55		06 25		06 45	06 55		07 15	07 25		07 45	07 55		08 15	08 25		08 45	08 55
Mitcham Eastfields	d				05 58		06 28		06 48	06 58		07 18	07 28		07 49	07 58		08 19	08 28		08 49	08 58
West Sutton	d					05 52		06 22			06 52			07 22			07 52			08 22		
Sutton Common	d					05 54		06 24			06 54			07 24			07 54			08 24		
St Helier	d					05 57		06 27			06 57			07 27			07 57			08 27		
Morden South	d					05 59		06 29			06 59			07 29			07 59			08 29		
South Merton	d					06 01		06 31			07 01			07 31			08 01			08 31		
Wimbledon Chase	d					06 03		06 33			07 03			07 33			08 03			08 33		
Wimbledon	a					06 06		06 36			07 06			07 36			08 06			08 36		
	d					06 07		06 37			07 07			07 37			08 07			08 37		
Haydons Road	d					06 10		06 40			07 10			07 40			08 10			08 40		
Tooting	d					06 13		06 43			07 13			07 43			08 13			08 43		
Streatham	d				06 03	06 18	06 33	06 48	06 53	07 03	07 18	07 23	07 33	07 48	07 53	08 03	08 18	08 23	08 33	08 48	08 53	09 03
Tulse Hill	a				06 07	06 22	06 37	06 52	06 56	07 07	07 22	07 26	07 37	07 52	07 56	08 07	08 22	08 26	08 37	08 52	08 56	09 07
	d				06 08	06 23	06 38	06 53	06 57	07 08	07 23	07 27	07 38	07 53	07 57	08 08	08 23	08 27	08 38	08 53	08 57	09 08
London Bridge	a								07 15			07 45			08 15			08 47			09 17	
Herne Hill	d				06 12	06 27	06 42	06 57		07 12	07 27		07 42	07 57		08 12	08 27		08 42	08 57		09 12
Loughborough Jn	d				06 15	06 30	06 45	07 00		07 15	07 30		07 45	08 00		08 15	08 30		08 45	09 00		09 15
Elephant & Castle	d			00 04	06 19	06 34	06 49	07 04		07 19	07 34		07 49	08 04		08 19	08 34		08 49	09 04		09 19
London Blackfriars	d		00 02	00 09	06 24	06 39	06 54	07 09		07 24	07 39		07 54	08 09		08 24	08 39		08 54	09 09		09 24
City Thameslink	d				06 26	06 41	06 56	07 11		07 26	07 41		07 56	08 11		08 26	08 41		08 56	09 11		09 26
Farringdon	d		00 06	00 13	06 29	06 44	06 59	07 14		07 29	07 44		07 59	08 14		08 29	08 44		08 59	09 14		09 29
St Pancras International	d		00 11	00 18	06 33	06 48	07 03	07 18		07 33	07 48		08 03	08 18		08 33	08 48		09 03	09 18		09 33
West Hampstead Thameslink	d	00 06	00 19	00 26	06 44	06 58	07 14	07 28		07 43	07 58		08 13	08 29		08 43	08 58		09 14	09 28		09 44
St Albans City	a	00 31	00 35	00 51	07 08	07 22	07 38	07 51		08 06	08 21		08 36	08 51		09 06	09 21		09 36	09 51		10 06

A To Bedford   **B** From Sutton (Surrey) to Bedford

For more London Bridge connections, refer to Table T173

Most Thameslink services from Blackfriars via Wimbledon and Hackbridge continue back towards Blackfriars.

Please note, Network Rail have stated that further updates to this timetable are possible during the validity period.

Table T179-R

Mondays to Fridays

23 July to 5 October

Wimbledon and Sutton - Thameslink

		TL	TL	TL	TL		TL	TL	TL	TL	TL	TL	TL	TL	TL	TL	TL	TL	TL	TL
Sutton	d	08 49	09 16	09 19	09 46		11 49	12 16	12 19	12 46	12 49	13 16	13 19	13 46	13 49	14 16	14 18	14 46	14 49	15 16
Carshalton	d		09 19		09 49			12 19		12 49		13 19		13 49		14 19		14 49		15 19
Hackbridge	d		09 22		09 52			12 22		12 52		13 22		13 52		14 22		14 52		15 22
Mitcham Junction	d		09 25		09 55			12 25		12 55		13 25		13 55		14 25		14 55		15 25
Mitcham Eastfields	d		09 28		09 58			12 28		12 58		13 28		13 58		14 28		14 58		15 28
West Sutton	d	08 52		09 22			11 52		12 22		12 52		13 22		13 52		14 21		14 52	
Sutton Common	d	08 54		09 24			11 54		12 24		12 54		13 24		13 54		14 23		14 54	
St Helier	d	08 57		09 27			11 57		12 27		12 57		13 27		13 57		14 26		14 57	
Morden South	d	08 59		09 29			11 59		12 29		12 59		13 29		13 59		14 28		14 59	
South Merton	d	09 01		09 31		and at the same minutes past each hour until	12 01		12 31		13 01		13 31		14 01		14 30		15 01	
Wimbledon Chase	d	09 03		09 33			12 03		12 33		13 03		13 33		14 03		14 32		15 03	
Wimbledon	a	09 06		09 36			12 06		12 36		13 06		13 36		14 06		14 35		15 06	
	d	09 07		09 37			12 07		12 37		13 07		13 37		14 07		14 36		15 07	
Haydons Road	d	09 10		09 40			12 10		12 40		13 10		13 40		14 10		14 38		15 10	
Tooting	d	09 13		09 43			12 13		12 43		13 13		13 43		14 13		14 41		15 13	
Streatham	d	09 18	09 33	09 48	10 03		12 18	12 33	12 48	13 03	13 18	13 33	13 48	14 03	14 18	14 33	14 46	15 03	15 18	15 33
Tulse Hill	a	09 22	09 37	09 52	10 07		12 22	12 37	12 52	13 07	13 22	13 37	13 52	14 07	14 22	14 37	14 50	15 07	15 22	15 37
	d	09 23	09 38	09 53	10 08		12 23	12 38	12 53	13 08	13 23	13 38	13 53	14 08	14 23	14 38	14 53	15 08	15 23	15 38
London Bridge	a																			
Herne Hill	d	09 27	09 42	09 57	10 12		12 27	12 42	12 57	13 12	13 27	13 42	13 57	14 12	14 27	14 42	14 57	15 12	15 27	15 42
Loughborough Jn	d	09 30	09 45	10 00	10 15		12 30	12 45	13 00	13 15	13 30	13 45	14 00	14 15	14 30	14 45	15 00	15 15	15 30	15 45
Elephant & Castle	d	09 34	09 49	10 04	10 19		12 34	12 49	13 04	13 19	13 34	13 49	14 04	14 19	14 34	14 49	15 04	15 19	15 34	15 49
London Blackfriars	d	09 39	09 54	10 09	10 24		12 39	12 54	13 09	13 24	13 39	13 54	14 09	14 24	14 39	14 54	15 09	15 24	15 39	15 54
City Thameslink	d	09 41	09 56	10 11	10 26		12 41	12 56	13 11	13 26	13 41	13 56	14 11	14 26	14 41	14 56	15 11	15 26	15 41	15 56
Farringdon	d	09 44	09 59	10 14	10 29		12 44	12 59	13 14	13 29	13 44	13 59	14 14	14 29	14 44	14 59	15 14	15 29	15 44	15 59
St Pancras International	d	09 48	10 03	10 18	10 33		12 48	13 03	13 18	13 33	13 48	14 03	14 18	14 33	14 48	15 03	15 18	15 33	15 48	16 03
West Hampstead Thameslink	d	09 59	10 14	10 29	10 44		12 59	13 14	13 29	13 44	13 59	14 14	14 29	14 44	14 59	15 14	15 29	15 44	15 59	16 14
St Albans City	a	10 23	10 38	10 53	11 08		13 23	13 38	13 53	14 08	14 23	14 38	14 53	15 08	15 23	15 38	15 53	16 08	16 23	16 38

		TL	TL	TL	TL	TL	TL	TL	TL	TL	TL	SN	TL	TL	SN	TL	TL	SN	TL	TL	SN
Sutton	d	15 19	15 46	15 49	16 16	16 19	16 46	16 49	17 16	17 19	17 46	17 38	17 49	18 16	18 08	18 19	18 46	18 38	18 49	19 16	19 08
Carshalton	d		15 49		16 19		16 49		17 19		17 49			18 19			18 49			19 19	
Hackbridge	d		15 52		16 22		16 52		17 22		17 52			18 22			18 52			19 22	
Mitcham Junction	d		15 55		16 25		16 55		17 25		17 55			18 25			18 55			19 25	
Mitcham Eastfields	d		15 58		16 28		16 58		17 28		17 58			18 28			18 58			19 28	
West Sutton	d	15 22		15 52		16 22		16 52		17 22		17 42	17 52		18 12	18 22		18 42	18 52		19 12
Sutton Common	d	15 24		15 54		16 24		16 54		17 24		17 44	17 54		18 14	18 24		18 44	18 54		19 14
St Helier	d	15 27		15 57		16 27		16 57		17 27		17 47	17 57		18 17	18 27		18 47	18 57		19 17
Morden South	d	15 29		15 59		16 29		16 59		17 29		17 49	17 59		18 19	18 29		18 49	18 59		19 19
South Merton	d	15 31		16 01		16 31		17 01		17 31		17 51	18 01		18 21	18 31		18 51	19 01		19 21
Wimbledon Chase	d	15 33		16 03		16 33		17 03		17 33		17 53	18 03		18 23	18 33		18 53	19 03		19 23
Wimbledon	a	15 36		16 06		16 36		17 06		17 36		17 58	18 06		18 28	18 36		18 58	19 06		19 28
	d	15 37		16 07		16 37		17 07		17 37		17 59	18 07		18 29	18 37		18 59	19 07		19 29
Haydons Road	d	15 40		16 10		16 40		17 10		17 40		18 01	18 10		18 31	18 40		19 01	19 10		19 31
Tooting	d	15 43		16 13		16 43		17 13		17 43		18 05	18 13		18 35	18 43		19 05	19 13		19 35
Streatham	d	15 48	16 03	16 18	16 33	16 48	17 03	17 18	17 33	17 48	18 03	18 10	18 18	18 33	18 40	18 48	19 03	19 10	19 18	19 33	19 40
Tulse Hill	a	15 52	16 07	16 22	16 37	16 52	17 07	17 22	17 37	17 52	18 07	18 14	18 22	18 37	18 43	18 52	19 07	19 13	19 22	19 37	19 43
	d	15 53	16 08	16 23	16 38	16 53	17 08	17 23	17 38	17 53	18 08	18 14	18 23	18 38	18 44	18 53	19 08	19 14	19 23	19 38	19 44
London Bridge	a											18 33			19 03			19 33			20 03
Herne Hill	d	15 57	16 12	16 27	16 42	16 57	17 12	17 27	17 42	17 57	18 12		18 27	18 42		18 57	19 12		19 27	19 42	
Loughborough Jn	d	16 00	16 15	16 30	16 45	17 00	17 15	17 30	17 45	18 00	18 15		18 30	18 45		19 00	19 15		19 30	19 45	
Elephant & Castle	d	16 04	16 19	16 34	16 49	17 04	17 19	17 34	17 49	18 04	18 19		18 34	18 49		19 04	19 19		19 34	19 49	
London Blackfriars	d	16 09	16 24	16 39	16 54	17 09	17 24	17 39	17 54	18 09	18 24		18 39	18 54		19 09	19 24		19 39	19 54	
City Thameslink	d	16 11	16 26	16 41	16 56	17 11	17 26	17 41	17 56	18 11	18 26		18 41	18 56		19 11	19 26		19 41	19 56	
Farringdon	d	16 14	16 29	16 44	16 59	17 14	17 29	17 44	17 59	18 14	18 29		18 44	18 59		19 14	19 29		19 44	19 59	
St Pancras International	d	16 18	16 33	16 48	17 03	17 18	17 33	17 48	18 03	18 18	18 33		18 48	19 03		19 18	19 33		19 48	20 03	
West Hampstead Thameslink	d	16 29	16 44	16 59	17 14	17 29	17 44	17 59	18 14	18 29	18 44		18 59	19 14		19 29	19 44		19 59	20 14	
St Albans City	a	16 52	17 07	17 22	17 37	17 52	18 07	18 23	18 37	18 52	19 07		19 22	19 37		19 53	20 08		20 23	20 38	

For more London Bridge connections, refer to Table T173

Most Thameslink services from Blackfriars via Wimbledon and Hackbridge continue back towards Blackfriars.

Table T179-R

Mondays to Fridays

23 July to 5 October

Wimbledon and Sutton - Thameslink

		TL	TL	TL	TL	TL	TL	TL	TL	TL	TL A	TL A	TL A	TL A	TL A	TL A	TL A	TL A
Sutton	d	19 19	19 46	19 49	20 16	20 21	20 46	20 49	21 16	21 19	21 46	21 49	22 18	22 19	22 48	22 49	23 18	23 19
Carshalton	d		19 49		20 19		20 49		21 19		21 49		22 21		22 51		23 21	
Hackbridge	d		19 52		20 22		20 52		21 22		21 52		22 24		22 54		23 24	
Mitcham Junction	d		19 55		20 25		20 55		21 25		21 55		22 27		22 57		23 27	
Mitcham Eastfields	d		19 58		20 28		20 58		21 28		21 58		22 30		23 00		23 30	
West Sutton	d	19 22		19 52		20 24		20 52		21 22		21 52		22 22		22 52		23 22
Sutton Common	d	19 24		19 54		20 26		20 54		21 24		21 54		22 24		22 54		23 24
St Helier	d	19 27		19 57		20 29		20 57		21 27		21 57		22 27		22 57		23 27
Morden South	d	19 29		19 59		20 31		20 59		21 29		21 59		22 29		22 59		23 29
South Merton	d	19 31		20 01		20 33		21 01		21 31		22 01		22 31		23 01		23 31
Wimbledon Chase	d	19 33		20 03		20 35		21 03		21 33		22 03		22 33		23 03		23 33
Wimbledon	a	19 36		20 06		20 41		21 06		21 36		22 06		22 36		23 06		23 36
	d	19 37		20 07		20 43		21 07		21 37		22 07		22 41		23 11		23 37
Haydons Road	d	19 40		20 10		20 46		21 10		21 40		22 10		22 44		23 14		23 40
Tooting	d	19 43		20 13		20 49		21 13		21 43		22 13		22 47		23 17		23 43
Streatham	d	19 48	20 03	20 18	20 33	20 54	21 03	21 18	21 33	21 48	22 03	22 18	22 35	22 52	23 05	23 22	23 35	23 48
Tulse Hill	a	19 52	20 07	20 22	20 37	20 58	21 07	21 22	21 37	21 52	22 07	22 22	22 39	22 56	23 09	23 26	23 39	23 52
	d	19 53	20 08	20 23	20 38	20 59	21 08	21 23	21 38	21 53	22 08	22 23	22 40	22 57	23 10	23 27	23 40	23 53
London Bridge	a																	
Herne Hill	d	19 57	20 12	20 27	20 42	21 04	21 12	21 27	21 42	21 57	22 12	22 27	22 44	23 04	23 14	23 34	23 44	23 57
Loughborough Jn	d	20 00	20 15	20 30	20 45	21 07	21 15	21 30	21 45	22 00	22 15	22 30	22 47	23 07	23 17	23 37	23 47	
Elephant & Castle	d	20 04	20 19	20 34	20 49	21 11	21 19	21 34	21 49	22 04	22 19	22 34	22 51	23 11	23 21	23 41	23 54	00 04
London Blackfriars	d	20 09	20 24	20 39	20 54	21 17	21 24	21 39	21 54	22 09	22 24	22 39	22 59	23 17	23 27	23 49	00 02	00 09
City Thameslink	d	20 11	20 26	20 41	20 56	21 19	21 26	21 41	21 56	22 11	22 26	22 41						
Farringdon	d	20 14	20 29	20 44	20 59	21 21	21 29	21 44	21 59	22 14	22 29	22 44	23 04	23 21	23 31	23 53	00 06	00 13
St Pancras International	d	20 18	20 33	20 48	21 03	21 26	21 33	21 48	22 03	22 18	22 33	22 48	23 08	23 26	23 36	23 58	00 11	00 18
West Hampstead Thameslink	d	20 29	20 44	20 59	21 14	21 34	21 44	21 59	22 14	22 29	22 44	23 02	23 17	23 34	23 44	00 06	00 19	00 26
St Albans City	a	20 53	21 08	21 23	21 38	21 54	22 08	22 23	22 38	22 53	23 08	23 26	23 41	23 58	00 09	00 31	00 35	00 51

Mondays to Fridays

8 October to 7 December

		TL MX B	TL MX B	TL MX B	TL	TL	TL	TL	SN	TL	TL	SN	TL	TL	SN	TL	TL	SN	TL	TL	SN	TL	TL
Sutton	d				05 46	05 49	06 16	06 19	06 36	06 46	06 49	07 06	07 16	07 19	07 36	07 46	07 49	08 06	08 16	08 19	08 36	08 46	08 49
Carshalton	d				05 49		06 19		06 39	06 49		07 09	07 19		07 39	07 49		08 09	08 19		08 39	08 49	
Hackbridge	d				05 52		06 22		06 42	06 52		07 12	07 22		07 42	07 52		08 12	08 22		08 42	08 52	
Mitcham Junction	d				05 55		06 25		06 45	06 55		07 15	07 25		07 45	07 55		08 15	08 25		08 45	08 55	
Mitcham Eastfields	d				05 58		06 28		06 48	06 58		07 18	07 28		07 49	07 58		08 19	08 28		08 49	08 58	
West Sutton	d					05 52		06 22			06 52			07 22			07 52			08 22			08 52
Sutton Common	d					05 54		06 24			06 54			07 24			07 54			08 24			08 54
St Helier	d					05 57		06 27			06 57			07 27			07 57			08 27			08 57
Morden South	d					05 59		06 29			06 59			07 29			07 59			08 29			08 59
South Merton	d					06 01		06 31			07 01			07 31			08 01			08 31			09 01
Wimbledon Chase	d					06 03		06 33			07 03			07 33			08 03			08 33			09 03
Wimbledon	a					06 06		06 36			07 06			07 36			08 06			08 36			09 06
	d					06 07		06 37			07 07			07 37			08 07			08 37			09 07
Haydons Road	d					06 10		06 40			07 10			07 40			08 10			08 40			09 10
Tooting	d					06 13		06 43			07 13			07 43			08 13			08 43			09 13
Streatham	d				06 03	06 18	06 33	06 48	06 53	07 03	07 18	07 23	07 33	07 48	07 53	08 03	08 18	08 23	08 33	08 48	08 53	09 03	09 18
Tulse Hill	a				06 07	06 22	06 37	06 52	06 56	07 07	07 22	07 26	07 37	07 52	07 56	08 07	08 22	08 26	08 37	08 52	08 56	09 07	09 22
	d				06 08	06 23	06 38	06 53	06 57	07 08	07 23	07 27	07 38	07 53	07 57	08 08	08 23	08 27	08 38	08 53	08 57	09 08	09 23
London Bridge	a								07 15			07 45			08 15			08 47			09 17		
Herne Hill	d				06 12	06 27	06 42	06 57		07 12	07 27		07 42	07 57		08 12	08 27		08 42	08 57		09 12	09 27
Loughborough Jn	d				06 15	06 30	06 45	07 00		07 15	07 30		07 45	08 00		08 15	08 30		08 45	09 00		09 15	09 30
Elephant & Castle	d			00 04	06 19	06 34	06 49	07 04		07 19	07 34		07 49	08 04		08 19	08 34		08 49	09 04		09 19	09 34
London Blackfriars	d		00 02	00 09	06 24	06 39	06 54	07 09		07 24	07 39		07 54	08 09		08 24	08 39		08 54	09 09		09 24	09 39
City Thameslink	d				06 26	06 41	06 56	07 11		07 26	07 41		07 56	08 11		08 26	08 41		08 56	09 11		09 26	09 41
Farringdon	d		00 06	00 13	06 29	06 44	06 59	07 14		07 29	07 44		07 59	08 14		08 29	08 44		08 59	09 14		09 29	09 44
St Pancras International	d		00 11	00 18	06 33	06 48	07 03	07 18		07 33	07 48		08 03	08 18		08 33	08 48		09 03	09 18		09 33	09 48
West Hampstead Thameslink	d	00 06	00 19	00 26	06 44	06 58	07 14	07 28		07 43	07 58		08 13	08 29		08 43	08 58		09 14	09 28		09 44	09 59
St Albans City	a	00 31	00 35	00 51	07 08	07 22	07 38	07 51		08 06	08 21		08 36	08 51		09 06	09 21		09 36	09 51		10 06	10 23

A To Bedford

B From Sutton (Surrey) to Bedford

For more London Bridge connections, refer to Table T173

Most Thameslink services from Blackfriars via Wimbledon and Hackbridge continue back towards Blackfriars.

Please note, Network Rail have stated that further updates to this timetable are possible during the validity period.

Wimbledon and Sutton - Thameslink

Mondays to Fridays

8 October to 7 December

		TL		TL	TL	TL	TL	TL	TL	TL	TL	TL		TL	TL	TL	TL	TL	TL	TL	TL	TL		TL	TL
Sutton 4	d	09 16		09 19	09 46	09 49	10 16	10 19	10 46	10 49	11 16	11 19		11 46	11 49	12 16	12 19	12 46	12 49	13 16	13 19	13 46		13 49	14 16
Carshalton	d	09 19			09 49		10 19		10 49		11 19			11 49		12 19		12 49		13 19		13 49			14 19
Hackbridge	d	09 22			09 52		10 22		10 52		11 22			11 52		12 22		12 52		13 22		13 52			14 22
Mitcham Junction	d	09 25			09 55		10 25		10 55		11 25			11 55		12 25		12 55		13 25		13 55			14 25
Mitcham Eastfields	d	09 28			09 58		10 28		10 58		11 28			11 58		12 28		12 58		13 28		13 58			14 28
West Sutton	d			09 22		09 52		10 22		10 52		11 22			11 52		12 22		12 52		13 22			13 52	
Sutton Common	d			09 24		09 54		10 24		10 54		11 24			11 54		12 24		12 54		13 24			13 54	
St Helier	d			09 27		09 57		10 27		10 57		11 27			11 57		12 27		12 57		13 27			13 57	
Morden South	d			09 29		09 59		10 29		10 59		11 29			11 59		12 29		12 59		13 29			13 59	
South Merton	d			09 31		10 01		10 31		11 01		11 31			12 01		12 31		13 01		13 31			14 01	
Wimbledon Chase	d			09 33		10 03		10 33		11 03		11 33			12 03		12 33		13 03		13 33			14 03	
Wimbledon 8 ⊖	a			09 36		10 06		10 36		11 06		11 36			12 06		12 36		13 06		13 36			14 06	
	d			09 37		10 07		10 37		11 07		11 37			12 07		12 37		13 07		13 37			14 07	
Haydons Road	d			09 40		10 10		10 40		11 10		11 40			12 10		12 40		13 10		13 40			14 10	
Tooting	d			09 43		10 13		10 43		11 13		11 43			12 13		12 43		13 13		13 43			14 13	
Streatham 4	d	09 33		09 48	10 03	10 18	10 33	10 48	11 03	11 18	11 33	11 48		12 03	12 18	12 33	12 48	13 03	13 18	13 33	13 48	14 03		14 18	14 33
Tulse Hill 3	a	09 37		09 52	10 07	10 22	10 37	10 52	11 07	11 22	11 37	11 52		12 07	12 22	12 37	12 52	13 07	13 22	13 37	13 52	14 07		14 22	14 37
	d	09 38		09 53	10 08	10 23	10 38	10 53	11 08	11 23	11 38	11 53		12 08	12 23	12 38	12 53	13 08	13 23	13 38	13 53	14 08		14 23	14 38
London Bridge 4 ⊖	a																								
Herne Hill 4	d	09 42		09 57	10 12	10 27	10 42	10 57	11 12	11 27	11 42	11 57		12 12	12 27	12 42	12 57	13 12	13 27	13 42	13 57	14 12		14 27	14 42
Loughborough Jn	d	09 45		10 00	10 15	10 30	10 45	11 00	11 15	11 30	11 45	12 00		12 15	12 30	12 45	13 00	13 15	13 30	13 45	14 00	14 15		14 30	14 45
Elephant & Castle ⊖	d	09 49		10 04	10 19	10 34	10 49	11 04	11 19	11 34	11 49	12 04		12 19	12 34	12 49	13 04	13 19	13 34	13 49	14 04	14 19		14 34	14 49
London Blackfriars 3 ⊖	d	09 54		10 09	10 24	10 39	10 54	11 09	11 24	11 39	11 54	12 09		12 24	12 39	12 54	13 09	13 24	13 39	13 54	14 09	14 24		14 39	14 54
City Thameslink 3	d	09 56		10 11	10 26	10 41	10 56	11 11	11 26	11 41	11 56	12 11		12 26	12 41	12 56	13 11	13 26	13 41	13 56	14 11	14 26		14 41	14 56
Farringdon 3 ⊖	d	09 59		10 14	10 29	10 44	10 59	11 14	11 29	11 44	11 59	12 14		12 29	12 44	12 59	13 14	13 29	13 44	13 59	14 14	14 29		14 44	14 59
St Pancras International 15 ⊖	d	10 03		10 18	10 33	10 48	11 03	11 18	11 33	11 48	12 03	12 18		12 33	12 48	13 03	13 18	13 33	13 48	14 03	14 18	14 33		14 48	15 03
West Hampstead Thameslink	d	10 14		10 29	10 44	10 59	11 14	11 29	11 42	11 59	12 14	12 29		12 44	12 59	13 14	13 29	13 42	13 59	14 14	14 29	14 44		14 59	15 14
St Albans City	a	10 38		10 53	11 08	11 23	11 37	11 53	12 05	12 23	12 38	12 53		13 08	13 23	13 37	13 53	14 05	14 23	14 38	14 53	15 08		15 23	15 38

		TL	TL	TL	TL	TL	TL	TL		TL	TL	TL	TL	TL	TL	TL	SN	TL		TL	SN	TL	TL	SN	TL
Sutton 4	d	14 18	14 46	14 49	15 16	15 19	15 46	15 49		16 16	16 19	16 46	16 49	17 16	17 19	17 46	17 38	17 49		18 16	18 08	18 19	18 46	18 38	18 49
Carshalton	d		14 49		15 19		15 49			16 19		16 49		17 19		17 49				18 19			18 49		
Hackbridge	d		14 52		15 22		15 52			16 22		16 52		17 22		17 52				18 22			18 52		
Mitcham Junction	d		14 55		15 25		15 55			16 25		16 55		17 25		17 55				18 25			18 55		
Mitcham Eastfields	d		14 58		15 28		15 58			16 28		16 58		17 28		17 58				18 28			18 58		
West Sutton	d	14 21		14 52		15 22		15 52			16 22		16 52		17 22		17 42	17 52			18 12	18 22		18 42	18 52
Sutton Common	d	14 23		14 54		15 24		15 54			16 24		16 54		17 24		17 44	17 54			18 14	18 24		18 44	18 54
St Helier	d	14 26		14 57		15 27		15 57			16 27		16 57		17 27		17 47	17 57			18 17	18 27		18 47	18 57
Morden South	d	14 28		14 59		15 29		15 59			16 29		16 59		17 29		17 49	17 59			18 19	18 29		18 49	18 59
South Merton	d	14 30		15 01		15 31		16 01			16 31		17 01		17 31		17 51	18 01			18 21	18 31		18 51	19 01
Wimbledon Chase	d	14 32		15 03		15 33		16 03			16 33		17 03		17 33		17 53	18 03			18 23	18 33		18 53	19 03
Wimbledon 8 ⊖	a	14 35		15 06		15 36		16 06			16 36		17 06		17 36		17 58	18 06			18 28	18 36		18 58	19 06
	d	14 36		15 07		15 37		16 07			16 37		17 07		17 37		17 59	18 07			18 29	18 37		18 59	19 07
Haydons Road	d	14 38		15 10		15 40		16 10			16 40		17 10		17 40		18 01	18 10			18 31	18 40		19 01	19 10
Tooting	d	14 41		15 13		15 43		16 13			16 43		17 13		17 43		18 05	18 13			18 35	18 43		19 05	19 13
Streatham 4	d	14 46	15 03	15 18	15 33	15 48	16 03	16 18		16 33	16 48	17 03	17 18	17 33	17 48	18 03	18 10	18 18		18 33	18 40	18 48	19 03	19 10	19 18
Tulse Hill 3	a	14 50	15 07	15 22	15 37	15 52	16 07	16 22		16 37	16 52	17 07	17 22	17 37	17 52	18 07	18 14	18 22		18 37	18 43	18 52	19 07	19 13	19 22
	d	14 53	15 08	15 23	15 38	15 53	16 08	16 23		16 38	16 53	17 08	17 23	17 38	17 53	18 08	18 14	18 23		18 38	18 44	18 53	19 08	19 14	19 23
London Bridge 4 ⊖	a																18 33				19 03			19 33	
Herne Hill 4	d	14 57	15 12	15 27	15 42	15 57	16 12	16 27		16 42	16 57	17 12	17 27	17 42	17 57	18 12		18 27		18 42		18 57	19 12		19 27
Loughborough Jn	d	15 00	15 15	15 30	15 45	16 00	16 15	16 30		16 45	17 00	17 15	17 30	17 45	18 00	18 15		18 30		18 45		19 00	19 15		19 30
Elephant & Castle ⊖	d	15 04	15 19	15 34	15 49	16 04	16 19	16 34		16 49	17 04	17 19	17 34	17 49	18 04	18 19		18 34		18 49		19 04	19 19		19 34
London Blackfriars 3 ⊖	d	15 09	15 24	15 39	15 54	16 09	16 24	16 39		16 54	17 09	17 24	17 39	17 54	18 09	18 24		18 39		18 54		19 09	19 24		19 39
City Thameslink 3	d	15 11	15 26	15 41	15 56	16 11	16 26	16 41		16 56	17 11	17 26	17 41	17 56	18 11	18 26		18 41		18 56		19 11	19 26		19 41
Farringdon 3 ⊖	d	15 14	15 29	15 44	15 59	16 14	16 29	16 44		16 59	17 14	17 29	17 44	17 59	18 14	18 29		18 44		18 59		19 14	19 29		19 44
St Pancras International 15 ⊖	d	15 18	15 33	15 48	16 03	16 18	16 33	16 48		17 03	17 18	17 33	17 48	18 03	18 18	18 33		18 48		19 03		19 18	19 33		19 48
West Hampstead Thameslink	d	15 29	15 44	15 59	16 14	16 29	16 44	16 59		17 14	17 29	17 44	17 59	18 14	18 29	18 44		18 59		19 14		19 29	19 44		19 59
St Albans City	a	15 53	16 08	16 23	16 38	16 52	17 07	17 22		17 37	17 52	18 07	18 23	18 37	18 52	19 07		19 22		19 37		19 53	20 08		20 23

		TL	SN	TL		TL	TL	TL	TL	TL	TL	TL	TL	TL A		TL A	TL A	TL A	TL A	TL A	TL A	TL A			
Sutton 4	d	19 16	19 08	19 19		19 46	19 49	20 16	20 21	20 46	20 49	21 16	21 19	21 46		21 49	22 18	22 19	22 48	22 49	23 18	23 19			
Carshalton	d	19 19				19 49		20 19		20 49		21 19		21 49			22 21		22 51		23 21				
Hackbridge	d	19 22				19 52		20 22		20 52		21 22		21 52			22 24		22 54		23 24				
Mitcham Junction	d	19 25				19 55		20 25		20 55		21 25		21 55			22 27		22 57		23 27				
Mitcham Eastfields	d	19 28				19 58		20 28		20 58		21 28		21 58			22 30		23 00		23 30				
West Sutton	d		19 12	19 22			19 52		20 24		20 52		21 22			21 52		22 22		22 52		23 22			
Sutton Common	d		19 14	19 24			19 54		20 26		20 54		21 24			21 54		22 24		22 54		23 24			
St Helier	d		19 17	19 27			19 57		20 29		20 57		21 27			21 57		22 27		22 57		23 27			
Morden South	d		19 19	19 29			19 59		20 31		20 59		21 29			21 59		22 29		22 59		23 29			
South Merton	d		19 21	19 31			20 01		20 33		21 01		21 31			22 01		22 31		23 01		23 31			
Wimbledon Chase	d		19 23	19 33			20 03		20 35		21 03		21 33			22 03		22 33		23 03		23 33			
Wimbledon 8 ⊖	a		19 28	19 36			20 06		20 41		21 06		21 36			22 06		22 36		23 06		23 36			
	d		19 29	19 37			20 07		20 43		21 07		21 37			22 07		22 41		23 11		23 37			
Haydons Road	d		19 31	19 40			20 10		20 46		21 10		21 40			22 10		22 44		23 14		23 40			
Tooting	d		19 35	19 43			20 13		20 49		21 13		21 43			22 13		22 47		23 17		23 43			
Streatham 4	d	19 33	19 40	19 48		20 03	20 18	20 33	20 54	21 03	21 18	21 33	21 48	22 03		22 18	22 35	22 52	23 05	23 22	23 35	23 48			
Tulse Hill 3	a	19 37	19 43	19 52		20 07	20 22	20 37	20 58	21 07	21 22	21 37	21 52	22 07		22 22	22 39	22 56	23 09	23 26	23 39	23 52			
	d	19 38	19 44	19 53		20 08	20 23	20 38	20 59	21 08	21 23	21 38	21 53	22 08		22 23	22 40	22 57	23 10	23 27	23 40	23 53			
London Bridge 4 ⊖	a		20 03																						
Herne Hill 4	d	19 42		19 57		20 12	20 27	20 42	21 04	21 12	21 27	21 42	21 57	22 12		22 27	22 44	23 04	23 14	23 34	23 44	23 57			
Loughborough Jn	d	19 45		20 00		20 15	20 30	20 45	21 07	21 15	21 30	21 45	22 00	22 15		22 30	22 47	23 07	23 17	23 37	23 47				
Elephant & Castle ⊖	d	19 49		20 04		20 19	20 34	20 49	21 11	21 19	21 34	21 49	22 04	22 19		22 34	22 51	23 11	23 21	23 41	23 54	00 04			
London Blackfriars 3 ⊖	d	19 54		20 09		20 24	20 39	20 54	21 17	21 24	21 39	21 54	22 09	22 24		22 39	22 59	23 17	23 27	23 49	00 02	00 09			
City Thameslink 3	d	19 56		20 11		20 26	20 41	20 56	21 19	21 26	21 41	21 56	22 11	22 26		22 41									
Farringdon 3 ⊖	d	19 59		20 14		20 29	20 44	20 59	21 21	21 29	21 44	21 59	22 14	22 29		22 44	23 04	23 21	23 31	23 53	00 06	00 13			
St Pancras International 15 ⊖	d	20 03		20 18		20 33	20 48	21 03	21 26	21 33	21 48	22 03	22 18	22 33		22 48	23 08	23 26	23 36	23 58	00 11	00 18			
West Hampstead Thameslink	d	20 14		20 29		20 44	20 59	21 14	21 34	21 44	21 59	22 14	22 29	22 44		23 02	23 17	23 34	23 44	00 06	00 19	00 26			
St Albans City	a	20 38		20 53		21 08	21 23	21 38	21 54	22 08	22 23	22 38	22 53	23 08		23 26	23 41	23 58	00 09	00 31	00 35	00 51			

A To Bedford

For more London Bridge connections, refer to Table T173

Most Thameslink services from Blackfriars via Wimbledon and Hackbridge continue back towards Blackfriars.

Wimbledon and Sutton - Thameslink

Saturdays

26 May to 8 December

		TL A	TL A	TL A	TL	TL	TL	TL	TL	TL		TL	TL	TL	TL	TL	TL	TL	TL	TL				
Sutton 4	d				05 46	05 49	06 16	06 19	06 46	06 49		07 16	07 19	07 46	07 49	08 16	08 19	08 46	08 49	09 16	and at the same minutes past each hour until			
Carshalton	d				05 49		06 19		06 49			07 19		07 49		08 19		08 49		09 19				
Hackbridge	d				05 52		06 22		06 52			07 22		07 52		08 22		08 52		09 22				
Mitcham Junction	d				05 55		06 25		06 55			07 25		07 55		08 25		08 55		09 25				
Mitcham Eastfields	d				05 58		06 28		06 58			07 28		07 58		08 28		08 58		09 28				
West Sutton	d					05 52		06 22		06 52			07 22		07 52		08 22		08 52					
Sutton Common	d					05 54		06 24		06 54			07 24		07 54		08 24		08 54					
St Helier	d					05 57		06 27		06 57			07 27		07 57		08 27		08 57					
Morden South	d					05 59		06 29		06 59			07 29		07 59		08 29		08 59					
South Merton	d					06 01		06 31		07 01			07 31		08 01		08 31		09 01					
Wimbledon Chase	d					06 03		06 33		07 03			07 33		08 03		08 33		09 03					
Wimbledon 8 ⊖	a					06 06		06 36		07 06			07 36		08 06		08 36		09 06					
	d					06 07		06 37		07 07			07 37		08 07		08 37		09 07					
Haydons Road	d					06 10		06 40		07 10			07 40		08 10		08 40		09 10					
Tooting	d					06 13		06 43		07 13			07 43		08 13		08 43		09 13					
Streatham 4	d				06 03	06 18	06 33	06 48	07 03	07 18		07 33	07 48	08 03	08 18	08 33	08 48	09 03	09 18	09 33				
Tulse Hill 3	a				06 07	06 22	06 37	06 52	07 07	07 22		07 37	07 52	08 07	08 22	08 37	08 52	09 07	09 22	09 37				
	d				06 08	06 23	06 38	06 53	07 08	07 23		07 38	07 53	08 08	08 23	08 38	08 53	09 08	09 23	09 38				
London Bridge 4 ⊖	a																							
Herne Hill 4	d				06 12	06 27	06 42	06 57	07 12	07 27		07 42	07 57	08 12	08 27	08 42	08 57	09 12	09 27	09 42				
Loughborough Jn	d				06 15	06 30	06 45	07 00	07 15	07 30		07 45	08 00	08 15	08 30	08 45	09 00	09 15	09 30	09 45				
Elephant & Castle ⊖	d			00 04	06 19	06 34	06 49	07 04	07 19	07 34		07 49	08 04	08 19	08 34	08 49	09 04	09 19	09 34	09 49				
London Blackfriars 3 ⊖	d		00 02	00 09	06 24	06 39	06 54	07 09	07 24	07 39		07 54	08 09	08 24	08 39	08 54	09 09	09 24	09 39	09 54				
City Thameslink 3	d																09 11	09 26	09 41	09 56				
Farringdon 3 ⊖	d		00 06	00 13	06 29	06 44	06 59	07 14	07 29	07 44		07 59	08 14	08 29	08 44	08 59	09 14	09 29	09 44	09 59				
St Pancras International 15 ⊖	d		00 11	00 18	06 33	06 48	07 03	07 18	07 33	07 48		08 03	08 18	08 33	08 48	09 03	09 18	09 33	09 48	10 03				
West Hampstead Thameslink	d	00 06	00 19	00 26	06 44	06 59	07 14	07 29	07 44	07 59		08 14	08 29	08 44	08 59	09 14	09 29	09 44	09 59	10 14				
St Albans City	a	00 31	00 35	00 51	07 08	07 23	07 38	07 53	08 08	08 23		08 38	08 53	09 08	09 23	09 38	09 53	10 08	10 23	10 38				

		TL	TL	TL	TL		TL	TL	TL	TL	TL	TL B	TL B	TL B	TL B		TL B	TL B	TL B	TL B				
Sutton 4	d	19 19	19 46	19 49	20 16		20 19	20 46	20 49	21 16	21 19	21 46	21 49	22 18	22 19		22 48	22 49	23 18	23 19				
Carshalton	d		19 49		20 19			20 49		21 19		21 49		22 21			22 51		23 21					
Hackbridge	d		19 52		20 22			20 52		21 22		21 52		22 24			22 54		23 24					
Mitcham Junction	d		19 55		20 25			20 55		21 25		21 55		22 27			22 57		23 27					
Mitcham Eastfields	d		19 58		20 28			20 58		21 28		21 58		22 30			23 00		23 30					
West Sutton	d	19 22		19 52			20 22		20 52		21 22		21 52		22 22			22 52		23 22				
Sutton Common	d	19 24		19 54			20 24		20 54		21 24		21 54		22 24			22 54		23 24				
St Helier	d	19 27		19 57			20 27		20 57		21 27		21 57		22 27			22 57		23 27				
Morden South	d	19 29		19 59			20 29		20 59		21 29		21 59		22 29			22 59		23 29				
South Merton	d	19 31		20 01			20 31		21 01		21 31		22 01		22 31			23 01		23 31				
Wimbledon Chase	d	19 33		20 03			20 33		21 03		21 33		22 03		22 33			23 03		23 33				
Wimbledon 8 ⊖	a	19 36		20 06			20 36		21 06		21 36		22 06		22 36			23 06		23 36				
	d	19 37		20 07			20 37		21 07		21 37		22 07		22 41			23 11		23 37				
Haydons Road	d	19 40		20 10			20 40		21 10		21 40		22 10		22 44			23 14		23 40				
Tooting	d	19 43		20 13			20 43		21 13		21 43		22 13		22 47			23 17		23 43				
Streatham 4	d	19 48	20 03	20 18	20 33		20 48	21 03	21 18	21 33	21 48	22 03	22 18	22 35	22 52		23 05	23 22	23 35	23 48				
Tulse Hill 3	a	19 52	20 07	20 22	20 37		20 52	21 07	21 22	21 37	21 52	22 07	22 22	22 39	22 56		23 09	23 26	23 39	23 52				
	d	19 53	20 08	20 23	20 38		20 53	21 08	21 23	21 38	21 53	22 08	22 23	22 40	22 57		23 10	23 27	23 40	23 53				
London Bridge 4 ⊖	a																							
Herne Hill 4	d	19 57	20 12	20 27	20 42		20 57	21 12	21 27	21 42	21 57	22 12	22 27	22 44	23 04		23 14	23 34	23 44	23 57				
Loughborough Jn	d	20 00	20 15	20 30	20 45		21 00	21 15	21 30	21 45	22 00	22 15	22 30	22 47	23 07		23 17	23 37	23 47					
Elephant & Castle ⊖	d	20 04	20 19	20 34	20 49		21 04	21 19	21 34	21 49	22 04	22 19	22 34	22 51	23 11		23 21	23 41	23 54	00 04				
London Blackfriars 3 ⊖	d	20 09	20 24	20 39	20 54		21 09	21 24	21 39	21 54	22 09	22 24	22 39	22 59	23 17		23 27	23 49	00 02	00 09				
City Thameslink 3	d	20 11	20 26	20 41	20 56																			
Farringdon 3 ⊖	d	20 14	20 29	20 44	20 59		21 14	21 29	21 44	21 59	22 14	22 29	22 44	23 04	23 21		23 31	23 53	00 06	00 13				
St Pancras International 15 ⊖	d	20 18	20 33	20 48	21 03		21 18	21 33	21 48	22 03	22 18	22 33	22 48	23 08	23 26		23 36	23 58	00 11	00 18				
West Hampstead Thameslink	d	20 29	20 44	20 59	21 14		21 29	21 44	21 59	22 14	22 29	22 44	23 02	23 17	23 34		23 44	00 06	00 19	00 26				
St Albans City	a	20 53	21 08	21 23	21 38		21 53	22 08	22 23	22 38	22 53	23 08	23 26	23 41	23 58		00 09	00 31	00 35	00 51				

A From Sutton (Surrey) to Bedford

B To Bedford

For more London Bridge connections, refer to Table T173

Most Thameslink services from Blackfriars via Wimbledon and Hackbridge continue back towards Blackfriars.

Table T179-R

Sundays

20 May to 2 December

Wimbledon and Sutton - Thameslink

		TL A	TL A	TL A	TL B	TL B		TL B	TL	TL B	TL	TL	TL B	TL	TL B	TL		TL B	TL	TL B	TL	TL B	TL	TL B	TL
Sutton	d				09 09	09 39		10 09	10 40	10 39	11 10	11 09	11 40	11 39	12 10	12 09		12 40	12 39	13 10	13 09	13 40	13 39	14 10	14 09
Carshalton	d								10 43		11 13		11 43		12 13			12 43		13 13		13 43		14 13	
Hackbridge	d								10 45		11 15		11 45		12 15			12 45		13 15		13 45		14 15	
Mitcham Junction	d								10 48		11 18		11 48		12 18			12 48		13 18		13 48		14 18	
Mitcham Eastfields	d								10 51		11 21		11 51		12 21			12 51		13 21		13 51		14 21	
West Sutton	d				09 12	09 42		10 12		10 42		11 12		11 42		12 12			12 42		13 12		13 42		14 12
Sutton Common	d				09 14	09 44		10 14		10 44		11 14		11 44		12 14			12 44		13 14		13 44		14 14
St Helier	d				09 17	09 47		10 17		10 47		11 17		11 47		12 17			12 47		13 17		13 47		14 17
Morden South	d				09 19	09 49		10 19		10 49		11 19		11 49		12 19			12 49		13 19		13 49		14 19
South Merton	d				09 21	09 51		10 21		10 51		11 21		11 51		12 21			12 51		13 21		13 51		14 21
Wimbledon Chase	d				09 23	09 53		10 23		10 53		11 23		11 53		12 23			12 53		13 23		13 53		14 23
Wimbledon	a				09 26	09 56		10 26		10 56		11 26		11 56		12 26			12 56		13 26		13 56		14 26
	d				09 27	09 57		10 27		10 57		11 27		11 57		12 27			12 57		13 27		13 57		14 27
Haydons Road	d				09 29	09 59		10 29		10 59		11 29		11 59		12 29			12 59		13 29		13 59		14 29
Tooting	d				09 32	10 02		10 32		11 02		11 32		12 02		12 32			13 02		13 32		14 02		14 32
Streatham	d				09 37	10 07		10 37	10 55	11 07	11 25	11 37	11 55	12 07	12 25	12 37		12 55	13 07	13 25	13 37	13 55	14 07	14 25	14 37
Tulse Hill	a				09 41	10 11		10 41	10 59	11 11	11 29	11 41	11 59	12 11	12 29	12 41		12 59	13 11	13 29	13 41	13 59	14 11	14 29	14 41
	d				09 41	10 11		10 41	10 59	11 11	11 29	11 41	11 59	12 11	12 29	12 41		12 59	13 11	13 29	13 41	13 59	14 11	14 29	14 41
London Bridge ⊖	a																								
Herne Hill	d				09 45	10 15		10 45	11 03	11 15	11 33	11 45	12 03	12 15	12 33	12 45		13 03	13 15	13 33	13 45	14 03	14 15	14 33	14 45
Loughborough Jn	d				09 48	10 18		10 48	11 06	11 18	11 36	11 48	12 06	12 18	12 36	12 48		13 06	13 18	13 36	13 48	14 06	14 18	14 36	14 48
Elephant & Castle ⊖	d			00 04	09 53	10 23		10 53	11 11	11 23	11 41	11 53	12 11	12 23	12 41	12 53		13 11	13 23	13 41	13 53	14 11	14 23	14 41	14 53
London Blackfriars ⊖	d		00 02	00 09	09 58	10 28		10 58	11a15	11 28	11a45	11 58	12 16	12 28	12 46	12 58		13 16	13 28	13 46	13 58	14 16	14 28	14 46	14 58
City Thameslink	d																								
Farringdon ⊖	d		00 06	00 13	10 02	10 32		11 02		11 32		12 02	12 20	12 32	12 50	13 02		13 20	13 32	13 50	14 02	14 20	14 32	14 50	15 02
St Pancras International ⊖	d		00 11	00 18	10 07	10 37		11 07		11 37		12 07	12 25	12 37	12 55	13 07		13 25	13 37	13 55	14 07	14 25	14 37	14 55	15 07
West Hampstead Thameslink	d	00 06	00 19	00 26	10 15	10 45		11 15		11 45		12 16	12 34	12 46	13 04	13 16		13 34	13 46	14 04	14 16	14 34	14 46	15 04	15 16
St Albans City	a	00 31	00 35	00 51	10 38	11 08		11 38		12 10		12 42	12 54	13 12	13 24	13 42		13 54	14 14	14 24	14 44	14 54	15 14	15 24	15 42

		TL B		TL	TL B	TL	TL B	TL	TL B	TL	TL B	TL		TL B	TL	TL B	TL	TL B	TL	TL B	TL	TL B		TL	TL B
Sutton	d	14 40		14 39	15 10	15 09	15 40	15 39	16 10	16 09	16 40	16 39		17 10	17 09	17 40	17 39	18 10	18 09	18 40	18 39	19 10		19 09	19 40
Carshalton	d	14 43			15 13		15 43		16 13		16 43			17 13		17 43		18 13		18 43		19 13			19 43
Hackbridge	d	14 45			15 15		15 45		16 15		16 45			17 15		17 45		18 15		18 45		19 15			19 45
Mitcham Junction	d	14 48			15 18		15 48		16 18		16 48			17 18		17 48		18 18		18 48		19 18			19 48
Mitcham Eastfields	d	14 51			15 21		15 51		16 21		16 51			17 21		17 51		18 21		18 51		19 21			19 51
West Sutton	d			14 42		15 12		15 42		16 12		16 42			17 12		17 42		18 12		18 42			19 12	
Sutton Common	d			14 44		15 14		15 44		16 14		16 44			17 14		17 44		18 14		18 44			19 14	
St Helier	d			14 47		15 17		15 47		16 17		16 47			17 17		17 47		18 17		18 47			19 17	
Morden South	d			14 49		15 19		15 49		16 19		16 49			17 19		17 49		18 19		18 49			19 19	
South Merton	d			14 51		15 21		15 51		16 21		16 51			17 21		17 51		18 21		18 51			19 21	
Wimbledon Chase	d			14 53		15 23		15 53		16 23		16 53			17 23		17 53		18 23		18 53			19 23	
Wimbledon	a			14 56		15 26		15 56		16 26		16 56			17 26		17 56		18 26		18 56			19 26	
	d			14 57		15 27		15 57		16 27		16 57			17 27		17 57		18 27		18 57			19 27	
Haydons Road	d			14 59		15 29		15 59		16 29		16 59			17 29		17 59		18 29		18 59			19 29	
Tooting	d			15 02		15 32		16 02		16 32		17 02			17 32		18 02		18 32		19 02			19 32	
Streatham	d	14 55		15 07	15 25	15 37	15 55	16 07	16 25	16 37	16 55	17 07		17 25	17 37	17 55	18 07	18 25	18 37	18 55	19 07	19 25		19 37	19 55
Tulse Hill	a	14 59		15 11	15 29	15 41	15 59	16 11	16 29	16 41	16 59	17 11		17 29	17 41	17 59	18 11	18 29	18 41	18 59	19 11	19 29		19 41	19 59
	d	14 59		15 11	15 29	15 41	15 59	16 11	16 29	16 41	16 59	17 11		17 29	17 41	17 59	18 11	18 29	18 41	18 59	19 11	19 29		19 41	19 59
London Bridge ⊖	a																								
Herne Hill	d	15 03		15 15	15 33	15 45	16 03	16 15	16 33	16 45	17 03	17 15		17 33	17 45	18 03	18 15	18 33	18 45	19 03	19 15	19 33		19 45	20 03
Loughborough Jn	d	15 06		15 18	15 36	15 48	16 06	16 18	16 36	16 48	17 06	17 18		17 36	17 48	18 06	18 18	18 36	18 48	19 06	19 18	19 36		19 48	20 06
Elephant & Castle ⊖	d	15 11		15 23	15 41	15 53	16 11	16 23	16 41	16 53	17 11	17 23		17 41	17 53	18 11	18 23	18 41	18 53	19 11	19 23	19 41		19 53	20 11
London Blackfriars ⊖	d	15 16		15 28	15 46	15 58	16 16	16 28	16 46	16 58	17 16	17 28		17 46	17 58	18 16	18 28	18 46	18 58	19 16	19 28	19 46		19 58	20 16
City Thameslink	d																								
Farringdon ⊖	d	15 20		15 32	15 50	16 02	16 20	16 32	16 50	17 02	17 20	17 32		17 50	18 02	18 20	18 32	18 50	19 02	19 20	19 32	19 50		20 02	20 20
St Pancras International ⊖	d	15 25		15 37	15 55	16 07	16 25	16 37	16 55	17 07	17 25	17 37		17 55	18 07	18 25	18 37	18 55	19 07	19 25	19 37	19 55		20 07	20 25
West Hampstead Thameslink	d	15 34		15 46	16 04	16 16	16 34	16 46	17 04	17 16	17 34	17 46		18 04	18 16	18 34	18 46	19 04	19 16	19 34	19 46	20 04		20 16	20 34
St Albans City	a	15 54		16 14	16 24	16 42	16 54	17 12	17 24	17 44	17 54	18 12		18 24	18 42	18 54	19 12	19 24	19 44	19 54	20 12	20 24		20 42	20 54

		TL	TL B	TL	TL B	TL	TL B	TL C		TL	TL	TL C	TL C
Sutton	d	19 39	20 10	20 09	20 40	20 39	21 10	21 09		21 40	22 10	22 09	22 40
Carshalton	d		20 13		20 43		21 13			21 43	22 13		22 43
Hackbridge	d		20 15		20 45		21 15			21 45	22 15		22 45
Mitcham Junction	d		20 18		20 48		21 18			21 48	22 18		22 48
Mitcham Eastfields	d		20 21		20 51		21 21			21 51	22 21		22 51
West Sutton	d	19 42		20 12		20 42		21 12				22 12	
Sutton Common	d	19 44		20 14		20 44		21 14				22 14	
St Helier	d	19 47		20 17		20 47		21 17				22 17	
Morden South	d	19 49		20 19		20 49		21 19				22 19	
South Merton	d	19 51		20 21		20 51		21 21				22 21	
Wimbledon Chase	d	19 53		20 23		20 53		21 23				22 23	
Wimbledon	a	19 56		20 26		20 56		21 26				22 26	
	d	19 57		20 27		20 57		21 27				22 27	
Haydons Road	d	19 59		20 29		20 59		21 29				22 29	
Tooting	d	20 02		20 32		21 02		21 32				22 32	
Streatham	d	20 07	20 25	20 37	20 55	21 07	21 25	21 37		21 55	22 25	22 37	22 55
Tulse Hill	a	20 11	20 29	20 41	20 59	21 11	21 29	21 41		21 59	22 29	22 41	22 59
	d	20 11	20 29	20 41	20 59	21 11	21 29	21 41		21 59	22 29	22 41	22 59
London Bridge ⊖	a												
Herne Hill	d	20 15	20 33	20 45	21 03	21 15	21 33	21 45		22 03	22 33	22 45	23 03
Loughborough Jn	d	20 18	20 36	20 48	21 06	21 18	21 36	21 48		22 06	22 36	22 48	23 06
Elephant & Castle ⊖	d	20 23	20 41	20 53	21 11	21 23	21 41	21 53		22 11	22 41	22 53	23 11
London Blackfriars ⊖	d	20 28	20 46	20 58	21 16	21 28	21 46	21 58		22 16	22a45	22 58	23 16
City Thameslink	d												
Farringdon ⊖	d	20 32	20 50	21 02	21 20	21 32	21 50	22 02		22 20		23 02	23 20
St Pancras International ⊖	d	20 37	20 55	21 07	21 25	21 37	21 55	22 07		22 25		23 07	23 25
West Hampstead Thameslink	d	20 46	21 04	21 16	21 34	21 46	22 04	22 15		22a33		23 15	23 33
St Albans City	a	21 12	21 24	21 42	21 54	22 12	22 24	22 40				23 40	23 58

A From Sutton (Surrey) to Bedford B To Luton C To Bedford

For more London Bridge connections, refer to Table T173

Most Thameslink services from Blackfriars via Wimbledon and Hackbridge continue back towards Blackfriars.

Table T180-F

Mondays to Fridays

21 May to 5 October

London - Hackbridge, Sutton, Epsom, Leatherhead, Dorking and Horsham

Miles	Miles	Miles	Miles			SN MO	TL MO	TL MX	SW MX	SW MX	SW	SN	TL	TL		SN	SW	TL	TL	SW	SN	SW	TL	TL
0	—	—	0	London Victoria ⊖	d							05 41				06 11			06 25		06 41			06 55
—	0	—	—	London Waterloo ⊖	d					00 15	05 47						06 24			06 39		06 54		
2¾	4¼	—	2¾	Clapham Junction	d					00 26	05 56	05 48				06 18	06 33		06 32	06 48	06 48	07 03		07 02
4½	—	—	4½	Balham ⊖	d							05 53				06 23					06 53			
—	—	0	—	St Pancras International	d									05 27				05 57					06 27	
—	—	1¼	—	Farringdon	d									05 32				06 02					06 32	
—	—	1¾	—	City Thameslink	d									05 34				06 04					06 34	
—	—	2¼	—	London Blackfriars	d									05 36				06 06					06 36	
—	—	3¾	—	Elephant & Castle	d									05 40				06 10					06 40	
—	—	5¾	—	Loughborough Jn	d									05 45				06 15					06 45	
—	—	6½	—	Herne Hill	d									05 50				06 20					06 50	
—	—	—	—	London Bridge	d								05 55											
—	—	7½	—	Tulse Hill	a									05 54				06 24					06 54	
—	—	—	—	Tulse Hill	d									05 56				06 26					06 56	
—	—	9¼	—	Streatham	d									06 00				06 30					07 00	
7¼	—	10¼	—	**Mitcham Eastfields**	d							06 00		06 04		06 30		06 34			07 00		07 04	
8¼	—	11¼	—	**Mitcham Junction**	d							06 03		06 07		06 33		06 37			07 03		07 07	
9½	—	12½	—	**Hackbridge**	d							06 06		06 10		06 36		06 40			07 06		07 10	
10¼	—	13¼	—	**Carshalton**	d							06 09		06 13		06 39		06 43	06 49		07 09		07 13	07 19
11½	—	14½	12¼	Sutton	a							06 13		06 17		06 43		06 47	06 53		07 13		07 17	07 23
—	—	—	—	Norwood Junction	d								06 09											
—	—	—	—	West Croydon	d								06 15											
—	—	—	—	Sutton	a								06 28											
—	—	—	—	Sutton	d							06 13	06 28			06 43			06 54		07 13			07 24
12¾	—	—	—	**Cheam**	d			00 02				06 16	06 31			06 46			06 57		07 16			07 27
14¼	—	—	—	**Ewell East**	d	00 01		00 05				06 19	06 34			06 49					07 19			
15¾	14¼	—	—	**Epsom**	a	00 05		00 09		00 50	06 20	06 23	06 38			06 53	06 57		07 03	07 11	07 23	07 27		07 33
—	—	—	—	**Epsom**	d			00 09	00 19		06 21		06 39				06 58		07 04	07 12		07 28		07 34
17¼	16½	—	—	**Ashtead**	d			00 14	00 23		06 25						07 02		07 09	07 16		07 32		07 39
19½	18½	—	—	**Leatherhead**	d		00 02	00 18	00a26		06a28		06a45				07 05		07 12	07a19		07 35		07 43
—	—	—	—	**Box Hill & Westhumble**	d		00 07	00 23											07 17					
23½	—	—	—	**Dorking**	a		00 09	00 26									07 12		07 20			07 42		07 50
—	—	—	—	**Dorking**	d			00 26											07 21					
28½	—	—	—	**Holmwood**	d			00s33											07 28					
30¾	—	—	—	**Ockley**	d			00s37											07 32					
35	—	—	—	**Warnham**	d			00s43											07 38					
37¼	—	—	—	Horsham	a			00 48											07 46					

		TL	SW	SN	SW	TL	TL	SW	SN	SW		TL	TL	TL	SW	SN	SW	TL	TL	TL		SW	SN	SW	TL
London Victoria ⊖	d			07 11			07 25		07 41				07 55			08 11			08 25				08 41		
London Waterloo ⊖	d		07 09		07 24			07 39		07 54					08 09		08 24					08 39		08 54	
Clapham Junction	d		07 18	07 18	07 33		07 32	07 48	07 48	08 03			08 02		08 18	08 18	08 33		08 32			08 48	08 48	09 03	
Balham ⊖	d			07 23					07 53							08 23							08 53		
St Pancras International	d					06 57						07 27						07 57							08 27
Farringdon	d					07 02						07 32						08 02							08 32
City Thameslink	d					07 04						07 34						08 04							08 34
London Blackfriars	d					07 06						07 36						08 06							08 36
Elephant & Castle	d					07 10						07 40						08 10							08 40
Loughborough Jn	d					07 15						07 45						08 15							08 45
Herne Hill	d					07 20						07 50						08 20							08 50
London Bridge	d	06 55												07 55						08 25					
Tulse Hill	a					07 24						07 54						08 24							08 54
Tulse Hill	d					07 26						07 56						08 27							08 57
Streatham	d					07 30						08 00						08 30							09 00
Mitcham Eastfields	d			07 30		07 34			08 00			08 04				08 30		08 34					09 00		09 04
Mitcham Junction	d			07 33		07 37			08 03			08 07				08 33		08 37					09 03		09 07
Hackbridge	d			07 36		07 40			08 06			08 10				08 36		08 40					09 06		09 10
Carshalton	d			07 39		07 43	07 50		08 09			08 13	08 19			08 39		08 43	08 49				09 09		09 13
Sutton	a			07 43		07 47	07 53		08 13			08 17	08 23			08 43		08 47	08 53				09 13		09 17
Norwood Junction	d	07 09												08 09						08 39					
West Croydon	d	07 16												08 16						08 45					
Sutton	a	07 28												08 28						08 58					
Sutton	d	07 28		07 43			07 54		08 13				08 24	08 28		08 43			08 54	08 58			09 13		
Cheam	d	07 31		07 46			07 57		08 16				08 27	08 31		08 46			08 57	09 01			09 16		
Ewell East	d	07 34		07 49					08 19					08 34		08 49				09 04			09 19		
Epsom	a	07 38	07 42	07 53	07 58		08 04	08 13	08 23	08 27			08 34	08 38	08 42	08 53	08 57		09 04	09 08		09 16	09 23	09 27	
Epsom	d				07 58		08 05	08 17		08 28			08 35		08 47		08 58		09 05			09 17		09 28	
Ashtead	d				08 02		08 10	08 21		08 32			08 40		08 51		09 02		09 10			09 21		09 32	
Leatherhead	d				08 05		08 14	08a24		08 35			08 44		08a54		09 05		09 14			09a24		09 35	
Box Hill & Westhumble	d						08 19												09 19						
Dorking	a				08 12		08 21			08 42			08 51				09 12		09 21					09 42	
Dorking	d						08 22												09 22						
Holmwood	d						08 29												09 29						
Ockley	d						08 33												09 33						
Warnham	d						08 39												09 39						
Horsham	a						08 43												09 43						

For faster trains from London and Clapham Junction to Horsham refer to Table T186

Please note, Network Rail have stated that further updates to this timetable are possible during the validity period.

London - Hackbridge, Sutton, Epsom, Leatherhead, Dorking and Horsham

		TL	TL	SW	SN	SW		TL	TL	TL	SW	SN	SW	TL	TL	TL		SW	SN	SW	TL	TL	TL	SW	SN
London Victoria ⊖	d	08 55			09 11				09 25			09 41			09 55				10 11			10 25			10 41
London Waterloo ⊖	d			09 09		09 24					09 39		09 54					10 09		10 24				10 39	
Clapham Junction	d	09 02		09 18	09 19	09 33			09 32		09 48	09 48	10 03		10 02			10 18	10 18	10 33		10 32		10 48	10 48
Balham ⊖	d				09 24							09 53							10 23						10 53
St Pancras International	d							08 57						09 27							09 57				
Farringdon	d							09 02						09 32							10 02				
City Thameslink	d							09 04						09 34							10 04				
London Blackfriars	d							09 06						09 36							10 06				
Elephant & Castle	d							09 10						09 40							10 10				
Loughborough Jn	d							09 15						09 45							10 15				
Herne Hill	d							09 20						09 50							10 20				
London Bridge	d		08 55							09 25						09 55							10 25		
Tulse Hill	a							09 24						09 54							10 24				
Tulse Hill	d							09 27						09 56							10 26				
Streatham	d							09 30						10 00							10 30				
Mitcham Eastfields	d				09 30			09 34				10 00		10 04					10 30		10 34				11 00
Mitcham Junction	d				09 33			09 37				10 03		10 07					10 33		10 37				11 03
Hackbridge	d				09 36			09 40				10 06		10 10					10 36		10 40				11 06
Carshalton	d	09 19			09 39			09 43	09 49			10 09		10 13	10 19				10 39		10 43	10 49			11 09
Sutton	a	09 23			09 43			09 47	09 53			10 13		10 17	10 23				10 43		10 47	10 53			11 13
Norwood Junction	d		09 09							09 39						10 09							10 39		
West Croydon	d		09 15							09 45						10 15							10 45		
Sutton	a		09 28							09 58						10 28							10 58		
Sutton	d	09 24	09 28		09 43				09 54	09 58		10 13			10 24	10 28			10 43			10 54	10 58		11 13
Cheam	d	09 27	09 31		09 46				09 57	10 01		10 16			10 27	10 31			10 46			10 57	11 01		11 16
Ewell East	d		09 34		09 49					10 04		10 19				10 34			10 49				11 04		11 19
Epsom	a	09 34	09 38	09 42	09 53	09 57			10 04	10 08	10 17	10 23	10 27		10 34	10 38		10 46	10 53	10 57		11 04	11 08	11 17	11 23
Epsom	d	09 35		09 47		09 58			10 05		10 18		10 28		10 35			10 47		10 58		11 05		11 17	
Ashtead	d	09 40		09 51		10 02			10 10		10 22		10 32		10 40			10 51		11 02		11 10		11 21	
Leatherhead	d	09 44		09a54		10 05			10 14		10a25		10 35		10 44			10a54		11 05		11 13		11a24	
Box Hill & Westhumble	d								10 19													11 18			
Dorking	a	09 51				10 12			10 21				10 42		10 51					11 12		11 21			
Dorking	d								10 22													11 22			
Holmwood	d								10 29													11 29			
Ockley	d								10 33													11 33			
Warnham	d								10 39													11 39			
Horsham	a								10 43													11 43			

		SW		TL	TL	TL	SW	SN	SW	TL	TL	TL		SW	SN	SW	TL	TL	TL	SW	SN	SW		TL	TL
London Victoria ⊖	d				10 55			11 11			11 25				11 41			11 55			12 11				12 25
London Waterloo ⊖	d	10 54					11 09		11 24					11 39		11 54				12 09		12 24			
Clapham Junction	d	11 03			11 02		11 18	11 18	11 33		11 32			11 48	11 48	12 03		12 02		12 18	12 18	12 33			12 32
Balham ⊖	d							11 23							11 53						12 23				
St Pancras International	d			10 27						10 57							11 27							11 57	
Farringdon	d			10 32						11 02							11 32							12 02	
City Thameslink	d			10 34						11 04							11 34							12 04	
London Blackfriars	d			10 36						11 06							11 36							12 06	
Elephant & Castle	d			10 40						11 10							11 40							12 10	
Loughborough Jn	d			10 45						11 15							11 45							12 15	
Herne Hill	d			10 50						11 20							11 50							12 20	
London Bridge	d					10 55						11 25							11 55						
Tulse Hill	a			10 54						11 24							11 54							12 24	
Tulse Hill	d			10 56						11 26							11 56							12 26	
Streatham	d			11 00						11 30							12 00							12 30	
Mitcham Eastfields	d			11 04				11 30		11 34					12 00		12 04				12 30			12 34	
Mitcham Junction	d			11 07				11 33		11 37					12 03		12 07				12 33			12 37	
Hackbridge	d			11 10				11 36		11 40					12 06		12 10				12 36			12 40	
Carshalton	d			11 13	11 19			11 39		11 43	11 49				12 09		12 13	12 19			12 39			12 43	12 49
Sutton	a			11 17	11 23			11 43		11 47	11 53				12 13		12 17	12 23			12 43			12 47	12 53
Norwood Junction	d					11 09						11 39							12 09						
West Croydon	d					11 15						11 45							12 15						
Sutton	a					11 28						11 58							12 28						
Sutton	d				11 24	11 28		11 43			11 54	11 58			12 13			12 24	12 28		12 43				12 54
Cheam	d				11 27	11 31		11 46			11 57	12 01			12 16			12 27	12 31		12 46				12 57
Ewell East	d					11 34		11 49				12 04			12 19				12 34		12 49				
Epsom	a	11 27			11 34	11 38	11 46	11 53	11 57		12 04	12 08		12 17	12 23	12 27		12 34	12 38	12 46	12 53	12 57			13 04
Epsom	d	11 28			11 35		11 47		11 58		12 05			12 17		12 28		12 35		12 47		12 58			13 05
Ashtead	d	11 32			11 40		11 51		12 02		12 10			12 21		12 32		12 40		12 51		13 02			13 10
Leatherhead	d	11 35			11 43		11a54		12 05		12 14			12a24		12 35		12 44		12a54		13 05			13 14
Box Hill & Westhumble	d										12 19														13 19
Dorking	a	11 42			11 51				12 12		12 21					12 42		12 51				13 12			13 21
Dorking	d										12 22														13 22
Holmwood	d										12 29														13 29
Ockley	d										12 33														13 33
Warnham	d										12 39														13 39
Horsham	a										12 43														13 43

For faster trains from London and Clapham Junction to Horsham refer to Table T186

Table T180-F

Mondays to Fridays

21 May to 5 October

London - Hackbridge, Sutton, Epsom, Leatherhead, Dorking and Horsham

		TL	SW	SN	SW	TL	TL	TL		SW	SN	SW	TL	TL	TL	SW	SN	SW		TL	TL	TL	SW	SN	SW
London Victoria ⊖	d			12 41			12 55				13 11			13 25			13 41				13 55			14 11	
London Waterloo ⊖	d		12 39		12 54					13 09		13 24				13 39		13 54					14 09		14 24
Clapham Junction	d		12 48	12 48	13 03		13 02			13 18	13 18	13 33		13 32		13 48	13 48	14 03			14 02		14 18	14 18	14 33
Balham ⊖	d			12 54							13 23						13 53							14 23	
St Pancras International	d					12 27							12 57							13 27					
Farringdon	d					12 32							13 02							13 32					
City Thameslink	d					12 34							13 04							13 34					
London Blackfriars	d					12 36							13 06							13 36					
Elephant & Castle	d					12 40							13 10							13 40					
Loughborough Jn	d					12 45							13 15							13 45					
Herne Hill	d					12 50							13 20							13 50					
London Bridge	d	12 25						12 55							13 25							13 55			
Tulse Hill	a					12 54							13 24							13 54					
Tulse Hill	d					12 56							13 26							13 56					
Streatham	d					13 00							13 30							14 00					
Mitcham Eastfields	d			13 01		13 04					13 30		13 34				14 00			14 04				14 30	
Mitcham Junction	d			13 04		13 07					13 33		13 37				14 03			14 07				14 33	
Hackbridge	d			13 07		13 10					13 36		13 40				14 06			14 10				14 36	
Carshalton	d			13 09		13 13	13 19				13 39		13 43	13 49			14 09			14 13	14 19			14 39	
Sutton	a			13 13		13 17	13 23				13 43		13 47	13 53			14 13			14 17	14 23			14 43	
Norwood Junction	d	12 39						13 09							13 39							14 09			
West Croydon	d	12 45						13 15							13 45							14 15			
Sutton	a	12 58						13 28							13 58							14 28			
Sutton	d	12 58		13 13			13 24	13 28			13 43			13 54	13 58		14 13				14 24	14 28		14 43	
Cheam	d	13 01		13 16			13 27	13 31			13 46			13 57	14 01		14 16				14 27	14 31		14 46	
Ewell East	d	13 04		13 19				13 34			13 49				14 04		14 19					14 34		14 49	
Epsom	a	13 08	13 17	13 23	13 27		13 34	13 38		13 46	13 53	13 57		14 04	14 08	14 17	14 23	14 27			14 34	14 38	14 46	14 53	14 57
Epsom	d		13 17		13 28		13 35			13 47		13 58		14 05		14 17		14 28			14 35		14 47		14 58
Ashtead	d		13 21		13 32		13 40			13 51		14 02		14 10		14 21		14 32			14 40		14 51		15 02
Leatherhead	d		13a24		13 35		13 44			13a54		14 05		14 14		14a24		14 35			14 44		14a54		15 05
Box Hill & Westhumble	d													14 19											
Dorking	a				13 42		13 51					14 12		14 21				14 42			14 51				15 12
Dorking	d													14 22											
Holmwood	d													14 29											
Ockley	d													14 33											
Warnham	d													14 39											
Horsham	a													14 43											

		TL	TL	TL		SW	SN	SW	TL	TL	TL	SW	SN	SW		TL	TL	TL	SW	SN	SW	TL	TL	TL	
London Victoria ⊖	d		14 25				14 41			14 55			15 11				15 25			15 41			15 55		
London Waterloo ⊖	d					14 39		14 54				15 09		15 24					15 39		15 54				
Clapham Junction	d		14 32			14 48	14 48	15 03		15 02		15 18	15 18	15 33			15 32		15 48	15 48	16 03		16 02		
Balham ⊖	d						14 53						15 23							15 53					
St Pancras International	d	13 57							14 27							14 57						15 27			
Farringdon	d	14 02							14 32							15 02						15 32			
City Thameslink	d	14 04							14 34							15 04						15 34			
London Blackfriars	d	14 06							14 36							15 06						15 36			
Elephant & Castle	d	14 10							14 40							15 10						15 40			
Loughborough Jn	d	14 15							14 45							15 15						15 45			
Herne Hill	d	14 20							14 50							15 20						15 50			
London Bridge	d			14 25							14 55							15 25						15 55	
Tulse Hill	a	14 24							14 54							15 24						15 54			
Tulse Hill	d	14 26							14 56							15 26						15 56			
Streatham	d	14 30							15 00							15 30						16 00			
Mitcham Eastfields	d	14 34					15 00		15 04				15 30			15 34				16 00		16 04			
Mitcham Junction	d	14 37					15 03		15 07				15 33			15 37				16 03		16 07			
Hackbridge	d	14 40					15 06		15 10				15 36			15 40				16 06		16 10			
Carshalton	d	14 43	14 49				15 09		15 13	15 19			15 39			15 43	15 49			16 09		16 13	16 19		
Sutton	a	14 47	14 53				15 13		15 17	15 23			15 43			15 47	15 53			16 13		16 17	16 23		
Norwood Junction	d			14 39							15 09							15 39						16 09	
West Croydon	d			14 45							15 15							15 45						16 15	
Sutton	a			14 58							15 28							15 58						16 28	
Sutton	d		14 54	14 58			15 13			15 24	15 28		15 43				15 54	15 58		16 13			16 24	16 28	
Cheam	d		14 57	15 01			15 16			15 27	15 31		15 46				15 57	16 01		16 16			16 27	16 31	
Ewell East	d			15 04			15 19				15 34		15 49					16 04		16 19				16 34	
Epsom	a		15 04	15 08		15 16	15 23	15 27		15 34	15 38	15 46	15 53	15 57			16 04	16 08	16 15	16 23	16 27		16 34	16 38	
Epsom	d		15 05			15 17		15 28		15 35		15 47		15 58			16 05		16 17		16 28		16 35		
Ashtead	d		15 10			15 21		15 32		15 40		15 51		16 02			16 10		16 21		16 32		16 40		
Leatherhead	d		15 14			15a24		15 35		15 44		15a54		16 05			16 14		16a24		16 35		16 44		
Box Hill & Westhumble	d		15 19														16 19								
Dorking	a		15 21					15 42		15 51				16 12			16 22				16 42		16 51		
Dorking	d		15 22														16 22								
Holmwood	d		15 29														16 29								
Ockley	d		15 33														16 33								
Warnham	d		15 39														16 39								
Horsham	a		15 43														16 43								

For faster trains from London and Clapham Junction to Horsham refer to Table T186

Please note, Network Rail have stated that further updates to this timetable are possible during the validity period.

Table T180-F

Mondays to Fridays

21 May to 5 October

London - Hackbridge, Sutton, Epsom, Leatherhead, Dorking and Horsham

		SW		SN	SW	TL	TL	TL	SW	SN		SW	TL	TL	SN	TL	SW	SN	SW	TL		TL	SN	SW	TL
London Victoria	⊖ d			16 12			16 25			16 41				16 55				17 11				17 25			
London Waterloo	⊖ d	16 09			16 24				16 39			16 54					17 09		17 24					17 31	
Clapham Junction	d	16 18		16 19	16 33		16 32		16 48	16 48		17 03		17 02			17 18	17 18	17 33			17 32		17 40	
Balham	⊖ d			16 24						16 53								17 23							
St Pancras International	d					15 57							16 27							16 57					
Farringdon	d					16 02							16 32							17 02					
City Thameslink	d					16 04							16 34							17 04					
London Blackfriars	d					16 06							16 36							17 06					
Elephant & Castle	d					16 10							16 40							17 10					
Loughborough Jn	d					16 15							16 45							17 15					
Herne Hill	d					16 20							16 50							17 20					
London Bridge	d							16 25							16 52	16 55							17 22		17 25
Tulse Hill	a					16 24							16 54		17 14					17 24			17 44		
Tulse Hill	d					16 26							16 56		17 16					17 26			17 46		
Streatham	d					16 30							17 00		17 20					17 30			17 50		
Mitcham Eastfields	d			16 30		16 34				17 00			17 04		17 24			17 30		17 34		17 43	17 54		
Mitcham Junction	d			16 33		16 37				17 03			17 07		17 27			17 33		17 37		17 46	17 57		
Hackbridge	d			16 36		16 40				17 06			17 10		17 30			17 36		17 40		17 49	18 00		
Carshalton	d			16 39		16 43	16 49			17 09			17 13	17 19	17 33			17 39		17 43		17 52	18 03		
Sutton	a			16 43		16 47	16 53			17 13			17 17	17 23	17 37			17 43		17 47		17 56	18 07		
Norwood Junction	d							16 39								17 09									17 39
West Croydon	d							16 46								17 16									17 46
Sutton	a							16 58								17 28									17 59
Sutton	d			16 43			16 54	16 58		17 13				17 24		17 28		17 43				17 56			18 00
Cheam	d			16 46			16 57	17 01		17 16				17 27		17 31		17 46				17 59			18 03
Ewell East	d			16 49				17 04		17 19						17 34		17 49							18 06
Epsom	a	16 46		16 53	16 57		17 04	17 08	17 12	17 23		17 27		17 34		17 38	17 42	17 53	17 57			18 05		18 08	18 10
Epsom	d	16 47			16 58		17 05		17 17			17 28		17 35		17 39	17 47		17 57			18 05			18 10
Ashtead	d	16 51			17 02		17 10		17 21			17 32		17 40		17 44	17 51		18 01			18 10			18 15
Leatherhead	d	16a54			17 05		17 14		17a24			17 35		17 44		17 48	17a54		18 04			18 14			18a18
Box Hill & Westhumble	d				17 10		17 19					17 40		17 49					18 09			18 19			
Dorking	a				17 14		17 22					17 44		17 52		17 55			18 15			18 21			
Dorking	d						17 22							17 52								18 22			
Holmwood	d						17 29							17 59								18 29			
Ockley	d						17 33							18 03								18 33			
Warnham	d						17 39							18 09								18 39			
Horsham	a						17 45							18 15								18 45			

		SW	SN	SW	TL	TL		SN	SW	TL	SW	SN	SW	TL	TL	SN		SW	TL	SW	SN	SW	TL	TL	SW
London Victoria	⊖ d		17 41			17 55						18 11			18 26						18 41			18 55	
London Waterloo	⊖ d	17 39		17 54					18 01		18 09		18 24					18 31		18 39		18 54			19 01
Clapham Junction	d	17 49	17 48	18 03		18 02			18 10		18 19	18 18	18 33		18 33			18 40		18 49	18 48	19 03		19 02	19 10
Balham	⊖ d		17 53									18 23									18 53				
St Pancras International	d				17 27									17 57									18 27		
Farringdon	d				17 32									18 02									18 32		
City Thameslink	d				17 34									18 04									18 34		
London Blackfriars	d				17 36									18 06									18 36		
Elephant & Castle	d				17 40									18 10									18 40		
Loughborough Jn	d				17 45									18 15									18 45		
Herne Hill	d				17 50									18 20									18 50		
London Bridge	d							17 52		17 55						18 22			18 25						
Tulse Hill	a				17 54			18 14						18 24		18 44							18 54		
Tulse Hill	d				17 56			18 16						18 26		18 46							18 56		
Streatham	d				18 00			18 20						18 30		18 50							19 00		
Mitcham Eastfields	d		18 00		18 04	18 13		18 24				18 30		18 34	18 43	18 54					19 00		19 04		
Mitcham Junction	d		18 03		18 07	18 16		18 27				18 33		18 37	18 46	18 57					19 03		19 07		
Hackbridge	d		18 06		18 10	18 19		18 30				18 36		18 40	18 49	19 00					19 06		19 10		
Carshalton	d		18 09		18 13	18 22		18 33				18 39		18 43	18 52	19 03					19 09		19 13	19 19	
Sutton	a		18 13		18 17	18 25		18 37				18 43		18 47	18 55	19 07					19 13		19 17	19 23	
Norwood Junction	d									18 09									18 39						
West Croydon	d									18 16									18 46						
Sutton	a									18 29									18 59						
Sutton	d		18 13			18 26				18 30		18 43			18 56				19 00		19 13			19 24	
Cheam	d		18 16			18 29				18 33		18 46			18 59				19 03		19 16			19 27	
Ewell East	d		18 19							18 36		18 49							19 06		19 19				
Epsom	a	18 17	18 23	18 27		18 35			18 38	18 40	18 49	18 53	18 57		19 05			19 07	19 10	19 16	19 23	19 27		19 34	19 36
Epsom	d	18 19		18 27		18 35				18 40	18 52		18 57		19 05				19 10	19 18		19 27		19 35	
Ashtead	d	18 23		18 31		18 40				18 45	18 56		19 01		19 10				19 15	19 22		19 31		19 40	
Leatherhead	d	18a26		18 34		18 44				18 49	18a59		19 04		19 14				19 19	19a25		19 34		19 44	
Box Hill & Westhumble	d			18 39		18 49							19 09		19 19							19 39			
Dorking	a			18 45		18 51				18 55			19 14		19 21				19 25			19 44		19 51	
Dorking	d					18 52									19 22										
Holmwood	d					18 59									19 29										
Ockley	d					19 03									19 33										
Warnham	d					19 09									19 39										
Horsham	a					19 15									19 45										

For faster trains from London and Clapham Junction to Horsham refer to Table T186

Table T180-F

Mondays to Fridays

21 May to 5 October

London - Hackbridge, Sutton, Epsom, Leatherhead, Dorking and Horsham

		TL		SW	SN	SW	TL	TL	TL	SW	SN	SW		TL	TL	TL	SW	SN	SW	TL	TL	TL		SW	SN
London Victoria	⊖ d				19 11			19 25			19 41				19 55			20 11			20 25				20 41
London Waterloo	⊖ d			19 09		19 24				19 39		19 54					20 09		20 24					20 39	
Clapham Junction	d			19 19	19 18	19 33		19 32		19 48	19 48	20 03			20 02		20 18	20 18	20 33		20 32			20 48	20 48
Balham	⊖ d				19 23						19 53							20 23							20 53
St Pancras International	d						18 57							19 27						19 57					
Farringdon	d						19 02							19 32						20 02					
City Thameslink	d						19 04							19 34						20 04					
London Blackfriars	d						19 06							19 36						20 06					
Elephant & Castle	d						19 10							19 40						20 10					
Loughborough Jn	d						19 15							19 45						20 15					
Herne Hill	d						19 20							19 50						20 20					
London Bridge	d	18 55							19 25							19 55						20 25			
Tulse Hill	a						19 24							19 54						20 24					
Tulse Hill	d						19 26							19 56						20 26					
Streatham	d						19 30							20 00						20 30					
Mitcham Eastfields	d				19 30		19 34				20 00			20 04				20 30		20 34					21 00
Mitcham Junction	d				19 33		19 37				20 03			20 07				20 33		20 37					21 03
Hackbridge	d				19 36		19 40				20 06			20 10				20 36		20 40					21 06
Carshalton	d				19 39		19 43	19 49			20 09			20 13	20 19			20 39		20 43	20 49				21 09
Sutton	a				19 43		19 47	19 53			20 13			20 17	20 24			20 43		20 47	20 53				21 13
Norwood Junction	d	19 09							19 39							20 09						20 39			
West Croydon	d	19 15							19 45							20 15						20 45			
Sutton	a	19 28							19 58							20 28						20 58			
Sutton	d	19 28			19 43			19 54	19 58		20 13				20 24	20 28		20 43			20 54	20 58			21 13
Cheam	d	19 31			19 46			19 57	20 01		20 16				20 27	20 31		20 46			20 57	21 01			21 16
Ewell East	d	19 34			19 49				20 04		20 19					20 34		20 49				21 04			21 19
Epsom	a	19 39		19 48	19 53	19 57		20 04	20 08	20 16	20 23	20 27			20 34	20 38	20 42	20 53	20 57		21 05	21 08		21 12	21 23
Epsom	d	19 40		19 52		19 58		20 05		20 17					20 35		20 43				21 05			21 13	
Ashtead	d	19 45		19 56		20 02		20 10		20 21					20 40		20 47				21 10			21 17	
Leatherhead	d	19a48		19a59		20 05		20 14		20a24					20 43		20 50				21 14			21a20	
Box Hill & Westhumble	d					20 10		20 19									20 55				21 19				
Dorking	a					20 14		20 22							20 51		20 57				21 22				
Dorking	d							20 22													21 22				
Holmwood	d							20 29													21 29				
Ockley	d							20 33													21 33				
Warnham	d							20 39													21 39				
Horsham	a							20 43													21 43				

		SW	TL	TL	TL	SW	SN	SW		TL	TL	TL	SW	SN	SW	TL	TL	TL		SW	SN	TL	TL	TL	SW
London Victoria	⊖ d			20 55			21 11				21 25			21 41			21 55				22 11		22 25		
London Waterloo	⊖ d	20 54				21 09		21 24					21 39		21 54					22 09					22 39
Clapham Junction	d	21 03		21 02		21 18	21 18	21 33			21 32		21 48	21 48	22 03		22 03			22 18	22 18		22 32		22 48
Balham	⊖ d						21 23							21 54							22 23				
St Pancras International	d		20 27							20 57						21 27						21 57			
Farringdon	d		20 32							21 02						21 32						22 02			
City Thameslink	d		20 34							21 04						21 34						22 04			
London Blackfriars	d		20 36							21 06						21 36						22 06			
Elephant & Castle	d		20 40							21 10						21 40						22 10			
Loughborough Jn	d		20 45							21 15						21 45						22 15			
Herne Hill	d		20 50							21 20						21 50						22 20			
London Bridge	d				20 55							21 25						21 55						22 25	
Tulse Hill	a		20 54							21 24						21 54						22 24			
Tulse Hill	d		20 56							21 26						21 56						22 26			
Streatham	d		21 00							21 30						22 00						22 30			
Mitcham Eastfields	d		21 04				21 30			21 34				22 01		22 04					22 30	22 34			
Mitcham Junction	d		21 07				21 33			21 37				22 04		22 07					22 33	22 37			
Hackbridge	d		21 10				21 36			21 40				22 07		22 10					22 36	22 40			
Carshalton	d		21 13	21 19			21 39			21 43	21 49			22 09		22 13	22 20				22 39	22 43	22 49		
Sutton	a		21 17	21 23			21 43			21 47	21 53			22 13		22 17	22 24				22 43	22 47	22 53		
Norwood Junction	d				21 09							21 39						22 09						22 39	
West Croydon	d				21 15							21 45						22 15						22 45	
Sutton	a				21 28							21 58						22 28						22 58	
Sutton	d			21 24	21 28		21 43				21 54	21 58		22 13			22 25	22 28			22 43		22 54	22 58	
Cheam	d			21 27	21 31		21 46				21 57	22 01		22 16			22 28	22 31			22 46		22 57	23 01	
Ewell East	d				21 34		21 49					22 04		22 19				22 34			22 49			23 04	
Epsom	a	21 27		21 34	21 38	21 42	21 53	21 57			22 04	22 08	22 12	22 23	22 27		22 34	22 38		22 42	22 53		23 04	23 08	23 12
Epsom	d			21 35		21 43					22 05		22 13				22 35			22 43			23 05		23 13
Ashtead	d			21 40		21 47					22 10		22 17				22 40			22 47			23 10		23 17
Leatherhead	d			21 44		21 50					22 14		22a20				22 44			22 50			23 14		23a20
Box Hill & Westhumble	d					21 55					22 19									22 55			23 19		
Dorking	a			21 51		21 57					22 22						22 51			22 57			23 22		
Dorking	d										22 22												23 22		
Holmwood	d										22 29												23 29		
Ockley	d										22 33												23 33		
Warnham	d										22 39												23 39		
Horsham	a										22 43												23 43		

For faster trains from London and Clapham Junction to Horsham refer to Table T186

Table T180-F

Mondays to Fridays
21 May to 5 October

London - Hackbridge, Sutton, Epsom, Leatherhead, Dorking and Horsham

		SN	TL	TL		TL	SW	SN	TL	TL	SW
London Victoria ⊖	d	22 41		22 55				23 11		23 25	
London Waterloo ⊖	d						23 09				23 42
Clapham Junction	d	22 48		23 02			23 18	23 18		23 32	23 51
Balham ⊖	d	22 53						23 23		23 37	
St Pancras International	d		22 27						22 57		
Farringdon	d		22 32						23 02		
City Thameslink	d		22 34								
London Blackfriars	d		22 36						23 06		
Elephant & Castle	d		22 40						23 10		
Loughborough Jn	d		22 45						23 15		
Herne Hill	d		22 50						23 20		
London Bridge	d					22 55					
Tulse Hill	a		22 54						23 24		
Tulse Hill	d		22 56						23 26		
Streatham	d		23 00						23 30		
Mitcham Eastfields	d	23 00	23 04					23 30	23 34	23 45	
Mitcham Junction	d	23 03	23 07					23 33	23 37	23 48	
Hackbridge	d	23 06	23 10					23 36	23 40	23 51	
Carshalton	d	23 09	23 13	23 19				23 39	23 43	23 54	
Sutton	a	23 13	23 17	23 23				23 43	23 47	23 58	
Norwood Junction	d					23 09					
West Croydon	d					23 15					
Sutton	a					23 28					
Sutton	d	23 13		23 24		23 28		23 43		23 59	
Cheam	d	23 16		23 27		23 31		23 46		00 02	
Ewell East	d	23 19				23 34		23 49		00 05	
Epsom	a	23 23		23 34		23 38	23 42	23 53		00 09	00 16
Epsom	d			23 35			23 43			00 09	00 19
Ashtead	d			23 40			23 47			00 14	00 23
Leatherhead	d			23 43			23 50			00 18	00a26
Box Hill & Westhumble	d						23 55			00 23	
Dorking	a			23 51			23 57			00 26	
Dorking	d									00 26	
Holmwood	d									00s33	
Ockley	d									00s37	
Warnham	d									00s43	
Horsham	a									00 48	

Mondays to Fridays
8 October to 7 December

		SN MO	TL MO	TL MX	SW MX	SW MX	SW	SN	TL	TL		SN	SW	TL	TL	SW	SN	SW	TL	TL		TL	SW	SN	SW
London Victoria ⊖	d							05 41				06 11			06 25		06 41			06 55				07 11	
London Waterloo ⊖	d					00 15	05 47						06 24			06 39		06 54					07 09		07 24
Clapham Junction	d					00 26	05 56	05 48				06 18	06 33		06 32	06 48	06 48	07 03		07 02			07 18	07 18	07 33
Balham ⊖	d							05 53				06 23					06 53							07 23	
St Pancras International	d									05 27				05 57					06 27						
Farringdon	d									05 32				06 02					06 32						
City Thameslink	d									05 34				06 04					06 34						
London Blackfriars	d									05 36				06 06					06 36						
Elephant & Castle	d									05 40				06 10					06 40						
Loughborough Jn	d									05 45				06 15					06 45						
Herne Hill	d									05 50				06 20					06 50						
London Bridge	d								05 55													06 55			
Tulse Hill	a									05 54				06 24					06 54						
Tulse Hill	d									05 56				06 26					06 56						
Streatham	d									06 00				06 30					07 00						
Mitcham Eastfields	d							06 00		06 04		06 30		06 34			07 00		07 04					07 30	
Mitcham Junction	d							06 03		06 07		06 33		06 37			07 03		07 07					07 33	
Hackbridge	d							06 06		06 10		06 36		06 40			07 06		07 10					07 36	
Carshalton	d							06 09		06 13		06 39		06 43	06 49		07 09		07 13	07 19				07 39	
Sutton	a							06 13		06 17		06 43		06 47	06 53		07 13		07 17	07 23				07 43	
Norwood Junction	d								06 09													07 09			
West Croydon	d								06 15													07 16			
Sutton	a								06 28													07 28			
Sutton	d							06 13	06 28			06 43			06 54		07 13			07 24		07 28		07 43	
Cheam	d			00 02				06 16	06 31			06 46			06 57		07 16			07 27		07 31		07 46	
Ewell East	d	00 01		00 05				06 19	06 34			06 49					07 19					07 34		07 49	
Epsom	a	00 05		00 09		00 50	06 20	06 23	06 38			06 53	06 57		07 03	07 11	07 23	07 27		07 33		07 38	07 42	07 53	07 58
Epsom	d			00 09	00 19		06 21		06 39				06 58		07 04	07 12		07 28		07 34					07 58
Ashtead	d			00 14	00 23		06 25						07 02		07 09	07 16		07 32		07 39					08 02
Leatherhead	d		00 02	00 18	00a26		06a28		06a45				07 05		07 12	07a19		07 35		07 43					08 05
Box Hill & Westhumble	d		00 07	00 23											07 17										
Dorking	a		00 09	00 26									07 14		07 20			07 44		07 50					08 14
Dorking	d			00 26											07 21										
Holmwood	d			00s33											07 28										
Ockley	d			00s37											07 32										
Warnham	d			00s43											07 38										
Horsham	a			00 48											07 46										

For faster trains from London and Clapham Junction to Horsham refer to Table T186

Table T180-F

Mondays to Fridays
8 October to 7 December

London - Hackbridge, Sutton, Epsom, Leatherhead, Dorking and Horsham

		TL	TL	SW	SN	SW		TL	TL	TL	SW	SN	SW	TL	TL	TL		SW	SN	SW	TL	TL	TL	SW	SN
London Victoria ⊖	d		07 25		07 41				07 55			08 11			08 25				08 41			08 55			09 11
London Waterloo ⊖	d			07 39		07 54					08 09		08 24					08 39		08 54				09 09	
Clapham Junction	d		07 32	07 48	07 48	08 03			08 02		08 18	08 18	08 33		08 32			08 48	08 48	09 03		09 02		09 18	09 19
Balham ⊖	d				07 53							08 23							08 53						09 24
St Pancras International	d	06 57						07 27						07 57							08 27				
Farringdon	d	07 02						07 32						08 02							08 32				
City Thameslink	d	07 04						07 34						08 04							08 34				
London Blackfriars	d	07 06						07 36						08 06							08 36				
Elephant & Castle	d	07 10						07 40						08 10							08 40				
Loughborough Jn	d	07 15						07 45						08 15							08 45				
Herne Hill	d	07 20						07 50						08 20							08 50				
London Bridge	d									07 55						08 25							08 55		
Tulse Hill	a	07 24						07 54						08 24							08 54				
Tulse Hill	d	07 26						07 56						08 27							08 57				
Streatham	d	07 30						08 00						08 30							09 00				
Mitcham Eastfields	d	07 34			08 00			08 04				08 30		08 34					09 00		09 04				09 30
Mitcham Junction	d	07 37			08 03			08 07				08 33		08 37					09 03		09 07				09 33
Hackbridge	d	07 40			08 06			08 10				08 36		08 40					09 06		09 10				09 36
Carshalton	d	07 43	07 50		08 09			08 13	08 19			08 39		08 43	08 49				09 09		09 13	09 19			09 39
Sutton	a	07 47	07 53		08 13			08 17	08 23			08 43		08 47	08 53				09 13		09 17	09 23			09 43
Norwood Junction	d									08 09						08 39							09 09		
West Croydon	d									08 16						08 45							09 15		
Sutton	a									08 28						08 58							09 28		
Sutton	d		07 54		08 13				08 24	08 28		08 43			08 54	08 58			09 13			09 24	09 28		09 43
Cheam	d		07 57		08 16				08 27	08 31		08 46			08 57	09 01			09 16			09 27	09 31		09 46
Ewell East	d				08 19					08 34		08 49				09 04			09 19				09 34		09 49
Epsom	a		08 04	08 13	08 23	08 27			08 34	08 38	08 42	08 53	08 57		09 04	09 08		09 16	09 23	09 27		09 34	09 38	09 42	09 53
Epsom	d		08 05	08 17		08 28			08 35		08 47		08 58		09 05			09 17		09 28		09 35		09 47	
Ashtead	d		08 10	08 21		08 32			08 40		08 51		09 02		09 10			09 21		09 32		09 40		09 51	
Leatherhead	d		08 14	08a24		08 35			08 44		08a54		09 05		09 14			09a24		09 35		09 44		09a54	
Box Hill & Westhumble	d		08 19												09 19										
Dorking	a		08 21			08 44			08 51				09 14		09 21					09 44		09 51			
Dorking	d		08 22												09 22										
Holmwood	d		08 29												09 29										
Ockley	d		08 33												09 33										
Warnham	d		08 39												09 39										
Horsham	a		08 43												09 43										

		SW		TL	TL	TL	SW	SN	SW	TL	TL	TL		SW	SN	SW	TL	TL	TL	SW	SN	SW		TL	TL
London Victoria ⊖	d				09 25			09 41			09 55				10 11			10 25			10 41				10 55
London Waterloo ⊖	d	09 24					09 39		09 54					10 09		10 24				10 39		10 54			
Clapham Junction	d	09 33			09 32		09 48	09 48	10 03		10 02			10 18	10 18	10 33		10 32		10 48	10 48	11 03			11 02
Balham ⊖	d							09 53							10 23						10 53				
St Pancras International	d			08 57						09 27							09 57							10 27	
Farringdon	d			09 02						09 32							10 02							10 32	
City Thameslink	d			09 04						09 34							10 04							10 34	
London Blackfriars	d			09 06						09 36							10 06							10 36	
Elephant & Castle	d			09 10						09 40							10 10							10 40	
Loughborough Jn	d			09 15						09 45							10 15							10 45	
Herne Hill	d			09 20						09 50							10 20							10 50	
London Bridge	d					09 25						09 55							10 25						
Tulse Hill	a			09 24						09 54							10 24							10 54	
Tulse Hill	d			09 27						09 56							10 26							10 56	
Streatham	d			09 30						10 00							10 30							11 00	
Mitcham Eastfields	d			09 34				10 00		10 04					10 30		10 34				11 00			11 04	
Mitcham Junction	d			09 37				10 03		10 07					10 33		10 37				11 03			11 07	
Hackbridge	d			09 40				10 06		10 10					10 36		10 40				11 06			11 10	
Carshalton	d			09 43	09 49			10 09		10 13	10 19				10 39		10 43	10 49			11 09			11 13	11 19
Sutton	a			09 47	09 53			10 13		10 17	10 23				10 43		10 47	10 53			11 13			11 17	11 23
Norwood Junction	d					09 39						10 09							10 39						
West Croydon	d					09 45						10 15							10 45						
Sutton	a					09 58						10 28							10 58						
Sutton	d				09 54	09 58		10 13			10 24	10 28			10 43			10 54	10 58		11 13				11 24
Cheam	d				09 57	10 01		10 16			10 27	10 31			10 46			10 57	11 01		11 16				11 27
Ewell East	d					10 04		10 19				10 34			10 49				11 04		11 19				
Epsom	a	09 57			10 04	10 08	10 17	10 23	10 27		10 34	10 38		10 46	10 53	10 57		11 04	11 08	11 17	11 23	11 27			11 34
Epsom	d	09 58			10 05		10 18		10 28		10 35			10 47		10 58		11 05		11 17		11 28			11 35
Ashtead	d	10 02			10 10		10 22		10 32		10 40			10 51		11 02		11 10		11 21		11 32			11 40
Leatherhead	d	10 05			10 14		10a25		10 35		10 44			10a54		11 05		11 13		11a24		11 35			11 43
Box Hill & Westhumble	d				10 19													11 18							
Dorking	a	10 14			10 21				10 44		10 51					11 14		11 21				11 44			11 51
Dorking	d				10 22													11 22							
Holmwood	d				10 29													11 29							
Ockley	d				10 33													11 33							
Warnham	d				10 39													11 39							
Horsham	a				10 43													11 43							

For faster trains from London and Clapham Junction to Horsham refer to Table T186

Please note, Network Rail have stated that further updates to this timetable are possible during the validity period.

Table T180-F

Mondays to Fridays

8 October to 7 December

London - Hackbridge, Sutton, Epsom, Leatherhead, Dorking and Horsham

		TL	SW	SN	SW	TL	TL	TL		SW	SN	SW	TL	TL	TL	SW	SN	SW		TL	TL	TL	SW	SN	SW
London Victoria ⊖	d			11 11			11 25				11 41			11 55			12 11				12 25			12 41	
London Waterloo ⊖	d		11 09		11 24					11 39		11 54				12 09		12 24					12 39		12 54
Clapham Junction	d		11 18	11 18	11 33		11 32			11 48	11 48	12 03		12 02		12 18	12 18	12 33			12 32		12 48	12 48	13 03
Balham ⊖	d			11 23							11 53						12 23							12 54	
St Pancras International	d					10 57							11 27							11 57					
Farringdon	d					11 02							11 32							12 02					
City Thameslink	d					11 04							11 34							12 04					
London Blackfriars	d					11 06							11 36							12 06					
Elephant & Castle	d					11 10							11 40							12 10					
Loughborough Jn	d					11 15							11 45							12 15					
Herne Hill	d					11 20							11 50							12 20					
London Bridge	d	10 55						11 25							11 55							12 25			
Tulse Hill	a					11 24							11 54							12 24					
Tulse Hill	d					11 26							11 56							12 26					
Streatham	d					11 30							12 00							12 30					
Mitcham Eastfields	d			11 30		11 34					12 00		12 04				12 30			12 34				13 01	
Mitcham Junction	d			11 33		11 37					12 03		12 07				12 33			12 37				13 04	
Hackbridge	d			11 36		11 40					12 06		12 10				12 36			12 40				13 07	
Carshalton	d			11 39		11 43	11 49				12 09		12 13	12 19			12 39			12 43	12 49			13 09	
Sutton	a			11 43		11 47	11 53				12 13		12 17	12 23			12 43			12 47	12 53			13 13	
Norwood Junction	d	11 09						11 39							12 09							12 39			
West Croydon	d	11 15						11 45							12 15							12 45			
Sutton	a	11 28						11 58							12 28							12 58			
Sutton	d	11 28		11 43			11 54	11 58			12 13			12 24	12 28		12 43				12 54	12 58		13 13	
Cheam	d	11 31		11 46			11 57	12 01			12 16			12 27	12 31		12 46				12 57	13 01		13 16	
Ewell East	d	11 34		11 49				12 04			12 19				12 34		12 49					13 04		13 19	
Epsom	a	11 38	11 46	11 53	11 57		12 04	12 08		12 17	12 23	12 27		12 34	12 38	12 46	12 53	12 57			13 04	13 08	13 17	13 23	13 27
Epsom	d		11 47		11 58		12 05			12 17		12 28		12 35		12 47		12 58			13 05		13 17		13 28
Ashtead	d		11 51		12 02		12 10			12 21		12 32		12 40		12 51		13 02			13 10		13 21		13 32
Leatherhead	d		11a54		12 05		12 14			12a24		12 35		12 44		12a54		13 05			13 14		13a24		13 35
Box Hill & Westhumble	d						12 19														13 19				
Dorking	a				12 14		12 21					12 44		12 51				13 14			13 21				13 44
Dorking	d						12 22														13 22				
Holmwood	d						12 29														13 29				
Ockley	d						12 33														13 33				
Warnham	d						12 39														13 39				
Horsham	a						12 43														13 43				

		TL	TL	TL		SW	SN	SW	TL	TL	TL	SW	SN	SW		TL	TL	TL	SW	SN	SW	TL	TL	TL	
London Victoria ⊖	d		12 55				13 11			13 25			13 41				13 55			14 11			14 25		
London Waterloo ⊖	d					13 09		13 24				13 39		13 54					14 09		14 24				
Clapham Junction	d		13 02			13 18	13 18	13 33		13 32		13 48	13 48	14 03			14 02		14 18	14 18	14 33		14 32		
Balham ⊖	d						13 23						13 53							14 23					
St Pancras International	d	12 27							12 57							13 27						13 57			
Farringdon	d	12 32							13 02							13 32						14 02			
City Thameslink	d	12 34							13 04							13 34						14 04			
London Blackfriars	d	12 36							13 06							13 36						14 06			
Elephant & Castle	d	12 40							13 10							13 40						14 10			
Loughborough Jn	d	12 45							13 15							13 45						14 15			
Herne Hill	d	12 50							13 20							13 50						14 20			
London Bridge	d			12 55							13 25							13 55						14 25	
Tulse Hill	a	12 54							13 24							13 54						14 24			
Tulse Hill	d	12 56							13 26							13 56						14 26			
Streatham	d	13 00							13 30							14 00						14 30			
Mitcham Eastfields	d	13 04					13 30		13 34				14 00			14 04				14 30		14 34			
Mitcham Junction	d	13 07					13 33		13 37				14 03			14 07				14 33		14 37			
Hackbridge	d	13 10					13 36		13 40				14 06			14 10				14 36		14 40			
Carshalton	d	13 13	13 19				13 39		13 43	13 49			14 09			14 13	14 19			14 39		14 43	14 49		
Sutton	a	13 17	13 23				13 43		13 47	13 53			14 13			14 17	14 23			14 43		14 47	14 53		
Norwood Junction	d			13 09							13 39							14 09						14 39	
West Croydon	d			13 15							13 45							14 15						14 45	
Sutton	a			13 28							13 58							14 28						14 58	
Sutton	d		13 24	13 28			13 43			13 54	13 58		14 13				14 24	14 28		14 43			14 54	14 58	
Cheam	d		13 27	13 31			13 46			13 57	14 01		14 16				14 27	14 31		14 46			14 57	15 01	
Ewell East	d			13 34			13 49				14 04		14 19					14 34		14 49				15 04	
Epsom	a		13 34	13 38		13 46	13 53	13 57		14 04	14 08	14 17	14 23	14 27			14 34	14 38	14 46	14 53	14 57		15 04	15 08	
Epsom	d		13 35			13 47		13 58		14 05		14 17		14 28			14 35		14 47		14 58		15 05		
Ashtead	d		13 40			13 51		14 02		14 10		14 21		14 32			14 40		14 51		15 02		15 10		
Leatherhead	d		13 44			13a54		14 05		14 14		14a24		14 35			14 44		14a54		15 05		15 14		
Box Hill & Westhumble	d									14 19													15 19		
Dorking	a		13 51					14 14		14 21				14 44			14 51				15 14		15 21		
Dorking	d									14 22													15 22		
Holmwood	d									14 29													15 29		
Ockley	d									14 33													15 33		
Warnham	d									14 39													15 39		
Horsham	a									14 43													15 43		

For faster trains from London and Clapham Junction to Horsham refer to Table T186

Table T180-F

Mondays to Fridays

8 October to 7 December

London - Hackbridge, Sutton, Epsom, Leatherhead, Dorking and Horsham

		SW	SN	SW	TL	TL	TL	SW	SN	SW		TL	TL	TL	SW	SN	SW	TL	TL	TL		SW	SN	SW	TL
London Victoria ⊖	d		14 41			14 55			15 11				15 25			15 41			15 55				16 12		
London Waterloo ⊖	d	14 39		14 54				15 09		15 24					15 39		15 54					16 09		16 24	
Clapham Junction	d	14 48	14 48	15 03		15 02		15 18	15 18	15 33			15 32		15 48	15 48	16 03		16 02			16 18	16 19	16 33	
Balham ⊖	d		14 53						15 23							15 53							16 24		
St Pancras International	d				14 27							14 57						15 27							15 57
Farringdon	d				14 32							15 02						15 32							16 02
City Thameslink	d				14 34							15 04						15 34							16 04
London Blackfriars	d				14 36							15 06						15 36							16 06
Elephant & Castle	d				14 40							15 10						15 40							16 10
Loughborough Jn	d				14 45							15 15						15 45							16 15
Herne Hill	d				14 50							15 20						15 50							16 20
London Bridge	d						14 55							15 25						15 55					
Tulse Hill	a				14 54							15 24						15 54							16 24
Tulse Hill	d				14 56							15 26						15 56							16 26
Streatham	d				15 00							15 30						16 00							16 30
Mitcham Eastfields	d		15 00		15 04				15 30			15 34				16 00		16 04					16 30		16 34
Mitcham Junction	d		15 03		15 07				15 33			15 37				16 03		16 07					16 33		16 37
Hackbridge	d		15 06		15 10				15 36			15 40				16 06		16 10					16 36		16 40
Carshalton	d		15 09		15 13	15 19			15 39			15 43	15 49			16 09		16 13	16 19				16 39		16 43
Sutton	a		15 13		15 17	15 23			15 43			15 47	15 53			16 13		16 17	16 23				16 43		16 47
Norwood Junction	d						15 09							15 39						16 09					
West Croydon	d						15 15							15 45						16 15					
Sutton	a						15 28							15 58						16 28					
Sutton	d		15 13			15 24	15 28		15 43				15 54	15 58		16 13			16 24	16 28			16 43		
Cheam	d		15 16			15 27	15 31		15 46				15 57	16 01		16 16			16 27	16 31			16 46		
Ewell East	d		15 19				15 34		15 49					16 04		16 19				16 34			16 49		
Epsom	a	15 16	15 23	15 27		15 34	15 38	15 46	15 53	15 57			16 04	16 08	16 15	16 23	16 27		16 34	16 38		16 46	16 53	16 57	
Epsom	d	15 17		15 28		15 35		15 47		15 58			16 05		16 17		16 28		16 35			16 47		16 58	
Ashtead	d	15 21		15 32		15 40		15 51		16 02			16 10		16 21		16 32		16 40			16 51		17 02	
Leatherhead	d	15a24		15 35		15 44		15a54		16 05			16 14		16a24		16 35		16 44			16a54		17 05	
Box Hill & Westhumble	d												16 19											17 10	
Dorking	a			15 44		15 51				16 14			16 22				16 44		16 51					17 16	
Dorking	d												16 22												
Holmwood	d												16 29												
Ockley	d												16 33												
Warnham	d												16 39												
Horsham	a												16 43												

		TL	TL	SW	SN	SW		TL	TL	SN	TL	SW	SN	SW	TL	TL		SN	SW	TL	SW	SN	SW	TL	TL
London Victoria ⊖	d	16 25			16 41				16 55				17 11			17 25						17 41			17 55
London Waterloo ⊖	d			16 39		16 54						17 09		17 24					17 31		17 39		17 54		
Clapham Junction	d	16 32		16 48	16 48	17 03			17 02			17 18	17 18	17 33		17 32			17 40		17 49	17 48	18 03		18 02
Balham ⊖	d				16 53								17 23									17 53			
St Pancras International	d							16 27							16 57									17 27	
Farringdon	d							16 32							17 02									17 32	
City Thameslink	d							16 34							17 04									17 34	
London Blackfriars	d							16 36							17 06									17 36	
Elephant & Castle	d							16 40							17 10									17 40	
Loughborough Jn	d							16 45							17 15									17 45	
Herne Hill	d							16 50							17 20									17 50	
London Bridge	d		16 25							16 52	16 55							17 22		17 25					
Tulse Hill	a							16 54		17 14					17 24			17 44						17 54	
Tulse Hill	d							16 56		17 16					17 26			17 46						17 56	
Streatham	d							17 00		17 20					17 30			17 50						18 00	
Mitcham Eastfields	d				17 00			17 04		17 24			17 30		17 34	17 43		17 54				18 00		18 04	18 13
Mitcham Junction	d				17 03			17 07		17 27			17 33		17 37	17 46		17 57				18 03		18 07	18 16
Hackbridge	d				17 06			17 10		17 30			17 36		17 40	17 49		18 00				18 06		18 10	18 19
Carshalton	d	16 49			17 09			17 13	17 19	17 33			17 39		17 43	17 52		18 03				18 09		18 13	18 22
Sutton	a	16 53			17 13			17 17	17 23	17 37			17 43		17 47	17 56		18 07				18 13		18 17	18 25
Norwood Junction	d		16 39								17 09									17 39					
West Croydon	d		16 46								17 16									17 46					
Sutton	a		16 58								17 28									17 59					
Sutton	d	16 54	16 58		17 13				17 24		17 28		17 43			17 56				18 00		18 13			18 26
Cheam	d	16 57	17 01		17 16				17 27		17 31		17 46			17 59				18 03		18 16			18 29
Ewell East	d		17 04		17 19						17 34		17 49							18 06		18 19			
Epsom	a	17 04	17 08	17 12	17 23	17 27			17 34		17 38	17 42	17 53	17 57		18 05			18 08	18 10	18 17	18 23	18 27		18 35
Epsom	d	17 05		17 17		17 28			17 35		17 39	17 47		17 57		18 05				18 10	18 19		18 27		18 35
Ashtead	d	17 10		17 21		17 32			17 40		17 44	17 51		18 01		18 10				18 15	18 23		18 31		18 40
Leatherhead	d	17 14		17a24		17 35			17 44		17 48	17a54		18 04		18 14				18a18	18a26		18 34		18 44
Box Hill & Westhumble	d	17 19				17 40			17 49					18 09		18 19							18 39		18 49
Dorking	a	17 22				17 46			17 52		17 55			18 17		18 21							18 47		18 51
Dorking	d	17 22							17 52							18 22									18 52
Holmwood	d	17 29							17 59							18 29									18 59
Ockley	d	17 33							18 03							18 33									19 03
Warnham	d	17 39							18 09							18 39									19 09
Horsham	a	17 45							18 15							18 45									19 15

For faster trains from London and Clapham Junction to Horsham refer to Table T186

Please note, Network Rail have stated that further updates to this timetable are possible during the validity period.

Table T180-F

Mondays to Fridays

8 October to 7 December

London - Hackbridge, Sutton, Epsom, Leatherhead, Dorking and Horsham

		SN		SW	TL	SW	SN	SW	TL	TL	SN	SW		TL	SW	SN	SW	TL	TL	SW	TL	SW		SN	SW
London Victoria ⊖	d						18 11			18 26						18 41			18 55					19 11	
London Waterloo ⊖	d			18 01		18 09		18 24				18 31			18 39		18 54			19 01		19 09			19 24
Clapham Junction	d			18 10		18 19	18 18	18 33		18 33		18 40			18 49	18 48	19 03		19 02	19 10		19 19		19 18	19 33
Balham ⊖	d						18 23									18 53								19 23	
St Pancras International	d								17 57									18 27							
Farringdon	d								18 02									18 32							
City Thameslink	d								18 04									18 34							
London Blackfriars	d								18 06									18 36							
Elephant & Castle	d								18 10									18 40							
Loughborough Jn	d								18 15									18 45							
Herne Hill	d								18 20									18 50							
London Bridge	d	17 52			17 55						18 22			18 25							18 55				
Tulse Hill	a	18 14							18 24		18 44							18 54							
Tulse Hill	d	18 16							18 26		18 46							18 56							
Streatham	d	18 20							18 30		18 50							19 00							
Mitcham Eastfields	d	18 24					18 30		18 34	18 43	18 54					19 00		19 04						19 30	
Mitcham Junction	d	18 27					18 33		18 37	18 46	18 57					19 03		19 07						19 33	
Hackbridge	d	18 30					18 36		18 40	18 49	19 00					19 06		19 10						19 36	
Carshalton	d	18 33					18 39		18 43	18 52	19 03					19 09		19 13	19 19					19 39	
Sutton	a	18 37					18 43		18 47	18 55	19 07					19 13		19 17	19 23					19 43	
Norwood Junction	d				18 09									18 39							19 09				
West Croydon	d				18 16									18 46							19 15				
Sutton	a				18 29									18 59							19 28				
Sutton	d				18 30		18 43			18 56				19 00		19 13			19 24		19 28			19 43	
Cheam	d				18 33		18 46			18 59				19 03		19 16			19 27		19 31			19 46	
Ewell East	d				18 36		18 49							19 06		19 19					19 34			19 49	
Epsom	a			18 38	18 40	18 49	18 53	18 57		19 05		19 07		19 10	19 16	19 23	19 27		19 34	19 36	19 39	19 48		19 53	19 57
Epsom	d				18 40	18 52		18 57		19 05				19 10	19 18		19 27		19 35		19 40	19 52			19 58
Ashtead	d				18 45	18 56		19 01		19 10				19 15	19 22		19 31		19 40		19 45	19 56			20 02
Leatherhead	d				18 49	18a59		19 04		19 14				19 19	19a25		19 34		19 44		19a48	19a59			20 05
Box Hill & Westhumble	d							19 09		19 19							19 39								20 10
Dorking	a				18 55			19 16		19 21				19 25			19 46		19 51						20 16
Dorking	d									19 22															
Holmwood	d									19 29															
Ockley	d									19 33															
Warnham	d									19 39															
Horsham	a									19 45															

		TL	TL	TL	SW	SN	SW	TL		TL	TL	SW	SN	SW	TL	TL	TL	SW		SN	SW	TL	TL	TL	SW
London Victoria ⊖	d		19 25			19 41				19 55			20 11			20 25				20 41			20 55		
London Waterloo ⊖	d				19 39		19 54					20 09		20 24				20 39			20 54				21 09
Clapham Junction	d		19 32		19 48	19 48	20 03			20 02		20 18	20 18	20 33		20 32		20 48		20 48	21 03		21 02		21 18
Balham ⊖	d					19 53							20 23							20 53					
St Pancras International	d	18 57						19 27							19 57							20 27			
Farringdon	d	19 02						19 32							20 02							20 32			
City Thameslink	d	19 04						19 34							20 04							20 34			
London Blackfriars	d	19 06						19 36							20 06							20 36			
Elephant & Castle	d	19 10						19 40							20 10							20 40			
Loughborough Jn	d	19 15						19 45							20 15							20 45			
Herne Hill	d	19 20						19 50							20 20							20 50			
London Bridge	d			19 25							19 55						20 25							20 55	
Tulse Hill	a	19 24						19 54							20 24							20 54			
Tulse Hill	d	19 26						19 56							20 26							20 56			
Streatham	d	19 30						20 00							20 30							21 00			
Mitcham Eastfields	d	19 34				20 00		20 04					20 30		20 34					21 00		21 04			
Mitcham Junction	d	19 37				20 03		20 07					20 33		20 37					21 03		21 07			
Hackbridge	d	19 40				20 06		20 10					20 36		20 40					21 06		21 10			
Carshalton	d	19 43	19 49			20 09		20 13		20 19			20 39		20 43	20 49				21 09		21 13	21 19		
Sutton	a	19 47	19 53			20 13		20 17		20 24			20 43		20 47	20 53				21 13		21 17	21 23		
Norwood Junction	d			19 39							20 09						20 39							21 09	
West Croydon	d			19 45							20 15						20 45							21 15	
Sutton	a			19 58							20 28						20 58							21 28	
Sutton	d		19 54	19 58		20 13				20 24	20 28		20 43			20 54	20 58			21 13			21 24	21 28	
Cheam	d		19 57	20 01		20 16				20 27	20 31		20 46			20 57	21 01			21 16			21 27	21 31	
Ewell East	d			20 04		20 19					20 34		20 49				21 04			21 19				21 34	
Epsom	a		20 04	20 08	20 16	20 23	20 27			20 34	20 38	20 42	20 53	20 57		21 05	21 08	21 12		21 23	21 27		21 34	21 38	21 42
Epsom	d		20 05		20 17					20 35		20 43				21 05		21 13					21 35		21 43
Ashtead	d		20 10		20 21					20 40		20 47				21 10		21 17					21 40		21 47
Leatherhead	d		20 14		20a24					20 43		20 50				21 14		21a20					21 44		21 50
Box Hill & Westhumble	d		20 19									20 55				21 19									21 55
Dorking	a		20 22							20 51		20 59				21 22							21 51		21 59
Dorking	d		20 22													21 22									
Holmwood	d		20 29													21 29									
Ockley	d		20 33													21 33									
Warnham	d		20 39													21 39									
Horsham	a		20 43													21 43									

For faster trains from London and Clapham Junction to Horsham refer to Table T186

Table T180-F

Mondays to Fridays

8 October to 7 December

London - Hackbridge, Sutton, Epsom, Leatherhead, Dorking and Horsham

		SN	SW	TL		TL	TL	SW	SN	SW	TL	TL	TL	SW		SN	TL	TL	TL	SW	SN	TL	TL	TL	
London Victoria ⊖	d	21 11				21 25			21 41			21 55				22 11		22 25			22 41		22 55		
London Waterloo ⊖	d		21 24					21 39		21 54				22 09						22 39					
Clapham Junction	d	21 18	21 33			21 32		21 48	21 48	22 03		22 03		22 18		22 18		22 32		22 48	22 48		23 02		
Balham ⊖	d	21 23							21 54							22 23					22 53				
St Pancras International	d			20 57							21 27						21 57					22 27			
Farringdon	d			21 02							21 32						22 02					22 32			
City Thameslink	d			21 04							21 34						22 04					22 34			
London Blackfriars	d			21 06							21 36						22 06					22 36			
Elephant & Castle	d			21 10							21 40						22 10					22 40			
Loughborough Jn	d			21 15							21 45						22 15					22 45			
Herne Hill	d			21 20							21 50						22 20					22 50			
London Bridge	d						21 25						21 55						22 25					22 55	
Tulse Hill	a			21 24							21 54						22 24					22 54			
Tulse Hill	d			21 26							21 56						22 26					22 56			
Streatham	d			21 30							22 00						22 30					23 00			
Mitcham Eastfields	d	21 30		21 34					22 01		22 04					22 30	22 34				23 00	23 04			
Mitcham Junction	d	21 33		21 37					22 04		22 07					22 33	22 37				23 03	23 07			
Hackbridge	d	21 36		21 40					22 07		22 10					22 36	22 40				23 06	23 10			
Carshalton	d	21 39		21 43		21 49			22 09		22 13	22 20				22 39	22 43	22 49			23 09	23 13	23 19		
Sutton	a	21 43		21 47		21 53			22 13		22 17	22 24				22 43	22 47	22 53			23 13	23 17	23 23		
Norwood Junction	d						21 39						22 09						22 39					23 09	
West Croydon	d						21 45						22 15						22 45					23 15	
Sutton	a						21 58						22 28						22 58					23 28	
Sutton	d	21 43				21 54	21 58		22 13			22 25	22 28			22 43		22 54	22 58		23 13		23 24	23 28	
Cheam	d	21 46				21 57	22 01		22 16			22 28	22 31			22 46		22 57	23 01		23 16		23 27	23 31	
Ewell East	d	21 49					22 04		22 19				22 34			22 49			23 04		23 19			23 34	
Epsom	a	21 53	21 57			22 04	22 08	22 12	22 23	22 27		22 34	22 38	22 42		22 53		23 04	23 08	23 12	23 23		23 34	23 38	
Epsom	d					22 05		22 13				22 35		22 43				23 05		23 13			23 35		
Ashtead	d					22 10		22 17				22 40		22 47				23 10		23 17			23 40		
Leatherhead	d					22 14		22a20				22 44		22 50				23 14		23a20			23 43		
Box Hill & Westhumble	d					22 19								22 55				23 19							
Dorking	a					22 22						22 51		22 59				23 22					23 51		
Dorking	d					22 22												23 22							
Holmwood	d					22 29												23 29							
Ockley	d					22 33												23 33							
Warnham	d					22 39												23 39							
Horsham	a					22 43												23 43							

		SW	SN	TL	TL	SW
London Victoria ⊖	d		23 11		23 25	
London Waterloo ⊖	d	23 09				23 42
Clapham Junction	d	23 18	23 18		23 32	23 51
Balham ⊖	d		23 23		23 37	
St Pancras International	d			22 57		
Farringdon	d			23 02		
City Thameslink	d					
London Blackfriars	d			23 06		
Elephant & Castle	d			23 10		
Loughborough Jn	d			23 15		
Herne Hill	d			23 20		
London Bridge	d					
Tulse Hill	a			23 24		
Tulse Hill	d			23 26		
Streatham	d			23 30		
Mitcham Eastfields	d		23 30	23 34	23 45	
Mitcham Junction	d		23 33	23 37	23 48	
Hackbridge	d		23 36	23 40	23 51	
Carshalton	d		23 39	23 43	23 54	
Sutton	a		23 43	23 47	23 58	
Norwood Junction	d					
West Croydon	d					
Sutton	a					
Sutton	d		23 43		23 59	
Cheam	d		23 46		00 02	
Ewell East	d		23 49		00 05	
Epsom	a	23 42	23 53		00 09	00 16
Epsom	d	23 43			00 09	00 19
Ashtead	d	23 47			00 14	00 23
Leatherhead	d	23 50			00 18	00a26
Box Hill & Westhumble	d	23 55			00 23	
Dorking	a	23 59			00 26	
Dorking	d				00 26	
Holmwood	d				00s33	
Ockley	d				00s37	
Warnham	d				00s43	
Horsham	a				00 48	

For faster trains from London and Clapham Junction to Horsham refer to Table T186

Table T180-F

Saturdays
26 May to 6 October

London - Hackbridge, Sutton, Epsom, Leatherhead, Dorking and Horsham

		TL	SW	SW	SN	TL	TL	TL	SW	SN		TL	TL	TL	SW	SN	SW	TL	TL	TL		SW	SN	SW	TL
London Victoria ⊖	d				00 20			06 25		06 41			06 55			07 11			07 25				07 41		
London Waterloo ⊖	d			00 15					06 39						07 09		07 24					07 39		07 54	
Clapham Junction	d			00 26	00 27			06 32	06 48	06 48			07 02		07 18	07 18	07 33		07 32			07 48	07 48	08 03	
Balham ⊖	d				00 33					06 53						07 23							07 53		
St Pancras International	d					05 27	05 57					06 27						06 57							07 27
Farringdon	d					05 32	06 02					06 32						07 02							07 32
City Thameslink	d																								
London Blackfriars	d					05 36	06 06					06 36						07 06							07 36
Elephant & Castle	d					05 40	06 10					06 40						07 10							07 40
Loughborough Jn	d					05 45	06 15					06 45						07 15							07 45
Herne Hill	d					05 50	06 20					06 50						07 20							07 50
London Bridge	d													06 55						07 25					
Tulse Hill	a					05 54	06 24					06 54						07 24							07 54
Tulse Hill	d					05 56	06 26					06 56						07 26							07 56
Streatham	d					06 00	06 30					07 00						07 30							08 00
Mitcham Eastfields	d				00 40	06 04	06 34			07 00		07 04				07 30		07 34					08 00		08 04
Mitcham Junction	d				00 43	06 07	06 37			07 03		07 07				07 33		07 37					08 03		08 07
Hackbridge	d				00 46	06 10	06 40			07 06		07 10				07 36		07 40					08 06		08 10
Carshalton	d				00 49	06 13	06 43	06 49		07 09		07 13	07 19			07 39		07 43	07 49				08 09		08 13
Sutton	a				00 53	06 17	06 47	06 53		07 13		07 17	07 23			07 43		07 47	07 53				08 13		08 17
Norwood Junction	d													07 09						07 39					
West Croydon	d													07 15						07 45					
Sutton	a													07 28						07 58					
Sutton	d				00 53			06 54		07 13			07 24	07 28		07 43			07 54	07 58			08 13		
Cheam	d	00 02			00 56			06 57		07 16			07 27	07 31		07 46			07 57	08 01			08 16		
Ewell East	d	00 05			00 59					07 19				07 34		07 49				08 04			08 19		
Epsom	a	00 09		00 50	01 03			07 04	07 12	07 23			07 34	07 38	07 42	07 53	07 57		08 04	08 08		08 12	08 23	08 27	
Epsom	d	00 09	00 19					07 05	07 13				07 35		07 43		07 58		08 05			08 13		08 28	
Ashtead	d	00 14	00 23					07 10	07 17				07 40		07 47		08 02		08 10			08 17		08 32	
Leatherhead	d	00 18	00a26					07 13	07a20				07 44		07a50		08 05		08 14			08a20		08 35	
Box Hill & Westhumble	d	00 23																	08 19						
Dorking	a	00 26						07 21					07 52				08 11		08 21					08 41	
Dorking	d	00 26																	08 22						
Holmwood	d	00s33																	08 29						
Ockley	d	00s37																	08 33						
Warnham	d	00s43																	08 39						
Horsham	a	00 48																	08 43						

		TL	TL	SW	SN	SW		TL	TL	TL	SW	SN	SW	TL	TL	TL		SW	SN	SW	TL	TL	TL	SW	SN
London Victoria ⊖	d	07 55			08 11				08 25			08 41			08 55				09 11			09 25			09 41
London Waterloo ⊖	d			08 09		08 24					08 39		08 54					09 09		09 24				09 39	
Clapham Junction	d	08 02		08 18	08 18	08 33			08 32		08 48	08 48	09 03		09 02			09 18	09 18	09 33		09 32		09 48	09 48
Balham ⊖	d				08 23							08 53							09 23						09 53
St Pancras International	d							07 57						08 27							08 57				
Farringdon	d							08 02						08 32							09 02				
City Thameslink	d																				09 04				
London Blackfriars	d							08 06						08 36							09 06				
Elephant & Castle	d							08 10						08 40							09 10				
Loughborough Jn	d							08 15						08 45							09 15				
Herne Hill	d							08 20						08 50							09 20				
London Bridge	d		07 55							08 25						08 55							09 25		
Tulse Hill	a							08 24						08 54							09 24				
Tulse Hill	d							08 26						08 56							09 26				
Streatham	d							08 30						09 00							09 30				
Mitcham Eastfields	d				08 30			08 34				09 00		09 04					09 30		09 34				10 00
Mitcham Junction	d				08 33			08 37				09 03		09 07					09 33		09 37				10 03
Hackbridge	d				08 36			08 40				09 06		09 10					09 36		09 40				10 06
Carshalton	d	08 19			08 39			08 43	08 49			09 09		09 13	09 19				09 39		09 43	09 49			10 09
Sutton	a	08 23			08 43			08 47	08 53			09 13		09 17	09 23				09 43		09 47	09 53			10 13
Norwood Junction	d		08 09							08 39						09 09							09 39		
West Croydon	d		08 15							08 45						09 15							09 45		
Sutton	a		08 28							08 58						09 28							09 58		
Sutton	d	08 24	08 28		08 43				08 54	08 58		09 13			09 24	09 28			09 43			09 54	09 58		10 13
Cheam	d	08 27	08 31		08 46				08 57	09 01		09 16			09 27	09 31			09 46			09 57	10 01		10 16
Ewell East	d		08 34		08 49					09 04		09 19				09 34			09 49				10 04		10 19
Epsom	a	08 34	08 38	08 42	08 53	08 57			09 04	09 08	09 12	09 23	09 27		09 34	09 38		09 42	09 53	09 57		10 04	10 08	10 12	10 23
Epsom	d	08 35		08 43		08 58			09 05		09 13		09 28		09 35			09 43		09 58		10 05		10 13	
Ashtead	d	08 40		08 47		09 02			09 10		09 17		09 32		09 40			09 47		10 02		10 10		10 17	
Leatherhead	d	08 44		08a50		09 05			09 14		09a20		09 35		09 44			09a50		10 05		10 14		10a20	
Box Hill & Westhumble	d								09 19													10 19			
Dorking	a	08 51				09 11			09 21				09 41		09 52					10 11		10 21			
Dorking	d								09 22													10 22			
Holmwood	d								09 29													10 29			
Ockley	d								09 33													10 33			
Warnham	d								09 39													10 39			
Horsham	a								09 43													10 43			

For faster trains from London and Clapham Junction to Horsham refer to Table T186

Table T180-F

Saturdays
26 May to 6 October

London - Hackbridge, Sutton, Epsom, Leatherhead, Dorking and Horsham

		SW		TL	TL	TL	SW	SN	SW	TL	TL	TL		SW	SN	SW	TL	TL	TL	SW	SN	SW		TL	TL
London Victoria ⊖	d				09 55			10 11			10 25				10 41			10 55			11 11				11 25
London Waterloo ⊖	d	09 54					10 09		10 24					10 39		10 54				11 09		11 24			
Clapham Junction	d	10 03			10 02		10 18	10 18	10 33		10 32			10 48	10 48	11 03		11 02		11 18	11 18	11 33			11 32
Balham ⊖	d							10 23							10 53						11 23				
St Pancras International	d			09 27						09 57							10 27							10 57	
Farringdon	d			09 32						10 02							10 32							11 02	
City Thameslink	d			09 34						10 04							10 34							11 04	
London Blackfriars	d			09 36						10 06							10 36							11 06	
Elephant & Castle	d			09 40						10 10							10 40							11 10	
Loughborough Jn	d			09 45						10 15							10 45							11 15	
Herne Hill	d			09 50						10 20							10 50							11 20	
London Bridge	d					09 55						10 25							10 55						
Tulse Hill	a			09 54						10 24							10 54							11 24	
Tulse Hill	d			09 56						10 26							10 56							11 26	
Streatham	d			10 00						10 30							11 00							11 30	
Mitcham Eastfields	d			10 04				10 30		10 34					11 00		11 04				11 30			11 34	
Mitcham Junction	d			10 07				10 33		10 37					11 03		11 07				11 33			11 37	
Hackbridge	d			10 10				10 36		10 40					11 06		11 10				11 36			11 40	
Carshalton	d			10 13	10 19			10 39		10 43	10 49				11 09		11 13	11 19			11 39			11 43	11 49
Sutton	a			10 17	10 23			10 43		10 47	10 53				11 13		11 17	11 23			11 43			11 47	11 53
Norwood Junction	d					10 09						10 39							11 09						
West Croydon	d					10 15						10 45							11 15						
Sutton	a					10 28						10 58							11 28						
Sutton	d				10 24	10 28		10 43			10 54	10 58			11 13			11 24	11 28		11 43				11 54
Cheam	d				10 27	10 31		10 46			10 57	11 01			11 16			11 27	11 31		11 46				11 57
Ewell East	d					10 34		10 49				11 04			11 19				11 34		11 49				
Epsom	a	10 27			10 34	10 38	10 42	10 53	10 57		11 04	11 08		11 12	11 23	11 27		11 34	11 38	11 42	11 53	11 57			12 04
Epsom	d	10 28			10 35		10 43		10 58		11 05			11 13		11 28		11 35		11 43		11 58			12 05
Ashtead	d	10 32			10 40		10 47		11 02		11 10			11 17		11 32		11 40		11 47		12 02			12 10
Leatherhead	d	10 35			10 44		10a50		11 05		11 14			11a20		11 35		11 44		11a50		12 05			12 14
Box Hill & Westhumble	d										11 19														12 19
Dorking	a	10 41			10 51				11 11		11 21					11 41		11 51				12 11			12 21
Dorking	d										11 22														12 22
Holmwood	d										11 29														12 29
Ockley	d										11 33														12 33
Warnham	d										11 39														12 39
Horsham	a										11 43														12 43

		TL	SW	SN	SW	TL	TL	TL		SW	SN	SW	TL	TL	TL	SW	SN	SW		TL	TL	TL	SW	SN	SW
London Victoria ⊖	d			11 41			11 55				12 11			12 25			12 41				12 55			13 11	
London Waterloo ⊖	d		11 39		11 54					12 09		12 24				12 39		12 54					13 09		13 24
Clapham Junction	d		11 48	11 48	12 03		12 02			12 18	12 18	12 33		12 32		12 48	12 48	13 03			13 02		13 18	13 18	13 33
Balham ⊖	d			11 53							12 23						12 53							13 23	
St Pancras International	d					11 27							11 57							12 27					
Farringdon	d					11 32							12 02							12 32					
City Thameslink	d					11 34							12 04							12 34					
London Blackfriars	d					11 36							12 06							12 36					
Elephant & Castle	d					11 40							12 10							12 40					
Loughborough Jn	d					11 45							12 15							12 45					
Herne Hill	d					11 50							12 20							12 50					
London Bridge	d	11 25						11 55							12 25							12 55			
Tulse Hill	a					11 54							12 24							12 54					
Tulse Hill	d					11 56							12 26							12 56					
Streatham	d					12 00							12 30							13 00					
Mitcham Eastfields	d			12 00		12 04					12 30		12 34				13 00			13 04				13 30	
Mitcham Junction	d			12 03		12 07					12 33		12 37				13 03			13 07				13 33	
Hackbridge	d			12 06		12 10					12 36		12 40				13 06			13 10				13 36	
Carshalton	d			12 09		12 13	12 19				12 39		12 43	12 49			13 09			13 13	13 19			13 39	
Sutton	a			12 13		12 17	12 23				12 43		12 47	12 53			13 13			13 17	13 23			13 43	
Norwood Junction	d	11 39						12 09							12 39							13 09			
West Croydon	d	11 45						12 15							12 45							13 15			
Sutton	a	11 58						12 28							12 58							13 28			
Sutton	d	11 58		12 13			12 24	12 28			12 43			12 54	12 58		13 13				13 24	13 28		13 43	
Cheam	d	12 01		12 16			12 27	12 31			12 46			12 57	13 01		13 16				13 27	13 31		13 46	
Ewell East	d	12 04		12 19				12 34			12 49				13 04		13 19					13 34		13 49	
Epsom	a	12 08	12 12	12 23	12 27		12 34	12 38		12 42	12 53	12 57		13 04	13 08	13 12	13 23	13 27			13 34	13 38	13 42	13 53	13 57
Epsom	d		12 13		12 28		12 35			12 43		12 58		13 05		13 13		13 28			13 35		13 43		13 58
Ashtead	d		12 17		12 32		12 40			12 47		13 02		13 10		13 17		13 32			13 40		13 47		14 02
Leatherhead	d		12a20		12 35		12 44			12a50		13 05		13 14		13a20		13 35			13 44		13a50		14 05
Box Hill & Westhumble	d													13 19											
Dorking	a				12 41		12 51					13 11		13 21				13 41			13 51				14 11
Dorking	d													13 22											
Holmwood	d													13 29											
Ockley	d													13 33											
Warnham	d													13 39											
Horsham	a													13 43											

For faster trains from London and Clapham Junction to Horsham refer to Table T186

Please note, Network Rail have stated that further updates to this timetable are possible during the validity period.

26 May to 6 October

London - Hackbridge, Sutton, Epsom, Leatherhead, Dorking and Horsham

		TL	TL	TL		SW	SN	SW	TL	TL	TL	SW	SN	SW		TL	TL	TL	SW	SN	SW	TL	TL	TL	
London Victoria ⊖	d		13 25				13 41			13 55			14 11				14 25			14 41			14 55		
London Waterloo ⊖	d					13 39		13 54				14 09		14 24					14 39		14 54				
Clapham Junction	d		13 32			13 48	13 48	14 03		14 02		14 18	14 18	14 33			14 32		14 48	14 48	15 03		15 02		
Balham ⊖	d						13 53						14 23							14 53					
St Pancras International	d	12 57							13 27							13 57						14 27			
Farringdon	d	13 02							13 32							14 02						14 32			
City Thameslink	d	13 04							13 34							14 04						14 34			
London Blackfriars	d	13 06							13 36							14 06						14 36			
Elephant & Castle	d	13 10							13 40							14 10						14 40			
Loughborough Jn	d	13 15							13 45							14 15						14 45			
Herne Hill	d	13 20							13 50							14 20						14 50			
London Bridge	d			13 25							13 55							14 25						14 55	
Tulse Hill	a	13 24							13 54							14 24						14 54			
Tulse Hill	d	13 26							13 56							14 26						14 56			
Streatham	d	13 30							14 00							14 30						15 00			
Mitcham Eastfields	d	13 34					14 00		14 04				14 30			14 34				15 00		15 04			
Mitcham Junction	d	13 37					14 03		14 07				14 33			14 37				15 03		15 07			
Hackbridge	d	13 40					14 06		14 10				14 36			14 40				15 06		15 10			
Carshalton	d	13 43	13 49				14 09		14 13	14 19			14 39			14 43	14 49			15 09		15 13	15 19		
Sutton	a	13 47	13 53				14 13		14 17	14 23			14 43			14 47	14 53			15 13		15 17	15 23		
Norwood Junction	d			13 39							14 09							14 39						15 09	
West Croydon	d			13 45							14 15							14 45						15 15	
Sutton	a			13 58							14 28							14 58						15 28	
Sutton	d		13 54	13 58			14 13			14 24	14 28		14 43				14 54	14 58		15 13			15 24	15 28	
Cheam	d		13 57	14 01			14 16			14 27	14 31		14 46				14 57	15 01		15 16			15 27	15 31	
Ewell East	d			14 04			14 19				14 34		14 49					15 04		15 19				15 34	
Epsom	a		14 04	14 08		14 12	14 23	14 27		14 34	14 38	14 42	14 53	14 57			15 04	15 08	15 12	15 23	15 27		15 34	15 38	
Epsom	d		14 05			14 13		14 28		14 35		14 43		14 58			15 05		15 13		15 28		15 35		
Ashtead	d		14 10			14 17		14 32		14 40		14 47		15 02			15 10		15 17		15 32		15 40		
Leatherhead	d		14 14			14a20		14 35		14 44		14a50		15 05			15 14		15a20		15 35		15 44		
Box Hill & Westhumble	d		14 19														15 19								
Dorking	a		14 21					14 41		14 51				15 11			15 21				15 41		15 51		
Dorking	d		14 22														15 22								
Holmwood	d		14 29														15 29								
Ockley	d		14 33														15 33								
Warnham	d		14 39														15 39								
Horsham	a		14 43														15 43								

		SW	SN	SW	TL	TL	TL	SW	SN	SW		TL	TL	TL	SW	SN	SW	TL	TL	TL		SW	SN	SW	TL
London Victoria ⊖	d		15 11			15 25			15 41				15 55			16 11			16 25				16 41		
London Waterloo ⊖	d	15 09		15 24				15 39		15 54					16 09		16 24					16 39		16 54	
Clapham Junction	d	15 18	15 18	15 33		15 32		15 48	15 48	16 03			16 02		16 18	16 18	16 33		16 32			16 48	16 48	17 03	
Balham ⊖	d		15 23						15 53							16 23							16 53		
St Pancras International	d				14 57							15 27						15 57							16 27
Farringdon	d				15 02							15 32						16 02							16 32
City Thameslink	d				15 04							15 34						16 04							16 34
London Blackfriars	d				15 06							15 36						16 06							16 36
Elephant & Castle	d				15 10							15 40						16 10							16 40
Loughborough Jn	d				15 15							15 45						16 15							16 45
Herne Hill	d				15 20							15 50						16 20							16 50
London Bridge	d						15 25							15 55						16 25					
Tulse Hill	a				15 24							15 54						16 24							16 54
Tulse Hill	d				15 26							15 56						16 26							16 56
Streatham	d				15 30							16 00						16 30							17 00
Mitcham Eastfields	d		15 30		15 34				16 00			16 04				16 30		16 34					17 00		17 04
Mitcham Junction	d		15 33		15 37				16 03			16 07				16 33		16 37					17 03		17 07
Hackbridge	d		15 36		15 40				16 06			16 10				16 36		16 40					17 06		17 10
Carshalton	d		15 39		15 43	15 49			16 09			16 13	16 19			16 39		16 43	16 49				17 09		17 13
Sutton	a		15 43		15 47	15 53			16 13			16 17	16 23			16 43		16 47	16 53				17 13		17 17
Norwood Junction	d						15 39							16 09						16 39					
West Croydon	d						15 45							16 15						16 45					
Sutton	a						15 58							16 28						16 58					
Sutton	d		15 43			15 54	15 58		16 13				16 24	16 28		16 43			16 54	16 58			17 13		
Cheam	d		15 46			15 57	16 01		16 16				16 27	16 31		16 46			16 57	17 01			17 16		
Ewell East	d		15 49				16 04		16 19					16 34		16 49				17 04			17 19		
Epsom	a	15 42	15 53	15 57		16 04	16 08	16 12	16 23	16 27			16 34	16 38	16 42	16 53	16 57		17 04	17 08		17 12	17 23	17 27	
Epsom	d	15 43		15 58		16 05		16 13		16 28			16 35		16 43		16 58		17 05			17 13		17 28	
Ashtead	d	15 47		16 02		16 10		16 17		16 32			16 40		16 47		17 02		17 10			17 17		17 32	
Leatherhead	d	15a50		16 05		16 14		16a20		16 35			16 44		16a50		17 05		17 14			17a20		17 35	
Box Hill & Westhumble	d					16 19													17 19						
Dorking	a			16 11		16 22				16 41			16 51				17 11		17 22					17 41	
Dorking	d					16 22													17 22						
Holmwood	d					16 29													17 29						
Ockley	d					16 33													17 33						
Warnham	d					16 39													17 39						
Horsham	a					16 43													17 43						

For faster trains from London and Clapham Junction to Horsham refer to Table T186

26 May to 6 October

London - Hackbridge, Sutton, Epsom, Leatherhead, Dorking and Horsham

		TL	TL	SW	SN	SW		TL	TL	TL	SW	SN	SW	TL	TL	TL		SW	SN	SW	TL	TL	TL	SW	SN
London Victoria ⊖	d	16 55			17 11				17 25			17 41			17 55				18 11			18 25			18 41
London Waterloo ⊖	d			17 09		17 24					17 39		17 54					18 09		18 24				18 39	
Clapham Junction	d	17 02		17 18	17 18	17 33			17 32		17 48	17 48	18 03		18 02			18 18	18 18	18 33		18 32		18 48	18 48
Balham ⊖	d				17 23							17 53							18 23						18 53
St Pancras International	d							16 57						17 27							17 57				
Farringdon	d							17 02						17 32							18 02				
City Thameslink	d							17 04						17 34							18 04				
London Blackfriars	d							17 06						17 36							18 06				
Elephant & Castle	d							17 10						17 40							18 10				
Loughborough Jn	d							17 15						17 45							18 15				
Herne Hill	d							17 20						17 50							18 20				
London Bridge	d		16 55							17 25						17 55							18 25		
Tulse Hill	a							17 24						17 54							18 24				
Tulse Hill	d							17 26						17 56							18 26				
Streatham	d							17 30						18 00							18 30				
Mitcham Eastfields	d				17 30			17 34				18 00		18 04					18 30		18 34				19 00
Mitcham Junction	d				17 33			17 37				18 03		18 07					18 33		18 37				19 03
Hackbridge	d				17 36			17 40				18 06		18 10					18 36		18 40				19 06
Carshalton	d	17 19			17 39			17 43	17 49			18 09		18 13	18 19				18 39		18 43	18 49			19 09
Sutton	a	17 23			17 43			17 47	17 53			18 13		18 17	18 23				18 43		18 47	18 53			19 13
Norwood Junction	d		17 09							17 39						18 09							18 39		
West Croydon	d		17 15							17 45						18 15							18 45		
Sutton	a		17 28							17 58						18 28							18 58		
Sutton	d	17 24	17 28		17 43				17 54	17 58		18 13			18 24	18 28			18 43			18 54	18 58		19 13
Cheam	d	17 27	17 31		17 46				17 57	18 01		18 16			18 27	18 31			18 46			18 57	19 01		19 16
Ewell East	d		17 34		17 49					18 04		18 19				18 34			18 49				19 04		19 19
Epsom	a	17 34	17 38	17 42	17 53	17 57			18 04	18 08	18 12	18 23	18 27		18 34	18 38		18 42	18 53	18 57		19 04	19 08	19 12	19 23
Epsom	d	17 35		17 43		17 58			18 05		18 13		18 28		18 35			18 43		18 58		19 05		19 13	
Ashtead	d	17 40		17 47		18 02			18 10		18 17		18 32		18 40			18 47		19 02		19 10		19 17	
Leatherhead	d	17 44		17a50		18 05			18 14		18a20		18 35		18 44			18a50		19 05		19 14		19a20	
Box Hill & Westhumble	d								18 19													19 19			
Dorking	a	17 51				18 11			18 22				18 41		18 51					19 11		19 21			
Dorking	d								18 22																
Holmwood	d								18 29																
Ockley	d								18 33																
Warnham	d								18 39																
Horsham	a								18 43																

		SW		TL	TL	TL	SW	SN	SW	TL	TL	TL		SW	SN	SW	TL	TL	TL	SW	SN	SW		TL	TL
London Victoria ⊖	d				18 55			19 11			19 25				19 41			19 55			20 11				20 25
London Waterloo ⊖	d	18 54					19 09		19 24					19 39		19 54				20 09		20 24			
Clapham Junction	d	19 03			19 02		19 18	19 18	19 33		19 32			19 48	19 48	20 03		20 02		20 18	20 18	20 33			20 32
Balham ⊖	d							19 23							19 53						20 23				
St Pancras International	d			18 27						18 57							19 27							19 57	
Farringdon	d			18 32						19 02							19 32							20 02	
City Thameslink	d			18 34						19 04							19 34							20 04	
London Blackfriars	d			18 36						19 06							19 36							20 06	
Elephant & Castle	d			18 40						19 10							19 40							20 10	
Loughborough Jn	d			18 45						19 15							19 45							20 15	
Herne Hill	d			18 50						19 20							19 50							20 20	
London Bridge	d					18 55						19 25							19 55						
Tulse Hill	a			18 54						19 24							19 54							20 24	
Tulse Hill	d			18 56						19 26							19 56							20 26	
Streatham	d			19 00						19 30							20 00							20 30	
Mitcham Eastfields	d			19 04				19 30		19 34					20 00		20 04				20 30			20 34	
Mitcham Junction	d			19 07				19 33		19 37					20 03		20 07				20 33			20 37	
Hackbridge	d			19 10				19 36		19 40					20 06		20 10				20 36			20 40	
Carshalton	d			19 13	19 19			19 39		19 43	19 49				20 09		20 13	20 19			20 39			20 43	20 49
Sutton	a			19 17	19 23			19 43		19 47	19 53				20 13		20 17	20 23			20 43			20 47	20 53
Norwood Junction	d					19 09						19 39							20 09						
West Croydon	d					19 15						19 45							20 15						
Sutton	a					19 28						19 58							20 28						
Sutton	d				19 24	19 28		19 43			19 54	19 58			20 13			20 24	20 28		20 43				20 54
Cheam	d				19 27	19 31		19 46			19 57	20 01			20 16			20 27	20 31		20 46				20 57
Ewell East	d					19 34		19 49				20 04			20 19				20 34		20 49				
Epsom	a	19 27			19 34	19 38	19 42	19 53	19 57		20 04	20 08		20 12	20 23	20 27		20 34	20 38	20 42	20 53	20 57			21 04
Epsom	d	19 28			19 35		19 43		19 58		20 05			20 13				20 35		20 43					21 05
Ashtead	d	19 32			19 40		19 47		20 02		20 10			20 17				20 40		20 47					21 10
Leatherhead	d	19 35			19 44		19a50		20 05		20 14			20a20				20 44		20 50					21 14
Box Hill & Westhumble	d										20 19														21 19
Dorking	a	19 41			19 51				20 11		20 21							20 51		20 57					21 21
Dorking	d																								
Holmwood	d																								
Ockley	d																								
Warnham	d																								
Horsham	a																								

For faster trains from London and Clapham Junction to Horsham refer to Table T186

Table T180-F

Saturdays

26 May to 6 October

London - Hackbridge, Sutton, Epsom, Leatherhead, Dorking and Horsham

		TL	SW	SN	SW	TL	TL	TL		SW	SN	SW	TL	TL	TL	SW	SN	SW		TL	TL	TL	SW	SN	TL
London Victoria ⊖	d			20 41			20 55				21 11			21 25			21 41				21 55			22 11	
London Waterloo ⊖	d		20 39		20 54					21 09		21 24				21 39		21 54					22 09		
Clapham Junction	d		20 48	20 48	21 03		21 02			21 18	21 18	21 33		21 32		21 48	21 48	22 03			22 02		22 18	22 18	
Balham ⊖	d			20 53							21 23						21 53							22 23	
St Pancras International	d					20 27							20 57							21 27					21 57
Farringdon	d					20 32							21 02							21 32					22 02
City Thameslink	d					20 34																			
London Blackfriars	d					20 36							21 06							21 36					22 06
Elephant & Castle	d					20 40							21 10							21 40					22 10
Loughborough Jn	d					20 45							21 15							21 45					22 15
Herne Hill	d					20 50							21 20							21 50					22 20
London Bridge	d	20 25						20 55							21 25							21 55			
Tulse Hill	a					20 54							21 24							21 54					22 24
Tulse Hill	d					20 56							21 26							21 56					22 26
Streatham	d					21 00							21 30							22 00					22 30
Mitcham Eastfields	d			21 00		21 04					21 30		21 34				22 00			22 04				22 30	22 34
Mitcham Junction	d			21 03		21 07					21 33		21 37				22 03			22 07				22 33	22 37
Hackbridge	d			21 06		21 10					21 36		21 40				22 06			22 10				22 36	22 40
Carshalton	d			21 09		21 13	21 19				21 39		21 43	21 49			22 09			22 13	22 19			22 39	22 43
Sutton	a			21 13		21 17	21 23				21 43		21 47	21 53			22 13			22 17	22 23			22 43	22 47
Norwood Junction	d	20 39						21 09							21 39							22 09			
West Croydon	d	20 45						21 15							21 45							22 15			
Sutton	a	20 58						21 28							21 58							22 28			
Sutton	d	20 58		21 13			21 24	21 28			21 43			21 54	21 58		22 13				22 24	22 28		22 43	
Cheam	d	21 01		21 16			21 27	21 31			21 46			21 57	22 01		22 16				22 27	22 31		22 46	
Ewell East	d	21 04		21 19				21 34			21 49				22 04		22 19					22 34		22 49	
Epsom	a	21 08	21 12	21 23	21 27		21 34	21 38		21 42	21 53	21 57		22 04	22 08	22 12	22 23	22 27			22 34	22 38	22 42	22 53	
Epsom	d		21 13				21 35			21 43				22 05		22 13					22 35		22 43		
Ashtead	d		21 17				21 40			21 47				22 10		22 17					22 40		22 47		
Leatherhead	d		21a20				21 44			21 50				22 14		22a20					22 44		22 50		
Box Hill & Westhumble	d													22 19											
Dorking	a						21 51			21 57				22 21							22 51		22 57		
Dorking	d																								
Holmwood	d																								
Ockley	d																								
Warnham	d																								
Horsham	a																								

		TL	TL	SW		SN	TL	TL	TL	SW	SN	TL	TL	SW		SN
London Victoria ⊖	d	22 25				22 41		22 55			23 11		23 25			23 45
London Waterloo ⊖	d			22 39						23 09				23 42		
Clapham Junction	d	22 33		22 48		22 49		23 02		23 18	23 18		23 32	23 51		23 53
Balham ⊖	d					22 53					23 23					23 57
St Pancras International	d						22 27					22 57				
Farringdon	d						22 32					23 02				
City Thameslink	d															
London Blackfriars	d						22 36					23 06				
Elephant & Castle	d						22 40					23 10				
Loughborough Jn	d						22 45					23 15				
Herne Hill	d						22 50					23 20				
London Bridge	d		22 25						22 55							
Tulse Hill	a						22 54					23 24				
Tulse Hill	d						22 56					23 26				
Streatham	d						23 00					23 30				
Mitcham Eastfields	d					23 00	23 04				23 30	23 34				00 04
Mitcham Junction	d					23 03	23 07				23 33	23 37				00 07
Hackbridge	d					23 06	23 10				23 36	23 40				00 10
Carshalton	d	22 49				23 09	23 13	23 19			23 39	23 43	23 52			00 13
Sutton	a	22 53				23 13	23 17	23 23			23 43	23 47	23 58			00 17
Norwood Junction	d		22 39						23 09							
West Croydon	d		22 45						23 15							
Sutton	a		22 58						23 28							
Sutton	d	22 54	22 58			23 13		23 24	23 28		23 43		23 59			00 17
Cheam	d	22 57	23 01			23 16		23 27	23 31		23 46		00 02			00 20
Ewell East	d		23 04			23 19			23 34		23 49					00 23
Epsom	a	23 04	23 08	23 12		23 23		23 34	23 38	23 42	23 53		00 07	00 15		00 27
Epsom	d	23 05		23 13				23 35		23 43			00 08	00 19		
Ashtead	d	23 10		23 17				23 40		23 47			00 13	00 23		
Leatherhead	d	23 14		23a20				23 43		23 50			00 16	00a26		
Box Hill & Westhumble	d	23 19											00 21			
Dorking	a	23 21						23 51		23 57			00 24			
Dorking	d															
Holmwood	d															
Ockley	d															
Warnham	d															
Horsham	a															

For faster trains from London and Clapham Junction to Horsham refer to Table T186

Table T180-F

Saturdays

13 October to 8 December

London - Hackbridge, Sutton, Epsom, Leatherhead, Dorking and Horsham

		TL	SW	SW	SN	TL	TL	TL	SW	SN		TL	TL	TL	SW	SN	SW	TL	TL	TL		SW	SN	SW	TL
London Victoria ⊖	d				00 20			06 25		06 41			06 55			07 11			07 25				07 41		
London Waterloo ⊖	d			00 15					06 39						07 09		07 24					07 39		07 54	
Clapham Junction	d			00 26	00 27			06 32	06 48	06 48			07 02		07 18	07 18	07 33		07 32			07 48	07 48	08 03	
Balham ⊖	d				00 33					06 53						07 23							07 53		
St Pancras International	d					05 27	05 57					06 27						06 57							07 27
Farringdon	d					05 32	06 02					06 32						07 02							07 32
City Thameslink	d																								
London Blackfriars	d					05 36	06 06					06 36						07 06							07 36
Elephant & Castle	d					05 40	06 10					06 40						07 10							07 40
Loughborough Jn	d					05 45	06 15					06 45						07 15							07 45
Herne Hill	d					05 50	06 20					06 50						07 20							07 50
London Bridge	d													06 55						07 25					
Tulse Hill	a					05 54	06 24					06 54						07 24							07 54
Tulse Hill	d					05 56	06 26					06 56						07 26							07 56
Streatham	d					06 00	06 30					07 00						07 30							08 00
Mitcham Eastfields	d				00 40	06 04	06 34			07 00		07 04				07 30		07 34					08 00		08 04
Mitcham Junction	d				00 43	06 07	06 37			07 03		07 07				07 33		07 37					08 03		08 07
Hackbridge	d				00 46	06 10	06 40			07 06		07 10				07 36		07 40					08 06		08 10
Carshalton	d				00 49	06 13	06 43	06 49		07 09		07 13	07 19			07 39		07 43	07 49				08 09		08 13
Sutton	a				00 53	06 17	06 47	06 53		07 13		07 17	07 23			07 43		07 47	07 53				08 13		08 17
Norwood Junction	d													07 09						07 39					
West Croydon	d													07 15						07 45					
Sutton	a													07 28						07 58					
Sutton	d				00 53			06 54		07 13			07 24	07 28		07 43			07 54	07 58			08 13		
Cheam	d	00 02			00 56			06 57		07 16			07 27	07 31		07 46			07 57	08 01			08 16		
Ewell East	d	00 05			00 59					07 19				07 34		07 49				08 04			08 19		
Epsom	a	00 09		00 50	01 03			07 04	07 12	07 23			07 34	07 38	07 42	07 53	07 57		08 04	08 08		08 12	08 23	08 27	
Epsom	d	00 09	00 19					07 05	07 13				07 35		07 43		07 58		08 05			08 13		08 28	
Ashtead	d	00 14	00 23					07 10	07 17				07 40		07 47		08 02		08 10			08 17		08 32	
Leatherhead	d	00 18	00a26					07 13	07a20				07 44		07a50		08 05		08 14			08a20		08 35	
Box Hill & Westhumble	d	00 23																	08 19						
Dorking	a	00 26						07 21					07 52				08 13		08 21					08 43	
Dorking	d	00 26																	08 22						
Holmwood	d	00s33																	08 29						
Ockley	d	00s37																	08 33						
Warnham	d	00s43																	08 39						
Horsham	a	00 48																	08 43						

		TL	TL	SW	SN	SW		TL	TL	TL	SW	SN	SW	TL	TL	TL		SW	SN	SW	TL	TL	TL	SW	SN
London Victoria ⊖	d	07 55			08 11				08 25			08 41			08 55				09 11			09 25			09 41
London Waterloo ⊖	d			08 09		08 24					08 39		08 54					09 09		09 24				09 39	
Clapham Junction	d	08 02		08 18	08 18	08 33			08 32		08 48	08 48	09 03		09 02			09 18	09 18	09 33		09 32		09 48	09 48
Balham ⊖	d				08 23							08 53							09 23						09 53
St Pancras International	d							07 57						08 27							08 57				
Farringdon	d							08 02						08 32							09 02				
City Thameslink	d																				09 04				
London Blackfriars	d							08 06						08 36							09 06				
Elephant & Castle	d							08 10						08 40							09 10				
Loughborough Jn	d							08 15						08 45							09 15				
Herne Hill	d							08 20						08 50							09 20				
London Bridge	d		07 55							08 25						08 55							09 25		
Tulse Hill	a							08 24						08 54							09 24				
Tulse Hill	d							08 26						08 56							09 26				
Streatham	d							08 30						09 00							09 30				
Mitcham Eastfields	d				08 30			08 34				09 00		09 04					09 30		09 34				10 00
Mitcham Junction	d				08 33			08 37				09 03		09 07					09 33		09 37				10 03
Hackbridge	d				08 36			08 40				09 06		09 10					09 36		09 40				10 06
Carshalton	d	08 19			08 39			08 43	08 49			09 09		09 13	09 19				09 39		09 43	09 49			10 09
Sutton	a	08 23			08 43			08 47	08 53			09 13		09 17	09 23				09 43		09 47	09 53			10 13
Norwood Junction	d		08 09							08 39						09 09							09 39		
West Croydon	d		08 15							08 45						09 15							09 45		
Sutton	a		08 28							08 58						09 28							09 58		
Sutton	d	08 24	08 28		08 43				08 54	08 58		09 13			09 24	09 28			09 43			09 54	09 58		10 13
Cheam	d	08 27	08 31		08 46				08 57	09 01		09 16			09 27	09 31			09 46			09 57	10 01		10 16
Ewell East	d		08 34		08 49					09 04		09 19				09 34			09 49				10 04		10 19
Epsom	a	08 34	08 38	08 42	08 53	08 57			09 04	09 08	09 12	09 23	09 27		09 34	09 38		09 42	09 53	09 57		10 04	10 08	10 12	10 23
Epsom	d	08 35		08 43		08 58			09 05		09 13		09 28		09 35			09 43		09 58		10 05		10 13	
Ashtead	d	08 40		08 47		09 02			09 10		09 17		09 32		09 40			09 47		10 02		10 10		10 17	
Leatherhead	d	08 44		08a50		09 05			09 14		09a20		09 35		09 44			09a50		10 05		10 14		10a20	
Box Hill & Westhumble	d								09 19													10 19			
Dorking	a	08 51				09 13			09 21				09 43		09 52					10 13		10 21			
Dorking	d								09 22													10 22			
Holmwood	d								09 29													10 29			
Ockley	d								09 33													10 33			
Warnham	d								09 39													10 39			
Horsham	a								09 43													10 43			

For faster trains from London and Clapham Junction to Horsham refer to Table T186

Table T180-F

Saturdays

13 October to 8 December

London - Hackbridge, Sutton, Epsom, Leatherhead, Dorking and Horsham

		SW		TL	TL	TL	SW	SN	SW	TL	TL	TL		SW	SN	SW	TL	TL	TL	SW	SN	SW		TL	TL
London Victoria ⊖	d				09 55			10 11			10 25				10 41			10 55			11 11				11 25
London Waterloo ⊖	d	09 54					10 09		10 24					10 39		10 54				11 09		11 24			
Clapham Junction	d	10 03			10 02		10 18	10 18	10 33		10 32			10 48	10 48	11 03		11 02		11 18	11 18	11 33			11 32
Balham ⊖	d							10 23							10 53						11 23				
St Pancras International	d			09 27						09 57							10 27							10 57	
Farringdon	d			09 32						10 02							10 32							11 02	
City Thameslink	d			09 34						10 04							10 34							11 04	
London Blackfriars	d			09 36						10 06							10 36							11 06	
Elephant & Castle	d			09 40						10 10							10 40							11 10	
Loughborough Jn	d			09 45						10 15							10 45							11 15	
Herne Hill	d			09 50						10 20							10 50							11 20	
London Bridge	d					09 55						10 25							10 55						
Tulse Hill	a			09 54						10 24							10 54							11 24	
Tulse Hill	d			09 56						10 26							10 56							11 26	
Streatham	d			10 00						10 30							11 00							11 30	
Mitcham Eastfields	d			10 04				10 30		10 34					11 00		11 04				11 30			11 34	
Mitcham Junction	d			10 07				10 33		10 37					11 03		11 07				11 33			11 37	
Hackbridge	d			10 10				10 36		10 40					11 06		11 10				11 36			11 40	
Carshalton	d			10 13	10 19			10 39		10 43	10 49				11 09		11 13	11 19			11 39			11 43	11 49
Sutton	a			10 17	10 23			10 43		10 47	10 53				11 13		11 17	11 23			11 43			11 47	11 53
Norwood Junction	d					10 09						10 39							11 09						
West Croydon	d					10 15						10 45							11 15						
Sutton	a					10 28						10 58							11 28						
Sutton	d				10 24	10 28		10 43			10 54	10 58			11 13			11 24	11 28		11 43				11 54
Cheam	d				10 27	10 31		10 46			10 57	11 01			11 16			11 27	11 31		11 46				11 57
Ewell East	d					10 34		10 49				11 04			11 19				11 34		11 49				
Epsom	a	10 27			10 34	10 38	10 42	10 53	10 57		11 04	11 08		11 12	11 23	11 27		11 34	11 38	11 42	11 53	11 57			12 04
Epsom	d	10 28			10 35		10 43		10 58		11 05			11 13		11 28		11 35		11 43		11 58			12 05
Ashtead	d	10 32			10 40		10 47		11 02		11 10			11 17		11 32		11 40		11 47		12 02			12 10
Leatherhead	d	10 35			10 44		10a50		11 05		11 14			11a20		11 35		11 44		11a50		12 05			12 14
Box Hill & Westhumble	d										11 19														12 19
Dorking	a	10 43			10 51				11 13		11 21					11 43		11 51				12 13			12 21
Dorking	d										11 22														12 22
Holmwood	d										11 29														12 29
Ockley	d										11 33														12 33
Warnham	d										11 39														12 39
Horsham	a										11 43														12 43

		TL	SW	SN	SW	TL	TL	TL		SW	SN	SW	TL	TL	TL	SW	SN	SW		TL	TL	TL	SW	SN	SW
London Victoria ⊖	d			11 41			11 55				12 11			12 25			12 41				12 55			13 11	
London Waterloo ⊖	d		11 39		11 54					12 09		12 24				12 39		12 54					13 09		13 24
Clapham Junction	d		11 48	11 48	12 03		12 02			12 18	12 18	12 33		12 32		12 48	12 48	13 03			13 02		13 18	13 18	13 33
Balham ⊖	d			11 53							12 23						12 53							13 23	
St Pancras International	d					11 27							11 57							12 27					
Farringdon	d					11 32							12 02							12 32					
City Thameslink	d					11 34							12 04							12 34					
London Blackfriars	d					11 36							12 06							12 36					
Elephant & Castle	d					11 40							12 10							12 40					
Loughborough Jn	d					11 45							12 15							12 45					
Herne Hill	d					11 50							12 20							12 50					
London Bridge	d	11 25						11 55							12 25							12 55			
Tulse Hill	a					11 54							12 24							12 54					
Tulse Hill	d					11 56							12 26							12 56					
Streatham	d					12 00							12 30							13 00					
Mitcham Eastfields	d			12 00		12 04					12 30		12 34				13 00			13 04				13 30	
Mitcham Junction	d			12 03		12 07					12 33		12 37				13 03			13 07				13 33	
Hackbridge	d			12 06		12 10					12 36		12 40				13 06			13 10				13 36	
Carshalton	d			12 09		12 13	12 19				12 39		12 43	12 49			13 09			13 13	13 19			13 39	
Sutton	a			12 13		12 17	12 23				12 43		12 47	12 53			13 13			13 17	13 23			13 43	
Norwood Junction	d	11 39						12 09							12 39							13 09			
West Croydon	d	11 45						12 15							12 45							13 15			
Sutton	a	11 58						12 28							12 58							13 28			
Sutton	d	11 58		12 13			12 24	12 28			12 43			12 54	12 58		13 13				13 24	13 28		13 43	
Cheam	d	12 01		12 16			12 27	12 31			12 46			12 57	13 01		13 16				13 27	13 31		13 46	
Ewell East	d	12 04		12 19				12 34			12 49				13 04		13 19					13 34		13 49	
Epsom	a	12 08	12 12	12 23	12 27		12 34	12 38		12 42	12 53	12 57		13 04	13 08	13 12	13 23	13 27			13 34	13 38	13 42	13 53	13 57
Epsom	d		12 13		12 28		12 35			12 43		12 58		13 05		13 13		13 28			13 35		13 43		13 58
Ashtead	d		12 17		12 32		12 40			12 47		13 02		13 10		13 17		13 32			13 40		13 47		14 02
Leatherhead	d		12a20		12 35		12 44			12a50		13 05		13 14		13a20		13 35			13 44		13a50		14 05
Box Hill & Westhumble	d													13 19											
Dorking	a				12 43		12 51					13 13		13 21				13 43			13 51				14 13
Dorking	d													13 22											
Holmwood	d													13 29											
Ockley	d													13 33											
Warnham	d													13 39											
Horsham	a													13 43											

For faster trains from London and Clapham Junction to Horsham refer to Table T186

Table T180-F

Saturdays

13 October to 8 December

London - Hackbridge, Sutton, Epsom, Leatherhead, Dorking and Horsham

		TL	TL	TL		SW	SN	SW	TL	TL	TL	SW	SN	SW		TL	TL	TL	SW	SN	SW	TL	TL	TL	
London Victoria ⊖	d		13 25				13 41			13 55			14 11				14 25			14 41			14 55		
London Waterloo ⊖	d					13 39		13 54				14 09		14 24					14 39		14 54				
Clapham Junction	d		13 32			13 48	13 48	14 03		14 02		14 18	14 18	14 33			14 32		14 48	14 48	15 03		15 02		
Balham ⊖	d						13 53						14 23							14 53					
St Pancras International	d	12 57							13 27							13 57						14 27			
Farringdon	d	13 02							13 32							14 02						14 32			
City Thameslink	d	13 04							13 34							14 04						14 34			
London Blackfriars	d	13 06							13 36							14 06						14 36			
Elephant & Castle	d	13 10							13 40							14 10						14 40			
Loughborough Jn	d	13 15							13 45							14 15						14 45			
Herne Hill	d	13 20							13 50							14 20						14 50			
London Bridge	d			13 25							13 55							14 25						14 55	
Tulse Hill	a	13 24							13 54							14 24						14 54			
Tulse Hill	d	13 26							13 56							14 26						14 56			
Streatham	d	13 30							14 00							14 30						15 00			
Mitcham Eastfields	d	13 34					14 00		14 04				14 30			14 34				15 00		15 04			
Mitcham Junction	d	13 37					14 03		14 07				14 33			14 37				15 03		15 07			
Hackbridge	d	13 40					14 06		14 10				14 36			14 40				15 06		15 10			
Carshalton	d	13 43	13 49				14 09		14 13	14 19			14 39			14 43	14 49			15 09		15 13	15 19		
Sutton	a	13 47	13 53				14 13		14 17	14 23			14 43			14 47	14 53			15 13		15 17	15 23		
Norwood Junction	d			13 39							14 09							14 39						15 09	
West Croydon	d			13 45							14 15							14 45						15 15	
Sutton	a			13 58							14 28							14 58						15 28	
Sutton	d		13 54	13 58			14 13			14 24	14 28		14 43				14 54	14 58		15 13			15 24	15 28	
Cheam	d		13 57	14 01			14 16			14 27	14 31		14 46				14 57	15 01		15 16			15 27	15 31	
Ewell East	d			14 04			14 19				14 34		14 49					15 04		15 19				15 34	
Epsom	a		14 04	14 08		14 12	14 23	14 27		14 34	14 38	14 42	14 53	14 57			15 04	15 08	15 12	15 23	15 27		15 34	15 38	
Epsom	d		14 05			14 13		14 28		14 35		14 43		14 58			15 05		15 13		15 28		15 35		
Ashtead	d		14 10			14 17		14 32		14 40		14 47		15 02			15 10		15 17		15 32		15 40		
Leatherhead	d		14 14			14a20		14 35		14 44		14a50		15 05			15 14		15a20		15 35		15 44		
Box Hill & Westhumble	d		14 19														15 19								
Dorking	a		14 21					14 43		14 51				15 13			15 21				15 43		15 51		
Dorking	d		14 22														15 22								
Holmwood	d		14 29														15 29								
Ockley	d		14 33														15 33								
Warnham	d		14 39														15 39								
Horsham	a		14 43														15 43								

		SW	SN	SW	TL	TL	TL	SW	SN	SW		TL	TL	TL	SW	SN	SW	TL	TL	TL		SW	SN	SW	TL
London Victoria ⊖	d		15 11			15 25			15 41				15 55			16 11			16 25				16 41		
London Waterloo ⊖	d	15 09		15 24				15 39		15 54					16 09		16 24					16 39		16 54	
Clapham Junction	d	15 18	15 18	15 33		15 32		15 48	15 48	16 03			16 02		16 18	16 18	16 33		16 32			16 48	16 48	17 03	
Balham ⊖	d		15 23						15 53							16 23							16 53		
St Pancras International	d				14 57							15 27						15 57							16 27
Farringdon	d				15 02							15 32						16 02							16 32
City Thameslink	d				15 04							15 34						16 04							16 34
London Blackfriars	d				15 06							15 36						16 06							16 36
Elephant & Castle	d				15 10							15 40						16 10							16 40
Loughborough Jn	d				15 15							15 45						16 15							16 45
Herne Hill	d				15 20							15 50						16 20							16 50
London Bridge	d						15 25							15 55						16 25					
Tulse Hill	a				15 24							15 54						16 24							16 54
Tulse Hill	d				15 26							15 56						16 26							16 56
Streatham	d				15 30							16 00						16 30							17 00
Mitcham Eastfields	d		15 30		15 34				16 00			16 04				16 30		16 34					17 00		17 04
Mitcham Junction	d		15 33		15 37				16 03			16 07				16 33		16 37					17 03		17 07
Hackbridge	d		15 36		15 40				16 06			16 10				16 36		16 40					17 06		17 10
Carshalton	d		15 39		15 43	15 49			16 09			16 13	16 19			16 39		16 43	16 49				17 09		17 13
Sutton	a		15 43		15 47	15 53			16 13			16 17	16 23			16 43		16 47	16 53				17 13		17 17
Norwood Junction	d						15 39							16 09						16 39					
West Croydon	d						15 45							16 15						16 45					
Sutton	a						15 58							16 28						16 58					
Sutton	d		15 43			15 54	15 58		16 13				16 24	16 28		16 43			16 54	16 58			17 13		
Cheam	d		15 46			15 57	16 01		16 16				16 27	16 31		16 46			16 57	17 01			17 16		
Ewell East	d		15 49				16 04		16 19					16 34		16 49				17 04			17 19		
Epsom	a	15 42	15 53	15 57		16 04	16 08	16 12	16 23	16 27			16 34	16 38	16 42	16 53	16 57		17 04	17 08		17 12	17 23	17 27	
Epsom	d	15 43		15 58		16 05		16 13		16 28			16 35		16 43		16 58		17 05			17 13		17 28	
Ashtead	d	15 47		16 02		16 10		16 17		16 32			16 40		16 47		17 02		17 10			17 17		17 32	
Leatherhead	d	15a50		16 05		16 14		16a20		16 35			16 44		16a50		17 05		17 14			17a20		17 35	
Box Hill & Westhumble	d					16 19													17 19						
Dorking	a			16 13		16 22				16 43			16 51				17 13		17 22					17 43	
Dorking	d					16 22													17 22						
Holmwood	d					16 29													17 29						
Ockley	d					16 33													17 33						
Warnham	d					16 39													17 39						
Horsham	a					16 43													17 43						

For faster trains from London and Clapham Junction to Horsham refer to Table T186

Please note, Network Rail have stated that further updates to this timetable are possible during the validity period.

Table T180-F

Saturdays

13 October to 8 December

London - Hackbridge, Sutton, Epsom, Leatherhead, Dorking and Horsham

		TL	TL	SW	SN	SW		TL	TL	TL	SW	SN	SW	TL	TL	TL		SW	SN	SW	TL	TL	TL	SW	SN
London Victoria 15 ⊖	d	16 55			17 11				17 25			17 41			17 55				18 11			18 25			18 41
London Waterloo 15 ⊖	d			17 09		17 24					17 39		17 54					18 09		18 24				18 39	
Clapham Junction 10	d	17 02		17 18	17 18	17 33			17 32		17 48	17 48	18 03		18 02			18 18	18 18	18 33		18 32		18 48	18 48
Balham 4 ⊖	d				17 23							17 53							18 23						18 53
St Pancras International	d							16 57						17 27							17 57				
Farringdon	d							17 02						17 32							18 02				
City Thameslink	d							17 04						17 34							18 04				
London Blackfriars	d							17 06						17 36							18 06				
Elephant & Castle	d							17 10						17 40							18 10				
Loughborough Jn	d							17 15						17 45							18 15				
Herne Hill	d							17 20						17 50							18 20				
London Bridge	d		16 55							17 25						17 55							18 25		
Tulse Hill	a							17 24						17 54							18 24				
Tulse Hill 3	d							17 26						17 56							18 26				
Streatham	d							17 30						18 00							18 30				
Mitcham Eastfields	d				17 30			17 34				18 00		18 04					18 30		18 34				19 00
Mitcham Junction	d				17 33			17 37				18 03		18 07					18 33		18 37				19 03
Hackbridge	d				17 36			17 40				18 06		18 10					18 36		18 40				19 06
Carshalton	d	17 19			17 39			17 43	17 49			18 09		18 13	18 19				18 39		18 43	18 49			19 09
Sutton	a	17 23			17 43			17 47	17 53			18 13		18 17	18 23				18 43		18 47	18 53			19 13
Norwood Junction	d		17 09							17 39						18 09							18 39		
West Croydon	d		17 15							17 45						18 15							18 45		
Sutton	a		17 28							17 58						18 28							18 58		
Sutton	d	17 24	17 28		17 43				17 54	17 58		18 13			18 24	18 28			18 43			18 54	18 58		19 13
Cheam	d	17 27	17 31		17 46				17 57	18 01		18 16			18 27	18 31			18 46			18 57	19 01		19 16
Ewell East	d		17 34		17 49					18 04		18 19				18 34			18 49				19 04		19 19
Epsom 3	a	17 34	17 38	17 42	17 53	17 57			18 04	18 08	18 12	18 23	18 27		18 34	18 38		18 42	18 53	18 57		19 04	19 08	19 12	19 23
Epsom	d	17 35		17 43		17 58			18 05		18 13		18 28		18 35			18 43		18 58		19 05		19 13	
Ashtead	d	17 40		17 47		18 02			18 10		18 17		18 32		18 40			18 47		19 02		19 10		19 17	
Leatherhead	d	17 44		17a50		18 05			18 14		18a20		18 35		18 44			18a50		19 05		19 14		19a20	
Box Hill & Westhumble	d								18 19													19 19			
Dorking 4	a	17 51				18 13			18 22				18 43		18 51					19 13		19 21			
Dorking	d								18 22																
Holmwood	d								18 29																
Ockley	d								18 33																
Warnham	d								18 39																
Horsham 4	a								18 43																

		SW		TL	TL	TL	SW	SN	SW	TL	TL	TL		SW	SN	SW	TL	TL	TL	SW	SN	SW		TL	TL
London Victoria 15 ⊖	d				18 55			19 11			19 25				19 41			19 55			20 11				20 25
London Waterloo 15 ⊖	d	18 54					19 09		19 24					19 39		19 54				20 09		20 24			
Clapham Junction 10	d	19 03			19 02		19 18	19 18	19 33		19 32			19 48	19 48	20 03		20 02		20 18	20 18	20 33			20 32
Balham 4 ⊖	d							19 23							19 53						20 23				
St Pancras International	d			18 27						18 57							19 27							19 57	
Farringdon	d			18 32						19 02							19 32							20 02	
City Thameslink	d			18 34						19 04							19 34							20 04	
London Blackfriars	d			18 36						19 06							19 36							20 06	
Elephant & Castle	d			18 40						19 10							19 40							20 10	
Loughborough Jn	d			18 45						19 15							19 45							20 15	
Herne Hill	d			18 50						19 20							19 50							20 20	
London Bridge	d					18 55						19 25							19 55						
Tulse Hill	a			18 54						19 24							19 54							20 24	
Tulse Hill 3	d			18 56						19 26							19 56							20 26	
Streatham	d			19 00						19 30							20 00							20 30	
Mitcham Eastfields	d			19 04				19 30		19 34					20 00		20 04				20 30			20 34	
Mitcham Junction	d			19 07				19 33		19 37					20 03		20 07				20 33			20 37	
Hackbridge	d			19 10				19 36		19 40					20 06		20 10				20 36			20 40	
Carshalton	d			19 13	19 19			19 39		19 43	19 49				20 09		20 13	20 19			20 39			20 43	20 49
Sutton	a			19 17	19 23			19 43		19 47	19 53				20 13		20 17	20 23			20 43			20 47	20 53
Norwood Junction	d					19 09						19 39							20 09						
West Croydon	d					19 15						19 45							20 15						
Sutton	a					19 28						19 58							20 28						
Sutton	d				19 24	19 28		19 43			19 54	19 58			20 13			20 24	20 28		20 43				20 54
Cheam	d				19 27	19 31		19 46			19 57	20 01			20 16			20 27	20 31		20 46				20 57
Ewell East	d					19 34		19 49				20 04			20 19				20 34		20 49				
Epsom 3	a	19 27			19 34	19 38	19 42	19 53	19 57		20 04	20 08		20 12	20 23	20 27		20 34	20 38	20 42	20 53	20 57			21 04
Epsom	d	19 28			19 35		19 43		19 58		20 05			20 13				20 35		20 43					21 05
Ashtead	d	19 32			19 40		19 47		20 02		20 10			20 17				20 40		20 47					21 10
Leatherhead	d	19 35			19 44		19a50		20 05		20 14			20a20				20 44		20 50					21 14
Box Hill & Westhumble	d										20 19														21 19
Dorking 4	a	19 43			19 51				20 13		20 21							20 51		20 59					21 21
Dorking	d																								
Holmwood	d																								
Ockley	d																								
Warnham	d																								
Horsham 4	a																								

For faster trains from London and Clapham Junction to Horsham refer to Table T186

Table T180-F

Saturdays

13 October to 8 December

London - Hackbridge, Sutton, Epsom, Leatherhead, Dorking and Horsham

		TL	SW	SN	SW	TL	TL	TL		SW	SN	SW	TL	TL	TL	SW	SN	SW		TL	TL	TL	SW	SN	TL
London Victoria 15 ⊖	d			20 41			20 55				21 11			21 25			21 41				21 55			22 11	
London Waterloo 15 ⊖	d		20 39		20 54					21 09		21 24				21 39		21 54					22 09		
Clapham Junction 10	d		20 48	20 48	21 03		21 02			21 18	21 18	21 33		21 32		21 48	21 48	22 03			22 02		22 18	22 18	
Balham 4 ⊖	d			20 53							21 23						21 53							22 23	
St Pancras International	d					20 27							20 57							21 27					21 57
Farringdon	d					20 32							21 02							21 32					22 02
City Thameslink	d					20 34																			
London Blackfriars	d					20 36							21 06							21 36					22 06
Elephant & Castle	d					20 40							21 10							21 40					22 10
Loughborough Jn	d					20 45							21 15							21 45					22 15
Herne Hill	d					20 50							21 20							21 50					22 20
London Bridge	d	20 25						20 55							21 25							21 55			
Tulse Hill	a					20 54							21 24							21 54					22 24
Tulse Hill 3	d					20 56							21 26							21 56					22 26
Streatham	d					21 00							21 30							22 00					22 30
Mitcham Eastfields	d			21 00		21 04					21 30		21 34				22 00			22 04				22 30	22 34
Mitcham Junction	d			21 03		21 07					21 33		21 37				22 03			22 07				22 33	22 37
Hackbridge	d			21 06		21 10					21 36		21 40				22 06			22 10				22 36	22 40
Carshalton	d			21 09		21 13	21 19				21 39		21 43	21 49			22 09			22 13	22 19			22 39	22 43
Sutton	a			21 13		21 17	21 23				21 43		21 47	21 53			22 13			22 17	22 23			22 43	22 47
Norwood Junction	d	20 39						21 09							21 39							22 09			
West Croydon	d	20 45						21 15							21 45							22 15			
Sutton	a	20 58						21 28							21 58							22 28			
Sutton	d	20 58		21 13			21 24	21 28			21 43			21 54	21 58		22 13				22 24	22 28		22 43	
Cheam	d	21 01		21 16			21 27	21 31			21 46			21 57	22 01		22 16				22 27	22 31		22 46	
Ewell East	d	21 04		21 19				21 34			21 49				22 04		22 19					22 34		22 49	
Epsom 3	a	21 08	21 12	21 23	21 27		21 34	21 38		21 42	21 53	21 57		22 04	22 08	22 12	22 23	22 27			22 34	22 38	22 42	22 53	
Epsom	d		21 13				21 35			21 43				22 05		22 13					22 35		22 43		
Ashtead	d		21 17				21 40			21 47				22 10		22 17					22 40		22 47		
Leatherhead	d		21a20				21 44			21 50				22 14		22a20					22 44		22 50		
Box Hill & Westhumble	d													22 19											
Dorking 4	a						21 51			21 59				22 21							22 51		22 59		
Dorking	d																								
Holmwood	d																								
Ockley	d																								
Warnham	d																								
Horsham 4	a																								

		TL	TL	SW		SN	TL	TL	TL	SW	SN	TL	TL	SW		SN
London Victoria 15 ⊖	d	22 25				22 41		22 55			23 11		23 25			23 45
London Waterloo 15 ⊖	d			22 39						23 09				23 42		
Clapham Junction 10	d	22 33		22 48		22 49		23 02		23 18	23 18		23 32	23 51		23 53
Balham 4 ⊖	d					22 53					23 23					23 57
St Pancras International	d						22 27					22 57				
Farringdon	d						22 32					23 02				
City Thameslink	d															
London Blackfriars	d						22 36					23 06				
Elephant & Castle	d						22 40					23 10				
Loughborough Jn	d						22 45					23 15				
Herne Hill	d						22 50					23 20				
London Bridge	d		22 25						22 55							
Tulse Hill	a						22 54					23 24				
Tulse Hill 3	d						22 56					23 26				
Streatham	d						23 00					23 30				
Mitcham Eastfields	d					23 00	23 04				23 30	23 34				00 04
Mitcham Junction	d					23 03	23 07				23 33	23 37				00 07
Hackbridge	d					23 06	23 10				23 36	23 40				00 10
Carshalton	d	22 49				23 09	23 13	23 19			23 39	23 43	23 52			00 13
Sutton	a	22 53				23 13	23 17	23 23			23 43	23 47	23 58			00 17
Norwood Junction	d		22 39						23 09							
West Croydon	d		22 45						23 15							
Sutton	a		22 58						23 28							
Sutton	d	22 54	22 58			23 13		23 24	23 28		23 43		23 59			00 17
Cheam	d	22 57	23 01			23 16		23 27	23 31		23 46		00 02			00 20
Ewell East	d		23 04			23 19			23 34		23 49					00 23
Epsom 3	a	23 04	23 08	23 12		23 23		23 34	23 38	23 42	23 53		00 07	00 15		00 27
Epsom	d	23 05		23 13				23 35		23 43			00 08	00 19		
Ashtead	d	23 10		23 17				23 40		23 47			00 13	00 23		
Leatherhead	d	23 14		23a20				23 43		23 50			00 16	00a26		
Box Hill & Westhumble	d	23 19											00 21			
Dorking 4	a	23 21						23 51		23 59			00 24			
Dorking	d															
Holmwood	d															
Ockley	d															
Warnham	d															
Horsham 4	a															

For faster trains from London and Clapham Junction to Horsham refer to Table T186

Table T180-F

Sundays

20 May to 30 September

London - Hackbridge, Sutton, Epsom, Leatherhead, Dorking and Horsham

		TL	SW	SN	SW	TL	TL	SW	TL	SW		TL	TL
London Victoria ⊖	d					06 40	07 10		07 40			08 10	
London Waterloo ⊖	d				00 15					08 02			
Clapham Junction	d				00 26	06 47	07 17		07 47	08 11		08 17	
Balham ⊖	d					06 53	07 23		07 53			08 23	
St Pancras International	d												
Farringdon	d												
City Thameslink	d												
London Blackfriars	d												
Elephant & Castle	d												
Loughborough Jn	d												
Herne Hill	d												
London Bridge	d												08 30
Tulse Hill	a												08 43
Tulse Hill	d												08 46
Streatham	d												08 50
Mitcham Eastfields	d			00 04		07 00	07 30		08 00			08 30	08 53
Mitcham Junction	d			00 07		07 03	07 33		08 03			08 33	08 56
Hackbridge	d			00 10		07 06	07 36		08 06			08 36	08 59
Carshalton	d			00 13		07 09	07 39		08 09			08 39	09 02
Sutton	a			00 17		07 12	07 42		08 12			08 42	09 05
Norwood Junction	d												
West Croydon	d												
Sutton	a												
Sutton	d			00 17		07 13	07 43		08 13			08 43	
Cheam	d	00 02		00 20		07 16	07 46		08 16			08 46	
Ewell East	d			00 23		07 19	07 49		08 19			08 49	
Epsom	a	00 07		00 27	00 50	07 23	07 53		08 23	08 36		08 53	
Epsom	d	00 08	00 19			07 23	07 53	08 08	08 23	08 38		08 53	
Ashtead	d	00 13	00 23			07 28	07 58	08 12	08 28	08 42		08 58	
Leatherhead	d	00 16	00a26			07 32	08 02	08a15	08 32	08 45		09 02	
Box Hill & Westhumble	d	00 21				07 37	08 07		08 37	08 50		09 07	
Dorking	a	00 24				07 39	08 09		08 39	08 52		09 09	
Dorking	d												
Holmwood	d												
Ockley	d												
Warnham	d												
Horsham	a												

		SW	TL	SN	TL	SW	TL	SN		TL	SW	TL	SN
London Victoria ⊖	d		08 42	08 52			09 12	09 22				09 42	09 52
London Waterloo ⊖	d	08 33				09 02					09 32		
Clapham Junction	d	08 41	08 50	08 58		09 11	09 20	09 28			09 41	09 50	09 58
Balham ⊖	d			09 03				09 33					10 03
St Pancras International	d												
Farringdon	d												
City Thameslink	d												
London Blackfriars	d									09 30			
Elephant & Castle	d									09 34			
Loughborough Jn	d									09 39			
Herne Hill	d									09 44			
London Bridge	d				09 00								
Tulse Hill	a				09 13					09 48			
Tulse Hill	d				09 16					09 48			
Streatham	d				09 20					09 52			
Mitcham Eastfields	d			09 10	09 23			09 40		09 55			10 10
Mitcham Junction	d			09 13	09 26			09 43		09 58			10 13
Hackbridge	d			09 16	09 29			09 46		10 01			10 16
Carshalton	d		09 09	09 19	09 32		09 39	09 49		10 04		10 09	10 19
Sutton	a		09 12	09 23	09 35		09 42	09 53		10 07		10 12	10 23
Norwood Junction	d												
West Croydon	d												
Sutton	a												
Sutton	d		09 13	09 24			09 43	09 54				10 13	10 24
Cheam	d		09 16	09 27			09 46	09 57				10 16	10 27
Ewell East	d		09 19	09 30			09 49	10 00				10 19	10 30
Epsom	a	09 07	09 23	09 34		09 36	09 53	10 04			10 06	10 23	10 34
Epsom	d	09 08	09 23			09 38	09 53				10 08	10 23	
Ashtead	d	09 12	09 28			09 42	09 58				10 12	10 28	
Leatherhead	d	09a15	09 32			09 45	10 02				10a15	10 32	
Box Hill & Westhumble	d		09 37			09 50	10 07					10 37	
Dorking	a		09 39			09 55	10 09					10 39	
Dorking	d												
Holmwood	d												
Ockley	d												
Warnham	d												
Horsham	a												

		TL	SW	TL	SN	TL		SW	TL	SN	TL	SW	TL
London Victoria ⊖	d			10 12	10 22				10 42	10 52			11 12
London Waterloo ⊖	d		10 02					10 32				11 02	
Clapham Junction	d		10 11	10 20	10 28			10 41	10 50	10 58		11 12	11 20
Balham ⊖	d				10 33					11 03			
St Pancras International	d												
Farringdon	d												
City Thameslink	d												
London Blackfriars	d	10 00				10 30					11 00		
Elephant & Castle	d	10 04				10 34					11 04		
Loughborough Jn	d	10 09				10 39					11 09		
Herne Hill	d	10 14				10 44					11 14		
London Bridge	d												
Tulse Hill	a	10 18				10 48					11 18		
Tulse Hill	d	10 18				10 48					11 18		
Streatham	d	10 22				10 52					11 22		
Mitcham Eastfields	d	10 25			10 40	10 55				11 10	11 25		
Mitcham Junction	d	10 28			10 43	10 58				11 13	11 28		
Hackbridge	d	10 31			10 46	11 01				11 16	11 31		
Carshalton	d	10 34		10 39	10 49	11 04			11 09	11 19	11 34		11 39
Sutton	a	10 37		10 42	10 53	11 07			11 12	11 23	11 37		11 42
Norwood Junction	d												
West Croydon	d												
Sutton	a												
Sutton	d			10 43	10 54				11 13	11 24			11 43
Cheam	d			10 46	10 57				11 16	11 27			11 46
Ewell East	d			10 49	11 00				11 19	11 30			11 49
Epsom	a		10 36	10 53	11 04			11 06	11 23	11 34		11 37	11 53
Epsom	d		10 38	10 53				11 08	11 23			11 38	11 53
Ashtead	d		10 42	10 58				11 12	11 28			11 42	11 58
Leatherhead	d		10 45	11 02				11a15	11 32			11 45	12 02
Box Hill & Westhumble	d		10 50	11 07					11 37			11 50	12 07
Dorking	a		10 52	11 09					11 39			11 52	12 09
Dorking	d												
Holmwood	d												
Ockley	d												
Warnham	d												
Horsham	a												

		SN	TL	SW		TL	SN	TL	SW	TL	SN	SW	TL
London Victoria ⊖	d	11 22				11 42	11 52			12 12	12 22		
London Waterloo ⊖	d			11 32					12 02			12 32	
Clapham Junction	d	11 28		11 42		11 50	11 58		12 11	12 20	12 28	12 42	
Balham ⊖	d	11 33					12 03				12 33		
St Pancras International	d												12 21
Farringdon	d												12 25
City Thameslink	d												
London Blackfriars	d		11 30					12 00					12 30
Elephant & Castle	d		11 34					12 04					12 34
Loughborough Jn	d		11 39					12 09					12 39
Herne Hill	d		11 44					12 14					12 44
London Bridge	d												
Tulse Hill	a		11 48					12 18					12 48
Tulse Hill	d		11 48					12 18					12 48
Streatham	d		11 52					12 22					12 52
Mitcham Eastfields	d	11 40	11 55				12 10	12 25			12 40		12 55
Mitcham Junction	d	11 43	11 58				12 13	12 28			12 43		12 58
Hackbridge	d	11 46	12 01				12 16	12 31			12 46		13 01
Carshalton	d	11 49	12 04			12 09	12 19	12 34		12 39	12 49		13 04
Sutton	a	11 53	12 07			12 12	12 23	12 37		12 42	12 53		13 07
Norwood Junction	d												
West Croydon	d												
Sutton	a												
Sutton	d	11 54				12 13	12 24			12 43	12 54		
Cheam	d	11 57				12 16	12 27			12 46	12 57		
Ewell East	d	12 00				12 19	12 30			12 49	13 00		
Epsom	a	12 04		12 06		12 23	12 34		12 37	12 53	13 04	13 06	
Epsom	d			12 08		12 23			12 38	12 53		13 08	
Ashtead	d			12 12		12 28			12 42	12 58		13 12	
Leatherhead	d			12a15		12 32			12 45	13 02		13a15	
Box Hill & Westhumble	d					12 37			12 50	13 07			
Dorking	a					12 39			12 52	13 09			
Dorking	d												
Holmwood	d												
Ockley	d												
Warnham	d												
Horsham	a												

For faster trains from London and Clapham Junction to Horsham refer to Table T186

Table T180-F

Sundays

20 May to 30 September

London - Hackbridge, Sutton, Epsom, Leatherhead, Dorking and Horsham

		TL		SN	SW	TL	TL	SN	SW	TL	TL	SN	
London Victoria ⊖	d	12 42		12 52			13 12	13 22			13 42	13 52	
London Waterloo ⊖	d				13 02				13 32				
Clapham Junction	d	12 50		12 58	13 11		13 20	13 28	13 41		13 50	13 58	
Balham ⊖	d			13 03				13 33				14 03	
St Pancras International	d					12 51				13 21			
Farringdon	d					12 55				13 25			
City Thameslink	d												
London Blackfriars	d					13 00				13 30			
Elephant & Castle	d					13 04				13 34			
Loughborough Jn	d					13 09				13 39			
Herne Hill	d					13 14				13 44			
London Bridge	d												
Tulse Hill	a					13 18				13 48			
Tulse Hill	d					13 18				13 48			
Streatham	d					13 22				13 52			
Mitcham Eastfields	d			13 10		13 25		13 40		13 55		14 10	
Mitcham Junction	d			13 13		13 28		13 43		13 58		14 13	
Hackbridge	d			13 16		13 31		13 46		14 01		14 16	
Carshalton	d	13 09		13 19		13 34	13 39	13 49		14 04	14 09	14 19	
Sutton	a	13 12		13 23		13 37	13 42	13 53		14 07	14 12	14 23	
Norwood Junction	d												
West Croydon	d												
Sutton	a												
Sutton	d	13 13		13 24			13 43	13 54			14 13	14 24	
Cheam	d	13 16		13 27			13 46	13 57			14 16	14 27	
Ewell East	d	13 19		13 30			13 49	14 00			14 19	14 30	
Epsom	a	13 23		13 34	13 36		13 53	14 04	14 06		14 23	14 34	
Epsom	d	13 23			13 38		13 53		14 08		14 23		
Ashtead	d	13 28			13 42		13 58		14 12		14 28		
Leatherhead	d	13 32			13 45		14 02		14a15		14 32		
Box Hill & Westhumble	d	13 37			13 50		14 07				14 37		
Dorking	a	13 39			13 52		14 09				14 39		
Dorking	d												
Holmwood	d												
Ockley	d												
Warnham	d												
Horsham	a												

		SW	TL	TL	SN	SW	TL	TL	SN	SW			
London Victoria ⊖	d			14 12	14 22			14 42	14 52				
London Waterloo ⊖	d	14 02				14 32				15 02			
Clapham Junction	d	14 11		14 20	14 28	14 41		14 50	14 58	15 11			
Balham ⊖	d				14 33				15 03				
St Pancras International	d		13 51				14 21						
Farringdon	d		13 55				14 25						
City Thameslink	d												
London Blackfriars	d		14 00				14 30						
Elephant & Castle	d		14 04				14 34						
Loughborough Jn	d		14 09				14 39						
Herne Hill	d		14 14				14 44						
London Bridge	d												
Tulse Hill	a		14 18				14 48						
Tulse Hill	d		14 18				14 48						
Streatham	d		14 22				14 52						
Mitcham Eastfields	d		14 25		14 40		14 55		15 10				
Mitcham Junction	d		14 28		14 43		14 58		15 13				
Hackbridge	d		14 31		14 46		15 01		15 16				
Carshalton	d		14 34	14 39	14 49		15 04	15 09	15 19				
Sutton	a		14 37	14 42	14 53		15 07	15 12	15 23				
Norwood Junction	d												
West Croydon	d												
Sutton	a												
Sutton	d			14 43	14 54			15 13	15 24				
Cheam	d			14 46	14 57			15 16	15 27				
Ewell East	d			14 49	15 00			15 19	15 30				
Epsom	a	14 36		14 53	15 04	15 06		15 23	15 34	15 36			
Epsom	d	14 38		14 53		15 08		15 23		15 38			
Ashtead	d	14 42		14 58		15 12		15 28		15 42			
Leatherhead	d	14 45		15 02		15a15		15 32		15 45			
Box Hill & Westhumble	d	14 50		15 07				15 37		15 50			
Dorking	a	14 52		15 09				15 39		15 52			
Dorking	d												
Holmwood	d												
Ockley	d												
Warnham	d												
Horsham	a												

		TL	TL	SN	SW	TL	TL	SN	SW	
London Victoria ⊖	d		15 12	15 22			15 42	15 52		
London Waterloo ⊖	d				15 32				16 02	
Clapham Junction	d		15 20	15 28	15 41		15 50	15 58	16 11	
Balham ⊖	d			15 33				16 03		
St Pancras International	d	14 51				15 21				
Farringdon	d	14 55				15 25				
City Thameslink	d									
London Blackfriars	d	15 00				15 30				
Elephant & Castle	d	15 04				15 34				
Loughborough Jn	d	15 09				15 39				
Herne Hill	d	15 14				15 44				
London Bridge	d									
Tulse Hill	a	15 18				15 48				
Tulse Hill	d	15 18				15 48				
Streatham	d	15 22				15 52				
Mitcham Eastfields	d	15 25		15 40		15 55		16 10		and at the same minutes past each hour until
Mitcham Junction	d	15 28		15 43		15 58		16 13		
Hackbridge	d	15 31		15 46		16 01		16 16		
Carshalton	d	15 34	15 39	15 49		16 04	16 09	16 19		
Sutton	a	15 37	15 42	15 53		16 07	16 12	16 23		
Norwood Junction	d									
West Croydon	d									
Sutton	a									
Sutton	d		15 43	15 54			16 13	16 24		
Cheam	d		15 46	15 57			16 16	16 27		
Ewell East	d		15 49	16 00			16 19	16 30		
Epsom	a		15 53	16 04	16 06		16 23	16 34	16 36	
Epsom	d		15 53		16 08		16 23		16 38	
Ashtead	d		15 58		16 12		16 28		16 42	
Leatherhead	d		16 02		16a15		16 32		16 45	
Box Hill & Westhumble	d		16 07				16 37			
Dorking	a		16 09				16 39		16 52	
Dorking	d									
Holmwood	d									
Ockley	d									
Warnham	d									
Horsham	a									

		TL	TL	SN	SW	TL	TL	SN	SW		TL	SN	SW	TL	SN
London Victoria ⊖	d		21 12	21 22			21 42	21 52			22 12	22 22		22 42	22 52
London Waterloo ⊖	d				21 32				22 02				22 32		
Clapham Junction	d		21 20	21 28	21 41		21 50	21 58	22 11		22 20	22 28	22 41	22 50	22 58
Balham ⊖	d			21 33				22 03				22 33			23 03
St Pancras International	d	20 51				21 21									
Farringdon	d	20 55				21 25									
City Thameslink	d														
London Blackfriars	d	21 00				21 30									
Elephant & Castle	d	21 04				21 34									
Loughborough Jn	d	21 09				21 39									
Herne Hill	d	21 14				21 44									
London Bridge	d														
Tulse Hill	a	21 18				21 48									
Tulse Hill	d	21 18				21 48									
Streatham	d	21 22				21 52									
Mitcham Eastfields	d	21 25		21 40		21 55		22 10				22 40			23 10
Mitcham Junction	d	21 28		21 43		21 58		22 13				22 43			23 13
Hackbridge	d	21 31		21 46		22 01		22 16				22 46			23 16
Carshalton	d	21 34	21 39	21 49		22 04	22 09	22 19			22 39	22 49		23 09	23 19
Sutton	a	21 37	21 42	21 53		22 07	22 12	22 23			22 42	22 53		23 12	23 23
Norwood Junction	d														
West Croydon	d														
Sutton	a														
Sutton	d		21 43	21 54			22 13	22 24			22 43	22 54		23 13	23 24
Cheam	d		21 46	21 57			22 16	22 27			22 46	22 57		23 16	23 27
Ewell East	d		21 49	22 00			22 19	22 30			22 49	23 00		23 19	23 30
Epsom	a		21 53	22 04	22 06		22 23	22 34	22 36		22 53	23 04	23 06	23 23	23 34
Epsom	d		21 53		22 08		22 23		22 38		22 53		23 08	23 23	
Ashtead	d		21 58		22 12		22 28		22 42		22 58		23 12	23 28	
Leatherhead	d		22 02		22a15		22 32		22 45		23 02		23a15	23 32	
Box Hill & Westhumble	d		22 07				22 37				23 07			23 37	
Dorking	a		22 09				22 39		22 52		23 09			23 39	
Dorking	d														
Holmwood	d														
Ockley	d														
Warnham	d														
Horsham	a														

For faster trains from London and Clapham Junction to Horsham refer to Table T186

Table T180-F

Sundays

20 May to 30 September

London - Hackbridge, Sutton, Epsom, Leatherhead, Dorking and Horsham

Station		SW	TL	SN	SW
London Victoria ⊖	d		23 12	23 22	
London Waterloo ⊖	d	23 02			23 32
Clapham Junction	d	23 11	23 20	23 29	23 41
Balham ⊖	d			23 35	
St Pancras International	d				
Farringdon	d				
City Thameslink	d				
London Blackfriars	d				
Elephant & Castle	d				
Loughborough Jn	d				
Herne Hill	d				
London Bridge	d				
Tulse Hill	a				
Tulse Hill	d				
Streatham	d				
Mitcham Eastfields	d			23 41	
Mitcham Junction	d			23 44	
Hackbridge	d			23 47	
Carshalton	d		23 39	23 50	
Sutton	a		23 42	23 54	
Norwood Junction	d				
West Croydon	d				
Sutton	a				
Sutton	d		23 43	23 54	
Cheam	d		23 46	23 57	
Ewell East	d		23 49	00 01	
Epsom	a	23 36	23 53	00 05	00 06
Epsom	d		23 53		
Ashtead	d		23 58		
Leatherhead	d		00 02		
Box Hill & Westhumble	d		00 07		
Dorking	a		00 09		
Dorking	d				
Holmwood	d				
Ockley	d				
Warnham	d				
Horsham	a				

Sundays

7 October to 2 December

Station		TL	SW	SN	SW	TL	TL	SW	TL	SW	TL	TL	SW	TL	SN	TL	SW	TL	SN	TL	SW	TL	SN
London Victoria ⊖	d					06 40	07 10		07 40		08 10			08 42	08 52			09 12	09 22			09 42	09 52
London Waterloo ⊖	d				00 15					08 02			08 33				09 02				09 32		
Clapham Junction	d				00 26	06 47	07 17		07 47	08 11	08 17		08 41	08 50	08 58		09 11	09 20	09 28		09 41	09 50	09 58
Balham ⊖	d					06 53	07 23		07 53		08 23				09 03				09 33				10 03
St Pancras International	d																						
Farringdon	d																						
City Thameslink	d																						
London Blackfriars	d																			09 30			
Elephant & Castle	d																			09 34			
Loughborough Jn	d																			09 39			
Herne Hill	d																			09 44			
London Bridge	d											08 30				09 00							
Tulse Hill	a											08 43				09 13				09 48			
Tulse Hill	d											08 46				09 16				09 48			
Streatham	d											08 50				09 20				09 52			
Mitcham Eastfields	d			00 04		07 00	07 30		08 00		08 30	08 53			09 10	09 23			09 40	09 55			10 10
Mitcham Junction	d			00 07		07 03	07 33		08 03		08 33	08 56			09 13	09 26			09 43	09 58			10 13
Hackbridge	d			00 10		07 06	07 36		08 06		08 36	08 59			09 16	09 29			09 46	10 01			10 16
Carshalton	d			00 13		07 09	07 39		08 09		08 39	09 02		09 09	09 19	09 32		09 39	09 49	10 04		10 09	10 19
Sutton	a			00 17		07 12	07 42		08 12		08 42	09 05		09 12	09 23	09 35		09 42	09 53	10 07		10 12	10 23
Norwood Junction	d																						
West Croydon	d																						
Sutton	a																						
Sutton	d			00 17		07 13	07 43		08 13		08 43			09 13	09 24			09 43	09 54			10 13	10 24
Cheam	d	00 02		00 20		07 16	07 46		08 16		08 46			09 16	09 27			09 46	09 57			10 16	10 27
Ewell East	d			00 23		07 19	07 49		08 19		08 49			09 19	09 30			09 49	10 00			10 19	10 30
Epsom	a	00 07		00 27	00 50	07 23	07 53		08 23	08 36	08 53		09 07	09 23	09 34		09 36	09 53	10 04		10 06	10 23	10 34
Epsom	d	00 08	00 19			07 23	07 53	08 08	08 23	08 38	08 53		09 08	09 23			09 38	09 53			10 08	10 23	
Ashtead	d	00 13	00 23			07 28	07 58	08 12	08 28	08 42	08 58		09 12	09 28			09 42	09 58			10 12	10 28	
Leatherhead	d	00 16	00a26			07 32	08 02	08a15	08 32	08 45	09 02		09a15	09 32			09 45	10 02			10a15	10 32	
Box Hill & Westhumble	d	00 21				07 37	08 07		08 37	08 50	09 07			09 37			09 50	10 07				10 37	
Dorking	a	00 24				07 39	08 09		08 39	08 54	09 09			09 39			09 54	10 09				10 39	
Dorking	d																						
Holmwood	d																						
Ockley	d																						
Warnham	d																						
Horsham	a																						

For faster trains from London and Clapham Junction to Horsham refer to Table T186

Table T180-F

Sundays

7 October to 2 December

London - Hackbridge, Sutton, Epsom, Leatherhead, Dorking and Horsham

Station		TL	SW	TL	SN	TL	SW	TL	SN	TL	SW	TL	SN	TL	SW	TL	SN	TL	SW	TL	SN	SW	TL
London Victoria ⊖	d			10 12	10 22			10 42	10 52			11 12	11 22			11 42	11 52			12 12	12 22		
London Waterloo ⊖	d		10 02				10 32				11 02				11 32				12 02			12 32	
Clapham Junction	d		10 11	10 20	10 28		10 41	10 50	10 58		11 12	11 20	11 28		11 42	11 50	11 58		12 11	12 20	12 28	12 42	
Balham ⊖	d				10 33				11 03				11 33				12 03				12 33		
St Pancras International	d																						12 21
Farringdon	d																						12 25
City Thameslink	d																						
London Blackfriars	d	10 00				10 30				11 00				11 30				12 00					12 30
Elephant & Castle	d	10 04				10 34				11 04				11 34				12 04					12 34
Loughborough Jn	d	10 09				10 39				11 09				11 39				12 09					12 39
Herne Hill	d	10 14				10 44				11 14				11 44				12 14					12 44
London Bridge	d																						
Tulse Hill	a	10 18				10 48				11 18				11 48				12 18					12 48
Tulse Hill	d	10 18				10 48				11 18				11 48				12 18					12 48
Streatham	d	10 22				10 52				11 22				11 52				12 22					12 52
Mitcham Eastfields	d	10 25			10 40	10 55			11 10	11 25			11 40	11 55			12 10	12 25			12 40		12 55
Mitcham Junction	d	10 28			10 43	10 58			11 13	11 28			11 43	11 58			12 13	12 28			12 43		12 58
Hackbridge	d	10 31			10 46	11 01			11 16	11 31			11 46	12 01			12 16	12 31			12 46		13 01
Carshalton	d	10 34		10 39	10 49	11 04		11 09	11 19	11 34		11 39	11 49	12 04		12 09	12 19	12 34		12 39	12 49		13 04
Sutton	a	10 37		10 42	10 53	11 07		11 12	11 23	11 37		11 42	11 53	12 07		12 12	12 23	12 37		12 42	12 53		13 07
Norwood Junction	d																						
West Croydon	d																						
Sutton	a																						
Sutton	d			10 43	10 54			11 13	11 24			11 43	11 54			12 13	12 24			12 43	12 54		
Cheam	d			10 46	10 57			11 16	11 27			11 46	11 57			12 16	12 27			12 46	12 57		
Ewell East	d			10 49	11 00			11 19	11 30			11 49	12 00			12 19	12 30			12 49	13 00		
Epsom	a		10 36	10 53	11 04		11 06	11 23	11 34		11 37	11 53	12 04		12 06	12 23	12 34		12 37	12 53	13 04	13 06	
Epsom	d		10 38	10 53			11 08	11 23			11 38	11 53			12 08	12 23			12 38	12 53		13 08	
Ashtead	d		10 42	10 58			11 12	11 28			11 42	11 58			12 12	12 28			12 42	12 58		13 12	
Leatherhead	d		10 45	11 02			11a15	11 32			11 45	12 02			12a15	12 32			12 45	13 02		13a15	
Box Hill & Westhumble	d		10 50	11 07				11 37			11 50	12 07				12 37			12 50	13 07			
Dorking	a		10 54	11 09				11 39			11 54	12 09				12 39			12 54	13 09			
Dorking	d																						
Holmwood	d																						
Ockley	d																						
Warnham	d																						
Horsham	a																						

Station		TL	SN	SW	TL	TL	SN	SW	TL	TL	SN	SW	TL	TL	SN	SW	TL	TL	SN	SW
London Victoria ⊖	d	12 42	12 52			13 12	13 22			13 42	13 52			14 12	14 22			14 42	14 52	
London Waterloo ⊖	d			13 02				13 32				14 02				14 32				15 02
Clapham Junction	d	12 50	12 58	13 11		13 20	13 28	13 41		13 50	13 58	14 11		14 20	14 28	14 41		14 50	14 58	15 11
Balham ⊖	d		13 03				13 33				14 03				14 33				15 03	
St Pancras International	d				12 51				13 21				13 51				14 21			
Farringdon	d				12 55				13 25				13 55				14 25			
City Thameslink	d																			
London Blackfriars	d				13 00				13 30				14 00				14 30			
Elephant & Castle	d				13 04				13 34				14 04				14 34			
Loughborough Jn	d				13 09				13 39				14 09				14 39			
Herne Hill	d				13 14				13 44				14 14				14 44			
London Bridge	d																			
Tulse Hill	a				13 18				13 48				14 18				14 48			
Tulse Hill	d				13 18				13 48				14 18				14 48			
Streatham	d				13 22				13 52				14 22				14 52			
Mitcham Eastfields	d		13 10		13 25		13 40		13 55		14 10		14 25		14 40		14 55		15 10	
Mitcham Junction	d		13 13		13 28		13 43		13 58		14 13		14 28		14 43		14 58		15 13	
Hackbridge	d		13 16		13 31		13 46		14 01		14 16		14 31		14 46		15 01		15 16	
Carshalton	d	13 09	13 19		13 34	13 39	13 49		14 04	14 09	14 19		14 34	14 39	14 49		15 04	15 09	15 19	
Sutton	a	13 12	13 23		13 37	13 42	13 53		14 07	14 12	14 23		14 37	14 42	14 53		15 07	15 12	15 23	
Norwood Junction	d																			
West Croydon	d																			
Sutton	a																			
Sutton	d	13 13	13 24			13 43	13 54			14 13	14 24			14 43	14 54			15 13	15 24	
Cheam	d	13 16	13 27			13 46	13 57			14 16	14 27			14 46	14 57			15 16	15 27	
Ewell East	d	13 19	13 30			13 49	14 00			14 19	14 30			14 49	15 00			15 19	15 30	
Epsom	a	13 23	13 34	13 36		13 53	14 04	14 06		14 23	14 34	14 36		14 53	15 04	15 06		15 23	15 34	15 36
Epsom	d	13 23		13 38		13 53		14 08		14 23		14 38		14 53		15 08		15 23		15 38
Ashtead	d	13 28		13 42		13 58		14 12		14 28		14 42		14 58		15 12		15 28		15 42
Leatherhead	d	13 32		13 45		14 02		14a15		14 32		14 45		15 02		15a15		15 32		15 45
Box Hill & Westhumble	d	13 37		13 50		14 07				14 37		14 50		15 07				15 37		15 50
Dorking	a	13 39		13 54		14 09				14 39		14 54		15 09				15 39		15 54
Dorking	d																			
Holmwood	d																			
Ockley	d																			
Warnham	d																			
Horsham	a																			

For faster trains from London and Clapham Junction to Horsham refer to Table T186

Please note, Network Rail have stated that further updates to this timetable are possible during the validity period.

Table T180-F

Sundays

7 October to 2 December

London - Hackbridge, Sutton, Epsom, Leatherhead, Dorking and Horsham

		TL	TL	SN	SW	TL	TL	SN	SW		TL	TL	SN	SW	TL	TL	SN	SW	TL	SN	SW	TL	SN
London Victoria 15 ⊖	d		15 12	15 22			15 42	15 52				21 12	21 22			21 42	21 52		22 12	22 22		22 42	22 52
London Waterloo 15 ⊖	d				15 32				16 02					21 32				22 02			22 32		
Clapham Junction 10	d		15 20	15 28	15 41		15 50	15 58	16 11			21 20	21 28	21 41		21 50	21 58	22 11	22 20	22 28	22 41	22 50	22 58
Balham 4 ⊖	d			15 33				16 03					21 33				22 03			22 33			23 03
St Pancras International	d	14 51				15 21					20 51				21 21								
Farringdon	d	14 55				15 25					20 55				21 25								
City Thameslink	d																						
London Blackfriars	d	15 00				15 30					21 00				21 30								
Elephant & Castle	d	15 04				15 34					21 04				21 34								
Loughborough Jn	d	15 09				15 39					21 09				21 39								
Herne Hill	d	15 14				15 44					21 14				21 44								
London Bridge	d																						
Tulse Hill	a	15 18				15 48					21 18				21 48								
Tulse Hill 3	d	15 18				15 48					21 18				21 48								
Streatham	d	15 22				15 52				and at	21 22				21 52								
Mitcham Eastfields	d	15 25		15 40		15 55		16 10		the same	21 25		21 40		21 55		22 10			22 40			23 10
Mitcham Junction	d	15 28		15 43		15 58		16 13		minutes	21 28		21 43		21 58		22 13			22 43			23 13
Hackbridge	d	15 31		15 46		16 01		16 16		past	21 31		21 46		22 01		22 16			22 46			23 16
Carshalton	d	15 34	15 39	15 49		16 04	16 09	16 19		each	21 34	21 39	21 49		22 04	22 09	22 19		22 39	22 49		23 09	23 19
Sutton	a	15 37	15 42	15 53		16 07	16 12	16 23		hour until	21 37	21 42	21 53		22 07	22 12	22 23		22 42	22 53		23 12	23 23
Norwood Junction	d																						
West Croydon	d																						
Sutton	a																						
Sutton	d		15 43	15 54			16 13	16 24				21 43	21 54			22 13	22 24		22 43	22 54		23 13	23 24
Cheam	d		15 46	15 57			16 16	16 27				21 46	21 57			22 16	22 27		22 46	22 57		23 16	23 27
Ewell East	d		15 49	16 00			16 19	16 30				21 49	22 00			22 19	22 30		22 49	23 00		23 19	23 30
Epsom 3	a		15 53	16 04	16 06		16 23	16 34	16 36			21 53	22 04	22 06		22 23	22 34	22 36	22 53	23 04	23 06	23 23	23 34
Epsom	d		15 53		16 08		16 23		16 38			21 53		22 08		22 23		22 38	22 53		23 08	23 23	
Ashtead	d		15 58		16 12		16 28		16 42			21 58		22 12		22 28		22 42	22 58		23 12	23 28	
Leatherhead	d		16 02		16a15		16 32		16 45			22 02		22a15		22 32		22 45	23 02		23a15	23 32	
Box Hill & Westhumble	d		16 07				16 37					22 07				22 37			23 07			23 37	
Dorking 4	a		16 09				16 39		16 54			22 09				22 39		22 54	23 09			23 39	
Dorking	d																						
Holmwood	d																						
Ockley	d																						
Warnham	d																						
Horsham 4	a																						

		SW	TL	SN	SW
London Victoria 15 ⊖	d		23 12	23 22	
London Waterloo 15 ⊖	d	23 02			23 32
Clapham Junction 10	d	23 11	23 20	23 29	23 41
Balham 4 ⊖	d			23 35	
St Pancras International	d				
Farringdon	d				
City Thameslink	d				
London Blackfriars	d				
Elephant & Castle	d				
Loughborough Jn	d				
Herne Hill	d				
London Bridge	d				
Tulse Hill	a				
Tulse Hill 3	d				
Streatham	d				
Mitcham Eastfields	d			23 41	
Mitcham Junction	d			23 44	
Hackbridge	d			23 47	
Carshalton	d		23 39	23 50	
Sutton	a		23 42	23 54	
Norwood Junction	d				
West Croydon	d				
Sutton	a				
Sutton	d		23 43	23 54	
Cheam	d		23 46	23 57	
Ewell East	d		23 49	00 01	
Epsom 3	a	23 36	23 53	00 05	00 06
Epsom	d		23 53		
Ashtead	d		23 58		
Leatherhead	d		00 02		
Box Hill & Westhumble	d		00 07		
Dorking 4	a		00 09		
Dorking	d				
Holmwood	d				
Ockley	d				
Warnham	d				
Horsham 4	a				

For faster trains from London and Clapham Junction to Horsham refer to Table T186

Table T180-R

Mondays to Fridays

21 May to 7 December

Horsham and Dorking, Leatherhead, Epsom, Sutton, Hackbridge - London

		TL	SW	TL	TL	TL	SN	SW	TL	TL		SW	TL	SN	SN	SW	TL	SW	TL	TL		SN	SN	SW	TL
Horsham 4	d												05 44							06 14					
Warnham	d												05 48							06 18					
Ockley	d												05 54							06 24					
Holmwood	d												05 58							06 28					
Dorking 4	a												06 06							06 36					
Dorking	d					05 37		05 47					06 07				06 27	06 30		06 37					
Box Hill & Westhumble	d					05 40		05 50					06 10					06 33		06 40					
Leatherhead	d		05 23			05 44		05 56					06 14			06 23	06 34	06 38		06 44				06 54	07 05
Ashtead	d		05 27			05 48		05 59					06 18			06 27	06 38	06 42		06 48				06 57	07 09
Epsom 3	a		05 31			05 53		06 04					06 23			06 31	06 43	06 46		06 53				07 02	07 13
Epsom	d	05 31	05 33	05 45		05 53	06 01	06 04	06 15			06 18	06 23		06 31	06 33	06 45	06 47		06 53			07 00	07 03	07 15
Ewell East	d	05 35		05 49			06 05		06 19						06 35		06 49						07 05		07 19
Cheam	d	05 38		05 52		05 59	06 08		06 22				06 29		06 38		06 52			06 59			07 08		07 22
Sutton	a	05 41		05 55		06 01	06 11		06 25				06 31		06 41		06 55			07 01			07 11		07 25
Sutton	d	05 42		05 56					06 26								06 56								07 26
West Croydon	a	05 55		06 09					06 39								07 09								07 39
Norwood Junction	a	06 02		06 15					06 45								07 15								07 45
Sutton	d				05 46	06 02	06 12			06 16			06 32	06 36	06 42				06 46	07 02		07 06	07 12		
Carshalton	d				05 49	06 05	06 15			06 19			06 35	06 39	06 45				06 49	07 05		07 09	07 15		
Hackbridge	d				05 52		06 18			06 22				06 42	06 48				06 52			07 12	07 18		
Mitcham Junction	d				05 55		06 21			06 25				06 45	06 51				06 55			07 15	07 21		
Mitcham Eastfields	a				05 58		06 24			06 28				06 48	06 54				06 58			07 18	07 24		
Streatham	d				06 03					06 33				06 53					07 03			07 23			
Tulse Hill 3	a				06 07					06 37				06 56					07 07			07 26			
Tulse Hill	d				06 08					06 38				06 57					07 08			07 27			
London Bridge	a	06 31		06 28					06 58					07 15			07 28					07 45			07 58
Herne Hill	a				06 11					06 41									07 11						
Loughborough Jn	a				06 15					06 45									07 15						
Elephant & Castle	a				06 19					06 49									07 19						
London Blackfriars	a				06 24					06 54									07 24						
City Thameslink	a				06 26					06 56									07 26						
Farringdon	a				06 28					06 58									07 28						
St Pancras International	a				06 33					07 03									07 33						
Balham 4 ⊖	a						06 33								07 03								07 32		
Clapham Junction 10	a		06 01			06 23	06 37	06 30				06 45	06 53		07 07	07 00		07 15		07 23			07 37	07 29	
London Waterloo 15 ⊖	a		06 11					06 40				06 56				07 12		07 27						07 41	
London Victoria 15 ⊖	a					06 32	06 45						07 02		07 15					07 32			07 46		

		SW	TL	SW	TL	SN		SN	SW	TL	SW	TL	SW	TL	SN	SN		SW	TL	SW	TL	SW	TL	SN	SN
Horsham 4	d				06 45									07 13											
Warnham	d				06 49									07 18											
Ockley	d				06 55									07 24											
Holmwood	d				06 59									07 28											
Dorking 4	a				07 06									07 36											
Dorking	d	07 01			07 07						07 32			07 37					07 56	08 00			08 07		
Box Hill & Westhumble	d	07 04			07 10						07 35			07 40						08 03					
Leatherhead	d	07 09			07 14				07 24	07 35	07 40			07 44				07 55	08 02	08 08			08 13		
Ashtead	d	07 13			07 18				07 27	07 39	07 43			07 48				07 58	08 06	08 12			08 17		
Epsom 3	a	07 17			07 23				07 32	07 44	07 48			07 53				08 03	08 11	08 16			08 23		
Epsom	d	07 18		07 22	07 23			07 30	07 34	07 45	07 48		07 52	07 53		08 01		08 04	08 15	08 17		08 22	08 23		08 31
Ewell East	d							07 35		07 49						08 05			08 19						08 35
Cheam	d				07 29			07 38		07 52				07 59		08 08			08 22				08 29		08 38
Sutton	a				07 31			07 41		07 55				08 01		08 11			08 25				08 31		08 41
Sutton	d									07 56									08 26						
West Croydon	a									08 09									08 39						
Norwood Junction	a									08 15									08 45						
Sutton	d		07 16		07 32	07 36		07 42				07 46		08 02	08 06	08 12					08 16		08 32	08 36	08 42
Carshalton	d		07 19		07 35	07 39		07 45				07 49		08 05	08 09	08 15					08 19		08 35	08 39	08 45
Hackbridge	d		07 22		07 38	07 42		07 48				07 52		08 08	08 12	08 18					08 22		08 38	08 42	08 48
Mitcham Junction	d		07 25		07 42	07 45		07 51				07 55		08 12	08 15	08 21					08 25		08 42	08 45	08 51
Mitcham Eastfields	a		07 28		07 45	07 48		07 54				07 58		08 15	08 18	08 24					08 28		08 45	08 48	08 54
Streatham	d		07 33			07 53						08 03			08 23						08 33			08 53	
Tulse Hill 3	a		07 37			07 56						08 07			08 26						08 37			08 56	
Tulse Hill	d		07 38			07 57						08 08			08 27						08 38			08 57	
London Bridge	a					08 15				08 28					08 47				08 58					09 17	
Herne Hill	a		07 41									08 11									08 41				
Loughborough Jn	a		07 45									08 15									08 45				
Elephant & Castle	a		07 49									08 19									08 49				
London Blackfriars	a		07 54									08 24									08 54				
City Thameslink	a		07 56									08 26									08 56				
Farringdon	a		07 58									08 28									08 58				
St Pancras International	a		08 03									08 33									09 03				
Balham 4 ⊖	a							08 02								08 32									09 03
Clapham Junction 10	a	07 42		07 48	07 54			08 07	08 01		08 12		08 18	08 24		08 37		08 31		08 42		08 48	08 54		09 07
London Waterloo 15 ⊖	a	07 56		08 00					08 13		08 24		08 30					08 43		08 54		09 00			
London Victoria 15 ⊖	a				08 04			08 16						08 33		08 45							09 03		09 19

Table T180-R

Mondays to Fridays

21 May to 7 December

Horsham and Dorking, Leatherhead, Epsom, Sutton, Hackbridge - London

		SW		TL	SW	TL	TL	SN	SW	TL	SW	TL		TL	SN	SW	TL	SW	TL	TL	SN	SW		TL	SW
Horsham	d						08 14													09 14					
Warnham	d						08 18													09 18					
Ockley	d						08 24													09 24					
Holmwood	d						08 28													09 28					
Dorking	a						08 36													09 36					
Dorking	d				08 30		08 37				09 00			09 07				09 33		09 37					10 03
Box Hill & Westhumble	d				08 33		08 40				09 03									09 40					
Leatherhead	d	08 24			08 38		08 44		08 54		09 08			09 13		09 23		09 39		09 44		09 53			10 09
Ashtead	d	08 27			08 41		08 48		08 57		09 11			09 17		09 27		09 43		09 48		09 57			10 13
Epsom	a	08 32			08 46		08 53		09 02		09 16			09 23		09 31		09 47		09 53		10 01			10 17
Epsom	d	08 34		08 45	08 47		08 53	09 01	09 04	09 15	09 17			09 23	09 31	09 34	09 45	09 49		09 53	10 01	10 04		10 15	10 19
Ewell East	d			08 49				09 05		09 19					09 35		09 49				10 05			10 19	
Cheam	d			08 52			08 59	09 08		09 22				09 29	09 38		09 52			09 59	10 08			10 22	
Sutton	a			08 55			09 01	09 11		09 25				09 31	09 41		09 55			10 01	10 11			10 25	
Sutton	d			08 56						09 26							09 56							10 26	
West Croydon	a			09 09						09 39							10 09							10 39	
Norwood Junction	a			09 15						09 45							10 15							10 45	
Sutton	d					08 46	09 02	09 12				09 16		09 32	09 42				09 46	10 02	10 12				
Carshalton	d					08 49	09 05	09 15				09 19		09 35	09 45				09 49	10 05	10 15				
Hackbridge	d					08 52		09 18				09 22			09 48				09 52		10 18				
Mitcham Junction	d					08 55		09 21				09 25			09 51				09 55		10 21				
Mitcham Eastfields	a					08 58		09 24				09 28			09 54				09 58		10 24				
Streatham	d					09 03						09 33							10 03						
Tulse Hill	a					09 07						09 37							10 07						
Tulse Hill	d					09 08						09 38							10 08						
London Bridge	a			09 28						09 58							10 28							10 58	
Herne Hill	a					09 11						09 41							10 11						
Loughborough Jn	a					09 15						09 45							10 15						
Elephant & Castle	a					09 19						09 49							10 19						
London Blackfriars	a					09 24						09 54							10 24						
City Thameslink	a					09 26						09 56							10 26						
Farringdon	a					09 28						09 58							10 28						
St Pancras International	a					09 33						10 03							10 33						
Balham ⊖	a							09 33							10 03						10 33				
Clapham Junction	a	09 01			09 15		09 23	09 37	09 30		09 45			09 53	10 07	10 00		10 15		10 23	10 37	10 30			10 45
London Waterloo ⊖	a	09 13			09 27				09 42		09 57					10 10		10 25				10 40			10 55
London Victoria ⊖	a						09 32	09 45						10 03	10 15					10 31	10 45				

		TL	TL	SN	SW	TL	SW	TL		TL	SN	SW	TL	SW	TL	TL	SN	SW		TL	SW	TL	TL	SN	SW
Horsham	d									10 14													11 14		
Warnham	d									10 18													11 18		
Ockley	d									10 24													11 24		
Holmwood	d									10 28													11 28		
Dorking	a									10 36													11 36		
Dorking	d		10 07				10 33			10 37				11 03		11 07					11 33		11 37		
Box Hill & Westhumble	d									10 40													11 40		
Leatherhead	d		10 13		10 23		10 39			10 44		10 53		11 09		11 13		11 23			11 39		11 44		11 53
Ashtead	d		10 17		10 27		10 43			10 48		10 57		11 13		11 17		11 27			11 43		11 48		11 57
Epsom	a		10 23		10 31		10 47			10 53		11 01		11 17		11 23		11 31			11 47		11 53		12 01
Epsom	d		10 23	10 31	10 34	10 45	10 49			10 53	11 01	11 04	11 15	11 19		11 23	11 31	11 34		11 45	11 49		11 53	12 01	12 04
Ewell East	d			10 35		10 49					11 05		11 19				11 35			11 49				12 05	
Cheam	d		10 29	10 38		10 52				10 59	11 08		11 22			11 29	11 38			11 52			11 59	12 08	
Sutton	a		10 31	10 41		10 55				11 01	11 11		11 25			11 31	11 41			11 55			12 01	12 11	
Sutton	d					10 56							11 26							11 56					
West Croydon	a					11 09							11 39							12 09					
Norwood Junction	a					11 15							11 45							12 15					
Sutton	d	10 16	10 32	10 42				10 46		11 02	11 12				11 16	11 32	11 42					11 46	12 02	12 12	
Carshalton	d	10 19	10 35	10 45				10 49		11 05	11 15				11 19	11 35	11 45					11 49	12 05	12 15	
Hackbridge	d	10 22		10 48				10 52			11 18				11 22		11 48					11 52		12 18	
Mitcham Junction	d	10 25		10 51				10 55			11 21				11 25		11 51					11 55		12 21	
Mitcham Eastfields	a	10 28		10 54				10 58			11 24				11 28		11 54					11 58		12 24	
Streatham	d	10 33						11 03							11 33							12 03			
Tulse Hill	a	10 37						11 07							11 37							12 07			
Tulse Hill	d	10 38						11 08							11 38							12 08			
London Bridge	a					11 28							11 58							12 28					
Herne Hill	a	10 41						11 11							11 41							12 11			
Loughborough Jn	a	10 45						11 15							11 45							12 15			
Elephant & Castle	a	10 49						11 19							11 49							12 19			
London Blackfriars	a	10 54						11 24							11 54							12 24			
City Thameslink	a	10 56						11 26							11 56							12 26			
Farringdon	a	10 58						11 28							11 58							12 28			
St Pancras International	a	11 03						11 33							12 03							12 33			
Balham ⊖	a			11 03							11 33						12 03							12 33	
Clapham Junction	a		10 53	11 07	11 00		11 15			11 23	11 37	11 30		11 45		11 53	12 07	12 00			12 15		12 23	12 37	12 30
London Waterloo ⊖	a				11 10		11 25					11 40		11 55				12 10			12 25				12 40
London Victoria ⊖	a		11 01	11 15						11 32	11 45					12 02	12 15						12 32	12 45	

Table T180-R

Mondays to Fridays

21 May to 7 December

Horsham and Dorking, Leatherhead, Epsom, Sutton, Hackbridge - London

		TL	SW	TL		TL	SN	SW	TL	SW	TL	TL	SN	SW		TL	SW	TL	TL	SN	SW	TL	SW	TL	
Horsham	d											12 14													
Warnham	d											12 18													
Ockley	d											12 24													
Holmwood	d											12 28													
Dorking	a											12 36													
Dorking	d		12 03			12 07				12 33		12 37					13 03		13 07				13 33		
Box Hill & Westhumble	d											12 40													
Leatherhead	d		12 09			12 13		12 23		12 39		12 44		12 53			13 09		13 13		13 23		13 39		
Ashtead	d		12 13			12 17		12 27		12 43		12 48		12 57			13 13		13 17		13 27		13 43		
Epsom	a		12 17			12 23		12 31		12 47		12 53		13 01			13 17		13 23		13 31		13 47		
Epsom	d	12 15	12 19			12 23	12 31	12 34	12 45	12 49		12 53	13 01	13 04		13 15	13 19		13 23	13 31	13 34	13 45	13 49		
Ewell East	d	12 19					12 35		12 49				13 05			13 19				13 35		13 49			
Cheam	d	12 22				12 29	12 38		12 52			12 59	13 08			13 22			13 29	13 38		13 52			
Sutton	a	12 25				12 31	12 41		12 55			13 01	13 11			13 25			13 31	13 41		13 55			
Sutton	d	12 26							12 56							13 26						13 56			
West Croydon	a	12 39							13 09							13 39						14 09			
Norwood Junction	a	12 45							13 15							13 45						14 15			
Sutton	d			12 16		12 32	12 42				12 46	13 02	13 12					13 16	13 32	13 42				13 46	
Carshalton	d			12 19		12 35	12 45				12 49	13 05	13 15					13 19	13 35	13 45				13 49	
Hackbridge	d			12 22			12 48				12 52		13 18					13 22		13 48				13 52	
Mitcham Junction	d			12 25			12 51				12 55		13 21					13 25		13 51				13 55	
Mitcham Eastfields	a			12 28			12 54				12 58		13 24					13 28		13 54				13 58	
Streatham	d			12 33							13 03							13 33						14 03	
Tulse Hill	a			12 37							13 07							13 37						14 07	
Tulse Hill	d			12 38							13 08							13 38						14 08	
London Bridge	a	12 58							13 28							13 58						14 28			
Herne Hill	a			12 41							13 11							13 41						14 11	
Loughborough Jn	a			12 45							13 15							13 45						14 15	
Elephant & Castle	a			12 49							13 19							13 49						14 19	
London Blackfriars	a			12 54							13 24							13 54						14 24	
City Thameslink	a			12 56							13 26							13 56						14 26	
Farringdon	a			12 58							13 28							13 58						14 28	
St Pancras International	a			13 03							13 33							14 03						14 33	
Balham ⊖	a						13 03						13 33							14 03					
Clapham Junction	a		12 45			12 53	13 07	13 00		13 15		13 23	13 37	13 30			13 45		13 53	14 07	14 00		14 15		
London Waterloo ⊖	a		12 55					13 10		13 25				13 40			13 55				14 10		14 25		
London Victoria ⊖	a					13 02	13 15					13 32	13 45						14 02	14 15					

		TL	SN	SW	TL	SW	TL	TL	SN	SW		TL	SW	TL	TL	SN	SW	TL	SW	TL		TL	SN	SW	TL
Horsham	d	13 14													14 14										
Warnham	d	13 18													14 18										
Ockley	d	13 24													14 24										
Holmwood	d	13 28													14 28										
Dorking	a	13 36													14 36										
Dorking	d	13 37				14 02		14 06					14 33		14 37				15 03			15 07			
Box Hill & Westhumble	d	13 40													14 40										
Leatherhead	d	13 44		13 53		14 08		14 12		14 23			14 39		14 44		14 53		15 09			15 13		15 23	
Ashtead	d	13 48		13 57		14 12		14 16		14 27			14 43		14 48		14 57		15 13			15 17		15 27	
Epsom	a	13 53		14 01		14 16		14 21		14 31			14 47		14 53		15 01		15 17			15 23		15 31	
Epsom	d	13 53	14 01	14 04	14 15	14 19		14 21	14 31	14 34		14 45	14 49		14 53	15 01	15 04	15 15	15 19			15 23	15 31	15 34	15 45
Ewell East	d		14 05		14 19				14 35			14 49				15 05		15 19					15 35		15 49
Cheam	d	13 59	14 08		14 22			14 27	14 38			14 52			14 59	15 08		15 22				15 29	15 38		15 52
Sutton	a	14 01	14 11		14 25			14 29	14 41			14 55			15 01	15 11		15 25				15 31	15 41		15 55
Sutton	d				14 26							14 56						15 26							15 56
West Croydon	a				14 39							15 09						15 39							16 09
Norwood Junction	a				14 45							15 15						15 45							16 15
Sutton	d	14 02	14 12				14 16	14 30	14 42					14 46	15 02	15 12				15 16		15 32	15 42		
Carshalton	d	14 05	14 15				14 19	14 33	14 45					14 49	15 05	15 15				15 19		15 35	15 45		
Hackbridge	d		14 18				14 22		14 48					14 52		15 18				15 22			15 48		
Mitcham Junction	d		14 21				14 25		14 51					14 55		15 21				15 25			15 51		
Mitcham Eastfields	a		14 24				14 28		14 54					14 58		15 24				15 28			15 54		
Streatham	d						14 33							15 03						15 33					
Tulse Hill	a						14 37							15 07						15 37					
Tulse Hill	d						14 38							15 08						15 38					
London Bridge	a				14 58							15 28						15 58							16 28
Herne Hill	a						14 41							15 11						15 41					
Loughborough Jn	a						14 45							15 15						15 45					
Elephant & Castle	a						14 49							15 19						15 49					
London Blackfriars	a						14 54							15 24						15 54					
City Thameslink	a						14 56							15 26						15 56					
Farringdon	a						14 58							15 28						15 58					
St Pancras International	a						15 03							15 33						16 03					
Balham ⊖	a		14 33						15 03							15 33							16 03		
Clapham Junction	a	14 23	14 37	14 30		14 45		14 53	15 07	15 00			15 15		15 23	15 37	15 30		15 45			15 53	16 07	16 00	
London Waterloo ⊖	a			14 40		14 55				15 10			15 25				15 40		15 55					16 10	
London Victoria ⊖	a	14 32	14 45					15 02	15 15						15 32	15 45						16 02	16 15		

Table T180-R

Mondays to Fridays

21 May to 7 December

Horsham and Dorking, Leatherhead, Epsom, Sutton, Hackbridge - London

		SW	TL	TL	SN	SW		TL	SW	TL	TL	SN	SW	TL	SW	TL		TL	SN	SW	TL	SW	TL	TL	SN
Horsham	d			15 14														16 14							
Warnham	d			15 18														16 18							
Ockley	d			15 24														16 24							
Holmwood	d			15 28														16 28							
Dorking	a			15 36														16 36							
Dorking	d	15 33		15 37					16 03		16 07				16 33			16 37				17 03		17 07	
Box Hill & Westhumble	d			15 40														16 40							
Leatherhead	d	15 39		15 44		15 53			16 09		16 13		16 23		16 39			16 44		16 53		17 09		17 13	
Ashtead	d	15 43		15 48		15 57			16 13		16 17		16 27		16 43			16 48		16 57		17 13		17 17	
Epsom	a	15 47		15 53		16 01			16 17		16 23		16 31		16 47			16 53		17 01		17 17		17 23	
Epsom	d	15 49		15 53	16 01	16 04		16 15	16 19		16 23	16 31	16 34	16 45	16 49			16 53	17 01	17 04	17 15	17 19		17 23	17 31
Ewell East	d				16 05			16 19				16 35		16 49					17 05		17 19				17 35
Cheam	d			15 59	16 08			16 22			16 29	16 38		16 52				16 59	17 08		17 22			17 29	17 38
Sutton	a			16 01	16 11			16 25			16 31	16 41		16 55				17 01	17 11		17 25			17 31	17 41
Sutton	d							16 26						16 56							17 26				
West Croydon	a							16 39						17 09							17 39				
Norwood Junction	a							16 45						17 15							17 45				
Sutton	d		15 46	16 02	16 12					16 16	16 32	16 42				16 46		17 02	17 12				17 16	17 32	17 42
Carshalton	d		15 49	16 05	16 15					16 19	16 35	16 45				16 49		17 05	17 15				17 19	17 35	17 45
Hackbridge	d		15 52		16 18					16 22		16 48				16 52			17 18				17 22		17 48
Mitcham Junction	d		15 55		16 21					16 25		16 51				16 55			17 21				17 25		17 51
Mitcham Eastfields	a		15 58		16 24					16 28		16 54				16 58			17 24				17 28		17 54
Streatham	d		16 03							16 33						17 03							17 33		
Tulse Hill	a		16 07							16 37						17 07							17 37		
Tulse Hill	d		16 08							16 38						17 08							17 38		
London Bridge	a							16 58						17 28							17 58				
Herne Hill	a		16 11							16 41						17 11							17 41		
Loughborough Jn	a		16 15							16 45						17 15							17 45		
Elephant & Castle	a		16 19							16 49						17 19							17 49		
London Blackfriars	a		16 24							16 54						17 24							17 54		
City Thameslink	a		16 26							16 56						17 26							17 56		
Farringdon	a		16 28							16 58						17 28							17 58		
St Pancras International	a		16 33							17 03						17 33							18 03		
Balham ⊖	a				16 33							17 03							17 33						18 03
Clapham Junction	a	16 15		16 23	16 37	16 30			16 45		16 53	17 07	17 00		17 15			17 23	17 37	17 30		17 45		17 53	18 07
London Waterloo ⊖	a	16 25				16 40			16 55				17 10		17 25					17 40		17 55			
London Victoria ⊖	a			16 32	16 45						17 03	17 15						17 32	17 45					18 02	18 19

		SW		SW	TL	TL	SN	SW	TL	SW	TL	TL		SN	SW	SW	TL	TL	SN	SW	TL	SW		TL	TL
Horsham	d					17 14						17 42						18 12							18 42
Warnham	d					17 18						17 46						18 16							18 46
Ockley	d					17 24						17 52						18 22							18 52
Holmwood	d					17 28						17 56						18 26							18 56
Dorking	a					17 36						18 03						18 33							19 03
Dorking	d			17 28		17 37				18 03		18 07				18 33		18 37		18 50					19 07
Box Hill & Westhumble	d					17 40						18 10						18 40							19 10
Leatherhead	d	17 23		17 35		17 44		17 53		18 09		18 14			18 23	18 39		18 44		18 56		19 08			19 14
Ashtead	d	17 27		17 38		17 48		17 57		18 13		18 18			18 27	18 43		18 48		18 59		19 12			19 18
Epsom	a	17 31		17 43		17 53		18 01		18 17		18 23			18 31	18 47		18 53		19 03		19 16			19 23
Epsom	d	17 34		17 49		17 53	18 01	18 04	18 15	18 19		18 23		18 31	18 34	18 49		18 53	19 01	19 04	19 15	19 19			19 23
Ewell East	d						18 05		18 19					18 35					19 05		19 19				
Cheam	d					17 59	18 08		18 22			18 29		18 38				18 59	19 08		19 22				19 29
Sutton	a					18 01	18 11		18 25			18 31		18 41				19 01	19 11		19 25				19 31
Sutton	d								18 26												19 26				
West Croydon	a								18 39												19 39				
Norwood Junction	a								18 45												19 45				
Sutton	d				17 46	18 02	18 12				18 16	18 32		18 42			18 46	19 02	19 12					19 16	19 32
Carshalton	d				17 49	18 05	18 15				18 19	18 35		18 45			18 49	19 05	19 15					19 19	19 35
Hackbridge	d				17 52		18 18				18 22			18 48			18 52		19 18					19 22	
Mitcham Junction	d				17 55		18 21				18 25			18 51			18 55		19 21					19 25	
Mitcham Eastfields	a				17 58		18 24				18 28			18 54			18 58		19 24					19 28	
Streatham	d				18 03						18 33						19 03							19 33	
Tulse Hill	a				18 07						18 37						19 07							19 37	
Tulse Hill	d				18 08						18 38						19 08							19 38	
London Bridge	a								18 58												19 58				
Herne Hill	a				18 11						18 41						19 11							19 41	
Loughborough Jn	a				18 15						18 45						19 15							19 45	
Elephant & Castle	a				18 19						18 49						19 19							19 49	
London Blackfriars	a				18 24						18 54						19 24							19 54	
City Thameslink	a				18 26						18 56						19 26							19 56	
Farringdon	a				18 28						18 58						19 28							19 58	
St Pancras International	a				18 33						19 03						19 33							20 03	
Balham ⊖	a						18 33							19 03					19 33						
Clapham Junction	a	18 00		18 14		18 23	18 37	18 30		18 45		18 53		19 07	19 00	19 16		19 23	19 37	19 30		19 45			19 53
London Waterloo ⊖	a	18 10		18 24				18 40		18 55					19 10	19 26				19 41		19 55			
London Victoria ⊖	a					18 34	18 45					19 02		19 15				19 33	19 45						20 02

Table T180-R

Mondays to Fridays

21 May to 7 December

Horsham and Dorking, Leatherhead, Epsom, Sutton, Hackbridge - London

		SN	SW	TL	SW	TL	TL	SN		SW	TL	SW	TL	TL	SN	SW	TL	SW		TL	TL	SN	SW	TL	SW
Horsham	d						19 12														20 14				
Warnham	d						19 16														20 18				
Ockley	d						19 22														20 24				
Holmwood	d						19 26														20 28				
Dorking	a						19 33														20 36				
Dorking	d				19 33		19 37					20 03		20 07				20 33			20 37				
Box Hill & Westhumble	d						19 40														20 40				
Leatherhead	d			19 29	19 39		19 44			19 53		20 09		20 13		20 23		20 39			20 44				21 11
Ashtead	d			19 34	19 43		19 48			19 57		20 13		20 17		20 27		20 42			20 48				21 14
Epsom	a			19 39	19 47		19 53			20 01		20 17		20 23		20 31		20 48			20 53				21 19
Epsom	d	19 31	19 34	19 42	19 49		19 53	20 01		20 04	20 15	20 19		20 23	20 31	20 34	20 45	20 49			20 53	21 01	21 04	21 15	21 19
Ewell East	d	19 35		19 49				20 05			20 19				20 35		20 49					21 05		21 19	
Cheam	d	19 38		19 52			19 59	20 08			20 22			20 29	20 38		20 52				20 59	21 08		21 22	
Sutton	a	19 41		19 55			20 01	20 11			20 25			20 31	20 41		20 55				21 01	21 11		21 25	
Sutton	d			19 56							20 26						20 56							21 26	
West Croydon	a			20 09							20 39						21 09							21 39	
Norwood Junction	a			20 15							20 45						21 15							21 45	
Sutton	d	19 42				19 46	20 02	20 12					20 16	20 32	20 42					20 46	21 02	21 12			
Carshalton	d	19 45				19 49	20 05	20 15					20 19	20 35	20 45					20 49	21 05	21 15			
Hackbridge	d	19 48				19 52		20 18					20 22		20 48					20 52		21 18			
Mitcham Junction	d	19 51				19 55		20 21					20 25		20 51					20 55		21 21			
Mitcham Eastfields	a	19 54				19 58		20 24					20 28		20 54					20 58		21 24			
Streatham	d					20 03							20 33							21 03					
Tulse Hill	a					20 07							20 37							21 07					
Tulse Hill	d					20 08							20 38							21 08					
London Bridge	a			20 28							20 58						21 28							21 58	
Herne Hill	a					20 11							20 41							21 11					
Loughborough Jn	a					20 15							20 45							21 15					
Elephant & Castle	a					20 19							20 49							21 19					
London Blackfriars	a					20 24							20 54							21 24					
City Thameslink	a					20 26							20 56							21 26					
Farringdon	a					20 28							20 58							21 28					
St Pancras International	a					20 33							21 03							21 33					
Balham ⊖	a	20 03						20 33							21 03							21 33			
Clapham Junction	a	20 07	20 00		20 15		20 23	20 37		20 30		20 45		20 55	21 07	21 00		21 15			21 23	21 37	21 31		21 45
London Waterloo ⊖	a		20 10		20 25					20 40		20 55				21 10		21 25					21 41		21 55
London Victoria ⊖	a	20 17					20 32	20 45						21 03	21 15						21 32	21 45			

		TL	TL	SN		SW	TL	SW	TL	TL	SN	TL	SW	TL		TL	SN	TL	SW	TL	SN	TL	SW	TL	
Horsham	d									21 14															
Warnham	d									21 18															
Ockley	d									21 24															
Holmwood	d									21 28															
Dorking	a									21 36															
Dorking	d		21 07					21 33		21 37						22 07			22 33			22 59			
Box Hill & Westhumble	d									21 40												23 02			
Leatherhead	d		21 13					21 40		21 44			22 11			22 13			22 39			23 06	23 11		
Ashtead	d		21 17					21 43		21 48			22 14			22 17			22 43			23 10	23 14		
Epsom	a		21 23					21 48		21 53			22 19			22 23			22 48			23 15	23 19		
Epsom	d		21 23	21 31		21 34	21 45	21 49		21 53	22 01	22 15	22 19			22 23	22 31	22 45	22 49		23 01	23 16	23 19		
Ewell East	d			21 35			21 49				22 05	22 19					22 35	22 49			23 05	23 20			
Cheam	d		21 29	21 38			21 52			21 59	22 08	22 22				22 29	22 38	22 52			23 08	23 23			
Sutton	a		21 31	21 41			21 55			22 01	22 11	22 25				22 31	22 41	22 55			23 11	23 26			
Sutton	d						21 56					22 26						22 56				23 26			
West Croydon	a						22 09					22 39						23 09				23 39			
Norwood Junction	a						22 15					22 45						23 15							
Sutton	d	21 16	21 32	21 42					21 46	22 02	22 12			22 18		22 32	22 42			22 48	23 12			23 18	
Carshalton	d	21 19	21 35	21 45					21 49	22 05	22 15			22 21		22 35	22 45			22 51	23 15			23 21	
Hackbridge	d	21 22		21 48					21 52		22 18			22 24			22 48			22 54	23 18			23 24	
Mitcham Junction	d	21 25		21 51					21 55		22 21			22 27			22 51			22 57	23 21			23 27	
Mitcham Eastfields	a	21 28		21 54					21 58		22 24			22 30			22 54			23 00	23 24			23 30	
Streatham	d	21 33							22 03					22 35						23 05				23 35	
Tulse Hill	a	21 37							22 07					22 39						23 09				23 39	
Tulse Hill	d	21 38							22 08					22 40						23 10				23 40	
London Bridge	a						22 28					22 58						23 28							
Herne Hill	a	21 41							22 11					22 43						23 13				23 43	
Loughborough Jn	a	21 45							22 15					22 47						23 17				23 47	
Elephant & Castle	a	21 49							22 19					22 51						23 21				23 51	
London Blackfriars	a	21 54							22 24					22 56						23 26				00 01	
City Thameslink	a	21 56							22 26																
Farringdon	a	21 58							22 28					23 03						23 31				00 06	
St Pancras International	a	22 03							22 33					23 08						23 35				00 10	
Balham ⊖	a			22 03							22 33						23 03				23 33				
Clapham Junction	a		21 53	22 07		22 00		22 15		22 23	22 37		22 45			22 53	23 07		23 15		23 37		23 48		
London Waterloo ⊖	a					22 10		22 25					22 55						23 28				23 58		
London Victoria ⊖	a		22 02	22 16						22 33	22 45					23 03	23 15				23 47				

Please note, Network Rail have stated that further updates to this timetable are possible during the validity period.

Horsham and Dorking, Leatherhead, Epsom, Sutton, Hackbridge - London

		SW	TL	SW	TL	SN	SW	TL	TL	SN		SW	TL	TL	TL	SN	SW	TL	TL	TL		SN	SW	TL	SW
Horsham	d																								
Warnham	d																								
Ockley	d																								
Holmwood	d																								
Dorking	a																								
Dorking	d									06 45					07 07					07 37					08 03
Box Hill & Westhumble	d																			07 40					
Leatherhead	d									06 52		06 55			07 13		07 23			07 44			07 53		08 09
Ashtead	d									06 56		06 59			07 17		07 27			07 48			07 57		08 13
Epsom	a									07 00		07 03			07 23		07 31			07 53			08 01		08 17
Epsom	d	05 34		06 04		06 31	06 34	06 45		07 01		07 04	07 15		07 23	07 31	07 34	07 45		07 53		08 01	08 04	08 15	08 19
Ewell East	d					06 35		06 49		07 05			07 19			07 35		07 49				08 05		08 19	
Cheam	d					06 38		06 52		07 08			07 22		07 29	07 38		07 52		07 59		08 08		08 22	
Sutton	a					06 41		06 55		07 11			07 25		07 31	07 41		07 55		08 01		08 11		08 25	
Sutton	d							06 56					07 26					07 56						08 26	
West Croydon	a							07 09					07 39					08 09						08 39	
Norwood Junction	a							07 15					07 45					08 15						08 45	
Sutton	d		05 46		06 16	06 42			06 46	07 12				07 16	07 32	07 42			07 46	08 02		08 12			
Carshalton	d		05 49		06 19	06 45			06 49	07 15				07 19	07 35	07 45			07 49	08 05		08 15			
Hackbridge	d		05 52		06 22	06 48			06 52	07 18				07 22		07 48			07 52			08 18			
Mitcham Junction	d		05 55		06 25	06 51			06 55	07 21				07 25		07 51			07 55			08 21			
Mitcham Eastfields	a		05 58		06 28	06 54			06 58	07 24				07 28		07 54			07 58			08 24			
Streatham	d		06 03		06 33				07 03					07 33					08 03						
Tulse Hill	a		06 07		06 37				07 07					07 37					08 07						
Tulse Hill	d		06 08		06 38				07 08					07 38					08 08						
London Bridge	a							07 28					07 58					08 28						08 58	
Herne Hill	a		06 11		06 41				07 11					07 41					08 11						
Loughborough Jn	a		06 15		06 45				07 15					07 45					08 15						
Elephant & Castle	a		06 19		06 49				07 19					07 49					08 19						
London Blackfriars	a		06 24		06 54				07 24					07 54					08 24						
City Thameslink	a																								
Farringdon	a		06 28		06 58				07 28					07 58					08 28						
St Pancras International	a		06 33		07 03				07 33					08 03					08 33						
Balham ⊖	a					07 03				07 33						08 03						08 33			
Clapham Junction	a	06 01		06 30		07 07	07 00			07 37		07 30			07 53	08 07	08 00			08 23		08 37	08 30		08 45
London Waterloo ⊖	a	06 11		06 40			07 10					07 40					08 10						08 40		08 55
London Victoria ⊖	a					07 15				07 45					08 02	08 15				08 32		08 45			

		TL	TL	SN	SW	TL		SW	TL	TL	SN	SW	TL	SW	TL	TL		SN	SW	TL	SW	TL	TL	SN	SW
Horsham	d									08 14													09 14		
Warnham	d									08 18													09 18		
Ockley	d									08 24													09 24		
Holmwood	d									08 28													09 28		
Dorking	a									08 36													09 36		
Dorking	d		08 07					08 33		08 37				09 03		09 07					09 33		09 37		
Box Hill & Westhumble	d									08 40													09 40		
Leatherhead	d		08 13		08 23			08 39		08 44		08 53		09 09		09 13			09 23		09 39		09 44		09 53
Ashtead	d		08 17		08 27			08 43		08 48		08 57		09 13		09 17			09 27		09 43		09 48		09 57
Epsom	a		08 23		08 31			08 47		08 53		09 01		09 17		09 23			09 31		09 47		09 53		10 01
Epsom	d		08 23	08 31	08 34	08 45		08 49		08 53	09 01	09 04	09 15	09 19		09 23		09 31	09 34	09 45	09 49		09 53	10 01	10 04
Ewell East	d			08 35		08 49					09 05		09 19					09 35		09 49				10 05	
Cheam	d		08 29	08 38		08 52				08 59	09 08		09 22			09 29		09 38		09 52			09 59	10 08	
Sutton	a		08 31	08 41		08 55				09 01	09 11		09 25			09 31		09 41		09 55			10 01	10 11	
Sutton	d					08 56							09 26							09 56					
West Croydon	a					09 09							09 39							10 09					
Norwood Junction	a					09 15							09 45							10 15					
Sutton	d	08 16	08 32	08 42					08 46	09 02	09 12				09 16	09 32		09 42				09 46	10 02	10 12	
Carshalton	d	08 19	08 35	08 45					08 49	09 05	09 15				09 19	09 35		09 45				09 49	10 05	10 15	
Hackbridge	d	08 22		08 48					08 52		09 18				09 22			09 48				09 52		10 18	
Mitcham Junction	d	08 25		08 51					08 55		09 21				09 25			09 51				09 55		10 21	
Mitcham Eastfields	a	08 28		08 54					08 58		09 24				09 28			09 54				09 58		10 24	
Streatham	d	08 33							09 03						09 33							10 03			
Tulse Hill	a	08 37							09 07						09 37							10 07			
Tulse Hill	d	08 38							09 08						09 38							10 08			
London Bridge	a					09 28							09 58							10 28					
Herne Hill	a	08 41							09 11						09 41							10 11			
Loughborough Jn	a	08 45							09 15						09 45							10 15			
Elephant & Castle	a	08 49							09 19						09 49							10 19			
London Blackfriars	a	08 54							09 24						09 54							10 24			
City Thameslink	a								09 26						09 56							10 26			
Farringdon	a	08 58							09 28						09 58							10 28			
St Pancras International	a	09 03							09 33						10 03							10 33			
Balham ⊖	a			09 03							09 33							10 03						10 33	
Clapham Junction	a		08 53	09 07	09 00			09 15		09 23	09 37	09 30		09 45		09 53		10 07	10 00		10 15		10 23	10 37	10 30
London Waterloo ⊖	a				09 10			09 25				09 40		09 55					10 10		10 25				10 40
London Victoria ⊖	a		09 02	09 15						09 32	09 45					10 02		10 15					10 32	10 45	

Table T180-R

Saturdays

26 May to 8 December

Horsham and Dorking, Leatherhead, Epsom, Sutton, Hackbridge - London

		TL		SW	TL	TL	SN	SW	TL	SW	TL	TL		SN	SW	TL	SW	TL	TL	SN	SW	TL		SW	TL
Horsham	d											10 14													
Warnham	d											10 18													
Ockley	d											10 24													
Holmwood	d											10 28													
Dorking	a											10 36													
Dorking	d			10 03		10 07				10 33		10 37					11 03		11 07					11 33	
Box Hill & Westhumble	d											10 40													
Leatherhead	d			10 09		10 13		10 23		10 39		10 44			10 53		11 09		11 13		11 23			11 39	
Ashtead	d			10 13		10 17		10 27		10 43		10 48			10 57		11 13		11 17		11 27			11 43	
Epsom	a			10 17		10 23		10 31		10 47		10 53			11 01		11 17		11 23		11 31			11 47	
Epsom	d	10 15		10 19		10 23	10 31	10 34	10 45	10 49		10 53		11 01	11 04	11 15	11 19		11 23	11 31	11 34	11 45		11 49	
Ewell East	d	10 19					10 35		10 49					11 05		11 19				11 35		11 49			
Cheam	d	10 22				10 29	10 38		10 52			10 59		11 08		11 22			11 29	11 38		11 52			
Sutton	a	10 25				10 31	10 41		10 55			11 01		11 11		11 25			11 31	11 41		11 55			
Sutton	d	10 26							10 56							11 26						11 56			
West Croydon	a	10 39							11 09							11 39						12 09			
Norwood Junction	a	10 45							11 15							11 45						12 15			
Sutton	d				10 16	10 32	10 42				10 46	11 02		11 12				11 16	11 32	11 42					11 46
Carshalton	d				10 19	10 35	10 45				10 49	11 05		11 15				11 19	11 35	11 45					11 49
Hackbridge	d				10 22		10 48				10 52			11 18				11 22		11 48					11 52
Mitcham Junction	d				10 25		10 51				10 55			11 21				11 25		11 51					11 55
Mitcham Eastfields	a				10 28		10 54				10 58			11 24				11 28		11 54					11 58
Streatham	d				10 33						11 03							11 33							12 03
Tulse Hill	a				10 37						11 07							11 37							12 07
Tulse Hill	d				10 38						11 08							11 38							12 08
London Bridge	a	10 58							11 28							11 58						12 28			
Herne Hill	a				10 41						11 11							11 41							12 11
Loughborough Jn	a				10 45						11 15							11 45							12 15
Elephant & Castle	a				10 49						11 19							11 49							12 19
London Blackfriars	a				10 54						11 24							11 54							12 24
City Thameslink	a				10 56						11 26							11 56							12 26
Farringdon	a				10 58						11 28							11 58							12 28
St Pancras International	a				11 03						11 33							12 03							12 33
Balham ⊖	a						11 03							11 33						12 03					
Clapham Junction	a			10 45		10 53	11 07	11 00		11 15		11 23		11 37	11 30		11 45		11 53	12 07	12 00			12 15	
London Waterloo ⊖	a			10 55				11 10		11 25					11 40		11 55				12 10			12 25	
London Victoria ⊖	a					11 02	11 15					11 32		11 45					12 02	12 15					

		TL	SN	SW	TL	SW	TL	TL		SN	SW	TL	SW	TL	TL	SN	SW	TL		SW	TL	TL	SN	SW	TL
Horsham	d	11 14													12 14										
Warnham	d	11 18													12 18										
Ockley	d	11 24													12 24										
Holmwood	d	11 28													12 28										
Dorking	a	11 36													12 36										
Dorking	d	11 37				12 03		12 07					12 33		12 37					13 03		13 07			
Box Hill & Westhumble	d	11 40													12 40										
Leatherhead	d	11 44		11 53		12 09		12 13			12 23		12 39		12 44		12 53			13 09		13 13		13 23	
Ashtead	d	11 48		11 57		12 13		12 17			12 27		12 43		12 48		12 57			13 13		13 17		13 27	
Epsom	a	11 53		12 01		12 17		12 23			12 31		12 47		12 53		13 01			13 17		13 23		13 31	
Epsom	d	11 53	12 01	12 04	12 15	12 19		12 23		12 31	12 34	12 45	12 49		12 53	13 01	13 04	13 15		13 19		13 23	13 31	13 34	13 45
Ewell East	d		12 05		12 19					12 35		12 49				13 05		13 19					13 35		13 49
Cheam	d	11 59	12 08		12 22			12 29		12 38		12 52			12 59	13 08		13 22				13 29	13 38		13 52
Sutton	a	12 01	12 11		12 25			12 31		12 41		12 55			13 01	13 11		13 25				13 31	13 41		13 55
Sutton	d				12 26							12 56						13 26							13 56
West Croydon	a				12 39							13 09						13 39							14 09
Norwood Junction	a				12 45							13 15						13 45							14 15
Sutton	d	12 02	12 12				12 16	12 32		12 42				12 46	13 02	13 12					13 16	13 32	13 42		
Carshalton	d	12 05	12 15				12 19	12 35		12 45				12 49	13 05	13 15					13 19	13 35	13 45		
Hackbridge	d		12 18				12 22			12 48				12 52		13 18					13 22		13 48		
Mitcham Junction	d		12 21				12 25			12 51				12 55		13 21					13 25		13 51		
Mitcham Eastfields	a		12 24				12 28			12 54				12 58		13 24					13 28		13 54		
Streatham	d						12 33							13 03							13 33				
Tulse Hill	a						12 37							13 07							13 37				
Tulse Hill	d						12 38							13 08							13 38				
London Bridge	a				12 58							13 28						13 58							14 28
Herne Hill	a						12 41							13 11							13 41				
Loughborough Jn	a						12 45							13 15							13 45				
Elephant & Castle	a						12 49							13 19							13 49				
London Blackfriars	a						12 54							13 24							13 54				
City Thameslink	a						12 56							13 26							13 56				
Farringdon	a						12 58							13 28							13 58				
St Pancras International	a						13 03							13 33							14 03				
Balham ⊖	a		12 33							13 03						13 33							14 03		
Clapham Junction	a	12 23	12 37	12 30		12 45		12 53		13 07	13 00		13 15		13 23	13 37	13 30			13 45		13 53	14 07	14 00	
London Waterloo ⊖	a			12 40		12 55					13 10		13 25				13 40			13 55				14 10	
London Victoria ⊖	a	12 32	12 45					13 02		13 15					13 32	13 45						14 02	14 15		

Please note, Network Rail have stated that further updates to this timetable are possible during the validity period.

Horsham and Dorking, Leatherhead, Epsom, Sutton, Hackbridge - London

		SW	TL	TL	SN	SW	TL	SW	TL	TL	SN	SW	TL	SW	TL	TL	SN	SW	TL	SW	TL	TL
Horsham 4	d			13 14												14 14						
Warnham	d			13 18												14 18						
Ockley	d			13 24												14 24						
Holmwood	d			13 28												14 28						
Dorking 4	a			13 36												14 36						
Dorking	d	13 33		13 37				14 03		14 07				14 33		14 37				15 03		15 07
Box Hill & Westhumble	d			13 40												14 40						
Leatherhead	d	13 39		13 44		13 53		14 09		14 13		14 23		14 39		14 44		14 53		15 09		15 13
Ashtead	d	13 43		13 48		13 57		14 13		14 17		14 27		14 43		14 48		14 57		15 13		15 17
Epsom 3	a	13 47		13 53		14 01		14 17		14 23		14 31		14 47		14 53		15 01		15 17		15 23
Epsom	d	13 49		13 53	14 01	14 04	14 15	14 19		14 23	14 31	14 34	14 45	14 49		14 53	15 01	15 04	15 15	15 19		15 23
Ewell East	d				14 05		14 19				14 35		14 49				15 05		15 19			
Cheam	d			13 59	14 08		14 22			14 29	14 38		14 52			14 59	15 08		15 22			15 29
Sutton	a			14 01	14 11		14 25			14 31	14 41		14 55			15 01	15 11		15 25			15 31
Sutton	d						14 26						14 56						15 26			
West Croydon	a						14 39						15 09						15 39			
Norwood Junction	a						14 45						15 15						15 45			
Sutton	d		13 46	14 02	14 12				14 16	14 32	14 42				14 46	15 02	15 12				15 16	15 32
Carshalton	d		13 49	14 05	14 15				14 19	14 35	14 45				14 49	15 05	15 15				15 19	15 35
Hackbridge	d		13 52		14 18				14 22		14 48				14 52		15 18				15 22	
Mitcham Junction	d		13 55		14 21				14 25		14 51				14 55		15 21				15 25	
Mitcham Eastfields	a		13 58		14 24				14 28		14 54				14 58		15 24				15 28	
Streatham	d		14 03						14 33						15 03						15 33	
Tulse Hill 3	a		14 07						14 37						15 07						15 37	
Tulse Hill	d		14 08						14 38						15 08						15 38	
London Bridge	a						14 58						15 28						15 58			
Herne Hill	a		14 11						14 41						15 11						15 41	
Loughborough Jn	a		14 15						14 45						15 15						15 45	
Elephant & Castle	a		14 19						14 49						15 19						15 49	
London Blackfriars	a		14 24						14 54						15 24						15 54	
City Thameslink	a		14 26						14 56						15 26						15 56	
Farringdon	a		14 28						14 58						15 28						15 58	
St Pancras International	a		14 33						15 03						15 33						16 03	
Balham 4 ⊖	a				14 33						15 03						15 33					
Clapham Junction 10	a	14 15		14 23	14 37	14 30		14 45		14 53	15 07	15 00		15 15		15 23	15 37	15 30		15 45		15 53
London Waterloo 15 ⊖	a	14 25				14 40		14 55				15 10		15 25				15 40		15 55		
London Victoria 15 ⊖	a			14 32	14 45					15 02	15 15					15 32	15 45					16 02

		SN	SW	TL	SW	TL	TL	SN	SW	TL	SW	TL	TL	SN	SW	TL	SW	TL	TL	SN	SW	TL	SW
Horsham 4	d						15 14												16 14				
Warnham	d						15 18												16 18				
Ockley	d						15 24												16 24				
Holmwood	d						15 28												16 28				
Dorking 4	a						15 36												16 36				
Dorking	d				15 33		15 37				16 03		16 07				16 33		16 37				17 03
Box Hill & Westhumble	d						15 40												16 40				
Leatherhead	d		15 23		15 39		15 44		15 53		16 09		16 13		16 23		16 39		16 44		16 53		17 09
Ashtead	d		15 27		15 43		15 48		15 57		16 13		16 17		16 27		16 43		16 48		16 57		17 13
Epsom 3	a		15 31		15 47		15 53		16 01		16 17		16 23		16 31		16 47		16 53		17 01		17 17
Epsom	d	15 31	15 34	15 45	15 49		15 53	16 01	16 04	16 15	16 19		16 23	16 31	16 34	16 45	16 49		16 53	17 01	17 04	17 15	17 19
Ewell East	d	15 35		15 49				16 05		16 19				16 35		16 49				17 05		17 19	
Cheam	d	15 38		15 52			15 59	16 08		16 22			16 29	16 38		16 52			16 59	17 08		17 22	
Sutton	a	15 41		15 55			16 01	16 11		16 25			16 31	16 41		16 55			17 01	17 11		17 25	
Sutton	d			15 56						16 26						16 56						17 26	
West Croydon	a			16 09						16 39						17 09						17 39	
Norwood Junction	a			16 15						16 45						17 15						17 45	
Sutton	d	15 42				15 46	16 02	16 12				16 16	16 32	16 42				16 46	17 02	17 12			
Carshalton	d	15 45				15 49	16 05	16 15				16 19	16 35	16 45				16 49	17 05	17 15			
Hackbridge	d	15 48				15 52		16 18				16 22		16 48				16 52		17 18			
Mitcham Junction	d	15 51				15 55		16 21				16 25		16 51				16 55		17 21			
Mitcham Eastfields	a	15 54				15 58		16 24				16 28		16 54				16 58		17 24			
Streatham	d					16 03						16 33						17 03					
Tulse Hill 3	a					16 07						16 37						17 07					
Tulse Hill	d					16 08						16 38						17 08					
London Bridge	a			16 28						16 58						17 28						17 58	
Herne Hill	a					16 11						16 41						17 11					
Loughborough Jn	a					16 15						16 45						17 15					
Elephant & Castle	a					16 19						16 49						17 19					
London Blackfriars	a					16 24						16 54						17 24					
City Thameslink	a					16 26						16 56						17 26					
Farringdon	a					16 28						16 58						17 28					
St Pancras International	a					16 33						17 03						17 33					
Balham 4 ⊖	a	16 03						16 33						17 03						17 33			
Clapham Junction 10	a	16 07	16 00		16 15		16 23	16 37	16 30		16 45		16 53	17 07	17 00		17 15		17 23	17 37	17 30		17 45
London Waterloo 15 ⊖	a		16 10		16 25				16 40		16 55				17 10		17 25				17 40		17 55
London Victoria 15 ⊖	a	16 15					16 32	16 45					17 02	17 15					17 32	17 45			

Table T180-R

Saturdays

26 May to 8 December

Horsham and Dorking, Leatherhead, Epsom, Sutton, Hackbridge - London

		TL	TL	SN	SW	TL	SW	TL	TL	SN	SW	TL	SW	TL	TL	SN	SW	TL	SW	TL	TL	SN	SW
Horsham 4	d								17 14												18 14		
Warnham	d								17 18												18 18		
Ockley	d								17 24												18 24		
Holmwood	d								17 28												18 28		
Dorking 4	a								17 36												18 36		
Dorking	d		17 07				17 33		17 37				18 03		18 07				18 33		18 37		
Box Hill & Westhumble	d								17 40												18 40		
Leatherhead	d		17 13		17 23		17 39		17 44		17 53		18 09		18 13		18 23		18 39		18 44		18 53
Ashtead	d		17 17		17 27		17 43		17 48		17 57		18 13		18 17		18 27		18 43		18 48		18 57
Epsom 3	a		17 23		17 31		17 47		17 53		18 01		18 17		18 23		18 31		18 47		18 53		19 01
Epsom	d		17 23	17 31	17 34	17 45	17 49		17 53	18 01	18 04	18 15	18 19		18 23	18 31	18 34	18 45	18 49		18 53	19 01	19 04
Ewell East	d			17 35		17 49				18 05		18 19				18 35		18 49				19 05	
Cheam	d		17 29	17 38		17 52			17 59	18 08		18 22			18 29	18 38		18 52			18 59	19 08	
Sutton	a		17 31	17 41		17 55			18 01	18 11		18 25			18 31	18 41		18 55			19 01	19 11	
Sutton	d					17 56						18 26						18 56					
West Croydon	a					18 09						18 39						19 09					
Norwood Junction	a					18 15						18 45						19 15					
Sutton	d	17 16	17 32	17 42				17 46	18 02	18 12				18 16	18 32	18 42				18 46	19 02	19 12	
Carshalton	d	17 19	17 35	17 45				17 49	18 05	18 15				18 19	18 35	18 45				18 49	19 05	19 15	
Hackbridge	d	17 22		17 48				17 52		18 18				18 22		18 48				18 52		19 18	
Mitcham Junction	d	17 25		17 51				17 55		18 21				18 25		18 51				18 55		19 21	
Mitcham Eastfields	a	17 28		17 54				17 58		18 24				18 28		18 54				18 58		19 24	
Streatham	d	17 33						18 03						18 33						19 03			
Tulse Hill 3	a	17 37						18 07						18 37						19 07			
Tulse Hill	d	17 38						18 08						18 38						19 08			
London Bridge	a					18 28						18 58						19 28					
Herne Hill	a	17 41						18 11						18 41						19 11			
Loughborough Jn	a	17 45						18 15						18 45						19 15			
Elephant & Castle	a	17 49						18 19						18 49						19 19			
London Blackfriars	a	17 54						18 24						18 54						19 24			
City Thameslink	a	17 56						18 26						18 56						19 26			
Farringdon	a	17 58						18 28						18 58						19 28			
St Pancras International	a	18 03						18 33						19 03						19 33			
Balham 4 ⊖	a			18 03						18 33						19 03						19 33	
Clapham Junction 10	a		17 53	18 07	18 00		18 15		18 23	18 37	18 30		18 45		18 53	19 07	19 00		19 15		19 23	19 37	19 30
London Waterloo 15 ⊖	a				18 10		18 25				18 40		18 55				19 10		19 25				19 40
London Victoria 15 ⊖	a		18 02	18 15					18 32	18 45					19 02	19 15					19 32	19 45	

		TL	SW	TL	TL	SN	SW	TL	SW	TL	TL	SN	SW	TL	SW	TL	TL	SN	SW	TL	SW	TL
Horsham 4	d																					
Warnham	d																					
Ockley	d																					
Holmwood	d																					
Dorking 4	a																					
Dorking	d		19 03		19 07				19 33		19 37				20 03		20 07				20 33	
Box Hill & Westhumble	d										19 40											
Leatherhead	d		19 10		19 13		19 23		19 40		19 44		19 53		20 10		20 13		20 23		20 40	
Ashtead	d		19 13		19 17		19 27		19 43		19 48		19 57		20 13		20 17		20 27		20 43	
Epsom 3	a		19 18		19 23		19 31		19 48		19 53		20 01		20 18		20 23		20 31		20 48	
Epsom	d	19 15	19 19		19 23	19 31	19 34	19 45	19 49		19 53	20 01	20 04	20 15	20 19		20 23	20 31	20 34	20 45	20 49	
Ewell East	d	19 19				19 35		19 49				20 05		20 19				20 35		20 49		
Cheam	d	19 22			19 29	19 38		19 52			19 59	20 08		20 22			20 29	20 38		20 52		
Sutton	a	19 25			19 31	19 41		19 55			20 01	20 11		20 25			20 31	20 41		20 55		
Sutton	d	19 26						19 56						20 26						20 56		
West Croydon	a	19 39						20 09						20 39						21 09		
Norwood Junction	a	19 45						20 15						20 45						21 15		
Sutton	d			19 16	19 32	19 42				19 46	20 02	20 12				20 16	20 32	20 42				20 46
Carshalton	d			19 19	19 35	19 45				19 49	20 05	20 15				20 19	20 35	20 45				20 49
Hackbridge	d			19 22		19 48				19 52		20 18				20 22		20 48				20 52
Mitcham Junction	d			19 25		19 51				19 55		20 21				20 25		20 51				20 55
Mitcham Eastfields	a			19 28		19 54				19 58		20 24				20 28		20 54				20 58
Streatham	d			19 33						20 03						20 33						21 03
Tulse Hill 3	a			19 37						20 07						20 37						21 07
Tulse Hill	d			19 38						20 08						20 38						21 08
London Bridge	a	19 58						20 28						20 58						21 28		
Herne Hill	a			19 41						20 11						20 41						21 11
Loughborough Jn	a			19 45						20 15						20 45						21 15
Elephant & Castle	a			19 49						20 19						20 49						21 19
London Blackfriars	a			19 54						20 24						20 54						21 24
City Thameslink	a			19 56						20 26						20 56						
Farringdon	a			19 58						20 28						20 58						21 28
St Pancras International	a			20 03						20 33						21 03						21 33
Balham 4 ⊖	a					20 03						20 33						21 03				
Clapham Junction 10	a		19 45		19 53	20 07	20 00		20 15		20 23	20 37	20 30		20 45		20 53	21 07	21 00		21 15	
London Waterloo 15 ⊖	a		19 55				20 10		20 25				20 40		20 55				21 11		21 25	
London Victoria 15 ⊖	a				20 02	20 15					20 32	20 45					21 02	21 15				

Table T180-R

Saturdays

26 May to 8 December

Horsham and Dorking, Leatherhead, Epsom, Sutton, Hackbridge - London

Station		TL	SN	SW	TL	SW	TL	TL	SN	SW	TL	SW
Horsham	d											
Warnham	d											
Ockley	d											
Holmwood	d											
Dorking	a											
Dorking	d	20 37						21 07				21 33
Box Hill & Westhumble	d	20 40										
Leatherhead	d	20 44				21 11		21 13				21 39
Ashtead	d	20 48				21 14		21 17				21 43
Epsom	a	20 53				21 19		21 23				21 47
Epsom	d	20 53	21 01	21 04	21 15	21 19		21 23	21 31	21 34	21 45	21 49
Ewell East	d		21 05		21 19				21 35		21 49	
Cheam	d	20 59	21 08		21 22			21 29	21 38		21 52	
Sutton	a	21 01	21 11		21 25			21 31	21 41		21 55	
Sutton	d				21 26						21 56	
West Croydon	a				21 39						22 09	
Norwood Junction	a				21 45						22 15	
Sutton	d	21 02	21 12				21 16	21 32	21 42			
Carshalton	d	21 05	21 15				21 19	21 35	21 45			
Hackbridge	d		21 18				21 22		21 48			
Mitcham Junction	d		21 21				21 25		21 51			
Mitcham Eastfields	a		21 24				21 28		21 54			
Streatham	d						21 33					
Tulse Hill	a						21 37					
Tulse Hill	d						21 38					
London Bridge	a				21 58						22 28	
Herne Hill	a						21 41					
Loughborough Jn	a						21 45					
Elephant & Castle	a						21 49					
London Blackfriars	a						21 54					
City Thameslink	a											
Farringdon	a						21 58					
St Pancras International	a						22 03					
Balham ⊖	a		21 33						22 03			
Clapham Junction	a	21 23	21 37	21 30		21 45		21 53	22 07	22 00		22 15
London Waterloo ⊖	a			21 40		21 55				22 10		22 25
London Victoria ⊖	a	21 32	21 45					22 01	22 15			

Station		TL	TL	SN	TL	SW	TL	TL	SN	TL	SW	TL
Horsham	d											
Warnham	d											
Ockley	d											
Holmwood	d											
Dorking	a											
Dorking	d		21 37					22 07			22 33	
Box Hill & Westhumble	d		21 40									
Leatherhead	d		21 44			22 11		22 13			22 39	
Ashtead	d		21 48			22 14		22 17			22 43	
Epsom	a		21 53			22 19		22 23			22 48	
Epsom	d		21 53	22 01	22 15	22 19		22 23	22 31	22 45	22 49	
Ewell East	d			22 05	22 19				22 35	22 49		
Cheam	d		21 59	22 08	22 22			22 29	22 38	22 52		
Sutton	a		22 01	22 11	22 25			22 31	22 41	22 55		
Sutton	d				22 26					22 56		
West Croydon	a				22 39					23 09		
Norwood Junction	a				22 45					23 15		
Sutton	d	21 46	22 02	22 12			22 18	22 32	22 42			22 48
Carshalton	d	21 49	22 05	22 15			22 21	22 35	22 45			22 51
Hackbridge	d	21 52		22 18			22 24		22 48			22 54
Mitcham Junction	d	21 55		22 21			22 27		22 51			22 57
Mitcham Eastfields	a	21 58		22 24			22 30		22 54			23 00
Streatham	d	22 03					22 35					23 05
Tulse Hill	a	22 07					22 39					23 09
Tulse Hill	d	22 08					22 40					23 10
London Bridge	a				22 58					23 28		
Herne Hill	a	22 11					22 43					23 13
Loughborough Jn	a	22 15					22 47					23 17
Elephant & Castle	a	22 19					22 51					23 21
London Blackfriars	a	22 24					22 59					23 26
City Thameslink	a											
Farringdon	a	22 28					23 03					23 31
St Pancras International	a	22 33					23 08					23 35
Balham ⊖	a			22 33					23 03			
Clapham Junction	a		22 23	22 37		22 45		22 53	23 07		23 15	
London Waterloo ⊖	a					22 55					23 25	
London Victoria ⊖	a		22 32	22 45				23 02	23 15			

Station		TL	SN	SW	TL	TL	TL
Horsham	d						
Warnham	d						
Ockley	d						
Holmwood	d						
Dorking	a						
Dorking	d	22 37			23 07		23 37
Box Hill & Westhumble	d	22 40			23 10		23 40
Leatherhead	d	22 44		23 11	23 14		23 44
Ashtead	d	22 48		23 14	23 18		23 48
Epsom	a	22 53		23 19	23 23		23 53
Epsom	d	22 53	23 01	23 19	23 23		23 53
Ewell East	d		23 05				
Cheam	d	22 59	23 08		23 29		23 59
Sutton	a	23 01	23 11		23 31		00 02
Sutton	d				23 32		00 03
West Croydon	a				23 45		00 15
Norwood Junction	a						
Sutton	d	23 02	23 12			23 18	
Carshalton	d	23 05	23 15			23 21	
Hackbridge	d		23 18			23 24	
Mitcham Junction	d		23 21			23 27	
Mitcham Eastfields	a		23 24			23 30	
Streatham	d					23 35	
Tulse Hill	a					23 39	
Tulse Hill	d					23 40	
London Bridge	a						
Herne Hill	a					23 43	
Loughborough Jn	a					23 47	
Elephant & Castle	a					23 51	
London Blackfriars	a					00 01	
City Thameslink	a						
Farringdon	a					00 06	
St Pancras International	a					00 10	
Balham ⊖	a		23 33				
Clapham Junction	a	23 23	23 37	23 48			
London Waterloo ⊖	a			23 58			
London Victoria ⊖	a	23 32	23 46				

Table T180-R

Sundays

20 May to 2 December

Horsham and Dorking, Leatherhead, Epsom, Sutton, Hackbridge - London

Station		TL A	SN	SN	SW	TL	SW	TL	SN	SW	TL	SN
Horsham	d											
Warnham	d											
Ockley	d											
Holmwood	d											
Dorking	a											
Dorking	d					07 16		07 46			08 16	
Box Hill & Westhumble	d					07 19		07 49			08 19	
Leatherhead	d					07 24		07 54			08 24	
Ashtead	d					07 28		07 58			08 28	
Epsom	a					07 32		08 02			08 32	
Epsom	d		06 43	07 03	07 24	07 33	07 54	08 03	08 14	08 24	08 33	08 44
Ewell East	d		06 47	07 07		07 37		08 07	08 18		08 37	08 48
Cheam	d		06 50	07 10		07 40		08 10	08 21		08 40	08 51
Sutton	a		06 53	07 13		07 43		08 13	08 24		08 43	08 54
Sutton	d	00 03	06 53									
West Croydon	a	00 15	07 06									
Norwood Junction	a											
Sutton	d			07 14		07 44		08 14	08 26		08 46	08 56
Carshalton	d			07 17		07 47		08 17	08 29		08 49	08 59
Hackbridge	d			07 20		07 50		08 20	08 32			09 02
Mitcham Junction	d			07 24		07 54		08 24	08 35			09 05
Mitcham Eastfields	a			07 27		07 57		08 27	08 38			09 08
Streatham	d											
Tulse Hill	a											
Tulse Hill	d											
London Bridge	a											
Herne Hill	a											
Loughborough Jn	a											
Elephant & Castle	a											
London Blackfriars	a											
City Thameslink	a											
Farringdon	a											
St Pancras International	a											
Balham ⊖	a		07 24	07 35		08 05		08 34	08 48			09 16
Clapham Junction	a		07 30	07 40	07 50	08 10	08 21	08 41	08 53	08 50	09 06	09 21
London Waterloo ⊖	a				08 04		08 39			09 05		
London Victoria ⊖	a		07 39	07 48		08 19		08 49	09 00		09 15	09 29

Station		SW	TL	SN	SW	TL	SN	SW	TL	SN	SW	TL
Horsham	d											
Warnham	d											
Ockley	d											
Holmwood	d											
Dorking	a											
Dorking	d		08 46		09 07	09 16			09 46		10 07	
Box Hill & Westhumble	d		08 49			09 19			09 49			
Leatherhead	d	08 45	08 54		09 15	09 24		09 45	09 54		10 15	
Ashtead	d	08 48	08 58		09 18	09 28		09 48	09 58		10 18	
Epsom	a	08 53	09 02		09 23	09 32		09 53	10 02		10 23	
Epsom	d	08 54	09 03	09 14	09 24	09 33	09 44	09 54	10 03	10 14	10 24	
Ewell East	d		09 07	09 18		09 37	09 48		10 07	10 18		
Cheam	d		09 10	09 21		09 40	09 51		10 10	10 21		
Sutton	a		09 13	09 24		09 43	09 54		10 13	10 24		
Sutton	d											
West Croydon	a											
Norwood Junction	a											
Sutton	d		09 16	09 26		09 46	09 56		10 16	10 26		10 40
Carshalton	d		09 19	09 29		09 49	09 59		10 19	10 29		10 43
Hackbridge	d			09 32			10 02			10 32		10 45
Mitcham Junction	d			09 35			10 05			10 35		10 48
Mitcham Eastfields	a			09 38			10 08			10 38		10 51
Streatham	d											10 55
Tulse Hill	a											10 59
Tulse Hill	d											10 59
London Bridge	a											
Herne Hill	a											11 03
Loughborough Jn	a											11 06
Elephant & Castle	a											11 10
London Blackfriars	a											11 15
City Thameslink	a											
Farringdon	a											
St Pancras International	a											
Balham ⊖	a			09 46			10 16			10 46		
Clapham Junction	a	09 20	09 36	09 51	09 49	10 06	10 21	10 19	10 36	10 51	10 49	
London Waterloo ⊖	a	09 35			10 04			10 29			11 04	
London Victoria ⊖	a		09 45	09 59		10 15	10 29		10 45	10 59		

Station		TL	SN	SW	TL	TL	SN	SW	TL
Horsham	d								
Warnham	d								
Ockley	d								
Holmwood	d								
Dorking	a								
Dorking	d	10 16				10 46		11 07	
Box Hill & Westhumble	d	10 19				10 49			
Leatherhead	d	10 24		10 45		10 54		11 15	
Ashtead	d	10 28		10 48		10 58		11 18	
Epsom	a	10 32		10 53		11 02		11 23	
Epsom	d	10 33	10 44	10 54		11 03	11 14	11 24	
Ewell East	d	10 37	10 48			11 07	11 18		
Cheam	d	10 40	10 51			11 10	11 21		
Sutton	a	10 43	10 54			11 13	11 24		
Sutton	d								
West Croydon	a								
Norwood Junction	a								
Sutton	d	10 46	10 56		11 10	11 16	11 26		11 40
Carshalton	d	10 49	10 59		11 13	11 19	11 29		11 43
Hackbridge	d		11 02		11 15		11 32		11 45
Mitcham Junction	d		11 05		11 18		11 35		11 48
Mitcham Eastfields	a		11 08		11 21		11 38		11 51
Streatham	d				11 25				11 55
Tulse Hill	a				11 29				11 59
Tulse Hill	d				11 29				11 59
London Bridge	a								
Herne Hill	a				11 33				12 03
Loughborough Jn	a				11 36				12 06
Elephant & Castle	a				11 40				12 10
London Blackfriars	a				11 45				12 15
City Thameslink	a								
Farringdon	a								12 20
St Pancras International	a								12 24
Balham ⊖	a		11 16				11 46		
Clapham Junction	a	11 06	11 21	11 19		11 36	11 51	11 49	
London Waterloo ⊖	a			11 29				12 04	
London Victoria ⊖	a	11 15	11 29			11 45	11 59		

Station		TL	SN	SW	TL	TL	SN	SW		TL	TL	SN	SW	TL	TL
Horsham	d														
Warnham	d														
Ockley	d														
Holmwood	d														
Dorking	a														
Dorking	d	11 16				11 46		12 07			16 16				16 46
Box Hill & Westhumble	d	11 19				11 49		12 10			16 19				16 49
Leatherhead	d	11 24		11 45		11 54		12 15			16 24		16 45		16 54
Ashtead	d	11 28		11 48		11 58		12 18			16 28		16 48		16 58
Epsom	a	11 32		11 53		12 02		12 23			16 32		16 53		17 02
Epsom	d	11 33	11 44	11 54		12 03	12 14	12 24			16 33	16 44	16 54		17 03
Ewell East	d	11 37	11 48			12 07	12 18				16 37	16 48			17 07
Cheam	d	11 40	11 51			12 10	12 21				16 40	16 51			17 10
Sutton	a	11 43	11 54			12 13	12 24				16 43	16 54			17 13
Sutton	d								and at						
West Croydon	a								the same						
Norwood Junction	a								minutes						
Sutton	d	11 46	11 56		12 10	12 16	12 26		past	16 40	16 46	16 56		17 10	17 16
Carshalton	d	11 49	11 59		12 13	12 19	12 29		each	16 43	16 49	16 59		17 13	17 19
Hackbridge	d		12 02		12 15		12 32		hour until	16 45		17 02		17 15	
Mitcham Junction	d		12 05		12 18		12 35			16 48		17 05		17 18	
Mitcham Eastfields	a		12 08		12 21		12 38			16 51		17 08		17 21	
Streatham	d				12 25					16 55				17 25	
Tulse Hill	a				12 29					16 59				17 29	
Tulse Hill	d				12 29					16 59				17 29	
London Bridge	a														
Herne Hill	a				12 33					17 03				17 33	
Loughborough Jn	a				12 36					17 06				17 36	
Elephant & Castle	a				12 40					17 10				17 40	
London Blackfriars	a				12 45					17 15				17 45	
City Thameslink	a														
Farringdon	a				12 50					17 20				17 50	
St Pancras International	a				12 54					17 24				17 54	
Balham ⊖	a		12 16				12 46					17 16			
Clapham Junction	a	12 06	12 21	12 19		12 36	12 51	12 49			17 06	17 21	17 19		17 36
London Waterloo ⊖	a			12 29				12 59					17 29		
London Victoria ⊖	a	12 15	12 29			12 45	12 59				17 15	17 29			17 45

A not 20 May

Table T180-R

Sundays
20 May to 2 December

Horsham and Dorking, Leatherhead, Epsom, Sutton, Hackbridge - London

		SN	SW		TL	TL	SN	SW	TL	TL	SN	SW	TL		TL	SN	SW	TL	TL	SN	SW	TL	TL		SN
Horsham	d																								
Warnham	d																								
Ockley	d																								
Holmwood	d																								
Dorking	a																								
Dorking	d		17 07			17 16				17 46		18 07			18 16				18 46		19 07		19 16		
Box Hill & Westhumble	d		17 10			17 19				17 49		18 10			18 19				18 49		19 10		19 19		
Leatherhead	d		17 15			17 24		17 45		17 54		18 15			18 24		18 45		18 54		19 15		19 24		
Ashtead	d		17 18			17 28		17 48		17 58		18 18			18 28		18 48		18 58		19 18		19 28		
Epsom	a		17 23			17 32		17 53		18 02		18 23			18 32		18 53		19 02		19 23		19 32		
Epsom	d	17 14	17 24			17 33	17 44	17 54		18 03	18 17	18 24			18 33	18 44	18 54		19 03	19 14	19 24		19 33		19 44
Ewell East	d	17 18				17 37	17 48			18 07	18 21				18 37	18 48			19 07	19 18			19 37		19 48
Cheam	d	17 21				17 40	17 51			18 10	18 24				18 40	18 51			19 10	19 21			19 40		19 51
Sutton	a	17 24				17 43	17 54			18 13	18 28				18 43	18 54			19 13	19 24			19 43		19 54
Sutton	d																								
West Croydon	a																								
Norwood Junction	a																								
Sutton	d	17 26			17 40	17 46	17 56		18 10	18 16	18 28		18 40		18 46	18 56		19 10	19 16	19 26		19 40	19 46		19 56
Carshalton	d	17 29			17 43	17 49	17 59		18 13	18 19	18 31		18 43		18 49	18 59		19 13	19 19	19 29		19 43	19 49		19 59
Hackbridge	d	17 32			17 45		18 02		18 15		18 34		18 45			19 02		19 15		19 32		19 45			20 02
Mitcham Junction	d	17 35			17 48		18 05		18 18		18 37		18 48			19 05		19 18		19 35		19 48			20 05
Mitcham Eastfields	a	17 38			17 51		18 08		18 21		18 40		18 51			19 08		19 21		19 38		19 51			20 08
Streatham	d				17 55				18 25				18 55					19 25				19 55			
Tulse Hill	a				17 59				18 29				18 59					19 29				19 59			
Tulse Hill	d				17 59				18 29				18 59					19 29				19 59			
London Bridge	a																								
Herne Hill	a				18 03				18 33				19 03					19 33				20 03			
Loughborough Jn	a				18 06				18 36				19 06					19 36				20 06			
Elephant & Castle	a				18 10				18 40				19 10					19 40				20 10			
London Blackfriars	a				18 15				18 45				19 15					19 45				20 15			
City Thameslink	a																								
Farringdon	a				18 20				18 50				19 20					19 50				20 20			
St Pancras International	a				18 24				18 54				19 24					19 54				20 24			
Balham ⊖	a	17 46					18 16				18 47					19 16				19 46					20 16
Clapham Junction	a	17 51	17 49			18 06	18 21	18 19		18 36	18 51	18 49			19 07	19 21	19 19		19 36	19 51	19 49		20 07		20 21
London Waterloo ⊖	a		17 59					18 29				18 59					19 29				19 59				
London Victoria ⊖	a	17 59				18 15	18 29			18 45	18 59				19 15	19 29			19 45	19 59			20 15		20 29

		SW	TL	TL	SN	SW	TL	TL	SN		SW	TL	TL	SN	SW	TL	TL	SN	SW		TL	TL	SN	SW	TL
Horsham	d																								
Warnham	d																								
Ockley	d																								
Holmwood	d																								
Dorking	a																								
Dorking	d			19 46		20 07		20 16					20 46		21 07		21 16					21 46		22 07	
Box Hill & Westhumble	d			19 49				20 19					20 49				21 19					21 49			
Leatherhead	d	19 45		19 54		20 15		20 24			20 45		20 54		21 15		21 24		21 45			21 54		22 15	
Ashtead	d	19 48		19 58		20 18		20 28			20 48		20 58		21 18		21 28		21 48			21 58		22 18	
Epsom	a	19 53		20 02		20 23		20 32			20 53		21 02		21 23		21 32		21 53			22 02		22 23	
Epsom	d	19 54		20 03	20 14	20 24		20 33	20 44		20 54		21 03	21 14	21 24		21 33	21 44	21 54			22 03	22 14	22 24	
Ewell East	d			20 07	20 18			20 37	20 48				21 07	21 18			21 37	21 48				22 07	22 18		
Cheam	d			20 10	20 21			20 40	20 51				21 10	21 21			21 40	21 51				22 10	22 21		
Sutton	a			20 13	20 24			20 43	20 54				21 13	21 24			21 43	21 54				22 13	22 24		
Sutton	d																								
West Croydon	a																								
Norwood Junction	a																								
Sutton	d		20 10	20 16	20 26		20 40	20 46	20 56			21 10	21 16	21 26		21 40	21 46	21 56			22 10	22 16	22 26		22 40
Carshalton	d		20 13	20 19	20 29		20 43	20 49	20 59			21 13	21 19	21 29		21 43	21 49	21 59			22 13	22 19	22 29		22 43
Hackbridge	d		20 15		20 32		20 45		21 02			21 15		21 32		21 45		22 02			22 15		22 32		22 45
Mitcham Junction	d		20 18		20 35		20 48		21 05			21 18		21 35		21 48		22 05			22 18		22 35		22 48
Mitcham Eastfields	a		20 21		20 38		20 51		21 08			21 21		21 38		21 51		22 08			22 21		22 38		22 51
Streatham	d		20 25				20 55					21 25				21 55					22 25				22 55
Tulse Hill	a		20 29				20 59					21 29				21 59					22 29				22 59
Tulse Hill	d		20 29				20 59					21 29				21 59					22 29				22 59
London Bridge	a																								
Herne Hill	a		20 33				21 03					21 33				22 03					22 33				23 03
Loughborough Jn	a		20 36				21 06					21 36				22 06					22 36				23 06
Elephant & Castle	a		20 40				21 10					21 40				22 10					22 40				23 10
London Blackfriars	a		20 45				21 15					21 45				22 15					22 45				23 15
City Thameslink	a																								
Farringdon	a		20 50				21 20					21 50				22 20									23 20
St Pancras International	a		20 54				21 24					21 54				22 24									23 24
Balham ⊖	a				20 46				21 16					21 46				22 16					22 46		
Clapham Junction	a	20 19		20 36	20 51	20 49		21 06	21 21		21 19		21 36	21 51	21 49		22 06	22 21	22 19			22 36	22 51	22 49	
London Waterloo ⊖	a	20 29				21 01					21 29				22 00				22 29					23 00	
London Victoria ⊖	a			20 45	20 59			21 15	21 29				21 45	21 59			22 15	22 29				22 45	22 59		

Table T180-R

Sundays
20 May to 2 December

Horsham and Dorking, Leatherhead, Epsom, Sutton, Hackbridge - London

		TL	SN	SW	TL		SW	TL
Horsham	d							
Warnham	d							
Ockley	d							
Holmwood	d							
Dorking	a							
Dorking	d	22 16			22 46		23 07	23 16
Box Hill & Westhumble	d	22 19			22 49			23 19
Leatherhead	d	22 24		22 45	22 54		23 15	23 24
Ashtead	d	22 28		22 48	22 58		23 18	23 28
Epsom	a	22 32		22 53	23 02		23 23	23 32
Epsom	d	22 33	22 44	22 54	23 03		23 24	23 33
Ewell East	d	22 37	22 48		23 07			23 37
Cheam	d	22 40	22 51		23 10			23 40
Sutton	a	22 43	22 54		23 13			23 43
Sutton	d							
West Croydon	a							
Norwood Junction	a							
Sutton	d	22 46	22 56		23 16			23 46
Carshalton	d	22 49	22 59		23 19			23 49
Hackbridge	d		23 02					23 52
Mitcham Junction	d		23 05					23 55
Mitcham Eastfields	a		23 08					23 58
Streatham	d							
Tulse Hill	a							
Tulse Hill	d							
London Bridge	a							
Herne Hill	a							
Loughborough Jn	a							
Elephant & Castle	a							
London Blackfriars	a							
City Thameslink	a							
Farringdon	a							
St Pancras International	a							
Balham ⊖	a		23 16					00 06
Clapham Junction	a	23 06	23 21	23 19	23 36		23 49	00 12
London Waterloo ⊖	a			23 29			00 01	
London Victoria ⊖	a	23 15	23 29		23 45			00 21

Please note, Network Rail have stated that further updates to this timetable are possible during the validity period.

London and Croydon - Purley, Caterham and Tattenham Corner

Miles	Miles	Miles			SN MO	TL MO ■	SN MX	SN MX		SN MO	SN MX	SN MX	SN MX	SN MX ■	SN MO	SN ■	SN MX	TL MO ■	TL MX ■	TL ■	TL ■	TL ■	SN ■
0	—	0	London Victoria ⊖	d												00 08							04 35
2¾	—	2¾	Clapham Junction	d												00 15							04 42
—	—	10	East Croydon	a												00 30							04 57
—	—	—	St Pancras International	d														00 51	00 52	01 32	02 32	03 32	
—	—	—	Farringdon	d																			
—	—	—	City Thameslink	d																			
—	—	—	London Blackfriars	d														01 01	01 02	01 40	02 40	03 40	
—	0	—	London Bridge ⊖	d													00 17						
—	8½	—	New Cross Gate ⊖	d																			
—	8¾	—	Norwood Junction	d											00 16		00 30						
10	10	—	East Croydon	a											00 19		00 34	01 27	01 28	02 06	03 06	04 06	
10	10	—	East Croydon	d		00 01		00 02		00 03				00 14	00 20	00 31	00 34	01 28	01 28	02 07	03 07	04 07	04 57
11½	11	—	South Croydon	d				00 04		00 05				00 17	00 22		00 37						
12½	12	—	Purley Oaks	d				00 07		00 08					00 25		00 40						
—	—	12½	Sanderstead	d							←	←		00 20									
13½	13	—	Purley	a		00 06		00 10		00 11	00 10	00 10			00 28	00 36	00 43	01 33	01 34	02 12	03 12	04 12	05 02
—	—	—	Purley	d				00 15	00 18	00 12	00 15	00 18	00 18		00 29		00 44						
—	14¼	—	Kenley	d				→	→	00 15	00 18				00 32		00 47						
—	15½	—	Whyteleafe	d						00 18	00 21				00 35		00 50						
—	—	15½	Upper Warlingham	a										00 27									
—	16	—	Whyteleafe South	d						00 20	00 23				00 37		00 52						
—	17¾	—	Caterham	a						00 25	00 28				00 42		00 57						
14¼	—	—	Reedham	d								00 20	00 20										
15	—	—	Coulsdon Town	d								00 23	00 23										
15¾	—	—	Woodmansterne	d								00 26	00 26										
16¾	—	—	Chipstead	d								00 29	00 29										
19¼	—	—	Kingswood	d			00 05					00 35	00 35										
20½	—	—	Tadworth	d	00 01		00 08					00 38	00 38										
21¼	—	—	Tattenham Corner	a	00 05		00 12					00 42	00 42										

		TL ■	SN ■	SN ■	TL ■	SN ■	SN		SN ■	TL ■	SN	TL ■	SN ■	SN		SN ■	TL ■	SN		TL ■	SN ■	SN	
London Victoria ⊖	d		05 21	05 32		05 39			05 51		06 02		06 09			06 21		06 32			06 39		
Clapham Junction	d		05 28	05 39		05 46			05 58		06 09		06 16			06 28		06 39			06 46		
East Croydon	a		05 41	05 51		05 55			06 09		06 19		06 26			06 39		06 49			06 56		
St Pancras International	d	04 32								05 45		05 55					06 15			06 25			
Farringdon	d									05 49		05 59					06 19			06 29			
City Thameslink	d									05 51		06 01					06 21			06 31			
London Blackfriars	d	04 40								05 54		06 04					06 24			06 34			
London Bridge ⊖	d				05 37		05 34			06 00		06 11		06 17			06 30			06 41		06 47	
New Cross Gate ⊖	d						05 40																
Norwood Junction	d				05 51		05 58			06 12							06 42						
East Croydon	a	05 06			05 54		06 02			06 16		06 24		06 31			06 46			06 54		07 01	
East Croydon	d	05 07	05 41	05 52	05 55	05 55	06 02		06 10	06 16	06 20	06 25	06 27	06 32		06 40	06 46	06 50		06 55	06 57	07 02	
South Croydon	d				05 58		06 05				06 23	06 28		06 35				06 53		06 58		07 05	
Purley Oaks	d						06 08				06 26			06 38				06 56				07 08	
Sanderstead	d		05 46		06a01				06 15			06a31				06 45				07a01			
Purley	a	05 12		05 56		06 01	06 11			06 22	06 29		06 32	06 41			06 53	06 59			07 02	07 11	
Purley	d						06 15	06 18			06 33			06 45	06 48			07 05	07 08			07 15	07 18
Kenley	d						06 18							06 48				07 08				07 18	
Whyteleafe	d						06 21							06 51				07 11				07 21	
Upper Warlingham	a		05 53						06 22							06 52							
Whyteleafe South	d						06 23							06 53				07 13				07 23	
Caterham	a						06 28							06 58				07 18				07 28	
Reedham	d							06 20			06 35				06 50				07 10				07 20
Coulsdon Town	d							06 23			06 38				06 53				07 13				07 23
Woodmansterne	d							06 26			06 41				06 56				07 16				07 26
Chipstead	d							06 29			06 44				06 59				07 19				07 29
Kingswood	d							06 35			06 50				07 05				07 25				07 35
Tadworth	d							06 38			06 53				07 08				07 28				07 38
Tattenham Corner	a							06 42			06 57				07 12				07 32				07 42

		SN ■	SN		TL ■	SN ■	SN		SN ■	SN	TL ■	SN ■	SN		SN ■	SN	TL ■	SN ■	SN		SN ■	SN	SN ■
London Victoria ⊖	d	06 51	07 02			07 09			07 21	07 32		07 39			07 51	08 01		08 09			08 21		08 39
Clapham Junction	d	06 58	07 09			07 16			07 28	07 39		07 46			07 58	08 08		08 16			08 28		08 46
East Croydon	a	07 09	07 19			07 27			07 39	07 49		07 57			08 09	08 19		08 27			08 39		08 57
St Pancras International	d				06 55						07 25						07 55						
Farringdon	d				06 59						07 29						07 59						
City Thameslink	d				07 01						07 31						08 01						
London Blackfriars	d				07 04						07 34						08 04						
London Bridge ⊖	d				07 11		07 17				07 41		07 47				08 11		08 17			08 10	
New Cross Gate ⊖	d																					08 18	
Norwood Junction	d																					08 39	
East Croydon	a				07 24		07 32				07 54		08 03				08 24		08 33			08 42	
East Croydon	d	07 10	07 20		07 25	07 27	07 33		07 40	07 50	07 55	07 57	08 04		08 10	08 20	08 25	08 27	08 34		08 40	08 43	08 57
South Croydon	d		07 23		07 28		07 35			07 53	07 58		08 06			08 23	08 28		08 36				
Purley Oaks	d		07 26				07 38			07 56			08 09			08 26			08 39				
Sanderstead	d	07 15			07a31				07 45		08a01				08 15		08a31				08 45		
Purley	a		07 29			07 32	07 41			07 59		08 02	08 12			08 29		08 32	08 42			08 50	09 02
Purley	d		07 35	07 38			07 45	07 48		08 05			08 15	08 18		08 32			08 45	08 48		08 53	
Kenley	d		07 38				07 48			08 08			08 18			08 35			08 48			08 56	
Whyteleafe	d		07 41				07 51			08 11			08 22			08 38			08 52			08 59	
Upper Warlingham	a	07 22							07 52						08 22						08 52		
Whyteleafe South	d		07 43				07 53			08 13			08 24			08 40			08 54			09 01	
Caterham	a		07 48				07 58			08 18			08 28			08 45			08 58			09 06	
Reedham	d			07 40				07 50						08 20						08 50			
Coulsdon Town	d			07 43				07 53						08 23						08 53			
Woodmansterne	d			07 46				07 56						08 26						08 56			
Chipstead	d			07 49				07 59						08 29						08 59			
Kingswood	d			07 55				08 05						08 35						09 05			
Tadworth	d			07 58				08 08						08 38						09 08			
Tattenham Corner	a			08 02				08 12						08 42						09 12			

London and Croydon - Purley, Caterham and Tattenham Corner

		SN		TL ■	SN ■	SN	SN ■	SN		TL ■	SN ■	SN	SN ■	SN		TL ■	SN ■	SN	SN	SN ■	SN	
London Victoria ⊖	d				08 51		09 09				09 21		09 39				09 51			10 09		
Clapham Junction	d				08 58		09 16				09 28		09 46				09 58			10 16		
East Croydon	a				09 09		09 26				09 39		09 56				10 09			10 26		
St Pancras International	d			08 35						09 05						09 35						
Farringdon	d			08 39						09 09						09 39						
City Thameslink	d			08 41						09 11						09 41						
London Blackfriars	d			08 44						09 14						09 44						
London Bridge ⊖	d	08 47		08 51		08 40		09 17		09 21		09 10		09 47		09 51		09 40	09 44		10 17	
New Cross Gate ⊖	d					08 48						09 18						09 48				
Norwood Junction	d			09 02		09 09				09 32		09 39				10 02		10 09				
East Croydon	a	09 03		09 06		09 12		09 32		09 36		09 42		10 02		10 06		10 13	10 24		10 31	
East Croydon	d	09 04		09 07	09 10	09 14	09 27	09 33		09 37	09 40	09 44	09 57	10 03		10 07	10 10	10 14	10 24	10 27	10 32	
South Croydon	d	09 06				09 17		09 35				09 47		10 06				10 17			10 35	
Purley Oaks	d	09 09				09 21		09 38				09 50		10 08				10 20			10 38	
Sanderstead	d				09 15						09 45						10 15					
Purley	a	09 12		09 14		09 24	09 33	09 41		09 43		09 54	10 03	10 11		10 13		10 24	10 31	10 33	10 41	
Purley	d	09 15	09 18			09 27		09 44	09 48			09 57		10 15	10 18			10 25	10 33		10 45	10 48
Kenley	d	09 18				09 30		09 47				10 00		10 18					10 36		10 48	
Whyteleafe	d	09 22				09 33		09 51				10 03		10 21					10 40		10 51	
Upper Warlingham	a				09 22						09 52						10 22					
Whyteleafe South	d	09 24				09 35		09 53				10 05		10 23					10 42		10 53	
Caterham	a	09 28				09 40		09 57				10 10		10 28					10 47		10 58	
Reedham	d		09 20						09 50						10 20			10 27				10 50
Coulsdon Town	d		09 23						09 53						10 23			10a31				10 53
Woodmansterne	d		09 26						09 56						10 26							10 56
Chipstead	d		09 29						09 59						10 29							10 59
Kingswood	d		09 35						10 05						10 35							11 05
Tadworth	d		09 38						10 08						10 38							11 08
Tattenham Corner	a		09 42						10 12						10 42							11 12

		TL ■	SN ■	SN	SN	SN ■	SN		TL ■	SN ■	SN	SN	SN ■	SN		TL ■	SN ■	SN	SN	SN ■	SN		TL ■
London Victoria ⊖	d		10 21			10 39				10 51			11 09				11 21			11 39			
Clapham Junction	d		10 28			10 46				10 58			11 16				11 28			11 46			
East Croydon	a		10 39			10 56				11 09			11 26				11 39			11 56			
St Pancras International	d	10 05							10 35							11 05							11 35
Farringdon	d	10 09							10 39							11 09							11 39
City Thameslink	d	10 11							10 41							11 11							11 41
London Blackfriars	d	10 14							10 44							11 14							11 44
London Bridge ⊖	d	10 21		10 10	10 14		10 47		10 51		10 40	10 44		11 17		11 21		11 10	11 14		11 47		11 51
New Cross Gate ⊖	d			10 18							10 48							11 18					
Norwood Junction	d	10 32		10 39					11 02		11 09					11 32		11 39					12 02
East Croydon	a	10 36		10 43	10 54		11 01		11 06		11 13	11 24		11 31		11 36		11 43	11 54		12 01		12 06
East Croydon	d	10 37	10 40	10 44	10 54	10 57	11 02		11 07	11 10	11 14	11 24	11 27	11 32		11 37	11 40	11 44	11 54	11 57	12 02		12 07
South Croydon	d			10 47			11 05				11 17			11 35				11 47			12 05		
Purley Oaks	d			10 50			11 08				11 20			11 38				11 50			12 08		
Sanderstead	d		10 45							11 15							11 45						
Purley	a	10 43		10 54	11 01	11 03	11 11		11 13		11 24	11 31	11 33	11 41		11 43		11 54	12 01	12 03	12 11		12 13
Purley	d			10 55	11 03		11 15	11 18			11 25	11 33		11 45	11 48			11 55	12 03		12 15	12 18	
Kenley	d				11 06		11 18					11 36		11 48					12 06		12 18		
Whyteleafe	d				11 10		11 21					11 40		11 51					12 10		12 21		
Upper Warlingham	a		10 52							11 22							11 52						
Whyteleafe South	d				11 12		11 23					11 42		11 53					12 12		12 23		
Caterham	a				11 17		11 28					11 47		11 58					12 17		12 28		
Reedham	d			10 57				11 20			11 27				11 50			11 57				12 20	
Coulsdon Town	d			11a01				11 23			11a31				11 53			12a01				12 23	
Woodmansterne	d							11 26							11 56							12 26	
Chipstead	d							11 29							11 59							12 29	
Kingswood	d							11 35							12 05							12 35	
Tadworth	d							11 38							12 08							12 38	
Tattenham Corner	a							11 42							12 12							12 42	

		SN ■	SN	SN	SN ■	SN		TL ■	SN ■	SN	SN	SN ■	SN		TL ■	SN ■	SN	SN	SN ■	SN		TL ■	SN ■
London Victoria ⊖	d	11 51			12 09				12 21			12 39				12 51			13 09				13 21
Clapham Junction	d	11 58			12 16				12 28			12 46				12 58			13 16				13 28
East Croydon	a	12 09			12 26				12 39			12 56				13 09			13 26				13 39
St Pancras International	d							12 05							12 35							13 05	
Farringdon	d							12 09							12 39							13 09	
City Thameslink	d							12 11							12 41							13 11	
London Blackfriars	d							12 14							12 44							13 14	
London Bridge ⊖	d		11 40	11 44		12 17		12 21		12 10	12 14		12 47		12 51		12 40	12 44		13 17		13 21	
New Cross Gate ⊖	d		11 48							12 18							12 48						
Norwood Junction	d		12 09					12 32		12 39					13 02		13 09					13 32	
East Croydon	a		12 13	12 24		12 31		12 36		12 43	12 54		13 01		13 06		13 13	13 24		13 31		13 36	
East Croydon	d	12 10	12 14	12 24	12 27	12 32		12 37	12 40	12 44	12 54	12 57	13 02		13 07	13 10	13 14	13 24	13 27	13 32		13 37	13 40
South Croydon	d		12 17			12 35				12 47			13 05				13 17			13 35			
Purley Oaks	d		12 20			12 38				12 50			13 08				13 21			13 38			
Sanderstead	d	12 15							12 45							13 15							13 45
Purley	a		12 24	12 31	12 33	12 41		12 43		12 54	13 01	13 03	13 11		13 13		13 24	13 31	13 33	13 41		13 43	
Purley	d		12 25	12 33		12 45	12 48			12 55	13 03		13 15	13 18			13 25	13 33		13 45	13 48		
Kenley	d			12 36		12 48					13 06		13 18					13 36		13 48			
Whyteleafe	d			12 40		12 51					13 10		13 21					13 40		13 51			
Upper Warlingham	a	12 22							12 52							13 22							13 52
Whyteleafe South	d			12 42		12 53					13 12		13 23					13 42		13 53			
Caterham	a			12 47		12 58					13 17		13 28					13 47		13 58			
Reedham	d		12 27				12 50			12 57				13 20			13 27				13 50		
Coulsdon Town	d		12a31				12 53			13a01				13 23			13a31				13 53		
Woodmansterne	d						12 56							13 26							13 56		
Chipstead	d						12 59							13 29							13 59		
Kingswood	d						13 05							13 35							14 05		
Tadworth	d						13 08							13 38							14 08		
Tattenham Corner	a						13 12							13 42							14 12		

London and Croydon - Purley, Caterham and Tattenham Corner

		SN	SN	SN ■	SN		TL ■	SN ■	SN	SN	SN ■	SN		TL ■	SN ■	SN	SN	SN ■	SN		TL ■	SN ■
London Victoria ⊖	d			13 39				13 51			14 09				14 21			14 39				14 51
Clapham Junction	d			13 46				13 58			14 16				14 28			14 46				14 58
East Croydon	a			13 56				14 09			14 26				14 39			14 56				15 09
St Pancras International	d						13 35							14 05							14 35	
Farringdon	d						13 39							14 09							14 39	
City Thameslink	d						13 41							14 11							14 41	
London Blackfriars	d						13 44							14 14							14 44	
London Bridge ⊖	d	13 10	13 14		13 47		13 51		13 40	13 44		14 17		14 21		14 10	14 14		14 47		14 51	
New Cross Gate ⊖	d	13 18							13 48							14 18						
Norwood Junction	d	13 39					14 02		14 09					14 32		14 39					15 02	
East Croydon	a	13 43	13 54		14 01		14 06		14 13	14 24		14 31		14 36		14 43	14 54		15 01		15 06	
East Croydon	d	13 44	13 54	13 57	14 02		14 07	14 10	14 14	14 24	14 27	14 32		14 37	14 40	14 44	14 54	14 57	15 02		15 07	15 10
South Croydon	d	13 47			14 05				14 17			14 35				14 47			15 05			
Purley Oaks	d	13 50			14 08				14 20			14 38				14 50			15 08			
Sanderstead	d							14 15							14 45							15 15
Purley	a	13 54	14 01	14 03	14 11		14 13		14 24	14 31	14 33	14 41		14 43		14 54	15 01	15 03	15 11		15 13	
Purley	d	13 55	14 03		14 15	14 18			14 25	14 33		14 45	14 48			14 55	15 03		15 15	15 18		
Kenley	d		14 06		14 18					14 36		14 48					15 06		15 18			
Whyteleafe	d		14 10		14 21					14 40		14 51					15 10		15 21			
Upper Warlingham	a							14 22							14 52							15 22
Whyteleafe South	d		14 12		14 23					14 42		14 53					15 12		15 23			
Caterham	a		14 17		14 28					14 47		14 58					15 17		15 28			
Reedham	d	13 57				14 20			14 27				14 50			14 57				15 20		
Coulsdon Town	d	14a01				14 23			14a31				14 53			15a01				15 23		
Woodmansterne	d					14 26							14 56							15 26		
Chipstead	d					14 29							14 59							15 29		
Kingswood	d					14 35							15 05							15 35		
Tadworth	d					14 38							15 08							15 38		
Tattenham Corner	a					14 42							15 12							15 42		

		SN	SN	SN ■	SN		TL ■	SN ■	SN	SN	SN ■	SN		TL ■	SN ■	SN	SN	SN ■	SN		TL ■	SN ■	SN
London Victoria ⊖	d			15 09				15 21			15 39				15 51			16 09				16 21	16 31
Clapham Junction	d			15 16				15 28			15 46				15 58			16 16				16 28	16 38
East Croydon	a			15 26				15 39			15 56				16 09			16 26				16 39	16 49
St Pancras International	d						15 05							15 35							16 05		
Farringdon	d						15 09							15 39							16 09		
City Thameslink	d						15 11							15 41							16 11		
London Blackfriars	d						15 14							15 44							16 14		
London Bridge ⊖	d	14 40	14 44		15 17		15 21		15 10	15 14		15 47		15 51		15 40	15 44		16 17		16 21		
New Cross Gate ⊖	d	14 48							15 18							15 48							
Norwood Junction	d	15 09					15 32		15 39					16 02		16 09					16 32		
East Croydon	a	15 13	15 24		15 31		15 36		15 43	15 54		16 02		16 06		16 13	16 24		16 32		16 36		
East Croydon	d	15 14	15 24	15 27	15 32		15 37	15 40	15 44	15 54	15 57	16 03		16 07	16 10	16 14	16 24	16 27	16 33		16 37	16 40	16 50
South Croydon	d	15 17			15 35			15 42	15 47			16 06			16 12	16 17			16 36			16 42	16 53
Purley Oaks	d	15 20			15 38				15 50			16 08				16 20			16 38				16 56
Sanderstead	d							15 45							16 15							16 45	
Purley	a	15 24	15 31	15 35	15 41		15 43		15 54	16 01	16 03	16 11		16 13		16 24	16 31	16 33	16 41		16 43		16 59
Purley	d	15 25	15 33		15 45	15 48			15 55	16 03		16 15	16 18			16 25	16 33		16 45	16 48			17 01
Kenley	d		15 36		15 48					16 06		16 18					16 36		16 48				17 04
Whyteleafe	d		15 40		15 51					16 10		16 21					16 40		16 51				17 07
Upper Warlingham	a							15 52							16 22							16 52	
Whyteleafe South	d		15 42		15 53					16 12		16 23					16 42		16 53				17 09
Caterham	a		15 47		15 58					16 17		16 28					16 47		16 58				17 14
Reedham	d	15 27				15 50			15 57				16 20			16 27				16 50			
Coulsdon Town	d	15a31				15 53			16a01				16 23			16a31				16 53			
Woodmansterne	d					15 56							16 26							16 56			
Chipstead	d					15 59							16 29							16 59			
Kingswood	d					16 05							16 35							17 05			
Tadworth	d					16 08							16 38							17 08			
Tattenham Corner	a					16 12							16 42							17 12			

		TL ■	SN ■	SN		TL ■	SN ■	SN		TL ■	SN		TL ■	SN ■	SN		TL ■	SN		TL ■	SN ■	SN	
London Victoria ⊖	d		16 39				16 51	17 02						17 21	17 32						17 51	18 02	
Clapham Junction	d		16 46				16 58	17 09						17 28	17 39						17 58	18 09	
East Croydon	a		16 56				17 09	17 19						17 39	17 49						18 09	18 19	
St Pancras International	d	16 25				16 35				16 55			17 05				17 25			17 35			
Farringdon	d	16 29				16 39				16 59			17 09				17 29			17 39			
City Thameslink	d	16 31				16 41				17 01			17 11				17 31			17 41			
London Blackfriars	d	16 34				16 44				17 04			17 14				17 34			17 44			
London Bridge ⊖	d	16 41		16 47		16 51				17 11	17 17		17 21				17 41	17 47		17 51			
New Cross Gate ⊖	d																						
Norwood Junction	d					17 02							17 32							18 02			
East Croydon	a	16 54		17 02		17 06				17 24	17 32		17 36				17 54	18 02		18 06			
East Croydon	d	16 55	16 57	17 03		17 07	17 10	17 20		17 25	17 33		17 37	17 40	17 50		17 56	18 03		18 07	18 10	18 20	
South Croydon	d	16 58		17 06				17 23		17 28	17 36				17 53		17 59	18 06				18 23	
Purley Oaks	d			17 08				17 26			17 38				17 56			18 08				18 26	
Sanderstead	d	17 02					17 15			17 32				17 45			18 02				18 15		
Purley	a		17 03	17 11		17 13		17 29			17 41		17 43		17 59			18 11		18 13		18 29	
Purley	d			17 15	17 18			17 35	17 38		17 45	17 48			18 05	18 08		18 15	18 18			18 35	18 38
Kenley	d			17 18				17 38			17 48				18 08			18 18				18 38	
Whyteleafe	d			17 21				17 41			17 51				18 11			18 21				18 41	
Upper Warlingham	a	17 09					17 22			17 39				17 52			18 09				18 22		
Whyteleafe South	d			17 23				17 43			17 53				18 13			18 23				18 43	
Caterham	a			17 28				17 48			17 58				18 18			18 28				18 48	
Reedham	d				17 20				17 40			17 50				18 10			18 20				18 40
Coulsdon Town	d				17 23				17 43			17 53				18 13			18 23				18 43
Woodmansterne	d				17 26				17 46			17 56				18 16			18 26				18 46
Chipstead	d				17 29				17 49			17 59				18 19			18 29				18 49
Kingswood	d				17 35				17 55			18 05				18 25			18 35				18 55
Tadworth	d				17 38				17 58			18 08				18 28			18 38				18 58
Tattenham Corner	a				17 42				18 02			18 12				18 32			18 42				19 02

London and Croydon - Purley, Caterham and Tattenham Corner

		TL ■	SN		TL ■	SN ■	SN		TL ■	SN		TL ■	SN ■	SN	TL ■	SN ■	SN		TL ■	SN ■	SN	SN
London Victoria ⊖	d					18 21	18 32						18 51			19 09				19 21		
Clapham Junction	d					18 28	18 39						18 58			19 16				19 28		
East Croydon	a					18 39	18 49						19 09			19 27				19 39		
St Pancras International	d	17 55			18 05				18 25			18 35			18 55				19 05			
Farringdon	d	17 59			18 09				18 29			18 39			18 59				19 09			
City Thameslink	d	18 01			18 11				18 31			18 41			19 01				19 11			
London Blackfriars	d	18 04			18 14				18 34			18 44			19 04				19 14			
London Bridge ⊖	d	18 11	18 17		18 21				18 41	18 47		18 51		18 40	19 11		19 17		19 21		19 10	19 14
New Cross Gate ⊖	d													18 48							19 18	
Norwood Junction	d				18 33							19 02		19 09					19 32		19 39	
East Croydon	a	18 24	18 33		18 36				18 54	19 03		19 06		19 13	19 24		19 32		19 36		19 42	19 54
East Croydon	d	18 25	18 33		18 37	18 40	18 50		18 55	19 03		19 07	19 10	19 13	19 25	19 27	19 33		19 37	19 40	19 44	19 54
South Croydon	d	18 28	18 36				18 53		18 58	19 06				19 16	19 28		19 35				19 47	
Purley Oaks	d		18 38				18 56			19 08				19 19			19 38				19 50	
Sanderstead	d	18 32				18 45			19 02				19 15		19 32					19 45		
Purley	a		18 41		18 43		18 59			19 11		19 13		19 22		19 32	19 41		19 43		19 54	20 01
Purley	d		18 45	18 48			19 05	19 08		19 15	19 18			19 25			19 45	19 48			19 55	20 03
Kenley	d		18 48				19 08			19 18							19 48					20 06
Whyteleafe	d		18 51				19 11			19 21							19 51					20 10
Upper Warlingham	a	18 39				18 52			19 09				19 22		19 39					19 52		
Whyteleafe South	d		18 53				19 13			19 23							19 53					20 12
Caterham	a		18 58				19 18			19 28							19 58					20 17
Reedham	d			18 50				19 10			19 20			19 27				19 50			19 57	
Coulsdon Town	d			18 53				19 13			19 23			19a31				19 53			20a01	
Woodmansterne	d			18 56				19 16			19 26							19 56				
Chipstead	d			18 59				19 19			19 29							19 59				
Kingswood	d			19 05				19 25			19 35							20 05				
Tadworth	d			19 08				19 28			19 38							20 08				
Tattenham Corner	a			19 12				19 32			19 42							20 12				

		SN ■	SN		TL ■	SN ■	SN	SN	SN ■	SN		TL ■	SN ■	SN	SN	SN ■	SN		TL ■	SN ■	SN	SN	SN ■
London Victoria ⊖	d	19 39				19 51			20 09				20 21			20 39				20 51			21 09
Clapham Junction	d	19 46				19 58			20 16				20 28			20 46				20 58			21 16
East Croydon	a	19 57				20 09			20 26				20 39			20 57				21 09			21 26
St Pancras International	d				19 35							20 05							20 35				
Farringdon	d				19 39							20 09							20 39				
City Thameslink	d				19 41							20 11							20 41				
London Blackfriars	d				19 44							20 14							20 44				
London Bridge ⊖	d		19 47		19 51		19 40	19 44		20 17		20 21		20 10	20 14		20 47		20 51		20 40	20 44	
New Cross Gate ⊖	d						19 48							20 18							20 48		
Norwood Junction	d				20 02		20 09					20 32		20 39					21 02		21 09		
East Croydon	a		20 02		20 06		20 13	20 24		20 31		20 36		20 43	20 53		21 02		21 06		21 13	21 24	
East Croydon	d	19 58	20 03		20 07	20 10	20 14	20 24	20 27	20 32		20 37	20 40	20 44	20 54	20 58	21 03		21 07	21 10	21 14	21 24	21 27
South Croydon	d		20 06				20 17			20 35				20 47			21 06				21 17		
Purley Oaks	d		20 08				20 20			20 38				20 50			21 08				21 20		
Sanderstead	d					20 15							20 45							21 15			
Purley	a	20 03	20 11		20 13		20 24	20 31	20 33	20 41		20 43		20 54	21 01	21 03	21 11		21 13		21 24	21 32	21 33
Purley	d		20 15	20 18			20 25	20 33		20 45	20 48			20 55	21 03		21 15	21 18			21 25	21 34	
Kenley	d		20 18					20 36		20 48					21 06		21 18					21 37	
Whyteleafe	d		20 21					20 40		20 51					21 10		21 21					21 41	
Upper Warlingham	a					20 22							20 52							21 22			
Whyteleafe South	d		20 23					20 42		20 53					21 12		21 23					21 43	
Caterham	a		20 28					20 47		20 58					21 17		21 28					21 47	
Reedham	d			20 20			20 27				20 50			20 57				21 20			21 27		
Coulsdon Town	d			20 23			20a31				20 53			21a01				21 23			21a31		
Woodmansterne	d			20 26							20 56							21 26					
Chipstead	d			20 29							20 59							21 29					
Kingswood	d			20 35							21 05							21 35					
Tadworth	d			20 38							21 08							21 38					
Tattenham Corner	a			20 42							21 12							21 42					

		SN		TL ■	SN ■	SN	SN	SN ■	SN		TL ■	SN ■	SN	SN	SN ■	SN		TL ■	SN ■	SN	SN	SN ■
London Victoria ⊖	d				21 21			21 39				21 51			22 09				22 21			22 39
Clapham Junction	d				21 28			21 46				21 58			22 16				22 28			22 46
East Croydon	a				21 39			21 56				22 09			22 26				22 39			22 56
St Pancras International	d			21 05							21 35							22 05				
Farringdon	d			21 09							21 39							22 09				
City Thameslink	d			21 11							21 41							22 11				
London Blackfriars	d			21 14							21 44							22 14				
London Bridge ⊖	d	21 17		21 21		21 10	21 14		21 47		21 51		21 40	21 44		22 17		22 21		22 10	22 14	
New Cross Gate ⊖	d					21 18							21 48							22 18		
Norwood Junction	d			21 32		21 39					22 02		22 09					22 32		22 39		
East Croydon	a	21 31		21 36		21 43	21 54		22 01		22 06		22 13	22 24		22 31		22 36		22 43	22 54	
East Croydon	d	21 32		21 37	21 40	21 44	21 54	21 57	22 02		22 07	22 10	22 14	22 24	22 27	22 32		22 37	22 40	22 44	22 54	22 57
South Croydon	d	21 35				21 47			22 05				22 17			22 35				22 47		
Purley Oaks	d	21 38				21 50			22 08				22 21			22 38				22 50		
Sanderstead	d				21 45							22 15							22 45			
Purley	a	21 41		21 43		21 54	22 01	22 03	22 11		22 13		22 24	22 31	22 33	22 41		22 43		22 54	23 01	23 03
Purley	d	21 45	21 48			21 55	22 03		22 15	22 18			22 25	22 33		22 45	22 48			22 55	23 03	
Kenley	d	21 48					22 06		22 18					22 36		22 48					23 06	
Whyteleafe	d	21 51					22 10		22 21					22 40		22 51					23 10	
Upper Warlingham	a				21 52							22 22							22 52			
Whyteleafe South	d	21 53					22 12		22 23					22 42		22 53					23 12	
Caterham	a	21 58					22 17		22 28					22 47		22 58					23 17	
Reedham	d		21 50			21 57				22 20			22 27				22 50			22 57		
Coulsdon Town	d		21 53			22a01				22 23			22a31				22 53			23a01		
Woodmansterne	d		21 56							22 26							22 56					
Chipstead	d		21 59							22 29							22 59					
Kingswood	d		22 05							22 35							23 05					
Tadworth	d		22 08							22 38							23 08					
Tattenham Corner	a		22 12							22 42							23 12					

Table T181-F

London and Croydon - Purley, Caterham and Tattenham Corner

Mondays to Fridays
21 May to 7 December

		SN		TL ■	SN ■	SN	SN ■	SN		TL ■	SN ■	SN ■	SN	SN FX	SN ■
London Victoria 15 ⊖	d				22 52		23 09				23 21	23 36			23 53
Clapham Junction 10	d				22 59		23 16				23 28	23 43			23 59
East Croydon	a				23 09		23 26				23 39	23 58			00 14
St Pancras International	d			22 35						23 05					
Farringdon	d			22 39						23 09					
City Thameslink	d			22 41											
London Blackfriars	d			22 44						23 14					
London Bridge 4 ⊖	d	22 47		22 51		22 40		23 17		23 21			23 47	23 47	
New Cross Gate 4 ⊖	d					22 48									
Norwood Junction 2	d			23 02		23 09				23 32					
East Croydon	a	23 01		23 06		23 13		23 31		23 36			00 01	00 01	
East Croydon ⇌	d	23 02		23 07	23 10	23 14	23 27	23 32		23 37	23 40	23 59	00 02	00 02	00 14
South Croydon 4	d	23 05				23 17		23 34					00 04	00 04	00 17
Purley Oaks	d	23 08				23 20		23 37					00 07	00 07	
Sanderstead	d				23 15						23 45				00 20
Purley 4	a	23 11		23 13		23 24	23 32	23 40		23 42		00 04	00 10	00 10	
Purley	d	23 15	23 18			23 25		23 45	23 48				00 15	00 18	
Kenley	d	23 18						23 48					00 18		
Whyteleafe	d	23 21						23 51					00 21		
Upper Warlingham	a				23 22						23 52				00 27
Whyteleafe South	d	23 23						23 53					00 23		
Caterham	a	23 28						23 58					00 28		
Reedham	d		23 20			23 27			23 50					00 20	
Coulsdon Town	d		23 23			23a31			23 53					00 23	
Woodmansterne	d		23 26						23 56					00 26	
Chipstead	d		23 29						23 59					00 29	
Kingswood	d		23 35						00 05					00 35	
Tadworth	d		23 38						00 08					00 38	
Tattenham Corner	a		23 42						00 12					00 42	

Saturdays
26 May to 8 December

		SN	SN	SN ■	SN	SN ■	SN	SN	SN	TL ■	SN ■	TL ■	SN ■	TL ■	SN ■	TL ■	SN ■	TL ■	SN ■	SN ■	TL ■	SN ■
London Victoria 15 ⊖	d					00 08					01 10		02 10		03 10		04 10		05 08	05 39		06 09
Clapham Junction 10	d					00 15					01 17		02 17		03 17		04 17		05 16	05 46		06 16
East Croydon	a					00 30					01 32		02 32		03 32		04 31		05 31	05 56		06 26
St Pancras International	d									00 52		01 32		02 32		03 32		04 32			05 45	
Farringdon	d																				05 49	
City Thameslink	d																					
London Blackfriars	d									01 02		01 40		02 40		03 40		04 40			05 54	
London Bridge 4 ⊖	d						00 17	00 17													06 00	
New Cross Gate 4 ⊖	d																					
Norwood Junction 2	d						00 30	00 30														
East Croydon	a						00 34	00 34		01 28		02 06		03 06		04 06		05 06			06 14	
East Croydon ⇌	d	00 02		00 14		00 31	00 34	00 34		01 28	01 33	02 07	02 32	03 07	03 32	04 07	04 31	05 07	05 31	05 57	06 16	06 27
South Croydon 4	d	00 04		00 17			00 37	00 37														
Purley Oaks	d	00 07					00 40	00 40														
Sanderstead	d			00 20																		
Purley 4	a	00 10				00 36	00 43	00 43		01 34	01 38	02 12	02 38	03 12	03 38	04 12	04 37	05 12	05 37	06 03	06 22	06 33
Purley	d	00 15			00 18		00 44	00 47	00 50													
Kenley	d	00 18					00 47	00 50														
Whyteleafe	d	00 21					00 50	00 53														
Upper Warlingham	a			00 27																		
Whyteleafe South	d	00 23					00 52	00 55														
Caterham	a	00 28					00 57	01 00														
Reedham	d				00 20				00 52													
Coulsdon Town	d				00 23				00 55													
Woodmansterne	d				00 26				00 58													
Chipstead	d				00 29				01 01													
Kingswood	d		00 05		00 35				01 07													
Tadworth	d		00 08		00 38				01 10													
Tattenham Corner	a		00 12		00 42				01 14													

Table T181-F

London and Croydon - Purley, Caterham and Tattenham Corner

Saturdays
26 May to 8 December

		SN		SN ■	SN	SN	SN ■	SN		SN ■	SN	SN	SN ■	SN		TL ■	SN ■	SN	SN	SN ■	SN	
London Victoria 15 ⊖	d			06 21			06 39			06 51			07 09				07 21			07 39		
Clapham Junction 10	d			06 28			06 46			06 58			07 16				07 28			07 46		
East Croydon	a			06 39			06 56			07 09			07 26				07 39			07 56		
St Pancras International	d															07 05						
Farringdon	d															07 09						
City Thameslink	d																					
London Blackfriars	d															07 14						
London Bridge 4 ⊖	d	06 17			06 11	06 14		06 47			06 40	06 44		07 17		07 22		07 10	07 14		07 47	
New Cross Gate 4 ⊖	d				06 18						06 48							07 18				
Norwood Junction 2	d				06 39						07 09					07 33		07 39				
East Croydon	a	06 31			06 43	06 54		07 01			07 13	07 24		07 31		07 36		07 43	07 54		08 01	
East Croydon ⇌	d	06 32		06 40	06 44	06 54	06 57	07 02		07 10	07 14	07 24	07 27	07 32		07 37	07 40	07 44	07 54	07 57	08 02	
South Croydon 4	d	06 35			06 47			07 05			07 17			07 35				07 47			08 05	
Purley Oaks	d	06 38			06 50			07 08			07 20			07 38				07 50			08 08	
Sanderstead	d			06 45						07 15							07 45					
Purley 4	a	06 41			06 54	07 01	07 03	07 11			07 24	07 31	07 33	07 41		07 43		07 54	08 01	08 03	08 11	
Purley	d	06 45	06 48		06 55	07 03		07 15	07 18		07 25	07 33		07 45	07 48			07 55	08 03		08 15	08 18
Kenley	d	06 48				07 06		07 18				07 36		07 48					08 06		08 18	
Whyteleafe	d	06 51				07 10		07 21				07 40		07 51					08 10		08 21	
Upper Warlingham	a			06 52						07 22							07 52					
Whyteleafe South	d	06 53				07 12		07 23				07 42		07 53					08 12		08 23	
Caterham	a	06 58				07 17		07 28				07 47		07 58					08 17		08 28	
Reedham	d		06 50		06 57				07 20		07 27				07 50			07 57				08 20
Coulsdon Town	d		06 53		07a01				07 23		07a31				07 53			08a01				08 23
Woodmansterne	d		06 56						07 26						07 56							08 26
Chipstead	d		06 59						07 29						07 59							08 29
Kingswood	d		07 05						07 35						08 05							08 35
Tadworth	d		07 08						07 38						08 08							08 38
Tattenham Corner	a		07 12						07 42						08 12							08 42

		TL ■	SN ■	SN	SN	SN ■	SN		TL ■	SN ■	SN	SN	SN ■	SN		TL ■	SN ■	SN	SN	SN ■	SN		TL ■
London Victoria 15 ⊖	d		07 51			08 09				08 21			08 39				08 51			09 09			
Clapham Junction 10	d		07 58			08 16				08 28			08 46				08 58			09 16			
East Croydon	a		08 09			08 26				08 39			08 56				09 09			09 26			
St Pancras International	d	07 35							08 05							08 35							09 05
Farringdon	d	07 39							08 09							08 39							09 09
City Thameslink	d																						09 11
London Blackfriars	d	07 44							08 14							08 44							09 14
London Bridge 4 ⊖	d	07 52		07 40	07 44		08 17		08 22		08 10	08 14		08 47		08 52		08 40	08 44		09 17		09 22
New Cross Gate 4 ⊖	d			07 48							08 18							08 48					
Norwood Junction 2	d	08 03		08 09					08 33		08 39					09 03		09 09					09 33
East Croydon	a	08 06		08 13	08 24		08 31		08 36		08 43	08 54		09 01		09 06		09 13	09 24		09 31		09 36
East Croydon ⇌	d	08 07	08 10	08 14	08 24	08 27	08 32		08 37	08 40	08 44	08 54	08 57	09 02		09 07	09 10	09 14	09 24	09 27	09 32		09 37
South Croydon 4	d			08 17			08 35				08 47			09 05				09 17			09 35		
Purley Oaks	d			08 20			08 38				08 50			09 08				09 20			09 38		
Sanderstead	d		08 15							08 45							09 15						
Purley 4	a	08 13		08 24	08 31	08 33	08 41		08 43		08 54	09 01	09 03	09 11		09 13		09 24	09 31	09 33	09 41		09 43
Purley	d			08 25	08 33		08 45	08 48			08 55	09 03		09 15	09 18			09 25	09 33		09 45	09 48	
Kenley	d				08 36		08 48					09 06		09 18					09 36		09 48		
Whyteleafe	d				08 40		08 51					09 10		09 21					09 40		09 51		
Upper Warlingham	a		08 22							08 52							09 22						
Whyteleafe South	d				08 42		08 53					09 12		09 23					09 42		09 53		
Caterham	a				08 47		08 58					09 17		09 28					09 47		09 58		
Reedham	d			08 27				08 50			08 57				09 20			09 27				09 50	
Coulsdon Town	d			08a31				08 53			09a01				09 23			09a31				09 53	
Woodmansterne	d							08 56							09 26							09 56	
Chipstead	d							08 59							09 29							09 59	
Kingswood	d							09 05							09 35							10 05	
Tadworth	d							09 08							09 38							10 08	
Tattenham Corner	a							09 12							09 42							10 12	

		SN ■	SN	SN	SN ■	SN		TL ■	SN ■	SN	SN	SN ■	SN		TL ■	SN ■	SN	SN	SN ■	SN		TL ■	SN ■
London Victoria 15 ⊖	d	09 21			09 39				09 51			10 09				10 21			10 39				10 51
Clapham Junction 10	d	09 28			09 46				09 58			10 16				10 28			10 46				10 58
East Croydon	a	09 39			09 56				10 09			10 26				10 39			10 56				11 09
St Pancras International	d							09 35							10 05							10 35	
Farringdon	d							09 39							10 09							10 39	
City Thameslink	d							09 41							10 11							10 41	
London Blackfriars	d							09 44							10 14							10 44	
London Bridge 4 ⊖	d		09 10	09 14		09 47		09 52		09 40	09 44		10 17		10 22		10 10	10 14		10 47		10 52	
New Cross Gate 4 ⊖	d		09 18							09 48							10 18						
Norwood Junction 2	d		09 39					10 03		10 09					10 33		10 39					11 03	
East Croydon	a		09 43	09 54		10 01		10 06		10 13	10 24		10 31		10 36		10 43	10 54		11 01		11 06	
East Croydon ⇌	d	09 40	09 44	09 54	09 57	10 02		10 07	10 10	10 14	10 24	10 27	10 32		10 37	10 40	10 44	10 54	10 57	11 02		11 07	11 10
South Croydon 4	d		09 47			10 05				10 17			10 35				10 47			11 05			
Purley Oaks	d		09 50			10 08				10 20			10 38				10 50			11 08			
Sanderstead	d	09 45							10 15							10 45							11 15
Purley 4	a		09 54	10 01	10 03	10 11		10 13		10 24	10 31	10 33	10 41		10 43		10 54	11 01	11 03	11 11		11 13	
Purley	d		09 55	10 03		10 15	10 18			10 25	10 33		10 45	10 48			10 55	11 03		11 15	11 18		
Kenley	d			10 06		10 18					10 36		10 48					11 06		11 18			
Whyteleafe	d			10 10		10 21					10 40		10 51					11 10		11 21			
Upper Warlingham	a	09 52							10 22							10 52							11 22
Whyteleafe South	d			10 12		10 23					10 42		10 53					11 12		11 23			
Caterham	a			10 17		10 28					10 47		10 58					11 17		11 28			
Reedham	d		09 57				10 20			10 27				10 50			10 57				11 20		
Coulsdon Town	d		10a01				10 23			10a31				10 53			11a01				11 23		
Woodmansterne	d						10 26							10 56							11 26		
Chipstead	d						10 29							10 59							11 29		
Kingswood	d						10 35							11 05							11 35		
Tadworth	d						10 38							11 08							11 38		
Tattenham Corner	a						10 42							11 12							11 42		

Table T181-F

Saturdays
26 May to 8 December

London and Croydon - Purley, Caterham and Tattenham Corner

		SN	SN	SN ■	SN		TL ■	SN ■	SN	SN	SN ■	SN		TL ■	SN ■	SN	SN	SN ■	SN		TL ■	SN ■
London Victoria ⊖	d			11 09				11 21			11 39				11 51			12 09				12 21
Clapham Junction	d			11 16				11 28			11 46				11 58			12 16				12 28
East Croydon	a			11 26				11 39			11 56				12 09			12 26				12 39
St Pancras International	d						11 05							11 35							12 05	
Farringdon	d						11 09							11 39							12 09	
City Thameslink	d						11 11							11 41							12 11	
London Blackfriars	d						11 14							11 44							12 14	
London Bridge ⊖	d	10 40	10 44		11 17		11 22		11 10	11 14		11 47		11 52		11 40	11 44		12 17		12 22	
New Cross Gate ⊖	d	10 48							11 18							11 48						
Norwood Junction	d	11 09					11 33		11 39					12 03		12 09					12 33	
East Croydon	a	11 13	11 24		11 31		11 36		11 43	11 54		12 01		12 06		12 13	12 24		12 31		12 36	
East Croydon	d	11 14	11 24	11 27	11 32		11 37	11 40	11 44	11 54	11 57	12 02		12 07	12 10	12 14	12 24	12 27	12 32		12 37	12 40
South Croydon	d	11 17			11 35				11 47			12 05				12 17			12 35			
Purley Oaks	d	11 20			11 38				11 50			12 08				12 20			12 38			
Sanderstead	d							11 45							12 15							12 45
Purley	a	11 24	11 31	11 33	11 41		11 43		11 54	12 01	12 03	12 11		12 13		12 24	12 31	12 33	12 41		12 43	
Purley	d	11 25	11 33		11 45	11 48			11 55	12 03		12 15	12 18			12 25	12 33		12 45	12 48		
Kenley	d		11 36		11 48					12 06		12 18					12 36		12 48			
Whyteleafe	d		11 39		11 51					12 10		12 21					12 40		12 51			
Upper Warlingham	a							11 52							12 22							12 52
Whyteleafe South	d		11 41		11 53					12 12		12 23					12 42		12 53			
Caterham	a		11 46		11 58					12 17		12 28					12 47		12 58			
Reedham	d	11 27				11 50			11 57				12 20			12 27				12 50		
Coulsdon Town	d	11a31				11 53			12a01				12 23			12a31				12 53		
Woodmansterne	d					11 56							12 26							12 56		
Chipstead	d					11 59							12 29							12 59		
Kingswood	d					12 05							12 35							13 05		
Tadworth	d					12 08							12 38							13 08		
Tattenham Corner	a					12 12							12 42							13 12		

		SN	SN	SN ■	SN		TL ■	SN ■	SN	SN	SN ■	SN		TL ■	SN ■	SN	SN	SN ■	SN		TL ■	SN ■	SN
London Victoria ⊖	d			12 39				12 51			13 09				13 21			13 39				13 51	
Clapham Junction	d			12 46				12 58			13 16				13 28			13 46				13 58	
East Croydon	a			12 56				13 09			13 26				13 39			13 56				14 09	
St Pancras International	d						12 35							13 05							13 35		
Farringdon	d						12 39							13 09							13 39		
City Thameslink	d						12 41							13 11							13 41		
London Blackfriars	d						12 44							13 14							13 44		
London Bridge ⊖	d	12 10	12 14		12 47		12 52		12 40	12 44		13 17		13 22		13 10	13 14		13 47		13 52		13 40
New Cross Gate ⊖	d	12 18							12 48							13 18							13 48
Norwood Junction	d	12 39					13 03		13 09					13 33		13 39					14 03		14 09
East Croydon	a	12 43	12 54		13 01		13 06		13 13	13 24		13 31		13 36		13 43	13 54		14 01		14 06		14 13
East Croydon	d	12 44	12 54	12 57	13 02		13 07	13 10	13 14	13 24	13 27	13 32		13 37	13 40	13 44	13 54	13 57	14 02		14 07	14 10	14 14
South Croydon	d	12 47			13 05				13 17			13 35				13 47			14 05				14 17
Purley Oaks	d	12 50			13 08				13 20			13 38				13 50			14 08				14 20
Sanderstead	d							13 15							13 45							14 15	
Purley	a	12 54	13 01	13 03	13 11		13 13		13 24	13 31	13 33	13 41		13 43		13 54	14 01	14 03	14 11		14 13		14 24
Purley	d	12 55	13 03		13 15	13 18			13 25	13 33		13 45	13 48			13 55	14 03		14 15	14 18			14 25
Kenley	d		13 06		13 18					13 36		13 48					14 06		14 18				
Whyteleafe	d		13 10		13 21					13 40		13 51					14 10		14 21				
Upper Warlingham	a							13 22							13 52							14 22	
Whyteleafe South	d		13 12		13 23					13 42		13 53					14 12		14 23				
Caterham	a		13 17		13 28					13 47		13 58					14 17		14 28				
Reedham	d	12 57				13 20			13 27				13 50			13 57				14 20			14 27
Coulsdon Town	d	13a01				13 23			13a31				13 53			14a01				14 23			14a31
Woodmansterne	d					13 26							13 56							14 26			
Chipstead	d					13 29							13 59							14 29			
Kingswood	d					13 35							14 05							14 35			
Tadworth	d					13 38							14 08							14 38			
Tattenham Corner	a					13 42							14 12							14 42			

		SN	SN ■	SN		TL ■	SN ■	SN	SN	SN ■	SN		TL ■	SN ■	SN	SN	SN ■	SN		TL ■	SN ■	SN	SN
London Victoria ⊖	d		14 09				14 21			14 39				14 51			15 09				15 21		
Clapham Junction	d		14 16				14 28			14 46				14 58			15 16				15 28		
East Croydon	a		14 26				14 39			14 56				15 09			15 26				15 39		
St Pancras International	d					14 05							14 35							15 05			
Farringdon	d					14 09							14 39							15 09			
City Thameslink	d					14 11							14 41							15 11			
London Blackfriars	d					14 14							14 44							15 14			
London Bridge ⊖	d	13 44		14 17		14 22		14 10	14 14		14 47		14 52		14 40	14 44		15 17		15 22		15 10	15 14
New Cross Gate ⊖	d							14 18							14 48							15 18	
Norwood Junction	d					14 33		14 39					15 03		15 09					15 33		15 39	
East Croydon	a	14 24		14 31		14 36		14 43	14 54		15 01		15 06		15 13	15 24		15 31		15 36		15 43	15 54
East Croydon	d	14 24	14 27	14 32		14 37	14 40	14 44	14 54	14 57	15 02		15 07	15 10	15 14	15 24	15 27	15 32		15 37	15 40	15 44	15 54
South Croydon	d			14 35				14 47			15 05				15 17			15 35				15 47	
Purley Oaks	d			14 38				14 50			15 08				15 20			15 38				15 50	
Sanderstead	d						14 45							15 15							15 45		
Purley	a	14 31	14 33	14 41		14 43		14 54	15 01	15 03	15 11		15 13		15 24	15 31	15 33	15 41		15 43		15 54	16 01
Purley	d	14 33		14 45	14 48			14 55	15 03		15 15	15 18			15 25	15 33		15 45	15 48			15 55	16 03
Kenley	d	14 36		14 48					15 06		15 18					15 36		15 48					16 06
Whyteleafe	d	14 40		14 51					15 10		15 21					15 40		15 51					16 10
Upper Warlingham	a						14 52							15 22							15 52		
Whyteleafe South	d	14 42		14 53					15 12		15 23					15 42		15 53					16 12
Caterham	a	14 47		14 58					15 17		15 28					15 47		15 58					16 17
Reedham	d				14 50			14 57				15 20			15 27				15 50			15 57	
Coulsdon Town	d				14 53			15a01				15 23			15a31				15 53			16a01	
Woodmansterne	d				14 56							15 26							15 56				
Chipstead	d				14 59							15 29							15 59				
Kingswood	d				15 05							15 35							16 05				
Tadworth	d				15 08							15 38							16 08				
Tattenham Corner	a				15 12							15 42							16 12				

Table T181-F

Saturdays
26 May to 8 December

London and Croydon - Purley, Caterham and Tattenham Corner

		SN ■	SN		TL ■	SN ■	SN	SN	SN ■	SN		TL ■	SN ■	SN	SN	SN ■	SN		TL ■	SN ■	SN	SN
London Victoria ⊖	d	15 39				15 51			16 09				16 21			16 39				16 51		
Clapham Junction	d	15 46				15 58			16 16				16 28			16 46				16 58		
East Croydon	a	15 56				16 09			16 26				16 39			16 56				17 09		
St Pancras International	d				15 35							16 05							16 35			
Farringdon	d				15 39							16 09							16 39			
City Thameslink	d				15 41							16 11							16 41			
London Blackfriars	d				15 44							16 14							16 44			
London Bridge ⊖	d		15 47		15 52		15 40	15 44		16 17		16 22		16 10	16 14		16 47		16 52		16 40	16 44
New Cross Gate ⊖	d						15 48							16 18							16 48	
Norwood Junction	d				16 03		16 09					16 33		16 39					17 03		17 09	
East Croydon	a		16 01		16 06		16 13	16 24		16 31		16 36		16 43	16 54		17 01		17 06		17 13	17 24
East Croydon	d	15 57	16 02		16 07	16 10	16 14	16 24	16 27	16 32		16 37	16 40	16 44	16 54	16 57	17 02		17 07	17 10	17 14	17 24
South Croydon	d		16 05				16 17			16 35				16 47			17 05				17 17	
Purley Oaks	d		16 08				16 20			16 38				16 50			17 08				17 20	
Sanderstead	d					16 15							16 45							17 15		
Purley	a	16 03	16 11		16 13		16 24	16 31	16 33	16 41		16 43		16 54	17 01	17 03	17 11		17 13		17 24	17 31
Purley	d		16 15	16 18			16 25	16 33		16 45	16 48			16 55	17 03		17 15	17 18			17 25	17 33
Kenley	d		16 18					16 36		16 48					17 06		17 18					17 36
Whyteleafe	d		16 21					16 40		16 51					17 10		17 21					17 40
Upper Warlingham	a					16 22							16 52							17 22		
Whyteleafe South	d		16 23					16 42		16 53					17 12		17 23					17 42
Caterham	a		16 28					16 47		16 58					17 17		17 28					17 47
Reedham	d			16 20			16 27				16 50			16 57				17 20			17 27	
Coulsdon Town	d			16 23			16a31				16 53			17a01				17 23			17a31	
Woodmansterne	d			16 26							16 56							17 26				
Chipstead	d			16 29							16 59							17 29				
Kingswood	d			16 35							17 05							17 35				
Tadworth	d			16 38							17 08							17 38				
Tattenham Corner	a			16 42							17 12							17 42				

		SN ■	SN		TL ■	SN ■	SN	SN	SN ■	SN		TL ■	SN ■	SN	SN	SN ■	SN		TL ■	SN ■	SN	SN	SN ■
London Victoria ⊖	d	17 09				17 21			17 39				17 51			18 09				18 21			18 39
Clapham Junction	d	17 16				17 28			17 46				17 58			18 16				18 28			18 46
East Croydon	a	17 26				17 39			17 56				18 09			18 26				18 39			18 56
St Pancras International	d				17 05							17 35							18 05				
Farringdon	d				17 09							17 39							18 09				
City Thameslink	d				17 11							17 41							18 11				
London Blackfriars	d				17 14							17 44							18 14				
London Bridge ⊖	d		17 17		17 22		17 10	17 14		17 47		17 52		17 40	17 44		18 17		18 22		18 10	18 14	
New Cross Gate ⊖	d						17 18							17 48							18 18		
Norwood Junction	d				17 33		17 39					18 03		18 09					18 33		18 39		
East Croydon	a		17 31		17 36		17 43	17 54		18 01		18 06		18 13	18 24		18 31		18 36		18 43	18 54	
East Croydon	d	17 27	17 32		17 37	17 40	17 44	17 54	17 57	18 02		18 07	18 10	18 14	18 24	18 27	18 32		18 37	18 40	18 44	18 54	18 57
South Croydon	d		17 35				17 47			18 05				18 17			18 35				18 47		
Purley Oaks	d		17 38				17 50			18 08				18 20			18 38				18 50		
Sanderstead	d					17 45							18 15							18 45			
Purley	a	17 33	17 41		17 43		17 54	18 01	18 03	18 11		18 13		18 24	18 31	18 33	18 41		18 43		18 54	19 01	19 03
Purley	d		17 45	17 48			17 55	18 03		18 15	18 18			18 25	18 33		18 45	18 48			18 55	19 03	
Kenley	d		17 48					18 06		18 18					18 36		18 48					19 06	
Whyteleafe	d		17 51					18 10		18 21					18 40		18 51					19 10	
Upper Warlingham	a					17 52							18 22							18 52			
Whyteleafe South	d		17 53					18 12		18 23					18 42		18 53					19 12	
Caterham	a		17 58					18 17		18 28					18 47		18 58					19 17	
Reedham	d			17 50			17 57				18 20			18 27				18 50			18 57		
Coulsdon Town	d			17 53			18a01				18 23			18a31				18 53			19a01		
Woodmansterne	d			17 56							18 26							18 56					
Chipstead	d			17 59							18 29							18 59					
Kingswood	d			18 05							18 35							19 05					
Tadworth	d			18 08							18 38							19 08					
Tattenham Corner	a			18 12							18 42							19 12					

		SN		TL ■	SN ■	SN	SN	SN ■	SN		TL ■	SN ■	SN	SN	SN ■	SN		TL ■	SN ■	SN	SN	SN ■
London Victoria ⊖	d				18 51			19 09				19 21			19 39				19 51			20 09
Clapham Junction	d				18 58			19 16				19 28			19 46				19 58			20 16
East Croydon	a				19 09			19 26				19 39			19 56				20 09			20 26
St Pancras International	d			18 35							19 05							19 35				
Farringdon	d			18 39							19 09							19 39				
City Thameslink	d			18 41							19 11							19 41				
London Blackfriars	d			18 44							19 14							19 44				
London Bridge ⊖	d	18 47		18 52		18 40	18 44		19 17		19 22		19 10	19 14		19 47		19 52		19 40	19 44	
New Cross Gate ⊖	d					18 48							19 18							19 48		
Norwood Junction	d			19 03		19 09					19 33		19 39					20 03		20 09		
East Croydon	a	19 01		19 06		19 13	19 24		19 31		19 36		19 43	19 54		20 01		20 06		20 13	20 24	
East Croydon	d	19 02		19 07	19 10	19 14	19 24	19 27	19 32		19 37	19 40	19 44	19 54	19 57	20 02		20 07	20 10	20 14	20 24	20 27
South Croydon	d	19 05				19 17			19 35				19 47			20 05				20 17		
Purley Oaks	d	19 08				19 20			19 38				19 50			20 08				20 20		
Sanderstead	d				19 15							19 45							20 15			
Purley	a	19 11		19 13		19 24	19 31	19 33	19 41		19 43		19 54	20 01	20 03	20 11		20 13		20 24	20 31	20 33
Purley	d	19 15	19 18			19 25	19 33		19 45	19 48			19 55	20 03		20 15	20 18			20 25	20 33	
Kenley	d	19 18					19 36		19 48					20 06		20 18					20 36	
Whyteleafe	d	19 21					19 40		19 51					20 10		20 21					20 40	
Upper Warlingham	a				19 22							19 52							20 22			
Whyteleafe South	d	19 23					19 42		19 53					20 12		20 23					20 42	
Caterham	a	19 28					19 47		19 58					20 17		20 28					20 47	
Reedham	d		19 20			19 27				19 50			19 57				20 20			20 27		
Coulsdon Town	d		19 23			19a31				19 53			20a01				20 23			20a31		
Woodmansterne	d		19 26							19 56							20 26					
Chipstead	d		19 29							19 59							20 29					
Kingswood	d		19 35							20 05							20 35					
Tadworth	d		19 38							20 08							20 38					
Tattenham Corner	a		19 42							20 12							20 42					

Table T181-F

Saturdays

26 May to 8 December

London and Croydon - Purley, Caterham and Tattenham Corner

		SN		TL ■	SN ■	SN	SN	SN ■	SN		TL ■	SN ■	SN	SN	SN ■	SN		TL ■	SN ■	SN	SN	SN ■
London Victoria	d				20 21			20 39				20 51			21 09				21 21			21 39
Clapham Junction	d				20 28			20 46				20 58			21 16				21 28			21 46
East Croydon	a				20 39			20 56				21 09			21 26				21 39			21 56
St Pancras International	d			20 05							20 35							21 05				
Farringdon	d			20 09							20 39							21 09				
City Thameslink	d			20 11							20 41											
London Blackfriars	d			20 14							20 44							21 14				
London Bridge	d	20 17		20 22		20 10	20 14		20 47		20 52		20 40	20 44		21 17		21 22		21 10	21 14	
New Cross Gate	d					20 18							20 48							21 18		
Norwood Junction	d			20 33		20 39					21 03		21 09					21 33		21 39		
East Croydon	a	20 31		20 36		20 43	20 54		21 01		21 06		21 13	21 24		21 31		21 36		21 43	21 54	
East Croydon	d	20 32		20 37	20 40	20 44	20 54	20 57	21 02		21 07	21 10	21 14	21 24	21 27	21 32		21 37	21 40	21 44	21 54	21 57
South Croydon	d	20 35				20 47			21 05				21 17			21 35				21 47		
Purley Oaks	d	20 38				20 50			21 08				21 20			21 38				21 50		
Sanderstead	d				20 45							21 15							21 45			
Purley	a	20 41		20 43		20 54	21 01	21 03	21 11		21 13		21 24	21 31	21 33	21 41		21 43		21 54	22 01	22 03
Purley	d	20 45	20 48			20 55	21 03		21 15	21 18			21 25	21 33		21 45	21 48			21 55	22 03	
Kenley	d	20 48					21 06		21 18					21 36		21 48					22 06	
Whyteleafe	d	20 51					21 10		21 21					21 40		21 51					22 10	
Upper Warlingham	a				20 52							21 22							21 52			
Whyteleafe South	d	20 53					21 12		21 23					21 42		21 53					22 12	
Caterham	a	20 58					21 17		21 28					21 47		21 58					22 17	
Reedham	d		20 50			20 57				21 20			21 27				21 50			21 57		
Coulsdon Town	d		20 53			21a02				21 23			21a31				21 53			22a01		
Woodmansterne	d		20 56							21 26							21 56					
Chipstead	d		20 59							21 29							21 59					
Kingswood	d		21 05							21 35							22 05					
Tadworth	d		21 08							21 38							22 08					
Tattenham Corner	a		21 12							21 42							22 12					

		SN		TL ■	SN ■	SN	SN	SN ■	SN		TL ■	SN ■	SN	SN	SN ■	SN		TL ■	SN ■	SN	SN ■
London Victoria	d				21 51			22 09				22 21			22 39				22 51		23 09
Clapham Junction	d				21 58			22 16				22 28			22 46				22 58		23 16
East Croydon	a				22 09			22 26				22 39			22 56				23 09		23 26
St Pancras International	d			21 35							22 05							22 35			
Farringdon	d			21 39							22 09							22 39			
City Thameslink	d																				
London Blackfriars	d			21 44							22 14							22 44			
London Bridge	d	21 47		21 52		21 40	21 44		22 17		22 22		22 10	22 14		22 47		22 52		22 40	
New Cross Gate	d					21 48							22 18							22 48	
Norwood Junction	d			22 03		22 09					22 33		22 39					23 03		23 09	
East Croydon	a	22 01		22 06		22 13	22 24		22 31		22 36		22 43	22 54		23 01		23 06		23 13	
East Croydon	d	22 02		22 07	22 10	22 14	22 24	22 27	22 32		22 37	22 40	22 44	22 54	22 57	23 02		23 07	23 10	23 14	23 27
South Croydon	d	22 05				22 17			22 35				22 47			23 05				23 17	
Purley Oaks	d	22 08				22 20			22 38				22 50			23 08				23 20	
Sanderstead	d				22 15							22 45							23 15		
Purley	a	22 11		22 13		22 24	22 31	22 33	22 41		22 43		22 54	23 01	23 03	23 11		23 13		23 24	23 33
Purley	d	22 15	22 18			22 25	22 33		22 45	22 48			22 55	23 03		23 15	23 18			23 25	
Kenley	d	22 18					22 36		22 48					23 06		23 18					
Whyteleafe	d	22 21					22 40		22 51					23 10		23 21					
Upper Warlingham	a				22 22							22 52							23 22		
Whyteleafe South	d	22 23					22 42		22 53					23 12		23 23					
Caterham	a	22 28					22 47		22 58					23 17		23 28					
Reedham	d		22 20			22 27				22 50			22 57				23 20			23 27	
Coulsdon Town	d		22 23			22a31				22 53			23a01				23 23			23a31	
Woodmansterne	d		22 26							22 56							23 26				
Chipstead	d		22 29							22 59							23 29				
Kingswood	d		22 35							23 05							23 35				
Tadworth	d		22 38							23 08							23 38				
Tattenham Corner	a		22 42							23 12							23 42				

		SN		TL ■	SN ■	SN ■	SN	SN ■
London Victoria	d				23 21	23 36		23 53
Clapham Junction	d				23 28	23 43		23 59
East Croydon	a				23 39	23 58		00 15
St Pancras International	d			23 05				
Farringdon	d			23 09				
City Thameslink	d							
London Blackfriars	d			23 14				
London Bridge	d	23 17		23 21			23 47	
New Cross Gate	d							
Norwood Junction	d			23 32				
East Croydon	a	23 31		23 36			00 01	
East Croydon	d	23 32		23 37	23 40	23 59	00 02	00 16
South Croydon	d	23 34					00 05	00 18
Purley Oaks	d	23 37					00 08	
Sanderstead	d				23 45			00 21
Purley	a	23 40		23 42		00 04	00 11	
Purley	d	23 45	23 48				00 15	
Kenley	d	23 48					00 18	
Whyteleafe	d	23 51					00 21	
Upper Warlingham	a				23 52			00 28
Whyteleafe South	d	23 53					00 23	
Caterham	a	23 58					00 28	
Reedham	d		23 50					
Coulsdon Town	d		23 53					
Woodmansterne	d		23 56					
Chipstead	d		23 59					
Kingswood	d		00 05					
Tadworth	d		00 08					
Tattenham Corner	a		00 12					

Table T181-F

Sundays

20 May to 2 December

London and Croydon - Purley, Caterham and Tattenham Corner

		SN	SN	SN ■	SN	SN ■	SN	TL ■	SN ■	SN ■	SN ■	SN ■	SN ■	SN	SN	SN	SN ■	SN		SN	SN	SN	
		A	A	A				A															
London Victoria	d					00 08			01 10	02 08	03 08	04 10	05 02	06 32		07 02				07 43	08 02		
Clapham Junction	d					00 15			01 17	02 17	03 17	04 17	05 10	06 40		07 10				07 51	08 10		
East Croydon	a					00 31			01 32	02 32	03 31	04 31	05 23	06 53		07 26				08 08	08 26		
St Pancras International	d							00 51															
Farringdon	d																						
City Thameslink	d																						
London Blackfriars	d							01 01															
London Bridge	d																07 19	07 31				08 01	
New Cross Gate	d																	07 38				08 08	
Norwood Junction	d																07 31	07 56				08 26	
East Croydon	a							01 27									07 35	08 02				08 32	
East Croydon	d	00 02		00 16		00 32		01 28	01 33	02 32	03 32	04 31	05 24	06 54	07 01	07 27	07 35	08 03		08 09	08 27	08 33	
South Croydon	d	00 05		00 18											07 03			08 05				08 35	
Purley Oaks	d	00 08													07 06			08 08				08 38	
Sanderstead	d			00 21																08 14			
Purley	a	00 11				00 37		01 33	01 38	02 38	03 37	04 37	05 29	06 58	07 09	07 32	07 40	08 11			08 32	08 41	
Purley	d	00 15			00 18		00 50								07 12			08 14	08 17			08 44	08 47
Kenley	d	00 18													07 15			08 17				08 47	
Whyteleafe	d	00 21													07 18			08 21				08 51	
Upper Warlingham	a			00 28																08 21			
Whyteleafe South	d	00 23													07 20			08 23				08 53	
Caterham	a	00 28													07 25			08 27				08 57	
Reedham	d																		08 19				08 49
Coulsdon Town	d																		08 22				08 52
Woodmansterne	d																		08 25				08 55
Chipstead	d																		08 28				08 58
Kingswood	d		00 05																08 34				09 04
Tadworth	d		00 08																08 37				09 07
Tattenham Corner	a		00 12		00 42		01 14												08 41				09 11

		SN ■	SN		SN	SN	SN		SN	TL ■	SN		SN	TL ■	SN	SN		SN	TL ■	SN		SN	TL ■
London Victoria	d				08 51	09 05			09 21				09 51		10 05			10 21				10 51	
Clapham Junction	d				08 58	09 12			09 28				09 58		10 12			10 28				10 58	
East Croydon	a				09 08	09 23			09 38				10 08		10 23			10 38				11 08	
St Pancras International	d													09 41					10 11				10 41
Farringdon	d													09 45					10 15				10 45
City Thameslink	d																						
London Blackfriars	d													09 50					10 20				10 50
London Bridge	d	08 19	08 24				08 54			09 27	09 24			09 56		09 54			10 26	10 24			10 56
New Cross Gate	d		08 30				09 00				09 30					10 00				10 30			
Norwood Junction	d	08 31	08 52				09 22				09 52					10 22				10 52			
East Croydon	a	08 35	08 55				09 25			09 41	09 55			10 10		10 25			10 40	10 55			11 10
East Croydon	d	08 37	08 56		09 09	09 23	09 26		09 39	09 41	09 56		10 09	10 11	10 23	10 26		10 39	10 41	10 56		11 09	11 11
South Croydon	d		08 59				09 29				09 59					10 29				10 59			
Purley Oaks	d		09 01				09 31				10 01					10 31				11 01			
Sanderstead	d				09 14				09 44				10 14					10 44				11 14	
Purley	a	08 42	09 04			09 28	09 34			09 46	10 04			10 16	10 28	10 34			10 46	11 04			11 16
Purley	d		09 08	09 11			09 38	09 41			10 08	10 11				10 38	10 41			11 08	11 11		
Kenley	d		09 11				09 41				10 11					10 41				11 11			
Whyteleafe	d		09 14				09 44				10 14					10 44				11 14			
Upper Warlingham	a				09 21				09 51				10 21					10 51				11 21	
Whyteleafe South	d		09 16				09 46				10 16					10 46				11 16			
Caterham	a		09 22				09 52				10 22					10 52				11 22			
Reedham	d			09 13				09 43				10 13					10 43				11 13		
Coulsdon Town	d			09 16				09 46				10 16					10 46				11 16		
Woodmansterne	d			09 19				09 49				10 19					10 49				11 19		
Chipstead	d			09 22				09 52				10 22					10 52				11 22		
Kingswood	d			09 28				09 58				10 28					10 58				11 28		
Tadworth	d			09 31				10 01				10 31					11 01				11 31		
Tattenham Corner	a			09 35				10 05				10 35					11 05				11 35		

		SN	SN		SN	TL ■	SN		SN	TL ■	SN	SN		SN	TL ■	SN		TL ■	SN	SN	SN	
London Victoria	d	11 05			11 21				11 51		12 05			12 21					12 51	13 05		
Clapham Junction	d	11 12			11 28				11 58		12 12			12 28					12 58	13 12		
East Croydon	a	11 23			11 38				12 08		12 23			12 38					13 11	13 23		
St Pancras International	d					11 11				11 41					12 11			12 41				
Farringdon	d					11 15				11 45					12 15			12 45				
City Thameslink	d																					
London Blackfriars	d					11 20				11 50					12 20			12 50				
London Bridge	d		10 54			11 26	11 24			11 56		11 54			12 26	12 24		12 56			12 54	
New Cross Gate	d		11 00				11 30					12 00				12 30					13 00	
Norwood Junction	d		11 22				11 52					12 22				12 52					13 22	
East Croydon	a		11 25			11 40	11 55			12 10		12 25			12 40	12 55		13 10			13 25	
East Croydon	d	11 23	11 26		11 39	11 41	11 56		12 09	12 11	12 23	12 26		12 39	12 41	12 56		13 11	13 12	13 23	13 26	
South Croydon	d		11 29				11 59					12 29				12 59					13 29	
Purley Oaks	d		11 31				12 01					12 31				13 01					13 31	
Sanderstead	d				11 44				12 14					12 44					13 17			
Purley	a	11 28	11 34			11 46	12 04			12 16	12 28	12 34			12 46	13 04		13 16		13 28	13 34	
Purley	d		11 38	11 41			12 08	12 11				12 38	12 41			13 08	13 11				13 38	13 41
Kenley	d		11 41				12 11					12 41				13 11					13 41	
Whyteleafe	d		11 44				12 14					12 44				13 14					13 44	
Upper Warlingham	a				11 51				12 21					12 51					13 24			
Whyteleafe South	d		11 46				12 16					12 46				13 16					13 46	
Caterham	a		11 52				12 22					12 52				13 22					13 52	
Reedham	d			11 43				12 13					12 43				13 13					13 43
Coulsdon Town	d			11 46				12 16					12 46				13 16					13 46
Woodmansterne	d			11 49				12 19					12 49				13 19					13 49
Chipstead	d			11 52				12 22					12 52				13 22					13 52
Kingswood	d			11 58				12 28					12 58				13 28					13 58
Tadworth	d			12 01				12 31					13 01				13 31					14 01
Tattenham Corner	a			12 05				12 35					13 05				13 35					14 05

A not 20 May

London and Croydon - Purley, Caterham and Tattenham Corner

		SN	TL	SN		SN	TL	SN	SN		SN	TL	SN		SN	TL	SN	SN		SN	TL	SN	
London Victoria ⊖	d	13 21				13 51		14 05			14 21				14 51		15 05			15 21			
Clapham Junction	d	13 28				13 58		14 12			14 28				14 58		15 12			15 28			
East Croydon	a	13 38				14 08		14 23			14 38				15 08		15 23			15 38			
St Pancras International	d		13 11				13 41					14 11				14 41					15 11		
Farringdon	d		13 15				13 45					14 15				14 45					15 15		
City Thameslink	d																						
London Blackfriars	d		13 20				13 50					14 20				14 50					15 20		
London Bridge ⊖	d		13 26	13 24			13 56		13 54			14 26	14 24			14 56		14 54			15 26	15 24	
New Cross Gate ⊖	d			13 30					14 00				14 30					15 00				15 30	
Norwood Junction	d			13 52					14 22				14 52					15 22				15 52	
East Croydon	a		13 40	13 55			14 10		14 25			14 40	14 55			15 10		15 25			15 40	15 55	
East Croydon	d	13 39	13 41	13 56		14 09	14 11	14 23	14 26		14 39	14 41	14 56		15 09	15 11	15 23	15 26		15 39	15 41	15 56	
South Croydon	d			13 59					14 29				14 59					15 29				15 59	
Purley Oaks	d			14 01					14 31				15 01					15 31				16 01	
Sanderstead	d	13 44				14 14					14 44				15 14					15 44			
Purley	a		13 46	14 04			14 16	14 28	14 34			14 46	15 04			15 16	15 28	15 34			15 46	16 04	
Purley	d			14 08	14 11				14 38	14 41			15 08	15 11				15 38	15 41			16 08	16 11
Kenley	d			14 11					14 41				15 11					15 41				16 11	
Whyteleafe	d			14 14					14 44				15 14					15 44				16 14	
Upper Warlingham	a	13 51				14 21					14 51				15 21					15 51			
Whyteleafe South	d			14 16					14 46				15 16					15 46				16 16	
Caterham	a			14 22					14 52				15 22					15 52				16 22	
Reedham	d				14 13					14 43				15 13					15 43				16 13
Coulsdon Town	d				14 16					14 46				15 16					15 46				16 16
Woodmansterne	d				14 19					14 49				15 19					15 49				16 19
Chipstead	d				14 22					14 52				15 22					15 52				16 22
Kingswood	d				14 28					14 58				15 28					15 58				16 28
Tadworth	d				14 31					15 01				15 31					16 01				16 31
Tattenham Corner	a				14 35					15 05				15 35					16 05				16 35

		TL	SN	SN	SN		SN	TL	SN		TL	SN	SN	SN		SN	TL	SN		SN	TL	
London Victoria ⊖	d		15 51	16 05			16 21					16 51	17 05			17 21				17 51		
Clapham Junction	d		15 58	16 12			16 28					16 58	17 12			17 28				17 58		
East Croydon	a		16 11	16 23			16 38					17 11	17 23			17 38				18 08		
St Pancras International	d	15 41						16 11			16 41						17 11				17 41	
Farringdon	d	15 45						16 15			16 45						17 15				17 45	
City Thameslink	d																					
London Blackfriars	d	15 50						16 20			16 50						17 20				17 50	
London Bridge ⊖	d	15 56			15 54			16 26	16 24		16 56			16 54			17 26	17 24			17 56	
New Cross Gate ⊖	d				16 00				16 30					17 00				17 30				
Norwood Junction	d				16 22				16 52					17 22				17 52				
East Croydon	a	16 10			16 25			16 40	16 55		17 10			17 25			17 40	17 55			18 10	
East Croydon	d	16 11	16 12	16 23	16 26		16 39	16 41	16 56		17 11	17 12	17 23	17 26		17 39	17 41	17 56		18 09	18 11	and at the same minutes past each hour until
South Croydon	d				16 29				16 59					17 29				17 59				
Purley Oaks	d				16 31				17 01					17 31				18 01				
Sanderstead	d		16 17				16 44					17 17				17 44				18 14		
Purley	a	16 16		16 28	16 34			16 46	17 04		17 16		17 28	17 34			17 46	18 04			18 16	
Purley	d				16 38	16 41			17 08	17 11				17 38	17 41			18 08	18 11			
Kenley	d				16 41				17 11					17 41				18 11				
Whyteleafe	d				16 44				17 14					17 44				18 14				
Upper Warlingham	a		16 24				16 51					17 24				17 51				18 21		
Whyteleafe South	d				16 46				17 16					17 46				18 16				
Caterham	a				16 52				17 22					17 52				18 22				
Reedham	d					16 43				17 13					17 43				18 13			
Coulsdon Town	d					16 46				17 16					17 46				18 16			
Woodmansterne	d					16 49				17 19					17 49				18 19			
Chipstead	d					16 52				17 22					17 52				18 22			
Kingswood	d					16 58				17 28					17 58				18 28			
Tadworth	d					17 01				17 31					18 01				18 31			
Tattenham Corner	a					17 05				17 35					18 05				18 35			

		SN	SN		SN	TL	SN		SN	TL	SN	SN		SN	TL	SN		TL	SN	SN	SN		SN
London Victoria ⊖	d	21 05			21 21				21 51		22 05			22 21					22 51	23 05			23 32
Clapham Junction	d	21 12			21 28				21 58		22 12			22 28					22 58	23 12			23 40
East Croydon	a	21 23			21 38				22 08		22 22			22 38					23 08	23 22			23 56
St Pancras International	d					21 11				21 41					22 11			22 35					
Farringdon	d					21 15				21 45					22 15			22 39					
City Thameslink	d																						
London Blackfriars	d					21 20				21 50					22 20			22 44					
London Bridge ⊖	d		20 54			21 26	21 24			21 56		21 54			22 26	22 24		22 51			22 54		
New Cross Gate ⊖	d		21 00				21 30					22 00				22 30					23 00		
Norwood Junction	d		21 22				21 52					22 22				22 52		23 03			23 22		
East Croydon	a		21 25			21 40	21 55			22 10		22 25			22 40	22 55		23 07			23 25		
East Croydon	d	21 23	21 26		21 39	21 41	21 56		22 09	22 11	22 23	22 26		22 39	22 41	22 56		23 08	23 09	23 23	23 26		23 57
South Croydon	d		21 29				21 59					22 29				22 59					23 29		
Purley Oaks	d		21 31				22 01					22 31				23 01					23 31		
Sanderstead	d				21 44				22 14					22 44					23 14				
Purley	a	21 28	21 34			21 46	22 04			22 16	22 27	22 34			22 46	23 04		23 13		23 27	23 34		00 02
Purley	d		21 38	21 41			22 08	22 11				22 38	22 41			23 08	23 11				23 38	23 41	
Kenley	d		21 41				22 11					22 41				23 11					23 41		
Whyteleafe	d		21 44				22 14					22 44				23 14					23 44		
Upper Warlingham	a				21 51				22 21					22 51					23 21				
Whyteleafe South	d		21 46				22 16					22 46				23 16					23 46		
Caterham	a		21 52				22 22					22 52				23 22					23 52		
Reedham	d			21 43				22 13					22 43				23 13					23 43	
Coulsdon Town	d			21 46				22 16					22 46				23 16					23 46	
Woodmansterne	d			21 49				22 19					22 49				23 19					23 49	
Chipstead	d			21 52				22 22					22 52				23 22					23 52	
Kingswood	d			21 58				22 28					22 58				23 28					23 58	
Tadworth	d			22 01				22 31					23 01				23 31					00 01	
Tattenham Corner	a			22 05				22 35					23 05				23 35					00 05	

London and Croydon - Purley, Caterham and Tattenham Corner

		TL	SN	SN
London Victoria ⊖	d			
Clapham Junction	d			
East Croydon	a			
St Pancras International	d			
Farringdon	d			
City Thameslink	d			
London Blackfriars	d			
London Bridge ⊖	d	23 45	23 31	23 50
New Cross Gate ⊖	d		23 39	23 57
Norwood Junction	d		23 58	00 16
East Croydon	a	23 59	00 02	00 19
East Croydon	d	00 01	00 03	00 20
South Croydon	d		00 05	00 22
Purley Oaks	d		00 08	00 25
Sanderstead	d			
Purley	a	00 06	00 11	00 28
Purley	d		00 12	00 29
Kenley	d		00 15	00 32
Whyteleafe	d		00 18	00 35
Upper Warlingham	a			
Whyteleafe South	d		00 20	00 37
Caterham	a		00 25	00 42
Reedham	d			
Coulsdon Town	d			
Woodmansterne	d			
Chipstead	d			
Kingswood	d			
Tadworth	d			
Tattenham Corner	a			

Table T181-R

Mondays to Fridays

21 May to 7 December

Tattenham Corner and Caterham, Purley - London and Croydon

Miles	Miles	Miles			TL MX ■	SN MO	TL ■	TL ■	TL ■	TL ■	TL ■	TL		SN ■	TL ■	SN ■	SN	SN	TL ■	SN	SN	TL ■		SN ■	SN ■
0	—	—	Tattenham Corner	d														05 39			05 49				
1¼	—	—	Tadworth	d														05 43			05 53				
2½	—	—	Kingswood	d														05 46			05 56				
5	—	—	Chipstead	d														05 52			06 02				
6	—	—	Woodmansterne	d														05 55			06 05				
6¾	—	—	Coulsdon Town	d														05 59			06 09				
7½	—	—	Reedham	d														06 02			06 12				
—	0	—	Caterham	d													05 50			06 00					
—	1¾	—	Whyteleafe South	d													05 53			06 03					
—	—	0	Upper Warlingham	d												06 02			06 11						06 32
—	2¼	—	Whyteleafe	d													05 55			06 05					
—	3½	—	Kenley	d													05 58			06 08					
—	—	—	Purley	a													06 02	06 05		06 12	06 15				
8¼	4¾	—	Purley [4]	d	00 03		01 03	02 04	03 03	04 03	05 01	05 11		05 52	05 58			06 09			06 19	06 24		06 28	
—	—	3¾	Sanderstead	d												06 09			06 18						06 39
9¼	5¾	—	Purley Oaks	d								05 14		05 54				06 12			06 22				
10¼	6¾	—	South Croydon [4]	d								05 17		05 57				06 15	06 21		06 25	06 28			
11¼	7¾	5¾	East Croydon	a	00 09		01 09	02 09	03 09	04 09	05 08	05 20		06 00	06 03	06 15		06 18	06 24		06 28	06 31		06 34	06 44
—	—	—	East Croydon	d	00 10		01 10	02 10	03 10	04 10	05 10	05 20			06 03			06 18	06 25			06 31			
—	9	—	Norwood Junction [2]	a								05 24			06 07							06 36			
—	15	—	New Cross Gate [4] ⊖	a							05 24	05 42			06 20				06 40			06 50			
—	17¾	—	London Bridge [4] ⊖	a								05 50						06 34							
—	—	—	London Blackfriars	a	00 36		01 36	02 36	03 36	04 36	05 31				06 26				06 46			06 56			
—	—	—	City Thameslink	a							05 33				06 28				06 48			06 58			
—	—	—	Farringdon	a	00 41						05 35				06 31				06 51			07 01			
—	—	—	St Pancras International	a	00 45		01 43	02 43	03 43	04 43	05 40				06 35				06 55			07 05			
—	—	—	East Croydon	d		00 06								06 00		06 15					06 28			06 34	06 45
19	—	13½	Clapham Junction [10]	a		00 18								06 11		06 25					06 39			06 44	06 55
21¾	—	15½	London Victoria [15] ⊖	a		00 27								06 18		06 32					06 49			06 52	07 03

		SN	SN	TL ■	SN	SN	TL ■	SN ■		SN ■	SN	SN	TL ■	SN	SN	TL ■	SN ■	SN ■		SN	SN	TL ■	SN	SN	TL ■
Tattenham Corner	d		06 09			06 19						06 39			06 49						07 09			07 19	
Tadworth	d		06 13			06 23						06 43			06 53						07 13			07 23	
Kingswood	d		06 16			06 26						06 46			06 56						07 16			07 26	
Chipstead	d		06 22			06 32						06 52			07 02						07 22			07 32	
Woodmansterne	d		06 25			06 35						06 55			07 05						07 25			07 35	
Coulsdon Town	d		06 29			06 39						06 59			07 09						07 29			07 39	
Reedham	d		06 32			06 42						07 02			07 12						07 32			07 42	
Caterham	d	06 20			06 30						06 50			07 00						07 20			07 30		
Whyteleafe South	d	06 23			06 33						06 53			07 03						07 23			07 33		
Upper Warlingham	d			06 39						07 02			07 11					07 32				07 41			
Whyteleafe	d	06 25			06 35						06 55			07 05						07 25			07 35		
Kenley	d	06 28			06 38						06 58			07 08						07 28			07 38		
Purley	a	06 32	06 35		06 42	06 45					07 02	07 05		07 12	07 15					07 32	07 35		07 42	07 45	
Purley [4]	d		06 39			06 49	06 54	06 58				07 09			07 19	07 24	07 28				07 39			07 49	07 54
Sanderstead	d			06 45						07 09			07 18					07 39				07 48			
Purley Oaks	d		06 42			06 52						07 12			07 22						07 42			07 52	
South Croydon [4]	d		06 45	06 48		06 55	06 58					07 15	07 21		07 25	07 28					07 45	07 51		07 55	07 58
East Croydon	a		06 48	06 51		06 58	07 01	07 04		07 15		07 18	07 24		07 28	07 31	07 34	07 45			07 48	07 54		07 58	08 01
East Croydon	d		06 48	06 51			07 01					07 18	07 25			07 31					07 48	07 55			08 01
Norwood Junction [2]	a						07 06									07 36									08 06
New Cross Gate [4] ⊖	a			07 05			07 20						07 40			07 50						08 10			08 20
London Bridge [4] ⊖	a		07 04									07 34									08 04				
London Blackfriars	a			07 11			07 26						07 46			07 56						08 16			08 26
City Thameslink	a			07 13			07 28						07 48			07 58						08 18			08 28
Farringdon	a			07 16			07 31						07 51			08 01						08 21			08 31
St Pancras International	a			07 20			07 35						07 55			08 05						08 25			08 35
East Croydon	d					06 58		07 04		07 15					07 28		07 34	07 45						07 58	
Clapham Junction [10]	a					07 10		07 14		07 25					07 40		07 44	07 57						08 10	
London Victoria [15] ⊖	a					07 19		07 22		07 32					07 49		07 52	08 06						08 19	

		SN ■	SN ■	SN	SN		TL ■	SN	SN	TL ■	SN ■	SN ■	SN	SN	TL ■		SN	SN	TL ■	SN ■	SN ■	SN	SN	SN	TL ■
Tattenham Corner	d				07 39				07 49					08 09				08 19					08 39		
Tadworth	d				07 43				07 53					08 13				08 23					08 43		
Kingswood	d				07 46				07 56					08 16				08 26					08 46		
Chipstead	d				07 52				08 02					08 22				08 32					08 52		
Woodmansterne	d				07 55				08 05					08 25				08 35					08 55		
Coulsdon Town	d				07 59				08 09					08 29				08 39					08 59		
Reedham	d				08 02				08 12					08 32				08 42					09 02		
Caterham	d			07 50				08 00					08 20				08 30					08 50		09 00	
Whyteleafe South	d			07 53				08 03					08 23				08 33					08 53		09 03	
Upper Warlingham	d		08 02				08 11					08 32			08 41						09 02				09 11
Whyteleafe	d			07 55				08 05					08 25				08 35					08 55		09 05	
Kenley	d			07 58				08 08					08 28				08 38					08 58		09 08	
Purley	a			08 02	08 05			08 12	08 15				08 32	08 35			08 42	08 45				09 02	09 05	09 12	
Purley [4]	d	07 58			08 09				08 19	08 24	08 28			08 39				08 49	08 54	08 58			09 09	09 15	
Sanderstead	d		08 09				08 18					08 39			08 48						09 09				09 18
Purley Oaks	d				08 12				08 22					08 42				08 52					09 12		
South Croydon [4]	d				08 15		08 21		08 25	08 28				08 45	08 51			08 55	08 58				09 15		09 22
East Croydon	a	08 04	08 15		08 18		08 24		08 28	08 31	08 34	08 45		08 48	08 54			08 58	09 01	09 04	09 15		09 18	09 21	09 24
East Croydon	d				08 18		08 25			08 31				08 48	08 55				09 01				09 18	09 21	09 25
Norwood Junction [2]	a									08 36									09 06						
New Cross Gate [4] ⊖	a						08 40			08 50					09 10				09 20						09 40
London Bridge [4] ⊖	a				08 34									09 04									09 34	10 06	
London Blackfriars	a						08 46			08 56					09 16				09 26						09 46
City Thameslink	a						08 48			08 58					09 18				09 28						09 48
Farringdon	a						08 51			09 01					09 21				09 31						09 51
St Pancras International	a						08 55			09 05					09 25				09 35						09 55
East Croydon	d	08 04	08 15						08 28		08 34	08 45						08 58		09 04	09 15				
Clapham Junction [10]	a	08 14	08 27						08 40		08 44	08 57						09 10		09 14	09 25				
London Victoria [15] ⊖	a	08 22	08 35						08 49		08 52	09 05						09 19		09 24	09 32				

Table T181-R

Mondays to Fridays

21 May to 7 December

Tattenham Corner and Caterham, Purley - London and Croydon

			TL ■	SN ■	SN ■	SN	SN	SN	TL ■	SN ■	TL ■		SN ■	SN	SN	SN	SN ■	TL ■	SN ■	SN	SN		SN	SN	SN ■
Tattenham Corner	d						09 09								09 39						10 09				
Tadworth	d						09 13								09 43						10 13				
Kingswood	d						09 16								09 46						10 16				
Chipstead	d						09 22								09 52						10 22				
Woodmansterne	d						09 25								09 55						10 25				
Coulsdon Town	d						09 29								09 59						10 29			10 42	
Reedham	d						09 32								10 02						10 32			10 45	
Caterham	d					09 20		09 30						09 50		10 00				10 20			10 30		
Whyteleafe South	d					09 23		09 33						09 53		10 03				10 23			10 33		
Upper Warlingham	d				09 32								10 02						10 32						
Whyteleafe	d					09 25		09 35						09 55		10 05				10 25			10 35		
Kenley	d					09 28		09 38						09 58		10 08				10 28			10 38		
Purley	a					09 32	09 35	09 42						10 02	10 05	10 12				10 32	10 35		10 42	10 47	
Purley [4]	d		09 24	09 28			09 39	09 45		09 55	09 58				10 09	10 15	10 25	10 28			10 39		10 45	10 48	10 55
Sanderstead	d				09 39				09 48				10 09						10 39						
Purley Oaks	d						09 42								10 12						10 42			10 51	
South Croydon [4]	d		09 28				09 45		09 51						10 15						10 45			10 54	
East Croydon	a		09 31	09 34	09 45		09 48	09 51	09 54	10 00	10 03		10 15		10 18	10 21	10 30	10 33	10 45		10 48		10 51	10 57	11 00
East Croydon	d		09 31				09 48	09 51	09 54		10 03				10 18	10 22		10 33			10 48		10 52	10 57	
Norwood Junction [2]	a		09 36								10 07							10 37						11 02	
New Cross Gate [4] ⊖	a		09 50								10 20							10 50						11 20	
London Bridge [4] ⊖	a						10 04	10 36	10 11						10 34	11 06					11 04		11 36	11 31	
London Blackfriars	a		09 56								10 26							10 56							
City Thameslink	a		09 58								10 28							10 58							
Farringdon	a		10 01								10 31							11 01							
St Pancras International	a		10 05								10 35							11 05							
East Croydon	d			09 34	09 45					10 00			10 15				10 30		10 45						11 00
Clapham Junction [10]	a			09 44	09 55					10 10			10 25				10 40		10 55						11 10
London Victoria [15] ⊖	a			09 52	10 02					10 18			10 32				10 48		11 02						11 18

		TL ■	SN ■	SN	SN	SN	SN		SN ■	TL ■	SN ■	SN	SN	SN	SN	SN ■	TL ■		SN ■	SN	SN	SN	SN	SN ■	TL ■
Tattenham Corner	d				10 39								11 09								11 39				
Tadworth	d				10 43								11 13								11 43				
Kingswood	d				10 46								11 16								11 46				
Chipstead	d				10 52								11 22								11 52				
Woodmansterne	d				10 55								11 25								11 55				
Coulsdon Town	d				10 59		11 12						11 29		11 42						11 59		12 12		
Reedham	d				11 02		11 15						11 32		11 45						12 02		12 15		
Caterham	d			10 50		11 00						11 20		11 30						11 50		12 00			
Whyteleafe South	d			10 53		11 03						11 23		11 33						11 53		12 03			
Upper Warlingham	d		11 02								11 32								12 02						
Whyteleafe	d			10 55		11 05						11 25		11 35						11 55		12 05			
Kenley	d			10 58		11 08						11 28		11 38						11 58		12 08			
Purley	a			11 02	11 05	11 12	11 17					11 32	11 35	11 42	11 47					12 02	12 05	12 12	12 17		
Purley [4]	d	10 58			11 09	11 15	11 18		11 25	11 28			11 39	11 45	11 48	11 55	11 58				12 09	12 15	12 18	12 25	12 28
Sanderstead	d		11 09								11 39								12 09						
Purley Oaks	d				11 12		11 21						11 42		11 51						12 12		12 21		
South Croydon [4]	d				11 15		11 24						11 45		11 54						12 15		12 24		
East Croydon	a	11 03	11 15		11 18	11 21	11 27		11 30	11 33	11 45		11 48	11 51	11 57	12 00	12 03		12 15		12 18	12 21	12 27	12 30	12 33
East Croydon	d	11 03			11 18	11 22	11 27			11 33			11 48	11 52	11 57		12 03				12 18	12 22	12 27		12 33
Norwood Junction [2]	a	11 07					11 32			11 37					12 02		12 07						12 32		12 37
New Cross Gate [4] ⊖	a	11 20					11 50			11 50					12 20		12 20						12 50		12 50
London Bridge [4] ⊖	a				11 34	12 06	12 01						12 04	12 36	12 31						12 34	13 06	13 01		
London Blackfriars	a	11 26								11 56							12 26								12 56
City Thameslink	a	11 28								11 58							12 28								12 58
Farringdon	a	11 31								12 01							12 31								13 01
St Pancras International	a	11 35								12 05							12 35								13 05
East Croydon	d		11 15						11 30		11 45					12 00			12 15					12 30	
Clapham Junction [10]	a		11 25						11 40		11 55					12 10			12 25					12 40	
London Victoria [15] ⊖	a		11 32						11 48		12 02					12 18			12 32					12 48	

		SN ■	SN	SN		SN	SN	SN ■	TL ■	SN ■	SN	SN	SN	SN		SN ■	TL ■	SN ■	SN	SN	SN	SN	SN ■	TL ■	
Tattenham Corner	d			12 09								12 39								13 09					
Tadworth	d			12 13								12 43								13 13					
Kingswood	d			12 16								12 46								13 16					
Chipstead	d			12 22								12 52								13 22					
Woodmansterne	d			12 25								12 55								13 25					
Coulsdon Town	d			12 29			12 42					12 59		13 12						13 29		13 42			
Reedham	d			12 32			12 45					13 02		13 15						13 32		13 45			
Caterham	d		12 20			12 30					12 50		13 00						13 20		13 30				
Whyteleafe South	d		12 23			12 33					12 53		13 03						13 23		13 33				
Upper Warlingham	d	12 32								13 02								13 32							
Whyteleafe	d		12 25			12 35					12 55		13 05						13 25		13 35				
Kenley	d		12 28			12 38					12 58		13 08						13 28		13 38				
Purley	a		12 32	12 35		12 42	12 47				13 02	13 05	13 12	13 17					13 32	13 35	13 42	13 47			
Purley [4]	d			12 39		12 45	12 48	12 55	12 58			13 09	13 15	13 18		13 25	13 28			13 39	13 45	13 48	13 55	13 58	
Sanderstead	d	12 39								13 09								13 39							
Purley Oaks	d			12 42			12 51					13 12		13 21						13 42		13 51			
South Croydon [4]	d			12 45			12 54					13 15		13 24						13 45		13 54			
East Croydon	a	12 45		12 48		12 51	12 57	13 00	13 03	13 15		13 18	13 21	13 27		13 30	13 33	13 45		13 48	13 51	13 57	14 00	14 03	
East Croydon	d			12 48		12 52	12 57		13 03			13 18	13 22	13 27			13 33			13 48	13 52	13 57		14 03	
Norwood Junction [2]	a						13 02		13 07					13 32			13 37					14 02		14 07	
New Cross Gate [4] ⊖	a						13 20		13 20					13 50			13 50					14 20		14 20	
London Bridge [4] ⊖	a			13 04		13 36	13 31					13 34	14 06	14 01						14 04	14 36	14 31			
London Blackfriars	a								13 26								13 56							14 26	
City Thameslink	a								13 28								13 58							14 28	
Farringdon	a								13 31								14 01							14 31	
St Pancras International	a								13 35								14 05							14 35	
East Croydon	d	12 45						13 00		13 15						13 30		13 45					14 00		
Clapham Junction [10]	a	12 55						13 10		13 25						13 40		13 55					14 10		
London Victoria [15] ⊖	a	13 02						13 18		13 32						13 48		14 02					14 18		

Table T181-R

Mondays to Fridays
21 May to 7 December

Tattenham Corner and Caterham, Purley - London and Croydon

	SN ■	SN	SN	SN	SN	SN ■	TL ■	SN ■	SN	SN	SN	SN	SN ■	TL ■	SN ■	SN	SN	SN	SN	SN ■	TL ■	SN ■ A
Tattenham Corner d			13 39							14 09							14 39					
Tadworth d			13 43							14 13							14 43					
Kingswood d			13 46							14 16							14 46					
Chipstead d			13 52							14 22							14 52					
Woodmansterne d			13 55							14 25							14 55					
Coulsdon Town d			13 59		14 12					14 29		14 42					14 59		15 12			
Reedham d			14 02		14 15					14 32		14 45					15 02		15 15			
Caterham d		13 50		14 00					14 20		14 30					14 50		15 00				
Whyteleafe South d		13 53		14 03					14 23		14 33					14 53		15 03				
Upper Warlingham d	14 02							14 32							15 02							
Whyteleafe d		13 55		14 05					14 25		14 35					14 55		15 05				
Kenley d		13 58		14 08					14 28		14 38					14 58		15 08				
Purley a		14 02	14 05	14 12	14 17				14 32	14 35	14 42	14 47				15 02	15 05	15 12	15 17			
Purley ■ d		14 09		14 15	14 18	14 25	14 28		14 39		14 45	14 48	14 55	14 58		15 09		15 15	15 18	15 25	15 28	
Sanderstead d	14 09							14 39							15 09							
Purley Oaks d		14 12			14 21				14 42			14 51				15 12			15 21			
South Croydon ■ d		14 15			14 24				14 45			14 54				15 15			15 24			15 36
East Croydon a	14 15	14 18		14 21	14 27	14 30	14 33	14 45	14 48		14 51	14 57	15 00	15 03	15 15	15 18		15 21	15 27	15 30	15 33	15 39
East Croydon d		14 18		14 22	14 27		14 33		14 48		14 52	14 57		15 03		15 18		15 22	15 27		15 33	
Norwood Junction ■ a					14 32		14 37					15 02		15 07					15 32		15 37	
New Cross Gate ■ ⊖ a					14 50		14 50					15 20		15 20					15 50		15 50	
London Bridge ■ ⊖ a		14 34		15 06	15 01				15 04		15 36	15 31				15 34		16 06	16 01			
London Blackfriars a							14 56							15 26							15 56	
City Thameslink a							14 58							15 28							15 58	
Farringdon a							15 01							15 31							16 01	
St Pancras International a							15 05							15 35							16 05	
East Croydon d	14 15					14 30		14 45					15 00		15 15					15 30		15 43
Clapham Junction ■ a	14 25					14 40		14 55					15 10		15 25					15 40		→
London Victoria ■ ⊖ a	14 32					14 48		15 02					15 18		15 32					15 49		

	SN ■ B	SN ■	SN ■ A	SN ■ B	SN	SN	SN	TL ■	SN	SN ■	TL ■	SN ■	SN	SN	SN	TL ■	SN	SN ■	TL ■	SN ■	SN	SN
Tattenham Corner d						15 09								15 39								16 09
Tadworth d						15 13								15 43								16 13
Kingswood d						15 16								15 46								16 16
Chipstead d						15 22								15 52								16 22
Woodmansterne d						15 25								15 55								16 25
Coulsdon Town d						15 29			15 42					15 59			16 12					16 29
Reedham d						15 32			15 45					16 02			16 15					16 32
Caterham d					15 20		15 30						15 50		16 00						16 20	
Whyteleafe South d					15 23		15 33						15 53		16 03						16 23	
Upper Warlingham d		15 32										16 02								16 32		
Whyteleafe d					15 25		15 35						15 55		16 05						16 25	
Kenley d					15 28		15 38						15 58		16 08						16 28	
Purley a					15 32	15 35	15 42		15 47				16 02	16 05	16 12		16 17				16 32	16 35
Purley ■ d					15 39		15 45	15 48	15 50	15 55	15 58		16 09		16 15	16 18	16 20	16 25	16 28		16 39	
Sanderstead d		15 39										16 09								16 39		
Purley Oaks d					15 42								16 12								16 42	
South Croydon ■ d	15 36				15 45				15 54				16 15				16 24				16 45	
East Croydon a	15 39	15 45			15 48		15 51	15 54	15 57	16 00	16 03	16 15	16 18		16 21	16 24	16 27	16 30	16 33	16 45	16 48	
East Croydon d					15 48		15 51	15 54	15 57		16 03		16 18		16 21	16 24	16 27		16 33		16 48	
Norwood Junction ■ a									16 02		16 07						16 32		16 37			
New Cross Gate ■ ⊖ a								16 10	16 20		16 20					16 40	16 50		16 50			
London Bridge ■ ⊖ a					16 04		16 36		16 31				16 34		17 06		17 01				17 04	
London Blackfriars a								16 16			16 26					16 46			16 56			
City Thameslink a								16 18			16 28					16 48			16 58			
Farringdon a								16 21			16 31					16 51			17 01			
St Pancras International a			←	←				16 25			16 35					16 55			17 05			
East Croydon d	15 43	15 46	15 43	15 43						16 00		16 15						16 30		16 45		
Clapham Junction ■ a	→	15 56	16 04	16 04						16 10		16 25						16 40		16 55		
London Victoria ■ ⊖ a		16 03	16 12	16 13						16 18		16 32						16 48		17 02		

A until 21 September

B from 24 September

Table T181-R

Mondays to Fridays
21 May to 7 December

Tattenham Corner and Caterham, Purley - London and Croydon

	SN	TL ■	SN	SN ■	TL ■	SN ■	SN	SN	SN	TL ■	SN ■	TL ■	SN ■	SN	SN	SN	TL ■	SN ■	TL ■	SN ■	SN	SN
Tattenham Corner d								16 39							17 09							17 39
Tadworth d								16 43							17 13							17 43
Kingswood d								16 46							17 16							17 46
Chipstead d								16 52							17 22							17 52
Woodmansterne d								16 55							17 25							17 55
Coulsdon Town d			16 42					16 59							17 29							17 59
Reedham d			16 45					17 02							17 32							18 02
Caterham d	16 30						16 50		17 00					17 20		17 30					17 50	
Whyteleafe South d	16 33						16 53		17 03					17 23		17 33					17 53	
Upper Warlingham d						17 02							17 32							18 02		
Whyteleafe d	16 35						16 55		17 05					17 25		17 35					17 55	
Kenley d	16 38						16 58		17 08					17 28		17 38					17 58	
Purley a	16 42		16 47				17 02	17 05	17 12					17 32	17 35	17 42					18 02	18 05
Purley ■ d	16 45	16 48	16 50	16 55	16 58		17 09		17 15	17 18	17 25	17 28		17 39		17 45	17 48	17 55	17 58		18 09	
Sanderstead d						17 09							17 39							18 09		
Purley Oaks d							17 12							17 42							18 12	
South Croydon ■ d			16 54				17 15							17 45							18 15	
East Croydon a	16 51	16 54	16 57	17 00	17 03	17 15	17 18		17 21	17 24	17 30	17 33	17 45	17 48		17 51	17 53	18 00	18 03	18 15	18 18	
East Croydon d	16 51	16 54	16 57		17 03		17 18		17 21	17 25		17 33		17 48		17 51	17 54		18 03		18 18	
Norwood Junction ■ a			17 03		17 07							17 37							18 07			
New Cross Gate ■ ⊖ a		17 10	17 20		17 20					17 40		17 50					18 10		18 20			
London Bridge ■ ⊖ a	17 36		17 31				17 34		18 06					18 04		18 36					18 34	
London Blackfriars a		17 16			17 26					17 46		17 56					18 16		18 26			
City Thameslink a		17 18			17 28					17 48		17 58					18 18		18 28			
Farringdon a		17 21			17 31					17 51		18 01					18 21		18 31			
St Pancras International a		17 25			17 35					17 55		18 05					18 25		18 35			
East Croydon d				17 00		17 15					17 30		17 45					18 00		18 15		
Clapham Junction ■ a				17 10		17 25					17 40		17 55					18 10		18 25		
London Victoria ■ ⊖ a				17 18		17 33					17 50		18 02					18 18		18 32		

	SN	TL ■	SN ■	TL ■	SN ■	SN	SN	SN	TL ■	SN ■	TL ■	SN ■	SN	SN	SN	TL ■	SN ■	TL ■	SN ■	SN	SN	TL ■
Tattenham Corner d							18 09							18 39							19 09	
Tadworth d							18 13							18 43							19 13	
Kingswood d							18 16							18 46							19 16	
Chipstead d							18 22							18 52							19 22	
Woodmansterne d							18 25							18 55							19 25	
Coulsdon Town d							18 29							18 59							19 29	
Reedham d							18 32							19 02							19 32	
Caterham d	18 00					18 20		18 30					18 50		19 00					19 20		
Whyteleafe South d	18 03					18 23		18 33					18 53		19 03					19 23		
Upper Warlingham d					18 32							19 02							19 32			
Whyteleafe d	18 05					18 25		18 35					18 55		19 05					19 25		
Kenley d	18 08					18 28		18 38					18 58		19 08					19 28		
Purley a	18 12					18 32	18 35	18 42					19 02	19 05	19 12					19 32	19 35	
Purley ■ d			18 25	18 28		18 39				18 55	18 58		19 09				19 25	19 28		19 39		
Sanderstead d		18 18			18 39				18 48			19 09				19 18			19 39			19 45
Purley Oaks d						18 42							19 12							19 42		
South Croydon ■ d						18 45							19 15							19 45		
East Croydon a		18 24	18 30	18 33	18 45	18 48			18 54	19 00	19 03	19 15	19 18			19 24	19 30	19 33	19 45	19 48		19 52
East Croydon d		18 25		18 33		18 48			18 55		19 03		19 18			19 24		19 33		19 48		19 52
Norwood Junction ■ a				18 37							19 07							19 37				
New Cross Gate ■ ⊖ a		18 40		18 50					19 10		19 20					19 40		19 50				
London Bridge ■ ⊖ a						19 04							19 34							20 04		20 11
London Blackfriars a		18 46		18 56					19 16		19 26					19 46		19 56				
City Thameslink a		18 48		18 58					19 18		19 28					19 48		19 58				
Farringdon a		18 51		19 01					19 21		19 31					19 51		20 01				
St Pancras International a		18 55		19 05					19 25		19 35					19 55		20 05				
East Croydon d			18 30		18 45					19 00		19 15					19 30		19 45			
Clapham Junction ■ a			18 40		18 55					19 10		19 25					19 40		19 55			
London Victoria ■ ⊖ a			18 48		19 03					19 18		19 32					19 49		20 02			

	SN	SN ■	TL ■	SN ■	SN	SN	TL ■	SN	SN ■	TL ■	SN ■	SN	SN	TL ■	SN	SN	SN ■	TL ■	SN ■	SN	SN
Tattenham Corner d						19 39							20 09								20 39
Tadworth d						19 43							20 13								20 43
Kingswood d						19 46							20 16								20 46
Chipstead d						19 52							20 22								20 52
Woodmansterne d						19 55							20 25								20 55
Coulsdon Town d	19 42					19 59		20 12					20 29			20 42					20 59
Reedham d	19 45					20 02		20 15					20 32			20 45					21 02
Caterham d					19 50							20 20			20 30					20 50	
Whyteleafe South d					19 53							20 23			20 33					20 53	
Upper Warlingham d				20 02							20 32								21 02		
Whyteleafe d					19 55							20 25			20 35					20 55	
Kenley d					19 58							20 28			20 38					20 58	
Purley a	19 47				20 02	20 05		20 17				20 32	20 35		20 42	20 47				21 02	21 05
Purley ■ d	19 48	19 55	19 58		20 09			20 18	20 25	20 28		20 39			20 45	20 48	20 55	20 58		21 09	
Sanderstead d				20 09			20 18				20 39			20 45					21 09		
Purley Oaks d	19 51				20 12			20 21				20 42				20 51				21 12	
South Croydon ■ d	19 54				20 15			20 24				20 45				20 54				21 15	
East Croydon a	19 57	20 00	20 03	20 15	20 18		20 24	20 27	20 30	20 33	20 45	20 48		20 52	20 54	20 57	21 00	21 03	21 15	21 18	
East Croydon d	19 57		20 03		20 18		20 24	20 27		20 33		20 48		20 52	20 54	20 57		21 03		21 18	
Norwood Junction ■ a	20 02		20 07					20 32		20 37						21 02		21 07			
New Cross Gate ■ ⊖ a	20 20		20 20					20 50		20 50						21 20		21 20			
London Bridge ■ ⊖ a	20 31				20 34		20 41	21 01				21 04		21 11	21 36	21 31				21 34	
London Blackfriars a			20 26							20 56								21 26			
City Thameslink a			20 28							20 58								21 28			
Farringdon a			20 31							21 01								21 31			
St Pancras International a			20 35							21 05								21 35			
East Croydon d		20 00		20 15					20 30		20 45						21 00		21 15		
Clapham Junction ■ a		20 10		20 25					20 40		20 58						21 12		21 25		
London Victoria ■ ⊖ a		20 18		20 32					20 48		21 05						21 19		21 32		

Table T181-R

Mondays to Fridays
21 May to 7 December

Tattenham Corner and Caterham, Purley - London and Croydon

		SN	SN	SN ■	TL ■	SN ■	SN	SN	SN	SN	SN ■	TL ■	SN ■	SN	SN	SN	SN	SN ■	SN ■	SN	SN	SN	SN
Tattenham Corner	d							21 09							21 39						22 09		
Tadworth	d							21 13							21 43						22 13		
Kingswood	d							21 16							21 46						22 16		
Chipstead	d							21 22							21 52						22 22		
Woodmansterne	d							21 25							21 55						22 25		
Coulsdon Town	d		21 12					21 29		21 42					21 59		22 12				22 29		22 42
Reedham	d		21 15					21 32		21 45					22 02		22 15				22 32		22 45
Caterham	d	21 00					21 20		21 30					21 50		22 00				22 20		22 30	
Whyteleafe South	d	21 03					21 23		21 33					21 53		22 03				22 23		22 33	
Upper Warlingham	d					21 32							22 02						22 32				
Whyteleafe	d	21 05					21 25		21 35					21 55		22 05				22 25		22 35	
Kenley	d	21 08					21 28		21 38					21 58		22 08				22 28		22 38	
Purley	a	21 12	21 17				21 32	21 35	21 42	21 47				22 02	22 05	22 12	22 17			22 32	22 35	22 42	22 47
Purley ■	d	21 15	21 18	21 25	21 28		21 39		21 45	21 48	21 55	21 58		22 09		22 15	22 18	22 25		22 39		22 45	22 48
Sanderstead	d					21 39							22 09						22 39				
Purley Oaks	d		21 21				21 42			21 51				22 12			22 21			22 42			22 51
South Croydon ■	d		21 24				21 45			21 54				22 15			22 24			22 45			22 54
East Croydon	a	21 21	21 27	21 30	21 33	21 45	21 48		21 51	21 57	22 00	22 03	22 15	22 18		22 21	22 27	22 30	22 45	22 48		22 51	22 57
East Croydon	d	21 22	21 27		21 33		21 48		21 52	21 57		22 03		22 18		22 22	22 27			22 48		22 52	22 57
Norwood Junction ■	a		21 32		21 37					22 02		22 07					22 32						23 02
New Cross Gate ■ ⊖	a		21 50		21 50					22 20		22 20					22 50						23 20
London Bridge ■ ⊖	a	22 06	22 01				22 04		22 36	22 31				22 34		23 06	23 01			23 04		23 36	23 31
London Blackfriars	a				21 56							22 26											
City Thameslink	a				21 58							22 28											
Farringdon	a				22 01							22 31											
St Pancras International	a				22 05							22 35											
East Croydon	d			21 30		21 45					22 00		22 15					22 30	22 45				
Clapham Junction ■	a			21 40		21 55					22 10		22 25					22 40	22 55				
London Victoria ■ ⊖	a			21 48		22 02					22 18		22 32					22 49	23 02				

		SN ■ A	SN ■	SN	SN	SN ■	SN ■
Tattenham Corner	d				22 39		
Tadworth	d				22 43		
Kingswood	d				22 46		
Chipstead	d				22 52		
Woodmansterne	d				22 55		
Coulsdon Town	d				22 59		
Reedham	d				23 02		
Caterham	d			22 50			
Whyteleafe South	d			22 53			
Upper Warlingham	d		23 02				23 32
Whyteleafe	d			22 55			
Kenley	d			22 58			
Purley	a			23 02	23 05		
Purley ■	d	22 55		23 09		23 25	
Sanderstead	d		23 09				23 39
Purley Oaks	d			23 12			
South Croydon ■	d			23 15			
East Croydon	a	23 00	23 15	23 18		23 30	23 45
East Croydon	d			23 18			
Norwood Junction ■	a						
New Cross Gate ■ ⊖	a						
London Bridge ■ ⊖	a			23 34			
London Blackfriars	a						
City Thameslink	a						
Farringdon	a						
St Pancras International	a						
East Croydon	d	23 00	23 15			23 30	23 45
Clapham Junction ■	a	23 10	23 25			23 44	23 59
London Victoria ■ ⊖	a	23 20	23 32			23 52	00 08

A not 7 December

Table T181-R

Saturdays
26 May to 8 December

Tattenham Corner and Caterham, Purley - London and Croydon

		TL ■	TL ■	TL ■	SN ■	TL ■	SN ■	TL ■	SN ■	TL ■	SN ■	SN ■	TL ■	TL ■	SN	SN	SN ■	TL ■	SN ■	SN	SN	SN	SN
Tattenham Corner	d															06 09					06 39		
Tadworth	d															06 13					06 43		
Kingswood	d															06 16					06 46		
Chipstead	d															06 22					06 52		
Woodmansterne	d															06 25					06 55		
Coulsdon Town	d															06 29					06 59		07 12
Reedham	d															06 32					07 02		07 15
Caterham	d														06 20					06 50		07 00	
Whyteleafe South	d														06 23					06 53		07 03	
Upper Warlingham	d																		07 02				
Whyteleafe	d														06 25					06 55		07 05	
Kenley	d														06 28					06 58		07 08	
Purley	a														06 32	06 35				07 02	07 05	07 12	07 17
Purley ■	d	00 03	01 03	02 04	02 29	03 03	03 29	04 03	04 29	05 01	05 24	05 55	05 58	06 28	06 39		06 55	06 58		07 09		07 15	07 18
Sanderstead	d																		07 09				
Purley Oaks	d														06 42					07 12			07 21
South Croydon ■	d														06 45					07 15			07 24
East Croydon	a	00 09	01 09	02 09	02 36	03 09	03 36	04 09	04 36	05 08	05 30	06 00	06 03	06 33	06 48		07 00	07 03	07 15	07 18		07 21	07 27
East Croydon	d	00 10	01 10	02 10		03 10		04 10		05 10			06 03	06 33	06 48			07 03		07 18		07 23	07 27
Norwood Junction ■	a												06 07	06 37				07 07					07 32
New Cross Gate ■ ⊖	a									05 25			06 20	06 50				07 20					07 50
London Bridge ■ ⊖	a														07 04					07 34		08 06	08 01
London Blackfriars	a	00 36	01 36	02 36		03 36		04 36		05 31			06 26	06 56				07 26					
City Thameslink	a																						
Farringdon	a	00 41								05 36			06 31	07 01				07 31					
St Pancras International	a	00 45	01 43	02 43		03 43		04 43		05 40			06 35	07 05				07 35					
East Croydon	d				02 36		03 36		04 36		05 30	06 00					07 00		07 15				
Clapham Junction ■	a				02 50		03 50		04 50		05 50	06 10					07 10		07 25				
London Victoria ■ ⊖	a				02 58		03 58		04 58		05 59	06 18					07 18		07 32				

		SN ■	TL ■	SN ■	SN	SN	SN	SN	SN ■	TL ■	SN ■	SN	SN	SN	SN	SN ■	TL ■	SN ■	SN	SN	SN	SN
Tattenham Corner	d					07 09							07 39							08 09		
Tadworth	d					07 13							07 43							08 13		
Kingswood	d					07 16							07 46							08 16		
Chipstead	d					07 22							07 52							08 22		
Woodmansterne	d					07 25							07 55							08 25		
Coulsdon Town	d					07 29		07 42					07 59		08 12					08 29		08 42
Reedham	d					07 32		07 45					08 02		08 15					08 32		08 45
Caterham	d				07 20		07 30					07 50		08 00					08 20		08 30	
Whyteleafe South	d				07 23		07 33					07 53		08 03					08 23		08 33	
Upper Warlingham	d			07 32							08 02							08 32				
Whyteleafe	d				07 25		07 35					07 55		08 05					08 25		08 35	
Kenley	d				07 28		07 38					07 58		08 08					08 28		08 38	
Purley	a				07 32	07 35	07 42	07 47				08 02	08 05	08 12	08 17				08 32	08 35	08 42	08 47
Purley ■	d	07 25	07 28		07 39		07 45	07 48	07 55	07 58		08 09		08 15	08 18	08 25	08 28		08 39		08 45	08 48
Sanderstead	d			07 39							08 09							08 39				
Purley Oaks	d				07 42			07 51				08 12			08 21				08 42			08 51
South Croydon ■	d				07 45			07 54				08 15			08 24				08 45			08 54
East Croydon	a	07 30	07 33	07 45	07 48		07 51	07 57	08 00	08 03	08 15	08 18		08 21	08 27	08 30	08 33	08 45	08 48		08 51	08 57
East Croydon	d		07 33		07 48		07 53	07 57		08 03		08 18		08 23	08 27		08 33		08 48		08 53	08 57
Norwood Junction ■	a		07 37					08 02		08 07					08 32		08 37					09 02
New Cross Gate ■ ⊖	a		07 50					08 20		08 20					08 50		08 50					09 20
London Bridge ■ ⊖	a				08 04		08 36	08 31				08 34		09 06	09 01				09 04		09 36	09 31
London Blackfriars	a		07 56							08 26							08 56					
City Thameslink	a																					
Farringdon	a		08 01							08 31							09 01					
St Pancras International	a		08 05							08 35							09 05					
East Croydon	d	07 30		07 45					08 00		08 15					08 30		08 45				
Clapham Junction ■	a	07 40		07 55					08 10		08 25					08 40		08 55				
London Victoria ■ ⊖	a	07 48		08 02					08 18		08 32					08 48		09 02				

		SN ■	TL ■	SN ■	SN	SN	SN	SN	SN ■	TL ■	SN ■	SN	SN	SN	SN	SN ■	TL ■	SN ■	SN	SN	SN	SN	SN ■
Tattenham Corner	d					08 39							09 09							09 39			
Tadworth	d					08 43							09 13							09 43			
Kingswood	d					08 46							09 16							09 46			
Chipstead	d					08 52							09 22							09 52			
Woodmansterne	d					08 55							09 25							09 55			
Coulsdon Town	d					08 59		09 12					09 29		09 42					09 59		10 12	
Reedham	d					09 02		09 15					09 32		09 45					10 02		10 15	
Caterham	d				08 50		09 00					09 20		09 30					09 50		10 00		
Whyteleafe South	d				08 53		09 03					09 23		09 33					09 53		10 03		
Upper Warlingham	d			09 02							09 32							10 02					
Whyteleafe	d				08 55		09 05					09 25		09 35					09 55		10 05		
Kenley	d				08 58		09 08					09 28		09 38					09 58		10 08		
Purley	a				09 02	09 05	09 12	09 17				09 32	09 35	09 42	09 47				10 02	10 05	10 12	10 17	
Purley ■	d	08 55	08 58		09 09		09 15	09 18	09 25	09 28		09 39		09 45	09 48	09 55	09 58		10 09		10 15	10 18	10 25
Sanderstead	d			09 09							09 39							10 09					
Purley Oaks	d				09 12			09 21				09 42			09 51				10 12			10 21	
South Croydon ■	d				09 15			09 24				09 45			09 54				10 15			10 24	
East Croydon	a	09 00	09 03	09 15	09 18		09 21	09 27	09 30	09 33	09 45	09 48		09 51	09 57	10 00	10 03	10 15	10 18		10 21	10 27	10 30
East Croydon	d		09 03		09 18		09 23	09 27		09 33		09 48		09 53	09 57		10 03		10 18		10 23	10 27	
Norwood Junction ■	a		09 07					09 32		09 37					10 02		10 07					10 32	
New Cross Gate ■ ⊖	a		09 20					09 50		09 50					10 20		10 20					10 50	
London Bridge ■ ⊖	a				09 34		10 06	10 01				10 04		10 36	10 31				10 34		11 06	11 01	
London Blackfriars	a		09 26							09 56							10 26						
City Thameslink	a		09 28							09 58							10 28						
Farringdon	a		09 31							10 01							10 31						
St Pancras International	a		09 35							10 05							10 35						
East Croydon	d	09 00		09 15					09 30		09 45					10 00		10 15					10 30
Clapham Junction ■	a	09 10		09 25					09 40		09 55					10 10		10 25					10 40
London Victoria ■ ⊖	a	09 18		09 32					09 48		10 02					10 18		10 32					10 48

Tattenham Corner and Caterham, Purley - London and Croydon

		TL 1	SN 1	SN	SN	SN	SN		SN 1	TL 1	SN 1	SN	SN	SN	SN	SN 1	TL 1		SN 1	SN	SN	SN	SN	SN 1	TL 1
Tattenham Corner	d				10 09								10 39								11 09				
Tadworth	d				10 13								10 43								11 13				
Kingswood	d				10 16								10 46								11 16				
Chipstead	d				10 22								10 52								11 22				
Woodmansterne	d				10 25								10 55								11 25				
Coulsdon Town	d				10 29		10 42						10 59		11 12						11 29		11 42		
Reedham	d				10 32		10 45						11 02		11 15						11 32		11 45		
Caterham	d			10 20		10 30						10 50		11 00						11 20		11 30			
Whyteleafe South	d			10 23		10 33						10 53		11 03						11 23		11 33			
Upper Warlingham	d		10 32								11 02								11 32						
Whyteleafe	d			10 25		10 35						10 55		11 05						11 25		11 35			
Kenley	d			10 28		10 38						10 58		11 08						11 28		11 38			
Purley	a			10 32	10 35	10 42	10 47					11 02	11 05	11 12	11 17					11 32	11 35	11 42	11 47		
Purley 4	d	10 28		10 39		10 45	10 48		10 55	10 58		11 09		11 15	11 18	11 25	11 28			11 39		11 45	11 48	11 55	11 58
Sanderstead	d		10 39								11 09								11 39						
Purley Oaks	d			10 42			10 51					11 12			11 21					11 42			11 51		
South Croydon 4	d			10 45			10 54					11 15			11 24					11 45			11 54		
East Croydon	a	10 33	10 45	10 48		10 51	10 57		11 00	11 03	11 15	11 18		11 21	11 27	11 30	11 33		11 45	11 48		11 51	11 57	12 00	12 03
East Croydon	d	10 33		10 48		10 53	10 57			11 03		11 18		11 23	11 27		11 33			11 48		11 53	11 57		12 03
Norwood Junction 2	a	10 37					11 02			11 07					11 32		11 37						12 02		12 07
New Cross Gate 4 ⊖	a	10 50					11 20			11 20					11 50		11 50						12 20		12 20
London Bridge 4 ⊖	a			11 04		11 36	11 31					11 34		12 06	12 01					12 04		12 36	12 31		
London Blackfriars	a	10 56								11 26							11 56								12 26
City Thameslink	a	10 58								11 28							11 58								12 28
Farringdon	a	11 01								11 31							12 01								12 31
St Pancras International	a	11 05								11 35							12 05								12 35
East Croydon	d		10 45						11 00		11 15					11 30			11 45					12 00	
Clapham Junction 10	a		10 55						11 10		11 25					11 40			11 55					12 10	
London Victoria 15 ⊖	a		11 02						11 18		11 32					11 48			12 02					12 18	

		SN 1	SN	SN		SN	SN	SN 1	TL 1	SN 1	SN	SN	SN	SN		SN 1	TL 1	SN 1	SN	SN	SN	SN	SN 1	TL 1	
Tattenham Corner	d			11 39								12 09								12 39					
Tadworth	d			11 43								12 13								12 43					
Kingswood	d			11 46								12 16								12 46					
Chipstead	d			11 52								12 22								12 52					
Woodmansterne	d			11 55								12 25								12 55					
Coulsdon Town	d			11 59			12 12					12 29		12 42						12 59		13 12			
Reedham	d			12 02			12 15					12 32		12 45						13 02		13 15			
Caterham	d		11 50			12 00					12 20		12 30						12 50		13 00				
Whyteleafe South	d		11 53			12 03					12 23		12 33						12 53		13 03				
Upper Warlingham	d	12 02								12 32								13 02							
Whyteleafe	d		11 55			12 05					12 25		12 35						12 55		13 05				
Kenley	d		11 58			12 08					12 28		12 38						12 58		13 08				
Purley	a		12 02	12 05		12 12	12 17				12 32	12 35	12 42	12 47					13 02	13 05	13 12	13 17			
Purley 4	d		12 09			12 15	12 18	12 25	12 28		12 39		12 45	12 48		12 55	12 58		13 09		13 15	13 18	13 25	13 28	
Sanderstead	d	12 09								12 39								13 09							
Purley Oaks	d		12 12				12 21				12 42			12 51					13 12			13 21			
South Croydon 4	d		12 15				12 24				12 45			12 54					13 15			13 24			
East Croydon	a	12 15	12 18			12 21	12 27	12 30	12 33	12 45	12 48		12 51	12 57		13 00	13 03	13 15	13 18		13 21	13 27	13 30	13 33	
East Croydon	d		12 18			12 23	12 27		12 33		12 48		12 53	12 57			13 03		13 18		13 23	13 27		13 33	
Norwood Junction 2	a						12 32		12 37					13 02			13 07					13 32		13 37	
New Cross Gate 4 ⊖	a						12 50		12 50					13 20			13 20					13 50		13 50	
London Bridge 4 ⊖	a		12 34			13 06	13 01				13 04		13 36	13 31					13 34		14 06	14 01			
London Blackfriars	a								12 56								13 26							13 56	
City Thameslink	a								12 58								13 28							13 58	
Farringdon	a								13 01								13 31							14 01	
St Pancras International	a								13 05								13 35							14 05	
East Croydon	d	12 15						12 30		12 45						13 00		13 15					13 30		
Clapham Junction 10	a	12 25						12 40		12 55						13 10		13 25					13 40		
London Victoria 15 ⊖	a	12 32						12 48		13 02						13 18		13 32					13 48		

		SN 1	SN	SN	SN	SN	SN 1	TL 1	SN 1	SN	SN		SN	SN	SN 1	TL 1	SN 1	SN	SN	SN	SN		SN 1	TL 1	SN 1
Tattenham Corner	d			13 09							13 39								14 09						
Tadworth	d			13 13							13 43								14 13						
Kingswood	d			13 16							13 46								14 16						
Chipstead	d			13 22							13 52								14 22						
Woodmansterne	d			13 25							13 55								14 25						
Coulsdon Town	d			13 29		13 42					13 59			14 12					14 29		14 42				
Reedham	d			13 32		13 45					14 02			14 15					14 32		14 45				
Caterham	d		13 20		13 30					13 50			14 00					14 20		14 30					
Whyteleafe South	d		13 23		13 33					13 53			14 03					14 23		14 33					
Upper Warlingham	d	13 32							14 02								14 32								15 02
Whyteleafe	d		13 25		13 35					13 55			14 05					14 25		14 35					
Kenley	d		13 28		13 38					13 58			14 08					14 28		14 38					
Purley	a		13 32	13 35	13 42	13 47				14 02	14 05		14 12	14 17				14 32	14 35	14 42	14 47				
Purley 4	d		13 39		13 45	13 48	13 55	13 58		14 09			14 15	14 18	14 25	14 28		14 39		14 45	14 48		14 55	14 58	
Sanderstead	d	13 39							14 09								14 39								15 09
Purley Oaks	d		13 42			13 51				14 12				14 21				14 42			14 51				
South Croydon 4	d		13 45			13 54				14 15				14 24				14 45			14 54				
East Croydon	a	13 45	13 48		13 51	13 57	14 00	14 03	14 15	14 18			14 21	14 27	14 30	14 33	14 45	14 48		14 51	14 57		15 00	15 03	15 15
East Croydon	d		13 48		13 53	13 57		14 03		14 18			14 23	14 27		14 33		14 48		14 53	14 57			15 03	
Norwood Junction 2	a					14 02		14 07						14 32		14 37					15 02			15 07	
New Cross Gate 4 ⊖	a					14 20		14 20						14 50		14 50					15 20			15 20	
London Bridge 4 ⊖	a		14 04		14 36	14 31				14 34			15 06	15 01				15 04		15 36	15 31				
London Blackfriars	a							14 26								14 56								15 26	
City Thameslink	a							14 28								14 58								15 28	
Farringdon	a							14 31								15 01								15 31	
St Pancras International	a							14 35								15 05								15 35	
East Croydon	d	13 45					14 00		14 15						14 30		14 45						15 00		15 15
Clapham Junction 10	a	13 55					14 10		14 25						14 40		14 55						15 10		15 25
London Victoria 15 ⊖	a	14 02					14 18		14 32						14 48		15 02						15 18		15 32

Tattenham Corner and Caterham, Purley - London and Croydon

		SN	SN	SN	SN	SN 1	TL 1		SN 1	SN	SN	SN	SN	SN 1	TL 1	SN 1	SN	SN		SN	SN	SN 1	TL 1	SN 1	
Tattenham Corner	d		14 39								15 09							15 39							
Tadworth	d		14 43								15 13							15 43							
Kingswood	d		14 46								15 16							15 46							
Chipstead	d		14 52								15 22							15 52							
Woodmansterne	d		14 55								15 25							15 55							
Coulsdon Town	d		14 59		15 12						15 29		15 42					15 59			16 12				
Reedham	d		15 02		15 15						15 32		15 45					16 02			16 15				
Caterham	d	14 50		15 00						15 20		15 30					15 50			16 00					
Whyteleafe South	d	14 53		15 03						15 23		15 33					15 53			16 03					
Upper Warlingham	d								15 32							16 02								16 32	
Whyteleafe	d	14 55		15 05						15 25		15 35					15 55			16 05					
Kenley	d	14 58		15 08						15 28		15 38					15 58			16 08					
Purley	a	15 02	15 05	15 12	15 17					15 32	15 35	15 42	15 47				16 02	16 05		16 12	16 17				
Purley 4	d	15 09		15 15	15 18	15 25	15 28			15 39		15 45	15 48	15 55	15 58		16 09			16 15	16 18	16 25	16 28		
Sanderstead	d								15 39							16 09								16 39	
Purley Oaks	d	15 12			15 21					15 42			15 51				16 12				16 21				
South Croydon 4	d	15 15			15 24					15 45			15 54				16 15				16 24				
East Croydon	a	15 18		15 21	15 27	15 30	15 33		15 45	15 48		15 51	15 57	16 00	16 03	16 15	16 18			16 21	16 27	16 30	16 33	16 45	
East Croydon	d	15 18		15 23	15 27		15 33			15 48		15 53	15 57		16 03		16 18			16 23	16 27		16 33		
Norwood Junction 2	a				15 32		15 37						16 02		16 07						16 32		16 37		
New Cross Gate 4 ⊖	a				15 50		15 50						16 20		16 20						16 50		16 50		
London Bridge 4 ⊖	a	15 34		16 06	16 01					16 04		16 36	16 31				16 34			17 06	17 01				
London Blackfriars	a						15 56								16 26								16 56		
City Thameslink	a						15 58								16 28								16 58		
Farringdon	a						16 01								16 31								17 01		
St Pancras International	a						16 05								16 35								17 05		
East Croydon	d					15 30			15 45					16 00		16 15						16 30		16 45	
Clapham Junction 10	a					15 40			15 55					16 10		16 25						16 40		16 55	
London Victoria 15 ⊖	a					15 48			16 02					16 18		16 32						16 48		17 02	

		SN	SN	SN	SN		SN 1	TL 1	SN 1	SN	SN	SN	SN	SN 1	TL 1		SN 1	SN	SN	SN	SN	SN 1	TL 1	SN 1	
Tattenham Corner	d		16 09								16 39								17 09						
Tadworth	d		16 13								16 43								17 13						
Kingswood	d		16 16								16 46								17 16						
Chipstead	d		16 22								16 52								17 22						
Woodmansterne	d		16 25								16 55								17 25						
Coulsdon Town	d		16 29		16 42						16 59		17 12						17 29		17 42				
Reedham	d		16 32		16 45						17 02		17 15						17 32		17 45				
Caterham	d	16 20		16 30						16 50		17 00						17 20		17 30					
Whyteleafe South	d	16 23		16 33						16 53		17 03						17 23		17 33					
Upper Warlingham	d								17 02								17 32							18 02	
Whyteleafe	d	16 25		16 35						16 55		17 05						17 25		17 35					
Kenley	d	16 28		16 38						16 58		17 08						17 28		17 38					
Purley	a	16 32	16 35	16 42	16 47					17 02	17 05	17 12	17 17					17 32	17 35	17 42	17 47				
Purley 4	d	16 39		16 45	16 48		16 55	16 58		17 09		17 15	17 18	17 25	17 28			17 39		17 45	17 48	17 55	17 58		
Sanderstead	d								17 09								17 39							18 09	
Purley Oaks	d	16 42			16 51					17 12			17 21					17 42			17 51				
South Croydon 4	d	16 45			16 54					17 15			17 24					17 45			17 54				
East Croydon	a	16 48		16 51	16 57		17 00	17 03	17 15	17 18		17 21	17 27	17 30	17 33		17 45	17 48		17 51	17 57	18 00	18 03	18 15	
East Croydon	d	16 48		16 53	16 57			17 03		17 18		17 23	17 27		17 33			17 48		17 53	17 57		18 03		
Norwood Junction 2	a				17 02			17 07					17 32		17 37						18 02		18 07		
New Cross Gate 4 ⊖	a				17 20			17 20					17 50		17 50						18 20		18 20		
London Bridge 4 ⊖	a	17 04		17 36	17 31					17 34		18 06	18 01					18 04		18 36	18 31				
London Blackfriars	a							17 26							17 56								18 26		
City Thameslink	a							17 28							17 58								18 28		
Farringdon	a							17 31							18 01								18 31		
St Pancras International	a							17 35							18 05								18 35		
East Croydon	d						17 00		17 15					17 30			17 45					18 00		18 15	
Clapham Junction 10	a						17 10		17 25					17 40			17 55					18 10		18 25	
London Victoria 15 ⊖	a						17 18		17 32					17 48			18 02					18 18		18 32	

		SN	SN		SN	SN	SN 1	TL 1	SN 1	SN	SN	SN	SN		SN 1	TL 1	SN 1	SN	SN	SN	SN	SN 1	TL 1		SN 1
Tattenham Corner	d		17 39								18 09								18 39						
Tadworth	d		17 43								18 13								18 43						
Kingswood	d		17 46								18 16								18 46						
Chipstead	d		17 52								18 22								18 52						
Woodmansterne	d		17 55								18 25								18 55						
Coulsdon Town	d		17 59			18 12					18 29		18 42						18 59		19 12				
Reedham	d		18 02			18 15					18 32		18 45						19 02		19 15				
Caterham	d	17 50			18 00					18 20		18 30						18 50		19 00					
Whyteleafe South	d	17 53			18 03					18 23		18 33						18 53		19 03					
Upper Warlingham	d								18 32								19 02								19 32
Whyteleafe	d	17 55			18 05					18 25		18 35						18 55		19 05					
Kenley	d	17 58			18 08					18 28		18 38						18 58		19 08					
Purley	a	18 02	18 05		18 12	18 17				18 32	18 35	18 42	18 47					19 02	19 05	19 12	19 17				
Purley 4	d	18 09			18 15	18 18	18 25	18 28		18 39		18 45	18 48		18 55	18 58		19 09		19 15	19 18	19 25	19 28		
Sanderstead	d								18 39								19 09								19 39
Purley Oaks	d	18 12				18 21				18 42			18 51					19 12			19 21				
South Croydon 4	d	18 15				18 24				18 45			18 54					19 15			19 24				
East Croydon	a	18 18			18 21	18 27	18 30	18 33	18 45	18 48		18 51	18 57		19 00	19 03	19 15	19 18		19 21	19 27	19 30	19 33		19 45
East Croydon	d	18 18			18 23	18 27		18 33		18 48		18 53	18 57			19 03		19 18		19 23	19 27		19 33		
Norwood Junction 2	a					18 32		18 37					19 02			19 07					19 32		19 37		
New Cross Gate 4 ⊖	a					18 50		18 50					19 20			19 20					19 50		19 50		
London Bridge 4 ⊖	a	18 34			19 06	19 01				19 04		19 36	19 31					19 34		20 06	20 01				
London Blackfriars	a							18 56								19 26							19 56		
City Thameslink	a							18 58								19 28							19 58		
Farringdon	a							19 01								19 31							20 01		
St Pancras International	a							19 05								19 35							20 05		
East Croydon	d						18 30		18 45						19 00		19 15					19 30			19 45
Clapham Junction 10	a						18 40		18 55						19 10		19 25					19 40			19 55
London Victoria 15 ⊖	a						18 48		19 02						19 18		19 32					19 48			20 02

Table T18I-R

Saturdays

26 May to 8 December

Tattenham Corner and Caterham, Purley - London and Croydon

	SN	SN	SN	SN	SN ■	TL ■	SN ■	SN	SN		SN	SN	SN ■	TL ■	SN ■	SN	SN	SN	SN		SN ■	TL ■	SN ■
Tattenham Corner d		19 09							19 39								20 09						
Tadworth d		19 13							19 43								20 13						
Kingswood d		19 16							19 46								20 16						
Chipstead d		19 22							19 52								20 22						
Woodmansterne d		19 25							19 55								20 25						
Coulsdon Town d		19 29		19 42					19 59			20 12					20 29		20 42				
Reedham d		19 32		19 45					20 02			20 15					20 32		20 45				
Caterham d	19 20		19 30					19 50			20 00					20 20		20 30					
Whyteleafe South d	19 23		19 33					19 53			20 03					20 23		20 33					
Upper Warlingham d							20 02								20 32								21 02
Whyteleafe d	19 25		19 35					19 55			20 05					20 25		20 35					
Kenley d	19 28		19 38					19 58			20 08					20 28		20 38					
Purley a	19 32	19 35	19 42	19 47				20 02	20 05		20 12	20 17				20 32	20 35	20 42	20 47				
Purley 4 d		19 39	19 45	19 48	19 55	19 58			20 09		20 15	20 18	20 25	20 28			20 39	20 45	20 48		20 55	20 58	
Sanderstead d							20 09								20 39								21 09
Purley Oaks d		19 42		19 51					20 12			20 21					20 42		20 51				
South Croydon 4 d		19 45		19 54					20 15			20 24					20 45		20 54				
East Croydon a		19 48	19 51	19 57	20 00	20 03	20 15		20 18		20 21	20 27	20 30	20 33	20 45		20 48	20 51	20 57		21 00	21 03	21 15
East Croydon d		19 48	19 53	19 57		20 03			20 18		20 23	20 27		20 33			20 48	20 53	20 57			21 03	
Norwood Junction 2 a				20 02		20 07						20 32		20 37					21 02			21 07	
New Cross Gate 4 ⊖ a				20 20		20 20						20 50		20 50					21 20			21 20	
London Bridge 4 ⊖ a		20 04	20 36	20 31					20 34		21 06	21 01					21 04	21 36	21 31				
London Blackfriars a						20 26								20 56								21 26	
City Thameslink a						20 28								20 58									
Farringdon a						20 31								21 01								21 31	
St Pancras International a						20 35								21 05								21 35	
East Croydon d					20 00		20 15						20 30		20 45						21 00		21 15
Clapham Junction 10 a					20 10		20 25						20 40		20 55						21 10		21 25
London Victoria 15 ⊖ a					20 18		20 32						20 48		21 02						21 18		21 32

	SN	SN	SN	SN	SN ■	TL ■		SN ■	SN	SN	SN	SN	SN ■	TL ■	SN ■	SN	SN		SN	SN	SN ■	SN ■	SN	SN
Tattenham Corner d		20 39								21 09							21 39							22 09
Tadworth d		20 43								21 13							21 43							22 13
Kingswood d		20 46								21 16							21 46							22 16
Chipstead d		20 52								21 22							21 52							22 22
Woodmansterne d		20 55								21 25							21 55							22 25
Coulsdon Town d		20 59		21 12						21 29		21 42					21 59			22 12				22 29
Reedham d		21 02		21 15						21 32		21 45					22 02			22 15				22 32
Caterham d	20 50		21 00						21 20		21 30					21 50			22 00				22 20	
Whyteleafe South d	20 53		21 03						21 23		21 33					21 53			22 03				22 23	
Upper Warlingham d								21 32							22 02							22 32		
Whyteleafe d	20 55		21 05						21 25		21 35					21 55			22 05				22 25	
Kenley d	20 58		21 08						21 28		21 38					21 58			22 08				22 28	
Purley a	21 02	21 05	21 12	21 17					21 32	21 35	21 42	21 47				22 02	22 05		22 12	22 17			22 32	22 35
Purley 4 d		21 09	21 15	21 18	21 25	21 28				21 39	21 45	21 48	21 55	21 58			22 09		22 15	22 18	22 25			22 39
Sanderstead d								21 39							22 09							22 39		
Purley Oaks d		21 12		21 21						21 42		21 51					22 12			22 21				22 42
South Croydon 4 d		21 15		21 24						21 45		21 54					22 15			22 24				22 45
East Croydon a		21 18	21 21	21 27	21 30	21 33		21 45		21 48	21 51	21 57	22 00	22 03	22 15		22 18		22 21	22 27	22 30	22 45		22 48
East Croydon d		21 18	21 23	21 27		21 33				21 48	21 53	21 57		22 03			22 18		22 23	22 27				22 48
Norwood Junction 2 a				21 32		21 37						22 02		22 07						22 32				
New Cross Gate 4 ⊖ a				21 50		21 50						22 20		22 20						22 50				
London Bridge 4 ⊖ a		21 34	22 06	22 01						22 04	22 36	22 31					22 34		23 06	23 01				23 04
London Blackfriars a						21 56								22 26										
City Thameslink a																								
Farringdon a						22 01								22 31										
St Pancras International a						22 05								22 35										
East Croydon d					21 30			21 45					22 00		22 15						22 30	22 45		
Clapham Junction 10 a					21 40			21 55					22 10		22 25						22 40	22 55		
London Victoria 15 ⊖ a					21 48			22 02					22 18		22 32						22 48	23 02		

	SN	SN	SN ■		SN ■	SN	SN	SN	SN ■	SN ■	SN	SN
Tattenham Corner d							22 39					23 09
Tadworth d							22 43					23 13
Kingswood d							22 46					23 16
Chipstead d							22 52					23 22
Woodmansterne d							22 55					23 25
Coulsdon Town d		22 42					22 59					23 29
Reedham d		22 45					23 02					23 32
Caterham d	22 30					22 50		23 00			23 20	
Whyteleafe South d	22 33					22 53		23 03			23 23	
Upper Warlingham d					23 02					23 32		
Whyteleafe d	22 35					22 55		23 05			23 25	
Kenley d	22 38					22 58		23 08			23 28	
Purley a	22 42	22 47				23 02	23 05	23 12			23 32	23 35
Purley 4 d	22 45	22 48	22 55				23 09	23 15	23 25			23 39
Sanderstead d					23 09					23 39		
Purley Oaks d		22 51					23 12					23 42
South Croydon 4 d		22 54					23 15					23 45
East Croydon a	22 51	22 57	23 00		23 15		23 18	23 21	23 30	23 45		23 48
East Croydon d	22 53	22 57					23 18	23 23				23 48
Norwood Junction 2 a		23 02										23 52
New Cross Gate 4 ⊖ a		23 20										
London Bridge 4 ⊖ a	23 36	23 31					23 34	00 06				00 06
London Blackfriars a												
City Thameslink a												
Farringdon a												
St Pancras International a												
East Croydon d			23 00		23 15				23 30	23 45		
Clapham Junction 10 a			23 10		23 25				23 41	00 04		
London Victoria 15 ⊖ a			23 18		23 32				23 50	00 12		

Table T18I-R

Sundays

20 May to 2 December

Tattenham Corner and Caterham, Purley - London and Croydon

	TL ■ A	TL ■	SN ■	SN ■	SN ■	TL ■	SN	SN	TL ■		SN	SN	SN	SN	TL ■	SN	SN	SN	TL ■		SN	SN	SN	SN
Tattenham Corner d														07 50				08 20					08 50	
Tadworth d														07 54				08 24					08 54	
Kingswood d														07 57				08 27					08 57	
Chipstead d														08 03				08 33					09 03	
Woodmansterne d														08 06				08 36					09 06	
Coulsdon Town d														08 10				08 40					09 10	
Reedham d														08 13				08 43					09 13	
Caterham d								07 05			07 35		08 02				08 32					09 02		
Whyteleafe South d								07 08			07 38		08 05				08 35					09 05		
Upper Warlingham d																08 38					09 08			
Whyteleafe d								07 10			07 40		08 07				08 37					09 07		
Kenley d								07 13			07 43		08 10				08 40					09 10		
Purley a								07 17			07 47		08 13	08 16			08 43	08 46				09 13	09 16	
Purley 4 d	00 03	01 03	03 30	04 29	05 23	06 25	07 16	07 20	07 25		07 50	08 16		08 20	08 25			08 50	09 12				09 20	09 25
Sanderstead d																08 45					09 15			
Purley Oaks d								07 22			07 52			08 22				08 52					09 23	
South Croydon 4 d								07 25			07 55			08 25				08 55					09 26	
East Croydon a	00 09	01 09	03 36	04 35	05 29	06 31	07 22	07 28	07 31		07 58	08 22		08 28	08 31	08 51		08 58	09 17		09 21		09 29	09 29
East Croydon d	00 10	01 10				06 32		07 29	07 32		07 59			08 29	08 32			08 59	09 18				09 31	
Norwood Junction 2 a						06 36		07 33	07 36		08 05			08 33	08 36			09 03					09 35	
New Cross Gate 4 ⊖ a								07 55			08 25			08 55				09 25	09 32				09 55	
London Bridge 4 ⊖ a						06 50		08 05	07 50		08 36			09 02	08 50			09 32					10 02	
London Blackfriars a	00 36	01 36																	09 38					
City Thameslink a																								
Farringdon a	00 41																		09 43					
St Pancras International a	00 45	01 45																	09 47					
East Croydon d			03 37	04 36	05 30		07 23					08 23				08 51					09 21			09 30
Clapham Junction 10 a			03 50	04 49	05 51		07 37					08 38				09 02					09 32			09 39
London Victoria 15 ⊖ a			03 58	04 58	05 59		07 46					08 46				09 09					09 39			09 47

	TL ■	SN	SN	SN	TL ■		SN	SN	SN	SN	TL ■	SN	SN	SN	TL ■		SN	SN	SN	SN	TL ■	SN	SN	SN
Tattenham Corner d				09 20					09 50					10 20					10 50					11 20
Tadworth d				09 24					09 54					10 24					10 54					11 24
Kingswood d				09 27					09 57					10 27					10 57					11 27
Chipstead d				09 33					10 03					10 33					11 03					11 33
Woodmansterne d				09 36					10 06					10 36					11 06					11 36
Coulsdon Town d				09 40					10 10					10 40					11 10					11 40
Reedham d				09 43					10 13					10 43					11 13					11 43
Caterham d			09 32					10 02					10 32					11 02					11 32	
Whyteleafe South d			09 35					10 05					10 35					11 05					11 35	
Upper Warlingham d		09 38					10 08					10 38					11 08					11 38		
Whyteleafe d			09 37					10 07					10 37					11 07					11 37	
Kenley d			09 40					10 10					10 40					11 10					11 40	
Purley a			09 43	09 46				10 13	10 16				10 43	10 46				11 13	11 16				11 43	11 46
Purley 4 d	09 42			09 50	10 12				10 20	10 25	10 42			10 50	11 12				11 20	11 25	11 42			11 50
Sanderstead d		09 45					10 15					10 45					11 15					11 45		
Purley Oaks d				09 53					10 23					10 53					11 23					11 53
South Croydon 4 d				09 56					10 26					10 56					11 26					11 56
East Croydon a	09 47	09 51		09 59	10 17		10 21		10 29	10 29	10 47	10 51		10 59	11 17		11 21		11 29	11 29	11 47	11 51		11 59
East Croydon d	09 48			10 01	10 18				10 31		10 48			11 01	11 18				11 31		11 48			12 01
Norwood Junction 2 a				10 05					10 35					11 05					11 35					12 05
New Cross Gate 4 ⊖ a	10 02			10 25	10 32				10 55		11 02			11 25	11 32				11 55		12 02			12 25
London Bridge 4 ⊖ a				10 32					11 02					11 32					12 02					12 32
London Blackfriars a	10 08				10 38						11 08				11 38						12 08			
City Thameslink a																								
Farringdon a	10 13				10 43						11 13				11 43						12 13			
St Pancras International a	10 17				10 47						11 17				11 47						12 17			
East Croydon d		09 51					10 21			10 30		10 51					11 21			11 30		11 51		
Clapham Junction 10 a		10 02					10 32			10 39		11 02					11 32			11 39		12 02		
London Victoria 15 ⊖ a		10 09					10 39			10 47		11 09					11 39			11 47		12 09		

	TL ■	SN	SN	SN	SN	TL ■	SN	SN	SN	TL ■		SN	SN	SN	SN	TL ■	SN	SN	SN	TL ■		SN
Tattenham Corner d				11 50					12 20					19 50					20 20			
Tadworth d				11 54					12 24					19 54					20 24			
Kingswood d				11 57					12 27					19 57					20 27			
Chipstead d				12 03					12 33					20 03					20 33			
Woodmansterne d				12 06					12 36					20 06					20 36			
Coulsdon Town d				12 10					12 40					20 10					20 40			
Reedham d				12 13					12 43					20 13					20 43			
Caterham d			12 02					12 32					20 02					20 32				
Whyteleafe South d			12 05					12 35					20 05					20 35				
Upper Warlingham d		12 08					12 38					20 08					20 38					21 08
Whyteleafe d			12 07					12 37					20 07					20 37				
Kenley d			12 10					12 40					20 10					20 40				
Purley a			12 13	12 16				12 43	12 46		and at the same minutes past each hour until		20 13	20 16				20 43	20 46			
Purley 4 d	12 12			12 20	12 25	12 42			12 50	13 12				20 20	20 25	20 42			20 50	21 12		
Sanderstead d		12 15					12 45					20 15					20 45					21 15
Purley Oaks d				12 23					12 53					20 23					20 53			
South Croydon 4 d				12 26					12 56					20 26					20 56			
East Croydon a	12 17	12 21		12 29	12 29	12 47	12 51		12 59	13 17		20 21		20 29	20 29	20 47	20 51		20 59	21 17		21 21
East Croydon d	12 18			12 31		12 48			13 01	13 18				20 31		20 48			21 01	21 18		
Norwood Junction 2 a				12 35					13 05					20 35					21 05			
New Cross Gate 4 ⊖ a	12 32			12 53		13 02			13 23	13 32				20 53		21 02			21 23	21 32		
London Bridge 4 ⊖ a				13 02					13 32					21 02					21 32			
London Blackfriars a	12 38					13 08				13 38						21 08				21 38		
City Thameslink a																						
Farringdon a	12 45					13 13				13 43						21 13				21 43		
St Pancras International a	12 49					13 17				13 47						21 17				21 47		
East Croydon d		12 21			12 30		12 51					20 21			20 30		20 51					21 21
Clapham Junction 10 a		12 32			12 39		13 02					20 32			20 39		21 02					21 32
London Victoria 15 ⊖ a		12 39			12 47		13 09					20 39			20 47		21 09					21 39

A not 20 May

Table T181-R

Sundays

20 May to 2 December

Tattenham Corner and Caterham, Purley - London and Croydon

		SN	SN	SN	TL	SN	SN	SN	SN	SN	SN	SN	TL	SN	SN	SN	TL	SN	SN	SN	SN	SN
Tattenham Corner	d		20 50					21 20			21 50					22 20				22 50		
Tadworth	d		20 54					21 24			21 54					22 24				22 54		
Kingswood	d		20 57					21 27			21 57					22 27				22 57		
Chipstead	d		21 03					21 33			22 03					22 33				23 03		
Woodmansterne	d		21 06					21 36			22 06					22 36				23 06		
Coulsdon Town	d		21 10					21 40			22 10					22 40				23 10		
Reedham	d		21 13					21 43			22 13					22 43				23 13		
Caterham	d	21 02					21 32			22 02					22 32				23 02			
Whyteleafe South	d	21 05					21 35			22 05					22 35				23 05			
Upper Warlingham	d					21 38			22 08					22 38				23 08			23 40	
Whyteleafe	d	21 07					21 37			22 07					22 37				23 07			
Kenley	d	21 10					21 40			22 10					22 40				23 10			
Purley	a	21 13	21 16				21 43	21 46		22 13	22 16				22 43	22 46			23 13	23 16		
Purley	d	21 20		21 25	21 42		21 50			22 20		22 25	22 38		22 50		23 07		23 20			23 59
Sanderstead	d					21 45			22 15					22 45				23 15			23 47	
Purley Oaks	d	21 23					21 53			22 23					22 53				23 23			
South Croydon	d	21 26					21 56			22 26					22 56				23 26			
East Croydon	a	21 29		21 29	21 47	21 51	21 59		22 21	22 29		22 29	22 45	22 51	22 59		23 12	23 21	23 29		23 54	00 05
East Croydon	d	21 31			21 48		22 01			22 31			22 47		23 01		23 12		23 31			
Norwood Junction	a	21 35					22 05			22 35			22 51		23 05		23 16		23 35			
New Cross Gate ⊖	a	21 53			22 02		22 23			22 53			23 04		23 23				23 53			
London Bridge ⊖	a	22 02					22 32			23 02					23 34		23 30		00 03			
London Blackfriars	a				22 08								23 10									
City Thameslink	a																					
Farringdon	a				22 13								23 16									
St Pancras International	a				22 17								23 20									
East Croydon	d			21 30		21 51			22 21			22 30		22 51				23 21			23 55	00 06
Clapham Junction	a			21 39		22 02			22 32			22 39		23 02				23 32			00 15	00 18
London Victoria ⊖	a			21 47		22 09			22 39			22 47		23 09				23 39			00 23	00 27

Table T182-F

Mondays to Fridays

21 May to 7 December

London - Oxted, East Grinstead and Uckfield

Miles	Miles			SN MX	SN MX	SN MX	SN	SN	TL	SN	SN	TL	SN	SN	TL	SN	SN	TL	SN	TL	SN	SN	TL
0	—	London Victoria ⊖175,177	d					05 21		05 51			06 21			06 51			07 21		07 51		
—	—	Clapham Junction	a					05 27		05 57			06 27			06 57			07 27		07 57		
—	—	Clapham Junction 175,177	d					05 28		05 58			06 28			06 58			07 28		07 58		
—	—	East Croydon	a					05 41		06 09			06 39			07 09			07 39		08 09		
—	—	St Pancras International	d									05 55			06 25			06 55		07 25			07 55
—	—	Farringdon	a									05 59			06 29			06 59		07 29			07 59
—	—	Farringdon	d									05 59			06 29			06 59		07 29			07 59
—	—	City Thameslink	a									06 01			06 31			07 01		07 31			08 01
—	—	City Thameslink	d									06 01			06 31			07 01		07 31			08 01
—	—	London Blackfriars	a									06 03			06 33			07 03		07 33			08 03
—	—		d																				
—	—	London Blackfriars	d									06 04			06 34			07 04		07 34			08 04
—	0	London Bridge ⊖175,177	a									06 10			06 40			07 10		07 40			08 10
—	—	London Bridge	d						05 37		06 07	06 11		06 37	06 41		07 07	07 11		07 41		08 07	08 11
10½	10¼	East Croydon 175,177	a						05 54		06 21	06 24		06 51	06 54		07 21	07 24		07 54		08 21	08 24
—	—	East Croydon	d			00 14	05 20	05 41	05 55	06 10	06 22	06 25	06 40	06 52	06 55	07 10	07 22	07 25	07 40	07 55	08 10	08 22	08 25
11½	—	South Croydon 175	d			00 17			05 58			06 28			06 58			07 28		07 58			08 28
12½	—	Sanderstead	d			00 20		05 46	06 02	06 15		06 32	06 45		07 02	07 15		07 32	07 45	08 02	08 15		08 32
13¾	—	Riddlesdown	d			00 23		05 49		06 18			06 48			07 18			07 48		08 18		
15½	—	Upper Warlingham	d			00 27		05 53		06 22			06 52			07 22			07 52		08 22		
17¼	—	Woldingham	d			00 31		05 57		06 26			06 56			07 26			07 56		08 26		
20½	20½	Oxted	a			00 37	05 33	06 02	06 13	06 31	06 35	06 43	07 01	07 05	07 13	07 31	07 35	07 43	08 01	08 13	08 31	08 35	08 43
—	—	Oxted	d	00 02			05 33	06 03	06 15	06 32	06 36	06 45	07 02	07 06	07 15	07 32	07 36	07 45	08 02	08 15	08 32	08 36	08 44
21½	21½	Hurst Green	d	00 05			05 36	06 06	06 18	06 35	06 39	06 48	07 05	07 09	07 18	07 35	07 39	07 48	08 05	08 18	08 35	08 39	08 47
26¼	—	Lingfield	d	00 11				06 12	06 24	06 41		06 54	07 11		07 24	07 41		07 54	08 11	08 24	08 41		08 53
28	—	Dormans	d	00 14				06 15	06 27	06 44		06 57	07 14		07 27	07 44		07 57	08 14	08 27	08 44		08 56
30¼	—	East Grinstead	a	00 20				06 20	06 33	06 50		07 03	07 20		07 33	07 50		08 03	08 20	08 33	08 50		09 02
—	25½	Edenbridge Town	d				05 42				06 45			07 15			07 45					08 45	
—	27½	Hever	d				05 46				06 49			07 19			07 49					08 49	
—	29¼	Cowden	d				05 50				06 53			07 23			07 53					08 53	
—	32¼	Ashurst	d				05 57				06 58			07 28			07 58					08 58	
—	35¾	Eridge	d				06 02				07 03			07 33			08 03					09 03	
—	39¼	Crowborough	d		00 04		06 09				07 10			07 40			08 10					09 10	
—	43¾	Buxted	d		00 10		06 15				07 16			07 46			08 16					09 16	
—	46¼	Uckfield	a		00 16		06 21				07 22			07 52			08 22					09 22	

		SN	SN	SN	SN	SN		SN	SN	SN	SN	SN	SN	SN	SN	SN	SN	TL	SN	SN	TL	SN
London Victoria ⊖175,177	d	08 21		08 51		09 21		13 51		14 21	14 51		15 21	15 51		16 21			16 51			17 21
Clapham Junction	a	08 27		08 57		09 27		13 57		14 27	14 57		15 27	15 57		16 27			16 57			17 27
Clapham Junction 175,177	d	08 28		08 58		09 28		13 58		14 28	14 58		15 28	15 58		16 28			16 58			17 28
East Croydon	a	08 39		09 09		09 39		14 09		14 39	15 09		15 39	16 09		16 39			17 09			17 39
St Pancras International	d																	16 25			16 55	
Farringdon	a																	16 29			16 59	
Farringdon	d																	16 29			16 59	
City Thameslink	a																	16 31			17 01	
City Thameslink	d																	16 31			17 01	
London Blackfriars	a																	16 33			17 03	
	d																					
London Blackfriars	d																	16 34			17 04	
London Bridge ⊖175,177	a																	16 40			17 10	
London Bridge	d		08 37		09 07		and at		14 07			15 07			16 07		16 37	16 41		17 07	17 11	
East Croydon 175,177	a		08 51		09 21		the same		14 21			15 21			16 21		16 51	16 54		17 21	17 24	
East Croydon	d	08 40	08 52	09 10	09 22	09 40	minutes	14 10	14 22	14 40	15 10	15 22	15 40	16 10	16 22	16 40	16 52	16 55	17 10	17 22	17 25	17 40
South Croydon 175	d						past						15 42	16 12		16 42		16 58			17 28	
Sanderstead	d	08 45		09 15		09 45	each	14 15		14 45	15 15		15 45	16 15		16 45		17 02	17 15		17 32	17 45
Riddlesdown	d	08 48		09 18		09 48	hour until	14 18		14 48	15 18		15 48	16 18		16 48		17 05	17 18		17 35	17 48
Upper Warlingham	d	08 52		09 22		09 52		14 22		14 52	15 22		15 52	16 22		16 52		17 09	17 22		17 39	17 52
Woldingham	d	08 56		09 26		09 56		14 26		14 56	15 26		15 56	16 26		16 56		17 13	17 26		17 43	17 56
Oxted	a	09 01	09 05	09 31	09 35	10 01		14 31	14 35	15 01	15 31	15 35	16 01	16 31	16 35	17 01	17 05	17 18	17 31	17 35	17 48	18 01
Oxted	d	09 02	09 06	09 32	09 36	10 02		14 32	14 36	15 02	15 32	15 36	16 02	16 32	16 36	17 02	17 06	17 19	17 32	17 36	17 49	18 02
Hurst Green	d	09 05	09 09	09 35	09 39	10 05		14 35	14 39	15 05	15 35	15 39	16 05	16 35	16 39	17 05	17 09	17 22	17 35	17 39	17 52	18 05
Lingfield	d	09 11		09 41		10 11		14 41		15 11	15 41		16 11	16 41		17 11		17 28	17 41		17 58	18 11
Dormans	d	09 14		09 44		10 14		14 44		15 14	15 44		16 14	16 44		17 14		17 31	17 44		18 01	18 14
East Grinstead	a	09 20		09 50		10 20		14 50		15 20	15 50		16 20	16 50		17 20		17 37	17 50		18 07	18 20
Edenbridge Town	d		09 15		09 45				14 45			15 45			16 45		17 15			17 45		
Hever	d		09 19		09 49				14 49			15 49			16 49		17 19			17 49		
Cowden	d		09 23		09 53				14 53			15 53			16 53		17 23			17 53		
Ashurst	d		09 28		09 58				14 58			15 58			16 58		17 28			17 58		
Eridge	d		09 33		10 03				15 03			16 03			17 03		17 33			18 03		
Crowborough	d		09 40		10 10				15 10			16 10			17 10		17 40			18 10		
Buxted	d		09 46		10 16				15 16			16 16			17 16		17 46			18 16		
Uckfield	a		09 52		10 22				15 22			16 22			17 22		17 52			18 22		

Table T182-F

London - Oxted, East Grinstead and Uckfield

Mondays to Fridays

21 May to 7 December

Station		SN	TL	SN	SN	TL	SN	TL	SN	SN	TL	SN
London Victoria ⊖175,177	d			17 51			18 21		18 51			19 21
Clapham Junction	a			17 57			18 27		18 57			19 27
Clapham Junction 175,177	d			17 58			18 28		18 58			19 28
East Croydon	a			18 09			18 39		19 09			19 39
St Pancras International	d		17 25			17 55		18 25			18 55	
Farringdon	a		17 29			17 59		18 29			18 59	
Farringdon	d		17 29			17 59		18 29			18 59	
City Thameslink	a		17 31			18 01		18 31			19 01	
City Thameslink	d		17 31			18 01		18 31			19 01	
London Blackfriars	a		17 33			18 03		18 33			19 03	
	d											
London Blackfriars	d		17 34			18 04		18 34			19 04	
London Bridge ⊖175,177	a		17 40			18 10		18 40			19 10	
London Bridge	d	17 37	17 41		18 07	18 11		18 41		19 07	19 11	
East Croydon 175,177 ⇌	a	17 51	17 54		18 21	18 24		18 54		19 21	19 24	
East Croydon	d	17 52	17 56	18 10	18 22	18 25	18 40	18 55	19 10	19 22	19 25	19 40
South Croydon 175	d		17 59			18 28		18 58			19 28	
Sanderstead	d		18 02	18 15		18 32	18 45	19 02	19 15		19 32	19 45
Riddlesdown	d		18 05	18 18		18 35	18 48	19 05	19 18		19 35	19 48
Upper Warlingham	d		18 09	18 22		18 39	18 52	19 09	19 22		19 39	19 52
Woldingham	d		18 13	18 26		18 43	18 56	19 13	19 26		19 43	19 56
Oxted	a	18 05	18 18	18 31	18 35	18 48	19 01	19 18	19 31	19 35	19 48	20 01
Oxted	d	18 06	18 19	18 32	18 36	18 49	19 02	19 19	19 32	19 36	19 49	20 02
Hurst Green	d	18 09	18 22	18 35	18 39	18 52	19 05	19 22	19 35	19 39	19 52	20 05
Lingfield	d		18 28	18 41		18 58	19 11	19 28	19 41		19 58	20 11
Dormans	d		18 31	18 44		19 01	19 14	19 31	19 44		20 01	20 14
East Grinstead	a		18 37	18 50		19 07	19 20	19 37	19 50		20 07	20 20
Edenbridge Town	d	18 15			18 45					19 45		
Hever	d	18 19			18 49					19 49		
Cowden	d	18 23			18 53					19 53		
Ashurst	d	18 28			18 58					19 58		
Eridge	d	18 33			19 03					20 03		
Crowborough	d	18 40			19 10					20 10		
Buxted	d	18 46			19 16					20 16		
Uckfield	a	18 52			19 22					20 22		

Station		SN	SN	SN	SN	SN	SN	SN	SN	SN	SN	SN
London Victoria ⊖175,177	d	19 51		20 21	20 51		21 21	21 51		22 21	22 52	
Clapham Junction	a	19 57		20 27	20 57		21 27	21 57		22 27	22 58	
Clapham Junction 175,177	d	19 58		20 28	20 58		21 28	21 58		22 28	22 59	
East Croydon	a	20 09		20 39	21 09		21 39	22 09		22 39	23 09	
St Pancras International	d											
Farringdon	a											
Farringdon	d											
City Thameslink	a											
City Thameslink	d											
London Blackfriars	a											
	d											
London Blackfriars	d											
London Bridge ⊖175,177	a											
London Bridge	d		20 07			21 07			22 07			23 07
East Croydon 175,177 ⇌	a		20 21			21 21			22 21			23 21
East Croydon	d	20 10	20 22	20 40	21 10	21 22	21 40	22 10	22 22	22 40	23 10	23 22
South Croydon 175	d											
Sanderstead	d	20 15		20 45	21 15		21 45	22 15		22 45	23 15	
Riddlesdown	d	20 18		20 48	21 18		21 48	22 18		22 48	23 18	
Upper Warlingham	d	20 22		20 52	21 22		21 52	22 22		22 52	23 22	
Woldingham	d	20 26		20 56	21 26		21 56	22 26		22 56	23 26	
Oxted	a	20 31	20 35	21 01	21 31	21 35	22 01	22 31	22 35	23 01	23 31	23 35
Oxted	d	20 32	20 36	21 02	21 32	21 36	22 02	22 32	22 36	23 02	23 32	23 36
Hurst Green	d	20 35	20 39	21 05	21 35	21 39	22 05	22 35	22 39	23 05	23 35	23 39
Lingfield	d	20 41		21 11	21 41		22 11	22 41		23 11	23 41	
Dormans	d	20 44		21 14	21 44		22 14	22 44		23 14	23 44	
East Grinstead	a	20 50		21 20	21 50		22 20	22 50		23 20	23 50	
Edenbridge Town	d		20 45			21 45			22 45			23 45
Hever	d		20 49			21 49			22 49			
Cowden	d		20 53			21 53			22 53			
Ashurst	d		20 58			21 58			22 58			
Eridge	d		21 03			22 03			23 03			23 57
Crowborough	d		21 10			22 10			23 10			00 04
Buxted	d		21 16			22 16			23 16			00 10
Uckfield	a		21 22			22 22			23 22			00 16

Station		SN	SN
London Victoria ⊖175,177	d	23 21	23 53
Clapham Junction	a	23 27	23 59
Clapham Junction 175,177	d	23 28	23 59
East Croydon	a	23 39	00 14
St Pancras International	d		
Farringdon	a		
Farringdon	d		
City Thameslink	a		
City Thameslink	d		
London Blackfriars	a		
	d		
London Blackfriars	d		
London Bridge ⊖175,177	a		
London Bridge	d		
East Croydon 175,177 ⇌	a		
East Croydon	d	23 40	00 14
South Croydon 175	d		00 17
Sanderstead	d	23 45	00 20
Riddlesdown	d	23 48	00 23
Upper Warlingham	d	23 52	00 27
Woldingham	d	23 56	00 31
Oxted	a	00 01	00 37
Oxted	d	00 02	
Hurst Green	d	00 05	
Lingfield	d	00 11	
Dormans	d	00 14	
East Grinstead	a	00 20	
Edenbridge Town	d		
Hever	d		
Cowden	d		
Ashurst	d		
Eridge	d		
Crowborough	d		
Buxted	d		
Uckfield	a		

Table T182-F

London - Oxted, East Grinstead and Uckfield

Saturdays

26 May to 8 December

Station		SN	SN	SN	SN	SN	SN	SN
London Victoria ⊖175,177	d				05 21		06 21	06 51
Clapham Junction	a				05 28		06 27	06 57
Clapham Junction 175,177	d				05 28		06 28	06 58
East Croydon	a				05 44		06 39	07 09
St Pancras International	d							
Farringdon	a							
Farringdon	d							
City Thameslink	a							
City Thameslink	d							
London Blackfriars	a							
	d							
London Blackfriars	d							
London Bridge ⊖175,177	a							
London Bridge	d					06 07		
East Croydon 175,177 ⇌	a					06 21		
East Croydon	d			00 14	05 45	06 22	06 40	07 10
South Croydon 175	d			00 17				
Sanderstead	d			00 20			06 45	07 15
Riddlesdown	d			00 23			06 48	07 18
Upper Warlingham	d			00 27			06 52	07 22
Woldingham	d			00 31			06 56	07 26
Oxted	a			00 37	05 58	06 35	07 01	07 31
Oxted	d	00 02			05 59	06 36	07 02	07 32
Hurst Green	d	00 05			06 02	06 39	07 05	07 35
Lingfield	d	00 11			06 08		07 11	07 41
Dormans	d	00 14			06 11		07 14	07 44
East Grinstead	a	00 20			06 17		07 20	07 50
Edenbridge Town	d					06 45		
Hever	d					06 49		
Cowden	d					06 53		
Ashurst	d					06 58		
Eridge	d					07 03		
Crowborough	d		00 04			07 10		
Buxted	d		00 10			07 16		
Uckfield	a		00 16			07 22		

Station			SN	SN	SN	SN	SN	SN	SN	SN	SN
London Victoria ⊖175,177	d			21 21	21 51		22 21	22 51		23 21	23 53
Clapham Junction	a			21 27	21 57		22 27	22 57		23 27	23 59
Clapham Junction 175,177	d			21 28	21 58		22 28	22 58		23 28	23 59
East Croydon	a			21 39	22 09		22 39	23 09		23 39	00 15
St Pancras International	d										
Farringdon	a										
Farringdon	d										
City Thameslink	a										
City Thameslink	d										
London Blackfriars	a										
	d										
London Blackfriars	d										
London Bridge ⊖175,177	a										
London Bridge	d	and at the same minutes past each hour until	21 07			22 07			23 07		
East Croydon 175,177 ⇌	a		21 21			22 21			23 21		
East Croydon	d		21 22	21 40	22 10	22 22	22 40	23 10	23 22	23 40	00 16
South Croydon 175	d										00 18
Sanderstead	d			21 45	22 15		22 45	23 15		23 45	00 21
Riddlesdown	d			21 48	22 18		22 48	23 18		23 48	00 24
Upper Warlingham	d			21 52	22 22		22 52	23 22		23 52	00 28
Woldingham	d			21 56	22 26		22 56	23 26		23 56	00 32
Oxted	a		21 35	22 01	22 31	22 35	23 01	23 31	23 35	00 01	00 37
Oxted	d		21 36	22 02	22 32	22 36	23 02	23 32	23 36	00 02	
Hurst Green	d		21 39	22 05	22 35	22 39	23 05	23 35	23 39	00 05	
Lingfield	d			22 11	22 41		23 11	23 41		00 11	
Dormans	d			22 14	22 44		23 14	23 44		00 14	
East Grinstead	a			22 20	22 50		23 20	23 50		00 20	
Edenbridge Town	d		21 45			22 45			23 45		
Hever	d		21 49			22 49			23 49		
Cowden	d		21 53			22 53			23 53		
Ashurst	d		21 58			22 58			23 58		
Eridge	d		22 03			23 03			00 03		
Crowborough	d		22 10			23 10			00 10		
Buxted	d		22 16			23 18			00 16		
Uckfield	a		22 22			23 24			00 22		

Sundays

20 May to 2 December

Station		SN A	SN A	SN A	SN	SN	SN	SN	SN	SN	SN	SN
London Victoria ⊖175,177	d				07 43		08 51		09 21	09 51		10 21
Clapham Junction	a				07 50		08 57		09 27	09 57		10 27
Clapham Junction 175,177	d				07 51		08 58		09 28	09 58		10 28
East Croydon	a				08 08		09 08		09 38	10 08		10 38
St Pancras International	d											
Farringdon	a											
Farringdon	d											
City Thameslink	a											
City Thameslink	d											
London Blackfriars	a											
	d											
London Blackfriars	d											
London Bridge ⊖175,177	a											
London Bridge	d											
East Croydon 175,177 ⇌	a											
East Croydon	d			00 16	08 09	08 17	09 09	09 23	09 39	10 09		10 39
South Croydon 175	d			00 18								
Sanderstead	d			00 21	08 14		09 14		09 44	10 14		10 44
Riddlesdown	d			00 24	08 17		09 17		09 47	10 17		10 47
Upper Warlingham	d			00 28	08 21		09 21		09 51	10 21		10 51
Woldingham	d			00 32	08 25		09 25		09 55	10 25		10 55
Oxted	a			00 37	08 30	08 36	09 30	09 36	10 00	10 33		11 00
Oxted	d	00 02			08 30	08 37	09 31	09 37	10 01	10 34	10 38	11 01
Hurst Green	d	00 05			08 33	08 40	09 34	09 40	10 04	10 37	10 41	11 04
Lingfield	d	00 11			08 39		09 40		10 10	10 43		11 10
Dormans	d	00 14			08 43		09 43		10 13	10 46		11 13
East Grinstead	a	00 20			08 48		09 48		10 18	10 51		11 18
Edenbridge Town	d					08 46		09 46			10 47	
Hever	d					08 50		09 50			10 51	
Cowden	d					08 54		09 54			10 55	
Ashurst	d					08 58		09 58			10 59	
Eridge	d		00 03			09 04		10 04			11 05	
Crowborough	d		00 10			09 11		10 11			11 12	
Buxted	d		00 16			09 17		10 17			11 18	
Uckfield	a		00 22			09 23		10 23			11 24	

Station		SN	SN	SN	SN	SN	SN	SN	SN	SN	SN	SN
London Victoria ⊖175,177	d	10 51		11 21	11 51		12 21	12 51		13 21	13 51	
Clapham Junction	a	10 57		11 27	11 57		12 27	12 57		13 27	13 57	
Clapham Junction 175,177	d	10 58		11 28	11 58		12 28	12 58		13 28	13 58	
East Croydon	a	11 08		11 38	12 08		12 38	13 11		13 38	14 08	
St Pancras International	d											
Farringdon	a											
Farringdon	d											
City Thameslink	a											
City Thameslink	d											
London Blackfriars	a											
	d											
London Blackfriars	d											
London Bridge ⊖175,177	a											
London Bridge	d											
East Croydon 175,177 ⇌	a											
East Croydon	d	11 09		11 39	12 09		12 39	13 12		13 39	14 09	
South Croydon 175	d											
Sanderstead	d	11 14		11 44	12 14		12 44	13 17		13 44	14 14	
Riddlesdown	d	11 17		11 47	12 17		12 47	13 20		13 47	14 17	
Upper Warlingham	d	11 21		11 51	12 21		12 51	13 24		13 51	14 21	
Woldingham	d	11 25		11 55	12 25		12 55	13 28		13 55	14 25	
Oxted	a	11 33		12 00	12 33		13 00	13 33		14 00	14 33	
Oxted	d	11 34	11 38	12 01	12 34	12 38	13 01	13 34	13 38	14 01	14 34	14 38
Hurst Green	d	11 37	11 41	12 04	12 37	12 41	13 04	13 37	13 41	14 04	14 37	14 41
Lingfield	d	11 43		12 10	12 43		13 10	13 43		14 10	14 43	
Dormans	d	11 46		12 13	12 46		13 13	13 46		14 13	14 46	
East Grinstead	a	11 51		12 18	12 51		13 18	13 51		14 18	14 51	
Edenbridge Town	d		11 47			12 47			13 47			14 47
Hever	d		11 51			12 51			13 51			14 51
Cowden	d		11 55			12 55			13 55			14 55
Ashurst	d		11 59			12 59			13 59			14 59
Eridge	d		12 05			13 05			14 05			15 05
Crowborough	d		12 12			13 12			14 12			15 12
Buxted	d		12 18			13 18			14 18			15 18
Uckfield	a		12 24			13 24			14 24			15 24

A not 20 May

Table T182-F

Sundays

20 May to 2 December

London - Oxted, East Grinstead and Uckfield

		SN	SN	SN	SN	SN	SN	SN	SN	SN	SN	SN		SN	SN	SN	SN	SN	SN
London Victoria 15 ⊖175,177	d	14 21	14 51		15 21	15 51		16 21	16 51		17 21	17 51	and at the same minutes past each hour until		21 21	21 51		22 21	22 51
Clapham Junction	a	14 27	14 57		15 27	15 57		16 27	16 57		17 27	17 57			21 27	21 57		22 27	22 57
Clapham Junction 10 175,177	d	14 28	14 58		15 28	15 58		16 28	16 58		17 28	17 58			21 28	21 58		22 28	22 58
East Croydon	a	14 38	15 08		15 38	16 11		16 38	17 11		17 38	18 08			21 38	22 08		22 38	23 08
St Pancras International	d																		
Farringdon	a																		
Farringdon	d																		
City Thameslink	a																		
City Thameslink	d																		
London Blackfriars	a																		
	d																		
London Blackfriars	d																		
London Bridge 4 ⊖175,177	a																		
London Bridge	d																		
East Croydon 175,177	a																		
East Croydon	d	14 39	15 09		15 39	16 12		16 39	17 12		17 39	18 09			21 39	22 09		22 39	23 09
South Croydon 4 175	d																		
Sanderstead	d	14 44	15 14		15 44	16 17		16 44	17 17		17 44	18 14			21 44	22 14		22 44	23 14
Riddlesdown	d	14 47	15 17		15 47	16 20		16 47	17 20		17 47	18 17			21 47	22 17		22 47	23 17
Upper Warlingham	d	14 51	15 21		15 51	16 24		16 51	17 24		17 51	18 21			21 51	22 21		22 51	23 21
Woldingham	d	14 55	15 25		15 55	16 28		16 55	17 28		17 55	18 25			21 55	22 25		22 55	23 25
Oxted 3	a	15 00	15 33		16 00	16 33		17 00	17 33		18 00	18 33			22 00	22 33		23 00	23 30
Oxted	d	15 01	15 34	15 38	16 01	16 34	16 38	17 01	17 34	17 38	18 01	18 34		21 38	22 01	22 34	22 38	23 01	23 31
Hurst Green	d	15 04	15 37	15 41	16 04	16 37	16 41	17 04	17 37	17 41	18 04	18 37		21 41	22 04	22 37	22 41	23 04	23 34
Lingfield	d	15 10	15 43		16 10	16 43		17 10	17 43		18 10	18 43			22 10	22 43		23 10	23 40
Dormans	d	15 13	15 46		16 13	16 46		17 13	17 46		18 13	18 46			22 13	22 46		23 13	23 43
East Grinstead	a	15 18	15 51		16 18	16 51		17 18	17 51		18 18	18 51			22 18	22 51		23 18	23 48
Edenbridge Town	d			15 47			16 47			17 47				21 47			22 47		
Hever	d			15 51			16 51			17 51				21 51			22 51		
Cowden	d			15 55			16 55			17 55				21 55			22 55		
Ashurst	d			15 59			16 59			17 59				21 59			22 59		
Eridge	d			16 05			17 05			18 05				22 05			23 05		
Crowborough	d			16 12			17 12			18 12				22 12			23 12		
Buxted	d			16 18			17 18			18 18				22 18			23 18		
Uckfield	a			16 24			17 24			18 24				22 24			23 24		

Table T182-R

Sundays

20 May to 2 December

Uckfield, East Grinstead and Oxted - London

		SN 1 A	SN		SN	SN	SN	SN		SN	SN	SN	SN	SN
Uckfield	d			and every 30 minutes until		09 34			and at the same minutes past each hour until	21 34			22 34	
Buxted	d					09 38				21 38			22 38	
Crowborough	d					09 45				21 45			22 45	
Eridge	d					09 51				21 51			22 51	
Ashurst	d					09 58				21 58			22 58	
Cowden	d					10 02				22 02			23 02	
Hever	d					10 07				22 07			23 07	
Edenbridge Town	a					10 10				22 10			23 10	
East Grinstead	d		08 12		09 42		10 12	10 42			22 12	22 42		23 14
Dormans	d		08 16		09 46		10 16	10 46			22 16	22 46		23 18
Lingfield	d		08 19		09 49		10 19	10 49			22 19	22 49		23 21
Hurst Green	d		08 26		09 56	10 17	10 26	10 56		22 17	22 26	22 56	23 17	23 28
Oxted	a		08 29		09 59	10 20	10 29	10 59		22 20	22 29	22 59	23 20	23 31
Oxted 3	d		08 29		09 59		10 29	10 59			22 29	22 59	23 21	23 31
Woldingham	d		08 35		10 05		10 35	11 05			22 35	23 05		23 37
Upper Warlingham	d		08 38		10 08		10 38	11 08			22 38	23 08		23 40
Riddlesdown	d		08 42		10 12		10 42	11 12			22 42	23 12		23 44
Sanderstead	d		08 45		10 15		10 45	11 15			22 45	23 15		23 47
South Croydon 4 175	d													
East Croydon	a		08 51		10 21		10 51	11 21			22 51	23 21	23 34	23 54
East Croydon 175,177	d													
London Bridge	a													
London Bridge 4 ⊖175,177	d													
London Blackfriars	d													
City Thameslink	d													
Farringdon	d													
St Pancras International	a													
East Croydon	d		08 51		10 21		10 51	11 21			22 51	23 21		23 55
Clapham Junction 10 175,177	d	00 05	09 02		10 32		11 02	11 32			23 02	23 32		00 16
London Victoria 15 ⊖175,177	a	00 12	09 09		10 39		11 09	11 39			23 09	23 39		00 23

A not 20 May

Table T182-R

Mondays to Fridays

21 May to 7 December

Uckfield, East Grinstead and Oxted - London

		SN MX 1	SN MO	SN	SN 1	TL 1	SN 1	SN 1	TL 1	SN 1	TL 1	SN 1	SN 1	TL 1	SN 1	SN 1	TL 1	SN 1	SN 1	TL 1	SN 1	SN 1	TL 1
Uckfield	d			05 10			05 31					06 33			07 03			07 33			08 03		
Buxted	d			05 14			05 35					06 37			07 07			07 37			08 07		
Crowborough	d			05 21			05 42					06 44			07 14			07 44			08 14		
Eridge	d			05 27			05 48					06 50			07 20			07 50			08 20		
Ashurst	d						05 54					06 56			07 26			07 56			08 26		
Cowden	d			05 35			05 58					07 00			07 30			08 00			08 30		
Hever	d						06 03					07 05			07 35			08 05			08 35		
Edenbridge Town	a			05 40			06 06					07 08			07 38			08 08			08 38		
East Grinstead	d				05 36	05 45		06 04	06 13	06 36	06 45		07 06	07 15		07 36	07 45		08 06	08 15		08 36	08 45
Dormans	d				05 40	05 49		06 08	06 17	06 40	06 49		07 10	07 19		07 40	07 49		08 10	08 19		08 40	08 49
Lingfield	d				05 43	05 52		06 11	06 20	06 43	06 52		07 13	07 22		07 43	07 52		08 13	08 22		08 43	08 52
Hurst Green	d				05 50	05 59	06 14	06 18	06 27	06 50	06 59	07 16	07 20	07 29	07 46	07 50	07 59	08 16	08 20	08 29	08 46	08 50	08 59
Oxted	a			05 48	05 53	06 02	06 17	06 22	06 29	06 53	07 02	07 19	07 23	07 32	07 49	07 53	08 02	08 19	08 23	08 32	08 49	08 53	09 02
Oxted 3	d			05 49	05 53	06 02	06 19	06 23	06 30	06 53	07 02	07 20	07 23	07 32	07 50	07 53	08 02	08 20	08 23	08 32	08 50	08 53	09 02
Woldingham	d				05 59	06 08		06 28	06 35	06 59	07 08		07 29	07 38		07 59	08 08		08 29	08 38		08 59	09 08
Upper Warlingham	d				06 02	06 11		06 32	06 39	07 02	07 11		07 32	07 41		08 02	08 11		08 32	08 41		09 02	09 11
Riddlesdown	d				06 06	06 15		06 35	06 42	07 06	07 15		07 36	07 45		08 06	08 15		08 36	08 45		09 06	09 15
Sanderstead	d				06 09	06 18		06 39	06 45	07 09	07 18		07 39	07 48		08 09	08 18		08 39	08 48		09 09	09 18
South Croydon 4 175	d					06 21			06 48		07 21			07 51			08 21			08 51			09 22
East Croydon	a			06 06	06 15	06 24	06 37	06 44	06 51	07 15	07 24	07 37	07 45	07 54	08 07	08 15	08 24	08 37	08 45	08 54	09 07	09 15	09 24
East Croydon 175,177	d			06 08		06 25	06 38		06 51		07 25	07 38		07 55	08 08		08 25	08 38		08 55	09 08		09 25
London Bridge	a			06 23		06 40	06 53		07 05		07 40	07 53		08 10	08 23		08 40	08 53		09 10	09 23		09 40
London Bridge 4 ⊖175,177	d					06 41			07 06		07 41			08 11			08 41			09 11			09 41
London Blackfriars	d					06 47			07 12		07 47			08 17			08 47			09 17			09 47
City Thameslink	d					06 49			07 14		07 49			08 19			08 49			09 19			09 49
Farringdon	d					06 51			07 16		07 51			08 21			08 51			09 21			09 51
St Pancras International	a					06 55			07 20		07 55			08 25			08 55			09 25			09 55
East Croydon	d				06 15			06 45		07 15			07 45			08 15			08 45			09 15	
Clapham Junction 10 175,177	d	00 01	00 16		06 26			06 56		07 26			07 58			08 28			08 58			09 26	
London Victoria 15 ⊖175,177	a	00 08	00 23		06 32			07 03		07 32			08 06			08 35			09 05			09 32	

		SN 1	SN 1	TL 1	SN 1	SN 1	SN 1	SN 1	SN 1	SN 1	SN 1		SN 1	SN 1	SN 1	SN 1	SN 1	SN 1	SN 1	SN 1	SN 1	SN 1
Uckfield	d	08 33				09 33		10 03		10 33		and at the same minutes past each hour until		13 33			14 33			15 33		
Buxted	d	08 37				09 37		10 07		10 37				13 37			14 37			15 37		
Crowborough	d	08 44				09 44		10 14		10 44				13 44			14 44			15 44		
Eridge	d	08 50				09 50		10 20		10 50				13 50			14 50			15 50		
Ashurst	d	08 56				09 56		10 26		10 56				13 56			14 56			15 56		
Cowden	d	09 00				10 00		10 30		11 00				14 00			15 00			16 00		
Hever	d	09 05				10 05		10 35		11 05				14 05			15 05			16 05		
Edenbridge Town	a	09 08				10 08		10 38		11 08				14 08			15 08			16 08		
East Grinstead	d		09 06	09 21	09 36		10 06		10 36		11 06		13 36		14 06	14 36		15 06	15 36		16 06	16 36
Dormans	d		09 10	09 25	09 40		10 10		10 40		11 10		13 40		14 10	14 40		15 10	15 40		16 10	16 40
Lingfield	d		09 13	09 28	09 43		10 13		10 43		11 13		13 43		14 13	14 43		15 13	15 43		16 13	16 43
Hurst Green	d	09 16	09 20	09 35	09 50	10 16	10 20	10 46	10 50	11 16	11 20		13 50	14 16	14 20	14 50	15 16	15 20	15 50	16 16	16 20	16 50
Oxted	a	09 19	09 23	09 38	09 53	10 19	10 23	10 49	10 53	11 19	11 23		13 53	14 19	14 23	14 53	15 19	15 23	15 53	16 19	16 23	16 53
Oxted 3	d	09 20	09 23	09 38	09 53	10 20	10 23	10 50	10 53	11 20	11 23		13 53	14 20	14 23	14 53	15 20	15 23	15 53	16 20	16 23	16 53
Woldingham	d		09 29		09 59		10 29		10 59		11 29		13 59		14 29	14 59		15 29	15 59		16 29	16 59
Upper Warlingham	d		09 32		10 02		10 32		11 02		11 32		14 02		14 32	15 02		15 32	16 02		16 32	17 02
Riddlesdown	d		09 36		10 06		10 36		11 06		11 36		14 06		14 36	15 06		15 36	16 06		16 36	17 06
Sanderstead	d		09 39	09 48	10 09		10 39		11 09		11 39		14 09		14 39	15 09		15 39	16 09		16 39	17 09
South Croydon 4 175	d			09 51																		
East Croydon	a	09 37	09 45	09 54	10 15	10 36	10 45	11 08	11 15	11 36	11 45		14 15	14 36	14 45	15 15	15 36	15 45	16 15	16 36	16 45	17 15
East Croydon 175,177	d	09 38		09 54		10 38				11 38				14 38			15 38			16 38		
London Bridge	a	09 53		10 11		10 53				11 53				14 53			15 53			16 54		
London Bridge 4 ⊖175,177	d																					
London Blackfriars	d																					
City Thameslink	d																					
Farringdon	d																					
St Pancras International	a																					
East Croydon	d		09 45		10 15		10 45		11 15		11 45		14 15		14 45	15 15		15 46	16 15		16 45	17 15
Clapham Junction 10 175,177	d		09 56		10 26		10 56		11 26		11 56		14 26		14 56	15 26		15 57	16 26		16 56	17 26
London Victoria 15 ⊖175,177	a		10 02		10 32		11 02		11 32		12 02		14 32		15 02	15 32		16 03	16 32		17 02	17 33

		SN 1	SN 1	SN 1	TL 1	SN 1	SN 1	TL 1	SN 1	SN 1	TL 1	SN 1	SN 1	TL 1	SN 1	SN 1	TL 1	SN 1	SN 1	TL 1	SN 1	SN 1
Uckfield	d	16 33				17 33			18 03			18 33			19 03			19 33				20 33
Buxted	d	16 37				17 37			18 07			18 37			19 07			19 37				20 37
Crowborough	d	16 44				17 44			18 14			18 44			19 14			19 44				20 44
Eridge	d	16 50				17 50			18 20			18 50			19 20			19 50				20 50
Ashurst	d	16 56				17 56			18 26			18 56			19 26			19 56				20 56
Cowden	d	17 00				18 00			18 30			19 00			19 30			20 00				21 00
Hever	d	17 05				18 05			18 35			19 05			19 35			20 05				21 05
Edenbridge Town	a	17 08				18 08			18 38			19 08			19 38			20 08				21 08
East Grinstead	d		17 06	17 36	17 51		18 06	18 21		18 36	18 51		19 06	19 17		19 36	19 51		20 06	20 17	20 36	
Dormans	d		17 10	17 40	17 55		18 10	18 25		18 40	18 55		19 10	19 21		19 40	19 55		20 10	20 21	20 40	
Lingfield	d		17 13	17 43	17 58		18 13	18 28		18 43	18 58		19 13	19 24		19 43	19 58		20 13	20 24	20 43	
Hurst Green	d	17 16	17 20	17 50	18 05	18 16	18 20	18 35	18 46	18 50	19 05	19 16	19 20	19 31	19 46	19 50	20 05	20 16	20 20	20 31	20 50	21 16
Oxted	a	17 19	17 23	17 53	18 08	18 19	18 23	18 38	18 49	18 53	19 08	19 19	19 23	19 34	19 49	19 53	20 08	20 19	20 23	20 34	20 53	21 19
Oxted 3	d	17 20	17 23	17 53	18 08	18 20	18 23	18 38	18 50	18 53	19 08	19 20	19 23	19 34	19 50	19 53	20 08	20 20	20 23	20 34	20 53	21 20
Woldingham	d		17 29	17 59			18 29			18 59			19 29			19 59			20 29		20 59	
Upper Warlingham	d		17 32	18 02			18 32			19 02			19 32			20 02			20 32		21 02	
Riddlesdown	d		17 36	18 06			18 36			19 06			19 36			20 06			20 36		21 06	
Sanderstead	d		17 39	18 09	18 18		18 39	18 48		19 09	19 18		19 39	19 45		20 09	20 18		20 39	20 45	21 09	
South Croydon 4 175	d																					
East Croydon	a	17 36	17 45	18 15	18 24	18 36	18 45	18 54	19 06	19 15	19 24	19 36	19 45	19 52	20 06	20 15	20 24	20 36	20 45	20 52	21 15	21 36
East Croydon 175,177	d	17 38			18 25	18 38		18 55	19 08		19 24	19 38		19 52	20 08		20 24	20 38		20 52		21 38
London Bridge	a	17 54			18 40	18 53		19 10	19 23		19 40	19 53		20 11	20 23		20 41	20 53		21 11		21 53
London Bridge 4 ⊖175,177	d				18 41			19 11			19 41											
London Blackfriars	d				18 47			19 17			19 47											
City Thameslink	d				18 49			19 19			19 49											
Farringdon	d				18 51			19 21			19 51											
St Pancras International	a				18 55			19 25			19 55											
East Croydon	d		17 45	18 15			18 45			19 15			19 45			20 15			20 45		21 15	
Clapham Junction 10 175,177	d		17 56	18 26			18 56			19 26			19 56			20 26			20 59		21 26	
London Victoria 15 ⊖175,177	a		18 02	18 32			19 03			19 32			20 02			20 32			21 05		21 32	

Table T182-R

Mondays to Fridays

21 May to 7 December

Uckfield, East Grinstead and Oxted - London

		SN ■	SN ■	SN ■	SN ■	SN ■	SN ■	SN ■
Uckfield	d			21 33			22 33	
Buxted	d			21 37			22 37	
Crowborough	d			21 44			22 44	
Eridge	d			21 50			22 50	
Ashurst	d			21 56			22 56	
Cowden	d			22 00			23 00	
Hever	d			22 05			23 05	
Edenbridge Town	a			22 08			23 08	
East Grinstead	d	21 06	21 36		22 06	22 36		23 06
Dormans	d	21 10	21 40		22 10	22 40		23 10
Lingfield	d	21 13	21 43		22 13	22 43		23 13
Hurst Green	d	21 20	21 50	22 16	22 20	22 50	23 16	23 20
Oxted	a	21 23	21 53	22 19	22 23	22 53	23 19	23 23
Oxted ■	d	21 23	21 53	22 20	22 23	22 53	23 20	23 23
Woldingham	d	21 29	21 59		22 29	22 59		23 29
Upper Warlingham	d	21 32	22 02		22 32	23 02		23 32
Riddlesdown	d	21 36	22 06		22 36	23 06		23 36
Sanderstead	d	21 39	22 09		22 39	23 09		23 39
South Croydon ■ 175	d							
East Croydon	a	21 45	22 15	22 36	22 45	23 15	23 36	23 45
East Croydon 175,177 ⇌	d			22 38			23 38	
London Bridge	a			22 53			23 53	
London Bridge ■ ⊖175,177	d							
London Blackfriars	d							
City Thameslink	d							
Farringdon	d							
St Pancras International	a							
East Croydon	d	21 45	22 15		22 45	23 15		23 45
Clapham Junction ■■ 175,177	d	21 56	22 26		22 56	23 26		00 01
London Victoria ■■ ⊖175,177	a	22 02	22 32		23 02	23 32		00 08

Saturdays

26 May to 8 December

		SN ■	SN ■	SN ■	SN ■		SN ■	SN ■	SN ■	SN ■	SN ■	SN ■
Uckfield	d			06 33				21 33			22 33	
Buxted	d			06 37				21 37			22 37	
Crowborough	d			06 44				21 44			22 44	
Eridge	d			06 50				21 50			22 50	
Ashurst	d			06 56				21 56			22 56	
Cowden	d			07 00				22 00			23 00	
Hever	d			07 05				22 05			23 05	
Edenbridge Town	a			07 08				22 08			23 08	
East Grinstead	d		06 36		07 06		21 36		22 06	22 36		23 06
Dormans	d		06 40		07 10		21 40		22 10	22 40		23 10
Lingfield	d		06 43		07 13	and at the same minutes past each hour until	21 43		22 13	22 43		23 13
Hurst Green	d		06 50	07 16	07 20		21 50	22 16	22 20	22 50	23 16	23 20
Oxted	a		06 53	07 19	07 23		21 53	22 19	22 23	22 53	23 19	23 23
Oxted ■	d		06 53	07 20	07 23		21 53	22 20	22 23	22 53	23 20	23 23
Woldingham	d		06 59		07 29		21 59		22 29	22 59		23 29
Upper Warlingham	d		07 02		07 32		22 02		22 32	23 02		23 32
Riddlesdown	d		07 06		07 36		22 06		22 36	23 06		23 36
Sanderstead	d		07 09		07 39		22 09		22 39	23 09		23 39
South Croydon ■ 175	d											
East Croydon	a		07 15	07 36	07 45		22 15	22 36	22 45	23 15	23 36	23 45
East Croydon 175,177 ⇌	d			07 37				22 37			23 38	
London Bridge	a			07 53				22 53			23 53	
London Bridge ■ ⊖175,177	d											
London Blackfriars	d											
City Thameslink	d											
Farringdon	d											
St Pancras International	a											
East Croydon	d		07 15		07 45		22 15		22 45	23 15		23 45
Clapham Junction ■■ 175,177	d	00 01	07 26		07 56		22 26		22 56	23 26		00 05
London Victoria ■■ ⊖175,177	a	00 08	07 32		08 02		22 32		23 02	23 32		00 12

For Sunday return journeys, see previous page

Table T183-F

Mondays to Fridays

21 May to 7 December

London - Redhill / Reigate / Tonbridge / Gatwick Airport - Horsham

Miles	Miles	Miles			SN MX	SN MO ■	SN MX ■	GW MX	TL MX ■	TL MO ■	TL MX ■	TL ■	TL ■	TL ■	SN ■	SN	GW	SN	TL ■	GW ⚲	SN ■	SN ■	GW
0	—	—	London Victoria	d		00 08	00 08								04 35							05 32	
2½	—	—	Clapham Junction	d		00 15	00 15								04 42							05 39	
10½	—	—	East Croydon	a		00 30	00 30								04 57							05 51	
—	—	0	St Pancras International	d					00 21	00 51	00 52	01 32	02 32	03 32					04 32				
—	—	1¼	Farringdon	d					00 26														
—	—	1¾	City Thameslink	d																			
—	—	2	London Blackfriars	d					00 31	01 01	01 02	01 40	02 40	03 40					04 40				
—	0	—	London Bridge	d																			
—	8½	—	Norwood Junction	d																			
—	—	—	East Croydon	a					00 57	01 27	01 28	02 06	03 06	04 06					05 06				
—	10¼	—	East Croydon	d		00 31	00 31		00 58	01 28	01 28	02 07	03 07	04 07	04 57				05 07			05 52	
13¼	13¼	—	Purley	d		00 37	00 37			01 34	01 34	02 13	03 13	04 13	05 03				05 13			05 56	
15¼	15¼	—	Coulsdon South	d		00 41	00 41								05 06								
19	19	—	Merstham	d		00 46	00 46								05 12								
20½	20½	—	Redhill	a		00 52	00 52		01 11		01 45				05 16							06 05	
—	—	—	Redhill	d	00 16											05 23	05 35	05 52					06 15
—	—	—	Reigate	a													05 39						06 19
—	22¾	—	Nutfield	a	00 20											05 27		05 56					
—	26¼	—	Godstone	a	00 26											05 33		06 02					
—	31	—	Edenbridge	a	00 32											05 38		06 08					
—	36	—	Penshurst	a	00 38											05 45		06 14					
—	37¾	—	Leigh (Kent)	a	00 42											05 48		06 18					
—	40¼	—	Tonbridge	a	00 46											05 53		06 23					
—	—	—	Tonbridge	d																			
—	—	—	Redhill	a																			
—	—	—	Reigate	d				00 45												05 35			
—	—	—	Redhill	a				00 49												05 39			
—	—	—	Redhill	d		00 53	00 53	00 57	01 11		01 46				05 17					05 41		06 05	
21	—	—	Earlswood (Surrey)	d																		06 08	
22½	—	—	Salfords	d																		06 11	
25¾	—	—	Horley	d		00 59	01 00			01 52	01 52	02 26	03 26	04 26	05 23				05 27			06 15	
26¼	—	—	Gatwick Airport	a		01 03	01 03	01 07	01 20	01 56	01 56	02 30	03 30	04 30	05 27				05 31	05 51		06 17	
—	—	—	Gatwick Airport	d					01 21	01 58	01 58	02 31	03 31	04 35					05 32		05 56	06 18	
29	—	—	Three Bridges	a					01 26	02 03	02 03	02 36	03 36	04 40					05 37		06 00	06 23	
—	—	—	Three Bridges	d																	06 01		
30¾	—	—	Crawley	d																	06 05		
32	—	—	Ifield	d																	06 08		
34½	—	—	Faygate	d																			
36¾	—	—	Littlehaven	d																	06 14		
38	—	—	Horsham	a																	06 17		

		SN ■	SN ■	SN	GW A	TL ■	SN ■	GW ⚲	SN	TL ■	GW	SN ■	SN ■	TL ■	SN	GW	TL ■	SN ■	GW ⚲	SN	SN ■		TL ■
London Victoria	d	05 39	05 54				06 09					06 36	06 39					07 06			07 09		
Clapham Junction	d	05 46	06 01				06 16					06 43	06 46					07 13			07 16		
East Croydon	a	05 55	06 10				06 26					06 52	06 56					07 22			07 27		
St Pancras International	d					05 45				06 15				06 35			06 45						07 15
Farringdon	d					05 49				06 19				06 39			06 49						07 19
City Thameslink	d					05 51				06 21				06 41			06 51						07 21
London Blackfriars	d					05 54				06 24				06 44			06 54						07 24
London Bridge	d					06 00				06 30				06 51			07 00						07 30
Norwood Junction	d					06 12				06 42				07 02			07 12						07 42
East Croydon	a					06 16				06 46				07 06			07 16						07 46
East Croydon	d	05 55	06 10			06 16	06 27			06 46		06 52	06 57	07 07			07 16	07 22			07 27		07 46
Purley	d	06 02				06 23	06 33			06 53			07 03								07 33		
Coulsdon South	d	06 06				06 27	06 37			06 57			07 07				07 24				07 37		07 55
Merstham	d	06 11				06 32	06 43			07 02			07 13				07 29				07 43		08 01
Redhill	a	06 15				06 36	06 47			07 06			07 17	07 20			07 33				07 47		08 05
Redhill	d	06 19		06 22	06 30		06 48		06 52		07 14		07 18		07 23	07 31				07 52		07 54	
Reigate	a	06 23			06 39		06 52				07 18		07 22			07 38						07 58	
Nutfield	a			06 26					06 56						07 27					07 56			
Godstone	a			06 32					07 02						07 33					08 02			
Edenbridge	a			06 38					07 08						07 38					08 08			
Penshurst	a			06 44					07 14						07 45					08 14			
Leigh (Kent)	a			06 48					07 18						07 48					08 18			
Tonbridge	a			06 53					07 23						07 53					08 23			
Tonbridge	d																						
Redhill	a																						
Reigate	d							06 32											07 32				
Redhill	a							06 37											07 37				
Redhill	d					06 37		06 42		07 07				07 21			07 34		07 43		07 57		08 06
Earlswood (Surrey)	d					06 39				07 09							07 36				08 00		
Salfords	d					06 43				07 13							07 40				08 04		
Horley	d					06 46				07 16							07 43				08 08		08 12
Gatwick Airport	a		06 25			06 50		06 54		07 19		07 07		07 28			07 46	07 37	07 51		08 12		08 15
Gatwick Airport	d		06 26			06 51				07 21		07 08					07 47	07 38					08 16
Three Bridges	a		06 31			06 56				07 26		07 13					07 52	07 42					08 21
Three Bridges	d		06 32			06 57				07 27		07 13					07 53	07 45					08 22
Crawley	d		06 36			07 01				07 31		07 17					07 57	07 49					08 26
Ifield	d		06 38			07 03				07 33							07 59						08 29
Faygate	d		06 42							07 37							08 03						08 33
Littlehaven	d		06 46			07 09				07 41		07 25					08 07						08 37
Horsham	a		06 50			07 13				07 45		07 28					08 11	07 57					08 41

A until 5 October

Table T183-F

Mondays to Fridays

21 May to 7 December

London - Redhill / Reigate / Tonbridge / Gatwick Airport - Horsham

Station		GW	SN 1	SN	SN 1		TL 1	SN 1	GW	GW A	SN 1		SN	TL 1	SN 1	TL 1	GW	SN 1	TL 1	SN	TL 1	GW	SN 1
London Victoria	d		07 36		07 39			08 06			08 09				08 36			08 39					09 06
Clapham Junction	d		07 43		07 46			08 13			08 16				08 43			08 46					09 13
East Croydon	a		07 52		07 57			08 22			08 27				08 52			08 57					09 22
St Pancras International	d						07 45							08 15		08 25			08 35		08 45		
Farringdon	d						07 49							08 19		08 29			08 39		08 49		
City Thameslink	d						07 51							08 21		08 31			08 41		08 51		
London Blackfriars	d						07 54							08 24		08 34			08 44		08 54		
London Bridge	d						08 00							08 30		08 41			08 51		09 00		
Norwood Junction	d						08 12							08 42					09 02				
East Croydon	a						08 16							08 46		08 54			09 06		09 14		
East Croydon	d		07 52		07 57		08 16	08 22			08 27			08 46	08 53	08 55		08 57	09 07		09 16		09 23
Purley	d				08 03						08 33							09 03	09 14				
Coulsdon South	d				08 07		08 25				08 37			08 56				09 07			09 23		
Merstham	d				08 13		08 31				08 43			09 01				09 13			09 28		
Redhill	a				08 17		08 35				08 49			09 05		09 09		09 19	09 22		09 32		
Redhill	d	08 14		08 22		08 24				08 51		08 55	08 55				09 14	09 21		09 25		09 33	
Reigate	a	08 18				08 28				08 55		09 00					09 18	09 25				09 37	
Nutfield	a			08 26									08 59							09 29			
Godstone	a			08 32									09 05							09 35			
Edenbridge	a			08 38									09 11							09 41			
Penshurst	a			08 44									09 17							09 47			
Leigh (Kent)	a			08 48									09 21							09 51			
Tonbridge	a			08 53									09 26							09 57			
Tonbridge	d																						
Redhill	a																						
Reigate	d								08 24														
Redhill	a								08 28														
Redhill	d				08 27		08 36		08 42		08 59			09 06		09 10			09 23		09 33		
Earlswood (Surrey)	d				08 30														09 25				
Salfords	d				08 34														09 29				
Horley	d				08 38		08 42				09 06			09 12					09 33		09 39		
Gatwick Airport	a		08 07		08 41		08 45	08 37	08 51		09 09			09 15	09 08	09 19			09 35		09 42		09 38
Gatwick Airport	d		08 08				08 46	08 38						09 16	09 09				09 36		09 44		09 39
Three Bridges	a		08 13				08 51	08 43						09 21	09 14				09 41		09 49		09 44
Three Bridges	d		08 14				08 52	08 44						09 22	09 15						09 50		09 44
Crawley	d		08 18				08 56	08 48						09 26	09 19						09 54		09 48
Ifield	d						08 59							09 29							09 56		
Faygate	d						09 03																
Littlehaven	d						09 07							09 35							10 02		
Horsham	a		08 27				09 11	08 57						09 39	09 27						10 08		09 57

Station		TL 1	SN 1	GW	TL 1	SN	TL 1	GW	SN 1	SN 1	TL 1	GW	TL 1	SN 1	SN 1	GW	TL 1	SN	TL 1	GW	SN 1	SN 1
London Victoria	d		09 09						09 36	09 39				10 06	10 09						10 36	10 39
Clapham Junction	d		09 16						09 43	09 46				10 13	10 16						10 43	10 46
East Croydon	a		09 26						09 52	09 56				10 22	10 26						10 52	10 56
St Pancras International	d	08 55			09 05		09 15				09 35		09 45				10 05		10 15			
Farringdon	d	08 59			09 09		09 19				09 39		09 49				10 09		10 19			
City Thameslink	d	09 01			09 11		09 21				09 41		09 51				10 11		10 21			
London Blackfriars	d	09 04			09 14		09 24				09 44		09 54				10 14		10 24			
London Bridge	d	09 11			09 21		09 30				09 51		10 00				10 21		10 30			
Norwood Junction	d				09 32						10 02						10 32					
East Croydon	a	09 24			09 36		09 44				10 06		10 14				10 36		10 44			
East Croydon	d	09 25	09 27		09 37		09 46		09 53	09 57	10 07		10 16	10 23	10 27		10 37		10 46		10 53	10 57
Purley	d		09 34		09 44					10 04	10 14				10 34		10 44					11 04
Coulsdon South	d		09 38				09 53			10 08			10 23		10 38				10 53			11 08
Merstham	d		09 44				09 58			10 14			10 28		10 44				10 58			11 14
Redhill	a	09 38	09 48		09 52		10 02			10 18	10 22		10 32		10 48		10 52		11 02			11 18
Redhill	d		09 49			10 00		10 14		10 19		10 30			10 49			11 00		11 14		11 19
Reigate	a		09 53					10 18		10 23		10 34			10 53					11 18		11 23
Nutfield	a					10 04												11 04				
Godstone	a					10 10												11 10				
Edenbridge	a					10 16												11 16				
Penshurst	a					10 22												11 22				
Leigh (Kent)	a					10 26												11 26				
Tonbridge	a					10 31												11 31				
Tonbridge	d																					
Redhill	a																					
Reigate	d			09 36												10 34						
Redhill	a			09 41												10 38						
Redhill	d	09 39		09 44	09 55		10 03				10 25		10 33			10 41	10 55		11 03			
Earlswood (Surrey)	d				09 57						10 27						10 57					
Salfords	d				10 01						10 31						11 01					
Horley	d				10 05		10 09				10 35		10 39				11 05		11 09			
Gatwick Airport	a	09 47		09 51	10 08		10 12		10 08		10 38		10 42	10 38		10 53	11 08		11 12		11 08	
Gatwick Airport	d						10 14		10 09				10 44	10 39					11 14		11 09	
Three Bridges	a						10 19		10 14				10 49	10 44					11 19		11 14	
Three Bridges	d						10 20		10 14				10 50	10 44					11 20		11 14	
Crawley	d						10 24		10 18				10 54	10 48					11 24		11 18	
Ifield	d						10 26						10 56						11 26			
Faygate	d																					
Littlehaven	d						10 32						11 02						11 32			
Horsham	a						10 38		10 27				11 08	10 57					11 38		11 27	

A until 5 October

Table T183-F

Mondays to Fridays

21 May to 7 December

London - Redhill / Reigate / Tonbridge / Gatwick Airport - Horsham

Station		TL 1	GW	TL 1	SN 1	SN 1	GW	TL 1	SN	TL 1	GW	SN 1	SN 1	TL 1	GW	TL 1	SN 1	SN 1	GW	TL 1	SN	TL 1	GW
London Victoria	d				11 06	11 09						11 36	11 39				12 06	12 09					
Clapham Junction	d				11 13	11 16						11 43	11 46				12 13	12 16					
East Croydon	a				11 22	11 26						11 52	11 56				12 22	12 26					
St Pancras International	d	10 35		10 45				11 05		11 15				11 35		11 45				12 05		12 15	
Farringdon	d	10 39		10 49				11 09		11 19				11 39		11 49				12 09		12 19	
City Thameslink	d	10 41		10 51				11 11		11 21				11 41		11 51				12 11		12 21	
London Blackfriars	d	10 44		10 54				11 14		11 24				11 44		11 54				12 14		12 24	
London Bridge	d	10 51		11 00				11 21		11 30				11 51		12 00				12 21		12 30	
Norwood Junction	d	11 02						11 32						12 02						12 32			
East Croydon	a	11 06		11 14				11 36		11 44				12 06		12 14				12 36		12 44	
East Croydon	d	11 07		11 16	11 23	11 27		11 37		11 46		11 53	11 57	12 07		12 16	12 23	12 27		12 37		12 46	
Purley	d	11 14				11 34		11 44					12 04	12 14				12 34		12 44			
Coulsdon South	d			11 23		11 38				11 53			12 08			12 23		12 38				12 53	
Merstham	d			11 28		11 44				11 58			12 14			12 28		12 44				12 58	
Redhill	a	11 22		11 32		11 48		11 52		12 02			12 18	12 22		12 32		12 48		12 52		13 02	
Redhill	d		11 30			11 49			12 00		12 14		12 19		12 30			12 49			13 00		13 14
Reigate	a		11 38			11 53					12 18		12 23		12 34			12 53					13 18
Nutfield	a								12 04												13 04		
Godstone	a								12 10												13 10		
Edenbridge	a								12 16												13 16		
Penshurst	a								12 22												13 22		
Leigh (Kent)	a								12 26												13 26		
Tonbridge	a								12 31												13 31		
Tonbridge	d																						
Redhill	a																						
Reigate	d						11 34												12 34				
Redhill	a						11 38												12 38				
Redhill	d	11 25		11 33			11 42	11 55		12 03				12 25		12 33			12 42	12 55		13 03	
Earlswood (Surrey)	d	11 27						11 57						12 27						12 57			
Salfords	d	11 31						12 01						12 31						13 01			
Horley	d	11 35		11 39				12 05		12 09				12 35		12 39				13 05		13 09	
Gatwick Airport	a	11 38		11 42	11 38		11 51	12 08		12 12		12 08		12 38		12 42	12 38		12 51	13 08		13 12	
Gatwick Airport	d			11 44	11 39					12 14		12 09				12 44	12 39					13 14	
Three Bridges	a			11 49	11 44					12 19		12 14				12 49	12 44					13 19	
Three Bridges	d			11 50	11 44					12 20		12 14				12 50	12 44					13 20	
Crawley	d			11 54	11 48					12 24		12 18				12 54	12 48					13 24	
Ifield	d			11 56						12 26						12 56						13 26	
Faygate	d			12 00																			
Littlehaven	d			12 04						12 32						13 02						13 32	
Horsham	a			12 08	11 57					12 38		12 27				13 08	12 57					13 38	

Station		SN 1	SN 1	TL 1	GW	TL 1	SN 1	SN 1	GW	TL 1	SN	TL 1	GW	SN 1	SN 1	TL 1	GW	TL 1	SN 1	SN 1	GW	TL 1
London Victoria	d	12 36	12 39				13 06	13 09						13 36	13 39				14 06	14 09		
Clapham Junction	d	12 43	12 46				13 13	13 16						13 43	13 46				14 13	14 16		
East Croydon	a	12 52	12 56				13 22	13 26						13 52	13 56				14 22	14 26		
St Pancras International	d			12 35		12 45				13 05		13 15				13 35		13 45				14 05
Farringdon	d			12 39		12 49				13 09		13 19				13 39		13 49				14 09
City Thameslink	d			12 41		12 51				13 11		13 21				13 41		13 51				14 11
London Blackfriars	d			12 44		12 54				13 14		13 24				13 44		13 54				14 14
London Bridge	d			12 51		13 00				13 21		13 30				13 51		14 00				14 21
Norwood Junction	d			13 02						13 32						14 02						14 32
East Croydon	a			13 06		13 14				13 36		13 44				14 06		14 14				14 36
East Croydon	d	12 53	12 57	13 07		13 16	13 23	13 27		13 37		13 46		13 53	13 57	14 07		14 16	14 23	14 27		14 37
Purley	d		13 04	13 14				13 34		13 44					14 04	14 14				14 34		14 44
Coulsdon South	d		13 08			13 23		13 38				13 53			14 08			14 23		14 38		
Merstham	d		13 14			13 28		13 44				13 58			14 14			14 28		14 44		
Redhill	a		13 18	13 22		13 32		13 48		13 52		14 02			14 18	14 22		14 32		14 48		14 52
Redhill	d		13 19		13 30			13 49			14 00		14 14		14 19		14 30			14 49		
Reigate	a		13 23		13 34			13 53					14 18		14 23		14 34			14 53		
Nutfield	a										14 04											
Godstone	a										14 10											
Edenbridge	a										14 16											
Penshurst	a										14 22											
Leigh (Kent)	a										14 26											
Tonbridge	a										14 31											
Tonbridge	d																					
Redhill	a																					
Reigate	d								13 38												14 34	
Redhill	a								13 42												14 39	
Redhill	d			13 25		13 33			13 46	13 55		14 03				14 25		14 33			14 42	14 55
Earlswood (Surrey)	d			13 27						13 57						14 27						14 57
Salfords	d			13 31						14 01						14 31						15 01
Horley	d			13 35		13 39				14 05		14 09				14 35		14 39				15 05
Gatwick Airport	a	13 08		13 38		13 42	13 38		13 53	14 08		14 12		14 08		14 38		14 42	14 38		14 51	15 08
Gatwick Airport	d	13 09				13 44	13 39					14 14		14 09				14 44	14 39			
Three Bridges	a	13 14				13 49	13 44					14 19		14 14				14 49	14 44			
Three Bridges	d	13 14				13 50	13 44					14 20		14 14				14 50	14 44			
Crawley	d	13 18				13 54	13 48					14 24		14 18				14 54	14 48			
Ifield	d					13 56						14 26						14 56				
Faygate	d																					
Littlehaven	d					14 02						14 32						15 02				
Horsham	a	13 27				14 08	13 57					14 38		14 27				15 08	14 57			

London - Redhill / Reigate / Tonbridge / Gatwick Airport - Horsham

		SN	TL ■	GW	SN ■	SN ■	TL ■	GW	SN	TL ■		SN ■	SN ■	GW	TL ■	SN	TL ■	GW	SN ■	SN ■		TL ■	SN	GW	TL ■
London Victoria	d				14 36	14 39						15 06	15 09						15 36	15 39					
Clapham Junction	d				14 43	14 46						15 13	15 16						15 43	15 46					
East Croydon	a				14 53	14 56						15 22	15 26						15 52	15 56					
St Pancras International	d		14 15				14 35			14 45					15 05		15 15					15 35			15 45
Farringdon	d		14 19				14 39			14 49					15 09		15 19					15 39			15 49
City Thameslink	d		14 21				14 41			14 51					15 11		15 21					15 41			15 51
London Blackfriars	d		14 24				14 44			14 54					15 14		15 24					15 44			15 54
London Bridge	d		14 30				14 51			15 00					15 21		15 30					15 51			16 00
Norwood Junction	d						15 02								15 32							16 02			
East Croydon	a		14 44				15 06			15 14					15 36		15 44					16 06			16 14
East Croydon	d		14 46		14 53	14 57	15 07			15 16		15 23	15 27		15 37		15 46		15 53	15 57		16 07			16 16
Purley	d					15 04	15 14						15 36		15 44					16 04		16 14			
Coulsdon South	d		14 53			15 08				15 23			15 40				15 53			16 08					16 23
Merstham	d		14 58			15 14				15 28			15 45				15 58			16 14					16 28
Redhill	a		15 02			15 18	15 22			15 32			15 49		15 52		16 02			16 18		16 23			16 32
Redhill	d	15 00		15 14		15 19		15 29	15 30				15 50			16 00		16 14		16 22			16 30	16 31	
Reigate	a			15 18		15 23		15 33					15 54					16 18		16 26				16 35	
Nutfield	a	15 04							15 34							16 04							16 34		
Godstone	a	15 10							15 40							16 10							16 40		
Edenbridge	a	15 16							15 46							16 16							16 46		
Penshurst	a	15 22							15 52							16 22							16 52		
Leigh (Kent)	a	15 26							15 56							16 26							16 56		
Tonbridge	a	15 31							16 01							16 31							17 01		
Tonbridge	d																								
Redhill	a																								
Reigate	d													15 34											
Redhill	a													15 38											
Redhill	d		15 03				15 25			15 33				15 42	15 55		16 03					16 25			16 33
Earlswood (Surrey)	d						15 27								15 57							16 27			
Salfords	d						15 31								16 01							16 31			
Horley	d		15 09				15 35			15 39					16 05		16 09					16 35			16 39
Gatwick Airport	a		15 12		15 08		15 38			15 42		15 38		15 51	16 08		16 12		16 08			16 38			16 42
Gatwick Airport	d		15 14		15 09					15 44		15 39					16 14		16 09						16 44
Three Bridges	a		15 19		15 14					15 49		15 44					16 19		16 14						16 49
Three Bridges	d		15 20		15 14					15 50		15 44					16 20		16 14						16 50
Crawley	d		15 24		15 18					15 54		15 48					16 24		16 18						16 54
Ifield	d		15 26							15 56							16 26								16 56
Faygate	d																								
Littlehaven	d		15 32							16 02							16 32								17 02
Horsham	a		15 38		15 27					16 08		15 57					16 38		16 27						17 10

		SN ■	GW	SN ■		TL ■		SN	TL ■	GW	SN ■	SN ■		SN ■	TL ■	SN		TL ■	GW	SN ■	SN ■	GW	SN ■		SN ■
London Victoria	d	16 06		16 09							16 36	16 39		16 45							17 06		17 09		17 15
Clapham Junction	d	16 13		16 16							16 43	16 46		16 52							17 13		17 16		17 22
East Croydon	a	16 23		16 26							16 52	16 56		17 01							17 22		17 26		17 31
St Pancras International	d					16 05			16 15						16 35			16 45							
Farringdon	d					16 09			16 19						16 39			16 49							
City Thameslink	d					16 11			16 21						16 41			16 51							
London Blackfriars	d					16 14			16 24						16 44			16 54							
London Bridge	d					16 21			16 30						16 51			17 00		17 03					
Norwood Junction	d					16 32									17 02										
East Croydon	a					16 36			16 44						17 06			17 14		17 16					
East Croydon	d	16 23		16 27		16 37			16 46		16 53	16 57		17 02	17 07			17 16		17 17	17 23		17 27		17 32
Purley	d			16 34		16 44						17 04			17 14										
Coulsdon South	d			16 38		16 48			16 56			17 08			17 18			17 25					17 35		
Merstham	d			16 44		16 53			17 02			17 14			17 23			17 30					17 41		
Redhill	a			16 48		16 57			17 06			17 18			17 27			17 34					17 45		
Redhill	d			16 52				17 00		17 14		17 22				17 30			17 45				17 51		
Reigate	a			16 56						17 18		17 26							17 49				17 55		
Nutfield	a							17 04								17 34									
Godstone	a							17 10								17 40									
Edenbridge	a							17 16								17 46									
Penshurst	a							17 22								17 52									
Leigh (Kent)	a							17 26								17 56									
Tonbridge	a							17 31								18 01									
Tonbridge	d																								
Redhill	a																								
Reigate	d		16 36																			17 34			
Redhill	a		16 40																			17 40			
Redhill	d		16 44		16 54	16 58			17 06				17 24		17 28			17 36				17 43		17 54	
Earlswood (Surrey)	d				16 57	17 00							17 27		17 30									17 56	
Salfords	d				17 00	17 04							17 30		17 34									18 00	
Horley	d				17 04	17 08							17 34	17 16	17 38									18 04	17 46
Gatwick Airport	a	16 38	16 52		17 07	17 11			17 15		17 08		17 37	17 19	17 41			17 45			17 38	17 51		18 07	17 49
Gatwick Airport	d	16 39							17 16		17 09							17 46			17 39			18 08	
Three Bridges	a	16 44							17 21		17 14							17 51		17 35	17 44			18 16	
Three Bridges	d	16 44							17 22		17 14							17 52		17 35	17 44				
Crawley	d	16 48							17 26		17 18							17 56		17 39	17 48				
Ifield	d								17 29									17 59			17 51				
Faygate	d								17 33									18 03							
Littlehaven	d								17 37									18 07		17 47	17 58				
Horsham	a	16 57							17 42		17 27							18 12		17 51	18 01				

London - Redhill / Reigate / Tonbridge / Gatwick Airport - Horsham

		TL ■		SN	TL ■	GW A	SN ■	SN ■		SN ■	TL ■	SN		TL ■	GW	SN ■	SN ■	GW	SN ■		SN ■	TL ■		SN	TL ■
London Victoria	d						17 36	17 39		17 45							18 06		18 09		18 15				
Clapham Junction	d						17 43	17 46		17 52							18 13		18 16		18 22				
East Croydon	a						17 52	17 56		18 01							18 22		18 27		18 31				
St Pancras International	d	17 05			17 15						17 35			17 45								18 05			18 15
Farringdon	d	17 09			17 19						17 39			17 49								18 09			18 19
City Thameslink	d	17 11			17 21						17 41			17 51								18 11			18 21
London Blackfriars	d	17 14			17 24						17 44			17 54								18 14			18 24
London Bridge	d	17 21			17 30						17 51			18 00		18 03						18 21			18 30
Norwood Junction	d	17 32									18 02											18 33			
East Croydon	a	17 36			17 44						18 06			18 14		18 16						18 36			18 44
East Croydon	d	17 37			17 46		17 53	17 57		18 02	18 07			18 16		18 17	18 23		18 27		18 32	18 37			18 46
Purley	d	17 44									18 14											18 44			
Coulsdon South	d	17 48			17 55			18 05			18 18			18 25					18 35			18 48			18 55
Merstham	d	17 53			18 00			18 11			18 23			18 30					18 41			18 53			19 00
Redhill	a	17 57			18 04			18 15			18 27			18 34					18 45			18 57			19 04
Redhill	d			18 00		18 14		18 21				18 30			18 43				18 51					19 00	
Reigate	a					18 18		18 25							18 47				18 55						
Nutfield	a			18 04								18 34												19 04	
Godstone	a			18 10								18 40												19 10	
Edenbridge	a			18 16								18 46												19 16	
Penshurst	a			18 22																				19 22	
Leigh (Kent)	a			18 26																				19 26	
Tonbridge	a			18 31								18 55												19 31	
Tonbridge	d																								
Redhill	a																								
Reigate	d																	18 35							
Redhill	a																	18 39							
Redhill	d	17 58			18 06				18 24		18 28			18 36				18 42		18 54		18 58			19 06
Earlswood (Surrey)	d	18 00							18 26		18 30									18 56		19 00			
Salfords	d	18 04							18 30		18 34									19 00		19 04			
Horley	d	18 08							18 34	18 16	18 38									19 04	18 46	19 08			
Gatwick Airport	a	18 11			18 15		18 08		18 37	18 19	18 41			18 45			18 38	18 50		19 07	18 49	19 11			19 15
Gatwick Airport	d				18 16		18 09		18 38					18 46			18 39			19 08					19 16
Three Bridges	a				18 21		18 14		18 43					18 51		18 35	18 44			19 16					19 21
Three Bridges	d				18 22		18 14							18 52		18 35	18 44								19 22
Crawley	d				18 26		18 18							18 56		18 39	18 48								19 26
Ifield	d				18 29									18 59			18 51								19 29
Faygate	d				18 33									19 03											19 33
Littlehaven	d				18 37									19 07		18 47	18 58								19 37
Horsham	a				18 42		18 27							19 12		18 51	19 01								19 42

		GW	SN ■	SN ■		SN ■	TL ■	SN		TL ■	SN ■	GW	SN ■		TL ■	SN	TL ■	GW A		SN ■	SN ■	TL ■	TL ■	GW	SN ■
London Victoria	d		18 36	18 39		18 45					19 06		19 09							19 36	19 39				20 06
Clapham Junction	d		18 43	18 46		18 52					19 13		19 16							19 43	19 46				20 13
East Croydon	a		18 52	18 57		19 01					19 22		19 27							19 52	19 57				20 22
St Pancras International	d						18 35			18 45					19 05		19 15					19 35	19 45		
Farringdon	d						18 39			18 49					19 09		19 19					19 39	19 49		
City Thameslink	d						18 41			18 51					19 11		19 21					19 41	19 51		
London Blackfriars	d						18 44			18 54					19 14		19 24					19 44	19 54		
London Bridge	d						18 51			19 00					19 21		19 30					19 51	20 00		
Norwood Junction	d						19 02								19 32							20 02			
East Croydon	a						19 06			19 14					19 36		19 44					20 06	20 14		
East Croydon	d		18 53	18 57		19 02	19 07			19 16	19 23		19 27		19 37		19 46			19 53	19 58	20 07	20 16		20 23
Purley	d						19 14						19 33		19 44						20 04	20 14			
Coulsdon South	d			19 06			19 18			19 23			19 37		19 48		19 53				20 08		20 23		
Merstham	d			19 12			19 23			19 28			19 43		19 53		19 58				20 14		20 28		
Redhill	a			19 16			19 27			19 32			19 47		19 57		20 02				20 18	20 22	20 32		
Redhill	d	19 13		19 21				19 30					19 51			20 00		20 13			20 19			20 34	
Reigate	a	19 17		19 25									19 55					20 17			20 23			20 38	
Nutfield	a							19 34								20 04									
Godstone	a							19 40								20 10									
Edenbridge	a							19 46								20 16									
Penshurst	a							19 52								20 22									
Leigh (Kent)	a							19 56								20 26									
Tonbridge	a							20 04								20 31									
Tonbridge	d																								
Redhill	a																								
Reigate	d											19 34													
Redhill	a											19 40													
Redhill	d				19 24		19 28			19 36		19 41		19 54	19 58		20 05					20 25	20 33		
Earlswood (Surrey)	d				19 26		19 30							19 56	20 00							20 27			
Salfords	d				19 30		19 34							20 00	20 04							20 31			
Horley	d				19 34	19 17	19 38							20 04	20 08		20 12					20 35	20 39		
Gatwick Airport	a		19 08		19 37	19 19	19 41			19 45	19 38	19 50		20 07	20 11		20 14			20 08		20 38	20 42		20 38
Gatwick Airport	d		19 09		19 38					19 46	19 39			20 08			20 16			20 09			20 44		20 39
Three Bridges	a		19 14		19 46					19 51	19 44			20 16			20 21			20 14			20 49		20 44
Three Bridges	d		19 14							19 52	19 44						20 22			20 14			20 50		20 44
Crawley	d		19 18							19 56	19 48						20 26			20 18			20 54		20 48
Ifield	d									19 59							20 29						20 56		
Faygate	d									20 03															
Littlehaven	d									20 07							20 35						21 02		
Horsham	a		19 27							20 12	19 57						20 39			20 27			21 08		20 57

A until 5 October

Table T183-F

Mondays to Fridays
21 May to 7 December

London - Redhill / Reigate / Tonbridge / Gatwick Airport - Horsham

	SN ■	GW 🚌	TL ■	SN	TL ■	GW	SN ■	SN ■	TL ■	TL ■	GW	SN ■	SN ■	GW 🚌	TL ■	SN	TL ■	GW	SN ■	SN ■	TL ■
London Victoria d	20 09						20 36	20 39				21 06	21 09						21 36	21 39	
Clapham Junction d	20 16						20 43	20 46				21 13	21 16						21 43	21 46	
East Croydon a	20 26						20 52	20 57				21 22	21 26						21 52	21 56	
St Pancras International d			20 05		20 15				20 35	20 45					21 05		21 15				21 35
Farringdon d			20 09		20 19				20 39	20 49					21 09		21 19				21 39
City Thameslink d			20 11		20 21				20 41	20 51					21 11		21 21				21 41
London Blackfriars d			20 14		20 24				20 44	20 54					21 14		21 24				21 44
London Bridge d			20 21		20 30				20 51	21 00					21 21		21 30				21 51
Norwood Junction d			20 32						21 02						21 32						22 02
East Croydon a			20 36		20 44				21 06	21 14					21 36		21 44				22 06
East Croydon d	20 27		20 37		20 46		20 53	20 58	21 07	21 16		21 23	21 27		21 37		21 46		21 53	21 57	22 07
Purley d	20 34		20 44					21 04	21 14				21 34		21 44					22 04	22 14
Coulsdon South d	20 38				20 53			21 08		21 23			21 38				21 53			22 08	
Merstham d	20 44				20 58			21 14		21 28			21 44				21 58			22 14	
Redhill a	20 48		20 52		21 02			21 18	21 22	21 32			21 48		21 52		22 02			22 18	22 22
Redhill d	20 49			21 00		21 13		21 19			21 35		21 49			22 00		22 12		22 19	
Reigate a	20 53					21 17		21 23			21 39		21 53					22 16		22 23	
Nutfield a				21 04												22 04					
Godstone a				21 10												22 10					
Edenbridge a				21 16												22 16					
Penshurst a				21 22												22 22					
Leigh (Kent) a				21 26												22 26					
Tonbridge a				21 31												22 31					
Tonbridge d																					
Redhill a																					
Reigate d		20 35												21 36							
Redhill a		20 39												21 40							
Redhill d		20 43	20 55		21 03				21 25	21 33				21 43	21 55		22 03				22 25
Earlswood (Surrey) d			20 57						21 27						21 57						22 27
Salfords d			21 01						21 31						22 01						22 31
Horley d			21 05		21 09				21 35	21 39					22 05		22 09				22 35
Gatwick Airport a		20 54	21 08		21 12		21 08		21 37	21 42		21 38		21 53	22 08		22 12		22 08		22 38
Gatwick Airport d					21 14		21 09			21 44		21 39					22 14		22 09		
Three Bridges a					21 19		21 14			21 49		21 44					22 19		22 14		
Three Bridges d					21 20		21 14			21 50		21 44					22 20		22 14		
Crawley d					21 24		21 18			21 54		21 48					22 24		22 18		
Ifield d					21 26					21 56							22 26				
Faygate d																					
Littlehaven d					21 32					22 02							22 32				
Horsham a					21 38		21 27			22 08		21 57					22 38		22 27		

	TL ■	SN ■	SN ■	GW A	TL ■	SN	TL ■	SN ■	SN ■	TL ■	GW	TL ■	SN ■	SN ■	TL ■	TL ■	TL ■	GW	SN ■
London Victoria d		22 06	22 09					22 36	22 39				23 06	23 09					23 36
Clapham Junction d		22 13	22 16					22 43	22 46				23 13	23 16					23 43
East Croydon a		22 22	22 26					22 52	22 56				23 22	23 26					23 58
St Pancras International d	21 45				22 05		22 15			22 35		22 45			23 05	23 15	23 22		
Farringdon d	21 49				22 09		22 19			22 39		22 49			23 09	23 19	23 27		
City Thameslink d	21 51				22 11		22 21			22 41		22 51							
London Blackfriars d	21 54				22 14		22 24			22 44		22 54			23 14	23 24	23 31		
London Bridge d	22 00				22 21		22 30			22 51		23 00			23 21	23 30	23 37		
Norwood Junction d					22 32					23 02					23 32				
East Croydon a	22 14				22 36		22 44			23 06		23 14			23 36	23 44	23 50		
East Croydon d	22 16	22 23	22 27		22 37		22 46	22 53	22 57	23 07		23 16	23 23	23 27	23 37	23 46	23 51		23 59
Purley d			22 34		22 44				23 04	23 14				23 33	23 43				00 05
Coulsdon South d	22 23		22 38				22 53		23 08			23 23		23 37			23 59		00 09
Merstham d	22 28		22 44				22 58		23 14			23 28		23 43			00 04		00 14
Redhill a	22 32		22 48		22 52		23 02		23 18	23 22		23 32		23 47	23 51	23 59	00 08		00 18
Redhill d			22 49			23 00			23 19		23 32			23 48					
Reigate a			22 53						23 23		23 36			23 52					
Nutfield a						23 04													
Godstone a						23 10													
Edenbridge a						23 16													
Penshurst a						23 22													
Leigh (Kent) a						23 26													
Tonbridge a						23 31													
Tonbridge d																			
Redhill a																			
Reigate d				22 36														23 55	
Redhill a				22 40														00 01	
Redhill d	22 33			22 43	22 55		23 03			23 25		23 33			23 52	23 59	00 09	00 12	00 19
Earlswood (Surrey) d					22 57					23 27						00 02			
Salfords d					23 01					23 31						00 05			
Horley d	22 39				23 05		23 09			23 35		23 39				00 09			00 25
Gatwick Airport a	22 42	22 38		22 52	23 08		23 12	23 08		23 37		23 41	23 38		00 01	00 12	00 17	00 20	00 29
Gatwick Airport d	22 44	22 39					23 14	23 09		23 38		23 42	23 39			00 14	00 18		00 31
Three Bridges a	22 49	22 44					23 19	23 14		23 43		23 47	23 44			00 19	00 23		00 36
Three Bridges d	22 50	22 44					23 20	23 14				23 49	23 44			00 20			00 36
Crawley d	22 54	22 48					23 24	23 18				23 53	23 48			00 24			00 40
Ifield d	22 56						23 26					23 55				00 26			
Faygate d																			
Littlehaven d	23 02						23 32					00 02				00 32			
Horsham a	23 08	22 57					23 38	23 27				00 06	23 57			00 36			00 49

A until 5 October

Table T183-F

Saturdays
26 May to 8 December

London - Redhill / Reigate / Tonbridge / Gatwick Airport - Horsham

	SN	SN ■	GW	TL ■	TL ■	SN ■	TL ■	SN ■	TL ■	SN ■	TL ■	SN ■	TL ■	GW	SN ■	SN ■	SN ■	SN	GW ■	TL ■	GW ■	SN ■
London Victoria d		00 08				01 10		02 10		03 10		04 10				05 08	05 39					06 06
Clapham Junction d		00 15				01 17		02 17		03 17		04 17				05 16	05 46					06 13
East Croydon a		00 30				01 32		02 32		03 32		04 31				05 31	05 56					06 22
St Pancras International d				00 21	00 52		01 32		02 32		03 32		04 32							05 45		
Farringdon d				00 26																05 49		
City Thameslink d																						
London Blackfriars d				00 31	01 02		01 40		02 40		03 40		04 40							05 54		
London Bridge d																				06 00		
Norwood Junction d																						
East Croydon a				00 57	01 28		02 06		03 06		04 06		05 06							06 14		
East Croydon d		00 31		00 58	01 28	01 33	02 07	02 32	03 07	03 32	04 07	04 31	05 07			05 31	05 57			06 16		06 23
Purley d		00 37			01 34	01 39	02 13	02 38	03 13	03 38	04 13	04 37	05 13			05 37	06 04			06 23		
Coulsdon South d		00 41				01s43										05 41	06 08			06 27		
Merstham d		00 46				01s48										05 46	06 14			06 32		
Redhill a		00 52		01 11	01 45	01s54						04 48				05 50	06 18			06 36		
Redhill d	00 16																06 19	06 25	06 27		06 44	
Reigate a																	06 23		06 33		06 48	
Nutfield a	00 20																	06 29				
Godstone a	00 26																	06 35				
Edenbridge a	00 32																	06 41				
Penshurst a	00 38																	06 47				
Leigh (Kent) a	00 42																	06 51				
Tonbridge a	00 46																	06 55				
Tonbridge d																						
Redhill a																						
Reigate d			00 45											05 35								
Redhill a			00 49											05 39								
Redhill d		00 53	00 57	01 11	01 46							04 49		05 43		05 51				06 37		
Earlswood (Surrey) d																				06 39		
Salfords d																				06 43		
Horley d		01 00			01 52	02 02	02 26	02 51	03 26	03 51	04 26	04 55	05 26			05 57				06 46		
Gatwick Airport a		01 03	01 07	01 20	01 56	02 06	02 30	02 55	03 30	03 55	04 30	04 59	05 29	05 51		06 00				06 50		06 38
Gatwick Airport d				01 21	01 58	02 13	02 31	02 56	03 31	03 56	04 35	05 00	05 30		05 56	06 01				06 51		06 39
Three Bridges a				01 26	02 03	02 18	02 36	03 01	03 36	04 01	04 40	05 05	05 35		06 02	06 06				06 56		06 44
Three Bridges d															06 02					06 58		06 44
Crawley d															06 06					07 02		06 48
Ifield d															06 09					07 04		
Faygate d																						
Littlehaven d															06 15					07 10		
Horsham a															06 18					07 14		06 57

	SN ■	GW	GW	SN	TL ■	SN ■	SN ■	GW	TL ■	GW ■	SN ■	SN ■	TL ■	GW	SN	TL ■	SN ■	SN ■	GW ■	TL ■	TL ■	GW ■
London Victoria d	06 09					06 36	06 39				07 06	07 09					07 36	07 39				
Clapham Junction d	06 16					06 43	06 46				07 13	07 16					07 43	07 46				
East Croydon a	06 26					06 52	06 56				07 22	07 26					07 52	07 56				
St Pancras International d					06 15				06 45				07 05			07 15				07 35	07 45	
Farringdon d					06 19				06 49				07 09			07 19				07 39	07 49	
City Thameslink d																						
London Blackfriars d					06 24				06 54				07 14			07 24				07 44	07 54	
London Bridge d					06 30				07 00				07 22			07 30				07 52	08 00	
Norwood Junction d													07 33							08 03		
East Croydon a					06 44				07 14				07 36			07 44				08 06	08 14	
East Croydon d	06 27				06 46	06 53	06 57		07 16		07 23	07 27	07 37			07 46	07 53	07 57		08 07	08 16	
Purley d	06 34						07 04					07 34	07 44					08 04		08 14		
Coulsdon South d	06 38				06 53		07 08		07 23			07 38				07 53		08 08			08 23	
Merstham d	06 44				06 58		07 14		07 28			07 44				07 58		08 14			08 28	
Redhill a	06 48				07 02		07 18		07 32			07 48	07 52			08 02		08 18		08 22	08 32	
Redhill d	06 49		06 58	07 00			07 19			07 44		07 49		07 58	08 00			08 19				08 44
Reigate a	06 53		07 03				07 23			07 48		07 53		08 03				08 23				08 48
Nutfield a				07 04											08 04							
Godstone a				07 10											08 10							
Edenbridge a				07 16											08 16							
Penshurst a				07 22											08 22							
Leigh (Kent) a				07 26											08 26							
Tonbridge a				07 34											08 31							
Tonbridge d																						
Redhill a																						
Reigate d		06 34						07 04											08 04			
Redhill a		06 38						07 09											08 08			
Redhill d		06 42			07 03			07 12	07 33				07 55			08 03			08 11	08 25	08 33	
Earlswood (Surrey) d													07 57							08 27		
Salfords d													08 01							08 31		
Horley d					07 09				07 39				08 05			08 09				08 35	08 39	
Gatwick Airport a		06 54			07 12	07 08		07 20	07 42		07 38		08 08			08 12	08 08		08 20	08 38	08 42	
Gatwick Airport d					07 14	07 09			07 44		07 39					08 14	08 09				08 44	
Three Bridges a					07 19	07 14			07 49		07 44					08 19	08 14				08 49	
Three Bridges d					07 20	07 14			07 50		07 44					08 20	08 14				08 50	
Crawley d					07 24	07 18			07 54		07 48					08 24	08 18				08 54	
Ifield d					07 26				07 56							08 26					08 56	
Faygate d																						
Littlehaven d					07 32				08 02							08 32					09 02	
Horsham a					07 38	07 27			08 08		07 57					08 38	08 27				09 08	

Table T183-F

Saturdays

26 May to 8 December

London - Redhill / Reigate / Tonbridge / Gatwick Airport - Horsham

		SN ■		SN ■	TL ■	SN	GW	TL ■	SN ■	SN ■	GW ■	TL ■		TL ■	GW ■	SN ■	SN ■	TL ■	SN	GW	TL ■	SN ■		SN ■	GW ■
London Victoria	d	08 06		08 09					08 36	08 39						09 06	09 09					09 36		09 39	
Clapham Junction	d	08 13		08 16					08 43	08 46						09 13	09 16					09 43		09 46	
East Croydon	a	08 22		08 26					08 52	08 56						09 22	09 26					09 52		09 56	
St Pancras International	d				08 05			08 15				08 35		08 45				09 05			09 15				
Farringdon	d				08 09			08 19				08 39		08 49				09 09			09 19				
City Thameslink	d																	09 11			09 21				
London Blackfriars	d				08 14			08 24				08 44		08 54				09 14			09 24				
London Bridge	d				08 22			08 30				08 52		09 00				09 22			09 30				
Norwood Junction	d				08 33							09 03						09 33							
East Croydon	a				08 36			08 44				09 06		09 14				09 36			09 44				
East Croydon	d	08 23		08 27	08 37			08 46	08 53	08 57		09 07		09 16		09 23	09 27	09 37			09 46	09 53		09 57	
Purley	d			08 34	08 44					09 04		09 14					09 34	09 44						10 04	
Coulsdon South	d			08 38				08 53		09 08				09 23			09 38				09 53			10 08	
Merstham	d			08 44				08 58		09 14				09 28			09 44				09 58			10 14	
Redhill	a			08 48	08 52			09 02		09 18		09 22		09 32			09 48	09 52			10 02			10 18	
Redhill	d			08 49		09 00	09 00			09 19					09 42		09 49		10 00	10 01				10 19	
Reigate	a			08 53			09 04			09 23					09 46		09 53			10 05				10 23	
Nutfield	a					09 04													10 04						
Godstone	a					09 10													10 10						
Edenbridge	a					09 16													10 16						
Penshurst	a					09 22													10 22						
Leigh (Kent)	a					09 26													10 26						
Tonbridge	a					09 31													10 31						
Tonbridge	d																								
Redhill	a																								
Reigate	d										09 04														10 04
Redhill	a										09 09														10 08
Redhill	d				08 55			09 03			09 12	09 25		09 33				09 55			10 03				10 12
Earlswood (Surrey)	d				08 57							09 27						09 57							
Salfords	d				09 01							09 31						10 01							
Horley	d				09 05			09 09				09 35		09 39				10 05			10 09				
Gatwick Airport	a	08 37			09 08			09 12	09 08		09 21	09 38		09 42		09 38		10 08			10 12	10 08			10 20
Gatwick Airport	d	08 39						09 14	09 09					09 44		09 39					10 14	10 09			
Three Bridges	a	08 44						09 19	09 14					09 49		09 44					10 19	10 14			
Three Bridges	d	08 44						09 20	09 14					09 50		09 44					10 20	10 14			
Crawley	d	08 48						09 24	09 18					09 54		09 48					10 24	10 18			
Ifield	d							09 26						09 56							10 26				
Faygate	d																								
Littlehaven	d							09 32						10 02							10 32				
Horsham	a	08 57						09 38	09 27					10 08		09 57					10 38	10 27			

		TL ■	TL ■	GW ■	SN ■	SN ■	TL ■	SN		GW	TL ■	SN ■	SN ■	GW ■	TL ■	TL ■	GW ■	SN ■		SN ■	TL ■	SN	GW	TL ■	SN ■
London Victoria	d				10 06	10 09						10 36	10 39					11 06		11 09					11 36
Clapham Junction	d				10 13	10 16						10 43	10 46					11 13		11 16					11 43
East Croydon	a				10 22	10 26						10 52	10 56					11 22		11 26					11 52
St Pancras International	d	09 35	09 45				10 05				10 15				10 35	10 45					11 05			11 15	
Farringdon	d	09 39	09 49				10 09				10 19				10 39	10 49					11 09			11 19	
City Thameslink	d	09 41	09 51				10 11				10 21				10 41	10 51					11 11			11 21	
London Blackfriars	d	09 44	09 54				10 14				10 24				10 44	10 54					11 14			11 24	
London Bridge	d	09 52	10 00				10 22				10 30				10 52	11 00					11 22			11 30	
Norwood Junction	d	10 03					10 33								11 03						11 33				
East Croydon	a	10 06	10 14				10 36				10 44				11 06	11 14					11 36			11 44	
East Croydon	d	10 07	10 16		10 23	10 27	10 37				10 46	10 53	10 57		11 07	11 16		11 23		11 27	11 37			11 46	11 53
Purley	d	10 14				10 34	10 44						11 04		11 14					11 34	11 44				
Coulsdon South	d		10 23			10 38					10 53		11 08			11 23				11 38				11 53	
Merstham	d		10 28			10 44					10 58		11 14			11 28				11 44				11 58	
Redhill	a	10 22	10 32			10 48	10 52				11 02		11 18		11 22	11 32				11 48	11 52			12 02	
Redhill	d			10 43		10 49		11 00		11 02			11 19				11 44			11 49		12 00	12 02		
Reigate	a			10 48		10 53				11 06			11 23				11 48			11 53			12 06		
Nutfield	a							11 04														12 04			
Godstone	a							11 10														12 10			
Edenbridge	a							11 16														12 16			
Penshurst	a							11 22														12 22			
Leigh (Kent)	a							11 26														12 26			
Tonbridge	a							11 31														12 31			
Tonbridge	d																								
Redhill	a																								
Reigate	d													11 04											
Redhill	a													11 08											
Redhill	d	10 25	10 33				10 55				11 03			11 12	11 23	11 33					11 55			12 03	
Earlswood (Surrey)	d	10 27					10 57								11 25						11 57				
Salfords	d	10 31					11 01								11 29						12 01				
Horley	d	10 35	10 39				11 05				11 09				11 33	11 39					12 05			12 09	
Gatwick Airport	a	10 38	10 42		10 38		11 08				11 12	11 08		11 20	11 37	11 42		11 38			12 08			12 12	12 08
Gatwick Airport	d		10 44		10 39						11 14	11 09				11 44		11 39						12 14	12 09
Three Bridges	a		10 49		10 44						11 19	11 14				11 49		11 44						12 19	12 14
Three Bridges	d		10 50		10 44						11 20	11 14				11 50		11 44						12 20	12 14
Crawley	d		10 54		10 48						11 24	11 18				11 54		11 48						12 24	12 18
Ifield	d		10 56								11 26					11 56								12 26	
Faygate	d																								
Littlehaven	d		11 02								11 32					12 02								12 32	
Horsham	a		11 08		10 57						11 38	11 27				12 08		11 57						12 38	12 27

Table T183-F

Saturdays

26 May to 8 December

London - Redhill / Reigate / Tonbridge / Gatwick Airport - Horsham

		SN ■	TL ■	TL ■		GW ■	SN ■	SN ■	TL ■	SN	GW	TL ■	SN ■	SN ■		GW ■	TL ■	TL ■	GW ■	SN ■	SN ■	TL ■	SN	GW	
London Victoria	d	11 39					12 06	12 09					12 36	12 39						13 06	13 09				
Clapham Junction	d	11 46					12 13	12 16					12 43	12 46						13 13	13 16				
East Croydon	a	11 56					12 22	12 26					12 52	12 56						13 22	13 26				
St Pancras International	d		11 35	11 45					12 05			12 15					12 35	12 45				13 05			
Farringdon	d		11 39	11 49					12 09			12 19					12 39	12 49				13 09			
City Thameslink	d		11 41	11 51					12 11			12 21					12 41	12 51				13 11			
London Blackfriars	d		11 44	11 54					12 14			12 24					12 44	12 54				13 14			
London Bridge	d		11 52	12 00					12 22			12 30					12 52	13 00				13 22			
Norwood Junction	d		12 03						12 33								13 03					13 33			
East Croydon	a		12 06	12 14					12 36			12 44					13 06	13 14				13 36			
East Croydon	d	11 57	12 07	12 16			12 23	12 27	12 37			12 46	12 53	12 57			13 07	13 16		13 23	13 27	13 37			
Purley	d	12 04	12 14					12 34	12 44					13 04			13 14				13 34	13 44			
Coulsdon South	d	12 08		12 23				12 38				12 53		13 08				13 23			13 38				
Merstham	d	12 14		12 28				12 44				12 58		13 14				13 28			13 44				
Redhill	a	12 18	12 22	12 32				12 48	12 52			13 02		13 18			13 22	13 32			13 48	13 52			
Redhill	d	12 19				12 44		12 49		13 00	13 02			13 19					13 44		13 49		14 00	14 02	
Reigate	a	12 23				12 48		12 53			13 06			13 23					13 48		13 53			14 06	
Nutfield	a									13 04													14 04		
Godstone	a									13 10													14 10		
Edenbridge	a									13 16													14 16		
Penshurst	a									13 22													14 22		
Leigh (Kent)	a									13 26													14 26		
Tonbridge	a									13 31													14 31		
Tonbridge	d																								
Redhill	a																								
Reigate	d															13 04									
Redhill	a															13 08									
Redhill	d		12 25	12 33					12 55			13 03				13 12	13 25	13 33				13 55			
Earlswood (Surrey)	d		12 27						12 57								13 27					13 57			
Salfords	d		12 31						13 01								13 31					14 01			
Horley	d		12 35	12 39					13 05			13 09					13 35	13 39				14 05			
Gatwick Airport	a		12 38	12 42			12 38		13 08			13 12	13 08			13 20	13 38	13 42		13 38		14 08			
Gatwick Airport	d			12 44			12 39					13 14	13 09					13 44		13 39					
Three Bridges	a			12 49			12 44					13 19	13 14					13 49		13 44					
Three Bridges	d			12 50			12 44					13 20	13 14					13 50		13 44					
Crawley	d			12 54			12 48					13 24	13 18					13 54		13 48					
Ifield	d			12 56								13 26						13 56							
Faygate	d																								
Littlehaven	d			13 02								13 32						14 02							
Horsham	a			13 08			12 57					13 38	13 27					14 08		13 57					

		TL ■	SN ■	SN ■	GW ■	TL ■	TL ■	GW ■	SN ■	SN ■		TL ■	GW	SN	TL ■	SN ■	SN ■	TL ■	TL ■	GW ■		SN ■	SN ■	TL ■	GW
London Victoria	d		13 36	13 39					14 06	14 09						14 36	14 39					15 06	15 09		
Clapham Junction	d		13 43	13 46					14 13	14 16						14 43	14 46					15 13	15 16		
East Croydon	a		13 52	13 56					14 22	14 26						14 52	14 56					15 22	15 26		
St Pancras International	d	13 15				13 35	13 45					14 05			14 15			14 35	14 45					15 05	
Farringdon	d	13 19				13 39	13 49					14 09			14 19			14 39	14 49					15 09	
City Thameslink	d	13 21				13 41	13 51					14 11			14 21			14 41	14 51					15 11	
London Blackfriars	d	13 24				13 44	13 54					14 14			14 24			14 44	14 54					15 14	
London Bridge	d	13 30				13 52	14 00					14 22			14 30			14 52	15 00					15 22	
Norwood Junction	d					14 03						14 33						15 03						15 33	
East Croydon	a	13 44				14 06	14 14					14 36			14 44			15 06	15 14					15 36	
East Croydon	d	13 46	13 53	13 57		14 07	14 16		14 23	14 27		14 37			14 46	14 53	14 57	15 07	15 16			15 23	15 27	15 37	
Purley	d			14 04		14 14				14 34		14 44					15 04	15 14					15 34	15 44	
Coulsdon South	d	13 53		14 08			14 23			14 38					14 53		15 08		15 23				15 38		
Merstham	d	13 58		14 14			14 28			14 44					14 58		15 14		15 28				15 44		
Redhill	a	14 02		14 18		14 22	14 32			14 48		14 52			15 02		15 18	15 22	15 32				15 48	15 52	
Redhill	d			14 19				14 44		14 49			14 59	15 00			15 19			15 44			15 49		15 59
Reigate	a			14 23				14 48		14 53			15 03				15 23			15 48			15 53		16 03
Nutfield	a													15 04											
Godstone	a													15 10											
Edenbridge	a													15 16											
Penshurst	a													15 22											
Leigh (Kent)	a													15 26											
Tonbridge	a													15 31											
Tonbridge	d																								
Redhill	a																								
Reigate	d				14 04																				
Redhill	a				14 08																				
Redhill	d	14 03			14 12	14 25	14 33					14 55			15 03			15 25	15 33					15 55	
Earlswood (Surrey)	d					14 27						14 57						15 27						15 57	
Salfords	d					14 31						15 01						15 31						16 01	
Horley	d	14 09				14 35	14 39					15 05			15 09			15 35	15 39					16 05	
Gatwick Airport	a	14 12	14 08		14 20	14 38	14 42		14 38			15 08			15 12	15 08		15 38	15 42			15 38		16 08	
Gatwick Airport	d	14 14	14 09				14 44		14 39						15 14	15 09			15 44			15 39			
Three Bridges	a	14 19	14 14				14 49		14 44						15 19	15 14			15 49			15 44			
Three Bridges	d	14 20	14 14				14 50		14 44						15 20	15 14			15 50			15 44			
Crawley	d	14 24	14 18				14 54		14 48						15 24	15 18			15 54			15 48			
Ifield	d	14 26					14 56								15 26				15 56						
Faygate	d																								
Littlehaven	d	14 32					15 02								15 32				16 02						
Horsham	a	14 38	14 27				15 08		14 57						15 38	15 27			16 08			15 57			

Table T183-F

Saturdays

26 May to 8 December

London - Redhill / Reigate / Tonbridge / Gatwick Airport - Horsham

		SN	TL	SN	SN	GW		TL	TL	GW	SN	SN	TL	GW	SN	TL		SN	SN	GW	TL	TL	GW	SN	SN
London Victoria	d			15 36	15 39						16 06	16 09						16 36	16 39					17 06	17 09
Clapham Junction	d			15 43	15 46						16 13	16 16						16 43	16 46					17 13	17 16
East Croydon	a			15 52	15 56						16 22	16 26						16 52	16 56					17 22	17 26
St Pancras International	d		15 15					15 35	15 45				16 05			16 15					16 35	16 45			
Farringdon	d		15 19					15 39	15 49				16 09			16 19					16 39	16 49			
City Thameslink	d		15 21					15 41	15 51				16 11			16 21					16 41	16 51			
London Blackfriars	d		15 24					15 44	15 54				16 14			16 24					16 44	16 54			
London Bridge	d		15 30					15 52	16 00				16 22			16 30					16 52	17 00			
Norwood Junction	d							16 03					16 33								17 03				
East Croydon	a		15 44					16 06	16 14				16 36			16 44					17 06	17 14			
East Croydon	d		15 46	15 53	15 57			16 07	16 16		16 23	16 27	16 37			16 46		16 53	16 57		17 07	17 16		17 23	17 27
Purley	d				16 04			16 14				16 34	16 44						17 04		17 14				17 34
Coulsdon South	d		15 53		16 08				16 23			16 38				16 53			17 08			17 23			17 38
Merstham	d		15 58		16 14				16 28			16 44				16 58			17 14			17 28			17 44
Redhill	a		16 02		16 18			16 22	16 32			16 48	16 52			17 02			17 18		17 22	17 32			17 48
Redhill	d	16 00			16 19					16 44		16 49		16 59	17 00				17 19				17 44		17 49
Reigate	a				16 23					16 48		16 53		17 03					17 23				17 48		17 53
Nutfield	a	16 04													17 04										
Godstone	a	16 10													17 10										
Edenbridge	a	16 16													17 16										
Penshurst	a	16 22													17 22										
Leigh (Kent)	a	16 26													17 26										
Tonbridge	a	16 31													17 31										
Tonbridge	d																								
Redhill	a																								
Reigate	d					16 04														17 04					
Redhill	a					16 08														17 09					
Redhill	d		16 03			16 12		16 25	16 33				16 55			17 03				17 12	17 23	17 33			
Earlswood (Surrey)	d							16 27					16 57								17 25				
Salfords	d							16 31					17 01								17 29				
Horley	d		16 09					16 35	16 39				17 05			17 09					17 33	17 39			
Gatwick Airport	a		16 12	16 08		16 21		16 38	16 42		16 38		17 08			17 12		17 08		17 21	17 38	17 42		17 38	
Gatwick Airport	d		16 14	16 09					16 44		16 39					17 14		17 09				17 44		17 39	
Three Bridges	a		16 19	16 14					16 49		16 44					17 19		17 14				17 49		17 44	
Three Bridges	d		16 20	16 14					16 50		16 44					17 20		17 14				17 50		17 44	
Crawley	d		16 24	16 18					16 54		16 48					17 24		17 18				17 54		17 48	
Ifield	d		16 26						16 56							17 26						17 56			
Faygate	d																								
Littlehaven	d		16 32						17 02							17 32						18 02			
Horsham	a		16 38	16 27					17 08		16 57					17 38		17 27				18 08		17 57	

		TL		GW	SN	TL	SN	SN	GW	TL	TL	GW		SN	SN	TL	GW	SN	TL	SN	SN	GW		TL	TL
London Victoria	d						17 36	17 39						18 06	18 09					18 36	18 39				
Clapham Junction	d						17 43	17 46						18 13	18 16					18 43	18 46				
East Croydon	a						17 52	17 56						18 22	18 26					18 52	18 56				
St Pancras International	d	17 05				17 15				17 35	17 45					18 05			18 15					18 35	18 45
Farringdon	d	17 09				17 19				17 39	17 49					18 09			18 19					18 39	18 49
City Thameslink	d	17 11				17 21				17 41	17 51					18 11			18 21					18 41	18 51
London Blackfriars	d	17 14				17 24				17 44	17 54					18 14			18 24					18 44	18 54
London Bridge	d	17 22				17 30				17 52	18 00					18 22			18 30					18 52	19 00
Norwood Junction	d	17 33								18 03						18 33								19 03	
East Croydon	a	17 36				17 44				18 06	18 14					18 36			18 44					19 06	19 14
East Croydon	d	17 37				17 46	17 53	17 57		18 07	18 16			18 23	18 27	18 37			18 46	18 53	18 57			19 07	19 16
Purley	d	17 44						18 04		18 14					18 34	18 44					19 04			19 14	
Coulsdon South	d					17 53		18 08			18 23				18 38				18 53		19 08				19 23
Merstham	d					17 58		18 14			18 28				18 44				18 58		19 14				19 28
Redhill	a	17 52				18 02		18 18		18 22	18 32				18 48	18 52			19 02		19 18			19 22	19 32
Redhill	d			17 59	18 00			18 19				18 44			18 49		18 59	19 00			19 19				
Reigate	a			18 03				18 23				18 48			18 53		19 03				19 23				
Nutfield	a				18 04													19 04							
Godstone	a				18 10													19 10							
Edenbridge	a				18 16													19 16							
Penshurst	a				18 22													19 22							
Leigh (Kent)	a				18 26													19 26							
Tonbridge	a				18 31													19 31							
Tonbridge	d																								
Redhill	a																								
Reigate	d								18 04													19 04			
Redhill	a								18 08													19 08			
Redhill	d	17 55				18 03			18 12	18 25	18 33					18 55			19 03			19 11		19 25	19 33
Earlswood (Surrey)	d	17 57								18 27						18 57								19 27	
Salfords	d	18 01								18 31						19 01								19 31	
Horley	d	18 05				18 09				18 35	18 39					19 05			19 09					19 35	19 39
Gatwick Airport	a	18 08				18 12	18 08		18 20	18 38	18 42			18 38		19 08			19 12	19 08		19 20		19 38	19 42
Gatwick Airport	d					18 14	18 09				18 44			18 39					19 14	19 09					19 44
Three Bridges	a					18 19	18 14				18 49			18 44					19 19	19 14					19 49
Three Bridges	d					18 20	18 14				18 50			18 44					19 20	19 14					19 50
Crawley	d					18 24	18 18				18 54			18 48					19 24	19 18					19 54
Ifield	d					18 26					18 56								19 26						19 56
Faygate	d																								
Littlehaven	d					18 32					19 02								19 32						20 02
Horsham	a					18 38	18 27				19 08			18 57					19 38	19 27					20 08

Table T183-F

Saturdays

26 May to 8 December

London - Redhill / Reigate / Tonbridge / Gatwick Airport - Horsham

		GW	SN	SN	TL	GW	SN	TL		SN	SN	GW	TL	TL	GW	SN	SN	GW		TL	SN	TL	GW	SN	SN
London Victoria	d		19 06	19 09						19 36	19 39					20 06	20 09							20 36	20 39
Clapham Junction	d		19 13	19 16						19 43	19 46					20 13	20 16							20 43	20 46
East Croydon	a		19 22	19 26						19 52	19 56					20 22	20 26							20 52	20 56
St Pancras International	d				19 05			19 15					19 35	19 45						20 05		20 15			
Farringdon	d				19 09			19 19					19 39	19 49						20 09		20 19			
City Thameslink	d				19 11			19 21					19 41	19 51						20 11		20 21			
London Blackfriars	d				19 14			19 24					19 44	19 54						20 14		20 24			
London Bridge	d				19 22			19 30					19 52	20 00						20 22		20 30			
Norwood Junction	d				19 33								20 03							20 33					
East Croydon	a				19 36			19 44					20 06	20 14						20 36		20 44			
East Croydon	d		19 23	19 27	19 37			19 46		19 53	19 57		20 07	20 16		20 23	20 27			20 37		20 46		20 53	20 57
Purley	d			19 34	19 44						20 04		20 14				20 34			20 44					21 04
Coulsdon South	d			19 38				19 53			20 08			20 23			20 38					20 53			21 08
Merstham	d			19 44				19 58			20 14			20 28			20 44					20 58			21 14
Redhill	a			19 48	19 52			20 02			20 18		20 22	20 32			20 48			20 52		21 02			21 18
Redhill	d	19 44		19 49		19 59	20 00				20 19				20 44		20 49				21 00		21 14		21 19
Reigate	a	19 48		19 53		20 03					20 23				20 48		20 53						21 18		21 23
Nutfield	a						20 04														21 04				
Godstone	a						20 10														21 10				
Edenbridge	a						20 16														21 16				
Penshurst	a						20 22														21 22				
Leigh (Kent)	a						20 26														21 26				
Tonbridge	a						20 31														21 31				
Tonbridge	d																								
Redhill	a																								
Reigate	d											20 04						20 34							
Redhill	a											20 08						20 38							
Redhill	d				19 55			20 03				20 11	20 25	20 33				20 42		20 55		21 03			
Earlswood (Surrey)	d				19 57								20 27							20 57					
Salfords	d				20 01								20 31							21 01					
Horley	d				20 05			20 09					20 35	20 39						21 05		21 09			
Gatwick Airport	a		19 38		20 08			20 12		20 08		20 20	20 38	20 42		20 38		20 50		21 08		21 12		21 07	
Gatwick Airport	d		19 39					20 14		20 09				20 44		20 39						21 14		21 09	
Three Bridges	a		19 44					20 19		20 14				20 49		20 44						21 19		21 14	
Three Bridges	d		19 44					20 20		20 14				20 50		20 44						21 20		21 14	
Crawley	d		19 48					20 24		20 18				20 54		20 48						21 24		21 18	
Ifield	d							20 26						20 56								21 26			
Faygate	d																								
Littlehaven	d							20 32						21 02								21 32			
Horsham	a		19 57					20 38		20 27				21 08		20 57						21 38		21 27	

		GW	TL	TL		GW	SN	SN	GW	TL	SN	TL	GW	SN		SN	TL	TL	SN	SN	GW	TL	SN	TL	
London Victoria	d						21 06	21 09						21 36		21 39			22 06	22 09					
Clapham Junction	d						21 13	21 16						21 43		21 46			22 13	22 16					
East Croydon	a						21 22	21 26						21 52		21 56			22 22	22 26					
St Pancras International	d		20 35	20 45						21 05		21 15					21 35	21 45				22 05		22 15	
Farringdon	d		20 39	20 49						21 09		21 19					21 39	21 49				22 09		22 19	
City Thameslink	d		20 41	20 51																					
London Blackfriars	d		20 44	20 54						21 14		21 24					21 44	21 54				22 14		22 24	
London Bridge	d		20 52	21 00						21 22		21 30					21 52	22 00				22 22		22 30	
Norwood Junction	d		21 03							21 33							22 03					22 33			
East Croydon	a		21 06	21 14						21 36		21 44					22 06	22 14				22 36		22 44	
East Croydon	d		21 07	21 16			21 23	21 27		21 37		21 46		21 53		21 57	22 07	22 16	22 23	22 27		22 37		22 46	
Purley	d		21 14					21 34		21 44						22 04	22 14			22 34		22 44			
Coulsdon South	d			21 23				21 38				21 53				22 08		22 23		22 38				22 53	
Merstham	d			21 28				21 44				21 58				22 14		22 28		22 44				22 58	
Redhill	a		21 22	21 32				21 48		21 52		22 02				22 18	22 22	22 32		22 48		22 52		23 02	
Redhill	d					21 35		21 49			22 00		22 12			22 19				22 49			23 00		
Reigate	a					21 39		21 53					22 16			22 23				22 53					
Nutfield	a										22 04												23 04		
Godstone	a										22 10												23 10		
Edenbridge	a										22 16												23 16		
Penshurst	a										22 22												23 22		
Leigh (Kent)	a										22 26												23 26		
Tonbridge	a										22 31												23 31		
Tonbridge	d																								
Redhill	a																								
Reigate	d	21 04							21 36												22 36				
Redhill	a	21 08							21 40												22 40				
Redhill	d	21 12	21 25	21 33					21 43	21 55		22 03					22 25	22 33			22 43	22 55		23 03	
Earlswood (Surrey)	d		21 27							21 57							22 27					22 57			
Salfords	d		21 31							22 01							22 31					23 01			
Horley	d		21 35	21 39						22 05		22 09					22 35	22 39				23 05		23 09	
Gatwick Airport	a	21 20	21 38	21 42			21 38		21 51	22 08		22 12		22 07			22 38	22 42	22 38		22 51	23 08		23 12	
Gatwick Airport	d			21 44			21 39			22 09		22 14		22 09			22 39	22 44	22 39			23 09		23 14	
Three Bridges	a			21 49			21 44			22 16		22 19		22 14			22 46	22 49	22 44			23 14		23 19	
Three Bridges	d			21 50			21 45					22 20		22 14				22 50	22 44					23 20	
Crawley	d			21 54			21 49					22 24		22 18				22 54	22 48					23 24	
Ifield	d			21 56								22 26						22 56						23 26	
Faygate	d																								
Littlehaven	d			22 02								22 32						23 02						23 32	
Horsham	a			22 08			21 57					22 38		22 27				23 08	22 57					23 38	

Table T183-F

London - Redhill / Reigate / Tonbridge / Gatwick Airport - Horsham

Saturdays
26 May to 8 December

		SN ■	SN ■	TL ■	GW ■	TL ■	SN ■	SN ■	TL ■	TL ■	TL ■	GW ■	SN ■
London Victoria	d	22 36	22 39				23 06	23 09					23 36
Clapham Junction	d	22 43	22 46				23 13	23 16					23 43
East Croydon	a	22 52	22 56				23 22	23 26					23 58
St Pancras International	d			22 35		22 45			23 05	23 15	23 22		
Farringdon	d			22 39		22 49			23 09	23 19	23 27		
City Thameslink	d												
London Blackfriars	d			22 44		22 54			23 14	23 24	23 31		
London Bridge	d			22 52		23 00			23 21	23 30	23 37		
Norwood Junction	d			23 03					23 32				
East Croydon	a			23 06		23 14			23 36	23 44	23 50		
East Croydon	d	22 53	22 57	23 07		23 16	23 23	23 27	23 37	23 46	23 51		23 59
Purley	d		23 04	23 14				23 34	23 43				00 05
Coulsdon South	d		23 08			23 23		23 38			23 59		00 09
Merstham	d		23 14			23 28		23 44			00 04		00 14
Redhill	a		23 18	23 22		23 32		23 48	23 51	23 59	00 08		00 18
Redhill	d		23 19		23 31			23 49					
Reigate	a		23 23		23 35			23 53					
Nutfield	a												
Godstone	a												
Edenbridge	a												
Penshurst	a												
Leigh (Kent)	a												
Tonbridge	a												
Tonbridge	d												
Redhill	a												
Reigate	d											23 55	
Redhill	a											23 59	
Redhill	d			23 25		23 33			23 52	23 59	00 09	00 12	00 19
Earlswood (Surrey)	d			23 27						00 02			
Salfords	d			23 31						00 05			
Horley	d			23 35		23 39				00 09			00 25
Gatwick Airport	a	23 08		23 37		23 41	23 38		00 01	00 12	00 17	00 20	00 29
Gatwick Airport	d	23 09		23 38		23 42	23 39			00 14	00 18		00 31
Three Bridges	a	23 14		23 43		23 47	23 44			00 19	00 23		00 36
Three Bridges	d	23 14				23 49	23 44			00 20			00 36
Crawley	d	23 18				23 53	23 48			00 24			00 40
Ifield	d					23 56				00 26			
Faygate	d												
Littlehaven	d					00 02				00 32			
Horsham	a	23 27				00 06	23 57			00 36			00 49

Sundays
20 May to 2 December

		SN ■	SN	GW ■ A	TL ■ A	SN ■	SN ■	SN ■	SN ■	SN ■	SN	SN	GW	GW	SN	SN	SN ■	SN	GW	GW	SN	GW ■	SN
London Victoria	d	00 08				01 10	02 08	03 08	04 10	05 02	05 45	06 32			07 02			07 32			08 02		
Clapham Junction	d	00 15				01 17	02 17	03 17	04 17	05 10	05 53	06 40			07 10			07 40			08 10		
East Croydon	a	00 31				01 32	02 32	03 31	04 31	05 23	06 08	06 53			07 26			07 56			08 26		
St Pancras International	d				00 51																		
Farringdon	d																						
City Thameslink	d																						
London Blackfriars	d				01 01																		
London Bridge	d																07 19						
Norwood Junction	d																07 31						
East Croydon	a				01 27												07 35						
East Croydon	d	00 32			01 28	01 33	02 32	03 32	04 31	05 24	06 09	06 54			07 27		07 35	07 57			08 27		
Purley	d	00 37			01 34	01 39	02 38	03 37	04 37	05 30		06 59			07 33		07 40				08 33		
Coulsdon South	d											07 03					07 44						
Merstham	d											07 08					07 49						
Redhill	a					01s50						07 12			07 42		07 53	08 10			08 42		
Redhill	d		00 15										07 20			07 50			08 29			08 43	08 48
Reigate	a												07 23						08 33			08 47	
Nutfield	a															07 54							08 52
Godstone	a															08 00							08 58
Edenbridge	a		00 26													08 05							09 03
Penshurst	a															08 12							09 10
Leigh (Kent)	a															08 16							09 14
Tonbridge	a		00 36													08 20							09 18
Tonbridge	d																						
Redhill	a																						
Reigate	d			00 45										07 04						08 13			
Redhill	a			00 49										07 08						08 17			
Redhill	d			00 57								07 13		07 16	07 42		07 53	08 10		08 18	08 42		
Earlswood (Surrey)	d																07 56						
Salfords	d																07 59						
Horley	d	00 57			01 52	02 02	02 51	03 50	04 53	05 46	06 28	07 19			07 49		08 03				08 49		
Gatwick Airport	a	01 01		01 05	01 56	02 06	02 55	03 54	04 57	05 50	06 32	07 23		07 27	07 52		08 06	08 19		08 28	08 52		
Gatwick Airport	d				01 58	02 08	02 56	03 55	04 58	05 51	06 33	07 24			07 53		08 09	08 20			08 54		
Three Bridges	a				02 03	02 13	03 01	04 00	05 03	05 56	06 37	07 28			07 58		08 14	08 24			08 58		
Three Bridges	d																08 15	08 25					
Crawley	d																08 19	08 29					
Ifield	d																08 21						
Faygate	d																						
Littlehaven	d																08 27						
Horsham	a																08 31	08 37					

A not 20 May

Table T183-F

London - Redhill / Reigate / Tonbridge / Gatwick Airport - Horsham

Sundays
20 May to 2 December

		SN ■	SN	SN	GW	GW	GW ■	SN	SN ■	TL ■	SN	SN	TL ■	GW	TL ■	GW	GW ■	SN	TL ■	TL ■	SN	SN	TL ■
London Victoria	d		08 32					09 05			09 33							10 05			10 33		
Clapham Junction	d		08 40					09 12			09 40							10 12			10 40		
East Croydon	a		08 51					09 23			09 49							10 23			10 49		
St Pancras International	d												09 35		09 41				10 05	10 11			10 35
Farringdon	d												09 39		09 45				10 09	10 15			10 39
City Thameslink	d																						
London Blackfriars	d												09 44		09 50				10 14	10 20			10 44
London Bridge	d	08 19							09 19	09 27			09 51		09 56				10 21	10 26			10 51
Norwood Junction	d	08 31							09 33				10 03						10 33				11 03
East Croydon	a	08 35							09 37	09 41			10 07		10 10				10 37	10 40			11 07
East Croydon	d	08 37	08 51					09 23	09 37	09 41	09 49		10 07		10 11			10 23	10 37	10 41	10 49		11 07
Purley	d	08 42						09 28		09 47					10 17			10 28		10 47			
Coulsdon South	d	08 46	08 58					09 32	09 44		09 56							10 32	10 44		10 56		
Merstham	d	08 51						09 37	09 49									10 37	10 49				
Redhill	a	08 55	09 05					09 41	09 53	09 56	10 03		10 19		10 25			10 41	10 53	10 56	11 03		11 19
Redhill	d			09 11		09 28	09 43	09 49				10 07				10 28	10 43	10 50				11 07	
Reigate	a					09 31	09 47	09 54								10 32	10 47	10 54					
Nutfield	a			09 15								10 11										11 11	
Godstone	a			09 21								10 17										11 17	
Edenbridge	a			09 26								10 22										11 22	
Penshurst	a			09 33								10 29										11 29	
Leigh (Kent)	a			09 37								10 33										11 33	
Tonbridge	a			09 41								10 37										11 37	
Tonbridge	d																						
Redhill	a																						
Reigate	d				09 17									10 17									
Redhill	a				09 24									10 24									
Redhill	d	08 55	09 06		09 26				09 53	09 57	10 04		10 19	10 26	10 29				10 53	10 57	11 04		11 19
Earlswood (Surrey)	d	08 58								09 59					10 31					10 59			
Salfords	d	09 01								10 03					10 35					11 03			
Horley	d	09 05							09 59	10 06					10 38				10 59	11 06			
Gatwick Airport	a	09 07	09 13		09 35				10 02	10 09	10 12		10 27	10 35	10 41				11 02	11 09	11 12		11 27
Gatwick Airport	d	09 09	09 14						10 03		10 13				10 42				11 03		11 13		
Three Bridges	a	09 14	09 19						10 08		10 18				10 47				11 08		11 18		
Three Bridges	d	09 15	09 19						10 09		10 19								11 09		11 18		
Crawley	d	09 19	09 23						10 13		10 23								11 13		11 22		
Ifield	d	09 21							10 15										11 15				
Faygate	d																						
Littlehaven	d	09 27							10 21										11 21				
Horsham	a	09 31	09 34						10 25		10 32								11 25		11 31		

		GW	TL ■	GW	GW ■	SN	TL ■	TL ■	SN	SN	TL ■	GW	TL ■	GW	GW ■	SN	TL ■	TL ■	SN	SN	TL ■	GW
London Victoria	d					11 05			11 33							12 05			12 33			
Clapham Junction	d					11 12			11 40							12 12			12 40			
East Croydon	a					11 23			11 49							12 23			12 49			
St Pancras International	d		10 41				11 05	11 11			11 35		11 41				12 05	12 11			12 35	
Farringdon	d		10 45				11 09	11 15			11 39		11 45				12 09	12 15			12 39	
City Thameslink	d																					
London Blackfriars	d		10 50				11 14	11 20			11 44		11 50				12 14	12 20			12 44	
London Bridge	d		10 56				11 21	11 26			11 51		11 56				12 21	12 26			12 51	
Norwood Junction	d						11 33				12 03						12 33				13 03	
East Croydon	a		11 10				11 37	11 40			12 07		12 10				12 37	12 40			13 07	
East Croydon	d		11 11			11 23	11 37	11 41	11 49		12 07		12 11			12 23	12 37	12 41	12 49		13 07	
Purley	d		11 17			11 28		11 47					12 17			12 28		12 47				
Coulsdon South	d					11 32	11 44		11 56							12 32	12 44		12 56			
Merstham	d					11 37	11 49									12 37	12 49					
Redhill	a		11 25			11 41	11 53	11 56	12 03		12 19		12 25			12 41	12 53	12 56	13 03		13 19	
Redhill	d			11 28	11 43	11 50				12 07				12 28	12 43	12 50				13 07		
Reigate	a			11 31	11 47	11 54								12 32	12 47	12 54						
Nutfield	a									12 11										13 11		
Godstone	a									12 17										13 17		
Edenbridge	a									12 22										13 22		
Penshurst	a									12 29										13 29		
Leigh (Kent)	a									12 33										13 33		
Tonbridge	a									12 37										13 37		
Tonbridge	d																					
Redhill	a																					
Reigate	d	11 17										12 17										13 17
Redhill	a	11 24										12 24										13 24
Redhill	d	11 26	11 29				11 53	11 57	12 04		12 19	12 26	12 29				12 53	12 57	13 04		13 19	13 26
Earlswood (Surrey)	d		11 31					11 59					12 31					12 59				
Salfords	d		11 35					12 03					12 35					13 03				
Horley	d		11 38				11 59	12 06					12 38				12 59	13 06				
Gatwick Airport	a	11 35	11 41				12 02	12 09	12 12		12 27	12 35	12 41				13 02	13 09	13 12		13 27	13 35
Gatwick Airport	d		11 42				12 03		12 13				12 42				13 03		13 13			
Three Bridges	a		11 47				12 08		12 18				12 47				13 08		13 18			
Three Bridges	d						12 09		12 18								13 09		13 18			
Crawley	d						12 13		12 22								13 13		13 22			
Ifield	d						12 15										13 15					
Faygate	d																					
Littlehaven	d						12 21										13 21					
Horsham	a						12 25		12 31								13 25		13 31			

Table T183-F

Sundays

20 May to 2 December

London - Redhill / Reigate / Tonbridge / Gatwick Airport - Horsham

		TL ■	GW	GW ■	SN	TL ■	TL ■	SN		SN	TL ■	GW	TL ■	GW	GW ■	SN	TL ■	TL ■		SN	SN	TL ■	GW	TL ■	GW
London Victoria	d				13 05			13 33								14 05				14 33					
Clapham Junction	d				13 12			13 40								14 12				14 40					
East Croydon	a				13 23			13 49								14 23				14 49					
St Pancras International	d	12 41				13 05	13 11				13 35		13 41				14 05	14 11				14 35		14 41	
Farringdon	d	12 45				13 09	13 15				13 39		13 45				14 09	14 15				14 39		14 45	
City Thameslink	d																								
London Blackfriars	d	12 50				13 14	13 20				13 44		13 50				14 14	14 20				14 44		14 50	
London Bridge	d	12 56				13 21	13 26				13 51		13 56				14 21	14 26				14 51		14 56	
Norwood Junction	d					13 33					14 03						14 33					15 03			
East Croydon	a	13 10				13 37	13 40				14 07		14 10				14 37	14 40				15 07		15 10	
East Croydon	d	13 11			13 23	13 37	13 41	13 49			14 07		14 11			14 23	14 37	14 41		14 49		15 07		15 11	
Purley	d	13 17			13 28		13 47						14 17			14 28		14 47						15 17	
Coulsdon South	d				13 32	13 44		13 56								14 32	14 44			14 56					
Merstham	d				13 37	13 49										14 37	14 49								
Redhill	a	13 25			13 41	13 53	13 56	14 03			14 19		14 25			14 41	14 53	14 56		15 03		15 19		15 25	
Redhill	d		13 28	13 43	13 50					14 07				14 28	14 43	14 50					15 07				15 28
Reigate	a		13 31	13 47	13 54									14 32	14 47	14 54									15 31
Nutfield	a									14 11											15 11				
Godstone	a									14 17											15 17				
Edenbridge	a									14 22											15 22				
Penshurst	a									14 29											15 29				
Leigh (Kent)	a									14 33											15 33				
Tonbridge	a									14 37											15 37				
Tonbridge	d																								
Redhill	a																								
Reigate	d											14 17											15 17		
Redhill	a											14 24											15 24		
Redhill	d	13 29				13 53	13 57	14 04			14 19	14 26	14 29				14 53	14 57		15 04		15 19	15 26	15 29	
Earlswood (Surrey)	d	13 31					13 59						14 31					14 59						15 31	
Salfords	d	13 35					14 03						14 35					15 03						15 35	
Horley	d	13 38				13 59	14 06						14 38				14 59	15 06						15 38	
Gatwick Airport	a	13 41				14 02	14 09	14 12			14 27	14 35	14 41				15 02	15 09		15 12		15 27	15 35	15 41	
Gatwick Airport	d	13 42				14 03		14 13					14 42				15 03			15 13				15 42	
Three Bridges	a	13 47				14 08		14 18					14 47				15 08			15 18				15 47	
Three Bridges	d					14 09		14 18									15 09			15 18					
Crawley	d					14 13		14 22									15 13			15 22					
Ifield	d					14 15											15 15								
Faygate	d																								
Littlehaven	d					14 21											15 21								
Horsham	a					14 25		14 31									15 25			15 31					

		GW ■	SN	TL ■		TL ■	SN	SN	TL ■	GW	TL ■	GW	GW ■	SN		TL ■	TL ■	SN	SN	TL ■	GW	TL ■	GW	GW ■	
London Victoria	d		15 05				15 33							16 05				16 33							
Clapham Junction	d		15 12				15 40							16 12				16 40							
East Croydon	a		15 23				15 49							16 23				16 49							
St Pancras International	d			15 05		15 11			15 35		15 41					16 05	16 11			16 35		16 41			
Farringdon	d			15 09		15 15			15 39		15 45					16 09	16 15			16 39		16 45			
City Thameslink	d																								
London Blackfriars	d			15 14		15 20			15 44		15 50					16 14	16 20			16 44		16 50			
London Bridge	d			15 21		15 26			15 51		15 56					16 21	16 26			16 51		16 56			
Norwood Junction	d			15 33					16 03							16 33				17 03					
East Croydon	a			15 37		15 40			16 07		16 10					16 37	16 40			17 07		17 10			
East Croydon	d		15 23	15 37		15 41	15 49		16 07		16 11			16 23		16 37	16 41	16 49		17 07		17 11			
Purley	d		15 28			15 47					16 17			16 28			16 47					17 17			
Coulsdon South	d		15 32	15 44			15 56							16 32		16 44		16 56							
Merstham	d		15 37	15 49										16 37		16 49									
Redhill	a		15 41	15 53		15 56	16 03		16 19		16 25			16 41		16 53	16 56	17 03		17 19		17 25			
Redhill	d	15 43	15 50					16 07				16 28	16 43	16 50					17 07				17 28	17 43	
Reigate	a	15 47	15 54									16 32	16 47	16 54									17 31	17 47	
Nutfield	a							16 11											17 11						
Godstone	a							16 17											17 17						
Edenbridge	a							16 22											17 22						
Penshurst	a							16 29											17 29						
Leigh (Kent)	a							16 33											17 33						
Tonbridge	a							16 37											17 37						
Tonbridge	d																								
Redhill	a																								
Reigate	d									16 17											17 17				
Redhill	a									16 24											17 24				
Redhill	d			15 53		15 57	16 04		16 19	16 26	16 29					16 53	16 57	17 04		17 19	17 26	17 29			
Earlswood (Surrey)	d					15 59					16 31						16 59					17 31			
Salfords	d					16 03					16 35						17 03					17 35			
Horley	d			15 59		16 06					16 38					16 59	17 06					17 38			
Gatwick Airport	a			16 02		16 09	16 12		16 27	16 35	16 41					17 02	17 09	17 12		17 27	17 35	17 41			
Gatwick Airport	d			16 03			16 13				16 42					17 03		17 13				17 42			
Three Bridges	a			16 08			16 18				16 47					17 08		17 18				17 47			
Three Bridges	d			16 09			16 18									17 09		17 18							
Crawley	d			16 13			16 22									17 13		17 22							
Ifield	d			16 15												17 15									
Faygate	d																								
Littlehaven	d			16 21												17 21									
Horsham	a			16 25			16 31									17 25		17 31							

Table T183-F

Sundays

20 May to 2 December

London - Redhill / Reigate / Tonbridge / Gatwick Airport - Horsham

		SN	TL ■	TL ■	SN	SN	TL ■	GW	TL ■	GW		GW ■	SN	TL ■	TL ■	SN	SN	TL ■	GW	TL ■		GW	GW ■	SN	TL ■
London Victoria	d	17 05			17 33								18 05			18 33								19 05	
Clapham Junction	d	17 12			17 40								18 12			18 40								19 12	
East Croydon	a	17 23			17 49								18 23			18 49								19 23	
St Pancras International	d		17 05	17 11			17 35		17 41					18 05	18 11			18 35		18 41					19 05
Farringdon	d		17 09	17 15			17 39		17 45					18 09	18 15			18 39		18 45					19 09
City Thameslink	d																								
London Blackfriars	d		17 14	17 20			17 44		17 50					18 14	18 20			18 44		18 50					19 14
London Bridge	d		17 21	17 26			17 51		17 56					18 21	18 26			18 51		18 56					19 21
Norwood Junction	d		17 33				18 03							18 33				19 03							19 33
East Croydon	a		17 37	17 40			18 07		18 10					18 37	18 40			19 07		19 10					19 37
East Croydon	d	17 23	17 37	17 41	17 49		18 07		18 11				18 23	18 37	18 41	18 49		19 07		19 11				19 23	19 37
Purley	d	17 28		17 47					18 17				18 28		18 47					19 17				19 28	
Coulsdon South	d	17 32	17 44		17 56								18 32	18 44		18 56								19 32	19 44
Merstham	d	17 37	17 49										18 37	18 49										19 37	19 49
Redhill	a	17 41	17 53	17 56	18 03		18 19		18 25				18 41	18 53	18 56	19 03		19 19		19 25				19 41	19 53
Redhill	d	17 50				18 07				18 28		18 43	18 50				19 07					19 28	19 43	19 50	
Reigate	a	17 54								18 32		18 47	18 54									19 31	19 47	19 54	
Nutfield	a					18 11											19 11								
Godstone	a					18 17											19 17								
Edenbridge	a					18 22											19 22								
Penshurst	a					18 29											19 29								
Leigh (Kent)	a					18 33											19 33								
Tonbridge	a					18 37											19 37								
Tonbridge	d																								
Redhill	a																								
Reigate	d							18 17											19 17						
Redhill	a							18 24											19 24						
Redhill	d		17 53	17 57	18 04		18 19	18 26	18 29					18 53	18 57	19 04		19 19	19 26	19 29					19 53
Earlswood (Surrey)	d			17 59					18 31						18 59					19 31					
Salfords	d			18 03					18 35						19 03					19 35					
Horley	d		17 59	18 06					18 38					18 59	19 06					19 38					19 59
Gatwick Airport	a		18 02	18 09	18 12		18 27	18 35	18 41					19 02	19 09	19 12		19 27	19 35	19 41					20 02
Gatwick Airport	d		18 03		18 13				18 42					19 03		19 13				19 42					20 03
Three Bridges	a		18 08		18 18				18 47					19 08		19 18				19 47					20 08
Three Bridges	d		18 09		18 18									19 09		19 18									20 09
Crawley	d		18 13		18 22									19 13		19 22									20 13
Ifield	d		18 15											19 15											20 15
Faygate	d																								
Littlehaven	d		18 21											19 21											20 21
Horsham	a		18 25		18 31									19 25		19 31									20 25

		TL ■	SN	SN	TL ■	GW		TL ■	GW	SN	TL ■	TL ■	SN	SN	GW ■	TL ■		TL ■	SN	GW ■	TL ■	TL ■	SN	SN	TL ■
London Victoria	d		19 33							20 05			20 33						21 05				21 33		
Clapham Junction	d		19 40							20 12			20 40						21 12				21 40		
East Croydon	a		19 49							20 23			20 49						21 23				21 49		
St Pancras International	d	19 11			19 35			19 41			20 05	20 11				20 35		20 41			21 05	21 11			21 35
Farringdon	d	19 15			19 39			19 45			20 09	20 15				20 39		20 45			21 09	21 15			21 39
City Thameslink	d																								
London Blackfriars	d	19 20			19 44			19 50			20 14	20 20				20 44		20 50			21 14	21 20			21 44
London Bridge	d	19 26			19 51			19 56			20 21	20 26				20 51		20 56			21 21	21 26			21 51
Norwood Junction	d				20 03						20 33					21 03					21 33				22 03
East Croydon	a	19 40			20 07			20 10			20 37	20 40				21 07		21 10			21 37	21 40			22 07
East Croydon	d	19 41	19 49		20 07			20 11		20 23	20 37	20 41	20 49			21 07		21 11	21 23		21 37	21 41	21 49		22 07
Purley	d	19 47						20 17		20 28		20 47						21 17	21 28			21 47			
Coulsdon South	d		19 56							20 32	20 44		20 56						21 32		21 44		21 56		
Merstham	d									20 37	20 49								21 37		21 49				
Redhill	a	19 56	20 03		20 19			20 25		20 41	20 53	20 56	21 03			21 19		21 25	21 41		21 53	21 56	22 03		22 19
Redhill	d			20 07					20 30	20 43				21 07	21 19				21 43					22 07	
Reigate	a								20 34	20 47					21 22				21 47						
Nutfield	a			20 11										21 11										22 11	
Godstone	a			20 17										21 17										22 17	
Edenbridge	a			20 22										21 22										22 22	
Penshurst	a			20 29										21 29										22 29	
Leigh (Kent)	a			20 33										21 33										22 33	
Tonbridge	a			20 37										21 37										22 37	
Tonbridge	d																								
Redhill	a																								
Reigate	d					20 17														21 37					
Redhill	a					20 24														21 43					
Redhill	d	19 57	20 04		20 19	20 26		20 29			20 53	20 57	21 04			21 19		21 27		21 44	21 53	21 57	22 04		22 19
Earlswood (Surrey)	d	19 59						20 31				20 59						21 29				21 59			
Salfords	d	20 03						20 35				21 03						21 33				22 03			
Horley	d	20 06						20 38			20 59	21 06						21 36			21 59	22 06			
Gatwick Airport	a	20 09	20 12		20 27	20 35		20 41			21 02	21 09	21 12			21 27		21 39		21 54	22 02	22 09	22 13		22 26
Gatwick Airport	d		20 13					20 42			21 03		21 13								22 03	22 10	22 14		22 27
Three Bridges	a		20 18					20 46			21 08		21 18								22 08	22 15	22 19		22 32
Three Bridges	d		20 18								21 09		21 18								22 09		22 20		
Crawley	d		20 22								21 13		21 22								22 13		22 24		
Ifield	d										21 15										22 15				
Faygate	d																								
Littlehaven	d										21 21										22 21				
Horsham	a		20 31								21 25		21 31								22 25		22 32		

Table T183-F

Sundays
20 May to 2 December

London - Redhill / Reigate / Tonbridge / Gatwick Airport - Horsham

		TL ■		GW	GW	SN	TL ■	TL ■	SN	SN	GW	TL ■		GW ■	SN	TL ■
London Victoria	d					22 05			22 35						23 05	
Clapham Junction	d					22 12			22 42						23 12	
East Croydon	a					22 22			22 51						23 22	
St Pancras International	d	21 41					22 05	22 11				22 35				
Farringdon	d	21 45					22 09	22 15				22 39				
City Thameslink	d															
London Blackfriars	d	21 50					22 14	22 20				22 44				
London Bridge	d	21 56					22 21	22 26				22 51				23 45
Norwood Junction	d						22 33					23 03				
East Croydon	a	22 10					22 37	22 40				23 07				23 59
East Croydon	d	22 11				22 23	22 37	22 41	22 51			23 08			23 23	00 01
Purley	d	22 17				22 28		22 47				23 13			23 28	00 06
Coulsdon South	d					22 31	22 44								23 32	
Merstham	d					22 37	22 49								23 37	
Redhill	a	22 25				22 41	22 53	22 56	23 03			23 22			23 41	00 15
Redhill	d			22 29						23 07	23 19					
Reigate	a			22 32							23 22					
Nutfield	a									23 11						
Godstone	a									23 17						
Edenbridge	a									23 22						
Penshurst	a									23 29						
Leigh (Kent)	a									23 33						
Tonbridge	a									23 37						
Tonbridge	d															
Redhill	a															
Reigate	d				22 29									23 29		
Redhill	a				22 35									23 35		
Redhill	d	22 27			22 38	22 43	22 53	22 57	23 04			23 23		23 38	23 42	00 16
Earlswood (Surrey)	d	22 29						22 59				23 25				00 18
Salfords	d	22 33						23 03				23 29				00 22
Horley	d	22 36					22 59	23 06				23 32				00 25
Gatwick Airport	a	22 39			22 47	22 50	23 02	23 09	23 12			23 35		23 48	23 50	00 29
Gatwick Airport	d	22 41				22 51	23 03		23 13			23 36			23 51	00 30
Three Bridges	a	22 45				22 55	23 08		23 18			23 40			23 56	00 35
Three Bridges	d					22 56	23 09		23 18						23 56	
Crawley	d					23 00	23 13		23 22						00 02	
Ifield	d						23 15								00 04	
Faygate	d															
Littlehaven	d						23 21								00 10	
Horsham	a					23 08	23 25		23 31						00 14	

Table T183-R

Mondays to Fridays
21 May to 7 December

Horsham / Gatwick Airport / Tonbridge / Reigate / Redhill - London

		SN MX	TL MO ■	GW MX	TL MX ■	TL ■		TL ■	TL ■	TL ■	SN	GW	TL ■	SN ■	SN	GW		TL ■	SN ■	TL ■	SN	SN	TL ■	GW	SN ■
Horsham	d																		05 15	05 25					05 41
Littlehaven	d																		05 18	05 29					05 45
Faygate	d																								
Ifield	d																		05 24	05 35					05 51
Crawley	d																		05 28	05 38					05 55
Three Bridges	a																		05 32	05 42					06 00
Three Bridges	d		00 37		00 37	01 41		02 41	03 41	04 35			05 14					05 27	05 33	05 43			05 51		06 02
Gatwick Airport	a		00 41		00 41	01 45		02 45	03 45	04 40			05 18					05 31	05 37	05 47			05 55		06 06
Gatwick Airport	d		00 42		00 42	01 46		02 46	03 46	04 41		05 10	05 19	05 28				05 33	05 38	05 49			05 56	06 00	06 08
Horley	d		00 45		00 45	01 49		02 49	03 49	04 43				05 31				05 35		05 51			05 59		
Salfords	d																	05 39					06 03		
Earlswood (Surrey)	d																	05 43					06 06		
Redhill	a				00 52					04 51		05 18	05 27	05 38				05 47		05 59			06 10	06 12	
Redhill	d											05 35												06 15	
Reigate	a											05 39												06 19	
Redhill	d	00 16													05 23							05 52			
Tonbridge	a																								
Tonbridge	d										04 40										05 28				
Leigh (Kent)	a										04 44										05 32				
Penshurst	a										04 48										05 36				
Edenbridge	a										04 55										05 43				
Godstone	a										05 01										05 49				
Nutfield	a	00 20									05 07				05 27						05 55	05 56			
Reigate	d			00 45												05 35									
Redhill	a			00 49							05 13					05 39					06 01				
Redhill	d				00 53					04 52			05 28	05 39				05 49		05 59			06 11		
Merstham	d													05 43						06 03			06 15		
Coulsdon South	d													05 48						06 09			06 20		
Purley	d		01 03		01 03	02 04		03 03	04 03	05 01				05 52				05 58					06 24		
East Croydon	a		01 09		01 09	02 09		03 09	04 09	05 08			05 39	06 00				06 03	05 53	06 15			06 31		06 23
East Croydon	d		01 10		01 10	02 10		03 10	04 10	05 10			05 40					06 03		06 16			06 31		
Norwood Junction	a																	06 07					06 36		
London Bridge	a									05 24			05 54					06 20		06 30			06 50		
London Blackfriars	a		01 36		01 36	02 36		03 36	04 36	05 31			06 01					06 26		06 36			06 56		
City Thameslink	a									05 33			06 03					06 28		06 38			06 58		
Farringdon	a									05 35			06 05					06 31		06 41			07 01		
St Pancras International	a		01 43		01 43	02 43		03 43	04 43	05 40			06 10					06 35		06 45			07 05		
East Croydon	d													06 00					05 53						06 24
Clapham Junction	a													06 11					06 02						06 33
London Victoria	a													06 18					06 10						06 42

		SN ■	SN ■		TL ■	SN	SN	GW	TL ■	SN ■	SN ■	SN ■	TL ■		SN	TL ■	SN	GW	SN ■	SN ■	SN ■	SN ■	GW		TL ■
Horsham	d								06 04	06 19						06 34			06 40	06 50					
Littlehaven	d								06 08							06 38			06 44	06 54					
Faygate	d								06 11							06 41									
Ifield	d								06 15							06 45			06 50						
Crawley	d								06 19	06 28						06 49			06 54	07 02					
Three Bridges	a								06 22	06 32						06 52			06 59	07 07					
Three Bridges	d				06 07				06 24	06 33						06 54			07 02	07 07					
Gatwick Airport	a				06 12				06 28	06 37						06 58			07 08						
Gatwick Airport	d	05 52			06 13				06 29	06 38	06 19		06 43			06 59		07 03	07 09		06 49				07 13
Horley	d	05 55			06 16						06 22		06 46								06 52				07 16
Salfords	d				06 20						06 26		06 50								06 56				07 20
Earlswood (Surrey)	d	06 00			06 24						06 30		06 54								07 00				07 24
Redhill	a	06 05			06 28				06 37		06 34		06 58			07 07		07 11			07 04				07 28
Redhill	d																	07 14							
Reigate	a																	07 18							
Redhill	d						06 22										06 52								
Tonbridge	a																								
Tonbridge	d					05 58									06 28										
Leigh (Kent)	a					06 02									06 32										
Penshurst	a					06 06									06 36										
Edenbridge	a					06 13									06 43										
Godstone	a					06 19									06 49										
Nutfield	a					06 25	06 26								06 55		06 56								
Reigate	d		06 06					06 32				06 36										07 06	07 20		
Redhill	a		06 11			06 31		06 37				06 41			07 01							07 11	07 24		
Redhill	d	06 15			06 29				06 39		06 45		06 59			07 09					07 15				07 29
Merstham	d	06 19			06 33				06 43		06 49		07 03			07 13					07 19				07 33
Coulsdon South	d	06 24			06 39				06 48		06 54		07 09			07 18					07 24				07 39
Purley	d	06 28							06 54		06 58					07 24					07 28				
East Croydon	a	06 34			06 45				07 01	06 53	07 04		07 15			07 31			07 23	07 26	07 34				07 45
East Croydon	d				06 46				07 01				07 16			07 31				07 27					07 46
Norwood Junction	a								07 06							07 36									
London Bridge	a				07 00				07 20				07 30			07 50				07 43					08 00
London Blackfriars	a				07 06				07 26				07 36			07 56									08 06
City Thameslink	a				07 08				07 28				07 38			07 58									08 08
Farringdon	a				07 11				07 31				07 41			08 01									08 11
St Pancras International	a				07 15				07 35				07 45			08 05									08 15
East Croydon	d	06 34								06 53	07 04								07 24		07 34				
Clapham Junction	a	06 44								07 02	07 14								07 33		07 44				
London Victoria	a	06 52								07 12	07 22								07 40		07 52				

Table T183-R

Mondays to Fridays
21 May to 7 December

Horsham / Gatwick Airport / Tonbridge / Reigate / Redhill - London

		SN	SN ■	SN	GW	TL ■	SN ■	SN ■	SN ■		TL ■	SN	SN	TL ■	SN	GW	SN ■	SN ■	SN ■	SN ■		GW	TL ■	SN	SN ■
Horsham	d					07 04	07 16							07 34			07 40	07 50							
Littlehaven	d					07 08	07 20							07 38			07 44	07 54							
Faygate	d					07 11								07 41											
Ifield	d					07 15								07 45			07 50								
Crawley	d					07 19	07 28							07 49			07 54	08 02							
Three Bridges	a					07 22	07 32							07 52			07 58	08 07							
Three Bridges	d					07 24	07 33							07 54			08 01	08 07							
Gatwick Airport	a					07 28	07 37							07 58			08 05								
Gatwick Airport	d		07 20			07 29	07 38	07 20			07 43		07 50	07 59		08 02	08 08		07 49				08 13		08 20
Horley	d		07 23					07 23			07 46		07 53						07 52				08 16		08 23
Salfords	d							07 27			07 50								07 56				08 20		
Earlswood (Surrey)	d							07 31			07 54								08 00				08 24		
Redhill	a					07 38		07 35			07 58			08 07		08 10			08 04				08 28		
Redhill	d															08 14									
Reigate	a															08 18									
Redhill	d			07 23											07 52										
Tonbridge	a																								
Tonbridge	d	06 58										07 28												07 58	
Leigh (Kent)	a	07 02										07 32												08 02	
Penshurst	a	07 06										07 36												08 06	
Edenbridge	a	07 13										07 43												08 13	
Godstone	a	07 19										07 49												08 19	
Nutfield	a	07 25		07 27								07 55			07 56									08 25	
Reigate	d				07 32				07 36											08 04		08 24			
Redhill	a	07 31			07 37				07 41			08 01								08 10		08 28		08 31	
Redhill	d					07 39			07 45		07 59			08 09						08 15			08 29		
Merstham	d					07 43			07 49		08 03			08 13						08 19			08 33		
Coulsdon South	d					07 48			07 54		08 09			08 18						08 24			08 39		
Purley	d					07 54			07 58					08 24						08 28					
East Croydon	a		07 37			08 01	07 53		08 04		08 15		08 07	08 31			08 23	08 26		08 34			08 45		08 37
East Croydon	d					08 01					08 16			08 31				08 27					08 46		
Norwood Junction	a					08 06								08 36											
London Bridge	a					08 20					08 30			08 50				08 43					09 00		
London Blackfriars	a					08 26					08 36			08 56									09 06		
City Thameslink	a					08 28					08 38			08 58									09 08		
Farringdon	a					08 31					08 41			09 01									09 11		
St Pancras International	a					08 35					08 45			09 05									09 15		
East Croydon	d		07 38				07 54		08 04				08 08				08 24			08 34					08 38
Clapham Junction	a		07 47				08 03		08 14				08 17				08 33			08 44					08 47
London Victoria	a		07 54				08 12		08 22				08 24				08 40			08 52					08 54

		TL ■	SN ■	SN	SN ■	SN ■		GW	TL ■	SN	SN ■	TL ■	SN	GW	SN ■	SN ■	SN ■		GW	TL ■	SN	SN ■	SN ■	SN	GW
Horsham	d	08 04	08 18									08 34			08 50					08 55					
Littlehaven	d	08 08										08 38								08 59					
Faygate	d	08 11										08 41													
Ifield	d	08 15										08 45								09 05					
Crawley	d	08 19	08 27									08 49			08 59					09 08					
Three Bridges	a	08 22	08 31									08 52			09 03					09 12					
Three Bridges	d	08 24	08 32									08 54			09 04					09 13					
Gatwick Airport	a	08 28	08 36									08 58			09 08					09 17					
Gatwick Airport	d	08 29	08 39		08 19				08 43		08 51	08 59		09 03	09 09	08 49				09 19		09 23			
Horley	d				08 22				08 46		08 54					08 52				09 21		09 26			
Salfords	d				08 26				08 50							08 56									
Earlswood (Surrey)	d				08 30				08 54							09 00						09 31			
Redhill	a	08 37			08 34				08 58			09 07		09 11		09 04				09 29		09 35			
Redhill	d													09 14											
Reigate	a													09 18											
Redhill	d			08 22									08 55											09 25	
Tonbridge	a																								
Tonbridge	d									08 28											08 58				
Leigh (Kent)	a									08 32											09 02				
Penshurst	a									08 36											09 06				
Edenbridge	a									08 43											09 13				
Godstone	a									08 49											09 19				
Nutfield	a			08 26						08 55			08 59								09 25			09 29	
Reigate	d					08 36		08 42									09 06		09 24				09 32		09 36
Redhill	a					08 41		08 46		09 02							09 11		09 28		09 31		09 37		09 41
Redhill	d	08 39				08 45			08 59			09 09					09 15			09 29			09 41		
Merstham	d	08 43				08 49			09 03			09 13					09 19			09 33			09 45		
Coulsdon South	d	08 48				08 54			09 09			09 18					09 24			09 39			09 50		
Purley	d	08 54				08 58						09 24					09 28						09 55		
East Croydon	a	09 01	08 54			09 04			09 15		09 09	09 31			09 24		09 34			09 45			10 00		
East Croydon	d	09 01							09 16			09 31								09 45					
Norwood Junction	a	09 06										09 36													
London Bridge	a	09 20							09 30			09 50								10 00					
London Blackfriars	a	09 26							09 36			09 56								10 06					
City Thameslink	a	09 28							09 38			09 58								10 08					
Farringdon	a	09 31							09 41			10 01								10 11					
St Pancras International	a	09 35							09 45			10 05								10 15					
East Croydon	d		08 54			09 04					09 09				09 24		09 34						10 00		
Clapham Junction	a		09 03			09 14					09 18				09 33		09 44						10 10		
London Victoria	a		09 10			09 24					09 26				09 40		09 52						10 18		

Table T183-R

Mondays to Fridays
21 May to 7 December

Horsham / Gatwick Airport / Tonbridge / Reigate / Redhill - London

		TL ■	SN ■		GW	TL ■	SN ■	SN	SN	GW	TL ■	SN ■	GW		TL ■	SN ■	SN	GW	TL ■	SN ■	TL ■	SN	SN ■		GW
					A																				
Horsham	d		09 20			09 25						09 50			09 55					10 20	10 25				
Littlehaven	d					09 29									09 59						10 29				
Faygate	d																								
Ifield	d					09 35									10 05						10 35				
Crawley	d		09 29			09 38						09 59			10 08					10 29	10 38				
Three Bridges	a		09 33			09 42						10 03			10 12					10 33	10 42				
Three Bridges	d		09 34			09 43						10 04			10 13					10 34	10 43				
Gatwick Airport	a		09 38			09 47						10 08			10 17					10 38	10 47				
Gatwick Airport	d	09 33	09 39			09 49				10 00	10 03	10 09			10 19				10 33	10 39	10 49				11 00
Horley	d	09 35				09 51					10 05				10 21				10 35		10 51				
Salfords	d	09 39									10 09								10 39						
Earlswood (Surrey)	d	09 43									10 13								10 43						
Redhill	a	09 48				09 59				10 08	10 17				10 29				10 47		10 59				11 08
Redhill	d									10 14															11 14
Reigate	a									10 18															11 18
Redhill	d								10 00													11 00			
Tonbridge	a																								
Tonbridge	d							09 31									10 01								
Leigh (Kent)	a							09 35									10 05								
Penshurst	a							09 39									10 09								
Edenbridge	a							09 46									10 16								
Godstone	a							09 52									10 22								
Nutfield	a							09 58	10 04								10 28					11 04			
Reigate	d				09 51		10 00						10 19			10 30		10 34					11 00		
Redhill	a				09 55		10 05	10 06					10 23			10 34	10 36	10 38					11 04		
Redhill	d	09 49				09 59	10 11				10 19				10 29	10 41			10 49		10 59		11 11		
Merstham	d					10 03	10 15								10 33	10 45					11 03		11 15		
Coulsdon South	d					10 09	10 20								10 39	10 50					11 09		11 20		
Purley	d	09 58					10 25				10 28					10 55			10 58				11 25		
East Croydon	a	10 03	09 54			10 15	10 30				10 33	10 24			10 45	11 00			11 03	10 54	11 15		11 30		
East Croydon	d	10 03				10 15					10 33				10 45				11 03		11 15				
Norwood Junction	a	10 07									10 37								11 07						
London Bridge	a	10 20				10 30					10 50				11 00				11 20		11 30				
London Blackfriars	a	10 26				10 36					10 56				11 06				11 26		11 36				
City Thameslink	a	10 28				10 38					10 58				11 08				11 28		11 38				
Farringdon	a	10 31				10 41					11 01				11 11				11 31		11 41				
St Pancras International	a	10 35				10 45					11 05				11 15				11 35		11 45				
East Croydon	d		09 54				10 30					10 24				11 00				10 54			11 30		
Clapham Junction	a		10 03				10 40					10 33				11 10				11 03			11 40		
London Victoria	a		10 11				10 48					10 41				11 18				11 11			11 48		

		TL ■	SN ■	GW	TL ■	SN ■	SN	GW	TL ■		SN ■	TL ■	SN	SN ■	GW	TL ■	SN ■	GW	TL ■		SN ■	SN	GW	TL ■	SN ■
Horsham	d		10 50		10 55						11 20	11 25					11 50		11 55						12 20
Littlehaven	d				10 59							11 29							11 59						
Faygate	d																								
Ifield	d				11 05							11 35							12 05						
Crawley	d		10 59		11 08						11 29	11 38					11 59		12 08						12 29
Three Bridges	a		11 03		11 12						11 33	11 42					12 03		12 12						12 33
Three Bridges	d		11 04		11 13						11 34	11 43					12 04		12 13						12 34
Gatwick Airport	a		11 08		11 17						11 38	11 47					12 08		12 17						12 38
Gatwick Airport	d	11 03	11 09		11 19				11 33		11 39	11 49			12 00	12 03	12 09		12 19					12 33	12 39
Horley	d	11 05			11 21				11 35			11 51				12 05			12 21					12 35	
Salfords	d	11 09							11 39							12 09								12 39	
Earlswood (Surrey)	d	11 13							11 43							12 13								12 43	
Redhill	a	11 17			11 29				11 47			11 59			12 08	12 17			12 29					12 47	
Redhill	d														12 14										
Reigate	a														12 18										
Redhill	d												12 00												
Tonbridge	a																								
Tonbridge	d						11 01															12 01			
Leigh (Kent)	a						11 05															12 05			
Penshurst	a						11 09															12 09			
Edenbridge	a						11 16															12 16			
Godstone	a						11 22															12 22			
Nutfield	a						11 28						12 04									12 28			
Reigate	d			11 19		11 30		11 34						12 00				12 19			12 30		12 34		
Redhill	a			11 25		11 34	11 36	11 38						12 04				12 23			12 34	12 36	12 38		
Redhill	d	11 19			11 29	11 41			11 49			11 59		12 11		12 19			12 29		12 41			12 49	
Merstham	d				11 33	11 45						12 03		12 15					12 33		12 45				
Coulsdon South	d				11 39	11 50						12 09		12 20					12 39		12 50				
Purley	d	11 28				11 55			11 58					12 25		12 28					12 55			12 58	
East Croydon	a	11 33	11 24		11 45	12 00			12 03		11 54	12 15		12 30		12 33	12 24		12 45		13 00			13 03	12 54
East Croydon	d	11 33			11 45				12 03			12 15				12 33			12 45					13 03	
Norwood Junction	a	11 37							12 07							12 37								13 07	
London Bridge	a	11 50			12 00				12 20			12 30				12 50			13 00					13 20	
London Blackfriars	a	11 56			12 06				12 26			12 36				12 56			13 06					13 26	
City Thameslink	a	11 58			12 08				12 28			12 38				12 58			13 08					13 28	
Farringdon	a	12 01			12 11				12 31			12 41				13 01			13 11					13 31	
St Pancras International	a	12 05			12 15				12 35			12 45				13 05			13 15					13 35	
East Croydon	d		11 24			12 00					11 54			12 30			12 24				13 00				12 54
Clapham Junction	a		11 33			12 10					12 03			12 40			12 33				13 10				13 03
London Victoria	a		11 41			12 18					12 11			12 48			12 41				13 18				13 11

A until 5 October

Table T183-R

Mondays to Fridays

21 May to 7 December

Horsham / Gatwick Airport / Tonbridge / Reigate / Redhill - London

		TL ■	SN	SN ■	GW		TL ■	SN ■	GW	TL ■	SN ■	SN	GW	TL ■	SN ■		TL ■	SN	SN ■	GW	TL ■	SN ■	GW	TL ■	SN ■
Horsham	d	12 23						12 50		12 55					13 20		13 25					13 50		13 55	
Littlehaven	d	12 27								12 59							13 29							13 59	
Faygate	d	12 30																							
Ifield	d	12 34								13 05							13 35							14 05	
Crawley	d	12 38						12 59		13 08					13 29		13 38					13 59		14 08	
Three Bridges	a	12 41						13 03		13 12					13 33		13 42					14 03		14 12	
Three Bridges	d	12 43						13 04		13 13					13 34		13 43					14 04		14 13	
Gatwick Airport	a	12 47						13 08		13 17					13 38		13 47					14 08		14 17	
Gatwick Airport	d	12 49			13 00		13 03	13 09		13 19				13 33	13 39		13 49			14 00	14 03	14 09		14 19	
Horley	d	12 51					13 05			13 21				13 35			13 51				14 05			14 21	
Salfords	d						13 09							13 39							14 09				
Earlswood (Surrey)	d						13 13							13 43							14 13				
Redhill	a	12 59			13 08		13 17			13 29				13 47			13 59			14 08	14 17			14 29	
Redhill	d				13 14															14 14					
Reigate	a				13 18															14 18					
Redhill	d		13 00															14 00							
Tonbridge	a																								
Tonbridge	d											13 01													
Leigh (Kent)	a											13 05													
Penshurst	a											13 09													
Edenbridge	a											13 16													
Godstone	a											13 22													
Nutfield	a		13 04									13 28						14 04							
Reigate	d			13 00					13 19		13 30		13 38						14 00			14 19			14 30
Redhill	a			13 04					13 23		13 34	13 36	13 42						14 04			14 23			14 34
Redhill	d	12 59		13 11			13 19			13 29	13 41			13 49			13 59		14 11		14 19			14 29	14 41
Merstham	d	13 03		13 15						13 33	13 45						14 03		14 15					14 33	14 45
Coulsdon South	d	13 09		13 20						13 39	13 50						14 09		14 20					14 39	14 50
Purley	d			13 25			13 28				13 55			13 58					14 25		14 28				14 55
East Croydon	a	13 15		13 30			13 33	13 24		13 45	14 00			14 03	13 54		14 15		14 30		14 33	14 24		14 45	15 00
East Croydon	d	13 15					13 33			13 45				14 03			14 15				14 33			14 45	
Norwood Junction	a						13 37							14 07							14 37				
London Bridge	a	13 30					13 50			14 00				14 20			14 30				14 50			15 00	
London Blackfriars	a	13 36					13 56			14 06				14 26			14 36				14 56			15 06	
City Thameslink	a	13 38					13 58			14 08				14 28			14 38				14 58			15 08	
Farringdon	a	13 41					14 01			14 11				14 31			14 41				15 01			15 11	
St Pancras International	a	13 45					14 05			14 15				14 35			14 45				15 05			15 15	
East Croydon	d			13 30				13 24			14 00				13 54				14 30			14 24			15 00
Clapham Junction	a			13 40				13 33			14 10				14 03				14 40			14 33			15 10
London Victoria	a			13 48				13 41			14 18				14 11				14 48			14 41			15 18

			SN	GW	TL ■	SN ■	TL ■	SN	SN ■	GW	TL ■		SN ■	GW	TL ■	TL ■	SN ■	SN	SN	GW	TL ■		SN ■	TL ■	TL ■
Horsham	d					14 20	14 25						14 50		14 55								15 20	15 25	
Littlehaven	d						14 29								14 59									15 29	
Faygate	d																								
Ifield	d						14 35								15 05									15 35	
Crawley	d					14 29	14 38						14 59		15 08								15 29	15 38	
Three Bridges	a					14 33	14 42						15 03		15 12								15 33	15 42	
Three Bridges	d					14 34	14 43						15 04		15 13								15 34	15 43	
Gatwick Airport	a					14 38	14 47						15 08		15 17								15 38	15 47	
Gatwick Airport	d				14 33	14 39	14 49			15 00	15 03		15 09		15 19	15 27					15 33		15 39	15 49	15 57
Horley	d				14 35		14 51				15 05				15 21						15 35			15 51	
Salfords	d				14 39						15 09										15 39				
Earlswood (Surrey)	d				14 43						15 13										15 43				
Redhill	a				14 47		14 59			15 08	15 17				15 29	15 35					15 47			15 59	16 05
Redhill	d									15 14															
Reigate	a									15 18															
Redhill	d							15 00											15 30						
Tonbridge	a																								
Tonbridge	d		14 01															15 01							
Leigh (Kent)	a		14 05															15 05							
Penshurst	a		14 09															15 09							
Edenbridge	a		14 16															15 16							
Godstone	a		14 22															15 22							
Nutfield	a		14 28					15 04										15 28	15 34						
Reigate	d			14 34					15 00					15 20			15 30			15 34					
Redhill	a		14 36	14 39					15 04					15 26			15 34	15 36		15 38					
Redhill	d				14 49		14 59		15 11		15 19				15 29	15 36	15 41				15 49			15 59	16 06
Merstham	d						15 03		15 15						15 33		15 45							16 03	
Coulsdon South	d						15 09		15 20						15 39		15 50							16 09	
Purley	d				14 58				15 25		15 28					15 48	15 55				15 58				16 18
East Croydon	a				15 03	14 54	15 15		15 30		15 33		15 24		15 45	15 54	16 00				16 03		15 54	16 15	16 24
East Croydon	d				15 03		15 15				15 33				15 45	15 54					16 03			16 15	16 24
Norwood Junction	a				15 07						15 37										16 07				
London Bridge	a				15 20		15 30				15 50				16 00	16 10					16 20			16 30	16 40
London Blackfriars	a				15 26		15 36				15 56				16 06	16 16					16 26			16 36	16 46
City Thameslink	a				15 28		15 38				15 58				16 08	16 18					16 28			16 38	16 48
Farringdon	a				15 31		15 41				16 01				16 11	16 21					16 31			16 41	16 51
St Pancras International	a				15 35		15 45				16 05				16 15	16 25					16 35			16 45	16 55
East Croydon	d					14 54			15 30				15 24				16 00						15 54		
Clapham Junction	a					15 03			15 40				15 33				16 10						16 03		
London Victoria	a					15 11			15 49				15 41				16 18						16 11		

Table T183-R

Mondays to Fridays

21 May to 7 December

Horsham / Gatwick Airport / Tonbridge / Reigate / Redhill - London

		SN	SN ■	GW	TL ■	SN	SN ■		GW	TL ■	TL ■	SN	SN ■	GW	TL ■	SN	SN ■		TL ■	TL ■	SN	SN ■	GW	TL ■	SN
Horsham	d						15 50			15 55							16 22		16 25						
Littlehaven	d									15 59									16 28						
Faygate	d																		16 32						
Ifield	d									16 05									16 36						
Crawley	d						15 59			16 08							16 31		16 39						
Three Bridges	a						16 03			16 12							16 35		16 43						
Three Bridges	d						16 04			16 13							16 36		16 44						
Gatwick Airport	a						16 08			16 17							16 40		16 48						
Gatwick Airport	d			16 00	16 03		16 09			16 19	16 27				16 33		16 41		16 49	16 57			17 00	17 03	
Horley	d				16 05					16 21					16 35				16 52					17 05	
Salfords	d				16 09										16 39									17 09	
Earlswood (Surrey)	d				16 13										16 43									17 13	
Redhill	a			16 08	16 17					16 29	16 35				16 47				16 59	17 05			17 08	17 17	
Redhill	d			16 14																			17 14		
Reigate	a			16 18																			17 18		
Redhill	d	16 00										16 30									17 00				
Tonbridge	a																								
Tonbridge	d					15 47										16 17									16 47
Leigh (Kent)	a					15 51										16 21									16 51
Penshurst	a					15 55										16 25									16 55
Edenbridge	a					16 02										16 32									17 02
Godstone	a					16 08										16 38									17 08
Nutfield	a	16 04				16 14						16 34				16 44					17 04				17 14
Reigate	d		16 00						16 23				16 30	16 36								17 00			
Redhill	a		16 04			16 20			16 27				16 34	16 40		16 50						17 04			17 20
Redhill	d		16 11		16 19					16 29	16 36		16 41		16 49				17 00	17 06		17 11		17 19	
Merstham	d		16 15							16 33			16 45						17 04			17 15			
Coulsdon South	d		16 20							16 39			16 50						17 09			17 20			
Purley	d		16 25		16 28						16 48		16 55		16 58					17 18		17 25		17 28	
East Croydon	a		16 30		16 33		16 24			16 45	16 54		17 00		17 03		16 55		17 15	17 24		17 30		17 33	
East Croydon	d				16 33					16 45	16 54				17 03				17 15	17 25				17 33	
Norwood Junction	a				16 37										17 07									17 37	
London Bridge	a				16 50					17 00	17 10				17 20				17 30	17 40				17 50	
London Blackfriars	a				16 56					17 06	17 16				17 26				17 36	17 46				17 56	
City Thameslink	a				16 58					17 08	17 18				17 28				17 38	17 48				17 58	
Farringdon	a				17 01					17 11	17 21				17 31				17 41	17 51				18 01	
St Pancras International	a				17 05					17 15	17 25				17 35				17 45	17 55				18 05	
East Croydon	d		16 30				16 24						17 00				16 56					17 30			
Clapham Junction	a		16 40				16 33						17 10				17 05					17 40			
London Victoria	a		16 48				16 41						17 18				17 12					17 50			

		SN ■	TL ■		GW	TL ■	SN	SN ■	GW	TL ■	SN	SN ■	TL ■		SN	SN ■	GW A	TL ■	SN	SN ■	TL ■	GW	SN		SN ■
Horsham	d	16 50	16 55									17 20	17 25							17 50	17 55				
Littlehaven	d		16 58										17 28								17 58				
Faygate	d		17 02										17 32								18 02				
Ifield	d		17 06										17 36								18 06				
Crawley	d	16 59	17 09									17 29	17 39							17 59	18 09				
Three Bridges	a	17 03	17 13									17 33	17 43							18 03	18 13				
Three Bridges	d	17 04	17 14									17 34	17 44							18 04	18 14				
Gatwick Airport	a	17 08	17 18									17 38	17 48							18 08	18 18				
Gatwick Airport	d	17 09	17 19			17 27				17 33		17 39	17 49				18 00	18 03		18 09	18 19				
Horley	d		17 22							17 35			17 52					18 05			18 22				
Salfords	d									17 39								18 09							
Earlswood (Surrey)	d									17 43								18 13							
Redhill	a		17 29			17 35				17 47			17 59				18 08	18 17			18 29				
Redhill	d																18 14								
Reigate	a																18 18								
Redhill	d						17 30								18 00								18 30		
Tonbridge	a																								
Tonbridge	d										17 17								17 47						
Leigh (Kent)	a										17 21								17 51						
Penshurst	a										17 25								17 55						
Edenbridge	a										17 32								18 02						
Godstone	a										17 38								18 08						
Nutfield	a						17 34				17 44				18 04				18 14				18 34		
Reigate	d				17 26			17 30	17 34							18 00						18 26			18 30
Redhill	a				17 32			17 36	17 40		17 50					18 04			18 20			18 30			18 35
Redhill	d		17 30			17 36		17 41		17 49			18 00			18 11		18 19			18 30				18 41
Merstham	d		17 34					17 45					18 04			18 15					18 34				18 45
Coulsdon South	d		17 39					17 50					18 09			18 20					18 39				18 50
Purley	d					17 48		17 55		17 58						18 25		18 28							18 55
East Croydon	a	17 24	17 45			17 53		18 00		18 03		17 54	18 15			18 30		18 33		18 24	18 45				19 00
East Croydon	d		17 45			17 54				18 03			18 15					18 33			18 45				
Norwood Junction	a									18 07								18 37							
London Bridge	a		18 00			18 10				18 20			18 30					18 50			19 00				
London Blackfriars	a		18 06			18 16				18 26			18 36					18 56			19 06				
City Thameslink	a		18 08			18 18				18 28			18 38					18 58			19 08				
Farringdon	a		18 11			18 21				18 31			18 41					19 01			19 11				
St Pancras International	a		18 15			18 25				18 35			18 45					19 05			19 15				
East Croydon	d	17 24						18 00				17 54				18 30				18 24					19 00
Clapham Junction	a	17 33						18 10				18 03				18 40				18 34					19 10
London Victoria	a	17 41						18 18				18 11				18 48				18 42					19 18

A until 5 October

Table T183-R

Mondays to Fridays

21 May to 7 December

Horsham / Gatwick Airport / Tonbridge / Reigate / Redhill - London

		GW	TL ■	SN	SN ■	TL ■	SN	SN ■	GW		TL ■	SN	SN ■	TL ■	GW	SN	SN ■	GW	TL ■		SN ■	SN	TL ■	SN	SN ■
Horsham	d				18 20	18 25							18 52	18 55							19 20		19 25		
Littlehaven	d					18 28								18 59									19 29		
Faygate	d					18 32																			
Ifield	d					18 36								19 05									19 35		
Crawley	d				18 29	18 39							19 01	19 08							19 29		19 38		
Three Bridges	a				18 33	18 43							19 05	19 12							19 33		19 42		
Three Bridges	d				18 34	18 44							19 06	19 13							19 34		19 43		
Gatwick Airport	a				18 38	18 48							19 10	19 17							19 38		19 47		
Gatwick Airport	d		18 33		18 39	18 49			19 00		19 03		19 11	19 19					19 33		19 39		19 49		
Horley	d		18 35			18 52					19 05			19 21					19 35				19 51		
Salfords	d		18 39								19 09								19 39						
Earlswood (Surrey)	d		18 43								19 13								19 43						
Redhill	a		18 47			18 59			19 08		19 17			19 29					19 47				19 59		
Redhill	d								19 13																
Reigate	a								19 17																
Redhill	d						19 00									19 30								20 00	
Tonbridge	a																								
Tonbridge	d			18 17								18 47										19 22			
Leigh (Kent)	a			18 21								18 51													
Penshurst	a			18 25								18 55													
Edenbridge	a			18 32								19 02										19 32			
Godstone	a			18 38								19 08										19 39			
Nutfield	a			18 44			19 04					19 14				19 34						19 44		20 04	
Reigate	d	18 35						19 00							19 26		19 30	19 34							20 00
Redhill	a	18 39		18 50				19 04				19 20			19 32		19 36	19 40				19 50			20 04
Redhill	d		18 49			19 00		19 11			19 19			19 29			19 41		19 49				19 59		20 11
Merstham	d					19 04		19 15						19 33			19 45						20 03		20 15
Coulsdon South	d					19 09		19 20						19 39			19 50						20 09		20 20
Purley	d		18 58					19 25			19 28						19 55		19 58						20 25
East Croydon	a		19 03		18 54	19 15		19 30			19 33		19 25	19 45			20 00		20 03		19 54		20 15		20 30
East Croydon	d		19 03			19 15					19 33			19 45					20 03				20 15		
Norwood Junction	a		19 07								19 37								20 07						
London Bridge	a		19 20			19 30					19 50			20 00					20 20				20 30		
London Blackfriars	a		19 26			19 36					19 56			20 06					20 26				20 36		
City Thameslink	a		19 28			19 38					19 58			20 08					20 28				20 38		
Farringdon	a		19 31			19 41					20 01			20 11					20 31				20 41		
St Pancras International	a		19 35			19 45					20 05			20 15					20 35				20 45		
East Croydon	d				18 54			19 30					19 26				20 00				19 54				20 30
Clapham Junction	a				19 03			19 40					19 35				20 10				20 04				20 40
London Victoria	a				19 11			19 49					19 42				20 18				20 11				20 48

		GW A	TL ■	SN ■	TL ■		SN ■	SN	GW	TL ■	SN ■	TL ■	SN	SN ■	GW		TL ■	SN ■	GW	TL ■	SN ■	SN	GW	TL ■	SN ■
Horsham	d			19 52	19 55						20 20	20 25						20 50		20 55					21 20
Littlehaven	d				19 59							20 29								20 59					
Faygate	d																								
Ifield	d				20 05							20 35								21 05					
Crawley	d			20 01	20 08						20 29	20 38						20 59		21 08					21 29
Three Bridges	a			20 05	20 12						20 33	20 42						21 03		21 12					21 33
Three Bridges	d			20 06	20 13						20 34	20 43						21 04		21 13					21 34
Gatwick Airport	a			20 10	20 18						20 38	20 47						21 08		21 17					21 38
Gatwick Airport	d	20 00	20 03	20 11	20 19					20 33	20 39	20 49			21 00		21 03	21 09		21 19				21 33	21 39
Horley	d		20 05		20 22					20 35		20 51					21 05			21 21				21 35	
Salfords	d		20 09							20 39							21 09							21 39	
Earlswood (Surrey)	d		20 13							20 43							21 13							21 43	
Redhill	a	20 08	20 17		20 29					20 47		20 59			21 08		21 17			21 29				21 47	
Redhill	d	20 13													21 13										
Reigate	a	20 17													21 17										
Redhill	d												21 00												
Tonbridge	a																								
Tonbridge	d							20 01														21 01			
Leigh (Kent)	a							20 05														21 05			
Penshurst	a							20 09														21 09			
Edenbridge	a							20 16														21 16			
Godstone	a							20 22														21 22			
Nutfield	a							20 28					21 04									21 28			
Reigate	d						20 30		20 35					21 00					21 24		21 30		21 36		
Redhill	a						20 34	20 36	20 39					21 04					21 28		21 34	21 36	21 40		
Redhill	d		20 19		20 30		20 41			20 49		20 59		21 11			21 19			21 29	21 41			21 49	
Merstham	d				20 34		20 45					21 03		21 15						21 33	21 45				
Coulsdon South	d				20 39		20 50					21 09		21 20						21 39	21 50				
Purley	d		20 28				20 55			20 58				21 25			21 28				21 55			21 58	
East Croydon	a		20 33	20 25	20 45		21 00			21 03	20 54	21 15		21 30			21 33	21 24		21 45	22 00			22 03	21 54
East Croydon	d		20 33		20 46					21 03		21 15					21 33			21 45				22 03	
Norwood Junction	a		20 37							21 07							21 37							22 07	
London Bridge	a		20 50		21 00					21 20		21 30					21 50			22 00				22 20	
London Blackfriars	a		20 56		21 06					21 26		21 36					21 56			22 06				22 26	
City Thameslink	a		20 58		21 08					21 28		21 38					21 58			22 08				22 28	
Farringdon	a		21 01		21 11					21 31		21 41					22 01			22 11				22 31	
St Pancras International	a		21 05		21 15					21 35		21 45					22 05			22 15				22 35	
East Croydon	d			20 26			21 00				20 54			21 30				21 24			22 00				21 54
Clapham Junction	a			20 35			21 12				21 06			21 40				21 33			22 10				22 03
London Victoria	a			20 42			21 19				21 13			21 48				21 41			22 18				22 11

A until 5 October

Table T183-R

Mondays to Fridays

21 May to 7 December

Horsham / Gatwick Airport / Tonbridge / Reigate / Redhill - London

			TL ■	SN	GW	SN ■	SN ■	TL ■	SN ■	SN ■ A	SN		GW B	TL ■	SN	SN ■	SN	GW	TL ■	SN ■	GW		SN		
Horsham	d		21 25			21 50		21 55	22 20					22 25					23 11	23 27					
Littlehaven	d		21 29					21 59						22 29					23 15						
Faygate	d																								
Ifield	d		21 35					22 05						22 35					23 21						
Crawley	d		21 38			21 59		22 08	22 29					22 38					23 24	23 36					
Three Bridges	a		21 42			22 03		22 12	22 33					22 42					23 28	23 40					
Three Bridges	d		21 43			22 04		22 13	22 34					22 43					23 29						
Gatwick Airport	a		21 47			22 08		22 17	22 38					22 47					23 33						
Gatwick Airport	d		21 49		22 00	22 09		22 19	22 39					22 49				23 18	23 35						
Horley	d		21 51					22 21						22 51					23 37						
Salfords	d																		23 41						
Earlswood (Surrey)	d																		23 45						
Redhill	a		21 59		22 08			22 29						22 59				23 26	23 49						
Redhill	d				22 12													23 32							
Reigate	a				22 16													23 36							
Redhill	d			22 00											23 00										
Tonbridge	a																								
Tonbridge	d										22 01						23 01						23 36		
Leigh (Kent)	a										22 05						23 05						23 40		
Penshurst	a										22 09						23 09						23 44		
Edenbridge	a										22 16						23 16						23 51		
Godstone	a										22 22						23 22						23 57		
Nutfield	a			22 04							22 28				23 04		23 28						00 03		
Reigate	d						22 00			22 30			22 36			23 00					23 55				
Redhill	a						22 04			22 34	22 36		22 40			23 04	23 36				00 01		00 09		
Redhill	d		21 59				22 11	22 29		22 41				22 59		23 11			23 49						
Merstham	d		22 03				22 15	22 33		22 45				23 03		23 15			23 53						
Coulsdon South	d		22 09				22 20	22 39		22 50				23 09		23 20			23 59						
Purley	d						22 25			22 55						23 25			00 03						
East Croydon	a		22 15			22 24	22 30	22 45	22 54	23 00				23 15		23 30			00 09						
East Croydon	d		22 15					22 45						23 15					00 10						
Norwood Junction	a																								
London Bridge	a		22 30					23 00						23 30											
London Blackfriars	a		22 36					23 06						23 36					00 36						
City Thameslink	a		22 38																						
Farringdon	a		22 41					23 11						23 41					00 41						
St Pancras International	a		22 45					23 15						23 45					00 45						
East Croydon	d					22 24	22 30		22 54	23 00						23 30									
Clapham Junction	a					22 33	22 40		23 03	23 10						23 44									
London Victoria	a					22 42	22 49		23 11	23 20						23 52									

Saturdays

26 May to 8 December

		SN	GW	TL ■	TL ■	SN ■	TL ■	SN ■	TL ■	SN ■		TL ■	SN ■	GW	SN ■	TL ■	TL ■	SN	TL ■	SN ■		GW ■	TL ■	SN	SN ■
Horsham	d																05 25			05 41			05 55		
Littlehaven	d																05 29			05 45			05 59		
Faygate	d																								
Ifield	d																05 35			05 51			06 05		
Crawley	d																05 38			05 55			06 08		
Three Bridges	a																05 42			06 00			06 12		
Three Bridges	d			00 37	01 41	02 08	02 41	03 08	03 41	04 08		04 35	04 58		05 22	05 27	05 43			06 03			06 13		
Gatwick Airport	a			00 41	01 45	02 12	02 45	03 12	03 45	04 12		04 40	05 02		05 26	05 31	05 47			06 08			06 17		
Gatwick Airport	d			00 42	01 46	02 13	02 46	03 13	03 46	04 13		04 41	05 03		05 28	05 33	05 49		06 03	06 09		06 12	06 19		
Horley	d			00 45	01 49	02 16	02 49	03 16	03 49	04 16		04 43	05 06		05 31	05 35	05 51		06 05				06 21		
Salfords	d																05 39		06 09						
Earlswood (Surrey)	d																05 43		06 13						
Redhill	a			00 52								04 51	05 14		05 39	05 47	05 59		06 17			06 22	06 29		
Redhill	d																					06 27			
Reigate	a																					06 33			
Redhill	d	00 16																						06 25	
Tonbridge	a																								
Tonbridge	d																	05 33							
Leigh (Kent)	a																	05 37							
Penshurst	a																	05 41							
Edenbridge	a																	05 48							
Godstone	a																	05 54							
Nutfield	a	00 20																06 00						06 29	
Reigate	d		00 45											05 35											06 30
Redhill	a		00 49											05 39				06 06							06 34
Redhill	d			00 53								04 52	05 14		05 41	05 49	05 59		06 19				06 29		06 41
Merstham	d														05 45		06 03						06 33		06 45
Coulsdon South	d														05 50		06 09						06 39		06 50
Purley	d			01 03	02 04	02 29	03 03	03 29	04 03	04 29		05 01	05 24		05 55	05 58			06 28						06 55
East Croydon	a			01 09	02 09	02 36	03 09	03 36	04 09	04 36		05 08	05 30		06 00	06 03	06 15		06 33	06 24			06 45		07 00
East Croydon	d			01 10	02 10		03 10		04 10			05 10				06 03	06 15		06 33				06 45		
Norwood Junction	a															06 07			06 37						
London Bridge	a											05 25				06 20	06 30		06 50				07 00		
London Blackfriars	a			01 36	02 36		03 36		04 36			05 31				06 26	06 36		06 56				07 06		
City Thameslink	a																								
Farringdon	a											05 36				06 31	06 41		07 01				07 11		
St Pancras International	a			01 43	02 43		03 43		04 43			05 40				06 35	06 45		07 05				07 15		
East Croydon	d					02 36		03 36		04 36			05 30		06 00					06 24					07 00
Clapham Junction	a					02 50		03 50		04 50			05 50		06 10					06 33					07 10
London Victoria	a					02 58		03 58		04 58			05 59		06 18					06 41					07 18

A not 7 December

B until 5 October

Table T183-R

Saturdays

26 May to 8 December

Horsham / Gatwick Airport / Tonbridge / Reigate / Redhill - London

		SN	GW ■	GW	TL ■	SN ■		GW	TL ■	SN	SN ■	GW	TL ■	SN ■	TL ■	SN ■		SN	GW ■	TL ■	SN ■	GW	TL ■	SN	SN ■
Horsham	d					06 20			06 25					06 50	06 55						07 20		07 25		
Littlehaven	d								06 29						06 59								07 29		
Faygate	d																								
Ifield	d								06 35						07 05								07 35		
Crawley	d					06 29			06 38					06 59	07 08						07 29		07 38		
Three Bridges	a					06 33			06 42					07 03	07 12						07 33		07 42		
Three Bridges	d					06 34			06 43					07 04	07 13						07 34		07 43		
Gatwick Airport	a					06 38			06 47					07 08	07 17						07 38		07 47		
Gatwick Airport	d		06 31		06 33	06 39			06 49				07 03	07 09	07 19				07 31	07 33	07 39		07 49		
Horley	d				06 35				06 51				07 05		07 21					07 35			07 51		
Salfords	d				06 39								07 09							07 39					
Earlswood (Surrey)	d				06 43								07 13							07 43					
Redhill	a		06 39		06 47				06 59				07 17		07 29				07 41	07 47			07 59		
Redhill	d		06 44																07 44						
Reigate	a		06 48																07 48						
Redhill	d									07 00														08 00	
Tonbridge	a																								
Tonbridge	d	06 03																07 01							
Leigh (Kent)	a	06 07																07 05							
Penshurst	a	06 11																07 09							
Edenbridge	a	06 18																07 16							
Godstone	a	06 24																07 22							
Nutfield	a	06 30								07 04								07 28						08 04	
Reigate	d			06 34				06 47			07 00	07 04				07 30						07 50			08 00
Redhill	a	06 36		06 38				06 51			07 04	07 09				07 34		07 36				07 54			08 04
Redhill	d				06 49				06 59		07 11		07 19		07 29	07 41				07 49			07 59		08 11
Merstham	d								07 03		07 15				07 33	07 45							08 03		08 15
Coulsdon South	d								07 09		07 20				07 39	07 50							08 09		08 20
Purley	d				06 58						07 25		07 28			07 55				07 58					08 25
East Croydon	a				07 03	06 54			07 15		07 30		07 33	07 24	07 45	08 00				08 03	07 54		08 15		08 30
East Croydon	d				07 03				07 15				07 33		07 45					08 03			08 15		
Norwood Junction	a				07 07								07 37							08 07					
London Bridge	a				07 20				07 30				07 50		08 00					08 20			08 30		
London Blackfriars	a				07 26				07 36				07 56		08 06					08 26			08 36		
City Thameslink	a																								
Farringdon	a				07 31				07 41				08 01		08 11					08 31			08 41		
St Pancras International	a				07 35				07 45				08 05		08 15					08 35			08 45		
East Croydon	d					06 54					07 30			07 24		08 00					07 54				08 30
Clapham Junction	a					07 03					07 40			07 33		08 10					08 03				08 40
London Victoria	a					07 11					07 48			07 41		08 18					08 11				08 48

		GW ■		TL ■	SN ■	TL ■	SN ■	SN	GW ■	TL ■	SN ■	GW		TL ■	SN	SN ■	GW ■	TL ■	SN ■	TL ■	SN ■	SN		GW ■	TL ■
Horsham	d				07 50	07 55					08 20			08 25					08 50	08 55					
Littlehaven	d					07 59								08 29						08 59					
Faygate	d																								
Ifield	d					08 05								08 35						09 05					
Crawley	d				07 59	08 08					08 29			08 38					08 59	09 08					
Three Bridges	a				08 03	08 12					08 33			08 42					09 03	09 12					
Three Bridges	d				08 04	08 13					08 34			08 43					09 04	09 13					
Gatwick Airport	a				08 08	08 17					08 38			08 47					09 08	09 17					
Gatwick Airport	d			08 03	08 09	08 19			08 31	08 33	08 39			08 49				09 03	09 09	09 19				09 30	09 33
Horley	d			08 05		08 21				08 35				08 51				09 05		09 21					09 35
Salfords	d			08 09						08 39								09 09							09 39
Earlswood (Surrey)	d			08 13						08 43								09 13							09 43
Redhill	a			08 17		08 29			08 40	08 47				08 59				09 17		09 29				09 39	09 47
Redhill	d								08 44															09 42	
Reigate	a								08 48															09 46	
Redhill	d														09 00										
Tonbridge	a																								
Tonbridge	d							08 01														09 01			
Leigh (Kent)	a							08 05														09 05			
Penshurst	a							08 09														09 09			
Edenbridge	a							08 16														09 16			
Godstone	a							08 22														09 22			
Nutfield	a							08 28							09 04							09 28			
Reigate	d	08 04					08 30					08 51				09 00	09 04				09 30				
Redhill	a	08 08					08 34	08 36				08 56				09 04	09 09				09 34	09 36			
Redhill	d			08 19		08 29	08 41			08 49				08 59		09 11		09 19		09 29	09 41				09 49
Merstham	d					08 33	08 45							09 03		09 15				09 33	09 45				
Coulsdon South	d					08 39	08 50							09 09		09 20				09 39	09 50				
Purley	d			08 28			08 55			08 58						09 25		09 28			09 55				09 58
East Croydon	a			08 33	08 24	08 45	09 00			09 03	08 54			09 15		09 30		09 33	09 24	09 45	10 00				10 03
East Croydon	d			08 33		08 45				09 03				09 15				09 33		09 45					10 03
Norwood Junction	a			08 37						09 07								09 37							10 07
London Bridge	a			08 50		09 00				09 20				09 30				09 50		10 00					10 20
London Blackfriars	a			08 56		09 06				09 26				09 36				09 56		10 06					10 26
City Thameslink	a					09 08				09 28				09 38				09 58		10 08					10 28
Farringdon	a			09 01		09 11				09 31				09 41				10 01		10 11					10 31
St Pancras International	a			09 05		09 15				09 35				09 45				10 05		10 15					10 35
East Croydon	d				08 24		09 00				08 54					09 30			09 24		10 00				
Clapham Junction	a				08 33		09 10				09 03					09 40			09 33		10 10				
London Victoria	a				08 41		09 18				09 11					09 48			09 41		10 18				

Table T183-R

Saturdays

26 May to 8 December

Horsham / Gatwick Airport / Tonbridge / Reigate / Redhill - London

		SN ■	GW	TL ■	SN	SN ■	GW ■	TL ■		SN ■	TL ■	SN ■	SN	GW ■	TL ■	SN ■	GW	TL ■		SN	SN ■	GW ■	TL ■	SN ■	TL ■
Horsham	d	09 20		09 25						09 50	09 55					10 20		10 25						10 50	10 55
Littlehaven	d			09 29							09 59							10 29							10 59
Faygate	d																								
Ifield	d			09 35							10 05							10 35							11 05
Crawley	d	09 29		09 38						09 59	10 08					10 29		10 38						10 59	11 08
Three Bridges	a	09 33		09 42						10 03	10 12					10 33		10 42						11 03	11 12
Three Bridges	d	09 34		09 43						10 04	10 13					10 34		10 43						11 04	11 13
Gatwick Airport	a	09 38		09 47						10 08	10 17					10 38		10 47						11 08	11 17
Gatwick Airport	d	09 39		09 49				10 03		10 09	10 19			10 30	10 33	10 39		10 49					11 03	11 09	11 19
Horley	d			09 51				10 05			10 21				10 35			10 51					11 05		11 21
Salfords	d							10 09							10 39								11 09		
Earlswood (Surrey)	d							10 13							10 43								11 13		
Redhill	a			09 59				10 17			10 29			10 39	10 47			10 59					11 17		11 29
Redhill	d													10 43											
Reigate	a													10 48											
Redhill	d				10 00															11 00					
Tonbridge	a																								
Tonbridge	d												10 01												
Leigh (Kent)	a												10 05												
Penshurst	a												10 09												
Edenbridge	a												10 16												
Godstone	a												10 22												
Nutfield	a				10 04								10 28							11 04					
Reigate	d		09 51			10 00	10 04					10 30					10 47				11 00	11 04			
Redhill	a		09 55			10 04	10 08					10 34	10 36				10 52				11 04	11 08			
Redhill	d			09 59		10 11		10 19			10 29	10 41			10 49			10 59			11 11		11 19		11 29
Merstham	d			10 03		10 15					10 33	10 45						11 03			11 15				11 33
Coulsdon South	d			10 09		10 20					10 39	10 50						11 09			11 20				11 39
Purley	d					10 25		10 28				10 55			10 58						11 25		11 28		
East Croydon	a	09 54		10 15		10 30		10 33		10 24	10 45	11 00			11 03	10 54		11 15			11 30		11 33	11 24	11 45
East Croydon	d			10 15				10 33			10 45				11 03			11 15					11 33		11 45
Norwood Junction	a							10 37							11 07								11 37		
London Bridge	a			10 30				10 50			11 00				11 20			11 30					11 50		12 00
London Blackfriars	a			10 36				10 56			11 06				11 26			11 36					11 56		12 06
City Thameslink	a			10 38				10 58			11 08				11 28			11 38					11 58		12 08
Farringdon	a			10 41				11 01			11 11				11 31			11 41					12 01		12 11
St Pancras International	a			10 45				11 05			11 15				11 35			11 45					12 05		12 15
East Croydon	d	09 54				10 30				10 24		11 00				10 54					11 30			11 24	
Clapham Junction	a	10 03				10 40				10 33		11 10				11 03					11 40			11 33	
London Victoria	a	10 11				10 48				10 41		11 18				11 11					11 48			11 41	

		SN ■	SN	GW ■		TL ■	SN ■	GW	TL ■	SN	SN ■	TL ■	SN ■	TL ■		SN ■	SN	GW ■	TL ■	SN ■	GW	TL ■	SN	SN ■	
Horsham	d						11 20		11 25				11 50	11 55						12 20		12 25			
Littlehaven	d								11 29					11 59								12 29			
Faygate	d																								
Ifield	d								11 35					12 05								12 35			
Crawley	d						11 29		11 38				11 59	12 08						12 29		12 38			
Three Bridges	a						11 33		11 42				12 03	12 12						12 33		12 42			
Three Bridges	d						11 34		11 43				12 04	12 13						12 34		12 43			
Gatwick Airport	a						11 38		11 47				12 08	12 17						12 38		12 47			
Gatwick Airport	d			11 30		11 33	11 39		11 49			12 03	12 09	12 19				12 30	12 33	12 39		12 49			
Horley	d					11 35			11 51			12 05		12 21					12 35			12 51			
Salfords	d					11 39						12 09							12 39						
Earlswood (Surrey)	d					11 43						12 13							12 43						
Redhill	a			11 39		11 47			11 59			12 17		12 29				12 39	12 47			12 59			
Redhill	d			11 44														12 44							
Reigate	a			11 48														12 48							
Redhill	d									12 00													13 00		
Tonbridge	a																								
Tonbridge	d		11 01														12 01								
Leigh (Kent)	a		11 05														12 05								
Penshurst	a		11 09														12 09								
Edenbridge	a		11 16														12 16								
Godstone	a		11 22														12 22								
Nutfield	a		11 28							12 04							12 28						13 04		
Reigate	d	11 30						11 47			12 00					12 30					12 48			13 00	
Redhill	a	11 34	11 36					11 52			12 04					12 34	12 36				12 52			13 04	
Redhill	d	11 41				11 49			11 59		12 11	12 19		12 29		12 41			12 49			12 59		13 11	
Merstham	d	11 45							12 03		12 15			12 33		12 45						13 03		13 15	
Coulsdon South	d	11 50							12 09		12 20			12 39		12 50						13 09		13 20	
Purley	d	11 55				11 58					12 25	12 28				12 55			12 58					13 25	
East Croydon	a	12 00				12 03	11 54		12 15		12 30	12 33	12 24	12 45		13 00			13 03	12 54		13 15		13 30	
East Croydon	d					12 03			12 15			12 33		12 45					13 03			13 15			
Norwood Junction	a					12 07						12 37							13 07						
London Bridge	a					12 20			12 30			12 50		13 00					13 20			13 30			
London Blackfriars	a					12 26			12 36			12 56		13 06					13 26			13 36			
City Thameslink	a					12 28			12 38			12 58		13 08					13 28			13 38			
Farringdon	a					12 31			12 41			13 01		13 11					13 31			13 41			
St Pancras International	a					12 35			12 45			13 05		13 15					13 35			13 45			
East Croydon	d	12 00					11 54				12 30		12 24			13 00				12 54				13 30	
Clapham Junction	a	12 10					12 03				12 40		12 33			13 10				13 03				13 40	
London Victoria	a	12 18					12 11				12 48		12 41			13 18				13 11				13 48	

Table T183-R

Saturdays

26 May to 8 December

Horsham / Gatwick Airport / Tonbridge / Reigate / Redhill - London

		GW ■	TL ■	SN ■	TL ■	SN ■	SN	GW ■	TL ■	SN ■		GW	TL ■	SN	SN ■	GW ■	TL ■	SN ■	TL ■	SN ■		SN	GW ■	TL ■	SN ■
Horsham	d			12 50	12 55					13 20			13 25					13 50	13 55						14 20
Littlehaven	d				12 59								13 29						13 59						
Faygate	d																								
Ifield	d				13 05								13 35						14 05						
Crawley	d			12 59	13 08					13 29			13 38					13 59	14 08						14 29
Three Bridges	a			13 03	13 12					13 33			13 42					14 03	14 12						14 33
Three Bridges	d			13 04	13 13					13 34			13 43					14 04	14 13						14 34
Gatwick Airport	a			13 08	13 17					13 38			13 47					14 08	14 17						14 38
Gatwick Airport	d		13 03	13 09	13 19			13 30	13 33	13 39			13 49				14 03	14 09	14 19				14 30	14 33	14 39
Horley	d		13 05		13 21				13 35				13 51				14 05		14 21					14 35	
Salfords	d		13 09						13 39								14 09							14 39	
Earlswood (Surrey)	d		13 13						13 43								14 13							14 43	
Redhill	a		13 17		13 29			13 39	13 47				13 59				14 17		14 29				14 39	14 47	
Redhill	d							13 44															14 44		
Reigate	a							13 48															14 48		
Redhill	d													14 00											
Tonbridge	a																								
Tonbridge	d						13 01															14 01			
Leigh (Kent)	a						13 05															14 05			
Penshurst	a						13 09															14 09			
Edenbridge	a						13 16															14 16			
Godstone	a						13 22															14 22			
Nutfield	a						13 28							14 04								14 28			
Reigate	d	13 04				13 30						13 48			14 00	14 04				14 30					
Redhill	a	13 08				13 34	13 36					13 52			14 04	14 08				14 34		14 36			
Redhill	d		13 19		13 29	13 41			13 49				13 59		14 11		14 19		14 29	14 41				14 49	
Merstham	d				13 33	13 45							14 03		14 15				14 33	14 45					
Coulsdon South	d				13 39	13 50							14 09		14 20				14 39	14 50					
Purley	d		13 28			13 55			13 58						14 25		14 28			14 55				14 58	
East Croydon	a		13 33	13 24	13 45	14 00			14 03	13 54			14 15		14 30		14 33	14 24	14 45	15 00				15 03	14 54
East Croydon	d		13 33		13 45				14 03				14 15				14 33		14 45					15 03	
Norwood Junction	a		13 37						14 07								14 37							15 07	
London Bridge	a		13 50		14 00				14 20				14 30				14 50		15 00					15 20	
London Blackfriars	a		13 56		14 06				14 26				14 36				14 56		15 06					15 26	
City Thameslink	a		13 58		14 08				14 28				14 38				14 58		15 08					15 28	
Farringdon	a		14 01		14 11				14 31				14 41				15 01		15 11					15 31	
St Pancras International	a		14 05		14 15				14 35				14 45				15 05		15 15					15 35	
East Croydon	d			13 24		14 00				13 54					14 30			14 24		15 00					14 54
Clapham Junction	a			13 33		14 10				14 03					14 40			14 33		15 10					15 03
London Victoria	a			13 41		14 18				14 11					14 48			14 41		15 18					15 11

		TL ■	SN	SN ■	TL ■	SN ■		TL ■	SN ■	SN	GW ■	TL ■	SN ■	GW	TL ■	SN		SN ■	GW ■	TL ■	SN ■	TL ■	SN ■	SN	GW ■
Horsham	d	14 25				14 50		14 55					15 20		15 25						15 50	15 55			
Littlehaven	d	14 29						14 59							15 29							15 59			
Faygate	d																								
Ifield	d	14 35						15 05							15 35							16 05			
Crawley	d	14 38				14 59		15 08					15 29		15 38						15 59	16 08			
Three Bridges	a	14 42				15 03		15 12					15 33		15 42						16 03	16 12			
Three Bridges	d	14 43				15 04		15 13					15 34		15 43						16 04	16 13			
Gatwick Airport	a	14 47				15 08		15 17					15 38		15 47						16 08	16 17			
Gatwick Airport	d	14 49			15 03	15 09		15 19			15 30	15 33	15 39		15 49					16 03	16 09	16 19			16 30
Horley	d	14 51			15 05			15 21				15 35			15 51					16 05		16 21			
Salfords	d				15 09							15 39								16 09					
Earlswood (Surrey)	d				15 13							15 43								16 13					
Redhill	a	14 59			15 17			15 29			15 40	15 47			15 59					16 17		16 29			16 39
Redhill	d										15 44														16 44
Reigate	a										15 48														16 48
Redhill	d		15 00													16 00									
Tonbridge	a																								
Tonbridge	d									15 01														16 01	
Leigh (Kent)	a									15 05														16 05	
Penshurst	a									15 09														16 09	
Edenbridge	a									15 16														16 16	
Godstone	a									15 22														16 22	
Nutfield	a		15 04							15 28						16 04								16 28	
Reigate	d			15 00					15 30					15 48				16 00	16 04				16 30		
Redhill	a			15 04					15 34	15 36				15 52				16 04	16 08				16 34	16 36	
Redhill	d	14 59		15 11	15 19			15 29	15 41			15 49			15 59			16 11		16 19		16 29	16 41		
Merstham	d	15 03		15 15				15 33	15 45						16 03			16 15				16 33	16 45		
Coulsdon South	d	15 09		15 20				15 39	15 50						16 09			16 20				16 39	16 50		
Purley	d			15 25	15 28				15 55			15 58						16 25		16 28			16 55		
East Croydon	a	15 15		15 30	15 33	15 24		15 45	16 00			16 03	15 54		16 15			16 30		16 33	16 24	16 45	17 00		
East Croydon	d	15 15			15 33			15 45				16 03			16 15					16 33		16 45			
Norwood Junction	a				15 37							16 07								16 37					
London Bridge	a	15 30			15 50			16 00				16 20			16 30					16 50		17 00			
London Blackfriars	a	15 36			15 56			16 06				16 26			16 36					16 56		17 06			
City Thameslink	a	15 38			15 58			16 08				16 28			16 38					16 58		17 08			
Farringdon	a	15 41			16 01			16 11				16 31			16 41					17 01		17 11			
St Pancras International	a	15 45			16 05			16 15				16 35			16 45					17 05		17 15			
East Croydon	d			15 30		15 24			16 00				15 54					16 30			16 24		17 00		
Clapham Junction	a			15 40		15 33			16 10				16 03					16 40			16 33		17 10		
London Victoria	a			15 48		15 41			16 18				16 11					16 48			16 41		17 18		

Table T183-R

Saturdays

26 May to 8 December

Horsham / Gatwick Airport / Tonbridge / Reigate / Redhill - London

		TL ■		SN ■	GW	TL ■	SN	SN ■	GW ■	TL ■	SN ■	TL ■		SN ■	SN	GW ■	TL ■	SN ■	GW	TL ■	SN	SN ■		GW ■	TL ■
Horsham	d			16 22		16 25					16 50	16 55						17 20		17 25					
Littlehaven	d					16 29						16 59								17 29					
Faygate	d																								
Ifield	d					16 35						17 05								17 35					
Crawley	d			16 31		16 38					16 59	17 08						17 29		17 38					
Three Bridges	a			16 35		16 42					17 03	17 12						17 33		17 42					
Three Bridges	d			16 36		16 43					17 04	17 13						17 34		17 43					
Gatwick Airport	a			16 40		16 47					17 08	17 17						17 38		17 47					
Gatwick Airport	d	16 33		16 41		16 49				17 03	17 09	17 19				17 30	17 33	17 39		17 49					18 03
Horley	d	16 35				16 51				17 05		17 21					17 35			17 51					18 05
Salfords	d	16 39								17 09							17 39								18 09
Earlswood (Surrey)	d	16 43								17 13							17 43								18 13
Redhill	a	16 47				16 59				17 17		17 29				17 39	17 47			17 59					18 17
Redhill	d															17 44									
Reigate	a															17 48									
Redhill	d						17 00														18 00				
Tonbridge	a																								
Tonbridge	d														17 01										
Leigh (Kent)	a														17 05										
Penshurst	a														17 09										
Edenbridge	a														17 16										
Godstone	a														17 22										
Nutfield	a						17 04								17 28						18 04				
Reigate	d				16 51			17 00	17 04					17 30					17 51			18 00		18 04	
Redhill	a				16 56			17 04	17 09					17 34	17 36				17 55			18 04		18 08	
Redhill	d	16 49				16 59		17 11		17 19		17 29		17 41			17 49			17 59		18 11			18 19
Merstham	d					17 03		17 15				17 33		17 45						18 03		18 15			
Coulsdon South	d					17 09		17 20				17 39		17 50						18 09		18 20			
Purley	d	16 58						17 25		17 28				17 55			17 58					18 25			18 28
East Croydon	a	17 03		16 55		17 15		17 30		17 33	17 24	17 45		18 00			18 03	17 54		18 15		18 30			18 33
East Croydon	d	17 03				17 15				17 33		17 45					18 03			18 15					18 33
Norwood Junction	a	17 07								17 37							18 07								18 37
London Bridge	a	17 20				17 30				17 50		18 00					18 20			18 30					18 50
London Blackfriars	a	17 26				17 36				17 56		18 06					18 26			18 36					18 56
City Thameslink	a	17 28				17 38				17 58		18 08					18 28			18 38					18 58
Farringdon	a	17 31				17 41				18 01		18 11					18 31			18 41					19 01
St Pancras International	a	17 35				17 45				18 05		18 15					18 35			18 45					19 05
East Croydon	d			16 56				17 30			17 24			18 00				17 54				18 30			
Clapham Junction	a			17 05				17 40			17 33			18 10				18 03				18 40			
London Victoria	a			17 12				17 48			17 41			18 18				18 11				18 48			

		SN ■	TL ■	SN ■	SN	GW ■	TL ■	SN ■		GW	TL ■	SN	SN ■	GW ■	TL ■	SN ■	TL ■	SN ■		SN	GW ■	TL ■	SN ■	TL ■	SN
Horsham	d	17 50	17 55					18 20			18 25					18 50	18 55						19 20	19 25	
Littlehaven	d		17 59								18 29						18 59							19 29	
Faygate	d																								
Ifield	d		18 05								18 35						19 05							19 35	
Crawley	d	17 59	18 08					18 29			18 38					18 59	19 08						19 29	19 38	
Three Bridges	a	18 03	18 12					18 33			18 42					19 03	19 12						19 33	19 42	
Three Bridges	d	18 04	18 13					18 34			18 43					19 04	19 13						19 34	19 43	
Gatwick Airport	a	18 08	18 17					18 38			18 47					19 08	19 17						19 38	19 47	
Gatwick Airport	d	18 09	18 19			18 30	18 33	18 39			18 49				19 03	19 09	19 19				19 30	19 33	19 39	19 49	
Horley	d		18 21				18 35				18 51				19 05		19 21					19 35		19 51	
Salfords	d						18 39								19 09							19 39			
Earlswood (Surrey)	d						18 43								19 13							19 43			
Redhill	a		18 29			18 39	18 47				18 59				19 17		19 29				19 39	19 47		19 59	
Redhill	d					18 44															19 44				
Reigate	a					18 48															19 48				
Redhill	d											19 00													20 00
Tonbridge	a																								
Tonbridge	d				18 01															19 01					
Leigh (Kent)	a				18 05															19 05					
Penshurst	a				18 09															19 09					
Edenbridge	a				18 16															19 16					
Godstone	a				18 22															19 22					
Nutfield	a				18 28							19 04								19 28					20 04
Reigate	d			18 30						18 51			19 00	19 04				19 30							
Redhill	a			18 34	18 36					18 55			19 04	19 08				19 34		19 36					
Redhill	d		18 29	18 41			18 49				18 59		19 11		19 19		19 29	19 41				19 49		19 59	
Merstham	d		18 33	18 45							19 03		19 15				19 33	19 45						20 03	
Coulsdon South	d		18 39	18 50							19 09		19 20				19 39	19 50						20 09	
Purley	d			18 55			18 58						19 25		19 28			19 55				19 58			
East Croydon	a	18 24	18 45	19 00			19 03	18 54			19 15		19 30		19 33	19 24	19 45	20 00				20 03	19 54	20 15	
East Croydon	d		18 45				19 03				19 15				19 33		19 45					20 03		20 15	
Norwood Junction	a						19 07								19 37							20 07			
London Bridge	a		19 00				19 20				19 30				19 50		20 00					20 20		20 30	
London Blackfriars	a		19 06				19 26				19 36				19 56		20 06					20 26		20 36	
City Thameslink	a		19 08				19 28				19 38				19 58		20 08					20 28		20 38	
Farringdon	a		19 11				19 31				19 41				20 01		20 11					20 31		20 41	
St Pancras International	a		19 15				19 35				19 45				20 05		20 15					20 35		20 45	
East Croydon	d	18 24		19 00				18 54					19 30			19 24		20 00					19 54		
Clapham Junction	a	18 33		19 10				19 03					19 40			19 33		20 10					20 03		
London Victoria	a	18 41		19 18				19 11					19 48			19 41		20 18					20 11		

Table T183-R

Horsham / Gatwick Airport / Tonbridge / Reigate / Redhill - London

Saturdays
26 May to 8 December

		SN	GW ■	TL ■	SN ■	TL ■	SN ■	SN	GW ■	GW ■	TL ■	SN ■	TL ■	GW	SN	SN ■	GW ■	GW ■	TL ■	SN ■	TL ■	SN ■
Horsham	d				19 50	19 55						20 20	20 25							20 50	20 55	
Littlehaven	d					19 59							20 29								20 59	
Faygate	d																					
Ifield	d					20 05							20 35								21 05	
Crawley	d				19 59	20 08						20 29	20 38							20 59	21 08	
Three Bridges	a				20 03	20 12						20 33	20 42							21 03	21 12	
Three Bridges	d				20 04	20 13						20 34	20 43							21 04	21 13	
Gatwick Airport	a				20 08	20 17						20 38	20 47							21 08	21 17	
Gatwick Airport	d			20 03	20 09	20 19			20 30		20 33	20 39	20 49				21 00		21 03	21 09	21 19	
Horley	d			20 05		20 21					20 35		20 51						21 05		21 21	
Salfords	d			20 09							20 39								21 09			
Earlswood (Surrey)	d			20 13							20 43								21 13			
Redhill	a			20 17		20 29			20 39		20 47		20 59				21 09		21 17		21 29	
Redhill	d								20 44								21 14					
Reigate	a								20 48								21 18					
Redhill	d														21 00							
Tonbridge	a																					
Tonbridge	d							20 01														
Leigh (Kent)	a							20 05														
Penshurst	a							20 09														
Edenbridge	a							20 16														
Godstone	a							20 22														
Nutfield	a							20 28							21 04							
Reigate	d	20 00	20 04				20 30			20 34				20 56		21 00		21 04				21 30
Redhill	a	20 04	20 08				20 34	20 36		20 38				21 00		21 04		21 08				21 34
Redhill	d	20 11		20 19		20 29	20 41				20 49		20 59			21 11			21 19		21 29	21 41
Merstham	d	20 15				20 33	20 45						21 03			21 15					21 33	21 45
Coulsdon South	d	20 20				20 39	20 50						21 09			21 20					21 39	21 50
Purley	d	20 25		20 28			20 55				20 58					21 25			21 28			21 55
East Croydon	a	20 30		20 33	20 24	20 45	21 00				21 03	20 54	21 15			21 30			21 33	21 24	21 45	22 00
East Croydon	d			20 33		20 45					21 03		21 15						21 33		21 45	
Norwood Junction	a			20 37							21 07								21 37			
London Bridge	a			20 50		21 00					21 20		21 30						21 50		22 00	
London Blackfriars	a			20 56		21 06					21 26		21 36						21 56		22 06	
City Thameslink	a			20 58																		
Farringdon	a			21 01		21 11					21 31		21 41						22 01		22 11	
St Pancras International	a			21 05		21 15					21 35		21 45						22 05		22 15	
East Croydon	d	20 30			20 24		21 00					20 54				21 30				21 24		22 00
Clapham Junction	a	20 40			20 33		21 10					21 03				21 40				21 33		22 10
London Victoria	a	20 48			20 41		21 18					21 11				21 48				21 41		22 18

		SN	GW ■	TL ■	SN ■	TL ■	SN	GW ■	SN ■	SN ■	TL ■	SN ■	SN ■	SN	GW ■	TL ■	SN	SN ■	SN	GW ■	TL ■	SN ■	GW ■
Horsham	d				21 20	21 25			21 50		21 55	22 20				22 25					23 11	23 27	
Littlehaven	d					21 29					21 59					22 29					23 15		
Faygate	d																						
Ifield	d					21 35					22 05					22 35					23 21		
Crawley	d				21 29	21 38			21 59		22 08	22 29				22 38					23 24	23 36	
Three Bridges	a				21 33	21 42			22 03		22 12	22 33				22 42					23 28	23 40	
Three Bridges	d				21 34	21 43			22 04		22 13	22 34				22 43					23 29		
Gatwick Airport	a				21 38	21 47			22 08		22 17	22 38				22 47					23 33		
Gatwick Airport	d			21 33	21 39	21 49		22 00	22 09		22 19	22 39				22 49				23 18	23 35		
Horley	d			21 35		21 51					22 21					22 51					23 37		
Salfords	d			21 39																	23 41		
Earlswood (Surrey)	d			21 43																	23 45		
Redhill	a			21 47		21 59		22 09			22 29					22 59				23 27	23 49		
Redhill	d							22 12												23 31			
Reigate	a							22 16												23 35			
Redhill	d						22 00										23 00						
Tonbridge	a																						
Tonbridge	d	21 01												22 01					23 03				
Leigh (Kent)	a	21 05												22 05					23 07				
Penshurst	a	21 09												22 09					23 11				
Edenbridge	a	21 16												22 16					23 18				
Godstone	a	21 22												22 22					23 24				
Nutfield	a	21 28					22 04							22 28			23 04		23 30				
Reigate	d		21 36							22 00			22 30		22 36			23 00					23 55
Redhill	a	21 36	21 40							22 04			22 34	22 36	22 40			23 04	23 36				23 59
Redhill	d			21 49		21 59				22 11	22 29		22 41			22 59		23 11			23 49		
Merstham	d					22 03				22 15	22 33		22 45			23 03		23 15			23 53		
Coulsdon South	d					22 09				22 20	22 39		22 50			23 09		23 20			23 59		
Purley	d			21 58						22 25			22 55					23 25			00 03		
East Croydon	a			22 03	21 54	22 15			22 24	22 30	22 45	22 54	23 00			23 15		23 30			00 09		
East Croydon	d			22 03		22 15					22 45					23 15					00 10		
Norwood Junction	a			22 07																			
London Bridge	a			22 20		22 30					23 00					23 30							
London Blackfriars	a			22 26		22 36					23 06					23 36					00 36		
City Thameslink	a																						
Farringdon	a			22 31		22 41					23 11					23 41					00 41		
St Pancras International	a			22 35		22 45					23 15					23 45					00 45		
East Croydon	d				21 54				22 24	22 30		22 54	23 00					23 30					
Clapham Junction	a				22 03				22 33	22 40		23 04	23 10					23 41					
London Victoria	a				22 11				22 41	22 48		23 11	23 18					23 50					

Table T183-R

Horsham / Gatwick Airport / Tonbridge / Reigate / Redhill - London

Sundays
20 May to 2 December

		SN	GW ■ A	TL ■	SN ■	SN ■	SN ■	TL ■	SN	SN	GW	TL ■	SN	GW	SN	SN	SN	SN	TL ■	GW	GW	SN	SN
Horsham	d								06 01	06 31		06 39			07 05				07 35				08 18
Littlehaven	d								06 04	06 34		06 42							07 38				
Faygate	d																						
Ifield	d								06 10	06 40		06 48							07 44				
Crawley	d								06 14	06 44		06 52			07 14				07 48				08 27
Three Bridges	a								06 19	06 47		06 55			07 19				07 51				08 30
Three Bridges	d			00 37	03 08	04 08	04 58	05 52	06 23	06 49		06 56			07 23				07 52				08 31
Gatwick Airport	a			00 41	03 12	04 12	05 02	05 56	06 27	06 53		07 01			07 27				07 57				08 35
Gatwick Airport	d			00 42	03 13	04 13	05 03	05 58	06 28	06 54		07 02		07 11	07 28			07 54	07 58		08 18	08 25	08 36
Horley	d			00 45	03 16	04 16	05 06	06 00				07 04							08 00				
Salfords	d							06 04				07 08							08 04				
Earlswood (Surrey)	d							06 08				07 12							08 08				
Redhill	a			00 52				06 12	06 36	07 03		07 16		07 17	07 36			08 03	08 12		08 26	08 34	08 44
Redhill	d													07 20							08 29		
Reigate	a													07 23							08 33		
Redhill	d	00 15														07 50							
Tonbridge	a																						
Tonbridge	d												07 00				07 29						
Leigh (Kent)	a												07 04				07 33						
Penshurst	a												07 08				07 37						
Edenbridge	a	00 26											07 14				07 43						
Godstone	a												07 21				07 50						
Nutfield	a												07 27			07 54	07 56						
Reigate	d		00 45								07 04									08 13			
Redhill	a		00 49								07 08		07 32				08 01			08 17			
Redhill	d			00 53				06 12	06 37	07 03		07 16			07 37			08 03	08 12			08 34	08 45
Merstham	d							06 16		07 07								08 07	08 16				
Coulsdon South	d							06 21		07 12								08 12	08 21				08 52
Purley	d			01 03	03 30	04 29	05 23	06 25		07 16		07 25						08 16	08 25				
East Croydon	a			01 09	03 36	04 35	05 29	06 31	06 50	07 22		07 31			07 50			08 22	08 31			08 45	08 58
East Croydon	d			01 10				06 32				07 32							08 32				
Norwood Junction	a							06 36				07 36							08 36				
London Bridge	a							06 50				07 50							08 50				
London Blackfriars	a			01 36																			
City Thameslink	a																						
Farringdon	a																						
St Pancras International	a			01 45																			
East Croydon	d				03 37	04 36	05 30		06 51	07 23					07 51			08 23				08 46	08 59
Clapham Junction	a				03 50	04 49	05 51		07 05	07 37					08 07			08 38				08 55	09 08
London Victoria	a				03 58	04 58	05 59		07 15	07 46					08 15			08 46				09 02	09 15

		TL ■	SN	SN	TL ■	GW ■	SN	TL ■	SN	GW	GW	TL ■	SN	TL ■	SN	TL ■	GW ■	SN	TL ■	SN	GW	GW	TL ■
Horsham	d							08 48					09 22						09 48				
Littlehaven	d							08 51											09 51				
Faygate	d																						
Ifield	d							08 57											09 57				
Crawley	d							09 01					09 31						10 01				
Three Bridges	a							09 04					09 35						10 04				
Three Bridges	d				08 43			09 05				09 13	09 35			09 43			10 05				
Gatwick Airport	a				08 47			09 10				09 17	09 40			09 47			10 10				
Gatwick Airport	d	08 46			08 49			09 11			09 17	09 19	09 41	09 46		09 49			10 11			10 17	10 19
Horley	d				08 51			09 13				09 21				09 51			10 13				10 21
Salfords	d				08 55							09 25				09 55							10 25
Earlswood (Surrey)	d				08 59							09 29				09 59							10 29
Redhill	a	08 54			09 03			09 21			09 26	09 33	09 49	09 54		10 03			10 21			10 26	10 33
Redhill	d										09 28											10 28	
Reigate	a										09 31											10 32	
Redhill	d		08 48						09 11											10 07			
Tonbridge	a																						
Tonbridge	d			08 29											09 29								
Leigh (Kent)	a			08 33											09 33								
Penshurst	a			08 37											09 37								
Edenbridge	a			08 43											09 43								
Godstone	a			08 50											09 50								
Nutfield	a		08 52	08 56					09 15						09 56					10 11			
Reigate	d					09 02	09 06			09 17							10 02	10 06			10 17		
Redhill	a			09 00		09 06	09 10			09 24					10 00		10 06	10 10			10 24		
Redhill	d	08 54			09 03		09 11	09 21				09 33	09 50	09 54		10 03		10 11	10 21				10 33
Merstham	d						09 15	09 25										10 15	10 25				
Coulsdon South	d						09 20	09 30					09 57					10 20	10 30				
Purley	d				09 12		09 25					09 42				10 12		10 25					10 42
East Croydon	a	09 06			09 17		09 29	09 37				09 47	10 03	10 07		10 17		10 29	10 37				10 47
East Croydon	d	09 07			09 18			09 37				09 48		10 07		10 18			10 37				10 48
Norwood Junction	a	09 11						09 41						10 11					10 41				
London Bridge	a	09 24			09 32			09 54				10 02		10 24		10 32			10 54				11 02
London Blackfriars	a	09 30			09 38			10 00				10 08		10 30		10 38			11 00				11 08
City Thameslink	a																						
Farringdon	a	09 35			09 43			10 05				10 13		10 35		10 43			11 05				11 13
St Pancras International	a	09 39			09 47			10 09				10 17		10 39		10 47			11 09				11 17
East Croydon	d						09 30						10 04					10 30					
Clapham Junction	a						09 39						10 14					10 39					
London Victoria	a						09 47						10 21					10 47					

A not 20 May

Horsham / Gatwick Airport / Tonbridge / Reigate / Redhill - London

		SN		TL ■	SN	TL ■	GW ■	SN	TL ■	SN	GW	GW		TL ■	SN	TL ■	SN	TL ■	GW ■	SN	TL ■	SN		GW	GW
Horsham	d	10 22							10 48						11 22						11 48				
Littlehaven	d								10 51												11 51				
Faygate	d																								
Ifield	d								10 57												11 57				
Crawley	d	10 31							11 01						11 31						12 01				
Three Bridges	a	10 35							11 04						11 35						12 04				
Three Bridges	d	10 35				10 43			11 05						11 35			11 43			12 05				
Gatwick Airport	a	10 40				10 47			11 10						11 40			11 47			12 10				
Gatwick Airport	d	10 41		10 46		10 49			11 11			11 17		11 19	11 41	11 46		11 49			12 11				12 17
Horley	d					10 51			11 13					11 21				11 51			12 13				
Salfords	d					10 55								11 25				11 55							
Earlswood (Surrey)	d					10 59								11 29				11 59							
Redhill	a	10 49		10 54		11 03			11 21			11 26		11 33	11 49	11 54		12 03			12 21				12 26
Redhill	d											11 28													12 28
Reigate	a											11 31													12 32
Redhill	d									11 07												12 07			
Tonbridge	a																								
Tonbridge	d				10 29												11 29								
Leigh (Kent)	a				10 33												11 33								
Penshurst	a				10 37												11 37								
Edenbridge	a				10 43												11 43								
Godstone	a				10 50												11 50								
Nutfield	a				10 56					11 11							11 56					12 11			
Reigate	d						11 02	11 06			11 17								12 02	12 06				12 17	
Redhill	a				11 00		11 06	11 10			11 24						12 00		12 06	12 10				12 24	
Redhill	d	10 50		10 54		11 03		11 11	11 21					11 33	11 50	11 54		12 03		12 11	12 21				
Merstham	d							11 15	11 25											12 15	12 25				
Coulsdon South	d	10 57						11 20	11 30						11 57					12 20	12 30				
Purley	d					11 12		11 25						11 42				12 12		12 25					
East Croydon	a	11 03		11 07		11 17		11 29	11 37					11 47	12 03	12 07		12 17		12 29	12 37				
East Croydon	d			11 07		11 18			11 37					11 48		12 07		12 18			12 37				
Norwood Junction	a			11 11					11 41							12 11					12 41				
London Bridge	a			11 24		11 32			11 54					12 02		12 24		12 32			12 54				
London Blackfriars	a			11 30		11 38			12 00					12 08		12 30		12 38			13 00				
City Thameslink	a																								
Farringdon	a			11 35		11 43			12 05					12 13		12 35		12 45			13 05				
St Pancras International	a			11 39		11 47			12 09					12 17		12 39		12 49			13 09				
East Croydon	d	11 04						11 30							12 04					12 30					
Clapham Junction	a	11 14						11 39							12 14					12 39					
London Victoria	a	11 21						11 47							12 21					12 47					

		TL ■	SN	TL ■	SN	TL ■	GW ■	SN		TL ■	SN	GW	GW	TL ■	SN	TL ■	SN	TL ■		GW ■	SN	TL ■	SN	GW	GW
Horsham	d		12 22							12 48					13 22							13 48			
Littlehaven	d									12 51												13 51			
Faygate	d																								
Ifield	d									12 57												13 57			
Crawley	d		12 31							13 01					13 31							14 01			
Three Bridges	a		12 35							13 04					13 35							14 04			
Three Bridges	d		12 35			12 43				13 05					13 35			13 43				14 05			
Gatwick Airport	a		12 40			12 47				13 10					13 40			13 47				14 10			
Gatwick Airport	d	12 19	12 41	12 46		12 49				13 11			13 17	13 19	13 41	13 46		13 49				14 11			14 17
Horley	d	12 21				12 51				13 13				13 21				13 51				14 13			
Salfords	d	12 25				12 55								13 25				13 55							
Earlswood (Surrey)	d	12 29				12 59								13 29				13 59							
Redhill	a	12 33	12 49	12 54		13 03				13 21			13 26	13 33	13 49	13 54		14 03				14 21			14 26
Redhill	d												13 28												14 28
Reigate	a												13 31												14 32
Redhill	d										13 07												14 07		
Tonbridge	a																								
Tonbridge	d				12 29												13 29								
Leigh (Kent)	a				12 33												13 33								
Penshurst	a				12 37												13 37								
Edenbridge	a				12 43												13 43								
Godstone	a				12 50												13 50								
Nutfield	a				12 56						13 11						13 56						14 11		
Reigate	d						13 02	13 06				13 17								14 02	14 06			14 17	
Redhill	a				13 00		13 06	13 10				13 24					14 00			14 06	14 10			14 24	
Redhill	d	12 33	12 50	12 54		13 03		13 11		13 21				13 33	13 50	13 54		14 03			14 11	14 21			
Merstham	d							13 15		13 25											14 15	14 25			
Coulsdon South	d		12 57					13 20		13 30					13 57						14 20	14 30			
Purley	d	12 42				13 12		13 25						13 42				14 12			14 25				
East Croydon	a	12 47	13 06	13 06		13 17		13 29		13 37				13 47	14 03	14 07		14 17			14 29	14 37			
East Croydon	d	12 48		13 07		13 18				13 37				13 48		14 07		14 18				14 37			
Norwood Junction	a			13 11						13 41						14 11						14 41			
London Bridge	a	13 02		13 24		13 32				13 54				14 02		14 24		14 32				14 54			
London Blackfriars	a	13 08		13 30		13 38				14 00				14 08		14 30		14 38				15 00			
City Thameslink	a																								
Farringdon	a	13 13		13 35		13 43				14 05				14 13		14 35		14 43				15 05			
St Pancras International	a	13 17		13 39		13 47				14 09				14 17		14 39		14 47				15 09			
East Croydon	d		13 06					13 30							14 04						14 30				
Clapham Junction	a		13 16					13 39							14 14						14 39				
London Victoria	a		13 23					13 47							14 21						14 47				

Table T183-R

Sundays

20 May to 2 December

Horsham / Gatwick Airport / Tonbridge / Reigate / Redhill - London

		TL ■	SN	TL ■		SN	TL ■	GW ■	SN	TL ■	SN	GW	GW	TL ■		SN	TL ■	SN	TL ■	GW ■	SN	TL ■	SN	GW	
Horsham	d		14 21							14 48						15 22						15 48			
Littlehaven	d									14 51												15 51			
Faygate	d																								
Ifield	d									14 57												15 57			
Crawley	d		14 30							15 01						15 31						16 01			
Three Bridges	a		14 35							15 04						15 35						16 04			
Three Bridges	d		14 35				14 43			15 05						15 35			15 43			16 05			
Gatwick Airport	a		14 40				14 47			15 10						15 40			15 47			16 10			
Gatwick Airport	d	14 19	14 41	14 46			14 49			15 11			15 17	15 19		15 41	15 46		15 49			16 11			
Horley	d	14 21					14 51			15 13				15 21					15 51			16 13			
Salfords	d	14 25					14 55							15 25					15 55						
Earlswood (Surrey)	d	14 29					14 59							15 29					15 59						
Redhill	a	14 33	14 49	14 54			15 03			15 21			15 26	15 33		15 49	15 54		16 03			16 21			
Redhill	d												15 28												
Reigate	a												15 31												
Redhill	d										15 07												16 07		
Tonbridge	a																								
Tonbridge	d					14 29												15 29							
Leigh (Kent)	a					14 33												15 33							
Penshurst	a					14 37												15 37							
Edenbridge	a					14 43												15 43							
Godstone	a					14 50												15 50							
Nutfield	a					14 56					15 11							15 56					16 11		
Reigate	d							15 02	15 06			15 17								16 02	16 06			16 17	
Redhill	a					15 00		15 06	15 10			15 24						16 00		16 06	16 10			16 24	
Redhill	d	14 33	14 50	14 54			15 03		15 11	15 21				15 33		15 50	15 54		16 03		16 11	16 21			
Merstham	d								15 15	15 25											16 15	16 25			
Coulsdon South	d		14 57						15 20	15 30						15 57					16 20	16 30			
Purley	d	14 42					15 12		15 25					15 42					16 12		16 25				
East Croydon	a	14 47	15 03	15 07			15 17		15 29	15 37				15 47		16 06	16 06		16 17		16 29	16 37			
East Croydon	d	14 48		15 07			15 18			15 37				15 48			16 07		16 18			16 37			
Norwood Junction	a			15 11						15 41							16 11					16 41			
London Bridge	a	15 02		15 24			15 32			15 54				16 02			16 24		16 32			16 54			
London Blackfriars	a	15 08		15 30			15 38			16 00				16 08			16 30		16 38			17 00			
City Thameslink	a																								
Farringdon	a	15 13		15 35			15 43			16 05				16 13			16 35		16 43			17 05			
St Pancras International	a	15 17		15 39			15 47			16 09				16 17			16 39		16 47			17 09			
East Croydon	d		15 04						15 30							16 06					16 30				
Clapham Junction	a		15 14						15 39							16 16					16 39				
London Victoria	a		15 21						15 47							16 23					16 47				

		GW	TL ■	SN	TL ■	SN	TL ■	GW ■	SN	TL ■		SN	GW	GW	TL ■	SN	TL ■	SN	TL ■	GW ■		SN	TL ■	SN	GW
Horsham	d			16 22						16 48						17 22							17 48		
Littlehaven	d									16 51													17 51		
Faygate	d																								
Ifield	d									16 57													17 57		
Crawley	d			16 31						17 01						17 31							18 01		
Three Bridges	a			16 35						17 04						17 35							18 04		
Three Bridges	d			16 35			16 43			17 05						17 35			17 43				18 05		
Gatwick Airport	a			16 40			16 47			17 10						17 40			17 47				18 10		
Gatwick Airport	d	16 17	16 19	16 41	16 46		16 49			17 11				17 17	17 19	17 41	17 46		17 49				18 11		
Horley	d		16 21				16 51			17 13					17 21				17 51				18 13		
Salfords	d		16 25				16 55								17 25				17 55						
Earlswood (Surrey)	d		16 29				16 59								17 29				17 59						
Redhill	a	16 26	16 33	16 49	16 54		17 03			17 21				17 26	17 33	17 49	17 54		18 03				18 21		
Redhill	d	16 28												17 28											
Reigate	a	16 32												17 31											
Redhill	d											17 07												18 07	
Tonbridge	a																								
Tonbridge	d					16 29												17 29							
Leigh (Kent)	a					16 33												17 33							
Penshurst	a					16 37												17 37							
Edenbridge	a					16 43												17 43							
Godstone	a					16 50												17 50							
Nutfield	a					16 56						17 11						17 56						18 11	
Reigate	d							17 02	17 06				17 17							18 02		18 06			18 17
Redhill	a					17 00		17 06	17 10				17 24					18 00		18 06		18 10			18 24
Redhill	d		16 33	16 50	16 54		17 03		17 11	17 21					17 33	17 50	17 54		18 03			18 11	18 21		
Merstham	d								17 15	17 25												18 15	18 25		
Coulsdon South	d			16 57					17 20	17 30						17 57						18 20	18 30		
Purley	d		16 42				17 12		17 25						17 42				18 12			18 25			
East Croydon	a		16 47	17 06	17 06		17 17		17 29	17 37					17 47	18 03	18 07		18 17			18 29	18 37		
East Croydon	d		16 48		17 07		17 18			17 37					17 48		18 07		18 18				18 37		
Norwood Junction	a				17 11					17 41							18 11						18 41		
London Bridge	a		17 02		17 24		17 32			17 54					18 02		18 24		18 32				18 54		
London Blackfriars	a		17 08		17 30		17 38			18 00					18 08		18 30		18 38				19 00		
City Thameslink	a																								
Farringdon	a		17 13		17 35		17 43			18 05					18 13		18 35		18 43				19 05		
St Pancras International	a		17 17		17 39		17 47			18 09					18 17		18 39		18 47				19 09		
East Croydon	d			17 06					17 30							18 04						18 30			
Clapham Junction	a			17 16					17 39							18 14						18 39			
London Victoria	a			17 23					17 47							18 21						18 47			

Table T183-R

Sundays

20 May to 2 December

Horsham / Gatwick Airport / Tonbridge / Reigate / Redhill - London

		GW	TL ■	SN	TL ■	SN		TL ■	GW ■	SN	TL ■	SN	GW	GW	TL ■	SN		TL ■	SN	TL ■	GW ■	SN	TL ■	SN	GW
Horsham	d			18 22							18 48					19 22							19 48		
Littlehaven	d										18 51												19 51		
Faygate	d																								
Ifield	d										18 57												19 57		
Crawley	d			18 31							19 01					19 31							20 01		
Three Bridges	a			18 35							19 04					19 35							20 04		
Three Bridges	d			18 35				18 43			19 05					19 35				19 43			20 05		
Gatwick Airport	a			18 40				18 47			19 10					19 40				19 47			20 10		
Gatwick Airport	d	18 17	18 19	18 41	18 46			18 49			19 11			19 17	19 19	19 41		19 46		19 49			20 11		
Horley	d		18 21					18 51			19 13				19 21					19 51			20 13		
Salfords	d		18 25					18 55							19 25					19 55					
Earlswood (Surrey)	d		18 29					18 59							19 29					19 59					
Redhill	a	18 26	18 33	18 49	18 54			19 03			19 21			19 26	19 33	19 49		19 54		20 03			20 21		
Redhill	d	18 28												19 28											
Reigate	a	18 32												19 31											
Redhill	d											19 07												20 07	
Tonbridge	a																								
Tonbridge	d					18 29													19 29						
Leigh (Kent)	a					18 33													19 33						
Penshurst	a					18 37													19 37						
Edenbridge	a					18 43													19 43						
Godstone	a					18 50													19 50						
Nutfield	a					18 56						19 11							19 56					20 11	
Reigate	d								19 02	19 06			19 17								20 02	20 06			20 17
Redhill	a					19 00			19 06	19 10			19 24						20 00		20 06	20 10			20 24
Redhill	d		18 33	18 50	18 54			19 03		19 11	19 21				19 33	19 50		19 54		20 03		20 11	20 21		
Merstham	d									19 15	19 25											20 15	20 25		
Coulsdon South	d			18 57						19 20	19 30					19 57						20 20	20 30		
Purley	d		18 42					19 12		19 25					19 42					20 12		20 25			
East Croydon	a		18 47	19 03	19 07			19 17		19 29	19 37				19 47	20 03		20 07		20 17		20 29	20 37		
East Croydon	d		18 48		19 07			19 18			19 37				19 48			20 07		20 18			20 37		
Norwood Junction	a				19 11						19 41							20 11					20 41		
London Bridge	a		19 02		19 24			19 32			19 54				20 02			20 24		20 32			20 54		
London Blackfriars	a		19 08		19 30			19 38			20 00				20 08			20 30		20 38			21 00		
City Thameslink	a																								
Farringdon	a		19 13		19 35			19 43			20 05				20 13			20 35		20 43			21 05		
St Pancras International	a		19 17		19 39			19 47			20 09				20 17			20 39		20 47			21 09		
East Croydon	d			19 04						19 30						20 04						20 30			
Clapham Junction	a			19 14						19 39						20 14						20 39			
London Victoria	a			19 21						19 47						20 21						20 47			

		GW		TL ■	SN	TL ■	SN	TL ■	SN	SN	GW ■	TL ■		TL ■	GW ■	SN	TL ■	SN	SN	TL ■	SN	GW		GW	TL ■
Horsham	d				20 22							20 48				21 22				21 48					
Littlehaven	d											20 51								21 51					
Faygate	d																								
Ifield	d											20 57								21 57					
Crawley	d				20 31							21 01				21 31				22 01					
Three Bridges	a				20 35							21 04				21 35				22 04					
Three Bridges	d				20 35			20 43				21 05				21 35				22 05					22 31
Gatwick Airport	a				20 40			20 47				21 10				21 40				22 10					22 35
Gatwick Airport	d	20 17		20 19	20 41	20 46		20 49			21 07	21 11		21 19		21 41	21 46			22 11		22 18			22 39
Horley	d			20 21				20 51				21 13		21 21						22 13					22 42
Salfords	d			20 25				20 55						21 25						22 17					22 46
Earlswood (Surrey)	d			20 29				20 59						21 29						22 21					22 49
Redhill	a	20 26		20 33	20 49	20 54		21 03			21 16	21 21		21 33		21 49	21 54			22 25		22 26			22 53
Redhill	d	20 30									21 19											22 29			
Reigate	a	20 34									21 22											22 32			
Redhill	d									21 07											22 07				
Tonbridge	a																								
Tonbridge	d						20 29											21 29							
Leigh (Kent)	a						20 33											21 33							
Penshurst	a						20 37											21 37							
Edenbridge	a						20 43											21 43							
Godstone	a						20 50											21 50							
Nutfield	a						20 56			21 11								21 56			22 11				
Reigate	d								21 06						21 37				22 06					22 29	
Redhill	a						21 00		21 10						21 43			22 00	22 10					22 35	
Redhill	d			20 33	20 50	20 54		21 03	21 11			21 21		21 33		21 50	21 54		22 11	22 25					22 54
Merstham	d								21 15			21 25							22 15	22 29					22 58
Coulsdon South	d				20 57				21 20			21 30				21 57			22 20	22 34					23 03
Purley	d			20 42				21 12	21 25					21 42					22 25	22 38					23 07
East Croydon	a			20 47	21 03	21 07		21 17	21 29			21 37		21 47		22 03	22 07		22 29	22 45					23 12
East Croydon	d			20 48		21 07		21 18				21 37		21 48			22 07			22 47					23 12
Norwood Junction	a					21 11						21 41					22 11			22 51					23 16
London Bridge	a			21 02		21 24		21 32				21 54		22 02			22 24			23 04					23 30
London Blackfriars	a			21 08		21 30		21 38				22 00		22 08			22 30			23 10					
City Thameslink	a																								
Farringdon	a			21 13		21 35		21 43				22 05		22 13			22 35			23 16					
St Pancras International	a			21 17		21 39		21 47				22 09		22 17			22 39			23 20					
East Croydon	d				21 04				21 30							22 04			22 30						
Clapham Junction	a				21 14				21 39							22 14			22 39						
London Victoria	a				21 21				21 47							22 21			22 47						

Table T183-R

Sundays

20 May to 2 December

Horsham / Gatwick Airport / Tonbridge / Reigate / Redhill - London

		SN	SN	TL ■	SN	GW	GW ■	SN		SN
Horsham	d	22 22		22 41						23 14
Littlehaven	d			22 44						23 17
Faygate	d									
Ifield	d			22 50						23 23
Crawley	d	22 31		22 54						23 27
Three Bridges	a	22 35		22 58						23 30
Three Bridges	d	22 35						23 25		23 31
Gatwick Airport	a	22 40						23 29		23 35
Gatwick Airport	d	22 41				23 08		23 30		23 36
Horley	d									23 38
Salfords	d									
Earlswood (Surrey)	d									
Redhill	a	22 49				23 16		23 38		23 46
Redhill	d					23 19				
Reigate	a					23 22				
Redhill	d				23 07					
Tonbridge	a									
Tonbridge	d		22 29							
Leigh (Kent)	a		22 33							
Penshurst	a		22 37							
Edenbridge	a		22 43							
Godstone	a		22 50							
Nutfield	a		22 56		23 11					
Reigate	d						23 29			
Redhill	a		23 00				23 35			
Redhill	d	22 50						23 38		23 47
Merstham	d									23 51
Coulsdon South	d	22 57								23 56
Purley	d									23 59
East Croydon	a	23 03						23 51		00 05
East Croydon	d									
Norwood Junction	a									
London Bridge	a									
London Blackfriars	a									
City Thameslink	a									
Farringdon	a									
St Pancras International	a									
East Croydon	d	23 04						23 52		00 06
Clapham Junction	a	23 14						00 08		00 18
London Victoria	a	23 21						00 17		00 27

Table T184-F

Mondays to Fridays

21 May to 7 December

London - Gatwick Airport - Haywards Heath - Brighton/Hove/Lewes

Miles	Miles			SN MX		TL MO	TL MX	TL	TL	TL	GX	TL	SN	GX	TL	GX	TL	GX	TL	GX	SN	GX	TL
0	—	London Victoria	d	00 02							05 14		05 32	06 00		06 13		06 30		06 43	06 46	07 00	
2¾	—	Clapham Junction	d	00 09									05 39								06 53		
10½	—	East Croydon	a	00 23									05 51								07 02		
—	0	St Pancras International	d			00 51	00 52	04 02	04 32	04 51		05 20			05 50		06 00		06 20				06 50
—	1¼	Farringdon	d							04 56		05 24			05 54		06 04		06 24				06 54
—	1¾	City Thameslink	d							04 58		05 26			05 56		06 06		06 26				06 56
—	2	London Blackfriars	d			01 01	01 02	04 10	04 40	05 01		05 29			05 59		06 09		06 29				06 59
—	—	London Bridge	d									05 35			06 05		06 15		06 35				07 05
—	—	East Croydon	a			01 27	01 28	04 36	05 06	05 27		05 48			06 18		06 28		06 48				07 18
—	12¾	East Croydon	d	00 24		01 28	01 28	04 37	05 07	05 28		05 49	05 52		06 19		06 29		06 49		07 03		07 19
26¾	29	Gatwick Airport	a	00 43		01 56	01 56	04 57	05 31	05 47	05 47	06 04	06 17	06 28	06 34	06 41	06 44	06 58	07 04	07 11	07 17	07 28	07 34
—	—	Gatwick Airport	d	00 44		01 58	01 58	04 58	05 32	05 48	05 51	06 05	06 18	06 31	06 35	06 42	06 45	07 00	07 05	07 12	07 20	07 31	07 35
29¼	31½	Three Bridges	a	00 48		02 03	02 03	05 03	05 37	05 53		06 09	06 23		06 39		06 49		07 09		07 24		07 39
—	—	Three Bridges	d	00 49		02 04	02 04	05 04	05 38	05 54		06 10	06 23		06 40		06 50		07 10		07 24		07 40
—	36	**Balcombe**	d							06 00		06 16			06 46				07 16				07 46
37¾	40	**Haywards Heath**	a	00 58		02 13	02 13	05 13	05 47	06 05		06 21	06 32		06 51		06 59		07 21		07 33		07 51
—	—	**Haywards Heath**	d	01 02	01 08	02 14	02 14	05 14	05 48	06 06		06 22	06 33		06 54		06 59		07 24		07 34		07 54
40¼	43	**Wivelsfield**	d						05 52	06 10		06 26	06 37		06 58				07 28				07 58
41½	43¾	**Burgess Hill**	d						05 54	06 12		06 28			07 00		07 05		07 30			07 44	08 00
43¾	46	**Hassocks**	d						05 58	06 16		06 32			07 04		07 08		07 34			07 47	
49½	51½	**Preston Park**	d						06 04	06 22		06 38			07 10		07 15		07 40			07 54	
—	53	**Brighton**	a	01s16		02 28	02 28	05 32	06 10	06 26	06 13	06 42		06 56	07 14	07 05	07 22	07 26	07 44	07 35		07 58	08 12
50¾	—	Hove	a	01s25																			
—	—	Lewes	a		01 23								06 53								07 54		

		GX	TL	SN	GX	TL	GX	SN		SN	TL	GX	TL	SN	TL	SN	TL	GX	SN		SN	TL	GX
London Victoria	d	07 13		07 16	07 30		07 43	07 46		07 55		08 13		08 16		08 25		08 43	08 46		08 55		09 14
Clapham Junction	d			07 23				07 53		08 02				08 23		08 32			08 53		09 02		
East Croydon	a			07 32				08 03		08 11				08 33		08 41			09 02		09 11		
St Pancras International	d		07 00			07 20					07 50		08 00		08 10		08 20					08 50	
Farringdon	d		07 04			07 24					07 54		08 04		08 14		08 24					08 54	
City Thameslink	d		07 06			07 26					07 56		08 06		08 16		08 26					08 56	
London Blackfriars	d		07 09			07 29					07 59		08 09		08 19		08 29					08 59	
London Bridge	d		07 15			07 35					08 05		08 15		08 25		08 35					09 05	
East Croydon	a		07 29			07 48					08 18		08 30		08 38		08 48					09 18	
East Croydon	d		07 30	07 33		07 49		08 03		08 11	08 19		08 30	08 33	08 38	08 41	08 49		09 03		09 11	09 19	
Gatwick Airport	a	07 41	07 44	07 47	07 58	08 04	08 11	08 18		08 26	08 34	08 41	08 45	08 48		08 56	09 04	09 11	09 17		09 26	09 34	09 41
Gatwick Airport	d	07 42	07 45	07 50	08 00	08 05	08 12	08 20		08 27	08 35	08 42	08 46	08 50		08 58	09 05	09 12	09 20		09 28	09 35	09 42
Three Bridges	a		07 49			08 09					08 39		08 50		08 57		09 09					09 39	
Three Bridges	d		07 50			08 10					08 40		08 51		08 57		09 10					09 40	
Balcombe	d					08 16					08 46						09 16					09 46	
Haywards Heath	a		07 59	08 01		08 21		08 31		08 38	08 51		09 00	09 02	09 06	09 09	09 21		09 31		09 41	09 51	
Haywards Heath	d		08 00	08 03		08 24		08 35	08 38	08 41	08 54		09 00	09 03	09 07	09 11	09 24		09 35	09 38	09 41	09 54	
Wivelsfield	d			08 08		08 28					08 58			09 07			09 28					09 58	
Burgess Hill	d		08 05			08 30				08 46	09 00		09 05			09 16	09 30				09 46	10 00	
Hassocks	d		08 08			08 33				08 50			09 09			09 20	09 33				09 50		
Preston Park	d		08 15			08 40							09 15		09 18		09 40						
Brighton	a	08 05	08 19		08 23	08 44	08 35			09 01	09 12	09 05	09 20			09 32	09 44	09 37			10 02	10 12	10 07
Hove	a								08 52						09 23					09 52			
Lewes	a			08 22				08 53						09 21					09 53				

		TL	SN		SN	TL	GX	SN		SN	TL	GX	TL	SN		SN	TL	GX	SN		SN	TL	GX
London Victoria	d		09 16		09 25		09 44	09 46		09 55		10 14		10 16		10 25		10 44	10 46		10 55		11 14
Clapham Junction	d		09 23		09 32			09 53		10 02				10 23		10 32			10 53		11 02		
East Croydon	a		09 32		09 41			10 02		10 11				10 32		10 41			11 02		11 11		
St Pancras International	d	09 00				09 20					09 50		10 00				10 20					10 50	
Farringdon	d	09 04				09 24					09 54		10 04				10 24					10 54	
City Thameslink	d	09 06				09 26					09 56		10 06				10 26					10 56	
London Blackfriars	d	09 09				09 29					09 59		10 09				10 29					10 59	
London Bridge	d	09 15				09 35					10 05		10 15				10 35					11 05	
East Croydon	a	09 28				09 48					10 18		10 28				10 48					11 18	
East Croydon	d	09 29	09 33		09 41	09 49		10 03		10 11	10 19		10 29	10 33		10 41	10 49		11 03		11 11	11 19	
Gatwick Airport	a	09 44	09 47		09 57	10 04	10 11	10 17		10 27	10 34	10 41	10 44	10 47		10 56	11 04	11 11	11 17		11 26	11 34	11 41
Gatwick Airport	d	09 45	09 50		10 01	10 05	10 12	10 20		10 31	10 35	10 42	10 45	10 50		10 58	11 05	11 12	11 20		11 28	11 35	11 42
Three Bridges	a	09 49				10 09					10 39		10 49				11 09					11 39	
Three Bridges	d	09 50				10 10					10 40		10 50				11 10					11 40	
Balcombe	d					10 16					10 46						11 16					11 46	
Haywards Heath	a	09 59	10 01		10 12	10 21		10 31		10 42	10 51		10 59	11 01		11 09	11 21		11 31		11 39	11 51	
Haywards Heath	d	10 00	10 05	10 07	10 13	10 24		10 35	10 38	10 43	10 54		10 59	11 05	11 07	11 11	11 24		11 35	11 38	11 41	11 54	
Wivelsfield	d			10 11		10 28					10 58				11 11		11 28					11 58	
Burgess Hill	d	10 06			10 18	10 30				10 48	11 00		11 05			11 16	11 30				11 46	12 00	
Hassocks	d	10 09			10 21	10 33				10 51			11 08			11 20	11 33				11 50		
Preston Park	d	10 16	10 18			10 40							11 15	11 18			11 40						
Brighton	a	10 20			10 32	10 44	10 37			11 02	11 12	11 07	11 19			11 32	11 44	11 37			12 02	12 12	12 07
Hove	a		10 22						10 52					11 22						11 52			
Lewes	a			10 25				10 53							11 23				11 53				

Table T184-F

Mondays to Fridays

21 May to 7 December

London - Gatwick Airport - Haywards Heath - Brighton/Hove/Lewes

		TL	SN		SN	TL	GX	SN		SN	TL A	TL B	GX	TL	SN		SN	TL	GX	SN		SN
London Victoria	d		11 16		11 25		11 44	11 46		11 55			12 14		12 16		12 25		12 44	12 46		12 55
Clapham Junction	d		11 23		11 32			11 53		12 02					12 23		12 32			12 53		13 02
East Croydon	a		11 32		11 41			12 02		12 11					12 32		12 41			13 02		13 11
St Pancras International	d	11 00				11 20					11 50	11 51		12 00				12 20				
Farringdon	d	11 04				11 24					11 54	11 55		12 04				12 24				
City Thameslink	d	11 06				11 26					11 56	11 57		12 06				12 26				
London Blackfriars	d	11 09				11 29					11 59	12 00		12 09				12 29				
London Bridge	d	11 15				11 35					12 05	12 06		12 15				12 35				
East Croydon	a	11 28				11 48					12 18	12 19		12 28				12 48				
East Croydon	d	11 29	11 33		11 41	11 49		12 03		12 11	12 19	12 19		12 29	12 33		12 41	12 49		13 03		13 11
Gatwick Airport	a	11 44	11 47		11 56	12 04	12 11	12 17		12 26	12 34	12 34	12 41	12 44	12 47		12 56	13 04	13 11	13 17		13 26
Gatwick Airport	d	11 45	11 50		11 58	12 05	12 12	12 20		12 28	12 35	12 35	12 42	12 45	12 50		12 58	13 05	13 12	13 20		13 28
Three Bridges	a	11 49				12 09					12 39	12 39		12 49				13 09				
Three Bridges	d	11 50				12 10					12 40	12 40		12 50				13 10				
Balcombe	d					12 16					12 46	12 46						13 16				
Haywards Heath	a	11 59	12 01		12 09	12 21		12 31		12 39	12 51	12 51		12 59	13 01		13 09	13 21		13 31		13 39
Haywards Heath	d	11 59	12 05	12 07	12 11	12 24		12 35	12 38	12 41	12 54	12 54		12 59	13 05	13 07	13 11	13 24		13 35	13 38	13 41
Wivelsfield	d			12 11		12 28					12 58	12 58				13 11		13 28				
Burgess Hill	d	12 05			12 16	12 30				12 46	13 00	13 00		13 05			13 16	13 30				13 46
Hassocks	d	12 08			12 20	12 33				12 50				13 08			13 20	13 33				13 50
Preston Park	d	12 15	12 18			12 40								13 15	13 18			13 40				
Brighton	a	12 19			12 32	12 44	12 37			13 02	13 12	13 12	13 07	13 19			13 32	13 44	13 37			14 02
Hove	a		12 22						12 52						13 22						13 52	
Lewes	a			12 23				12 53								13 23				13 53		

		TL	GX	TL	SN		SN	TL	GX	SN		SN	TL A	TL B	GX	TL	SN		SN	TL	GX	SN	
London Victoria	d		13 14		13 16		13 25		13 44	13 46		13 55			14 14		14 16		14 25		14 44	14 46	
Clapham Junction	d				13 23		13 32			13 53		14 02					14 23		14 32			14 53	
East Croydon	a				13 32		13 41			14 02		14 11					14 32		14 41			15 02	
St Pancras International	d	12 50		13 00				13 20					13 50	13 51		14 00				14 20			
Farringdon	d	12 54		13 04				13 24					13 54	13 55		14 04				14 24			
City Thameslink	d	12 56		13 06				13 26					13 56	13 57		14 06				14 26			
London Blackfriars	d	12 59		13 09				13 29					13 59	14 00		14 09				14 29			
London Bridge	d	13 05		13 15				13 35					14 05	14 06		14 15				14 35			
East Croydon	a	13 18		13 28				13 48					14 18	14 19		14 28				14 48			
East Croydon	d	13 19		13 29	13 33		13 41	13 49		14 03		14 11	14 19	14 19		14 29	14 33		14 41	14 49		15 03	
Gatwick Airport	a	13 34	13 41	13 44	13 47		13 56	14 04	14 11	14 17		14 26	14 34	14 34	14 41	14 44	14 47		14 56	15 04	15 11	15 17	
Gatwick Airport	d	13 35	13 42	13 45	13 50		13 58	14 05	14 12	14 20		14 28	14 35	14 35	14 42	14 45	14 50		14 58	15 05	15 12	15 20	
Three Bridges	a	13 39		13 49				14 09					14 39	14 39		14 49				15 09			
Three Bridges	d	13 40		13 50				14 10					14 40	14 40		14 50				15 10			
Balcombe	d	13 46						14 16					14 46	14 46						15 16			
Haywards Heath	a	13 51		13 59	14 01		14 09	14 21		14 31		14 39	14 51	14 51		14 59	15 01		15 09	15 21		15 31	
Haywards Heath	d	13 54		13 59	14 05	14 07	14 11	14 24		14 35	14 38	14 41	14 54	14 54		14 59	15 05	15 07	15 11	15 24		15 35	15 38
Wivelsfield	d	13 58				14 11		14 28					14 58	14 58				15 11		15 28			
Burgess Hill	d	14 00		14 05			14 16	14 30				14 46	15 00	15 00		15 05			15 16	15 30			
Hassocks	d			14 08			14 20	14 33				14 50				15 08			15 20	15 33			
Preston Park	d			14 15	14 18			14 40								15 15	15 18			15 40			
Brighton	a	14 12	14 07	14 19			14 32	14 44	14 37			15 02	15 12	15 12	15 07	15 19			15 32	15 44	15 37		
Hove	a				14 22						14 52						15 22						15 52
Lewes	a					14 23				14 53								15 23				15 53	

		SN	TL C	TL D	GX	TL	SN		SN	TL	GX	SN		SN	TL	GX	TL	SN		SN	TL	GX	SN
London Victoria	d	14 55			15 14		15 16		15 25		15 44	15 46		15 55		16 14		16 16		16 25		16 43	16 45
Clapham Junction	d	15 02					15 23		15 32			15 53		16 02				16 23		16 32			16 52
East Croydon	a	15 11					15 32		15 41			16 02		16 11				16 32		16 41			17 01
St Pancras International	d		14 50	14 51		15 00				15 20					15 50		16 00				16 20		
Farringdon	d		14 54	14 55		15 04				15 24					15 54		16 04				16 24		
City Thameslink	d		14 56	14 57		15 06				15 26					15 56		16 06				16 26		
London Blackfriars	d		14 59	15 00		15 09				15 29					15 59		16 09				16 29		
London Bridge	d		15 05	15 06		15 15				15 35					16 05		16 15				16 35		
East Croydon	a		15 18	15 19		15 28				15 48					16 19		16 29				16 49		
East Croydon	d	15 11	15 19	15 19		15 29	15 33		15 41	15 49		16 03		16 11	16 20		16 29	16 33		16 41	16 50		17 02
Gatwick Airport	a	15 26	15 34	15 34	15 41	15 44	15 47		15 56	16 04	16 11	16 17		16 26	16 35	16 41	16 44	16 47		16 56	17 04	17 11	17 19
Gatwick Airport	d	15 28	15 35	15 35	15 42	15 45	15 50		15 58	16 05	16 12	16 20		16 28	16 36	16 42	16 45	16 50		16 58	17 06	17 12	17 20
Three Bridges	a		15 39	15 39		15 49				16 09					16 40		16 49				17 10		
Three Bridges	d		15 40	15 40		15 50				16 10					16 41		16 50				17 11		
Balcombe	d		15 46	15 46						16 16					16 47						17 17		
Haywards Heath	a	15 39	15 51	15 51		15 59	16 01		16 09	16 21		16 31		16 39	16 52		16 59	17 01		17 09	17 22		17 32
Haywards Heath	d	15 41	15 54	15 54		15 59	16 05	16 07	16 11	16 24		16 35	16 38	16 41	16 54		16 59	17 05	17 07	17 12	17 24		17 33
Wivelsfield	d		15 58	15 58				16 11		16 28					16 59				17 11		17 29		17 37
Burgess Hill	d	15 46	16 00	16 00		16 05			16 16	16 30				16 46	17 01		17 05			17 17	17 31		
Hassocks	d	15 50				16 08			16 20	16 33				16 50			17 09			17 21	17 35		
Preston Park	d					16 15	16 18			16 40							17 16	17 20			17 42		
Brighton	a	16 02	16 12	16 12	16 07	16 19			16 32	16 44	16 37			17 02	17 13	17 07	17 21			17 32	17 46	17 37	
Hove	a						16 22						16 52					17 24					
Lewes	a							16 23				16 53							17 25				17 52

A from 23 July until 5 October
B until 20 July, from 8 October
C from 30 July
D until 27 July

London - Gatwick Airport - Haywards Heath - Brighton/Hove/Lewes

		TL 1	SN 1	GX	TL 1	GX	TL 1	TL 1	SN 1	SN 1	GX	SN 1	TL 1	GX	TL 1	SN 1	TL 1	SN 1	GX	TL 1	GX	TL 1
London Victoria	d		16 54	16 59		17 13			17 15	17 24	17 29			17 43		17 45		17 54	17 59		18 13	
Clapham Junction	d		17 02						17 22	17 32						17 52		18 02				
East Croydon	a		17 11						17 31	17 41						18 01		18 11				
St Pancras International	d	16 40			16 50			17 00					17 20				17 40			17 50		
Farringdon	d	16 44			16 54			17 04					17 24				17 44			17 54		
City Thameslink	d	16 46			16 56			17 06					17 26				17 46			17 56		
London Blackfriars	d	16 49			16 59			17 09					17 29				17 49			17 59		
London Bridge	d	16 55			17 05			17 15				17 33	17 35				17 55			18 05		
East Croydon	a	17 08			17 19			17 29				17 47	17 49				18 08			18 19		
East Croydon	d	17 08	17 11		17 20			17 29	17 32	17 41		17 48	17 50			18 02	18 08	18 11		18 20		
Gatwick Airport	a		17 26	17 29	17 35	17 41		17 44	17 49	17 56	17 59	18 02	18 05	18 11		18 19		18 26	18 29	18 35	18 41	
Gatwick Airport	d		17 27	17 33	17 36	17 42	←	17 45	17 50	17 57	18 00	18 03	18 06	18 12	←	18 20		18 27	18 33	18 36	18 42	←
Three Bridges	a	17 27			17 40		17 40	17 49					18 10		18 10		18 27			18 40		18 40
Three Bridges	d	17 28			17 41		17 41	17 50					18 11		18 11		18 28			18 41		18 41
Balcombe	d				→		17 47						→		18 17					→		18 47
Haywards Heath	a	17 37	17 39	17 44			17 52	17 59	18 02	18 09	18 12	18 15			18 22	18 32	18 37	18 39	18 44			18 52
Haywards Heath	d	17 37	17 40	17 45			17 54	18 00	18 03	18 10	18 14	18 16			18 24	18 33	18 37	18 40	18 45			18 54
Wivelsfield	d						17 59		18 07			18 21			18 29	18 37						18 59
Burgess Hill	d		17 46			17 56	18 01	18 05		18 16				18 26	18 31			18 46			18 56	19 01
Hassocks	d			17 52		18 00		18 09			18 22			18 30	18 35				18 52		19 00	
Preston Park	d	17 50	17 55					18 16		18 25					18 42		18 50	18 55				
Brighton	a			18 02		18 12	18 15	18 21			18 32			18 42	18 46				19 02		19 12	19 15
Hove	a	17 54	18 00							18 30							18 54	19 00				
Lewes	a								18 22			18 38				18 52						

		TL 1	SN 1	SN 1	GX	SN 1	TL 1	GX	TL 1	SN 1	SN 1	GX	TL 1	GX	TL 1	SN 1		SN 1	TL 1	GX	SN 1		SN 1
London Victoria	d		18 15	18 24	18 29			18 43		18 45	18 54	18 59		19 14		19 16		19 25		19 44	19 46		19 55
Clapham Junction	d		18 22	18 32						18 52	19 02					19 23		19 32			19 53		20 02
East Croydon	a		18 31	18 41						19 01	19 11					19 32		19 41			20 02		20 11
St Pancras International	d	18 00					18 20						18 50		19 00				19 20				
Farringdon	d	18 04					18 24						18 54		19 04				19 24				
City Thameslink	d	18 06					18 26						18 56		19 06				19 26				
London Blackfriars	d	18 09					18 29						18 59		19 09				19 29				
London Bridge	d	18 15				18 33	18 35						19 05		19 15				19 35				
East Croydon	a	18 29				18 47	18 49						19 19		19 29				19 48				
East Croydon	d	18 29	18 32	18 41		18 48	18 50			19 02	19 11		19 20		19 29	19 33		19 41	19 49		20 03		20 11
Gatwick Airport	a	18 44	18 49	18 56	18 59	19 02	19 05	19 11		19 19	19 26	19 29	19 35	19 41	19 44	19 47		19 56	20 04	20 11	20 17		20 26
Gatwick Airport	d	18 45	18 50	18 57	19 00	19 03	19 06	19 12	←	19 20	19 27	19 30	19 36	19 42	19 45	19 50		19 58	20 05	20 12	20 20		20 28
Three Bridges	a	18 49					19 10		19 10				19 40		19 49				20 09				
Three Bridges	d	18 50					19 11		19 11				19 41		19 50				20 10				
Balcombe	d						→		19 17				19 47						20 16				
Haywards Heath	a	18 59	19 02	19 08	19 11	19 15			19 22	19 32	19 38	19 41	19 52		19 59	20 01		20 09	20 21		20 31		20 39
Haywards Heath	d	19 00	19 03	19 10	19 13	19 16			19 24	19 33	19 40	19 43	19 54		20 00	20 05	20 07	20 11	20 24		20 35	20 38	20 41
Wivelsfield	d		19 07			19 21			19 29	19 37			19 59				20 11		20 28				
Burgess Hill	d	19 06		19 16				19 26	19 31		19 46		20 01		20 05			20 17	20 30				20 47
Hassocks	d	19 10			19 22			19 30	19 35			19 52			20 09			20 21	20 33				20 51
Preston Park	d	19 17		19 25					19 42		19 55				20 15	20 18			20 40				
Brighton	a	19 21			19 32			19 42	19 46			20 02	20 13	20 07	20 19			20 32	20 44	20 37			21 02
Hove	a			19 30							20 00					20 22						20 52	
Lewes	a		19 22			19 38				19 52							20 25				20 53		

		TL 1 A	TL 1 B	GX	TL 1	SN 1		SN 1	TL 1	GX	SN 1		SN 1	TL 1	GX	TL 1	SN 1		SN 1	TL 1	GX	SN 1	
London Victoria	d			20 14		20 16		20 25		20 44	20 46		20 55		21 14		21 16		21 25		21 44	21 46	
Clapham Junction	d					20 23		20 32			20 53		21 02				21 23		21 32			21 53	
East Croydon	a					20 32		20 41			21 02		21 11				21 32		21 41			22 02	
St Pancras International	d	19 50	19 51		20 00				20 20					20 50		21 00				21 20			
Farringdon	d	19 54	19 55		20 04				20 24					20 54		21 04				21 24			
City Thameslink	d	19 56	19 57		20 06				20 26					20 56		21 06				21 26			
London Blackfriars	d	19 59	20 00		20 09				20 29					20 59		21 09				21 29			
London Bridge	d	20 05	20 06		20 15				20 35					21 05		21 15				21 35			
East Croydon	a	20 18	20 19		20 28				20 48					21 18		21 28				21 48			
East Croydon	d	20 19	20 19		20 29	20 33		20 41	20 49		21 03		21 11	21 19		21 29	21 33		21 41	21 49		22 03	
Gatwick Airport	a	20 34	20 34	20 41	20 44	20 47		20 56	21 04	21 11	21 17		21 26	21 34	21 41	21 44	21 47		21 56	22 04	22 11	22 17	
Gatwick Airport	d	20 35	20 35	20 42	20 45	20 50		20 58	21 05	21 12	21 20		21 28	21 35	21 42	21 45	21 50		21 58	22 05	22 12	22 20	
Three Bridges	a	20 39	20 39		20 49				21 09					21 39		21 49				22 09			
Three Bridges	d	20 40	20 40		20 50				21 10					21 40		21 50				22 10			
Balcombe	d	20 46	20 46						21 16					21 46						22 16			
Haywards Heath	a	20 51	20 51		20 59	21 01		21 09	21 21		21 31		21 39	21 51		21 59	22 01		22 09	22 21		22 31	
Haywards Heath	d	20 54	20 54		20 59	21 05	21 07	21 11	21 24		21 35	21 38	21 41	21 54		21 59	22 05	22 07	22 11	22 24		22 35	22 38
Wivelsfield	d	20 58	20 58				21 11		21 28					21 58				22 11		22 28			
Burgess Hill	d	21 00	21 00		21 05			21 17	21 30				21 47	22 00		22 05			22 17	22 30			
Hassocks	d				21 08			21 21	21 33				21 51			22 08			22 21	22 33			
Preston Park	d				21 15	21 18			21 40							22 15	22 18			22 40			
Brighton	a	21 12	21 12	21 07	21 19			21 32	21 44	21 37			22 02	22 12	22 07	22 19			22 32	22 44	22 37		
Hove	a					21 22						21 52					22 22						22 52
Lewes	a						21 25				21 53							22 25				22 53	

A from 30 July

B until 27 July

Table T184-F

Mondays to Fridays

21 May to 7 December

London - Gatwick Airport - Haywards Heath - Brighton/Hove/Lewes

		SN 1	TL 1	GX A	TL 1	SN 1 A		SN 1	SN 1	TL 1	GX	SN 1		SN FX 1	SN FO 1	TL 1	TL 1	SN 1	SN 1	TL 1	TL 1
London Victoria	d	21 55		22 14		22 16			22 25		22 44	22 46		22 55	22 55			23 16	23 25		
Clapham Junction	d	22 02				22 23			22 32			22 53		23 02	23 02			23 23	23 32		
East Croydon	a	22 11				22 32			22 41			23 02		23 11	23 11			23 32	23 41		
St Pancras International	d		21 51		22 00					22 20						22 50	23 00			23 22	23 51
Farringdon	d		21 55		22 04					22 24						22 54	23 04			23 27	23 56
City Thameslink	d		21 57		22 06					22 26						22 56					
London Blackfriars	d		22 00		22 09					22 29						22 59	23 09			23 31	00 01
London Bridge	d		22 06		22 15					22 35						23 05	23 15			23 37	
East Croydon	a		22 19		22 28					22 48						23 18	23 28			23 50	00 27
East Croydon	d	22 11	22 19		22 29	22 33			22 41	22 49		23 03		23 11	23 11	23 19	23 29	23 33	23 43	23 51	00 28
Gatwick Airport	a	22 26	22 34	22 41	22 44	22 47			22 56	23 04	23 11	23 17		23 26	23 26	23 34	23 47	23 52	00 03	00 17	00 48
Gatwick Airport	d	22 28	22 35	22 42	22 45	22 50			22 58	23 05	23 12	23 20		23 28	23 28	23 35	23 48	23 54	00 04	00 18	00 49
Three Bridges	a		22 39		22 49					23 09						23 39	23 53			00 23	00 54
Three Bridges	d		22 40		22 50					23 10						23 40	23 54			00 24	00 55
Balcombe	d		22 46							23 16						23 46				00 30	
Haywards Heath	a	22 39	22 51		22 59	23 01			23 09	23 21		23 31		23 39	23 39	23 51	00 03	00 05	00 17	00 35	01 04
Haywards Heath	d	22 41	22 54		22 59	23 05	23 07	23 07	23 11	23 24		23 35	23 38	23 41	23 41	23 54	00 04	00 09	00 17	00 36	01 04
Wivelsfield	d		22 58				23 11	23 11		23 28		23 39				23 58		00 13		00 40	01 08
Burgess Hill	d	22 47	23 00		23 05				23 17	23 30				23 46	23 46	00 01	00 09		00 22	00 42	01 10
Hassocks	d	22 51			23 08				23 21	23 33				23 50	23 50		00 12		00 26	00 45	01 14
Preston Park	d				23 15	23 18				23 40							00 19	00 22		00 52	01 20
Brighton	a	23 03	23 12	23 07	23 19				23 32	23 44	23 37			00 02	00 02	00 12	00 23		00 35	00 56	01 24
Hove	a					23 22							23 52					00 26			
Lewes	a						23 25	23 25				23 55									

Saturdays

26 May to 8 December

		SN 1		TL 1	SN 1	SN 1	TL 1	TL 1	TL 1	SN 1	TL 1	GX 1	TL 1	SN 1	TL 1	GX 1	TL 1	TL 1	GX 1	SN 1	SN 1	SN 1	TL 1
London Victoria	d	00 02			01 10	04 10				05 08		05 44				06 14			06 44			06 55	
Clapham Junction	d	00 09			01 17	04 17				05 16												07 02	
East Croydon	a	00 23			01 32	04 31				05 31												07 11	
St Pancras International	d			00 52			04 02	04 32	04 51		05 20				05 50		06 00	06 20					06 50
Farringdon	d								04 56		05 24				05 54		06 04	06 24					06 54
City Thameslink	d																						
London Blackfriars	d			01 02			04 10	04 40	05 01		05 29				05 59		06 09	06 29					06 59
London Bridge	d										05 35				06 05		06 15	06 35					07 05
East Croydon	a			01 28			04 36	05 06	05 27		05 48				06 18		06 28	06 48					07 18
East Croydon	d	00 24		01 28	01 33	04 31	04 37	05 07	05 28	05 31	05 49				06 19		06 29	06 49				07 11	07 19
Gatwick Airport	a	00 43		01 56	02 06	04 59	05 02	05 29	05 47	06 00	06 04	06 11			06 34	06 41	06 44	07 04	07 11			07 26	07 34
Gatwick Airport	d	00 44		01 58	02 13	05 00	05 04	05 30	05 48	06 01	06 05	06 12		06 13	06 35	06 42	06 45	07 05	07 12			07 28	07 35
Three Bridges	a	00 48		02 03	02 18	05 05	05 09	05 35	05 53	06 06	06 09			06 19	06 39		06 49	07 09					07 39
Three Bridges	d	00 49		02 04	02 19	05 06	05 09	05 36	05 54	06 07	06 10			06 20	06 40		06 50	07 10					07 40
Balcombe	d								06 00		06 16		←		06 46			07 16					07 46
Haywards Heath	a	00 58		02 13	02 28	05 15	05 20	05 45	06 05	06 16	06 21	06 23	06 21	06 29	06 51	06 53	06 59	07 21				07 39	07 51
Haywards Heath	d	01 02	01 08	02 14	02 29	05 17	05 20	05 45	06 06	06 17	06 25	06 23	06 25	06 31	06 52	06 55	06 59	07 24		07 35	07 38	07 41	07 54
Wivelsfield	d							05 49	06 10		→		06 29				07 03	07 28					07 58
Burgess Hill	d							05 51	06 12	06 22			06 32				07 06	07 30				07 46	08 00
Hassocks	d							05 55	06 16	06 26			06 35				07 09	07 33				07 50	
Preston Park	d							06 01	06 22				06 42				07 16	07 40					
Brighton	a	01s16		02 28	02 43	05 35	05 38	06 07	06 26	06 36		06 39	06 46		07 06	07 09	07 22	07 44	07 37			08 01	08 12
Hove	a	01s25																			07 52		
Lewes	a		01 23											06 49						07 53			

		GX 1	TL 1	SN 1	TL 1	GX 1	SN 1		SN 1	TL 1	GX 1	TL 1	SN 1		SN 1	TL 1	GX 1	SN 1		SN 1	TL 1
London Victoria	d	07 14		07 25		07 44	07 46		07 55		08 14		08 16		08 25		08 44	08 46		08 55	
Clapham Junction	d			07 32			07 53		08 02				08 23		08 32			08 53		09 02	
East Croydon	a			07 41			08 02		08 11				08 32		08 41			09 02		09 11	
St Pancras International	d		07 00		07 20					07 50		08 00				08 20					08 50
Farringdon	d		07 04		07 24					07 54		08 04				08 24					08 54
City Thameslink	d																				
London Blackfriars	d		07 09		07 29					07 59		08 09				08 29					08 59
London Bridge	d		07 15		07 35					08 05		08 15				08 35					09 05
East Croydon	a		07 28		07 48					08 18		08 28				08 48					09 18
East Croydon	d		07 30	07 41	07 49		08 03		08 11	08 19		08 29	08 33		08 41	08 49		09 03		09 11	09 19
Gatwick Airport	a	07 41	07 44	07 56	08 04	08 11	08 18		08 26	08 34	08 41	08 44	08 47		08 56	09 04	09 11	09 18		09 26	09 34
Gatwick Airport	d	07 42	07 45	07 58	08 05	08 12	08 20		08 28	08 35	08 42	08 45	08 50		08 58	09 05	09 12	09 20		09 28	09 35
Three Bridges	a		07 49		08 09					08 39		08 49				09 09					09 39
Three Bridges	d		07 50		08 10					08 40		08 50				09 10					09 40
Balcombe	d				08 16					08 46						09 16					09 46
Haywards Heath	a		07 59	08 09	08 21		08 31		08 39	08 51		08 59	09 01		09 09	09 21		09 31		09 39	09 51
Haywards Heath	d		08 00	08 11	08 24		08 35	08 38	08 41	08 54		09 00	09 05	09 07	09 11	09 24		09 35	09 38	09 41	09 54
Wivelsfield	d				08 28					08 58				09 11		09 28					09 58
Burgess Hill	d		08 05	08 16	08 30				08 46	09 00		09 05			09 16	09 30				09 46	10 00
Hassocks	d		08 08	08 20	08 33				08 50			09 08			09 20	09 33				09 50	
Preston Park	d		08 15		08 40							09 15	09 18			09 40					
Brighton	a	08 07	08 19	08 31	08 44	08 37			09 01	09 12	09 07	09 19			09 31	09 44	09 37			10 01	10 12
Hove	a							08 52					09 22						09 52		
Lewes	a						08 53							09 23				09 53			

A not 7 December

Table T184-F

Saturdays

26 May to 8 December

London - Gatwick Airport - Haywards Heath - Brighton/Hove/Lewes

		GX	TL	SN		SN	TL	GX	SN		SN	TL		GX	TL	SN		SN	TL	GX	SN		SN	TL
London Victoria	d	09 14		09 16		09 25		09 44	09 46		09 55		and at the same minutes past each hour until	20 14		20 16		20 25		20 44	20 46		20 55	
Clapham Junction	d			09 23		09 32			09 53		10 02					20 23		20 32			20 53		21 02	
East Croydon	a			09 32		09 41			10 02		10 11					20 32		20 41			21 02		21 11	
St Pancras International	d		09 00				09 20					09 50			20 00				20 20					20 50
Farringdon	d		09 04				09 24					09 54			20 04				20 24					20 54
City Thameslink	d		09 06				09 26					09 56			20 06				20 26					20 56
London Blackfriars	d		09 09				09 29					09 59			20 09				20 29					20 59
London Bridge	d		09 15				09 35					10 05			20 15				20 35					21 05
East Croydon	a		09 28				09 48					10 18			20 28				20 48					21 18
East Croydon	d		09 29	09 33		09 41	09 49		10 03		10 11	10 19			20 29	20 33		20 41	20 49		21 03		21 11	21 19
Gatwick Airport	a	09 41	09 44	09 47		09 56	10 04	10 11	10 18		10 26	10 34		20 41	20 44	20 47		20 56	21 04	21 11	21 18		21 26	21 34
Gatwick Airport	d	09 42	09 45	09 50		09 58	10 05	10 12	10 20		10 28	10 35		20 42	20 45	20 50		20 58	21 05	21 12	21 20		21 28	21 35
Three Bridges	a		09 49				10 09					10 39			20 49				21 09					21 39
Three Bridges	d		09 50				10 10					10 40			20 50				21 10					21 40
Balcombe	d						10 16					10 46							21 16					21 46
Haywards Heath	a		09 59	10 01		10 09	10 21		10 31		10 39	10 51			20 59	21 01		21 09	21 21		21 31		21 39	21 51
Haywards Heath	d		10 00	10 05	10 07	10 11	10 24		10 35	10 38	10 41	10 54			21 00	21 05	21 07	21 11	21 24		21 35	21 38	21 41	21 54
Wivelsfield	d				10 11		10 28					10 58					21 11		21 28					21 58
Burgess Hill	d		10 05			10 16	10 30				10 46	11 00			21 05			21 16	21 30				21 46	22 00
Hassocks	d		10 08			10 20	10 33				10 50				21 08			21 20	21 33				21 50	
Preston Park	d		10 15	10 18			10 40								21 15	21 18			21 40					
Brighton	a	10 07	10 19			10 31	10 44	10 37			11 01	11 12		21 07	21 19			21 31	21 44	21 37			22 01	22 12
Hove	a			10 22						10 52						21 22						21 52		
Lewes	a				10 23				10 53								21 23				21 53			

			GX	TL	SN		SN	TL	GX	SN			SN	TL	GX	TL	SN		SN	TL	GX		TL	SN	
London Victoria	d		21 14		21 16		21 25		21 44	21 46			21 55		22 14		22 16		22 25		22 44			22 46	
Clapham Junction	d				21 23		21 32			21 53			22 02				22 23		22 32					22 53	
East Croydon	a				21 32		21 41			22 02			22 11				22 32		22 41					23 02	
St Pancras International	d			21 00				21 20						21 50		22 00				22 20			22 30		
Farringdon	d			21 04				21 24						21 54		22 04				22 24			22 34		
City Thameslink	d																								
London Blackfriars	d			21 09				21 29						21 59		22 09				22 29			22 39		
London Bridge	d			21 15				21 35						22 05		22 15				22 35			22 45		
East Croydon	a			21 28				21 48						22 18		22 28				22 48			22 58		
East Croydon	d			21 29	21 33		21 41	21 49		22 03			22 11	22 19		22 29	22 33		22 41	22 49			22 59	23 03	
Gatwick Airport	a		21 41	21 44	21 47		21 56	22 04	22 11	22 18			22 26	22 34	22 41	22 44	22 47		22 56	23 04	23 11		23 14	23 18	
Gatwick Airport	d		21 42	21 45	21 50		21 58	22 05	22 12	22 20			22 28	22 35	22 42	22 45	22 50		22 58	23 05	23 12		23 15	23 20	
Three Bridges	a			21 49				22 09						22 39		22 49				23 09			23 19		
Three Bridges	d			21 50				22 10						22 40		22 50				23 10			23 20		
Balcombe	d							22 16						22 46						23 16					
Haywards Heath	a			21 59	22 01		22 09	22 21		22 31			22 39	22 51		22 59	23 01		23 09	23 21			23 29	23 31	
Haywards Heath	d			22 00	22 05	22 07	22 11	22 24		22 35	22 38		22 41	22 54		23 00	23 05	23 07	23 11	23 24			23 30	23 35	23 38
Wivelsfield	d					22 11		22 28						22 58				23 11		23 28					
Burgess Hill	d			22 05			22 16	22 30					22 46	23 00		23 05			23 16	23 30			23 35		
Hassocks	d			22 08			22 20	22 33					22 50			23 08			23 20	23 33			23 38		
Preston Park	d			22 15	22 18			22 40								23 15	23 18			23 40			23 45		
Brighton	a		22 07	22 19			22 31	22 44	22 37				23 01	23 12	23 07	23 19			23 31	23 44	23 37		23 49		
Hove	a				22 22						22 52						23 22								23 52
Lewes	a					22 23				22 53								23 23						23 53	

		SN	TL	TL	SN	SN	TL		TL
London Victoria	d	22 55			23 16	23 25			
Clapham Junction	d	23 02			23 23	23 32			
East Croydon	a	23 11			23 32	23 41			
St Pancras International	d		22 50	23 00			23 22		23 51
Farringdon	d		22 54	23 04			23 27		23 56
City Thameslink	d								
London Blackfriars	d		22 59	23 09			23 31		00 01
London Bridge	d		23 05	23 15			23 37		
East Croydon	a		23 18	23 28			23 50		00 27
East Croydon	d	23 11	23 19	23 29	23 33	23 43	23 51		00 28
Gatwick Airport	a	23 26	23 34	23 47	23 52	00 04	00 17		00 48
Gatwick Airport	d	23 28	23 35	23 48	23 54	00 05	00 18		00 49
Three Bridges	a		23 39	23 53			00 23		00 54
Three Bridges	d		23 40	23 54			00 24		00 55
Balcombe	d		23 46				00 30		
Haywards Heath	a	23 39	23 51	00 03	00 05	00 17	00 35		01 04
Haywards Heath	d	23 41	23 54	00 04	00 09	00 17	00 36		01 04
Wivelsfield	d		23 58				00 40		01 08
Burgess Hill	d	23 46	00 01	00 09		00 22	00 42		01 10
Hassocks	d	23 50		00 12		00 26	00 45		01 14
Preston Park	d			00 19	00 21		00 52		01 20
Brighton	a	00 01	00 12	00 23		00 35	00 56		01 24
Hove	a				00 25				
Lewes	a								

Table T184-F

Sundays

20 May to 2 December

London - Gatwick Airport - Haywards Heath - Brighton/Hove/Lewes

		SN	SN	TL A	SN	SN	SN	SN	SN	TL		SN	TL	TL	SN	SN	SN	TL	SN	SN		TL	SN	SN	TL
London Victoria	d		00 02		01 10	04 10	05 02	05 45	06 32			07 02			08 02	08 14			08 46	08 55			09 16	09 25	
Clapham Junction	d		00 09		01 17	04 17	05 10	05 53	06 40			07 10			08 10	08 21			08 53	09 02			09 23	09 32	
East Croydon	a		00 23		01 32	04 31	05 23	06 08	06 53			07 26			08 26	08 39			09 02	09 11			09 32	09 41	
St Pancras International	d			00 51																					09 26
Farringdon	d																								09 30
City Thameslink	d																								
London Blackfriars	d			01 01																					09 35
London Bridge	d									07 11			07 41	08 11				08 41				09 11			09 41
East Croydon	a			01 27						07 24			07 54	08 24				08 54				09 24			09 54
East Croydon	d		00 24	01 28	01 33	04 31	05 24	06 09	06 54	07 25		07 27	07 55	08 25	08 27	08 40		08 55	09 03	09 12		09 25	09 33	09 42	09 55
Gatwick Airport	a		00 43	01 56	02 06	04 57	05 50	06 32	07 23	07 43		07 52	08 14	08 43	08 52	08 58		09 09	09 18	09 26		09 39	09 47	09 56	10 09
Gatwick Airport	d		00 44	01 58	02 08	04 58	05 51	06 33	07 24	07 45		07 53	08 15	08 44	08 54	08 59	←	09 10	09 20	09 28		09 40	09 50	09 58	10 10
Three Bridges	a		00 48	02 03	02 13	05 03	05 56	06 37	07 28	07 50		07 58	08 19	08 48	08 58		08 58	09 14		09 32		09 44			10 14
Three Bridges	d		00 49	02 04	02 14	05 04	05 57	06 38	07 29	07 51		07 58	08 20	08 49	09 03		09 03	09 15		09 32		09 45			10 15
Balcombe	d								07 35				08 26		→			09 21							10 21
Haywards Heath	a		00 58	02 13	02 23	05 13	06 06	06 47	07 40	08 00		08 07	08 31	09 00		09 09	09 12	09 26	09 30	09 41		09 54	10 00	10 09	10 26
Haywards Heath	d	00 11	01 02	02 14	02 24	05 13	06 07	06 48	07 40	08 01		08 08	08 32	09 01		09 10	09 13	09 27	09 31	09 42		09 55	10 02	10 12	10 27
Wivelsfield	d	00 15						06 52	07 44	08 05		08 12	08 36	09 05			09 17	09 31	09 35			09 59			10 31
Burgess Hill	d							06 54	07 47	08 07		08 14	08 38	09 07			09 19	09 33		09 47		10 01		10 17	10 33
Hassocks	d							06 58	07 50	08 10		08 18	08 41	09 10			09 22	09 36		09 51		10 04		10 21	10 36
Preston Park	d							07 05	07 57	08 17		08 24	08 48	09 17		09 22	09 29	09 43				10 11	10 14		10 43
Brighton	a		01s16	02 28	02 38	05 28	06 21	07 11	08 01	08 21		08 30	08 52	09 21			09 33	09 47		10 01		10 15		10 31	10 47
Hove	a		01s25													09 25							10 17		
Lewes	a	00 27																	09 49						

		SN	SN	TL	SN	SN		TL	SN	SN	TL	SN	SN	TL	SN	SN		TL	SN	SN	TL	SN	SN	TL	SN
London Victoria	d	09 46	09 55		10 16	10 25			10 46	10 55		11 16	11 25		11 46	11 55			12 16	12 25		12 46	12 55		13 16
Clapham Junction	d	09 53	10 02		10 23	10 32			10 53	11 02		11 23	11 32		11 53	12 02			12 23	12 32		12 53	13 02		13 23
East Croydon	a	10 02	10 11		10 32	10 41			11 02	11 11		11 32	11 41		12 02	12 11			12 32	12 41		13 02	13 12		13 32
St Pancras International	d			09 56				10 26			10 56			11 26				11 56			12 26			12 56	
Farringdon	d			10 00				10 30			11 00			11 30				12 00			12 30			13 00	
City Thameslink	d																								
London Blackfriars	d			10 05				10 35			11 05			11 35				12 05			12 35			13 05	
London Bridge	d			10 11				10 41			11 11			11 41				12 11			12 41			13 11	
East Croydon	a			10 24				10 54			11 24			11 54				12 24			12 54			13 24	
East Croydon	d	10 03	10 12	10 25	10 33	10 42		10 55	11 03	11 12	11 25	11 33	11 42	11 55	12 03	12 12		12 25	12 33	12 42	12 55	13 03	13 13	13 25	13 33
Gatwick Airport	a	10 18	10 26	10 39	10 47	10 56		11 09	11 18	11 26	11 39	11 47	11 56	12 09	12 18	12 26		12 39	12 47	12 56	13 09	13 18	13 27	13 39	13 47
Gatwick Airport	d	10 20	10 28	10 40	10 50	10 58		11 10	11 20	11 28	11 40	11 50	11 58	12 10	12 20	12 28		12 40	12 50	12 58	13 10	13 20	13 28	13 40	13 50
Three Bridges	a		10 32	10 44				11 14		11 32	11 44			12 14		12 32		12 44			13 14		13 32	13 44	
Three Bridges	d		10 32	10 45				11 15		11 32	11 45			12 15		12 32		12 45			13 15		13 33	13 45	
Balcombe	d							11 21						12 21							13 21				
Haywards Heath	a	10 30	10 41	10 54	11 00	11 09		11 26	11 30	11 41	11 54	12 00	12 09	12 26	12 30	12 41		12 54	13 00	13 09	13 26	13 30	13 42	13 54	14 00
Haywards Heath	d	10 31	10 42	10 55	11 02	11 12		11 27	11 31	11 42	11 55	12 02	12 12	12 27	12 31	12 42		12 55	13 02	13 12	13 27	13 31	13 42	13 55	14 02
Wivelsfield	d	10 35		10 59				11 31	11 35		11 59			12 31	12 35			12 59			13 31	13 35		13 59	
Burgess Hill	d		10 47	11 01		11 17		11 33		11 47	12 01		12 17	12 33		12 47		13 01		13 17	13 33		13 48	14 01	
Hassocks	d		10 51	11 04		11 21		11 36		11 51	12 04		12 21	12 36		12 51		13 04		13 21	13 36		13 52	14 04	
Preston Park	d			11 11	11 14			11 43			12 11	12 14		12 43				13 11	13 14		13 43			14 11	14 14
Brighton	a		11 01	11 15		11 31		11 47		12 01	12 15		12 31	12 47		13 01		13 15		13 31	13 47		14 01	14 15	
Hove	a				11 17							12 17							13 17						14 17
Lewes	a	10 49							11 49						12 49							13 49			

		SN		TL	SN	SN	TL	SN	SN	TL	SN	SN		TL	SN	SN	TL	SN	SN	TL	SN	SN		TL	SN
London Victoria	d	13 25			13 46	13 55		14 16	14 25		14 46	14 55			15 16	15 25		15 46	15 55		16 16	16 25			16 46
Clapham Junction	d	13 32			13 53	14 02		14 23	14 32		14 53	15 02			15 23	15 32		15 53	16 02		16 23	16 32			16 53
East Croydon	a	13 41			14 02	14 11		14 32	14 41		15 02	15 11			15 32	15 41		16 02	16 12		16 32	16 41			17 02
St Pancras International	d			13 26			13 56			14 26				14 56			15 26			15 56				16 26	
Farringdon	d			13 30			14 00			14 30				15 00			15 30			16 00				16 30	
City Thameslink	d																								
London Blackfriars	d			13 35			14 05			14 35				15 05			15 35			16 05				16 35	
London Bridge	d			13 41			14 11			14 41				15 11			15 41			16 11				16 41	
East Croydon	a			13 54			14 24			14 54				15 24			15 54			16 24				16 54	
East Croydon	d	13 42		13 55	14 03	14 12	14 25	14 33	14 42	14 55	15 03	15 12		15 25	15 33	15 42	15 55	16 03	16 13	16 25	16 33	16 42		16 55	17 03
Gatwick Airport	a	13 56		14 09	14 18	14 26	14 39	14 47	14 56	15 09	15 18	15 26		15 39	15 47	15 56	16 09	16 18	16 27	16 39	16 47	16 56		17 09	17 18
Gatwick Airport	d	13 58		14 10	14 20	14 28	14 40	14 50	14 58	15 10	15 20	15 28		15 40	15 50	15 58	16 10	16 20	16 28	16 40	16 50	16 58		17 10	17 20
Three Bridges	a			14 14		14 32	14 44			15 14		15 32		15 44			16 14		16 32	16 44				17 14	
Three Bridges	d			14 15		14 32	14 45			15 15		15 32		15 45			16 15		16 33	16 45				17 15	
Balcombe	d			14 21						15 21							16 21							17 21	
Haywards Heath	a	14 09		14 26	14 30	14 41	14 54	15 00	15 09	15 26	15 30	15 41		15 54	16 00	16 09	16 26	16 30	16 42	16 54	17 00	17 09		17 26	17 30
Haywards Heath	d	14 12		14 27	14 31	14 42	14 55	15 02	15 12	15 27	15 31	15 42		15 55	16 02	16 12	16 27	16 31	16 42	16 55	17 02	17 12		17 27	17 31
Wivelsfield	d			14 31	14 35		14 59			15 31	15 35			15 59			16 31	16 35		16 59				17 31	17 35
Burgess Hill	d	14 17		14 33		14 47	15 01		15 17	15 33		15 47		16 01		16 17	16 33		16 48	17 01		17 17		17 33	
Hassocks	d	14 21		14 36		14 51	15 04		15 21	15 36		15 51		16 04		16 21	16 36		16 52	17 04		17 21		17 36	
Preston Park	d			14 43			15 11	15 14		15 43				16 11	16 14		16 43			17 11	17 14			17 43	
Brighton	a	14 31		14 47		15 01	15 15		15 31	15 47		16 01		16 15		16 31	16 47		17 01	17 15		17 31		17 47	
Hove	a							15 17							16 17						17 17				
Lewes	a				14 49						15 49							16 49							17 49

A not 20 May

Table T184-F

Sundays

20 May to 2 December

London - Gatwick Airport - Haywards Heath - Brighton/Hove/Lewes

Station		SN	TL ■	SN	SN	TL ■	SN	SN		TL ■	SN	SN	TL ■	SN	SN		TL ■	SN	SN	TL ■	SN	TL ■	SN	TL ■
London Victoria	d	16 55		17 16	17 25		17 46	17 55			21 16	21 25		21 46	21 55			22 16	22 25		22 46		23 16	
Clapham Junction	d	17 02		17 23	17 32		17 53	18 02			21 23	21 32		21 53	22 02			22 23	22 32		22 53		23 23	
East Croydon	a	17 12		17 32	17 41		18 02	18 11			21 32	21 41		22 02	22 11			22 32	22 41		23 02		23 32	
St Pancras International	d		16 56			17 26				20 56			21 26				21 56			22 26		22 56		23 26
Farringdon	d		17 00			17 30				21 00			21 30				22 00			22 30		23 00		23 30
City Thameslink	d																							
London Blackfriars	d		17 05			17 35				21 05			21 35				22 05			22 35		23 05		23 35
London Bridge	d		17 11			17 41				21 11			21 41				22 11			22 41		23 11		23 41
East Croydon	a		17 24			17 54				21 24			21 54				22 24			22 54		23 24		23 54
East Croydon	d	17 13	17 25	17 33	17 42	17 55	18 03	18 12	and at the same minutes past each hour until	21 25	21 33	21 42	21 55	22 03	22 12		22 25	22 33	22 42	22 55	23 03	23 25	23 33	23 55
Gatwick Airport	a	17 27	17 39	17 47	17 56	18 09	18 18	18 26		21 39	21 47	21 56	22 09	22 18	22 26		22 39	22 47	22 56	23 09	23 18	23 42	23 54	00 17
Gatwick Airport	d	17 28	17 40	17 50	17 58	18 10	18 20	18 28		21 40	21 50	21 58	22 10	22 20	22 28		22 40	22 50	22 58	23 10	23 20	23 44	23 55	00 18
Three Bridges	a	17 32	17 44			18 14		18 32		21 44			22 14		22 32		22 44			23 14		23 48		00 22
Three Bridges	d	17 33	17 45			18 15		18 32		21 45			22 15		22 32		22 45			23 15		23 49		00 23
Balcombe	d					18 21							22 21							23 21				00 29
Haywards Heath	a	17 42	17 54	18 00	18 09	18 26	18 30	18 41		21 54	22 00	22 09	22 26	22 30	22 41		22 54	23 00	23 09	23 26	23 30	23 58	00 07	00 34
Haywards Heath	d	17 42	17 55	18 02	18 12	18 27	18 31	18 42		21 55	22 02	22 12	22 27	22 31	22 42		22 55	23 02	23 12	23 27	23 31	23 59	00 08	00 35
Wivelsfield	d		17 59			18 31	18 35			21 59			22 31	22 35			22 59			23 31	23 35	00 03		
Burgess Hill	d	17 48	18 01		18 17	18 33		18 47		22 01		22 17	22 33		22 47		23 01		23 17	23 33		00 05		00 40
Hassocks	d	17 52	18 04		18 21	18 36		18 51		22 04		22 21	22 36		22 51		23 04		23 21	23 36		00 08		00 43
Preston Park	d		18 11	18 14		18 43				22 11	22 14		22 43				23 11	23 14		23 43		00 15	00 19	00 50
Brighton	a	18 01	18 15		18 31	18 47		19 01		22 15		22 31	22 47		23 01		23 15		23 31	23 47		00 19		00 54
Hove	a			18 17							22 17							23 17					00 23	
Lewes	a						18 49							22 49							23 49			

Station		SN		TL ■
London Victoria	d	23 32		
Clapham Junction	d	23 40		
East Croydon	a	23 56		
St Pancras International	d			23 51
Farringdon	d			23 56
City Thameslink	d			
London Blackfriars	d			00 01
London Bridge	d			
East Croydon	a			00 27
East Croydon	d	23 57		00 28
Gatwick Airport	a	00 21		00 47
Gatwick Airport	d	00 23		00 48
Three Bridges	a	00 27		00 53
Three Bridges	d	00 28		00 54
Balcombe	d	00 34		
Haywards Heath	a	00 39		01 03
Haywards Heath	d	00 39		01 04
Wivelsfield	d	00 43		01 08
Burgess Hill	d	00 45		01 10
Hassocks	d	00 49		01 13
Preston Park	d	00 55		01 20
Brighton	a	00 59		01 24
Hove	a			
Lewes	a			

Table T184-R

Mondays to Fridays

21 May to 7 December

Brighton/Hove/Lewes - Haywards Heath - Gatwick Airport - London

Station		TL ■	TL ■	TL ■	SN ■	SN ■		TL ■	SN ■	SN ■	TL ■	SN ■	SN ■	TL ■	GX ■	TL ■		SN ■	TL ■	SN ■	GX ■	SN ■	SN ■	SN ■	GX ■
Lewes	d				05 11				05 46				06 00					06 16							
Hove	d									05 53										06 23				06 32	
Brighton	d	00 04	04 12	05 06		05 19		05 26			05 52			06 05	06 14				06 22		06 29				06 44
Preston Park	d	00 08		05 10				05 30		05 58				06 09						06 29				06 38	
Hassocks	d	00 14		05 16				05 36						06 16	06 23						06 38				06 53
Burgess Hill	d	00 18		05 20		05 29		05 40		06 07	06 03			06 20	06 27	←			06 33	06 38					06 57
Wivelsfield	d	00 20		05 22				05 42	06 02		06 06	←	06 20	06 23		06 23		06 33	06 36			←	←		
Haywards Heath	a	00 24	04 25	05 27	05 31	05 35		05 46	06 07	06 13	06 10	06 07	06 24	→		06 28		06 37	06 40	06 44	06 46	06 37	06 44	06 50	
Haywards Heath	d	00 25	04 26	05 28	05 39			05 47	06 17		06 11	06 17	06 25			06 31		06 49	06 41	06 49	06 47	06 49		06 51	
Balcombe	d	00 30		05 34				05 52	→				06 30					→		→				06 57	
Three Bridges	a	00 36	04 34	05 39	05 47			05 58			06 19	06 25				06 40			06 49			06 57		07 02	
Three Bridges	d	00 37	04 35	05 40	05 48			05 59			06 20	06 26				06 41			06 50			06 58		07 03	
Gatwick Airport	a	00 41	04 40	05 44	05 52			06 03			06 24	06 31	06 40		06 41	06 45			06 54		06 58	07 02			07 11
Gatwick Airport	d	00 42	04 41	05 46	05 53			06 06			06 25	06 33	06 41		06 44	06 46			06 55		06 59	07 03			07 14
East Croydon	a	01 09	05 08	06 00	06 07			06 21			06 40	06 48	06 56			07 01			07 10			07 18		07 20	
East Croydon	d	01 10	05 10	06 01				06 21			06 40		06 57			07 01			07 10					07 21	
London Bridge	d		05 25	06 16				06 35			06 54		07a13			07 16			07 24					07 35	
London Blackfriars	d	01 36	05 31	06 22				06 42			07 02					07 22			07 32					07 42	
City Thameslink	d		05 33	06 24				06 44			07 04					07 24			07 34					07 44	
Farringdon	d		05 36	06 26				06 46			07 06					07 26			07 36					07 46	
St Pancras International	a	01 43	05 40	06 30				06 50			07 10					07 30			07 40					07 50	
East Croydon	d				06 08							06 49										07 19			
Clapham Junction	a				06 19							06 58										07 28			
London Victoria	a				06 27							07 05			07 14						07 28	07 35			07 43

Station		SN ■		TL ■	GX ■	SN ■	SN ■	TL ■	GX ■	TL ■	SN	TL ■		GX ■	SN ■	SN ■	GX ■	SN ■	GX ■	SN ■	TL ■	TL ■		GX ■	TL ■
Lewes	d	06 46					07 02				07 16							07 46							
Hove	d					06 57									07 27	07 32				07 52					
Brighton	d			06 48	06 57			07 07	07 14			07 18		07 27			07 44		07 54		07 59	08 07		08 14	
Preston Park	d			06 52		07 03		07 11				07 22			07 33	07 38				07 59		08 11			
Hassocks	d			06 59	07 06			07 18	07 23			07 29		07 36			07 53		08 03		08 08	08 18		08 23	
Burgess Hill	d			07 03		07 12		07 22	07 27			07 33			07 42		07 57			08 08	08 12	08 22		08 27	
Wivelsfield	d	07 02		07 06			07 21			←	07 32	07 36						08 02			08 14				←
Haywards Heath	a	07 06		07 10	07 13	07 17	07 26	07 28		07 28	07 36	07 40		07 43	07 47	07 50		08 06	08 10	08 14	08 19	08 28			08 28
Haywards Heath	d	07 07		07 11	07 14	07 17	07 26	07 31		07 31	07 37	07 41		07 44	07 47	07 50		08 07	08 11	08 16	08 19	08 31			08 31
Balcombe	d							→								07 56					08 25	→			
Three Bridges	a			07 19		07 26				07 40		07 49			07 56	08 02				08 24	08 30				08 40
Three Bridges	d			07 20		07 27				07 41		07 50			07 57	08 03				08 25	08 31				08 41
Gatwick Airport	a	07 19		07 24	07 27	07 32	07 41		07 41	07 45	07 49	07 54		07 58	08 02		08 11	08 19	08 23	08 31	08 35			08 41	08 45
Gatwick Airport	d	07 20		07 25	07 28	07 33	07 42		07 44	07 46	07 50	07 55		07 59	08 03		08 14	08 20	08 28	08 33	08 36			08 44	08 46
East Croydon	a	07 37		07 40		07 48	07 56			08 01	08 07	08 10			08 18	08 20		08 37		08 48	08 51				09 01
East Croydon	d			07 40			07 57			08 01		08 10				08 21					08 51				09 01
London Bridge	d			07 54			08a13			08 16		08 24				08 35					09 05				09 16
London Blackfriars	d			08 02						08 22		08 32				08 42					09 12				09 22
City Thameslink	d			08 04						08 24		08 34				08 44					09 14				09 24
Farringdon	d			08 06						08 26		08 36				08 46					09 16				09 26
St Pancras International	a			08 10						08 30		08 40				08 50					09 20				09 30
East Croydon	d	07 38				07 50					08 08				08 20			08 38		08 50					
Clapham Junction	a	07 47				08 00					08 17				08 30			08 47		09 00					
London Victoria	a	07 54			07 58	08 08			08 13		08 24			08 28	08 37		08 43	08 54	08 58	09 08				09 13	

Station		SN ■	GX ■	SN ■	TL ■	GX ■	GX ■	SN ■	SN ■		TL ■	TL ■	GX ■	TL ■	SN ■	SN ■	TL ■	SN ■	TL ■		GX ■	SN ■	SN ■	TL ■	SN ■
Lewes	d	08 14						08 46								09 21						09 45			
Hove	d			08 24					08 52						09 21								09 51		
Brighton	d		08 24		08 28	08 44	08 57				09 02	09 08	09 18	←			09 25	09 33			09 48			09 58	10 03
Preston Park	d			08 29	08 32				08 57			09 12		09 12			09 29						09 57		
Hassocks	d		08 33			08 53	09 07					→		09 18			09 35	09 41							10 11
Burgess Hill	d			08 38	08 41	08 57					09 12			09 22			09 39	09 45						10 08	10 15
Wivelsfield	d	08 33			08 43			09 03			09 14						09 41					10 01		10 10	
Haywards Heath	a	08 38	08 40	08 44	08 48			09 07	09 11		09 18			09 27	09 36	09 40	09 45	09 50				10 06	10 10	10 15	10 20
Haywards Heath	d	08 38	08 41	08 46	08 48			09 15			09 19			09 31	09 44		09 46	09 51	←			10 14		10 16	10 21
Balcombe	d				08 54						09 24						09 52		09 52					10 22	
Three Bridges	a			08 54	08 59						09 30			09 39			→		09 57					→	
Three Bridges	d			08 55	09 00						09 31			09 40					09 59						
Gatwick Airport	a	08 50	08 54	09 01	09 05	09 11	09 23	09 27			09 35		09 41	09 44	09 56			10 02	10 03		10 11	10 26			10 32
Gatwick Airport	d	08 51	08 58	09 03	09 06	09 12	09 24	09 28			09 36		09 42	09 46	09 57			10 03	10 06		10 12	10 27			10 33
East Croydon	a	09 09		09 18	09 21			09 42			09 51			10 01	10 11			10 18	10 21			10 41			10 48
East Croydon	d				09 21						09 51			10 01					10 21						
London Bridge	d				09 35						10 05			10 16					10 35						
London Blackfriars	d				09 42						10 12			10 22					10 42						
City Thameslink	d				09 44						10 14			10 24					10 44						
Farringdon	d				09 46						10 16			10 26					10 46						
St Pancras International	a				09 50						10 20			10 30					10 50						
East Croydon	d	09 09		09 19				09 43							10 12			10 19				10 42			10 49
Clapham Junction	a	09 18		09 28				09 52							10 21			10 28				10 51			10 58
London Victoria	a	09 26	09 28	09 35		09 43	09 54	09 59					10 13		10 29			10 35			10 43	10 59			11 05

Brighton/Hove/Lewes - Haywards Heath - Gatwick Airport - London

		TL	TL	GX	TL		SN	SN	TL	SN	TL	GX	SN	TL	TL		SN	TL	TL	GX	TL	SN	SN	TL	SN
Lewes	d							10 21					10 45										11 21		
Hove	d						10 21							10 51								11 21			
Brighton	d		10 08	10 18	←				10 26	10 33		10 48			10 58		11 03		11 08	11 18	←			11 26	11 33
Preston Park	d		10 12		10 12				10 30					10 57					11 12		11 12			11 30	
Hassocks	d		→		10 18				10 36	10 41							11 11		→		11 18			11 36	11 41
Burgess Hill	d				10 22				10 40	10 45					11 08		11 15				11 22			11 40	11 45
Wivelsfield	d								10 42				11 01		11 10									11 42	
Haywards Heath	a				10 27		10 36	10 40	10 46	10 50			11 06	11 09	11 15		11 20				11 27	11 36	11 40	11 46	11 50
Haywards Heath	d	←			10 31		10 44		10 47	10 51	←		11 14		11 17		11 21	←			11 31	11 44		11 47	11 51
Balcombe	d	10 22							10 52		10 52				11 22			11 22						11 52	
Three Bridges	a	10 27			10 39				→		10 58				→			11 28			11 39			→	
Three Bridges	d	10 29			10 40						10 59							11 29			11 40				
Gatwick Airport	a	10 33		10 41	10 44		10 56			11 02	11 03	11 11	11 26				11 32	11 33		11 41	11 44	11 56			12 02
Gatwick Airport	d	10 36		10 42	10 46		10 57			11 03	11 06	11 12	11 27				11 33	11 36		11 42	11 46	11 57			12 03
East Croydon	a	10 51			11 01		11 11			11 18	11 21		11 41				11 48	11 51			12 01	12 11			12 18
East Croydon	d	10 51			11 01						11 21							11 51			12 01				
London Bridge	d	11 05			11 16						11 35							12 05			12 16				
London Blackfriars	d	11 12			11 22						11 42							12 12			12 22				
City Thameslink	d	11 14			11 24						11 44							12 14			12 24				
Farringdon	d	11 16			11 26						11 46							12 16			12 26				
St Pancras International	a	11 20			11 30						11 50							12 20			12 30				
East Croydon	d						11 12			11 19			11 42				11 49					12 12			12 19
Clapham Junction	a						11 21			11 28			11 51				11 58					12 22			12 28
London Victoria	a			11 13			11 29			11 35		11 43	11 59				12 05			12 13		12 29			12 35

			TL	GX	SN	SN	TL	SN	TL	TL	GX		TL	SN	SN	TL	SN	TL	GX	SN	SN		TL	SN	TL
Lewes	d				11 48										12 21					12 48					
Hove	d					11 51								12 21							12 51				
Brighton	d			11 48			11 58	12 03		12 08	12 18		←			12 26	12 33		12 48				12 58	13 03	
Preston Park	d					11 57				12 12			12 12			12 30					12 57				
Hassocks	d							12 11		→			12 18			12 36	12 41							13 11	
Burgess Hill	d						12 08	12 15					12 22			12 40	12 45						13 08	13 15	
Wivelsfield	d				12 01		12 10									12 42				13 01			13 10		
Haywards Heath	a				12 06	12 10	12 15	12 20					12 27	12 36	12 40	12 46	12 50			13 06	13 10		13 15	13 20	
Haywards Heath	d		←		12 14		12 16	12 21	←				12 31	12 44		12 47	12 51	←		13 14			13 16	13 21	←
Balcombe	d		11 52				12 22		12 22							12 52		12 52					13 22		13 22
Three Bridges	a		11 58				→		12 27				12 39			→		12 58					→		13 27
Three Bridges	d		11 59						12 29				12 40					12 59							13 29
Gatwick Airport	a		12 03	12 11	12 26			12 32	12 33		12 41		12 44	12 56			13 02	13 03	13 11	13 26				13 32	13 33
Gatwick Airport	d		12 06	12 12	12 27			12 33	12 36		12 42		12 46	12 57			13 03	13 06	13 12	13 27				13 33	13 36
East Croydon	a		12 21		12 41			12 48	12 51				13 01	13 11			13 18	13 21		13 41				13 48	13 51
East Croydon	d		12 21						12 51				13 01					13 21							13 51
London Bridge	d		12 35						13 05				13 16					13 35							14 05
London Blackfriars	d		12 42						13 12				13 22					13 42							14 12
City Thameslink	d		12 44						13 14				13 24					13 44							14 14
Farringdon	d		12 46						13 16				13 26					13 46							14 16
St Pancras International	a		12 50						13 20				13 30					13 50							14 20
East Croydon	d				12 42			12 49						13 12			13 19			13 42				13 49	
Clapham Junction	a				12 51			12 58						13 21			13 28			13 51				13 58	
London Victoria	a			12 43	12 59			13 05			13 13			13 29			13 35		13 43	13 59				14 05	

		TL	GX	TL	SN	SN	TL		SN	TL	GX	SN	SN	TL	SN	TL	TL		GX	TL	SN	SN	TL	SN	TL
Lewes	d					13 21						13 48										14 21			
Hove	d				13 21								13 51								14 21				
Brighton	d	13 08	13 18	←			13 26		13 33		13 48			13 58	14 03		14 08		14 18	←			14 26	14 33	
Preston Park	d	13 12		13 12			13 30						13 57				14 12			14 12			14 30		
Hassocks	d	→		13 18			13 36		13 41						14 11		→			14 18			14 36	14 41	
Burgess Hill	d			13 22			13 40		13 45					14 08	14 15					14 22			14 40	14 45	
Wivelsfield	d						13 42					14 01		14 10									14 42		
Haywards Heath	a			13 27	13 36	13 40	13 46		13 50			14 06	14 10	14 15	14 20					14 27	14 36	14 40	14 46	14 50	
Haywards Heath	d			13 31	13 44		13 47		13 51	←		14 14		14 16	14 21	←				14 31	14 44		14 47	14 51	←
Balcombe	d						13 52			13 52				14 22		14 22							14 52		14 52
Three Bridges	a			13 39			→			13 58				→		14 27				14 39			→		14 58
Three Bridges	d			13 40						13 59						14 29				14 40					14 59
Gatwick Airport	a		13 41	13 44	13 56				14 02	14 03	14 11	14 26			14 32	14 33			14 41	14 44	14 56			15 02	15 03
Gatwick Airport	d		13 42	13 46	13 57				14 03	14 06	14 12	14 27			14 33	14 36			14 42	14 46	14 57			15 03	15 06
East Croydon	a			14 01	14 11				14 18	14 21		14 41			14 48	14 51				15 01	15 11			15 18	15 21
East Croydon	d			14 01						14 21						14 52				15 01					15 21
London Bridge	d			14 16						14 35						15 05				15 16					15 35
London Blackfriars	d			14 22						14 42						15 12				15 22					15 42
City Thameslink	d			14 24						14 44						15 14				15 24					15 44
Farringdon	d			14 26						14 46						15 16				15 26					15 46
St Pancras International	a			14 30						14 50						15 20				15 30					15 50
East Croydon	d				14 12				14 19			14 42			14 49						15 12			15 19	
Clapham Junction	a				14 21				14 28			14 51			14 58						15 21			15 28	
London Victoria	a		14 13		14 29				14 35		14 43	14 59			15 05				15 13		15 29			15 35	

Table T184-R

Mondays to Fridays

21 May to 7 December

Brighton/Hove/Lewes - Haywards Heath - Gatwick Airport - London

		GX	SN	SN		TL	SN	TL	TL	GX	TL	SN	SN	TL		SN	TL	GX	SN	SN	TL	SN	TL	TL	
Lewes	d		14 45										15 21						15 45						
Hove	d			14 51								15 21								15 52					
Brighton	d	14 48				14 56	15 03		15 08	15 18	←			15 26		15 33		15 48			15 58	16 03		16 08	
Preston Park	d			14 57		15 00			15 12		15 12			15 30						15 58				16 12	
Hassocks	d					15 06	15 11		→		15 18			15 36		15 41						16 11		→	
Burgess Hill	d					15 10	15 15				15 22			15 40		15 45					16 08	16 15			
Wivelsfield	d		15 01			15 12								15 42					16 01		16 10				
Haywards Heath	a		15 06	15 10		15 16	15 20				15 27	15 36	15 40	15 46		15 50			16 06	16 10	16 15	16 20			
Haywards Heath	d		15 14			15 17	15 21	←			15 31	15 44		15 47		15 51	←		16 14		16 16	16 21	←		
Balcombe	d					15 22		15 22						15 52			15 52				16 22		16 22		
Three Bridges	a					→		15 28			15 39			→			15 58				→		16 28		
Three Bridges	d							15 29			15 40						15 59						16 29		
Gatwick Airport	a	15 11	15 26				15 32	15 33		15 41	15 44	15 56				16 02	16 03	16 11	16 26			16 32	16 33		
Gatwick Airport	d	15 12	15 27				15 33	15 36		15 42	15 46	15 57				16 03	16 06	16 12	16 27			16 33	16 36		
East Croydon	a		15 41				15 48	15 51			16 01	16 11				16 18	16 21		16 42			16 48	16 51		
East Croydon	d							15 51			16 01						16 21						16 51		
London Bridge	d							16 05			16 16						16 35						17 05		
London Blackfriars	d							16 12			16 22						16 42						17 12		
City Thameslink	d							16 14			16 24						16 44						17 14		
Farringdon	d							16 16			16 26						16 46						17 16		
St Pancras International	a							16 20			16 30						16 50						17 20		
East Croydon	d		15 42				15 49					16 12				16 19			16 42			16 49			
Clapham Junction	a		15 51				15 59					16 21				16 28			16 51			16 58			
London Victoria	a	15 43	16 00				16 09			16 15		16 29				16 35		16 43	16 59			17 05			

		GX	TL	SN	SN	TL	SN	TL	GX	SN	SN		TL	SN	TL	TL	GX	TL	SN	SN	TL		SN	TL	GX
Lewes	d				16 21					16 45										17 21					
Hove	d			16 21							16 51								17 21						
Brighton	d	16 18	←			16 26	16 33		16 48				16 58	17 03		17 08	17 16	←			17 26		17 33		17 46
Preston Park	d		16 12			16 30					16 57					17 12		17 12			17 30				
Hassocks	d		16 18			16 36	16 41							17 11		→		17 18			17 36		17 41		
Burgess Hill	d		16 22			16 40	16 45						17 08	17 15				17 22			17 40		17 45		
Wivelsfield	d					16 42				17 02			17 10								17 42				
Haywards Heath	a		16 27	16 36	16 40	16 46	16 50			17 07	17 11		17 15	17 20				17 27	17 36	17 40	17 46		17 50		
Haywards Heath	d		16 31	16 44		16 47	16 51	←		17 15			17 17	17 21	←			17 31	17 44		17 47		17 51	←	
Balcombe	d					16 52		16 52					17 22		17 22						17 52			17 52	
Three Bridges	a		16 39			→		16 58					→		17 28			17 39			→			17 58	
Three Bridges	d		16 40					16 59							17 29			17 40						17 59	
Gatwick Airport	a	16 43	16 44	16 56			17 02	17 03	17 11	17 26				17 32	17 34		17 41	17 44	17 56				18 02	18 03	18 11
Gatwick Airport	d	16 44	16 46	16 57			17 03	17 06	17 12	17 27				17 33	17 36		17 42	17 46	17 57				18 03	18 06	18 12
East Croydon	a		17 01	17 12			17 18	17 21		17 42				17 48	17 51			18 01	18 12				18 18	18 21	
East Croydon	d		17 01					17 21							17 51			18 01						18 21	
London Bridge	d		17 16					17 35							18 05			18 16						18 35	
London Blackfriars	d		17 22					17 42							18 12			18 22						18 42	
City Thameslink	d		17 24					17 44							18 14			18 24						18 44	
Farringdon	d		17 26					17 46							18 16			18 26						18 46	
St Pancras International	a		17 30					17 50							18 20			18 30						18 50	
East Croydon	d			17 12			17 18			17 42				17 48					18 12				18 18		
Clapham Junction	a			17 21			17 28			17 51				17 58					18 21				18 28		
London Victoria	a	17 14		17 29			17 35		17 43	17 59				18 05			18 13		18 29				18 35		18 44

		SN	SN	TL	SN	TL	TL		GX	TL	SN	SN	TL	SN	TL	GX	SN	SN		TL	SN	TL	TL	GX	TL
Lewes	d	17 45										18 21					18 45								
Hove	d		17 51								18 21							18 53							
Brighton	d			17 58	18 03		18 08		18 16	←			18 26	18 33		18 46				18 58	19 03		19 08	19 16	←
Preston Park	d		17 57				18 12			18 12			18 30					18 58					19 12		19 12
Hassocks	d				18 11		→			18 18			18 36	18 41							19 11		→		19 18
Burgess Hill	d			18 08	18 15					18 22			18 40	18 45						19 08	19 15				19 22
Wivelsfield	d	18 02		18 10									18 42				19 02			19 10					
Haywards Heath	a	18 07	18 11	18 15	18 20					18 27	18 36	18 40	18 46	18 50			19 07	19 11		19 15	19 20				19 27
Haywards Heath	d	18 15		18 17	18 21	←				18 31	18 44		18 47	18 51	←		19 15			19 17	19 21	←			19 31
Balcombe	d			18 22		18 22							18 52		18 52					19 22		19 22			
Three Bridges	a			→		18 28				18 39			→		18 58					→		19 28			19 39
Three Bridges	d					18 29				18 40					18 59							19 29			19 40
Gatwick Airport	a	18 26			18 32	18 33			18 41	18 44	18 56			19 02	19 03	19 12	19 26				19 32	19 33		19 41	19 44
Gatwick Airport	d	18 27			18 33	18 36			18 42	18 46	18 57			19 03	19 06	19 13	19 27				19 33	19 36		19 42	19 46
East Croydon	a	18 42			18 48	18 51				19 01	19 11			19 18	19 21		19 42				19 48	19 51			20 01
East Croydon	d					18 51				19 01					19 21							19 51			20 01
London Bridge	d					19 05				19 16					19 35							20 05			20 16
London Blackfriars	d					19 12				19 22					19 42							20 12			20 22
City Thameslink	d					19 14				19 24					19 44							20 14			20 24
Farringdon	d					19 16				19 26					19 46							20 16			20 26
St Pancras International	a					19 20				19 30					19 50							20 20			20 30
East Croydon	d	18 42			18 48						19 12			19 18			19 42				19 49				
Clapham Junction	a	18 51			18 58						19 21			19 28			19 51				19 58				
London Victoria	a	18 59			19 05				19 14		19 29			19 35		19 44	19 59				20 05			20 14	

Table T184-R

Mondays to Fridays

21 May to 7 December

Brighton/Hove/Lewes - Haywards Heath - Gatwick Airport - London

		SN	SN	TL		SN	TL	GX	SN	SN	TL	SN	TL	TL		GX	TL	SN	SN	TL	SN	TL	GX	SN	SN
Lewes	d		19 21						19 46										20 21					20 48	
Hove	d	19 21								19 52								20 21							20 51
Brighton	d			19 26		19 33		19 48			19 58	20 03		20 08		20 18	←			20 26	20 33		20 48		
Preston Park	d			19 30						19 58				20 12			20 12			20 30					20 57
Hassocks	d			19 36		19 41						20 11		→			20 18			20 36	20 41				
Burgess Hill	d			19 40		19 45					20 08	20 15					20 22			20 40	20 45				
Wivelsfield	d			19 42					20 02		20 10									20 42				21 02	
Haywards Heath	a	19 36	19 40	19 46		19 50			20 07	20 11	20 15	20 20					20 27	20 36	20 40	20 46	20 50			21 06	21 10
Haywards Heath	d	19 44		19 47		19 51	←		20 15		20 16	20 21	←				20 31	20 44		20 47	20 51	←		21 14	
Balcombe	d			19 52			19 52				20 22		20 22							20 52		20 52			
Three Bridges	a			→			19 58				→		20 27				20 39			→		20 58			
Three Bridges	d						19 59						20 29				20 40					20 59			
Gatwick Airport	a	19 56				20 02	20 03	20 12	20 27			20 32	20 33			20 41	20 44	20 56			21 02	21 03	21 11	21 26	
Gatwick Airport	d	19 57				20 03	20 06	20 13	20 28			20 33	20 36			20 42	20 46	20 57			21 03	21 06	21 12	21 27	
East Croydon	a	20 11				20 18	20 21		20 42			20 48	20 51				21 01	21 11			21 18	21 21		21 41	
East Croydon	d						20 21						20 51				21 01					21 21			
London Bridge	d						20 35						21 05				21 16					21 35			
London Blackfriars	d						20 42						21 12				21 22					21 42			
City Thameslink	d						20 44						21 14				21 24					21 44			
Farringdon	d						20 46						21 16				21 26					21 46			
St Pancras International	a						20 50						21 20				21 30					21 50			
East Croydon	d	20 12				20 19			20 43			20 49						21 12			21 19			21 42	
Clapham Junction	a	20 21				20 28			20 52			21 01						21 21			21 28			21 51	
London Victoria	a	20 30				20 35		20 44	20 59			21 08				21 15		21 29			21 35		21 43	21 59	

			TL	SN	TL	TL	GX	TL	SN	SN	TL		SN	TL	GX	SN	SN	TL	SN	TL	TL		GX	TL	
Lewes	d									21 21						21 48									
Hove	d								21 21								21 51								
Brighton	d		20 58	21 03		21 08	21 18	←			21 26		21 33		21 48			21 58	22 03		22 08		22 18	←	
Preston Park	d					21 12		21 12			21 30						21 57				22 12			22 12	
Hassocks	d			21 11		→		21 18			21 36		21 41						22 11		→			22 18	
Burgess Hill	d		21 08	21 15				21 22			21 40		21 45					22 08	22 15					22 22	
Wivelsfield	d		21 10								21 42					22 02		22 10							
Haywards Heath	a		21 15	21 20				21 27	21 36	21 40	21 46		21 50			22 07	22 11	22 15	22 20					22 27	
Haywards Heath	d		21 16	21 21	←			21 31	21 44		21 47		21 51	←		22 15		22 17	22 21	←				22 31	
Balcombe	d		21 22		21 22						21 52			21 52				22 22		22 22					
Three Bridges	a		→		21 27			21 39			→			21 58				→		22 28				22 39	
Three Bridges	d				21 29			21 40						21 59						22 29				22 40	
Gatwick Airport	a			21 32	21 33		21 41	21 44	21 56				22 02	22 03	22 11	22 27			22 32	22 33			22 41	22 44	
Gatwick Airport	d			21 33	21 36		21 42	21 46	21 57				22 03	22 06	22 12	22 28			22 33	22 36			22 42	22 46	
East Croydon	a			21 48	21 51			22 01	22 12				22 18	22 21		22 42			22 48	22 51				23 01	
East Croydon	d				21 51			22 01						22 21						22 51				23 01	
London Bridge	d				22 05			22 16						22 35						23 05				23 16	
London Blackfriars	d				22 12			22 22						22 42						23 12				23 22	
City Thameslink	d				22 14			22 24						22 44											
Farringdon	d				22 16			22 26						22 46						23 16				23 26	
St Pancras International	a				22 20			22 30						22 50						23 20				23 30	
East Croydon	d			21 49					22 12				22 19			22 43			22 49						
Clapham Junction	a			21 58					22 21				22 28			22 52			22 58						
London Victoria	a			22 05			22 13		22 29				22 35		22 43	23 00			23 05				23 13		

		SN	SN	TL	SN	TL	GX A	SN	SN		TL	SN	TL	TL
Lewes	d		22 21					22 48						
Hove	d	22 21							22 51					
Brighton	d			22 26	22 33		22 48				22 56	23 13	23 24	23 42
Preston Park	d			22 30					22 57		23 00		23 28	23 46
Hassocks	d			22 36	22 41						23 06	23 21	23 34	23 52
Burgess Hill	d			22 40	22 45						23 10	23 25	23 38	23 56
Wivelsfield	d			22 42				23 01			23 12		23 40	23 58
Haywards Heath	a	22 36	22 40	22 46	22 50			23 06	23 10		23 16	23 30	23 45	00 02
Haywards Heath	d	22 44		22 47	22 51	←		23 14			23 17	23 30	23 46	00 03
Balcombe	d			22 52		22 52					23 22		23 52	00 08
Three Bridges	a			→		22 58					23 28		23 57	00 14
Three Bridges	d					22 59					23 29		23 58	00 15
Gatwick Airport	a	22 56			23 02	23 03	23 11	23 26			23 33	23 45	00 03	00 19
Gatwick Airport	d	22 57			23 03	23 06	23 12	23 27			23 34	23 55	00 04	00 21
East Croydon	a	23 12			23 18	23 21		23 42			23 52	00 15	00 22	00 39
East Croydon	d					23 21					23 53		00 23	00 40
London Bridge	d					23 35								
London Blackfriars	d					23 42					00 22		00 50	01 08
City Thameslink	d													
Farringdon	d					23 46					00 25			
St Pancras International	a					23 50					00 29		00 59	01 15
East Croydon	d	23 12			23 19			23 42				00 16		
Clapham Junction	a	23 21			23 28			23 57				00 33		
London Victoria	a	23 30			23 35		23 43	00 05				00 41		

A not 7 December

Table T184-R

Saturdays

26 May to 8 December

Brighton/Hove/Lewes - Haywards Heath - Gatwick Airport - London

		TL	TL	SN	TL	SN	TL	SN	TL	SN	SN		TL	SN	TL	TL	GX	TL	SN	SN	TL		SN	TL	GX
Lewes	d					05 24														06 21					
Hove	d										05 54								06 21						
Brighton	d	00 04	04 12	04 33	05 06		05 26	05 33		05 44			05 58	06 03		06 08	06 18	←			06 26		06 33		06 48
Preston Park	d	00 08			05 10		05 30			05 48						06 12		06 12			06 30				
Hassocks	d	00 14			05 16		05 36	05 41		05 54				06 11		→		06 18			06 36		06 41		
Burgess Hill	d	00 18			05 20		05 40	05 45		05 58			06 08	06 15				06 22			06 40		06 45		
Wivelsfield	d	00 20			05 22		05 42			06 01			06 10								06 42				
Haywards Heath	a	00 24	04 25	04 46	05 27	05 40	05 46	05 50		06 06	06 10		06 15	06 20				06 27	06 36	06 40	06 46		06 50		
Haywards Heath	d	00 25	04 26	04 47	05 28	05 43	05 47	05 51	←	06 14			06 16	06 21	←			06 31	06 44		06 47		06 51	←	
Balcombe	d	00 30			05 34		05 52		05 52				06 22		06 22						06 52			06 52	
Three Bridges	a	00 36	04 34	04 56	05 39	05 52	→		05 58				→		06 27			06 39			→			06 58	
Three Bridges	d	00 37	04 35	04 58	05 40	05 53			05 59						06 29			06 40						06 59	
Gatwick Airport	a	00 41	04 40	05 02	05 44	05 57		06 02	06 05	06 26				06 32	06 33		06 41	06 44	06 56				07 02	07 05	07 11
Gatwick Airport	d	00 42	04 41	05 03	05 46			06 03	06 06	06 27				06 33	06 36		06 42	06 46	06 57				07 03	07 06	07 12
East Croydon	a	01 09	05 08	05 30	06 00			06 18	06 21	06 41				06 48	06 51			07 01	07 11				07 18	07 21	
East Croydon	d	01 10	05 10		06 01				06 21						06 51			07 01						07 21	
London Bridge	d		05 26		06 16				06 35						07 05			07 16						07 35	
London Blackfriars	d	01 36	05 32		06 22				06 42						07 12			07 22						07 42	
City Thameslink	d																								
Farringdon	d		05 36		06 26				06 46						07 16			07 26						07 46	
St Pancras International	a	01 43	05 40		06 30				06 50						07 20			07 30						07 50	
East Croydon	d			05 30				06 19		06 42				06 49					07 12				07 19		
Clapham Junction	a			05 50				06 28		06 51				06 58					07 21				07 28		
London Victoria	a			05 59				06 35		06 59				07 05			07 13		07 29				07 35		07 43

		SN	SN	TL	SN	TL	TL		GX	TL	SN	SN	TL	SN	TL	GX	SN	SN		TL	SN	TL	TL	GX	TL
Lewes	d	06 48										07 21					07 48								
Hove	d		06 51								07 21							07 51							
Brighton	d			06 58	07 03		07 08		07 18	←			07 26	07 33		07 48				07 58	08 03		08 08	08 18	←
Preston Park	d		06 57				07 12			07 12			07 30					07 57					08 12		08 12
Hassocks	d				07 11		→			07 18			07 36	07 41							08 11		→		08 18
Burgess Hill	d			07 08	07 15					07 22			07 40	07 45						08 08	08 15				08 22
Wivelsfield	d	07 01		07 10									07 42				08 01			08 10					
Haywards Heath	a	07 06	07 10	07 15	07 20					07 27	07 36	07 40	07 46	07 50			08 06	08 10		08 15	08 20				08 27
Haywards Heath	d	07 14		07 16	07 21	←				07 31	07 44		07 47	07 51	←		08 14			08 16	08 21	←			08 31
Balcombe	d			07 22		07 22							07 52		07 52					08 22		08 22			
Three Bridges	a			→		07 27				07 39			→		07 58					→		08 27			08 39
Three Bridges	d					07 29				07 40					07 59							08 29			08 40
Gatwick Airport	a	07 26			07 32	07 33			07 41	07 44	07 56			08 02	08 05	08 11	08 26				08 32	08 33		08 41	08 44
Gatwick Airport	d	07 27			07 33	07 36			07 42	07 46	07 57			08 03	08 06	08 12	08 27				08 33	08 36		08 42	08 46
East Croydon	a	07 41			07 48	07 51				08 01	08 11			08 18	08 21		08 41				08 48	08 51			09 01
East Croydon	d					07 51				08 01					08 21							08 51			09 01
London Bridge	d					08 05				08 16					08 35							09 05			09 16
London Blackfriars	d					08 12				08 22					08 42							09 12			09 22
City Thameslink	d																					09 14			09 24
Farringdon	d					08 16				08 26					08 46							09 16			09 26
St Pancras International	a					08 20				08 30					08 50							09 20			09 30
East Croydon	d	07 42			07 49						08 12			08 19			08 42				08 49				
Clapham Junction	a	07 51			07 58						08 21			08 28			08 51				08 58				
London Victoria	a	07 59			08 05				08 13		08 29			08 35		08 43	08 59				09 05			09 13	

		SN	SN	TL		SN	TL	GX	SN	SN	TL	SN	TL	TL		GX	TL	SN	SN	TL	SN	TL	GX	SN	SN
Lewes	d		08 21						08 48										09 21					09 48	
Hove	d	08 21								08 51								09 21							09 51
Brighton	d			08 26		08 33		08 48			08 58	09 03		09 08		09 18	←			09 26	09 33		09 48		
Preston Park	d			08 30						08 57				09 12			09 12			09 30					09 57
Hassocks	d			08 36		08 41						09 11		→			09 18			09 36	09 41				
Burgess Hill	d			08 40		08 45					09 08	09 15					09 22			09 40	09 45				
Wivelsfield	d			08 42					09 01		09 10									09 42				10 01	
Haywards Heath	a	08 36	08 40	08 46		08 50			09 06	09 10	09 15	09 20					09 27	09 36	09 40	09 46	09 50			10 06	10 10
Haywards Heath	d	08 44		08 47		08 51	←		09 14		09 16	09 21	←				09 31	09 44		09 47	09 51	←		10 14	
Balcombe	d			08 52			08 52				09 22		09 22							09 52		09 52			
Three Bridges	a			→			08 58				→		09 27				09 39			→		09 58			
Three Bridges	d						08 59						09 29				09 40					09 59			
Gatwick Airport	a	08 56				09 02	09 05	09 11	09 26			09 32	09 33			09 41	09 44	09 56			10 02	10 05	10 11	10 26	
Gatwick Airport	d	08 57				09 03	09 06	09 12	09 27			09 33	09 36			09 42	09 46	09 57			10 03	10 06	10 12	10 27	
East Croydon	a	09 11				09 18	09 21		09 41			09 48	09 51				10 01	10 11			10 18	10 21		10 41	
East Croydon	d						09 21						09 51				10 01					10 21			
London Bridge	d						09 35						10 05				10 16					10 35			
London Blackfriars	d						09 42						10 12				10 22					10 42			
City Thameslink	d						09 44						10 14				10 24					10 44			
Farringdon	d						09 46						10 16				10 26					10 46			
St Pancras International	a						09 50						10 20				10 30					10 50			
East Croydon	d	09 12				09 19			09 42			09 49						10 12			10 19			10 42	
Clapham Junction	a	09 21				09 28			09 51			09 58						10 21			10 28			10 51	
London Victoria	a	09 29				09 35		09 43	09 59			10 05				10 13		10 29			10 35		10 43	10 59	

Table T184-R

Saturdays

26 May to 8 December

Brighton/Hove/Lewes - Haywards Heath - Gatwick Airport - London

		TL	SN	TL	TL	GX	TL	SN	SN	TL	SN	TL	GX	SN	SN	TL	SN	TL	TL	GX	TL
Lewes	d								10 21					10 48							
Hove	d							10 21							10 51						
Brighton	d	09 58	10 03		10 08	10 18	←			10 26	10 33		10 48			10 58	11 03		11 08	11 18	←
Preston Park	d				10 12		10 12			10 30					10 57				11 12		11 12
Hassocks	d		10 11		→		10 18			10 36	10 41						11 11		→		11 18
Burgess Hill	d	10 08	10 15				10 22			10 40	10 45					11 08	11 15				11 22
Wivelsfield	d	10 10								10 42				11 01		11 10					
Haywards Heath	a	10 15	10 20				10 27	10 36	10 40	10 46	10 50			11 06	11 10	11 15	11 20				11 27
Haywards Heath	d	10 16	10 21	←			10 31	10 44		10 47	10 51	←		11 14		11 16	11 21	←			11 31
Balcombe	d	10 22		10 22						10 52		10 52				11 22		11 22			
Three Bridges	a	→		10 27			10 39			→		10 58				→		11 27			11 39
Three Bridges	d			10 29			10 40					10 59						11 29			11 40
Gatwick Airport	a		10 32	10 33		10 41	10 44	10 56			11 02	11 05	11 11	11 26			11 32	11 33		11 41	11 44
Gatwick Airport	d		10 33	10 36		10 42	10 46	10 57			11 03	11 06	11 12	11 27			11 33	11 36		11 42	11 46
East Croydon	a		10 48	10 51			11 01	11 11			11 18	11 21		11 41			11 48	11 51			12 01
East Croydon	d			10 51			11 01					11 21						11 51			12 01
London Bridge	d			11 05			11 16					11 35						12 05			12 16
London Blackfriars	d			11 12			11 22					11 42						12 12			12 22
City Thameslink	d			11 14			11 24					11 44						12 14			12 24
Farringdon	d			11 16			11 26					11 46						12 16			12 26
St Pancras International	a			11 20			11 30					11 50						12 20			12 30
East Croydon	d		10 49					11 12			11 19			11 42			11 49				
Clapham Junction	a		10 58					11 21			11 28			11 51			11 58				
London Victoria	a		11 05			11 13		11 29			11 35		11 43	11 59			12 05			12 13	

		SN	SN	TL	SN	TL	GX	SN	SN	TL	SN	TL	TL	GX	TL	SN	SN	TL	SN	TL	GX	SN	SN
Lewes	d		11 21					11 48									12 21					12 48	
Hove	d	11 21							11 51							12 21							12 51
Brighton	d			11 26	11 33		11 48			11 58	12 03		12 08	12 18	←			12 26	12 33		12 48		
Preston Park	d			11 30					11 57				12 12		12 12			12 30					12 57
Hassocks	d			11 36	11 41						12 11		→		12 18			12 36	12 41				
Burgess Hill	d			11 40	11 45					12 08	12 15				12 22			12 40	12 45				
Wivelsfield	d			11 42				12 01		12 10								12 42				13 01	
Haywards Heath	a	11 36	11 40	11 46	11 50			12 06	12 10	12 15	12 20				12 27	12 36	12 40	12 46	12 50			13 06	13 10
Haywards Heath	d	11 44		11 47	11 51	←		12 14		12 16	12 21	←			12 31	12 44		12 47	12 51	←		13 14	
Balcombe	d			11 52		11 52				12 22		12 22						12 52		12 52			
Three Bridges	a			→		11 58				→		12 27			12 39			→		12 58			
Three Bridges	d					11 59						12 29			12 40					12 59			
Gatwick Airport	a	11 56			12 02	12 05	12 11	12 26			12 32	12 33		12 41	12 44	12 56			13 02	13 05	13 11	13 26	
Gatwick Airport	d	11 57			12 03	12 06	12 12	12 27			12 33	12 36		12 42	12 46	12 57			13 03	13 06	13 12	13 27	
East Croydon	a	12 11			12 18	12 21		12 41			12 48	12 51			13 01	13 11			13 18	13 21		13 41	
East Croydon	d					12 21						12 51			13 01					13 21			
London Bridge	d					12 35						13 05			13 16					13 35			
London Blackfriars	d					12 42						13 12			13 22					13 42			
City Thameslink	d					12 44						13 14			13 24					13 44			
Farringdon	d					12 46						13 16			13 26					13 46			
St Pancras International	a					12 50						13 20			13 30					13 50			
East Croydon	d	12 12			12 19			12 42			12 49					13 12			13 19			13 42	
Clapham Junction	a	12 21			12 28			12 51			12 58					13 21			13 28			13 51	
London Victoria	a	12 29			12 35		12 43	12 59			13 05			13 13		13 29			13 35		13 43	13 59	

		TL	SN	TL	TL	GX	TL	SN	SN	TL	SN	TL	GX	SN	SN	TL	SN	TL	TL	GX	TL	SN	SN
Lewes	d								13 21					13 48									14 21
Hove	d							13 21							13 51							14 21	
Brighton	d	12 58	13 03		13 08	13 18	←			13 26	13 33		13 48			13 58	14 03		14 08	14 18	←		
Preston Park	d				13 12		13 12			13 30					13 57				14 12		14 12		
Hassocks	d		13 11		→		13 18			13 36	13 41						14 11		→		14 18		
Burgess Hill	d	13 08	13 15				13 22			13 40	13 45					14 08	14 15				14 22		
Wivelsfield	d	13 10								13 42				14 01		14 10							
Haywards Heath	a	13 15	13 20				13 27	13 36	13 40	13 46	13 50			14 06	14 10	14 15	14 20				14 27	14 36	14 40
Haywards Heath	d	13 16	13 21	←			13 31	13 44		13 47	13 51	←		14 14		14 16	14 21	←			14 31	14 44	
Balcombe	d	13 22		13 22						13 52		13 52				14 22		14 22					
Three Bridges	a	→		13 27			13 39			→		13 58				→		14 27			14 39		
Three Bridges	d			13 29			13 40					13 59						14 29			14 40		
Gatwick Airport	a		13 32	13 33		13 41	13 44	13 56			14 02	14 05	14 11	14 26			14 32	14 33		14 41	14 44	14 56	
Gatwick Airport	d		13 33	13 36		13 42	13 46	13 57			14 03	14 06	14 12	14 27			14 33	14 36		14 42	14 46	14 57	
East Croydon	a		13 48	13 51			14 01	14 11			14 18	14 21		14 41			14 48	14 51			15 01	15 11	
East Croydon	d			13 51			14 01					14 21						14 51			15 01		
London Bridge	d			14 05			14 16					14 35						15 05			15 16		
London Blackfriars	d			14 12			14 22					14 42						15 12			15 22		
City Thameslink	d			14 14			14 24					14 44						15 14			15 24		
Farringdon	d			14 16			14 26					14 46						15 16			15 26		
St Pancras International	a			14 20			14 30					14 50						15 20			15 30		
East Croydon	d		13 49					14 12			14 19			14 42			14 49					15 12	
Clapham Junction	a		13 58					14 21			14 28			14 51			14 58					15 21	
London Victoria	a		14 05			14 13		14 29			14 35		14 43	14 59			15 05			15 13		15 29	

Table T184-R

Saturdays

26 May to 8 December

Brighton/Hove/Lewes - Haywards Heath - Gatwick Airport - London

		TL	SN	TL	GX	SN	SN	TL	SN	TL	TL	GX	TL	SN	SN	TL	SN	TL	GX	SN	SN	TL
Lewes	d					14 48									15 21					15 48		
Hove	d						14 51							15 21							15 51	
Brighton	d	14 26	14 33		14 48			14 58	15 03		15 08	15 18	←			15 26	15 33		15 48			15 58
Preston Park	d	14 30					14 57				15 12		15 12			15 30					15 57	
Hassocks	d	14 36	14 41						15 11		→		15 18			15 36	15 41					
Burgess Hill	d	14 40	14 45					15 08	15 15				15 22			15 40	15 45					16 08
Wivelsfield	d	14 42				15 01		15 10								15 42				16 01		16 10
Haywards Heath	a	14 46	14 50			15 06	15 10	15 15	15 20				15 27	15 36	15 40	15 46	15 50			16 06	16 10	16 15
Haywards Heath	d	14 47	14 51	←		15 14		15 16	15 21	←			15 31	15 44		15 47	15 51	←		16 14		16 16
Balcombe	d	14 52		14 52				15 22		15 22						15 52		15 52				16 22
Three Bridges	a	→		14 58				→		15 27			15 39			→		15 58				→
Three Bridges	d			14 59						15 29			15 40					15 59				
Gatwick Airport	a		15 02	15 05	15 11	15 26			15 32	15 33		15 41	15 44	15 56			16 02	16 05	16 11	16 26		
Gatwick Airport	d		15 03	15 06	15 12	15 27			15 33	15 36		15 42	15 46	15 57			16 03	16 06	16 12	16 27		
East Croydon	a		15 18	15 21		15 41			15 48	15 51			16 01	16 11			16 18	16 21		16 41		
East Croydon	d			15 21						15 51			16 01					16 21				
London Bridge	d			15 35						16 05			16 16					16 35				
London Blackfriars	d			15 42						16 12			16 22					16 42				
City Thameslink	d			15 44						16 14			16 24					16 44				
Farringdon	d			15 46						16 16			16 26					16 46				
St Pancras International	a			15 50						16 20			16 30					16 50				
East Croydon	d		15 19			15 42			15 49					16 12			16 19			16 42		
Clapham Junction	a		15 28			15 51			15 58					16 21			16 28			16 51		
London Victoria	a		15 35		15 43	15 59			16 05			16 13		16 29			16 35		16 43	16 59		

		SN	TL	TL	GX	TL	SN	SN	TL	SN	TL	GX	SN	SN	TL	SN	TL	TL	GX	TL	SN	SN	TL
Lewes	d							16 21					16 48									17 21	
Hove	d						16 21							16 51							17 21		
Brighton	d	16 03		16 08	16 18	←			16 26	16 33		16 48			16 58	17 03		17 08	17 18	←			17 26
Preston Park	d			16 12		16 12			16 30					16 57				17 12		17 12			17 30
Hassocks	d	16 11		→		16 18			16 36	16 41						17 11		→		17 18			17 36
Burgess Hill	d	16 15				16 22			16 40	16 45					17 08	17 15				17 22			17 40
Wivelsfield	d								16 42				17 01		17 10								17 42
Haywards Heath	a	16 20				16 27	16 36	16 40	16 46	16 50			17 06	17 10	17 15	17 20				17 27	17 36	17 40	17 46
Haywards Heath	d	16 21	←			16 31	16 44		16 47	16 51	←		17 14		17 16	17 21	←			17 31	17 44		17 47
Balcombe	d		16 22						16 52		16 52				17 22		17 22						17 52
Three Bridges	a		16 27			16 39			→		16 58				→		17 27			17 39			→
Three Bridges	d		16 29			16 40					16 59						17 29			17 40			
Gatwick Airport	a	16 32	16 33		16 43	16 44	16 56			17 02	17 05	17 11	17 26			17 32	17 33		17 41	17 44	17 56		
Gatwick Airport	d	16 33	16 36		16 44	16 46	16 57			17 03	17 06	17 12	17 27			17 33	17 36		17 42	17 46	17 57		
East Croydon	a	16 48	16 51			17 01	17 11			17 18	17 21		17 41			17 48	17 51			18 01	18 11		
East Croydon	d		16 51			17 01					17 21						17 51			18 01			
London Bridge	d		17 05			17 16					17 35						18 05			18 16			
London Blackfriars	d		17 12			17 22					17 42						18 12			18 22			
City Thameslink	d		17 14			17 24					17 44						18 14			18 24			
Farringdon	d		17 16			17 26					17 46						18 16			18 26			
St Pancras International	a		17 20			17 30					17 50						18 20			18 30			
East Croydon	d	16 49					17 12			17 19			17 42			17 49					18 12		
Clapham Junction	a	16 58					17 21			17 28			17 51			17 58					18 21		
London Victoria	a	17 05			17 14		17 29			17 35		17 43	17 59			18 05			18 13		18 29		

		SN	TL	GX	SN	SN	TL	SN	TL	TL	GX	TL	SN	SN	TL	SN	TL	GX	SN	SN	TL	SN	TL
Lewes	d				17 48									18 21					18 48				
Hove	d					17 51							18 21							18 51			
Brighton	d	17 33		17 48			17 58	18 03		18 08	18 18	←			18 26	18 33		18 48			18 58	19 03	
Preston Park	d					17 57				18 12		18 12			18 30					18 57			
Hassocks	d	17 41						18 11		→		18 18			18 36	18 41						19 11	
Burgess Hill	d	17 45					18 08	18 15				18 22			18 40	18 45					19 08	19 15	
Wivelsfield	d				18 01		18 10								18 42				19 01		19 10		
Haywards Heath	a	17 50			18 06	18 10	18 15	18 20				18 27	18 36	18 40	18 46	18 50			19 06	19 10	19 15	19 20	
Haywards Heath	d	17 51	←		18 14		18 16	18 21	←			18 31	18 44		18 47	18 51	←		19 14		19 16	19 21	←
Balcombe	d		17 52				18 22		18 22						18 52		18 52				19 22		19 22
Three Bridges	a		17 58				→		18 27			18 39			→		18 58				→		19 27
Three Bridges	d		17 59						18 29			18 40					18 59						19 29
Gatwick Airport	a	18 02	18 05	18 11	18 26			18 32	18 33		18 41	18 44	18 56			19 02	19 05	19 11	19 26			19 32	19 33
Gatwick Airport	d	18 03	18 06	18 12	18 27			18 33	18 36		18 42	18 46	18 57			19 03	19 06	19 12	19 27			19 33	19 36
East Croydon	a	18 18	18 21		18 41			18 48	18 51			19 01	19 11			19 18	19 21		19 41			19 48	19 51
East Croydon	d		18 21						18 51			19 01					19 21						19 51
London Bridge	d		18 35						19 05			19 16					19 35						20 05
London Blackfriars	d		18 42						19 12			19 22					19 42						20 12
City Thameslink	d		18 44						19 14			19 24					19 44						20 14
Farringdon	d		18 46						19 16			19 26					19 46						20 16
St Pancras International	a		18 50						19 20			19 30					19 50						20 20
East Croydon	d	18 19			18 42			18 49					19 12			19 19			19 42			19 49	
Clapham Junction	a	18 28			18 51			18 58					19 21			19 28			19 51			19 58	
London Victoria	a	18 35		18 43	18 59			19 05			19 13		19 29			19 35		19 43	19 59			20 05	

Table T184-R

Saturdays

26 May to 8 December

Brighton/Hove/Lewes - Haywards Heath - Gatwick Airport - London

		TL ■		GX ■	TL ■	SN ■	SN ■	TL ■	SN ■	TL ■	GX ■	SN ■	SN ■		TL ■	SN ■	TL ■	TL ■	GX ■	TL ■	SN ■	SN ■	TL ■		SN ■
Lewes	d						19 21					19 48										20 21			
Hove	d					19 21							19 51								20 21				
Brighton	d	19 08		19 18	←			19 26	19 33		19 48				19 58	20 03		20 08	20 18	←			20 26		20 33
Preston Park	d	19 12			19 12			19 30					19 57					20 12		20 12			20 30		
Hassocks	d	→			19 18			19 36	19 41							20 11		→		20 18			20 36		20 41
Burgess Hill	d				19 22			19 40	19 45						20 08	20 15				20 22			20 40		20 45
Wivelsfield	d							19 42				20 01			20 10								20 42		
Haywards Heath	a				19 27	19 36	19 40	19 46	19 50			20 06	20 10		20 15	20 20				20 27	20 36	20 40	20 46		20 50
Haywards Heath	d				19 31	19 44		19 47	19 51	←		20 14			20 16	20 21	←			20 31	20 44		20 47		20 51
Balcombe	d							19 52		19 52					20 22		20 22						20 52		
Three Bridges	a				19 39			→		19 58					→		20 27			20 39			→		
Three Bridges	d				19 40					19 59							20 29			20 40					
Gatwick Airport	a			19 41	19 44	19 56			20 02	20 05	20 11	20 26				20 32	20 33		20 41	20 44	20 56				21 02
Gatwick Airport	d			19 42	19 46	19 57			20 03	20 06	20 12	20 27				20 33	20 36		20 42	20 46	20 57				21 03
East Croydon	a				20 01	20 11			20 18	20 21		20 41				20 48	20 51			21 01	21 11				21 18
East Croydon	d				20 01					20 21							20 51			21 01					
London Bridge	d				20 16					20 35							21 05			21 16					
London Blackfriars	d				20 22					20 42							21 12			21 22					
City Thameslink	d				20 24					20 44															
Farringdon	d				20 26					20 46							21 16			21 26					
St Pancras International	a				20 30					20 50							21 20			21 30					
East Croydon	d					20 12			20 19			20 42				20 49					21 12				21 19
Clapham Junction	a					20 21			20 28			20 51				20 58					21 21				21 28
London Victoria	a			20 13		20 29			20 35		20 43	20 59				21 05			21 13		21 29				21 35

		TL ■	GX ■	SN ■	SN ■	TL ■	SN ■	TL ■	TL ■		GX ■	TL ■	SN ■	SN ■	TL ■	SN ■	TL ■	GX ■	SN ■	SN ■		TL ■	SN ■	TL ■	TL ■
Lewes	d			20 48										21 21					21 48						
Hove	d				20 51								21 21							21 51					
Brighton	d		20 48			20 58	21 03		21 08		21 18	←			21 26	21 33		21 48				21 58	22 03		22 08
Preston Park	d				20 57				21 12			21 12			21 30					21 57					22 12
Hassocks	d						21 11		→			21 18			21 36	21 41							22 11		→
Burgess Hill	d					21 08	21 15					21 22			21 40	21 45						22 08	22 15		
Wivelsfield	d			21 01		21 10									21 42				22 01			22 10			
Haywards Heath	a			21 06	21 10	21 15	21 20					21 27	21 36	21 40	21 46	21 50			22 06	22 10		22 15	22 20		
Haywards Heath	d	←		21 14		21 16	21 21	←				21 31	21 44		21 47	21 51	←		22 14			22 16	22 21	←	
Balcombe	d	20 52				21 22		21 22							21 52		21 52					22 22		22 22	
Three Bridges	a	20 58				→		21 27				21 39			→		21 58					→		22 27	
Three Bridges	d	20 59						21 29				21 40					21 59							22 29	
Gatwick Airport	a	21 05	21 11	21 26			21 32	21 33			21 41	21 44	21 56			22 02	22 05	22 11	22 26				22 32	22 33	
Gatwick Airport	d	21 06	21 12	21 27			21 33	21 36			21 42	21 46	21 57			22 03	22 06	22 12	22 27				22 33	22 36	
East Croydon	a	21 21		21 41			21 48	21 51				22 01	22 12			22 18	22 21		22 41				22 48	22 51	
East Croydon	d	21 21						21 51				22 01					22 21							22 51	
London Bridge	d	21 35						22 05				22 16					22 35							23 05	
London Blackfriars	d	21 42						22 12				22 22					22 42							23 12	
City Thameslink	d																								
Farringdon	d	21 46						22 16				22 26					22 46							23 16	
St Pancras International	a	21 50						22 20				22 30					22 50							23 20	
East Croydon	d			21 42			21 49						22 12			22 19			22 42				22 49		
Clapham Junction	a			21 51			21 58						22 21			22 28			22 51				22 58		
London Victoria	a		21 43	21 59			22 05				22 13		22 29			22 35		22 43	22 59				23 05		

		GX ■	TL ■	SN ■	SN ■	TL ■		SN ■	TL ■	GX ■	TL ■	SN ■	TL ■	TL ■
Lewes	d				22 21									
Hove	d			22 21										
Brighton	d	22 18	←			22 28		22 33		22 48	22 54	23 13	23 24	23 42
Preston Park	d		22 12								22 58		23 28	23 46
Hassocks	d		22 18					22 41			23 04	23 21	23 34	23 52
Burgess Hill	d		22 22			22 38		22 45			23 08	23 25	23 38	23 56
Wivelsfield	d					22 40					23 10		23 40	23 58
Haywards Heath	a		22 27	22 36	22 40	22 45		22 50			23 15	23 30	23 45	00 02
Haywards Heath	d		22 31	22 44		22 46		22 51	←		23 16	23 30	23 46	00 03
Balcombe	d					22 52			22 52		23 22		23 52	00 08
Three Bridges	a		22 39			→			22 57		23 27		23 57	00 14
Three Bridges	d		22 40						22 59		23 28		23 58	00 15
Gatwick Airport	a	22 41	22 44	22 56				23 02	23 03	23 11	23 33	23 45	00 03	00 19
Gatwick Airport	d	22 42	22 46	22 57				23 03	23 06	23 12	23 34	23 55	00 04	00 21
East Croydon	a		23 01	23 11				23 18	23 21		23 54	00 16	00 22	00 39
East Croydon	d		23 01						23 21		23 54		00 23	00 40
London Bridge	d		23 16						23 35					
London Blackfriars	d		23 22						23 42		00 22		00 50	01 06
City Thameslink	d													
Farringdon	d		23 26						23 46		00 26			
St Pancras International	a		23 30						23 50		00 30		00 59	01 15
East Croydon	d			23 12				23 19				00 16		
Clapham Junction	a			23 21				23 28				00 33		
London Victoria	a	23 13		23 29				23 35		23 43		00 41		

Table T184-R

Sundays

20 May to 2 December

Brighton/Hove/Lewes - Haywards Heath - Gatwick Airport - London

		TL ■	SN ■	TL ■	SN	TL ■	TL ■	SN	TL ■	SN	SN		TL ■	SN	SN	TL ■	SN	SN	TL ■	SN	SN		TL ■	SN	SN
Lewes	d										07 19						08 18							09 21	
Hove	d														07 52					08 52					
Brighton	d	00 04	04 33	05 42	05 47	06 08	06 42	06 47	07 08	07 17			07 42	07 47		08 08		08 27	08 42		08 57		09 08		09 27
Preston Park	d	00 08		05 46	05 51	06 12	06 46	06 51	07 12				07 46		07 57	08 12			08 46	08 57			09 12		
Hassocks	d	00 14		05 52	05 57	06 18	06 52	06 57	07 18	07 25			07 52	07 56		08 18		08 36	08 52		09 06		09 18		09 36
Burgess Hill	d	00 18		05 56	06 01	06 22	06 56	07 01	07 22	07 29			07 56	08 00		08 22		08 40	08 56		09 10		09 22		09 40
Wivelsfield	d	00 20		05 58	06 03	06 24	06 58	07 03	07 24				07 58			08 24	08 35		08 58				09 24	09 36	
Haywards Heath	a	00 24	04 46	06 03	06 07	06 29	07 03	07 07	07 29	07 34	07 38		08 03	08 06	08 09	08 29	08 39	08 45	09 03	09 08	09 15		09 29	09 41	09 45
Haywards Heath	d	00 25	04 47	06 04	06 08	06 30	07 04	07 08	07 30	07 42			08 04	08 13		08 30	08 41	08 46	09 04	09 11	09 16		09 30	09 41	09 46
Balcombe	d	00 30				06 36			07 36							08 35							09 36		
Three Bridges	a	00 36	04 56	06 12	06 16	06 42	07 12	07 16	07 42				08 12			08 41			09 12		09 24		09 42		
Three Bridges	d	00 37	04 58	06 13	06 23	06 43	07 13	07 23	07 43				08 13			08 42			09 13		09 25		09 43		
Gatwick Airport	a	00 41	05 02	06 18	06 27	06 48	07 18	07 27	07 48	07 53			08 17	08 24		08 46	08 52	08 58	09 17	09 24	09 29		09 47	09 53	09 58
Gatwick Airport	d	00 42	05 03	06 21	06 28	06 51	07 21	07 28	07 51	07 54			08 21	08 25		08 47	08 56	09 00	09 19	09 25	09 30		09 49	09 56	10 00
East Croydon	a	01 09	05 29	06 39	06 50	07 09	07 39	07 50	08 09	08 22			08 39	08 45		09 02	09 10	09 14	09 33	09 40	09 44		10 03	10 10	10 14
East Croydon	d	01 10		06 40		07 10	07 40		08 10				08 40			09 02			09 34				10 04		
London Bridge	d			06a55		07a25	07a58		08a25				08a55			09a17			09 49				10 19		
London Blackfriars	d	01 36																	09 55				10 25		
City Thameslink	d																								
Farringdon	d																		09 59				10 29		
St Pancras International	a	01 45																	10 03				10 33		
East Croydon	d		05 30		06 51			07 51		08 23				08 46			09 11	09 15		09 41	09 45			10 11	10 15
Clapham Junction	a		05 51		07 05			08 07		08 38				08 55			09 20	09 24		09 50	09 54			10 20	10 24
London Victoria	a		05 59		07 15			08 15		08 46				09 02			09 28	09 32		09 58	10 02			10 28	10 32

		TL ■	SN	SN	TL ■	SN	SN		TL ■	SN	SN	TL ■	SN	SN	TL ■	SN	SN		TL ■	SN	SN	TL ■	SN	SN	TL ■
Lewes	d					10 21							11 21							12 21					
Hove	d		09 52							10 52						11 52							12 52		
Brighton	d	09 42		09 57	10 08		10 27		10 42		10 57	11 08		11 27	11 42		11 57		12 08		12 27	12 42		12 57	13 08
Preston Park	d	09 46	09 57		10 12				10 46	10 57		11 12			11 46	11 57			12 12			12 46	12 57		13 12
Hassocks	d	09 52		10 06	10 18		10 36		10 52		11 06	11 18		11 36	11 52		12 06		12 18		12 36	12 52		13 06	13 18
Burgess Hill	d	09 56		10 10	10 22		10 40		10 56		11 10	11 22		11 40	11 56		12 10		12 22		12 40	12 56		13 10	13 22
Wivelsfield	d	09 58			10 24	10 36			10 58			11 24	11 36		11 58				12 24	12 36		12 58			13 24
Haywards Heath	a	10 03	10 08	10 15	10 29	10 41	10 45		11 03	11 08	11 15	11 29	11 41	11 45	12 03	12 08	12 15		12 29	12 41	12 45	13 03	13 08	13 15	13 29
Haywards Heath	d	10 04	10 11	10 16	10 30	10 41	10 46		11 04	11 11	11 16	11 30	11 41	11 46	12 04	12 11	12 16		12 30	12 41	12 46	13 04	13 11	13 16	13 30
Balcombe	d				10 36							11 36							12 36						13 36
Three Bridges	a	10 12		10 24	10 42				11 12		11 24	11 42			12 12		12 24		12 42			13 12		13 24	13 42
Three Bridges	d	10 13		10 25	10 43				11 13		11 25	11 43			12 13		12 25		12 43			13 13		13 25	13 43
Gatwick Airport	a	10 17	10 24	10 29	10 47	10 53	10 58		11 17	11 23	11 29	11 47	11 53	11 58	12 17	12 24	12 29		12 47	12 53	12 58	13 17	13 24	13 29	13 47
Gatwick Airport	d	10 19	10 25	10 30	10 49	10 56	11 00		11 19	11 25	11 30	11 49	11 56	12 00	12 19	12 25	12 30		12 49	12 56	13 00	13 19	13 25	13 30	13 49
East Croydon	a	10 33	10 40	10 44	11 03	11 10	11 14		11 33	11 39	11 44	12 03	12 10	12 14	12 33	12 40	12 44		13 03	13 10	13 14	13 33	13 40	13 44	14 03
East Croydon	d	10 34			11 04				11 34			12 04			12 34				13 04			13 34			14 04
London Bridge	d	10 49			11 19				11 49			12 19			12 49				13 19			13 49			14 19
London Blackfriars	d	10 55			11 25				11 55			12 25			12 55				13 25			13 55			14 25
City Thameslink	d																								
Farringdon	d	10 59			11 29				11 59			12 29			12 59				13 29			13 59			14 29
St Pancras International	a	11 03			11 33				12 03			12 33			13 03				13 33			14 03			14 33
East Croydon	d		10 41	10 45		11 11	11 15			11 40	11 45		12 11	12 15		12 41	12 45			13 11	13 15		13 41	13 45	
Clapham Junction	a		10 50	10 54		11 20	11 24			11 50	11 54		12 20	12 24		12 50	12 54			13 22	13 25		13 50	13 54	
London Victoria	a		10 58	11 02		11 28	11 32			11 58	12 02		12 28	12 32		12 58	13 02			13 30	13 32		13 58	14 02	

		SN	SN		TL ■	SN	SN	TL ■	SN	SN	TL ■	SN	SN		TL ■	SN	SN	TL ■	SN	SN	TL ■	SN	SN		
Lewes	d	13 21							14 21							15 21						16 21			
Hove	d					13 52						14 52							15 52						
Brighton	d		13 27		13 42		13 57	14 08		14 27	14 42		14 57		15 08		15 27	15 42		15 57	16 08		16 27		
Preston Park	d				13 46	13 57		14 12			14 46	14 57			15 12			15 46	15 57		16 12				
Hassocks	d		13 36		13 52		14 06	14 18		14 36	14 52		15 06		15 18		15 36	15 52		16 06	16 18		16 36		
Burgess Hill	d		13 40		13 56		14 10	14 22		14 40	14 56		15 10		15 22		15 40	15 56		16 10	16 22		16 40		
Wivelsfield	d	13 36			13 58			14 24	14 36		14 58				15 24	15 36		15 58			16 24	16 36			
Haywards Heath	a	13 41	13 45		14 03	14 08	14 15	14 29	14 41	14 45	15 03	15 08	15 15		15 29	15 41	15 45	16 03	16 08	16 15	16 29	16 41	16 45		
Haywards Heath	d	13 41	13 46		14 04	14 11	14 16	14 30	14 41	14 46	15 04	15 11	15 16		15 30	15 41	15 46	16 04	16 11	16 16	16 30	16 41	16 46		
Balcombe	d							14 36							15 36						16 36				
Three Bridges	a				14 12		14 24	14 42			15 12		15 24		15 42			16 12		16 24	16 42				
Three Bridges	d				14 13		14 25	14 43			15 13		15 25		15 43			16 13		16 25	16 43				
Gatwick Airport	a	13 53	13 58		14 17	14 24	14 29	14 47	14 53	14 58	15 17	15 24	15 29		15 47	15 53	15 58	16 17	16 24	16 29	16 47	16 53	16 58		
Gatwick Airport	d	13 56	14 00		14 19	14 25	14 30	14 49	14 56	15 00	15 19	15 25	15 30		15 49	15 56	16 00	16 19	16 25	16 30	16 49	16 56	17 00		
East Croydon	a	14 10	14 14		14 33	14 40	14 44	15 03	15 10	15 14	15 33	15 40	15 44		16 03	16 10	16 14	16 33	16 40	16 44	17 03	17 10	17 14		
East Croydon	d				14 34			15 04			15 34				16 04			16 34			17 04				
London Bridge	d				14 49			15 19			15 49				16 19			16 49			17 19				
London Blackfriars	d				14 55			15 25			15 55				16 25			16 55			17 25				
City Thameslink	d																								
Farringdon	d				14 59			15 29			15 59				16 29			16 59			17 29				
St Pancras International	a				15 03			15 33			16 03				16 33			17 03			17 33				
East Croydon	d	14 11	14 15			14 41	14 45		15 11	15 15		15 41	15 45			16 11	16 15		16 41	16 45		17 11	17 15		
Clapham Junction	a	14 20	14 24			14 50	14 54		15 20	15 24		15 50	15 54			16 22	16 24		16 50	16 54		17 22	17 25		
London Victoria	a	14 28	14 32			14 58	15 02		15 28	15 32		15 58	16 02			16 30	16 32		16 58	17 02		17 30	17 32		

Table T184-R

Sundays

20 May to 2 December

Brighton/Hove/Lewes - Haywards Heath - Gatwick Airport - London

		TL 1	SN	SN	TL 1	SN	SN		TL 1	SN	SN	TL 1	SN	SN	TL 1	SN	SN	TL 1	SN	SN	TL 1	SN	TL 1
Lewes	d					17 21							20 21						21 21				
Hove	d		16 52							19 52						20 52							
Brighton	d	16 42		16 57	17 08		17 27		19 42		19 57	20 08		20 27	20 42		20 57	21 08		21 27	21 42	21 54	22 08
Preston Park	d	16 46	16 57		17 12				19 46	19 57		20 12			20 46	20 57		21 12			21 46	21 58	22 12
Hassocks	d	16 52		17 06	17 18		17 36		19 52		20 06	20 18		20 36	20 52		21 06	21 18		21 36	21 52	22 05	22 18
Burgess Hill	d	16 56		17 10	17 22		17 40		19 56		20 10	20 22		20 40	20 56		21 10	21 22		21 40	21 56	22 09	22 22
Wivelsfield	d	16 58			17 24	17 36			19 58			20 24	20 36		20 58			21 24	21 36		21 58	22 11	22 24
Haywards Heath	a	17 03	17 08	17 15	17 29	17 41	17 45	and at the same minutes past each hour until	20 03	20 08	20 15	20 29	20 41	20 45	21 03	21 08	21 15	21 29	21 41	21 45	22 03	22 15	22 29
Haywards Heath	d	17 04	17 11	17 16	17 30	17 41	17 46		20 04	20 11	20 16	20 30	20 41	20 46	21 04	21 10	21 16	21 30	21 41	21 46	22 04	22 16	22 30
Balcombe	d				17 36							20 36						21 36					22 36
Three Bridges	a	17 12		17 24	17 42				20 12		20 24	20 42			21 12		21 24	21 42			22 12	22 24	22 42
Three Bridges	d	17 13		17 25	17 43				20 13		20 25	20 43			21 13		21 25	21 43			22 13	22 25	22 43
Gatwick Airport	a	17 17	17 24	17 29	17 47	17 53	17 58		20 17	20 24	20 29	20 47	20 53	20 58	21 17	21 24	21 29	21 48	21 53	21 58	22 17	22 29	22 47
Gatwick Airport	d	17 19	17 25	17 30	17 49	17 56	18 00		20 19	20 25	20 30	20 49	20 56	21 00	21 19	21 25	21 30	21 49	21 56	22 00	22 19	22 30	22 49
East Croydon	a	17 33	17 40	17 44	18 03	18 10	18 14		20 33	20 40	20 44	21 03	21 10	21 14	21 33	21 39	21 44	22 03	22 10	22 14	22 33	22 44	23 03
East Croydon	d	17 34			18 04				20 34			21 04			21 34			22 04			22 34		23 04
London Bridge	d	17 49			18 19				20 49			21 19			21 49			22 19			22 49		23 19
London Blackfriars	d	17 55			18 25				20 55			21 25			21 55			22 25			22 55		23 27
City Thameslink	d																						
Farringdon	d	17 59			18 29				20 59			21 29			21 59			22 29			22 59		23 31
St Pancras International	a	18 03			18 33				21 03			21 33			22 03			22 33			23 03		23 35
East Croydon	d		17 41	17 45		18 11	18 15			20 41	20 45		21 11	21 15		21 40	21 45		22 11	22 15		22 45	
Clapham Junction	a		17 50	17 54		18 20	18 24			20 50	20 54		21 20	21 24		21 49	21 54		22 20	22 24		22 54	
London Victoria	a		17 58	18 02		18 28	18 32			20 58	21 02		21 28	21 32		21 58	22 02		22 28	22 32		23 02	

		SN	TL 1	SN	TL 1	TL 1
Lewes	d					
Hove	d					
Brighton	d	22 27	22 42	22 54	23 08	23 42
Preston Park	d		22 46	22 58	23 12	23 46
Hassocks	d	22 36	22 52	23 05	23 18	23 52
Burgess Hill	d	22 40	22 56	23 09	23 22	23 56
Wivelsfield	d		22 58	23 11	23 24	23 58
Haywards Heath	a	22 45	23 03	23 15	23 29	00 03
Haywards Heath	d	22 46	23 04	23 16	23 30	00 04
Balcombe	d				23 36	
Three Bridges	a	22 54	23 13	23 24	23 42	00 13
Three Bridges	d	22 55	23 15	23 25	23 45	00 15
Gatwick Airport	a	22 59	23 19	23 29	23 49	00 19
Gatwick Airport	d	23 00	23 21	23 30	23 51	00 21
East Croydon	a	23 14	23 39	23 51	00 09	00 39
East Croydon	d		23 40		00 10	00 40
London Bridge	d					
London Blackfriars	d		00 06		00 36	01 06
City Thameslink	d					
Farringdon	d		00 11			
St Pancras International	a		00 15		00 45	01 15
East Croydon	d	23 15		23 52		
Clapham Junction	a	23 24		00 08		
London Victoria	a	23 32		00 17		

Table T185-F

Mondays to Fridays

21 May to 7 December

London - Gatwick Airport - Three Bridges - Horsham : Summary of Fast Trains

		SN MX 1	SN 1	TL 1	TL MO 1	TL MX 1	TL 1	TL 1	TL 1	TL 1	TL 1	SN 1	TL 1	GX 1	GX 1	TL 1	GX 1	TL 1	SN 1	GX 1	SN 1	GX 1	TL 1
London Victoria	d	00 02	00 08									04 35		05 00	05 14		05 30		05 32	05 44	05 54	06 00	
Clapham Junction	d	00 09	00 15									04 42							05 39		06 01		
East Croydon	a	00 23	00 30									04 57							05 51		06 10		
St Pancras International	d			00 21	00 51	00 52	01 32	02 32	03 02	03 32	04 02		04 32			04 51		05 20					05 45
Farringdon	d			00 26												04 56		05 24					05 49
City Thameslink	d															04 58		05 26					05 51
London Blackfriars	d			00 31	01 01	01 02	01 40	02 40	03 10	03 40	04 10		04 40			05 01		05 29					05 54
London Bridge	d																	05 35					06 00
East Croydon	a			00 57	01 27	01 28	02 06	03 06	03 36	04 06	04 36		05 06			05 27		05 48					06 16
East Croydon	d	00 24	00 31	00 58	01 28	01 28	02 07	03 07	03 37	04 07	04 37	04 57	05 07			05 28		05 49	05 52		06 10		06 16
Gatwick Airport	a	00 43	01 03	01 20	01 56	01 56	02 30	03 30	03 56	04 30	04 57	05 27	05 31	05 39	05 47	05 47	05 59	06 04	06 17	06 12	06 25	06 28	06 50
Three Bridges	a	00 48		01 26	02 03	02 03	02 36	03 36	04 02	04 40	05 03		05 37			05 53		06 09	06 23		06 31		↪
Crawley	a																				06 35		
Horsham	a																				06 50		

		TL 1	GX 1	TL 1	TL 1	TL	GX 1	TL 1	TL 1	SN 1	GX 1	SN 1	TL 1	GX 1	TL 1	TL 1	TL 1	SN 1	SN 1	GX 1	TL 1	TL 1	SN 1
London Victoria	d		06 13			06 25	06 30			06 36	06 43	06 46		07 00				07 06	07 09	07 13			07 16
Clapham Junction	d					06 32				06 43		06 53						07 13	07 16				07 23
East Croydon	a									06 52		07 02						07 22	07 27				07 32
St Pancras International	d	05 50		06 00				06 15	06 20						06 35	06 45	06 50				07 00		
Farringdon	d	05 54		06 04				06 19	06 24						06 39	06 49	06 54				07 04		
City Thameslink	d	05 56		06 06				06 21	06 26						06 41	06 51	06 56				07 06		
London Blackfriars	d	05 59		06 09				06 24	06 29						06 44	06 54	06 59				07 09		
London Bridge	d	06 05		06 15				06 30	06 35						06 51	07 00	07 05				07 15		
East Croydon	a	06 18		06 28				06 46	06 48						07 06	07 16	07 18				07 29		
East Croydon	d	06 19		06 29	←			06 46	06 49	06 52		07 03	←		07 07	07 16	07 19	07 22	07 27		07 30	←	07 33
Gatwick Airport	a	06 34	06 41	06 44	06 50		06 58	07 19	07 04	07 07	07 11	07 17	07 19	07 28	07 28	07 46	07 34	07 37	08 12	07 41	07 44	07 46	07 47
Three Bridges	a	06 39		06 49	06 56			↪	07 09	07 13		07 24	07 26			↪	07 39	07 42			07 49	07 52	
Crawley	a				07 00					07 17			07 30					07 48				07 56	
Horsham	a				07 13	07 46				07 28			07 45					07 57				08 11	

		TL	TL 1	GX 1	TL 1	TL 1	SN 1	SN 1	GX 1	TL 1	SN 1	TL 1	SN 1	GX 1	TL 1	TL 1	SN 1	SN 1	GX 1	TL 1	TL 1	SN 1
London Victoria	d	07 25		07 30			07 36	07 39	07 43		07 46		07 55	07 59			08 06	08 09	08 13			08 16
Clapham Junction	d	07 32					07 43	07 46			07 53		08 02				08 13	08 16				08 23
East Croydon	a						07 52	07 57			08 03		08 11				08 22	08 27				08 33
St Pancras International	d		07 10		07 15	07 20						07 40			07 45	07 50				08 00		
Farringdon	d		07 14		07 19	07 24						07 44			07 49	07 54				08 04		
City Thameslink	d		07 16		07 21	07 26						07 46			07 51	07 56				08 06		
London Blackfriars	d		07 19		07 24	07 29						07 49			07 54	07 59				08 09		
London Bridge	d		07 25		07 30	07 35						07 55			08 00	08 05				08 15		
East Croydon	a		07 38		07 46	07 48						08 08			08 16	08 18				08 30		
East Croydon	d		07 38		07 46	07 49	07 52	07 57		←	08 03	08 08	08 11		08 16	08 19	08 22	08 27		08 30	←	08 33
Gatwick Airport	a		07 53	07 58	08 15	08 04	08 07	08 41	08 11	08 15	08 18	08 23	08 26	08 30	08 45	08 34	08 37	09 09	08 41	08 45	08 45	08 48
Three Bridges	a				↪	08 09	08 13			08 21					↪	08 39	08 43			08 50	08 51	
Crawley	a						08 18			08 26							08 48				08 56	
Horsham	a	08 43					08 27			08 41							08 57				09 11	

		SN 1	TL	GX 1	TL 1	TL 1	SN 1	GX 1	TL 1	TL 1	SN 1	TL 1	TL 1	SN 1	GX 1	TL 1	TL 1	TL 1	SN 1	GX 1	TL 1	TL 1	TL 1
London Victoria	d	08 25	08 25	08 30			08 36	08 43			08 46			08 55	09 00				09 06	09 14			
Clapham Junction	d	08 32	08 32				08 43				08 53			09 02					09 13				
East Croydon	a	08 41					08 52				09 02			09 11					09 22				
St Pancras International	d				08 15	08 20				08 25		08 35	08 40			08 45	08 50					08 55	09 00
Farringdon	d				08 19	08 24				08 29		08 39	08 44			08 49	08 54					08 59	09 04
City Thameslink	d				08 21	08 26				08 31		08 41	08 46			08 51	08 56					09 01	09 06
London Blackfriars	d				08 24	08 29				08 34		08 44	08 49			08 54	08 59					09 04	09 09
London Bridge	d				08 30	08 35				08 41		08 51	08 55			09 00	09 05					09 11	09 15
East Croydon	a				08 46	08 48				08 54		09 06	09 08			09 14	09 18					09 24	09 28
East Croydon	d	08 41			08 46	08 49	08 53		←	08 55	09 03	09 07	09 08	09 11		09 16	09 19	←	09 23		←	09 25	09 29
Gatwick Airport	a	08 56		08 59	09 15	09 04	09 08	09 11	09 15	09 19	09 17	09 35	09 23	09 26	09 29	09 42	09 34	09 35	09 38	09 41	09 42	09 47	09 44
Three Bridges	a				↪	09 09	09 14		09 21			↪	09 28			↪	09 39	09 41	09 44		09 49		09 49
Crawley	a						09 18		09 26										09 48		09 53		
Horsham	a		09 43				09 27		09 39										09 57		10 08		

		SN 1	TL	TL 1	TL 1	SN 1	GX 1	TL 1	TL 1	SN 1	GX 1	TL 1	SN 1	TL 1	TL 1	SN 1	GX 1	TL 1	TL 1	SN 1	GX 1	TL 1
London Victoria	d	09 16	09 25			09 25	09 30			09 36	09 44		09 46			09 55	10 00			10 06	10 14	
Clapham Junction	d	09 23	09 32			09 32				09 43			09 53			10 02				10 13		
East Croydon	a	09 32				09 41				09 52			10 02			10 11				10 22		
St Pancras International	d			09 05	09 10			09 15	09 20					09 35	09 40			09 45	09 50			
Farringdon	d			09 09	09 14			09 19	09 24					09 39	09 44			09 49	09 54			
City Thameslink	d			09 11	09 16			09 21	09 26					09 41	09 46			09 51	09 56			
London Blackfriars	d			09 14	09 19			09 24	09 29					09 44	09 49			09 54	09 59			
London Bridge	d			09 21	09 25			09 30	09 35					09 51	09 55			10 00	10 05			
East Croydon	a			09 36	09 38			09 44	09 48					10 06	10 08			10 14	10 18			
East Croydon	d	09 33		09 37	09 38	09 41		09 46	09 49	09 53		←	10 03	10 07	10 08	10 11		10 16	10 19	10 23		←
Gatwick Airport	a	09 47		10 08	09 53	09 57	10 00	10 12	10 04	10 08	10 11	10 12	10 17	10 38	10 23	10 27	10 30	10 42	10 34	10 38	10 41	10 42
Three Bridges	a				10 02			↪	10 09	10 14		10 19			10 32			↪	10 39	10 44		10 49
Crawley	a									10 18		10 23								10 48		10 53
Horsham	a		10 43							10 27		10 38								10 57		11 08

21 May to 7 December

London - Gatwick Airport - Three Bridges - Horsham : Summary of Fast Trains

		TL	SN	TL	TL	TL	SN	GX	TL	TL	SN	GX	TL	SN	TL	SN	GX	TL	TL	SN	GX	TL	TL
London Victoria	d		10 16	10 25			10 25	10 30			10 36	10 44		10 46		10 55	11 00			11 06	11 14		
Clapham Junction	d		10 23	10 32			10 32				10 43			10 53		11 02				11 13			
East Croydon	a		10 32				10 41				10 52			11 02		11 11				11 22			
St Pancras International	d	10 00			10 05				10 15	10 20					10 35			10 45	10 50				11 00
Farringdon	d	10 04			10 09				10 19	10 24					10 39			10 49	10 54				11 04
City Thameslink	d	10 06			10 11				10 21	10 26					10 41			10 51	10 56				11 06
London Blackfriars	d	10 09			10 14				10 24	10 29					10 44			10 54	10 59				11 09
London Bridge	d	10 15			10 21	10 22			10 30	10 35					10 51			11 00	11 05				11 15
East Croydon	a	10 28			10 36	10 38			10 44	10 48					11 06			11 14	11 18				11 28
East Croydon	d	10 29	10 33		10 37	10 38	10 41		10 46	10 49	10 53		←	11 03	11 07	11 11		11 16	11 19	11 23		←	11 29
Gatwick Airport	a	10 44	10 47		11 08	10 53	10 56	10 59	11 12	11 04	11 08	11 11	11 12	11 17	11 38	11 26	11 29	11 42	11 34	11 38	11 41	11 42	11 44
Three Bridges	a	10 49				10 59			→	11 09	11 14		11 19					→	11 39	11 44		11 49	11 49
Crawley	a										11 18		11 23							11 48		11 53	
Horsham	a			11 43							11 27		11 38							11 57		12 08	

		SN	TL	TL	SN	GX	TL	TL	SN	GX	TL	SN	TL	SN	GX	TL	TL A	TL B	SN	GX	TL	TL
London Victoria	d	11 16	11 25		11 25	11 30			11 36	11 44		11 46		11 55	12 00				12 06	12 14		
Clapham Junction	d	11 23	11 32		11 32				11 43			11 53		12 02					12 13			
East Croydon	a	11 32			11 41				11 52			12 02		12 11					12 22			
St Pancras International	d			11 05			11 15	11 20					11 35			11 45	11 50	11 51				12 00
Farringdon	d			11 09			11 19	11 24					11 39			11 49	11 54	11 55				12 04
City Thameslink	d			11 11			11 21	11 26					11 41			11 51	11 56	11 57				12 06
London Blackfriars	d			11 14			11 24	11 29					11 44			11 54	11 59	12 00				12 09
London Bridge	d			11 21			11 30	11 35					11 51			12 00	12 05	12 06				12 15
East Croydon	a			11 36			11 44	11 48					12 06			12 14	12 18	12 19				12 28
East Croydon	d	11 33		11 37	11 41		11 46	11 49	11 53		←	12 03	12 07	12 11		12 16	12 19	12 19	12 23		←	12 29
Gatwick Airport	a	11 47		12 08	11 56	11 59	12 12	12 04	12 08	12 11	12 12	12 17	12 38	12 26	12 29	12 42	12 34	12 34	12 38	12 41	12 42	12 44
Three Bridges	a						→	12 09	12 14		12 19					→	12 39	12 39	12 44		12 49	12 49
Crawley	a								12 18		12 23								12 48		12 53	
Horsham	a		12 43						12 27		12 38								12 57		13 08	

		SN	TL	TL	SN	GX	TL	TL	SN	GX	TL	SN	TL	SN	GX	TL	TL	SN	GX	TL	TL	SN	TL
London Victoria	d	12 16	12 25		12 25	12 30			12 36	12 44		12 46		12 55	13 00			13 06	13 14			13 16	13 25
Clapham Junction	d	12 23	12 32		12 32				12 43			12 53		13 02				13 13				13 23	13 32
East Croydon	a	12 32			12 41				12 52			13 02		13 11				13 22				13 32	
St Pancras International	d			12 05			12 15	12 20					12 35			12 45	12 50				13 00		
Farringdon	d			12 09			12 19	12 24					12 39			12 49	12 54				13 04		
City Thameslink	d			12 11			12 21	12 26					12 41			12 51	12 56				13 06		
London Blackfriars	d			12 14			12 24	12 29					12 44			12 54	12 59				13 09		
London Bridge	d			12 21			12 30	12 35					12 51			13 00	13 05				13 15		
East Croydon	a			12 36			12 44	12 48					13 06			13 14	13 18				13 28		
East Croydon	d	12 33		12 37	12 41		12 46	12 49	12 53		←	13 03	13 07	13 11		13 16	13 19	13 23		←	13 29	13 33	
Gatwick Airport	a	12 47		13 08	12 56	12 59	13 12	13 04	13 08	13 11	13 12	13 17	13 38	13 26	13 29	13 42	13 34	13 38	13 41	13 42	13 44	13 47	
Three Bridges	a						→	13 09	13 14		13 19					→	13 39	13 44		13 49	13 49		
Crawley	a								13 18		13 23							13 48		13 53			
Horsham	a		13 43						13 27		13 38							13 57		14 08			14 43

		TL	SN	GX	TL	TL	SN	GX	TL	SN	TL	SN	GX	TL	TL A	TL B	SN	GX	TL	TL	SN	TL
London Victoria	d		13 25	13 30			13 36	13 44		13 46		13 55	14 00				14 06	14 14			14 16	14 25
Clapham Junction	d		13 32				13 43			13 53		14 02					14 13				14 23	14 32
East Croydon	a		13 41				13 52			14 02		14 11					14 22				14 32	
St Pancras International	d	13 05			13 15	13 20					13 35			13 45	13 50	13 51				14 00		
Farringdon	d	13 09			13 19	13 24					13 39			13 49	13 54	13 55				14 04		
City Thameslink	d	13 11			13 21	13 26					13 41			13 51	13 56	13 57				14 06		
London Blackfriars	d	13 14			13 24	13 29					13 44			13 54	13 59	14 00				14 09		
London Bridge	d	13 21			13 30	13 35					13 51			14 00	14 05	14 06				14 15		
East Croydon	a	13 36			13 44	13 48					14 06			14 14	14 18	14 19				14 28		
East Croydon	d	13 37	13 41		13 46	13 49	13 53		←	14 03	14 07	14 11		14 16	14 19	14 19	14 23		←	14 29	14 33	
Gatwick Airport	a	14 08	13 56	13 59	14 12	14 04	14 08	14 11	14 12	14 17	14 38	14 26	14 29	14 42	14 34	14 34	14 38	14 41	14 42	14 44	14 47	
Three Bridges	a				→	14 09	14 14		14 19					→	14 39	14 39	14 44		14 49	14 49		
Crawley	a						14 18		14 23								14 48		14 53			
Horsham	a						14 27		14 38								14 57		15 08			15 43

		TL	SN	GX	TL	TL	SN	GX	TL	SN	TL	SN	GX	TL	TL C	TL D	SN	GX	TL	TL	SN	TL	TL
London Victoria	d		14 25	14 30			14 36	14 44		14 46		14 55	15 00				15 06	15 14			15 16	15 25	
Clapham Junction	d		14 32				14 43			14 53		15 02					15 13				15 23	15 32	
East Croydon	a		14 41				14 53			15 02		15 11					15 22				15 32		
St Pancras International	d	14 05			14 15	14 20					14 35			14 45	14 50	14 51				15 00			15 05
Farringdon	d	14 09			14 19	14 24					14 39			14 49	14 54	14 55				15 04			15 09
City Thameslink	d	14 11			14 21	14 26					14 41			14 51	14 56	14 57				15 06			15 11
London Blackfriars	d	14 14			14 24	14 29					14 44			14 54	14 59	15 00				15 09			15 14
London Bridge	d	14 21			14 30	14 35					14 51			15 00	15 05	15 06				15 15			15 21
East Croydon	a	14 36			14 44	14 48					15 06			15 14	15 18	15 19				15 28			15 36
East Croydon	d	14 37	14 41		14 46	14 49	14 53		←	15 03	15 07	15 11		15 16	15 19	15 19	15 23		←	15 29	15 33		15 37
Gatwick Airport	a	15 08	14 56	14 59	15 12	15 04	15 08	15 11	15 12	15 17	15 38	15 26	15 29	15 42	15 34	15 34	15 38	15 41	15 42	15 44	15 47		16 08
Three Bridges	a				→	15 09	15 14		15 19					→	15 39	15 39	15 44		15 49	15 49			
Crawley	a						15 18		15 23								15 48		15 53				
Horsham	a						15 27		15 38								15 57		16 08			16 43	

A from 23 July until 5 October
B until 20 July, from 8 October
C from 30 July
D until 27 July

Table T185-F

Mondays to Fridays

21 May to 7 December

London - Gatwick Airport - Three Bridges - Horsham : Summary of Fast Trains

		SN	GX	TL	TL	SN	GX	TL	SN	TL	SN	GX	TL	TL	SN	SN	GX	TL	TL	SN	TL	TL
London Victoria	d	15 25	15 30			15 36	15 44		15 46		15 55	16 00			16 06	16 09	16 14			16 16	16 25	
Clapham Junction	d	15 32				15 43			15 53		16 02				16 13	16 16				16 23	16 32	
East Croydon	a	15 41				15 52			16 02		16 11				16 23	16 26				16 32		
St Pancras International	d			15 15	15 20					15 35			15 45	15 50					16 00			16 05
Farringdon	d			15 19	15 24					15 39			15 49	15 54					16 04			16 09
City Thameslink	d			15 21	15 26					15 41			15 51	15 56					16 06			16 11
London Blackfriars	d			15 24	15 29					15 44			15 54	15 59					16 09			16 14
London Bridge	d			15 30	15 35					15 51			16 00	16 05					16 15			16 21
East Croydon	a			15 44	15 48					16 06			16 14	16 19					16 29			16 36
East Croydon	d	15 41		15 46	15 49	15 53		←	16 03	16 07	16 11		16 16	16 20	16 23	16 27		←	16 29	16 33		16 37
Gatwick Airport	a	15 56	15 59	16 12	16 04	16 08	16 11	16 12	16 17	16 38	16 26	16 29	16 42	16 35	16 38	17 07	16 41	16 42	16 44	16 47		17 11
Three Bridges	a			→	16 09	16 14		16 19					→	16 40	16 44			16 49	16 49			
Crawley	a					16 18		16 23							16 48			16 53				
Horsham	a					16 27		16 38							16 57			17 10			17 45	

		SN	GX	TL	TL	SN	SN	GX	TL	SN	TL	SN	TL	SN	TL	GX	TL	SN	SN	GX	TL	TL	SN
London Victoria	d	16 25	16 29			16 36	16 39	16 43		16 45		16 54			16 55	16 59		17 06	17 09	17 13			17 15
Clapham Junction	d	16 32				16 43	16 46			16 52		17 02			17 02			17 13	17 16				17 22
East Croydon	a	16 41				16 52	16 56			17 01		17 11						17 22	17 26				17 31
St Pancras International	d			16 15	16 20						16 35		16 45				16 50				17 00		
Farringdon	d			16 19	16 24						16 39		16 49				16 54				17 04		
City Thameslink	d			16 21	16 26						16 41		16 51				16 56				17 06		
London Blackfriars	d			16 24	16 29						16 44		16 54				16 59				17 09		
London Bridge	d			16 30	16 35						16 51		17 00	17 03			17 05				17 15		
East Croydon	a			16 44	16 49						17 06		17 14	17 16			17 19				17 29		
East Croydon	d	16 41		16 46	16 50	16 53	16 57		←	17 02	17 07	17 11	17 16	17 17			17 20	17 23	17 27		17 29	←	17 32
Gatwick Airport	a	16 56	16 59	17 15	17 04	17 08	17 37	17 11	17 15	17 19	17 41	17 26	17 45			17 29	17 35	17 38	18 07	17 41	17 44	17 45	17 49
Three Bridges	a			→	17 10	17 14			17 21				→	17 35			17 40	17 44	→		17 49	17 51	
Crawley	a					17 18			17 26					17 39				17 48				17 56	
Horsham	a					17 27			17 42					17 51	18 15			18 01				18 12	

		TL	SN	TL	GX	TL	SN	TL	SN	SN	SN	GX	TL	SN	TL	SN	TL	SN	TL	GX	TL	SN
London Victoria	d		17 24	17 25	17 29					17 36	17 39	17 43		17 45		17 54			17 55	17 59		
Clapham Junction	d		17 32	17 32						17 43	17 46			17 52		18 02			18 02			
East Croydon	a		17 41							17 52	17 56			18 01		18 11						
St Pancras International	d	17 05				17 15		17 20							17 35		17 45				17 50	
Farringdon	d	17 09				17 19		17 24							17 39		17 49				17 54	
City Thameslink	d	17 11				17 21		17 26							17 41		17 51				17 56	
London Blackfriars	d	17 14				17 24		17 29							17 44		17 54				17 59	
London Bridge	d	17 21				17 30	17 33	17 35							17 51		18 00	18 03			18 05	
East Croydon	a	17 36				17 44	17 47	17 49							18 06		18 14	18 16			18 19	
East Croydon	d	17 37	17 41			17 46	17 48	17 50	←	17 53	17 57		←	18 02	18 07	18 11	18 16	18 17			18 20	←
Gatwick Airport	a	18 11	17 56		17 59	18 15	18 02	18 05	18 07	18 08	18 37	18 11	18 15	18 19	18 41	18 26	18 45			18 29	18 35	18 37
Three Bridges	a					→		18 10	18 16	18 14	→		18 21				→	18 35			18 40	18 43
Crawley	a									18 18			18 26					18 39				
Horsham	a			18 45						18 27			18 42					18 51	19 15			

		SN	SN	GX	TL	TL	SN	TL	SN	TL	GX	TL	SN	TL	SN	SN	SN	GX	TL	SN	TL	SN	GX
London Victoria	d	18 06	18 09	18 13			18 15		18 24	18 26	18 29					18 36	18 39	18 43		18 45		18 54	18 59
Clapham Junction	d	18 13	18 16				18 22		18 32	18 33						18 43	18 46			18 52		19 02	
East Croydon	a	18 22	18 27				18 31		18 41							18 52	18 57			19 01		19 11	
St Pancras International	d				18 00			18 05				18 15		18 20							18 35		
Farringdon	d				18 04			18 09				18 19		18 24							18 39		
City Thameslink	d				18 06			18 11				18 21		18 26							18 41		
London Blackfriars	d				18 09			18 14				18 24		18 29							18 44		
London Bridge	d				18 15			18 21				18 30	18 33	18 35							18 51		
East Croydon	a				18 29			18 36				18 44	18 47	18 49							19 06		
East Croydon	d	18 23	18 27		18 29	←	18 32	18 37	18 41			18 46	18 48	18 50	←	18 53	18 57		←	19 02	19 07	19 11	
Gatwick Airport	a	18 38	19 07	18 41	18 44	18 45	18 49	19 11	18 56		18 59	19 15	19 02	19 05	19 07	19 08	19 37	19 11	19 15	19 19	19 41	19 26	19 29
Three Bridges	a	18 44	→		18 49	18 51						→		19 10	19 16	19 14	→		19 21				
Crawley	a	18 48				18 56										19 18			19 26				
Horsham	a	19 01				19 12				19 45						19 27			19 42				

		TL	TL	SN	SN	SN	GX	TL	TL	SN	TL	TL	SN	GX	TL	TL	SN	SN	GX	TL	SN	TL	SN
London Victoria	d				19 06	19 09	19 14			19 16	19 25		19 25	19 30				19 36	19 44		19 46		19 55
Clapham Junction	d				19 13	19 16				19 23	19 32		19 32					19 43			19 53		20 02
East Croydon	a				19 22	19 27				19 32			19 41					19 52			20 02		20 11
St Pancras International	d	18 45	18 50					19 00				19 05			19 15	19 20						19 35	
Farringdon	d	18 49	18 54					19 04				19 09			19 19	19 24						19 39	
City Thameslink	d	18 51	18 56					19 06				19 11			19 21	19 26						19 41	
London Blackfriars	d	18 54	18 59					19 09				19 14			19 24	19 29						19 44	
London Bridge	d	19 00	19 05					19 15				19 21			19 30	19 35						19 51	
East Croydon	a	19 14	19 19					19 29				19 36			19 44	19 48						20 06	
East Croydon	d	19 16	19 20	←	19 23	19 27		19 29	←	19 33		19 37	19 41		19 46	19 49	←	19 53		←	20 03	20 07	20 11
Gatwick Airport	a	19 45	19 35	19 37	19 38	20 07	19 41	19 44	19 45	19 47		20 11	19 56	19 59	20 14	20 04	20 07	20 08	20 11	20 14	20 17	20 38	20 26
Three Bridges	a	→	19 40	19 46	19 44	→		19 49	19 51						→	20 09	20 16	20 14		20 21			
Crawley	a				19 48				19 56									20 18		20 26			
Horsham	a				19 57				20 12		20 43							20 27		20 39			

Table T185-F

London - Gatwick Airport - Three Bridges - Horsham : Summary of Fast Trains

Mondays to Fridays
21 May to 7 December

	GX	TL	TL	TL	SN	GX	TL		TL	SN	TL	TL	TL	SN	GX	TL	TL		SN	GX	TL	SN	TL	TL
			A	B																				
London Victoria d	20 00				20 06	20 14				20 16	20 25			20 25	20 30				20 36	20 44		20 46		
Clapham Junction d					20 13					20 23	20 32			20 32					20 43			20 53		
East Croydon a					20 22					20 32				20 41					20 52			21 02		
St Pancras International d		19 45	19 50	19 51					20 00			20 05				20 15	20 20						20 35	
Farringdon d		19 49	19 54	19 55					20 04			20 09				20 19	20 24						20 39	
City Thameslink d		19 51	19 56	19 57					20 06			20 11				20 21	20 26						20 41	
London Blackfriars d		19 54	19 59	20 00					20 09			20 14				20 24	20 29						20 44	
London Bridge d		20 00	20 05	20 06					20 15			20 21	20 22			20 30	20 35						20 51	20 52
East Croydon a		20 14	20 18	20 19					20 28			20 36	20 38			20 44	20 48						21 06	21 08
East Croydon d		20 16	20 19	20 19	20 23		←		20 29	20 33		20 37	20 38	20 41		20 46	20 49		20 53		←	21 03	21 07	21 08
Gatwick Airport a	20 29	20 42	20 34	20 34	20 38	20 41	20 42		20 44	20 47		21 08	20 53	20 56	20 59	21 12	21 04		21 08	21 11	21 12	21 17	21 37	21 23
Three Bridges a		→	20 39	20 39	20 44		20 49		20 49				20 59			→	21 09		21 14		21 19			21 29
Crawley a					20 48		20 53												21 18		21 23			
Horsham a					20 57		21 08				21 43								21 27		21 38			

	SN	GX	TL		TL	SN	GX	TL	TL	SN	TL	TL	TL		SN	GX	TL	TL	SN	GX	TL	SN	TL	
London Victoria d	20 55	21 00				21 06	21 14			21 16	21 25				21 25	21 30			21 36	21 44		21 46		
Clapham Junction d	21 02					21 13				21 23	21 32				21 32				21 43			21 53		
East Croydon a	21 11					21 22				21 32					21 41				21 52			22 02		
St Pancras International d			20 45		20 50				21 00			21 05					21 15	21 20					21 35	
Farringdon d			20 49		20 54				21 04			21 09					21 19	21 24					21 39	
City Thameslink d			20 51		20 56				21 06			21 11					21 21	21 26					21 41	
London Blackfriars d			20 54		20 59				21 09			21 14					21 24	21 29					21 44	
London Bridge d			21 00		21 05				21 15			21 21	21 22				21 30	21 35					21 51	
East Croydon a			21 14		21 18				21 28			21 36	21 38				21 44	21 48					22 06	
East Croydon d	21 11		21 16		21 19	21 23		←	21 29	21 33		21 37	21 38		21 41		21 46	21 49	21 53		←	22 03	22 07	
Gatwick Airport a	21 26	21 29	21 42		21 34	21 38	21 41	21 42	21 44	21 47		22 08	21 53		21 56	21 59	22 12	22 04	22 08	22 11	22 12	22 17	22 38	
Three Bridges a			→		21 39	21 44		21 49	21 49				21 59				→	22 09	22 14		22 19			
Crawley a						21 48		21 53											22 18		22 23			
Horsham a						21 57		22 08			22 43								22 27		22 38			

	SN	GX	TL	TL	SN	GX	TL	TL	SN		TL	TL	SN	TL	TL	SN	GX	TL	SN		TL	SN	SN	TL
						C			C													FX	FO	
London Victoria d	21 55	22 00			22 06	22 14			22 16		22 25		22 25			22 36	22 44		22 46			22 55	22 55	
Clapham Junction d	22 02				22 13				22 23		22 32		22 32			22 43			22 53			23 02	23 02	
East Croydon a	22 11				22 22				22 32				22 41			22 52			23 02			23 11	23 11	
St Pancras International d			21 45	21 51				22 00				22 05		22 15	22 20						22 35			22 45
Farringdon d			21 49	21 55				22 04				22 09		22 19	22 24						22 39			22 49
City Thameslink d			21 51	21 57				22 06				22 11		22 21	22 26						22 41			22 51
London Blackfriars d			21 54	22 00				22 09				22 14		22 24	22 29						22 44			22 54
London Bridge d			22 00	22 06				22 15				22 21		22 30	22 35						22 51			23 00
East Croydon a			22 14	22 19				22 28				22 36		22 44	22 48						23 06			23 14
East Croydon d	22 11		22 16	22 19	22 23		←	22 29	22 33			22 37	22 41	22 46	22 49	22 53		←	23 03		23 07	23 11	23 11	23 16
Gatwick Airport a	22 26	22 29	22 42	22 34	22 38	22 41	22 42	22 44	22 47			23 08	22 56	23 12	23 04	23 08	23 11	23 12	23 17		23 37	23 26	23 26	23 41
Three Bridges a			→	22 39	22 44		22 49	22 49						→	23 09	23 14		23 19			→			→
Crawley a					22 48		22 53									23 18		23 23						
Horsham a					22 57		23 08				23 43					23 27		23 38						

	TL	TL	SN	TL	TL		SN	TL	SN	TL	TL	TL	SN	TL
London Victoria d			23 06				23 16		23 25		23 25		23 36	
Clapham Junction d			23 13				23 23		23 32		23 32		23 43	
East Croydon a			23 22				23 32		23 41				23 58	
St Pancras International d	22 50				23 00			23 05		23 15		23 22		23 51
Farringdon d	22 54				23 04			23 09		23 19		23 27		23 56
City Thameslink d	22 56													
London Blackfriars d	22 59				23 09			23 14		23 24		23 31		00 01
London Bridge d	23 05				23 15			23 21		23 30		23 37		
East Croydon a	23 18				23 28			23 36		23 44		23 50		00 27
East Croydon d	23 19	←	23 23	←	23 29		23 33	23 37	23 43	23 46		23 51	23 59	00 28
Gatwick Airport a	23 34	23 37	23 38	23 41	23 47		23 52	00 01	00 03	00 12		00 17	00 29	00 48
Three Bridges a	23 39	23 43	23 44	23 47	23 53					00 19		00 23	00 36	00 54
Crawley a			23 48	23 53						00 23			00 40	
Horsham a			23 57	00 06						00 36	00 48		00 49	

Saturdays
26 May to 8 December

	SN	SN	TL	TL	SN	TL	SN	TL	SN		TL	TL	SN	TL	TL	GX	TL	SN	GX		GX	TL	GX	GX
London Victoria d	00 02	00 08			01 10		02 10		03 10				04 10			05 00		05 08	05 15		05 30		05 44	06 00
Clapham Junction d	00 09	00 15			01 17		02 17		03 17				04 17					05 16						
East Croydon a	00 23	00 30			01 32		02 32		03 32				04 31					05 31						
St Pancras International d			00 21	00 52		01 32		02 32			03 02	03 32		04 02	04 32		04 51					05 20		
Farringdon d			00 26														04 56					05 24		
City Thameslink d																								
London Blackfriars d			00 31	01 02		01 40		02 40			03 10	03 40		04 10	04 40		05 01					05 29		
London Bridge d																						05 35		
East Croydon a			00 57	01 28		02 06		03 06			03 36	04 06		04 36	05 06		05 27					05 48		
East Croydon d	00 24	00 31	00 58	01 28	01 33	02 07	02 32	03 07	03 32		03 37	04 07	04 31	04 37	05 07		05 28	05 31				05 49		
Gatwick Airport a	00 43	01 03	01 20	01 56	02 06	02 30	02 55	03 30	03 55		03 58	04 30	04 59	05 02	05 29	05 36	05 47	06 00	05 49		05 59	06 04	06 11	06 29
Three Bridges a	00 48		01 26	02 03	02 18	02 36	03 01	03 36	04 01		04 06	04 40	05 05	05 09	05 35		05 53	06 06				06 09		
Crawley a																								
Horsham a																								

A from 30 July B until 27 July C not 7 December

Table T185-F

London - Gatwick Airport - Three Bridges - Horsham : Summary of Fast Trains

Saturdays
26 May to 8 December

	TL		TL	SN	GX	TL	TL	GX	TL	TL	SN		GX	TL	SN	GX	TL	TL	SN	GX	TL		TL	TL
London Victoria d				06 06	06 14			06 30			06 36		06 44		06 55	07 00			07 06	07 14			07 25	
Clapham Junction d				06 13							06 43				07 02				07 13				07 32	
East Croydon a				06 22							06 52				07 11				07 22					
St Pancras International d	05 45		05 50			06 00			06 15	06 20							06 45	06 50						07 00
Farringdon d	05 49		05 54			06 04			06 19	06 24							06 49	06 54						07 04
City Thameslink d																								
London Blackfriars d	05 54		05 59			06 09			06 24	06 29							06 54	06 59						07 09
London Bridge d	06 00		06 05			06 15			06 30	06 35							07 00	07 05						07 15
East Croydon a	06 14		06 18			06 28			06 44	06 48							07 14	07 18						07 28
East Croydon d	06 16		06 19	06 23		06 29	←		06 46	06 49	06 53			←	07 11		07 16	07 19	07 23		←			07 30
Gatwick Airport a	06 50		06 34	06 38	06 41	06 44	06 50	06 59	07 12	07 04	07 08		07 11	07 12	07 26	07 29	07 42	07 34	07 38	07 41	07 42			07 44
Three Bridges a	→		06 39	06 44		06 49	06 56		→	07 09	07 14			07 19			→	07 39	07 44		07 49			07 49
Crawley a				06 48			07 01				07 18			07 23					07 48		07 53			
Horsham a				06 57			07 14				07 27			07 38					07 57		08 08		08 43	

	TL	SN	GX	TL	TL	SN	GX		TL	SN	TL	SN	GX	TL	TL	SN	GX		TL	TL	SN	TL	TL	SN
London Victoria d		07 25	07 30			07 36	07 44			07 46		07 55	08 00			08 06	08 14				08 16	08 25		08 25
Clapham Junction d		07 32				07 43				07 53		08 02				08 13					08 23	08 32		08 32
East Croydon a		07 41				07 52				08 02		08 11				08 22					08 32			08 41
St Pancras International d	07 05			07 15	07 20						07 35			07 45	07 50					08 00			08 05	
Farringdon d	07 09			07 19	07 24						07 39			07 49	07 54					08 04			08 09	
City Thameslink d																								
London Blackfriars d	07 14			07 24	07 29						07 44			07 54	07 59					08 09			08 14	
London Bridge d	07 22			07 30	07 35						07 52			08 00	08 05					08 15			08 22	
East Croydon a	07 36			07 44	07 48						08 06			08 14	08 18					08 28			08 36	
East Croydon d	07 37	07 41		07 46	07 49	07 53			←	08 03	08 07	08 11		08 16	08 19	08 23			←	08 29	08 33		08 37	08 41
Gatwick Airport a	08 08	07 56	07 59	08 12	08 04	08 08	08 11		08 12	08 18	08 38	08 26	08 29	08 42	08 34	08 37	08 41		08 42	08 44	08 47		09 08	08 56
Three Bridges a				→	08 09	08 14			08 19					→	08 39	08 44			08 49	08 49				
Crawley a						08 18			08 23							08 48			08 53					
Horsham a						08 27			08 38							08 57			09 08			09 43		

	GX	TL	TL		SN	GX	TL	SN	TL	SN	GX	TL	TL		SN	GX	TL	TL	SN	TL	TL	SN	GX	
London Victoria d	08 30				08 36	08 44		08 46		08 55	09 00				09 06	09 14			09 16	09 25		09 25	09 30	
Clapham Junction d					08 43			08 53		09 02					09 13				09 23	09 32		09 32		
East Croydon a					08 52			09 02		09 11					09 22				09 32			09 41		
St Pancras International d		08 15	08 20						08 35			08 45	08 50					09 00			09 05			
Farringdon d		08 19	08 24						08 39			08 49	08 54					09 04			09 09			
City Thameslink d																		09 06			09 11			
London Blackfriars d		08 24	08 29						08 44			08 54	08 59					09 09			09 14			
London Bridge d		08 30	08 35						08 52			09 00	09 05					09 15			09 22			
East Croydon a		08 44	08 48						09 06			09 14	09 18					09 28			09 36			
East Croydon d		08 46	08 49		08 53		←	09 03	09 07	09 11		09 16	09 19		09 23		←	09 29	09 33		09 37	09 41		
Gatwick Airport a	08 59	09 12	09 04		09 08	09 11	09 12	09 18	09 38	09 26	09 29	09 42	09 34		09 38	09 41	09 42	09 44	09 47		10 08	09 56	09 59	
Three Bridges a		→	09 09		09 14		09 19					→	09 39		09 44		09 49	09 49						
Crawley a					09 18		09 23								09 48		09 53							
Horsham a					09 27		09 38								09 57		10 08			10 43				

	TL	TL	SN	GX	TL	SN	TL	SN	GX		TL	TL	SN	GX	TL	TL	SN	TL	TL		SN	GX	TL	TL
London Victoria d			09 36	09 44		09 46		09 55	10 00				10 06	10 14			10 16	10 25			10 25	10 30		
Clapham Junction d			09 43			09 53		10 02					10 13				10 23	10 32			10 32			
East Croydon a			09 52			10 02		10 11					10 22				10 32				10 41			
St Pancras International d	09 15	09 20					09 35				09 45	09 50				10 00			10 05				10 15	10 20
Farringdon d	09 19	09 24					09 39				09 49	09 54				10 04			10 09				10 19	10 24
City Thameslink d	09 21	09 26					09 41				09 51	09 56				10 06			10 11				10 21	10 26
London Blackfriars d	09 24	09 29					09 44				09 54	09 59				10 09			10 14				10 24	10 29
London Bridge d	09 30	09 35					09 52				10 00	10 05				10 15			10 22				10 30	10 35
East Croydon a	09 44	09 48					10 06				10 14	10 18				10 28			10 36				10 44	10 48
East Croydon d	09 46	09 49	09 53		←	10 03	10 07	10 11			10 16	10 19	10 23		←	10 29	10 33		10 37		10 41		10 46	10 49
Gatwick Airport a	10 12	10 04	10 08	10 11	10 12	10 18	10 38	10 26	10 29		10 42	10 34	10 38	10 41	10 42	10 44	10 47		11 08		10 56	10 59	11 12	11 04
Three Bridges a	→	10 09	10 14		10 19						→	10 39	10 44		10 49	10 49							→	11 09
Crawley a			10 18		10 23								10 48		10 53									
Horsham a			10 27		10 38								10 57		11 08			11 43						

	SN	GX	TL	SN	TL		SN	GX	TL	TL	SN	GX	TL	TL	SN		TL	TL	SN	GX	TL	TL	SN	GX
London Victoria d	10 36	10 44		10 46			10 55	11 00			11 06	11 14			11 16		11 25		11 25	11 30			11 36	11 44
Clapham Junction d	10 43			10 53			11 02				11 13				11 23		11 32		11 32				11 43	
East Croydon a	10 52			11 02			11 11				11 22				11 32				11 41				11 52	
St Pancras International d					10 35				10 45	10 50				11 00				11 05			11 15	11 20		
Farringdon d					10 39				10 49	10 54				11 04				11 09			11 19	11 24		
City Thameslink d					10 41				10 51	10 56				11 06				11 11			11 21	11 26		
London Blackfriars d					10 44				10 54	10 59				11 09				11 14			11 24	11 29		
London Bridge d					10 52				11 00	11 05				11 15				11 22			11 30	11 35		
East Croydon a					11 06				11 14	11 18				11 28				11 36			11 44	11 48		
East Croydon d	10 53		←	11 03	11 07		11 11		11 16	11 19	11 23		←	11 29	11 33			11 37	11 41		11 46	11 49	11 53	
Gatwick Airport a	11 08	11 11	11 12	11 18	11 37		11 26	11 29	11 42	11 34	11 38	11 41	11 42	11 44	11 47			12 08	11 56	11 59	12 12	12 04	12 08	12 11
Three Bridges a	11 14		11 19						→	11 39	11 44		11 49	11 49							→	12 09	12 14	
Crawley a	11 18		11 23								11 48		11 53										12 18	
Horsham a	11 27		11 38								11 57		12 08				12 43						12 27	

London - Gatwick Airport - Three Bridges - Horsham : Summary of Fast Trains

		TL	SN	TL	SN	GX	TL	TL		SN	GX	TL	TL	SN	TL	TL	SN	GX		TL	TL	SN	GX	TL	SN
London Victoria	d		11 46		11 55	12 00				12 06	12 14			12 16	12 25		12 25	12 30				12 36	12 44		12 46
Clapham Junction	d		11 53		12 02					12 13				12 23	12 32		12 32					12 43			12 53
East Croydon	a		12 02		12 11					12 22				12 32			12 41					12 52			13 02
St Pancras International	d			11 35			11 45	11 50					12 00			12 05				12 15	12 20				
Farringdon	d			11 39			11 49	11 54					12 04			12 09				12 19	12 24				
City Thameslink	d			11 41			11 51	11 56					12 06			12 11				12 21	12 26				
London Blackfriars	d			11 44			11 54	11 59					12 09			12 14				12 24	12 29				
London Bridge	d			11 52			12 00	12 05					12 15			12 22				12 30	12 35				
East Croydon	a			12 06			12 14	12 18					12 28			12 36				12 44	12 48				
East Croydon	d	←	12 03	12 07	12 11		12 16	12 19		12 23		←	12 29	12 33		12 37	12 41			12 46	12 49	12 53		←	13 03
Gatwick Airport	a	12 12	12 18	12 38	12 26	12 29	12 42	12 34		12 38	12 41	12 42	12 44	12 47		13 08	12 56	12 59		13 12	13 04	13 08	13 11	13 12	13 18
Three Bridges	a	12 19					→	12 39		12 44		12 49	12 49							→	13 09	13 14		13 19	
Crawley	a	12 23								12 48		12 53										13 18		13 23	
Horsham	a	12 38								12 57		13 08			13 43							13 27		13 38	

		TL	SN	GX		TL	TL	SN	GX	TL	TL	SN	TL	TL		SN	GX	TL	TL	SN	GX	TL	SN	TL	
London Victoria	d		12 55	13 00				13 06	13 14			13 16	13 25			13 25	13 30			13 36	13 44		13 46		
Clapham Junction	d		13 02					13 13				13 23	13 32			13 32				13 43			13 53		
East Croydon	a		13 11					13 22				13 32				13 41				13 52			14 02		
St Pancras International	d	12 35				12 45	12 50				13 00			13 05				13 15	13 20					13 35	
Farringdon	d	12 39				12 49	12 54				13 04			13 09				13 19	13 24					13 39	
City Thameslink	d	12 41				12 51	12 56				13 06			13 11				13 21	13 26					13 41	
London Blackfriars	d	12 44				12 54	12 59				13 09			13 14				13 24	13 29					13 44	
London Bridge	d	12 52				13 00	13 05				13 15			13 22				13 30	13 35					13 52	
East Croydon	a	13 06				13 14	13 18				13 28			13 36				13 44	13 48					14 06	
East Croydon	d	13 07	13 11			13 16	13 19	13 23		←	13 29	13 33		13 37		13 41		13 46	13 49	13 53		←	14 03	14 07	
Gatwick Airport	a	13 38	13 26	13 29		13 42	13 34	13 38	13 41	13 42	13 44	13 47		14 08		13 56	13 59	14 12	14 04	14 08	14 11	14 12	14 18	14 38	
Three Bridges	a					→	13 39	13 44		13 49	13 49							→	14 09	14 14		14 19			
Crawley	a							13 48		13 53										14 18		14 23			
Horsham	a							13 57		14 08			14 43							14 27		14 38			

		SN	GX	TL	TL	SN	GX	TL	TL	SN		TL	TL	SN	GX	TL	TL	SN	GX	TL		SN	TL	SN	GX
London Victoria	d	13 55	14 00			14 06	14 14			14 16		14 25		14 25	14 30			14 36	14 44			14 46		14 55	15 00
Clapham Junction	d	14 02				14 13				14 23		14 32		14 32				14 43				14 53		15 02	
East Croydon	a	14 11				14 22				14 32				14 41				14 52				15 02		15 11	
St Pancras International	d			13 45	13 50				14 00				14 05			14 15	14 20						14 35		
Farringdon	d			13 49	13 54				14 04				14 09			14 19	14 24						14 39		
City Thameslink	d			13 51	13 56				14 06				14 11			14 21	14 26						14 41		
London Blackfriars	d			13 54	13 59				14 09				14 14			14 24	14 29						14 44		
London Bridge	d			14 00	14 05				14 15				14 22			14 30	14 35						14 52		
East Croydon	a			14 14	14 18				14 28				14 36			14 44	14 48						15 06		
East Croydon	d	14 11		14 16	14 19	14 23		←	14 29	14 33			14 37	14 41		14 46	14 49	14 53		←		15 03	15 07	15 11	
Gatwick Airport	a	14 26	14 29	14 42	14 34	14 38	14 41	14 42	14 44	14 47			15 08	14 56	14 59	15 12	15 04	15 08	15 11	15 12		15 18	15 38	15 26	15 29
Three Bridges	a			→	14 39	14 44		14 49	14 49							→	15 09	15 14		15 19					
Crawley	a					14 48		14 53										15 18		15 23					
Horsham	a					14 57		15 08				15 43						15 27		15 38					

		TL	TL	SN	GX	TL		TL	SN	TL	TL	SN	GX	TL	TL	SN		GX	TL	SN	TL	SN	GX	TL	TL
London Victoria	d			15 06	15 14				15 16	15 25		15 25	15 30			15 36		15 44		15 46		15 55	16 00		
Clapham Junction	d			15 13					15 23	15 32		15 32				15 43				15 53		16 02			
East Croydon	a			15 22					15 32			15 41				15 52				16 02		16 11			
St Pancras International	d	14 45	14 50					15 00			15 05			15 15	15 20						15 35			15 45	15 50
Farringdon	d	14 49	14 54					15 04			15 09			15 19	15 24						15 39			15 49	15 54
City Thameslink	d	14 51	14 56					15 06			15 11			15 21	15 26						15 41			15 51	15 56
London Blackfriars	d	14 54	14 59					15 09			15 14			15 24	15 29						15 44			15 54	15 59
London Bridge	d	15 00	15 05					15 15			15 22			15 30	15 35						15 52			16 00	16 05
East Croydon	a	15 14	15 18					15 28			15 36			15 44	15 48						16 06			16 14	16 18
East Croydon	d	15 16	15 19	15 23		←		15 29	15 33		15 37	15 41		15 46	15 49	15 53			←	16 03	16 07	16 11		16 16	16 19
Gatwick Airport	a	15 42	15 34	15 38	15 41	15 42		15 44	15 47		16 08	15 56	15 59	16 12	16 04	16 08		16 11	16 12	16 18	16 38	16 26	16 29	16 42	16 34
Three Bridges	a	→	15 39	15 44		15 49		15 49						→	16 09	16 14			16 19					→	16 39
Crawley	a			15 48		15 53										16 18			16 23						
Horsham	a			15 57		16 08				16 43						16 27			16 38						

		SN		GX	TL	TL	SN	TL	TL	SN	GX	TL		TL	SN	GX	TL	SN	TL	SN	GX	TL		TL	SN
London Victoria	d	16 06		16 14			16 16	16 25		16 25	16 30				16 36	16 44		16 46		16 55	17 00				17 06
Clapham Junction	d	16 13					16 23	16 32		16 32					16 43			16 53		17 02					17 13
East Croydon	a	16 22					16 32			16 41					16 52			17 02		17 11					17 22
St Pancras International	d					16 00			16 05			16 15		16 20					16 35			16 45		16 50	
Farringdon	d					16 04			16 09			16 19		16 24					16 39			16 49		16 54	
City Thameslink	d					16 06			16 11			16 21		16 26					16 41			16 51		16 56	
London Blackfriars	d					16 09			16 14			16 24		16 29					16 44			16 54		16 59	
London Bridge	d					16 15			16 22			16 30		16 35					16 52			17 00		17 05	
East Croydon	a					16 28			16 36			16 44		16 48					17 06			17 14		17 18	
East Croydon	d	16 23			←	16 29	16 33		16 37	16 41		16 46		16 49	16 53		←	17 03	17 07	17 11		17 16		17 19	17 23
Gatwick Airport	a	16 38		16 41	16 42	16 44	16 47		17 08	16 56	16 59	17 12		17 04	17 08	17 11	17 12	17 18	17 38	17 26	17 29	17 42		17 34	17 38
Three Bridges	a	16 44			16 49	16 49						→		17 09	17 14		17 19					→		17 39	17 44
Crawley	a	16 48			16 53										17 18		17 23								17 48
Horsham	a	16 57			17 08			17 43							17 27		17 38								17 57

		GX	TL	TL		SN	TL	TL	SN	GX	TL	TL	SN	GX		TL	SN	TL	SN	GX	TL	TL	SN	GX	
London Victoria	d	17 14				17 16	17 25		17 25	17 30			17 36	17 44			17 46		17 55	18 00			18 06	18 14	
Clapham Junction	d					17 23	17 32		17 32				17 43				17 53		18 02				18 13		
East Croydon	a					17 32			17 41				17 52				18 02		18 11				18 22		
St Pancras International	d			17 00				17 05			17 15	17 20						17 35			17 45	17 50			
Farringdon	d			17 04				17 09			17 19	17 24						17 39			17 49	17 54			
City Thameslink	d			17 06				17 11			17 21	17 26						17 41			17 51	17 56			
London Blackfriars	d			17 09				17 14			17 24	17 29						17 44			17 54	17 59			
London Bridge	d			17 15				17 22			17 30	17 35						17 52			18 00	18 05			
East Croydon	a			17 28				17 36			17 44	17 48						18 06			18 14	18 18			
East Croydon	d		←	17 29		17 33		17 37	17 41		17 46	17 49	17 53			←	18 03	18 07	18 11		18 16	18 19	18 23		
Gatwick Airport	a	17 41	17 42	17 44		17 47		18 08	17 56	17 59	18 12	18 04	18 08	18 11		18 12	18 18	18 38	18 26	18 29	18 42	18 34	18 38	18 41	
Three Bridges	a		17 49	17 49							→	18 09	18 14			18 19					→	18 39	18 44		
Crawley	a		17 53										18 18			18 23							18 48		
Horsham	a		18 08				18 43						18 27			18 38							18 57		

		TL	TL	SN	TL	SN	GX	TL	TL	SN		GX	TL	SN	TL	SN	GX	TL	TL	SN		GX	TL	TL	SN
London Victoria	d			18 16		18 25	18 30			18 36		18 44		18 46		18 55	19 00			19 06		19 14			19 16
Clapham Junction	d			18 23		18 32				18 43				18 53		19 02				19 13					19 23
East Croydon	a			18 32		18 41				18 52				19 02		19 11				19 22					19 32
St Pancras International	d		18 00		18 05			18 15	18 20						18 35			18 45	18 50					19 00	
Farringdon	d		18 04		18 09			18 19	18 24						18 39			18 49	18 54					19 04	
City Thameslink	d		18 06		18 11			18 21	18 26						18 41			18 51	18 56					19 06	
London Blackfriars	d		18 09		18 14			18 24	18 29						18 44			18 54	18 59					19 09	
London Bridge	d		18 15		18 22			18 30	18 35						18 52			19 00	19 05					19 15	
East Croydon	a		18 28		18 36			18 44	18 48						19 06			19 14	19 18					19 28	
East Croydon	d	←	18 29	18 33	18 37	18 41		18 46	18 49	18 53			←	19 03	19 07	19 11		19 16	19 19	19 23			←	19 29	19 33
Gatwick Airport	a	18 42	18 44	18 47	19 08	18 56	18 59	19 12	19 04	19 08		19 11	19 12	19 18	19 38	19 26	19 29	19 42	19 34	19 38		19 41	19 42	19 44	19 47
Three Bridges	a	18 49	18 49					→	19 09	19 14			19 19					→	19 39	19 44			19 49	19 49	
Crawley	a	18 53								19 18			19 23							19 48			19 53		
Horsham	a	19 08								19 27			19 38							19 57			20 08		

		TL	SN	GX	TL	TL		SN	GX	TL	SN	TL	SN	GX	TL	TL		SN	GX	TL	TL	SN	TL	SN	GX
London Victoria	d		19 25	19 30				19 36	19 44		19 46		19 55	20 00				20 06	20 14			20 16		20 25	20 30
Clapham Junction	d		19 32					19 43			19 53		20 02					20 13				20 23		20 32	
East Croydon	a		19 41					19 52			20 02		20 11					20 22				20 32		20 41	
St Pancras International	d	19 05			19 15	19 20						19 35			19 45	19 50					20 00		20 05		
Farringdon	d	19 09			19 19	19 24						19 39			19 49	19 54					20 04		20 09		
City Thameslink	d	19 11			19 21	19 26						19 41			19 51	19 56					20 06		20 11		
London Blackfriars	d	19 14			19 24	19 29						19 44			19 54	19 59					20 09		20 14		
London Bridge	d	19 22			19 30	19 35						19 52			20 00	20 05					20 15		20 22		
East Croydon	a	19 36			19 44	19 48						20 06			20 14	20 18					20 28		20 36		
East Croydon	d	19 37	19 41		19 46	19 49		19 53		←	20 03	20 07	20 11		20 16	20 19		20 23		←	20 29	20 33	20 37	20 41	
Gatwick Airport	a	20 08	19 56	19 59	20 12	20 04		20 08	20 11	20 12	20 18	20 38	20 26	20 29	20 42	20 34		20 38	20 41	20 42	20 44	20 47	21 08	20 56	20 59
Three Bridges	a				→	20 09		20 14		20 19					→	20 39		20 44		20 49	20 49				
Crawley	a							20 18		20 23								20 48		20 53					
Horsham	a							20 27		20 38								20 57		21 08					

		TL		TL	SN	GX	TL	SN	TL	SN	GX	TL		TL	SN	GX	TL	TL	SN	TL	SN	GX		TL	TL
London Victoria	d				20 36	20 44		20 46		20 55	21 00				21 06	21 14			21 16		21 25	21 30			
Clapham Junction	d				20 43			20 53		21 02					21 13				21 23		21 32				
East Croydon	a				20 52			21 02		21 11					21 22				21 32		21 41				
St Pancras International	d	20 15		20 20					20 35			20 45		20 50				21 00		21 05				21 15	21 20
Farringdon	d	20 19		20 24					20 39			20 49		20 54				21 04		21 09				21 19	21 24
City Thameslink	d	20 21		20 26					20 41			20 51		20 56											
London Blackfriars	d	20 24		20 29					20 44			20 54		20 59				21 09		21 14				21 24	21 29
London Bridge	d	20 30		20 35					20 52			21 00		21 05				21 15		21 22				21 30	21 35
East Croydon	a	20 44		20 48					21 06			21 14		21 18				21 28		21 36				21 44	21 48
East Croydon	d	20 46		20 49	20 53		←	21 03	21 07	21 11		21 16		21 19	21 23		←	21 29	21 33	21 37	21 41			21 46	21 49
Gatwick Airport	a	21 12		21 04	21 07	21 11	21 12	21 18	21 38	21 26	21 29	21 42		21 34	21 38	21 41	21 42	21 44	21 47	22 08	21 56	21 59		22 12	22 04
Three Bridges	a	→		21 09	21 14		21 19					→		21 39	21 44		21 49	21 49		→				→	22 09
Crawley	a				21 18		21 23								21 48		21 53								
Horsham	a				21 27		21 38								21 57		22 08								

		SN	TL	GX	TL	SN	TL	SN		GX	TL	TL	SN	TL	GX	TL	TL	SN		TL	SN	TL	TL	TL	SN
London Victoria	d	21 36		21 44		21 46		21 55		22 00			22 06		22 14			22 16			22 25				22 36
Clapham Junction	d	21 43				21 53		22 02					22 13					22 23			22 32				22 43
East Croydon	a	21 52				22 02		22 11					22 22					22 32			22 41				22 52
St Pancras International	d						21 35				21 45	21 50					22 00			22 05		22 15	22 20		
Farringdon	d						21 39				21 49	21 54					22 04			22 09		22 19	22 24		
City Thameslink	d																								
London Blackfriars	d						21 44				21 54	21 59					22 09			22 14		22 24	22 29		
London Bridge	d						21 52				22 00	22 05					22 15			22 22		22 30	22 35		
East Croydon	a						22 06				22 14	22 18					22 28			22 36		22 44	22 48		
East Croydon	d	21 53	←		←	22 03	22 07	22 11			22 16	22 19	22 23	←		←	22 29	22 33		22 37	22 41	22 46	22 49	←	22 53
Gatwick Airport	a	22 07	22 08	22 11	22 12	22 18	22 38	22 26		22 29	22 42	22 34	22 38	22 38	22 41	22 42	22 44	22 47		23 08	22 56	23 12	23 04	23 08	23 08
Three Bridges	a	22 14	22 16		22 19		→				→	22 39	22 44	22 46		22 49	22 49			→		→	23 09	23 14	23 14
Crawley	a	22 18			22 23								22 48			22 53									23 18
Horsham	a	22 27			22 38								22 57			23 08									23 27

Table T185-F

Saturdays

26 May to 8 December

London - Gatwick Airport - Three Bridges - Horsham : Summary of Fast Trains

	GX ■	TL ■	TL ■	SN ■	TL ■	SN ■	TL ■	TL ■	TL ■	SN ■	TL ■	TL ■	SN ■	TL ■	SN ■	TL ■	TL ■	SN ■	TL ■
London Victoria d	22 44			22 46		22 55				23 06			23 16		23 25			23 36	
Clapham Junction d				22 53		23 02				23 13			23 23		23 32			23 43	
East Croydon a				23 02		23 11				23 22			23 32		23 41			23 58	
St Pancras International d			22 30		22 35		22 45	22 50				23 00		23 05		23 15	23 22		23 51
Farringdon d			22 34		22 39		22 49	22 54				23 04		23 09		23 19	23 27		23 56
City Thameslink d																			
London Blackfriars d			22 39		22 44		22 54	22 59				23 09		23 14		23 24	23 31		00 01
London Bridge d			22 45		22 52		23 00	23 05				23 15		23 21		23 30	23 37		
East Croydon a			22 58		23 06		23 14	23 18				23 28		23 36		23 44	23 50		00 27
East Croydon d		←	22 59	23 03	23 07	23 11	23 16	23 19	←	23 23	←	23 29	23 33	23 37	23 43	23 46	23 51	23 59	00 28
Gatwick Airport a	23 11	23 12	23 14	23 18	23 37	23 26	23 41	23 34	23 37	23 38	23 41	23 47	23 52	00 01	00 04	00 12	00 17	00 29	00 48
Three Bridges a		23 19	23 19		→		→	23 39	23 43	23 44	23 47	23 53				00 19	00 23	00 36	00 54
Crawley a		23 23								23 48	23 53					00 23		00 40	
Horsham a		23 38								23 57	00 06					00 36		00 49	

Sundays

20 May to 2 December

	SN ■	SN ■	TL ■ A	TL ■ A	SN ■	SN ■	SN ■	SN ■	GX	SN ■	GX	SN	GX	GX	SN	GX	TL ■	SN	SN ■	GX	TL ■	SN
London Victoria d	00 02	00 08			01 10	02 08	03 08	04 10	05 00	05 02	05 30	05 45	06 00	06 30	06 32	07 00		07 02		07 30		07 32
Clapham Junction d	00 09	00 15			01 17	02 17	03 17	04 17		05 10		05 53			06 40			07 10				07 40
East Croydon a	00 23	00 31			01 32	02 32	03 31	04 31		05 23		06 08			06 53			07 26				07 56
St Pancras International d			00 21	00 51																		
Farringdon d			00 26																			
City Thameslink d																						
London Blackfriars d			00 31	01 01																		
London Bridge d																	07 11		07 19		07 41	
East Croydon a			00 57	01 27													07 24		07 35		07 54	
East Croydon d	00 24	00 32	00 58	01 28	01 33	02 32	03 32	04 31		05 24		06 09			06 54		07 25	07 27	07 35		07 55	07 57
Gatwick Airport a	00 43	01 01	01 20	01 56	02 06	02 55	03 54	04 57	05 36	05 50	06 06	06 32	06 37	07 06	07 23	07 37	07 43	07 52	08 06	08 09	08 14	08 19
Three Bridges a	00 48		01 26	02 03	02 13	03 01	04 00	05 03		05 56		06 37			07 28		07 50	07 58	08 14		08 19	08 24
Crawley a																			08 18			08 28
Horsham a																			08 31			08 37

	GX	TL ■	SN	SN ■	SN	GX	SN	TL ■	SN	SN	SN	GX	TL ■	GX	SN	SN ■	TL ■	SN	GX	SN	TL ■	SN
London Victoria d	08 00		08 02		08 14	08 30	08 32			08 46	08 55	09 00		09 14	09 16			09 25	09 30	09 33		
Clapham Junction d			08 10		08 21		08 40			08 53	09 02				09 23			09 32		09 40		
East Croydon a			08 26		08 39		08 51			09 02	09 11				09 32			09 41		09 49		
St Pancras International d																					09 26	
Farringdon d																					09 30	
City Thameslink d																						
London Blackfriars d																					09 35	
London Bridge d		08 11		08 19				08 41					09 11			09 19	09 27				09 41	
East Croydon a		08 24		08 35				08 54					09 24			09 37	09 41				09 54	
East Croydon d		08 25	08 27	08 37	08 40		08 51	08 55	←	09 03	09 12		09 25		09 33	09 37	09 41	09 42		09 49	09 55	←
Gatwick Airport a	08 39	08 43	08 52	09 07	08 58	09 00	09 13	09 09	09 13	09 18	09 26	09 29	09 39	09 43	09 47	10 02	10 09	09 56	09 59	10 12	10 09	10 12
Three Bridges a		08 48	08 58	09 14			→	09 14	09 19		09 32		09 44			10 08				→	10 14	10 18
Crawley a				09 18					09 23							10 12						10 22
Horsham a				09 31					09 34							10 25						10 32

	GX	SN	TL ■	TL ■	SN	GX	TL ■	TL ■	GX	SN	TL ■	TL ■	SN	GX	SN	TL ■	SN	GX	SN	TL ■	TL ■
London Victoria d	09 44	09 46			09 55	10 00			10 14	10 16			10 25	10 30	10 33			10 44	10 46		
Clapham Junction d		09 53			10 02					10 23			10 32		10 40				10 53		
East Croydon a		10 02			10 11					10 32			10 41		10 49				11 02		
St Pancras International d			09 35	09 41			09 56				10 05	10 11				10 26				10 35	10 41
Farringdon d			09 39	09 45			10 00				10 09	10 15				10 30				10 39	10 45
City Thameslink d																					
London Blackfriars d			09 44	09 50			10 05				10 14	10 20				10 35				10 44	10 50
London Bridge d			09 51	09 56			10 11				10 21	10 26				10 41				10 51	10 56
East Croydon a			10 07	10 10			10 24				10 37	10 40				10 54				11 07	11 10
East Croydon d		10 03	10 07	10 11	10 12		10 25	←		10 33	10 37	10 41	10 42		10 49	10 55	←		11 03	11 07	11 11
Gatwick Airport a	10 13	10 18	10 27	10 41	10 26	10 29	10 39	10 41	10 43	10 47	11 02	11 09	10 56	10 59	11 12	11 09	11 12	11 13	11 18	11 27	11 41
Three Bridges a				→	10 32		10 44	10 47			11 08				→	11 14	11 18				→
Crawley a											11 12						11 22				
Horsham a											11 25						11 31				

	SN	GX	TL ■	TL ■	GX	SN	TL ■	TL ■	SN	GX	SN	TL ■	SN	GX	SN	TL ■	TL ■	SN	GX	TL ■	TL ■	GX
London Victoria d	10 55	11 00			11 14	11 16			11 25	11 30	11 33			11 44	11 46			11 55	12 00			12 14
Clapham Junction d	11 02					11 23			11 32		11 40				11 53			12 02				
East Croydon a	11 11					11 32			11 41		11 49				12 02			12 11				
St Pancras International d			10 56				11 05	11 11				11 26				11 35	11 41			11 56		
Farringdon d			11 00				11 09	11 15				11 30				11 39	11 45			12 00		
City Thameslink d																						
London Blackfriars d			11 05				11 14	11 20				11 35				11 44	11 50			12 05		
London Bridge d			11 11				11 21	11 26				11 41				11 51	11 56			12 11		
East Croydon a			11 24				11 37	11 40				11 54				12 07	12 10			12 24		
East Croydon d	11 12		11 25	←		11 33	11 37	11 41	11 42		11 49	11 55	←		12 03	12 07	12 11	12 12		12 25	←	
Gatwick Airport a	11 26	11 29	11 39	11 41	11 43	11 47	12 02	12 09	11 56	11 59	12 12	12 09	12 12	12 13	12 18	12 27	12 41	12 26	12 29	12 39	12 41	12 43
Three Bridges a	11 32		11 44	11 47			12 08				→	12 14	12 18				→	12 32		12 44	12 47	
Crawley a							12 12						12 22									
Horsham a							12 25						12 31									

A not 20 May

Table T185-F

Sundays

20 May to 2 December

London - Gatwick Airport - Three Bridges - Horsham : Summary of Fast Trains

	SN	TL ■	TL ■	SN	GX	SN	TL ■	SN	GX	SN	TL ■	TL ■	SN	GX	TL ■	TL ■	GX	SN	TL ■	TL ■	SN	GX
London Victoria d	12 16			12 25	12 30	12 33			12 44	12 46			12 55	13 00			13 14	13 16			13 25	13 30
Clapham Junction d	12 23			12 32		12 40				12 53			13 02					13 23			13 32	
East Croydon a	12 32			12 41		12 49				13 02			13 12					13 32			13 41	
St Pancras International d		12 05	12 11				12 26				12 35	12 41			12 56				13 05	13 11		
Farringdon d		12 09	12 15				12 30				12 39	12 45			13 00				13 09	13 15		
City Thameslink d																						
London Blackfriars d		12 14	12 20				12 35				12 44	12 50			13 05				13 14	13 20		
London Bridge d		12 21	12 26				12 41				12 51	12 56			13 11				13 21	13 26		
East Croydon a		12 37	12 40				12 54				13 07	13 10			13 24				13 37	13 40		
East Croydon d	12 33	12 37	12 41	12 42		12 49	12 55	←		13 03	13 07	13 11	13 13		13 25	←		13 33	13 37	13 41	13 42	
Gatwick Airport a	12 47	13 02	13 09	12 56	12 59	13 12	13 09	13 12	13 14	13 18	13 27	13 41	13 27	13 30	13 39	13 41	13 43	13 47	14 02	14 09	13 56	13 59
Three Bridges a		13 08				→	13 14	13 18				→	13 32		13 44	13 47			14 08			
Crawley a		13 12						13 22											14 12			
Horsham a		13 25						13 31											14 25			

	SN	TL ■	SN	GX	SN	TL ■	TL ■	SN	GX	TL ■	TL ■	GX	SN	TL ■	TL ■	SN	GX	SN	TL ■	SN	GX	SN
London Victoria d	13 33			13 44	13 46			13 55	14 00			14 14	14 16			14 25	14 30	14 33			14 44	14 46
Clapham Junction d	13 40				13 53			14 02					14 23			14 32		14 40				14 53
East Croydon a	13 49				14 02			14 11					14 32			14 41		14 49				15 02
St Pancras International d		13 26				13 35	13 41			13 56				14 05	14 11				14 26			
Farringdon d		13 30				13 39	13 45			14 00				14 09	14 15				14 30			
City Thameslink d																						
London Blackfriars d		13 35				13 44	13 50			14 05				14 14	14 20				14 35			
London Bridge d		13 41				13 51	13 56			14 11				14 21	14 26				14 41			
East Croydon a		13 54				14 07	14 10			14 24				14 37	14 40				14 54			
East Croydon d	13 49	13 55	←		14 03	14 07	14 11	14 12		14 25	←		14 33	14 37	14 41	14 42		14 49	14 55	←		15 03
Gatwick Airport a	14 12	14 09	14 12	14 13	14 18	14 27	14 41	14 26	14 29	14 39	14 41	14 43	14 47	15 02	15 09	14 56	14 59	15 12	15 09	15 12	15 13	15 18
Three Bridges a	→	14 14	14 18				→	14 32		14 44	14 47			15 08				→	15 14	15 18		
Crawley a			14 22											15 12						15 22		
Horsham a			14 31											15 25						15 31		

	TL ■	TL ■	SN	GX	TL ■	TL ■	GX	SN	TL ■	TL ■	SN	GX	SN	TL ■	SN	GX	SN	TL ■	TL ■	SN	GX
London Victoria d			14 55	15 00			15 14	15 16			15 25	15 30	15 33			15 44	15 46			15 55	16 00
Clapham Junction d			15 02					15 23			15 32		15 40				15 53			16 02	
East Croydon a			15 11					15 32			15 41		15 49				16 02			16 12	
St Pancras International d	14 35	14 41			14 56				15 05	15 11				15 26				15 35	15 41		
Farringdon d	14 39	14 45			15 00				15 09	15 15				15 30				15 39	15 45		
City Thameslink d																					
London Blackfriars d	14 44	14 50			15 05				15 14	15 20				15 35				15 44	15 50		
London Bridge d	14 51	14 56			15 11				15 21	15 26				15 41				15 51	15 56		
East Croydon a	15 07	15 10			15 24				15 37	15 40				15 54				16 07	16 10		
East Croydon d	15 07	15 11	15 12		15 25	←		15 33	15 37	15 41	15 42		15 49	15 55	←		16 03	16 07	16 11	16 13	
Gatwick Airport a	15 27	15 41	15 26	15 29	15 39	15 41	15 43	15 47	16 02	16 09	15 56	15 59	16 12	16 09	16 12	16 14	16 18	16 27	16 41	16 27	16 30
Three Bridges a		→	15 32		15 44	15 47			16 08				→	16 14	16 18				→	16 32	
Crawley a									16 12						16 22						
Horsham a									16 25						16 31						

	TL ■	TL ■	GX	SN	TL ■	TL ■	SN	GX	SN	TL ■	SN	GX	SN	TL ■	TL ■	SN	GX	TL ■	TL ■	GX	SN	TL ■
London Victoria d			16 14	16 16			16 25	16 30	16 33			16 44	16 46			16 55	17 00			17 14	17 16	
Clapham Junction d				16 23			16 32		16 40				16 53			17 02					17 23	
East Croydon a				16 32			16 41		16 49				17 02			17 12					17 32	
St Pancras International d	15 56				16 05	16 11				16 26				16 35	16 41			16 56				17 05
Farringdon d	16 00				16 09	16 15				16 30				16 39	16 45			17 00				17 09
City Thameslink d																						
London Blackfriars d	16 05				16 14	16 20				16 35				16 44	16 50			17 05				17 14
London Bridge d	16 11				16 21	16 26				16 41				16 51	16 56			17 11				17 21
East Croydon a	16 24				16 37	16 40				16 54				17 07	17 10			17 24				17 37
East Croydon d	16 25	←		16 33	16 37	16 41	16 42		16 49	16 55	←		17 03	17 07	17 11	17 13		17 25	←		17 33	17 37
Gatwick Airport a	16 39	16 41	16 43	16 47	17 02	17 09	16 56	16 59	17 12	17 09	17 12	17 14	17 18	17 27	17 41	17 27	17 30	17 39	17 41	17 43	17 47	18 02
Three Bridges a	16 44	16 47			17 08				→	17 14	17 18				→	17 32		17 44	17 47			18 08
Crawley a					17 12						17 22											18 12
Horsham a					17 25						17 31											18 25

	TL ■	SN	GX	SN	TL ■	SN	GX	SN	TL ■	TL ■	SN	GX	TL ■	TL ■	GX	SN	TL ■	TL ■	SN	GX	SN
London Victoria d		17 25	17 30	17 33			17 44	17 46			17 55	18 00			18 14	18 16			18 25	18 30	18 33
Clapham Junction d		17 32		17 40				17 53			18 02					18 23			18 32		18 40
East Croydon a		17 41		17 49				18 02			18 11					18 32			18 41		18 49
St Pancras International d	17 11				17 26				17 35	17 41			17 56				18 05	18 11			
Farringdon d	17 15				17 30				17 39	17 45			18 00				18 09	18 15			
City Thameslink d																					
London Blackfriars d	17 20				17 35				17 44	17 50			18 05				18 14	18 20			
London Bridge d	17 26				17 41				17 51	17 56			18 11				18 21	18 26			
East Croydon a	17 40				17 54				18 07	18 10			18 24				18 37	18 40			
East Croydon d	17 41	17 42		17 49	17 55	←		18 03	18 07	18 11	18 12		18 25	←		18 33	18 37	18 41	18 42		18 49
Gatwick Airport a	18 09	17 56	17 59	18 12	18 09	18 12	18 13	18 18	18 27	18 41	18 26	18 29	18 39	18 41	18 43	18 47	19 02	19 09	18 56	18 59	19 12
Three Bridges a				→	18 14	18 18				→	18 32		18 44	18 47			19 08				→
Crawley a						18 22											19 12				
Horsham a						18 31											19 25				

Table T185-F

Sundays

20 May to 2 December

London - Gatwick Airport - Three Bridges - Horsham : Summary of Fast Trains

		TL ■	SN	GX	SN	TL ■		TL ■	SN	GX	TL ■	TL ■	GX	SN	TL ■	TL ■		SN	GX	SN	TL ■	SN	GX	SN	TL ■
London Victoria	d			18 44	18 46				18 55	19 00			19 14	19 16				19 25	19 30	19 33			19 44	19 46	
Clapham Junction	d				18 53				19 02					19 23				19 32		19 40				19 53	
East Croydon	a				19 02				19 11					19 32				19 41		19 49				20 02	
St Pancras International	d	18 26				18 35		18 41			18 56				19 05	19 11					19 26				19 35
Farringdon	d	18 30				18 39		18 45			19 00				19 09	19 15					19 30				19 39
City Thameslink	d																								
London Blackfriars	d	18 35				18 44		18 50			19 05				19 14	19 20					19 35				19 44
London Bridge	d	18 41				18 51		18 56			19 11				19 21	19 26					19 41				19 51
East Croydon	a	18 54				19 07		19 10			19 24				19 37	19 40					19 54				20 07
East Croydon	d	18 55	←		19 03	19 07		19 11	19 12		19 25	←		19 33	19 37	19 41		19 42		19 49	19 55	←		20 03	20 07
Gatwick Airport	a	19 09	19 12	19 13	19 18	19 27		19 41	19 26	19 29	19 39	19 41	19 43	19 47	20 02	20 09		19 56	19 59	20 12	20 09	20 12	20 13	20 18	20 27
Three Bridges	a	19 14	19 18					→	19 32		19 44	19 47			20 08					→	20 14	20 18			
Crawley	a		19 22												20 12							20 22			
Horsham	a		19 31												20 25							20 31			

		TL ■		SN	GX	TL ■	TL ■	GX	SN	TL ■	TL ■	SN		GX	SN	TL ■	SN	GX	SN	TL ■	TL ■	SN		GX	TL ■
London Victoria	d			19 55	20 00			20 14	20 16			20 25		20 30	20 33			20 44	20 46			20 55		21 00	
Clapham Junction	d			20 02					20 23			20 32			20 40				20 53			21 02			
East Croydon	a			20 11					20 32			20 41			20 49				21 02			21 11			
St Pancras International	d	19 41				19 56				20 05	20 11					20 26				20 35	20 41				20 56
Farringdon	d	19 45				20 00				20 09	20 15					20 30				20 39	20 45				21 00
City Thameslink	d																								
London Blackfriars	d	19 50				20 05				20 14	20 20					20 35				20 44	20 50				21 05
London Bridge	d	19 56				20 11				20 21	20 26					20 41				20 51	20 56				21 11
East Croydon	a	20 10				20 24				20 37	20 40					20 54				21 07	21 10				21 24
East Croydon	d	20 11		20 12		20 25	←		20 33	20 37	20 41	20 42			20 49	20 55	←		21 03	21 07	21 11	21 12			21 25
Gatwick Airport	a	20 41		20 26	20 29	20 39	20 41	20 43	20 47	21 02	21 09	20 56		20 59	21 12	21 09	21 12	21 13	21 18	21 27	21 39	21 26		21 29	21 39
Three Bridges	a	→		20 32		20 44	20 46			21 08					→	21 14	21 18					21 32			21 44
Crawley	a									21 12							21 22								
Horsham	a									21 25							21 31								

		SN	TL ■	TL ■	SN	GX	SN	TL ■		SN	SN	TL ■	TL ■	SN	GX	SN	TL ■	TL ■		SN	SN	TL ■	TL ■	SN	GX
London Victoria	d	21 16			21 25	21 30	21 33				21 46			21 55	22 00	22 05				22 16				22 25	22 30
Clapham Junction	d	21 23			21 32		21 40				21 53			22 02		22 12				22 23				22 32	
East Croydon	a	21 32			21 41		21 49				22 02			22 11		22 22				22 32				22 41	
St Pancras International	d		21 05	21 11				21 26				21 35	21 41				21 56					22 05	22 11		
Farringdon	d		21 09	21 15				21 30				21 39	21 45				22 00					22 09	22 15		
City Thameslink	d																								
London Blackfriars	d		21 14	21 20				21 35				21 44	21 50				22 05					22 14	22 20		
London Bridge	d		21 21	21 26				21 41				21 51	21 56				22 11					22 21	22 26		
East Croydon	a		21 37	21 40				21 54				22 07	22 10				22 24					22 37	22 40		
East Croydon	d	21 33	21 37	21 41	21 42		21 49	21 55		←	22 03	22 07	22 11	22 12		22 23	22 25	←		22 33	←	22 37	22 41	22 42	
Gatwick Airport	a	21 47	22 02	22 09	21 56	21 59	22 13	22 09		22 13	22 18	22 26	22 39	22 26	22 29	22 50	22 39	22 39		22 47	22 50	23 02	23 09	22 56	22 59
Three Bridges	a		22 08	22 15			→	22 14		22 19		22 32	→	22 32		→	22 44	22 45			22 55	23 08			
Crawley	a		22 12							22 23											22 59	23 12			
Horsham	a		22 25							22 32											23 08	23 25			

		SN	TL ■	SN		SN	TL ■	SN	TL ■	SN	SN	TL ■	SN	TL ■		TL ■
London Victoria	d	22 35				22 46		23 05			23 16		23 32			
Clapham Junction	d	22 42				22 53		23 12			23 23		23 40			
East Croydon	a	22 51				23 02		23 22			23 32		23 56			
St Pancras International	d		22 26				22 35		22 56			23 26				23 51
Farringdon	d		22 30				22 39		23 00			23 30				23 56
City Thameslink	d															
London Blackfriars	d		22 35				22 44		23 05			23 35				00 01
London Bridge	d		22 41				22 51		23 11			23 41		23 45		
East Croydon	a		22 54				23 07		23 24			23 54		23 59		00 27
East Croydon	d	22 51	22 55	←		23 03	23 08	23 23	23 25	←	23 33	23 55	23 57	00 01		00 28
Gatwick Airport	a	23 12	23 09	23 12		23 18	23 35	23 50	23 42	23 50	23 54	00 17	00 21	00 29		00 47
Three Bridges	a	→	23 14	23 18			23 40	→	23 48	23 56		00 22	00 27	00 35		00 53
Crawley	a			23 22						00 01						
Horsham	a			23 31						00 14						

Table T185-R

Mondays to Fridays

21 May to 7 December

Horsham - Three Bridges - Gatwick Airport - London : Summary of Fast Trains

		TL MO ■	TL MX ■	TL ■	TL ■	TL ■		TL ■	TL ■	TL ■	TL ■	TL ■	TL ■	SN ■	TL ■	SN ■		SN ■	TL ■	TL ■	SN ■	SN ■	TL ■	GX ■	TL ■
Horsham	d															05 15				05 25					
Crawley	d															05 28				05 38					
Three Bridges	d	00 15	00 15	00 37	01 41	02 15		02 41	03 15	03 41	04 15	04 35	05 14		05 27	05 33			05 40	05 43		05 48	05 51		05 59
Gatwick Airport	d	00 21	00 21	00 42	01 46	02 21		02 46	03 21	03 46	04 21	04 41	05 19	05 28	05 33	05 38			05 46	05 49	05 52	05 53	05 56	05 59	06 06
East Croydon	a	00 39	00 39	01 09	02 09	02 39		03 09	03 39	04 09	04 39	05 08	05 39	06 00	06 03	05 53			06 00	06 15	06 34	06 07	06 31		06 21
East Croydon	d	00 40	00 40	01 10	02 10	02 40		03 10	03 40	04 10	04 40	05 10	05 40		06 03				06 01	06 16			06 31		06 21
London Bridge	d											05 25	05 55		06 21				06 16	06 31			06 51		06 35
London Blackfriars	d	01 06	01 08	01 36	02 36	03 06		03 36	04 06	04 36	05 06	05 31	06 01		06 27				06 22	06 37			06 57		06 42
City Thameslink	d										05 08	05 33	06 03		06 29				06 24	06 39			06 59		06 44
Farringdon	d										05 11	05 36	06 06		06 31				06 26	06 41			07 01		06 46
St Pancras International	a	01 15	01 15	01 43	02 43	03 13		03 43	04 13	04 43	05 15	05 40	06 10		06 35			←	06 30	06 45			07 05		06 50
East Croydon	d													06 00		05 53		06 00			06 34	06 08			
Clapham Junction	a													→		06 02		06 11			→	06 19			
London Victoria	a															06 10		06 18				06 27		06 29	

		SN ■		TL ■	GX ■	SN ■	SN ■	TL ■	GX ■	TL	TL ■	SN ■		TL	SN ■	SN ■	TL ■	GX ■	SN ■	TL ■	SN ■	TL ■		TL ■	GX ■
Horsham	d	05 41								05 44	06 04			06 14	06 19									06 34	
Crawley	d	05 55									06 19				06 28									06 49	
Three Bridges	d	06 02		06 07				06 20			06 24	06 26			06 33					06 41		06 50		06 54	
Gatwick Airport	d	06 08		06 13	06 14		06 19	06 25	06 28		06 29	06 33			06 38	06 41	06 43	06 44		06 46	06 49	06 55		06 59	06 59
East Croydon	a	06 23		06 45			07 04	06 40			07 01	06 48			06 53	06 56	07 15			07 01	07 34	07 10		07 31	
East Croydon	d			06 46				06 40			07 01					06 57	07 16			07 01		07 10		07 31	
London Bridge	d			07 01				06 54			07 21					07a13	07 31			07 16		07 24		07 51	
London Blackfriars	d			07 07				07 02			07 27						07 37			07 22		07 32		07 57	
City Thameslink	d			07 09				07 04			07 29						07 39			07 24		07 34		07 59	
Farringdon	d			07 11				07 06			07 31						07 41			07 26		07 36		08 01	
St Pancras International	a			07 15		←		07 10			07 35						07 45		←	07 30		07 40		08 05	
East Croydon	d	06 24				06 34	07 04					06 49			06 53				07 04		07 34				
Clapham Junction	a	06 33				06 44	→			06 53		06 58		07 23	07 02				07 14		→				
London Victoria	a	06 42			06 43	06 52			06 58	07 02		07 05		07 32	07 12			07 14	07 22						07 28

		SN ■	SN ■	TL ■	GX ■	SN ■	SN ■	SN ■		TL ■	GX ■	TL	SN ■	TL ■	SN ■	TL	SN ■	SN ■		TL ■	GX ■	SN ■	TL ■	SN ■	SN
Horsham	d		06 40									06 45	06 50	07 04		07 13	07 16								
Crawley	d		06 54										07 02	07 19			07 28								
Three Bridges	d	06 58	07 02							07 20			07 07	07 24	07 27		07 33						07 41		
Gatwick Airport	d	07 03	07 09	07 13	07 14		07 20	07 20		07 25	07 28			07 29	07 33		07 38	07 42		07 43	07 44		07 46	07 49	07 50
East Croydon	a	07 18	07 23	07 45			07 37	08 04		07 40			07 26	08 01	07 48		07 53	07 56		08 15			08 01	08 34	08 07
East Croydon	d			07 46						07 40			07 27	08 01				07 57		08 16			08 01		
London Bridge	d			08 01						07 54			07a43	08 21				08a13		08 31			08 16		
London Blackfriars	d			08 07						08 02				08 27						08 37			08 22		
City Thameslink	d			08 09						08 04				08 29						08 39			08 24		
Farringdon	d			08 11						08 06				08 31						08 41			08 26		
St Pancras International	a			08 15		←				08 10				08 35						08 45		←	08 30		
East Croydon	d	07 19	07 24			07 34	07 38	08 04							07 50		07 54					08 04		08 34	08 08
Clapham Junction	a	07 28	07 33			07 44	07 47	→				07 54			08 00	08 24	08 03					08 14		→	08 17
London Victoria	a	07 35	07 40		07 43	07 52	07 54				07 58	08 04			08 08	08 33	08 12				08 13	08 22			08 24

		TL ■	TL ■	GX ■		SN ■	SN ■	SN ■	TL ■	GX ■	SN ■	SN ■	SN ■	GX ■		TL ■	SN ■	TL	TL ■	SN ■	TL ■	GX ■	SN ■	TL ■	
Horsham	d		07 34				07 40	07 50								08 04		08 14		08 18					
Crawley	d		07 49				07 54	08 02								08 19				08 27					
Three Bridges	d	07 50	07 54			07 57	08 01	08 07								08 24	08 25		08 31	08 32				08 41	
Gatwick Airport	d	07 55	07 59	07 59		08 03	08 08		08 13	08 14		08 19	08 20	08 28		08 29	08 33		08 36	08 39	08 43	08 44		08 46	
East Croydon	a	08 10	08 31			08 18	08 23	08 26	08 45			09 04	08 37			09 01	08 48		08 51	08 54	09 15			09 01	
East Croydon	d	08 10	08 31					08 27	08 46							09 01			08 51		09 16			09 01	
London Bridge	d	08 24	08 51					08a43	09 01							09 21			09 05		09 31			09 16	
London Blackfriars	d	08 32	08 57						09 07							09 27			09 12		09 37			09 22	
City Thameslink	d	08 34	08 59						09 09							09 29			09 14		09 39			09 24	
Farringdon	d	08 36	09 01						09 11							09 31			09 16		09 41			09 26	
St Pancras International	a	08 40	09 05						09 15		←					09 35			09 20		09 45		←	09 30	
East Croydon	d					08 20	08 24				08 34	09 04	08 38				08 50			08 54			09 04		
Clapham Junction	a					08 30	08 33				08 44	→	08 47				09 00	09 23		09 03			09 14		
London Victoria	a			08 28		08 37	08 40			08 43	08 52		08 54	08 58			09 08	09 32		09 10		09 13	09 24		

		SN ■	SN ■	GX ■	TL ■	SN ■	TL ■	SN ■	GX ■	SN ■		TL ■	SN ■	GX ■	SN ■	TL	TL ■	TL ■	SN ■	GX ■		SN ■	TL ■	TL ■	GX ■
Horsham	d				08 34			08 50				08 55				09 14			09 20					09 25	
Crawley	d				08 49			08 59				09 08							09 29					09 38	
Three Bridges	d				08 54	08 55	09 00	09 04				09 13						09 31	09 34				09 40	09 43	
Gatwick Airport	d	08 49	08 51	08 58	08 59	09 03	09 06	09 09	09 12	←		09 19	09 23	09 24	09 28		09 33	09 36	09 39	09 42			09 46	09 49	09 53
East Croydon	a	09 34	09 09		09 31	09 18	09 21	09 24		09 34		09 45	10 00		09 42		10 03	09 51	09 54				10 01	10 15	
East Croydon	d	→			09 31		09 21					09 45					10 03	09 51					10 01	10 15	
London Bridge	d				09 51		09 35					10 01					10 21	10 05					10 16	10 31	
London Blackfriars	d				09 57		09 42					10 07					10 27	10 12					10 22	10 37	
City Thameslink	d				09 59		09 44					10 09					10 29	10 14					10 24	10 39	
Farringdon	d				10 01		09 46					10 11					10 31	10 16					10 26	10 41	
St Pancras International	a				10 05		09 50					10 15					10 35	10 20				←	10 30	10 45	
East Croydon	d		09 09			09 19		09 24		09 34			10 00		09 43				09 54			10 00			
Clapham Junction	a		09 18			09 28		09 33		09 44			→		09 52	10 23			10 03			10 10			
London Victoria	a		09 26	09 28		09 35		09 40	09 43	09 52				09 54	09 59	10 31			10 11	10 13		10 18			10 20

Table T185-R

Mondays to Fridays

21 May to 7 December

Horsham - Three Bridges - Gatwick Airport - London : Summary of Fast Trains

		SN [1]		SN [1]	TL [1]	TL [1]	SN [1]	GX [1]	TL [1]	GX [1]	SN [1]	SN [1]		TL	TL [1]	TL [1]	SN [1]	GX [1]	TL [1]	TL [1]	GX [1]	SN [1]		SN [1]	TL [1]
Horsham	d						09 50		09 55					10 14			10 20			10 25					
Crawley	d						09 59		10 08								10 29			10 38					
Three Bridges	d					09 59	10 04		10 13							10 29	10 34		10 40	10 43					
Gatwick Airport	d	09 57		10 03	10 03	10 06	10 09	10 12	10 19	10 23	10 27	10 33			10 33	10 36	10 39	10 42	10 46	10 49	10 54	10 57		11 03	11 03
East Croydon	a	10 11		10 18	10 33	10 21	10 24		10 45		10 41	10 48			11 03	10 51	10 54		11 01	11 15		11 11		11 18	11 33
East Croydon	d				10 33	10 21			10 45						11 03	10 51			11 01	11 15					11 33
London Bridge	d				10 51	10 35			11 01						11 21	11 05			11 16	11 31					11 51
London Blackfriars	d				10 57	10 42			11 07						11 27	11 12			11 22	11 37					11 57
City Thameslink	d				10 59	10 44			11 09						11 29	11 14			11 24	11 39					11 59
Farringdon	d				11 01	10 46			11 11						11 31	11 16			11 26	11 41					12 01
St Pancras International	a				11 05	10 50			11 15						11 35	11 20			11 30	11 45					12 05
East Croydon	d	10 12		10 19			10 24				10 42	10 49					10 54					11 12		11 19	
Clapham Junction	a	10 21		10 28			10 33				10 51	10 58		11 23			11 03					11 21		11 28	
London Victoria	a	10 29		10 35			10 41	10 43		10 50	10 59	11 05		11 32			11 11	11 13			11 20	11 29		11 35	

		TL [1]	SN [1]	GX [1]	TL [1]	GX [1]	SN [1]	SN [1]		TL	TL [1]	TL [1]	SN [1]	GX [1]	TL [1]	TL [1]	GX [1]	SN [1]		SN [1]	TL [1]	TL [1]	SN [1]	GX [1]	TL [1]
Horsham	d		10 50		10 55					11 14			11 20			11 25							11 50		11 55
Crawley	d		10 59		11 08								11 29			11 38							11 59		12 08
Three Bridges	d	10 59	11 04		11 13							11 29	11 34		11 40	11 43						11 59	12 04		12 13
Gatwick Airport	d	11 06	11 09	11 12	11 19	11 23	11 27	11 33			11 33	11 36	11 39	11 42	11 46	11 49	11 53	11 57		12 03	12 03	12 06	12 09	12 12	12 19
East Croydon	a	11 21	11 24		11 45		11 41	11 48			12 03	11 51	11 54		12 01	12 15		12 11		12 18	12 33	12 21	12 24		12 45
East Croydon	d	11 21			11 45						12 03	11 51			12 01	12 15					12 33	12 21			12 45
London Bridge	d	11 35			12 01						12 21	12 05			12 16	12 31					12 51	12 35			13 01
London Blackfriars	d	11 42			12 07						12 27	12 12			12 22	12 37					12 57	12 42			13 07
City Thameslink	d	11 44			12 09						12 29	12 14			12 24	12 39					12 59	12 44			13 09
Farringdon	d	11 46			12 11						12 31	12 16			12 26	12 41					13 01	12 46			13 11
St Pancras International	a	11 50			12 15						12 35	12 20			12 30	12 45					13 05	12 50			13 15
East Croydon	d		11 24				11 42	11 49					11 54					12 12		12 19			12 24		
Clapham Junction	a		11 33				11 51	11 58		12 23			12 03					12 22		12 28			12 33		
London Victoria	a		11 41	11 43		11 50	11 59	12 05		12 32			12 11	12 13			12 20	12 29		12 35			12 41	12 43	

		GX [1]	SN [1]	SN [1]		TL	TL [1]	TL [1]	SN [1]	GX [1]	TL [1]	TL [1]	GX [1]	SN [1]		SN [1]	TL [1]	TL [1]	SN [1]	GX [1]	TL [1]	GX [1]	SN [1]	SN [1]	
Horsham	d					12 14			12 20			12 23							12 50		12 55				
Crawley	d								12 29			12 38							12 59		13 08				
Three Bridges	d							12 29	12 34		12 40	12 43						12 59	13 04		13 13				
Gatwick Airport	d	12 23	12 27	12 33			12 33	12 36	12 39	12 42	12 46	12 49	12 53	12 57		13 03	13 03	13 06	13 09	13 12	13 19	13 23	13 27	13 33	
East Croydon	a		12 41	12 48			13 03	12 51	12 54		13 01	13 15		13 11		13 18	13 33	13 21	13 24		13 45		13 41	13 48	
East Croydon	d						13 03	12 51			13 01	13 15					13 33	13 21			13 45				
London Bridge	d						13 21	13 05			13 16	13 31					13 51	13 35			14 01				
London Blackfriars	d						13 27	13 12			13 22	13 37					13 57	13 42			14 07				
City Thameslink	d						13 29	13 14			13 24	13 39					13 59	13 44			14 09				
Farringdon	d						13 31	13 16			13 26	13 41					14 01	13 46			14 11				
St Pancras International	a						13 35	13 20			13 30	13 45					14 05	13 50			14 15				
East Croydon	d		12 42	12 49					12 54					13 12		13 19			13 24				13 42	13 49	
Clapham Junction	a		12 51	12 58		13 23			13 03					13 21		13 28			13 33				13 51	13 58	
London Victoria	a	12 50	12 59	13 05		13 32			13 11	13 13			13 20	13 29		13 35			13 41	13 43		13 50	13 59	14 05	

		TL	TL [1]	TL [1]	SN [1]	GX [1]	TL [1]	TL [1]	GX [1]	SN [1]		SN [1]	TL [1]	TL [1]	SN [1]	GX [1]	TL [1]	GX [1]	SN [1]	SN [1]		TL	TL [1]	TL [1]	SN [1]
Horsham	d	13 14			13 20			13 25							13 50		13 55					14 14			14 20
Crawley	d				13 29			13 38							13 59		14 08								14 29
Three Bridges	d			13 29	13 34		13 40	13 43						13 59	14 04		14 13							14 29	14 34
Gatwick Airport	d		13 33	13 36	13 39	13 42	13 46	13 49	13 53	13 57		14 03	14 03	14 06	14 09	14 12	14 19	14 23	14 27	14 33			14 33	14 36	14 39
East Croydon	a		14 03	13 51	13 54		14 01	14 15		14 11		14 18	14 33	14 21	14 24		14 45		14 41	14 48			15 03	14 51	14 54
East Croydon	d		14 03	13 51			14 01	14 15					14 33	14 21			14 45						15 03	14 52	
London Bridge	d		14 21	14 05			14 16	14 31					14 51	14 35			15 01						15 21	15 05	
London Blackfriars	d		14 27	14 12			14 22	14 37					14 57	14 42			15 07						15 27	15 12	
City Thameslink	d		14 29	14 14			14 24	14 39					14 59	14 44			15 09						15 29	15 14	
Farringdon	d		14 31	14 16			14 26	14 41					15 01	14 46			15 11						15 31	15 16	
St Pancras International	a		14 35	14 20			14 30	14 45					15 05	14 50			15 15						15 35	15 20	
East Croydon	d				13 54					14 12		14 19			14 24				14 42	14 49					14 54
Clapham Junction	a	14 23			14 03					14 21		14 28			14 33				14 51	14 58		15 23			15 03
London Victoria	a	14 32			14 11	14 13			14 20	14 29		14 35			14 41	14 43		14 50	14 59	15 05		15 32			15 11

		GX [1]	TL [1]	TL [1]	GX [1]	SN [1]		SN [1]	TL [1]	TL [1]	SN [1]	GX [1]	TL [1]	GX [1]	SN [1]	TL [1]		SN [1]	TL	TL [1]	TL [1]	SN [1]	GX [1]	TL [1]	TL [1]
Horsham	d			14 25							14 50		14 55						15 14			15 20			15 25
Crawley	d			14 38							14 59		15 08									15 29			15 38
Three Bridges	d		14 40	14 43						14 59	15 04		15 13								15 29	15 34		15 40	15 43
Gatwick Airport	d	14 42	14 46	14 49	14 53	14 57		15 03	15 03	15 06	15 09	15 12	15 19	15 23	15 27	15 27		15 33		15 33	15 36	15 39	15 42	15 46	15 49
East Croydon	a		15 01	15 15		15 11		15 18	15 33	15 21	15 24		15 45		15 41	15 54		15 48		16 03	15 51	15 54		16 01	16 15
East Croydon	d		15 01	15 15					15 33	15 21			15 45			15 54				16 03	15 51			16 01	16 15
London Bridge	d		15 16	15 31					15 51	15 35			16 01			16 11				16 21	16 05			16 16	16 31
London Blackfriars	d		15 22	15 37					15 57	15 42			16 07			16 17				16 27	16 12			16 22	16 37
City Thameslink	d		15 24	15 39					15 59	15 44			16 09			16 19				16 29	16 14			16 24	16 39
Farringdon	d		15 26	15 41					16 01	15 46			16 11			16 21				16 31	16 16			16 26	16 41
St Pancras International	a		15 30	15 45					16 05	15 50			16 15			16 25				16 35	16 20			16 30	16 45
East Croydon	d					15 12		15 19			15 24				15 42			15 49				15 54			
Clapham Junction	a					15 21		15 28			15 33				15 51			15 59	16 23			16 03			
London Victoria	a	15 13			15 20	15 29		15 35			15 41	15 43		15 50	16 00			16 09	16 32			16 11	16 15		

Table T185-R

Mondays to Fridays

21 May to 7 December

Horsham - Three Bridges - Gatwick Airport - London : Summary of Fast Trains

		GX [1]	SN [1]	TL [1]	SN [1]	TL [1]	TL [1]	SN [1]		GX [1]	TL [1]	GX [1]	SN [1]	TL [1]	SN [1]	TL	TL [1]	TL [1]		SN [1]	GX [1]	TL [1]	TL [1]	GX [1]	TL [1]
Horsham	d							15 50			15 55					16 14				16 22			16 25		
Crawley	d							15 59			16 08									16 31			16 39		
Three Bridges	d						15 59	16 04			16 13							16 29		16 36		16 40	16 44		16 49
Gatwick Airport	d	15 53	15 57	15 57	16 03	16 03	16 06	16 09		16 12	16 19	16 22	16 27	16 27	16 33		16 33	16 36		16 41	16 44	16 46	16 49	16 52	16 54
East Croydon	a		16 11	16 24	16 18	16 33	16 21	16 24			16 45		16 42	16 54	16 48		17 03	16 51		16 55		17 01	17 15		17 09
East Croydon	d			16 24		16 33	16 21				16 45			16 54			17 03	16 51				17 01	17 15		17 10
London Bridge	d			16 41		16 51	16 35				17 01			17 11			17 21	17 05				17 16	17 31		17 24
London Blackfriars	d			16 47		16 57	16 42				17 07			17 17			17 27	17 12				17 22	17 37		17 32
City Thameslink	d			16 49		16 59	16 44				17 09			17 19			17 29	17 14				17 24	17 39		17 34
Farringdon	d			16 51		17 01	16 46				17 11			17 21			17 31	17 16				17 26	17 41		17 36
St Pancras International	a			16 55		17 05	16 50				17 15			17 25			17 35	17 20				17 30	17 45		17 40
East Croydon	d		16 12		16 19			16 24					16 42		16 49					16 56					
Clapham Junction	a		16 21		16 28			16 33					16 51		16 58	17 23				17 05					
London Victoria	a	16 20	16 29		16 35			16 41		16 43		16 50	16 59		17 05	17 32				17 12	17 14			17 20	

		SN [1]	TL [1]	SN [1]		TL [1]	TL [1]	SN [1]	GX [1]	TL [1]	GX [1]	TL [1]	SN [1]	TL [1]		SN [1]	TL	TL [1]	TL [1]	SN [1]	GX [1]	TL [1]	TL [1]	GX	
Horsham	d							16 50		16 55							17 14			17 20			17 25		
Crawley	d							16 59		17 09										17 29			17 39		
Three Bridges	d						16 59	17 04		17 14		17 19							17 29	17 34		17 40	17 44		
Gatwick Airport	d	16 57	16 57	17 03		17 03	17 06	17 09	17 12	17 19	17 22	17 24	17 27	17 27		17 33		17 33	17 36	17 39	17 42	17 46	17 49	17 52	
East Croydon	a	17 12	17 24	17 18		17 33	17 21	17 24		17 45		17 39	17 42	17 53		17 48		18 03	17 51	17 54		18 01	18 15		
East Croydon	d		17 25			17 33	17 21			17 45		17 40		17 54				18 03	17 51			18 01	18 15		
London Bridge	d		17 41			17 51	17 35			18 01		17 54		18 11				18 21	18 05			18 16	18 31		
London Blackfriars	d		17 47			17 57	17 42			18 07		18 02		18 17				18 27	18 12			18 22	18 37		
City Thameslink	d		17 49			17 59	17 44			18 09		18 04		18 19				18 29	18 14			18 24	18 39		
Farringdon	d		17 51			18 01	17 46			18 11		18 06		18 21				18 31	18 16			18 26	18 41		
St Pancras International	a		17 55			18 05	17 50			18 15		18 10		18 25				18 35	18 20			18 30	18 45		
East Croydon	d	17 12		17 18				17 24					17 42			17 48				17 54					
Clapham Junction	a	17 21		17 28				17 33					17 51			17 58	18 23			18 03					
London Victoria	a	17 29		17 35				17 41	17 43		17 50		17 59			18 05	18 34			18 11	18 13			18 20	

		SN [1]	SN [1]	TL	TL [1]	TL [1]	SN [1]	GX	TL [1]	GX		SN [1]	SN [1]	TL	TL [1]	TL [1]	SN [1]	GX	TL [1]	TL [1]		GX	SN [1]	SN [1]	TL
Horsham	d			17 42			17 50		17 55					18 12			18 20			18 25					18 42
Crawley	d						17 59		18 09								18 29			18 39					
Three Bridges	d					17 59	18 04		18 14							18 29	18 34		18 40	18 44					
Gatwick Airport	d	17 57	18 03		18 03	18 06	18 09	18 12	18 19	18 22		18 27	18 33		18 33	18 36	18 39	18 42	18 46	18 49		18 53	18 57	19 03	
East Croydon	a	18 12	18 18		18 33	18 21	18 24		18 45			18 42	18 48		19 03	18 51	18 54		19 01	19 15			19 11	19 18	
East Croydon	d				18 33	18 21			18 45						19 03	18 51			19 01	19 15					
London Bridge	d				18 51	18 35			19 01						19 21	19 05			19 16	19 31					
London Blackfriars	d				18 57	18 42			19 07						19 27	19 12			19 22	19 37					
City Thameslink	d				18 59	18 44			19 09						19 29	19 14			19 24	19 39					
Farringdon	d				19 01	18 46			19 11						19 31	19 16			19 26	19 41					
St Pancras International	a				19 05	18 50			19 15						19 35	19 20			19 30	19 45					
East Croydon	d	18 12	18 18				18 24					18 42	18 48				18 54						19 12	19 18	
Clapham Junction	a	18 21	18 28	18 53			18 34					18 51	18 58	19 23			19 03						19 21	19 28	19 53
London Victoria	a	18 29	18 35	19 02			18 42	18 44		18 50		18 59	19 05	19 33			19 11	19 14				19 20	19 29	19 35	20 02

		TL [1]	TL [1]	SN [1]	GX	TL [1]		GX	SN [1]	SN [1]	TL	TL [1]	TL [1]	SN [1]	GX	TL [1]		TL [1]	GX	SN [1]	SN [1]	TL [1]	TL [1]	SN [1]	GX
Horsham	d			18 52		18 55					19 12			19 20				19 25						19 52	
Crawley	d			19 01		19 08								19 29				19 38						20 01	
Three Bridges	d		18 59	19 06		19 13							19 29	19 34		19 40		19 43					19 59	20 06	
Gatwick Airport	d	19 03	19 06	19 11	19 13	19 19		19 23	19 27	19 33		19 33	19 36	19 39	19 42	19 46		19 49	19 53	19 57	20 03	20 03	20 06	20 11	20 13
East Croydon	a	19 33	19 21	19 25		19 45			19 42	19 48		20 03	19 51	19 54		20 01		20 15		20 11	20 18	20 33	20 21	20 25	
East Croydon	d	19 33	19 21			19 45						20 03	19 51			20 01		20 15				20 33	20 21		
London Bridge	d	19 51	19 35			20 01						20 21	20 05			20 16		20 31				20 51	20 35		
London Blackfriars	d	19 57	19 42			20 07						20 27	20 12			20 22		20 37				20 57	20 42		
City Thameslink	d	19 59	19 44			20 09						20 29	20 14			20 24		20 39				20 59	20 44		
Farringdon	d	20 01	19 46			20 11						20 31	20 16			20 26		20 41				21 01	20 46		
St Pancras International	a	20 05	19 50			20 15						20 35	20 20			20 30		20 45				21 05	20 50		
East Croydon	d			19 26					19 42	19 49				19 54						20 12	20 19			20 26	
Clapham Junction	a			19 35					19 51	19 58	20 23			20 04						20 21	20 28			20 35	
London Victoria	a			19 42	19 44			19 50	19 59	20 05	20 32			20 11	20 14				20 20	20 30	20 35			20 42	20 44

		TL [1]		GX	SN [1]	SN [1]	TL	TL [1]	TL [1]	SN [1]	GX	TL [1]		TL [1]	GX	SN [1]	SN [1]	TL [1]	TL [1]	SN [1]	GX	TL [1]		GX	SN [1]
Horsham	d	19 55					20 14			20 20				20 25						20 50		20 55			
Crawley	d	20 08								20 29				20 38						20 59		21 08			
Three Bridges	d	20 13							20 29	20 34		20 40		20 43					20 59	21 04		21 13			
Gatwick Airport	d	20 19		20 23	20 28	20 33		20 33	20 36	20 39	20 42	20 46		20 49	20 54	20 57	21 03	21 03	21 06	21 09	21 12	21 19		21 24	21 27
East Croydon	a	20 45			20 42	20 48		21 03	20 51	20 54		21 01		21 15		21 11	21 18	21 33	21 21	21 24		21 45			21 41
East Croydon	d	20 46						21 03	20 51			21 01		21 15				21 33	21 21			21 45			
London Bridge	d	21 01						21 21	21 05			21 16		21 31				21 51	21 35			22 01			
London Blackfriars	d	21 07						21 27	21 12			21 22		21 37				21 57	21 42			22 07			
City Thameslink	d	21 09						21 29	21 14			21 24		21 39				21 59	21 44			22 09			
Farringdon	d	21 11						21 31	21 16			21 26		21 41				22 01	21 46			22 11			
St Pancras International	a	21 15						21 35	21 20			21 30		21 45				22 05	21 50			22 15			
East Croydon	d				20 43	20 49				20 54						21 12	21 19			21 24					21 42
Clapham Junction	a				20 52	21 01	21 23			21 06						21 21	21 28			21 33					21 51
London Victoria	a			20 50	20 59	21 08	21 32			21 13	21 15				21 24	21 29	21 35			21 41	21 43			21 50	21 59

Table T185-R

Mondays to Fridays

21 May to 7 December

Horsham - Three Bridges - Gatwick Airport - London : Summary of Fast Trains

		SN ■	TL	TL ■	TL ■	SN ■	GX	TL ■	TL ■	GX	SN ■	SN ■	TL ■	SN ■	GX	TL ■	GX A	SN ■	SN ■	TL ■	SN ■	GX
Horsham	d		21 14			21 20			21 25					21 50		21 55					22 20	
Crawley	d					21 29			21 38					21 59		22 08					22 29	
Three Bridges	d				21 29	21 34		21 40	21 43				21 59	22 04		22 13				22 29	22 34	
Gatwick Airport	d	21 33		21 33	21 36	21 39	21 42	21 46	21 49	21 54	21 57	22 03	22 06	22 09	22 12	22 19	22 23	22 28	22 33	22 36	22 39	22 42
East Croydon	a	21 48		22 03	21 51	21 54		22 01	22 15		22 12	22 18	22 21	22 24		22 45		22 42	22 48	22 51	22 54	
East Croydon	d			22 03	21 51			22 01	22 15				22 21			22 45				22 51		
London Bridge	d			22 21	22 05			22 16	22 31				22 35			23 01				23 05		
London Blackfriars	d			22 27	22 12			22 22	22 37				22 42			23 07				23 12		
City Thameslink	d			22 29	22 14			22 24	22 39				22 44									
Farringdon	d			22 31	22 16			22 26	22 41				22 46			23 11				23 16		
St Pancras International	a			22 35	22 20			22 30	22 45				22 50			23 15				23 20		
East Croydon	d	21 49				21 54					22 12	22 19		22 24				22 43	22 49		22 54	
Clapham Junction	a	21 58	22 23			22 03					22 21	22 28		22 33				22 52	22 58		23 03	
London Victoria	a	22 05	22 33			22 11	22 13			22 20	22 29	22 35		22 42	22 43		22 51	23 00	23 05		23 11	23 13

		TL ■	TL ■	GX A	SN ■	SN ■	TL ■	GX A	SN ■	TL ■	TL ■	SN ■	SN ■	TL ■
Horsham	d		22 25								23 11	23 27		
Crawley	d		22 38								23 24	23 36		
Three Bridges	d	22 40	22 43				22 59			23 29	23 29	23a40		23 58
Gatwick Airport	d	22 46	22 49	22 53	22 57	23 03	23 06	23 12	23 27	23 34	23 35		23 55	00 04
East Croydon	a	23 01	23 15		23 12	23 18	23 21		23 42	23 52	00 09		00 15	00 22
East Croydon	d	23 01	23 15				23 21			23 53	00 10			00 23
London Bridge	d	23 16	23 31				23 35							
London Blackfriars	d	23 22	23 37				23 42			00 22	00 37			00 50
City Thameslink	d													
Farringdon	d	23 26	23 41				23 46			00 25	00 41			
St Pancras International	a	23 30	23 45				23 50			00 29	00 45			00 59
East Croydon	d				23 12	23 19			23 42				00 16	
Clapham Junction	a				23 21	23 28			23 57				00 33	
London Victoria	a			23 20	23 30	23 35		23 43	00 05				00 41	

Saturdays

26 May to 8 December

		TL ■	TL ■	TL ■	SN ■	TL ■	TL ■	SN ■	TL ■	TL ■	SN ■	TL ■	TL ■	SN ■	TL ■	SN ■	TL ■	TL ■	TL ■	GX ■	SN ■	TL ■	TL ■
Horsham	d																		05 25				
Crawley	d																		05 38				
Three Bridges	d	00 15	00 37	01 41	02 08	02 15	02 41	03 08	03 15	03 41	04 08	04 15	04 35	04 58	05 15	05 22	05 27	05 40	05 43				05 59
Gatwick Airport	d	00 21	00 42	01 46	02 13	02 21	02 46	03 13	03 21	03 46	04 13	04 21	04 41	05 03	05 20	05 28	05 33	05 46	05 49	05 58	06 03	06 03	06 06
East Croydon	a	00 39	01 09	02 09	02 36	02 39	03 09	03 36	03 39	04 09	04 36	04 39	05 08	05 30	05 38	06 00	06 03	06 00	06 15		06 18	06 33	06 21
East Croydon	d	00 40	01 10	02 10		02 40	03 10		03 40	04 10		04 40	05 10		05 39		06 03	06 01	06 15			06 33	06 21
London Bridge	d												05 26		05 55		06 21	06 16	06 31			06 51	06 35
London Blackfriars	d	01 08	01 36	02 36		03 06	03 36		04 06	04 36		05 06	05 32		06 02		06 27	06 22	06 37			06 57	06 42
City Thameslink	d																						
Farringdon	d											05 11	05 36		06 06		06 31	06 26	06 41			07 01	06 46
St Pancras International	a	01 15	01 43	02 43		03 13	03 43		04 13	04 43		05 15	05 40		06 10		06 35	06 30	06 45			07 05	06 50
East Croydon	d				02 36			03 36			04 36			05 30		06 00					06 19		
Clapham Junction	a				02 50			03 50			04 50			05 50		06 10					06 28		
London Victoria	a				02 58			03 58			04 58			05 59		06 18				06 25	06 35		

		SN ■	GX ■	TL ■	GX ■	SN ■	SN ■	TL ■	TL ■	SN ■	GX ■	TL ■	TL ■	GX ■	SN ■	SN ■	TL ■	TL ■	SN ■	GX ■	TL ■	GX ■	SN ■
Horsham	d	05 41		05 55						06 20			06 25						06 50		06 55		
Crawley	d	05 55		06 08						06 29			06 38						06 59		07 08		
Three Bridges	d	06 03		06 13					06 29	06 34		06 40	06 43					06 59	07 04		07 13		
Gatwick Airport	d	06 09	06 12	06 19	06 23	06 27	06 33	06 33	06 36	06 39	06 42	06 46	06 49	06 53	06 57	07 03	07 03	07 06	07 09	07 12	07 19	07 23	07 27
East Croydon	a	06 24		06 45		06 41	06 48	07 03	06 51	06 54		07 01	07 15		07 11	07 18	07 33	07 21	07 24		07 45		07 41
East Croydon	d			06 45				07 03	06 51			07 01	07 15				07 33	07 21			07 45		
London Bridge	d			07 01				07 21	07 05			07 16	07 31				07 51	07 35			08 01		
London Blackfriars	d			07 07				07 27	07 12			07 22	07 37				07 57	07 42			08 07		
City Thameslink	d																						
Farringdon	d			07 11				07 31	07 16			07 26	07 41				08 01	07 46			08 11		
St Pancras International	a			07 15				07 35	07 20			07 30	07 45				08 05	07 50			08 15		
East Croydon	d	06 24				06 42	06 49			06 54					07 12	07 19			07 24				07 42
Clapham Junction	a	06 33				06 51	06 58			07 03					07 21	07 28			07 33				07 51
London Victoria	a	06 41	06 43		06 50	06 59	07 05			07 11	07 13			07 20	07 29	07 35			07 41	07 43		07 50	07 59

		SN ■	TL ■	TL ■	SN ■	GX ■	TL ■	TL ■	GX ■	SN ■	SN ■	TL ■	TL ■	SN ■	GX ■	TL ■	GX ■	SN ■	SN ■	TL	TL ■	TL ■
Horsham	d				07 20			07 25						07 50		07 55				08 14		
Crawley	d				07 29			07 38						07 59		08 08						
Three Bridges	d			07 29	07 34		07 40	07 43					07 59	08 04		08 13						08 29
Gatwick Airport	d	07 33	07 33	07 36	07 39	07 42	07 46	07 49	07 53	07 57	08 03	08 03	08 06	08 09	08 12	08 19	08 23	08 27	08 33		08 33	08 36
East Croydon	a	07 48	08 03	07 51	07 54		08 01	08 15		08 11	08 18	08 33	08 21	08 24		08 45		08 41	08 48		09 03	08 51
East Croydon	d		08 03	07 51			08 01	08 15				08 33	08 21			08 45					09 03	08 51
London Bridge	d		08 21	08 05			08 16	08 31				08 51	08 35			09 01					09 21	09 05
London Blackfriars	d		08 27	08 12			08 22	08 37				08 57	08 42			09 07					09 27	09 12
City Thameslink	d															09 09					09 29	09 14
Farringdon	d		08 31	08 16			08 26	08 41				09 01	08 46			09 11					09 31	09 16
St Pancras International	a		08 35	08 20			08 30	08 45				09 05	08 50			09 15					09 35	09 20
East Croydon	d	07 49			07 54					08 12	08 19			08 24				08 42	08 49			
Clapham Junction	a	07 58			08 03					08 21	08 28			08 33				08 51	08 58	09 23		
London Victoria	a	08 05			08 11	08 13			08 20	08 29	08 35			08 41	08 43		08 50	08 59	09 05	09 32		

A not 7 December

Table T185-R

Saturdays

26 May to 8 December

Horsham - Three Bridges - Gatwick Airport - London : Summary of Fast Trains

		SN ■	GX ■	TL ■	TL ■	GX ■	SN ■	SN ■	TL ■	TL ■	SN ■	GX ■	TL ■	GX ■	SN ■	SN ■	TL	TL ■	TL ■	SN ■	GX ■	TL ■
Horsham	d	08 20			08 25						08 50		08 55				09 14			09 20		
Crawley	d	08 29			08 38						08 59		09 08							09 29		
Three Bridges	d	08 34		08 40	08 43					08 59	09 04		09 13						09 29	09 34		09 40
Gatwick Airport	d	08 39	08 42	08 46	08 49	08 53	08 57	09 03	09 03	09 06	09 09	09 12	09 19	09 23	09 27	09 33		09 33	09 36	09 39	09 42	09 46
East Croydon	a	08 54		09 01	09 15		09 11	09 18	09 33	09 21	09 24		09 45		09 41	09 48		10 03	09 51	09 54		10 01
East Croydon	d			09 01	09 15				09 33	09 21			09 45					10 03	09 51			10 01
London Bridge	d			09 16	09 31				09 51	09 35			10 01					10 21	10 05			10 16
London Blackfriars	d			09 22	09 37				09 57	09 42			10 07					10 27	10 12			10 22
City Thameslink	d			09 24	09 39				09 59	09 44			10 09					10 29	10 14			10 24
Farringdon	d			09 26	09 41				10 01	09 46			10 11					10 31	10 16			10 26
St Pancras International	a			09 30	09 45				10 05	09 50			10 15					10 35	10 20			10 30
East Croydon	d	08 54					09 12	09 19			09 24				09 42	09 49				09 54		
Clapham Junction	a	09 03					09 21	09 28			09 33				09 51	09 58	10 23			10 03		
London Victoria	a	09 11	09 13			09 20	09 29	09 35			09 41	09 43		09 50	09 59	10 05	10 32			10 11	10 13	

		TL ■	GX ■	SN ■	SN ■	TL ■	TL ■	SN ■	GX ■	TL ■	GX ■	SN ■	SN ■	TL	TL ■	TL ■	SN ■	GX ■	TL ■	TL ■	GX ■	SN ■	SN ■
Horsham	d	09 25						09 50		09 55				10 14			10 20			10 25			
Crawley	d	09 38						09 59		10 08							10 29			10 38			
Three Bridges	d	09 43					09 59	10 04		10 13						10 29	10 34		10 40	10 43			
Gatwick Airport	d	09 49	09 53	09 57	10 03	10 03	10 06	10 09	10 12	10 19	10 23	10 27	10 33		10 33	10 36	10 39	10 42	10 46	10 49	10 53	10 57	11 03
East Croydon	a	10 15		10 11	10 18	10 33	10 21	10 24		10 45		10 41	10 48		11 03	10 51	10 54		11 01	11 15		11 11	11 18
East Croydon	d	10 15				10 33	10 21			10 45					11 03	10 51			11 01	11 15			
London Bridge	d	10 31				10 51	10 35			11 01					11 21	11 05			11 16	11 31			
London Blackfriars	d	10 37				10 57	10 42			11 07					11 27	11 12			11 22	11 37			
City Thameslink	d	10 39				10 59	10 44			11 09					11 29	11 14			11 24	11 39			
Farringdon	d	10 41				11 01	10 46			11 11					11 31	11 16			11 26	11 41			
St Pancras International	a	10 45				11 05	10 50			11 15					11 35	11 20			11 30	11 45			
East Croydon	d			10 12	10 19			10 24				10 42	10 49				10 54					11 12	11 19
Clapham Junction	a			10 21	10 28			10 33				10 51	10 58	11 23			11 03					11 21	11 28
London Victoria	a		10 20	10 29	10 35			10 41	10 43		10 50	10 59	11 05	11 32			11 11	11 13			11 20	11 29	11 35

		TL ■	TL ■	SN ■	GX ■	TL ■	GX ■	SN ■	SN ■	TL	TL ■	TL ■	SN ■	GX ■	TL ■	TL ■	GX ■	SN ■	SN ■	TL ■	TL ■	SN ■	GX ■
Horsham	d			10 50		10 55				11 14			11 20			11 25						11 50	
Crawley	d			10 59		11 08							11 29			11 38						11 59	
Three Bridges	d		10 59	11 04		11 13						11 29	11 34		11 40	11 43					11 59	12 04	
Gatwick Airport	d	11 03	11 06	11 09	11 12	11 19	11 23	11 27	11 33		11 33	11 36	11 39	11 42	11 46	11 49	11 53	11 57	12 03	12 03	12 06	12 09	12 12
East Croydon	a	11 33	11 21	11 24		11 45		11 41	11 48		12 03	11 51	11 54		12 01	12 15		12 11	12 18	12 33	12 21	12 24	
East Croydon	d	11 33	11 21			11 45					12 03	11 51			12 01	12 15				12 33	12 21		
London Bridge	d	11 51	11 35			12 01					12 21	12 05			12 16	12 31				12 51	12 35		
London Blackfriars	d	11 57	11 42			12 07					12 27	12 12			12 22	12 37				12 57	12 42		
City Thameslink	d	11 59	11 44			12 09					12 29	12 14			12 24	12 39				12 59	12 44		
Farringdon	d	12 01	11 46			12 11					12 31	12 16			12 26	12 41				13 01	12 46		
St Pancras International	a	12 05	11 50			12 15					12 35	12 20			12 30	12 45				13 05	12 50		
East Croydon	d			11 24				11 42	11 49				11 54					12 12	12 19			12 24	
Clapham Junction	a			11 33				11 51	11 58	12 23			12 03					12 21	12 28			12 33	
London Victoria	a			11 41	11 43		11 50	11 59	12 05	12 32			12 11	12 13			12 20	12 29	12 35			12 41	12 43

		TL ■	GX ■	SN ■	SN ■	TL	TL ■	TL ■	SN ■	GX ■	TL ■	TL ■	GX ■	SN ■	SN ■	TL ■	TL ■	SN ■	GX ■	TL ■	GX ■	SN ■
Horsham	d	11 55				12 14			12 20			12 25						12 50		12 55		
Crawley	d	12 08							12 29			12 38						12 59		13 08		
Three Bridges	d	12 13						12 29	12 34		12 40	12 43					12 59	13 04		13 13		
Gatwick Airport	d	12 19	12 23	12 27	12 33		12 33	12 36	12 39	12 42	12 46	12 49	12 53	12 57	13 03	13 03	13 06	13 09	13 12	13 19	13 23	13 27
East Croydon	a	12 45		12 41	12 48		13 03	12 51	12 54		13 01	13 15		13 11	13 18	13 33	13 21	13 24		13 45		13 41
East Croydon	d	12 45					13 03	12 51			13 01	13 15				13 33	13 21			13 45		
London Bridge	d	13 01					13 21	13 05			13 16	13 31				13 51	13 35			14 01		
London Blackfriars	d	13 07					13 27	13 12			13 22	13 37				13 57	13 42			14 07		
City Thameslink	d	13 09					13 29	13 14			13 24	13 39				13 59	13 44			14 09		
Farringdon	d	13 11					13 31	13 16			13 26	13 41				14 01	13 46			14 11		
St Pancras International	a	13 15					13 35	13 20			13 30	13 45				14 05	13 50			14 15		
East Croydon	d			12 42	12 49				12 54					13 12	13 19			13 24				13 42
Clapham Junction	a			12 51	12 58	13 23			13 03					13 21	13 28			13 33				13 51
London Victoria	a		12 50	12 59	13 05	13 32			13 11	13 13			13 20	13 29	13 35			13 41	13 43		13 50	13 59

		SN ■	TL	TL ■	TL ■	SN ■	GX ■	TL ■	TL ■	GX ■	SN ■	SN ■	TL ■	TL ■	SN ■	GX ■	TL ■	GX ■	SN ■	SN ■	TL	TL ■	TL ■
Horsham	d		13 14			13 20			13 25						13 50		13 55				14 14		
Crawley	d					13 29			13 38						13 59		14 08						
Three Bridges	d				13 29	13 34		13 40	13 43					13 59	14 04		14 13						14 29
Gatwick Airport	d	13 33		13 33	13 36	13 39	13 42	13 46	13 49	13 53	13 57	14 03	14 03	14 06	14 09	14 12	14 19	14 23	14 27	14 33		14 33	14 36
East Croydon	a	13 48		14 03	13 51	13 54		14 01	14 15		14 11	14 18	14 33	14 21	14 24		14 45		14 41	14 48		15 03	14 51
East Croydon	d			14 03	13 51			14 01	14 15				14 33	14 21			14 45					15 03	14 51
London Bridge	d			14 21	14 05			14 16	14 31				14 51	14 35			15 01					15 21	15 05
London Blackfriars	d			14 27	14 12			14 22	14 37				14 57	14 42			15 07					15 27	15 12
City Thameslink	d			14 29	14 14			14 24	14 39				14 59	14 44			15 09					15 29	15 14
Farringdon	d			14 31	14 16			14 26	14 41				15 01	14 46			15 11					15 31	15 16
St Pancras International	a			14 35	14 20			14 30	14 45				15 05	14 50			15 15					15 35	15 20
East Croydon	d	13 49				13 54					14 12	14 19			14 24				14 42	14 49			
Clapham Junction	a	13 58	14 23			14 03					14 21	14 28			14 33				14 51	14 58	15 23		
London Victoria	a	14 05	14 32			14 11	14 13			14 20	14 29	14 35			14 41	14 43		14 50	14 59	15 05	15 32		

Table T185-R

Saturdays
26 May to 8 December

Horsham - Three Bridges - Gatwick Airport - London : Summary of Fast Trains

	SN ■	GX ■	TL ■	TL ■	GX ■	SN ■	SN ■	TL ■	TL ■		SN ■	GX ■	TL ■	GX ■	SN ■	SN ■	TL	TL ■	TL ■		SN ■	GX ■	TL ■	TL ■
Horsham d	14 20			14 25							14 50		14 55				15 14				15 20			15 25
Crawley d	14 29			14 38							14 59		15 08								15 29			15 38
Three Bridges d	14 34		14 40	14 43					14 59		15 04		15 13						15 29		15 34		15 40	15 43
Gatwick Airport d	14 39	14 42	14 46	14 49	14 53	14 57	15 03	15 03	15 06		15 09	15 12	15 19	15 23	15 27	15 33		15 33	15 36		15 39	15 42	15 46	15 49
East Croydon a	14 54		15 01	15 15		15 11	15 18	15 33	15 21		15 24		15 45		15 41	15 48		16 03	15 51		15 54		16 01	16 15
East Croydon d			15 01	15 15				15 33	15 21				15 45					16 03	15 51				16 01	16 15
London Bridge d			15 16	15 31				15 51	15 35				16 01					16 21	16 05				16 16	16 31
London Blackfriars d			15 22	15 37				15 57	15 42				16 07					16 27	16 12				16 22	16 37
City Thameslink d			15 24	15 39				15 59	15 44				16 09					16 29	16 14				16 24	16 39
Farringdon d			15 26	15 41				16 01	15 46				16 11					16 31	16 16				16 26	16 41
St Pancras International a			15 30	15 45				16 05	15 50				16 15					16 35	16 20				16 30	16 45
East Croydon d	14 54					15 12	15 19				15 24				15 42	15 49					15 54			
Clapham Junction a	15 03					15 21	15 28				15 33				15 51	15 58	16 23				16 03			
London Victoria a	15 11	15 13			15 20	15 29	15 35				15 41	15 43		15 50	15 59	16 05	16 32				16 11	16 13		

	GX ■	SN ■	SN ■	TL ■	TL ■		SN ■	GX ■	TL ■	GX ■	SN ■	SN ■	TL	TL ■	TL ■		SN ■	GX ■	TL ■	TL ■	GX ■	SN ■	SN ■	TL ■
Horsham d							15 50		15 55				16 14				16 22			16 25				
Crawley d							15 59		16 08								16 31			16 38				
Three Bridges d					15 59		16 04		16 13						16 29		16 36		16 40	16 43				
Gatwick Airport d	15 53	15 57	16 03	16 03	16 06		16 09	16 12	16 19	16 23	16 27	16 33		16 33	16 36		16 41	16 44	16 46	16 49	16 53	16 57	17 03	17 03
East Croydon a		16 11	16 18	16 33	16 21		16 24		16 45		16 41	16 48		17 03	16 51		16 55		17 01	17 15		17 11	17 18	17 33
East Croydon d				16 33	16 21				16 45					17 03	16 51				17 01	17 15				17 33
London Bridge d				16 51	16 35				17 01					17 21	17 05				17 16	17 31				17 51
London Blackfriars d				16 57	16 42				17 07					17 27	17 12				17 22	17 37				17 57
City Thameslink d				16 59	16 44				17 09					17 29	17 14				17 24	17 39				17 59
Farringdon d				17 01	16 46				17 11					17 31	17 16				17 26	17 41				18 01
St Pancras International a				17 05	16 50				17 15					17 35	17 20				17 30	17 45				18 05
East Croydon d		16 12	16 19				16 24				16 42	16 49					16 56					17 12	17 19	
Clapham Junction a		16 21	16 28				16 33				16 51	16 58	17 23				17 05					17 21	17 28	
London Victoria a	16 20	16 29	16 35				16 41	16 43		16 50	16 59	17 05	17 32				17 12	17 14			17 20	17 29	17 35	

	TL ■		SN ■	GX ■	TL ■	GX ■	SN ■	SN ■	TL	TL ■	TL ■		SN ■	GX ■	TL ■	TL ■	GX ■	SN ■	SN ■	TL ■	TL ■		SN ■	GX ■
Horsham d			16 50		16 55				17 14				17 20			17 25							17 50	
Crawley d			16 59		17 08								17 29			17 38							17 59	
Three Bridges d	16 59		17 04		17 13						17 29		17 34		17 40	17 43					17 59		18 04	
Gatwick Airport d	17 06		17 09	17 12	17 19	17 23	17 27	17 33		17 33	17 36		17 39	17 42	17 46	17 49	17 53	17 57	18 03	18 03	18 06		18 09	18 12
East Croydon a	17 21		17 24		17 45		17 41	17 48		18 03	17 51		17 54		18 01	18 15		18 11	18 18	18 33	18 21		18 24	
East Croydon d	17 21				17 45					18 03	17 51				18 01	18 15				18 33	18 21			
London Bridge d	17 35				18 01					18 21	18 05				18 16	18 31				18 51	18 35			
London Blackfriars d	17 42				18 07					18 27	18 12				18 22	18 37				18 57	18 42			
City Thameslink d	17 44				18 09					18 29	18 14				18 24	18 39				18 59	18 44			
Farringdon d	17 46				18 11					18 31	18 16				18 26	18 41				19 01	18 46			
St Pancras International a	17 50				18 15					18 35	18 20				18 30	18 45				19 05	18 50			
East Croydon d			17 24				17 42	17 49					17 54					18 12	18 19				18 24	
Clapham Junction a			17 33				17 51	17 58	18 23				18 03					18 21	18 28				18 33	
London Victoria a			17 41	17 43		17 50	17 59	18 05	18 32				18 11	18 13			18 20	18 29	18 35				18 41	18 43

	TL ■	GX ■	SN ■	SN ■	TL	TL ■	TL ■		SN ■	GX ■	TL ■	TL ■	GX ■	SN ■	SN ■	TL ■	TL ■		SN ■	GX ■	TL ■	GX ■	SN ■	SN ■
Horsham d	17 55				18 14				18 20			18 25							18 50		18 55			
Crawley d	18 08								18 29			18 38							18 59		19 08			
Three Bridges d	18 13						18 29		18 34		18 40	18 43					18 59		19 04		19 13			
Gatwick Airport d	18 19	18 23	18 27	18 33		18 33	18 36		18 39	18 42	18 46	18 49	18 53	18 57	19 03	19 03	19 06		19 09	19 12	19 19	19 23	19 27	19 33
East Croydon a	18 45		18 41	18 48		19 03	18 51		18 54		19 01	19 15		19 11	19 18	19 33	19 21		19 24		19 45		19 41	19 48
East Croydon d	18 45					19 03	18 51				19 01	19 15				19 33	19 21				19 45			
London Bridge d	19 01					19 21	19 05				19 16	19 31				19 51	19 35				20 01			
London Blackfriars d	19 07					19 27	19 12				19 22	19 37				19 57	19 42				20 07			
City Thameslink d	19 09					19 29	19 14				19 24	19 39				19 59	19 44				20 09			
Farringdon d	19 11					19 31	19 16				19 26	19 41				20 01	19 46				20 11			
St Pancras International a	19 15					19 35	19 20				19 30	19 45				20 05	19 50				20 15			
East Croydon d			18 42	18 49					18 54					19 12	19 19				19 24				19 42	19 49
Clapham Junction a			18 51	18 58	19 23				19 03					19 21	19 28				19 33				19 51	19 58
London Victoria a		18 50	18 59	19 05	19 32				19 11	19 13			19 20	19 29	19 35				19 41	19 43		19 50	19 59	20 05

	TL ■	TL ■	SN ■		GX ■	TL ■	TL ■	GX ■	SN ■	SN ■	TL ■	TL ■	SN ■		GX ■	TL ■	GX ■	SN ■	SN ■	TL ■	TL ■	SN ■	GX ■	
Horsham d			19 20				19 25						19 50			19 55						20 20		
Crawley d			19 29				19 38						19 59			20 08						20 29		
Three Bridges d		19 29	19 34			19 40	19 43					19 59	20 04			20 13					20 29	20 34		
Gatwick Airport d	19 33	19 36	19 39		19 42	19 46	19 49	19 53	19 57	20 03	20 03	20 06	20 09		20 12	20 19	20 23	20 27	20 33	20 33	20 36	20 39	20 42	
East Croydon a	20 03	19 51	19 54			20 01	20 15		20 11	20 18	20 33	20 21	20 24			20 45		20 41	20 48	21 03	20 51	20 54		
East Croydon d	20 03	19 51				20 01	20 15				20 33	20 21				20 45				21 03	20 51			
London Bridge d	20 21	20 05				20 16	20 31				20 51	20 35				21 01				21 21	21 05			
London Blackfriars d	20 27	20 12				20 22	20 37				20 57	20 42				21 07				21 27	21 12			
City Thameslink d	20 29	20 14				20 24	20 39				20 59	20 44												
Farringdon d	20 31	20 16				20 26	20 41				21 01	20 46				21 11				21 31	21 16			
St Pancras International a	20 35	20 20				20 30	20 45				21 05	20 50				21 15				21 35	21 20			
East Croydon d			19 54						20 12	20 19			20 24					20 42	20 49			20 54		
Clapham Junction a			20 03						20 21	20 28			20 33					20 51	20 58			21 03		
London Victoria a			20 11		20 13			20 20	20 29	20 35			20 41		20 43		20 50	20 59	21 05			21 11	21 13	

Table T185-R

Saturdays
26 May to 8 December

Horsham - Three Bridges - Gatwick Airport - London : Summary of Fast Trains

	TL ■	TL ■	GX ■	SN ■	SN ■		TL ■	TL ■	SN ■	GX ■	TL ■	GX ■	SN ■	SN ■	TL ■		TL ■	SN ■	GX ■	TL ■	TL ■	GX ■	SN ■	SN ■
Horsham d		20 25							20 50		20 55							21 20			21 25			
Crawley d		20 38							20 59		21 08							21 29			21 38			
Three Bridges d	20 40	20 43						20 59	21 04		21 13						21 29	21 34		21 40	21 43			
Gatwick Airport d	20 46	20 49	20 53	20 57	21 03		21 03	21 06	21 09	21 12	21 19	21 23	21 27	21 33	21 33		21 36	21 39	21 42	21 46	21 49	21 53	21 57	22 03
East Croydon a	21 01	21 15		21 11	21 18		21 33	21 21	21 24		21 45		21 41	21 48	22 03		21 51	21 54		22 01	22 15		22 12	22 18
East Croydon d	21 01	21 15					21 33	21 21			21 45				22 03		21 51			22 01	22 15			
London Bridge d	21 16	21 31					21 51	21 35			22 01				22 21		22 05			22 16	22 31			
London Blackfriars d	21 22	21 37					21 57	21 42			22 07				22 27		22 12			22 22	22 37			
City Thameslink d																								
Farringdon d	21 26	21 41					22 01	21 46			22 11				22 31		22 16			22 26	22 41			
St Pancras International a	21 30	21 45					22 05	21 50			22 15				22 35		22 20			22 30	22 45			
East Croydon d				21 12	21 19				21 24				21 42	21 49				21 54					22 12	22 19
Clapham Junction a				21 21	21 28				21 33				21 51	21 58				22 03					22 21	22 28
London Victoria a			21 20	21 29	21 35				21 41	21 43		21 50	21 59	22 05				22 11	22 13			22 20	22 29	22 35

	TL ■		SN ■	GX ■	TL ■	GX ■	SN ■	SN ■	TL ■	SN ■	GX ■		TL ■	TL ■	GX ■	SN ■	SN ■	TL ■	GX ■	TL ■	TL ■		SN ■	SN ■
Horsham d			21 50		21 55					22 20				22 25							23 11		23 27	
Crawley d			21 59		22 08					22 29				22 38							23 24		23 36	
Three Bridges d	21 59		22 04		22 13				22 29	22 34			22 40	22 43				22 59		23 28	23 29		23a40	
Gatwick Airport d	22 06		22 09	22 12	22 19	22 23	22 27	22 33	22 36	22 39	22 42		22 46	22 49	22 53	22 57	23 03	23 06	23 12	23 34	23 35			23 55
East Croydon a	22 21		22 24		22 45		22 41	22 48	22 51	22 54			23 01	23 15		23 11	23 18	23 21		23 54	00 09			00 16
East Croydon d	22 21				22 45				22 51				23 01	23 15				23 21		23 54	00 10			
London Bridge d	22 35				23 01				23 05				23 16	23 31				23 35						
London Blackfriars d	22 42				23 07				23 12				23 22	23 37				23 42		00 22	00 37			
City Thameslink d																								
Farringdon d	22 46				23 11				23 16				23 26	23 41				23 46		00 26	00 41			
St Pancras International a	22 50				23 15				23 20				23 30	23 45				23 50		00 30	00 45			
East Croydon d			22 24				22 42	22 49		22 54						23 12	23 19							00 16
Clapham Junction a			22 33				22 51	22 58		23 04						23 21	23 28							00 33
London Victoria a			22 41	22 43		22 50	22 59	23 05		23 11	23 13				23 20	23 29	23 35		23 43					00 41

	TL ■
Horsham d	
Crawley d	
Three Bridges d	23 58
Gatwick Airport d	00 04
East Croydon a	00 22
East Croydon d	00 23
London Bridge d	
London Blackfriars d	00 50
City Thameslink d	
Farringdon d	
St Pancras International a	00 59
East Croydon d	
Clapham Junction a	
London Victoria a	

Sundays
20 May to 2 December

	TL ■ A	TL ■	SN ■	SN ■	SN ■	GX	TL ■	GX	TL ■		SN	GX	TL ■	SN	TL ■	GX	TL ■	SN	GX		TL ■	SN	TL ■	GX
Horsham d											06 01			06 31	06 39			07 05					07 35	
Crawley d											06 14			06 44	06 52			07 14					07 48	
Three Bridges d	00 15	00 37	03 08	04 08	04 58		05 52		06 13		06 23		06 43	06 49	06 56		07 13	07 23			07 43		07 52	
Gatwick Airport d	00 21	00 42	03 13	04 13	05 03	05 48	05 58	06 18	06 21		06 28	06 48	06 51	06 54	07 02	07 18	07 21	07 28	07 48		07 51	07 54	07 58	08 15
East Croydon a	00 39	01 09	03 36	04 35	05 29		06 31		06 39		06 50		07 09	07 22	07 31		07 39	07 50			08 09	08 22	08 31	
East Croydon d	00 40	01 10					06 32		06 40				07 10		07 32		07 40				08 10		08 32	
London Bridge d							06a50		06a55				07a25		07a50		07a58				08a25		08a50	
London Blackfriars d	01 06	01 36																						
City Thameslink d																								
Farringdon d																								
St Pancras International a	01 15	01 45																						
East Croydon d			03 37	04 36	05 30						06 51			07 23				07 51				08 23		
Clapham Junction a			03 50	04 49	05 51						07 05			07 37				08 07				08 38		
London Victoria a			03 58	04 58	05 59	06 24		06 58			07 15	07 28		07 46		07 58		08 15	08 28			08 46		08 54

	TL ■	SN	SN	TL ■	TL ■		TL ■	GX	SN	SN	TL ■	TL ■	TL ■	GX	SN		SN	SN	TL ■	TL ■	TL ■	GX	SN	SN
Horsham d			08 18								08 48							09 22						
Crawley d			08 27								09 01							09 31						
Three Bridges d	08 13		08 31		08 42		08 43				09 05	09 13	09 13				09 25	09 35		09 43	09 43			
Gatwick Airport d	08 21	08 25	08 36	08 46	08 47		08 49	08 53	08 56	09 00	09 11	09 19	09 19	09 22	09 25		09 30	09 41	09 46	09 49	09 49	09 52	09 56	10 00
East Croydon a	08 39	08 45	08 58	09 06	09 02		09 17		09 10	09 14	09 37	09 33	09 47		09 40		09 44	10 03	10 07	10 03	10 17		10 10	10 14
East Croydon d	08 40			09 07	09 02		09 18				09 37	09 34	09 48						10 07	10 04	10 18			
London Bridge d	08a55			09 25	09a17		09 33				09 55	09 49	10 03						10 25	10 19	10 33			
London Blackfriars d				09 31			09 39				10 01	09 55	10 09						10 31	10 25	10 39			
City Thameslink d																								
Farringdon d				09 35			09 43				10 05	09 59	10 13						10 35	10 29	10 43			
St Pancras International a				09 39			09 47				10 09	10 03	10 17						10 39	10 33	10 47			
East Croydon d		08 46	08 59						09 11	09 15					09 41		09 45	10 04					10 11	10 15
Clapham Junction a		08 55	09 08						09 20	09 24					09 50		09 54	10 14					10 20	10 24
London Victoria a		09 02	09 15					09 20	09 28	09 32				09 50	09 58		10 02	10 21				10 24	10 28	10 32

A not 20 May

Table T185-R

Sundays

20 May to 2 December

Horsham - Three Bridges - Gatwick Airport - London : Summary of Fast Trains

	GX	TL ■	TL ■	TL ■	GX	SN	SN		GX	SN	TL ■	TL ■	TL ■	GX	SN	SN	GX		TL ■	TL ■	TL ■	GX	SN	SN
Horsham d		09 48								10 22									10 48					
Crawley d		10 01								10 31									11 01					
Three Bridges d		10 05	10 13				10 25			10 35		10 43	10 43						11 05	11 13				11 25
Gatwick Airport d	10 06	10 11	10 19	10 19	10 22	10 25	10 30		10 36	10 41	10 46	10 49	10 49	10 52	10 56	11 00	11 06		11 11	11 19	11 19	11 22	11 25	11 30
East Croydon a		10 37	10 33	10 47		10 40	10 44			11 03	11 07	11 03	11 17		11 10	11 14			11 37	11 33	11 47		11 39	11 44
East Croydon d		10 37	10 34	10 48							11 07	11 04	11 18						11 37	11 34	11 48			
London Bridge d		10 55	10 49	11 03							11 25	11 19	11 33						11 55	11 49	12 03			
London Blackfriars d		11 01	10 55	11 09							11 31	11 25	11 39						12 01	11 55	12 09			
City Thameslink d																								
Farringdon d		11 05	10 59	11 13							11 35	11 29	11 43						12 05	11 59	12 13			
St Pancras International a		11 09	11 03	11 17							11 39	11 33	11 47						12 09	12 03	12 17			
East Croydon d						10 41	10 45			11 04					11 11	11 15							11 40	11 45
Clapham Junction a						10 50	10 54			11 14					11 20	11 24							11 50	11 54
London Victoria a	10 36				10 50	10 58	11 02		11 05	11 21				11 24	11 28	11 32	11 36					11 50	11 58	12 02

	GX	SN	TL ■		TL ■	TL ■	GX	SN	SN	GX	TL ■	TL ■	TL ■		GX	SN	SN	GX	SN	TL ■	TL ■	TL ■	GX	
Horsham d		11 22									11 48								12 22					
Crawley d		11 31									12 01								12 31					
Three Bridges d		11 35			11 43	11 43					12 05	12 13					12 25		12 35		12 43	12 43		
Gatwick Airport d	11 36	11 41	11 46		11 49	11 49	11 52	11 56	12 00	12 06	12 11	12 19	12 19		12 22	12 25	12 30	12 36	12 41	12 46	12 49	12 49	12 52	
East Croydon a		12 03	12 07		12 03	12 17		12 10	12 14		12 37	12 33	12 47			12 40	12 44		13 06	13 06	13 03	13 17		
East Croydon d			12 07		12 04	12 18					12 37	12 34	12 48							13 07	13 04	13 18		
London Bridge d			12 25		12 19	12 33					12 55	12 49	13 03							13 25	13 19	13 33		
London Blackfriars d			12 31		12 25	12 41					13 01	12 55	13 09							13 31	13 25	13 39		
City Thameslink d																								
Farringdon d			12 35		12 29	12 45					13 05	12 59	13 13							13 35	13 29	13 43		
St Pancras International a			12 39		12 33	12 49					13 09	13 03	13 17							13 39	13 33	13 47		
East Croydon d		12 04						12 11	12 15							12 41	12 45		13 06					
Clapham Junction a		12 14						12 20	12 24							12 50	12 54		13 16					
London Victoria a	12 05	12 21					12 24	12 28	12 32	12 36					12 50	12 58	13 02	13 05	13 23				13 28	

	SN	SN	GX	TL ■	TL ■	TL ■	GX	SN	SN		GX	SN	TL ■	TL ■	TL ■	GX	SN	SN	GX		TL ■	TL ■	TL ■	GX
Horsham d				12 48								13 22									13 48			
Crawley d				13 01								13 31									14 01			
Three Bridges d				13 05	13 13				13 25			13 35		13 43	13 43						14 05	14 13		
Gatwick Airport d	12 56	13 00	13 06	13 11	13 19	13 19	13 22	13 25	13 30		13 36	13 41	13 46	13 49	13 49	13 52	13 56	14 00	14 06		14 11	14 19	14 19	14 22
East Croydon a	13 10	13 14		13 37	13 33	13 47		13 40	13 44			14 03	14 07	14 03	14 17		14 10	14 14			14 37	14 33	14 47	
East Croydon d				13 37	13 34	13 48							14 07	14 04	14 18						14 37	14 34	14 48	
London Bridge d				13 55	13 49	14 03							14 25	14 19	14 33						14 55	14 49	15 03	
London Blackfriars d				14 01	13 55	14 09							14 31	14 25	14 39						15 01	14 55	15 09	
City Thameslink d																								
Farringdon d				14 05	13 59	14 13							14 35	14 29	14 43						15 05	14 59	15 13	
St Pancras International a				14 09	14 03	14 17							14 39	14 33	14 47						15 09	15 03	15 17	
East Croydon d	13 11	13 15						13 41	13 45			14 04					14 11	14 15						
Clapham Junction a	13 22	13 25						13 50	13 54			14 14					14 20	14 24						
London Victoria a	13 30	13 32	13 36				13 50	13 58	14 02		14 05	14 21				14 24	14 28	14 32	14 36					14 50

	SN	SN	GX	SN	TL ■		TL ■	TL ■	GX	SN	SN	GX	TL ■	TL ■	TL ■		GX	SN	SN	GX	SN	TL ■	TL ■	TL ■
Horsham d				14 21									14 48								15 22			
Crawley d				14 30									15 01								15 31			
Three Bridges d		14 25		14 35			14 43	14 43					15 05	15 13					15 25		15 35		15 43	15 43
Gatwick Airport d	14 25	14 30	14 36	14 41	14 46		14 49	14 49	14 52	14 56	15 00	15 06	15 11	15 19	15 19		15 22	15 25	15 30	15 36	15 41	15 46	15 49	15 49
East Croydon a	14 40	14 44		15 03	15 07		15 03	15 17		15 10	15 14		15 37	15 33	15 47			15 40	15 44		16 06	16 06	16 03	16 17
East Croydon d					15 07		15 04	15 18					15 37	15 34	15 48							16 07	16 04	16 18
London Bridge d					15 25		15 19	15 33					15 55	15 49	16 03							16 25	16 19	16 33
London Blackfriars d					15 31		15 25	15 39					16 01	15 55	16 09							16 31	16 25	16 39
City Thameslink d																								
Farringdon d					15 35		15 29	15 43					16 05	15 59	16 13							16 35	16 29	16 43
St Pancras International a					15 39		15 33	15 47					16 09	16 03	16 17							16 39	16 33	16 47
East Croydon d	14 41	14 45		15 04						15 11	15 15							15 41	15 45		16 06			
Clapham Junction a	14 50	14 54		15 14						15 20	15 24							15 50	15 54		16 16			
London Victoria a	14 58	15 02	15 05	15 21					15 24	15 28	15 32	15 36					15 50	15 58	16 02	16 05	16 23			

	GX		SN	SN	GX	TL ■	TL ■	TL ■	GX	SN	SN		GX	SN	TL ■	TL ■	TL ■	GX	SN	SN	GX		TL ■	TL ■
Horsham d						15 48								16 22									16 48	
Crawley d						16 01								16 31									17 01	
Three Bridges d						16 05	16 13				16 25			16 35		16 43	16 43						17 05	17 13
Gatwick Airport d	15 52		15 56	16 00	16 06	16 11	16 19	16 19	16 22	16 25	16 30		16 36	16 41	16 46	16 49	16 49	16 52	16 56	17 00	17 06		17 11	17 19
East Croydon a			16 10	16 14		16 37	16 33	16 47		16 40	16 44			17 06	17 06	17 03	17 17		17 10	17 14			17 37	17 33
East Croydon d						16 37	16 34	16 48							17 07	17 04	17 18						17 37	17 34
London Bridge d						16 55	16 49	17 03							17 25	17 19	17 33						17 55	17 49
London Blackfriars d						17 01	16 55	17 09							17 31	17 25	17 39						18 01	17 55
City Thameslink d																								
Farringdon d						17 05	16 59	17 13							17 35	17 29	17 43						18 05	17 59
St Pancras International a						17 09	17 03	17 17							17 39	17 33	17 47						18 09	18 03
East Croydon d			16 11	16 15						16 41	16 45			17 06					17 11	17 15				
Clapham Junction a			16 22	16 24						16 50	16 54			17 16					17 22	17 25				
London Victoria a	16 28		16 30	16 32	16 36				16 50	16 58	17 02		17 05	17 23				17 28	17 30	17 32	17 36			

Table T185-R

Sundays

20 May to 2 December

Horsham - Three Bridges - Gatwick Airport - London : Summary of Fast Trains

	TL ■	GX	SN		SN	GX	SN	TL ■	TL ■	TL ■	GX	SN	SN		GX	TL ■	TL ■	TL ■	GX	SN	SN	GX	SN	
Horsham d							17 22									17 48							18 22	
Crawley d							17 31									18 01							18 31	
Three Bridges d					17 25		17 35		17 43	17 43						18 05	18 13				18 25		18 35	
Gatwick Airport d	17 19	17 22	17 25		17 30	17 36	17 41	17 46	17 49	17 49	17 52	17 56	18 00		18 06	18 11	18 19	18 19	18 22	18 25	18 30	18 36	18 41	
East Croydon a	17 47		17 40		17 44		18 03	18 07	18 03	18 17		18 10	18 14			18 37	18 33	18 47		18 40	18 44		19 03	
East Croydon d	17 48							18 07	18 04	18 18						18 37	18 34	18 48						
London Bridge d	18 03							18 25	18 19	18 33						18 55	18 49	19 03						
London Blackfriars d	18 09							18 31	18 25	18 39						19 01	18 55	19 09						
City Thameslink d																								
Farringdon d	18 13							18 35	18 29	18 43						19 05	18 59	19 13						
St Pancras International a	18 17							18 39	18 33	18 47						19 09	19 03	19 17						
East Croydon d			17 41		17 45		18 04					18 11	18 15							18 41	18 45		19 04	
Clapham Junction a			17 50		17 54		18 14					18 20	18 24							18 50	18 54		19 14	
London Victoria a		17 50	17 58		18 02	18 05	18 21				18 24	18 28	18 32		18 36				18 50	18 58	19 02	19 05	19 21	

	TL ■	TL ■	TL ■	GX	SN	SN	GX	TL ■	TL ■		TL ■	GX	SN	SN	GX	SN	TL ■	TL ■	TL ■		GX	SN	SN	GX
Horsham d								18 48								19 22								
Crawley d								19 01								19 31								
Three Bridges d		18 43	18 43					19 05	19 13					19 25		19 35		19 43	19 43					
Gatwick Airport d	18 46	18 49	18 49	18 52	18 56	19 00	19 06	19 11	19 19		19 19	19 22	19 25	19 30	19 36	19 41	19 46	19 49	19 49		19 52	19 56	20 00	20 06
East Croydon a	19 07	19 03	19 17		19 10	19 14		19 37	19 33		19 47		19 40	19 44		20 03	20 07	20 03	20 17			20 10	20 14	
East Croydon d	19 07	19 04	19 18					19 37	19 34		19 48						20 07	20 04	20 18					
London Bridge d	19 25	19 19	19 33					19 55	19 49		20 03						20 25	20 19	20 33					
London Blackfriars d	19 31	19 25	19 39					20 01	19 55		20 09						20 31	20 25	20 39					
City Thameslink d																								
Farringdon d	19 35	19 29	19 43					20 05	19 59		20 13						20 35	20 29	20 43					
St Pancras International a	19 39	19 33	19 47					20 09	20 03		20 17						20 39	20 33	20 47					
East Croydon d					19 11	19 15							19 41	19 45		20 04						20 11	20 15	
Clapham Junction a					19 20	19 24							19 50	19 54		20 14						20 20	20 24	
London Victoria a				19 24	19 28	19 32	19 36					19 50	19 58	20 02	20 05	20 21					20 24	20 28	20 32	20 36

	TL ■	TL ■	TL ■	GX	SN		SN	GX	SN	TL ■	TL ■	TL ■	GX	SN	SN		GX	TL ■	TL ■	TL ■	GX	SN	SN	GX
Horsham d	19 48								20 22									20 48						
Crawley d	20 01								20 31									21 01						
Three Bridges d	20 05	20 13					20 25		20 35		20 43	20 43						21 05	21 13				21 25	
Gatwick Airport d	20 11	20 19	20 19	20 22	20 25		20 30	20 36	20 41	20 46	20 49	20 49	20 52	20 56	21 00		21 06	21 11	21 19	21 19	21 22	21 25	21 30	21 36
East Croydon a	20 37	20 33	20 47		20 40		20 44		21 03	21 07	21 03	21 17		21 10	21 14			21 37	21 33	21 47		21 39	21 44	
East Croydon d	20 37	20 34	20 48							21 07	21 04	21 18						21 37	21 34	21 48				
London Bridge d	20 55	20 49	21 03							21 25	21 19	21 33						21 55	21 49	22 03				
London Blackfriars d	21 01	20 55	21 09							21 31	21 25	21 39						22 01	21 55	22 09				
City Thameslink d																								
Farringdon d	21 05	20 59	21 13							21 35	21 29	21 43						22 05	21 59	22 13				
St Pancras International a	21 09	21 03	21 17							21 39	21 33	21 47						22 09	22 03	22 17				
East Croydon d					20 41		20 45		21 04					21 11	21 15							21 40	21 45	
Clapham Junction a					20 50		20 54		21 14					21 20	21 24							21 49	21 54	
London Victoria a				20 50	20 58		21 02	21 05	21 21				21 24	21 28	21 32		21 36				21 50	21 58	22 02	22 05

	SN		TL ■	TL ■	GX	SN	SN	TL ■	TL ■	GX	SN		TL ■	SN	TL ■	GX	SN	TL ■	GX	TL ■	SN		SN	TL ■
Horsham d	21 22							21 48						22 22				22 41					23 14	
Crawley d	21 31							22 01						22 31				22 54					23 27	
Three Bridges d	21 35			21 43				22 05	22 13		22 25		22 31	22 35	22 43		22 55	22a58		23 15	23 25		23 31	23 45
Gatwick Airport d	21 41		21 46	21 49	21 52	21 56	22 00	22 11	22 19	22 22	22 30		22 39	22 41	22 49	22 52	23 00		23 18	23 21	23 30		23 36	23 51
East Croydon a	22 03		22 07	22 03		22 10	22 14	22 45	22 33		22 44		23 12	23 03	23 03		23 14			23 39	23 51		00 05	00 09
East Croydon d			22 07	22 04				22 47	22 34				23 12		23 04					23 40				00 10
London Bridge d			22 25	22 19				23 05	22 49				23a30		23 19									
London Blackfriars d			22 31	22 25				23 12	22 55						23 27					00 06				00 36
City Thameslink d																								
Farringdon d			22 35	22 29				23 16	22 59						23 31					00 11				
St Pancras International a			22 39	22 33				23 20	23 03						23 35					00 15				00 45
East Croydon d	22 04					22 11	22 15				22 45			23 04			23 15				23 52		00 06	
Clapham Junction a	22 14					22 20	22 24				22 54			23 14			23 24				00 08		00 18	
London Victoria a	22 21				22 24	22 28	22 32			22 50	23 02			23 21		23 25	23 32		23 49		00 17		00 27	

Table T186-F

Mondays to Fridays
21 May to 7 December

London, Gatwick Airport, Arun Valley and Brighton - Bognor Regis, Chichester, Portsmouth and Southampton

Miles	Miles	Miles			SN MX	SN ■	SN	SN ■	SN	SN	SN	SN	SN ■		SN	SN	SN ■	SN	SN	SN	SN ■	SN	SN ■		SN
0	—	—	London Victoria	d																					
2¾	—	—	Clapham Junction	d																					
10½	—	—	East Croydon	a																					
—	0	—	London Bridge	d																					
—	10½	—	East Croydon	a																					
—	—	—	East Croydon	d																					
26¾	26¾	—	Gatwick Airport	d																	05 56				
29¼	29¼	—	Three Bridges	a																	06 00				
—	—	—		d																	06 01				
30¾	—	—	Crawley	d																	06 05				
38	—	—	Horsham	a																	06 17				
—	—	—		d																	06 18				
39¼	—	—	**Christs Hospital**	d																	06 22				
41½	—	—	**Billingshurst**	d																	06 28				
43	—	—	**Pulborough**	d																	06 34				
44¼	—	—	**Amberley**	d																	06 40				
48	—	—	**Arundel**	d																	06 45				
—	50½	0	Brighton	d								05 00					05 27	06 02					06 32		
—	—	1	Hove	d								05 05					05 32	06 06					06 36		
—	—	2½	Portslade	d								05 08					05 37	06 09					06 39		
—	—	3¾	Southwick	d								05 11					05 41	06 12					06 42		
—	—	5½	Shoreham-by-Sea	d								05 14					05 44	06 16					06 46		
—	—	7¾	Lancing	d								05 18					05 48	06 20					06 50		
—	—	10¼	Worthing	d								05 22					05 54	06 24					06 55		
—	—	10¾	West Worthing	d								05 24					05 56	06 27					06 57		
—	—	11¾	Durrington-on-Sea	d								05 27					05 59	06 29					06 59		
—	—	12½	Goring-by-Sea	d								05 29					06 01	06 32					07 02		
—	—	15¼	Angmering	d								05 33					06 05	06 36					07 06		
51¼	—	—	Littlehampton	d				05 04			05 29				05 56	06 00			06 43						07 08
53½	—	19½	**Ford**	d				05 09			05 34				06 01	06 05	06 13		06 48		06 52		07 13		07 17
56¼	—	21¾	**Barnham**	a				05 13			05 39	05 44			06 05	06 09	06 17	06 47	06 52		06 57		07 18		07 22
—	—	—	**Barnham**	d	00 36				05 28		05 52					06 11				06 55					
—	—	—	**Bognor Regis**	a	00 43				05 35		05 59					06 18				07 01		←			
—	—	—	**Barnham**	d		04 59	05 03	05 15		05 21		05 45	06 03		06 06		06 19	06 48	07 02		06 58	07 02	07 19		07 22
62¼	—	28¾	**Chichester**	a		05 06	05 10	05 22		05 28		05 52	06 10		06 13		06 26	06 56	→		07 05	07 09	07 26		07 30
—	—	—		d		05 07	05 11	05 23		05 29		05 53	06 11		06 14		06 27	06 56			07 06	07 10	07 27		07 30
64	—	29¾	**Fishbourne (Sussex)**	d											06 17							07 13			07 33
65¾	—	31¼	**Bosham**	d											06 20							07 16			07 36
66¾	—	32¾	**Nutbourne**	d											06 23							07 19			07 40
67¾	—	33¾	**Southbourne**	d								06 00			06 26		06 34	07 03			07 13	07 22			07 42
69½	—	35¼	**Emsworth**	d								06 03			06 29		06 37	07 06			07 16	07 25	07 35		07 45
70¾	—	36½	**Warblington**	d											06 32							07 28			
71¼	—	37¾	Havant	a		05 17	05 21	05 33		05 39		06 06	06 21		06 34		06 40	07 10			07 19	07 30	07 38		07 49
72	—	—	Bedhampton	a											06 37							07 35			07 52
—	—	41¼	Hilsea	a											06 43							07 40			07 57
—	—	43½	Fratton	a			05 30			05 48		06 15			06 47			07 21				07 44			08 01
—	—	44½	Portsmouth & Southsea	a			05 33			05 52		06 20			06 51			07 25				07 48			08 05
—	—	45¼	Portsmouth Harbour	a			05 37			05 56		06 24			06 57										
75¼	—	—	Cosham	a		05 24		05 41					06 29				06 49				07 26		07 45		
78½	—	—	Portchester	a		05 28		05 46									06 54				07 31				
81¼	—	—	Fareham	a		05 33		05 51					06 38				06 59				07 36		07 55		
84¾	—	—	Swanwick	a		05 40		05 58					06 44				07 06				07 43		08 02		
95¾	—	—	Southampton Central	a		06 00		06 18					07 02				07 25				08 03		08 19		

Table T186-F

Mondays to Fridays
21 May to 7 December

London, Gatwick Airport, Arun Valley and Brighton - Bognor Regis, Chichester, Portsmouth and Southampton

		SN	SN ■	SN	SN	SN	SN ■	SN ■	SN		SN	SN	SN ■	SN	SN	SN	SN ■		SN ■		SN	GW ◇	SN ■		SN
London Victoria	d		05 54				06 36						07 06				07 36						08 06		
Clapham Junction	d		06 01				06 43						07 13				07 43						08 13		
East Croydon	a		06 10				06 52						07 22				07 52						08 22		
London Bridge	d																								
East Croydon	a																								
East Croydon	d		06 10				06 52						07 22				07 52						08 22		
Gatwick Airport	d		06 26				07 08						07 38				08 08						08 38		
Three Bridges	a		06 31				07 13						07 42				08 13						08 43		
	d		06 32				07 13						07 45				08 14						08 44		
Crawley	d		06 36				07 17						07 49				08 18						08 48		
Horsham	a		06 50				07 28						07 57				08 27						08 57		
	d		06 51				07 29						08 00				08 31	08 34					09 01	09 04	
Christs Hospital	d		06 55				07 33						08 04					08 38						09 08	
Billingshurst	d		07 02				07 39						08 10					08 44						09 14	
Pulborough	d		07 08				07 46						08 17					08 51						09 21	
Amberley	d		07 14				07 52						08 23					08 57						09 27	
Arundel	d		07 19				07 57						08 28					09 01						09 32	
Brighton	d				07 02			07 32			07 41			08 00					08 32			08 59			09 05
Hove	d				07 06			07 36			07 45			08 04					08 36			09 03			09 09
Portslade	d				07 09			07 39			07 48			08 07					08 39						09 12
Southwick	d				07 12			07 42			07 51			08 10					08 42						09 16
Shoreham-by-Sea	d				07 16			07 46			07 55			08 14					08 46			09 13			09 20
Lancing	d				07 20			07 50			07 59			08 18					08 50						09 24
Worthing	d				07 25			07 55			08 04			08 25					08 55			09 22			09 29
West Worthing	d							07 57			08 06			08 27					08 57						
Durrington-on-Sea	d							07 59			08 08			08 29					08 59						
Goring-by-Sea	d							08 02			08 11			08 32					09 02						
Angmering	d				07 31			08 06			08 15			08 36					09 06						09 35
Littlehampton	d			07 26		07 53			08 10			08 24				08 55					09 10				
Ford	d		07 26	07 31		07 58	08 03	08 13	08 17		08 23	08 29	08 34			09 00		09 07	09 13		09 17			09 39	
Barnham	a		07 32	07 36	07 42	08 02	08 08	08 18	08 22		08 28	08 33	08 39	08 47		09 04	08 58	09 12	09 18		09 22	09 36	09 28	09 43	09 47
Barnham	d	07 30		07 44			08 10		08 23				08 40		08 52			09 13			09 23			09 44	
Bognor Regis	a	07 36		07 51			08 17		08 30				08 46		08 59			09 20			09 30			09 50	
Barnham	d		07 35		07 43	08 04		08 19			08 28	08 36		08 48		09 05	08 59		09 19			09 37	09 29		09 48
Chichester	a		07 43		07 51	08 11		08 26			08 36	08 44		08 55		09 12	09 06		09 26			09 45	09 37		09 55
	d		07 44		07 51	08 12		08 27			08 36			08 56		09 13	09 07		09 27			09 46	09 37		09 56
Fishbourne (Sussex)	d					08 15										09 16									
Bosham	d					08 18										09 19									
Nutbourne	d					08 21										09 22									
Southbourne	d		07 51		07 58	08 24								09 03		09 25	09 14								10 03
Emsworth	d		07 54		08 01	08 27		08 35						09 06		09 28	09 17		09 35						10 06
Warblington	d		07 57			08 30										09 31									
Havant	a		07 59		08 05	08 32		08 38			08 46			09 09		09 33	09 22		09 39			09 57	09 47		10 09
Bedhampton	a					08 36										09 36									
Hilsea	a					08 41										09 42									
Fratton	a				08 16	08 45					08 56			09 18		09 46							09 56		10 18
Portsmouth & Southsea	a				08 19	08 49					08 59			09 23		09 50							10 00		10 23
Portsmouth Harbour	a				08 23						09 04												10 04		
Cosham	a		08 08					08 46									09 29		09 47			10 04			
Portchester	a		08 13														09 34								
Fareham	a		08 18					08 54									09 39		09 55			10 12			
Swanwick	a		08 25					09 00									09 46		10 01						
Southampton Central	a		08 52					09 20									10 05		10 19			10 40			

Table T186-F

Mondays to Fridays

21 May to 7 December

London, Gatwick Airport, Arun Valley and Brighton - Bognor Regis, Chichester, Portsmouth and Southampton

		SN	SN	SN ■			SN ■	SN	SN ■		SN	SN	SN	SN ■		SN ■	SN	SN ■			SN ■	SN	SN	SN
London Victoria	d			08 36					09 06					09 36				10 06			12 06			
Clapham Junction	d			08 43					09 13					09 43				10 13			12 13			
East Croydon	a			08 52					09 22					09 52				10 22			12 22			
London Bridge	d																							
East Croydon	a																							
East Croydon	d			08 53					09 23					09 53				10 23			12 23			
Gatwick Airport	d			09 09					09 39					10 09				10 39			12 39			
Three Bridges	a			09 14					09 44					10 14				10 44			12 44			
	d			09 15					09 44					10 14				10 44			12 44			
Crawley	d			09 19					09 48					10 18				10 48			12 48			
Horsham	a			09 27					09 57					10 27				10 57			12 57			
	d			09 31	09 34				10 01	10 04				10 31	10 34			11 01	11 04		13 04			
Christs Hospital	d				09 38										10 38									
Billingshurst	d				09 44					10 12					10 44				11 12		13 12			
Pulborough	d				09 51					10 19					10 51				11 19		13 19			
Amberley	d				09 57										10 57									
Arundel	d				10 01					10 28					11 01				11 28		13 28			
Brighton	d						09 32				10 02					10 32						13 02		
Hove	d						09 36				10 06					10 36						13 06		
Portslade	d						09 39				10 09					10 39						13 09		
Southwick	d						09 42				10 12					10 42						13 12		
Shoreham-by-Sea	d						09 46				10 16					10 46				and at the same minutes past each hour until		13 16		
Lancing	d						09 50				10 20					10 50						13 20		
Worthing	d						09 55				10 25					10 55						13 25		
West Worthing	d						09 57									10 57								
Durrington-on-Sea	d						09 59									10 59								
Goring-by-Sea	d						10 02									11 02								
Angmering	d						10 06				10 32					11 06						13 32		
Littlehampton	d		09 55					10 10					10 55				11 10							13 55
Ford	d		10 00		10 07		10 13	10 17		10 34			11 00		11 07	11 13	11 17		11 34		13 34			14 00
Barnham	a		10 04	09 58	10 12		10 18	10 22	10 28	10 39	10 43		11 04	10 58	11 12	11 18	11 22	11 28	11 39		13 39	13 43		14 04
Barnham	d	09 52			10 13			10 23		10 40		10 52			11 13		11 23		11 40		13 40		13 52	
Bognor Regis	a	09 59			10 20			10 30		10 46		10 59			11 20		11 30		11 46		13 46		13 59	
Barnham	d		10 05	09 59			10 19		10 29		10 44		11 05	10 59		11 19		11 29				13 44		14 05
Chichester	a		10 12	10 06			10 26		10 37		10 51		11 12	11 06		11 26		11 37				13 51		14 12
	d		10 13	10 07			10 27		10 37		10 52		11 13	11 07		11 27		11 37				13 52		14 13
Fishbourne (Sussex)	d		10 16										11 16											14 16
Bosham	d		10 19										11 19											14 19
Nutbourne	d		10 22										11 22											14 22
Southbourne	d		10 25	10 14							10 59		11 25	11 14								13 59		14 25
Emsworth	d		10 28	10 17			10 35				11 02		11 28	11 17		11 35						14 02		14 28
Warblington	d		10 31										11 31											14 31
Havant	a		10 33	10 20			10 38		10 47		11 05		11 33	11 20		11 38		11 48				14 05		14 33
Bedhampton	a		10 36										11 36											14 36
Hilsea	a		10 42										11 42											14 42
Fratton	a		10 46						10 56		11 14		11 46					11 57				14 14		14 46
Portsmouth & Southsea	a		10 50						11 00		11 18		11 50					12 01				14 18		14 50
Portsmouth Harbour	a								11 04		11 22							12 05				14 22		
Cosham	a			10 28			10 46							11 28		11 46								
Portchester	a			10 33										11 33										
Fareham	a			10 38			10 54							11 38		11 54								
Swanwick	a			10 45			11 01							11 45		12 01								
Southampton Central	a			11 03			11 19							12 03		12 19								

Table T186-F

Mondays to Fridays

21 May to 7 December

London, Gatwick Airport, Arun Valley and Brighton - Bognor Regis, Chichester, Portsmouth and Southampton

		SN ■		SN ■	SN	SN ■			SN	SN	SN	SN ■		SN ■	SN	SN ■			SN	SN	SN	SN ■		SN ■	SN
London Victoria	d	12 36				13 06						13 36				14 06						14 36			
Clapham Junction	d	12 43				13 13						13 43				14 13						14 43			
East Croydon	a	12 52				13 22						13 52				14 22						14 53			
London Bridge	d																								
East Croydon	a																								
East Croydon	d	12 53				13 23						13 53				14 23						14 53			
Gatwick Airport	d	13 09				13 39						14 09				14 39						15 09			
Three Bridges	a	13 14				13 44						14 14				14 44						15 14			
	d	13 14				13 44						14 14				14 44						15 14			
Crawley	d	13 18				13 48						14 18				14 48						15 18			
Horsham	a	13 27				13 57						14 27				14 57						15 27			
	d	13 31	13 34			14 01	14 04					14 31	14 34			15 01	15 04					15 31	15 34		
Christs Hospital	d		13 38										14 38				15 08						15 38		
Billingshurst	d		13 44				14 12						14 44				15 14						15 44		
Pulborough	d		13 51				14 19						14 51				15 21						15 51		
Amberley	d		13 57										14 57										15 57		
Arundel	d		14 01				14 28						15 01				15 30						16 01		
Brighton	d			13 32					14 02					14 32					15 02					15 32	
Hove	d			13 36					14 06					14 36					15 06					15 36	
Portslade	d			13 39					14 09					14 39					15 09					15 39	
Southwick	d			13 42					14 12					14 42					15 12					15 42	
Shoreham-by-Sea	d			13 46					14 16					14 46					15 16					15 46	
Lancing	d			13 50					14 20					14 50					15 20					15 50	
Worthing	d			13 55					14 25					14 55					15 26					15 55	
West Worthing	d			13 57										14 57										15 57	
Durrington-on-Sea	d			13 59										14 59										15 59	
Goring-by-Sea	d			14 02										15 02										16 02	
Angmering	d			14 06					14 32					15 06					15 34					16 06	
Littlehampton	d				14 10						14 55				15 09						15 55				16 10
Ford	d		14 07	14 13	14 17		14 34				15 00		15 07	15 13	15 17		15 36		15 41		16 00		16 07	16 13	16 17
Barnham	a	13 58	14 12	14 18	14 22	14 28	14 39		14 43		15 04	14 58	15 12	15 18	15 22	15 28	15 40		15 46		16 04	15 58	16 12	16 18	16 22
Barnham	d		14 13		14 23		14 40			14 54			15 13		15 23		15 41			15 52			16 13		16 23
Bognor Regis	a		14 20		14 30		14 46			15 00			15 20		15 30		15 48			15 59			16 20		16 30
Barnham	d	13 59		14 19		14 29			14 44		15 05	14 59		15 19		15 29			15 47		16 05	15 59		16 19	
Chichester	a	14 06		14 26		14 37			14 51		15 12	15 06		15 26		15 37			15 54		16 12	16 06		16 26	
	d	14 07		14 27		14 37			14 52		15 13	15 07		15 27		15 37			15 55		16 13	16 07		16 27	
Fishbourne (Sussex)	d										15 16										16 16				
Bosham	d										15 19										16 19				
Nutbourne	d										15 22										16 22				
Southbourne	d	14 14							14 59		15 25	15 14							16 02		16 25	16 14			
Emsworth	d	14 17		14 35					15 02		15 28	15 17		15 35					16 05		16 28	16 17		16 35	
Warblington	d										15 31										16 31				
Havant	a	14 20		14 38		14 48			15 05		15 33	15 20		15 38		15 47			16 08		16 33	16 20		16 38	
Bedhampton	a										15 36										16 36				
Hilsea	a										15 42										16 42				
Fratton	a					14 57			15 14		15 46					15 56			16 17		16 46				
Portsmouth & Southsea	a					15 01			15 18		15 50					16 00			16 23		16 50				
Portsmouth Harbour	a					15 05			15 22							16 04									
Cosham	a	14 28		14 46								15 28		15 46								16 28		16 46	
Portchester	a	14 33										15 33										16 33			
Fareham	a	14 38		14 54								15 38		15 54								16 38		16 54	
Swanwick	a	14 45		15 01								15 45		16 01								16 45		17 01	
Southampton Central	a	15 03		15 19								16 03		16 20								17 02		17 19	

Table T186-F

Mondays to Fridays

21 May to 7 December

London, Gatwick Airport, Arun Valley and Brighton - Bognor Regis, Chichester, Portsmouth and Southampton

		SN 1			SN	SN	SN	SN 1		SN 1	SN	GW ◇	SN 1			SN	SN	SN	SN 1		SN 1	SN	SN 1		
London Victoria	d	15 06						15 36					16 06						16 36						
Clapham Junction	d	15 13						15 43					16 13						16 43						
East Croydon	a	15 22						15 52					16 23						16 52						
London Bridge	d																						17 03		
East Croydon	a																						17 16		
East Croydon	d	15 23						15 53					16 23						16 53				17 17		
Gatwick Airport	d	15 39						16 09					16 39						17 09						
Three Bridges	a	15 44						16 14					16 44						17 14				17 35		
	d	15 44						16 14					16 44						17 14				17 35		
Crawley	d	15 48						16 18					16 48						17 18				17 39		
Horsham	a	15 57						16 27					16 57						17 27				17 51		
	d	16 01	16 04					16 31	16 34				17 01	17 04					17 31	17 34			17 54	17 58	
Christs Hospital	d		16 08						16 38					17 08						17 38				18 02	
Billingshurst	d		16 14						16 44					17 14						17 44				18 08	
Pulborough	d		16 21						16 51					17 21						17 51				18 15	
Amberley	d								16 57					17 27						17 57					
Arundel	d		16 30						17 01					17 32						18 01				18 25	
Brighton	d				16 02					16 32		17 02				17 05					17 32				
Hove	d				16 06					16 36		17 06				17 10					17 37				
Portslade	d				16 09					16 39						17 13					17 40				
Southwick	d				16 12					16 42						17 16					17 43				
Shoreham-by-Sea	d				16 16					16 46		17 12				17 20					17 47				
Lancing	d				16 20					16 50						17 24					17 51				
Worthing	d				16 26					16 55		17 23				17 28					17 56				
West Worthing	d									16 57						17 30					17 58				
Durrington-on-Sea	d									16 59						17 33					18 00				
Goring-by-Sea	d									17 02						17 35					18 03				
Angmering	d				16 34					17 06						17 39					18 07				
Littlehampton	d						16 55				17 10							17 55				18 18			
Ford	d		16 36		16 41		17 00		17 07	17 13	17 17			17 38		17 47		18 00		18 07	18 14	18 23			
Barnham	a	16 28	16 40		16 46		17 04	16 58	17 12	17 18	17 22	17 38	17 28	17 43		17 51		18 04	17 58	18 12	18 19	18 27	18 23	18 34	
Barnham	d		16 41			16 52			17 13		17 23			17 44			17 53			18 14		18 28		18 35	
Bognor Regis	a		16 48			16 59			17 20		17 30			17 50			18 00			18 20		18 34		18 42	
Barnham	d	16 29			16 47		17 05	16 59		17 19		17 38	17 29			17 52		18 05	17 59		18 19		18 23		
Chichester	a	16 37			16 54		17 12	17 06		17 26		17 46	17 36			18 00		18 12	18 06		18 27		18 31		
	d	16 37			16 55		17 13	17 07		17 27		17 46	17 37			18 00		18 13	18 07		18 27		18 31		
Fishbourne (Sussex)	d						17 16						17 40					18 16					18 34		
Bosham	d						17 19						17 43					18 19					18 37		
Nutbourne	d						17 22											18 22							
Southbourne	d				17 02		17 25	17 14					17 47			18 07		18 25	18 14				18 42		
Emsworth	d				17 05		17 28	17 17		17 35			17 50			18 10		18 28	18 17		18 36		18 45		
Warblington	d						17 31											18 31							
Havant	a	16 47			17 08		17 33	17 20		17 38		17 57	17 54			18 14		18 33	18 22		18 39		18 48		
Bedhampton	a						17 36											18 36							
Hilsea	a						17 42											18 44							
Fratton	a	16 56			17 18		17 46						18 03			18 23		18 48					18 57		
Portsmouth & Southsea	a	17 00			17 23		17 50						18 08			18 26		18 52					19 01		
Portsmouth Harbour	a	17 04																					19 05		
Cosham	a							17 28		17 46		18 04							18 29		18 46				
Portchester	a							17 33											18 34						
Fareham	a							17 38		17 54		18 12							18 39		18 54				
Swanwick	a							17 45		18 01									18 46		19 01				
Southampton Central	a							18 05		18 19		18 39							19 03		19 20				

Table T186-F

Mondays to Fridays

21 May to 7 December

London, Gatwick Airport, Arun Valley and Brighton - Bognor Regis, Chichester, Portsmouth and Southampton

		SN 1	SN	SN	SN	SN 1		SN 1	SN	SN 1			SN 1	SN	SN	SN	SN 1		SN 1	SN	SN 1			SN	SN
London Victoria	d	17 06				17 36							18 06				18 36				19 06				
Clapham Junction	d	17 13				17 43							18 13				18 43				19 13				
East Croydon	a	17 22				17 52							18 22				18 52				19 22				
London Bridge	d									18 03															
East Croydon	a									18 16															
East Croydon	d	17 23				17 53				18 17			18 23				18 53				19 23				
Gatwick Airport	d	17 39				18 09							18 39				19 09				19 39				
Three Bridges	a	17 44				18 14				18 35			18 44				19 14				19 44				
	d	17 44				18 14				18 35			18 44				19 14				19 44				
Crawley	d	17 48				18 18				18 39			18 48				19 18				19 48				
Horsham	a	18 01				18 27				18 51			19 01				19 27				19 57				
	d	18 02				18 31	18 34			18 54	18 58		19 02				19 31	19 34			20 01	20 04			
Christs Hospital	d	18 06					18 38				19 02		19 06					19 38				20 08			
Billingshurst	d	18 13					18 44				19 08		19 13					19 44				20 14			
Pulborough	d	18 20					18 51				19 15		19 20					19 51				20 21			
Amberley	d	18 26					18 57				19 21							19 57				20 27			
Arundel	d	18 31					19 02				19 26		19 31					20 01				20 31			
Brighton	d		18 02					18 32						19 02					19 32					20 02	
Hove	d		18 07					18 37						19 07					19 37					20 07	
Portslade	d		18 10					18 40						19 10					19 40					20 10	
Southwick	d		18 13					18 43						19 13					19 43					20 13	
Shoreham-by-Sea	d		18 16					18 47						19 16					19 47					20 16	
Lancing	d		18 20					18 51						19 20					19 51					20 20	
Worthing	d		18 25					18 56						19 25					19 56					20 25	
West Worthing	d		18 27					18 58											19 58					20 27	
Durrington-on-Sea	d		18 29					19 00						19 29					20 00					20 29	
Goring-by-Sea	d		18 32					19 03						19 31					20 03					20 32	
Angmering	d		18 36					19 07						19 35					20 07					20 36	
Littlehampton	d				18 55				19 18							19 55				20 14					20 44
Ford	d	18 37	18 43		19 00		19 08	19 14	19 23				19 38	19 43		20 00		20 07	20 14	20 19		20 37		20 43	20 49
Barnham	a	18 42	18 48		19 04	18 58	19 13	19 19	19 27	19 23	19 36		19 42	19 47		20 04	19 58	20 12	20 19	20 24	20 28	20 42		20 48	20 54
Barnham	d	18 43		18 52			19 14		19 28		19 36		19 43		19 52			20 13		20 24		20 43			20 54
Bognor Regis	a	18 49		18 59			19 20		19 34		19 43		19 49		19 59			20 20		20 31		20 50			21 01
Barnham	d		18 49		19 05	18 59		19 20		19 23				19 48		20 05	19 59		20 20		20 29			20 49	
Chichester	a		18 56		19 12	19 06		19 27		19 31				19 56		20 12	20 06		20 27		20 37			20 56	
	d		18 57		19 13	19 07		19 28		19 31				19 56		20 13	20 07		20 28		20 37			20 57	
Fishbourne (Sussex)	d				19 16					19 34						20 16									
Bosham	d				19 19					19 37						20 19									
Nutbourne	d				19 22											20 22									
Southbourne	d		19 04		19 25	19 14				19 42				20 03		20 25	20 14							21 04	
Emsworth	d		19 07		19 28	19 17		19 36		19 45				20 06		20 28	20 17		20 36					21 07	
Warblington	d				19 31											20 31									
Havant	a		19 10		19 33	19 20		19 39		19 48				20 10		20 35	20 20		20 39		20 47			21 10	
Bedhampton	a				19 36											20 38									
Hilsea	a				19 42											20 44									
Fratton	a		19 19		19 46					19 57				20 19		20 48					20 56			21 19	
Portsmouth & Southsea	a		19 23		19 50					20 01				20 23		20 53					21 00			21 23	
Portsmouth Harbour	a									20 05											21 04				
Cosham	a					19 29		19 46									20 28		20 46						
Portchester	a					19 33											20 33								
Fareham	a					19 38		19 54									20 38		20 54						
Swanwick	a					19 45		20 01									20 45		21 01						
Southampton Central	a					20 03		20 19									21 03		21 19						

Table T186-F

Mondays to Fridays

21 May to 7 December

London, Gatwick Airport, Arun Valley and Brighton - Bognor Regis, Chichester, Portsmouth and Southampton

		SN ■		SN ■	SN	SN ■		SN		SN	SN ■		SN	SN	SN ■		SN	SN		SN ■	SN	SN	SN ■		SN ■ A
London Victoria	d	19 36				20 06					20 36				21 06					21 36			22 06		22 16
Clapham Junction	d	19 43				20 13					20 43				21 13					21 43			22 13		22 23
East Croydon	a	19 52				20 22					20 52				21 22					21 52			22 22		22 32
London Bridge	d																								
East Croydon	a																								
East Croydon	d	19 53				20 23					20 53				21 23					21 53			22 23		22 33
Gatwick Airport	d	20 09				20 39					21 09				21 39					22 09			22 39		22 50
Three Bridges	a	20 14				20 44					21 14				21 44					22 14			22 44		
	d	20 14				20 44					21 14				21 44					22 14			22 44		
Crawley	d	20 18				20 48					21 18				21 48					22 18			22 48		
Horsham	a	20 27				20 57					21 27				21 57					22 27			22 57		
	d	20 31	20 34			21 01	21 04				21 31	21 34			22 01	22 04				22 28			22 58		
Christs Hospital	d		20 38				21 08					21 38				22 08				22 32			23 02		
Billingshurst	d		20 44				21 14					21 44				22 14				22 38			23 08		
Pulborough	d		20 51				21 21					21 51				22 21				22 45			23 15		
Amberley	d		20 57				21 27					21 57				22 27				22 51			23 21		
Arundel	d		21 01				21 31					22 01				22 31				22 55			23 25		
Brighton	d			20 32				21 02					21 32				22 02				22 32				
Hove	d			20 36				21 07					21 37				22 07				22 37				23 22
Portslade	d			20 39				21 10					21 40				22 10				22 41				23 25
Southwick	d			20 42				21 13					21 43				22 13				22 45				23 28
Shoreham-by-Sea	d			20 46				21 16					21 46				22 16				22 49				23 32
Lancing	d			20 50				21 20					21 50				22 20				22 53				23 36
Worthing	d			20 55				21 25					21 55				22 25				22 59				23 41
West Worthing	d			20 57				21 27					21 57				22 27				23 01				23 43
Durrington-on-Sea	d			20 59				21 29					21 59				22 29				23 03				23 45
Goring-by-Sea	d			21 02				21 32					22 02				22 32				23 06				23 48
Angmering	d			21 06				21 36					22 06				22 36				23 10				23 52
Littlehampton	d				21 10					21 40				22 10								23 16			
Ford	d		21 07	21 13	21 17		21 37	21 43		21 47		22 07	22 13	22 17		22 37	22 43			23 02	23 17	23 21	23 32		23 59
Barnham	a	20 58	21 12	21 18	21 22	21 28	21 42	21 48		21 52	21 58	22 12	22 18	22 23	22 28	22 42	22 48			23 06	23 22	23 26	23 36		00 04
Barnham	d		21 13		21 23		21 43			21 53		22 13		22 25		22 43		22 52				23 28		23 43	00 12
Bognor Regis	a		21 20		21 32		21 50			22 00		22 20		22 32		22 50		22 59				23 35		23 49	00 19
Barnham	d	21 03		21 19		21 29		21 49			21 59		22 19		22 30		22 49			23 07	23 22		23 40		
Chichester	a	21 10		21 26		21 37		21 56			22 06		22 27		22 37		22 56			23 15	23 30		23 48		
	d	21 11		21 27		21 37		21 57			22 07				22 38		22 57			23 15	23 30				
Fishbourne (Sussex)	d	21 14									22 10									23 18					
Bosham	d	21 17									22 13									23 21					
Nutbourne	d	21 20									22 16									23 25					
Southbourne	d	21 23						22 04			22 19				22 45		23 04			23 27					
Emsworth	d	21 26		21 35				22 07			22 22				22 48		23 07			23 30					
Warblington	d	21 29									22 25									23 33					
Havant	a	21 33		21 38		21 50		22 10			22 27				22 52		23 10			23 36	23 41				
Bedhampton	a																								
Hilsea	a																								
Fratton	a					21 59		22 19							23 02		23 19			23 48					
Portsmouth & Southsea	a					22 03		22 23							23 07		23 23			23 54					
Portsmouth Harbour	a					22 07		22 27							23 11		23 28								
Cosham	a	21 40		21 45							22 34														
Portchester	a	21 45									22 39														
Fareham	a	21 50		21 55							22 44														
Swanwick	a	21 57		22 02							22 50														
Southampton Central	a	22 15		22 23							23 08														

A not 7 December

Table T186-F

Mondays to Fridays

21 May to 7 December

London, Gatwick Airport, Arun Valley and Brighton - Bognor Regis, Chichester, Portsmouth and Southampton

		SN ■
London Victoria	d	22 36
Clapham Junction	d	22 43
East Croydon	a	22 52
London Bridge	d	
East Croydon	a	
East Croydon	d	22 53
Gatwick Airport	d	23 09
Three Bridges	a	23 14
	d	23 14
Crawley	d	23 18
Horsham	a	23 27
	d	23 30
Christs Hospital	d	23 34
Billingshurst	d	23 40
Pulborough	d	23 47
Amberley	d	23 53
Arundel	d	23 57
Brighton	d	
Hove	d	
Portslade	d	
Southwick	d	
Shoreham-by-Sea	d	
Lancing	d	
Worthing	d	
West Worthing	d	
Durrington-on-Sea	d	
Goring-by-Sea	d	
Angmering	d	
Littlehampton	d	
Ford	d	00 03
Barnham	a	00 08
Barnham	d	
Bognor Regis	a	
Barnham	d	00 09
Chichester	a	00 17
	d	
Fishbourne (Sussex)	d	
Bosham	d	
Nutbourne	d	
Southbourne	d	
Emsworth	d	
Warblington	d	
Havant	a	
Bedhampton	a	
Hilsea	a	
Fratton	a	
Portsmouth & Southsea	a	
Portsmouth Harbour	a	
Cosham	a	
Portchester	a	
Fareham	a	
Swanwick	a	
Southampton Central	a	

Saturdays
26 May to 8 December

London, Gatwick Airport, Arun Valley and Brighton - Bognor Regis, Chichester, Portsmouth and Southampton

		SN	SN ■	SN	SN ■	SN ■	SN	SN ■	SN	SN ■		SN	SN ■	SN	SN	SN ■	SN	SN ■	SN	SN ■			SN	SN	SN
London Victoria	d																			06 06					
Clapham Junction	d																			06 13					
East Croydon	a																			06 22					
London Bridge	d																								
East Croydon	a																								
East Croydon	d																			06 23					
Gatwick Airport	d															05 56				06 39					
Three Bridges	a															06 02				06 44					
	d															06 02				06 44					
Crawley	d															06 06				06 48					
Horsham	a															06 18				06 57					
	d															06 19				07 01	07 04				
Christs Hospital	d															06 23									
Billingshurst	d															06 29					07 12				
Pulborough	d															06 35					07 19				
Amberley	d															06 41									
Arundel	d															06 46					07 28				
Brighton	d							05 14		05 32				06 02				06 32					07 02		
Hove	d							05 20		05 36				06 06				06 36					07 06		
Portslade	d							05 23		05 39				06 09				06 39					07 09		
Southwick	d							05 26		05 42				06 12				06 42					07 12		
Shoreham-by-Sea	d							05 29		05 46				06 16				06 46					07 16		
Lancing	d							05 33		05 50				06 20				06 50					07 20		
Worthing	d							05 37		05 55				06 25				06 55					07 25		
West Worthing	d							05 39		05 57								06 57							
Durrington-on-Sea	d							05 42		05 59								06 59							
Goring-by-Sea	d							05 44		06 02								07 02							
Angmering	d							05 48		06 06				06 32				07 06					07 32		
Littlehampton	d								05 55				06 19				06 55		07 10						07 55
Ford	d							05 56	06 00	06 13						06 53	07 00	07 13	07 17		07 34				08 00
Barnham	a							06 00	06 04	06 18			06 27	06 43		06 57	07 04	07 18	07 22	07 28	07 39		07 43		08 04
Barnham	d	00 36										06 22			06 52				07 23		07 40			07 52	
Bognor Regis	a	00 43										06 29			06 59				07 30		07 46			07 59	
Barnham	d		05 00	05 05	05 19	05 29	05 44	06 01	06 05	06 19			06 29	06 44		06 58	07 05	07 19		07 29			07 44		08 05
Chichester	a		05 07	05 12	05 26	05 36	05 51	06 08	06 12	06 26			06 36	06 51		07 05	07 12	07 26		07 37			07 51		08 12
	d		05 08	05 13	05 27	05 37	05 52	06 09	06 13	06 27			06 37	06 52		07 06	07 13	07 27		07 37			07 52		08 13
Fishbourne (Sussex)	d			05 16					06 16								07 16								08 16
Bosham	d			05 19					06 19								07 19								08 19
Nutbourne	d			05 22					06 22								07 22								08 22
Southbourne	d			05 25			05 59		06 25					06 59		07 13	07 25						07 59		08 25
Emsworth	d		05 16	05 28	05 35		06 02	06 17	06 28	06 35				07 02		07 16	07 28	07 35					08 02		08 28
Warblington	d			05 31					06 31								07 31								08 31
Havant	a		05 19	05 33	05 38	05 47	06 05	06 20	06 33	06 38			06 47	07 05		07 19	07 33	07 38		07 47			08 05		08 33
Bedhampton	a			05 36					06 36								07 36								08 36
Hilsea	a			05 42					06 42								07 42								08 42
Fratton	a			05 46		05 56	06 16		06 46				06 56	07 14			07 46			07 56			08 16		08 46
Portsmouth & Southsea	a			05 50		06 00	06 21		06 50				07 00	07 18			07 50			08 00			08 20		08 50
Portsmouth Harbour	a					06 04	06 25						07 04	07 22						08 04			08 24		
Cosham	a		05 27		05 46			06 28		06 46						07 27		07 46							
Portchester	a															07 31									
Fareham	a		05 35		05 54			06 36		06 54						07 36		07 54							
Swanwick	a		05 42		06 01			06 43		07 01						07 43		08 01							
Southampton Central	a		06 01		06 19			07 01		07 19						08 03		08 19							

Table T186-F

Saturdays
26 May to 8 December

London, Gatwick Airport, Arun Valley and Brighton - Bognor Regis, Chichester, Portsmouth and Southampton

		SN ■		SN ■	SN	SN ■			SN	SN	SN	SN ■		SN ■	SN	SN ■			GW ◇	SN	SN	SN			
London Victoria	d	06 36				07 06						07 36				08 06									
Clapham Junction	d	06 43				07 13						07 43				08 13									
East Croydon	a	06 52				07 22						07 52				08 22									
London Bridge	d																								
East Croydon	a																								
East Croydon	d	06 53				07 23						07 53				08 23									
Gatwick Airport	d	07 09				07 39						08 09				08 39									
Three Bridges	a	07 14				07 44						08 14				08 44									
	d	07 14				07 44						08 14				08 44									
Crawley	d	07 18				07 48						08 18				08 48									
Horsham	a	07 27				07 57						08 27				08 57									
	d	07 31	07 34			08 01	08 04					08 31	08 34			09 01	09 04								
Christs Hospital	d		07 38										08 38												
Billingshurst	d		07 44				08 12						08 44				09 12								
Pulborough	d		07 51				08 19						08 51				09 19								
Amberley	d		07 57										08 57												
Arundel	d		08 02				08 28						09 01				09 28								
Brighton	d			07 32					08 02					08 32					09 00	09 04					
Hove	d			07 36					08 06					08 36					09 04	09 08					
Portslade	d			07 39					08 09					08 39						09 11					
Southwick	d			07 42					08 12					08 42						09 14					
Shoreham-by-Sea	d			07 46					08 16					08 46					09 13	09 18					
Lancing	d			07 50					08 20					08 50						09 22					
Worthing	d			07 55					08 25					08 55					09 22	09 27					
West Worthing	d			07 57										08 57											
Durrington-on-Sea	d			07 59										08 59											
Goring-by-Sea	d			08 02										09 02											
Angmering	d			08 06					08 32					09 06						09 34					
Littlehampton	d				08 10						08 55				09 10							09 55			
Ford	d		08 08	08 13	08 17		08 34				09 00		09 07	09 13	09 17		09 34					10 00			
Barnham	a	07 58	08 13	08 18	08 22	08 28	08 39		08 43		09 04	08 58	09 12	09 18	09 22	09 28	09 39		09 42	09 46		10 04			
Barnham	d		08 14		08 23		08 40			08 52			09 13		09 23		09 40				09 52				
Bognor Regis	a		08 20		08 30		08 46			08 59			09 20		09 30		09 46				09 59				
Barnham	d	07 59		08 19		08 29			08 44		09 05	08 59		09 19		09 29			09 43	09 47		10 05			
Chichester	a	08 06		08 26		08 37			08 51		09 12	09 06		09 26		09 37			09 50	09 55		10 12			
	d	08 07		08 27		08 37			08 52		09 13	09 07		09 27		09 37			09 51	09 55		10 13			
Fishbourne (Sussex)	d										09 16											10 16			
Bosham	d										09 19											10 19			
Nutbourne	d										09 22											10 22			
Southbourne	d	08 14							08 59		09 25	09 14								10 02		10 25			
Emsworth	d	08 17		08 35					09 02		09 28	09 17		09 35						10 05		10 28			
Warblington	d										09 31											10 31			
Havant	a	08 20		08 38		08 47			09 05		09 33	09 20		09 38		09 47			10 01	10 09		10 33			
Bedhampton	a										09 36											10 36			
Hilsea	a										09 42											10 42			
Fratton	a					08 56			09 14		09 46					09 56				10 18		10 46			
Portsmouth & Southsea	a					09 00			09 18		09 50					10 00				10 21		10 50			
Portsmouth Harbour	a					09 04			09 22							10 04				10 26					
Cosham	a	08 28		08 46								09 28		09 46					10 08						
Portchester	a	08 33										09 33													
Fareham	a	08 38		08 54								09 38		09 54					10 16						
Swanwick	a	08 45		09 01								09 45		10 01											
Southampton Central	a	09 03		09 19								10 03		10 19					10 40						

Table T186-F

Saturdays

26 May to 8 December

London, Gatwick Airport, Arun Valley and Brighton - Bognor Regis, Chichester, Portsmouth and Southampton

		SN ■		SN ■	SN	SN ■		SN	
London Victoria	d	08 36				09 06			
Clapham Junction	d	08 43				09 13			
East Croydon	a	08 52				09 22			
London Bridge	d								
East Croydon	a								
East Croydon	d	08 53				09 23			
Gatwick Airport	d	09 09				09 39			
Three Bridges	a	09 14				09 44			
	d	09 14				09 44			
Crawley	d	09 18				09 48			
Horsham	a	09 27				09 57			
	d	09 31	09 34			10 01	10 04		
Christs Hospital	d		09 38						
Billingshurst	d		09 44				10 12		
Pulborough	d		09 51				10 19		
Amberley	d		09 57						
Arundel	d		10 01				10 28		
Brighton	d			09 32				10 02	
Hove	d			09 36				10 06	
Portslade	d			09 39				10 09	
Southwick	d			09 42				10 12	
Shoreham-by-Sea	d			09 46				10 16	and at the same minutes past each hour until
Lancing	d			09 50				10 20	
Worthing	d			09 55				10 25	
West Worthing	d			09 57					
Durrington-on-Sea	d			09 59					
Goring-by-Sea	d			10 02					
Angmering	d			10 06				10 32	
Littlehampton	d				10 10				
Ford	d		10 07	10 13	10 17		10 34		
Barnham	a	09 58	10 12	10 18	10 22	10 28	10 39	10 43	
Barnham	d		10 13		10 23		10 40		
Bognor Regis	a		10 20		10 30		10 46		
Barnham	d	09 59		10 19		10 29		10 44	
Chichester	a	10 06		10 26		10 37		10 51	
	d	10 07		10 27		10 37		10 52	
Fishbourne (Sussex)	d								
Bosham	d								
Nutbourne	d								
Southbourne	d	10 14						10 59	
Emsworth	d	10 17		10 35				11 02	
Warblington	d								
Havant	a	10 20		10 38		10 47		11 05	
Bedhampton	a								
Hilsea	a								
Fratton	a					10 56		11 14	
Portsmouth & Southsea	a					11 00		11 18	
Portsmouth Harbour	a					11 04		11 22	
Cosham	a	10 28		10 46					
Portchester	a	10 33							
Fareham	a	10 38		10 54					
Swanwick	a	10 45		11 01					
Southampton Central	a	11 03		11 19					

		SN	SN	SN ■		SN ■	SN	SN ■		SN		SN	SN	SN ■		SN ■
London Victoria	d			14 36				15 06						15 36		
Clapham Junction	d			14 43				15 13						15 43		
East Croydon	a			14 52				15 22						15 52		
London Bridge	d															
East Croydon	a															
East Croydon	d			14 53				15 23						15 53		
Gatwick Airport	d			15 09				15 39						16 09		
Three Bridges	a			15 14				15 44						16 14		
	d			15 14				15 44						16 14		
Crawley	d			15 18				15 48						16 18		
Horsham	a			15 27				15 57						16 27		
	d			15 31	15 34			16 01	16 04					16 31	16 34	
Christs Hospital	d				15 38										16 38	
Billingshurst	d				15 44				16 12						16 44	
Pulborough	d				15 51				16 19						16 51	
Amberley	d				15 57										16 57	
Arundel	d				16 01				16 28						17 01	
Brighton	d					15 32				16 02						16 32
Hove	d					15 36				16 06						16 36
Portslade	d					15 39				16 09						16 39
Southwick	d					15 42				16 12						16 42
Shoreham-by-Sea	d					15 46				16 16						16 46
Lancing	d					15 50				16 20						16 50
Worthing	d					15 55				16 25						16 55
West Worthing	d					15 57										16 57
Durrington-on-Sea	d					15 59										16 59
Goring-by-Sea	d					16 02										17 02
Angmering	d					16 06				16 32						17 06
Littlehampton	d		15 55				16 10						16 55			
Ford	d		16 00		16 07	16 13	16 17		16 34				17 00		17 07	17 13
Barnham	a		16 04	15 58	16 12	16 18	16 22	16 28	16 39	16 43			17 04	16 58	17 12	17 18
Barnham	d	15 52			16 13		16 23		16 40			16 52			17 13	
Bognor Regis	a	15 59			16 20		16 30		16 46			16 59			17 20	
Barnham	d		16 05	15 59		16 19		16 29		16 44			17 05	16 59		17 19
Chichester	a		16 12	16 06		16 26		16 37		16 51			17 12	17 06		17 26
	d		16 13	16 07		16 27		16 37		16 52			17 13	17 07		17 27
Fishbourne (Sussex)	d		16 16										17 16			
Bosham	d		16 19										17 19			
Nutbourne	d		16 22										17 22			
Southbourne	d		16 25	16 14						16 59			17 25	17 14		
Emsworth	d		16 28	16 17		16 35				17 02			17 28	17 17		17 35
Warblington	d		16 31										17 31			
Havant	a		16 33	16 20		16 38		16 47		17 05			17 33	17 20		17 38
Bedhampton	a		16 36										17 36			
Hilsea	a		16 42										17 42			
Fratton	a		16 46					16 56		17 14			17 46			
Portsmouth & Southsea	a		16 50					17 00		17 18			17 50			
Portsmouth Harbour	a							17 04		17 22						
Cosham	a			16 28		16 46								17 28		17 46
Portchester	a			16 33										17 33		
Fareham	a			16 38		16 54								17 38		17 54
Swanwick	a			16 45		17 01								17 45		18 01
Southampton Central	a			17 03		17 19								18 03		18 20

Table T186-F

Saturdays

26 May to 8 December

London, Gatwick Airport, Arun Valley and Brighton - Bognor Regis, Chichester, Portsmouth and Southampton

		SN	SN ■		GW ◇		SN	SN	SN	SN ■		SN ■	SN
London Victoria	d		16 06							16 36			
Clapham Junction	d		16 13							16 43			
East Croydon	a		16 22							16 52			
London Bridge	d												
East Croydon	a												
East Croydon	d		16 23							16 53			
Gatwick Airport	d		16 39							17 09			
Three Bridges	a		16 44							17 14			
	d		16 44							17 14			
Crawley	d		16 48							17 18			
Horsham	a		16 57							17 27			
	d		17 01	17 04						17 31	17 34		
Christs Hospital	d										17 38		
Billingshurst	d			17 12							17 44		
Pulborough	d			17 19							17 51		
Amberley	d										17 57		
Arundel	d			17 28							18 01		
Brighton	d				17 00		17 04					17 32	
Hove	d				17 04		17 08					17 36	
Portslade	d						17 11					17 39	
Southwick	d						17 14					17 42	
Shoreham-by-Sea	d				17 13		17 18					17 46	
Lancing	d						17 22					17 50	
Worthing	d				17 22		17 27					17 55	
West Worthing	d											17 57	
Durrington-on-Sea	d											17 59	
Goring-by-Sea	d											18 02	
Angmering	d						17 34					18 06	
Littlehampton	d	17 10							17 55				18 10
Ford	d	17 17		17 34					18 00		18 07	18 13	18 17
Barnham	a	17 22	17 28	17 39	17 42		17 46		18 04	17 58	18 12	18 18	18 22
Barnham	d	17 23		17 40				17 52			18 13		18 23
Bognor Regis	a	17 30		17 46				17 59			18 20		18 30
Barnham	d		17 29		17 42		17 47		18 05	17 59		18 19	
Chichester	a		17 37		17 50		17 55		18 12	18 06		18 26	
	d		17 37		17 50		17 55		18 13	18 07		18 27	
Fishbourne (Sussex)	d								18 16				
Bosham	d								18 19				
Nutbourne	d								18 22				
Southbourne	d						18 02		18 25	18 14			
Emsworth	d						18 05		18 28	18 17		18 35	
Warblington	d								18 31				
Havant	a		17 47		18 01		18 09		18 33	18 20		18 38	
Bedhampton	a								18 36				
Hilsea	a								18 42				
Fratton	a		17 56				18 18		18 46				
Portsmouth & Southsea	a		18 00				18 21		18 50				
Portsmouth Harbour	a		18 04				18 26						
Cosham	a				18 08					18 28		18 46	
Portchester	a									18 33			
Fareham	a				18 16					18 38		18 54	
Swanwick	a									18 45		19 01	
Southampton Central	a				18 43					19 03		19 19	

		SN ■			SN	SN	SN	SN ■		SN ■	SN	SN ■	
London Victoria	d	17 06						17 36				18 06	
Clapham Junction	d	17 13						17 43				18 13	
East Croydon	a	17 22						17 52				18 22	
London Bridge	d												
East Croydon	a												
East Croydon	d	17 23						17 53				18 23	
Gatwick Airport	d	17 39						18 09				18 39	
Three Bridges	a	17 44						18 14				18 44	
	d	17 44						18 14				18 44	
Crawley	d	17 48						18 18				18 48	
Horsham	a	17 57						18 27				18 57	
	d	18 01	18 04					18 31	18 34			19 01	19 04
Christs Hospital	d								18 38				
Billingshurst	d		18 12						18 44				19 12
Pulborough	d		18 19						18 51				19 19
Amberley	d								18 57				
Arundel	d		18 28						19 01				19 28
Brighton	d				18 02					18 32			
Hove	d				18 06					18 36			
Portslade	d				18 09					18 39			
Southwick	d				18 12					18 42			
Shoreham-by-Sea	d				18 16					18 46			
Lancing	d				18 20					18 50			
Worthing	d				18 25					18 55			
West Worthing	d									18 57			
Durrington-on-Sea	d									18 59			
Goring-by-Sea	d									19 02			
Angmering	d				18 32					19 06			
Littlehampton	d						18 55				19 10		
Ford	d		18 34				19 00		19 07	19 13	19 17		19 34
Barnham	a	18 28	18 39		18 43		19 04	18 58	19 12	19 18	19 22	19 28	19 39
Barnham	d		18 40			18 52			19 13		19 23		19 40
Bognor Regis	a		18 46			18 59			19 20		19 30		19 46
Barnham	d	18 29			18 44		19 05	18 59		19 19		19 29	
Chichester	a	18 37			18 51		19 12	19 06		19 26		19 37	
	d	18 37			18 52		19 13	19 07		19 27		19 37	
Fishbourne (Sussex)	d						19 16						
Bosham	d						19 19						
Nutbourne	d						19 22						
Southbourne	d				18 59		19 25	19 14					
Emsworth	d				19 02		19 28	19 17		19 35			
Warblington	d						19 31						
Havant	a	18 47			19 05		19 33	19 20		19 38		19 47	
Bedhampton	a						19 36						
Hilsea	a						19 42						
Fratton	a	18 56			19 14		19 46					19 56	
Portsmouth & Southsea	a	19 00			19 18		19 50					20 00	
Portsmouth Harbour	a	19 04			19 22							20 04	
Cosham	a							19 28		19 46			
Portchester	a							19 33					
Fareham	a							19 38		19 54			
Swanwick	a							19 45		20 01			
Southampton Central	a							20 03		20 19			

London, Gatwick Airport, Arun Valley and Brighton - Bogner Regis, Chichester, Portsmouth and Southampton

		SN	SN	SN	SN ■	SN ■	SN ■	SN	SN ■	SN ■	SN	SN	SN ■	SN ■	SN ■	SN	SN ■	SN ■	SN	SN	SN ■	SN ■
London Victoria	d				18 36				19 06				19 36				20 06				20 36	
Clapham Junction	d				18 43				19 13				19 43				20 13				20 43	
East Croydon	a				18 52				19 22				19 52				20 22				20 52	
London Bridge	d																					
East Croydon	a																					
East Croydon	d				18 53				19 23				19 53				20 23				20 53	
Gatwick Airport	d				19 09				19 39				20 09				20 39				21 09	
Three Bridges	a				19 14				19 44				20 14				20 44				21 14	
	d				19 14				19 44				20 14				20 44				21 14	
Crawley	d				19 18				19 48				20 18				20 48				21 18	
Horsham	a				19 27				19 57				20 27				20 57				21 27	
	d				19 31	19 34			20 01	20 04			20 31	20 34			21 01	21 04			21 31	21 34
Christs Hospital	d					19 38								20 38								21 38
Billingshurst	d					19 44				20 12				20 44				21 12				21 44
Pulborough	d					19 51				20 19				20 51				21 19				21 51
Amberley	d					19 57								20 57								21 57
Arundel	d					20 01				20 28				21 01				21 28				22 01
Brighton	d	19 02					19 32				20 02				20 32				21 02			
Hove	d	19 06					19 36				20 06				20 36				21 06			
Portslade	d	19 09					19 39				20 09				20 39				21 09			
Southwick	d	19 12					19 42				20 12				20 42				21 12			
Shoreham-by-Sea	d	19 16					19 46				20 16				20 46				21 16			
Lancing	d	19 20					19 50				20 20				20 50				21 20			
Worthing	d	19 25					19 55				20 25				20 55				21 25			
West Worthing	d						19 57								20 57							
Durrington-on-Sea	d						19 59								20 59							
Goring-by-Sea	d						20 02								21 02							
Angmering	d	19 32					20 06				20 32				21 06				21 32			
Littlehampton	d			19 55				20 10								21 10				21 40		
Ford	d			20 00		20 07	20 13	20 17		20 34				21 07	21 13	21 17		21 34		21 45		22 07
Barnham	a	19 43		20 04	19 58	20 12	20 18	20 22	20 28	20 39	20 43		20 58	21 12	21 18	21 22	21 28	21 39	21 43	21 50	21 58	22 12
Barnham	d		19 52			20 13		20 23		20 40		20 52		21 13		21 23		21 40		21 53		22 13
Bognor Regis	a		19 59			20 20		20 30		20 46		20 59		21 20		21 30		21 46		22 00		22 19
Barnham	d	19 44		20 05	19 59		20 19		20 29		20 44		21 03		21 19		21 29		21 44		21 59	
Chichester	a	19 51		20 12	20 06		20 26		20 37		20 51		21 10		21 26		21 37		21 51		22 06	
	d	19 52		20 13	20 07		20 27		20 37		20 52		21 11		21 27		21 37		21 52		22 07	
Fishbourne (Sussex)	d			20 16									21 14								22 10	
Bosham	d			20 19									21 17								22 13	
Nutbourne	d			20 22									21 20								22 16	
Southbourne	d	19 59		20 25	20 14						20 59		21 23						21 59		22 19	
Emsworth	d	20 02		20 28	20 17		20 35				21 02		21 26		21 35				22 02		22 22	
Warblington	d			20 31									21 29								22 25	
Havant	a	20 05		20 33	20 20		20 38		20 47		21 05		21 31		21 38		21 48		22 05		22 27	
Bedhampton	a			20 36									21 34									
Hilsea	a			20 42																		
Fratton	a	20 14		20 47					20 56		21 14						21 58		22 14			
Portsmouth & Southsea	a	20 18		20 50					21 00		21 18						22 03		22 18			
Portsmouth Harbour	a	20 22							21 04		21 22						22 07		22 22			
Cosham	a				20 28		20 46						21 40		21 46						22 34	
Portchester	a				20 33								21 44								22 39	
Fareham	a				20 38		20 54						21 49		21 54						22 44	
Swanwick	a				20 45		21 01						21 56		22 02						22 51	
Southampton Central	a				21 03		21 19						22 15		22 19						23 08	

London, Gatwick Airport, Arun Valley and Brighton - Bognor Regis, Chichester, Portsmouth and Southampton

		SN	SN	SN ■	SN	SN ■	SN	SN	SN ■	SN ■	SN ■	SN ■	SN ■
London Victoria	d			21 06		21 36			22 06		22 16	22 36	23 16
Clapham Junction	d			21 13		21 43			22 13		22 23	22 43	23 23
East Croydon	a			21 22		21 52			22 22		22 32	22 52	23 32
London Bridge	d												
East Croydon	a												
East Croydon	d			21 23		21 53			22 23		22 33	22 53	23 33
Gatwick Airport	d			21 39		22 09			22 39		22 50	23 09	23 54
Three Bridges	a			21 44		22 14			22 44			23 14	
	d			21 45		22 14			22 44			23 14	
Crawley	d			21 49		22 18			22 48			23 18	
Horsham	a			21 57		22 27			22 57			23 27	
	d			21 58		22 28			22 58			23 30	
Christs Hospital	d			22 02		22 32			23 02			23 34	
Billingshurst	d			22 08		22 38			23 08			23 40	
Pulborough	d			22 15		22 45			23 15			23 47	
Amberley	d			22 21		22 51			23 21			23 53	
Arundel	d			22 26		22 55			23 25			23 57	
Brighton	d	21 32			22 02		22 32						
Hove	d	21 36			22 06		22 37				23 22		00 25
Portslade	d	21 39			22 09		22 41				23 25		00 28
Southwick	d	21 42			22 12		22 45				23 28		00 31
Shoreham-by-Sea	d	21 46			22 16		22 49				23 32		00 35
Lancing	d	21 50			22 20		22 53				23 36		00 39
Worthing	d	21 55			22 25		22 59				23 41		00 43
West Worthing	d						23 01				23 43		00 45
Durrington-on-Sea	d						23 03				23 45		00 48
Goring-by-Sea	d						23 06				23 48		00 50
Angmering	d	22 02			22 32		23 10				23 52		00 54
Littlehampton	d		22 12					23 17					
Ford	d		22 17			23 02	23 17	23 23	23 32		23 59	00 03	01 02
Barnham	a	22 16	22 22	22 36	22 43	23 06	23 22	23 27	23 36		00 04	00 08	01 06
Barnham	d		22 25	22 37				23 28		23 43	00 12		
Bognor Regis	a		22 32	22 43				23 35		23 49	00 19		
Barnham	d	22 17			22 44	23 07	23 24		23 40			00 09	01 08
Chichester	a	22 24			22 51	23 15	23 31		23 48			00 17	01 15
	d	22 25			22 52	23 15							
Fishbourne (Sussex)	d					23 18							
Bosham	d					23 21							
Nutbourne	d					23 25							
Southbourne	d	22 32			22 59	23 27							
Emsworth	d	22 35			23 02	23 30							
Warblington	d					23 33							
Havant	a	22 38			23 05	23 36							
Bedhampton	a												
Hilsea	a												
Fratton	a	22 48			23 14	23 48							
Portsmouth & Southsea	a	22 52			23 18	23 55							
Portsmouth Harbour	a	22 56			23 22								
Cosham	a												
Portchester	a												
Fareham	a												
Swanwick	a												
Southampton Central	a												

Table T186-F

Sundays
20 May to 2 December

London, Gatwick Airport, Arun Valley and Brighton - Bognor Regis, Chichester, Portsmouth and Southampton

		SN	SN	SN	SN	SN	SN	SN	SN	SN	SN	SN	SN	SN	SN	SN	SN	SN	SN	SN	SN	SN	SN
London Victoria	d										07 32				08 32					09 33			
Clapham Junction	d										07 40				08 40					09 40			
East Croydon	a										07 56				08 51					09 49			
London Bridge	d																						
East Croydon	a																						
East Croydon	d										07 57				08 51					09 49			
Gatwick Airport	d										08 20				09 14					10 13			
Three Bridges	a										08 24				09 19					10 18			
	d										08 25				09 19					10 19			
Crawley	d										08 29				09 23					10 23			
Horsham	a										08 37				09 34					10 32			
	d										08 38				09 35					10 35			
Christs Hospital	d										08 42				09 39					10 39			
Billingshurst	d										08 48				09 45					10 45			
Pulborough	d										08 55				09 52					10 52			
Amberley	d										09 01				09 58					10 58			
Arundel	d										09 06				10 02					11 02			
Brighton	d					07 15	07 30		08 00	08 20		08 30		09 00			09 30		10 00			10 30	
Hove	d					07 19	07 34		08 04	08 24		08 34		09 04			09 34		10 04			10 34	
Portslade	d						07 39		08 09			08 39		09 09			09 39		10 09			10 39	
Southwick	d						07 43		08 13			08 43		09 13			09 43		10 13			10 43	
Shoreham-by-Sea	d					07 26	07 47		08 17	08 31		08 47		09 17			09 47		10 17			10 47	
Lancing	d						07 51		08 21			08 51		09 21			09 51		10 21			10 51	
Worthing	d					07 33	07 57		08 27	08 38		08 57		09 27			09 57		10 27			10 57	
West Worthing	d						07 59		08 29			08 59		09 29			09 59		10 29			10 59	
Durrington-on-Sea	d						08 01		08 31			09 01		09 31			10 01		10 31			11 01	
Goring-by-Sea	d						08 04		08 34			09 04		09 34			10 04		10 34			11 04	
Angmering	d					07 40	08 08		08 38	08 45		09 08		09 38			10 08		10 38			11 08	
Littlehampton	d		06 42	07 31	07 39			08 31					09 31					10 31					11 31
Ford	d		06 47	07 36	07 44	07 49	08 16	08 36	08 46	08 52	09 12	09 16	09 36	09 46	10 08		10 16	10 36	10 46	11 08		11 16	11 36
Barnham	a		06 51	07 41	07 48	07 53	08 20	08 41	08 50	08 57	09 16	09 21	09 41	09 50	10 13		10 20	10 41	10 50	11 13		11 20	11 41
Barnham	d	06 45		07 43				08 43			09 17		09 43			10 18		10 43			11 18		11 43
Bognor Regis	a	06 51		07 49				08 49			09 24		09 49			10 24		10 49			11 24		11 49
Barnham	d		06 52		07 49	07 54	08 21		08 51	08 57		09 22		09 51	10 13		10 21		10 51	11 13		11 21	
Chichester	a		06 59		07 56	08 02	08 28		08 58	09 05		09 29		09 58	10 21		10 28		10 58	11 21		11 28	
	d		07 00		07 57	08 02	08 29		08 59	09 05		09 30		09 59	10 22		10 29		10 59	11 22		11 29	
Fishbourne (Sussex)	d						08 32					09 33					10 32					11 32	
Bosham	d						08 35					09 36					10 35					11 35	
Nutbourne	d						08 38					09 39					10 38					11 38	
Southbourne	d		07 07			08 09	08 41			09 12		09 42			10 29		10 41			11 29		11 41	
Emsworth	d		07 10		08 05	08 12	08 44		09 07	09 15		09 45		10 07	10 33		10 44		11 07	11 33		11 44	
Warblington	d						08 47					09 48					10 47					11 47	
Havant	a		07 14		08 09	08 16	08 49		09 10	09 19		09 50		10 10	10 36		10 49		11 10	11 36		11 49	
Bedhampton	a						08 52					09 53					10 52					11 52	
Hilsea	a																						
Fratton	a		07 23			08 25	09 00			09 28		10 01			10 47		11 00			11 47		12 00	
Portsmouth & Southsea	a		07 27			08 28	09 03			09 31		10 04			10 52		11 03			11 50		12 03	
Portsmouth Harbour	a		07 31			08 32	09 07			09 35		10 08			10 56		11 07			11 55		12 07	
Cosham	a				08 17				09 17					10 17					11 17				
Portchester	a																						
Fareham	a				08 25				09 25					10 25					11 25				
Swanwick	a				08 32				09 32					10 32					11 32				
Southampton Central	a				08 50				09 50					10 50					11 50				

Table T186-F

Sundays
20 May to 2 December

London, Gatwick Airport, Arun Valley and Brighton - Bognor Regis, Chichester, Portsmouth and Southampton

		SN	GW ◇	SN		SN		SN	SN	SN		SN	SN	SN	SN			SN	SN	SN	SN		SN	SN	SN
London Victoria	d			10 33						11 33					12 33						13 33				
Clapham Junction	d			10 40						11 40					12 40						13 40				
East Croydon	a			10 49						11 49					12 49						13 49				
London Bridge	d																								
East Croydon	a																								
East Croydon	d			10 49						11 49					12 49						13 49				
Gatwick Airport	d			11 13						12 13					13 13						14 13				
Three Bridges	a			11 18						12 18					13 18						14 18				
	d			11 18						12 18					13 18						14 18				
Crawley	d			11 22						12 22					13 22						14 22				
Horsham	a			11 31						12 31					13 31						14 31				
	d			11 31						12 31					13 31						14 31				
Christs Hospital	d			11 35						12 35					13 35						14 35				
Billingshurst	d			11 42						12 42					13 42						14 42				
Pulborough	d			11 48						12 48					13 48						14 48				
Amberley	d			11 54						12 54					13 54						14 54				
Arundel	d			11 59						12 59					13 59						14 59				
Brighton	d	11 00	11 10			11 30			12 00			12 30		13 00				13 30		14 00			14 30		15 00
Hove	d	11 04	11 14			11 34			12 04			12 34		13 04				13 34		14 04			14 34		15 04
Portslade	d	11 09				11 39			12 09			12 39		13 09				13 39		14 09			14 39		15 09
Southwick	d	11 13				11 43			12 13			12 43		13 13				13 43		14 13			14 43		15 13
Shoreham-by-Sea	d	11 17	11 21			11 47			12 17			12 47		13 17				13 47		14 17			14 47		15 17
Lancing	d	11 21				11 51			12 21			12 51		13 21				13 51		14 21			14 51		15 21
Worthing	d	11 27	11 31			11 57			12 27			12 57		13 27				13 57		14 27			14 57		15 27
West Worthing	d	11 29				11 59			12 29			12 59		13 29				13 59		14 29			14 59		15 29
Durrington-on-Sea	d	11 31				12 01			12 31			13 01		13 31				14 01		14 31			15 01		15 31
Goring-by-Sea	d	11 34				12 04			12 34			13 04		13 34				14 04		14 34			15 04		15 34
Angmering	d	11 38				12 08			12 38			13 08		13 38				14 08		14 38			15 08		15 38
Littlehampton	d							12 31					13 31						14 31					15 31	
Ford	d	11 46		12 05		12 16		12 36	12 46	13 05		13 16	13 36	13 46	14 05			14 16	14 36	14 46	15 05		15 16	15 36	15 46
Barnham	a	11 50	11 55	12 09		12 20		12 41	12 50	13 09		13 20	13 41	13 50	14 09			14 20	14 41	14 50	15 09		15 20	15 41	15 50
Barnham	d			12 16				12 43		13 16			13 43		14 16				14 43		15 16			15 43	
Bognor Regis	a			12 23				12 49		13 23			13 49		14 23				14 49		15 23			15 49	
Barnham	d	11 51	11 56		12 13	12 21			12 51		13 13	13 21		13 51		14 13		14 21		14 51		15 13	15 21		15 51
Chichester	a	11 58	12 03		12 20	12 28			12 58		13 20	13 28		13 58		14 20		14 28		14 58		15 20	15 28		15 58
	d	11 59	12 04		12 21	12 29			12 59		13 21	13 29		13 59		14 21		14 29		14 59		15 21	15 29		15 59
Fishbourne (Sussex)	d					12 32						13 32						14 32					15 32		
Bosham	d					12 35						13 35						14 35					15 35		
Nutbourne	d					12 38						13 38						14 38					15 38		
Southbourne	d				12 28	12 41					13 28	13 41				14 28		14 41				15 28	15 41		
Emsworth	d	12 07			12 32	12 44			13 07		13 32	13 44		14 07		14 32		14 44		15 07		15 32	15 44		16 07
Warblington	d					12 47						13 47						14 47					15 47		
Havant	a	12 10	12 15		12 36	12 49			13 10		13 36	13 49		14 10		14 36		14 49		15 10		15 36	15 49		16 10
Bedhampton	a					12 52						13 52						14 52					15 52		
Hilsea	a																								
Fratton	a				12 47	13 00					13 45	14 00				14 47		15 00				15 45	16 00		
Portsmouth & Southsea	a				12 52	13 03					13 49	14 03				14 51		15 03				15 49	16 03		
Portsmouth Harbour	a				12 56	13 07					13 53	14 07				14 56		15 07				15 53	16 07		
Cosham	a	12 17	12 25						13 17					14 17						15 17					16 17
Portchester	a																								
Fareham	a	12 25	12 33						13 25					14 25						15 25					16 25
Swanwick	a	12 32							13 32					14 32						15 32					16 32
Southampton Central	a	12 50	12 55						13 50					14 50						15 50					16 50

Table T186-F

Sundays

20 May to 2 December

London, Gatwick Airport, Arun Valley and Brighton - Bognor Regis, Chichester, Portsmouth and Southampton

		SN	SN	SN	GW	GW	SN	SN	SN	SN	SN	SN	SN	SN	SN	SN	SN	GW	SN	SN	SN
					◇ A	◇ B												◇			
London Victoria	d	14 33								15 33					16 33						
Clapham Junction	d	14 40								15 40					16 40						
East Croydon	a	14 49								15 49					16 49						
London Bridge	d																				
East Croydon	a																				
East Croydon	d	14 49								15 49					16 49						
Gatwick Airport	d	15 13								16 13					17 13						
Three Bridges	a	15 18								16 18					17 18						
	d	15 18								16 18					17 18						
Crawley	d	15 22								16 22					17 22						
Horsham	a	15 31								16 31					17 31						
	d	15 31								16 31					17 31						
Christs Hospital	d	15 35								16 35					17 35						
Billingshurst	d	15 42								16 42					17 42						
Pulborough	d	15 48								16 48					17 48						
Amberley	d	15 54								16 54					17 54						
Arundel	d	15 59								16 59					17 59						
Brighton	d			15 30	15 47	15 47			16 00			16 30		17 00			17 30	17 46			18 00
Hove	d			15 34	15 51	15 51			16 04			16 34		17 04			17 34	17 50			18 04
Portslade	d			15 39					16 09			16 39		17 09			17 39				18 09
Southwick	d			15 43					16 13			16 43		17 13			17 43				18 13
Shoreham-by-Sea	d			15 47	15 57	15 57			16 17			16 47		17 17			17 47	17 56			18 17
Lancing	d			15 51					16 21			16 51		17 21			17 51				18 21
Worthing	d			15 57	16 09	16 09			16 27			16 57		17 27			17 57	18 08			18 27
West Worthing	d			15 59					16 29			16 59		17 29			17 59				18 29
Durrington-on-Sea	d			16 01					16 31			17 01		17 31			18 01				18 31
Goring-by-Sea	d			16 04					16 34			17 04		17 34			18 04				18 34
Angmering	d			16 08					16 38			17 08		17 38			18 08				18 38
Littlehampton	d							16 31					17 31							18 31	
Ford	d	16 05		16 16				16 36	16 46	17 05		17 16	17 36	17 46	18 05		18 16			18 36	18 46
Barnham	a	16 09		16 20	16 26	16 26		16 41	16 50	17 09		17 20	17 41	17 50	18 09		18 20	18 26		18 41	18 50
Barnham	d	16 16						16 43		17 16			17 43		18 16					18 43	
Bognor Regis	a	16 23					←	16 49		17 23			17 49		18 23				←	18 49	
Barnham	d		16 13	16 31	16 27	16 27	16 31		16 51		17 13	17 21		17 51		18 13	18 31	18 27	18 31		18 51
Chichester	a		16 20	→	16 34	16 34	16 38		16 58		17 20	17 28		17 58		18 20	→	18 34	18 38		18 58
	d		16 21		16 35	16 35	16 39		16 59		17 21	17 29		17 59		18 21		18 35	18 39		18 59
Fishbourne (Sussex)	d						16 42					17 32							18 42		
Bosham	d						16 45					17 35							18 45		
Nutbourne	d						16 48					17 38							18 48		
Southbourne	d		16 28				16 51				17 28	17 41				18 28			18 51		
Emsworth	d		16 32				16 54		17 07		17 32	17 44		18 07		18 32			18 54		19 07
Warblington	d						16 57					17 47							18 57		
Havant	a		16 36		16 44	16 45	16 59		17 10		17 36	17 49		18 10		18 36		18 50	18 59		19 10
Bedhampton	a						17 02					17 52							19 02		
Hilsea	a																				
Fratton	a		16 47				17 11				17 47	18 00				18 48			19 14		
Portsmouth & Southsea	a		16 51								17 50	18 03				18 51					
Portsmouth Harbour	a		16 55								17 54	18 07				18 55					
Cosham	a				16 51	16 52			17 17					18 17				18 56			19 17
Portchester	a																				
Fareham	a				16 59	16 59			17 25					18 25				19 04			19 25
Swanwick	a								17 32					18 32							19 32
Southampton Central	a				17 20	17 20			17 50					18 50				19 26			19 50

A until 9 September

B from 16 September

Table T186-F

Sundays

20 May to 2 December

London, Gatwick Airport, Arun Valley and Brighton - Bognor Regis, Chichester, Portsmouth and Southampton

		SN	SN	SN	SN	SN	SN	SN	SN	SN	SN	SN	SN	SN	SN	SN	SN	SN	SN	GW	SN	SN	SN
London Victoria	d	17 33					18 33					19 33					20 33						21 16
Clapham Junction	d	17 40					18 40					19 40					20 40						21 23
East Croydon	a	17 49					18 49					19 49					20 49						21 32
London Bridge	d																						
East Croydon	a																						
East Croydon	d	17 49					18 49					19 49					20 49						21 33
Gatwick Airport	d	18 13					19 13					20 13					21 13						21 50
Three Bridges	a	18 18					19 18					20 18					21 18						
	d	18 18					19 18					20 18					21 18						
Crawley	d	18 22					19 22					20 22					21 22						
Horsham	a	18 31					19 31					20 31					21 31						
	d	18 31					19 31					20 31					21 31						
Christs Hospital	d	18 35					19 35					20 35					21 35						
Billingshurst	d	18 42					19 42					20 42					21 42						
Pulborough	d	18 48					19 48					20 48					21 48						
Amberley	d	18 54					19 54					20 54					21 54						
Arundel	d	18 59					19 59					20 59					21 59						
Brighton	d			18 30		19 00			19 30		20 00			20 30		21 00			21 30	21 46			
Hove	d			18 34		19 04			19 34		20 04			20 34		21 04			21 34	21 50			22 19
Portslade	d			18 39		19 09			19 39		20 09			20 39		21 09			21 39				22 23
Southwick	d			18 43		19 13			19 43		20 13			20 43		21 13			21 43				22 27
Shoreham-by-Sea	d			18 47		19 17			19 47		20 17			20 47		21 17			21 47	21 56			22 31
Lancing	d			18 51		19 21			19 51		20 21			20 51		21 21			21 51				22 35
Worthing	d			18 57		19 27			19 57		20 27			20 57		21 27			21 57	22 03			22 44
West Worthing	d			18 59		19 29			19 59		20 29			20 59		21 29			21 59				
Durrington-on-Sea	d			19 01		19 31			20 01		20 31			21 01		21 31			22 01				
Goring-by-Sea	d			19 04		19 34			20 04		20 34			21 04		21 34			22 04				
Angmering	d			19 08		19 38			20 08		20 38			21 08		21 38			22 08				
Littlehampton	d				19 31					20 31					21 31							22 31	
Ford	d	19 05		19 16	19 36	19 46	20 05		20 16	20 36	20 46	21 05		21 16	21 36	21 46	22 05		22 16			22 36	22 56
Barnham	a	19 09		19 20	19 41	19 50	20 09		20 20	20 41	20 50	21 09		21 20	21 41	21 50	22 09		22 20	22 24		22 41	23 00
Barnham	d	19 16			19 43		20 16			20 43		21 16			21 43		22 16					22 43	
Bognor Regis	a	19 23			19 49		20 23			20 49		21 23			21 49		22 23				←	22 49	
Barnham	d		19 13	19 21		19 51		20 13	20 21		20 51		21 13	21 21		21 51		22 13	22 29	22 24	22 29		23 01
Chichester	a		19 20	19 28		19 58		20 20	20 28		20 58		21 20	21 28		21 58		22 20	→	22 32	22 36		23 08
	d		19 21	19 29		19 59		20 21	20 29		20 59		21 21	21 29		21 59		22 21		22 32	22 37		23 09
Fishbourne (Sussex)	d			19 32					20 32					21 32							22 40		
Bosham	d			19 35					20 35					21 35							22 43		23 13
Nutbourne	d			19 38					20 38					21 38							22 46		23 17
Southbourne	d		19 28	19 41				20 28	20 41				21 28	21 41				22 28			22 49		23 19
Emsworth	d		19 32	19 44		20 07		20 32	20 44		21 07		21 32	21 44		22 07		22 32			22 52		23 22
Warblington	d			19 47					20 47					21 47							22 55		
Havant	a		19 36	19 49		20 10		20 36	20 49		21 10		21 36	21 49		22 10		22 36		22 44	22 57		23 26
Bedhampton	a			19 52					20 52					21 52							23 01		
Hilsea	a																						
Fratton	a		19 47	20 00				20 47	21 00				21 45	22 00				22 47		22 59	23 11		23 35
Portsmouth & Southsea	a		19 51	20 03				20 51	21 03				21 49	22 03				22 52		23 02	23 15		23 38
Portsmouth Harbour	a		19 55	20 07				20 55	21 07				21 54	22 07				22 56		23 07	23 20		23 42
Cosham	a					20 17					21 17					22 17							
Portchester	a																						
Fareham	a					20 25					21 25					22 25							
Swanwick	a					20 32					21 32					22 32							
Southampton Central	a					20 50					21 50					22 50							

Table T186-F

Sundays

20 May to 2 December

London, Gatwick Airport, Arun Valley and Brighton - Bognor Regis, Chichester, Portsmouth and Southampton

		SN	SN	SN
London Victoria	d	21 33		22 35
Clapham Junction	d	21 40		22 42
East Croydon	a	21 49		22 51
London Bridge	d			
East Croydon	a			
East Croydon	d	21 49		22 51
Gatwick Airport	d	22 14		23 13
Three Bridges	a	22 19		23 18
	d	22 20		23 18
Crawley	d	22 24		23 22
Horsham	a	22 32		23 31
	d	22 33		23 31
Christs Hospital	d	22 37		23 35
Billingshurst	d	22 43		23 42
Pulborough	d	22 50		23 48
Amberley	d	22 56		23 54
Arundel	d	23 00		23 59
Brighton	d		22 47	
Hove	d		22 52	
Portslade	d		22 56	
Southwick	d		23 00	
Shoreham-by-Sea	d		23 04	
Lancing	d		23 08	
Worthing	d		23 14	
West Worthing	d		23 16	
Durrington-on-Sea	d		23 19	
Goring-by-Sea	d		23 21	
Angmering	d		23 26	
Littlehampton	d		23 42	
Ford	d	23 10	23 47	00 05
Barnham	a	23 14	23 51	00 09
Barnham	d	23 20		00 11
Bognor Regis	a	23 26		00 17
Barnham	d		23 52	
Chichester	a		23 59	
	d			
Fishbourne (Sussex)	d			
Bosham	d			
Nutbourne	d			
Southbourne	d			
Emsworth	d			
Warblington	d			
Havant	a			
Bedhampton	a			
Hilsea	a			
Fratton	a			
Portsmouth & Southsea	a			
Portsmouth Harbour	a			
Cosham	a			
Portchester	a			
Fareham	a			
Swanwick	a			
Southampton Central	a			

Table T186-R

Mondays to Fridays

21 May to 7 December

Bognor Regis, Chichester, Portsmouth and Southampton - London, Gatwick Airport, Arun Valley and Brighton

Miles	Miles	Miles			SN	SN	SN	SN	SN ■	SN	SN	SN ■	SN ■		SN	SN	SN ■	SN ■	SN	SN	SN ■	SN ■	SN		SN
0	—	—	Southampton Central	d																	05 46				
11	—	—	Swanwick	d																	06 04				
14½	—	—	Fareham	d																	06 11				
17¼	—	—	Portchester	d																	06 16				
20½	—	—	Cosham	d																	06 20				
—	—	0	Portsmouth Harbour	d									05 28					05 57					06 12		06 32
—	—	0¾	Portsmouth & Southsea	d									05 32					06 01					06 16		06 36
—	—	1¾	Fratton	d									05 36					06 05					06 20		06 40
—	—	4	Hilsea	d									05 40										06 24		
23¼	—	—	Bedhampton	d									05 45										06 29		
24½	—	8	Havant	d					05 20				05 48					06 14			06 28		06 32		06 51
25¼	—	8¾	**Warblington**	d									05 50										06 34		
26½	—	10	**Emsworth**	d									05 53					06 18			06 31		06 37		06 54
28¼	—	11½	**Southbourne**	d									05 56					06 22			06 34		06 40		06 57
29¼	—	14½	**Nutbourne**	d									05 59										06 42		
30¾	—	16	**Bosham**	d									06 02					06 26			06 39		06 45		
32	—	15½	**Fishbourne (Sussex)**	d									06 05					06 29					06 48		
33½	—	17	**Chichester**	a					05 30				06 08					06 32			06 43		06 51		07 04
—	—	—		d	04 54		05 25		05 31		05 50		06 09			06 16		06 33			06 44		06 54		07 05
39½	—	23½	**Barnham**	a	05 01		05 32		05 39		05 57		06 16			06 24		06 41			06 52		07 01		07 12
—	—	—	**Bognor Regis**	d		04 55		05 29		05 38		05 56			06 09		06 21		06 35	06 44		06 51			
—	—	—	**Barnham**	a		05 02		05 35		05 44		06 02			06 16		06 28		06 42	06 51		06 57			
—	—	—	**Barnham**	d	05 02	05 06	05 33	05 37	05 41	05 45	05 58	06 03	06 17		06 20	06 24	06 29	06 43	06 47		06 55	06 59	07 03		07 13
42½	—	25¾	**Ford**	d	05 07	05 11	05 37	05 41		05 49	06 03	06 08			06 26	06 29	06 33		06 51		06 59	07 03	07 07		07 17
44½	—	—	Littlehampton	a		05 16		05 46		05 54					06 31				06 57				07 15		
—	—	30	Angmering	a	05 14		05 44				06 10					06 36					07 06				07 25
—	—	32¾	Goring-by-Sea	a	05 18		05 48				06 14					06 40					07 11				07 29
—	—	34	Durrington-on-Sea	a	05 20		05 51				06 16					06 43					07 13				07 32
—	—	34½	West Worthing	a	05 23		05 53				06 19					06 46					07 16				07 35
—	—	35	Worthing	a	05 25		05 56				06 21					06 49					07 18				07 38
—	—	37½	Lancing	a	05 31		06 02				06 27					06 53					07 23				07 43
—	—	39¾	Shoreham-by-Sea	a	05 36		06 06				06 32					06 57					07 27				07 47
—	—	41½	Southwick	a	05 39		06 09				06 35					07 01					07 30				07 51
—	—	42¾	Portslade	a	05 43		06 13				06 39					07 05					07 34				07 54
—	—	44¼	Hove	a	05 48		06 18				06 44					07 08					07 37				07 58
—	0	45¼	Brighton	a	05 54		06 24				06 49					07 14					07 44				08 03
48	—	—	**Arundel**	d					05 50			06 14					06 39					07 09			
51¾	—	—	**Amberley**	d					05 54			06 19					06 44					07 14			
53	—	—	**Pulborough**	d					06 01			06 26					06 50					07 21			
53¾	—	—	**Billingshurst**	d					06 08			06 33					06 57					07 28			
55¾	—	—	**Christs Hospital**	d					06 14			06 39					07 04					07 34			
57	—	—	Horsham	a					06 18			06 43	06 46				07 08	07 12				07 38			
—	—	—																							
—	—	—		d					06 19			06 50					07 16					07 40			
64¼	—	—	Crawley	a					06 27			07 02					07 27					07 53			
65¾	21¼	—	Three Bridges	a					06 32			07 07					07 32					07 58			
—	—	—		d					06 33			07 07					07 33					08 01			
68¾	23¾	—	Gatwick Airport	a					06 37								07 37					08 05			
—	—	—	East Croydon	a					06 53			07 26					07 53					08 23			
—	40¼	—	East Croydon	d								07 27													
—	50½	—	London Bridge	a								07 43													
84½	—	—	East Croydon	d					06 53								07 54					08 24			
93	—	—	Clapham Junction	a					07 02								08 03					08 33			
95¾	—	—	London Victoria	a					07 12								08 12					08 40			

21 May to 7 December

Bognor Regis, Chichester, Portsmouth and Southampton - London, Gatwick Airport, Arun Valley and Brighton

		SN ■	SN ■	SN	SN ■	SN ■	GW	SN	SN	SN	SN ■	SN ■	SN	SN ■	SN	SN	SN ■	SN ■	SN	SN	SN ■	SN ■	SN ■
Southampton Central	d		06 10			06 36						07 12		07 33								08 10	08 26
Swanwick	d		06 28			06 56						07 31		07 51								08 28	08 48
Fareham	d		06 36			07 03						07 38		07 57								08 35	08 56
Portchester	d		06 41			07 08						07 43										08 40	
Cosham	d		06 46			07 12						07 47		08 06								08 44	09 04
Portsmouth Harbour	d						07 09		07 18										08 29				
Portsmouth & Southsea	d						07 13		07 22	07 32					07 57			08 14	08 33				
Fratton	d						07 17		07 26	07 36					08 01			08 18	08 37				
Hilsea	d								07 30						08 05								
Bedhampton	d								07 35									08 25					
Havant	d		06 54			07 19	07 27		07 38	07 46		07 55		08 12	08 15			08 28	08 46			08 52	09 11
Warblington	d								07 40						08 17								
Emsworth	d		06 58			07 22	07 32		07 43	07 49		07 58			08 20				08 49			08 56	09 14
Southbourne	d		07 01			07 25	07 36		07 46	07 52		08 01			08 23				08 52			08 59	
Nutbourne	d								07 49						08 26								
Bosham	d					07 30			07 52						08 29								
Fishbourne (Sussex)	d					07 33			07 55						08 32								
Chichester	a		07 08			07 36	07 42		07 58	08 01		08 08		08 23	08 35			08 38	09 00			09 06	09 22
	d		07 09			07 37	07 43		07 58	08 02		08 09		08 23	08 35			08 39	09 00			09 09	09 23
Barnham	a		07 16			07 44	07 51		08 06	08 09		08 16		08 31	08 43			08 46	09 08			09 16	09 30
Bognor Regis	d	07 00		07 07	07 26			07 41			07 54		08 14			08 36	08 28			09 05	08 56		
Barnham	a	07 06		07 14	07 32			07 47			08 00		08 21			08 43	08 34			09 11	09 02		
Barnham	d	07 07	07 17	07 23	07 33	07 45	07 52	07 54	08 06	08 10	08 01	08 17	08 22	08 31	08 43		08 35	08 47	09 09	09 12	09 03	09 17	09 31
Ford	d			07 28				07 59	08 11	08 14	08 06		08 27	08 36	08 48		08 40			09 17	09 07		09 36
Littlehampton	a			07 33				08 04		08 19			08 32		08 53					09 23			
Angmering	a						08 01		08 18					08 43					09 19				09 43
Goring-by-Sea	a													08 48									09 47
Durrington-on-Sea	a													08 51									09 50
West Worthing	a													08 53									09 52
Worthing	a						08 10		08 25					08 56					09 26				09 55
Lancing	a								08 31					09 00					09 30				10 00
Shoreham-by-Sea	a						08 18		08 35					09 05					09 35				10 04
Southwick	a								08 39					09 08					09 38				10 08
Portslade	a						08 24		08 43					09 12					09 42				10 11
Hove	a						08 28		08 48					09 16					09 45				10 15
Brighton	a						08 35		08 54					09 21					09 51				10 21
Arundel	d	07 16			07 42						08 12						08 45				09 13		
Amberley	d				07 46						08 17						08 50				09 17		
Pulborough	d	07 26			07 53						08 23						08 56				09 24		
Billingshurst	d	07 33			08 00						08 30						09 03				09 31		
Christs Hospital	d	07 39			08 06						08 37										09 37		
Horsham	a	07 43	07 46		08 10	08 14					08 41	08 46					09 11	09 16			09 41	09 46	
	d	07 50			08 18						08 50						09 20				09 50		
Crawley	a	08 02			08 26						08 58						09 28				09 58		
Three Bridges	a	08 07			08 31						09 03						09 33				10 03		
	d	08 07			08 32						09 04						09 34				10 04		
Gatwick Airport	a				08 36						09 08						09 38				10 08		
East Croydon	a	08 26			08 54						09 24						09 54				10 24		
East Croydon	d	08 27																					
London Bridge	a	08 43																					
East Croydon	d				08 54						09 24						09 54				10 24		
Clapham Junction	a				09 03						09 33						10 03				10 33		
London Victoria	a				09 10						09 40						10 11				10 41		

21 May to 7 December

Bognor Regis, Chichester, Portsmouth and Southampton - London, Gatwick Airport, Arun Valley and Brighton

		SN	SN	SN ■	SN ■	SN	SN	SN ■	SN ■	SN	SN	SN	SN ■	SN ■	SN	SN	SN ■	SN ■	SN ■	SN	SN	SN ■	SN ■
Southampton Central	d								09 13	09 26								10 13	10 26				
Swanwick	d								09 32									10 32	10 46				
Fareham	d								09 39									10 39	10 53				
Portchester	d								09 44									10 44					
Cosham	d								09 48	10 02								10 48	11 02				
Portsmouth Harbour	d				09 11									10 11									11 11
Portsmouth & Southsea	d	08 57			09 15	09 33					09 57			10 15	10 33					10 57			11 15
Fratton	d	09 01			09 19	09 37					10 01			10 19	10 37					11 01			11 19
Hilsea	d	09 05									10 05									11 05			
Bedhampton	d	09 12									10 10									11 10			
Havant	d	09 15			09 29	09 46			09 55	10 10	10 14			10 28	10 46			10 55	11 10	11 14			11 28
Warblington	d	09 17									10 16									11 16			
Emsworth	d	09 20				09 49			09 58	10 13	10 19				10 49			10 58	11 13	11 19			
Southbourne	d	09 23				09 52			10 01		10 22				10 52			11 01		11 22			
Nutbourne	d	09 25									10 24									11 24			
Bosham	d	09 28									10 27									11 27			
Fishbourne (Sussex)	d	09 31									10 30									11 30			
Chichester	a	09 34			09 39	09 59			10 08	10 21	10 33			10 38	10 59			11 08	11 21	11 33			11 38
	d	09 35			09 39	10 00			10 09	10 22	10 34			10 39	11 00			11 09	11 22	11 34			11 39
Barnham	a	09 42			09 47	10 07			10 16	10 30	10 41			10 46	11 07			11 16	11 30	11 41			11 46
Bognor Regis	d		09 36	09 29			10 05	09 56				10 36	10 29			11 05	10 56				11 36	11 29	
Barnham	a		09 43	09 35			10 11	10 02				10 43	10 35			11 11	11 02				11 43	11 35	
Barnham	d	09 43		09 36	09 48	10 09	10 12	10 03	10 17	10 31	10 42		10 36	10 47	11 09	11 12	11 03	11 17	11 31	11 42		11 36	11 47
Ford	d	09 47		09 41			10 17	10 07		10 36	10 47		10 41			11 17	11 07		11 36	11 47		11 41	
Littlehampton	a	09 53					10 23				10 53					11 23				11 53			
Angmering	a					10 19				10 43					11 19				11 43				
Goring-by-Sea	a									10 47									11 47				
Durrington-on-Sea	a									10 50									11 50				
West Worthing	a									10 52									11 52				
Worthing	a					10 26				10 55					11 26				11 55				
Lancing	a					10 30				11 00					11 30				12 00				
Shoreham-by-Sea	a					10 35				11 04					11 35				12 04				
Southwick	a					10 38				11 08					11 38				12 08				
Portslade	a					10 42				11 11					11 42				12 11				
Hove	a					10 45				11 15					11 45				12 15				
Brighton	a					10 51				11 21					11 51				12 21				
Arundel	d			09 46				10 13					10 46				11 13					11 46	
Amberley	d							10 17									11 17						
Pulborough	d			09 55				10 24					10 55				11 24					11 55	
Billingshurst	d			10 02				10 31					11 02				11 31					12 02	
Christs Hospital	d							10 37									11 37						
Horsham	a			10 11	10 16			10 41	10 46				11 11	11 16			11 41	11 46				12 11	12 16
	d			10 20				10 50					11 20				11 50					12 20	
Crawley	a			10 28				10 58					11 28				11 58					12 28	
Three Bridges	a			10 33				11 03					11 33				12 03					12 33	
	d			10 34				11 04					11 34				12 04					12 34	
Gatwick Airport	a			10 38				11 08					11 38				12 08					12 38	
East Croydon	a			10 54				11 24					11 54				12 24					12 54	
East Croydon	d																						
London Bridge	a																						
East Croydon	d			10 54				11 24					11 54				12 24					12 54	
Clapham Junction	a			11 03				11 33					12 03				12 33					13 03	
London Victoria	a			11 11				11 41					12 11				12 41					13 11	

Table T186-R

Mondays to Fridays

21 May to 7 December

Bognor Regis, Chichester, Portsmouth and Southampton - London, Gatwick Airport, Arun Valley and Brighton

		SN	SN	SN	SN	SN	SN	SN	SN	SN	SN	SN	SN	SN	SN	SN	SN	SN	SN	SN	SN
				1	1				1	1			1	1	1			1	1		
Southampton Central	d				11 13	11 26								12 13	12 29						
Swanwick	d				11 32									12 32	12 46						
Fareham	d				11 39									12 39	12 53						
Portchester	d				11 44									12 44							
Cosham	d				11 48	12 01								12 48	13 02						
Portsmouth Harbour	d	11 29								12 11	12 29								13 11	13 29	
Portsmouth & Southsea	d	11 33					11 57			12 15	12 33					12 57			13 15	13 33	
Fratton	d	11 37					12 01			12 19	12 37					13 01			13 19	13 37	
Hilsea	d						12 05									13 05					
Bedhampton	d						12 10									13 10					
Havant	d	11 46			11 55	12 10	12 14			12 28	12 46			12 55	13 10	13 14			13 28	13 46	
Warblington	d						12 16									13 16					
Emsworth	d	11 49			11 58	12 13	12 19				12 49			12 58	13 13	13 19				13 49	
Southbourne	d	11 52			12 01		12 22				12 52			13 01		13 22				13 52	
Nutbourne	d						12 24									13 24					
Bosham	d						12 27									13 27					
Fishbourne (Sussex)	d						12 30									13 30					
Chichester	a	11 59			12 08	12 21	12 33			12 38	12 59			13 08	13 21	13 33			13 38	13 59	
	d	12 00			12 09	12 22	12 34			12 39	13 00			13 09	13 22	13 34			13 39	14 00	
Barnham	a	12 07			12 16	12 30	12 41			12 46	13 07			13 16	13 30	13 41			13 46	14 07	
Bognor Regis	d		12 05	11 56				12 36	12 29			13 05	12 56				13 36	13 29			14 05
Barnham	a		12 11	12 02				12 43	12 35			13 11	13 02				13 43	13 35			14 11
Barnham	d	12 09	12 12	12 03	12 17	12 31	12 42		12 36	12 47	13 09	13 12	13 03	13 17	13 31	13 42		13 36	13 47	14 09	14 12
Ford	d		12 17	12 07		12 36	12 47		12 41			13 17	13 07		13 36	13 47		13 41			14 17
Littlehampton	a		12 23				12 53					13 23				13 53					14 23
Angmering	a	12 19				12 43					13 19				13 43					14 19	
Goring-by-Sea	a					12 47									13 47						
Durrington-on-Sea	a					12 50									13 50						
West Worthing	a					12 52									13 52						
Worthing	a	12 26				12 55					13 26				13 55					14 26	
Lancing	a	12 30				13 00					13 30				14 00					14 30	
Shoreham-by-Sea	a	12 35				13 04					13 35				14 04					14 35	
Southwick	a	12 38				13 08					13 38				14 08					14 38	
Portslade	a	12 42				13 11					13 42				14 11					14 42	
Hove	a	12 45				13 15					13 45				14 15					14 45	
Brighton	a	12 51				13 21					13 51				14 21					14 51	
Arundel	d			12 13					12 46				13 13					13 46			
Amberley	d			12 17									13 17								
Pulborough	d			12 24					12 55				13 24					13 55			
Billingshurst	d			12 31					13 02				13 31					14 02			
Christs Hospital	d			12 37									13 37								
Horsham	a			12 41	12 46				13 11	13 16			13 41	13 46				14 11	14 16		
	d			12 50					13 20				13 50					14 20			
Crawley	a			12 58					13 28				13 58					14 28			
Three Bridges	a			13 03					13 33				14 03					14 33			
	d			13 04					13 34				14 04					14 34			
Gatwick Airport	a			13 08					13 38				14 08					14 38			
East Croydon	a			13 24					13 54				14 24					14 54			
East Croydon	d																				
London Bridge	a																				
East Croydon	d			13 24					13 54				14 24					14 54			
Clapham Junction	a			13 33					14 03				14 33					15 03			
London Victoria	a			13 41					14 11				14 41					15 11			

Table T186-R

Mondays to Fridays

21 May to 7 December

Bognor Regis, Chichester, Portsmouth and Southampton - London, Gatwick Airport, Arun Valley and Brighton

		SN	SN	SN	SN	SN	SN	SN	SN	SN	SN	SN	SN	GW	SN	SN	SN	SN	SN	SN	SN	SN	SN
		1	1	1			1	1			1	1	1		1			1	1			1	1
Southampton Central	d		13 13	13 26								14 13	14 26	14 34									15 13
Swanwick	d		13 32	13 46								14 32	14 46										15 32
Fareham	d		13 39	13 53								14 39	14 53	14 56									15 39
Portchester	d		13 44									14 44											15 44
Cosham	d		13 48	14 02								14 48	15 01	15 04									15 49
Portsmouth Harbour	d							14 11	14 29										15 11	15 29			
Portsmouth & Southsea	d				13 57			14 15	14 33							14 57			15 15	15 33			
Fratton	d				14 01			14 19	14 37							15 01			15 19	15 37			
Hilsea	d				14 05											15 05							
Bedhampton	d				14 10											15 13							
Havant	d		13 55	14 10	14 14			14 28	14 46			14 55	15 09	15 12		15 16			15 28	15 46			15 55
Warblington	d				14 16											15 18							
Emsworth	d		13 58	14 13	14 19				14 49			14 58				15 21				15 49			15 59
Southbourne	d		14 01		14 22				14 52			15 01				15 24				15 52			16 02
Nutbourne	d				14 24											15 27							
Bosham	d				14 27											15 30							
Fishbourne (Sussex)	d				14 30											15 33							
Chichester	a		14 08	14 21	14 33			14 38	14 59			15 08	15 19	15 23		15 36			15 40	15 59			16 09
	d		14 09	14 22	14 34			14 39	15 00			15 09	15 19	15 27		15 36			15 40	16 00			16 09
Barnham	a		14 16	14 30	14 41			14 46	15 07			15 16	15 27	15 35		15 44			15 48	16 07			16 17
Bognor Regis	d	13 56				14 36	14 29			15 05	14 56						15 36	15 26			16 05	15 56	
Barnham	a	14 02				14 43	14 35			15 11	15 02						15 44	15 32			16 11	16 02	
Barnham	d	14 03	14 17	14 31	14 42		14 36	14 47	15 09	15 12	15 03	15 17	15 27	15 37		15 44		15 33	15 49	16 09	16 12	16 03	16 17
Ford	d	14 07		14 36	14 47		14 41			15 17	15 07		15 32			15 49		15 37			16 17	16 07	
Littlehampton	a				14 53					15 23						15 54					16 23		
Angmering	a			14 43					15 19				15 39							16 19			
Goring-by-Sea	a			14 47									15 43										
Durrington-on-Sea	a			14 50									15 45										
West Worthing	a			14 52									15 48										
Worthing	a			14 55					15 26				15 51	15 53	←					16 26			
Lancing	a			15 00					15 30				16 03		16 03					16 30			
Shoreham-by-Sea	a			15 04					15 35				→	16 00	16 07					16 35			
Southwick	a			15 08					15 38						16 10					16 38			
Portslade	a			15 11					15 42						16 14					16 42			
Hove	a			15 15					15 45					16 08	16 17					16 45			
Brighton	a			15 21					15 51					16 14	16 22					16 51			
Arundel	d	14 13					14 46				15 13							15 43				16 13	
Amberley	d	14 17									15 17											16 17	
Pulborough	d	14 24					14 55				15 24							15 53				16 24	
Billingshurst	d	14 31					15 02				15 31							16 00				16 31	
Christs Hospital	d	14 37									15 37							16 06				16 37	
Horsham	a	14 41	14 46				15 11	15 16			15 41	15 46						16 11	16 18			16 41	16 46
	d	14 50					15 20				15 50							16 22				16 50	
Crawley	a	14 58					15 28				15 58							16 30				16 58	
Three Bridges	a	15 03					15 33				16 03							16 35				17 03	
	d	15 04					15 34				16 04							16 36				17 04	
Gatwick Airport	a	15 08					15 38				16 08							16 40				17 08	
East Croydon	a	15 24					15 54				16 24							16 55				17 24	
East Croydon	d																						
London Bridge	a																						
East Croydon	d	15 24					15 54				16 24							16 56				17 24	
Clapham Junction	a	15 33					16 03				16 33							17 05				17 33	
London Victoria	a	15 41					16 11				16 41							17 12				17 41	

Table T186-R

Mondays to Fridays
21 May to 7 December

Bognor Regis, Chichester, Portsmouth and Southampton - London, Gatwick Airport, Arun Valley and Brighton

		SN ■	SN	SN		SN ■	SN ■	SN	SN	SN ■	SN ■	SN ■	SN	SN		SN ■	SN ■	SN	SN	SN ■	SN ■	SN ■	SN	SN
Southampton Central	d	15 26									16 12	16 26									17 14	17 26		
Swanwick	d	15 46									16 32	16 46									17 32	17 46		
Fareham	d	15 53									16 39	16 53									17 39	17 53		
Portchester	d										16 44										17 44			
Cosham	d	16 02									16 48	17 02									17 48	18 02		
Portsmouth Harbour	d						16 11										17 11							
Portsmouth & Southsea	d		15 57				16 15	16 33					16 57				17 15	17 33					17 57	
Fratton	d		16 01				16 19	16 37					17 01				17 19	17 37					18 02	
Hilsea	d		16 05										17 05										18 06	
Bedhampton	d		16 10										17 10										18 11	
Havant	d	16 10	16 14				16 28	16 46			16 55	17 10	17 13				17 28	17 46			17 55	18 10	18 14	
Warblington	d		16 16										17 15										18 16	
Emsworth	d	16 13	16 19					16 49			16 58	17 13	17 18					17 49			17 58	18 13	18 19	
Southbourne	d		16 22					16 52			17 01		17 21					17 52			18 01		18 22	
Nutbourne	d		16 24										17 24										18 24	
Bosham	d		16 27										17 27										18 27	
Fishbourne (Sussex)	d		16 30										17 30										18 30	
Chichester	a	16 21	16 33				16 38	16 59			17 08	17 21	17 33				17 38	17 59			18 08	18 21	18 33	
	d	16 22	16 34				16 39	17 00			17 09	17 22	17 34				17 39	18 00			18 09	18 22	18 34	
Barnham	a	16 30	16 41				16 46	17 07			17 16	17 30	17 41				17 46	18 07			18 16	18 30	18 41	
Bognor Regis	d			16 36		16 29			17 05	16 56				17 36		17 29			18 05	17 56				18 39
Barnham	a			16 44		16 35			17 11	17 02				17 43		17 35			18 11	18 02				18 46
Barnham	d	16 31	16 42			16 36	16 47	17 09	17 12	17 03	17 17	17 31	17 42			17 36	17 47	18 09	18 14	18 03	18 19	18 31	18 42	
Ford	d	16 36	16 47			16 41			17 17	17 07		17 36	17 47			17 41			18 20	18 07		18 36	18 47	
Littlehampton	a		16 53						17 23				17 53						18 25				18 53	
Angmering	a	16 43						17 19				17 43						18 19				18 43		
Goring-by-Sea	a	16 47										17 47										18 47		
Durrington-on-Sea	a	16 50										17 50										18 50		
West Worthing	a	16 52										17 52										18 52		
Worthing	a	16 55						17 26				17 55						18 26				18 55		
Lancing	a	17 00						17 30				18 00						18 30				19 00		
Shoreham-by-Sea	a	17 04						17 35				18 04						18 35				19 04		
Southwick	a	17 08						17 38				18 08						18 38				19 08		
Portslade	a	17 11						17 42				18 11						18 42				19 11		
Hove	a	17 15						17 45				18 15						18 45				19 15		
Brighton	a	17 21						17 51				18 21						18 51				19 21		
Arundel	d					16 46				17 13						17 46				18 13				
Amberley	d									17 17										18 17				
Pulborough	d					16 55				17 24						17 55				18 24				
Billingshurst	d					17 02				17 31						18 02				18 31				
Christs Hospital	d									17 37										18 37				
Horsham	a					17 11	17 16			17 41	17 46					18 11	18 16			18 41	18 48			
	d					17 20				17 50						18 20				18 52				
Crawley	a					17 28				17 58						18 28				19 00				
Three Bridges	a					17 33				18 03						18 33				19 05				
	d					17 34				18 04						18 34				19 06				
Gatwick Airport	a					17 38				18 08						18 38				19 10				
East Croydon	a					17 54				18 24						18 54				19 25				
East Croydon	d																							
London Bridge	a																							
East Croydon	d					17 54				18 24						18 54				19 26				
Clapham Junction	a					18 03				18 34						19 03				19 35				
London Victoria	a					18 11				18 42						19 11				19 42				

Table T186-R

Mondays to Fridays
21 May to 7 December

Bognor Regis, Chichester, Portsmouth and Southampton - London, Gatwick Airport, Arun Valley and Brighton

		SN ■	SN ■	SN	SN	SN ■	SN ■	SN ■	SN	SN		SN ■	SN ■	SN	SN	SN ■	SN ■	SN ■	SN	SN ■	SN ■		SN	SN
Southampton Central	d						18 13	18 26									19 12	19 26						
Swanwick	d						18 32	18 46									19 32	19 46						
Fareham	d						18 39	18 53									19 39	19 53						
Portchester	d						18 44										19 44							
Cosham	d						18 48	19 02									19 48	20 02						
Portsmouth Harbour	d												19 11								20 11			
Portsmouth & Southsea	d		18 15	18 33					18 57				19 15	19 33					19 57		20 15		20 33	
Fratton	d		18 19	18 37					19 01				19 19	19 37					20 01		20 19		20 37	
Hilsea	d								19 05										20 05					
Bedhampton	d								19 10										20 10					
Havant	d		18 28	18 47			18 55	19 10	19 13				19 28	19 46			19 55	20 10	20 13		20 28		20 46	
Warblington	d								19 15										20 15					
Emsworth	d			18 50			18 58	19 13	19 18					19 49			19 58	20 13	20 18				20 49	
Southbourne	d			18 53			19 01		19 21					19 52			20 01		20 21				20 52	
Nutbourne	d								19 24										20 24					
Bosham	d								19 27										20 27					
Fishbourne (Sussex)	d								19 30										20 30					
Chichester	a		18 38	19 00			19 08	19 21	19 33				19 38	19 59			20 08	20 21	20 33		20 38		20 59	
	d		18 39	19 01			19 09	19 22	19 34				19 39	20 00			20 09	20 22	20 34		20 39		21 00	
Barnham	a		18 46	19 08			19 16	19 30	19 41				19 46	20 07			20 16	20 30	20 41		20 46		21 07	
Bognor Regis	d	18 29			19 05	18 56				19 38		19 29			20 05	19 56				20 29				21 05
Barnham	a	18 35			19 11	19 02				19 44		19 35			20 11	20 02				20 35				21 11
Barnham	d	18 36	18 47	19 09	19 14	19 03	19 19	19 31	19 42			19 36	19 47	20 09	20 12	20 03	20 17	20 31	20 42	20 36	20 47		21 09	21 12
Ford	d	18 41			19 20	19 07		19 36	19 47			19 41			20 17	20 07		20 36	20 47	20 41				21 17
Littlehampton	a				19 25				19 53						20 23				20 53					21 23
Angmering	a			19 19				19 43						20 19				20 43					21 19	
Goring-by-Sea	a							19 47										20 47						
Durrington-on-Sea	a							19 50										20 50						
West Worthing	a							19 52										20 52						
Worthing	a			19 26				19 55						20 26				20 55					21 26	
Lancing	a			19 30				20 00						20 30				21 00					21 30	
Shoreham-by-Sea	a			19 35				20 04						20 35				21 04					21 35	
Southwick	a			19 38				20 08						20 38				21 08					21 38	
Portslade	a			19 42				20 11						20 42				21 11					21 42	
Hove	a			19 45				20 15						20 45				21 15					21 45	
Brighton	a			19 51				20 21						20 51				21 21					21 51	
Arundel	d	18 46				19 13						19 46				20 13				20 46				
Amberley	d					19 17										20 17								
Pulborough	d	18 55				19 24						19 55				20 24				20 55				
Billingshurst	d	19 02				19 31						20 02				20 31				21 02				
Christs Hospital	d					19 37										20 37								
Horsham	a	19 11	19 16			19 41	19 48					20 11	20 16			20 41	20 46			21 11	21 16			
	d	19 20				19 52						20 20				20 50				21 20				
Crawley	a	19 28				20 00						20 28				20 58				21 28				
Three Bridges	a	19 33				20 05						20 33				21 03				21 33				
	d	19 34				20 06						20 34				21 04				21 34				
Gatwick Airport	a	19 38				20 10						20 38				21 08				21 38				
East Croydon	a	19 54				20 25						20 54				21 24				21 54				
East Croydon	d																							
London Bridge	a																							
East Croydon	d	19 54				20 26						20 54				21 24				21 54				
Clapham Junction	a	20 04				20 35						21 06				21 33				22 03				
London Victoria	a	20 11				20 42						21 13				21 41				22 11				

Table T186-R

Bognor Regis, Chichester, Portsmouth and Southampton - London, Gatwick Airport, Arun Valley and Brighton

Mondays to Fridays

21 May to 7 December

		SN ■	SN ■	SN ■	SN	SN ■	SN ■	SN		SN	SN	SN	SN ■	SN	SN	SN	SN	SN ■		SN	SN
Southampton Central	d		20 13	20 26							21 13		21 32			22 21		22 33			23 12
Swanwick	d		20 32	20 46							21 33		21 50			22 40		22 51			
Fareham	d		20 39	20 54							21 40		21 57			22 47		22 57			23 38
Portchester	d		20 44								21 45		22 02			22 52					
Cosham	d		20 48	21 02							21 49		22 06			22 56		23 06			23 47
Portsmouth Harbour	d						21 11							22 15	22 40					23 16	
Portsmouth & Southsea	d				20 57		21 15	21 33						22 19	22 44					23 20	
Fratton	d				21 01		21 19	21 37						22 23	22 48					23 24	
Hilsea	d				21 05									22 27	22 52					23 28	
Bedhampton	d				21 10									22 32	22 57					23 33	
Havant	d		20 55	21 10	21 13		21 30	21 47			21 56		22 14	22 35	23 00	23 04		23 12		23 36	23 54
Warblington	d				21 15								22 16							23 38	
Emsworth	d		20 58	21 13	21 18			21 50					22 19	22 38		23 07				23 41	
Southbourne	d		21 01		21 21			21 53					22 22	22 41		23 10				23 44	
Nutbourne	d				21 24								22 24							23 46	
Bosham	d				21 27								22 27							23 49	
Fishbourne (Sussex)	d				21 30								22 30							23 52	
Chichester	a		21 08	21 21	21 33		21 40	22 00			22 06		22 33	22 48	23 10	23 17		23 22		23 56	00 05
	d		21 09	21 22	21 34		21 40	22 01			22 07		22 40	22 49	23 10	23 18		23 23		23 57	00 06
Barnham	a		21 16	21 30	21 41		21 48	22 08			22 14		22 47	22 56	23 18	23 25		23 31		00 04	00 13
Bognor Regis	d	20 55				21 29				22 05		22 36					23 20				
Barnham	a	21 02				21 35				22 12		22 43					23 27				
Barnham	d	21 03	21 17	21 31	21 42	21 36	21 48	22 09			22 16		22 48	22 58	23 19	23 26		23 32		00 06	
Ford	d	21 07		21 36	21 47	21 41					22 20		22 53	23 02	23 23	23 31				00 10	
Littlehampton	a				21 53						22 25				23 28	23 37		23 41		00 16	
Angmering	a			21 43				22 19			22 42			23 09	23 51						
Goring-by-Sea	a			21 47							22 46			23 13	23 55						
Durrington-on-Sea	a			21 50							22 49			23 16	23 57						
West Worthing	a			21 52							22 51			23 18	23 59						
Worthing	a			21 55				22 26			22 54			23 21	00 02						
Lancing	a			22 00				22 30			23 00			23 27	00 08						
Shoreham-by-Sea	a			22 04				22 35			23 04			23 31	00 12						
Southwick	a			22 08				22 38			23 07			23 35	00 16						
Portslade	a			22 11				22 42			23 11			23 39	00 20						
Hove	a			22 15				22 46			23 15			23 44	00 25						
Brighton	a			22 21				22 51			23 20			23 49	00 30						
Arundel	d	21 13				21 46							22 58								
Amberley	d	21 17											23 03								
Pulborough	d	21 24				21 55							23 09								
Billingshurst	d	21 31				22 02							23 16								
Christs Hospital	d	21 37											23 22								
Horsham	a	21 41	21 46			22 11	22 16						23 26								
	d	21 50				22 20							23 27								
Crawley	a	21 58				22 28							23 35								
Three Bridges	a	22 03				22 33							23 40								
	d	22 04				22 34															
Gatwick Airport	a	22 08				22 38															
East Croydon	a	22 24				22 54															
East Croydon	d																				
London Bridge	a																				
East Croydon	d	22 24				22 54															
Clapham Junction	a	22 33				23 03															
London Victoria	a	22 42				23 11															

Table T186-R

Bognor Regis, Chichester, Portsmouth and Southampton - London, Gatwick Airport, Arun Valley and Brighton

Saturdays

26 May to 8 December

		SN ■	SN	SN ■	SN	SN ■	SN	SN ■	SN	SN		SN ■	SN ■	SN	SN	SN ■	SN ■	GW	SN ■	SN		SN	SN ■	SN ■	SN
Southampton Central	d																06 13		06 26						
Swanwick	d																06 32		06 43						
Fareham	d																06 39		06 51						
Portchester	d																06 44								
Cosham	d																06 48		07 00						
Portsmouth Harbour	d												06 11	06 29				06 50						07 11	07 29
Portsmouth & Southsea	d			04 55					05 57				06 15	06 33				06 54		06 57				07 15	07 33
Fratton	d			04 59					06 01				06 19	06 37				06 58		07 01				07 19	07 37
Hilsea	d								06 05											07 05					
Bedhampton	d								06 10											07 11					
Havant	d			05 07		05 50			06 13				06 28	06 46			06 55	07 08	07 11	07 14				07 28	07 46
Warblington	d								06 15											07 16					
Emsworth	d					05 53			06 18					06 49			06 58		07 14	07 19					07 49
Southbourne	d					05 56			06 21					06 52			07 01			07 22					07 52
Nutbourne	d								06 24											07 25					
Bosham	d								06 27											07 28					
Fishbourne (Sussex)	d								06 30											07 31					
Chichester	a			05 18		06 03			06 33				06 38	06 59			07 08	07 18	07 23	07 34				07 38	07 59
	d			05 18		06 04		06 23	06 34				06 39	07 00			07 09	07 19	07 24	07 34				07 39	08 00
Barnham	a			05 26		06 11		06 30	06 41				06 46	07 07			07 16	07 27	07 32	07 42				07 46	08 07
Bognor Regis	d		05 05		05 37		06 00			06 36		06 29			07 05	06 56						07 36	07 29		
Barnham	a		05 11		05 43		06 06			06 43		06 35			07 11	07 02						07 43	07 35		
Barnham	d	04 48	05 12	05 26	05 45	06 12	06 16	06 31	06 42			06 36	06 47	07 08	07 12	07 03	07 17	07 27	07 32	07 42			07 36	07 47	08 09
Ford	d	04 53	05 17		05 50	06 16	06 20	06 36	06 47			06 41			07 17	07 07			07 37	07 47			07 41		
Littlehampton	a	04 58	05 23				06 26		06 53						07 23					07 53					
Angmering	a	05 13			05 57			06 43						07 18					07 44						08 19
Goring-by-Sea	a	05 18			06 01			06 47											07 48						
Durrington-on-Sea	a	05 20			06 03			06 50											07 51						
West Worthing	a	05 23			06 06			06 52											07 53						
Worthing	a	05 25		05 42	06 08			06 55						07 26				07 49	07 56						08 26
Lancing	a	05 30			06 14			07 00						07 30					08 01						08 30
Shoreham-by-Sea	a	05 35			06 19			07 04						07 35				08 00	08 05						08 35
Southwick	a	05 38			06 22			07 08						07 38					08 09						08 38
Portslade	a	05 42			06 26			07 11						07 42					08 12						08 42
Hove	a	05 45		05 54	06 31			07 15						07 45				08 12	08 16						08 45
Brighton	a	05 50			06 36			07 21						07 51				08 17	08 24						08 51
Arundel	d					06 22						06 46				07 13							07 46		
Amberley	d					06 26										07 17									
Pulborough	d					06 32						06 55				07 24							07 55		
Billingshurst	d					06 39						07 02				07 31							08 02		
Christs Hospital	d					06 45										07 37									
Horsham	a					06 49						07 11	07 16			07 41	07 46						08 11	08 16	
	d					06 50						07 20				07 50							08 20		
Crawley	a					06 58						07 28				07 58							08 28		
Three Bridges	a					07 03						07 33				08 03							08 33		
	d					07 04						07 34				08 04							08 34		
Gatwick Airport	a			06 26		07 08						07 38				08 08							08 38		
East Croydon	a			06 41		07 24						07 54				08 24							08 54		
East Croydon	d																								
London Bridge	a																								
East Croydon	d			06 42		07 24						07 54				08 24							08 54		
Clapham Junction	a			06 51		07 33						08 03				08 33							09 03		
London Victoria	a			06 59		07 41						08 11				08 41							09 11		

Table T186-R

Saturdays

26 May to 8 December

Bognor Regis, Chichester, Portsmouth and Southampton - London, Gatwick Airport, Arun Valley and Brighton

		SN	SN ■	SN ■	SN ■	SN		SN	SN ■	SN ■	SN	SN	SN ■	SN ■	SN ■	SN	SN	SN ■	SN ■	SN	SN
Southampton Central	d			07 13	07 26									08 13	08 27						
Swanwick	d			07 32	07 46									08 32	08 46						
Fareham	d			07 39	07 53									08 39	08 53						
Portchester	d			07 44										08 44							
Cosham	d			07 48	08 02									08 48	09 02						
Portsmouth Harbour	d									08 11	08 29								09 11	09 29	
Portsmouth & Southsea	d					07 57				08 15	08 33					08 57			09 15	09 33	
Fratton	d					08 01				08 19	08 37					09 01			09 19	09 37	
Hilsea	d					08 05										09 05					
Bedhampton	d					08 10										09 10					
Havant	d			07 55	08 10	08 13				08 28	08 46			08 55	09 10	09 13			09 28	09 46	
Warblington	d					08 15										09 15					
Emsworth	d			07 58	08 13	08 18					08 49			08 58	09 13	09 18				09 49	
Southbourne	d			08 01		08 21					08 52			09 01		09 21				09 52	
Nutbourne	d					08 24										09 24					
Bosham	d					08 27										09 27					
Fishbourne (Sussex)	d					08 30										09 30					
Chichester	a			08 08	08 21	08 33				08 38	08 59			09 08	09 21	09 33			09 38	09 59	
	d			08 09	08 22	08 34				08 39	09 00			09 09	09 22	09 34			09 39	10 00	
Barnham	a			08 16	08 30	08 41				08 46	09 07			09 16	09 30	09 41			09 46	10 07	
Bognor Regis	d	08 05	07 56					08 36	08 29			09 05	08 56				09 36	09 29			10 05
Barnham	a	08 11	08 02					08 43	08 35			09 11	09 02				09 43	09 35			10 11
Barnham	d	08 12	08 03	08 17	08 31	08 42			08 36	08 47	09 09	09 12	09 03	09 17	09 31	09 42		09 36	09 47	10 09	10 12
Ford	d	08 17	08 07		08 36	08 47			08 41			09 17	09 07		09 36	09 47		09 41			10 17
Littlehampton	a	08 23				08 53						09 23				09 53					10 23
Angmering	a				08 43						09 19				09 43					10 19	
Goring-by-Sea	a				08 47										09 47						
Durrington-on-Sea	a				08 50										09 50						
West Worthing	a				08 52										09 52						
Worthing	a				08 55						09 26				09 55					10 26	
Lancing	a				09 00						09 30				10 00					10 30	
Shoreham-by-Sea	a				09 04						09 35				10 04					10 35	
Southwick	a				09 08						09 38				10 08					10 38	
Portslade	a				09 11						09 42				10 11					10 42	
Hove	a				09 15						09 45				10 15					10 45	
Brighton	a				09 21						09 51				10 21					10 51	
Arundel	d		08 13						08 46				09 13					09 46			
Amberley	d		08 17										09 17								
Pulborough	d		08 24						08 55				09 24					09 55			
Billingshurst	d		08 31						09 02				09 31					10 02			
Christs Hospital	d		08 37										09 37								
Horsham	a		08 41	08 46					09 11	09 16			09 41	09 46				10 11	10 16		
	d		08 50						09 20				09 50					10 20			
Crawley	a		08 58						09 28				09 58					10 28			
Three Bridges	a		09 03						09 33				10 03					10 33			
	d		09 04						09 34				10 04					10 34			
Gatwick Airport	a		09 08						09 38				10 08					10 38			
East Croydon	a		09 24						09 54				10 24					10 54			
East Croydon	d																				
London Bridge	a																				
East Croydon	d		09 24						09 54				10 24					10 54			
Clapham Junction	a		09 33						10 03				10 33					11 03			
London Victoria	a		09 41						10 11				10 41					11 11			

Table T186-R

Saturdays

26 May to 8 December

Bognor Regis, Chichester, Portsmouth and Southampton - London, Gatwick Airport, Arun Valley and Brighton

		SN ■	SN ■	SN ■		SN	SN	SN ■	SN ■	SN	SN	SN ■	SN ■	SN ■		SN	SN	SN ■	SN ■	SN	SN	SN ■	SN ■	SN ■
Southampton Central	d		09 13	09 26									13 13	13 26									14 13	14 26
Swanwick	d		09 32	09 46									13 32	13 46									14 32	
Fareham	d		09 39	09 53									13 39	13 53									14 39	15 00
Portchester	d		09 44										13 44										14 44	→
Cosham	d		09 48	10 02									13 48	14 02									14 48	
Portsmouth Harbour	d								13 11	13 29									14 11	14 29				
Portsmouth & Southsea	d					12 57			13 15	13 33						13 57			14 15	14 33				
Fratton	d					13 01			13 19	13 37						14 01			14 19	14 37				
Hilsea	d					13 05										14 05								
Bedhampton	d					13 10										14 10								
Havant	d		09 55	10 10		13 13			13 28	13 46			13 55	14 10		14 13			14 28	14 46			14 55	
Warblington	d					13 15										14 15								
Emsworth	d		09 58	10 13		13 18				13 49			13 58	14 13		14 18				14 49			14 58	
Southbourne	d		10 01			13 21				13 52			14 01			14 21				14 52			15 01	
Nutbourne	d					13 24										14 24								
Bosham	d					13 27										14 27								
Fishbourne (Sussex)	d					13 30										14 30								
Chichester	a		10 08	10 21		13 33			13 38	13 59			14 08	14 21		14 33			14 38	14 59			15 08	
	d		10 09	10 22		13 34			13 39	14 00			14 09	14 22		14 34			14 39	15 00			15 09	
Barnham	a		10 16	10 30		13 41			13 46	14 07			14 16	14 30		14 41			14 46	15 07			15 16	
Bognor Regis	d	09 56					13 36	13 29			14 05	13 56					14 36	14 29			15 05	14 56		
Barnham	a	10 02					13 43	13 35			14 11	14 02					14 43	14 35			15 11	15 02		
Barnham	d	10 03	10 17	10 31	and at	13 42		13 36	13 47	14 09	14 12	14 03	14 17	14 31		14 42		14 36	14 47	15 09	15 12	15 03	15 17	
Ford	d	10 07		10 36	the same	13 47		13 41			14 17	14 07		14 36		14 47		14 41			15 17	15 07		
Littlehampton	a				minutes	13 53					14 23					14 53					15 23			
Angmering	a			10 43	past					14 19				14 43						15 19				
Goring-by-Sea	a			10 47	each									14 47										
Durrington-on-Sea	a			10 50	hour until									14 50										
West Worthing	a			10 52										14 52										
Worthing	a			10 55						14 26				14 55						15 26				
Lancing	a			11 00						14 30				15 00						15 30				
Shoreham-by-Sea	a			11 04						14 35				15 04						15 35				
Southwick	a			11 08						14 38				15 08						15 38				
Portslade	a			11 11						14 42				15 11						15 42				
Hove	a			11 15						14 45				15 15						15 45				
Brighton	a			11 21						14 51				15 21						15 51				
Arundel	d	10 13						13 46				14 13						14 46				15 13		
Amberley	d	10 17										14 17										15 17		
Pulborough	d	10 24						13 55				14 24						14 55				15 24		
Billingshurst	d	10 31						14 02				14 31						15 02				15 31		
Christs Hospital	d	10 37										14 37										15 37		
Horsham	a	10 41	10 46					14 11	14 16			14 41	14 46					15 11	15 16			15 41	15 46	
	d	10 50						14 20				14 50						15 20				15 50		
Crawley	a	10 58						14 28				14 58						15 28				15 58		
Three Bridges	a	11 03						14 33				15 03						15 33				16 03		
	d	11 04						14 34				15 04						15 34				16 04		
Gatwick Airport	a	11 08						14 38				15 08						15 38				16 08		
East Croydon	a	11 24						14 54				15 24						15 54				16 24		
East Croydon	d																							
London Bridge	a																							
East Croydon	d	11 24						14 54				15 24						15 54				16 24		
Clapham Junction	a	11 33						15 03				15 33						16 03				16 33		
London Victoria	a	11 41						15 11				15 41						16 11				16 41		

Bognor Regis, Chichester, Portsmouth and Southampton - London, Gatwick Airport, Arun Valley and Brighton

		GW	SN	SN	SN	SN	SN	SN	SN	SN	SN	SN	SN	SN	SN	SN		SN	SN
		R	■			■	■			■	■	■			■	■			
Southampton Central	d	14 34									15 13	15 26							
Swanwick	d		←								15 32	15 46							
Fareham	d	14 56	15 00								15 39	15 53							
Portchester	d										15 44								
Cosham	d	15 04									15 48	16 02							
Portsmouth Harbour	d						15 11	15 29								16 11		19 29	
Portsmouth & Southsea	d				14 57		15 15	15 33					15 57			16 15		19 33	
Fratton	d				15 01		15 19	15 37					16 01			16 19		19 37	
Hilsea	d				15 08								16 05						
Bedhampton	d				15 14								16 10						
Havant	d	15 10	15 14		15 17		15 28	15 46			15 55	16 10	16 13			16 28		19 46	
Warblington	d				15 19								16 15						
Emsworth	d				15 22			15 49			15 58	16 13	16 18					19 49	
Southbourne	d				15 25			15 52			16 01		16 21					19 52	
Nutbourne	d				15 27								16 24						
Bosham	d				15 30								16 27						
Fishbourne (Sussex)	d				15 33								16 30						
Chichester	a	15 21	15 24		15 36		15 40	15 59			16 08	16 21	16 33			16 38		19 59	
	d	15 21	15 25		15 37		15 40	16 00			16 09	16 22	16 34			16 39		20 00	
Barnham	a	15 29	15 33		15 44		15 48	16 07			16 16	16 30	16 41			16 46		20 07	
Bognor Regis	d			15 36		15 29			16 05	15 56				16 36	16 29				20 05
Barnham	a			15 43		15 37			16 11	16 02				16 43	16 35		and at		20 11
Barnham	d	15 29	15 33		15 45	15 37	15 49	16 09	16 12	16 03	16 17	16 31	16 42		16 36	16 47	the same	20 09	20 12
Ford	d		15 38		15 49	15 42			16 17	16 07		16 36	16 47		16 41		minutes		20 17
Littlehampton	a				15 55				16 23				16 53				past		20 23
Angmering	a		15 45					16 19				16 43					each	20 19	
Goring-by-Sea	a		15 49									16 47					hour until		
Durrington-on-Sea	a		15 52									16 50							
West Worthing	a		15 54									16 52							
Worthing	a	15 51	15 57					16 26				16 55						20 26	
Lancing	a		16 01					16 30				17 00						20 30	
Shoreham-by-Sea	a	16 00	16 05					16 35				17 04						20 35	
Southwick	a		16 09					16 38				17 08						20 38	
Portslade	a		16 12					16 42				17 11						20 42	
Hove	a	16 12	16 15					16 45				17 15						20 45	
Brighton	a	16 18	16 24					16 51				17 21						20 51	
Arundel	d					15 47				16 13					16 46				
Amberley	d									16 17									
Pulborough	d					15 56				16 24					16 55				
Billingshurst	d					16 03				16 31					17 02				
Christs Hospital	d									16 37									
Horsham	a					16 12	16 18			16 41	16 46				17 11	17 16			
	d					16 22				16 50					17 20				
Crawley	a					16 30				16 58					17 28				
Three Bridges	a					16 35				17 03					17 33				
	d					16 36				17 04					17 34				
Gatwick Airport	a					16 40				17 08					17 38				
East Croydon	a					16 55				17 24					17 54				
East Croydon	d																		
London Bridge	a																		
East Croydon	d					16 56				17 24					17 54				
Clapham Junction	a					17 05				17 33					18 03				
London Victoria	a					17 12				17 41					18 11				

Table T186-R

Saturdays
26 May to 8 December

Bognor Regis, Chichester, Portsmouth and Southampton - London, Gatwick Airport, Arun Valley and Brighton

		SN	SN	SN	SN	SN	SN	SN	SN	SN	SN	SN	SN	SN	SN	SN	SN	SN	SN	SN	SN	SN	SN
		■	■	■			■	■			■	■	■			■	■					■	
Southampton Central	d		19 13	19 26								20 13	20 26						21 13			21 32	
Swanwick	d		19 32	19 46								20 32	20 46						21 33			21 51	
Fareham	d		19 39	19 53								20 39	20 53						21 40			21 58	
Portchester	d		19 44									20 44							21 45			22 03	
Cosham	d		19 48	20 02								20 48	21 02						21 49			22 07	
Portsmouth Harbour	d							20 11	20 29								21 11			21 40			22 15
Portsmouth & Southsea	d				19 57			20 15	20 33					20 57			21 15			21 44			22 19
Fratton	d				20 01			20 19	20 37					21 01			21 19			21 48			22 23
Hilsea	d				20 05									21 05						21 52			22 27
Bedhampton	d				20 10									21 10						21 57			22 32
Havant	d		19 55	20 10	20 13			20 28	20 46			20 55	21 10	21 13			21 28		21 56	22 00		22 14	22 35
Warblington	d				20 15									21 15								22 16	
Emsworth	d		19 58	20 13	20 18				20 49			20 58	21 13	21 18								22 19	22 39
Southbourne	d		20 01		20 21				20 52			21 01		21 21								22 22	22 42
Nutbourne	d				20 24									21 24								22 24	
Bosham	d				20 27									21 27								22 27	
Fishbourne (Sussex)	d				20 30									21 30								22 30	
Chichester	a		20 08	20 21	20 33			20 38	20 59			21 08	21 21	21 33			21 38		22 06	22 10		22 33	22 49
	d		20 09	20 22	20 34			20 39	21 00			21 09	21 22	21 34			21 39		22 07	22 12		22 40	22 52
Barnham	a		20 16	20 30	20 41			20 46	21 07			21 16	21 30	21 41			21 46		22 14	22 19		22 47	22 59
Bognor Regis	d	19 56				20 36	20 29			21 05	20 56				21 36	21 29		22 05			22 35		
Barnham	a	20 02				20 43	20 35			21 11	21 02				21 43	21 35		22 11			22 41		
Barnham	d	20 03	20 17	20 31	20 42		20 36	20 47	21 09	21 12	21 03	21 17	21 31	21 42		21 36	21 47		22 16	22 20	22 42	22 48	23 00
Ford	d	20 07		20 36	20 47		20 41			21 17	21 07		21 36	21 47		21 41			22 20	22 24	22 46	22 53	23 04
Littlehampton	a				20 53					21 23				21 53					22 25	22 29	22 51		
Angmering	a			20 43					21 19				21 43						22 42				23 11
Goring-by-Sea	a			20 47									21 47						22 46				23 15
Durrington-on-Sea	a			20 50									21 50						22 49				23 18
West Worthing	a			20 52									21 52						22 51				23 20
Worthing	a			20 55					21 26				21 55						22 54				23 23
Lancing	a			21 00					21 30				22 00						23 00				23 27
Shoreham-by-Sea	a			21 04					21 35				22 04						23 04				23 31
Southwick	a			21 08					21 38				22 08						23 07				23 35
Portslade	a			21 11					21 42				22 11						23 11				23 39
Hove	a			21 15					21 45				22 15						23 15				23 43
Brighton	a			21 21					21 51				22 21						23 20				23 49
Arundel	d	20 13					20 46				21 13					21 46						22 58	
Amberley	d	20 17									21 17											23 03	
Pulborough	d	20 24					20 55				21 24					21 55						23 09	
Billingshurst	d	20 31					21 02				21 31					22 02						23 16	
Christs Hospital	d	20 37									21 37											23 22	
Horsham	a	20 41	20 46				21 11	21 16			21 41	21 46				22 11	22 16					23 26	
	d	20 50					21 20				21 50					22 20						23 27	
Crawley	a	20 58					21 28				21 58					22 28						23 35	
Three Bridges	a	21 03					21 33				22 03					22 33						23 40	
	d	21 04					21 34				22 04					22 34							
Gatwick Airport	a	21 08					21 38				22 08					22 38							
East Croydon	a	21 24					21 54				22 24					22 54							
East Croydon	d																						
London Bridge	a																						
East Croydon	d	21 24					21 54				22 24					22 54							
Clapham Junction	a	21 33					22 03				22 33					23 04							
London Victoria	a	21 41					22 11				22 41					23 11							

Table T186-R

Saturdays
26 May to 8 December

Bognor Regis, Chichester, Portsmouth and Southampton - London, Gatwick Airport, Arun Valley and Brighton

		SN	SN	SN	SN [1]	SN	SN
Southampton Central	d			22 21	22 26		23 16
Swanwick	d			22 40	22 46		
Fareham	d			22 47	22 53		23 38
Portchester	d			22 52			
Cosham	d			22 56	23 02		23 47
Portsmouth Harbour	d	22 40				23 15	
Portsmouth & Southsea	d	22 44				23 19	
Fratton	d	22 48				23 23	
Hilsea	d	22 52				23 27	
Bedhampton	d	22 57				23 32	
Havant	d	23 00		23 04	23 10	23 35	23 54
Warblington	d					23 37	
Emsworth	d			23 07	23 13	23 40	
Southbourne	d			23 10		23 43	
Nutbourne	d					23 45	
Bosham	d					23 48	
Fishbourne (Sussex)	d					23 51	
Chichester	a	23 10		23 17	23 21	23 55	00 05
	d	23 10		23 18	23 22	23 56	00 06
Barnham	a	23 18		23 25	23 30	00 03	00 13
Bognor Regis	d		23 15				
Barnham	a		23 21				
Barnham	d	23 19		23 26	23 31	00 05	00 14
Ford	d	23 23		23 31	23 36	00 10	00 18
Littlehampton	a	23 28		23 37	23 41	00 16	00 24
Angmering	a	23 51					
Goring-by-Sea	a	23 55					
Durrington-on-Sea	a	23 57					
West Worthing	a	23 59					
Worthing	a	00 02					
Lancing	a	00 09					
Shoreham-by-Sea	a	00 13					
Southwick	a	00 16					
Portslade	a	00 20					
Hove	a	00 25					
Brighton	a	00 30					
Arundel	d						
Amberley	d						
Pulborough	d						
Billingshurst	d						
Christs Hospital	d						
Horsham	a						
	d						
Crawley	a						
Three Bridges	a						
	d						
Gatwick Airport	a						
East Croydon	a						
East Croydon	d						
London Bridge	a						
East Croydon	d						
Clapham Junction	a						
London Victoria	a						

Table T186-R

Sundays
20 May to 2 December

Bognor Regis, Chichester, Portsmouth and Southampton - London, Gatwick Airport, Arun Valley and Brighton

		SN	SN	SN	SN	SN	SN	SN	SN	SN	SN	SN	SN	GW	SN	SN	SN	SN	SN	SN	SN	SN	SN
Southampton Central	d							07 30					08 21	08 31						09 30			
Swanwick	d							07 47					08 40							09 47			
Fareham	d							07 54					08 47	08 54						09 54			
Portchester	d																						
Cosham	d							08 03					08 56	09 02						10 03			
Portsmouth Harbour	d					07 14			08 01		08 14				09 01		09 14				10 01		10 14
Portsmouth & Southsea	d					07 18			08 05		08 18				09 05		09 18				10 05		10 18
Fratton	d					07 22			08 09		08 22				09 09		09 22				10 09		10 22
Hilsea	d																						
Bedhampton	d					07 30					08 30						09 30						10 30
Havant	d			07 11		07 33		08 10	08 18		08 33		09 02	09 13	09 18		09 33			10 10	10 18		10 33
Warblington	d					07 35					08 35						09 35						10 35
Emsworth	d			07 15		07 38		08 14	08 21		08 38		09 06		09 21		09 38			10 14	10 21		10 38
Southbourne	d			07 18		07 41			08 24		08 41				09 24		09 41				10 24		10 41
Nutbourne	d					07 44					08 44						09 44						10 44
Bosham	d					07 47					08 47						09 47						10 47
Fishbourne (Sussex)	d					07 50					08 50						09 50						10 50
Chichester	a			07 25		07 53		08 22	08 31		08 53		09 14	09 24	09 31		09 53			10 22	10 31		10 53
	d			07 26		07 53		08 22	08 32		08 53		09 14	09 24	09 32		09 53			10 22	10 32		10 53
Barnham	a			07 35		08 01		08 30	08 40		09 01		09 22	09 32	09 40		10 01			10 30	10 40		11 01
Bognor Regis	d		07 00		07 26		08 00			08 31		09 00				09 31		10 00	10 06			10 31	
Barnham	a		07 06		07 32		08 06			08 37		09 06				09 37		10 06	10 13			10 37	
Barnham	d	06 10	07 07	07 39		08 02	08 07	08 31	08 44		09 02	09 07	09 23	09 32	09 44		10 02	10 07		10 31	10 44		11 02
Ford	d	06 14	07 11	07 43		08 06	08 11	08 35	08 48		09 06	09 11	09 27		09 48		10 06	10 11		10 35	10 48		11 06
Littlehampton	a	06 19	07 16				08 16					09 16						10 16					
Angmering	a					08 13		08 42			09 13		09 34				10 13			10 42			11 13
Goring-by-Sea	a					08 18		08 47			09 18		09 39				10 18			10 47			11 18
Durrington-on-Sea	a					08 20		08 49			09 20		09 41				10 20			10 49			11 20
West Worthing	a					08 23		08 52			09 23		09 44				10 23			10 52			11 23
Worthing	a	06 37				08 25		08 54			09 25		09 46	09 58			10 25			10 54			11 25
Lancing	a	06 42				08 31		09 00			09 31		10 00				10 31			11 00			11 31
Shoreham-by-Sea	a	06 46				08 35		09 04			09 35		10 04	10 08			10 35			11 04			11 35
Southwick	a	06 49				08 39		09 08			09 39		10 08				10 39			11 08			11 39
Portslade	a	06 53				08 43		09 12			09 43		10 12				10 43			11 12			11 43
Hove	a	06 56				08 47		09 16			09 47		10 16	10 22			10 47			11 16			11 47
Brighton	a	07 00				08 52		09 22			09 52		10 22	10 26			10 52			11 22			11 52
Arundel	d			07 49					08 54						09 54						10 54		
Amberley	d			07 53					08 58						09 58						10 58		
Pulborough	d			08 00					09 05						10 05						11 05		
Billingshurst	d			08 07					09 12						10 12						11 12		
Christs Hospital	d			08 13					09 18						10 18						11 18		
Horsham	a			08 17					09 22						10 22						11 22		
	d			08 18					09 22						10 22						11 22		
Crawley	a			08 26					09 31						10 31						11 31		
Three Bridges	a			08 30					09 35						10 35						11 35		
	d			08 31					09 35						10 35						11 35		
Gatwick Airport	a			08 35					09 40						10 40						11 40		
East Croydon	a			08 58					10 03						11 03						12 03		
East Croydon	d																						
London Bridge	a																						
East Croydon	d			08 59					10 04						11 04						12 04		
Clapham Junction	a			09 08					10 14						11 14						12 14		
London Victoria	a			09 15					10 21						11 21						12 21		

Table T186-R

Sundays
20 May to 2 December

Bognor Regis, Chichester, Portsmouth and Southampton - London, Gatwick Airport, Arun Valley and Brighton

		SN	SN	SN	SN	SN	SN	SN	SN	SN	SN	SN	SN	SN	SN	SN	SN	GW	SN	SN	SN	SN	SN
																		◇					
Southampton Central	d			10 30					11 30					12 30				13 04			13 30		
Swanwick	d			10 47					11 47					12 47							13 47		
Fareham	d			10 54					11 54					12 54				13 30			13 54		
Portchester	d																						
Cosham	d			11 03					12 03					13 03				13 38			14 03		
Portsmouth Harbour	d				11 01		11 14			12 01		12 13			13 01		13 14					14 01	
Portsmouth & Southsea	d				11 05		11 18			12 05		12 17			13 05		13 18					14 05	
Fratton	d				11 09		11 22			12 09		12 21			13 09		13 22					14 09	
Hilsea	d																						
Bedhampton	d						11 30					12 29					13 30						
Havant	d			11 10	11 18		11 33		12 10	12 18		12 33		13 10	13 18		13 33	13 46			14 10	14 18	
Warblington	d						11 35					12 35					13 35						
Emsworth	d			11 14	11 21		11 38		12 14	12 21		12 38		13 14	13 21		13 38				14 14	14 21	
Southbourne	d				11 24		11 41			12 24		12 41			13 24		13 41					14 24	
Nutbourne	d						11 44					12 44					13 44						
Bosham	d						11 47					12 47					13 47						
Fishbourne (Sussex)	d						11 50					12 50					13 50						
Chichester	a			11 22	11 31		11 53		12 22	12 31		12 53		13 22	13 31		13 53	13 57			14 22	14 31	
	d			11 22	11 32		11 53		12 22	12 32		12 53		13 22	13 32		13 53	13 58			14 22	14 32	
Barnham	a			11 30	11 40		12 01		12 30	12 40		13 01		13 30	13 40		14 01	14 08			14 30	14 40	
Bognor Regis	d	11 00	11 06			11 31		12 00			12 31		13 00			13 31				14 00			14 31
Barnham	a	11 06	11 13			11 37		12 06			12 37		13 06			13 37				14 12			14 37
Barnham	d	11 07		11 31	11 44		12 02	12 07	12 31	12 44		13 02	13 07	13 31	13 44		14 02	14 08		14 12	14 31	14 44	
Ford	d	11 11		11 35	11 48		12 06	12 11	12 35	12 48		13 06	13 11	13 35	13 48		14 06			14 20	14 35	14 48	
Littlehampton	a	11 16						12 16					13 16							14 25			
Angmering	a			11 42			12 13		12 42			13 13		13 42			14 13				14 42		
Goring-by-Sea	a			11 47			12 18		12 47			13 18		13 47			14 18				14 47		
Durrington-on-Sea	a			11 49			12 20		12 49			13 20		13 49			14 20				14 49		
West Worthing	a			11 52			12 23		12 52			13 23		13 52			14 23				14 52		
Worthing	a			11 54			12 25		12 54			13 25		13 54			14 25	14 26	←		14 54		
Lancing	a			12 00			12 31		13 00			13 31		14 00			14 44		14 44		15 00		
Shoreham-by-Sea	a			12 04			12 35		13 04			13 35		14 04			→	14 35	14 48		15 04		
Southwick	a			12 08			12 39		13 08			13 39		14 08					14 52		15 08		
Portslade	a			12 12			12 43		13 12			13 43		14 12					14 56		15 12		
Hove	a			12 16			12 47		13 16			13 47		14 16				14 47	15 00		15 16		
Brighton	a			12 22			12 52		13 22			13 52		14 22				14 53	15 05		15 22		
Arundel	d				11 54					12 54					13 54							14 54	
Amberley	d				11 58					12 58					13 58							14 58	
Pulborough	d				12 05					13 05					14 04							15 05	
Billingshurst	d				12 12					13 12					14 11							15 12	
Christs Hospital	d				12 18					13 18					14 17							15 18	
Horsham	a				12 22					13 22					14 21							15 22	
	d				12 22					13 22					14 21							15 22	
Crawley	a				12 31					13 31					14 30							15 31	
Three Bridges	a				12 35					13 35					14 35							15 35	
	d				12 35					13 35					14 35							15 35	
Gatwick Airport	a				12 40					13 40					14 40							15 40	
East Croydon	a				13 06					14 03					15 03							16 06	
East Croydon	d																						
London Bridge	a																						
East Croydon	d				13 06					14 04					15 04							16 06	
Clapham Junction	a				13 16					14 14					15 14							16 16	
London Victoria	a				13 23					14 21					15 21							16 23	

Table T186-R

Sundays
20 May to 2 December

Bognor Regis, Chichester, Portsmouth and Southampton - London, Gatwick Airport, Arun Valley and Brighton

		SN	SN	SN	SN	SN	SN	GW	SN	SN	SN	SN	SN	SN	SN	SN	SN	SN	SN	SN	SN	SN	SN
								◇															
Southampton Central	d			14 30				15 06			15 30					16 30					17 30		
Swanwick	d			14 47							15 47					16 47					17 47		
Fareham	d			14 54				15 28			15 54					16 54					17 54		
Portchester	d																						
Cosham	d			15 03				15 36			16 03					17 03					18 03		
Portsmouth Harbour	d	14 14			15 01		15 14					16 01		16 14			17 01					18 01	
Portsmouth & Southsea	d	14 18			15 05		15 18					16 05		16 18			17 05					18 05	
Fratton	d	14 22			15 09		15 22					16 09		16 22			17 09		17 22			18 09	
Hilsea	d																						
Bedhampton	d	14 30					15 30							16 30					17 30				
Havant	d	14 33		15 10	15 18		15 33	15 43			16 10	16 18		16 33		17 10	17 18		17 33		18 10	18 18	
Warblington	d	14 35					15 35							16 35					17 35				
Emsworth	d	14 38		15 14	15 21		15 38				16 14	16 21		16 38		17 14	17 21		17 38		18 14	18 21	
Southbourne	d	14 41			15 24		15 41					16 24		16 41			17 24		17 41			18 24	
Nutbourne	d	14 44					15 44							16 44					17 44				
Bosham	d	14 47					15 47							16 47					17 47				
Fishbourne (Sussex)	d	14 50					15 50							16 50					17 50				
Chichester	a	14 53		15 22	15 31		15 53	15 53		←	16 22	16 31		16 53		17 22	17 31		17 53		18 22	18 31	
	d	14 53		15 22	15 32		15 53	15 54			16 22	16 32		16 53		17 22	17 32		17 53		18 22	18 32	
Barnham	a	15 01		15 30	15 40		16 01	16 01		16 01	16 30	16 40		17 01		17 30	17 40		18 01		18 30	18 40	
Bognor Regis	d		15 00			15 31	→		16 02				16 31		17 00			17 31		18 00			18 31
Barnham	a		15 06			15 37			16 09				16 37		17 06			17 37		18 06			18 37
Barnham	d	15 02	15 07	15 31	15 44			16 02	16 09	16 14	16 31	16 44		17 02	17 07	17 31	17 44		18 02	18 07	18 31	18 44	
Ford	d	15 06	15 11	15 35	15 48				16 14	16 18	16 35	16 48		17 06	17 11	17 35	17 48		18 06	18 11	18 35	18 48	
Littlehampton	a		15 16						16 19						17 16					18 16			
Angmering	a	15 13		15 42						16 27	16 42			17 13		17 42			18 13		18 42		
Goring-by-Sea	a	15 18		15 47						16 31	16 47			17 18		17 47			18 18		18 47		
Durrington-on-Sea	a	15 20		15 49						16 33	16 49			17 20		17 49			18 20		18 49		
West Worthing	a	15 23		15 52						16 36	16 52			17 23		17 52			18 23		18 52		
Worthing	a	15 25		15 54				16 19		16 38	16 54			17 25		17 54			18 25		18 54		
Lancing	a	15 31		16 00						16 44	17 00			17 31		18 00			18 31		19 00		
Shoreham-by-Sea	a	15 35		16 04				16 29		16 48	17 04			17 35		18 04			18 35		19 04		
Southwick	a	15 39		16 08						16 51	17 08			17 39		18 08			18 39		19 08		
Portslade	a	15 43		16 12						16 55	17 12			17 43		18 12			18 43		19 12		
Hove	a	15 47		16 16				16 40		17 00	17 16			17 47		18 16			18 47		19 16		
Brighton	a	15 53		16 22				16 47		17 04	17 22			17 52		18 22			18 52		19 22		
Arundel	d				15 54							16 54					17 54					18 54	
Amberley	d				15 58							16 58					17 58					18 58	
Pulborough	d				16 05							17 05					18 05					19 05	
Billingshurst	d				16 12							17 12					18 12					19 12	
Christs Hospital	d				16 18							17 18					18 18					19 18	
Horsham	a				16 22							17 22					18 22					19 22	
	d				16 22							17 22					18 22					19 22	
Crawley	a				16 31							17 31					18 31					19 31	
Three Bridges	a				16 35							17 35					18 35					19 35	
	d				16 35							17 35					18 35					19 35	
Gatwick Airport	a				16 40							17 40					18 40					19 40	
East Croydon	a				17 06							18 03					19 03					20 03	
East Croydon	d																						
London Bridge	a																						
East Croydon	d				17 06							18 04					19 04					20 04	
Clapham Junction	a				17 16							18 14					19 14					20 14	
London Victoria	a				17 23							18 21					19 21					20 21	

Table T186-R

Sundays

20 May to 2 December

Bognor Regis, Chichester, Portsmouth and Southampton - London, Gatwick Airport, Arun Valley and Brighton

		SN	SN	SN	SN	SN	SN	SN	SN	GW	SN	SN	SN	SN	SN	SN	SN	SN	SN	SN	SN	SN
										◇												
Southampton Central	d			18 30					19 21	19 28						20 28					21 30	
Swanwick	d			18 47					19 41							20 46					21 47	
Fareham	d			18 54					19 49	19 54						20 53					21 54	
Portchester	d																					
Cosham	d			19 03					19 57	20 02						21 03					22 03	
Portsmouth Harbour	d	18 14			19 01							20 01		20 14			21 01		21 14			22 01
Portsmouth & Southsea	d	18 18			19 05							20 05		20 18			21 05		21 18			22 05
Fratton	d	18 22			19 09		19 22					20 09		20 22			21 09		21 22			22 09
Hilsea	d																					
Bedhampton	d	18 30					19 30							20 30					21 30			
Havant	d	18 33		19 10	19 18		19 33		20 04	20 11		20 18		20 33		21 10	21 18		21 33		22 10	22 17
Warblington	d	18 35					19 35							20 35					21 35			
Emsworth	d	18 38		19 14	19 21		19 38		20 07			20 21		20 38		21 14	21 21		21 38		22 14	22 21
Southbourne	d	18 41			19 24		19 41					20 24		20 41			21 24		21 41			22 24
Nutbourne	d	18 44					19 44							20 44					21 44			
Bosham	d	18 47					19 47							20 47					21 47			
Fishbourne (Sussex)	d	18 50					19 50							20 50					21 50			
Chichester	a	18 53		19 22	19 31		19 53		20 15	20 21		20 31		20 53		21 22	21 31		21 53		22 22	22 31
	d	18 53		19 22	19 32		19 53		20 16	20 22		20 32		20 53		21 22	21 32		21 53		22 22	22 32
Barnham	a	19 01		19 30	19 40		20 01		20 23	20 29		20 40		21 01		21 30	21 40		22 01		22 30	22 39
Bognor Regis	d		19 00			19 31		20 00					20 31		21 00			21 31		22 00		
Barnham	a		19 06			19 37		20 06					20 37		21 06			21 37		22 06		
Barnham	d	19 02	19 07	19 31	19 44		20 02	20 07	20 24	20 30		20 44		21 02	21 07	21 31	21 44		22 02	22 07	22 31	22 40
Ford	d	19 06	19 11	19 35	19 48		20 06	20 11	20 28			20 48		21 06	21 11	21 35	21 48		22 06	22 11	22 35	22 44
Littlehampton	a		19 16					20 16						21 11	21 16	21 40				22 16		22 50
Angmering	a	19 13		19 42			20 13		20 35					21 25		21 55			22 13		22 42	23 04
Goring-by-Sea	a	19 18		19 47			20 18		20 40					21 29		21 59			22 18		22 47	23 09
Durrington-on-Sea	a	19 20		19 49			20 20		20 42					21 32		22 02			22 20		22 49	23 11
West Worthing	a	19 23		19 52			20 23		20 45					21 34		22 04			22 23		22 52	23 14
Worthing	a	19 25		19 54			20 25		20 47	20 50	←			21 37		22 07			22 25		22 54	23 16
Lancing	a	19 31		20 00			20 31		21 02		21 02			21 43		22 13			22 31		23 00	23 22
Shoreham-by-Sea	a	19 35		20 04			20 35		→	20 57	21 06			21 47		22 17			22 35		23 04	23 26
Southwick	a	19 39		20 08			20 39				21 09			21 50		22 20			22 39		23 08	23 30
Portslade	a	19 43		20 12			20 43				21 13			21 54		22 24			22 43		23 12	23 34
Hove	a	19 47		20 16			20 47			21 05	21 18			21 59		22 29			22 47		23 16	23 38
Brighton	a	19 52		20 22			20 52			21 10	21 22			22 04		22 34			22 52		23 22	23 43
Arundel	d				19 54							20 54					21 54					
Amberley	d				19 58							20 58					21 58					
Pulborough	d				20 05							21 05					22 05					
Billingshurst	d				20 12							21 12					22 12					
Christs Hospital	d				20 18							21 18					22 18					
Horsham	a				20 22							21 22					22 22					
	d				20 22							21 22					22 22					
Crawley	a				20 31							21 31					22 31					
Three Bridges	a				20 35							21 35					22 35					
	d				20 35							21 35					22 35					
Gatwick Airport	a				20 40							21 40					22 40					
East Croydon	a				21 03							22 03					23 03					
East Croydon	d																					
London Bridge	a																					
East Croydon	d				21 04							22 04					23 04					
Clapham Junction	a				21 14							22 14					23 14					
London Victoria	a				21 21							22 21					23 21					

Table T186-R

Sundays

20 May to 2 December

Bognor Regis, Chichester, Portsmouth and Southampton - London, Gatwick Airport, Arun Valley and Brighton

		SN	SN	SN	SN	SN
Southampton Central	d			22 30		22 58
Swanwick	d			22 47		23 15
Fareham	d			22 54		23 22
Portchester	d					
Cosham	d			23 04		23 31
Portsmouth Harbour	d		22 14		23 01	
Portsmouth & Southsea	d		22 18		23 05	
Fratton	d		22 22		23 09	
Hilsea	d					
Bedhampton	d					
Havant	d		22 31	23 12	23 18	23 38
Warblington	d					
Emsworth	d		22 35		23 22	23 42
Southbourne	d		22 38		23 25	
Nutbourne	d					
Bosham	d					
Fishbourne (Sussex)	d					
Chichester	a		22 45	23 22	23 32	23 50
	d		22 46	23 22	23 32	23 50
Barnham	a		22 53	23 30	23 40	23 58
Bognor Regis	d	22 28				
Barnham	a	22 34				
Barnham	d	22 43	22 57	23 30	23 40	23 59
Ford	d	22 47	23 01		23 45	00 03
Littlehampton	a	22 52	23 06	23 40	23 50	00 09
Angmering	a					
Goring-by-Sea	a					
Durrington-on-Sea	a					
West Worthing	a					
Worthing	a					
Lancing	a					
Shoreham-by-Sea	a					
Southwick	a					
Portslade	a					
Hove	a					
Brighton	a					
Arundel	d					
Amberley	d					
Pulborough	d					
Billingshurst	d					
Christs Hospital	d					
Horsham	a					
	d					
Crawley	a					
Three Bridges	a					
	d					
Gatwick Airport	a					
East Croydon	a					
East Croydon	d					
London Bridge	a					
East Croydon	d					
Clapham Junction	a					
London Victoria	a					

Table T188-F

Mondays to Fridays

21 May to 7 December

London - Gatwick Airport and Brighton - Worthing - Southampton Central

		SN MX ■ A	SN MX	SN MO	SN MX	SN MO A	SN MX ■ A	SN MX ■	SN MX ■ A	SN	SN ■	SN	SN	SN	SN	SN	SN ■	SN	SN	SN	SN	SN	SN ■
London Victoria ■ ⊖	d							00 02															
Clapham Junction ■	d							00 09															
East Croydon	a							00 23															
St Pancras International	d																						
Farringdon	d																						
City Thameslink	d																						
London Blackfriars	d																						
London Bridge	d																						
East Croydon	a																						
East Croydon	d							00 24															
Gatwick Airport ■ ✈	d							00 44															
Haywards Heath ■	d					00 08	00 09	01 02															
Preston Park	d					00 19	00 22																
Brighton ■	d		00 04	00 10	00 12			01s16		05 00	05 27	05 39	05 51	06 02	06 11	06 21	06 32	06 41	06 50	07 02	07 11	07 20	07 32
Hove ■	a		00 08	00 14	00 17	00 23	00 26	01s25		05 04	05 31	05 44	05 55	06 06	06 16	06 25	06 36	06 45	06 54	07 06	07 15	07 24	07 36
	d		00 09			00 23	00 26			05 05	05 32		05 55	06 06		06 25	06 36	06 45	06 54	07 06	07 15	07 24	07 36
Aldrington	d		00 11								05 34		05 57			06 27			06 56			07 26	
Portslade	d		00 14			00 26	00 29	01s28		05 08	05 37		06 00	06 09		06 30	06 39	06 48	06 59	07 09	07 18	07 29	07 39
Fishersgate	d		00 16								05 39		06 02			06 32			07 01			07 31	
Southwick	d		00 18				00 32	01s31		05 11	05 41		06 04	06 12		06 34	06 42	06 51	07 03	07 12	07 21	07 33	07 42
Shoreham-by-Sea	d	00 02	00 22			00 31	00 36	01s34		05 14	05 44		06 08	06 16		06 38	06 46	06 55	07 07	07 16	07 25	07 37	07 46
Lancing	d	00 06	00 26			00 35	00 40	01s38		05 18	05 48		06 12	06 20		06 42	06 50	06 59	07 11	07 20	07 29	07 41	07 50
East Worthing	d		00 29								05 51		06 15			06 45			07 14			07 44	
Worthing ■	a	00 11	00 31			00 39	00 45	01 43		05 22	05 54		06 18	06 24		06 48	06 54	07 03	07 17	07 24	07 33	07 47	07 54
	d		00 32							05 22	05 54		06 18	06 24		06 48	06 55	07 04	07 17	07 25	07 34	07 47	07 55
West Worthing	d		00a34							05 24	05 56		06a21	06 27		06 50	06 57	07a06	07 19		07a36	07 49	07 57
Durrington-on-Sea	d									05 27	05 59			06 29		06 53	06 59		07 22			07 52	07 59
Goring-by-Sea	d									05 29	06 01			06 32		06 55	07 02		07 24			07 54	08 02
Angmering ■	d									05 33	06 05			06 36		06 59	07 06		07 28	07 31		07 58	08 06
Littlehampton ■	a															07 11			07 41			08 08	
Barnham	a									05 44	06 17			06 47			07 18			07 42			08 18
Barnham	d								00 12														
Bognor Regis	a								00 19														
Barnham	d									05 45	06 19			06 48			07 19			07 43			08 19
Chichester ■	a									05 52	06 26			06 56			07 26			07 51			08 26
Havant	a									06 06	06 40			07 10			07 38			08 05			08 38
Havant	d									06 07				07 11						08 06			
Portsmouth & Southsea	a									06 20				07 25						08 19			
Portsmouth Harbour ⛴	a									06 24										08 23			
Havant	d										06 42						07 39						08 39
Fareham	a										06 59						07 55						08 54
Southampton Central ⛴	a										07 25						08 19						09 20

		SN	SN	SN	SN	SN	SN ■	SN	SN ■	SN	GW ◇ B	SN	SN	TL ■ C	SN	SN ■	SN	SN ■	SN	SN	SN	SN ■	SN
London Victoria ■ ⊖	d								07 46									08 46				09 16	
Clapham Junction ■	d								07 53									08 53				09 23	
East Croydon	a								08 03									09 02				09 32	
St Pancras International	d													08 10									
Farringdon	d													08 14									
City Thameslink	d													08 16									
London Blackfriars	d													08 19									
London Bridge	d													08 25									
East Croydon	a													08 38									
East Croydon	d								08 03					08 38				09 03				09 33	
Gatwick Airport ■ ✈	d								08 20									09 20				09 50	
Haywards Heath ■	d								08 38					09 07				09 38				10 05	
Preston Park	d													09 18								10 18	
Brighton ■	d	07 41	07 51	08 00	08 14	08 22	08 32	08 40		08 51	08 59	09 05	09 09		09 21	09 32	09 39		09 51	10 02	10 09		10 21
Hove ■	a	07 45	07 55	08 04	08 18	08 26	08 36	08 45	08 52	08 55	09 02	09 09	09 14	09 23	09 26	09 36	09 44	09 52	09 55	10 06	10 14	10 22	10 25
	d	07 45	07 55	08 04	08 19	08 26	08 36		08 53	08 56	09 03	09 09		09 23	09 26	09 36		09 52	09 55	10 06		10 22	10 25
Aldrington	d		07 57			08 28				08 58					09 28				09 57				10 27
Portslade	d	07 48	08 00	08 07	08 22	08 31	08 39		08 56	09 00		09 12		09 27	09 31	09 39		09 55	10 00	10 09		10 25	10 30
Fishersgate	d		08 02			08 33				09 02					09 33				10 02				10 32
Southwick	d	07 51	08 04	08 10	08 25	08 35	08 42			09 04		09 16			09 35	09 42			10 04	10 12			10 34
Shoreham-by-Sea	d	07 55	08 08	08 14	08 29	08 39	08 46		09 01	09 08	09 13	09 20		09 32	09 39	09 46		10 00	10 08	10 16		10 30	10 38
Lancing	d	07 59	08 12	08 18	08 33	08 43	08 50		09 05	09 12		09 24		09 36	09 43	09 50		10 04	10 12	10 20			10 42
East Worthing	d		08 15			08 46				09 15					09 46				10 15				10 45
Worthing ■	a	08 03	08 18	08 22	08 37	08 49	08 54		09 09	09 17	09 20	09 28		09 40	09 48	09 54		10 08	10 18	10 24		10 36	10 48
	d	08 04	08 18	08 25	08 38	08 49	08 55		09 09	09 18	09 22	09 29		09 40	09 49	09 55		10 09	10 18	10 25		10 39	10 48
West Worthing	d	08 06	08a21	08 27	08 40	08a52	08 57		09 11	09a20				09 43	09a51	09 57		10 11	10a21			10 41	10a51
Durrington-on-Sea	d	08 08		08 29	08 43		08 59		09 14					09 46		09 59		10 13				10 43	
Goring-by-Sea	d	08 11		08 32	08 45		09 02		09 16					09 49		10 02		10 16				10 46	
Angmering ■	d	08 15		08 36	08 50		09 06		09 20			09 35		09 53		10 06		10 20		10 32		10 50	
Littlehampton ■	a				09 00				09 31					10 03				10 31				11 01	
Barnham	a	08 28		08 47			09 18				09 36	09 47				10 18				10 43			
Barnham	d																						
Bognor Regis	a																						
Barnham	d	08 28		08 48			09 19				09 37	09 48				10 19				10 44			
Chichester ■	a	08 36		08 55			09 26				09 45	09 55				10 26				10 51			
Havant	a	08 46		09 09			09 39				09 57	10 09				10 38				11 05			
Havant	d	08 47		09 10								10 10								11 06			
Portsmouth & Southsea	a	08 59		09 23								10 23								11 18			
Portsmouth Harbour ⛴	a	09 04																		11 22			
Havant	d						09 40				09 58					10 39							
Fareham	a						09 55				10 12					10 54							
Southampton Central ⛴	a						10 19				10 40					11 19							

A From London Victoria B To Great Malvern C From Bedford

Table T188-F

Mondays to Fridays

21 May to 7 December

London - Gatwick Airport and Brighton - Worthing - Southampton Central

		SN ■	SN	SN ■	SN	SN	SN	SN ■	SN	SN ■	SN	SN ■	SN	SN	SN	SN ■	SN	SN ■	SN	SN ■	SN	SN
London Victoria ■ ⊖	d			09 46				10 16				10 46				11 16				11 46		
Clapham Junction ■	d			09 53				10 23				10 53				11 23				11 53		
East Croydon	a			10 02				10 32				11 02				11 32				12 02		
St Pancras International	d																					
Farringdon	d																					
City Thameslink	d																					
London Blackfriars	d																					
London Bridge	d																					
East Croydon	a																					
East Croydon	d			10 03				10 33				11 03				11 33				12 03		
Gatwick Airport ■ ✈	d			10 20				10 50				11 20				11 50				12 20		
Haywards Heath ■	d			10 38				11 05				11 38				12 05				12 38		
Preston Park	d							11 18								12 18						
Brighton ■	d	10 32	10 39		10 51	11 02	11 09		11 21	11 32	11 39		11 51	12 02	12 09		12 21	12 32	12 39		12 51	13 02
Hove ■	a	10 36	10 44	10 52	10 55	11 06	11 14	11 22	11 25	11 36	11 44	11 52	11 55	12 06	12 14	12 22	12 25	12 36	12 44	12 52	12 55	13 06
	d	10 36		10 52	10 55	11 06		11 22	11 25	11 36		11 52	11 55	12 06		12 22	12 25	12 36		12 52	12 55	13 06
Aldrington	d				10 57				11 27				11 57				12 27				12 57	
Portslade	d	10 39		10 55	11 00	11 09		11 25	11 30	11 39		11 55	12 00	12 09		12 25	12 30	12 39		12 55	13 00	13 09
Fishersgate	d				11 02				11 32				12 02				12 32				13 02	
Southwick	d	10 42			11 04	11 12			11 34	11 42			12 04	12 12			12 34	12 42			13 04	13 12
Shoreham-by-Sea	d	10 46		11 00	11 08	11 16		11 30	11 38	11 46		12 00	12 08	12 16		12 30	12 38	12 46		13 00	13 08	13 16
Lancing	d	10 50		11 04	11 12	11 20			11 42	11 50		12 04	12 12	12 20			12 42	12 50		13 04	13 12	13 20
East Worthing	d				11 15				11 45				12 15				12 45				13 15	
Worthing ■	a	10 54		11 08	11 18	11 24		11 36	11 48	11 54		12 08	12 18	12 24		12 36	12 48	12 54		13 08	13 18	13 24
	d	10 55		11 09	11 18	11 25		11 39	11 48	11 55		12 09	12 18	12 25		12 39	12 48	12 55		13 09	13 18	13 25
West Worthing	d	10 57		11 11	11a21			11 41	11a51	11 57		12 11	12a21			12 41	12a51	12 57		13 11	13a21	
Durrington-on-Sea	d	10 59		11 13				11 43		11 59		12 13				12 43		12 59		13 13		
Goring-by-Sea	d	11 02		11 16				11 46		12 02		12 16				12 46		13 02		13 16		
Angmering ■	d	11 06		11 20		11 32		11 50		12 06		12 20		12 32		12 50		13 06		13 20		13 32
Littlehampton ■	a			11 31				12 01				12 31				13 01				13 31		
Barnham	a	11 18				11 43				12 18				12 43				13 18				13 43
Barnham	d																					
Bognor Regis	a																					
Barnham	d	11 19				11 44				12 19				12 44				13 19				13 44
Chichester ■	a	11 26				11 51				12 26				12 51				13 26				13 51
Havant	a	11 38				12 05				12 38				13 05				13 38				14 05
Havant	d					12 06								13 06								14 06
Portsmouth & Southsea	a					12 18								13 18								14 18
Portsmouth Harbour ⛴	a					12 22								13 22								14 22
Havant	d	11 39								12 39								13 39				
Fareham	a	11 54								12 54								13 54				
Southampton Central ⛴	a	12 19								13 19								14 19				

		SN	SN ■	SN	SN ■	SN	SN ■	SN	SN	SN	SN ■	SN	SN ■	SN	SN ■	SN	SN	SN	SN ■	SN	SN ■	SN	SN ■
London Victoria ■ ⊖	d		12 16				12 46				13 16				13 46				14 16				14 46
Clapham Junction ■	d		12 23				12 53				13 23				13 53				14 23				14 53
East Croydon	a		12 32				13 02				13 32				14 02				14 32				15 02
St Pancras International	d																						
Farringdon	d																						
City Thameslink	d																						
London Blackfriars	d																						
London Bridge	d																						
East Croydon	a																						
East Croydon	d		12 33				13 03				13 33				14 03				14 33				15 03
Gatwick Airport ■ ✈	d		12 50				13 20				13 50				14 20				14 50				15 20
Haywards Heath ■	d		13 05				13 38				14 05				14 38				15 05				15 38
Preston Park	d		13 18								14 18								15 18				
Brighton ■	d	13 09		13 21	13 32	13 39		13 51	14 02	14 09		14 21	14 32	14 39		14 51	15 02	15 09		15 21	15 32	15 39	
Hove ■	a	13 14	13 22	13 25	13 36	13 44	13 52	13 55	14 06	14 14	14 22	14 25	14 36	14 44	14 52	14 55	15 06	15 14	15 22	15 25	15 36	15 44	15 52
	d		13 22	13 25	13 36		13 52	13 55	14 06		14 22	14 25	14 36		14 52	14 55	15 06		15 22	15 25	15 36		15 52
Aldrington	d			13 27				13 57				14 27				14 57				15 27			
Portslade	d		13 25	13 30	13 39		13 55	14 00	14 09		14 25	14 30	14 39		14 55	15 00	15 09		15 25	15 30	15 39		15 55
Fishersgate	d			13 32				14 02				14 32				15 02				15 32			
Southwick	d			13 34	13 42			14 04	14 12			14 34	14 42			15 04	15 12			15 34	15 42		
Shoreham-by-Sea	d		13 30	13 38	13 46		14 00	14 08	14 16		14 30	14 38	14 46		15 00	15 08	15 16		15 30	15 38	15 46		16 00
Lancing	d			13 42	13 50		14 04	14 12	14 20			14 42	14 50		15 04	15 12	15 20		15 34	15 42	15 50		16 04
East Worthing	d			13 45				14 15				14 45				15 16				15 45			
Worthing ■	a		13 36	13 48	13 54		14 08	14 18	14 24		14 36	14 48	14 54		15 08	15 18	15 24		15 38	15 48	15 54		16 08
	d		13 39	13 48	13 55		14 09	14 18	14 25		14 39	14 48	14 55		15 09	15 19	15 26		15 39	15 48	15 55		16 09
West Worthing	d		13 41	13a51	13 57		14 11	14a21			14 41	14a51	14 57		15 11	15 21			15 41	15 51	15 57		16 11
Durrington-on-Sea	d		13 43		13 59		14 13				14 43		14 59		15 13	15 23			15 43		15 59		16 13
Goring-by-Sea	d		13 46		14 02		14 16				14 46		15 02		15 16	15 26			15 46		16 02		16 16
Angmering ■	d		13 50		14 06		14 20		14 32		14 50		15 06		15 20	15 30	15 34		15 50		16 06		16 20
Littlehampton ■	a		14 01				14 31				15 01				15 31	15 41			16 01	16 05			16 31
Barnham	a				14 18				14 43				15 18				15 46				16 18		
Barnham	d																						
Bognor Regis	a																						
Barnham	d				14 19				14 44				15 19				15 47				16 19		
Chichester ■	a				14 26				14 51				15 26				15 54				16 26		
Havant	a				14 38				15 05				15 38				16 08				16 38		
Havant	d								15 06								16 09						
Portsmouth & Southsea	a								15 18								16 23						
Portsmouth Harbour ⛴	a								15 22														
Havant	d				14 39								15 39								16 39		
Fareham	a				14 54								15 54								16 54		
Southampton Central ⛴	a				15 19								16 20								17 19		

21 May to 7 December

London - Gatwick Airport and Brighton - Worthing - Southampton Central

	SN	SN	SN	SN 1	SN	SN 1	SN	SN 1	SN	GW ◇ A	SN	SN	SN 1	SN	SN 1	SN	TL 1 B	SN	SN 1	SN	SN
London Victoria 15 d				15 16				15 46					16 16						16 54		
Clapham Junction 10 d				15 23				15 53					16 23						17 02		
East Croydon a				15 32				16 02					16 32						17 11		
St Pancras International d																	16 40				
Farringdon d																	16 44				
City Thameslink d																	16 46				
London Blackfriars d																	16 49				
London Bridge d																	16 55				
East Croydon a																	17 08				
East Croydon d				15 33				16 03					16 33				17 08		17 11		
Gatwick Airport 10 d				15 50				16 20					16 50						17 27		
Haywards Heath 3 d				16 05				16 38					17 05				17 37		17 40		
Preston Park d				16 18									17 20				17 50		17 55		
Brighton 10 d	15 51	16 02	16 09		16 21	16 32	16 39		16 51	17 02	17 05	17 12		17 21	17 32	17 42		17 52		18 02	18 10
Hove 2 a	15 55	16 06	16 14	16 22	16 25	16 36	16 44	16 52	16 55	17 05	17 10	17 16	17 24	17 25	17 36	17 46	17 54	17 57	18 00	18 06	18 14
d	15 55	16 06		16 22	16 25	16 36		16 52	16 55	17 06	17 10	17 16	17 27		17 37	17 46	17 54		18 01	18 07	18 14
Aldrington d	15 57				16 27				16 57			17 18				17 48					18 16
Portslade d	16 00	16 09		16 25	16 30	16 39		16 55	17 00		17 13	17 21	17 30		17 40	17 51	17 58		18 04	18 10	18 19
Fishersgate d	16 02				16 32				17 02			17 23				17 53					18 21
Southwick d	16 04	16 12			16 34	16 42			17 04		17 16	17 25			17 43	17 55				18 13	18 23
Shoreham-by-Sea d	16 08	16 16		16 30	16 38	16 46		17 00	17 08	17 12	17 20	17 29	17 35		17 47	17 59	18 03		18 09	18 16	18 27
Lancing d	16 12	16 20			16 42	16 50		17 04	17 12		17 24	17 33	17 39		17 51	18 03	18 07		18 14	18 20	18 31
East Worthing d	16 15				16 45				17 15			17 36				18 06					18 34
Worthing 4 a	16 18	16 24		16 36	16 48	16 54		17 08	17 18	17 21	17 28	17 39	17 43		17 55	18 08	18 11		18 18	18 24	18 36
d	16 18	16 26		16 39	16 48	16 55		17 09	17 18	17 23	17 28	17 39	17 43		17 56	18 09	18 12		18 18	18 25	18 37
West Worthing d	16 21			16 41	16 51	16 57		17 11	17 21		17 30	17 42	17 45		17 58		18 15		18 21	18 27	18a39
Durrington-on-Sea d	16 23			16 43		16 59		17 13			17 33	17 44	17 48		18 00		18 18		18 24	18 29	
Goring-by-Sea d	16 26			16 46		17 02		17 16			17 35	17 47	17 50		18 03		18 21		18 27	18 32	
Angmering 3 d	16 30	16 34		16 50		17 06		17 20			17 39	17 51	17 55		18 07		18 25		18 31	18 36	
Littlehampton 4 a	16 41			17 01	17 05			17 31	17 35			18 01	18 05			18 28	18 35		18 43		
Barnham a		16 46				17 18				17 38	17 51				18 19					18 48	
Barnham d																					
Bognor Regis a																					
Barnham d		16 47				17 19				17 38	17 52				18 19					18 49	
Chichester 4 a		16 54				17 26				17 46	18 00				18 27					18 56	
Havant a		17 08				17 38				17 57	18 14				18 39					19 10	
Havant d		17 09									18 14									19 11	
Portsmouth & Southsea a		17 23									18 26									19 23	
Portsmouth Harbour a																					
Havant d						17 39				17 58					18 40						
Fareham a						17 54				18 12					18 54						
Southampton Central a						18 19				18 39					19 20						

	SN	SN 1	SN 1	SN	TL 1 B	SN	SN 1	SN	SN	SN	SN 1	SN 1	SN	SN	SN 1	SN	SN	SN 1	SN	SN 1	SN	SN 1
London Victoria 15 d		17 24					17 54				18 24				18 54			19 16				19 46
Clapham Junction 10 d		17 32					18 02				18 32				19 02			19 23				19 53
East Croydon a		17 41					18 11				18 41				19 11			19 32				20 02
St Pancras International d					17 40																	
Farringdon d					17 44																	
City Thameslink d					17 46																	
London Blackfriars d					17 49																	
London Bridge d					17 55																	
East Croydon a					18 08																	
East Croydon d		17 41			18 08		18 11				18 41				19 11			19 33				20 03
Gatwick Airport 10 d		17 57					18 27				18 57				19 27			19 50				20 20
Haywards Heath 3 d		18 10			18 37		18 40				19 10				19 40			20 05				20 38
Preston Park d		18 25			18 50		18 55				19 25				19 55			20 18				
Brighton 10 d	18 22		18 32	18 40		18 52		19 02	19 10	19 22		19 32	19 40	19 52		20 02	20 12		20 21	20 32	20 42	
Hove 2 a	18 27	18 30	18 36	18 44	18 54	18 57	19 00	19 06	19 14	19 27	19 30	19 36	19 44	19 57	20 00	20 06	20 17	20 22	20 25	20 36	20 47	20 52
d		18 31	18 37	18 44	18 54		19 01	19 07	19 14		19 31	19 37	19 44		20 01	20 07		20 22	20 25	20 36		20 52
Aldrington d				18 46					19 16				19 46						20 27			
Portslade d		18 34	18 40	18 49	18 58		19 04	19 10	19 19		19 34	19 40	19 49		20 04	20 10		20 25	20 30	20 39		20 55
Fishersgate d				18 51					19 21				19 51						20 32			
Southwick d			18 43	18 53				19 13	19 23			19 43	19 53			20 13			20 34	20 42		20 58
Shoreham-by-Sea d		18 39	18 47	18 57	19 03		19 09	19 16	19 27		19 39	19 47	19 57		20 09	20 16		20 30	20 38	20 46		21 02
Lancing d		18 44	18 51	19 01	19 07		19 14	19 20	19 31		19 44	19 51	20 01		20 14	20 20		20 34	20 42	20 50		21 06
East Worthing d				19 04					19 34				20 04						20 45			
Worthing 4 a		18 48	18 55	19 06	19 11		19 18	19 24	19 36		19 48	19 55	20 06		20 18	20 24		20 38	20 48	20 54		21 10
d		18 48	18 56	19 07	19 12		19 18	19 25	19 37		19 48	19 56	20 07		20 18	20 25		20 39	20 48	20 55		21 11
West Worthing d		18 51	18 58	19a09	19 15		19 21		19a39		19 51	19 58	20a09		20 21	20 27		20 41	20a51	20 57		21 13
Durrington-on-Sea d		18 54	19 00		19 18		19 24	19 29			19 54	20 00			20 24	20 29		20 43		20 59		21 15
Goring-by-Sea d		18 57	19 03		19 21		19 27	19 31			19 57	20 03			20 27	20 32		20 46		21 02		21 18
Angmering 3 d		19 01	19 07		19 25		19 31	19 35			20 01	20 07			20 31	20 36		20 50		21 06		21 22
Littlehampton 4 a		19 13			19 35		19 43				20 13				20 43			21 01				21 32
Barnham a			19 19					19 47				20 19				20 48				21 18		
Barnham d																						
Bognor Regis a																						
Barnham d			19 20					19 48				20 20				20 49				21 19		
Chichester 4 a			19 27					19 56				20 27				20 56				21 26		
Havant a			19 39					20 10				20 39				21 10				21 38		
Havant d								20 10								21 11						
Portsmouth & Southsea a								20 23								21 23						
Portsmouth Harbour a																						
Havant d			19 40									20 40								21 39		
Fareham a			19 54									20 54								21 55		
Southampton Central a			20 19									21 19								22 23		

A To Bristol Temple Meads
B From Bedford

Table T188-F

Mondays to Fridays

21 May to 7 December

London - Gatwick Airport and Brighton - Worthing - Southampton Central

	SN	SN	SN	SN 1	SN	SN	SN	SN 1	SN	SN	SN	SN 1	SN	SN	SN 1	SN	SN	SN 1 A	SN	SN 1	SN 1
London Victoria 15 d				20 16				20 46				21 16			21 46			22 16		22 46	23 16
Clapham Junction 10 d				20 23				20 53				21 23			21 53			22 23		22 53	23 23
East Croydon a				20 32				21 02				21 32			22 02			22 32		23 02	23 32
St Pancras International d																					
Farringdon d																					
City Thameslink d																					
London Blackfriars d																					
London Bridge d																					
East Croydon a																					
East Croydon d				20 33				21 03				21 33			22 03			22 33		23 03	23 33
Gatwick Airport 10 d				20 50				21 20				21 50			22 20			22 50		23 20	23 54
Haywards Heath 3 d				21 05				21 38				22 05			22 38			23 05		23 38	00 09
Preston Park d				21 18								22 18						23 18			00 22
Brighton 10 d	20 51	21 02	21 12		21 21	21 32	21 42		21 51	22 02	22 12		22 32	22 42		22 57	23 12		23 42		
Hove 2 a	20 55	21 06	21 17	21 22	21 25	21 36	21 47	21 52	21 55	22 06	22 17	22 22	22 36	22 47	22 52	23 01	23 17	23 22	23 47	23 52	00 26
d	20 55	21 07		21 22	21 25	21 37		21 52	21 55	22 07		22 22	22 37		22 52	23 01		23 22		23 52	00 26
Aldrington d	20 57				21 27				21 57				22 39			23 03					
Portslade d	21 00	21 10		21 25	21 30	21 40		21 55	22 00	22 10		22 25	22 41		22 55	23 06		23 25		23 55	00 29
Fishersgate d	21 02				21 32				22 02				22 43			23 08					
Southwick d	21 04	21 13		21 28	21 34	21 43		21 58	22 04	22 13		22 28	22 45		22 58	23 10		23 28		23 58	00 32
Shoreham-by-Sea d	21 08	21 16		21 32	21 38	21 46		22 02	22 08	22 16		22 32	22 49		23 02	23 14		23 32		00 02	00 36
Lancing d	21 12	21 20		21 36	21 42	21 50		22 06	22 12	22 20		22 36	22 53		23 06	23 18		23 36		00 06	00 40
East Worthing d	21 15				21 45				22 15				22 56			23 21					
Worthing 4 a	21 18	21 24		21 40	21 48	21 54		22 10	22 18	22 24		22 40	22 58		23 10	23 24		23 40		00 11	00 45
d	21 18	21 25		21 41	21 48	21 55		22 11	22 18	22 25		22 41	22 59		23 11	23 24		23 41			
West Worthing d	21a21	21 27		21 43	21a51	21 57		22 13	22a21	22 27		22 43	23 01		23 13	23a27		23 43			
Durrington-on-Sea d		21 29		21 45		21 59		22 15		22 29		22 45	23 03		23 15			23 45			
Goring-by-Sea d		21 32		21 48		22 02		22 18		22 32		22 48	23 06		23 18			23 48			
Angmering 3 d		21 36		21 52		22 06		22 22		22 36		22 52	23 10		23 22			23 52			
Littlehampton 4 a				22 02				22 32				23 02			23 32						
Barnham a		21 48				22 18				22 48			23 22					00 04			
Barnham d																		00 12			
Bognor Regis a																		00 19			
Barnham d		21 49				22 19				22 49			23 22								
Chichester 4 a		21 56				22 27				22 56			23 30								
Havant a		22 10								23 10			23 41								
Havant d		22 11								23 11											
Portsmouth & Southsea a		22 23								23 23											
Portsmouth Harbour a		22 27								23 28											
Havant d																					
Fareham a																					
Southampton Central a																					

Saturdays

26 May to 8 December

	SN 1 B	SN	SN	SN 1 B	SN 1	SN 1 C	SN 1	SN 1	SN	SN	SN	SN	SN	SN 1	SN	SN 1	SN	SN	SN	SN	SN 1	SN
London Victoria 15 d					00 02																	
Clapham Junction 10 d					00 09																	
East Croydon a					00 23																	
St Pancras International d																						
Farringdon d																						
City Thameslink d																						
London Blackfriars d																						
London Bridge d																						
East Croydon a																						
East Croydon d					00 24																	
Gatwick Airport 10 d					00 44																	
Haywards Heath 3 d				00 09	01 02																	
Preston Park d				00 22																		
Brighton 10 d		00 04	00 12		01s16		05 14	05 32	05 39	05 51	06 02	06 09	06 21	06 32	06 39	06 47	06 51	07 02	07 09	07 21	07 32	07 39
Hove 2 a		00 08	00 17	00 26	01s25		05 18	05 36	05 44	05 55	06 06	06 14	06 25	06 36	06 44	06 51	06 55	07 06	07 14	07 25	07 36	07 44
d		00 09		00 26			05 20	05 36		05 55	06 06		06 25	06 36		06 52	06 55	07 06		07 25	07 36	
Aldrington d		00 11								05 57			06 27				06 57			07 27		
Portslade d		00 14		00 29	01s28		05 23	05 39		06 00	06 09		06 30	06 39		06 55	07 00	07 09		07 30	07 39	
Fishersgate d		00 16								06 02			06 32				07 02			07 32		
Southwick d		00 18		00 32	01s31		05 26	05 42		06 04	06 12		06 34	06 42			07 04	07 12		07 34	07 42	
Shoreham-by-Sea d	00 02	00 22		00 36	01s34		05 29	05 46		06 08	06 16		06 38	06 46		07 00	07 08	07 16		07 38	07 46	
Lancing d	00 06	00 26		00 40	01s38		05 33	05 50		06 12	06 20		06 42	06 50		07 04	07 12	07 20		07 42	07 50	
East Worthing d		00 29								06 15			06 45				07 15			07 45		
Worthing 4 a	00 11	00 31		00 45	01 43		05 37	05 54		06 18	06 24		06 48	06 54		07 08	07 18	07 24		07 48	07 54	
d		00 32					05 37	05 55		06 18	06 25		06 48	06 55		07 09	07 18	07 25		07 48	07 55	
West Worthing d		00a34					05 39	05 57		06a21			06a51	06 57		07 11	07a21			07a51	07 57	
Durrington-on-Sea d							05 42	05 59						06 59		07 13					07 59	
Goring-by-Sea d							05 44	06 02						07 02		07 16					08 02	
Angmering 3 d							05 48	06 06			06 32			07 06		07 20		07 32			08 06	
Littlehampton 4 a																07 31						
Barnham a							06 00	06 18			06 43			07 18				07 43			08 18	
Barnham d						00 12																
Bognor Regis a						00 19																
Barnham d							06 01	06 19			06 44			07 19				07 44			08 19	
Chichester 4 a							06 08	06 26			06 51			07 26				07 51			08 26	
Havant a							06 20	06 38			07 05			07 38				08 05			08 38	
Havant d											07 06							08 06				
Portsmouth & Southsea a											07 18							08 20				
Portsmouth Harbour a											07 22							08 24				
Havant d							06 21	06 39						07 39							08 39	
Fareham a							06 36	06 54						07 54							08 54	
Southampton Central a							07 01	07 19						08 19							09 19	

A not 7 December
B From London Victoria
C not 8 December. From London Victoria

Saturdays
26 May to 8 December

London - Gatwick Airport and Brighton - Worthing - Southampton Central

		SN ■	SN	SN	SN	SN		SN ■	SN	SN ■	SN	GW ◇ A	SN	SN	SN ■	SN		SN ■	SN	SN ■	SN	SN	SN	SN ■	SN
London Victoria ■ ⊖	d									07 46					08 16					08 46				09 16	
Clapham Junction ■	d									07 53					08 23					08 53				09 23	
East Croydon	a									08 02					08 32					09 02				09 32	
St Pancras International	d																								
Farringdon	d																								
City Thameslink	d																								
London Blackfriars	d																								
London Bridge	d																								
East Croydon	a																								
East Croydon	d									08 03					08 33					09 03				09 33	
Gatwick Airport ■ ✈	d									08 20					08 50					09 20				09 50	
Haywards Heath ■	d	07 38								08 38					09 05					09 38				10 05	
Preston Park	d														09 18									10 18	
Brighton ■	d		07 51	08 02	08 09	08 21		08 32	08 39		08 51	09 00	09 04	09 09		09 21		09 32	09 39		09 51	10 02	10 09		10 21
Hove ■	a	07 52	07 55	08 06	08 14	08 25		08 36	08 44	08 52	08 55	09 03	09 08	09 14	09 22	09 25		09 36	09 44	09 52	09 55	10 06	10 14	10 22	10 25
	d	07 52	07 55	08 06		08 25		08 36		08 52	08 55	09 04	09 08		09 22	09 25		09 36		09 52	09 55	10 06		10 22	10 25
Aldrington	d		07 57			08 27					08 57					09 27					09 57				10 27
Portslade	d	07 55	08 00	08 09		08 30		08 39		08 55	09 00		09 11		09 25	09 30		09 39		09 55	10 00	10 09		10 25	10 30
Fishersgate	d		08 02			08 32					09 02					09 32					10 02				10 32
Southwick	d		08 04	08 12		08 34		08 42			09 04		09 14			09 34		09 42			10 04	10 12			10 34
Shoreham-by-Sea	d	08 00	08 08	08 16		08 38		08 46		09 00	09 08	09 13	09 18		09 30	09 38		09 46		10 00	10 08	10 16		10 30	10 38
Lancing	d	08 04	08 12	08 20		08 42		08 50		09 04	09 12		09 22			09 42		09 50		10 04	10 12	10 20			10 42
East Worthing	d		08 15			08 45					09 15					09 45					10 15				10 45
Worthing ■	a	08 08	08 18	08 24		08 48		08 54		09 08	09 18	09 22	09 26		09 36	09 48		09 54		10 08	10 18	10 24		10 36	10 48
	d	08 09	08 18	08 25		08 48		08 55		09 09	09 18	09 22	09 27		09 39	09 48		09 55		10 09	10 18	10 25		10 39	10 48
West Worthing	d	08 11	08a21			08a51		08 57		09 11	09a21				09 41	09a51		09 57		10 11	10a21			10 41	10a51
Durrington-on-Sea	d	08 13						08 59		09 13					09 43			09 59		10 13				10 43	
Goring-by-Sea	d	08 16						09 02		09 16					09 46			10 02		10 16				10 46	
Angmering ■	d	08 20		08 32				09 06		09 20			09 34		09 50			10 06		10 20		10 32		10 50	
Littlehampton ■	a	08 31								09 31					10 01					10 31				11 01	
Barnham	a			08 43				09 18				09 42	09 46					10 18				10 43			
Barnham	d																								
Bognor Regis	a																								
Barnham	d			08 44				09 19				09 43	09 47					10 19				10 44			
Chichester ■	a			08 51				09 26				09 50	09 55					10 26				10 51			
Havant	a			09 05				09 38				10 01	10 09					10 38				11 05			
Havant	d			09 06									10 09									11 06			
Portsmouth & Southsea	a			09 18									10 21									11 18			
Portsmouth Harbour ⛴	a			09 22									10 26									11 22			
Havant	d							09 39				10 02						10 39							
Fareham	a							09 54				10 16						10 54							
Southampton Central ⛴	a							10 19				10 40						11 19							

		SN ■		SN	SN ■	SN	SN	SN	SN ■	SN	SN ■	SN		SN ■	SN	SN	SN	SN ■	SN	SN ■	SN	SN ■		SN	SN
London Victoria ■ ⊖	d				09 46				10 16					10 46				11 16				11 46			
Clapham Junction ■	d				09 53				10 23					10 53				11 23				11 53			
East Croydon	a				10 02				10 32					11 02				11 32				12 02			
St Pancras International	d																								
Farringdon	d																								
City Thameslink	d																								
London Blackfriars	d																								
London Bridge	d																								
East Croydon	a																								
East Croydon	d				10 03				10 33					11 03				11 33				12 03			
Gatwick Airport ■ ✈	d				10 20				10 50					11 20				11 50				12 20			
Haywards Heath ■	d				10 38				11 05					11 38				12 05				12 38			
Preston Park	d								11 18									12 18							
Brighton ■	d	10 32		10 39		10 51	11 02	11 09		11 21	11 32	11 39			11 51	12 02	12 09		12 21	12 32	12 39			12 51	13 02
Hove ■	a	10 36		10 44	10 52	10 55	11 06	11 14	11 22	11 25	11 36	11 44		11 52	11 55	12 06	12 14	12 22	12 25	12 36	12 44	12 52		12 55	13 06
	d	10 36			10 52	10 55	11 06		11 22	11 25	11 36			11 52	11 55	12 06		12 22	12 25	12 36		12 52		12 55	13 06
Aldrington	d					10 57				11 27					11 57				12 27					12 57	
Portslade	d	10 39			10 55	11 00	11 09		11 25	11 30	11 39			11 55	12 00	12 09		12 25	12 30	12 39		12 55		13 00	13 09
Fishersgate	d					11 02				11 32					12 02				12 32					13 02	
Southwick	d	10 42				11 04	11 12			11 34	11 42				12 04	12 12			12 34	12 42				13 04	13 12
Shoreham-by-Sea	d	10 46			11 00	11 08	11 16		11 30	11 38	11 46			12 00	12 08	12 16		12 30	12 38	12 46		13 00		13 08	13 16
Lancing	d	10 50			11 04	11 12	11 20			11 42	11 50			12 04	12 12	12 20			12 42	12 50		13 04		13 12	13 20
East Worthing	d					11 15				11 45					12 15				12 45					13 15	
Worthing ■	a	10 54			11 08	11 18	11 24		11 36	11 48	11 54			12 08	12 18	12 24		12 36	12 48	12 54		13 08		13 18	13 24
	d	10 55			11 09	11 18	11 25		11 39	11 48	11 55			12 09	12 18	12 25		12 39	12 48	12 55		13 09		13 18	13 25
West Worthing	d	10 57			11 11	11a21			11 41	11a51	11 57			12 11	12a21			12 41	12a51	12 57		13 11		13a21	
Durrington-on-Sea	d	10 59			11 13				11 43		11 59			12 13				12 43		12 59		13 13			
Goring-by-Sea	d	11 02			11 16				11 46		12 02			12 16				12 46		13 02		13 16			
Angmering ■	d	11 06			11 20		11 32		11 50		12 06			12 20		12 32		12 50		13 06		13 20			13 32
Littlehampton ■	a				11 31				12 01					12 31				13 01				13 31			
Barnham	a	11 18					11 43				12 18					12 43				13 18					13 43
Barnham	d																								
Bognor Regis	a																								
Barnham	d	11 19					11 44				12 19					12 44				13 19					13 44
Chichester ■	a	11 26					11 51				12 26					12 51				13 26					13 51
Havant	a	11 38					12 05				12 38					13 05				13 38					14 05
Havant	d						12 06									13 06									14 06
Portsmouth & Southsea	a						12 18									13 18									14 18
Portsmouth Harbour ⛴	a						12 22									13 22									14 22
Havant	d	11 39									12 39									13 39					
Fareham	a	11 54									12 54									13 54					
Southampton Central ⛴	a	12 19									13 19									14 19					

A To Great Malvern

Saturdays
26 May to 8 December

London - Gatwick Airport and Brighton - Worthing - Southampton Central

		SN	SN ■	SN	SN ■	SN	SN ■	SN		SN	SN	SN ■	SN	SN ■	SN	SN ■	SN	SN		SN	SN ■	SN	SN ■	SN	SN ■
London Victoria ■ ⊖	d		12 16				12 46					13 16				13 46					14 16				14 46
Clapham Junction ■	d		12 23				12 53					13 23				13 53					14 23				14 53
East Croydon	a		12 32				13 02					13 32				14 02					14 32				15 02
St Pancras International	d																								
Farringdon	d																								
City Thameslink	d																								
London Blackfriars	d																								
London Bridge	d																								
East Croydon	a																								
East Croydon	d		12 33				13 03					13 33				14 03					14 33				15 03
Gatwick Airport ■ ✈	d		12 50				13 20					13 50				14 20					14 50				15 20
Haywards Heath ■	d		13 05				13 38					14 05				14 38					15 05				15 38
Preston Park	d		13 18									14 18									15 18				
Brighton ■	d	13 09		13 21	13 32	13 39		13 51		14 02	14 09		14 21	14 32	14 39		14 51	15 02		15 09		15 21	15 32	15 39	
Hove ■	a	13 14	13 22	13 25	13 36	13 44	13 52	13 56		14 06	14 14	14 22	14 25	14 36	14 44	14 52	14 55	15 06		15 14	15 22	15 25	15 36	15 44	15 52
	d		13 22	13 25	13 36		13 52	13 56		14 06		14 22	14 25	14 36		14 52	14 55	15 06			15 22	15 25	15 36		15 52
Aldrington	d			13 27				13 58					14 27				14 57					15 27			
Portslade	d		13 25	13 30	13 39		13 55	14 01		14 09		14 25	14 30	14 39		14 55	15 00	15 09			15 25	15 30	15 39		15 55
Fishersgate	d			13 32				14 03					14 32				15 02					15 32			
Southwick	d			13 34	13 42			14 05		14 12			14 34	14 42			15 04	15 12				15 34	15 42		
Shoreham-by-Sea	d		13 30	13 38	13 46		14 00	14 09		14 16		14 30	14 38	14 46		15 00	15 08	15 16			15 30	15 38	15 46		16 00
Lancing	d			13 42	13 50		14 04	14 13		14 20			14 42	14 50		15 04	15 12	15 20				15 42	15 50		16 04
East Worthing	d			13 45				14 16					14 45				15 15					15 45			
Worthing ■	a		13 36	13 48	13 54		14 08	14 19		14 24		14 36	14 48	14 54		15 08	15 18	15 24			15 36	15 48	15 54		16 08
	d		13 39	13 48	13 55		14 09	14 19		14 25		14 39	14 48	14 55		15 09	15 18	15 25			15 39	15 48	15 55		16 09
West Worthing	d		13 41	13a51	13 57		14 11	14a22				14 41	14a51	14 57		15 11	15a21				15 41	15a51	15 57		16 11
Durrington-on-Sea	d		13 43		13 59		14 13					14 43		14 59		15 13					15 43		15 59		16 13
Goring-by-Sea	d		13 46		14 02		14 16					14 46		15 02		15 16					15 46		16 02		16 16
Angmering ■	d		13 50		14 06		14 20			14 32		14 50		15 06		15 20		15 32			15 50		16 06		16 20
Littlehampton ■	a		14 01				14 31					15 01				15 31					16 01				16 31
Barnham	a				14 18					14 43				15 18				15 43					16 18		
Barnham	d																								
Bognor Regis	a																								
Barnham	d				14 19					14 44				15 19				15 44					16 19		
Chichester ■	a				14 26					14 51				15 26				15 51					16 26		
Havant	a				14 38					15 05				15 38				16 05					16 38		
Havant	d									15 06								16 06							
Portsmouth & Southsea	a									15 18								16 18							
Portsmouth Harbour ⛴	a									15 22								16 22							
Havant	d				14 39									15 39									16 39		
Fareham	a				14 54									15 54									16 54		
Southampton Central ⛴	a				15 19									16 19									17 19		

		SN	SN	SN		SN ■	SN	SN ■	SN	SN ■	SN	GW ◇ A	SN	SN		SN ■	SN	SN ■	SN	SN ■	SN	SN	SN	SN ■	
London Victoria ■ ⊖	d					15 16				15 46						16 16				16 46				17 16	
Clapham Junction ■	d					15 23				15 53						16 23				16 53				17 23	
East Croydon	a					15 32				16 02						16 32				17 02				17 32	
St Pancras International	d																								
Farringdon	d																								
City Thameslink	d																								
London Blackfriars	d																								
London Bridge	d																								
East Croydon	a																								
East Croydon	d					15 33				16 03						16 33				17 03				17 33	
Gatwick Airport ■ ✈	d					15 50				16 20						16 50				17 20				17 50	
Haywards Heath ■	d					16 05				16 38						17 05				17 38				18 05	
Preston Park	d					16 18										17 18								18 18	
Brighton ■	d	15 51	16 02	16 09			16 21	16 32	16 39		16 51	17 00	17 04	17 09			17 21	17 32	17 39		17 51	18 02	18 09		
Hove ■	a	15 55	16 06	16 14		16 22	16 25	16 36	16 44	16 52	16 55	17 03	17 08	17 14		17 22	17 25	17 36	17 44	17 52	17 55	18 06	18 14	18 22	
	d	15 55	16 06			16 22	16 25	16 36		16 52	16 55	17 04	17 08			17 22	17 25	17 36		17 52	17 55	18 06		18 22	
Aldrington	d	15 57					16 27				16 57						17 27				17 57				
Portslade	d	16 00	16 09			16 25	16 30	16 39		16 55	17 00		17 11			17 25	17 30	17 39		17 55	18 00	18 09		18 25	
Fishersgate	d	16 02					16 32				17 02						17 32				18 02				
Southwick	d	16 04	16 12				16 34	16 42			17 04		17 14				17 34	17 42			18 04	18 12			
Shoreham-by-Sea	d	16 08	16 16			16 30	16 38	16 46		17 00	17 08	17 13	17 18			17 30	17 38	17 46		18 00	18 08	18 16		18 30	
Lancing	d	16 12	16 20				16 42	16 50		17 04	17 12		17 22				17 42	17 50		18 04	18 12	18 20			
East Worthing	d	16 15					16 45				17 15						17 45				18 15				
Worthing ■	a	16 18	16 24			16 36	16 48	16 54		17 08	17 18	17 22	17 26			17 36	17 48	17 54		18 08	18 18	18 24		18 36	
	d	16 18	16 25			16 39	16 48	16 55		17 09	17 18	17 22	17 27			17 39	17 48	17 55		18 09	18 18	18 25		18 39	
West Worthing	d	16a21				16 41	16a51	16 57		17 11	17a21					17 41	17a51	17 57		18 11	18a21			18 41	
Durrington-on-Sea	d					16 43		16 59		17 13						17 43		17 59		18 13				18 43	
Goring-by-Sea	d					16 46		17 02		17 16						17 46		18 02		18 16				18 46	
Angmering ■	d		16 32			16 50		17 06		17 20			17 34			17 50		18 06		18 20		18 32		18 50	
Littlehampton ■	a					17 01				17 31						18 01				18 31				19 01	
Barnham	a		16 43					17 18				17 42	17 46					18 18				18 43			
Barnham	d																								
Bognor Regis	a																								
Barnham	d		16 44					17 19				17 42	17 47					18 19				18 44			
Chichester ■	a		16 51					17 26				17 50	17 55					18 26				18 51			
Havant	a		17 05					17 38				18 01	18 09					18 38				19 05			
Havant	d		17 06										18 09									19 06			
Portsmouth & Southsea	a		17 18										18 21									19 18			
Portsmouth Harbour ⛴	a		17 22										18 26									19 22			
Havant	d							17 39				18 02						18 39							
Fareham	a							17 54				18 16						18 54							
Southampton Central ⛴	a							18 20				18 43						19 19							

A To Bristol Temple Meads

Table T188-F

Saturdays 26 May to 8 December

London - Gatwick Airport and Brighton - Worthing - Southampton Central

		SN	SN ■	SN	SN ■	SN	SN	SN	SN ■	SN	SN ■	SN	SN ■	SN	SN	SN	SN ■	SN	SN ■	SN	SN ■	SN	SN
London Victoria ⊖	d				17 46				18 16				18 46				19 16				19 46		
Clapham Junction	d				17 53				18 23				18 53				19 23				19 53		
East Croydon	a				18 02				18 32				19 02				19 32				20 02		
St Pancras International	d																						
Farringdon	d																						
City Thameslink	d																						
London Blackfriars	d																						
London Bridge	d																						
East Croydon	a																						
East Croydon	d				18 03				18 33				19 03				19 33				20 03		
Gatwick Airport ✈	d				18 20				18 50				19 20				19 50				20 20		
Haywards Heath	d				18 38				19 05				19 38				20 05				20 38		
Preston Park	d								19 18								20 18						
Brighton	d	18 21	18 32	18 39		18 51	19 02	19 09		19 21	19 32	19 39		19 51	20 02	20 09		20 21	20 32	20 39		20 51	21 02
Hove	a	18 25	18 36	18 44	18 52	18 55	19 06	19 14	19 22	19 25	19 36	19 44	19 52	19 55	20 06	20 14	20 22	20 25	20 36	20 44	20 52	20 55	21 06
	d	18 25	18 36		18 52	18 55	19 06		19 22	19 25	19 36		19 52	19 55	20 06		20 22	20 25	20 36		20 52	20 55	21 06
Aldrington	d	18 27				18 57				19 27				19 57				20 27				20 57	
Portslade	d	18 30	18 39		18 55	19 00	19 09		19 25	19 30	19 39		19 55	20 00	20 09		20 25	20 30	20 39		20 55	21 00	21 09
Fishersgate	d	18 32				19 02				19 32				20 02				20 32				21 02	
Southwick	d	18 34	18 42			19 04	19 12			19 34	19 42			20 04	20 12			20 34	20 42		20 58	21 04	21 12
Shoreham-by-Sea	d	18 38	18 46		19 00	19 08	19 16		19 30	19 38	19 46		20 00	20 08	20 16		20 30	20 38	20 46		21 02	21 08	21 16
Lancing	d	18 42	18 50		19 04	19 12	19 20			19 42	19 50		20 04	20 12	20 20			20 42	20 50		21 06	21 12	21 20
East Worthing	d	18 45				19 15				19 45				20 15				20 45				21 15	
Worthing	a	18 48	18 54		19 08	19 18	19 24		19 36	19 48	19 54		20 08	20 18	20 24		20 36	20 48	20 54		21 10	21 18	21 24
	d	18 48	18 55		19 09	19 18	19 25		19 39	19 48	19 55		20 09	20 18	20 25		20 39	20 48	20 55		21 11	21 18	21 25
West Worthing	d	18a51	18 57		19 11	19a21			19 41	19a51	19 57		20 11	20a21			20 41	20a51	20 57		21 13	21a21	
Durrington-on-Sea	d		18 59		19 13				19 43		19 59		20 13				20 43		20 59		21 15		
Goring-by-Sea	d		19 02		19 16				19 46		20 02		20 16				20 46		21 02		21 18		
Angmering	d		19 06		19 20		19 32		19 50		20 06		20 20		20 32		20 50		21 06		21 22		21 32
Littlehampton	a				19 31				20 01				20 31				21 01				21 32		
Barnham	a		19 18				19 43				20 18				20 43				21 18				21 43
Barnham	d																						
Bognor Regis	a																						
Barnham	d		19 19				19 44				20 19				20 44				21 19				21 44
Chichester	a		19 26				19 51				20 26				20 51				21 26				21 51
Havant	a		19 38				20 05				20 38				21 05				21 38				22 05
Havant	d						20 06								21 06								22 06
Portsmouth & Southsea	a						20 18								21 18								22 18
Portsmouth Harbour	a						20 22								21 22								22 22
Havant	d		19 39								20 39								21 39				
Fareham	a		19 54								20 54								21 54				
Southampton Central	a		20 19								21 19								22 19				

		SN	SN ■	SN	SN	SN	SN ■	SN	SN	SN	SN ■	SN	SN	SN ■	SN	SN ■	SN	SN ■	SN ■
London Victoria ⊖	d		20 16				20 46				21 16			21 46		22 16		22 46	23 16
Clapham Junction	d		20 23				20 53				21 23			21 53		22 23		22 53	23 23
East Croydon	a		20 32				21 02				21 32			22 02		22 32		23 02	23 32
St Pancras International	d																		
Farringdon	d																		
City Thameslink	d																		
London Blackfriars	d																		
London Bridge	d																		
East Croydon	a																		
East Croydon	d		20 33				21 03				21 33			22 03		22 33		23 03	23 33
Gatwick Airport ✈	d		20 50				21 20				21 50			22 20		22 50		23 20	23 54
Haywards Heath	d		21 05				21 38				22 05			22 38		23 05		23 38	00 09
Preston Park	d		21 18								22 18					23 18			00 21
Brighton	d	21 09		21 21	21 32	21 39		21 51	22 02	22 09		22 32	22 39		23 02		23 39		
Hove	a	21 14	21 22	21 25	21 36	21 44	21 52	21 55	22 06	22 14	22 22	22 36	22 44	22 52	23 07	23 22	23 44	23 52	00 25
	d		21 22	21 25	21 36		21 52	21 55	22 06		22 22	22 37		22 52	23 07	23 22		23 52	00 25
Aldrington	d			21 27				21 57				22 39			23 09				
Portslade	d		21 25	21 30	21 39		21 55	22 00	22 09		22 25	22 41		22 55	23 12	23 25		23 55	00 28
Fishersgate	d			21 32				22 02				22 43			23 14				
Southwick	d		21 28	21 34	21 42		21 58	22 04	22 12		22 28	22 45		22 58	23 16	23 28		23 58	00 31
Shoreham-by-Sea	d		21 32	21 38	21 46		22 02	22 08	22 16		22 32	22 49		23 02	23 20	23 32		00 02	00 35
Lancing	d		21 36	21 42	21 50		22 06	22 12	22 20		22 36	22 53		23 06	23 24	23 36		00 06	00 39
East Worthing	d			21 45				22 15				22 56			23 27				
Worthing	a		21 40	21 48	21 54		22 10	22 18	22 24		22 40	22 58		23 10	23 30	23 40		00 11	00 43
	d		21 41	21 48	21 55		22 11	22 18	22 25		22 41	22 59		23 11	23 30	23 41			00 43
West Worthing	d		21 43	21a51			22 13	22a21			22 43	23 01		23 13	23a33	23 43			00 45
Durrington-on-Sea	d		21 45				22 15				22 45	23 03		23 15		23 45			00 48
Goring-by-Sea	d		21 48				22 18				22 48	23 06		23 18		23 48			00 50
Angmering	d		21 52		22 02		22 22		22 32		22 52	23 10		23 22		23 52			00 54
Littlehampton	a		22 02				22 33				23 02			23 32					
Barnham	a				22 16				22 43			23 22				00 04			01 06
Barnham	d															00 12			
Bognor Regis	a															00 19			
Barnham	d				22 17				22 44			23 24							01 08
Chichester	a				22 24				22 51			23 31							01 15
Havant	a				22 38				23 05										
Havant	d				22 39				23 06										
Portsmouth & Southsea	a				22 52				23 18										
Portsmouth Harbour	a				22 56				23 22										
Havant	d																		
Fareham	a																		
Southampton Central	a																		

Table T188-F

Sundays 20 May to 2 December

London - Gatwick Airport and Brighton - Worthing - Southampton Central

		SN ■ A	SN	SN ■ A	SN ■ A	SN ■	SN	SN	SN	SN	SN	SN	SN	SN	SN	SN	SN	SN	SN	SN	SN	SN	GW ◇ B
London Victoria ⊖	d					00 02										08 14				09 16			
Clapham Junction	d					00 09										08 21				09 23			
East Croydon	a					00 23										08 39				09 32			
St Pancras International	d																						
Farringdon	d																						
City Thameslink	d																						
London Blackfriars	d																						
London Bridge	d																						
East Croydon	a																						
East Croydon	d					00 24										08 40				09 33			
Gatwick Airport ✈	d					00 44										08 59				09 50			
Haywards Heath	d				00 09	01 02										09 10				10 02			
Preston Park	d				00 21											09 22				10 14			
Brighton	d		00 04			01s16	07 15	07 30	07 46	08 00	08 09	08 20	08 30	09 00	09 09		09 30	10 00	10 09		10 30	11 00	11 10
Hove	a		00 08		00 25	01s25	07 19	07 34	07 50	08 04	08 13	08 24	08 34	09 04	09 13	09 25	09 34	10 04	10 13	10 17	10 34	11 04	11 13
	d		00 09		00 25		07 19	07 34		08 04		08 24	08 34	09 04		09 26	09 34	10 04		10 19	10 34	11 04	11 14
Aldrington	d		00 11					07 36		08 06			08 36	09 06			09 36	10 06			10 36	11 06	
Portslade	d		00 14		00 28	01s28		07 39		08 09			08 39	09 09		09 29	09 39	10 09		10 22	10 39	11 09	
Fishersgate	d		00 16					07 41		08 11			08 41	09 11			09 41	10 11			10 41	11 11	
Southwick	d		00 18		00 31	01s31		07 43		08 13			08 43	09 13			09 43	10 13			10 43	11 13	
Shoreham-by-Sea	d	00 02	00 22		00 35	01s34	07 26	07 47		08 17		08 31	08 47	09 17		09 34	09 47	10 17		10 27	10 47	11 17	11 21
Lancing	d	00 06	00 26		00 39	01s38		07 51		08 21			08 51	09 21		09 38	09 51	10 21		10 31	10 51	11 21	
East Worthing	d		00 29					07 54		08 24			08 54	09 24			09 54	10 24			10 54	11 24	
Worthing	a	00 11	00 31		00 43	01 43	07 32	07 56		08 26		08 37	08 56	09 26		09 42	09 56	10 26		10 35	10 56	11 26	11 31
	d		00 32		00 43		07 33	07 57		08 27		08 38	08 57	09 27		09 42	09 57	10 27		10 35	10 57	11 27	11 31
West Worthing	d		00a34		00 45			07 59		08 29			08 59	09 29		09 44	09 59	10 29		10 37	10 59	11 29	
Durrington-on-Sea	d				00 48			08 01		08 31			09 01	09 31		09 47	10 01	10 31		10 40	11 01	11 31	
Goring-by-Sea	d				00 50			08 04		08 34			09 04	09 34		09 49	10 04	10 34		10 42	11 04	11 34	
Angmering	d				00 54		07 40	08 08		08 38		08 45	09 08	09 38		09 53	10 08	10 38		10 46	11 08	11 38	
Littlehampton	a															10 03				10 56			
Barnham	a				01 06		07 53	08 20		08 50		08 57	09 21	09 50			10 20	10 50			11 20	11 50	11 55
Barnham	d			00 12																			
Bognor Regis	a			00 19																			
Barnham	d				01 08		07 54	08 21		08 51		08 57	09 22	09 51			10 21	10 51			11 21	11 51	11 56
Chichester	a				01 15		08 02	08 28		08 58		09 05	09 29	09 58			10 28	10 58			11 28	11 58	12 03
Havant	a						08 16	08 49		09 10		09 19	09 50	10 10			10 49	11 10			11 49	12 10	12 15
Havant	d						08 16	08 50				09 19	09 51				10 50				11 50		
Portsmouth & Southsea	a						08 28	09 03				09 31	10 04				11 03				12 03		
Portsmouth Harbour	a						08 32	09 07				09 35	10 08				11 07				12 07		
Havant	d									09 11				10 11				11 11				12 11	12 15
Fareham	a									09 25				10 25				11 25				12 25	12 33
Southampton Central	a									09 50				10 50				11 50				12 50	12 55

		SN	SN	SN	SN	SN	SN	SN	SN	SN	SN	SN	SN	SN	SN	SN	SN	SN	SN	SN C	GW ◇ D	GW ◇ E	SN
London Victoria ⊖	d	10 16					11 16				12 16				13 16				14 16				
Clapham Junction	d	10 23					11 23				12 23				13 23				14 23				
East Croydon	a	10 32					11 32				12 32				13 32				14 32				
St Pancras International	d																						
Farringdon	d																						
City Thameslink	d																						
London Blackfriars	d																						
London Bridge	d																						
East Croydon	a																						
East Croydon	d	10 33					11 33				12 33				13 33				14 33				
Gatwick Airport ✈	d	10 50					11 50				12 50				13 50				14 50				
Haywards Heath	d	11 02					12 02				13 02				14 02				15 02				
Preston Park	d	11 14					12 14				13 14				14 14				15 14				
Brighton	d		11 13	11 30	12 00	12 09		12 30	13 00	13 09		13 30	14 00	14 09		14 30	15 00	15 09		15 30	15 47	15 47	16 00
Hove	a	11 17	11 17	11 34	12 04	12 13	12 17	12 34	13 04	13 13	13 17	13 34	14 04	14 13	14 17	14 34	15 04	15 13	15 17	15 34	15 50	15 50	16 04
	d	11 19		11 34	12 04		12 19	12 34	13 04		13 19	13 34	14 04		14 19	14 34	15 04		15 19	15 34	15 51	15 51	16 04
Aldrington	d			11 36	12 06			12 36	13 06			13 36	14 06			14 36	15 06			15 36			16 06
Portslade	d	11 22		11 39	12 09		12 22	12 39	13 09		13 22	13 39	14 09		14 22	14 39	15 09		15 22	15 39			16 09
Fishersgate	d			11 41	12 11			12 41	13 11			13 41	14 11			14 41	15 11			15 41			16 11
Southwick	d			11 43	12 13			12 43	13 13			13 43	14 13			14 43	15 13			15 43			16 13
Shoreham-by-Sea	d	11 27		11 47	12 17		12 27	12 47	13 17		13 27	13 47	14 17		14 27	14 47	15 17		15 27	15 47	15 57	15 57	16 17
Lancing	d	11 31		11 51	12 21		12 31	12 51	13 21		13 31	13 51	14 21		14 31	14 51	15 21		15 31	15 51			16 21
East Worthing	d			11 54	12 24			12 54	13 24			13 54	14 24			14 54	15 24			15 54			16 24
Worthing	a	11 35		11 56	12 26		12 35	12 56	13 26		13 35	13 56	14 26		14 35	14 56	15 26		15 35	15 56	16 04	16 04	16 26
	d	11 35		11 57	12 27		12 35	12 57	13 27		13 35	13 57	14 27		14 35	14 57	15 27		15 35	15 57	16 09	16 09	16 27
West Worthing	d	11 37		11 59	12 29		12 37	12 59	13 29		13 37	13 59	14 29		14 37	14 59	15 29		15 37	15 59			16 29
Durrington-on-Sea	d	11 40		12 01	12 31		12 40	13 01	13 31		13 40	14 01	14 31		14 40	15 01	15 31		15 40	16 01			16 31
Goring-by-Sea	d	11 42		12 04	12 34		12 42	13 04	13 34		13 42	14 04	14 34		14 42	15 04	15 34		15 42	16 04			16 34
Angmering	d	11 46		12 08	12 38		12 46	13 08	13 38		13 46	14 08	14 38		14 46	15 08	15 38		15 46	16 08			16 38
Littlehampton	a	11 56					12 56				13 56				14 56				15 56				
Barnham	a			12 20	12 50			13 20	13 50			14 20	14 50			15 20	15 50			16 20	16 26	16 26	16 50
Barnham	d																						
Bognor Regis	a																						
Barnham	d			12 21	12 51			13 21	13 51			14 21	14 51			15 21	15 51			16 31	16 27	16 27	16 51
Chichester	a			12 28	12 58			13 28	13 58			14 28	14 58			15 28	15 58			16 38	16 34	16 34	16 58
Havant	a			12 49	13 10			13 49	14 10			14 49	15 10			15 49	16 10			16 59	16 44	16 45	17 10
Havant	d			12 50				13 50				14 50				15 50							
Portsmouth & Southsea	a			13 03				14 03				15 03				16 03							
Portsmouth Harbour	a			13 07				14 07				15 07				16 07							
Havant	d				13 11				14 11				15 11				16 11				16 45	16 46	17 11
Fareham	a				13 25				14 25				15 25				16 25				16 59	16 59	17 25
Southampton Central	a				13 50				14 50				15 50				16 50				17 20	17 20	17 50

A not 20 May. From London Victoria
B To Cardiff Central
C To Fratton
D until 9 September. To Bristol Temple Meads
E from 16 September. To Bristol Temple Meads

Table T188-F

Sundays
20 May to 2 December

London - Gatwick Airport and Brighton - Worthing - Southampton Central

	SN	SN	SN	SN	SN	SN	SN A	GW ◇ B	SN	SN
London Victoria ■ ⊖ d		15 16				16 16				
Clapham Junction ■ d		15 23				16 23				
East Croydon a		15 32				16 32				
St Pancras International d										
Farringdon d										
City Thameslink d										
London Blackfriars d										
London Bridge d										
East Croydon a										
East Croydon d		15 33				16 33				
Gatwick Airport ■ ✈ d		15 50				16 50				
Haywards Heath ■ d		16 02				17 02				
Preston Park d		16 14				17 14				
Brighton ■ d	16 09		16 30	17 00	17 09		17 30	17 46	18 00	18 09
Hove ■ a	16 13	16 17	16 34	17 04	17 13	17 17	17 34	17 49	18 04	18 13
d		16 19	16 34	17 04		17 19	17 34	17 50	18 04	
Aldrington d			16 36	17 06			17 36		18 06	
Portslade d		16 22	16 39	17 09		17 22	17 39		18 09	
Fishersgate d			16 41	17 11			17 41		18 11	
Southwick d			16 43	17 13			17 43		18 13	
Shoreham-by-Sea d		16 27	16 47	17 17		17 27	17 47	17 56	18 17	
Lancing d		16 31	16 51	17 21		17 31	17 51		18 21	
East Worthing d			16 54	17 24			17 54		18 24	
Worthing ■ a		16 35	16 56	17 26		17 35	17 56	18 03	18 26	
d		16 35	16 57	17 27		17 35	17 57	18 08	18 27	
West Worthing d		16 37	16 59	17 29		17 37	17 59		18 29	
Durrington-on-Sea d		16 40	17 01	17 31		17 40	18 01		18 31	
Goring-by-Sea d		16 42	17 04	17 34		17 42	18 04		18 34	
Angmering ■ d		16 46	17 08	17 38		17 46	18 08		18 38	
Littlehampton ■ a		16 56				17 56				
Barnham a			17 20	17 50			18 20	18 26	18 50	
Barnham d										
Bognor Regis a										
Barnham d			17 21	17 51			18 31	18 27	18 51	
Chichester ■ a			17 28	17 58			18 38	18 34	18 58	
Havant a			17 49	18 10			18 59	18 50	19 10	
Havant d			17 50							
Portsmouth & Southsea a			18 03							
Portsmouth Harbour ⛴ a			18 07							
Havant d				18 11				18 50	19 11	
Fareham a				18 25				19 04	19 25	
Southampton Central ⛴ a				18 50				19 26	19 50	

	SN	SN	SN	SN	SN	SN	SN	SN	SN	SN	SN
London Victoria ■ ⊖ d	17 16				18 16				19 16		
Clapham Junction ■ d	17 23				18 23				19 23		
East Croydon a	17 32				18 32				19 32		
St Pancras International d											
Farringdon d											
City Thameslink d											
London Blackfriars d											
London Bridge d											
East Croydon a											
East Croydon d	17 33				18 33				19 33		
Gatwick Airport ■ ✈ d	17 50				18 50				19 50		
Haywards Heath ■ d	18 02				19 02				20 02		
Preston Park d	18 14				19 14				20 14		
Brighton ■ d		18 30	19 00	19 09		19 30	20 00	20 09		20 30	21 00
Hove ■ a	18 17	18 34	19 04	19 13	19 17	19 34	20 04	20 13	20 17	20 34	21 04
d	18 19	18 34	19 04		19 19	19 34	20 04		20 19	20 34	21 04
Aldrington d		18 36	19 06			19 36	20 06			20 36	21 06
Portslade d	18 22	18 39	19 09		19 22	19 39	20 09		20 22	20 39	21 09
Fishersgate d		18 41	19 11			19 41	20 11			20 41	21 11
Southwick d		18 43	19 13			19 43	20 13			20 43	21 13
Shoreham-by-Sea d	18 27	18 47	19 17		19 27	19 47	20 17		20 27	20 47	21 17
Lancing d	18 31	18 51	19 21		19 31	19 51	20 21		20 31	20 51	21 21
East Worthing d		18 54	19 24			19 54	20 24			20 54	21 24
Worthing ■ a	18 35	18 56	19 26		19 35	19 56	20 26		20 35	20 56	21 26
d	18 35	18 57	19 27		19 35	19 57	20 27		20 35	20 57	21 27
West Worthing d	18 37	18 59	19 29		19 37	19 59	20 29		20 37	20 59	21 29
Durrington-on-Sea d	18 40	19 01	19 31		19 40	20 01	20 31		20 40	21 01	21 31
Goring-by-Sea d	18 42	19 04	19 34		19 42	20 04	20 34		20 42	21 04	21 34
Angmering ■ d	18 46	19 08	19 38		19 46	20 08	20 38		20 46	21 08	21 38
Littlehampton ■ a	18 56				19 56				20 56		
Barnham a		19 20	19 50			20 20	20 50			21 20	21 50
Barnham d											
Bognor Regis a											
Barnham d		19 21	19 51			20 21	20 51			21 21	21 51
Chichester ■ a		19 28	19 58			20 28	20 58			21 28	21 58
Havant a		19 49	20 10			20 49	21 10			21 49	22 10
Havant d		19 50				20 50				21 50	
Portsmouth & Southsea a		20 03				21 03				22 03	
Portsmouth Harbour ⛴ a		20 07				21 07				22 07	
Havant d			20 11				21 11				22 11
Fareham a			20 25				21 25				22 25
Southampton Central ⛴ a			20 50				21 50				22 50

	SN	SN	SN	GW	SN	SN	SN	SN	SN	SN	SN	SN
London Victoria ■ ⊖ d		20 16					21 16				22 16	23 16
Clapham Junction ■ d		20 23					21 23				22 23	23 23
East Croydon a		20 32					21 32				22 32	23 32
St Pancras International d												
Farringdon d												
City Thameslink d												
London Blackfriars d												
London Bridge d												
East Croydon a												
East Croydon d		20 33					21 33				22 33	23 33
Gatwick Airport ■ ✈ d		20 50					21 50				22 50	23 55
Haywards Heath ■ d		21 02					22 02				23 02	00 08
Preston Park d		21 14					22 14				23 14	00 19
Brighton ■ d	21 10		21 30	21 46	21 55	22 10			22 47	23 05		
Hove ■ a	21 14	21 17	21 34	21 49	21 59	22 14	22 17		22 51	23 09	23 17	00 23
d		21 19	21 34	21 50	22 00		22 19		22 52		23 19	00 23
Aldrington d			21 36		22 02		22 21		22 54			
Portslade d		21 22	21 39		22 04		22 23		22 56		23 22	00 26
Fishersgate d			21 41		22 06		22 25		22 58			
Southwick d			21 43		22 08		22 27		23 00			
Shoreham-by-Sea d		21 27	21 47	21 56	22 12		22 31		23 04		23 27	00 31
Lancing d		21 31	21 51		22 16		22 35		23 08		23 31	00 35
East Worthing d			21 54		22 19		22 38		23 11			
Worthing ■ a		21 35	21 56	22 02	22 22		22 40		23 14		23 35	00 39
d		21 35	21 57	22 03	22 22		22 44	22 48	23 14			
West Worthing d		21 37	21 59		22 24			22 50	23 16			
Durrington-on-Sea d		21 40	22 01		22 27			22 52	23 19			
Goring-by-Sea d		21 42	22 04		22 29			22 55	23 21			
Angmering ■ d		21 46	22 08		22 34			22 59	23 26			
Littlehampton ■ a		21 56			22 44			23 10	23 36			
Barnham a			22 20	22 24			23 00		23 51			
Barnham d												
Bognor Regis a												
Barnham d			22 29	22 24			23 01		23 52			
Chichester ■ a			22 36	22 32			23 08		23 59			
Havant a			22 57	22 44			23 26					
Havant d			22 58	22 44			23 26					
Portsmouth & Southsea a			23 15	23 02			23 38					
Portsmouth Harbour ⛴ a			23 20	23 07			23 42					
Havant d												
Fareham a												
Southampton Central ⛴ a												

A To Fratton
B To Bristol Temple Meads

Table T188-R

Mondays to Fridays
21 May to 7 December

Southampton Central - Worthing - Brighton and Gatwick Airport - London

	SN MX A	SN	SN ■	SN	SN	SN ■	SN ■ B	SN	SN	SN ■	SN
Southampton Central ⛴ d											
Fareham d											
Havant a											
Portsmouth Harbour ⛴ d											
Portsmouth & Southsea d											
Havant a											
Havant d											
Chichester ■ d		04 54			05 25				05 50		06 16
Barnham a		05 01			05 32				05 57		06 24
Bognor Regis d											
Barnham a											
Barnham d		05 02			05 33				05 58		06 24
Littlehampton ■ d			05 14			05 44	05 52			06 16	
Angmering ■ d		05 14	05 23		05 44	05 54	06 01		06 10	06 26	06 36
Goring-by-Sea d		05 18	05 27		05 48	05 58	06 06		06 14	06 31	06 40
Durrington-on-Sea d		05 20	05 30		05 51	06 00	06 09		06 16	06 34	06 43
West Worthing d		05 23	05 32		05 53	06 03	06 12		06 19	06 37	06 46
Worthing ■ a		05 25	05 35		05 56	06 05	06 14		06 21	06 39	06 49
d	00 03	05 26	05 35		05 56	06 06	06 15		06 22	06 40	06 49
East Worthing d	00 05	05 28			05 59				06 24		
Lancing d	00 08	05 31	05 40		06 02	06 10	06 19		06 27	06 44	06 53
Shoreham-by-Sea d	00 13	05 36	05 44		06 06	06 15	06 24		06 32	06 49	06 58
Southwick d	00 16	05 39			06 09				06 35		07 01
Fishersgate d	00 18	05 41			06 11				06 37		07 03
Portslade d	00 20	05 44	05 49		06 14	06 20	06 29		06 40	06 54	07 05
Aldrington d	00 23	05 46			06 16				06 42		
Hove ■ a	00 25	05 48	05 52		06 18	06 23	06 32		06 44	06 57	07 08
d	00 26	05 49	05 53	06 01	06 19	06 23	06 32	06 36	06 45	06 57	07 09
Brighton ■ a	00 30	05 54		06 05	06 24			06 40	06 49		07 14
Preston Park a			05 58			06 28	06 37			07 02	
Haywards Heath ■ a			06 13			06 44	06 50			07 17	
Gatwick Airport ■ ✈ a			06 31			07 02				07 32	
East Croydon a			06 48			07 18	07 20			07 48	
East Croydon d							07 21				
London Bridge a							07 34				
London Blackfriars a							07 41				
City Thameslink a							07 43				
Farringdon a							07 46				
St Pancras International a							07 50				
East Croydon d			06 49			07 19				07 50	
Clapham Junction ■ a			06 58			07 28				08 00	
London Victoria ■ ⊖ a			07 05			07 35				08 08	

	SN	SN	SN ■	SN ■ B	SN ■	SN	SN ■	SN	SN	SN	SN ■
Southampton Central ⛴ d					05 46						
Fareham d					06 11						
Havant a					06 27						
Portsmouth Harbour ⛴ d								06 32			
Portsmouth & Southsea d								06 36			
Havant a								06 50			
Havant d					06 28			06 51			
Chichester ■ d					06 44			07 05			
Barnham a					06 52			07 12			
Bognor Regis d											
Barnham a											
Barnham d					06 55			07 13			
Littlehampton ■ d			06 47	06 52			07 12		07 22		07 42
Angmering ■ d			06 56	07 01	07 07		07 21	07 25	07 31		07 53
Goring-by-Sea d			07 01	07 06	07 11		07 26	07 30	07 36		07 57
Durrington-on-Sea d			07 04	07 09	07 13		07 29	07 33	07 39		08 00
West Worthing d	06 52		07 07	07 12	07 16	07 22	07 32	07 36	07 42	07 52	08 03
Worthing ■ a	06 55		07 09	07 14	07 18	07 25	07 34	07 38	07 44	07 55	08 06
d	06 55		07 10	07 15	07 19	07 25	07 35	07 39	07 45	07 55	08 06
East Worthing d	06 58					07 28			07 48	07 58	
Lancing d	07 01		07 14	07 19	07 23	07 31	07 39	07 43	07 51	08 01	08 11
Shoreham-by-Sea d	07 06		07 19	07 24	07 27	07 36	07 44	07 48	07 56	08 06	08 15
Southwick d	07 09				07 30	07 39		07 51	07 59	08 09	
Fishersgate d	07 11					07 41				08 11	
Portslade d	07 14		07 24	07 29	07 34	07 44	07 49	07 55	08 03	08 14	08 20
Aldrington d	07 16					07 46				08 16	
Hove ■ a	07 18		07 27	07 32	07 37	07 48	07 52	07 58	08 06	08 18	08 23
d	07 19	07 26	07 27	07 32	07 39	07 49	07 52	07 59	08 07	08 19	08 24
Brighton ■ a	07 23	07 30			07 44	07 54		08 03	08 11	08 25	
Preston Park a			07 32	07 37			07 57				08 29
Haywards Heath ■ a			07 47	07 50			08 14				08 44
Gatwick Airport ■ ✈ a			08 02				08 31				09 01
East Croydon a			08 18	08 20			08 48				09 18
East Croydon d				08 21							
London Bridge a				08 34							
London Blackfriars a				08 41							
City Thameslink a				08 43							
Farringdon a				08 46							
St Pancras International a				08 50							
East Croydon d			08 20				08 50				09 19
Clapham Junction ■ a			08 30				09 00				09 28
London Victoria ■ ⊖ a			08 37				09 08				09 35

	GW	SN	SN	SN ■	SN	SN	SN ■	SN ■	SN	SN	SN
Southampton Central ⛴ d							07 33				
Fareham d							07 57				
Havant a							08 12				
Portsmouth Harbour ⛴ d	07 09		07 18								08 29
Portsmouth & Southsea d	07 13		07 22								08 33
Havant a	07 25		07 38								08 45
Havant d	07 27		07 38				08 12				08 46
Chichester ■ d	07 43		07 58				08 23				09 00
Barnham a	07 51		08 06				08 31				09 08
Bognor Regis d											
Barnham a											
Barnham d	07 52		08 06				08 31				09 09
Littlehampton ■ d		07 59		08 14				08 44			
Angmering ■ d	08 01	08 08	08 18	08 23			08 44	08 53			09 19
Goring-by-Sea d		08 12		08 27			08 48	08 57			
Durrington-on-Sea d		08 14		08 30			08 51	08 59			
West Worthing d		08 17		08 32		08 38	08 53	09 02		09 12	
Worthing ■ a	08 10	08 19	08 25	08 35		08 41	08 56	09 04		09 15	09 26
d	08 11	08 20	08 25	08 35		08 41	08 56	09 05		09 15	09 26
East Worthing d		08 23	08 28			08 44				09 18	
Lancing d		08 26	08 31	08 39		08 47	09 00			09 21	09 30
Shoreham-by-Sea d	08 20	08 30	08 36	08 44		08 52	09 05	09 12		09 26	09 35
Southwick d		08 33	08 39			08 55	09 08			09 29	09 38
Fishersgate d			08 41			08 57				09 31	
Portslade d	08 25	08 37	08 43	08 48		09 00	09 12	09 17		09 34	09 42
Aldrington d			08 46			09 02				09 36	
Hove ■ a	08 28	08 40	08 48	08 51		09 04	09 16	09 20		09 38	09 45
d	08 30	08 41	08 48	08 52	09 00	09 07	09 16	09 21	09 26	09 39	09 46
Brighton ■ a	08 35	08 45	08 54		09 04	09 12	09 21		09 30	09 44	09 51
Preston Park a				08 57							
Haywards Heath ■ a				09 11				09 36			
Gatwick Airport ■ ✈ a				09 27				09 56			
East Croydon a				09 42				10 11			
East Croydon d											
London Bridge a											
London Blackfriars a											
City Thameslink a											
Farringdon a											
St Pancras International a											
East Croydon d				09 43				10 12			
Clapham Junction ■ a				09 52				10 21			
London Victoria ■ ⊖ a				09 59				10 29			

	SN ■	SN	SN	SN ■	SN ■	SN	SN	SN	TL ■	SN	SN
Southampton Central ⛴ d				08 26							
Fareham d				08 56							
Havant a				09 10							
Portsmouth Harbour ⛴ d											
Portsmouth & Southsea d								09 33			
Havant a								09 45			
Havant d				09 11				09 46			
Chichester ■ d				09 23				10 00			
Barnham a				09 30				10 07			
Bognor Regis d											
Barnham a											
Barnham d				09 31				10 09			
Littlehampton ■ d	09 14				09 44				10 14		
Angmering ■ d	09 23			09 43	09 53			10 19	10 23		
Goring-by-Sea d	09 27			09 47	09 57				10 27		
Durrington-on-Sea d	09 29			09 50	09 59				10 29		
West Worthing d	09 32		09 42	09 52	10 02		10 12		10 32		10 42
Worthing ■ a	09 34		09 45	09 55	10 04		10 15	10 26	10 34		10 45
d	09 35		09 45	09 56	10 05		10 15	10 26	10 35		10 45
East Worthing d			09 48				10 18				10 48
Lancing d	09 39		09 51	10 00			10 21	10 30	10 39		10 51
Shoreham-by-Sea d	09 43		09 56	10 05	10 12		10 26	10 35	10 43		10 56
Southwick d			09 59	10 08			10 29	10 38			10 59
Fishersgate d			10 01				10 31				11 01
Portslade d	09 48		10 04	10 11	10 17		10 34	10 42	10 48		11 04
Aldrington d			10 06				10 36				11 06
Hove ■ a	09 51		10 08	10 15	10 20		10 38	10 45	10 51		11 08
d	09 51	09 56	10 09	10 16	10 21	10 26	10 39	10 46	10 51	10 56	11 09
Brighton ■ a		10 01	10 14	10 21		10 31	10 44	10 51		11 01	11 14
Preston Park a	09 56								10 56		
Haywards Heath ■ a	10 10				10 36				11 09		
Gatwick Airport ■ ✈ a	10 26				10 56						
East Croydon a	10 41				11 11						
East Croydon d											
London Bridge a											
London Blackfriars a											
City Thameslink a											
Farringdon a											
St Pancras International a											
East Croydon d	10 42				11 12						
Clapham Junction ■ a	10 51				11 21						
London Victoria ■ ⊖ a	10 59				11 29						

A From Portsmouth Harbour
B To Bedford

Table T188-R

Mondays to Fridays

21 May to 7 December

Southampton Central - Worthing - Brighton and Gatwick Airport - London

		SN		SN ■	SN	SN	SN	SN ■	SN	SN	SN ■	SN ■		SN	SN	SN	SN ■	SN	SN	SN	SN ■	SN		SN	SN
Southampton Central	d	09 26									10 26									11 26					
Fareham	d										10 53														
Havant	a	10 09									11 09									12 09					
Portsmouth Harbour	d															11 29									12 29
Portsmouth & Southsea	d						10 33									11 33									12 33
Havant	a						10 45									11 45									12 45
Havant	d	10 10					10 46				11 10					11 46				12 10					12 46
Chichester	d	10 22					11 00				11 22					12 00				12 22					13 00
Barnham	a	10 30					11 07				11 30					12 07				12 30					13 07
Bognor Regis	d																								
Barnham	a																								
Barnham	d	10 31					11 09				11 31					12 09				12 31					13 09
Littlehampton	d			10 44				11 14				11 44					12 14				12 44				
Angmering	d	10 43		10 53			11 19	11 23			11 43	11 53				12 19	12 23			12 43	12 53				13 19
Goring-by-Sea	d	10 47		10 57				11 27			11 47	11 57					12 27			12 47	12 57				
Durrington-on-Sea	d	10 50		10 59				11 29			11 50	11 59					12 29			12 50	12 59				
West Worthing	d	10 52		11 02		11 12		11 32		11 42	11 52	12 02			12 12		12 32		12 42	12 52	13 02			13 12	
Worthing	a	10 55		11 04		11 15	11 26	11 34		11 45	11 55	12 04			12 15	12 26	12 34		12 45	12 55	13 04			13 15	13 26
	d	10 56		11 05		11 15	11 26	11 35		11 45	11 56	12 05			12 15	12 26	12 35		12 45	12 56	13 05			13 15	13 26
East Worthing	d					11 18				11 48					12 18				12 48					13 18	
Lancing	d	11 00				11 21	11 30	11 39		11 51	12 00				12 21	12 30	12 39		12 51	13 00				13 21	13 30
Shoreham-by-Sea	d	11 05		11 12		11 26	11 35	11 43		11 56	12 05	12 12			12 26	12 35	12 43		12 56	13 05	13 12			13 26	13 35
Southwick	d	11 08				11 29	11 38			11 59	12 08				12 29	12 38			12 59	13 08				13 29	13 38
Fishersgate	d					11 31				12 01					12 31				13 01					13 31	
Portslade	d	11 11		11 17		11 34	11 42	11 48		12 04	12 11	12 17			12 34	12 42	12 48		13 04	13 11	13 17			13 34	13 42
Aldrington	d					11 36				12 06					12 36				13 06					13 36	
Hove	a	11 15		11 20		11 38	11 45	11 51		12 08	12 15	12 20			12 38	12 45	12 51		13 08	13 15	13 20			13 38	13 45
	d	11 16		11 21	11 26	11 39	11 46	11 51	11 56	12 09	12 16	12 21		12 26	12 39	12 46	12 51	12 56	13 09	13 16	13 21	13 26		13 39	13 46
Brighton	a	11 21			11 31	11 44	11 51		12 01	12 14	12 21			12 31	12 44	12 51		13 01	13 14	13 21		13 31		13 44	13 51
Preston Park	a							11 56									12 56								
Haywards Heath	a			11 36				12 10				12 36					13 10				13 36				
Gatwick Airport	a			11 56				12 26				12 56					13 26				13 56				
East Croydon	a			12 11				12 41				13 11					13 41				14 11				
East Croydon	d																								
London Bridge	a																								
London Blackfriars	a																								
City Thameslink	a																								
Farringdon	a																								
St Pancras International	a																								
East Croydon	d			12 12				12 42				13 12					13 42				14 12				
Clapham Junction	a			12 22				12 51				13 21					13 51				14 21				
London Victoria	a			12 29				12 59				13 29					13 59				14 29				

		SN ■	SN	SN	SN ■	SN ■	SN	SN		SN	SN ■	SN	SN	SN ■	SN ■	SN	SN	SN		SN ■	SN	SN	SN ■ A	GW ■ B	SN ■ C
Southampton Central	d				12 29									13 26									14 26	14 34	
Fareham	d				12 53									13 53									14 53	14 56	
Havant	a				13 09									14 09									15 08	15 10	
Portsmouth Harbour	d									13 29								14 29							
Portsmouth & Southsea	d									13 33								14 33							
Havant	a									13 45								14 45							
Havant	d				13 10					13 46				14 10				14 46					15 09	15 12	
Chichester	d				13 22					14 00				14 22				15 00					15 19	15 27	
Barnham	a				13 30					14 07				14 30				15 07					15 27	15 35	
Bognor Regis	d																								
Barnham	a																								
Barnham	d				13 31					14 09				14 31				15 09					15 27	15 37	
Littlehampton	d	13 14				13 44					14 14				14 44					15 13					
Angmering	d	13 23			13 43	13 53				14 19	14 23			14 43	14 53			15 19		15 22			15 39		
Goring-by-Sea	d	13 27			13 47	13 57					14 27			14 47	14 57					15 26			15 43		
Durrington-on-Sea	d	13 29			13 50	13 59					14 29			14 50	14 59					15 28			15 45		
West Worthing	d	13 32		13 42	13 52	14 02		14 12			14 32		14 42	14 52	15 02		15 12			15 31		15 39	15 48		←
Worthing	a	13 34		13 45	13 55	14 04		14 15		14 26	14 34		14 45	14 55	15 04		15 15	15 26		15 33		15 42	15 51	15 53	15 51
	d	13 35		13 45	13 56	14 05		14 15		14 26	14 35		14 45	14 56	15 05		15 15	15 26		15 34		15 42	15 59	15 54	15 59
East Worthing	d			13 48				14 18					14 48				15 18			15 37		15 45	→		
Lancing	d	13 39		13 51	14 00			14 21		14 30	14 39		14 51	15 00			15 21	15 30		15 40		15 48			16 03
Shoreham-by-Sea	d	13 43		13 56	14 05	14 12		14 26		14 35	14 43		14 56	15 05	15 12		15 26	15 35		15 44		15 53		16 01	16 07
Southwick	d			13 59	14 08			14 29		14 38			14 59	15 08			15 29	15 38				15 56			16 10
Fishersgate	d			14 01				14 31					15 01				15 31					15 58			
Portslade	d	13 48		14 04	14 11	14 17		14 34		14 42	14 48		15 04	15 11	15 17		15 34	15 42		15 49		16 01			16 14
Aldrington	d			14 06				14 36					15 06				15 36					16 03			
Hove	a	13 51		14 08	14 15	14 20		14 38		14 45	14 51		15 08	15 15	15 20		15 38	15 45		15 52		16 05		16 08	16 17
	d	13 51	13 56	14 09	14 16	14 21	14 26	14 39		14 46	14 51	14 56	15 09	15 16	15 21	15 26	15 39	15 46		15 52	15 56	16 06		16 10	16 17
Brighton	a		14 01	14 14	14 21		14 31	14 44		14 51		15 01	15 14	15 21		15 31	15 44	15 51			16 01	16 10		16 14	16 22
Preston Park	a	13 56									14 56									15 57					
Haywards Heath	a	14 10				14 36					15 10				15 36					16 10					
Gatwick Airport	a	14 26				14 56					15 26				15 56					16 26					
East Croydon	a	14 41				15 11					15 41				16 11					16 42					
East Croydon	d																								
London Bridge	a																								
London Blackfriars	a																								
City Thameslink	a																								
Farringdon	a																								
St Pancras International	a																								
East Croydon	d	14 42				15 12					15 42				16 12					16 42					
Clapham Junction	a	14 51				15 21					15 51				16 21					16 51					
London Victoria	a	14 59				15 29					16 00				16 29					16 59					

A To Brighton

B From Great Malvern

C From Southampton Central

Table T188-R

Mondays to Fridays

21 May to 7 December

Southampton Central - Worthing - Brighton and Gatwick Airport - London

		SN ■	SN	SN		SN	SN ■	SN	SN	SN ■	SN ■	SN	SN	SN		SN ■	SN	SN	SN ■	SN ■	SN	SN	SN	SN ■	
Southampton Central	d									15 26									16 26						
Fareham	d									15 53									16 53						
Havant	a									16 09									17 09						
Portsmouth Harbour	d					15 29																			
Portsmouth & Southsea	d					15 33								16 33									17 33		
Havant	a					15 45								16 45									17 45		
Havant	d					15 46				16 10				16 46					17 10				17 46		
Chichester	d					16 00				16 22				17 00					17 22				18 00		
Barnham	a					16 07				16 30				17 07					17 30				18 07		
Bognor Regis	d																								
Barnham	a																								
Barnham	d					16 09				16 31				17 09					17 31				18 09		
Littlehampton	d	15 44		15 51			16 14		16 21		16 44		16 51			17 14		17 21		17 44		17 51		18 14	
Angmering	d	15 53		16 02		16 19	16 23		16 32	16 43	16 53		17 02	17 19		17 23		17 32	17 43	17 53		18 02	18 19	18 24	
Goring-by-Sea	d	15 57		16 06			16 27		16 36	16 47	16 57		17 06			17 27		17 36	17 47	17 57		18 06		18 28	
Durrington-on-Sea	d	15 59		16 09			16 29		16 39	16 50	16 59		17 09			17 29		17 39	17 50	17 59		18 09		18 31	
West Worthing	d	16 02		16 12			16 32		16 42	16 52	17 02		17 12			17 32		17 42	17 52	18 02		18 12		18 33	
Worthing	a	16 04		16 15		16 26	16 34		16 45	16 55	17 04		17 15	17 26		17 34		17 45	17 55	18 04		18 15	18 26	18 36	
	d	16 05		16 15		16 26	16 35		16 45	16 56	17 05		17 15	17 26		17 35		17 45	17 56	18 05		18 15	18 26	18 36	
East Worthing	d			16 18					16 48				17 18					17 48				18 18			
Lancing	d			16 21		16 30	16 39		16 51	17 00			17 21	17 30		17 39		17 51	18 00			18 21	18 30	18 40	
Shoreham-by-Sea	d	16 12		16 26		16 35	16 43		16 56	17 05	17 12		17 26	17 35		17 43		17 56	18 05	18 12		18 26	18 35	18 45	
Southwick	d			16 29		16 38			16 59	17 08			17 29	17 38				17 59	18 08			18 29	18 38		
Fishersgate	d			16 31					17 01				17 31					18 01				18 31			
Portslade	d	16 17		16 34		16 42	16 48		17 04	17 11	17 17		17 34	17 42		17 48		18 04	18 11	18 17		18 34	18 42	18 49	
Aldrington	d			16 36					17 06				17 36					18 06				18 36			
Hove	a	16 20		16 38		16 45	16 51		17 08	17 15	17 20		17 38	17 45		17 51		18 08	18 15	18 20		18 38	18 45	18 52	
	d	16 21	16 26	16 39		16 46	16 51	17 01	17 09	17 16	17 21	17 31	17 39	17 46		17 51	18 01	18 09	18 16	18 21	18 31	18 39	18 46	18 53	
Brighton	a		16 31	16 44		16 51		17 05	17 15	17 21		17 36	17 45	17 51			18 05	18 14	18 21		18 35	18 44	18 51		
Preston Park	a						16 56									17 56								18 58	
Haywards Heath	a	16 36					17 11				17 36					18 11				18 36				19 11	
Gatwick Airport	a	16 56					17 26				17 56					18 26				18 56				19 26	
East Croydon	a	17 12					17 42				18 12					18 42				19 11				19 42	
East Croydon	d																								
London Bridge	a																								
London Blackfriars	a																								
City Thameslink	a																								
Farringdon	a																								
St Pancras International	a																								
East Croydon	d	17 12					17 42				18 12					18 42				19 12				19 42	
Clapham Junction	a	17 21					17 51				18 21					18 51				19 21				19 51	
London Victoria	a	17 29					17 59				18 29					18 59				19 29				19 59	

		SN	SN	SN ■	SN ■	SN	SN	SN	SN ■	SN		SN	SN ■	SN ■	SN	SN	SN	SN ■	SN	SN		SN ■	SN ■	SN	SN
Southampton Central	d			17 26									18 26									19 26			
Fareham	d			17 53									18 53									19 53			
Havant	a			18 09									19 09									20 09			
Portsmouth Harbour	d																								
Portsmouth & Southsea	d							18 33									19 33								
Havant	a							18 46									19 45								
Havant	d			18 10				18 47					19 10				19 46					20 10			
Chichester	d			18 22				19 01					19 22				20 00					20 22			
Barnham	a			18 30				19 08					19 30				20 07					20 30			
Bognor Regis	d																								
Barnham	a																								
Barnham	d			18 31				19 09					19 31				20 09					20 31			
Littlehampton	d		18 27		18 40				19 10					19 40				20 10					20 40		
Angmering	d		18 36	18 43	18 53			19 19	19 24				19 43	19 53			20 19	20 23				20 43	20 53		
Goring-by-Sea	d			18 47	18 57				19 28				19 47	19 57				20 27				20 47	20 57		
Durrington-on-Sea	d			18 50	18 59				19 30				19 50	19 59				20 29				20 50	20 59		
West Worthing	d		18 42	18 52	19 02		19 12		19 33			19 42	19 52	20 02		20 12		20 32		20 42		20 52	21 02		21 12
Worthing	a		18 45	18 55	19 04		19 15	19 26	19 35			19 45	19 55	20 04		20 15	20 26	20 34		20 45		20 55	21 04		21 15
	d		18 45	18 56	19 05		19 15	19 26	19 36			19 45	19 56	20 05		20 15	20 26	20 35		20 45		20 56	21 05		21 15
East Worthing	d		18 48				19 18					19 48				20 18				20 48					21 18
Lancing	d		18 51	19 00			19 21	19 30	19 40			19 51	20 00			20 21	20 30	20 39		20 51		21 00			21 21
Shoreham-by-Sea	d		18 56	19 05	19 12		19 26	19 35	19 44			19 56	20 05	20 12		20 26	20 35	20 43		20 56		21 05	21 12		21 26
Southwick	d		18 59	19 08			19 29	19 38				19 59	20 08			20 29	20 38			20 59		21 08			21 29
Fishersgate	d		19 01				19 31					20 01				20 31				21 01					21 31
Portslade	d		19 04	19 11	19 17		19 34	19 42	19 49			20 04	20 11	20 17		20 34	20 42	20 48		21 04		21 11	21 17		21 34
Aldrington	d		19 06				19 36					20 06				20 36				21 06					21 36
Hove	a		19 08	19 15	19 20		19 38	19 45	19 52			20 08	20 15	20 20		20 38	20 45	20 51		21 08		21 15	21 20		21 38
	d	19 01	19 09	19 16	19 21	19 31	19 39	19 46	19 52	20 01		20 10	20 16	20 21	20 26	20 40	20 46	20 51	20 56	21 10		21 16	21 21	21 26	21 40
Brighton	a	19 05	19 14	19 21		19 35	19 44	19 51		20 05		20 15	20 21		20 31	20 45	20 51		21 01	21 15		21 21		21 31	21 45
Preston Park	a								19 57									20 56							
Haywards Heath	a				19 36				20 11					20 36				21 10					21 36		
Gatwick Airport	a				19 56				20 27					20 56				21 26					21 56		
East Croydon	a				20 11				20 42					21 11				21 41					22 12		
East Croydon	d																								
London Bridge	a																								
London Blackfriars	a																								
City Thameslink	a																								
Farringdon	a																								
St Pancras International	a																								
East Croydon	d				20 12				20 43					21 12				21 42					22 12		
Clapham Junction	a				20 21				20 52					21 21				21 51					22 21		
London Victoria	a				20 30				20 59					21 29				21 59					22 29		

Table T188-R

Mondays to Fridays

21 May to 7 December

Southampton Central - Worthing - Brighton and Gatwick Airport - London

	SN	SN ■	SN	SN	SN ■	SN ■	SN	SN	SN	SN ■	SN	SN	SN	SN	SN	SN
Southampton Central d					20 26							21 13				
Fareham d					20 54							21 40				
Havant a					21 09							21 55				
Portsmouth Harbour d														22 15		22 40
Portsmouth & Southsea d	20 33								21 33					22 19		22 44
Havant a	20 45								21 46					22 34		22 59
Havant d	20 46				21 10				21 47			21 56		22 35		23 00
Chichester d	21 00				21 22				22 01			22 07		22 49		23 10
Barnham a	21 07				21 30				22 08			22 14		22 56		23 18
Bognor Regis d																
Barnham a																
Barnham d	21 09				21 31				22 09			22 16		22 58		23 19
Littlehampton d		21 14				21 44				22 14		22 33				23 42
Angmering d	21 19	21 23			21 43	21 53			22 19	22 23		22 42		23 09		23 51
Goring-by-Sea d		21 27			21 47	21 57				22 27		22 46		23 13		23 55
Durrington-on-Sea d		21 29			21 50	21 59				22 29		22 49		23 16		23 57
West Worthing d		21 32		21 42	21 52	22 02		22 12		22 32		22 51		23 18		23 59
Worthing a	21 26	21 34		21 45	21 55	22 04		22 15	22 26	22 34		22 54		23 21		00 02
Worthing d	21 26	21 35		21 45	21 56	22 05		22 15	22 26	22 35		22 54		23 21		00 03
East Worthing d				21 48				22 18				22 57		23 24		00 05
Lancing d	21 30	21 39		21 51	22 00			22 21	22 30	22 39		23 00		23 27		00 08
Shoreham-by-Sea d	21 35	21 43		21 56	22 05	22 12		22 26	22 35	22 43		23 04		23 32		00 13
Southwick d	21 38			21 59	22 08			22 29	22 38			23 07		23 35		00 16
Fishersgate d				22 01				22 31				23 09		23 37		00 18
Portslade d	21 42	21 48		22 04	22 12	22 17		22 34	22 42	22 48		23 11		23 39		00 20
Aldrington d				22 06				22 36	22 44			23 13		23 42		00 23
Hove a	21 45	21 51		22 08	22 15	22 20		22 38	22 46	22 51		23 15		23 44		00 25
Hove d	21 46	21 51	21 56	22 10	22 16	22 21	22 26	22 40	22 47	22 51	22 56	23 16	23 26	23 44	23 56	00 26
Brighton a	21 51		22 01	22 15	22 21		22 31	22 45	22 51		23 01	23 20	23 31	23 49	00 01	00 30
Preston Park a		21 56								22 56						
Haywards Heath a		22 11				22 36				23 10						
Gatwick Airport a		22 27				22 56				23 26						
East Croydon a		22 42				23 12				23 42						
East Croydon d																
London Bridge a																
London Blackfriars a																
City Thameslink a																
Farringdon a																
St Pancras International a																
East Croydon d		22 43				23 12				23 42						
Clapham Junction a		22 52				23 21				23 57						
London Victoria a		23 00				23 30				00 05						

Saturdays

26 May to 8 December

	SN A	SN ■	SN ■	SN	SN ■	SN	SN	SN ■	SN	SN	SN ■	SN ■	SN	SN	SN	SN ■	SN	SN	GW	SN ■	SN ■	SN
Southampton Central d																				06 26		
Fareham d																				06 51		
Havant a																				07 10		
Portsmouth Harbour d															06 29				06 50			
Portsmouth & Southsea d			04 55												06 33				06 54			
Havant a			05 07												06 45				07 07			
Havant d			05 07												06 46				07 08	07 11		
Chichester d			05 18								06 23				07 00				07 19	07 24		
Barnham a			05 26								06 30				07 07				07 27	07 32		
Bognor Regis d							05 37															
Barnham a							05 43															
Barnham d		04 48	05 26				05 45				06 31				07 08				07 27	07 32		
Littlehampton d		05 04			05 44			06 14				06 44				07 14					07 44	
Angmering d		05 14			05 53		05 57	06 23			06 43	06 53			07 19	07 23				07 44	07 53	
Goring-by-Sea d		05 18			05 57		06 01	06 27			06 47	06 57				07 27				07 48	07 57	
Durrington-on-Sea d		05 20			05 59		06 03	06 29			06 50	06 59				07 29				07 51	07 59	
West Worthing d		05 23			06 02		06 06	06 32		06 42	06 52	07 02		07 12		07 32		07 42		07 53	08 02	
Worthing a		05 25	05 42		06 04		06 08	06 34		06 45	06 55	07 04		07 15	07 26	07 34		07 45	07 49	07 56	08 04	
Worthing d	00 03	05 26	05 43		06 05		06 09	06 35		06 45	06 56	07 05		07 15	07 26	07 35		07 45	07 49	07 57	08 05	
East Worthing d	00 05						06 11			06 48				07 18				07 48				
Lancing d	00 08	05 30					06 14	06 39		06 51	07 00			07 21	07 30	07 39		07 51		08 01		
Shoreham-by-Sea d	00 13	05 35			06 12		06 19	06 43		06 56	07 05	07 12		07 26	07 35	07 43		07 56	08 01	08 06	08 12	
Southwick d	00 16	05 38					06 22			06 59	07 08			07 29	07 38			07 59		08 09		
Fishersgate d	00 18						06 24			07 01				07 31				08 01				
Portslade d	00 20	05 42			06 17		06 26	06 48		07 04	07 11	07 17		07 34	07 42	07 48		08 04		08 12	08 17	
Aldrington d	00 23						06 29			07 06				07 36				08 06				
Hove a	00 25	05 45	05 54		06 20		06 31	06 51		07 08	07 15	07 20		07 38	07 45	07 51		08 08	08 12	08 16	08 20	
Hove d	00 26	05 46	05 54	05 56	06 21	06 26	06 32	06 51	06 56	07 09	07 16	07 21	07 26	07 39	07 46	07 51	07 56	08 09	08 12	08 17	08 21	08 26
Brighton a	00 30	05 50		06 01		06 31	06 36		07 01	07 14	07 21		07 31	07 44	07 51		08 01	08 14	08 17	08 24		08 31
Preston Park a								06 56								07 56						
Haywards Heath a			06 10		06 36			07 10				07 36				08 10					08 36	
Gatwick Airport a			06 26		06 56			07 26				07 56				08 26					08 56	
East Croydon a			06 41		07 11			07 41				08 11				08 41					09 11	
East Croydon d																						
London Bridge a																						
London Blackfriars a																						
City Thameslink a																						
Farringdon a																						
St Pancras International a																						
East Croydon d			06 42		07 12			07 42				08 12				08 42					09 12	
Clapham Junction a			06 51		07 21			07 51				08 21				08 51					09 21	
London Victoria a			06 59		07 29			07 59				08 29				08 59					09 29	

A From Portsmouth Harbour

Table T188-R

Saturdays

26 May to 8 December

Southampton Central - Worthing - Brighton and Gatwick Airport - London

	SN	SN	SN ■	SN	SN	SN ■	SN ■	SN	SN	SN	SN ■	SN	SN	SN ■	SN ■	SN	SN	SN	SN ■	SN	SN	SN ■
Southampton Central d						07 26								08 27								09 26
Fareham d						07 53								08 53								09 53
Havant a						08 09								09 09								10 09
Portsmouth Harbour d		07 29								08 29								09 29				
Portsmouth & Southsea d		07 33								08 33								09 33				
Havant a		07 45								08 45								09 45				
Havant d		07 46				08 10				08 46				09 10				09 46				10 10
Chichester d		08 00				08 22				09 00				09 22				10 00				10 22
Barnham a		08 07				08 30				09 07				09 30				10 07				10 30
Bognor Regis d																						
Barnham a																						
Barnham d		08 09				08 31				09 09				09 31				10 09				10 31
Littlehampton d			08 14				08 44				09 14				09 44				10 14			
Angmering d		08 19	08 23			08 43	08 53			09 19	09 23			09 43	09 53			10 19	10 23			10 43
Goring-by-Sea d			08 27			08 47	08 57				09 27			09 47	09 57				10 27			10 47
Durrington-on-Sea d			08 29			08 50	08 59				09 29			09 50	09 59				10 29			10 50
West Worthing d	08 12		08 32		08 42	08 52	09 02		09 12		09 32		09 42	09 52	10 02		10 12		10 32		10 42	10 52
Worthing a	08 17	08 26	08 34		08 45	08 55	09 04		09 15	09 26	09 34		09 45	09 55	10 04		10 15	10 26	10 34		10 45	10 55
Worthing d	08 17	08 26	08 35		08 45	08 56	09 05		09 15	09 26	09 35		09 45	09 56	10 05		10 15	10 26	10 35		10 45	10 56
East Worthing d	08 20				08 48				09 18				09 48				10 18				10 48	
Lancing d	08 23	08 30	08 39		08 51	09 00			09 21	09 30	09 39		09 51	10 00			10 21	10 30	10 39		10 51	11 00
Shoreham-by-Sea d	08 28	08 35	08 43		08 56	09 05	09 12		09 26	09 35	09 43		09 56	10 05	10 12		10 26	10 35	10 43		10 56	11 05
Southwick d	08 31	08 38			08 59	09 08			09 29	09 38			09 59	10 08			10 29	10 38			10 59	11 08
Fishersgate d	08 33				09 01				09 31				10 01				10 31				11 01	
Portslade d	08 36	08 42	08 48		09 04	09 11	09 17		09 34	09 42	09 48		10 04	10 11	10 17		10 34	10 42	10 48		11 04	11 11
Aldrington d	08 38				09 06				09 36				10 06				10 36				11 06	
Hove a	08 40	08 45	08 51		09 08	09 15	09 20		09 38	09 45	09 51		10 08	10 15	10 20		10 38	10 45	10 51		11 08	11 15
Hove d	08 41	08 46	08 51	08 58	09 09	09 16	09 21	09 26	09 39	09 46	09 51	09 56	10 09	10 16	10 21	10 26	10 39	10 46	10 51	10 56	11 09	11 16
Brighton a	08 46	08 51		09 03	09 14	09 21		09 31	09 44	09 51		10 01	10 14	10 21		10 31	10 44	10 51		11 01	11 14	11 21
Preston Park a			08 56								09 56								10 56			
Haywards Heath a			09 10				09 36				10 10				10 36				11 10			
Gatwick Airport a			09 26				09 56				10 26				10 56				11 26			
East Croydon a			09 41				10 11				10 41				11 11				11 41			
East Croydon d																						
London Bridge a																						
London Blackfriars a																						
City Thameslink a																						
Farringdon a																						
St Pancras International a																						
East Croydon d			09 42				10 12				10 42				11 12				11 42			
Clapham Junction a			09 51				10 21				10 51				11 21				11 51			
London Victoria a			09 59				10 29				10 59				11 29				11 59			

	SN ■	SN	SN	SN	SN ■	SN	SN	SN ■	SN ■	SN	SN	SN	SN ■	SN	SN	SN ■	SN ■	SN	SN	SN	SN ■
Southampton Central d								10 26								11 26					
Fareham d								10 53								11 53					
Havant a								11 09								12 09					
Portsmouth Harbour d				10 29								11 29								12 29	
Portsmouth & Southsea d				10 33								11 33								12 33	
Havant a				10 45								11 45								12 45	
Havant d				10 46				11 10				11 46				12 10				12 46	
Chichester d				11 00				11 22				12 00				12 22				13 00	
Barnham a				11 07				11 30				12 07				12 30				13 07	
Bognor Regis d																					
Barnham a																					
Barnham d				11 09				11 31				12 09				12 31				13 09	
Littlehampton d	10 44				11 14				11 44				12 14				12 44				13 14
Angmering d	10 53			11 19	11 23			11 43	11 53			12 19	12 23			12 43	12 53			13 19	13 23
Goring-by-Sea d	10 57				11 27			11 47	11 57				12 27			12 47	12 57				13 27
Durrington-on-Sea d	10 59				11 29			11 50	11 59				12 29			12 50	12 59				13 29
West Worthing d	11 02		11 12		11 32		11 42	11 52	12 02		12 12		12 32		12 42	12 52	13 02		13 12		13 32
Worthing a	11 04		11 15	11 26	11 34		11 45	11 55	12 04		12 15	12 26	12 34		12 45	12 55	13 04		13 15	13 26	13 34
Worthing d	11 05		11 15	11 26	11 35		11 45	11 56	12 05		12 15	12 26	12 35		12 45	12 56	13 05		13 15	13 26	13 35
East Worthing d			11 18				11 48				12 18				12 48				13 18		
Lancing d			11 21	11 30	11 39		11 51	12 00			12 21	12 30	12 39		12 51	13 00			13 21	13 30	13 39
Shoreham-by-Sea d	11 12		11 26	11 35	11 43		11 56	12 05	12 12		12 26	12 35	12 43		12 56	13 05	13 12		13 26	13 35	13 43
Southwick d			11 29	11 38			11 59	12 08			12 29	12 38			12 59	13 08			13 29	13 38	
Fishersgate d			11 31				12 01				12 31				13 01				13 31		
Portslade d	11 17		11 34	11 42	11 48		12 04	12 11	12 17		12 34	12 42	12 48		13 04	13 11	13 17		13 34	13 42	13 48
Aldrington d			11 36				12 06				12 36				13 06				13 36		
Hove a	11 20		11 38	11 45	11 51		12 08	12 15	12 20		12 38	12 45	12 51		13 08	13 15	13 20		13 38	13 45	13 51
Hove d	11 21	11 26	11 39	11 46	11 51	11 56	12 09	12 16	12 21	12 26	12 39	12 46	12 51	12 56	13 09	13 16	13 21	13 26	13 39	13 46	13 51
Brighton a		11 31	11 44	11 51		12 01	12 14	12 21		12 31	12 44	12 51		13 01	13 14	13 21		13 31	13 44	13 51	
Preston Park a					11 56								12 56								13 56
Haywards Heath a	11 36				12 10				12 36				13 10				13 36				14 10
Gatwick Airport a	11 56				12 26				12 56				13 26				13 56				14 26
East Croydon a	12 11				12 41				13 11				13 41				14 11				14 41
East Croydon d																					
London Bridge a																					
London Blackfriars a																					
City Thameslink a																					
Farringdon a																					
St Pancras International a																					
East Croydon d	12 12				12 42				13 12				13 42				14 12				14 42
Clapham Junction a	12 21				12 51				13 21				13 51				14 21				14 51
London Victoria a	12 29				12 59				13 29				13 59				14 29				14 59

Southampton Central - Worthing - Brighton and Gatwick Airport - London

		SN	SN	SN 1	SN 1	SN	SN	SN		SN 1	SN	SN	SN 1	SN 1	SN	SN	SN	SN 1		SN	SN	GW A	SN 1	SN 1	SN
Southampton Central	d			12 26									13 26									14 34	14 26		
Fareham	d			12 53									13 53									14 56	15 00		
Havant	a			13 09									14 09									15 10	15 13		
Portsmouth Harbour	d							13 29									14 29								
Portsmouth & Southsea	d							13 33									14 33								
Havant	a							13 45									14 45								
Havant	d			13 10				13 46					14 10				14 46					15 10	15 14		
Chichester	d			13 22				14 00					14 22				15 00					15 21	15 25		
Barnham	a			13 30				14 07					14 30				15 07					15 29	15 33		
Bognor Regis	d																								
Barnham	a																								
Barnham	d			13 31				14 09					14 31				15 09					15 29	15 33		
Littlehampton	d				13 44					14 14				14 44				15 14						15 44	
Angmering	d			13 43	13 53			14 19		14 23			14 43	14 53			15 19	15 23					15 45	15 53	
Goring-by-Sea	d			13 47	13 57					14 27			14 47	14 57				15 27					15 49	15 57	
Durrington-on-Sea	d			13 50	13 59					14 29			14 50	14 59				15 29					15 52	15 59	
West Worthing	d		13 42	13 52	14 02		14 12			14 32		14 42	14 52	15 02		15 12		15 32			15 42		15 54	16 02	
Worthing	a		13 45	13 55	14 04		14 15	14 26		14 34		14 45	14 55	15 04		15 15	15 26	15 34			15 45	15 51	15 57	16 04	
	d		13 45	13 56	14 05		14 15	14 26		14 35		14 45	14 56	15 05		15 15	15 26	15 35			15 45	15 52	15 57	16 05	
East Worthing	d		13 48				14 18					14 48				15 18					15 48				
Lancing	d		13 51	14 00			14 21	14 30		14 39		14 51	15 00			15 21	15 30	15 39			15 51		16 01		
Shoreham-by-Sea	d		13 56	14 05	14 12		14 26	14 35		14 43		14 56	15 05	15 12		15 26	15 35	15 43			15 56	16 01	16 06	16 12	
Southwick	d		13 59	14 08			14 29	14 38				14 59	15 08			15 29	15 38				15 59		16 09		
Fishersgate	d		14 01				14 31					15 01				15 31					16 01				
Portslade	d		14 04	14 11	14 17		14 34	14 42		14 48		15 04	15 11	15 17		15 34	15 42	15 48			16 04		16 12	16 17	
Aldrington	d		14 06				14 36					15 06				15 36					16 06				
Hove	a		14 08	14 15	14 20		14 38	14 45		14 51		15 08	15 15	15 20		15 38	15 45	15 51			16 08	16 12	16 15	16 20	
	d	13 56	14 09	14 16	14 21	14 26	14 39	14 46		14 51	14 56	15 09	15 16	15 21	15 26	15 39	15 46	15 51		15 56	16 09	16 13	16 16	16 21	16 26
Brighton	a	14 01	14 14	14 21		14 31	14 44	14 51			15 01	15 14	15 21		15 31	15 44	15 51			16 01	16 14	16 18	16 24		16 31
Preston Park	a									14 56								15 56							
Haywards Heath	a				14 36					15 10				15 36				16 10						16 36	
Gatwick Airport	a				14 56					15 26				15 56				16 26						16 56	
East Croydon	a				15 11					15 41				16 11				16 41						17 11	
East Croydon	d																								
London Bridge	a																								
London Blackfriars	a																								
City Thameslink	a																								
Farringdon	a																								
St Pancras International	a																								
East Croydon	d				15 12					15 42				16 12				16 42						17 12	
Clapham Junction	a				15 21					15 51				16 21				16 51						17 21	
London Victoria	a				15 29					15 59				16 29				16 59						17 29	

		SN	SN	SN 1		SN	SN	SN 1	SN 1	SN	SN	SN	SN 1	SN		SN	SN 1	SN 1	SN	SN	SN	SN 1	SN	SN
Southampton Central	d							15 26									16 26							
Fareham	d							15 53									16 53							
Havant	a							16 09									17 09							
Portsmouth Harbour	d		15 29									16 29									17 29			
Portsmouth & Southsea	d		15 33									16 33									17 33			
Havant	a		15 45									16 45									17 45			
Havant	d		15 46					16 10				16 46					17 10				17 46			
Chichester	d		16 00					16 22				17 00					17 22				18 00			
Barnham	a		16 07					16 30				17 07					17 30				18 07			
Bognor Regis	d																							
Barnham	a																							
Barnham	d		16 09					16 31				17 09					17 31				18 09			
Littlehampton	d			16 14					16 44				17 14					17 44				18 14		
Angmering	d		16 19	16 23				16 43	16 53			17 19	17 23				17 43	17 53			18 19	18 23		
Goring-by-Sea	d			16 27				16 47	16 57				17 27				17 47	17 57				18 27		
Durrington-on-Sea	d			16 29				16 50	16 59				17 29				17 50	17 59				18 29		
West Worthing	d	16 12		16 32			16 42	16 52	17 02		17 12		17 32			17 42	17 52	18 02		18 12		18 32		18 42
Worthing	a	16 15	16 26	16 34			16 45	16 55	17 04		17 15	17 26	17 34			17 45	17 55	18 04		18 15	18 26	18 34		18 45
	d	16 15	16 26	16 35			16 45	16 56	17 05		17 15	17 26	17 35			17 45	17 56	18 05		18 15	18 26	18 35		18 45
East Worthing	d	16 18					16 48				17 18					17 48				18 18				18 48
Lancing	d	16 21	16 30	16 39			16 51	17 00			17 21	17 30	17 39			17 51	18 00			18 21	18 30	18 39		18 51
Shoreham-by-Sea	d	16 26	16 35	16 43			16 56	17 05	17 12		17 26	17 35	17 43			17 56	18 05	18 12		18 26	18 35	18 43		18 56
Southwick	d	16 29	16 38				16 59	17 08			17 29	17 38				17 59	18 08			18 29	18 38			18 59
Fishersgate	d	16 31					17 01				17 31					18 01				18 31				19 01
Portslade	d	16 34	16 42	16 48			17 04	17 11	17 17		17 34	17 42	17 48			18 04	18 11	18 17		18 34	18 42	18 48		19 04
Aldrington	d	16 36					17 06				17 36					18 06				18 36				19 06
Hove	a	16 38	16 45	16 51			17 08	17 15	17 20		17 38	17 45	17 51			18 08	18 15	18 20		18 38	18 45	18 51		19 08
	d	16 39	16 46	16 51		16 58	17 09	17 16	17 21	17 26	17 39	17 46	17 51	17 56		18 09	18 16	18 21	18 26	18 39	18 46	18 51	18 56	19 09
Brighton	a	16 44	16 51			17 03	17 14	17 21		17 31	17 44	17 51		18 01		18 14	18 21		18 31	18 44	18 51		19 01	19 14
Preston Park	a			16 56									17 56									18 56		
Haywards Heath	a			17 10					17 36				18 10					18 36				19 10		
Gatwick Airport	a			17 26					17 56				18 26					18 56				19 26		
East Croydon	a			17 41					18 11				18 41					19 11				19 41		
East Croydon	d																							
London Bridge	a																							
London Blackfriars	a																							
City Thameslink	a																							
Farringdon	a																							
St Pancras International	a																							
East Croydon	d			17 42					18 12				18 42					19 12				19 42		
Clapham Junction	a			17 51					18 21				18 51					19 21				19 51		
London Victoria	a			17 59					18 29				18 59					19 29				19 59		

A From Great Malvern

Table T188-R

Saturdays

26 May to 8 December

Southampton Central - Worthing - Brighton and Gatwick Airport - London

		SN 1	SN 1	SN	SN	SN	SN 1	SN	SN	SN 1		SN 1	SN	SN	SN	SN 1	SN	SN	SN 1	SN 1		SN	SN	SN	SN 1
Southampton Central	d	17 26								18 26									19 26						
Fareham	d	17 53								18 53									19 53						
Havant	a	18 09								19 09									20 09						
Portsmouth Harbour	d					18 29									19 29									20 29	
Portsmouth & Southsea	d					18 33									19 33									20 33	
Havant	a					18 45									19 45									20 45	
Havant	d	18 10				18 46				19 10					19 46				20 10					20 46	
Chichester	d	18 22				19 00				19 22					20 00				20 22					21 00	
Barnham	a	18 30				19 07				19 30					20 07				20 30					21 07	
Bognor Regis	d																								
Barnham	a																								
Barnham	d	18 31				19 09				19 31					20 09				20 31					21 09	
Littlehampton	d		18 44				19 14					19 44				20 14				20 44					21 14
Angmering	d	18 43	18 53			19 19	19 23			19 43		19 53			20 19	20 23			20 43	20 53				21 19	21 23
Goring-by-Sea	d	18 47	18 57				19 27			19 47		19 57				20 27			20 47	20 57					21 27
Durrington-on-Sea	d	18 50	18 59				19 29			19 50		19 59				20 29			20 50	20 59					21 29
West Worthing	d	18 52	19 02		19 12		19 32		19 42	19 52		20 02		20 12		20 32		20 42	20 52	21 02			21 12		21 32
Worthing	a	18 55	19 04		19 15	19 26	19 34		19 45	19 55		20 04		20 15	20 26	20 34		20 45	20 55	21 04			21 15	21 26	21 34
	d	18 56	19 05		19 15	19 26	19 35		19 45	19 56		20 05		20 15	20 26	20 35		20 45	20 56	21 05			21 15	21 26	21 35
East Worthing	d				19 18				19 48					20 18				20 48					21 18		
Lancing	d	19 00			19 21	19 30	19 39		19 51	20 00				20 21	20 30	20 39		20 51	21 00				21 21	21 30	21 39
Shoreham-by-Sea	d	19 05	19 12		19 26	19 35	19 43		19 56	20 05		20 12		20 26	20 35	20 43		20 56	21 05	21 12			21 26	21 35	21 43
Southwick	d	19 08			19 29	19 38			19 59	20 08				20 29	20 38			20 59	21 08				21 29	21 38	
Fishersgate	d				19 31				20 01					20 31				21 01					21 31		
Portslade	d	19 11	19 17		19 34	19 42	19 48		20 04	20 11		20 17		20 34	20 42	20 48		21 04	21 11	21 17			21 34	21 42	21 48
Aldrington	d				19 36				20 06					20 36				21 06					21 36		
Hove	a	19 15	19 20		19 38	19 45	19 51		20 08	20 15		20 20		20 38	20 45	20 51		21 08	21 15	21 20			21 38	21 45	21 51
	d	19 16	19 21	19 26	19 39	19 46	19 51	19 56	20 09	20 16		20 21	20 26	20 39	20 46	20 51	20 56	21 09	21 16	21 21		21 26	21 39	21 46	21 51
Brighton	a	19 21		19 31	19 44	19 51		20 01	20 14	20 21			20 31	20 44	20 51		21 01	21 14	21 21			21 31	21 44	21 51	
Preston Park	a						19 56									20 56									21 56
Haywards Heath	a		19 36				20 10					20 36				21 10				21 36					22 10
Gatwick Airport	a		19 56				20 26					20 56				21 26				21 56					22 26
East Croydon	a		20 11				20 41					21 11				21 41				22 12					22 41
East Croydon	d																								
London Bridge	a																								
London Blackfriars	a																								
City Thameslink	a																								
Farringdon	a																								
St Pancras International	a																								
East Croydon	d		20 12				20 42					21 12				21 42				22 12					22 42
Clapham Junction	a		20 21				20 51					21 21				21 51				22 21					22 51
London Victoria	a		20 29				20 59					21 29				21 59				22 29					22 59

		SN	SN	SN 1	SN 1	SN		SN	SN	SN	SN	SN	SN	SN
Southampton Central	d			20 26							21 13			
Fareham	d			20 53							21 40			
Havant	a			21 09							21 55			
Portsmouth Harbour	d											22 15		22 40
Portsmouth & Southsea	d											22 19		22 44
Havant	a											22 35		22 59
Havant	d			21 10							21 56	22 35		23 00
Chichester	d			21 22							22 07	22 52		23 10
Barnham	a			21 30							22 14	22 59		23 18
Bognor Regis	d													
Barnham	a													
Barnham	d			21 31							22 16	23 00		23 19
Littlehampton	d				21 44						22 33			23 42
Angmering	d			21 43	21 53						22 42	23 11		23 51
Goring-by-Sea	d			21 47	21 57						22 46	23 15		23 55
Durrington-on-Sea	d			21 50	21 59						22 49	23 18		23 57
West Worthing	d		21 42	21 52	22 02			22 12		22 42	22 51	23 20		23 59
Worthing	a		21 45	21 55	22 04			22 15		22 45	22 54	23 23		00 02
	d		21 45	21 56	22 05			22 15		22 45	22 54	23 23		00 03
East Worthing	d		21 48					22 18		22 48	22 57			00 06
Lancing	d		21 51	22 00				22 21		22 51	23 00	23 27		00 09
Shoreham-by-Sea	d		21 56	22 05	22 12			22 26		22 56	23 04	23 32		00 13
Southwick	d		21 59	22 08				22 29		22 59	23 07	23 35		00 16
Fishersgate	d		22 01					22 31		23 01	23 09	23 37		00 18
Portslade	d		22 04	22 11	22 17			22 34		23 04	23 11	23 39		00 21
Aldrington	d		22 06					22 36		23 06	23 13	23 41		00 23
Hove	a		22 08	22 15	22 20			22 38		23 08	23 15	23 43		00 25
	d	21 56	22 09	22 16	22 21	22 26		22 39	22 56	23 09	23 16	23 45	23 56	00 26
Brighton	a	22 01	22 14	22 21		22 31		22 44	23 01	23 14	23 20	23 49	00 01	00 30
Preston Park	a													
Haywards Heath	a				22 36									
Gatwick Airport	a				22 56									
East Croydon	a				23 11									
East Croydon	d													
London Bridge	a													
London Blackfriars	a													
City Thameslink	a													
Farringdon	a													
St Pancras International	a													
East Croydon	d				23 12									
Clapham Junction	a				23 21									
London Victoria	a				23 29									

Table T188-R

Sundays

20 May to 2 December

Southampton Central - Worthing - Brighton and Gatwick Airport - London

		SN A	SN	SN	SN	SN	SN	SN	SN	SN	SN	SN	SN	SN	GW B	SN	SN	SN	SN	SN	SN	SN	SN
Southampton Central	d									07 30				08 21	08 31				09 30				10 30
Fareham	d									07 54				08 47	08 54				09 54				10 54
Havant	a									08 10				09 02	09 13				10 10				11 10
Portsmouth Harbour	d						07 14				08 14					09 14				10 14			
Portsmouth & Southsea	d						07 18				08 18					09 18				10 18			
Havant	a						07 33				08 33					09 33				10 33			
Havant	d						07 33			08 10	08 33			09 02	09 13	09 33			10 10	10 33			11 10
Chichester	d						07 53			08 22	08 53			09 14	09 24	09 53			10 22	10 53			11 22
Barnham	a						08 01			08 30	09 01			09 22	09 32	10 01			10 30	11 01			11 30
Bognor Regis	d																						
Barnham	a																						
Barnham	d		06 10				08 02			08 31	09 02			09 23	09 32	10 02			10 31	11 02			11 31
Littlehampton	d		06 24	07 14		07 35		08 14				09 14					10 14				11 14		
Angmering	d			07 23		07 44	08 14	08 23		08 43	09 14	09 23		09 35		10 14	10 23		10 43	11 14	11 23		11 43
Goring-by-Sea	d			07 27		07 48	08 18	08 27		08 47	09 18	09 27		09 39		10 18	10 27		10 47	11 18	11 27		11 47
Durrington-on-Sea	d			07 29		07 51	08 20	08 29		08 49	09 20	09 29		09 41		10 20	10 29		10 49	11 20	11 29		11 49
West Worthing	d			07 32		07 53	08 23	08 32		08 52	09 23	09 32		09 44		10 23	10 32		10 52	11 23	11 32		11 52
Worthing	a		06 37	07 34		07 56	08 25	08 34		08 54	09 25	09 34		09 46	09 58	10 25	10 34		10 54	11 25	11 34		11 54
	d	00 03	06 38	07 35		07 56	08 26	08 35		08 55	09 26	09 35		09 55	09 58	10 26	10 35		10 55	11 26	11 35		11 55
East Worthing	d	00 06				07 59	08 28			08 57	09 28			09 57		10 28			10 57	11 28			11 57
Lancing	d	00 09	06 42	07 39		08 02	08 31	08 39		09 00	09 31	09 39		10 00		10 31	10 39		11 00	11 31	11 39		12 00
Shoreham-by-Sea	d	00 13	06 46	07 43		08 06	08 36	08 43		09 05	09 36	09 43		10 05	10 09	10 36	10 43		11 05	11 36	11 43		12 05
Southwick	d	00 16	06 49			08 09	08 39			09 08	09 39			10 08		10 39			11 08	11 39			12 08
Fishersgate	d	00 18				08 11	08 41			09 10	09 41			10 10		10 41			11 10	11 41			12 10
Portslade	d	00 21	06 53	07 48		08 13	08 43	08 48		09 12	09 43	09 48		10 12		10 43	10 48		11 12	11 43	11 48		12 12
Aldrington	d	00 23				08 16	08 45			09 14	09 45			10 14		10 45			11 14	11 45			12 14
Hove	a	00 25	06 56	07 51		08 18	08 47	08 51		09 16	09 47	09 51		10 16	10 22	10 47	10 51		11 16	11 47	11 51		12 16
	d	00 26	06 56	07 52	07 59	08 20	08 48	08 52	08 59	09 18	09 48	09 52	09 59	10 18	10 22	10 48	10 52	10 59	11 18	11 48	11 52	11 59	12 18
Brighton	a	00 30	07 00		08 03	08 24	08 52		09 03	09 22	09 52		10 03	10 22	10 26	10 52		11 03	11 22	11 52		12 03	12 22
Preston Park	a			07 57				08 57				09 57					10 57				11 57		
Haywards Heath	a			08 09				09 08				10 08					11 08				12 08		
Gatwick Airport	a			08 24				09 24				10 24					11 23				12 24		
East Croydon	a			08 45				09 40				10 40					11 39				12 40		
East Croydon	d																						
London Bridge	a																						
London Blackfriars	a																						
City Thameslink	a																						
Farringdon	a																						
St Pancras International	a																						
East Croydon	d			08 46				09 41				10 41					11 40				12 41		
Clapham Junction	a			08 55				09 50				10 50					11 50				12 50		
London Victoria	a			09 02				09 58				10 58					11 58				12 58		

		SN	SN	SN	SN	SN	SN	SN	SN	SN C	GW ◇ D	SN	SN	SN E	SN	SN	SN	SN	SN	GW ◇ D	SN	SN	SN
Southampton Central	d				11 30				12 30		13 04				13 30				14 30	15 06			
Fareham	d				11 54				12 54		13 30				13 54				14 54	15 28			
Havant	a				12 10				13 10		13 45				14 10				15 10	15 42			
Portsmouth Harbour	d	11 14				12 13				13 14						14 14							15 14
Portsmouth & Southsea	d	11 18				12 17				13 18						14 18							15 18
Havant	a	11 33				12 32				13 33						14 33							15 33
Havant	d	11 33			12 10	12 33			13 10	13 33	13 46				14 10	14 33			15 10	15 43			15 33
Chichester	d	11 53			12 22	12 53			13 22	13 53	13 58				14 22	14 53			15 22	15 54			15 53
Barnham	a	12 01			12 30	13 01			13 30	14 01	14 08				14 30	15 01			15 30	16 01			16 01
Bognor Regis	d																						
Barnham	a																						
Barnham	d	12 02			12 31	13 02			13 31	14 02	14 08				14 31	15 02			15 31	16 02			16 14
Littlehampton	d		12 14				13 14						14 14				15 14					16 14	
Angmering	d	12 14	12 23		12 43	13 14	13 23		13 43	14 14			14 23		14 43	15 14	15 23		15 43			16 23	16 27
Goring-by-Sea	d	12 18	12 27		12 47	13 18	13 27		13 47	14 18			14 27		14 47	15 18	15 27		15 47			16 27	16 31
Durrington-on-Sea	d	12 20	12 29		12 49	13 20	13 29		13 49	14 20			14 29		14 49	15 20	15 29		15 49			16 29	16 33
West Worthing	d	12 23	12 32		12 52	13 23	13 32		13 52	14 23			14 32	←	14 52	15 23	15 32		15 52			16 32	16 36
Worthing	a	12 25	12 34		12 54	13 25	13 34		13 54	14 25	14 26		14 34	14 25	14 54	15 25	15 34		15 54	16 19		16 34	16 38
	d	12 26	12 35		12 55	13 26	13 35		13 55	14 39	14 27		14 35	14 39	14 55	15 26	15 35		15 55	16 22		16 35	16 39
East Worthing	d	12 28			12 57	13 28			13 57	→				14 41	14 57	15 28			15 57				16 41
Lancing	d	12 31	12 39		13 00	13 31	13 39		14 00				14 39	14 44	15 00	15 31	15 39		16 00			16 39	16 44
Shoreham-by-Sea	d	12 36	12 43		13 05	13 36	13 43		14 05		14 36		14 43	14 49	15 05	15 36	15 43		16 05	16 29		16 43	16 48
Southwick	d	12 39			13 08	13 39			14 08					14 52	15 08	15 39			16 08				16 51
Fishersgate	d	12 41			13 10	13 41			14 10					14 54	15 10	15 41			16 10				16 53
Portslade	d	12 43	12 48		13 12	13 43	13 48		14 12				14 48	14 56	15 12	15 43	15 48		16 12			16 48	16 55
Aldrington	d	12 45			13 14	13 45			14 14					14 58	15 14	15 45			16 14				16 58
Hove	a	12 47	12 51		13 16	13 47	13 51		14 16		14 47		14 51	15 00	15 16	15 47	15 51		16 16	16 40		16 51	17 00
	d	12 48	12 52	12 59	13 18	13 48	13 52	13 59	14 18		14 47	14 48	14 52	15 01	15 18	15 48	15 52	15 59	16 18	16 42	16 48	16 52	17 00
Brighton	a	12 52		13 03	13 22	13 52		14 03	14 22		14 53	14 52		15 05	15 22	15 53		16 03	16 22	16 47	16 52		17 04
Preston Park	a		12 57				13 57						14 57				15 57					16 57	
Haywards Heath	a		13 08				14 08						15 08				16 08					17 08	
Gatwick Airport	a		13 24				14 24						15 24				16 24					17 24	
East Croydon	a		13 40				14 40						15 40				16 40					17 40	
East Croydon	d																						
London Bridge	a																						
London Blackfriars	a																						
City Thameslink	a																						
Farringdon	a																						
St Pancras International	a																						
East Croydon	d		13 41				14 41						15 41				16 41					17 41	
Clapham Junction	a		13 50				14 50						15 50				16 50					17 50	
London Victoria	a		13 58				14 58						15 58				16 58					17 58	

A not 20 May. From Portsmouth Harbour
B From Romsey
C To Brighton
D From Cardiff Central
E From Portsmouth Harbour

Table T188-R

Sundays

20 May to 2 December

Southampton Central - Worthing - Brighton and Gatwick Airport - London

		SN	SN	SN	SN	SN	SN A	SN	SN	SN	SN	SN	SN	SN	SN A	SN	SN	SN B	GW ◇ C	SN D	SN	SN
Southampton Central	d	15 30				16 30				17 30				18 30				19 21	19 28			20 28
Fareham	d	15 54				16 54				17 54				18 54				19 49	19 54			20 53
Havant	a	16 10				17 10				18 10				19 10				20 03	20 10			21 10
Portsmouth Harbour	d		16 14								18 14										20 14	
Portsmouth & Southsea	d		16 18								18 18										20 18	
Havant	a		16 33								18 33										20 33	
Havant	d	16 10	16 33			17 10	17 33			18 10	18 33			19 10	19 33			20 04	20 11		20 33	21 10
Chichester	d	16 22	16 53			17 22	17 53			18 22	18 53			19 22	19 53			20 16	20 22		20 53	21 22
Barnham	a	16 30	17 01			17 30	18 01			18 30	19 01			19 30	20 01			20 23	20 29		21 01	21 30
Bognor Regis	d																					
Barnham	a																					
Barnham	d	16 31	17 02			17 31	18 02			18 31	19 02			19 31	20 02			20 24	20 30		21 02	21 31
Littlehampton	d			17 14				18 14				19 14				20 14					21 15	21 45
Angmering	d	16 43	17 14	17 23		17 43	18 14	18 23		18 43	19 14	19 23		19 43	20 14	20 23		20 36			21 25	21 55
Goring-by-Sea	d	16 47	17 18	17 27		17 47	18 18	18 27		18 47	19 18	19 27		19 47	20 18	20 27		20 40			21 29	21 59
Durrington-on-Sea	d	16 49	17 20	17 29		17 49	18 20	18 29		18 49	19 20	19 29		19 49	20 20	20 29		20 42			21 32	22 02
West Worthing	d	16 52	17 23	17 32		17 52	18 23	18 32		18 52	19 23	19 32		19 52	20 23	20 32		20 45		←	21 34	22 04
Worthing	a	16 54	17 25	17 34		17 54	18 25	18 34		18 54	19 25	19 34		19 54	20 25	20 34		20 47	20 50	20 47	21 37	22 07
	d	16 55	17 26	17 35		17 55	18 26	18 35		18 55	19 26	19 35		19 55	20 26	20 35		20 56	20 51	20 56	21 37	22 07
East Worthing	d	16 57	17 28			17 57	18 28			18 57	19 28			19 57	20 28			→		20 59	21 40	22 10
Lancing	d	17 00	17 31	17 39		18 00	18 31	18 39		19 00	19 31	19 39		20 00	20 31	20 39				21 02	21 43	22 13
Shoreham-by-Sea	d	17 05	17 36	17 43		18 05	18 36	18 43		19 05	19 36	19 43		20 05	20 36	20 43			20 57	21 06	21 47	22 17
Southwick	d	17 08	17 39			18 08	18 39			19 08	19 39			20 08	20 39					21 09	21 50	22 20
Fishersgate	d	17 10	17 41			18 10	18 41			19 10	19 41			20 10	20 41					21 11	21 52	22 22
Portslade	d	17 12	17 43	17 48		18 12	18 43	18 48		19 12	19 43	19 48		20 12	20 43	20 48				21 13	21 54	22 24
Aldrington	d	17 14	17 45			18 14	18 45			19 14	19 45			20 14	20 45					21 16	21 57	22 27
Hove	a	17 16	17 47	17 51		18 16	18 47	18 51		19 16	19 47	19 51		20 16	20 47	20 51			21 05	21 18	21 59	22 29
	d	17 18	17 48	17 52	17 59	18 18	18 48	18 52	18 59	19 18	19 48	19 52	19 59	20 18	20 48	20 52	20 59		21 06	21 18	22 00	22 30
Brighton	a	17 22	17 52		18 03	18 22	18 52		19 03	19 22	19 52		20 03	20 22	20 52		21 03		21 10	21 22	22 04	22 34
Preston Park	a			17 57				18 57				19 57				20 57						
Haywards Heath	a			18 08				19 08				20 08				21 08						
Gatwick Airport	a			18 24				19 24				20 24				21 24						
East Croydon	a			18 40				19 40				20 40				21 39						
East Croydon	d																					
London Bridge	a																					
London Blackfriars	a																					
City Thameslink	a																					
Farringdon	a																					
St Pancras International	a																					
East Croydon	d			18 41				19 41				20 41				21 40						
Clapham Junction	a			18 50				19 50				20 50				21 49						
London Victoria	a			18 58				19 58				20 58				21 58						

		SN	SN	SN
Southampton Central	d		21 30	
Fareham	d		21 54	
Havant	a		22 10	
Portsmouth Harbour	d	21 14		22 01
Portsmouth & Southsea	d	21 18		22 05
Havant	a	21 33		22 17
Havant	d	21 33	22 10	22 17
Chichester	d	21 53	22 22	22 32
Barnham	a	22 01	22 30	22 39
Bognor Regis	d			
Barnham	a			
Barnham	d	22 02	22 31	22 40
Littlehampton	d			22 55
Angmering	d	22 14	22 43	23 05
Goring-by-Sea	d	22 18	22 47	23 09
Durrington-on-Sea	d	22 20	22 49	23 11
West Worthing	d	22 23	22 52	23 14
Worthing	a	22 25	22 54	23 16
	d	22 26	22 55	23 17
East Worthing	d	22 28	22 57	23 19
Lancing	d	22 31	23 00	23 22
Shoreham-by-Sea	d	22 36	23 05	23 27
Southwick	d	22 39	23 08	23 30
Fishersgate	d	22 41	23 10	23 32
Portslade	d	22 43	23 12	23 34
Aldrington	d	22 45	23 14	23 36
Hove	a	22 47	23 16	23 38
	d	22 48	23 18	23 39
Brighton	a	22 52	23 22	23 43
Preston Park	a			
Haywards Heath	a			
Gatwick Airport	a			
East Croydon	a			
East Croydon	d			
London Bridge	a			
London Blackfriars	a			
City Thameslink	a			
Farringdon	a			
St Pancras International	a			
East Croydon	d			
Clapham Junction	a			
London Victoria	a			

A From Fratton
B To Brighton
C From Cardiff Central
D From Southampton Central

Table T189-F

Brighton - Falmer - Lewes - Newhaven - Seaford with London connections

Miles	Miles			TL ■	SN MX	TL ■	SN ■	TL ■	SN ■	SN	TL ■	SN ■	SN	SN	TL ■	SN ■	TL ■	SN	GX ■	SN	TL ■	GX ■	SN ■
—	—	Brighton	d	00 04		04 12	05 01	05 06	05 19	05 21	05 26	05 31	05 41	05 47	05 52	05 58	06 05	06 07	06 14	06 21	06 22	06 29	06 31
0¾	—	London Road (Brighton)	d							05 24			05 44	05 50				06 10		06 24			
1¾	—	Moulsecoomb	d							05 27			05 47	05 53				06 13		06 27			
3½	—	Falmer	d							05 31		05 38	05 51	05 57		06 05		06 17		06 31			06 38
8	12¼	Lewes ■	a				05 13			05 38		05 45	05 58	06 04		06 12		06 24		06 38			06 45
—	—	London Victoria	d																				
—	—	Clapham Junction	d																				
—	—	East Croydon	a																				
—	—	London Bridge	d																				
—	—	East Croydon	a																				
—	—	East Croydon	d																				
—	—	Gatwick Airport	a																06 41				
—	—	Haywards Heath	a	00 24		04 25		05 27	05 35		05 46				06 10		06 28				06 40	06 46	
—	—	Lewes	a																				
—	—	Lewes	d										06 00					06 25					
—	15¾	Southease	d		00 06																		
—	18½	Newhaven Town	d		00 11								06 10					06 35					
—	18¾	Newhaven Harbour	d		00 12								06 12					06 36					
—	20¾	Bishopstone	d		00 15								06 15					06 39					
—	21¼	Seaford	a		00 19								06 19					06 43					

		SN	GX ■	TL ■	SN	GX ■	SN ■	TL ■	SN	GX ■	TL ■	SN	GX ■	SN ■	SN	GX ■	SN	GX ■	TL ■	SN ■	TL ■	SN	GX ■
Brighton	d	06 41	06 44	06 48	06 51	06 57	07 01	07 07	07 11	07 14	07 18	07 21	07 27	07 31	07 41	07 44	07 51	07 54	07 59	08 01	08 07	08 11	08 14
London Road (Brighton)	d	06 44			06 54				07 14			07 24			07 44		07 54					08 14	
Moulsecoomb	d	06 47			06 57				07 17			07 27		07 35	07 47		07 57					08 17	
Falmer	d	06 51			07 01		07 08		07 21			07 31		07 40	07 51		08 01			08 08		08 21	
Lewes ■	a	06 58			07 08		07 15		07 28			07 38		07 47	07 58		08 08			08 15		08 28	
London Victoria	d																						
Clapham Junction	d																						
East Croydon	a																						
London Bridge	d																						
East Croydon	a																						
East Croydon	d																						
Gatwick Airport	a		07 11							07 41						08 11							08 41
Haywards Heath	a			07 10		07 13		07 28			07 40		07 43					08 10	08 19		08 28		
Lewes	a																						
Lewes	d	06 59							07 29						07 59							08 29	
Southease	d																						
Newhaven Town	d	07 09							07 39						08 09							08 39	
Newhaven Harbour	d	07 10							07 40						08 10							08 40	
Bishopstone	d	07 13							07 43						08 13							08 43	
Seaford	a	07 17							07 47						08 17							08 47	

		SN	GX ■	TL ■	SN ■	SN	GX ■	SN	GX ■	SN ■	TL ■	TL ■	SN	GX ■	SN	TL ■	SN ■	SN ■	SN	GX ■	SN	TL ■
Brighton	d	08 21	08 24	08 28	08 31	08 41	08 44	08 51	08 57	09 01	09 02	09 08	09 11	09 18	09 21	09 25	09 31	09 33	09 41	09 48	09 51	09 58
London Road (Brighton)	d	08 24				08 44		08 54					09 14		09 24				09 44		09 54	
Moulsecoomb	d	08 27			08 35	08 47		08 57					09 17		09 27		09 35		09 47		09 57	
Falmer	d	08 31			08 40	08 51		09 01		09 08			09 21		09 31		09 40		09 51		10 01	
Lewes ■	a	08 38			08 47	08 58		09 08		09 15			09 28		09 38		09 47		09 58		10 08	
London Victoria	d																					
Clapham Junction	d																					
East Croydon	a																					
London Bridge	d																					
East Croydon	a																					
East Croydon	d																					
Gatwick Airport	a						09 11		09 23					09 41						10 11		
Haywards Heath	a		08 40	08 48							09 18	09 27				09 45		09 50				10 15
Lewes	a																					
Lewes	d					08 59							09 29						09 59			
Southease	d					09 06													10 06			
Newhaven Town	d					09 11							09 39						10 11			
Newhaven Harbour	d					09 12							09 40						10 12			
Bishopstone	d					09 15							09 43						10 15			
Seaford	a					09 19							09 47						10 19			

		SN ■	SN ■	TL ■	SN	GX ■	SN	TL ■	SN ■	SN ■	SN	GX ■	SN	TL ■	SN ■	SN ■	TL ■	SN	GX ■	SN	TL ■	SN ■	SN ■
Brighton	d	10 01	10 03	10 08	10 11	10 18	10 21	10 26	10 31	10 33	10 41	10 48	10 51	10 58	11 01	11 03	11 08	11 11	11 18	11 21	11 26	11 31	11 33
London Road (Brighton)	d				10 14		10 24				10 44		10 54					11 14		11 24			
Moulsecoomb	d				10 17		10 27		10 35		10 47		10 57					11 17		11 27		11 35	
Falmer	d	10 08			10 21		10 31		10 40		10 51		11 01		11 08			11 21		11 31		11 40	
Lewes ■	a	10 15			10 28		10 38		10 47		10 58		11 08		11 15			11 28		11 38		11 47	
London Victoria	d																						
Clapham Junction	d																						
East Croydon	a																						
London Bridge	d																						
East Croydon	a																						
East Croydon	d																						
Gatwick Airport	a					10 41						11 11							11 41				
Haywards Heath	a		10 20	10 27				10 46		10 50				11 15		11 20	11 27				11 46		11 50
Lewes	a																						
Lewes	d				10 29						10 59							11 29					
Southease	d										11 06												
Newhaven Town	d				10 39						11 11							11 39					
Newhaven Harbour	d				10 40						11 12							11 40					
Bishopstone	d				10 43						11 15							11 43					
Seaford	a				10 47						11 19							11 47					

Table T189-F

Mondays to Fridays

21 May to 7 December

Brighton - Falmer - Lewes - Newhaven - Seaford with London connections

		SN	GX ■	SN	TL ■	SN ■	SN ■	TL ■	SN	GX ■	SN	TL ■	SN ■	SN ■	SN	GX ■	SN	TL ■	SN ■	SN ■	TL ■	SN	GX ■
Brighton	d	11 41	11 48	11 51	11 58	12 01	12 03	12 08	12 11	12 18	12 21	12 26	12 31	12 33	12 41	12 48	12 51	12 58	13 01	13 03	13 08	13 11	13 18
London Road (Brighton)	d	11 44		11 54					12 14		12 24				12 44		12 54					13 14	
Moulsecoomb	d	11 47		11 57					12 17		12 27		12 35		12 47		12 57					13 17	
Falmer	d	11 51		12 01		12 08			12 21		12 31		12 40		12 51		13 01		13 08			13 21	
Lewes ■	a	11 58		12 08		12 15			12 28		12 38		12 47		12 58		13 08		13 15			13 28	
London Victoria	d																						
Clapham Junction	d																						
East Croydon	a																						
London Bridge	d																						
East Croydon	a																						
East Croydon	d																						
Gatwick Airport	a		12 11							12 41						13 11							13 41
Haywards Heath	a				12 15		12 20	12 27				12 46		12 50				13 15		13 20	13 27		
Lewes	a																						
Lewes	d	11 59							12 29						12 59							13 29	
Southease	d	12 06													13 06								
Newhaven Town	d	12 11							12 39						13 11							13 39	
Newhaven Harbour	d	12 12							12 40						13 12							13 40	
Bishopstone	d	12 15							12 43						13 15							13 43	
Seaford	a	12 19							12 47						13 19							13 47	

		SN	TL ■	SN ■	SN ■	SN	GX ■	SN	TL ■	SN ■	SN ■	TL ■	SN	GX ■	SN	TL ■	SN ■	SN ■	SN	GX ■	SN	TL ■
Brighton	d	13 21	13 26	13 31	13 33	13 41	13 48	13 51	13 58	14 01	14 03	14 08	14 11	14 18	14 21	14 26	14 31	14 33	14 41	14 48	14 51	14 56
London Road (Brighton)	d	13 24				13 44		13 54					14 14		14 24				14 44		14 54	
Moulsecoomb	d	13 27		13 35		13 47		13 57					14 17		14 27		14 35		14 47		14 57	
Falmer	d	13 31		13 40		13 51		14 01		14 08			14 21		14 31		14 40		14 51		15 01	
Lewes ■	a	13 38		13 47		13 58		14 08		14 15			14 28		14 38		14 47		14 58		15 08	
London Victoria	d																					
Clapham Junction	d																					
East Croydon	a																					
London Bridge	d																					
East Croydon	a																					
East Croydon	d																					
Gatwick Airport	a						14 11							14 41						15 11		
Haywards Heath	a		13 46		13 50				14 15		14 20	14 27				14 46		14 50				15 16
Lewes	a																					
Lewes	d					13 59							14 29						14 59			
Southease	d					14 06													15 06			
Newhaven Town	d					14 11							14 39						15 11			
Newhaven Harbour	d					14 12							14 40						15 12			
Bishopstone	d					14 15							14 43						15 15			
Seaford	a					14 19							14 47						15 19			

		SN ■	SN ■	TL ■	SN	GX ■	SN	TL ■	SN ■	SN ■	SN	GX ■	SN	TL ■	SN ■	SN ■	TL ■	SN	GX ■	SN	TL ■	SN ■	SN ■
Brighton	d	15 01	15 03	15 08	15 11	15 18	15 21	15 26	15 31	15 33	15 41	15 48	15 51	15 58	16 01	16 03	16 08	16 11	16 18	16 21	16 26	16 31	16 33
London Road (Brighton)	d				15 14		15 24				15 44		15 54					16 14		16 24			
Moulsecoomb	d				15 17		15 27		15 35		15 47		15 57		16 05			16 17		16 27		16 35	
Falmer	d	15 08			15 21		15 31		15 40		15 51		16 01		16 10			16 21		16 31		16 40	
Lewes ■	a	15 15			15 28		15 38		15 47		15 58		16 08		16 17			16 28		16 38		16 47	
London Victoria	d																						
Clapham Junction	d																						
East Croydon	a																						
London Bridge	d																						
East Croydon	a																						
East Croydon	d																						
Gatwick Airport	a					15 41						16 11							16 43				
Haywards Heath	a		15 20	15 27				15 46		15 50				16 15		16 20	16 27				16 46		16 50
Lewes	a																						
Lewes	d				15 29						15 59							16 29					
Southease	d										16 06							16 36					
Newhaven Town	d				15 39						16 11							16 41					
Newhaven Harbour	d				15 40						16 12							16 42					
Bishopstone	d				15 43						16 15							16 45					
Seaford	a				15 47						16 19							16 49					

		SN	GX ■	SN	TL ■	SN ■	SN ■	TL ■	SN	GX ■	SN	TL ■	SN ■	SN ■	SN	GX	SN	TL ■	SN ■	SN ■	TL ■	SN
Brighton	d	16 41	16 48	16 51	16 58	17 01	17 03	17 08	17 11	17 16	17 21	17 26	17 31	17 33	17 41	17 46	17 51	17 58	18 01	18 03	18 08	18 11
London Road (Brighton)	d	16 44		16 54					17 14		17 24				17 44		17 54					18 14
Moulsecoomb	d	16 47		16 57		17 05			17 17		17 27		17 35		17 47		17 57		18 05			18 17
Falmer	d	16 51		17 01		17 10			17 21		17 31		17 40		17 51		18 01		18 10			18 21
Lewes ■	a	16 58		17 08		17 17			17 28		17 38		17 47		17 58		18 08		18 17			18 28
London Victoria	d																					
Clapham Junction	d																					
East Croydon	a																					
London Bridge	d																					
East Croydon	a																					
East Croydon	d																					
Gatwick Airport	a		17 11							17 41						18 11						
Haywards Heath	a				17 15		17 20	17 27				17 46		17 50				18 15		18 20	18 27	
Lewes	a																					
Lewes	d	16 59							17 29						17 59							18 29
Southease	d	17 06							17 36						18 06							18 36
Newhaven Town	d	17 11							17 41						18 11							18 41
Newhaven Harbour	d	17 12							17 42						18 12							18 42
Bishopstone	d	17 15							17 45						18 15							18 45
Seaford	a	17 19							17 49						18 19							18 49

Table T189-F

Mondays to Fridays

21 May to 7 December

Brighton - Falmer - Lewes - Newhaven - Seaford with London connections

		SN ■ A	GX	SN	TL ■	SN ■	SN ■	SN	GX	SN		TL ■	SN ■	SN ■	TL ■	SN	GX	SN	TL ■	SN ■		SN ■	SN	GX	SN
Brighton	d		18 16	18 21	18 26	18 31	18 33	18 38	18 46	18 51		18 58	19 01	19 03	19 08	19 11	19 16	19 21	19 26	19 31		19 33	19 41	19 48	19 51
London Road (Brighton)	d			18 24				18 41		18 54						19 14		19 24					19 44		19 54
Moulsecoomb	d			18 27		18 35		18 44		18 57						19 17		19 27		19 35			19 47		19 57
Falmer	d			18 31		18 40		18 48		19 01			19 08			19 21		19 31		19 40			19 51		20 01
Lewes ■	a			18 38		18 47		18 55		19 08			19 15			19 28		19 39		19 47			19 58		20 08
London Victoria	d	17 45																							
Clapham Junction	d	17 52																							
East Croydon	a	18 01																							
London Bridge	d																								
East Croydon	a																								
East Croydon	d	18 02																							
Gatwick Airport	a	18 19	18 41						19 12								19 41							20 12	
Haywards Heath	a	18 32			18 46		18 50					19 15		19 20	19 27				19 46			19 50			
Lewes	a	18 52																							
Lewes	d	18 59						19 05								19 29							19 59		
Southease	d							19 12															20 06		
Newhaven Town	d	19 09						19 17								19 39							20 11		
Newhaven Harbour	d	19 10						19a18								19 40							20 12		
Bishopstone	d	19 13														19 43							20 15		
Seaford	a	19 17														19 47							20 19		

		TL ■	SN ■	SN ■	TL ■	SN		GX	SN	TL ■	SN ■	SN ■	SN	GX	SN	TL ■		SN ■	SN ■	TL ■	SN	GX	SN	TL ■	SN ■
Brighton	d	19 58	20 01	20 03	20 08	20 11		20 18	20 21	20 26	20 31	20 33	20 41	20 48	20 51	20 58		21 01	21 03	21 08	21 11	21 18	21 21	21 26	21 31
London Road (Brighton)	d					20 14			20 24				20 44		20 54						21 14		21 24		
Moulsecoomb	d					20 17			20 27		20 35		20 47		20 57						21 17		21 27		21 35
Falmer	d		20 08			20 21			20 31		20 40		20 51		21 01			21 08			21 21		21 31		21 40
Lewes ■	a		20 15			20 28			20 38		20 47		20 58		21 08			21 15			21 28		21 38		21 47
London Victoria	d																								
Clapham Junction	d																								
East Croydon	a																								
London Bridge	d																								
East Croydon	a																								
East Croydon	d																								
Gatwick Airport	a							20 41						21 11								21 41			
Haywards Heath	a	20 15		20 20	20 27					20 46		20 50				21 15			21 20	21 27				21 46	
Lewes	a																								
Lewes	d					20 29							20 59								21 29				
Southease	d												21 06												
Newhaven Town	d					20 39							21 11								21 39				
Newhaven Harbour	d					20 40							21 12								21 40				
Bishopstone	d					20 43							21 15								21 43				
Seaford	a					20 47							21 19								21 47				

		SN ■		SN	GX	SN	TL ■	SN ■	SN ■	TL ■	SN	GX		SN	TL ■	SN ■	SN ■	SN	GX B	SN	TL ■	SN ■		SN	SN ■
Brighton	d	21 33		21 41	21 48	21 51	21 58	22 01	22 03	22 08	22 11	22 18		22 21	22 26	22 32	22 33	22 41	22 48	22 51	22 56	23 02		23 11	23 13
London Road (Brighton)	d			21 44		21 54					22 14			22 24				22 44		22 54				23 14	
Moulsecoomb	d			21 47		21 57					22 17			22 27				22 47		22 57				23 17	
Falmer	d			21 51		22 01		22 08			22 21			22 31		22 39		22 51		23 01		23 09		23 21	
Lewes ■	a			21 58		22 08		22 15			22 28			22 38		22 46		22 58		23 08		23 16		23 28	
London Victoria	d																								
Clapham Junction	d																								
East Croydon	a																								
London Bridge	d																								
East Croydon	a																								
East Croydon	d																								
Gatwick Airport	a				22 11							22 41							23 11						
Haywards Heath	a	21 50					22 15		22 20	22 27					22 46		22 50				23 16				23 30
Lewes	a																								
Lewes	d			21 59							22 29							22 59						23 29	
Southease	d			22 06														23 06							
Newhaven Town	d			22 11							22 39							23 11						23 39	
Newhaven Harbour	d			22 12							22 40							23 12						23 40	
Bishopstone	d			22 15							22 43							23 15						23 43	
Seaford	a			22 19							22 47							23 19						23 47	

		SN	TL ■	SN ■	SN	TL ■
Brighton	d	23 21	23 24	23 32	23 41	23 42
London Road (Brighton)	d	23 24			23 44	
Moulsecoomb	d	23 27			23 47	
Falmer	d	23 31		23 39	23 51	
Lewes ■	a	23 38		23 46	23 58	
London Victoria	d					
Clapham Junction	d					
East Croydon	a					
London Bridge	d					
East Croydon	a					
East Croydon	d					
Gatwick Airport	a					
Haywards Heath	a		23 45			00 02
Lewes	a					
Lewes	d				23 59	
Southease	d				00 06	
Newhaven Town	d				00 11	
Newhaven Harbour	d				00 12	
Bishopstone	d				00 15	
Seaford	a				00 19	

A ■ to Lewes

B not 7 December

Table T189-F

Saturdays

26 May to 8 December

Brighton - Falmer - Lewes - Newhaven - Seaford with London connections

		TL ■	SN	TL ■	SN ■	TL ■	SN ■	TL ■	SN ■	SN		SN ■	TL ■	SN ■	TL ■	SN	GX ■	SN	TL ■	SN ■		SN ■	SN	GX ■	SN
Brighton	d	00 04		04 12	04 33	05 06	05 10	05 26	05 33	05 41		05 44	05 58	06 03	06 08	06 11	06 18	06 21	06 26	06 31		06 33	06 41	06 48	06 51
London Road (Brighton)	d									05 44						06 14		06 24					06 44		06 54
Moulsecoomb	d									05 47						06 17		06 27		06 35			06 47		06 57
Falmer	d									05 51						06 21		06 31		06 40			06 51		07 01
Lewes ■	a						05 22			05 58						06 28		06 38		06 47			06 58		07 08
London Victoria	d																								
Clapham Junction	d																								
East Croydon	a																								
London Bridge	d																								
East Croydon	a																								
East Croydon	d																								
Gatwick Airport	a																06 41							07 11	
Haywards Heath	a	00 24		04 25	04 46	05 27		05 46	05 50			06 06	06 15	06 20	06 27				06 46			06 50			
Lewes	a																								
Lewes	d									05 59						06 29							06 59		
Southease	d		00 06																				07 06		
Newhaven Town	d		00 11							06 09						06 39							07 11		
Newhaven Harbour	d		00 12							06 10						06 40							07 12		
Bishopstone	d		00 15							06 13						06 43							07 15		
Seaford	a		00 19							06 17						06 47							07 19		

		TL ■	SN ■	SN ■	TL ■	SN		GX ■	SN	TL ■	SN ■	SN ■	SN	GX ■	SN	TL ■		SN ■	SN ■	TL ■	SN	GX ■	SN	TL ■	SN ■
Brighton	d	06 58	07 01	07 03	07 08	07 11		07 18	07 21	07 26	07 31	07 33	07 41	07 48	07 51	07 58		08 01	08 03	08 08	08 11	08 18	08 21	08 26	08 31
London Road (Brighton)	d					07 14			07 24				07 44		07 54						08 14		08 24		
Moulsecoomb	d					07 17			07 27		07 35		07 47		07 57						08 17		08 27		08 35
Falmer	d		07 08			07 21			07 31		07 40		07 51		08 01			08 08			08 21		08 31		08 40
Lewes ■	a		07 15			07 28			07 38		07 47		07 58		08 08			08 15			08 28		08 38		08 47
London Victoria	d																								
Clapham Junction	d																								
East Croydon	a																								
London Bridge	d																								
East Croydon	a																								
East Croydon	d																								
Gatwick Airport	a							07 41						08 11								08 41			
Haywards Heath	a	07 15		07 20	07 27					07 46		07 50				08 15			08 20	08 27				08 46	
Lewes	a																								
Lewes	d					07 29							07 59								08 29				
Southease	d												08 06												
Newhaven Town	d					07 39							08 11								08 39				
Newhaven Harbour	d					07 40							08 12								08 40				
Bishopstone	d					07 43							08 15								08 43				
Seaford	a					07 47							08 19								08 47				

		SN ■		SN	GX ■	SN	TL ■	SN ■	SN ■	TL ■	SN	GX ■		SN	TL ■	SN ■	SN ■	SN	GX ■	SN	TL ■	SN ■		SN ■	TL ■
Brighton	d	08 33		08 41	08 48	08 51	08 58	09 01	09 03	09 08	09 11	09 18		09 21	09 26	09 31	09 33	09 41	09 48	09 51	09 58	10 01		10 03	10 08
London Road (Brighton)	d			08 44		08 54					09 14			09 24				09 44		09 54					
Moulsecoomb	d			08 47		08 57					09 17			09 27		09 35		09 47		09 57					
Falmer	d			08 51		09 01		09 08			09 21			09 31		09 40		09 51		10 01		10 08			
Lewes ■	a			08 58		09 08		09 15			09 28			09 38		09 47		09 58		10 08		10 15			
London Victoria	d																								
Clapham Junction	d																								
East Croydon	a																								
London Bridge	d																								
East Croydon	a																								
East Croydon	d																								
Gatwick Airport	a				09 11							09 41							10 11						
Haywards Heath	a	08 50					09 15		09 20	09 27					09 46		09 50				10 15			10 20	10 27
Lewes	a																								
Lewes	d			08 59							09 28							09 59							
Southease	d			09 06														10 06							
Newhaven Town	d			09 11							09 38							10 11							
Newhaven Harbour	d			09 12							09 40							10 12							
Bishopstone	d			09 15							09 43							10 15							
Seaford	a			09 19							09 47							10 19							

		SN	GX ■	SN	TL ■	SN ■	SN ■	SN		GX ■	SN	TL ■	SN ■	SN ■	TL ■	SN	GX ■	SN		TL ■	SN ■	SN ■	SN	GX ■	SN
Brighton	d	10 11	10 18	10 21	10 26	10 31	10 33	10 41		10 48	10 51	10 58	11 01	11 03	11 08	11 11	11 18	11 21		11 26	11 31	11 33	11 41	11 48	11 51
London Road (Brighton)	d	10 14		10 24				10 44			10 54					11 14		11 24					11 44		11 54
Moulsecoomb	d	10 17		10 27		10 35		10 47			10 57					11 17		11 27			11 35		11 47		11 57
Falmer	d	10 21		10 31		10 40		10 51			11 01		11 08			11 21		11 31			11 40		11 51		12 01
Lewes ■	a	10 28		10 38		10 47		10 58			11 08		11 15			11 28		11 38			11 47		11 58		12 08
London Victoria	d																								
Clapham Junction	d																								
East Croydon	a																								
London Bridge	d																								
East Croydon	a																								
East Croydon	d																								
Gatwick Airport	a		10 41							11 11							11 41							12 11	
Haywards Heath	a				10 46		10 50					11 15		11 20	11 27					11 46		11 50			
Lewes	a																								
Lewes	d	10 29						10 59								11 29							11 59		
Southease	d							11 06															12 06		
Newhaven Town	d	10 39						11 11								11 39							12 11		
Newhaven Harbour	d	10 40						11 12								11 40							12 12		
Bishopstone	d	10 43						11 15								11 43							12 15		
Seaford	a	10 47						11 19								11 47							12 19		

Table T189-F

Saturdays

26 May to 8 December

Brighton - Falmer - Lewes - Newhaven - Seaford with London connections

		TL	SN	SN	TL	SN	GX	SN	TL	SN	SN	SN	GX	SN	TL	SN	SN	TL	SN	GX	SN	TL
Brighton	d	11 58	12 01	12 03	12 08	12 11	12 18	12 21	12 26	12 31	12 33	12 41	12 48	12 51	12 58	13 01	13 03	13 08	13 11	13 18	13 21	13 26
London Road (Brighton)	d					12 14		12 24				12 44		12 54					13 14		13 24	
Moulsecoomb	d					12 17		12 27		12 35		12 47		12 57					13 17		13 27	
Falmer	d		12 08			12 21		12 31		12 40		12 51		13 01		13 08			13 21		13 31	
Lewes	a		12 15			12 28		12 38		12 47		12 58		13 08		13 15			13 28		13 38	
London Victoria	d																					
Clapham Junction	d																					
East Croydon	a																					
London Bridge	d																					
East Croydon	a																					
East Croydon	d																					
Gatwick Airport	a						12 41						13 11							13 41		
Haywards Heath	a	12 15		12 20	12 27				12 46		12 50				13 15		13 20	13 27				13 46
Lewes	a																					
Lewes	d					12 29						12 59							13 29			
Southease	d											13 06										
Newhaven Town	d					12 39						13 11							13 39			
Newhaven Harbour	d					12 40						13 12							13 40			
Bishopstone	d					12 43						13 15							13 43			
Seaford	a					12 47						13 19							13 47			

		SN	SN	SN	GX	SN	TL	SN	SN	TL	SN	GX	SN	TL	SN	SN	SN	GX	SN	TL	SN	SN	TL
Brighton	d	13 31	13 33	13 41	13 48	13 51	13 58	14 01	14 03	14 08	14 11	14 18	14 21	14 26	14 31	14 33	14 41	14 48	14 51	14 58	15 01	15 03	15 08
London Road (Brighton)	d			13 44		13 54					14 14		14 24				14 44		14 54				
Moulsecoomb	d	13 35		13 47		13 57					14 17		14 27		14 35		14 47		14 57				
Falmer	d	13 40		13 51		14 01		14 08			14 21		14 31		14 40		14 51		15 01		15 08		
Lewes	a	13 47		13 58		14 08		14 15			14 28		14 38		14 47		14 58		15 08		15 15		
London Victoria	d																						
Clapham Junction	d																						
East Croydon	a																						
London Bridge	d																						
East Croydon	a																						
East Croydon	d																						
Gatwick Airport	a				14 11							14 41						15 11					
Haywards Heath	a		13 50				14 15		14 20	14 27				14 46		14 50				15 15		15 20	15 27
Lewes	a																						
Lewes	d			13 59							14 29						14 59						
Southease	d			14 06													15 06						
Newhaven Town	d			14 11							14 39						15 11						
Newhaven Harbour	d			14 12							14 40						15 12						
Bishopstone	d			14 15							14 43						15 15						
Seaford	a			14 19							14 47						15 19						

		SN	GX	SN	TL	SN	SN	SN	GX	SN	TL	SN	SN	TL	SN	GX	SN	TL	SN	SN	SN	GX	SN
Brighton	d	15 11	15 18	15 21	15 26	15 31	15 33	15 41	15 48	15 51	15 58	16 01	16 03	16 08	16 11	16 18	16 21	16 26	16 31	16 33	16 41	16 48	16 51
London Road (Brighton)	d	15 14		15 24				15 44		15 54					16 14		16 24				16 44		16 54
Moulsecoomb	d	15 17		15 27		15 35		15 47		15 57					16 17		16 27		16 35		16 47		16 57
Falmer	d	15 21		15 31		15 40		15 51		16 01		16 08			16 21		16 31		16 40		16 51		17 01
Lewes	a	15 28		15 38		15 47		15 58		16 08		16 15			16 28		16 38		16 47		16 58		17 08
London Victoria	d																						
Clapham Junction	d																						
East Croydon	a																						
London Bridge	d																						
East Croydon	a																						
East Croydon	d																						
Gatwick Airport	a		15 41						16 11							16 43						17 11	
Haywards Heath	a				15 46		15 50				16 15		16 20	16 27				16 46		16 50			
Lewes	a																						
Lewes	d	15 29						15 59							16 29						16 59		
Southease	d							16 06													17 06		
Newhaven Town	d	15 39						16 11							16 39						17 11		
Newhaven Harbour	d	15 40						16 12							16 40						17 12		
Bishopstone	d	15 43						16 15							16 43						17 15		
Seaford	a	15 47						16 19							16 47						17 19		

		TL	SN	SN	TL	SN	GX	SN	TL	SN	SN	SN	GX	SN	TL	SN	SN	TL	SN	GX	SN	TL
Brighton	d	16 58	17 01	17 03	17 08	17 11	17 18	17 21	17 26	17 31	17 33	17 41	17 48	17 51	17 58	18 01	18 03	18 08	18 11	18 18	18 21	18 26
London Road (Brighton)	d					17 14		17 24				17 44		17 54					18 14		18 24	
Moulsecoomb	d					17 17		17 27		17 35		17 47		17 57					18 17		18 27	
Falmer	d		17 08			17 21		17 31		17 40		17 51		18 01		18 08			18 21		18 31	
Lewes	a		17 15			17 28		17 38		17 47		17 58		18 08		18 15			18 28		18 38	
London Victoria	d																					
Clapham Junction	d																					
East Croydon	a																					
London Bridge	d																					
East Croydon	a																					
East Croydon	d																					
Gatwick Airport	a						17 41						18 11							18 41		
Haywards Heath	a	17 15		17 20	17 27				17 46		17 50				18 15		18 20	18 27				18 46
Lewes	a																					
Lewes	d					17 29						17 59							18 29			
Southease	d											18 06										
Newhaven Town	d					17 39						18 11							18 39			
Newhaven Harbour	d					17 40						18 12							18 40			
Bishopstone	d					17 43						18 15							18 43			
Seaford	a					17 47						18 19							18 47			

Table T189-F

Saturdays

26 May to 8 December

Brighton - Falmer - Lewes - Newhaven - Seaford with London connections

		SN	SN	SN	GX	SN	TL	SN	SN	TL	SN	GX	SN	TL	SN	SN	SN	GX	SN	TL	SN	SN	TL
Brighton	d	18 31	18 33	18 41	18 48	18 51	18 58	19 01	19 03	19 08	19 11	19 18	19 21	19 26	19 31	19 33	19 41	19 48	19 51	19 58	20 01	20 03	20 08
London Road (Brighton)	d			18 44		18 54					19 14		19 24				19 44		19 54				
Moulsecoomb	d	18 35		18 47		18 57					19 17		19 27		19 35		19 47		19 57				
Falmer	d	18 40		18 51		19 01		19 08			19 21		19 31		19 40		19 51		20 01		20 08		
Lewes	a	18 47		18 58		19 08		19 15			19 28		19 38		19 47		19 58		20 08		20 15		
London Victoria	d																						
Clapham Junction	d																						
East Croydon	a																						
London Bridge	d																						
East Croydon	a																						
East Croydon	d																						
Gatwick Airport	a				19 11							19 41						20 11					
Haywards Heath	a		18 50				19 15		19 20	19 27				19 46		19 50				20 15		20 20	20 27
Lewes	a																						
Lewes	d			18 59							19 29						19 59						
Southease	d			19 06													20 06						
Newhaven Town	d			19 11							19 39						20 11						
Newhaven Harbour	d			19 12							19 40						20 12						
Bishopstone	d			19 15							19 43						20 15						
Seaford	a			19 19							19 47						20 19						

		SN	GX	SN	TL	SN	SN	SN	GX	SN	TL	SN	SN	TL	SN	GX	SN	TL	SN	SN	SN	GX
Brighton	d	20 11	20 18	20 21	20 26	20 31	20 33	20 41	20 48	20 51	20 58	21 01	21 03	21 08	21 11	21 18	21 21	21 26	21 31	21 33	21 41	21 48
London Road (Brighton)	d	20 14		20 24				20 44		20 54					21 14		21 24				21 44	
Moulsecoomb	d	20 17		20 27		20 35		20 47		20 57					21 17		21 27		21 35		21 47	
Falmer	d	20 21		20 31		20 40		20 51		21 01		21 08			21 21		21 31		21 40		21 51	
Lewes	a	20 28		20 38		20 47		20 58		21 08		21 15			21 28		21 38		21 47		21 58	
London Victoria	d																					
Clapham Junction	d																					
East Croydon	a																					
London Bridge	d																					
East Croydon	a																					
East Croydon	d																					
Gatwick Airport	a		20 41						21 11							21 41						22 11
Haywards Heath	a				20 46		20 50				21 15		21 20	21 27				21 46		21 50		
Lewes	a																					
Lewes	d	20 29						20 59							21 29						21 59	
Southease	d							21 06													22 06	
Newhaven Town	d	20 39						21 11							21 39						22 11	
Newhaven Harbour	d	20 40						21 12							21 40						22 12	
Bishopstone	d	20 43						21 15							21 43						22 15	
Seaford	a	20 47						21 19							21 47						22 19	

		SN	TL	SN	SN	TL	SN	GX	SN	TL	SN	SN	SN	GX	SN	TL	SN	SN	SN	SN	TL	SN	SN
Brighton	d	21 51	21 58	22 01	22 03	22 08	22 11	22 18	22 21	22 28	22 32	22 33	22 41	22 48	22 51	22 54	23 02	23 11	23 13	23 21	23 24	23 32	23 41
London Road (Brighton)	d	21 54					22 14		22 24				22 44		22 54			23 14		23 24			23 44
Moulsecoomb	d	21 57					22 17		22 27				22 47		22 57			23 17		23 27			23 47
Falmer	d	22 01		22 08			22 21		22 31		22 39		22 51		23 01		23 09	23 21		23 31		23 39	23 51
Lewes	a	22 08		22 15			22 28		22 38		22 46		22 58		23 08		23 16	23 28		23 38		23 46	23 58
London Victoria	d																						
Clapham Junction	d																						
East Croydon	a																						
London Bridge	d																						
East Croydon	a																						
East Croydon	d																						
Gatwick Airport	a							22 41						23 11									
Haywards Heath	a		22 15		22 20	22 27				22 45		22 50				23 15			23 30		23 45		
Lewes	a																						
Lewes	d						22 29						22 59					23 29					23 59
Southease	d												23 06										00 06
Newhaven Town	d						22 39						23 11					23 39					00 11
Newhaven Harbour	d						22 40						23 12					23 40					00 12
Bishopstone	d						22 43						23 15					23 43					00 15
Seaford	a						22 47						23 19					23 47					00 19

		TL
Brighton	d	23 42
London Road (Brighton)	d	
Moulsecoomb	d	
Falmer	d	
Lewes	a	
London Victoria	d	
Clapham Junction	d	
East Croydon	a	
London Bridge	d	
East Croydon	a	
East Croydon	d	
Gatwick Airport	a	
Haywards Heath	a	00 02
Lewes	a	
Lewes	d	
Southease	d	
Newhaven Town	d	
Newhaven Harbour	d	
Bishopstone	d	
Seaford	a	

Table T189-F

Sundays

20 May to 2 December

Brighton - Falmer - Lewes - Newhaven - Seaford with London connections

	TL ■	SN A	SN ■	TL ■	SN	TL ■	TL ■	SN	SN		SN	TL ■	SN	SN	SN	TL ■	SN	SN	SN		TL ■	SN	SN	SN
Brighton d	00 04		04 33	05 42	05 47	06 08	06 42	06 47	06 55		07 05	07 08	07 15	07 17	07 35	07 42	07 47	07 47	08 05		08 08	08 17	08 27	08 35
London Road (Brighton) d									06 58				07 18		07 38		07 50					08 20		08 38
Moulsecoomb d									07 01				07 21		07 41		07 53					08 23		08 41
Falmer d									07 05		07 12		07 25		07 45		07 57		08 12			08 27		08 45
Lewes ■ a									07 12		07 19		07 32		07 52		08 04		08 19			08 34		08 52
London Victoria d																								
Clapham Junction d																								
East Croydon a				06 39		07 09	07 39					08 09				08 39					09 02			
London Bridge d				06a55		07a25	07a58					08a25				08a55					09a17			
East Croydon a																								
East Croydon d																								
Gatwick Airport a																								
Haywards Heath a	00 24		04 46		06 07			07 07						07 34				08 06					08 45	
Lewes a																								
Lewes d													07 33				08 05					08 35		
Southease d		00 06															08 12							
Newhaven Town d		00 11											07 42				08 16					08 44		
Newhaven Harbour d		00 12											07 44				08 17					08 45		
Bishopstone d		00 15											07 47				08 20					08 48		
Seaford a		00 19											07 51				08 24					08 52		

	TL ■	SN	SN	SN	TL ■	SN	SN			TL ■	SN	SN	SN	TL ■	SN	SN		TL ■	SN	SN	TL ■	SN	SN	SN
Brighton d	08 42	08 47	08 57	09 05	09 08	09 17	09 27	and at the same minutes past each hour until		20 42	20 47	20 57	21 05	21 08	21 17	21 27		21 42	21 47	21 54	22 08	22 10	22 17	22 27
London Road (Brighton) d		08 50				09 20					20 50				21 20				21 50				22 20	
Moulsecoomb d		08 53				09 23					20 53				21 23				21 53				22 23	
Falmer d		08 57		09 12		09 27					20 57		21 12		21 27				21 57			22 17	22 27	
Lewes ■ a		09 04		09 19		09 34					21 04		21 19		21 34				22 04			22 24	22 34	
London Victoria d																								
Clapham Junction d																								
East Croydon a																								
London Bridge d																								
East Croydon a																								
East Croydon d																								
Gatwick Airport a																								
Haywards Heath a	09 03		09 15		09 29		09 45			21 03		21 15		21 29		21 45		22 03		22 15	22 29			22 45
Lewes a																								
Lewes d		09 05				09 35					21 05				21 35				22 05				22 35	
Southease d		09 12									21 12								22 12					
Newhaven Town d		09 16				09 44					21 16				21 44				22 16				22 44	
Newhaven Harbour d		09 17				09 45					21 17				21 45				22 17				22 45	
Bishopstone d		09 20				09 48					21 20				21 48				22 20				22 48	
Seaford a		09 24				09 52					21 24				21 52				22 24				22 52	

	TL ■	SN		SN	TL ■	SN	SN	TL ■
Brighton d	22 42	22 47		22 54	23 08	23 20	23 35	23 42
London Road (Brighton) d		22 50					23 38	
Moulsecoomb d		22 53					23 41	
Falmer d		22 57				23 27	23 45	
Lewes ■ a		23 04				23 34	23 53	
London Victoria d								
Clapham Junction d								
East Croydon a								
London Bridge d								
East Croydon a								
East Croydon d								
Gatwick Airport a								
Haywards Heath a	23 03			23 15	23 29			00 03
Lewes a								
Lewes d		23 05						
Southease d		23 12						
Newhaven Town d		23 16						
Newhaven Harbour d		23 17						
Bishopstone d		23 20						
Seaford a		23 24						

A not 20 May

Table T189-R

Mondays to Fridays

21 May to 7 December

Seaford with London connections - Newhaven - Lewes - Falmer - Brighton

	SN MX	SN MX	SN MX ■	SN MX ■	TL ■		TL ■	TL ■	SN	SN	TL ■	SN	SN ■	TL ■	SN		SN	TL ■	SN	SN	TL ■	SN ■	TL ■	SN
Seaford d									04 50	05 25					05 55				06 25					06 50
Bishopstone d									04 52	05 27					05 57				06 27					06 52
Newhaven Harbour d									04 56	05 31					06 01				06 31					06 56
Newhaven Town d		00 02							04 58	05 33					06 03				06 33					06 57
Southease d		00 06																						
Lewes a		00 12							05 07	05 42					06 12				06 42					07 07
Lewes d																								07 16
Haywards Heath a																								07 36
Gatwick Airport a																								07 49
East Croydon a																								08 07
East Croydon d																								
London Bridge a																								
East Croydon d				00 24	00 28		01 28	04 37			05 07			05 28				05 49			06 19		06 29	08 08
Clapham Junction d																								08 18
London Victoria a																								08 24
Lewes ■ d		00 13	00 27						05 15	05 42		05 53	06 07		06 13		06 23		06 42	06 53		07 00		
Falmer d	00 01	00 20	00 35						05 22	05 50		06 00	06 14		06 20		06 30		06 50	07 00		07 07		
Moulsecoomb d	00 05	00 24	00 39						05 26	05 54		06 04	06 18		06 24		06 34		06 54	07 04		07 12		
London Road (Brighton) d	00 07	00 27	00 41						05 29	05 56		06 07	06 21		06 27		06 37		06 56	07 07				
Brighton a	00 12	00 30	00 45	01s16	01 24		02 28	05 32	05 33	06 00	06 10	06 10	06 24	06 26	06 30		06 40	06 42	07 00	07 10	07 14	07 17	07 22	

	SN		SN	TL ■	SN ■	SN	SN	TL ■	TL ■	SN ■	SN		SN	TL ■	SN ■	SN	SN ■	SN	TL ■	TL ■	SN ■		SN	SN ■
Seaford d						07 23					07 53					08 23							08 53	
Bishopstone d						07 25					07 55					08 25							08 55	
Newhaven Harbour d	07 03					07 29					07 59					08 29							08 59	
Newhaven Town d	07 05					07 31					08 01					08 31							09 01	
Southease d	07 09					07 35										08 35							09 05	
Lewes a	07 15					07 41					08 10					08 41							09 11	
Lewes d																								
Haywards Heath a																								
Gatwick Airport a																								
East Croydon a																								
East Croydon d																								
London Bridge a																								
East Croydon d				06 49				07 19	07 30					07 49			08 11		08 19	08 30				08 41
Clapham Junction d																								
London Victoria a																								
Lewes ■ d	07 16		07 23		07 33	07 43	07 53			08 03	08 13		08 23		08 33	08 43		08 53			09 03		09 13	
Falmer d	07 23		07 30		07 40	07 50	08 00			08 11	08 20		08 30		08 40	08 50		09 00			09 11		09 20	
Moulsecoomb d	07 27		07 34		07 44	07 54	08 04			08 15	08 24		08 34		08 44	08 54		09 04			09 15		09 24	
London Road (Brighton) d	07 30		07 37			07 57	08 07				08 27		08 37			08 57		09 07					09 27	
Brighton a	07 33		07 40	07 44	07 49	08 00	08 10	08 12	08 19	08 20	08 30		08 40	08 44	08 49	09 00	09 01	09 10	09 12	09 20	09 20		09 30	09 32

	SN	TL ■	SN ■	SN	SN ■	SN	TL ■		TL ■	SN ■	SN	SN ■	SN	TL ■	SN ■	SN	SN ■		SN	TL ■	TL ■	SN ■	SN	SN ■
Seaford d				09 25							09 53					10 25							10 53	
Bishopstone d				09 27							09 55					10 27							10 55	
Newhaven Harbour d				09 31							09 59					10 31							10 59	
Newhaven Town d				09 33							10 01					10 33							11 01	
Southease d											10 05												11 05	
Lewes a				09 41							10 11					10 41							11 11	
Lewes d																								
Haywards Heath a																								
Gatwick Airport a																								
East Croydon a																								
East Croydon d																								
London Bridge a																								
East Croydon d		08 49			09 11		09 19		09 29			09 41		09 49			10 11			10 19	10 29			10 41
Clapham Junction d																								
London Victoria a																								
Lewes ■ d	09 23		09 33	09 43		09 53				10 03	10 13		10 23		10 33	10 43			10 53			11 03	11 13	
Falmer d	09 30		09 41	09 50		10 00				10 11	10 20		10 30		10 41	10 50			11 00			11 10	11 20	
Moulsecoomb d	09 34		09 45	09 54		10 04				10 15	10 24		10 34			10 54			11 04			11 14	11 24	
London Road (Brighton) d	09 37			09 57		10 07					10 27		10 37			10 57			11 07				11 27	
Brighton a	09 40	09 44	09 49	10 00	10 02	10 10	10 12		10 20	10 20	10 30	10 32	10 40	10 44	10 48	11 00	11 02		11 10	11 12	11 19	11 19	11 30	11 32

	SN	TL ■	SN ■		SN	SN ■	SN	TL ■	TL ■	SN ■	SN	SN ■	SN		TL ■	SN ■	SN	SN ■	SN	TL ■	TL ■	SN ■	SN	
Seaford d					11 25						11 53						12 25						12 53	
Bishopstone d					11 27						11 55						12 27						12 55	
Newhaven Harbour d					11 31						11 59						12 31						12 59	
Newhaven Town d					11 33						12 01						12 33						13 01	
Southease d											12 05												13 05	
Lewes a					11 42						12 11						12 42						13 11	
Lewes d																								
Haywards Heath a																								
Gatwick Airport a																								
East Croydon a																								
East Croydon d																								
London Bridge a																								
East Croydon d		10 49				11 11		11 19	11 29			11 41			11 49			12 11		12 19	12 29			
Clapham Junction d																								
London Victoria a																								
Lewes ■ d	11 23		11 33		11 43		11 53			12 03	12 13		12 23			12 33	12 43		12 53			13 03	13 13	
Falmer d	11 30		11 41		11 50		12 00			12 10	12 20		12 30			12 41	12 50		13 00			13 10	13 20	
Moulsecoomb d	11 34				11 54		12 04			12 14	12 24		12 34				12 54		13 04			13 14	13 24	
London Road (Brighton) d	11 37				11 57		12 07				12 27		12 37				12 57		13 07				13 27	
Brighton a	11 40	11 44	11 48		12 00	12 02	12 10	12 12	12 19	12 19	12 30	12 32	12 40		12 44	12 48	13 00	13 02	13 10	13 12	13 19	13 19	13 30	

21 May to 7 December

Seaford with London connections - Newhaven - Lewes - Falmer - Brighton

		SN ■	SN	TL ■	SN ■	SN	SN ■	SN	TL ■	TL ■		SN ■	SN	SN ■	SN	TL ■	SN ■	SN	SN ■	SN		TL ■	TL ■	SN ■	SN
Seaford	d					13 25							13 53					14 25							14 53
Bishopstone	d					13 27							13 55					14 27							14 55
Newhaven Harbour	d					13 31							13 59					14 31							14 59
Newhaven Town	d					13 33							14 01					14 33							15 01
Southease	d												14 05												15 05
Lewes	a					13 42							14 11					14 41							15 11
Lewes	d																								
Haywards Heath	a																								
Gatwick Airport	a																								
East Croydon	a																								
East Croydon	d																								
London Bridge	a																								
East Croydon	d	12 41		12 49			13 11		13 19	13 29				13 41		13 49			14 11			14 19	14 29		
Clapham Junction	d																								
London Victoria	a																								
Lewes ■	d		13 23		13 33	13 43		13 53				14 03	14 13		14 23		14 33	14 43		14 53				15 03	15 13
Falmer	d		13 30		13 41	13 50		14 00				14 10	14 20		14 30		14 41	14 50		15 00				15 10	15 20
Moulsecoomb	d		13 34			13 54		14 04				14 14	14 24		14 34			14 54		15 04				15 14	15 24
London Road (Brighton)	d		13 37			13 57		14 07					14 27		14 37			14 57		15 07					15 27
Brighton	a	13 32	13 40	13 44	13 48	14 00	14 02	14 10	14 12	14 19		14 19	14 30	14 32	14 40	14 44	14 48	15 00	15 02	15 10		15 12	15 19	15 19	15 30

		SN ■	SN	TL ■	SN ■	SN		SN ■	SN	TL ■	TL ■	SN ■	SN	SN ■	SN	TL ■		SN ■	SN	SN ■	SN	TL ■	SN ■	TL ■	SN
Seaford	d					15 25							15 53						16 25						16 55
Bishopstone	d					15 27							15 55						16 27						16 57
Newhaven Harbour	d					15 31							15 59						16 31						17 01
Newhaven Town	d					15 33							16 01						16 33						17 03
Southease	d												16 05												17 07
Lewes	a					15 41							16 11						16 41						17 13
Lewes	d																								
Haywards Heath	a																								
Gatwick Airport	a																								
East Croydon	a																								
East Croydon	d																								
London Bridge	a																								
East Croydon	d	14 41		14 49				15 11		15 19	15 29			15 41		15 49				16 11		16 20		16 29	
Clapham Junction	d																								
London Victoria	a																								
Lewes ■	d		15 23		15 33	15 43			15 53			16 03	16 13		16 23			16 33	16 43		16 53		17 03		17 14
Falmer	d		15 30		15 41	15 50			16 00			16 10	16 20		16 30			16 41	16 50		17 00		17 10		17 21
Moulsecoomb	d		15 34			15 54			16 04			16 14	16 24		16 34				16 54		17 04		17 14		17 25
London Road (Brighton)	d		15 37			15 57			16 07				16 27		16 37				16 57		17 07				17 28
Brighton	a	15 32	15 40	15 44	15 48	16 00		16 02	16 10	16 12	16 19	16 19	16 30	16 32	16 40	16 44		16 48	17 00	17 02	17 10	17 13	17 19	17 21	17 31

		SN ■		SN	TL ■	SN ■	SN	SN	TL ■	SN ■	TL ■	SN		SN	TL ■	SN ■	SN	SN	TL ■	SN ■	TL ■	SN		SN	TL ■
Seaford	d						17 25					17 55					18 25					18 55			
Bishopstone	d						17 27					17 57					18 27					18 57			
Newhaven Harbour	d						17 31					18 01					18 31					19 01			
Newhaven Town	d						17 33					18 03					18 33					19 03			
Southease	d											18 07										19 07			
Lewes	a						17 41					18 13					18 41					19 13			
Lewes	d																								
Haywards Heath	a																								
Gatwick Airport	a																								
East Croydon	a																								
East Croydon	d																								
London Bridge	a																								
East Croydon	d	16 41			16 50				17 20		17 29				17 50				18 20		18 29				18 50
Clapham Junction	d																								
London Victoria	a																								
Lewes ■	d			17 23		17 33	17 43	17 53		18 03		18 14		18 23		18 33	18 43	18 53		19 03		19 14		19 23	
Falmer	d			17 30		17 41	17 50	18 00		18 10		18 21		18 30		18 41	18 50	19 00		19 10		19 21		19 30	
Moulsecoomb	d			17 34			17 54	18 04		18 14		18 25		18 34			18 54	19 04		19 14		19 25		19 34	
London Road (Brighton)	d			17 37			17 57	18 07				18 28		18 37			18 57	19 07				19 28		19 37	
Brighton	a	17 32		17 40	17 46	17 48	18 00	18 10	18 15	18 19	18 21	18 31		18 41	18 46	18 48	19 00	19 10	19 15	19 19	19 21	19 31		19 40	19 46

		SN ■	SN	SN	TL ■	TL ■	SN ■	SN		SN ■	SN	TL ■	SN ■	SN ■	SN	SN	TL ■	TL ■		SN ■	SN	SN ■	SN	TL ■	SN ■
Seaford	d		19 25					19 53							20 25						20 53				
Bishopstone	d		19 27					19 55							20 27						20 55				
Newhaven Harbour	d		19 31					19 59							20 31						20 59				
Newhaven Town	d		19 33					20 01							20 33						21 01				
Southease	d							20 05													21 05				
Lewes	a		19 42					20 11							20 43						21 11				
Lewes	d																								
Haywards Heath	a																								
Gatwick Airport	a																								
East Croydon	a																								
East Croydon	d																								
London Bridge	a																								
East Croydon	d				19 20	19 29				19 41		19 49		20 11			20 19	20 29				20 41		20 49	
Clapham Junction	d																								
London Victoria	a																								
Lewes ■	d	19 36	19 43	19 53			20 03	20 13			20 23		20 39		20 46	20 53				21 06	21 13		21 23		21 33
Falmer	d	19 43	19 50	20 01			20 10	20 20			20 30		20 46		20 53	21 00				21 13	21 20		21 30		21 41
Moulsecoomb	d		19 54	20 05			20 14	20 24			20 34				20 57	21 04				21 17	21 24		21 34		
London Road (Brighton)	d		19 57	20 08				20 27			20 37				21 00	21 07					21 27		21 37		
Brighton	a	19 51	20 00	20 12	20 13	20 19	20 19	20 31		20 32	20 40	20 44	20 54	21 02	21 04	21 10	21 12	21 19		21 24	21 30	21 32	21 40	21 44	21 48

Table T189-R

Mondays to Fridays

21 May to 7 December

Seaford with London connections - Newhaven - Lewes - Falmer - Brighton

		SN	SN ■	SN		TL ■	TL ■	SN ■	SN	SN ■	SN	TL ■	SN ■	SN		SN ■	SN	TL ■	TL ■	SN ■	SN	SN ■	SN	TL ■
Seaford	d	21 25							21 53					22 25							22 53			
Bishopstone	d	21 27							21 55					22 27							22 55			
Newhaven Harbour	d	21 31							21 59					22 31							22 59			
Newhaven Town	d	21 33							22 01					22 33							23 01			
Southease	d								22 05												23 05			
Lewes	a	21 42							22 11					22 42							23 11			
Lewes	d																							
Haywards Heath	a																							
Gatwick Airport	a																							
East Croydon	a																							
East Croydon	d																							
London Bridge	a																							
East Croydon	d		21 11			21 19	21 29			21 41		21 49				22 11		22 19	22 29			22 41		22 49
Clapham Junction	d																							
London Victoria	a																							
Lewes ■	d	21 43		21 53				22 03	22 13		22 23		22 33	22 43			22 53			23 03	23 13		23 23	
Falmer	d	21 50		22 00				22 10	22 20		22 30		22 41	22 50			23 00			23 10	23 20		23 30	
Moulsecoomb	d	21 54		22 04				22 14	22 24		22 34			22 54			23 04			23 14	23 24		23 34	
London Road (Brighton)	d	21 57		22 07					22 27		22 37			22 57			23 07				23 27		23 37	
Brighton	a	22 00	22 02	22 10		22 12	22 19	22 19	22 30	22 32	22 40	22 44	22 48	23 00		23 03	23 10	23 12	23 19	23 19	23 30	23 32	23 40	23 44

		SN ■	SN	SN FO ■	SN FX ■	TL ■	SN	TL ■	SN	SN ■		TL ■
Seaford	d		23 25						23 53			
Bishopstone	d		23 27						23 55			
Newhaven Harbour	d		23 31						23 59			
Newhaven Town	d		23 33						00 02			
Southease	d								00 06			
Lewes	a		23 42						00 12			
Lewes	d											
Haywards Heath	a											
Gatwick Airport	a											
East Croydon	a											
East Croydon	d											
London Bridge	a											
East Croydon	d			23 11	23 11	23 19		23 29		23 43		23 51
Clapham Junction	d											
London Victoria	a											
Lewes ■	d	23 34	23 43				23 53		00 13			
Falmer	d	23 41	23 50				00 01		00 20			
Moulsecoomb	d		23 54				00 05		00 24			
London Road (Brighton)	d		23 57				00 07		00 27			
Brighton	a	23 49	00 01	00 02	00 02	00 12	00 12	00 23	00 30	00 35		00 56

Saturdays

26 May to 8 December

		SN	SN	SN ■	SN ■	TL ■	TL ■	SN ■	SN ■	TL ■		SN	TL ■	SN ■	TL ■	SN ■	TL ■	SN	TL ■	SN		SN ■	TL ■	SN	SN
Seaford	d											05 04						06 25						06 53	
Bishopstone	d											05 06						06 27						06 55	
Newhaven Harbour	d											05 10						06 31						06 59	
Newhaven Town	d		00 02									05 11						06 33						07 01	
Southease	d		00 06																					07 05	
Lewes	a		00 12									05 20						06 42						07 11	
Lewes	d																								
Haywards Heath	a																								
Gatwick Airport	a																								
East Croydon	a																								
East Croydon	d																								
London Bridge	a																								
East Croydon	d				00 24	00 28	01 28	01 33	04 31	04 37			05 07		05 28	05 31	05 49		06 19				06 29		
Clapham Junction	d																								
London Victoria	a																								
Lewes ■	d		00 13	00 27								05 27		06 08				06 43		06 53		07 03		07 13	07 23
Falmer	d	00 01	00 20	00 35								05 34		06 15				06 50		07 00		07 10		07 20	07 30
Moulsecoomb	d	00 05	00 24	00 39								05 38		06 19				06 54		07 04		07 14		07 24	07 34
London Road (Brighton)	d	00 07	00 27	00 41								05 41		06 22				06 57		07 07				07 27	07 37
Brighton	a	00 12	00 30	00 45	01s16	01 24	02 28	02 43	05 35	05 38		05 44	06 07	06 25	06 26	06 36	06 46	07 00	07 06	07 10		07 19	07 22	07 30	07 40

		TL ■	SN ■	SN	SN ■	SN		TL ■	SN ■	TL ■	SN	SN ■	SN	TL ■	SN ■	SN	SN ■	SN	TL ■	SN ■	TL ■	
Seaford	d			07 25							07 53					08 25						and at the same minutes past each hour until
Bishopstone	d			07 27							07 55					08 27						
Newhaven Harbour	d			07 31							07 59					08 31						
Newhaven Town	d			07 33							08 01					08 33						
Southease	d										08 05											
Lewes	a			07 42							08 11					08 42						
Lewes	d																					
Haywards Heath	a																					
Gatwick Airport	a																					
East Croydon	a																					
East Croydon	d																					
London Bridge	a																					
East Croydon	d	06 49			07 11			07 19		07 30		07 41		07 49			08 11		08 19		08 29	
Clapham Junction	d																					
London Victoria	a																					
Lewes ■	d		07 33	07 43		07 53			08 03		08 13		08 23		08 33	08 43		08 53		09 03		
Falmer	d		07 41	07 50		08 00			08 10		08 20		08 30		08 41	08 50		09 00		09 10		
Moulsecoomb	d			07 54		08 04					08 24		08 34			08 54		09 04				
London Road (Brighton)	d			07 57		08 07					08 27		08 37			08 57		09 07				
Brighton	a	07 44	07 48	08 00	08 01	08 10		08 12	08 18	08 19	08 30	08 31	08 40	08 44	08 48	09 00	09 01	09 10	09 12	09 18	09 19	

Seaford with London connections - Newhaven - Lewes - Falmer - Brighton

Saturdays

26 May to 8 December

		SN	SN ■	SN	TL ■	SN ■	SN	SN ■	SN	TL ■	SN ■	TL ■	SN	SN ■	SN	TL ■	TL ■	SN ■	SN ■	SN	SN	TL ■	TL ■
Seaford	d	21 53					22 25						22 53							23 25			
Bishopstone	d	21 55					22 27						22 55							23 27			
Newhaven Harbour	d	21 59					22 31						22 59							23 31			
Newhaven Town	d	22 01					22 33						23 01							23 33			
Southease	d	22 05											23 05										
Lewes	a	22 11					22 42						23 11							23 42			
Lewes	d																						
Haywards Heath	a																						
Gatwick Airport	a																						
East Croydon	a																						
East Croydon	d																						
London Bridge	a																						
East Croydon	d		21 41		21 49			22 11		22 19		22 29		22 41		22 49	22 59		23 11			23 19	23 29
Clapham Junction	d																						
London Victoria	a																						
Lewes ■	d	22 13		22 23		22 33	22 43		22 53		23 03		23 13		23 23			23 35		23 43	23 53		
Falmer	d	22 20		22 30		22 41	22 50		23 00		23 10		23 20		23 30			23 42		23 50	00 01		
Moulsecoomb	d	22 24		22 34			22 54		23 04				23 24		23 34					23 54	00 05		
London Road (Brighton)	d	22 27		22 37			22 57		23 07				23 27		23 37					23 57	00 07		
Brighton	a	22 30	22 31	22 40	22 44	22 48	23 00	23 01	23 10	23 12	23 18	23 19	23 30	23 31	23 40	23 44	23 49	23 50	00 01	00 01	00 11	00 12	00 23

		SN	SN ■	TL ■
Seaford	d	23 53		
Bishopstone	d	23 55		
Newhaven Harbour	d	23 59		
Newhaven Town	d	00 02		
Southease	d	00 06		
Lewes	a	00 12		
Lewes	d			
Haywards Heath	a			
Gatwick Airport	a			
East Croydon	a			
East Croydon	d			
London Bridge	a			
East Croydon	d		23 43	23 51
Clapham Junction	d			
London Victoria	a			
Lewes ■	d	00 13		
Falmer	d	00 20		
Moulsecoomb	d	00 24		
London Road (Brighton)	d	00 27		
Brighton	a	00 30	00 35	00 56

Sundays

20 May to 2 December

		SN	SN	SN ■	SN ■	TL ■	TL ■	SN ■	SN ■	SN ■	SN	SN	SN	SN	TL ■	SN	SN	TL ■	SN	SN	TL ■	SN	SN
		A	A	A		A	A																
Seaford	d																07 57			08 29			08 59
Bishopstone	d																07 59			08 31			09 01
Newhaven Harbour	d																08 03			08 35			09 05
Newhaven Town	d		00 02														08 04			08 36			09 06
Southease	d		00 06														08 08						09 10
Lewes	a		00 12														08 14			08 45			09 17
Lewes	d																						
Haywards Heath	a																						
Gatwick Airport	a																						
East Croydon	a																						
East Croydon	d																						
London Bridge	a																						
East Croydon	d				00 24	00 28	01 28	01 33	04 31	05 24	06 09			06 54	07 25	07 27		07 55			08 25	08 27	
Clapham Junction	d																						
London Victoria	a																						
Lewes ■	d		00 13	00 27								07 23	07 38				08 23		08 38	08 46			09 24
Falmer	d	00 01	00 20	00 35								07 30	07 45				08 30		08 45	08 53			09 31
Moulsecoomb	d	00 05	00 24	00 39								07 34	07 49				08 34		08 49	08 57			09 35
London Road (Brighton)	d	00 07	00 27	00 41								07 37	07 52				08 37		08 52	09 00			09 38
Brighton	a	00 11	00 30	00 45	01s16	01 24	02 28	02 38	05 28	06 21	07 11	07 40	07 56	08 01	08 21	08 30	08 41	08 52	08 56	09 04	09 21	09 33	09 41

		TL ■	SN	SN	SN	TL ■	SN	SN	SN	TL ■	SN	SN	TL ■	SN	SN	SN	TL ■	SN	SN	TL ■	SN	SN	SN
Seaford	d				09 29				09 59			10 29				10 59			11 29				11 59
Bishopstone	d				09 31				10 01			10 31				11 01			11 31				12 01
Newhaven Harbour	d				09 35				10 05			10 35				11 05			11 35				12 05
Newhaven Town	d				09 36				10 06			10 36				11 06			11 36				12 06
Southease	d								10 10							11 10							12 10
Lewes	a				09 45				10 17			10 45				11 17			11 45				12 17
Lewes	d																						
Haywards Heath	a																						
Gatwick Airport	a																						
East Croydon	a																						
East Croydon	d																						
London Bridge	a																						
East Croydon	d	08 55		09 12		09 25		09 42		09 55	10 12		10 25		10 42		10 55	11 12		11 25		11 42	
Clapham Junction	d																						
London Victoria	a																						
Lewes ■	d		09 36		09 46		10 09		10 24			10 46		11 07		11 24			11 46		12 07		12 24
Falmer	d		09 44		09 53		10 16		10 31			10 53		11 14		11 31			11 53		12 14		12 31
Moulsecoomb	d				09 57				10 35			10 57				11 35			11 57				12 35
London Road (Brighton)	d				10 00				10 38			11 00				11 38			12 00				12 38
Brighton	a	09 47	09 51	10 01	10 04	10 15	10 24	10 31	10 41	10 47	11 01	11 04	11 15	11 22	11 31	11 41	11 47	12 01	12 04	12 15	12 22	12 31	12 41

A not 20 May

Please check the 'Additional Notes to Individual Tables' [illegible]

Table T189-R

Seaford with London connections - Newhaven - Lewes - Falmer - Brighton

Sundays

20 May to 2 December

		TL ■	SN	SN	TL ■	SN	SN	SN	TL ■	SN	SN	TL ■	SN	SN	SN	TL ■	SN	SN	TL ■	SN	SN	SN
Seaford	d			12 29				12 59			13 29				13 59			14 29				14 59
Bishopstone	d			12 31				13 01			13 31				14 01			14 31				15 01
Newhaven Harbour	d			12 35				13 05			13 35				14 05			14 35				15 05
Newhaven Town	d			12 36				13 06			13 36				14 06			14 36				15 06
Southease	d							13 10							14 10							15 10
Lewes	a			12 45				13 17			13 45				14 17			14 45				15 17
Lewes	d																					
Haywards Heath	a																					
Gatwick Airport	a																					
East Croydon	a																					
East Croydon	d																					
London Bridge	a																					
East Croydon	d	11 55	12 12		12 25		12 42		12 55	13 13		13 25		13 42		13 55	14 12		14 25		14 42	
Clapham Junction	d																					
London Victoria	a																					
Lewes ■	d			12 46		13 07		13 24			13 46		14 07		14 24			14 46		15 07		15 24
Falmer	d			12 53		13 14		13 31			13 53		14 14		14 31			14 53		15 14		15 31
Moulsecoomb	d			12 57				13 35			13 57				14 35			14 57				15 35
London Road (Brighton)	d			13 00				13 38			14 00				14 38			15 00				15 38
Brighton	a	12 47	13 01	13 04	13 15	13 22	13 31	13 41	13 47	14 01	14 04	14 15	14 22	14 31	14 41	14 47	15 01	15 04	15 15	15 22	15 31	15 41

		TL ■	SN	SN	TL ■	SN	SN	SN	TL ■	SN	SN	TL ■	SN	SN	SN	TL ■	SN	SN	TL ■	SN	SN	SN	TL ■
Seaford	d			15 29				15 59			16 29				16 59			17 29				17 59	
Bishopstone	d			15 31				16 01			16 31				17 01			17 31				18 01	
Newhaven Harbour	d			15 35				16 05			16 35				17 05			17 35				18 05	
Newhaven Town	d			15 36				16 06			16 36				17 06			17 36				18 06	
Southease	d							16 10							17 10							18 10	
Lewes	a			15 45				16 17			16 45				17 17			17 45				18 17	
Lewes	d																						
Haywards Heath	a																						
Gatwick Airport	a																						
East Croydon	a																						
East Croydon	d																						
London Bridge	a																						
East Croydon	d	14 55	15 12		15 25		15 42		15 55	16 13		16 25		16 42		16 55	17 13		17 25		17 42		17 55
Clapham Junction	d																						
London Victoria	a																						
Lewes ■	d			15 46		16 07		16 24			16 46		17 07		17 24			17 46		18 07		18 24	
Falmer	d			15 53		16 14		16 31			16 53		17 14		17 31			17 53		18 14		18 31	
Moulsecoomb	d			15 57				16 35			16 57				17 35			17 57				18 35	
London Road (Brighton)	d			16 00				16 38			17 00				17 38			18 00				18 38	
Brighton	a	15 47	16 01	16 04	16 15	16 22	16 31	16 41	16 47	17 01	17 04	17 15	17 22	17 31	17 41	17 47	18 01	18 04	18 15	18 22	18 31	18 41	18 47

		SN		SN	TL ■	SN	SN	SN	TL ■	SN	SN	TL ■	SN	SN	SN	SN	TL ■	SN	SN	TL ■	SN	SN
Seaford	d			20 29				20 59			21 29				21 57				22 29			
Bishopstone	d			20 31				21 01			21 31				21 59				22 31			
Newhaven Harbour	d			20 35				21 05			21 35				22 03				22 35			
Newhaven Town	d			20 36				21 06			21 36				22 04				22 36			
Southease	d							21 10							22 08							
Lewes	a		and at the same minutes past each hour until	20 45				21 17			21 45				22 15				22 45			
Lewes	d																					
Haywards Heath	a																					
Gatwick Airport	a																					
East Croydon	a																					
East Croydon	d																					
London Bridge	a																					
East Croydon	d	18 12			20 25		20 42		20 55	21 12		21 25		21 42			21 55	22 12		22 25		22 42
Clapham Junction	d																					
London Victoria	a																					
Lewes ■	d			20 46		21 07		21 24			21 46		22 07		22 15	22 23			22 46		23 07	
Falmer	d			20 53		21 14		21 31			21 53		22 14		22 23	22 30			22 53		23 14	
Moulsecoomb	d			20 57				21 35			21 57				22 27	22 34			22 57			
London Road (Brighton)	d			21 00				21 38			22 00				22 29	22 37			23 00			
Brighton	a	19 01		21 04	21 15	21 22	21 31	21 41	21 47	22 01	22 04	22 15	22 22	22 31	22 33	22 41	22 47	23 01	23 04	23 15	23 23	23 31

		SN	SN	TL ■	TL ■	TL ■	SN
Seaford	d	22 57					
Bishopstone	d	22 59					
Newhaven Harbour	d	23 03					
Newhaven Town	d	23 04					
Southease	d	23 08					
Lewes	a	23 15					
Lewes	d						
Haywards Heath	a						
Gatwick Airport	a						
East Croydon	a						
East Croydon	d						
London Bridge	a						
East Croydon	d			22 55	23 25	23 55	23 57
Clapham Junction	d						
London Victoria	a						
Lewes ■	d	23 15	23 23				
Falmer	d	23 23	23 31				
Moulsecoomb	d	23 27	23 35				
London Road (Brighton)	d	23 29	23 37				
Brighton	a	23 33	23 42	23 47	00 19	00 54	00 59

Table T190-F

Mondays to Fridays

21 May to 7 December

London and Brighton - Eastbourne - Bexhill - Hastings

Miles	Miles			SN MX ■	SN MX ■	SN MO	SN MX ■	SN ■	SN ■	SN ■	SN ■	SN ■	SN ■	SN ■	SN ■	SN ■	SN ■	SN ■	SN ■	SN ■	SN ■	SN ■	SN ■
—	—	London Victoria ⊖	d				00 02									05 32				06 46		07 16	
—	—	Clapham Junction	d				00 09									05 39				06 53		07 23	
—	—	East Croydon	a				00 23									05 51				07 02		07 32	
—	—	London Bridge ⊖	d																				
—	—	East Croydon	a																				
—	—	East Croydon	d				00 24									05 52				07 03		07 33	
—	—	Gatwick Airport ✈	d				00 44									06 18				07 20		07 50	
—	0	Haywards Heath	d				01 08									06 33				07 34		08 03	
—	3	Wivelsfield	d													06 37						08 08	
—	6¾	**Plumpton**	d													06 44				07 44			
—	9½	**Cooksbridge**	d													06 48				07 49		08 17	
—	—	**Lewes**	a				01 23									06 53				07 54		08 22	
0	—	Brighton	d							05 01		05 31	05 58		06 31		07 01		07 31		08 01		
0¾	—	London Road (Brighton)	d																				
1¾	—	Moulsecoomb	d																07 35				
3½	—	Falmer	d									05 38	06 05		06 38		07 08		07 40		08 08		
8	12¼	Lewes	a							05 13		05 45	06 12		06 45		07 15		07 47		08 15		
—	—	**Lewes**	d				01 23			05 14		05 46	06 12		06 46	06 54	07 15		07 47	07 54	08 15	08 26	
11	—	**Glynde**	d										06 18			06 59	07 21				08 21		
15½	—	**Berwick**	d		00 05							05 55			06 55	07 05			07 56				
19¾	—	**Polegate**	d	00 02	00 10	00 10	01s35			05 26		06 00	06 27		07 00	07 10	07 30		08 02	08 07	08 30	08 38	
21¾	—	Hampden Park	d	00 06	00 14	00 15	01s40			05 31		06 05			07 05	07 15			08 06			08 43	
23¾	—	Eastbourne	a	00 11	00 19	00 19	01 44			05 37		06 09	06 35		07 09	07 19	07 38		08 11	08 15	08 38	08 48	
—	—		d		00 25			04 58	05 10	05 42	05 47	06 15	06 41	06 46	07 15	07 25	07 43	07 49	08 16	08 21	08 43		08 49
25¾	—	Hampden Park	d						05 14	05 46	05 51	06 19	06 45	06 50	07 19	07 29	07 47	07 53		08 25	08 47		08 53
28¾	—	**Pevensey & Westham**	d		00 32				05 19		05 57		06 51	06 56		07 34	07 52	07 59	08 24	08 30	08 52		08 59
29½	—	**Pevensey Bay**	d															08 01					09 01
31½	—	**Normans Bay**	d								06 02			07 01				08 05		08 35			09 05
33¼	—	**Cooden Beach**	d		00 39						06 06			07 05		07 41	07 59	08 10	08 30	08 39	08 59		09 10
34¾	—	**Collington**	d		00 42						06 10			07 09		07 44	08 02	08 13	08 34	08 43	09 02		09 13
35½	—	**Bexhill**	d		00 45			05 14	05 28	05 58	06 13	06 31	07 02	07 13	07 31	07 48	08 07	08 16	08 37	08 45	09 05		09 16
39¼	—	St Leonards Warrior Sq	d		00 51			05 21	05 34	06 04	06 20	06 39	07 09	07 19	07 39	07 55	08 13	08 23	08 43	08 52	09 11		09 23
40	0	Hastings	a		00 54			05 24	05 37	06 07	06 23	06 42	07 12	07 23	07 42	07 58	08 16	08 26	08 46	08 55	09 14		09 26
—	1	Ore	a					05 28		06 11	06 27		07 17	07 27		08 02	08 20	08 30		08 59	09 18		09 31
—	11¼	Rye	a					05 44			06 44			07 44				08 47					09 47
—	26½	Ashford International	a					06 07			07 08			08 09				09 10					10 10

		SN ■	SN ■	SN ■	SN ■	SN ■	SN ■	SN ■	SN ■	SN ■	SN ■	SN ■	SN ■	SN ■	SN ■	SN ■	SN ■	SN ■	SN ■	SN ■	SN ■	SN ■	SN ■
London Victoria ⊖	d		07 46		08 16			08 46		09 16			09 46		10 16			10 46		11 16			11 46
Clapham Junction	d		07 53		08 23			08 53		09 23			09 53		10 23			10 53		11 23			11 53
East Croydon	a		08 03		08 33			09 02		09 32			10 02		10 32			11 02		11 32			12 02
London Bridge ⊖	d																						
East Croydon	a																						
East Croydon	d		08 03		08 33			09 03		09 33			10 03		10 33			11 03		11 33			12 03
Gatwick Airport ✈	d		08 20		08 50			09 20		09 50			10 20		10 50			11 20		11 50			12 20
Haywards Heath	d		08 35		09 03			09 35		10 07			10 35		11 07			11 35		12 07			12 35
Wivelsfield	d				09 07					10 11					11 11					12 11			
Plumpton	d		08 45					09 45					10 45					11 45					12 45
Cooksbridge	d				09 16					10 20													
Lewes	a		08 53		09 21			09 53		10 25			10 53		11 23			11 53		12 23			12 53
Brighton	d	08 31		09 01			09 31		10 01			10 31		11 01			11 31		12 01			12 31	
London Road (Brighton)	d																						
Moulsecoomb	d	08 35					09 35					10 35					11 35					12 35	
Falmer	d	08 40		09 08			09 40		10 08			10 40		11 08			11 40		12 08			12 40	
Lewes	a	08 47		09 15			09 47		10 15			10 47		11 15			11 47		12 15			12 47	
Lewes	d	08 47	08 53	09 15	09 24		09 47	09 54	10 15	10 26		10 47	10 54	11 15	11 24		11 47	11 54	12 15	12 24		12 47	12 54
Glynde	d			09 21					10 21					11 21					12 21				
Berwick	d	08 56					09 56					10 56					11 56					12 56	
Polegate	d	09 02	09 06	09 30	09 37		10 02	10 06	10 30	10 38		11 02	11 06	11 30	11 36		12 02	12 06	12 30	12 36		13 02	13 06
Hampden Park	d	09 06			09 42		10 06			10 43		11 06			11 41		12 06			12 41		13 06	
Eastbourne	a	09 11	09 14	09 38	09 47		10 11	10 14	10 38	10 48		11 11	11 14	11 38	11 46		12 11	12 14	12 38	12 46		13 11	13 14
	d	09 16	09 20	09 43		09 49	10 16	10 20	10 44		10 49	11 16	11 20	11 43		11 49	12 16	12 20	12 43		12 49	13 16	13 20
Hampden Park	d		09 24	09 47		09 53		10 24	10 48		10 53		11 24	11 47		11 53		12 24	12 47		12 53		13 24
Pevensey & Westham	d		09 29	09 52		09 59		10 29	10 53		10 59		11 29	11 52		11 59		12 29	12 52		12 59		13 29
Pevensey Bay	d																						
Normans Bay	d					10 04					11 04					12 04					13 04		
Cooden Beach	d		09 36	09 59		10 08		10 36			11 08		11 36			12 08		12 36			13 08		13 36
Collington	d		09 39	10 02		10 12		10 39			11 12		11 39			12 12		12 39			13 12		13 39
Bexhill	d	09 34	09 42	10 06		10 15	10 30	10 42	11 02		11 15	11 30	11 42	12 02		12 15	12 30	12 42	13 02		13 15	13 30	13 42
St Leonards Warrior Sq	d	09 40	09 49	10 13		10 22	10 37	10 49	11 08		11 22	11 37	11 50	12 08		12 22	12 37	12 49	13 08		13 22	13 37	13 49
Hastings	a	09 43	09 53	10 16		10 25	10 40	10 53	11 11		11 25	11 40	11 53	12 11		12 25	12 40	12 53	13 11		13 25	13 40	13 53
Ore	a		09 57	10 20		10 29		10 57	11 15		11 29		11 57	12 15		12 29		12 57	13 15		13 29		13 57
Rye	a					10 46					11 45					12 46					13 45		
Ashford International	a					11 09					12 09					13 09					14 09		

Table T190-F

Mondays to Fridays

21 May to 7 December

London and Brighton - Eastbourne - Bexhill - Hastings

		SN ■	SN ■	SN ■	SN ■	SN ■	SN ■	SN ■	SN ■	SN ■	SN ■	SN ■	SN ■	SN ■	SN ■	SN ■	SN ■	SN ■	SN ■	SN ■	SN ■	SN ■
London Victoria ⊖	d		12 16			12 46		13 16			13 46		14 16			14 46		15 16			15 46	
Clapham Junction	d		12 23			12 53		13 23			13 53		14 23			14 53		15 23			15 53	
East Croydon	a		12 32			13 02		13 32			14 02		14 32			15 02		15 32			16 02	
London Bridge ⊖	d																					
East Croydon	a																					
East Croydon	d		12 33			13 03		13 33			14 03		14 33			15 03		15 33			16 03	
Gatwick Airport ✈	d		12 50			13 20		13 50			14 20		14 50			15 20		15 50			16 20	
Haywards Heath	d		13 07			13 35		14 07			14 35		15 07			15 35		16 07			16 35	
Wivelsfield	d		13 11					14 11					15 11					16 11				
Plumpton	d					13 45					14 45					15 45					16 45	
Cooksbridge	d																					
Lewes	a		13 23			13 53		14 23			14 53		15 23			15 53		16 23			16 53	
Brighton	d	13 01			13 31		14 01			14 31		15 01			15 31		16 01			16 31		17 01
London Road (Brighton)	d																					
Moulsecoomb	d				13 35					14 35					15 35		16 05			16 35		17 05
Falmer	d	13 08			13 40		14 08			14 40		15 08			15 40		16 10			16 40		17 10
Lewes	a	13 15			13 47		14 15			14 47		15 15			15 47		16 17			16 47		17 17
Lewes	d	13 15	13 24		13 47	13 54	14 15	14 24		14 47	14 54	15 15	15 24		15 47	15 54	16 17	16 24		16 47	16 54	17 17
Glynde	d	13 21					14 21					15 21					16 23					17 23
Berwick	d				13 56					14 56					15 56					16 56		
Polegate	d	13 30	13 36		14 02	14 06	14 30	14 36		15 02	15 06	15 30	15 36		16 02	16 06	16 32	16 36		17 02	17 06	17 32
Hampden Park	d		13 41		14 06			14 41		15 06			15 41		16 06		16 37	16 43		17 07		17 37
Eastbourne	a	13 38	13 46		14 11	14 14	14 38	14 46		15 11	15 14	15 38	15 46		16 11	16 14	16 41	16 48		17 11	17 14	17 41
	d	13 43		13 49	14 16	14 20	14 43		14 49	15 16	15 20	15 43		15 49	16 16	16 20	16 46		16 52	17 16	17 20	17 46
Hampden Park	d	13 47		13 53		14 24	14 47		14 53		15 24	15 47		15 53		16 24			16 56		17 24	
Pevensey & Westham	d	13 52		13 59		14 29	14 52		14 59		15 29	15 52		15 59		16 29	16 54		17 02		17 29	17 53
Pevensey Bay	d													16 01			16 56					
Normans Bay	d			14 04					15 04					16 05			17 00					17 58
Cooden Beach	d			14 08		14 36			15 08		15 36	15 58		16 10		16 36	17 05		17 09		17 36	18 03
Collington	d			14 12		14 39			15 12		15 39	16 02		16 13		16 39	17 09		17 13		17 39	18 06
Bexhill	d	14 02		14 15	14 30	14 42	15 02		15 15	15 30	15 42	16 04		16 16	16 31	16 42	17 11		17 16	17 32	17 42	18 09
St Leonards Warrior Sq	d	14 08		14 22	14 37	14 49	15 08		15 22	15 37	15 49	16 11		16 23	16 37	16 49	17 18		17 23	17 38	17 49	18 15
Hastings	a	14 11		14 25	14 40	14 53	15 11		15 25	15 40	15 53	16 14		16 26	16 40	16 53	17 21		17 26	17 43	17 53	18 18
Ore	a	14 15		14 29		14 57	15 15		15 29		15 57	16 18		16 30		16 57	17 25		17 30		17 57	18 22
Rye	a			14 46					15 45					16 47					17 46			
Ashford International	a			15 09					16 09					17 10					18 09			

		SN ■	SN ■	SN ■	SN ■	SN ■	SN ■	SN ■	SN ■	SN ■	SN ■	SN ■	SN ■	SN ■	SN ■	SN ■	SN ■	SN ■	SN ■	SN ■	SN ■	SN ■	SN ■
London Victoria ⊖	d	16 16			16 45		17 15			17 45		17 45		18 15				18 45		19 16			19 46
Clapham Junction	d	16 23			16 52		17 22			17 52		17 52		18 22				18 52		19 23			19 53
East Croydon	a	16 32			17 01		17 31			18 01		18 01		18 31				19 01		19 32			20 02
London Bridge ⊖	d								17 33							18 33							
East Croydon	a								17 47							18 47							
East Croydon	d	16 33			17 02		17 32		17 48	18 02		18 02		18 32		18 48		19 02		19 33			20 03
Gatwick Airport ✈	d	16 50			17 20		17 50		18 03	18 20		18 20		18 50		19 03		19 20		19 50			20 20
Haywards Heath	d	17 07			17 33		18 03		18 16	18 33		18 33		19 03		19 16		19 33		20 07			20 35
Wivelsfield	d	17 11			17 37		18 07		18 21	18 37		18 37		19 07		19 21		19 37		20 11			
Plumpton	d				17 45				18 28	18 45		18 45				19 28		19 45					20 45
Cooksbridge	d	17 20					18 17		18 33					19 17		19 33				20 20			
Lewes	a	17 25			17 52		18 22		18 38	18 52		18 52		19 22		19 38		19 52		20 25			20 53
Brighton	d			17 31		18 01					18 31		19 01				19 31		20 01			20 31	
London Road (Brighton)	d																						
Moulsecoomb	d			17 35		18 05					18 35						19 35					20 35	
Falmer	d			17 40		18 10					18 40		19 08				19 40		20 08			20 40	
Lewes	a			17 47		18 17					18 47		19 15				19 47		20 15			20 47	
Lewes	d	17 26		17 47	17 53	18 17	18 22		18 39		18 47	18 56	19 15	19 22		19 39	19 47	19 53	20 15	20 26		20 47	20 54
Glynde	d					18 23	18 28		18 45				19 21	19 28		19 45			20 21				
Berwick	d			17 56			18 33		18 51		18 56			19 33		19 51	19 56					20 57	
Polegate	d	17 38		18 02	18 06	18 32	18 39		18 56		19 02	19 08	19 30	19 39		19 56	20 02	20 06	20 30	20 38		21 02	21 06
Hampden Park	d	17 43		18 07	18 11	18 37	18 45		19 01		19 08	19 13		19 44		20 01	20 07	20 11		20 43		21 07	
Eastbourne	a	17 48		18 11	18 15	18 41	18 49		19 06		19 12	19 18	19 38	19 48		20 06	20 12	20 18	20 38	20 48		21 11	21 14
	d		17 52	18 16	18 21	18 46		18 52			19 21	19 27	19 43		19 49		20 17	20 24	20 43		20 49	21 16	21 20
Hampden Park	d		17 56		18 25			18 56				19 31	19 47		19 53			20 28	20 47		20 53		21 24
Pevensey & Westham	d		18 02		18 30	18 53		19 02				19 36	19 52		19 59			20 33	20 52		20 59		21 29
Pevensey Bay	d		18 04																				
Normans Bay	d					18 58									20 04						21 04		
Cooden Beach	d		18 10		18 37	19 03		19 09				19 43			20 08			20 40			21 08		21 36
Collington	d		18 13		18 40	19 06		19 13				19 46			20 12			20 43			21 12		21 39
Bexhill	d		18 17	18 35	18 44	19 09		19 19			19 38	19 49	20 02		20 15		20 31	20 46	21 02		21 15	21 31	21 42
St Leonards Warrior Sq	d		18 24	18 41	18 50	19 15		19 25			19 44	19 55	20 08		20 22		20 37	20 52	21 08		21 21	21 37	21 49
Hastings	a		18 27	18 45	18 53	19 18		19 29			19 47	19 58	20 11		20 25		20 40	20 55	21 11		21 25	21 40	21 53
Ore	a		18 31		18 57	19 23		19 33				20 02	20 17		20 29			20 59	21 15		21 29		21 57
Rye	a		18 48					19 48							20 46						21 45		
Ashford International	a		19 10					20 10							21 09						22 09		

Table T190-F

Mondays to Fridays
21 May to 7 December

London and Brighton - Eastbourne - Bexhill - Hastings

		SN	SN	SN	SN	SN	SN	SN	SN	SN	SN	SN	SN	SN	SN
London Victoria 15 ⊖	d		20 16			20 46		21 16		21 46		22 16			22 46
Clapham Junction 10	d		20 23			20 53		21 23		21 53		22 23			22 53
East Croydon	a		20 32			21 02		21 32		22 02		22 32			23 02
London Bridge 4 ⊖	d														
East Croydon	a														
East Croydon	d		20 33			21 03		21 33		22 03		22 33			23 03
Gatwick Airport 10 ✈	d		20 50			21 20		21 50		22 20		22 50			23 20
Haywards Heath 3	d		21 07			21 35		22 07		22 35		23 07	23 07		23 35
Wivelsfield 4	d		21 11					22 11				23 11	23 11		23 39
Plumpton	d					21 45				22 45					23 46
Cooksbridge	d		21 20					22 20				23 20	23 20		23 50
Lewes	a		21 25			21 53		22 25		22 53		23 25	23 25		23 55
Brighton 10	d	21 01			21 31		22 01		22 32		23 02			23 32	
London Road (Brighton)	d														
Moulsecoomb	d				21 35										
Falmer	d	21 08			21 40		22 08		22 39		23 09			23 39	
Lewes 4	a	21 15			21 47		22 15		22 46		23 16			23 46	
Lewes	d	21 15	21 26		21 47	21 54	22 15	22 26	22 48	22 54	23 16	23 26	23 26	23 48	23 56
Glynde	d	21 21					22 21				23 22				
Berwick	d				21 56						23 27				00 05
Polegate	d	21 30	21 38		22 02	22 06	22 30	22 38	23 01	23 06	23 33	23 38	23 38	00 02	00 10
Hampden Park 4	d		21 43		22 06			22 43	23 06		23 37	23 43	23 43	00 06	00 14
Eastbourne 4	a	21 38	21 48		22 11	22 14	22 38	22 48	23 11	23 14	23 42	23 48	23 48	00 11	00 19
	d	21 43		21 49	22 16	22 20	22 44			23 20					00 25
Hampden Park 4	d	21 47		21 53		22 24	22 48			23 24					
Pevensey & Westham	d	21 52		21 59		22 29	22 53			23 29					00 32
Pevensey Bay	d														
Normans Bay	d			22 04											
Cooden Beach	d			22 08		22 36				23 36					00 39
Collington	d			22 12		22 39				23 39					00 42
Bexhill 4	d	22 02		22 15	22 31	22 42	23 03			23 42					00 45
St Leonards Warrior Sq 4	d	22 08		22 21	22 37	22 49	23 09			23 49					00 51
Hastings 4	a	22 11		22 25	22 40	22 53	23 13			23 53					00 54
Ore	a	22 15		22 29											
Rye	a			22 48											
Ashford International	a			23 10											

Saturdays
26 May to 8 December

		SN	SN	SN	SN	SN	SN	SN	SN	SN	SN	SN	SN	SN	SN	SN	SN	SN	SN	SN	SN	SN	SN
London Victoria 15 ⊖	d			00 02																07 46		08 16	
Clapham Junction 10	d			00 09																07 53		08 23	
East Croydon	a			00 23																08 02		08 32	
London Bridge 4 ⊖	d																						
East Croydon	a																						
East Croydon	d			00 24																08 03		08 33	
Gatwick Airport 10 ✈	d			00 44								06 13								08 20		08 50	
Haywards Heath 3	d			01 08								06 31				07 35				08 35		09 07	
Wivelsfield 4	d																					09 11	
Plumpton	d											06 42				07 46				08 46			
Cooksbridge	d																						
Lewes	a			01 23								06 49				07 53				08 53		09 23	
Brighton 10	d					05 10					06 31		07 01		07 31		08 01		08 31		09 01		
London Road (Brighton)	d																						
Moulsecoomb	d										06 35				07 35				08 35				
Falmer	d										06 40		07 08		07 40		08 08		08 40		09 08		
Lewes 4	a					05 22					06 47		07 15		07 47		08 15		08 47		09 15		
Lewes	d			01 23		05 24					06 47	06 50	07 15		07 47	07 54	08 15		08 47	08 54	09 15	09 24	
Glynde	d												07 21				08 21				09 21		
Berwick	d		00 05									06 59			07 56				08 56				
Polegate	d	00 02	00 10	01s35		05 36					07 00	07 05	07 30		08 02	08 06	08 30		09 02	09 06	09 30	09 36	
Hampden Park 4	d	00 06	00 14	01s40		05 41					07 04	07 10			08 06	08 11			09 06			09 41	
Eastbourne 4	a	00 11	00 19	01 44		05 45					07 09	07 14	07 38		08 11	08 15	08 38		09 11	09 14	09 38	09 46	
	d		00 25		05 30		05 46	05 49	06 43	06 49	07 15	07 22	07 43	07 49	08 16	08 22	08 43	08 49	09 16	09 20	09 43		09 49
Hampden Park 4	d						05 50	05 53	06 47	06 53	07 19	07 26	07 47	07 53		08 26	08 47	08 53		09 24	09 47		09 53
Pevensey & Westham	d		00 32				05 55	05 59	06 52	06 59		07 31	07 52	07 59		08 31	08 52	08 59		09 29	09 52		09 59
Pevensey Bay	d																						
Normans Bay	d							06 04		07 04				08 04				09 04					10 04
Cooden Beach	d		00 39					06 09		07 08		07 38	07 59	08 08	08 28	08 38	08 58	09 08		09 36	09 58		10 09
Collington	d		00 42					06 12		07 12		07 41	08 02	08 12	08 32	08 41	09 02	09 12		09 39	10 02		10 12
Bexhill 4	d		00 45		05 44		06 07	06 16	07 02	07 15	07 30	07 44	08 05	08 15	08 34	08 44	09 04	09 15	09 30	09 42	10 04		10 15
St Leonards Warrior Sq 4	d		00 51		05 51		06 14	06 22	07 08	07 22	07 37	07 50	08 11	08 22	08 41	08 50	09 11	09 22	09 37	09 49	10 11		10 22
Hastings 4	a		00 54		05 54		06 17	06 26	07 11	07 25	07 40	07 53	08 14	08 25	08 44	08 53	09 14	09 25	09 40	09 53	10 14		10 25
Ore	a				05 58		06 20	06 30	07 15	07 29		07 57	08 18	08 29		08 57	09 18	09 29		09 57	10 18		10 29
Rye	a							06 47		07 45				08 46				09 45					10 46
Ashford International	a							07 09		08 09				09 09				10 09					11 09

Table T190-F

Saturdays
26 May to 8 December

London and Brighton - Eastbourne - Bexhill - Hastings

		SN	SN	SN	SN	SN	SN	SN	SN	SN	SN	SN	SN	SN	SN	SN	SN	SN	SN	SN	SN	SN	SN
London Victoria 15 ⊖	d		08 46		09 16			09 46		10 16			10 46		11 16			11 46		12 16			12 46
Clapham Junction 10	d		08 53		09 23			09 53		10 23			10 53		11 23			11 53		12 23			12 53
East Croydon	a		09 02		09 32			10 02		10 32			11 02		11 32			12 02		12 32			13 02
London Bridge 4 ⊖	d																						
East Croydon	a																						
East Croydon	d		09 03		09 33			10 03		10 33			11 03		11 33			12 03		12 33			13 03
Gatwick Airport 10 ✈	d		09 20		09 50			10 20		10 50			11 20		11 50			12 20		12 50			13 20
Haywards Heath 3	d		09 35		10 07			10 35		11 07			11 35		12 07			12 35		13 07			13 35
Wivelsfield 4	d				10 11					11 11					12 11					13 11			
Plumpton	d		09 46					10 46					11 46					12 46					13 46
Cooksbridge	d																						
Lewes	a		09 53		10 23			10 53		11 23			11 53		12 23			12 53		13 23			13 53
Brighton 10	d	09 31		10 01			10 31		11 01			11 31		12 01			12 31		13 01			13 31	
London Road (Brighton)	d																						
Moulsecoomb	d	09 35					10 35					11 35					12 35					13 35	
Falmer	d	09 40		10 08			10 40		11 08			11 40		12 08			12 40		13 08			13 40	
Lewes 4	a	09 47		10 15			10 47		11 15			11 47		12 15			12 47		13 15			13 47	
Lewes	d	09 47	09 54	10 15	10 24		10 47	10 54	11 15	11 24		11 47	11 54	12 15	12 24		12 47	12 54	13 15	13 24		13 47	13 54
Glynde	d			10 21					11 21					12 21					13 21				
Berwick	d	09 56					10 56					11 56					12 56					13 56	
Polegate	d	10 02	10 06	10 30	10 36		11 02	11 06	11 30	11 36		12 02	12 06	12 30	12 36		13 02	13 06	13 30	13 36		14 02	14 06
Hampden Park 4	d	10 06			10 41		11 06			11 41		12 06			12 41		13 06			13 41		14 06	
Eastbourne 4	a	10 11	10 14	10 38	10 46		11 11	11 14	11 38	11 46		12 11	12 14	12 38	12 46		13 11	13 14	13 38	13 46		14 11	14 14
	d	10 16	10 20	10 43		10 49	11 16	11 20	11 43		11 49	12 16	12 20	12 43		12 49	13 16	13 20	13 43		13 49	14 16	14 20
Hampden Park 4	d		10 24	10 47		10 53		11 24	11 47		11 53		12 24	12 47		12 53		13 24	13 47		13 53		14 24
Pevensey & Westham	d		10 29	10 52		10 59		11 29	11 52		11 59		12 29	12 52		12 59		13 29	13 52		13 59		14 29
Pevensey Bay	d																						
Normans Bay	d					11 04					12 04					13 04					14 04		
Cooden Beach	d		10 36			11 08		11 36			12 08		12 36			13 08		13 36			14 08		14 36
Collington	d		10 39			11 12		11 39			12 12		12 39			13 12		13 39			14 12		14 39
Bexhill 4	d	10 30	10 42	11 02		11 15	11 30	11 42	12 02		12 15	12 30	12 42	13 02		13 15	13 30	13 42	14 02		14 15	14 30	14 42
St Leonards Warrior Sq 4	d	10 37	10 49	11 08		11 22	11 37	11 49	12 08		12 22	12 37	12 49	13 08		13 22	13 37	13 49	14 08		14 22	14 37	14 49
Hastings 4	a	10 40	10 53	11 11		11 25	11 40	11 53	12 11		12 25	12 40	12 53	13 11		13 25	13 40	13 53	14 11		14 25	14 40	14 53
Ore	a		10 57	11 15		11 29		11 57	12 15		12 29		12 57	13 15		13 29		13 57	14 15		14 29		14 57
Rye	a					11 45					12 46					13 45					14 46		
Ashford International	a					12 09					13 09					14 09					15 09		

		SN	SN	SN	SN	SN	SN	SN	SN	SN	SN	SN	SN	SN	SN	SN	SN	SN	SN	SN	SN	SN
London Victoria 15 ⊖	d		13 16			13 46		14 16			14 46		15 16			15 46		16 16			16 46	
Clapham Junction 10	d		13 23			13 53		14 23			14 53		15 23			15 53		16 23			16 53	
East Croydon	a		13 32			14 02		14 32			15 02		15 32			16 02		16 32			17 02	
London Bridge 4 ⊖	d																					
East Croydon	a																					
East Croydon	d		13 33			14 03		14 33			15 03		15 33			16 03		16 33			17 03	
Gatwick Airport 10 ✈	d		13 50			14 20		14 50			15 20		15 50			16 20		16 50			17 20	
Haywards Heath 3	d		14 07			14 35		15 07			15 35		16 07			16 35		17 07			17 35	
Wivelsfield 4	d		14 11					15 11					16 11					17 11				
Plumpton	d					14 46					15 46					16 46					17 46	
Cooksbridge	d																					
Lewes	a		14 23			14 53		15 23			15 53		16 23			16 53		17 23			17 53	
Brighton 10	d	14 01			14 31		15 01			15 31		16 01			16 31		17 01			17 31		18 01
London Road (Brighton)	d																					
Moulsecoomb	d				14 35					15 35					16 35					17 35		
Falmer	d	14 08			14 40		15 08			15 40		16 08			16 40		17 08			17 40		18 08
Lewes 4	a	14 15			14 47		15 15			15 47		16 15			16 47		17 15			17 47		18 15
Lewes	d	14 15	14 24		14 47	14 54	15 15	15 24		15 47	15 54	16 15	16 24		16 47	16 54	17 15	17 24		17 47	17 54	18 15
Glynde	d	14 21					15 21					16 21					17 21					18 21
Berwick	d				14 56					15 56					16 56					17 56		
Polegate	d	14 30	14 36		15 02	15 06	15 30	15 36		16 02	16 06	16 30	16 36		17 02	17 06	17 30	17 36		18 02	18 06	18 30
Hampden Park 4	d		14 41		15 06			15 41		16 06			16 41		17 06			17 41		18 06		
Eastbourne 4	a	14 38	14 46		15 11	15 14	15 38	15 46		16 11	16 14	16 38	16 46		17 11	17 14	17 38	17 46		18 11	18 14	18 38
	d	14 43		14 49	15 16	15 20	15 43		15 49	16 16	16 20	16 43		16 49	17 16	17 20	17 43		17 49	18 16	18 20	18 43
Hampden Park 4	d	14 47		14 53		15 24	15 47		15 53		16 24	16 47		16 53		17 24	17 47		17 53		18 24	18 47
Pevensey & Westham	d	14 52		14 59		15 29	15 52		15 59		16 29	16 52		16 59		17 29	17 52		17 59		18 29	18 52
Pevensey Bay	d																					
Normans Bay	d			15 04					16 04					17 04					18 04			
Cooden Beach	d			15 08		15 36	15 58		16 08		16 36	16 58		17 08		17 36	17 58		18 08		18 36	18 58
Collington	d			15 12		15 39	16 02		16 12		16 39	17 02		17 12		17 39	18 02		18 12		18 39	19 02
Bexhill 4	d	15 02		15 15	15 30	15 42	16 04		16 15	16 30	16 42	17 04		17 15	17 30	17 42	18 04		18 15	18 30	18 42	19 04
St Leonards Warrior Sq 4	d	15 08		15 22	15 37	15 49	16 11		16 22	16 37	16 49	17 11		17 22	17 37	17 49	18 11		18 22	18 37	18 49	19 11
Hastings 4	a	15 11		15 25	15 40	15 53	16 14		16 25	16 40	16 53	17 14		17 25	17 40	17 53	18 14		18 25	18 40	18 53	19 14
Ore	a	15 15		15 29		15 57	16 18		16 29		16 57	17 18		17 29		17 57	18 18		18 29		18 57	19 18
Rye	a			15 45					16 46					17 45					18 46			
Ashford International	a			16 09					17 09					18 09					19 09			

Table T190-F

Saturdays

26 May to 8 December

London and Brighton - Eastbourne - Bexhill - Hastings

		SN ■	SN ■	SN ■	SN ■	SN ■	SN ■	SN ■	SN ■	SN ■	SN ■	SN ■
London Victoria ⊖	d	17 16			17 46		18 16			18 46		19 16
Clapham Junction	d	17 23			17 53		18 23			18 53		19 23
East Croydon	a	17 32			18 02		18 32			19 02		19 32
London Bridge ⊖	d											
East Croydon	a											
East Croydon	d	17 33			18 03		18 33			19 03		19 33
Gatwick Airport	d	17 50			18 20		18 50			19 20		19 50
Haywards Heath	d	18 07			18 35		19 07			19 35		20 07
Wivelsfield	d	18 11					19 11					20 11
Plumpton	d				18 46					19 46		
Cooksbridge	d											
Lewes	a	18 23			18 53		19 23			19 53		20 23
Brighton	d			18 31		19 01			19 31		20 01	
London Road (Brighton)	d											
Moulsecoomb	d			18 35					19 35			
Falmer	d			18 40		19 08			19 40		20 08	
Lewes	a			18 47		19 15			19 47		20 15	
Lewes	d	18 24		18 47	18 54	19 15	19 24		19 47	19 54	20 15	20 24
Glynde	d					19 21					20 21	
Berwick	d			18 56					19 56			
Polegate	d	18 36		19 02	19 06	19 30	19 36		20 02	20 06	20 30	20 36
Hampden Park	d	18 41		19 06			19 41		20 06			20 41
Eastbourne	a	18 46		19 11	19 14	19 38	19 46		20 11	20 14	20 38	20 46
	d		18 49	19 16	19 20	19 43		19 49	20 16	20 20	20 43	
Hampden Park	d		18 53		19 24	19 47		19 53		20 24	20 47	
Pevensey & Westham	d		18 59		19 29	19 52		19 59		20 29	20 52	
Pevensey Bay	d											
Normans Bay	d		19 04					20 04				
Cooden Beach	d		19 08		19 36			20 08		20 36		
Collington	d		19 12		19 39			20 12		20 39		
Bexhill	d		19 15	19 30	19 42	20 02		20 15	20 30	20 42	21 02	
St Leonards Warrior Sq	d		19 22	19 37	19 49	20 08		20 22	20 37	20 49	21 08	
Hastings	a		19 25	19 40	19 53	20 11		20 25	20 40	20 53	21 11	
Ore	a		19 29		19 57	20 15		20 29		20 57	21 15	
Rye	a		19 45					20 46				
Ashford International	a		20 09					21 09				

		SN ■	SN ■	SN ■	SN ■	SN ■	SN ■	SN ■	SN ■	SN ■	SN ■	SN ■
London Victoria ⊖	d			19 46		20 16			20 46		21 16	
Clapham Junction	d			19 53		20 23			20 53		21 23	
East Croydon	a			20 02		20 32			21 02		21 32	
London Bridge ⊖	d											
East Croydon	a											
East Croydon	d			20 03		20 33			21 03		21 33	
Gatwick Airport	d			20 20		20 50			21 20		21 50	
Haywards Heath	d			20 35		21 07			21 35		22 07	
Wivelsfield	d					21 11					22 11	
Plumpton	d			20 46					21 46			
Cooksbridge	d											
Lewes	a			20 53		21 23			21 53		22 23	
Brighton	d		20 31		21 01			21 31		22 01		22 32
London Road (Brighton)	d											
Moulsecoomb	d		20 35					21 35				
Falmer	d		20 40		21 08			21 40		22 08		22 39
Lewes	a		20 47		21 15			21 47		22 15		22 46
Lewes	d		20 47	20 54	21 15	21 24		21 47	21 54	22 15	22 24	22 47
Glynde	d				21 21					22 21		
Berwick	d		20 56					21 56				
Polegate	d		21 02	21 06	21 30	21 36		22 02	22 06	22 30	22 36	23 00
Hampden Park	d		21 06			21 41		22 06			22 41	
Eastbourne	a		21 11	21 14	21 38	21 46		22 11	22 14	22 38	22 46	23 08
	d	20 49	21 16	21 20	21 43		21 49	22 16	22 20	22 43		23 15
Hampden Park	d	20 53		21 24	21 47		21 53		22 24	22 47		
Pevensey & Westham	d	20 59		21 29	21 52		21 59		22 29	22 52		
Pevensey Bay	d											
Normans Bay	d	21 04					22 04					
Cooden Beach	d	21 08		21 36			22 08		22 36			
Collington	d	21 12		21 39			22 12		22 39			
Bexhill	d	21 15	21 30	21 42	22 02		22 15	22 30	22 42	23 02		23 29
St Leonards Warrior Sq	d	21 22	21 37	21 49	22 08		22 21	22 37	22 49	23 08		23 36
Hastings	a	21 25	21 40	21 53	22 11		22 25	22 40	22 53	23 11		23 39
Ore	a	21 29		21 57	22 15		22 29			23 15		
Rye	a	21 48					22 48					
Ashford International	a	22 10					23 10					

		SN ■	SN ■	SN ■	SN ■	SN ■
London Victoria ⊖	d	21 46		22 16		22 46
Clapham Junction	d	21 53		22 23		22 53
East Croydon	a	22 02		22 32		23 02
London Bridge ⊖	d					
East Croydon	a					
East Croydon	d	22 03		22 33		23 03
Gatwick Airport	d	22 20		22 50		23 20
Haywards Heath	d	22 35		23 07		23 35
Wivelsfield	d			23 11		
Plumpton	d	22 46				23 46
Cooksbridge	d					
Lewes	a	22 53		23 23		23 53
Brighton	d		23 02		23 32	
London Road (Brighton)	d					
Moulsecoomb	d					
Falmer	d		23 09		23 39	
Lewes	a		23 16		23 46	
Lewes	d	22 54	23 16	23 26	23 48	23 55
Glynde	d		23 22			
Berwick	d		23 27			00 04
Polegate	d	23 06	23 33	23 38	00 01	00 09
Hampden Park	d		23 37	23 43	00 06	00 14
Eastbourne	a	23 14	23 42	23 48	00 10	00 18
	d	23 20				00 23
Hampden Park	d	23 24				
Pevensey & Westham	d	23 29				00 31
Pevensey Bay	d					
Normans Bay	d					
Cooden Beach	d	23 36				00 37
Collington	d	23 39				00 41
Bexhill	d	23 42				00 43
St Leonards Warrior Sq	d	23 49				00 50
Hastings	a	23 53				00 53
Ore	a					
Rye	a					
Ashford International	a					

Table T190-F

Sundays

20 May to 2 December

London and Brighton - Eastbourne - Bexhill - Hastings

		SN ■	SN ■	SN	SN	SN	SN	SN	SN	SN	SN	SN
London Victoria ⊖	d											
Clapham Junction	d											
East Croydon	a											
London Bridge ⊖	d											
East Croydon	a											
East Croydon	d											
Gatwick Airport	d											
Haywards Heath	d			00 11								
Wivelsfield	d			00 15								
Plumpton	d											
Cooksbridge	d											
Lewes	a			00 27								
Brighton	d					07 05		07 35	08 05		08 35	09 05
London Road (Brighton)	d							07 38			08 38	
Moulsecoomb	d							07 41			08 41	
Falmer	d					07 12		07 45	08 12		08 45	09 12
Lewes	a					07 19		07 52	08 19		08 52	09 19
Lewes	d			00 27		07 21		07 55	08 21		08 55	09 21
Glynde	d					07 26			08 26			09 26
Berwick	d		00 04			07 32			08 32			09 32
Polegate	d	00 01	00 09	00s39		07 37		08 07	08 37		09 07	09 37
Hampden Park	d	00 06	00 14	00s44		07 42			08 42			09 42
Eastbourne	a	00 10	00 18	00 48		07 47			08 47			09 46
	d		00 23		07 26		07 59			08 56		
Hampden Park	d				07 30			08 27			09 27	
Pevensey & Westham	d		00 31		07 35			08 32			09 32	
Pevensey Bay	d											
Normans Bay	d							08 37			09 37	
Cooden Beach	d		00 37		07 42			08 42			09 42	
Collington	d		00 41		07 45			08 45			09 45	
Bexhill	d		00 43		07 48		08 16	08 48		09 14	09 48	
St Leonards Warrior Sq	d		00 50		07 55		08 22	08 55		09 21	09 55	
Hastings	a		00 53		07 58		08 26	08 58		09 25	09 58	
Ore	a				08 02		08 30	09 02		09 30	10 02	
Rye	a						08 47			09 47		
Ashford International	a						09 10			10 11		

		SN	SN	SN	SN	SN	SN	SN	and at the same minutes past each hour until	SN	SN	SN
London Victoria ⊖	d		08 46			09 46				17 46		
Clapham Junction	d		08 53			09 53				17 53		
East Croydon	a		09 02			10 02				18 02		
London Bridge ⊖	d											
East Croydon	a											
East Croydon	d		09 03			10 03				18 03		
Gatwick Airport	d		09 20			10 20				18 20		
Haywards Heath	d		09 31			10 31				18 31		
Wivelsfield	d		09 35			10 35				18 35		
Plumpton	d		09 42			10 42				18 42		
Cooksbridge	d											
Lewes	a		09 49			10 49				18 49		
Brighton	d			10 05			11 05				19 05	
London Road (Brighton)	d											
Moulsecoomb	d											
Falmer	d			10 12			11 12				19 12	
Lewes	a			10 19			11 19				19 19	
Lewes	d		09 50	10 21		10 50	11 21			18 50	19 21	
Glynde	d			10 26			11 26				19 26	
Berwick	d			10 32			11 32				19 32	
Polegate	d		10 02	10 37		11 02	11 37			19 02	19 37	
Hampden Park	d			10 42			11 42				19 42	
Eastbourne	a		10 10	10 47		11 10	11 47			19 10	19 47	
	d	09 56	10 17		10 56	11 17		11 56		19 17		19 56
Hampden Park	d		10 21			11 21				19 21		
Pevensey & Westham	d		10 26			11 26				19 26		
Pevensey Bay	d											
Normans Bay	d		10 31			11 31				19 31		
Cooden Beach	d		10 36			11 36				19 36		
Collington	d		10 39			11 39				19 39		
Bexhill	d	10 14	10 43		11 14	11 43		12 14		19 43		20 14
St Leonards Warrior Sq	d	10 21	10 50		11 21	11 50		12 21		19 50		20 21
Hastings	a	10 24	10 53		11 26	11 53		12 24		19 53		20 24
Ore	a	10 29	10 57		11 30	11 57		12 29		19 57		20 29
Rye	a	10 46			11 46			12 46				20 46
Ashford International	a	11 10			12 10			13 10				21 10

		SN	SN	SN	SN	SN	SN	SN	SN	SN	SN
London Victoria ⊖	d	18 46			19 46		20 46		21 46		22 46
Clapham Junction	d	18 53			19 53		20 53		21 53		22 53
East Croydon	a	19 02			20 02		21 02		22 02		23 02
London Bridge ⊖	d										
East Croydon	a										
East Croydon	d	19 03			20 03		21 03		22 03		23 03
Gatwick Airport	d	19 20			20 20		21 20		22 20		23 20
Haywards Heath	d	19 31			20 31		21 31		22 31		23 31
Wivelsfield	d	19 35			20 35		21 35		22 35		23 35
Plumpton	d	19 42			20 42		21 42		22 42		23 42
Cooksbridge	d										
Lewes	a	19 49			20 49		21 49		22 49		23 49
Brighton	d		20 05			21 05		22 10		23 20	
London Road (Brighton)	d										
Moulsecoomb	d										
Falmer	d		20 12			21 12		22 17		23 27	
Lewes	a		20 19			21 19		22 24		23 34	
Lewes	d	19 50	20 21		20 50	21 21	21 50	22 25	22 50	23 35	23 58
Glynde	d		20 26			21 26		22 30		23 40	
Berwick	d		20 32			21 32		22 36		23 46	
Polegate	d	20 02	20 37		21 02	21 37	22 02	22 41	23 02	23 51	00 10
Hampden Park	d		20 42			21 42				23 56	00 15
Eastbourne	a	20 10	20 47		21 10	21 46	22 10	22 49	23 10	00 01	00 19
	d	20 17		20 56	21 17	21 51	22 17	22 55	23 17		
Hampden Park	d	20 21			21 21	21 55	22 21	22 59	23 21		
Pevensey & Westham	d	20 26			21 26		22 26		23 26		
Pevensey Bay	d										
Normans Bay	d										
Cooden Beach	d	20 32			21 32		22 32		23 32		
Collington	d	20 36			21 36		22 36		23 36		
Bexhill	d	20 38		21 14	21 38	22 06	22 38	23 10	23 38		
St Leonards Warrior Sq	d	20 45		21 21	21 45	22 13	22 45	23 17	23 45		
Hastings	a	20 48		21 24	21 48	22 16	22 48	23 20	23 48		
Ore	a	20 52		21 28	21 52	22 20					
Rye	a			21 47							
Ashford International	a			22 10							

Table T190-R

Mondays to Fridays

21 May to 7 December

Hastings - Bexhill - Eastbourne - Brighton and London

Miles	Miles			SN MX 1	SN 1	SN 1	SN 1	SN 1	SN 1	SN 1	SN 1	SN 1	SN 1	SN 1	SN 1	SN 1	SN 1	SN 1	SN 1	SN 1	SN 1	SN 1	SN 1
—	0	Ashford International	d														06 22					07 22	
—	15¼	Rye	d														06 45					07 45	
—	25½	Ore	d											06 33			07 04	07 12	07 35			08 04	08 18
0	26½	Hastings	d						05 08		05 53		06 10	06 37		06 49	07 09	07 15	07 39		07 53	08 08	08 22
0¾	—	St Leonards Warrior Sq	d						05 11		05 56		06 13	06 40		06 52	07 12	07 19	07 42		07 56	08 11	08 25
4½	—	**Bexhill**	d						05 18		06 03		06 20	06 47		06 59	07 20	07 26	07 49		08 03	08 19	08 33
5¼	—	**Collington**	d						05 21		06 06		06 23			07 02	07 22	07 28			08 06	08 22	08 35
6¼	—	**Cooden Beach**	d						05 24		06 09		06 26			07 06	07 25	07 31			08 09	08 25	08 38
8½	—	**Normans Bay**	d													07 10					08 13		
10½	—	**Pevensey Bay**	d																		08 16		
11¼	—	**Pevensey & Westham**	d						05 31		06 16		06 32			07 15	07 32	07 38			08 19	08 32	08 45
14¼	—	Hampden Park	d						05 36		06 21		06 37			07 20	07 38				08 24	08 38	08 50
16¼	—	Eastbourne	a						05 40		06 25		06 42	07 03		07 28	07 42	07 46	08 04		08 28	08 42	08 54
—	—		d	00 06	04 49	05 20	05 34	05 39	05 54	06 20	06 32	06 36	06 49	07 09	07 20	07 37		07 52	08 09	08 24	08 37		09 00
18¼	—	Hampden Park	d	00 10	04 53	05 24	05 39	05 43	05 58	06 24	06 36	06 40	06 53		07 24	07 42		07 56		08 28	08 42		
20¼	—	**Polegate**	d	00 14	04 58	05 29	05 44	05 48	06 03	06 29	06 41	06 45	06 58	07 16	07 29	07 47		08 01	08 16	08 33	08 47		09 07
24¼	—	**Berwick**	d			05 34	05 49	05 53		06 34	06 46	06 50		07 21	07 34	07 52			08 21		08 52		
29	—	**Glynde**	d			05 40	05 54	05 59		06 40	06 51	06 56		07 27	07 40	07 57			08 27		08 57		
32	9	**Lewes**	a	00 27	05 11	05 45	06 00	06 06	06 16	06 45	06 57	07 01	07 12	07 32	07 45	08 03		08 14	08 32	08 46	09 03		09 20
—	—	Lewes	d	00 27				06 07			07 00			07 33		08 03			08 33		09 03		
36½	—	Falmer	d	00 35				06 14			07 07			07 40		08 11			08 40		09 11		
38¼	—	Moulsecoomb	d	00 39				06 18			07 12			07 44		08 15			08 44		09 15		
39¼	—	London Road (Brighton)	d	00 41				06 21															
40	—	Brighton	a	00 45				06 24			07 17			07 49		08 20			08 49		09 20		
—	—	**Lewes**	d		05 11	05 46	06 00		06 16	06 46		07 02	07 16		07 46			08 14		08 46			09 21
—	11¾	**Cooksbridge**	d				06 06		06 22			07 07	07 21					08 20		08 52			
—	14½	**Plumpton**	d		05 20	05 54	06 12			06 54		07 13			07 54			08 25					09 29
—	18¾	Wivelsfield	d			06 02	06 20		06 33	07 02		07 21	07 32		08 02			08 33		09 03			
—	21¼	Haywards Heath	d		05 39	06 17	06 25		06 49	07 07		07 26	07 37		08 07			08 38		09 15			09 44
—	—	Gatwick Airport	d		05 53	06 33	06 41		07 03	07 20		07 42	07 50		08 20			08 51		09 28			09 57
—	—	East Croydon	a		06 07	06 48	06 56		07 18	07 37		07 56	08 07		08 37			09 09		09 42			10 11
—	—	East Croydon	d				06 57					07 57											
—	—	London Bridge	a				07 13					08 13											
—	—	East Croydon	d		06 08	06 49			07 19	07 38			08 08		08 38			09 09		09 43			10 12
—	—	Clapham Junction	d		06 20	06 59			07 29	07 48			08 18		08 48			09 19		09 53			10 22
—	—	London Victoria	a		06 27	07 05			07 35	07 54			08 24		08 54			09 26		09 59			10 29

		SN 1	SN 1	SN 1	SN 1	SN 1	SN 1	SN 1	SN 1	SN 1	SN 1	SN 1	SN 1	SN 1	SN 1	SN 1	SN 1	SN 1	SN 1	SN 1	SN 1	SN 1	SN 1
Ashford International	d				08 24					09 24					10 24					11 24			
Rye	d				08 48					09 47					10 47					11 47			
Ore	d	08 36			09 05	09 18	09 33			10 03	10 18	10 33			11 03	11 18	11 33			12 03	12 18	12 33	
Hastings	d	08 40		08 53	09 09	09 22	09 37		10 00	10 07	10 22	10 37		11 00	11 07	11 22	11 37		12 00	12 07	12 22	12 37	
St Leonards Warrior Sq	d	08 43		08 56	09 12	09 25	09 40		10 04	10 10	10 25	10 40		11 04	11 10	11 25	11 40		12 04	12 10	12 25	12 40	
Bexhill	d	08 50		09 03	09 20	09 33	09 47		10 11	10 18	10 33	10 47		11 11	11 18	11 33	11 47		12 11	12 18	12 33	12 47	
Collington	d			09 06	09 22	09 35				10 20	10 35				11 20	11 35				12 20	12 35		
Cooden Beach	d			09 09	09 25	09 38				10 23	10 38				11 23	11 38				12 23	12 38		
Normans Bay	d			09 13						10 27					11 27					12 27			
Pevensey Bay	d			09 16																			
Pevensey & Westham	d			09 19	09 32	09 45			10 19	10 32	10 45			11 19	11 32	11 45			12 19	12 32	12 45		
Hampden Park	d			09 24	09 38	09 50			10 25	10 38	10 50			11 25	11 38	11 50			12 25	12 38	12 50		
Eastbourne	a	09 05		09 28	09 42	09 54	10 03		10 29	10 42	10 54	11 03		11 29	11 42	11 54	12 03		12 29	12 42	12 54	13 03	
	d	09 11	09 24	09 37		10 00	10 11	10 24	10 38		11 00	11 11	11 25	11 38		12 00	12 11	12 25	12 38		13 00	13 11	13 25
Hampden Park	d		09 28	09 42				10 28	10 42				11 29	11 42				12 29	12 42				13 29
Polegate	d	09 18	09 32	09 47		10 07	10 18	10 32	10 47		11 07	11 18	11 34	11 47		12 07	12 18	12 34	12 47		13 07	13 18	13 34
Berwick	d			09 52					10 52					11 52					12 52				
Glynde	d	09 27		09 57			10 27					11 27					12 27					13 27	
Lewes	a	09 33	09 45	10 03		10 20	10 33	10 45	11 01		11 20	11 33	11 46	12 01		12 20	12 33	12 46	13 01		13 20	13 33	13 46
Lewes	d	09 33		10 03			10 33		11 03			11 33		12 03			12 33		13 03			13 33	
Falmer	d	09 41		10 11			10 41		11 10			11 41		12 10			12 41		13 10			13 41	
Moulsecoomb	d	09 45		10 15					11 14					12 14					13 14				
London Road (Brighton)	d																						
Brighton	a	09 49		10 20			10 48		11 19			11 48		12 19			12 48		13 19			13 48	
Lewes	d		09 45			10 21		10 45			11 21		11 48			12 21		12 48			13 21		13 48
Cooksbridge	d		09 51					10 51															
Plumpton	d					10 29					11 29					12 29					13 29		
Wivelsfield	d		10 01					11 01					12 01					13 01					14 01
Haywards Heath	d		10 14			10 44		11 14			11 44		12 14			12 44		13 14			13 44		14 14
Gatwick Airport	d		10 27			10 57		11 27			11 57		12 27			12 57		13 27			13 57		14 27
East Croydon	a		10 41			11 11		11 41			12 11		12 41			13 11		13 41			14 11		14 41
East Croydon	d																						
London Bridge	a																						
East Croydon	d		10 42			11 12		11 42			12 12		12 42			13 12		13 42			14 12		14 42
Clapham Junction	d		10 52			11 22		11 52			12 23		12 52			13 22		13 52			14 22		14 52
London Victoria	a		10 59			11 29		11 59			12 29		12 59			13 29		13 59			14 29		14 59

Table T190-R

Mondays to Fridays

21 May to 7 December

Hastings - Bexhill - Eastbourne - Brighton and London

		SN 1	SN 1	SN 1	SN 1	SN 1	SN 1	SN 1	SN 1	SN 1	SN 1	SN 1	SN 1	SN 1	SN 1	SN 1	SN 1	SN 1	SN 1	SN 1	SN 1	SN 1
Ashford International	d		12 24					13 24					14 24					15 24				
Rye	d		12 47					13 47					14 47					15 47				
Ore	d		13 03	13 18	13 33			14 03	14 18	14 33			15 03	15 18	15 33			16 03	16 11	16 33		
Hastings	d	13 00	13 07	13 22	13 37		14 00	14 07	14 22	14 37		14 55	15 07	15 22	15 37		15 54	16 07	16 15	16 37		16 54
St Leonards Warrior Sq	d	13 04	13 10	13 25	13 40		14 04	14 10	14 25	14 40		14 58	15 10	15 25	15 40		15 57	16 10	16 18	16 40		16 57
Bexhill	d	13 11	13 18	13 33	13 47		14 11	14 18	14 33	14 47		15 05	15 18	15 32	15 47		16 04	16 20	16 29	16 47		17 04
Collington	d		13 20	13 35				14 20	14 35			15 08	15 20	15 35			16 07	16 23	16 32			17 07
Cooden Beach	d		13 23	13 38				14 23	14 38			15 11	15 23	15 38			16 10	16 26	16 35			17 10
Normans Bay	d		13 27					14 27				15 15		15 42			16 14					17 14
Pevensey Bay	d											15 18					16 17					
Pevensey & Westham	d	13 19	13 32	13 45			14 19	14 32	14 45			15 21	15 32	15 46			16 20	16 33	16 42			17 19
Hampden Park	d	13 25	13 38	13 50			14 25	14 38	14 50			15 26	15 38	15 51			16 25	16 40	16 47			17 24
Eastbourne	a	13 29	13 42	13 54	14 03		14 29	14 42	14 54	15 03		15 30	15 42	15 55	16 04		16 29	16 44	16 51	17 03		17 28
	d	13 38		14 00	14 11	14 24	14 38		15 00	15 11	15 24	15 38		16 01	16 11	16 24	16 38		17 00	17 11	17 24	17 38
Hampden Park	d	13 42				14 28	14 42				15 28	15 42				16 28	16 44		17 04		17 28	17 44
Polegate	d	13 47		14 07	14 18	14 32	14 47		15 07	15 18	15 32	15 47		16 08	16 18	16 32	16 49		17 08	17 18	17 32	17 49
Berwick	d	13 52					14 52					15 52					16 54					17 54
Glynde	d				14 27					15 27					16 27					17 27		
Lewes	a	14 01		14 20	14 33	14 45	15 01		15 20	15 33	15 45	16 01		16 20	16 33	16 45	17 02		17 21	17 33	17 45	18 02
Lewes	d	14 03			14 33		15 03			15 33		16 03			16 33		17 03			17 33		18 03
Falmer	d	14 10			14 41		15 10			15 41		16 10			16 41		17 10			17 41		18 10
Moulsecoomb	d	14 14					15 14					16 14					17 14					18 14
London Road (Brighton)	d																					
Brighton	a	14 19			14 48		15 19			15 48		16 19			16 48		17 19			17 48		18 19
Lewes	d			14 21		14 45			15 21		15 45			16 21		16 45			17 21		17 45	
Cooksbridge	d					14 51					15 51					16 51					17 51	
Plumpton	d			14 29					15 29					16 29					17 29			
Wivelsfield	d					15 01					16 01					17 02					18 02	
Haywards Heath	d			14 44		15 14			15 44		16 14			16 44		17 15			17 44		18 15	
Gatwick Airport	d			14 57		15 27			15 57		16 27			16 57		17 27			17 57		18 27	
East Croydon	a			15 11		15 41			16 11		16 42			17 12		17 42			18 12		18 42	
East Croydon	d																					
London Bridge	a																					
East Croydon	d			15 12		15 42			16 12		16 42			17 12		17 42			18 12		18 42	
Clapham Junction	d			15 22		15 52			16 22		16 52			17 22		17 52			18 22		18 52	
London Victoria	a			15 29		16 00			16 29		16 59			17 29		17 59			18 29		18 59	

		SN 1	SN 1	SN 1	SN 1	SN 1	SN 1	SN 1	SN 1	SN 1	SN 1	SN 1	SN 1	SN 1	SN 1	SN 1	SN 1	SN 1	SN 1	SN 1	SN 1	SN 1	SN 1
Ashford International	d	16 24					17 24					18 24					19 24					20 24	
Rye	d	16 48					17 47					18 48					19 47					20 47	
Ore	d	17 05	17 13	17 36			18 03	18 11	18 37			19 03	19 18	19 37			20 03	20 18	20 35			21 03	21 18
Hastings	d	17 09	17 17	17 40		17 55	18 07	18 15	18 41		18 54	19 07	19 22	19 41		20 00	20 07	20 22	20 40		21 01	21 07	21 22
St Leonards Warrior Sq	d	17 12	17 20	17 43		17 58	18 10	18 18	18 44		18 57	19 10	19 25	19 44		20 04	20 10	20 25	20 43		21 05	21 10	21 25
Bexhill	d	17 20	17 29	17 50		18 05	18 20	18 29	18 52		19 04	19 18	19 33	19 52		20 11	20 18	20 33	20 50		21 12	21 18	21 33
Collington	d	17 23	17 32			18 08	18 23	18 32			19 07	19 20	19 35				20 20	20 35				21 20	21 35
Cooden Beach	d	17 26	17 35			18 11	18 26	18 35			19 10	19 23	19 38				20 23	20 38				21 23	21 38
Normans Bay	d					18 15					19 14						20 27					21 27	
Pevensey Bay	d																						
Pevensey & Westham	d	17 33	17 42			18 20	18 33	18 42			19 19	19 32	19 45			20 19	20 32	20 45			21 20	21 32	21 45
Hampden Park	d	17 40	17 47			18 25	18 40	18 47			19 24	19 38	19 50			20 25	20 38	20 50			21 26	21 38	21 50
Eastbourne	a	17 44	17 51	18 05		18 29	18 44	18 51	19 09		19 28	19 42	19 54	20 09		20 29	20 42	20 54	21 05		21 30	21 42	21 54
	d		18 00	18 11	18 24	18 38		19 00	19 14	19 24	19 38		20 00	20 14	20 27	20 38		21 00	21 11	21 25	21 39		22 00
Hampden Park	d		18 04		18 28	18 44		19 04		19 28	19 42				20 31	20 42				21 29	21 43		
Polegate	d		18 08	18 18	18 32	18 49		19 08	19 21	19 33	19 47		20 07	20 21	20 35	20 47		21 07	21 18	21 34	21 48		22 07
Berwick	d					18 54					19 52					20 52					21 53		
Glynde	d			18 27					19 30					20 30					21 27				
Lewes	a		18 21	18 33	18 45	19 02		19 21	19 35	19 45	20 01		20 20	20 37	20 48	21 01		21 20	21 33	21 46	22 02		22 20
Lewes	d			18 33		19 03			19 36		20 03			20 39		21 06			21 33		22 03		
Falmer	d			18 41		19 10			19 43		20 10			20 46		21 13			21 41		22 10		
Moulsecoomb	d					19 14					20 14					21 17					22 14		
London Road (Brighton)	d																						
Brighton	a			18 48		19 19			19 51		20 19			20 54		21 24			21 48		22 19		
Lewes	d		18 21		18 45			19 21		19 46			20 21		20 48			21 21		21 48			22 21
Cooksbridge	d				18 51					19 52													
Plumpton	d		18 29					19 29					20 29					21 29					22 29
Wivelsfield	d				19 02					20 02					21 02					22 02			
Haywards Heath	d		18 44		19 15			19 44		20 15			20 44		21 14			21 44		22 15			22 44
Gatwick Airport	d		18 57		19 27			19 57		20 28			20 57		21 27			21 57		22 28			22 57
East Croydon	a		19 11		19 42			20 11		20 42			21 11		21 41			22 12		22 42			23 12
East Croydon	d																						
London Bridge	a																						
East Croydon	d		19 12		19 42			20 12		20 43			21 12		21 42			22 12		22 43			23 12
Clapham Junction	d		19 22		19 52			20 22		20 52			21 22		21 52			22 22		22 53			23 22
London Victoria	a		19 29		19 59			20 30		20 59			21 29		21 59			22 29		23 00			23 30

Table T190-R

Hastings - Bexhill - Eastbourne - Brighton and London

Mondays to Fridays
21 May to 7 December

		SN	SN	SN	SN	SN	SN	SN
Ashford International	d				21 24			
Rye	d				21 48			
Ore	d	21 35			22 05	22 15	22 27	
Hastings	d	21 39		22 00	22 09	22 19	22 30	23 29
St Leonards Warrior Sq	d	21 42		22 04	22 12	22 22	22 34	23 32
Bexhill	d	21 49		22 11	22 20	22 29	22 41	23 39
Collington	d				22 22	22 32	22 43	23 42
Cooden Beach	d				22 25	22 35	22 46	23 45
Normans Bay	d				22 29		22 50	
Pevensey Bay	d							
Pevensey & Westham	d			22 19	22 34	22 42	22 55	23 52
Hampden Park	d			22 25	22 40	22 47	23 00	23 57
Eastbourne	a	22 04		22 29	22 44	22 52	23 04	00 01
	d	22 11	22 25	22 38			23 09	00 06
Hampden Park	d		22 29	22 44			23 13	00 10
Polegate	d	22 18	22 34	22 49			23 17	00 14
Berwick	d			22 54			23 22	
Glynde	d	22 27					23 28	
Lewes	a	22 33	22 46	23 02			23 33	00 27
Lewes	d	22 33		23 03			23 34	00 27
Falmer	d	22 41		23 10			23 41	00 35
Moulsecoomb	d			23 14				00 39
London Road (Brighton)	d							00 41
Brighton	a	22 48		23 19			23 49	00 45
Lewes	d		22 48					
Cooksbridge	d							
Plumpton	d							
Wivelsfield	d		23 01					
Haywards Heath	d		23 14					
Gatwick Airport	d		23 27					
East Croydon	a		23 42					
East Croydon	d							
London Bridge	a							
East Croydon	d		23 42					
Clapham Junction	d		23 57					
London Victoria	a		00 05					

Saturdays
26 May to 8 December

		SN	SN	SN	SN	SN	SN	SN	SN	SN
Ashford International	d									
Rye	d									
Ore	d							06 20	06 33	
Hastings	d						06 00	06 24	06 37	
St Leonards Warrior Sq	d						06 04	06 27	06 40	
Bexhill	d						06 11	06 34	06 47	
Collington	d						06 13	06 37		
Cooden Beach	d						06 16	06 40		
Normans Bay	d									
Pevensey Bay	d									
Pevensey & Westham	d						06 23	06 46		
Hampden Park	d						06 28	06 51		
Eastbourne	a						06 32	06 55	07 04	
	d	00 06	05 02	05 42	05 58	06 25	06 38	07 01	07 11	07 25
Hampden Park	d	00 10	05 06	05 46	06 02	06 29	06 42			07 29
Polegate	d	00 14	05 11	05 51	06 07	06 34	06 47	07 08	07 18	07 34
Berwick	d			05 56			06 52			
Glynde	d			06 02					07 27	
Lewes	a	00 27	05 23	06 07	06 20	06 46	07 01	07 20	07 33	07 46
Lewes	d	00 27		06 08			07 03		07 33	
Falmer	d	00 35		06 15			07 10		07 41	
Moulsecoomb	d	00 39		06 19			07 14			
London Road (Brighton)	d	00 41		06 22						
Brighton	a	00 45		06 25			07 19		07 48	
Lewes	d		05 24		06 21	06 48		07 21		07 48
Cooksbridge	d									
Plumpton	d				06 29			07 29		
Wivelsfield	d					07 01				08 01
Haywards Heath	d		05 43		06 44	07 14		07 44		08 14
Gatwick Airport	d		05a57		06 57	07 27		07 57		08 27
East Croydon	a				07 11	07 41		08 11		08 41
East Croydon	d									
London Bridge	a									
East Croydon	d				07 12	07 42		08 12		08 42
Clapham Junction	d				07 22	07 52		08 22		08 52
London Victoria	a				07 29	07 59		08 29		08 59

		SN	SN	SN	SN	SN	SN	SN	SN	SN	SN	SN
Ashford International	d		06 24					07 24				
Rye	d		06 47					07 47				
Ore	d		07 07	07 20	07 33			08 03	08 20	08 33		
Hastings	d	07 00	07 11	07 24	07 37		08 00	08 07	08 24	08 37		09 00
St Leonards Warrior Sq	d	07 04	07 14	07 27	07 40		08 04	08 10	08 27	08 40		09 04
Bexhill	d	07 11	07 23	07 34	07 47		08 11	08 18	08 34	08 47		09 11
Collington	d	07 13		07 37			08 13	08 20	08 37			09 13
Cooden Beach	d	07 16		07 40			08 16	08 23	08 40			09 16
Normans Bay	d							08 27				
Pevensey Bay	d											
Pevensey & Westham	d	07 23	07 31	07 46			08 23	08 32	08 46			09 23
Hampden Park	d	07 28	07 38	07 51			08 28	08 38	08 51			09 28
Eastbourne	a	07 32	07 42	07 55	08 04		08 32	08 42	08 55	09 04		09 32
	d	07 38		08 01	08 11	08 25	08 38		09 01	09 11	09 25	09 38
Hampden Park	d	07 42				08 29	08 42				09 29	09 42
Polegate	d	07 47		08 08	08 18	08 34	08 47		09 08	09 18	09 34	09 47
Berwick	d	07 52					08 52					09 52
Glynde	d				08 27					09 27		
Lewes	a	08 01		08 20	08 33	08 46	09 01		09 20	09 33	09 46	10 01
Lewes	d	08 03			08 33		09 03			09 33		10 03
Falmer	d	08 10			08 41		09 10			09 41		10 10
Moulsecoomb	d											
London Road (Brighton)	d											
Brighton	a	08 18			08 48		09 18			09 48		10 18
Lewes	d			08 21		08 48			09 21		09 48	
Cooksbridge	d											
Plumpton	d			08 29					09 29			
Wivelsfield	d					09 01					10 01	
Haywards Heath	d			08 44		09 14			09 44		10 14	
Gatwick Airport	d			08 57		09 27			09 57		10 27	
East Croydon	a			09 11		09 41			10 11		10 41	
East Croydon	d											
London Bridge	a											
East Croydon	d			09 12		09 42			10 12		10 42	
Clapham Junction	d			09 22		09 52			10 22		10 52	
London Victoria	a			09 29		09 59			10 29		10 59	

Table T190-R

Hastings - Bexhill - Eastbourne - Brighton and London

Saturdays
26 May to 8 December

		SN	SN	SN	SN	SN		SN	SN	SN	SN	SN
Ashford International	d	08 24						12 24				
Rye	d	08 47						12 47				
Ore	d	09 03	09 18	09 33				13 03	13 18	13 33		
Hastings	d	09 07	09 22	09 37		10 00		13 07	13 22	13 37		14 00
St Leonards Warrior Sq	d	09 10	09 25	09 40		10 04		13 10	13 25	13 40		14 04
Bexhill	d	09 18	09 33	09 47		10 11		13 18	13 33	13 47		14 11
Collington	d	09 20	09 35					13 20	13 35			
Cooden Beach	d	09 23	09 38					13 23	13 38			
Normans Bay	d	09 27						13 27				
Pevensey Bay	d											
Pevensey & Westham	d	09 32	09 45			10 19		13 32	13 45			14 19
Hampden Park	d	09 38	09 50			10 25		13 38	13 50			14 25
Eastbourne	a	09 42	09 54	10 03		10 29		13 42	13 54	14 03		14 29
	d		10 00	10 11	10 25	10 38	and at the same minutes past each hour until		14 00	14 11	14 25	14 38
Hampden Park	d				10 29	10 42					14 29	14 42
Polegate	d		10 07	10 18	10 34	10 47			14 07	14 18	14 34	14 47
Berwick	d					10 52						14 52
Glynde	d			10 27						14 27		
Lewes	a		10 20	10 33	10 46	11 01			14 20	14 33	14 46	15 01
Lewes	d			10 33		11 03				14 33		15 03
Falmer	d			10 41		11 10				14 41		15 10
Moulsecoomb	d											
London Road (Brighton)	d											
Brighton	a			10 48		11 18				14 48		15 18
Lewes	d		10 21		10 48				14 21		14 48	
Cooksbridge	d											
Plumpton	d		10 29						14 29			
Wivelsfield	d				11 01						15 01	
Haywards Heath	d		10 44		11 14				14 44		15 14	
Gatwick Airport	d		10 57		11 27				14 57		15 27	
East Croydon	a		11 11		11 41				15 11		15 41	
East Croydon	d											
London Bridge	a											
East Croydon	d		11 12		11 42				15 12		15 42	
Clapham Junction	d		11 22		11 52				15 22		15 52	
London Victoria	a		11 29		11 59				15 29		15 59	

		SN	SN	SN	SN	SN	SN	SN	SN	SN	SN
Ashford International	d	13 24					14 24				
Rye	d	13 47					14 47				
Ore	d	14 03	14 18	14 33			15 03	15 18	15 33		
Hastings	d	14 07	14 22	14 37		15 00	15 07	15 22	15 37		16 00
St Leonards Warrior Sq	d	14 10	14 25	14 40		15 04	15 10	15 25	15 40		16 04
Bexhill	d	14 18	14 33	14 47		15 11	15 18	15 33	15 47		16 11
Collington	d	14 20	14 35			15 13	15 20	15 35			16 13
Cooden Beach	d	14 23	14 38			15 16	15 23	15 38			16 16
Normans Bay	d	14 27					15 27				
Pevensey Bay	d										
Pevensey & Westham	d	14 32	14 45			15 23	15 32	15 45			16 23
Hampden Park	d	14 38	14 50			15 28	15 38	15 50			16 28
Eastbourne	a	14 42	14 54	15 03		15 32	15 42	15 54	16 03		16 32
	d		15 00	15 11	15 25	15 38		16 00	16 11	16 25	16 38
Hampden Park	d				15 29	15 42				16 29	16 42
Polegate	d		15 07	15 18	15 34	15 47		16 07	16 18	16 34	16 47
Berwick	d					15 52					16 52
Glynde	d			15 27					16 27		
Lewes	a		15 20	15 33	15 46	16 01		16 20	16 33	16 46	17 01
Lewes	d			15 33		16 03			16 33		17 03
Falmer	d			15 41		16 10			16 41		17 10
Moulsecoomb	d										
London Road (Brighton)	d										
Brighton	a			15 48		16 18			16 48		17 18
Lewes	d		15 21		15 48			16 21		16 48	
Cooksbridge	d										
Plumpton	d		15 29					16 29			
Wivelsfield	d				16 01					17 01	
Haywards Heath	d		15 44		16 14			16 44		17 14	
Gatwick Airport	d		15 57		16 27			16 57		17 27	
East Croydon	a		16 11		16 41			17 11		17 41	
East Croydon	d										
London Bridge	a										
East Croydon	d		16 12		16 42			17 12		17 42	
Clapham Junction	d		16 22		16 52			17 22		17 52	
London Victoria	a		16 29		16 59			17 29		17 59	

		SN	SN	SN	SN	SN	SN	SN	SN	SN	SN	SN
Ashford International	d	15 24					16 24					17 24
Rye	d	15 47					16 47					17 47
Ore	d	16 03	16 18	16 33			17 03	17 20	17 33			18 03
Hastings	d	16 07	16 22	16 37		16 55	17 07	17 24	17 37		18 00	18 07
St Leonards Warrior Sq	d	16 10	16 25	16 40		16 59	17 10	17 27	17 40		18 04	18 10
Bexhill	d	16 18	16 33	16 47		17 11	17 18	17 34	17 47		18 11	18 18
Collington	d	16 20	16 35			17 13	17 20	17 37			18 13	18 20
Cooden Beach	d	16 23	16 38			17 16	17 23	17 40			18 16	18 23
Normans Bay	d	16 27					17 27					18 27
Pevensey Bay	d											
Pevensey & Westham	d	16 32	16 45			17 23	17 32	17 46			18 23	18 32
Hampden Park	d	16 38	16 50			17 28	17 38	17 51			18 28	18 38
Eastbourne	a	16 42	16 54	17 03		17 32	17 42	17 55	18 04		18 32	18 42
	d		17 00	17 11	17 25	17 38		18 01	18 11	18 25	18 38	
Hampden Park	d				17 29	17 42				18 29	18 42	
Polegate	d		17 07	17 18	17 34	17 47		18 08	18 18	18 34	18 47	
Berwick	d					17 52					18 52	
Glynde	d			17 27					18 27			
Lewes	a		17 20	17 33	17 46	18 01		18 20	18 33	18 46	19 01	
Lewes	d			17 33		18 03			18 33		19 03	
Falmer	d			17 41		18 10			18 41		19 10	
Moulsecoomb	d											
London Road (Brighton)	d											
Brighton	a			17 48		18 18			18 48		19 18	
Lewes	d		17 21		17 48			18 21		18 48		
Cooksbridge	d											
Plumpton	d		17 29					18 29				
Wivelsfield	d				18 01					19 01		
Haywards Heath	d		17 44		18 14			18 44		19 14		
Gatwick Airport	d		17 57		18 27			18 57		19 27		
East Croydon	a		18 11		18 41			19 11		19 41		
East Croydon	d											
London Bridge	a											
East Croydon	d		18 12		18 42			19 12		19 42		
Clapham Junction	d		18 22		18 52			19 22		19 52		
London Victoria	a		18 29		18 59			19 29		19 59		

		SN	SN	SN	SN	SN	SN	SN	SN	SN	SN	SN
Ashford International	d					18 24					19 24	
Rye	d					18 47					19 47	
Ore	d	18 20	18 33			19 03	19 18	19 33			20 03	20 18
Hastings	d	18 24	18 37		19 00	19 07	19 22	19 37		20 00	20 07	20 22
St Leonards Warrior Sq	d	18 27	18 40		19 04	19 10	19 25	19 40		20 04	20 10	20 25
Bexhill	d	18 34	18 47		19 11	19 18	19 33	19 47		20 11	20 18	20 33
Collington	d	18 37				19 20	19 35				20 20	20 35
Cooden Beach	d	18 40				19 23	19 38				20 23	20 38
Normans Bay	d					19 27					20 27	
Pevensey Bay	d											
Pevensey & Westham	d	18 46			19 19	19 32	19 45			20 19	20 32	20 45
Hampden Park	d	18 51			19 25	19 38	19 50			20 25	20 38	20 50
Eastbourne	a	18 55	19 04		19 29	19 42	19 54	20 03		20 29	20 42	20 54
	d	19 01	19 11	19 25	19 38		20 00	20 11	20 25	20 38		21 00
Hampden Park	d			19 29	19 42				20 29	20 42		
Polegate	d	19 08	19 18	19 34	19 47		20 07	20 18	20 34	20 47		21 07
Berwick	d				19 52					20 52		
Glynde	d		19 27					20 27				
Lewes	a	19 20	19 33	19 46	20 01		20 20	20 33	20 46	21 01		21 20
Lewes	d		19 33		20 03			20 33		21 03		
Falmer	d		19 41		20 10			20 41		21 10		
Moulsecoomb	d											
London Road (Brighton)	d											
Brighton	a		19 48		20 18			20 48		21 18		
Lewes	d	19 21		19 48			20 21		20 48			21 21
Cooksbridge	d											
Plumpton	d	19 29					20 29					21 29
Wivelsfield	d			20 01					21 01			
Haywards Heath	d	19 44		20 14			20 44		21 14			21 44
Gatwick Airport	d	19 57		20 27			20 57		21 27			21 57
East Croydon	a	20 11		20 41			21 11		21 41			22 12
East Croydon	d											
London Bridge	a											
East Croydon	d	20 12		20 42			21 12		21 42			22 12
Clapham Junction	d	20 22		20 52			21 22		21 52			22 22
London Victoria	a	20 29		20 59			21 29		21 59			22 29

Table T190-R

Saturdays
26 May to 8 December

Hastings - Bexhill - Eastbourne - Brighton and London

		SN	SN	SN	SN	SN	SN	SN	SN	SN	SN	SN	SN
		1	1	1	1	1	1	1	1	1	1	1	1
Ashford International	d				20 24				21 24			22 24	
Rye	d				20 47				21 47			22 47	
Ore	d	20 33			21 03	21 18	21 33		22 03	22 15	22 27	23 03	23 26
Hastings	d	20 37		21 00	21 07	21 22	21 37	22 00	22 07	22 19	22 30	23 07	23 29
St Leonards Warrior Sq	d	20 40		21 04	21 10	21 25	21 40	22 04	22 10	22 22	22 34	23 10	23 33
Bexhill	d	20 47		21 11	21 18	21 33	21 47	22 11	22 18	22 29	22 41	23 18	23 40
Collington	d				21 20	21 35			22 20	22 32	22 43	23 20	23 42
Cooden Beach	d				21 23	21 38			22 23	22 35	22 46	23 23	23 45
Normans Bay	d				21 27				22 27		22 50	23 27	
Pevensey Bay	d												
Pevensey & Westham	d			21 19	21 32	21 45		22 19	22 32	22 42	22 55	23 34	23 52
Hampden Park	d			21 25	21 38	21 50		22 25	22 38	22 47	23 00	23 40	23 57
Eastbourne	a	21 03		21 29	21 42	21 54	22 03	22 29	22 42	22 51	23 04	23 45	00 01
	d	21 11	21 25	21 38		22 00	22 11	22 38			23 09		00 06
Hampden Park	d		21 29	21 42				22 42			23 13		00 10
Polegate	d	21 18	21 34	21 47		22 07	22 18	22 47			23 18		00 14
Berwick	d			21 52				22 52			23 23		
Glynde	d	21 27					22 27				23 28		
Lewes	a	21 33	21 46	22 01		22 20	22 33	23 01			23 34		00 27
Lewes	d	21 33		22 03			22 33	23 03			23 35		00 27
Falmer	d	21 41		22 10			22 41	23 10			23 42		00 35
Moulsecoomb	d												00 39
London Road (Brighton)	d												00 41
Brighton	a	21 48		22 18			22 48	23 18			23 50		00 45
Lewes	d		21 48			22 21							
Cooksbridge	d												
Plumpton	d					22 29							
Wivelsfield	d		22 01										
Haywards Heath	d		22 14			22 44							
Gatwick Airport	d		22 27			22 57							
East Croydon	a		22 41			23 11							
East Croydon	d												
London Bridge	a												
East Croydon	d		22 42			23 12							
Clapham Junction	d		22 52			23 22							
London Victoria	a		22 59			23 29							

Sundays
20 May to 2 December

		SN	SN	SN	SN	SN	SN	SN	SN	SN
		1								
Ashford International	d								08 25	
Rye	d								08 48	
Ore	d						08 15	08 35	09 07	
Hastings	d						08 19	08 38	09 11	
St Leonards Warrior Sq	d						08 22	08 42	09 14	
Bexhill	d						08 30	08 49	09 22	
Collington	d						08 32			
Cooden Beach	d						08 35			
Normans Bay	d						08 39			
Pevensey Bay	d									
Pevensey & Westham	d						08 44			
Hampden Park	d						08 49	09 00		
Eastbourne	a						08 54	09 05	09 39	
	d	00 06	06 57	07 12	07 55	08 12	09 00	09 11		09 43
Hampden Park	d	00 10	07 01	07 16	07 59	08 16		09 15		09 47
Polegate	d	00 14	07 06	07 21	08 05	08 21	09 07	09 20		09 52
Berwick	d			07 26		08 26		09 25		09 57
Glynde	d			07 31		08 31		09 30		10 02
Lewes	a	00 27	07 18	07 37	08 18	08 37	09 20	09 36		10 08
Lewes	d	00 27		07 38		08 38		09 36		10 09
Falmer	d	00 35		07 45		08 45		09 44		10 16
Moulsecoomb	d	00 39		07 49		08 49				
London Road (Brighton)	d	00 41		07 52		08 52				
Brighton	a	00 45		07 56		08 56		09 51		10 24
Lewes	d		07 19		08 18		09 21			
Cooksbridge	d									
Plumpton	d		07 27		08 27		09 29			
Wivelsfield	d				08 35		09 36			
Haywards Heath	d		07 42		08 41		09 41			
Gatwick Airport	d		07 54		08 56		09 56			
East Croydon	a		08 22		09 10		10 10			
East Croydon	d									
London Bridge	a									
East Croydon	d		08 23		09 11		10 11			
Clapham Junction	d		08 39		09 21		10 21			
London Victoria	a		08 46		09 28		10 28			

		SN	SN	SN	SN	SN	SN	SN	SN	SN	SN	SN	SN	SN
Ashford International	d		09 25			10 25			11 25			12 25		
Rye	d		09 48			10 48			11 48			12 48		
Ore	d	09 15	10 04		10 15	11 04		11 15	12 04		12 15	13 04		13 15
Hastings	d	09 19	10 08		10 19	11 08		11 19	12 08		12 19	13 08		13 19
St Leonards Warrior Sq	d	09 22	10 11		10 22	11 11		11 22	12 11		12 22	13 11		13 22
Bexhill	d	09 30	10 19		10 30	11 19		11 30	12 19		12 30	13 19		13 30
Collington	d	09 32			10 32			11 32			12 32			13 32
Cooden Beach	d	09 35			10 35			11 35			12 35			13 35
Normans Bay	d	09 39			10 39			11 39			12 39			13 39
Pevensey Bay	d													
Pevensey & Westham	d	09 44			10 44			11 44			12 44			13 44
Hampden Park	d	09 49			10 49			11 49			12 49			13 49
Eastbourne	a	09 54	10 36		10 54	11 36		11 54	12 36		12 54	13 36		13 54
	d	10 00		10 41	11 00		11 41	12 00		12 41	13 00		13 41	14 00
Hampden Park	d			10 45			11 45			12 45			13 45	
Polegate	d	10 07		10 50	11 07		11 50	12 07		12 50	13 07		13 50	14 07
Berwick	d			10 55			11 55			12 55			13 55	
Glynde	d			11 00			12 00			13 00			14 00	
Lewes	a	10 20		11 06	11 20		12 06	12 20		13 06	13 20		14 06	14 20
Lewes	d			11 07			12 07			13 07			14 07	
Falmer	d			11 14			12 14			13 14			14 14	
Moulsecoomb	d													
London Road (Brighton)	d													
Brighton	a			11 22			12 22			13 22			14 22	
Lewes	d	10 21			11 21			12 21			13 21			14 21
Cooksbridge	d													
Plumpton	d	10 29			11 29			12 29			13 29			14 29
Wivelsfield	d	10 36			11 36			12 36			13 36			14 36
Haywards Heath	d	10 41			11 41			12 41			13 41			14 41
Gatwick Airport	d	10 56			11 56			12 56			13 56			14 56
East Croydon	a	11 10			12 10			13 10			14 10			15 10
East Croydon	d													
London Bridge	a													
East Croydon	d	11 11			12 11			13 11			14 11			15 11
Clapham Junction	d	11 21			12 21			13 23			14 21			15 21
London Victoria	a	11 28			12 28			13 30			14 28			15 28

Table T190-R

Sundays
20 May to 2 December

Hastings - Bexhill - Eastbourne - Brighton and London

		SN	SN	SN	SN	SN	SN	SN	SN	SN	
Ashford International	d	13 25			14 25			15 25			
Rye	d	13 48			14 48			15 48			
Ore	d	14 04		14 15	15 04		15 15	16 04		16 15	
Hastings	d	14 08		14 19	15 08		15 19	16 08		16 19	
St Leonards Warrior Sq	d	14 11		14 22	15 11		15 22	16 11		16 22	
Bexhill	d	14 19		14 30	15 19		15 30	16 19		16 30	
Collington	d			14 32			15 32			16 32	
Cooden Beach	d			14 35			15 35			16 35	
Normans Bay	d			14 39			15 39			16 39	
Pevensey Bay	d										
Pevensey & Westham	d			14 44			15 44			16 44	
Hampden Park	d			14 49			15 49			16 49	
Eastbourne	a	14 36		14 54	15 36		15 54	16 36		16 54	
	d		14 41	15 00		15 41	16 00		16 41	17 00	
Hampden Park	d		14 45			15 45			16 45		and at
Polegate	d		14 50	15 07		15 50	16 07		16 50	17 07	the same
Berwick	d		14 55			15 55			16 55		minutes
Glynde	d		15 00			16 00			17 00		past
Lewes	a		15 06	15 20		16 06	16 20		17 06	17 20	each
Lewes	d		15 07			16 07			17 07		hour until
Falmer	d		15 14			16 14			17 14		
Moulsecoomb	d										
London Road (Brighton)	d										
Brighton	a		15 22			16 22			17 22		
Lewes	d			15 21			16 21			17 21	
Cooksbridge	d										
Plumpton	d			15 29			16 29			17 29	
Wivelsfield	d			15 36			16 36			17 36	
Haywards Heath	d			15 41			16 41			17 41	
Gatwick Airport	d			15 56			16 56			17 56	
East Croydon	a			16 10			17 10			18 10	
East Croydon	d										
London Bridge	a										
East Croydon	d			16 11			17 11			18 11	
Clapham Junction	d			16 23			17 23			18 21	
London Victoria	a			16 30			17 30			18 28	

		SN	SN	SN	SN	SN	SN	SN	SN	SN	SN	SN
Ashford International	d	18 25			19 25			20 25			21 25	
Rye	d	18 48			19 48			20 48			21 48	
Ore	d	19 04		19 15	20 04		20 18	21 04		21 14	22 04	
Hastings	d	19 08		19 19	20 08		20 22	21 08		21 17	22 08	
St Leonards Warrior Sq	d	19 11		19 22	20 11		20 25	21 11		21 21	22 11	
Bexhill	d	19 19		19 30	20 19		20 33	21 19		21 28	22 19	
Collington	d			19 32			20 35			21 30		
Cooden Beach	d			19 35			20 38			21 33		
Normans Bay	d			19 39								
Pevensey Bay	d											
Pevensey & Westham	d			19 44			20 45			21 40		
Hampden Park	d			19 49			20 49					
Eastbourne	a	19 36		19 54	20 36		20 54	21 36			22 36	
	d		19 41	20 00		20 41	21 00		21 41			22 41
Hampden Park	d		19 45			20 45			21 45	21 44		22 45
Polegate	d		19 50	20 07		20 50	21 07		21 50	22 06		22 50
Berwick	d		19 55			20 55			21 55			22 55
Glynde	d		20 00			21 00			22 00			23 00
Lewes	a		20 06	20 20		21 06	21 20		22 06	22 19		23 06
Lewes	d		20 07			21 07			22 07	22 23		23 07
Falmer	d		20 14			21 14			22 14	22 30		23 14
Moulsecoomb	d									22 34		
London Road (Brighton)	d									22 37		
Brighton	a		20 22			21 22			22 22	22 41		23 23
Lewes	d			20 21			21 21					
Cooksbridge	d											
Plumpton	d			20 29			21 29					
Wivelsfield	d			20 36			21 36					
Haywards Heath	d			20 41			21 41					
Gatwick Airport	d			20 56			21 56					
East Croydon	a			21 10			22 10					
East Croydon	d											
London Bridge	a											
East Croydon	d			21 11			22 11					
Clapham Junction	d			21 21			22 21					
London Victoria	a			21 28			22 28					

		SN	SN	SN
Ashford International	d			
Rye	d			
Ore	d	22 14	22 35	
Hastings	d	22 17	22 38	23 25
St Leonards Warrior Sq	d	22 21	22 42	23 28
Bexhill	d	22 30	22 49	23 35
Collington	d	22 32		23 38
Cooden Beach	d	22 35		23 41
Normans Bay	d			
Pevensey Bay	d			
Pevensey & Westham	d	22 43		23 48
Hampden Park	d	22 49	23 00	23 52
Eastbourne	a	22 54	23 05	23 57
	d	22 59		
Hampden Park	d			
Polegate	d	23 07		
Berwick	d			
Glynde	d			
Lewes	a	23 19		
Lewes	d	23 23		
Falmer	d	23 31		
Moulsecoomb	d	23 35		
London Road (Brighton)	d	23 37		
Brighton	a	23 42		
Lewes	d			
Cooksbridge	d			
Plumpton	d			
Wivelsfield	d			
Haywards Heath	d			
Gatwick Airport	d			
East Croydon	a			
East Croydon	d			
London Bridge	a			
East Croydon	d			
Clapham Junction	d			
London Victoria	a			

Table T191-F

Mondays to Fridays
21 May to 7 December

Eastbourne - Hampden Park

Miles			SN MX ■	SN ■	SN ■	SN ■	SN ■	SN ■	SN ■	SN ■	SN ■		SN ■	SN ■	SN ■	SN ■	SN ■	SN ■	SN ■	SN ■	SN ■		SN ■	SN ■	SN ■
0	Eastbourne	d	00 06	04 49	05 10	05 20	05 34	05 39	05 42	05 47	05 54	....	06 15	06 20	06 32	06 36	06 41	06 46	06 49	07 15	07 20	....	07 25	07 37	07 43
2	Hampden Park	a	00 10	04 53	05 14	05 24	05 38	05 43	05 46	05 51	05 58		06 19	06 24	06 36	06 40	06 45	06 50	06 53	07 19	07 24		07 29	07 41	07 47

		SN ■	SN ■	SN ■	SN ■	SN ■	SN ■		SN ■	SN ■	SN ■	SN ■	SN ■	SN ■	SN ■	SN ■	SN ■		SN ■	SN ■	SN ■	SN ■	SN ■	SN ■	SN ■
Eastbourne	d	07 49	07 52	08 21	08 24	08 37	08 43	....	08 49	09 20	09 24	09 37	09 43	09 49	10 20	10 24	10 38	....	10 44	10 49	11 20	11 25	11 38	11 43	11 49
Hampden Park	a	07 53	07 56	08 25	08 28	08 41	08 47		08 53	09 24	09 28	09 41	09 47	09 53	10 24	10 28	10 42		10 48	10 53	11 24	11 29	11 42	11 47	11 53

		SN ■	SN ■		SN ■	SN ■	SN ■	SN ■	SN ■	SN ■	SN ■	SN ■	SN ■		SN ■	SN ■	SN ■	SN ■	SN ■	SN ■	SN ■	SN ■	SN ■		SN ■
Eastbourne	d	12 20	12 25	....	12 38	12 43	12 49	13 20	13 25	13 38	13 43	13 49	14 20	....	14 24	14 38	14 43	14 49	15 20	15 24	15 38	15 43	15 49	....	16 20
Hampden Park	a	12 24	12 29		12 42	12 47	12 53	13 24	13 29	13 42	13 47	13 53	14 24		14 28	14 42	14 47	14 53	15 24	15 28	15 42	15 47	15 53		16 24

		SN ■	SN ■	SN ■	SN ■	SN ■	SN ■	SN ■	SN ■		SN ■	SN ■	SN ■	SN ■	SN ■	SN ■	SN ■	SN ■	SN ■		SN ■	SN ■	SN ■	SN ■	SN ■
Eastbourne	d	16 24	16 38	16 52	17 00	17 20	17 24	17 38	17 52	....	18 00	18 21	18 24	18 38	18 52	19 00	19 24	19 27	19 38	....	19 43	19 49	20 24	20 27	20 38
Hampden Park	a	16 28	16 42	16 56	17 04	17 24	17 28	17 42	17 56		18 04	18 25	18 28	18 42	18 56	19 04	19 28	19 31	19 42		19 47	19 53	20 28	20 31	20 42

		SN ■	SN ■	SN ■	SN ■		SN ■	SN ■	SN ■	SN ■	SN ■	SN ■	SN ■	SN ■	SN ■
Eastbourne	d	20 43	20 49	21 20	21 25	....	21 39	21 43	21 49	22 20	22 25	22 38	22 44	23 09	23 20
Hampden Park	a	20 47	20 53	21 24	21 29		21 43	21 47	21 53	22 24	22 29	22 42	22 48	23 13	23 24

Saturdays
26 May to 8 December

		SN ■	SN ■	SN ■	SN ■	SN ■	SN ■	SN ■	SN ■	SN ■		SN ■	SN ■	SN ■	SN ■	SN ■	SN ■	SN ■	SN ■	SN ■	SN ■	SN ■	SN ■
Eastbourne	d	00 06	05 02	05 42	05 46	05 49	05 58	06 25	06 38	06 43	....	06 49	07 15	07 22	07 25	07 38	07 43	07 49	08 22	08 25	08 38	08 43	08 49
Hampden Park	a	00 10	05 06	05 46	05 50	05 53	06 02	06 29	06 42	06 47		06 53	07 19	07 26	07 29	07 42	07 47	07 53	08 26	08 29	08 42	08 47	08 53

		SN ■		SN ■	SN ■	SN ■	SN ■	SN ■		SN ■	SN ■	SN ■	SN ■
Eastbourne	d	09 20	and at the same minutes past each hour until	21 25	21 38	21 43	21 49	22 20	....	22 38	22 43	23 09	23 20
Hampden Park	a	09 24		21 29	21 42	21 47	21 53	22 24		22 42	22 47	23 13	23 24

Sundays
20 May to 2 December

		SN ■	SN	SN	SN	SN	SN	SN	SN	SN	SN		SN	SN		SN	SN	SN	SN	SN
Eastbourne	d	00 06	06 57	07 12	07 26	07 55	08 12	09 11	09 43	10 17	10 41	and at the same minutes past each hour until	21 17	21 41	....	21 51	22 17	22 41	22 55	23 17
Hampden Park	a	00 10	07 01	07 16	07 30	07 59	08 16	09 15	09 47	10 21	10 45		21 21	21 45		21 55	22 21	22 45	22 59	23 21

Table T191-R

Mondays to Fridays
21 May to 7 December

Hampden Park - Eastbourne

Miles			SN MX ■	SN MX ■	SN MO	SN ■	SN ■	SN ■		SN ■	SN ■	SN ■	SN ■	SN ■	SN ■	SN ■	SN ■	SN ■		SN ■	SN ■	SN ■	SN ■	SN ■	SN ■
0	Hampden Park	d	00 06	00 14	00 15	05 31	05 36	06 05	....	06 21	06 37	07 05	07 15	07 20	07 38	08 06	08 24	08 38	....	08 43	08 50	09 06	09 24	09 38	09 42
2	Eastbourne	a	00 11	00 19	00 19	05 37	05 40	06 09		06 25	06 42	07 09	07 19	07 28	07 42	08 11	08 28	08 42		08 48	08 54	09 11	09 28	09 42	09 47

		SN ■	SN ■	SN ■		SN ■	SN ■	SN ■	SN ■	SN ■	SN ■	SN ■		SN ■	SN ■	SN ■	SN ■	SN ■		SN ■	SN ■	SN ■	SN ■	SN ■
Hampden Park	d	09 50	10 06	10 25	....	10 38	10 43	10 50	11 06	11 25	11 38	11 41	and at the same minutes past each hour until	13 50	14 06	14 25	14 38	14 41	....	14 50	15 06	15 26	15 38	15 41
Eastbourne	a	09 54	10 11	10 29		10 42	10 48	10 54	11 11	11 29	11 42	11 46		13 54	14 11	14 29	14 42	14 46		14 54	15 11	15 30	15 42	15 46

		SN ■	SN ■	SN ■	SN ■		SN ■	SN ■	SN ■	SN ■	SN ■	SN ■	SN ■	SN ■	SN ■		SN ■	SN ■	SN ■	SN ■	SN ■	SN ■	SN ■	SN ■	SN ■
Hampden Park	d	15 51	16 06	16 25	16 37	....	16 40	16 43	16 47	17 07	17 24	17 37	17 40	17 43	17 47	....	18 07	18 11	18 25	18 37	18 40	18 45	18 47	19 01	19 08
Eastbourne	a	15 55	16 11	16 29	16 41		16 44	16 48	16 51	17 11	17 28	17 41	17 44	17 48	17 51		18 11	18 15	18 29	18 41	18 44	18 49	18 51	19 06	19 12

			SN ■	SN ■	SN ■	SN ■	SN ■	SN ■	SN ■	SN ■	SN ■		SN ■	SN ■	SN ■	SN ■	SN ■	SN ■	SN ■	SN ■	SN ■		SN ■	SN ■	SN ■
Hampden Park	d	....	19 13	19 24	19 38	19 44	19 50	20 01	20 07	20 11	20 25	....	20 38	20 43	20 50	21 07	21 26	21 38	21 43	21 50	22 06	....	22 25	22 40	22 43
Eastbourne	a		19 18	19 28	19 42	19 48	19 54	20 06	20 12	20 18	20 29		20 42	20 48	20 54	21 11	21 30	21 42	21 48	21 54	22 11		22 29	22 44	22 48

		SN ■	SN ■	SN ■	SN ■	SN ■	SN ■
Hampden Park	d	22 47	23 00	23 06	23 37	23 43	23 57
Eastbourne	a	22 52	23 04	23 11	23 42	23 48	00 01

Saturdays
26 May to 8 December

		SN ■	SN ■	SN ■	SN ■	SN ■	SN ■	SN ■	SN ■	SN ■		SN ■	SN ■	SN ■	SN ■	SN ■	SN ■	SN ■	SN ■	SN ■	SN ■	SN ■	SN ■
Hampden Park	d	00 06	00 14	05 41	06 28	06 51	07 04	07 10	07 28	07 38	....	07 51	08 06	08 11	08 28	08 38	08 51	09 06	09 28	09 38	09 41	09 50	10 06
Eastbourne	a	00 11	00 19	05 45	06 32	06 55	07 09	07 14	07 32	07 42		07 55	08 11	08 15	08 32	08 42	08 55	09 11	09 32	09 42	09 46	09 54	10 11

		SN ■		SN ■	SN ■	SN ■	SN ■	SN ■		SN ■	SN ■	SN ■	SN ■	SN ■	SN ■	SN ■	SN ■	SN ■		SN ■	SN ■	SN ■	SN ■	SN ■
Hampden Park	d	10 25	and at the same minutes past each hour until	13 38	13 41	13 50	14 06	14 25	....	14 38	14 41	14 50	15 06	15 28	15 38	15 41	15 50	16 06	....	16 28	16 38	16 41	16 50	17 06
Eastbourne	a	10 29		13 42	13 46	13 54	14 11	14 29		14 42	14 46	14 54	15 11	15 32	15 42	15 46	15 54	16 11		16 32	16 42	16 46	16 54	17 11

		SN ■	SN ■	SN ■	SN ■		SN ■	SN ■	SN ■	SN ■	SN ■	SN ■	SN ■	SN ■	SN ■		SN ■	SN ■	SN ■	SN ■	SN ■	SN ■	SN ■	SN ■	SN ■
Hampden Park	d	17 28	17 38	17 41	17 51	....	18 06	18 28	18 38	18 41	18 51	19 06	19 25	19 38	19 41	....	19 50	20 06	20 25	20 38	20 41	20 50	21 06	21 25	21 38
Eastbourne	a	17 32	17 42	17 46	17 55		18 11	18 32	18 42	18 46	18 55	19 11	19 29	19 42	19 46		19 54	20 11	20 29	20 42	20 46	20 54	21 11	21 29	21 42

			SN ■	SN ■	SN ■	SN ■	SN ■	SN ■	SN ■	SN ■	SN ■		SN ■	SN ■	SN ■
Hampden Park	d	....	21 41	21 50	22 06	22 25	22 38	22 41	22 47	23 00	23 37	....	23 40	23 43	23 57
Eastbourne	a		21 46	21 54	22 11	22 29	22 42	22 46	22 51	23 04	23 42		23 45	23 48	00 01

Sundays
20 May to 2 December

		SN ■	SN ■	SN	SN	SN	SN	SN	SN	SN		SN	SN		SN	SN	SN	SN	SN	SN
Hampden Park	d	00 06	00 14	07 42	08 42	08 49	09 00	09 42	09 49	10 42	and at the same minutes past each hour until	19 49	20 42	....	20 49	21 42	22 49	23 00	23 52	23 56
Eastbourne	a	00 10	00 18	07 47	08 47	08 54	09 05	09 46	09 54	10 47		19 54	20 47		20 54	21 46	22 54	23 05	23 57	00 01

Table T192-F

Mondays to Fridays

21 May to 7 December

Eastbourne - Hastings - Rye - Ashford with Brighton and London connect

		SN	SN	SN	SN	SN	SN	SN	SN	SN		SN	SN	SN	SN	SN	SN	SN	SN	SN		SN	SN	SN	SN
		■	■	■	■	■	■	■	■	■		■	■	■	■	■	■	■	■	■		■	■	■	■
Brighton	d																								
Lewes	d																								
Eastbourne	a																								
Eastbourne	d	04 58		05 47		06 46		07 49	08 49	09 49		10 49	11 49	12 49	13 49	14 49	15 49		16 52			17 52		18 52	19 49
Hampden Park	d			05 51		06 50		07 53	08 53	09 53		10 53	11 53	12 53	13 53	14 53	15 53		16 56			17 56		18 56	19 53
Pevensey & Westham	d			05 57		06 56		07 59	08 59	09 59		10 59	11 59	12 59	13 59	14 59	15 59		17 02			18 02		19 02	19 59
Pevensey Bay	d							08 01	09 01								16 01					18 04			
Normans Bay	d			06 02		07 01		08 05	09 05	10 04		11 04	12 04	13 04	14 04	15 04	16 05								20 04
Cooden Beach	d			06 06		07 05		08 10	09 10	10 08		11 08	12 08	13 08	14 08	15 08	16 10		17 09			18 10		19 09	20 08
Collington	d			06 10		07 09		08 13	09 13	10 12		11 12	12 12	13 12	14 12	15 12	16 13		17 13			18 13		19 13	20 12
Bexhill	d	05 14		06 13		07 13		08 16	09 16	10 15		11 15	12 15	13 15	14 15	15 15	16 16		17 16			18 17		19 19	20 15
St Leonards Warrior Sq	d	05 21		06 20		07 19		08 23	09 23	10 22		11 22	12 22	13 22	14 22	15 22	16 23		17 23			18 24		19 25	20 22
Hastings	d	05 25	05 45	06 24		07 23		08 27	09 28	10 26		11 26	12 26	13 26	14 26	15 26	16 27	17 05	17 27			18 28		19 29	20 26
Ore	d	05 29	05 49	06 28		07 27		08 31	09 32	10 30		11 30	12 30	13 30	14 30	15 30	16 31	17 09	17 31			18 31		19 33	20 30
Three Oaks	d		05 55	06 34		07 33		08 37		10 36			12 36		14 36		16 37	17 15				18 37			20 36
Doleham	d		05 58															17 18							
Winchelsea	d		06 04			07 41			09 43			11 42		13 42		15 42		17 24	17 42					19 44	
Rye	a	05 44	06 07	06 44		07 44		08 47	09 47	10 46		11 45	12 46	13 45	14 46	15 45	16 47	17 27	17 46			18 48		19 48	20 46
	d	05 45	06 08	06 46	07 16	07 47	08 16	08 48	09 48	10 47		11 47	12 47	13 47	14 47	15 47	16 48	17 28	17 47	18 26		18 48	19 26	19 48	20 47
Appledore (Kent)	d	05 54	06 17	06 55	07 25	07 56	08 25	08 57	09 57	10 56		11 56	12 56	13 56	14 56	15 56	16 57	17 37	17 56	18 35		18 57	19 35	19 57	20 56
Ham Street	a	05 59	06 22	07 00	07 30	08 01	08 30	09 02	10 02	11 01		12 01	13 01	14 01	15 01	16 01	17 02	17 42	18 01	18 40		19 02	19 40	20 02	21 01
Ashford International	a	06 07	06 30	07 08	07 38	08 09	08 38	09 10	10 10	11 09		12 09	13 09	14 09	15 09	16 09	17 10	17 50	18 09	18 48		19 10	19 48	20 10	21 09
Ashford International	d	*06 36*	*06 36*	*07 16*	*07 44*	*08 16*	*08 43*	*09 16*	*10 16*	*11 16*		*12 16*	*13 16*	*14 16*	*15 16*	*16 16*	*17 16*	*18 16*	*18 43*	*19 16*		*19 16*	*20 16*	*20 16*	*21 16*
Ebbsfleet International	a	*06 55*	*06 55*	*07 35*		*08 35*	*09 02*	*09 35*	*10 35*	*11 35*		*12 35*	*13 35*	*14 35*	*15 35*	*16 35*	*17 35*	*18 35*	*19 02*	*19 35*		*19 35*	*20 35*	*20 35*	*21 35*
Stratford International	a	*07 07*	*07 07*	*07 47*	*08 12*	*08 47*	*09 14*	*09 47*	*10 47*	*11 47*		*12 47*	*13 47*	*14 47*	*15 47*	*16 47*	*17 47*	*18 47*	*19 14*	*19 47*		*19 47*	*20 47*	*20 47*	*21 47*
St Pancras International	a	*07 14*	*07 14*	*07 54*	*08 20*	*08 54*	*09 21*	*09 54*	*10 55*	*11 54*		*12 55*	*13 54*	*14 54*	*15 54*	*16 54*	*17 54*	*18 54*	*19 21*	*19 54*		*19 54*	*20 54*	*20 54*	*21 54*

		SN	SN	SE	SE	SE		SE	SE	SE	SE	SE	SE	SE	SE	SE		SE	SE	SE	SE	SE	SE	SE	SE
		■	■	◇	◇	◇		◇	◇	◇	◇	◇	◇	◇	◇	◇		◇	◇	◇	◇	◇	◇	◇	◇
Brighton	d																								
Lewes	d																								
Eastbourne	a																								
Eastbourne	d	20 49	21 49																						
Hampden Park	d	20 53	21 53																						
Pevensey & Westham	d	20 59	21 59																						
Pevensey Bay	d																								
Normans Bay	d	21 04	22 04																						
Cooden Beach	d	21 08	22 08																						
Collington	d	21 12	22 12																						
Bexhill	d	21 15	22 15																						
St Leonards Warrior Sq	d	21 21	22 21																						
Hastings	d	21 26	22 26																						
Ore	d	21 30	22 29																						
Three Oaks	d		22 35																						
Doleham	d		22 38																						
Winchelsea	d	21 42	22 44																						
Rye	a	21 45	22 48																						
	d	21 47	22 48																						
Appledore (Kent)	d	21 56	22 57																						
Ham Street	a	22 01	23 02																						
Ashford International	a	22 09	23 10																						
Ashford International	d	*22 16*	*23 16*																						
Ebbsfleet International	a	*22 35*	*23 35*																						
Stratford International	a	*22 47*	*23 47*																						
St Pancras International	a	*22 54*	*23 54*																						

Table T192-F

Saturdays

26 May to 8 December

Eastbourne - Hastings - Rye - Ashford with Brighton and London connect

		SN	SN	SN	SN	SN	SN	SN	SN	SN		SN	SN	SN	SN	SN	SN	SN	SN	SE		SE	SE	SE	SE
		■	■	■	■	■	■	■	■	■		■	■	■	■	■	■	■	■	◇		◇	◇	◇	◇
Brighton	d																								
Lewes	d																								
Eastbourne	a																								
Eastbourne	d		05 49	06 49	07 49	08 49	09 49	10 49	11 49	12 49		13 49	14 49	15 49	16 49	17 49	18 49	19 49	20 49						
Hampden Park	d		05 53	06 53	07 53	08 53	09 53	10 53	11 53	12 53		13 53	14 53	15 53	16 53	17 53	18 53	19 53	20 53						
Pevensey & Westham	d		05 59	06 59	07 59	08 59	09 59	10 59	11 59	12 59		13 59	14 59	15 59	16 59	17 59	18 59	19 59	20 59						
Pevensey Bay	d																								
Normans Bay	d		06 04	07 04	08 04	09 04	10 04	11 04	12 04	13 04		14 04	15 04	16 04	17 04	18 04	19 04	20 04	21 04						
Cooden Beach	d		06 09	07 08	08 08	09 08	10 09	11 08	12 08	13 08		14 08	15 08	16 08	17 08	18 08	19 08	20 08	21 08						
Collington	d		06 12	07 12	08 12	09 12	10 12	11 12	12 12	13 12		14 12	15 12	16 12	17 12	18 12	19 12	20 12	21 12						
Bexhill	d		06 16	07 15	08 15	09 15	10 15	11 15	12 15	13 15		14 15	15 15	16 15	17 15	18 15	19 15	20 15	21 15						
St Leonards Warrior Sq	d		06 22	07 22	08 22	09 22	10 22	11 22	12 22	13 22		14 22	15 22	16 22	17 22	18 22	19 22	20 22	21 22						
Hastings	d	05 20	06 26	07 26	08 26	09 26	10 26	11 26	12 26	13 26		14 26	15 26	16 26	17 26	18 26	19 26	20 26	21 26						
Ore	d	05 24	06 30	07 30	08 30	09 30	10 30	11 30	12 30	13 30		14 30	15 30	16 30	17 30	18 30	19 30	20 30	21 29						
Three Oaks	d	05 30	06 36		08 36		10 36		12 36			14 36		16 36		18 36		20 36	21 35						
Doleham	d	05 33																	21 38						
Winchelsea	d	05 39		07 42		09 42		11 42		13 42			15 42		17 42		19 42		21 44						
Rye	a	05 42	06 47	07 45	08 46	09 45	10 46	11 45	12 46	13 45		14 46	15 45	16 46	17 45	18 46	19 45	20 46	21 48						
	d	05 44	06 47	07 47	08 47	09 47	10 47	11 47	12 47	13 47		14 47	15 47	16 47	17 47	18 47	19 47	20 47	21 48						
Appledore (Kent)	d	05 53	06 56	07 56	08 56	09 56	10 56	11 56	12 56	13 56		14 56	15 56	16 56	17 56	18 56	19 56	20 56	21 57						
Ham Street	a	05 58	07 01	08 01	09 01	10 01	11 01	12 01	13 01	14 01		15 01	16 01	17 01	18 01	19 01	20 01	21 01	22 02						
Ashford International	a	06 06	07 09	08 09	09 09	10 09	11 09	12 09	13 09	14 09		15 09	16 09	17 09	18 09	19 09	20 09	21 09	22 10						
Ashford International	d	*06 16*	*07 16*	*08 16*	*09 16*	*10 16*	*11 16*	*12 16*	*13 16*	*14 16*		*15 16*	*16 16*	*17 16*	*18 16*	*19 16*	*20 16*	*21 16*	*22 16*						
Ebbsfleet International	a	*06 35*	*07 35*	*08 35*	*09 35*	*10 35*	*11 35*	*12 35*	*13 35*	*14 35*		*15 35*	*16 35*	*17 35*	*18 35*	*19 35*	*20 35*	*21 35*	*22 35*						
Stratford International	a	*06 47*	*07 47*	*08 47*	*09 47*	*10 47*	*11 47*	*12 47*	*13 47*	*14 47*		*15 47*	*16 47*	*17 47*	*18 47*	*19 47*	*20 47*	*21 47*	*22 47*						
St Pancras International	a	*06 54*	*07 54*	*08 55*	*09 54*	*10 55*	*11 54*	*12 55*	*13 54*	*14 54*		*15 54*	*16 54*	*17 54*	*18 54*	*19 54*	*20 54*	*21 54*	*22 54*						

Sundays

20 May to 2 December

Eastbourne - Hastings - Rye - Ashford with Brighton and London connect

		SN	SN	SN	SN	SN	SN	SN	SN	SN		SN	SN	SN	SN	SN	SN	SE	SE	SE		SE	SE	SE	SE
																		◇	◇	◇		◇	◇	◇	◇
Brighton	d																								
Lewes	d																								
Eastbourne	a																								
Eastbourne	d		07 59	08 56	09 56	10 56	11 56	12 56	13 56	14 56		15 56	16 56	17 56	18 56	19 56	20 56								
Hampden Park	d																								
Pevensey & Westham	d																								
Pevensey Bay	d																								
Normans Bay	d																								
Cooden Beach	d																								
Collington	d																								
Bexhill	d		08 16	09 14	10 14	11 14	12 14	13 14	14 14	15 14		16 14	17 14	18 14	19 14	20 14	21 14								
St Leonards Warrior Sq	d		08 22	09 21	10 21	11 21	12 21	13 21	14 21	15 21		16 21	17 21	18 21	19 21	20 21	21 21								
Hastings	d	07 24	08 26	09 26	10 26	11 27	12 26	13 26	14 26	15 26		16 26	17 26	18 26	19 26	20 26	21 25								
Ore	d	07 28	08 30	09 30	10 30	11 31	12 30	13 30	14 30	15 30		16 30	17 30	18 30	19 30	20 30	21 29								
Three Oaks	d	07 34	08 36		10 36		12 36		14 36			16 36		18 36		20 36	21 35								
Doleham	d	07 37															21 38								
Winchelsea	d	07 43		09 42		11 43		13 42		15 42			17 42		19 42		21 44								
Rye	a	07 46	08 47	09 46	10 46	11 46	12 46	13 46	14 46	15 46		16 46	17 46	18 46	19 46	20 46	21 47								
	d	07 48	08 48	09 48	10 48	11 48	12 48	13 48	14 48	15 48		16 48	17 48	18 48	19 48	20 48	21 48								
Appledore (Kent)	d	07 57	08 57	09 57	10 57	11 57	12 57	13 57	14 57	15 57		16 57	17 57	18 57	19 57	20 57	21 57								
Ham Street	a	08 02	09 02	10 02	11 02	12 02	13 02	14 02	15 02	16 02		17 02	18 02	19 02	20 02	21 02	22 02								
Ashford International	a	08 10	09 10	10 10	11 10	12 10	13 10	14 10	15 10	16 10		17 10	18 10	19 10	20 10	21 10	22 10								
Ashford International	d	*08 16*	*09 16*	*10 16*	*11 16*	*12 16*	*13 16*	*14 16*	*15 16*	*16 16*		*17 16*	*18 16*	*19 16*	*20 16*	*21 16*	*22 16*								
Ebbsfleet International	a	*08 35*	*09 35*	*10 35*	*11 35*	*12 35*	*13 35*	*14 35*	*15 35*	*16 35*		*17 35*	*18 35*	*19 35*	*20 35*	*21 35*	*22 35*								
Stratford International	a	*08 47*	*09 47*	*10 47*	*11 47*	*12 47*	*13 47*	*14 47*	*15 47*	*16 47*		*17 47*	*18 47*	*19 47*	*20 47*	*21 47*	*22 47*								
St Pancras International	a	*08 54*	*09 54*	*10 54*	*11 54*	*12 54*	*13 54*	*14 54*	*15 54*	*16 54*		*17 55*	*18 54*	*19 54*	*20 54*	*21 54*	*22 54*								

Table T192-R

Mondays to Fridays
21 May to 7 December

London connect and Brighton with Ashford - Rye - Hastings - Eastbourne

		SN		SN	SN	SN	SN	SN	SN	SN	SN	SN	SN	SN	SN	SN	SN	SN
St Pancras International	d				06 40	07 04	07 25	07 37	08 37	09 37	10 37	11 37	12 37	13 37	14 37	15 37	16 37	17 07
Stratford International	d				06 47	07 11	07 32	07 44	08 44	09 44	10 44	11 44	12 44	13 44	14 44	15 44	16 44	17 14
Ebbsfleet International	d				06 59	07 22	07 46	07 55	08 55	09 55	10 55	11 55	12 55	13 55	14 55	15 55	16 55	17 26
Ashford International	a				07 19	07 41	08 05	08 15	09 14	10 14	11 14	12 14	13 14	14 14	15 14	16 14	17 14	17 45
Ashford International	d	06 22		06 45	07 22	07 45	08 24	08 45	09 24	10 24	11 24	12 24	13 24	14 24	15 24	16 24	17 24	17 55
Ham Street	d	06 30		06 53	07 30	07 53	08 32	08 53	09 32	10 32	11 32	12 32	13 32	14 32	15 32	16 32	17 32	18 03
Appledore (Kent)	d	06 34		06 57	07 34	07 57	08 36	08 57	09 36	10 36	11 36	12 36	13 36	14 36	15 36	16 36	17 37	18 07
Rye	a	06 43		07 06	07 43	08 06	08 45	09 06	09 45	10 45	11 45	12 45	13 45	14 45	15 45	16 45	17 46	18 16
	d	06 45			07 45		08 48	09 07	09 47	10 47	11 47	12 47	13 47	14 47	15 47	16 48	17 47	
Winchelsea	d	06 48			07 48		08 51	09 10		10 50		12 50		14 50		16 51		
Doleham	d	06 55			07 55			09 17										
Three Oaks	d	06 58			07 58		08 59	09 20	09 58		11 57		13 57		15 57	16 59	17 57	
Ore	d	07 04			08 04		09 05	09 26	10 03	11 03	12 03	13 03	14 03	15 03	16 03	17 05	18 03	
Hastings	d	07 09			08 08		09 09	09a29	10 07	11 07	12 07	13 07	14 07	15 07	16 07	17 09	18 07	
St Leonards Warrior Sq	d	07 12			08 11		09 12		10 10	11 10	12 10	13 10	14 10	15 10	16 10	17 12	18 10	
Bexhill	d	07 20			08 19		09 20		10 18	11 18	12 18	13 18	14 18	15 18	16 20	17 20	18 20	
Collington	d	07 22			08 22		09 22		10 20	11 20	12 20	13 20	14 20	15 20	16 23	17 23	18 23	
Cooden Beach	d	07 25			08 25		09 25		10 23	11 23	12 23	13 23	14 23	15 23	16 26	17 26	18 26	
Normans Bay	d								10 27	11 27	12 27	13 27	14 27					
Pevensey Bay	d																	
Pevensey & Westham	d	07 32			08 32		09 32		10 32	11 32	12 32	13 32	14 32	15 32	16 33	17 33	18 33	
Hampden Park	d	07 38			08 38		09 38		10 38	11 38	12 38	13 38	14 38	15 38	16 40	17 40	18 40	
Eastbourne	a	07 42			08 42		09 42		10 42	11 42	12 42	13 42	14 42	15 42	16 44	17 44	18 44	
Eastbourne	d																	
Lewes	d																	
Brighton	a																	

		SN	SN	SN		SN	SN	SN	SN	SN
St Pancras International	d	17 37	18 07	18 37		19 07	19 37	20 37	21 37	22 37
Stratford International	d	17 44	18 14	18 45		19 14	19 44	20 44	21 44	22 44
Ebbsfleet International	d	17 56	18 26	18 56		19 26	19 55	20 55	21 55	22 55
Ashford International	a	18 15	18 45	19 15		19 45	20 14	21 14	22 14	23 14
Ashford International	d	18 24	18 55	19 24		19 52	20 24	21 24	22 25	23 25
Ham Street	d	18 32	19 03	19 32		20 00	20 32	21 32	22 33	23 33
Appledore (Kent)	d	18 36	19 07	19 36		20 04	20 36	21 36	22 37	23 37
Rye	a	18 45	19 16	19 45		20 13	20 45	21 45	22 46	23 46
	d	18 48		19 48		20 14	20 47	21 48	22 49	23 47
Winchelsea	d	18 52					20 50	21 51	22 53	23 50
Doleham	d								22 59	
Three Oaks	d			19 59				21 59	23 03	23 58
Ore	d	19 03		20 04		20 30	21 03	22 05	23 09	00 04
Hastings	d	19 07		20 08		20a33	21 07	22 09	23a12	00a08
St Leonards Warrior Sq	d	19 10		20 11			21 10	22 12		
Bexhill	d	19 18		20 19			21 18	22 20		
Collington	d	19 20		20 21			21 20	22 22		
Cooden Beach	d	19 23		20 24			21 23	22 25		
Normans Bay	d			20 28			21 27	22 29		
Pevensey Bay	d									
Pevensey & Westham	d	19 32		20 33			21 32	22 34		
Hampden Park	d	19 38		20 39			21 38	22 40		
Eastbourne	a	19 42		20 43			21 42	22 44		
Eastbourne	d									
Lewes	d									
Brighton	a									

Saturdays
26 May to 8 December

		SN	SN	SN	SN	SN	SN	SN		SN	SN	SN	SN	SN	SN	SN	SN	SN		SN	SN
St Pancras International	d		06 37	07 37	08 37	09 34	10 37	11 37		12 37	13 37	14 37	15 37	16 37	17 37	18 37	19 37	20 37		21 37	22 37
Stratford International	d		06 44	07 44	08 44	09 41	10 44	11 44		12 44	13 44	14 44	15 44	16 44	17 44	18 45	19 44	20 44		21 44	22 44
Ebbsfleet International	d		06 55	07 55	08 55	09 52	10 55	11 55		12 55	13 55	14 55	15 55	16 55	17 56	18 56	19 55	20 55		21 55	22 55
Ashford International	a		07 14	08 14	09 14	10 11	11 14	12 14		13 14	14 14	15 14	16 14	17 14	18 15	19 15	20 14	21 14		22 14	23 14
Ashford International	d	06 24	07 24	08 24	09 24	10 24	11 24	12 24		13 24	14 24	15 24	16 24	17 24	18 24	19 24	20 24	21 24		22 24	23 25
Ham Street	d	06 32	07 32	08 32	09 32	10 32	11 32	12 32		13 32	14 32	15 32	16 32	17 32	18 32	19 32	20 32	21 32		22 32	23 33
Appledore (Kent)	d	06 36	07 36	08 36	09 36	10 36	11 36	12 36		13 36	14 36	15 36	16 36	17 36	18 36	19 36	20 36	21 36		22 36	23 37
Rye	a	06 45	07 45	08 45	09 45	10 45	11 45	12 45		13 45	14 45	15 45	16 45	17 45	18 45	19 45	20 45	21 45		22 45	23 46
	d	06 47	07 47	08 47	09 47	10 47	11 47	12 47		13 47	14 47	15 47	16 47	17 47	18 47	19 47	20 47	21 47		22 47	23 47
Winchelsea	d	06 50		08 50		10 50		12 50			14 50		16 50		18 50		20 50			22 50	23 50
Doleham	d	06 57																			23 57
Three Oaks	d	07 00	07 57		09 57		11 57			13 57		15 57		17 57		19 57		21 57			00 01
Ore	d	07 07	08 03	09 03	10 03	11 03	12 03	13 03		14 03	15 03	16 03	17 03	18 03	19 03	20 03	21 03	22 03		23 03	00 07
Hastings	d	07 11	08 07	09 07	10 07	11 07	12 07	13 07		14 07	15 07	16 07	17 07	18 07	19 07	20 07	21 07	22 07		23 07	00a10
St Leonards Warrior Sq	d	07 14	08 10	09 10	10 10	11 10	12 10	13 10		14 10	15 10	16 10	17 10	18 10	19 10	20 10	21 10	22 10		23 10	
Bexhill	d	07 23	08 18	09 18	10 18	11 18	12 18	13 18		14 18	15 18	16 18	17 18	18 18	19 18	20 18	21 18	22 18		23 18	
Collington	d		08 20	09 20	10 20	11 20	12 20	13 20		14 20	15 20	16 20	17 20	18 20	19 20	20 20	21 20	22 20		23 20	
Cooden Beach	d		08 23	09 23	10 23	11 23	12 23	13 23		14 23	15 23	16 23	17 23	18 23	19 23	20 23	21 23	22 23		23 23	
Normans Bay	d		08 27	09 27	10 27	11 27	12 27	13 27		14 27	15 27	16 27	17 27	18 27	19 27	20 27	21 27	22 27		23 27	
Pevensey Bay	d																				
Pevensey & Westham	d	07 31	08 32	09 32	10 32	11 32	12 32	13 32		14 32	15 32	16 32	17 32	18 32	19 32	20 32	21 32	22 32		23 34	
Hampden Park	d	07 38	08 38	09 38	10 38	11 38	12 38	13 38		14 38	15 38	16 38	17 38	18 38	19 38	20 38	21 38	22 38		23 40	
Eastbourne	a	07 42	08 42	09 42	10 42	11 42	12 42	13 42		14 42	15 42	16 42	17 42	18 42	19 42	20 42	21 42	22 42		23 45	
Eastbourne	d																				
Lewes	d																				
Brighton	a																				

Table T192-R

Sundays
20 May to 2 December

London connect and Brighton with Ashford - Rye - Hastings - Eastbourne

		SN	SN	SN	SN	SN	SN	SN	SN		SN	SN	SN	SN			
St Pancras International	d		08 37	09 37	10 37	11 37	12 37	11 25	14 37		15 37	16 37	17 37	18 37	19 37	20 37	21 37
Stratford International	d		08 44	09 44	10 44	11 44	12 44	11 32	14 44		15 44	16 44	17 44	18 45	19 44	20 44	21 44
Ebbsfleet International	d		08 55	09 55	10 55	11 55	12 55	11 43	14 55		15 55	16 55	17 56	18 56	19 55	20 55	21 55
Ashford International	a		09 14	10 14	11 14	12 14	13 14	14 15	15 14		16 14	17 14	18 15	19 15	20 14	21 14	22 14
Ashford International	d	08 25	09 25	10 25	11 25	12 25	13 25	14 25	15 25		16 25	17 25	18 25	19 25	20 25	21 25	22 34
Ham Street	d	08 33	09 33	10 33	11 33	12 33	13 33	14 33	15 33		16 33	17 33	18 33	19 33	20 33	21 33	22 42
Appledore (Kent)	d	08 37	09 37	10 37	11 37	12 37	13 37	14 37	15 37		16 37	17 37	18 37	19 37	20 37	21 37	22 46
Rye	a	08 46	09 46	10 46	11 46	12 46	13 46	14 46	15 46		16 46	17 46	18 46	19 46	20 46	21 46	22 55
	d	08 48	09 48	10 48	11 48	12 48	13 48	14 48	15 48		16 48	17 48	18 48	19 48	20 48	21 48	22 56
Winchelsea	d	08 51		10 51		12 51		14 51			16 51		18 51		20 51		22 59
Doleham	d	08 58															23 06
Three Oaks	d	09 01	09 58		11 58		13 58		15 58			17 58		19 58		21 58	23 09
Ore	d	09 07	10 04	11 04	12 04	13 04	14 04	15 04	16 04		17 04	18 04	19 04	20 04	21 04	22 04	23 15
Hastings	d	09 11	10 08	11 08	12 08	13 08	14 08	15 08	16 08		17 08	18 08	19 08	20 08	21 08	22 08	23a19
St Leonards Warrior Sq	d	09 14	10 11	11 11	12 11	13 11	14 11	15 11	16 11		17 11	18 11	19 11	20 11	21 11	22 11	
Bexhill	d	09 22	10 19	11 19	12 19	13 19	14 19	15 19	16 19		17 19	18 19	19 19	20 19	21 19	22 19	
Collington	d																
Cooden Beach	d																
Normans Bay	d																
Pevensey Bay	d																
Pevensey & Westham	d																
Hampden Park	d																
Eastbourne	a	09 39	10 36	11 36	12 36	13 36	14 36	15 36	16 36		17 36	18 36	19 36	20 36	21 36	22 36	
Eastbourne	d																
Lewes	d																
Brighton	a																

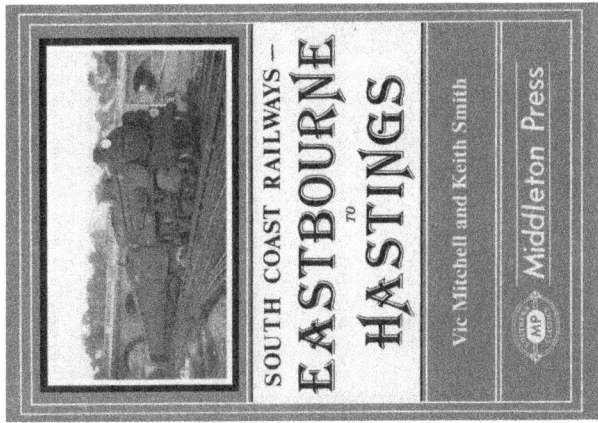

Table T194-F

Mondays to Fridays
21 May to 7 December

St Pancras International - Kent High Speed Domestic Services

Miles	Miles	Miles	Miles			SE MX ◇ A	SE MO ◇ A	SE MX ◇ A	SE TTh FO ◇ A	SE MX ◇■ B	SE MO ◇■ B	SE MO ◇ A	SE WO ◇ A	SE ThFO ◇ A	SE TO ◇ A	SE TTh FO ◇ A	SE WO ◇ A	SE MX ◇	SE MX ◇■ B	SE WTh FO	SE ◇■ C	SE ◇■ D	SE ■	SE ■ E
0	0	0	0	**St Pancras International** ⊖	d													00 12						
6	6	6	6	**Stratford International** ⊖	d			00 02										00 19						
22¼	22¼	22¼	22¼	**Ebbsfleet International**	a			00 12										00 30						
—	—	—	—		d			00 13										00 30						
24¾	—	—	24¾	Gravesend	d			00 18																
32	—	—	32	Strood	d			00 29																
—	—	—	44¼	Maidstone West	d																			
33	—	—	—	Rochester	d	00 02	00 02	00 32																
33½	—	—	—	Chatham	d	00 06	00 06	00 36																
35½	—	—	—	Gillingham (Kent)	d	00 10	00 10	00 40																
38½	—	—	—	Rainham (Kent)	d	00 15	00 15	00 45																
44	—	—	—	Sittingbourne	d	00 23	00 23	00 53																
51½	—	—	—	**Faversham**	a	00 31	00 32	01 03																
58¾	—	—	—	Whitstable	d																			
62½	—	—	—	Herne Bay	d																			
70½	—	—	—	Birchington-on-Sea	d																			
73½	—	—	—	Margate	d				00 04															
76¾	—	—	—	**Broadstairs**	a				00 09															
—	—	—	—	Ramsgate	d				00a17												04 51	05 20		
—	56	56	—	**Ashford International**	a													00 50						
—	—	—	—		d					00 04	00 05					00 15	00 15		01 05	01 07			05 25	06 05
—	69¼	—	—	Folkestone West	d					00 21	00 21					00 28	00 28		01s22				05 42	
—	70	—	—	Folkestone Central	d					00 24	00 24					00 30	00 30		01s24				05 45	
—	77¼	—	—	**Dover Priory**	d					00a35	00a35					00 42	00 42		01a38				06 05	
—	—	—	—	Deal	a											00s59	01s02						06 22	
—	—	—	—	Sandwich	a											01s06	01s08				05 05	05 33	06 28	
—	—	—	—	Dover Priory	a																05 29	05 57		
—	—	70¼	—	**Canterbury West**	a															01 30				06 26
—	—	—	—		d							00 09	00 09	00 09										06 27
—	—	87¾	—	Ramsgate	d							00 28	00a30	00 31	00 44	01a23	01a23						06a43	06a51
—	—	87¾	—	Broadstairs	d							00s33		00s36	00s49									
—	—	91	—	**Margate**	a							00 39		00 42	00 58									

		SE ◇ F	SE ◇	SE ◇■ C	SE ◇ G	SE ■	SE	SE ◇■ B	SE ■ H	SE ◇■ C	SE I	SE ◇	SE ◇	SE ◇	SE ◇■ J	SE ◇■ C	SE ■ H	SE ■ H	SE ◇ F	SE ◇	SE ◇ F	SE ◇ K
St Pancras International ⊖	d		06 25									06 40	06 55	07 04					07 22	07 25	07 37	
Stratford International ⊖	d		06 32									06 47	07 02	07 11					07 29	07 32	07 44	
Ebbsfleet International	a		06 42									06 58	07 12	07 22					07 39	07 42	07 54	←
	d		06 43									06 59	07 13	07 22					07 40	07 46	07 55	
Gravesend	d		06 48										07 19						07 44			07 44
Strood	d		07 01										07 31						→			07 54
Maidstone West	d		07a16																			
Rochester	d												07 34									07 58
Chatham	d												07 38									08 02
Gillingham (Kent)	d												07 43									08 06
Rainham (Kent)	d												07 47									08 11
Sittingbourne	d												07 55									08 18
Faversham	a												08 03									08 26
Whitstable	d				06 31				07 01								07 32	08 01				08 35
Herne Bay	d				06 38				07 08								07 39	08 08				08 42
Birchington-on-Sea	d				06 46				07 16								07 47	08 16				08 51
Margate	d				06 54				07 24								07 55	08 24				08 59
Broadstairs	a				06 59				07 29								08 00	08 29				09 04
Ramsgate	d	06 14		06 50	07 10				07a36	07 42						08 05	08a07	08a36				09 12
Ashford International	a											07 19		07 41						08 05	08 15	
	d					06 28	06 30	07 00			07 05			07 42	07 58					08 09	08 16	
Folkestone West	d					06 45		07 17												08 25	08 29	
Folkestone Central	d					06 48		07 20												08 28	08 31	
Dover Priory	d					07 10		07 36												08a39	08 44	
Deal	a	06 32				07 27		07 54													09 01	
Sandwich	a			07 02	07 22	07 33		08 01		08 01						08 24					09 07	09 24
Dover Priory	a	06 47		07 24	07 45					08 24						08 52						09 47
Canterbury West	a						06 51				07 27			07 58	08 16							
	d						06 52							07 59	08 17							
Ramsgate	d					07a46	07 14	08a20						08 25	08a41						09 20	
Broadstairs	d						07 20							08 30							09 25	
Margate	a						07 26							08 36							09 29	

A From St Pancras International
B From London Charing Cross
C To London Charing Cross
D To London Cannon Street
E From Tonbridge
F To St Pancras International
G From Faversham to St Pancras International
H From Faversham
I From Maidstone East
J From London Cannon Street
K From St Pancras International to Dover Priory continues to St Pancras International

Table T194-F

Mondays to Fridays
21 May to 7 December

St Pancras International - Kent High Speed Domestic Services

		SE ◇	SE ◇■ A	SE ◇■ A	SE ◇	SE ◇■ A	SE ◇■ A	SE ◇ B	SE ◇ B	SE ◇ C	SE ◇	SE ◇■ A	SE ◇	SE ◇■ A	SE ◇ B	SE ◇ B	SE ◇ C	SE ◇	SE ◇■ A	SE ◇	SE ◇■ A	SE ◇ B	SE ◇ B
St Pancras International ⊖	d	08 07			08 12			08 25	08 37		08 58		09 09		09 25	09 37		09 55		10 08		10 27	10 37
Stratford International ⊖	d	08 14			08 19			08 32	08 44		09 05		09 16		09 32	09 44		10 02		10 15		10 34	10 44
Ebbsfleet International	a	08 25			08 30			08 42	08 54	←	09 15		09 27		09 43	09 54	←	10 12		10 26		10 44	10 54
	d	08 26			08 30			08 43	08 55		09 16		09 27		09 44	09 55		10 13		10 26		10 45	10 55
Gravesend	d	08 30						08 48		08 48	09 20				09 48		09 48	10 18				10 49	
Strood	d	08 40						→		08 59	09 30				→		09 59	10 29				→	
Maidstone West	d																						
Rochester	d	08 44								09 02	09 34						10 02	10 32					
Chatham	d	08 47								09 06	09 37						10 06	10 36					
Gillingham (Kent)	d	08 53								09 10	09 42						10 10	10 40					
Rainham (Kent)	d	08 58								09 15	09 47						10 15	10 45					
Sittingbourne	d	09 05								09 23	09 54						10 23	10 54					
Faversham	a	09 14								09 31	10 05						10 31	11 05					
Whitstable	d									09 40							10 40						
Herne Bay	d									09 45							10 45						
Birchington-on-Sea	d									09 54							10 54						
Margate	d									09 59							10 59						
Broadstairs	a									10 05							11 05						
Ramsgate	d									10 12							11 12						
Ashford International	a				08 50				09 14				09 47			10 14				10 46			11 14
	d		08 33	08 38	08 52	09 05	09 08		09 15			09 35	09 52	10 05		10 15			10 35	10 52	11 02		11 15
Folkestone West	d			08 55		09 21			09 28					10 22		10 28					11 19		11 28
Folkestone Central	d			08 58		09 24			09 30					10 25		10 30					11 22		11 30
Dover Priory	d			09a10		09a38			09 43					10a38		10 42					11a33		11 42
Deal	a								10 00							10 59							11 59
Sandwich	a								10 06	10 24						11 06	11 24						12 06
Dover Priory	a									10 47							11 47						
Canterbury West	a		08 54		09 08		09 30					09 53	10 08						10 53	11 08			
	d		08 55		09 09							09 54	10 09						10 54	11 09			
Ramsgate	d		09a18		09 31				10 20			10a18	10 28			11 20			11a19	11 28			12 20
Broadstairs	d				09 36				10 25				10 33			11 25				11 33			12 25
Margate	a				09 42				10 29				10 39			11 29				11 39			12 29

		SE ◇ C	SE ◇	SE ◇■ A	SE ◇	SE ◇■ A	SE ◇ B	SE ◇ B	SE ◇ C	SE ◇	SE ◇■ A	SE ◇	SE ◇■ A	SE ◇ B	SE ◇ B	SE ◇ C	SE ◇	SE ◇■ A	SE ◇	SE ◇■ A	SE ◇ B	SE ◇ B	SE ◇ C
St Pancras International ⊖	d		10 52		11 12		11 25	11 37		11 55		12 12		12 27	12 37		12 52		13 12		13 25	13 37	
Stratford International ⊖	d		10 59		11 19		11 32	11 44		12 02		12 19		12 34	12 44		12 59		13 19		13 32	13 44	
Ebbsfleet International	a	←	11 09		11 30		11 42	11 54	←	12 12		12 30		12 44	12 54	←	13 09		13 30		13 42	13 54	←
	d		11 13		11 30		11 43	11 55		12 13		12 30		12 45	12 55		13 13		13 30		13 43	13 55	
Gravesend	d	10 49	11 18				11 48		11 48	12 18				12 49		12 49	13 18				13 48		13 48
Strood	d	10 59	11 29				→		11 59	12 29				→		12 59	13 29				→		13 59
Maidstone West	d																						
Rochester	d	11 02	11 32						12 02	12 32						13 02	13 32						14 02
Chatham	d	11 06	11 36						12 06	12 36						13 06	13 36						14 06
Gillingham (Kent)	d	11 10	11 40						12 10	12 40						13 10	13 40						14 10
Rainham (Kent)	d	11 15	11 45						12 15	12 45						13 15	13 45						14 15
Sittingbourne	d	11 23	11 54						12 23	12 54						13 23	13 54						14 23
Faversham	a	11 31	12 05						12 31	13 05						13 31	14 05						14 31
Whitstable	d	11 40							12 40							13 40							14 40
Herne Bay	d	11 45							12 45							13 45							14 45
Birchington-on-Sea	d	11 54							12 54							13 54							14 54
Margate	d	11 59							12 59							13 59							14 59
Broadstairs	a	12 05							13 05							14 05							15 05
Ramsgate	d	12 12							13 12							14 12							15 12
Ashford International	a				11 50			12 14				12 50			13 14				13 50			14 14	
	d			11 35	11 52	12 02		12 15			12 35	12 52	13 02		13 15			13 35	13 52	14 02		14 15	
Folkestone West	d					12 19		12 28					13 19		13 28					14 19		14 28	
Folkestone Central	d					12 22		12 30					13 22		13 30					14 22		14 30	
Dover Priory	d					12a33		12 42					13a33		13 42					14a33		14 42	
Deal	a							12 59							13 59							14 59	
Sandwich	a	12 24						13 06	13 24						14 06	14 24						15 06	15 24
Dover Priory	a	12 47							13 47							14 47							15 47
Canterbury West	a			11 53	12 08						12 53	13 08						13 53	14 08				
	d			11 54	12 09						12 54	13 09						13 54	14 09				
Ramsgate	d			12a16	12 28			13 20			13a16	13 28			14 20			14a16	14 28			15 20	
Broadstairs	d				12 33			13 25				13 33			14 25				14 33			15 25	
Margate	a				12 39			13 29				13 39			14 29				14 39			15 29	

A From London Charing Cross
B To St Pancras International
C From St Pancras International to Dover Priory continues to St Pancras International

Table T194-F

Mondays to Fridays

21 May to 7 December

St Pancras International - Kent
High Speed Domestic Services

		SE ◇	SE ◇1 A	SE ◇1 B	SE ◇1 A	SE ◇	SE ◇1 A	SE ◇1 B	SE ◇ C	SE ◇ C	SE ◇ D	SE ◇	SE ◇1 A	SE 1 A	SE ◇	SE ◇1 A	SE ◇1 B	SE ◇ C	SE ◇ C	SE ◇ D	SE ◇	SE ◇1 A	SE ◇1 A
St Pancras International ⊖	d	13 55				14 09			14 25	14 37		14 55			15 12			15 25	15 37		15 55		
Stratford International ⊖	d	14 02				14 16			14 32	14 44		15 02			15 19			15 32	15 44		16 02		
Ebbsfleet International	a	14 12				14 27			14 42	14 54	←	15 12			15 30			15 42	15 54	←	16 12		
	d	14 13				14 27			14 43	14 55		15 13			15 30			15 43	15 55		16 13		
Gravesend	d	14 18							14 48		14 48	15 18						15 48		15 48	16 18		
Strood	d	14 29							→		14 59	15 29						→		15 59	16 29		
Maidstone West	d																						
Rochester	d	14 32									15 02	15 32								16 02	16 32		
Chatham	d	14 36									15 05	15 36								16 05	16 36		
Gillingham (Kent)	d	14 40									15 10	15 40								16 10	16 40		
Rainham (Kent)	d	14 45									15 14	15 45								16 14	16 45		
Sittingbourne	d	14 54									15 22	15 54								16 22	16 53		
Faversham	a	15 05									15 30	16 05								16 30	17 01		
Whitstable	d										15 39									16 39			
Herne Bay	d										15 46									16 46			
Birchington-on-Sea	d										15 54									16 54			
Margate	d										16 02									17 02			
Broadstairs	a										16 07									17 07			
Ramsgate	d			15 21				15 50			16 13						16 50			17 13			
Ashford International	a					14 47				15 14					15 50				16 14				
	d		14 35		14 38	14 52	15 02			15 15			15 35	15 38	15 52	16 02			16 15			16 35	16 38
Folkestone West	d				14 55		15 19			15 28				15 55		16 19			16 28				16 55
Folkestone Central	d				14 58		15 22			15 30				15 58		16 22			16 30				16 58
Dover Priory	d				15 25		15a33			15 42				16 10		16a33			16 42				17 11
Deal	a				15 42					15 59				16 27					16 59				17 28
Sandwich	a			15 33	15 48			16 02		16 06	16 25			16 34			17 02		17 06	17 25			17 34
Dover Priory	a			15 57				16 24			16 48						17 24			17 48			
Canterbury West	a		14 53			15 08							15 53		16 08							16 56	
	d		14 54			15 09							15 54		16 09							16 57	
Ramsgate	d		15a16		16a11	15 28				16 20			16a16	16a54	16 28				17 20			17a24	17a49
Broadstairs	d					15 33				16 25					16 33				17 25				
Margate	a					15 39				16 29					16 39				17 29				

		SE ◇	SE ◇1 A	SE ◇	SE ◇1 B	SE ◇1 E	SE ◇ F	SE ◇	SE ◇	SE ◇1 A	SE ◇ G	SE ◇1 B	SE ◇1 A	SE ◇	SE ◇	SE ◇	SE ◇	SE ◇1 A	SE ◇1 A	SE ◇	SE ◇	SE ◇1 A	SE ◇
St Pancras International ⊖	d	16 12		16 25			16 37	16 50	16 55					17 07	17 16	17 20	17 25			17 37	17 46		17 50
Stratford International ⊖	d	16 19		16 32			16 44	16 57	17 02					17 14	17 23	17 27	17 32			17 44	17 53		17 57
Ebbsfleet International	a	16 30		16 42			16 54		17 12					17 25	17 33		17 42			17 55	18 03		
	d	16 30		16 43			16 55		17 13					17 26	17 35		17 43			17 56	18 05		
Gravesend	d			16 48					17 18						17 39						18 09		
Strood	d			16 59					17 28						17 50						18 20		
Maidstone West	d														18a08						18a38		
Rochester	d			17 02					17 31								17 58						
Chatham	d			17 06					17 35								18 02						
Gillingham (Kent)	d			17 10					17 41								18 07						
Rainham (Kent)	d			17 15					17 46								18 12						
Sittingbourne	d			17 23					17 54								18 19						
Faversham	a			17 31					18 02								18 27						
Whitstable	d					17 44											18 37						
Herne Bay	d					17 51											18 43						
Birchington-on-Sea	d					18 00											18 52						
Margate	d					18 08											18 58						
Broadstairs	a					18 13											19 03						
Ramsgate	d				17 50	18a22						18 23					19a13						
Ashford International	a	16 50					17 14	17 24			←			17 45		17 54				18 15			18 24
	d	16 52	17 03				17 18	17 26		17 35			17 38	17 47		17 56		18 03	18 05	18 17		18 20	18 26
Folkestone West	d		17 20				17 30				17 30		17 55	18 00					18 22	18 30		18 38	
Folkestone Central	d		17 23				→				17 33		17 58	18 03					18 25	18 35		18a43	
Dover Priory	d		17a34								17 45		18 12	18a15					18a39	18 46			
Deal	a										18 02		18 29							19 04			
Sandwich	a				18 02						18 08	18 35	18 36							19 10			
Dover Priory	a				18 24							18 57											
Canterbury West	a	17 08						17 41		17 56						18 11		18 24					18 41
	d	17 09						17 42		17 57						18 12		18 25					18 42
Ramsgate	d	17 32						18 02		18a21	18 26		18a53			18 32		18a49		19a25			19 02
Broadstairs	d	17 37						18 07			18 32					18 37							19 07
Margate	a	17 42						18 15			18 37					18 45							19 15

A From London Charing Cross
B To London Charing Cross
C To St Pancras International
D From St Pancras International to Dover Priory continues to St Pancras International
E From Faversham
F To Faversham
G From St Pancras International to Faversham

Table T194-F

Mondays to Fridays

21 May to 7 December

St Pancras International - Kent
High Speed Domestic Services

		SE ◇	SE ◇1 A	SE ◇	SE ◇	SE ◇1 B	SE ◇1 C	SE ◇	SE ◇	SE ◇1 A	SE ◇1 C	SE ◇	SE ◇1 A	SE ◇	SE ◇1 C	SE ◇1 B	SE ◇1 C	SE ◇	SE ◇	SE ◇1 C	SE ◇	SE ◇1 A	SE ◇ D
St Pancras International ⊖	d	17 55		18 07	18 16			18 20	18 25			18 37		18 50				18 55	19 07		19 20		
Stratford International ⊖	d	18 02		18 14	18 23			18 27	18 32			18 45		18 57				19 02	19 14		19 27		
Ebbsfleet International	a	18 12		18 25	18 33				18 42			18 55						19 12	19 25				
	d	18 13		18 26	18 35				18 43			18 56						19 13	19 26				
Gravesend	d	18 18			18 39													19 18					
Strood	d	18 31			18 51													19 30					
Maidstone West	d				19a09																		
Rochester	d	18 36							19 01								19 26	19 35					
Chatham	d	18 40							19 05								19 30	19 39					
Gillingham (Kent)	d	18 45							19 10								19 35	19 44					
Rainham (Kent)	d	18 50							19 15								19 40	19 49					
Sittingbourne	d	18 58							19 25								19 49	19 56					
Faversham	a	19 06							19 33								20 00	20 05					
Whitstable	d	19 15							19 42								20 09						
Herne Bay	d	19 21							19 48								20 16						
Birchington-on-Sea	d	19 30							19 57								20 25						
Margate	d	19 36							20 02								20 33						21 00
Broadstairs	a	19 45							20 10								20 38						21 05
Ramsgate	d					19 23										20 23	20a48						21 12
Ashford International	a			18 45				18 54				19 15		19 25					19 45		19 54		
	d		18 33	18 47			18 51	18 56		19 02	19 06	19 17	19 22	19 27	19 32				19 47	19 52	19 56	20 07	
Folkestone West	d			19 00			19 09				19 23	19 31	19 40						20 00	20 09			
Folkestone Central	d			19 03			19 12				19a28	19 34	19 43						20 03	20 12			
Dover Priory	d			19a15			19 25					19 46	19 55						20a14	20a27			
Deal	a						19 43					20 04	20 14										
Sandwich	a					19 35	19 50					20 13	20 21			20 35							21 24
Dover Priory	a					19 57										20 57							→
Canterbury West	a		18 55					19 11		19 24				19 42	19 54						20 11	20 29	
	d		18 56					19 12		19 25				19 43	19 55						20 12	20 30	
Ramsgate	d		19a21				20a08	19 32		19a52			20a38	20 03	20a21						20 32	20a57	
Broadstairs	d							19 37						20 08							20 37		
Margate	a							19 45						20 16							20 45		

		SE ◇	SE ◇ D	SE ◇ D	SE ◇ E	SE ◇	SE ◇1 A	SE ◇1 A	SE ◇	SE ◇1 A	SE ◇	SE 1 F	SE ◇	SE ◇ G	SE ◇	SE ◇1 A	SE ◇	SE ◇1 A	SE ◇	SE ◇	SE 1 F	SE ◇
St Pancras International ⊖	d	19 25		19 37		19 55			20 12		20 25		20 37		20 55		21 12		21 25	21 37		21 55
Stratford International ⊖	d	19 32		19 44		20 02			20 19		20 32		20 44		21 02		21 19		21 32	21 44		22 02
Ebbsfleet International	a	19 42		19 54		20 12			20 30		20 42		20 54		21 12		21 30		21 42	21 54		22 12
	d	19 43		19 55		20 13			20 30		20 43		20 55		21 13		21 30		21 43	21 55		22 13
Gravesend	d	19 48				20 18					20 48				21 18				21 48			22 18
Strood	d	19 59				20 29					20 59				21 29				21 59			22 29
Maidstone West	d																					
Rochester	d	20 02				20 32					21 02				21 32				22 02			22 32
Chatham	d	20 06				20 36					21 06				21 36				22 06			22 36
Gillingham (Kent)	d	20 11				20 40					21 10				21 40				22 10			22 40
Rainham (Kent)	d	20 16				20 45					21 15				21 45				22 15			22 45
Sittingbourne	d	20 23				20 54					21 23				21 53				22 23			22 53
Faversham	a	20 31				21 05					21 31				22 01				22 31			23 01
Whitstable	d	20 40									21 40								22 40			
Herne Bay	d	20 47									21 47								22 47			
Birchington-on-Sea	d	20 56									21 56								22 56			
Margate	d	21 04									22 04								23 04			
Broadstairs	a	21 09									22 09								23 09		←	
Ramsgate	d	21a17	22 12								22a17	23 12							23a17		23 12	
Ashford International	a			20 14					20 50			→	21 14				21 50			22 14		
	d			20 15			20 35	20 38	20 52	21 05			21 15			21 32	21 52	22 04		22 15		
Folkestone West	d			20 28				20 55		21 21			21 28					22 21		22 28		
Folkestone Central	d			20 30				20 58		21 24			21 30					22 24		22 30		
Dover Priory	d			20 42				21 10		21a37			21 42					22a35		22 42		
Deal	a			20 59	←			21 27					21 59	←						22 59		
Sandwich	a		22 24	21 06	21 24			21 33					22 06	22 24						23 06	23 24	
Dover Priory	a		→		21 47									22 47							23 47	
Canterbury West	a						20 56		21 08							21 53	22 08					
	d						20 57		21 10							21 53	22 09					
Ramsgate	d			21 20			21a23	21a50	21 32				22a19			22a17	22 28			23a22		
Broadstairs	d			21 25					21 38								22 33					
Margate	a			21 29					21 43								22 39					

A From London Charing Cross
B To London Charing Cross
C From London Cannon Street
D To St Pancras International
E From Margate to St Pancras International
F To Ashford International
G From Ramsgate to St Pancras International

Table T194-F

Mondays to Fridays
21 May to 7 December

St Pancras International - Kent High Speed Domestic Services

		SE ◇■ A	SE TO ◇	SE TX ◇	SE ◇■ A	SE TX ◇	SE TO ◇	SE ◇	SE ◇	SE MX ◇■ A	SE MO ◇■ A	SE TO ◇	SE WThFO ◇	SE MO ◇	SE ◇	SE TX ◇	SE TO ◇	SE ◇
St Pancras International ⊖	d		22 12	22 12		22 25	22 25	22 37	22 55			23 12	23 12	23 12	23 25	23 37	23 37	23 55
Stratford International ⊖	d		22 19	22 19		22 32	22 32	22 44	23 02			23 19	23 19	23 19	23 32	23 44	23 44	00 02
Ebbsfleet International	a		22 30	22 30		22 42	22 42	22 54	23 12			23 30	23 30	23 30	23 42	23 54	23 54	00 12
	d		22 30	22 30		22 43	22 43	22 55	23 13			23 30	23 30	23 30	23 43	23 55	23 55	00 13
Gravesend	d					22 48	22 48		23 18						23 48			00 18
Strood	d					22 59	22 59		23 29						23 59			00 29
Maidstone West	d																	
Rochester	d					23 02	23 02		23 32						00 02			00 32
Chatham	d					23 06	23 06		23 36						00 06			00 36
Gillingham (Kent)	d					23 10	23 10		23 40						00 10			00 40
Rainham (Kent)	d					23 15	23 15		23 45						00 15			00 45
Sittingbourne	d					23 23	23 23		23 53						00 23			00 53
Faversham	a					23 31	23 31		00 05						00 31			01 03
Whitstable	d					23 40												
Herne Bay	d					23 47												
Birchington-on-Sea	d					23 56												
Margate	d					00 04												
Broadstairs	a					00 09												
Ramsgate	d					00a17	00a39											
Ashford International	a		22 50	22 50				23 14				23 50	23 50	23 50		00 14	00 14	
	d	22 34	22 52	22 52	23 04			23 15		23 34	23 34	23 52	23 52	23 52		00 15	00 15	
Folkestone West	d				23 21			23 28								00 28	00 28	
Folkestone Central	d				23 24			23 30								00 30	00 30	
Dover Priory	d				23a35			23 44								00 42	00 42	
Deal	a							00 01								00s59	01s02	
Sandwich	a							00 07								01s06	01s08	
Dover Priory	a																	
Canterbury West	a	22 55	23 08	23 08						23 55		00 08	00 08					
	d	22 56	23 09	23 09						23 56		00 09	00 09					
Ramsgate	d	23a18	23a30	23 30				00a21		00a18	00a29	00a30	00 31	00 44		01a23	01a23	
Broadstairs	d			23 35									00s36	00s49				
Margate	a			23 40									00 42	00 58				

Saturdays
26 May to 8 December

		SE ◇ B	SE ◇ B	SE ◇ B	SE ◇■ A	SE ◇ B	SE ◇ B	SE ◇	SE ◇■ A	SE ◇ C	SE ◇ C	SE ◇ D	SE	SE ◇ E	SE ■ F	SE ■ G	SE ◇ C	SE ■ H	SE ◇ C	SE ■	SE ◇■ A	SE ◇	SE ■ F
St Pancras International ⊖	d							00 12									06 37					07 08	
Stratford International ⊖	d		00 02					00 19									06 44					07 15	
Ebbsfleet International	a		00 12					00 30									06 54					07 26	
	d		00 13					00 30									06 55					07 26	
Gravesend	d		00 18																				
Strood	d		00 29																				
Maidstone West	d																						
Rochester	d	00 02	00 32																				
Chatham	d	00 06	00 36																				
Gillingham (Kent)	d	00 10	00 40																	07 28			
Rainham (Kent)	d	00 15	00 45																	07 33			
Sittingbourne	d	00 23	00 53																	07 42			
Faversham	a	00 31	01 03																	07 52			
Whitstable	d											06 32						07 32		08 02			
Herne Bay	d											06 39						07 39		08 09			
Birchington-on-Sea	d											06 48						07 48		08 18			
Margate	d			00 04								06 57						07 57		08 25			
Broadstairs	a			00 09								07 02						08 02		08 31			
Ramsgate	d			00a17						06 12		07 12						08a09	08 12	08a38			
Ashford International	a							00 50									07 14					07 46	
	d				00 04		00 15		01 05		06 15		06 35		07 02	07 05	07 15				07 35	07 52	08 02
Folkestone West	d				00 21		00 28		01s22		06 28				07 19		07 28						08 19
Folkestone Central	d				00 24		00 30		01s24		06 30				07 22		07 30						08 22
Dover Priory	d				00a35		00 42		01a38		06 42				07a33		07 42						08a33
Deal	a						00s59				06 59						07 59						
Sandwich	a						01s06			06 24	07 06	07 24					08 06		08 24				
Dover Priory	a									06 47		07 47							08 47				
Canterbury West	a												06 53	←		07 27					07 53	08 08	
	d					00 09							06 54								07 54	08 09	
Ramsgate	d					00 31	01a23				07 20		07 16	07 20			08 20				08a16	08 28	
Broadstairs	d					00s36					→		07 21	07 25			08 25					08 33	
Margate	a					00 42							07 26	07 29			08 29					08 39	

A From London Charing Cross
B From St Pancras International
C To St Pancras International
D From Faversham to St Pancras International
E From Ashford International to St Pancras International
F From Tonbridge
G From Maidstone East
H From Faversham

Table T194-F

Saturdays
26 May to 8 December

St Pancras International - Kent High Speed Domestic Services

		SE ◇ A	SE ◇ A	SE ◇ B	SE ◇	SE ◇■ C	SE ◇	SE ◇■ C	SE ◇ A	SE ◇ A	SE ◇ B	SE ◇	SE ◇■ C	SE ◇	SE ◇■ C	SE ◇ A	SE ◇ A	SE ◇ B	SE ◇	SE ◇■ C	SE ◇	SE ◇■ C	SE ◇ A
St Pancras International ⊖	d	07 25	07 37		07 55		08 12		08 25	08 37		08 52		09 09		09 25	09 34		09 55		10 08		10 22
Stratford International ⊖	d	07 32	07 44		08 02		08 19		08 32	08 44		08 59		09 16		09 32	09 41		10 02		10 15		10 32
Ebbsfleet International	a	07 42	07 54	←	08 12		08 30		08 42	08 54	←	09 09		09 27		09 43	09 51	←	10 12		10 26		10 43
	d	07 43	07 55		08 13		08 30		08 43	08 55		09 13		09 27		09 44	09 52		10 13		10 26		10 44
Gravesend	d	07 48		07 48	08 18				08 48		08 48	09 18				09 48		09 48	10 18				10 48
Strood	d	→		07 59	08 29				→		08 59	09 29				→		09 59	10 29				→
Maidstone West	d																						
Rochester	d			08 02	08 32						09 02	09 32						10 02	10 32				
Chatham	d			08 06	08 36						09 06	09 36						10 06	10 36				
Gillingham (Kent)	d			08 10	08 40						09 10	09 40						10 10	10 40				
Rainham (Kent)	d			08 15	08 45						09 15	09 45						10 15	10 45				
Sittingbourne	d			08 23	08 54						09 23	09 54						10 23	10 54				
Faversham	a			08 31	09 05						09 31	10 05						10 31	11 05				
Whitstable	d			08 40							09 40							10 40					
Herne Bay	d			08 45							09 45							10 45					
Birchington-on-Sea	d			08 54							09 54							10 54					
Margate	d			08 59							09 59							10 59					
Broadstairs	a			09 05							10 05							11 05					
Ramsgate	d			09 12							10 12							11 12					
Ashford International	a		08 14				08 50			09 14				09 47			10 11				10 46		
	d		08 15			08 35	08 52	09 02		09 15			09 35	09 52	10 02		10 15			10 35	10 52	11 02	
Folkestone West	d		08 28					09 19		09 28					10 19		10 28					11 19	
Folkestone Central	d		08 30					09 22		09 30					10 22		10 30					11 22	
Dover Priory	d		08 42					09a33		09 42					10a33		10 42					11a33	
Deal	a		08 59							09 59							10 59						
Sandwich	a		09 06	09 24						10 06	10 24						11 06	11 24					
Dover Priory	a			09 47							10 47							11 47					
Canterbury West	a					08 53	09 08						09 53	10 08						10 53	11 08		
	d					08 54	09 09						09 54	10 09						10 54	11 09		
Ramsgate	d		09 20			09a16	09 28			10 20			10a16	10 28			11 20			11a16	11 28		
Broadstairs	d		09 25				09 33			10 25				10 33			11 25				11 33		
Margate	a		09 29				09 39			10 29				10 39			11 29				11 39		

		SE ◇ A	SE ◇ B	SE ◇	SE ◇■ C	SE ◇	SE ◇■ C	SE ◇ A	SE ◇ A	SE ◇ B	SE ◇	SE ◇■ C	SE ◇	SE ◇■ C	SE ◇ A	SE ◇ A	SE ◇ B	SE ◇	SE ◇■ C	SE ◇	SE ◇■ C	SE ◇ A	SE ◇ A
St Pancras International ⊖	d	10 37		10 52		11 12		11 25	11 37		11 55		12 12		12 27	12 37		12 52		13 12		13 25	13 37
Stratford International ⊖	d	10 44		10 59		11 19		11 32	11 44		12 02		12 19		12 34	12 44		12 59		13 19		13 32	13 44
Ebbsfleet International	a	10 54	←	11 09		11 30		11 42	11 54	←	12 12		12 30		12 44	12 54	←	13 09		13 30		13 42	13 54
	d	10 55		11 13		11 30		11 43	11 55		12 13		12 30		12 45	12 55		13 13		13 30		13 43	13 55
Gravesend	d		10 48	11 18				11 48		11 48	12 18				12 49		12 49	13 18				13 48	
Strood	d		10 59	11 29				→		11 59	12 29				→		12 59	13 29				→	
Maidstone West	d																						
Rochester	d		11 02	11 32						12 02	12 32						13 02	13 32					
Chatham	d		11 06	11 36						12 06	12 36						13 06	13 36					
Gillingham (Kent)	d		11 10	11 40						12 10	12 40						13 10	13 40					
Rainham (Kent)	d		11 15	11 45						12 15	12 45						13 15	13 45					
Sittingbourne	d		11 23	11 54						12 23	12 54						13 23	13 54					
Faversham	a		11 31	12 05						12 31	13 05						13 31	14 05					
Whitstable	d		11 40							12 40							13 40						
Herne Bay	d		11 45							12 45							13 45						
Birchington-on-Sea	d		11 54							12 54							13 54						
Margate	d		11 59							12 59							13 59						
Broadstairs	a		12 05							13 05							14 05						
Ramsgate	d		12 12							13 12							14 12						
Ashford International	a	11 14				11 50			12 14				12 50			13 14				13 50			14 14
	d	11 15			11 35	11 52	12 02		12 15			12 35	12 52	13 02		13 15			13 35	13 52	14 02		14 15
Folkestone West	d	11 28					12 19		12 28					13 19		13 28					14 19		14 28
Folkestone Central	d	11 30					12 22		12 30					13 22		13 30					14 22		14 30
Dover Priory	d	11 42					12a33		12 42					13a33		13 42					14a33		14 42
Deal	a	11 59							12 59							13 59							14 59
Sandwich	a	12 06	12 24						13 06	13 24						14 06	14 24						15 06
Dover Priory	a		12 47							13 47							14 47						
Canterbury West	a				11 53	12 08						12 53	13 08						13 53	14 08			
	d				11 54	12 09						12 54	13 09						13 54	14 09			
Ramsgate	d	12 20			12a16	12 28			13 20			13a16	13 28			14 20			14a16	14 28			15 20
Broadstairs	d	12 25				12 33			13 25				13 33			14 25				14 33			15 25
Margate	a	12 29				12 39			13 29				13 39			14 29				14 39			15 29

A To St Pancras International
B From St Pancras International to Dover Priory continues to St Pancras International
C From London Charing Cross

Table T194-F

Saturdays
26 May to 8 December

St Pancras International - Kent High Speed Domestic Services

		SE ◇ A	SE ◇	SE ◇1 B	SE ◇	SE ◇1 B	SE ◇ C	SE ◇ C	SE ◇ A	SE ◇	SE ◇1 B	SE ◇	and at the same minutes past each hour until	SE ◇1 B	SE ◇ C	SE ◇ C	SE ◇ A	SE ◇	SE ◇1 B	SE ◇	SE ◇1 B	SE ◇ C	SE ◇ C
St Pancras International 15 ⊖	d		13 55		14 09		14 25	14 37		14 55		15 12			18 25	18 37		18 55		19 12		19 25	19 37
Stratford International ⊖	d		14 02		14 16		14 32	14 44		15 02		15 19			18 32	18 44		19 02		19 19		19 32	19 44
Ebbsfleet International	a	←	14 12		14 27		14 42	14 54	←	15 12		15 30			18 42	18 54	←	19 12		19 30		19 42	19 54
	d		14 13		14 27		14 43	14 55		15 13		15 30			18 43	18 55		19 13		19 30		19 43	19 55
Gravesend 4	d	13 48	14 18				14 48		14 48	15 18					18 48		18 48	19 18				19 48	
Strood 4	d	13 59	14 29				→		14 59	15 29					→		18 59	19 29				→	
Maidstone West	d																						
Rochester 4	d	14 02	14 32						15 02	15 32							19 02	19 32					
Chatham 4	d	14 06	14 36						15 06	15 36							19 06	19 36					
Gillingham (Kent) 4	d	14 10	14 40						15 10	15 40							19 10	19 40					
Rainham (Kent)	d	14 15	14 45						15 15	15 45							19 15	19 45					
Sittingbourne 4	d	14 23	14 54						15 23	15 54							19 23	19 54					
Faversham 2	a	14 31	15 05						15 31	16 05							19 31	20 05					
Whitstable	d	14 40							15 40								19 40						
Herne Bay	d	14 45							15 45								19 45						
Birchington-on-Sea	d	14 54							15 54								19 54						
Margate 4	d	14 59							15 59								19 59						
Broadstairs	a	15 05							16 05								20 05						
Ramsgate	d	15 12							16 12								20 12						
Ashford International	a				14 47			15 14				15 50				19 14				19 50			20 14
	d			14 35	14 52	15 02		15 15			15 35	15 52		19 02		19 15			19 35	19 52	20 02		20 15
Folkestone West	d					15 19		15 28						19 19		19 28					20 19		20 28
Folkestone Central	d					15 22		15 30						19 22		19 30					20 22		20 30
Dover Priory 4	d					15a33		15 42						19a33		19 42					20a33		20 42
Deal	a							15 59								19 59							20 59
Sandwich	a	15 24						16 06	16 24							20 06	20 24						21 06
Dover Priory	a	15 47							16 47								20 47						
Canterbury West 4	a			14 53	15 08						15 53	16 08							19 53	20 08			
	d			14 54	15 09						15 54	16 09							19 54	20 09			
Ramsgate 4	d			15a16	15 28			16 20			16a16	16 28				20 20			20a16	20 28			21 20
Broadstairs	d				15 33			16 25				16 33				20 25				20 33			21 25
Margate 4	a				15 39			16 29				16 39				20 29				20 39			21 29

		SE ◇ A	SE ◇	SE ◇1 B	SE ◇	SE ◇1 B	SE ◇ C	SE ◇	SE ◇ A	SE ◇	SE ◇1 B	SE ◇	SE ◇1 B	SE ◇	SE ◇	SE ◇	SE ◇1 B	SE ◇	SE ◇1 B	SE 1 D	SE ◇	SE ◇	SE ◇
St Pancras International 15 ⊖	d		19 55		20 12		20 25	20 37		20 55		21 12		21 25	21 37	21 55		22 12			22 25	22 37	22 55
Stratford International ⊖	d		20 02		20 19		20 32	20 44		21 02		21 19		21 32	21 44	22 02		22 19			22 32	22 44	23 02
Ebbsfleet International	a	←	20 12		20 30		20 42	20 54	←	21 12		21 30		21 42	21 54	22 12		22 30			22 42	22 54	23 12
	d		20 13		20 30		20 43	20 55		21 13		21 30		21 43	21 55	22 13		22 30			22 43	22 55	23 13
Gravesend 4	d	19 48	20 18				20 48		20 48	21 18				21 48		22 18					22 48		23 18
Strood 4	d	19 59	20 29				→		20 59	21 29				21 59		22 29					22 59		23 29
Maidstone West	d																						
Rochester 4	d	20 02	20 32						21 02	21 32				22 02		22 32					23 02		23 32
Chatham 4	d	20 06	20 36						21 06	21 36				22 06		22 36					23 06		23 36
Gillingham (Kent) 4	d	20 10	20 40						21 10	21 40				22 10		22 40					23 10		23 40
Rainham (Kent)	d	20 15	20 45						21 15	21 45				22 15		22 45					23 15		23 45
Sittingbourne 4	d	20 23	20 54						21 23	21 53				22 23		22 53					23 23		23 53
Faversham 2	a	20 31	21 05						21 31	22 01				22 31		23 01					23 31		00 01
Whitstable	d	20 40							21 40					22 40							23 40		
Herne Bay	d	20 45							21 45					22 45							23 45		
Birchington-on-Sea	d	20 54							21 54					22 54							23 54		
Margate 4	d	20 59							21 59					22 59							23 59		
Broadstairs	a	21 05							22 05					23 05							00 05		
Ramsgate	d	21 12							22 12					23a11						23 12	00a11		
Ashford International	a				20 50			21 14				21 50			22 14			22 50				23 14	
	d			20 32	20 52	21 02		21 15			21 32	21 52	22 02		22 15		22 34	22 52	23 04			23 15	
Folkestone West	d					21 19		21 28					22 19		22 28				23 21			23 28	
Folkestone Central	d					21 22		21 30					22 22		22 30				23 24			23 30	
Dover Priory 4	d					21a33		21 42					22a33		22 42				23a35			23 42	
Deal	a							21 59							22 59							23 58	
Sandwich	a	21 24						22 06	22 24						23 06					23 24		00 06	
Dover Priory	a	21 47							22 47											23 47			
Canterbury West 4	a			20 53	21 08						21 53	22 08					22 55	23 08					
	d			20 54	21 09						21 54	22 09					22 56	23 09					
Ramsgate 4	d			21a16	21 28			22a19			22a16	22 28			23a21		23a18	23 29				00a21	
Broadstairs	d				21 33							22 33						23 35					
Margate 4	a				21 39							22 39						23 40					

A From St Pancras International to Dover Priory continues to St Pancras International
B From London Charing Cross
C To St Pancras International
D To Ashford International

Table T194-F

Saturdays
26 May to 8 December

St Pancras International - Kent High Speed Domestic Services

		SE ◇1 A	SE ◇	SE ◇	SE ◇	SE ◇
St Pancras International 15 ⊖	d		23 12	23 25	23 37	23 55
Stratford International ⊖	d		23 19	23 32	23 44	00 02
Ebbsfleet International	a		23 30	23 42	23 54	00 12
	d		23 30	23 43	23 55	00 13
Gravesend 4	d			23 48		00 18
Strood 4	d			23 59		00 29
Maidstone West	d					
Rochester 4	d			00 02		00 32
Chatham 4	d			00 06		00 36
Gillingham (Kent) 4	d			00 10		00 40
Rainham (Kent)	d			00 15		00 45
Sittingbourne 4	d			00 23		00 53
Faversham 2	a			00 31		01 01
Whitstable	d					
Herne Bay	d					
Birchington-on-Sea	d					
Margate 4	d					
Broadstairs	a					
Ramsgate	d					
Ashford International	a		23 50		00 14	
	d	23 34	23 52		00 15	
Folkestone West	d				00 28	
Folkestone Central	d				00 30	
Dover Priory 4	d				00 42	
Deal	a				00s59	
Sandwich	a				01s06	
Dover Priory	a					
Canterbury West 4	a	23 55	00 08			
	d	23 56	00 09			
Ramsgate 4	d	00a18	00 28		01a23	
Broadstairs	d		00s33			
Margate 4	a		00 39			

Sundays
20 May to 2 December

		SE ◇ B	SE ◇ B	SE ◇1 C	SE ◇ B	SE ◇ B	SE ◇1 C	SE ◇	SE ◇1 C	SE ◇ D	SE 1	SE ◇ D	SE ◇ D	SE 1	SE 1 E	SE ◇ D	SE ◇ D	SE ◇ D	SE ◇ F	SE ◇1 A	SE ◇	SE ◇1 A	SE ◇ D
St Pancras International 15 ⊖	d							00 12									08 25	08 37			09 09		09 25
Stratford International ⊖	d		00 02					00 19									08 32	08 44			09 16		09 32
Ebbsfleet International	a		00 12					00 30									08 42	08 54	←		09 27		09 43
	d		00 13					00 30									08 43	08 55			09 27		09 44
Gravesend 4	d		00 18														08 48		08 48				09 48
Strood 4	d		00 29														→		08 59				→
Maidstone West	d																						
Rochester 4	d	00 02	00 32																09 02				
Chatham 4	d	00 06	00 36																09 06				
Gillingham (Kent) 4	d	00 10	00 40																09 10				
Rainham (Kent)	d	00 15	00 45																09 15				
Sittingbourne 4	d	00 23	00 53																09 23				
Faversham 2	a	00 31	01 01																09 31				
Whitstable	d																		09 40				
Herne Bay	d																		09 45				
Birchington-on-Sea	d																		09 54				
Margate 4	d																		09 59				
Broadstairs	a																		10 05				
Ramsgate	d									07 12		08 12				09 12			10 12				
Ashford International	a							00 50										09 14			09 47		
	d			00 04		00 15	00 34		01 05		08 08		08 15	08 32	09 05			09 15		09 32	09 52	10 05	
Folkestone West	d			00 21		00 28			01s22				08 28		09 21			09 28				10 21	
Folkestone Central	d			00 24		00 30			01s24				08 30		09 24			09 30				10 24	
Dover Priory 4	d			00a35		00 42			01a38				08 42		09a35			09 42				10a35	
Deal	a					00s59							08 59					09 59					
Sandwich	a					01s06				07 24		08 24	09 06			09 24		10 06	10 24				
Dover Priory	a									07 47		08 47				09 47			10 47				
Canterbury West 4	a						00 55				08 30			08 50						09 50	10 08		
	d				00 09		00 56							08 51						09 51	10 09		
Ramsgate 4	d				00 28	01a23	01a20						09 20	09a15				10 20		10a15	10 28		
Broadstairs	d				00s33								09 25					10 25			10 33		
Margate 4	a				00 39								09 29					10 29			10 39		

A From London Charing Cross
B not 20 May. From St Pancras International
C not 20 May. From London Charing Cross
D To St Pancras International
E From Tonbridge
F From St Pancras International to Dover Priory continues to St Pancras International

Table T194-F

Sundays

20 May to 2 December

St Pancras International - Kent High Speed Domestic Services

	SE	SE	SE	SE	SE	SE	SE	SE	SE	SE	SE	SE	SE	SE	SE	SE	SE	SE	SE	SE	SE	SE
	◇	◇	◇■1	◇	◇■1	◇	◇	◇	◇■1	◇	◇■1	◇	◇	◇	◇■1	◇	◇■1	◇	◇	◇	◇	◇■1
	A	B	C		C	A	A	B	C		C	A	A	B	C		C	A	A	B	A	C
St Pancras International ⊖ d	09 37			10 08		10 27	10 37			11 12		11 25	11 37			12 12		12 27	12 37		12 52	
Stratford International ⊖ d	09 44			10 15		10 34	10 44			11 19		11 32	11 44			12 19		12 34	12 44		12 59	
Ebbsfleet International a	09 54	←		10 26		10 44	10 54	←		11 30		11 42	11 54	←		12 30		12 44	12 54	←	13 09	
d	09 55			10 26		10 45	10 55			11 30		11 43	11 55			12 30		12 45	12 55		13 13	
Gravesend d		09 48				10 49		10 49				11 48		11 48				12 49		12 49	13 18	
Strood d		09 59				→		10 59				→		11 59				→		12 59	13 29	
Maidstone West d																						
Rochester d		10 02						11 03						12 02						13 03	13 32	
Chatham d		10 06						11 06						12 06						13 06	13 36	
Gillingham (Kent) d		10 10						11 11						12 10						13 11	13 40	
Rainham (Kent) d		10 15						11 15						12 15						13 15	13 45	
Sittingbourne d		10 23						11 23						12 23						13 23	13 53	
Faversham a		10 31						11 31						12 31						13 31	14 02	
Whitstable d		10 40						11 40						12 40						13 40		
Herne Bay d		10 45						11 45						12 45						13 45		
Birchington-on-Sea d		10 54						11 54						12 54						13 54		
Margate d		10 59						11 59						12 59						13 59		
Broadstairs a		11 05						12 05						13 05						14 05		
Ramsgate d		11 12						12 12						13 12						14 12		
Ashford International a	10 14			10 46			11 14			11 50			12 14			12 50			13 14			
d	10 15		10 32	10 52	11 05		11 15		11 32	11 52	12 05		12 15		12 32	12 52	13 05		13 15			13 32
Folkestone West d	10 28				11 21		11 28				12 21		12 28				13 21		13 28			
Folkestone Central d	10 30				11 24		11 30				12 24		12 30				13 24		13 30			
Dover Priory d	10 42				11a35		11 42				12a35		12 42				13a35		13 42			
Deal a	10 59						11 59						12 59						13 59			
Sandwich a	11 06	11 24					12 06	12 24					13 06	13 24					14 06	14 24		
Dover Priory a		11 47						12 47						13 47						14 47		
Canterbury West a			10 50	11 08					11 50	12 08					12 50	13 08						13 50
d			10 51	11 09					11 51	12 09					12 51	13 09						13 51
Ramsgate d	11 20		11a15	11 28			12 20		12a15	12 28			13 20		13a15	13 28			14 20			14a15
Broadstairs d	11 25			11 33			12 25			12 33			13 25			13 33			14 25			
Margate a	11 29			11 39			12 29			12 39			13 29			13 39			14 29			

	SE	SE	SE	SE	SE	SE	SE	SE	SE	SE	SE	SE	SE	SE	SE	SE	SE	SE	SE	SE	SE	SE
	◇	◇■1	◇	◇	◇	◇	◇■1	◇	◇■1	◇	◇	◇	◇	◇■1	◇	◇■1	◇	◇	◇	◇	◇■1	◇
		C	A	A	B	A	C		C	A	A	B	A	C		C	A	A	B		C	
St Pancras International ⊖ d	13 12		13 25	13 37		13 55		14 09		14 25	14 37		14 55		15 12		15 25	15 37		15 55		16 12
Stratford International ⊖ d	13 19		13 32	13 44		14 02		14 16		14 32	14 44		15 02		15 19		15 32	15 44		16 02		16 19
Ebbsfleet International a	13 30		13 42	13 54	←	14 12		14 27		14 42	14 54	←	15 12		15 30		15 42	15 54	←	16 12		16 30
d	13 30		13 43	13 55		14 13		14 27		14 43	14 55		15 13		15 30		15 43	15 55		16 13		16 31
Gravesend d			13 48		13 48	14 18				14 48		14 48	15 18				15 48		15 48	16 18		
Strood d			→		13 59	14 29				→		14 59	15 29				→		15 59	16 29		
Maidstone West d																						
Rochester d					14 02	14 32						15 02	15 32						16 02	16 32		
Chatham d					14 06	14 36						15 06	15 36						16 06	16 36		
Gillingham (Kent) d					14 10	14 40						15 10	15 40						16 10	16 40		
Rainham (Kent) d					14 15	14 45						15 15	15 45						16 15	16 45		
Sittingbourne d					14 23	14 53						15 23	15 53						16 23	16 53		
Faversham a					14 31	15 02						15 31	16 02						16 31	17 02		
Whitstable d					14 40							15 40							16 40			
Herne Bay d					14 45							15 45							16 45			
Birchington-on-Sea d					14 54							15 54							16 54			
Margate d					14 59							15 59							16 59			
Broadstairs a					15 05							16 05							17 05			
Ramsgate d					15 12							16 12							17 12			
Ashford International a	13 50			14 14				14 47			15 14				15 50			16 14				16 50
d	13 52	14 05		14 15			14 32	14 52	15 07		15 15			15 32	15 52	16 05		16 15			16 32	16 52
Folkestone West d		14 21		14 28					15 23		15 28					16 21		16 28				
Folkestone Central d		14 24		14 30					15 26		15 30					16 24		16 30				
Dover Priory d		14a35		14 42					15a37		15 42					16a35		16 42				
Deal a				14 59							15 59							16 59				
Sandwich a				15 06	15 24						16 06	16 24						17 06	17 24			
Dover Priory a					15 47							16 47							17 47			
Canterbury West a	14 08						14 50	15 08						15 50	16 08						16 50	17 08
d	14 09						14 51	15 09						15 51	16 09						16 51	17 09
Ramsgate d	14 28			15 20			15a15	15 28			16 20			16a15	16 28			17 20			17a15	17 28
Broadstairs d	14 33			15 25				15 33			16 25				16 33			17 25				17 33
Margate a	14 39			15 29				15 39			16 29				16 39			17 29				17 39

A To St Pancras International
B From St Pancras International to Dover Priory continues to St Pancras International
C From London Charing Cross

Table T194-F

Sundays

20 May to 2 December

St Pancras International - Kent High Speed Domestic Services

	SE	SE	SE	SE	SE	SE	SE	SE	SE	SE	SE	SE	SE	SE	SE	SE	SE	SE	SE	SE	SE	SE
	◇■1	◇	◇	◇	◇	◇■1	◇	◇■1	◇	◇	◇	◇	◇■1	◇	◇■1	◇	◇	◇	◇	◇■1	◇	◇■1
	A	B	B	C	B	A		A	B	B	C	B	A		A	B	B	C		A		A
St Pancras International ⊖ d		16 25	16 37		16 55		17 12		17 25	17 37		17 52		18 12		18 25	18 37		18 55		19 12	
Stratford International ⊖ d		16 32	16 44		17 02		17 19		17 32	17 44		18 02		18 19		18 32	18 44		19 02		19 19	
Ebbsfleet International a		16 42	16 54	←	17 12		17 30		17 42	17 54	←	18 13		18 30		18 42	18 54	←	19 12		19 30	
d		16 43	16 55		17 13		17 30		17 43	17 55		18 13		18 30		18 43	18 55		19 13		19 30	
Gravesend d		16 48		16 48	17 18				17 48		17 48	18 18				18 48		18 48	19 18			
Strood d		→		16 59	17 29				→		17 59	18 29				→		18 59	19 29			
Maidstone West d																						
Rochester d				17 02	17 32						18 02	18 32						19 02	19 32			
Chatham d				17 06	17 36						18 06	18 36						19 06	19 36			
Gillingham (Kent) d				17 10	17 40						18 10	18 40						19 10	19 40			
Rainham (Kent) d				17 15	17 45						18 15	18 45						19 15	19 45			
Sittingbourne d				17 23	17 53						18 23	18 53						19 23	19 53			
Faversham a				17 31	18 02						18 31	19 02						19 31	20 02			
Whitstable d				17 40							18 40							19 40				
Herne Bay d				17 45							18 45							19 45				
Birchington-on-Sea d				17 54							18 54							19 54				
Margate d				17 59							18 59							19 59				
Broadstairs a				18 05							19 05							20 05				
Ramsgate d				18 12							19 12							20 12				
Ashford International a			17 14				17 50			18 14				18 50			19 14				19 50	
d	17 05		17 15			17 32	17 52	18 05		18 15			18 32	18 52	19 05		19 15			19 32	19 52	20 05
Folkestone West d	17 21		17 28					18 21		18 28					19 21		19 28					20 21
Folkestone Central d	17 24		17 30					18 24		18 30					19 24		19 30					20 24
Dover Priory d	17a35		17 42					18a35		18 42					19a35		19 42					20a35
Deal a			17 59							18 59							19 59					
Sandwich a			18 06	18 24						19 06	19 24						20 06	20 24				
Dover Priory a				18 47							19 47							20 47				
Canterbury West a						17 50	18 08						18 53	19 08						19 53	20 08	
d						17 51	18 09						18 54	19 09						19 54	20 09	
Ramsgate d			18 20			18a15	18 28			19 20			19a15	19 28			20 20			20a15	20 28	
Broadstairs d			18 25				18 33			19 25				19 33			20 25				20 33	
Margate a			18 29				18 39			19 29				19 39			20 29				20 39	

	SE	SE	SE	SE	SE	SE	SE	SE	SE	SE	SE	SE	SE	SE	SE	SE	SE	SE	SE	SE	SE	SE
	◇	◇	◇	◇	◇■1	◇	◇■1	◇	◇	◇	◇	◇■1	◇	◇■1	◇	◇	◇	◇■1	◇	◇■1	◇	◇
	B	B	C	B	A		A	D		E		A		A				A		A		
St Pancras International ⊖ d	19 25	19 37		19 55		20 12		20 25	20 37		20 55		21 12		21 25	21 37	21 55		22 12		22 25	22 37
Stratford International ⊖ d	19 32	19 44		20 02		20 19		20 32	20 44		21 02		21 19		21 32	21 44	22 02		22 19		22 32	22 44
Ebbsfleet International a	19 42	19 54	←	20 12		20 30		20 42	20 54	←	21 12		21 30		21 42	21 54	22 12		22 30		22 42	22 54
d	19 43	19 55		20 13		20 30		20 43	20 55		21 13		21 30		21 43	21 55	22 13		22 30		22 43	22 55
Gravesend d	19 48		19 48	20 18				20 48		20 48	21 18				21 48		22 18				22 48	
Strood d	→		19 59	20 29				→		20 59	21 29				21 59		22 29				22 59	
Maidstone West d																						
Rochester d			20 02	20 32						21 02	21 32				22 02		22 32				23 02	
Chatham d			20 06	20 36						21 06	21 36				22 06		22 36				23 06	
Gillingham (Kent) d			20 10	20 40						21 10	21 40				22 10		22 40				23 10	
Rainham (Kent) d			20 15	20 45						21 15	21 45				22 15		22 45				23 15	
Sittingbourne d			20 23	20 53						21 23	21 53				22 23		22 53				23 23	
Faversham a			20 31	21 02						21 31	22 02				22 31		23 02				23 31	
Whitstable d			20 40							21 40					22 40						23 40	
Herne Bay d			20 45							21 45					22 45						23 45	
Birchington-on-Sea d			20 54							21 54					22 54						23 54	
Margate d			20 59							21 59					22 59						23 59	
Broadstairs a			21 05							22 05					23 05						00 05	
Ramsgate d			21 12							22 12					23a11						00a11	
Ashford International a		20 14				20 50			21 14				21 50			22 14			22 50			23 14
d		20 15			20 32	20 52	21 05		21 15			21 32	21 52	22 05		22 15		22 32	22 52	23 05		23 15
Folkestone West d		20 28					21 21		21 28					22 21		22 28				23 21		23 28
Folkestone Central d		20 30					21 24		21 30					22 24		22 30				23 24		23 30
Dover Priory d		20 42					21a35		21 42					22a35		22 42				23a35		23 42
Deal a		20 59							21 59							22 59						23 58
Sandwich a		21 06	21 24						22 06	22 24						23 06						00 06
Dover Priory a			21 47							22 47												
Canterbury West a					20 53	21 08						21 53	22 08					22 53	23 08			
d					20 54	21 09						21 54	22 09					22 54	23 09			
Ramsgate d		21 20			21a15	21 28			22a18			22a15	22 28			23a18		23a15	23 28			00a18
Broadstairs d		21 25				21 33							22 33						23 33			
Margate a		21 29				21 39							22 39						23 39			

A From London Charing Cross
B To St Pancras International
C From St Pancras International to Dover Priory continues to St Pancras International
D To Ashford International
E From St Pancras International to Ashford International

Table T194-F

Sundays
20 May to 2 December

St Pancras International - Kent High Speed Domestic Services

		SE	SE	SE	SE	SE
		◇	◇■	◇	◇	◇
			A			
St Pancras International ■ ⊖	d	22 55		23 12	23 25	23 37
Stratford International ⊖	d	23 02		23 19	23 32	23 44
Ebbsfleet International	a	23 12		23 30	23 42	23 54
	d	23 13		23 30	23 43	23 55
Gravesend ■	d	23 18			23 48	
Strood ■	d	23 29			23 59	
Maidstone West	d					
Rochester ■	d	23 32			00 02	
Chatham ■	d	23 36			00 06	
Gillingham (Kent) ■	d	23 40			00 10	
Rainham (Kent)	d	23 45			00 15	
Sittingbourne ■	d	23 53			00 23	
Faversham ■	a	00 02			00 32	
Whitstable	d					
Herne Bay	d					
Birchington-on-Sea	d					
Margate ■	d					
Broadstairs	a					
Ramsgate	d					
Ashford International	a			23 50		00 15
	d		23 32	23 52		
Folkestone West	d					
Folkestone Central	d					
Dover Priory ■	d					
Deal	a					
Sandwich	a					
Dover Priory	a					
Canterbury West ■	a		23 53	00 08		
	d		23 54	00 09		
Ramsgate ■	d		00a15	00 28		
Broadstairs	d			00s33		
Margate ■	a			00 39		

A From London Charing Cross

Table T194-R

Mondays to Fridays
21 May to 7 December

Kent - St Pancras International High Speed Domestic Services

Miles	Miles	Miles	Miles			SE		SE	SE	SE	SE	SE	SE	SE	SE	SE	SE		SE	SE	SE	SE	SE	SE	SE
						MO		TTh FO	TTh FO	MO	ThFO	TO	TTh FO												
						◇		◇	◇■	◇■	◇	◇	◇■	◇■	◇	◇	◇■		◇■	◇	◇	◇■	◇■	◇	◇
—	—	—	—	St Pancras International	d																				
—	—	0	—	Margate ■	d			00 04	00 25	00 27			01 08											05 46	
—	—	3¼	—	Broadstairs	d	00 05		00 10	00 31	00 33			01 14											05 52	
—	—	5½	—	Ramsgate ■	d	00a11		00a17	00a38	00a40			01a21			04 55	04 51					05 38	05 20	05 58	
—	—	20¾	—	**Canterbury West**	a											05 17						06 00		06 17	
—	—	—	—		d											05 18						06 01		06 18	
—	—	—	—	Dover Priory	d																				
—	—	—	—	Sandwich	d												05 06						05 34		05 54
—	—	—	—	Deal	d												05 12						05 40		06 00
—	0	—	—	**Dover Priory**	d									04 30			05 29				05 45		05 59		06 18
—	7¼	—	—	Folkestone Central	d									04 42			05 41				05 56		06 10		06 29
—	8	—	—	Folkestone West	d									04 44			05 43				05 58		06 12		06 31
—	21¼	—	—	**Ashford International**	a									05 01		05 41	06 01				06 11	06 23	06 30	06 34	06 44
—	—	—	—		d											05 43					06 13			06 36	06 46
—	—	—	—	Ramsgate	d						00 31	00 44													
0	—	—	—	**Broadstairs**	d						00s36	00s49													
3¼	—	—	—	Margate ■	d						00a42	00a58													
6¼	—	—	—	Birchington-on-Sea	d																				
14¼	—	—	—	Herne Bay	d																				
18¼	—	—	—	Whitstable	d																				
25	—	—	—	**Faversham** ■	a																				
—	—	—	—		d										04 58					05 28					
32¾	—	—	—	Sittingbourne ■	d										05 07					05 37					
38½	—	—	—	Rainham (Kent)	d										05 15					05 45					
41½	—	—	—	Gillingham (Kent) ■	d										05 20				05 40	05 50					
43¼	—	—	—	Chatham ■	d										05 24				05 44	05 54					
43¾	—	—	—	Rochester ■	d										05 28				05a47	05 58					
—	—	—	0	Maidstone West	d																				
44¾	—	—	12¼	Strood ■	d										05 31					06 01					
52	—	—	19½	Gravesend	d										05 41					06 11					
54	54½	68¼	21½	**Ebbsfleet International**	a										05 45	06 02				06 15	06 32			06 55	07 05
—	—	—	—		d										05 46	06 02				06 16	06 32			06 55	07 06
70¾	71¼	85	38¼	**Stratford International** ⊖	a										05 57	06 14				06 27	06 44			07 07	07 17
76¾	77¼	91	44¼	**St Pancras International** ■ ⊖	a										06 05	06 21				06 35	06 51			07 14	07 25

		SE	SE	SE		SE	SE	SE	SE	SE	SE	SE	SE	SE	SE		SE	SE	SE	SE	SE	SE	SE	SE	SE
		◇■	◇■	◇■		◇	◇	◇■	◇	◇	◇	◇■	◇	◇	◇		◇	◇	◇	◇■	◇■	◇	◇	◇	■
St Pancras International	d																		07 04						
Margate ■	d						06 16						06 46									07 16		06 54	07 24
Broadstairs	d						06 22						06 52									07 22		07 00	07 30
Ramsgate ■	d		06 10				06 28			06 14			06 58							06 50	07 05	07 28		07 10	07a36
Canterbury West	a		06 33				06 47						07 17								07 31	07 47			
	d		06 34				06 48					07 03	07 18								07 36	07 48			
Dover Priory	d																								
Sandwich	d			06 05						06 26					06 50					07 02				07 22	
Deal	d			06 11						06 32					06 56					07 08				07 28	
Dover Priory	d			06 30						06 48					07 13					07 25				07 46	
Folkestone Central	d			06 42						06 59					07 24					07 36				07 57	
Folkestone West	d			06 44						07 01					07 27					07 38				07 59	
Ashford International	a		06 55	07 01			07 04			07 14		07 25	07 34		07 40				07 41	07 55	07 57	08 04		08 12	
	d						07 06			07 16			07 36		07 44				07 42			08 06		08 16	
Ramsgate	d																		08 25						
Broadstairs	d							06 23			06 29							06 58	08 30						
Margate ■	d							06 28			06 34							07 03	08a36						
Birchington-on-Sea	d							06 33			06 39							07 08							
Herne Bay	d							06 42			06 48							07 17							
Whitstable	d							06 48			06 53							07 23							
Faversham ■	a							06 56			07 01							07 31							
	d	06 07				06 28		06 57			07 02							07 31							
Sittingbourne ■	d	06 18				06 36		07 05			07 10							07 39							
Rainham (Kent)	d	06 28				06 44		07 12			07 17							07 47							
Gillingham (Kent) ■	d	06 33				06 49		07 17			07 22							07 52							
Chatham ■	d	06 37				06 53		07 22			07 27							07 56							
Rochester ■	d	06a40				06 57		07a25			07 30							08 00							
Maidstone West	d								06 53					07 25									07 53		
Strood ■	d								07 10		07 34			07 43				08 03					08 11		
Gravesend	d								07 21		07 44			07 53				08 14					08 21		
Ebbsfleet International	a					07 11			07 25	07 35	07 48			07 56				08 17					08 25	08 35	
	d					07 12			07 26	07 36	07 49			07 57			08 09	08 18					08 26	08 36	
Stratford International ⊖	a					07 24	07 34		07 39	07 47	08 00		08 04	08 09	08 12		08 20	08 30				08 34	08 39	08 47	
St Pancras International ■ ⊖	a					07 31	07 42		07 46	07 54	08 08		08 12	08 16	08 20		08 28	08 38				08 42	08 46	08 54	

Table T194-R

Mondays to Fridays

21 May to 7 December

Kent - St Pancras International High Speed Domestic Services

	SE		SE	SE	SE	SE	SE	SE	SE	SE	SE	SE		SE	SE	SE	SE	SE	SE	SE	SE	SE	SE	
	◇ 1		◇	◇	◇	◇ 1	◇ 1	◇	◇	◇ 1	1	1		◇	◇	◇	◇ 1	◇ 1	◇	◇	◇	◇	◇ 1	
St Pancras International d					08 12											09 09					07 22	07 37		
Margate d				07 48							07 55	08 24			08 51						08 59		09 33	
Broadstairs d				07 54							08 01	08 30			08 57						09 05		09 39	
Ramsgate d				08 01		07 42	08 14			08 05	08a07	08a36			09 03			09 15		09 35	09 12		09a45	
Canterbury West a				08 24			08 35								09 22			09 37		09 54				
d				08 25			08 36								09 23			09 38		09 54				
Dover Priory d																						08 44		
Sandwich d						08 02				08 30											09 25	09 08		
Deal d						08 08				08 36											09 31			
Dover Priory d	07 58					08 25			08 49	08 58							09 25				09 49			
Folkestone Central d	08 09					08 36			09 00	09 09							09 36				10 00			
Folkestone West d	08 11					08 38			09 02	09 11							09 38				10 02			
Ashford International a	08 28			08 41	08 50	08 55	08 58		09 15	09 28					09 39	09 47	09 55	09 58		10 10	10 15			
d				08 43	08 52				09 16						09 43	09 52				10 11	10 16			
Ramsgate d					09 31											10 28						09 20		
Broadstairs d					09 36											10 33						09 25		
Margate d					09a42											10a39						09 30		
Birchington-on-Sea d																						09 35		
Herne Bay d																						09 44		
Whitstable d																						09 49		
Faversham a																						09 57		
d			07 59					08 28						08 59					09 30			09 58		
Sittingbourne d			08 07					08 38						09 08					09 38			10 08		
Rainham (Kent) d			08 14					08 46						09 16					09 46			10 16		
Gillingham (Kent) d			08 19					08 51						09 21					09 51			10 21		
Chatham d			08 24					08 55						09 25					09 55			10 25		
Rochester d			08 27					08 59						09 29					09 59			10 29		
Maidstone West d																								
Strood d			08 32					09 02						09 32					10 02			10 32		
Gravesend d			08 43					09 12						09 42					10 12			10 42		
Ebbsfleet International a			08 46	09 02				09 16	09 35					09 46	10 02				10 16		10 35	10 46		
d			08 48	09 02				09 17	09 35					09 48	10 02				10 16		10 35	10 48		
Stratford International ⊖ a			08 59	09 14				09 28	09 47					09 59	10 14				10 28	10 39	10 47	10 59		
St Pancras International ⊖ a			09 07	09 21				09 36	09 54					10 06	10 21				10 35	10 47	10 55	11 07		

	SE	SE	SE	SE	SE	SE	SE	SE	SE	SE		SE	SE	SE	SE	SE	SE	SE	SE	SE	SE		SE	SE
	◇ 1	◇	◇	◇ 1	◇	◇	◇	◇ 1	◇ 1	◇		◇	◇ 1	◇	◇	◇	◇ 1	◇ 1	◇	◇	◇ 1		◇	◇
St Pancras International d			10 08			08 25	08 37					11 12			09 25	09 37				12 12				10 27
Margate d		09 53				09 59		10 25		10 53					10 59		11 25		11 53					11 59
Broadstairs d		09 59				10 05		10 31		10 59					11 05		11 31		11 59					12 05
Ramsgate d		10 05		10 19		10 12		10a38		11 05			11 19		11 12		11a38		12 05		12 19			12 12
Canterbury West a		10 24		10 41						11 24			11 41						12 24		12 41			
d		10 25		10 42						11 25			11 42						12 25		12 42			
Dover Priory d							09 43									10 42								
Sandwich d						10 25	10 07								11 25	11 06								12 25
Deal d						10 31									11 31									12 31
Dover Priory d	09 58					10 49			10 58						11 49			11 58						12 49
Folkestone Central d	10 09					11 00			11 09						12 00			12 09						13 00
Folkestone West d	10 11					11 02			11 11						12 02			12 11						13 02
Ashford International a	10 28	10 41	10 46	11 00		11 15			11 28	11 41		11 50	12 00		12 15			12 28	12 41	12 50	13 00			13 15
d		10 43	10 52			11 16				11 43		11 52			12 16				12 43	12 52				13 16
Ramsgate d			11 28				10 20					12 28				11 20				13 28				
Broadstairs d			11 33				10 25					12 33				11 25				13 33				
Margate d			11a39				10 30					12a39				11 30				13a39				
Birchington-on-Sea d							10 35									11 35								
Herne Bay d							10 44									11 44								
Whitstable d							10 49									11 49								
Faversham a							10 57									11 57								
d					10 30		10 58							11 30		11 58							12 30	
Sittingbourne d					10 38		11 08							11 38		12 08							12 38	
Rainham (Kent) d					10 46		11 16							11 46		12 16							12 46	
Gillingham (Kent) d					10 51		11 21							11 51		12 21							12 51	
Chatham d					10 55		11 25							11 55		12 25							12 55	
Rochester d					10 59		11 29							11 59		12 29							12 59	
Maidstone West d																								
Strood d					11 02		11 32							12 02		12 32							13 02	
Gravesend d					11 12		11 42							12 12		12 42							13 12	
Ebbsfleet International a		11 02			11 16	11 35	11 46			12 02				12 16	12 35	12 46			13 02				13 16	13 35
d		11 02			11 18	11 36	11 47			12 02				12 17	12 35	12 47			13 02				13 18	13 35
Stratford International ⊖ a		11 14			11 29	11 47	11 58			12 14				12 28	12 47	12 58			13 14				13 29	13 47
St Pancras International ⊖ a		11 21			11 40	11 54	12 05			12 21				12 36	12 55	13 06			13 21				13 37	13 54

Table T194-R

Mondays to Fridays

21 May to 7 December

Kent - St Pancras International High Speed Domestic Services

	SE	SE	SE	SE	SE	SE	SE	SE		SE	SE	SE	SE	SE	SE	SE	SE	SE	SE		SE	SE	SE	SE
	◇	◇ 1	◇ 1	◇	◇	◇ 1	◇	◇		◇	◇ 1	◇ 1	◇	◇	◇ 1	◇	◇	◇	◇ 1		◇ 1	◇	◇	◇ 1
St Pancras International d	10 37				13 12			11 25		11 37				14 09			12 27	12 37					15 12	
Margate d		12 25		12 53				12 59			13 25		13 53				13 59		14 25			14 53		
Broadstairs d		12 31		12 59				13 05			13 31		13 59				14 05		14 31			14 59		
Ramsgate d		12a38		13 05		13 19		13 12			13a38		14 05		14 19		14 12		14a38			15 05		15 17
Canterbury West a				13 24		13 41							14 24		14 41							15 24		15 39
d				13 25		13 42							14 25		14 42							15 25		15 42
Dover Priory d	11 42									12 42								13 42						
Sandwich d	12 06							13 25		13 06							14 25	14 06						
Deal d								13 31									14 31							
Dover Priory d			12 58					13 49				13 58					14 49				14 58			
Folkestone Central d			13 09					14 00				14 09					15 00				15 09			
Folkestone West d			13 11					14 02				14 11					15 02				15 11			
Ashford International a			13 28	13 41	13 50	14 00		14 15				14 28	14 41	14 47	15 00		15 15				15 28	15 41	15 50	16 00
d				13 43	13 52			14 16					14 43	14 52			15 16					15 43	15 52	
Ramsgate d	12 20				14 28					13 20				15 28				14 20					16 28	
Broadstairs d	12 25				14 33					13 25				15 33				14 25					16 33	
Margate d	12 30				14a39					13 30				15a39				14 30					16a39	
Birchington-on-Sea d	12 35									13 35								14 35						
Herne Bay d	12 44									13 44								14 44						
Whitstable d	12 49									13 49								14 49						
Faversham a	12 57									13 57								14 57						
d	12 58						13 30			13 58						14 30		14 58						
Sittingbourne d	13 08						13 38			14 08						14 38		15 08						
Rainham (Kent) d	13 16						13 46			14 16						14 46		15 16						
Gillingham (Kent) d	13 21						13 51			14 21						14 51		15 21						
Chatham d	13 25						13 55			14 25						14 55		15 25						
Rochester d	13 29						13 59			14 29						14 59		15 29						
Maidstone West d																								
Strood d	13 32						14 02			14 32						15 02		15 32						
Gravesend d	13 42						14 12			14 42						15 12		15 42						
Ebbsfleet International a	13 46			14 02			14 16	14 35		14 46			15 02			15 16	15 35	15 46				16 02		
d	13 51			14 02			14 17	14 35		14 47			15 02			15 17	15 35	15 51				16 02		
Stratford International ⊖ a	14 02			14 14			14 28	14 47		14 58			15 14			15 28	15 47	16 02				16 14		
St Pancras International ⊖ a	14 10			14 21			14 36	14 54		15 06			15 21			15 36	15 54	16 10				16 21		

	SE	SE	SE	SE	SE	SE		SE	SE	SE	SE	SE	SE	SE	SE	SE	SE		SE	SE	SE	SE	SE	SE
	◇	◇	◇	◇ 1	◇ 1	◇		◇	◇ 1	◇ 1	◇	◇	◇	◇ 1	◇ 1	◇	◇ 1		◇ 1	◇	◇	◇	◇	◇
St Pancras International d		13 25	13 37					16 12				14 25	14 37								15 25	15 37	16 50	17 20
Margate d		14 59			15 25	15 53						16 02		16 28		16 53					17 02			
Broadstairs d		15 05			15 31	15 59						16 08		16 34		16 59					17 08			
Ramsgate d		15 12		15 21	15a38	16 05			15 50	16 18		16 13		16a40		17 05	16 50		17 18		17 13			
Canterbury West a						16 24				16 40						17 24			17 39				17 41	18 11
d						16 25				16 41						17 25			17 40				17 42	18 12
Dover Priory d			14 42										15 42									16 42		
Sandwich d		15 25	15 06	15 34					16 02			16 26	16 06				17 02				17 26	17 06		
Deal d		15 31		15 41					16 08			16 32					17 08				17 32			
Dover Priory d		15 49		15 58					16 25			16 49			16 58		17 25				17 49			
Folkestone Central d		16 00		16 09					16 36			17 00			17 09		17 36				18 00			
Folkestone West d		16 02		16 11					16 38			17 02			17 11		17 38				18 02			
Ashford International a		16 15		16 28		16 41		16 50	16 55	16 59		17 15			17 28	17 41	17 55		17 58		18 15			
d		16 16				16 45		16 52				17 16				17 43					18 16			
Ramsgate d			15 20					17 32					16 20									17 20	18 02	18 32
Broadstairs d			15 25					17 37					16 25									17 25	18 07	18 37
Margate d			15 30					17a42					16 30									17 30	18a15	18a45
Birchington-on-Sea d			15 35										16 35									17 35		
Herne Bay d			15 44										16 44									17 44		
Whitstable d			15 49										16 49									17 49		
Faversham a			15 57										16 57									17 57		
d	15 28		15 58								16 25		16 58							17 28		17 58		
Sittingbourne d	15 38		16 08								16 37		17 08							17 38		18 08		
Rainham (Kent) d	15 46		16 16								16 46		17 16							17 46		18 16		
Gillingham (Kent) d	15 51		16 21								16 51		17 21							17 51		18 21		
Chatham d	15 55		16 25								16 55		17 25							17 55		18 25		
Rochester d	15 59		16 29								16 59		17 29							17 59		18 29		
Maidstone West d																								
Strood d	16 02		16 32								17 02		17 32							18 03		18 35		
Gravesend d	16 12		16 42								17 12		17 42							18 13		18 45		
Ebbsfleet International a	16 16	16 35	16 46			17 04					17 16	17 35	17 46			18 02				18 17	18 35	18 49		
d	16 17	16 35	16 48			17 04					17 17	17 35	17 47			18 02				18 18	18 35	18 51		
Stratford International ⊖ a	16 28	16 47	17 00			17 16					17 28	17 47	17 58			18 14				18 29	18 47	19 02		
St Pancras International ⊖ a	16 36	16 54	17 10			17 23					17 36	17 54	18 10			18 23				18 37	18 54	19 10		

Table T194-R

Mondays to Fridays

21 May to 7 December

Kent - St Pancras International High Speed Domestic Services

		SE	SE	SE	SE	SE	SE	SE	SE	SE	SE	SE	SE	SE	SE	SE	SE	SE	SE	SE	SE	SE	SE
		◇[1]	◇[1]	◇[1]	◇	◇	◇	◇[1]	◇	◇	◇	◇[1]	◇[1]	◇	◇	◇	◇	◇	◇[1]	◇	◇[1]	◇	◇
St Pancras International	d				17 25	17 37	17 50			17 55	18 20			18 25				18 50					
Margate [4]	d	17 32	18 08	18 26	18 58				17 53	19 36				20 02						18 53			
Broadstairs	d	17 38	18 14	18 32	19 04				17 59	19a45				20a10						18 59			
Ramsgate [4]	d	17a46	18a22	18a41	19a13				18 05			17 50	18 10						18 23	19 05	19 16		
Canterbury West	a								18 24				18 35							19 24	19 38		
	d								18 25				18 36							19 25	19 39		
Dover Priory	d					18 46																	
Sandwich	d					19 11						18 02							18 35				
Deal	d											18 08							18 41				
Dover Priory	d							17 58				18 25					18 49		18 58				19 49
Folkestone Central	d							18 09				18 36					19 00		19 09				20 00
Folkestone West	d							18 11				18 38					19 02		19 11				20 02
Ashford International	a						18 24	18 28	18 41		18 54	18 55	18 58				19 15	19 25	19 28	19 41	20 00		20 15
	d						18 26		18 43		18 56						19 16	19 27		19 43			20 16
Ramsgate	d					19a25	19 02				19 32							20 03					
Broadstairs	d						19 07				19 37							20 08					
Margate [4]	d						19a15				19a45							20a16					
Birchington-on-Sea	d																						
Herne Bay	d																						
Whitstable	d																						
Faversham [2]	a																						
	d															18 28						19 30	
Sittingbourne [4]	d															18 38						19 38	
Rainham (Kent)	d															18 46						19 46	
Gillingham (Kent) [4]	d															18 51						19 51	
Chatham [4]	d															18 55						19 55	
Rochester [4]	d															18 59						19 59	
Maidstone West	d														18 42								
Strood [4]	d														18 58	19 02						20 02	
Gravesend	d														19 08	19 12						20 12	
Ebbsfleet International	a								19 02						19 12	19 16	19 35			20 02		20 16	20 35
	d								19 02						19 13	19 17	19 35			20 02		20 17	20 35
Stratford International ⊖	a								19 14						19 24	19 28	19 47			20 14		20 28	20 47
St Pancras International [4] ⊖	a								19 21						19 31	19 36	19 54			20 21		20 36	20 54

		SE	SE	SE	SE	SE	SE	SE	SE	SE	SE	SE	SE	SE	SE	SE	SE	SE	SE	SE	SE	SE	SE
		◇	◇	◇[1]	◇[1]	◇[1]	◇	◇[1]	◇	◇[1]	◇	◇	◇[1]	◇	◇	◇[1]	◇	◇	◇[1]	◇	◇	◇	◇[1]
St Pancras International	d		19 20								19 25	20 12						21 12				19 37	
Margate [4]	d				19 26	19 30	19 53	19 57		20 33	21 04						20 53				21 00		21 28
Broadstairs	d				19 32	19a39	19 59	20 03		20 39	21 10						20 59				21 06		21 34
Ramsgate [4]	d			19 23	19a39		20 05	20a12		20a48	21a17		20 16			20 23	21 05		21 16		21 12		21a42
Canterbury West	a		20 11				20 24						20 38				21 24		21 38				
	d		20 12				20 25						20 39				21 25		21 39				
Dover Priory	d																					20 42	
Sandwich	d			19 35												20 35					21 25	21 06	
Deal	d			19 41												20 41					21 31		
Dover Priory	d			19 58										20 49		20 58					21 49		
Folkestone Central	d			20 09										21 00		21 09					22 00		
Folkestone West	d			20 11										21 02		21 11					22 02		
Ashford International	a			20 28			20 41					20 50	21 00	21 15		21 28	21 41	21 50	22 00		22 15		
	d						20 43					20 52		21 16			21 43	21 52			22 16		
Ramsgate	d	19 20	20 32									21 32			20 20			22 28				21 20	
Broadstairs	d	19 25	20 37									21 38			20 25			22 33				21 25	
Margate [4]	d	19 30	20a45									21a43			20 30			22a39				21 30	
Birchington-on-Sea	d	19 35													20 35							21 35	
Herne Bay	d	19 44													20 44							21 44	
Whitstable	d	19 49													20 49							21 49	
Faversham [2]	a	19 57													20 57							21 57	
	d	19 58							20 30						20 58					21 30		21 58	
Sittingbourne [4]	d	20 08							20 38						21 08					21 38		22 08	
Rainham (Kent)	d	20 16							20 46						21 16					21 46		22 16	
Gillingham (Kent) [4]	d	20 21							20 51						21 21					21 51		22 21	
Chatham [4]	d	20 25							20 55						21 25					21 55		22 25	
Rochester [4]	d	20 29							20 59						21 29					21 59		22 29	
Maidstone West	d																						
Strood [4]	d	20 32							21 02						21 32					22 02		22 32	
Gravesend	d	20 42							21 12						21 42					22 12		22 42	
Ebbsfleet International	a	20 46					21 02		21 16					21 35	21 46		22 02			22 16	22 35	22 46	
	d	20 51					21 02		21 21					21 35	21 47		22 02			22 17	22 35	22 47	
Stratford International ⊖	a	21 02					21 14		21 32					21 47	21 58		22 14			22 28	22 47	22 58	
St Pancras International [4] ⊖	a	21 10					21 21		21 39					21 54	22 06		22 21			22 36	22 54	23 06	

Table T194-R

Mondays to Fridays

21 May to 7 December

Kent - St Pancras International High Speed Domestic Services

		SE	SE	SE	SE	SE	SE	SE	SE	SE	SE	SE	SE	SE	SE	SE	SE	SE	SE	SE
									TX					TX		TO	WTh FO	MO		
		◇[1]	◇	◇	◇	◇[1]	◇	◇	◇	[1]	◇		◇[1]	◇	◇	◇	◇	◇	[1]	◇
St Pancras International	d			20 25	20 37		21 25	21 37	22 12					22 25	22 37	23 12	23 12	23 12		23 37
Margate [4]	d		21 53	22 04		22 25	23 04					22 53	23 25	00 04						
Broadstairs	d		21 59	22 10		22 31	23 10					22 59	23 31	00 10						
Ramsgate [4]	d		22 05	22a17		22a38	23a17			22 16	22 12	23 05	23a38	00a17					23 12	
Canterbury West	a		22 24							22 38		23 24				00 08				
	d		22 25							22 39		23 25				00 09				
Dover Priory	d				21 42			22 42							23 44					00 42
Sandwich	d				22 06			23 06			22 25				00 08				23 25	01s06
Deal	d										22 31								23 31	
Dover Priory	d	21 58									22 49								23 49	
Folkestone Central	d	22 09									23 00								23 59	
Folkestone West	d	22 11									23 02								00 02	
Ashford International	a	22 28	22 41						22 50	23 00	23 15	23 41					23 50	23 50	00 20	
	d		22 43						22 52		23 16						23 52	23 52		
Ramsgate	d				22a19			23a22	23 30						00a21	00a30	00 31	00 44		01a23
Broadstairs	d								23 35								00s36	00s49		
Margate [4]	d								23a40								00a42	00a58		
Birchington-on-Sea	d																			
Herne Bay	d																			
Whitstable	d																			
Faversham [2]	a																			
	d																			
Sittingbourne [4]	d																			
Rainham (Kent)	d																			
Gillingham (Kent) [4]	d																			
Chatham [4]	d																			
Rochester [4]	d																			
Maidstone West	d																			
Strood [4]	d																			
Gravesend	d																			
Ebbsfleet International	a		23 02								23 35									
	d		23 02								23 35									
Stratford International ⊖	a		23 14								23 47									
St Pancras International [4] ⊖	a		23 21								23 54									

Saturdays

26 May to 8 December

		SE	SE	SE	SE	SE	SE	SE	SE	SE	SE	SE	SE	SE	SE	SE	SE	SE	SE	SE	SE	SE	SE
		◇	◇[1]	◇	◇[1]	◇[1]	◇	◇[1]	◇	◇	◇[1]	◇	◇[1]	◇	◇	◇	◇[1]	◇	◇	◇[1]	◇	◇	◇
St Pancras International	d																		07 08				
Margate [4]	d	00 04	00 25		01 08							05 53						06 53				06 57	
Broadstairs	d	00 10	00 31		01 14							05 59						06 59				07 03	
Ramsgate [4]	d	00a17	00a38		01a21		05 05	05 15				06 05	06 15		06 12			07 05		07 15		07 12	
Canterbury West	a						05 24	05 36				06 24	06 36					07 24		07 36			
	d						05 25	05 37				06 25	06 37					07 25		07 37			
Dover Priory	d																						06 42
Sandwich	d														06 25							07 25	07 06
Deal	d														06 31							07 31	
Dover Priory	d					04 58				05 49	05 58				06 49		06 58					07 49	
Folkestone Central	d					05 09				06 00	06 09				07 00		07 09					08 00	
Folkestone West	d					05 11				06 02	06 11				07 02		07 11					08 02	
Ashford International	a					05 28	05 41	05 58		06 15	06 28	06 41	06 58		07 15		07 28	07 41	07 46	07 58		08 15	
	d						05 43			06 16		06 43			07 16			07 43	07 52			08 16	
Ramsgate	d			00 31												06 20			08 28				07 20
Broadstairs	d			00s36												06 25			08 33				07 25
Margate [4]	d			00a42												06 30			08a39				07 30
Birchington-on-Sea	d															06 35							07 35
Herne Bay	d															06 44							07 44
Whitstable	d															06 49							07 49
Faversham [2]	a															06 57							07 57
	d								05 30					06 30		06 58					07 30		07 58
Sittingbourne [4]	d								05 38					06 38		07 08					07 38		08 08
Rainham (Kent)	d								05 46					06 46		07 16					07 46		08 16
Gillingham (Kent) [4]	d								05 51					06 51		07 21					07 51		08 21
Chatham [4]	d								05 55					06 55		07 25					07 55		08 25
Rochester [4]	d								05 59					06 59		07 29					07 59		08 29
Maidstone West	d																						
Strood [4]	d								06 02					07 02		07 32					08 02		08 32
Gravesend	d								06 12					07 12		07 42					08 12		08 42
Ebbsfleet International	a						06 02		06 16	06 35		07 02		07 16	07 35	07 46		08 02			08 16	08 35	08 46
	d						06 02		06 17	06 35		07 02		07 17	07 35	07 47		08 02			08 18	08 35	08 47
Stratford International ⊖	a						06 14		06 28	06 47		07 14		07 28	07 47	07 58		08 14			08 29	08 47	08 58
St Pancras International [4] ⊖	a						06 21		06 36	06 54		07 21		07 36	07 54	08 06		08 21			08 36	08 55	09 06

Table T194-R

Saturdays

26 May to 8 December

Kent - St Pancras International
High Speed Domestic Services

		SE ◇■	SE ◇	SE ■	SE ◇	SE ◇■	SE ◇	SE ◇	SE ◇	SE ■	SE ◇■	SE ◇	SE ◇	SE ◇■	SE ◇	SE ◇	SE ◇	SE ◇■	SE ◇■	SE ◇	SE ◇	SE ◇■	SE ◇
St Pancras International	d				08 12				06 37				09 09			07 25	07 37				10 08		
Margate ■	d		07 53	07 57						08 25		08 53				08 59		09 25		09 53			
Broadstairs	d		07 59	08 03						08 31		08 59				09 05		09 31		09 59			
Ramsgate ■	d		08 05	08a09		08 17		08 12		08a38		09 05		09 17		09 12		09a38		10 05		10 19	
Canterbury West	a		08 24			08 39						09 24		09 39						10 24		10 41	
	d		08 25			08 40						09 25		09 40						10 25		10 42	
Dover Priory	d								07 42								08 42						
Sandwich	d							08 25	08 06							09 25	09 06						
Deal	d							08 31								09 31							
Dover Priory	d	07 58						08 49			08 58					09 49			09 58				
Folkestone Central	d	08 09						09 00			09 09					10 00			10 09				
Folkestone West	d	08 11						09 02			09 11					10 02			10 11				
Ashford International	a	08 30	08 41		08 50	08 58		09 15			09 30	09 41	09 47	09 58		10 15			10 30	10 41	10 46	11 00	
	d		08 43		08 52			09 16				09 43	09 52			10 16				10 43	10 52		
Ramsgate	d				09 28				08 20				10 28				09 20				11 28		
Broadstairs	d				09 33				08 25				10 33				09 25				11 33		
Margate ■	d				09a39				08 30				10a39				09 30				11a39		
Birchington-on-Sea	d								08 35								09 35						
Herne Bay	d								08 44								09 44						
Whitstable	d								08 49								09 49						
Faversham ■	a								08 57								09 57						
	d						08 30		08 58						09 30		09 58						10 30
Sittingbourne ■	d						08 38		09 08						09 38		10 08						10 38
Rainham (Kent)	d						08 46		09 16						09 46		10 16						10 46
Gillingham (Kent) ■	d						08 51		09 21						09 51		10 21						10 51
Chatham ■	d						08 55		09 25						09 55		10 25						10 55
Rochester ■	d						08 59		09 29						09 59		10 29						10 59
Maidstone West	d																						
Strood ■	d						09 02		09 32						10 02		10 32						11 02
Gravesend	d						09 12		09 42						10 12		10 42						11 12
Ebbsfleet International	a		09 02				09 16	09 35	09 46			10 02			10 16	10 35	10 46			11 02			11 16
	d		09 02				09 18	09 35	09 47			10 02			10 16	10 35	10 48			11 02			11 18
Stratford International ⊖	a		09 14				09 29	09 47	09 58			10 14			10 28	10 47	10 59			11 14			11 29
St Pancras International ■ ⊖	a		09 21				09 36	09 54	10 06			10 21			10 35	10 55	11 06			11 21			11 37

		SE ◇	SE ◇	SE ◇■	SE ◇■	SE ◇	SE ◇	SE ◇■	SE ◇	SE ◇	SE ◇	SE ◇■	SE ◇■	SE ◇	SE ◇	SE ◇■	SE ◇	SE ◇	SE ◇	SE ◇■	SE ◇■	SE ◇	SE ◇
St Pancras International	d	08 25	08 37				11 12			09 25	09 34				12 12			10 22	10 37				13 12
Margate ■	d	09 59		10 25		10 53				10 59		11 25		11 53				11 59		12 25		12 53	
Broadstairs	d	10 05		10 31		10 59				11 05		11 31		11 59				12 05		12 31		12 59	
Ramsgate ■	d	10 12		10a38		11 05		11 19		11 12		11a38		12 05		12 19		12 12		12a38		13 05	
Canterbury West	a					11 24		11 41						12 24		12 41						13 24	
	d					11 25		11 42						12 25		12 42						13 25	
Dover Priory	d		09 42								10 42								11 42				
Sandwich	d	10 25	10 06							11 25	11 06							12 25	12 06				
Deal	d	10 31								11 31								12 31					
Dover Priory	d	10 49			10 58					11 49			11 58					12 49			12 58		
Folkestone Central	d	11 00			11 09					12 00			12 09					13 00			13 09		
Folkestone West	d	11 02			11 11					12 02			12 11					13 02			13 11		
Ashford International	a	11 15			11 28	11 41	11 50	12 00		12 15			12 29	12 41	12 50	13 00		13 15			13 28	13 41	13 50
	d	11 16				11 43	11 52			12 16				12 43	12 52			13 16				13 43	13 52
Ramsgate	d		10 20				12 28				11 20				13 28				12 20				14 28
Broadstairs	d		10 25				12 33				11 25				13 33				12 25				14 33
Margate ■	d		10 30				12a39				11 30				13a39				12 30				14a39
Birchington-on-Sea	d		10 35								11 35								12 35				
Herne Bay	d		10 44								11 44								12 44				
Whitstable	d		10 49								11 49								12 49				
Faversham ■	a		10 57								11 57								12 57				
	d		10 58					11 30		11 58					12 30		12 58						
Sittingbourne ■	d		11 08					11 38		12 08					12 38		13 08						
Rainham (Kent)	d		11 16					11 46		12 16					12 46		13 16						
Gillingham (Kent) ■	d		11 21					11 51		12 21					12 51		13 21						
Chatham ■	d		11 25					11 55		12 25					12 55		13 25						
Rochester ■	d		11 29					11 59		12 29					12 59		13 29						
Maidstone West	d																						
Strood ■	d		11 32					12 02		12 32					13 02		13 32						
Gravesend	d		11 42					12 12		12 42					13 12		13 42						
Ebbsfleet International	a	11 35	11 46			12 02			12 16	12 35	12 46			13 02			13 16	13 35	13 46			14 02	
	d	11 35	11 47			12 02			12 17	12 35	12 47			13 02			13 18	13 35	13 51			14 02	
Stratford International ⊖	a	11 47	11 58			12 14			12 28	12 47	12 58			13 14			13 29	13 47	14 02			14 14	
St Pancras International ■ ⊖	a	11 54	12 06			12 21			12 36	12 55	13 06			13 21			13 37	13 54	14 09			14 21	

Table T194-R

Saturdays

26 May to 8 December

Kent - St Pancras International
High Speed Domestic Services

		SE ◇■	SE ◇	SE ◇	SE ◇	SE ◇■	SE ◇■	SE ◇	SE ◇	SE ◇■	SE ◇	SE ◇	SE ◇	SE ◇■	SE ◇■	SE ◇	SE ◇	SE ◇■	SE ◇	SE ◇	SE ◇	SE ◇■	SE ◇■
St Pancras International	d			11 25	11 37				14 09			12 27	12 37				15 12			13 25	13 37		
Margate ■	d			12 59		13 25		13 53				13 59		14 25		14 53				14 59		15 25	
Broadstairs	d			13 05		13 31		13 59				14 05		14 31		14 59				15 05		15 31	
Ramsgate ■	d	13 19		13 12		13a38		14 05		14 19		14 12		14a38		15 05		15 19		15 12		15a38	
Canterbury West	a	13 41						14 24		14 41						15 24		15 41					
	d	13 42						14 25		14 42						15 25		15 42					
Dover Priory	d				12 42								13 42								14 42		
Sandwich	d			13 25	13 06							14 25	14 06							15 25	15 06		
Deal	d			13 31								14 31								15 31			
Dover Priory	d			13 49			13 58					14 49			14 58					15 49			15 58
Folkestone Central	d			14 00			14 09					15 00			15 09					16 00			16 09
Folkestone West	d			14 02			14 11					15 02			15 11					16 02			16 11
Ashford International	a	14 00		14 15			14 28	14 41	14 47	15 00		15 15			15 28	15 41	15 50	16 00		16 15			16 28
	d			14 16				14 43	14 52			15 16				15 46	15 52			16 16			
Ramsgate	d				13 20				15 28				14 20				16 28				15 20		
Broadstairs	d				13 25				15 33				14 25				16 33				15 25		
Margate ■	d				13 30				15a39				14 30				16a39				15 30		
Birchington-on-Sea	d				13 35								14 35								15 35		
Herne Bay	d				13 44								14 44								15 44		
Whitstable	d				13 49								14 49								15 49		
Faversham ■	a				13 57								14 57								15 57		
	d		13 30		13 58						14 30		14 58						15 30		15 58		
Sittingbourne ■	d		13 38		14 08						14 38		15 08						15 38		16 08		
Rainham (Kent)	d		13 46		14 16						14 46		15 16						15 46		16 16		
Gillingham (Kent) ■	d		13 51		14 21						14 51		15 21						15 51		16 21		
Chatham ■	d		13 55		14 25						14 55		15 25						15 55		16 25		
Rochester ■	d		13 59		14 29						14 59		15 29						15 59		16 29		
Maidstone West	d																						
Strood ■	d		14 02		14 32						15 02		15 32						16 02		16 32		
Gravesend	d		14 12		14 42						15 12		15 42						16 12		16 42		
Ebbsfleet International	a		14 16	14 35	14 46			15 02			15 16	15 35	15 46			16 05			16 16	16 35	16 46		
	d		14 17	14 35	14 48			15 02			15 18	15 35	15 51			16 05			16 17	16 35	16 47		
Stratford International ⊖	a		14 28	14 47	14 59			15 14			15 29	15 47	16 02			16 17			16 28	16 47	16 58		
St Pancras International ■ ⊖	a		14 36	14 54	15 07			15 21			15 40	15 54	16 09			16 24			16 36	16 54	17 06		

		SE ◇	SE ◇	SE ◇■	SE ◇	SE ◇	SE ◇	SE ◇■	SE ◇■	SE ◇	SE ◇	SE ◇■	SE ◇	SE ◇	SE ◇	SE ◇■	SE ◇■	SE ◇	SE ◇	SE ◇■	SE ◇	SE ◇	SE ◇
St Pancras International	d		16 12			14 25	14 37				17 12			15 25	15 37				18 12			16 25	16 37
Margate ■	d	15 53				15 59		16 25		16 53				16 59		17 25		17 53				17 59	
Broadstairs	d	15 59				16 05		16 31		16 59				17 05		17 31		17 59				18 05	
Ramsgate ■	d	16 05		16 19		16 12		16a38		17 05		17 19		17 12		17a38		18 05		18 19		18 12	
Canterbury West	a	16 24		16 41						17 24		17 41						18 24		18 41			
	d	16 25		16 42						17 25		17 42						18 25		18 42			
Dover Priory	d						15 42								16 42								17 42
Sandwich	d					16 25	16 06							17 25	17 06							18 25	18 06
Deal	d					16 31								17 31								18 31	
Dover Priory	d					16 49			16 58					17 49			17 58					18 49	
Folkestone Central	d					17 00			17 09					18 00			18 09					19 00	
Folkestone West	d					17 02			17 11					18 02			18 11					19 02	
Ashford International	a	16 41	16 50	17 00		17 15			17 28	17 41	17 50	18 00		18 15			18 28	18 41	18 50	19 00		19 15	
	d	16 43	16 52			17 16				17 43	17 52			18 16				18 43	18 52			19 16	
Ramsgate	d		17 28				16 20				18 28				17 20				19 28				18 20
Broadstairs	d		17 33				16 25				18 33				17 25				19 33				18 25
Margate ■	d		17a39				16 30				18a39				17 30				19a39				18 30
Birchington-on-Sea	d						16 35								17 35								18 35
Herne Bay	d						16 44								17 44								18 44
Whitstable	d						16 49								17 49								18 49
Faversham ■	a						16 57								17 57								18 57
	d				16 30		16 58						17 30		17 58						18 30		18 58
Sittingbourne ■	d				16 38		17 08						17 38		18 08						18 38		19 08
Rainham (Kent)	d				16 46		17 16						17 46		18 16						18 46		19 16
Gillingham (Kent) ■	d				16 51		17 21						17 51		18 21						18 51		19 21
Chatham ■	d				16 55		17 25						17 55		18 25						18 55		19 25
Rochester ■	d				16 59		17 29						17 59		18 29						18 59		19 29
Maidstone West	d																						
Strood ■	d				17 02		17 32						18 02		18 32						19 02		19 32
Gravesend	d				17 12		17 42						18 12		18 42						19 12		19 42
Ebbsfleet International	a	17 02			17 16	17 35	17 46			18 02			18 16	18 35	18 46			19 02			19 16	19 35	19 46
	d	17 02			17 17	17 35	17 47			18 02			18 18	18 35	18 47			19 02			19 17	19 35	19 47
Stratford International ⊖	a	17 14			17 28	17 47	17 58			18 14			18 29	18 47	18 58			19 14			19 28	19 47	19 58
St Pancras International ■ ⊖	a	17 21			17 36	17 54	18 09			18 21			18 36	18 54	19 06			19 21			19 36	19 54	20 06

Kent - St Pancras International High Speed Domestic Services

Saturdays
26 May to 8 December

		SE	SE	SE	SE	SE	SE	SE	SE	SE	SE	SE	SE	SE	SE	SE	SE	SE	SE	SE	SE	SE
		◇■	◇■	◇	◇	◇■	◇	◇	◇	◇■	◇■	◇	◇	◇■	◇	◇	◇	◇■	◇■	◇	◇	◇■
St Pancras International	d				19 12			17 25	17 37				20 12			18 25	18 37				21 12	
Margate ■	d	18 25		18 53				18 59		19 25		19 53				19 59		20 25		20 53		
Broadstairs	d	18 31		18 59				19 05		19 31		19 59				20 05		20 31		20 59		
Ramsgate ■	d	18a38		19 05		19 19		19 12		19a38		20 05		20 19		20 12		20a38		21 05		21 16
Canterbury West	a			19 24		19 41						20 24		20 41						21 24		21 38
	d			19 25		19 42						20 25		20 42						21 25		21 39
Dover Priory	d								18 42								19 42					
Sandwich	d							19 25	19 06							20 25	20 06					
Deal	d							19 31								20 31						
Dover Priory	d		18 58					19 49			19 58					20 49			20 58			
Folkestone Central	d		19 09					20 00			20 09					21 00			21 09			
Folkestone West	d		19 11					20 02			20 11					21 02			21 11			
Ashford International	a		19 28	19 41	19 50	20 00		20 15			20 28	20 41	20 50	21 00		21 15			21 28	21 41	21 50	22 00
	d			19 43	19 52			20 16				20 43	20 52			21 16				21 43	21 52	
Ramsgate	d				20 28				19 20				21 28				20 20				22 28	
Broadstairs	d				20 33				19 25				21 33				20 25				22 33	
Margate ■	d				20a39				19 30				21a39				20 30				22a39	
Birchington-on-Sea	d								19 35								20 35					
Herne Bay	d								19 44								20 44					
Whitstable	d								19 49								20 49					
Faversham ■	a								19 57								20 57					
	d						19 30		19 58						20 30		20 58					
Sittingbourne ■	d						19 38		20 08						20 38		21 08					
Rainham (Kent)	d						19 46		20 16						20 46		21 16					
Gillingham (Kent) ■	d						19 51		20 21						20 51		21 21					
Chatham ■	d						19 55		20 25						20 55		21 25					
Rochester ■	d						19 59		20 29						20 59		21 29					
Maidstone West	d																					
Strood ■	d						20 02		20 32						21 02		21 32					
Gravesend	d						20 12		20 42						21 12		21 42					
Ebbsfleet International	a			20 02			20 16	20 35	20 46			21 02			21 16	21 35	21 46			22 02		
	d			20 02			20 17	20 35	20 51			21 02			21 17	21 35	21 47			22 02		
Stratford International ⊖	a			20 14			20 28	20 47	21 02			21 14			21 28	21 47	21 58			22 14		
St Pancras International ■ ⊖	a			20 21			20 36	20 54	21 09			21 21			21 36	21 54	22 06			22 21		

		SE	SE	SE	SE	SE	SE	SE	SE	SE	SE	SE	SE	SE	SE	SE	SE	SE	SE	SE	SE	SE
		◇	◇	◇	◇■	◇■	◇	◇	■	◇	◇	◇■			◇	◇	■	◇■	◇	◇	◇	◇
St Pancras International	d		19 25	19 37				22 12		20 25	20 37				21 25	21 37			22 25	22 37	23 12	23 37
Margate ■	d		20 59		21 25		21 53			21 59		22 25		22 53	22 59			23 25	23 59			
Broadstairs	d		21 05		21 31		21 59			22 05		22 31		22 59	23 05			23 31	00 05			
Ramsgate ■	d		21 12		21a38		22 05		22 16	22 12		22a38		23 05	23a11		23 12	23a38	00a11			
Canterbury West	a						22 24		22 38					23 24							00 08	
	d						22 25		22 39					23 25							00 09	
Dover Priory	d			20 42							21 42					22 42				23 42		00 42
Sandwich	d		21 25	21 06						22 25	22 06					23 06	23 25			00 06		01s06
Deal	d		21 31							22 31							23 31					
Dover Priory	d		21 49			21 58				22 49			22 58				23 49					
Folkestone Central	d		22 00			22 09				23 00			23 09				23 59					
Folkestone West	d		22 02			22 11				23 02			23 11				00 02					
Ashford International	a		22 15			22 28	22 41	22 50	23 00	23 15			23 29	23 41			00 20					
	d		22 16				22 43	22 52		23 16												
Ramsgate	d			21 20				23 29			22a19					23a21				00a21	00 28	01a23
Broadstairs	d			21 25				23 35													00s33	
Margate ■	d			21 30				23a40													00a39	
Birchington-on-Sea	d			21 35																		
Herne Bay	d			21 44																		
Whitstable	d			21 49																		
Faversham ■	a			21 57																		
	d	21 30		21 58																		
Sittingbourne ■	d	21 38		22 08																		
Rainham (Kent)	d	21 46		22 16																		
Gillingham (Kent) ■	d	21 51		22 21																		
Chatham ■	d	21 55		22 25																		
Rochester ■	d	21 59		22 29																		
Maidstone West	d																					
Strood ■	d	22 02		22 32																		
Gravesend	d	22 12		22 42																		
Ebbsfleet International	a	22 16	22 35	22 46			23 02			23 35												
	d	22 17	22 35	22 47			23 02			23 35												
Stratford International ⊖	a	22 28	22 47	22 58			23 14			23 47												
St Pancras International ■ ⊖	a	22 36	22 54	23 06			23 21			23 54												

Kent - St Pancras International High Speed Domestic Services

Sundays
20 May to 2 December

		SE	SE	SE	SE	SE	SE	SE	SE	SE	SE	SE	SE	SE	SE	SE	SE	SE	SE	SE	SE	SE	SE
		◇	◇■	◇■	◇■	◇	◇	◇■	◇	◇	◇■	◇	◇	◇■	◇	◇■	◇	◇	◇■	◇■	◇	◇■	◇
		A	A	A																			
St Pancras International	d																						08 25
Margate ■	d		00 25	01 07						07 53					08 53				09 24		09 53		09 59
Broadstairs	d	00 05	00 31	01 13						07 59					08 59				09 30		09 59		10 05
Ramsgate ■	d	00a11	00a38	01a20	07 16		07 12			08 05	08 16	08 12			09 05	09 20	09 12		09a37		10 05	10 20	10 12
Canterbury West	a				07 38					08 24	08 38				09 24	09 42					10 24	10 42	
	d				07 39					08 25	08 39				09 25	09 43					10 25	10 43	
Dover Priory	d																	08 42					
Sandwich	d						07 25					08 25					09 25	09 06					10 25
Deal	d						07 31					08 31					09 31						10 31
Dover Priory	d						07 49	07 58				08 49		08 58			09 49			09 58			10 49
Folkestone Central	d						08 00	08 09				09 00		09 09			10 00			10 09			11 00
Folkestone West	d						08 02	08 11				09 02		09 11			10 02			10 11			11 02
Ashford International	a				08 01		08 15	08 28		08 41	09 01	09 15		09 28	09 41	10 01	10 15			10 28	10 41	11 01	11 15
	d						08 16			08 43		09 16			09 43		10 16				10 43		11 16
Ramsgate	d												08 20					09 20					
Broadstairs	d												08 25					09 25					
Margate ■	d												08 30					09 30					
Birchington-on-Sea	d												08 35					09 35					
Herne Bay	d												08 44					09 44					
Whitstable	d												08 49					09 49					
Faversham ■	a												08 57					09 57					
	d					07 00			08 00				08 58					09 58					
Sittingbourne ■	d					07 08			08 08				09 08					10 08					
Rainham (Kent)	d					07 16			08 16				09 16					10 16					
Gillingham (Kent) ■	d					07 21			08 21				09 21					10 21					
Chatham ■	d					07 25			08 25				09 25					10 25					
Rochester ■	d					07 29			08 29				09 29					10 29					
Maidstone West	d																						
Strood ■	d					07 32			08 32				09 32					10 32					
Gravesend	d					07 42			08 42				09 42					10 42					
Ebbsfleet International	a					07 46	08 35		08 46	09 02		09 35	09 46		10 02		10 35	10 46			11 02		11 35
	d					07 47	08 35		08 47	09 02		09 35	09 47		10 02		10 35	10 47			11 02		11 35
Stratford International ⊖	a					07 58	08 47		08 58	09 14		09 47	09 58		10 14		10 47	10 58			11 14		11 47
St Pancras International ■ ⊖	a					08 06	08 54		09 06	09 21		09 54	10 06		10 21		10 54	11 06			11 21		11 54

		SE	SE	SE	SE	SE	SE	SE	SE	SE	SE	SE	SE	SE	SE	SE	SE	SE	SE	SE	SE	SE	SE
		◇	◇	◇■	◇■	◇	◇■	◇	◇	◇	◇	◇■	◇■	◇	◇■	◇	◇	◇	◇	◇■	◇■	◇	◇■
St Pancras International	d	08 37	09 09						09 25	09 37	10 08						10 27	10 37	11 12				
Margate ■	d			10 24		10 53			10 59			11 24		11 53			11 59			12 24		12 53	
Broadstairs	d			10 30		10 59			11 05			11 30		11 59			12 05			12 30		12 59	
Ramsgate ■	d			10a37		11 05	11 20		11 12			11a37		12 05	12 20		12 12			12a37		13 05	13 20
Canterbury West	a		10 08			11 24	11 42				11 08			12 24	12 42				12 08			13 24	13 42
	d		10 09			11 25	11 43				11 09			12 25	12 43				12 09			13 25	13 43
Dover Priory	d	09 42								10 42								11 42					
Sandwich	d	10 06							11 25	11 06							12 25	12 06					
Deal	d								11 31								12 31						
Dover Priory	d				10 58				11 49				11 58				12 49				12 58		
Folkestone Central	d				11 09				12 00				12 09				13 00				13 09		
Folkestone West	d				11 11				12 02				12 11				13 02				13 11		
Ashford International	a				11 29	11 41	12 01		12 15				12 28	12 41	13 01		13 15				13 28	13 41	14 01
	d					11 43			12 16					12 43			13 16					13 43	
Ramsgate	d	10 20	10 28							11 20	11 28							12 20	12 28				
Broadstairs	d	10 25	10 33							11 25	11 33							12 25	12 33				
Margate ■	d	10 30	10a39							11 30	11a39							12 30	12a39				
Birchington-on-Sea	d	10 35								11 35								12 35					
Herne Bay	d	10 44								11 44								12 44					
Whitstable	d	10 49								11 49								12 49					
Faversham ■	a	10 57								11 57								12 57					
	d	10 58						11 30		11 58						12 30		12 58					
Sittingbourne ■	d	11 08						11 38		12 08						12 38		13 08					
Rainham (Kent)	d	11 16						11 46		12 16						12 46		13 16					
Gillingham (Kent) ■	d	11 21						11 51		12 21						12 51		13 21					
Chatham ■	d	11 25						11 55		12 25						12 55		13 25					
Rochester ■	d	11 29						11 59		12 29						12 59		13 29					
Maidstone West	d																						
Strood ■	d	11 32						12 02		12 32						13 02		13 32					
Gravesend	d	11 42						12 12		12 42						13 12		13 42					
Ebbsfleet International	a	11 46				12 02		12 16	12 35	12 46				13 02		13 16	13 35	13 46				14 02	
	d	11 47				12 02		12 17	12 35	12 47				13 02		13 18	13 35	13 47				14 02	
Stratford International ⊖	a	11 58				12 14		12 28	12 47	12 58				13 14		13 29	13 47	13 58				14 14	
St Pancras International ■ ⊖	a	12 05				12 21		12 36	12 54	13 06				13 21		13 37	13 54	14 06				14 21	

A not 20 May

Kent - St Pancras International
High Speed Domestic Services

		SE	SE	SE	SE	SE	SE	SE	SE	SE	SE	SE	SE	SE	SE	SE	SE	SE	SE	SE	SE	SE	SE
		◇	◇	◇	◇	◇1	◇1	◇	◇	◇	◇1	◇	◇	◇	◇1	◇1	◇	◇	◇	◇1	◇	◇	◇
St Pancras International	d		11 25	11 37	12 12				12 52			12 27	12 37	13 12				13 55			13 25	13 37	14 09
Margate 4	d		12 59			13 24		13 53				13 59			14 24		14 53				14 59		
Broadstairs	d		13 05			13 30		13 59				14 05			14 30		14 59				15 05		
Ramsgate 4	d		13 12			13a37		14 05			14 20	14 12			14a37		15 05			15 20	15 12		
Canterbury West	a				13 08			14 24			14 42			14 08			15 24			15 42			15 08
	d				13 09			14 25			14 43			14 09			15 25			15 43			15 09
Dover Priory	d			12 42									13 42									14 42	
Sandwich	d		13 25	13 06								14 25	14 06								15 25	15 06	
Deal	d		13 31									14 31									15 31		
Dover Priory	d		13 49				13 58					14 49				14 58					15 49		
Folkestone Central	d		14 00				14 09					15 00				15 09					16 00		
Folkestone West	d		14 02				14 11					15 02				15 11					16 02		
Ashford International	a		14 15				14 28	14 41			15 01	15 15				15 28	15 41			16 01	16 15		
	d		14 16					14 43				15 16					15 43				16 16		
Ramsgate	d			13 20	13 28								14 20	14 28								15 20	15 28
Broadstairs	d			13 25	13 33								14 25	14 33								15 25	15 33
Margate 4	d			13 30	13a39								14 30	14a39								15 30	15a39
Birchington-on-Sea	d			13 35									14 35									15 35	
Herne Bay	d			13 44									14 44									15 44	
Whitstable	d			13 49									14 49									15 49	
Faversham 2	a			13 57					14 02				14 57					15 02				15 57	
	d	13 30		13 58					14 30	14 30			14 58					15 30	15 30			15 58	
Sittingbourne 4	d	13 38		14 08					14 38	14 38			15 08					15 38	15 38			16 08	
Rainham (Kent)	d	13 46		14 16					14 46	14 46			15 16					15 46	15 46			16 16	
Gillingham (Kent) 4	d	13 51		14 21					14 51	14 51			15 21					15 51	15 51			16 21	
Chatham 4	d	13 55		14 25					14 55	14 55			15 25					15 55	15 55			16 25	
Rochester 4	d	13 59		14 29					14 59	14 59			15 29					15 59	15 59			16 29	
Maidstone West	d																						
Strood 4	d	14 02		14 32					15 02	15 02			15 32					16 02	16 02			16 32	
Gravesend	d	14 12		14 42					15 12	15 12			15 42					16 12	16 12			16 42	
Ebbsfleet International	a	14 16	14 35	14 46				15 02	15 16	15 16		15 35	15 46				16 02	16 16	16 16		16 35	16 46	
	d	14 17	14 35	14 48				15 02	15 18	15 18		15 35	15 51				16 02	16 17	16 17		16 35	16 47	
Stratford International ⊖	a	14 28	14 47	14 59				15 14	15 29	15 29		15 47	16 02				16 14	16 28	16 28		16 47	16 58	
St Pancras International 4 ⊖	a	14 36	14 54	15 06				15 21	15 40	15 40		15 54	16 10				16 21	16 36	16 36		16 54	17 06	

		SE	SE	SE	SE	SE	SE	SE	SE	SE	SE	SE	SE	SE	SE	SE	SE	SE	SE	SE	SE	SE	SE
		◇1	◇1	◇	◇	◇	◇1	◇	◇	◇	◇1	◇1	◇	◇1	◇	◇	◇	◇	◇1	◇1	◇	◇	◇
St Pancras International	d				14 55			14 25	14 37	15 12						15 25	15 37	16 12				16 55	
Margate 4	d	15 24		15 53				15 59			16 24		16 53			16 59			17 24		17 53		
Broadstairs	d	15 30		15 59				16 05			16 30		16 59			17 05			17 30		17 59		
Ramsgate 4	d	15a37		16 05			16 20	16 12			16a37		17 05	17 20		17 12			17a37		18 05		
Canterbury West	a			16 24			16 42			16 08			17 24	17 42				17 08			18 24		
	d			16 25			16 43			16 09			17 25	17 43				17 09			18 25		
Dover Priory	d								15 42								16 42						
Sandwich	d							16 25	16 06							17 25	17 06						
Deal	d							16 31								17 31							
Dover Priory	d		15 58					16 49				16 58				17 49				17 58			
Folkestone Central	d		16 09					17 00				17 09				18 00				18 09			
Folkestone West	d		16 11					17 02				17 11				18 02				18 11			
Ashford International	a		16 28	16 41			17 01	17 15				17 28	17 41	18 01		18 15				18 28	18 41		
	d			16 43				17 16					17 43			18 16					18 43		
Ramsgate	d								16 20	16 28							17 20	17 28					
Broadstairs	d								16 25	16 33							17 25	17 33					
Margate 4	d								16 30	16a39							17 30	17a39					
Birchington-on-Sea	d								16 35								17 35						
Herne Bay	d								16 44								17 44						
Whitstable	d								16 49								17 49						
Faversham 2	a				16 02				16 57								17 57					18 02	
	d				16 30	16 30			16 58						17 30		17 58					18 30	18 30
Sittingbourne 4	d				16 38	16 38			17 08						17 38		18 08					18 38	18 38
Rainham (Kent)	d				16 46	16 46			17 16						17 46		18 16					18 46	18 46
Gillingham (Kent) 4	d				16 51	16 51			17 21						17 51		18 21					18 51	18 51
Chatham 4	d				16 55	16 55			17 25						17 55		18 25					18 55	18 55
Rochester 4	d				16 59	16 59			17 29						17 59		18 29					18 59	18 59
Maidstone West	d																						
Strood 4	d				17 02	17 02			17 32						18 02		18 32					19 02	19 02
Gravesend	d				17 12	17 12			17 42						18 12		18 42					19 12	19 12
Ebbsfleet International	a			17 02	17 16	17 16		17 35	17 46				18 02		18 16	18 35	18 46				19 02	19 16	19 16
	d			17 02	17 17	17 17		17 35	17 53				18 02		18 18	18 35	18 51				19 02	19 17	19 17
Stratford International ⊖	a			17 14	17 28	17 28		17 47	18 04				18 14		18 29	18 47	19 02				19 14	19 28	19 28
St Pancras International 4 ⊖	a			17 21	17 36	17 36		17 55	18 11				18 21		18 37	18 54	19 10				19 21	19 36	19 36

Table T194-R

Sundays

20 May to 2 December

Kent - St Pancras International
High Speed Domestic Services

		SE	SE	SE	SE	SE	SE	SE	SE	SE	SE	SE	SE	SE	SE	SE	SE	SE	SE	SE	SE	SE	SE
		◇1	◇	◇	◇	◇1	◇1	◇	◇	◇	◇1	◇	◇	◇	◇1	◇1	◇	◇1	◇	◇	◇	◇	◇1
St Pancras International	d		16 25	16 37	17 12				17 52			17 25	17 37	18 12						18 25	18 37	19 12	
Margate 4	d		17 59			18 24		18 53				18 59			19 24		19 53			19 59			20 24
Broadstairs	d		18 05			18 30		18 59				19 05			19 30		19 59			20 05			20 30
Ramsgate 4	d	18 20	18 12			18a37		19 05			19 16	19 12			19a37		20 05	20 16		20 12			20a37
Canterbury West	a	18 42			18 08			19 24			19 38			19 08			20 24	20 38				20 08	
	d	18 43			18 09			19 25			19 39			19 09			20 25	20 39				20 09	
Dover Priory	d			17 42									18 42								19 42		
Sandwich	d		18 25	18 06								19 25	19 06							20 25	20 06		
Deal	d		18 31									19 31								20 31			
Dover Priory	d		18 49				18 58					19 49				19 58				20 49			
Folkestone Central	d		19 00				19 09					20 00				20 09				21 00			
Folkestone West	d		19 02				19 11					20 02				20 11				21 02			
Ashford International	a	19 01	19 15				19 28	19 41			20 01	20 15				20 28	20 41	21 01		21 15			
	d		19 16					19 43				20 16					20 43			21 16			
Ramsgate	d			18 20	18 28								19 20	19 28							20 20	20 28	
Broadstairs	d			18 25	18 33								19 25	19 33							20 25	20 33	
Margate 4	d			18 30	18a39								19 30	19a39							20 30	20a39	
Birchington-on-Sea	d			18 35									19 35								20 35		
Herne Bay	d			18 44									19 44								20 44		
Whitstable	d			18 49									19 49								20 49		
Faversham 2	a			18 57					19 02				19 57								20 57		
	d			18 58					19 30	19 30			19 58						20 30		20 58		
Sittingbourne 4	d			19 08					19 38	19 38			20 08						20 38		21 08		
Rainham (Kent)	d			19 16					19 46	19 46			20 16						20 46		21 16		
Gillingham (Kent) 4	d			19 21					19 51	19 51			20 21						20 51		21 21		
Chatham 4	d			19 25					19 55	19 55			20 25						20 55		21 25		
Rochester 4	d			19 29					19 59	19 59			20 29						20 59		21 29		
Maidstone West	d																						
Strood 4	d			19 32					20 02	20 02			20 32						21 02		21 32		
Gravesend	d			19 42					20 12	20 12			20 42						21 12		21 42		
Ebbsfleet International	a		19 35	19 46				20 02	20 16	20 16		20 35	20 46				21 02		21 16	21 35	21 46		
	d		19 35	19 51				20 02	20 17	20 17		20 35	20 47				21 02		21 17	21 35	21 48		
Stratford International ⊖	a		19 47	20 02				20 14	20 28	20 28		20 47	20 58				21 14		21 28	21 47	21 59		
St Pancras International 4 ⊖	a		19 54	20 09				20 21	20 36	20 36		20 54	21 05				21 21		21 36	21 54	22 07		

		SE	SE	SE	SE	SE	SE	SE	SE	SE	SE	SE	SE	SE	SE	SE	SE	SE	SE	SE	SE	SE
		◇1	◇	◇	◇	◇1	◇	◇	◇	◇1	1	◇	1	◇	◇	◇	◇1		◇	◇	◇	◇1
St Pancras International	d			19 55			19 25	19 37	20 12					20 25	20 37	21 12			21 25	21 37	22 12	
Margate 4	d		20 53				20 59			21 24		21 53		21 59			22 24	22 53	22 59			23 24
Broadstairs	d		20 59				21 05			21 30		21 59		22 05			22 30	22 59	23 05			23 30
Ramsgate 4	d		21 05			21 16	21 12			21a37		22 05	22 16	22 12			22a37	23 05	23a11			23a37
Canterbury West	a		21 24			21 38			21 08			22 24	22 38			22 08		23 24			23 08	
	d		21 25			21 39			21 09			22 25	22 39			22 09		23 25			23 09	
Dover Priory	d							20 42							21 42					22 42		
Sandwich	d						21 25	21 06						22 25	22 06					23 06		
Deal	d						21 31							22 31								
Dover Priory	d	20 58					21 49				21 58			22 49								
Folkestone Central	d	21 09					22 00				22 09			23 00								
Folkestone West	d	21 11					22 02				22 11			23 02								
Ashford International	a	21 28	21 41			22 01	22 15				22 28	22 41	23 01	23 15				23 41				
	d		21 43				22 16					22 43										
Ramsgate	d							21 20	21 28						22a18	22 28				23a18	23 28	
Broadstairs	d							21 25	21 33							22 33					23 33	
Margate 4	d							21 30	21a39							22a39					23a39	
Birchington-on-Sea	d							21 35														
Herne Bay	d							21 44														
Whitstable	d							21 49														
Faversham 2	a			21 02				21 57														
	d			21 30	21 30			21 58														
Sittingbourne 4	d			21 38	21 38			22 08														
Rainham (Kent)	d			21 46	21 46			22 16														
Gillingham (Kent) 4	d			21 51	21 51			22 21														
Chatham 4	d			21 55	21 55			22 25														
Rochester 4	d			21 59	21 59			22 29														
Maidstone West	d																					
Strood 4	d			22 02	22 02			22 32														
Gravesend	d			22 12	22 12			22 42														
Ebbsfleet International	a		22 02	22 16	22 16		22 35	22 46				23 02										
	d		22 02	22 17	22 17		22 35	22 47				23 02										
Stratford International ⊖	a		22 14	22 28	22 28		22 47	22 58				23 14										
St Pancras International 4 ⊖	a		22 21	22 36	22 36		22 54	23 06				23 21										

Table T194-R

Sundays
20 May to 2 December

Kent - St Pancras International High Speed Domestic Services

		SE ◇	SE ◇	SE ◇
St Pancras International	d	22 25	22 37	23 12
Margate ■	d	23 59		
Broadstairs	d	00 05		
Ramsgate ■	d	00a11		
Canterbury West	a			00 08
	d			00 09
Dover Priory	d		23 42	
Sandwich	d		00 06	
Deal	d			
Dover Priory	d			
Folkestone Central	d			
Folkestone West	d			
Ashford International	a			
	d			
Ramsgate	d		00a18	00 28
Broadstairs	d			00s33
Margate ■	d			00a39
Birchington-on-Sea	d			
Herne Bay	d			
Whitstable	d			
Faversham ■	a			
	d			
Sittingbourne ■	d			
Rainham (Kent)	d			
Gillingham (Kent) ■	d			
Chatham ■	d			
Rochester ■	d			
Maidstone West	d			
Strood ■	d			
Gravesend	d			
Ebbsfleet International	a			
	d			
Stratford International ⊖	a			
St Pancras International ■ ⊖	a			

Table T195-F

Mondays to Fridays
21 May to 7 December

London - Catford, Beckenham Junction, Bromley South, Orpington, Otford and Sevenoaks

Miles	Miles	Miles			TL MX A	TL MO B	TL MX B	SE MO ◇■ C	SE MX D	SE MX E	SE MX ◇■ F	TL MO B	TL MX B	SE MO E	SE MX E	SE MX G	SE WO ■ H	SE MX ◇■ I	SE MX	SE ◇ J	TL	SE ◇■ K	TL
—	—	—	**London Victoria** ■ ⊖	d												00 06	00 10	00 25	00 28	00 40		05 12	
3¼	—	—	Brixton ⊖	d										00 05	00 05				00 35				
—	—	—	Kentish Town ⊖	d																			
—	—	—	St Pancras International ■ ⊖	d																			
—	—	—	Farringdon ⊖	d																			
—	—	—	City Thameslink ■	d																			
—	—	—	**London Blackfriars** ■ ⊖	d																	04 56		05 16
—	—	—	Elephant & Castle ⊖	d																	05 00		05 20
—	—	—	Loughborough Jn	d	00 02																		
—	—	—	Herne Hill ■	d	00a06									00 07	00 08				00 37				
5	—	—	West Dulwich	d										00 10	00 11				00 40				
5¾	—	—	Sydenham Hill	d										00 12	00 13				00 42				
7¼	—	—	Penge East	d										00 15	00 16				00 45				
7¾	—	—	Kent House ■	d						00 02				00 17	00 18				00 47				
8¾	—	—	**Beckenham Junction** ■	d						00 05				00 20	00 21				00 50				
—	3¾	4¼	Denmark Hill ■	d												00 16					05 08	05 22	05 28
—	4½	5	Peckham Rye ■	d									00 01			00 18					05 11		05 31
—	5¼	5¾	Nunhead ■	d									00 04			00 21					05 14		05 34
—	—	7½	Lewisham ■	a												00 26							
—	6½	—	Crofton Park	d								00 02	00 07								05 17		05 37
—	7½	—	Catford	d								00 05	00 10								05 20		05 40
—	8¼	—	Bellingham	d								00 08	00 13								05 23		05 43
—	9	—	Beckenham Hill	d								00 10	00 15								05 25		05 45
—	9¾	—	Ravensbourne	d								00 13	00 17								05 27		05 47
10	10½	—	Shortlands ■	d						00 09		00 15	00 20	00 23	00 24				00 53		05 30		05 50
11	11½	—	**Bromley South** ■	d					00 05	00a12	00 12	00 18	00 23	00 26	00 27		00s33	00 42	00 56	00 57	05 33	05 35	05 53
12	12½	—	Bickley ■	d								00 21	00 26	00 28	00 29				00 58		05 36		05 56
13¾	—	—	Petts Wood ■	d										00 33	00 34				01 03		05 40		
15	—	—	**Orpington** ■	d										00a36	00a38				01a07		05a44		
—	14¾	—	St Mary Cray	d			00 01	00 03	00 11		00 18	00 25	00 31					00 48		01s02		05 40	06 01
—	17½	—	**Swanley** ■	d			00 06	00a07	00a15		00 22	00 30	00 36					00 52		01s06		05a44	06 06
—	20½	—	Eynsford	d		00 05	00 11					00 35	00 41										06 11
—	22¾	—	Shoreham (Kent)	d		00 09	00 15					00 39	00 45										06 15
—	24	—	Otford ■	d		00 12	00 18				00a30	00 42	00 48					01a00					06 18
—	25¾	—	Bat & Ball	d		00 15	00 21					00 45	00 51										06 21
—	27	—	**Sevenoaks** ■	a		00 19	00 25					00 49	00 55										06 25

		TL L	SE	TL	TL M	SE ◇■ K	SE ◇■ I	TL	TL L	SE	TL N	TL O	SE ◇■ K	SE	SE G	SE ◇■ P	TL	TL L	SE	SE ◇■ K	TL N	TL L	SE G
London Victoria ■ ⊖	d		05 28			05 42	05 50			05 58			06 12	06 12	06 15	06 25			06 28	06 40			06 42
Brixton ⊖	d		05 35							06 05				06 19					06 35				
Kentish Town ⊖	d	05 04			05 21				05 36		05 41	05 51						06 04			06 11	06 21	
St Pancras International ■ ⊖	d	05 12			05 27				05 42		05 47	05 57						06 12			06 17	06 27	
Farringdon ⊖	d	05 17			05 32				05 47		05 52	06 02						06 17			06 22	06 32	
City Thameslink ■	d	05 19			05 34				05 49		05 54	06 04						06 19			06 24	06 34	
London Blackfriars ■ ⊖	d	05 21		05 26	05 36			05 46	05 51		05 56	06 06					06 16	06 21			06 26	06 36	
Elephant & Castle ⊖	d	05 25		05 30	05 40			05 50	05 55		06 00	06 10					06 20	06 25			06 30	06 40	
Loughborough Jn	d	05 30			05 45				06 00			06 15						06 30				06 45	
Herne Hill ■	d	05a34	05 37		05a49				06a04	06 07		06a19		06 22				06a34	06 37			06a49	
West Dulwich	d		05 40							06 10				06 24					06 40				
Sydenham Hill	d		05 42							06 12				06 26					06 42				
Penge East	d		05 45							06 15				06 29					06 45				
Kent House ■	d		05 47							06 17				06 31					06 47				
Beckenham Junction ■	d		05 50							06 20				06 34					06 50				
Denmark Hill ■	d			05 38		05 52		05 58			06 08		06 22		06 25		06 28				06 38		06 52
Peckham Rye ■	d			05 41				06 01			06 11				06 28		06 31				06 41		06 55
Nunhead ■	d			05 44				06 04			06 14				06 30		06 34				06 44		
Lewisham ■	a														06 35								07 01
Crofton Park	d			05 47				06 07			06 17						06 37				06 47		
Catford	d			05 50				06 10			06 20						06 40				06 50		
Bellingham	d			05 53				06 13			06 23						06 43				06 53		
Beckenham Hill	d			05 55				06 15			06 25						06 45				06 55		
Ravensbourne	d			05 57				06 17			06 27						06 47				06 57		
Shortlands ■	d		05 53	06 00				06 20		06 23	06 30			06 37			06 50		06 53		07 00		
Bromley South ■	d		05 56	06 03		06 05	06 12	06 23		06 26	06 33		06 36	06a41		06 42	06 53		06 56	06 58	07 03		
Bickley ■	d		05 58	06 06				06 26		06 28	06 36						06 56		06 58		07 06		
Petts Wood ■	d		06 03	06 10						06 33	06 40								07 03		07 10		
Orpington ■	d		06a07	06a14						06a37	06a44								07a07		07a14		
St Mary Cray	d					06 10	06 18	06 31					06 41			06 48	07 01			07 04			
Swanley ■	d					06a14	06 22	06 36					06a45			06 52	07 06			07a08			
Eynsford	d							06 41									07 11						
Shoreham (Kent)	d							06 45									07 15						
Otford ■	d						06a30	06 48								07a00	07 18						
Bat & Ball	d							06 51									07 21						
Sevenoaks ■	a							06 55									07 25						

A From St Albans City to Sutton (Surrey)
B From London Blackfriars
C From London Victoria to Faversham
D From London Victoria to Gillingham (Kent)
E From London Victoria
F From London Victoria to Ashford International
G To Dartford
H To Ramsgate
I To Ashford International
J To Gillingham (Kent)
K To Dover Priory
L From Luton to Sutton (Surrey)
M From West Hampstead Thameslink to Sutton (Surrey)
N From West Hampstead Thameslink
O To Sutton (Surrey)
P To Canterbury West

London - Catford, Beckenham Junction, Bromley South, Orpington, Otford and Sevenoaks

		SE	SE 1 A	TL	TL B	SE	TL C	TL B	SE D	SE ◇1 E	SE	TL F	TL B	SE ◇1 G	TL H	SE	SE ◇1 I	TL J	SE	TL B	SE ◇1 K	TL C	SE
London Victoria ⊖	d	06 43	06 55			06 58			07 08	07 10	07 13					07 28	07 40				07 42		07 43
Brixton ⊖	d	06 50				07 05					07 20					07 35							07 50
Kentish Town ⊖	d				06 36			06 51					07 06							07 21			
St Pancras International ⊖	d				06 42		06 47	06 57					07 12					07 17		07 27			
Farringdon ⊖	d				06 47		06 52	07 02					07 17					07 22		07 32			
City Thameslink	d				06 49		06 54	07 04					07 19					07 24		07 34			
London Blackfriars ⊖	d			06 46	06 51		06 56	07 06				07 16	07 21	07 23				07 26	07 34	07 36			
Elephant & Castle ⊖	d			06 50	06 55		07 00	07 10				07 20	07 25	07 27				07 30		07 40			
Loughborough Jn	d				07 00			07 15					07 30							07 45			
Herne Hill	d	06 53			07a04	07 07		07a19			07 23		07a34			07 37			07 43	07a49			07 53
West Dulwich	d	06 55				07 10					07 25					07 40							07 55
Sydenham Hill	d	06 57				07 12					07 27					07 42							07 57
Penge East	d	07 01				07 15					07 31					07 45							08 01
Kent House	d	07 03				07 17					07 33					07 47							08 03
Beckenham Junction	d	07 05				07 20					07 35					07 50			07a53				08 05
Denmark Hill	d			06 58			07 08			07 20		07 28		07 36	←			07 39			07 52	←	
Peckham Rye	d			07 01			07 11					07 31			07 31			07 42				07 42	
Nunhead	d			07 04			07 14					→			07 34			→				07 45	
Lewisham	a								07 25														
Crofton Park	d			07 07			07 17								07 37							07 48	
Catford	d			07 10			07 20								07 40							07 51	
Bellingham	d			07 13			07 23								07 43							07 54	
Beckenham Hill	d			07 15			07 25								07 45							07 56	
Ravensbourne	d			07 17			07 27								07 47							07 58	
Shortlands	d	07 09		07 20		07 23	07 30				07 38				07 50	07 53						08 01	08 08
Bromley South	d	07a12	07 13	07 23		07 26	07 33			07 33	07a42			07 53	07 53	07 56	07a58				08 05	08 07	08a12
Bickley	d			07 26		07 28	07 36								07 56	07 58						08 10	
Petts Wood	d					07 34	07 41									08 03						08 15	
Orpington	d					07a38	07a45									08a07						08a18	
St Mary Cray	d		07 19	07 32						07 39				07 59	08 02						08 10		
Swanley	d		07 23	07 37						07a43				08 04	08 08						08a14		
Eynsford	d			07 42											08 13								
Shoreham (Kent)	d			07 46											08 17								
Otford	d		07a31	07 49										08a12	08 20								
Bat & Ball	d			07 52											08 23								
Sevenoaks	a			07 56											08 26								

		SE L	SE ◇1 A	TL	TL B	SE	TL C	SE	TL B	SE L	SE ◇1 K	SE 1 M	SE	SE ◇1 N	TL	TL B	SE	TL C	SE	TL B	SE L	SE ◇1 I
London Victoria ⊖	d	07 45	07 55			07 58				08 06	08 10	08 12	08 13	08 25			08 28				08 38	08 40
Brixton ⊖	d					08 05							08 20				08 35					
Kentish Town ⊖	d				07 36				07 51							08 06				08 21		
St Pancras International ⊖	d				07 42		07 47		07 57							08 12		08 17		08 27		
Farringdon ⊖	d				07 47		07 52		08 02							08 17		08 22		08 32		
City Thameslink	d				07 49		07 54		08 04							08 19		08 24		08 34		
London Blackfriars ⊖	d			07 46	07 51		07 56	08 04	08 06						08 16	08 21		08 26	08 34	08 36		
Elephant & Castle ⊖	d			07 50	07 55		08 00		08 10						08 20	08 25		08 30		08 40		
Loughborough Jn	d				08 00				08 15							08 30				08 45		
Herne Hill	d				08a04	08 07		08 13	08a19				08 23			08a34	08 37		08 43	08a49		
West Dulwich	d					08 10							08 25				08 40					
Sydenham Hill	d					08 12							08 27				08 42					
Penge East	d					08 15							08 31				08 45					
Kent House	d					08 17							08 33				08 47					
Beckenham Junction	d					08 20		08a23					08 35				08 50		08a53			
Denmark Hill	d	07 55		07 58			08 08			08 16		08 22			08 28			08 38			08 47	
Peckham Rye	d	07 58		08 01			08 11			08 18					08 31			08 41			08 50	
Nunhead	d	08 00		08 04			08 14			08 21					08 34			08 44			08 52	
Lewisham	a	08 06								08 28											09 00	
Crofton Park	d			08 07			08 17								08 37			08 47				
Catford	d			08 10			08 20								08 40			08 50				
Bellingham	d			08 13			08 23								08 43			08 53				
Beckenham Hill	d			08 15			08 25								08 45			08 55				
Ravensbourne	d			08 17			08 27								08 47			08 57				
Shortlands	d			08 20		08 23	08 30						08 38		08 50		08 54	09 00				
Bromley South	d		08 12	08 23		08 26	08 33				08a27	08 36	08a42	08 42	08 53		08 57	09 03				08a57
Bickley	d			08 26		08 28	08 36								08 56		08 59	09 06				
Petts Wood	d					08 33	08 43										09 03	09 10				
Orpington	d					08a37	08a47										09a07	09a14				
St Mary Cray	d		08 18	08 31								08 41			09 01							
Swanley	d		08 22	08 36								08a45		08 50	09 06							
Eynsford	d			08 41											09 11							
Shoreham (Kent)	d			08 45											09 15							
Otford	d		08a30	08 48										08a58	09 18							
Bat & Ball	d			08 51											09 21							
Sevenoaks	a			08 55											09 25							

A To Ashford International
B From St Albans City to Sutton (Surrey)
C From Luton
D To Dartford
E To Gillingham (Kent)
F To Sevenoaks
G To Maidstone East
H From London Blackfriars
I To Ramsgate
J From Luton to Orpington
K To Dover Priory
L To Gravesend
M To Rochester
N To Canterbury West

Table T195-F

Mondays to Fridays

21 May to 7 December

London - Catford, Beckenham Junction, Bromley South, Orpington, Otford and Sevenoaks

		SE ◇1 A	SE	SE ◇1 B	TL	TL C	SE	TL D	TL C	SE E	SE ◇1 A	SE	SE ◇1 F	TL	TL C	SE	TL D	TL C	SE E	SE ◇1 G	SE ◇1 A	SE	SE 1 B
London Victoria ⊖	d	08 42	08 43	08 55			08 58			09 06	09 10	09 13	09 25			09 28			09 36	09 37	09 42	09 43	09 55
Brixton ⊖	d		08 50				09 05					09 20				09 35						09 50	
Kentish Town ⊖	d					08 36			08 51						09 06			09 21					
St Pancras International ⊖	d					08 42		08 47	08 57						09 12		09 17	09 27					
Farringdon ⊖	d					08 47		08 52	09 02						09 17		09 22	09 32					
City Thameslink	d					08 49		08 54	09 04						09 19		09 24	09 34					
London Blackfriars ⊖	d				08 46	08 51		08 56	09 06					09 16	09 21		09 26	09 36					
Elephant & Castle ⊖	d				08 50	08 55		09 00	09 10					09 20	09 25		09 30	09 40					
Loughborough Jn	d					09 00			09 15						09 30			09 45					
Herne Hill	d		08 53			09a04	09 07		09a19			09 22			09a34	09 37		09a49				09 52	
West Dulwich	d		08 55				09 10					09 25				09 40						09 55	
Sydenham Hill	d		08 57				09 12					09 27				09 42						09 57	
Penge East	d		09 01				09 15					09 30				09 45						10 00	
Kent House	d		09 03				09 17					09 32				09 47						10 02	
Beckenham Junction	d		09 05				09 20					09 35				09 50						10 05	
Denmark Hill	d	08 52			08 58			09 08		09 16				09 28			09 38		09 46		09 52		
Peckham Rye	d				09 01			09 12		09 18				09 31			09 41		09 48				
Nunhead	d				09 04			09 15		09 21				09 34			09 44		09 51				
Lewisham	a									09 26									09 56				
Crofton Park	d				09 07			09 18						09 37			09 47						
Catford	d				09 10			09 21						09 40			09 50						
Bellingham	d				09 13			09 24						09 43			09 53						
Beckenham Hill	d				09 15			09 26						09 45			09 55						
Ravensbourne	d				09 17			09 28						09 47			09 57						
Shortlands	d		09 08		09 20		09 23	09 31				09 38		09 50		09 53	10 00					10 08	
Bromley South	d	09 05	09a12	09 12	09 23		09 26	09 34			09a26	09a42	09 42	09 53		09 56	10 03			09a56	10 05	10a12	10 12
Bickley	d				09 26		09 28	09 37						09 56		09 58	10 06						
Petts Wood	d						09 33	09 42								10 03	10 10						
Orpington	d						09a37	09a46								10a07	10a14						
St Mary Cray	d	09 10		09 18	09 32									10 01							10 10		10 18
Swanley	d	09a14		09 22	09 37								09 50	10 06							10a14		10 22
Eynsford	d				09 42									10 11									
Shoreham (Kent)	d				09 46									10 15									
Otford	d			09a30	09 49								09a58	10 18									10a30
Bat & Ball	d				09 52									10 21									
Sevenoaks	a				09 56									10 25									

		TL	TL C	SE	TL D	TL C	SE E	SE ◇1 A	SE	SE ◇1 F	TL	TL C	SE	TL	TL C	SE E	SE ◇1 G	SE ◇1 A	SE	SE ◇1 B	TL	TL C
London Victoria ⊖	d			09 58			10 06	10 10	10 13	10 25			10 28			10 36	10 40	10 42	10 43	10 55		
Brixton ⊖	d			10 05					10 20				10 35						10 50			
Kentish Town ⊖	d		09 36			09 51						10 06		10 11	10 21							10 36
St Pancras International ⊖	d		09 42		09 47	09 57						10 12		10 17	10 27							10 42
Farringdon ⊖	d		09 47		09 52	10 02						10 17		10 22	10 32							10 47
City Thameslink	d		09 49		09 54	10 04						10 19		10 24	10 34							10 49
London Blackfriars ⊖	d	09 46	09 51		09 56	10 06					10 16	10 21		10 26	10 36						10 46	10 51
Elephant & Castle ⊖	d	09 50	09 55		10 00	10 10					10 20	10 25		10 30	10 40						10 50	10 55
Loughborough Jn	d		10 00			10 15						10 30			10 45							11 00
Herne Hill	d		10a04	10 07		10a19			10 22			10a34	10 37		10a49				10 52			11a04
West Dulwich	d			10 10					10 25				10 40						10 55			
Sydenham Hill	d			10 12					10 27				10 42						10 57			
Penge East	d			10 15					10 30				10 45						11 00			
Kent House	d			10 17					10 32				10 47						11 02			
Beckenham Junction	d			10 20					10 35				10 50						11 05			
Denmark Hill	d	09 58			10 08		10 16				10 28			10 38		10 46		10 52			10 58	
Peckham Rye	d	10 01			10 11		10 18				10 31			10 41		10 48					11 01	
Nunhead	d	10 04			10 14		10 21				10 34			10 44		10 51					11 04	
Lewisham	a						10 26									10 56						
Crofton Park	d	10 07			10 17						10 37			10 47							11 07	
Catford	d	10 10			10 20						10 40			10 50							11 10	
Bellingham	d	10 13			10 23						10 43			10 53							11 13	
Beckenham Hill	d	10 15			10 25						10 45			10 55							11 15	
Ravensbourne	d	10 17			10 27						10 47			10 57							11 17	
Shortlands	d	10 20		10 23	10 30				10 38		10 50		10 53	11 00					11 08		11 20	
Bromley South	d	10 23		10 26	10 33			10a26	10a42	10 42	10 53		10 56	11 03			10a56	11 05	11a12	11 12	11 23	
Bickley	d	10 26		10 28	10 37						10 56		10 58	11 06							11 26	
Petts Wood	d			10 33	10 42								11 03	11 10								
Orpington	d			10a37	10a45								11a07	11a14								
St Mary Cray	d	10 31									11 01							11 10		11 18	11 31	
Swanley	d	10 36								10 50	11 06							11a14		11 22	11 36	
Eynsford	d	10 41									11 11										11 41	
Shoreham (Kent)	d	10 45									11 15										11 45	
Otford	d	10 48								10a58	11 18									11a30	11 48	
Bat & Ball	d	10 51									11 21										11 51	
Sevenoaks	a	10 55									11 25										11 55	

A To Dover Priory
B To Ashford International
C From St Albans City to Sutton (Surrey)
D From Luton
E To Gravesend
F To Canterbury West
G To Ramsgate

London - Catford, Beckenham Junction, Bromley South, Orpington, Otford and Sevenoaks

		SE	TL	TL A	SE B	SE ◇1 C	SE	SE ◇1 D	TL	TL A	SE	TL	TL A	SE B	SE ◇1 E	SE ◇1 C	SE	SE ◇1 F	TL	TL A	SE	and at the same minutes past each hour until
London Victoria 15	d	10 58			11 06	11 10	11 13	11 25			11 28			11 36	11 40	11 42	11 43	11 55			11 58	
Brixton	d	11 05					11 20				11 35						11 50				12 05	
Kentish Town	d		10 41	10 51						11 06		11 11	11 21							11 36		
St Pancras International 15	d		10 47	10 57						11 12		11 17	11 27							11 42		
Farringdon	d		10 52	11 02						11 17		11 22	11 32							11 47		
City Thameslink 3	d		10 54	11 04						11 19		11 24	11 34							11 49		
London Blackfriars 3	d		10 56	11 06					11 16	11 21		11 26	11 36						11 46	11 51		
Elephant & Castle	d		11 00	11 10					11 20	11 25		11 30	11 40						11 50	11 55		
Loughborough Jn.	d			11 15						11 30			11 45							12 00		
Herne Hill 4	d	11 07		11a19			11 22			11a34	11 37		11a49				11 52			12a04	12 07	
West Dulwich	d	11 10					11 25				11 40						11 55				12 10	
Sydenham Hill	d	11 12					11 27				11 42						11 57				12 12	
Penge East	d	11 15					11 30				11 45						12 00				12 15	
Kent House 4	d	11 17					11 32				11 47						12 02				12 17	
Beckenham Junction 4	d	11 20					11 35				11 50						12 05				12 20	
Denmark Hill 4	d		11 08		11 16				11 28			11 38		11 46		11 52			11 58			
Peckham Rye 4	d		11 11		11 18				11 31			11 41		11 48					12 01			
Nunhead 4	d		11 14		11 21				11 34			11 44		11 51					12 04			
Lewisham 4	a				11 26									11 56								
Crofton Park	d		11 17						11 37			11 47							12 07			
Catford	d		11 20						11 40			11 50							12 10			
Bellingham	d		11 23						11 43			11 53							12 13			
Beckenham Hill	d		11 25						11 45			11 55							12 15			
Ravensbourne	d		11 27						11 47			11 57							12 17			
Shortlands 4	d	11 23	11 30				11 38		11 50		11 53	12 00					12 08		12 20		12 23	
Bromley South 4	d	11 26	11 33			11a26	11a42	11 42	11 53		11 56	12 03			11a56	12 05	12a12	12 12	12 23		12 26	
Bickley 4	d	11 28	11 36						11 56		11 58	12 06							12 26		12 28	
Petts Wood 4	d	11 33	11 40								12 03	12 10									12 33	
Orpington 4	d	11a39	11a44								12a07	12a14									12a37	
St Mary Cray	d								12 01							12 10		12 18	12 31			
Swanley 4	d							11 50	12 06							12a14		12 22	12 36			
Eynsford	d								12 11										12 41			
Shoreham (Kent)	d								12 15										12 45			
Otford 4	d							11a58	12 18									12a30	12 48			
Bat & Ball	d								12 21										12 51			
Sevenoaks 4	a								12 25										12 55			

		TL	TL A	SE B	SE ◇1 C	SE	SE ◇1 D	TL	TL A	SE	TL	TL A	SE B	SE ◇1 E	SE ◇1 G	SE	SE ◇1 F	TL	TL A	SE	TL	TL A	SE B	SE ◇1 C
London Victoria 15	d			14 06	14 10	14 13	14 25			14 28			14 36	14 40	14 42	14 43	14 55			14 58			15 06	15 10
Brixton	d					14 20				14 35						14 50				15 05				
Kentish Town	d	13 41	13 51						14 06		14 11	14 21							14 36		14 41	14 51		
St Pancras International 15	d	13 47	13 57						14 12		14 17	14 27							14 42		14 47	14 57		
Farringdon	d	13 52	14 02						14 17		14 22	14 32							14 47		14 52	15 02		
City Thameslink 3	d	13 54	14 04						14 19		14 24	14 34							14 49		14 54	15 04		
London Blackfriars 3	d	13 56	14 06					14 16	14 21		14 26	14 36						14 46	14 51		14 56	15 06		
Elephant & Castle	d	14 00	14 10					14 20	14 25		14 30	14 40						14 50	14 55		15 00	15 10		
Loughborough Jn.	d		14 15						14 30			14 45							15 00			15 15		
Herne Hill 4	d		14a19			14 22			14a34	14 37		14a49				14 52			15a04	15 07		15a19		
West Dulwich	d					14 25				14 40						14 55				15 10				
Sydenham Hill	d					14 27				14 42						14 57				15 12				
Penge East	d					14 30				14 45						15 00				15 15				
Kent House 4	d					14 32				14 47						15 02				15 17				
Beckenham Junction 4	d					14 35				14 50						15 05				15 20				
Denmark Hill 4	d	14 08		14 16				14 28			14 38		14 46		14 52			14 58			15 08		15 16	
Peckham Rye 4	d	14 11		14 18				14 31			14 41		14 48					15 01			15 11		15 18	
Nunhead 4	d	14 14		14 21				14 34			14 44		14 51					15 04			15 14		15 21	
Lewisham 4	a			14 26									14 56										15 26	
Crofton Park	d	14 17						14 37			14 47							15 07			15 17			
Catford	d	14 20						14 40			14 50							15 10			15 20			
Bellingham	d	14 23						14 43			14 53							15 13			15 23			
Beckenham Hill	d	14 25						14 45			14 55							15 15			15 25			
Ravensbourne	d	14 27						14 47			14 57							15 17			15 27			
Shortlands 4	d	14 30				14 38		14 50		14 53	15 00					15 08		15 20		15 23	15 30			
Bromley South 4	d	14 33			14a26	14a42	14 42	14 53		14 56	15 03			14a56	15 05	15a12	15 12	15 23		15 26	15 33			15a26
Bickley 4	d	14 36						14 56		14 58	15 06							15 26		15 28	15 36			
Petts Wood 4	d	14 40								15 03	15 10									15 33	15 40			
Orpington 4	d	14a44								15a07	15a14									15a37	15a44			
St Mary Cray	d							15 01							15 10		15 18	15 31						
Swanley 4	d						14 50	15 06							15a14		15 22	15 36						
Eynsford	d							15 11										15 41						
Shoreham (Kent)	d							15 15										15 45						
Otford 4	d						14a58	15 18									15a30	15 48						
Bat & Ball	d							15 21										15 51						
Sevenoaks 4	a							15 25										15 55						

A From St Albans City to Sutton (Surrey)
B To Gravesend
C To Dover Priory
D To Canterbury West
E To Ramsgate
F To Ashford International
G To Gillingham (Kent)

Table T195-F
Mondays to Fridays
21 May to 7 December

London - Catford, Beckenham Junction, Bromley South, Orpington, Otford and Sevenoaks

		SE	SE ◇1 A	TL	TL B	SE	TL	TL B	SE C	SE ◇1 D	SE ◇1 E	SE	SE ◇1 F	TL	TL B	SE	TL	TL B	SE C	SE ◇1 D	SE 1 E	SE	SE ◇1 F
London Victoria 15	d	15 13	15 25			15 28			15 36	15 40	15 42	15 43	15 55			15 58			16 06	16 10	16 12	16 13	16 25
Brixton	d	15 20				15 35						15 50				16 05						16 20	
Kentish Town	d				15 06		15 11	15 21							15 36		15 41	15 51					
St Pancras International 15	d				15 12		15 17	15 27							15 42		15 47	15 57					
Farringdon	d				15 17		15 22	15 32							15 47		15 52	16 02					
City Thameslink 3	d				15 19		15 24	15 34							15 49		15 54	16 04					
London Blackfriars 3	d			15 16	15 21		15 26	15 36						15 46	15 51		15 56	16 06					
Elephant & Castle	d			15 20	15 25		15 30	15 40						15 50	15 55		16 00	16 10					
Loughborough Jn.	d				15 30			15 45							16 00			16 15					
Herne Hill 4	d	15 22			15a34	15 37		15a49				15 52			16a04	16 07		16a19				16 22	
West Dulwich	d	15 25				15 40						15 55				16 10						16 25	
Sydenham Hill	d	15 27				15 42						15 57				16 12						16 27	
Penge East	d	15 30				15 45						16 00				16 15						16 30	
Kent House 4	d	15 32				15 47						16 02				16 17						16 32	
Beckenham Junction 4	d	15 35				15 50						16 05				16 20						16 35	
Denmark Hill 4	d			15 28			15 38		15 46		15 52			15 58			16 08		16 16		16 22		
Peckham Rye 4	d			15 31			15 41		15 48					16 01			16 11		16 18				
Nunhead 4	d			15 34			15 44		15 51					16 04			16 14		16 21				
Lewisham 4	a								15 56										16 26				
Crofton Park	d			15 37			15 47							16 07			16 17						
Catford	d			15 40			15 50							16 10			16 20						
Bellingham	d			15 43			15 53							16 13			16 23						
Beckenham Hill	d			15 45			15 55							16 15			16 25						
Ravensbourne	d			15 47			15 58							16 17			16 27						
Shortlands 4	d	15 38		15 50		15 53	16 00					16 08		16 20		16 23	16 30					16 38	
Bromley South 4	d	15a42	15 42	15 53		15 56	16 03			15a56	16 05	16a12	16 12	16 23		16 26	16 33			16a26	16 35	16a43	16 42
Bickley 4	d			15 56		15 58	16 06							16 26		16 28	16 36						
Petts Wood 4	d					16 03	16 11									16 33	16 40						
Orpington 4	d					16a07	16a14									16a37	16a44						
St Mary Cray	d			16 01							16 10		16 18	16 31							16 40		
Swanley 4	d		15 50	16 06							16a14		16 22	16 36							16a44		16 50
Eynsford	d			16 11										16 41									
Shoreham (Kent)	d			16 15										16 45									
Otford 4	d		15a58	16 18									16a30	16 48									16a58
Bat & Ball	d			16 21										16 51									
Sevenoaks 4	a			16 25										16 55									

		TL	TL B	SE	TL	TL B	SE G	SE ◇1 H	SE ◇1 I	SE	SE ◇1 F	TL	SE	TL B	SE	TL J	SE ◇1 I	TL B	SE G	SE 1 K	SE ◇1 D	TL L
London Victoria 15	d			16 28			16 36	16 40	16 42	16 43	16 52				16 58				17 06	17 09	17 10	
Brixton	d			16 35						16 50					17 05							
Kentish Town	d		16 06		16 11	16 22								16 37		16 41		16 52				
St Pancras International 15	d		16 12		16 17	16 27								16 42		16 47		16 57				
Farringdon	d		16 17		16 22	16 32								16 47		16 52		17 02				
City Thameslink 3	d		16 19		16 24	16 34								16 49		16 54		17 04				
London Blackfriars 3	d	16 16	16 21		16 26	16 36						16 46	16 49	16 51		16 56	17 05	17 06				
Elephant & Castle	d	16 20	16 25		16 30	16 40						16 50	16 53	16 55		17 00	17 09	17 10				
Loughborough Jn.	d		16 30			16 45							16 57	17 00				17 15				
Herne Hill 4	d		16a34	16 37		16a49				16 52			17 01	17a04	17 07			17a19				
West Dulwich	d			16 40						16 55			17 04		17 10							
Sydenham Hill	d			16 42						16 57			17 06		17 12							
Penge East	d			16 45						17 00			17 09		17 15							
Kent House 4	d			16 47						17 02			17 12		17 17							
Beckenham Junction 4	d			16 50						17 05			17a16		17 20							
Denmark Hill 4	d	16 28			16 38		16 46		16 52			16 58				17 08			17 16			
Peckham Rye 4	d	16 31			16 41		16 48					17 01				17 11			17 19			
Nunhead 4	d	16 34			16 44		16 51					17 04				17 14			17 21			
Lewisham 4	a						16 56												17 26			
Crofton Park	d	16 37			16 47							17 07				17 17						
Catford	d	16 40			16 50							17 10				17 20						
Bellingham	d	16 43			16 53							17 13				17 23						
Beckenham Hill	d	16 45			16 55							17 15				17 25						
Ravensbourne	d	16 47			16 57							17 17				17 27						
Shortlands 4	d	16 50		16 53	17 00					17 08		17 20			17 23	17 30						←
Bromley South 4	d	16 53		16 56	17 03			16a56	17 05	17a13	17 12	17 23			17 26	17 33	17 29			17 34	17a29	17 33
Bickley 4	d	16 56		16 58	17 06							17 26			17 28	→						17 36
Petts Wood 4	d			17 06	17 10										17 33							17 42
Orpington 4	d			17a11	17a14										17a37							17a45
St Mary Cray	d	17 01							17 11		17 18	17 31					17 36					
Swanley 4	d	17 06							17a15		17 22	17 36					17a40					
Eynsford	d	17 11										17 41										
Shoreham (Kent)	d	17 15										17 45										
Otford 4	d	17 18									17a30	17 48								17a51		
Bat & Ball	d	17 21										17 51										
Sevenoaks 4	a	17 25										17 55										

A To Canterbury West
B From St Albans City to Sutton (Surrey)
C To Gravesend
D To Dover Priory
E To Gillingham (Kent)
F To Ashford International
G To Dartford
H To Ramsgate
I To Rochester
J From West Hampstead Thameslink to Orpington
K To Maidstone East
L From West Hampstead Thameslink

London - Catford, Beckenham Junction, Bromley South, Orpington, Otford and Sevenoaks

		SE ◇ A	SE	SE ◇■ B	TL	SE	TL C	SE	TL D	TL C	SE E	SE ◇■ F	SE ◇■ B	SE ◇■ G	SE	SE ◇■ B	TL	SE	TL C	SE E	SE	SE ■ H	SE ◇■ F
London Victoria ⊖	d	17 12	17 13	17 22				17 28			17 34	17 40		17 42	17 43	17 52				17 55	17 58	18 07	18 10
Brixton ⊖	d		17 20					17 35							17 50						18 05		
Kentish Town ⊖	d						17 07		17 11	17 22									17 37				
St Pancras International ⊖	d						17 12		17 17	17 27									17 42				
Farringdon ⊖	d						17 17		17 22	17 32									17 47				
City Thameslink	d						17 19		17 24	17 34									17 49				
London Blackfriars ⊖	d				17 16	17 19	17 21		17 26	17 36			17 38				17 46	17 49	17 51				
Elephant & Castle ⊖	d				17 20	17 23	17 25		17 30	17 40			17 42				17 50	17 53	17 55				
Loughborough Jn.	d					17 27	17 30			17 45								17 57	18 00				
Herne Hill	d		17 22			17 31	17a34	17 37		17a49					17 52			18 01	18a04		18 07		
West Dulwich	d		17 25			17 34		17 40							17 55			18 04			18 10		
Sydenham Hill	d		17 27			17 36		17 42							17 57			18 06			18 12		
Penge East	d		17 30			17 39		17 45							18 00			18 09			18 15		
Kent House	d		17 32			17 42		17 47							18 02			18 12			18 17		
Beckenham Junction	d		17 35			17a46		17 50							18 05			18a16			18 20		
Denmark Hill	d	17 22			17 28				17 38		17 44			17 52			17 58			18 05			
Peckham Rye	d				17 31				17 41		17 47						18 01			18 08			
Nunhead	d				17 34				17 44		17 50						18 04			18 11			
Lewisham	a										17 59									18 18			
Crofton Park	d				17 37				17 47								18 07						
Catford	d				17 40				17 50								18 10						
Bellingham	d				17 43				17 53								18 13						
Beckenham Hill	d				17 45				17 55								18 15						
Ravensbourne	d				17 47				17 57								18 17						
Shortlands	d		17 38		17 50			17 53	18 00						18 08		18 20				18 23		
Bromley South	d	17 37	17a43	17 42	17 53			17 56	18 03			17a56	18 03	18 07	18a13	18 12	18 23				18 26	18 33	18a29
Bickley	d				17 56			17 58	18 06								18 26				18 28	→	
Petts Wood	d							18 06	18 12												18 33		
Orpington	d							18a12	18a16												18a38		
St Mary Cray	d	17 43			18 01								18 10	18 14		18 18	18 30						
Swanley	d	17a47		17 51	18 06								18 14	18a18		18 22	18 35						
Eynsford	d				18 11												18 40						
Shoreham (Kent)	d				18 15												18 44						
Otford	d			17a59	18 18								18a22			18a30	18 47						
Bat & Ball	d				18 21												18 50						
Sevenoaks	a				18 25												18 55						

		TL I	SE ◇ G	SE ■ J	TL D	TL C	SE ◇■ A	SE	TL K	SE	TL C	SE E	SE ◇■ B	TL L	SE	TL M	TL C	SE ◇ G	SE ◇■ N	SE E	SE	SE ◇■ B
London Victoria ⊖	d						18 12	18 13				18 21	18 22		18 28			18 39	18 40	18 42	18 43	18 52
Brixton ⊖	d							18 20							18 35						18 50	
Kentish Town ⊖	d	17 41				17 52					18 06					18 11	18 22					
St Pancras International ⊖	d	17 47				17 57					18 12					18 17	18 27					
Farringdon ⊖	d	17 52				18 02					18 17					18 22	18 32					
City Thameslink	d	17 54				18 04					18 19					18 24	18 34					
London Blackfriars ⊖	d	17 56	18 05			18 06			18 16	18 19	18 21					18 26	18 36					
Elephant & Castle ⊖	d	18 00	18 09			18 10			18 20	18 23	18 25					18 30	18 40					
Loughborough Jn.	d					18 15				18 27	18 30						18 45					
Herne Hill	d					18a19		18 22		18 31	18a34				18 37		18a49				18 52	
West Dulwich	d							18 25		18 34					18 40						18 55	
Sydenham Hill	d							18 27		18 36					18 42						18 57	
Penge East	d							18 30		18 39					18 45						19 00	
Kent House	d							18 32		18 42					18 47						19 02	
Beckenham Junction	d				←			18 35		18a46					18 50						19 05	
Denmark Hill	d	18 08			18 08		18 22		18 28			18 31				18 38		18 49		18 52		
Peckham Rye	d	→			18 11				18 31			18 34				18 41				18 55		
Nunhead	d				18 14				18 34			18 37				18 44				18 58		
Lewisham	a											18 43		←						19 05		
Crofton Park	d				18 17				18 37					18 37		18 47						
Catford	d				18 20				→					18 40		18 50						
Bellingham	d				18 23									18 43		18 53						
Beckenham Hill	d				18 25									18 45		18 55						
Ravensbourne	d				18 27									18 47		18 57						
Shortlands	d			←	18 30			18 38						18 50	18 53	19 00					19 08	
Bromley South	d		18 29	18 33	18 33		18 37	18a43					18 42	18 53	18 56	19 03		19 04	18a56		19a13	19 12
Bickley	d				18 36									18 56	18 58	19 06						
Petts Wood	d				18 44										19 06	19 10						
Orpington	d				18a48										19a11	19a14						
St Mary Cray	d		18 36				18 43							19 01				19 10				19 18
Swanley	d		18a40				18a47						18 51	19 06				19a14				19 22
Eynsford	d													19 11								
Shoreham (Kent)	d													19 15								
Otford	d			18a52									18a59	19 18								19a30
Bat & Ball	d													19 21								
Sevenoaks	a													19 25								

A To Sheerness-on-Sea
B To Ashford International
C From St Albans City to Sutton (Surrey)
D From West Hampstead Thameslink
E To Dartford
F To Ramsgate
G To Rochester
H To Maidstone East
I From West Hampstead Thameslink to Orpington
J From London Victoria to Maidstone East
K To Sevenoaks
L From London Blackfriars
M From Luton
N To Dover Priory

Table T195-F

Mondays to Fridays
21 May to 7 December

London - Catford, Beckenham Junction, Bromley South, Orpington, Otford and Sevenoaks

		TL	SE	TL A	SE	TL B	SE ◇■ C	TL A	SE D	SE ◇■ E	TL F	SE ■ G	SE	SE ◇■ H	TL	TL A	SE	TL F	TL A	SE D	SE ◇■ I	SE ◇ G	SE
London Victoria ⊖	d				18 58				19 06	19 10		19 12	19 13	19 25			19 28			19 36	19 40	19 42	19 43
Brixton ⊖	d				19 05								19 20				19 35						19 50
Kentish Town ⊖	d			18 36		18 41		18 52								19 05		19 11	19 21				
St Pancras International ⊖	d			18 42		18 47		18 57								19 12		19 17	19 27				
Farringdon ⊖	d			18 47		18 52		19 02								19 17		19 22	19 32				
City Thameslink	d			18 49		18 54		19 04								19 19		19 24	19 34				
London Blackfriars ⊖	d	18 46	18 49	18 51		18 56	19 05	19 06							19 16	19 21		19 26	19 36				
Elephant & Castle ⊖	d	18 50	18 53	18 55		19 00	19 09	19 10							19 20	19 25		19 30	19 40				
Loughborough Jn.	d		18 57	19 00				19 15								19 30			19 45				
Herne Hill	d		19 01	19a04	19 07			19a19					19 22			19a34	19 37		19a49				19 52
West Dulwich	d		19 04		19 10								19 25				19 40						19 55
Sydenham Hill	d		19 06		19 12								19 27				19 42						19 57
Penge East	d		19 09		19 15								19 30				19 45						20 00
Kent House	d		19 12		19 17								19 32				19 47						20 02
Beckenham Junction	d		19a16		19 20								19 35				19 50						20 05
Denmark Hill	d	18 58				19 08			19 16			19 22			19 28			19 39		19 46		19 52	
Peckham Rye	d	19 01				19 11			19 18						19 31			19 42		19 48			
Nunhead	d	19 04				19 14			19 21						19 34			19 45		19 51			
Lewisham	a								19 26		←									19 56			
Crofton Park	d	19 07				19 17					19 17				19 37			19 48					
Catford	d	19 10				→					19 20				19 40			19 51					
Bellingham	d	19 13									19 23				19 43			19 54					
Beckenham Hill	d	19 15									19 25				19 45			19 56					
Ravensbourne	d	19 17									19 27				19 47			19 58					
Shortlands	d	19 20			19 23						19 30		19 38		19 50		19 53	20 01					20 08
Bromley South	d	19 23			19 26		19 27			19a29	19 33	19 35	19a42	19 42	19 53		19 56	20 04			19a56	20 05	20a12
Bickley	d	19 26			19 28						19 36				19 56		19 58	20 06					
Petts Wood	d				19 33						19 40						20 03	20 11					
Orpington	d				19a38						19a44						20a07	20a14					
St Mary Cray	d	19 31					19 34					19 41			20 01							20 10	
Swanley	d	19 36					19 40					19a45		19 50	20 06							20a14	
Eynsford	d	19 41													20 11								
Shoreham (Kent)	d	19 45													20 15								
Otford	d	19 48					19a51							19a58	20 18								
Bat & Ball	d	19 51													20 21								
Sevenoaks	a	19 55													20 25								

		SE ◇■ J	TL	TL A	SE	TL F	TL A	SE D	SE ◇■ E	SE ◇ G	SE	SE ◇■ J	TL	TL A	SE	TL F	TL A	SE D	SE ◇■ I	SE ◇ K	SE	SE ◇■ J	TL
London Victoria ⊖	d	19 55			19 58			20 06	20 10	20 12	20 13	20 25			20 28			20 36	20 40	20 42	20 43	20 55	
Brixton ⊖	d				20 05						20 20				20 35						20 50		
Kentish Town ⊖	d			19 36		19 41	19 51							20 06		20 11	20 21						
St Pancras International ⊖	d			19 42		19 47	19 57							20 12		20 17	20 27						
Farringdon ⊖	d			19 47		19 52	20 02							20 17		20 22	20 32						
City Thameslink	d			19 49		19 54	20 04							20 19		20 24	20 34						
London Blackfriars ⊖	d		19 46	19 51		19 56	20 06						20 16	20 21		20 26	20 36						20 46
Elephant & Castle ⊖	d		19 50	19 55		20 00	20 10						20 20	20 25		20 30	20 40						20 50
Loughborough Jn.	d			20 00			20 15							20 30			20 45						
Herne Hill	d			20a04	20 07		20a19				20 22			20a34	20 37		20a49				20 52		
West Dulwich	d				20 10						20 25				20 40						20 55		
Sydenham Hill	d				20 12						20 27				20 42						20 57		
Penge East	d				20 15						20 30				20 45						21 00		
Kent House	d				20 17						20 32				20 47						21 02		
Beckenham Junction	d				20 20						20 35				20 50						21 05		
Denmark Hill	d		19 58			20 08		20 16		20 22			20 28			20 38		20 46		20 52			20 58
Peckham Rye	d		20 01			20 11		20 18					20 31			20 41		20 48					21 01
Nunhead	d		20 04			20 14		20 21					20 34			20 44		20 51					21 04
Lewisham	a							20 26										20 56					
Crofton Park	d		20 07			20 17							20 37			20 47							21 07
Catford	d		20 10			20 20							20 40			20 50							21 10
Bellingham	d		20 13			20 23							20 43			20 53							21 13
Beckenham Hill	d		20 15			20 25							20 45			20 55							21 15
Ravensbourne	d		20 17			20 27							20 47			20 57							21 17
Shortlands	d		20 20		20 23	20 30					20 38		20 50		20 53	21 00					21 08		21 20
Bromley South	d	20 12	20 23		20 26	20 33			20a26	20 37	20a42	20 42	20 53		20 56	21 03			20a56	21 05	21a12	21 12	21 23
Bickley	d		20 26		20 28	20 36							20 56		20 58	21 06							21 26
Petts Wood	d				20 33	20 40									21 03	21 10							
Orpington	d				20a37	20a44									21a07	21a14							
St Mary Cray	d	20 18	20 31							20 42			21 01							21 10		21 18	21 31
Swanley	d	20 22	20 36							20a46		20 51	21 06							21a14		21 22	21 36
Eynsford	d		20 41										21 11										21 41
Shoreham (Kent)	d		20 45										21 15										21 45
Otford	d	20a30	20 48									20a59	21 18									21a30	21 48
Bat & Ball	d		20 51										21 21										21 51
Sevenoaks	a		20 55										21 25										21 55

A From St Albans City to Sutton (Surrey)
B From Luton to Orpington
C To Maidstone East
D To Gravesend
E To Dover Priory
F From Luton
G To Gillingham (Kent)
H To Canterbury West
I To Ramsgate
J To Ashford International
K To Canterbury East

Table T195-F

Mondays to Fridays

21 May to 7 December

London - Catford, Beckenham Junction, Bromley South, Orpington, Otford and Sevenoaks

	TL A		SE	TL	TL A	SE B	SE ◇1 C	SE	SE ◇1 D	TL	TL A		SE	TL	TL A	SE B	SE ◇1 E	SE ◇ F	SE	SE ◇1 D	TL		TL A	SE
London Victoria ⊖ d			20 58			21 06	21 10	21 13	21 25				21 28			21 36	21 40	21 42	21 43	21 55				21 58
Brixton ⊖ d			21 05					21 20					21 35						21 50					22 05
Kentish Town ⊖ d	20 36			20 41	20 51						21 06			21 11	21 21								21 36	
St Pancras International ⊖ d	20 42			20 47	20 57						21 12			21 17	21 27								21 42	
Farringdon ⊖ d	20 47			20 52	21 02						21 17			21 22	21 32								21 47	
City Thameslink d	20 49			20 54	21 04						21 19			21 24	21 34								21 49	
London Blackfriars ⊖ d	20 51			20 56	21 06					21 16	21 21			21 26	21 36						21 46		21 51	
Elephant & Castle ⊖ d	20 55			21 00	21 10					21 20	21 25			21 30	21 40						21 50		21 55	
Loughborough Jn. d	21 00				21 15						21 30				21 45								22 00	
Herne Hill d	21a04		21 07		21a19			21 22			21a34		21 37		21a49				21 52				22a04	22 07
West Dulwich d			21 10					21 25					21 40						21 55					22 10
Sydenham Hill d			21 12					21 27					21 42						21 57					22 12
Penge East d			21 15					21 30					21 45						22 00					22 15
Kent House d			21 17					21 32					21 47						22 02					22 17
Beckenham Junction d			21 20					21 35					21 50						22 05					22 20
Denmark Hill d				21 08		21 16				21 28				21 38		21 46		21 52			21 58			
Peckham Rye d				21 11		21 18				21 31				21 41		21 48					22 01			
Nunhead d				21 14		21 21				21 34				21 44		21 51					22 04			
Lewisham a						21 26										21 56								
Crofton Park d				21 17						21 37				21 47							22 07			
Catford d				21 20						21 40				21 50							22 10			
Bellingham d				21 23						21 43				21 53							22 13			
Beckenham Hill d				21 25						21 45				21 55							22 15			
Ravensbourne d				21 27						21 47				21 57							22 17			
Shortlands d			21 23	21 30				21 38		21 50			21 53	22 00					22 08		22 20			22 23
Bromley South d			21 26	21 33			21a26	21a42	21 42	21 53			21 56	22 03			21a56	22 05	22a12	22 12	22 23			22 26
Bickley d			21 28	21 36						21 56			21 58	22 06							22 26			22 28
Petts Wood d			21 33	21 40									22 03	22 10										22 33
Orpington d			21a37	21a44									22a07	22a14										22a37
St Mary Cray d										22 01								22 10		22 18	22 31			
Swanley d									21 50	22 06								22a14		22 22	22 36			
Eynsford d										22 11											22 41			
Shoreham (Kent) d										22 15											22 45			
Otford d									21a58	22 18										22a30	22 48			
Bat & Ball d										22 21											22 51			
Sevenoaks a										22 25											22 55			

	TL	TL A	SE B	SE ◇1 C	SE	SE ◇1 D	TL		TL A	SE	TL	TL A	SE B	SE ◇1 E	SE ◇ G	SE	SE ◇1 D		TL	TL A	SE	TL	TL A	SE H
London Victoria ⊖ d			22 06	22 10	22 13	22 25				22 28			22 36	22 40	22 42	22 43	22 55				22 58			23 06
Brixton ⊖ d					22 20					22 35						22 50					23 05			
Kentish Town ⊖ d	21 41	21 51							22 06		22 11	22 21								22 36		22 41	22 51	
St Pancras International ⊖ d	21 47	21 57							22 12		22 17	22 27								22 42		22 47	22 57	
Farringdon ⊖ d	21 52	22 02							22 17		22 22	22 32								22 47		22 52	23 02	
City Thameslink d	21 54	22 04							22 19		22 24	22 34								22 49		22 54		
London Blackfriars ⊖ d	21 56	22 06					22 16		22 21		22 26	22 36							22 46	22 51		22 56	23 06	
Elephant & Castle ⊖ d	22 00	22 10					22 20		22 25		22 30	22 40							22 50	22 55		23 00	23 10	
Loughborough Jn. d		22 15							22 30			22 45								23 00			23 15	
Herne Hill d		22a19			22 22				22a34	22 37		22a49				22 52				23a04	23 07		23a19	
West Dulwich d					22 25					22 40						22 55					23 10			
Sydenham Hill d					22 27					22 42						22 57					23 12			
Penge East d					22 30					22 45						23 00					23 15			
Kent House d					22 32					22 47						23 02					23 17			
Beckenham Junction d					22 35					22 50						23 05					23 20			
Denmark Hill d	22 08		22 16				22 28				22 38		22 46		22 52				22 58			23 08		23 16
Peckham Rye d	22 11		22 18				22 31				22 41		22 48						23 01			23 11		23 18
Nunhead d	22 14		22 21				22 34				22 44		22 51						23 04			23 14		23 21
Lewisham a			22 26										22 56											23 26
Crofton Park d	22 17						22 37				22 47								23 07			23 17		
Catford d	22 20						22 40				22 50								23 10			23 20		
Bellingham d	22 23						22 43				22 53								23 13			23 23		
Beckenham Hill d	22 25						22 45				22 55								23 15			23 25		
Ravensbourne d	22 27						22 47				22 57								23 17			23 27		
Shortlands d	22 30				22 38		22 50			22 53	23 00					23 08			23 20		23 23	23 30		
Bromley South d	22 33			22a26	22a42	22 42	22 53			22 56	23 03			22a56	23 05	23a12	23 12		23 23		23 26	23 33		
Bickley d	22 36						22 56			22 58	23 06								23 26		23 28	23 36		
Petts Wood d	22 40									23 03	23 10										23 33	23 40		
Orpington d	22a44									23a07	23a14										23a37	23a44		
St Mary Cray d							23 01								23 10		23 18		23 31					
Swanley d						22 50	23 06								23a14		23 22		23 36					
Eynsford d							23 11												23 41					
Shoreham (Kent) d							23 15												23 45					
Otford d						22a58	23 18										23a30		23 48					
Bat & Ball d							23 21												23 51					
Sevenoaks a							23 25												23 55					

A From St Albans City to Sutton (Surrey)
B To Gravesend
C To Dover Priory
D To Ashford International
E To Ramsgate
F To Canterbury East
G To Gillingham (Kent)
H To Dartford

Table T195-F

Mondays to Fridays

21 May to 7 December

London - Catford, Beckenham Junction, Bromley South, Orpington, Otford and Sevenoaks

	SE ◇1 A	SE	SE ◇1 B		TL	TL C	SE	SE D	SE E	SE	SE ◇1 B	TL	TL C		SE
London Victoria ⊖ d	23 10	23 13	23 25				23 28	23 36	23 42	23 43	23 55				23 58
Brixton ⊖ d		23 20					23 35			23 50					00 05
Kentish Town ⊖ d						23 06							23 38		
St Pancras International ⊖ d						23 12							23 44		
Farringdon ⊖ d						23 17							23 49		
City Thameslink d															
London Blackfriars ⊖ d					23 16	23 21						23 46	23 53		
Elephant & Castle ⊖ d					23 20	23 25						23 50	23 57		
Loughborough Jn. d						23 30							00 02		
Herne Hill d		23 22				23a34	23 37			23 52			00a06		00 08
West Dulwich d		23 25					23 40			23 55					00 11
Sydenham Hill d		23 27					23 42			23 57					00 13
Penge East d		23 30					23 45			23 59					00 16
Kent House d		23 32					23 47			00 02					00 18
Beckenham Junction d		23 35					23 50			00 05					00 21
Denmark Hill d					23 28			23 46	23 52			23 58			
Peckham Rye d					23 31			23 48				00 01			
Nunhead d					23 34			23 51				00 04			
Lewisham a								23 56							
Crofton Park d					23 37							00 07			
Catford d					23 40							00 10			
Bellingham d					23 43							00 13			
Beckenham Hill d					23 45							00 15			
Ravensbourne d					23 47							00 17			
Shortlands d		23 38			23 50		23 53			00 09		00 20			00 24
Bromley South d	23a26	23a42	23 42		23 53		23 56		00 05	00a12	00 12	00 23			00 27
Bickley d					23 56		23 58					00 26			00 29
Petts Wood d							00 03								00 34
Orpington d							00a07								00a38
St Mary Cray d					00 01				00 11		00 18	00 31			
Swanley d			23 50		00 06				00a15		00 22	00 36			
Eynsford d					00 11							00 41			
Shoreham (Kent) d					00 15							00 45			
Otford d			23a58		00 18						00a30	00 48			
Bat & Ball d					00 21							00 51			
Sevenoaks a					00 25							00 55			

Saturdays

26 May to 8 December

	TL F	TL C	SE G	SE H	SE ◇1 I	TL F	SE H	SE D	SE ◇1 B		SE	TL	TL J	SE	TL K	SE ◇1 L	SE	TL	TL J		SE	TL K	SE	SE ◇1 M
London Victoria ⊖ d								00 06	00 25		00 28			05 28		05 42	05 43				05 58		06 13	06 25
Brixton ⊖ d							00 05				00 35			05 35			05 50				06 05		06 20	
Kentish Town ⊖ d													05 04		05 21				05 34			05 51		
St Pancras International ⊖ d													05 12		05 27				05 42			05 57		
Farringdon ⊖ d													05 17		05 32				05 47			06 02		
City Thameslink d																								
London Blackfriars ⊖ d												05 16	05 21		05 36			05 46	05 51			06 06		
Elephant & Castle ⊖ d												05 20	05 25		05 40			05 50	05 55			06 10		
Loughborough Jn. d		00 02											05 30		05 45				06 00			06 15		
Herne Hill d		00a06					00 08				00 37		05a34	05 37	05a49		05 52		06a04		06 07	06a19	06 22	
West Dulwich d							00 11				00 40			05 40			05 55				06 10		06 25	
Sydenham Hill d							00 13				00 42			05 42			05 57				06 12		06 27	
Penge East d							00 16				00 45			05 45			06 00				06 15		06 30	
Kent House d				00 02			00 18				00 47			05 47			06 02				06 17		06 32	
Beckenham Junction d				00 05			00 21				00 50			05 50			06 05				06 20		06 35	
Denmark Hill d								00 16				05 28				05 52		05 58						
Peckham Rye d						00 01		00 18				05 31						06 01						
Nunhead d						00 04		00 21				05 34						06 04						
Lewisham a								00 26																
Crofton Park d						00 07						05 37						06 07						
Catford d						00 10						05 40						06 10						
Bellingham d						00 13						05 43						06 13						
Beckenham Hill d						00 15						05 45						06 15						
Ravensbourne d						00 17						05 47						06 17						
Shortlands d				00 09		00 20	00 24				00 53	05 50		05 53			06 08	06 20			06 23		06 38	
Bromley South d			00 05	00a12	00 12	00 23	00 27		00 42		00 56	05 53		05 56		06 05	06a11	06 23			06 26		06a41	06 42
Bickley d						00 26	00 29				00 58	05 56		05 58				06 26			06 28			
Petts Wood d							00 34				01 03			06 03							06 33			
Orpington d							00a38				01a07			06a06							06a36			
St Mary Cray d	00 01		00 11		00 18	00 31			00 48			06 01				06 10		06 31						06 48
Swanley d	00 06		00a15		00 22	00 36			00 52			06 06				06a14		06 36						06 52
Eynsford d	00 11					00 41						06 11						06 41						
Shoreham (Kent) d	00 15					00 45						06 15						06 45						
Otford d	00 18				00a30	00 48			01a00			06 18						06 48						07a00
Bat & Ball d	00 21					00 51						06 21						06 51						
Sevenoaks a	00 25					00 55						06 25						06 55						

A To Ramsgate
B To Ashford International
C From St Albans City to Sutton (Surrey)
D To Dartford
E To Gillingham (Kent)
F From London Blackfriars
G From London Victoria to Gillingham (Kent)
H From London Victoria
I From London Victoria to Ashford International
J From Luton to Sutton (Surrey)
K From West Hampstead Thameslink to Sutton (Surrey)
L To Dover Priory
M To Canterbury West

London - Catford, Beckenham Junction, Bromley South, Orpington, Otford and Sevenoaks

	TL	TL	SE	TL	SE		SE	TL	TL	SE	TL	TL	SE	SE	SE		SE	TL	TL	SE	TL	TL	SE	SE
		A		A	◇ B				C			C	D	◇ B			◇ E		C			C	D	◇ F
London Victoria ⊖ d			06 28		06 42		06 43			06 58			07 06	07 10	07 13		07 25			07 28			07 36	07 40
Brixton ⊖ d			06 35				06 50			07 05					07 20					07 35				
Kentish Town ⊖ d		06 04		06 21					06 36			06 51							07 06		07 11	07 21		
St Pancras International ⊖ d		06 12		06 27					06 42			06 57							07 12		07 17	07 27		
Farringdon ⊖ d		06 17		06 32					06 47			07 02							07 17		07 22	07 32		
City Thameslink d																								
London Blackfriars ⊖ d	06 16	06 21		06 36				06 46	06 51		06 56	07 06						07 16	07 21		07 26	07 36		
Elephant & Castle ⊖ d	06 20	06 25		06 40				06 50	06 55		07 00	07 10						07 20	07 25		07 30	07 40		
Loughborough Jn. d		06 30		06 45					07 00			07 15							07 30			07 45		
Herne Hill d		06a34	06 37	06a49			06 52		07a04	07 07		07a19			07 22				07a34	07 37		07a49		
West Dulwich d			06 40				06 55			07 10					07 25					07 40				
Sydenham Hill d			06 42				06 57			07 12					07 27					07 42				
Penge East d			06 45				07 00			07 15					07 30					07 45				
Kent House d			06 47				07 02			07 17					07 32					07 47				
Beckenham Junction d			06 50				07 05			07 20					07 35					07 50				
Denmark Hill d	06 28				06 52			06 58			07 08		07 16					07 28			07 38		07 46	
Peckham Rye d	06 31							07 01			07 11		07 18					07 31			07 41		07 48	
Nunhead d	06 34							07 04			07 14		07 21					07 34			07 44		07 51	
Lewisham a													07 26										07 56	
Crofton Park d	06 37							07 07			07 17							07 37			07 47			
Catford d	06 40							07 10			07 20							07 40			07 50			
Bellingham d	06 43							07 13			07 23							07 43			07 53			
Beckenham Hill d	06 45							07 15			07 25							07 45			07 55			
Ravensbourne d	06 47							07 17			07 27							07 47			07 57			
Shortlands d	06 50		06 53				07 08	07 20		07 23	07 30				07 38			07 50		07 53	08 00			
Bromley South d	06 53		06 56		07 05		07a11	07 23		07 26	07 33			07a26	07a41		07 42	07 53		07 56	08 03			07a56
Bickley d	06 56		06 58					07 26		07 28	07 36							07 56		07 58	08 06			
Petts Wood d			07 03							07 33	07 40									08 03	08 10			
Orpington d			07a06							07a36	07a44									08a06	08a14			
St Mary Cray d	07 01				07 10			07 31									07 48	08 01						
Swanley d	07 06				07a14			07 36									07 52	08 06						
Eynsford d	07 11							07 41										08 11						
Shoreham (Kent) d	07 15							07 45										08 15						
Otford d	07 18							07 48									08a00	08 18						
Bat & Ball d	07 21							07 51										08 21						
Sevenoaks a	07 25							07 55										08 25						

	SE		SE	SE	TL	TL	SE	TL	TL	SE	SE		SE	SE	TL	TL	SE	TL	TL	SE	SE		SE	SE
	◇ B			◇ G		C			C	D	◇ B			◇ E		C			C	D	◇ F		◇ B	
London Victoria ⊖ d	07 42		07 43	07 55			07 58			08 06	08 10		08 13	08 25			08 28			08 36	08 40		08 42	08 43
Brixton ⊖ d			07 50				08 05						08 20				08 35							08 50
Kentish Town ⊖ d						07 36		07 41	07 51							08 06		08 11	08 21					
St Pancras International ⊖ d						07 42		07 47	07 57							08 12		08 17	08 27					
Farringdon ⊖ d						07 47		07 52	08 02							08 17		08 22	08 32					
City Thameslink d																								
London Blackfriars ⊖ d					07 46	07 51		07 56	08 06						08 16	08 21		08 26	08 36					
Elephant & Castle ⊖ d					07 50	07 55		08 00	08 10						08 20	08 25		08 30	08 40					
Loughborough Jn. d						08 00			08 15							08 30			08 45					
Herne Hill d			07 52			08a04	08 07		08a19				08 22			08a34	08 37		08a49					08 52
West Dulwich d			07 55				08 10						08 25				08 40							08 55
Sydenham Hill d			07 57				08 12						08 27				08 42							08 57
Penge East d			08 00				08 15						08 30				08 45							09 00
Kent House d			08 02				08 17						08 32				08 47							09 02
Beckenham Junction d			08 05				08 20						08 35				08 50							09 05
Denmark Hill d	07 52				07 58			08 08		08 16					08 28			08 38		08 46			08 52	
Peckham Rye d					08 01			08 11		08 18					08 31			08 41		08 48				
Nunhead d					08 04			08 14		08 21					08 34			08 44		08 51				
Lewisham a										08 26										08 56				
Crofton Park d					08 07			08 17							08 37			08 47						
Catford d					08 10			08 20							08 40			08 50						
Bellingham d					08 13			08 23							08 43			08 53						
Beckenham Hill d					08 15			08 25							08 45			08 55						
Ravensbourne d					08 17			08 27							08 47			08 57						
Shortlands d			08 08		08 20		08 23	08 30					08 38		08 50		08 53	09 00						09 08
Bromley South d	08 05		08a11	08 12	08 23		08 26	08 33			08a26		08a41	08 42	08 53		08 56	09 03			08a56		09 05	09a11
Bickley d					08 26		08 28	08 36							08 56		08 58	09 06						
Petts Wood d							08 33	08 40									09 03	09 10						
Orpington d							08a36	08a44									09a06	09a14						
St Mary Cray d	08 10			08 18	08 31										09 01								09 10	
Swanley d	08a14			08 22	08 36									08 50	09 06								09a14	
Eynsford d					08 41										09 11									
Shoreham (Kent) d					08 45										09 15									
Otford d				08a30	08 48									08a58	09 18									
Bat & Ball d					08 51										09 21									
Sevenoaks a					08 55										09 25									

A From Luton to Sutton (Surrey)
B To Dover Priory
C From St Albans City to Sutton (Surrey)
D To Gravesend
E To Canterbury West
F To Ramsgate
G To Ashford International

Table T195-F

Saturdays
26 May to 8 December

London - Catford, Beckenham Junction, Bromley South, Orpington, Otford and Sevenoaks

	SE	TL	TL	SE	TL	TL	SE	SE	SE	SE	TL	TL	SE	TL	TL	SE	SE	SE	SE	SE	TL	TL	SE	
	◇ A		B			B	C	◇ D		◇ E		B			B	C	◇ F	◇ D		◇ A		B		
London Victoria ⊖ d	08 55			08 58			09 06	09 10	09 13	09 25			09 28			09 36	09 40	09 42	09 43	09 55			09 58	
Brixton ⊖ d				09 05					09 20				09 35						09 50				10 05	
Kentish Town ⊖ d			08 36		08 41	08 51						09 06		09 11	09 21							09 36		
St Pancras International ⊖ d			08 42		08 47	08 57						09 12		09 17	09 27							09 42		
Farringdon ⊖ d			08 47		08 52	09 02						09 17		09 22	09 32							09 47		
City Thameslink d						09 04						09 19		09 24	09 34							09 49		
London Blackfriars ⊖ d		08 46	08 51		08 56	09 06					09 16	09 21		09 26	09 36						09 46	09 51		
Elephant & Castle ⊖ d		08 50	08 55		09 00	09 10					09 20	09 25		09 30	09 40						09 50	09 55		
Loughborough Jn. d			09 00			09 15						09 30			09 45							10 00		
Herne Hill d			09a04	09 07		09a19			09 22			09a34	09 37		09a49				09 52			10a04	10 07	
West Dulwich d				09 10					09 25				09 40						09 55				10 10	
Sydenham Hill d				09 12					09 27				09 42						09 57				10 12	
Penge East d				09 15					09 30				09 45						10 00				10 15	
Kent House d				09 17					09 32				09 47						10 02				10 17	
Beckenham Junction d				09 20					09 35				09 50						10 05				10 20	
Denmark Hill d		08 58			09 08		09 16				09 28			09 38		09 46		09 52			09 58			
Peckham Rye d		09 01			09 11		09 18				09 31			09 41		09 48					10 01			
Nunhead d		09 04			09 14		09 21				09 34			09 44		09 51					10 04			
Lewisham a							09 26									09 56								
Crofton Park d		09 07			09 17						09 37			09 47							10 07			
Catford d		09 10			09 20						09 40			09 50							10 10			
Bellingham d		09 13			09 23						09 43			09 53							10 13			
Beckenham Hill d		09 15			09 25						09 45			09 55							10 15			
Ravensbourne d		09 17			09 27						09 47			09 57							10 17			
Shortlands d		09 20		09 23	09 30				09 38		09 50		09 53	10 00					10 08		10 20		10 23	
Bromley South d	09 12	09 23		09 26	09 33			09a26	09a41	09 42	09 53		09 56	10 03			09a56	10 05	10a11	10 12	10 23		10 26	
Bickley d		09 26		09 28	09 36						09 56		09 58	10 06							10 26		10 28	
Petts Wood d				09 33	09 40								10 03	10 10									10 33	
Orpington d				09a36	09a44								10a06	10a14									10a36	
St Mary Cray d	09 18	09 32									10 01							10 10		10 18	10 31			
Swanley d	09 22	09 37								09 50	10 06							10a14		10 22	10 36			
Eynsford d		09 42									10 11										10 41			
Shoreham (Kent) d		09 46									10 15										10 45			
Otford d	09a30	09 49								09a58	10 18									10a30	10 48			
Bat & Ball d		09 52									10 21										10 51			
Sevenoaks a		09 56									10 25										10 55			

	TL		TL	SE	SE	SE	SE	TL	TL	SE	TL	TL	SE	SE	SE	SE	SE	TL	TL	SE	TL		TL
		and at the same minutes past each hour until	B	C	◇ D		◇ E		B			B	C	◇ F	◇ D		◇ A		B				B
London Victoria ⊖ d				12 06	12 10	12 13	12 25			12 28			12 36	12 40	12 42	12 43	12 55			12 58			
Brixton ⊖ d						12 20				12 35						12 50				13 05			
Kentish Town ⊖ d	09 41		11 51						12 06		12 11	12 21							12 36		12 41		12 51
St Pancras International ⊖ d	09 47		11 57						12 12		12 17	12 27							12 42		12 47		12 57
Farringdon ⊖ d	09 52		12 02						12 17		12 22	12 32							12 47		12 52		13 02
City Thameslink d	09 54		12 04						12 19		12 24	12 34							12 49		12 54		13 04
London Blackfriars ⊖ d	09 56		12 06					12 16	12 21		12 26	12 36						12 46	12 51		12 56		13 06
Elephant & Castle ⊖ d	10 00		12 10					12 20	12 25		12 30	12 40						12 50	12 55		13 00		13 10
Loughborough Jn. d			12 15						12 30			12 45							13 00				13 15
Herne Hill d			12a19			12 22			12a34	12 37		12a49				12 52			13a04	13 07			13a19
West Dulwich d						12 25				12 40						12 55				13 10			
Sydenham Hill d						12 27				12 42						12 57				13 12			
Penge East d						12 30				12 45						13 00				13 15			
Kent House d						12 32				12 47						13 02				13 17			
Beckenham Junction d						12 35				12 50						13 05				13 20			
Denmark Hill d	10 08			12 16				12 28			12 38		12 46		12 52			12 58			13 08		
Peckham Rye d	10 11			12 18				12 31			12 41		12 48					13 01			13 11		
Nunhead d	10 14			12 21				12 34			12 44		12 51					13 04			13 14		
Lewisham a				12 26									12 56										
Crofton Park d	10 17							12 37			12 47							13 07			13 17		
Catford d	10 20							12 40			12 50							13 10			13 20		
Bellingham d	10 23							12 43			12 53							13 13			13 23		
Beckenham Hill d	10 25							12 45			12 55							13 15			13 25		
Ravensbourne d	10 27							12 47			12 57							13 17			13 27		
Shortlands d	10 30					12 38		12 50		12 53	13 00					13 08		13 20		13 23	13 30		
Bromley South d	10 33				12a26	12a41	12 42	12 53		12 56	13 03			12a56	13 05	13a11	13 12	13 23		13 26	13 33		
Bickley d	10 36							12 56		12 58	13 06							13 26		13 28	13 36		
Petts Wood d	10 40									13 03	13 10									13 33	13 40		
Orpington d	10a44									13a06	13a14									13a36	13a44		
St Mary Cray d								13 01							13 10		13 18	13 31					
Swanley d							12 50	13 06							13a14		13 22	13 36					
Eynsford d								13 11										13 41					
Shoreham (Kent) d								13 15										13 45					
Otford d							12a58	13 18									13a30	13 48					
Bat & Ball d								13 21										13 51					
Sevenoaks a								13 25										13 55					

A To Ashford International
B From St Albans City to Sutton (Surrey)
C To Gravesend
D To Dover Priory
E To Canterbury West
F To Ramsgate

Table T195-F

Saturdays
26 May to 8 December

London - Catford, Beckenham Junction, Bromley South, Orpington, Otford and Sevenoaks

		SE	SE	SE	SE	TL	TL	SE	TL		TL	SE	SE	SE	SE	SE	TL	TL	SE		TL	TL	SE	SE	SE
		A	◇1 B		◇1 C		D				D	A	◇1 E	◇1 B		◇1 F		D				D	A	◇1 B	
London Victoria ⊖	d	13 06	13 10	13 13	13 25			13 28				13 36	13 40	13 42	13 43	13 55			13 58				14 06	14 10	14 13
Brixton ⊖	d			13 20				13 35							13 50				14 05						14 20
Kentish Town ⊖	d						13 06		13 11		13 21							13 36			13 41	13 51			
St Pancras International ⊖	d						13 12		13 17		13 27							13 42			13 47	13 57			
Farringdon ⊖	d						13 17		13 22		13 32							13 47			13 52	14 02			
City Thameslink	d						13 19		13 24		13 34							13 49			13 54	14 04			
London Blackfriars ⊖	d					13 16	13 21		13 26		13 36						13 46	13 51			13 56	14 06			
Elephant & Castle ⊖	d					13 20	13 25		13 30		13 40						13 50	13 55			14 00	14 10			
Loughborough Jn.	d						13 30				13 45							14 00				14 15			
Herne Hill	d			13 22			13a34	13 37			13a49				13 52			14a04	14 07			14a19			14 22
West Dulwich	d			13 25				13 40							13 55				14 10						14 25
Sydenham Hill	d			13 27				13 42							13 57				14 12						14 27
Penge East	d			13 30				13 45							14 00				14 15						14 30
Kent House	d			13 32				13 47							14 02				14 17						14 32
Beckenham Junction	d			13 35				13 50							14 05				14 20						14 35
Denmark Hill	d	13 16				13 28			13 38			13 46		13 52			13 58				14 08		14 16		
Peckham Rye	d	13 18				13 31			13 41			13 48					14 01				14 11		14 18		
Nunhead	d	13 21				13 34			13 44			13 51					14 04				14 14		14 21		
Lewisham	a	13 26										13 56											14 26		
Crofton Park	d					13 37			13 47								14 07				14 17				
Catford	d					13 40			13 50								14 10				14 20				
Bellingham	d					13 43			13 53								14 13				14 23				
Beckenham Hill	d					13 45			13 55								14 15				14 25				
Ravensbourne	d					13 47			13 57								14 17				14 28				
Shortlands	d			13 38		13 50		13 53	14 00						14 08		14 20		14 23		14 30				14 38
Bromley South	d		13a26	13a41	13 42	13 53		13 56	14 03				13a56	14 05	14a11	14 12	14 23		14 26		14 33			14a26	14a41
Bickley	d					13 56		13 58	14 06								14 26		14 28		14 36				
Petts Wood	d							14 03	14 10										14 33		14 40				
Orpington	d							14a06	14a14										14a36		14a44				
St Mary Cray	d					14 01								14 10		14 18	14 31								
Swanley	d				13 50	14 06								14a14		14 22	14 36								
Eynsford	d					14 11											14 41								
Shoreham (Kent)	d					14 15											14 45								
Otford	d				13a58	14 18										14a30	14 48								
Bat & Ball	d					14 21											14 51								
Sevenoaks	a					14 25											14 55								

		SE	TL	TL	SE	TL	TL	SE	SE	SE	SE	SE	TL	TL	SE	TL		TL	SE	SE	SE	SE	TL	TL
		◇1 C		D			D	A	◇1 E	◇1 B		◇1 F		D				D	A	◇1 B		◇1 F		D
London Victoria ⊖	d	14 25			14 28			14 36	14 40	14 42	14 43	14 55			14 58				20 06	20 10	20 13	20 25		
Brixton ⊖	d				14 35						14 50				15 05						20 20			
Kentish Town ⊖	d			14 06		14 11	14 21							14 36		14 41		19 51						20 06
St Pancras International ⊖	d			14 12		14 17	14 27							14 42		14 47		19 57						20 12
Farringdon ⊖	d			14 17		14 22	14 32							14 47		14 52		20 02						20 17
City Thameslink	d			14 19		14 24	14 34							14 49		14 54		20 04						20 19
London Blackfriars ⊖	d		14 16	14 21		14 26	14 36						14 46	14 51		14 56		20 06					20 16	20 21
Elephant & Castle ⊖	d		14 20	14 25		14 30	14 40						14 50	14 55		15 00		20 10					20 20	20 25
Loughborough Jn.	d			14 30			14 45							15 00				20 15						20 30
Herne Hill	d			14a34	14 37		14a49				14 52			15a04	15 07			20a19			20 22			20a34
West Dulwich	d				14 40						14 55				15 10						20 25			
Sydenham Hill	d				14 42						14 57				15 12						20 27			
Penge East	d				14 45						15 00				15 15		and at the same minutes past each hour until				20 30			
Kent House	d				14 47						15 02				15 17						20 32			
Beckenham Junction	d				14 50						15 05				15 20						20 35			
Denmark Hill	d		14 28			14 38		14 46		14 52			14 58			15 08			20 16				20 28	
Peckham Rye	d		14 31			14 41		14 48					15 01			15 11			20 18				20 31	
Nunhead	d		14 34			14 44		14 51					15 04			15 14			20 21				20 34	
Lewisham	a							14 56											20 26					
Crofton Park	d		14 37			14 47							15 07			15 17							20 37	
Catford	d		14 40			14 50							15 10			15 20							20 40	
Bellingham	d		14 43			14 53							15 13			15 23							20 43	
Beckenham Hill	d		14 45			14 55							15 15			15 25							20 45	
Ravensbourne	d		14 47			14 57							15 17			15 27							20 47	
Shortlands	d		14 50		14 53	15 00					15 08		15 20		15 23	15 30					20 38		20 50	
Bromley South	d	14 42	14 53		14 56	15 03			14a56	15 05	15a11	15 12	15 23		15 26	15 33				20a26	20a41	20 42	20 53	
Bickley	d		14 56		14 58	15 06							15 26		15 28	15 36							20 56	
Petts Wood	d				15 03	15 10									15 33	15 40								
Orpington	d				15a06	15a14									15a36	15a44								
St Mary Cray	d		15 01							15 10		15 18	15 31										21 01	
Swanley	d	14 50	15 06							15a14		15 22	15 36									20 50	21 06	
Eynsford	d		15 11										15 41										21 11	
Shoreham (Kent)	d		15 15										15 45										21 15	
Otford	d	14a58	15 18									15a30	15 48									20a58	21 18	
Bat & Ball	d		15 21										15 51										21 21	
Sevenoaks	a		15 25										15 55										21 25	

A To Gravesend
B To Dover Priory
C To Canterbury West
D From St Albans City to Sutton (Surrey)
E To Ramsgate
F To Ashford International

Table T195-F

Saturdays
26 May to 8 December

London - Catford, Beckenham Junction, Bromley South, Orpington, Otford and Sevenoaks

		SE	TL	TL	SE	SE	SE	SE	SE	TL	TL	SE	TL		TL	SE	SE	SE	SE	TL	TL	SE	TL		TL
				A	B	◇1 C	◇1 D		◇1 E		A				A	B	◇1 F		◇1 E		A				A
London Victoria ⊖	d	20 28			20 36	20 40	20 42	20 43	20 55			20 58				21 06	21 10	21 13	21 25			21 28			
Brixton ⊖	d	20 35						20 50				21 05						21 20				21 35			
Kentish Town ⊖	d		20 11	20 21							20 36		20 41		20 51						21 06		21 11		21 21
St Pancras International ⊖	d		20 17	20 27							20 42		20 47		20 57						21 12		21 17		21 27
Farringdon ⊖	d		20 22	20 32							20 47		20 52		21 02						21 17		21 22		21 32
City Thameslink	d		20 24	20 34							20 49		20 54												
London Blackfriars ⊖	d		20 26	20 36						20 46	20 51		20 56		21 06					21 16	21 21		21 26		21 36
Elephant & Castle ⊖	d		20 30	20 40						20 50	20 55		21 00		21 10					21 20	21 25		21 30		21 40
Loughborough Jn.	d			20 45							21 00				21 15						21 30				21 45
Herne Hill	d	20 37		20a49				20 52			21a04	21 07			21a19			21 22			21a34	21 37			21a49
West Dulwich	d	20 40						20 55				21 10						21 25				21 40			
Sydenham Hill	d	20 42						20 57				21 12						21 27				21 42			
Penge East	d	20 45						21 00				21 15						21 30				21 45			
Kent House	d	20 47						21 02				21 17						21 32				21 47			
Beckenham Junction	d	20 50						21 05				21 20						21 35				21 50			
Denmark Hill	d		20 38		20 46		20 52			20 58			21 08			21 16				21 28			21 38		
Peckham Rye	d		20 41		20 48					21 01			21 11			21 18				21 31			21 41		
Nunhead	d		20 44		20 51					21 04			21 14			21 21				21 34			21 44		
Lewisham	a				20 56											21 26									
Crofton Park	d		20 47							21 07			21 17							21 37			21 47		
Catford	d		20 50							21 10			21 20							21 40			21 50		
Bellingham	d		20 53							21 13			21 23							21 43			21 53		
Beckenham Hill	d		20 55							21 15			21 25							21 45			21 55		
Ravensbourne	d		20 57							21 17			21 27							21 47			21 57		
Shortlands	d	20 53	21 00					21 08		21 20		21 23	21 30					21 38		21 50		21 53	22 00		
Bromley South	d	20 56	21 03			20a56	21 05	21a11	21 12	21 23		21 26	21 33				21a26	21a41	21 42	21 53		21 56	22 03		
Bickley	d	20 58	21 06							21 26		21 28	21 36							21 56		21 58	22 06		
Petts Wood	d	21 03	21 10									21 33	21 40									22 03	22 10		
Orpington	d	21a06	21a14									21a36	21a44									22a06	22a14		
St Mary Cray	d						21 10		21 18	21 31										22 01					
Swanley	d						21a14		21 22	21 36									21 50	22 06					
Eynsford	d									21 41										22 11					
Shoreham (Kent)	d									21 45										22 15					
Otford	d								21a30	21 48									21a58	22 18					
Bat & Ball	d									21 51										22 21					
Sevenoaks	a									21 55										22 25					

		SE	SE	SE	SE	SE	TL	TL	SE		TL	TL	SE	SE	SE	SE	TL	TL	SE		TL	TL	SE	SE	SE
		B	◇1 C	◇1 D		◇1 E		A				A	B	◇1 F		◇1 E		A				A	B	◇1 C	◇1 G
London Victoria ⊖	d	21 36	21 40	21 42	21 43	21 55			21 58				22 06	22 10	22 13	22 25			22 28				22 36	22 40	22 42
Brixton ⊖	d				21 50				22 05						22 20				22 35						
Kentish Town ⊖	d							21 36			21 41	21 51						22 06			22 11	22 21			
St Pancras International ⊖	d							21 42			21 47	21 57						22 12			22 17	22 27			
Farringdon ⊖	d							21 47			21 52	22 02						22 17			22 22	22 32			
City Thameslink	d																								
London Blackfriars ⊖	d						21 46	21 51			21 56	22 06					22 16	22 21			22 26	22 36			
Elephant & Castle ⊖	d						21 50	21 55			22 00	22 10					22 20	22 25			22 30	22 40			
Loughborough Jn.	d							22 00				22 15						22 30				22 45			
Herne Hill	d				21 52			22a04	22 07			22a19			22 22			22a34	22 37			22a49			
West Dulwich	d				21 55				22 10						22 25				22 40						
Sydenham Hill	d				21 57				22 12						22 27				22 42						
Penge East	d				22 00				22 15						22 30				22 45						
Kent House	d				22 02				22 17						22 32				22 47						
Beckenham Junction	d				22 05				22 20						22 35				22 50						
Denmark Hill	d	21 46		21 52			21 58				22 08		22 16				22 28				22 38		22 46		22 52
Peckham Rye	d	21 48					22 01				22 11		22 18				22 31				22 41		22 48		
Nunhead	d	21 51					22 04				22 14		22 21				22 34				22 44		22 51		
Lewisham	a	21 56											22 26										22 56		
Crofton Park	d						22 07				22 17						22 37				22 47				
Catford	d						22 10				22 20						22 40				22 50				
Bellingham	d						22 13				22 23						22 43				22 53				
Beckenham Hill	d						22 15				22 25						22 45				22 55				
Ravensbourne	d						22 17				22 27						22 47				22 57				
Shortlands	d				22 08		22 20		22 23		22 30				22 38		22 50		22 53		23 00				
Bromley South	d		21a56	22 05	22a11	22 12	22 23		22 26		22 33			22a26	22a41	22 42	22 53		22 56		23 03			22a56	23 05
Bickley	d						22 26		22 28		22 36						22 56		22 58		23 06				
Petts Wood	d								22 33		22 40								23 03		23 10				
Orpington	d								22a36		22a44								23a06		23a14				
St Mary Cray	d			22 10		22 18	22 31										23 01								23 10
Swanley	d			22a14		22 22	22 36									22 50	23 06								23a14
Eynsford	d						22 41										23 11								
Shoreham (Kent)	d						22 45										23 15								
Otford	d					22a30	22 48									22a58	23 18								
Bat & Ball	d						22 51										23 21								
Sevenoaks	a						22 55										23 25								

A From St Albans City to Sutton (Surrey)
B To Gravesend
C To Ramsgate
D To Canterbury East
E To Ashford International
F To Dover Priory
G To Gillingham (Kent)

Table T195-F

London - Catford, Beckenham Junction, Bromley South, Orpington, Otford and Sevenoaks

Saturdays
26 May to 8 December

		SE	SE ◇1 A	TL	TL B	SE	TL	TL B	SE C	SE ◇1 D	SE	SE ◇1 A	TL	TL B	SE	SE C	SE ◇1 E	SE	SE ◇1 A	TL	TL B	SE
London Victoria	⊖ d	22 43	22 55			22 58			23 06	23 10	23 13	23 25			23 28	23 36	23 42	23 43	23 55			23 58
Brixton	⊖ d	22 50				23 05					23 20				23 35			23 50				00 05
Kentish Town	⊖ d				22 36		22 41	22 51						23 06							23 38	
St Pancras International	⊖ d				22 42		22 47	22 57						23 12							23 44	
Farringdon	⊖ d				22 47		22 52	23 02						23 17							23 49	
City Thameslink	d																					
London Blackfriars	⊖ d			22 46	22 51		22 56	23 06					23 16	23 21						23 46	23 53	
Elephant & Castle	⊖ d			22 50	22 55		23 00	23 10					23 20	23 25						23 50	23 57	
Loughborough Jn.	d				23 00			23 15						23 30							00 02	
Herne Hill	d	22 52			23a04	23 07		23a19			23 22			23a34	23 37			23 52			00a06	00 08
West Dulwich	d	22 55				23 10					23 25				23 40			23 55				00 11
Sydenham Hill	d	22 57				23 12					23 27				23 42			23 57				00 13
Penge East	d	23 00				23 15					23 30				23 45			23 59				00 16
Kent House	d	23 02				23 17					23 32				23 47			00 02				00 18
Beckenham Junction	d	23 05				23 20					23 35				23 50			00 05				00 21
Denmark Hill	d			22 58			23 08		23 16				23 28			23 46	23 52			23 58		
Peckham Rye	d			23 01			23 11		23 18				23 31			23 48				00 01		
Nunhead	d			23 04			23 14		23 21				23 34			23 51				00 04		
Lewisham	a								23 26							23 56						
Crofton Park	d			23 07			23 17						23 37							00 07		
Catford	d			23 10			23 20						23 40							00 10		
Bellingham	d			23 13			23 23						23 43							00 13		
Beckenham Hill	d			23 15			23 25						23 45							00 15		
Ravensbourne	d			23 17			23 27						23 47							00 17		
Shortlands	d	23 08		23 20		23 23	23 30				23 38		23 50		23 53			00 09		00 20		00 24
Bromley South	d	23a11	23 12	23 23		23 26	23 33			23a26	23a41	23 42	23 53		23 56		00 05	00a12	00 12	00 23		00 27
Bickley	d			23 26		23 28	23 36						23 56		23 58					00 26		00 29
Petts Wood	d					23 33	23 40								00 03							00 34
Orpington	d					23a37	23a44								00a06							00a37
St Mary Cray	d		23 18	23 31									00 01				00 10		00 18	00 31		
Swanley	d		23 22	23 36								23 50	00 06				00a14		00 22	00 36		
Eynsford	d			23 41									00 11							00 41		
Shoreham (Kent)	d			23 45									00 15							00 45		
Otford	d		23a30	23 48								23a58	00 18						00a30	00 48		
Bat & Ball	d			23 51									00 21							00 51		
Sevenoaks	a			23 55									00 25							00 55		

Sundays
20 May to 2 December

		TL F	TL G	SE ◇1 H	SE I	SE ◇1 J	TL F	SE I	SE C	SE ◇1 A	SE	SE E	TL K	SE ◇1 L	TL M	SE	SE C	SE ◇1 N	TL	SE	SE C	SE ◇1 O	TL K
London Victoria	⊖ d								00 06	00 25	00 28	00 40	07 12	07 25		07 28	07 36	07 40	07 44	07 58	08 06	08 10	08 14
Brixton	⊖ d							00 05			00 35					07 35				08 05			
Kentish Town	⊖ d																						
St Pancras International	⊖ d																						
Farringdon	⊖ d																						
City Thameslink	d																						
London Blackfriars	⊖ d																						
Elephant & Castle	⊖ d																						
Loughborough Jn.	d		00 02																				
Herne Hill	d		00a06					00 08			00 37					07 37				08 07			
West Dulwich	d							00 11			00 40					07 40				08 10			
Sydenham Hill	d							00 13			00 42					07 42				08 12			
Penge East	d							00 16			00 45					07 45				08 15			
Kent House	d				00 02			00 18			00 47					07 47				08 17			
Beckenham Junction	d				00 05			00 21			00 50				←	07 50				08 20			
Denmark Hill	d								00 16				07 23		07 23		07 46		07 53		08 16	08 20	08 23
Peckham Rye	d						00 01		00 18				→		07 26		07 48		07 56		08 18		→
Nunhead	d						00 04		00 21						07 29		07 51		07 59		08 21		
Lewisham	a								00 26								07 56				08 26		
Crofton Park	d						00 07								07 32				08 02				
Catford	d						00 10								07 35				08 05				
Bellingham	d						00 13								07 38				08 08				
Beckenham Hill	d						00 15								07 40				08 10				
Ravensbourne	d						00 17								07 43				08 13				
Shortlands	d				00 09		00 20	00 24			00 53				07 45	07 53			08 15	08 23			
Bromley South	d			00 05	00a12	00 12	00 23	00 27		00 42	00 56	00 57		07 42	07 48	07 56		07a57	08 18	08 26		08 34	
Bickley	d						00 26	00 29			00 58				07 51	07 58			08 21	08 28			
Petts Wood	d							00 34			01 03					08 03				08 33			
Orpington	d							00a37			01a06					08a07				08a37			
St Mary Cray	d	00 01		00 10		00 18	00 31			00 48		01s02		07 47	07 55				08 25			08 39	
Swanley	d	00 06		00a14		00 22	00 36			00 52		01s06		07 52	08 00				08 30			08a43	
Eynsford	d	00 11					00 41								08 05				08 35				
Shoreham (Kent)	d	00 15					00 45								08 09				08 39				
Otford	d	00 18				00a30	00 48			01a00				08a00	08 12				08 42				
Bat & Ball	d	00 21					00 51								08 15				08 45				
Sevenoaks	a	00 25					00 55								08 19				08 49				

A To Ashford International
B From St Albans City to Sutton (Surrey)
C To Dartford
D To Ramsgate
E To Gillingham (Kent)
F not 20 May. From London Blackfriars
G not 20 May. From St Albans City to Sutton (Surrey)
H not 20 May. From London Victoria to Gillingham (Kent)
I not 20 May. From London Victoria
J not 20 May. From London Victoria to Ashford International
K To Sevenoaks
L To Canterbury West
M From London Victoria
N To Dover Priory
O To Canterbury East

Table T195-F

London - Catford, Beckenham Junction, Bromley South, Orpington, Otford and Sevenoaks

Sundays
20 May to 2 December

		SE ◇1 A	TL B	SE	SE C	SE ◇1 D	TL	SE	SE C	SE ◇1 E	TL F	SE ◇1 A	TL B	SE	TL G	SE C	SE ◇1 D	TL	TL H	SE	TL G	SE C	SE ◇1 E
London Victoria	⊖ d	08 25		08 28	08 36	08 40	08 44	08 58	09 06	09 10	09 14	09 25		09 28		09 36	09 40			09 58		10 06	10 10
Brixton	⊖ d			08 35				09 05						09 35						10 05			
Kentish Town	⊖ d																		09 31				
St Pancras International	⊖ d																		09 38				
Farringdon	⊖ d																		09 42				
City Thameslink	d																						
London Blackfriars	⊖ d														09 30			09 42	09 47		10 00		
Elephant & Castle	⊖ d														09 34			09 46	09 51		10 04		
Loughborough Jn.	d														09 39				09 56		10 09		
Herne Hill	d			08 37				09 07						09 37	09a42				09a59	10 07	10a12		
West Dulwich	d			08 40				09 10						09 40						10 10			
Sydenham Hill	d			08 42				09 12						09 42						10 12			
Penge East	d			08 45				09 15						09 45						10 15			
Kent House	d			08 47				09 17						09 47						10 17			
Beckenham Junction	d		←	08 50				09 20					←	09 50						10 20			
Denmark Hill	d		08 23		08 46		08 53		09 16	09 20	09 23		09 23			09 46		09 53				10 16	10 20
Peckham Rye	d		08 26		08 48		08 56		09 18		→		09 26			09 48		09 56				10 18	
Nunhead	d		08 29		08 51		08 59		09 21				09 29			09 51		09 59				10 21	
Lewisham	a				08 56				09 26							09 56						10 26	
Crofton Park	d		08 32				09 02						09 32					10 02					
Catford	d		08 35				09 05						09 35					10 05					
Bellingham	d		08 38				09 08						09 38					10 08					
Beckenham Hill	d		08 40				09 10						09 40					10 10					
Ravensbourne	d		08 43				09 13						09 43					10 13					
Shortlands	d		08 45	08 53			09 15	09 23					09 45	09 53				10 15		10 23			
Bromley South	d	08 42	08 48	08 56		08a57	09 18	09 26		09 34		09 42	09 48	09 56			09a57	10 18		10 26			10 34
Bickley	d		08 51	08 58			09 21	09 28					09 51	09 58				10 21		10 28			
Petts Wood	d			09 03				09 33						10 03						10 33			
Orpington	d			09a07				09a37						10a07						10a37			
St Mary Cray	d	08 47	08 55				09 25			09 39		09 47	09 55					10 25					10 39
Swanley	d	08 52	09 00				09 30			09a43		09 52	10 00					10 30					10a43
Eynsford	d		09 05				09 35						10 05					10 35					
Shoreham (Kent)	d		09 09				09 39						10 09					10 39					
Otford	d	09a00	09 12				09 42					10a00	10 12					10 42					
Bat & Ball	d		09 15				09 45						10 15					10 45					
Sevenoaks	a		09 19				09 49						10 19					10 49					

		SE ◇1 A	TL	TL H	SE	TL G	SE C	SE ◇1 D	TL	TL H	SE	TL G	SE C	SE ◇1 E	SE ◇1 A	TL	TL H	SE	TL G	SE C	SE ◇1 D	TL
London Victoria	⊖ d	10 25			10 28		10 36	10 40			10 58		11 06	11 10	11 25			11 28		11 36	11 40	
Brixton	⊖ d				10 35						11 05							11 35				
Kentish Town	⊖ d			10 01						10 31							11 01					
St Pancras International	⊖ d			10 08						10 38							11 08					
Farringdon	⊖ d			10 12						10 42							11 12					
City Thameslink	d																					
London Blackfriars	⊖ d		10 12	10 17		10 30			10 42	10 47		11 00				11 12	11 17		11 30			11 42
Elephant & Castle	⊖ d		10 16	10 21		10 34			10 46	10 51		11 04				11 16	11 21		11 34			11 46
Loughborough Jn.	d			10 26		10 39				10 56		11 09					11 26		11 39			
Herne Hill	d			10a29	10 37	10a42				10a59	11 07	11a12					11a29	11 37	11a42			
West Dulwich	d				10 40						11 10							11 40				
Sydenham Hill	d				10 42						11 12							11 42				
Penge East	d				10 45						11 15							11 45				
Kent House	d				10 47						11 17							11 47				
Beckenham Junction	d				10 50						11 20							11 50				
Denmark Hill	d		10 23				10 46		10 53				11 16	11 20		11 23				11 46		11 53
Peckham Rye	d		10 26				10 48		10 56				11 18			11 26				11 48		11 56
Nunhead	d		10 29				10 51		10 59				11 21			11 29				11 51		11 59
Lewisham	a						10 56						11 26							11 56		
Crofton Park	d		10 32						11 02							11 32						12 02
Catford	d		10 35						11 05							11 35						12 05
Bellingham	d		10 38						11 08							11 38						12 08
Beckenham Hill	d		10 40						11 10							11 40						12 10
Ravensbourne	d		10 43						11 13							11 43						12 13
Shortlands	d		10 45		10 53				11 15		11 23					11 45		11 53				12 15
Bromley South	d	10 42	10 48		10 56			10a57	11 18		11 26			11 34	11 42	11 48		11 56			11a57	12 18
Bickley	d		10 51		10 58				11 21		11 28					11 51		11 58				12 21
Petts Wood	d				11 03						11 33							12 03				
Orpington	d				11a07						11a37							12a07				
St Mary Cray	d	10 47	10 55						11 25					11 39	11 47	11 55						12 25
Swanley	d	10 52	11 00						11 30					11a43	11 52	12 00						12 30
Eynsford	d		11 05						11 35							12 05						12 35
Shoreham (Kent)	d		11 09						11 39							12 09						12 39
Otford	d	11a00	11 12						11 42						12a00	12 12						12 42
Bat & Ball	d		11 15						11 45							12 15						12 45
Sevenoaks	a		11 19						11 49							12 19						12 49

A To Canterbury West
B From London Victoria
C To Dartford
D To Dover Priory
E To Canterbury East
F To Sevenoaks
G To Sutton (Surrey)
H From Luton to Sutton (Surrey)

Table T195-F

Sundays

20 May to 2 December

London - Catford, Beckenham Junction, Bromley South, Orpington, Otford and Sevenoaks

	TL A	SE	TL B	SE C	SE ◇1 D	SE ◇1 E	TL		TL A	SE	TL B	SE C	SE ◇1 F	TL	TL A	SE	TL A	SE C	SE ◇1 D	SE ◇1 E	TL	TL A	SE	TL G
London Victoria ⊖ d		11 58		12 06	12 10	12 25				12 28		12 36	12 40			12 58		13 06	13 10	13 25			13 28	
Brixton ⊖ d		12 05								12 35						13 05							13 35	
Kentish Town ⊖ d	11 31								12 01						12 31		12 44							13 14
St Pancras International ⊖ d	11 38								12 08		12 21				12 38		12 51					13 08		13 21
Farringdon ⊖ d	11 42								12 12		12 25				12 42		12 55					13 12		13 25
City Thameslink d																								
London Blackfriars ⊖ d	11 47		12 00				12 12		12 17		12 30			12 42	12 47		13 00				13 12	13 17		13 30
Elephant & Castle ⊖ d	11 51		12 04				12 16		12 21		12 34			12 46	12 51		13 04				13 16	13 21		13 34
Loughborough Jn d	11 56		12 09						12 26		12 39				12 56		13 09					13 26		13 39
Herne Hill d	11a59	12 07	12a12						12a29	12 37	12a42				12a59	13 07	13a12					13a29	13 37	13a42
West Dulwich d		12 10								12 40						13 10							13 40	
Sydenham Hill d		12 12								12 42						13 12							13 42	
Penge East d		12 15								12 45						13 15							13 45	
Kent House d		12 17								12 47						13 17							13 47	
Beckenham Junction d		12 20								12 50						13 20							13 50	
Denmark Hill d				12 16	12 20		12 23					12 46		12 53				13 16	13 20		13 23			
Peckham Rye d				12 18			12 26					12 48		12 56				13 18			13 26			
Nunhead d				12 21			12 29					12 51		12 59				13 21			13 29			
Lewisham a				12 26								12 56						13 26						
Crofton Park d							12 32							13 02							13 32			
Catford d							12 35							13 05							13 35			
Bellingham d							12 38							13 08							13 38			
Beckenham Hill d							12 40							13 10							13 40			
Ravensbourne d							12 43							13 13							13 43			
Shortlands d		12 23					12 45			12 53				13 15		13 23					13 45		13 53	
Bromley South d		12 26			12 34	12 42	12 48			12 56			12a57	13 18		13 26			13 34	13 42	13 48		13 56	
Bickley d		12 28					12 51			12 58				13 21		13 28					13 51		13 58	
Petts Wood d		12 33								13 03						13 33							14 03	
Orpington d		12a37								13a07						13a37							14a07	
St Mary Cray d					12 39	12 47	12 55							13 25					13 39	13 47	13 55			
Swanley d					12a43	12 52	13 00							13 30					13a43	13 52	14 00			
Eynsford d							13 05							13 35							14 05			
Shoreham (Kent) d							13 09							13 39							14 09			
Otford d						13a00	13 12							13 42						14a00	14 12			
Bat & Ball d							13 15							13 45							14 15			
Sevenoaks a							13 19							13 49							14 19			

	SE C	SE ◇1 F	TL	TL A		SE	TL G	SE C	SE ◇1 D	SE ◇1 H	TL	TL A	SE	TL G	SE C	SE ◇1 F	TL	TL A		SE	TL G	SE C	SE ◇1 D
London Victoria ⊖ d	13 36	13 40			and at the same minutes past each hour until	18 58		19 06	19 10	19 25			19 28		19 36	19 40				19 58		20 06	20 10
Brixton ⊖ d						19 05							19 35							20 05			
Kentish Town ⊖ d							18 44							19 14							19 44		
St Pancras International ⊖ d				13 38			18 51					19 08		19 21				19 38			19 51		
Farringdon ⊖ d				13 42			18 55					19 12		19 25				19 42			19 55		
City Thameslink d																							
London Blackfriars ⊖ d			13 42	13 47			19 00				19 12	19 17		19 30			19 42	19 47			20 00		
Elephant & Castle ⊖ d			13 46	13 51			19 04				19 16	19 21		19 34			19 46	19 51			20 04		
Loughborough Jn d				13 56			19 09					19 26		19 39				19 56			20 09		
Herne Hill d				13a59		19 07	19a12					19a29	19 37	19a42				19a59		20 07	20a12		
West Dulwich d						19 10							19 40							20 10			
Sydenham Hill d						19 12							19 42							20 12			
Penge East d						19 15							19 45							20 15			
Kent House d						19 17							19 47							20 17			
Beckenham Junction d						19 20							19 50							20 20			
Denmark Hill d	13 46		13 53					19 16	19 20		19 23				19 46		19 53					20 16	20 20
Peckham Rye d	13 48		13 56					19 18			19 26				19 48		19 56					20 18	
Nunhead d	13 51		13 59					19 21			19 29				19 51		19 59					20 21	
Lewisham a	13 56							19 26							19 56							20 26	
Crofton Park d			14 02								19 32						20 02						
Catford d			14 05								19 35						20 05						
Bellingham d			14 08								19 38						20 08						
Beckenham Hill d			14 10								19 40						20 10						
Ravensbourne d			14 13								19 43						20 13						
Shortlands d			14 15			19 23					19 45		19 53				20 15			20 23			
Bromley South d		13a57	14 18			19 26			19 34	19 42	19 48		19 56			19a57	20 18			20 26			20 34
Bickley d			14 21			19 28					19 51		19 58				20 21			20 28			
Petts Wood d						19 33							20 03							20 33			
Orpington d						19a37							20a07							20a37			
St Mary Cray d			14 25						19 39	19 47	19 55						20 25						20 39
Swanley d			14 30						19a43	19 52	20 00						20 30						20a43
Eynsford d			14 35								20 05						20 35						
Shoreham (Kent) d			14 39								20 09						20 39						
Otford d			14 42							20a00	20 12						20 42						
Bat & Ball d			14 45								20 15						20 45						
Sevenoaks a			14 49								20 19						20 49						

A From Luton to Sutton (Surrey)
B To Sutton (Surrey)
C To Dartford
D To Canterbury East
E To Canterbury West
F To Dover Priory
G From St Albans City to Sutton (Surrey)
H To Ashford International

Table T195-F

Sundays

20 May to 2 December

London - Catford, Beckenham Junction, Bromley South, Orpington, Otford and Sevenoaks

	SE ◇1 A	TL	TL B	SE	TL C		SE D	SE ◇1 E	TL	TL B	SE	TL C	SE D	SE ◇1 F	SE ◇1 A		TL	TL B	SE	TL C	SE D	SE ◇1 E	TL	TL B
London Victoria ⊖ d	20 25			20 28			20 36	20 40			20 58		21 06	21 10	21 25				21 28		21 36	21 40		
Brixton ⊖ d				20 35							21 05								21 35					
Kentish Town ⊖ d					20 14							20 44								21 14				
St Pancras International ⊖ d			20 08		20 21					20 38		20 51						21 08		21 21				21 38
Farringdon ⊖ d			20 12		20 25					20 42		20 55						21 12		21 25				21 42
City Thameslink d																								
London Blackfriars ⊖ d		20 12	20 17		20 30				20 42	20 47		21 00					21 12	21 17		21 30			21 42	21 47
Elephant & Castle ⊖ d		20 16	20 21		20 34				20 46	20 51		21 04					21 16	21 21		21 34			21 46	21 51
Loughborough Jn d			20 26		20 39					20 56		21 09						21 26		21 39				21 56
Herne Hill d			20a29	20 37	20a42					20a59	21 07	21a12						21a29	21 37	21a42				21a59
West Dulwich d				20 40							21 10								21 40					
Sydenham Hill d				20 42							21 12								21 42					
Penge East d				20 45							21 15								21 45					
Kent House d				20 47							21 17								21 47					
Beckenham Junction d				20 50							21 20								21 50					
Denmark Hill d		20 23					20 46		20 53				21 16	21 20			21 23				21 46		21 53	
Peckham Rye d		20 26					20 48		20 56				21 18				21 26				21 48		21 56	
Nunhead d		20 29					20 51		20 59				21 21				21 29				21 51		21 59	
Lewisham a							20 56						21 26								21 56			
Crofton Park d		20 32							21 02								21 32						22 02	
Catford d		20 35							21 05								21 35						22 05	
Bellingham d		20 38							21 08								21 38						22 08	
Beckenham Hill d		20 40							21 10								21 40						22 10	
Ravensbourne d		20 43							21 13								21 43						22 13	
Shortlands d		20 45		20 53					21 15		21 23						21 45		21 53				22 15	
Bromley South d	20 42	20 48		20 56				20a57	21 18		21 26			21 34	21 42		21 48		21 56			21a57	22 18	
Bickley d		20 51		20 58					21 21		21 28						21 51		21 58				22 21	
Petts Wood d				21 03							21 33								22 03					
Orpington d				21a07							21a37								22a07					
St Mary Cray d	20 47	20 55							21 25					21 39	21 47		21 55						22 25	
Swanley d	20 52	21 01							21 30					21a43	21 52		22 00						22 30	
Eynsford d		21 06							21 35								22 05						22 35	
Shoreham (Kent) d		21 10							21 39								22 09						22 39	
Otford d	21a00	21 13							21 42						22a00		22 12						22 42	
Bat & Ball d		21 16							21 45								22 15						22 45	
Sevenoaks a		21 20							21 49								22 19						22 49	

	SE		SE D	SE ◇1 F	SE ◇1 A	TL	SE	SE D	SE ◇1 G	TL	SE		SE D	SE ◇1 H	SE ◇1 A	TL	SE	SE D	SE ◇1 F	TL	SE
London Victoria ⊖ d	21 58		22 06	22 10	22 25		22 28	22 36	22 40		22 58		23 06	23 10	23 25		23 28	23 36	23 40		23 58
Brixton ⊖ d	22 05						22 35				23 05						23 35				00 05
Kentish Town ⊖ d																					
St Pancras International ⊖ d																					
Farringdon ⊖ d																					
City Thameslink d																					
London Blackfriars ⊖ d						22 12				22 42						23 12				23 42	
Elephant & Castle ⊖ d						22 16				22 46						23 16				23 46	
Loughborough Jn d																					
Herne Hill d	22 07						22 37				23 07						23 37				00 07
West Dulwich d	22 10						22 40				23 10						23 40				00 10
Sydenham Hill d	22 12						22 42				23 12						23 42				00 12
Penge East d	22 15						22 45				23 15						23 45				00 15
Kent House d	22 17						22 47				23 17						23 47				00 17
Beckenham Junction d	22 20						22 50				23 20						23 50				00 20
Denmark Hill d			22 16	22 20		22 23		22 46		22 53			23 16	23 20		23 23		23 46		23 53	
Peckham Rye d			22 18			22 26		22 48		22 56			23 18			23 26		23 48		23 56	
Nunhead d			22 21			22 29		22 51		22 59			23 21			23 29		23 51		23 59	
Lewisham a			22 26					22 56					23 26					23 56			
Crofton Park d						22 32				23 02						23 32				00 02	
Catford d						22 35				23 05						23 35				00 05	
Bellingham d						22 38				23 08						23 38				00 08	
Beckenham Hill d						22 40				23 10						23 40				00 10	
Ravensbourne d						22 43				23 13						23 43				00 13	
Shortlands d	22 23					22 45	22 53			23 15	23 23					23 45	23 53			00 15	00 23
Bromley South d	22 26			22 34	22 42	22 48	22 56		22a57	23 18	23 26			23 34	23 42	23 48	23 56		23 57	00 18	00 26
Bickley d	22 28					22 51	22 58			23 21	23 28					23 51	23 58			00 21	00 28
Petts Wood d	22 33						23 03				23 33						00 03				00 33
Orpington d	22a37						23a07				23a37						00a06				00a36
St Mary Cray d				22 39	22 47	22 55				23 25				23 39	23 47	23 55			00 03	00 25	
Swanley d				22a43	22 52	23 00				23 30				23a43	23 52	23 59			00a07	00 30	
Eynsford d						23 05				23 35						00 05				00 35	
Shoreham (Kent) d						23 09				23 39						00 09				00 39	
Otford d					23a00	23 12				23 42					23a59	00 12				00 42	
Bat & Ball d						23 15				23 45						00 15				00 45	
Sevenoaks a						23 19				23 49						00 19				00 49	

A To Ashford International
B From Luton to Sutton (Surrey)
C From St Albans City to Sutton (Surrey)
D To Dartford
E To Dover Priory
F To Faversham
G To Ramsgate
H To Gillingham (Kent)

Table 195R

Sevenoaks and Otford, Orpington, Bromley South, Beckenham Junction, Catford - London

Miles	Miles	Miles			TL	SE	SE	TL	TL	SE	SE	TL	TL		TL	TL	TL	TL	TL	TL	TL	TL	TL		TL
					MX	MX	MX	MO	MX	MX	MO	MX	MX		MX	MO	MX	MX	MO	MX					
						◇■		■			◇■	■				■	■	■	■	■	■	■	■		■
					A	B	C	D	A		E	D	F		G	D	H	D	D	D	D	I	I		I
—	0	—	**Sevenoaks**	d																					
—	1¼	—	Bat & Ball	d																					
—	3	—	Otford	d																					
—	4¼	—	Shoreham (Kent)	d																					
—	6½	—	Eynsford	d																					
—	9½	—	**Swanley**	d																					
—	12¼	—	St Mary Cray	d																					
0	—	—	**Orpington**	d																					
1¼	—	—	Petts Wood	d																					
3	14½	—	Bickley	d			00 01																		
4	15½	—	**Bromley South**	d		00 04	00 04			00 19	00 20														
5	16½	—	Shortlands	d			00 07																		
—	17¼	—	Ravensbourne	d																					
—	18	—	Beckenham Hill	d									00 01		00 01										
—	18¾	—	Bellingham	d									00 03		00 03										
—	19½	—	Catford	d									00 06		00 06										
—	20½	—	Crofton Park	d									00 08		00 08										
—	—	0	Lewisham	a																					
—	—	—		d																					
—	21¾	1¾	Nunhead	d									00 11		00 11										
—	22½	2½	Peckham Rye	d									00 14		00 14										
—	23¼	3¼	Denmark Hill	d									00 17		00 17										
6¼	—	—	**Beckenham Junction**	d			00 10																		
7¼	—	—	Kent House	d			00 12																		
7¾	—	—	Penge East	d			00 14																		
9¼	—	—	Sydenham Hill	d			00 18																		
10	—	—	West Dulwich	d			00 20																		
11	—	—	Herne Hill	d			00 23																		
—	—	—	Loughborough Jn	d																					
—	25¾	—	Elephant & Castle ⊖	d					00 04				00 24		00 24										
—	27	—	**London Blackfriars** ⊖	d	00 02			00 06	00 09			00 22	00 29		00a33	00 36	00 37	00 50	01 06	01 08	01 36	02 36	03 06		03 36
—	—	—	City Thameslink	a									00 31												
—	—	—	Farringdon ⊖	a	00 06			00 10	00 13			00 25	00 33				00 41								
—	—	—	St Pancras International ⊖	a	00 10			00 15	00 17			00 29	00 38			00 45	00 45	00 59	01 15	01 15	01 43	02 43	03 13		03 43
—	—	—	Kentish Town ⊖	a				00 20	00 22							00 50		01 05			01 48	02 48			03 48
11¾	—	—	Brixton ⊖	d			00 26																		
15	—	7½	**London Victoria** ⊖	a		00 24	00 34			00 39	00 36														

		TL	TL	TL	TL	SE	SE	SE	TL		TL	SE	SE	SE	TL	TL	TL	TL	TL		TL	TL	TL	SE	SE
		■	■	■					■			■			■			■			■			◇■	■
		I	I	I	J			K	D		J	L		K	I	M	J	N	O		I		P	Q	R
Sevenoaks	d											05 02		05 17								05 22		05 40	
Bat & Ball	d																					05 25			
Otford	d																					05 29			
Shoreham (Kent)	d																					05 32			
Eynsford	d																					05 36			
Swanley	d					04 38																05 41			05 47
St Mary Cray	d					04 42																05 45			05 52
Orpington	d				04 33		04 54	05 00			05 03	05a12	05 24	05 33			05 33							05a50	
Petts Wood	d				04 36		04 57	05 03			05 06		05 27	05 36			05 36								
Bickley	d				04 40	04 46	05 01				05 10		05 31				05 40					05 50			
Bromley South	d				04 43	04 49	05 04				05 13		05 34				05 43					05 53			05 59
Shortlands	d				04 45	04 52	05 07				05 15		05 37				05 45					05 55			
Ravensbourne	d				04 48						05 18						05 48					05 58			
Beckenham Hill	d				04 50						05 20						05 50					06 00			
Bellingham	d				04 52						05 22						05 52					06 02			
Catford	d				04 55						05 25						05 55					06 05			
Crofton Park	d				04 58						05 28						05 58					06 08			
Lewisham	a							05 20						05 53											
	d																								
Nunhead	d				05 01						05 31						06 01					06 11			
Peckham Rye	d				05 04						05 34						06 04					06 14			
Denmark Hill	d				05 07						05 37						06 07					06 17			
Beckenham Junction	d					04 55	05 10						05 40												
Kent House	d					04 57	05 12						05 42												
Penge East	d					04 59	05 14						05 44												
Sydenham Hill	d					05 03	05 18						05 48												
West Dulwich	d					05 05	05 20						05 50												
Herne Hill	d					05 08	05 23						05 53						06 12						
Loughborough Jn	d																		06 15						
Elephant & Castle ⊖	d				05 14						05 44						06 14		06 19			06 24			
London Blackfriars ⊖	d	04 06	04 36	05 06	05 19				05 31		05 49				06 01	06 04	06 19	06 22	06 24		06 27	06a29	06 34		
City Thameslink	a			05 08	05 21				05 33		05 51				06 03	06 06	06 21	06 23	06 26		06 28		06 36		
Farringdon ⊖	a			05 10	05 23				05 35		05 53				06 05	06 08	06 23	06 26	06 28		06 31		06 38		
St Pancras International ⊖	a	04 13	04 43	05 15	05 28				05 40		05 58				06 10	06 13	06 28	06 30	06 33		06 35		06 43		
Kentish Town ⊖	a		04 48		05 33						06 03					06 18			06 38						
Brixton ⊖	d					05 11	05 26						05 56												
London Victoria ⊖	a					05 20	05 35						06 05												06 20

A From Sutton (Surrey) to Bedford
B From Dover Priory
C From Orpington
D From Brighton to Bedford
E From Ramsgate
F From Sevenoaks to Finsbury Park
G From Sevenoaks
H From Horsham to Peterborough
I From Three Bridges to Bedford
J To Luton
K To London Charing Cross
L From Tonbridge to London Charing Cross
M From Gillingham (Kent) to St Albans City
N From Brighton to Cambridge
O From Sutton (Surrey) to St Albans City
P From Gillingham (Kent) to Luton
Q From Tunbridge Wells to London Charing Cross
R From Gillingham (Kent)

Table 195R

Sevenoaks and Otford, Orpington, Bromley South, Beckenham Junction, Catford - London

		SE	SE	SE	SE		SE	TL	TL	TL	TL	TL	SE	TL	TL		TL	TL	SE	SE	SE	SE	SE	SE	SE
		◇■		◇■				■		■	■				■			■		◇■			◇■		◇■
		A		B	C		D	E	F	G	H	I		F	J			G	K	L	C	M	N		O
Sevenoaks	d			05 50													05 52					06 01	06 09		
Bat & Ball	d																05 55								
Otford	d																05 59								06 17
Shoreham (Kent)	d																06 02								
Eynsford	d																06 05								
Swanley	d																06 11		06 19						06 26
St Mary Cray	d																06 15		06 23						
Orpington	d		05 52	05a58			06 00					06 03										06 18	06a20	06 24	
Petts Wood	d		05 55				06 03					06 06										06 21		06 27	
Bickley	d		05 59									06 10					06 20							06 31	
Bromley South	d	06 02	06 04									06 13	06 16				06 23		06 30	06 33				06 35	06 36
Shortlands	d		06 07									06 15	06 19				06 25							06 38	
Ravensbourne	d											06 18					06 28								
Beckenham Hill	d											06 20					06 30								
Bellingham	d											06 22					06 32								
Catford	d											06 25					06 35								
Crofton Park	d											06 28					06 38								
Lewisham	a						06 20															06 40			
	d				06 11																06 36				
Nunhead	d				06 17							06 31					06 41				06 44				
Peckham Rye	d				06 20							06 34					06 44				06 47				
Denmark Hill	d				06 24							06 37					06 47				06 50				
Beckenham Junction	d		06 10										06 22											06 42	
Kent House	d		06 12										06 24											06 44	
Penge East	d		06 14										06 26											06 46	
Sydenham Hill	d		06 18										06 30											06 50	
West Dulwich	d		06 20										06 32											06 52	
Herne Hill	d		06 23						06 27				06 35	06 42										06 55	
Loughborough Jn	d								06 30					06 45											
Elephant & Castle ⊖	d								06 34			06 44		06 49			06 54								
London Blackfriars ⊖	d							06 37	06 39	06 42	06 47	06 49		06 54	06 57		06a59	07 02							
City Thameslink	a							06 38	06 41	06 43	06 48	06 51		06 56	06 58			07 03							
Farringdon ⊖	a							06 41	06 43	06 46	06 51	06 53		06 58	07 01			07 06							
St Pancras International ⊖	a							06 45	06 48	06 50	06 55	06 58		07 03	07 05			07 10							
Kentish Town ⊖	a								06 53					07 08											
Brixton ⊖	d		06 26										06 38											06 58	
London Victoria ⊖	a	06 23	06 35		06 37								06 48						06 51	06 54	07 02			07 07	06 57

			SE	TL	TL	SE	TL	TL	TL	SE	TL		TL	TL	SE	TL	TL	SE	SE	SE	SE		SE	SE	SE
			◇■		■	◇■		■			■			■			■	◇■			◇■		◇■		■
			P	Q	R	O	F	H	I		S		F	T			G	U	M	D	V		O		K
Sevenoaks	d		06 17													06 22		06 31		06 34	06 41				
Bat & Ball	d															06 25									
Otford	d					06 25										06 29							06 48		
Shoreham (Kent)	d															06 32									
Eynsford	d															06 35									
Swanley	d					06 34										06 41									06 56
St Mary Cray	d															06 45									07 00
Orpington	d		06a25						06 29									06a39	06 41	06 49	06a52			06 54	
Petts Wood	d								06 32										06 44	06a52				06 57	
Bickley	d								06 40							06 50								07 01	
Bromley South	d					06 42			06 43	06 49						06 53							07 04	07 04	07 07
Shortlands	d								06 45	06 52						06 55								07 07	
Ravensbourne	d								06 48							06 58									
Beckenham Hill	d								06 50							07 00									
Bellingham	d								06 52							07 02									
Catford	d								06 55							07 05									
Crofton Park	d								06 58							07 08									
Lewisham	a																		07 03						
	d																								
Nunhead	d								07 01							07 11									07 16
Peckham Rye	d								07 04							07 14									
Denmark Hill	d								07 07							07 17									07 22
Beckenham Junction	d									06 55					07 01									07 10	
Kent House	d									06 57					07 04									07 13	
Penge East	d									06 59					07 06									07 15	
Sydenham Hill	d									07 03					07 10								07 14		
West Dulwich	d									07 05					07 12									07 20	
Herne Hill	d						06 57			07 08			07 12		07 15									07 23	
Loughborough Jn	d						07 00						07 15		07 19										
Elephant & Castle ⊖	d					07 03	07 04		07 14				07 19		07 23	07 24									
London Blackfriars ⊖	d			07 04	07 07	07a09	07 09	07 12	07 19		07 22		07 24	07 27	07a29	07a29	07 32								
City Thameslink	a			07 06	07 08		07 11	07 13	07 21		07 23		07 26	07 28			07 33								
Farringdon ⊖	a			07 08	07 11		07 13	07 16	07 23		07 26		07 28	07 31			07 36								
St Pancras International ⊖	a			07 13	07 15		07 18	07 20	07 28		07 30		07 33	07 35			07 40								
Kentish Town ⊖	a						07 23		07 33																
Brixton ⊖	d									07 11														07 26	
London Victoria ⊖	a									07 20													07 29	07 35	07 34

A From Ramsgate
B From Dover Priory to London Cannon Street
C From Dartford
D To London Cannon Street
E From Horsham to Peterborough
F From Sutton (Surrey) to St Albans City
G From Brighton to Bedford
H From East Grinstead to Bedford
I To Luton
J From Three Bridges to Bedford
K From Gillingham (Kent)
L From Dover Priory
M To London Charing Cross
N From Tunbridge Wells to London Cannon Street
O From Ashford International
P From Ashford International to London Charing Cross
Q From Rainham Kt to Luton
R From Three Bridges to Peterborough
S From Brighton to Cambridge
T From Horsham to Bedford
U From Hastings to London Charing Cross
V From Tunbridge Wells to London Charing Cross

Sevenoaks and Otford, Orpington, Bromley South, Beckenham Junction, Catford - London

		SE ◇■ A	SE B	TL C	TL ■ D	TL E	SN ■ F	TL G	SE H	SE ◇■ I	TL ■ J	TL K	SE ◇ L	SE	TL E	TL ■ M	SE	TL	TL ■ N	SE ◇■ O	SE P	SE ◇■ Q	SE H
Sevenoaks ■	d																	06 52		06 54	06 56	07 03	
Bat & Ball	d																	06 55					
Otford ■	d												06 56					06 59					
Shoreham (Kent)	d																	07 02					
Eynsford	d																	07 05					
Swanley ■	d												07 07					07 11					
St Mary Cray	d												07 11					07 15					
Orpington ■	d							06 59	07 02											07a02	07 11	07a14	07 20
Petts Wood ■	d							07 02	07 05												07a14		07 23
Bickley ■	d							07 06										07 20					
Bromley South ■	d	07 12						07 13		07 16		←	07 19	07 19				07 23					
Shortlands ■	d							07 15				07 15		07 22				07 25					
Ravensbourne	d							→				07 18						07 28					
Beckenham Hill	d											07 20						07 30					
Bellingham	d											07 22						07 32					
Catford	d											07 25						07 35					
Crofton Park	d											07 28						07 38					
Lewisham ■	a								07 23														07 43
	d		07 15																				
Nunhead ■	d											07 31						07 41					
Peckham Rye ■	d		07 21									07 34						07 44					
Denmark Hill ■	d		07 26									07 37						07 47					
Beckenham Junction ■ ⇌	d													07 25			07 31						
Kent House ■	d													07 28			07 34						
Penge East	d													07 30			07 36						
Sydenham Hill	d													07 34			07 40						
West Dulwich	d												07 30				07 42						
Herne Hill ■	d					07 27								07 38	07 42		07 45						
Loughborough Jn	d					07 30									07 45		07 49						
Elephant & Castle ⊖	d					07 34				07 39		07 44			07 49		07 53	07 54					
London Blackfriars ■ ⊖	d			07 34	07 37	07 39	07 42			07a45	07 47	07 49			07 54	07 57	07a59	07a59	08 02				
City Thameslink ■	a			07 36	07 38	07 41	07 43				07 48	07 51			07 56	07 58			08 03				
Farringdon ⊖	a			07 38	07 41	07 43	07 46				07 51	07 53			07 58	08 01			08 06				
St Pancras International ■ ⊖	a			07 43	07 45	07 48	07 50				07 55	07 58			08 03	08 05			08 10				
Kentish Town ⊖	a			07 48								08 03											
Brixton ⊖	d													07 41									
London Victoria ■ ⊖	a	07 38	07 38										07 45	07 50									

		SE L	SE	SE R	SE S	TL C	TL ■ D	SE ◇■ L	TL E	TL ■ J	TL G	SE P	SE H	SE ◇■ T	SE	TL ■ U	TL E	TL ■ M	TL V	SE ■ L	SE P	SE ■ W
Sevenoaks ■	d											07 17							07 18		07 37	
Bat & Ball	d																		07 21			
Otford ■	d	07 16						07 22											07 25	07 34		
Shoreham (Kent)	d																		07 28			
Eynsford	d																		07 31			
Swanley ■	d			07 27				07 32											07 37			07 41
St Mary Cray	d			07 32															07 41			07 45
Orpington ■	d		07 24								07 30	07 33	07 42								07 51	
Petts Wood ■	d		07 27								07 33	07a36	07 46								07a54	
Bickley ■	d		07 31								07 40								07 46			
Bromley South ■	d	07 33	07 34	07 39				07 42			07 43			07 46	07 49				→	07 50		07 53
Shortlands ■	d		07 36								07 45				07 52							
Ravensbourne	d										07 48											
Beckenham Hill	d										07 50											
Bellingham	d										07 52											07 58
Catford	d										07 55											
Crofton Park	d			07 46							07 58											
Lewisham ■	a												08 05									
	d				07 46																	
Nunhead ■	d				07 54						08 01											
Peckham Rye ■	d				07 57						08 04											
Denmark Hill ■	d			07 55	08 00						08 07											08 10
Beckenham Junction ■ ⇌	d		07 40												07 56							
Kent House ■	d		07 43																	07 55		
Penge East	d	07 39													08 00							
Sydenham Hill	d		07 47												08 03							
West Dulwich	d		07 49												08 06							
Herne Hill ■	d		07 53						07 57						08 09		08 12					
Loughborough Jn	d								08 00								08 15					
Elephant & Castle ⊖	d							08 02	08 04		08 14						08 19					
London Blackfriars ■ ⊖	d					08 04	08 07	08a09	08 09	08 17	08 19					08 22	08 24	08 27				
City Thameslink ■	a					08 06	08 08		08 11	08 18	08 21					08 23	08 26	08 28				
Farringdon ⊖	a					08 08	08 11		08 13	08 21	08 23					08 26	08 28	08 31				
St Pancras International ■ ⊖	a					08 13	08 15		08 18	08 25	08 28					08 30	08 33	08 35				
Kentish Town ⊖	a					08 18					08 33											
Brixton ⊖	d		07 56												08 12							
London Victoria ■ ⊖	a	07 58	08 05	08 07	08 13									08 09	08 21					08 12		08 25

A From Dover Priory
B From Barnehurst
C From Rainham Kt to Luton
D From Gatwick Airport to Peterborough
E From Sutton (Surrey) to St Albans City
F From Littlehampton to Bedford
G To Luton
H To London Charing Cross
I From Broadstairs
J From East Grinstead to Bedford
K From Orpington to Luton
L From Ashford International
M From Horsham to Bedford
N From Brighton to Bedford
O From Hastings to London Cannon Street
P To London Cannon Street
Q From Tunbridge Wells to London Charing Cross
R From Sheerness-on-Sea
S From Dartford
T From Ramsgate
U From Brighton to Cambridge
V To London Blackfriars
W From Rochester

Sevenoaks and Otford, Orpington, Bromley South, Beckenham Junction, Catford - London

		SE	TL A	TL ■ B	SE C	SE	SE D	TL E	SE ■ F	TL ■ G	SE ■ H	TL I	SN ■ J	TL ■ K	TL L	SE ◇■ M	SE ◇ N	SE	TL I	SE C	TL ■ O	SE	TL
Sevenoaks ■	d																						07 52
Bat & Ball	d																						07 55
Otford ■	d																07 56						07 59
Shoreham (Kent)	d																						08 02
Eynsford	d																						08 05
Swanley ■	d								07 54		07 58						08 07						08 11
St Mary Cray	d								07 59		08 02												08 15
Orpington ■	d					07 54	08 03								08 03								
Petts Wood ■	d		←			07 57	08 06								08 06								
Bickley ■	d		07 46			08 01									08 10								08 20
Bromley South ■	d		07 53			08 04			08 06		08 09				08 13	08 14	08 17	08 19					08 23
Shortlands ■	d		07 55			08 06									08 15			08 22					08 25
Ravensbourne	d		07 58												08 18								08 28
Beckenham Hill	d		08 00												08 20								08 30
Bellingham	d		08 02												08 22								08 32
Catford	d		08 05												08 25								08 35
Crofton Park	d		08 08								08 18				08 28								08 38
Lewisham ■	a						08 23																
	d				08 06															08 27			
Nunhead ■	d		08 11		08 14										08 31					08 34			08 41
Peckham Rye ■	d		08 14		08 17										08 34					08 37			08 44
Denmark Hill ■	d		08 17		08 20				08 23						08 37					08 42			08 47
Beckenham Junction ■ ⇌	d	08 01				08 10												08 25				08 31	
Kent House ■	d	08 04				08 12												08 28				08 34	
Penge East	d	08 06				08 14												08 30				08 36	
Sydenham Hill	d	08 10				08 17											08 27					08 40	
West Dulwich	d	08 12				08 20												08 35				08 42	
Herne Hill ■	d	08 15				08 23						08 27						08 38	08 42			08 45	
Loughborough Jn	d	08 19										08 30							08 45			08 49	
Elephant & Castle ⊖	d	08 23	08 24						08 31			08 34			08 44				08 49			08 53	08 54
London Blackfriars ■ ⊖	d	08a29	08a29	08 32				08 34	08a37	08 37		08 39	08 42	08 47	08 49				08 54		08 57	08a59	08a59
City Thameslink ■	a			08 33				08 36		08 38		08 41	08 43	08 48	08 51				08 56		08 58		
Farringdon ⊖	a			08 36				08 38		08 41		08 43	08 46	08 51	08 53				08 58		09 01		
St Pancras International ■ ⊖	a			08 40				08 43		08 45		08 48	08 50	08 55	08 58				09 03		09 05		
Kentish Town ⊖	a							08 48							09 03								
Brixton ⊖	d					08 26												08 41					
London Victoria ■ ⊖	a				08 33	08 35					08 36					08 39	08 42	08 51		08 55			

		TL E	SE P	SE D	SE ■ Q	SE	SE R	TL ■ G	TL I	TL ■ B	TL ■ K	TL L	SE P	SE ◇ N	SE D	SE ◇■ S	SE	TL ■ T	TL I	TL ■ O	SE	TL	TL U
Sevenoaks ■	d		07 57										08 17									08 22	
Bat & Ball	d																					08 25	
Otford ■	d													08 26								08 29	
Shoreham (Kent)	d																					08 32	
Eynsford	d																					08 35	
Swanley ■	d				08 23									08 35								08 41	
St Mary Cray	d				08 27									08 39								08 45	
Orpington ■	d		08 12	08 21		08 24						08 29	08 34		08 42								
Petts Wood ■	d		08a15	08 24		08 27						08 32	08a37		08 45								
Bickley ■	d					08 31						08 36										08 50	
Bromley South ■	d				08 34	08 34						08 43		08 46		08 49	08 49					08 53	
Shortlands ■	d					08 36						08 45					08 52					08 55	
Ravensbourne	d											08 48										08 58	
Beckenham Hill	d											08 50										09 00	
Bellingham	d				08 40							08 52										09 02	
Catford	d											08 55										09 05	
Crofton Park	d											08 58										09 08	
Lewisham ■	a			08 43											09 04								
	d						08 46																
Nunhead ■	d						08 52					09 01										09 11	
Peckham Rye ■	d						08 55					09 04										09 14	
Denmark Hill ■	d				08 50		08 59					09 07										09 17	
Beckenham Junction ■ ⇌	d					08 40											08 56				09 01		
Kent House ■	d					08 42											08 58				09 04		
Penge East	d					08 44											09 01				09 06		
Sydenham Hill	d					08 47											09 04				09 10		
West Dulwich	d					08 50											09 07				09 12		
Herne Hill ■	d					08 53			08 57								09 10		09 12		09 15		
Loughborough Jn	d								09 00										09 15		09 19		
Elephant & Castle ⊖	d								09 04			09 14							09 19		09 23	09 24	
London Blackfriars ■ ⊖	d	09 04						09 07	09 09	09 12	09 17	09 19						09 22	09 24	09 27	09a29	09a29	09 34
City Thameslink ■	a	09 06						09 08	09 11	09 13	09 18	09 21						09 23	09 26	09 28			09 36
Farringdon ⊖	a	09 08						09 11	09 13	09 16	09 21	09 23						09 26	09 28	09 31			09 38
St Pancras International ■ ⊖	a	09 13						09 15	09 18	09 20	09 25	09 28						09 30	09 33	09 35			09 43
Kentish Town ⊖	a	09 18										09 33											09 48
Brixton ⊖	d					08 56											09 13						
London Victoria ■ ⊖	a				09 03	09 05	09 11							09 10		09 13	09 22						

A From Sevenoaks
B From Brighton to Bedford
C From Dartford
D To London Charing Cross
E From Rainham Kt to West Hampstead Thameslink
F From Sole Street
G From Gatwick Airport to Peterborough
H From Sheerness-on-Sea
I From Sutton (Surrey) to St Albans City
J From Littlehampton to Bedford
K From East Grinstead to Bedford
L To Luton
M From Ramsgate
N From Ashford International
O From Horsham to Bedford
P To London Cannon Street
Q From Rochester
R From Barnehurst
S From Dover Priory
T From Brighton to Cambridge
U From Rainham Kt to Luton

Sevenoaks and Otford, Orpington, Bromley South, Beckenham Junction, Catford - London

			SE	SE	SE	SE	SE	TL	TL	TL	TL		TL	SE	SE	TL	SE	TL	TL	SE	SE		SE	SE	SE
			A			B	■ C	■ D	E	■ F	■ G			◇ H		E	I	■ J	K	◇■ L	M		A	◇■ N	◇■ O
Sevenoaks ■	d		08 37																08 52	08 56			09 06	09 13	
Bat & Ball	d																		08 55						
Otford ■	d													08 56					08 59						
Shoreham (Kent)	d																		09 02						
Eynsford	d																		09 05						
Swanley ■	d			08 51			09 01							09 05					09 11						
St Mary Cray	d			08 56			09 06							09 09					09 15						
Orpington ■	d		08 52		08 55								09 03							09a04	09 11		09 21	09a23	
Petts Wood ■	d		08a55		08 58								09 06								09 14		09a24		
Bickley ■	d				09 02								09 10						09 20						
Bromley South ■	d			09 03	09 05		09 12						09 13	09 17	09 19				09 23						09 33
Shortlands ■	d				09 07								09 15		09 22				09 25						
Ravensbourne	d												09 18						09 28						
Beckenham Hill	d												09 20						→						
Bellingham	d						09 18						09 22												
Catford	d												09 25												
Crofton Park	d						09 22						09 28												
Lewisham ■	a																				09 32				
	d					09 07											09 32								
Nunhead ■	d					09 14							09 31				09 37								
Peckham Rye ■	d					09 17							09 34				09 40								
Denmark Hill ■	d					09 22	09 28						09 37				09 44								
Beckenham Junction ■	d			09 07	09 11										09 25										
Kent House ■	d				09 13										09 27										
Penge East	d			09 11											09 29										
Sydenham Hill	d				09 17										09 33										
West Dulwich	d				09 20										09 35										
Herne Hill ■	d				09 23				09 27						09 38	09 42									
Loughborough Jn.	d								09 30							09 45									
Elephant & Castle ⊖	d								09 34				09 44			09 49									
London Blackfriars ■ ⊖	d							09 37	09 39	09 42	09 47		09 49			09 54		09 57							
City Thameslink ■	a							09 38	09 41	09 43	09 48		09 51			09 56		09 58							
Farringdon ⊖	a							09 41	09 43	09 46	09 51		09 53			09 58		10 01							
St Pancras International ■ ⊖	a							09 45	09 48	09 50	09 55		09 58			10 03		10 05							
Kentish Town ⊖	a								09 53				10 03			10 08									
Brixton ⊖	d				09 26										09 41										
London Victoria ■ ⊖	a			09 28	09 35	09 35	09 41							09 40	09 50		09 57								09 56

		SE	SE	TL	TL	TL	TL		TL	TL	SE	SE	SE	TL	TL	TL	TL		TL	SE	SE	SE	SE	SE	SE
			◇■ P	Q	R	■ S	E		■ F		◇■ T		I	■ U	E	■ V			R	◇■ L	M	A	◇■ N	■ W	◇■ O
Sevenoaks ■	d																09 22			09 29		09 35	09 43		
Bat & Ball	d																09 25								
Otford ■	d		09 15								09 26						09 29								
Shoreham (Kent)	d																09 32								
Eynsford	d																09 35								
Swanley ■	d		09 24								09 35						09 41							09 47	
St Mary Cray	d		09 28								09 39						09 45							09 52	
Orpington ■	d	09 24								09 33										09a37	09 41	09 50	09a51		
Petts Wood ■	d	09 27								09 36											09 44	09a53			
Bickley ■	d	09 32								09 40							09 50								
Bromley South ■	d	09 35	09 36							09 43	09 47	09 49					09 53							10 00	10 03
Shortlands ■	d	09 38		←						09 45		09 52					09 55								
Ravensbourne	d			09 28						09 48							09 58								
Beckenham Hill	d			09 30						09 50							10 00								
Bellingham	d			09 32						09 52							10 02								
Catford	d			09 35						09 55							10 05								
Crofton Park	d			09 38						09 58							10 08								
Lewisham ■	a																				10 02				
	d												10 02												
Nunhead ■	d			09 41						10 01			10 07				10 11								
Peckham Rye ■	d			09 44						10 04			10 10				10 14								
Denmark Hill ■	d			09 47						10 07			10 14				10 17							10 20	
Beckenham Junction ■	d	09 43										09 55													
Kent House ■	d	09 45										09 57													
Penge East	d	09 47										09 59													
Sydenham Hill	d	09 50										10 03													
West Dulwich	d	09 52										10 05													
Herne Hill ■	d	09 55					09 57					10 08			10 12										
Loughborough Jn.	d						10 00								10 15										
Elephant & Castle ⊖	d		09 53	09 54			10 04			10 14					10 19		10 24								
London Blackfriars ■ ⊖	d		10a00	09a59	10 04	10 07	10 09		10 12	10 19				10 22	10 24	10 27	10a29		10 34						
City Thameslink ■	a				10 06	10 08	10 11		10 13	10 21				10 23	10 26	10 28			10 36						
Farringdon ⊖	a				10 08	10 11	10 13		10 16	10 23				10 26	10 28	10 31			10 38						
St Pancras International ■ ⊖	a				10 13	10 15	10 18		10 20	10 28				10 30	10 33	10 35			10 43						
Kentish Town ⊖	a						10 23			10 33					10 38										
Brixton ⊖	d	09 58										10 11													
London Victoria ■ ⊖	a	10 05									10 08	10 20	10 25											10 32	10 25

A To London Charing Cross
B From Dartford
C From Gillingham (Kent)
D From Gatwick Airport to Peterborough
E From Sutton (Surrey) to St Albans City
F From Brighton to Bedford
G From East Grinstead to Bedford
H From Ashford International
I From Gravesend
J From Horsham to Bedford
K To London Blackfriars
L From Hastings to London Charing Cross
M To London Cannon Street
N From Tunbridge Wells to London Charing Cross
O From Ramsgate
P From Maidstone East
Q From Sevenoaks
R From Rainham Kt to Luton
S From Horsham to Peterborough
T From Canterbury West
U From Brighton to Cambridge
V From Gatwick Airport to Bedford
W From Rochester

Sevenoaks and Otford, Orpington, Bromley South, Beckenham Junction, Catford - London

		SE	TL		TL	TL	TL	SE	SE	TL	SE	TL	TL		TL	SE	SE	SE	SE	SE	SE	SE	TL		TL
			■ A		B	■ C		◇■ D		B	E	■ F			G	◇■ H	I	J	◇■ K	◇■ L	◇■ M		■ A		B
Sevenoaks ■	d												09 52			09 59		10 05	10 13						
Bat & Ball	d												09 55												
Otford ■	d							09 56					09 59												
Shoreham (Kent)	d												10 02												
Eynsford	d												10 05												
Swanley ■	d							10 05					10 11							10 17					
St Mary Cray	d							10 09					10 15							10 22					
Orpington ■	d	09 54					10 03									10a07	10 11	10 20	10a21			10 24			
Petts Wood ■	d	09 57					10 06										10 14	10a23				10 27			
Bickley ■	d	10 01					10 10						10 20									10 31			
Bromley South ■	d	10 04					10 13	10 17	10 19				10 23							10 30	10 33	10 34			
Shortlands ■	d	10 07					10 15		10 22				10 25									10 37			
Ravensbourne	d						10 18						10 28												
Beckenham Hill	d						10 20						10 30												
Bellingham	d						10 22						10 32												
Catford	d						10 25						10 35												
Crofton Park	d						10 28						10 38												
Lewisham ■	a																10 32								
	d										10 32														
Nunhead ■	d						10 31				10 37		10 41												
Peckham Rye ■	d						10 34				10 40		10 44												
Denmark Hill ■	d						10 37				10 44		10 47							10 50					
Beckenham Junction ■	d	10 10							10 25													10 40			
Kent House ■	d	10 12							10 27													10 42			
Penge East	d	10 14							10 29													10 44			
Sydenham Hill	d	10 18							10 33													10 48			
West Dulwich	d	10 20							10 35													10 50			
Herne Hill ■	d	10 23			10 27				10 38	10 42												10 53			10 57
Loughborough Jn.	d				10 30					10 45															11 00
Elephant & Castle ⊖	d				10 34		10 44			10 49			10 54												11 04
London Blackfriars ■ ⊖	d		10 37		10 39	10 42	10 49			10 54		10 57	10a59		11 04								11 07		11 09
City Thameslink ■	a		10 38		10 41	10 43	10 51			10 56		10 58			11 06								11 08		11 11
Farringdon ⊖	a		10 41		10 43	10 46	10 53			10 58		11 01			11 08								11 11		11 13
St Pancras International ■ ⊖	a		10 45		10 48	10 50	10 58			11 03		11 05			11 13								11 15		11 18
Kentish Town ⊖	a				10 53		11 03			11 08															11 23
Brixton ⊖	d	10 26							10 41													10 56			
London Victoria ■ ⊖	a	10 33						10 38	10 48		10 55									11 00	10 53	11 03			

		TL	TL	SE	SE	SE	TL	TL	TL		TL	TL	SE	SE	SE	SE	SE	SE	TL		TL	TL	TL	SE	SE
		■ C		◇■ N		E	■ O	B	■ F			G	◇■ H	I	J	◇■ K	◇■ L		■ A		B	■ C		◇■ D	
Sevenoaks ■	d										10 22		10 29		10 35	10 43									
Bat & Ball	d										10 25														
Otford ■	d			10 26							10 29													10 56	
Shoreham (Kent)	d										10 32														
Eynsford	d										10 35														
Swanley ■	d			10 37							10 41													11 05	
St Mary Cray	d										10 45													11 09	
Orpington ■	d		10 33										10a37	10 41	10 50	10a51		10 54					11 03		
Petts Wood ■	d		10 36											10 44	10a53			10 57					11 06		
Bickley ■	d		10 40								10 50							11 01					11 10		
Bromley South ■	d		10 43	10 47	10 49						10 53						11 03	11 04					11 13	11 17	11 19
Shortlands ■	d		10 45		10 52						10 55							11 07					11 15		11 22
Ravensbourne	d		10 48								10 58												11 18		
Beckenham Hill	d		10 50								11 00												11 20		
Bellingham	d		10 52								11 02												11 22		
Catford	d		10 55								11 05												11 25		
Crofton Park	d		10 58								11 08												11 28		
Lewisham ■	a													11 02											
	d					11 02																			
Nunhead ■	d		11 01			11 07					11 11												11 31		
Peckham Rye ■	d		11 04			11 10					11 14												11 34		
Denmark Hill ■	d		11 07			11 14					11 17												11 37		
Beckenham Junction ■	d				10 55													11 10							11 25
Kent House ■	d				10 57													11 12							11 27
Penge East	d				10 59													11 14							11 29
Sydenham Hill	d				11 03													11 18							11 33
West Dulwich	d				11 05													11 20							11 35
Herne Hill ■	d				11 08			11 12										11 23			11 27				11 38
Loughborough Jn.	d							11 15													11 30				
Elephant & Castle ⊖	d		11 14					11 19			11 24										11 34		11 44		
London Blackfriars ■ ⊖	d	11 12	11 19				11 22	11 24	11 27		11a29	11 34							11 37		11 39	11 42	11 49		
City Thameslink ■	a	11 13	11 21				11 23	11 26	11 28			11 36							11 38		11 41	11 43	11 51		
Farringdon ⊖	a	11 16	11 23				11 26	11 28	11 31			11 38							11 41		11 43	11 46	11 53		
St Pancras International ■ ⊖	a	11 20	11 28				11 30	11 33	11 35			11 43							11 45		11 48	11 50	11 58		
Kentish Town ⊖	a		11 33					11 38													11 53		12 03		
Brixton ⊖	d				11 11													11 26							11 41
London Victoria ■ ⊖	a			11 08	11 18	11 25											11 25	11 33						11 38	11 48

A From Horsham to Peterborough
B From Sutton (Surrey) to St Albans City
C From Brighton to Bedford
D From Ashford International
E From Gravesend
F From Gatwick Airport to Bedford
G From Rainham Kt to Luton
H From Hastings to London Charing Cross
I To London Cannon Street
J To London Charing Cross
K From Tunbridge Wells to London Charing Cross
L From Dover Priory
M From Ramsgate
N From Canterbury West
O From Brighton to Cambridge

Table 195R

Mondays to Fridays
21 May to 7 December

Sevenoaks and Otford, Orpington, Bromley South, Beckenham Junction, Catford - London

	TL A	SE B	TL 1 C	TL		TL D	SE ◇1 E	SE F	SE G	SE ◇1 H	SE ◇1 I	SE 1 J	SE	TL 1 K		TL A	TL 1 L	TL	SE ◇1 M	SE B	TL 1 N	TL A	TL 1 C	TL
Sevenoaks d				10 52			10 59		11 05	11 13														11 22
Bat & Ball d				10 55																				11 25
Otford d				10 59															11 26					11 29
Shoreham (Kent) d				11 02																				11 32
Eynsford d				11 05																				11 35
Swanley d				11 11							11 17								11 37					11 41
St Mary Cray d				11 15							11 22													11 45
Orpington d							11a07	11 11	11 20	11a21			11 24					11 33						
Petts Wood d								11 14	11a23				11 27					11 36						
Bickley d				11 20									11 31					11 40						11 50
Bromley South d				11 23							11 30	11 33	11 34					11 43	11 47					11 53
Shortlands d				11 25									11 37					11 45						11 55
Ravensbourne d				11 28														11 48						11 58
Beckenham Hill d				11 30														11 50						12 00
Bellingham d				11 32														11 52						12 02
Catford d				11 35														11 55						12 05
Crofton Park d				11 38														11 58						12 08
Lewisham a								11 32																
d		11 32																		12 02				
Nunhead d		11 37		11 41														12 01		12 07				12 11
Peckham Rye d		11 40		11 44														12 04		12 10				12 14
Denmark Hill d		11 44		11 47							11 50							12 07		12 14				12 17
Beckenham Junction d													11 40											
Kent House d													11 42											
Penge East d													11 44											
Sydenham Hill d													11 48											
West Dulwich d													11 50											
Herne Hill d	11 42												11 53			11 57						12 12		
Loughborough Jn. d	11 45															12 00						12 15		
Elephant & Castle ⊖ d	11 49			11 54												12 04		12 14				12 19		12 24
London Blackfriars ⊖ d	11 54		11 57	11a59		12 04								12 07		12 09	12 12	12 19			12 22	12 24	12 27	12a29
City Thameslink a	11 56		11 58			12 06								12 08		12 11	12 13	12 21			12 23	12 26	12 28	
Farringdon ⊖ a	11 58		12 01			12 08								12 11		12 13	12 16	12 23			12 26	12 28	12 31	
St Pancras International ⊖ a	12 03		12 05			12 13								12 15		12 18	12 20	12 28			12 30	12 33	12 35	
Kentish Town ⊖ a	12 08															12 23		12 33				12 38		
Brixton ⊖ d													11 56											
London Victoria ⊖ a		11 55									12 00	11 53	12 03						12 08	12 25				

		TL D	SE ◇1 E	SE F	SE G	SE ◇1 H	SE ◇1 I	SE	TL 1 K	TL A		TL 1 L	TL	SE ◇1 O	SE	TL A	SE B	TL 1 C	TL	TL D		SE ◇1 E	SE F	SE G
Sevenoaks d			11 29		11 35	11 43													11 52			11 59		12 05
Bat & Ball d																			11 55					
Otford d														11 56					11 59					
Shoreham (Kent) d																			12 02					
Eynsford d																			12 05					
Swanley d														12 05					12 11					
St Mary Cray d														12 09					12 15					
Orpington d			11a37	11 41	11 50	11a51		11 54					12 03									12a07	12 11	12 20
Petts Wood d				11 44	11a53			11 57					12 06										12 14	12a23
Bickley d								12 01					12 10						12 20					
Bromley South d							12 03	12 04					12 13	12 17	12 19				12 23					
Shortlands d								12 07					12 15		12 22				12 25					
Ravensbourne d													12 18						12 28					
Beckenham Hill d													12 20						12 30					
Bellingham d													12 22						12 32					
Catford d													12 25						12 35					
Crofton Park d													12 28						12 38					
Lewisham a				12 02																			12 32	
d																	12 32							
Nunhead d													12 31				12 37		12 41					
Peckham Rye d													12 34				12 40		12 44					
Denmark Hill d													12 37				12 44		12 47					
Beckenham Junction d								12 10							12 25									
Kent House d								12 12							12 27									
Penge East d								12 14							12 29									
Sydenham Hill d								12 18							12 33									
West Dulwich d								12 20							12 35									
Herne Hill d								12 23		12 27					12 38	12 42								
Loughborough Jn. d										12 30						12 45								
Elephant & Castle ⊖ d										12 34			12 44			12 49			12 54					
London Blackfriars ⊖ d		12 34							12 37	12 39		12 42	12 49			12 54		12 57	12a59	13 04				
City Thameslink a		12 36							12 38	12 41		12 43	12 51			12 56		12 58		13 06				
Farringdon ⊖ a		12 38							12 41	12 43		12 46	12 53			12 58		13 01		13 08				
St Pancras International ⊖ a		12 43							12 45	12 48		12 50	12 58			13 03		13 05		13 13				
Kentish Town ⊖ a										12 53			13 03			13 08								
Brixton ⊖ d								12 26							12 41									
London Victoria ⊖ a							12 25	12 33						12 38	12 48		12 55							

A From Sutton (Surrey) to St Albans City
B From Gravesend
C From Gatwick Airport to Bedford
D From Rainham Kt to Luton
E From Hastings to London Charing Cross
F To London Cannon Street
G To London Charing Cross
H From Tunbridge Wells to London Charing Cross
I From Dover Priory
J From Ramsgate
K From Horsham to Peterborough
L From Brighton to Bedford
M From Canterbury West
N From Brighton to Cambridge
O From Ashford International

Table 195R

Mondays to Fridays
21 May to 7 December

Sevenoaks and Otford, Orpington, Bromley South, Beckenham Junction, Catford - London

	SE ◇1 A	SE ◇1 B	SE ◇1 C	SE	TL 1 D	TL E		TL 1 F	TL	SE ◇1 G	SE	SE H	TL 1 I	TL E	TL 1 J	TL		TL K	SE ◇1 L	SE M	SE N	SE ◇1 A	SE ◇1 B	SE
Sevenoaks d	12 13															12 22			12 29		12 35	12 43		
Bat & Ball d																12 25								
Otford d										12 26						12 29								
Shoreham (Kent) d																12 32								
Eynsford d																12 35								
Swanley d		12 17								12 37						12 41								
St Mary Cray d		12 22														12 45								
Orpington d	12a21			12 24					12 33										12a37	12 41	12 50	12a51		12 54
Petts Wood d				12 27					12 36											12 44	12a53			12 57
Bickley d				12 31					12 40							12 50								13 01
Bromley South d		12 30	12 33	12 34					12 43	12 47	12 49					12 53							13 03	13 04
Shortlands d				12 37					12 45		12 52					12 55								13 07
Ravensbourne d									12 48							12 58								
Beckenham Hill d									12 50							13 00								
Bellingham d									12 52							13 02								
Catford d									12 55							13 05								
Crofton Park d									12 58							13 08								
Lewisham a																				13 02				
d												13 02												
Nunhead d									13 01			13 07				13 11								
Peckham Rye d									13 04			13 10				13 14								
Denmark Hill d		12 50							13 07			13 14				13 17								
Beckenham Junction d				12 40							12 55													13 10
Kent House d				12 42							12 57													13 12
Penge East d				12 44							12 59													13 14
Sydenham Hill d				12 48							13 03													13 18
West Dulwich d				12 50							13 05													13 20
Herne Hill d				12 53		12 57					13 08			13 12										13 23
Loughborough Jn. d						13 00								13 15										
Elephant & Castle ⊖ d						13 04			13 14					13 19		13 24								
London Blackfriars ⊖ d					13 07	13 09		13 12	13 19				13 22	13 24	13 27	13a29		13 34						
City Thameslink a					13 08	13 11		13 13	13 21				13 23	13 26	13 28			13 36						
Farringdon ⊖ a					13 11	13 13		13 16	13 23				13 26	13 28	13 31			13 38						
St Pancras International ⊖ a					13 15	13 18		13 20	13 28				13 30	13 33	13 35			13 43						
Kentish Town ⊖ a						13 23			13 33					13 38										
Brixton ⊖ d				12 56							13 11													13 26
London Victoria ⊖ a		13 00	12 53	13 03						13 08	13 18	13 25											13 26	13 33

	TL 1 D	TL E		TL 1 F	TL	SE ◇1 O	SE	TL E	SE H	TL 1 J	TL	TL K		SE ◇1 L	SE M	SE N	SE ◇1 A	SE ◇1 B	SE ◇1 C	SE	TL 1 D	TL E		TL 1 F
Sevenoaks d											12 52			12 59		13 05	13 13							
Bat & Ball d											12 55													
Otford d						12 56					12 59													
Shoreham (Kent) d											13 02													
Eynsford d											13 05													
Swanley d						13 05					13 11							13 17						
St Mary Cray d						13 09					13 15							13 22						
Orpington d					13 03									13a07	13 11	13 20	13a21			13 24				
Petts Wood d					13 06										13 14	13a23				13 27				
Bickley d					13 10						13 20									13 31				
Bromley South d					13 13	13 17	13 19				13 23							13 30	13 33	13 34				
Shortlands d					13 15		13 22				13 25									13 37				
Ravensbourne d					13 18						13 28													
Beckenham Hill d					13 20						13 30													
Bellingham d					13 22						13 32													
Catford d					13 25						13 35													
Crofton Park d					13 28						13 38													
Lewisham a															13 32									
d									13 32															
Nunhead d					13 31				13 37		13 41													
Peckham Rye d					13 34				13 40		13 44													
Denmark Hill d					13 37				13 44		13 47							13 50						
Beckenham Junction d							13 25													13 40				
Kent House d							13 27													13 42				
Penge East d							13 29													13 44				
Sydenham Hill d							13 33													13 48				
West Dulwich d							13 35													13 50				
Herne Hill d		13 27					13 38	13 42												13 53		13 57		
Loughborough Jn. d		13 30						13 45														14 00		
Elephant & Castle ⊖ d		13 34			13 44			13 49			13 54											14 04		
London Blackfriars ⊖ d	13 37	13 39		13 42	13 49			13 54		13 57	13a59	14 04									14 07	14 09		14 12
City Thameslink a	13 38	13 41		13 43	13 51			13 56		13 58		14 06									14 08	14 11		14 13
Farringdon ⊖ a	13 41	13 43		13 46	13 53			13 58		14 01		14 08									14 11	14 13		14 16
St Pancras International ⊖ a	13 45	13 48		13 50	13 58			14 03		14 05		14 13									14 15	14 18		14 20
Kentish Town ⊖ a		13 53			14 03			14 08														14 23		
Brixton ⊖ d							13 41													13 56				
London Victoria ⊖ a						13 38	13 48		13 55									14 01	13 53	14 03				

A From Tunbridge Wells to London Charing Cross
B From Dover Priory
C From Ramsgate
D From Horsham to Peterborough
E From Sutton (Surrey) to St Albans City
F From Brighton to Bedford
G From Canterbury West
H From Gravesend
I From Brighton to Cambridge
J From Gatwick Airport to Bedford
K From Rainham Kt to Luton
L From Hastings to London Charing Cross
M To London Cannon Street
N To London Charing Cross
O From Ashford International

Sevenoaks and Otford, Orpington, Bromley South, Beckenham Junction, Catford - London

		TL	SE	SE	SE	TL	TL	TL	TL	TL	SE	SE	SE	SE	SE	SE	TL	TL	TL	TL	SE	SE	TL
			◇1			1		1			◇1			◇1	◇1		1		1		◇1		
			A		B	C	D	E		F	G	H	I	J	K		L	D	M		N		D
Sevenoaks	d								13 22		13 29		13 35	13 43									
Bat & Ball	d								13 25														
Otford	d		13 26						13 29												13 56		
Shoreham (Kent)	d								13 32														
Eynsford	d								13 35														
Swanley	d		13 37						13 41												14 05		
St Mary Cray	d								13 45												14 09		
Orpington	d	13 33									13a37	13 41	13 50	13a51		13 54				14 03			
Petts Wood	d	13 36										13 44	13a53			13 57				14 06			
Bickley	d	13 40							13 50							14 01				14 10			
Bromley South	d	13 43	13 47	13 49					13 53						14 03	14 04				14 13	14 17	14 19	
Shortlands	d	13 45		13 52					13 55							14 07				14 15		14 22	
Ravensbourne	d	13 48							13 58											14 18			
Beckenham Hill	d	13 50							14 00											14 20			
Bellingham	d	13 52							14 02											14 22			
Catford	d	13 55							14 05											14 25			
Crofton Park	d	13 58							14 08											14 28			
Lewisham	a											14 02											
	d				14 02																		
Nunhead	d	14 01			14 07				14 11											14 31			
Peckham Rye	d	14 04			14 10				14 14											14 34			
Denmark Hill	d	14 07			14 14				14 17											14 37			
Beckenham Junction	d			13 55												14 10						14 25	
Kent House	d			13 57												14 12						14 27	
Penge East	d			13 59												14 14						14 29	
Sydenham Hill	d			14 03												14 18						14 33	
West Dulwich	d			14 05												14 20						14 35	
Herne Hill	d			14 08			14 12									14 23		14 27				14 38	14 42
Loughborough Jn.	d						14 15											14 30					14 45
Elephant & Castle	⊖ d	14 14					14 19		14 24									14 34		14 44			14 49
London Blackfriars	⊖ d	14 19				14 22	14 24	14 27	14a29	14 34							14 37	14 39	14 42	14 49			14 54
City Thameslink	a	14 21				14 23	14 26	14 28		14 36							14 38	14 41	14 43	14 51			14 56
Farringdon	⊖ a	14 23				14 26	14 28	14 31		14 38							14 41	14 43	14 46	14 53			14 58
St Pancras International	⊖ a	14 28				14 30	14 33	14 35		14 43							14 45	14 48	14 50	14 58			15 03
Kentish Town	⊖ a	14 33					14 38											14 53		15 03			15 08
Brixton	⊖ d			14 11												14 26						14 41	
London Victoria	⊖ a		14 08	14 18	14 25										14 25	14 33					14 39	14 48	

		SE	TL	TL	TL	SE	SE	SE	SE	SE	SE	SE	TL	TL	TL	TL	SE	SE	SE	TL	TL	TL	TL
			1			◇1			◇1	◇1	◇1		1		1		◇1			1		1	
		B	E		F	G	H	I	J	K	O		L	D	M		A		B	C	D	E	
Sevenoaks	d			13 52		13 59		14 05	14 13														14 22
Bat & Ball	d			13 55																			14 25
Otford	d			13 59													14 26						14 29
Shoreham (Kent)	d			14 02																			14 32
Eynsford	d			14 05																			14 35
Swanley	d			14 11						14 17							14 37						14 41
St Mary Cray	d			14 15						14 22													14 45
Orpington	d					14a07	14 11	14 20	14a21			14 24				14 33							
Petts Wood	d						14 14	14a23				14 27				14 36							
Bickley	d			14 20								14 31				14 40							14 50
Bromley South	d			14 23						14 30	14 33	14 34				14 43	14 47	14 49					14 53
Shortlands	d			14 25								14 37				14 45		14 52					14 55
Ravensbourne	d			14 28												14 48							14 58
Beckenham Hill	d			14 30												14 50							15 00
Bellingham	d			14 32												14 52							15 02
Catford	d			14 35												14 55							15 05
Crofton Park	d			14 38												14 58							15 08
Lewisham	a						14 32																
	d	14 32																	15 02				
Nunhead	d	14 37		14 41												15 01			15 07				15 11
Peckham Rye	d	14 40		14 44												15 04			15 10				15 14
Denmark Hill	d	14 44		14 47						14 50						15 07			15 14				15 17
Beckenham Junction	d											14 40						14 55					
Kent House	d											14 42						14 57					
Penge East	d											14 44						14 59					
Sydenham Hill	d											14 48						15 03					
West Dulwich	d											14 50						15 05					
Herne Hill	d											14 53		14 57				15 08			15 12		
Loughborough Jn.	d													15 00							15 15		
Elephant & Castle	⊖ d			14 54										15 04		15 14					15 19		15 24
London Blackfriars	⊖ d		14 57	14a59	15 04								15 07	15 09	15 12	15 19				15 22	15 24	15 27	15a29
City Thameslink	a		14 58		15 06								15 08	15 11	15 13	15 21				15 23	15 26	15 28	
Farringdon	⊖ a		15 01		15 08								15 11	15 13	15 16	15 23				15 26	15 28	15 31	
St Pancras International	⊖ a		15 05		15 13								15 15	15 18	15 20	15 28				15 30	15 33	15 35	
Kentish Town	⊖ a													15 23		15 33					15 38		
Brixton	⊖ d											14 56						15 11					
London Victoria	⊖ a	14 55								15 00	14 53	15 04					15 08	15 18	15 25				

A From Canterbury West
B From Gravesend
C From Brighton to Cambridge
D From Sutton (Surrey) to St Albans City
E From Gatwick Airport to Bedford
F From Rainham Kt to Luton
G From Hastings to London Charing Cross
H To London Cannon Street
I To London Charing Cross
J From Tunbridge Wells to London Charing Cross
K From Dover Priory
L From Horsham to Peterborough
M From Brighton to Bedford
N From Ashford International
O From Ramsgate

Sevenoaks and Otford, Orpington, Bromley South, Beckenham Junction, Catford - London

		TL	SE	SE	SE	SE	SE	SE	TL	TL	TL	TL	SE	SE	TL	SE	TL	TL	TL	SE	SE	SE
			◇1			◇1	◇1		1		1		◇1				1			◇1		
		A	B	C	D	E	F		G	H	I		J		H	K	L		A	B	C	D
Sevenoaks	d		14 29		14 35	14 43												14 52		14 59		15 05
Bat & Ball	d																	14 55				
Otford	d												14 56					14 59				
Shoreham (Kent)	d																	15 02				
Eynsford	d																	15 05				
Swanley	d												15 05					15 11				
St Mary Cray	d												15 09					15 15				
Orpington	d		14a37	14 41	14 50	14a51		14 54				15 03								15a07	15 11	15 20
Petts Wood	d			14 44	14a53			14 57				15 06									15 14	15a23
Bickley	d							15 01				15 10						15 20				
Bromley South	d						15 03	15 04				15 13	15 17	15 19				15 23				
Shortlands	d							15 07				15 15		15 22				15 25				
Ravensbourne	d											15 18						15 28				
Beckenham Hill	d											15 20						15 30				
Bellingham	d											15 22						15 32				
Catford	d											15 25						15 35				
Crofton Park	d											15 28						15 38				
Lewisham	a			15 02																	15 32	
	d															15 32						
Nunhead	d											15 31				15 37		15 41				
Peckham Rye	d											15 34				15 40		15 44				
Denmark Hill	d											15 37				15 44		15 47				
Beckenham Junction	d							15 10						15 25								
Kent House	d							15 12						15 27								
Penge East	d							15 14						15 29								
Sydenham Hill	d							15 18						15 33								
West Dulwich	d							15 20						15 35								
Herne Hill	d							15 23		15 27				15 38	15 42							
Loughborough Jn.	d									15 30					15 45							
Elephant & Castle	⊖ d									15 34		15 44			15 49			15 54				
London Blackfriars	⊖ d	15 34							15 37	15 39	15 42	15 49			15 54		15 57	15a59	16 04			
City Thameslink	a	15 36							15 38	15 41	15 43	15 51			15 56		15 58		16 06			
Farringdon	⊖ a	15 38							15 41	15 43	15 46	15 53			15 58		16 01		16 08			
St Pancras International	⊖ a	15 43							15 45	15 48	15 50	15 58			16 03		16 05		16 13			
Kentish Town	⊖ a									15 53		16 03			16 08				16 18			
Brixton	⊖ d							15 26						15 41								
London Victoria	⊖ a						15 25	15 34					15 38	15 49		15 55						

		SE	SE	SE	SE	TL	TL	TL	TL	TL	SE	SE	SE	TL	TL	TL	TL	TL	SE	SE	SE	SE	SE
		◇1	◇1	◇1		1		1	1		◇1			1		1			◇1			◇1	◇1
		E	F	M		G	H	I	L	N	O		K	P	H	L		A	B	C	D	E	F
Sevenoaks	d	15 13															15 22		15 29		15 35	15 43	
Bat & Ball	d																15 25						
Otford	d										15 26						15 29						
Shoreham (Kent)	d																15 32						
Eynsford	d																15 35						
Swanley	d		15 17								15 35						15 41						
St Mary Cray	d		15 22								15 39						15 45						
Orpington	d	15a21			15 24					15 33									15a37	15 41	15 50	15a51	
Petts Wood	d				15 27					15 36										15 44	15a53		
Bickley	d				15 31					15 40							15 50						
Bromley South	d		15 30	15 33	15 34					15 43	15 47	15 49					15 53						16 03
Shortlands	d				15 37					15 45		15 52					15 55						
Ravensbourne	d									15 48							15 58						
Beckenham Hill	d									15 50							16 00						
Bellingham	d									15 52							16 02						
Catford	d									15 55							16 05						
Crofton Park	d									15 58							16 08						
Lewisham	a																			16 02			
	d												16 02										
Nunhead	d									16 01			16 08				16 11						
Peckham Rye	d									16 04			16 11				16 14						
Denmark Hill	d		15 50							16 07			16 14				16 17						
Beckenham Junction	d				15 40							15 55											
Kent House	d				15 42							15 57											
Penge East	d				15 44							15 59											
Sydenham Hill	d				15 48							16 03											
West Dulwich	d				15 50							16 05											
Herne Hill	d				15 53		15 57					16 08			16 12								
Loughborough Jn.	d						16 00								16 15								
Elephant & Castle	⊖ d						16 04			16 14					16 19		16 24						
London Blackfriars	⊖ d					16 07	16 09	16 12	16 17	16 19				16 22	16 24	16 27	16a29	16 34					
City Thameslink	a					16 08	16 11	16 13	16 18	16 21				16 23	16 26	16 28		16 36					
Farringdon	⊖ a					16 11	16 13	16 16	16 21	16 23				16 26	16 28	16 31		16 38					
St Pancras International	⊖ a					16 15	16 18	16 20	16 25	16 28				16 30	16 33	16 35		16 43					
Kentish Town	⊖ a									16 33								16 48					
Brixton	⊖ d				15 56							16 11											
London Victoria	⊖ a		16 01	15 53	16 03						16 09	16 18	16 25										16 25

A From Rainham Kt to Luton
B From Hastings to London Charing Cross
C To London Cannon Street
D To London Charing Cross
E From Tunbridge Wells to London Charing Cross
F From Dover Priory
G From Horsham to Peterborough
H From Sutton (Surrey) to St Albans City
I From Brighton to Bedford
J From Ashford International
K From Gravesend
L From Gatwick Airport to Bedford
M From Ramsgate
N To Luton
O From Canterbury West
P From Brighton to Cambridge

Table 195R

Mondays to Fridays

21 May to 7 December

Sevenoaks and Otford, Orpington, Bromley South, Beckenham Junction, Catford - London

Station		SE	TL ■ A		TL B	TL ■ C	TL ■ D	TL E	SE ◇■ F	SE	TL B	SE G	TL ■ D		TL	TL H	SE ◇■ I	SE J	SE K	SE ◇■ L	SE ◇ M	SE ◇■ N	SE		TL ■ A
Sevenoaks	d														15 52		15 59		16 05	16 13					
Bat & Ball	d														15 55										
Otford	d								15 56						15 59										
Shoreham (Kent)	d														16 02										
Eynsford	d														16 05										
Swanley	d								16 05						16 11						16 17				
St Mary Cray	d								16 09						16 15						16 22				
Orpington	d	15 54						16 03									16a07	16 11	16 20	16a23			16 24		
Petts Wood	d	15 57						16 06										16 14	16a23				16 27		
Bickley	d	16 01						16 10							16 20								16 31		
Bromley South	d	16 04						16 13	16 17	16 19					16 23						16 30	16 33	16 34		
Shortlands	d	16 07						16 15		16 22					16 25								16 37		
Ravensbourne	d							16 18							16 28										
Beckenham Hill	d							16 20							16 30										
Bellingham	d							16 22							16 32										
Catford	d							16 25							16 35										
Crofton Park	d							16 28							16 38										
Lewisham	a																	16 32							
	d											16 32													
Nunhead	d							16 31				16 37			16 41										
Peckham Rye	d							16 34				16 40			16 44										
Denmark Hill	d							16 37				16 44			16 47						16 50				
Beckenham Junction	d	16 10								16 25													16 40		
Kent House	d	16 12								16 27													16 42		
Penge East	d	16 14								16 29													16 44		
Sydenham Hill	d	16 18								16 33													16 48		
West Dulwich	d	16 20								16 35													16 50		
Herne Hill	d	16 23			16 27					16 38	16 42												16 53		
Loughborough Jn.	d				16 30						16 45														
Elephant & Castle	⊖ d				16 34			16 44			16 49				16 54										
London Blackfriars	⊖ d		16 37		16 39	16 42	16 47	16 49			16 54		16 57		16a59	17 03									17 07
City Thameslink	a		16 38		16 41	16 43	16 48	16 51			16 56		16 58			17 04									17 08
Farringdon	⊖ a		16 41		16 43	16 46	16 51	16 53			16 58		17 01			17 07									17 11
St Pancras International	⊖ a		16 45		16 48	16 50	16 55	16 58			17 03		17 05			17 11									17 15
Kentish Town	⊖ a							17 03																	
Brixton	⊖ d	16 26								16 41													16 56		
London Victoria	⊖ a	16 34							16 38	16 48		16 55									17 01	16 54	17 05		

Station		TL B	TL ■ C	TL ■ D	TL E	SE ◇■ O	SE	SE G	TL ■ P		TL B	TL ■ D	TL	TL ■ Q	SE ◇■ I	SE J	SE K	SE ◇■ L	SE ◇■ M		SE	SE ◇■ R	TL S	TL ■ A	TL B
Sevenoaks	d												16 22		16 29		16 35	16 43				16 49			
Bat & Ball	d												16 25												
Otford	d					16 26							16 29												
Shoreham (Kent)	d												16 32												
Eynsford	d												16 35												
Swanley	d					16 35							16 41												
St Mary Cray	d					16 39							16 45												
Orpington	d				16 33										16a37	16 41	16 50	16a51			16 54	16a57			
Petts Wood	d				16 36											16 44	16a53				16 57				
Bickley	d				16 40								16 50								17 01				
Bromley South	d				16 43	16 47	16 49						16 53						17 03		17 04				
Shortlands	d				16 45		16 52						16 55								17 07				
Ravensbourne	d				16 48								16 58												
Beckenham Hill	d				16 50								17 00												
Bellingham	d				16 52								17 02												
Catford	d				16 55								17 05												
Crofton Park	d				16 58								17 08												
Lewisham	a															17 03									
	d							17 02																	
Nunhead	d				17 01			17 07					17 11												
Peckham Rye	d				17 04			17 10					17 14												
Denmark Hill	d				17 07			17 14					17 17												
Beckenham Junction	d						16 55														17 10				
Kent House	d						16 57														17 12				
Penge East	d						16 59														17 14				
Sydenham Hill	d						17 03														17 18				
West Dulwich	d						17 05														17 20				
Herne Hill	d	16 57					17 08				17 12										17 23				17 27
Loughborough Jn.	d	17 00									17 15														17 30
Elephant & Castle	⊖ d	17 04			17 14						17 19		17 24												17 34
London Blackfriars	⊖ d	17 09	17 12	17 17	17 19				17 22		17 24	17 27	17a29	17 32									17 34	17 37	17 39
City Thameslink	a	17 11	17 13	17 18	17 21				17 23		17 26	17 28		17 33									17 36	17 38	17 41
Farringdon	⊖ a	17 13	17 16	17 21	17 23				17 26		17 28	17 31		17 36									17 38	17 41	17 43
St Pancras International	⊖ a	17 18	17 20	17 25	17 28				17 30		17 33	17 35		17 40									17 43	17 45	17 48
Kentish Town	⊖ a				17 33																		17 48		
Brixton	⊖ d						17 11														17 26				
London Victoria	⊖ a					17 08	17 18	17 25											17 24		17 34				

A From Horsham to Peterborough
B From Sutton (Surrey) to St Albans City
C From Brighton to Bedford
D From Gatwick Airport to Bedford
E To Luton
F From Ashford International
G From Gravesend
H From Rainham Kt to Bedford
I From Hastings to London Charing Cross
J To London Cannon Street
K To London Charing Cross
L From Tunbridge Wells to London Charing Cross
M From Dover Priory
N From Ramsgate
O From Canterbury West
P From Brighton to Cambridge
Q From Three Bridges to Bedford
R From Ramsgate to London Charing Cross
S From Rainham Kt to Luton

Table 195R

Mondays to Fridays

21 May to 7 December

Sevenoaks and Otford, Orpington, Bromley South, Beckenham Junction, Catford - London

Station		TL ■ A	SE	TL ■ B	TL C		SE ◇■ D	SE	TL E	SE F	TL ■ B	TL	TL ■ G	SE ◇■ H	SE I		SE J	SE ◇■ K	SE ■ L	SE ◇■ M	SE	TL N	TL ■ O	TL E	TL ■ A
Sevenoaks	d											16 52		16 59			17 05	17 11							
Bat & Ball	d											16 55													
Otford	d						16 56					16 59													
Shoreham (Kent)	d											17 02													
Eynsford	d											17 05													
Swanley	d						17 05					17 11							17 17						
St Mary Cray	d						17 09					17 15							17 22						
Orpington	d				17 03									17a07	17 11		17 18	17a22			17 24				
Petts Wood	d				17 06										17 14		17a21				17 27				
Bickley	d				17 10							17 20									17 31				
Bromley South	d				17 13		17 17	17 19				17 23							17 30	17 33	17 34				
Shortlands	d				17 15			17 22				17 25									17 37				
Ravensbourne	d				17 18							17 28													
Beckenham Hill	d				17 20							17 30													
Bellingham	d				17 22							17 32													
Catford	d				17 25							17 35													
Crofton Park	d				17 28							17 38													
Lewisham	a														17 33										
	d									17 32															
Nunhead	d				17 31					17 37		17 41													
Peckham Rye	d				17 34					17 40		17 44													
Denmark Hill	d				17 37					17 44		17 47							17 50						
Beckenham Junction	d		17 24					17 25													17 40				
Kent House	d							17 27													17 42				
Penge East	d							17 29													17 44				
Sydenham Hill	d							17 33													17 48				
West Dulwich	d							17 35													17 50				
Herne Hill	d		17 32					17 38	17 42												17 53			17 57	
Loughborough Jn.	d								17 45															18 00	
Elephant & Castle	⊖ d				17 44				17 49			17 54												18 04	
London Blackfriars	⊖ d	17 42	17a43	17 47	17 49				17 54		17 57	17a59	18 02									18 04	18 07	18 09	18 12
City Thameslink	a	17 43		17 48	17 51				17 56		17 58		18 03									18 06	18 08	18 11	18 13
Farringdon	⊖ a	17 46		17 51	17 53				17 58		18 01		18 06									18 08	18 11	18 13	18 16
St Pancras International	⊖ a	17 50		17 55	17 58				18 03		18 05		18 10									18 13	18 15	18 18	18 20
Kentish Town	⊖ a				18 03																	18 18			
Brixton	⊖ d							17 41													17 56				
London Victoria	⊖ a						17 38	17 48		17 55									18 00	17 53	18 03				

Station			SE	TL ■ B	TL C	SE ◇■ P	SE	SE F	SE I	TL ■ Q	TL E		TL ■ B	TL	TL N	SE ◇■ R	SE J	SE ■ L	SE ◇■ S	SE	SE ◇■ T		TL ■ O	TL E	TL ■ A
Sevenoaks	d													17 22		17 32	17 34				17 50				
Bat & Ball	d													17 25											
Otford	d					17 26								17 29											
Shoreham (Kent)	d													17 32											
Eynsford	d													17 35											
Swanley	d					17 35								17 41				17 47							
St Mary Cray	d					17 39								17 45				17 52							
Orpington	d				17 33				17 40							17a40	17 48			17 54	17a58				
Petts Wood	d				17 36				17 44								17a52			17 57					
Bickley	d				17 40									17 50						18 01					
Bromley South	d				17 43	17 47	17 49							17 53				18 00	18 03	18 04					
Shortlands	d				17 45		17 52							17 55						18 07					
Ravensbourne	d				17 48									17 58											
Beckenham Hill	d				17 50									18 00											
Bellingham	d				17 52									18 02											
Catford	d				17 55									18 05											
Crofton Park	d				17 58									18 08											
Lewisham	a								18 01																
	d							18 00																	
Nunhead	d				18 01			18 07						18 11											
Peckham Rye	d				18 04			18 10						18 14											
Denmark Hill	d				18 07			18 14						18 17				18 20							
Beckenham Junction	d		17 54				17 55													18 10					
Kent House	d						17 57													18 12					
Penge East	d						17 59													18 14					
Sydenham Hill	d						18 03													18 18					
West Dulwich	d						18 05													18 20					
Herne Hill	d		18 02				18 08				18 12									18 23				18 27	
Loughborough Jn.	d										18 15													18 30	
Elephant & Castle	⊖ d				18 14						18 19			18 24										18 34	
London Blackfriars	⊖ d		18a13	18 17	18 19					18 22	18 24		18 27	18a29	18 34								18 37	18 39	18 42
City Thameslink	a			18 18	18 21					18 23	18 26		18 28		18 36								18 38	18 41	18 43
Farringdon	⊖ a			18 21	18 23					18 26	18 28		18 31		18 38								18 41	18 43	18 46
St Pancras International	⊖ a			18 25	18 28					18 30	18 33		18 35		18 43								18 45	18 48	18 50
Kentish Town	⊖ a				18 33										18 48										
Brixton	⊖ d						18 11													18 26					
London Victoria	⊖ a					18 08	18 18	18 25										18 30	18 25	18 33					

A From Brighton to Bedford
B From Gatwick Airport to Bedford
C To Luton
D From Ashford International
E From Sutton (Surrey) to St Albans City
F From Gravesend
G From Three Bridges to Bedford
H From Hastings to London Cannon Street
I To London Cannon Street
J To London Charing Cross
K From Tunbridge Wells to London Charing Cross
L From Gillingham (Kent)
M From Ramsgate
N From Rainham Kt to Luton
O From Horsham to Peterborough
P From Canterbury West
Q From Brighton to Cambridge
R From Hastings to London Charing Cross
S From Dover Priory
T From Ramsgate to London Charing Cross

Sevenoaks and Otford, Orpington, Bromley South, Beckenham Junction, Catford - London

		SE	TL ■ A	TL B	SE ◇■ C	SE	TL D		SE E	TL ■ F	TL	TL G	SE ◇■ H	SE I	SE J	SE ◇■ K	SE ■ L		SE ◇■ M	SE	TL ■ N	TL D	TL ■ O	TL ■ A	TL P
Sevenoaks ■	d										17 52		17 59		18 02	18 13									
Bat & Ball	d										17 55														
Otford ■	d				17 56						17 59														
Shoreham (Kent)	d										18 02														
Eynsford	d										18 05														
Swanley ■	d				18 05						18 11						18 17								
St Mary Cray	d				18 09						18 15						18 22								
Orpington ■	d			18 02									18a07	18 09	18 20	18a21				18 23					18 33
Petts Wood ■	d			18 05										18 14	18a23					18 27					18 36
Bickley ■	d			18 10							18 20									18 31					18 40
Bromley South ■	d			18 13	18 17	18 19					18 23						18 30		18 33	18 34					18 43
Shortlands ■	d			18 15		18 22					18 25									18 37					18 45
Ravensbourne	d			18 18							18 28														18 48
Beckenham Hill	d			18 20							18 30														18 50
Bellingham	d			18 22							18 32														18 52
Catford	d			18 25							18 35														18 55
Crofton Park	d			18 28							18 38														18 58
Lewisham ■	a													18 32											
	d								18 32																
Nunhead ■	d			18 31					18 37		18 41														19 01
Peckham Rye ■	d			18 34					18 40		18 44														19 04
Denmark Hill ■	d			18 37					18 43		18 47						18 50								19 07
Beckenham Junction ■	d	18 24				18 25														18 40					
Kent House ■	d					18 27														18 42					
Penge East	d					18 29														18 44					
Sydenham Hill	d					18 33														18 48					
West Dulwich	d					18 35														18 50					
Herne Hill ■	d	18 32				18 38	18 42													18 53		18 57			
Loughborough Jn.	d						18 45															19 00			
Elephant & Castle ⊖	d			18 44			18 49				18 54											19 04			19 14
London Blackfriars ■ ⊖	d	18a43	18 47	18 49			18 54			18 57	18a59	19 04									19 07	19 09	19 12	19 17	19 19
City Thameslink ■	a		18 48	18 51			18 56			18 58		19 06									19 08	19 11	19 13	19 18	19 21
Farringdon ⊖	a		18 51	18 53			18 58			19 01		19 08									19 11	19 13	19 16	19 21	19 23
St Pancras International ■ ⊖	a		18 55	18 58			19 03			19 05		19 13									19 15	19 18	19 20	19 25	19 28
Kentish Town ⊖	a			19 03								19 18													
Brixton ⊖	d					18 41														18 56					
London Victoria ■ ⊖	a				18 38	18 48			18 57								19 00		18 55	19 03					

		SE ◇■ Q	SE		SE	SE E	TL ■ R	TL D	TL ■ F	TL	TL G	SE ◇■ H	SE I		SE J	SE ◇■ S	SE ◇■ T	SE U	SE	TL ■ N	TL D	TL ■ O	TL ■ A		TL P
Sevenoaks ■	d									18 22		18 31			18 35	18 43									
Bat & Ball	d									18 25															
Otford ■	d	18 26								18 29															
Shoreham (Kent)	d									18 32															
Eynsford	d									18 35															
Swanley ■	d	18 35								18 41															
St Mary Cray	d	18 39								18 45															
Orpington ■	d											18a39	18 41		18 50	18a51			18 54						19 03
Petts Wood ■	d												18 44		18a53				18 57						19 06
Bickley ■	d									18 50									19 01						19 10
Bromley South ■	d	18 47	18 49							18 53							19 03		19 04						19 13
Shortlands ■	d		18 52							18 55									19 07						19 15
Ravensbourne	d									18 58															19 18
Beckenham Hill	d									19 00															19 20
Bellingham	d									19 02															19 22
Catford	d									19 05															19 25
Crofton Park	d									19 08															19 28
Lewisham ■	a												19 01												
	d					19 00												19 14							
Nunhead ■	d					19 07				19 11															19 31
Peckham Rye ■	d					19 09				19 14															19 34
Denmark Hill ■	d					19 14				19 17															19 37
Beckenham Junction ■	d		18 55		19 01														19 10						
Kent House ■	d		18 57																19 12						
Penge East	d		18 59																19 14						
Sydenham Hill	d		19 03																19 18						
West Dulwich	d		19 05																19 20						
Herne Hill ■	d		19 08					19 12											19 23		19 27				
Loughborough Jn.	d							19 15													19 30				
Elephant & Castle ⊖	d							19 19		19 24											19 34				19 44
London Blackfriars ■ ⊖	d						19 22	19 24	19 27	19a29	19 34									19 37	19 39	19 42	19 47		19 49
City Thameslink ■	a						19 23	19 26	19 28		19 36									19 38	19 41	19 43	19 48		19 51
Farringdon ⊖	a						19 26	19 28	19 31		19 38									19 41	19 43	19 46	19 51		19 53
St Pancras International ■ ⊖	a						19 30	19 33	19 35		19 43									19 45	19 48	19 50	19 55		19 58
Kentish Town ⊖	a							19 38													19 53				
Brixton ⊖	d		19 11																19 26						
London Victoria ■ ⊖	a	19 08	19 18		19 24	19 28											19 24	19 33	19 34						

A From East Grinstead to Bedford
B To Luton
C From Ashford International
D From Sutton (Surrey) to St Albans City
E From Dartford
F From Gatwick Airport to Bedford
G From Rainham Kt to Luton
H From Hastings to London Charing Cross
I To London Cannon Street
J To London Charing Cross
K From Tunbridge Wells to London Cannon Street
L From Gillingham (Kent)
M From Ramsgate
N From Horsham to Peterborough
O From Brighton to Bedford
P To West Hampstead Thameslink
Q From Canterbury West
R From Brighton to Cambridge
S From Tunbridge Wells to London Charing Cross
T From Dover Priory
U From Barnehurst

Sevenoaks and Otford, Orpington, Bromley South, Beckenham Junction, Catford - London

		SE ◇■ A	SE	TL B	SE	SE C	TL ■ D	TL	TL E		SE ◇■ F	SE G	SE H	SE ◇■ I	SE J	SE ◇■ K	SE	TL ■ L	TL B		TL ■ M	TL	SE ◇■ N	SE	SE O
Sevenoaks ■	d							18 52			19 00		19 05	19 14											
Bat & Ball	d							18 55																	
Otford ■	d	18 56						18 59															19 26		
Shoreham (Kent)	d							19 02																	
Eynsford	d							19 05																	
Swanley ■	d	19 05						19 11							19 18								19 35		
St Mary Cray	d	19 09						19 15							19 23								19 39		
Orpington ■	d										19a08	19 11	19 20	19a22			19 24					19 33			
Petts Wood ■	d											19 14	19a23				19 27					19 36			
Bickley ■	d							19 20									19 31					19 40			
Bromley South ■	d	19 17	19 19					19 23							19 30	19 33	19 34					19 43	19 47	19 49	
Shortlands ■	d		19 22					19 25									19 37					19 45		19 52	
Ravensbourne	d							19 28														19 48			
Beckenham Hill	d							19 30														19 50			
Bellingham	d							19 32														19 52			
Catford	d							19 35														19 55			
Crofton Park	d							19 38														19 58			
Lewisham ■	a											19 32													
	d					19 32																			20 02
Nunhead ■	d					19 37		19 41														20 01			20 07
Peckham Rye ■	d					19 40		19 44														20 04			20 10
Denmark Hill ■	d					19 44		19 47							19 50							20 07			20 14
Beckenham Junction ■	d		19 25		19 31												19 40							19 55	
Kent House ■	d		19 27														19 42							19 57	
Penge East	d		19 29														19 44							19 59	
Sydenham Hill	d		19 33														19 48							20 03	
West Dulwich	d		19 35														19 50							20 05	
Herne Hill ■	d		19 38	19 42													19 53		19 57					20 08	
Loughborough Jn.	d			19 45															20 00						
Elephant & Castle ⊖	d			19 49				19 54											20 04			20 14			
London Blackfriars ■ ⊖	d			19 54			19 57	19a59	20 04									20 07	20 09		20 12	20 19			
City Thameslink ■	a			19 56			19 58		20 06									20 08	20 11		20 13	20 21			
Farringdon ⊖	a			19 58			20 01		20 08									20 11	20 13		20 16	20 23			
St Pancras International ■ ⊖	a			20 03			20 05		20 13									20 15	20 18		20 20	20 28			
Kentish Town ⊖	a			20 08															20 23			20 33			
Brixton ⊖	d		19 41														19 56							20 11	
London Victoria ■ ⊖	a	19 38	19 48		19 54	19 55									20 00	19 54	20 03						20 08	20 18	20 25

		TL ■ P	TL B	TL ■ D	TL		TL E	SE ◇■ F	SE G	SE H	SE ◇■ I	SE ◇■ Q	SE	TL ■ L	TL B		TL ■ M	TL	SE ◇■ A	SE	TL B	SE C	TL ■ D	TL	TL E
Sevenoaks ■	d				19 22			19 29		19 35	19 43													19 52	
Bat & Ball	d				19 25																			19 55	
Otford ■	d				19 29														19 56					19 59	
Shoreham (Kent)	d				19 32																			20 02	
Eynsford	d				19 35																			20 05	
Swanley ■	d				19 41														20 05					20 11	
St Mary Cray	d				19 45														20 09					20 15	
Orpington ■	d							19a37	19 41	19 50	19a51		19 54					20 03							
Petts Wood ■	d								19 44	19a53			19 57					20 06							
Bickley ■	d				19 50								20 01					20 10						20 20	
Bromley South ■	d				19 53							20 03	20 04					20 13	20 17	20 19				20 23	
Shortlands ■	d				19 55								20 07					20 15		20 22				20 25	
Ravensbourne	d				19 58													20 18						20 28	
Beckenham Hill	d				20 00													20 20						20 30	
Bellingham	d				20 02													20 22						20 32	
Catford	d				20 05													20 25						20 35	
Crofton Park	d				20 08													20 28						20 38	
Lewisham ■	a								20 02																
	d																					20 32			
Nunhead ■	d				20 11													20 31				20 37		20 41	
Peckham Rye ■	d				20 14													20 34				20 40		20 44	
Denmark Hill ■	d				20 17													20 37				20 44		20 47	
Beckenham Junction ■	d												20 10							20 25					
Kent House ■	d												20 12							20 27					
Penge East	d												20 14							20 29					
Sydenham Hill	d												20 18							20 33					
West Dulwich	d												20 20							20 35					
Herne Hill ■	d		20 12										20 23		20 27					20 38	20 42				
Loughborough Jn.	d		20 15												20 30						20 45				
Elephant & Castle ⊖	d		20 19		20 24										20 34			20 44			20 49			20 54	
London Blackfriars ■ ⊖	d	20 22	20 24	20 27	20a29		20 34							20 37	20 39		20 42	20 49			20 54		20 57	20a59	21 04
City Thameslink ■	a	20 23	20 26	20 28			20 36							20 38	20 41		20 43	20 51			20 56		20 58		21 06
Farringdon ⊖	a	20 26	20 28	20 31			20 38							20 41	20 43		20 46	20 53			20 58		21 01		21 08
St Pancras International ■ ⊖	a	20 30	20 33	20 35			20 43							20 45	20 48		20 50	20 58			21 03		21 05		21 13
Kentish Town ⊖	a		20 38												20 53			21 03			21 08				21 18
Brixton ⊖	d												20 26							20 41					
London Victoria ■ ⊖	a											20 23	20 33						20 38	20 48		20 55			

A From Ashford International
B From Sutton (Surrey) to St Albans City
C From Dartford
D From Gatwick Airport to Bedford
E From Rainham Kt to Luton
F From Hastings to London Charing Cross
G To London Cannon Street
H To London Charing Cross
I From Tunbridge Wells to London Charing Cross
J From Rochester
K From Ramsgate
L From Horsham to Peterborough
M From Brighton to Bedford
N From Canterbury West
O From Gravesend
P From Brighton to Cambridge
Q From Dover Priory

Sevenoaks and Otford, Orpington, Bromley South, Beckenham Junction, Catford - London

Station			SE ◇1 A	SE B	SE C	SE ◇1 D	SE 1 E	SE ◇1 F	SE	TL 1 G	TL 1 H		TL I	TL	SE ◇1 J	SE	SE B	SE K	TL 1 L	TL I	TL 1 M		TL	TL N	SE C
Sevenoaks	d		19 59		20 05	20 13																	20 22		20 35
Bat & Ball	d																						20 25		
Otford	d														20 26								20 29		
Shoreham (Kent)	d																						20 32		
Eynsford	d																						20 35		
Swanley	d						20 18								20 37								20 41		
St Mary Cray	d						20 23																20 45		
Orpington	d		20a07	20 11	20 20	20a21			20 24					20 33			20 41								20 50
Petts Wood	d			20 14	20a23				20 27					20 36			20 44								20a53
Bickley	d								20 31					20 40									20 50		
Bromley South	d						20 30	20 33	20 34					20 43	20 47	20 49							20 53		
Shortlands	d								20 37					20 45		20 52							20 55		
Ravensbourne	d													20 48									20 58		
Beckenham Hill	d													20 50									21 00		
Bellingham	d													20 52									21 02		
Catford	d													20 55									21 05		
Crofton Park	d													20 58									21 08		
Lewisham	a			20 32													21 02								
	d																	21 02							
Nunhead	d													21 01				21 07					21 11		
Peckham Rye	d													21 04				21 10					21 14		
Denmark Hill	d						20 50							21 07				21 14					21 17		
Beckenham Junction	d								20 40							20 55									
Kent House	d								20 42							20 57									
Penge East	d								20 44							20 59									
Sydenham Hill	d								20 48							21 03									
West Dulwich	d								20 50							21 05									
Herne Hill	d								20 53				21 04			21 08				21 12					
Loughborough Jn.	d												21 07							21 15					
Elephant & Castle ⊖	d												21 11	21 14						21 19			21 24		
London Blackfriars ⊖	d									21 07	21 12		21 17	21 19					21 22	21 24	21 27		21a29	21 34	
City Thameslink	a									21 08	21 13		21 18	21 21					21 23	21 26	21 28			21 36	
Farringdon ⊖	a									21 11	21 16		21 21	21 23					21 26	21 28	21 31			21 38	
St Pancras International ⊖	a									21 15	21 20		21 25	21 28					21 30	21 33	21 35			21 43	
Kentish Town ⊖	a													21 33						21 38					
Brixton ⊖	d								20 56							21 11									
London Victoria ⊖	a						21 00	20 53	21 03						21 08	21 19		21 25							

Station		SE ◇1 D	SE ◇1 O	SE	TL 1 G	TL I	TL 1 H		TL	SE ◇1 J	SE	TL I	SE K	TL 1 M	TL	TL P	SE ◇1 A		SE B	SE C	SE ◇1 D	SE 1 Q	SE ◇1 F	SE	TL 1 G
Sevenoaks	d	20 43													20 52		20 59			21 05	21 13				
Bat & Ball	d														20 55										
Otford	d									20 56					20 59										
Shoreham (Kent)	d														21 02										
Eynsford	d														21 05										
Swanley	d									21 05					21 11							21 17			
St Mary Cray	d									21 09					21 15							21 22			
Orpington	d	20a51		20 54					21 03								21a07		21 11	21 20	21a21			21 24	
Petts Wood	d			20 57					21 06										21 14	21a23				21 27	
Bickley	d			21 01					21 10						21 20									21 31	
Bromley South	d		21 03	21 04					21 13	21 17	21 19				21 23							21 30	21 33	21 34	
Shortlands	d			21 07					21 15		21 22				21 25									21 37	
Ravensbourne	d								21 18						21 28										
Beckenham Hill	d								21 20						21 30										
Bellingham	d								21 22						21 32										
Catford	d								21 25						21 35										
Crofton Park	d								21 28						21 38										
Lewisham	a																		21 32						
	d												21 32												
Nunhead	d								21 31				21 37		21 41										
Peckham Rye	d								21 34				21 40		21 44										
Denmark Hill	d								21 37				21 44		21 47							21 50			
Beckenham Junction	d			21 10							21 25													21 40	
Kent House	d			21 12							21 27													21 42	
Penge East	d			21 14							21 29													21 44	
Sydenham Hill	d			21 18							21 33													21 48	
West Dulwich	d			21 20							21 35													21 50	
Herne Hill	d			21 23		21 27					21 38	21 42												21 53	
Loughborough Jn.	d					21 30						21 45													
Elephant & Castle ⊖	d					21 34			21 44			21 49			21 54										
London Blackfriars ⊖	d				21 37	21 39	21 42		21 49			21 54		21 57	21a59	22 04									22 07
City Thameslink	a				21 38	21 41	21 43		21 51			21 56		21 58		22 06									22 08
Farringdon ⊖	a				21 41	21 43	21 46		21 53			21 58		22 01		22 08									22 11
St Pancras International ⊖	a				21 45	21 48	21 50		21 58			22 03		22 05		22 13									22 15
Kentish Town ⊖	a					21 53			22 03			22 08													
Brixton ⊖	d			21 26							21 41													21 56	
London Victoria ⊖	a		21 25	21 34						21 38	21 48		21 55									22 00	21 53	22 03	

A From Hastings to London Charing Cross
B To London Cannon Street
C To London Charing Cross
D From Tunbridge Wells to London Charing Cross
E From Rochester
F From Ramsgate
G From Horsham to Peterborough
H From Brighton to Bedford
I From Sutton (Surrey) to St Albans City
J From Ashford International
K From Gravesend
L From Brighton to Cambridge
M From Gatwick Airport to Bedford
N From Rainham Kt to Bedford
O From Dover Priory
P From Rainham Kt to Luton
Q From Gillingham (Kent)

Sevenoaks and Otford, Orpington, Bromley South, Beckenham Junction, Catford - London

Station		TL A	TL 1 B		TL	SE ◇1 C	SE	SE D	SE E	TL 1 F	TL G	TL 1 H	TL		TL I	SE J	SE ◇1 K	SE ◇1 L	SE	TL 1 M	TL G	TL 1 B	TL N		SE ◇1 C
Sevenoaks	d												21 22			21 35	21 43								
Bat & Ball	d												21 25												
Otford	d					21 26							21 29												21 56
Shoreham (Kent)	d												21 32												
Eynsford	d												21 35												
Swanley	d					21 37							21 41												22 05
St Mary Cray	d												21 45												22 09
Orpington	d				21 33			21 41								21 50	21a51		21 54				22 03		
Petts Wood	d				21 36			21 44								21a53			21 57				22 06		
Bickley	d				21 40								21 50						22 01				22 10		
Bromley South	d				21 43	21 47	21 49						21 53					22 03	22 04				22 13		22 17
Shortlands	d				21 45		21 52						21 55						22 07				22 15		
Ravensbourne	d				21 48								21 58										22 18		
Beckenham Hill	d				21 50								22 00										22 20		
Bellingham	d				21 52								22 02										22 22		
Catford	d				21 55								22 05										22 25		
Crofton Park	d				21 58								22 08										22 28		
Lewisham	a							22 02																	
	d								22 02																
Nunhead	d				22 01				22 07				22 11										22 31		
Peckham Rye	d				22 04				22 10				22 14										22 34		
Denmark Hill	d				22 07				22 14				22 17										22 37		
Beckenham Junction	d						21 55												22 10						
Kent House	d						21 57												22 12						
Penge East	d						21 59												22 14						
Sydenham Hill	d						22 03												22 18						
West Dulwich	d						22 05												22 20						
Herne Hill	d	21 57					22 08				22 12								22 23		22 27				
Loughborough Jn.	d	22 00									22 15										22 30				
Elephant & Castle ⊖	d	22 04			22 14						22 19		22 24								22 34		22 44		
London Blackfriars ⊖	d	22 09	22 12		22 19					22 22	22 24	22 27	22a29		22 34					22 37	22 39	22 42	22 49		
City Thameslink	a	22 11	22 13		22 21					22 23	22 26	22 28			22 36					22 38	22 41	22 43	22 51		
Farringdon ⊖	a	22 13	22 16		22 23					22 26	22 28	22 31			22 38					22 41	22 43	22 46	22 53		
St Pancras International ⊖	a	22 18	22 20		22 28					22 30	22 33	22 35			22 43					22 45	22 48	22 50	22 58		
Kentish Town ⊖	a	22 23			22 33						22 38										22 53				
Brixton ⊖	d						22 11												22 26						
London Victoria ⊖	a					22 08	22 18		22 25									22 23	22 33						22 39

Station		SE	TL G	SE E	TL	TL I	SE ◇1 O	SE D	SE J		SE ◇1 K	SE ◇1 P	SE ◇1 Q	SE	TL 1 M	TL 1 B	TL G	TL	TL 1 F		SE ◇1 C	SE D	SE E	TL G	TL
Sevenoaks	d				21 52		21 59		22 05		22 13														22 22
Bat & Ball	d				21 55																				22 25
Otford	d				21 59																22 27				22 29
Shoreham (Kent)	d				22 02																				22 32
Eynsford	d				22 05																				22 35
Swanley	d				22 11							22 17									22 37				22 41
St Mary Cray	d				22 15							22 22													22 45
Orpington	d						22a07	22 11	22 20		22a21			22 24				22 33				22 41			
Petts Wood	d							22 14	22a23					22 27				22 36				22 44			
Bickley	d				22 20									22 31				22 40							22 50
Bromley South	d	22 19			22 23							22 30	22 33	22 34				22 43			22 47				22 53
Shortlands	d	22 22			22 25									22 37				22 45							22 55
Ravensbourne	d				22 28													22 48							22 58
Beckenham Hill	d				22 30													22 50							23 00
Bellingham	d				22 32													22 52							23 02
Catford	d				22 35													22 55							23 05
Crofton Park	d				22 38													22 58							23 08
Lewisham	a							22 32														23 02			
	d			22 32																			23 02		
Nunhead	d			22 37	22 41													23 01					23 07		23 11
Peckham Rye	d			22 40	22 44													23 04					23 10		23 14
Denmark Hill	d			22 44	22 47							22 50						23 07					23 14		23 17
Beckenham Junction	d	22 25												22 40											
Kent House	d	22 27												22 42											
Penge East	d	22 29												22 44											
Sydenham Hill	d	22 33												22 48											
West Dulwich	d	22 35												22 50											
Herne Hill	d	22 38	22 44											22 53			23 04							23 14	
Loughborough Jn.	d		22 47														23 07							23 17	
Elephant & Castle ⊖	d		22 51		22 54												23 11	23 14						23 21	23 24
London Blackfriars ⊖	d		22 59		22a59	23 04									23 07	23 12	23 17	23a19	23 22					23 27	23a29
City Thameslink	a																								
Farringdon ⊖	a		23 03			23 08									23 11	23 16	23 21		23 26					23 31	
St Pancras International ⊖	a		23 08			23 13									23 15	23 20	23 25		23 30					23 35	
Kentish Town ⊖	a		23 13														23 30							23 40	
Brixton ⊖	d	22 41												22 56											
London Victoria ⊖	a	22 49		22 55								23 00	22 53	23 03							23 08		23 25		

A From Sutton (Surrey) to St Albans City
B From Brighton to Bedford
C From Ashford International
D To London Cannon Street
E From Gravesend
F From Brighton to Cambridge
G From Sutton (Surrey) to Bedford
H From Gatwick Airport to Bedford
I From Rainham Kt to West Hampstead Thameslink
J To London Charing Cross
K From Tunbridge Wells to London Charing Cross
L From Dover Priory
M From Horsham to Peterborough
N To West Hampstead Thameslink
O From Hastings to London Charing Cross
P From Gillingham (Kent)
Q From Ramsgate

Table 195R

Mondays to Fridays

21 May to 7 December

Sevenoaks and Otford, Orpington, Bromley South, Beckenham Junction, Catford - London

		TL	SE	SE	SE	SE	TL	TL	TL	TL	SE	SE	SE	TL	SE	SE MT FO	SE MTO	SE WTh FO	TL	SE	TL	TL	TL
				◇1	◇1		1	1			1				◇1								
		A	B	C	D		E	F	G		H		I		J	K	K	B	G		G		L
Sevenoaks	d		22 35	22 43										22 52	22 59		23 05	23 05				23 22	23 22
Bat & Ball	d													22 55								23 25	23 25
Otford	d										22 56			22 59								23 29	23 29
Shoreham (Kent)	d													23 02								23 32	23 32
Eynsford	d													23 05								23 35	23 36
Swanley	d				22 47						23 05			23 11								23 41	23 41
St Mary Cray	d				22 52						23 09			23 15								23 45	23 45
Orpington	d		22 50	22a51		22 54				23 03					23a07	23 11	23 20	23 20		23 24			
Petts Wood	d		22a53			22 57				23 06						23 14	23 23	23a23		23 27			
Bickley	d					23 01				23 10				23 20						23 31		23 50	23 50
Bromley South	d				23 00	23 04				23 13	23 17	23 19		23 23						23 34		23 53	23 53
Shortlands	d					23 07				23 15		23 22		23 25						23 37		23 55	23 55
Ravensbourne	d									23 18				23 28								23 58	23 58
Beckenham Hill	d									23 20				23 30								00 01	00 01
Bellingham	d									23 22				23 32								00 03	00 03
Catford	d									23 25				23 35								00 06	00 06
Crofton Park	d									23 28				23 38								00 08	00 08
Lewisham	a															23 32	23 40						
	d												23 32										
Nunhead	d									23 31			23 37	23 41								00 11	00 11
Peckham Rye	d									23 34			23 40	23 44								00 14	00 14
Denmark Hill	d				23 20					23 37			23 44	23 47								00 17	00 17
Beckenham Junction	d					23 10						23 25								23 40			
Kent House	d					23 12						23 27								23 42			
Penge East	d					23 14						23 29								23 44			
Sydenham Hill	d					23 18						23 33								23 48			
West Dulwich	d					23 20						23 35								23 50			
Herne Hill	d					23 23			23 34			23 38							23 44	23 53	23 57		
Loughborough Jn.	d								23 37										23 47				
Elephant & Castle ⊖	d								23 41	23 44				23 54					23 54		00 04	00 24	00 24
London Blackfriars ⊖	d	23 34					23 37	23 42	23 49	23a49				23a59					00 02		00 09	00a33	00 29
City Thameslink	a																						00 31
Farringdon ⊖	a	23 38					23 41	23 46	23 53										00 06		00 13		00 33
St Pancras International ⊖	a	23 43					23 45	23 50	23 57										00 10		00 17		00 38
Kentish Town ⊖	a								00 01												00 22		
Brixton ⊖	d					23 26						23 41								23 56			
London Victoria ⊖	a				23 31	23 34					23 38	23 48	23 55							00 03			

		SE	SE WTh FO	SE MTO	SE	SE	SE
		◇1			◇1	◇1	
		M	B	K	H	D	
Sevenoaks	d	23 27	23 35	23 35			
Bat & Ball	d						
Otford	d				23 36		
Shoreham (Kent)	d						
Eynsford	d						
Swanley	d				23 45	23 53	
St Mary Cray	d				23 50	23 57	
Orpington	d	23a35	23 50	23 50			23 54
Petts Wood	d		23 53	23 53			23 57
Bickley	d						00 01
Bromley South	d				23 57	00 04	00 04
Shortlands	d						00 07
Ravensbourne	d						
Beckenham Hill	d						
Bellingham	d						
Catford	d						
Crofton Park	d						
Lewisham	a		00 10	00 12			
	d						
Nunhead	d						
Peckham Rye	d						
Denmark Hill	d						
Beckenham Junction	d						00 10
Kent House	d						00 12
Penge East	d						00 14
Sydenham Hill	d						00 18
West Dulwich	d						00 20
Herne Hill	d						00 23
Loughborough Jn.	d						
Elephant & Castle ⊖	d						
London Blackfriars ⊖	d						
City Thameslink	a						
Farringdon ⊖	a						
St Pancras International ⊖	a						
Kentish Town ⊖	a						
Brixton ⊖	d						00 26
London Victoria ⊖	a				00 18	00 24	00 34

A From Rainham Kt to West Hampstead Thameslink
B To London Charing Cross
C From Tunbridge Wells to London Charing Cross
D From Dover Priory
E From Horsham to Peterborough
F From Brighton to Bedford
G From Sutton (Surrey) to Bedford
H From Ashford International
I From Gravesend
J From Hastings to London Charing Cross
K To London Cannon Street
L To Finsbury Park
M From Tunbridge Wells to London Cannon Street

Table 195R

Saturdays

26 May to 8 December

Sevenoaks and Otford, Orpington, Bromley South, Beckenham Junction, Catford - London

		TL	SE	SE	TL	SE	TL	TL	TL	TL	TL	TL	TL	TL	TL	TL	TL	TL	SE	TL	SE	TL	TL
			◇1				1			1	1	1	1	1	1	1	1	1		1			1
		A	B	C	A		D	E	F	G	D	D	D	H	H	H	H	H		H		I	D
Sevenoaks	d																						
Bat & Ball	d																						
Otford	d																						
Shoreham (Kent)	d																						
Eynsford	d																						
Swanley	d																		04 37				
St Mary Cray	d																		04 41				
Orpington	d																				05 24		
Petts Wood	d																				05 27		
Bickley	d			00 01															04 45		05 31		
Bromley South	d		00 04	00 04		00 19													04 49		05 34		
Shortlands	d			00 07															04 52		05 37		
Ravensbourne	d																						
Beckenham Hill	d							00 01	00 01														
Bellingham	d							00 03	00 03														
Catford	d							00 06	00 06														
Crofton Park	d							00 08	00 08														
Lewisham	a																						
	d																						
Nunhead	d							00 11	00 11														
Peckham Rye	d							00 14	00 14														
Denmark Hill	d							00 17	00 17														
Beckenham Junction	d			00 10															04 55		05 40		
Kent House	d			00 12															04 57		05 42		
Penge East	d			00 14															04 59		05 44		
Sydenham Hill	d			00 18															05 03		05 48		
West Dulwich	d			00 20															05 05		05 50		
Herne Hill	d			00 23															05 08		05 53		
Loughborough Jn.	d																						
Elephant & Castle ⊖	d				00 04			00 24	00 24														
London Blackfriars ⊖	d	00 02			00 09		00 22	00 29	00a33	00 37	00 50	01 08	01 36	02 36	03 06	03 36	04 06	04 36		05 06		05 27	05 32
City Thameslink	a							00 31															
Farringdon ⊖	a	00 06			00 13		00 25	00 33		00 41										05 10		05 31	05 36
St Pancras International ⊖	a	00 10			00 17		00 29	00 38		00 45	00 59	01 15	01 43	02 43	03 13	03 43	04 13	04 43		05 15		05 35	05 40
Kentish Town ⊖	a				00 22						01 05		01 48	02 48		03 48	04 18	04 48				05 40	
Brixton ⊖	d			00 26															05 11		05 56		
London Victoria ⊖	a		00 24	00 34		00 39													05 18		06 03		

		SE	TL	TL	TL	TL	TL	TL	TL	SE	SE	SE	SE	TL	TL	SE	TL	TL	TL	TL	TL	SE	SE
			1		1		1					◇1		1			1		1				◇1
		J	H	K	L	M	H		K	N		O	J	G	M		D	M	P		Q	N	R
Sevenoaks	d							05 22		05 35										05 52		06 05	06 13
Bat & Ball	d							05 25												05 55			
Otford	d							05 29												05 59			
Shoreham (Kent)	d							05 32												06 02			
Eynsford	d							05 36												06 05			
Swanley	d							05 41				06 02								06 11			
St Mary Cray	d							05 45				06 06								06 15			
Orpington	d	05 41								05 50	05 54		06 11									06 20	06a21
Petts Wood	d	05 44								05a53	05 57		06 14									06a23	
Bickley	d							05 50			06 01									06 20			
Bromley South	d							05 53			06 04	06 14				06 19				06 23			
Shortlands	d							05 55			06 07					06 22				06 25			
Ravensbourne	d							05 58												06 28			
Beckenham Hill	d							06 00												06 30			
Bellingham	d							06 02												06 32			
Catford	d							06 05												06 35			
Crofton Park	d							06 08												06 38			
Lewisham	a	06 02											06 32										
	d																						
Nunhead	d							06 11												06 41			
Peckham Rye	d							06 14												06 44			
Denmark Hill	d							06 17				06 27								06 47			
Beckenham Junction	d										06 10					06 25							
Kent House	d										06 12					06 27							
Penge East	d										06 14					06 29							
Sydenham Hill	d										06 18					06 33							
West Dulwich	d										06 20					06 35							
Herne Hill	d					06 12					06 23				06 27	06 38		06 42					
Loughborough Jn.	d					06 15									06 30			06 45					
Elephant & Castle ⊖	d					06 19		06 24							06 34			06 49		06 54			
London Blackfriars ⊖	d		06 02	06 04	06 22	06 24	06 27	06a29	06 34					06 37	06 39		06 42	06 54	06 57	06a59	07 04		
City Thameslink	a																						
Farringdon ⊖	a		06 06	06 08	06 26	06 28	06 31		06 38					06 41	06 43		06 46	06 58	07 01		07 08		
St Pancras International ⊖	a		06 10	06 13	06 30	06 33	06 35		06 43					06 45	06 48		06 50	07 03	07 05		07 13		
Kentish Town ⊖	a			06 18		06 38									06 53			07 08					
Brixton ⊖	d										06 26					06 41							
London Victoria ⊖	a										06 33	06 38				06 48							

A From Sutton (Surrey) to Bedford
B From Dover Priory
C From Orpington
D From Brighton to Bedford
E From Sevenoaks to Finsbury Park
F From Sevenoaks
G From Horsham to Peterborough
H From Three Bridges to Bedford
I To St Albans City
J To London Cannon Street
K From Gillingham (Kent) to Luton
L From Brighton to Cambridge
M From Sutton (Surrey) to St Albans City
N To London Charing Cross
O From Ramsgate
P From Gatwick Airport to Bedford
Q From Rainham Kt to Luton
R From Tunbridge Wells to London Charing Cross

Table 195R

Saturdays
26 May to 8 December

Sevenoaks and Otford, Orpington, Bromley South, Beckenham Junction, Catford - London

		SE		TL ■ A	TL B	TL ■ C	TL	SE ◇■ D	SE	SE E	SE F	TL ■ G		TL B	TL ■ H	TL	TL I	SE J	SE	TL ■ A	TL B	TL ■ C		TL	SE ◇■ D
Sevenoaks	d															06 22		06 35							
Bat & Ball	d															06 25									
Otford	d							06 26								06 29									06 56
Shoreham (Kent)	d															06 32									
Eynsford	d															06 35									
Swanley	d							06 35								06 41									07 05
St Mary Cray	d							06 39								06 45									07 09
Orpington	d	06 24					06 33			06 41								06 50	06 54					07 03	
Petts Wood	d	06 27					06 36			06 44								06a53	06 57					07 06	
Bickley	d	06 31					06 40									06 50			07 01					07 10	
Bromley South	d	06 34					06 43	06 47	06 49							06 53			07 04					07 13	07 17
Shortlands	d	06 37					06 45		06 52							06 55			07 07					07 15	
Ravensbourne	d						06 48									06 58								07 18	
Beckenham Hill	d						06 50									07 00								07 20	
Bellingham	d						06 52									07 02								07 22	
Catford	d						06 55									07 05								07 25	
Crofton Park	d						06 58									07 08								07 28	
Lewisham	a									07 02															
	d										07 02														
Nunhead	d						07 01				07 07					07 11								07 31	
Peckham Rye	d						07 04				07 10					07 14								07 34	
Denmark Hill	d						07 07				07 14					07 17								07 37	
Beckenham Junction	d	06 40							06 55										07 10						
Kent House	d	06 42							06 57										07 12						
Penge East	d	06 44							06 59										07 14						
Sydenham Hill	d	06 48							07 03										07 18						
West Dulwich	d	06 50							07 05										07 20						
Herne Hill	d	06 53			06 57				07 08					07 12					07 23		07 27				
Loughborough Jn.	d				07 00									07 15							07 30				
Elephant & Castle	d				07 04		07 14							07 19		07 24					07 34			07 44	
London Blackfriars	d			07 07	07 09	07 12	07 19					07 22		07 24	07 27	07a29	07 34			07 37	07 39	07 42		07 49	
City Thameslink	a																								
Farringdon	a			07 11	07 13	07 16	07 23					07 26		07 28	07 31		07 38			07 41	07 43	07 46		07 53	
St Pancras International	a			07 15	07 18	07 20	07 28					07 30		07 33	07 35		07 43			07 45	07 48	07 50		07 58	
Kentish Town	a				07 23		07 33							07 38							07 53			08 03	
Brixton	d	06 56							07 11										07 26						
London Victoria	a	07 03						07 08	07 18		07 25								07 33						07 38

		SE	TL B	SE K	TL ■ H	TL	TL I	SE ◇■ L		SE E	SE J	SE ◇■ M	SE ◇■ N	SE	TL ■ A	TL B	TL ■ C	TL		SE ◇■ D	SE	SE K	TL ■ G	TL B	TL ■ H
Sevenoaks	d					06 52		06 59			07 05														
Bat & Ball	d					06 55																			
Otford	d					06 59														07 26					
Shoreham (Kent)	d					07 02																			
Eynsford	d					07 05																			
Swanley	d					07 11						07 17								07 37					
St Mary Cray	d					07 15						07 22													
Orpington	d							07a07		07 11	07 20			07 24				07 33							
Petts Wood	d									07 14	07a23			07 27				07 36							
Bickley	d					07 20								07 31				07 40							
Bromley South	d	07 19				07 23						07 30	07 33	07 34				07 43		07 47	07 49				
Shortlands	d	07 22				07 25								07 37				07 45			07 52				
Ravensbourne	d					07 28												07 48							
Beckenham Hill	d					07 30												07 50							
Bellingham	d					07 32												07 52							
Catford	d					07 35												07 55							
Crofton Park	d					07 38												07 58							
Lewisham	a									07 32															
	d			07 32																		08 02			
Nunhead	d			07 37		07 41												08 01				08 07			
Peckham Rye	d			07 40		07 44												08 04				08 10			
Denmark Hill	d			07 44		07 47						07 50						08 07				08 14			
Beckenham Junction	d	07 25												07 40							07 55				
Kent House	d	07 27												07 42							07 57				
Penge East	d	07 29												07 44							07 59				
Sydenham Hill	d	07 33												07 48							08 03				
West Dulwich	d	07 35												07 50							08 05				
Herne Hill	d	07 38	07 42											07 53		07 57					08 08			08 12	
Loughborough Jn.	d		07 45													08 00								08 15	
Elephant & Castle	d		07 49			07 54										08 04		08 14						08 19	
London Blackfriars	d		07 54		07 57	07a59	08 04								08 07	08 09	08 12	08 19					08 22	08 24	08 27
City Thameslink	a																								
Farringdon	a		07 58		08 01		08 08								08 11	08 13	08 16	08 23					08 26	08 28	08 31
St Pancras International	a		08 03		08 05		08 13								08 15	08 18	08 20	08 28					08 30	08 33	08 35
Kentish Town	a		08 08													08 23		08 33						08 38	
Brixton	d	07 41												07 56							08 11				
London Victoria	a	07 48		07 55								08 00	07 53	08 03						08 08	08 18	08 25			

A From Horsham to Peterborough
B From Sutton (Surrey) to St Albans City
C From Brighton to Bedford
D From Ashford International
E To London Cannon Street
F From Dartford
G From Brighton to Cambridge
H From Gatwick Airport to Bedford
I From Rainham Kt to Luton
J To London Charing Cross
K From Gravesend
L From Hastings to London Charing Cross
M From Gillingham (Kent)
N From Ramsgate

Table 195R

Saturdays
26 May to 8 December

Sevenoaks and Otford, Orpington, Bromley South, Beckenham Junction, Catford - London

		TL	TL A	SE ◇■ B		SE C	SE D	SE ◇■ E	SE ◇■ F	SE	TL ■ G	TL H	TL ■ I	TL		SE ◇■ J	SE	TL H	SE K	TL ■ L	TL	TL A	SE ◇■ B	SE C	
Sevenoaks	d	07 22		07 29			07 35	07 43													07 52		07 59		
Bat & Ball	d	07 25																			07 55				
Otford	d	07 29														07 56					07 59				
Shoreham (Kent)	d	07 32																			08 02				
Eynsford	d	07 35																			08 05				
Swanley	d	07 41														08 05					08 11				
St Mary Cray	d	07 45														08 09					08 15				
Orpington	d			07a37		07 41	07 50	07a51		07 54				08 03									08a07	08 11	
Petts Wood	d					07 44	07a53			07 57				08 06										08 14	
Bickley	d	07 50								08 01				08 10							08 20				
Bromley South	d	07 53							08 03	08 04				08 13		08 17	08 19				08 23				
Shortlands	d	07 55								08 07				08 15			08 22				08 25				
Ravensbourne	d	07 58												08 18							08 28				
Beckenham Hill	d	08 00												08 20							08 30				
Bellingham	d	08 02												08 22							08 32				
Catford	d	08 05												08 25							08 35				
Crofton Park	d	08 08												08 28							08 38				
Lewisham	a					08 02																		08 32	
	d																		08 32						
Nunhead	d	08 11												08 31					08 37		08 41				
Peckham Rye	d	08 14												08 34					08 40		08 44				
Denmark Hill	d	08 17												08 37					08 44		08 47				
Beckenham Junction	d									08 10							08 25								
Kent House	d									08 12							08 27								
Penge East	d									08 14							08 29								
Sydenham Hill	d									08 18							08 33								
West Dulwich	d									08 20							08 35								
Herne Hill	d									08 23		08 27					08 38	08 42							
Loughborough Jn.	d											08 30						08 45							
Elephant & Castle	d	08 24										08 34		08 44				08 49			08 54				
London Blackfriars	d	08a29	08 34								08 37	08 39	08 42	08 49				08 54		08 57	08a59	09 04			
City Thameslink	a																					09 06			
Farringdon	a		08 38								08 41	08 43	08 46	08 53				08 58		09 01		09 08			
St Pancras International	a		08 43								08 45	08 48	08 50	08 58				09 03		09 05		09 13			
Kentish Town	a											08 53		09 03				09 08							
Brixton	d									08 26							08 41								
London Victoria	a								08 23	08 33						08 38	08 48		08 55						

		SE D	SE ◇■ E	SE ◇■ F	SE ◇■ M	SE	TL ■ G	TL H	TL ■ I	TL		SE ◇■ J	SE	SE K	TL ■ N	TL H	TL ■ L	TL	TL A	SE ◇■ B		SE C	SE D	SE ◇■ E	SE ◇■ F
Sevenoaks	d	08 05	08 13															08 22		08 29			08 35	08 43	
Bat & Ball	d																	08 25							
Otford	d											08 26						08 29							
Shoreham (Kent)	d																	08 32							
Eynsford	d																	08 35							
Swanley	d			08 17								08 37						08 41							
St Mary Cray	d			08 22														08 45							
Orpington	d	08 20	08a21			08 24				08 33										08a37		08 41	08 50	08a51	
Petts Wood	d	08a23				08 27				08 36												08 44	08a53		
Bickley	d					08 31				08 40								08 50							
Bromley South	d			08 30	08 33	08 34				08 43		08 47	08 49					08 53							09 03
Shortlands	d					08 37				08 45			08 52					08 55							
Ravensbourne	d									08 48								08 58							
Beckenham Hill	d									08 50								09 00							
Bellingham	d									08 52								09 02							
Catford	d									08 55								09 05							
Crofton Park	d									08 58								09 08							
Lewisham	a																					09 02			
	d													09 02											
Nunhead	d									09 01				09 07				09 11							
Peckham Rye	d									09 04				09 10				09 14							
Denmark Hill	d			08 50						09 07				09 14				09 17							
Beckenham Junction	d					08 40							08 55												
Kent House	d					08 42							08 57												
Penge East	d					08 44							08 59												
Sydenham Hill	d					08 48							09 03												
West Dulwich	d					08 50							09 05												
Herne Hill	d					08 53		08 57					09 08			09 12									
Loughborough Jn.	d							09 00								09 15									
Elephant & Castle	d							09 04		09 14						09 19		09 24							
London Blackfriars	d						09 07	09 09	09 12	09 19					09 22	09 24	09 27	09a29	09 34						
City Thameslink	a						09 08	09 11	09 13	09 21					09 23	09 26	09 28		09 36						
Farringdon	a						09 11	09 13	09 16	09 23					09 26	09 28	09 31		09 38						
St Pancras International	a						09 15	09 18	09 20	09 28					09 30	09 33	09 35		09 43						
Kentish Town	a							09 23		09 33						09 38									
Brixton	d					08 56							09 11												
London Victoria	a			09 00	08 53	09 03						09 08	09 18	09 25											09 23

A From Rainham Kt to Luton
B From Hastings to London Charing Cross
C To London Cannon Street
D To London Charing Cross
E From Tunbridge Wells to London Charing Cross
F From Dover Priory
G From Horsham to Peterborough
H From Sutton (Surrey) to St Albans City
I From Brighton to Bedford
J From Ashford International
K From Gravesend
L From Gatwick Airport to Bedford
M From Ramsgate
N From Brighton to Cambridge

Sevenoaks and Otford, Orpington, Bromley South, Beckenham Junction, Catford - London

		SE	TL	TL	TL	TL		SE	SE	TL	SE	TL	TL	TL	SE	SE		SE	SE	SE	SE	SE	TL	TL	TL
			1 A	B	1 C			◇1 D		B	E	1 F		G	◇1 H	I		J	◇1 K	◇1 L	◇1 M		1 A	B	1 C
Sevenoaks 4	d												08 52		08 59			09 05	09 13						
Bat & Ball	d												08 55												
Otford 4	d							08 56					08 59												
Shoreham (Kent)	d												09 02												
Eynsford	d												09 05												
Swanley 4	d							09 05					09 11							09 17					
St Mary Cray	d							09 09					09 15							09 22					
Orpington 4	d	08 54				09 03									09a07	09 11		09 20	09a21			09 24			
Petts Wood 4	d	08 57				09 06										09 14		09a23				09 27			
Bickley 4	d	09 01				09 10							09 20									09 31			
Bromley South 4	d	09 04				09 13		09 17	09 19				09 23							09 30	09 33	09 34			
Shortlands 4	d	09 07				09 15			09 22				09 25									09 37			
Ravensbourne	d					09 18							09 28												
Beckenham Hill	d					09 20							09 30												
Bellingham	d					09 22							09 32												
Catford	d					09 25							09 35												
Crofton Park	d					09 28							09 38												
Lewisham 4	a															09 32									
	d										09 32														
Nunhead 4	d					09 31					09 37		09 41												
Peckham Rye 4	d					09 34					09 40		09 44												
Denmark Hill 4	d					09 37					09 44		09 47							09 50					
Beckenham Junction 4	d	09 10							09 25													09 40			
Kent House 4	d	09 12							09 27													09 42			
Penge East	d	09 14							09 29													09 44			
Sydenham Hill	d	09 18							09 33													09 48			
West Dulwich	d	09 20							09 35													09 50			
Herne Hill 4	d	09 23		09 27					09 38	09 42												09 53		09 57	
Loughborough Jn.	d			09 30						09 45														10 00	
Elephant & Castle	d			09 34		09 44				09 49			09 54											10 04	
London Blackfriars 3	d		09 37	09 39	09 42	09 49				09 54		09 57	09a59	10 04									10 07	10 09	10 12
City Thameslink 3	a		09 38	09 41	09 43	09 51				09 56		09 58		10 06									10 08	10 11	10 13
Farringdon	a		09 41	09 43	09 46	09 53				09 58		10 01		10 08									10 11	10 13	10 16
St Pancras International 15	a		09 45	09 48	09 50	09 58				10 03		10 05		10 13									10 15	10 18	10 20
Kentish Town	a			09 53		10 03				10 08														10 23	
Brixton	d	09 26							09 41													09 56			
London Victoria 15	a	09 33						09 38	09 48		09 55									10 00	09 53	10 03			

		TL		SE	SE	SE	TL	TL	TL	TL	TL	SE		SE	SE	SE	SE	SE	TL	TL	TL	TL		SE	SE
				◇1 N		E	1 O	B	1 F		G	◇1 H		I	J	◇1 K	◇1 L		1 A	B	1 C			◇1 D	
Sevenoaks 4	d									09 22		09 29			09 35	09 43									
Bat & Ball	d									09 25															
Otford 4	d			09 26						09 29														09 56	
Shoreham (Kent)	d									09 32															
Eynsford	d									09 35															
Swanley 4	d			09 37						09 41														10 05	
St Mary Cray	d									09 45														10 09	
Orpington 4	d	09 33										09a37		09 41	09 50	09a51		09 54				10 03			
Petts Wood 4	d	09 36												09 44	09a53			09 57				10 06			
Bickley 4	d	09 40								09 50								10 01				10 10			
Bromley South 4	d	09 43		09 47	09 49					09 53							10 03	10 04				10 13		10 17	10 19
Shortlands 4	d	09 45			09 52					09 55								10 07				10 15			10 22
Ravensbourne	d	09 48								09 58												10 18			
Beckenham Hill	d	09 50								10 00												10 20			
Bellingham	d	09 52								10 02												10 22			
Catford	d	09 55								10 05												10 25			
Crofton Park	d	09 58								10 08												10 28			
Lewisham 4	a													10 02											
	d					10 02																			
Nunhead 4	d	10 01				10 07				10 11												10 31			
Peckham Rye 4	d	10 04				10 10				10 14												10 34			
Denmark Hill 4	d	10 07				10 14				10 17												10 37			
Beckenham Junction 4	d				09 55													10 10							10 25
Kent House 4	d				09 57													10 12							10 27
Penge East	d				09 59													10 14							10 29
Sydenham Hill	d				10 03													10 18							10 33
West Dulwich	d				10 05													10 20							10 35
Herne Hill 4	d				10 08			10 12										10 23		10 27					10 38
Loughborough Jn.	d							10 15												10 30					
Elephant & Castle	d	10 14						10 19		10 24										10 34		10 44			
London Blackfriars 3	d	10 19					10 22	10 24	10 27	10a29	10 34								10 37	10 39	10 42	10 49			
City Thameslink 3	a	10 21					10 23	10 26	10 28		10 36								10 38	10 41	10 43	10 51			
Farringdon	a	10 23					10 26	10 28	10 31		10 38								10 41	10 43	10 46	10 53			
St Pancras International 15	a	10 28					10 30	10 33	10 35		10 43								10 45	10 48	10 50	10 58			
Kentish Town	a	10 33						10 38												10 53		11 03			
Brixton	d				10 11													10 26							10 41
London Victoria 15	a			10 08	10 18	10 25											10 23	10 33						10 38	10 48

A From Horsham to Peterborough
B From Sutton (Surrey) to St Albans City
C From Brighton to Bedford
D From Ashford International
E From Gravesend
F From Gatwick Airport to Bedford
G From Rainham Kt to Luton
H From Hastings to London Charing Cross
I To London Cannon Street
J To London Charing Cross
K From Tunbridge Wells to London Charing Cross
L From Dover Priory
M From Ramsgate
N From Canterbury West
O From Brighton to Cambridge

Sevenoaks and Otford, Orpington, Bromley South, Beckenham Junction, Catford - London

		TL	SE	TL	TL	TL	SE	SE		SE	SE	SE	SE	SE	TL	TL	TL	TL		SE	SE	SE	TL	TL	TL
		A	B	1 C		D	◇1 E	F		G	◇1 H	◇1 I	◇1 J		1 K	A	1 L			◇1 M		B	1 N	A	1 C
Sevenoaks 4	d				09 52		09 59			10 05	10 13														
Bat & Ball	d				09 55																				
Otford 4	d				09 59															10 26					
Shoreham (Kent)	d				10 02																				
Eynsford	d				10 05																				
Swanley 4	d				10 11							10 17								10 37					
St Mary Cray	d				10 15							10 22													
Orpington 4	d						10a07	10 11		10 20	10a21			10 24				10 33							
Petts Wood 4	d							10 14		10a23				10 27				10 36							
Bickley 4	d				10 20									10 31				10 40							
Bromley South 4	d				10 23							10 30	10 33	10 34				10 43		10 47	10 49				
Shortlands 4	d				10 25									10 37				10 45			10 52				
Ravensbourne	d				10 28													10 48							
Beckenham Hill	d				10 30													10 50							
Bellingham	d				10 32													10 52							
Catford	d				10 35													10 55							
Crofton Park	d				10 38													10 58							
Lewisham 4	a							10 32																	
	d		10 32																			11 02			
Nunhead 4	d		10 37		10 41													11 01				11 07			
Peckham Rye 4	d		10 40		10 44													11 04				11 10			
Denmark Hill 4	d		10 44		10 47							10 50						11 07				11 14			
Beckenham Junction 4	d													10 40							10 55				
Kent House 4	d													10 42							10 57				
Penge East	d													10 44							10 59				
Sydenham Hill	d													10 48							11 03				
West Dulwich	d													10 50							11 05				
Herne Hill 4	d	10 42												10 53		10 57					11 08			11 12	
Loughborough Jn.	d	10 45														11 00								11 15	
Elephant & Castle	d	10 49			10 54											11 04		11 14						11 19	
London Blackfriars 3	d	10 54		10 57	10a59	11 04									11 07	11 09	11 12	11 19					11 22	11 24	11 27
City Thameslink 3	a	10 56		10 58		11 06									11 08	11 11	11 13	11 21					11 23	11 26	11 28
Farringdon	a	10 58		11 01		11 08									11 11	11 13	11 16	11 23					11 26	11 28	11 31
St Pancras International 15	a	11 03		11 05		11 13									11 15	11 18	11 20	11 28					11 30	11 33	11 35
Kentish Town	a	11 08														11 23		11 33						11 38	
Brixton	d													10 56							11 11				
London Victoria 15	a		10 55									11 00	10 53	11 03						11 08	11 18	11 25			

		TL	TL	SE		SE	SE	SE	SE	SE	TL	TL	TL	TL		SE	SE	TL	SE	TL	TL	TL	SE	SE	
			D	◇1 E		F	G	◇1 H	◇1 I		1 K	A	1 L			◇1 O		A	B	1 C		D	◇1 E	F	
Sevenoaks 4	d	10 22		10 29			10 35	10 43													10 52		10 59		
Bat & Ball	d	10 25																			10 55				
Otford 4	d	10 29														10 56					10 59				
Shoreham (Kent)	d	10 32																			11 02				
Eynsford	d	10 35																			11 05				
Swanley 4	d	10 41														11 05					11 11				
St Mary Cray	d	10 45														11 09					11 15				
Orpington 4	d			10a37		10 41	10 50	10a51		10 54				11 03									11a07	11 11	
Petts Wood 4	d					10 44	10a53			10 57				11 06										11 14	
Bickley 4	d	10 50								11 01				11 10							11 20				
Bromley South 4	d	10 53							11 03	11 04				11 13		11 17	11 19				11 23				
Shortlands 4	d	10 55								11 07				11 15			11 22				11 25				
Ravensbourne	d	10 58												11 18							11 28				
Beckenham Hill	d	11 00												11 20							11 30				
Bellingham	d	11 02												11 22							11 32				
Catford	d	11 05												11 25							11 35				
Crofton Park	d	11 08												11 28							11 38				
Lewisham 4	a					11 02																		11 32	
	d																		11 32						
Nunhead 4	d	11 11												11 31					11 37		11 41				
Peckham Rye 4	d	11 14												11 34					11 40		11 44				
Denmark Hill 4	d	11 17												11 37					11 44		11 47				
Beckenham Junction 4	d									11 10							11 25								
Kent House 4	d									11 12							11 27								
Penge East	d									11 14							11 29								
Sydenham Hill	d									11 18							11 33								
West Dulwich	d									11 20							11 35								
Herne Hill 4	d									11 23		11 27					11 38	11 42							
Loughborough Jn.	d											11 30						11 45							
Elephant & Castle	d	11 24										11 34		11 44				11 49			11 54				
London Blackfriars 3	d	11a29	11 34								11 37	11 39	11 42	11 49				11 54		11 57	11a59	12 04			
City Thameslink 3	a		11 36								11 38	11 41	11 43	11 51				11 56		11 58		12 06			
Farringdon	a		11 38								11 41	11 43	11 46	11 53				11 58		12 01		12 08			
St Pancras International 15	a		11 43								11 45	11 48	11 50	11 58				12 03		12 05		12 13			
Kentish Town	a											11 53		12 03				12 08							
Brixton	d									11 26							11 41								
London Victoria 15	a								11 23	11 33						11 38	11 48		11 55						

A From Sutton (Surrey) to St Albans City
B From Gravesend
C From Gatwick Airport to Bedford
D From Rainham Kt to Luton
E From Hastings to London Charing Cross
F To London Cannon Street
G To London Charing Cross
H From Tunbridge Wells to London Charing Cross
I From Dover Priory
J From Ramsgate
K From Horsham to Peterborough
L From Brighton to Bedford
M From Canterbury West
N From Brighton to Cambridge
O From Ashford International

Table 195R

Saturdays

26 May to 8 December

Sevenoaks and Otford, Orpington, Bromley South, Beckenham Junction, Catford - London

		SE A	SE ◇1 B	SE ◇1 C	SE ◇1 D	SE	TL 1 E	TL F	TL 1 G	TL		SE ◇1 H	SE	SE I	TL 1 J	TL F	TL 1 K	TL	TL L	SE ◇1 M		SE N	SE A	SE ◇1 B	SE ◇1 C
Sevenoaks	d	11 05	11 13															11 22		11 29			11 35	11 43	
Bat & Ball	d																	11 25							
Otford	d											11 26						11 29							
Shoreham (Kent)	d																	11 32							
Eynsford	d																	11 35							
Swanley	d			11 17								11 37						11 41							
St Mary Cray	d			11 22														11 45							
Orpington	d	11 20	11a21			11 24				11 33										11a37		11 41	11 50	11a51	
Petts Wood	d	11a23				11 27				11 36												11 44	11a53		
Bickley	d					11 31				11 40								11 50							
Bromley South	d			11 30	11 33	11 34				11 43		11 47	11 49					11 53							12 03
Shortlands	d					11 37				11 45			11 52					11 55							
Ravensbourne	d									11 48								11 58							
Beckenham Hill	d									11 50								12 00							
Bellingham	d									11 52								12 02							
Catford	d									11 55								12 05							
Crofton Park	d									11 58								12 08							
Lewisham	a																					12 02			
	d													12 02											
Nunhead	d									12 01				12 07				12 11							
Peckham Rye	d									12 04				12 10				12 14							
Denmark Hill	d			11 50						12 07				12 14				12 17							
Beckenham Junction	d					11 40							11 55												
Kent House	d					11 42							11 57												
Penge East	d					11 44							11 59												
Sydenham Hill	d					11 48							12 03												
West Dulwich	d					11 50							12 05												
Herne Hill	d					11 53		11 57					12 08			12 12									
Loughborough Jn.	d							12 00								12 15									
Elephant & Castle	d							12 04		12 14						12 19		12 24							
London Blackfriars	d						12 07	12 09	12 12	12 19					12 22	12 24	12 27	12a29	12 34						
City Thameslink	a						12 08	12 11	12 13	12 21					12 23	12 26	12 28		12 36						
Farringdon	a						12 11	12 13	12 16	12 23					12 26	12 28	12 31		12 38						
St Pancras International	a						12 15	12 18	12 20	12 28					12 30	12 33	12 35		12 43						
Kentish Town	a							12 23		12 33						12 38									
Brixton	d					11 56							12 11												
London Victoria	a			12 00	11 53	12 03						12 08	12 18	12 25											12 23

		SE	TL 1 E	TL F	TL 1 G	TL		SE ◇1 O	SE	TL F	SE I	TL 1 K	TL	TL L	SE ◇1 M	SE N		SE A	SE ◇1 B	SE ◇1 C	SE ◇1 D	SE	TL 1 E	TL F	TL 1 G
Sevenoaks	d												11 52		11 59			12 05	12 13						
Bat & Ball	d												11 55												
Otford	d							11 56					11 59												
Shoreham (Kent)	d												12 02												
Eynsford	d												12 05												
Swanley	d							12 05					12 11							12 17					
St Mary Cray	d							12 09					12 15							12 22					
Orpington	d	11 54				12 03									12a07	12 11		12 20	12a21			12 24			
Petts Wood	d	11 57				12 06										12 14		12a23				12 27			
Bickley	d	12 01				12 10							12 20									12 31			
Bromley South	d	12 04				12 13		12 17	12 19				12 23							12 30	12 33	12 34			
Shortlands	d	12 07				12 15			12 22				12 25									12 37			
Ravensbourne	d					12 18							12 28												
Beckenham Hill	d					12 20							12 30												
Bellingham	d					12 22							12 32												
Catford	d					12 25							12 35												
Crofton Park	d					12 28							12 38												
Lewisham	a															12 32									
	d										12 32														
Nunhead	d					12 31					12 37		12 41												
Peckham Rye	d					12 34					12 40		12 44												
Denmark Hill	d					12 37					12 44		12 47							12 50					
Beckenham Junction	d	12 10							12 25													12 40			
Kent House	d	12 12							12 27													12 42			
Penge East	d	12 14							12 29													12 44			
Sydenham Hill	d	12 18							12 33													12 48			
West Dulwich	d	12 20							12 35													12 50			
Herne Hill	d	12 23		12 27					12 38	12 42												12 53		12 57	
Loughborough Jn.	d			12 30						12 45														13 00	
Elephant & Castle	d			12 34		12 44				12 49			12 54											13 04	
London Blackfriars	d		12 37	12 39	12 42	12 49				12 54		12 57	12a59	13 04									13 07	13 09	13 12
City Thameslink	a		12 38	12 41	12 43	12 51				12 56		12 58		13 06									13 08	13 11	13 13
Farringdon	a		12 41	12 43	12 46	12 53				12 58		13 01		13 08									13 11	13 13	13 16
St Pancras International	a		12 45	12 48	12 50	12 58				13 03		13 05		13 13									13 15	13 18	13 20
Kentish Town	a			12 53		13 03				13 08														13 23	
Brixton	d	12 26							12 41													12 56			
London Victoria	a	12 33						12 38	12 48		12 55									13 00	12 53	13 03			

A To London Charing Cross
B From Tunbridge Wells to London Charing Cross
C From Dover Priory
D From Ramsgate
E From Horsham to Peterborough
F From Sutton (Surrey) to St Albans City
G From Brighton to Bedford
H From Canterbury West
I From Gravesend
J From Brighton to Cambridge
K From Gatwick Airport to Bedford
L From Rainham Kt to Luton
M From Hastings to London Charing Cross
N To London Cannon Street
O From Ashford International

Table 195R

Saturdays

26 May to 8 December

Sevenoaks and Otford, Orpington, Bromley South, Beckenham Junction, Catford - London

		TL		SE ◇1 A	SE	SE B	TL 1 C	TL D	TL 1 E	TL	TL F	SE ◇1 G		SE H	SE I	SE ◇1 J	SE ◇1 K	SE	TL 1 L	TL D	TL 1 M	TL		SE ◇1 N	SE
Sevenoaks	d									12 22		12 29			12 35	12 43									
Bat & Ball	d									12 25															
Otford	d			12 26						12 29														12 56	
Shoreham (Kent)	d									12 32															
Eynsford	d									12 35															
Swanley	d			12 37						12 41														13 05	
St Mary Cray	d									12 45														13 09	
Orpington	d	12 33										12a37		12 41	12 50	12a51		12 54				13 03			
Petts Wood	d	12 36												12 44	12a53			12 57				13 06			
Bickley	d	12 40								12 50								13 01				13 10			
Bromley South	d	12 43		12 47	12 49					12 53							13 03	13 04				13 13		13 17	13 19
Shortlands	d	12 45			12 52					12 55								13 07				13 15			13 22
Ravensbourne	d	12 48								12 58												13 18			
Beckenham Hill	d	12 50								13 00												13 20			
Bellingham	d	12 52								13 02												13 22			
Catford	d	12 55								13 05												13 25			
Crofton Park	d	12 58								13 08												13 28			
Lewisham	a													13 02											
	d					13 02																			
Nunhead	d	13 01				13 07				13 11												13 31			
Peckham Rye	d	13 04				13 10				13 14												13 34			
Denmark Hill	d	13 07				13 14				13 17												13 37			
Beckenham Junction	d				12 55													13 10							13 25
Kent House	d				12 57													13 12							13 27
Penge East	d				12 59													13 14							13 29
Sydenham Hill	d				13 03													13 18							13 33
West Dulwich	d				13 05													13 20							13 35
Herne Hill	d				13 08			13 12										13 23		13 27					13 38
Loughborough Jn.	d							13 15												13 30					
Elephant & Castle	d	13 14						13 19		13 24										13 34		13 44			
London Blackfriars	d	13 19					13 22	13 24	13 27	13a29	13 34								13 37	13 39	13 42	13 49			
City Thameslink	a	13 21					13 23	13 26	13 28		13 36								13 38	13 41	13 43	13 51			
Farringdon	a	13 23					13 26	13 28	13 31		13 38								13 41	13 43	13 46	13 53			
St Pancras International	a	13 28					13 30	13 33	13 35		13 43								13 45	13 48	13 50	13 58			
Kentish Town	a	13 33						13 38												13 53		14 03			
Brixton	d				13 11													13 26							13 41
London Victoria	a			13 08	13 18	13 25											13 23	13 33						13 38	13 48

		TL D	SE B	TL 1 E	TL	TL F	SE ◇1 G	SE H		SE I	SE ◇1 J	SE ◇1 K	SE ◇1 O	SE	TL 1 L	TL D	TL 1 M	TL		SE ◇1 A	SE	SE B	TL 1 C	TL D	TL 1 E
Sevenoaks	d				12 52		12 59			13 05	13 13														
Bat & Ball	d				12 55																				
Otford	d				12 59															13 26					
Shoreham (Kent)	d				13 02																				
Eynsford	d				13 05																				
Swanley	d				13 11							13 17								13 37					
St Mary Cray	d				13 15							13 22													
Orpington	d						13a07	13 11		13 20	13a21			13 24				13 33							
Petts Wood	d							13 14		13a23				13 27				13 36							
Bickley	d				13 20									13 31				13 40							
Bromley South	d				13 23							13 30	13 33	13 34				13 43		13 47	13 49				
Shortlands	d				13 25									13 37				13 45			13 52				
Ravensbourne	d				13 28													13 48							
Beckenham Hill	d				13 30													13 50							
Bellingham	d				13 32													13 52							
Catford	d				13 35													13 55							
Crofton Park	d				13 38													13 58							
Lewisham	a							13 32																	
	d		13 32																			14 02			
Nunhead	d		13 37		13 41													14 01				14 07			
Peckham Rye	d		13 40		13 44													14 04				14 10			
Denmark Hill	d		13 44		13 47							13 50						14 07				14 14			
Beckenham Junction	d													13 40							13 55				
Kent House	d													13 42							13 57				
Penge East	d													13 44							13 59				
Sydenham Hill	d													13 48							14 03				
West Dulwich	d													13 50							14 05				
Herne Hill	d	13 42												13 53		13 57					14 08			14 12	
Loughborough Jn.	d	13 45														14 00								14 15	
Elephant & Castle	d	13 49			13 54											14 04		14 14						14 19	
London Blackfriars	d	13 54		13 57	13a59	14 04									14 07	14 09	14 12	14 19					14 22	14 24	14 27
City Thameslink	a	13 56		13 58		14 06									14 08	14 11	14 13	14 21					14 23	14 26	14 28
Farringdon	a	13 58		14 01		14 08									14 11	14 13	14 16	14 23					14 26	14 28	14 31
St Pancras International	a	14 03		14 05		14 13									14 15	14 18	14 20	14 28					14 30	14 33	14 35
Kentish Town	a	14 08														14 23		14 33						14 38	
Brixton	d													13 56							14 11				
London Victoria	a		13 55									14 00	13 53	14 03						14 08	14 18	14 25			

A From Canterbury West
B From Gravesend
C From Brighton to Cambridge
D From Sutton (Surrey) to St Albans City
E From Gatwick Airport to Bedford
F From Rainham Kt to Luton
G From Hastings to London Charing Cross
H To London Cannon Street
I To London Charing Cross
J From Tunbridge Wells to London Charing Cross
K From Dover Priory
L From Horsham to Peterborough
M From Brighton to Bedford
N From Ashford International
O From Ramsgate

Table 195R

Saturdays
26 May to 8 December

Sevenoaks and Otford, Orpington, Bromley South, Beckenham Junction, Catford - London

Station		TL	TL A	SE ◇1 B	SE C	SE D	SE ◇1 E	SE ◇1 F	SE	TL 1 G	TL H	TL 1 I	TL	SE ◇1 J	SE	TL H	SE K	TL 1 L	TL	TL A	SE ◇1 B	SE C
Sevenoaks	d	13 22		13 29		13 35	13 43												13 52		13 59	
Bat & Ball	d	13 25																	13 55			
Otford	d	13 29												13 56					13 59			
Shoreham (Kent)	d	13 32																	14 02			
Eynsford	d	13 35																	14 05			
Swanley	d	13 41												14 05					14 11			
St Mary Cray	d	13 45												14 09					14 15			
Orpington	d			13a37	13 41	13 50	13a51		13 54				14 03								14a07	14 11
Petts Wood	d				13 44	13a53			13 57				14 06									14 14
Bickley	d	13 50							14 01				14 10						14 20			
Bromley South	d	13 53						14 03	14 04				14 13	14 17	14 19				14 23			
Shortlands	d	13 55							14 07				14 15		14 22				14 25			
Ravensbourne	d	13 58											14 18						14 28			
Beckenham Hill	d	14 00											14 20						14 30			
Bellingham	d	14 02											14 22						14 32			
Catford	d	14 05											14 25						14 35			
Crofton Park	d	14 08											14 28						14 38			
Lewisham	a				14 02																	14 32
	d																14 32					
Nunhead	d	14 11											14 31				14 37		14 41			
Peckham Rye	d	14 14											14 34				14 40		14 44			
Denmark Hill	d	14 17											14 37				14 44		14 47			
Beckenham Junction	d								14 10						14 25							
Kent House	d								14 12						14 27							
Penge East	d								14 14						14 29							
Sydenham Hill	d								14 18						14 33							
West Dulwich	d								14 20						14 35							
Herne Hill	d								14 23		14 27				14 38	14 42						
Loughborough Jn	d										14 30					14 45						
Elephant & Castle	d	14 24									14 34		14 44			14 49			14 54			
London Blackfriars	d	14a29	14 34							14 37	14 39	14 42	14 49			14 54		14 57	14a59	15 04		
City Thameslink	a		14 36							14 38	14 41	14 43	14 51			14 56		14 58		15 06		
Farringdon	a		14 38							14 41	14 43	14 46	14 53			14 58		15 01		15 08		
St Pancras International	a		14 43							14 45	14 48	14 50	14 58			15 03		15 05		15 13		
Kentish Town	a										14 53		15 03			15 08						
Brixton	d								14 26						14 41							
London Victoria	a							14 23	14 33					14 38	14 48		14 55					

Station		SE D	SE ◇1 E	SE ◇1 F	SE ◇1 M	SE	TL 1 G	TL H	TL 1 I	TL	SE ◇1 N	SE	SE K	TL 1 O	TL H	TL 1 L	TL	TL A	SE ◇1 B	SE C	SE D	SE ◇1 E	SE ◇1 F
Sevenoaks	d	14 05	14 13														14 22		14 29		14 35	14 43	
Bat & Ball	d																14 25						
Otford	d										14 26						14 29						
Shoreham (Kent)	d																14 32						
Eynsford	d																14 35						
Swanley	d			14 17							14 37						14 41						
St Mary Cray	d			14 22													14 45						
Orpington	d	14 20	14a21			14 24				14 33									14a37	14 41	14 50	14a51	
Petts Wood	d	14a23				14 27				14 36										14 44	14a53		
Bickley	d					14 31				14 40							14 50						
Bromley South	d			14 30	14 33	14 34				14 43	14 47	14 49					14 53						15 03
Shortlands	d					14 37				14 45		14 52					14 55						
Ravensbourne	d									14 48							14 58						
Beckenham Hill	d									14 50							15 00						
Bellingham	d									14 52							15 02						
Catford	d									14 55							15 05						
Crofton Park	d									14 58							15 08						
Lewisham	a																			15 02			
	d												15 02										
Nunhead	d									15 01			15 07				15 11						
Peckham Rye	d									15 04			15 10				15 14						
Denmark Hill	d			14 50						15 07			15 14				15 17						
Beckenham Junction	d					14 40						14 55											
Kent House	d					14 42						14 57											
Penge East	d					14 44						14 59											
Sydenham Hill	d					14 48						15 03											
West Dulwich	d					14 50						15 05											
Herne Hill	d					14 53		14 57				15 08			15 12								
Loughborough Jn	d							15 00							15 15								
Elephant & Castle	d							15 04		15 14					15 19		15 24						
London Blackfriars	d						15 07	15 09	15 12	15 19				15 22	15 24	15 27	15a29	15 34					
City Thameslink	a						15 08	15 11	15 13	15 21				15 23	15 26	15 28		15 36					
Farringdon	a						15 11	15 13	15 16	15 23				15 26	15 28	15 31		15 38					
St Pancras International	a						15 15	15 18	15 20	15 28				15 30	15 33	15 35		15 43					
Kentish Town	a							15 23		15 33					15 38								
Brixton	d					14 56						15 11											
London Victoria	a			15 00	14 53	15 03					15 08	15 18	15 25										15 23

A From Rainham Kt to Luton
B From Hastings to London Charing Cross
C To London Cannon Street
D To London Charing Cross
E From Tunbridge Wells to London Charing Cross
F From Dover Priory
G From Horsham to Peterborough
H From Sutton (Surrey) to St Albans City
I From Brighton to Bedford
J From Ashford International
K From Gravesend
L From Gatwick Airport to Bedford
M From Ramsgate
N From Canterbury West
O From Brighton to Cambridge

Table 195R

Saturdays
26 May to 8 December

Sevenoaks and Otford, Orpington, Bromley South, Beckenham Junction, Catford - London

Station		SE	TL 1 A	TL B	TL 1 C	TL	SE ◇1 D	SE	TL B	SE E	TL 1 F	TL	TL G	SE ◇1 H	SE I	SE J	SE ◇1 K	SE ◇1 L	SE ◇1 M	SE	TL 1 A	TL B	TL 1 C
Sevenoaks	d											14 52		14 59		15 05	15 13						
Bat & Ball	d											14 55											
Otford	d						14 56					14 59											
Shoreham (Kent)	d											15 02											
Eynsford	d											15 05											
Swanley	d						15 05					15 11						15 17					
St Mary Cray	d						15 09					15 15						15 22					
Orpington	d	14 54				15 03								15a07	15 11	15 20	15a21			15 24			
Petts Wood	d	14 57				15 06									15 14	15a23				15 27			
Bickley	d	15 01				15 10						15 20								15 31			
Bromley South	d	15 04				15 13	15 17	15 19				15 23						15 30	15 33	15 34			
Shortlands	d	15 07				15 15		15 22				15 25								15 37			
Ravensbourne	d					15 18						15 28											
Beckenham Hill	d					15 20						15 30											
Bellingham	d					15 22						15 32											
Catford	d					15 25						15 35											
Crofton Park	d					15 28						15 38											
Lewisham	a														15 32								
	d									15 32													
Nunhead	d					15 31				15 37		15 41											
Peckham Rye	d					15 34				15 40		15 44											
Denmark Hill	d					15 37				15 44		15 47						15 50					
Beckenham Junction	d	15 10						15 25												15 40			
Kent House	d	15 12						15 27												15 42			
Penge East	d	15 14						15 29												15 44			
Sydenham Hill	d	15 18						15 33												15 48			
West Dulwich	d	15 20						15 35												15 50			
Herne Hill	d	15 23		15 27				15 38	15 42											15 53		15 57	
Loughborough Jn	d			15 30					15 45													16 00	
Elephant & Castle	d			15 34		15 44			15 49			15 54										16 04	
London Blackfriars	d		15 37	15 39	15 42	15 49			15 54		15 57	15a59	16 04								16 07	16 09	16 12
City Thameslink	a		15 38	15 41	15 43	15 51			15 56		15 58		16 06								16 08	16 11	16 13
Farringdon	a		15 41	15 43	15 46	15 53			15 58		16 01		16 08								16 11	16 13	16 16
St Pancras International	a		15 45	15 48	15 50	15 58			16 03		16 05		16 13								16 15	16 18	16 20
Kentish Town	a			15 53		16 03			16 08													16 23	
Brixton	d	15 26						15 41												15 56			
London Victoria	a	15 33					15 38	15 48		15 55								16 00	15 53	16 03			

Station		TL	SE ◇1 N	SE	SE E	TL 1 O	TL B	TL 1 F	TL	TL G	SE ◇1 H	SE I	SE J	SE ◇1 K	SE ◇1 L	SE	TL 1 A	TL B	TL 1 C	TL	SE ◇1 D	SE
Sevenoaks	d								15 22		15 29		15 35	15 43								
Bat & Ball	d								15 25													
Otford	d		15 26						15 29												15 56	
Shoreham (Kent)	d								15 32													
Eynsford	d								15 35													
Swanley	d		15 37						15 41												16 05	
St Mary Cray	d								15 45												16 09	
Orpington	d	15 33									15a37	15 41	15 50	15a51		15 54				16 03		
Petts Wood	d	15 36										15 44	15a53			15 57				16 06		
Bickley	d	15 40							15 50							16 01				16 10		
Bromley South	d	15 43	15 47	15 49					15 53						16 03	16 04				16 13	16 17	16 19
Shortlands	d	15 45		15 52					15 55							16 07				16 15		16 22
Ravensbourne	d	15 48							15 58											16 18		
Beckenham Hill	d	15 50							16 00											16 20		
Bellingham	d	15 52							16 02											16 22		
Catford	d	15 55							16 05											16 25		
Crofton Park	d	15 58							16 08											16 28		
Lewisham	a											16 02										
	d				16 02																	
Nunhead	d	16 01			16 07				16 11											16 31		
Peckham Rye	d	16 04			16 10				16 14											16 34		
Denmark Hill	d	16 07			16 14				16 17											16 37		
Beckenham Junction	d			15 55												16 10						16 25
Kent House	d			15 57												16 12						16 27
Penge East	d			15 59												16 14						16 29
Sydenham Hill	d			16 03												16 18						16 33
West Dulwich	d			16 05												16 20						16 35
Herne Hill	d			16 08			16 12									16 23		16 27				16 38
Loughborough Jn	d						16 15											16 30				
Elephant & Castle	d	16 14					16 19		16 24									16 34		16 44		
London Blackfriars	d	16 19				16 22	16 24	16 27	16a29	16 34							16 37	16 39	16 42	16 49		
City Thameslink	a	16 21				16 23	16 26	16 28		16 36							16 38	16 41	16 43	16 51		
Farringdon	a	16 23				16 26	16 28	16 31		16 38							16 41	16 43	16 46	16 53		
St Pancras International	a	16 28				16 30	16 33	16 35		16 43							16 45	16 48	16 50	16 58		
Kentish Town	a	16 33					16 38											16 53		17 03		
Brixton	d			16 11												16 26						16 41
London Victoria	a		16 08	16 18	16 25										16 23	16 33					16 38	16 48

A From Horsham to Peterborough
B From Sutton (Surrey) to St Albans City
C From Brighton to Bedford
D From Ashford International
E From Gravesend
F From Gatwick Airport to Bedford
G From Rainham Kt to Luton
H From Hastings to London Charing Cross
I To London Cannon Street
J To London Charing Cross
K From Tunbridge Wells to London Charing Cross
L From Dover Priory
M From Ramsgate
N From Canterbury West
O From Brighton to Cambridge

Saturdays

26 May to 8 December

Sevenoaks and Otford, Orpington, Bromley South, Beckenham Junction, Catford - London

Station		TL A	SE B	TL 1 C	TL	TL D	SE ◇1 E	SE F	SE G	SE ◇1 H	SE ◇1 I	SE ◇1 J	SE	TL 1 K	TL A	TL 1 L	TL	SE ◇1 M	SE	SE B	TL 1 N	TL A	TL 1 C
Sevenoaks	d				15 52		15 59		16 05	16 13													
Bat & Ball	d				15 55																		
Otford	d				15 59													16 26					
Shoreham (Kent)	d				16 02																		
Eynsford	d				16 05																		
Swanley	d				16 11						16 17							16 37					
St Mary Cray	d				16 15						16 22												
Orpington	d						16a07	16 11	16 20	16a21			16 24				16 33						
Petts Wood	d							16 14	16a23				16 27				16 36						
Bickley	d				16 20								16 31				16 40						
Bromley South	d				16 23						16 30	16 33	16 34				16 43	16 47	16 49				
Shortlands	d				16 25								16 37				16 45		16 52				
Ravensbourne	d				16 28												16 48						
Beckenham Hill	d				16 30												16 50						
Bellingham	d				16 32												16 52						
Catford	d				16 35												16 55						
Crofton Park	d				16 38												16 58						
Lewisham	a							16 32															
	d		16 32																	17 02			
Nunhead	d		16 37		16 41												17 01			17 07			
Peckham Rye	d		16 40		16 44												17 04			17 10			
Denmark Hill	d		16 44		16 47						16 50						17 07			17 14			
Beckenham Junction	d												16 40						16 55				
Kent House	d												16 42						16 57				
Penge East	d												16 44						16 59				
Sydenham Hill	d												16 48						17 03				
West Dulwich	d												16 50						17 05				
Herne Hill	d	16 42											16 53		16 57				17 08			17 12	
Loughborough Jn.	d	16 45													17 00							17 15	
Elephant & Castle ⊖	d	16 49			16 54										17 04		17 14					17 19	
London Blackfriars ⊖	d	16 54		16 57	16a59	17 04								17 07	17 09	17 12	17 19				17 22	17 24	17 27
City Thameslink	a	16 56		16 58		17 06								17 08	17 11	17 13	17 21				17 23	17 26	17 28
Farringdon ⊖	a	16 58		17 01		17 08								17 11	17 13	17 16	17 23				17 26	17 28	17 31
St Pancras International ⊖	a	17 03		17 05		17 13								17 15	17 18	17 20	17 28				17 30	17 33	17 35
Kentish Town ⊖	a	17 08													17 23		17 33					17 38	
Brixton ⊖	d												16 56						17 11				
London Victoria ⊖	a		16 55								17 00	16 53	17 03					17 08	17 18	17 25			

Station		TL	TL D	SE ◇1 E	SE F	SE G	SE ◇1 H	SE ◇1 I	SE	TL 1 K	TL A	TL 1 L	TL	SE ◇1 O	SE	TL A	SE B	TL 1 C	TL	TL D	SE ◇1 E	SE F
Sevenoaks	d	16 22		16 29		16 35	16 43												16 52		16 59	
Bat & Ball	d	16 25																	16 55			
Otford	d	16 29												16 56					16 59			
Shoreham (Kent)	d	16 32																	17 02			
Eynsford	d	16 35																	17 05			
Swanley	d	16 41												17 05					17 11			
St Mary Cray	d	16 45												17 09					17 15			
Orpington	d			16a37	16 41	16 50	16a51		16 54				17 03								17a07	17 11
Petts Wood	d				16 44	16a53			16 57				17 06									17 14
Bickley	d	16 50							17 01				17 10						17 20			
Bromley South	d	16 53						17 03	17 04				17 13	17 17	17 19				17 23			
Shortlands	d	16 55							17 07				17 15		17 22				17 25			
Ravensbourne	d	16 58											17 18						17 28			
Beckenham Hill	d	17 00											17 20						17 30			
Bellingham	d	17 02											17 22						17 32			
Catford	d	17 05											17 25						17 35			
Crofton Park	d	17 08											17 28						17 38			
Lewisham	a				17 02																	17 32
	d																17 32					
Nunhead	d	17 11											17 31				17 37		17 41			
Peckham Rye	d	17 14											17 34				17 40		17 44			
Denmark Hill	d	17 17											17 37				17 44		17 47			
Beckenham Junction	d								17 10						17 25							
Kent House	d								17 12						17 27							
Penge East	d								17 14						17 29							
Sydenham Hill	d								17 18						17 33							
West Dulwich	d								17 20						17 35							
Herne Hill	d								17 23		17 27				17 38	17 42						
Loughborough Jn.	d										17 30					17 45						
Elephant & Castle ⊖	d	17 24									17 34		17 44			17 49			17 54			
London Blackfriars ⊖	d	17a29	17 34							17 37	17 39	17 42	17 49			17 54		17 57	17a59	18 04		
City Thameslink	a		17 36							17 38	17 41	17 43	17 51			17 56		17 58		18 06		
Farringdon ⊖	a		17 38							17 41	17 43	17 46	17 53			17 58		18 01		18 08		
St Pancras International ⊖	a		17 43							17 45	17 48	17 50	17 58			18 03		18 05		18 13		
Kentish Town ⊖	a										17 53		18 03			18 08						
Brixton ⊖	d								17 26						17 41							
London Victoria ⊖	a							17 23	17 33					17 38	17 48		17 55					

A From Sutton (Surrey) to St Albans City
B From Gravesend
C From Gatwick Airport to Bedford
D From Rainham Kt to Luton
E From Hastings to London Charing Cross
F To London Cannon Street
G To London Charing Cross
H From Tunbridge Wells to London Charing Cross
I From Dover Priory
J From Ramsgate
K From Horsham to Peterborough
L From Brighton to Bedford
M From Canterbury West
N From Brighton to Cambridge
O From Ashford International

Saturdays

26 May to 8 December

Sevenoaks and Otford, Orpington, Bromley South, Beckenham Junction, Catford - London

Station		SE A	SE ◇1 B	SE ◇1 C	SE ◇1 D	SE	TL 1 E	TL F	TL 1 G	TL	SE ◇1 H	SE	SE I	TL 1 J	TL F	TL 1 K	TL	TL L	SE ◇1 M	SE N	SE A	SE ◇1 B	SE ◇1 C
Sevenoaks	d	17 05	17 13														17 22		17 29		17 35	17 43	
Bat & Ball	d																17 25						
Otford	d										17 26						17 29						
Shoreham (Kent)	d																17 32						
Eynsford	d																17 35						
Swanley	d			17 17							17 37						17 41						
St Mary Cray	d			17 22													17 45						
Orpington	d	17 20	17a21			17 24				17 33									17a37	17 41	17 50	17a51	
Petts Wood	d	17a23				17 27				17 36										17 44	17a53		
Bickley	d					17 31				17 40							17 50						
Bromley South	d			17 30	17 33	17 34				17 43	17 47	17 49					17 53						18 03
Shortlands	d					17 37				17 45		17 52					17 55						
Ravensbourne	d									17 48							17 58						
Beckenham Hill	d									17 50							18 00						
Bellingham	d									17 52							18 02						
Catford	d									17 55							18 05						
Crofton Park	d									17 58							18 08						
Lewisham	a																			18 02			
	d												18 02										
Nunhead	d									18 01			18 07				18 11						
Peckham Rye	d									18 04			18 10				18 14						
Denmark Hill	d			17 50						18 07			18 14				18 17						
Beckenham Junction	d					17 40						17 55											
Kent House	d					17 42						17 57											
Penge East	d					17 44						17 59											
Sydenham Hill	d					17 48						18 03											
West Dulwich	d					17 50						18 05											
Herne Hill	d					17 53		17 57				18 08			18 12								
Loughborough Jn.	d							18 00							18 15								
Elephant & Castle ⊖	d							18 04		18 14					18 19		18 24						
London Blackfriars ⊖	d						18 07	18 09	18 12	18 19				18 22	18 24	18 27	18a29	18 34					
City Thameslink	a						18 08	18 11	18 13	18 21				18 23	18 26	18 28		18 36					
Farringdon ⊖	a						18 11	18 13	18 16	18 23				18 26	18 28	18 31		18 38					
St Pancras International ⊖	a						18 15	18 18	18 20	18 28				18 30	18 33	18 35		18 43					
Kentish Town ⊖	a							18 23		18 33					18 38								
Brixton ⊖	d					17 56						18 11											
London Victoria ⊖	a			18 00	17 53	18 03					18 08	18 18	18 25										18 23

Station		SE	TL 1 E	TL F	TL 1 G	TL	SE ◇1 O	SE	TL F	SE I	TL 1 K	TL	TL L	SE ◇1 M	SE N	SE A	SE ◇1 B	SE ◇1 C	SE ◇1 D	SE	TL 1 E	TL F	TL 1 G
Sevenoaks	d											17 52		17 59		18 05	18 13						
Bat & Ball	d											17 55											
Otford	d						17 56					17 59											
Shoreham (Kent)	d											18 02											
Eynsford	d											18 05											
Swanley	d						18 05					18 11						18 17					
St Mary Cray	d						18 09					18 15						18 22					
Orpington	d	17 54				18 03								18a07	18 11	18 20	18a21			18 24			
Petts Wood	d	17 57				18 06									18 14	18a23				18 27			
Bickley	d	18 01				18 10						18 20								18 31			
Bromley South	d	18 04				18 13	18 17	18 19				18 23						18 30	18 33	18 34			
Shortlands	d	18 07				18 15		18 22				18 25								18 37			
Ravensbourne	d					18 18						18 28											
Beckenham Hill	d					18 20						18 30											
Bellingham	d					18 22						18 32											
Catford	d					18 25						18 35											
Crofton Park	d					18 28						18 38											
Lewisham	a														18 32								
	d									18 32													
Nunhead	d					18 31				18 37		18 41											
Peckham Rye	d					18 34				18 40		18 44											
Denmark Hill	d					18 37				18 44		18 47						18 50					
Beckenham Junction	d	18 10						18 25												18 40			
Kent House	d	18 12						18 27												18 42			
Penge East	d	18 14						18 29												18 44			
Sydenham Hill	d	18 18						18 33												18 48			
West Dulwich	d	18 20						18 35												18 50			
Herne Hill	d	18 23		18 27				18 38	18 42											18 53		18 57	
Loughborough Jn.	d			18 30					18 45													19 00	
Elephant & Castle ⊖	d			18 34		18 44			18 49			18 54										19 04	
London Blackfriars ⊖	d		18 37	18 39	18 42	18 49			18 54		18 57	18a59	19 04								19 07	19 09	19 12
City Thameslink	a		18 38	18 41	18 43	18 51			18 56		18 58		19 06								19 08	19 11	19 13
Farringdon ⊖	a		18 41	18 43	18 46	18 53			18 58		19 01		19 08								19 11	19 13	19 16
St Pancras International ⊖	a		18 45	18 48	18 50	18 58			19 03		19 05		19 13								19 15	19 18	19 20
Kentish Town ⊖	a			18 53		19 03			19 08													19 23	
Brixton ⊖	d	18 26						18 41												18 56			
London Victoria ⊖	a	18 33					18 38	18 48		18 55								19 00	18 53	19 03			

A To London Charing Cross
B From Tunbridge Wells to London Charing Cross
C From Dover Priory
D From Ramsgate
E From Horsham to Peterborough
F From Sutton (Surrey) to St Albans City
G From Brighton to Bedford
H From Canterbury West
I From Gravesend
J From Brighton to Cambridge
K From Gatwick Airport to Bedford
L From Rainham Kt to Luton
M From Hastings to London Charing Cross
N To London Cannon Street
O From Ashford International

Table 195R

Saturdays

26 May to 8 December

Sevenoaks and Otford, Orpington, Bromley South, Beckenham Junction, Catford - London

		TL		SE ◇1 A	SE	SE B	TL 1 C	TL D	TL 1 E	TL	TL F	SE ◇1 G		SE H	SE I	SE ◇1 J	SE ◇1 K	SE	TL 1 L	TL D	TL 1 M	TL		SE ◇1 N	SE
Sevenoaks	d									18 22		18 29			18 35	18 43									
Bat & Ball	d									18 25															
Otford	d			18 26						18 29														18 56	
Shoreham (Kent)	d									18 32															
Eynsford	d									18 35															
Swanley	d			18 37						18 41														19 05	
St Mary Cray	d									18 45														19 09	
Orpington	d	18 33										18a37		18 41	18 50	18a51		18 54				19 03			
Petts Wood	d	18 36												18 44	18a53			18 57				19 06			
Bickley	d	18 40								18 50								19 01				19 10			
Bromley South	d	18 43		18 47	18 49					18 53							19 03	19 04				19 13		19 17	19 19
Shortlands	d	18 45			18 52					18 55								19 07				19 15			19 22
Ravensbourne	d	18 48								18 58												19 18			
Beckenham Hill	d	18 50								19 00												19 20			
Bellingham	d	18 52								19 02												19 22			
Catford	d	18 55								19 05												19 25			
Crofton Park	d	18 58								19 08												19 28			
Lewisham	a													19 02											
	d					19 02																			
Nunhead	d	19 01				19 07				19 11												19 31			
Peckham Rye	d	19 04				19 10				19 14												19 34			
Denmark Hill	d	19 07				19 14				19 17												19 37			
Beckenham Junction	d				18 55													19 10							19 25
Kent House	d				18 57													19 12							19 27
Penge East	d				18 59													19 14							19 29
Sydenham Hill	d				19 03													19 18							19 33
West Dulwich	d				19 05													19 20							19 35
Herne Hill	d				19 08			19 12										19 23		19 27					19 38
Loughborough Jn.	d							19 15												19 30					
Elephant & Castle ⊖	d	19 14						19 19		19 24										19 34		19 44			
London Blackfriars ⊖	d	19 19					19 22	19 24	19 27	19a29	19 34								19 37	19 39	19 42	19 49			
City Thameslink	a	19 21					19 23	19 26	19 28		19 36								19 38	19 41	19 43	19 51			
Farringdon ⊖	a	19 23					19 26	19 28	19 31		19 38								19 41	19 43	19 46	19 53			
St Pancras International ⊖	a	19 28					19 30	19 33	19 35		19 43								19 45	19 48	19 50	19 58			
Kentish Town ⊖	a	19 33						19 38												19 53		20 03			
Brixton ⊖	d				19 11													19 26							19 41
London Victoria ⊖	a			19 08	19 18	19 25											19 23	19 33						19 38	19 48

		TL D	SE B	TL 1 E	TL	TL F	SE ◇1 G	SE H		SE I	SE ◇1 J	SE ◇1 K	SE ◇1 O	SE	TL 1 L	TL D	TL 1 M	TL		SE ◇1 A	SE	SE B	TL 1 C	TL D	TL 1 E
Sevenoaks	d				18 52		18 59			19 05	19 13														
Bat & Ball	d				18 55																				
Otford	d				18 59															19 26					
Shoreham (Kent)	d				19 02																				
Eynsford	d				19 05																				
Swanley	d				19 11							19 17								19 37					
St Mary Cray	d				19 15							19 22													
Orpington	d						19a07	19 11		19 20	19a21			19 24				19 33							
Petts Wood	d							19 14		19a23				19 27				19 36							
Bickley	d				19 20									19 31				19 40							
Bromley South	d				19 23							19 30	19 33	19 34				19 43		19 47	19 49				
Shortlands	d				19 25									19 37				19 45			19 52				
Ravensbourne	d				19 28													19 48							
Beckenham Hill	d				19 30													19 50							
Bellingham	d				19 32													19 52							
Catford	d				19 35													19 55							
Crofton Park	d				19 38													19 58							
Lewisham	a							19 32																	
	d		19 32																			20 02			
Nunhead	d		19 37		19 41													20 01				20 07			
Peckham Rye	d		19 40		19 44													20 04				20 10			
Denmark Hill	d		19 44		19 47							19 50						20 07				20 14			
Beckenham Junction	d													19 40							19 55				
Kent House	d													19 42							19 57				
Penge East	d													19 44							19 59				
Sydenham Hill	d													19 48							20 03				
West Dulwich	d													19 50							20 05				
Herne Hill	d	19 42												19 53		19 57					20 08			20 12	
Loughborough Jn.	d	19 45														20 00								20 15	
Elephant & Castle ⊖	d	19 49			19 54											20 04		20 14						20 19	
London Blackfriars ⊖	d	19 54		19 57	19a59	20 04									20 07	20 09	20 12	20 19					20 22	20 24	20 27
City Thameslink	a	19 56		19 58		20 06									20 08	20 11	20 13	20 21					20 23	20 26	20 28
Farringdon ⊖	a	19 58		20 01		20 08									20 11	20 13	20 16	20 23					20 26	20 28	20 31
St Pancras International ⊖	a	20 03		20 05		20 13									20 15	20 18	20 20	20 28					20 30	20 33	20 35
Kentish Town ⊖	a	20 08														20 23		20 33						20 38	
Brixton ⊖	d													19 56							20 11				
London Victoria ⊖	a		19 55									20 00	19 53	20 03						20 08	20 18	20 25			

A From Canterbury West
B From Gravesend
C From Brighton to Cambridge
D From Sutton (Surrey) to St Albans City
E From Gatwick Airport to Bedford
F From Rainham Kt to Luton
G From Hastings to London Charing Cross
H To London Cannon Street
I To London Charing Cross
J From Tunbridge Wells to London Charing Cross
K From Dover Priory
L From Horsham to Peterborough
M From Brighton to Bedford
N From Ashford International
O From Ramsgate

Table 195R

Saturdays

26 May to 8 December

Sevenoaks and Otford, Orpington, Bromley South, Beckenham Junction, Catford - London

		TL	TL A	SE ◇1 B		SE C	SE D	SE ◇1 E	SE ◇1 F	SE	TL 1 G	TL H	TL 1 I	TL		SE ◇1 J	SE	TL H	SE K	TL 1 L	TL	TL A	SE ◇1 B	SE C	
Sevenoaks	d	19 22		19 29			19 35	19 43													19 52		19 59		
Bat & Ball	d	19 25																			19 55				
Otford	d	19 29														19 56					19 59				
Shoreham (Kent)	d	19 32																			20 02				
Eynsford	d	19 35																			20 05				
Swanley	d	19 41														20 05					20 11				
St Mary Cray	d	19 45														20 09					20 15				
Orpington	d			19a37		19 41	19 50	19a51		19 54				20 03									20a07	20 11	
Petts Wood	d					19 44	19a53			19 57				20 06										20 14	
Bickley	d	19 50								20 01				20 10							20 20				
Bromley South	d	19 53							20 03	20 04				20 13		20 17	20 19				20 23				
Shortlands	d	19 55								20 07				20 15			20 22				20 25				
Ravensbourne	d	19 58												20 18							20 28				
Beckenham Hill	d	20 00												20 20							20 30				
Bellingham	d	20 02												20 22							20 32				
Catford	d	20 05												20 25							20 35				
Crofton Park	d	20 08												20 28							20 38				
Lewisham	a					20 02																		20 32	
	d																		20 32						
Nunhead	d	20 11												20 31					20 37		20 41				
Peckham Rye	d	20 14												20 34					20 40		20 44				
Denmark Hill	d	20 17												20 37					20 44		20 47				
Beckenham Junction	d									20 10							20 25								
Kent House	d									20 12							20 27								
Penge East	d									20 14							20 29								
Sydenham Hill	d									20 18							20 33								
West Dulwich	d									20 20							20 35								
Herne Hill	d									20 23		20 27					20 38	20 42							
Loughborough Jn.	d											20 30						20 45							
Elephant & Castle ⊖	d	20 24										20 34		20 44				20 49			20 54				
London Blackfriars ⊖	d	20a29	20 34								20 37	20 39	20 42	20 49				20 54		20 57	20a59	21 04			
City Thameslink	a		20 36								20 38	20 41	20 43	20 51				20 56		20 58					
Farringdon ⊖	a		20 38								20 41	20 43	20 46	20 53				20 58		21 01		21 08			
St Pancras International ⊖	a		20 43								20 45	20 48	20 50	20 58				21 03		21 05		21 13			
Kentish Town ⊖	a											20 53		21 03				21 08							
Brixton ⊖	d									20 26							20 41								
London Victoria ⊖	a								20 23	20 33						20 38	20 48		20 55						

		SE D	SE ◇1 E	SE ◇1 F	SE ◇1 M	SE	TL 1 G	TL H	TL 1 I	TL		SE ◇1 N	SE	SE C	SE K	TL 1 O	TL H	TL 1 L	TL	TL A		SE D	SE ◇1 E	SE ◇1 F	SE
Sevenoaks	d	20 05	20 13																20 22			20 35	20 43		
Bat & Ball	d																		20 25						
Otford	d											20 26							20 29						
Shoreham (Kent)	d																		20 32						
Eynsford	d																		20 35						
Swanley	d			20 17								20 37							20 41						
St Mary Cray	d			20 22															20 45						
Orpington	d	20 20	20a21			20 24				20 33				20 41								20 50	20a51		20 54
Petts Wood	d	20a23				20 27				20 36				20 44								20a53			20 57
Bickley	d					20 31				20 40									20 50						21 01
Bromley South	d			20 30	20 33	20 34				20 43		20 47	20 49						20 53					21 03	21 04
Shortlands	d					20 37				20 45			20 52						20 55						21 07
Ravensbourne	d									20 48									20 58						
Beckenham Hill	d									20 50									21 00						
Bellingham	d									20 52									21 02						
Catford	d									20 55									21 05						
Crofton Park	d									20 58									21 08						
Lewisham	a													21 02											
	d														21 02										
Nunhead	d									21 01					21 07				21 11						
Peckham Rye	d									21 04					21 10				21 14						
Denmark Hill	d			20 50						21 07					21 14				21 17						
Beckenham Junction	d					20 40							20 55												21 10
Kent House	d					20 42							20 57												21 12
Penge East	d					20 44							20 59												21 14
Sydenham Hill	d					20 48							21 03												21 18
West Dulwich	d					20 50							21 05												21 20
Herne Hill	d					20 53		20 57					21 08				21 12								21 23
Loughborough Jn.	d							21 00									21 15								
Elephant & Castle ⊖	d							21 04		21 14							21 19		21 24						
London Blackfriars ⊖	d						21 07	21 09	21 12	21 19						21 22	21 24	21 27	21a29	21 34					
City Thameslink	a																								
Farringdon ⊖	a						21 11	21 13	21 16	21 23						21 26	21 28	21 31		21 38					
St Pancras International ⊖	a						21 15	21 18	21 20	21 28						21 30	21 33	21 35		21 43					
Kentish Town ⊖	a							21 23		21 33							21 38								
Brixton ⊖	d					20 56							21 11												21 26
London Victoria ⊖	a			21 00	20 53	21 03						21 08	21 18		21 25									21 23	21 33

A From Rainham Kt to Luton
B From Hastings to London Charing Cross
C To London Cannon Street
D To London Charing Cross
E From Tunbridge Wells to London Charing Cross
F From Dover Priory
G From Horsham to Peterborough
H From Sutton (Surrey) to St Albans City
I From Brighton to Bedford
J From Ashford International
K From Gravesend
L From Gatwick Airport to Bedford
M From Ramsgate
N From Canterbury West
O From Brighton to Cambridge

Sevenoaks and Otford, Orpington, Bromley South, Beckenham Junction, Catford - London

		TL ■ A	TL B	TL ■ C	TL	SE ◇■ D		SE	TL B	SE E	TL ■ F	TL	TL G	SE ◇■ H	SE I	SE J		SE ◇■ K	SE ◇■ L	SE ◇■ M	SE	TL ■ A	TL B	TL ■ C	TL
Sevenoaks ■	d											20 52		20 59		21 05		21 13							
Bat & Ball	d											20 55													
Otford ■	d					20 56						20 59													
Shoreham (Kent)	d											21 02													
Eynsford	d											21 05													
Swanley ■	d					21 05						21 11							21 17						
St Mary Cray	d					21 09						21 15							21 22						
Orpington ■	d				21 03									21a07	21 11	21 20		21a21			21 24				21 33
Petts Wood ■	d				21 06										21 14	21a23					21 27				21 36
Bickley ■	d				21 10							21 20									21 31				21 40
Bromley South ■	d				21 13	21 17		21 19				21 23							21 30	21 33	21 34				21 43
Shortlands ■	d				21 15			21 22				21 25									21 37				21 45
Ravensbourne	d				21 18							21 28													21 48
Beckenham Hill	d				21 20							21 30													21 50
Bellingham	d				21 22							21 32													21 52
Catford	d				21 25							21 35													21 55
Crofton Park	d				21 28							21 38													21 58
Lewisham ■	a														21 32										
	d									21 32															
Nunhead ■	d				21 31					21 37		21 41													22 01
Peckham Rye ■	d				21 34					21 40		21 44													22 04
Denmark Hill ■	d				21 37					21 44		21 47							21 50						22 07
Beckenham Junction ■	d							21 25													21 40				
Kent House ■	d							21 27													21 42				
Penge East	d							21 29													21 44				
Sydenham Hill	d							21 33													21 48				
West Dulwich	d							21 35													21 50				
Herne Hill ■	d		21 27					21 38	21 42												21 53		21 57		
Loughborough Jn	d		21 30						21 45														22 00		
Elephant & Castle ⊖	d		21 34		21 44				21 49			21 54											22 04		22 14
London Blackfriars ■ ⊖	d	21 37	21 39	21 42	21 49				21 54		21 57	21a59	22 04									22 07	22 09	22 12	22 19
City Thameslink ■	a																								
Farringdon ⊖	a	21 41	21 43	21 46	21 53				21 58		22 01		22 08									22 11	22 13	22 16	22 23
St Pancras International ■ ⊖	a	21 45	21 48	21 50	21 58				22 03		22 05		22 13									22 15	22 18	22 20	22 28
Kentish Town ⊖	a		21 53		22 03				22 08														22 23		22 33
Brixton ⊖	d							21 41													21 56				
London Victoria ■ ⊖	a					21 38		21 48		21 55									22 00	21 53	22 03				

		SE ◇■ N		SE	SE I	SE E	TL ■ O	TL P	TL ■ F	TL	TL Q	SE J		SE ◇■ K	SE ◇■ L	SE	TL ■ A	TL P	TL ■ C	TL R	SE ◇■ D	SE		TL P	SE E
Sevenoaks ■	d									21 22		21 35		21 43											
Bat & Ball	d									21 25															
Otford ■	d	21 26								21 29											21 56				
Shoreham (Kent)	d									21 32															
Eynsford	d									21 35															
Swanley ■	d	21 37								21 41											22 05				
St Mary Cray	d									21 45											22 09				
Orpington ■	d				21 41							21 50		21a51		21 54				22 03					
Petts Wood ■	d				21 44							21a53				21 57				22 06					
Bickley ■	d									21 50						22 01				22 10					
Bromley South ■	d	21 47		21 49						21 53					22 03	22 04				22 13	22 17	22 19			
Shortlands ■	d			21 52						21 55						22 07				22 15		22 22			
Ravensbourne	d									21 58										22 18					
Beckenham Hill	d									22 00										22 20					
Bellingham	d									22 02										22 22					
Catford	d									22 05										22 25					
Crofton Park	d									22 08										22 28					
Lewisham ■	a				22 02																				
	d					22 02																			22 32
Nunhead ■	d					22 07				22 11										22 31					22 37
Peckham Rye ■	d					22 10				22 14										22 34					22 40
Denmark Hill ■	d					22 14				22 17										22 37					22 44
Beckenham Junction ■	d			21 55												22 10						22 25			
Kent House ■	d			21 57												22 12						22 27			
Penge East	d			21 59												22 14						22 29			
Sydenham Hill	d			22 03												22 18						22 33			
West Dulwich	d			22 05												22 20						22 35			
Herne Hill ■	d			22 08				22 12								22 23		22 27				22 38		22 44	
Loughborough Jn	d							22 15										22 30						22 47	
Elephant & Castle ⊖	d							22 19		22 24								22 34		22 44				22 51	
London Blackfriars ■ ⊖	d						22 22	22 24	22 27	22a29	22 34						22 37	22 39	22 42	22 49				22 59	
City Thameslink ■	a																								
Farringdon ⊖	a						22 26	22 28	22 31		22 38						22 41	22 43	22 46	22 53				23 03	
St Pancras International ■ ⊖	a						22 30	22 33	22 35		22 43						22 45	22 48	22 50	22 58				23 08	
Kentish Town ⊖	a							22 38										22 53						23 13	
Brixton ⊖	d			22 11												22 26						22 41			
London Victoria ■ ⊖	a	22 08		22 18		22 25									22 23	22 33					22 38	22 48			22 55

A From Horsham to Peterborough
B From Sutton (Surrey) to St Albans City
C From Brighton to Bedford
D From Ashford International
E From Gravesend
F From Gatwick Airport to Bedford
G From Rainham Kt to Luton
H From Hastings to London Charing Cross
I To London Cannon Street
J To London Charing Cross
K From Tunbridge Wells to London Charing Cross
L From Dover Priory
M From Ramsgate
N From Canterbury West
O From Brighton to Cambridge
P From Sutton (Surrey) to Bedford
Q From Rainham Kt to West Hampstead Thameslink
R To West Hampstead Thameslink

Sevenoaks and Otford, Orpington, Bromley South, Beckenham Junction, Catford - London

		TL	TL A	SE ◇■ B	SE C	SE D	SE ◇■ E	SE ◇■ F		SE	TL ■ G	TL ■ H	TL I	TL	TL ■ J	SE ◇■ K	SE	TL I		SE C	SE L	TL	TL A	SE D	SE ◇■ E
Sevenoaks ■	d	21 52		21 59		22 05	22 13															22 22		22 35	22 43
Bat & Ball	d	21 55																				22 25			
Otford ■	d	21 59														22 26						22 29			
Shoreham (Kent)	d	22 02																				22 32			
Eynsford	d	22 05																				22 35			
Swanley ■	d	22 11														22 37						22 41			
St Mary Cray	d	22 15																				22 45			
Orpington ■	d			22a07	22 11	22 20	22a22			22 24				22 33						22 41				22 50	22a51
Petts Wood ■	d				22 14	22a23				22 27				22 36						22 44				22a53	
Bickley ■	d	22 20								22 31				22 40								22 50			
Bromley South ■	d	22 23						22 33		22 34				22 43		22 47	22 49					22 53			
Shortlands ■	d	22 25								22 37				22 45			22 52					22 55			
Ravensbourne	d	22 28												22 48								22 58			
Beckenham Hill	d	22 30												22 50								23 00			
Bellingham	d	22 32												22 52								23 02			
Catford	d	22 35												22 55								23 05			
Crofton Park	d	22 38												22 58								23 08			
Lewisham ■	a				22 32															23 02					
	d																				23 02				
Nunhead ■	d	22 41												23 01							23 07	23 11			
Peckham Rye ■	d	22 44												23 04							23 10	23 14			
Denmark Hill ■	d	22 47												23 07							23 14	23 17			
Beckenham Junction ■	d									22 40							22 55								
Kent House ■	d									22 42							22 57								
Penge East	d									22 44							22 59								
Sydenham Hill	d									22 48							23 03								
West Dulwich	d									22 50							23 05								
Herne Hill ■	d									22 53			23 04				23 08	23 14							
Loughborough Jn	d												23 07					23 17							
Elephant & Castle ⊖	d	22 54											23 11	23 15				23 21				23 24			
London Blackfriars ■ ⊖	d	22a59	23 04								23 07	23 12	23 17	23a19	23 22			23 27				23a29	23 34		
City Thameslink ■	a																								
Farringdon ⊖	a		23 08								23 11	23 16	23 21		23 26			23 31					23 38		
St Pancras International ■ ⊖	a		23 13								23 15	23 20	23 25		23 30			23 35					23 43		
Kentish Town ⊖	a												23 30					23 40							
Brixton ⊖	d									22 56							23 11								
London Victoria ■ ⊖	a							22 52		23 03						23 08	23 18				23 25				

		SE ◇■ M	SE	TL ■ G		TL ■ H	TL I	TL	SE ◇■ N	SE	TL I	SE L	TL	SE ◇■ B		SE C	SE D	SE ◇■ F	SE	TL I	TL	SE ◇■ E	SE D	SE ◇■ N	
Sevenoaks ■	d												22 52	22 59			23 05				23 22	23 27	23 35		
Bat & Ball	d												22 55								23 25				
Otford ■	d								22 56				22 59								23 29			23 36	
Shoreham (Kent)	d												23 02								23 32				
Eynsford	d												23 05								23 35				
Swanley ■	d	22 47							23 05				23 11								23 41			23 45	
St Mary Cray	d	22 52							23 09				23 15								23 45			23 49	
Orpington ■	d		22 54					23 03						23a07		23 11	23 20		23 24			23a35	23 50		
Petts Wood ■	d		22 57					23 06								23 14	23a23		23 27				23 53		
Bickley ■	d		23 01					23 10					23 20						23 31		23 50				
Bromley South ■	d	23 00	23 04					23 13	23 17	23 19			23 23					23 33	23 34		23 53			23 56	
Shortlands ■	d		23 07					23 15		23 22			23 25						23 37		23 55				
Ravensbourne	d							23 18					23 28								23 58				
Beckenham Hill	d							23 20					23 30								00 01				
Bellingham	d							23 22					23 32								00 03				
Catford	d							23 25					23 35								00 06				
Crofton Park	d							23 28					23 38								00 08				
Lewisham ■	a															23 32							00 10		
	d											23 32													
Nunhead ■	d							23 31				23 37	23 41								00 11				
Peckham Rye ■	d							23 34				23 40	23 44								00 14				
Denmark Hill ■	d	23 20						23 37				23 44	23 47								00 17				
Beckenham Junction ■	d		23 10							23 25									23 40						
Kent House ■	d		23 12							23 27									23 42						
Penge East	d		23 14							23 29									23 44						
Sydenham Hill	d		23 18							23 33									23 48						
West Dulwich	d		23 20							23 35									23 50						
Herne Hill ■	d		23 23				23 34			23 38	23 44								23 53	23 57					
Loughborough Jn	d						23 37				23 47														
Elephant & Castle ⊖	d						23 41	23 44			23 54		23 55							00 04	00 24				
London Blackfriars ■ ⊖	d			23 37		23 42	23 49	23a49			00 02		23a59							00 09	00a29				
City Thameslink ■	a																								
Farringdon ⊖	a			23 41		23 46	23 53				00 06									00 13					
St Pancras International ■ ⊖	a			23 45		23 50	23 57				00 10									00 17					
Kentish Town ⊖	a						00 01													00 22					
Brixton ⊖	d		23 26							23 41									23 56						
London Victoria ■ ⊖	a	23 30	23 33						23 39	23 48		23 55						23 52	00 03					00 15	

A From Rainham Kt to West Hampstead Thameslink
B From Hastings to London Charing Cross
C To London Cannon Street
D To London Charing Cross
E From Tunbridge Wells to London Charing Cross
F From Ramsgate
G From Horsham to Peterborough
H From Brighton to Bedford
I From Sutton (Surrey) to Bedford
J From Brighton to Cambridge
K From Canterbury West
L From Gravesend
M From Dover Priory
N From Ashford International

Table 195R

Saturdays
26 May to 8 December

Sevenoaks and Otford, Orpington, Bromley South, Beckenham Junction, Catford - London

		SE ◇■ A	SE
Sevenoaks	d		
Bat & Ball	d		
Otford	d		
Shoreham (Kent)	d		
Eynsford	d		
Swanley	d	23 53	
St Mary Cray	d	23 57	
Orpington	d		23 54
Petts Wood	d		23 57
Bickley	d		00 01
Bromley South	d	00 04	00 04
Shortlands	d		00 07
Ravensbourne	d		
Beckenham Hill	d		
Bellingham	d		
Catford	d		
Crofton Park	d		
Lewisham	a		
	d		
Nunhead	d		
Peckham Rye	d		
Denmark Hill	d		
Beckenham Junction	d		00 10
Kent House	d		00 12
Penge East	d		00 14
Sydenham Hill	d		00 18
West Dulwich	d		00 20
Herne Hill	d		00 23
Loughborough Jn.	d		
Elephant & Castle ⊖	d		
London Blackfriars ⊖	d		
City Thameslink	a		
Farringdon ⊖	a		
St Pancras International ⊖	a		
Kentish Town ⊖	a		
Brixton ⊖	d		00 26
London Victoria ⊖	a	00 24	00 33

Sundays
20 May to 2 December

		TL B	SE ◇■ C	SE D	TL B	SE	TL ■ E	TL F	TL ■ G	TL ■ E		TL ■ E	TL ■ H	TL	SE I	SE	SE ◇■ J	SE K	TL	SE I		SE	SE ◇■ L	SE ◇■ M	SE K
Sevenoaks	d																			07 04			07 17		
Bat & Ball	d																								
Otford	d																								
Shoreham (Kent)	d																								
Eynsford	d																								
Swanley	d																07 13								
St Mary Cray	d																07 18								
Orpington	d													06 46	06 49	06 54			07 16	07 19		07 24	07a25		
Petts Wood	d													06 49	06 52	06 57			07 19	07 22		07 27			
Bickley	d			00 01										06 57		07 01			07 26			07 31			
Bromley South	d		00 04	00 04		00 19								07 01		07 04	07 26		07 29			07 34		07 48	
Shortlands	d			00 07										07 03		07 07			07 31			07 37			
Ravensbourne	d													07 06					07 34						
Beckenham Hill	d							00 01						07 08					07 36						
Bellingham	d							00 03						07 10					07 38						
Catford	d							00 06						07 13					07 41						
Crofton Park	d							00 08						07 16					07 44						
Lewisham	a														07 09					07 39					
	d																	07 32							08 02
Nunhead	d							00 11						07 19				07 37	07 47						08 07
Peckham Rye	d							00 14						07 22				07 40	07 50						08 10
Denmark Hill	d							00 17						07 25			07 38	07 42	07 53						08 12
Beckenham Junction	d			00 10												07 10						07 40			
Kent House	d			00 12												07 12						07 42			
Penge East	d			00 14												07 14						07 44			
Sydenham Hill	d			00 18												07 18						07 48			
West Dulwich	d			00 20												07 20						07 50			
Herne Hill	d			00 23												07 23						07 53			
Loughborough Jn.	d																								
Elephant & Castle ⊖	d				00 04			00 24																	
London Blackfriars ⊖	d	00 02			00 09		00 22	00a29	00 37	00 50		01 06	01 36												
City Thameslink	a																								
Farringdon ⊖	a	00 06			00 13		00 26		00 41																
St Pancras International ⊖	a	00 10			00 17		00 30		00 45	00 59		01 15	01 45												
Kentish Town ⊖	a				00 22					01 05			01 50												
Brixton ⊖	d			00 26												07 26						07 56			
London Victoria ⊖	a		00 24	00 33		00 37								07 36		07 35	07 48	07 54	08 06			08 04		08 09	08 24

A From Dover Priory
B not 20 May. From Sutton (Surrey) to Bedford
C not 20 May. From Dover Priory
D not 20 May. From Orpington
E not 20 May. From Brighton to Bedford
F not 20 May. From Sevenoaks
G not 20 May. From Horsham to Hitchin
H From Brighton to Bedford
I To London Charing Cross
J From Gillingham (Kent)
K From Dartford
L From Ashford International to London Charing Cross
M From Faversham

Table 195R

Sundays
20 May to 2 December

Sevenoaks and Otford, Orpington, Bromley South, Beckenham Junction, Catford - London

		TL	SE ◇■ A	SE B	SE	SE ◇■ C		SE ◇■ D	SE E	TL	SE B	SE	SE ◇■ C	SE ◇■ F	SE ◇■ G	SE H		TL ■ I	TL	TL ■ J	SE ◇■ K	SE B	SE	SE ◇■ L	SE ◇■ M
Sevenoaks	d	07 28	07 31	07 34		07 47				07 58	08 04		08 17						08 28		08 31	08 34		08 47	
Bat & Ball	d	07 31								08 01									08 31						
Otford	d	07 35								08 05					08 31				08 35						
Shoreham (Kent)	d	07 38								08 08									08 38						
Eynsford	d	07 41								08 11									08 41						
Swanley	d	07 47						08 13		08 17					08 42				08 47						09 13
St Mary Cray	d	07 51						08 18		08 21					08 46				08 51						09 18
Orpington	d		07a39	07 49	07 54	07a55					08 19	08 24	08a25								08a39	08 49	08 54	08a55	
Petts Wood	d			07 52	07 57						08 22	08 27										08 52	08 57		
Bickley	d	07 56			08 01					08 26		08 31							08 56				09 01		
Bromley South	d	07 59			08 04			08 26		08 29		08 34		08 48	08 52				08 59				09 04		09 26
Shortlands	d	08 01			08 07					08 31		08 37							09 01				09 07		
Ravensbourne	d	08 04								08 34									09 04						
Beckenham Hill	d	08 06								08 36									09 06						
Bellingham	d	08 08								08 38									09 08						
Catford	d	08 11								08 41									09 11						
Crofton Park	d	08 14								08 44									09 14						
Lewisham	a			08 09							08 39											09 09			
	d								08 32							09 02									
Nunhead	d	08 17							08 37	08 47						09 07			09 17						
Peckham Rye	d	08 20							08 40	08 50						09 10			09 20						
Denmark Hill	d	08 23						08 38	08 42	08 53						09 12			09 23						09 38
Beckenham Junction	d				08 10							08 40											09 10		
Kent House	d				08 12							08 42											09 12		
Penge East	d				08 14							08 44											09 14		
Sydenham Hill	d				08 18							08 48											09 18		
West Dulwich	d				08 20							08 50											09 20		
Herne Hill	d				08 23							08 53											09 23		
Loughborough Jn.	d																								
Elephant & Castle ⊖	d																		09 30						
London Blackfriars ⊖	d																	09 31	09a34	09 39					
City Thameslink	a																								
Farringdon ⊖	a																	09 35		09 43					
St Pancras International ⊖	a																	09 39		09 47					
Kentish Town ⊖	a																								
Brixton ⊖	d				08 26							08 56											09 26		
London Victoria ⊖	a	08 36			08 34			08 48	08 54	09 06		09 04		09 09	09 13	09 24							09 34		09 48

		SE H		TL ■ N	TL O	TL ■ P	TL	TL Q	SE ◇■ K	SE B	SE	SE ◇■ R		SE ◇■ F	SE ◇■ G	SE H	TL ■ J	TL ■ N	TL O	TL ■ I	TL	TL Q		SE ◇■ K	SE B
Sevenoaks	d						08 58		09 01	09 04		09 17									09 28			09 31	09 34
Bat & Ball	d						09 01														09 31				
Otford	d						09 05								09 31						09 35				
Shoreham (Kent)	d						09 08														09 38				
Eynsford	d						09 11														09 41				
Swanley	d						09 17								09 42						09 47				
St Mary Cray	d						09 21								09 46						09 51				
Orpington	d								09a09	09 19	09 24	09a25												09a39	09 49
Petts Wood	d									09 22	09 27														09 52
Bickley	d						09 26				09 31										09 56				
Bromley South	d						09 29				09 34			09 48	09 52						09 59				
Shortlands	d						09 31				09 37										10 01				
Ravensbourne	d						09 34														10 04				
Beckenham Hill	d						09 36														10 06				
Bellingham	d						09 38														10 08				
Catford	d						09 41														10 11				
Crofton Park	d						09 44														10 14				
Lewisham	a									09 39															10 09
	d	09 32														10 02									
Nunhead	d	09 37					09 47									10 07					10 17				
Peckham Rye	d	09 40					09 50									10 10					10 20				
Denmark Hill	d	09 42					09 53									10 12					10 23				
Beckenham Junction	d										09 40														
Kent House	d										09 42														
Penge East	d										09 44														
Sydenham Hill	d										09 48														
West Dulwich	d										09 50														
Herne Hill	d				09 45						09 53								10 15						
Loughborough Jn.	d				09 48														10 18						
Elephant & Castle ⊖	d				09 53		10 00												10 23		10 30				
London Blackfriars ⊖	d			09 55	09 58	10 01	10a04	10 05									10 09	10 25	10 28	10 31	10a34	10 35			
City Thameslink	a																								
Farringdon ⊖	a			09 59	10 02	10 05		10 09									10 13	10 29	10 32	10 35		10 39			
St Pancras International ⊖	a			10 03	10 06	10 09		10 13									10 17	10 33	10 36	10 39		10 43			
Kentish Town ⊖	a				10 11			10 18											10 41			10 48			
Brixton ⊖	d										09 56														
London Victoria ⊖	a	09 54									10 04			10 05	10 13	10 24									

A From Tonbridge to London Charing Cross
B To London Charing Cross
C From Ashford International to London Charing Cross
D From Faversham
E From Grove Park C.S.D.
F From Dover Priory
G From Ashford International
H From Dartford
I From Gatwick Airport to Cambridge
J From Three Bridges to Bedford
K From Hastings to London Charing Cross
L From Ramsgate to London Charing Cross
M From Faversham Down Reception
N From Brighton to Bedford
O From Sutton (Surrey) to Luton
P From Horsham to Peterborough
Q From Rainham Kt
R From Dover Priory to London Charing Cross

Sevenoaks and Otford, Orpington, Bromley South, Beckenham Junction, Catford - London

	SE	SE	SE	SE	TL	TL	TL	TL	TL	TL	SE	SE	SE	SE	SE	SE	SE	TL	TL	TL	TL	TL
		◇■	◇■		■	■		■			◇■			◇■	◇■	◇■		■	■		■	
		A	B	C	D	E	F	G		H	I	J		K	L	M	C	N	E	F	O	
Sevenoaks d		09 47							09 58		10 01	10 04		10 17								10 28
Bat & Ball d									10 01													10 31
Otford d									10 05							10 31						10 35
Shoreham (Kent) d									10 08													10 38
Eynsford d									10 11													10 41
Swanley d			10 13						10 17							10 42						10 47
St Mary Cray d			10 18						10 21							10 46						10 51
Orpington d	09 54	09a55									10a09	10 19	10 24	10a25								
Petts Wood d	09 57											10 22	10 27									
Bickley d	10 01								10 26				10 31									10 56
Bromley South d	10 04		10 26						10 29				10 34		10 48	10 52						10 59
Shortlands d	10 07								10 31				10 37									11 01
Ravensbourne d									10 34													11 04
Beckenham Hill d									10 36													11 06
Bellingham d									10 38													11 08
Catford d									10 41													11 11
Crofton Park d									10 44													11 14
Lewisham a												10 39										
d				10 32													11 02					
Nunhead d				10 37					10 47								11 07					11 17
Peckham Rye d				10 40					10 50								11 10					11 20
Denmark Hill d			10 38	10 42					10 53								11 12					11 23
Beckenham Junction d	10 10												10 40									
Kent House d	10 12												10 42									
Penge East d	10 14												10 44									
Sydenham Hill d	10 18												10 48									
West Dulwich d	10 20												10 50									
Herne Hill d	10 23						10 45						10 53							11 15		
Loughborough Jn. d							10 48													11 18		
Elephant & Castle ⊖ d							10 53		11 00											11 23		11 30
London Blackfriars ⊖ d					10 39	10 55	10 58	11 01	11a04	11 05								11 09	11 25	11 28	11 31	11a34
City Thameslink a																						
Farringdon ⊖ a					10 43	10 59	11 02	11 05		11 09								11 13	11 29	11 32	11 35	
St Pancras International ⊖ a					10 47	11 03	11 06	11 09		11 13								11 17	11 33	11 36	11 39	
Kentish Town ⊖ a							11 11			11 18										11 41		
Brixton ⊖ d	10 26												10 56									
London Victoria ⊖ a	10 34		10 48	10 54									11 04		11 05	11 13	11 24					

	TL	SE	SE	SE	SE	SE	SE	TL	TL	TL	TL	TL	TL	SE	SE	SE	SE	SE	SE	SE	TL
		◇■			◇■	◇■		■	■		■			◇■			◇■	◇■	◇■		■
	H	I	J		A	B	C	D	E	P	G		H	I	J		K	L	M	C	N
Sevenoaks d		10 31	10 34		10 47							10 58		11 01	11 04		11 17				
Bat & Ball d												11 01									
Otford d												11 05							11 31		
Shoreham (Kent) d												11 08									
Eynsford d												11 11									
Swanley d						11 13						11 17							11 42		
St Mary Cray d						11 18						11 21							11 46		
Orpington d		10a39	10 49	10 54	10a55									11a09	11 19	11 24	11a25				
Petts Wood d			10 52	10 57											11 22	11 27					
Bickley d				11 01								11 26				11 31					
Bromley South d				11 04		11 26						11 29				11 34		11 48	11 52		
Shortlands d				11 07								11 31				11 37					
Ravensbourne d												11 34									
Beckenham Hill d												11 36									
Bellingham d												11 38									
Catford d												11 41									
Crofton Park d												11 44									
Lewisham a			11 09												11 39						
d							11 32													12 02	
Nunhead d							11 37					11 47								12 07	
Peckham Rye d							11 40					11 50								12 10	
Denmark Hill d						11 38	11 42					11 53								12 12	
Beckenham Junction d				11 10												11 40					
Kent House d				11 12												11 42					
Penge East d				11 14												11 44					
Sydenham Hill d				11 18												11 48					
West Dulwich d				11 20												11 50					
Herne Hill d				11 23						11 45						11 53					
Loughborough Jn. d										11 48											
Elephant & Castle ⊖ d										11 53		12 00									
London Blackfriars ⊖ d	11 35							11 39	11 55	11 58	12 01	12a04	12 05								12 09
City Thameslink a																					
Farringdon ⊖ a	11 39							11 43	11 59	12 02	12 05		12 09								12 13
St Pancras International ⊖ a	11 43							11 47	12 03	12 06	12 09		12 13								12 17
Kentish Town ⊖ a	11 48									12 11			12 18								
Brixton ⊖ d				11 26												11 56					
London Victoria ⊖ a				11 34		11 48	11 54									12 04		12 05	12 13	12 24	

A From Ramsgate to London Charing Cross
B From Canterbury East
C From Dartford
D From Three Bridges to Bedford
E From Brighton to Bedford
F From Sutton (Surrey) to Luton
G From Horsham to Peterborough
H From Rainham Kt
I From Hastings to London Charing Cross
J To London Charing Cross
K From Dover Priory to London Charing Cross
L From Dover Priory
M From Canterbury West
N From Gatwick Airport to Bedford
O From Gatwick Airport to Cambridge
P From Sutton (Surrey) to St Albans City

Table 195R

Sundays

20 May to 2 December

Sevenoaks and Otford, Orpington, Bromley South, Beckenham Junction, Catford - London

	TL	TL	TL	TL	TL	TL	SE	SE	SE	SE	SE	SE	TL	TL	TL	TL	TL	TL	TL	SE	SE	SE
		■		■			◇■			◇■	◇■		■		■		■			◇■		
	A	B	C	D		E	F	G		H	I	J	K	A	B	C	L		E	F	G	
Sevenoaks d					11 28		11 31	11 34		11 47								11 58		12 01	12 04	
Bat & Ball d					11 31													12 01				
Otford d					11 35													12 05				
Shoreham (Kent) d					11 38													12 08				
Eynsford d					11 41													12 11				
Swanley d					11 47						12 13							12 17				
St Mary Cray d					11 51						12 18							12 21				
Orpington d							11a39	11 49	11 54	11a55										12a09	12 19	12 24
Petts Wood d								11 52	11 57												12 22	12 27
Bickley d					11 56				12 01									12 26				12 31
Bromley South d					11 59				12 04		12 26							12 29				12 34
Shortlands d					12 01				12 07									12 31				12 37
Ravensbourne d					12 04													12 34				
Beckenham Hill d					12 06													12 36				
Bellingham d					12 08													12 38				
Catford d					12 11													12 41				
Crofton Park d					12 14													12 44				
Lewisham a								12 09													12 39	
d												12 32										
Nunhead d					12 17							12 37						12 47				
Peckham Rye d					12 20							12 40						12 50				
Denmark Hill d					12 23						12 38	12 42						12 53				
Beckenham Junction d									12 10													12 40
Kent House d									12 12													12 42
Penge East d									12 14													12 44
Sydenham Hill d									12 18													12 48
West Dulwich d									12 20													12 50
Herne Hill d	12 03		12 15						12 23					12 33		12 45						12 53
Loughborough Jn. d	12 06		12 18											12 36		12 48						
Elephant & Castle ⊖ d	12 11		12 23		12 30									12 41		12 53		13 00				
London Blackfriars ⊖ d	12 16	12 25	12 28	12 31	12a34	12 35							12 41	12 46	12 55	12 58	13 01	13a04	13 05			
City Thameslink a																						
Farringdon ⊖ a	12 20	12 29	12 32	12 35		12 39							12 45	12 50	12 59	13 02	13 05		13 09			
St Pancras International ⊖ a	12 24	12 33	12 36	12 39		12 43							12 49	12 54	13 03	13 06	13 09		13 13			
Kentish Town ⊖ a			12 41			12 48										13 11			13 18			
Brixton ⊖ d									12 26													12 56
London Victoria ⊖ a									12 34		12 48	12 54										13 04

	SE	SE	SE	SE	TL	TL	TL	TL	TL	TL	TL	SE	SE	SE	SE	SE	SE	TL	TL	TL	TL	TL
	◇■	◇■	◇■		■		■		■			◇■			◇■	◇■		■		■		■
	M	N	O	J	P	A	B	C	D		E	F	G		H	I	J	K	A	B	C	L
Sevenoaks d	12 17									12 28		12 31	12 34		12 47							
Bat & Ball d										12 31												
Otford d			12 31							12 35												
Shoreham (Kent) d										12 38												
Eynsford d										12 41												
Swanley d			12 42							12 47						13 13						
St Mary Cray d			12 46							12 51						13 18						
Orpington d	12a25											12a39	12 49	12 54	12a55							
Petts Wood d													12 52	12 57								
Bickley d										12 56				13 01								
Bromley South d		12 48	12 52							12 59				13 04		13 26						
Shortlands d										13 01				13 07								
Ravensbourne d										13 04												
Beckenham Hill d										13 06												
Bellingham d										13 08												
Catford d										13 11												
Crofton Park d										13 14												
Lewisham a													13 09									
d				13 02													13 32					
Nunhead d				13 07						13 17							13 37					
Peckham Rye d				13 10						13 20							13 40					
Denmark Hill d				13 12						13 23						13 38	13 42					
Beckenham Junction d														13 10								
Kent House d														13 12								
Penge East d														13 14								
Sydenham Hill d														13 18								
West Dulwich d														13 20								
Herne Hill d						13 03		13 15						13 23					13 33		13 45	
Loughborough Jn. d						13 06		13 18											13 36		13 48	
Elephant & Castle ⊖ d						13 11		13 23		13 30									13 41		13 53	
London Blackfriars ⊖ d					13 09	13 16	13 25	13 28	13 31	13a34	13 35							13 39	13 46	13 55	13 58	14 01
City Thameslink a																						
Farringdon ⊖ a					13 13	13 20	13 29	13 32	13 35		13 39							13 43	13 50	13 59	14 02	14 05
St Pancras International ⊖ a					13 17	13 24	13 33	13 36	13 39		13 43							13 47	13 54	14 03	14 06	14 09
Kentish Town ⊖ a								13 41			13 48										14 11	
Brixton ⊖ d														13 26								
London Victoria ⊖ a		13 05	13 13	13 24										13 34		13 48	13 54					

A From Sutton (Surrey) to Luton
B From Brighton to Bedford
C From Sutton (Surrey) to St Albans City
D From Gatwick Airport to Cambridge
E From Rainham Kt
F From Hastings to London Charing Cross
G To London Charing Cross
H From Ramsgate to London Charing Cross
I From Canterbury East
J From Dartford
K From Three Bridges to Bedford
L From Horsham to Peterborough
M From Dover Priory to London Charing Cross
N From Dover Priory
O From Canterbury West
P From Gatwick Airport to Bedford

Sevenoaks and Otford, Orpington, Bromley South, Beckenham Junction, Catford - London

		TL		TL	SE	SE	SE	SE	SE	SE	SE	TL		TL	TL	TL	TL	TL	TL	SE	SE	SE		SE	SE
					◇■			◇■	◇■	◇■		■			■		■			◇■				◇■	◇■
				A	B	C		D	E	F	G	H		I	J	K	L		A	B	C			M	N
Sevenoaks	d	12 58			13 01	13 04		13 17										13 28		13 31	13 34			13 47	
Bat & Ball	d	13 01																13 31							
Otford	d	13 05								13 31								13 35							
Shoreham (Kent)	d	13 08																13 38							
Eynsford	d	13 11																13 41							
Swanley	d	13 17								13 42								13 47							14 13
St Mary Cray	d	13 21								13 46								13 51							14 18
Orpington	d				13a09	13 19	13 24	13a25												13a39	13 49	13 54		13a55	
Petts Wood	d					13 22	13 27														13 52	13 57			
Bickley	d	13 26					13 31											13 56				14 01			
Bromley South	d	13 29					13 34		13 48	13 52								13 59				14 04			14 26
Shortlands	d	13 31					13 37											14 01				14 07			
Ravensbourne	d	13 34																14 04							
Beckenham Hill	d	13 36																14 06							
Bellingham	d	13 38																14 08							
Catford	d	13 41																14 11							
Crofton Park	d	13 44																14 14							
Lewisham	a					13 39															14 09				
	d										14 02														
Nunhead	d	13 47									14 07							14 17							
Peckham Rye	d	13 50									14 10							14 20							
Denmark Hill	d	13 53									14 12							14 23							14 38
Beckenham Junction	d						13 40															14 10			
Kent House	d						13 42															14 12			
Penge East	d						13 44															14 14			
Sydenham Hill	d						13 48															14 18			
West Dulwich	d						13 50															14 20			
Herne Hill	d						13 53							14 03		14 15						14 23			
Loughborough Jn.	d													14 06		14 18									
Elephant & Castle ⊖	d	14 00												14 11		14 23		14 30							
London Blackfriars ⊖	d	14a04		14 05								14 09		14 16	14 25	14 28	14 31	14a34	14 35						
City Thameslink	a																								
Farringdon ⊖	a			14 09								14 13		14 20	14 29	14 32	14 35		14 39						
St Pancras International ⊖	a			14 13								14 17		14 24	14 33	14 36	14 39		14 43						
Kentish Town ⊖	a			14 18												14 41			14 48						
Brixton ⊖	d						13 56															14 26			
London Victoria ⊖	a						14 04		14 05	14 13	14 24											14 34			14 48

		SE	TL	TL	TL	TL	TL	TL		TL	SE	SE	SE	SE	SE	SE	SE	TL		TL	TL	TL	TL	TL	TL
			■		■		■				◇■			◇■	◇■	◇■		■			■		■		
		G	O	I	J	K	P			A	B	C		D	E	F	G	H		I	J	K	L		A
Sevenoaks	d							13 58			14 01	14 04		14 17										14 28	
Bat & Ball	d							14 01																14 31	
Otford	d							14 05								14 31								14 35	
Shoreham (Kent)	d							14 08																14 38	
Eynsford	d							14 11																14 41	
Swanley	d							14 17								14 42								14 47	
St Mary Cray	d							14 21								14 46								14 51	
Orpington	d										14a09	14 19	14 24	14a25											
Petts Wood	d											14 22	14 27												
Bickley	d							14 26					14 31											14 56	
Bromley South	d							14 29					14 34		14 48	14 52								14 59	
Shortlands	d							14 31					14 37											15 01	
Ravensbourne	d							14 34																15 04	
Beckenham Hill	d							14 36																15 06	
Bellingham	d							14 38																15 08	
Catford	d							14 41																15 11	
Crofton Park	d							14 44																15 14	
Lewisham	a											14 39													
	d	14 32															15 02								
Nunhead	d	14 37						14 47									15 07							15 17	
Peckham Rye	d	14 40						14 50									15 10							15 20	
Denmark Hill	d	14 42						14 53									15 12							15 23	
Beckenham Junction	d												14 40												
Kent House	d												14 42												
Penge East	d												14 44												
Sydenham Hill	d												14 48												
West Dulwich	d												14 50												
Herne Hill	d			14 33		14 45							14 53							15 03		15 15			
Loughborough Jn.	d			14 36		14 48														15 06		15 18			
Elephant & Castle ⊖	d			14 41		14 53		15 00												15 11		15 23		15 30	
London Blackfriars ⊖	d		14 39	14 46	14 55	14 58	15 01	15a04		15 05								15 09		15 16	15 25	15 28	15 31	15a34	15 35
City Thameslink	a																								
Farringdon ⊖	a		14 43	14 50	14 59	15 02	15 05			15 09								15 13		15 20	15 29	15 32	15 35		15 39
St Pancras International ⊖	a		14 47	14 54	15 03	15 06	15 09			15 13								15 17		15 24	15 33	15 36	15 39		15 43
Kentish Town ⊖	a					15 11				15 18												15 41			15 48
Brixton ⊖	d												14 56												
London Victoria ⊖	a	14 54											15 04		15 05	15 13	15 24								

A From Rainham Kt
B From Hastings to London Charing Cross
C To London Charing Cross
D From Dover Priory to London Charing Cross
E From Dover Priory
F From Canterbury West
G From Dartford
H From Gatwick Airport to Bedford
I From Sutton (Surrey) to Luton
J From Brighton to Bedford
K From Sutton (Surrey) to St Albans City
L From Gatwick Airport to Cambridge
M From Ramsgate to London Charing Cross
N From Canterbury East
O From Three Bridges to Bedford
P From Horsham to Peterborough

Sevenoaks and Otford, Orpington, Bromley South, Beckenham Junction, Catford - London

		SE	SE	SE		SE	SE	SE	TL	TL	TL	TL	TL	TL		TL	SE	SE	SE	SE	SE	SE	SE	TL	
		◇■				◇■	◇■		■		■		■				◇■			◇■	◇■	◇■		■	
		A	B			C	D	E	F	G	H	I	J			K	A	B		L	M	N	E	O	
Sevenoaks	d	14 31	14 34			14 47								14 58			15 01	15 04		15 17					
Bat & Ball	d													15 01											
Otford	d													15 05								15 31			
Shoreham (Kent)	d													15 08											
Eynsford	d													15 11											
Swanley	d						15 13							15 17								15 42			
St Mary Cray	d						15 18							15 21								15 46			
Orpington	d	14a39	14 49	14 54		14a55											15a09	15 19	15 24	15a25					
Petts Wood	d		14 52	14 57														15 22	15 27						
Bickley	d			15 01										15 26					15 31						
Bromley South	d			15 04			15 26							15 29					15 34		15 48	15 52			
Shortlands	d			15 07										15 31					15 37						
Ravensbourne	d													15 34											
Beckenham Hill	d													15 36											
Bellingham	d													15 38											
Catford	d													15 41											
Crofton Park	d													15 44											
Lewisham	a		15 09															15 39							
	d							15 32															16 02		
Nunhead	d							15 37						15 47									16 07		
Peckham Rye	d							15 40						15 50									16 10		
Denmark Hill	d						15 38	15 42						15 53									16 12		
Beckenham Junction	d			15 10															15 40						
Kent House	d			15 12															15 42						
Penge East	d			15 14															15 44						
Sydenham Hill	d			15 18															15 48						
West Dulwich	d			15 20															15 50						
Herne Hill	d			15 23						15 33		15 45							15 53						
Loughborough Jn.	d									15 36		15 48													
Elephant & Castle ⊖	d									15 41		15 53		16 00											
London Blackfriars ⊖	d								15 39	15 46	15 55	15 58	16 01	16a04		16 05								16 09	
City Thameslink	a																								
Farringdon ⊖	a								15 43	15 50	15 59	16 02	16 05			16 09								16 13	
St Pancras International ⊖	a								15 47	15 54	16 03	16 06	16 09			16 13								16 17	
Kentish Town ⊖	a											16 11				16 18									
Brixton ⊖	d			15 26															15 56						
London Victoria ⊖	a			15 34			15 48	15 54											16 04		16 05	16 13	16 24		

		TL	TL	TL	TL	TL	TL	SE	SE	SE		SE	SE	SE	TL	TL	TL	TL	TL	TL		TL	SE	SE	SE
			■		■			◇■				◇■	◇■		■		■		■				◇■		
		G	H	I	P		K	A	B			C	D	E	F	G	H	I	J			K	A	B	
Sevenoaks	d					15 28		15 31	15 34			15 47								15 58			16 01	16 04	
Bat & Ball	d					15 31														16 01					
Otford	d					15 35														16 05					
Shoreham (Kent)	d					15 38														16 08					
Eynsford	d					15 41														16 11					
Swanley	d					15 47							16 13							16 17					
St Mary Cray	d					15 51							16 18							16 21					
Orpington	d							15a39	15 49	15 54		15a55											16a09	16 19	16 24
Petts Wood	d								15 52	15 57														16 22	16 27
Bickley	d					15 56				16 01										16 26					16 31
Bromley South	d					15 59				16 04			16 26							16 29					16 34
Shortlands	d					16 01				16 07										16 31					16 37
Ravensbourne	d					16 04														16 34					
Beckenham Hill	d					16 06														16 36					
Bellingham	d					16 08														16 38					
Catford	d					16 11														16 41					
Crofton Park	d					16 14														16 44					
Lewisham	a								16 09															16 39	
	d													16 32											
Nunhead	d					16 17								16 37						16 47					
Peckham Rye	d					16 20								16 40						16 50					
Denmark Hill	d					16 23							16 38	16 42						16 53					
Beckenham Junction	d									16 10															16 40
Kent House	d									16 12															16 42
Penge East	d									16 14															16 44
Sydenham Hill	d									16 18															16 48
West Dulwich	d									16 20															16 50
Herne Hill	d	16 03		16 15						16 23						16 33		16 45							16 53
Loughborough Jn.	d	16 06		16 18												16 36		16 48							
Elephant & Castle ⊖	d	16 11		16 23		16 30										16 41		16 53		17 00					
London Blackfriars ⊖	d	16 16	16 25	16 28	16 31	16a34	16 35								16 39	16 46	16 55	16 58	17 01	17a04		17 05			
City Thameslink	a																								
Farringdon ⊖	a	16 20	16 29	16 32	16 35		16 39								16 43	16 50	16 59	17 02	17 05			17 09			
St Pancras International ⊖	a	16 24	16 33	16 36	16 39		16 43								16 47	16 54	17 03	17 06	17 09			17 13			
Kentish Town ⊖	a			16 41			16 48											17 11				17 18			
Brixton ⊖	d									16 26															16 56
London Victoria ⊖	a									16 34			16 48	16 54											17 04

A From Hastings to London Charing Cross
B To London Charing Cross
C From Ramsgate to London Charing Cross
D From Canterbury East
E From Dartford
F From Three Bridges to Bedford
G From Sutton (Surrey) to Luton
H From Brighton to Bedford
I From Sutton (Surrey) to St Albans City
J From Horsham to Peterborough
K From Rainham Kt
L From Dover Priory to London Charing Cross
M From Dover Priory
N From Canterbury West
O From Gatwick Airport to Bedford
P From Gatwick Airport to Cambridge

Sevenoaks and Otford, Orpington, Bromley South, Beckenham Junction, Catford - London

		SE	SE	SE	SE	TL		TL	TL	TL	TL	TL	TL	SE	SE	SE		SE	SE	SE	TL	TL	TL	TL	TL
		◇1	◇1	◇1		1			1		1			◇1				◇1	◇1		1		1		1
		A	B	C	D	E		F	G	H	I		J	K	L			M	N	D	O	F	G	H	P
Sevenoaks	d	16 17										16 28		16 31	16 34			16 47							
Bat & Ball	d											16 31													
Otford	d			16 31								16 35													
Shoreham (Kent)	d											16 38													
Eynsford	d											16 41													
Swanley	d			16 42								16 47							17 13						
St Mary Cray	d			16 46								16 51							17 18						
Orpington	d	16a25												16a39	16 49	16 54		16a55							
Petts Wood	d														16 52	16 57									
Bickley	d											16 56				17 01									
Bromley South	d		16 48	16 52								16 59				17 04			17 26						
Shortlands	d											17 01				17 07									
Ravensbourne	d											17 04													
Beckenham Hill	d											17 06													
Bellingham	d											17 08													
Catford	d											17 11													
Crofton Park	d											17 14													
Lewisham	a														17 09										
	d				17 02															17 32					
Nunhead	d				17 07							17 17								17 37					
Peckham Rye	d				17 10							17 20								17 40					
Denmark Hill	d				17 12							17 23							17 38	17 42					
Beckenham Junction	d															17 10									
Kent House	d															17 12									
Penge East	d															17 14									
Sydenham Hill	d															17 18									
West Dulwich	d															17 20									
Herne Hill	d							17 03		17 15						17 23						17 33		17 45	
Loughborough Jn.	d							17 06		17 18												17 36		17 48	
Elephant & Castle ⊖	d							17 11		17 23		17 30										17 41		17 53	
London Blackfriars ⊖	d					17 09		17 16	17 25	17 28	17 31	17a34	17 35								17 39	17 46	17 55	17 58	18 01
City Thameslink	a																								
Farringdon ⊖	a					17 13		17 20	17 29	17 32	17 35		17 39								17 43	17 50	17 59	18 02	18 05
St Pancras International ⊖	a					17 17		17 24	17 33	17 36	17 39		17 43								17 47	17 54	18 03	18 06	18 09
Kentish Town ⊖	a									17 41			17 48											18 11	
Brixton ⊖	d															17 26									
London Victoria ⊖	a		17 05	17 13	17 24											17 34			17 48	17 54					

		TL		TL	SE	SE	SE	SE	SE	SE	SE	TL		TL	TL	TL	TL	TL	TL	SE	SE	SE		SE	SE
					◇1			◇1	◇1	◇1		1			1		1			◇1				◇1	◇1
				J	K	L		A	B	C	D	E		F	G	H	I		J	K	L			M	N
Sevenoaks	d	16 58			17 01	17 04		17 17										17 28		17 31	17 34			17 47	
Bat & Ball	d	17 01																17 31							
Otford	d	17 05								17 31								17 35							
Shoreham (Kent)	d	17 08																17 38							
Eynsford	d	17 11																17 41							
Swanley	d	17 17								17 42								17 47							18 13
St Mary Cray	d	17 21								17 46								17 51							18 18
Orpington	d				17a09	17 19	17 24	17a25												17a39	17 49	17 54		17a55	
Petts Wood	d					17 22	17 27														17 52	17 57			
Bickley	d	17 26					17 31											17 56				18 01			
Bromley South	d	17 29					17 34		17 48	17 52								17 59				18 04			18 26
Shortlands	d	17 31					17 37											18 01				18 07			
Ravensbourne	d	17 34																18 04							
Beckenham Hill	d	17 36																18 06							
Bellingham	d	17 38																18 08							
Catford	d	17 41																18 11							
Crofton Park	d	17 44																18 14							
Lewisham	a					17 39															18 09				
	d										18 02														
Nunhead	d	17 47									18 07							18 17							
Peckham Rye	d	17 50									18 10							18 20							
Denmark Hill	d	17 53									18 12							18 23							18 38
Beckenham Junction	d						17 40															18 10			
Kent House	d						17 42															18 12			
Penge East	d						17 44															18 14			
Sydenham Hill	d						17 48															18 18			
West Dulwich	d						17 50															18 20			
Herne Hill	d						17 53							18 03		18 15						18 23			
Loughborough Jn.	d													18 06		18 18									
Elephant & Castle ⊖	d	18 00												18 11		18 23		18 30							
London Blackfriars ⊖	d	18a04		18 05								18 09		18 16	18 25	18 28	18 31	18a34	18 35						
City Thameslink	a																								
Farringdon ⊖	a			18 09								18 13		18 20	18 29	18 32	18 35		18 39						
St Pancras International ⊖	a			18 13								18 17		18 24	18 33	18 36	18 39		18 43						
Kentish Town ⊖	a			18 18												18 41			18 48						
Brixton ⊖	d						17 56															18 26			
London Victoria ⊖	a						18 04		18 05	18 13	18 24											18 34			18 48

A From Dover Priory to London Charing Cross
B From Dover Priory
C From Canterbury West
D From Dartford
E From Gatwick Airport to Bedford
F From Sutton (Surrey) to Luton
G From Brighton to Bedford
H From Sutton (Surrey) to St Albans City
I From Gatwick Airport to Cambridge
J From Rainham Kt
K From Hastings to London Charing Cross
L To London Charing Cross
M From Ramsgate to London Charing Cross
N From Canterbury East
O From Three Bridges to Bedford
P From Horsham to Peterborough

Sevenoaks and Otford, Orpington, Bromley South, Beckenham Junction, Catford - London

		SE	TL	TL	TL	TL	TL	TL		TL	SE	SE	SE	SE	SE	SE	SE	TL		TL	TL	TL	TL	TL	TL
			1		1		1				◇1			◇1	◇1	◇1		1			1		1		
		A	B	C	D	E	F			G	H	I		J	K	L	A	M		C	D	E	N		G
Sevenoaks	d							17 58			18 01	18 04		18 17										18 28	
Bat & Ball	d							18 01																18 31	
Otford	d							18 05								18 31								18 35	
Shoreham (Kent)	d							18 08																18 38	
Eynsford	d							18 11																18 41	
Swanley	d							18 17								18 42								18 47	
St Mary Cray	d							18 21								18 46								18 51	
Orpington	d										18a09	18 19	18 24	18a25											
Petts Wood	d											18 22	18 27												
Bickley	d							18 26					18 31											18 56	
Bromley South	d							18 29					18 34		18 48	18 52								18 59	
Shortlands	d							18 31					18 37											19 01	
Ravensbourne	d							18 34																19 04	
Beckenham Hill	d							18 36																19 06	
Bellingham	d							18 38																19 08	
Catford	d							18 41																19 11	
Crofton Park	d							18 44																19 14	
Lewisham	a											18 39													
	d	18 32															19 02								
Nunhead	d	18 37						18 47									19 07							19 17	
Peckham Rye	d	18 40						18 50									19 10							19 20	
Denmark Hill	d	18 42						18 53									19 12							19 23	
Beckenham Junction	d												18 40												
Kent House	d												18 42												
Penge East	d												18 44												
Sydenham Hill	d												18 48												
West Dulwich	d												18 50												
Herne Hill	d			18 33		18 45							18 53							19 03		19 15			
Loughborough Jn.	d			18 36		18 48														19 06		19 18			
Elephant & Castle ⊖	d			18 41		18 53		19 00												19 11		19 23		19 30	
London Blackfriars ⊖	d		18 39	18 46	18 55	18 58	19 01	19a04		19 05								19 09		19 16	19 25	19 28	19 31	19a34	19 35
City Thameslink	a																								
Farringdon ⊖	a		18 43	18 50	18 59	19 02	19 05			19 09								19 13		19 20	19 29	19 32	19 35		19 39
St Pancras International ⊖	a		18 47	18 54	19 03	19 06	19 09			19 13								19 17		19 24	19 33	19 36	19 39		19 43
Kentish Town ⊖	a					19 11				19 18												19 41			19 48
Brixton ⊖	d												18 56												
London Victoria ⊖	a	18 54											19 04		19 05	19 13	19 24								

		SE	SE	SE		SE	SE	SE	TL	TL	TL	TL	TL	TL		TL	SE	SE	SE	SE	SE	SE	SE	TL	
		◇1				◇1	◇1		1		1		1				◇1			◇1	◇1	◇1		1	
		H	I			O	P	A	B	C	D	E	F			G	H	I		J	K	L	A	M	
Sevenoaks	d	18 31	18 34			18 47								18 58			19 01	19 04		19 17					
Bat & Ball	d													19 01											
Otford	d													19 05								19 31			
Shoreham (Kent)	d													19 08											
Eynsford	d													19 11											
Swanley	d						19 13							19 17								19 42			
St Mary Cray	d						19 18							19 21								19 46			
Orpington	d	18a39	18 49	18 54		18a55											19a09	19 19	19 24	19a25					
Petts Wood	d		18 52	18 57														19 22	19 27						
Bickley	d			19 01										19 26					19 31						
Bromley South	d			19 04			19 26							19 29					19 34		19 48	19 52			
Shortlands	d			19 07										19 31					19 37						
Ravensbourne	d													19 34											
Beckenham Hill	d													19 36											
Bellingham	d													19 38											
Catford	d													19 41											
Crofton Park	d													19 44											
Lewisham	a		19 09															19 39							
	d							19 32															20 02		
Nunhead	d							19 37						19 47									20 07		
Peckham Rye	d							19 40						19 50									20 10		
Denmark Hill	d						19 38	19 42						19 53									20 12		
Beckenham Junction	d			19 10															19 40						
Kent House	d			19 12															19 42						
Penge East	d			19 14															19 44						
Sydenham Hill	d			19 18															19 48						
West Dulwich	d			19 20															19 50						
Herne Hill	d			19 23						19 33		19 45							19 53						
Loughborough Jn.	d									19 36		19 48													
Elephant & Castle ⊖	d									19 41		19 53		20 00											
London Blackfriars ⊖	d								19 39	19 46	19 55	19 58	20 01	20a04		20 05								20 09	
City Thameslink	a																								
Farringdon ⊖	a								19 43	19 50	19 59	20 02	20 05			20 09								20 13	
St Pancras International ⊖	a								19 47	19 54	20 03	20 06	20 09			20 13								20 17	
Kentish Town ⊖	a											20 11				20 18									
Brixton ⊖	d			19 26															19 56						
London Victoria ⊖	a			19 34			19 48	19 54											20 04		20 05	20 13	20 24		

A From Dartford
B From Three Bridges to Bedford
C From Sutton (Surrey) to Luton
D From Brighton to Bedford
E From Sutton (Surrey) to St Albans City
F From Horsham to Peterborough
G From Rainham Kt
H From Hastings to London Charing Cross
I To London Charing Cross
J From Dover Priory to London Charing Cross
K From Dover Priory
L From Canterbury West
M From Gatwick Airport to Bedford
N From Gatwick Airport to Cambridge
O From Ramsgate to London Charing Cross
P From Canterbury East

Sevenoaks and Otford, Orpington, Bromley South, Beckenham Junction, Catford - London

		TL A	TL ■ B	TL C	TL ■ D	TL	TL E	SE ◇■ F	SE G	SE		SE ◇■ H	SE ◇■ I	SE J	TL ■ K	TL A	TL ■ B	TL C	TL ■ L	TL		TL E	SE ◇■ F	SE G	SE
Sevenoaks	d					19 28		19 31	19 34			19 47								19 58			20 01	20 04	
Bat & Ball	d					19 31														20 01					
Otford	d					19 35														20 05					
Shoreham (Kent)	d					19 38														20 08					
Eynsford	d					19 41														20 11					
Swanley	d					19 47							20 13							20 17					
St Mary Cray	d					19 51							20 18							20 21					
Orpington	d							19a39	19 49	19 54		19a55											20a09	20 19	20 24
Petts Wood	d								19 52	19 57														20 22	20 27
Bickley	d					19 56				20 01										20 26					20 31
Bromley South	d					19 59				20 04			20 26							20 29					20 34
Shortlands	d					20 01				20 07										20 31					20 37
Ravensbourne	d					20 04														20 34					
Beckenham Hill	d					20 06														20 36					
Bellingham	d					20 08														20 38					
Catford	d					20 11														20 41					
Crofton Park	d					20 14														20 44					
Lewisham	a								20 09															20 39	
	d													20 32											
Nunhead	d					20 17								20 37						20 47					
Peckham Rye	d					20 20								20 40						20 50					
Denmark Hill	d					20 23							20 38	20 42						20 53					
Beckenham Junction	d									20 10															20 40
Kent House	d									20 12															20 42
Penge East	d									20 14															20 44
Sydenham Hill	d									20 18															20 48
West Dulwich	d									20 20															20 50
Herne Hill	d	20 03		20 15						20 23						20 33		20 45							20 53
Loughborough Jn	d	20 06		20 18												20 36		20 48							
Elephant & Castle	d	20 11		20 23		20 30										20 41		20 53		21 00					
London Blackfriars	d	20 16	20 25	20 28	20 31	20a34	20 35								20 39	20 46	20 55	20 58	21 01	21a04		21 05			
City Thameslink	a																								
Farringdon	a	20 20	20 29	20 32	20 35		20 39								20 43	20 50	20 59	21 02	21 05			21 09			
St Pancras International	a	20 24	20 33	20 36	20 39		20 43								20 47	20 54	21 03	21 06	21 09			21 13			
Kentish Town	a			20 41			20 48											21 11				21 18			
Brixton	d									20 26															20 56
London Victoria	a									20 34			20 48	20 54											21 04

		SE ◇■ M	SE ◇■ N	SE ◇■ O	SE J	TL ■ P		TL A	TL ■ B	TL C	TL ■ D	TL	TL E	SE G	SE	SE ◇■ H		SE ◇■ I	SE J	TL ■ K	TL A	TL ■ B	TL Q	TL ■ L	TL
Sevenoaks	d	20 17										20 28		20 34		20 47									20 58
Bat & Ball	d											20 31													21 01
Otford	d			20 31								20 35													21 05
Shoreham (Kent)	d											20 38													21 08
Eynsford	d											20 41													21 11
Swanley	d			20 42								20 47						21 13							21 17
St Mary Cray	d			20 46								20 51						21 18							21 21
Orpington	d	20a25												20 49	20 54	20a55									
Petts Wood	d													20 52	20 57										
Bickley	d											20 56			21 01										21 26
Bromley South	d		20 48	20 52								20 59			21 04			21 26							21 29
Shortlands	d											21 01			21 07										21 31
Ravensbourne	d											21 04													21 34
Beckenham Hill	d											21 06													21 36
Bellingham	d											21 08													21 38
Catford	d											21 11													21 41
Crofton Park	d											21 14													21 44
Lewisham	a													21 09											
	d				21 02														21 32						
Nunhead	d				21 07							21 17							21 37						21 47
Peckham Rye	d				21 10							21 20							21 40						21 50
Denmark Hill	d				21 12							21 23						21 38	21 42						21 53
Beckenham Junction	d														21 10										
Kent House	d														21 12										
Penge East	d														21 14										
Sydenham Hill	d														21 18										
West Dulwich	d														21 20										
Herne Hill	d							21 03		21 15					21 23						21 33		21 45		
Loughborough Jn	d							21 06		21 18											21 36		21 48		
Elephant & Castle	d							21 11		21 23		21 30									21 41		21 53		22 00
London Blackfriars	d					21 09		21 16	21 25	21 28	21 31	21a34	21 35							21 39	21 46	21 55	21 58	22 01	22a04
City Thameslink	a																								
Farringdon	a					21 13		21 20	21 29	21 32	21 35		21 39							21 43	21 50	21 59	22 02	22 05	
St Pancras International	a					21 17		21 24	21 33	21 36	21 39		21 43							21 47	21 54	22 03	22 06	22 09	
Kentish Town	a									21 41			21 48										22 11		
Brixton	d														21 26										
London Victoria	a		21 05	21 13	21 24										21 34			21 48	21 54						

A From Sutton (Surrey) to Luton
B From Brighton to Bedford
C From Sutton (Surrey) to St Albans City
D From Gatwick Airport to Cambridge
E From Rainham Kt
F From Hastings to London Charing Cross
G To London Charing Cross
H From Ramsgate to London Charing Cross
I From Canterbury East
J From Dartford
K From Three Bridges to Bedford
L From Horsham to Peterborough
M From Dover Priory to London Charing Cross
N From Dover Priory
O From Canterbury West
P From Gatwick Airport to Bedford
Q From Sutton (Surrey) to Bedford

Sevenoaks and Otford, Orpington, Bromley South, Beckenham Junction, Catford - London

		TL A		SE ◇■ B	SE C	SE	SE ◇■ D	SE ◇■ E	SE ◇■ F	SE G	TL ■ H	TL I		TL ■ J	TL ■ K	TL	TL A	SE C	SE	SE ◇■ L	SE ◇■ M	SE G		TL ■ J	TL N
Sevenoaks	d			21 01	21 04		21 17									21 28		21 34		21 47					
Bat & Ball	d															21 31									
Otford	d								21 31							21 35									
Shoreham (Kent)	d															21 38									
Eynsford	d															21 41									
Swanley	d								21 42							21 47					22 13				
St Mary Cray	d								21 46							21 51					22 18				
Orpington	d			21a09	21 19	21 24	21a25											21 49	21 54	21a55					
Petts Wood	d				21 22	21 27												21 52	21 57						
Bickley	d					21 31										21 56			22 01						
Bromley South	d					21 34		21 48	21 52							21 59			22 04		22 26				
Shortlands	d					21 37										22 01			22 07						
Ravensbourne	d															22 04									
Beckenham Hill	d															22 06									
Bellingham	d															22 08									
Catford	d															22 11									
Crofton Park	d															22 14									
Lewisham	a				21 39													22 09							
	d									22 02												22 32			
Nunhead	d									22 07						22 17						22 37			
Peckham Rye	d									22 10						22 20						22 40			
Denmark Hill	d									22 12						22 23					22 38	22 42			
Beckenham Junction	d					21 40													22 10						
Kent House	d					21 42													22 12						
Penge East	d					21 44													22 14						
Sydenham Hill	d					21 48													22 18						
West Dulwich	d					21 50													22 20						
Herne Hill	d					21 53						22 03							22 23						22 45
Loughborough Jn	d											22 06													22 48
Elephant & Castle	d											22 11				22 30									22 53
London Blackfriars	d	22 05									22 09	22 16		22 25	22 31	22a34	22 35							22 55	22 58
City Thameslink	a																								
Farringdon	a	22 09									22 13	22 20		22 29	22 35		22 39							22 59	23 02
St Pancras International	a	22 13									22 17	22 24		22 33	22 39		22 43							23 03	23 06
Kentish Town	a	22 18															22 48								23 11
Brixton	d					21 56													22 26						
London Victoria	a					22 04		22 05	22 13	22 24									22 34		22 48	22 54			

		TL	TL O	SE ◇■ B	SE C	SE	SE ◇■ D	SE ◇■ E		SE ◇■ F	SE G	TL ■ P	TL N	TL ■ J	TL	TL Q	SE C	SE		SE ◇■ L	SE C	SE ◇■ M	SE	SE C	
Sevenoaks	d	21 58		22 01	22 04		22 17								22 28		22 34			22 47	23 04			23 34	
Bat & Ball	d	22 01													22 31										
Otford	d	22 05								22 31					22 35										
Shoreham (Kent)	d	22 08													22 38										
Eynsford	d	22 11													22 41										
Swanley	d	22 17								22 42					22 47							23 13			
St Mary Cray	d	22 21								22 46					22 51							23 18			
Orpington	d			22a09	22 19	22 24	22a25										22 49	22 54		22a55	23 19		23 24	23 49	
Petts Wood	d				22 22	22 27											22 52	22 57			23 22		23 27	23 52	
Bickley	d	22 26				22 31									22 56			23 01					23 31		
Bromley South	d	22 29				22 34		22 48		22 52					22 59			23 04				23 26	23 34		
Shortlands	d	22 31				22 37									23 01			23 07					23 37		
Ravensbourne	d	22 34													23 04										
Beckenham Hill	d	22 36													23 06										
Bellingham	d	22 38													23 08										
Catford	d	22 41													23 11										
Crofton Park	d	22 44													23 14										
Lewisham	a				22 39												23 09				23 39			00 09	
	d										23 02														
Nunhead	d	22 47									23 07				23 17										
Peckham Rye	d	22 50									23 10				23 20										
Denmark Hill	d	22 53									23 12				23 23							23 38			
Beckenham Junction	d					22 40												23 10					23 40		
Kent House	d					22 42												23 12					23 42		
Penge East	d					22 44												23 14					23 44		
Sydenham Hill	d					22 48												23 18					23 48		
West Dulwich	d					22 50												23 20					23 50		
Herne Hill	d					22 53							23 03					23 23					23 53		
Loughborough Jn	d												23 06												
Elephant & Castle	d	23 00											23 11		23 30										
London Blackfriars	d	23a04	23 05									23 12	23 16	23 27	23a34	23 37									
City Thameslink	a																								
Farringdon	a		23 09									23 16	23 20	23 31		23 41									
St Pancras International	a		23 13									23 20	23 24	23 35		23 45									
Kentish Town	a		23 18										23 29			23 50									
Brixton	d					22 56												23 26					23 56		
London Victoria	a					23 04		23 05		23 13	23 24							23 34				23 48	00 04		

A From Rainham Kt
B From Hastings to London Charing Cross
C To London Charing Cross
D From Dover Priory to London Charing Cross
E From Dover Priory
F From Ashford International
G From Dartford
H From Gatwick Airport to Bedford
I From Sutton (Surrey) to West Hampstead Thameslink
J From Brighton to Bedford
K From Gatwick Airport to Cambridge
L From Ramsgate to London Charing Cross
M From Canterbury East
N From Sutton (Surrey) to Bedford
O From Rainham Kt to West Hampstead Thameslink
P From Horsham to Peterborough
Q From Rainham Kt to Bedford

Table T196-F

Mondays to Fridays
21 May to 7 December

Cambridge, Kentish Town and London Thameslink-Denmark Hill-Catford-Bromley South-Swanley-Otford-Maidstone and Orpington and Sevenoaks

		TL	TL	TL	TL	TL	TL	TL	TL	TL		TL	SE ◇1	TL	TL	TL	TL	TL	TL	TL		TL	TL	TL	TL
Cambridge	d																								
Stevenage	d																								
Welwyn Garden City	d																								
Finsbury Park	d																								
Kentish Town	d					05 41		06 11																	
St Pancras International	d					05 47		06 17		06 47					07 17		07 47		08 17			08 47		09 17	
Farringdon	d					05 52		06 22		06 52					07 22		07 52		08 22			08 52		09 22	
City Thameslink	d					05 54		06 24		06 54					07 24		07 54		08 24			08 54		09 24	
London Blackfriars	d	04 56	05 16	05 26	05 46	05 56	06 16	06 26	06 46	06 56		07 16	07 23		07 26	07 46	07 56	08 16	08 26	08 46		08 56	09 16	09 26	09 46
London Bridge	a																								
Elephant & Castle	d	05 00	05 20	05 30	05 50	06 00	06 20	06 30	06 50	07 00		07 20	07 27		07 30	07 50	08 00	08 20	08 30	08 50		09 00	09 20	09 30	09 50
Denmark Hill	d	05 08	05 28	05 38	05 58	06 08	06 28	06 38	06 58	07 08		07 28	07 36	←	07 39	07 58	08 08	08 28	08 38	08 58		09 08	09 28	09 38	09 58
Peckham Rye	d	05 11	05 31	05 41	06 01	06 11	06 31	06 41	07 01	07 11		07 31		07 31	07 42	08 01	08 11	08 31	08 41	09 01		09 12	09 31	09 41	10 01
Nunhead	d	05 14	05 34	05 44	06 04	06 14	06 34	06 44	07 04	07 14		→		07 34	07 45	08 04	08 14	08 34	08 44	09 04		09 15	09 34	09 44	10 04
Crofton Park	d	05 17	05 37	05 47	06 07	06 17	06 37	06 47	07 07	07 17				07 37	07 48	08 07	08 17	08 37	08 47	09 07		09 18	09 37	09 47	10 07
Catford	d	05 20	05 40	05 50	06 10	06 20	06 40	06 50	07 10	07 20				07 40	07 51	08 10	08 20	08 40	08 50	09 10		09 21	09 40	09 50	10 10
Bellingham	d	05 23	05 43	05 53	06 13	06 23	06 43	06 53	07 13	07 23				07 43	07 54	08 13	08 23	08 43	08 53	09 13		09 24	09 43	09 53	10 13
Beckenham Hill	d	05 25	05 45	05 55	06 15	06 25	06 45	06 55	07 15	07 25				07 45	07 56	08 15	08 25	08 45	08 55	09 15		09 26	09 45	09 55	10 15
Ravensbourne	d	05 27	05 47	05 57	06 17	06 27	06 47	06 57	07 17	07 27				07 47	07 58	08 17	08 27	08 47	08 57	09 17		09 28	09 47	09 57	10 17
Shortlands	d	05 30	05 50	06 00	06 20	06 30	06 50	07 00	07 20	07 30				07 50	08 01	08 20	08 30	08 50	09 00	09 20		09 31	09 50	10 00	10 20
Bromley South	d	05 33	05 53	06 03	06 23	06 33	06 53	07 03	07 23	07 33			07 53	07 53	08 07	08 23	08 33	08 53	09 03	09 23		09 34	09 53	10 03	10 23
Bickley	d	05 36	05 56	06 06	06 26	06 36	06 56	07 06	07 26	07 36				07 56	08 10	08 26	08 36	08 56	09 06	09 26		09 37	09 56	10 06	10 26
Petts Wood	d	05 40		06 10		06 40		07 10		07 41					08 15		08 43		09 10			09 42		10 10	
Orpington	a	05 44		06 14		06 44		07 14		07 45					08 18		08 47		09 14			09 46		10 14	
St Mary Cray	d		06 01		06 31		07 01		07 32				07 59	08 02		08 31		09 01		09 32			10 01		10 31
Swanley	d		06 06		06 36		07 06		07 37				08 04	08 08		08 36		09 06		09 37			10 06		10 36
Eynsford	d		06 11		06 41		07 11		07 42					08 13		08 41		09 11		09 42			10 11		10 41
Shoreham (Kent)	d		06 15		06 45		07 15		07 46					08 17		08 45		09 15		09 46			10 15		10 45
Otford	d		06 18		06 48		07 18		07 49				08 12	08 20		08 48		09 18		09 49			10 18		10 48
Bat & Ball	d		06 21		06 51		07 21		07 52					08 23		08 51		09 21		09 52			10 21		10 51
Sevenoaks	a		06 25		06 55		07 25		07 56					08 26		08 55		09 25		09 56			10 25		10 55
Borough Green & Wrotham	d												08 22												
West Malling	d												08 28												
Maidstone East	a												08 42												
Bearsted	a																								
Ashford International	a																								

		TL	TL	TL	TL	TL		TL	TL	TL	TL		TL	TL	TL	TL	TL	TL	TL	TL	TL		TL	SE ◇1
Cambridge	d																							
Stevenage	d																							
Welwyn Garden City	d																							
Finsbury Park	d																							
Kentish Town	d			10 11		10 41			14 11		14 41			15 11		15 41		16 11		16 41			17 11	
St Pancras International	d	09 47		10 17		10 47			14 17		14 47			15 17		15 47		16 17		16 47			17 17	
Farringdon	d	09 52		10 22		10 52			14 22		14 52			15 22		15 52		16 22		16 52			17 22	
City Thameslink	d	09 54		10 24		10 54			14 24		14 54			15 24		15 54		16 24		16 54			17 24	
London Blackfriars	d	09 56	10 16	10 26	10 46	10 56		14 16	14 26	14 46	14 56		15 16	15 26	15 46	15 56	16 16	16 26	16 46	16 56	17 16		17 26	17 38
London Bridge	a																							
Elephant & Castle	d	10 00	10 20	10 30	10 50	11 00		14 20	14 30	14 50	15 00		15 20	15 30	15 50	16 00	16 20	16 30	16 50	17 00	17 20		17 30	17 42
Denmark Hill	d	10 08	10 28	10 38	10 58	11 08		14 28	14 38	14 58	15 08		15 28	15 38	15 58	16 08	16 28	16 38	16 58	17 08	17 28		17 38	
Peckham Rye	d	10 11	10 31	10 41	11 01	11 11		14 31	14 41	15 01	15 11		15 31	15 41	16 01	16 11	16 31	16 41	17 01	17 11	17 31		17 41	
Nunhead	d	10 14	10 34	10 44	11 04	11 14	and at	14 34	14 44	15 04	15 14		15 34	15 44	16 04	16 14	16 34	16 44	17 04	17 14	17 34		17 44	
Crofton Park	d	10 17	10 37	10 47	11 07	11 17	the same	14 37	14 47	15 07	15 17		15 37	15 47	16 07	16 17	16 37	16 47	17 07	17 17	17 37		17 47	
Catford	d	10 20	10 40	10 50	11 10	11 20	minutes	14 40	14 50	15 10	15 20		15 40	15 50	16 10	16 20	16 40	16 50	17 10	17 20	17 40		17 50	
Bellingham	d	10 23	10 43	10 53	11 13	11 23	past	14 43	14 53	15 13	15 23		15 43	15 53	16 13	16 23	16 43	16 53	17 13	17 23	17 43		17 53	
Beckenham Hill	d	10 25	10 45	10 55	11 15	11 25	each	14 45	14 55	15 15	15 25		15 45	15 55	16 15	16 25	16 45	16 55	17 15	17 25	17 45		17 55	
Ravensbourne	d	10 27	10 47	10 57	11 17	11 27	hour until	14 47	14 57	15 17	15 27		15 47	15 58	16 17	16 27	16 47	16 57	17 17	17 27	17 47		17 57	
Shortlands	d	10 30	10 50	11 00	11 20	11 30		14 50	15 00	15 20	15 30		15 50	16 00	16 20	16 30	16 50	17 00	17 20	17 30	17 50		18 00	
Bromley South	d	10 33	10 53	11 03	11 23	11 33		14 53	15 03	15 23	15 33		15 53	16 03	16 23	16 33	16 53	17 03	17 23	17 33	17 53		18 03	18 03
Bickley	d	10 37	10 56	11 06	11 26	11 36		14 56	15 06	15 26	15 36		15 56	16 06	16 26	16 36	16 56	17 06	17 26	17 36	17 56		18 06	
Petts Wood	d	10 42		11 10		11 40			15 10		15 40			16 11		16 40		17 10		17 42			18 12	
Orpington	a	10 45		11 14		11 44			15 14		15 44			16 14		16 44		17 14		17 45			18 16	
St Mary Cray	d		11 01		11 31			15 01		15 31			16 01		16 31		17 01		17 31		18 01			18 10
Swanley	d		11 06		11 36			15 06		15 36			16 06		16 36		17 06		17 36		18 06			18 14
Eynsford	d		11 11		11 41			15 11		15 41			16 11		16 41		17 11		17 41		18 11			
Shoreham (Kent)	d		11 15		11 45			15 15		15 45			16 15		16 45		17 15		17 45		18 15			
Otford	d		11 18		11 48			15 18		15 48			16 18		16 48		17 18		17 48		18 18			18 23
Bat & Ball	d		11 21		11 51			15 21		15 51			16 21		16 51		17 21		17 51		18 21			
Sevenoaks	a		11 25		11 55			15 25		15 55			16 25		16 55		17 25		17 55		18 25			
Borough Green & Wrotham	d																							18 33
West Malling	d																							18 39
Maidstone East	a																							18 50
Bearsted	a																							18 56
Ashford International	a																							19 24

Maidstone to Cambridge Service will be introduced in December 2019

Please note, Network Rail have stated that further updates to this timetable are possible during the validity period.

Table T196-F

Mondays to Fridays
21 May to 7 December

Cambridge, Kentish Town and London Thameslink-Denmark Hill-Catford-Bromley South-Swanley-Otford-Maidstone and Orpington and Sevenoaks

		TL	TL	TL	TL	TL	TL	SE ◇1		TL	TL	TL	TL	TL	TL	TL	TL	TL		TL	TL	TL	TL	TL	TL
Cambridge	d																								
Stevenage	d																								
Welwyn Garden City	d																								
Finsbury Park	d																								
Kentish Town	d		17 41		18 11		18 41					19 11		19 41		20 11		20 41			21 11		21 41		22 11
St Pancras International	d		17 47		18 17		18 47					19 17		19 47		20 17		20 47			21 17		21 47		22 17
Farringdon	d		17 52		18 22		18 52					19 22		19 52		20 22		20 52			21 22		21 52		22 22
City Thameslink	d		17 54		18 24		18 54					19 24		19 54		20 24		20 54			21 24		21 54		22 24
London Blackfriars	d	17 46	17 56	18 16	18 26	18 46	18 56	19 05			19 16	19 26	19 46	19 56	20 16	20 26	20 46	20 56		21 16	21 26	21 46	21 56	22 16	22 26
London Bridge	a																								
Elephant & Castle	d	17 50	18 00	18 20	18 30	18 50	19 00	19 09		←	19 20	19 30	19 50	20 00	20 20	20 30	20 50	21 00		21 20	21 30	21 50	22 00	22 20	22 30
Denmark Hill	d	17 58	18 08	18 28	18 38	18 58	19 08			19 08	19 28	19 39	19 58	20 08	20 28	20 38	20 58	21 08		21 28	21 38	21 58	22 08	22 28	22 38
Peckham Rye	d	18 01	18 11	18 31	18 41	19 01	→			19 11	19 31	19 42	20 01	20 11	20 31	20 41	21 01	21 11		21 31	21 41	22 01	22 11	22 31	22 41
Nunhead	d	18 04	18 14	18 34	18 44	19 04				19 14	19 34	19 45	20 04	20 14	20 34	20 44	21 04	21 14		21 34	21 44	22 04	22 14	22 34	22 44
Crofton Park	d	18 07	18 17	18 37	18 47	19 07				19 17	19 37	19 48	20 07	20 17	20 37	20 47	21 07	21 17		21 37	21 47	22 07	22 17	22 37	22 47
Catford	d	18 10	18 20	18 40	18 50	19 10				19 20	19 40	19 51	20 10	20 20	20 40	20 50	21 10	21 20		21 40	21 50	22 10	22 20	22 40	22 50
Bellingham	d	18 13	18 23	18 43	18 53	19 13				19 23	19 43	19 54	20 13	20 23	20 43	20 53	21 13	21 23		21 43	21 53	22 13	22 23	22 43	22 53
Beckenham Hill	d	18 15	18 25	18 45	18 55	19 15				19 25	19 45	19 56	20 15	20 25	20 45	20 55	21 15	21 25		21 45	21 55	22 15	22 25	22 45	22 55
Ravensbourne	d	18 17	18 27	18 47	18 57	19 17				19 27	19 47	19 58	20 17	20 27	20 47	20 57	21 17	21 27		21 47	21 57	22 17	22 27	22 47	22 57
Shortlands	d	18 20	18 30	18 50	19 00	19 20				19 30	19 50	20 01	20 20	20 30	20 50	21 00	21 20	21 30		21 50	22 00	22 20	22 30	22 50	23 00
Bromley South	d	18 23	18 33	18 53	19 03	19 23		19 27		19 33	19 53	20 04	20 23	20 33	20 53	21 03	21 23	21 33		21 53	22 03	22 23	22 33	22 53	23 03
Bickley	d	18 26	18 36	18 56	19 06	19 26				19 36	19 56	20 06	20 26	20 36	20 56	21 06	21 26	21 36		21 56	22 06	22 26	22 36	22 56	23 06
Petts Wood	d		18 44		19 10					19 40		20 11		20 40		21 10		21 40			22 10		22 40		23 10
Orpington	a		18 48		19 14					19 44		20 14		20 44		21 14		21 44			22 14		22 44		23 14
St Mary Cray	d	18 30		19 01		19 31		19 34			20 01		20 31		21 01		21 31			22 01		22 31		23 01	
Swanley	d	18 35		19 06		19 36		19 40			20 06		20 36		21 06		21 36			22 06		22 36		23 06	
Eynsford	d	18 40		19 11		19 41					20 11		20 41		21 11		21 41			22 11		22 41		23 11	
Shoreham (Kent)	d	18 44		19 15		19 45					20 15		20 45		21 15		21 45			22 15		22 45		23 15	
Otford	d	18 47		19 18		19 48		19 52			20 18		20 48		21 18		21 48			22 18		22 48		23 18	
Bat & Ball	d	18 50		19 21		19 51					20 21		20 51		21 21		21 51			22 21		22 51		23 21	
Sevenoaks	a	18 55		19 25		19 55					20 25		20 55		21 25		21 55			22 25		22 55		23 25	
Borough Green & Wrotham	d							19 59																	
West Malling	d							20 06																	
Maidstone East	a							20 16																	
Bearsted	a																								
Ashford International	a																								

		TL	TL	TL		TL
Cambridge	d					
Stevenage	d					
Welwyn Garden City	d					
Finsbury Park	d					
Kentish Town	d		22 41			
St Pancras International	d		22 47			
Farringdon	d		22 52			
City Thameslink	d		22 54			
London Blackfriars	d	22 46	22 56	23 16		23 46
London Bridge	a					
Elephant & Castle	d	22 50	23 00	23 20		23 50
Denmark Hill	d	22 58	23 08	23 28		23 58
Peckham Rye	d	23 01	23 11	23 31		00 01
Nunhead	d	23 04	23 14	23 34		00 04
Crofton Park	d	23 07	23 17	23 37		00 07
Catford	d	23 10	23 20	23 40		00 10
Bellingham	d	23 13	23 23	23 43		00 13
Beckenham Hill	d	23 15	23 25	23 45		00 15
Ravensbourne	d	23 17	23 27	23 47		00 17
Shortlands	d	23 20	23 30	23 50		00 20
Bromley South	d	23 23	23 33	23 53		00 23
Bickley	d	23 26	23 36	23 56		00 26
Petts Wood	d		23 40			
Orpington	a		23 44			
St Mary Cray	d	23 31		00 01		00 31
Swanley	d	23 36		00 06		00 36
Eynsford	d	23 41		00 11		00 41
Shoreham (Kent)	d	23 45		00 15		00 45
Otford	d	23 48		00 18		00 48
Bat & Ball	d	23 51		00 21		00 51
Sevenoaks	a	23 55		00 25		00 55
Borough Green & Wrotham	d					
West Malling	d					
Maidstone East	a					
Bearsted	a					
Ashford International	a					

Maidstone to Cambridge Service will be introduced in December 2019

Table T196-F

Saturdays
26 May to 8 December

Cambridge, Kentish Town and London Thameslink-Denmark Hill-Catford-Bromley South-Swanley-Otford-Maidstone and Orpington and Sevenoaks

		TL	and every 30 minutes until	TL	TL	TL	TL	TL	TL	TL	
Cambridge	d										
Stevenage	d										
Welwyn Garden City	d										
Finsbury Park	d										
Kentish Town	d						07 11		07 41		
St Pancras International	d						07 17		07 47		
Farringdon	d						07 22		07 52		
City Thameslink	d										
London Blackfriars	d	05 16		06 46	06 56	07 16	07 26	07 46	07 56	08 16	
London Bridge	a										
Elephant & Castle	d	05 20		06 50	07 00	07 20	07 30	07 50	08 00	08 20	
Denmark Hill	d	05 28		06 58	07 08	07 28	07 38	07 58	08 08	08 28	
Peckham Rye	d	05 31		07 01	07 11	07 31	07 41	08 01	08 11	08 31	
Nunhead	d	05 34		07 04	07 14	07 34	07 44	08 04	08 14	08 34	
Crofton Park	d	05 37		07 07	07 17	07 37	07 47	08 07	08 17	08 37	
Catford	d	05 40		07 10	07 20	07 40	07 50	08 10	08 20	08 40	
Bellingham	d	05 43		07 13	07 23	07 43	07 53	08 13	08 23	08 43	
Beckenham Hill	d	05 45		07 15	07 25	07 45	07 55	08 15	08 25	08 45	
Ravensbourne	d	05 47		07 17	07 27	07 47	07 57	08 17	08 27	08 47	
Shortlands	d	05 50		07 20	07 30	07 50	08 00	08 20	08 30	08 50	
Bromley South	d	05 53		07 23	07 33	07 53	08 03	08 23	08 33	08 53	
Bickley	d	05 56		07 26	07 36	07 56	08 06	08 26	08 36	08 56	
Petts Wood	d				07 40		08 10		08 40		
Orpington	a				07 44		08 14		08 44		
St Mary Cray	d	06 01		07 31		08 01		08 31		09 01	
Swanley	d	06 06		07 36		08 06		08 36		09 06	
Eynsford	d	06 11		07 41		08 11		08 41		09 11	
Shoreham (Kent)	d	06 15		07 45		08 15		08 45		09 15	
Otford	d	06 18		07 48		08 18		08 48		09 18	
Bat & Ball	d	06 21		07 51		08 21		08 51		09 21	
Sevenoaks	a	06 25		07 55		08 25		08 55		09 25	
Borough Green & Wrotham	d										
West Malling	d										
Maidstone East	a										
Bearsted	a										
Ashford International	a										

		TL	TL	TL	TL	TL	TL	TL	and at the same minutes past each hour until	TL	TL	TL	TL
Cambridge	d												
Stevenage	d												
Welwyn Garden City	d												
Finsbury Park	d												
Kentish Town	d	08 11		08 41		09 11		09 41			12 11		12 41
St Pancras International	d	08 17		08 47		09 17		09 47			12 17		12 47
Farringdon	d	08 22		08 52		09 22		09 52			12 22		12 52
City Thameslink	d					09 24		09 54			12 24		12 54
London Blackfriars	d	08 26	08 46	08 56	09 16	09 26	09 46	09 56		12 16	12 26	12 46	12 56
London Bridge	a												
Elephant & Castle	d	08 30	08 50	09 00	09 20	09 30	09 50	10 00		12 20	12 30	12 50	13 00
Denmark Hill	d	08 38	08 58	09 08	09 28	09 38	09 58	10 08		12 28	12 38	12 58	13 08
Peckham Rye	d	08 41	09 01	09 11	09 31	09 41	10 01	10 11		12 31	12 41	13 01	13 11
Nunhead	d	08 44	09 04	09 14	09 34	09 44	10 04	10 14		12 34	12 44	13 04	13 14
Crofton Park	d	08 47	09 07	09 17	09 37	09 47	10 07	10 17		12 37	12 47	13 07	13 17
Catford	d	08 50	09 10	09 20	09 40	09 50	10 10	10 20		12 40	12 50	13 10	13 20
Bellingham	d	08 53	09 13	09 23	09 43	09 53	10 13	10 23		12 43	12 53	13 13	13 23
Beckenham Hill	d	08 55	09 15	09 25	09 45	09 55	10 15	10 25		12 45	12 55	13 15	13 25
Ravensbourne	d	08 57	09 17	09 27	09 47	09 57	10 17	10 27		12 47	12 57	13 17	13 27
Shortlands	d	09 00	09 20	09 30	09 50	10 00	10 20	10 30		12 50	13 00	13 20	13 30
Bromley South	d	09 03	09 23	09 33	09 53	10 03	10 23	10 33		12 53	13 03	13 23	13 33
Bickley	d	09 06	09 26	09 36	09 56	10 06	10 26	10 36		12 56	13 06	13 26	13 36
Petts Wood	d	09 10		09 40		10 10		10 40			13 10		13 40
Orpington	a	09 14		09 44		10 14		10 44			13 14		13 44
St Mary Cray	d		09 32		10 01		10 31			13 01		13 31	
Swanley	d		09 37		10 06		10 36			13 06		13 36	
Eynsford	d		09 42		10 11		10 41			13 11		13 41	
Shoreham (Kent)	d		09 46		10 15		10 45			13 15		13 45	
Otford	d		09 49		10 18		10 48			13 18		13 48	
Bat & Ball	d		09 52		10 21		10 51			13 21		13 51	
Sevenoaks	a		09 56		10 25		10 55			13 25		13 55	
Borough Green & Wrotham	d												
West Malling	d												
Maidstone East	a												
Bearsted	a												
Ashford International	a												

			TL	TL	TL	TL	TL	TL	TL	TL	and at the same minutes past each hour until	TL	TL	TL	TL
Cambridge	d														
Stevenage	d														
Welwyn Garden City	d														
Finsbury Park	d														
Kentish Town	d			13 11		13 41		14 11		14 41			20 11		20 41
St Pancras International	d			13 17		13 47		14 17		14 47			20 17		20 47
Farringdon	d			13 22		13 52		14 22		14 52			20 22		20 52
City Thameslink	d			13 24		13 54		14 24		14 54			20 24		20 54
London Blackfriars	d		13 16	13 26	13 46	13 56	14 16	14 26	14 46	14 56		20 16	20 26	20 46	20 56
London Bridge	a														
Elephant & Castle	d		13 20	13 30	13 50	14 00	14 20	14 30	14 50	15 00		20 20	20 30	20 50	21 00
Denmark Hill	d		13 28	13 38	13 58	14 08	14 28	14 38	14 58	15 08		20 28	20 38	20 58	21 08
Peckham Rye	d		13 31	13 41	14 01	14 11	14 31	14 41	15 01	15 11		20 31	20 41	21 01	21 11
Nunhead	d		13 34	13 44	14 04	14 14	14 34	14 44	15 04	15 14		20 34	20 44	21 04	21 14
Crofton Park	d		13 37	13 47	14 07	14 17	14 37	14 47	15 07	15 17		20 37	20 47	21 07	21 17
Catford	d		13 40	13 50	14 10	14 20	14 40	14 50	15 10	15 20		20 40	20 50	21 10	21 20
Bellingham	d		13 43	13 53	14 13	14 23	14 43	14 53	15 13	15 23		20 43	20 53	21 13	21 23
Beckenham Hill	d		13 45	13 55	14 15	14 25	14 45	14 55	15 15	15 25		20 45	20 55	21 15	21 25
Ravensbourne	d		13 47	13 57	14 17	14 28	14 47	14 57	15 17	15 27		20 47	20 57	21 17	21 27
Shortlands	d		13 50	14 00	14 20	14 30	14 50	15 00	15 20	15 30		20 50	21 00	21 20	21 30
Bromley South	d		13 53	14 03	14 23	14 33	14 53	15 03	15 23	15 33		20 53	21 03	21 23	21 33
Bickley	d		13 56	14 06	14 26	14 36	14 56	15 06	15 26	15 36		20 56	21 06	21 26	21 36
Petts Wood	d			14 10		14 40		15 10		15 40			21 10		21 40
Orpington	a			14 14		14 44		15 14		15 44			21 14		21 44
St Mary Cray	d		14 01		14 31		15 01		15 31			21 01		21 31	
Swanley	d		14 06		14 36		15 06		15 36			21 06		21 36	
Eynsford	d		14 11		14 41		15 11		15 41			21 11		21 41	
Shoreham (Kent)	d		14 15		14 45		15 15		15 45			21 15		21 45	
Otford	d		14 18		14 48		15 18		15 48			21 18		21 48	
Bat & Ball	d		14 21		14 51		15 21		15 51			21 21		21 51	
Sevenoaks	a		14 25		14 55		15 25		15 55			21 25		21 55	
Borough Green & Wrotham	d														
West Malling	d														
Maidstone East	a														
Bearsted	a														
Ashford International	a														

			TL	TL	TL	TL	TL	TL	TL	TL
Cambridge	d									
Stevenage	d									
Welwyn Garden City	d									
Finsbury Park	d									
Kentish Town	d			21 11		21 41		22 11		22 41
St Pancras International	d			21 17		21 47		22 17		22 47
Farringdon	d			21 22		21 52		22 22		22 52
City Thameslink	d									
London Blackfriars	d		21 16	21 26	21 46	21 56	22 16	22 26	22 46	22 56
London Bridge	a									
Elephant & Castle	d		21 20	21 30	21 50	22 00	22 20	22 30	22 50	23 00
Denmark Hill	d		21 28	21 38	21 58	22 08	22 28	22 38	22 58	23 08
Peckham Rye	d		21 31	21 41	22 01	22 11	22 31	22 41	23 01	23 11
Nunhead	d		21 34	21 44	22 04	22 14	22 34	22 44	23 04	23 14
Crofton Park	d		21 37	21 47	22 07	22 17	22 37	22 47	23 07	23 17
Catford	d		21 40	21 50	22 10	22 20	22 40	22 50	23 10	23 20
Bellingham	d		21 43	21 53	22 13	22 23	22 43	22 53	23 13	23 23
Beckenham Hill	d		21 45	21 55	22 15	22 25	22 45	22 55	23 15	23 25
Ravensbourne	d		21 47	21 57	22 17	22 27	22 47	22 57	23 17	23 27
Shortlands	d		21 50	22 00	22 20	22 30	22 50	23 00	23 20	23 30
Bromley South	d		21 53	22 03	22 23	22 33	22 53	23 03	23 23	23 33
Bickley	d		21 56	22 06	22 26	22 36	22 56	23 06	23 26	23 36
Petts Wood	d			22 10		22 40		23 10		23 40
Orpington	a			22 14		22 44		23 14		23 44
St Mary Cray	d		22 01		22 31		23 01		23 31	
Swanley	d		22 06		22 36		23 06		23 36	
Eynsford	d		22 11		22 41		23 11		23 41	
Shoreham (Kent)	d		22 15		22 45		23 15		23 45	
Otford	d		22 18		22 48		23 18		23 48	
Bat & Ball	d		22 21		22 51		23 21		23 51	
Sevenoaks	a		22 25		22 55		23 25		23 55	
Borough Green & Wrotham	d									
West Malling	d									
Maidstone East	a									
Bearsted	a									
Ashford International	a									

Maidstone to Cambridge Service will be introduced in December 2019

Table T196-F

Saturdays
26 May to 8 December

Cambridge, Kentish Town and London Thameslink-Denmark Hill-Catford-Bromley South-Swanley-Otford-Maidstone and Orpington and Sevenoaks

		TL		TL
Cambridge	d			
Stevenage	d			
Welwyn Garden City	d			
Finsbury Park	d			
Kentish Town	d			
St Pancras International	d			
Farringdon	d			
City Thameslink	d			
London Blackfriars	d	23 16		23 46
London Bridge	a			
Elephant & Castle	d	23 20		23 50
Denmark Hill	d	23 28		23 58
Peckham Rye	d	23 31		00 01
Nunhead	d	23 34		00 04
Crofton Park	d	23 37		00 07
Catford	d	23 40		00 10
Bellingham	d	23 43		00 13
Beckenham Hill	d	23 45		00 15
Ravensbourne	d	23 47		00 17
Shortlands	d	23 50		00 20
Bromley South	d	23 53		00 23
Bickley	d	23 56		00 26
Petts Wood	d			
Orpington	a			
St Mary Cray	d	00 01		00 31
Swanley	d	00 06		00 36
Eynsford	d	00 11		00 41
Shoreham (Kent)	d	00 15		00 45
Otford	d	00 18		00 48
Bat & Ball	d	00 21		00 51
Sevenoaks	a	00 25		00 55
Borough Green & Wrotham	d			
West Malling	d			
Maidstone East	a			
Bearsted	a			
Ashford International	a			

Sundays
20 May to 2 December

		TL	and every 30 minutes until	TL	TL	TL	and every 30 minutes until	TL	TL	TL
Cambridge	d									
Stevenage	d									
Welwyn Garden City	d									
Finsbury Park	d									
Kentish Town	d									
St Pancras International	d									
Farringdon	d									
City Thameslink	d									
London Blackfriars	d	09 42		19 42	20 12	20 42		22 42	23 12	23 42
London Bridge	a									
Elephant & Castle	d	09 46		19 46	20 16	20 46		22 46	23 16	23 46
Denmark Hill	d	09 53		19 53	20 23	20 53		22 53	23 23	23 53
Peckham Rye	d	09 56		19 56	20 26	20 56		22 56	23 26	23 56
Nunhead	d	09 59		19 59	20 29	20 59		22 59	23 29	23 59
Crofton Park	d	10 02		20 02	20 32	21 02		23 02	23 32	00 02
Catford	d	10 05		20 05	20 35	21 05		23 05	23 35	00 05
Bellingham	d	10 08		20 08	20 38	21 08		23 08	23 38	00 08
Beckenham Hill	d	10 10		20 10	20 40	21 10		23 10	23 40	00 10
Ravensbourne	d	10 13		20 13	20 43	21 13		23 13	23 43	00 13
Shortlands	d	10 15		20 15	20 45	21 15		23 15	23 45	00 15
Bromley South	d	10 18		20 18	20 48	21 18		23 18	23 48	00 18
Bickley	d	10 21		20 21	20 51	21 21		23 21	23 51	00 21
Petts Wood	d									
Orpington	a									
St Mary Cray	d	10 25		20 25	20 55	21 25		23 25	23 55	00 25
Swanley	d	10 30		20 30	21 01	21 30		23 30	23 59	00 30
Eynsford	d	10 35		20 35	21 06	21 35		23 35	00 05	00 35
Shoreham (Kent)	d	10 39		20 39	21 10	21 39		23 39	00 09	00 39
Otford	d	10 42		20 42	21 13	21 42		23 42	00 12	00 42
Bat & Ball	d	10 45		20 45	21 16	21 45		23 45	00 15	00 45
Sevenoaks	a	10 49		20 49	21 20	21 49		23 49	00 19	00 49
Borough Green & Wrotham	d									
West Malling	d									
Maidstone East	a									
Bearsted	a									
Ashford International	a									

Maidstone to Cambridge Service will be introduced in December 2019

Please note, Network Rail have stated that further updates to this timetable are possible during the validity period.

Table T196-R

Mondays to Fridays
21 May to 7 December

Sevenoaks and Orpington and Maidstone-Otford-Swanley-Bromley South-Catford-Denmark Hill-London Thameslink and Kentish Town, Cambridge

		TL	TL	TL	TL	TL	TL	SE ◇1	TL	TL	TL	TL	SE ◇1	TL	TL	TL	TL	TL	TL	TL	TL	SE ◇1	TL
Ashford International	d							05 30					06 22										
Bearsted	d							05 55					06 47										
Maidstone East	d							06 02					06 54									08 52	
West Malling	d							06 09					07 05									08 59	
Borough Green & Wrotham	d							06 16					07 12									09 06	
Sevenoaks	d				05 22		05 52			06 22		06 52			07 18		07 52		08 22		08 52		
Bat & Ball	d				05 25		05 55			06 25		06 55			07 21		07 55		08 25		08 55		
Otford	d				05 29		05 59	06 25		06 29		06 59	07 22		07 25		07 59		08 29		08 59	09 15	
Shoreham (Kent)	d				05 32		06 02			06 32		07 02			07 28		08 02		08 32		09 02		
Eynsford	d				05 36		06 05			06 35		07 05			07 31		08 05		08 35		09 05		
Swanley	d				05 41		06 11	06 34		06 41		07 11	07 32		07 37		08 11		08 41		09 11	09 24	
St Mary Cray	d				05 45		06 15			06 45		07 15			07 41		08 15		08 45		09 15	09 28	
Orpington	d	04 33	05 03	05 33		06 03			06 29		06 59			07 30		08 03		08 29		09 03			
Petts Wood	d	04 36	05 06	05 36		06 06			06 32		07 02			07 33		08 06		08 32		09 06			
Bickley	d	04 40	05 10	05 40	05 50	06 10	06 20		06 40	06 50	07 06	07 20		07 40	07 46	08 10	08 20	08 36	08 50	09 10	09 20		
Bromley South	d	04 43	05 13	05 43	05 53	06 13	06 23	06 42	06 43	06 53	07 13	07 23	07 42	07 43	07 53	08 13	08 23	08 43	08 53	09 13	09 23	09 36	←
Shortlands	d	04 45	05 15	05 45	05 55	06 15	06 25		06 45	06 55	07 15	07 25		07 45	07 55	08 15	08 25	08 45	08 55	09 15	09 25		09 25
Ravensbourne	d	04 48	05 18	05 48	05 58	06 18	06 28		06 48	06 58	07 18	07 28		07 48	07 58	08 18	08 28	08 48	08 58	09 18	→		09 28
Beckenham Hill	d	04 50	05 20	05 50	06 00	06 20	06 30		06 50	07 00	07 20	07 30		07 50	08 00	08 20	08 30	08 50	09 00	09 20			09 30
Bellingham	d	04 52	05 22	05 52	06 02	06 22	06 32		06 52	07 02	07 22	07 32		07 52	08 02	08 22	08 32	08 52	09 02	09 22			09 32
Catford	d	04 55	05 25	05 55	06 05	06 25	06 35		06 55	07 05	07 25	07 35		07 55	08 05	08 25	08 35	08 55	09 05	09 25			09 35
Crofton Park	d	04 58	05 28	05 58	06 08	06 28	06 38		06 58	07 08	07 28	07 38		07 58	08 08	08 28	08 38	08 58	09 08	09 28			09 38
Nunhead	d	05 01	05 31	06 01	06 11	06 31	06 41		07 01	07 11	07 31	07 41		08 01	08 11	08 31	08 41	09 01	09 11	09 31			09 41
Peckham Rye	d	05 04	05 34	06 04	06 14	06 34	06 44		07 04	07 14	07 34	07 44		08 04	08 14	08 34	08 44	09 04	09 14	09 34			09 44
Denmark Hill	d	05 07	05 37	06 07	06 17	06 37	06 47		07 07	07 17	07 37	07 47		08 07	08 17	08 37	08 47	09 07	09 17	09 37			09 47
Elephant & Castle	a	05 14	05 44	06 14	06 24	06 44	06 54	07 02	07 14	07 24	07 44	07 54	08 01	08 14	08 24	08 44	08 54	09 14	09 24	09 44		09 53	09 54
London Bridge	a																						
London Blackfriars	a	05 19	05 49	06 19	06 29	06 49	06 59	07 09	07 19	07 29	07 49	07 59	08 09	08 19	08 29	08 49	08 59	09 19	09 29	09 49		10 00	09 59
City Thameslink	a	05 21	05 51	06 21		06 51			07 21		07 51			08 21		08 51		09 21		09 51			
Farringdon	a	05 23	05 53	06 23		06 53			07 23		07 53			08 23		08 53		09 23		09 53			
St Pancras International	a	05 28	05 58	06 28		06 58			07 28		07 58			08 28		08 58		09 28		09 58			
Kentish Town	a	05 33	06 03						07 33		08 03			08 33		09 03		09 33		10 03			
Finsbury Park	a																						
Welwyn Garden City	a																						
Stevenage	a																						
Cambridge	a																						

		TL	TL	TL	TL		TL	TL	TL	TL	TL	TL	TL	TL	TL	TL	TL	TL	TL	TL	TL	TL
Ashford International	d																					
Bearsted	d																					
Maidstone East	d																					
West Malling	d																					
Borough Green & Wrotham	d																					
Sevenoaks	d		09 22		09 52			16 22		16 52		17 22		17 52		18 22		18 52		19 22		19 52
Bat & Ball	d		09 25		09 55			16 25		16 55		17 25		17 55		18 25		18 55		19 25		19 55
Otford	d		09 29		09 59			16 29		16 59		17 29		17 59		18 29		18 59		19 29		19 59
Shoreham (Kent)	d		09 32		10 02			16 32		17 02		17 32		18 02		18 32		19 02		19 32		20 02
Eynsford	d		09 35		10 05			16 35		17 05		17 35		18 05		18 35		19 05		19 35		20 05
Swanley	d		09 41		10 11			16 41		17 11		17 41		18 11		18 41		19 11		19 41		20 11
St Mary Cray	d		09 45		10 15			16 45		17 15		17 45		18 15		18 45		19 15		19 45		20 15
Orpington	d	09 33		10 03			16 33		17 03		17 33		18 02		18 33		19 03		19 33		20 03	
Petts Wood	d	09 36		10 06			16 36		17 06		17 36		18 05		18 36		19 06		19 36		20 06	
Bickley	d	09 40	09 50	10 10	10 20	and at the same minutes past each hour until	16 40	16 50	17 10	17 20	17 40	17 50	18 10	18 20	18 40	18 50	19 10	19 20	19 40	19 50	20 10	20 20
Bromley South	d	09 43	09 53	10 13	10 23		16 43	16 53	17 13	17 23	17 43	17 53	18 13	18 23	18 43	18 53	19 13	19 23	19 43	19 53	20 13	20 23
Shortlands	d	09 45	09 55	10 15	10 25		16 45	16 55	17 15	17 25	17 45	17 55	18 15	18 25	18 45	18 55	19 15	19 25	19 45	19 55	20 15	20 25
Ravensbourne	d	09 48	09 58	10 18	10 28		16 48	16 58	17 18	17 28	17 48	17 58	18 18	18 28	18 48	18 58	19 18	19 28	19 48	19 58	20 18	20 28
Beckenham Hill	d	09 50	10 00	10 20	10 30		16 50	17 00	17 20	17 30	17 50	18 00	18 20	18 30	18 50	19 00	19 20	19 30	19 50	20 00	20 20	20 30
Bellingham	d	09 52	10 02	10 22	10 32		16 52	17 02	17 22	17 32	17 52	18 02	18 22	18 32	18 52	19 02	19 22	19 32	19 52	20 02	20 22	20 32
Catford	d	09 55	10 05	10 25	10 35		16 55	17 05	17 25	17 35	17 55	18 05	18 25	18 35	18 55	19 05	19 25	19 35	19 55	20 05	20 25	20 35
Crofton Park	d	09 58	10 08	10 28	10 38		16 58	17 08	17 28	17 38	17 58	18 08	18 28	18 38	18 58	19 08	19 28	19 38	19 58	20 08	20 28	20 38
Nunhead	d	10 01	10 11	10 31	10 41		17 01	17 11	17 31	17 41	18 01	18 11	18 31	18 41	19 01	19 11	19 31	19 41	20 01	20 11	20 31	20 41
Peckham Rye	d	10 04	10 14	10 34	10 44		17 04	17 14	17 34	17 44	18 04	18 14	18 34	18 44	19 04	19 14	19 34	19 44	20 04	20 14	20 34	20 44
Denmark Hill	d	10 07	10 17	10 37	10 47		17 07	17 17	17 37	17 47	18 07	18 17	18 37	18 47	19 07	19 17	19 37	19 47	20 07	20 17	20 37	20 47
Elephant & Castle	a	10 14	10 24	10 44	10 54		17 14	17 24	17 44	17 54	18 14	18 24	18 44	18 54	19 14	19 24	19 44	19 54	20 14	20 24	20 44	20 54
London Bridge	a																					
London Blackfriars	a	10 19	10 29	10 49	10 59		17 19	17 29	17 49	17 59	18 19	18 29	18 49	18 59	19 19	19 29	19 49	19 59	20 19	20 29	20 49	20 59
City Thameslink	a	10 21		10 51			17 21		17 51		18 21		18 51		19 21		19 51		20 21		20 51	
Farringdon	a	10 23		10 53			17 23		17 53		18 23		18 53		19 23		19 53		20 23		20 53	
St Pancras International	a	10 28		10 58			17 28		17 58		18 28		18 58		19 28		19 58		20 28		20 58	
Kentish Town	a	10 33		11 03			17 33		18 03		18 33		19 03						20 33		21 03	
Finsbury Park	a																					
Welwyn Garden City	a																					
Stevenage	a																					
Cambridge	a																					

Maidstone to Cambridge Service will be introduced in December 2019

Table T196-R

Mondays to Fridays
21 May to 7 December

Sevenoaks and Orpington and Maidstone-Otford-Swanley-Bromley South-Catford-Denmark Hill-London Thameslink and Kentish Town, Cambridge

		TL	TL	TL	TL	TL	TL	TL	TL	TL	TL	TL	TL	TL	TL
Ashford International	d														
Bearsted	d														
Maidstone East	d														
West Malling	d														
Borough Green & Wrotham	d														
Sevenoaks	d		20 22		20 52		21 22		21 52		22 22		22 52	23 22	23 22
Bat & Ball	d		20 25		20 55		21 25		21 55		22 25		22 55	23 25	23 25
Otford	d		20 29		20 59		21 29		21 59		22 29		22 59	23 29	23 29
Shoreham (Kent)	d		20 32		21 02		21 32		22 02		22 32		23 02	23 32	23 32
Eynsford	d		20 35		21 05		21 35		22 05		22 35		23 05	23 35	23 36
Swanley	d		20 41		21 11		21 41		22 11		22 41		23 11	23 41	23 41
St Mary Cray	d		20 45		21 15		21 45		22 15		22 45		23 15	23 45	23 45
Orpington	d	20 33		21 03		21 33		22 03		22 33		23 03			
Petts Wood	d	20 36		21 06		21 36		22 06		22 36		23 06			
Bickley	d	20 40	20 50	21 10	21 20	21 40	21 50	22 10	22 20	22 40	22 50	23 10	23 20	23 50	23 50
Bromley South	d	20 43	20 53	21 13	21 23	21 43	21 53	22 13	22 23	22 43	22 53	23 13	23 23	23 53	23 53
Shortlands	d	20 45	20 55	21 15	21 25	21 45	21 55	22 15	22 25	22 45	22 55	23 15	23 25	23 55	23 55
Ravensbourne	d	20 48	20 58	21 18	21 28	21 48	21 58	22 18	22 28	22 48	22 58	23 18	23 28	23 58	23 58
Beckenham Hill	d	20 50	21 00	21 20	21 30	21 50	22 00	22 20	22 30	22 50	23 00	23 20	23 30	00 01	00 01
Bellingham	d	20 52	21 02	21 22	21 32	21 52	22 02	22 22	22 32	22 52	23 02	23 22	23 32	00 03	00 03
Catford	d	20 55	21 05	21 25	21 35	21 55	22 05	22 25	22 35	22 55	23 05	23 25	23 35	00 06	00 06
Crofton Park	d	20 58	21 08	21 28	21 38	21 58	22 08	22 28	22 38	22 58	23 08	23 28	23 38	00 08	00 08
Nunhead	d	21 01	21 11	21 31	21 41	22 01	22 11	22 31	22 41	23 01	23 11	23 31	23 41	00 11	00 11
Peckham Rye	d	21 04	21 14	21 34	21 44	22 04	22 14	22 34	22 44	23 04	23 14	23 34	23 44	00 14	00 14
Denmark Hill	d	21 07	21 17	21 37	21 47	22 07	22 17	22 37	22 47	23 07	23 17	23 37	23 47	00 17	00 17
Elephant & Castle	a	21 14	21 24	21 44	21 54	22 14	22 24	22 44	22 54	23 14	23 24	23 44	23 54	00 24	00 24
London Bridge	a														
London Blackfriars	a	21 19	21 29	21 49	21 59	22 19	22 29	22 49	22 59	23 19	23 29	23 49	23 59	00 33	00 29
City Thameslink	a	21 21		21 51		22 21		22 51							00 31
Farringdon	a	21 23		21 53		22 23		22 53							00 33
St Pancras International	a	21 28		21 58		22 28		22 58							00 38
Kentish Town	a	21 33		22 03		22 33									
Finsbury Park	a														00 44
Welwyn Garden City	a														
Stevenage	a														
Cambridge	a														

Saturdays
26 May to 8 December

		TL	TL	TL	TL	TL	TL	TL	TL	TL	TL	TL	TL	TL		TL	TL	TL	TL	TL	TL	TL	TL
Ashford International	d																						
Bearsted	d																						
Maidstone East	d																						
West Malling	d																						
Borough Green & Wrotham	d																						
Sevenoaks	d	05 22	05 52		06 22		06 52		07 22		07 52		08 22			18 52		19 22		19 52		20 22	
Bat & Ball	d	05 25	05 55		06 25		06 55		07 25		07 55		08 25			18 55		19 25		19 55		20 25	
Otford	d	05 29	05 59		06 29		06 59		07 29		07 59		08 29			18 59		19 29		19 59		20 29	
Shoreham (Kent)	d	05 32	06 02		06 32		07 02		07 32		08 02		08 32			19 02		19 32		20 02		20 32	
Eynsford	d	05 36	06 05		06 35		07 05		07 35		08 05		08 35			19 05		19 35		20 05		20 35	
Swanley	d	05 41	06 11		06 41		07 11		07 41		08 11		08 41			19 11		19 41		20 11		20 41	
St Mary Cray	d	05 45	06 15		06 45		07 15		07 45		08 15		08 45			19 15		19 45		20 15		20 45	
Orpington	d			06 33		07 03		07 33		08 03		08 33		09 03			19 33		20 03		20 33		21 03
Petts Wood	d			06 36		07 06		07 36		08 06		08 36		09 06			19 36		20 06		20 36		21 06
Bickley	d	05 50	06 20	06 40	06 50	07 10	07 20	07 40	07 50	08 10	08 20	08 40	08 50	09 10	and at the same minutes past each hour until	19 20	19 40	19 50	20 10	20 20	20 40	20 50	21 10
Bromley South	d	05 53	06 23	06 43	06 53	07 13	07 23	07 43	07 53	08 13	08 23	08 43	08 53	09 13		19 23	19 43	19 53	20 13	20 23	20 43	20 53	21 13
Shortlands	d	05 55	06 25	06 45	06 55	07 15	07 25	07 45	07 55	08 15	08 25	08 45	08 55	09 15		19 25	19 45	19 55	20 15	20 25	20 45	20 55	21 15
Ravensbourne	d	05 58	06 28	06 48	06 58	07 18	07 28	07 48	07 58	08 18	08 28	08 48	08 58	09 18		19 28	19 48	19 58	20 18	20 28	20 48	20 58	21 18
Beckenham Hill	d	06 00	06 30	06 50	07 00	07 20	07 30	07 50	08 00	08 20	08 30	08 50	09 00	09 20		19 30	19 50	20 00	20 20	20 30	20 50	21 00	21 20
Bellingham	d	06 02	06 32	06 52	07 02	07 22	07 32	07 52	08 02	08 22	08 32	08 52	09 02	09 22		19 32	19 52	20 02	20 22	20 32	20 52	21 02	21 22
Catford	d	06 05	06 35	06 55	07 05	07 25	07 35	07 55	08 05	08 25	08 35	08 55	09 05	09 25		19 35	19 55	20 05	20 25	20 35	20 55	21 05	21 25
Crofton Park	d	06 08	06 38	06 58	07 08	07 28	07 38	07 58	08 08	08 28	08 38	08 58	09 08	09 28		19 38	19 58	20 08	20 28	20 38	20 58	21 08	21 28
Nunhead	d	06 11	06 41	07 01	07 11	07 31	07 41	08 01	08 11	08 31	08 41	09 01	09 11	09 31		19 41	20 01	20 11	20 31	20 41	21 01	21 11	21 31
Peckham Rye	d	06 14	06 44	07 04	07 14	07 34	07 44	08 04	08 14	08 34	08 44	09 04	09 14	09 34		19 44	20 04	20 14	20 34	20 44	21 04	21 14	21 34
Denmark Hill	d	06 17	06 47	07 07	07 17	07 37	07 47	08 07	08 17	08 37	08 47	09 07	09 17	09 37		19 47	20 07	20 17	20 37	20 47	21 07	21 17	21 37
Elephant & Castle	a	06 24	06 54	07 14	07 24	07 44	07 54	08 14	08 24	08 44	08 54	09 14	09 24	09 44		19 54	20 14	20 24	20 44	20 54	21 14	21 24	21 44
London Bridge	a																						
London Blackfriars	a	06 29	06 59	07 19	07 29	07 49	07 59	08 19	08 29	08 49	08 59	09 19	09 29	09 49		19 59	20 19	20 29	20 49	20 59	21 19	21 29	21 49
City Thameslink	a											09 21		09 51			20 21		20 51				
Farringdon	a			07 23		07 53		08 23		08 53		09 23		09 53			20 23		20 53		21 23		21 53
St Pancras International	a			07 28		07 58		08 28		08 58		09 28		09 58			20 28		20 58		21 28		21 58
Kentish Town	a			07 33		08 03		08 33		09 03		09 33		10 03			20 33		21 03		21 33		22 03
Finsbury Park	a																						
Welwyn Garden City	a																						
Stevenage	a																						
Cambridge	a																						

Maidstone to Cambridge Service will be introduced in December 2019

Table T196-R

Saturdays

26 May to 8 December

Sevenoaks and Orpington and Maidstone-Otford-Swanley-Bromley South-Catford-Denmark Hill-London Thameslink and Kentish Town, Cambridge

		TL	TL	TL	TL	TL	TL	TL	TL	TL	TL
Ashford International	d										
Bearsted	d										
Maidstone East	d										
West Malling	d										
Borough Green & Wrotham	d										
Sevenoaks	d	20 52		21 22		21 52		22 22		22 52	23 22
Bat & Ball	d	20 55		21 25		21 55		22 25		22 55	23 25
Otford	d	20 59		21 29		21 59		22 29		22 59	23 29
Shoreham (Kent)	d	21 02		21 32		22 02		22 32		23 02	23 32
Eynsford	d	21 05		21 35		22 05		22 35		23 05	23 35
Swanley	d	21 11		21 41		22 11		22 41		23 11	23 41
St Mary Cray	d	21 15		21 45		22 15		22 45		23 15	23 45
Orpington	d		21 33		22 03		22 33		23 03		
Petts Wood	d		21 36		22 06		22 36		23 06		
Bickley	d	21 20	21 40	21 50	22 10	22 20	22 40	22 50	23 10	23 20	23 50
Bromley South	d	21 23	21 43	21 53	22 13	22 23	22 43	22 53	23 13	23 23	23 53
Shortlands	d	21 25	21 45	21 55	22 15	22 25	22 45	22 55	23 15	23 25	23 55
Ravensbourne	d	21 28	21 48	21 58	22 18	22 28	22 48	22 58	23 18	23 28	23 58
Beckenham Hill	d	21 30	21 50	22 00	22 20	22 30	22 50	23 00	23 20	23 30	00 01
Bellingham	d	21 32	21 52	22 02	22 22	22 32	22 52	23 02	23 22	23 32	00 03
Catford	d	21 35	21 55	22 05	22 25	22 35	22 55	23 05	23 25	23 35	00 06
Crofton Park	d	21 38	21 58	22 08	22 28	22 38	22 58	23 08	23 28	23 38	00 08
Nunhead	d	21 41	22 01	22 11	22 31	22 41	23 01	23 11	23 31	23 41	00 11
Peckham Rye	d	21 44	22 04	22 14	22 34	22 44	23 04	23 14	23 34	23 44	00 14
Denmark Hill	d	21 47	22 07	22 17	22 37	22 47	23 07	23 17	23 37	23 47	00 17
Elephant & Castle	a	21 54	22 14	22 24	22 44	22 54	23 14	23 24	23 44	23 54	00 24
London Bridge	a										
London Blackfriars	a	21 59	22 19	22 29	22 49	22 59	23 19	23 29	23 49	23 59	00 29
City Thameslink	a										
Farringdon	a		22 23		22 53						
St Pancras International	a		22 28		22 58						
Kentish Town	a		22 33								
Finsbury Park	a										
Welwyn Garden City	a										
Stevenage	a										
Cambridge	a										

Sundays

20 May to 2 December

		TL		TL
Ashford International	d			
Bearsted	d			
Maidstone East	d			
West Malling	d			
Borough Green & Wrotham	d			
Sevenoaks	d	08 28		22 28
Bat & Ball	d	08 31		22 31
Otford	d	08 35		22 35
Shoreham (Kent)	d	08 38		22 38
Eynsford	d	08 41		22 41
Swanley	d	08 47		22 47
St Mary Cray	d	08 51		22 51
Orpington	d			
Petts Wood	d			
Bickley	d	08 56		22 56
Bromley South	d	08 59	and	22 59
Shortlands	d	09 01	every 30	23 01
Ravensbourne	d	09 04	minutes	23 04
Beckenham Hill	d	09 06	until	23 06
Bellingham	d	09 08		23 08
Catford	d	09 11		23 11
Crofton Park	d	09 14		23 14
Nunhead	d	09 17		23 17
Peckham Rye	d	09 20		23 20
Denmark Hill	d	09 23		23 23
Elephant & Castle	a	09 29		23 29
London Bridge	a			
London Blackfriars	a	09 34		23 34
City Thameslink	a			
Farringdon	a			
St Pancras International	a			
Kentish Town	a			
Finsbury Park	a			
Welwyn Garden City	a			
Stevenage	a			
Cambridge	a			

Maidstone to Cambridge Service will be introduced in December 2019

Table T197-F

Mondays to Fridays

21 May to 7 December

London - Maidstone East and Ashford International

Miles			SE MX ◇■ A	SE MX ◇■ A	SE MO ◇■ A	SE MX ◇■ A	SE MX ◇■	SE	SE ◇■	SE ◇■	SE ■	SE ◇■	SE ◇■	SE ◇■	SE ◇■		SE ◇■	SE ◇■	SE ◇■	SE ◇■	SE ◇■	SE ◇■
—	London Victoria	d					00 25		05 50	06 25	06 55		07 55	08 25	08 55		13 25	13 55	14 25	14 55	15 25	15 55
—	St Pancras International	d																				
—	Farringdon	d																				
—	City Thameslink	d																				
—	London Blackfriars	d										07 23										
—	Bromley South	d				00 12	00 42		06 12	06 42	07 13	07 53	08 12	08 42	09 12		13 42	14 12	14 42	15 12	15 42	16 12
14¾	St Mary Cray 195	d				00 18	00 48		06 18	06 48	07 19	07 59	08 18		09 18			14 18		15 18		16 18
17½	Swanley ■ 195	d				00 22	00 52		06 22	06 52	07 23	08 04	08 22	08 50	09 22	and at	13 50	14 22	14 50	15 22	15 50	16 22
24	Otford ■ 195	d				00 30	01 00		06 30	07 00	07 31	08 12	08 30	08 58	09 30	the same	13 58	14 30	14 58	15 30	15 58	16 30
27	**Kemsing**	d				00s35			06 35	07 05	07 36	08 17	08 35		09 35	minutes		14 35		15 35		16 35
29½	**Borough Green & Wrotham**	d		00 06		00s40	01s08		06 40	07 10	07 41	08 22	08 40	09 06	09 40	past	14 06	14 40	15 06	15 40	16 06	16 40
34¾	**West Malling**	d		00 12		00s46	01s14		06 46	07 16	07 47	08 28	08 46	09 12	09 46	each	14 12	14 46	15 12	15 46	16 12	16 46
35¾	**East Malling**	d				00s49	01s17		06 49	07 19	07 50	08 31	08 49		09 49	hour until		14 49		15 49		16 49
37½	**Barming**	d				00s53	01s21		06 53	07 23	07 54	08 35	08 53		09 53			14 53		15 53		16 53
40	**Maidstone East ■**	a		00 20		00 57	01 25		06 57	07 27	07 58	08 42	08 57	09 20	09 57		14 20	14 57	15 20	15 57	16 20	16 57
—	**Maidstone East**	d		00 22	00 27	00 59	01 27	06 22	06 59	07 29	07 59		08 59	09 22	09 59		14 22	14 59	15 22	15 59	16 22	16 59
42¾	**Bearsted**	d	00 04	00s27	00s32	01s04	01s32	06 27	07 04	07 34	08 04		09 04	09 27	10 04		14 27	15 04	15 27	16 04	16 27	17 04
45	**Hollingbourne**	d	00 08	00s31	00s36		01s36	06 31	07 08	07 38	08 08		09 08	09 31			14 31		15 31	16 08	16 31	17 08
47½	**Harrietsham**	d	00 11	00s34	00s39		01s39	06 35	07 12	07 42	08 12		09 12	09 34			14 34		15 34	16 11	16 34	17 11
49¾	**Lenham**	d	00 15	00s38	00s43		01s43	06 39	07 16	07 46	08 16		09 16	09 38			14 38		15 38	16 15	16 38	17 15
53¼	**Charing**	d	00 20	00s43	00s48		01s48	06 44	07 21	07 51	08 21		09 21	09 43			14 43		15 43	16 20	16 43	17 20
—	Ashford International	a	00 29	00 53	00 57	01 23	02 01	06 53	07 31	08 01	08 31		09 30	09 53	10 23		14 53	15 23	15 53	16 29	16 53	17 29
—	Wye	a						07 11		08 11				10 11			15 11		16 11		17 11	
—	Chilham	a						07 17		08 18				10 17			15 17		16 17		17 17	
—	Chartham	a						07 21		08 21				10 21			15 21		16 21		17 21	
—	Canterbury West	a						07 27		08 29				10 27			15 27		16 27		17 27	

		SE ◇■	SE ◇■	SE ■	SE ◇■	SE ◇■	SE ◇■	SE ■	SE ◇■	SE ◇■	SE ◇■	SE ◇■	SE ◇■	SE ◇■	SE ◇■	SE ◇■	SE ◇■	SE ◇■	SE ◇■	SE ◇■	SE ◇■
London Victoria	d	16 25	16 52	17 09	17 22		17 52	18 07	18 22	18 52		19 25	19 55	20 25	20 55	21 25	21 55	22 25	22 55	23 25	23 55
St Pancras International	d																				
Farringdon	d																				
City Thameslink	d																				
London Blackfriars	d					17 38					19 05										
Bromley South	d	16 42	17 12	17 34	17 42	18 03	18 12	18 33	18 42	19 12	19 27	19 42	20 12	20 42	21 12	21 42	22 12	22 42	23 12	23 42	00 12
St Mary Cray 195	d		17 18			18 10	18 18			19 18	19 34		20 18		21 18		22 18		23 18		00 18
Swanley ■ 195	d	16 50	17 22		17 51	18 14	18 22		18 51	19 22	19 40	19 50	20 22	20 51	21 22	21 50	22 22	22 50	23 22	23 50	00 22
Otford ■ 195	d	16 59	17 31	17 52	17 59	18 23	18 31	18 52	18 59	19 31	19 52	19 58	20 30	20 59	21 30	21 58	22 30	22 58	23 30	23 58	00 30
Kemsing	d		17 36			18 28	18 36			19 36			20 35		21 35		22 35		23 35		00s35
Borough Green & Wrotham	d	17 07	17 41	18 00	18 07	18 33	18 41	19 00	19 07	19 41	19 59	20 06	20 40	21 06	21 40	22 06	22 40	23 06	23 40	00 06	00s40
West Malling	d	17 13	17 47	18 06	18 14	18 39	18 47	19 06	19 14	19 47	20 06	20 12	20 46	21 13	21 46	22 12	22 46	23 12	23 46	00 12	00s46
East Malling	d		17 50	18 09		18 42	18 50	19 09		19 50		20 15	20 49		21 49		22 49		23 49		00s49
Barming	d		17 54	18 13		18 46	18 54	19 13		19 54		20 19	20 53		21 53		22 53		23 53		00s53
Maidstone East ■	a	17 21	17 58	18 20	18 22	18 50	18 58	19 20	19 22	19 58	20 16	20 24	20 57	21 21	21 57	22 20	22 57	23 20	23 57	00 20	00 57
Maidstone East	d	17 23	18 00		18 23	18 51	18 59		19 23	20 00		20 25	20 59	21 23	21 59	22 22	22 59	23 22	23 59	00 22	00 59
Bearsted	d	17 28	18 05		18 28	18 56	19 05		19 28	20 05		20 30	21 04	21 28	22 04	22 27	23 04	23 27	00 04	00s27	01s04
Hollingbourne	d	17 32	18 09		18 32	19 00	19 08		19 32	20 09		20 34	21 08	21 32	22 08	22 31	23 08	23 31	00 08	00s31	
Harrietsham	d	17 35	18 12		18 36	19 04	19 12		19 36	20 12		20 37	21 11	21 35	22 11	22 34	23 11	23 34	00 11	00s34	
Lenham	d	17 39	18 16		18 40	19 07	19 16		19 40	20 16		20 41	21 15	21 39	22 15	22 38	23 15	23 38	00 15	00s38	
Charing	d	17 44	18 21		18 45	19 13	19 21		19 45	20 21		20 46	21 20	21 45	22 20	22 43	23 20	23 43	00 20	00s43	
Ashford International	a	17 56	18 32		18 59	19 24	19 34		19 57	20 32		20 56	21 29	21 54	22 29	22 53	23 29	23 53	00 29	00 53	01 23
Wye	a											21 11									
Chilham	a											21 17									
Chartham	a											21 21									
Canterbury West	a											21 27									

Saturdays

26 May to 8 December

		SE ◇■ A	SE ◇■ A	SE ◇■ A	SE ◇■	SE ■	SE ◇■	SE ◇■	SE ◇■	SE ◇■		SE ◇■	SE ◇■	SE ◇■	SE ◇■	SE ◇■	SE ◇■	SE ◇■	SE ◇■	SE ◇■	SE ◇■	SE ◇■
London Victoria	d				00 25		06 25	07 25	07 55	08 25		17 55	18 25	18 55	19 25	19 55	20 25	20 55	21 25	21 55	22 25	22 55
St Pancras International	d																					
Farringdon	d																					
City Thameslink	d																					
London Blackfriars	d																					
Bromley South	d			00 12	00 42		06 42	07 42	08 12	08 42		18 12	18 42	19 12	19 42	20 12	20 42	21 12	21 42	22 12	22 42	23 12
St Mary Cray 195	d			00 18	00 48		06 48	07 48	08 18			18 18		19 18		20 18		21 18		22 18		23 18
Swanley ■ 195	d			00 22	00 52		06 52	07 52	08 22	08 50	and at	18 22	18 50	19 22	19 50	20 22	20 50	21 22	21 50	22 22	22 50	23 22
Otford ■ 195	d			00 30	01 00		07 00	08 00	08 30	08 58	the same	18 30	18 58	19 30	19 58	20 30	20 58	21 30	21 58	22 30	22 58	23 30
Kemsing	d			00s35			07 05	08 05	08 35		minutes	18 35		19 35		20 35		21 35		22 35		23 35
Borough Green & Wrotham	d		00 06	00s40	01s08		07 10	08 10	08 40	09 06	past	18 40	19 06	19 40	20 06	20 40	21 06	21 40	22 06	22 40	23 06	23 40
West Malling	d		00 12	00s46	01s14		07 16	08 16	08 46	09 12	each	18 46	19 12	19 46	20 12	20 46	21 12	21 46	22 12	22 46	23 12	23 46
East Malling	d			00s49	01s17		07 19	08 19	08 49		hour until	18 49		19 49		20 49		21 49		22 49		23 49
Barming	d			00s53	01s21		07 23	08 23	08 53			18 53		19 53		20 53		21 53		22 53		23 53
Maidstone East ■	a		00 20	00 57	01 25		07 27	08 27	08 57	09 20		18 57	19 20	19 57	20 20	20 57	21 20	21 57	22 20	22 57	23 20	23 57
Maidstone East	d		00 22	00 59	01 27	06 22	07 28	08 28	08 59	09 22		18 59	19 22	19 59	20 22	20 59	21 22	21 59	22 22	22 59	23 22	23 59
Bearsted	d	00 04	00s27	01s04	01s32	06 27	07 34	08 34	09 04	09 27		19 04	19 27	20 04	20 27	21 04	21 27	22 04	22 27	23 04	23 27	00 04
Hollingbourne	d	00 08	00s31		01s36	06 31	07 37	08 37		09 31			19 31		20 31		21 31		22 31		23 31	
Harrietsham	d	00 11	00s34		01s39	06 34	07 41	08 41		09 34			19 34		20 34		21 34		22 34		23 34	
Lenham	d	00 15	00s38		01s43	06 38	07 45	08 45		09 38			19 38		20 38		21 38		22 38		23 38	
Charing	d	00 20	00s43		01s48	06 43	07 50	08 50		09 43			19 43		20 43		21 43		22 43		23 43	
Ashford International	a	00 29	00 53	01 23	02 01	06 53	07 58	08 58	09 23	09 53		19 23	19 53	20 23	20 53	21 23	21 53	22 23	22 53	23 23	23 55	00 23
Wye	a					07 11	08 11	09 11		10 11			20 11									
Chilham	a					07 17	08 17	09 17		10 17			20 17									
Chartham	a					07 21	08 21	09 21		10 21			20 21									
Canterbury West	a					07 27	08 27	09 27		10 27			20 27									

A From London Victoria

Table T197-F

London - Maidstone East and Ashford International

Saturdays
26 May to 8 December

		SE ◇1	SE ◇1
London Victoria	d	23 25	23 55
St Pancras International	d		
Farringdon	d		
City Thameslink	d		
London Blackfriars	d		
Bromley South	d	23 42	00 12
St Mary Cray 195	d		00 18
Swanley ■ 195	d	23 50	00 22
Otford ■ 195	d	23 58	00 30
Kemsing	d		00s35
Borough Green & Wrotham	d	00 06	00s40
West Malling	d	00 12	00s46
East Malling	d		00s49
Barming	d		00s53
Maidstone East ■	a	00 20	00 57
Maidstone East	d	00 22	00 59
Bearsted	d	00s27	01s04
Hollingbourne	d	00s31	
Harrietsham	d	00s34	
Lenham	d	00s38	
Charing	d	00s43	
Ashford International	a	00 53	01 23
Wye	a		
Chilham	a		
Chartham	a		
Canterbury West	a		

Sundays
20 May to 2 December

		SE ◇1 A	SE ◇1 A	SE ◇1 A	SE ◇1	SE ◇1		SE ◇1	SE ◇1		SE ◇1	SE ◇1
London Victoria	d				00 25	07 25		16 25	17 25		22 25	23 25
St Pancras International	d											
Farringdon	d											
City Thameslink	d											
London Blackfriars	d											
Bromley South	d			00 12	00 42	07 42		16 42	17 42		22 42	23 42
St Mary Cray 195	d			00 18	00 48	07 47		16 47	17 47		22 47	23 47
Swanley ■ 195	d			00 22	00 52	07 52		16 52	17 52		22 52	23 52
Otford ■ 195	d			00 30	01 00	08 00		17 00	18 00		23 00	23 59
Kemsing	d			00s35			and hourly until			and hourly until		
Borough Green & Wrotham	d		00 06	00s40	01s08	08 07		17 07	18 07		23 07	00s07
West Malling	d		00 12	00s46	01s14	08 14		17 14	18 14		23 14	00s13
East Malling	d			00s49	01s17	08 17		17 17	18 17		23 17	00s17
Barming	d			00s53	01s21	08 20		17 20	18 20		23 20	00s20
Maidstone East ■	a		00 20	00 57	01 25	08 25		17 25	18 25		23 25	00 25
Maidstone East	d		00 22	00 59	01 27	08 27		17 27	18 27		23 27	00 27
Bearsted	d	00 04	00s27	01s04	01s32	08 32		17 32	18 32		23 32	00s32
Hollingbourne	d		00s31		01s36	08 36		17 36	18 36		23 36	00s36
Harrietsham	d		00s34		01s39	08 39		17 39	18 39		23 39	00s39
Lenham	d		00s38		01s43	08 43		17 43	18 43		23 43	00s43
Charing	d		00s43		01s48	08 48		17 48	18 48		23 48	00s48
Ashford International	a	00 23	00 53	01 23	01 58	08 58		17 58	18 57		23 57	00 57
Wye	a					09 14		18 14				
Chilham	a					09 20		18 20				
Chartham	a					09 24		18 24				
Canterbury West	a					09 30		18 30				

A not 20 May. From London Victoria

Table T197-R

Canterbury West - Ashford International - Maidstone East - London

Mondays to Fridays
21 May to 7 December

		SE ◇1 A	SE ◇1 A	SE ◇1 A	SE ◇ A	SE A	SE ◇1 A	SE 1 A	SE ◇ A	SE ◇ A	SE ◇ A	SE ◇1	SE ◇1	SE ◇1 A	SE ◇1		SE ◇1 A	SE ◇1	SE ◇1 A	SE ◇1	SE ◇1 A	SE ◇1
Canterbury West	d												08 04		09 05			12 05		13 05		14 05
Chartham	d												08 09		09 10			12 10		13 10		14 10
Chilham	d												08 12		09 13			12 13		13 13		14 13
Wye	d												08 19		09 20			12 20		13 20		14 20
Ashford International	a												08 26		09 27			12 27		13 27		14 27
Charing	d	05 27	05 39	05 56	06 09	06 25	06 31	06 48	07 05	07 35	08 05		08 38		09 41			12 41		13 41		14 41
Lenham	d	05 32	05 44	06 01	06 14	06 30	06 36	06 53	07 10	07 40	08 10		08 43		09 46			12 46		13 46		14 46
Harrietsham	d	05 35	05 47	06 04	06 17	06 33	06 39	06 56	07 13	07 44	08 14		08 47		09 50			12 50		13 50		14 50
Hollingbourne	d	05 39	05 51	06 08	06 21	06 37	06 43	07 00	07 17	07 48	08 18		08 51		09 54	and at the same minutes past each hour until		12 54		13 54		14 54
Bearsted	a	05 43	05 55	06 12	06 25	06 41	06 47	07 04	07 21	07 51	08 21		08 54		09 57			12 57		13 57		14 57
Maidstone East	a	05 49	06 01	06 18	06 31	06 47	06 53	07 10	07 27	07 58	08 28		09 00		10 03			13 03		14 03		15 03
Maidstone East ■	d	05 50	06 02	06 19	06 32	06 48	06 54	07 11	07 28	07 59	08 29	08 52	09 00	09 29	10 04		12 29	13 04	13 29	14 04	14 29	15 04
Barming	d	05 54		06 23		06 52	06 59		07 32	08 03	08 33		09 05	09 33			12 33		13 33		14 33	
East Malling	d	05 58		06 27		06 56	07 02		07 36	08 07	08 37		09 08	09 37			12 37		13 37		14 37	
West Malling	d	06 01	06 09	06 30	06 39	06 59	07 05	07 18	07 39	08 10	08 40	08 59	09 11	09 40	10 11		12 40	13 11	13 40	14 11	14 40	15 11
Borough Green & Wrotham	d	06 08	06 16	06 37	06 46	07 06	07 12	07 25	07 46	08 16	08 46	09 06	09 18	09 46	10 18		12 46	13 18	13 46	14 18	14 46	15 18
Kemsing	d			06 41		07 10	07 16		07 50	08 20	08 50			09 50			12 50		13 50		14 50	
Otford ■ 195	d	06 17	06 25	06 48	06 56	07 16	07 22	07 34	07 56	08 26	08 56	09 15	09 26	09 56	10 26		12 56	13 26	13 56	14 26	14 56	15 26
Swanley ■ 195	d	06 26	06 34		07 07		07 32		08 07	08 35	09 05	09 24	09 35	10 05	10 37		13 05	13 37	14 05	14 37	15 05	15 35
St Mary Cray 195	d				07 11					08 39	09 09	09 28	09 39	10 09			13 09		14 09		15 09	15 39
Bromley South	a	06 35	06 42	07 03	07 18	07 31	07 41	07 49	08 16	08 45	09 16	09 36	09 46	10 16	10 45		13 16	13 45	14 16	14 45	15 16	15 46
London Bridge	d																					
London Blackfriars	d		07a09				08a09					10a00										
City Thameslink	d																					
Farringdon	d																					
St Pancras International	d																					
London Victoria	a	06 57		07 29	07 45	07 58		08 12	08 42	09 10	09 40		10 08	10 38	11 08		13 38	14 08	14 39	15 08	15 38	16 09

		SE ◇1 A	SE ◇1	SE ◇1 A	SE ◇1	SE ◇1 A	SE ◇1	SE ◇1 A	SE ◇1	SE ◇1 A	SE ◇1 A	SE ◇1 A	SE ◇1 A	SE ◇1 A	SE ◇1 A	SE 1 A	SE ◇1 A
Canterbury West	d		15 05		16 05		17 05		18 05								
Chartham	d		15 10		16 10		17 10		18 10								
Chilham	d		15 13		16 13		17 13		18 13								
Wye	d		15 20		16 20		17 20		18 20								
Ashford International	a		15 27		16 27		17 28		18 27								
Charing	d		15 41	16 05	16 41	17 05	17 41	18 05	18 41	19 05	19 43		20 43		21 43		22 48
Lenham	d		15 46	16 10	16 46	17 10	17 46	18 10	18 46	19 10	19 48		20 48		21 48		22 53
Harrietsham	d		15 50	16 14	16 50	17 14	17 50	18 14	18 50	19 14	19 51		20 51		21 51		22 57
Hollingbourne	d		15 54	16 18	16 54	17 18	17 54	18 18	18 54	19 18	19 55		20 55		21 55		23 01
Bearsted	a		15 57	16 21	16 57	17 21	17 57	18 21	18 57	19 21	19 59		20 59		21 59		23 04
Maidstone East	a		16 03	16 28	17 03	17 28	18 03	18 28	19 03	19 28	20 04		21 04		22 04		23 10
Maidstone East ■	d	15 29	16 04	16 29	17 04	17 29	18 04	18 29	19 04	19 29	20 05	20 29	21 05	21 29	22 05	22 29	23 11
Barming	d	15 33		16 33		17 33		18 33		19 33		20 33		21 33		22 33	23 15
East Malling	d	15 37		16 37		17 37		18 37		19 37		20 37		21 37		22 37	23 19
West Malling	d	15 40	16 11	16 40	17 11	17 40	18 11	18 40	19 11	19 40	20 12	20 40	21 12	21 40	22 12	22 40	23 22
Borough Green & Wrotham	d	15 46	16 18	16 46	17 18	17 46	18 18	18 46	19 18	19 46	20 18	20 46	21 18	21 46	22 19	22 46	23 28
Kemsing	d	15 50		16 50		17 50		18 50		19 50		20 50		21 50		22 50	
Otford ■ 195	d	15 56	16 26	16 56	17 26	17 56	18 26	18 56	19 26	19 56	20 26	20 56	21 26	21 56	22 27	22 56	23 36
Swanley ■ 195	d	16 05	16 35	17 05	17 35	18 05	18 35	19 05	19 35	20 05	20 37	21 05	21 37	22 05	22 37	23 05	23 45
St Mary Cray 195	d	16 09	16 39	17 09	17 39	18 09	18 39	19 09	19 39	20 09		21 09		22 09		23 09	23 50
Bromley South	a	16 16	16 46	17 16	17 46	18 16	18 46	19 16	19 46	20 16	20 45	21 16	21 45	22 16	22 45	23 16	23 56
London Bridge	d																
London Blackfriars	d																
City Thameslink	d																
Farringdon	d																
St Pancras International	d																
London Victoria	a	16 38	17 08	17 38	18 08	18 38	19 08	19 38	20 08	20 38	21 08	21 38	22 08	22 39	23 08	23 38	00 18

Saturdays
26 May to 8 December

		SE ◇1 A	SE ◇1 A	SE ◇1 A	SE ◇1 A	SE ◇1 A	SE ◇1 A	SE ◇1		SE ◇1 A	SE ◇1	SE ◇1 A	SE ◇1 A
Canterbury West	d							08 05			21 05		
Chartham	d							08 10			21 10		
Chilham	d							08 13			21 13		
Wye	d							08 20			21 20		
Ashford International	a							08 27			21 27		
Charing	d	05 36		06 41		07 41		08 41			21 41		22 48
Lenham	d	05 41		06 46		07 46		08 46			21 46		22 53
Harrietsham	d	05 44		06 50		07 50		08 50			21 50		22 57
Hollingbourne	d	05 48		06 54		07 54		08 54	and at the same minutes past each hour until		21 54		23 01
Bearsted	a	05 53		06 57		07 57		08 57			21 57		23 04
Maidstone East	a	05 58		07 03		08 03		09 03			22 03		23 10
Maidstone East ■	d	05 59	06 29	07 04	07 29	08 04	08 29	09 04		21 29	22 04	22 29	23 11
Barming	d	06 03	06 33		07 33		08 33			21 33		22 33	23 15
East Malling	d	06 07	06 37		07 37		08 37			21 37		22 37	23 19
West Malling	d	06 10	06 40	07 11	07 40	08 11	08 40	09 11		21 40	22 11	22 40	23 22
Borough Green & Wrotham	d	06 16	06 46	07 18	07 46	08 18	08 46	09 18		21 46	22 18	22 46	23 28
Kemsing	d	06 20	06 50		07 50		08 50			21 50		22 50	
Otford ■ 195	d	06 26	06 56	07 26	07 56	08 26	08 56	09 26		21 56	22 26	22 56	23 36
Swanley ■ 195	d	06 35	07 05	07 37	08 05	08 37	09 05	09 37		22 05	22 37	23 05	23 45
St Mary Cray 195	d	06 39	07 09		08 09		09 09			22 09		23 09	23 49
Bromley South	a	06 46	07 16	07 45	08 16	08 45	09 16	09 45		22 16	22 45	23 16	23 56
London Bridge	d												
London Blackfriars	d												
City Thameslink	d												
Farringdon	d												
St Pancras International	d												
London Victoria	a	07 08	07 38	08 08	08 38	09 08	09 38	10 08		22 38	23 08	23 39	00 15

A From Ashford International

Table T197-R

Sundays
20 May to 2 December

Canterbury West - Ashford International - Maidstone East - London

		SE ◇1 A	SE ◇1 A	SE ◇1		SE ◇1	SE ◇1 A	SE ◇1 A
Canterbury West	d			09 04		19 04		
Chartham	d			09 09		19 09		
Chilham	d			09 12		19 12		
Wye	d			09 19		19 19		
Ashford International	a			09 26		19 26		
Charing	d	07 44	08 44	09 44		19 44	20 44	21 44
Lenham	d	07 49	08 49	09 49		19 49	20 49	21 49
Harrietsham	d	07 52	08 52	09 52		19 52	20 52	21 52
Hollingbourne	d	07 56	08 56	09 56		19 56	20 56	21 56
Bearsted	a	07 59	08 59	09 59		19 59	20 59	21 59
Maidstone East	a	08 05	09 05	10 05	and hourly until	20 05	21 05	22 05
Maidstone East	d	08 06	09 06	10 06		20 06	21 06	22 06
Barming	d	08 11	09 11	10 11		20 11	21 11	22 11
East Malling	d	08 14	09 14	10 14		20 14	21 14	22 14
West Malling	d	08 17	09 17	10 17		20 17	21 17	22 17
Borough Green & Wrotham	d	08 24	09 24	10 24		20 24	21 24	22 24
Kemsing	d							
Otford 195	d	08 31	09 31	10 31		20 31	21 31	22 31
Swanley 195	d	08 42	09 42	10 42		20 42	21 42	22 42
St Mary Cray 195	d	08 46	09 46	10 46		20 46	21 46	22 46
Bromley South	a	08 52	09 52	10 52		20 52	21 52	22 52
London Bridge	d							
London Blackfriars	d							
City Thameslink	d							
Farringdon	d							
St Pancras International	d							
London Victoria	a	09 13	10 13	11 13		21 13	22 13	23 13

A From Ashford International

Table T199-F

Mondays to Fridays
21 May to 7 December

London - Lewisham, Hither Green, Petts Wood and Orpington (Summary of Services)

		SE TWO	SE MX	SE MO	SE ThFO	SE ThFO	SE ThFO	SE MX	SE MO	SE ThFO		SE TWO	SE MO	SE ThFO	SE TWO	SE ThFO	SE MX	SE ThFO	SE MO A	SE ThFO		SE MThFO	SE TWO	TL	SE
London Charing Cross ⊖	d				00 02	00 05	00 07		00 12	00 15			00 16	00 18		00 26		00 32	00 46	00 50		04 50			05 20
London Waterloo (East) ⊖	d				00 05	00 08	00 10		00 15	00 18			00 19	00 21		00 29		00 35	00 49	00 53		04 53			05 23
London Cannon Street ⊖	d											00 20			00 27								04 54		
London Blackfriars ⊖	d																							04 56	
London Bridge ⊖	d		00 01	00 01	00 11	00 14	00 16		00 21	00 24		00 24	00 25	00 28	00 32	00 35		00 41	00 55	00 59		04 59	04 59		05 29
London Victoria ⊖	d							00 06									00 28								
New Cross ⊖	d											00 30			00 38										
St Johns	d	00 02										00 32			00 40										
Lewisham	a	00 04	00 09				00 24	00 26	00 30			00 34	00 34	00 36	00 42	00 44		00 49	01 03	01 07		05 07	05 07		05 37
Hither Green	a	00 09		00 12	00 21	00 23						00 39	00 39	00 41				00 54	01 09	01 12		05 12	05 12		05 42
Petts Wood	a	00 22				00 36						00 52	00 51	00 54			01 03		01 21	01 25				05 40	
Orpington	a	00 25				00 42				00 50		00 57	00 55	01 00			01 07		01 27	01 32				05 44	

		SE	SE ◇1	SE	SE	SE		TL	SE	TL	SE	SE	SE	SE	SE	SE ◇1		SE	SE	SE	TL	TL	SE	SE	SE
London Charing Cross ⊖	d	05 26	05 30			05 32					05 42	05 48		05 52	05 54	05 56				06 05				06 12	
London Waterloo (East) ⊖	d	05 29	05 33			05 35					05 45	05 51		05 55	05 57	05 59				06 08				06 15	
London Cannon Street ⊖	d				05 35				05 39				05 55						06 09				06 16		
London Blackfriars ⊖	d							05 26		05 41											05 56	06 11			
London Bridge ⊖	d	05 35	05 39		05 39	05 41			05 43	05a47	05 51	05 57	05 59	06 01	06 03	06 05			06 13	06 14		06a17	06 20	06 21	
London Victoria ⊖	d			05 28														05 58							06 15
New Cross ⊖	d				06a58				05 49				07a21						06 19				06 26		
St Johns	d								05 51										06 21				06 28		
Lewisham	a	05 43				05 49			05 53		06 00	06 07			06 11				06 23				06 31	06 29	06 35
Hither Green	a					05 54			05 58					06 12					06 28	06 23			06 36		
Petts Wood	a			06 03		06 06		06 10										06 33		06 36	06 40		06 48		
Orpington	a		05 55	06 07		06 11		06 14								06 22		06 37		06 40	06 44		06 54		

		SE		SE	SE	SE	SE ◇1	SE	SE	SE	SE	TL		TL	SE	SE	SE	SE	SE	SE	SE	SE ◇1		SE	SE
London Charing Cross ⊖	d			06 23		06 25	06 28				06 35				06 41				06 53		06 56	07 00			
London Waterloo (East) ⊖	d			06 26		06 28	06 31				06 38				06 44				06 56		06 59	07 03			
London Cannon Street ⊖	d	06 25			06 28				06 35	06 39							06 49	06 55		07 00					07 05
London Blackfriars ⊖	d											06 26		06 41											
London Bridge ⊖	d	06 29		06 32	06 32	06 35	06 37		06 39	06 43	06 44			06a47	06 50		06 53	06 59	07 02	07 04	07 05	07 09			07 09
London Victoria ⊖	d							06 28								06 42								06 58	
New Cross ⊖	d	07a38			06 38				08a05	06 49							06 59	08a20		07 10					
St Johns	d				06 40					06 51							07 01			07 12					
Lewisham	a				06 42	06 44				06 53					06 58	07 01	07 03			07 17	07 13				
Hither Green	a			06 43						06 58	06 53						07 08		07 13						08 26
Petts Wood	a							07 03			07 06	07 10					07 20							07 34	
Orpington	a						06 53	07 07			07 09	07 14					07 25					07 25		07 38	

		SE	TL	SE	SE	TL	SE	SE		SE	SE ◇1	SE	SE	SE	SE	SE	SE ◇1	SE		SE	SE	SE	SE ◇1	TL	TL
London Charing Cross ⊖	d	07 06						07 12			07 15				07 21	07 25	07 27				07 33				
London Waterloo (East) ⊖	d	07 09						07 15			07 18				07 24	07 28	07 30				07 36				
London Cannon Street ⊖	d				07 11		07 15			07 19		07 22	07 22	07 25						07 36		07 40	07 42		
London Blackfriars ⊖	d		06 56			07 11																		07 26	07 41
London Bridge ⊖	d	07 15			07 15	07a17	07 19	07 21		07 23	07 24	07 26	07 26	07 29	07 30	07 34	07 36			07 40	07 42		07 46		07a47
London Victoria ⊖	d			07 08														07 28							
New Cross ⊖	d				07 21		07 26			07 29		07 32	07 32	08a39						09a01		07 50			
St Johns	d				07 23					07 31		07 34	07 34									07 52			
Lewisham	a			07 25	07 27			07 29		07 33		07 36	07 36			07 43						07 54			
Hither Green	a	07 25			07 34		07 31						08 31		07 40						07 53	08 00			
Petts Wood	a	07 38	07 41				07 44											08 03			08 06			08 15	
Orpington	a	07 41	07 45				07 48				07 40						07 55	08 07			08 10		08 07	08 18	

		SE	SE	SE		SE	SE	SE	SE	SE	SE ◇1	SE	SE	TL		SE	TL 1	SE	SE	SE	SE	SE	SE ◇1	SE	
London Charing Cross ⊖	d	07 39		07 47			07 53		07 56		08 00		08 06						08 10	08 12		08 14	08 18		
London Waterloo (East) ⊖	d	07 42		07 50			07 56		07 59		08 05		08 09						08 13	08 15		08 17	08 21		
London Cannon Street ⊖	d					07 53		08 00		08 05								08 14			08 17			08 19	
London Blackfriars ⊖	d													07 56			08 12								
London Bridge ⊖	d	07 48		07 56		07 57	08 02		08 05	08 09	08 11		08 15				08a17	08 18	08 19	08 21	08 21	08 23	08 27		
London Victoria ⊖	d		07 45									07 58				08 06									
New Cross ⊖	d					08 03				09a33											08 28			08 31	
St Johns	d					08 05															08 30			08 33	
Lewisham	a	07 59	08 06			08 08		08 10	08 17							08 28				08 31	08 33			08 35	
Hither Green	a					08 14	08 12						08 27					08 29			08 38	08 33			
Petts Wood	a					08 27						08 33	08 40	08 43							08 51				
Orpington	a			08 17		08 33					08 29	08 37	08 45	08 47					08 42		08 58		08 43		

		SE	SE	SE	SE	SE	SE	SE ◇1	SE	SE		SE	SE	SE ◇1	TL	SE	SE	TL	SE	SE		SE	SE	SE	SE
London Charing Cross ⊖	d			08 20	08 22	08 24	08 26	08 28				08 32				08 38			08 42	08 44			08 46	08 50	
London Waterloo (East) ⊖	d			08 23	08 25	08 27	08 29	08 31				08 35				08 41			08 45	08 47			08 49	08 53	
London Cannon Street ⊖	d	08 22	08 24							08 34			08 37	08 40								08 52			08 54
London Blackfriars ⊖	d														08 26			08 41							
London Bridge ⊖	d		08 28	08 29	08 31	08 33	08 35	08 37		08 38		08 41	08 41	08 44		08 47		08a47	08 51	08 53		08 56	08 57	08 59	08 59
London Victoria ⊖	d								08 28								08 38								
New Cross ⊖	d	08 34	09a46							10a01			08 47									09 02			10a16
St Johns	d	08 36											08 49									09 04			
Lewisham	a	08 38					08 43						08 54			08 57	09 00		09 03			09 06		09 09	
Hither Green	a				08 41							08 52	08 59									09 12	09 10		
Petts Wood	a								09 03			09 06			09 10							09 25			
Orpington	a			08 52		08 55		08 56	09 07			09 09		09 05	09 14					09 16		09 31			

A from 4 June, not 25 June

Table T199-F

Mondays to Fridays
21 May to 7 December

London - Lewisham, Hither Green, Petts Wood and Orpington (Summary of Services)

		SE		SE	SE	SE	SE	SE	SE	TL	SE	TL		SE	SE	SE	SE	SE	SE	SE	SE	SE		SE	SE
				◇1		◇1								◇1						◇1		◇1			
London Charing Cross	d			08 58		09 02			09 06						09 12				09 20	09 22		09 24		09 26	
London Waterloo (East)	d			09 01		09 05			09 09						09 15				09 23	09 25		09 27		09 29	
London Cannon Street	d	08 58			09 05			09 08						09 14		09 17	09 20	09 24			09 27				
London Blackfriars	d									08 56		09 11													
London Bridge	d	09 02		09 07	09 09	09 11		09 13	09 15			09a17		09 18	09 21	09 21	09 24	09 28	09 29	09 31	09 31	09 33		09 35	
London Victoria	d						08 58				09 06														09 28
New Cross	d	09 08			10a33			09 19								09 28	09 31	10a46			09 37				
St Johns	d	09 10						09 21								09 30	09 33				09 39				
Lewisham	a	09 12						09 23			09 26				09 31	09 34	09 36				09 41			09 44	
Hither Green	a							09 29	09 24								09 41		09 38						
Petts Wood	a						09 33		09 36	09 42							09 54								10 03
Orpington	a			09 24		09 30	09 37		09 40	09 46				09 38			09 59			09 48		09 53			10 07

		SE	SE	TL	SE	SE	TL	SE		SE	SE	SE	SE	SE	SE	SE	SE	SE		SE	SE	SE	TL	SE	TL
											◇1						◇1								
London Charing Cross	d		09 34					09 42			09 45		09 48			09 54	10 00					10 05			
London Waterloo (East)	d		09 37					09 45			09 48		09 51			09 58	10 03					10 08			
London Cannon Street	d	09 35			09 38					09 47		09 50		09 54	09 57					10 05	10 08				
London Blackfriars	d			09 26			09 41																09 56		10 11
London Bridge	d	09 39	09 43		09 43		09a47	09 51		09 51	09 54	09 54	09 57	09 58	10 01	10 05	10 09			10 09	10 13	10 14			10a17
London Victoria	d					09 36												09 58						10 06	
New Cross	d	11a03			09 49					09 57		10 00		11a16	10 07					11a31	10 19				
St Johns	d				09 51					09 59		10 02			10 09						10 21				
Lewisham	a				09 53	09 56		10 00		10 02		10 04			10 11	10 14					10 23			10 26	
Hither Green	a		09 52		09 58							10 09	10 07								10 28	10 23			
Petts Wood	a		10 06	10 10								10 22						10 33				10 36	10 42		
Orpington	a		10 09	10 14							10 09	10 28					10 25	10 37				10 39	10 45		

		SE	SE	SE		SE	SE	SE	SE	SE	SE	SE	SE	SE		SE	TL	SE	TL	SE	SE	SE	SE	SE	
				◇1							◇1											◇1			
London Charing Cross	d	10 12		10 15			10 18			10 24	10 30					10 35				10 42		10 45		10 48	
London Waterloo (East)	d	10 15		10 18			10 21			10 28	10 33					10 38				10 45		10 48		10 51	
London Cannon Street	d		10 17			10 20		10 24	10 27				10 35	10 38							10 47		10 50		
London Blackfriars	d																10 26		10 41						
London Bridge	d	10 21	10 21	10 24		10 24	10 27	10 28	10 31	10 35	10 39		10 39	10 43		10 44			10a47	10 51	10 51	10 54	10 54	10 57	
London Victoria	d											10 28						10 36							
New Cross	d		10 27			10 30		11a46	10 37				12a01	10 49							10 57		11 00		
St Johns	d		10 29			10 32			10 39					10 51							10 59		11 02		
Lewisham	a	10 29	10 32			10 34			10 41	10 44				10 53				10 56		10 59	11 02		11 04		
Hither Green	a					10 39	10 36							10 58		10 53							11 09	11 06	
Petts Wood	a					10 52						11 03				11 06	11 10						11 22		
Orpington	a			10 39		10 55					10 55	11 07				11 09	11 14					11 09	11 25		

		SE	SE	SE	SE	SE	SE	SE	SE	TL		SE	TL	SE	SE	SE	SE	SE	SE	SE		SE	SE	SE	SE
					◇1											◇1							◇1		
London Charing Cross	d			10 54	11 00				11 05					11 12		11 15		11 18				11 24	11 30		
London Waterloo (East)	d			10 58	11 03				11 08					11 15		11 18		11 21				11 28	11 33		
London Cannon Street	d	10 54	10 57				11 05	11 08							11 17		11 20		11 24	11 27					11 35
London Blackfriars	d									10 56			11 11												
London Bridge	d	10 58	11 01	11 05	11 09		11 09	11 13	11 14				11a17	11 21	11 21	11 24	11 24	11 27	11 28	11 31		11 35	11 39		11 39
London Victoria	d					10 58						11 06												11 28	
New Cross	d	12a16	11 07				12a31	11 19							11 27		11 30		12a46	11 37					13a01
St Johns	d		11 09					11 21							11 29		11 32			11 39					
Lewisham	a		11 11	11 14				11 23				11 26		11 29	11 32		11 34			11 41		11 44			
Hither Green	a							11 28	11 23								11 39	11 36							
Petts Wood	a					11 33			11 36	11 40							11 52							12 03	
Orpington	a				11 25	11 39			11 40	11 44						11 39	11 57						11 55	12 07	

		SE	SE	TL	SE	TL		SE	SE	SE	SE	SE	SE	SE	SE	SE		SE	SE	SE	SE	TL	SE	TL	SE
										◇1						◇1									
London Charing Cross	d		11 35					11 42		11 45		11 48			11 54	12 00					12 05				12 12
London Waterloo (East)	d		11 38					11 45		11 48		11 51			11 58	12 03					12 08				12 15
London Cannon Street	d	11 38							11 47		11 50		11 54	11 57					12 05	12 08					
London Blackfriars	d			11 26		11 41																11 56		12 11	
London Bridge	d	11 43	11 44			11a47		11 51	11 51	11 54	11 54	11 57	11 58	12 01	12 05	12 09			12 09	12 13	12 14			12a17	12 21
London Victoria	d				11 36													11 58					12 06		
New Cross	d	11 49							11 57		12 00		13a16	12 07					13a31	12 19					
St Johns	d	11 51							11 59		12 02			12 09						12 21					
Lewisham	a	11 53			11 56			11 59	12 02		12 04			12 11	12 14					12 23			12 26		12 29
Hither Green	a	11 58	11 53								12 09	12 06								12 28	12 23				
Petts Wood	a		12 06	12 10							12 22							12 33			12 36	12 40			
Orpington	a		12 09	12 14						12 09	12 25					12 25		12 37			12 39	12 44			

		SE		SE	SE	SE	SE	SE	SE	SE	SE	SE		SE	SE	TL	SE	TL	SE	SE	SE	SE		SE	SE
				◇1						◇1											◇1				
London Charing Cross	d			12 15		12 18			12 24	12 30					12 35				12 42		12 45			12 48	
London Waterloo (East)	d			12 18		12 21			12 28	12 33					12 38				12 45		12 48			12 51	
London Cannon Street	d	12 17			12 20		12 24	12 27				12 35		12 38						12 47		12 50			12 54
London Blackfriars	d															12 26		12 41							
London Bridge	d	12 21		12 24	12 24	12 27	12 28	12 31	12 35	12 39		12 39		12 43	12 44			12a47	12 51	12 51	12 54	12 54		12 57	12 58
London Victoria	d										12 28						12 36								
New Cross	d	12 27			12 30		13a46	12 37				14a01		12 49						12 57		13 00			14a16
St Johns	d	12 29			12 32			12 39						12 51						12 59		13 02			
Lewisham	a	12 32			12 34			12 41	12 44					12 53			12 56		12 59	13 02		13 04			
Hither Green	a				12 39	12 36								12 58	12 53							13 09		13 06	
Petts Wood	a				12 52						13 03				13 06	13 10						13 22			
Orpington	a			12 39	12 55					12 55	13 07				13 09	13 14					13 09	13 25			

NRT MAY 2018 EDITION

Table T199-F

Mondays to Fridays
21 May to 7 December

London - Lewisham, Hither Green, Petts Wood and Orpington (Summary of Services)

		SE	SE	SE		SE	SE	SE	SE	TL	SE	TL	SE	SE		SE	SE	SE	SE	SE	SE	SE	SE	SE	
				◇1												◇1						◇1			
London Charing Cross	d		12 54	13 00					13 05				13 12			13 15		13 18			13 24	13 30			
London Waterloo (East)	d		12 58	13 03					13 08				13 15			13 18		13 21			13 28	13 33			
London Cannon Street	d	12 57					13 05	13 08						13 17			13 20		13 24	13 27				13 35	
London Blackfriars	d									12 56		13 11													
London Bridge	d	13 01	13 05	13 09			13 09	13 13	13 14			13a17	13 21	13 21		13 24	13 24	13 27	13 28	13 31	13 35	13 39		13 39	
London Victoria	d					12 58					13 06												13 28		
New Cross	d	13 07					14a31	13 19						13 27			13 30		14a46	13 37				15a01	
St Johns	d	13 09						13 21						13 29			13 32			13 39					
Lewisham	a	13 11	13 14					13 23			13 26		13 29	13 32			13 34			13 41	13 44				
Hither Green	a							13 28	13 23								13 39	13 36							
Petts Wood	a					13 33			13 36	13 40							13 52						14 03		
Orpington	a			13 25		13 37			13 39	13 44						13 39	13 55					13 55	14 07		

		SE	SE	TL	SE	TL	SE	SE	SE	SE		SE	SE	SE	SE	SE	SE	SE	SE	SE		TL	SE	TL	SE
									◇1							◇1									
London Charing Cross	d		13 35				13 42		13 45			13 48			13 54	14 00				14 05					14 12
London Waterloo (East)	d		13 38				13 45		13 48			13 51			13 58	14 03				14 08					14 15
London Cannon Street	d	13 38						13 47		13 50			13 54	13 57				14 05	14 08						
London Blackfriars	d			13 26		13 41																13 56		14 11	
London Bridge	d	13 43	13 44			13a47	13 51	13 51	13 54	13 54		13 57	13 58	14 01	14 05	14 09		14 09	14 13	14 14				14a17	14 21
London Victoria	d				13 36												13 58						14 06		
New Cross	d	13 49						13 57		14 00			15a16	14 07				15a31	14 19						
St Johns	d	13 51						13 59		14 02				14 09					14 21						
Lewisham	a	13 53			13 56		13 59	14 02		14 04				14 11	14 14				14 23				14 26		14 29
Hither Green	a	13 58	13 53							14 09		14 06							14 28	14 23					
Petts Wood	a		14 06	14 10						14 22							14 33			14 36		14 40			
Orpington	a		14 09	14 14					14 09	14 25						14 25	14 37			14 39		14 44			

		SE	SE	SE	SE	SE		SE	SE	SE	SE	SE	SE	SE	TL	SE		TL	SE	SE	SE	SE	SE	SE	SE
			◇1							◇1											◇1				
London Charing Cross	d		14 15		14 18				14 24	14 30				14 35					14 42		14 45		14 48		
London Waterloo (East)	d		14 18		14 21				14 28	14 33				14 38					14 45		14 48		14 51		
London Cannon Street	d	14 17		14 20		14 24		14 27				14 35	14 38							14 47		14 50		14 54	14 57
London Blackfriars	d														14 26			14 41							
London Bridge	d	14 21	14 24	14 24	14 27	14 28		14 31	14 35	14 39		14 39	14 43	14 44				14a47	14 51	14 51	14 54	14 54	14 57	14 58	15 01
London Victoria	d										14 28					14 36									
New Cross	d	14 27		14 30		15a46		14 37				16a02	14 49							14 57		15 00		16a16	15 07
St Johns	d	14 29		14 32				14 39					14 51							14 59		15 02			15 09
Lewisham	a	14 32		14 34				14 41	14 44				14 53			14 56			14 59	15 02		15 04			15 11
Hither Green	a			14 39	14 36								14 58	14 53								15 09	15 06		
Petts Wood	a			14 52							15 03			15 06	15 10							15 22			
Orpington	a		14 39	14 55						14 55	15 07			15 09	15 14						15 09	15 27			

		SE		SE	SE	SE	SE	SE	TL	SE	TL	SE		SE	SE	SE	SE	SE	SE	SE	SE	SE		SE	SE
				◇1											◇1						◇1				
London Charing Cross	d	14 54		15 00				15 05				15 12			15 15		15 18			15 24	15 30				
London Waterloo (East)	d	14 58		15 03				15 08				15 15			15 18		15 21			15 28	15 33				
London Cannon Street	d					15 05	15 08							15 17		15 20		15 24	15 27					15 35	15 38
London Blackfriars	d								14 56		15 11														
London Bridge	d	15 05		15 09		15 09	15 13	15 14			15a17	15 21		15 21	15 24	15 24	15 27	15 28	15 31	15 35	15 39			15 39	15 43
London Victoria	d				14 58					15 06												15 28			
New Cross	d					16a31	15 19							15 27		15 30		16a41	15 37					17a04	15 49
St Johns	d						15 21							15 29		15 32			15 39						15 51
Lewisham	a	15 14					15 23			15 26		15 29		15 32		15 34			15 41	15 44					15 53
Hither Green	a						15 28	15 23								15 39	15 36								15 58
Petts Wood	a				15 33			15 36	15 40							15 52						16 03			
Orpington	a			15 25	15 37			15 39	15 44						15 39	15 55					15 55	16 07			

		SE	TL	SE	TL	SE	SE	SE		SE	SE	SE	SE	SE	SE	SE	SE	SE		SE	TL	SE	TL	SE	SE
								◇1							◇1										
London Charing Cross	d	15 35				15 42		15 45			15 48			15 54	16 00					16 05					16 12
London Waterloo (East)	d	15 38				15 45		15 48			15 51			15 58	16 03					16 08					16 15
London Cannon Street	d						15 47			15 50		15 54	15 57				16 05	16 08						16 15	
London Blackfriars	d		15 26		15 41																15 56		16 11		
London Bridge	d	15 44			15a47	15 51	15 51	15 54		15 54	15 57	15 58	16 01	16 05	16 09		16 10	16 13		16 14			16a17	16 20	16 21
London Victoria	d			15 36												15 58						16 06			
New Cross	d						15 57			16 01		17a13	16 07				17a33	16 19						16 26	
St Johns	d						15 59			16 03			16 09					16 21						16 28	
Lewisham	a			15 56		16 00	16 03			16 05			16 11	16 14				16 23				16 26		16 32	16 29
Hither Green	a	15 53								16 10	16 06							16 28		16 23					
Petts Wood	a	16 06	16 11							16 23						16 33				16 36	16 40				
Orpington	a	16 09	16 14					16 10		16 29					16 25	16 37				16 40	16 44				

		SE	SE	SE		SE	SE	SE	SE	SE	SE	TL	SE	SE		SE	TL	SE	SE	SE	SE	SE	SE	SE	
		◇1							◇1															◇1	
London Charing Cross	d	16 14		16 18				16 24	16 28	16 30								16 41		16 45		16 48		16 51	
London Waterloo (East)	d	16 17		16 21				16 28	16 31	16 33								16 44		16 48		16 51		16 54	
London Cannon Street	d		16 18			16 25	16 27						16 37	16 39					16 45		16 50		16 52		
London Blackfriars	d											16 26					16 41								
London Bridge	d	16 23	16 23	16 27		16 30	16 32	16 35	16 37	16 39			16 42	16 44			16a47	16 50	16 50	16 54	16 55	16 57	16 57	17 00	
London Victoria	d										16 28					16 36									
New Cross	d		16 29			16 36	17a41						17a58	16 50					16 56		17 01		17 04		
St Johns	d		16 31			16 38								16 52					16 58		17 03				
Lewisham	a		16 34			16 40		16 44						16 54		16 56		16 59	17 00	17 03	17 05				
Hither Green	a		16 41	16 38						16 48				16 59				17 04				17 07	17 09		
Petts Wood	a		16 54							17 02	17 05	17 10						17 18					17 23		
Orpington	a	16 39	17 00						16 54	17 06	17 11	17 14						17 24					17 27	17 17	

Table T199-F

Mondays to Fridays
21 May to 7 December

London - Lewisham, Hither Green, Petts Wood and Orpington (Summary of Services)

	SE	SE	SE	SE	SE		SE	TL	SE	SE	SE	SE	TL	SE	SE		SE	SE	SE	SE	SE	SE	SE	SE
London Charing Cross ⊖ d	16 53						17 03		17 06			17 08			17 13			17 17		17 26	17 28			17 34
London Waterloo (East) ⊖ d	16 56						17 06		17 09			17 11			17 16			17 20		17 29	17 31			17 37
London Cannon Street ⊖ d			16 58	17 03	17 05						17 11			17 16			17 19		17 27				17 32	
London Blackfriars ⊖ d								16 56					17 11											
London Bridge ⊖ d	17 02		17 03	17 08	17 10		17 12		17 15		17 16	17 17	17a17	17 21	17 22		17 24	17 26	17 32	17 35	17 37		17 37	17 43
London Victoria ⊖ d		16 58								17 06												17 28		
New Cross ⊖ d			17 09	17 15	18a36						17 22						17 30		17 37				17 43	
St Johns d			17 11								17 24						17 32						17 45	
Lewisham a	17 11		17 13	17 18			17 20		17 23	17 26	17 28				17 30		17 34		17 41	17 44			17 47	17 51
Hither Green a			17 19				17 25					17 28		17 31			17 40	17 36		17 49	17 47			18 57
Petts Wood a		17 33					17 38	17 41						17 45						18 03		18 06		
Orpington a		17 37					17 45	17 45						17 49						18 09		18 12		

	SE		TL	SE	SE	SE	TL	SE	SE	SE	SE		SE	SE	SE	SE	SE	SE	SE	TL	SE		SE	SE
London Charing Cross ⊖ d				17 36				17 41		17 47	17 51			17 53		17 55					17 59			
London Waterloo (East) ⊖ d				17 39				17 44		17 50	17 54			17 56		17 58					18 02			
London Cannon Street ⊖ d	17 39				17 41				17 47				17 55		17 58		18 00						18 04	18 09
London Blackfriars ⊖ d			17 26				17 41													17 56				
London Bridge ⊖ d	17 44			17 45	17 46		17a47	17 50	17 52	17 56	18 00		18 00	18 02	18 03	18 04	18 05				18 08		18 09	18 14
London Victoria ⊖ d						17 34												17 55	17 58					
New Cross ⊖ d	17 50				17 53				17 58				18 06		18 09		18 11						19a31	18 20
St Johns d					17 55								18 08				18 13							
Lewisham a				17 54	17 57	17 59			18 02	18 04	18 09		18 11			18 13	18 16	18 18						18 23
Hither Green a	17 55				18 03			18 00						18 12	18 14		18 21				18 18			
Petts Wood a	18 09		18 12							18 21					18 27				18 33	18 43				
Orpington a	18 12		18 16							18 28					18 32				18 38	18 48				

	TL	SE	SE	SE	SE	SE	SE		SE	SE	SE	SE	SE ◇■	SE	TL	SE	SE		SE	SE	SE	TL	SE	SE
London Charing Cross ⊖ d		18 09	18 11		18 15		18 17				18 29		18 31						18 36		18 38		18 43	
London Waterloo (East) ⊖ d		18 12	18 14		18 18		18 20				18 32		18 34						18 39		18 41		18 46	
London Cannon Street ⊖ d				18 15		18 20			18 22			18 33				18 35	18 38			18 41				18 48
London Blackfriars ⊖ d	18 11														18 26							18 41		
London Bridge ⊖ d	18a17	18 18	18 20	18 20	18 24	18 25	18 26		18 27		18 38	18 38	18 40			18 40	18 43		18 45	18 46	18 47	18a47	18 52	18 53
London Victoria ⊖ d										18 21				18 28										
New Cross ⊖ d				18 26		18 31			18 34			18 44				20a01	18 49			18 52				18 59
St Johns d				18 28					18 36			18 46					18 51			18 54				19 01
Lewisham a			18 28	18 30		18 36	18 34		18 39	18 43		18 48					18 53			18 57	18 55		19 00	19 03
Hither Green a					18 35	18 41			18 46		18 48								18 55	19 03				19 09
Petts Wood a		18 40				18 55					19 02			19 05	19 10									19 24
Orpington a		18 47				18 59					19 08		18 56	19 11	19 14									19 30

	SE	SE ◇■	SE		SE	SE	SE	SE	SE ◇■	SE	SE	SE	SE		SE	TL	SE	TL	SE	SE	SE ◇■	SE	SE	
London Charing Cross ⊖ d		18 45	18 48					18 56	19 00			19 02			19 05					19 12	19 15		19 18	
London Waterloo (East) ⊖ d		18 49	18 51					18 59	19 03			19 05			19 08					19 15	19 18		19 21	
London Cannon Street ⊖ d					18 53	18 55	18 57				19 05		19 08						19 16			19 22		
London Blackfriars ⊖ d																18 56		19 11						
London Bridge ⊖ d		18 55	18 57		18 58	19 00	19 02	19 05	19 09		19 09	19 11	19 13		19 14			19a17	19 20	19 21	19 24	19 26	19 27	
London Victoria ⊖ d	18 42									18 58							19 06							
New Cross ⊖ d					19 04	20a16	19 08				20a31		19 19						19 26			19 32		
St Johns d					19 06		19 10						19 21						19 28			19 34		
Lewisham a	19 05				19 08		19 12	19 14					19 23				19 26		19 32	19 29		19 36		
Hither Green a			19 06									19 21	19 28		19 23							19 41	19 38	
Petts Wood a			19 20							19 33					19 36	19 40						19 54		
Orpington a		19 11	19 26						19 26	19 38					19 39	19 44					19 39	19 59		

	SE	SE	SE	SE ◇■	SE	SE	SE	SE	TL		SE	TL	SE	SE	SE ◇■	SE	SE	SE	SE		SE ◇■	SE	SE	SE
London Charing Cross ⊖ d			19 24	19 30				19 35					19 42		19 45		19 48		19 54		20 00			
London Waterloo (East) ⊖ d			19 28	19 33				19 38					19 45		19 48		19 51		19 58		20 03			
London Cannon Street ⊖ d	19 24	19 27				19 35	19 38							19 47		19 50		19 57					20 05	20 08
London Blackfriars ⊖ d									19 26			19 41												
London Bridge ⊖ d	19 28	19 31	19 35	19 39		19 39	19 43	19 44				19a47	19 51	19 51	19 54	19 54	19 57	20 01	20 05		20 09		20 09	20 13
London Victoria ⊖ d					19 28						19 36											19 58		
New Cross ⊖ d	20a46	19 37				21a01	19 49							19 57		20 00		20 07					21a31	20 19
St Johns d		19 39					19 51							19 59		20 02		20 09						20 21
Lewisham a		19 41	19 44				19 53				19 56		19 59	20 02		20 04		20 11	20 14					20 23
Hither Green a							19 58	19 53								20 09	20 06							20 28
Petts Wood a					20 03			20 06	20 11							20 22						20 33		
Orpington a				19 55	20 07			20 09	20 14						20 09	20 25					20 25	20 37		

	SE	TL	SE	TL	SE		SE	SE ◇■	SE	SE	SE	SE	SE ◇■	SE	SE		SE	SE	TL	SE	TL	SE	SE	SE ◇■
London Charing Cross ⊖ d	20 05				20 12			20 15		20 18		20 24	20 30					20 35				20 42		20 45
London Waterloo (East) ⊖ d	20 08				20 15			20 18		20 21		20 28	20 33					20 38				20 45		20 48
London Cannon Street ⊖ d							20 17		20 20		20 27				20 35		20 38						20 47	
London Blackfriars ⊖ d		19 56		20 11															20 26		20 41			
London Bridge ⊖ d	20 14			20a17	20 21		20 21	20 24	20 24	20 27	20 31	20 35	20 39		20 39		20 43	20 44			20a47	20 51	20 51	20 54
London Victoria ⊖ d			20 06											20 28						20 36				
New Cross ⊖ d							20 27		20 30		20 37				22a01		20 49						20 57	
St Johns d							20 29		20 32		20 39						20 51						20 59	
Lewisham a			20 26		20 29		20 32		20 34		20 41	20 44					20 53			20 56		20 59	21 02	
Hither Green a	20 23								20 39	20 36							20 58	20 53						
Petts Wood a	20 36	20 40							20 52					21 03				21 06	21 10					
Orpington a	20 39	20 44						20 39	20 55				20 55	21 07				21 09	21 14					21 09

Table T199-F

Mondays to Fridays
21 May to 7 December

London - Lewisham, Hither Green, Petts Wood and Orpington (Summary of Services)

	SE	SE	SE	SE	SE ◇■	SE	SE		SE	SE	TL	SE	TL	SE ◇■	SE	SE	SE		SE	SE	SE	SE ◇■	SE	SE
London Charing Cross ⊖ d		20 48		20 54	21 00					21 05				21 10	21 12		21 18			21 24		21 30		
London Waterloo (East) ⊖ d		20 51		20 58	21 03					21 08				21 13	21 15		21 21			21 28		21 33		
London Cannon Street ⊖ d	20 50		20 57				21 05		21 08							21 20			21 27		21 32			21 38
London Blackfriars ⊖ d											20 56		21 11											
London Bridge ⊖ d	20 54	20 57	21 01	21 05	21 09		21 09		21 13	21 14			21a17	21 19	21 21	21 24	21 27		21 31	21 35	21 36	21 39		21 43
London Victoria ⊖ d						20 58						21 06											21 28	
New Cross ⊖ d	21 00		21 07				22a31		21 19							21 30			21 37		23a01			21 49
St Johns d	21 02		21 09						21 21							21 32			21 39					21 51
Lewisham a	21 04		21 11	21 14					21 23			21 26			21 29	21 34			21 41	21 44				21 53
Hither Green a	21 09	21 06							21 28	21 23						21 39	21 36							21 58
Petts Wood a	21 22					21 33				21 36	21 40					21 52							22 03	
Orpington a	21 25				21 25	21 37				21 39	21 44			21 34		21 55						21 55	22 07	

	SE	TL	SE		TL	SE	SE ◇■	SE	SE	SE	SE	SE	SE ◇■		SE	SE	SE	TL	SE	TL	SE ◇■	SE	SE	
London Charing Cross ⊖ d	21 35					21 42	21 45		21 48		21 54		22 00				22 05				22 10	22 12		
London Waterloo (East) ⊖ d	21 38					21 45	21 48		21 51		21 58		22 03				22 08				22 13	22 15		
London Cannon Street ⊖ d								21 50		21 57		22 02				22 08							22 20	
London Blackfriars ⊖ d		21 26			21 41													21 56		22 11				
London Bridge ⊖ d	21 44				21a47	21 51	21 54	21 54	21 57	22 01	22 05	22 06	22 09			22 13	22 14			22a17	22 19	22 21	22 24	
London Victoria ⊖ d			21 36												21 58				22 06					
New Cross ⊖ d								22 00		22 07		23a31				22 19							22 30	
St Johns d								22 02		22 09						22 21							22 32	
Lewisham a			21 56			21 59		22 04		22 11	22 14					22 23			22 26			22 29	22 34	
Hither Green a	21 53							22 09	22 06							22 28	22 23						22 39	
Petts Wood a	22 06	22 10						22 22							22 33		22 36	22 40					22 52	
Orpington a	22 09	22 14					22 09	22 25					22 25		22 37		22 39	22 44			22 34		22 55	

	SE	SE	SE	SE MT FO	SE ◇■	SE	SE	SE	TL		SE	TL	SE	SE ◇■	SE MT FO	SE W ThO	SE	SE	SE		SE ◇■	SE	SE	SE
London Charing Cross ⊖ d	22 18		22 24		22 30			22 35					22 42	22 45			22 48		22 54		23 00		23 02	23 05
London Waterloo (East) ⊖ d	22 21		22 28		22 33			22 38					22 45	22 48			22 51		22 58		23 03		23 05	23 08
London Cannon Street ⊖ d		22 27		22 32			22 38								22 50	22 50		22 57						
London Blackfriars ⊖ d									22 26			22 41												
London Bridge ⊖ d	22 27	22 31	22 35	22 36	22 39		22 43	22 44				22a47	22 51	22 54	22 54	22 54	22 57	23 01	23 05		23 09		23 11	23 14
London Victoria ⊖ d						22 28					22 36											22 58		
New Cross ⊖ d		22 37		00a01			22 49								23 00	23 00		23 07						
St Johns d		22 39					22 51								23 02	23 02		23 09						
Lewisham a		22 41	22 44				22 53				22 56		22 59		23 04	23 04		23 11	23 14					
Hither Green a	22 36						22 58	22 53							23 09	23 09	23 06						23 21	23 23
Petts Wood a						23 03		23 06	23 10						23 22	23 22						23 33		23 36
Orpington a					22 55	23 07		23 09	23 14					23 09	23 25	23 27					23 25	23 37		23 39

	TL	SE	TL	SE	SE		SE	SE	SE	SE ◇■	SE	SE	SE	SE	SE W ThO		SE	SE ◇■	SE MT FO	SE	SE	SE FO	SE	
London Charing Cross ⊖ d				23 12			23 20		23 24	23 30		23 32	23 35				23 42	23 45		23 50	23 52			
London Waterloo (East) ⊖ d				23 15			23 23		23 28	23 33		23 35	23 38				23 45	23 48		23 53	23 55			
London Cannon Street ⊖ d					23 20			23 27							23 45				23 50			23 57		
London Blackfriars ⊖ d	22 56		23 11																					
London Bridge ⊖ d			23a17	23 21	23 24		23 29	23 31	23 35	23 39		23 41	23 44		23 49		23 51	23 54	23 54	23 59	00 01	00 01		
London Victoria ⊖ d		23 06									23 28			23 36									23 58	
New Cross ⊖ d					23 30			23 37							23 54				23 59			00 07		
St Johns d					23 32			23 39							23 57				00 02			00 09		
Lewisham a		23 26		23 29	23 34		23 37	23 41	23 44					23 56	00 01		23 59		00 04	00 07	00 09	00 11		
Hither Green a					23 39		23 42					23 51	23 53		00 09				00 09	00 12				
Petts Wood a	23 40				23 52						00 03		00 06		00 22				00 22				00 34	
Orpington a	23 44				23 55					23 55	00 07		00 12		00 25			00 09	00 25				00 38	

Saturdays
26 May to 8 December

	SE	SE	SE	SE	SE	SE	SE	SE	SE		SE	SE	SE	SE	SE	SE	TL	SE	SE		SE	SE ◇■	SE	SE
London Charing Cross ⊖ d					00 26		00 50	04 50			05 20	05 24			05 35	05 37			05 50		05 54	06 00		
London Waterloo (East) ⊖ d					00 29		00 53	04 53			05 23	05 28			05 38	05 40			05 53		05 58	06 03		
London Cannon Street ⊖ d									05 05					05 35				05 50						06 05
London Blackfriars ⊖ d																	05 41							
London Bridge ⊖ d		00 01	00 01		00 35		00 59	04 59	05 09		05 29	05 35		05 39	05 44	05 46	05a47	05 54	05 59		06 05	06 09		06 09
London Victoria ⊖ d				00 06		00 28							05 28										05 58	
New Cross ⊖ d			00 07						06a31					07a01				06 00						07a31
St Johns d	00 02		00 09															06 02						
Lewisham a	00 04	00 09	00 11	00 26	00 44		01 07	05 07			05 37	05 44				05 56		06 04	06 07		06 14			
Hither Green a	00 09						01 12	05 14			05 44				05 53			06 09	06 14					
Petts Wood a	00 22					01 03	01 25						06 03		06 06			06 22					06 33	
Orpington a	00 25					01 07	01 32						06 06		06 09			06 25				06 25	06 36	

London - Lewisham, Hither Green, Petts Wood and Orpington (Summary of Services)

	SE		SE	SE	TL	SE	SE	SE	SE	SE	SE		SE	SE	SE	TL	SE	SE	SE	SE	SE		SE	SE
London Charing Cross ⊖ d			06 05	06 07		06 12		06 18	06 24					06 35	06 37		06 42		06 48		06 54			
London Waterloo (East) ⊖ d			06 08	06 10		06 15		06 21	06 28					06 38	06 40		06 45		06 51		06 58			
London Cannon Street ⊖ d	06 08						06 20				06 35		06 38					06 50		06 57				07 05
London Blackfriars ⊖ d					06 11											06 41								
London Bridge ⊖ d	06 13		06 14	06 16	06a17	06 21	06 24	06 27	06 35		06 39		06 43	06 44	06 46	06a47	06 51	06 54	06 57	07 01	07 05			07 09
London Victoria ⊖ d										06 28													06 58	
New Cross ⊖ d	06 19						06 30				08a01		06 49					07 00		07 07				08a31
St Johns d	06 21						06 32						06 51					07 02		07 09				
Lewisham a	06 23			06 26		06 29	06 34		06 44				06 53		06 56		06 59	07 04		07 11	07 14			
Hither Green a	06 28		06 23				06 39	06 36					06 58	06 53				07 09	07 06					
Petts Wood a			06 36				06 52			07 03				07 06				07 22					07 33	
Orpington a			06 39				06 55			07 06				07 09				07 25					07 36	

	SE	SE	TL	SE	TL	SE	SE		SE ◇1	SE	SE	SE	SE	SE	SE	SE	SE		TL	SE	TL	SE	SE	SE ◇1
London Charing Cross ⊖ d		07 05				07 12			07 15		07 18		07 24				07 35					07 42		07 45
London Waterloo (East) ⊖ d		07 08				07 15			07 18		07 21		07 28				07 38					07 45		07 48
London Cannon Street ⊖ d	07 08						07 17			07 20		07 27			07 35	07 38							07 47	
London Blackfriars ⊖ d			06 56		07 11														07 26		07 41			
London Bridge ⊖ d	07 13	07 14			07a17	07 21	07 21		07 24	07 24	07 27	07 31	07 35		07 39	07 43	07 44				07a47	07 51	07 51	07 54
London Victoria ⊖ d				07 06										07 28						07 36				
New Cross ⊖ d	07 19						07 27			07 30		07 37			09a01	07 49							07 57	
St Johns d	07 21						07 29			07 32		07 39				07 51							07 59	
Lewisham a	07 23			07 26		07 29	07 32			07 34		07 41	07 44			07 53				07 56		07 59	08 02	
Hither Green a	07 28	07 23								07 39	07 36					07 58	07 53							
Petts Wood a		07 36	07 40							07 52				08 03			08 06		08 10					
Orpington a		07 39	07 44						07 39	07 55				08 06			08 09		08 14					08 09

	SE	SE	SE		SE	SE	SE	SE	SE	SE	TL	SE	TL	SE	SE	SE ◇1	SE	SE	SE	SE	SE	SE ◇1	SE	SE
London Charing Cross ⊖ d		07 48				07 54				08 05				08 12		08 15		08 18			08 24	08 30		
London Waterloo (East) ⊖ d		07 51				07 58				08 08				08 15		08 18		08 21			08 28	08 33		
London Cannon Street ⊖ d	07 50		07 54		07 57			08 05	08 08						08 17		08 20		08 24	08 27				08 35
London Blackfriars ⊖ d											07 56		08 11											
London Bridge ⊖ d	07 54	07 57	07 58		08 01	08 05		08 09	08 13	08 14			08a17	08 21	08 21	08 24	08 24	08 27	08 28	08 31	08 35	08 39		08 39
London Victoria ⊖ d							07 58					08 06											08 28	
New Cross ⊖ d	08 00		09a16		08 07			09a31	08 19						08 27		08 30		09a46	08 37				10a01
St Johns d	08 02				08 09				08 21						08 29		08 32			08 39				
Lewisham a	08 04				08 11	08 14			08 23			08 26		08 29	08 32		08 34			08 41	08 44			
Hither Green a	08 09	08 06							08 28	08 23							08 39	08 36						
Petts Wood a	08 22						08 33			08 36	08 40						08 52						09 03	
Orpington a	08 25						08 36			08 39	08 44					08 39	08 55					08 55	09 06	

	SE	SE	TL	SE	TL	SE	SE	SE ◇1	SE	SE	SE	SE	SE	SE ◇1		SE	SE	SE	SE	TL	SE	TL	SE
London Charing Cross ⊖ d		08 35				08 42		08 45		08 48			08 54	09 00					13 05				13 12
London Waterloo (East) ⊖ d		08 38				08 45		08 48		08 51			08 58	09 03	and at				13 08				13 15
London Cannon Street ⊖ d	08 38						08 47		08 50		08 54	08 57			the same		13 05	13 08					
London Blackfriars ⊖ d			08 26		08 41										minutes					12 56		13 11	
London Bridge ⊖ d	08 43	08 44			08a47	08 51	08 51	08 54	08 54	08 57	08 58	09 01	09 05	09 09	past		13 09	13 13	13 14			13a17	13 21
London Victoria ⊖ d				08 36											each	12 58					13 06		
New Cross ⊖ d	08 49						08 57		09 00		10a16	09 07			hour until		14a31	13 19					
St Johns d	08 51						08 59		09 02			09 09						13 21					
Lewisham a	08 53			08 56		08 59	09 02		09 04			09 11	09 14					13 23			13 26		13 29
Hither Green a	08 58	08 53							09 09	09 06								13 28	13 23				
Petts Wood a		09 06	09 10						09 22							13 33			13 36	13 40			
Orpington a		09 09	09 14					09 09	09 25					09 25		13 36			13 39	13 44			

	SE	SE ◇1	SE	SE	SE	SE	SE	SE ◇1	SE	SE	SE	SE	TL	SE	TL	SE	SE	SE ◇1	SE	SE	SE	SE	SE	SE ◇1
London Charing Cross ⊖ d		13 15		13 18			13 24	13 30				13 35				13 42		13 45		13 48			13 54	14 00
London Waterloo (East) ⊖ d		13 18		13 21			13 28	13 33				13 38				13 45		13 48		13 51			13 58	14 03
London Cannon Street ⊖ d	13 17		13 20		13 24	13 27				13 35	13 38						13 47		13 50		13 54	13 57		
London Blackfriars ⊖ d													13 26		13 41									
London Bridge ⊖ d	13 21	13 24	13 24	13 27	13 28	13 31	13 35	13 39		13 39	13 43	13 44			13a47	13 51	13 51	13 54	13 54	13 57	13 58	14 01	14 05	14 09
London Victoria ⊖ d									13 28					13 36										
New Cross ⊖ d	13 27		13 30		14a46	13 37				15a01	13 49						13 57		14 00		15a16	14 07		
St Johns d	13 29		13 32			13 39					13 51						13 59		14 02			14 09		
Lewisham a	13 32		13 34			13 41	13 44				13 53			13 56		13 59	14 02		14 04			14 11	14 14	
Hither Green a			13 39	13 36							13 58	13 53							14 09	14 06				
Petts Wood a			13 52						14 03			14 06	14 10						14 22					
Orpington a		13 39	13 55					13 55	14 06			14 09	14 14					14 09	14 25					14 25

		SE	SE	SE	SE	TL	SE	TL	SE	SE	SE ◇1	SE	SE	SE	SE	SE	SE ◇1	SE	SE	SE	SE	TL	SE	TL
London Charing Cross ⊖ d					14 05				14 12		14 15		14 18			14 24	14 30				14 35			
London Waterloo (East) ⊖ d					14 08				14 15		14 18		14 21			14 28	14 33				14 38			
London Cannon Street ⊖ d			14 05	14 08						14 17		14 20		14 24	14 27				14 35	14 38				
London Blackfriars ⊖ d						13 56		14 11														14 26		14 41
London Bridge ⊖ d			14 09	14 13	14 14			14a17	14 21	14 21	14 24	14 24	14 27	14 28	14 31	14 35	14 39		14 39	14 43	14 44			14a47
London Victoria ⊖ d		13 58					14 06											14 28					14 36	
New Cross ⊖ d			15a31	14 19						14 27		14 30		15a46	14 37				16a01	14 49				
St Johns d				14 21						14 29		14 32			14 39					14 51				
Lewisham a				14 23			14 26		14 29	14 32		14 34			14 41	14 44				14 53			14 56	
Hither Green a				14 30	14 23							14 39	14 36							14 58	14 53			
Petts Wood a		14 33			14 36	14 40						14 52						15 03			15 06	15 10		
Orpington a		14 36			14 39	14 44					14 39	14 55					14 55	15 06			15 09	15 14		

Table T199-F

Saturdays
26 May to 8 December

London - Lewisham, Hither Green, Petts Wood and Orpington (Summary of Services)

	SE	SE	SE ◇1	SE	SE	SE	SE	SE	SE ◇1	SE	SE	SE		SE	TL	SE	TL	SE	SE	SE ◇1	SE	SE	SE
London Charing Cross ⊖ d	14 42		14 45		14 48			14 54	15 00					18 05				18 12		18 15		18 18	
London Waterloo (East) ⊖ d	14 45		14 48		14 51			14 58	15 03				and at	18 08				18 15		18 18		18 21	
London Cannon Street ⊖ d		14 47		14 50		14 54	14 57				15 05	15 08	the same						18 17		18 20		18 24
London Blackfriars ⊖ d													minutes		17 56		18 11						
London Bridge ⊖ d	14 51	14 51	14 54	14 54	14 57	14 58	15 01	15 05	15 09		15 09	15 13	past	18 14			18a17	18 21	18 21	18 24	18 24	18 27	18 28
London Victoria ⊖ d										14 58			each			18 06							
New Cross ⊖ d		14 57		15 00		16a16	15 07				16a31	15 19	hour until						18 27		18 30		19a46
St Johns d		14 59		15 02			15 09					15 21							18 29		18 32		
Lewisham a	14 59	15 02		15 04			15 11	15 14				15 23				18 26		18 29	18 32		18 34		
Hither Green a				15 09	15 06							15 28		18 23							18 39	18 36	
Petts Wood a				15 22						15 33				18 36	18 40						18 52		
Orpington a			15 09	15 25					15 25	15 36				18 39	18 44					18 39	18 55		

	SE	SE	SE ◇1	SE	SE	SE	SE	TL	SE	TL	SE	SE	SE ◇1	SE	SE	SE	SE	SE	SE ◇1	SE	SE	SE		SE
London Charing Cross ⊖ d		18 24	18 30				18 35				18 42		18 45		18 48			18 54	19 00					19 05
London Waterloo (East) ⊖ d		18 28	18 33				18 38				18 45		18 48		18 51			18 58	19 03					19 08
London Cannon Street ⊖ d	18 27				18 35	18 38						18 47		18 50		18 54	18 57				19 05	19 08		
London Blackfriars ⊖ d								18 26		18 41														
London Bridge ⊖ d	18 31	18 35	18 39		18 39	18 43	18 44			18a47	18 51	18 51	18 54	18 54	18 57	18 58	19 01	19 05	19 09		19 09	19 13		19 14
London Victoria ⊖ d				18 28					18 36											18 58				
New Cross ⊖ d	18 37				20a01	18 49						18 57		19 00		20a16	19 07				20a31	19 19		
St Johns d	18 39					18 51						18 59		19 02			19 09					19 21		
Lewisham a	18 41	18 44				18 53			18 56		18 59	19 02		19 04			19 11	19 14				19 23		
Hither Green a						18 58	18 53							19 09	19 06							19 28		19 23
Petts Wood a				19 03			19 06	19 10						19 22						19 33				19 36
Orpington a			18 55	19 06			19 09	19 14					19 09	19 25					19 25	19 36				19 39

	TL	SE	TL	SE	SE	SE ◇1	SE	SE		SE	SE	SE	SE ◇1	SE	SE	SE	SE	TL		SE	TL	SE	SE	SE ◇1
London Charing Cross ⊖ d				19 12		19 15		19 18				19 24	19 30				19 35					19 42		19 45
London Waterloo (East) ⊖ d				19 15		19 18		19 21				19 28	19 33				19 38					19 45		19 48
London Cannon Street ⊖ d					19 17		19 20			19 24	19 27				19 35	19 38							19 47	
London Blackfriars ⊖ d	18 56		19 11															19 26			19 41			
London Bridge ⊖ d			19a17	19 21	19 21	19 24	19 24	19 27		19 28	19 31	19 35	19 39		19 39	19 43	19 44				19a47	19 51	19 51	19 54
London Victoria ⊖ d		19 06												19 28						19 36				
New Cross ⊖ d					19 27		19 30			20a46	19 37				21a01	19 49							19 57	
St Johns d					19 29		19 32				19 39					19 51							19 59	
Lewisham a		19 26		19 29	19 32		19 34				19 41	19 44				19 53				19 56		19 59	20 02	
Hither Green a							19 39	19 36								19 58	19 53							
Petts Wood a	19 40						19 52							20 03			20 06	20 10						
Orpington a	19 44					19 39	19 55						19 55	20 06			20 09	20 14						20 09

	SE	SE	SE	SE		SE ◇1	SE	SE	SE	SE	TL	SE	TL	SE		SE	SE ◇1	SE	SE	SE	SE	SE	SE ◇1	SE
London Charing Cross ⊖ d		19 48		19 54		20 00				20 05				20 12			20 15		20 18		20 24		20 30	
London Waterloo (East) ⊖ d		19 51		19 58		20 03				20 08				20 15			20 18		20 21		20 28		20 33	
London Cannon Street ⊖ d	19 50		19 57					20 05	20 08							20 17		20 20		20 27		20 32		
London Blackfriars ⊖ d											19 56		20 11											
London Bridge ⊖ d	19 54	19 57	20 01	20 05		20 09		20 09	20 13	20 14			20a17	20 21		20 21	20 24	20 24	20 27	20 31	20 35	20 36	20 39	
London Victoria ⊖ d							19 58					20 06												20 28
New Cross ⊖ d	20 00		20 07					21a31	20 19							20 27		20 30		20 37		22a01		
St Johns d	20 02		20 09						20 21							20 29		20 32		20 39				
Lewisham a	20 04		20 11	20 14					20 23			20 26		20 29		20 32		20 34		20 41	20 44			
Hither Green a	20 09	20 06							20 28	20 23								20 39	20 36					
Petts Wood a	20 22						20 33			20 36	20 40							20 52						21 03
Orpington a	20 25					20 25	20 36			20 39	20 44						20 39	20 55					20 55	21 06

		SE	SE	TL	SE	TL	SE	SE	SE ◇1	SE		SE	SE	SE	SE	SE ◇1	SE	SE	SE	TL		SE	TL	SE ◇1
London Charing Cross ⊖ d			20 35				20 42		20 45			20 48		20 54		21 00			21 05					21 10
London Waterloo (East) ⊖ d			20 38				20 45		20 48			20 51		20 58		21 03			21 08					21 13
London Cannon Street ⊖ d		20 38						20 47		20 50			20 57		21 02			21 08						
London Blackfriars ⊖ d				20 26		20 41														20 56			21 11	
London Bridge ⊖ d		20 43	20 44			20a47	20 51	20 51	20 54	20 54		20 57	21 01	21 05	21 06	21 09		21 13	21 14				21a17	21 19
London Victoria ⊖ d					20 36												20 58					21 06		
New Cross ⊖ d		20 49						20 57		21 00			21 07		22a31			21 19						
St Johns d		20 51						20 59		21 02			21 09					21 21						
Lewisham a		20 53			20 56		20 59	21 02		21 04			21 11	21 14				21 23				21 26		
Hither Green a		20 58	20 53							21 09		21 06						21 28	21 23					
Petts Wood a			21 06	21 10						21 22							21 33		21 36	21 40				
Orpington a			21 09	21 14					21 09	21 25						21 25	21 36		21 39	21 44				21 34

	SE	SE	SE	SE	SE	SE		SE ◇1	SE	SE	SE	TL	SE	TL	SE	SE ◇1		SE	SE	SE	SE	SE	SE ◇1	SE
London Charing Cross ⊖ d	21 12		21 18		21 24			21 30			21 35				21 42	21 45			21 48		21 54		22 00	
London Waterloo (East) ⊖ d	21 15		21 21		21 28			21 33			21 38				21 45	21 48			21 51		21 58		22 03	
London Cannon Street ⊖ d		21 20		21 27		21 32				21 38								21 50		21 57		22 02		
London Blackfriars ⊖ d												21 26		21 41										
London Bridge ⊖ d	21 21	21 24	21 27	21 31	21 35	21 36		21 39		21 43	21 44			21a47	21 51	21 54		21 54	21 57	22 01	22 05	22 06	22 09	
London Victoria ⊖ d									21 28				21 36											21 58
New Cross ⊖ d		21 30		21 37		23a01				21 49								22 00		22 07		23a31		
St Johns d		21 32		21 39						21 51								22 02		22 09				
Lewisham a	21 29	21 34		21 41	21 44					21 53			21 56		21 59			22 04		22 11	22 14			
Hither Green a		21 39	21 36							21 58	21 53							22 09	22 06					
Petts Wood a		21 52							22 03		22 06	22 10						22 22						22 33
Orpington a		21 55						21 55	22 06		22 09	22 14				22 09		22 25					22 25	22 36

Table T199-F

Saturdays
26 May to 8 December

London - Lewisham, Hither Green, Petts Wood and Orpington (Summary of Services)

Station	SE	SE	TL	SE	TL	SE ◇1	SE	SE		SE	SE	SE	SE	SE ◇1	SE	SE	SE	TL		SE	TL	SE	SE ◇1	SE
London Charing Cross 4 ⊖ d		22 05				22 10	22 12			22 18		22 24		22 30			22 35					22 42	22 45	
London Waterloo (East) 4 ⊖ d		22 08				22 13	22 15			22 21		22 28		22 33			22 38					22 45	22 48	
London Cannon Street 4 ⊖ d	22 08							22 20			22 27		22 32			22 38								22 50
London Blackfriars 3 ⊖ d			21 56		22 11													22 26			22 41			
London Bridge 4 ⊖ d	22 13	22 14			22a17	22 19	22 21	22 24		22 27	22 31	22 35	22 36	22 39		22 43	22 44				22a47	22 51	22 54	22 54
London Victoria 15 ⊖ d				22 06											22 28					22 36				
New Cross 4 ⊖ d	22 19							22 30			22 37		00a02			22 49								23 00
St Johns d	22 21							22 32			22 39					22 51								23 02
Lewisham 4 a	22 23			22 26			22 29	22 34			22 41	22 44				22 53				22 56		22 59		23 04
Hither Green 4 a	22 28	22 23						22 39		22 36						22 58	22 53							23 09
Petts Wood 4 a		22 36	22 40					22 52							23 03		23 06	23 10						23 22
Orpington 4 a		22 39	22 44			22 34		22 55						22 55	23 06		23 09	23 14					23 09	23 25

Station	SE	SE	SE	SE ◇1		SE	SE	SE	TL	SE	TL	SE ◇1	SE	SE		SE	SE	SE	SE ◇1	SE	SE	SE	SE	SE ◇1
London Charing Cross 4 ⊖ d	22 48		22 54	23 00			23 02	23 05				23 10	23 12			23 20		23 24	23 30		23 32	23 35		23 45
London Waterloo (East) 4 ⊖ d	22 51		22 58	23 03			23 05	23 08				23 13	23 15			23 23		23 28	23 33		23 35	23 38		23 48
London Cannon Street 4 ⊖ d		22 57												23 20			23 27							
London Blackfriars 3 ⊖ d									22 56		23 11													
London Bridge 4 ⊖ d	22 57	23 01	23 05	23 09			23 11	23 14			23a17	23 19	23 21	23 24		23 29	23 31	23 35	23 39		23 41	23 44		23 54
London Victoria 15 ⊖ d						22 58				23 06										23 28			23 36	
New Cross 4 ⊖ d		23 07												23 30			23 37							
St Johns d		23 10												23 32			23 40							
Lewisham 4 a		23 12	23 14							23 26			23 29	23 34		23 37	23 42	23 44					23 56	
Hither Green 4 a	23 06						23 21	23 23						23 39		23 42					23 51	23 53		
Petts Wood 4 a						23 33		23 36	23 40					23 52						00 03		00 06		
Orpington 4 a				23 25		23 37		23 39	23 44			23 34		23 55					23 55	00 06		00 09		00 09

Station		SE	SE	SE	SE	SE
London Charing Cross 4 ⊖ d			23 50		23 54	
London Waterloo (East) 4 ⊖ d			23 53		23 58	
London Cannon Street 4 ⊖ d		23 50		23 57		
London Blackfriars 3 ⊖ d						
London Bridge 4 ⊖ d		23 54	23 59	00 01	00 05	
London Victoria 15 ⊖ d						23 58
New Cross 4 ⊖ d		23 59		00 07		
St Johns d		00 02		00 09		
Lewisham 4 a		00 04	00 07	00 11	00 14	
Hither Green 4 a		00 09	00 12			
Petts Wood 4 a		00 22				00 34
Orpington 4 a		00 25				00 37

Sundays
20 May to 2 December

Station	SE A	SE A	SE A	SE	SE	SE	SE	SE	SE		SE	SE	SE	SE	SE	SE	SE	SE	SE		SE	SE	SE	SE
London Charing Cross 4 ⊖ d				00 02	00 05			00 26			00 32	00 50						07 42	07 46		07 52			
London Waterloo (East) 4 ⊖ d				00 05	00 08			00 29			00 35	00 53						07 45	07 49		07 55			
London Cannon Street 4 ⊖ d							00 20							07 29	07 33		07 42						07 59	08 03
London Blackfriars 3 ⊖ d																								
London Bridge 4 ⊖ d		00 01	00 05	00 11	00 14		00 24	00 35			00 41	00 58		07 33	07 37		07 46	07 51	07 55		08 01		08 03	08 07
London Victoria 15 ⊖ d						00 06			00 28				07 28			07 36						07 58		
New Cross 4 ⊖ d		00 07					00 30							08a52	07 43		07 52						09a22	08 13
St Johns d	00 02	00 09					00 32								07 45		07 54							08 15
Lewisham 4 a	00 04	00 11	00 14			00 26	00 34	00 44			00 49	01 07			07 47	07 56	07 58	08 00	08 04					08 17
Hither Green 4 a	00 09			00 21	00 23		00 39				00 54	01 12					08 03		08 09		08 12			
Petts Wood 4 a	00 22				00 37		00 52		01 03			01 25	08 03						08 21			08 33		
Orpington 4 a	00 25				00 42		00 55		01 06			01 29	08 07						08 27			08 37		

Station	SE	SE	SE ◇1	SE	SE		SE	SE	SE ◇1	SE	SE	SE	SE	SE ◇1	SE		SE	SE	SE	SE ◇1	SE	SE	SE	
London Charing Cross 4 ⊖ d			08 10	08 12	08 16		08 22		08 25					08 40	08 42		08 46	08 52		08 55				
London Waterloo (East) 4 ⊖ d			08 13	08 15	08 19		08 25		08 28					08 43	08 45		08 49	08 55		08 58				
London Cannon Street 4 ⊖ d		08 12						08 29			08 33		08 42						08 59			09 03		
London Blackfriars 3 ⊖ d																								
London Bridge 4 ⊖ d		08 16	08 19	08 21	08 25		08 31	08 33	08 34		08 37		08 46	08 49	08 51		08 55	09 01	09 03	09 04		09 07		
London Victoria 15 ⊖ d	08 06									08 28		08 36									08 58		09 06	
New Cross 4 ⊖ d		08 22						09a52			08 43		08 52						10a22			09 13		
St Johns d		08 24									08 45		08 54									09 15		
Lewisham 4 a	08 26	08 28		08 30	08 34						08 47	08 56	08 58		09 00		09 04					09 17	09 26	
Hither Green 4 a		08 33			08 39		08 42						09 03				09 09	09 12						
Petts Wood 4 a					08 51					09 03							09 21				09 33			
Orpington 4 a			08 36		08 57				08 50	09 07				09 06			09 27			09 20	09 37			

Station	SE	SE ◇1	SE	SE	SE	SE	SE ◇1	SE	SE	SE	TL	SE	SE ◇1	SE	SE	SE	SE	SE ◇1	SE	SE	SE	TL	
London Charing Cross 4 ⊖ d		09 10	09 12	09 16	09 22		09 25						09 40	09 42	09 46	09 52		09 55					
London Waterloo (East) 4 ⊖ d		09 13	09 15	09 19	09 25		09 28						09 43	09 45	09 49	09 55		09 58					and at
London Cannon Street 4 ⊖ d	09 12					09 29			09 33			09 42					09 59			10 03			the same
London Blackfriars 3 ⊖ d											09 41											10 11	minutes
London Bridge 4 ⊖ d	09 16	09 19	09 21	09 25	09 31	09 33	09 34		09 37		09a46	09 46	09 49	09 51	09 55	10 01	10 03	10 04		10 07		10a16	past
London Victoria 15 ⊖ d								09 28		09 36									09 58		10 06		each
New Cross 4 ⊖ d	09 22					10a52			09 43			09 52					11a22			10 13			hour until
St Johns d	09 24								09 45			09 54								10 15			
Lewisham 4 a	09 28		09 30	09 34					09 47	09 56		09 58		10 00	10 04					10 17	10 26		
Hither Green 4 a	09 33			09 39	09 42							10 03			10 09	10 12							
Petts Wood 4 a				09 51				10 03							10 21				10 33				
Orpington 4 a		09 36		09 57			09 50	10 07					10 06		10 27			10 20	10 37				

A not 20 May

Please check the 'Additional Notes to Individual Tables' section f...

Table T199-F

Sundays
20 May to 2 December

London - Lewisham, Hither Green, Petts Wood and Orpington (Summary of Services)

Station	SE	SE ◇1	SE	SE	SE	SE	SE ◇1	SE	SE	SE	TL	SE	SE ◇1	SE	SE	SE	SE	SE ◇1	SE	SE	SE	TL		SE
London Charing Cross 4 ⊖ d		19 10	19 12	19 16	19 22		19 25						19 40	19 42	19 46	19 52		19 55						
London Waterloo (East) 4 ⊖ d		19 13	19 15	19 19	19 25		19 28						19 43	19 45	19 49	19 55		19 58						
London Cannon Street 4 ⊖ d	19 12					19 29			19 33			19 42					19 59			20 03				20 12
London Blackfriars 3 ⊖ d											19 41											20 11		
London Bridge 4 ⊖ d	19 16	19 19	19 21	19 25	19 31	19 33	19 34		19 37		19a46	19 46	19 49	19 51	19 55	20 01	20 03	20 04		20 07		20a16		20 16
London Victoria 15 ⊖ d								19 28		19 36									19 58		20 06			
New Cross 4 ⊖ d	19 22					20a52			19 43			19 52					21a22			20 13				20 22
St Johns d	19 24								19 45			19 54								20 15				20 24
Lewisham 4 a	19 28		19 30	19 34					19 47	19 56		19 58		20 00	20 04					20 17	20 26			20 28
Hither Green 4 a	19 33			19 39	19 42							20 03			20 09	20 12								20 33
Petts Wood 4 a				19 51				20 03							20 21				20 33					
Orpington 4 a		19 36		19 57			19 50	20 07					20 06		20 27			20 20	20 37					

Station	SE ◇1	SE	SE	SE	SE	SE ◇1	SE	SE		SE	TL	SE	SE ◇1	SE	SE	SE	SE	SE		SE	SE	TL	SE	SE ◇1
London Charing Cross 4 ⊖ d	20 10	20 12	20 16	20 22		20 25							20 40	20 42	20 46	20 52								21 10
London Waterloo (East) 4 ⊖ d	20 13	20 15	20 19	20 25		20 28							20 43	20 45	20 49	20 55								21 13
London Cannon Street 4 ⊖ d					20 29			20 33				20 42						20 59		21 03			21 12	
London Blackfriars 3 ⊖ d											20 41											21 11		
London Bridge 4 ⊖ d	20 19	20 21	20 25	20 31	20 33	20 34		20 37			20a46	20 46	20 49	20 51	20 55	21 01		21 03		21 07		21a16	21 16	21 19
London Victoria 15 ⊖ d							20 28			20 36							20 58				21 06			
New Cross 4 ⊖ d					21a52			20 43				20 52						22a22		21 13			21 22	
St Johns d								20 45				20 54								21 15			21 24	
Lewisham 4 a		20 30	20 34					20 47		20 56		20 58		21 00	21 04					21 17	21 26		21 28	
Hither Green 4 a			20 39	20 42								21 03			21 09	21 12							21 33	
Petts Wood 4 a			20 51				21 03								21 21		21 33							
Orpington 4 a	20 36		20 57			20 50	21 07						21 06		21 27		21 37							21 36

Station	SE	SE	SE	SE		SE ◇1	SE	SE	SE	TL	SE	SE ◇1	SE	SE		SE	SE	SE	SE	SE	TL	SE	SE ◇1	SE
London Charing Cross 4 ⊖ d	21 12	21 16	21 22			21 25						21 40	21 42	21 46		21 52							22 10	22 12
London Waterloo (East) 4 ⊖ d	21 15	21 19	21 25			21 28						21 43	21 45	21 49		21 55							22 13	22 15
London Cannon Street 4 ⊖ d				21 29				21 33			21 42							21 59	22 03			22 12		
London Blackfriars 3 ⊖ d										21 41											22 11			
London Bridge 4 ⊖ d	21 21	21 25	21 31	21 33		21 34		21 37		21a46	21 46	21 49	21 51	21 55		22 01		22 03	22 07		22a16	22 16	22 19	22 21
London Victoria 15 ⊖ d							21 28		21 36								21 58			22 06				
New Cross 4 ⊖ d				22a52				21 43			21 52							23a22	22 13			22 22		
St Johns d								21 45			21 54								22 15			22 24		
Lewisham 4 a	21 30	21 34						21 47	21 56		21 58		22 00	22 04					22 17	22 26		22 28		22 30
Hither Green 4 a		21 39	21 42								22 03			22 09		22 12						22 33		
Petts Wood 4 a		21 51					22 03							22 21			22 33							
Orpington 4 a		21 57				21 50	22 07					22 06		22 27			22 37						22 36	

Station		SE	SE	SE	SE ◇1	SE	SE	SE	TL	SE		SE ◇1	SE	SE	SE	SE	SE	SE	TL	SE		SE ◇1	SE	SE
London Charing Cross 4 ⊖ d		22 16	22 22		22 25							22 40	22 42	22 46	22 52							23 10	23 12	23 16
London Waterloo (East) 4 ⊖ d		22 19	22 25		22 28							22 43	22 45	22 49	22 55							23 13	23 15	23 19
London Cannon Street 4 ⊖ d				22 29			22 33			22 42							23 03			23 12				
London Blackfriars 3 ⊖ d									22 41										23 11					
London Bridge 4 ⊖ d		22 25	22 31	22 33	22 34		22 37		22a46	22 46		22 49	22 51	22 55	23 01		23 07		23a16	23 16		23 19	23 21	23 25
London Victoria 15 ⊖ d						22 28		22 36								22 58		23 06						
New Cross 4 ⊖ d				23a52			22 43			22 52							23 13			23 22				
St Johns d							22 45			22 54							23 15			23 24				
Lewisham 4 a		22 34					22 47	22 56		22 58			23 00	23 04			23 17	23 26		23 28			23 30	23 34
Hither Green 4 a		22 39	22 42							23 03				23 09	23 12					23 33				23 39
Petts Wood 4 a		22 51				23 03								23 21		23 33								23 51
Orpington 4 a		22 57			22 50	23 07						23 06		23 27		23 37						23 36		23 57

Station	SE	SE ◇1	SE	SE	SE	SE ◇1		SE	SE	SE	SE
London Charing Cross 4 ⊖ d	23 22	23 25				23 40		23 42	23 46	23 52	
London Waterloo (East) 4 ⊖ d	23 25	23 28				23 43		23 45	23 49	23 55	
London Cannon Street 4 ⊖ d				23 33							
London Blackfriars 3 ⊖ d											
London Bridge 4 ⊖ d	23 31	23 34		23 37		23 49		23 51	23 55	00 01	
London Victoria 15 ⊖ d			23 28		23 36						23 58
New Cross 4 ⊖ d				23 43							
St Johns d				23 45							
Lewisham 4 a				23 47	23 56			00 01	00 05		
Hither Green 4 a	23 42								00 09	00 12	
Petts Wood 4 a			00 03						00 21		00 33
Orpington 4 a		23 50	00 06			00 06			00 27		00 36

Table T199-R

Mondays to Fridays

21 May to 7 December

Orpington, Petts Wood, Hither Green and Lewisham - London (Summary of Services)

		SE	SE	SE	SE	SE		SE	SE	SE	SE	SE	SE	SE	TL	SE		SE	SE	TL	SE	SE	SE	SE	SE
		TWO	MO	TWO	TWO	MO		ThFO	TWO	TWO	ThFO	TWO	TWO	ThFO							1				
Orpington	d														04 33	04 54			05 00	05 03	05 13		05 24		
Petts Wood	d														04 36	04 57			05 03	05 06			05 27		
Hither Green	d					00 05		00 06	00 06				00 16	00 16				05 10	05 16			05 22			05 37
Lewisham	d				00 05	00 11		00 11	00 13	00 15	00 15	00 16						05 16	05 21			05 27		05 35	05 43
St Johns	d			00 02																		05 29			
New Cross	⊖ d	00 01	00 02	00 05																		05 31			
London Victoria	⊖ a															05 35							06 05		
London Bridge	⊖ d	00 09	00 09	00 12	00a13	00 21		00 21	00 21	00 25	00 25	00 26	00a29	00 29				05 26	05 30		05 37	05 38		05 45	05 53
London Blackfriars	⊖ a														05 19					05 49					
London Cannon Street	⊖ a	00 13	00 13	00 18					00 27	00 33												05 44			
London Waterloo (East)	⊖ d					00 26		00 26			00 30	00 31		00 34				05 31	05 36		05 42			05 50	05 58
London Charing Cross	⊖ a					00 29		00 31			00 35	00 34		00 39				05 37	05 41		05 48			05 57	06 03

		TL		TL	SE	SE	SE	SE	SE	SE	SE	SE		SE	SE	SE	SE	SE	SE	SE	TL	SE		TL	SE
									◇1											◇1					
Orpington	d			05 33			05 33		05 51		05 52								05 55	05 59		06 00		06 03	
Petts Wood	d			05 36			05 36				05 55								05 58			06 03		06 06	
Hither Green	d				05 42		05 49			05 52							05 58	06 09	06 11			06 16			
Lewisham	d				05 47	05 50	05 54	05 56		05 58		06 03		06 09	06 11	06 19	07 08					06 21			06 26
St Johns	d				05 49					06 00		06 05		06 11								06 23			
New Cross	⊖ d				05 52					06 02		06 07		06 13								06 25			
London Victoria	⊖ a										06 35				06 37										
London Bridge	⊖ d	05 58			06 00	05 59	06 03	06 06	06 08	06 09		06 14		06 20		06 29	07 18	06 20	06 22	06 18	06 28	06 33			06 35
London Blackfriars	⊖ a	06 04		06 19																	06 34			06 49	
London Cannon Street	⊖ a				06 06					06 15		06 20		06 26						06 24		06 39			
London Waterloo (East)	⊖ d					06 05	06 08	06 11	06 13							06 35	07 23	06 25	06 27						06 40
London Charing Cross	⊖ a					06 10	06 14	06 16	06 19							06 40	07 29	06 31	06 33						06 46

		SE	SE	SE	SE	SE	SE	SE		SE	SE	SE	TL	SE	SE	SE	SE	SE		SE	SE	TL	SE	SE	SE
										◇1		◇1									◇1				
Orpington	d							06 18		06 21	06 24	06 27	06 29							06 33	06 40				06 41
Petts Wood	d							06 21			06 27		06 32							06 36					06 44
Hither Green	d	06 25	06 29				06 30	06 36										06 48		06 50			06 56		06 58
Lewisham	d	06 31		06 33	06 36	06 38	07 40	06 41						06 44		06 48	06 50	06 54						06 59	07 04
St Johns	d			06 35												06 50		06 56						07 01	
New Cross	⊖ d	06 36		06 37						06 33					06 49	06 52		06 58		06 55				07 03	
London Victoria	⊖ a				07 02						07 07														
London Bridge	⊖ d	06 42	06 41	06 44		06 47	07 53	06 52		06 39		06 45		06 54	08 17	07 00	07 00	07 05		07 03	06 57	06 58	07 07	07 10	07 14
London Blackfriars	⊖ a												07 19									07 04			
London Cannon Street	⊖ a	06 48		06 50						06 46					08 23	07 06		07 11		07 09				07 16	
London Waterloo (East)	⊖ d		06 46			06 53	07 58	06 57				06 50		06 59			07 05				07 02		07 12		07 19
London Charing Cross	⊖ a		06 52			06 58	08 04	07 03				06 56		07 05			07 12				07 08		07 18		07 25

		SE	SE	SE		TL	SE	SE	SE	SE	SE	SE	SE	SE		SE	SE	TL	SE	SE	SE	SE	SE	SE	
			◇1														◇1			◇1					
Orpington	d	06 49	06 53	06 54		06 59										07 02	07 04		07 11	07 15					
Petts Wood	d	06 52		06 57		07 02										07 05			07 14						
Hither Green	d	07 06									07 11	07 16				07 19			07 29				07 31	07 36	
Lewisham	d						07 08	07 12	07 15		07 17		07 21	07 23		07 25					07 31	07 35	07 38		
St Johns	d										07 19			07 25									07 40		
New Cross	⊖ d	07 12								07 21	07 22		07 24	07 28					07 34			07 38	07 43		
London Victoria	⊖ a			07 35					07 38																
London Bridge	⊖ d	07 19	07 10				07 18	07 22		08 39	07 30	07 27	07 32	07 35		07 35	07 25	07 28	07 42	07 32	07 41	07 45	07 50	07 47	
London Blackfriars	⊖ a					07 49												07 34							
London Cannon Street	⊖ a	07 25								08 45	07 35		07 38	07 41			07 31		07 48			07 51	07 56		
London Waterloo (East)	⊖ d		07 15				07 23	07 27				07 32				07 40				07 37	07 47			07 52	
London Charing Cross	⊖ a		07 21				07 29	07 33				07 38				07 46				07 44	07 53			07 58	

		SE	SE	TL	SE	TL	SE	SE	SE	SE		SE	SE	SE	SE	SE	SE	SE	SE	SE		SE	SE	SE	SE
Orpington	d		07 20		07 24	07 30						07 33					07 42		07 51	07 54			07 57		
Petts Wood	d		07 23		07 27	07 33						07 36					07 46		07 54	07 57			08 00		
Hither Green	d		07 38									07 50		07 53			08 00	08 02							
Lewisham	d	07 40	07 44				07 46		07 48	07 51			07 55	08 00	08 02	08 06	08 08					08 11		08 13	08 15
St Johns	d								07 50				07 57	08 03										08 15	08 18
New Cross	⊖ d							07 50	07 53			07 56	08 00	08 06					08 11					08 18	08 21
London Victoria	⊖ a				08 05		08 13									08 33				08 35					
London Bridge	⊖ d	07 53	07 55	07 58				09 08	08 00	08 02		08 03	08 07	08 13	08 13		08 19	08 15	08 19			08 21	08 23	08 25	08 30
London Blackfriars	⊖ a			08 04		08 19																			
London Cannon Street	⊖ a							09 14	08 06			08 09	08 13	08 19					08 25					08 31	08 36
London Waterloo (East)	⊖ d	07 58	08 00							08 07					08 18		08 24	08 20				08 26	08 28		
London Charing Cross	⊖ a	08 04	08 06							08 13					08 24		08 30	08 26				08 32	08 34		

		SE	SE	TL	TL	SE		SE	SE	SE	SE	SE	SE	SE	SE	SE		SE	SE	SE	SE	SE	TL	TL	SE
Orpington	d				08 03			08 03						08 12						08 21	08 24			08 29	
Petts Wood	d				08 06			08 06						08 15						08 24	08 27			08 32	
Hither Green	d	08 11	08 15					08 19		08 27				08 30		08 30		08 32	08 35	08 38		08 42			
Lewisham	d	08 19				08 22		08 24	08 27			08 29	08 31		08 36			08 39		08 44					08 46
St Johns	d	08 21										08 31						08 41							
New Cross	⊖ d	08 24									08 31	08 34		08 37	08 39			08 44							
London Victoria	⊖ a								08 55												09 05				09 11
London Bridge	⊖ d	08 32	08 27	08 28		08 33		08 35		08 39	09 47	08 41	08 43	08 44	08 47	09 38		08 51	08 47	08 54		08 56	08 58		
London Blackfriars	⊖ a			08 34	08 49																		09 04	09 19	
London Cannon Street	⊖ a	08 38									09 55	08 47		08 50	08 53	09 44		08 57							
London Waterloo (East)	⊖ d		08 32			08 38		08 40		08 44			08 48						08 52	09 00		09 02			
London Charing Cross	⊖ a		08 38			08 44		08 46		08 50			08 54						08 58	09 05		09 07			

Table T199-R

Mondays to Fridays

21 May to 7 December

Orpington, Petts Wood, Hither Green and Lewisham - London (Summary of Services)

		SE	SE	SE	SE	SE	SE	SE		SE	SE	SE	SE	SE	SE	SE	SE	SE		TL	SE	SE	TL	SE	SE
															◇						◇1				
Orpington	d					08 34							08 42		08 46		08 52	08 55		09 03	09 05				
Petts Wood	d					08 37							08 45				08 55	08 58		09 06					
Hither Green	d				08 50	08 52		08 55					08 59			09 03	09 09							09 16	
Lewisham	d		08 48	08 51	08 55		08 56			09 01	09 04	09 04	09 05	09 07		09 10						09 15			
St Johns	d		08 50		08 59						09 06					09 12									
New Cross	⊖ d	08 47	08 53		09 01	08 58					09 08					09 15									09 19
London Victoria	⊖ a													09 35				09 35							
London Bridge	⊖ d	10 07	09 00	09 01	09 10	09 06	09 06	09 08		09 11	09 15	10 17	09 15		09 04	09 22	09 20				09 22	09 25	09 28	09 29	10 37
London Blackfriars	⊖ a																			09 49			09 34		
London Cannon Street	⊖ a	10 13	09 07		09 16	09 12					09 21	10 21				09 28									10 41
London Waterloo (East)	⊖ d			09 06			09 12	09 14		09 16			09 20		09 09		09 25				09 27	09 30		09 34	
London Charing Cross	⊖ a			09 12			09 18	09 20		09 22			09 27		09 15		09 31				09 33	09 37		09 40	

		SE	SE	SE		SE	SE	SE	SE	SE	SE	SE	TL	SE		SE	SE	SE	TL	SE	SE	SE	SE	SE	
											◇1						◇1								
Orpington	d							09 11		09 21	09 24	09 24	09 33				09 38								
Petts Wood	d							09 14		09 24		09 27	09 36												
Hither Green	d					09 22		09 27	09 34	09 37													09 52		
Lewisham	d	09 17	09 26			09 29	09 32	09 34						09 39		09 42		09 46		09 55			09 57	10 02	
St Johns	d	09 20				09 31		09 36						09 41		09 44							09 59		
New Cross	⊖ d	09 22		09 28		09 33		09 38						09 44		09 47					09 49	09 57	10 01		
London Victoria	⊖ a						09 57					10 05												10 25	
London Bridge	⊖ d	09 30	09 36	10 47		09 40		09 45	09 45	09 48	09 41			09 51		09 54	09 55	09 57	09 58	10 05	11 07	11 17	10 09		
London Blackfriars	⊖ a												10 19						10 04						
London Cannon Street	⊖ a	09 36		10 51		09 46		09 51						09 57		10 02					11 11	11 21	10 15		
London Waterloo (East)	⊖ d		09 41						09 50	09 53	09 46						10 00	10 02		10 10					
London Charing Cross	⊖ a		09 47						09 56	09 59	09 52						10 06	10 05		10 15					

		SE	SE	SE	SE	SE	TL	SE	SE	SE		SE	TL	SE	SE	SE	SE	SE	SE	SE		SE	SE	SE	TL
					◇1					◇1													◇1		
Orpington	d	09 41		09 50	09 52	09 54	10 03			10 08									10 11			10 20	10 22	10 24	10 33
Petts Wood	d	09 44		09 53		09 57	10 06												10 14			10 23		10 27	10 36
Hither Green	d	09 57	10 03	10 06													10 22		10 27	10 33		10 36			
Lewisham	d	10 04						10 09	10 12			10 16		10 25			10 27	10 32	10 34						
St Johns	d	10 06						10 11	10 14								10 31		10 36						
New Cross	⊖ d	10 08						10 14	10 17						10 19	10 27	10 33		10 38						
London Victoria	⊖ a					10 33												10 55						11 03	
London Bridge	⊖ d	10 14	10 15	10 17	10 09			10 20	10 24	10 25		10 27	10 28	10 35	11 37	11 47	10 39		10 44	10 45		10 47	10 39		
London Blackfriars	⊖ a						10 49						10 34												11 19
London Cannon Street	⊖ a	10 18						10 24	10 30						11 41	11 51	10 43		10 48						
London Waterloo (East)	⊖ d		10 20	10 22	10 14					10 30		10 32		10 40						10 50		10 52	10 44		
London Charing Cross	⊖ a		10 23	10 27	10 20					10 36		10 35		10 43						10 53		10 57	10 48		

		SE	SE	SE	SE	TL		SE	SE	SE	SE	SE	SE	SE	SE	SE		SE	TL	SE	SE	SE	SE	TL	SE
				◇1												◇1						◇1			
Orpington	d			10 38									10 41		10 50	10 52		10 54	11 03			11 08			
Petts Wood	d												10 44		10 53			10 57	11 06						
Hither Green	d										10 52		10 57	11 03	11 06										
Lewisham	d	10 39	10 42		10 46			10 55			10 57	11 02	11 04							11 09	11 12		11 16		11 25
St Johns	d	10 41	10 44								11 01		11 06							11 11	11 14				
New Cross	⊖ d	10 44	10 47						10 49	10 57	11 03		11 08							11 14	11 17				
London Victoria	⊖ a											11 25						11 33							
London Bridge	⊖ d	10 50	10 54	10 55	10 57	10 58		11 05	12 07	12 17	11 09		11 14	11 15	11 17	11 09				11 20	11 24	11 25	11 27	11 28	11 35
London Blackfriars	⊖ a					11 04													11 49					11 34	
London Cannon Street	⊖ a	10 54	11 00						12 11	12 21	11 13		11 18							11 24	11 30				
London Waterloo (East)	⊖ d			11 00	11 02			11 10						11 20	11 22	11 14						11 30	11 32		11 40
London Charing Cross	⊖ a			11 04	11 05			11 13						11 23	11 27	11 18						11 34	11 35		11 43

		SE		SE	SE	SE	SE	SE	SE	SE	SE	TL		SE	SE	SE	SE	TL	SE	SE	SE	SE		SE	SE
										◇1						◇1									
Orpington	d						11 11		11 20	11 22	11 24	11 33				11 38									11 41
Petts Wood	d						11 14		11 23		11 27	11 36													11 44
Hither Green	d				11 22		11 27	11 33	11 36													11 52			11 57
Lewisham	d				11 27	11 32	11 34							11 39	11 42		11 46		11 55			11 57		12 02	12 04
St Johns	d				11 29		11 36							11 41	11 44							11 59			12 06
New Cross	⊖ d	11 19		11 27	11 31		11 38							11 44	11 47					11 49	11 57	12 01			12 08
London Victoria	⊖ a					11 55					12 03													12 25	
London Bridge	⊖ d	12 37		12 47	11 39		11 44	11 45	11 47	11 39				11 50	11 54	11 55	11 57	11 58	12 05	13 07	13 17	12 09			12 14
London Blackfriars	⊖ a											12 19						12 04							
London Cannon Street	⊖ a	12 41		12 51	11 43		11 48							11 54	12 00					13 11	13 21	12 13			12 18
London Waterloo (East)	⊖ d							11 50	11 52	11 44						12 00	12 02		12 10						
London Charing Cross	⊖ a							11 53	11 57	11 48						12 04	12 05		12 13						

		SE	SE	SE	SE	TL	SE	SE		SE	SE	TL	SE	SE	SE	SE	SE	SE		SE	SE	SE	SE	TL	SE
				◇1						◇1												◇1			
Orpington	d		11 50	11 52	11 54	12 03				12 08								12 11			12 20	12 22	12 24	12 33	
Petts Wood	d		11 53		11 57	12 06												12 14			12 23		12 27	12 36	
Hither Green	d	12 03	12 06													12 22		12 27		12 33	12 36				
Lewisham	d						12 09	12 12			12 16		12 25			12 27	12 32	12 34							12 39
St Johns	d						12 11	12 14								12 29		12 36							12 41
New Cross	⊖ d						12 14	12 17						12 19	12 27	12 31		12 38							12 44
London Victoria	⊖ a				12 33												12 55						13 03		
London Bridge	⊖ d	12 15	12 17	12 09			12 20	12 24		12 25	12 27	12 28	12 35	13 37	13 47	12 39		12 44		12 45	12 47	12 39			12 50
London Blackfriars	⊖ a					12 49						12 34												13 19	
London Cannon Street	⊖ a						12 24	12 30						13 41	13 51	12 43		12 48							12 54
London Waterloo (East)	⊖ d	12 20	12 22	12 14						12 30	12 32		12 40							12 50	12 52	12 44			
London Charing Cross	⊖ a	12 23	12 27	12 18						12 34	12 35		12 43							12 53	12 57	12 48			

Orpington, Petts Wood, Hither Green and Lewisham - London (Summary of Services)

		SE	SE	SE	TL	SE	SE	SE	SE	SE		SE	SE	SE	SE	SE	TL	SE	SE	SE		SE	TL	SE	SE
			◇1												◇1					◇1					
Orpington	d		12 38									12 41		12 50	12 52	12 54	13 03			13 08					
Petts Wood	d											12 44		12 53		12 57	13 06								
Hither Green	d								12 52			12 57	13 03	13 06											
Lewisham	d	12 42		12 46		12 55			12 57	13 02		13 04						13 09	13 12			13 16		13 25	
St Johns	d	12 44							12 59			13 06						13 11	13 14						
New Cross	d	12 47					12 49	12 57	13 01			13 08						13 14	13 17						13 19
London Victoria	a									13 25						13 33									
London Bridge	d	12 54	12 55	12 57	12 58	13 05	14 07	14 17	13 09			13 14	13 15	13 17	13 09			13 20	13 24	13 25		13 27	13 28	13 35	14 37
London Blackfriars	a				13 04												13 49						13 34		
London Cannon Street	a	13 00					14 11	14 21	13 13			13 18						13 24	13 30						14 41
London Waterloo (East)	d		13 00	13 02		13 10							13 20	13 22	13 14					13 30		13 32		13 40	
London Charing Cross	a		13 04	13 05		13 13							13 23	13 27	13 18					13 34		13 35		13 43	

		SE	SE	SE	SE	SE		SE	SE	SE	TL	SE	SE	SE	SE	TL		SE	SE	SE	SE	SE	SE	SE	SE
									◇1					◇1											
Orpington	d				13 11			13 20	13 22	13 24	13 33			13 38									13 41		13 50
Petts Wood	d				13 14			13 23		13 27	13 36												13 44		13 53
Hither Green	d		13 22		13 27	13 33		13 36													13 52		13 57	14 03	14 06
Lewisham	d		13 27	13 32	13 34							13 39	13 42		13 46			13 55			13 57	14 02	14 04		
St Johns	d		13 29		13 36							13 41	13 44								13 59		14 06		
New Cross	d	13 27	13 31		13 38							13 44	13 47						13 49	13 57	14 01		14 08		
London Victoria	a			13 55						14 03												14 25			
London Bridge	d	14 47	13 39		13 44	13 45		13 47	13 39			13 50	13 54	13 55	13 57	13 58		14 05	15 07	15 17	14 09		14 14	14 15	14 17
London Blackfriars	a										14 19					14 04									
London Cannon Street	a	14 51	13 43		13 48							13 54	14 00						15 11	15 21	14 13		14 18		
London Waterloo (East)	d					13 50		13 52	13 44					14 00	14 02			14 10						14 20	14 22
London Charing Cross	a					13 53		13 57	13 48					14 04	14 05			14 13						14 23	14 27

		SE		SE	TL	SE	SE	SE	SE	TL	SE	SE		SE	SE	SE	SE	SE	SE	SE	SE	TL		SE	SE
		◇1						◇1												◇1					
Orpington	d	13 52		13 54	14 03			14 08									14 11		14 20	14 22	14 24	14 33			
Petts Wood	d			13 57	14 06												14 14		14 23		14 27	14 36			
Hither Green	d														14 22		14 27	14 33	14 36						
Lewisham	d					14 09	14 12		14 16		14 25				14 27	14 32	14 34							14 39	14 42
St Johns	d					14 11	14 14								14 29		14 36							14 41	14 44
New Cross	d					14 14	14 17					14 19		14 27	14 31		14 38							14 44	14 47
London Victoria	a			14 33												14 55					15 04				
London Bridge	d	14 09				14 20	14 24	14 25	14 27	14 28	14 35	15 37		15 47	14 39		14 44	14 45	14 47	14 39				14 50	14 54
London Blackfriars	a				14 49					14 34												15 19			
London Cannon Street	a					14 24	14 30					15 41		15 51	14 43		14 48							14 55	15 00
London Waterloo (East)	d	14 14						14 30	14 32		14 40							14 50	14 52	14 44					
London Charing Cross	a	14 18						14 34	14 35		14 43							14 53	14 57	14 48					

		SE	SE	TL	SE	SE	SE	SE		SE	SE	SE	SE	SE	SE	TL	SE	SE		SE	SE	TL	SE	SE	SE
		◇1												◇1						◇1					
Orpington	d	14 38									14 41		14 50	14 52	14 54	15 03				15 08					
Petts Wood	d										14 44		14 53		14 57	15 06									
Hither Green	d							14 52			14 57	15 03	15 06												
Lewisham	d		14 46		14 55			14 57		15 02	15 04						15 09	15 12			15 16		15 25		
St Johns	d							14 59			15 06						15 11	15 14							
New Cross	d					14 49	14 57	15 01			15 08						15 14	15 17						15 19	15 27
London Victoria	a									15 25					15 34										
London Bridge	d	14 55	14 57	14 58	15 05	16 06	16 17	15 09			15 14	15 15	15 17	15 09			15 20	15 24		15 25	15 27	15 28	15 35	16 34	16 47
London Blackfriars	a			15 04												15 49						15 34			
London Cannon Street	a					16 12	16 23	15 13			15 18						15 24	15 30						16 40	16 53
London Waterloo (East)	d	15 00	15 02		15 10							15 20	15 22	15 14						15 30	15 32		15 40		
London Charing Cross	a	15 04	15 05		15 13							15 23	15 27	15 18						15 34	15 35		15 43		

		SE	SE	SE		SE	SE	SE	SE	TL	SE	SE	SE	SE		TL	SE	SE	SE	SE	SE	SE	SE	SE	
								◇1					◇1												
Orpington	d			15 11			15 20	15 22	15 24	15 33			15 38									15 41		15 50	
Petts Wood	d			15 14			15 23		15 27	15 36												15 44		15 53	
Hither Green	d	15 22		15 27		15 33	15 36													15 52		15 57	16 03	16 06	
Lewisham	d	15 27	15 32	15 34							15 39	15 42		15 46			15 56			15 58	16 02	16 04			
St Johns	d	15 29		15 36							15 41	15 44								16 00		16 06			
New Cross	d	15 31		15 38							15 44	15 47						15 49	15 57	16 02		16 08			
London Victoria	a		15 55						16 03												16 25				
London Bridge	d	15 39		15 44		15 45	15 47	15 39			15 50	15 54	15 55	15 57		15 58	16 05	17 08	17 19	16 09		16 14	16 15	16 17	
London Blackfriars	a									16 19						16 04									
London Cannon Street	a	15 43		15 48							15 54	16 00						17 14	17 25	16 15		16 19			
London Waterloo (East)	d					15 50	15 52	15 44					16 00	16 02			16 10						16 20	16 22	
London Charing Cross	a					15 53	15 57	15 48					16 04	16 05			16 15						16 23	16 27	

		SE	SE	TL	SE	SE	SE	SE	TL	SE		SE	SE	SE	SE	SE	SE	SE	SE	SE		SE	TL	SE	SE
		◇1					◇1			1										◇1					◇1
Orpington	d	15 52	15 54	16 03			16 08			16 11							16 11		16 20	16 24		16 24	16 33		16 38
Petts Wood	d		15 57	16 06													16 14		16 23			16 27	16 36		
Hither Green	d														16 22		16 27	16 33	16 36						
Lewisham	d				16 09	16 12		16 16				16 25			16 27	16 32	16 34							16 37	
St Johns	d				16 11	16 14									16 29		16 36							16 39	
New Cross	d				16 14	16 17							16 19	16 26	16 31		16 38							16 42	
London Victoria	a		16 34													16 55						17 05			
London Bridge	d	16 09			16 20	16 23	16 25	16 27	16 28	16 29		16 35	17 36	17 39	16 38		16 44	16 45	16 47	16 41				16 50	16 55
London Blackfriars	a			16 49					16 34														17 19		
London Cannon Street	a				16 24	16 29							17 42	17 45	16 44		16 50							16 56	
London Waterloo (East)	d	16 14					16 30	16 32		16 34		16 41						16 52	16 53	16 46					17 00
London Charing Cross	a	16 18					16 34	16 36		16 38		16 46						16 57	16 58	16 51					17 07

Table T199-R

Mondays to Fridays
21 May to 7 December

Orpington, Petts Wood, Hither Green and Lewisham - London (Summary of Services)

		SE		TL	SE	SE	SE	SE	SE	SE	SE	SE		SE	SE	SE	SE	SE	SE	SE	SE	SE		TL	TL
																	◇1		◇1						
Orpington	d											16 41				16 50	16 52	16 54	16 59						17 03
Petts Wood	d											16 44				16 53		16 57							17 06
Hither Green	d								16 53			16 58			17 02	17 09									
Lewisham	d	16 42			16 46	16 55			17 00	17 02		17 05		17 09							17 13	17 15			
St Johns	d	16 46							17 02					17 11							17 16				
New Cross	d	16 48					16 50	16 56	17 05		17 09	17 10		17 14						17 15	17 19				
London Victoria	a									17 25								17 34							
London Bridge	d	16 55		16 57	16 57	17 05	18 04	18 18	17 11		18 31	17 16			17 15	17 20	17 11		17 18	18 38	17 26	17 25		17 28	
London Blackfriars	a			17 02																				17 34	17 49
London Cannon Street	a	17 02					18 10	18 24	17 17		18 37	17 23		17 27						18 44	17 32				
London Waterloo (East)	d				17 02	17 10									17 20	17 28	17 16		17 25			17 32			
London Charing Cross	a				17 06	17 16									17 25	17 31	17 21		17 30			17 39			

		SE	SE	SE	SE	SE	SE	SE		SE	SE	SE	SE	SE	SE	SE	TL	TL		SE	SE	SE	SE	SE	SE
		◇1									◇1														
Orpington	d	17 09				17 11	17 15			17 18	17 23	17 24	17 28					17 33							
Petts Wood	d					17 14				17 24		17 27						17 36							
Hither Green	d			17 27		17 29		17 31		17 40														17 52	
Lewisham	d		17 25		17 32	17 34								17 38	17 42	17 45				17 48	17 55				17 56
St Johns	d			17 31		17 37									17 44									17 56	
New Cross	d			17 34		17 39								17 41	17 47							17 53	17 58	17 59	
London Victoria	a				17 55							18 03													
London Bridge	d	17 31	17 35			17 45	17 37	17 42		17 50	17 40		17 46	17 48	17 53	17 54	17 58			17 58	18 05	19 25	19 20	18 07	19 09
London Blackfriars	a																18 04	18 19							
London Cannon Street	a	17 37		17 47		17 51								17 52	18 00							19 30	19 24	18 13	19 15
London Waterloo (East)	d		17 40				17 43	17 47		17 55	17 45		17 51			17 59				18 03	18 11				
London Charing Cross	a		17 46				17 48	17 52		18 00	17 50		17 54			18 05				18 08	18 17				

		SE	SE	SE		SE	SE	SE	SE	TL	SE	SE	SE	TL		SE	SE	SE	SE	SE	SE	SE	SE	SE	
				◇1					◇1				◇1												
Orpington	d		17 40	17 41			17 48	17 54	18 00	18 02			18 09									18 09			
Petts Wood	d		17 44				17 52	17 57		18 05												18 14			
Hither Green	d		17 57			18 03	18 05													18 24		18 27	18 33	18 36	
Lewisham	d	18 00	18 02			18 09						18 14				18 17	18 19	18 23		18 30	18 32	18 35			
St Johns	d		18 07														18 22			18 34		18 41			
New Cross	d		18 09								18 11	18 17					18 26		18 34	18 37		18 44			
London Victoria	a	18 25						18 33													18 57				
London Bridge	d			18 00		18 19	18 17		18 21		19 37	18 23	18 26	18 28		18 28	18 34	18 33	20 07	18 44		18 52	18 45	19 47	
London Blackfriars	a									18 49				18 34											
London Cannon Street	a		18 20								19 43	18 27					18 40		20 11	18 50		18 56		19 51	
London Waterloo (East)	d			18 06		18 25	18 22		18 27				18 31			18 33		18 38					18 50		
London Charing Cross	a			18 12		18 30	18 27		18 33				18 37			18 38		18 41					18 53		

		SE	SE	SE	SE	TL	SE	SE	TL	SE		SE	SE	SE	SE	SE	SE	SE	SE	SE		SE	SE	TL	SE
			◇1					◇1												◇1					◇1
Orpington	d	18 20	18 22	18 23	18 29	18 33		18 40								18 41			18 50	18 52			18 54	19 03	19 09
Petts Wood	d	18 23		18 27		18 36										18 44			18 53				18 57	19 06	
Hither Green	d	18 39														18 57	18 59	19 02	19 06						
Lewisham	d						18 41			18 48		18 50	18 55	18 57	19 00	19 03	19 07					19 14			
St Johns	d						18 44					18 52				19 06	19 09								
New Cross	d						18 47					18 54				19 08	19 11								
London Victoria	a			19 03											19 28							19 33	19 34		
London Bridge	d	18 50	18 41		18 47		18 55	18 56	18 58	19 00		19 01	19 05	20 17		19 14	19 17	19 13	19 19	19 10					19 26
London Blackfriars	a					19 19			19 04															19 49	
London Cannon Street	a		18 47				19 01					19 05		20 21		19 19	19 21								
London Waterloo (East)	d	18 55			18 54			19 01		19 06			19 10					19 20	19 24	19 15					19 31
London Charing Cross	a	19 02			18 57			19 05		19 09			19 13					19 23	19 28	19 19					19 35

		TL	SE	SE	SE	SE		SE	SE	SE	SE	SE	SE	SE	SE	TL		SE	SE	SE	SE	TL	SE	SE	SE
														◇1						◇1					
Orpington	d										19 11		19 20	19 23	19 24	19 33				19 38					
Petts Wood	d										19 14		19 23		19 27	19 36									
Hither Green	d								19 22		19 27	19 34	19 36												19 52
Lewisham	d			19 16	19 17	19 25			19 27	19 32	19 34							19 39	19 42		19 46		19 55		19 57
St Johns	d			19 19					19 29		19 36							19 41	19 44						19 59
New Cross	d		19 19	19 22				19 26	19 32		19 38							19 44	19 47					19 49	20 01
London Victoria	a									19 55					20 03										
London Bridge	d	19 28	20 37	19 29	19 28	19 35		20 47	19 40		19 44	19 45	19 47	19 40				19 50	19 54	19 55	19 57	19 58	20 05	21 07	20 09
London Blackfriars	a	19 34														20 19						20 04			
London Cannon Street	a		20 41	19 33				20 51	19 46		19 48							19 54	19 58					21 11	20 15
London Waterloo (East)	d				19 33	19 40						19 50	19 52	19 45						20 00	20 02		20 10		
London Charing Cross	a				19 36	19 43						19 53	19 57	19 49						20 04	20 05		20 13		

		SE		SE	SE	SE	SE	SE	TL	SE	SE	SE		SE	TL	SE	SE	SE	SE	SE	SE	SE		SE	SE
							◇1					◇1												◇1	
Orpington	d			19 41		19 50	19 52	19 54	20 03			20 08								20 11		20 20		20 22	20 24
Petts Wood	d			19 44		19 53		19 57	20 06											20 14		20 23			20 27
Hither Green	d			19 57	20 03	20 06												20 22		20 27	20 33	20 36			
Lewisham	d	20 02		20 04						20 09	20 12			20 17		20 25		20 27	20 32	20 34					
St Johns	d			20 06						20 11	20 14							20 29		20 36					
New Cross	d			20 08						20 14	20 17						20 19	20 31		20 38					
London Victoria	a	20 25						20 33											20 55						21 03
London Bridge	d			20 14	20 15	20 17	20 09			20 20	20 24	20 25		20 27	20 28	20 35	21 37	20 39		20 44	20 45	20 47		20 39	
London Blackfriars	a								20 49						20 34										
London Cannon Street	a			20 18						20 24	20 30						21 41	20 43		20 48					
London Waterloo (East)	d				20 20	20 22	20 14					20 30		20 32		20 40					20 50	20 52		20 44	
London Charing Cross	a				20 23	20 27	20 18					20 34		20 35		20 43					20 53	20 57		20 48	

Table T199-R

Mondays to Fridays

21 May to 7 December

Orpington, Petts Wood, Hither Green and Lewisham - London (Summary of Services)

		SE	SE	SE		TL	TL	SE	SE	SE	SE	SE	SE	SE		SE ◇1	SE	TL	SE	SE ◇1	SE	TL	SE	SE	
Orpington	d						20 33					20 41		20 50		20 52	20 54	21 03		21 08					
Petts Wood	d						20 36					20 44		20 53			20 57	21 06							
Hither Green	d									20 52		20 57	21 03	21 06											
Lewisham	d	20 39	20 42	20 46				20 55		20 57	21 02	21 04							21 09		21 16		21 25		
St Johns	d	20 41	20 44							20 59		21 06							21 11						
New Cross	d	20 44	20 47						20 49	21 01		21 08							21 14					21 19	
London Victoria	a										21 25						21 34								
London Bridge	d	20 50	20 54	20 57		20 58		21 05	22 07	21 09		21 14	21 15	21 17		21 09			21 20	21 25	21 27	21 28	21 35	22 37	
London Blackfriars	a					21 04	21 19											21 49				21 34			
London Cannon Street	a	20 54	21 00						22 11	21 13		21 18							21 25					22 41	
London Waterloo (East)	d			21 02				21 10					21 20	21 22		21 14				21 30	21 32		21 40		
London Charing Cross	a			21 05				21 13					21 23	21 27		21 18				21 34	21 35		21 43		

		SE	SE	SE	SE	SE	SE ◇1	SE	SE	SE		TL	TL	SE	SE	SE	SE	SE	SE	SE		SE ◇1	SE	TL	SE
Orpington	d			21 11		21 20	21 22	21 24					21 33					21 41		21 50		21 52	21 54	22 03	
Petts Wood	d			21 14		21 23		21 27					21 36					21 44		21 53			21 57	22 06	
Hither Green	d	21 22		21 27	21 33	21 36										21 52		21 57	22 03	22 06					
Lewisham	d	21 27	21 32	21 34					21 39	21 46				21 55		21 57	22 02	22 04							22 09
St Johns	d	21 29		21 36					21 41							21 59		22 06							22 11
New Cross	d	21 31		21 38					21 44						21 49	22 01		22 08							22 14
London Victoria	a		21 55					22 03									22 25						22 33		
London Bridge	d	21 39		21 44	21 45	21 47	21 39		21 50	21 57		21 58		22 05	23 07	22 09		22 14	22 15	22 17		22 09			22 20
London Blackfriars	a											22 04	22 19											22 49	
London Cannon Street	a	21 43		21 48					21 54						23 11	22 13		22 18							22 24
London Waterloo (East)	d				21 50	21 52	21 44			22 02				22 10					22 20	22 22		22 14			
London Charing Cross	a				21 53	21 57	21 48			22 05				22 13					22 23	22 27		22 18			

		SE ◇1	SE	TL	SE	SE		SE	SE	SE	SE	SE	SE ◇1	SE	SE	SE		TL	TL	SE	TL	SE MT FO	SE	SE	SE
Orpington	d	22 08								22 11		22 20	22 22	22 24					22 33						22 41
Petts Wood	d									22 14		22 23		22 27					22 36						22 44
Hither Green	d							22 22		22 27	22 33	22 36											22 52		22 57
Lewisham	d		22 16		22 25			22 27	22 32	22 34					22 39	22 46				22 55			22 57	23 02	23 04
St Johns	d							22 29		22 36					22 41								22 59		23 06
New Cross	d					22 19		22 31		22 38					22 44							22 49	23 01		23 08
London Victoria	a								22 55					23 03										23 25	
London Bridge	d	22 25	22 27	22 28	22 35	23 37		22 39		22 44	22 45	22 47	22 39		22 50	22 57		22 58		23 05	23 28	00 07	23 09		23 14
London Blackfriars	a			22 34														23 04	23 19		23 34				
London Cannon Street	a					23 41		22 43		22 48					22 54							00 11	23 13		23 18
London Waterloo (East)	d	22 30	22 32		22 40						22 50	22 52	22 44			23 02				23 10					
London Charing Cross	a	22 34	22 35		22 43						22 53	22 57	22 48			23 05				23 13					

		SE		SE	SE ◇1	SE	TL	SE	SE ◇1	SE	SE WTh FO	SE MTO		SE MT FO	SE W ThO	SE	SE MT FO	SE WTh FO	SE FO	SE W ThO	SE MTO	SE		SE WTh FO ◇1	SE MTO ◇1
Orpington	d			22 50	22 52	22 54	23 03		23 08								23 11	23 20			23 20	23 24		23 36	23 36
Petts Wood	d			22 53		22 57	23 06										23 14	23 23			23 23	23 27			
Hither Green	d	23 03		23 06										23 22	23 22		23 27	23 36			23 36				
Lewisham	d							23 09		23 16	23 25	23 25		23 27	23 27	23 32	23 34		23 39	23 40	23 41				
St Johns	d							23 11						23 29	23 29		23 36		23 41		23 43				
New Cross	d							23 14						23 31	23 31		23 38		23 44		23 45				
London Victoria	a					23 34										23 55						00 03			
London Bridge	d	23 15		23 17	23 09			23 20	23 25	23 27	23 35	23 35		23 39	23a41		23 44	23 47	23 50	23 50	23 52			23 54	23 56
London Blackfriars	a						23 49																		
London Cannon Street	a							23 24						23 43			23 48		23 54		23 58				00 03
London Waterloo (East)	d	23 20		23 22	23 14				23 30	23 32	23 40	23 40					23 52		23 55				23 59		
London Charing Cross	a	23 23		23 27	23 18				23 34	23 35	23 43	23 44					23 57		00 01				00 03		

		SE	SE WTh FO	SE MT FO	SE W ThO	SE MTO	SE WTh FO	SE MTO		SE
Orpington	d						23 50	23 50		23 54
Petts Wood	d						23 53	23 53		23 57
Hither Green	d			23 52	23 52		00 06	00 06		
Lewisham	d	23 46	23 55	23 57	23 58	23 59	00 11	00 13		
St Johns	d			23 59		00 02				
New Cross	d			00 01		00 05				
London Victoria	a									00 34
London Bridge	d	23 57	00 05	00 09	00a08	00 12	00 21	00 21		
London Blackfriars	a									
London Cannon Street	a			00 13		00 18		00 27		
London Waterloo (East)	d	00 02	00 10				00 26			
London Charing Cross	a	00 05	00 13				00 31			

Table T199-R

Saturdays

26 May to 8 December

Orpington, Petts Wood, Hither Green and Lewisham - London (Summary of Services)

		SE	SE	SE	SE	SE		SE	SE	SE	SE	TL	SE	SE	SE	SE		SE	SE	SE	SE	TL	SE	SE	SE
Orpington	d									05 20			05 24			05 41			05 50	05 54					
Petts Wood	d									05 23			05 27			05 44			05 53	05 57					
Hither Green	d		00 06		00 16	05 25		05 29	05 33	05 36	05 40			05 44		05 57		06 03	06 06						06 17
Lewisham	d		00 11	00 15		05 30		05 34			05 46			05 49	05 55	06 04					06 16		06 20		
St Johns	d							05 36						05 51		06 06									06 21
New Cross	d	00 01						05 38						05 53		06 08								06 19	06 23
London Victoria	a												06 03							06 33					
London Bridge	d	00 09	00 21	00 25	00 29	05 40		05 45	05 45	05 47	05 56	05 58		06 00	06 05	06 14		06 15	06 17		06 27	06 28	06 30	07 37	06 30
London Blackfriars	a											06 04										06 34			
London Cannon Street	a	00 13						05 49						06 04		06 18								07 41	06 34
London Waterloo (East)	d		00 26	00 30	00 34	05 45			05 50	05 53	06 01				06 10			06 20	06 22		06 32		06 35		
London Charing Cross	a		00 31	00 35	00 39	05 49			05 53	05 57	06 04				06 13			06 23	06 27		06 35		06 39		

		SE		SE	SE	SE	SE	SE ◇1	SE	SE	TL	TL		SE	SE	SE	SE	SE	SE	SE	SE	SE		SE	TL
Orpington	d				06 11		06 20	06 22	06 24			06 33								06 41		06 50		06 54	07 03
Petts Wood	d				06 14		06 23		06 27			06 36								06 44		06 53		06 57	07 06
Hither Green	d			06 22	06 27	06 33	06 36									06 47		06 52		06 57	07 03	07 06			
Lewisham	d	06 25		06 27	06 34					06 46				06 50			06 55	06 57	07 02	07 04					
St Johns	d			06 29	06 36											06 51		06 59		07 06					
New Cross	d			06 31	06 38										06 49	06 53		07 01		07 08					
London Victoria	a								07 03										07 25					07 33	
London Bridge	d	06 35		06 39	06 44	06 45	06 47	06 39		06 57	06 58			07 00	08 07	07 00	07 05	07 09		07 14	07 15	07 17			
London Blackfriars	a										07 04	07 19													07 49
London Cannon Street	a			06 43	06 48										08 11	07 04		07 13		07 18					
London Waterloo (East)	d	06 40				06 50	06 52	06 44		07 02				07 05			07 10				07 20	07 22			
London Charing Cross	a	06 43				06 53	06 57	06 48		07 05				07 09			07 13				07 23	07 27			

		SE ◇1	SE	TL	SE	SE	SE	SE		SE	SE	SE	SE	SE	SE	SE	TL	SE	SE ◇1	SE	TL	SE	SE	SE	SE
Orpington	d	07 08											07 11		07 20	07 24	07 33		07 38						
Petts Wood	d												07 14		07 23	07 27	07 36								
Hither Green	d						07 17				07 22		07 27	07 33	07 36										07 52
Lewisham	d		07 16		07 20			07 25			07 27	07 32	07 34					07 39		07 46		07 55			07 57
St Johns	d						07 21				07 29		07 36					07 41							07 59
New Cross	d					07 19	07 23			07 27	07 31		07 38					07 44					07 49	07 57	08 01
London Victoria	a											07 55				08 03									
London Bridge	d	07 25	07 27	07 28	07 30	08 37	07 30	07 35		08 47	07 39		07 44	07 45	07 47			07 50	07 55	07 57	07 58	08 05	09 07	09 17	08 09
London Blackfriars	a			07 34													08 19				08 04				
London Cannon Street	a					08 41	07 34			08 51	07 43		07 48					07 54					09 11	09 21	08 13
London Waterloo (East)	d	07 30	07 32		07 35			07 40						07 50	07 52				08 00	08 02		08 10			
London Charing Cross	a	07 34	07 35		07 39			07 43						07 53	07 57				08 04	08 05		08 13			

		SE	SE	SE	SE	SE ◇1	SE	TL	SE	SE	SE ◇1	SE	TL	SE	SE	SE	SE	SE	SE	SE	SE	SE ◇1	SE	TL	SE
Orpington	d		07 41		07 50	07 52	07 54	08 03			08 08								08 11		08 20	08 22	08 24	08 33	
Petts Wood	d		07 44		07 53		07 57	08 06											08 14		08 23		08 27	08 36	
Hither Green	d		07 57	08 03	08 06												08 22		08 27	08 33	08 36				
Lewisham	d	08 02	08 04						08 09	08 12		08 16		08 25			08 27	08 32	08 34						08 39
St Johns	d		08 06						08 11	08 14							08 29		08 36						08 41
New Cross	d		08 08						08 14	08 17					08 19	08 27	08 31		08 38						08 44
London Victoria	a	08 25					08 33											08 55					09 03		
London Bridge	d		08 14	08 15	08 17	08 09			08 20	08 24	08 25	08 27	08 28	08 35	09 37	09 47	08 39		08 44	08 45	08 47	08 39			08 50
London Blackfriars	a							08 49					08 34											09 19	
London Cannon Street	a		08 18						08 24	08 30					09 41	09 51	08 43		08 48						08 54
London Waterloo (East)	d			08 20	08 22	08 14					08 30	08 32		08 40						08 50	08 52	08 44			
London Charing Cross	a			08 23	08 27	08 18					08 34	08 35		08 43						08 53	08 57	08 48			

		SE	and at the same minutes past each hour until	SE ◇1	SE	TL	SE	SE	SE	SE	SE	SE	SE	SE	SE ◇1	SE	TL	SE	SE	SE ◇1	SE	TL	SE	SE
Orpington	d			11 38								11 41		11 50	11 52	11 54	12 03			12 08				
Petts Wood	d											11 44		11 53		11 57	12 06							
Hither Green	d									11 52		11 57	12 03	12 06										
Lewisham	d	08 42			11 46		11 55			11 57	12 02	12 04						12 09	12 12		12 16		12 25	
St Johns	d	08 44								11 59		12 06						12 11	12 14					
New Cross	d	08 47						11 49	11 57	12 01		12 08						12 14	12 17					12 19
London Victoria	a										12 25					12 33								
London Bridge	d	08 54		11 55	11 57	11 58	12 05	13 07	13 17	12 09		12 14	12 15	12 17	12 09			12 20	12 24	12 25	12 27	12 28	12 35	13 37
London Blackfriars	a					12 04											12 49					12 34		
London Cannon Street	a	09 00						13 11	13 21	12 13		12 18						12 24	12 30					13 41
London Waterloo (East)	d			12 00	12 02		12 10						12 20	12 22	12 14					12 30	12 32		12 40	
London Charing Cross	a			12 04	12 05		12 13						12 23	12 27	12 18					12 34	12 35		12 43	

		SE	SE	SE	SE	SE	SE	SE ◇1	SE	TL	SE	SE		SE ◇1	SE	TL	SE	SE	SE	SE	SE	SE	SE	SE	SE ◇1
Orpington	d				12 11		12 20	12 22	12 24	12 33				12 38								12 41		12 50	12 52
Petts Wood	d				12 14		12 23		12 27	12 36												12 44		12 53	
Hither Green	d		12 22		12 27	12 33	12 36													12 52		12 57	13 03	13 06	
Lewisham	d		12 27	12 32	12 34						12 39	12 42			12 45		12 55			12 57	13 02	13 04			
St Johns	d		12 29		12 36						12 41	12 44								12 59		13 06			
New Cross	d	12 27	12 31		12 38						12 44	12 47						12 49	12 57	13 01		13 08			
London Victoria	a			12 55					13 03												13 25				
London Bridge	d	13 47	12 39		12 44	12 45	12 47	12 39			12 50	12 54		12 55	12 57	12 58	13 05	14 07	14 17	13 09		13 14	13 15	13 17	13 09
London Blackfriars	a									13 19						13 04									
London Cannon Street	a	13 51	12 43		12 48						12 54	13 00						14 11	14 21	13 13		13 18			
London Waterloo (East)	d					12 50	12 52	12 44						13 00	13 02		13 10						13 20	13 22	13 14
London Charing Cross	a					12 53	12 57	12 48						13 04	13 05		13 13						13 23	13 27	13 18

Saturdays

26 May to 8 December

Orpington, Petts Wood, Hither Green and Lewisham - London (Summary of Services)

		SE	TL	SE	SE	SE	SE	TL	SE	SE	SE	SE	SE	SE	SE	SE	SE	SE	TL	SE	SE	SE	SE	
						◇1											◇1					◇1		
Orpington	d	12 54	13 03			13 08								13 11		13 20	13 22	13 24	13 33			13 38		and at
Petts Wood	d	12 57	13 06											13 14		13 23		13 27	13 36					the same
Hither Green	d											13 22		13 27	13 33	13 36								minutes
Lewisham	d			13 09	13 12		13 16		13 25			13 27	13 32	13 34						13 39	13 42		13 46	past
St Johns	d			13 11	13 14							13 29		13 36						13 41	13 44			each
New Cross	d			13 14	13 17					13 19	13 27	13 31		13 38						13 44	13 47			hour until
London Victoria	a	13 33											13 55					14 03						
London Bridge	d			13 20	13 24	13 25	13 27	13 28	13 35	14 37	14 47	13 39		13 44	13 45	13 47	13 39			13 50	13 54	13 55	13 57	
London Blackfriars	a		13 49					13 34											14 19					
London Cannon Street	a			13 24	13 30					14 41	14 51	13 43		13 48						13 54	14 00			
London Waterloo (East)	d					13 30	13 32		13 40						13 50	13 52	13 44					14 00	14 02	
London Charing Cross	a					13 34	13 35		13 43						13 53	13 57	13 48					14 04	14 05	

		TL	SE	SE	SE	SE	SE	SE	SE	SE	SE	SE	TL	SE	SE	SE	SE	TL	SE	SE	SE	SE	SE	SE	SE
											◇1					◇1									
Orpington	d							17 41		17 50	17 52	17 54	18 03			18 08								18 11	
Petts Wood	d							17 44		17 53		17 57	18 06											18 14	
Hither Green	d					17 52		17 57	18 03	18 06												18 22		18 27	18 33
Lewisham	d		17 55			17 57	18 02	18 04						18 09	18 12		18 16		18 25			18 27	18 32	18 34	
St Johns	d					17 59		18 06						18 11	18 14							18 29		18 36	
New Cross	d			17 49	17 57	18 01		18 08						18 14	18 17					18 19	18 27	18 31		18 38	
London Victoria	a						18 25					18 33											18 55		
London Bridge	d	17 58	18 05	19 07	19 17	18 09		18 14	18 15	18 17	18 09			18 20	18 24	18 25	18 27	18 28	18 35	19 37	19 47	18 39		18 44	18 45
London Blackfriars	a	18 04											18 49					18 34							
London Cannon Street	a			19 11	19 21	18 13		18 18						18 24	18 30					19 41	19 51	18 43		18 48	
London Waterloo (East)	d		18 10						18 20	18 22	18 14					18 30	18 32		18 40						18 50
London Charing Cross	a		18 13						18 23	18 27	18 18					18 34	18 35		18 43						18 53

		SE	SE	SE	TL	SE	SE	SE	SE		TL	SE	SE	SE	SE	SE	SE	SE	SE		SE	TL	SE	SE	SE
			◇1					◇1											◇1						◇1
Orpington	d	18 20	18 22	18 24	18 33			18 38								18 41		18 50	18 52		18 54	19 03			19 08
Petts Wood	d	18 23		18 27	18 36											18 44		18 53			18 57	19 06			
Hither Green	d	18 36												18 52		18 57	19 03	19 06							
Lewisham	d					18 39	18 42		18 46			18 55		18 57	19 02	19 04							19 09	19 12	
St Johns	d					18 41	18 44							18 59		19 06							19 11	19 14	
New Cross	d					18 44	18 47						18 49	19 01		19 08							19 14	19 17	
London Victoria	a			19 03											19 25						19 33				
London Bridge	d	18 47	18 39			18 50	18 54	18 55	18 57		18 58	19 05	20 07	19 09		19 14	19 15	19 17	19 09				19 20	19 24	19 25
London Blackfriars	a				19 19						19 04											19 49			
London Cannon Street	a					18 54	19 00						20 11	19 13		19 18							19 24	19 30	
London Waterloo (East)	d	18 52	18 44					19 00	19 02			19 10					19 20	19 22	19 14						19 30
London Charing Cross	a	18 57	18 48					19 04	19 05			19 13					19 23	19 27	19 18						19 34

		SE	TL	SE	SE		SE	SE	SE	SE	SE	SE	SE	TL	SE		SE	SE	SE	TL	SE	SE	SE	SE	SE
												◇1						◇1							
Orpington	d								19 11		19 20	19 22	19 24	19 33				19 38							19 41
Petts Wood	d								19 14		19 23		19 27	19 36											19 44
Hither Green	d						19 22		19 27	19 33	19 36												19 52		19 57
Lewisham	d	19 16		19 25			19 27	19 32	19 34						19 39		19 42		19 46		19 55		19 57	20 02	20 04
St Johns	d						19 29		19 36						19 41		19 44						19 59		20 06
New Cross	d				19 19		19 31		19 38						19 44		19 47					19 49	20 01		20 08
London Victoria	a							19 55					20 03											20 25	
London Bridge	d	19 27	19 28	19 35	20 37		19 39		19 44	19 45	19 47	19 39			19 50		19 54	19 55	19 57	19 58	20 05	21 07	20 09		20 14
London Blackfriars	a		19 34											20 19						20 04					
London Cannon Street	a				20 41		19 43		19 48						19 54		20 00					21 11	20 13		20 18
London Waterloo (East)	d	19 32		19 40						19 50	19 52	19 44						20 00	20 02		20 10				
London Charing Cross	a	19 35		19 43						19 53	19 57	19 48						20 04	20 05		20 13				

			SE	SE	SE	SE	TL	SE	SE	SE	SE		TL	SE	SE	SE	SE	SE	SE	SE	SE		SE	SE	SE
					◇1					◇1											◇1				
Orpington	d			19 50	19 52	19 54	20 03			20 08								20 11		20 20	20 22		20 24		
Petts Wood	d			19 53		19 57	20 06											20 14		20 23			20 27		
Hither Green	d		20 03	20 06												20 22		20 27	20 33	20 36					
Lewisham	d							20 09	20 12		20 16			20 25		20 27	20 32	20 34						20 39	20 42
St Johns	d							20 11	20 14							20 29		20 36						20 41	20 44
New Cross	d							20 14	20 17						20 19	20 31		20 38						20 44	20 47
London Victoria	a					20 33											20 55						21 03		
London Bridge	d		20 15	20 17	20 09			20 20	20 24	20 25	20 27		20 28	20 35	21 37	20 39		20 44	20 45	20 47	20 39			20 50	20 54
London Blackfriars	a						20 49						20 34												
London Cannon Street	a							20 24	20 30						21 41	20 43		20 48						20 54	21 00
London Waterloo (East)	d		20 20	20 22	20 14					20 30	20 32			20 40					20 50	20 52	20 44				
London Charing Cross	a		20 23	20 27	20 18					20 34	20 35			20 43					20 53	20 57	20 48				

		SE	TL	TL	SE	SE	SE		SE	SE	SE	SE	SE	SE	TL	SE	SE		SE	TL	SE	SE	SE	SE	SE
													◇1				◇1								
Orpington	d			20 33						20 41		20 50	20 52	20 54	21 03		21 08								21 11
Petts Wood	d			20 36						20 44		20 53		20 57	21 06										21 14
Hither Green	d						20 52			20 57	21 03	21 06											21 22		21 27
Lewisham	d	20 46			20 55		20 57		21 02	21 04						21 09			21 16		21 25		21 27	21 32	21 34
St Johns	d						20 59			21 06						21 11							21 29		21 36
New Cross	d					20 49	21 01			21 08						21 14						21 19	21 31		21 38
London Victoria	a								21 25					21 33										21 55	
London Bridge	d	20 57	20 58		21 05	22 07	21 09			21 14	21 15	21 17	21 09			21 20	21 25		21 27	21 28	21 35	22 37	21 39		21 44
London Blackfriars	a		21 04	21 19											21 49					21 34					
London Cannon Street	a					22 11	21 13			21 18						21 24						22 41	21 43		21 48
London Waterloo (East)	d	21 02			21 10						21 20	21 22	21 14				21 30		21 32		21 40				
London Charing Cross	a	21 05			21 13						21 23	21 27	21 18				21 34		21 35		21 43				

Saturdays

26 May to 8 December

Orpington, Petts Wood, Hither Green and Lewisham - London (Summary of Services)

		SE	SE	SE	SE	SE	SE	TL	TL		SE	SE	SE	SE	SE	SE	SE	SE	SE		TL	SE	SE	SE	TL
				◇1														◇1					◇1		
Orpington	d		21 20	21 22	21 24				21 33						21 41		21 50	21 52	21 54		22 03		22 08		
Petts Wood	d		21 23		21 27				21 36						21 44		21 53		21 57		22 06				
Hither Green	d	21 33	21 36										21 52		21 57	22 03	22 06								
Lewisham	d					21 39	21 46				21 55		21 57	22 02	22 04							22 09		22 16	
St Johns	d					21 41							21 59		22 06							22 11			
New Cross	d					21 44						21 49	22 01		22 08							22 14			
London Victoria	a				22 03									22 25					22 33						
London Bridge	d	21 45	21 47	21 39		21 50	21 57	21 58			22 05	23 07	22 09		22 14	22 15	22 17	22 09				22 20	22 25	22 27	22 28
London Blackfriars	a							22 04	22 19												22 49				22 34
London Cannon Street	a					21 54						23 11	22 13		22 18							22 24			
London Waterloo (East)	d	21 50	21 52	21 44			22 02				22 10					22 20	22 22	22 14					22 30	22 32	
London Charing Cross	a	21 53	21 57	21 48			22 05				22 13					22 23	22 27	22 18					22 34	22 35	

		SE	SE	SE	SE		SE	SE	SE	SE	SE	SE	SE	TL	TL		SE	SE	SE	SE	SE	SE	SE	SE	SE
										◇1														◇1	
Orpington	d						22 11		22 20	22 22	22 24				22 33						22 41		22 50	22 52	22 54
Petts Wood	d						22 14		22 23		22 27				22 36						22 44		22 53		22 57
Hither Green	d			22 22			22 27	22 33	22 36										22 52		22 57	23 03	23 06		
Lewisham	d	22 25		22 27	22 32		22 34					22 39	22 46				22 55		22 57	23 02	23 04				
St Johns	d			22 29			22 36					22 41							22 59		23 06				
New Cross	d		22 19	22 31			22 38					22 44						22 49	23 01		23 08				
London Victoria	a				22 55						23 03									23 25					23 33
London Bridge	d	22 35	23 37	22 39			22 44	22 45	22 47	22 39		22 50	22 57	22 58			23 05	00 07	23 09		23 14	23 15	23 17	23 09	
London Blackfriars	a													23 04	23 19										
London Cannon Street	a		23 41	22 43			22 48					22 54						00 11	23 13		23 18				
London Waterloo (East)	d	22 40						22 50	22 52	22 44			23 02				23 10					23 20	23 22	23 14	
London Charing Cross	a	22 43						22 53	22 57	22 48			23 05				23 13					23 23	23 27	23 18	

			TL	SE	SE	SE	TL	SE	SE	SE	SE		SE	SE	SE	SE	SE	SE	SE	SE	SE		SE
					◇1												◇1						
Orpington	d		23 03		23 08						23 11			23 20	23 24		23 36				23 50		23 54
Petts Wood	d		23 06								23 14			23 23	23 27						23 53		23 57
Hither Green	d								23 22		23 27		23 33	23 36						23 52	00 06		
Lewisham	d			23 09		23 16		23 25	23 27	23 32	23 34					23 39		23 46	23 55	23 57	00 12		
St Johns	d			23 11					23 29		23 36					23 41				23 59			
New Cross	d			23 14					23 31		23 38					23 44				00 02			
London Victoria	a									23 55					00 03								00 33
London Bridge	d			23 20	23 25	23 27	23 28	23 35	23 39		23 44		23 45	23 47		23 50	23 54	23 56	00 05	00 09	00 22		
London Blackfriars	a		23 49				23 34																
London Cannon Street	a			23 24					23 43		23 48					23 54				00 13			
London Waterloo (East)	d				23 30	23 32		23 40					23 50	23 52			23 59	00 01	00 10		00 27		
London Charing Cross	a				23 34	23 35		23 43					23 53	23 57			00 03	00 05	00 13		00 30		

Sundays

20 May to 2 December

		SE	SE	SE	SE	TL	SE	SE	SE	SE		SE	SE	TL	SE	SE	SE	SE	SE	SE		SE	SE	SE	SE
																	◇1	◇1							
		A	A	A	A																				
Orpington	d					06 46	06 49	06 54						07 16	07 19	07 24	07 26	07 40							
Petts Wood	d					06 49	06 52	06 57						07 19	07 22	07 27									
Hither Green	d		00 06		00 16		07 05		07 12			07 29			07 35					07 42				07 59	
Lewisham	d		00 12	00 16			07 11		07 18	07 25			07 32		07 41					07 48		07 55	07 58		08 02
St Johns	d								07 20											07 50			08 00		
New Cross	d	00 02							07 23										07 52	07 53			08 02		
London Victoria	a					07 36		07 35					07 54	08 06		08 04									08 24
London Bridge	d	00 09	00 22	00 26	00 28		07 21		07 30	07 35		07 41			07 51		07 43	07 56	09 13	08 00		08 05	08 09	08 11	
London Blackfriars	a																								
London Cannon Street	a	00 13							07 34										09 17	08 04			08 13		
London Waterloo (East)	d		00 27	00 31	00 33		07 26			07 40		07 46			07 56		07 48	08 01				08 10		08 16	
London Charing Cross	a		00 30	00 35	00 36		07 29			07 43		07 49			07 59		07 52	08 05				08 13		08 19	

		SE	SE	SE	SE	SE		SE	SE	SE	SE	SE	SE	SE	SE	SE		SE	SE	SE	SE	SE	SE	SE	SE
				◇1										◇1	◇1										◇1
Orpington	d	07 49	07 54	07 56								08 19	08 24	08 26	08 40								08 49	08 54	08 56
Petts Wood	d	07 52	07 57									08 22	08 27										08 52	08 57	
Hither Green	d	08 05				08 12				08 29		08 35						08 42			08 59		09 05		
Lewisham	d	08 11				08 18		08 25	08 28		08 32	08 41						08 48	08 55	08 58		09 02	09 11		
St Johns	d					08 20			08 30									08 50		09 00					
New Cross	d				08 22	08 23			08 32							08 52		08 53		09 02					
London Victoria	a		08 34								08 54		09 04									09 24		09 34	
London Bridge	d	08 21		08 13	09 43	08 30		08 35	08 39	08 41		08 51		08 43	08 56	10 13		09 00	09 05	09 09	09 11		09 21		09 13
London Blackfriars	a																								
London Cannon Street	a				09 47	08 34			08 43							10 17		09 04		09 13					
London Waterloo (East)	d	08 26		08 18				08 40		08 46		08 56		08 48	09 01				09 10		09 16		09 26		09 18
London Charing Cross	a	08 29		08 22				08 43		08 49		08 59		08 52	09 05				09 13		09 19		09 29		09 22

A not 20 May

Table T199-R

Sundays

20 May to 2 December

Orpington, Petts Wood, Hither Green and Lewisham - London (Summary of Services)

			SE ◇1	SE	SE	SE	SE	SE	SE	SE	SE	SE ◇1	SE ◇1	TL	SE	SE	SE	SE	SE	SE	SE	SE	SE ◇1	SE ◇1	
Orpington	d		09 10							09 19	09 24	09 26	09 40								09 49	09 54	09 56	10 10	
Petts Wood	d									09 22	09 27										09 52	09 57			
Hither Green	d				09 12			09 29		09 35						09 42			09 59		10 05				
Lewisham	d				09 18	09 25	09 28		09 32	09 41						09 48	09 55	09 58		10 02	10 11				
St Johns	d				09 20		09 30									09 50		10 00							
New Cross	d			09 22	09 23		09 32								09 52	09 53		10 02							
London Victoria	a								09 54		10 04									10 24		10 34			
London Bridge	d		09 26	10 43	09 30	09 35	09 39	09 41		09 51		09 43	09 56	09 58	11 13	10 00	10 05	10 09	10 11		10 21		10 13	10 26	
London Blackfriars	a													10 04											
London Cannon Street	a			10 47	09 34		09 43								11 17	10 04		10 13							
London Waterloo (East)	d		09 31			09 40		09 46		09 56		09 48	10 01				10 10		10 16		10 26		10 18	10 31	
London Charing Cross	a		09 35			09 43		09 49		09 59		09 52	10 05				10 13		10 19		10 29		10 22	10 35	

		TL			SE	SE	SE	SE	SE	SE	SE	SE	SE ◇1	SE ◇1	TL	SE	SE	SE	SE	SE	SE	SE	SE	SE ◇1	SE ◇1
Orpington	d		and at the same minutes past each hour until								19 19	19 24	19 26	19 40								19 49	19 54	19 56	20 10
Petts Wood	d										19 22	19 27										19 52	19 57		
Hither Green	d					19 12			19 29		19 35						19 42			19 59		20 05			
Lewisham	d					19 18	19 25	19 28		19 32	19 41						19 48	19 55	19 58		20 02	20 11			
St Johns	d					19 20		19 30									19 50		20 00						
New Cross	d				19 22	19 23		19 32								19 52	19 53		20 02						
London Victoria	a									19 54		20 04									20 24		20 34		
London Bridge	d	10 28			20 43	19 30	19 35	19 39	19 41		19 51		19 43	19 56	19 58	21 13	20 00	20 05	20 09	20 11		20 21		20 13	20 26
London Blackfriars	a	10 34													20 04										
London Cannon Street	a				20 47	19 34		19 43								21 17	20 04		20 13						
London Waterloo (East)	d						19 40		19 46		19 56		19 48	20 01				20 10		20 16		20 26		20 18	20 31
London Charing Cross	a						19 43		19 49		19 59		19 52	20 05				20 13		20 19		20 29		20 22	20 35

		TL		SE	SE	SE	SE	SE	SE	SE	SE	SE ◇1		TL	SE	SE	SE	SE	SE	SE	SE	SE		SE ◇1	SE ◇1
Orpington	d									20 19	20 24	20 26									20 49	20 54		20 56	21 10
Petts Wood	d									20 22	20 27										20 52	20 57			
Hither Green	d				20 12			20 29		20 35						20 42			20 59		21 05				
Lewisham	d				20 18	20 25	20 28		20 32	20 41						20 48	20 55	20 58		21 02	21 11				
St Johns	d				20 20		20 30									20 50		21 00							
New Cross	d			20 22	20 23		20 32								20 52	20 53		21 02							
London Victoria	a								20 54		21 04									21 24		21 34			
London Bridge	d	20 28		21 43	20 30	20 35	20 39	20 41		20 51		20 43		20 58	22 13	21 00	21 05	21 09	21 11		21 21			21 13	21 26
London Blackfriars	a	20 34												21 04											
London Cannon Street	a			21 47	20 34		20 43								22 17	21 04		21 13							
London Waterloo (East)	d					20 40		20 46		20 56		20 48					21 10		21 16		21 26			21 18	21 31
London Charing Cross	a					20 43		20 49		20 59		20 52					21 13		21 19		21 29			21 22	21 35

		TL	SE	SE	SE	SE	SE	SE		SE	SE	SE ◇1	TL	SE	SE	SE	SE	SE		SE	SE	SE	SE ◇1	SE ◇1	TL
Orpington	d									21 19	21 24	21 26									21 49	21 54	21 56	22 10	
Petts Wood	d									21 22	21 27										21 52	21 57			
Hither Green	d			21 12			21 29			21 35					21 42			21 59			22 05				
Lewisham	d			21 18	21 25	21 28		21 32		21 41					21 48	21 55	21 58			22 02	22 11				
St Johns	d			21 20		21 30									21 50		22 00								
New Cross	d		21 22	21 23		21 32								21 52	21 53		22 02								
London Victoria	a							21 54			22 04									22 24		22 34			
London Bridge	d	21 28	22 43	21 30	21 35	21 39	21 41			21 51		21 43	21 58	23 13	22 00	22 05	22 09	22 11			22 21		22 13	22 26	22 28
London Blackfriars	a	21 34											22 04												22 34
London Cannon Street	a		22 47	21 34		21 43								23 17	22 04		22 13								
London Waterloo (East)	d				21 40		21 46			21 56		21 48				22 10		22 16			22 26		22 18	22 31	
London Charing Cross	a				21 43		21 49			21 59		21 52				22 13		22 19			22 29		22 22	22 35	

		SE	SE	SE		SE	SE	SE	SE	SE	SE ◇1	TL	SE	SE		SE	SE	SE	SE	SE	SE ◇1	TL	SE	SE	
Orpington	d								22 19	22 24	22 26								22 49	22 54	22 56				
Petts Wood	d								22 22	22 27									22 52	22 57					
Hither Green	d		22 12				22 29		22 35				22 42				22 59		23 05				23 12		
Lewisham	d		22 18	22 25		22 28		22 32	22 41				22 48	22 55		22 58		23 02	23 11				23 18	23 25	
St Johns	d		22 20			22 30							22 50			23 00							23 20		
New Cross	d	22 22	22 23			22 32							22 53			23 02							23 23		
London Victoria	a							22 54		23 04								23 24		23 34					
London Bridge	d	23 43	22 30	22 35		22 39	22 41		22 51		22 43	22 58	23 00	23 05		23 09	23 11		23 21		23 13	23 28	23 30	23 35	
London Blackfriars	a											23 04										23 34			
London Cannon Street	a	23 47	22 34			22 43							23 04			23 13							23 34		
London Waterloo (East)	d			22 40			22 46		22 56		22 48			23 10			23 16		23 26		23 18			23 40	
London Charing Cross	a			22 43			22 49		22 59		22 52			23 13			23 19		23 29		23 22			23 43	

		SE	SE	SE	SE	SE	SE	SE	SE	SE
Orpington	d			23 19	23 24					23 49
Petts Wood	d			23 22	23 27					23 52
Hither Green	d		23 29	23 35		23 42			23 59	00 05
Lewisham	d	23 28		23 41		23 48	23 55	23 58		00 11
St Johns	d	23 30				23 50		23 59		
New Cross	d	23 32				23 53		00 02		
London Victoria	a				00 04					
London Bridge	d	23 39	23 41	23 51		23 59	00 05	00 09	00 11	00 21
London Blackfriars	a									
London Cannon Street	a	23 43				00 04		00 13		
London Waterloo (East)	d		23 46	23 56			00 10		00 16	00 26
London Charing Cross	a		23 49	23 59			00 13		00 19	00 29

Table T200-F

Mondays to Fridays

21 May to 7 December

London - Dartford and Gillingham

Miles	Miles	Miles	Miles	Miles			SE MO	TL	SE ◇	TL MO	TL MX	SE MX ◇	SE MO	SE MX	SE MX	SE MO	SE MX	SE MX	SE MX	SE MO	TL MX		SE MO	SE MX	SE MO
—	—	—	—	0	St Pancras Int'l	d																			
—	—	—	—	6	Stratford International	d						00 02													
—	—	—	—	22¾	Ebbsfleet International	d						00 13													
0	—	0	0	—	London Charing Cross	d																			
0¾	—	0¾	0¾	—	London Waterloo (East)	d																			
—	0	—	—	—	London Cannon Street	d																			
1¾	1¾	1¾	1¾	—	London Bridge	d																			00 01
—	3¾	—	—	—	Deptford	d																			
—	4¼	—	—	—	Greenwich	d																			
—	5¼	—	—	—	Maze Hill	d																			
—	5¾	—	—	—	Westcombe Park	d																			
—	—	—	—	0	London Victoria	d																			
—	—	—	—	4¼	Denmark Hill	d																			
—	—	—	—	5	Peckham Rye	d																			
—	—	—	—	5¾	Nunhead	d																			
—	—	4¾	4¾	—	New Cross	d																			
—	—	5½	5½	—	St Johns	d																			
6	—	6	6	7½	Lewisham	d																	00 01		
7	—	7	—	8½	Blackheath	d																	00 03	00 03	
—	—	8	—	9½	Kidbrooke	d													00 02	00 02					
—	—	9	—	10½	Eltham	d													00 06	00 06					
—	—	10¼	—	11¾	Falconwood	d													00 09	00 09					
—	—	11¼	—	12¾	Welling	d													00 11	00 11					
—	—	12¾	—	14¼	Bexleyheath	d									00 03				00 15	00 15					
—	—	14	—	15½	Barnehurst	d									00 06				00 17	00 18					
—	—	—	7¼	—	Hither Green	d																			00 12
—	—	—	8	—	Lee	d																			00 14
—	—	—	9½	—	Mottingham	d																			00 17
—	—	—	10½	—	New Eltham	d																			00 20
—	—	—	12	—	Sidcup	d											00 03								00 24
—	—	—	13	—	Albany Park	d											00 06								00 26
—	—	—	14	—	Bexley	d											00 08								00 29
—	—	—	15½	—	Crayford	d							00 02	00 03			00 12								00 32
9	6½	—	—	—	Charlton	d																	00 08	00 08	
10	7½	—	—	—	Woolwich Dockyard	d																	00 11	00 11	
10¾	8¼	—	—	—	Woolwich Arsenal	d																	00 14	00 14	
11¼	8¾	—	—	—	Plumstead	d																	00 16	00 16	
12¾	10¼	—	—	—	Abbey Wood	d												00 03					00 20	00 20	
14¼	11¾	—	—	—	Belvedere	d										00 03		00 06					00 23	00 23	
15½	13	—	—	—	Erith	d										00 06		00 09					00 25	00 25	
16¾	14¼	—	—	—	Slade Green	d	00 01									00 10		00 14					00 31	00 31	
18¾	16¼	17	17¼	18½	Dartford	a	00 06						00 08	00 08	00 14	00 15	00 17	00 21	00 25	00 24			00 36	00 36	00 38
—	—	—	—	—		d							00 09				00 18				00 28				00 39
20¾	—	—	19¼	—	Stone Crossing	d				00 02	00 02		00 13				00 22				00 32				00s43
21½	—	—	20	—	Greenhithe for Bluewater	d				00 04	00 04		00 15				00 24				00 34				00s45
22¾	—	—	21¼	—	Swanscombe	d				00 07	00 07		00 18				00 27				00 37				00s48
23½	—	—	22	—	Northfleet	d				00 09	00 09		00 20				00 29				00 39				00s50
25½	—	—	24	24¾	Gravesend	d				00 13	00 13	00 18	00a25				00a36				00 43				00a55
30	—	—	28½	29¼	Higham	d				00 19	00 19										00 49				
32¾	—	—	31¼	32	Strood	d				00 25	00 25	00 29									00 56				
—	—	—	—	—	Maidstone West	d																			
33¾	—	—	32¼	33	Rochester	d			00 02	00 28	00 28	00 32									00 59				
34½	—	—	32¾	33½	Chatham	d		00 02	00 06	00 31	00 32	00 36									01 03				
36	—	—	34½	35¼	Gillingham (Kent)	a		00 06	00 10	00 36	00 36	00 40									01 07				
—	—	—	—	—	Rainham Kt.	a			00 15			00 45													

Please note, Network Rail have stated that further updates to this timetable are possible during the validity period.

Table T200-F

Mondays to Fridays

21 May to 7 December

London - Dartford and Gillingham

Station		SE MX	SE MO	SE TWO	SE MX	TL MO	SE MO	SE ThFO	SE TWO	TL MX	TL	SE TWO	SE MThFO		SE	TL	SE	SE	SE	SE	SE	TL	SE	SE	SE
St Pancras Int'l ⊖	d																								
Stratford International ⊖	d																								
Ebbsfleet International	d																								
London Charing Cross ⊖	d						00 12	00 26					04 50				05 20	05 26					05 42		05 52
London Waterloo (East) ⊖	d						00 15	00 29					04 53				05 23	05 29					05 45		05 55
London Cannon Street ⊖	d			00 02					00 32			04 54			05 05				05 35	05 39	05 39			05 55	
London Bridge ⊖	d	00 01	00 03	00 06			00 21	00 35	00 36			04 59	04 59		05 09		05 29	05 35	05 39	05 43	05 43	05 48	05 51	05 59	06 01
Deptford	d		00 09	00 12					00 42						05 15				05 45			05 55		06 05	
Greenwich	d		00 11	00 14					00 44						05 17				05 47			05 57		06 07	
Maze Hill	d		00 14	00 17					00 47						05 20				05 50			06 00		06 10	
Westcombe Park	d		00 16	00 19					00 49						05 22				05 52			06 02		06 12	
London Victoria ⊖	d				00 06																				
Denmark Hill	d				00 16																				
Peckham Rye	d				00 18																				
Nunhead	d				00 21																				
New Cross ⊖	d																			05 49	05 49				
St Johns	d																			05 51	05 51				
Lewisham	d	00 10			00 26		00 31	00 45				05 08	05 08				05 38	05 44		05 54	05 54		06 01		
Blackheath	d	00 13			00 29		00 33	00 48										05 47					06 03		
Kidbrooke	d	00 16			00 32			00 51										05 50							
Eltham	d	00 19			00 36			00 54										05 53							
Falconwood	d	00 22			00 39			00 57										05 56							
Welling	d	00 25			00 41			01 00										05 59							
Bexleyheath	d	00 28			00 45			01 03										06 02							
Barnehurst	d	00 31			00 47			01 06										06 05							
Hither Green	d											05 13	05 13				05 43			05 58	05 58				06 13
Lee	d											05 15	05 15				05 45			06 00	06 00				06 15
Mottingham	d											05 18	05 18				05 48			06 03	06 03				06 18
New Eltham	d											05 20	05 20				05 50			06 06	06 06				06 20
Sidcup	d											05 24	05 24				05 54			06 09	06 09				06 24
Albany Park	d											05 26	05 26				05 56			06 12	06 12				06 26
Bexley	d											05 29	05 29				05 59			06 15	06 15				06 29
Crayford	d											05 32	05 33				06 03			06 22	06 22				06 32
Charlton	d		00 19	00 22			00 38		00 52						05 25				05 55		06a59	06 05	06 08	06 15	
Woolwich Dockyard	d		00 22	00 25			00 41		00 55						05 28				05 58				06 11	06 18	
Woolwich Arsenal	d		00 25	00 28			00 44		00 58						05 31				06 01			06 10	06 14	06 21	
Plumstead	d		00 27	00 30			00 46		01 00						05 33				06 03			06 13	06 16	06 23	
Abbey Wood	d		00 30	00 33			00 50		01 03						05 36				06 06			06 16	06 19	06 26	
Belvedere	d		00 33	00 36			00 53		01 06						05 39				06 09				06 22	06 29	
Erith	d		00 36	00 39			00 55		01 09						05 42				06 12				06 25	06 32	
Slade Green	d		00 40	00 44			01 01		01 12						05 47				06a16	06a34		06 22	06 28	06a35	
Dartford	a	00 41	00 45	00 49	00 56		01 06	01 16	01 20			05 38	05 38		05 52		06 08	06 14				06 27	06 34		06 37
	d					00 58				01 24	04 58	05 39	05 39			05 58	06 09					06 28			
Stone Crossing	d					01s02				01s28	05 02	05 43	05 43			06 02	06 13					06 32			
Greenhithe for Bluewater	d					01s04				01s30	05 04	05 45	05 45			06 04	06 15					06 34			
Swanscombe	d					01s07				01s33	05 07	05 48	05 48			06 07	06 18					06 37			
Northfleet	d					01s09				01s35	05 09	05 50	05 50			06 09	06 20					06 39			
Gravesend	d					01 13				01 39	05 13	05a56	05a56			06 13	06a25					06 43			
Higham	d					01s19				01s45	05 19					06 19						06 49			
Strood	d					01s24				01s50	05 25					06 25						06 55			
Maidstone West	d																								
Rochester	d					01s27				01s53	05 28					06 28						06 58			
Chatham	d					01s31				01s57	05 31					06 31						07 01			
Gillingham (Kent)	a					01 36				02 02	05 35					06 35						07 05			
Rainham Kt	a										05 41					06 41						07 11			

Table T200-F

Mondays to Fridays

21 May to 7 December

London - Dartford and Gillingham

Station		SE	SE	SE	SE ◇		TL	SE	SE	SE	SE ◇	SE	SE	SE	SE	SE ◇	TL	SE	SE	SE	SE		SE	SE	SE
St Pancras Int'l ⊖	d				06 25						06 55					07 22									
Stratford International ⊖	d				06 32						07 02					07 29									
Ebbsfleet International	d				06 43						07 13					07 40									
London Charing Cross ⊖	d	05 54						06 12				06 23	06 25					06 41			06 53		06 56		
London Waterloo (East) ⊖	d	05 57						06 15				06 26	06 28					06 44			06 56		06 59		
London Cannon Street ⊖	d		06 09	06 09						06 25				06 35	06 39					06 55				07 05	
London Bridge ⊖	d	06 03	06 13	06 13			06 18	06 21		06 29		06 32	06 35	06 39	06 43		06 48	06 50		06 59	07 02		07 05	07 09	
Deptford	d						06 25			06 35				06 45			06 55			07 05				07 15	
Greenwich	d						06 27			06 37				06 47			06 57			07 07				07 17	
Maze Hill	d						06 30			06 40				06 50			07 00			07 10				07 20	
Westcombe Park	d						06 32			06 42				06 52			07 02			07 12				07 22	
London Victoria ⊖	d								06 15										06 42						07 08
Denmark Hill	d								06 25										06 52						
Peckham Rye	d								06 28										06 55						
Nunhead	d								06 30																
New Cross ⊖	d		06 19	06 19											06 49										
St Johns	d		06 21	06 21											06 51										
Lewisham	d	06 14	06 24	06 24				06 30	06 37				06 45		06 54			06 59	07 02				07 15		07 26
Blackheath	d	06 17						06 33	06 40				06 48					07 02	07 05				07 18		07 29
Kidbrooke	d	06 20							06 43				06 51						07 08				07 21		
Eltham	d	06 23							06 46				06 54						07 11				07 24		
Falconwood	d	06 26							06 49				06 57										07 27		
Welling	d	06 29							06 52				07 00										07 30		
Bexleyheath	d	06 32							06 55				07 03						07 17				07 33		
Barnehurst	d	06 35							06 58				07 08						07 20				07 36		
Hither Green	d		06 30	06 30								06 43			06 59						07 13				
Lee	d		06 32	06 32								06 45			07 01						07 15				
Mottingham	d		06 35	06 35								06 48			07 04						07 18				
New Eltham	d		06 38	06 38								06 51			07 07						07 21				
Sidcup	d		06 41	06 41								06 54			07 10						07 24				
Albany Park	d		06 44	06 44								06 57			07 13						07 27				
Bexley	d		06 47	06 47								06 59			07 16						07 29				
Crayford	d		06 56	06 56								07 03			07 25						07 33				
Charlton	d			07a30			06 35	06 38		06 45				06 55	07a57		07 05	07 08		07 15				07 25	
Woolwich Dockyard	d							06 41		06 48				06 58				07 11		07 18				07 28	
Woolwich Arsenal	d						06 40	06 44		06 51				07 01			07 10	07 14		07 21				07 31	
Plumstead	d						06 43	06 46		06 53				07 03			07 13	07 16		07 23				07 33	
Abbey Wood	d						06 46	06 49		06 56				07 06			07 16	07 20		07 26				07 36	
Belvedere	d							06 52		06 59				07 09				07 23		07 29				07 39	
Erith	d							06 55		07 02				07 12				07 25		07 32				07 42	
Slade Green	d		07a07				06 52	06 58		07a05				07a16			07 22	07 29		07a36				07a46	
Dartford	a	06 44					06 57	07 05	07 05			07 07	07 18				07 29	07 36	07 29		07 37		07 46		07 50
	d						06 58					07 09					07 30				07 39				
Stone Crossing	d						07 02					07 13					07 34				07 43				
Greenhithe for Bluewater	d						07 04					07 15					07 36				07 45				
Swanscombe	d						07 07					07 18					07 39				07 48				
Northfleet	d						07 09					07 20					07 41				07 50				
Gravesend	d				06 48		07 13				07 19	07a27				07 44	07 47				07a56				
Higham	d						07 19										07 53								
Strood	d				07 01		07 25				07 31					07 54	07 59								
Maidstone West	d				07a16																				
Rochester	d						07 28				07 34					07 58	08 02								
Chatham	d						07 31				07 38					08 02	08 06								
Gillingham (Kent)	a						07 35				07 42					08 06	08 10								
Rainham Kt	a						07 42				07 47					08 11	08 21								

Please note, Network Rail have stated that further updates to this timetable are possible during the validity period.

Table T200-F

Mondays to Fridays

21 May to 7 December

London - Dartford and Gillingham

		SE	TL	SE	SE	SE	SE	SE	SE	SE	SE	SE	SE ◇	SE	TL	SE	SE	SE	SE ◇	SE	SE	SE	SE	TL
St Pancras Int'l	d												08 07						08 25					
Stratford International	d												08 14						08 32					
Ebbsfleet International	d												08 26						08 43					
London Charing Cross	d			07 12				07 21	07 25			07 39								07 53	07 56			
London Waterloo (East)	d			07 15				07 24	07 28			07 42								07 56	07 59			
London Cannon Street	d	07 11			07 22	07 22	07 25			07 36	07 40					07 47	07 57	08 00				08 05		
London Bridge	d	07 15	07 18	07 21	07 26	07 26	07 29	07 30	07 34	07 40		07 48			07 48		08 01			08 02	08 05	08 09		08 18
Deptford	d		07 25				07 35			07 46					07 55		08 07					08 15		08 25
Greenwich	d		07 27				07 37			07 48					07 57		08 09					08 17		08 27
Maze Hill	d		07 30				07 40			07 51					08 00		08 12					08 20		08 30
Westcombe Park	d		07 32				07 42			07 53					08 02		08 14					08 22		08 32
London Victoria	d													07 45									08 06	
Denmark Hill	d													07 55									08 16	
Peckham Rye	d													07 58									08 18	
Nunhead	d													08 00									08 21	
New Cross	d	07 21			07 32	07 32					07 50													
St Johns	d	07 23			07 34	07 34					07 52													
Lewisham	d	07 28		07 30	07 37	07 37			07 45		07 56	08 00		08 07				08 11			08 18		08 29	
Blackheath	d			07 33	07 40	07 40			07 48			08 03						08 14			08 21		08 32	
Kidbrooke	d				07 43	07 43			07 51									08 17			08 24		08 35	
Eltham	d				07 46	07 46			07 54							08 04		08 20			08 27		08 38	
Falconwood	d				07 49	07 49			07 57									08 24			08 30			
Welling	d				07 52	07 52			08 00							08 08		08 26			08 33			
Bexleyheath	d				07 55	07 55			08 03							08 11		08 30			08 36		08 44	
Barnehurst	d				07 58	07 58			08 06							08 14		08 35			08 39		08 47	
Hither Green	d	07 34				08a31		07 41			08 01									08 14				
Lee	d							07 43			08 03									08 16				
Mottingham	d							07 46			08 06									08 19				
New Eltham	d	07 39						07 49			08 08									08 21				
Sidcup	d	07 43						07 52			08 12									08 25				
Albany Park	d	07 45						07 55			08 14									08 27				
Bexley	d	07 48						07 57			08 17									08 30				
Crayford	d	07 51			08a09			08 01			08 21									08 33				
Charlton	d	08a19	07 35	07 38			07 45			07 56	08a50	08 08			08 05		08 17					08 25		08 35
Woolwich Dockyard	d			07 41						07 59		08 11					08 20					08 28		
Woolwich Arsenal	d		07 40	07 44			07 50			08 02		08 14			08 10		08 23					08 31		08 40
Plumstead	d		07 43	07 46						08 04		08 16			08 13		08 25					08 33		08 43
Abbey Wood	d		07 46	07 50			07 55			08 07		08 20			08 16		08 28					08 36		08 46
Belvedere	d			07 53						08 10		08 23					08 31					08 39		
Erith	d			07 55						08 13		08 25					08 34					08 42		
Slade Green	d		07 52	07 59			08a02			08a16		08 29			08 22	08a24	08 37	08a44				08a45		08 52
Dartford	a		07 57	08 06				08 06	08 16			08 37		08 24	08 27		08 45			08 38	08 48		08 54	08 57
	d		08 01					08 09						08 24	08 28					08 39			08 54	08 58
Stone Crossing	d		08 05					08 13							08 32					08 43				09 02
Greenhithe for Bluewater	d		08 07					08 15						08 30	08 34					08 45			09 00	09 04
Swanscombe	d		08 10					08 18							08 37					08 48				09 07
Northfleet	d		08 12					08 20							08 39					08 50				09 09
Gravesend	d		08 19					08a27					08 30	08a41	08 43				08 48	08a57			09a09	09 13
Higham	d		08 25												08 49									09 19
Strood	d		08 31										08 40		08 55				08 59					09 25
Maidstone West	d																							
Rochester	d		08 34										08 44		08 58				09 02					09 28
Chatham	d		08 37										08 47		09 01				09 06					09 31
Gillingham (Kent)	a		08 41										08 51		09 05				09 10					09 35
Rainham Kt	a		08 49										08 57		09 11				09 15					09 41

Table T200-F

Mondays to Fridays

21 May to 7 December

London - Dartford and Gillingham

		SE	SE	SE	SE	SE	SE ◇	SE	SE	SE	SE	SE	SE	TL	SE	SE	SE	SE	SE	SE ◇	SE	SE	SE
St Pancras Int'l	d						08 58													09 25			
Stratford International	d						09 05													09 32			
Ebbsfleet International	d						09 16													09 44			
London Charing Cross	d		08 12	08 14				08 22	08 26			08 38			08 42	08 46	08 50				09 00		
London Waterloo (East)	d		08 15	08 17				08 25	08 29			08 41			08 45	08 49	08 53				09 03		
London Cannon Street	d	08 14			08 19	08 24				08 34	08 37							08 54	09 05			09 08	
London Bridge	d	08 18	08 21	08 23		08 28		08 31	08 35	08 38	08 41	08 47		08 48	08 51	08 57	08 59	08 59	09 09		09 09	09 13	
Deptford	d					08 35				08 45				08 55				09 05	09 15				
Greenwich	d					08 37				08 47				08 57				09 07	09 17				
Maze Hill	d					08 40				08 50				09 00				09 10	09 20				
Westcombe Park	d					08 42				08 52				09 02				09 12	09 22				
London Victoria	d												08 38										09 06
Denmark Hill	d												08 47										09 16
Peckham Rye	d												08 50										09 18
Nunhead	d												08 52										09 21
New Cross	d				08 31						08 47											09 19	
St Johns	d				08 33						08 49											09 21	
Lewisham	d		08 32		08 36				08 45		08 55	08 58	09 01		09 04		09 12					09 24	09 26
Blackheath	d		08 35		08 39				08 48			09 01	09 04		09 07		09 15						09 29
Kidbrooke	d				08 42				08 51						09 10		09 18						09 32
Eltham	d				08 45				08 54				09 10		09 13		09 22						09 36
Falconwood	d				08 48				08 57						09 16		09 25						09 39
Welling	d				08 51				09 00						09 19		09 27						09 41
Bexleyheath	d				08 54				09 03				09 16		09 22		09 31						09 45
Barnehurst	d				09 00				09 06						09 30		09 35						09 47
Hither Green	d	08 30		08 34				08 42			09 00					09 11						09 30	
Lee	d	08 32		08 36				08 44			09 02											09 32	
Mottingham	d	08 35		08 39				08 47			09 05											09 35	
New Eltham	d	08 38		08 42				08 50			09 08					09 16					09 25	09 38	
Sidcup	d	08 41		08 45				08 53			09 11					09 20					09 29	09 41	
Albany Park	d	08 44		08 48				08 56			09 14											09 44	
Bexley	d	08 46		08 51				08 58			09 16					09 23					09 32	09 46	
Crayford	d	08 50		08 55				09 02			09 21					09 27					09 36	09 51	
Charlton	d	09a19	08 43			08 46				08 55	09a49	09 08		09 05				09 16	09 25			10a19	
Woolwich Dockyard	d		08 46			08 49				08 58		09 11						09 19	09 28				
Woolwich Arsenal	d		08 49			08 52				09 01		09 14		09 10				09 22	09 31				
Plumstead	d		08 51			08 54				09 03		09 16		09 13				09 24	09 33				
Abbey Wood	d		08 54			08 58				09 06		09 19		09 16				09 27	09 36				
Belvedere	d		08 57			09 01				09 09		09 22						09 30	09 39				
Erith	d		09 00			09 03				09 12		09 25						09 33	09 42				
Slade Green	d		09 04		09a07	09a06				09a15		09 30		09 22	09a39			09a36	09a46				
Dartford	a		09 12	09 03				09 07	09 17			09 40	09 24	09 27		09 34	09 46				09 40		09 54
	d							09 08					09 24	09 28							09 41		09 54
Stone Crossing	d							09 12						09 32							09 45		
Greenhithe for Bluewater	d							09 15					09 30	09 34							09 47		10 00
Swanscombe	d							09 18						09 37							09 50		
Northfleet	d							09 20						09 39							09 52		
Gravesend	d						09 20	09a26					09a41	09 43						09 48	09a56		10a09
Higham	d													09 49									
Strood	d						09 30							09 55						09 59			
Maidstone West	d																						
Rochester	d						09 34							09 58						10 02			
Chatham	d						09 37							10 01						10 06			
Gillingham (Kent)	a						09 41							10 05						10 10			
Rainham Kt	a						09 46							10 11						10 15			

Table T200-F

21 May to 7 December

London - Dartford and Gillingham

		TL	SE	SE	SE	SE	SE	SE ◇	SE	SE	SE	SE	TL	SE	SE	SE	SE	SE	SE	SE ◇	SE	SE	SE	TL
St Pancras Int'l ⊖	d							09 55												10 27				
Stratford International ⊖	d							10 02												10 34				
Ebbsfleet International	d							10 13												10 45				
London Charing Cross ⊖	d		09 12			09 20	09 26		09 28					09 42		09 48		09 54			10 02			
London Waterloo (East) ⊖	d		09 15			09 23	09 29		09 31					09 45		09 51		09 58			10 05			
London Cannon Street ⊖	d			09 17	09 24					09 35	09 38				09 47		09 54		10 05			10 08		
London Bridge ⊖	d	09 18	09 21	09 21	09 28	09 29	09 35		09 37	09 39	09 43		09 48	09 51	09 51	09 57	09 58	10 05	10 09		10 11	10 13		10 18
Deptford	d	09 25			09 35					09 45			09 55				10 05		10 15					10 25
Greenwich	d	09 27			09 37					09 47			09 57				10 07		10 17					10 27
Maze Hill	d	09 30			09 40					09 50			10 00				10 10		10 20					10 30
Westcombe Park	d	09 32			09 42					09 52			10 02				10 12		10 22					10 32
London Victoria ⊖	d											09 36											10 06	
Denmark Hill	d											09 46											10 16	
Peckham Rye	d											09 48											10 18	
Nunhead	d											09 51											10 21	
New Cross ⊖	d			09 28							09 49				09 57							10 19		
St Johns	d			09 30							09 51				09 59							10 21		
Lewisham	d		09 32	09 35			09 45				09 54	09 56		10 01	10 04			10 15				10 24	10 26	
Blackheath	d		09 35	09 38			09 48					09 59		10 04	10 07			10 18					10 29	
Kidbrooke	d			09 41			09 51					10 02			10 10			10 21					10 32	
Eltham	d			09 44			09 54					10 06			10 13			10 24					10 36	
Falconwood	d			09 47			09 57					10 09			10 16			10 27					10 39	
Welling	d			09 50			10 00					10 11			10 19			10 30					10 41	
Bexleyheath	d			09 53			10 03					10 15			10 22			10 33					10 45	
Barnehurst	d			09 59			10 06					10 17			10 28			10 36					10 47	
Hither Green	d					09 39					09 59					10 07						10 29		
Lee	d					09 41					10 01					10 09						10 31		
Mottingham	d					09 44					10 04					10 12						10 34		
New Eltham	d					09 46			09 55		10 07					10 15					10 25	10 37		
Sidcup	d					09 50			09 58		10 10					10 19					10 28	10 40		
Albany Park	d					09 52					10 13					10 21						10 43		
Bexley	d					09 55			10 02		10 15					10 24					10 32	10 45		
Crayford	d					09 58			10 05		10 21					10 27					10 35	10 51		
Charlton	d	09 35	09 40		09 45					09 55	10a49		10 05	10 08			10 15		10 25			11a19		10 35
Woolwich Dockyard	d		09 43		09 48					09 58				10 11			10 18		10 28					
Woolwich Arsenal	d	09 40	09 46		09 51					10 01			10 10	10 14			10 21		10 31					10 40
Plumstead	d	09 43	09 48		09 53					10 03			10 13	10 16			10 23		10 33					10 43
Abbey Wood	d	09 46	09 51		09 56					10 06			10 16	10 20			10 26		10 36					10 46
Belvedere	d		09 54		09 59					10 09				10 23			10 29		10 39					
Erith	d		09 57		10 02					10 12				10 25			10 32		10 42					
Slade Green	d	09 52	10 03	10a05	10a06					10a15			10 22	10 31	10a35		10a36		10a45					10 52
Dartford	a	09 57	10 08			10 05	10 14		10 10			10 24	10 27	10 38		10 32		10 44			10 40		10 54	10 57
	d	09 58							10 11			10 24	10 28								10 41		10 54	10 58
Stone Crossing	d	10 02							10 15				10 32								10 45			11 02
Greenhithe for Bluewater	d	10 04							10 17			10 30	10 34								10 47		11 00	11 04
Swanscombe	d	10 07							10 20				10 37								10 50			11 07
Northfleet	d	10 09							10 22				10 39								10 52			11 09
Gravesend	d	10 13						10 18	10a26			10a38	10 43							10 49	10a56		11a09	11 13
Higham	d	10 19											10 49											11 19
Strood	d	10 25						10 29					10 55							10 59				11 25
Maidstone West	d																							
Rochester	d	10 28						10 32					10 58							11 02				11 28
Chatham	d	10 31						10 36					11 01							11 06				11 31
Gillingham (Kent)	a	10 35						10 40					11 05							11 10				11 35
Rainham Kt	a	10 41						10 45					11 11							11 15				11 41

Table T200-F

21 May to 7 December

London - Dartford and Gillingham

		SE	SE	SE	SE	SE	SE	SE ◇	SE	SE	SE	TL	SE	SE	SE	SE	SE	SE	SE ◇	SE	SE	SE	TL
St Pancras Int'l ⊖	d							10 52											11 25				
Stratford International ⊖	d							10 59											11 32				
Ebbsfleet International	d							11 13											11 43				
London Charing Cross ⊖	d	10 12		10 18		10 24			10 32				10 42		10 48		10 54			11 02			
London Waterloo (East) ⊖	d	10 15		10 21		10 28			10 35				10 45		10 51		10 58			11 05			
London Cannon Street ⊖	d		10 17		10 24		10 35			10 38				10 47		10 54		11 05			11 08		
London Bridge ⊖	d	10 21	10 21	10 27	10 28	10 35	10 39		10 41	10 43		10 48	10 51	10 51	10 57	10 58	11 05	11 09		11 11	11 13		11 18
Deptford	d				10 35		10 45					10 55				11 05		11 15					11 25
Greenwich	d				10 37		10 47					10 57				11 07		11 17					11 27
Maze Hill	d				10 40		10 50					11 00				11 10		11 20					11 30
Westcombe Park	d				10 42		10 52					11 02				11 12		11 22					11 32
London Victoria ⊖	d										10 36											11 06	
Denmark Hill	d										10 46											11 16	
Peckham Rye	d										10 48											11 18	
Nunhead	d										10 51											11 21	
New Cross ⊖	d		10 27							10 49				10 57							11 19		
St Johns	d		10 29							10 51				10 59							11 21		
Lewisham	d	10 30	10 34			10 45				10 54	10 56		11 00	11 04			11 15				11 24	11 26	
Blackheath	d	10 33	10 37			10 48					10 59		11 03	11 07			11 18					11 29	
Kidbrooke	d		10 40			10 51					11 02			11 10			11 21					11 32	
Eltham	d		10 43			10 54					11 06			11 13			11 24					11 36	
Falconwood	d		10 46			10 57					11 09			11 16			11 27					11 39	
Welling	d		10 49			11 00					11 11			11 19			11 30					11 41	
Bexleyheath	d		10 52			11 03					11 15			11 22			11 33					11 45	
Barnehurst	d		10 58			11 06					11 17			11 28			11 36					11 47	
Hither Green	d			10 37						10 59					11 07						11 29		
Lee	d			10 39						11 01					11 09						11 31		
Mottingham	d			10 42						11 04					11 12						11 34		
New Eltham	d			10 45					10 55	11 07					11 15					11 25	11 37		
Sidcup	d			10 48					10 58	11 10					11 18					11 28	11 40		
Albany Park	d			10 51						11 13					11 21						11 43		
Bexley	d			10 53					11 02	11 15					11 23					11 32	11 45		
Crayford	d			10 57					11 05	11 21					11 27					11 35	11 51		
Charlton	d	10 38			10 45		10 55			11a49		11 05	11 08			11 15		11 25			12a19		11 35
Woolwich Dockyard	d	10 41			10 48		10 58						11 11			11 18		11 28					
Woolwich Arsenal	d	10 44			10 51		11 01					11 10	11 14			11 21		11 31					11 40
Plumstead	d	10 46			10 53		11 03					11 13	11 16			11 23		11 33					11 43
Abbey Wood	d	10 50			10 56		11 06					11 16	11 20			11 26		11 36					11 46
Belvedere	d	10 53			10 59		11 09						11 23			11 29		11 39					
Erith	d	10 55			11 02		11 12						11 25			11 32		11 42					
Slade Green	d	11 01	11a05		11a06		11a15					11 22	11 31	11a35		11a36		11a45					11 52
Dartford	a	11 08		11 02		11 14			11 10		11 24	11 27	11 38		11 32		11 44			11 40		11 54	11 57
	d								11 11		11 24	11 28								11 41		11 54	11 58
Stone Crossing	d								11 15			11 32								11 45			12 02
Greenhithe for Bluewater	d								11 17		11 30	11 34								11 47		12 00	12 04
Swanscombe	d								11 20			11 37								11 50			12 07
Northfleet	d								11 22			11 39								11 52			12 09
Gravesend	d							11 18	11a26		11a39	11 43							11 48	11a56		12a09	12 13
Higham	d											11 49											12 19
Strood	d							11 29				11 55							11 59				12 25
Maidstone West	d																						
Rochester	d							11 32				11 58							12 02				12 28
Chatham	d							11 36				12 01							12 06				12 31
Gillingham (Kent)	a							11 40				12 05							12 10				12 35
Rainham Kt	a							11 45				12 11							12 15				12 41

Please note, Network Rail have stated that further updates to this timetable are possible during the validity period.

Table T200-F

Mondays to Fridays

21 May to 7 December

London - Dartford and Gillingham

		SE	SE	SE	SE	SE	SE	SE ◇	SE	SE	SE	TL	SE	SE	SE	SE	SE	SE	SE ◇	SE	SE	SE	TL	SE
St Pancras Int'l	d							11 55											12 27					
Stratford International	d							12 02											12 34					
Ebbsfleet International	d							12 13											12 45					
London Charing Cross	d	11 12		11 18		11 24			11 32				11 42		11 48		11 54			12 02				12 12
London Waterloo (East)	d	11 15		11 21		11 28			11 35				11 45		11 51		11 58			12 05				12 15
London Cannon Street	d		11 17		11 24		11 35			11 38				11 47		11 54		12 05			12 08			
London Bridge	d	11 21	11 21	11 27	11 28	11 35	11 39		11 41	11 43		11 48	11 51	11 51	11 57	11 58	12 05	12 09		12 11	12 13		12 18	12 21
Deptford	d				11 35		11 45					11 55				12 05		12 15					12 25	
Greenwich	d				11 37		11 47					11 57				12 07		12 17					12 27	
Maze Hill	d				11 40		11 50					12 00				12 10		12 20					12 30	
Westcombe Park	d				11 42		11 52					12 02				12 12		12 22					12 32	
London Victoria	d										11 36											12 06		
Denmark Hill	d										11 46											12 16		
Peckham Rye	d										11 48											12 18		
Nunhead	d										11 51											12 21		
New Cross	d		11 27							11 49				11 57							12 19			
St Johns	d		11 29							11 51				11 59							12 21			
Lewisham	d	11 30	11 34			11 45				11 54	11 56		12 00	12 04			12 15				12 24	12 26		12 30
Blackheath	d	11 33	11 37			11 48					11 59		12 03	12 07			12 18					12 29		12 33
Kidbrooke	d		11 40			11 51					12 02			12 10			12 21					12 32		
Eltham	d		11 43			11 54					12 06			12 13			12 24					12 36		
Falconwood	d		11 46			11 57					12 09			12 16			12 27					12 39		
Welling	d		11 49			12 00					12 11			12 19			12 30					12 41		
Bexleyheath	d		11 52			12 03					12 15			12 22			12 33					12 45		
Barnehurst	d		11 58			12 06					12 17			12 28			12 36					12 47		
Hither Green	d			11 37						11 59					12 07						12 29			
Lee	d			11 39						12 01					12 09						12 31			
Mottingham	d			11 42						12 04					12 12						12 34			
New Eltham	d			11 45					11 55	12 07					12 15					12 25	12 37			
Sidcup	d			11 48					11 58	12 10					12 18					12 28	12 40			
Albany Park	d			11 51						12 13					12 21						12 43			
Bexley	d			11 53					12 02	12 15					12 23					12 32	12 45			
Crayford	d			11 57					12 05	12 21					12 27					12 35	12 51			
Charlton	d	11 38			11 45		11 55			12a49		12 05	12 08			12 15		12 25			13a19		12 35	12 38
Woolwich Dockyard	d	11 41			11 48		11 58						12 11			12 18		12 28						12 41
Woolwich Arsenal	d	11 44			11 51		12 01					12 10	12 14			12 21		12 31					12 40	12 44
Plumstead	d	11 46			11 53		12 03					12 13	12 16			12 23		12 33					12 43	12 46
Abbey Wood	d	11 50			11 56		12 06					12 16	12 20			12 26		12 36					12 46	12 50
Belvedere	d	11 53			11 59		12 09						12 23			12 29		12 39						12 53
Erith	d	11 55			12 02		12 12						12 25			12 32		12 42						12 55
Slade Green	d	12 01	12a05		12a06		12a15					12 22	12 31	12a35		12a36		12a45					12 52	13 01
Dartford	a	12 08		12 02		12 14			12 10		12 24	12 27	12 38		12 32		12 44			12 40		12 54	12 57	13 08
	d								12 11		12 24	12 28								12 41		12 54	12 58	
Stone Crossing	d								12 15			12 32								12 45			13 02	
Greenhithe for Bluewater	d								12 17		12 30	12 34								12 47		13 00	13 04	
Swanscombe	d								12 20			12 37								12 50			13 07	
Northfleet	d								12 22			12 39								12 52			13 09	
Gravesend	d							12 18	12a26		12a39	12 43							12 49	12a56		13a09	13 13	
Higham	d											12 49											13 19	
Strood	d							12 29				12 55							12 59				13 25	
Maidstone West	d																							
Rochester	d							12 32				12 58							13 02				13 28	
Chatham	d							12 36				13 01							13 06				13 31	
Gillingham (Kent)	a							12 40				13 05							13 10				13 35	
Rainham Kt	a							12 45				13 11							13 15				13 41	

Table T200-F

Mondays to Fridays

21 May to 7 December

London - Dartford and Gillingham

		SE	SE	SE	SE	SE	SE ◇	SE	SE	SE	TL	SE	SE	SE	SE	SE	SE	SE ◇	SE	SE	SE	TL	SE
St Pancras Int'l	d						12 52											13 25					
Stratford International	d						12 59											13 32					
Ebbsfleet International	d						13 13											13 43					
London Charing Cross	d		12 18		12 24			12 32				12 42		12 48		12 54			13 02				13 12
London Waterloo (East)	d		12 21		12 28			12 35				12 45		12 51		12 58			13 05				13 15
London Cannon Street	d	12 17		12 24		12 35			12 38				12 47		12 54		13 05			13 08			
London Bridge	d	12 21	12 27	12 28	12 35	12 39		12 41	12 43		12 48	12 51	12 51	12 57	12 58	13 05	13 09		13 11	13 13		13 18	13 21
Deptford	d			12 35		12 45					12 55				13 05		13 15					13 25	
Greenwich	d			12 37		12 47					12 57				13 07		13 17					13 27	
Maze Hill	d			12 40		12 50					13 00				13 10		13 20					13 30	
Westcombe Park	d			12 42		12 52					13 02				13 12		13 22					13 32	
London Victoria	d									12 36											13 06		
Denmark Hill	d									12 46											13 16		
Peckham Rye	d									12 48											13 18		
Nunhead	d									12 51											13 21		
New Cross	d	12 27							12 49				12 57							13 19			
St Johns	d	12 29							12 51				12 59							13 21			
Lewisham	d	12 34			12 45				12 54	12 56		13 00	13 04			13 15				13 24	13 26		13 30
Blackheath	d	12 37			12 48					12 59		13 03	13 07			13 18					13 29		13 33
Kidbrooke	d	12 40			12 51					13 02			13 10			13 21					13 32		
Eltham	d	12 43			12 54					13 06			13 13			13 24					13 36		
Falconwood	d	12 46			12 57					13 09			13 16			13 27					13 39		
Welling	d	12 49			13 00					13 11			13 19			13 30					13 41		
Bexleyheath	d	12 52			13 03					13 15			13 22			13 33					13 45		
Barnehurst	d	12 58			13 06					13 17			13 28			13 36					13 47		
Hither Green	d		12 37						12 59					13 07						13 29			
Lee	d		12 39						13 01					13 09						13 31			
Mottingham	d		12 42						13 04					13 12						13 34			
New Eltham	d		12 45					12 55	13 07					13 15					13 25	13 37			
Sidcup	d		12 48					12 58	13 10					13 18					13 28	13 40			
Albany Park	d		12 51						13 13					13 21						13 43			
Bexley	d		12 53					13 02	13 15					13 23					13 32	13 45			
Crayford	d		12 57					13 05	13 21					13 27					13 35	13 51			
Charlton	d			12 45		12 55			13a49		13 05	13 08			13 15		13 25			14a19		13 35	13 38
Woolwich Dockyard	d			12 48		12 58						13 11			13 18		13 28						13 41
Woolwich Arsenal	d			12 51		13 01					13 10	13 14			13 21		13 31					13 40	13 44
Plumstead	d			12 53		13 03					13 13	13 16			13 23		13 33					13 43	13 46
Abbey Wood	d			12 56		13 06					13 16	13 20			13 26		13 36					13 46	13 50
Belvedere	d			12 59		13 09						13 23			13 29		13 39						13 53
Erith	d			13 02		13 12						13 25			13 32		13 42						13 55
Slade Green	d	13a05		13a06		13a15					13 22	13 31	13a35		13a36		13a45					13 52	14 01
Dartford	a		13 02		13 14			13 10		13 24	13 27	13 38		13 32		13 44			13 40		13 54	13 57	14 08
	d							13 11		13 24	13 28								13 41		13 54	13 58	
Stone Crossing	d							13 15			13 32								13 45			14 02	
Greenhithe for Bluewater	d							13 17		13 30	13 34								13 47		14 00	14 04	
Swanscombe	d							13 20			13 37								13 50			14 07	
Northfleet	d							13 22			13 39								13 52			14 09	
Gravesend	d						13 18	13a26		13a39	13 43							13 48	13a56		14a09	14 13	
Higham	d										13 49											14 19	
Strood	d						13 29				13 55							13 59				14 25	
Maidstone West	d																						
Rochester	d						13 32				13 58							14 02				14 28	
Chatham	d						13 36				14 01							14 06				14 31	
Gillingham (Kent)	a						13 40				14 05							14 10				14 35	
Rainham Kt	a						13 45				14 11							14 15				14 41	

Table T200-F

Mondays to Fridays

21 May to 7 December

London - Dartford and Gillingham

		SE	SE	SE	SE	SE	SE ◇	SE	SE	SE	TL	SE	SE	SE	SE	SE	SE	SE ◇	SE	SE	SE	TL	SE	SE
St Pancras Int'l ⊖	d						13 55											14 25						
Stratford International ⊖	d						14 02											14 32						
Ebbsfleet International	d						14 13											14 43						
London Charing Cross ⊖	d		13 18		13 24			13 32				13 42		13 48		13 54			14 02				14 12	
London Waterloo (East) ⊖	d		13 21		13 28			13 35				13 45		13 51		13 58			14 05				14 15	
London Cannon Street ⊖	d	13 17		13 24		13 35			13 38				13 47		13 54		14 05			14 08				14 17
London Bridge ⊖	d	13 21	13 27	13 28	13 35	13 39		13 41	13 43		13 48	13 51	13 51	13 57	13 58	14 05	14 09		14 11	14 13		14 18	14 21	14 21
Deptford	d			13 35		13 45					13 55				14 05		14 15					14 25		
Greenwich	d			13 37		13 47					13 57				14 07		14 17					14 27		
Maze Hill	d			13 40		13 50					14 00				14 10		14 20					14 30		
Westcombe Park	d			13 42		13 52					14 02				14 12		14 22					14 32		
London Victoria ⊖	d									13 36											14 06			
Denmark Hill	d									13 46											14 16			
Peckham Rye	d									13 48											14 18			
Nunhead	d									13 51											14 21			
New Cross ⊖	d	13 27							13 49				13 57							14 19				14 27
St Johns	d	13 29							13 51				13 59							14 21				14 29
Lewisham	d	13 34			13 45				13 54	13 56		14 00	14 04			14 15				14 24	14 26		14 30	14 34
Blackheath	d	13 37			13 48					13 59		14 03	14 07			14 18					14 29		14 33	14 37
Kidbrooke	d	13 40			13 51					14 02			14 10			14 21					14 32			14 40
Eltham	d	13 43			13 54					14 06			14 13			14 24					14 36			14 43
Falconwood	d	13 46			13 57					14 09			14 16			14 27					14 39			14 46
Welling	d	13 49			14 00					14 11			14 19			14 30					14 41			14 49
Bexleyheath	d	13 52			14 03					14 15			14 22			14 33					14 45			14 52
Barnehurst	d	13 58			14 06					14 17			14 28			14 36					14 47			14 58
Hither Green	d		13 37						13 59					14 07						14 29				
Lee	d		13 39						14 01					14 09						14 31				
Mottingham	d		13 42						14 04					14 12						14 34				
New Eltham	d		13 45					13 55	14 07					14 15					14 25	14 37				
Sidcup	d		13 48					13 58	14 10					14 18					14 28	14 40				
Albany Park	d		13 51						14 13					14 21						14 43				
Bexley	d		13 53					14 02	14 15					14 23					14 32	14 45				
Crayford	d		13 57					14 05	14 21					14 27					14 35	14 51				
Charlton	d			13 45		13 55			14a49		14 05	14 08			14 15		14 25			15a19		14 35	14 38	
Woolwich Dockyard	d			13 48		13 58						14 11			14 18		14 28						14 41	
Woolwich Arsenal	d			13 51		14 01					14 10	14 14			14 21		14 31					14 40	14 44	
Plumstead	d			13 53		14 03					14 13	14 16			14 23		14 33					14 43	14 46	
Abbey Wood	d			13 56		14 06					14 16	14 20			14 26		14 36					14 46	14 50	
Belvedere	d			13 59		14 09						14 23			14 29		14 39						14 53	
Erith	d			14 02		14 12						14 25			14 32		14 42						14 55	
Slade Green	d	14a05		14a06		14a15					14 22	14 31	14a35		14a36		14a45					14 52	15 01	15a05
Dartford	a		14 02		14 14			14 10		14 24	14 27	14 38		14 32		14 44			14 40		14 54	14 57	15 08	
	d							14 11		14 24	14 28								14 41		14 54	14 58		
Stone Crossing	d							14 15			14 32								14 45			15 02		
Greenhithe for Bluewater	d							14 17		14 30	14 34								14 47		15 00	15 04		
Swanscombe	d							14 20			14 37								14 50			15 07		
Northfleet	d							14 22			14 39								14 52			15 09		
Gravesend	d						14 18	14a26		14a39	14 43							14 48	14a56		15a09	15 13		
Higham	d										14 49											15 19		
Strood	d						14 29				14 55							14 59				15 25		
Maidstone West	d																							
Rochester	d						14 32				14 58							15 02				15 28		
Chatham	d						14 36				15 01							15 05				15 31		
Gillingham (Kent)	a						14 40				15 05							15 09				15 35		
Rainham Kt	a						14 45				15 11							15 14				15 41		

Table T200-F

Mondays to Fridays

21 May to 7 December

London - Dartford and Gillingham

		SE	SE	SE	SE	SE ◇	SE	SE	SE	TL	SE	SE	SE	SE	SE	SE	SE ◇	SE	SE	SE	TL	SE	SE
St Pancras Int'l ⊖	d					14 55											15 25						
Stratford International ⊖	d					15 02											15 32						
Ebbsfleet International	d					15 13											15 43						
London Charing Cross ⊖	d	14 18		14 24			14 32				14 42		14 48		14 54			15 02				15 12	
London Waterloo (East) ⊖	d	14 21		14 28			14 35				14 45		14 51		14 58			15 05				15 15	
London Cannon Street ⊖	d		14 24		14 35			14 38				14 47		14 54		15 05			15 08				15 17
London Bridge ⊖	d	14 27	14 28	14 35	14 39		14 41	14 43		14 48	14 51	14 51	14 57	14 58	15 05	15 09		15 11	15 13		15 18	15 21	15 21
Deptford	d		14 35		14 45					14 55				15 05		15 15					15 25		
Greenwich	d		14 37		14 47					14 57				15 07		15 17					15 27		
Maze Hill	d		14 40		14 50					15 00				15 10		15 20					15 30		
Westcombe Park	d		14 42		14 52					15 02				15 12		15 22					15 32		
London Victoria ⊖	d								14 36											15 06			
Denmark Hill	d								14 46											15 16			
Peckham Rye	d								14 48											15 18			
Nunhead	d								14 51											15 21			
New Cross ⊖	d							14 49				14 57							15 19				15 27
St Johns	d							14 51				14 59							15 21				15 29
Lewisham	d			14 45				14 54	14 56		15 00	15 04			15 15				15 24	15 26		15 30	15 34
Blackheath	d			14 48					14 59		15 03	15 07			15 18					15 29		15 33	15 37
Kidbrooke	d			14 51					15 02			15 10			15 21					15 32			15 40
Eltham	d			14 54					15 06			15 13			15 24					15 36			15 43
Falconwood	d			14 57					15 09			15 16			15 27					15 39			15 46
Welling	d			15 00					15 11			15 19			15 30					15 41			15 49
Bexleyheath	d			15 03					15 15			15 22			15 33					15 45			15 52
Barnehurst	d			15 06					15 17			15 28			15 36					15 47			15 58
Hither Green	d	14 37						14 59					15 07						15 29				
Lee	d	14 39						15 01					15 09						15 31				
Mottingham	d	14 42						15 04					15 12						15 34				
New Eltham	d	14 45					14 55	15 07					15 15					15 25	15 37				
Sidcup	d	14 48					14 58	15 10					15 18					15 28	15 40				
Albany Park	d	14 51						15 13					15 21						15 43				
Bexley	d	14 53					15 02	15 15					15 23					15 32	15 45				
Crayford	d	14 57					15 05	15 21					15 27					15 35	15 51				
Charlton	d		14 45		14 55			15a49		15 05	15 08			15 15		15 25			16a17		15 35	15 38	
Woolwich Dockyard	d		14 48		14 58						15 11			15 18		15 28						15 41	
Woolwich Arsenal	d		14 51		15 01					15 10	15 14			15 21		15 31					15 40	15 44	
Plumstead	d		14 53		15 03					15 13	15 16			15 23		15 33					15 43	15 46	
Abbey Wood	d		14 56		15 06					15 16	15 20			15 26		15 36					15 46	15 50	
Belvedere	d		14 59		15 09						15 23			15 29		15 39						15 53	
Erith	d		15 02		15 12						15 25			15 32		15 42						15 55	
Slade Green	d		15a06		15a15					15 22	15 31	15a35		15a36		15a45					15 52	16 01	16a05
Dartford	a	15 02		15 14			15 10		15 24	15 27	15 38		15 32		15 44			15 40		15 54	15 57	16 08	
	d						15 11		15 24	15 28								15 41		15 54	15 58		
Stone Crossing	d						15 15			15 32								15 45			16 02		
Greenhithe for Bluewater	d						15 17		15 30	15 34								15 47		16 00	16 04		
Swanscombe	d						15 20			15 37								15 50			16 07		
Northfleet	d						15 22			15 39								15 52			16 09		
Gravesend	d					15 18	15a26		15a39	15 43							15 48	15a56		16a09	16 13		
Higham	d									15 49											16 19		
Strood	d					15 29				15 55							15 59				16 25		
Maidstone West	d																						
Rochester	d					15 32				15 58							16 02				16 28		
Chatham	d					15 36				16 01							16 05				16 31		
Gillingham (Kent)	a					15 40				16 05							16 09				16 35		
Rainham Kt	a					15 45				16 11							16 14				16 41		

Please note, Network Rail have stated that further updates to this timetable are possible during the validity period.

Table T200-F

Mondays to Fridays

21 May to 7 December

London - Dartford and Gillingham

		SE	SE	SE	SE	SE ◇	SE	SE	SE	TL	SE	SE	SE	SE	SE	SE	SE ◇	SE	SE	SE	TL	SE	SE	SE
St Pancras Int'l ⊖	d					15 55											16 25							
Stratford International ⊖ ⛴	d					16 02											16 32							
Ebbsfleet International	d					16 13											16 43							
London Charing Cross ⊖	d	15 18		15 24			15 32				15 42		15 48		15 54			16 02					16 12	16 18
London Waterloo (East) ⊖	d	15 21		15 28			15 35				15 45		15 51		15 58			16 05					16 15	16 21
London Cannon Street ⊖	d		15 24		15 35			15 38				15 47		15 54		16 05			16 08			16 15		
London Bridge ⊖	d	15 27	15 28	15 35	15 39		15 41	15 43		15 48	15 51	15 51	15 57	15 58	16 05	16 10		16 11	16 13		16 18	16 20	16 21	16 27
Deptford	d		15 35		15 45					15 55				16 05		16 16					16 25			
Greenwich ⛴	d		15 37		15 47					15 57				16 07		16 18					16 27			
Maze Hill	d		15 40		15 50					16 00				16 10		16 21					16 30			
Westcombe Park	d		15 42		15 52					16 02				16 12		16 23					16 32			
London Victoria ⊖	d								15 36											16 06				
Denmark Hill	d								15 46											16 16				
Peckham Rye	d								15 48											16 18				
Nunhead	d								15 51											16 21				
New Cross ⊖	d							15 49				15 57							16 19			16 26		
St Johns	d							15 51				15 59							16 21			16 28		
Lewisham ⛴	d			15 45				15 54	15 56		16 01	16 04			16 15				16 24	16 26		16 33	16 30	
Blackheath	d			15 48					15 59		16 03	16 07			16 18					16 29		16 36	16 33	
Kidbrooke	d			15 51					16 02			16 10			16 21					16 32		16 39		
Eltham	d			15 54					16 06			16 13			16 24					16 36		16 42		
Falconwood	d			15 57					16 09			16 16			16 27					16 39		16 45		
Welling	d			16 00					16 11			16 19			16 30					16 41		16 48		
Bexleyheath	d			16 03					16 15			16 22			16 33					16 45		16 51		
Barnehurst	d			16 06					16 17			16 28			16 36					16 47		16 54		
Hither Green	d	15 37						15 59					16 07						16 29					16 39
Lee	d	15 39						16 01					16 09						16 31					16 41
Mottingham	d	15 42						16 04					16 12						16 34					16 44
New Eltham	d	15 45					15 55	16 07					16 15					16 25	16 37					16 47
Sidcup	d	15 48					15 58	16 10					16 18					16 28	16 40					16 50
Albany Park	d	15 51						16 13					16 21						16 43					16 53
Bexley	d	15 53					16 02	16 15					16 23					16 32	16 45					16 55
Crayford	d	15 57					16 05	16 21					16 27					16 35	16 50					16 59
Charlton	d		15 45		15 55			16a50		16 05	16 08			16 15		16 26			17a18		16 35		16 38	
Woolwich Dockyard	d		15 48		15 58						16 11			16 18		16 29							16 41	
Woolwich Arsenal ⛴	d		15 51		16 01					16 10	16 14			16 21		16 32					16 40		16 44	
Plumstead	d		15 53		16 03					16 13	16 16			16 23		16 34					16 43		16 46	
Abbey Wood	d		15 56		16 06					16 16	16 20			16 26		16 37					16 46		16 50	
Belvedere	d		15 59		16 09						16 23			16 29		16 40							16 53	
Erith	d		16 02		16 12						16 25			16 32		16 43							16 55	
Slade Green	d		16a06		16a15					16 22	16 32	16a35		16a36		16a46					16 52	17a05	17 01	
Dartford	a	16 02		16 14			16 10		16 24	16 27	16 38		16 32		16 44			16 40		16 54	16 57		17 10	17 04
	d						16 11		16 24	16 28								16 41		16 54	16 58			
Stone Crossing	d						16 15			16 32								16 45			17 02			
Greenhithe for Bluewater	d						16 17		16 30	16 34								16 47		17 00	17 04			
Swanscombe	d						16 20			16 37								16 50			17 07			
Northfleet	d						16 22			16 39								16 52			17 09			
Gravesend	d					16 18	16a26		16a39	16 43							16 48	16a58		17a09	17 13			
Higham	d									16 49											17 19			
Strood	d					16 29				16 55							16 59				17 25			
Maidstone West	d																							
Rochester	d					16 32				16 58							17 02				17 28			
Chatham	d					16 36				17 01							17 06				17 32			
Gillingham (Kent)	a					16 40				17 05							17 10				17 36			
Rainham Kt	a					16 45				17 11							17 15				17 42			

Table T200-F

Mondays to Fridays

21 May to 7 December

London - Dartford and Gillingham

		SE	SE	SE	SE ◇	SE	SE	SE ◇	TL	SE	SE	SE	SE	SE	SE	SE	SE	SE	SE	SE	SE ◇	TL	SE
St Pancras Int'l ⊖	d				16 55			17 16													17 46		
Stratford International ⊖ ⛴	d				17 02			17 23													17 53		
Ebbsfleet International	d				17 13			17 35													18 05		
London Charing Cross ⊖	d		16 24			16 33						16 45	16 48		16 53				17 06	17 08			
London Waterloo (East) ⊖	d		16 28			16 36						16 48	16 51		16 56				17 09	17 11			
London Cannon Street ⊖	d	16 27		16 37			16 39				16 45			16 54		16 58	17 03	17 05					
London Bridge ⊖	d	16 32	16 35	16 42		16 42	16 44		16 48		16 50	16 54	16 57	16 59	17 02	17 03	17 08	17 10	17 15	17 17		17 18	
Deptford	d	16 38		16 48					16 55					17 05				17 16				17 25	
Greenwich ⛴	d	16 40		16 50					16 57					17 08				17 19				17 27	
Maze Hill	d	16 43		16 53					17 00					17 11				17 22				17 30	
Westcombe Park	d	16 45		16 55					17 02					17 14				17 24				17 32	
London Victoria ⊖	d									16 36													17 06
Denmark Hill	d									16 46													17 16
Peckham Rye	d									16 48													17 19
Nunhead	d									16 51													17 21
New Cross ⊖	d						16 50				16 56					17 09	17 15						
St Johns	d						16 52				16 58					17 11							
Lewisham ⛴	d		16 45				16 55			16 57	17 01	17 04			17 12	17 15	17 19		17 24				17 27
Blackheath	d		16 48							17 00	17 04	17 07			17 15		17 22		17 27				17 30
Kidbrooke	d		16 51							17 03	17 07				17 18		17 25		17 30				17 33
Eltham	d		16 54							17 07	17 11				17 21		17 29		17 34				17 38
Falconwood	d		16 57							17 10	17 14				17 24		17 32		17 37				17 41
Welling	d		17 00							17 13	17 17				17 27		17 35		17 40				17 44
Bexleyheath	d		17 03							17 16	17 20				17 31		17 38		17 44				17 48
Barnehurst	d		17 06							17 19	17 28				17 34		17 43		17 47				17 51
Hither Green	d						17 00						17 08			17 20				17 28			
Lee	d						17 02						17 10			17 22				17 31			
Mottingham	d						17 05						17 14			17 26				17 34			
New Eltham	d					16 55	17 08						17 17			17 29				17 37			
Sidcup	d					16 58	17 12						17 21			17 32				17a42			
Albany Park	d						17 14						17 24			17 35							
Bexley	d					17 02	17 17						17 27			17 38							
Crayford	d					17 05	17 22						17 30			17 45							
Charlton	d	16 48		16 58			17a47		17 05			17 13		17 17		18a14		17 26				17 35	
Woolwich Dockyard	d	16 51		17 01								17 16		17 20				17 29					
Woolwich Arsenal ⛴	d	16 54		17 04					17 10			17 19		17 23				17 32				17 40	
Plumstead	d	16 56		17 06					17 13			17 21		17 25				17 34				17 43	
Abbey Wood	d	16 59		17 09					17 16			17 24		17 29				17 38				17 46	
Belvedere	d	17 02		17 12								17 27		17 32				17 41					
Erith	d	17 05		17 15								17 30		17 35				17 43					
Slade Green	d	17a09		17a18					17 22		17a39	17a33		17 39			18a00	17a46				17 52	
Dartford	a		17 16			17 10			17 27	17 32			17 36	17 50	17 44				17 58			17 57	18 02
	d					17 11			17 32				17 37									17 58	
Stone Crossing	d					17 15			17 36				17 41									18 02	
Greenhithe for Bluewater	d					17 17			17 38				17 43									18 04	
Swanscombe	d					17 20			17 41				17 46									18 07	
Northfleet	d					17 22			17 44				17 49									18 09	
Gravesend	d				17 18	17a28		17 39	17 50				17a56								18 09	18 13	
Higham	d								17 56													18 19	
Strood	d				17 28			17 50	18 01												18 20	18 25	
Maidstone West	d							18a08													18a38		
Rochester	d				17 31				18 05													18 28	
Chatham	d				17 35				18 08													18 32	
Gillingham (Kent)	a				17 40				18 12													18 36	
Rainham Kt	a				17 46				18 19													18 42	

Table T200-F

Mondays to Fridays

21 May to 7 December

London - Dartford and Gillingham

		SE	SE	SE ◇	SE	SE	SE	SE	SE	SE	SE	SE	SE	SE ◇	SE	TL	SE	SE	SE	SE	SE	SE	SE	SE
St Pancras Int'l	d			17 55										18 16										
Stratford International	d			18 02										18 23										
Ebbsfleet International	d			18 13										18 35										
London Charing Cross	d	17 13			17 17			17 28		17 32	17 34	17 36			17 41					17 49	17 51	17 53	17 55	
London Waterloo (East)	d	17 16			17 20			17 31		17 35	17 37	17 39			17 44					17 52	17 54	17 56	17 58	
London Cannon Street	d		17 19			17 25	17 27		17 34				17 41					17 47	17 49					18 00
London Bridge	d	17 22	17 24		17 26	17 30	17 32	17 37	17 39	17 41	17 43	17 45	17 46		17 50	17 48		17 52	17 54	17 58	18 00	18 02	18 04	18 05
Deptford	d					17 36			17 45							17 55			18 00					
Greenwich	d					17 39			17 48							17 57			18 03					
Maze Hill	d					17 43			17 51							18 00			18 06					
Westcombe Park	d					17 45			17 54							18 02			18 09					
London Victoria	d																17 34							
Denmark Hill	d																17 44							
Peckham Rye	d																17 47							
Nunhead	d																17 50							
New Cross	d		17 30				17 37						17 53					17 58						18 11
St Johns	d		17 32										17 55											18 13
Lewisham	d	17 31	17 36				17 43				17 52	17 56	17 59				18 00	18 03			18 10		18 14	18 17
Blackheath	d	17 34					17 46			17 52	17 55	17 59					18 03	18 06		18 09	18 13		18 17	
Kidbrooke	d						17 49			17 56		18 02					18 06	18 09		18 12			18 20	
Eltham	d						17 53			17 59		18 06					18 10	18 13		18 16			18 24	
Falconwood	d						17 56			18 03		18 09					18 13	18 16		18 19			18 27	
Welling	d						17 59			18 06		18 12					18 16	18 19		18 22			18 30	
Bexleyheath	d						18 03			18 09		18 15					18 20	18 23		18 26			18 33	
Barnehurst	d						18 08			18 12		18 19					18 23	18 26		18a31			18 37	
Hither Green	d		17 41		17 37			17 48					18 04		18 00							18 13		18 22
Lee	d		17 43					17 50					18 06									18 15		18 25
Mottingham	d		17 47					17 54					18 10									18 19		18 28
New Eltham	d		17 50		17 43			17 57					18 13		18 06							18 22		18 31
Sidcup	d		17 53		17 47			18a03					18 16		18 10							18 26		18 35
Albany Park	d		17 56		17 50								18 19		18 13									18 38
Bexley	d		17 59		17 53								18 22		18 16									18 41
Crayford	d		18 03		17 56								18 28		18 19							18a32		18 48
Charlton	d	17 39				17 48			17 56		18 00		19a03			18 05			18 11		18 18			19a19
Woolwich Dockyard	d	17 42							17 59		18 03								18 14		18 21			
Woolwich Arsenal	d	17 45				17 53			18 02		18 06					18 10			18 17		18 24			
Plumstead	d	17 47							18 04		18 09					18 13			18 20		18 26			
Abbey Wood	d	17 50				17 58			18 08		18 12					18 16			18 23		18 30			
Belvedere	d	17 53							18 11		18 15								18 27		18 33			
Erith	d	17 56							18 13		18 18								18 30		18 36			
Slade Green	d	17a59					18a16		18 17		18a21	18a28				18 24		18a35	18 34		18a42			
Dartford	a		18 13		18 01	18 08			18 26	18 22					18 24	18 29	18 33		18 39				18 48	
	d				18 03	18 09									18 25	18 32			18 40					
Stone Crossing	d				18 07										18 29	18 36								
Greenhithe for Bluewater	d				18 09	18 15									18 31	18 38			18 45					
Swanscombe	d				18 12										18 34	18 41								
Northfleet	d				18 15										18 37	18 44								
Gravesend	d			18 18	18 22	18a25								18 39	18a43	18 50			18a56					
Higham	d				18 28											18 56								
Strood	d			18 31	18a36									18 51		19 01								
Maidstone West	d													19a09										
Rochester	d			18 36												19 05								
Chatham	d			18 40												19 08								
Gillingham (Kent)	a			18 44												19 12								
Rainham Kt	a			18 50												19 19								

Table T200-F

Mondays to Fridays

21 May to 7 December

London - Dartford and Gillingham

		SE	SE	SE	SE	TL	SE	SE	SE	SE	SE ◇	SE	SE	SE	SE	SE	SE	SE	SE	TL	SE	SE	SE
St Pancras Int'l	d										18 55												
Stratford International	d										19 02												
Ebbsfleet International	d										19 13												
London Charing Cross	d	17 59					18 11	18 15	18 17			18 25					18 36		18 38		18 43		
London Waterloo (East)	d	18 02					18 14	18 18	18 20			18 28					18 39		18 41		18 46		
London Cannon Street	d			18 04	18 09					18 22			18 24		18 33	18 35		18 41					18 53
London Bridge	d	18 08		18 09	18 14	18 18	18 20	18 24	18 26	18 27		18 34	18 29		18 38	18 40	18 45	18 46	18 47	18 48	18 52		18 58
Deptford	d			18 15		18 25							18 35			18 46				18 55			
Greenwich	d			18 18		18 27							18 38			18 49				18 57			
Maze Hill	d			18 21		18 30							18 42			18 52				19 00			
Westcombe Park	d			18 24		18 32							18 44			18 55				19 02			
London Victoria	d		17 55											18 21								18 42	
Denmark Hill	d		18 05											18 31								18 52	
Peckham Rye	d		18 08											18 34								18 55	
Nunhead	d		18 11											18 37								18 58	
New Cross	d				18 20					18 34					18 44			18 52					19 04
St Johns	d									18 36					18 46			18 54					19 06
Lewisham	d		18 19		18 24		18 30		18 35	18 41				18 44	18 49			18 59	18 57		19 01	19 06	19 10
Blackheath	d		18 22		18 27		18 33		18 39					18 47	18 52				19 00		19 04	19 09	19 13
Kidbrooke	d		18 25		18 31				18 42					18 50	18 55				19 03			19 12	19 16
Eltham	d		18 29		18 34				18 46					18 54	18 59				19 07			19 16	19 20
Falconwood	d		18 32		18 38				18 49					18 57	19 02				19 10			19 19	19 23
Welling	d		18 34		18 41				18 52					19 00	19 05				19 13			19 22	19 26
Bexleyheath	d		18 38		18 44				18 56					19 03	19 09				19 17			19 25	19 29
Barnehurst	d		18 41		18 54				19 02					19 06	19a15				19 23			19 28	19 32
Hither Green	d	18 19						18 36		18 47							18 56	19 04					
Lee	d							18 38		18 49							18 58	19 06					
Mottingham	d							18 41		18 53							19 02	19 09					
New Eltham	d	18 26						18 44		18 56		18 48					19 05	19 12					
Sidcup	d	18 30						18 47		18 59		18 51					19 09	19 16					
Albany Park	d	18 33						18 50		19 02		18 54					19 12	19 18					
Bexley	d	18 36						18 53		19 05		18 57					19 15	19 21					
Crayford	d	18 39						18 57		19 14		19 01					19 18	19 25					19a47
Charlton	d			18 26		18 35	18 38	19a29		19a49			18 47			18 57				19 05	19 09		
Woolwich Dockyard	d			18 29			18 41									19 00					19 12		
Woolwich Arsenal	d			18 32		18 40	18 44						18 52			19 03				19 10	19 15		
Plumstead	d			18 35		18 43	18 46									19 06				19 13	19 17		
Abbey Wood	d			18 38		18 46	18 50						18 57			19 09				19 16	19 21		
Belvedere	d			18 41			18 53									19 13					19 24		
Erith	d			18 44			18 56									19 16					19 27		
Slade Green	d			18a47	19a12	18 52	18a59									19a19			19a36	19 22	19a33		
Dartford	a	18 44	18 51			18 57			19 12			19 06	19 08	19 16			19 26	19 33		19 27		19 40	
	d	18 46				18 58						19 07	19 10							19 28			
Stone Crossing	d					19 02						19 11	19 14							19 32			
Greenhithe for Bluewater	d	18 51				19 04						19 13	19 16							19 34			
Swanscombe	d					19 07							19 19							19 37			
Northfleet	d					19 09							19 21							19 39			
Gravesend	d	19 00				19 13					19 18	19a23	19 26							19 43			
Higham	d	19 06				19 19							19 32							19 49			
Strood	d	19a14				19 27					19 30		19a40							19 55			
Maidstone West	d																						
Rochester	d					19 30					19 35									19 58			
Chatham	d					19 34					19 39									20 02			
Gillingham (Kent)	a					19 38					19 43									20 06			
Rainham Kt	a					19 44					19 48									20 12			

Please note, Network Rail have stated that further updates to this timetable are possible during the validity period.

Table T200-F

Mondays to Fridays

21 May to 7 December

London - Dartford and Gillingham

		SE	SE ◇	SE	SE	SE	SE	SE	SE	TL	SE	SE	SE		SE	SE	SE	SE ◇	SE	SE	SE	TL	SE	SE	SE
St Pancras Int'l ⊖	d		19 25															19 55							
Stratford International ⊖ ⛴	d		19 32															20 02							
Ebbsfleet International	d		19 43															20 13							
London Charing Cross ⊖	d			18 54	18 56		19 02					19 12	19 18			19 24			19 32				19 42		19 48
London Waterloo (East) ⊖	d			18 57	18 59		19 05					19 15	19 21			19 28			19 35				19 45		19 51
London Cannon Street ⊖	d	18 55				19 05		19 08			19 16				19 24		19 35			19 38				19 47	
London Bridge ⊖	d	19 00		19 03	19 05	19 09	19 11	19 13		19 18	19 20	19 21	19 27		19 28	19 35	19 39		19 41	19 43		19 48	19 51	19 51	19 57
Deptford	d	19 06				19 15				19 25					19 35		19 45					19 55			
Greenwich ⛴	d	19 09				19 17				19 27					19 37		19 47					19 57			
Maze Hill	d	19 12				19 20				19 30					19 40		19 50					20 00			
Westcombe Park	d	19 15				19 22				19 32					19 42		19 52					20 02			
London Victoria ⊖	d								19 06												19 36				
Denmark Hill	d								19 16												19 46				
Peckham Rye	d								19 18												19 48				
Nunhead	d								19 21												19 51				
New Cross ⊖	d							19 19			19 26									19 49				19 57	
St Johns	d							19 21			19 28									19 51				19 59	
Lewisham ⛴	d				19 15			19 24	19 26		19 34	19 30				19 45				19 54	19 56		20 00	20 04	
Blackheath	d				19 18				19 29		19 37	19 33				19 48					19 59		20 03	20 07	
Kidbrooke	d				19 21				19 32		19 40					19 51					20 02			20 10	
Eltham	d				19 25				19 36		19 43					19 55					20 06			20 13	
Falconwood	d				19 28				19 39		19 46					19 58					20 09			20 16	
Welling	d				19 31				19 41		19 49					20 01					20 11			20 19	
Bexleyheath	d				19 35				19 45		19 52					20 05					20 15			20 22	
Barnehurst	d				19 38				19 47		19 58					20 08					20 17			20a26	
Hither Green	d						19 22	19 29					19 38							19 59					20 07
Lee	d						19 24	19 31					19 41							20 01					20 09
Mottingham	d						19 28	19 34					19 44							20 04					20 12
New Eltham	d			19 17			19 31	19 37					19 47						19 55	20 07					20 15
Sidcup	d			19 21			19 34	19 40					19 50						19 58	20 10					20 18
Albany Park	d						19 37	19 43					19 53							20 13					20 21
Bexley	d			19 25			19 40	19 45					19 55						20 02	20 15					20 23
Crayford	d			19 29			19 47	19 51					19 59						20 05	20 21					20 27
Charlton	d	19 17				19 25		20a19		19 35		19 38			19 45		19 55			20a49		20 05	20 08		
Woolwich Dockyard	d	19 20				19 28						19 41			19 48		19 58						20 11		
Woolwich Arsenal ⛴	d	19 23				19 31				19 40		19 44			19 51		20 01					20 10	20 14		
Plumstead	d	19 25				19 33				19 43		19 46			19 53		20 03					20 13	20 16		
Abbey Wood	d	19 29				19 36				19 46		19 50			19 56		20 06					20 16	20 20		
Belvedere	d	19 32				19 39						19 53			19 59		20 09						20 23		
Erith	d	19 35				19 42						19 55			20 02		20 12						20 25		
Slade Green	d	19a39				19a45				19 52	20a07	20 01			20a06		20a15					20 22	20 31		
Dartford	a			19 34	19 48		19 56		19 54	19 57		20 08	20 06			20 18			20 10		20 24	20 27	20 38		20 34
	d			19 35					19 54	19 58									20 11		20 24	20 28			
Stone Crossing	d			19 39						20 02									20 15			20 32			
Greenhithe for Bluewater	d			19 41					20 00	20 04									20 17		20 30	20 34			
Swanscombe	d			19 44						20 07									20 20			20 37			
Northfleet	d			19 46						20 09									20 22			20 39			
Gravesend	d		19 48	19a55					20a09	20 13								20 18	20a26		20a39	20 43			
Higham	d									20 19												20 49			
Strood	d		19 59							20 25								20 29				20 55			
Maidstone West	d																								
Rochester	d		20 02							20 28								20 32				20 58			
Chatham	d		20 06							20 31								20 36				21 01			
Gillingham (Kent)	a		20 10							20 35								20 40				21 05			
Rainham Kt	a		20 15							20 41								20 45				21 11			

Table T200-F

Mondays to Fridays

21 May to 7 December

London - Dartford and Gillingham

		SE	SE	SE	SE ◇		SE	SE	SE	TL	SE	SE	SE	SE	SE	SE	SE ◇	SE	SE	SE	TL		SE	SE	SE
St Pancras Int'l ⊖	d				20 25												20 55								
Stratford International ⊖ ⛴	d				20 32												21 02								
Ebbsfleet International	d				20 43												21 13								
London Charing Cross ⊖	d		19 54				20 02				20 12		20 18		20 24			20 32					20 42		20 48
London Waterloo (East) ⊖	d		19 58				20 05				20 15		20 21		20 28			20 35					20 45		20 51
London Cannon Street ⊖	d	19 54		20 05				20 08				20 17		20 24		20 35			20 38					20 47	
London Bridge ⊖	d	19 58	20 05	20 09			20 11	20 13		20 18	20 21	20 21	20 27	20 28	20 35	20 39		20 41	20 43		20 48		20 51	20 51	20 57
Deptford	d	20 05		20 15						20 25				20 35		20 45					20 55				
Greenwich ⛴	d	20 07		20 17						20 27				20 37		20 47					20 57				
Maze Hill	d	20 10		20 20						20 30				20 40		20 50					21 00				
Westcombe Park	d	20 12		20 22						20 32				20 42		20 52					21 02				
London Victoria ⊖	d								20 06											20 36					
Denmark Hill	d								20 16											20 46					
Peckham Rye	d								20 18											20 48					
Nunhead	d								20 21											20 51					
New Cross ⊖	d							20 19				20 27							20 49					20 57	
St Johns	d							20 21				20 29							20 51					20 59	
Lewisham ⛴	d		20 15					20 24	20 26		20 30	20 34			20 45				20 54	20 56			21 00	21 04	
Blackheath	d		20 18						20 29		20 33	20 37			20 48					20 59			21 03	21 07	
Kidbrooke	d		20 21						20 32			20 40			20 51					21 02				21 10	
Eltham	d		20 24						20 36			20 43			20 54					21 06				21 13	
Falconwood	d		20 27						20 39			20 46			20 57					21 09				21 16	
Welling	d		20 30						20 41			20 49			21 00					21 11				21 19	
Bexleyheath	d		20 33						20 45			20 52			21 03					21 15				21 22	
Barnehurst	d		20 36						20 47			20a56			21 06					21 17				21a26	
Hither Green	d							20 29					20 37						20 59						21 07
Lee	d							20 31					20 39						21 01						21 09
Mottingham	d							20 34					20 42						21 04						21 12
New Eltham	d						20 25	20 37					20 45					20 55	21 07						21 15
Sidcup	d						20 28	20 40					20 48					20 58	21 10						21 18
Albany Park	d							20 43					20 51						21 13						21 21
Bexley	d						20 32	20 45					20 53					21 02	21 15						21 23
Crayford	d						20 35	20 51					20 57					21 05	21 21						21 27
Charlton	d	20 15		20 25				21a19		20 35	20 38			20 45		20 55			21a49		21 05		21 08		
Woolwich Dockyard	d	20 18		20 28							20 41			20 48		20 58							21 11		
Woolwich Arsenal ⛴	d	20 21		20 31						20 40	20 44			20 51		21 01					21 10		21 14		
Plumstead	d	20 23		20 33						20 43	20 46			20 53		21 03					21 13		21 16		
Abbey Wood	d	20 26		20 36						20 46	20 50			20 56		21 06					21 16		21 20		
Belvedere	d	20 29		20 39							20 53			20 59		21 09							21 23		
Erith	d	20 32		20 42							20 55			21 02		21 12							21 25		
Slade Green	d	20a38		20a45						20 52	21 01			21a06		21a15					21 22		21 31		
Dartford	a		20 44				20 40		20 54	20 57	21 08		21 02		21 14			21 10		21 24	21 27		21 38		21 32
	d						20 41		20 54	20 58								21 11		21 24	21 28				
Stone Crossing	d						20 45			21 02								21 15			21 32				
Greenhithe for Bluewater	d						20 47		21 00	21 04								21 17		21 30	21 34				
Swanscombe	d						20 50			21 07								21 20			21 37				
Northfleet	d						20 52			21 09								21 22			21 39				
Gravesend	d				20 48		20a56		21a09	21 13							21 18	21a26		21a39	21 43				
Higham	d									21 19											21 49				
Strood	d				20 59					21 25							21 29				21 55				
Maidstone West	d																								
Rochester	d				21 02					21 28							21 32				21 58				
Chatham	d				21 06					21 31							21 36				22 01				
Gillingham (Kent)	a				21 10					21 35							21 40				22 05				
Rainham Kt	a				21 15					21 41							21 45				22 12				

Table T200-F

Mondays to Fridays

21 May to 7 December

London - Dartford and Gillingham

		SE	SE	SE	SE ◇	SE	SE	SE	TL	SE	SE	SE	SE		SE ◇	SE	SE	SE	TL	SE	SE	SE	SE	SE ◇	SE
St Pancras Int'l	d				21 25										21 55									22 25	
Stratford International	d				21 32										22 02									22 32	
Ebbsfleet International	d				21 43										22 13									22 43	
London Charing Cross	d		20 54			21 02				21 12	21 18	21 24				21 32				21 42	21 48	21 54			22 02
London Waterloo (East)	d		20 58			21 05				21 15	21 21	21 28				21 35				21 45	21 51	21 58			22 05
London Cannon Street	d	20 54		21 05			21 08						21 32				21 38						22 02		
London Bridge	d	20 58	21 05	21 09		21 11	21 13		21 18	21 21	21 27	21 35	21 36			21 41	21 43		21 48	21 51	21 57	22 05	22 06		22 11
Deptford	d	21 05		21 15					21 25				21 42						21 55				22 12		
Greenwich	d	21 07		21 17					21 27				21 44						21 57				22 14		
Maze Hill	d	21 10		21 20					21 30				21 47						22 00				22 17		
Westcombe Park	d	21 12		21 22					21 32				21 49						22 02				22 19		
London Victoria	d							21 06										21 36							
Denmark Hill	d							21 16										21 46							
Peckham Rye	d							21 18										21 48							
Nunhead	d							21 21										21 51							
New Cross	d						21 19										21 49								
St Johns	d						21 21										21 51								
Lewisham	d		21 15				21 24	21 26		21 30		21 45					21 54	21 56		22 00		22 15			
Blackheath	d		21 18					21 29		21 33		21 48						21 59		22 03		22 18			
Kidbrooke	d		21 21					21 32				21 51						22 02				22 21			
Eltham	d		21 24					21 36				21 54						22 06				22 24			
Falconwood	d		21 27					21 39				21 57						22 09				22 27			
Welling	d		21 30					21 41				22 00						22 11				22 30			
Bexleyheath	d		21 33					21 45				22 03						22 15				22 33			
Barnehurst	d		21 36					21 47				22 06						22 17				22 36			
Hither Green	d						21 29				21 37						21 59				22 07				
Lee	d						21 31				21 39						22 01				22 09				
Mottingham	d						21 34				21 42						22 04				22 12				
New Eltham	d					21 25	21 37				21 45					21 55	22 07				22 15				22 25
Sidcup	d					21 28	21 40				21 48					21 58	22 10				22 18				22 28
Albany Park	d						21 43				21 51						22 13				22 21				
Bexley	d					21 32	21 45				21 53					22 02	22 15				22 23				22 32
Crayford	d					21 35	21 51				21 57					22 05	22 21				22 27				22 35
Charlton	d	21 15		21 25			22a19		21 35	21 38			21 52				22a49		22 05	22 08			22 22		
Woolwich Dockyard	d	21 18		21 28						21 41			21 55							22 11			22 25		
Woolwich Arsenal	d	21 21		21 31					21 40	21 44			21 58						22 10	22 14			22 28		
Plumstead	d	21 23		21 33					21 43	21 46			22 00						22 13	22 16			22 30		
Abbey Wood	d	21 26		21 36					21 46	21 50			22 03						22 16	22 20			22 33		
Belvedere	d	21 29		21 39						21 53			22 06							22 23			22 36		
Erith	d	21 32		21 42						21 55			22 09							22 25			22 39		
Slade Green	d	21a36		21a45					21 52	22 01			22a13						22 22	22 31			22a43		
Dartford	a		21 44			21 40		21 54	21 57	22 08	22 02	22 14				22 10		22 24	22 27	22 38	22 32	22 44			22 40
	d					21 41		21 54	21 58							22 11		22 24	22 28						22 41
Stone Crossing	d					21 45			22 02							22 15			22 32						22 45
Greenhithe for Bluewater	d					21 47		22 00	22 04							22 17		22 30	22 34						22 47
Swanscombe	d					21 50			22 07							22 20			22 37						22 50
Northfleet	d					21 52			22 09							22 22			22 39						22 52
Gravesend	d				21 48	21a56		22a09	22 13						22 18	22a26		22a39	22 43					22 48	22a56
Higham	d								22 19										22 49						
Strood	d				21 59				22 25						22 29				22 55					22 59	
Maidstone West	d																								
Rochester	d				22 02				22 28						22 32				22 58					23 02	
Chatham	d				22 06				22 31						22 36				23 01					23 06	
Gillingham (Kent)	a				22 10				22 35						22 40				23 05					23 10	
Rainham Kt	a				22 15				22 41						22 45				23 11					23 15	

Table T200-F

Mondays to Fridays

21 May to 7 December

London - Dartford and Gillingham

		SE	SE	TL	SE		SE	SE	SE MT FO	SE ◇	SE	SE MT FO	SE	TL	SE	SE	SE	SE	SE ◇	SE	SE		TL	SE	SE
St Pancras Int'l	d									22 55									23 25						
Stratford International	d									23 02									23 32						
Ebbsfleet International	d									23 13									23 43						
London Charing Cross	d				22 12		22 18	22 24			22 32				22 42	22 48	22 54			23 02				23 12	23 20
London Waterloo (East)	d				22 15		22 21	22 28			22 35				22 45	22 51	22 58			23 05				23 15	23 23
London Cannon Street	d	22 08							22 32			22 38						23 02							
London Bridge	d	22 13		22 18	22 21		22 27	22 35	22 36		22 41	22 43		22 48	22 51	22 57	23 05	23 06		23 11			23 18	23 21	23 29
Deptford	d			22 25					22 42					22 55				23 12					23 25		
Greenwich	d			22 27					22 44					22 57				23 14					23 27		
Maze Hill	d			22 30					22 47					23 00				23 17					23 30		
Westcombe Park	d			22 32					22 49					23 02				23 19					23 32		
London Victoria	d		22 06										22 36								23 06				
Denmark Hill	d		22 16										22 46								23 16				
Peckham Rye	d		22 18										22 48								23 18				
Nunhead	d		22 21										22 51								23 21				
New Cross	d	22 19										22 49													
St Johns	d	22 21										22 51													
Lewisham	d	22 24	22 26		22 30			22 45				22 54	22 56		23 00		23 15				23 26			23 30	23 38
Blackheath	d		22 29		22 33			22 48					22 59		23 03		23 18				23 29			23 33	
Kidbrooke	d		22 32					22 51					23 02				23 21				23 32				
Eltham	d		22 36					22 54					23 06				23 24				23 36				
Falconwood	d		22 39					22 57					23 09				23 27				23 39				
Welling	d		22 41					23 00					23 11				23 30				23 41				
Bexleyheath	d		22 45					23 03					23 15				23 33				23 45				
Barnehurst	d		22 47					23 06					23 17				23 36				23 47				
Hither Green	d	22 29					22 37					22 59				23 07				23 22					23 43
Lee	d	22 31					22 39					23 01				23 09				23 24					23 45
Mottingham	d	22 34					22 42					23 04				23 12				23 27					23 48
New Eltham	d	22 37					22 45				22 55	23 07				23 15				23 30					23 51
Sidcup	d	22 40					22 48				22 58	23 10				23 18				23 33					23 54
Albany Park	d	22 43					22 51					23 13				23 21				23 36					23 57
Bexley	d	22 45					22 53				23 02	23 15				23 23				23 38					23 59
Crayford	d	22 51					22 57				23 05	23 21				23 27				23 42					00 03
Charlton	d	23a19		22 35	22 38				22 52			23a49		23 05	23 08			23 22					23 35	23 38	
Woolwich Dockyard	d				22 41				22 55						23 11			23 25						23 41	
Woolwich Arsenal	d			22 40	22 44				22 58					23 10	23 14			23 28					23 40	23 44	
Plumstead	d			22 43	22 46				23 00					23 13	23 16			23 30					23 43	23 46	
Abbey Wood	d			22 46	22 50				23 03					23 16	23 20			23 33					23 46	23 50	
Belvedere	d				22 53				23 06						23 23			23 36						23 53	
Erith	d				22 55				23 09						23 25			23 39						23 55	
Slade Green	d			22 52	23 01				23a13					23 22	23 31			23 44					23 52	23 59	
Dartford	a		22 54	22 57	23 08		23 02	23 14			23 10		23 24	23 27	23 38	23 32	23 44	23 51		23 47	23 54		23 57	00 05	00 08
	d		22 54	22 58							23 11		23 24	23 28						23 48			23 58		
Stone Crossing	d			23 02							23 15			23 32						23 52			00 02		
Greenhithe for Bluewater	d		23 00	23 04							23 17		23 30	23 34						23 54			00 04		
Swanscombe	d			23 07							23 20			23 37						23 57			00 07		
Northfleet	d			23 09							23 22			23 39						23 59			00 09		
Gravesend	d		23a09	23 13						23 18	23a26		23a39	23 43					23 48	00a06			00 13		
Higham	d			23 19										23 49									00 19		
Strood	d			23 25						23 29				23 55					23 59				00 25		
Maidstone West	d																								
Rochester	d			23 28						23 32				23 58					00 02				00 28		
Chatham	d			23 31						23 36				00 02					00 06				00 32		
Gillingham (Kent)	a			23 35						23 40				00 06					00 10				00 36		
Rainham Kt	a			23 41						23 45									00 15						

Please note, Network Rail have stated that further updates to this timetable are possible during the validity period.

Table T200-F

Mondays to Fridays

21 May to 7 December

London - Dartford and Gillingham

		SE	SE	SE ◇	SE	SE	SE	SE
St Pancras Int'l	d			23 55				
Stratford International	d			00 02				
Ebbsfleet International	d			00 13				
London Charing Cross	d	23 24			23 32		23 42	23 52
London Waterloo (East)	d	23 28			23 35		23 45	23 55
London Cannon Street	d		23 32					
London Bridge	d	23 35	23 36		23 41		23 51	00 01
Deptford	d		23 42					
Greenwich	d		23 44					
Maze Hill	d		23 47					
Westcombe Park	d		23 49					
London Victoria	d					23 36		
Denmark Hill	d					23 46		
Peckham Rye	d					23 48		
Nunhead	d					23 51		
New Cross	d							
St Johns	d							
Lewisham	d	23 45				23 56	23 59	00 10
Blackheath	d	23 48				23 59	00 03	00 13
Kidbrooke	d	23 51				00 02		00 16
Eltham	d	23 54				00 06		00 19
Falconwood	d	23 57				00 09		00 22
Welling	d	23 59				00 11		00 25
Bexleyheath	d	00 03				00 15		00 28
Barnehurst	d	00 06				00 17		00 31
Hither Green	d				23 52			
Lee	d				23 54			
Mottingham	d				23 57			
New Eltham	d				23 59			
Sidcup	d				00 03			
Albany Park	d				00 06			
Bexley	d				00 08			
Crayford	d				00 12			
Charlton	d		23 52				00 08	
Woolwich Dockyard	d		23 55				00 11	
Woolwich Arsenal	d		23 58				00 14	
Plumstead	d		23 59				00 16	
Abbey Wood	d		00 03				00 20	
Belvedere	d		00 06				00 23	
Erith	d		00 09				00 25	
Slade Green	d		00 14				00 31	
Dartford	a	00 14	00 21		00 17	00 25	00 36	00 41
	d				00 18			
Stone Crossing	d				00 22			
Greenhithe for Bluewater	d				00 24			
Swanscombe	d				00 27			
Northfleet	d				00 29			
Gravesend	d			00 18	00a36			
Higham	d							
Strood	d			00 29				
Maidstone West	d							
Rochester	d			00 32				
Chatham	d			00 36				
Gillingham (Kent)	a			00 40				
Rainham Kt	a			00 45				

Table T200-F

Saturdays

26 May to 8 December

London - Dartford and Gillingham

		TL	SE ◇	TL	SE ◇	SE	SE	SE	SE	SE	TL	SE	SE	SE	SE	SE		SE	TL	TL	SE	SE	TL	SE	SE
St Pancras Int'l	d																								
Stratford International	d				00 02																				
Ebbsfleet International	d				00 13																				
London Charing Cross	d															00 26					04 50			05 20	05 24
London Waterloo (East)	d															00 29					04 53			05 23	05 28
London Cannon Street	d													00 02				00 32				05 05			
London Bridge	d												00 01	00 06		00 35		00 36			04 59	05 09		05 29	05 35
Deptford	d													00 12				00 42				05 15			
Greenwich	d													00 14				00 44				05 17			
Maze Hill	d													00 17				00 47				05 20			
Westcombe Park	d													00 19				00 49				05 22			
London Victoria	d														00 06										
Denmark Hill	d														00 16										
Peckham Rye	d														00 18										
Nunhead	d														00 21										
New Cross	d																								
St Johns	d																								
Lewisham	d												00 10		00 26	00 45					05 10			05 40	05 45
Blackheath	d											00 03	00 13		00 29	00 48									05 48
Kidbrooke	d									00 02			00 16		00 32	00 51									05 51
Eltham	d									00 06			00 19		00 36	00 54									05 54
Falconwood	d									00 09			00 22		00 39	00 57									05 57
Welling	d									00 11			00 25		00 41	01 00									06 00
Bexleyheath	d						00 03			00 15			00 28		00 45	01 03									06 03
Barnehurst	d						00 06			00 17			00 31		00 47	01 06									06 06
Hither Green	d																				05 15			05 45	
Lee	d																				05 17			05 47	
Mottingham	d																				05 20			05 50	
New Eltham	d																				05 23			05 53	
Sidcup	d							00 03													05 26			05 56	
Albany Park	d							00 06													05 29			05 59	
Bexley	d							00 08													05 31			06 01	
Crayford	d					00 03		00 12													05 35			06 05	
Charlton	d											00 08		00 22				00 52				05 25			
Woolwich Dockyard	d											00 11		00 25				00 55				05 28			
Woolwich Arsenal	d											00 14		00 28				00 58				05 31			
Plumstead	d											00 16		00 30				01 00				05 33			
Abbey Wood	d								00 03			00 20		00 33				01 03				05 36			
Belvedere	d								00 06			00 23		00 36				01 06				05 39			
Erith	d								00 09			00 25		00 39				01 09				05 42			
Slade Green	d								00 14			00 31		00 44				01 12				05a45			
Dartford	a					00 08	00 14	00 17	00 21	00 25		00 36	00 41	00 51	00 56	01 16		01 20			05 40			06 10	06 14
	d							00 18			00 28								01 24	04 58	05 41		05 58	06 11	
Stone Crossing	d			00 02				00 22			00 32								01s28	05 02	05 45		06 02	06 15	
Greenhithe for Bluewater	d			00 04				00 24			00 34								01s30	05 04	05 47		06 04	06 17	
Swanscombe	d			00 07				00 27			00 37								01s33	05 07	05 50		06 07	06 20	
Northfleet	d			00 09				00 29			00 39								01s35	05 09	05 52		06 09	06 22	
Gravesend	d			00 13	00 18			00a36			00 43								01 39	05 13	05a56		06 13	06a26	
Higham	d			00 19							00 49								01s45	05 19			06 19		
Strood	d			00 25	00 29						00 56								01s50	05 25			06 25		
Maidstone West	d																								
Rochester	d		00 02	00 28	00 32						00 59								01s53	05 28			06 28		
Chatham	d	00 02	00 06	00 32	00 36						01 03								01s57	05 31			06 31		
Gillingham (Kent)	a	00 06	00 10	00 36	00 40						01 07								02 02	05 35			06 35		
Rainham Kt	a		00 15		00 45															05 42			06 41		

Table T200-F

London - Dartford and Gillingham

Saturdays
26 May to 8 December

		SE	TL	SE	SE	SE	SE	TL	SE	SE	SE	SE	SE	TL	SE	SE ◇	SE	SE	SE	SE	SE	TL	SE
St Pancras Int'l	d															07 25							
Stratford International	d															07 32							
Ebbsfleet International	d															07 43							
London Charing Cross	d			05 50	05 54				06 12	06 18	06 24				06 42		06 48	06 54					07 12
London Waterloo (East)	d			05 53	05 58				06 15	06 21	06 28				06 45		06 51	06 58					07 15
London Cannon Street	d	05 35				06 05	06 08					06 35	06 38						07 05	07 08			
London Bridge	d	05 39	05 48	05 59	06 05	06 09	06 13	06 18	06 21	06 27	06 35	06 39	06 43	06 48	06 51		06 57	07 05	07 09	07 13		07 18	07 21
Deptford	d	05 45	05 55			06 15		06 25				06 45		06 55					07 15			07 25	
Greenwich	d	05 47	05 57			06 17		06 27				06 47		06 57					07 17			07 27	
Maze Hill	d	05 50	06 00			06 20		06 30				06 50		07 00					07 20			07 30	
Westcombe Park	d	05 52	06 02			06 22		06 32				06 52		07 02					07 22			07 32	
London Victoria	d																				07 06		
Denmark Hill	d																				07 16		
Peckham Rye	d																				07 18		
Nunhead	d																				07 21		
New Cross	d						06 19						06 49							07 19			
St Johns	d						06 21						06 51							07 21			
Lewisham	d			06 10	06 15		06 24		06 30		06 45		06 54		07 00			07 15		07 24	07 26		07 30
Blackheath	d				06 18				06 33		06 48				07 03			07 18			07 29		07 33
Kidbrooke	d				06 21						06 51							07 21			07 32		
Eltham	d				06 24						06 54							07 24			07 36		
Falconwood	d				06 27						06 57							07 27			07 39		
Welling	d				06 30						07 00							07 30			07 41		
Bexleyheath	d				06 33						07 03							07 33			07 45		
Barnehurst	d				06 36						07 06							07 36			07 47		
Hither Green	d			06 15			06 29			06 37			06 59				07 07			07 29			
Lee	d			06 17			06 31			06 39			07 01				07 09			07 31			
Mottingham	d			06 20			06 34			06 42			07 04				07 12			07 34			
New Eltham	d			06 23			06 37			06 45			07 07				07 15			07 37			
Sidcup	d			06 26			06 40			06 48			07 10				07 18			07 40			
Albany Park	d			06 29			06 43			06 51			07 13				07 21			07 43			
Bexley	d			06 31			06 45			06 53			07 15				07 23			07 45			
Crayford	d			06 35			06 51			06 57			07 21				07 27			07 51			
Charlton	d	05 55	06 05			06 25	07a19	06 35	06 38			06 55	07a49	07 05	07 08				07 25	08a19		07 35	07 38
Woolwich Dockyard	d	05 58				06 28			06 41			06 58			07 11				07 28				07 41
Woolwich Arsenal	d	06 01	06 10			06 31		06 40	06 44			07 01		07 10	07 14				07 31			07 40	07 44
Plumstead	d	06 03	06 13			06 33		06 43	06 46			07 03		07 13	07 16				07 33			07 43	07 46
Abbey Wood	d	06 06	06 16			06 36		06 46	06 50			07 06		07 16	07 20				07 36			07 46	07 50
Belvedere	d	06 09				06 39			06 53			07 09			07 23				07 39				07 53
Erith	d	06 12				06 42			06 55			07 12			07 25				07 42				07 55
Slade Green	d	06a15	06 22			06a45		06 52	07 01			07a15		07 22	07 31				07a45			07 52	08 01
Dartford	a		06 27	06 40	06 44			06 57	07 08	07 02	07 14			07 27	07 38		07 32	07 44			07 54	07 57	08 08
	d		06 28	06 41				06 58		07 04				07 28			07 34				07 54	07 58	
Stone Crossing	d		06 32	06 45				07 02		07 08				07 32			07 38					08 02	
Greenhithe for Bluewater	d		06 34	06 47				07 04		07 11				07 34			07 41				08 00	08 04	
Swanscombe	d		06 37	06 50				07 07		07 14				07 37			07 44					08 07	
Northfleet	d		06 39	06 52				07 09		07 17				07 39			07 47					08 09	
Gravesend	d		06 43	06a56				07 13		07a23				07 43		07 48	07a53				08a09	08 13	
Higham	d		06 49					07 19						07 49								08 19	
Strood	d		06 55					07 25						07 55		07 59						08 25	
Maidstone West	d																						
Rochester	d		06 58					07 28						07 58		08 02						08 28	
Chatham	d		07 01					07 31						08 01		08 06						08 31	
Gillingham (Kent)	a		07 05					07 35						08 05		08 10						08 35	
Rainham Kt	a		07 11					07 41						08 11		08 15						08 41	

Table T200-F

London - Dartford and Gillingham

Saturdays
26 May to 8 December

		SE	SE	SE	SE	SE ◇	SE	SE	SE	TL	SE	SE	SE	SE	SE	SE	SE ◇	SE	SE	SE	TL	SE	SE	SE
St Pancras Int'l	d					07 55											08 25							
Stratford International	d					08 02											08 32							
Ebbsfleet International	d					08 13											08 43							
London Charing Cross	d		07 18	07 24			07 32				07 42		07 48		07 54			08 02				08 12		08 18
London Waterloo (East)	d		07 21	07 28			07 35				07 45		07 51		07 58			08 05				08 15		08 21
London Cannon Street	d	07 17			07 35			07 38				07 47		07 54		08 05			08 08				08 17	
London Bridge	d	07 21	07 27	07 35	07 39		07 41	07 43		07 48	07 51	07 51	07 57	07 58	08 05	08 09		08 11	08 13		08 18	08 21	08 21	08 27
Deptford	d				07 45					07 55				08 05		08 15					08 25			
Greenwich	d				07 47					07 57				08 07		08 17					08 27			
Maze Hill	d				07 50					08 00				08 10		08 20					08 30			
Westcombe Park	d				07 52					08 02				08 12		08 22					08 32			
London Victoria	d								07 36											08 06				
Denmark Hill	d								07 46											08 16				
Peckham Rye	d								07 48											08 18				
Nunhead	d								07 51											08 21				
New Cross	d	07 27						07 49				07 57							08 19				08 27	
St Johns	d	07 29						07 51				07 59							08 21				08 29	
Lewisham	d	07 34		07 45				07 54	07 56		08 00	08 04			08 15				08 24	08 26		08 30	08 34	
Blackheath	d	07 37		07 48					07 59		08 03	08 07			08 18					08 29		08 33	08 37	
Kidbrooke	d	07 40		07 51					08 02			08 10			08 21					08 32			08 40	
Eltham	d	07 43		07 54					08 06			08 13			08 24					08 36			08 43	
Falconwood	d	07 46		07 57					08 09			08 16			08 27					08 39			08 46	
Welling	d	07 49		08 00					08 11			08 19			08 30					08 41			08 49	
Bexleyheath	d	07 52		08 03					08 15			08 22			08 33					08 45			08 52	
Barnehurst	d	07 58		08 06					08 17			08 28			08 36					08 47			08 58	
Hither Green	d		07 37					07 59					08 07						08 29					08 37
Lee	d		07 39					08 01					08 09						08 31					08 39
Mottingham	d		07 42					08 04					08 12						08 34					08 42
New Eltham	d		07 45				07 55	08 07					08 15					08 25	08 37					08 45
Sidcup	d		07 48				07 58	08 10					08 18					08 28	08 40					08 48
Albany Park	d		07 51					08 13					08 21						08 43					08 51
Bexley	d		07 53				08 02	08 15					08 23					08 32	08 45					08 53
Crayford	d		07 57				08 05	08 21					08 27					08 35	08 51					08 57
Charlton	d				07 55			08a49		08 05	08 08			08 15		08 25			09a19		08 35	08 38		
Woolwich Dockyard	d				07 58						08 11			08 18		08 28						08 41		
Woolwich Arsenal	d				08 01					08 10	08 14			08 21		08 31					08 40	08 44		
Plumstead	d				08 03					08 13	08 16			08 23		08 33					08 43	08 46		
Abbey Wood	d				08 06					08 16	08 20			08 26		08 36					08 46	08 50		
Belvedere	d				08 09						08 23			08 29		08 39						08 53		
Erith	d				08 12						08 25			08 32		08 42						08 55		
Slade Green	d	08a05			08a15					08 22	08 31	08a35		08a36		08a45					08 52	09 01	09a05	
Dartford	a		08 02	08 14			08 10		08 24	08 27	08 38		08 32		08 44			08 40		08 54	08 57	09 08		09 02
	d						08 11		08 24	08 28								08 41		08 54	08 58			
Stone Crossing	d						08 15			08 32								08 45			09 02			
Greenhithe for Bluewater	d						08 17		08 30	08 34								08 47		09 00	09 04			
Swanscombe	d						08 20			08 37								08 50			09 07			
Northfleet	d						08 22			08 39								08 52			09 09			
Gravesend	d					08 18	08a26		08a39	08 43							08 48	08a56		09a09	09 13			
Higham	d									08 49											09 19			
Strood	d					08 29				08 55							08 59				09 25			
Maidstone West	d																							
Rochester	d					08 32				08 58							09 02				09 28			
Chatham	d					08 36				09 01							09 06				09 31			
Gillingham (Kent)	a					08 40				09 05							09 10				09 35			
Rainham Kt	a					08 45				09 11							09 15				09 41			

Please note, Network Rail have stated that further updates to this timetable are possible during the validity period.

Table T200-F

Saturdays

26 May to 8 December

London - Dartford and Gillingham

		SE	SE	SE	SE ◇	SE	SE	SE	TL	SE	SE	SE	SE	SE	SE	SE ◇	SE	SE	SE	TL	SE	SE	SE
St Pancras Int'l 15 ⊖	d				08 52											09 25							
Stratford International ⊖ ⛴	d				08 59											09 32							
Ebbsfleet International	d				09 13											09 44							
London Charing Cross 4 ⊖	d		08 24			08 32				08 42		08 48		08 54			09 02				09 12		09 18
London Waterloo (East) 4 ⊖	d		08 28			08 35				08 45		08 51		08 58			09 05				09 15		09 21
London Cannon Street 4 ⊖	d	08 24		08 35			08 38				08 47		08 54		09 05			09 08				09 17	
London Bridge 4 ⊖	d	08 28	08 35	08 39		08 41	08 43		08 48	08 51	08 51	08 57	08 58	09 05	09 09		09 11	09 13		09 18	09 21	09 21	09 27
Deptford	d	08 35		08 45					08 55				09 05		09 15					09 25			
Greenwich 4 ⛴	d	08 37		08 47					08 57				09 07		09 17					09 27			
Maze Hill	d	08 40		08 50					09 00				09 10		09 20					09 30			
Westcombe Park	d	08 42		08 52					09 02				09 12		09 22					09 32			
London Victoria 15 ⊖	d							08 36											09 06				
Denmark Hill 4	d							08 46											09 16				
Peckham Rye 4	d							08 48											09 18				
Nunhead 4	d							08 51											09 21				
New Cross 4 ⊖	d						08 49				08 57							09 19				09 27	
St Johns	d						08 51				08 59							09 21				09 29	
Lewisham 4 ⛴	d		08 45				08 54	08 56		09 00	09 04			09 15				09 24	09 26		09 30	09 34	
Blackheath 4	d		08 48					08 59		09 03	09 07			09 18					09 29		09 33	09 37	
Kidbrooke	d		08 51					09 02			09 10			09 21					09 32			09 40	
Eltham	d		08 54					09 06			09 13			09 24					09 36			09 43	
Falconwood	d		08 57					09 09			09 16			09 27					09 39			09 46	
Welling	d		09 00					09 11			09 19			09 30					09 41			09 49	
Bexleyheath	d		09 03					09 15			09 22			09 33					09 45			09 52	
Barnehurst 4	d		09 06					09 17			09 28			09 36					09 47			09 58	
Hither Green 4	d						08 59					09 07						09 29					09 37
Lee	d						09 01					09 09						09 31					09 39
Mottingham	d						09 04					09 12						09 34					09 42
New Eltham	d					08 55	09 07					09 15					09 25	09 37					09 45
Sidcup 4	d					08 58	09 10					09 18					09 28	09 40					09 48
Albany Park	d						09 13					09 21						09 43					09 51
Bexley	d					09 02	09 15					09 23					09 32	09 45					09 53
Crayford	d					09 05	09 21					09 27					09 35	09 51					09 57
Charlton 4	d	08 45		08 55			09a49		09 05	09 08			09 15		09 25			10a19		09 35	09 38		
Woolwich Dockyard	d	08 48		08 58						09 11			09 18		09 28						09 41		
Woolwich Arsenal 4 ⛴	d	08 51		09 01					09 10	09 14			09 21		09 31					09 40	09 44		
Plumstead	d	08 53		09 03					09 13	09 16			09 23		09 33					09 43	09 46		
Abbey Wood	d	08 56		09 06					09 16	09 20			09 26		09 36					09 46	09 50		
Belvedere	d	08 59		09 09						09 23			09 29		09 39						09 53		
Erith	d	09 02		09 12						09 25			09 32		09 42						09 55		
Slade Green 4	d	09a06		09a15					09 22	09 31	09a35		09a36		09a45					09 52	10 01	10a05	
Dartford 4	a		09 14			09 10		09 24	09 27	09 38		09 32		09 44			09 40		09 54	09 57	10 08		10 02
	d					09 11		09 24	09 28								09 41		09 54	09 58			
Stone Crossing	d					09 15			09 32								09 45			10 02			
Greenhithe for Bluewater	d					09 17		09 30	09 34								09 47		10 00	10 04			
Swanscombe	d					09 20			09 37								09 50			10 07			
Northfleet	d					09 22			09 39								09 52			10 09			
Gravesend 4	d				09 18	09a26		09a39	09 43							09 48	09a56		10a09	10 13			
Higham	d								09 49											10 19			
Strood 4	d				09 29				09 55							09 59				10 25			
Maidstone West	d																						
Rochester 4	d				09 32				09 58							10 02				10 28			
Chatham 4	d				09 36				10 01							10 06				10 31			
Gillingham (Kent) 4	a				09 40				10 05							10 10				10 35			
Rainham Kt	a				09 45				10 11							10 15				10 41			

Table T200-F

Saturdays

26 May to 8 December

London - Dartford and Gillingham

		SE	SE	SE	SE ◇	SE	SE	SE	TL	SE	SE	SE	SE	SE	SE	SE ◇	SE	SE	SE	TL	SE	SE	SE	SE
St Pancras Int'l 15 ⊖	d				09 55											10 22								
Stratford International ⊖ ⛴	d				10 02											10 32								
Ebbsfleet International	d				10 13											10 44								
London Charing Cross 4 ⊖	d		09 24			09 32				09 42		09 48		09 54			10 02				10 12		10 18	
London Waterloo (East) 4 ⊖	d		09 28			09 35				09 45		09 51		09 58			10 05				10 15		10 21	
London Cannon Street 4 ⊖	d	09 24		09 35			09 38				09 47		09 54		10 05			10 08				10 17		10 24
London Bridge 4 ⊖	d	09 28	09 35	09 39		09 41	09 43		09 48	09 51	09 51	09 57	09 58	10 05	10 09		10 11	10 13		10 18	10 21	10 21	10 27	10 28
Deptford	d	09 36		09 45					09 55				10 05		10 15					10 25				10 35
Greenwich 4 ⛴	d	09 38		09 47					09 57				10 07		10 17					10 27				10 37
Maze Hill	d	09 41		09 50					10 00				10 10		10 20					10 30				10 40
Westcombe Park	d	09 43		09 52					10 02				10 12		10 22					10 32				10 42
London Victoria 15 ⊖	d							09 36											10 06					
Denmark Hill 4	d							09 46											10 16					
Peckham Rye 4	d							09 48											10 18					
Nunhead 4	d							09 51											10 21					
New Cross 4 ⊖	d						09 49				09 57							10 19				10 27		
St Johns	d						09 51				09 59							10 21				10 29		
Lewisham 4 ⛴	d		09 45				09 54	09 56		10 00	10 04			10 15				10 24	10 26		10 30	10 34		
Blackheath 4	d		09 48					09 59		10 03	10 07			10 18					10 29		10 33	10 37		
Kidbrooke	d		09 51					10 02			10 10			10 21					10 32			10 40		
Eltham	d		09 54					10 06			10 13			10 24					10 36			10 43		
Falconwood	d		09 57					10 09			10 16			10 27					10 39			10 46		
Welling	d		10 00					10 11			10 19			10 30					10 41			10 49		
Bexleyheath	d		10 03					10 15			10 22			10 33					10 45			10 52		
Barnehurst 4	d		10 06					10 17			10 28			10 36					10 47			10 58		
Hither Green 4	d						09 59					10 07						10 29					10 37	
Lee	d						10 01					10 09						10 31					10 39	
Mottingham	d						10 04					10 12						10 34					10 42	
New Eltham	d					09 55	10 07					10 15					10 25	10 37					10 45	
Sidcup 4	d					09 58	10 10					10 18					10 28	10 40					10 48	
Albany Park	d						10 13					10 21						10 43					10 51	
Bexley	d					10 02	10 15					10 23					10 32	10 45					10 53	
Crayford	d					10 05	10 21					10 27					10 35	10 51					10 57	
Charlton 4	d	09 46		09 55			10a49		10 05	10 08			10 15		10 25			11a19		10 35	10 38			10 45
Woolwich Dockyard	d	09 49		09 58						10 11			10 18		10 28						10 41			10 48
Woolwich Arsenal 4 ⛴	d	09 52		10 01					10 10	10 14			10 21		10 31					10 40	10 44			10 51
Plumstead	d	09 54		10 03					10 13	10 16			10 23		10 33					10 43	10 46			10 53
Abbey Wood	d	09 57		10 06					10 16	10 20			10 26		10 36					10 46	10 50			10 56
Belvedere	d	10 00		10 09						10 23			10 29		10 39						10 53			10 59
Erith	d	10 03		10 12						10 25			10 32		10 42						10 55			11 02
Slade Green 4	d	10a07		10a15					10 22	10 31	10a35		10a36		10a45					10 52	11 01	11a05		11a06
Dartford 4	a		10 14			10 10		10 24	10 27	10 38		10 32		10 44			10 40		10 54	10 57	11 08		11 02	
	d					10 11		10 24	10 28								10 41		10 54	10 58				
Stone Crossing	d					10 15			10 32								10 45			11 02				
Greenhithe for Bluewater	d					10 17		10 30	10 34								10 47		11 00	11 04				
Swanscombe	d					10 20			10 37								10 50			11 07				
Northfleet	d					10 22			10 39								10 52			11 09				
Gravesend 4	d				10 18	10a26		10a39	10 43							10 48	10a56		11a09	11 13				
Higham	d								10 49											11 19				
Strood 4	d				10 29				10 55							10 59				11 25				
Maidstone West	d																							
Rochester 4	d				10 32				10 58							11 02				11 28				
Chatham 4	d				10 36				11 01							11 06				11 31				
Gillingham (Kent) 4	a				10 40				11 05							11 10				11 35				
Rainham Kt	a				10 45				11 11							11 15				11 41				

Table T200-F

Saturdays

26 May to 8 December

London - Dartford and Gillingham

		SE	SE	SE ◇	SE	SE	SE	TL	SE	SE	SE	SE	SE	SE	SE ◇	SE	SE	SE	TL	SE	SE	SE	SE
St Pancras Int'l ⊖	d			10 52											11 25								
Stratford International ⊖ ⛴	d			10 59											11 32								
Ebbsfleet International	d			11 13											11 43								
London Charing Cross ⊖	d	10 24			10 32				10 42		10 48		10 54			11 02				11 12		11 18	
London Waterloo (East) ⊖	d	10 28			10 35				10 45		10 51		10 58			11 05				11 15		11 21	
London Cannon Street ⊖	d		10 35			10 38				10 47		10 54		11 05			11 08				11 17		11 24
London Bridge ⊖	d	10 35	10 39		10 41	10 43		10 48	10 51	10 51	10 57	10 58	11 05	11 09		11 11	11 13		11 18	11 21	11 21	11 27	11 28
Deptford	d		10 45					10 55				11 05		11 15					11 25				11 35
Greenwich ⛴	d		10 47					10 57				11 07		11 17					11 27				11 37
Maze Hill	d		10 50					11 00				11 10		11 20					11 30				11 40
Westcombe Park	d		10 52					11 02				11 12		11 22					11 32				11 42
London Victoria ⊖	d						10 36											11 06					
Denmark Hill	d						10 46											11 16					
Peckham Rye	d						10 48											11 18					
Nunhead	d						10 51											11 21					
New Cross ⊖	d					10 49				10 57							11 19				11 27		
St Johns	d					10 51				10 59							11 21				11 29		
Lewisham ⛴	d	10 45				10 54	10 56		11 00	11 04			11 15				11 24	11 26		11 30	11 34		
Blackheath	d	10 48					10 59		11 03	11 07			11 18					11 29		11 33	11 37		
Kidbrooke	d	10 51					11 02			11 10			11 21					11 32			11 40		
Eltham	d	10 54					11 06			11 13			11 24					11 36			11 43		
Falconwood	d	10 57					11 09			11 16			11 27					11 39			11 46		
Welling	d	11 00					11 11			11 19			11 30					11 41			11 49		
Bexleyheath	d	11 03					11 15			11 22			11 33					11 45			11 52		
Barnehurst	d	11 06					11 17			11 28			11 36					11 47			11 58		
Hither Green	d					10 59					11 07						11 29					11 37	
Lee	d					11 01					11 09						11 31					11 39	
Mottingham	d					11 04					11 12						11 34					11 42	
New Eltham	d				10 55	11 07					11 15					11 25	11 37					11 45	
Sidcup	d				10 58	11 10					11 18					11 28	11 40					11 48	
Albany Park	d					11 13					11 21						11 43					11 51	
Bexley	d				11 02	11 15					11 23					11 32	11 45					11 53	
Crayford	d				11 05	11 21					11 27					11 35	11 51					11 57	
Charlton	d		10 55			11a49		11 05	11 08			11 15		11 25			12a19		11 35	11 38			11 45
Woolwich Dockyard	d		10 58						11 11			11 18		11 28						11 41			11 48
Woolwich Arsenal ⛴	d		11 01					11 10	11 14			11 21		11 31					11 40	11 44			11 51
Plumstead	d		11 03					11 13	11 16			11 23		11 33					11 43	11 46			11 53
Abbey Wood	d		11 06					11 16	11 20			11 26		11 36					11 46	11 50			11 56
Belvedere	d		11 09						11 23			11 29		11 39						11 53			11 59
Erith	d		11 12						11 25			11 32		11 42						11 55			12 02
Slade Green	d		11a15					11 22	11 31	11a35		11a36		11a45					11 52	12 01	12a05		12a06
Dartford	a	11 14			11 10		11 24	11 27	11 38		11 32		11 44			11 40		11 54	11 57	12 08		12 02	
	d				11 11		11 24	11 28								11 41		11 54	11 58				
Stone Crossing	d				11 15			11 32								11 45			12 02				
Greenhithe for Bluewater	d				11 17		11 30	11 34								11 47		12 00	12 04				
Swanscombe	d				11 20			11 37								11 50			12 07				
Northfleet	d				11 22			11 39								11 52			12 09				
Gravesend	d			11 18	11a26		11a39	11 43							11 48	11a56		12a09	12 13				
Higham	d							11 49											12 19				
Strood	d			11 29				11 55							11 59				12 25				
Maidstone West	d																						
Rochester	d			11 32				11 58							12 02				12 28				
Chatham	d			11 36				12 01							12 06				12 31				
Gillingham (Kent)	a			11 40				12 05							12 10				12 35				
Rainham Kt	a			11 45				12 11							12 15				12 41				

Table T200-F

Saturdays

26 May to 8 December

London - Dartford and Gillingham

		SE	SE	SE ◇	SE	SE	SE	TL	SE	SE	SE	SE	SE	SE	SE ◇	SE	SE	SE	TL	SE	SE	SE	SE	SE
St Pancras Int'l ⊖	d			11 55											12 27									
Stratford International ⊖ ⛴	d			12 02											12 34									
Ebbsfleet International	d			12 13											12 45									
London Charing Cross ⊖	d	11 24			11 32				11 42		11 48		11 54			12 02				12 12		12 18		12 24
London Waterloo (East) ⊖	d	11 28			11 35				11 45		11 51		11 58			12 05				12 15		12 21		12 28
London Cannon Street ⊖	d		11 35			11 38				11 47		11 54		12 05			12 08				12 17		12 24	
London Bridge ⊖	d	11 35	11 39		11 41	11 43		11 48	11 51	11 51	11 57	11 58	12 05	12 09		12 11	12 13		12 18	12 21	12 21	12 27	12 28	12 35
Deptford	d		11 45					11 55				12 05		12 15					12 25				12 35	
Greenwich ⛴	d		11 47					11 57				12 07		12 17					12 27				12 37	
Maze Hill	d		11 50					12 00				12 10		12 20					12 30				12 40	
Westcombe Park	d		11 52					12 02				12 12		12 22					12 32				12 42	
London Victoria ⊖	d						11 36											12 06						
Denmark Hill	d						11 46											12 16						
Peckham Rye	d						11 48											12 18						
Nunhead	d						11 51											12 21						
New Cross ⊖	d					11 49				11 57							12 19				12 27			
St Johns	d					11 51				11 59							12 21				12 29			
Lewisham ⛴	d	11 45				11 54	11 56		12 00	12 04			12 15				12 24	12 26		12 30	12 34			12 45
Blackheath	d	11 48					11 59		12 03	12 07			12 18					12 29		12 33	12 37			12 48
Kidbrooke	d	11 51					12 02			12 10			12 21					12 32			12 40			12 51
Eltham	d	11 54					12 06			12 13			12 24					12 36			12 43			12 54
Falconwood	d	11 57					12 09			12 16			12 27					12 39			12 46			12 57
Welling	d	12 00					12 11			12 19			12 30					12 41			12 49			13 00
Bexleyheath	d	12 03					12 15			12 22			12 33					12 45			12 52			13 03
Barnehurst	d	12 06					12 17			12 28			12 36					12 47			12 58			13 06
Hither Green	d					11 59					12 07						12 29					12 37		
Lee	d					12 01					12 09						12 31					12 39		
Mottingham	d					12 04					12 12						12 34					12 42		
New Eltham	d				11 55	12 07					12 15					12 25	12 37					12 45		
Sidcup	d				11 58	12 10					12 18					12 28	12 40					12 48		
Albany Park	d					12 13					12 21						12 43					12 51		
Bexley	d				12 02	12 15					12 23					12 32	12 45					12 53		
Crayford	d				12 05	12 21					12 27					12 35	12 51					12 57		
Charlton	d		11 55			12a49		12 05	12 08			12 15		12 25			13a19		12 35	12 38			12 45	
Woolwich Dockyard	d		11 58						12 11			12 18		12 28						12 41			12 48	
Woolwich Arsenal ⛴	d		12 01					12 10	12 14			12 21		12 31					12 40	12 44			12 51	
Plumstead	d		12 03					12 13	12 16			12 23		12 33					12 43	12 46			12 53	
Abbey Wood	d		12 06					12 16	12 20			12 26		12 36					12 46	12 50			12 56	
Belvedere	d		12 09						12 23			12 29		12 39						12 53			12 59	
Erith	d		12 12						12 25			12 32		12 42						12 55			13 02	
Slade Green	d		12a15					12 22	12 31	12a35		12a36		12a45					12 52	13 01	13a05		13a06	
Dartford	a	12 14			12 10		12 24	12 27	12 38		12 32		12 44			12 40		12 54	12 57	13 08		13 02		13 14
	d				12 11		12 24	12 28								12 41		12 54	12 58					
Stone Crossing	d				12 15			12 32								12 45			13 02					
Greenhithe for Bluewater	d				12 17		12 30	12 34								12 47		13 00	13 04					
Swanscombe	d				12 20			12 37								12 50			13 07					
Northfleet	d				12 22			12 39								12 52			13 09					
Gravesend	d			12 18	12a26		12a39	12 43							12 49	12a56		13a09	13 13					
Higham	d							12 49											13 19					
Strood	d			12 29				12 55							12 59				13 25					
Maidstone West	d																							
Rochester	d			12 32				12 58							13 02				13 28					
Chatham	d			12 36				13 01							13 06				13 31					
Gillingham (Kent)	a			12 40				13 05							13 10				13 35					
Rainham Kt	a			12 45				13 11							13 15				13 41					

Please note, Network Rail have stated that further updates to this timetable are possible during the validity period.

Table T200-F

Saturdays

26 May to 8 December

London - Dartford and Gillingham

		SE	SE ◇	SE	SE	SE	TL	SE	SE	SE	SE	SE	SE	SE ◇	SE	SE	SE	TL	SE	SE	SE	SE	SE
St Pancras Int'l	d		12 52											13 25									
Stratford International	d		12 59											13 32									
Ebbsfleet International	d		13 13											13 43									
London Charing Cross	d			12 32				12 42		12 48		12 54			13 02				13 12		13 18		13 24
London Waterloo (East)	d			12 35				12 45		12 51		12 58			13 05				13 15		13 21		13 28
London Cannon Street	d	12 35			12 38				12 47		12 54		13 05			13 08				13 17		13 24	
London Bridge	d	12 39		12 41	12 43		12 48	12 51	12 51	12 57	12 58	13 05	13 09		13 11	13 13		13 18	13 21	13 21	13 27	13 28	13 35
Deptford	d	12 45					12 55				13 05		13 15					13 25				13 35	
Greenwich	d	12 47					12 57				13 07		13 17					13 27				13 37	
Maze Hill	d	12 50					13 00				13 10		13 20					13 30				13 40	
Westcombe Park	d	12 52					13 02				13 12		13 22					13 32				13 42	
London Victoria	d					12 36											13 06						
Denmark Hill	d					12 46											13 16						
Peckham Rye	d					12 48											13 18						
Nunhead	d					12 51											13 21						
New Cross	d				12 49				12 57							13 19				13 27			
St Johns	d				12 51				12 59							13 21				13 29			
Lewisham	d				12 54	12 56		13 00	13 04			13 15				13 24	13 26		13 30	13 34			13 45
Blackheath	d					12 59		13 03	13 07			13 18					13 29		13 33	13 37			13 48
Kidbrooke	d					13 02			13 10			13 21					13 32			13 40			13 51
Eltham	d					13 06			13 13			13 24					13 36			13 43			13 54
Falconwood	d					13 09			13 16			13 27					13 39			13 46			13 57
Welling	d					13 11			13 19			13 30					13 41			13 49			14 00
Bexleyheath	d					13 15			13 22			13 33					13 45			13 52			14 03
Barnehurst	d					13 17			13 28			13 36					13 47			13 58			14 06
Hither Green	d				12 59					13 07						13 29					13 37		
Lee	d				13 01					13 09						13 31					13 39		
Mottingham	d				13 04					13 12						13 34					13 42		
New Eltham	d			12 55	13 07					13 15					13 25	13 37					13 45		
Sidcup	d			12 58	13 10					13 18					13 28	13 40					13 48		
Albany Park	d				13 13					13 21						13 43					13 51		
Bexley	d			13 02	13 15					13 23					13 32	13 45					13 53		
Crayford	d			13 05	13 21					13 27					13 35	13 51					13 57		
Charlton	d	12 55			13a49		13 05	13 08			13 15		13 25			14a19		13 35	13 38			13 45	
Woolwich Dockyard	d	12 58						13 11			13 18		13 28						13 41			13 48	
Woolwich Arsenal	d	13 01					13 10	13 14			13 21		13 31					13 40	13 44			13 51	
Plumstead	d	13 03					13 13	13 16			13 23		13 33					13 43	13 46			13 53	
Abbey Wood	d	13 06					13 16	13 20			13 26		13 36					13 46	13 50			13 56	
Belvedere	d	13 09						13 23			13 29		13 39						13 53			13 59	
Erith	d	13 12						13 25			13 32		13 42						13 55			14 02	
Slade Green	d	13a15					13 22	13 31	13a35		13a36		13a45					13 52	14 01	14a05		14a06	
Dartford	a			13 10		13 24	13 27	13 38		13 32		13 44			13 40		13 54	13 57	14 08		14 02		14 14
	d			13 11		13 24	13 28								13 41		13 54	13 58					
Stone Crossing	d			13 15			13 32								13 45			14 02					
Greenhithe for Bluewater	d			13 17		13 30	13 34								13 47		14 00	14 04					
Swanscombe	d			13 20			13 37								13 50			14 07					
Northfleet	d			13 22			13 39								13 52			14 09					
Gravesend	d		13 18	13a26		13a39	13 43							13 48	13a56		14a09	14 13					
Higham	d						13 49											14 19					
Strood	d		13 29				13 55							13 59				14 25					
Maidstone West	d																						
Rochester	d		13 32				13 58							14 02				14 28					
Chatham	d		13 36				14 01							14 06				14 31					
Gillingham (Kent)	a		13 40				14 05							14 10				14 35					
Rainham Kt	a		13 45				14 11							14 15				14 41					

Table T200-F

Saturdays

26 May to 8 December

London - Dartford and Gillingham

		SE	SE ◇	SE	SE	SE	TL	SE	SE	SE	SE	SE	SE	SE ◇	SE	SE	SE	TL	SE	SE	SE	SE	SE	SE
St Pancras Int'l	d		13 55											14 25										
Stratford International	d		14 02											14 32										
Ebbsfleet International	d		14 13											14 43										
London Charing Cross	d			13 32				13 42		13 48		13 54			14 02				14 12		14 18		14 24	
London Waterloo (East)	d			13 35				13 45		13 51		13 58			14 05				14 15		14 21		14 28	
London Cannon Street	d	13 35			13 38				13 47		13 54		14 05			14 08				14 17		14 24		14 35
London Bridge	d	13 39		13 41	13 43		13 48	13 51	13 51	13 57	13 58	14 05	14 09		14 11	14 13		14 18	14 21	14 21	14 27	14 28	14 35	14 39
Deptford	d	13 45					13 55				14 05		14 15					14 25				14 35		14 45
Greenwich	d	13 47					13 57				14 07		14 17					14 27				14 37		14 47
Maze Hill	d	13 50					14 00				14 10		14 20					14 30				14 40		14 50
Westcombe Park	d	13 52					14 02				14 12		14 22					14 32				14 42		14 52
London Victoria	d					13 36											14 06							
Denmark Hill	d					13 46											14 16							
Peckham Rye	d					13 48											14 18							
Nunhead	d					13 51											14 21							
New Cross	d				13 49				13 57							14 19				14 27				
St Johns	d				13 51				13 59							14 21				14 29				
Lewisham	d				13 54	13 56		14 00	14 04			14 15				14 24	14 26		14 30	14 34			14 45	
Blackheath	d					13 59		14 03	14 07			14 18					14 29		14 33	14 37			14 48	
Kidbrooke	d					14 02			14 10			14 21					14 32			14 40			14 51	
Eltham	d					14 06			14 13			14 24					14 36			14 43			14 54	
Falconwood	d					14 09			14 16			14 27					14 39			14 46			14 57	
Welling	d					14 11			14 19			14 30					14 41			14 49			15 00	
Bexleyheath	d					14 15			14 22			14 33					14 45			14 52			15 03	
Barnehurst	d					14 17			14 28			14 36					14 47			14 58			15 06	
Hither Green	d				13 59					14 07						14 31					14 37			
Lee	d				14 01					14 09						14 33					14 39			
Mottingham	d				14 04					14 12						14 36					14 42			
New Eltham	d			13 55	14 07					14 15					14 25	14 39					14 45			
Sidcup	d			13 58	14 10					14 18					14 28	14 42					14 48			
Albany Park	d				14 13					14 21						14 45					14 51			
Bexley	d			14 02	14 15					14 23					14 32	14 47					14 53			
Crayford	d			14 05	14 21					14 27					14 35	14 52					14 57			
Charlton	d	13 55			14a49		14 05	14 08			14 15		14 25			15a19		14 35	14 38			14 45		14 55
Woolwich Dockyard	d	13 58						14 11			14 18		14 28						14 41			14 48		14 58
Woolwich Arsenal	d	14 01					14 10	14 14			14 21		14 31					14 40	14 44			14 51		15 01
Plumstead	d	14 03					14 13	14 16			14 23		14 33					14 43	14 46			14 53		15 03
Abbey Wood	d	14 06					14 16	14 20			14 26		14 36					14 46	14 50			14 56		15 06
Belvedere	d	14 09						14 23			14 29		14 39						14 53			14 59		15 09
Erith	d	14 12						14 25			14 32		14 42						14 55			15 02		15 12
Slade Green	d	14a15					14 22	14 31	14a35		14a36		14a45					14 52	15 01	15a05		15a06		15a15
Dartford	a			14 10		14 24	14 27	14 38		14 32		14 44			14 40		14 54	14 57	15 08		15 02		15 14	
	d			14 11		14 24	14 28								14 41		14 54	14 58						
Stone Crossing	d			14 15			14 32								14 45			15 02						
Greenhithe for Bluewater	d			14 17		14 30	14 34								14 47		15 00	15 04						
Swanscombe	d			14 20			14 37								14 50			15 07						
Northfleet	d			14 22			14 39								14 52			15 09						
Gravesend	d		14 18	14a26		14a39	14 43							14 48	14a56		15a09	15 13						
Higham	d						14 49											15 19						
Strood	d		14 29				14 55							14 59				15 25						
Maidstone West	d																							
Rochester	d		14 32				14 58							15 02				15 28						
Chatham	d		14 36				15 01							15 06				15 31						
Gillingham (Kent)	a		14 40				15 05							15 10				15 35						
Rainham Kt	a		14 45				15 11							15 15				15 41						

Table T200-F

Saturdays

26 May to 8 December

London - Dartford and Gillingham

		SE ◇	SE	SE	SE	TL	SE	SE	SE	SE	SE	SE	SE ◇	SE	SE	SE	TL	SE	SE	SE	SE	SE	SE
St Pancras Int'l ⊖	d	14 55											15 25										
Stratford International ⊖	d	15 02											15 32										
Ebbsfleet International	d	15 13											15 43										
London Charing Cross ⊖	d		14 32				14 42		14 48		14 54			15 02				15 12		15 18		15 24	
London Waterloo (East) ⊖	d		14 35				14 45		14 51		14 58			15 05				15 15		15 21		15 28	
London Cannon Street ⊖	d			14 38				14 47		14 54		15 05			15 08				15 17		15 24		15 35
London Bridge ⊖	d		14 41	14 43		14 48	14 51	14 51	14 57	14 58	15 05	15 09		15 11	15 13		15 18	15 21	15 21	15 27	15 28	15 35	15 39
Deptford	d					14 55				15 05		15 15					15 25				15 35		15 45
Greenwich	d					14 57				15 07		15 17					15 27				15 37		15 47
Maze Hill	d					15 00				15 10		15 20					15 30				15 40		15 50
Westcombe Park	d					15 02				15 12		15 22					15 32				15 42		15 52
London Victoria ⊖	d				14 36											15 06							
Denmark Hill	d				14 46											15 16							
Peckham Rye	d				14 48											15 18							
Nunhead	d				14 51											15 21							
New Cross ⊖	d			14 49				14 57							15 19				15 27				
St Johns	d			14 51				14 59							15 21				15 29				
Lewisham	d			14 54	14 56		15 00	15 04			15 15				15 24	15 26		15 30	15 34			15 45	
Blackheath	d				14 59		15 03	15 07			15 18					15 29		15 33	15 37			15 48	
Kidbrooke	d				15 02			15 10			15 21					15 32			15 40			15 51	
Eltham	d				15 06			15 13			15 24					15 36			15 43			15 54	
Falconwood	d				15 09			15 16			15 27					15 39			15 46			15 57	
Welling	d				15 11			15 19			15 30					15 41			15 49			16 00	
Bexleyheath	d				15 15			15 22			15 33					15 45			15 52			16 03	
Barnehurst	d				15 17			15 28			15 36					15 47			15 58			16 06	
Hither Green	d			14 59					15 07						15 29					15 37			
Lee	d			15 01					15 09						15 31					15 39			
Mottingham	d			15 04					15 12						15 34					15 42			
New Eltham	d		14 55	15 07					15 15					15 25	15 37					15 45			
Sidcup	d		14 58	15 10					15 18					15 28	15 40					15 48			
Albany Park	d			15 13					15 21						15 43					15 51			
Bexley	d		15 02	15 15					15 23					15 32	15 45					15 53			
Crayford	d		15 05	15 21					15 27					15 35	15 51					15 57			
Charlton	d			15a49		15 05	15 08			15 15		15 25			16a19		15 35	15 38			15 45		15 55
Woolwich Dockyard	d						15 11			15 18		15 28						15 41			15 48		15 58
Woolwich Arsenal	d					15 10	15 14			15 21		15 31					15 40	15 44			15 51		16 01
Plumstead	d					15 13	15 16			15 23		15 33					15 43	15 46			15 53		16 03
Abbey Wood	d					15 16	15 20			15 26		15 36					15 46	15 50			15 56		16 06
Belvedere	d						15 23			15 29		15 39						15 53			15 59		16 09
Erith	d						15 25			15 32		15 42						15 55			16 02		16 12
Slade Green	d					15 22	15 31	15a35		15a36		15a45					15 52	16 01	16a05		16a06		16a15
Dartford	a		15 10		15 24	15 27	15 38		15 32		15 44			15 40		15 54	15 57	16 08		16 02		16 14	
	d		15 11		15 24	15 28								15 41		15 54	15 58						
Stone Crossing	d		15 15			15 32								15 45			16 02						
Greenhithe for Bluewater	d		15 17		15 30	15 34								15 47		16 00	16 04						
Swanscombe	d		15 20			15 37								15 50			16 07						
Northfleet	d		15 22			15 39								15 52			16 09						
Gravesend	d	15 18	15a26		15a39	15 43							15 48	15a56		16a09	16 13						
Higham	d					15 49											16 19						
Strood	d	15 29				15 55							15 59				16 25						
Maidstone West	d																						
Rochester	d	15 32				15 58							16 02				16 28						
Chatham	d	15 36				16 01							16 06				16 31						
Gillingham (Kent)	a	15 40				16 05							16 10				16 35						
Rainham Kt	a	15 45				16 11							16 15				16 41						

Table T200-F

Saturdays

26 May to 8 December

London - Dartford and Gillingham

		SE ◇	SE	SE	SE	TL	SE	SE	SE	SE	SE	SE	SE ◇	SE	SE	SE	TL	SE	SE	SE	SE	SE	SE	SE ◇
St Pancras Int'l ⊖	d	15 55											16 25											16 55
Stratford International ⊖	d	16 02											16 32											17 02
Ebbsfleet International	d	16 13											16 43											17 13
London Charing Cross ⊖	d		15 32				15 42		15 48		15 54			16 02				16 12		16 18		16 24		
London Waterloo (East) ⊖	d		15 35				15 45		15 51		15 58			16 05				16 15		16 21		16 28		
London Cannon Street ⊖	d			15 38				15 47		15 54		16 05			16 08				16 17		16 24		16 35	
London Bridge ⊖	d		15 41	15 43		15 48	15 51	15 51	15 57	15 58	16 05	16 09		16 11	16 13		16 18	16 21	16 21	16 27	16 28	16 35	16 39	
Deptford	d					15 55				16 05		16 15					16 25				16 35		16 45	
Greenwich	d					15 57				16 07		16 17					16 27				16 37		16 47	
Maze Hill	d					16 00				16 10		16 20					16 30				16 40		16 50	
Westcombe Park	d					16 02				16 12		16 22					16 32				16 42		16 52	
London Victoria ⊖	d				15 36											16 06								
Denmark Hill	d				15 46											16 16								
Peckham Rye	d				15 48											16 18								
Nunhead	d				15 51											16 21								
New Cross ⊖	d			15 49				15 57							16 19				16 27					
St Johns	d			15 51				15 59							16 21				16 29					
Lewisham	d			15 54	15 56		16 00	16 04			16 15				16 24	16 26		16 30	16 34			16 45		
Blackheath	d				15 59		16 03	16 07			16 18					16 29		16 33	16 37			16 48		
Kidbrooke	d				16 02			16 10			16 21					16 32			16 40			16 51		
Eltham	d				16 06			16 13			16 24					16 36			16 43			16 54		
Falconwood	d				16 09			16 16			16 27					16 39			16 46			16 57		
Welling	d				16 11			16 19			16 30					16 41			16 49			17 00		
Bexleyheath	d				16 15			16 22			16 33					16 45			16 52			17 03		
Barnehurst	d				16 17			16 28			16 36					16 47			16 58			17 06		
Hither Green	d			15 59					16 07						16 29					16 37				
Lee	d			16 01					16 09						16 31					16 39				
Mottingham	d			16 04					16 12						16 34					16 42				
New Eltham	d		15 55	16 07					16 15					16 25	16 37					16 45				
Sidcup	d		15 58	16 10					16 18					16 28	16 40					16 48				
Albany Park	d			16 13					16 21						16 43					16 51				
Bexley	d		16 02	16 15					16 23					16 32	16 45					16 53				
Crayford	d		16 05	16 21					16 27					16 35	16 51					16 57				
Charlton	d			16a49		16 05	16 08			16 15		16 25			17a19		16 35	16 38			16 45		16 55	
Woolwich Dockyard	d						16 11			16 18		16 28						16 41			16 48		16 58	
Woolwich Arsenal	d					16 10	16 14			16 21		16 31					16 40	16 44			16 51		17 01	
Plumstead	d					16 13	16 16			16 23		16 33					16 43	16 46			16 53		17 03	
Abbey Wood	d					16 16	16 20			16 26		16 36					16 46	16 50			16 56		17 06	
Belvedere	d						16 23			16 29		16 39						16 53			16 59		17 09	
Erith	d						16 25			16 32		16 42						16 55			17 02		17 12	
Slade Green	d					16 22	16 31	16a35		16a36		16a45					16 52	17 01	17a05		17a06		17a15	
Dartford	a		16 10		16 24	16 27	16 38		16 32		16 44			16 40		16 54	16 57	17 08		17 02		17 14		
	d		16 11		16 24	16 28								16 41		16 54	16 58							
Stone Crossing	d		16 15			16 32								16 45			17 02							
Greenhithe for Bluewater	d		16 17		16 30	16 34								16 47		17 00	17 04							
Swanscombe	d		16 20			16 37								16 50			17 07							
Northfleet	d		16 22			16 39								16 52			17 09							
Gravesend	d	16 18	16a26		16a39	16 43							16 48	16a56		17a09	17 13							17 18
Higham	d					16 49											17 19							
Strood	d	16 29				16 55							16 59				17 25							17 29
Maidstone West	d																							
Rochester	d	16 32				16 58							17 02				17 28							17 32
Chatham	d	16 36				17 01							17 06				17 31							17 36
Gillingham (Kent)	a	16 40				17 05							17 10				17 35							17 40
Rainham Kt	a	16 45				17 11							17 15				17 41							17 45

Table T200-F

Saturdays

26 May to 8 December

London - Dartford and Gillingham

		SE	SE	SE	TL	SE	SE	SE	SE	SE	SE	SE ◇	SE	SE	SE	TL	SE	SE	SE	SE	SE	SE	SE ◇
St Pancras Int'l ⊖	d											17 25											17 55
Stratford International ⊖	d											17 32											18 02
Ebbsfleet International	d											17 43											18 13
London Charing Cross ⊖	d	16 32				16 42		16 48		16 54			17 02				17 12		17 18		17 24		
London Waterloo (East) ⊖	d	16 35				16 45		16 51		16 58			17 05				17 15		17 21		17 28		
London Cannon Street ⊖	d		16 38				16 47		16 54		17 05			17 08				17 17		17 24		17 35	
London Bridge ⊖	d	16 41	16 43		16 48	16 51	16 51	16 57	16 58	17 05	17 09		17 11	17 13		17 18	17 21	17 21	17 27	17 28	17 35	17 39	
Deptford	d				16 55				17 05		17 15					17 25				17 35		17 45	
Greenwich	d				16 57				17 07		17 17					17 27				17 37		17 47	
Maze Hill	d				17 00				17 10		17 20					17 30				17 40		17 50	
Westcombe Park	d				17 02				17 12		17 22					17 32				17 42		17 52	
London Victoria ⊖	d			16 36											17 06								
Denmark Hill	d			16 46											17 16								
Peckham Rye	d			16 48											17 18								
Nunhead	d			16 51											17 21								
New Cross ⊖	d		16 49				16 57							17 19				17 27					
St Johns	d		16 51				16 59							17 21				17 29					
Lewisham	d		16 54	16 56		17 00	17 04			17 15				17 24	17 26		17 30	17 34			17 45		
Blackheath	d			16 59		17 03	17 07			17 18					17 29		17 33	17 37			17 48		
Kidbrooke	d			17 02			17 10			17 21					17 32			17 40			17 51		
Eltham	d			17 06			17 13			17 24					17 36			17 43			17 54		
Falconwood	d			17 09			17 16			17 27					17 39			17 46			17 57		
Welling	d			17 11			17 19			17 30					17 41			17 49			18 00		
Bexleyheath	d			17 15			17 22			17 33					17 45			17 52			18 03		
Barnehurst	d			17 17			17 28			17 36					17 47			17 58			18 06		
Hither Green	d		16 59					17 07						17 29					17 37				
Lee	d		17 01					17 09						17 31					17 39				
Mottingham	d		17 04					17 12						17 34					17 42				
New Eltham	d	16 55	17 07					17 15					17 25	17 37					17 45				
Sidcup	d	16 58	17 10					17 18					17 28	17 40					17 48				
Albany Park	d		17 13					17 21						17 43					17 51				
Bexley	d	17 02	17 15					17 23					17 32	17 45					17 53				
Crayford	d	17 05	17 21					17 27					17 35	17 51					17 57				
Charlton	d		17a49		17 05	17 08			17 15		17 25			18a19		17 35	17 38			17 45		17 55	
Woolwich Dockyard	d					17 11			17 18		17 28						17 41			17 48		17 58	
Woolwich Arsenal	d				17 10	17 14			17 21		17 31					17 40	17 44			17 51		18 01	
Plumstead	d				17 13	17 16			17 23		17 33					17 43	17 46			17 53		18 03	
Abbey Wood	d				17 16	17 20			17 26		17 36					17 46	17 50			17 56		18 06	
Belvedere	d					17 23			17 29		17 39						17 53			17 59		18 09	
Erith	d					17 25			17 32		17 42						17 55			18 02		18 12	
Slade Green	d				17 22	17 31	17a35		17a36		17a45					17 52	18 01	18a05		18a06		18a15	
Dartford	a	17 10		17 24	17 27	17 38		17 32		17 44			17 40		17 54	17 57	18 08		18 02		18 14		
	d	17 11		17 24	17 28								17 41		17 54	17 58							
Stone Crossing	d	17 15			17 32								17 45			18 02							
Greenhithe for Bluewater	d	17 17		17 30	17 34								17 47		18 00	18 04							
Swanscombe	d	17 20			17 37								17 50			18 07							
Northfleet	d	17 22			17 39								17 52			18 09							
Gravesend	d	17a26		17a39	17 43							17 48	17a56		18a09	18 13							18 18
Higham	d				17 49											18 19							
Strood	d				17 55							17 59				18 25							18 29
Maidstone West	d																						
Rochester	d				17 58							18 02				18 28							18 32
Chatham	d				18 01							18 06				18 31							18 36
Gillingham (Kent)	a				18 05							18 10				18 35							18 40
Rainham Kt	a				18 11							18 15				18 41							18 45

Table T200-F

Saturdays

26 May to 8 December

London - Dartford and Gillingham

		SE	SE	SE	TL	SE	SE	SE	SE	SE	SE	SE ◇	SE	SE	SE	TL	SE	SE	SE	SE	SE	SE	SE ◇	SE
St Pancras Int'l ⊖	d											18 25											18 55	
Stratford International ⊖	d											18 32											19 02	
Ebbsfleet International	d											18 43											19 13	
London Charing Cross ⊖	d	17 32				17 42		17 48		17 54			18 02				18 12		18 18		18 24			18 32
London Waterloo (East) ⊖	d	17 35				17 45		17 51		17 58			18 05				18 15		18 21		18 28			18 35
London Cannon Street ⊖	d		17 38				17 47		17 54		18 05			18 08				18 17		18 24		18 35		
London Bridge ⊖	d	17 41	17 43		17 48	17 51	17 51	17 57	17 58	18 05	18 09		18 11	18 13		18 18	18 21	18 21	18 27	18 28	18 35	18 39		18 41
Deptford	d				17 55				18 05		18 15					18 25				18 35		18 45		
Greenwich	d				17 57				18 07		18 17					18 27				18 37		18 47		
Maze Hill	d				18 00				18 10		18 20					18 30				18 40		18 50		
Westcombe Park	d				18 02				18 12		18 22					18 32				18 42		18 52		
London Victoria ⊖	d			17 36											18 06									
Denmark Hill	d			17 46											18 16									
Peckham Rye	d			17 48											18 18									
Nunhead	d			17 51											18 21									
New Cross ⊖	d		17 49				17 57							18 19				18 27						
St Johns	d		17 51				17 59							18 21				18 29						
Lewisham	d		17 54	17 56		18 00	18 04			18 15				18 24	18 26		18 30	18 34			18 45			
Blackheath	d			17 59		18 03	18 07			18 18					18 29		18 33	18 37			18 48			
Kidbrooke	d			18 02			18 10			18 21					18 32			18 40			18 51			
Eltham	d			18 06			18 13			18 24					18 36			18 43			18 54			
Falconwood	d			18 09			18 16			18 27					18 39			18 46			18 57			
Welling	d			18 11			18 19			18 30					18 41			18 49			19 00			
Bexleyheath	d			18 15			18 22			18 33					18 45			18 52			19 03			
Barnehurst	d			18 17			18 28			18 36					18 47			18 58			19 06			
Hither Green	d		17 59					18 07						18 29					18 37					
Lee	d		18 01					18 09						18 31					18 39					
Mottingham	d		18 04					18 12						18 34					18 42					
New Eltham	d	17 55	18 07					18 15					18 25	18 37					18 45					18 55
Sidcup	d	17 58	18 10					18 18					18 28	18 40					18 48					18 58
Albany Park	d		18 13					18 21						18 43					18 51					
Bexley	d	18 02	18 15					18 23					18 32	18 45					18 53					19 02
Crayford	d	18 05	18 21					18 27					18 35	18 51					18 57					19 05
Charlton	d		18a49		18 05	18 08			18 15		18 25			19a19		18 35	18 38			18 45		18 55		
Woolwich Dockyard	d					18 11			18 18		18 28						18 41			18 48		18 58		
Woolwich Arsenal	d				18 10	18 14			18 21		18 31					18 40	18 44			18 51		19 01		
Plumstead	d				18 13	18 16			18 23		18 33					18 43	18 46			18 53		19 03		
Abbey Wood	d				18 16	18 20			18 26		18 36					18 46	18 50			18 56		19 06		
Belvedere	d					18 23			18 29		18 39						18 53			18 59		19 09		
Erith	d					18 25			18 32		18 42						18 55			19 02		19 12		
Slade Green	d				18 22	18 31	18a35		18a36		18a45					18 52	19 01	19a05		19a06		19a15		
Dartford	a	18 10		18 24	18 27	18 38		18 32		18 44			18 40		18 54	18 57	19 08		19 02		19 14			19 10
	d	18 11		18 24	18 28								18 41		18 54	18 58								19 11
Stone Crossing	d	18 15			18 32								18 45			19 02								19 15
Greenhithe for Bluewater	d	18 17		18 30	18 34								18 47		19 00	19 04								19 17
Swanscombe	d	18 20			18 37								18 50			19 07								19 20
Northfleet	d	18 22			18 39								18 52			19 09								19 22
Gravesend	d	18a26		18a39	18 43							18 48	18a56		19a09	19 13							19 18	19a26
Higham	d				18 49											19 19								
Strood	d				18 55							18 59				19 25							19 29	
Maidstone West	d																							
Rochester	d				18 58							19 02				19 28							19 32	
Chatham	d				19 01							19 06				19 31							19 36	
Gillingham (Kent)	a				19 05							19 10				19 35							19 40	
Rainham Kt	a				19 11							19 15				19 41							19 45	

Please note, Network Rail have stated that further updates to this timetable are possible during the validity period.

Table T200-F

Saturdays

26 May to 8 December

London - Dartford and Gillingham

		SE	SE	TL	SE	SE	SE	SE	SE	SE	SE ◇	SE	SE	SE	TL	SE	SE	SE	SE	SE	SE	SE ◇	SE
St Pancras Int'l	d										19 25											19 55	
Stratford International	d										19 32											20 02	
Ebbsfleet International	d										19 43											20 13	
London Charing Cross	d				18 42		18 48		18 54			19 02				19 12		19 18		19 24			19 32
London Waterloo (East)	d				18 45		18 51		18 58			19 05				19 15		19 21		19 28			19 35
London Cannon Street	d	18 38				18 47		18 54		19 05			19 08				19 17		19 24		19 35		
London Bridge	d	18 43		18 48	18 51	18 51	18 57	18 58	19 05	19 09		19 11	19 13		19 18	19 21	19 21	19 27	19 28	19 35	19 39		19 41
Deptford	d			18 55				19 05		19 15					19 25				19 35		19 45		
Greenwich	d			18 57				19 07		19 17					19 27				19 37		19 47		
Maze Hill	d			19 00				19 10		19 20					19 30				19 40		19 50		
Westcombe Park	d			19 02				19 12		19 22					19 32				19 42		19 52		
London Victoria	d		18 36											19 06									
Denmark Hill	d		18 46											19 16									
Peckham Rye	d		18 48											19 18									
Nunhead	d		18 51											19 21									
New Cross	d	18 49				18 57							19 19				19 27						
St Johns	d	18 51				18 59							19 21				19 29						
Lewisham	d	18 54	18 56		19 00	19 04			19 15				19 24	19 26		19 30	19 34			19 45			
Blackheath	d		18 59		19 03	19 07			19 18					19 29		19 33	19 37			19 48			
Kidbrooke	d		19 02			19 10			19 21					19 32			19 40			19 51			
Eltham	d		19 06			19 13			19 24					19 36			19 43			19 54			
Falconwood	d		19 09			19 16			19 27					19 39			19 46			19 57			
Welling	d		19 11			19 19			19 30					19 41			19 49			20 00			
Bexleyheath	d		19 15			19 22			19 33					19 45			19 52			20 03			
Barnehurst	d		19 17			19a25			19 36					19 47			19a55			20 06			
Hither Green	d	18 59					19 07						19 29					19 37					
Lee	d	19 01					19 09						19 31					19 39					
Mottingham	d	19 04					19 12						19 34					19 42					
New Eltham	d	19 07					19 15					19 25	19 37					19 45					19 55
Sidcup	d	19 10					19 18					19 28	19 40					19 48					19 58
Albany Park	d	19 13					19 21						19 43					19 51					
Bexley	d	19 15					19 23					19 32	19 45					19 53					20 02
Crayford	d	19 21					19 27					19 35	19 51					19 57					20 05
Charlton	d	19a49		19 05	19 08			19 15		19 25			20a19		19 35	19 38			19 45		19 55		
Woolwich Dockyard	d				19 11			19 18		19 28						19 41			19 48		19 58		
Woolwich Arsenal	d			19 10	19 14			19 21		19 31					19 40	19 44			19 51		20 01		
Plumstead	d			19 13	19 16			19 23		19 33					19 43	19 46			19 53		20 03		
Abbey Wood	d			19 16	19 20			19 26		19 36					19 46	19 50			19 56		20 06		
Belvedere	d				19 23			19 29		19 39						19 53			19 59		20 09		
Erith	d				19 25			19 32		19 42						19 55			20 02		20 12		
Slade Green	d			19 22	19 31			19a36		19a45					19 52	20 01			20a06		20a15		
Dartford	a		19 24	19 27	19 38		19 32		19 44			19 40		19 54	19 57	20 08		20 02		20 14			20 10
	d		19 24	19 28								19 41		19 54	19 58								20 11
Stone Crossing	d			19 32								19 45			20 02								20 15
Greenhithe for Bluewater	d		19 30	19 34								19 47		20 00	20 04								20 17
Swanscombe	d			19 37								19 50			20 07								20 20
Northfleet	d			19 39								19 52			20 09								20 22
Gravesend	d		19a39	19 43							19 48	19a56		20a09	20 13							20 18	20a26
Higham	d			19 49											20 19								
Strood	d			19 55							19 59				20 25							20 29	
Maidstone West	d																						
Rochester	d			19 58							20 02				20 28							20 32	
Chatham	d			20 01							20 06				20 31							20 36	
Gillingham (Kent)	a			20 05							20 10				20 35							20 40	
Rainham Kt	a			20 11							20 15				20 41							20 45	

Table T200-F

Saturdays

26 May to 8 December

London - Dartford and Gillingham

		SE	SE	TL	SE	SE	SE	SE	SE	SE	SE ◇	SE	SE	SE	TL	SE	SE	SE	SE	SE	SE ◇	SE	SE	SE
St Pancras Int'l	d										20 25										20 55			
Stratford International	d										20 32										21 02			
Ebbsfleet International	d										20 43										21 13			
London Charing Cross	d				19 42		19 48		19 54			20 02				20 12		20 18	20 24			20 32		
London Waterloo (East)	d				19 45		19 51		19 58			20 05				20 15		20 21	20 28			20 35		
London Cannon Street	d	19 38				19 47		19 54		20 05			20 08				20 17			20 32			20 38	
London Bridge	d	19 43		19 48	19 51	19 51	19 57	19 58	20 05	20 09		20 11	20 13		20 18	20 21	20 21	20 27	20 35	20 36		20 41	20 43	
Deptford	d			19 55				20 05		20 15					20 25					20 42				
Greenwich	d			19 57				20 07		20 17					20 27					20 44				
Maze Hill	d			20 00				20 10		20 20					20 30					20 47				
Westcombe Park	d			20 02				20 12		20 22					20 32					20 49				
London Victoria	d		19 36											20 06										20 36
Denmark Hill	d		19 46											20 16										20 46
Peckham Rye	d		19 48											20 18										20 48
Nunhead	d		19 51											20 21										20 51
New Cross	d	19 49				19 57							20 19				20 27						20 49	
St Johns	d	19 51				19 59							20 21				20 29						20 51	
Lewisham	d	19 54	19 56		20 00	20 04			20 15				20 24	20 26		20 30	20 34		20 45				20 54	20 56
Blackheath	d		19 59		20 03	20 07			20 18					20 29		20 33	20 37		20 48					20 59
Kidbrooke	d		20 02			20 10			20 21					20 32			20 40		20 51					21 02
Eltham	d		20 06			20 13			20 24					20 36			20 43		20 54					21 06
Falconwood	d		20 09			20 16			20 27					20 39			20 46		20 57					21 09
Welling	d		20 11			20 19			20 30					20 41			20 49		21 00					21 11
Bexleyheath	d		20 15			20 22			20 33					20 45			20 52		21 03					21 15
Barnehurst	d		20 17			20a25			20 36					20 47			20a55		21 06					21 17
Hither Green	d	19 59					20 07						20 29					20 37					20 59	
Lee	d	20 01					20 09						20 31					20 39					21 01	
Mottingham	d	20 04					20 12						20 34					20 42					21 04	
New Eltham	d	20 07					20 15					20 25	20 37					20 45				20 55	21 07	
Sidcup	d	20 10					20 18					20 28	20 40					20 48				20 58	21 10	
Albany Park	d	20 13					20 21						20 43					20 51					21 13	
Bexley	d	20 15					20 23					20 32	20 45					20 53				21 02	21 15	
Crayford	d	20 21					20 27					20 35	20 51					20 57				21 05	21 21	
Charlton	d	20a49		20 05	20 08			20 15		20 25			21a19		20 35	20 38				20 52			21a49	
Woolwich Dockyard	d				20 11			20 18		20 28						20 41				20 55				
Woolwich Arsenal	d			20 10	20 14			20 21		20 31					20 40	20 44				20 58				
Plumstead	d			20 13	20 16			20 23		20 33					20 43	20 46				21 00				
Abbey Wood	d			20 16	20 20			20 26		20 36					20 46	20 50				21 03				
Belvedere	d				20 23			20 29		20 39						20 53				21 06				
Erith	d				20 25			20 32		20 42						20 55				21 09				
Slade Green	d			20 22	20 31			20a36		20a45					20 52	21 01				21a13				
Dartford	a		20 24	20 27	20 38		20 32		20 44			20 40		20 54	20 57	21 08		21 02	21 14			21 10		21 24
	d		20 24	20 28								20 41		20 54	20 58							21 11		21 24
Stone Crossing	d			20 32								20 45			21 02							21 15		
Greenhithe for Bluewater	d		20 30	20 34								20 47		21 00	21 04							21 17		21 30
Swanscombe	d			20 37								20 50			21 07							21 20		
Northfleet	d			20 39								20 52			21 09							21 22		
Gravesend	d		20a39	20 43							20 48	20a56		21a09	21 13						21 18	21a26		21a39
Higham	d			20 49											21 19									
Strood	d			20 55							20 59				21 25						21 29			
Maidstone West	d																							
Rochester	d			20 58							21 02				21 28						21 32			
Chatham	d			21 01							21 06				21 31						21 36			
Gillingham (Kent)	a			21 05							21 10				21 35						21 40			
Rainham Kt	a			21 11							21 15				21 41						21 45			

Please note, Network Rail have stated that further updates to this timetable are possible during the validity period.

Saturdays

26 May to 8 December

London - Dartford and Gillingham

		TL	SE	SE	SE	SE	SE	SE ◇	SE	SE	SE	TL	SE	SE	SE	SE	SE ◇	SE	SE	SE	TL	SE	SE
St Pancras Int'l ⊖	d							21 25									21 55						
Stratford International ⊖	d							21 32									22 02						
Ebbsfleet International	d							21 43									22 13						
London Charing Cross ⊖	d		20 42		20 48	20 54			21 02				21 12	21 18	21 24			21 32				21 42	21 48
London Waterloo (East) ⊖	d		20 45		20 51	20 58			21 05				21 15	21 21	21 28			21 35				21 45	21 51
London Cannon Street ⊖	d			20 47			21 02			21 08						21 32			21 38				
London Bridge ⊖	d	20 48	20 51	20 51	20 57	21 05	21 06		21 11	21 13		21 18	21 21	21 27	21 35	21 36		21 41	21 43		21 48	21 51	21 57
Deptford	d	20 55					21 12					21 25				21 42					21 55		
Greenwich	d	20 57					21 14					21 27				21 44					21 57		
Maze Hill	d	21 00					21 17					21 30				21 47					22 00		
Westcombe Park	d	21 02					21 19					21 32				21 49					22 02		
London Victoria ⊖	d										21 06									21 36			
Denmark Hill	d										21 16									21 46			
Peckham Rye	d										21 18									21 48			
Nunhead	d										21 21									21 51			
New Cross ⊖	d			20 57						21 19									21 49				
St Johns	d			20 59						21 21									21 51				
Lewisham	d		21 00	21 04		21 15				21 24	21 26		21 30		21 45				21 54	21 56		22 00	
Blackheath	d		21 03	21 07		21 18					21 29		21 33		21 48					21 59		22 03	
Kidbrooke	d			21 10		21 21					21 32				21 51					22 02			
Eltham	d			21 13		21 24					21 36				21 54					22 06			
Falconwood	d			21 16		21 27					21 39				21 57					22 09			
Welling	d			21 19		21 30					21 41				22 00					22 11			
Bexleyheath	d			21 22		21 33					21 45				22 03					22 15			
Barnehurst	d			21a25		21 36					21 47				22 06					22 17			
Hither Green	d				21 07					21 29				21 37					21 59				22 07
Lee	d				21 09					21 31				21 39					22 01				22 09
Mottingham	d				21 12					21 34				21 42					22 04				22 12
New Eltham	d				21 15				21 25	21 37				21 45				21 55	22 07				22 15
Sidcup	d				21 18				21 28	21 40				21 48				21 58	22 10				22 18
Albany Park	d				21 21					21 43				21 51					22 13				22 21
Bexley	d				21 23				21 32	21 45				21 53				22 02	22 15				22 23
Crayford	d				21 27				21 35	21 51				21 57				22 05	22 21				22 27
Charlton	d	21 05	21 08				21 22			22a19		21 35	21 38			21 52			22a49		22 05	22 08	
Woolwich Dockyard	d		21 11				21 25						21 41			21 55						22 11	
Woolwich Arsenal	d	21 10	21 14				21 28					21 40	21 44			21 58					22 10	22 14	
Plumstead	d	21 13	21 16				21 30					21 43	21 46			22 00					22 13	22 16	
Abbey Wood	d	21 16	21 20				21 33					21 46	21 50			22 03					22 16	22 20	
Belvedere	d		21 23				21 36						21 53			22 06						22 23	
Erith	d		21 25				21 39						21 55			22 09						22 25	
Slade Green	d	21 22	21 31				21a43					21 52	22 01			22a13					22 22	22 31	
Dartford	a	21 27	21 38		21 32	21 44			21 40		21 54	21 57	22 08	22 02	22 14			22 10		22 24	22 27	22 38	22 32
	d	21 28							21 41		21 54	21 58						22 11		22 24	22 28		
Stone Crossing	d	21 32							21 45			22 02						22 15			22 32		
Greenhithe for Bluewater	d	21 34							21 47		22 00	22 04						22 17		22 30	22 34		
Swanscombe	d	21 37							21 50			22 07						22 20			22 37		
Northfleet	d	21 39							21 52			22 09						22 22			22 39		
Gravesend	d	21 43						21 48	21a56		22a09	22 13					22 18	22a26		22a39	22 43		
Higham	d	21 49										22 19									22 49		
Strood	d	21 55						21 59				22 25					22 29				22 55		
Maidstone West	d																						
Rochester	d	21 58						22 02				22 28					22 32				22 58		
Chatham	d	22 01						22 06				22 31					22 36				23 01		
Gillingham (Kent)	a	22 05						22 10				22 35					22 40				23 05		
Rainham Kt	a	22 11						22 15				22 41					22 45				23 11		

Saturdays

26 May to 8 December

London - Dartford and Gillingham

		SE	SE	SE ◇	SE	SE	SE	TL	SE	SE	SE	SE	SE ◇	SE	SE	SE	TL	SE	SE	SE	SE	SE ◇	SE	TL
St Pancras Int'l ⊖	d			22 25									22 55									23 25		
Stratford International ⊖	d			22 32									23 02									23 32		
Ebbsfleet International	d			22 43									23 13									23 43		
London Charing Cross ⊖	d	21 54			22 02				22 12	22 18	22 24			22 32				22 42	22 48	22 54			23 02	
London Waterloo (East) ⊖	d	21 58			22 05				22 15	22 21	22 28			22 35				22 45	22 51	22 58			23 05	
London Cannon Street ⊖	d		22 02			22 08						22 32			22 38						23 02			
London Bridge ⊖	d	22 05	22 06		22 11	22 13		22 18	22 21	22 27	22 35	22 36		22 41	22 43		22 48	22 51	22 57	23 05	23 06		23 11	23 18
Deptford	d		22 12					22 25				22 42					22 55				23 12			23 25
Greenwich	d		22 14					22 27				22 44					22 57				23 14			23 27
Maze Hill	d		22 17					22 30				22 47					23 00				23 17			23 30
Westcombe Park	d		22 19					22 32				22 49					23 02				23 19			23 32
London Victoria ⊖	d						22 06									22 36								
Denmark Hill	d						22 16									22 46								
Peckham Rye	d						22 18									22 48								
Nunhead	d						22 21									22 51								
New Cross ⊖	d					22 19									22 49									
St Johns	d					22 21									22 51									
Lewisham	d	22 15				22 24	22 26		22 30		22 45				22 54	22 56		23 00		23 15				
Blackheath	d	22 18					22 29		22 33		22 48					22 59		23 03		23 18				
Kidbrooke	d	22 21					22 32				22 51					23 02				23 21				
Eltham	d	22 24					22 36				22 54					23 06				23 24				
Falconwood	d	22 27					22 39				22 57					23 09				23 27				
Welling	d	22 30					22 41				23 00					23 11				23 30				
Bexleyheath	d	22 33					22 45				23 03					23 15				23 33				
Barnehurst	d	22 36					22 47				23 06					23 17				23 36				
Hither Green	d					22 29				22 37					22 59				23 07				23 22	
Lee	d					22 31				22 39					23 01				23 09				23 24	
Mottingham	d					22 34				22 42					23 04				23 12				23 27	
New Eltham	d				22 25	22 37				22 45				22 55	23 07				23 15				23 30	
Sidcup	d				22 28	22 40				22 48				22 58	23 10				23 18				23 33	
Albany Park	d					22 43				22 51					23 13				23 21				23 36	
Bexley	d				22 32	22 45				22 53				23 02	23 15				23 23				23 38	
Crayford	d				22 35	22 51				22 57				23 05	23 21				23 27				23 42	
Charlton	d		22 22			23a19		22 35	22 38			22 52			23a49		23 05	23 08			23 22			23 35
Woolwich Dockyard	d		22 25						22 41			22 55						23 11			23 25			
Woolwich Arsenal	d		22 28					22 40	22 44			22 58					23 10	23 14			23 28			23 40
Plumstead	d		22 30					22 43	22 46			23 00					23 13	23 16			23 30			23 43
Abbey Wood	d		22 33					22 46	22 50			23 03					23 16	23 20			23 33			23 46
Belvedere	d		22 36						22 53			23 06						23 23			23 36			
Erith	d		22 39						22 55			23 09						23 25			23 39			
Slade Green	d		22a43					22 52	23 01			23a13					23 22	23 31			23 44			23 52
Dartford	a	22 44			22 40		22 54	22 57	23 08	23 02	23 14			23 10		23 24	23 27	23 38	23 32	23 44	23 50		23 47	23 57
	d				22 41		22 54	22 58						23 11		23 24	23 28						23 48	23 58
Stone Crossing	d				22 45			23 02						23 15			23 32						23 52	00 02
Greenhithe for Bluewater	d				22 47		23 00	23 04						23 17		23 30	23 34						23 54	00 04
Swanscombe	d				22 50			23 07						23 20			23 37						23 57	00 07
Northfleet	d				22 52			23 09						23 22			23 39						23 59	00 09
Gravesend	d			22 48	22a56		23a09	23 13					23 18	23a26		23a39	23 43					23 48	00a04	00 13
Higham	d							23 19									23 49							00 19
Strood	d			22 59				23 25					23 29				23 55					23 59		00 25
Maidstone West	d																							
Rochester	d			23 02				23 28					23 32				23 58					00 02		00 28
Chatham	d			23 06				23 31					23 36				00 02					00 06		00 32
Gillingham (Kent)	a			23 10				23 35					23 40				00 06					00 10		00 36
Rainham Kt	a			23 15				23 41					23 45									00 15		

Table T200-F

Saturdays
26 May to 8 December

London - Dartford and Gillingham

		SE	SE	SE	SE	SE ◇	SE	SE	SE	SE
St Pancras Int'l	d					23 55				
Stratford International	d					00 02				
Ebbsfleet International	d					00 13				
London Charing Cross	d		23 12	23 20	23 24		23 32		23 50	23 54
London Waterloo (East)	d		23 15	23 23	23 28		23 35		23 53	23 58
London Cannon Street	d									
London Bridge	d		23 21	23 29	23 35		23 41		23 59	00 05
Deptford	d									
Greenwich	d									
Maze Hill	d									
Westcombe Park	d									
London Victoria	d	23 06						23 36		
Denmark Hill	d	23 16						23 46		
Peckham Rye	d	23 18						23 48		
Nunhead	d	23 21						23 51		
New Cross	d									
St Johns	d									
Lewisham	d	23 26	23 30	23 38	23 45			23 56	00 08	00 15
Blackheath	d	23 29	23 33		23 48			23 59		00 18
Kidbrooke	d	23 32			23 51			00 02		00 21
Eltham	d	23 36			23 54			00 06		00 24
Falconwood	d	23 39			23 57			00 09		00 27
Welling	d	23 41			23 59			00 11		00 30
Bexleyheath	d	23 45			00 03			00 15		00 33
Barnehurst	d	23 47			00 06			00 17		00 36
Hither Green	d			23 43			23 52		00 13	
Lee	d			23 45			23 54		00 15	
Mottingham	d			23 48			23 57		00 18	
New Eltham	d			23 51			23 59		00 21	
Sidcup	d			23 54			00 03		00 24	
Albany Park	d			23 57			00 06		00 27	
Bexley	d			23 59			00 08		00 29	
Crayford	d			00 03			00 12		00 33	
Charlton	d		23 38							
Woolwich Dockyard	d		23 41							
Woolwich Arsenal	d		23 44							
Plumstead	d		23 46							
Abbey Wood	d		23 50							
Belvedere	d		23 53							
Erith	d		23 55							
Slade Green	d		00 01							
Dartford	a	23 57	00 08	00 10	00 14		00 17	00 24	00 38	00 44
	d						00 18			
Stone Crossing	d						00 22			
Greenhithe for Bluewater	d						00 24			
Swanscombe	d						00 27			
Northfleet	d						00 29			
Gravesend	d					00 18	00a34			
Higham	d									
Strood	d					00 29				
Maidstone West	d									
Rochester	d					00 32				
Chatham	d					00 36				
Gillingham (Kent)	a					00 40				
Rainham Kt	a					00 45				

Table T200-F

Sundays
20 May to 2 December

London - Dartford and Gillingham

		SE A	TL A	SE ◇ A	TL A	SE ◇ A	SE A	SE A	SE A	SE A	TL	SE A	SE A
St Pancras Int'l	d												
Stratford International	d					00 02							
Ebbsfleet International	d					00 13							
London Charing Cross	d												
London Waterloo (East)	d												
London Cannon Street	d												
London Bridge	d												00 05
Deptford	d												
Greenwich	d												
Maze Hill	d												
Westcombe Park	d												
London Victoria	d												
Denmark Hill	d												
Peckham Rye	d												
Nunhead	d												
New Cross	d												
St Johns	d												
Lewisham	d											00 08	00 15
Blackheath	d												00 18
Kidbrooke	d									00 02			00 21
Eltham	d									00 06			00 24
Falconwood	d									00 09			00 27
Welling	d									00 11			00 30
Bexleyheath	d							00 03		00 15			00 33
Barnehurst	d							00 06		00 17			00 36
Hither Green	d											00 13	
Lee	d											00 15	
Mottingham	d											00 18	
New Eltham	d											00 21	
Sidcup	d								00 03			00 24	
Albany Park	d								00 06			00 27	
Bexley	d								00 08			00 29	
Crayford	d						00 03		00 12			00 33	
Charlton	d												
Woolwich Dockyard	d												
Woolwich Arsenal	d												
Plumstead	d												
Abbey Wood	d												
Belvedere	d												
Erith	d												
Slade Green	d	00 01											
Dartford	a	00 08					00 10	00 14	00 17	00 24		00 38	00 44
	d								00 18		00 28		
Stone Crossing	d				00 02				00 22		00 32		
Greenhithe for Bluewater	d				00 04				00 24		00 34		
Swanscombe	d				00 07				00 27		00 37		
Northfleet	d				00 09				00 29		00 39		
Gravesend	d				00 13	00 18			00a34		00 43		
Higham	d				00 19						00 49		
Strood	d				00 25	00 29					00 55		
Maidstone West	d												
Rochester	d			00 02	00 28	00 32					00 58		
Chatham	d		00 02	00 06	00 32	00 36					01 02		
Gillingham (Kent)	a		00 06	00 10	00 36	00 40					01 06		
Rainham Kt	a			00 15		00 45							

		SE	SE	SE	SE	TL	SE	TL	SE	SE	TL	SE
St Pancras Int'l	d											
Stratford International	d											
Ebbsfleet International	d											
London Charing Cross	d	00 02		00 26	00 32							
London Waterloo (East)	d	00 05		00 29	00 35							
London Cannon Street	d						07 29					07 42
London Bridge	d	00 11		00 35	00 41		07 33					07 46
Deptford	d						07 39					
Greenwich	d						07 41					
Maze Hill	d						07 44					
Westcombe Park	d						07 46					
London Victoria	d		00 06							07 36		
Denmark Hill	d		00 16							07 46		
Peckham Rye	d		00 18							07 48		
Nunhead	d		00 21							07 51		
New Cross	d											07 52
St Johns	d											07 54
Lewisham	d		00 26	00 45	00 50					07 56		07 59
Blackheath	d		00 29	00 48						07 59		
Kidbrooke	d		00 32	00 51						08 02		
Eltham	d		00 36	00 54						08 06		
Falconwood	d		00 39	00 57						08 09		
Welling	d		00 41	01 00						08 11		
Bexleyheath	d		00 45	01 03						08 15		
Barnehurst	d		00 47	01 06						08 18		
Hither Green	d	00 22			00 55							08 04
Lee	d	00 24			00 57							08 06
Mottingham	d	00 27			01 00							08 09
New Eltham	d	00 30			01 03							08 12
Sidcup	d	00 33			01 06							08 16
Albany Park	d	00 36			01 09							08 18
Bexley	d	00 38			01 11							08 21
Crayford	d	00 42			01 15							08 25
Charlton	d						07 49					08a55
Woolwich Dockyard	d						07 52					
Woolwich Arsenal	d						07 55					
Plumstead	d						07 57					
Abbey Wood	d						08 00					
Belvedere	d						08 03					
Erith	d						08 06					
Slade Green	d						08a09					
Dartford	a	00 47	00 55	01 14	01 19					08 24		
	d	00 48			01 20	01 24		07 58	08 09		08 28	
Stone Crossing	d	00 52				01 28		08 02	08 13		08 32	
Greenhithe for Bluewater	d	00 54			01s25	01 30		08 04	08 15		08 34	
Swanscombe	d	00s57				01 33		08 07	08 18		08 37	
Northfleet	d	00s59				01 35		08 09	08 20		08 39	
Gravesend	d	01a04			01a35	01 39		08 13	08a25		08 43	
Higham	d					01 45		08 19			08 49	
Strood	d					01 50		08 25			08 55	
Maidstone West	d											
Rochester	d					01 54		08 28			08 58	
Chatham	d					01 57		08 31			09 01	
Gillingham (Kent)	a					02 02		08 35			09 05	
Rainham Kt	a							08 41			09 11	

A not 20 May

Please note, Network Rail have stated that further updates to this timetable are possible during the validity period.

Table T200-F

Sundays

20 May to 2 December

London - Dartford and Gillingham

		SE	SE	SE	SE	SE	SE	TL	SE	SE	SE	SE	SE	TL	SE	SE	SE	SE	SE	SE	TL	SE	SE
			◇													◇							
St Pancras Int'l ⊖	d		08 25													09 25							
Stratford International ⊖	d		08 32													09 32							
Ebbsfleet International	d		08 43													09 44							
London Charing Cross ⊖	d	07 42		07 52					08 12	08 22					08 42		08 52					09 12	09 22
London Waterloo (East) ⊖	d	07 45		07 55					08 15	08 25					08 45		08 55					09 15	09 25
London Cannon Street ⊖	d				07 59		08 12				08 29		08 42					08 59		09 12			
London Bridge ⊖	d	07 51		08 01	08 03		08 16	08 18	08 21	08 31	08 33		08 46	08 48	08 51		09 01	09 03		09 16	09 18	09 21	09 31
Deptford	d				08 09			08 25			08 39			08 55				09 09			09 25		
Greenwich	d				08 11			08 27			08 41			08 57				09 11			09 27		
Maze Hill	d				08 14			08 30			08 44			09 00				09 14			09 30		
Westcombe Park	d				08 16			08 32			08 46			09 02				09 16			09 32		
London Victoria ⊖	d					08 06						08 36							09 06				
Denmark Hill	d					08 16						08 46							09 16				
Peckham Rye	d					08 18						08 48							09 18				
Nunhead	d					08 21						08 51							09 21				
New Cross ⊖	d						08 22						08 52							09 22			
St Johns	d						08 24						08 54							09 24			
Lewisham	d	08 01				08 26	08 29		08 31			08 56	08 59		09 01				09 26	09 29		09 31	
Blackheath	d	08 03				08 29			08 33			08 59			09 03				09 29			09 33	
Kidbrooke	d					08 32						09 02							09 32				
Eltham	d					08 36						09 06							09 36				
Falconwood	d					08 39						09 09							09 39				
Welling	d					08 41						09 11							09 41				
Bexleyheath	d					08 45						09 15							09 45				
Barnehurst	d					08 48						09 18							09 48				
Hither Green	d			08 12			08 34			08 42			09 04				09 12			09 34			09 42
Lee	d			08 14			08 36			08 44			09 06				09 14			09 36			09 44
Mottingham	d			08 17			08 39			08 47			09 09				09 17			09 39			09 47
New Eltham	d			08 20			08 42			08 50			09 12				09 20			09 42			09 50
Sidcup	d			08 24			08 46			08 54			09 16				09 24			09 46			09 54
Albany Park	d			08 26			08 48			08 56			09 18				09 26			09 48			09 56
Bexley	d			08 29			08 51			08 59			09 21				09 29			09 51			09 59
Crayford	d			08 32			08 55			09 02			09 25				09 32			09 55			10 02
Charlton	d	08 08			08 19		09a25	08 35	08 38		08 49		09a55	09 05	09 08			09 19		10a25	09 35	09 38	
Woolwich Dockyard	d	08 11			08 22				08 41		08 52				09 11			09 22				09 41	
Woolwich Arsenal	d	08 14			08 25			08 40	08 44		08 55			09 10	09 14			09 25			09 40	09 44	
Plumstead	d	08 16			08 27			08 43	08 46		08 57			09 13	09 16			09 27			09 43	09 46	
Abbey Wood	d	08 20			08 30			08 46	08 50		09 00			09 16	09 20			09 30			09 46	09 50	
Belvedere	d	08 23			08 33				08 53		09 03				09 23			09 33				09 53	
Erith	d	08 25			08 36				08 55		09 06				09 25			09 36				09 55	
Slade Green	d	08 31			08a39			08 52	09 01		09a09			09 22	09 31			09a39			09 52	10 01	
Dartford	a	08 36		08 38		08 54		08 57	09 06	09 08		09 24		09 27	09 36		09 38		09 54		09 57	10 06	10 08
	d			08 39				08 58		09 09				09 28			09 39				09 58		10 09
Stone Crossing	d			08 43				09 02		09 13				09 32			09 43				10 02		10 13
Greenhithe for Bluewater	d			08 45				09 04		09 15				09 34			09 45				10 04		10 15
Swanscombe	d			08 48				09 07		09 18				09 37			09 48				10 07		10 18
Northfleet	d			08 50				09 09		09 20				09 39			09 50				10 09		10 20
Gravesend	d		08 48	08a55				09 13		09a25				09 43		09 48	09a55				10 13		10a25
Higham	d							09 19						09 49							10 19		
Strood	d		08 59					09 25						09 55		09 59					10 25		
Maidstone West	d																						
Rochester	d		09 02					09 28						09 58		10 02					10 28		
Chatham	d		09 06					09 31						10 01		10 06					10 31		
Gillingham (Kent)	a		09 10					09 35						10 05		10 10					10 35		
Rainham Kt	a		09 15					09 41						10 11		10 15					10 41		

Table T200-F

Sundays

20 May to 2 December

London - Dartford and Gillingham

		SE	SE	SE	TL	SE	SE	SE	SE	SE	SE	TL	SE	SE	SE	SE	SE	TL	SE	SE	SE	SE	SE	SE
							◇													◇				
St Pancras Int'l ⊖	d						10 27													11 25				
Stratford International ⊖	d						10 34													11 32				
Ebbsfleet International	d						10 45													11 43				
London Charing Cross ⊖	d					09 42		09 52					10 12	10 22					10 42		10 52			
London Waterloo (East) ⊖	d					09 45		09 55					10 15	10 25					10 45		10 55			
London Cannon Street ⊖	d	09 29		09 42					09 59		10 12				10 29		10 42					10 59		11 12
London Bridge ⊖	d	09 33		09 46	09 48	09 51		10 01	10 03		10 16	10 18	10 21	10 31	10 33		10 46	10 48	10 51		11 01	11 03		11 16
Deptford	d	09 39			09 55				10 09			10 25			10 39			10 55				11 09		
Greenwich	d	09 41			09 57				10 11			10 27			10 41			10 57				11 11		
Maze Hill	d	09 44			10 00				10 14			10 30			10 44			11 00				11 14		
Westcombe Park	d	09 46			10 02				10 16			10 32			10 46			11 02				11 16		
London Victoria ⊖	d		09 36							10 06						10 36							11 06	
Denmark Hill	d		09 46							10 16						10 46							11 16	
Peckham Rye	d		09 48							10 18						10 48							11 18	
Nunhead	d		09 51							10 21						10 51							11 21	
New Cross ⊖	d			09 52							10 22						10 52							11 22
St Johns	d			09 54							10 24						10 54							11 24
Lewisham	d		09 56	09 59		10 01				10 26	10 29		10 31			10 56	10 59		11 01				11 26	11 29
Blackheath	d		09 59			10 03				10 29			10 33			10 59			11 03				11 29	
Kidbrooke	d		10 02							10 32						11 02							11 32	
Eltham	d		10 06							10 36						11 06							11 36	
Falconwood	d		10 09							10 39						11 09							11 39	
Welling	d		10 11							10 41						11 11							11 41	
Bexleyheath	d		10 15							10 45						11 15							11 45	
Barnehurst	d		10 18							10 48						11 18							11 48	
Hither Green	d			10 04				10 12			10 34			10 42			11 04				11 12			11 34
Lee	d			10 06				10 14			10 36			10 44			11 06				11 14			11 36
Mottingham	d			10 09				10 17			10 39			10 47			11 09				11 17			11 39
New Eltham	d			10 12				10 20			10 42			10 50			11 12				11 20			11 42
Sidcup	d			10 16				10 24			10 46			10 54			11 16				11 24			11 46
Albany Park	d			10 18				10 26			10 48			10 56			11 18				11 26			11 48
Bexley	d			10 21				10 29			10 51			10 59			11 21				11 29			11 51
Crayford	d			10 25				10 32			10 55			11 02			11 25				11 32			11 55
Charlton	d	09 49		10a55	10 05	10 08			10 19		11a25	10 35	10 38		10 49		11a55	11 05	11 08			11 19		12a25
Woolwich Dockyard	d	09 52				10 11			10 22				10 41		10 52				11 11			11 22		
Woolwich Arsenal	d	09 55			10 10	10 14			10 25			10 40	10 44		10 55			11 10	11 14			11 25		
Plumstead	d	09 57			10 13	10 16			10 27			10 43	10 46		10 57			11 13	11 16			11 27		
Abbey Wood	d	10 00			10 16	10 20			10 30			10 46	10 50		11 00			11 16	11 20			11 30		
Belvedere	d	10 03				10 23			10 33				10 53		11 03				11 23			11 33		
Erith	d	10 06				10 25			10 36				10 55		11 06				11 25			11 36		
Slade Green	d	10a09			10 22	10 31			10a39			10 52	11 01		11a09			11 22	11 31			11a39		
Dartford	a		10 24		10 27	10 36		10 38		10 54		10 57	11 06	11 08		11 24		11 27	11 36		11 38		11 54	
	d				10 28			10 39				10 58		11 09				11 28			11 39			
Stone Crossing	d				10 32			10 43				11 02		11 13				11 32			11 43			
Greenhithe for Bluewater	d				10 34			10 45				11 04		11 15				11 34			11 45			
Swanscombe	d				10 37			10 48				11 07		11 18				11 37			11 48			
Northfleet	d				10 39			10 50				11 09		11 20				11 39			11 50			
Gravesend	d				10 43		10 49	10a55				11 13		11a25				11 43		11 48	11a55			
Higham	d				10 49							11 19						11 49						
Strood	d				10 55		10 59					11 25						11 55		11 59				
Maidstone West	d																							
Rochester	d				10 58		11 03					11 28						11 58		12 02				
Chatham	d				11 01		11 06					11 31						12 01		12 06				
Gillingham (Kent)	a				11 05		11 10					11 35						12 05		12 10				
Rainham Kt	a				11 11		11 15					11 41						12 11		12 15				

Table T200-F

Sundays

20 May to 2 December

London - Dartford and Gillingham

		TL	SE	SE	SE	SE	SE	TL	SE	SE ◇	SE	SE	SE	SE	TL	SE	SE ◇	SE	SE	SE	SE	TL	SE
St Pancras Int'l	d									12 27							12 52						
Stratford International	d									12 34							12 59						
Ebbsfleet International	d									12 45							13 13						
London Charing Cross	d		11 12	11 22					11 42		11 52					12 12		12 22					12 42
London Waterloo (East)	d		11 15	11 25					11 45		11 55					12 15		12 25					12 45
London Cannon Street	d				11 29		11 42					11 59		12 12					12 29		12 42		
London Bridge	d	11 18	11 21	11 31	11 33		11 46	11 48	11 51		12 01	12 03		12 16	12 18	12 21		12 31	12 33		12 46	12 48	12 51
Deptford	d	11 25			11 39			11 55				12 09			12 25				12 39			12 55	
Greenwich	d	11 27			11 41			11 57				12 11			12 27				12 41			12 57	
Maze Hill	d	11 30			11 44			12 00				12 14			12 30				12 44			13 00	
Westcombe Park	d	11 32			11 46			12 02				12 16			12 32				12 46			13 02	
London Victoria	d					11 36							12 06							12 36			
Denmark Hill	d					11 46							12 16							12 46			
Peckham Rye	d					11 48							12 18							12 48			
Nunhead	d					11 51							12 21							12 51			
New Cross	d						11 52							12 22							12 52		
St Johns	d						11 54							12 24							12 54		
Lewisham	d		11 31			11 56	11 59		12 01				12 26	12 29		12 31				12 56	12 59		13 01
Blackheath	d		11 33			11 59			12 03				12 29			12 33				12 59			13 03
Kidbrooke	d					12 02							12 32							13 02			
Eltham	d					12 06							12 36							13 06			
Falconwood	d					12 09							12 39							13 09			
Welling	d					12 11							12 41							13 11			
Bexleyheath	d					12 15							12 45							13 15			
Barnehurst	d					12 18							12 48							13 18			
Hither Green	d			11 42			12 04				12 12			12 34				12 42			13 04		
Lee	d			11 44			12 06				12 14			12 36				12 44			13 06		
Mottingham	d			11 47			12 09				12 17			12 39				12 47			13 09		
New Eltham	d			11 50			12 12				12 20			12 42				12 50			13 12		
Sidcup	d			11 54			12 16				12 24			12 46				12 54			13 16		
Albany Park	d			11 56			12 18				12 26			12 48				12 56			13 18		
Bexley	d			11 59			12 21				12 29			12 51				12 59			13 21		
Crayford	d			12 02			12 25				12 32			12 55				13 02			13 25		
Charlton	d	11 35	11 38		11 49		12a55	12 05	12 08			12 19		13a25	12 35	12 38			12 49		13a55	13 05	13 08
Woolwich Dockyard	d		11 41		11 52				12 11			12 22				12 41			12 52				13 11
Woolwich Arsenal	d	11 40	11 44		11 55			12 10	12 14			12 25			12 40	12 44			12 55			13 10	13 14
Plumstead	d	11 43	11 46		11 57			12 13	12 16			12 27			12 43	12 46			12 57			13 13	13 16
Abbey Wood	d	11 46	11 50		12 00			12 16	12 20			12 30			12 46	12 50			13 00			13 16	13 20
Belvedere	d		11 53		12 03				12 23			12 33				12 53			13 03				13 23
Erith	d		11 55		12 06				12 25			12 36				12 55			13 06				13 25
Slade Green	d	11 52	12 01		12a09			12 22	12 31			12a39			12 52	13 01			13a09			13 22	13 31
Dartford	a	11 57	12 06	12 08		12 24		12 27	12 36		12 38		12 54		12 57	13 06		13 08		13 24		13 27	13 36
	d	11 58		12 09				12 28			12 39				12 58			13 09				13 28	
Stone Crossing	d	12 02		12 13				12 32			12 43				13 02			13 13				13 32	
Greenhithe for Bluewater	d	12 04		12 15				12 34			12 45				13 04			13 15				13 34	
Swanscombe	d	12 07		12 18				12 37			12 48				13 07			13 18				13 37	
Northfleet	d	12 09		12 20				12 39			12 50				13 09			13 20				13 39	
Gravesend	d	12 13		12a25				12 43		12 49	12a55				13 13		13 18	13a25				13 43	
Higham	d	12 19						12 49							13 19							13 49	
Strood	d	12 25						12 55		12 59					13 25		13 29					13 55	
Maidstone West	d																						
Rochester	d	12 28						12 58		13 03					13 28		13 32					13 58	
Chatham	d	12 31						13 01		13 06					13 31		13 36					14 01	
Gillingham (Kent)	a	12 35						13 05		13 10					13 35		13 40					14 05	
Rainham Kt	a	12 41						13 11		13 15					13 41		13 45					14 11	

Table T200-F

Sundays

20 May to 2 December

London - Dartford and Gillingham

		SE ◇	SE	SE	SE	SE	TL	SE	SE ◇	SE	SE	SE	SE	TL	SE	SE ◇	SE	SE	SE	SE	TL	SE	SE ◇	SE
St Pancras Int'l	d	13 25							13 55							14 25							14 55	
Stratford International	d	13 32							14 02							14 32							15 02	
Ebbsfleet International	d	13 43							14 13							14 43							15 13	
London Charing Cross	d		12 52					13 12		13 22					13 42		13 52					14 12		14 22
London Waterloo (East)	d		12 55					13 15		13 25					13 45		13 55					14 15		14 25
London Cannon Street	d			12 59		13 12					13 29		13 42					13 59		14 12				
London Bridge	d		13 01	13 03		13 16	13 18	13 21		13 31	13 33		13 46	13 48	13 51		14 01	14 03		14 16	14 18	14 21		14 31
Deptford	d			13 09			13 25				13 39			13 55				14 09			14 25			
Greenwich	d			13 11			13 27				13 41			13 57				14 11			14 27			
Maze Hill	d			13 14			13 30				13 44			14 00				14 14			14 30			
Westcombe Park	d			13 16			13 32				13 46			14 02				14 16			14 32			
London Victoria	d				13 06							13 36							14 06					
Denmark Hill	d				13 16							13 46							14 16					
Peckham Rye	d				13 18							13 48							14 18					
Nunhead	d				13 21							13 51							14 21					
New Cross	d					13 22							13 52							14 22				
St Johns	d					13 24							13 54							14 24				
Lewisham	d				13 26	13 29		13 31				13 56	13 59		14 01				14 26	14 29		14 31		
Blackheath	d				13 29			13 33				13 59			14 03				14 29			14 33		
Kidbrooke	d				13 32							14 02							14 32					
Eltham	d				13 36							14 06							14 36					
Falconwood	d				13 39							14 09							14 39					
Welling	d				13 41							14 11							14 41					
Bexleyheath	d				13 45							14 15							14 45					
Barnehurst	d				13 48							14 18							14 48					
Hither Green	d		13 12			13 34				13 42			14 04				14 12			14 34				14 42
Lee	d		13 14			13 36				13 44			14 06				14 14			14 36				14 44
Mottingham	d		13 17			13 39				13 47			14 09				14 17			14 39				14 47
New Eltham	d		13 20			13 42				13 50			14 12				14 20			14 42				14 50
Sidcup	d		13 24			13 46				13 54			14 16				14 24			14 46				14 54
Albany Park	d		13 26			13 48				13 56			14 18				14 26			14 48				14 56
Bexley	d		13 29			13 51				13 59			14 21				14 29			14 51				14 59
Crayford	d		13 32			13 55				14 02			14 25				14 32			14 55				15 02
Charlton	d			13 19		14a25	13 35	13 38			13 49		14a55	14 05	14 08			14 19		15a25	14 35	14 38		
Woolwich Dockyard	d			13 22				13 41			13 52				14 11			14 22				14 41		
Woolwich Arsenal	d			13 25			13 40	13 44			13 55			14 10	14 14			14 25			14 40	14 44		
Plumstead	d			13 27			13 43	13 46			13 57			14 13	14 16			14 27			14 43	14 46		
Abbey Wood	d			13 30			13 46	13 50			14 00			14 16	14 20			14 30			14 46	14 50		
Belvedere	d			13 33				13 53			14 03				14 23			14 33				14 53		
Erith	d			13 36				13 55			14 06				14 25			14 36				14 55		
Slade Green	d			13a39			13 52	14 01			14a09			14 22	14 31			14a39			14 52	15 01		
Dartford	a		13 38		13 54		13 57	14 06		14 08		14 24		14 27	14 36		14 38		14 54		14 57	15 06		15 08
	d		13 39				13 58			14 09				14 28			14 39				14 58			15 09
Stone Crossing	d		13 43				14 02			14 13				14 32			14 43				15 02			15 13
Greenhithe for Bluewater	d		13 45				14 04			14 15				14 34			14 45				15 04			15 15
Swanscombe	d		13 48				14 07			14 18				14 37			14 48				15 07			15 18
Northfleet	d		13 50				14 09			14 20				14 39			14 50				15 09			15 20
Gravesend	d	13 48	13a55				14 13		14 18	14a25				14 43		14 48	14a55				15 13		15 18	15a25
Higham	d						14 19							14 49							15 19			
Strood	d	13 59					14 25		14 29					14 55		14 59					15 25		15 29	
Maidstone West	d																							
Rochester	d	14 02					14 28		14 32					14 58		15 02					15 28		15 32	
Chatham	d	14 06					14 31		14 36					15 01		15 06					15 31		15 36	
Gillingham (Kent)	a	14 10					14 35		14 40					15 05		15 10					15 35		15 40	
Rainham Kt	a	14 15					14 41		14 45					15 11		15 15					15 41		15 45	

Please note, Network Rail have stated that further updates to this timetable are possible during the validity period.

Table T200-F

Sundays

20 May to 2 December

London - Dartford and Gillingham

Station		SE	SE	SE	TL	SE	SE ◇	SE	SE	SE	SE	TL	SE	SE ◇	SE	SE	SE	SE	TL	SE	SE ◇	SE	SE
St Pancras Int'l	d						15 25							15 55							16 25		
Stratford International	d						15 32							16 02							16 32		
Ebbsfleet International	d						15 43							16 13							16 43		
London Charing Cross	d					14 42		14 52					15 12		15 22					15 42		15 52	
London Waterloo (East)	d					14 45		14 55					15 15		15 25					15 45		15 55	
London Cannon Street	d	14 29		14 42					14 59		15 12					15 29		15 42					15 59
London Bridge	d	14 33		14 46	14 48	14 51		15 01	15 03		15 16	15 18	15 21		15 31	15 33		15 46	15 48	15 51		16 01	16 03
Deptford	d	14 39			14 55				15 09			15 25				15 39			15 55				16 09
Greenwich	d	14 41			14 57				15 11			15 27				15 41			15 57				16 11
Maze Hill	d	14 44			15 00				15 14			15 30				15 44			16 00				16 14
Westcombe Park	d	14 46			15 02				15 16			15 32				15 46			16 02				16 16
London Victoria	d		14 36							15 06							15 36						
Denmark Hill	d		14 46							15 16							15 46						
Peckham Rye	d		14 48							15 18							15 48						
Nunhead	d		14 51							15 21							15 51						
New Cross	d			14 52							15 22							15 52					
St Johns	d			14 54							15 24							15 54					
Lewisham	d		14 56	14 59		15 01				15 26	15 29		15 31				15 56	15 59		16 01			
Blackheath	d		14 59			15 03				15 29			15 33				15 59			16 03			
Kidbrooke	d		15 02							15 32							16 02						
Eltham	d		15 06							15 36							16 06						
Falconwood	d		15 09							15 39							16 09						
Welling	d		15 11							15 41							16 11						
Bexleyheath	d		15 15							15 45							16 15						
Barnehurst	d		15 18							15 48							16 18						
Hither Green	d			15 04				15 12			15 34				15 42			16 04				16 12	
Lee	d			15 06				15 14			15 36				15 44			16 06				16 14	
Mottingham	d			15 09				15 17			15 39				15 47			16 09				16 17	
New Eltham	d			15 12				15 20			15 42				15 50			16 12				16 20	
Sidcup	d			15 16				15 24			15 46				15 54			16 16				16 24	
Albany Park	d			15 18				15 26			15 48				15 56			16 18				16 26	
Bexley	d			15 21				15 29			15 51				15 59			16 21				16 29	
Crayford	d			15 25				15 32			15 55				16 02			16 25				16 32	
Charlton	d	14 49		15a55	15 05	15 08			15 19		16a25	15 35	15 38			15 49		16a55	16 05	16 08			16 19
Woolwich Dockyard	d	14 52				15 11			15 22				15 41			15 52				16 11			16 22
Woolwich Arsenal	d	14 55			15 10	15 14			15 25			15 40	15 44			15 55			16 10	16 14			16 25
Plumstead	d	14 57			15 13	15 16			15 27			15 43	15 46			15 57			16 13	16 16			16 27
Abbey Wood	d	15 00			15 16	15 20			15 30			15 46	15 50			16 00			16 16	16 20			16 30
Belvedere	d	15 03				15 23			15 33				15 53			16 03				16 23			16 33
Erith	d	15 06				15 25			15 36				15 55			16 06				16 25			16 36
Slade Green	d	15a09			15 22	15 31			15a39			15 52	16 01			16a09			16 22	16 31			16a39
Dartford	a		15 24		15 27	15 36		15 38		15 54		15 57	16 06		16 08		16 24		16 27	16 36		16 38	
	d				15 28			15 39				15 58			16 09				16 28			16 39	
Stone Crossing	d				15 32			15 43				16 02			16 13				16 32			16 43	
Greenhithe for Bluewater	d				15 34			15 45				16 04			16 15				16 34			16 45	
Swanscombe	d				15 37			15 48				16 07			16 18				16 37			16 48	
Northfleet	d				15 39			15 50				16 09			16 20				16 39			16 50	
Gravesend	d				15 43		15 48	15a55				16 13		16 18	16a25				16 43		16 48	16a55	
Higham	d				15 49							16 19							16 49				
Strood	d				15 55		15 59					16 25		16 29					16 55		16 59		
Maidstone West	d																						
Rochester	d				15 58		16 02					16 28		16 32					16 58		17 02		
Chatham	d				16 01		16 06					16 31		16 36					17 01		17 06		
Gillingham (Kent)	a				16 05		16 10					16 35		16 40					17 05		17 10		
Rainham Kt	a				16 11		16 15					16 41		16 45					17 11		17 15		

Table T200-F

Sundays

20 May to 2 December

London - Dartford and Gillingham

Station		SE	SE	TL	SE	SE ◇	SE	SE	SE	SE	TL	SE	SE ◇	SE	SE	SE	SE	TL	SE	SE ◇	SE	SE	SE	SE
St Pancras Int'l	d					16 55							17 25							17 52				
Stratford International	d					17 02							17 32							18 02				
Ebbsfleet International	d					17 13							17 43							18 13				
London Charing Cross	d				16 12		16 22					16 42		16 52					17 12		17 22			
London Waterloo (East)	d				16 15		16 25					16 45		16 55					17 15		17 25			
London Cannon Street	d		16 12					16 29		16 42					16 59		17 12					17 29		17 42
London Bridge	d		16 16	16 18	16 21		16 31	16 33		16 46	16 48	16 51		17 01	17 03		17 16	17 18	17 21		17 31	17 33		17 46
Deptford	d			16 25				16 39			16 55				17 09			17 25				17 39		
Greenwich	d			16 27				16 41			16 57				17 11			17 27				17 41		
Maze Hill	d			16 30				16 44			17 00				17 14			17 30				17 44		
Westcombe Park	d			16 32				16 46			17 02				17 16			17 32				17 46		
London Victoria	d	16 06							16 36							17 06							17 36	
Denmark Hill	d	16 16							16 46							17 16							17 46	
Peckham Rye	d	16 18							16 48							17 18							17 48	
Nunhead	d	16 21							16 51							17 21							17 51	
New Cross	d		16 22							16 52							17 22							17 52
St Johns	d		16 24							16 54							17 24							17 54
Lewisham	d	16 26	16 29		16 31				16 56	16 59		17 01				17 26	17 29		17 31				17 56	17 59
Blackheath	d	16 29			16 33				16 59			17 03				17 29			17 33				17 59	
Kidbrooke	d	16 32							17 02							17 32							18 02	
Eltham	d	16 36							17 06							17 36							18 06	
Falconwood	d	16 39							17 09							17 39							18 09	
Welling	d	16 41							17 11							17 41							18 11	
Bexleyheath	d	16 45							17 15							17 45							18 15	
Barnehurst	d	16 48							17 18							17 48							18 18	
Hither Green	d		16 34				16 42			17 04				17 12			17 34				17 42			18 04
Lee	d		16 36				16 44			17 06				17 14			17 36				17 44			18 06
Mottingham	d		16 39				16 47			17 09				17 17			17 39				17 47			18 09
New Eltham	d		16 42				16 50			17 12				17 20			17 42				17 50			18 12
Sidcup	d		16 46				16 54			17 16				17 24			17 46				17 54			18 16
Albany Park	d		16 48				16 56			17 18				17 26			17 48				17 56			18 18
Bexley	d		16 51				16 59			17 21				17 29			17 51				17 59			18 21
Crayford	d		16 55				17 02			17 25				17 32			17 55				18 02			18 25
Charlton	d		17a25	16 35	16 38			16 49		17a55	17 05	17 08			17 19		18a25	17 35	17 38			17 49		18a55
Woolwich Dockyard	d				16 41			16 52				17 11			17 22				17 41			17 52		
Woolwich Arsenal	d			16 40	16 44			16 55			17 10	17 14			17 25			17 40	17 44			17 55		
Plumstead	d			16 43	16 46			16 57			17 13	17 16			17 27			17 43	17 46			17 57		
Abbey Wood	d			16 46	16 50			17 00			17 16	17 20			17 30			17 46	17 50			18 00		
Belvedere	d				16 53			17 03				17 23			17 33				17 53			18 03		
Erith	d				16 55			17 06				17 25			17 36				17 55			18 06		
Slade Green	d			16 52	17 01			17a09			17 22	17 31			17a39			17 52	18 01			18a09		
Dartford	a	16 54		16 57	17 06		17 08		17 24		17 27	17 36		17 38		17 54		17 57	18 06		18 08		18 24	
	d			16 58			17 09				17 28			17 39				17 58			18 09			
Stone Crossing	d			17 02			17 13				17 32			17 43				18 02			18 13			
Greenhithe for Bluewater	d			17 04			17 15				17 34			17 45				18 04			18 15			
Swanscombe	d			17 07			17 18				17 37			17 48				18 07			18 18			
Northfleet	d			17 09			17 20				17 39			17 50				18 09			18 20			
Gravesend	d			17 13		17 18	17a25				17 43		17 48	17a55				18 13		18 18	18a25			
Higham	d			17 19							17 49							18 19						
Strood	d			17 25		17 29					17 55		17 59					18 25		18 29				
Maidstone West	d																							
Rochester	d			17 28		17 32					17 58		18 02					18 28		18 32				
Chatham	d			17 31		17 36					18 01		18 06					18 31		18 36				
Gillingham (Kent)	a			17 35		17 40					18 05		18 10					18 35		18 40				
Rainham Kt	a			17 41		17 45					18 11		18 15					18 41		18 45				

Table T200-F

London - Dartford and Gillingham

Sundays

20 May to 2 December

		TL	SE	SE ◇	SE	SE	SE	SE	TL	SE	SE ◇	SE	SE	SE	SE	TL	SE	SE ◇	SE	SE	SE	SE	TL
St Pancras Int'l ⊖	d			18 25							18 55							19 25					
Stratford International ⊖	d			18 32							19 02							19 32					
Ebbsfleet International	d			18 43							19 13							19 43					
London Charing Cross ⊖	d		17 42		17 52					18 12		18 22					18 42		18 52				
London Waterloo (East) ⊖	d		17 45		17 55					18 15		18 25					18 45		18 55				
London Cannon Street ⊖	d					17 59		18 12					18 29		18 42					18 59		19 12	
London Bridge ⊖	d	17 48	17 51		18 01	18 03		18 16	18 18	18 21		18 31	18 33		18 46	18 48	18 51		19 01	19 03		19 16	19 18
Deptford	d	17 55				18 09			18 25				18 39			18 55				19 09			19 25
Greenwich	d	17 57				18 11			18 27				18 41			18 57				19 11			19 27
Maze Hill	d	18 00				18 14			18 30				18 44			19 00				19 14			19 30
Westcombe Park	d	18 02				18 16			18 32				18 46			19 02				19 16			19 32
London Victoria ⊖	d						18 06							18 36							19 06		
Denmark Hill	d						18 16							18 46							19 16		
Peckham Rye	d						18 18							18 48							19 18		
Nunhead	d						18 21							18 51							19 21		
New Cross ⊖	d							18 22							18 52							19 22	
St Johns	d							18 24							18 54							19 24	
Lewisham	d		18 01				18 26	18 29		18 31				18 56	18 59		19 01				19 26	19 29	
Blackheath	d		18 03				18 29			18 33				18 59			19 03				19 29		
Kidbrooke	d						18 32							19 02							19 32		
Eltham	d						18 36							19 06							19 36		
Falconwood	d						18 39							19 09							19 39		
Welling	d						18 41							19 11							19 41		
Bexleyheath	d						18 45							19 15							19 45		
Barnehurst	d						18 48							19 18							19 48		
Hither Green	d				18 12			18 34				18 42			19 04				19 12			19 34	
Lee	d				18 14			18 36				18 44			19 06				19 14			19 36	
Mottingham	d				18 17			18 39				18 47			19 09				19 17			19 39	
New Eltham	d				18 20			18 42				18 50			19 12				19 20			19 42	
Sidcup	d				18 24			18 46				18 54			19 16				19 24			19 46	
Albany Park	d				18 26			18 48				18 56			19 18				19 26			19 48	
Bexley	d				18 29			18 51				18 59			19 21				19 29			19 51	
Crayford	d				18 32			18 55				19 02			19 25				19 32			19 55	
Charlton	d	18 05	18 08			18 19		19a25	18 35	18 38			18 49		19a55	19 05	19 08			19 19		20a25	19 35
Woolwich Dockyard	d		18 11			18 22				18 41			18 52				19 11			19 22			
Woolwich Arsenal	d	18 10	18 14			18 25			18 40	18 44			18 55			19 10	19 14			19 25			19 40
Plumstead	d	18 13	18 16			18 27			18 43	18 46			18 57			19 13	19 16			19 27			19 43
Abbey Wood	d	18 16	18 20			18 30			18 46	18 50			19 00			19 16	19 20			19 30			19 46
Belvedere	d		18 23			18 33				18 53			19 03				19 23			19 33			
Erith	d		18 25			18 36				18 55			19 06				19 25			19 36			
Slade Green	d	18 22	18 31			18a39			18 52	19 01			19a09			19 22	19 31			19a39			19 52
Dartford	a	18 27	18 36		18 38		18 54		18 57	19 06		19 08		19 24		19 27	19 36		19 38		19 54		19 57
	d	18 28			18 39				18 58			19 09				19 28			19 39				19 58
Stone Crossing	d	18 32			18 43				19 02			19 13				19 32			19 43				20 02
Greenhithe for Bluewater	d	18 34			18 45				19 04			19 15				19 34			19 45				20 04
Swanscombe	d	18 37			18 48				19 07			19 18				19 37			19 48				20 07
Northfleet	d	18 39			18 50				19 09			19 20				19 39			19 50				20 09
Gravesend	d	18 43		18 48	18a55				19 13		19 18	19a25				19 43		19 48	19a55				20 13
Higham	d	18 49							19 19							19 49							20 19
Strood	d	18 55		18 59					19 25		19 29					19 55		19 59					20 25
Maidstone West	d																						
Rochester	d	18 58		19 02					19 28		19 32					19 58		20 02					20 28
Chatham	d	19 01		19 06					19 31		19 36					20 01		20 06					20 31
Gillingham (Kent)	a	19 05		19 10					19 35		19 40					20 05		20 10					20 35
Rainham Kt	a	19 11		19 15					19 41		19 45					20 11		20 15					20 41

Table T200-F

London - Dartford and Gillingham

Sundays

20 May to 2 December

		SE	SE ◇	SE	SE	SE	SE	TL	SE	SE ◇	SE	SE	SE	SE	TL	SE	SE ◇	SE	SE	SE	SE	TL	SE	SE ◇
St Pancras Int'l ⊖	d		19 55							20 25							20 55							21 25
Stratford International ⊖	d		20 02							20 32							21 02							21 32
Ebbsfleet International	d		20 13							20 43							21 13							21 43
London Charing Cross ⊖	d	19 12		19 22					19 42		19 52					20 12		20 22					20 42	
London Waterloo (East) ⊖	d	19 15		19 25					19 45		19 55					20 15		20 25					20 45	
London Cannon Street ⊖	d				19 29		19 42					19 59		20 12					20 29		20 42			
London Bridge ⊖	d	19 21		19 31	19 33		19 46	19 48	19 51		20 01	20 03		20 16	20 18	20 21		20 31	20 33		20 46	20 48	20 51	
Deptford	d				19 39			19 55				20 09			20 25				20 39			20 55		
Greenwich	d				19 41			19 57				20 11			20 27				20 41			20 57		
Maze Hill	d				19 44			20 00				20 14			20 30				20 44			21 00		
Westcombe Park	d				19 46			20 02				20 16			20 32				20 46			21 02		
London Victoria ⊖	d					19 36							20 06							20 36				
Denmark Hill	d					19 46							20 16							20 46				
Peckham Rye	d					19 48							20 18							20 48				
Nunhead	d					19 51							20 21							20 51				
New Cross ⊖	d						19 52							20 22							20 52			
St Johns	d						19 54							20 24							20 54			
Lewisham	d	19 31				19 56	19 59		20 01				20 26	20 29		20 31				20 56	20 59		21 01	
Blackheath	d	19 33				19 59			20 03				20 29			20 33				20 59			21 03	
Kidbrooke	d					20 02							20 32							21 02				
Eltham	d					20 06							20 36							21 06				
Falconwood	d					20 09							20 39							21 09				
Welling	d					20 11							20 41							21 11				
Bexleyheath	d					20 15							20 45							21 15				
Barnehurst	d					20 18							20 48							21 18				
Hither Green	d			19 42			20 04				20 12			20 34				20 42			21 04			
Lee	d			19 44			20 06				20 14			20 36				20 44			21 06			
Mottingham	d			19 47			20 09				20 17			20 39				20 47			21 09			
New Eltham	d			19 50			20 12				20 20			20 42				20 50			21 12			
Sidcup	d			19 54			20 16				20 24			20 46				20 54			21 16			
Albany Park	d			19 56			20 18				20 26			20 48				20 56			21 18			
Bexley	d			19 59			20 21				20 29			20 51				20 59			21 21			
Crayford	d			20 02			20 25				20 32			20 55				21 02			21 25			
Charlton	d	19 38			19 49		20a55	20 05	20 08			20 19		21a25	20 35	20 38			20 49		21a55	21 05	21 08	
Woolwich Dockyard	d	19 41			19 52				20 11			20 22				20 41			20 52				21 11	
Woolwich Arsenal	d	19 44			19 55			20 10	20 14			20 25			20 40	20 44			20 55			21 10	21 14	
Plumstead	d	19 46			19 57			20 13	20 16			20 27			20 43	20 46			20 57			21 13	21 16	
Abbey Wood	d	19 50			20 00			20 16	20 20			20 30			20 46	20 50			21 00			21 16	21 20	
Belvedere	d	19 53			20 03				20 23			20 33				20 53			21 03				21 23	
Erith	d	19 55			20 06				20 25			20 36				20 55			21 06				21 25	
Slade Green	d	20 01			20a09			20 22	20 31			20a39			20 52	21 01			21a09			21 22	21 31	
Dartford	a	20 06		20 08		20 24		20 27	20 36		20 38		20 54		20 57	21 06		21 08		21 24		21 27	21 36	
	d			20 09				20 28			20 39				20 58			21 09				21 28		
Stone Crossing	d			20 13				20 32			20 43				21 02			21 13				21 32		
Greenhithe for Bluewater	d			20 15				20 34			20 45				21 04			21 15				21 34		
Swanscombe	d			20 18				20 37			20 48				21 07			21 18				21 37		
Northfleet	d			20 20				20 39			20 50				21 09			21 20				21 39		
Gravesend	d		20 18	20a25				20 43		20 48	20a55				21 13		21 18	21a25				21 43		21 48
Higham	d							20 49							21 19							21 49		
Strood	d		20 29					20 55		20 59					21 25		21 29					21 55		21 59
Maidstone West	d																							
Rochester	d		20 32					20 58		21 02					21 28		21 32					21 58		22 02
Chatham	d		20 36					21 01		21 06					21 31		21 36					22 01		22 06
Gillingham (Kent)	a		20 40					21 05		21 10					21 35		21 40					22 05		22 10
Rainham Kt	a		20 45					21 11		21 15					21 41		21 45					22 11		22 15

Please note, Network Rail have stated that further updates to this timetable are possible during the validity period.

Table T200-F

Sundays
20 May to 2 December

London - Dartford and Gillingham

		SE	SE	SE	SE	TL	SE	SE		SE	SE	SE	SE	TL	SE	SE	SE	SE	SE	SE	TL	SE	SE	SE
								◇								◇							◇	
St Pancras Int'l ⊖	d							21 55								22 25							22 55	
Stratford International ⊖	d							22 02								22 32							23 02	
Ebbsfleet International	d							22 13								22 43							23 13	
London Charing Cross ⊖	d	20 52					21 12			21 22					21 42		21 52					22 12		22 22
London Waterloo (East) ⊖	d	20 55					21 15			21 25					21 45		21 55					22 15		22 25
London Cannon Street ⊖	d		20 59		21 12						21 29		21 42					21 59		22 12				
London Bridge ⊖	d	21 01	21 03		21 16	21 18	21 21			21 31	21 33		21 46	21 48	21 51		22 01	22 03		22 16	22 18	22 21		22 31
Deptford	d		21 09			21 25					21 39			21 55				22 09			22 25			
Greenwich	d		21 11			21 27					21 41			21 57				22 11			22 27			
Maze Hill	d		21 14			21 30					21 44			22 00				22 14			22 30			
Westcombe Park	d		21 16			21 32					21 46			22 02				22 16			22 32			
London Victoria ⊖	d			21 06								21 36							22 06					
Denmark Hill	d			21 16								21 46							22 16					
Peckham Rye	d			21 18								21 48							22 18					
Nunhead	d			21 21								21 51							22 21					
New Cross ⊖	d				21 22								21 52							22 22				
St Johns	d				21 24								21 54							22 24				
Lewisham	d			21 26	21 29		21 31					21 56	21 59		22 01				22 26	22 29		22 31		
Blackheath	d			21 29			21 33					21 59			22 03				22 29			22 33		
Kidbrooke	d			21 32								22 02							22 32					
Eltham	d			21 36								22 06							22 36					
Falconwood	d			21 39								22 09							22 39					
Welling	d			21 41								22 11							22 41					
Bexleyheath	d			21 45								22 15							22 45					
Barnehurst	d			21 48								22 18							22 48					
Hither Green	d	21 12			21 34					21 42			22 04				22 12			22 34				22 42
Lee	d	21 14			21 36					21 44			22 06				22 14			22 36				22 44
Mottingham	d	21 17			21 39					21 47			22 09				22 17			22 39				22 47
New Eltham	d	21 20			21 42					21 50			22 12				22 20			22 42				22 50
Sidcup	d	21 24			21 46					21 54			22 16				22 24			22 46				22 54
Albany Park	d	21 26			21 48					21 56			22 18				22 26			22 48				22 56
Bexley	d	21 29			21 51					21 59			22 21				22 29			22 51				22 59
Crayford	d	21 32			21 55					22 02			22 25				22 32			22 55				23 02
Charlton	d		21 19		22a25	21 35	21 38				21 49		22a55	22 05	22 08			22 19		23a25	22 35	22 38		
Woolwich Dockyard	d		21 22				21 41				21 52				22 11			22 22				22 41		
Woolwich Arsenal	d		21 25			21 40	21 44				21 55			22 10	22 14			22 25			22 40	22 44		
Plumstead	d		21 27			21 43	21 46				21 57			22 13	22 16			22 27			22 43	22 46		
Abbey Wood	d		21 30			21 46	21 50				22 00			22 16	22 20			22 30			22 46	22 50		
Belvedere	d		21 33				21 53				22 03				22 23			22 33				22 53		
Erith	d		21 36				21 55				22 06				22 25			22 36				22 55		
Slade Green	d		21a39			21 52	22 01				22a09			22 22	22 31			22a39			22 52	23 01		
Dartford	a	21 38		21 54		21 57	22 06			22 08		22 24		22 27	22 36		22 38		22 54		22 57	23 06		23 08
	d	21 39				21 58				22 09				22 28			22 39				22 58			23 09
Stone Crossing	d	21 43				22 02				22 13				22 32			22 43				23 02			23 13
Greenhithe for Bluewater	d	21 45				22 04				22 15				22 34			22 45				23 04			23 15
Swanscombe	d	21 48				22 07				22 18				22 37			22 48				23 07			23 18
Northfleet	d	21 50				22 09				22 20				22 39			22 50				23 09			23 20
Gravesend	d	21a55				22 13		22 18		22a25				22 43		22 48	22a55				23 13		23 18	23a25
Higham	d					22 19								22 49							23 19			
Strood	d					22 25		22 29						22 55		22 59					23 25		23 29	
Maidstone West	d																							
Rochester	d					22 28		22 32						22 58		23 02					23 28		23 32	
Chatham	d					22 31		22 36						23 01		23 06					23 31		23 36	
Gillingham (Kent)	a					22 35		22 40						23 05		23 10					23 35		23 40	
Rainham Kt	a					22 41		22 45						23 11		23 15					23 41		23 45	

Table T200-F

Sundays
20 May to 2 December

London - Dartford and Gillingham

		SE	SE	SE	TL	SE	SE	SE	SE	SE	SE	TL	SE	SE	SE	SE		SE	SE	SE
							◇													
St Pancras Int'l ⊖	d						23 25													
Stratford International ⊖	d						23 32													
Ebbsfleet International	d						23 43													
London Charing Cross ⊖	d					22 42		22 52					23 12	23 22				23 42	23 52	
London Waterloo (East) ⊖	d					22 45		22 55					23 15	23 25				23 45	23 55	
London Cannon Street ⊖	d	22 29		22 42					22 59		23 12				23 29					23 59
London Bridge ⊖	d	22 33		22 46	22 48	22 51		23 01	23 03		23 16	23 18	23 21	23 31	23 33			23 51	00 01	00 03
Deptford	d	22 39			22 55				23 09			23 25			23 39					00 09
Greenwich	d	22 41			22 57				23 11			23 27			23 41					00 11
Maze Hill	d	22 44			23 00				23 14			23 30			23 44					00 14
Westcombe Park	d	22 46			23 02				23 16			23 32			23 46					00 16
London Victoria ⊖	d		22 36							23 06						23 36				
Denmark Hill	d		22 46							23 16						23 46				
Peckham Rye	d		22 48							23 18						23 48				
Nunhead	d		22 51							23 21						23 51				
New Cross ⊖	d			22 52							23 22									
St Johns	d			22 54							23 24									
Lewisham	d		22 56	22 59		23 01				23 26	23 29		23 31			23 56		00 01		
Blackheath	d		22 59			23 03				23 29			23 33			23 59		00 03		
Kidbrooke	d		23 02							23 32						00 02				
Eltham	d		23 06							23 36						00 06				
Falconwood	d		23 09							23 39						00 09				
Welling	d		23 11							23 41						00 11				
Bexleyheath	d		23 15							23 45						00 15				
Barnehurst	d		23 18							23 48						00 18				
Hither Green	d			23 03				23 12			23 33			23 42					00 12	
Lee	d			23 06				23 14			23 36			23 44					00 14	
Mottingham	d			23 09				23 17			23 39			23 47					00 17	
New Eltham	d			23 12				23 20			23 42			23 50					00 20	
Sidcup	d			23 15				23 24			23 45			23 54					00 24	
Albany Park	d			23 18				23 26			23 48			23 56					00 26	
Bexley	d			23 20				23 29			23 50			23 59					00 29	
Crayford	d			23 24				23 32			23 54			00 02					00 32	
Charlton	d	22 49			23 05	23 08			23 19			23 35	23 38		23 49			00 08		00 19
Woolwich Dockyard	d	22 52				23 11			23 22				23 41		23 52			00 11		00 22
Woolwich Arsenal	d	22 55			23 10	23 14			23 25			23 40	23 44		23 55			00 14		00 25
Plumstead	d	22 57			23 13	23 16			23 27			23 43	23 46		23 57			00 16		00 27
Abbey Wood	d	23 00			23 16	23 20			23 30			23 46	23 50		23 59			00 20		00 30
Belvedere	d	23 03				23 23			23 33				23 53		00 03			00 23		00 33
Erith	d	23 06				23 25			23 36				23 55		00 06			00 25		00 36
Slade Green	d	23a09			23 22	23 31			23 40			23 52	00 01		00 10			00 31		00 40
Dartford	a		23 24	23 29	23 27	23 36		23 38	23 45	23 54	23 59	23 57	00 06	00 08	00 15	00 24		00 36	00 38	00 45
	d				23 28			23 39				23 58		00 09					00 39	
Stone Crossing	d				23 32			23 43				00 02		00 13					00s43	
Greenhithe for Bluewater	d				23 34			23 45				00 04		00 15					00s45	
Swanscombe	d				23 37			23 48				00 07		00 18					00s48	
Northfleet	d				23 39			23 50				00 09		00 20					00s50	
Gravesend	d				23 43		23 48	23a55				00 13		00a25					00a55	
Higham	d				23 49							00 19								
Strood	d				23 55		23 59					00 25								
Maidstone West	d																			
Rochester	d				23 58		00 02					00 28								
Chatham	d				00 02		00 06					00 31								
Gillingham (Kent)	a				00 06		00 10					00 36								
Rainham Kt	a						00 15													

Table T200-R

Mondays to Fridays

21 May to 7 December

Gillingham and Dartford - London

Miles	Miles	Miles	Miles	Miles			SE TWO	SE MO	SE TWO	TL	SE TWO	SE TWO	SE ThFO	SE TWO	SE TWO	TL	SE	SE	SE	TL	SE		SE	SE	SE
—	—	—	—	—	Rainham Kt	d																			
0	—	—	0	0	**Gillingham (Kent)**	d										04 00				04 36					
1¾	—	—	1¾	1¾	**Chatham**	d										04 04				04 40					
2¼	—	—	2¼	2¼	Rochester	d										04 08				04 44					
—	—	—	—	—	Maidstone West	d																			
3¼	—	—	3¼	3¼	Strood	d										04 11				04 47					
6	—	—	6	6	Higham	d										04 16				04 52					
10½	—	—	10½	10½	**Gravesend**	d										04 23	04 32			04 59					
12½	—	—	12½	—	Northfleet	d				00 03						04 27				05 03					
13¼	—	—	13¼	—	Swanscombe	d				00 05						04 29				05 05					
14½	—	—	14½	—	Greenhithe for Bluewater	d				00 08						04 32	04 38			05 08					
15¼	—	—	15¼	—	Stone Crossing	d				00 10						04 34				05 10					
17¼	0	0	17¼	0	**Dartford**	a				00 15						04 39	04 44			05 14					
—	—	—	—	—		d											04 45	05 03	05 12	05 15	05 18				
19¼	2	—	—	—	Slade Green	d												05 08		05 21			05 26		
20½	3¼	—	—	—	Erith	d												05 11					05 29		
21¾	4½	—	—	—	Belvedere	d												05 13					05 31		
23¼	6	—	—	—	Abbey Wood	d												05 17		05 28			05 35		
24¾	7½	—	—	—	Plumstead	d												05 20		05 31			05 38		
25¼	8	—	—	—	**Woolwich Arsenal**	d												05 23		05 34			05 41		
26	8¾	—	—	—	Woolwich Dockyard	d						00 03	00 03	00 03				05 25							
27	9¾	—	—	—	Charlton	d						00 06	00 06	00 06				05 29		05 40			05 47		
—	—	—	19	—	Crayford	d											04 50		05 17					05 32	
—	—	—	20½	—	Bexley	d											04 53		05 20					05 35	
—	—	—	21½	—	Albany Park	d									00 01		04 55		05 22					05 37	
—	—	—	22½	—	Sidcup	d									00 04		04 58		05 25					05 40	
—	—	—	24	—	New Eltham	d									00 08		05 02		05 29					05 43	
—	—	—	25	—	Mottingham	d									00 10		05 04		05 31					05 46	
—	—	—	26½	—	Lee	d									00 13		05 07		05 34					05 49	
—	—	—	27¼	—	Hither Green	d									00 16		05 10		05 37					05 52	
—	—	3	—	3	Barnehurst	d															05 27				05 42
—	—	4¼	—	4¼	Bexleyheath	d															05 30				05 44
—	—	5¾	—	5¾	Welling	d															05 33				05 47
—	—	6¾	—	6¾	Falconwood	d															05 35				05 50
—	—	8	—	8	Eltham	d															05 38				05 53
—	—	9	—	9	Kidbrooke	d															05 42				05 56
29	—	10	—	10	Blackheath	d						00 11	00 11	00 11							05 46		05 52		05 59
30	—	11	28½	11	Lewisham	d					00 05	00 15	00 15	00 16			05 16		05 43		05 50		05 56	05 58	06 03
—	—	11½	29	—	St Johns	d			00 02															06 00	06 05
—	—	12¼	29¾	—	New Cross ⊖	d	00 01	00 02	00 05															06 02	06 07
—	—	—	—	12¾	Nunhead	d																			
—	—	—	—	13½	Peckham Rye	d																			
—	—	—	—	14¼	Denmark Hill	d																			
—	—	—	—	18½	**London Victoria** ⊖	a																			
—	10½	—	—	—	Westcombe Park	d												05 31		05 42					
—	11	—	—	—	Maze Hill	d												05 33		05 44					
—	12	—	—	—	Greenwich	d												05 36		05 47					
—	12½	—	—	—	**Deptford**	a												05 38		05 49					
34¼	15½	15¼	32¾	—	London Bridge ⊖	a	00 07	00 07	00 10		00 13	00 23	00 23	00 24	00 29		05 24	05 44	05 51	05 57	05 58		06 04	06 07	06 13
—	16¼	—	—	—	**London Cannon Street** ⊖	a	00 13	00 13	00 18			00 33						05 52						06 15	06 20
35¼	—	16¼	33¼	—	**London Waterloo (East)** ⊖	a							00 29	00 30			05 30		05 57		06 04		06 10		
—	—	—	—	—	**London Charing Cross** ⊖	a							00 35	00 34			05 37		06 03		06 10		06 16		
—	—	—	—	12½	**Ebbsfleet International**	a																			
—	—	—	—	29¾	**Stratford International** ⊖	a																			
—	—	—	—	35¼	**St Pancras Int'l** ⊖	a																			

Table T200-R

Mondays to Fridays

21 May to 7 December

Gillingham and Dartford - London

		SE	SE ◇	SE	SE	SE	SE	SE	TL	SE ◇	SE	SE	SE		SE	SE	SE	SE	SE	TL	SE ◇	SE ◇	SE	SE	SE
Rainham Kt	d									05 15										05 30		05 45			
Gillingham (Kent)	d								05 06	05 20										05 36	05 40	05 50			
Chatham	d								05 10	05 24										05 40	05 44	05 54			
Rochester	d								05 14	05 28										05 44	05 48	05 58			
Maidstone West	d																								
Strood	d								05 17	05 31										05 47		06 01			
Higham	d								05 22											05 52					
Gravesend	d				05 46				05 29	05 41										05 59		06 11		06 15	
Northfleet	d				05 50				05 33											06 03					
Swanscombe	d				05 52				05 35											06 05					
Greenhithe for Bluewater	d				05 55				05 38											06 08				06 21	
Stone Crossing	d				05 57				05 40											06 10					
Dartford	a				06 01				05 44											06 14				06 26	
	d	05 42			06 03		05 33	05 40	05 45		05 48	06 30					06 01	06 06		06 15			06 20	06 27	
Slade Green	d						05 38		05 51						05 56		06 07		06 14	06 21					
Erith	d						05 41								05 59		06 10		06 17						
Belvedere	d						05 43								06 01		06 12		06 19						
Abbey Wood	d						05 47		05 58						06 05		06 16		06 23	06 28				06 37	
Plumstead	d						05 50		06 01						06 08		06 19		06 26	06 31					
Woolwich Arsenal	d						05 53		06 04						06 11		06 22		06 29	06 34				06 41	
Woolwich Dockyard	d						05 55								06 13		06 25		06 31						
Charlton	d					05 55	05 59		06 10				06 15		06 17		06 28		06 35	06 40				06 47	
Crayford	d	05 47		06 04	06 08	06 26						06 35	06 49												
Bexley	d	05 50		06 07	06 11	06 29						06 38	06 52												
Albany Park	d	05 53		06 10	06 14	06 32						06 40	06 55												
Sidcup	d	05 56		06 13	06 17	06 35						06 43	06 58												
New Eltham	d	05 59		06 16	06 20	06 38						06 47	07 01												
Mottingham	d	06 02		06 19	06 23	06 41						06 49	07 04												
Lee	d	06 05		06 22	06 26	06 44						06 53	07 07												
Hither Green	d	06 09		06 25	06 29	06 48						06 56	07 11												
Barnehurst	d							05 48			05 56					06 10		06 14					06 28		06 36
Bexleyheath	d							05 51			05 59					06 13		06 17					06 31		06 39
Welling	d							05 54			06 02					06 16		06 20					06 34		06 42
Falconwood	d							05 56			06 04					06 18		06 22					06 36		06 44
Eltham	d							05 59			06 07					06 21		06 25					06 39		06 47
Kidbrooke	d							06 02			06 11					06 25		06 28					06 42		06 51
Blackheath	d							06 06			06 15				06 22	06 29		06 32	06 40				06 46		06 55
Lewisham	d			06 31		06 54		06 11			06 19		07 17		06 26	06 33		06 36	06 44				06 50		06 59
St Johns	d					06 56							07 19			06 35									07 01
New Cross ⊖	d		06 33	06 36		06 58							07 22			06 37									07 03
Nunhead	d							06 17										06 44							
Peckham Rye	d							06 20										06 47							
Denmark Hill	d							06 24										06 50							
London Victoria ⊖	a							06 37										07 02							
Westcombe Park	d						06 01		06 12								06 31			06 42				06 49	
Maze Hill	d						06 03		06 14								06 33			06 44				06 52	
Greenwich	d						06 06		06 17								06 37			06 47				06 56	
Deptford	a						06 08		06 19								06 39			06 49				06 58	
London Bridge ⊖	a	06 18	06 38	06 41	06 39	07 04	06 14		06 27		06 27	07 06	07 28		06 34	06 43	06 46		06 52	06 57	06 25		06 58	07 05	07 09
London Cannon Street ⊖	a		06 46	06 48		07 11	06 22						07 35			06 50	06 54				06 33			07 13	07 16
London Waterloo (East) ⊖	a	06 24			06 45						06 34	07 12			06 40				06 58				07 04		
London Charing Cross ⊖	a	06 31			06 52						06 40	07 18			06 46				07 05				07 12		
Ebbsfleet International	a									05 45												06 15			
Stratford International ⊖	a									05 57												06 27			
St Pancras Int'l ⊖	a									06 05												06 35			

Table T200-R

Mondays to Fridays

21 May to 7 December

Gillingham and Dartford - London

		SE	SE	SE	SE	SE	SE	SE	TL	SE	SE	SE	SE	SE	SE	SE	SE	SE	SE	SE	SE	SE	SE
										◇	◇■												
Rainham Kt	d								06 00	06 11	06 28												
Gillingham (Kent) ■	d								06 06	06 17	06 33												
Chatham ■	d								06 10	06 21	06 37												
Rochester ■	d								06 14	06 25	06 41												
Maidstone West	d																						
Strood ■	d	06 23							06 18	06 28									07 03				
Higham	d	06 28							06 23										07 08				
Gravesend ■	d	06 35		06 50					06 30	06 39									07 15			07 39	
Northfleet	d			06 54					06 33										07 18				
Swanscombe	d			06 56					06 35										07 20				
Greenhithe for Bluewater	d	06 42		06 59					06 39										07 24			07 45	
Stone Crossing	d	06 44		07 01					06 41										07 26				
Dartford ■	a	06 48		07 06					06 45										07 30			07 50	
	d	06 49		07 07			06 38	06 41	06 46					06 55	06 59				07 31			07 51	
Slade Green ■	d					06 38	06 43		06 51					07 00		07 06		07 06					
Erith	d					06 41	06 46							07 03									
Belvedere	d					06 43	06 48							07 05									
Abbey Wood	d					06 47	06 52		06 58					07 09									
Plumstead	d					06 50	06 55		07 01					07 12									
Woolwich Arsenal ■ ⛴	d					06 53	06 58		07 04					07 15									
Woolwich Dockyard	d					06 56	07 01							07 17									
Charlton ■	d				06 55	06 59	07 04		07 10					07 21									07 25
Crayford	d	06 54	07 08	07 12	07 31														07 36	07 40	07 49	07 56	08 04
Bexley	d	06 57	07 11	07 16	07 34														07 39	07 43	07 52	07 59	08 07
Albany Park	d	07 00	07 14	07 19	07 37														07 42	07 46	07 55	08 02	08 10
Sidcup ■	d	07 03	07 17	07 22	07 40														07 45	07 49	07 58	08 05	08 13
New Eltham	d	07 06	07 21	07 26	07 43														07 49	07 52	08 01	08 09	08 17
Mottingham	d	07 09	07 24	07 29	07 46															07 55	08 04		08 20
Lee	d	07 12	07 27	07 32	07 49															07 59	08 08		08 23
Hither Green ■	d	07 16	07 31	07 36	07 53															08 02	08 11	08 15	08 27
Barnehurst ■	d							06 49				06 53	07 00		07 07	07a11	07 12	07 12					
Bexleyheath	d							06 52				06 56	07 03		07 10		07 15	07 15					
Welling	d							06 55				06 59	07 06		07 13		07 18	07 18					
Falconwood	d							06 57				07 01	07 08		07 16		07 20	07 20					
Eltham	d							07 00				07 04	07 11		07 19		07 23	07 23					
Kidbrooke	d							07 04				07 07	07 15		07 23		07 27	07 27					
Blackheath ■	d					07 04		07 08				07 11	07 19		07 27		07 31	07 31					
Lewisham ■ ⛴	d		07 38		08 00	07 08		07 12				07 15	07 23		07 31		07 35	07 35			08 19		
St Johns	d		07 40		08 03								07 25								08 21		
New Cross ■ ⊖	d		07 43		08 06								07 28				07 38	07 38			08 24		
Nunhead ■	d																						
Peckham Rye ■	d											07 21											
Denmark Hill ■	d											07 26											
London Victoria ■ ⊖	a											07 38											
Westcombe Park	d						07 07		07 12					07 23									
Maze Hill	d						07 09		07 14					07 26									
Greenwich ■ ⛴	d						07 13		07 17					07 30									
Deptford	a						07 15		07 19					07 32									
London Bridge ■ ⊖	a	07 25	07 48	07 45	08 11	07 16	07 21	07 20	07 27		07 19		07 33	07 38	07 39		07 44	07 44	08 05	08 13	08 30	08 25	08 37
London Cannon Street ■ ⊖	a		07 56		08 19		07 29				07 27		07 41	07 46			07 51	07 51			08 38		
London Waterloo (East) ■ ⊖	a	07 31		07 51		07 22		07 26							07 46				08 11	08 19		08 31	08 43
London Charing Cross ■ ⊖	a	07 38		07 58		07 29		07 33							07 53				08 18	08 26		08 38	08 50
Ebbsfleet International	a									06 42													
Stratford International ⊖ ⛴	a									06 55													
St Pancras Int'l ■ ⊖	a									07 02													

Table T200-R

Mondays to Fridays

21 May to 7 December

Gillingham and Dartford - London

		SE	SE	SE	TL	SE	SE	SE	SE	SE	SE	SE	SE	SE	SE	SE	SE	SE	SE	SE	SE	SE	SE	TL
						◇																		
Rainham Kt	d				06 30																			06 56
Gillingham (Kent) ■	d				06 36																			07 03
Chatham ■	d				06 40																			07 07
Rochester ■	d				06 44																			07 11
Maidstone West	d					06 53																		
Strood ■	d		06 44		06 47	07 10											07 38							07 17
Higham	d		06 49		06 52												07 43							07 22
Gravesend ■	d		06 56		06 59	07 21											07 50							07 29
Northfleet	d				07 03												07 55							07 32
Swanscombe	d				07 05												07 57							07 34
Greenhithe for Bluewater	d		07 03		07 08												08 01							07 38
Stone Crossing	d		07 05		07 10												08 03							07 40
Dartford ■	a		07 10		07 14												08 08							07 44
	d		07 11	07 13	07 15		07 19				07 28	07 35		07 39			08 09							07 45
Slade Green ■	d	07 10			07 21			07 25			07 33									07 36	07 37	07 37	07 49	07 50
Erith	d	07 12						07 28			07 35									07 39				
Belvedere	d	07 15						07 30			07 38									07 41				
Abbey Wood	d	07 18	07 23		07 28			07 34			07 41									07 45				07 57
Plumstead	d	07 21			07 31			07 37			07 44									07 48				08 01
Woolwich Arsenal ■ ⛴	d	07 24	07 28		07 34			07 40			07 47									07 51				08 04
Woolwich Dockyard	d	07 27						07 43												07 54				
Charlton ■	d	07 30	07 33		07 40			07 46			07 53								07 56	07 57				08 10
Crayford	d														08 04	08 10	08 14		08 28				08a00	
Bexley	d														08 07	08 13	08 17		08 31					
Albany Park	d														08 10	08 16	08 20		08 34					
Sidcup ■	d														08 13	08 19	08 24	08 29	08 37					
New Eltham	d														08 17	08 22	08 28	08 32	08 40					
Mottingham	d														08 20	08 25		08 35	08 43					
Lee	d														08 23	08 29		08 38	08 46					
Hither Green ■	d														08 27	08 32	08 35	08 42	08 50					
Barnehurst ■	d			07 21			07 27		07 32	07 36		07 43		07 47							07a50	07 52		
Bexleyheath	d			07 24			07 30		07 35	07 39		07 46		07 50								07 55		
Welling	d			07 28			07 34		07 38	07 42		07 49		07 54								07 58		
Falconwood	d			07 31			07 36		07 40	07 44		07 51		07 56								08 00		
Eltham	d			07 34			07 39		07 43	07 47		07 54		07 59								08 03		
Kidbrooke	d			07 37			07 43		07 47	07 51		07 57		08 03								08 07		
Blackheath ■	d	07 36		07 42			07 47		07 51	07 55	07 58	08 02		08 07								08 11		
Lewisham ■ ⛴	d	07 40		07 46			07 51		07 55		08 02	08 06		08 11		08 39			08 55			08 15		
St Johns	d								07 57							08 41			08 59			08 18		
New Cross ■ ⊖	d								08 00				08 11			08 44			09 01			08 21		
Nunhead ■	d			07 54								08 14												
Peckham Rye ■	d			07 57								08 17												
Denmark Hill ■	d			08 00								08 20												
London Victoria ■ ⊖	a			08 13								08 33												
Westcombe Park	d		07 36		07 42			07 49												08 00				08 12
Maze Hill	d		07 38		07 44			07 51												08 02				08 14
Greenwich ■ ⛴	d		07 42		07 47			07 55												08 06				08 17
Deptford	a		07 44		07 49			07 57												08 08				08 19
London Bridge ■ ⊖	a	07 51	07 50		07 57		08 00	08 03	08 05	08 07	08 11		08 17	08 19	08 37	08 49	08 45	08 54	09 08	08 15		08 28		08 27
London Cannon Street ■ ⊖	a		07 59					08 11	08 13				08 25			08 57			09 16	08 23		08 36		
London Waterloo (East) ■ ⊖	a	07 57					08 06			08 13	08 17			08 25	08 43		08 51	09 01						
London Charing Cross ■ ⊖	a	08 04					08 13			08 20	08 24			08 32	08 50		08 58	09 07						
Ebbsfleet International	a					07 25																		
Stratford International ⊖ ⛴	a					07 39																		
St Pancras Int'l ■ ⊖	a					07 46																		

Table T200-R

Mondays to Fridays

21 May to 7 December

Gillingham and Dartford - London

		SE ◇■	SE ◇	SE ◇	SE		SE	SE	SE	SE	SE	SE	SE	SE	SE	SE	SE	SE	SE	SE	TL		SE ◇■	SE ◇	SE ◇
Rainham Kt	d	07 12	07 17																		07 30		07 39	07 47	
Gillingham (Kent) ■	d	07 17	07 22																		07 36		07 44	07 52	
Chatham ■	d	07 22	07 27																		07 40		07 49	07 56	
Rochester ■	d	07 26	07 30																		07 44		07 52	08 00	
Maidstone West	d			07 25																					07 53
Strood ■	d		07 34	07 43																	07 47			08 03	08 11
Higham	d																				07 52				
Gravesend ■	d		07 44	07 53											08 11			08 34			07 59			08 14	08 21
Northfleet	d														08 15			08 38			08 03				
Swanscombe	d														08 17			08 40			08 05				
Greenhithe for Bluewater	d														08 20			08 43			08 08				
Stone Crossing	d														08 22			08 45			08 10				
Dartford ■	a														08 27			08 49			08 14				
	d								07 56		07 59				08 28			08 50		08 04	08 15				
Slade Green ■	d							07 54		07 59		08 03		08 03						08 09	08 21				
Erith	d							07 56		08 02										08 12					
Belvedere	d							07 59		08 04										08 14					
Abbey Wood	d							08 02		08 08										08 18	08 28				
Plumstead	d							08 05		08 11										08 21	08 31				
Woolwich Arsenal ■ ⛴	d							08 08		08 14										08 24	08 34				
Woolwich Dockyard	d									08 16										08 26					
Charlton ■	d							08 13		08 20									08 25	08 30	08 40				
Crayford	d														08 33			08 55	09 00						
Bexley	d														08 36			08 58	09 03						
Albany Park	d														08 39			09 01	09 06						
Sidcup ■	d														08 42		08 50	09 04	09 09						
New Eltham	d														08 45		08 53	09 07	09 12						
Mottingham	d														08 48		08 56	09 10	09 15						
Lee	d														08 51		08 59	09 13	09 18						
Hither Green ■	d														08 55		09 03	09 16	09 22						
Barnehurst ■	d				07 52		07 56		08 04		08 07	08a10	08 12	08 12		08 23									
Bexleyheath	d				07 55		07 59		08 07		08 10		08 15	08 15		08 26									
Welling	d				07 58		08 02		08 10		08 13		08 18	08 18		08 29									
Falconwood	d				08 00		08 04		08 12		08 16		08 21	08 21		08 31									
Eltham	d				08 03		08 07		08 15		08 19		08 24	08 24		08 34									
Kidbrooke	d				08 07		08 11		08 19		08 23		08 28	08 28		08 37									
Blackheath ■	d				08 11		08 15	08 18	08 23		08 27		08 32	08 32		08 42									
Lewisham ■ ⛴	d				08 15			08 22	08 27		08 31		08 36	08 36		08 46	09 10		09 29						
St Johns	d				08 18												09 12		09 31						
New Cross ■ ⊖	d				08 21								08 39	08 39			09 15		09 33						
Nunhead ■	d								08 34							08 52									
Peckham Rye ■	d								08 37							08 55									
Denmark Hill ■	d								08 42							08 59									
London Victoria ■ ⊖	a								08 55							09 11									
Westcombe Park	d									08 22										08 32	08 42				
Maze Hill	d									08 25										08 35	08 44				
Greenwich ■ ⛴	d									08 28										08 38	08 47				
Deptford	a									08 30										08 40	08 49				
London Bridge ■ ⊖	a	08 07			08 28		08 27	08 31		08 37	08 41		08 45	08 45	09 06		09 20	09 27	09 39	08 47	08 57		08 32		
London Cannon Street ■ ⊖	a	08 15			08 36					08 45			08 53	08 53			09 28		09 46	08 55			08 40		
London Waterloo (East) ■ ⊖	a						08 33	08 37			08 47				09 13			09 33							
London Charing Cross ■ ⊖	a						08 40	08 44			08 54				09 20			09 40							
Ebbsfleet International	a		07 48	07 56																				08 17	08 25
Stratford International ⊖ ⛴	a		08 00	08 09																				08 30	08 39
St Pancras Int'l ■ ⊖	a		08 08	08 16																				08 38	08 46

Table T200-R

Mondays to Fridays

21 May to 7 December

Gillingham and Dartford - London

		SE ◇■	SE	SE	SE	SE	SE	SE	SE	SE	SE	SE	TL		SE ◇	SE ◇■	SE	SE	SE	SE	SE	SE	SE	SE	SE
Rainham Kt	d	07 57											08 01		08 14	08 18									
Gillingham (Kent) ■	d	08 03											08 07		08 19	08 24									
Chatham ■	d	08 07											08 11		08 24	08 28									
Rochester ■	d	08 11											08 15		08 27	08 32									
Maidstone West	d																								
Strood ■	d												08 18		08 32										
Higham	d												08 23												
Gravesend ■	d							09 05					08 30		08 43			08 50						09 35	
Northfleet	d							09 08					08 34											09 38	
Swanscombe	d							09 10					08 36											09 40	
Greenhithe for Bluewater	d							09 14					08 39					08 56						09 44	
Stone Crossing	d							09 16					08 41											09 46	
Dartford ■	a							09 20					08 45					09 01						09 50	
	d		08 20				09 05	09 21		08 32	08 37		08 46				08 54	09 02					09 35	09 51	
Slade Green ■	d			08 26	08 30					08 39		08 45	08 51						08 59	09 07		09 07			
Erith	d			08 29	08 32					08 42		08 48							09 02						
Belvedere	d			08 31	08 35					08 44		08 50							09 04						
Abbey Wood	d			08 35	08 38					08 48		08 54	08 58						09 08						
Plumstead	d			08 38	08 41					08 51		08 57	09 01						09 11						
Woolwich Arsenal ■ ⛴	d			08 41	08 44					08 54		09 00	09 04						09 14						
Woolwich Dockyard	d			08 44	08 47					08 57		09 02							09 16						
Charlton ■	d			08 47	08 50				08 55	09 00		09 06	09 10						09 20						09 25
Crayford	d						09 12	09 26	09 32														09 42	09 56	10 02
Bexley	d						09 15	09 29	09 35														09 45	09 59	10 05
Albany Park	d						09 17		09 37														09 47		10 07
Sidcup ■	d						09 20	09 33	09 40														09 50	10 03	10 10
New Eltham	d						09 24	09 36	09 44														09 54	10 06	10 14
Mottingham	d						09 26		09 46														09 56		10 16
Lee	d						09 29		09 49														09 59		10 19
Hither Green ■	d						09 34		09 52														10 03		10 22
Barnehurst ■	d		08 28			08 41					08 45						09 02	09 09		09a15	09 20	09 20			
Bexleyheath	d		08 31			08 44					08 47						09 05	09 12			09 23	09 23			
Welling	d		08 34			08 47					08 50						09 08	09 15			09 26	09 26			
Falconwood	d		08 36			08 49					08 53						09 11	09 18			09 28	09 28			
Eltham	d		08 39			08 52					08 56						09 14	09 21			09 31	09 31			
Kidbrooke	d		08 43			08 56					08 59						09 18	09 24			09 34	09 34			
Blackheath ■	d		08 47	08 52		09 00					09 03	09 11					09 22	09 28			09 38	09 38			
Lewisham ■ ⛴	d		08 51	08 56		09 04			09 57		09 07	09 15					09 26	09 32			09 42	09 42			10 27
St Johns	d					09 06			09 59												09 44	09 44			10 31
New Cross ■ ⊖	d					09 08			10 01												09 47	09 47			10 33
Nunhead ■	d										09 14							09 37							
Peckham Rye ■	d										09 17							09 40							
Denmark Hill ■	d										09 22							09 44							
London Victoria ■ ⊖	a										09 35							09 57							
Westcombe Park	d				08 52					09 03			09 12						09 22						
Maze Hill	d				08 54					09 05			09 14						09 24						
Greenwich ■ ⛴	d				08 58					09 09			09 17						09 28						
Deptford	a				09 00					09 11			09 19						09 30						
London Bridge ■ ⊖	a	08 51	08 59	09 04	09 06	09 14	09 43	09 51	10 07	09 18		09 23	09 27			09 10	09 34		09 36		09 52	09 52	10 13	10 20	10 38
London Cannon Street ■ ⊖	a	08 59			09 14	09 21			10 15	09 26						09 18			09 44		10 02	10 02			10 43
London Waterloo (East) ■ ⊖	a		09 05	09 11			09 49	09 57				09 29					09 40						10 19	10 26	
London Charing Cross ■ ⊖	a		09 12	09 18			09 56	10 03				09 37					09 47						10 23	10 30	
Ebbsfleet International	a														08 46										
Stratford International ⊖ ⛴	a														08 59										
St Pancras Int'l ■ ⊖	a														09 07										

Please note, Network Rail have stated that further updates to this timetable are possible during the validity period.

Table T200-R

Mondays to Fridays

21 May to 7 December

Gillingham and Dartford - London

		SE	SE	TL	SE ◇		SE	SE	SE	SE	SE	SE	SE	SE	SE	SE	SE	TL	SE ◇	SE	SE		SE	SE	SE
Rainham Kt	d			08 30	08 46													09 00	09 16						
Gillingham (Kent)	d			08 36	08 51													09 06	09 21						
Chatham	d			08 40	08 55													09 10	09 25						
Rochester	d			08 44	08 59													09 14	09 29						
Maidstone West	d																								
Strood	d			08 47	09 02													09 17	09 32						
Higham	d			08 52														09 22							
Gravesend	d			08 59	09 12			09 20						10 05				09 29	09 42		09 50				
Northfleet	d			09 03										10 08				09 33							
Swanscombe	d			09 05										10 10				09 35							
Greenhithe for Bluewater	d			09 08				09 26						10 14				09 38			09 56				
Stone Crossing	d			09 10										10 16				09 40							
Dartford	a			09 14				09 31						10 20				09 44			10 01				
	d		09 11	09 15			09 25	09 32					10 05	10 21			09 41	09 45		09 54	10 02				
Slade Green	d	09 09	09 16	09 21					09 29	09 37		09 37				09 39	09 46	09 51					09 59	10 07	
Erith	d	09 12	09 18						09 32							09 42	09 48						10 02		
Belvedere	d	09 14	09 21						09 34							09 44	09 51						10 04		
Abbey Wood	d	09 18	09 24	09 28					09 38							09 48	09 54	09 58					10 08		
Plumstead	d	09 21	09 27	09 31					09 41							09 51	09 57	10 01					10 11		
Woolwich Arsenal	d	09 24	09 30	09 34					09 44							09 54	10 00	10 04					10 14		
Woolwich Dockyard	d	09 26	09 33						09 46							09 56	10 03						10 16		
Charlton	d	09 30	09 36	09 40					09 50						09 55	10 00	10 06	10 10					10 20		
Crayford	d												10 12	10 26	10 32										
Bexley	d												10 15	10 29	10 35										
Albany Park	d												10 17		10 37										
Sidcup	d												10 20	10 33	10 40										
New Eltham	d												10 24	10 36	10 44										
Mottingham	d												10 26		10 46										
Lee	d												10 29		10 49										
Hither Green	d												10 33		10 52										
Barnehurst	d						09 33	09 39		09a45	09 50	09 50								10 03	10 09			10a15	10 20
Bexleyheath	d						09 36	09 42			09 53	09 53								10 06	10 12				10 23
Welling	d						09 39	09 45			09 56	09 56								10 09	10 15				10 26
Falconwood	d						09 41	09 48			09 58	09 58								10 11	10 18				10 28
Eltham	d						09 44	09 51			10 01	10 01								10 14	10 21				10 31
Kidbrooke	d						09 47	09 54			10 04	10 04								10 17	10 24				10 34
Blackheath	d		09 41				09 51	09 58			10 08	10 08					10 11			10 21	10 28				10 38
Lewisham	d		09 46				09 55	10 02			10 12	10 12			10 57		10 16			10 25	10 32				10 42
St Johns	d										10 14	10 14			11 01										10 44
New Cross	d										10 17	10 17			11 03										10 47
Nunhead	d							10 07													10 37				
Peckham Rye	d							10 10													10 40				
Denmark Hill	d							10 14													10 44				
London Victoria	a							10 25													10 55				
Westcombe Park	d	09 32		09 42					09 52							10 02		10 12					10 22		
Maze Hill	d	09 34		09 44					09 54							10 04		10 14					10 24		
Greenwich	d	09 37		09 47					09 57							10 07		10 17					10 27		
Deptford	a	09 39		09 49					09 59							10 09		10 19					10 29		
London Bridge	a	09 45	09 55	09 57			10 03		10 05		10 22	10 22	10 43	10 50	11 08	10 15	10 25	10 27		10 33			10 35		10 52
London Cannon Street	a	09 55							10 13		10 30	10 30			11 13	10 21							10 41		11 00
London Waterloo (East)	a		10 01				10 09						10 49	10 56			10 31			10 39					
London Charing Cross	a		10 05				10 15						10 53	11 00			10 35			10 43					
Ebbsfleet International	a				09 16														09 46						
Stratford International	a				09 28														09 59						
St Pancras Int'l	a				09 36														10 06						

Table T200-R

Mondays to Fridays

21 May to 7 December

Gillingham and Dartford - London

		SE	SE	SE	SE	SE	SE	TL	SE ◇	SE	SE	SE	SE		SE	SE	SE	SE	SE	SE	SE	TL	SE ◇	SE	SE
Rainham Kt	d							09 28	09 46													09 58	10 16		
Gillingham (Kent)	d							09 34	09 51													10 04	10 21		
Chatham	d							09 38	09 55													10 08	10 25		
Rochester	d							09 42	09 59													10 12	10 29		
Maidstone West	d																								
Strood	d							09 45	10 02													10 15	10 32		
Higham	d							09 50														10 20			
Gravesend	d			10 35				09 59	10 12		10 20							11 05				10 29	10 42		10 50
Northfleet	d			10 38				10 02										11 08				10 32			
Swanscombe	d			10 40				10 04										11 10				10 34			
Greenhithe for Bluewater	d			10 44				10 08			10 26							11 14				10 38			10 56
Stone Crossing	d			10 46				10 10										11 16				10 40			
Dartford	a			10 50				10 14			10 31							11 20				10 44			11 01
	d		10 35	10 51			10 11	10 15		10 25	10 32						11 05	11 21			10 41	10 45		10 55	11 02
Slade Green	d	10 07				10 09	10 16	10 21				10 29	10 37			10 37				10 39	10 46	10 51			
Erith	d					10 12	10 18					10 32								10 42	10 48				
Belvedere	d					10 14	10 21					10 34								10 44	10 51				
Abbey Wood	d					10 18	10 24	10 28				10 38								10 48	10 54	10 58			
Plumstead	d					10 21	10 27	10 31				10 41								10 51	10 57	11 01			
Woolwich Arsenal	d					10 24	10 30	10 34				10 44								10 54	11 00	11 04			
Woolwich Dockyard	d					10 26	10 33					10 46								10 56	11 03				
Charlton	d				10 25	10 30	10 36	10 40				10 50							10 55	11 00	11 06	11 10			
Crayford	d		10 42	10 56	11 02												11 12	11 26	11 32						
Bexley	d		10 45	10 59	11 05												11 15	11 29	11 35						
Albany Park	d		10 47		11 07												11 17		11 37						
Sidcup	d		10 50	11 03	11 10												11 20	11 33	11 40						
New Eltham	d		10 54	11 06	11 14												11 24	11 36	11 44						
Mottingham	d		10 56		11 16												11 26		11 46						
Lee	d		10 59		11 19												11 29		11 49						
Hither Green	d		11 03		11 22												11 33		11 52						
Barnehurst	d	10 20								10 33	10 39		10a45		10 50	10 50								11 03	11 09
Bexleyheath	d	10 23								10 36	10 42				10 53	10 53								11 06	11 12
Welling	d	10 26								10 39	10 45				10 56	10 56								11 09	11 15
Falconwood	d	10 28								10 41	10 48				10 58	10 58								11 11	11 18
Eltham	d	10 31								10 44	10 51				11 01	11 01								11 14	11 21
Kidbrooke	d	10 34								10 47	10 54				11 04	11 04								11 17	11 24
Blackheath	d	10 38					10 41			10 51	10 58				11 08	11 08					11 11			11 21	11 28
Lewisham	d	10 42			11 27		10 46			10 55	11 02				11 12	11 12			11 57		11 16			11 25	11 32
St Johns	d	10 44			11 29										11 14	11 14			11 59						
New Cross	d	10 47			11 31										11 17	11 17			12 01						
Nunhead	d										11 07														11 37
Peckham Rye	d										11 10														11 40
Denmark Hill	d										11 14														11 44
London Victoria	a										11 25														11 55
Westcombe Park	d					10 32		10 42				10 52								11 02		11 12			
Maze Hill	d					10 34		10 44				10 54								11 04		11 14			
Greenwich	d					10 37		10 47				10 57								11 07		11 17			
Deptford	a					10 39		10 49				10 59								11 09		11 19			
London Bridge	a	10 52	11 13	11 21	11 37	10 45	10 55	10 57		11 03		11 05			11 22	11 22	11 43	11 50	12 07	11 15	11 25	11 27		11 33	
London Cannon Street	a	11 00			11 43	10 51						11 11			11 30	11 30			12 13	11 21					
London Waterloo (East)	a		11 19	11 26			11 01			11 09							11 49	11 56			11 31			11 39	
London Charing Cross	a		11 23	11 30			11 05			11 13							11 53	12 00			11 35			11 43	
Ebbsfleet International	a								10 16														10 46		
Stratford International	a								10 28														10 59		
St Pancras Int'l	a								10 35														11 07		

Table T200-R

Mondays to Fridays

21 May to 7 December

Gillingham and Dartford - London

		SE	SE	SE	SE		SE	SE	SE	SE	SE	TL	SE	SE	SE	SE	SE	SE	SE	SE	SE		SE	SE	SE
													◇												
Rainham Kt	d											10 28	10 46												
Gillingham (Kent)	d											10 34	10 51												
Chatham	d											10 38	10 55												
Rochester	d											10 42	10 59												
Maidstone West	d																								
Strood	d											10 45	11 02												
Higham	d											10 50													
Gravesend	d							11 35				10 59	11 12		11 20						12 05				
Northfleet	d							11 38				11 02									12 08				
Swanscombe	d							11 40				11 04									12 10				
Greenhithe for Bluewater	d							11 44				11 08			11 26						12 14				
Stone Crossing	d							11 46				11 10									12 16				
Dartford	a							11 50				11 14			11 31						12 20				
	d						11 35	11 51			11 11	11 15		11 25	11 32					12 05	12 21				11 41
Slade Green	d	10 59	11 07		11 07					11 09	11 16	11 21				11 29	11 37		11 37					11 39	11 46
Erith	d	11 02								11 12	11 18					11 32								11 42	11 48
Belvedere	d	11 04								11 14	11 21					11 34								11 44	11 51
Abbey Wood	d	11 08								11 18	11 24	11 28				11 38								11 48	11 54
Plumstead	d	11 11								11 21	11 27	11 31				11 41								11 51	11 57
Woolwich Arsenal	d	11 14								11 24	11 30	11 34				11 44								11 54	12 00
Woolwich Dockyard	d	11 16								11 26	11 33					11 46								11 56	12 03
Charlton	d	11 20							11 25	11 30	11 36	11 40				11 50							11 55	12 00	12 06
Crayford	d						11 42	11 56	12 02											12 12	12 26		12 32		
Bexley	d						11 45	11 59	12 05											12 15	12 29		12 35		
Albany Park	d						11 47		12 07											12 17			12 37		
Sidcup	d						11 50	12 03	12 10											12 20	12 33		12 40		
New Eltham	d						11 54	12 06	12 14											12 24	12 36		12 44		
Mottingham	d						11 56		12 16											12 26			12 46		
Lee	d						11 59		12 19											12 29			12 49		
Hither Green	d						12 03		12 22											12 33			12 52		
Barnehurst	d		11a15	11 20	11 20									11 33	11 39		11a45	11 50	11 50						
Bexleyheath	d			11 23	11 23									11 36	11 42			11 53	11 53						
Welling	d			11 26	11 26									11 39	11 45			11 56	11 56						
Falconwood	d			11 28	11 28									11 41	11 48			11 58	11 58						
Eltham	d			11 31	11 31									11 44	11 51			12 01	12 01						
Kidbrooke	d			11 34	11 34									11 47	11 54			12 04	12 04						
Blackheath	d			11 38	11 38						11 41			11 51	11 58			12 08	12 08						12 11
Lewisham	d			11 42	11 42				12 27		11 46			11 55	12 02			12 12	12 12				12 57		12 16
St Johns	d			11 44	11 44				12 29									12 14	12 14				12 59		
New Cross	d			11 47	11 47				12 31									12 17	12 17				13 01		
Nunhead	d														12 07										
Peckham Rye	d														12 10										
Denmark Hill	d														12 14										
London Victoria	a														12 25										
Westcombe Park	d	11 22								11 32		11 42				11 52								12 02	
Maze Hill	d	11 24								11 34		11 44				11 54								12 04	
Greenwich	d	11 27								11 37		11 47				11 57								12 07	
Deptford	a	11 29								11 39		11 49				11 59								12 09	
London Bridge	a	11 35		11 52	11 52		12 13	12 20	12 37	11 45	11 55	11 57		12 03		12 05		12 22	12 22	12 43	12 50		13 07	12 15	12 25
London Cannon Street	a	11 41		12 00	12 00				12 43	11 51						12 11		12 30	12 30				13 13	12 21	
London Waterloo (East)	a						12 19	12 26			12 01			12 09						12 49	12 56				12 31
London Charing Cross	a						12 23	12 30			12 05			12 13						12 53	13 00				12 35
Ebbsfleet International	a												11 16												
Stratford International	a												11 29												
St Pancras Int'l	a												11 40												

Table T200-R

Mondays to Fridays

21 May to 7 December

Gillingham and Dartford - London

		TL	SE	SE	SE	SE	SE	SE	SE	SE	SE	SE	SE		SE	TL	SE	SE	SE	SE	SE	SE	SE	SE	SE
			◇														◇								
Rainham Kt	d	10 58	11 16													11 28	11 46								
Gillingham (Kent)	d	11 04	11 21													11 34	11 51								
Chatham	d	11 08	11 25													11 38	11 55								
Rochester	d	11 12	11 29													11 42	11 59								
Maidstone West	d																								
Strood	d	11 15	11 32													11 45	12 02								
Higham	d	11 20														11 50									
Gravesend	d	11 29	11 42		11 50						12 35					11 59	12 12		12 20						13 05
Northfleet	d	11 32									12 38					12 02									13 08
Swanscombe	d	11 34									12 40					12 04									13 10
Greenhithe for Bluewater	d	11 38			11 56						12 44					12 08			12 26						13 14
Stone Crossing	d	11 40									12 46					12 10									13 16
Dartford	a	11 44			12 01						12 50					12 14			12 31						13 20
	d	11 45		11 54	12 02					12 35	12 51				12 11	12 15		12 25	12 32					13 05	13 21
Slade Green	d	11 51				11 59	12 07		12 07				12 09		12 16	12 21				12 29	12 37		12 37		
Erith	d					12 02							12 12		12 18					12 32					
Belvedere	d					12 04							12 14		12 21					12 34					
Abbey Wood	d	11 58				12 08							12 18		12 24	12 28				12 38					
Plumstead	d	12 01				12 11							12 21		12 27	12 31				12 41					
Woolwich Arsenal	d	12 04				12 14							12 24		12 30	12 34				12 44					
Woolwich Dockyard	d					12 16							12 26		12 33					12 46					
Charlton	d	12 10				12 20						12 25	12 30		12 36	12 40				12 50					
Crayford	d									12 42	12 56	13 02												13 12	13 26
Bexley	d									12 45	12 59	13 05												13 15	13 29
Albany Park	d									12 47		13 07												13 17	
Sidcup	d									12 50	13 03	13 10												13 20	13 33
New Eltham	d									12 54	13 06	13 14												13 24	13 36
Mottingham	d									12 56		13 16												13 26	
Lee	d									12 59		13 19												13 29	
Hither Green	d									13 03		13 22												13 33	
Barnehurst	d			12 03	12 09		12a15	12 20	12 20									12 33	12 39		12a45	12 50	12 50		
Bexleyheath	d			12 06	12 12			12 23	12 23									12 36	12 42			12 53	12 53		
Welling	d			12 09	12 15			12 26	12 26									12 39	12 45			12 56	12 56		
Falconwood	d			12 11	12 18			12 28	12 28									12 41	12 48			12 58	12 58		
Eltham	d			12 14	12 21			12 31	12 31									12 44	12 51			13 01	13 01		
Kidbrooke	d			12 17	12 24			12 34	12 34									12 47	12 54			13 04	13 04		
Blackheath	d			12 21	12 28			12 38	12 38						12 41			12 51	12 58			13 08	13 08		
Lewisham	d			12 25	12 32			12 42	12 42			13 27			12 46			12 55	13 02			13 12	13 12		
St Johns	d							12 44	12 44			13 29										13 14	13 14		
New Cross	d							12 47	12 47			13 31										13 17	13 17		
Nunhead	d				12 37														13 07						
Peckham Rye	d				12 40														13 10						
Denmark Hill	d				12 44														13 14						
London Victoria	a				12 55														13 25						
Westcombe Park	d	12 12				12 22							12 32			12 42				12 52					
Maze Hill	d	12 14				12 24							12 34			12 44				12 54					
Greenwich	d	12 17				12 27							12 37			12 47				12 57					
Deptford	a	12 19				12 29							12 39			12 49				12 59					
London Bridge	a	12 27		12 33		12 35		12 52	12 52	13 13	13 20	13 37	12 45		12 55	12 57		13 03		13 05		13 22	13 22	13 43	13 50
London Cannon Street	a					12 41		13 00	13 00			13 43	12 51							13 11		13 30	13 30		
London Waterloo (East)	a			12 39						13 19	13 26				13 01			13 09						13 49	13 56
London Charing Cross	a			12 43						13 23	13 30				13 05			13 13						13 53	14 00
Ebbsfleet International	a		11 46														12 16								
Stratford International	a		11 58														12 28								
St Pancras Int'l	a		12 05														12 36								

Please note, Network Rail have stated that further updates to this timetable are possible during the validity period.

Table T200-R

Mondays to Fridays

21 May to 7 December

Gillingham and Dartford - London

		SE	SE	SE	TL	SE	SE	SE	SE	SE	SE	SE	SE	SE	SE	SE	SE	TL	SE	SE	SE	SE	SE
						◇													◇				
Rainham Kt	d				11 58	12 16												12 28	12 46				
Gillingham (Kent)	d				12 04	12 21												12 34	12 51				
Chatham	d				12 08	12 25												12 38	12 55				
Rochester	d				12 12	12 29												12 42	12 59				
Maidstone West	d																						
Strood	d				12 15	12 32												12 45	13 02				
Higham	d				12 20													12 50					
Gravesend	d				12 29	12 42		12 50						13 35				12 59	13 12		13 20		
Northfleet	d				12 32									13 38				13 02					
Swanscombe	d				12 34									13 40				13 04					
Greenhithe for Bluewater	d				12 38			12 56						13 44				13 08			13 26		
Stone Crossing	d				12 40									13 46				13 10					
Dartford	a				12 44			13 01						13 50				13 14			13 31		
	d			12 41	12 45		12 55	13 02					13 35	13 51			13 11	13 15		13 25	13 32		
Slade Green	d		12 39	12 46	12 51				12 59	13 07		13 07				13 09	13 16	13 21				13 29	13 37
Erith	d		12 42	12 48					13 02							13 12	13 18					13 32	
Belvedere	d		12 44	12 51					13 04							13 14	13 21					13 34	
Abbey Wood	d		12 48	12 54	12 58				13 08							13 18	13 24	13 28				13 38	
Plumstead	d		12 51	12 57	13 01				13 11							13 21	13 27	13 31				13 41	
Woolwich Arsenal	d		12 54	13 00	13 04				13 14							13 24	13 30	13 34				13 44	
Woolwich Dockyard	d		12 56	13 03					13 16							13 26	13 33					13 46	
Charlton	d	12 55	13 00	13 06	13 10				13 20						13 25	13 30	13 36	13 40				13 50	
Crayford	d	13 32											13 42	13 56	14 02								
Bexley	d	13 35											13 45	13 59	14 05								
Albany Park	d	13 37											13 47		14 07								
Sidcup	d	13 40											13 50	14 03	14 10								
New Eltham	d	13 44											13 54	14 06	14 14								
Mottingham	d	13 46											13 56		14 16								
Lee	d	13 49											13 59		14 19								
Hither Green	d	13 52											14 03		14 22								
Barnehurst	d						13 03	13 09		13a15	13 20	13 20								13 33	13 39		13a45
Bexleyheath	d						13 06	13 12			13 23	13 23								13 36	13 42		
Welling	d						13 09	13 15			13 26	13 26								13 39	13 45		
Falconwood	d						13 11	13 18			13 28	13 28								13 41	13 48		
Eltham	d						13 14	13 21			13 31	13 31								13 44	13 51		
Kidbrooke	d						13 17	13 24			13 34	13 34								13 47	13 54		
Blackheath	d			13 11			13 21	13 28			13 38	13 38					13 41			13 51	13 58		
Lewisham	d	13 57		13 16			13 25	13 32			13 42	13 42			14 27		13 46			13 55	14 02		
St Johns	d	13 59									13 44	13 44			14 29								
New Cross	d	14 01									13 47	13 47			14 31								
Nunhead	d							13 37													14 07		
Peckham Rye	d							13 40													14 10		
Denmark Hill	d							13 44													14 14		
London Victoria	a							13 55													14 25		
Westcombe Park	d		13 02		13 12				13 22							13 32		13 42				13 52	
Maze Hill	d		13 04		13 14				13 24							13 34		13 44				13 54	
Greenwich	d		13 07		13 17				13 27							13 37		13 47				13 57	
Deptford	a		13 09		13 19				13 29							13 39		13 49				13 59	
London Bridge	a	14 07	13 15	13 25	13 27		13 33		13 35		13 52	13 52	14 13	14 20	14 37	13 45	13 55	13 57		14 03		14 05	
London Cannon Street	a	14 13	13 21						13 41		14 00	14 00			14 43	13 51						14 11	
London Waterloo (East)	a			13 31			13 39						14 19	14 26			14 01			14 09			
London Charing Cross	a			13 35			13 43						14 23	14 30			14 05			14 13			
Ebbsfleet International	a					12 46													13 16				
Stratford International	a					12 58													13 29				
St Pancras Int'l	a					13 06													13 37				

Table T200-R

Mondays to Fridays

21 May to 7 December

Gillingham and Dartford - London

		SE	SE	SE	SE	SE	SE	SE	TL	SE	SE	SE	SE	SE	SE	SE	SE	SE	SE	SE	SE	TL	SE	SE
										◇													◇	
Rainham Kt	d								12 58	13 16												13 28	13 46	
Gillingham (Kent)	d								13 04	13 21												13 34	13 51	
Chatham	d								13 08	13 25												13 38	13 55	
Rochester	d								13 12	13 29												13 42	13 59	
Maidstone West	d																							
Strood	d								13 15	13 32												13 45	14 02	
Higham	d								13 20													13 50		
Gravesend	d				14 05				13 29	13 42		13 50						14 35				13 59	14 12	
Northfleet	d				14 08				13 32									14 38				14 02		
Swanscombe	d				14 10				13 34									14 40				14 04		
Greenhithe for Bluewater	d				14 14				13 38			13 56						14 44				14 08		
Stone Crossing	d				14 16				13 40									14 46				14 10		
Dartford	a				14 20				13 44			14 01						14 50				14 14		
	d			14 05	14 21			13 41	13 45		13 55	14 02					14 35	14 51			14 11	14 15		14 25
Slade Green	d		13 37				13 39	13 46	13 51				13 59	14 07		14 07				14 09	14 16	14 21		
Erith	d						13 42	13 48					14 02							14 12	14 18			
Belvedere	d						13 44	13 51					14 04							14 14	14 21			
Abbey Wood	d						13 48	13 54	13 58				14 08							14 18	14 24	14 28		
Plumstead	d						13 51	13 57	14 01				14 11							14 21	14 27	14 31		
Woolwich Arsenal	d						13 54	14 00	14 04				14 14							14 24	14 30	14 34		
Woolwich Dockyard	d						13 56	14 03					14 16							14 26	14 33			
Charlton	d					13 55	14 00	14 06	14 10				14 20						14 25	14 30	14 36	14 40		
Crayford	d			14 12	14 26	14 32											14 42	14 56	15 02					
Bexley	d			14 15	14 29	14 35											14 45	14 59	15 05					
Albany Park	d			14 17		14 37											14 47		15 07					
Sidcup	d			14 20	14 33	14 40											14 50	15 03	15 10					
New Eltham	d			14 24	14 36	14 44											14 54	15 06	15 14					
Mottingham	d			14 26		14 46											14 56		15 16					
Lee	d			14 29		14 49											14 59		15 19					
Hither Green	d			14 33		14 52											15 03		15 22					
Barnehurst	d	13 50	13 50								14 03	14 09		14a15	14 20	14 20								14 33
Bexleyheath	d	13 53	13 53								14 06	14 12			14 23	14 23								14 36
Welling	d	13 56	13 56								14 09	14 15			14 26	14 26								14 39
Falconwood	d	13 58	13 58								14 11	14 18			14 28	14 28								14 41
Eltham	d	14 01	14 01								14 14	14 21			14 31	14 31								14 44
Kidbrooke	d	14 04	14 04								14 17	14 24			14 34	14 34								14 47
Blackheath	d	14 08	14 08					14 11			14 21	14 28			14 38	14 38					14 41			14 51
Lewisham	d	14 12	14 12			14 57		14 16			14 25	14 32			14 42	14 42			15 27		14 46			14 55
St Johns	d	14 14	14 14			14 59									14 44	14 44			15 29					
New Cross	d	14 17	14 17			15 01									14 47	14 47			15 31					
Nunhead	d											14 37												
Peckham Rye	d											14 40												
Denmark Hill	d											14 44												
London Victoria	a											14 55												
Westcombe Park	d						14 02		14 12				14 22							14 32		14 42		
Maze Hill	d						14 04		14 14				14 24							14 34		14 44		
Greenwich	d						14 07		14 17				14 27							14 37		14 47		
Deptford	a						14 09		14 19				14 29							14 39		14 49		
London Bridge	a	14 22	14 22	14 43	14 50	15 07	14 15	14 25	14 27		14 33		14 35		14 52	14 52	15 13	15 20	15 37	14 46	14 55	14 57		15 03
London Cannon Street	a	14 30	14 30			15 13	14 21						14 41		15 00	15 00			15 43	14 51				
London Waterloo (East)	a			14 49	14 56			14 31			14 39						15 19	15 26			15 01			15 09
London Charing Cross	a			14 53	15 00			14 35			14 43						15 23	15 30			15 05			15 13
Ebbsfleet International	a									13 46													14 16	
Stratford International	a									14 02													14 28	
St Pancras Int'l	a									14 10													14 36	

Table T200-R

Mondays to Fridays

21 May to 7 December

Gillingham and Dartford - London

		SE	SE	SE	SE		SE	SE	SE	SE	SE	SE	TL	SE	SE	SE	SE	SE	SE	SE	SE		SE	SE	SE
														◇											
Rainham Kt	d												13 58	14 16											
Gillingham (Kent)	d												14 04	14 21											
Chatham	d												14 08	14 25											
Rochester	d												14 12	14 29											
Maidstone West	d																								
Strood	d												14 15	14 32											
Higham	d												14 20												
Gravesend	d	14 20							15 05				14 29	14 42		14 50							15 35		
Northfleet	d								15 08				14 32										15 38		
Swanscombe	d								15 10				14 34										15 40		
Greenhithe for Bluewater	d	14 26							15 14				14 38			14 56							15 44		
Stone Crossing	d								15 16				14 40										15 46		
Dartford	a	14 31							15 20				14 44			15 01							15 50		
	d	14 32						15 05	15 21			14 41	14 45		14 55	15 02					15 35		15 51		
Slade Green	d		14 29	14 37			14 37				14 39	14 46	14 51				14 59	15 07		15 07					15 09
Erith	d		14 32								14 42	14 48					15 02								15 12
Belvedere	d		14 34								14 44	14 51					15 04								15 14
Abbey Wood	d		14 38								14 48	14 54	14 58				15 08								15 18
Plumstead	d		14 41								14 51	14 57	15 01				15 11								15 21
Woolwich Arsenal	d		14 44								14 54	15 00	15 04				15 14								15 24
Woolwich Dockyard	d		14 46								14 56	15 03					15 16								15 26
Charlton	d		14 50							14 55	15 00	15 06	15 10				15 20							15 25	15 30
Crayford	d							15 12	15 26	15 32											15 42		15 56	16 02	
Bexley	d							15 15	15 29	15 35											15 45		15 59	16 05	
Albany Park	d							15 17		15 37											15 47			16 07	
Sidcup	d							15 20	15 33	15 40											15 50		16 03	16 10	
New Eltham	d							15 24	15 36	15 44											15 54		16 06	16 14	
Mottingham	d							15 26		15 46											15 56			16 16	
Lee	d							15 29		15 49											15 59			16 19	
Hither Green	d							15 33		15 52											16 03			16 22	
Barnehurst	d	14 39		14a45	14 50		14 50								15 03	15 09		15a15	15 20	15 20					
Bexleyheath	d	14 42			14 53		14 53								15 06	15 12			15 23	15 23					
Welling	d	14 45			14 56		14 56								15 09	15 15			15 26	15 26					
Falconwood	d	14 48			14 58		14 58								15 11	15 18			15 28	15 28					
Eltham	d	14 51			15 01		15 01								15 14	15 21			15 31	15 31					
Kidbrooke	d	14 54			15 04		15 04								15 17	15 24			15 34	15 34					
Blackheath	d	14 58			15 08		15 08					15 11			15 21	15 28			15 38	15 38					
Lewisham	d	15 02			15 12		15 12			15 58		15 16			15 25	15 32			15 42	15 42				16 27	
St Johns	d				15 14		15 14			16 00									15 44	15 44				16 29	
New Cross ⊖	d				15 17		15 17			16 02									15 47	15 47				16 31	
Nunhead	d	15 07														15 37									
Peckham Rye	d	15 10														15 40									
Denmark Hill	d	15 14														15 44									
London Victoria ⊖	a	15 25														15 55									
Westcombe Park	d		14 52								15 02		15 12				15 22								15 32
Maze Hill	d		14 54								15 04		15 14				15 24								15 34
Greenwich	d		14 57								15 07		15 17				15 27								15 37
Deptford	a		14 59								15 09		15 19				15 29								15 39
London Bridge ⊖	a		15 05		15 22		15 22	15 43	15 50	16 08	15 15	15 25	15 27		15 33		15 35		15 52	15 52	16 13		16 20	16 37	15 45
London Cannon Street ⊖	a		15 11		15 30		15 30			16 15	15 21						15 41		16 00	16 00				16 44	15 51
London Waterloo (East) ⊖	a							15 49	15 56			15 31			15 39						16 19		16 25		
London Charing Cross ⊖	a							15 53	16 00			15 35			15 43						16 23		16 30		
Ebbsfleet International	a													14 46											
Stratford International ⊖	a													14 58											
St Pancras Int'l ⊖	a													15 06											

Table T200-R

Mondays to Fridays

21 May to 7 December

Gillingham and Dartford - London

		SE	TL	SE	SE	SE	SE	SE	SE	SE	SE	SE	SE		SE	SE	TL	SE	SE	SE	SE	SE	SE	SE	SE
				◇															◇			◇			
Rainham Kt	d		14 28	14 46													14 58		15 16			15 46			
Gillingham (Kent)	d		14 34	14 51													15 04		15 21			15 51			
Chatham	d		14 38	14 55													15 08		15 25			15 55			
Rochester	d		14 42	14 59													15 12		15 29			15 59			
Maidstone West	d																								
Strood	d		14 45	15 02													15 15		15 32			16 02			
Higham	d		14 50														15 20								
Gravesend	d		14 59	15 12		15 20						16 03					15 29		15 42		15 50	16 12			
Northfleet	d		15 02									16 06					15 32								
Swanscombe	d		15 04									16 08					15 34								
Greenhithe for Bluewater	d		15 08			15 26						16 12					15 38				15 56				
Stone Crossing	d		15 10									16 14					15 40								
Dartford	a		15 14			15 31						16 18					15 44				16 01				
	d	15 11	15 15		15 25	15 32					16 05	16 19				15 41	15 45			15 55	16 02				16 25
Slade Green	d	15 16	15 21				15 29	15 37		15 37					15 39	15 46	15 51	15 57					16 07		
Erith	d	15 18					15 32								15 42	15 48		16 00							
Belvedere	d	15 21					15 34								15 44	15 51		16 02							
Abbey Wood	d	15 24	15 28				15 38								15 48	15 54	15 58	16 06							
Plumstead	d	15 27	15 31				15 41								15 51	15 57	16 01	16 09							
Woolwich Arsenal	d	15 30	15 34				15 44								15 54	16 00	16 04	16 12							
Woolwich Dockyard	d	15 33					15 46								15 56	16 03		16 14							
Charlton	d	15 36	15 40				15 50						15 55		16 00	16 06	16 10	16 18							
Crayford	d										16 12	16 24	16 32												
Bexley	d										16 15	16 27	16 35												
Albany Park	d										16 17		16 37												
Sidcup	d										16 20	16 31	16 40												
New Eltham	d										16 24	16 34	16 44												
Mottingham	d										16 26		16 46												
Lee	d										16 29		16 49												
Hither Green	d										16 33		16 53												
Barnehurst	d				15 33	15 39		15a45	15 50	15 50										16 03	16 09		16 15	16 15	16 33
Bexleyheath	d				15 36	15 42			15 53	15 53										16 06	16 12		16 18	16 18	16 36
Welling	d				15 39	15 45			15 56	15 56										16 09	16 15		16 21	16 21	16 39
Falconwood	d				15 41	15 48			15 58	15 58										16 11	16 18		16 23	16 23	16 41
Eltham	d				15 44	15 51			16 01	16 01										16 14	16 21		16 26	16 26	16 44
Kidbrooke	d				15 47	15 54			16 04	16 04										16 17	16 24		16 29	16 29	16 47
Blackheath	d	15 41			15 51	15 58			16 08	16 08						16 11				16 21	16 28		16 33	16 33	16 51
Lewisham	d	15 46			15 56	16 02			16 12	16 12			17 00			16 16				16 25	16 32		16 37	16 37	16 55
St Johns	d								16 14	16 14			17 02										16 39	16 39	
New Cross ⊖	d								16 17	16 17			17 05										16 42	16 42	
Nunhead	d					16 08															16 37				
Peckham Rye	d					16 11															16 40				
Denmark Hill	d					16 14															16 44				
London Victoria ⊖	a					16 25															16 55				
Westcombe Park	d		15 42				15 52								16 02		16 12	16 20							
Maze Hill	d		15 44				15 54								16 04		16 14	16 22							
Greenwich	d		15 47				15 57								16 07		16 17	16 25							
Deptford	a		15 49				15 59								16 09		16 19	16 27							
London Bridge ⊖	a	15 55	15 57		16 04		16 05		16 22	16 22	16 43	16 49	17 10		16 16	16 25	16 27	16 33		16 33			16 49	16 49	17 03
London Cannon Street ⊖	a						16 12		16 29	16 29			17 17		16 23			16 40					16 56	16 56	
London Waterloo (East) ⊖	a	16 01			16 10						16 51	16 55				16 31				16 40					17 09
London Charing Cross ⊖	a	16 05			16 15						16 57	17 01				16 36				16 46					17 16
Ebbsfleet International	a			15 16															15 46			16 16			
Stratford International ⊖	a			15 28															16 02			16 28			
St Pancras Int'l ⊖	a			15 36															16 10			16 36			

Please note, Network Rail have stated that further updates to this timetable are possible during the validity period.

Table T200-R

Mondays to Fridays

21 May to 7 December

Gillingham and Dartford - London

		SE	SE	SE	SE	SE	SE	SE	SE	SE	SE	SE	SE	SE	SE	SE	TL	SE ◇	SE	SE	SE	SE	SE
Rainham Kt	d																16 00	16 16					
Gillingham (Kent)	d																16 06	16 21					
Chatham	d																16 10	16 25					
Rochester	d																16 14	16 29					
Maidstone West	d																						
Strood	d																16 17	16 32					
Higham	d																16 22						
Gravesend	d	16 20		16 35									17 05				16 29	16 42		16 50			
Northfleet	d			16 38									17 08				16 33						
Swanscombe	d			16 40									17 10				16 35						
Greenhithe for Bluewater	d	16 26		16 44									17 14				16 38			16 56			
Stone Crossing	d			16 46									17 16				16 40						
Dartford	a	16 31		16 50									17 20				16 44			17 01			
	d	16 32	16 35	16 51			16 11					17 05	17 21			16 41	16 45		16 55	17 02			
Slade Green	d					16 09	16 16	16 30	16 37		16 37				16 39	16 46	16 51				16 58	17 06	17 10
Erith	d					16 12	16 18	16 32							16 42	16 48					17 00		
Belvedere	d					16 14	16 21	16 35							16 44	16 51					17 03		
Abbey Wood	d					16 18	16 24	16 38							16 48	16 54	16 58				17 06	17 12	
Plumstead	d					16 21	16 27	16 41							16 51	16 57	17 01				17 09		
Woolwich Arsenal	d					16 24	16 30	16 44							16 54	17 00	17 04				17 12	17 16	
Woolwich Dockyard	d					16 26	16 33	16 47							16 56	17 03					17 15		
Charlton	d				16 26	16 30	16 36	16 50						16 58	17 00	17 06	17 10				17 18	17 22	
Crayford	d		16 41	16 56	17 04							17 10	17 26	17 31									
Bexley	d		16 44	16 59	17 07							17 13	17 29	17 34									
Albany Park	d		16 46		17 09							17 15		17 36									
Sidcup	d		16 49	17 03	17 12							17 18	17 33	17 39									
New Eltham	d		16 53	17 06	17 16							17 22	17 36	17 43									
Mottingham	d		16 55		17 18							17 24		17 45									
Lee	d		16 58		17 21							17 27		17 48									
Hither Green	d		17 02		17 27							17 31		17 52									
Barnehurst	d	16 40							16a45	16 47	16 47								17 03	17 09			17 18
Bexleyheath	d	16 43								16 50	16 50								17 06	17 12			17 21
Welling	d	16 46								16 53	16 53								17 09	17 15			
Falconwood	d	16 48								16 55	16 55								17 11	17 18			
Eltham	d	16 51								16 58	16 58								17 14	17 21			17 27
Kidbrooke	d	16 54								17 01	17 01								17 17	17 24			17 30
Blackheath	d	16 58					16 41			17 05	17 05					17 11			17 21	17 28			17 34
Lewisham	d	17 02					16 46			17 09	17 09					17 15			17 25	17 32			17 38
St Johns	d				17 31					17 11	17 11			17 56									
New Cross	d				17 34					17 14	17 14			17 59									17 41
Nunhead	d	17 07																		17 37			
Peckham Rye	d	17 10																		17 40			
Denmark Hill	d	17 14																		17 44			
London Victoria	a	17 25																		17 55			
Westcombe Park	d					16 32		16 52							17 02		17 12				17 20	17 24	
Maze Hill	d					16 34		16 54							17 04		17 14				17 22	17 26	
Greenwich	d					16 37		16 58							17 08		17 17				17 26	17 29	
Deptford	a					16 39		17 00							17 10		17 19				17 28	17 31	
London Bridge	a		17 13	17 20		16 46	16 55	17 07				17 40	17 51	18 06	17 18	17 23	17 27		17 34		17 35	17 38	17 47
London Cannon Street	a				17 47	16 53		17 14		17 27	17 27			18 13	17 25						17 42	17 45	17 52
London Waterloo (East)	a		17 20	17 28			17 01					17 46	17 56			17 30			17 39				
London Charing Cross	a		17 25	17 34			17 06					17 52	18 03			17 39			17 46				
Ebbsfleet International	a																	16 46					
Stratford International	a																	17 00					
St Pancras Int'l	a																	17 10					

Table T200-R

Mondays to Fridays

21 May to 7 December

Gillingham and Dartford - London

		SE	SE	SE	SE	SE	SE	SE	TL	SE	SE ◇	SE	SE	SE	SE	SE	SE	SE	SE	SE	TL	SE	SE ◇	SE
Rainham Kt	d								16 30		16 46										17 00		17 16	
Gillingham (Kent)	d								16 36		16 51										17 06		17 21	
Chatham	d								16 40		16 55										17 10		17 25	
Rochester	d								16 44		16 59										17 14		17 29	
Maidstone West	d																							
Strood	d								16 47		17 02										17 17		17 32	
Higham	d								16 52												17 22			
Gravesend	d					17 35			16 59		17 12		17 18				18 05				17 29		17 42	
Northfleet	d					17 38			17 03								18 08				17 33			
Swanscombe	d					17 40			17 05								18 10				17 35			
Greenhithe for Bluewater	d					17 44			17 08				17 24				18 14				17 38			
Stone Crossing	d					17 46			17 10								18 16				17 40			
Dartford	a					17 50			17 14				17 29				18 20				17 44			
	d			17 35		17 51		17 11	17 15			17 25	17 30			18 06	18 21			17 39	17 45			17 53
Slade Green	d							17 16	17 21	17 29				17 34					17 40	17 46	17 51	17 54		
Erith	d							17 18		17 32									17 43	17 48		17 57		
Belvedere	d							17 21		17 34									17 45	17 51		17 59		
Abbey Wood	d							17 24	17 28	17 38									17 49	17 54	17 58	18 03		
Plumstead	d							17 27	17 31										17 52	17 57	18 01	18 06		
Woolwich Arsenal	d							17 30	17 34	17 42									17 55	18 00	18 04	18 09		
Woolwich Dockyard	d							17 33											17 57	18 03		18 11		
Charlton	d						17 26	17 36	17 40	17 48								18 00	18 01	18 06	18 10	18 15		
Crayford	d			17 42		17 56	18 03									18 12	18 26	18 37						
Bexley	d			17 45		17 59	18 06									18 15	18 29	18 40						
Albany Park	d			17 47			18 08									18 17		18 42						
Sidcup	d			17 50		18 03	18 11									18 20	18 33	18 45						
New Eltham	d			17 54		18 06	18 15									18 24	18 36	18 49						
Mottingham	d			17 56			18 17									18 26		18 51						
Lee	d			17 59			18 20									18 29		18 54						
Hither Green	d			18 03	18 13		18 24									18 33		18 59						
Barnehurst	d	17 18	17 25		18a49							17 34	17 38	17 50	17 50									18 01
Bexleyheath	d	17 21	17 28									17 36	17 41	17 53	17 53									18 04
Welling	d		17 31									17 39	17 44	17 56	17 56									18 07
Falconwood	d		17 33									17 42	17 46	17 58	17 58									18 09
Eltham	d	17 27	17 36									17 44	17 49	18 01	18 01									18 12
Kidbrooke	d	17 30	17 40									17 47	17 52	18 04	18 04									18 15
Blackheath	d	17 34	17 44					17 41				17 51	17 56	18 08	18 08					18 13				18 19
Lewisham	d	17 38	17 48	18 09			18 30	17 45				17 55	18 00	18 14	18 14			19 07		18 17				18 23
St Johns	d						18 34											19 09						
New Cross	d	17 41					18 37							18 17	18 17			19 11						
Nunhead	d												18 07											
Peckham Rye	d												18 10											
Denmark Hill	d												18 14											
London Victoria	a												18 25											
Westcombe Park	d								17 42	17 50									18 03		18 12	18 17		
Maze Hill	d								17 44	17 52									18 05		18 14	18 19		
Greenwich	d								17 47	17 55									18 08		18 17	18 22		
Deptford	a								17 49	17 57									18 10		18 19	18 24		
London Bridge	a	17 47	17 56	18 17		18 22	18 43	17 53	17 57	18 03		18 03		18 22	18 22	18 44	18 52	19 16	18 17	18 26	18 27	18 30		18 31
London Cannon Street	a	17 52					18 50			18 10				18 27	18 27			19 21	18 24			18 37		
London Waterloo (East)	a		18 02	18 24		18 28		17 58				18 09				18 50	18 57			18 32				18 37
London Charing Cross	a		18 08	18 30		18 34		18 05				18 17				18 53	19 02			18 38				18 41
Ebbsfleet International	a										17 16												17 46	
Stratford International	a										17 28												17 58	
St Pancras Int'l	a										17 36												18 10	

Table T200-R

Gillingham and Dartford - London

		SE	SE	SE	SE		SE	SE	SE	SE	SE	SE	TL	SE	SE	SE	SE	SE	SE	SE	SE		SE	SE	SE
														◇											
Rainham Kt	d												17 28	17 46											
Gillingham (Kent)	d												17 34	17 51											
Chatham	d												17 38	17 55											
Rochester	d												17 42	17 59											
Maidstone West	d																								
Strood	d												17 47	18 03											
Higham	d												17 52												
Gravesend	d						18 35						17 59	18 13				18 51		19 05					
Northfleet	d						18 38						18 03							19 08					
Swanscombe	d						18 40						18 05							19 10					
Greenhithe for Bluewater	d						18 44						18 08					18 58		19 14					
Stone Crossing	d						18 46						18 10							19 16					
Dartford	a						18 51						18 14					19 03		19 20					
	d				18 35		18 52		18 02	18 08			18 15		18 25		18 38	19 07		19 21					18 42
Slade Green	d	18 00	18 00						18 09			18 16	18 21			18 29							18 39	18 43	18 48
Erith	d	18 03							18 11			18 18				18 32							18 42	18 46	18 50
Belvedere	d	18 05							18 14			18 21				18 34							18 44	18 48	18 53
Abbey Wood	d	18 09							18 17			18 24	18 28			18 38							18 48	18 52	18 56
Plumstead	d	18 12							18 20			18 27	18 31			18 41							18 51	18 55	18 59
Woolwich Arsenal	d	18 15							18 23			18 30	18 34			18 44							18 54	18 58	19 02
Woolwich Dockyard	d	18 17							18 26			18 33				18 46							18 56	19 00	19 04
Charlton	d	18 21						18 26	18 29			18 36	18 40			18 50					18 57		19 00	19 04	19 07
Crayford	d			18 37	18 41		18 56	19 02										19 12		19 26	19 32				
Bexley	d			18 40	18 44		18 59	19 05										19 15		19 29	19 35				
Albany Park	d			18 42	18 46			19 07										19 17			19 37				
Sidcup	d			18 45	18 49		19 03	19 10										19 20		19 33	19 40				
New Eltham	d			18 49	18 53		19 06	19 14										19 24		19 36	19 44				
Mottingham	d			18 51	18 55			19 16										19 26			19 46				
Lee	d			18 54	18 59			19 19										19 29			19 49				
Hither Green	d			18 59	19 02			19 22										19 34			19 52				
Barnehurst	d		18a18								18 19				18 33				18 52						
Bexleyheath	d									18 16	18 22				18 36				18 55						
Welling	d										18 25				18 39				18 58						
Falconwood	d										18 27				18 41				19 00						
Eltham	d									18 23	18 30				18 44				19 03						
Kidbrooke	d										18 33				18 47				19 06						
Blackheath	d									18 28	18 37	18 42			18 51		18 55		19 10						19 13
Lewisham	d			19 07				19 27		18 32	18 41	18 48			18 55		19 00		19 14		19 57				19 17
St Johns	d			19 09				19 29			18 44										19 59				
New Cross	d			19 11				19 32			18 47										20 01				
Nunhead	d									18 37							19 07								
Peckham Rye	d									18 40							19 09								
Denmark Hill	d									18 43							19 14								
London Victoria	a									18 57							19 28		19 33						
Westcombe Park	d	18 23							18 31				18 42			18 52							19 02	19 06	
Maze Hill	d	18 25							18 33				18 44			18 54							19 04	19 09	
Greenwich	d	18 28							18 37				18 47			18 57							19 08	19 13	
Deptford	a	18 30							18 39				18 49			18 59							19 10	19 15	
London Bridge	a	18 37		19 16	19 11		19 21	19 39	18 48		18 54	18 58	18 57		19 03	19 08		19 43		19 51	20 07		19 19	19 23	19 26
London Cannon Street	a	18 44		19 21				19 46	18 54		19 01					19 15					20 15		19 24	19 30	
London Waterloo (East)	a				19 19		19 27					19 05			19 09			19 49		19 57					19 32
London Charing Cross	a				19 23		19 31					19 09			19 13			19 53		20 01					19 36
Ebbsfleet International	a													18 17											
Stratford International	a													18 29											
St Pancras Int'l	a													18 37											

Table T200-R

Gillingham and Dartford - London

		TL	SE	SE	SE	SE	SE	SE	SE	SE	SE	SE	SE		TL	SE	SE	SE	SE	SE	SE	SE	SE	SE	SE
			◇													◇	◇								
Rainham Kt	d	18 00	18 16												18 30		18 46								
Gillingham (Kent)	d	18 06	18 21												18 36		18 51								
Chatham	d	18 10	18 25												18 40		18 55								
Rochester	d	18 14	18 29												18 44		18 59								
Maidstone West	d															18 42									
Strood	d	18 18	18 35												18 47	18 58	19 02								
Higham	d	18 23													18 52										
Gravesend	d	18 30	18 45							19 35					18 59	19 08	19 12		19 18					20 05	
Northfleet	d	18 33								19 38					19 03									20 08	
Swanscombe	d	18 35								19 40					19 05									20 10	
Greenhithe for Bluewater	d	18 39								19 44					19 08				19 26					20 14	
Stone Crossing	d	18 41								19 46					19 10									20 16	
Dartford	a	18 45								19 50					19 14				19 31					20 20	
	d	18 46		18 55		19 02			19 35	19 51					19 15			19 25	19 32				20 05	20 21	
Slade Green	d	18 51			18 59		19 01					19 09	19 16		19 21					19 29	19 39				
Erith	d				19 02							19 12	19 18							19 32					
Belvedere	d				19 04							19 14	19 21							19 34					
Abbey Wood	d	18 59			19 08							19 18	19 24		19 28					19 38					
Plumstead	d	19 02			19 11							19 21	19 27		19 31					19 41					
Woolwich Arsenal	d	19 05			19 14							19 24	19 30		19 34					19 44					
Woolwich Dockyard	d				19 16							19 26	19 33							19 46					
Charlton	d	19 10			19 20						19 25	19 30	19 36		19 40					19 50					19 55
Crayford	d								19 42	19 56	20 02												20 12	20 26	20 32
Bexley	d								19 45	19 59	20 05												20 15	20 29	20 35
Albany Park	d								19 47		20 07												20 17		20 37
Sidcup	d								19 50	20 03	20 10												20 20	20 33	20 40
New Eltham	d								19 54	20 06	20 14												20 24	20 36	20 44
Mottingham	d								19 56		20 16												20 26		20 46
Lee	d								19 59		20 19												20 29		20 49
Hither Green	d								20 03		20 22												20 33		20 52
Barnehurst	d			19 03		19 09	19 20	19 20										19 33	19 39		19 50	19 50			
Bexleyheath	d			19 06		19 12	19 23	19 23										19 36	19 42		19 53	19 53			
Welling	d			19 09		19 15	19 26	19 26										19 39	19 45		19 56	19 56			
Falconwood	d			19 11		19 18	19 28	19 28										19 41	19 48		19 58	19 58			
Eltham	d			19 14		19 21	19 31	19 31										19 44	19 51		20 01	20 01			
Kidbrooke	d			19 17		19 24	19 34	19 34										19 47	19 54		20 04	20 04			
Blackheath	d			19 21		19 28	19 38	19 38					19 41					19 51	19 58		20 08	20 08			
Lewisham	d			19 25		19 32	19 42	19 42			20 27		19 46					19 55	20 02		20 12	20 12			20 57
St Johns	d						19 44	19 44			20 29										20 14	20 14			20 59
New Cross	d						19 47	19 47			20 31										20 17	20 17			21 01
Nunhead	d					19 37													20 07						
Peckham Rye	d					19 40													20 10						
Denmark Hill	d					19 44													20 14						
London Victoria	a					19 55													20 25						
Westcombe Park	d	19 12			19 22							19 32			19 42					19 52					
Maze Hill	d	19 14			19 24							19 34			19 44					19 54					
Greenwich	d	19 18			19 27							19 37			19 47					19 57					
Deptford	a	19 20			19 29							19 39			19 49					19 59					
London Bridge	a	19 27		19 33	19 36		19 52	19 52	20 13	20 20	20 37	19 46	19 55		19 57			20 03		20 05	20 22	20 22	20 43	20 50	21 07
London Cannon Street	a				19 43		19 58	19 58			20 43	19 51								20 11	20 30	20 30			21 13
London Waterloo (East)	a			19 39					20 19	20 26			20 01					20 09					20 49	20 56	
London Charing Cross	a			19 43					20 23	20 30			20 05					20 13					20 53	21 00	
Ebbsfleet International	a		18 49													19 12	19 16								
Stratford International	a		19 02													19 24	19 28								
St Pancras Int'l	a		19 10													19 31	19 36								

Table T200-R

Mondays to Fridays

21 May to 7 December

Gillingham and Dartford - London

Station		SE	SE	TL	SE		SE	SE	SE	SE	SE	SE	SE	SE	SE	SE	TL	SE	SE	SE	SE		SE	SE	SE
					◇													◇							
Rainham Kt	d			18 58	19 16												19 28	19 46							
Gillingham (Kent)	d			19 04	19 21												19 34	19 51							
Chatham	d			19 08	19 25												19 38	19 55							
Rochester	d			19 12	19 29												19 42	19 59							
Maidstone West	d																								
Strood	d			19 15	19 32												19 45	20 02							
Higham	d			19 20													19 50								
Gravesend	d			19 29	19 42								20 35				19 59	20 12		20 20				21 05	
Northfleet	d			19 32									20 38				20 02							21 08	
Swanscombe	d			19 34									20 40				20 04							21 10	
Greenhithe for Bluewater	d			19 38									20 44				20 08			20 26				21 14	
Stone Crossing	d			19 40									20 46				20 10							21 16	
Dartford	a			19 44									20 50				20 14			20 31				21 20	
	d		19 41	19 45			19 55		20 02			20 35	20 51			20 11	20 15		20 25	20 32			21 05	21 21	
Slade Green	d	19 39	19 46	19 51				19 59		20 07					20 09	20 16	20 21				20 29				
Erith	d	19 42	19 48					20 02							20 12	20 18					20 32				
Belvedere	d	19 44	19 51					20 04							20 14	20 21					20 34				
Abbey Wood	d	19 48	19 54	19 58				20 08							20 18	20 24	20 28				20 38				
Plumstead	d	19 51	19 57	20 01				20 11							20 21	20 27	20 31				20 41				
Woolwich Arsenal	d	19 54	20 00	20 04				20 14							20 24	20 30	20 34				20 44				
Woolwich Dockyard	d	19 56	20 03					20 16							20 26	20 33					20 46				
Charlton	d	20 00	20 06	20 10				20 20						20 25	20 30	20 36	20 40				20 50				20 55
Crayford	d											20 43	20 56	21 02									21 12	21 26	21 32
Bexley	d											20 46	20 59	21 05									21 15	21 29	21 35
Albany Park	d											20 49		21 07									21 17		21 37
Sidcup	d											20 51	21 03	21 10									21 20	21 33	21 40
New Eltham	d											20 54	21 06	21 14									21 24	21 36	21 44
Mottingham	d											20 57		21 16									21 26		21 46
Lee	d											21 00		21 19									21 29		21 49
Hither Green	d											21 03		21 22									21 33		21 52
Barnehurst	d						20 03		20 09	20 20	20 20								20 33	20 39					
Bexleyheath	d						20 06		20 12	20 23	20 23								20 36	20 42					
Welling	d						20 09		20 15	20 26	20 26								20 39	20 45					
Falconwood	d						20 11		20 18	20 28	20 28								20 41	20 48					
Eltham	d						20 14		20 21	20 31	20 31								20 44	20 51					
Kidbrooke	d						20 17		20 24	20 34	20 34								20 47	20 54					
Blackheath	d		20 11				20 21		20 28	20 38	20 38					20 41			20 51	20 58					
Lewisham	d		20 17				20 25		20 32	20 42	20 42			21 27		20 46			20 55	21 02					21 57
St Johns	d									20 44	20 44			21 29											21 59
New Cross ⊖	d									20 47	20 47			21 31											22 01
Nunhead	d								20 37											21 07					
Peckham Rye	d								20 40											21 10					
Denmark Hill	d								20 44											21 14					
London Victoria ⊖	a								20 55											21 25					
Westcombe Park	d	20 02		20 12				20 22							20 32		20 42				20 52				
Maze Hill	d	20 04		20 14				20 24							20 34		20 44				20 54				
Greenwich	d	20 07		20 17				20 27							20 37		20 47				20 57				
Deptford	a	20 09		20 19				20 29							20 39		20 49				20 59				
London Bridge ⊖	a	20 15	20 25	20 27			20 33	20 35		20 52	20 52	21 13	21 20	21 37	20 45	20 55	20 57		21 03		21 05		21 43	21 50	22 07
London Cannon Street ⊖	a	20 21						20 41		21 00	21 00			21 43	20 51						21 11				22 13
London Waterloo (East) ⊖	a		20 31				20 39					21 19	21 26			21 01			21 09				21 49	21 56	
London Charing Cross ⊖	a		20 35				20 43					21 23	21 30			21 05			21 13				21 53	22 00	
Ebbsfleet International	a				19 46													20 16							
Stratford International ⊖	a				19 59													20 28							
St Pancras Int'l ⊖	a				20 07													20 36							

Table T200-R

Mondays to Fridays

21 May to 7 December

Gillingham and Dartford - London

Station		SE	TL	SE	SE	SE	SE	SE	SE	SE	SE	TL	SE		SE	SE	SE	SE	SE	SE	SE	TL	SE	SE	SE
				◇									◇										◇		
Rainham Kt	d		19 58	20 16								20 28	20 46									20 58	21 16		
Gillingham (Kent)	d		20 04	20 21								20 34	20 51									21 04	21 21		
Chatham	d		20 08	20 25								20 38	20 55									21 08	21 25		
Rochester	d		20 12	20 29								20 42	20 59									21 12	21 29		
Maidstone West	d																								
Strood	d		20 15	20 32								20 45	21 02									21 15	21 32		
Higham	d		20 20									20 50										21 20			
Gravesend	d		20 29	20 42		20 50			21 35			20 59	21 12			21 20			22 05			21 29	21 42		21 50
Northfleet	d		20 32						21 38			21 02							22 08			21 32			
Swanscombe	d		20 34						21 40			21 04							22 10			21 34			
Greenhithe for Bluewater	d		20 38			20 56			21 44			21 08				21 26			22 14			21 38			21 56
Stone Crossing	d		20 40						21 46			21 10							22 16			21 40			
Dartford	a		20 44			21 01			21 50			21 14				21 31			22 20			21 44			22 01
	d	20 41	20 45		20 55	21 02		21 35	21 51		21 11	21 15			21 25	21 32		22 05	22 21		21 41	21 45		21 55	22 02
Slade Green	d	20 46	20 51				20 59				21 16	21 21					21 29				21 46	21 51			
Erith	d	20 48					21 02				21 18						21 32				21 48				
Belvedere	d	20 51					21 04				21 21						21 34				21 51				
Abbey Wood	d	20 54	20 58				21 08				21 24	21 28					21 38				21 54	21 58			
Plumstead	d	20 57	21 01				21 11				21 27	21 31					21 41				21 57	22 01			
Woolwich Arsenal	d	21 00	21 04				21 14				21 30	21 34					21 44				22 00	22 04			
Woolwich Dockyard	d	21 03					21 16				21 33						21 46				22 03				
Charlton	d	21 06	21 10				21 20			21 25	21 36	21 40					21 50			21 52	22 06	22 10			
Crayford	d							21 42	21 56	22 02								22 12	22 26	22 32					
Bexley	d							21 45	21 59	22 05								22 15	22 29	22 35					
Albany Park	d							21 47		22 07								22 17		22 37					
Sidcup	d							21 50	22 03	22 10								22 20	22 33	22 40					
New Eltham	d							21 54	22 06	22 14								22 24	22 36	22 44					
Mottingham	d							21 56		22 16								22 26		22 46					
Lee	d							21 59		22 19								22 29		22 49					
Hither Green	d							22 03		22 22								22 33		22 52					
Barnehurst	d				21 03	21 09									21 33	21 39								22 03	22 09
Bexleyheath	d				21 06	21 12									21 36	21 42								22 06	22 12
Welling	d				21 09	21 15									21 39	21 45								22 09	22 15
Falconwood	d				21 11	21 18									21 41	21 48								22 11	22 18
Eltham	d				21 14	21 21									21 44	21 51								22 14	22 21
Kidbrooke	d				21 17	21 24									21 47	21 54								22 17	22 24
Blackheath	d	21 11			21 21	21 28					21 41				21 51	21 58					22 11			22 21	22 28
Lewisham	d	21 16			21 25	21 32				22 27	21 46				21 55	22 02				22 57	22 16			22 25	22 32
St Johns	d									22 29										22 59					
New Cross ⊖	d									22 31										23 01					
Nunhead	d					21 37										22 07									22 37
Peckham Rye	d					21 40										22 10									22 40
Denmark Hill	d					21 44										22 14									22 44
London Victoria ⊖	a					21 55										22 25									22 55
Westcombe Park	d		21 12				21 22					21 42					21 52					22 12			
Maze Hill	d		21 14				21 24					21 44					21 54					22 14			
Greenwich	d		21 17				21 27					21 47					21 57					22 17			
Deptford	a		21 19				21 29					21 49					21 59					22 19			
London Bridge ⊖	a	21 25	21 27		21 33		21 35	22 13	22 21	22 37	21 55	21 57			22 03		22 05	22 43	22 50	23 07	22 25	22 27		22 33	
London Cannon Street ⊖	a						21 41			22 43							22 11			23 13					
London Waterloo (East) ⊖	a	21 31			21 39			22 19	22 26		22 01				22 09			22 49	22 56		22 31			22 39	
London Charing Cross ⊖	a	21 35			21 43			22 23	22 30		22 05				22 13			22 53	23 00		22 35			22 43	
Ebbsfleet International	a			20 46									21 16										21 46		
Stratford International ⊖	a			21 02									21 32										21 58		
St Pancras Int'l ⊖	a			21 10									21 39										22 06		

Please note, Network Rail have stated that further updates to this timetable are possible during the validity period.

Table T200-R

Mondays to Fridays

21 May to 7 December

Gillingham and Dartford - London

		SE	SE	SE	SE MT FO		SE W ThO	SE	TL	SE ◇	SE	SE	SE	SE WTh FO	SE MTO	SE	SE MT FO	SE	TL	SE	SE ◇		SE	SE	TL
Rainham Kt	d								21 28	21 46									22 00		22 16				22 30
Gillingham (Kent)	d								21 34	21 51									22 06		22 21				22 36
Chatham	d								21 38	21 55									22 10		22 25				22 40
Rochester	d								21 42	21 59									22 14		22 29				22 44
Maidstone West	d																								
Strood	d								21 45	22 02									22 17		22 32				22 47
Higham	d								21 50										22 22						22 52
Gravesend	d			22 35					21 59	22 12		22 20				23 05			22 29		22 42		22 50		22 59
Northfleet	d			22 38					22 02							23 08			22 33						23 03
Swanscombe	d			22 40					22 04							23 10			22 35						23 05
Greenhithe for Bluewater	d			22 44					22 08			22 26				23 14			22 38				22 56		23 08
Stone Crossing	d			22 46					22 10							23 16			22 40						23 10
Dartford	a			22 50					22 14			22 31				23 20			22 44				23 01		23 15
	d		22 35	22 51				22 11	22 15		22 25	22 32		22 55	22 55	23 21		22 41	22 45				23 02	23 11	
Slade Green	d	21 59						22 16	22 21				22 29					22 46	22 51	22 59				23 16	
Erith	d	22 02						22 18					22 32					22 48		23 02				23 18	
Belvedere	d	22 04						22 21					22 34					22 51		23 04				23 21	
Abbey Wood	d	22 08						22 24	22 28				22 38					22 54	22 58	23 08				23 24	
Plumstead	d	22 11						22 27	22 31				22 41					22 57	23 01	23 11				23 27	
Woolwich Arsenal	d	22 14						22 30	22 34				22 44					23 00	23 04	23 14				23 30	
Woolwich Dockyard	d	22 16						22 33					22 46					23 03		23 16				23 33	
Charlton	d	22 20			22 22		22 22	22 36	22 40				22 50				22 52	23 06	23 10	23 20				23 36	
Crayford	d		22 42	22 56	23 02		23 02									23 26	23 32								
Bexley	d		22 45	22 59	23 05		23 05									23 29	23 35								
Albany Park	d		22 47		23 07		23 07										23 37								
Sidcup	d		22 50	23 03	23 10		23 10									23 33	23 40								
New Eltham	d		22 54	23 06	23 14		23 14									23 36	23 44								
Mottingham	d		22 56		23 16		23 16										23 46								
Lee	d		22 59		23 19		23 19										23 49								
Hither Green	d		23 03		23 22		23 22										23 52								
Barnehurst	d										22 33	22 39		23 03	23 03								23 09		
Bexleyheath	d										22 36	22 42		23 06	23 06								23 12		
Welling	d										22 39	22 45		23 09	23 09								23 15		
Falconwood	d										22 41	22 48		23 11	23 11								23 18		
Eltham	d										22 44	22 51		23 14	23 14								23 21		
Kidbrooke	d										22 47	22 54		23 17	23 17								23 24		
Blackheath	d							22 41			22 51	22 58		23 21	23 21			23 11					23 28	23 41	
Lewisham	d				23 27		23 27	22 46			22 55	23 02		23 25	23 25		23 57	23 16					23 32	23 46	
St Johns	d				23 29		23 29										23 59								
New Cross	d				23 31		23 31										00 01								
Nunhead	d											23 07											23 37		
Peckham Rye	d											23 10											23 40		
Denmark Hill	d											23 14											23 44		
London Victoria	a											23 25											23 55		
Westcombe Park	d	22 22							22 42				22 52						23 12	23 22					
Maze Hill	d	22 24							22 44				22 54						23 14	23 24					
Greenwich	d	22 27							22 47				22 57						23 17	23 27					
Deptford	a	22 29							22 49				22 59						23 19	23 29					
London Bridge	a	22 35	23 13	23 20	23 37		23 41	22 55	22 57		23 03		23 05	23 33	23 33	23 50	00 07	23 25	23 27	23 35				23 55	
London Cannon Street	a	22 41			23 43								23 11				00 13			23 41					
London Waterloo (East)	a		23 19	23 26				23 01			23 09			23 39	23 39	23 56		23 31						00 01	
London Charing Cross	a		23 23	23 30				23 05			23 13			23 43	23 44	00 01		23 35						00 05	
Ebbsfleet International	a									22 16											22 46				
Stratford International	a									22 28											22 58				
St Pancras Int'l	a									22 36											23 06				

Table T200-R

Mondays to Fridays

21 May to 7 December

Gillingham and Dartford - London

		SE WTh FO	SE MT FO	SE W ThO	SE MTO	SE MTO	SE WTh FO	SE MTO	TL	SE MTO	TL
Rainham Kt	d								23 00		23 30
Gillingham (Kent)	d								23 06		23 36
Chatham	d								23 10		23 40
Rochester	d								23 14		23 44
Maidstone West	d										
Strood	d								23 17		23 47
Higham	d								23 22		23 52
Gravesend	d								23 29	23 35	23 59
Northfleet	d								23 33	23 38	00 03
Swanscombe	d								23 35	23 40	00 05
Greenhithe for Bluewater	d								23 38	23 44	00 08
Stone Crossing	d								23 40	23 46	00 10
Dartford	a								23 45	23 50	00 15
	d	23 25			23 25	23 41	23 41	23 41		23 51	
Slade Green	d		23 29			23 46	23 46	23 46			
Erith	d		23 32			23 48	23 48	23 48			
Belvedere	d		23 34			23 51	23 51	23 51			
Abbey Wood	d		23 38			23 54	23 54	23 54			
Plumstead	d		23 41			23 57	23 57	23 57			
Woolwich Arsenal	d		23 44			23 59	23 59	23 59			
Woolwich Dockyard	d		23 46			00 03	00 03	00 03			
Charlton	d		23 50			00 06	00 06	00 06			
Crayford	d			23 32						23 56	
Bexley	d			23 35						23 59	
Albany Park	d			23 37						00 01	
Sidcup	d			23 40						00 04	
New Eltham	d			23 44						00 08	
Mottingham	d			23 46						00 10	
Lee	d			23 49						00 13	
Hither Green	d			23 52						00 16	
Barnehurst	d	23 33			23 33						
Bexleyheath	d	23 36			23 36						
Welling	d	23 39			23 39						
Falconwood	d	23 41			23 41						
Eltham	d	23 44			23 44						
Kidbrooke	d	23 47			23 47						
Blackheath	d	23 51			23 51	00 11	00 11	00 11			
Lewisham	d	23 55		23 58	00 05	00 15	00 15	00 16			
St Johns	d										
New Cross	d										
Nunhead	d										
Peckham Rye	d										
Denmark Hill	d										
London Victoria	a										
Westcombe Park	d		23 52								
Maze Hill	d		23 54								
Greenwich	d		23 57								
Deptford	a		23 59								
London Bridge	a	00 03	00 05	00 08	00 13	00 23	00 23	00 24		00 29	
London Cannon Street	a		00 11			00 33					
London Waterloo (East)	a	00 09					00 29	00 30			
London Charing Cross	a	00 13					00 35	00 34			
Ebbsfleet International	a										
Stratford International	a										
St Pancras Int'l	a										

Please note, Network Rail have stated that further updates to this timetable are possible during the validity period.

Table T200-R

Saturdays

26 May to 8 December

Gillingham and Dartford - London

		SE	TL	SE	TL	SE	SE	SE	SE	TL	SE	SE	SE	SE	SE	TL		SE	SE	SE	SE	SE	SE	TL	SE
																									◇
Rainham Kt	d																							05 28	05 46
Gillingham (Kent)	d				04 06					04 36						05 06								05 34	05 51
Chatham	d				04 10					04 40						05 10								05 38	05 55
Rochester	d				04 14					04 44						05 14								05 42	05 59
Maidstone West	d																								
Strood	d				04 17					04 47						05 17								05 45	06 02
Higham	d				04 22					04 52						05 22								05 50	
Gravesend	d				04 29		05 18			04 59		05 48				05 29			06 18	06 35				05 59	06 12
Northfleet	d		00 03		04 33		05 22			05 03		05 52				05 33			06 22	06 38				06 02	
Swanscombe	d		00 05		04 35		05 24			05 05		05 54				05 35			06 24	06 40				06 04	
Greenhithe for Bluewater	d		00 08		04 38		05 27			05 08		05 57				05 38			06 27	06 44				06 08	
Stone Crossing	d		00 10		04 40		05 29			05 10		05 59				05 40			06 29	06 46				06 10	
Dartford	a		00 15		04 45		05 34			05 14		06 04				05 44			06 34	06 50				06 14	
	d					05 05	05 35		05 03	05 15	05 25	06 05			05 41	05 45		05 55	06 35	06 51			06 11	06 15	
Slade Green	d								05 09	05 21				05 39	05 46	05 51						06 09	06 16	06 21	
Erith	d								05 12					05 42	05 48							06 12	06 18		
Belvedere	d								05 14					05 44	05 51							06 14	06 21		
Abbey Wood	d								05 18	05 28				05 48	05 54	05 58						06 18	06 24	06 28	
Plumstead	d								05 21	05 31				05 51	05 57	06 01						06 21	06 27	06 31	
Woolwich Arsenal	d								05 24	05 34				05 54	06 00	06 04						06 24	06 30	06 34	
Woolwich Dockyard	d			00 03					05 26					05 56	06 03							06 26	06 33		
Charlton	d			00 06				05 25	05 30	05 40			05 55	06 00	06 06	06 10					06 25	06 30	06 36	06 40	
Crayford	d					05 12	05 42	06 02				06 12	06 32						06 42	06 56	07 02				
Bexley	d					05 15	05 45	06 05				06 15	06 35						06 45	06 59	07 05				
Albany Park	d					05 17	05 47	06 07				06 17	06 37						06 47		07 07				
Sidcup	d					05 20	05 50	06 10				06 20	06 40						06 50	07 03	07 10				
New Eltham	d					05 24	05 54	06 14				06 24	06 44						06 54	07 06	07 14				
Mottingham	d					05 26	05 56	06 16				06 26	06 46						06 56		07 16				
Lee	d					05 29	05 59	06 19				06 29	06 49						06 59		07 19				
Hither Green	d					05 33	06 03	06 22				06 33	06 52						07 03		07 22				
Barnehurst	d										05 33							06 03							
Bexleyheath	d										05 36							06 06							
Welling	d										05 39							06 09							
Falconwood	d										05 41							06 11							
Eltham	d										05 44							06 14							
Kidbrooke	d										05 47							06 17							
Blackheath	d			00 11							05 51				06 11			06 21					06 41		
Lewisham	d			00 15				06 27			05 55		06 57		06 16			06 25			07 27		06 46		
St Johns	d							06 29					06 59								07 29				
New Cross	d	00 01						06 31					07 01								07 31				
Nunhead	d																								
Peckham Rye	d																								
Denmark Hill	d																								
London Victoria	a																								
Westcombe Park	d								05 32	05 42				06 02		06 12						06 32		06 42	
Maze Hill	d								05 34	05 44				06 04		06 14						06 34		06 44	
Greenwich	d								05 37	05 47				06 07		06 17						06 37		06 47	
Deptford	a								05 39	05 49				06 09		06 19						06 39		06 49	
London Bridge	a	00 07		00 23		05 43	06 13	06 37	05 45	05 57	06 03	06 43	07 07	06 15	06 25	06 27		06 33	07 13	07 20	07 37	06 45	06 55	06 57	
London Cannon Street	a	00 13						06 43	05 51				07 13	06 21							07 43	06 51			
London Waterloo (East)	a			00 29		05 49	06 19				06 09	06 49			06 31			06 39	07 19	07 26			07 01		
London Charing Cross	a			00 35		05 53	06 23				06 13	06 53			06 35			06 43	07 23	07 30			07 05		
Ebbsfleet International	a																								06 16
Stratford International	a																								06 28
St Pancras Int'l	a																								06 36

Table T200-R

Saturdays

26 May to 8 December

Gillingham and Dartford - London

		SE	SE	SE	SE	SE	SE	SE		TL	SE	SE	SE	SE	SE	SE	SE	SE	TL	SE	SE	SE	SE	SE	
																				◇					
Rainham Kt	d									05 58									06 28	06 46					
Gillingham (Kent)	d									06 04									06 34	06 51					
Chatham	d									06 08									06 38	06 55					
Rochester	d									06 12									06 42	06 59					
Maidstone West	d																								
Strood	d									06 15									06 45	07 02					
Higham	d									06 20									06 50						
Gravesend	d				07 05					06 29		06 50			07 35				06 59	07 12		07 20			
Northfleet	d				07 08					06 32					07 38				07 02						
Swanscombe	d				07 10					06 34					07 40				07 04						
Greenhithe for Bluewater	d				07 14					06 38		06 56			07 44				07 08			07 26			
Stone Crossing	d				07 16					06 40					07 46				07 10						
Dartford	a				07 20					06 44		07 01			07 50				07 14			07 31			
	d	06 25	06 32	07 05	07 21			06 41		06 45	06 55	07 02		07 35	07 51			07 11	07 15		07 25	07 32			
Slade Green	d						06 39	06 46		06 51			06 59				07 09	07 16	07 21				07 29		
Erith	d						06 42	06 48					07 02				07 12	07 18					07 32		
Belvedere	d						06 44	06 51					07 04				07 14	07 21					07 34		
Abbey Wood	d						06 48	06 54		06 58			07 08				07 18	07 24	07 28				07 38		
Plumstead	d						06 51	06 57		07 01			07 11				07 21	07 27	07 31				07 41		
Woolwich Arsenal	d						06 54	07 00		07 04			07 14				07 24	07 30	07 34				07 44		
Woolwich Dockyard	d						06 56	07 03					07 16				07 26	07 33					07 46		
Charlton	d					06 55	07 00	07 06		07 10			07 20			07 25	07 30	07 36	07 40				07 50		
Crayford	d			07 12	07 26	07 32								07 42	07 56	08 02									
Bexley	d			07 15	07 29	07 35								07 45	07 59	08 05									
Albany Park	d			07 17		07 37								07 47		08 07									
Sidcup	d			07 20	07 33	07 40								07 50	08 03	08 10									
New Eltham	d			07 24	07 36	07 44								07 54	08 06	08 14									
Mottingham	d			07 26		07 46								07 56		08 16									
Lee	d			07 29		07 49								07 59		08 19									
Hither Green	d			07 33		07 52								08 03		08 22									
Barnehurst	d	06 33	06 39								07 03	07 09									07 33	07 39		07 50	
Bexleyheath	d	06 36	06 42								07 06	07 12									07 36	07 42		07 53	
Welling	d	06 39	06 45								07 09	07 15									07 39	07 45		07 56	
Falconwood	d	06 41	06 48								07 11	07 18									07 41	07 48		07 58	
Eltham	d	06 44	06 51								07 14	07 21									07 44	07 51		08 01	
Kidbrooke	d	06 47	06 54								07 17	07 24									07 47	07 54		08 04	
Blackheath	d	06 51	06 58					07 11			07 21	07 28						07 41			07 51	07 58		08 08	
Lewisham	d	06 55	07 02			07 57		07 16			07 25	07 32				08 27		07 46			07 55	08 02		08 12	
St Johns	d					07 59										08 29								08 14	
New Cross	d					08 01										08 31								08 17	
Nunhead	d		07 07									07 37										08 07			
Peckham Rye	d		07 10									07 40										08 10			
Denmark Hill	d		07 14									07 44										08 14			
London Victoria	a		07 25									07 55										08 25			
Westcombe Park	d						07 02			07 12			07 22				07 32		07 42				07 52		
Maze Hill	d						07 04			07 14			07 24				07 34		07 44				07 54		
Greenwich	d						07 07			07 17			07 27				07 37		07 47				07 57		
Deptford	a						07 09			07 19			07 29				07 39		07 49				07 59		
London Bridge	a	07 03		07 43	07 50	08 07	07 15	07 25		07 27	07 33		07 35	08 13	08 20	08 37	07 45	07 55	07 57		08 03		08 05	08 22	
London Cannon Street	a					08 13	07 21						07 41			08 43	07 51						08 11	08 30	
London Waterloo (East)	a	07 09		07 49	07 56			07 31			07 39			08 19	08 26			08 01			08 09				
London Charing Cross	a	07 13		07 53	08 00			07 35			07 43			08 23	08 30			08 05			08 13				
Ebbsfleet International	a																			07 16					
Stratford International	a																			07 28					
St Pancras Int'l	a																			07 36					

Table T200-R

Saturdays

26 May to 8 December

Gillingham and Dartford - London

		SE	SE	SE	SE	SE	TL	SE	SE	SE	SE	SE	SE	SE	SE	SE		SE	TL	SE	SE	SE	SE	SE	SE
								◇												◇					
Rainham Kt	d						06 58	07 16											07 28	07 46					
Gillingham (Kent)	d						07 04	07 21											07 34	07 51					
Chatham	d						07 08	07 25											07 38	07 55					
Rochester	d						07 12	07 29											07 42	07 59					
Maidstone West	d																								
Strood	d						07 15	07 32											07 45	08 02					
Higham	d						07 20												07 50						
Gravesend	d		08 05				07 29	07 42		07 50				08 35					07 59	08 12		08 20			
Northfleet	d		08 08				07 32							08 38					08 02						
Swanscombe	d		08 10				07 34							08 40					08 04						
Greenhithe for Bluewater	d		08 14				07 38			07 56				08 44					08 08			08 26			
Stone Crossing	d		08 16				07 40							08 46					08 10						
Dartford	a		08 20				07 44			08 01				08 50					08 14			08 31			
	d	08 05	08 21			07 41	07 45		07 55	08 02			08 35	08 51				08 11	08 15		08 25	08 32			
Slade Green	d				07 39	07 46	07 51				07 59					08 09		08 16	08 21				08 29	08 37	
Erith	d				07 42	07 48					08 02					08 12		08 18					08 32		
Belvedere	d				07 44	07 51					08 04					08 14		08 21					08 34		
Abbey Wood	d				07 48	07 54	07 58				08 08					08 18		08 24	08 28				08 38		
Plumstead	d				07 51	07 57	08 01				08 11					08 21		08 27	08 31				08 41		
Woolwich Arsenal	d				07 54	08 00	08 04				08 14					08 24		08 30	08 34				08 44		
Woolwich Dockyard	d				07 56	08 03					08 16					08 26		08 33					08 46		
Charlton	d			07 55	08 00	08 06	08 10				08 20				08 25	08 30		08 36	08 40				08 50		
Crayford	d	08 12	08 26	08 32									08 42	08 56	09 02										
Bexley	d	08 15	08 29	08 35									08 45	08 59	09 05										
Albany Park	d	08 17		08 37									08 47		09 07										
Sidcup	d	08 20	08 33	08 40									08 50	09 03	09 10										
New Eltham	d	08 24	08 36	08 44									08 54	09 06	09 14										
Mottingham	d	08 26		08 46									08 56		09 16										
Lee	d	08 29		08 49									08 59		09 19										
Hither Green	d	08 33		08 52									09 03		09 22										
Barnehurst	d								08 03	08 09		08 20									08 33	08 39		08a45	08 50
Bexleyheath	d								08 06	08 12		08 23									08 36	08 42			08 53
Welling	d								08 09	08 15		08 26									08 39	08 45			08 56
Falconwood	d								08 11	08 18		08 28									08 41	08 48			08 58
Eltham	d								08 14	08 21		08 31									08 44	08 51			09 01
Kidbrooke	d								08 17	08 24		08 34									08 47	08 54			09 04
Blackheath	d					08 11			08 21	08 28		08 38						08 41			08 51	08 58			09 08
Lewisham	d			08 57		08 16			08 25	08 32		08 42			09 27			08 46			08 55	09 02			09 12
St Johns	d			08 59								08 44			09 29										09 14
New Cross	d			09 01								08 47			09 31										09 17
Nunhead	d									08 37												09 07			
Peckham Rye	d									08 40												09 10			
Denmark Hill	d									08 44												09 14			
London Victoria	a									08 55												09 25			
Westcombe Park	d				08 02		08 12				08 22					08 32			08 42				08 52		
Maze Hill	d				08 04		08 14				08 24					08 34			08 44				08 54		
Greenwich	d				08 07		08 17				08 27					08 37			08 47				08 57		
Deptford	a				08 09		08 19				08 29					08 39			08 49				08 59		
London Bridge	a	08 43	08 50	09 07	08 15	08 25	08 27		08 33		08 35	08 52	09 13	09 20	09 37	08 45		08 55	08 57		09 03		09 05		09 22
London Cannon Street	a			09 13	08 21						08 41	09 00			09 43	08 51							09 11		09 30
London Waterloo (East)	a	08 49	08 56			08 31			08 39				09 19	09 26				09 01			09 09				
London Charing Cross	a	08 53	09 00			08 35			08 43				09 23	09 30				09 05			09 13				
Ebbsfleet International	a							07 46												08 16					
Stratford International	a							07 58												08 29					
St Pancras Int'l	a							08 06												08 36					

Table T200-R

Saturdays

26 May to 8 December

Gillingham and Dartford - London

		SE	SE	SE	SE	SE	SE	TL		SE	SE	SE	SE	SE	SE	SE	SE	SE	SE	SE	SE	TL	SE	SE	
										◇													◇		
Rainham Kt	d							07 58		08 16												08 28	08 46		
Gillingham (Kent)	d							08 04		08 21												08 34	08 51		
Chatham	d							08 08		08 25												08 38	08 55		
Rochester	d							08 12		08 29												08 42	08 59		
Maidstone West	d																								
Strood	d							08 15		08 32												08 45	09 02		
Higham	d							08 20														08 50			
Gravesend	d			09 05				08 29		08 42		08 50						09 35				08 59	09 12		
Northfleet	d			09 08				08 32										09 38				09 02			
Swanscombe	d			09 10				08 34										09 40				09 04			
Greenhithe for Bluewater	d			09 14				08 38				08 56						09 44				09 08			
Stone Crossing	d			09 16				08 40										09 46				09 10			
Dartford	a			09 20				08 44				09 01						09 50				09 14			
	d		09 05	09 21			08 41	08 45			08 55	09 02					09 35	09 51			09 11	09 15		09 25	
Slade Green	d	08 37				08 39	08 46	08 51					08 59	09 07		09 07				09 09	09 16	09 21			
Erith	d					08 42	08 48						09 02							09 12	09 18				
Belvedere	d					08 44	08 51						09 04							09 14	09 21				
Abbey Wood	d					08 48	08 54	08 58					09 08							09 18	09 24	09 28			
Plumstead	d					08 51	08 57	09 01					09 11							09 21	09 27	09 31			
Woolwich Arsenal	d					08 54	09 00	09 04					09 14							09 24	09 30	09 34			
Woolwich Dockyard	d					08 56	09 03						09 16							09 26	09 33				
Charlton	d				08 55	09 00	09 06	09 10					09 20						09 25	09 30	09 36	09 40			
Crayford	d		09 12	09 26	09 32												09 42	09 56	10 02						
Bexley	d		09 15	09 29	09 35												09 45	09 59	10 05						
Albany Park	d		09 17		09 37												09 47		10 07						
Sidcup	d		09 20	09 33	09 40												09 50	10 03	10 10						
New Eltham	d		09 24	09 36	09 44												09 54	10 06	10 14						
Mottingham	d		09 26		09 46												09 56		10 16						
Lee	d		09 29		09 49												09 59		10 19						
Hither Green	d		09 33		09 52												10 03		10 22						
Barnehurst	d	08 50									09 03	09 09		09a15	09 20	09 20								09 33	
Bexleyheath	d	08 53									09 06	09 12			09 23	09 23								09 36	
Welling	d	08 56									09 09	09 15			09 26	09 26								09 39	
Falconwood	d	08 58									09 11	09 18			09 28	09 28								09 41	
Eltham	d	09 01									09 14	09 21			09 31	09 31								09 44	
Kidbrooke	d	09 04									09 17	09 24			09 34	09 34								09 47	
Blackheath	d	09 08					09 11				09 21	09 28			09 38	09 38				09 41				09 51	
Lewisham	d	09 12			09 57		09 16				09 25	09 32			09 42	09 42			10 27	09 46				09 55	
St Johns	d	09 14			09 59										09 44	09 44			10 29						
New Cross	d	09 17			10 01										09 47	09 47			10 31						
Nunhead	d											09 37													
Peckham Rye	d											09 40													
Denmark Hill	d											09 44													
London Victoria	a											09 55													
Westcombe Park	d					09 02		09 12					09 22							09 32		09 42			
Maze Hill	d					09 04		09 14					09 24							09 34		09 44			
Greenwich	d					09 07		09 17					09 27							09 37		09 47			
Deptford	a					09 09		09 19					09 29							09 39		09 49			
London Bridge	a	09 22	09 43	09 50	10 07	09 15	09 25	09 27			09 33		09 35		09 52	09 52	10 13	10 20	10 37	09 45	09 55	09 57		10 03	
London Cannon Street	a	09 30			10 13	09 21							09 41		10 00	10 00			10 43	09 51					
London Waterloo (East)	a		09 49	09 56			09 31				09 39						10 19	10 26			10 01			10 09	
London Charing Cross	a		09 53	10 00			09 35				09 43						10 23	10 30			10 05			10 13	
Ebbsfleet International	a									08 46													09 16		
Stratford International	a									08 58													09 29		
St Pancras Int'l	a									09 06													09 36		

Please note, Network Rail have stated that further updates to this timetable are possible during the validity period.

Table T200-R

Saturdays

26 May to 8 December

Gillingham and Dartford - London

		SE	SE	SE	SE	SE	SE	SE	SE	SE	SE	TL	SE	SE	SE	SE		SE	SE	SE	SE	SE	SE	SE	SE
													◇												
Rainham Kt	d											08 58	09 16												
Gillingham (Kent)	d											09 04	09 21												
Chatham	d											09 08	09 25												
Rochester	d											09 12	09 29												
Maidstone West	d																								
Strood	d											09 15	09 32												
Higham	d											09 20													
Gravesend	d	09 20						10 05				09 29	09 42		09 50							10 35			
Northfleet	d							10 08				09 32										10 38			
Swanscombe	d							10 10				09 34										10 40			
Greenhithe for Bluewater	d	09 26						10 14				09 38			09 56							10 44			
Stone Crossing	d							10 16				09 40										10 46			
Dartford	a	09 31						10 20				09 44			10 01							10 50			
	d	09 32					10 05	10 21			09 41	09 45		09 55	10 02						10 35	10 51			10 11
Slade Green	d		09 29	09 37		09 37				09 39	09 46	09 51				09 59		10 08		10 08				10 09	10 16
Erith	d		09 32							09 42	09 48					10 02								10 12	10 18
Belvedere	d		09 34							09 44	09 51					10 04								10 14	10 21
Abbey Wood	d		09 38							09 48	09 54	09 58				10 08								10 18	10 24
Plumstead	d		09 41							09 51	09 57	10 01				10 11								10 21	10 27
Woolwich Arsenal	d		09 44							09 54	10 00	10 04				10 14								10 24	10 30
Woolwich Dockyard	d		09 46							09 56	10 03					10 16								10 26	10 33
Charlton	d		09 50						09 55	10 00	10 06	10 10				10 20							10 25	10 30	10 36
Crayford	d						10 12	10 26	10 32												10 42	10 56	11 02		
Bexley	d						10 15	10 29	10 35												10 45	10 59	11 05		
Albany Park	d						10 17		10 37												10 47		11 07		
Sidcup	d						10 20	10 33	10 40												10 50	11 03	11 10		
New Eltham	d						10 24	10 36	10 44												10 54	11 06	11 14		
Mottingham	d						10 26		10 46												10 56		11 16		
Lee	d						10 29		10 49												10 59		11 19		
Hither Green	d						10 33		10 52												11 03		11 22		
Barnehurst	d	09 39		09a45	09 50	09 50								10 03	10 09			10a16	10 20	10 20					
Bexleyheath	d	09 42			09 53	09 53								10 06	10 12				10 23	10 23					
Welling	d	09 45			09 56	09 56								10 09	10 15				10 26	10 26					
Falconwood	d	09 48			09 58	09 58								10 11	10 18				10 28	10 28					
Eltham	d	09 51			10 01	10 01								10 14	10 21				10 31	10 31					
Kidbrooke	d	09 54			10 04	10 04								10 17	10 24				10 34	10 34					
Blackheath	d	09 58			10 08	10 08					10 11			10 21	10 28				10 38	10 38					10 41
Lewisham	d	10 02			10 12	10 12			10 57		10 16			10 25	10 32				10 42	10 42			11 27		10 46
St Johns	d				10 14	10 14			10 59										10 44	10 44			11 29		
New Cross	d				10 17	10 17			11 01										10 47	10 47			11 31		
Nunhead	d	10 07													10 37										
Peckham Rye	d	10 10													10 40										
Denmark Hill	d	10 14													10 44										
London Victoria	a	10 25													10 55										
Westcombe Park	d		09 52							10 02		10 12				10 22								10 32	
Maze Hill	d		09 54							10 04		10 14				10 24								10 34	
Greenwich	d		09 57							10 07		10 17				10 27								10 37	
Deptford	a		09 59							10 09		10 19				10 29								10 39	
London Bridge	a		10 05		10 22	10 22	10 43	10 50	11 07	10 15	10 25	10 27		10 33		10 35			10 52	10 52	11 13	11 20	11 37	10 45	10 55
London Cannon Street	a		10 11		10 30	10 30			11 13	10 21						10 41			11 00	11 00			11 43	10 51	
London Waterloo (East)	a						10 49	10 56			10 31			10 39							11 19	11 26			11 01
London Charing Cross	a						10 53	11 00			10 35			10 43							11 23	11 30			11 05
Ebbsfleet International	a												09 46												
Stratford International	a												09 58												
St Pancras Int'l	a												10 06												

Table T200-R

Saturdays

26 May to 8 December

Gillingham and Dartford - London

		TL	SE	SE	SE	SE	SE	SE		SE	SE	SE	SE	SE	SE	TL	SE	SE	SE	SE	SE	SE	SE	SE	
			◇														◇								
Rainham Kt	d	09 28	09 46													09 58	10 16								
Gillingham (Kent)	d	09 34	09 51													10 04	10 21								
Chatham	d	09 38	09 55													10 08	10 25								
Rochester	d	09 42	09 59													10 12	10 29								
Maidstone West	d																								
Strood	d	09 45	10 02													10 15	10 32								
Higham	d	09 50														10 20									
Gravesend	d	09 59	10 12		10 20							11 05				10 29	10 42		10 50						
Northfleet	d	10 02										11 08				10 32									
Swanscombe	d	10 04										11 10				10 34									
Greenhithe for Bluewater	d	10 08			10 26							11 14				10 38			10 56						
Stone Crossing	d	10 10										11 16				10 40									
Dartford	a	10 14			10 31							11 20				10 44			11 01						
	d	10 15		10 25	10 32						11 05	11 21			10 41	10 45		10 55	11 02					11 35	
Slade Green	d	10 21				10 29	10 37			10 37				10 39	10 46	10 51				10 59	11 07		11 07		
Erith	d					10 32								10 42	10 48					11 02					
Belvedere	d					10 34								10 44	10 51					11 04					
Abbey Wood	d	10 28				10 38								10 48	10 54	10 58				11 08					
Plumstead	d	10 31				10 41								10 51	10 57	11 01				11 11					
Woolwich Arsenal	d	10 34				10 44								10 54	11 00	11 04				11 14					
Woolwich Dockyard	d					10 46								10 56	11 03					11 16					
Charlton	d	10 40				10 50							10 55	11 00	11 06	11 10				11 20					
Crayford	d										11 12	11 26	11 32											11 42	
Bexley	d										11 15	11 29	11 35											11 45	
Albany Park	d										11 17		11 37											11 47	
Sidcup	d										11 20	11 33	11 40											11 50	
New Eltham	d										11 24	11 36	11 44											11 54	
Mottingham	d										11 26		11 46											11 56	
Lee	d										11 29		11 49											11 59	
Hither Green	d										11 33		11 52											12 03	
Barnehurst	d			10 33	10 39		10a45	10 50		10 50								11 03	11 09		11a15	11 20	11 20		
Bexleyheath	d			10 36	10 42			10 53		10 53								11 06	11 12			11 23	11 23		
Welling	d			10 39	10 45			10 56		10 56								11 09	11 15			11 26	11 26		
Falconwood	d			10 41	10 48			10 58		10 58								11 11	11 18			11 28	11 28		
Eltham	d			10 44	10 51			11 01		11 01								11 14	11 21			11 31	11 31		
Kidbrooke	d			10 47	10 54			11 04		11 04								11 17	11 24			11 34	11 34		
Blackheath	d			10 51	10 58			11 08		11 08					11 11			11 21	11 28			11 38	11 38		
Lewisham	d			10 55	11 02			11 12		11 12			11 57		11 16			11 25	11 32			11 42	11 42		
St Johns	d							11 14		11 14			11 59									11 44	11 44		
New Cross	d							11 17		11 17			12 01									11 47	11 47		
Nunhead	d				11 07														11 37						
Peckham Rye	d				11 10														11 40						
Denmark Hill	d				11 14														11 44						
London Victoria	a				11 25														11 55						
Westcombe Park	d	10 42				10 52								11 02		11 12				11 22					
Maze Hill	d	10 44				10 54								11 04		11 14				11 24					
Greenwich	d	10 47				10 57								11 07		11 17				11 27					
Deptford	a	10 49				10 59								11 09		11 19				11 29					
London Bridge	a	10 57		11 03		11 05		11 22		11 22	11 43	11 50	12 07	11 15	11 25	11 27		11 33		11 35		11 52	11 52	12 13	
London Cannon Street	a					11 11		11 30		11 30			12 13	11 21						11 41		12 00	12 00		
London Waterloo (East)	a			11 09							11 49	11 56			11 31			11 39						12 19	
London Charing Cross	a			11 13							11 53	12 00			11 35			11 43						12 23	
Ebbsfleet International	a		10 16														10 46								
Stratford International	a		10 28														10 59								
St Pancras Int'l	a		10 35														11 06								

Table T200-R

Saturdays

26 May to 8 December

Gillingham and Dartford - London

		SE	SE	SE	SE	TL	SE	SE	SE	SE	SE	SE	SE	SE	SE	SE		SE	SE	TL	SE	SE	SE	SE	SE
							◇														◇				
Rainham Kt	d					10 28	10 46													10 58	11 16				
Gillingham (Kent)	d					10 34	10 51													11 04	11 21				
Chatham	d					10 38	10 55													11 08	11 25				
Rochester	d					10 42	10 59													11 12	11 29				
Maidstone West	d																								
Strood	d					10 45	11 02													11 15	11 32				
Higham	d					10 50														11 20					
Gravesend	d	11 35				10 59	11 12		11 20						12 05					11 29	11 42		11 50		
Northfleet	d	11 38				11 02									12 08					11 32					
Swanscombe	d	11 40				11 04									12 10					11 34					
Greenhithe for Bluewater	d	11 44				11 08			11 26						12 14					11 38			11 56		
Stone Crossing	d	11 46				11 10									12 16					11 40					
Dartford	a	11 50				11 14			11 31						12 20					11 44			12 01		
	d	11 51			11 11	11 15		11 25	11 32					12 05	12 21				11 41	11 45		11 55	12 02		
Slade Green	d			11 09	11 16	11 21				11 29	11 37		11 37					11 39	11 46	11 51				11 59	12 07
Erith	d			11 12	11 18					11 32								11 42	11 48					12 02	
Belvedere	d			11 14	11 21					11 34								11 44	11 51					12 04	
Abbey Wood	d			11 18	11 24	11 28				11 38								11 48	11 54	11 58				12 08	
Plumstead	d			11 21	11 27	11 31				11 41								11 51	11 57	12 01				12 11	
Woolwich Arsenal	d			11 24	11 30	11 34				11 44								11 54	12 00	12 04				12 14	
Woolwich Dockyard	d			11 26	11 33					11 46								11 56	12 03					12 16	
Charlton	d		11 25	11 30	11 36	11 40				11 50						11 55		12 00	12 06	12 10				12 20	
Crayford	d	11 56	12 02											12 12	12 26	12 32									
Bexley	d	11 59	12 05											12 15	12 29	12 35									
Albany Park	d		12 07											12 17		12 37									
Sidcup	d	12 03	12 10											12 20	12 33	12 40									
New Eltham	d	12 06	12 14											12 24	12 36	12 44									
Mottingham	d		12 16											12 26		12 46									
Lee	d		12 19											12 29		12 49									
Hither Green	d		12 22											12 33		12 52									
Barnehurst	d							11 33	11 39		11a45	11 50	11 50									12 03	12 09		12a15
Bexleyheath	d							11 36	11 42			11 53	11 53									12 06	12 12		
Welling	d							11 39	11 45			11 56	11 56									12 09	12 15		
Falconwood	d							11 41	11 48			11 58	11 58									12 11	12 18		
Eltham	d							11 44	11 51			12 01	12 01									12 14	12 21		
Kidbrooke	d							11 47	11 54			12 04	12 04									12 17	12 24		
Blackheath	d				11 41			11 51	11 58			12 08	12 08						12 11			12 21	12 28		
Lewisham	d		12 27		11 46			11 55	12 02			12 12	12 12			12 57			12 16			12 25	12 32		
St Johns	d		12 29									12 14	12 14			12 59									
New Cross ⊖	d		12 31									12 17	12 17			13 01									
Nunhead	d								12 07														12 37		
Peckham Rye	d								12 10														12 40		
Denmark Hill	d								12 14														12 44		
London Victoria ⊖	a								12 25														12 55		
Westcombe Park	d			11 32		11 42				11 52								12 02		12 12				12 22	
Maze Hill	d			11 34		11 44				11 54								12 04		12 14				12 24	
Greenwich	d			11 37		11 47				11 57								12 07		12 17				12 27	
Deptford	a			11 39		11 49				11 59								12 09		12 19				12 29	
London Bridge ⊖	a	12 20	12 37	11 45	11 55	11 57		12 03		12 05		12 22	12 22	12 43	12 50	13 07		12 15	12 25	12 27		12 33		12 35	
London Cannon Street ⊖	a		12 43	11 51						12 11		12 30	12 30			13 13		12 21						12 41	
London Waterloo (East) ⊖	a	12 26			12 01			12 09						12 49	12 56				12 31			12 39			
London Charing Cross ⊖	a	12 30			12 05			12 13						12 53	13 00				12 35			12 43			
Ebbsfleet International	a						11 16														11 46				
Stratford International ⊖	a						11 29														11 58				
St Pancras Int'l ⊖	a						11 37														12 06				

Table T200-R

Saturdays

26 May to 8 December

Gillingham and Dartford - London

		SE	SE	SE	SE	SE	SE	SE		TL	SE	SE	SE	SE	SE	SE	SE	SE	SE	SE	SE	SE	TL	SE	
											◇													◇	
Rainham Kt	d									11 28	11 46												11 58	12 16	
Gillingham (Kent)	d									11 34	11 51												12 04	12 21	
Chatham	d									11 38	11 55												12 08	12 25	
Rochester	d									11 42	11 59												12 12	12 29	
Maidstone West	d																								
Strood	d									11 45	12 02												12 15	12 32	
Higham	d									11 50													12 20		
Gravesend	d				12 35					11 59	12 12		12 20						13 05				12 29	12 42	
Northfleet	d				12 38					12 02									13 08				12 32		
Swanscombe	d				12 40					12 04									13 10				12 34		
Greenhithe for Bluewater	d				12 44					12 08			12 26						13 14				12 38		
Stone Crossing	d				12 46					12 10									13 16				12 40		
Dartford	a				12 50					12 14			12 31						13 20				12 44		
	d			12 35	12 51			12 11		12 15		12 25	12 32					13 05	13 21			12 41	12 45		
Slade Green	d		12 07				12 09	12 16		12 21				12 29	12 37		12 37				12 39	12 46	12 51		
Erith	d						12 12	12 18						12 32							12 42	12 48			
Belvedere	d						12 14	12 21						12 34							12 44	12 51			
Abbey Wood	d						12 18	12 24		12 28				12 38							12 48	12 54	12 58		
Plumstead	d						12 21	12 27		12 31				12 41							12 51	12 57	13 01		
Woolwich Arsenal	d						12 24	12 30		12 34				12 44							12 54	13 00	13 04		
Woolwich Dockyard	d						12 26	12 33						12 46							12 56	13 03			
Charlton	d					12 25	12 30	12 36		12 40				12 50						12 55	13 00	13 06	13 10		
Crayford	d			12 42	12 56	13 02												13 12	13 26	13 32					
Bexley	d			12 45	12 59	13 05												13 15	13 29	13 35					
Albany Park	d			12 47		13 07												13 17		13 37					
Sidcup	d			12 50	13 03	13 10												13 20	13 33	13 40					
New Eltham	d			12 54	13 06	13 14												13 24	13 36	13 44					
Mottingham	d			12 56		13 16												13 26		13 46					
Lee	d			12 59		13 19												13 29		13 49					
Hither Green	d			13 03		13 22												13 33		13 52					
Barnehurst	d	12 20	12 20									12 33	12 39		12a45	12 50	12 50								
Bexleyheath	d	12 23	12 23									12 36	12 42			12 53	12 53								
Welling	d	12 26	12 26									12 39	12 45			12 56	12 56								
Falconwood	d	12 28	12 28									12 41	12 48			12 58	12 58								
Eltham	d	12 31	12 31									12 44	12 51			13 01	13 01								
Kidbrooke	d	12 34	12 34									12 47	12 54			13 04	13 04								
Blackheath	d	12 38	12 38					12 41				12 51	12 58			13 08	13 08					13 11			
Lewisham	d	12 42	12 42			13 27		12 45				12 55	13 02			13 12	13 12			13 57		13 16			
St Johns	d	12 44	12 44			13 29										13 14	13 14			13 59					
New Cross ⊖	d	12 47	12 47			13 31										13 17	13 17			14 01					
Nunhead	d												13 07												
Peckham Rye	d												13 10												
Denmark Hill	d												13 14												
London Victoria ⊖	a												13 25												
Westcombe Park	d						12 32			12 42				12 52							13 02		13 12		
Maze Hill	d						12 34			12 44				12 54							13 04		13 14		
Greenwich	d						12 37			12 47				12 57							13 07		13 17		
Deptford	a						12 39			12 49				12 59							13 09		13 19		
London Bridge ⊖	a	12 52	12 52	13 13	13 20	13 37	12 45	12 55		12 57		13 03		13 05		13 22	13 22	13 43	13 50	14 07	13 15	13 25	13 27		
London Cannon Street ⊖	a	13 00	13 00			13 43	12 51							13 11		13 30	13 30			14 13	13 21				
London Waterloo (East) ⊖	a			13 19	13 26			13 01				13 09						13 49	13 56			13 31			
London Charing Cross ⊖	a			13 23	13 30			13 05				13 13						13 53	14 00			13 35			
Ebbsfleet International	a										12 16													12 46	
Stratford International ⊖	a										12 28													12 58	
St Pancras Int'l ⊖	a										12 36													13 06	

NRT MAY 2018 EDITION

Table T200-R

Saturdays
26 May to 8 December

Gillingham and Dartford - London

Station		SE	SE	SE	SE	SE	SE	SE	SE	SE	SE	SE	TL	SE ◇	SE	SE	SE	SE	SE	SE	SE	SE	SE	SE
Rainham Kt	d												12 28	12 46										
Gillingham (Kent)	d												12 34	12 51										
Chatham	d												12 38	12 55										
Rochester	d												12 42	12 59										
Maidstone West	d																							
Strood	d												12 45	13 02										
Higham	d												12 50											
Gravesend	d		12 50						13 35				12 59	13 12		13 20						14 05		
Northfleet	d								13 38				13 02									14 08		
Swanscombe	d								13 40				13 04									14 10		
Greenhithe for Bluewater	d		12 56						13 44				13 08			13 26						14 14		
Stone Crossing	d								13 46				13 10									14 16		
Dartford	a		13 01						13 50				13 14			13 31						14 20		
	d	12 55	13 02					13 35	13 51			13 11	13 15		13 25	13 32					14 05	14 21		
Slade Green	d			12 59	13 07		13 07				13 09	13 16	13 21				13 29	13 37		13 37				13 39
Erith	d			13 02							13 12	13 18					13 32							13 42
Belvedere	d			13 04							13 14	13 21					13 34							13 44
Abbey Wood	d			13 08							13 18	13 24	13 28				13 38							13 48
Plumstead	d			13 11							13 21	13 27	13 31				13 41							13 51
Woolwich Arsenal	d			13 14							13 24	13 30	13 34				13 44							13 54
Woolwich Dockyard	d			13 16							13 26	13 33					13 46							13 56
Charlton	d			13 20						13 25	13 30	13 36	13 40				13 50						13 55	14 00
Crayford	d							13 42	13 56	14 02											14 12	14 26	14 32	
Bexley	d							13 45	13 59	14 05											14 15	14 29	14 35	
Albany Park	d							13 47		14 07											14 17		14 37	
Sidcup	d							13 50	14 03	14 10											14 20	14 33	14 40	
New Eltham	d							13 54	14 06	14 14											14 24	14 36	14 44	
Mottingham	d							13 56		14 16											14 26		14 46	
Lee	d							13 59		14 19											14 29		14 49	
Hither Green	d							14 03		14 22											14 33		14 52	
Barnehurst	d	13 03	13 09		13a15	13 20	13 20								13 33	13 39		13a45	13 50	13 50				
Bexleyheath	d	13 06	13 12			13 23	13 23								13 36	13 42			13 53	13 53				
Welling	d	13 09	13 15			13 26	13 26								13 39	13 45			13 56	13 56				
Falconwood	d	13 11	13 18			13 28	13 28								13 41	13 48			13 58	13 58				
Eltham	d	13 14	13 21			13 31	13 31								13 44	13 51			14 01	14 01				
Kidbrooke	d	13 17	13 24			13 34	13 34								13 47	13 54			14 04	14 04				
Blackheath	d	13 21	13 28			13 38	13 38					13 41			13 51	13 58			14 08	14 08				
Lewisham	d	13 25	13 32			13 42	13 42			14 27		13 46			13 55	14 02			14 12	14 12			14 57	
St Johns	d					13 44	13 44			14 29									14 14	14 14			14 59	
New Cross ⊖	d					13 47	13 47			14 31									14 17	14 17			15 01	
Nunhead	d		13 37													14 07								
Peckham Rye	d		13 40													14 10								
Denmark Hill	d		13 44													14 14								
London Victoria ⊖	a		13 55													14 25								
Westcombe Park	d			13 22							13 32		13 42				13 52							14 02
Maze Hill	d			13 24							13 34		13 44				13 54							14 04
Greenwich	d			13 27							13 37		13 47				13 57							14 07
Deptford	a			13 29							13 39		13 49				13 59							14 09
London Bridge ⊖	a	13 33		13 35		13 52	13 52	14 13	14 20	14 37	13 45	13 55	13 57		14 03		14 05		14 22	14 22	14 43	14 50	15 07	14 15
London Cannon Street ⊖	a			13 41		14 00	14 00			14 43	13 51						14 11		14 30	14 30			15 13	14 21
London Waterloo (East) ⊖	a	13 39						14 19	14 26			14 01			14 09						14 49	14 56		
London Charing Cross ⊖	a	13 43						14 23	14 30			14 05			14 13						14 53	15 00		
Ebbsfleet International	a													13 16										
Stratford International ⊖	a													13 29										
St Pancras Int'l ⊖	a													13 37										

Table T200-R

Saturdays
26 May to 8 December

Gillingham and Dartford - London

Station		SE	TL	SE ◇	SE	SE	SE	SE	SE	SE	SE	SE	SE	SE	SE	TL	SE ◇	SE	SE	SE	SE	SE	SE
Rainham Kt	d		12 58	13 16												13 28	13 46						
Gillingham (Kent)	d		13 04	13 21												13 34	13 51						
Chatham	d		13 08	13 25												13 38	13 55						
Rochester	d		13 12	13 29												13 42	13 59						
Maidstone West	d																						
Strood	d		13 15	13 32												13 45	14 02						
Higham	d		13 20													13 50							
Gravesend	d		13 29	13 42		13 50						14 35				13 59	14 12		14 20				
Northfleet	d		13 32									14 38				14 02							
Swanscombe	d		13 34									14 40				14 04							
Greenhithe for Bluewater	d		13 38			13 56						14 44				14 08			14 26				
Stone Crossing	d		13 40									14 46				14 10							
Dartford	a		13 44			14 01						14 50				14 14			14 31				
	d	13 41	13 45		13 55	14 02					14 35	14 51			14 11	14 15		14 25	14 32				
Slade Green	d	13 46	13 51				13 59	14 07		14 07				14 09	14 16	14 21				14 29	14 37		14 37
Erith	d	13 48					14 02							14 12	14 18					14 32			
Belvedere	d	13 51					14 04							14 14	14 21					14 34			
Abbey Wood	d	13 54	13 58				14 08							14 18	14 24	14 28				14 38			
Plumstead	d	13 57	14 01				14 11							14 21	14 27	14 31				14 41			
Woolwich Arsenal	d	14 00	14 04				14 14							14 24	14 30	14 34				14 44			
Woolwich Dockyard	d	14 03					14 16							14 26	14 33					14 46			
Charlton	d	14 06	14 10				14 20						14 25	14 30	14 36	14 40				14 50			
Crayford	d										14 42	14 56	15 02										
Bexley	d										14 45	14 59	15 05										
Albany Park	d										14 47		15 07										
Sidcup	d										14 50	15 03	15 10										
New Eltham	d										14 54	15 06	15 14										
Mottingham	d										14 56		15 16										
Lee	d										14 59		15 19										
Hither Green	d										15 03		15 22										
Barnehurst	d				14 03	14 09		14a15	14 20	14 20								14 33	14 39		14a45	14 50	14 50
Bexleyheath	d				14 06	14 12			14 23	14 23								14 36	14 42			14 53	14 53
Welling	d				14 09	14 15			14 26	14 26								14 39	14 45			14 56	14 56
Falconwood	d				14 11	14 18			14 28	14 28								14 41	14 48			14 58	14 58
Eltham	d				14 14	14 21			14 31	14 31								14 44	14 51			15 01	15 01
Kidbrooke	d				14 17	14 24			14 34	14 34								14 47	14 54			15 04	15 04
Blackheath	d	14 11			14 21	14 28			14 38	14 38					14 41			14 51	14 58			15 08	15 08
Lewisham	d	14 16			14 25	14 32			14 42	14 42			15 27		14 46			14 55	15 02			15 12	15 12
St Johns	d								14 44	14 44			15 29									15 14	15 14
New Cross ⊖	d								14 47	14 47			15 31									15 17	15 17
Nunhead	d					14 37													15 07				
Peckham Rye	d					14 40													15 10				
Denmark Hill	d					14 44													15 14				
London Victoria ⊖	a					14 55													15 25				
Westcombe Park	d		14 12				14 22							14 32		14 42				14 52			
Maze Hill	d		14 14				14 24							14 34		14 44				14 54			
Greenwich	d		14 17				14 27							14 37		14 47				14 57			
Deptford	a		14 19				14 29							14 39		14 49				14 59			
London Bridge ⊖	a	14 25	14 27		14 33		14 35		14 52	14 52	15 13	15 20	15 37	14 45	14 55	14 57		15 03		15 05		15 22	15 22
London Cannon Street ⊖	a						14 41		15 00	15 00			15 43	14 51						15 11		15 30	15 30
London Waterloo (East) ⊖	a	14 31			14 39						15 19	15 26			15 01			15 09					
London Charing Cross ⊖	a	14 35			14 43						15 23	15 30			15 05			15 13					
Ebbsfleet International	a			13 46													14 16						
Stratford International ⊖	a			14 02													14 28						
St Pancras Int'l ⊖	a			14 09													14 36						

Please note, Network Rail have stated that further updates to this timetable are possible during the validity period.

Table T200-R

Saturdays

26 May to 8 December

Gillingham and Dartford - London

		SE	SE	SE	SE	SE	TL	SE ◇	SE	SE	SE	SE	SE	SE	SE	SE	SE	SE	SE	TL	SE ◇	SE	SE	SE
Rainham Kt	d						13 58	14 16												14 28	14 46			
Gillingham (Kent)	d						14 04	14 21												14 34	14 51			
Chatham	d						14 08	14 25												14 38	14 55			
Rochester	d						14 12	14 29												14 42	14 59			
Maidstone West	d																							
Strood	d						14 15	14 32												14 45	15 02			
Higham	d						14 20													14 50				
Gravesend	d		15 05				14 29	14 42		14 50						15 35				14 59	15 12		15 20	
Northfleet	d		15 08				14 32									15 38				15 02				
Swanscombe	d		15 10				14 34									15 40				15 04				
Greenhithe for Bluewater	d		15 14				14 38			14 56						15 44				15 08			15 26	
Stone Crossing	d		15 16				14 40									15 46				15 10				
Dartford	a		15 20				14 44			15 01						15 50				15 14			15 31	
	d	15 05	15 21			14 41	14 45		14 55	15 02					15 35	15 51			15 11	15 15		15 25	15 32	
Slade Green	d				14 39	14 46	14 51				14 59	15 07		15 07				15 09	15 16	15 21				15 29
Erith	d				14 42	14 48					15 02							15 12	15 18					15 32
Belvedere	d				14 44	14 51					15 04							15 14	15 21					15 34
Abbey Wood	d				14 48	14 54	14 58				15 08							15 18	15 24	15 28				15 38
Plumstead	d				14 51	14 57	15 01				15 11							15 21	15 27	15 31				15 41
Woolwich Arsenal	d				14 54	15 00	15 04				15 14							15 24	15 30	15 34				15 44
Woolwich Dockyard	d				14 56	15 03					15 16							15 26	15 33					15 46
Charlton	d			14 55	15 00	15 06	15 10				15 20						15 25	15 30	15 36	15 40				15 50
Crayford	d	15 12	15 26	15 32											15 42	15 56	16 02							
Bexley	d	15 15	15 29	15 35											15 45	15 59	16 05							
Albany Park	d	15 17		15 37											15 47		16 07							
Sidcup	d	15 20	15 33	15 40											15 50	16 03	16 10							
New Eltham	d	15 24	15 36	15 44											15 54	16 06	16 14							
Mottingham	d	15 26		15 46											15 56		16 16							
Lee	d	15 29		15 49											15 59		16 19							
Hither Green	d	15 33		15 52											16 03		16 22							
Barnehurst	d								15 03	15 09		15a15	15 20	15 20								15 33	15 39	
Bexleyheath	d								15 06	15 12			15 23	15 23								15 36	15 42	
Welling	d								15 09	15 15			15 26	15 26								15 39	15 45	
Falconwood	d								15 11	15 18			15 28	15 28								15 41	15 48	
Eltham	d								15 14	15 21			15 31	15 31								15 44	15 51	
Kidbrooke	d								15 17	15 24			15 34	15 34								15 47	15 54	
Blackheath	d					15 11			15 21	15 28			15 38	15 38					15 41			15 51	15 58	
Lewisham	d			15 57		15 16			15 25	15 32			15 42	15 42			16 27		15 46			15 55	16 02	
St Johns	d			15 59									15 44	15 44			16 29							
New Cross	d			16 01									15 47	15 47			16 31							
Nunhead	d									15 37													16 07	
Peckham Rye	d									15 40													16 10	
Denmark Hill	d									15 44													16 14	
London Victoria	a									15 55													16 25	
Westcombe Park	d				15 02		15 12				15 22							15 32		15 42				15 52
Maze Hill	d				15 04		15 14				15 24							15 34		15 44				15 54
Greenwich	d				15 07		15 17				15 27							15 37		15 47				15 57
Deptford	a				15 09		15 19				15 29							15 39		15 49				15 59
London Bridge	a	15 43	15 50	16 07	15 15	15 25	15 27		15 33		15 35		15 52	15 52	16 13	16 20	16 37	15 45	15 55	15 57		16 03		16 05
London Cannon Street	a			16 13	15 21						15 41		16 00	16 00			16 43	15 51						16 11
London Waterloo (East)	a	15 49	15 56			15 31			15 39						16 19	16 26			16 01			16 09		
London Charing Cross	a	15 53	16 00			15 35			15 43						16 23	16 30			16 05			16 13		
Ebbsfleet International	a							14 46													15 16			
Stratford International	a							14 59													15 29			
St Pancras Int'l	a							15 07													15 40			

Table T200-R

Saturdays

26 May to 8 December

Gillingham and Dartford - London

		SE	SE	SE	SE	SE	SE	SE	SE	TL	SE ◇	SE	SE	SE	SE	SE	SE	SE	SE	SE	SE	SE	TL
Rainham Kt	d									14 58	15 16												15 28
Gillingham (Kent)	d									15 04	15 21												15 34
Chatham	d									15 08	15 25												15 38
Rochester	d									15 12	15 29												15 42
Maidstone West	d																						
Strood	d									15 15	15 32												15 45
Higham	d									15 20													15 50
Gravesend	d					16 05				15 29	15 42		15 50						16 35				15 59
Northfleet	d					16 08				15 32									16 38				16 02
Swanscombe	d					16 10				15 34									16 40				16 04
Greenhithe for Bluewater	d					16 14				15 38			15 56						16 44				16 08
Stone Crossing	d					16 16				15 40									16 46				16 10
Dartford	a					16 20				15 44			16 01						16 50				16 14
	d				16 05	16 21			15 41	15 45		15 55	16 02					16 35	16 51			16 11	16 15
Slade Green	d	15 37		15 37				15 39	15 46	15 51				15 59	16 07		16 07				16 09	16 16	16 21
Erith	d							15 42	15 48					16 02							16 12	16 18	
Belvedere	d							15 44	15 51					16 04							16 14	16 21	
Abbey Wood	d							15 48	15 54	15 58				16 08							16 18	16 24	16 28
Plumstead	d							15 51	15 57	16 01				16 11							16 21	16 27	16 31
Woolwich Arsenal	d							15 54	16 00	16 04				16 14							16 24	16 30	16 34
Woolwich Dockyard	d							15 56	16 03					16 16							16 26	16 33	
Charlton	d						15 55	16 00	16 06	16 10				16 20						16 25	16 30	16 36	16 40
Crayford	d				16 12	16 26	16 32											16 42	16 56	17 02			
Bexley	d				16 15	16 29	16 35											16 45	16 59	17 05			
Albany Park	d				16 17		16 37											16 47		17 07			
Sidcup	d				16 20	16 33	16 40											16 50	17 03	17 10			
New Eltham	d				16 24	16 36	16 44											16 54	17 06	17 14			
Mottingham	d				16 26		16 46											16 56		17 16			
Lee	d				16 29		16 49											16 59		17 19			
Hither Green	d				16 33		16 52											17 03		17 22			
Barnehurst	d	15a45	15 50	15 50								16 03	16 09		16a15	16 20	16 20						
Bexleyheath	d		15 53	15 53								16 06	16 12			16 23	16 23						
Welling	d		15 56	15 56								16 09	16 15			16 26	16 26						
Falconwood	d		15 58	15 58								16 11	16 18			16 28	16 28						
Eltham	d		16 01	16 01								16 14	16 21			16 31	16 31						
Kidbrooke	d		16 04	16 04								16 17	16 24			16 34	16 34						
Blackheath	d		16 08	16 08					16 11			16 21	16 28			16 38	16 38					16 41	
Lewisham	d		16 12	16 12			16 57		16 16			16 25	16 32			16 42	16 42			17 27		16 46	
St Johns	d		16 14	16 14			16 59									16 44	16 44			17 29			
New Cross	d		16 17	16 17			17 01									16 47	16 47			17 31			
Nunhead	d												16 37										
Peckham Rye	d												16 40										
Denmark Hill	d												16 44										
London Victoria	a												16 55										
Westcombe Park	d							16 02		16 12				16 22							16 32		16 42
Maze Hill	d							16 04		16 14				16 24							16 34		16 44
Greenwich	d							16 07		16 17				16 27							16 37		16 47
Deptford	a							16 09		16 19				16 29							16 39		16 49
London Bridge	a		16 22	16 22	16 43	16 50	17 07	16 15	16 25	16 27		16 33		16 35		16 52	16 52	17 13	17 20	17 37	16 45	16 55	16 57
London Cannon Street	a		16 30	16 30			17 13	16 21						16 41		17 00	17 00			17 43	16 51		
London Waterloo (East)	a				16 49	16 56			16 31			16 39						17 19	17 26			17 01	
London Charing Cross	a				16 53	17 00			16 35			16 43						17 23	17 30			17 05	
Ebbsfleet International	a										15 46												
Stratford International	a										16 02												
St Pancras Int'l	a										16 09												

Please note, Network Rail have stated that further updates to this timetable are possible during the validity period.

Table T200-R

Saturdays

26 May to 8 December

Gillingham and Dartford - London

		SE ◇	SE	SE	SE	SE	SE	SE	SE	SE	SE	SE	SE	TL	SE ◇	SE		SE	SE	SE	SE	SE	SE	SE	SE
Rainham Kt	d	15 46												15 58	16 16										
Gillingham (Kent)	d	15 51												16 04	16 21										
Chatham	d	15 55												16 08	16 25										
Rochester	d	15 59												16 12	16 29										
Maidstone West	d																								
Strood	d	16 02												16 16	16 32										
Higham	d													16 21											
Gravesend	d	16 12		16 20						17 05				16 29	16 42			16 50						17 35	
Northfleet	d									17 08				16 32										17 38	
Swanscombe	d									17 10				16 34										17 40	
Greenhithe for Bluewater	d			16 26						17 14				16 38				16 56						17 44	
Stone Crossing	d									17 16				16 40										17 46	
Dartford	a			16 31						17 20				16 44				17 01						17 50	
	d		16 25	16 32					17 05	17 21			16 41	16 45		16 55		17 02					17 35	17 51	
Slade Green	d				16 29	16 37		16 37				16 39	16 46	16 51					16 59	17 07		17 07			
Erith	d				16 32							16 42	16 48						17 02						
Belvedere	d				16 34							16 44	16 51						17 04						
Abbey Wood	d				16 38							16 48	16 54	16 58					17 08						
Plumstead	d				16 41							16 51	16 57	17 01					17 11						
Woolwich Arsenal	d				16 44							16 54	17 00	17 04					17 14						
Woolwich Dockyard	d				16 46							16 56	17 03						17 16						
Charlton	d				16 50						16 55	17 00	17 06	17 10					17 20						17 25
Crayford	d								17 12	17 26	17 32												17 42	17 56	18 02
Bexley	d								17 15	17 29	17 35												17 45	17 59	18 05
Albany Park	d								17 17		17 37												17 47		18 07
Sidcup	d								17 20	17 33	17 40												17 50	18 03	18 10
New Eltham	d								17 24	17 36	17 44												17 54	18 06	18 14
Mottingham	d								17 26		17 46												17 56		18 16
Lee	d								17 29		17 49												17 59		18 19
Hither Green	d								17 33		17 52												18 03		18 22
Barnehurst	d		16 33	16 39		16a45	16 50	16 50								17 03		17 09		17a15	17 20	17 20			
Bexleyheath	d		16 36	16 42			16 53	16 53								17 06		17 12			17 23	17 23			
Welling	d		16 39	16 45			16 56	16 56								17 09		17 15			17 26	17 26			
Falconwood	d		16 41	16 48			16 58	16 58								17 11		17 18			17 28	17 28			
Eltham	d		16 44	16 51			17 01	17 01								17 14		17 21			17 31	17 31			
Kidbrooke	d		16 47	16 54			17 04	17 04								17 17		17 24			17 34	17 34			
Blackheath	d		16 51	16 58			17 08	17 08					17 11			17 21		17 28			17 38	17 38			
Lewisham	d		16 55	17 02			17 12	17 12			17 57		17 16			17 25		17 32			17 42	17 42			18 27
St Johns	d						17 14	17 14			17 59										17 44	17 44			18 29
New Cross	d						17 17	17 17			18 01										17 47	17 47			18 31
Nunhead	d			17 07														17 37							
Peckham Rye	d			17 10														17 40							
Denmark Hill	d			17 14														17 44							
London Victoria	a			17 25														17 55							
Westcombe Park	d				16 52							17 02		17 12					17 22						
Maze Hill	d				16 54							17 04		17 14					17 24						
Greenwich	d				16 57							17 07		17 17					17 27						
Deptford	a				16 59							17 09		17 19					17 29						
London Bridge	a		17 03		17 05		17 22	17 22	17 43	17 50	18 07	17 15	17 25	17 27		17 33			17 35		17 52	17 52	18 13	18 20	18 37
London Cannon Street	a				17 11		17 30	17 30			18 13	17 21							17 41		18 00	18 00			18 43
London Waterloo (East)	a		17 09						17 49	17 56			17 31			17 39							18 19	18 26	
London Charing Cross	a		17 13						17 53	18 00			17 35			17 43							18 23	18 30	
Ebbsfleet International	a	16 16													16 46										
Stratford International	a	16 28													16 58										
St Pancras Int'l	a	16 36													17 06										

Table T200-R

Saturdays

26 May to 8 December

Gillingham and Dartford - London

		SE	SE	TL	SE ◇	SE	SE	SE		SE	SE	SE	SE	SE	SE	SE	SE	TL	SE ◇	SE	SE	SE	SE	SE	
Rainham Kt	d			16 28	16 46													16 58	17 16						
Gillingham (Kent)	d			16 34	16 51													17 04	17 21						
Chatham	d			16 38	16 55													17 08	17 25						
Rochester	d			16 42	16 59													17 12	17 29						
Maidstone West	d																								
Strood	d			16 45	17 02													17 15	17 32						
Higham	d			16 50														17 20							
Gravesend	d			16 59	17 12		17 20							18 05				17 29	17 42		17 50				
Northfleet	d			17 02										18 08				17 32							
Swanscombe	d			17 04										18 10				17 34							
Greenhithe for Bluewater	d			17 08			17 26							18 14				17 38			17 56				
Stone Crossing	d			17 10										18 16				17 40							
Dartford	a			17 14			17 31							18 20				17 44			18 01				
	d		17 11	17 15		17 25	17 32						18 05	18 21			17 41	17 45		17 55	18 02				
Slade Green	d	17 09	17 16	17 21				17 29		17 37		17 37				17 39	17 46	17 51				17 59	18 07		
Erith	d	17 12	17 18					17 32								17 42	17 48					18 02			
Belvedere	d	17 14	17 21					17 34								17 44	17 51					18 04			
Abbey Wood	d	17 18	17 24	17 28				17 38								17 48	17 54	17 58				18 08			
Plumstead	d	17 21	17 27	17 31				17 41								17 51	17 57	18 01				18 11			
Woolwich Arsenal	d	17 24	17 30	17 34				17 44								17 54	18 00	18 04				18 14			
Woolwich Dockyard	d	17 26	17 33					17 46								17 56	18 03					18 16			
Charlton	d	17 30	17 36	17 40				17 50							17 55	18 00	18 06	18 10				18 20			
Crayford	d												18 12	18 26	18 32										
Bexley	d												18 15	18 29	18 35										
Albany Park	d												18 17		18 37										
Sidcup	d												18 20	18 33	18 40										
New Eltham	d												18 24	18 36	18 44										
Mottingham	d												18 26		18 46										
Lee	d												18 29		18 49										
Hither Green	d												18 33		18 52										
Barnehurst	d					17 33	17 39			17a45	17 50	17 50								18 03	18 09		18a15	18 20	
Bexleyheath	d					17 36	17 42				17 53	17 53								18 06	18 12			18 23	
Welling	d					17 39	17 45				17 56	17 56								18 09	18 15			18 26	
Falconwood	d					17 41	17 48				17 58	17 58								18 11	18 18			18 28	
Eltham	d					17 44	17 51				18 01	18 01								18 14	18 21			18 31	
Kidbrooke	d					17 47	17 54				18 04	18 04								18 17	18 24			18 34	
Blackheath	d		17 41			17 51	17 58				18 08	18 08					18 11			18 21	18 28			18 38	
Lewisham	d		17 46			17 55	18 02				18 12	18 12			18 57		18 16			18 25	18 32			18 42	
St Johns	d										18 14	18 14			18 59									18 44	
New Cross	d										18 17	18 17			19 01									18 47	
Nunhead	d						18 07														18 37				
Peckham Rye	d						18 10														18 40				
Denmark Hill	d						18 14														18 44				
London Victoria	a						18 25														18 55				
Westcombe Park	d	17 32		17 42				17 52								18 02		18 12				18 22			
Maze Hill	d	17 34		17 44				17 54								18 04		18 14				18 24			
Greenwich	d	17 37		17 47				17 57								18 07		18 17				18 27			
Deptford	a	17 39		17 49				17 59								18 09		18 19				18 29			
London Bridge	a	17 45	17 55	17 57		18 03		18 05			18 22	18 22	18 43	18 50	19 07	18 15	18 25	18 27		18 33		18 35		18 52	
London Cannon Street	a	17 51						18 11			18 30	18 30			19 13	18 21						18 41		19 00	
London Waterloo (East)	a		18 01			18 09							18 49	18 56			18 31			18 39					
London Charing Cross	a		18 05			18 13							18 53	19 00			18 35			18 43					
Ebbsfleet International	a				17 16														17 46						
Stratford International	a				17 28														17 58						
St Pancras Int'l	a				17 36														18 09						

Table T200-R

Saturdays

26 May to 8 December

Gillingham and Dartford - London

		SE	SE	SE	SE	SE	SE	TL	SE	SE	SE	SE	SE	SE	SE	SE		SE	SE	SE	SE	TL	SE	SE	SE
									◇														◇		
Rainham Kt	d							17 28	17 46													17 58	18 16		
Gillingham (Kent)	d							17 34	17 51													18 04	18 21		
Chatham	d							17 38	17 55													18 08	18 25		
Rochester	d							17 42	17 59													18 12	18 29		
Maidstone West	d																								
Strood	d							17 45	18 02													18 15	18 32		
Higham	d							17 50														18 20			
Gravesend	d			18 35				17 59	18 12		18 20							19 05				18 29	18 42		18 50
Northfleet	d			18 38				18 02										19 08				18 32			
Swanscombe	d			18 40				18 04										19 10				18 34			
Greenhithe for Bluewater	d			18 44				18 08			18 26							19 14				18 38			18 56
Stone Crossing	d			18 46				18 10										19 16				18 40			
Dartford	a			18 50				18 14			18 31							19 20				18 44			19 01
	d		18 35	18 51			18 11	18 15		18 25	18 32					19 05		19 21			18 41	18 45		18 55	19 02
Slade Green	d	18 07				18 09	18 16	18 21				18 29	18 37		18 37					18 39	18 46	18 51			
Erith	d					18 12	18 18					18 32								18 42	18 48				
Belvedere	d					18 14	18 21					18 34								18 44	18 51				
Abbey Wood	d					18 18	18 24	18 28				18 38								18 48	18 54	18 58			
Plumstead	d					18 21	18 27	18 31				18 41								18 51	18 57	19 01			
Woolwich Arsenal	d					18 24	18 30	18 34				18 44								18 54	19 00	19 04			
Woolwich Dockyard	d					18 26	18 33					18 46								18 56	19 03				
Charlton	d				18 25	18 30	18 36	18 40				18 50							18 55	19 00	19 06	19 10			
Crayford	d		18 42	18 56	19 02											19 12		19 26	19 32						
Bexley	d		18 45	18 59	19 05											19 15		19 29	19 35						
Albany Park	d		18 47		19 07											19 17			19 37						
Sidcup	d		18 50	19 03	19 10											19 20		19 33	19 40						
New Eltham	d		18 54	19 06	19 14											19 24		19 36	19 44						
Mottingham	d		18 56		19 16											19 26			19 46						
Lee	d		18 59		19 19											19 29			19 49						
Hither Green	d		19 03		19 22											19 33			19 52						
Barnehurst	d	18 20								18 33	18 39		18a45	18 50	18 50									19 03	19 09
Bexleyheath	d	18 23								18 36	18 42			18 53	18 53									19 06	19 12
Welling	d	18 26								18 39	18 45			18 56	18 56									19 09	19 15
Falconwood	d	18 28								18 41	18 48			18 58	18 58									19 11	19 18
Eltham	d	18 31								18 44	18 51			19 01	19 01									19 14	19 21
Kidbrooke	d	18 34								18 47	18 54			19 04	19 04									19 17	19 24
Blackheath	d	18 38					18 41			18 51	18 58			19 08	19 08						19 11			19 21	19 28
Lewisham	d	18 42			19 27		18 46			18 55	19 02			19 12	19 12				19 57		19 16			19 25	19 32
St Johns	d	18 44			19 29									19 14	19 14				19 59						
New Cross	d	18 47			19 31									19 17	19 17				20 01						
Nunhead	d										19 07														19 37
Peckham Rye	d										19 10														19 40
Denmark Hill	d										19 14														19 44
London Victoria	a										19 25														19 55
Westcombe Park	d					18 32		18 42				18 52								19 02		19 12			
Maze Hill	d					18 34		18 44				18 54								19 04		19 14			
Greenwich	d					18 37		18 47				18 57								19 07		19 17			
Deptford	a					18 39		18 49				18 59								19 09		19 19			
London Bridge	a	18 52	19 13	19 20	19 37	18 45	18 55	18 57		19 03		19 05		19 22	19 22	19 43		19 50	20 07	19 15	19 25	19 27		19 33	
London Cannon Street	a	19 00			19 43	18 51						19 11		19 30	19 30				20 13	19 21					
London Waterloo (East)	a		19 19	19 26			19 01			19 09						19 49		19 56			19 31			19 39	
London Charing Cross	a		19 23	19 30			19 05			19 13						19 53		20 00			19 35			19 43	
Ebbsfleet International	a								18 16														18 46		
Stratford International	a								18 29														18 58		
St Pancras Int'l	a								18 36														19 06		

Table T200-R

Saturdays

26 May to 8 December

Gillingham and Dartford - London

		SE	SE	SE	SE	SE	SE	SE		SE	SE	TL	SE	SE	SE	SE	SE	SE	SE	SE	SE	SE	SE	TL	
													◇												
Rainham Kt	d											18 28	18 46											18 58	
Gillingham (Kent)	d											18 34	18 51											19 04	
Chatham	d											18 38	18 55											19 08	
Rochester	d											18 42	18 59											19 12	
Maidstone West	d																								
Strood	d											18 45	19 02											19 15	
Higham	d											18 50												19 20	
Gravesend	d						19 35					18 59	19 12		19 20						20 05			19 29	
Northfleet	d						19 38					19 02									20 08			19 32	
Swanscombe	d						19 40					19 04									20 10			19 34	
Greenhithe for Bluewater	d						19 44					19 08			19 26						20 14			19 38	
Stone Crossing	d						19 46					19 10									20 16			19 40	
Dartford	a						19 50					19 14			19 31						20 20			19 44	
	d					19 35	19 51				19 11	19 15		19 25	19 32					20 05	20 21		19 41	19 45	
Slade Green	d	18 59	19 07		19 07					19 09	19 16	19 21				19 29	19 37		19 37				19 46	19 51	
Erith	d	19 02								19 12	19 18					19 32							19 48		
Belvedere	d	19 04								19 14	19 21					19 34							19 51		
Abbey Wood	d	19 08								19 18	19 24	19 28				19 38							19 54	19 58	
Plumstead	d	19 11								19 21	19 27	19 31				19 41							19 57	20 01	
Woolwich Arsenal	d	19 14								19 24	19 30	19 34				19 44							20 00	20 04	
Woolwich Dockyard	d	19 16								19 26	19 33					19 46							20 03		
Charlton	d	19 20						19 25		19 30	19 36	19 40				19 50						19 55	20 06	20 10	
Crayford	d					19 42	19 56	20 02												20 12	20 26	20 32			
Bexley	d					19 45	19 59	20 05												20 15	20 29	20 35			
Albany Park	d					19 47		20 07												20 17		20 37			
Sidcup	d					19 50	20 03	20 10												20 20	20 33	20 40			
New Eltham	d					19 54	20 06	20 14												20 24	20 36	20 44			
Mottingham	d					19 56		20 16												20 26		20 46			
Lee	d					19 59		20 19												20 29		20 49			
Hither Green	d					20 03		20 22												20 33		20 52			
Barnehurst	d		19a15	19 20	19 20									19 33	19 39		19a45	19 50	19 50						
Bexleyheath	d			19 23	19 23									19 36	19 42			19 53	19 53						
Welling	d			19 26	19 26									19 39	19 45			19 56	19 56						
Falconwood	d			19 28	19 28									19 41	19 48			19 58	19 58						
Eltham	d			19 31	19 31									19 44	19 51			20 01	20 01						
Kidbrooke	d			19 34	19 34									19 47	19 54			20 04	20 04						
Blackheath	d			19 38	19 38						19 41			19 51	19 58			20 08	20 08				20 11		
Lewisham	d			19 42	19 42			20 27			19 46			19 55	20 02			20 12	20 12			20 57	20 16		
St Johns	d			19 44	19 44			20 29										20 14	20 14			20 59			
New Cross	d			19 47	19 47			20 31										20 17	20 17			21 01			
Nunhead	d														20 07										
Peckham Rye	d														20 10										
Denmark Hill	d														20 14										
London Victoria	a														20 25										
Westcombe Park	d	19 22								19 32		19 42				19 52								20 12	
Maze Hill	d	19 24								19 34		19 44				19 54								20 14	
Greenwich	d	19 27								19 37		19 47				19 57								20 17	
Deptford	a	19 29								19 39		19 49				19 59								20 19	
London Bridge	a	19 35		19 52	19 52	20 13	20 20	20 37		19 45	19 55	19 57		20 03		20 05		20 22	20 22	20 43	20 50	21 07	20 25	20 27	
London Cannon Street	a	19 41		20 00	20 00			20 43		19 51						20 11		20 30	20 30			21 13			
London Waterloo (East)	a					20 19	20 26				20 01			20 09						20 49	20 56		20 31		
London Charing Cross	a					20 23	20 30				20 05			20 13						20 53	21 00		20 35		
Ebbsfleet International	a												19 16												
Stratford International	a												19 28												
St Pancras Int'l	a												19 36												

Please note, Network Rail have stated that further updates to this timetable are possible during the validity period.

Table T200-R

Saturdays
26 May to 8 December

Gillingham and Dartford - London

		SE ◇	SE	SE	SE	SE	SE	SE	SE	SE	SE	SE	TL	SE ◇	SE	SE		SE	SE	SE	SE	SE	TL	SE ◇	SE
Rainham Kt	d	19 16											19 28	19 46									19 58	20 16	
Gillingham (Kent)	d	19 21											19 34	19 51									20 04	20 21	
Chatham	d	19 25											19 38	19 55									20 08	20 25	
Rochester	d	19 29											19 42	19 59									20 12	20 29	
Maidstone West	d																								
Strood	d	19 32											19 45	20 02									20 15	20 32	
Higham	d												19 50										20 20		
Gravesend	d	19 42		19 50						20 35			19 59	20 12		20 20				21 05			20 29	20 42	
Northfleet	d									20 38			20 02							21 08			20 32		
Swanscombe	d									20 40			20 04							21 10			20 34		
Greenhithe for Bluewater	d			19 56						20 44			20 08			20 26				21 14			20 38		
Stone Crossing	d									20 46			20 10							21 16			20 40		
Dartford	a			20 01						20 50			20 14			20 31				21 20			20 44		
	d		19 55	20 02					20 35	20 51		20 11	20 15		20 25	20 32			21 05	21 21		20 41	20 45		20 55
Slade Green	d				19 59	20 07		20 07				20 16	20 21					20 29				20 46	20 51		
Erith	d				20 02							20 18						20 32				20 48			
Belvedere	d				20 04							20 21						20 34				20 51			
Abbey Wood	d				20 08							20 24	20 28					20 38				20 54	20 58		
Plumstead	d				20 11							20 27	20 31					20 41				20 57	21 01		
Woolwich Arsenal	d				20 14							20 30	20 34					20 44				21 00	21 04		
Woolwich Dockyard	d				20 16							20 33						20 46				21 03			
Charlton	d				20 20						20 25	20 36	20 40					20 50			20 52	21 06	21 10		
Crayford	d								20 42	20 56	21 02								21 12	21 26	21 32				
Bexley	d								20 45	20 59	21 05								21 15	21 29	21 35				
Albany Park	d								20 47		21 07								21 17		21 37				
Sidcup	d								20 50	21 03	21 10								21 20	21 33	21 40				
New Eltham	d								20 54	21 06	21 14								21 24	21 36	21 44				
Mottingham	d								20 56		21 16								21 26		21 46				
Lee	d								20 59		21 19								21 29		21 49				
Hither Green	d								21 03		21 22								21 33		21 52				
Barnehurst	d		20 03	20 09		20a15	20 20	20 20							20 33	20 39									21 03
Bexleyheath	d		20 06	20 12			20 23	20 23							20 36	20 42									21 06
Welling	d		20 09	20 15			20 26	20 26							20 39	20 45									21 09
Falconwood	d		20 11	20 18			20 28	20 28							20 41	20 48									21 11
Eltham	d		20 14	20 21			20 31	20 31							20 44	20 51									21 14
Kidbrooke	d		20 17	20 24			20 34	20 34							20 47	20 54									21 17
Blackheath	d		20 21	20 28			20 38	20 38				20 41			20 51	20 58						21 11			21 21
Lewisham	d		20 25	20 32			20 42	20 42			21 27	20 46			20 55	21 02					21 57	21 16			21 25
St Johns	d						20 44	20 44			21 29										21 59				
New Cross	d						20 47	20 47			21 31										22 01				
Nunhead	d			20 37												21 07									
Peckham Rye	d			20 40												21 10									
Denmark Hill	d			20 44												21 14									
London Victoria	a			20 55												21 25									
Westcombe Park	d				20 22								20 42					20 52					21 12		
Maze Hill	d				20 24								20 44					20 54					21 14		
Greenwich	d				20 27								20 47					20 57					21 17		
Deptford	a				20 29								20 49					20 59					21 19		
London Bridge	a		20 33		20 35		20 52	20 52	21 13	21 20	21 37	20 55	20 57		21 03			21 05	21 43	21 50	22 07	21 25	21 27		21 33
London Cannon Street	a				20 41		21 00	21 00			21 43							21 11			22 13				
London Waterloo (East)	a		20 39						21 19	21 26		21 01			21 09				21 49	21 56		21 31			21 39
London Charing Cross	a		20 43						21 23	21 30		21 05			21 13				21 53	22 00		21 35			21 43
Ebbsfleet International	a	19 46												20 16										20 46	
Stratford International	a	19 58												20 28										21 02	
St Pancras Int'l	a	20 06												20 36										21 09	

Table T200-R

Saturdays
26 May to 8 December

Gillingham and Dartford - London

		SE	SE	SE	SE	SE	SE	TL		SE ◇	SE	SE	SE	SE	SE	SE	SE	TL	SE ◇	SE	SE	SE	SE	SE	
Rainham Kt	d							20 28		20 46								20 58	21 16						
Gillingham (Kent)	d							20 34		20 51								21 04	21 21						
Chatham	d							20 38		20 55								21 08	21 25						
Rochester	d							20 42		20 59								21 12	21 29						
Maidstone West	d																								
Strood	d							20 45		21 02								21 15	21 32						
Higham	d							20 50										21 20							
Gravesend	d	20 50			21 35			20 59		21 12		21 20			22 05			21 29	21 42		21 50			22 35	
Northfleet	d				21 38			21 02							22 08			21 32						22 38	
Swanscombe	d				21 40			21 04							22 10			21 34						22 40	
Greenhithe for Bluewater	d	20 56			21 44			21 08				21 26			22 14			21 38			21 56			22 44	
Stone Crossing	d				21 46			21 10							22 16			21 40						22 46	
Dartford	a	21 01			21 50			21 14				21 31			22 20			21 44			22 01			22 50	
	d	21 02		21 35	21 51		21 11	21 15			21 25	21 32		22 05	22 21		21 41	21 45		21 55	22 02		22 35	22 51	
Slade Green	d		20 59				21 16	21 21					21 29				21 46	21 51				21 59			
Erith	d		21 02				21 18						21 32				21 48					22 02			
Belvedere	d		21 04				21 21						21 34				21 51					22 04			
Abbey Wood	d		21 08				21 24	21 28					21 38				21 54	21 58				22 08			
Plumstead	d		21 11				21 27	21 31					21 41				21 57	22 01				22 11			
Woolwich Arsenal	d		21 14				21 30	21 34					21 44				22 00	22 04				22 14			
Woolwich Dockyard	d		21 16				21 33						21 46				22 03					22 16			
Charlton	d		21 20			21 22	21 36	21 40					21 50			21 52	22 06	22 10				22 20			
Crayford	d			21 42	21 56	22 02								22 12	22 26	22 32							22 42	22 56	
Bexley	d			21 45	21 59	22 05								22 15	22 29	22 35							22 45	22 59	
Albany Park	d			21 47		22 07								22 17		22 37							22 47		
Sidcup	d			21 50	22 03	22 10								22 20	22 33	22 40							22 50	23 03	
New Eltham	d			21 54	22 06	22 14								22 24	22 36	22 44							22 54	23 06	
Mottingham	d			21 56		22 16								22 26		22 46							22 56		
Lee	d			21 59		22 19								22 29		22 49							22 59		
Hither Green	d			22 03		22 22								22 33		22 52							23 03		
Barnehurst	d	21 09									21 33	21 39								22 03	22 09				
Bexleyheath	d	21 12									21 36	21 42								22 06	22 12				
Welling	d	21 15									21 39	21 45								22 09	22 15				
Falconwood	d	21 18									21 41	21 48								22 11	22 18				
Eltham	d	21 21									21 44	21 51								22 14	22 21				
Kidbrooke	d	21 24									21 47	21 54								22 17	22 24				
Blackheath	d	21 28					21 41				21 51	21 58					22 11			22 21	22 28				
Lewisham	d	21 32				22 27	21 46				21 55	22 02				22 57	22 16			22 25	22 32				
St Johns	d					22 29										22 59									
New Cross	d					22 31										23 01									
Nunhead	d	21 37										22 07									22 37				
Peckham Rye	d	21 40										22 10									22 40				
Denmark Hill	d	21 44										22 14									22 44				
London Victoria	a	21 55										22 25									22 55				
Westcombe Park	d		21 22					21 42					21 52					22 12				22 22			
Maze Hill	d		21 24					21 44					21 54					22 14				22 24			
Greenwich	d		21 27					21 47					21 57					22 17				22 27			
Deptford	a		21 29					21 49					21 59					22 19				22 29			
London Bridge	a		21 35	22 13	22 20	22 37	21 55	21 57			22 03		22 05	22 43	22 50	23 07	22 25	22 27		22 33		22 35	23 13	23 20	
London Cannon Street	a		21 41			22 43							22 11			23 13						22 41			
London Waterloo (East)	a			22 19	22 26		22 01				22 09			22 49	22 56		22 31			22 39			23 19	23 26	
London Charing Cross	a			22 23	22 30		22 05				22 13			22 53	23 00		22 35			22 43			23 23	23 30	
Ebbsfleet International	a									21 16									21 46						
Stratford International	a									21 28									21 58						
St Pancras Int'l	a									21 36									22 06						

Table T200-R

Saturdays

26 May to 8 December

Gillingham and Dartford - London

Station		SE	SE	TL	SE ◇	SE	SE	SE	SE	SE	SE	SE	SE	TL	SE	SE ◇	SE	SE	TL	SE	SE	SE	TL	SE
Rainham Kt	d			21 28	21 46									21 58		22 16			22 28				22 58	
Gillingham (Kent)	d			21 34	21 51									22 04		22 21			22 34				23 04	
Chatham	d			21 38	21 55									22 08		22 25			22 38				23 08	
Rochester	d			21 42	21 59									22 12		22 29			22 42				23 12	
Maidstone West	d																							
Strood	d			21 45	22 02									22 15		22 32			22 45				23 15	
Higham	d			21 50										22 20					22 50				23 20	
Gravesend	d			21 59	22 12		22 20				23 05			22 29		22 42	22 50		22 59				23 27	23 35
Northfleet	d			22 02							23 08			22 32					23 02				23 31	23 38
Swanscombe	d			22 04							23 10			22 34					23 04				23 33	23 40
Greenhithe for Bluewater	d			22 08			22 26				23 14			22 38			22 56		23 08				23 36	23 44
Stone Crossing	d			22 10							23 16			22 40					23 10				23 38	23 46
Dartford	a			22 14			22 31				23 20			22 44			23 01		23 14				23 43	23 50
	d		22 11	22 15		22 25	22 32		22 55	23 05	23 21		22 41	22 45			23 02	23 11		23 25		23 41		23 51
Slade Green	d		22 16	22 21				22 29					22 46	22 51	22 59			23 16			23 29	23 46		
Erith	d		22 18					22 32					22 48		23 02			23 18			23 32	23 48		
Belvedere	d		22 21					22 34					22 51		23 04			23 21			23 34	23 51		
Abbey Wood	d		22 24	22 28				22 38					22 54	22 58	23 08			23 24			23 38	23 54		
Plumstead	d		22 27	22 31				22 41					22 57	23 01	23 11			23 27			23 41	23 57		
Woolwich Arsenal	d		22 30	22 34				22 44					23 00	23 04	23 14			23 30			23 44	23 59		
Woolwich Dockyard	d		22 33					22 46					23 03		23 16			23 33			23 46	00 03		
Charlton	d	22 22	22 36	22 40				22 50				22 52	23 06	23 10	23 20			23 36			23 50	00 06		
Crayford	d	23 02								23 12	23 26	23 32												23 56
Bexley	d	23 05								23 15	23 29	23 35												23 59
Albany Park	d	23 07								23 17		23 37												00 01
Sidcup	d	23 10								23 20	23 33	23 40												00 04
New Eltham	d	23 14								23 24	23 36	23 44												00 08
Mottingham	d	23 16								23 26		23 46												00 10
Lee	d	23 19								23 29		23 49												00 13
Hither Green	d	23 22								23 33		23 52												00 16
Barnehurst	d					22 33	22 39		23 03								23 09			23 33				
Bexleyheath	d					22 36	22 42		23 06								23 12			23 36				
Welling	d					22 39	22 45		23 09								23 15			23 39				
Falconwood	d					22 41	22 48		23 11								23 18			23 41				
Eltham	d					22 44	22 51		23 14								23 21			23 44				
Kidbrooke	d					22 47	22 54		23 17								23 24			23 47				
Blackheath	d		22 41			22 51	22 58		23 21				23 11				23 28	23 41		23 51		00 11		
Lewisham	d	23 27	22 46			22 55	23 02		23 25			23 57	23 16				23 32	23 46		23 55		00 16		
St Johns	d	23 29										23 59												
New Cross	d	23 31										00 02												
Nunhead	d						23 07										23 37							
Peckham Rye	d						23 10										23 40							
Denmark Hill	d						23 14										23 44							
London Victoria ⊖	a						23 25										23 55							
Westcombe Park	d			22 42				22 52						23 12	23 22						23 52			
Maze Hill	d			22 44				22 54						23 14	23 24						23 54			
Greenwich	d			22 47				22 57						23 17	23 27						23 57			
Deptford	a			22 49				22 59						23 19	23 29						23 59			
London Bridge ⊖	a	23 37	22 55	22 57		23 03		23 05	23 33	23 43	23 50	00 07	23 25	23 27	23 35			23 54		00 03	00 05	00 24		00 26
London Cannon Street ⊖	a	23 43						23 11				00 13			23 41						00 11			
London Waterloo (East) ⊖	a		23 01			23 09			23 39	23 49	23 56		23 31					00 01		00 09		00 30		00 32
London Charing Cross ⊖	a		23 05			23 13			23 43	23 53	00 01		23 35					00 05		00 13		00 35		00 36
Ebbsfleet International	a				22 16											22 46								
Stratford International ⊖	a				22 28											22 58								
St Pancras Int'l ⊖	a				22 36											23 06								

Table T200-R

Saturdays

26 May to 8 December

Gillingham and Dartford - London

Station		TL
Rainham Kt	d	23 28
Gillingham (Kent)	d	23 34
Chatham	d	23 38
Rochester	d	23 42
Maidstone West	d	
Strood	d	23 45
Higham	d	23 50
Gravesend	d	23 57
Northfleet	d	00 01
Swanscombe	d	00 03
Greenhithe for Bluewater	d	00 06
Stone Crossing	d	00 08
Dartford	a	00 13
	d	
Slade Green	d	
Erith	d	
Belvedere	d	
Abbey Wood	d	
Plumstead	d	
Woolwich Arsenal	d	
Woolwich Dockyard	d	
Charlton	d	
Crayford	d	
Bexley	d	
Albany Park	d	
Sidcup	d	
New Eltham	d	
Mottingham	d	
Lee	d	
Hither Green	d	
Barnehurst	d	
Bexleyheath	d	
Welling	d	
Falconwood	d	
Eltham	d	
Kidbrooke	d	
Blackheath	d	
Lewisham	d	
St Johns	d	
New Cross ⊖	d	
Nunhead	d	
Peckham Rye	d	
Denmark Hill	d	
London Victoria ⊖	a	
Westcombe Park	d	
Maze Hill	d	
Greenwich	d	
Deptford	a	
London Bridge ⊖	a	
London Cannon Street ⊖	a	
London Waterloo (East) ⊖	a	
London Charing Cross ⊖	a	
Ebbsfleet International	a	
Stratford International ⊖	a	
St Pancras Int'l ⊖	a	

Please note, Network Rail have stated that further updates to this timetable are possible during the validity period.

Table T200-R

Sundays

20 May to 2 December

Gillingham and Dartford - London

		TL	SE	SE	SE	SE	SE	SE	SE	SE	SE	TL	SE	SE	SE	SE		SE	SE	SE	SE	TL	SE	SE	SE
		A	A	A	A																		◇		
Rainham Kt	d																						07 16		
Gillingham (Kent)	d											06 36										07 06	07 21		
Chatham	d											06 40										07 10	07 25		
Rochester	d											06 44										07 14	07 29		
Maidstone West	d																								
Strood	d											06 47										07 17	07 32		
Higham	d											06 52										07 22			
Gravesend	d											06 59				07 18			07 48			07 29	07 42		
Northfleet	d	00 01										07 03				07 21			07 51			07 33			
Swanscombe	d	00 03										07 05				07 23			07 53			07 35			
Greenhithe for Bluewater	d	00 06										07 08				07 27			07 57			07 38			
Stone Crossing	d	00 08										07 10				07 29			07 59			07 40			
Dartford	a	00 13										07 14				07 33			08 03			07 44			
	d							06 50	07 02	07 04		07 15		07 20	07 32	07 34			08 04			07 45		07 50	08 02
Slade Green	d					06 35		06 55			07 05	07 21		07 25							07 35	07 51		07 55	
Erith	d					06 37		06 57			07 07			07 27							07 37			07 57	
Belvedere	d					06 40		07 00			07 10			07 30							07 40			08 00	
Abbey Wood	d					06 43		07 03			07 13	07 28		07 33							07 43	07 58		08 03	
Plumstead	d					06 46		07 06			07 16	07 31		07 36							07 46	08 01		08 06	
Woolwich Arsenal	d					06 49		07 09			07 19	07 34		07 39							07 49	08 04		08 09	
Woolwich Dockyard	d			00 03		06 52		07 12			07 22			07 42							07 52			08 12	
Charlton	d			00 06		06 55		07 15			07 25	07 40		07 45						07 49	07 55	08 10		08 15	
Crayford	d						06 52			07 09			07 22			07 39		07 52	08 09	08 22					
Bexley	d						06 55			07 12			07 25			07 42		07 55	08 12	08 25					
Albany Park	d				00 01		06 57			07 14			07 27			07 44		07 57	08 14	08 27					
Sidcup	d				00 04		07 00			07 17			07 30			07 47		08 00	08 17	08 30					
New Eltham	d				00 08		07 04			07 21			07 34			07 51		08 04	08 21	08 34					
Mottingham	d				00 10		07 06			07 23			07 36			07 53		08 06	08 23	08 36					
Lee	d				00 13		07 09			07 26			07 39			07 56		08 09	08 26	08 39					
Hither Green	d				00 16		07 12			07 29			07 42			07 59		08 12	08 29	08 42					
Barnehurst	d								07 09						07 39										08 09
Bexleyheath	d								07 12						07 42										08 12
Welling	d								07 15						07 45										08 15
Falconwood	d								07 18						07 48										08 18
Eltham	d								07 21						07 51										08 21
Kidbrooke	d								07 24						07 54										08 24
Blackheath	d			00 11				07 20	07 28					07 50	07 58									08 20	08 28
Lewisham	d			00 16			07 18	07 25	07 32				07 48	07 55	08 02			08 18		08 48				08 25	08 32
St Johns	d						07 20						07 50					08 20		08 50					
New Cross	d		00 02				07 23						07 53					08 23		08 53					
Nunhead	d								07 37						08 07										08 37
Peckham Rye	d								07 40						08 10										08 40
Denmark Hill	d								07 42						08 12										08 42
London Victoria	a								07 54						08 24										08 54
Westcombe Park	d					06 57					07 27	07 42									07 57	08 12			
Maze Hill	d					06 59					07 29	07 44									07 59	08 14			
Greenwich	d					07 03					07 33	07 47									08 03	08 17			
Deptford	a					07 05					07 35	07 49									08 05	08 19			
London Bridge	a		00 07	00 24	00 26	07 11	07 28	07 33		07 39	07 41	07 57	07 58	08 03		08 09		08 28	08 39	08 58	08 11	08 27		08 33	
London Cannon Street	a		00 13			07 17	07 34				07 47		08 04					08 34		09 04	08 17				
London Waterloo (East)	a			00 30	00 32			07 39		07 45				08 09		08 15			08 45					08 39	
London Charing Cross	a			00 35	00 36			07 43		07 49				08 13		08 19			08 49					08 43	
Ebbsfleet International	a																						07 46		
Stratford International	a																						07 58		
St Pancras Int'l	a																						08 06		

A not 20 May

Table T200-R

Sundays

20 May to 2 December

Gillingham and Dartford - London

		SE	SE	SE	TL	SE	SE	SE		SE	SE	SE	SE	SE	SE	SE	SE	TL	SE	SE	SE	SE	SE	TL
						◇																		
Rainham Kt	d				07 30	08 16												08 30						09 00
Gillingham (Kent)	d				07 36	08 21												08 36						09 06
Chatham	d				07 40	08 25												08 40						09 10
Rochester	d				07 44	08 29												08 44						09 14
Maidstone West	d																							
Strood	d				07 47	08 32												08 47						09 17
Higham	d				07 52													08 52						09 22
Gravesend	d	08 18			07 59	08 42				08 48					09 18			08 59			09 48			09 29
Northfleet	d	08 21			08 03					08 51					09 21			09 03			09 51			09 33
Swanscombe	d	08 23			08 05					08 53					09 23			09 05			09 53			09 35
Greenhithe for Bluewater	d	08 27			08 08					08 57					09 27			09 08			09 57			09 38
Stone Crossing	d	08 29			08 10					08 59					09 29			09 10			09 59			09 40
Dartford	a	08 33			08 14					09 03					09 33			09 14			10 03			09 44
	d	08 34			08 15		08 20	08 32		09 04			08 50	09 02	09 34			09 15	09 20	09 32	10 04			09 45
Slade Green	d			08 05	08 21		08 25					08 35	08 55				09 05	09 21	09 25				09 35	09 51
Erith	d			08 07			08 27					08 37	08 57				09 07		09 27				09 37	
Belvedere	d			08 10			08 30					08 40	09 00				09 10		09 30				09 40	
Abbey Wood	d			08 13	08 28		08 33					08 43	09 03				09 13	09 28	09 33				09 43	09 58
Plumstead	d			08 16	08 31		08 36					08 46	09 06				09 16	09 31	09 36				09 46	10 01
Woolwich Arsenal	d			08 19	08 34		08 39					08 49	09 09				09 19	09 34	09 39				09 49	10 04
Woolwich Dockyard	d			08 22			08 42					08 52	09 12				09 22		09 42				09 52	
Charlton	d		08 19	08 25	08 40		08 45				08 49	08 55	09 15			09 19	09 25	09 40	09 45			09 49	09 55	10 10
Crayford	d	08 39	08 52							09 09	09 22				09 39	09 52					10 09	10 22		
Bexley	d	08 42	08 55							09 12	09 25				09 42	09 55					10 12	10 25		
Albany Park	d	08 44	08 57							09 14	09 27				09 44	09 57					10 14	10 27		
Sidcup	d	08 47	09 00							09 17	09 30				09 47	10 00					10 17	10 30		
New Eltham	d	08 51	09 04							09 21	09 34				09 51	10 04					10 21	10 34		
Mottingham	d	08 53	09 06							09 23	09 36				09 53	10 06					10 23	10 36		
Lee	d	08 56	09 09							09 26	09 39				09 56	10 09					10 26	10 39		
Hither Green	d	08 59	09 12							09 29	09 42				09 59	10 12					10 29	10 42		
Barnehurst	d							08 39						09 09						09 39				
Bexleyheath	d							08 42						09 12						09 42				
Welling	d							08 45						09 15						09 45				
Falconwood	d							08 48						09 18						09 48				
Eltham	d							08 51						09 21						09 51				
Kidbrooke	d							08 54						09 24						09 54				
Blackheath	d						08 50	08 58					09 20	09 28					09 50	09 58				
Lewisham	d		09 18				08 55	09 02			09 48		09 25	09 32		10 18			09 55	10 02		10 48		
St Johns	d		09 20								09 50					10 20						10 50		
New Cross	d		09 23								09 53					10 23						10 53		
Nunhead	d							09 07						09 37						10 07				
Peckham Rye	d							09 10						09 40						10 10				
Denmark Hill	d							09 12						09 42						10 12				
London Victoria	a							09 24						09 54						10 24				
Westcombe Park	d			08 27	08 42							08 57					09 27	09 42					09 57	10 12
Maze Hill	d			08 29	08 44							08 59					09 29	09 44					09 59	10 14
Greenwich	d			08 33	08 47							09 03					09 33	09 47					10 03	10 17
Deptford	a			08 35	08 49							09 05					09 35	09 49					10 05	10 19
London Bridge	a	09 09	09 28	08 41	08 57		09 03			09 39	09 58	09 11	09 33		10 09	10 28	09 41	09 57	10 03		10 39	10 58	10 11	10 27
London Cannon Street	a		09 34	08 47							10 04	09 17				10 34	09 47					11 04	10 17	
London Waterloo (East)	a	09 15					09 09			09 45			09 39		10 15				10 09		10 45			
London Charing Cross	a	09 19					09 13			09 49			09 43		10 19				10 13		10 49			
Ebbsfleet International	a					08 46																		
Stratford International	a					08 58																		
St Pancras Int'l	a					09 06																		

Table T200-R

Sundays

20 May to 2 December

Gillingham and Dartford - London

		SE	SE	SE	SE	SE	SE	TL	SE	SE	SE	SE	SE	TL	SE	SE	SE	SE	SE	SE	TL	SE	SE	SE
		◇													◇									
Rainham Kt	d	09 16						09 30						10 00	10 16						10 30			
Gillingham (Kent)	d	09 21						09 36						10 06	10 21						10 36			
Chatham	d	09 25						09 40						10 10	10 25						10 40			
Rochester	d	09 29						09 44						10 14	10 29						10 44			
Maidstone West	d																							
Strood	d	09 32						09 47						10 17	10 32						10 47			
Higham	d							09 52						10 22							10 52			
Gravesend	d	09 42			10 18			09 59			10 48			10 29	10 42			11 18			10 59			11 48
Northfleet	d				10 21			10 03			10 51			10 33				11 21			11 03			11 51
Swanscombe	d				10 23			10 05			10 53			10 35				11 23			11 05			11 53
Greenhithe for Bluewater	d				10 27			10 08			10 57			10 38				11 27			11 08			11 57
Stone Crossing	d				10 29			10 10			10 59			10 40				11 29			11 10			11 59
Dartford	a				10 33			10 14			11 03			10 44				11 33			11 14			12 03
	d		09 50	10 02	10 34			10 15	10 20	10 32	11 04			10 46		10 50	11 02	11 34			11 15	11 20	11 32	12 04
Slade Green	d		09 55				10 05	10 21	10 25				10 35	10 51		10 55				11 05	11 21	11 25		
Erith	d		09 57				10 07		10 27				10 37			10 57				11 07		11 27		
Belvedere	d		10 00				10 10		10 30				10 40			11 00				11 10		11 30		
Abbey Wood	d		10 03				10 13	10 28	10 33				10 43	10 58		11 03				11 13	11 28	11 33		
Plumstead	d		10 06				10 16	10 31	10 36				10 46	11 01		11 06				11 16	11 31	11 36		
Woolwich Arsenal	d		10 09				10 19	10 34	10 39				10 49	11 04		11 09				11 19	11 34	11 39		
Woolwich Dockyard	d		10 12				10 22		10 42				10 52			11 12				11 22		11 42		
Charlton	d		10 15			10 19	10 25	10 40	10 45			10 49	10 55	11 10		11 15			11 19	11 25	11 40	11 45		
Crayford	d				10 39	10 52					11 09	11 22						11 39	11 52					12 09
Bexley	d				10 42	10 55					11 12	11 25						11 42	11 55					12 12
Albany Park	d				10 44	10 57					11 14	11 27						11 44	11 57					12 14
Sidcup	d				10 47	11 00					11 17	11 30						11 47	12 00					12 17
New Eltham	d				10 51	11 04					11 21	11 34						11 51	12 04					12 21
Mottingham	d				10 53	11 06					11 23	11 36						11 53	12 06					12 23
Lee	d				10 56	11 09					11 26	11 39						11 56	12 09					12 26
Hither Green	d				10 59	11 12					11 29	11 42						11 59	12 12					12 29
Barnehurst	d			10 09						10 39							11 09						11 39	
Bexleyheath	d			10 12						10 42							11 12						11 42	
Welling	d			10 15						10 45							11 15						11 45	
Falconwood	d			10 18						10 48							11 18						11 48	
Eltham	d			10 21						10 51							11 21						11 51	
Kidbrooke	d			10 24						10 54							11 24						11 54	
Blackheath	d		10 20	10 28					10 50	10 58						11 20	11 28					11 50	11 58	
Lewisham	d		10 25	10 32		11 18			10 55	11 02		11 48				11 25	11 32		12 18			11 55	12 02	
St Johns	d					11 20						11 50							12 20					
New Cross ⊖	d					11 23						11 53							12 23					
Nunhead	d			10 37						11 07							11 37						12 07	
Peckham Rye	d			10 40						11 10							11 40						12 10	
Denmark Hill	d			10 42						11 12							11 42						12 12	
London Victoria ⊖	a			10 54						11 24							11 54						12 24	
Westcombe Park	d						10 27	10 42					10 57	11 12						11 27	11 42			
Maze Hill	d						10 29	10 44					10 59	11 14						11 29	11 44			
Greenwich	d						10 33	10 47					11 03	11 17						11 33	11 47			
Deptford	a						10 35	10 49					11 05	11 19						11 35	11 49			
London Bridge ⊖	a		10 33		11 09	11 28	10 41	10 57	11 03		11 39	11 58	11 11	11 27		11 33		12 09	12 28	11 41	11 57	12 03		12 39
London Cannon Street ⊖	a					11 34	10 47					12 04	11 17						12 34	11 47				
London Waterloo (East) ⊖	a		10 39		11 15				11 09		11 45					11 39		12 15				12 09		12 45
London Charing Cross ⊖	a		10 43		11 19				11 13		11 49					11 43		12 19				12 13		12 49
Ebbsfleet International	a	09 46													10 46									
Stratford International ⊖	a	09 58													10 58									
St Pancras Int'l ⊖	a	10 06													11 06									

Table T200-R

Sundays

20 May to 2 December

Gillingham and Dartford - London

		SE	SE	TL	SE	SE	SE	SE	SE	SE	TL	SE	SE	SE	SE	SE	SE	TL	SE	SE	SE	SE	SE
					◇							◇							◇				
Rainham Kt	d			11 00	11 16						11 30	11 46						12 00	12 16				
Gillingham (Kent)	d			11 06	11 21						11 36	11 51						12 06	12 21				
Chatham	d			11 10	11 25						11 40	11 55						12 10	12 25				
Rochester	d			11 14	11 29						11 44	11 59						12 14	12 29				
Maidstone West	d																						
Strood	d			11 17	11 32						11 47	12 02						12 17	12 32				
Higham	d			11 22							11 52							12 22					
Gravesend	d			11 29	11 42			12 18			11 59	12 12			12 48			12 29	12 42			13 18	
Northfleet	d			11 33				12 21			12 03				12 51			12 33				13 21	
Swanscombe	d			11 35				12 23			12 05				12 53			12 35				13 23	
Greenhithe for Bluewater	d			11 38				12 27			12 08				12 57			12 38				13 27	
Stone Crossing	d			11 40				12 29			12 10				12 59			12 40				13 29	
Dartford	a			11 44				12 33			12 14				13 03			12 44				13 33	
	d			11 45		11 50	12 02	12 34			12 15		12 20	12 32	13 04			12 45		12 50	13 02	13 34	
Slade Green	d		11 35	11 51		11 55				12 05	12 21		12 25				12 35	12 51		12 55			
Erith	d		11 37			11 57				12 07			12 27				12 37			12 57			
Belvedere	d		11 40			12 00				12 10			12 30				12 40			13 00			
Abbey Wood	d		11 43	11 58		12 03				12 13	12 28		12 33				12 43	12 58		13 03			
Plumstead	d		11 46	12 01		12 06				12 16	12 31		12 36				12 46	13 01		13 06			
Woolwich Arsenal	d		11 49	12 04		12 09				12 19	12 34		12 39				12 49	13 04		13 09			
Woolwich Dockyard	d		11 52			12 12				12 22			12 42				12 52			13 12			
Charlton	d	11 49	11 55	12 10		12 15			12 19	12 25	12 40		12 45			12 49	12 55	13 10		13 15			13 19
Crayford	d	12 22						12 39	12 52						13 09	13 22						13 39	13 52
Bexley	d	12 25						12 42	12 55						13 12	13 25						13 42	13 55
Albany Park	d	12 27						12 44	12 57						13 14	13 27						13 44	13 57
Sidcup	d	12 30						12 47	13 00						13 17	13 30						13 47	14 00
New Eltham	d	12 34						12 51	13 04						13 21	13 34						13 51	14 04
Mottingham	d	12 36						12 53	13 06						13 23	13 36						13 53	14 06
Lee	d	12 39						12 56	13 09						13 26	13 39						13 56	14 09
Hither Green	d	12 42						12 59	13 12						13 29	13 42						13 59	14 12
Barnehurst	d						12 09							12 39							13 09		
Bexleyheath	d						12 12							12 42							13 12		
Welling	d						12 15							12 45							13 15		
Falconwood	d						12 18							12 48							13 18		
Eltham	d						12 21							12 51							13 21		
Kidbrooke	d						12 24							12 54							13 24		
Blackheath	d					12 20	12 28						12 50	12 58						13 20	13 28		
Lewisham	d	12 48				12 25	12 32		13 18				12 55	13 02		13 48				13 25	13 32		14 18
St Johns	d	12 50							13 20							13 50							14 20
New Cross ⊖	d	12 53							13 23							13 53							14 23
Nunhead	d						12 37							13 07							13 37		
Peckham Rye	d						12 40							13 10							13 40		
Denmark Hill	d						12 42							13 12							13 42		
London Victoria ⊖	a						12 54							13 24							13 54		
Westcombe Park	d		11 57	12 12						12 27	12 42						12 57	13 12					
Maze Hill	d		11 59	12 14						12 29	12 44						12 59	13 14					
Greenwich	d		12 03	12 17						12 33	12 47						13 03	13 17					
Deptford	a		12 05	12 19						12 35	12 49						13 05	13 19					
London Bridge ⊖	a	12 58	12 11	12 27		12 33		13 09	13 28	12 41	12 57		13 03		13 39	13 58	13 11	13 27		13 33		14 09	14 28
London Cannon Street ⊖	a	13 04	12 17						13 34	12 47						14 04	13 17						14 34
London Waterloo (East) ⊖	a					12 39		13 15					13 09		13 45					13 39		14 15	
London Charing Cross ⊖	a					12 43		13 19					13 13		13 49					13 43		14 19	
Ebbsfleet International	a				11 46							12 16							12 46				
Stratford International ⊖	a				11 58							12 28							12 58				
St Pancras Int'l ⊖	a				12 05							12 36							13 06				

Please note, Network Rail have stated that further updates to this timetable are possible during the validity period.

Table T200-R

Sundays

20 May to 2 December

Gillingham and Dartford - London

		SE	TL	SE ◇	SE	SE	SE	SE	SE	TL	SE ◇	SE	SE	SE	SE	SE	TL	SE ◇	SE	SE	SE	SE	SE	TL
Rainham Kt	d		12 30	12 46						13 00	13 16						13 30	13 46						14 00
Gillingham (Kent)	d		12 36	12 51						13 06	13 21						13 36	13 51						14 06
Chatham	d		12 40	12 55						13 10	13 25						13 40	13 55						14 10
Rochester	d		12 44	12 59						13 14	13 29						13 44	13 59						14 14
Maidstone West	d																							
Strood	d		12 47	13 02						13 17	13 32						13 47	14 02						14 17
Higham	d		12 52							13 22							13 52							14 22
Gravesend	d		12 59	13 12			13 48			13 29	13 42			14 18			13 59	14 12			14 48			14 29
Northfleet	d		13 03				13 51			13 33				14 21			14 03				14 51			14 33
Swanscombe	d		13 05				13 53			13 35				14 23			14 05				14 53			14 35
Greenhithe for Bluewater	d		13 08				13 57			13 38				14 27			14 08				14 57			14 38
Stone Crossing	d		13 10				13 59			13 40				14 29			14 10				14 59			14 40
Dartford	a		13 14				14 03			13 44				14 33			14 14				15 03			14 44
	d		13 15		13 20	13 32	14 04			13 45		13 50	14 02	14 34			14 15		14 20	14 32	15 04			14 45
Slade Green	d	13 05	13 21		13 25				13 35	13 51		13 55				14 05	14 21		14 25				14 35	14 51
Erith	d	13 07			13 27				13 37			13 57				14 07			14 27				14 37	
Belvedere	d	13 10			13 30				13 40			14 00				14 10			14 30				14 40	
Abbey Wood	d	13 13	13 28		13 33				13 43	13 58		14 03				14 13	14 28		14 33				14 43	14 58
Plumstead	d	13 16	13 31		13 36				13 46	14 01		14 06				14 16	14 31		14 36				14 46	15 01
Woolwich Arsenal	d	13 19	13 34		13 39				13 49	14 04		14 09				14 19	14 34		14 39				14 49	15 04
Woolwich Dockyard	d	13 22			13 42				13 52			14 12				14 22			14 42				14 52	
Charlton	d	13 25	13 40		13 45			13 49	13 55	14 10		14 15			14 19	14 25	14 40		14 45			14 49	14 55	15 10
Crayford	d						14 09	14 22						14 39	14 52						15 09	15 22		
Bexley	d						14 12	14 25						14 42	14 55						15 12	15 25		
Albany Park	d						14 14	14 27						14 44	14 57						15 14	15 27		
Sidcup	d						14 17	14 30						14 47	15 00						15 17	15 30		
New Eltham	d						14 21	14 34						14 51	15 04						15 21	15 34		
Mottingham	d						14 23	14 36						14 53	15 06						15 23	15 36		
Lee	d						14 26	14 39						14 56	15 09						15 26	15 39		
Hither Green	d						14 29	14 42						14 59	15 12						15 29	15 42		
Barnehurst	d					13 39							14 09							14 39				
Bexleyheath	d					13 42							14 12							14 42				
Welling	d					13 45							14 15							14 45				
Falconwood	d					13 48							14 18							14 48				
Eltham	d					13 51							14 21							14 51				
Kidbrooke	d					13 54							14 24							14 54				
Blackheath	d				13 50	13 58						14 20	14 28						14 50	14 58				
Lewisham	d				13 55	14 02		14 48				14 25	14 32		15 18				14 55	15 02		15 48		
St Johns	d							14 50							15 20							15 50		
New Cross	d							14 53							15 23							15 53		
Nunhead	d					14 07							14 37							15 07				
Peckham Rye	d					14 10							14 40							15 10				
Denmark Hill	d					14 12							14 42							15 12				
London Victoria	a					14 24							14 54							15 24				
Westcombe Park	d	13 27	13 42						13 57	14 12						14 27	14 42						14 57	15 12
Maze Hill	d	13 29	13 44						13 59	14 14						14 29	14 44						14 59	15 14
Greenwich	d	13 33	13 47						14 03	14 17						14 33	14 47						15 03	15 17
Deptford	a	13 35	13 49						14 05	14 19						14 35	14 49						15 05	15 19
London Bridge	a	13 41	13 57		14 03		14 39	14 58	14 11	14 27		14 33		15 09	15 28	14 41	14 57		15 03		15 39	15 58	15 11	15 27
London Cannon Street	a	13 47						15 04	14 17						15 34	14 47						16 04	15 17	
London Waterloo (East)	a				14 09		14 45					14 39		15 15					15 09		15 45			
London Charing Cross	a				14 13		14 49					14 43		15 19					15 13		15 49			
Ebbsfleet International	a			13 16							13 46							14 16						
Stratford International	a			13 29							13 58							14 28						
St Pancras Int'l	a			13 37							14 06							14 36						

Table T200-R

Sundays

20 May to 2 December

Gillingham and Dartford - London

		SE ◇	SE	SE	SE	SE	SE	TL	SE ◇	SE	SE	SE	SE	SE	TL	SE ◇	SE	SE	SE	SE	SE	TL	SE ◇
Rainham Kt	d	14 16						14 30	14 46						15 00	15 16						15 30	15 46
Gillingham (Kent)	d	14 21						14 36	14 51						15 06	15 21						15 36	15 51
Chatham	d	14 25						14 40	14 55						15 10	15 25						15 40	15 55
Rochester	d	14 29						14 44	14 59						15 14	15 29						15 44	15 59
Maidstone West	d																						
Strood	d	14 32						14 47	15 02						15 17	15 32						15 47	16 02
Higham	d							14 52							15 22							15 52	
Gravesend	d	14 42			15 18			14 59	15 12			15 48			15 29	15 42			16 18			15 59	16 12
Northfleet	d				15 21			15 03				15 51			15 33				16 21			16 03	
Swanscombe	d				15 23			15 05				15 53			15 35				16 23			16 05	
Greenhithe for Bluewater	d				15 27			15 08				15 57			15 38				16 27			16 08	
Stone Crossing	d				15 29			15 10				15 59			15 40				16 29			16 10	
Dartford	a				15 33			15 14				16 03			15 44				16 33			16 14	
	d		14 50	15 02	15 34			15 15		15 20	15 32	16 04			15 45		15 50	16 02	16 34			16 15	
Slade Green	d		14 55				15 05	15 21		15 25				15 35	15 51		15 55				16 05	16 21	
Erith	d		14 57				15 07			15 27				15 37			15 57				16 07		
Belvedere	d		15 00				15 10			15 30				15 40			16 00				16 10		
Abbey Wood	d		15 03				15 13	15 28		15 33				15 43	15 58		16 03				16 13	16 28	
Plumstead	d		15 06				15 16	15 31		15 36				15 46	16 01		16 06				16 16	16 31	
Woolwich Arsenal	d		15 09				15 19	15 34		15 39				15 49	16 04		16 09				16 19	16 34	
Woolwich Dockyard	d		15 12				15 22			15 42				15 52			16 12				16 22		
Charlton	d		15 15			15 19	15 25	15 40		15 45			15 49	15 55	16 10		16 15			16 19	16 25	16 40	
Crayford	d				15 39	15 52						16 09	16 22						16 39	16 52			
Bexley	d				15 42	15 55						16 12	16 25						16 42	16 55			
Albany Park	d				15 44	15 57						16 14	16 27						16 44	16 57			
Sidcup	d				15 47	16 00						16 17	16 30						16 47	17 00			
New Eltham	d				15 51	16 04						16 21	16 34						16 51	17 04			
Mottingham	d				15 53	16 06						16 23	16 36						16 53	17 06			
Lee	d				15 56	16 09						16 26	16 39						16 56	17 09			
Hither Green	d				15 59	16 12						16 29	16 42						16 59	17 12			
Barnehurst	d			15 09							15 39							16 09					
Bexleyheath	d			15 12							15 42							16 12					
Welling	d			15 15							15 45							16 15					
Falconwood	d			15 18							15 48							16 18					
Eltham	d			15 21							15 51							16 21					
Kidbrooke	d			15 24							15 54							16 24					
Blackheath	d		15 20	15 28						15 50	15 58						16 20	16 28					
Lewisham	d		15 25	15 32		16 18				15 55	16 02		16 48				16 25	16 32		17 18			
St Johns	d					16 20							16 50							17 20			
New Cross	d					16 23							16 53							17 23			
Nunhead	d			15 37							16 07							16 37					
Peckham Rye	d			15 40							16 10							16 40					
Denmark Hill	d			15 42							16 12							16 42					
London Victoria	a			15 54							16 24							16 54					
Westcombe Park	d						15 27	15 42						15 57	16 12						16 27	16 42	
Maze Hill	d						15 29	15 44						15 59	16 14						16 29	16 44	
Greenwich	d						15 33	15 47						16 03	16 17						16 33	16 47	
Deptford	a						15 35	15 49						16 05	16 19						16 35	16 49	
London Bridge	a		15 33		16 09	16 28	15 41	15 57		16 03		16 39	16 58	16 11	16 27		16 33		17 09	17 28	16 41	16 57	
London Cannon Street	a					16 34	15 47						17 04	16 17						17 34	16 47		
London Waterloo (East)	a		15 39		16 15					16 09		16 45					16 39		17 15				
London Charing Cross	a		15 43		16 19					16 13		16 49					16 43		17 19				
Ebbsfleet International	a	14 46							15 16							15 46							16 16
Stratford International	a	14 59							15 29							16 02							16 28
St Pancras Int'l	a	15 06							15 40							16 10							16 36

Table T200-R

Sundays

20 May to 2 December

Gillingham and Dartford - London

		SE	SE	SE	SE	SE	TL	SE ◇	SE	SE	SE	SE	SE	TL	SE ◇	SE		SE	SE	SE	SE	TL	SE ◇	SE	SE
Rainham Kt	d						16 00	16 16						16 30	16 46							17 00	17 16		
Gillingham (Kent)	d						16 06	16 21						16 36	16 51							17 06	17 21		
Chatham	d						16 10	16 25						16 40	16 55							17 10	17 25		
Rochester	d						16 14	16 29						16 44	16 59							17 14	17 29		
Maidstone West	d																								
Strood	d						16 17	16 32						16 47	17 02							17 17	17 32		
Higham	d						16 22							16 52								17 22			
Gravesend	d			16 48			16 29	16 42			17 18			16 59	17 12				17 48			17 29	17 42		
Northfleet	d			16 51			16 33				17 21			17 03					17 51			17 33			
Swanscombe	d			16 53			16 35				17 23			17 05					17 53			17 35			
Greenhithe for Bluewater	d			16 57			16 38				17 27			17 08					17 57			17 38			
Stone Crossing	d			16 59			16 40				17 29			17 10					17 59			17 40			
Dartford	a			17 03			16 44				17 33			17 14					18 03			17 44			
	d	16 20	16 32	17 04			16 45		16 50	17 02	17 34			17 15		17 20		17 32	18 04			17 45		17 50	18 02
Slade Green	d	16 25				16 35	16 51		16 55				17 05	17 21		17 25					17 35	17 51		17 55	
Erith	d	16 27				16 37			16 57				17 07			17 27					17 37			17 57	
Belvedere	d	16 30				16 40			17 00				17 10			17 30					17 40			18 00	
Abbey Wood	d	16 33				16 43	16 58		17 03				17 13	17 28		17 33					17 43	17 58		18 03	
Plumstead	d	16 36				16 46	17 01		17 06				17 16	17 31		17 36					17 46	18 01		18 06	
Woolwich Arsenal	d	16 39				16 49	17 04		17 09				17 19	17 34		17 39					17 49	18 04		18 09	
Woolwich Dockyard	d	16 42				16 52			17 12				17 22			17 42					17 52			18 12	
Charlton	d	16 45			16 49	16 55	17 10		17 15			17 19	17 25	17 40		17 45				17 49	17 55	18 10		18 15	
Crayford	d			17 09	17 22						17 39	17 52							18 09	18 22					
Bexley	d			17 12	17 25						17 42	17 55							18 12	18 25					
Albany Park	d			17 14	17 27						17 44	17 57							18 14	18 27					
Sidcup	d			17 17	17 30						17 47	18 00							18 17	18 30					
New Eltham	d			17 21	17 34						17 51	18 04							18 21	18 34					
Mottingham	d			17 23	17 36						17 53	18 06							18 23	18 36					
Lee	d			17 26	17 39						17 56	18 09							18 26	18 39					
Hither Green	d			17 29	17 42						17 59	18 12							18 29	18 42					
Barnehurst	d		16 39							17 09								17 39							18 09
Bexleyheath	d		16 42							17 12								17 42							18 12
Welling	d		16 45							17 15								17 45							18 15
Falconwood	d		16 48							17 18								17 48							18 18
Eltham	d		16 51							17 21								17 51							18 21
Kidbrooke	d		16 54							17 24								17 54							18 24
Blackheath	d	16 50	16 58						17 20	17 28						17 50		17 58						18 20	18 28
Lewisham	d	16 55	17 02		17 48				17 25	17 32		18 18				17 55		18 02		18 48				18 25	18 32
St Johns	d				17 50							18 20								18 50					
New Cross ⊖	d				17 53							18 23								18 53					
Nunhead	d		17 07							17 37								18 07							18 37
Peckham Rye	d		17 10							17 40								18 10							18 40
Denmark Hill	d		17 12							17 42								18 12							18 42
London Victoria ⊖	a		17 24							17 54								18 24							18 54
Westcombe Park	d					16 57	17 12						17 27	17 42							17 57	18 12			
Maze Hill	d					16 59	17 14						17 29	17 44							17 59	18 14			
Greenwich	d					17 03	17 17						17 33	17 47							18 03	18 17			
Deptford	a					17 05	17 19						17 35	17 49							18 05	18 19			
London Bridge ⊖	a	17 03		17 39	17 58	17 11	17 27		17 33		18 09	18 28	17 41	17 57		18 03			18 39	18 58	18 11	18 27		18 33	
London Cannon Street ⊖	a				18 04	17 17						18 34	17 47							19 04	18 17				
London Waterloo (East) ⊖	a	17 09		17 45					17 39		18 15					18 09			18 45					18 39	
London Charing Cross ⊖	a	17 13		17 49					17 43		18 19					18 13			18 49					18 43	
Ebbsfleet International	a							16 46							17 16								17 46		
Stratford International ⊖	a							16 58							17 28								18 04		
St Pancras Int'l ⊖	a							17 06							17 36								18 11		

Table T200-R

Sundays

20 May to 2 December

Gillingham and Dartford - London

		SE	SE	SE	TL	SE ◇	SE	SE		SE	SE	SE	TL	SE ◇	SE	SE	SE	SE	SE	TL	SE ◇	SE	SE	SE
Rainham Kt	d				17 30	17 46							18 00	18 16						18 30	18 46			
Gillingham (Kent)	d				17 36	17 51							18 06	18 21						18 36	18 51			
Chatham	d				17 40	17 55							18 10	18 25						18 40	18 55			
Rochester	d				17 44	17 59							18 14	18 29						18 44	18 59			
Maidstone West	d																							
Strood	d				17 47	18 02							18 17	18 32						18 47	19 02			
Higham	d				17 52								18 22							18 52				
Gravesend	d	18 18			17 59	18 12				18 48			18 29	18 42			19 18			18 59	19 12			19 48
Northfleet	d	18 21			18 03					18 51			18 33				19 21			19 03				19 51
Swanscombe	d	18 23			18 05					18 53			18 35				19 23			19 05				19 53
Greenhithe for Bluewater	d	18 27			18 08					18 57			18 38				19 27			19 08				19 57
Stone Crossing	d	18 29			18 10					18 59			18 40				19 29			19 10				19 59
Dartford	a	18 33			18 14					19 03			18 44				19 33			19 14				20 03
	d	18 34			18 15		18 20	18 32		19 04			18 45		18 50	19 02	19 34			19 15		19 20	19 32	20 04
Slade Green	d			18 05	18 21		18 25					18 35	18 51		18 55				19 05	19 21		19 25		
Erith	d			18 07			18 27					18 37			18 57				19 07			19 27		
Belvedere	d			18 10			18 30					18 40			19 00				19 10			19 30		
Abbey Wood	d			18 13	18 28		18 33					18 43	18 58		19 03				19 13	19 28		19 33		
Plumstead	d			18 16	18 31		18 36					18 46	19 01		19 06				19 16	19 31		19 36		
Woolwich Arsenal	d			18 19	18 34		18 39					18 49	19 04		19 09				19 19	19 34		19 39		
Woolwich Dockyard	d			18 22			18 42					18 52			19 12				19 22			19 42		
Charlton	d		18 19	18 25	18 40		18 45				18 49	18 55	19 10		19 15			19 19	19 25	19 40		19 45		
Crayford	d	18 39	18 52							19 09	19 22						19 39	19 52						20 09
Bexley	d	18 42	18 55							19 12	19 25						19 42	19 55						20 12
Albany Park	d	18 44	18 57							19 14	19 27						19 44	19 57						20 14
Sidcup	d	18 47	19 00							19 17	19 30						19 47	20 00						20 17
New Eltham	d	18 51	19 04							19 21	19 34						19 51	20 04						20 21
Mottingham	d	18 53	19 06							19 23	19 36						19 53	20 06						20 23
Lee	d	18 56	19 09							19 26	19 39						19 56	20 09						20 26
Hither Green	d	18 59	19 12							19 29	19 42						19 59	20 12						20 29
Barnehurst	d							18 39								19 09							19 39	
Bexleyheath	d							18 42								19 12							19 42	
Welling	d							18 45								19 15							19 45	
Falconwood	d							18 48								19 18							19 48	
Eltham	d							18 51								19 21							19 51	
Kidbrooke	d							18 54								19 24							19 54	
Blackheath	d						18 50	18 58							19 20	19 28						19 50	19 58	
Lewisham	d		19 18				18 55	19 02			19 48				19 25	19 32		20 18				19 55	20 02	
St Johns	d		19 20								19 50							20 20						
New Cross ⊖	d		19 23								19 53							20 23						
Nunhead	d							19 07								19 37							20 07	
Peckham Rye	d							19 10								19 40							20 10	
Denmark Hill	d							19 12								19 42							20 12	
London Victoria ⊖	a							19 24								19 54							20 24	
Westcombe Park	d			18 27	18 42							18 57	19 12						19 27	19 42				
Maze Hill	d			18 29	18 44							18 59	19 14						19 29	19 44				
Greenwich	d			18 33	18 47							19 03	19 17						19 33	19 47				
Deptford	a			18 35	18 49							19 05	19 19						19 35	19 49				
London Bridge ⊖	a	19 09	19 28	18 41	18 57		19 03			19 39	19 58	19 11	19 27		19 33		20 09	20 28	19 41	19 57		20 03		20 39
London Cannon Street ⊖	a		19 34	18 47							20 04	19 17						20 34	19 47					
London Waterloo (East) ⊖	a	19 15					19 09			19 45					19 39		20 15					20 09		20 45
London Charing Cross ⊖	a	19 19					19 13			19 49					19 43		20 19					20 13		20 49
Ebbsfleet International	a					18 16								18 46							19 16			
Stratford International ⊖	a					18 29								19 02							19 28			
St Pancras Int'l ⊖	a					18 37								19 10							19 36			

Please note, Network Rail have stated that further updates to this timetable are possible during the validity period.

Table T200-R

Sundays

20 May to 2 December

Gillingham and Dartford - London

		SE	SE	TL	SE	SE	SE	SE	SE	SE	TL	SE	SE	SE	SE	SE		SE	TL	SE	SE	SE	SE	SE	SE
					◇							◇								◇					
Rainham Kt	d			19 00	19 16						19 30	19 46							20 00	20 16					
Gillingham (Kent)	d			19 06	19 21						19 36	19 51							20 06	20 21					
Chatham	d			19 10	19 25						19 40	19 55							20 10	20 25					
Rochester	d			19 14	19 29						19 44	19 59							20 14	20 29					
Maidstone West	d																								
Strood	d			19 17	19 32						19 47	20 02							20 17	20 32					
Higham	d			19 22							19 52								20 22						
Gravesend	d			19 29	19 42			20 18			19 59	20 12			20 48				20 29	20 42			21 18		
Northfleet	d			19 33				20 21			20 03				20 51				20 33				21 21		
Swanscombe	d			19 35				20 23			20 05				20 53				20 35				21 23		
Greenhithe for Bluewater	d			19 38				20 27			20 08				20 57				20 38				21 27		
Stone Crossing	d			19 40				20 29			20 10				20 59				20 40				21 29		
Dartford	a			19 44				20 33			20 14				21 03				20 44				21 33		
	d			19 45		19 50	20 02	20 34			20 15		20 20	20 32	21 04				20 45		20 50	21 02	21 34		
Slade Green	d		19 35	19 51		19 55				20 05	20 21		20 25					20 35	20 51		20 55				21 05
Erith	d		19 37			19 57				20 07			20 27					20 37			20 57				21 07
Belvedere	d		19 40			20 00				20 10			20 30					20 40			21 00				21 10
Abbey Wood	d		19 43	19 58		20 03				20 13	20 28		20 33					20 43	20 58		21 03				21 13
Plumstead	d		19 46	20 01		20 06				20 16	20 31		20 36					20 46	21 01		21 06				21 16
Woolwich Arsenal	d		19 49	20 04		20 09				20 19	20 34		20 39					20 49	21 04		21 09				21 19
Woolwich Dockyard	d		19 52			20 12				20 22			20 42					20 52			21 12				21 22
Charlton	d	19 49	19 55	20 10		20 15			20 19	20 25	20 40		20 45			20 49		20 55	21 10		21 15			21 19	21 25
Crayford	d	20 22						20 39	20 52						21 09	21 22							21 39	21 52	
Bexley	d	20 25						20 42	20 55						21 12	21 25							21 42	21 55	
Albany Park	d	20 27						20 44	20 57						21 14	21 27							21 44	21 57	
Sidcup	d	20 30						20 47	21 00						21 17	21 30							21 47	22 00	
New Eltham	d	20 34						20 51	21 04						21 21	21 34							21 51	22 04	
Mottingham	d	20 36						20 53	21 06						21 23	21 36							21 53	22 06	
Lee	d	20 39						20 56	21 09						21 26	21 39							21 56	22 09	
Hither Green	d	20 42						20 59	21 12						21 29	21 42							21 59	22 12	
Barnehurst	d						20 09							20 39								21 09			
Bexleyheath	d						20 12							20 42								21 12			
Welling	d						20 15							20 45								21 15			
Falconwood	d						20 18							20 48								21 18			
Eltham	d						20 21							20 51								21 21			
Kidbrooke	d						20 24							20 54								21 24			
Blackheath	d					20 20	20 28						20 50	20 58							21 20	21 28			
Lewisham	d	20 48				20 25	20 32		21 18				20 55	21 02		21 48					21 25	21 32		22 18	
St Johns	d	20 50							21 20							21 50								22 20	
New Cross	d	20 53							21 23							21 53								22 23	
Nunhead	d						20 37							21 07								21 37			
Peckham Rye	d						20 40							21 10								21 40			
Denmark Hill	d						20 42							21 12								21 42			
London Victoria	a						20 54							21 24								21 54			
Westcombe Park	d		19 57	20 12						20 27	20 42							20 57	21 12						21 27
Maze Hill	d		19 59	20 14						20 29	20 44							20 59	21 14						21 29
Greenwich	d		20 03	20 17						20 33	20 47							21 03	21 17						21 33
Deptford	a		20 05	20 19						20 35	20 49							21 05	21 19						21 35
London Bridge	a	20 58	20 11	20 27		20 33		21 09	21 28	20 41	20 57		21 03		21 39	21 58		21 11	21 27		21 33		22 09	22 28	21 41
London Cannon Street	a	21 04	20 17						21 34	20 47						22 04		21 17						22 34	21 47
London Waterloo (East)	a					20 39		21 15					21 09		21 45						21 39		22 15		
London Charing Cross	a					20 43		21 19					21 13		21 49						21 43		22 19		
Ebbsfleet International	a				19 46							20 16								20 46					
Stratford International	a				20 02							20 28								20 58					
St Pancras Int'l	a				20 09							20 36								21 05					

Table T200-R

Sundays

20 May to 2 December

Gillingham and Dartford - London

		TL	SE	SE	SE	SE	SE	SE		TL	SE	SE	SE	SE	SE	SE	TL	SE	SE	SE	SE	SE	SE	TL	
			◇								◇							◇							
Rainham Kt	d	20 30	20 46							21 00	21 16						21 30	21 46						22 00	
Gillingham (Kent)	d	20 36	20 51							21 06	21 21						21 36	21 51						22 06	
Chatham	d	20 40	20 55							21 10	21 25						21 40	21 55						22 10	
Rochester	d	20 44	20 59							21 14	21 29						21 44	21 59						22 14	
Maidstone West	d																								
Strood	d	20 47	21 02							21 17	21 32						21 47	22 02						22 17	
Higham	d	20 52								21 22							21 52							22 22	
Gravesend	d	20 59	21 12			21 48				21 29	21 42			22 18			21 59	22 12			22 48			22 29	
Northfleet	d	21 03				21 51				21 33				22 21			22 03				22 51			22 33	
Swanscombe	d	21 05				21 53				21 35				22 23			22 05				22 53			22 35	
Greenhithe for Bluewater	d	21 08				21 57				21 38				22 27			22 08				22 57			22 38	
Stone Crossing	d	21 10				21 59				21 40				22 29			22 10				22 59			22 40	
Dartford	a	21 14				22 03				21 44				22 33			22 14				23 03			22 44	
	d	21 15		21 20	21 32	22 04				21 45		21 50	22 02	22 34			22 15		22 20	22 32	23 04			22 45	
Slade Green	d	21 21		21 25				21 35		21 51		21 55				22 05	22 21		22 25				22 35	22 51	
Erith	d			21 27				21 37				21 57				22 07			22 27				22 37		
Belvedere	d			21 30				21 40				22 00				22 10			22 30				22 40		
Abbey Wood	d	21 28		21 33				21 43		21 58		22 03				22 13	22 28		22 33				22 43	22 58	
Plumstead	d	21 31		21 36				21 46		22 01		22 06				22 16	22 31		22 36				22 46	23 01	
Woolwich Arsenal	d	21 34		21 39				21 49		22 04		22 09				22 19	22 34		22 39				22 49	23 04	
Woolwich Dockyard	d			21 42				21 52				22 12				22 22			22 42				22 52		
Charlton	d	21 40		21 45			21 49	21 55		22 10		22 15			22 19	22 25	22 40		22 45			22 49	22 55	23 10	
Crayford	d					22 09	22 22							22 39	22 52						23 09	23 22			
Bexley	d					22 12	22 25							22 42	22 55						23 12	23 25			
Albany Park	d					22 14	22 27							22 44	22 57						23 14	23 27			
Sidcup	d					22 17	22 30							22 47	23 00						23 17	23 30			
New Eltham	d					22 21	22 34							22 51	23 04						23 21	23 34			
Mottingham	d					22 23	22 36							22 53	23 06						23 23	23 36			
Lee	d					22 26	22 39							22 56	23 09						23 26	23 39			
Hither Green	d					22 29	22 42							22 59	23 12						23 29	23 42			
Barnehurst	d				21 39								22 09							22 39					
Bexleyheath	d				21 42								22 12							22 42					
Welling	d				21 45								22 15							22 45					
Falconwood	d				21 48								22 18							22 48					
Eltham	d				21 51								22 21							22 51					
Kidbrooke	d				21 54								22 24							22 54					
Blackheath	d			21 50	21 58							22 20	22 28						22 50	22 58					
Lewisham	d			21 55	22 02		22 48					22 25	22 32		23 18				22 55	23 02		23 48			
St Johns	d						22 50								23 20							23 50			
New Cross	d						22 53								23 23							23 53			
Nunhead	d				22 07								22 37							23 07					
Peckham Rye	d				22 10								22 40							23 10					
Denmark Hill	d				22 12								22 42							23 12					
London Victoria	a				22 24								22 54							23 24					
Westcombe Park	d	21 42						21 57		22 12						22 27	22 42						22 57	23 12	
Maze Hill	d	21 44						21 59		22 14						22 29	22 44						22 59	23 14	
Greenwich	d	21 47						22 03		22 17						22 33	22 47						23 03	23 17	
Deptford	a	21 49						22 05		22 19						22 35	22 49						23 05	23 19	
London Bridge	a	21 57		22 03		22 39	22 58	22 11		22 27		22 33		23 09	23 28	22 41	22 57		23 03		23 39	23 58	23 11	23 27	
London Cannon Street	a						23 04	22 17							23 34	22 47						00 04	23 17		
London Waterloo (East)	a			22 09		22 45						22 39		23 15					23 09		23 45				
London Charing Cross	a			22 13		22 49						22 43		23 19					23 13		23 49				
Ebbsfleet International	a		21 16								21 46							22 16							
Stratford International	a		21 28								21 59							22 28							
St Pancras Int'l	a		21 36								22 07							22 36							

Table T200-R

Sundays

20 May to 2 December

Gillingham and Dartford - London

		SE ◇	SE	TL	SE	SE	SE	TL	TL
Rainham Kt	d	22 16		22 30				23 00	23 30
Gillingham (Kent)	d	22 21		22 36				23 06	23 36
Chatham	d	22 25		22 40				23 10	23 40
Rochester	d	22 29		22 44				23 14	23 44
Maidstone West	d								
Strood	d	22 32		22 47				23 17	23 47
Higham	d			22 52				23 22	23 52
Gravesend	d	22 42		22 59			23 18	23 29	23 59
Northfleet	d			23 03			23 21	23 33	00 03
Swanscombe	d			23 05			23 23	23 35	00 05
Greenhithe for Bluewater	d			23 08			23 27	23 38	00 08
Stone Crossing	d			23 10			23 29	23 40	00 10
Dartford	a			23 15			23 33	23 45	00 15
	d		22 50			23 20	23 34		
Slade Green	d		22 55		23 05	23 25			
Erith	d		22 57		23 07	23 27			
Belvedere	d		23 00		23 10	23 30			
Abbey Wood	d		23 03		23 13	23 33			
Plumstead	d		23 06		23 16	23 36			
Woolwich Arsenal	d		23 09		23 19	23 39			
Woolwich Dockyard	d		23 12		23 22	23 42			
Charlton	d		23 15		23 25	23 45			
Crayford	d						23 39		
Bexley	d						23 42		
Albany Park	d						23 44		
Sidcup	d						23 47		
New Eltham	d						23 51		
Mottingham	d						23 53		
Lee	d						23 56		
Hither Green	d						23 59		
Barnehurst	d								
Bexleyheath	d								
Welling	d								
Falconwood	d								
Eltham	d								
Kidbrooke	d								
Blackheath	d		23 20			23 50			
Lewisham	d		23 25			23 55			
St Johns	d								
New Cross	d								
Nunhead	d								
Peckham Rye	d								
Denmark Hill	d								
London Victoria	a								
Westcombe Park	d				23 27				
Maze Hill	d				23 29				
Greenwich	d				23 33				
Deptford	a				23 35				
London Bridge	a		23 33		23 41	00 04	00 09		
London Cannon Street	a				23 47				
London Waterloo (East)	a		23 39			00 09	00 15		
London Charing Cross	a		23 43			00 13	00 19		
Ebbsfleet International	a	22 46							
Stratford International	a	22 58							
St Pancras Int'l	a	23 06							

Table T201-F

Mondays to Fridays

21 May to 7 December

London Thameslink - Greenwich - Woolwich - Medway

		TL MX	SE TWO	TL MO	SE MO	SE TWO	TL MX	TL	SE MThFO	SE TWO		SE	TL	SE	SE	TL	SE	SE	SE ◇	TL		SE	SE	SE ◇	SE
Luton	d																								
Luton Airport Parkway	d																								
St Albans	d																								
West Hampstead Thameslink	d															05 22				05 52					
St Pancras International	d															05 32			06 25	06 02				06 55	
Farringdon	d															05 37				06 07					
City Thameslink	d															05 39				06 09					
London Blackfriars	a															05 41				06 11					
London Charing Cross	d				00 12				04 50					05 20			05 42					06 12			06 23
Waterloo East	a				00 14				04 52					05 22			05 44					06 14			06 25
London Cannon Street	d		00 02			00 32				04 54		05 05			05 35			05 55					06 25		
London Bridge	d		00 06		00 21	00 36			04 59	04 59		05 09		05 29	05 39	05 48	05 51	05 59		06 18		06 21	06 29		06 32
London Victoria	d																								
Deptford	d		00 12			00 42						05 15			05 45	05 55		06 05		06 25			06 35		
Greenwich	d		00 14			00 44						05 17			05 47	05 57		06 07		06 27			06 37		
Maze Hill	d		00 17			00 47						05 20			05 50	06 00		06 10		06 30			06 40		
Westcombe Park	d		00 19			00 49						05 22			05 52	06 02		06 12		06 32			06 42		
Charlton	d		00 22		00 38	00 52						05 25			05 55	06 05	06 08	06 15		06 35		06 38	06 45		
Woolwich Dockyard	d		00 25		00 41	00 55						05 28			05 58		06 11	06 18				06 41	06 48		
Woolwich Arsenal	d		00 28		00 44	00 58						05 31			06 01	06 10	06 14	06 21		06 40		06 44	06 51		
Plumstead	d		00 30		00 46	01 00						05 33			06 03	06 13	06 16	06 23		06 43		06 46	06 53		
Abbey Wood	d		00 33		00 50	01 03						05 36			06 06	06 16	06 19	06 26		06 46		06 49	06 56		
Belvedere	d		00 36		00 53	01 06						05 39			06 09		06 22	06 29				06 52	06 59		
Erith	d		00 39		00 55	01 09						05 42			06 12		06 25	06 32				06 55	07 02		
Slade Green	d		00 44		01 01	01 12						05 47			06a16	06 22	06 28	06a35		06 52		06 58	07a05		
Dartford	d	00 28	00a49	00 58	01a06	01a20	01 24	04 58	05 39	05 39		05a52	05 58	06 09		06 28	06a34			06 58		07a05			07 09
Stone Crossing	d	00 32		01s02			01s28	05 02	05 43	05 43			06 02	06 13		06 32				07 02					07 13
Greenhithe	d	00 34		01s04			01s30	05 04	05 45	05 45			06 04	06 15		06 34				07 04					07 15
Swanscombe	d	00 37		01s07			01s33	05 07	05 48	05 48			06 07	06 18		06 37				07 07					07 18
Northfleet	d	00 39		01s09			01s35	05 09	05 50	05 50			06 09	06 20		06 39				07 09					07 20
Gravesend	d	00 43		01 13			01 39	05 13	05a56	05a56			06 13	06a25		06 43			06 48	07 13				07 19	07a27
Higham	d	00 49		01s19			01s45	05 19					06 19			06 49				07 19					
Strood	d	00 56		01s24			01s50	05 25					06 25			06 55			06a58	07 25				07 31	
Rochester	d	00 59		01s27			01s53	05 28					06 28			06 58				07 28				07 34	
Chatham	d	01 03		01s31			01s57	05 31					06 31			07 01				07 31				07 38	
Gillingham	d	01a07		01a36			02a02	05 36					06 36			07 06				07 36				07 43	
Rainham	a							05 41					06 41			07 11				07 42				07 47	

		SE	SE ◇	TL	SE	SE		SE	SE	TL	SE	SE	SE	SE	SE ◇	SE		TL	SE	SE	SE ◇	SE	SE	SE	TL 1 A
Luton	d									06 25								06 55							07 25
Luton Airport Parkway	d									06 28								06 58							07 28
St Albans	d									06 38								07 10							07 39
West Hampstead Thameslink	d			06 21																					
St Pancras International	d		07 22	06 32						07 02					08 07			07 32			08 25				08 03
Farringdon	d			06 37						07 07								07 37							08 07
City Thameslink	d			06 39						07 09								07 39							08 09
London Blackfriars	a			06 41						07 11								07 41							08 11
London Charing Cross	d				06 41			06 53			07 12		07 21						07 39			07 53			
Waterloo East	a				06 43			06 55			07 14		07 23						07 41			07 55			
London Cannon Street	d	06 35				06 55			07 05			07 25		07 36						07 57			08 05		
London Bridge	d	06 39		06 48	06 50	06 59		07 02	07 09	07 18	07 21	07 29	07 30	07 40				07 48	07 48	08 01		08 02	08 09		08 18
London Victoria	d															07 45								08 06	
Deptford	d	06 45		06 55		07 05			07 15	07 25		07 35		07 46				07 55		08 07			08 15		08 25
Greenwich	d	06 47		06 57		07 07			07 17	07 27		07 37		07 48				07 57		08 09			08 17		08 27
Maze Hill	d	06 50		07 00		07 10			07 20	07 30		07 40		07 51				08 00		08 12			08 20		08 30
Westcombe Park	d	06 52		07 02		07 12			07 22	07 32		07 42		07 53				08 02		08 14			08 22		08 32
Charlton	d	06 55		07 05	07 08	07 15			07 25	07 35	07 38	07 45		07 56				08 05	08 08	08 17			08 25		08 35
Woolwich Dockyard	d	06 58			07 11	07 18			07 28		07 41			07 59					08 11	08 20			08 28		
Woolwich Arsenal	d	07 01		07 10	07 14	07 21			07 31	07 40	07 44	07 50		08 02				08 10	08 14	08 23			08 31		08 40
Plumstead	d	07 03		07 13	07 16	07 23			07 33	07 43	07 46			08 04				08 13	08 16	08 25			08 33		08 43
Abbey Wood	d	07 06		07 16	07 20	07 26			07 36	07 46	07 50	07 55		08 07				08 16	08 20	08 28			08 36		08 46
Belvedere	d	07 09			07 23	07 29			07 39		07 53			08 10					08 23	08 31			08 39		
Erith	d	07 12			07 25	07 32			07 42		07 55			08 13					08 25	08 34			08 42		
Slade Green	d	07a16		07 22	07 29	07a36			07a46	07 52	07 59	08a02		08a16				08 22	08 29	08 37			08a45		08 52
Dartford	d			07 30	07a36			07 39		08 01	08a06		08 09			08 24		08 28	08a37	08a45		08 39		08 54	08 58
Stone Crossing	d			07 34				07 43		08 05			08 13					08 32				08 43			09 02
Greenhithe	d			07 36				07 45		08 07			08 15			08 30		08 34				08 45		09 00	09 04
Swanscombe	d			07 39				07 48		08 10			08 18					08 37				08 48			09 07
Northfleet	d			07 41				07 50		08 12			08 20					08 39				08 50			09 09
Gravesend	d		07 44	07 47				07a56		08 19			08a27		08 30	08a41		08 43			08 48	08a57		09a09	09 13
Higham	d			07 53						08 25								08 49							09 19
Strood	d		07 54	07 59						08 31					08 40			08 55			08 59				09 25
Rochester	d		07 58	08 02						08 34					08 44			08 58			09 02				09 28
Chatham	d		08 02	08 06						08 37					08 47			09 01			09 06				09 31
Gillingham	d		08 06	08 16						08 44					08 53			09 06			09 10				09 36
Rainham	a		08 11	08 21						08 49					08 57			09 11			09 15				09 41

A 1 from London Blackfriars

Please note, Network Rail have stated that further updates to this timetable are possible during the validity period.

NRT MAY 2018 EDITION

Table T201-F

Mondays to Fridays
21 May to 7 December

London Thameslink - Greenwich - Woolwich - Medway

		SE		SE	SE ◇	SE	SE	SE	SE	TL	SE	SE		SE	SE ◇	SE	SE	TL	SE	SE	SE ◇	SE		SE	SE
Luton	d									07 46								08 16							
Luton Airport Parkway	d									07 49								08 19							
St Albans	d									08 00								08 30							
West Hampstead Thameslink	d									08 21								08 51							
St Pancras International	d				08 58					08 32					09 25			09 02			09 55				
Farringdon	d									08 37								09 07							
City Thameslink	d									08 39								09 09							
London Blackfriars	a									08 41								09 11							
London Charing Cross	d	08 12				08 22			08 38							09 00			09 12			09 28			
Waterloo East	a	08 14				08 24			08 40							09 02			09 14			09 30			
London Cannon Street	d			08 24			08 34					08 54		09 05						09 24				09 35	
London Bridge	d	08 21		08 28		08 31	08 38		08 47	08 48		08 59		09 09		09 09		09 18	09 21	09 28		09 37		09 39	
London Victoria	d							08 38									09 06								09 36
Deptford	d			08 35			08 45			08 55		09 05		09 15				09 25		09 35				09 45	
Greenwich	d			08 37			08 47			08 57		09 07		09 17				09 27		09 37				09 47	
Maze Hill	d			08 40			08 50			09 00		09 10		09 20				09 30		09 40				09 50	
Westcombe Park	d			08 42			08 52			09 02	←	09 12		09 22				09 32		09 42				09 52	
Charlton	d	08 43		08 46			08 55		09 08	09 05	09 08	09 16		09 25				09 35	09 40	09 45				09 55	
Woolwich Dockyard	d	08 46		08 49			08 58		→		09 11	09 19		09 28					09 43	09 48				09 58	
Woolwich Arsenal	d	08 49		08 52			09 01			09 10	09 14	09 22		09 31				09 40	09 46	09 51				10 01	
Plumstead	d	08 51		08 54			09 03			09 13	09 16	09 24		09 33				09 43	09 48	09 53				10 03	
Abbey Wood	d	08 54		08 58			09 06			09 16	09 19	09 27		09 36				09 46	09 51	09 56				10 06	
Belvedere	d	08 57		09 01			09 09				09 22	09 30		09 39					09 54	09 59				10 09	
Erith	d	09 00		09 03			09 12				09 25	09 33		09 42					09 57	10 02				10 12	
Slade Green	d	09 04		09a06			09a15			09 22	09 30	09a36		09a46				09 52	10 03	10a06				10a15	
Dartford	d	09a12				09 08		09 24		09 28	09a40					09 41	09 54	09 58	10a08			10 11			10 24
Stone Crossing	d					09 12				09 32						09 45		10 02				10 15			
Greenhithe	d					09 15		09 30		09 34						09 47	10 00	10 04				10 17			10 30
Swanscombe	d					09 18				09 37						09 50		10 07				10 20			
Northfleet	d					09 20				09 39						09 52		10 09				10 22			
Gravesend	d				09 20	09a26		09a41		09 43					09 48	09a56	10a09	10 13			10 18	10a26			10a38
Higham	d									09 49								10 19							
Strood	d				09 30					09 55					09 59			10 25			10 29				
Rochester	d				09 34					09 58					10 02			10 28			10 32				
Chatham	d				09 37					10 01					10 06			10 31			10 36				
Gillingham	d				09 42					10 06					10 10			10 36			10 40				
Rainham	a				09 46					10 11					10 15			10 41			10 45				

		TL	SE	SE	SE	SE ◇	SE	SE		TL	SE	SE	SE	SE ◇	SE	SE	TL	SE		SE	SE	SE ◇	SE	SE	TL
Luton	d	08 46								09 16							09 46								10 16
Luton Airport Parkway	d	08 49								09 19							09 51								10 21
St Albans	d	09 00								09 30							10 01								10 31
West Hampstead Thameslink	d	09 21								09 51							10 21								10 51
St Pancras International	d	09 32				10 27				10 02				10 52			10 32					11 25			11 02
Farringdon	d	09 37								10 07							10 37								11 07
City Thameslink	d	09 39								10 09							10 39								11 09
London Blackfriars	a	09 41								10 11							10 41								11 11
London Charing Cross	d		09 42				10 02				10 12				10 32			10 42					11 02		
Waterloo East	a		09 44				10 04				10 14				10 34			10 44					11 04		
London Cannon Street	d			09 54	10 05							10 24	10 35							10 54	11 05				
London Bridge	d	09 48	09 51	09 58	10 09		10 11			10 18	10 21	10 28	10 39		10 41		10 48	10 51		10 58	11 09		11 11		11 18
London Victoria	d							10 06								10 36								11 06	
Deptford	d	09 55		10 05	10 15					10 25		10 35	10 45				10 55			11 05	11 15				11 25
Greenwich	d	09 57		10 07	10 17					10 27		10 37	10 47				10 57			11 07	11 17				11 27
Maze Hill	d	10 00		10 10	10 20					10 30		10 40	10 50				11 00			11 10	11 20				11 30
Westcombe Park	d	10 02		10 12	10 22					10 32		10 42	10 52				11 02			11 12	11 22				11 32
Charlton	d	10 05	10 08	10 15	10 25					10 35	10 38	10 45	10 55				11 05	11 08		11 15	11 25				11 35
Woolwich Dockyard	d		10 11	10 18	10 28						10 41	10 48	10 58					11 11		11 18	11 28				
Woolwich Arsenal	d	10 10	10 14	10 21	10 31					10 40	10 44	10 51	11 01				11 10	11 14		11 21	11 31				11 40
Plumstead	d	10 13	10 16	10 23	10 33					10 43	10 46	10 53	11 03				11 13	11 16		11 23	11 33				11 43
Abbey Wood	d	10 16	10 20	10 26	10 36					10 46	10 50	10 56	11 06				11 16	11 20		11 26	11 36				11 46
Belvedere	d		10 23	10 29	10 39						10 53	10 59	11 09					11 23		11 29	11 39				
Erith	d		10 25	10 32	10 42						10 55	11 02	11 12					11 25		11 32	11 42				
Slade Green	d	10 22	10 31	10a36	10a45					10 52	11 01	11a06	11a15				11 22	11 31		11a36	11a45				11 52
Dartford	d	10 28	10a38				10 41	10 54		10 58	11a08				11 11	11 24	11 28	11a38					11 41	11 54	11 58
Stone Crossing	d	10 32					10 45			11 02					11 15		11 32						11 45		12 02
Greenhithe	d	10 34					10 47	11 00		11 04					11 17	11 30	11 34						11 47	12 00	12 04
Swanscombe	d	10 37					10 50			11 07					11 20		11 37						11 50		12 07
Northfleet	d	10 39					10 52			11 09					11 22		11 39						11 52		12 09
Gravesend	d	10 43				10 49	10a56	11a09		11 13				11 18	11a26	11a39	11 43					11 48	11a56	12a09	12 13
Higham	d	10 49								11 19							11 49								12 19
Strood	d	10 55				10 59				11 25				11 29			11 55					11 59			12 25
Rochester	d	10 58				11 02				11 28				11 32			11 58					12 02			12 28
Chatham	d	11 01				11 06				11 31				11 36			12 01					12 06			12 31
Gillingham	d	11 06				11 10				11 36				11 40			12 06					12 10			12 36
Rainham	a	11 11				11 15				11 41				11 45			12 11					12 15			12 41

Table T201-F

Mondays to Fridays
21 May to 7 December

London Thameslink - Greenwich - Woolwich - Medway

		SE	SE	SE		SE ◇	SE	SE	TL	SE	SE	SE	SE ◇	SE		SE	TL	SE	SE	SE	SE ◇	SE	SE	TL	
Luton	d								10 48								11 18							11 48	
Luton Airport Parkway	d								10 51								11 21							11 51	
St Albans	d								11 01								11 31							12 01	
West Hampstead Thameslink	d								11 21								11 51							12 21	
St Pancras International	d					11 55			11 32				12 27				12 02				12 52			12 32	
Farringdon	d								11 37								12 07							12 37	
City Thameslink	d								11 39								12 09							12 39	
London Blackfriars	a								11 41								12 11							12 41	
London Charing Cross	d	11 12					11 32			11 42				12 02				12 12				12 32			
Waterloo East	a	11 14					11 34			11 44				12 04				12 14				12 34			
London Cannon Street	d		11 24	11 35							11 54	12 05							12 24	12 35					
London Bridge	d	11 21	11 28	11 39			11 41		11 48	11 51	11 58	12 09		12 11			12 18	12 21	12 28	12 39		12 41		12 48	
London Victoria	d							11 36								12 06							12 36		
Deptford	d		11 35	11 45					11 55		12 05	12 15					12 25		12 35	12 45				12 55	
Greenwich	d		11 37	11 47					11 57		12 07	12 17					12 27		12 37	12 47				12 57	
Maze Hill	d		11 40	11 50					12 00		12 10	12 20					12 30		12 40	12 50				13 00	
Westcombe Park	d		11 42	11 52					12 02		12 12	12 22					12 32		12 42	12 52				13 02	
Charlton	d	11 38	11 45	11 55					12 05	12 08	12 15	12 25					12 35	12 38	12 45	12 55				13 05	
Woolwich Dockyard	d	11 41	11 48	11 58						12 11	12 18	12 28						12 41	12 48	12 58					
Woolwich Arsenal	d	11 44	11 51	12 01					12 10	12 14	12 21	12 31					12 40	12 44	12 51	13 01				13 10	
Plumstead	d	11 46	11 53	12 03					12 13	12 16	12 23	12 33					12 43	12 46	12 53	13 03				13 13	
Abbey Wood	d	11 50	11 56	12 06					12 16	12 20	12 26	12 36					12 46	12 50	12 56	13 06				13 16	
Belvedere	d	11 53	11 59	12 09						12 23	12 29	12 39						12 53	12 59	13 09					
Erith	d	11 55	12 02	12 12						12 25	12 32	12 42						12 55	13 02	13 12					
Slade Green	d	12 01	12a06	12a15					12 22	12 31	12a36	12a45					12 52	13 01	13a06	13a15				13 22	
Dartford	d	12a08					12 11	12 24	12 28	12a38				12 41		12 54	12 58	13a08				13 11	13 24	13 28	
Stone Crossing	d						12 15		12 32					12 45			13 02					13 15		13 32	
Greenhithe	d						12 17	12 30	12 34					12 47		13 00	13 04					13 17	13 30	13 34	
Swanscombe	d						12 20		12 37					12 50			13 07					13 20		13 37	
Northfleet	d						12 22		12 39					12 52			13 09					13 22		13 39	
Gravesend	d					12 18	12a26	12a39	12 43				12 49	12a56		13a09	13 13				13 18	13a26	13a39	13 43	
Higham	d								12 49								13 19							13 49	
Strood	d					12 29			12 55				12 59				13 25				13 29			13 55	
Rochester	d					12 32			12 58				13 02				13 28				13 32			13 58	
Chatham	d					12 36			13 01				13 06				13 31				13 36			14 01	
Gillingham	d					12 40			13 06				13 10				13 36				13 40			14 06	
Rainham	a					12 45			13 11				13 15				13 41				13 45			14 11	

		SE	SE	SE	SE ◇	SE	SE	TL	SE	SE		SE	SE ◇	SE	SE	TL	SE	SE	SE	SE ◇		SE	SE	TL	SE
Luton	d							12 18								12 48								13 18	
Luton Airport Parkway	d							12 21								12 51								13 21	
St Albans	d							12 31								13 01								13 31	
West Hampstead Thameslink	d							12 51								13 21								13 51	
St Pancras International	d				13 25			13 02					13 55			13 32				14 25				14 02	
Farringdon	d							13 07								13 37								14 07	
City Thameslink	d							13 09								13 39								14 09	
London Blackfriars	a							13 11								13 41								14 11	
London Charing Cross	d	12 42				13 02			13 12					13 32			13 42					14 02			14 12
Waterloo East	a	12 44				13 04			13 14					13 34			13 44					14 04			14 14
London Cannon Street	d		12 54	13 05						13 24		13 35						13 54	14 05						
London Bridge	d	12 51	12 58	13 09		13 11		13 18	13 21	13 28		13 39		13 41		13 48	13 51	13 58	14 09			14 11		14 18	14 21
London Victoria	d						13 06								13 36								14 06		
Deptford	d		13 05	13 15				13 25		13 35		13 45				13 55		14 05	14 15					14 25	
Greenwich	d		13 07	13 17				13 27		13 37		13 47				13 57		14 07	14 17					14 27	
Maze Hill	d		13 10	13 20				13 30		13 40		13 50				14 00		14 10	14 20					14 30	
Westcombe Park	d		13 12	13 22				13 32		13 42		13 52				14 02		14 12	14 22					14 32	
Charlton	d	13 08	13 15	13 25				13 35	13 38	13 45		13 55				14 05	14 08	14 15	14 25					14 35	14 38
Woolwich Dockyard	d	13 11	13 18	13 28					13 41	13 48		13 58					14 11	14 18	14 28						14 41
Woolwich Arsenal	d	13 14	13 21	13 31				13 40	13 44	13 51		14 01				14 10	14 14	14 21	14 31					14 40	14 44
Plumstead	d	13 16	13 23	13 33				13 43	13 46	13 53		14 03				14 13	14 16	14 23	14 33					14 43	14 46
Abbey Wood	d	13 20	13 26	13 36				13 46	13 50	13 56		14 06				14 16	14 20	14 26	14 36					14 46	14 50
Belvedere	d	13 23	13 29	13 39					13 53	13 59		14 09					14 23	14 29	14 39						14 53
Erith	d	13 25	13 32	13 42					13 55	14 02		14 12					14 25	14 32	14 42						14 55
Slade Green	d	13 31	13a36	13a45				13 52	14 01	14a06		14a15				14 22	14 31	14a36	14a45					14 52	15 01
Dartford	d	13a38				13 41	13 54	13 58	14a08					14 11	14 24	14 28	14a38					14 41	14 54	14 58	15a08
Stone Crossing	d					13 45		14 02						14 15		14 32						14 45		15 02	
Greenhithe	d					13 47	14 00	14 04						14 17	14 30	14 34						14 47	15 00	15 04	
Swanscombe	d					13 50		14 07						14 20		14 37						14 50		15 07	
Northfleet	d					13 52		14 09						14 22		14 39						14 52		15 09	
Gravesend	d				13 48	13a56	14a09	14 13					14 18	14a26	14a39	14 43				14 48		14a56	15a09	15 13	
Higham	d							14 19								14 49								15 19	
Strood	d				13 59			14 25					14 29			14 55				14 59				15 25	
Rochester	d				14 02			14 28					14 32			14 58				15 02				15 28	
Chatham	d				14 06			14 31					14 36			15 01				15 05				15 31	
Gillingham	d				14 10			14 36					14 40			15 06				15 10				15 36	
Rainham	a				14 15			14 41					14 45			15 11				15 14				15 41	

Please note, Network Rail have stated that further updates to this timetable are possible during the validity period.

Table T201-F

Mondays to Fridays

21 May to 7 December

London Thameslink - Greenwich - Woolwich - Medway

		SE	SE	SE ◇	SE	SE	TL	SE	SE	SE	SE ◇	SE	SE	TL	SE	SE	SE	SE ◇	SE	SE	TL	SE	SE
Luton	d						13 48							14 18							14 48		
Luton Airport Parkway	d						13 51							14 21							14 51		
St Albans	d						14 01							14 31							15 01		
West Hampstead Thameslink	d						14 21							14 51							15 21		
St Pancras International	d			14 55			14 32				15 25			15 02				15 55			15 32		
Farringdon	d						14 37							15 07							15 37		
City Thameslink	d						14 39							15 09							15 39		
London Blackfriars	a						14 41							15 11							15 41		
London Charing Cross	d				14 32			14 42				15 02			15 12				15 32			15 42	
Waterloo East	a				14 34			14 44				15 04			15 14				15 34			15 44	
London Cannon Street	d	14 24	14 35						14 54	15 05						15 24	15 35						15 54
London Bridge	d	14 28	14 39		14 41		14 48	14 51	14 58	15 09		15 11		15 18	15 21	15 28	15 39		15 41		15 48	15 51	15 58
London Victoria	d					14 36							15 06							15 36			
Deptford	d	14 35	14 45				14 55		15 05	15 15				15 25		15 35	15 45				15 55		16 05
Greenwich	d	14 37	14 47				14 57		15 07	15 17				15 27		15 37	15 47				15 57		16 07
Maze Hill	d	14 40	14 50				15 00		15 10	15 20				15 30		15 40	15 50				16 00		16 10
Westcombe Park	d	14 42	14 52				15 02		15 12	15 22				15 32		15 42	15 52				16 02		16 12
Charlton	d	14 45	14 55				15 05	15 08	15 15	15 25				15 35	15 38	15 45	15 55				16 05	16 08	16 15
Woolwich Dockyard	d	14 48	14 58					15 11	15 18	15 28					15 41	15 48	15 58					16 11	16 18
Woolwich Arsenal	d	14 51	15 01				15 10	15 14	15 21	15 31				15 40	15 44	15 51	16 01				16 10	16 14	16 21
Plumstead	d	14 53	15 03				15 13	15 16	15 23	15 33				15 43	15 46	15 53	16 03				16 13	16 16	16 23
Abbey Wood	d	14 56	15 06				15 16	15 20	15 26	15 36				15 46	15 50	15 56	16 06				16 16	16 20	16 26
Belvedere	d	14 59	15 09					15 23	15 29	15 39					15 53	15 59	16 09					16 23	16 29
Erith	d	15 02	15 12					15 25	15 32	15 42					15 55	16 02	16 12					16 25	16 32
Slade Green	d	15a06	15a15				15 22	15 31	15a36	15a45				15 52	16 01	16a06	16a15				16 22	16 32	16a36
Dartford	d				15 11	15 24	15 28	15a38				15 41	15 54	15 58	16a08				16 11	16 24	16 28	16a38	
Stone Crossing	d				15 15		15 32					15 45		16 02					16 15		16 32		
Greenhithe	d				15 17	15 30	15 34					15 47	16 00	16 04					16 17	16 30	16 34		
Swanscombe	d				15 20		15 37					15 50		16 07					16 20		16 37		
Northfleet	d				15 22		15 39					15 52		16 09					16 22		16 39		
Gravesend	d			15 18	15a26	15a39	15 43				15 48	15a56	16a09	16 13				16 18	16a26	16a39	16 43		
Higham	d						15 49							16 19							16 49		
Strood	d			15 29			15 55				15 59			16 25				16 29			16 55		
Rochester	d			15 32			15 58				16 02			16 28				16 32			16 58		
Chatham	d			15 36			16 01				16 05			16 31				16 36			17 01		
Gillingham	d			15 40			16 06				16 10			16 36				16 40			17 06		
Rainham	a			15 45			16 11				16 14			16 41				16 45			17 11		

		SE	SE ◇	SE	SE	TL	SE	SE	SE	SE ◇	SE	SE ◇	TL	SE	SE	SE	SE	SE ◇	TL	SE	SE ◇	SE
Luton	d					15 18							15 48						16 18			
Luton Airport Parkway	d					15 21							15 51						16 21			
St Albans	d					15 31							16 01						16 31			
West Hampstead Thameslink	d					15 51							16 21						16 51			
St Pancras International	d		16 25			16 02				16 55		17 16	16 32					17 46	17 02		17 55	
Farringdon	d					16 07							16 37						17 07			
City Thameslink	d					16 09							16 39						17 09			
London Blackfriars	a					16 11							16 41						17 11			
London Charing Cross	d			16 02			16 12				16 33			16 45	16 48					17 13		17 17
Waterloo East	a			16 04			16 14				16 35			16 47	16 50					17 15		17 19
London Cannon Street	d	16 05						16 27	16 37							16 54	17 05					
London Bridge	d	16 10		16 11		16 18	16 21	16 32	16 42		16 42		16 48	16 54	16 57	16 59	17 10		17 18	17 22		17 26
London Victoria	d				16 06																	
Deptford	d	16 16				16 25		16 38	16 48				16 55			17 05	17 16		17 25			
Greenwich	d	16 18				16 27		16 40	16 50				16 57			17 08	17 19		17 27			
Maze Hill	d	16 21				16 30		16 43	16 53				17 00			17 11	17 22		17 30			
Westcombe Park	d	16 23				16 32		16 45	16 55				17 02			17 14	17 24		17 32			
Charlton	d	16 26				16 35	16 38	16 48	16 58				17 05	17 13		17 17	17 26		17 35	17 39		
Woolwich Dockyard	d	16 29					16 41	16 51	17 01					17 16		17 20	17 29			17 42		
Woolwich Arsenal	d	16 32				16 40	16 44	16 54	17 04				17 10	17 19		17 23	17 32		17 40	17 45		
Plumstead	d	16 34				16 43	16 46	16 56	17 06				17 13	17 21		17 25	17 34		17 43	17 47		
Abbey Wood	d	16 37				16 46	16 50	16 59	17 09				17 16	17 24		17 29	17 38		17 46	17 50		
Belvedere	d	16 40					16 53	17 02	17 12					17 27		17 32	17 41			17 53		
Erith	d	16 43					16 55	17 05	17 15					17 30		17 35	17 43			17 56		
Slade Green	d	16a46				16 52	17 01	17a09	17a18				17 22	17a33		17 39	17a46		17 52	17a59		
Dartford	d			16 41	16 54	16 58	17a10				17 11		17 32		17 37	17a50			17 58			18 03
Stone Crossing	d			16 45		17 02					17 15		17 36		17 41				18 02			18 07
Greenhithe	d			16 47	17 00	17 04					17 17		17 38		17 43				18 04			18 09
Swanscombe	d			16 50		17 07					17 20		17 41		17 46				18 07			18 12
Northfleet	d			16 52		17 09					17 22		17 44		17 49				18 09			18 15
Gravesend	d		16 48	16a58	17a09	17 13				17 18	17a28	17 39	17 50		17a56			18 09	18 13		18 18	18 22
Higham	d					17 19							17 56						18 19			18 28
Strood	d		16 59			17 25				17 28		17a49	18 01					18a19	18 25		18 31	18a36
Rochester	d		17 02			17 28				17 31			18 05						18 28		18 36	
Chatham	d		17 06			17 32				17 35			18 08						18 32		18 40	
Gillingham	d		17 10			17 37				17 41			18 13						18 37		18 45	
Rainham	a		17 15			17 42				17 46			18 19						18 42		18 50	

Table T201-F

Mondays to Fridays

21 May to 7 December

London Thameslink - Greenwich - Woolwich - Medway

		SE	SE	SE	SE ◇	TL	SE	TL	SE	SE	SE	SE	TL	SE	SE ◇	SE	SE	SE	SE	TL	SE	SE	SE ◇
Luton	d					16 46							17 16							17 46			
Luton Airport Parkway	d					16 49							17 19							17 49			
St Albans	d					17 00							17 30							18 00			
West Hampstead Thameslink	d					17 21							17 51							18 21			
St Pancras International	d				18 16	17 32							18 02		18 55					18 32			19 25
Farringdon	d					17 37							18 07							18 37			
City Thameslink	d					17 39							18 09							18 39			
London Blackfriars	a					17 41							18 11							18 41			
London Charing Cross	d			17 34			17 41			17 51	17 59			18 11			18 25				18 43		
Waterloo East	a			17 36			17 43			17 53	18 01			18 13			18 27				18 45		
London Cannon Street	d	17 25	17 34						17 49			18 04				18 24			18 35			18 55	
London Bridge	d	17 30	17 39	17 43		17 48	17 50		17 54	18 00	18 08	18 09	18 18	18 20		18 29	18 34		18 40	18 48	18 52	19 00	
London Victoria	d							←										←					
Deptford	d	17 36	17 45			17 55		17 55	18 00			18 15	18 25			18 35		18 35	18 46	18 55		19 06	
Greenwich	d	17 39	17 48			→		17 57	18 03			18 18	18 27			→		18 38	18 49	18 57		19 09	
Maze Hill	d	17 43	17 51					18 00	18 06			18 21	18 30					18 42	18 52	19 00		19 12	
Westcombe Park	d	17 45	17 54					18 02	18 09			18 24	18 32					18 44	18 55	19 02		19 15	
Charlton	d	17 48	17 56	18 00				18 05	18 11	18 18		18 26	18 35	18 38				18 47	18 57	19 05	19 09	19 17	
Woolwich Dockyard	d		17 59	18 03					18 14	18 21		18 29		18 41					19 00		19 12	19 20	
Woolwich Arsenal	d	17 53	18 02	18 06				18 10	18 17	18 24		18 32	18 40	18 44				18 52	19 03	19 10	19 15	19 23	
Plumstead	d		18 04	18 09				18 13	18 20	18 26		18 35	18 43	18 46					19 06	19 13	19 17	19 25	
Abbey Wood	d	17 58	18 08	18 12				18 16	18 23	18 30		18 38	18 46	18 50				18 57	19 09	19 16	19 21	19 29	
Belvedere	d		18 11	18 15					18 27	18 33		18 41		18 53					19 13		19 24	19 32	
Erith	d		18 13	18 18					18 30	18 36		18 44		18 56					19 16		19 27	19 35	
Slade Green	d		18 17	18a21				18 24	18 34	18a42		18a47	18 52	18a59					19a19	19 22	19a33	19a39	
Dartford	d	18 09	18a26				18 25	18 32	18 40		18 46		18 58				19 07	19 10		19 28			
Stone Crossing	d						18 29	18 36					19 02				19 11	19 14		19 32			
Greenhithe	d	18 15					18 31	18 38	18 45		18 51		19 04				19 13	19 16		19 34			
Swanscombe	d						18 34	18 41					19 07					19 19		19 37			
Northfleet	d						18 37	18 44					19 09					19 21		19 39			
Gravesend	d	18a25			18 39		18a43	18 50	18a56		19 00		19 13		19 18		19a23	19 26		19 43			19 48
Higham	d							18 56			19 06		19 19					19 32		19 49			
Strood	d				18a49			19 01			19a14		19 27		19 30			19a40		19 55			19 59
Rochester	d							19 05					19 30		19 35					19 58			20 02
Chatham	d							19 08					19 34		19 39					20 02			20 06
Gillingham	d							19 13					19 39		19 44					20 07			20 11
Rainham	a							19 19					19 44		19 48					20 12			20 15

		SE	SE	SE	TL	SE	SE	SE	SE ◇	SE	SE	TL	SE	SE	SE	SE ◇	SE	SE	TL	SE	SE	SE
Luton	d				18 16							18 46							19 18			
Luton Airport Parkway	d				18 19							18 49							19 21			
St Albans	d				18 30							19 00							19 31			
West Hampstead Thameslink	d				18 51							19 21							19 51			
St Pancras International	d				19 02				19 55			19 32				20 25			20 02			
Farringdon	d				19 07							19 37							20 07			
City Thameslink	d				19 09							19 39							20 09			
London Blackfriars	a				19 11							19 41							20 11			
London Charing Cross	d	18 54				19 12				19 32			19 42				20 02			20 12		
Waterloo East	a	18 56				19 14				19 34			19 44				20 04			20 14		
London Cannon Street	d		19 05				19 24	19 35						19 54	20 05						20 24	20 35
London Bridge	d	19 03	19 09		19 18	19 21	19 28	19 39		19 41		19 48	19 51	19 58	20 09		20 11		20 18	20 21	20 28	20 39
London Victoria	d			19 06							19 36							20 06				
Deptford	d		19 15		19 25		19 35	19 45				19 55		20 05	20 15				20 25		20 35	20 45
Greenwich	d		19 17		19 27		19 37	19 47				19 57		20 07	20 17				20 27		20 37	20 47
Maze Hill	d		19 20		19 30		19 40	19 50				20 00		20 10	20 20				20 30		20 40	20 50
Westcombe Park	d		19 22		19 32		19 42	19 52				20 02		20 12	20 22				20 32		20 42	20 52
Charlton	d		19 25		19 35	19 38	19 45	19 55				20 05	20 08	20 15	20 25				20 35	20 38	20 45	20 55
Woolwich Dockyard	d		19 28			19 41	19 48	19 58					20 11	20 18	20 28					20 41	20 48	20 58
Woolwich Arsenal	d		19 31		19 40	19 44	19 51	20 01				20 10	20 14	20 21	20 31				20 40	20 44	20 51	21 01
Plumstead	d		19 33		19 43	19 46	19 53	20 03				20 13	20 16	20 23	20 33				20 43	20 46	20 53	21 03
Abbey Wood	d		19 36		19 46	19 50	19 56	20 06				20 16	20 20	20 26	20 36				20 46	20 50	20 56	21 06
Belvedere	d		19 39			19 53	19 59	20 09					20 23	20 29	20 39					20 53	20 59	21 09
Erith	d		19 42			19 55	20 02	20 12					20 25	20 32	20 42					20 55	21 02	21 12
Slade Green	d		19a45		19 52	20 01	20a06	20a15				20 22	20 31	20a38	20a45				20 52	21 01	21a06	21a15
Dartford	d	19 35		19 54	19 58	20a08				20 11	20 24	20 28	20a38				20 41	20 54	20 58	21a08		
Stone Crossing	d	19 39			20 02					20 15		20 32					20 45		21 02			
Greenhithe	d	19 41		20 00	20 04					20 17	20 30	20 34					20 47	21 00	21 04			
Swanscombe	d	19 44			20 07					20 20		20 37					20 50		21 07			
Northfleet	d	19 46			20 09					20 22		20 39					20 52		21 09			
Gravesend	d	19a55		20a09	20 13				20 18	20a26	20a39	20 43				20 48	20a56	21a09	21 13			
Higham	d				20 19							20 49							21 19			
Strood	d				20 25				20 29			20 55				20 59			21 25			
Rochester	d				20 28				20 32			20 58				21 02			21 28			
Chatham	d				20 31				20 36			21 01				21 06			21 31			
Gillingham	d				20 36				20 40			21 06				21 10			21 36			
Rainham	a				20 41				20 45			21 11				21 15			21 41			

Please note, Network Rail have stated that further updates to this timetable are possible during the validity period.

Table T201-F

Mondays to Fridays

21 May to 7 December

London Thameslink - Greenwich - Woolwich - Medway

		SE ◇	SE	SE	TL	SE	SE	SE	SE ◇	SE		SE	TL	SE	SE	SE ◇	SE	SE	TL	SE		SE	SE ◇	SE	SE
Luton	d				19 48								20 18						20 48						
Luton Airport Parkway	d				19 51								20 21						20 51						
St Albans	d				20 01								20 31						21 01						
West Hampstead Thameslink	d				20 21								20 51						21 21						
St Pancras International	d	20 55			20 32				21 25				21 02			21 55			21 32				22 25		
Farringdon	d				20 37								21 07						21 37						
City Thameslink	d				20 39								21 09						21 39						
London Blackfriars	a				20 41								21 11						21 41						
London Charing Cross	d		20 32			20 42				21 02				21 12			21 32			21 42				22 02	
Waterloo East	a		20 34			20 44				21 04				21 14			21 34			21 44				22 04	
London Cannon Street	d						20 54	21 05							21 32							22 02			
London Bridge	d		20 41		20 48	20 51	20 58	21 09		21 11			21 18	21 21	21 36		21 41		21 48	21 51		22 06		22 11	
London Victoria	d			20 36								21 06						21 36							22 06
Deptford	d				20 55		21 05	21 15					21 25		21 42				21 55			22 12			
Greenwich	d				20 57		21 07	21 17					21 27		21 44				21 57			22 14			
Maze Hill	d				21 00		21 10	21 20					21 30		21 47				22 00			22 17			
Westcombe Park	d				21 02		21 12	21 22					21 32		21 49				22 02			22 19			
Charlton	d				21 05	21 08	21 15	21 25					21 35	21 38	21 52				22 05	22 08		22 22			
Woolwich Dockyard	d					21 11	21 18	21 28						21 41	21 55					22 11		22 25			
Woolwich Arsenal	d				21 10	21 14	21 21	21 31					21 40	21 44	21 58				22 10	22 14		22 28			
Plumstead	d				21 13	21 16	21 23	21 33					21 43	21 46	22 00				22 13	22 16		22 30			
Abbey Wood	d				21 16	21 20	21 26	21 36					21 46	21 50	22 03				22 16	22 20		22 33			
Belvedere	d					21 23	21 29	21 39						21 53	22 06					22 23		22 36			
Erith	d					21 25	21 32	21 42						21 55	22 09					22 25		22 39			
Slade Green	d				21 22	21 31	21a36	21a45					21 52	22 01	22a13				22 22	22 31		22a43			
Dartford	d		21 11	21 24	21 28	21a38				21 41		21 54	21 58	22a08			22 11	22 24	22 28	22a38				22 41	22 54
Stone Crossing	d		21 15		21 32					21 45			22 02				22 15		22 32					22 45	
Greenhithe	d		21 17	21 30	21 34					21 47		22 00	22 04				22 17	22 30	22 34					22 47	23 00
Swanscombe	d		21 20		21 37					21 50			22 07				22 20		22 37					22 50	
Northfleet	d		21 22		21 39					21 52			22 09				22 22		22 39					22 52	
Gravesend	d	21 18	21a26	21a39	21 43				21 48	21a56		22a09	22 13			22 18	22a26	22a39	22 43				22 48	22a56	23a09
Higham	d				21 49								22 19						22 49						
Strood	d	21 29			21 55				21 59				22 25			22 29			22 55				22 59		
Rochester	d	21 32			21 58				22 02				22 28			22 32			22 58				23 02		
Chatham	d	21 36			22 01				22 06				22 31			22 36			23 01				23 06		
Gillingham	d	21 40			22 06				22 10				22 36			22 40			23 06				23 10		
Rainham	a	21 45			22 12				22 15				22 41			22 45			23 11				23 15		

		TL	SE	SE MT FO	SE ◇	SE		SE	TL	SE	SE	SE ◇	SE	TL	SE	SE		SE ◇	SE	SE					
Luton	d	21 18							21 48					22 18											
Luton Airport Parkway	d	21 21							21 51					22 21											
St Albans	d	21 31							22 01					22 31											
West Hampstead Thameslink	d	21 51							22 21					22 51											
St Pancras International	d	22 02			22 55				22 32			23 25		23 02				23 55							
Farringdon	d	22 07							22 37					23 07											
City Thameslink	d	22 09							22 39																
London Blackfriars	a	22 11							22 41					23 11											
London Charing Cross	d		22 12			22 32				22 42			23 02		23 12				23 32	23 42					
Waterloo East	a		22 14			22 34				22 44			23 04		23 14				23 34	23 44					
London Cannon Street	d			22 32							23 02					23 32									
London Bridge	d	22 18	22 21	22 36		22 41			22 48	22 51	23 06		23 11	23 18	23 21	23 36			23 41	23 51					
London Victoria	d							22 36																	
Deptford	d	22 25		22 42					22 55		23 12			23 25		23 42									
Greenwich	d	22 27		22 44					22 57		23 14			23 27		23 44									
Maze Hill	d	22 30		22 47					23 00		23 17			23 30		23 47									
Westcombe Park	d	22 32		22 49					23 02		23 19			23 32		23 49									
Charlton	d	22 35	22 38	22 52					23 05	23 08	23 22			23 35	23 38	23 52				00 08					
Woolwich Dockyard	d		22 41	22 55						23 11	23 25				23 41	23 55				00 11					
Woolwich Arsenal	d	22 40	22 44	22 58					23 10	23 14	23 28			23 40	23 44	23 58				00 14					
Plumstead	d	22 43	22 46	23 00					23 13	23 16	23 30			23 43	23 46	23 59				00 16					
Abbey Wood	d	22 46	22 50	23 03					23 16	23 20	23 33			23 46	23 50	00 03				00 20					
Belvedere	d		22 53	23 06						23 23	23 36				23 53	00 06				00 23					
Erith	d		22 55	23 09						23 25	23 39				23 55	00 09				00 25					
Slade Green	d	22 52	23 01	23a13					23 22	23 31	23 44			23 52	23 59	00 14				00 31					
Dartford	d	22 58	23a08			23 11		23 24	23 28	23a38	23a51		23 48	23 58	00a05	00a21			00 18	00a36					
Stone Crossing	d	23 02				23 15			23 32				23 52	00 02					00 22						
Greenhithe	d	23 04				23 17		23 30	23 34				23 54	00 04					00 24						
Swanscombe	d	23 07				23 20			23 37				23 57	00 07					00 27						
Northfleet	d	23 09				23 22			23 39				23 59	00 09					00 29						
Gravesend	d	23 13			23 18	23a26		23a39	23 43			23 48	00a06	00 13				00 18	00a36						
Higham	d	23 19							23 49					00 19											
Strood	d	23 25			23 29				23 55			23 59		00 25				00 29							
Rochester	d	23 28			23 32				23 58			00 02		00 28				00 32							
Chatham	d	23 31			23 36				00 02			00 06		00 32				00 36							
Gillingham	d	23 36			23 40				00a06			00 10		00a36				00 40							
Rainham	a	23 41			23 45							00 15						00 45							

Table T201-F

Saturdays

26 May to 8 December

London Thameslink - Greenwich - Woolwich - Medway

		TL	SE	SE	TL	TL	SE	SE	TL	SE		SE	TL	SE	SE	TL	SE	SE	SE	TL		SE	SE ◇	SE	SE
Luton	d																								
Luton Airport Parkway	d																								
St Albans	d																								
West Hampstead Thameslink	d												05 22			05 52				06 22					
St Pancras International	d												05 32			06 02				06 32			07 25		
Farringdon	d												05 37			06 07				06 37					
City Thameslink	d																								
London Blackfriars	a												05 41			06 11				06 41					
London Charing Cross	d						04 50			05 20				05 50			06 12	06 18				06 42		06 48	
Waterloo East	a						04 52			05 22				05 52			06 14	06 20				06 44		06 50	
London Cannon Street	d		00 02	00 32				05 05				05 35			06 05				06 35						07 05
London Bridge	d		00 06	00 36			04 59	05 09		05 29		05 39	05 48	05 59	06 09	06 18	06 21	06 27	06 39	06 48		06 51		06 57	07 09
London Victoria	d																								
Deptford	d		00 12	00 42				05 15				05 45	05 55		06 15	06 25			06 45	06 55					07 15
Greenwich	d		00 14	00 44				05 17				05 47	05 57		06 17	06 27			06 47	06 57					07 17
Maze Hill	d		00 17	00 47				05 20				05 50	06 00		06 20	06 30			06 50	07 00					07 20
Westcombe Park	d		00 19	00 49				05 22				05 52	06 02		06 22	06 32			06 52	07 02					07 22
Charlton	d		00 22	00 52				05 25				05 55	06 05		06 25	06 35	06 38		06 55	07 05		07 08			07 25
Woolwich Dockyard	d		00 25	00 55				05 28				05 58			06 28		06 41		06 58			07 11			07 28
Woolwich Arsenal	d		00 28	00 58				05 31				06 01	06 10		06 31	06 40	06 44		07 01	07 10		07 14			07 31
Plumstead	d		00 30	01 00				05 33				06 03	06 13		06 33	06 43	06 46		07 03	07 13		07 16			07 33
Abbey Wood	d		00 33	01 03				05 36				06 06	06 16		06 36	06 46	06 50		07 06	07 16		07 20			07 36
Belvedere	d		00 36	01 06				05 39				06 09			06 39		06 53		07 09			07 23			07 39
Erith	d		00 39	01 09				05 42				06 12			06 42		06 55		07 12			07 25			07 42
Slade Green	d		00 44	01 12				05a45				06a15	06 22		06a45	06 52	07 01		07a15	07 22		07 31			07a45
Dartford	d	00 28	00a51	01a20	01 24	04 58	05 41		05 58	06 11			06 28	06 41		06 58	07a08	07 04		07 28		07a38		07 34	
Stone Crossing	d	00 32			01s28	05 02	05 45		06 02	06 15			06 32	06 45		07 02		07 08		07 32				07 38	
Greenhithe	d	00 34			01s30	05 04	05 47		06 04	06 17			06 34	06 47		07 04		07 11		07 34				07 41	
Swanscombe	d	00 37			01s33	05 07	05 50		06 07	06 20			06 37	06 50		07 07		07 14		07 37				07 44	
Northfleet	d	00 39			01s35	05 09	05 52		06 09	06 22			06 39	06 52		07 09		07 17		07 39				07 47	
Gravesend	d	00 43			01 39	05 13	05a56		06 13	06a26			06 43	06a56		07 13		07a23		07 43			07 48	07a53	
Higham	d	00 49			01s45	05 19			06 19				06 49			07 19				07 49					
Strood	d	00 56			01s50	05 25			06 25				06 55			07 25				07 55			07 59		
Rochester	d	00 59			01s53	05 28			06 28				06 58			07 28				07 58			08 02		
Chatham	d	01 03			01s57	05 31			06 31				07 01			07 31				08 01			08 06		
Gillingham	d	01a07			02a02	05 36			06 36				07 06			07 36				08 06			08 10		
Rainham	a					05 42			06 41				07 11			07 41				08 11			08 15		

		SE	TL	SE	SE	SE ◇		SE	SE	TL	SE	SE	SE	SE ◇	SE	SE		TL	SE	SE	SE	SE ◇	SE	SE	TL
Luton	d		06 18							06 48								07 18							07 48
Luton Airport Parkway	d		06 21							06 51								07 21							07 51
St Albans	d		06 31							07 01								07 31							08 01
West Hampstead Thameslink	d		06 51							07 21								07 51							08 21
St Pancras International	d		07 02			07 55				07 32				08 25				08 02				08 52			08 32
Farringdon	d		07 07							07 37								08 07							08 37
City Thameslink	d																								
London Blackfriars	a		07 11							07 41								08 11							08 41
London Charing Cross	d			07 12				07 32			07 42				08 02				08 12				08 32		
Waterloo East	a			07 14				07 34			07 44				08 04				08 14				08 34		
London Cannon Street	d				07 35							07 54	08 05							08 24	08 35				
London Bridge	d		07 18	07 21	07 39			07 41		07 48	07 51	07 58	08 09		08 11			08 18	08 21	08 28	08 39		08 41		08 48
London Victoria	d	07 06							07 36							08 06								08 36	
Deptford	d		07 25		07 45					07 55		08 05	08 15					08 25		08 35	08 45				08 55
Greenwich	d		07 27		07 47					07 57		08 07	08 17					08 27		08 37	08 47				08 57
Maze Hill	d		07 30		07 50					08 00		08 10	08 20					08 30		08 40	08 50				09 00
Westcombe Park	d		07 32		07 52					08 02		08 12	08 22					08 32		08 42	08 52				09 02
Charlton	d		07 35	07 38	07 55					08 05	08 08	08 15	08 25					08 35	08 38	08 45	08 55				09 05
Woolwich Dockyard	d			07 41	07 58						08 11	08 18	08 28						08 41	08 48	08 58				
Woolwich Arsenal	d		07 40	07 44	08 01					08 10	08 14	08 21	08 31					08 40	08 44	08 51	09 01				09 10
Plumstead	d		07 43	07 46	08 03					08 13	08 16	08 23	08 33					08 43	08 46	08 53	09 03				09 13
Abbey Wood	d		07 46	07 50	08 06					08 16	08 20	08 26	08 36					08 46	08 50	08 56	09 06				09 16
Belvedere	d			07 53	08 09						08 23	08 29	08 39						08 53	08 59	09 09				
Erith	d			07 55	08 12						08 25	08 32	08 42						08 55	09 02	09 12				
Slade Green	d		07 52	08 01	08a15					08 22	08 31	08a36	08a45					08 52	09 01	09a06	09a15				09 22
Dartford	d	07 54	07 58	08a08				08 11	08 24	08 28	08a38				08 41	08 54		08 58	09a08				09 11	09 24	09 28
Stone Crossing	d		08 02					08 15		08 32					08 45			09 02					09 15		09 32
Greenhithe	d	08 00	08 04					08 17	08 30	08 34					08 47	09 00		09 04					09 17	09 30	09 34
Swanscombe	d		08 07					08 20		08 37					08 50			09 07					09 20		09 37
Northfleet	d		08 09					08 22		08 39					08 52			09 09					09 22		09 39
Gravesend	d	08a09	08 13			08 18		08a26	08a39	08 43				08 48	08a56	09a09		09 13				09 18	09a26	09a39	09 43
Higham	d		08 19							08 49								09 19							09 49
Strood	d		08 25			08 29				08 55				08 59				09 25				09 29			09 55
Rochester	d		08 28			08 32				08 58				09 02				09 28				09 32			09 58
Chatham	d		08 31			08 36				09 01				09 06				09 31				09 36			10 01
Gillingham	d		08 36			08 40				09 06				09 10				09 36				09 40			10 06
Rainham	a		08 41			08 45				09 11				09 15				09 41				09 45			10 11

Table T201-F

London Thameslink - Greenwich - Woolwich - Medway

Saturdays

26 May to 8 December

		SE		SE	SE	SE ◇	SE	SE	TL	SE	SE	SE		SE ◇	SE	SE	TL	SE	SE	SE	SE ◇	SE		SE	TL
Luton	d								08 18								08 48								09 18
Luton Airport Parkway	d								08 21								08 51								09 21
St Albans	d								08 31								09 01								09 31
West Hampstead Thameslink	d								08 51								09 21								09 51
St Pancras International	d					09 25			09 02					09 55			09 32				10 22				10 02
Farringdon	d								09 07								09 37								10 07
City Thameslink	d								09 09								09 39								10 09
London Blackfriars	a								09 11								09 41								10 11
London Charing Cross	d	08 42					09 02			09 12					09 32			09 42				10 02			
Waterloo East	a	08 44					09 04			09 14					09 34			09 44				10 04			
London Cannon Street	d			08 54	09 05						09 24	09 35							09 54	10 05					
London Bridge	d	08 51		08 58	09 09		09 11		09 18	09 21	09 28	09 39			09 41		09 48	09 51	09 58	10 09		10 11			10 18
London Victoria	d							09 06								09 36								10 06	
Deptford	d			09 05	09 15				09 25		09 36	09 45					09 55		10 05	10 15					10 25
Greenwich	d			09 07	09 17				09 27		09 38	09 47					09 57		10 07	10 17					10 27
Maze Hill	d			09 10	09 20				09 30		09 41	09 50					10 00		10 10	10 20					10 30
Westcombe Park	d			09 12	09 22				09 32		09 43	09 52					10 02		10 12	10 22					10 32
Charlton	d	09 08		09 15	09 25				09 35	09 38	09 46	09 55					10 05	10 08	10 15	10 25					10 35
Woolwich Dockyard	d	09 11		09 18	09 28					09 41	09 49	09 58						10 11	10 18	10 28					
Woolwich Arsenal	d	09 14		09 21	09 31				09 40	09 44	09 52	10 01					10 10	10 14	10 21	10 31					10 40
Plumstead	d	09 16		09 23	09 33				09 43	09 46	09 54	10 03					10 13	10 16	10 23	10 33					10 43
Abbey Wood	d	09 20		09 26	09 36				09 46	09 50	09 57	10 06					10 16	10 20	10 26	10 36					10 46
Belvedere	d	09 23		09 29	09 39					09 53	10 00	10 09						10 23	10 29	10 39					
Erith	d	09 25		09 32	09 42					09 55	10 03	10 12						10 25	10 32	10 42					
Slade Green	d	09 31		09a36	09a45				09 52	10 01	10a07	10a15					10 22	10 31	10a36	10a45					10 52
Dartford	d	09a38					09 41	09 54	09 58	10a08					10 11	10 24	10 28	10a38				10 41		10 54	10 58
Stone Crossing	d						09 45		10 02						10 15		10 32					10 45			11 02
Greenhithe	d						09 47	10 00	10 04						10 17	10 30	10 34					10 47		11 00	11 04
Swanscombe	d						09 50		10 07						10 20		10 37					10 50			11 07
Northfleet	d						09 52		10 09						10 22		10 39					10 52			11 09
Gravesend	d					09 48	09a56	10a09	10 13					10 18	10a26	10a39	10 43				10 48	10a56		11a09	11 13
Higham	d								10 19								10 49								11 19
Strood	d					09 59			10 25					10 29			10 55				10 59				11 25
Rochester	d					10 02			10 28					10 32			10 58				11 02				11 28
Chatham	d					10 06			10 31					10 36			11 01				11 06				11 31
Gillingham	d					10 10			10 36					10 40			11 06				11 10				11 36
Rainham	a					10 15			10 41					10 45			11 11				11 15				11 41

		SE	SE	SE	SE ◇	SE	SE	TL		SE	SE	SE	SE ◇	SE	SE	TL	SE	SE		SE	SE ◇	SE	SE	TL	SE
Luton	d							09 48								10 18								10 48	
Luton Airport Parkway	d							09 51								10 21								10 51	
St Albans	d							10 01								10 31								11 01	
West Hampstead Thameslink	d							10 21								10 51								11 21	
St Pancras International	d				10 52			10 32					11 25			11 02					11 55			11 32	
Farringdon	d							10 37								11 07								11 37	
City Thameslink	d							10 39								11 09								11 39	
London Blackfriars	a							10 41								11 11								11 41	
London Charing Cross	d	10 12				10 32				10 42				11 02			11 12					11 32			11 42
Waterloo East	a	10 14				10 34				10 44				11 04			11 14					11 34			11 44
London Cannon Street	d		10 24	10 35							10 54	11 05						11 24		11 35					
London Bridge	d	10 21	10 28	10 39		10 41		10 48		10 51	10 58	11 09		11 11		11 18	11 21	11 28		11 39		11 41		11 48	11 51
London Victoria	d						10 36								11 06								11 36		
Deptford	d		10 35	10 45				10 55			11 05	11 15				11 25		11 35		11 45				11 55	
Greenwich	d		10 37	10 47				10 57			11 07	11 17				11 27		11 37		11 47				11 57	
Maze Hill	d		10 40	10 50				11 00			11 10	11 20				11 30		11 40		11 50				12 00	
Westcombe Park	d		10 42	10 52				11 02			11 12	11 22				11 32		11 42		11 52				12 02	
Charlton	d	10 38	10 45	10 55				11 05		11 08	11 15	11 25				11 35	11 38	11 45		11 55				12 05	12 08
Woolwich Dockyard	d	10 41	10 48	10 58						11 11	11 18	11 28					11 41	11 48		11 58					12 11
Woolwich Arsenal	d	10 44	10 51	11 01				11 10		11 14	11 21	11 31				11 40	11 44	11 51		12 01				12 10	12 14
Plumstead	d	10 46	10 53	11 03				11 13		11 16	11 23	11 33				11 43	11 46	11 53		12 03				12 13	12 16
Abbey Wood	d	10 50	10 56	11 06				11 16		11 20	11 26	11 36				11 46	11 50	11 56		12 06				12 16	12 20
Belvedere	d	10 53	10 59	11 09						11 23	11 29	11 39					11 53	11 59		12 09					12 23
Erith	d	10 55	11 02	11 12						11 25	11 32	11 42					11 55	12 02		12 12					12 25
Slade Green	d	11 01	11a06	11a15				11 22		11 31	11a36	11a45				11 52	12 01	12a06		12a15				12 22	12 31
Dartford	d	11a08				11 11	11 24	11 28		11a38				11 41	11 54	11 58	12a08					12 11	12 24	12 28	12a38
Stone Crossing	d					11 15		11 32						11 45		12 02						12 15		12 32	
Greenhithe	d					11 17	11 30	11 34						11 47	12 00	12 04						12 17	12 30	12 34	
Swanscombe	d					11 20		11 37						11 50		12 07						12 20		12 37	
Northfleet	d					11 22		11 39						11 52		12 09						12 22		12 39	
Gravesend	d				11 18	11a26	11a39	11 43					11 48	11a56	12a09	12 13					12 18	12a26	12a39	12 43	
Higham	d							11 49								12 19								12 49	
Strood	d				11 29			11 55					11 59			12 25					12 29			12 55	
Rochester	d				11 32			11 58					12 02			12 28					12 32			12 58	
Chatham	d				11 36			12 01					12 06			12 31					12 36			13 01	
Gillingham	d				11 40			12 06					12 10			12 36					12 40			13 06	
Rainham	a				11 45			12 11					12 15			12 41					12 45			13 11	

Table T201-F

London Thameslink - Greenwich - Woolwich - Medway

Saturdays

26 May to 8 December

		SE	SE	SE ◇		SE	SE	TL	SE	SE	SE	SE ◇	SE	SE		TL	SE	SE	SE	SE ◇	SE	SE	TL	SE	
Luton	d							11 18								11 48							12 18		
Luton Airport Parkway	d							11 21								11 51							12 21		
St Albans	d							11 31								12 01							12 31		
West Hampstead Thameslink	d							11 51								12 21							12 51		
St Pancras International	d			12 27				12 02				12 52				12 32				13 25			13 02		
Farringdon	d							12 07								12 37							13 07		
City Thameslink	d							12 09								12 39							13 09		
London Blackfriars	a							12 11								12 41							13 11		
London Charing Cross	d					12 02			12 12				12 32				12 42				13 02			13 12	
Waterloo East	a					12 04			12 14				12 34				12 44				13 04			13 14	
London Cannon Street	d	11 54	12 05							12 24	12 35							12 54	13 05						
London Bridge	d	11 58	12 09			12 11		12 18	12 21	12 28	12 39		12 41			12 48	12 51	12 58	13 09		13 11		13 18	13 21	
London Victoria	d						12 06							12 36								13 06			
Deptford	d	12 05	12 15					12 25		12 35	12 45					12 55		13 05	13 15				13 25		
Greenwich	d	12 07	12 17					12 27		12 37	12 47					12 57		13 07	13 17				13 27		
Maze Hill	d	12 10	12 20					12 30		12 40	12 50					13 00		13 10	13 20				13 30		
Westcombe Park	d	12 12	12 22					12 32		12 42	12 52					13 02		13 12	13 22				13 32		
Charlton	d	12 15	12 25					12 35	12 38	12 45	12 55					13 05	13 08	13 15	13 25				13 35	13 38	
Woolwich Dockyard	d	12 18	12 28						12 41	12 48	12 58						13 11	13 18	13 28					13 41	
Woolwich Arsenal	d	12 21	12 31					12 40	12 44	12 51	13 01					13 10	13 14	13 21	13 31				13 40	13 44	
Plumstead	d	12 23	12 33					12 43	12 46	12 53	13 03					13 13	13 16	13 23	13 33				13 43	13 46	
Abbey Wood	d	12 26	12 36					12 46	12 50	12 56	13 06					13 16	13 20	13 26	13 36				13 46	13 50	
Belvedere	d	12 29	12 39						12 53	12 59	13 09						13 23	13 29	13 39					13 53	
Erith	d	12 32	12 42						12 55	13 02	13 12						13 25	13 32	13 42					13 55	
Slade Green	d	12a36	12a45					12 52	13 01	13a06	13a15					13 22	13 31	13a36	13a45				13 52	14 01	
Dartford	d					12 41	12 54	12 58	13a08				13 11	13 24		13 28	13a38				13 41	13 54	13 58	14a08	
Stone Crossing	d					12 45		13 02					13 15			13 32					13 45		14 02		
Greenhithe	d					12 47	13 00	13 04					13 17	13 30		13 34					13 47	14 00	14 04		
Swanscombe	d					12 50		13 07					13 20			13 37					13 50		14 07		
Northfleet	d					12 52		13 09					13 22			13 39					13 52		14 09		
Gravesend	d			12 49		12a56	13a09	13 13				13 18	13a26	13a39		13 43				13 48	13a56	14a09	14 13		
Higham	d							13 19								13 49							14 19		
Strood	d			12 59				13 25				13 29				13 55				13 59			14 25		
Rochester	d			13 02				13 28				13 32				13 58				14 02			14 28		
Chatham	d			13 06				13 31				13 36				14 01				14 06			14 31		
Gillingham	d			13 10				13 36				13 40				14 06				14 10			14 36		
Rainham	a			13 15				13 41				13 45				14 11				14 15			14 41		

		SE	SE	SE ◇	SE	SE	TL	SE	SE	SE		SE ◇	SE	SE	TL	SE	SE	SE	SE ◇	SE		SE	TL	SE	SE
Luton	d						12 48								13 18								13 48		
Luton Airport Parkway	d						12 51								13 21								13 51		
St Albans	d						13 01								13 31								14 01		
West Hampstead Thameslink	d						13 21								13 51								14 21		
St Pancras International	d			13 55			13 32					14 25			14 02				14 55				14 32		
Farringdon	d						13 37								14 07								14 37		
City Thameslink	d						13 39								14 09								14 39		
London Blackfriars	a						13 41								14 11								14 41		
London Charing Cross	d				13 32			13 42					14 02			14 12				14 32				14 42	
Waterloo East	a				13 34			13 44					14 04			14 14				14 34				14 44	
London Cannon Street	d	13 24	13 35						13 54	14 05							14 24	14 35							14 54
London Bridge	d	13 28	13 39		13 41		13 48	13 51	13 58	14 09			14 11		14 18	14 21	14 28	14 39		14 41			14 48	14 51	14 58
London Victoria	d					13 36								14 06								14 36			
Deptford	d	13 35	13 45				13 55		14 05	14 15					14 25		14 35	14 45					14 55		15 05
Greenwich	d	13 37	13 47				13 57		14 07	14 17					14 27		14 37	14 47					14 57		15 07
Maze Hill	d	13 40	13 50				14 00		14 10	14 20					14 30		14 40	14 50					15 00		15 10
Westcombe Park	d	13 42	13 52				14 02		14 12	14 22					14 32		14 42	14 52					15 02		15 12
Charlton	d	13 45	13 55				14 05	14 08	14 15	14 25					14 35	14 38	14 45	14 55					15 05	15 08	15 15
Woolwich Dockyard	d	13 48	13 58					14 11	14 18	14 28						14 41	14 48	14 58						15 11	15 18
Woolwich Arsenal	d	13 51	14 01				14 10	14 14	14 21	14 31					14 40	14 44	14 51	15 01					15 10	15 14	15 21
Plumstead	d	13 53	14 03				14 13	14 16	14 23	14 33					14 43	14 46	14 53	15 03					15 13	15 16	15 23
Abbey Wood	d	13 56	14 06				14 16	14 20	14 26	14 36					14 46	14 50	14 56	15 06					15 16	15 20	15 26
Belvedere	d	13 59	14 09					14 23	14 29	14 39						14 53	14 59	15 09						15 23	15 29
Erith	d	14 02	14 12					14 25	14 32	14 42						14 55	15 02	15 12						15 25	15 32
Slade Green	d	14a06	14a15				14 22	14 31	14a36	14a45					14 52	15 01	15a06	15a15					15 22	15 31	15a36
Dartford	d				14 11	14 24	14 28	14a38					14 41	14 54	14 58	15a08				15 11		15 24	15 28	15a38	
Stone Crossing	d				14 15		14 32						14 45		15 02					15 15			15 32		
Greenhithe	d				14 17	14 30	14 34						14 47	15 00	15 04					15 17		15 30	15 34		
Swanscombe	d				14 20		14 37						14 50		15 07					15 20			15 37		
Northfleet	d				14 22		14 39						14 52		15 09					15 22			15 39		
Gravesend	d			14 18	14a26	14a39	14 43					14 48	14a56	15a09	15 13				15 18	15a26		15a39	15 43		
Higham	d						14 49								15 19								15 49		
Strood	d			14 29			14 55					14 59			15 25				15 29				15 55		
Rochester	d			14 32			14 58					15 02			15 28				15 32				15 58		
Chatham	d			14 36			15 01					15 06			15 31				15 36				16 01		
Gillingham	d			14 40			15 06					15 10			15 36				15 40				16 06		
Rainham	a			14 45			15 11					15 15			15 41				15 45				16 11		

Table T201-F

Saturdays

26 May to 8 December

London Thameslink - Greenwich - Woolwich - Medway

		SE	SE	SE	SE	TL		SE	SE	SE	SE	SE	SE	TL	SE	SE		SE	SE	SE	SE	TL	SE	SE	SE
			◇								◇								◇						
Luton	d					14 18								14 48								15 18			
Luton Airport Parkway	d					14 21								14 51								15 21			
St Albans	d					14 31								15 01								15 31			
West Hampstead Thameslink	d					14 51								15 21								15 51			
St Pancras International	d		15 25			15 02					15 55			15 32					16 25			16 02			
Farringdon	d					15 07								15 37								16 07			
City Thameslink	d					15 09								15 39								16 09			
London Blackfriars	a					15 11								15 41								16 11			
London Charing Cross	d			15 02				15 12				15 32			15 42					16 02			16 12		
Waterloo East	a			15 04				15 14				15 34			15 44					16 04			16 14		
London Cannon Street	d	15 05							15 24	15 35						15 54		16 05						16 24	16 35
London Bridge	d	15 09		15 11		15 18		15 21	15 28	15 39		15 41		15 48	15 51	15 58		16 09		16 11		16 18	16 21	16 28	16 39
London Victoria	d				15 06								15 36								16 06				
Deptford	d	15 15				15 25			15 35	15 45				15 55		16 05		16 15				16 25		16 35	16 45
Greenwich	d	15 17				15 27			15 37	15 47				15 57		16 07		16 17				16 27		16 37	16 47
Maze Hill	d	15 20				15 30			15 40	15 50				16 00		16 10		16 20				16 30		16 40	16 50
Westcombe Park	d	15 22				15 32			15 42	15 52				16 02		16 12		16 22				16 32		16 42	16 52
Charlton	d	15 25				15 35		15 38	15 45	15 55				16 05	16 08	16 15		16 25				16 35	16 38	16 45	16 55
Woolwich Dockyard	d	15 28						15 41	15 48	15 58					16 11	16 18		16 28					16 41	16 48	16 58
Woolwich Arsenal	d	15 31				15 40		15 44	15 51	16 01				16 10	16 14	16 21		16 31				16 40	16 44	16 51	17 01
Plumstead	d	15 33				15 43		15 46	15 53	16 03				16 13	16 16	16 23		16 33				16 43	16 46	16 53	17 03
Abbey Wood	d	15 36				15 46		15 50	15 56	16 06				16 16	16 20	16 26		16 36				16 46	16 50	16 56	17 06
Belvedere	d	15 39						15 53	15 59	16 09					16 23	16 29		16 39					16 53	16 59	17 09
Erith	d	15 42						15 55	16 02	16 12					16 25	16 32		16 42					16 55	17 02	17 12
Slade Green	d	15a45				15 52		16 01	16a06	16a15				16 22	16 31	16a36		16a45				16 52	17 01	17a06	17a15
Dartford	d			15 41	15 54	15 58		16a08				16 11	16 24	16 28	16a38					16 41	16 54	16 58	17a08		
Stone Crossing	d			15 45		16 02						16 15		16 32						16 45		17 02			
Greenhithe	d			15 47	16 00	16 04						16 17	16 30	16 34						16 47	17 00	17 04			
Swanscombe	d			15 50		16 07						16 20		16 37						16 50		17 07			
Northfleet	d			15 52		16 09						16 22		16 39						16 52		17 09			
Gravesend	d		15 48	15a56	16a09	16 13					16 18	16a26	16a39	16 43					16 48	16a56	17a09	17 13			
Higham	d					16 19								16 49								17 19			
Strood	d		15 59			16 25					16 29			16 55					16 59			17 25			
Rochester	d		16 02			16 28					16 32			16 58					17 02			17 28			
Chatham	d		16 06			16 31					16 36			17 01					17 06			17 31			
Gillingham	d		16 10			16 36					16 40			17 06					17 10			17 36			
Rainham	a		16 15			16 41					16 45			17 11					17 15			17 41			

		SE		SE	SE	TL	SE	SE	SE	SE	SE	SE		TL	SE	SE	SE	SE	SE	SE	TL	SE		SE	SE
		◇								◇								◇							
Luton	d					15 48								16 18							16 48				
Luton Airport Parkway	d					15 51								16 21							16 51				
St Albans	d					16 01								16 31							17 01				
West Hampstead Thameslink	d					16 21								16 51							17 21				
St Pancras International	d	16 55				16 32				17 25				17 02				17 55			17 32				
Farringdon	d					16 37								17 07							17 37				
City Thameslink	d					16 39								17 09							17 39				
London Blackfriars	a					16 41								17 11							17 41				
London Charing Cross	d			16 32			16 42				17 02				17 12				17 32			17 42			
Waterloo East	a			16 34			16 44				17 04				17 14				17 34			17 44			
London Cannon Street	d							16 54	17 05							17 24	17 35							17 54	18 05
London Bridge	d			16 41		16 48	16 51	16 58	17 09		17 11			17 18	17 21	17 28	17 39		17 41		17 48	17 51		17 58	18 09
London Victoria	d				16 36							17 06								17 36					
Deptford	d					16 55		17 05	17 15					17 25		17 35	17 45				17 55			18 05	18 15
Greenwich	d					16 57		17 07	17 17					17 27		17 37	17 47				17 57			18 07	18 17
Maze Hill	d					17 00		17 10	17 20					17 30		17 40	17 50				18 00			18 10	18 20
Westcombe Park	d					17 02		17 12	17 22					17 32		17 42	17 52				18 02			18 12	18 22
Charlton	d					17 05	17 08	17 15	17 25					17 35	17 38	17 45	17 55				18 05	18 08		18 15	18 25
Woolwich Dockyard	d						17 11	17 18	17 28						17 41	17 48	17 58					18 11		18 18	18 28
Woolwich Arsenal	d					17 10	17 14	17 21	17 31					17 40	17 44	17 51	18 01				18 10	18 14		18 21	18 31
Plumstead	d					17 13	17 16	17 23	17 33					17 43	17 46	17 53	18 03				18 13	18 16		18 23	18 33
Abbey Wood	d					17 16	17 20	17 26	17 36					17 46	17 50	17 56	18 06				18 16	18 20		18 26	18 36
Belvedere	d						17 23	17 29	17 39						17 53	17 59	18 09					18 23		18 29	18 39
Erith	d						17 25	17 32	17 42						17 55	18 02	18 12					18 25		18 32	18 42
Slade Green	d					17 22	17 31	17a36	17a45					17 52	18 01	18a06	18a15				18 22	18 31		18a36	18a45
Dartford	d			17 11	17 24	17 28	17a38				17 41	17 54		17 58	18a08				18 11	18 24	18 28	18a38			
Stone Crossing	d			17 15		17 32					17 45			18 02					18 15		18 32				
Greenhithe	d			17 17	17 30	17 34					17 47	18 00		18 04					18 17	18 30	18 34				
Swanscombe	d			17 20		17 37					17 50			18 07					18 20		18 37				
Northfleet	d			17 22		17 39					17 52			18 09					18 22		18 39				
Gravesend	d	17 18		17a26	17a39	17 43				17 48	17a56	18a09		18 13				18 18	18a26	18a39	18 43				
Higham	d					17 49								18 19							18 49				
Strood	d	17 29				17 55				17 59				18 25				18 29			18 55				
Rochester	d	17 32				17 58				18 02				18 28				18 32			18 58				
Chatham	d	17 36				18 01				18 06				18 31				18 36			19 01				
Gillingham	d	17 40				18 06				18 10				18 36				18 40			19 06				
Rainham	a	17 45				18 11				18 15				18 41				18 45			19 11				

Table T201-F

Saturdays

26 May to 8 December

London Thameslink - Greenwich - Woolwich - Medway

		SE	SE	SE	TL	SE	SE	SE		SE	SE	SE	TL	SE	SE	SE	SE	SE		SE	TL	SE	SE	SE	SE
		◇								◇							◇								◇
Luton	d				17 18								17 48								18 18				
Luton Airport Parkway	d				17 21								17 51								18 21				
St Albans	d				17 31								18 01								18 31				
West Hampstead Thameslink	d				17 51								18 21								18 51				
St Pancras International	d	18 25			18 02					18 55			18 32				19 25				19 02				19 55
Farringdon	d				18 07								18 37								19 07				
City Thameslink	d				18 09								18 39								19 09				
London Blackfriars	a				18 11								18 41								19 11				
London Charing Cross	d		18 02			18 12					18 32			18 42				19 02				19 12			
Waterloo East	a		18 04			18 14					18 34			18 44				19 04				19 14			
London Cannon Street	d						18 24	18 35							18 54	19 05							19 24	19 35	
London Bridge	d		18 11		18 18	18 21	18 28	18 39			18 41		18 48	18 51	18 58	19 09		19 11			19 18	19 21	19 28	19 39	
London Victoria	d			18 06								18 36								19 06					
Deptford	d				18 25		18 35	18 45					18 55		19 05	19 15					19 25		19 35	19 45	
Greenwich	d				18 27		18 37	18 47					18 57		19 07	19 17					19 27		19 37	19 47	
Maze Hill	d				18 30		18 40	18 50					19 00		19 10	19 20					19 30		19 40	19 50	
Westcombe Park	d				18 32		18 42	18 52					19 02		19 12	19 22					19 32		19 42	19 52	
Charlton	d				18 35	18 38	18 45	18 55					19 05	19 08	19 15	19 25					19 35	19 38	19 45	19 55	
Woolwich Dockyard	d					18 41	18 48	18 58						19 11	19 18	19 28						19 41	19 48	19 58	
Woolwich Arsenal	d				18 40	18 44	18 51	19 01					19 10	19 14	19 21	19 31					19 40	19 44	19 51	20 01	
Plumstead	d				18 43	18 46	18 53	19 03					19 13	19 16	19 23	19 33					19 43	19 46	19 53	20 03	
Abbey Wood	d				18 46	18 50	18 56	19 06					19 16	19 20	19 26	19 36					19 46	19 50	19 56	20 06	
Belvedere	d					18 53	18 59	19 09						19 23	19 29	19 39						19 53	19 59	20 09	
Erith	d					18 55	19 02	19 12						19 25	19 32	19 42						19 55	20 02	20 12	
Slade Green	d				18 52	19 01	19a06	19a15					19 22	19 31	19a36	19a45					19 52	20 01	20a06	20a15	
Dartford	d		18 41	18 54	18 58	19a08					19 11	19 24	19 28	19a38				19 41		19 54	19 58	20a08			
Stone Crossing	d		18 45		19 02						19 15		19 32					19 45			20 02				
Greenhithe	d		18 47	19 00	19 04						19 17	19 30	19 34					19 47		20 00	20 04				
Swanscombe	d		18 50		19 07						19 20		19 37					19 50			20 07				
Northfleet	d		18 52		19 09						19 22		19 39					19 52			20 09				
Gravesend	d	18 48	18a56	19a09	19 13					19 18	19a26	19a39	19 43				19 48	19a56		20a09	20 13				20 18
Higham	d				19 19								19 49								20 19				
Strood	d	18 59			19 25					19 29			19 55				19 59				20 25				20 29
Rochester	d	19 02			19 28					19 32			19 58				20 02				20 28				20 32
Chatham	d	19 06			19 31					19 36			20 01				20 06				20 31				20 36
Gillingham	d	19 10			19 36					19 40			20 06				20 10				20 36				20 40
Rainham	a	19 15			19 41					19 45			20 11				20 15				20 41				20 45

		SE	SE	TL		SE	SE	SE	SE	SE	SE	TL	SE	SE		SE	SE	SE	TL	SE	SE	SE	SE	SE	
									◇							◇						◇			
Luton	d			18 48								19 18							19 48						
Luton Airport Parkway	d			18 51								19 21							19 51						
St Albans	d			19 01								19 31							20 01						
West Hampstead Thameslink	d			19 21								19 51							20 21						
St Pancras International	d			19 32					20 25			20 02				20 55			20 32			21 25			
Farringdon	d			19 37								20 07							20 37						
City Thameslink	d			19 39								20 09							20 39						
London Blackfriars	a			19 41								20 11							20 41						
London Charing Cross	d	19 32				19 42				20 02			20 12				20 32			20 42			21 02		
Waterloo East	a	19 34				19 44				20 04			20 14				20 34			20 44			21 04		
London Cannon Street	d						19 54	20 05						20 32							21 02				
London Bridge	d	19 41		19 48		19 51	19 58	20 09		20 11		20 18	20 21	20 36			20 41		20 48	20 51	21 06		21 11		
London Victoria	d		19 36								20 06							20 36						21 06	
Deptford	d			19 55			20 05	20 15				20 25		20 42					20 55		21 12				
Greenwich	d			19 57			20 07	20 17				20 27		20 44					20 57		21 14				
Maze Hill	d			20 00			20 10	20 20				20 30		20 47					21 00		21 17				
Westcombe Park	d			20 02			20 12	20 22				20 32		20 49					21 02		21 19				
Charlton	d			20 05		20 08	20 15	20 25				20 35	20 38	20 52					21 05	21 08	21 22				
Woolwich Dockyard	d					20 11	20 18	20 28					20 41	20 55						21 11	21 25				
Woolwich Arsenal	d			20 10		20 14	20 21	20 31				20 40	20 44	20 58					21 10	21 14	21 28				
Plumstead	d			20 13		20 16	20 23	20 33				20 43	20 46	21 00					21 13	21 16	21 30				
Abbey Wood	d			20 16		20 20	20 26	20 36				20 46	20 50	21 03					21 16	21 20	21 33				
Belvedere	d					20 23	20 29	20 39					20 53	21 06						21 23	21 36				
Erith	d					20 25	20 32	20 42					20 55	21 09						21 25	21 39				
Slade Green	d			20 22		20 31	20a36	20a45				20 52	21 01	21a13					21 22	21 31	21a43				
Dartford	d	20 11	20 24	20 28		20a38				20 41	20 54	20 58	21a08				21 11	21 24	21 28	21a38			21 41	21 54	
Stone Crossing	d	20 15		20 32						20 45		21 02					21 15		21 32				21 45		
Greenhithe	d	20 17	20 30	20 34						20 47	21 00	21 04					21 17	21 30	21 34				21 47	22 00	
Swanscombe	d	20 20		20 37						20 50		21 07					21 20		21 37				21 50		
Northfleet	d	20 22		20 39						20 52		21 09					21 22		21 39				21 52		
Gravesend	d	20a26	20a39	20 43					20 48	20a56	21a09	21 13				21 18	21a26	21a39	21 43			21 48	21a56	22a09	
Higham	d			20 49								21 19							21 49						
Strood	d			20 55					20 59			21 25				21 29			21 55			21 59			
Rochester	d			20 58					21 02			21 28				21 32			21 58			22 02			
Chatham	d			21 01					21 06			21 31				21 36			22 01			22 06			
Gillingham	d			21 06					21 10			21 36				21 40			22 06			22 10			
Rainham	a			21 11					21 15			21 41				21 45			22 11			22 15			

Please note, Network Rail have stated that further updates to this timetable are possible during the validity period.

Table T201-F

Saturdays

26 May to 8 December

London Thameslink - Greenwich - Woolwich - Medway

		TL	SE	SE	SE ◇	SE	SE	TL	SE	SE	SE ◇	SE	SE	TL	SE	SE	SE ◇	SE	SE	TL	SE	SE	SE ◇
Luton	d	20 18						20 48						21 18						21 48			
Luton Airport Parkway	d	20 21						20 51						21 21						21 51			
St Albans	d	20 31						21 01						21 31						22 01			
West Hampstead Thameslink	d	20 51						21 21						21 51						22 21			
St Pancras International	d	21 02			21 55			21 32			22 25			22 02			22 55			22 32			23 25
Farringdon	d	21 07						21 37						22 07						22 37			
City Thameslink	d																						
London Blackfriars	a	21 11						21 41						22 11						22 41			
London Charing Cross	d		21 12			21 32			21 42			22 02			22 12			22 32			22 42		
Waterloo East	a		21 14			21 34			21 44			22 04			22 14			22 34			22 44		
London Cannon Street	d			21 32						22 02						22 32						23 02	
London Bridge	d	21 18	21 21	21 36		21 41		21 48	21 51	22 06		22 11		22 18	22 21	22 36		22 41		22 48	22 51	23 06	
London Victoria	d						21 36						22 06						22 36				
Deptford	d	21 25		21 42				21 55		22 12				22 25		22 42				22 55		23 12	
Greenwich	d	21 27		21 44				21 57		22 14				22 27		22 44				22 57		23 14	
Maze Hill	d	21 30		21 47				22 00		22 17				22 30		22 47				23 00		23 17	
Westcombe Park	d	21 32		21 49				22 02		22 19				22 32		22 49				23 02		23 19	
Charlton	d	21 35	21 38	21 52				22 05	22 08	22 22				22 35	22 38	22 52				23 05	23 08	23 22	
Woolwich Dockyard	d		21 41	21 55					22 11	22 25					22 41	22 55					23 11	23 25	
Woolwich Arsenal	d	21 40	21 44	21 58				22 10	22 14	22 28				22 40	22 44	22 58				23 10	23 14	23 28	
Plumstead	d	21 43	21 46	22 00				22 13	22 16	22 30				22 43	22 46	23 00				23 13	23 16	23 30	
Abbey Wood	d	21 46	21 50	22 03				22 16	22 20	22 33				22 46	22 50	23 03				23 16	23 20	23 33	
Belvedere	d		21 53	22 06					22 23	22 36					22 53	23 06					23 23	23 36	
Erith	d		21 55	22 09					22 25	22 39					22 55	23 09					23 25	23 39	
Slade Green	d	21 52	22 01	22a13				22 22	22 31	22a43				22 52	23 01	23a13				23 22	23 31	23 44	
Dartford	d	21 58	22a08			22 11	22 24	22 28	22a38			22 41	22 54	22 58	23a08			23 11	23 24	23 28	23a38	23a50	
Stone Crossing	d	22 02				22 15		22 32				22 45		23 02				23 15		23 32			
Greenhithe	d	22 04				22 17	22 30	22 34				22 47	23 00	23 04				23 17	23 30	23 34			
Swanscombe	d	22 07				22 20		22 37				22 50		23 07				23 20		23 37			
Northfleet	d	22 09				22 22		22 39				22 52		23 09				23 22		23 39			
Gravesend	d	22 13			22 18	22a26	22a39	22 43			22 48	22a56	23a09	23 13			23 18	23a26	23a39	23 43			23 48
Higham	d	22 19						22 49						23 19						23 49			
Strood	d	22 25			22 29			22 55			22 59			23 25			23 29			23 55			23 59
Rochester	d	22 28			22 32			22 58			23 02			23 28			23 32			23 58			00 02
Chatham	d	22 31			22 36			23 01			23 06			23 31			23 36			00 02			00 06
Gillingham	d	22 36			22 40			23 06			23 10			23 36			23 40			00a06			00 10
Rainham	a	22 41			22 45			23 11			23 15			23 41			23 45						00 15

		SE	TL	SE	SE ◇	SE
Luton	d		22 18			
Luton Airport Parkway	d		22 21			
St Albans	d		22 31			
West Hampstead Thameslink	d		22 51			
St Pancras International	d		23 02		23 55	
Farringdon	d		23 07			
City Thameslink	d					
London Blackfriars	a		23 11			
London Charing Cross	d	23 02		23 12		23 32
Waterloo East	a	23 04		23 14		23 34
London Cannon Street	d					
London Bridge	d	23 11	23 18	23 21		23 41
London Victoria	d					
Deptford	d		23 25			
Greenwich	d		23 27			
Maze Hill	d		23 30			
Westcombe Park	d		23 32			
Charlton	d		23 35	23 38		
Woolwich Dockyard	d			23 41		
Woolwich Arsenal	d		23 40	23 44		
Plumstead	d		23 43	23 46		
Abbey Wood	d		23 46	23 50		
Belvedere	d			23 53		
Erith	d			23 55		
Slade Green	d		23 52	00 01		
Dartford	d	23 48	23 58	00a08		00 18
Stone Crossing	d	23 52	00 02			00 22
Greenhithe	d	23 54	00 04			00 24
Swanscombe	d	23 57	00 07			00 27
Northfleet	d	23 59	00 09			00 29
Gravesend	d	00a04	00 13		00 18	00a34
Higham	d		00 19			
Strood	d		00 25		00 29	
Rochester	d		00 28		00 32	
Chatham	d		00 32		00 36	
Gillingham	d		00a36		00 40	
Rainham	a				00 45	

Table T201-F

Sundays

20 May to 2 December

London Thameslink - Greenwich - Woolwich - Medway

		TL	SE	TL	SE	TL	SE	TL	SE	SE ◇	SE	SE	TL	SE	SE	SE	TL	SE	SE ◇	SE	SE	TL	SE
Luton	d																						
Luton Airport Parkway	d																						
St Albans	d																						
West Hampstead Thameslink	d																						
St Pancras International	d									08 25									09 25				
Farringdon	d																						
City Thameslink	d																						
London Blackfriars	a																						
London Charing Cross	d		00 02						07 42		07 52			08 12	08 22			08 42		08 52			09 12
Waterloo East	a		00 04						07 44		07 54			08 14	08 24			08 44		08 54			09 14
London Cannon Street	d				07 29							07 59				08 29					08 59		
London Bridge	d		00 11		07 33				07 51		08 01	08 03	08 18	08 21	08 31	08 33	08 48	08 51		09 01	09 03	09 18	09 21
London Victoria	d																						
Deptford	d				07 39							08 09	08 25			08 39	08 55				09 09	09 25	
Greenwich	d				07 41							08 11	08 27			08 41	08 57				09 11	09 27	
Maze Hill	d				07 44							08 14	08 30			08 44	09 00				09 14	09 30	
Westcombe Park	d				07 46							08 16	08 32			08 46	09 02				09 16	09 32	
Charlton	d				07 49				08 08			08 19	08 35	08 38		08 49	09 05	09 08			09 19	09 35	09 38
Woolwich Dockyard	d				07 52				08 11			08 22		08 41		08 52		09 11			09 22		09 41
Woolwich Arsenal	d				07 55				08 14			08 25	08 40	08 44		08 55	09 10	09 14			09 25	09 40	09 44
Plumstead	d				07 57				08 16			08 27	08 43	08 46		08 57	09 13	09 16			09 27	09 43	09 46
Abbey Wood	d				08 00				08 20			08 30	08 46	08 50		09 00	09 16	09 20			09 30	09 46	09 50
Belvedere	d				08 03				08 23			08 33		08 53		09 03		09 23			09 33		09 53
Erith	d				08 06				08 25			08 36		08 55		09 06		09 25			09 36		09 55
Slade Green	d				08a09				08 31			08a39	08 52	09 01		09a09	09 22	09 31			09a39	09 52	10 01
Dartford	d	00 28	00 48	01 24		07 58	08 09	08 28	08a36		08 39		08 58	09a06	09 09		09 28	09a36		09 39		09 58	10a06
Stone Crossing	d	00 32	00 52	01 28		08 02	08 13	08 32			08 43		09 02		09 13		09 32			09 43		10 02	
Greenhithe	d	00 34	00 54	01 30		08 04	08 15	08 34			08 45		09 04		09 15		09 34			09 45		10 04	
Swanscombe	d	00 37	00s57	01 33		08 07	08 18	08 37			08 48		09 07		09 18		09 37			09 48		10 07	
Northfleet	d	00 39	00s59	01 35		08 09	08 20	08 39			08 50		09 09		09 20		09 39			09 50		10 09	
Gravesend	d	00 43	01a04	01 39		08 13	08a25	08 43		08 48	08a55		09 13		09a25		09 43		09 48	09a55		10 13	
Higham	d	00 49		01 45		08 19		08 49					09 19				09 49					10 19	
Strood	d	00 55		01 50		08 25		08 55		08 59			09 25				09 55		09 59			10 25	
Rochester	d	00 58		01 54		08 28		08 58		09 02			09 28				09 58		10 02			10 28	
Chatham	d	01 02		01 57		08 31		09 01		09 06			09 31				10 01		10 06			10 31	
Gillingham	d	01a06		02a02		08 36		09 06		09 10			09 36				10 06		10 10			10 36	
Rainham	a					08 41		09 11		09 15			09 41				10 11		10 15			10 41	

		SE	SE	TL	SE	SE ◇	SE	SE	TL	SE	SE	SE	TL	SE	SE ◇	SE	SE	TL	SE	SE	SE	TL	SE
Luton	d																						
Luton Airport Parkway	d																						
St Albans	d																						
West Hampstead Thameslink	d			09 20					09 50														
St Pancras International	d			09 32		10 27			10 02				10 32		11 25			11 02				11 32	
Farringdon	d			09 36					10 06				10 36					11 06				11 36	
City Thameslink	d																						
London Blackfriars	a			09 40					10 10				10 40					11 10				11 40	
London Charing Cross	d	09 22			09 42		09 52			10 12	10 22			10 42		10 52			11 12	11 22			11 42
Waterloo East	a	09 24			09 44		09 54			10 14	10 24			10 44		10 54			11 14	11 24			11 44
London Cannon Street	d		09 29					09 59				10 29					10 59				11 29		
London Bridge	d	09 31	09 33	09 48	09 51		10 01	10 03	10 18	10 21	10 31	10 33	10 48	10 51		11 01	11 03	11 18	11 21	11 31	11 33	11 48	11 51
London Victoria	d																						
Deptford	d		09 39	09 55				10 09	10 25			10 39	10 55				11 09	11 25			11 39	11 55	
Greenwich	d		09 41	09 57				10 11	10 27			10 41	10 57				11 11	11 27			11 41	11 57	
Maze Hill	d		09 44	10 00				10 14	10 30			10 44	11 00				11 14	11 30			11 44	12 00	
Westcombe Park	d		09 46	10 02				10 16	10 32			10 46	11 02				11 16	11 32			11 46	12 02	
Charlton	d		09 49	10 05	10 08			10 19	10 35	10 38		10 49	11 05	11 08			11 19	11 35	11 38		11 49	12 05	12 08
Woolwich Dockyard	d		09 52		10 11			10 22		10 41		10 52		11 11			11 22		11 41		11 52		12 11
Woolwich Arsenal	d		09 55	10 10	10 14			10 25	10 40	10 44		10 55	11 10	11 14			11 25	11 40	11 44		11 55	12 10	12 14
Plumstead	d		09 57	10 13	10 16			10 27	10 43	10 46		10 57	11 13	11 16			11 27	11 43	11 46		11 57	12 13	12 16
Abbey Wood	d		10 00	10 16	10 20			10 30	10 46	10 50		11 00	11 16	11 20			11 30	11 46	11 50		12 00	12 16	12 20
Belvedere	d		10 03		10 23			10 33		10 53		11 03		11 23			11 33		11 53		12 03		12 23
Erith	d		10 06		10 25			10 36		10 55		11 06		11 25			11 36		11 55		12 06		12 25
Slade Green	d		10a09	10 22	10 31			10a39	10 52	11 01		11a09	11 22	11 31			11a39	11 52	12 01		12a09	12 22	12 31
Dartford	d	10 09		10 28	10a36		10 39		10 58	11a06	11 09		11 28	11a36		11 39		11 58	12a06	12 09		12 28	12a36
Stone Crossing	d	10 13		10 32			10 43		11 02		11 13		11 32			11 43		12 02		12 13		12 32	
Greenhithe	d	10 15		10 34			10 45		11 04		11 15		11 34			11 45		12 04		12 15		12 34	
Swanscombe	d	10 18		10 37			10 48		11 07		11 18		11 37			11 48		12 07		12 18		12 37	
Northfleet	d	10 20		10 39			10 50		11 09		11 20		11 39			11 50		12 09		12 20		12 39	
Gravesend	d	10a25		10 43		10 49	10a55		11 13		11a25		11 43		11 48	11a55		12 13		12a25		12 43	
Higham	d			10 49					11 19				11 49					12 19				12 49	
Strood	d			10 55		10 59			11 25				11 55		11 59			12 25				12 55	
Rochester	d			10 58		11 03			11 28				11 58		12 02			12 28				12 58	
Chatham	d			11 01		11 06			11 31				12 01		12 06			12 31				13 01	
Gillingham	d			11 06		11 11			11 36				12 06		12 10			12 36				13 06	
Rainham	a			11 11		11 15			11 41				12 11		12 15			12 41				13 11	

Table T201-F

Sundays

20 May to 2 December

London Thameslink - Greenwich - Woolwich - Medway

		SE ◇		SE	SE	TL	SE	SE ◇	SE	SE	TL	SE	SE ◇	SE	SE	TL	SE	SE ◇		SE	SE	TL	SE	SE ◇
Luton	d																		and at the same minutes past each hour until					
Luton Airport Parkway	d																							
St Albans	d																							
West Hampstead Thameslink	d																							
St Pancras International	d	12 27				12 02		12 52			12 32		13 25			13 02		13 55				15 32		16 25
Farringdon	d					12 06					12 36					13 06						15 36		
City Thameslink	d																							
London Blackfriars	a					12 10					12 40					13 10						15 40		
London Charing Cross	d			11 52			12 12		12 22			12 42		12 52			13 12			15 22			15 42	
Waterloo East	a			11 54			12 14		12 24			12 44		12 54			13 14			15 24			15 44	
London Cannon Street	d				11 59					12 29					12 59						15 29			
London Bridge	d			12 01	12 03	12 18	12 21		12 31	12 33	12 48	12 51		13 01	13 03	13 18	13 21			15 31	15 33	15 48	15 51	
London Victoria	d																							
Deptford	d				12 09	12 25				12 39	12 55				13 09	13 25					15 39	15 55		
Greenwich	d				12 11	12 27				12 41	12 57				13 11	13 27					15 41	15 57		
Maze Hill	d				12 14	12 30				12 44	13 00				13 14	13 30					15 44	16 00		
Westcombe Park	d				12 16	12 32				12 46	13 02				13 16	13 32					15 46	16 02		
Charlton	d				12 19	12 35	12 38			12 49	13 05	13 08			13 19	13 35	13 38				15 49	16 05	16 08	
Woolwich Dockyard	d				12 22		12 41			12 52		13 11			13 22		13 41				15 52		16 11	
Woolwich Arsenal	d				12 25	12 40	12 44			12 55	13 10	13 14			13 25	13 40	13 44				15 55	16 10	16 14	
Plumstead	d				12 27	12 43	12 46			12 57	13 13	13 16			13 27	13 43	13 46				15 57	16 13	16 16	
Abbey Wood	d				12 30	12 46	12 50			13 00	13 16	13 20			13 30	13 46	13 50				16 00	16 16	16 20	
Belvedere	d				12 33		12 53			13 03		13 23			13 33		13 53				16 03		16 23	
Erith	d				12 36		12 55			13 06		13 25			13 36		13 55				16 06		16 25	
Slade Green	d				12a39	12 52	13 01			13a09	13 22	13 31			13a39	13 52	14 01				16a09	16 22	16 31	
Dartford	d			12 39		12 58	13a06		13 09		13 28	13a36		13 39		13 58	14a06			16 09		16 28	16a36	
Stone Crossing	d			12 43		13 02			13 13		13 32			13 43		14 02				16 13		16 32		
Greenhithe	d			12 45		13 04			13 15		13 34			13 45		14 04				16 15		16 34		
Swanscombe	d			12 48		13 07			13 18		13 37			13 48		14 07				16 18		16 37		
Northfleet	d			12 50		13 09			13 20		13 39			13 50		14 09				16 20		16 39		
Gravesend	d	12 49		12a55		13 13		13 18	13a25		13 43		13 48	13a55		14 13		14 18		16a25		16 43		16 48
Higham	d					13 19					13 49					14 19						16 49		
Strood	d	12 59				13 25		13 29			13 55		13 59			14 25		14 29				16 55		16 59
Rochester	d	13 03				13 28		13 32			13 58		14 02			14 28		14 32				16 58		17 02
Chatham	d	13 06				13 31		13 36			14 01		14 06			14 31		14 36				17 01		17 06
Gillingham	d	13 11				13 36		13 40			14 06		14 10			14 36		14 40				17 06		17 10
Rainham	a	13 15				13 41		13 45			14 11		14 15			14 41		14 45				17 11		17 15

		SE	SE	TL	SE	SE ◇		SE	SE	TL	SE	SE ◇	SE	SE	TL	SE		SE ◇	SE	SE	TL	SE	SE ◇	SE	SE
Luton	d																								
Luton Airport Parkway	d																								
St Albans	d																								
West Hampstead Thameslink	d																								
St Pancras International	d			16 02		16 55				16 32		17 25			17 02			17 52			17 32		18 25		
Farringdon	d			16 06						16 36					17 06						17 36				
City Thameslink	d																								
London Blackfriars	a			16 10						16 40					17 10						17 40				
London Charing Cross	d	15 52			16 12			16 22			16 42		16 52			17 12			17 22			17 42		17 52	
Waterloo East	a	15 54			16 14			16 24			16 44		16 54			17 14			17 24			17 44		17 54	
London Cannon Street	d		15 59						16 29					16 59						17 29					17 59
London Bridge	d	16 01	16 03	16 18	16 21			16 31	16 33	16 48	16 51		17 01	17 03	17 18	17 21			17 31	17 33	17 48	17 51		18 01	18 03
London Victoria	d																								
Deptford	d		16 09	16 25					16 39	16 55				17 09	17 25					17 39	17 55				18 09
Greenwich	d		16 11	16 27					16 41	16 57				17 11	17 27					17 41	17 57				18 11
Maze Hill	d		16 14	16 30					16 44	17 00				17 14	17 30					17 44	18 00				18 14
Westcombe Park	d		16 16	16 32					16 46	17 02				17 16	17 32					17 46	18 02				18 16
Charlton	d		16 19	16 35	16 38				16 49	17 05	17 08			17 19	17 35	17 38				17 49	18 05	18 08			18 19
Woolwich Dockyard	d		16 22		16 41				16 52		17 11			17 22		17 41				17 52		18 11			18 22
Woolwich Arsenal	d		16 25	16 40	16 44				16 55	17 10	17 14			17 25	17 40	17 44				17 55	18 10	18 14			18 25
Plumstead	d		16 27	16 43	16 46				16 57	17 13	17 16			17 27	17 43	17 46				17 57	18 13	18 16			18 27
Abbey Wood	d		16 30	16 46	16 50				17 00	17 16	17 20			17 30	17 46	17 50				18 00	18 16	18 20			18 30
Belvedere	d		16 33		16 53				17 03		17 23			17 33		17 53				18 03		18 23			18 33
Erith	d		16 36		16 55				17 06		17 25			17 36		17 55				18 06		18 25			18 36
Slade Green	d		16a39	16 52	17 01				17a09	17 22	17 31			17a39	17 52	18 01				18a09	18 22	18 31			18a39
Dartford	d	16 39		16 58	17a06			17 09		17 28	17a36		17 39		17 58	18a06			18 09		18 28	18a36		18 39	
Stone Crossing	d	16 43		17 02				17 13		17 32			17 43		18 02				18 13		18 32			18 43	
Greenhithe	d	16 45		17 04				17 15		17 34			17 45		18 04				18 15		18 34			18 45	
Swanscombe	d	16 48		17 07				17 18		17 37			17 48		18 07				18 18		18 37			18 48	
Northfleet	d	16 50		17 09				17 20		17 39			17 50		18 09				18 20		18 39			18 50	
Gravesend	d	16a55		17 13		17 18		17a25		17 43		17 48	17a55		18 13			18 18	18a25		18 43		18 48	18a55	
Higham	d			17 19						17 49					18 19						18 49				
Strood	d			17 25		17 29				17 55		17 59			18 25			18 29			18 55		18 59		
Rochester	d			17 28		17 32				17 58		18 02			18 28			18 32			18 58		19 02		
Chatham	d			17 31		17 36				18 01		18 06			18 31			18 36			19 01		19 06		
Gillingham	d			17 36		17 40				18 06		18 10			18 36			18 40			19 06		19 10		
Rainham	a			17 41		17 45				18 11		18 15			18 41			18 45			19 11		19 15		

Table T201-F

Sundays

20 May to 2 December

London Thameslink - Greenwich - Woolwich - Medway

		TL	SE	SE ◇		SE	SE	TL	SE	SE ◇	SE	SE	TL	SE	SE ◇		SE	SE	TL	SE	SE ◇	SE	SE	TL
Luton	d				and at the same minutes past each hour until																			
Luton Airport Parkway	d																							
St Albans	d																							21 27
West Hampstead Thameslink	d																							21 50
St Pancras International	d	18 02		18 55				20 32		21 25			21 02		21 55				21 32		22 25			22 02
Farringdon	d	18 06						20 36					21 06						21 36					22 06
City Thameslink	d																							
London Blackfriars	a	18 10						20 40					21 10						21 40					22 10
London Charing Cross	d		18 12			20 22			20 42		20 52			21 12			21 22			21 42		21 52		
Waterloo East	a		18 14			20 24			20 44		20 54			21 14			21 24			21 44		21 54		
London Cannon Street	d						20 29					20 59						21 29					21 59	
London Bridge	d	18 18	18 21			20 31	20 33	20 48	20 51		21 01	21 03	21 18	21 21			21 31	21 33	21 48	21 51		22 01	22 03	22 18
London Victoria	d																							
Deptford	d	18 25					20 39	20 55				21 09	21 25					21 39	21 55				22 09	22 25
Greenwich	d	18 27					20 41	20 57				21 11	21 27					21 41	21 57				22 11	22 27
Maze Hill	d	18 30					20 44	21 00				21 14	21 30					21 44	22 00				22 14	22 30
Westcombe Park	d	18 32					20 46	21 02				21 16	21 32					21 46	22 02				22 16	22 32
Charlton	d	18 35	18 38				20 49	21 05	21 08			21 19	21 35	21 38				21 49	22 05	22 08			22 19	22 35
Woolwich Dockyard	d		18 41				20 52		21 11			21 22		21 41				21 52		22 11			22 22	
Woolwich Arsenal	d	18 40	18 44				20 55	21 10	21 14			21 25	21 40	21 44				21 55	22 10	22 14			22 25	22 40
Plumstead	d	18 43	18 46				20 57	21 13	21 16			21 27	21 43	21 46				21 57	22 13	22 16			22 27	22 43
Abbey Wood	d	18 46	18 50				21 00	21 16	21 20			21 30	21 46	21 50				22 00	22 16	22 20			22 30	22 46
Belvedere	d		18 53				21 03		21 23			21 33		21 53				22 03		22 23			22 33	
Erith	d		18 55				21 06		21 25			21 36		21 55				22 06		22 25			22 36	
Slade Green	d	18 52	19 01				21a09	21 22	21 31			21a39	21 52	22 01				22a09	22 22	22 31			22a39	22 52
Dartford	d	18 58	19a06			21 09		21 28	21a36		21 39		21 58	22a06			22 09		22 28	22a36		22 39		22 58
Stone Crossing	d	19 02				21 13		21 32			21 43		22 02				22 13		22 32			22 43		23 02
Greenhithe	d	19 04				21 15		21 34			21 45		22 04				22 15		22 34			22 45		23 04
Swanscombe	d	19 07				21 18		21 37			21 48		22 07				22 18		22 37			22 48		23 07
Northfleet	d	19 09				21 20		21 39			21 50		22 09				22 20		22 39			22 50		23 09
Gravesend	d	19 13		19 18		21a25		21 43		21 48	21a55		22 13		22 18		22a25		22 43		22 48	22a55		23 13
Higham	d	19 19						21 49					22 19						22 49					23 19
Strood	d	19 25		19 29				21 55		21 59			22 25		22 29				22 55		22 59			23 25
Rochester	d	19 28		19 32				21 58		22 02			22 28		22 32				22 58		23 02			23 28
Chatham	d	19 31		19 36				22 01		22 06			22 31		22 36				23 01		23 06			23 31
Gillingham	d	19 36		19 40				22 06		22 10			22 36		22 40				23 06		23 10			23 36
Rainham	a	19 41		19 45				22 11		22 15			22 41		22 45				23 11		23 15			23 41

		SE		SE ◇	SE	SE	TL	SE	SE ◇	SE	SE	TL		SE	SE	SE	SE	SE
Luton	d																	
Luton Airport Parkway	d																	
St Albans	d						21 57					22 27						
West Hampstead Thameslink	d						22 20					22 50						
St Pancras International	d			22 55			22 32		23 25			23 02						
Farringdon	d						22 36					23 06						
City Thameslink	d																	
London Blackfriars	a						22 40					23 10						
London Charing Cross	d	22 12			22 22			22 42		22 52				23 12	23 22		23 42	
Waterloo East	a	22 14			22 24			22 44		22 54				23 14	23 24		23 44	
London Cannon Street	d					22 29					22 59					23 29		23 59
London Bridge	d	22 21			22 31	22 33	22 48	22 51		23 01	23 03	23 18		23 21	23 31	23 33	23 51	00 03
London Victoria	d																	
Deptford	d					22 39	22 55				23 09	23 25				23 39		00 09
Greenwich	d					22 41	22 57				23 11	23 27				23 41		00 11
Maze Hill	d					22 44	23 00				23 14	23 30				23 44		00 14
Westcombe Park	d					22 46	23 02				23 16	23 32				23 46		00 16
Charlton	d	22 38				22 49	23 05	23 08			23 19	23 35		23 38		23 49	00 08	00 19
Woolwich Dockyard	d	22 41				22 52		23 11			23 22			23 41		23 52	00 11	00 22
Woolwich Arsenal	d	22 44				22 55	23 10	23 14			23 25	23 40		23 44		23 55	00 14	00 25
Plumstead	d	22 46				22 57	23 13	23 16			23 27	23 43		23 46		23 57	00 16	00 27
Abbey Wood	d	22 50				23 00	23 16	23 20			23 30	23 46		23 50		23 59	00 20	00 30
Belvedere	d	22 53				23 03		23 23			23 33			23 53		00 03	00 23	00 33
Erith	d	22 55				23 06		23 25			23 36			23 55		00 06	00 25	00 36
Slade Green	d	23 01				23a09	23 22	23 31			23 40	23 52		00 01		00 10	00 31	00 40
Dartford	d	23a06			23 09		23 28	23a36		23 39	23a45	23 58		00a06	00 09	00a15	00a36	00a45
Stone Crossing	d				23 13		23 32			23 43		00 02			00 13			
Greenhithe	d				23 15		23 34			23 45		00 04			00 15			
Swanscombe	d				23 18		23 37			23 48		00 07			00 18			
Northfleet	d				23 20		23 39			23 50		00 09			00 20			
Gravesend	d			23 18	23a25		23 43		23 48	23a55		00 13			00a25			
Higham	d						23 49					00 19						
Strood	d			23 29			23 55		23 59			00 25						
Rochester	d			23 32			23 58		00 02			00 28						
Chatham	d			23 36			00 02		00 06			00 31						
Gillingham	d			23 40			00a06		00 10			00a36						
Rainham	a			23 45					00 15									

Please note, Network Rail have stated that further updates to this timetable are possible during the validity period.

Table T201-R

Mondays to Fridays

21 May to 7 December

Medway - Woolwich - Greenwich - London Thameslink

		TL	SE	SE	TL	SE	SE	SE	SE	TL		SE	SE ◇	SE	SE	SE	SE	TL	SE	SE ◇		SE	SE	SE	SE
Rainham	d												05 15					05 30		05 45					
Gillingham	d	04 00			04 36					05 06			05 20					05 36		05 50					
Chatham	d	04 04			04 40					05 10			05 24					05 40		05 54					
Rochester	d	04 08			04 44					05 14			05 28					05 44		05 58					
Strood	d	04 11			04 47					05 17			05 31					05 47		06 01					
Higham	d	04 16			04 52					05 22								05 52							
Gravesend	d	04 23	04 32		04 59					05 29			05 41		05 46			05 59		06 11			06 15		
Northfleet	d	04 27			05 03					05 33					05 50			06 03							
Swanscombe	d	04 29			05 05					05 35					05 52			06 05							
Greenhithe	d	04 32	04 38		05 08					05 38					05 55			06 08					06 21		
Stone Crossing	d	04 34			05 10					05 40					05 57			06 10							
Dartford	d	04a39	04 45	05 03	05 15			05 33		05 45				06 01	06 03	←		06 15					06 27		06 38
Slade Green	d			05 08	05 21	05 26		05 38		05 51		05 56		06 07		06 07	06 14	06 21						06 38	06 43
Erith	d			05 11		05 29		05 41				05 59		→		06 10	06 17							06 41	06 46
Belvedere	d			05 13		05 31		05 43				06 01				06 12	06 19							06 43	06 48
Abbey Wood	d			05 17	05 28	05 35		05 47		05 58		06 05				06 16	06 23	06 28					06 37	06 47	06 52
Plumstead	d			05 20	05 31	05 38		05 50		06 01		06 08				06 19	06 26	06 31						06 50	06 55
Woolwich Arsenal	d			05 23	05 34	05 41		05 53		06 04		06 11				06 22	06 29	06 34					06 41	06 53	06 58
Woolwich Dockyard	d			05 25				05 55				06 13				06 25	06 31							06 56	07 01
Charlton	d			05 29	05 40	05 47		05 59		06 10		06 17				06 28	06 35	06 40					06 47	06 59	07 04
Westcombe Park	d			05 31	05 42			06 01		06 12						06 31		06 42					06 49		07 07
Maze Hill	d			05 33	05 44			06 03		06 14						06 33		06 44					06 52		07 09
Greenwich	d			05 36	05 47		05 47	06 06	06 07	06 17						06 37		06 47				06 47	06 56		07 13
Deptford	a			05 38	05 49			06 08		06 19						06 39		06 49					06 58		07 15
London Victoria	d																		←						
London Bridge	d		05 26	05 46	05 58	06 06	07 05	06 16	07 30	06 28		06 35			06 41	06 48	06 54	06 58	07 05			08 13	07 07	07 18	07 23
London Cannon Street	d			05a52			→	06a22	→							06a54			07a11			→	07a13		07a29
Waterloo East	d		05 31			06 11						06 40			06 46		06 59							07 23	
London Charing Cross	a		05 37			06 16						06 46			06 52		07 05							07 29	
London Blackfriars	d				06 04					06 34								07 04							
City Thameslink	d				06 06					06 36								07 06							
Farringdon	d				06 09					06 39								07 09							
St Pancras International	d				06 13					06 43			06a05					07 13		06a35					
West Hampstead Thameslink	d				06 22					06 52								07 22							
St Albans	d				06a46					07 17								07 47							
Luton Airport Parkway	d									07 32								08 02							
Luton	a									07 36								08 06							

		TL	SE	TL	SE	SE ◇		SE	SE	SE	SE	SE	SE	SE	TL	SE		SE	SE	SE	SE	SE	SE ◇	SE	SE
Rainham	d	06 00				06 11									06 30										
Gillingham	d	06 06				06 17									06 36										
Chatham	d	06 10				06 21									06 40										
Rochester	d	06 14				06 25									06 44										
Strood	d	06 18	06 23			06 28							06 44		06 47					07 03			07 10		
Higham	d	06 23	06 28										06 49		06 52					07 08					
Gravesend	d	06 30	06 35			06 39					06 50		06 56		06 59					07 15			07 21		
Northfleet	d	06 33									06 54				07 03					07 18					
Swanscombe	d	06 35									06 56				07 05					07 20					
Greenhithe	d	06 39	06 42								06 59		07 03		07 08					07 24					
Stone Crossing	d	06 41	06 44								07 01		07 05		07 10					07 26					
Dartford	d	06 46	06 49	←					06 55		07 07		07 11		07 15				07 28	07 31		←			
Slade Green	d	06 51		06 51					07 00	07 06		07 10			07 21			07 25	07 33			07 33		07 36	07 37
Erith	d	→							07 03			07 12						07 28	→			07 35		07 39	
Belvedere	d								07 05			07 15						07 30				07 38		07 41	
Abbey Wood	d			06 58					07 09			07 18	07 23		07 28			07 34				07 41		07 45	
Plumstead	d			07 01					07 12			07 21			07 31			07 37				07 44		07 48	
Woolwich Arsenal	d			07 04					07 15			07 24	07 28		07 34			07 40				07 47		07 51	
Woolwich Dockyard	d								07 17			07 27						07 43						07 54	
Charlton	d			07 10					07 21			07 30	07 33		07 40			07 46				07 53		07 57	
Westcombe Park	d			07 12					07 23				07 36		07 42			07 49						08 00	
Maze Hill	d			07 14					07 26				07 38		07 44			07 51						08 02	
Greenwich	d			07 17				07 17	07 30				07 42		07 47	07 48		07 55						08 06	
Deptford	a			07 19					07 32				07 44		07 49			07 57						08 08	
London Victoria	d				←									←							←				
London Bridge	d		07 27	07 28	07 30			08 39	07 40	07 45	07 47	07 53	07 52	07 53	07 58	09 10		08 05		08 07	08 13	08 13		08 17	08 30
London Cannon Street	d				07a35			→	07a46	07a51		→	07a59			→		08a11			08a19			08a23	→
Waterloo East	d		07 32								07 52			07 58						08 12		08 18			
London Charing Cross	a		07 38								07 58			08 04						08 18		08 24			
London Blackfriars	d			07 34											08 04										
City Thameslink	d			07 36											08 06										
Farringdon	d			07 39											08 09										
St Pancras International	d			07 43		07a02									08 13								07a46		
West Hampstead Thameslink	d			07 52											08 22										
St Albans	d			08 17											08 47										
Luton Airport Parkway	d			08 30											09 01										
Luton	a			08 34											09 04										

Table T201-R

Mondays to Fridays

21 May to 7 December

Medway - Woolwich - Greenwich - London Thameslink

		TL		SE	TL	SE	SE ◇	SE	SE	SE	SE	SE		SE	SE	SE	SE ◇	TL	SE	SE ◇	SE	SE ◇		SE ◇	SE
Rainham	d	06 56					07 17											07 30				07 47			
Gillingham	d	07 03					07 22											07 36				07 52			
Chatham	d	07 07					07 27											07 40				07 56			
Rochester	d	07 11					07 30											07 44				08 00			
Strood	d	07 17					07 34								07 38		07 43	07 47		07 54		08 03		08 11	
Higham	d	07 22													07 43			07 52							
Gravesend	d	07 29		07 39			07 44								07 50		07 53	07 59			08 11	08 14		08 21	
Northfleet	d	07 32													07 55			08 03			08 15				
Swanscombe	d	07 34													07 57			08 05			08 17				
Greenhithe	d	07 38		07 45											08 01			08 08			08 20				
Stone Crossing	d	07 40													08 03			08 10			08 22				
Dartford	d	07 45		07 51	←									08 04	08 09	←		08 15			08 28				
Slade Green	d	07 50			07 50			07 54			07 59	08 03		08 09		08 09		08 21	08 26						
Erith	d	→						07 56			08 02			→		08 12			08 29						
Belvedere	d							07 59			08 04					08 14			08 31						
Abbey Wood	d				07 57			08 02			08 08					08 18		08 28	08 35						
Plumstead	d				08 01			08 05			08 11					08 21		08 31	08 38						
Woolwich Arsenal	d				08 04			08 08			08 14					08 24		08 34	08 41						
Woolwich Dockyard	d										08 16					08 26			08 44						
Charlton	d				08 10			08 13			08 20					08 30		08 40	08 47						
Westcombe Park	d				08 12						08 22					08 32		08 42							
Maze Hill	d				08 14						08 25					08 35		08 44							
Greenwich	d				08 17					08 17	08 28					08 38		08 47							08 47
Deptford	a				08 19						08 30					08 40		08 49							
London Victoria	d					←			←																
London Bridge	d			08 27	08 28	08 30		08 33	08 39	09 40	08 39	08 47			08 47	08 49		08 58	09 06		09 08				10 09
London Cannon Street	d					08a36				→	08a45	08a53				08a55									→
Waterloo East	d			08 32				08 38	08 44						08 52				09 12		09 14				
London Charing Cross	a			08 38				08 44	08 50						08 58				09 18		09 20				
London Blackfriars	d				08 34													09 04							
City Thameslink	d				08 36													09 06							
Farringdon	d				08 39													09 09							
St Pancras International	d				08 43		08a08										08a16	09 13		10a55		08a38		08a46	
West Hampstead Thameslink	d				08a52													09a22							
St Albans	d																								
Luton Airport Parkway	d																								
Luton	a																								

		SE	SE	SE	SE	TL	SE	SE ◇		SE	SE	SE	SE	SE	SE	SE	TL	SE ◇		SE	SE	SE	TL	SE ◇	SE
Rainham	d					08 01		08 14									08 30							08 46	
Gillingham	d					08 07		08 19									08 36							08 51	
Chatham	d					08 11		08 24									08 40							08 55	
Rochester	d					08 15		08 27									08 44							08 59	
Strood	d					08 18		08 32									08 47	08 59						09 02	
Higham	d					08 23											08 52								
Gravesend	d					08 30	08 34	08 43		08 50							08 59			09 05				09 12	09 20
Northfleet	d					08 34	08 38										09 03			09 08					
Swanscombe	d					08 36	08 40										09 05			09 10					
Greenhithe	d					08 39	08 43			08 56							09 08			09 14					09 26
Stone Crossing	d					08 41	08 45										09 10			09 16					
Dartford	d			08 32		08 46	08 50			09 02						09 11	09 15			09 21			←		09 32
Slade Green	d	08 30		08 39	08 45	08 51						08 59		09 07	09 09	09 16	09 21					←	09 21		
Erith	d	08 32		08 42	08 48							09 02			09 12	09 18	→					09 18			
Belvedere	d	08 35		08 44	08 50							09 04			09 14	→						09 21			
Abbey Wood	d	08 38		08 48	08 54	08 58						09 08			09 18							09 24	09 28		
Plumstead	d	08 41		08 51	08 57	09 01						09 11			09 21							09 27	09 31		
Woolwich Arsenal	d	08 44		08 54	09 00	09 04						09 14			09 24							09 30	09 34		
Woolwich Dockyard	d	08 47		08 57	09 02							09 16			09 26							09 33			
Charlton	d	08 50		09 00	09 06	09 10						09 20			09 30							09 36	09 40		
Westcombe Park	d	08 52		09 03		09 12						09 22			09 32								09 42		
Maze Hill	d	08 54		09 05		09 14						09 24			09 34								09 44		
Greenwich	d	08 58		09 09		09 17					09 17	09 28			09 37								09 47		
Deptford	a	09 00		09 11		09 19						09 30			09 39								09 49		
London Victoria	d		←							09a57			←								←				10a25
London Bridge	d	09 08	09 10	09 20	09 25	09 28	09 29				10 39	09 38	09 40	09 54	09 47					09 53	09 54	09 57	09 58		
London Cannon Street	d	09a14	09a16	09a26							→	09a44	09a46	→	09a55						10a02				
Waterloo East	d				09 30		09 34													09 58		10 02			
London Charing Cross	a				09 37		09 40													10 03		10 05			
London Blackfriars	d					09 34																	10 04		
City Thameslink	d					09 36																	10 06		
Farringdon	d					09 39																	10 09		
St Pancras International	d					09 43		09a07										11a54					10 13	09a36	
West Hampstead Thameslink	d					09 52																	10 22		
St Albans	d					10 20																	10 45		
Luton Airport Parkway	d					10 32																	10 57		
Luton	a					10 36																	11 01		

Please note, Network Rail have stated that further updates to this timetable are possible during the validity period.

Table T201-R

Mondays to Fridays

21 May to 7 December

Medway - Woolwich - Greenwich - London Thameslink

		SE	SE	SE		SE	SE	SE	TL	SE	SE	SE	TL	SE		SE	SE	SE	SE	SE	SE	SE	TL	SE	
														◇										◇	
Rainham	d								09 00					09 16									09 28		
Gillingham	d								09 06					09 21									09 34		
Chatham	d								09 10					09 25									09 38		
Rochester	d								09 14					09 29									09 42		
Strood	d								09 17					09 32									09 45	09 59	
Higham	d								09 22														09 50		
Gravesend	d								09 29	09 35				09 42		09 50							09 59		
Northfleet	d								09 33	09 38													10 02		
Swanscombe	d								09 35	09 40													10 04		
Greenhithe	d								09 38	09 44						09 56							10 08		
Stone Crossing	d								09 40	09 46													10 10		
Dartford	d							09 41	09 45	09 51			←			10 02						10 11	10 15		
Slade Green	d		09 29			09 37	09 39	09 46	09 51			←	09 51					09 59		10 07	10 09	10 16	10 21		
Erith	d		09 32				09 42	09 48	→			09 48						10 02			10 12	10 18	→		
Belvedere	d		09 34				09 44	→				09 51						10 04			10 14	→			
Abbey Wood	d		09 38				09 48					09 54	09 58					10 08			10 18				
Plumstead	d		09 41				09 51					09 57	10 01					10 11			10 21				
Woolwich Arsenal	d		09 44				09 54					10 00	10 04					10 14			10 24				
Woolwich Dockyard	d		09 46				09 56					10 03						10 16			10 26				
Charlton	d		09 50				10 00					10 06	10 10					10 20			10 30				
Westcombe Park	d		09 52				10 02						10 12					10 22			10 32				
Maze Hill	d		09 54				10 04						10 14					10 24			10 34				
Greenwich	d	09 47	09 57				10 07						10 17				10 17	10 27			10 37				
Deptford	a		09 59				10 09						10 19					10 29			10 39				
London Victoria	d			←							←					10a55			←						
London Bridge	d	11 09	10 07	10 09		10 24	10 17			10 22	10 24	10 27	10 28				11 39	10 37	10 39	10 54	10 47				
London Cannon Street	d	→	10a13	10a15		→	10a21				10a30						→	10a41	10a43	→	10a51				
Waterloo East	d									10 27		10 32													
London Charing Cross	a									10 30		10 35													
London Blackfriars	d												10 34												
City Thameslink	d												10 36												
Farringdon	d												10 39												
St Pancras International	d												10 43	10a06										12a55	
West Hampstead Thameslink	d												10 52												
St Albans	d												11 15												
Luton Airport Parkway	d												11 27												
Luton	a												11 31												

		SE	SE	SE	TL	SE	SE	SE	SE	SE		SE	SE	SE	TL	SE	SE	SE	TL	SE		SE	SE	SE	SE
						◇														◇					
Rainham	d					09 46									09 58					10 16					
Gillingham	d					09 51									10 04					10 21					
Chatham	d					09 55									10 08					10 25					
Rochester	d					09 59									10 12					10 29					
Strood	d					10 02									10 15					10 32					
Higham	d														10 20										
Gravesend	d	10 05				10 12	10 20								10 29	10 35				10 42		10 50			
Northfleet	d	10 08													10 32	10 38									
Swanscombe	d	10 10													10 34	10 40									
Greenhithe	d	10 14					10 26								10 38	10 44						10 56			
Stone Crossing	d	10 16													10 40	10 46									
Dartford	d	10 21			←		10 32							10 41	10 45	10 51			←			11 02			
Slade Green	d			←	10 21				10 29			10 37	10 39	10 46	10 51			←	10 51					10 59	
Erith	d			10 18					10 32				10 42	10 48	→			10 48						11 02	
Belvedere	d			10 21					10 34				10 44	→				10 51						11 04	
Abbey Wood	d			10 24	10 28				10 38				10 48					10 54	10 58					11 08	
Plumstead	d			10 27	10 31				10 41				10 51					10 57	11 01					11 11	
Woolwich Arsenal	d			10 30	10 34				10 44				10 54					11 00	11 04					11 14	
Woolwich Dockyard	d			10 33					10 46				10 56					11 03						11 16	
Charlton	d			10 36	10 40				10 50				11 00					11 06	11 10					11 20	
Westcombe Park	d				10 42				10 52				11 02						11 12					11 22	
Maze Hill	d				10 44				10 54				11 04						11 14					11 24	
Greenwich	d				10 47			10 47	10 57				11 07						11 17				11 17	11 27	
Deptford	a				10 49				10 59				11 09						11 19					11 29	
London Victoria	d		←				11a25			←							←					11a55			←
London Bridge	d	10 52	10 54	10 57	10 58			12 09	11 07	11 09		11 24	11 17			11 22	11 24	11 27	11 28				12 39	11 37	11 39
London Cannon Street	d		11a00					→	11a11	11a13		→	11a21				11a30						→	11a41	11a43
Waterloo East	d	10 57		11 02												11 27		11 32							
London Charing Cross	a	11 00		11 05												11 30		11 35							
London Blackfriars	d				11 04														11 34						
City Thameslink	d				11 06														11 36						
Farringdon	d				11 09														11 39						
St Pancras International	d				11 13	10a35													11 43	11a07					
West Hampstead Thameslink	d				11 22														11 52						
St Albans	d				11 45														12 15						
Luton Airport Parkway	d				11 57														12 27						
Luton	a				12 01														12 31						

Table T201-R

Mondays to Fridays

21 May to 7 December

Medway - Woolwich - Greenwich - London Thameslink

		SE	SE	SE	TL	SE		SE	SE	SE	TL	SE	SE	SE	SE	SE		SE	SE	SE	TL	SE	SE	SE	TL
						◇						◇													
Rainham	d				10 28							10 46									10 58				
Gillingham	d				10 34							10 51									11 04				
Chatham	d				10 38							10 55									11 08				
Rochester	d				10 42							10 59									11 12				
Strood	d				10 45	10 59						11 02									11 15				
Higham	d				10 50																11 20				
Gravesend	d				10 59			11 05				11 12	11 20								11 29	11 35			
Northfleet	d				11 02			11 08													11 32	11 38			
Swanscombe	d				11 04			11 10													11 34	11 40			
Greenhithe	d				11 08			11 14					11 26								11 38	11 44			
Stone Crossing	d				11 10			11 16													11 40	11 46			
Dartford	d			11 11	11 15			11 21			←		11 32							11 41	11 45	11 51			←
Slade Green	d	11 07	11 09	11 16	11 21					←	11 21				11 29			11 37	11 39	11 46	11 51			←	11 51
Erith	d		11 12	11 18	→					11 18					11 32				11 42	11 48	→			11 48	
Belvedere	d		11 14	→						11 21					11 34				11 44	→				11 51	
Abbey Wood	d		11 18							11 24	11 28				11 38				11 48					11 54	11 58
Plumstead	d		11 21							11 27	11 31				11 41				11 51					11 57	12 01
Woolwich Arsenal	d		11 24							11 30	11 34				11 44				11 54					12 00	12 04
Woolwich Dockyard	d		11 26							11 33					11 46				11 56					12 03	
Charlton	d		11 30							11 36	11 40				11 50				12 00					12 06	12 10
Westcombe Park	d		11 32								11 42				11 52				12 02						12 12
Maze Hill	d		11 34								11 44				11 54				12 04						12 14
Greenwich	d		11 37								11 47			11 47	11 57				12 07						12 17
Deptford	a		11 39								11 49				11 59				12 09						12 19
London Victoria	d								←				12a25			←							←		
London Bridge	d	11 54	11 47					11 52	11 54	11 57	11 58			13 09	12 07	12 09		12 24	12 17			12 22	12 24	12 27	12 28
London Cannon Street	d	→	11a51						12a00					→	12a11	12a13		→	12a21				12a30		
Waterloo East	d							11 57		12 02												12 27		12 32	
London Charing Cross	a							12 00		12 05												12 30		12 35	
London Blackfriars	d										12 04														12 34
City Thameslink	d										12 06														12 36
Farringdon	d										12 09														12 39
St Pancras International	d					13a54					12 13	11a40													12 43
West Hampstead Thameslink	d										12 22														12 52
St Albans	d										12 45														13 15
Luton Airport Parkway	d										12 57														13 27
Luton	a										13 01														13 31

		SE		SE	SE	SE	SE	SE	SE	SE	TL	SE		SE	SE	SE	TL	SE	SE	SE	SE	SE		SE	SE
		◇										◇						◇							
Rainham	d	11 16									11 28							11 46							
Gillingham	d	11 21									11 34							11 51							
Chatham	d	11 25									11 38							11 55							
Rochester	d	11 29									11 42							11 59							
Strood	d	11 32									11 45	11 59						12 02							
Higham	d										11 50														
Gravesend	d	11 42		11 50							11 59			12 05				12 12	12 20						
Northfleet	d										12 02			12 08											
Swanscombe	d										12 04			12 10											
Greenhithe	d			11 56							12 08			12 14					12 26						
Stone Crossing	d										12 10			12 16											
Dartford	d			12 02						12 11	12 15			12 21			←		12 32						
Slade Green	d					11 59		12 07	12 09	12 16	12 21					←	12 21				12 29			12 37	12 39
Erith	d					12 02			12 12	12 18	→					12 18					12 32				12 42
Belvedere	d					12 04			12 14	→						12 21					12 34				12 44
Abbey Wood	d					12 08			12 18							12 24	12 28				12 38				12 48
Plumstead	d					12 11			12 21							12 27	12 31				12 41				12 51
Woolwich Arsenal	d					12 14			12 24							12 30	12 34				12 44				12 54
Woolwich Dockyard	d					12 16			12 26							12 33					12 46				12 56
Charlton	d					12 20			12 30							12 36	12 40				12 50				13 00
Westcombe Park	d					12 22			12 32								12 42				12 52				13 02
Maze Hill	d					12 24			12 34								12 44				12 54				13 04
Greenwich	d				12 17	12 27			12 37								12 47			12 47	12 57				13 07
Deptford	a					12 29			12 39								12 49				12 59				13 09
London Victoria	d			12a55			←								←				13a25			←			
London Bridge	d				13 39	12 37	12 39	12 54	12 47					12 52	12 54	12 57	12 58			14 09	13 07	13 09		13 24	13 17
London Cannon Street	d				→	12a41	12a43	→	12a51						13a00					→	13a11	13a13		→	13a21
Waterloo East	d													12 57		13 02									
London Charing Cross	a													13 00		13 05									
London Blackfriars	d																13 04								
City Thameslink	d																13 06								
Farringdon	d																13 09								
St Pancras International	d	12a05										14a54					13 13	12a36							
West Hampstead Thameslink	d																13 22								
St Albans	d																13 45								
Luton Airport Parkway	d																13 57								
Luton	a																14 01								

Table T201-R

Mondays to Fridays

21 May to 7 December

Medway - Woolwich - Greenwich - London Thameslink

		SE	TL	SE	SE	SE	TL	SE ◇	SE	SE	SE	SE	SE	SE	SE	TL	SE ◇	SE	SE	SE	TL	SE ◇	SE
Rainham	d		11 58					12 16								12 28						12 46	
Gillingham	d		12 04					12 21								12 34						12 51	
Chatham	d		12 08					12 25								12 38						12 55	
Rochester	d		12 12					12 29								12 42						12 59	
Strood	d		12 15					12 32								12 45	12 59					13 02	
Higham	d		12 20													12 50							
Gravesend	d		12 29	12 35				12 42	12 50							12 59		13 05				13 12	13 20
Northfleet	d		12 32	12 38												13 02		13 08					
Swanscombe	d		12 34	12 40												13 04		13 10					
Greenhithe	d		12 38	12 44					12 56							13 08		13 14					13 26
Stone Crossing	d		12 40	12 46												13 10		13 16					
Dartford	d	12 41	12 45	12 51			←		13 02						13 11	13 15		13 21			←		13 32
Slade Green	d	12 46	12 51			←	12 51				12 59		13 07	13 09	13 16	13 21				←	13 21		
Erith	d	12 48	→			12 48					13 02			13 12	13 18	→				13 18			
Belvedere	d	→				12 51					13 04			13 14	→					13 21			
Abbey Wood	d					12 54	12 58				13 08			13 18						13 24	13 28		
Plumstead	d					12 57	13 01				13 11			13 21						13 27	13 31		
Woolwich Arsenal	d					13 00	13 04				13 14			13 24						13 30	13 34		
Woolwich Dockyard	d					13 03					13 16			13 26						13 33			
Charlton	d					13 06	13 10				13 20			13 30						13 36	13 40		
Westcombe Park	d						13 12				13 22			13 32							13 42		
Maze Hill	d						13 14				13 24			13 34							13 44		
Greenwich	d						13 17			13 17	13 27			13 37							13 47		
Deptford	a						13 19				13 29			13 39							13 49		
London Victoria	d				←				13a55			←							←				14a25
London Bridge	d			13 22	13 24	13 27	13 28			14 39	13 37	13 39	13 54	13 47				13 52	13 54	13 57	13 58		
London Cannon Street	d				13a30					→	13a41	13a43	→	13a51					14a00				
Waterloo East	d			13 27		13 32												13 57		14 02			
London Charing Cross	a			13 30		13 35												14 00		14 05			
London Blackfriars	d						13 34														14 04		
City Thameslink	d						13 36														14 06		
Farringdon	d						13 39														14 09		
St Pancras International	d						13 43	13a06									15a54				14 13	13a37	
West Hampstead Thameslink	d						13 52														14 22		
St Albans	d						14 15														14 45		
Luton Airport Parkway	d						14 27														14 57		
Luton	a						14 31														15 01		

		SE	SE	SE	SE	SE	SE	TL	SE	SE	SE	TL	SE ◇	SE	SE	SE	SE	SE	SE	SE	TL	SE ◇
Rainham	d							12 58					13 16								13 28	
Gillingham	d							13 04					13 21								13 34	
Chatham	d							13 08					13 25								13 38	
Rochester	d							13 12					13 29								13 42	
Strood	d							13 15					13 32								13 45	13 59
Higham	d							13 20													13 50	
Gravesend	d							13 29	13 35				13 42	13 50							13 59	
Northfleet	d							13 32	13 38												14 02	
Swanscombe	d							13 34	13 40												14 04	
Greenhithe	d							13 38	13 44					13 56							14 08	
Stone Crossing	d							13 40	13 46												14 10	
Dartford	d						13 41	13 45	13 51			←		14 02						14 11	14 15	
Slade Green	d		13 29		13 37	13 39	13 46	13 51			←	13 51				13 59		14 07	14 09	14 16	14 21	
Erith	d		13 32			13 42	13 48	→			13 48					14 02			14 12	14 18	→	
Belvedere	d		13 34			13 44	→				13 51					14 04			14 14	→		
Abbey Wood	d		13 38			13 48					13 54	13 58				14 08			14 18			
Plumstead	d		13 41			13 51					13 57	14 01				14 11			14 21			
Woolwich Arsenal	d		13 44			13 54					14 00	14 04				14 14			14 24			
Woolwich Dockyard	d		13 46			13 56					14 03					14 16			14 26			
Charlton	d		13 50			14 00					14 06	14 10				14 20			14 30			
Westcombe Park	d		13 52			14 02						14 12				14 22			14 32			
Maze Hill	d		13 54			14 04						14 14				14 24			14 34			
Greenwich	d	13 47	13 57			14 07						14 17			14 17	14 27			14 37			
Deptford	a		13 59			14 09						14 19				14 29			14 39			
London Victoria	d			←						←				14a55			←					
London Bridge	d	15 09	14 07	14 09	14 24	14 17			14 22	14 24	14 27	14 28			15 39	14 37	14 39	14 54	14 47			
London Cannon Street	d	→	14a11	14a13	→	14a21				14a30					→	14a41	14a43	→	14a51			
Waterloo East	d								14 27		14 32											
London Charing Cross	a								14 30		14 35											
London Blackfriars	d											14 34										
City Thameslink	d											14 36										
Farringdon	d											14 39										
St Pancras International	d											14 43	14a10									16a54
West Hampstead Thameslink	d											14 52										
St Albans	d											15 15										
Luton Airport Parkway	d											15 27										
Luton	a											15 31										

Table T201-R

Mondays to Fridays

21 May to 7 December

Medway - Woolwich - Greenwich - London Thameslink

		SE	SE	SE	TL	SE ◇	SE	SE	SE	SE	SE	SE	SE	TL	SE	SE	SE	TL	SE ◇	SE	SE	SE	SE
Rainham	d					13 46								13 58					14 16				
Gillingham	d					13 51								14 04					14 21				
Chatham	d					13 55								14 08					14 25				
Rochester	d					13 59								14 12					14 29				
Strood	d					14 02								14 15					14 32				
Higham	d													14 20									
Gravesend	d	14 05				14 12	14 20							14 29	14 35				14 42	14 50			
Northfleet	d	14 08												14 32	14 38								
Swanscombe	d	14 10												14 34	14 40								
Greenhithe	d	14 14					14 26							14 38	14 44					14 56			
Stone Crossing	d	14 16												14 40	14 46								
Dartford	d	14 21			←		14 32						14 41	14 45	14 51			←		15 02			
Slade Green	d			←	14 21				14 29		14 37	14 39	14 46	14 51			←	14 51				14 59	
Erith	d			14 18					14 32			14 42	14 48	→			14 48					15 02	
Belvedere	d			14 21					14 34			14 44	→				14 51					15 04	
Abbey Wood	d			14 24	14 28				14 38			14 48					14 54	14 58				15 08	
Plumstead	d			14 27	14 31				14 41			14 51					14 57	15 01				15 11	
Woolwich Arsenal	d			14 30	14 34				14 44			14 54					15 00	15 04				15 14	
Woolwich Dockyard	d			14 33					14 46			14 56					15 03					15 16	
Charlton	d			14 36	14 40				14 50			15 00					15 06	15 10				15 20	
Westcombe Park	d				14 42				14 52			15 02						15 12				15 22	
Maze Hill	d				14 44				14 54			15 04						15 14				15 24	
Greenwich	d				14 47			14 47	14 57			15 07						15 17			15 17	15 27	
Deptford	a				14 49				14 59			15 09						15 19				15 29	
London Victoria	d		←				15a25			←						←				15a55			←
London Bridge	d	14 52	14 54	14 57	14 58			16 09	15 07	15 09	15 24	15 17			15 22	15 24	15 27	15 28			16 38	15 37	15 39
London Cannon Street	d		15a00					→	15a11	15a13	→	15a21				15a30					→	15a41	15a43
Waterloo East	d	14 57		15 02											15 27		15 32						
London Charing Cross	a	15 00		15 05											15 30		15 35						
London Blackfriars	d				15 04													15 34					
City Thameslink	d				15 06													15 36					
Farringdon	d				15 09													15 39					
St Pancras International	d				15 13	14a36												15 43	15a06				
West Hampstead Thameslink	d				15 22													15 52					
St Albans	d				15 45													16 19					
Luton Airport Parkway	d				15 57													16 32					
Luton	a				16 01													16 36					

		SE	SE	SE	TL	SE ◇	SE	SE	SE	TL	SE ◇	SE	SE	SE	SE	SE	SE	SE	TL	SE	SE	SE	TL
Rainham	d				14 28						14 46								14 58				
Gillingham	d				14 34						14 51								15 04				
Chatham	d				14 38						14 55								15 08				
Rochester	d				14 42						14 59								15 12				
Strood	d				14 45	14 59					15 02								15 15				
Higham	d				14 50														15 20				
Gravesend	d				14 59		15 05				15 12	15 20							15 29	15 35			
Northfleet	d				15 02		15 08												15 32	15 38			
Swanscombe	d				15 04		15 10												15 34	15 40			
Greenhithe	d				15 08		15 14					15 26							15 38	15 44			
Stone Crossing	d				15 10		15 16												15 40	15 46			
Dartford	d			15 11	15 15		15 21			←		15 32						15 41	15 45	15 51			←
Slade Green	d	15 07	15 09	15 16	15 21				←	15 21				15 29		15 37	15 39	15 46	15 51			←	15 51
Erith	d		15 12	15 18	→				15 18					15 32			15 42	15 48	→			15 48	
Belvedere	d		15 14	→					15 21					15 34			15 44	→				15 51	
Abbey Wood	d		15 18						15 24	15 28				15 38			15 48					15 54	15 58
Plumstead	d		15 21						15 27	15 31				15 41			15 51					15 57	16 01
Woolwich Arsenal	d		15 24						15 30	15 34				15 44			15 54					16 00	16 04
Woolwich Dockyard	d		15 26						15 33					15 46			15 56					16 03	
Charlton	d		15 30						15 36	15 40				15 50			16 00					16 06	16 10
Westcombe Park	d		15 32							15 42				15 52			16 02						16 12
Maze Hill	d		15 34							15 44				15 54			16 04						16 14
Greenwich	d		15 37							15 47			15 47	15 57			16 07						16 17
Deptford	a		15 39							15 49				15 59			16 09						16 19
London Victoria	d							←				16a25			←						←		
London Bridge	d	15 54	15 47				15 52	15 54	15 57	15 58			17 11	16 06	16 09	16 23	16 17			16 21	16 23	16 27	16 28
London Cannon Street	d	→	15a51					16a00					→	16a12	16a15	→	16a23				16a29		
Waterloo East	d						15 57		16 02											16 26		16 32	
London Charing Cross	a						16 00		16 05											16 30		16 36	
London Blackfriars	d									16 04													16 34
City Thameslink	d									16 06													16 36
Farringdon	d									16 09													16 39
St Pancras International	d					17a54				16 13	15a36												16 43
West Hampstead Thameslink	d									16 22													16 52
St Albans	d									16 47													17 17
Luton Airport Parkway	d									17 01													17 32
Luton	a									17 05													17 36

Please note, Network Rail have stated that further updates to this timetable are possible during the validity period.

Table T201-R

Mondays to Fridays

21 May to 7 December

Medway - Woolwich - Greenwich - London Thameslink

		SE		SE	SE	SE	SE	SE	SE	SE	SE	SE		SE	SE	SE	SE	SE	SE	SE	SE	SE		TL	SE
		◇					◇								◇										
Rainham	d	15 16													15 46									16 00	
Gillingham	d	15 21													15 51									16 06	
Chatham	d	15 25													15 55									16 10	
Rochester	d	15 29													15 59									16 14	
Strood	d	15 32					15 59								16 02									16 17	
Higham	d																							16 22	
Gravesend	d	15 42		15 50								16 03			16 12	16 20								16 29	16 35
Northfleet	d											16 06												16 33	16 38
Swanscombe	d											16 08												16 35	16 40
Greenhithe	d			15 56								16 12				16 26								16 38	16 44
Stone Crossing	d											16 14												16 40	16 46
Dartford	d			16 02							16 11	16 19		←		16 32					16 41			16 45	16 51
Slade Green	d				15 57			16 07	16 09		16 16			16 16			16 30		16 37	16 39	16 46	16 47		16 51	
Erith	d				16 00				16 12		→			16 18			16 32			16 42	16 48			→	
Belvedere	d				16 02				16 14					16 21			16 35			16 44	→				
Abbey Wood	d				16 06				16 18					16 24			16 38			16 48					
Plumstead	d				16 09				16 21					16 27			16 41			16 51					
Woolwich Arsenal	d				16 12				16 24					16 30			16 44			16 54					
Woolwich Dockyard	d				16 14				16 26					16 33			16 47			16 56					
Charlton	d				16 18				16 30					16 36			16 50			17 00					
Westcombe Park	d				16 20				16 32								16 52			17 02					
Maze Hill	d				16 22				16 34								16 54			17 04					
Greenwich	d				16 25				16 37								16 58			17 08					
Deptford	a				16 27				16 39								17 00			17 10					
London Victoria	d			16a55		←				←						17a25		←							
London Bridge	d				16 34	16 38		16 50	16 47	16 50		16 51		16 57			17 08	17 11		17 19					17 22
London Cannon Street	d				16a40	16a44		→	16a53	16a56							17a14	17a17	17a27	17a25		17a47			
Waterloo East	d											16 56		17 02											17 29
London Charing Cross	a											17 01		17 06											17 34
London Blackfriars	d																								
City Thameslink	d																								
Farringdon	d																								
St Pancras International	d	16a10					18a54								16a36										
West Hampstead Thameslink	d																								
St Albans	d																								
Luton Airport Parkway	d																								
Luton	a																								

		SE	TL	SE	SE	SE	SE	SE		SE	SE	SE	TL	SE	SE	TL	SE	SE		SE	SE	SE	SE	SE	SE
				◇													◇								
Rainham	d			16 16									16 30				16 46								
Gillingham	d			16 21									16 36				16 51								
Chatham	d			16 25									16 40				16 55								
Rochester	d			16 29									16 44				16 59								
Strood	d			16 32									16 47				17 02								
Higham	d												16 52												
Gravesend	d			16 42	16 50								16 59	17 05			17 12	17 18							
Northfleet	d												17 03	17 08											
Swanscombe	d												17 05	17 10											
Greenhithe	d				16 56								17 08	17 14				17 24							
Stone Crossing	d												17 10	17 16											
Dartford	d		←		17 02						17 11		17 15	17 21		←		17 30							17 39
Slade Green	d	←	16 51				16 58	17 06		17 10	17 16	17 19	17 21			17 21				17 29		17 34	17 40		17 46
Erith	d	16 48					17 00				17 18		→							17 32			17 43		17 48
Belvedere	d	16 51					17 03				17 21									17 34			17 45		→
Abbey Wood	d	16 54	16 58				17 06	17 12			17 24					17 28				17 38			17 49		
Plumstead	d	16 57	17 01				17 09				17 27					17 31							17 52		
Woolwich Arsenal	d	17 00	17 04				17 12	17 16			17 30					17 34				17 42			17 55		
Woolwich Dockyard	d	17 03					17 15				17 33												17 57		
Charlton	d	17 06	17 10				17 18	17 22			17 36					17 40				17 48			18 01		
Westcombe Park	d		17 12				17 20	17 24								17 42				17 50			18 03		
Maze Hill	d		17 14				17 22	17 26								17 44				17 52			18 05		
Greenwich	d		17 17			17 19	17 26	17 29								17 47				17 55			18 08		
Deptford	a		17 19				17 28	17 31								17 49				17 57			18 10		
London Victoria	d				17a55										←			18a25			←			←	
London Bridge	d	17 25	17 28			18 44	17 36	17 39		17 48	17 54	18 07		17 52	17 54	17 58				18 04	18 07	18 23	18 18	18 23	
London Cannon Street	d					→	17a42	17a45		17a52	→	→								18a10	18a13	→	18a24	18a27	
Waterloo East	d	17 32												17 57	17 59										
London Charing Cross	a	17 39												18 03	18 05										
London Blackfriars	d		17 34													18 04									
City Thameslink	d		17 36													18 06									
Farringdon	d		17 39													18 09									
St Pancras International	d		17 43	17a10												18 13	17a36								
West Hampstead Thameslink	d		17 52													18 22									
St Albans	d		18 20													18 47									
Luton Airport Parkway	d		18 31													19 01									
Luton	a		18 35													19 05									

Table T201-R

Mondays to Fridays

21 May to 7 December

Medway - Woolwich - Greenwich - London Thameslink

		TL	SE	SE		TL	SE	SE	SE	SE	SE	SE	SE	TL		SE	TL	SE	SE	SE	SE	SE	SE	SE
							◇												◇					
Rainham	d	17 00					17 16							17 28					17 46					
Gillingham	d	17 06					17 21							17 34					17 51					
Chatham	d	17 10					17 25							17 38					17 55					
Rochester	d	17 14					17 29							17 42					17 59					
Strood	d	17 17					17 32							17 47					18 03					
Higham	d	17 22												17 52										
Gravesend	d	17 29	17 35				17 42							17 59		18 05			18 13					
Northfleet	d	17 33	17 38											18 03		18 08								
Swanscombe	d	17 35	17 40											18 05		18 10								
Greenhithe	d	17 38	17 44											18 08		18 14								
Stone Crossing	d	17 40	17 46											18 10		18 16								
Dartford	d	17 45	17 51			←						18 02		18 15		18 21	←							
Slade Green	d	17 51		←		17 51			17 54	18 00		18 09	18 16	18 21			18 21			18 22		18 29		18 39
Erith	d	→		17 48					17 57	18 03		18 11	18 18	→								18 32		18 42
Belvedere	d			17 51					17 59	18 05		18 14	18 21									18 34		18 44
Abbey Wood	d			17 54		17 58			18 03	18 09		18 17	18 24				18 28					18 38		18 48
Plumstead	d			17 57		18 01			18 06	18 12		18 20	18 27				18 31					18 41		18 51
Woolwich Arsenal	d			18 00		18 04			18 09	18 15		18 23	18 30				18 34					18 44		18 54
Woolwich Dockyard	d			18 03					18 11	18 17		18 26	18 33									18 46		18 56
Charlton	d			18 06		18 10			18 15	18 21		18 29	18 36				18 40					18 50		19 00
Westcombe Park	d					18 12			18 17	18 23		18 31					18 42					18 52		19 02
Maze Hill	d					18 14			18 19	18 25		18 33					18 44					18 54		19 04
Greenwich	d					18 17		18 18	18 22	18 28		18 37					18 47				18 49	18 57		19 08
Deptford	a					18 19			18 24	18 30		18 39					18 49					18 59		19 10
London Victoria	d										←							←					←	
London Bridge	d		18 24	18 28		18 28		19 40	18 31	18 38	18 44	18 49	19 00			18 53	18 58	19 00		19 17	20 09	19 09	19 17	19 20
London Cannon Street	d							→	18a37	18a44	18a50	18a54	→							→	→	19a15	19a21	19a24
Waterloo East	d		18 29	18 33												18 58		19 06						
London Charing Cross	a		18 34	18 38												19 02		19 09						
London Blackfriars	d					18 34											19 04							
City Thameslink	d					18 36											19 06							
Farringdon	d					18 39											19 09							
St Pancras International	d					18 43	18a10										19 13		18a37					
West Hampstead Thameslink	d					18 52											19 22							
St Albans	d					19 17											19 50							
Luton Airport Parkway	d					19 32											20 02							
Luton	a					19 36											20 06							

		SE	SE	SE	TL	SE	SE	SE	TL	SE		SE	SE	SE	SE	SE	SE	TL	SE	SE		SE	TL	SE	SE
										◇														◇	◇
Rainham	d				18 00					18 16								18 30							18 46
Gillingham	d				18 06					18 21								18 36							18 51
Chatham	d				18 10					18 25								18 40							18 55
Rochester	d				18 14					18 29								18 44							18 59
Strood	d				18 18					18 35								18 47						18 58	19 02
Higham	d				18 23													18 52							
Gravesend	d				18 30	18 35				18 45				18 51				18 59	19 05					19 08	19 12
Northfleet	d				18 33	18 38												19 03	19 08						
Swanscombe	d				18 35	18 40												19 05	19 10						
Greenhithe	d				18 39	18 44								18 58				19 08	19 14						
Stone Crossing	d				18 41	18 46												19 10	19 16						
Dartford	d		18 42		18 46	18 52			←					19 07				19 15	19 21				←		
Slade Green	d	18 43	18 48		18 51				18 51			18 59			19 01	19 09	19 16	19 21				←	19 21		
Erith	d	18 46	18 50		→							19 02				19 12	19 18	→				19 18			
Belvedere	d	18 48	18 53									19 04				19 14	→					19 21			
Abbey Wood	d	18 52	18 56						18 59			19 08				19 18						19 24	19 28		
Plumstead	d	18 55	18 59						19 02			19 11				19 21						19 27	19 31		
Woolwich Arsenal	d	18 58	19 02						19 05			19 14				19 24						19 30	19 34		
Woolwich Dockyard	d	19 00	19 04									19 16				19 26						19 33			
Charlton	d	19 04	19 07						19 10			19 20				19 30						19 36	19 40		
Westcombe Park	d	19 06							19 12			19 22				19 32							19 42		
Maze Hill	d	19 09							19 14			19 24				19 34							19 44		
Greenwich	d	19 13		19 17					19 18			19 27				19 37							19 47		
Deptford	a	19 15							19 20			19 29				19 39							19 49		
London Victoria	d						←	←					←							←					
London Bridge	d	19 25	19 28	20 39		19 23	19 25	19 28	19 28			19 37	19 40	19 45	19 54	19 47			19 53	19 54		19 57	19 58		
London Cannon Street	d	→	→	→			19a30					19a43	19a46		→	19a51				19a58					
Waterloo East	d					19 28		19 33						19 50					19 58			20 02			
London Charing Cross	a					19 31		19 36						19 53					20 01			20 05			
London Blackfriars	d								19 34														20 04		
City Thameslink	d								19 36														20 06		
Farringdon	d								19 39														20 09		
St Pancras International	d								19 43	19a10													20 13	19a31	19a36
West Hampstead Thameslink	d								19 52														20 22		
St Albans	d								20 17														20 45		
Luton Airport Parkway	d								20 32														20 57		
Luton	a								20 36														21 01		

Table T201-R

Mondays to Fridays
21 May to 7 December

Medway - Woolwich - Greenwich - London Thameslink

		SE	SE	SE	SE	SE	SE	SE	TL	SE	SE	SE	TL	SE ◇	SE	SE	SE	SE	SE	SE	TL	SE	SE
Rainham	d								18 58					19 16							19 28		
Gillingham	d								19 04					19 21							19 34		
Chatham	d								19 08					19 25							19 38		
Rochester	d								19 12					19 29							19 42		
Strood	d								19 15					19 32							19 45		
Higham	d								19 20												19 50		
Gravesend	d	19 18							19 29	19 35				19 42							19 59	20 05	
Northfleet	d								19 32	19 38											20 02	20 08	
Swanscombe	d								19 34	19 40											20 04	20 10	
Greenhithe	d	19 26							19 38	19 44											20 08	20 14	
Stone Crossing	d								19 40	19 46											20 10	20 16	
Dartford	d	19 32						19 41	19 45	19 51			←							20 11	20 15	20 21	
Slade Green	d			19 29		19 39	19 39	19 46	19 51			←	19 51			19 59		20 07	20 09	20 16	20 21		
Erith	d			19 32		19 42		19 48	→			19 48				20 02			20 12	20 18	→		
Belvedere	d			19 34		19 44		→				19 51				20 04			20 14	→			
Abbey Wood	d			19 38		19 48						19 54	19 58			20 08			20 18				
Plumstead	d			19 41		19 51						19 57	20 01			20 11			20 21				
Woolwich Arsenal	d			19 44		19 54						20 00	20 04			20 14			20 24				
Woolwich Dockyard	d			19 46		19 56						20 03				20 16			20 26				
Charlton	d			19 50		20 00						20 06	20 10			20 20			20 30				
Westcombe Park	d			19 52		20 02							20 12			20 22			20 32				
Maze Hill	d			19 54		20 04							20 14			20 24			20 34				
Greenwich	d		19 47	19 57		20 07							20 17		20 17	20 27			20 37				
Deptford	a			19 59		20 09							20 19			20 29			20 39				
London Victoria	d	20a25			←						←						←						←
London Bridge	d		21 09	20 07	20 09	20 17	20 24			20 22	20 24	20 27	20 28		21 39	20 37	20 39	20 54	20 47			20 52	20 54
London Cannon Street	d		→	20a11	20a15	20a21	→				20a30				→	20a41	20a43	→	20a51				21a00
Waterloo East	d									20 27		20 32										20 57	
London Charing Cross	a									20 30		20 35										21 00	
London Blackfriars	d												20 34										
City Thameslink	d												20 36										
Farringdon	d												20 39										
St Pancras International	d												20 43	20a07									
West Hampstead Thameslink	d												20 52										
St Albans	d												21 15										
Luton Airport Parkway	d												21 27										
Luton	a												21 31										

		SE	TL	SE ◇	SE	SE	SE	SE	SE	TL	SE	SE	TL	SE ◇	SE	SE	SE	SE	SE	SE	TL	SE
Rainham	d			19 46						19 58				20 16							20 28	
Gillingham	d			19 51						20 04				20 21							20 34	
Chatham	d			19 55						20 08				20 25							20 38	
Rochester	d			19 59						20 12				20 29							20 42	
Strood	d			20 02						20 15				20 32							20 45	
Higham	d									20 20											20 50	
Gravesend	d			20 12	20 20					20 29	20 35			20 42	20 50						20 59	21 05
Northfleet	d									20 32	20 38										21 02	21 08
Swanscombe	d									20 34	20 40										21 04	21 10
Greenhithe	d				20 26					20 38	20 44				20 56						21 08	21 14
Stone Crossing	d									20 40	20 46										21 10	21 16
Dartford	d		←		20 32				20 41	20 45	20 51		←		21 02				21 11		21 15	21 21
Slade Green	d	←	20 21				20 29		20 46	20 51		←	20 51				20 59		21 16		21 21	
Erith	d	20 18					20 32		20 48	→		20 48					21 02		21 18		→	
Belvedere	d	20 21					20 34		→			20 51					21 04		21 21			
Abbey Wood	d	20 24	20 28				20 38					20 54	20 58				21 08		21 24			
Plumstead	d	20 27	20 31				20 41					20 57	21 01				21 11		21 27			
Woolwich Arsenal	d	20 30	20 34				20 44					21 00	21 04				21 14		21 30			
Woolwich Dockyard	d	20 33					20 46					21 03					21 16		21 33			
Charlton	d	20 36	20 40				20 50					21 06	21 10				21 20		21 36			
Westcombe Park	d		20 42				20 52						21 12				21 22					
Maze Hill	d		20 44				20 54						21 14				21 24					
Greenwich	d		20 47			20 47	20 57						21 17			21 17	21 27			21 44		
Deptford	a		20 49				20 59						21 19				21 29					
London Victoria	d				21a25			←							21a55			←				
London Bridge	d	20 57	20 58			22 09	21 07	21 09			21 22	21 27	21 28			22 39	21 37	21 39	21 57	23 09		21 52
London Cannon Street	d					→	21a11	21a13								→	21a41	21a43	→	→		
Waterloo East	d	21 02									21 27	21 32										21 57
London Charing Cross	a	21 05									21 30	21 35										22 00
London Blackfriars	d		21 04										21 34									
City Thameslink	d		21 06										21 36									
Farringdon	d		21 09										21 39									
St Pancras International	d		21 13	20a36									21 43	21a10								
West Hampstead Thameslink	d		21 24										21 52									
St Albans	d		21 48										22 15									
Luton Airport Parkway	d		22 02										22 27									
Luton	a		22 06										22 30									

Table T201-R

Mondays to Fridays
21 May to 7 December

Medway - Woolwich - Greenwich - London Thameslink

		SE	TL	SE ◇	SE	SE	SE	SE	SE MT FO	TL	SE	SE	TL	SE ◇	SE	SE	SE	SE	SE MT FO	TL	SE	SE	TL
Rainham	d			20 46						20 58				21 16						21 28			
Gillingham	d			20 51						21 04				21 21						21 34			
Chatham	d			20 55						21 08				21 25						21 38			
Rochester	d			20 59						21 12				21 29						21 42			
Strood	d			21 02						21 15				21 32						21 45			
Higham	d									21 20										21 50			
Gravesend	d			21 12	21 20					21 29	21 35			21 42	21 50					21 59	22 05		
Northfleet	d									21 32	21 38									22 02	22 08		
Swanscombe	d									21 34	21 40									22 04	22 10		
Greenhithe	d				21 26					21 38	21 44				21 56					22 08	22 14		
Stone Crossing	d									21 40	21 46									22 10	22 16		
Dartford	d		←		21 32			21 41		21 45	21 51		←		22 02			22 11		22 15	22 21		←
Slade Green	d		21 21			21 29		21 46		21 51			21 51			21 59		22 16		22 21			22 21
Erith	d					21 32		21 48		→						22 02		22 18		→			
Belvedere	d					21 34		21 51								22 04		22 21					
Abbey Wood	d		21 28			21 38		21 54					21 58			22 08		22 24					22 28
Plumstead	d		21 31			21 41		21 57					22 01			22 11		22 27					22 31
Woolwich Arsenal	d		21 34			21 44		22 00					22 04			22 14		22 30					22 34
Woolwich Dockyard	d					21 46		22 03								22 16		22 33					
Charlton	d		21 40			21 50		22 06					22 10			22 20		22 36					22 40
Westcombe Park	d		21 42			21 52							22 12			22 22							22 42
Maze Hill	d		21 44			21 54							22 14			22 24							22 44
Greenwich	d		21 47			21 57			22 14				22 17			22 27			22 44				22 47
Deptford	a		21 49			21 59							22 19			22 29							22 49
London Victoria	d	←			22a25		←					←			22a55		←					←	
London Bridge	d	21 57	21 58			22 07	22 09	22 27	23 39		22 22	22 27	22 28			22 37	22 39	22 57	00 09		22 52	22 57	22 58
London Cannon Street	d					22a11	22a13	→	→							22a41	22a43	→	→				
Waterloo East	d	22 02									22 27	22 32									22 57	23 02	
London Charing Cross	a	22 05									22 30	22 35									23 00	23 05	
London Blackfriars	d		22 04										22 34										23 04
City Thameslink	d		22 06										22 36										
Farringdon	d		22 09										22 39										23 09
St Pancras International	d		22 13	21a39									22 43	22a06									23 13
West Hampstead Thameslink	d		22 22										22a51										23a21
St Albans	d		22 45																				
Luton Airport Parkway	d		22 57																				
Luton	a		23 01																				

		SE ◇	SE	SE	SE	SE	SE W ThO	TL	SE	SE	TL	SE ◇	SE	SE	SE MT FO	SE W ThO	SE	TL	SE	SE	SE MT FO	SE MT FO
Rainham	d	21 46						22 00				22 16						22 30				
Gillingham	d	21 51						22 06				22 21						22 36				
Chatham	d	21 55						22 10				22 25						22 40				
Rochester	d	21 59						22 14				22 29						22 44				
Strood	d	22 02						22 17				22 32						22 47				
Higham	d							22 22										22 52				
Gravesend	d	22 12	22 20					22 29	22 35			22 42	22 50					22 59	23 05			
Northfleet	d							22 33	22 38									23 03	23 08			
Swanscombe	d							22 35	22 40									23 05	23 10			
Greenhithe	d		22 26					22 38	22 44				22 56					23 08	23 14			
Stone Crossing	d							22 40	22 46									23 10	23 16			
Dartford	d		22 32			22 41		22 45	22 51		←		23 02				23 11	23a15	23 21	←		
Slade Green	d			22 29		22 46	22 46	22 51		←	22 51			22 59			23 16			23 16	23 29	
Erith	d			22 32		22 48		→		22 48				23 02			→			23 18	23 32	
Belvedere	d			22 34		→				22 51				23 04						23 21	23 34	
Abbey Wood	d			22 38						22 54	22 58			23 08						23 24	23 38	
Plumstead	d			22 41						22 57	23 01			23 11						23 27	23 41	
Woolwich Arsenal	d			22 44						23 00	23 04			23 14						23 30	23 44	
Woolwich Dockyard	d			22 46						23 03				23 16						23 33	23 46	
Charlton	d			22 50						23 06	23 10			23 20						23 36	23 50	
Westcombe Park	d			22 52							23 12			23 22							23 52	
Maze Hill	d			22 54							23 14			23 24							23 54	
Greenwich	d			22 57							23 17			23 27							23 57	
Deptford	a			22 59							23 19			23 29							23 59	
London Victoria	d		23a25		←								23a55		←	←						←
London Bridge	d			23 07	23 09		23a41		23 22	23 27	23 28			23 37	23 39	23a41			23 52	23 57	00 07	00 09
London Cannon Street	d			23a11	23a13		→							23a41	23a43						00a11	00a13
Waterloo East	d								23 27	23 32									23 57	00 02		
London Charing Cross	a								23 30	23 35									00 01	00 05		
London Blackfriars	d										23 34											
City Thameslink	d																					
Farringdon	d										23 39											
St Pancras International	d	22a36									23 43	23a06										
West Hampstead Thameslink	d										23a51											
St Albans	d																					
Luton Airport Parkway	d																					
Luton	a																					

Please note, Network Rail have stated that further updates to this timetable are possible during the validity period.

Table T201-R

Mondays to Fridays
21 May to 7 December

Medway - Woolwich - Greenwich - London Thameslink

		SE MTO	SE WThFO	SE MTO	TL	SE MTO	TL
Rainham	d				23 00		23 30
Gillingham	d				23 06		23 36
Chatham	d				23 10		23 40
Rochester	d				23 14		23 44
Strood	d				23 17		23 47
Higham	d				23 22		23 52
Gravesend	d				23 29	23 35	23 59
Northfleet	d				23 33	23 38	00 03
Swanscombe	d				23 35	23 40	00 05
Greenhithe	d				23 38	23 44	00 08
Stone Crossing	d				23 40	23 46	00 10
Dartford	d	23 41	23 41	23 41	23a45	23 51	00a15
Slade Green	d	23 46	23 46	23 46			
Erith	d	23 48	23 48	23 48			
Belvedere	d	23 51	23 51	23 51			
Abbey Wood	d	23 54	23 54	23 54			
Plumstead	d	23 57	23 57	23 57			
Woolwich Arsenal	d	23 59	23 59	23 59			
Woolwich Dockyard	d	00 03	00 03	00 03			
Charlton	d	00 06	00 06	00 06			
Westcombe Park	d						
Maze Hill	d						
Greenwich	d						
Deptford	a						
London Victoria	d						
London Bridge	d	00 25	00 25	00 26		00a29	
London Cannon Street	d	00a33					
Waterloo East	d		00 30	00 31			
London Charing Cross	a		00 35	00 34			
London Blackfriars	d						
City Thameslink	d						
Farringdon	d						
St Pancras International	d						
West Hampstead Thameslink	d						
St Albans	d						
Luton Airport Parkway	d						
Luton	a						

Saturdays
26 May to 8 December

		TL	SE	SE	TL	SE	SE	SE	SE	TL
Rainham	d									
Gillingham	d	04 06			04 36					05 06
Chatham	d	04 10			04 40					05 10
Rochester	d	04 14			04 44					05 14
Strood	d	04 17			04 47					05 17
Higham	d	04 22			04 52					05 22
Gravesend	d	04 29			04 59	05 18				05 29
Northfleet	d	04 33			05 03	05 22				05 33
Swanscombe	d	04 35			05 05	05 24				05 35
Greenhithe	d	04 38			05 08	05 27				05 38
Stone Crossing	d	04 40			05 10	05 29				05 40
Dartford	d	04a45		05 03	05 15	05 35			05 41	05 45
Slade Green	d			05 09	05 21			05 39	05 46	05 51
Erith	d			05 12				05 42	05 48	
Belvedere	d			05 14				05 44	05 51	
Abbey Wood	d			05 18	05 28			05 48	05 54	05 58
Plumstead	d			05 21	05 31			05 51	05 57	06 01
Woolwich Arsenal	d			05 24	05 34			05 54	06 00	06 04
Woolwich Dockyard	d			05 26				05 56	06 03	
Charlton	d			05 30	05 40			06 00	06 06	06 10
Westcombe Park	d			05 32	05 42			06 02		06 12
Maze Hill	d			05 34	05 44			06 04		06 14
Greenwich	d		05 17	05 37	05 47		05 47	06 07		06 17
Deptford	a			05 39	05 49			06 09		06 19
London Victoria	d									
London Bridge	d		06 39	05 47	05 58	06 15	07 09	06 17	06 27	06 28
London Cannon Street	d		→	05a51			→	06a21		
Waterloo East	d					06 20			06 32	
London Charing Cross	a					06 23			06 35	
London Blackfriars	d				06 04					06 34
City Thameslink	d									
Farringdon	d				06 09					06 39
St Pancras International	d				06 13					06 43
West Hampstead Thameslink	d				06 22					06 52
St Albans	d				06 46					07 15
Luton Airport Parkway	d				06 57					07 27
Luton	a				07 01					07 31

		SE	SE	SE	SE	SE	TL	SE	SE ◇	SE	SE	SE	SE	TL
Rainham	d						05 28		05 46					05 58
Gillingham	d						05 34		05 51					06 04
Chatham	d						05 38		05 55					06 08
Rochester	d						05 42		05 59					06 12
Strood	d						05 45		06 02					06 15
Higham	d						05 50							06 20
Gravesend	d		05 48				05 59		06 12	06 18				06 29
Northfleet	d		05 52				06 02			06 22				06 32
Swanscombe	d		05 54				06 04			06 24				06 34
Greenhithe	d		05 57				06 08			06 27				06 38
Stone Crossing	d		05 59				06 10			06 29				06 40
Dartford	d		06 05			06 11	06 15			06 35			06 41	06 45
Slade Green	d				06 09	06 16	06 21					06 39	06 46	06 51
Erith	d				06 12	06 18						06 42	06 48	→
Belvedere	d				06 14	06 21						06 44	→	
Abbey Wood	d				06 18	06 24	06 28					06 48		
Plumstead	d				06 21	06 27	06 31					06 51		
Woolwich Arsenal	d				06 24	06 30	06 34					06 54		
Woolwich Dockyard	d				06 26	06 33						06 56		
Charlton	d				06 30	06 36	06 40					07 00		
Westcombe Park	d				06 32		06 42					07 02		
Maze Hill	d				06 34		06 44					07 04		
Greenwich	d			06 17	06 37		06 47				06 47	07 07		
Deptford	a				06 39		06 49					07 09		
London Victoria	d	←						←						
London Bridge	d	06 39	06 45	07 39	06 47	06 57	06 58	07 09		07 15	08 09	07 17		
London Cannon Street	d	06a43		→	06a51			07a13			→	07a21		
Waterloo East	d		06 50			07 02				07 20				
London Charing Cross	a		06 53			07 05				07 23				
London Blackfriars	d						07 04							
City Thameslink	d													
Farringdon	d						07 09							
St Pancras International	d						07 13		06a36					
West Hampstead Thameslink	d						07 22							
St Albans	d						07 45							
Luton Airport Parkway	d						07 57							
Luton	a						08 01							

Table T201-R

Saturdays
26 May to 8 December

Medway - Woolwich - Greenwich - London Thameslink

		SE	SE	TL	SE	SE	SE	SE	SE	SE	TL	SE
Rainham	d										06 28	
Gillingham	d										06 34	
Chatham	d										06 38	
Rochester	d										06 42	
Strood	d										06 45	
Higham	d										06 50	
Gravesend	d	06 35			06 50						06 59	07 05
Northfleet	d	06 38									07 02	07 08
Swanscombe	d	06 40									07 04	07 10
Greenhithe	d	06 44			06 56						07 08	07 14
Stone Crossing	d	06 46									07 10	07 16
Dartford	d	06 51		←	07 02					07 11	07 15	07 21
Slade Green	d		←	06 51			06 59		07 09	07 16	07 21	
Erith	d		06 48				07 02		07 12	07 18	→	
Belvedere	d		06 51				07 04		07 14	→		
Abbey Wood	d		06 54	06 58			07 08		07 18			
Plumstead	d		06 57	07 01			07 11		07 21			
Woolwich Arsenal	d		07 00	07 04			07 14		07 24			
Woolwich Dockyard	d		07 03				07 16		07 26			
Charlton	d		07 06	07 10			07 20		07 30			
Westcombe Park	d			07 12			07 22		07 32			
Maze Hill	d			07 14			07 24		07 34			
Greenwich	d			07 17		07 17	07 27		07 37			
Deptford	a			07 19			07 29		07 39			
London Victoria	d				07a55			←				
London Bridge	d	07 22	07 27	07 28		08 39	07 37	07 39	07 47			07 52
London Cannon Street	d					→	07a41	07a43	07a51			
Waterloo East	d	07 27	07 32									07 57
London Charing Cross	a	07 30	07 35									08 00
London Blackfriars	d			07 34								
City Thameslink	d											
Farringdon	d			07 39								
St Pancras International	d			07 43								
West Hampstead Thameslink	d			07 52								
St Albans	d			08 15								
Luton Airport Parkway	d			08 27								
Luton	a			08 31								

		SE	TL	SE ◇	SE	SE	SE	SE	SE	SE	TL	SE
Rainham	d			06 46							06 58	
Gillingham	d			06 51							07 04	
Chatham	d			06 55							07 08	
Rochester	d			06 59							07 12	
Strood	d			07 02							07 15	
Higham	d										07 20	
Gravesend	d			07 12	07 20						07 29	07 35
Northfleet	d										07 32	07 38
Swanscombe	d										07 34	07 40
Greenhithe	d				07 26						07 38	07 44
Stone Crossing	d										07 40	07 46
Dartford	d		←		07 32					07 41	07 45	07 51
Slade Green	d	←	07 21				07 29		07 39	07 46	07 51	
Erith	d	07 18					07 32		07 42	07 48	→	
Belvedere	d	07 21					07 34		07 44	→		
Abbey Wood	d	07 24	07 28				07 38		07 48			
Plumstead	d	07 27	07 31				07 41		07 51			
Woolwich Arsenal	d	07 30	07 34				07 44		07 54			
Woolwich Dockyard	d	07 33					07 46		07 56			
Charlton	d	07 36	07 40				07 50		08 00			
Westcombe Park	d		07 42				07 52		08 02			
Maze Hill	d		07 44				07 54		08 04			
Greenwich	d		07 47			07 47	07 57		08 07			
Deptford	a		07 49				07 59		08 09			
London Victoria	d				08a25			←				
London Bridge	d	07 57	07 58			09 09	08 07	08 09	08 17			08 22
London Cannon Street	d					→	08a11	08a13	08a21			
Waterloo East	d	08 02										08 27
London Charing Cross	a	08 05										08 30
London Blackfriars	d		08 04									
City Thameslink	d											
Farringdon	d		08 09									
St Pancras International	d		08 13	07a36								
West Hampstead Thameslink	d		08 22									
St Albans	d		08 45									
Luton Airport Parkway	d		08 57									
Luton	a		09 01									

		SE	TL	SE ◇	SE	SE	SE	SE	SE	SE	TL
Rainham	d			07 16							07 28
Gillingham	d			07 21							07 34
Chatham	d			07 25							07 38
Rochester	d			07 29							07 42
Strood	d			07 32							07 45
Higham	d										07 50
Gravesend	d			07 42	07 50						07 59
Northfleet	d										08 02
Swanscombe	d										08 04
Greenhithe	d				07 56						08 08
Stone Crossing	d										08 10
Dartford	d		←		08 02					08 11	08 15
Slade Green	d	←	07 51				07 59		08 09	08 16	08 21
Erith	d	07 48					08 02		08 12	08 18	→
Belvedere	d	07 51					08 04		08 14	→	
Abbey Wood	d	07 54	07 58				08 08		08 18		
Plumstead	d	07 57	08 01				08 11		08 21		
Woolwich Arsenal	d	08 00	08 04				08 14		08 24		
Woolwich Dockyard	d	08 03					08 16		08 26		
Charlton	d	08 06	08 10				08 20		08 30		
Westcombe Park	d		08 12				08 22		08 32		
Maze Hill	d		08 14				08 24		08 34		
Greenwich	d		08 17			08 17	08 27		08 37		
Deptford	a		08 19				08 29		08 39		
London Victoria	d				08a55			←			
London Bridge	d	08 27	08 28			09 39	08 37	08 39	08 47		
London Cannon Street	d					→	08a41	08a43	08a51		
Waterloo East	d	08 32									
London Charing Cross	a	08 35									
London Blackfriars	d		08 34								
City Thameslink	d										
Farringdon	d		08 39								
St Pancras International	d		08 43	08a06							
West Hampstead Thameslink	d		08 52								
St Albans	d		09 15								
Luton Airport Parkway	d		09 27								
Luton	a		09 31								

		SE ◇	SE	SE	TL	SE ◇	SE	SE	SE	SE	SE	SE
Rainham	d					07 46						
Gillingham	d					07 51						
Chatham	d					07 55						
Rochester	d					07 59						
Strood	d	07 59				08 02						
Higham	d											
Gravesend	d		08 05			08 12	08 20					
Northfleet	d		08 08									
Swanscombe	d		08 10									
Greenhithe	d		08 14				08 26					
Stone Crossing	d		08 16									
Dartford	d		08 21		←		08 32					
Slade Green	d			←	08 21				08 29		08 37	08 39
Erith	d			08 18					08 32			08 42
Belvedere	d			08 21					08 34			08 44
Abbey Wood	d			08 24	08 28				08 38			08 48
Plumstead	d			08 27	08 31				08 41			08 51
Woolwich Arsenal	d			08 30	08 34				08 44			08 54
Woolwich Dockyard	d			08 33					08 46			08 56
Charlton	d			08 36	08 40				08 50			09 00
Westcombe Park	d				08 42				08 52			09 02
Maze Hill	d				08 44				08 54			09 04
Greenwich	d				08 47			08 47	08 57			09 07
Deptford	a				08 49				08 59			09 09
London Victoria	d						09a25			←		
London Bridge	d		08 52	08 57	08 58			10 09	09 07	09 09	09 24	09 17
London Cannon Street	d							→	09a11	09a13	→	09a21
Waterloo East	d		08 57	09 02								
London Charing Cross	a		09 00	09 05								
London Blackfriars	d				09 04							
City Thameslink	d				09 06							
Farringdon	d				09 09							
St Pancras International	d	10a55			09 13	08a36						
West Hampstead Thameslink	d				09 22							
St Albans	d				09 45							
Luton Airport Parkway	d				09 57							
Luton	a				10 01							

Table T201-R

Saturdays

26 May to 8 December

Medway - Woolwich - Greenwich - London Thameslink

		SE	TL	SE	SE	SE	TL	SE		SE	SE	SE	SE	SE	SE	SE	TL	SE		SE	SE	SE	TL	SE	SE
								◇										◇						◇	
Rainham	d		07 58					08 16									08 28							08 46	
Gillingham	d		08 04					08 21									08 34							08 51	
Chatham	d		08 08					08 25									08 38							08 55	
Rochester	d		08 12					08 29									08 42							08 59	
Strood	d		08 15					08 32									08 45	08 59						09 02	
Higham	d		08 20														08 50								
Gravesend	d		08 29	08 35				08 42		08 50							08 59			09 05				09 12	09 20
Northfleet	d		08 32	08 38													09 02			09 08					
Swanscombe	d		08 34	08 40													09 04			09 10					
Greenhithe	d		08 38	08 44						08 56							09 08			09 14					09 26
Stone Crossing	d		08 40	08 46													09 10			09 16					
Dartford	d	08 41	08 45	08 51			←			09 02						09 11	09 15			09 21			←		09 32
Slade Green	d	08 46	08 51			←	08 51					08 59		09 07	09 09	09 16	09 21					←	09 21		
Erith	d	08 48	→			08 48						09 02			09 12	09 18	→					09 18			
Belvedere	d	→				08 51						09 04			09 14	→						09 21			
Abbey Wood	d					08 54	08 58					09 08			09 18							09 24	09 28		
Plumstead	d					08 57	09 01					09 11			09 21							09 27	09 31		
Woolwich Arsenal	d					09 00	09 04					09 14			09 24							09 30	09 34		
Woolwich Dockyard	d					09 03						09 16			09 26							09 33			
Charlton	d					09 06	09 10					09 20			09 30							09 36	09 40		
Westcombe Park	d						09 12					09 22			09 32								09 42		
Maze Hill	d						09 14					09 24			09 34								09 44		
Greenwich	d						09 17				09 17	09 27			09 37								09 47		
Deptford	a						09 19					09 29			09 39								09 49		
London Victoria	d				←					09a55			←								←				10a25
London Bridge	d			09 22	09 24	09 27	09 28				10 39	09 37	09 39	09 54	09 47					09 52	09 54	09 57	09 58		
London Cannon Street	d				09a30						→	09a41	09a43	→	09a51						10a00				
Waterloo East	d			09 27		09 32														09 57		10 02			
London Charing Cross	a			09 30		09 35														10 00		10 05			
London Blackfriars	d						09 34																10 04		
City Thameslink	d						09 36																10 06		
Farringdon	d						09 39																10 09		
St Pancras International	d						09 43	09a06										11a54					10 13	09a36	
West Hampstead Thameslink	d						09 52																10 22		
St Albans	d						10 15																10 45		
Luton Airport Parkway	d						10 27																10 57		
Luton	a						10 31																11 01		

		SE	SE	SE		SE	SE	SE	TL	SE	SE	SE	TL	SE		SE	SE	SE	SE	SE	SE	SE	TL	SE	
														◇										◇	
Rainham	d								08 58					09 16									09 28		
Gillingham	d								09 04					09 21									09 34		
Chatham	d								09 08					09 25									09 38		
Rochester	d								09 12					09 29									09 42		
Strood	d								09 15					09 32									09 45	09 59	
Higham	d								09 20														09 50		
Gravesend	d								09 29	09 35				09 42		09 50							09 59		
Northfleet	d								09 32	09 38													10 02		
Swanscombe	d								09 34	09 40													10 04		
Greenhithe	d								09 38	09 44						09 56							10 08		
Stone Crossing	d								09 40	09 46													10 10		
Dartford	d							09 41	09 45	09 51			←			10 02						10 11	10 15		
Slade Green	d		09 29			09 37	09 39	09 46	09 51			←	09 51					09 59		10 08	10 09	10 16	10 21		
Erith	d		09 32				09 42	09 48	→			09 48						10 02			10 12	10 18	→		
Belvedere	d		09 34				09 44	→				09 51						10 04			10 14	→			
Abbey Wood	d		09 38				09 48					09 54	09 58					10 08			10 18				
Plumstead	d		09 41				09 51					09 57	10 01					10 11			10 21				
Woolwich Arsenal	d		09 44				09 54					10 00	10 04					10 14			10 24				
Woolwich Dockyard	d		09 46				09 56					10 03						10 16			10 26				
Charlton	d		09 50				10 00					10 06	10 10					10 20			10 30				
Westcombe Park	d		09 52				10 02						10 12					10 22			10 32				
Maze Hill	d		09 54				10 04						10 14					10 24			10 34				
Greenwich	d	09 47	09 57				10 07						10 17				10 17	10 27			10 37				
Deptford	a		09 59				10 09						10 19					10 29			10 39				
London Victoria	d			←							←					10a55			←						
London Bridge	d	11 09	10 07	10 09		10 24	10 17			10 22	10 24	10 27	10 28				11 39	10 37	10 39	10 54	10 47				
London Cannon Street	d	→	10a11	10a13		→	10a21				10a30						→	10a41	10a43	→	10a51				
Waterloo East	d									10 27		10 32													
London Charing Cross	a									10 30		10 35													
London Blackfriars	d												10 34												
City Thameslink	d												10 36												
Farringdon	d												10 39												
St Pancras International	d												10 43	10a06										12a55	
West Hampstead Thameslink	d												10 52												
St Albans	d												11 15												
Luton Airport Parkway	d												11 27												
Luton	a												11 31												

Table T201-R

Saturdays

26 May to 8 December

Medway - Woolwich - Greenwich - London Thameslink

		SE	SE	SE	TL	SE	SE	SE	SE	SE		SE	SE	SE	TL	SE	SE	SE	TL	SE		SE	SE	SE	SE
						◇														◇					
Rainham	d					09 46									09 58					10 16					
Gillingham	d					09 51									10 04					10 21					
Chatham	d					09 55									10 08					10 25					
Rochester	d					09 59									10 12					10 29					
Strood	d					10 02									10 15					10 32					
Higham	d														10 20										
Gravesend	d	10 05				10 12	10 20								10 29	10 35				10 42		10 50			
Northfleet	d	10 08													10 32	10 38									
Swanscombe	d	10 10													10 34	10 40									
Greenhithe	d	10 14					10 26								10 38	10 44						10 56			
Stone Crossing	d	10 16													10 40	10 46									
Dartford	d	10 21			←		10 32							10 41	10 45	10 51			←			11 02			
Slade Green	d			←	10 21				10 29			10 37	10 39	10 46	10 51			←	10 51					10 59	
Erith	d			10 18					10 32				10 42	10 48	→			10 48						11 02	
Belvedere	d			10 21					10 34				10 44	→				10 51						11 04	
Abbey Wood	d			10 24	10 28				10 38				10 48					10 54	10 58					11 08	
Plumstead	d			10 27	10 31				10 41				10 51					10 57	11 01					11 11	
Woolwich Arsenal	d			10 30	10 34				10 44				10 54					11 00	11 04					11 14	
Woolwich Dockyard	d			10 33					10 46				10 56					11 03						11 16	
Charlton	d			10 36	10 40				10 50				11 00					11 06	11 10					11 20	
Westcombe Park	d				10 42				10 52				11 02						11 12					11 22	
Maze Hill	d				10 44				10 54				11 04						11 14					11 24	
Greenwich	d				10 47			10 47	10 57				11 07						11 17				11 17	11 27	
Deptford	a				10 49				10 59				11 09						11 19					11 29	
London Victoria	d		←				11a25			←							←					11a55			←
London Bridge	d	10 52	10 54	10 57	10 58			12 09	11 07	11 09		11 24	11 17			11 22	11 24	11 27	11 28				12 39	11 37	11 39
London Cannon Street	d		11a00					→	11a11	11a13		→	11a21				11a30						→	11a41	11a43
Waterloo East	d	10 57		11 02												11 27		11 32							
London Charing Cross	a	11 00		11 05												11 30		11 35							
London Blackfriars	d				11 04														11 34						
City Thameslink	d				11 06														11 36						
Farringdon	d				11 09														11 39						
St Pancras International	d				11 13	10a35													11 43	11a06					
West Hampstead Thameslink	d				11 22														11 52						
St Albans	d				11 45														12 15						
Luton Airport Parkway	d				11 57														12 27						
Luton	a				12 01														12 31						

		SE	SE	SE	TL	SE		SE	SE	SE	TL	SE	SE	SE	SE	SE		SE	SE	SE	TL	SE	SE	SE	TL
						◇						◇													
Rainham	d				10 28							10 46									10 58				
Gillingham	d				10 34							10 51									11 04				
Chatham	d				10 38							10 55									11 08				
Rochester	d				10 42							10 59									11 12				
Strood	d				10 45	10 59						11 02									11 15				
Higham	d				10 50																11 20				
Gravesend	d				10 59			11 05				11 12	11 20								11 29	11 35			
Northfleet	d				11 02			11 08													11 32	11 38			
Swanscombe	d				11 04			11 10													11 34	11 40			
Greenhithe	d				11 08			11 14					11 26								11 38	11 44			
Stone Crossing	d				11 10			11 16													11 40	11 46			
Dartford	d			11 11	11 15			11 21			←		11 32							11 41	11 45	11 51			←
Slade Green	d	11 07	11 09	11 16	11 21					←	11 21				11 29			11 37	11 39	11 46	11 51			←	11 51
Erith	d		11 12	11 18	→					11 18					11 32				11 42	11 48	→			11 48	
Belvedere	d		11 14	→						11 21					11 34				11 44	→				11 51	
Abbey Wood	d		11 18							11 24	11 28				11 38				11 48					11 54	11 58
Plumstead	d		11 21							11 27	11 31				11 41				11 51					11 57	12 01
Woolwich Arsenal	d		11 24							11 30	11 34				11 44				11 54					12 00	12 04
Woolwich Dockyard	d		11 26							11 33					11 46				11 56					12 03	
Charlton	d		11 30							11 36	11 40				11 50				12 00					12 06	12 10
Westcombe Park	d		11 32								11 42				11 52				12 02						12 12
Maze Hill	d		11 34								11 44				11 54				12 04						12 14
Greenwich	d		11 37								11 47			11 47	11 57				12 07						12 17
Deptford	a		11 39								11 49				11 59				12 09						12 19
London Victoria	d								←				12a25			←							←		
London Bridge	d	11 54	11 47					11 52	11 54	11 57	11 58			13 09	12 07	12 09		12 24	12 17			12 22	12 24	12 27	12 28
London Cannon Street	d	→	11a51						12a00					→	12a11	12a13		→	12a21				12a30		
Waterloo East	d							11 57		12 02												12 27		12 32	
London Charing Cross	a							12 00		12 05												12 30		12 35	
London Blackfriars	d										12 04														12 34
City Thameslink	d										12 06														12 36
Farringdon	d										12 09														12 39
St Pancras International	d					13a54					12 13	11a37													12 43
West Hampstead Thameslink	d										12 22														12 52
St Albans	d										12 45														13 15
Luton Airport Parkway	d										12 57														13 27
Luton	a										13 01														13 31

Please note, Network Rail have stated that further updates to this timetable are possible during the validity period.

Table T201-R

Saturdays

26 May to 8 December

Medway - Woolwich - Greenwich - London Thameslink

		SE		SE	SE	SE	SE	SE	SE	SE	TL	SE		SE	SE	SE	TL	SE	SE	SE	SE	SE		SE	SE
		◇										◇						◇							
Rainham	d	11 16									11 28							11 46							
Gillingham	d	11 21									11 34							11 51							
Chatham	d	11 25									11 38							11 55							
Rochester	d	11 29									11 42							11 59							
Strood	d	11 32									11 45	11 59						12 02							
Higham	d										11 50														
Gravesend	d	11 42		11 50							11 59			12 05				12 12	12 20						
Northfleet	d										12 02			12 08											
Swanscombe	d										12 04			12 10											
Greenhithe	d			11 56							12 08			12 14					12 26						
Stone Crossing	d										12 10			12 16											
Dartford	d			12 02						12 11	12 15			12 21			←		12 32						
Slade Green	d					11 59		12 07	12 09	12 16	12 21					←	12 21				12 29			12 37	12 39
Erith	d					12 02			12 12	12 18	→					12 18					12 32				12 42
Belvedere	d					12 04			12 14	→						12 21					12 34				12 44
Abbey Wood	d					12 08			12 18							12 24	12 28				12 38				12 48
Plumstead	d					12 11			12 21							12 27	12 31				12 41				12 51
Woolwich Arsenal	d					12 14			12 24							12 30	12 34				12 44				12 54
Woolwich Dockyard	d					12 16			12 26							12 33					12 46				12 56
Charlton	d					12 20			12 30							12 36	12 40				12 50				13 00
Westcombe Park	d					12 22			12 32								12 42				12 52				13 02
Maze Hill	d					12 24			12 34								12 44				12 54				13 04
Greenwich	d				12 17	12 27			12 37								12 47			12 47	12 57				13 07
Deptford	a					12 29			12 39								12 49				12 59				13 09
London Victoria	d			12a55			←								←				13a25			←			
London Bridge	d				13 39	12 37	12 39	12 54	12 47					12 52	12 54	12 57	12 58			14 09	13 07	13 09		13 24	13 17
London Cannon Street	d				→	12a41	12a43	→	12a51						13a00					→	13a11	13a13		→	13a21
Waterloo East	d													12 57		13 02									
London Charing Cross	a													13 00		13 05									
London Blackfriars	d																13 04								
City Thameslink	d																13 06								
Farringdon	d																13 09								
St Pancras International	d	12a06										14a54					13 13	12a36							
West Hampstead Thameslink	d																13 22								
St Albans	d																13 45								
Luton Airport Parkway	d																13 57								
Luton	a																14 01								

		SE	TL	SE	SE	SE	TL	SE		SE	SE	SE	SE	SE	SE	SE	TL	SE		SE	SE	SE	TL	SE	SE
								◇										◇						◇	
Rainham	d		11 58					12 16									12 28							12 46	
Gillingham	d		12 04					12 21									12 34							12 51	
Chatham	d		12 08					12 25									12 38							12 55	
Rochester	d		12 12					12 29									12 42							12 59	
Strood	d		12 15					12 32									12 45	12 59						13 02	
Higham	d		12 20														12 50								
Gravesend	d		12 29	12 35				12 42		12 50							12 59			13 05				13 12	13 20
Northfleet	d		12 32	12 38													13 02			13 08					
Swanscombe	d		12 34	12 40													13 04			13 10					
Greenhithe	d		12 38	12 44						12 56							13 08			13 14					13 26
Stone Crossing	d		12 40	12 46													13 10			13 16					
Dartford	d	12 41	12 45	12 51			←			13 02						13 11	13 15			13 21			←		13 32
Slade Green	d	12 46	12 51			←	12 51					12 59		13 07	13 09	13 16	13 21					←	13 21		
Erith	d	12 48	→			12 48						13 02			13 12	13 18	→					13 18			
Belvedere	d	→				12 51						13 04			13 14	→						13 21			
Abbey Wood	d					12 54	12 58					13 08			13 18							13 24	13 28		
Plumstead	d					12 57	13 01					13 11			13 21							13 27	13 31		
Woolwich Arsenal	d					13 00	13 04					13 14			13 24							13 30	13 34		
Woolwich Dockyard	d					13 03						13 16			13 26							13 33			
Charlton	d					13 06	13 10					13 20			13 30							13 36	13 40		
Westcombe Park	d						13 12					13 22			13 32								13 42		
Maze Hill	d						13 14					13 24			13 34								13 44		
Greenwich	d						13 17				13 17	13 27			13 37								13 47		
Deptford	a						13 19					13 29			13 39								13 49		
London Victoria	d				←					13a55			←								←				14a25
London Bridge	d			13 22	13 24	13 27	13 28				14 39	13 37	13 39	13 54	13 47					13 52	13 54	13 57	13 58		
London Cannon Street	d				13a30						→	13a41	13a43	→	13a51						14a00				
Waterloo East	d			13 27		13 32														13 57		14 02			
London Charing Cross	a			13 30		13 35														14 00		14 05			
London Blackfriars	d						13 34																14 04		
City Thameslink	d						13 36																14 06		
Farringdon	d						13 39																14 09		
St Pancras International	d						13 43	13a06										15a54					14 13	13a37	
West Hampstead Thameslink	d						13 52																14 22		
St Albans	d						14 15																14 45		
Luton Airport Parkway	d						14 27																14 57		
Luton	a						14 31																15 01		

Table T201-R

Saturdays

26 May to 8 December

Medway - Woolwich - Greenwich - London Thameslink

		SE	SE	SE		SE	SE	SE	TL	SE	SE	SE	TL	SE		SE	SE	SE	SE	SE	SE	SE	TL	SE	
														◇										◇	
Rainham	d								12 58					13 16									13 28		
Gillingham	d								13 04					13 21									13 34		
Chatham	d								13 08					13 25									13 38		
Rochester	d								13 12					13 29									13 42		
Strood	d								13 15					13 32									13 45	13 59	
Higham	d								13 20														13 50		
Gravesend	d								13 29	13 35				13 42		13 50							13 59		
Northfleet	d								13 32	13 38													14 02		
Swanscombe	d								13 34	13 40													14 04		
Greenhithe	d								13 38	13 44						13 56							14 08		
Stone Crossing	d								13 40	13 46													14 10		
Dartford	d							13 41	13 45	13 51			←			14 02						14 11	14 15		
Slade Green	d		13 29			13 37	13 39	13 46	13 51			←	13 51					13 59		14 07	14 09	14 16	14 21		
Erith	d		13 32				13 42	13 48	→			13 48						14 02			14 12	14 18	→		
Belvedere	d		13 34				13 44	→				13 51						14 04			14 14	→			
Abbey Wood	d		13 38				13 48					13 54	13 58					14 08			14 18				
Plumstead	d		13 41				13 51					13 57	14 01					14 11			14 21				
Woolwich Arsenal	d		13 44				13 54					14 00	14 04					14 14			14 24				
Woolwich Dockyard	d		13 46				13 56					14 03						14 16			14 26				
Charlton	d		13 50				14 00					14 06	14 10					14 20			14 30				
Westcombe Park	d		13 52				14 02						14 12					14 22			14 32				
Maze Hill	d		13 54				14 04						14 14					14 24			14 34				
Greenwich	d	13 47	13 57				14 07						14 17				14 17	14 27			14 37				
Deptford	a		13 59				14 09						14 19					14 29			14 39				
London Victoria	d			←							←					14a55			←						
London Bridge	d	15 09	14 07	14 09		14 24	14 17			14 22	14 24	14 27	14 28				15 39	14 37	14 39	14 54	14 47				
London Cannon Street	d	→	14a11	14a13		→	14a21				14a30						→	14a41	14a43	→	14a51				
Waterloo East	d									14 27		14 32													
London Charing Cross	a									14 30		14 35													
London Blackfriars	d												14 34												
City Thameslink	d												14 36												
Farringdon	d												14 39												
St Pancras International	d												14 43	14a09										16a54	
West Hampstead Thameslink	d												14 52												
St Albans	d												15 15												
Luton Airport Parkway	d												15 27												
Luton	a												15 31												

		SE	SE	SE	TL	SE	SE	SE	SE	SE		SE	SE	SE	TL	SE	SE	SE	TL	SE		SE	SE	SE	SE
						◇														◇					
Rainham	d					13 46									13 58					14 16					
Gillingham	d					13 51									14 04					14 21					
Chatham	d					13 55									14 08					14 25					
Rochester	d					13 59									14 12					14 29					
Strood	d					14 02									14 15					14 32					
Higham	d														14 20										
Gravesend	d	14 05				14 12	14 20								14 29	14 35				14 42		14 50			
Northfleet	d	14 08													14 32	14 38									
Swanscombe	d	14 10													14 34	14 40									
Greenhithe	d	14 14					14 26								14 38	14 44						14 56			
Stone Crossing	d	14 16													14 40	14 46									
Dartford	d	14 21			←		14 32							14 41	14 45	14 51			←			15 02			
Slade Green	d			←	14 21				14 29			14 37	14 39	14 46	14 51			←	14 51					14 59	
Erith	d			14 18					14 32				14 42	14 48	→			14 48						15 02	
Belvedere	d			14 21					14 34				14 44	→				14 51						15 04	
Abbey Wood	d			14 24	14 28				14 38				14 48					14 54	14 58					15 08	
Plumstead	d			14 27	14 31				14 41				14 51					14 57	15 01					15 11	
Woolwich Arsenal	d			14 30	14 34				14 44				14 54					15 00	15 04					15 14	
Woolwich Dockyard	d			14 33					14 46				14 56					15 03						15 16	
Charlton	d			14 36	14 40				14 50				15 00					15 06	15 10					15 20	
Westcombe Park	d				14 42				14 52				15 02						15 12					15 22	
Maze Hill	d				14 44				14 54				15 04						15 14					15 24	
Greenwich	d				14 47			14 47	14 57				15 07						15 17				15 17	15 27	
Deptford	a				14 49				14 59				15 09						15 19					15 29	
London Victoria	d		←				15a25			←							←					15a55			←
London Bridge	d	14 52	14 54	14 57	14 58			16 09	15 07	15 09		15 24	15 17			15 22	15 24	15 27	15 28				16 39	15 37	15 39
London Cannon Street	d		15a00					→	15a11	15a13		→	15a21				15a30						→	15a41	15a43
Waterloo East	d	14 57		15 02												15 27		15 32							
London Charing Cross	a	15 00		15 05												15 30		15 35							
London Blackfriars	d				15 04														15 34						
City Thameslink	d				15 06														15 36						
Farringdon	d				15 09														15 39						
St Pancras International	d				15 13	14a36													15 43	15a07					
West Hampstead Thameslink	d				15 22														15 52						
St Albans	d				15 45														16 15						
Luton Airport Parkway	d				15 57														16 27						
Luton	a				16 01														16 31						

Table T201-R

Saturdays

26 May to 8 December

Medway - Woolwich - Greenwich - London Thameslink

		SE	SE	SE	TL	SE ◇		SE	SE	SE	TL	SE ◇	SE	SE	SE	SE		SE	SE	SE	TL	SE	SE	SE	TL
Rainham	d				14 28							14 46									14 58				
Gillingham	d				14 34							14 51									15 04				
Chatham	d				14 38							14 55									15 08				
Rochester	d				14 42							14 59									15 12				
Strood	d				14 45	14 59						15 02									15 15				
Higham	d				14 50																15 20				
Gravesend	d				14 59			15 05				15 12	15 20								15 29	15 35			
Northfleet	d				15 02			15 08													15 32	15 38			
Swanscombe	d				15 04			15 10													15 34	15 40			
Greenhithe	d				15 08			15 14					15 26								15 38	15 44			
Stone Crossing	d				15 10			15 16													15 40	15 46			
Dartford	d			15 11	15 15			15 21			←		15 32							15 41	15 45	15 51			←
Slade Green	d	15 07	15 09	15 16	15 21					←	15 21				15 29			15 37	15 39	15 46	15 51			←	15 51
Erith	d		15 12	15 18	→					15 18					15 32				15 42	15 48	→			15 48	
Belvedere	d		15 14	→						15 21					15 34				15 44	→				15 51	
Abbey Wood	d		15 18							15 24	15 28				15 38				15 48					15 54	15 58
Plumstead	d		15 21							15 27	15 31				15 41				15 51					15 57	16 01
Woolwich Arsenal	d		15 24							15 30	15 34				15 44				15 54					16 00	16 04
Woolwich Dockyard	d		15 26							15 33					15 46				15 56					16 03	
Charlton	d		15 30							15 36	15 40				15 50				16 00					16 06	16 10
Westcombe Park	d		15 32								15 42				15 52				16 02						16 12
Maze Hill	d		15 34								15 44				15 54				16 04						16 14
Greenwich	d		15 37								15 47			15 47	15 57				16 07						16 17
Deptford	a		15 39								15 49				15 59				16 09						16 19
London Victoria	d								←				16a25			←							←		
London Bridge	d	15 54	15 47					15 52	15 54	15 57	15 58			17 09	16 07	16 09		16 24	16 17			16 22	16 24	16 27	16 28
London Cannon Street	d	→	15a51						16a00					→	16a11	16a13		→	16a21				16a30		
Waterloo East	d							15 57		16 02												16 27		16 32	
London Charing Cross	a							16 00		16 05												16 30		16 35	
London Blackfriars	d										16 04														16 34
City Thameslink	d										16 06														16 36
Farringdon	d										16 09														16 39
St Pancras International	d					17a54					16 13	15a40													16 43
West Hampstead Thameslink	d										16 22														16 52
St Albans	d										16 45														17 15
Luton Airport Parkway	d										16 57														17 27
Luton	a										17 01														17 31

		SE ◇		SE	SE	SE	SE	SE	SE	SE	TL	SE ◇		SE	SE	SE	TL	SE ◇	SE	SE	SE	SE		SE	SE
Rainham	d	15 16									15 28							15 46							
Gillingham	d	15 21									15 34							15 51							
Chatham	d	15 25									15 38							15 55							
Rochester	d	15 29									15 42							15 59							
Strood	d	15 32									15 45	15 59						16 02							
Higham	d										15 50														
Gravesend	d	15 42		15 50							15 59			16 05				16 12	16 20						
Northfleet	d										16 02			16 08											
Swanscombe	d										16 04			16 10											
Greenhithe	d			15 56							16 08			16 14					16 26						
Stone Crossing	d										16 10			16 16											
Dartford	d			16 02						16 11	16 15			16 21			←		16 32						
Slade Green	d					15 59		16 07	16 09	16 16	16 21					←	16 21				16 29			16 37	16 39
Erith	d					16 02			16 12	16 18	→					16 18					16 32				16 42
Belvedere	d					16 04			16 14	→						16 21					16 34				16 44
Abbey Wood	d					16 08			16 18							16 24	16 28				16 38				16 48
Plumstead	d					16 11			16 21							16 27	16 31				16 41				16 51
Woolwich Arsenal	d					16 14			16 24							16 30	16 34				16 44				16 54
Woolwich Dockyard	d					16 16			16 26							16 33					16 46				16 56
Charlton	d					16 20			16 30							16 36	16 40				16 50				17 00
Westcombe Park	d					16 22			16 32								16 42				16 52				17 02
Maze Hill	d					16 24			16 34								16 44				16 54				17 04
Greenwich	d				16 17	16 27			16 37								16 47			16 47	16 57				17 07
Deptford	a					16 29			16 39								16 49				16 59				17 09
London Victoria	d			16a55			←								←				17a25			←			
London Bridge	d				17 39	16 37	16 39	16 54	16 47					16 52	16 54	16 57	16 58			18 09	17 07	17 09		17 24	17 17
London Cannon Street	d				→	16a41	16a43	→	16a51						17a00					→	17a11	17a13		→	17a21
Waterloo East	d													16 57		17 02									
London Charing Cross	a													17 00		17 05									
London Blackfriars	d																17 04								
City Thameslink	d																17 06								
Farringdon	d																17 09								
St Pancras International	d	16a09										18a54					17 13	16a36							
West Hampstead Thameslink	d																17 22								
St Albans	d																17 45								
Luton Airport Parkway	d																17 57								
Luton	a																18 01								

Table T201-R

Saturdays

26 May to 8 December

Medway - Woolwich - Greenwich - London Thameslink

		SE	TL	SE	SE	SE	TL	SE ◇		SE	SE	SE	SE	SE	SE	SE	TL	SE ◇		SE	SE	SE	TL	SE ◇	SE
Rainham	d		15 58					16 16									16 28							16 46	
Gillingham	d		16 04					16 21									16 34							16 51	
Chatham	d		16 08					16 25									16 38							16 55	
Rochester	d		16 12					16 29									16 42							16 59	
Strood	d		16 16					16 32									16 45	16 59						17 02	
Higham	d		16 21														16 50								
Gravesend	d		16 29	16 35				16 42		16 50							16 59			17 05				17 12	17 20
Northfleet	d		16 32	16 38													17 02			17 08					
Swanscombe	d		16 34	16 40													17 04			17 10					
Greenhithe	d		16 38	16 44						16 56							17 08			17 14					17 26
Stone Crossing	d		16 40	16 46													17 10			17 16					
Dartford	d	16 41	16 45	16 51			←			17 02						17 11	17 15			17 21			←		17 32
Slade Green	d	16 46	16 51			←	16 51					16 59		17 07	17 09	17 16	17 21					←	17 21		
Erith	d	16 48	→			16 48						17 02			17 12	17 18	→					17 18			
Belvedere	d	→				16 51						17 04			17 14	→						17 21			
Abbey Wood	d					16 54	16 58					17 08			17 18							17 24	17 28		
Plumstead	d					16 57	17 01					17 11			17 21							17 27	17 31		
Woolwich Arsenal	d					17 00	17 04					17 14			17 24							17 30	17 34		
Woolwich Dockyard	d					17 03						17 16			17 26							17 33			
Charlton	d					17 06	17 10					17 20			17 30							17 36	17 40		
Westcombe Park	d						17 12					17 22			17 32								17 42		
Maze Hill	d						17 14					17 24			17 34								17 44		
Greenwich	d						17 17				17 17	17 27			17 37								17 47		
Deptford	a						17 19					17 29			17 39								17 49		
London Victoria	d				←					17a55			←								←				18a25
London Bridge	d			17 22	17 24	17 27	17 28				18 39	17 37	17 39	17 54	17 47					17 52	17 54	17 57	17 58		
London Cannon Street	d				17a30						→	17a41	17a43	→	17a51						18a00				
Waterloo East	d			17 27		17 32														17 57		18 02			
London Charing Cross	a			17 30		17 35														18 00		18 05			
London Blackfriars	d						17 34																18 04		
City Thameslink	d						17 36																18 06		
Farringdon	d						17 39																18 09		
St Pancras International	d						17 43	17a06										19a54					18 13	17a36	
West Hampstead Thameslink	d						17 52																18 22		
St Albans	d						18 15																18 45		
Luton Airport Parkway	d						18 27																18 57		
Luton	a						18 31																19 01		

		SE	SE	SE		SE	SE	SE	TL	SE	SE	SE	TL	SE ◇		SE	SE	SE	SE	SE	SE	SE	TL	SE ◇	
Rainham	d								16 58					17 16									17 28		
Gillingham	d								17 04					17 21									17 34		
Chatham	d								17 08					17 25									17 38		
Rochester	d								17 12					17 29									17 42		
Strood	d								17 15					17 32									17 45	17 59	
Higham	d								17 20														17 50		
Gravesend	d								17 29	17 35				17 42		17 50							17 59		
Northfleet	d								17 32	17 38													18 02		
Swanscombe	d								17 34	17 40													18 04		
Greenhithe	d								17 38	17 44						17 56							18 08		
Stone Crossing	d								17 40	17 46													18 10		
Dartford	d							17 41	17 45	17 51			←			18 02						18 11	18 15		
Slade Green	d		17 29			17 37	17 39	17 46	17 51			←	17 51					17 59		18 07	18 09	18 16	18 21		
Erith	d		17 32				17 42	17 48	→			17 48						18 02			18 12	18 18	→		
Belvedere	d		17 34				17 44	→				17 51						18 04			18 14	→			
Abbey Wood	d		17 38				17 48					17 54	17 58					18 08			18 18				
Plumstead	d		17 41				17 51					17 57	18 01					18 11			18 21				
Woolwich Arsenal	d		17 44				17 54					18 00	18 04					18 14			18 24				
Woolwich Dockyard	d		17 46				17 56					18 03						18 16			18 26				
Charlton	d		17 50				18 00					18 06	18 10					18 20			18 30				
Westcombe Park	d		17 52				18 02						18 12					18 22			18 32				
Maze Hill	d		17 54				18 04						18 14					18 24			18 34				
Greenwich	d	17 47	17 57				18 07						18 17				18 17	18 27			18 37				
Deptford	a		17 59				18 09						18 19					18 29			18 39				
London Victoria	d			←							←					18a55			←						
London Bridge	d	19 09	18 07	18 09		18 24	18 17			18 22	18 24	18 27	18 28				19 39	18 37	18 39	18 54	18 47				
London Cannon Street	d	→	18a11	18a13		→	18a21				18a30						→	18a41	18a43	→	18a51				
Waterloo East	d									18 27		18 32													
London Charing Cross	a									18 30		18 35													
London Blackfriars	d												18 34												
City Thameslink	d												18 36												
Farringdon	d												18 39												
St Pancras International	d												18 43	18a09										20a54	
West Hampstead Thameslink	d												18 52												
St Albans	d												19 15												
Luton Airport Parkway	d												19 27												
Luton	a												19 31												

Please note, Network Rail have stated that further updates to this timetable are possible during the validity period.

Table T201-R

Saturdays

26 May to 8 December

Medway - Woolwich - Greenwich - London Thameslink

		SE	SE	SE	TL	SE ◇	SE	SE	SE	SE		SE	SE	SE	TL	SE	SE	SE	TL	SE ◇		SE	SE	SE	SE
Rainham	d					17 46									17 58					18 16					
Gillingham	d					17 51									18 04					18 21					
Chatham	d					17 55									18 08					18 25					
Rochester	d					17 59									18 12					18 29					
Strood	d					18 02									18 15					18 32					
Higham	d														18 20										
Gravesend	d	18 05				18 12	18 20								18 29	18 35				18 42		18 50			
Northfleet	d	18 08													18 32	18 38									
Swanscombe	d	18 10													18 34	18 40									
Greenhithe	d	18 14					18 26								18 38	18 44						18 56			
Stone Crossing	d	18 16													18 40	18 46									
Dartford	d	18 21			←		18 32							18 41	18 45	18 51			←			19 02			
Slade Green	d			←	18 21				18 29			18 37	18 39	18 46	18 51			←	18 51					18 59	
Erith	d			18 18					18 32				18 42	18 48	→			18 48						19 02	
Belvedere	d			18 21					18 34				18 44	→				18 51						19 04	
Abbey Wood	d			18 24	18 28				18 38				18 48					18 54	18 58					19 08	
Plumstead	d			18 27	18 31				18 41				18 51					18 57	19 01					19 11	
Woolwich Arsenal	d			18 30	18 34				18 44				18 54					19 00	19 04					19 14	
Woolwich Dockyard	d			18 33					18 46				18 56					19 03						19 16	
Charlton	d			18 36	18 40				18 50				19 00					19 06	19 10					19 20	
Westcombe Park	d				18 42				18 52				19 02						19 12					19 22	
Maze Hill	d				18 44				18 54				19 04						19 14					19 24	
Greenwich	d				18 47			18 47	18 57				19 07						19 17				19 17	19 27	
Deptford	a				18 49				18 59				19 09						19 19					19 29	
London Victoria	d		←				19a25			←							←					19a55			←
London Bridge	d	18 52	18 54	18 57	18 58			20 09	19 07	19 09		19 24	19 17			19 22	19 24	19 27	19 28				20 39	19 37	19 39
London Cannon Street	d		19a00					→	19a11	19a13		→	19a21				19a30						→	19a41	19a43
Waterloo East	d	18 57		19 02												19 27		19 32							
London Charing Cross	a	19 00		19 05												19 30		19 35							
London Blackfriars	d				19 04														19 34						
City Thameslink	d				19 06														19 36						
Farringdon	d				19 09														19 39						
St Pancras International	d				19 13	18a36													19 43	19a06					
West Hampstead Thameslink	d				19 22														19 52						
St Albans	d				19 45														20 15						
Luton Airport Parkway	d				19 57														20 27						
Luton	a				20 01														20 31						

		SE	SE	SE	TL	SE ◇		SE	SE	SE	TL	SE ◇	SE	SE	SE	SE		SE	SE	TL	SE	SE	SE	TL	SE ◇
Rainham	d				18 28							18 46								18 58					19 16
Gillingham	d				18 34							18 51								19 04					19 21
Chatham	d				18 38							18 55								19 08					19 25
Rochester	d				18 42							18 59								19 12					19 29
Strood	d				18 45	18 59						19 02								19 15					19 32
Higham	d				18 50															19 20					
Gravesend	d				18 59			19 05				19 12	19 20							19 29	19 35				19 42
Northfleet	d				19 02			19 08												19 32	19 38				
Swanscombe	d				19 04			19 10												19 34	19 40				
Greenhithe	d				19 08			19 14					19 26							19 38	19 44				
Stone Crossing	d				19 10			19 16												19 40	19 46				
Dartford	d			19 11	19 15			19 21			←		19 32						19 41	19 45	19 51			←	
Slade Green	d	19 07	19 09	19 16	19 21					←	19 21				19 29			19 37	19 46	19 51			←	19 51	
Erith	d		19 12	19 18	→					19 18					19 32				19 48	→			19 48		
Belvedere	d		19 14	→						19 21					19 34				→				19 51		
Abbey Wood	d		19 18							19 24	19 28				19 38								19 54	19 58	
Plumstead	d		19 21							19 27	19 31				19 41								19 57	20 01	
Woolwich Arsenal	d		19 24							19 30	19 34				19 44								20 00	20 04	
Woolwich Dockyard	d		19 26							19 33					19 46								20 03		
Charlton	d		19 30							19 36	19 40				19 50								20 06	20 10	
Westcombe Park	d		19 32								19 42				19 52									20 12	
Maze Hill	d		19 34								19 44				19 54									20 14	
Greenwich	d		19 37								19 47			19 47	19 57									20 17	
Deptford	a		19 39								19 49				19 59									20 19	
London Victoria	d								←				20a25			←						←			
London Bridge	d	19 54	19 47					19 52	19 54	19 57	19 58			21 09	20 07	20 09		20 24			20 22	20 24	20 27	20 28	
London Cannon Street	d	→	19a51						20a00					→	20a11	20a13		→				20a30			
Waterloo East	d							19 57		20 02											20 27		20 32		
London Charing Cross	a							20 00		20 05											20 30		20 35		
London Blackfriars	d										20 04													20 34	
City Thameslink	d										20 06													20 36	
Farringdon	d										20 09													20 39	
St Pancras International	d					21a54					20 13	19a36												20 43	20a06
West Hampstead Thameslink	d										20 22													20 52	
St Albans	d										20 45													21 15	
Luton Airport Parkway	d										20 57													21 27	
Luton	a										21 01													21 31	

Table T201-R

Saturdays

26 May to 8 December

Medway - Woolwich - Greenwich - London Thameslink

		SE		SE	SE	SE	SE	SE	SE	TL	SE ◇	SE		SE	SE	TL	SE ◇	SE	SE	SE	SE	SE		TL	SE
Rainham	d									19 28							19 46							19 58	
Gillingham	d									19 34							19 51							20 04	
Chatham	d									19 38							19 55							20 08	
Rochester	d									19 42							19 59							20 12	
Strood	d									19 45	19 59						20 02							20 15	
Higham	d									19 50														20 20	
Gravesend	d	19 50								19 59		20 05					20 12	20 20						20 29	20 35
Northfleet	d									20 02		20 08												20 32	20 38
Swanscombe	d									20 04		20 10												20 34	20 40
Greenhithe	d	19 56								20 08		20 14						20 26						20 38	20 44
Stone Crossing	d									20 10		20 16												20 40	20 46
Dartford	d	20 02						20 11		20 15		20 21				←		20 32			20 41			20 45	20 51
Slade Green	d				19 59		20 07	20 16		20 21						20 21			20 29		20 46			20 51	
Erith	d				20 02			20 18		→									20 32		20 48			→	
Belvedere	d				20 04			20 21											20 34		20 51				
Abbey Wood	d				20 08			20 24								20 28			20 38		20 54				
Plumstead	d				20 11			20 27								20 31			20 41		20 57				
Woolwich Arsenal	d				20 14			20 30								20 34			20 44		21 00				
Woolwich Dockyard	d				20 16			20 33											20 46		21 03				
Charlton	d				20 20			20 36								20 40			20 50		21 06				
Westcombe Park	d				20 22											20 42			20 52						
Maze Hill	d				20 24											20 44			20 54						
Greenwich	d			20 17	20 27				20 44							20 47			20 57			21 14			
Deptford	a				20 29											20 49			20 59						
London Victoria	d	20a55				←								←	←			21a25		←					
London Bridge	d			21 39	20 37	20 39	20 54	20 57	22 09			20 52		20 54	20 57	20 58			21 07	21 09	21 27	22 39			21 22
London Cannon Street	d			→	20a41	20a43	→	→	→					21a00					21a11	21a13	→	→			
Waterloo East	d											20 57			21 02										21 27
London Charing Cross	a											21 00			21 05										21 30
London Blackfriars	d															21 04									
City Thameslink	d																								
Farringdon	d															21 09									
St Pancras International	d										22a54					21 13	20a36								
West Hampstead Thameslink	d															21 22									
St Albans	d															21 45									
Luton Airport Parkway	d															21 57									
Luton	a															22 01									

		SE	TL	SE ◇	SE	SE	SE	SE		SE	TL	SE ◇	SE	SE	TL	SE ◇	SE	SE		SE	SE	SE	TL	SE	SE
Rainham	d			20 16							20 28					20 46							20 58		
Gillingham	d			20 21							20 34					20 51							21 04		
Chatham	d			20 25							20 38					20 55							21 08		
Rochester	d			20 29							20 42					20 59							21 12		
Strood	d			20 32							20 45	20 59				21 02							21 15		
Higham	d										20 50												21 20		
Gravesend	d			20 42	20 50						20 59		21 05			21 12	21 20						21 29	21 35	
Northfleet	d										21 02		21 08										21 32	21 38	
Swanscombe	d										21 04		21 10										21 34	21 40	
Greenhithe	d				20 56						21 08		21 14				21 26						21 38	21 44	
Stone Crossing	d										21 10		21 16										21 40	21 46	
Dartford	d		←		21 02			21 11			21 15		21 21		←		21 32				21 41		21 45	21 51	
Slade Green	d		20 51			20 59		21 16			21 21				21 21			21 29			21 46		21 51		
Erith	d					21 02		21 18			→							21 32			21 48		→		
Belvedere	d					21 04		21 21										21 34			21 51				
Abbey Wood	d		20 58			21 08		21 24							21 28			21 38			21 54				
Plumstead	d		21 01			21 11		21 27							21 31			21 41			21 57				
Woolwich Arsenal	d		21 04			21 14		21 30							21 34			21 44			22 00				
Woolwich Dockyard	d					21 16		21 33										21 46			22 03				
Charlton	d		21 10			21 20		21 36							21 40			21 50			22 06				
Westcombe Park	d		21 12			21 22									21 42			21 52							
Maze Hill	d		21 14			21 24									21 44			21 54							
Greenwich	d		21 17			21 27				21 44					21 47			21 57				22 14			
Deptford	a		21 19			21 29									21 49			21 59							
London Victoria	d	←			21a55		←							←			22a25			←					←
London Bridge	d	21 27	21 28			21 37	21 39	21 57		23 09			21 52	21 57	21 58			22 07		22 09	22 27	23 39		22 22	22 27
London Cannon Street	d					21a41	21a43	→		→								22a11		22a13	→	→			
Waterloo East	d	21 32											21 57	22 02										22 27	22 32
London Charing Cross	a	21 35											22 00	22 05										22 30	22 35
London Blackfriars	d		21 34												22 04										
City Thameslink	d																								
Farringdon	d		21 39												22 09										
St Pancras International	d		21 43	21a09								23a54			22 13	21a36									
West Hampstead Thameslink	d		21 52												22 22										
St Albans	d		22 15												22 45										
Luton Airport Parkway	d		22 27												22 57										
Luton	a		22 31												23 02										

Table T201-R

Saturdays
26 May to 8 December

Medway - Woolwich - Greenwich - London Thameslink

		TL	SE ◇	SE		SE	SE	SE	SE	TL	SE	SE	TL	SE ◇		SE	SE	SE	SE	TL	SE	SE	TL	SE ◇
Rainham	d		21 16							21 28				21 46						21 58				22 16
Gillingham	d		21 21							21 34				21 51						22 04				22 21
Chatham	d		21 25							21 38				21 55						22 08				22 25
Rochester	d		21 29							21 42				21 59						22 12				22 29
Strood	d		21 32							21 45				22 02						22 15				22 32
Higham	d									21 50										22 20				
Gravesend	d		21 42	21 50						21 59	22 05			22 12		22 20				22 29	22 35			22 42
Northfleet	d									22 02	22 08									22 32	22 38			
Swanscombe	d									22 04	22 10									22 34	22 40			
Greenhithe	d			21 56						22 08	22 14					22 26				22 38	22 44			
Stone Crossing	d									22 10	22 16									22 40	22 46			
Dartford	d	←		22 02				22 11		22 15	22 21		←			22 32			22 41	22 45	22 51		←	
Slade Green	d	21 51				21 59		22 16		22 21			22 21				22 29		22 46	22 51		←	22 51	
Erith	d					22 02		22 18		→							22 32		22 48	→		22 48		
Belvedere	d					22 04		22 21									22 34		→			22 51		
Abbey Wood	d	21 58				22 08		22 24					22 28				22 38					22 54	22 58	
Plumstead	d	22 01				22 11		22 27					22 31				22 41					22 57	23 01	
Woolwich Arsenal	d	22 04				22 14		22 30					22 34				22 44					23 00	23 04	
Woolwich Dockyard	d					22 16		22 33									22 46					23 03		
Charlton	d	22 10				22 20		22 36					22 40				22 50					23 06	23 10	
Westcombe Park	d	22 12				22 22							22 42				22 52						23 12	
Maze Hill	d	22 14				22 24							22 44				22 54						23 14	
Greenwich	d	22 17				22 27			22 44				22 47				22 57						23 17	
Deptford	a	22 19				22 29							22 49				22 59						23 19	
London Victoria	d			22a55			←					←				23a25		←						
London Bridge	d	22 28				22 37	22 39	22 57	00 09		22 52	22 57	22 58				23 07	23 09			23 22	23 27	23 28	
London Cannon Street	d					22a41	22a43	→	→								23a11	23a13						
Waterloo East	d										22 57	23 02									23 27	23 32		
London Charing Cross	a										23 00	23 05									23 30	23 35		
London Blackfriars	d	22 34											23 04										23 34	
City Thameslink	d																							
Farringdon	d	22 39											23 09										23 39	
St Pancras International	d	22 43	22a06										23 13	22a36									23 43	23a06
West Hampstead Thameslink	d	22a51											23a21										23a51	
St Albans	d																							
Luton Airport Parkway	d																							
Luton	a																							

		SE	SE	SE	SE	TL	SE	SE	SE	SE		SE	TL	SE	TL
Rainham	d					22 28							22 58		23 28
Gillingham	d					22 34							23 04		23 34
Chatham	d					22 38							23 08		23 38
Rochester	d					22 42							23 12		23 42
Strood	d					22 45							23 15		23 45
Higham	d					22 50							23 20		23 50
Gravesend	d	22 50				22 59	23 05						23 27	23 35	23 57
Northfleet	d					23 02	23 08						23 31	23 38	00 01
Swanscombe	d					23 04	23 10						23 33	23 40	00 03
Greenhithe	d	22 56				23 08	23 14						23 36	23 44	00 06
Stone Crossing	d					23 10	23 16						23 38	23 46	00 08
Dartford	d	23 02			23 11	23a14	23 21	←				23 41	23a43	23 51	00a13
Slade Green	d		22 59		23 16			23 16	23 29			23 46			
Erith	d		23 02		→			23 18	23 32			23 48			
Belvedere	d		23 04					23 21	23 34			23 51			
Abbey Wood	d		23 08					23 24	23 38			23 54			
Plumstead	d		23 11					23 27	23 41			23 57			
Woolwich Arsenal	d		23 14					23 30	23 44			23 59			
Woolwich Dockyard	d		23 16					23 33	23 46			00 03			
Charlton	d		23 20					23 36	23 50			00 06			
Westcombe Park	d		23 22						23 52						
Maze Hill	d		23 24						23 54						
Greenwich	d		23 27						23 57						
Deptford	a		23 29						23 59						
London Victoria	d	23a55		←						←					
London Bridge	d		23 37	23 39			23 52	23 56	00 07	00 09		00 26		00 28	
London Cannon Street	d		23a41	23a43					00a11	00a13					
Waterloo East	d						23 57	00 01				00 31		00 33	
London Charing Cross	a						00 01	00 05				00 35		00 36	
London Blackfriars	d														
City Thameslink	d														
Farringdon	d														
St Pancras International	d														
West Hampstead Thameslink	d														
St Albans	d														
Luton Airport Parkway	d														
Luton	a														

Table T201-R

Sundays
20 May to 2 December

Medway - Woolwich - Greenwich - London Thameslink

		SE	SE	SE	SE	TL	SE	SE	SE	SE		TL	SE ◇	SE	SE	SE	SE	TL	SE	SE		SE	SE ◇	SE	SE
Rainham	d												07 16					07 30					08 16		
Gillingham	d					06 36						07 06	07 21					07 36					08 21		
Chatham	d					06 40						07 10	07 25					07 40					08 25		
Rochester	d					06 44						07 14	07 29					07 44					08 29		
Strood	d					06 47						07 17	07 32					07 47					08 32		
Higham	d					06 52						07 22						07 52							
Gravesend	d					06 59		07 18				07 29	07 42		07 48			07 59				08 18	08 42		
Northfleet	d					07 03		07 21				07 33			07 51			08 03				08 21			
Swanscombe	d					07 05		07 23				07 35			07 53			08 05				08 23			
Greenhithe	d					07 08		07 27				07 38			07 57			08 08				08 27			
Stone Crossing	d					07 10		07 29				07 40			07 59			08 10				08 29			
Dartford	d		06 50			07 15	07 20	07 34				07 45		07 50	08 04			08 15		08 20		08 34			
Slade Green	d	06 35	06 55	07 05		07 21	07 25		07 35			07 51		07 55		08 05		08 21		08 25				08 35	
Erith	d	06 37	06 57	07 07			07 27		07 37					07 57		08 07				08 27				08 37	
Belvedere	d	06 40	07 00	07 10			07 30		07 40					08 00		08 10				08 30				08 40	
Abbey Wood	d	06 43	07 03	07 13		07 28	07 33		07 43			07 58		08 03		08 13		08 28		08 33				08 43	
Plumstead	d	06 46	07 06	07 16		07 31	07 36		07 46			08 01		08 06		08 16		08 31		08 36				08 46	
Woolwich Arsenal	d	06 49	07 09	07 19		07 34	07 39		07 49			08 04		08 09		08 19		08 34		08 39				08 49	
Woolwich Dockyard	d	06 52	07 12	07 22			07 42		07 52					08 12		08 22				08 42				08 52	
Charlton	d	06 55	07 15	07 25		07 40	07 45		07 55			08 10		08 15		08 25		08 40		08 45				08 55	
Westcombe Park	d	06 57		07 27		07 42			07 57			08 12				08 27		08 42						08 57	
Maze Hill	d	06 59		07 29		07 44			07 59			08 14				08 29		08 44						08 59	
Greenwich	d	07 03		07 33	07 41	07 47			08 03	08 11		08 17				08 33	08 41	08 47						09 03	
Deptford	a	07 05		07 35		07 49			08 05			08 19				08 35		08 49						09 05	
London Victoria	d																		←						←
London Bridge	d	07 13	07 35	07 43	09 00	07a57	08 05	08 11	08 13	09 30		08a27		08 35	08 41	08 43	10 00	08a57	09 00	09 05		09 11		09 13	09 30
London Cannon Street	d	07a17		07a47	→				08a17	→						08a47	→		09a04					09a17	09a34
Waterloo East	d		07 40				08 10	08 16						08 40	08 46					09 10		09 16			
London Charing Cross	a		07 43				08 13	08 19						08 43	08 49					09 13		09 19			
London Blackfriars	d																								
City Thameslink	d																								
Farringdon	d																								
St Pancras International	d												08a06										09a06		
West Hampstead Thameslink	d																								
St Albans	d																								
Luton Airport Parkway	d																								
Luton	a																								

		SE	SE	SE	SE	SE		TL	SE	SE ◇	SE	SE	SE	SE	TL	SE		SE ◇	SE	SE	SE	SE	TL	SE	SE ◇
Rainham	d							08 30							09 00			09 16					09 30		
Gillingham	d							08 36							09 06			09 21					09 36		
Chatham	d							08 40							09 10			09 25					09 40		
Rochester	d							08 44							09 14			09 29					09 44		
Strood	d							08 47		08 59					09 17			09 32					09 47		09 59
Higham	d							08 52							09 22								09 52		
Gravesend	d		08 48					08 59				09 18			09 29			09 42		09 48			09 59		
Northfleet	d		08 51					09 03				09 21			09 33					09 51			10 03		
Swanscombe	d		08 53					09 05				09 23			09 35					09 53			10 05		
Greenhithe	d		08 57					09 08				09 27			09 38					09 57			10 08		
Stone Crossing	d		08 59					09 10				09 29			09 40					09 59			10 10		
Dartford	d	08 50	09 04					09 15			09 20	09 34			09 45				09 50	10 04			10 15		
Slade Green	d	08 55			09 05			09 21			09 25		09 35		09 51				09 55		10 05		10 21		
Erith	d	08 57			09 07						09 27		09 37						09 57		10 07				
Belvedere	d	09 00			09 10						09 30		09 40						10 00		10 10				
Abbey Wood	d	09 03			09 13			09 28			09 33		09 43		09 58				10 03		10 13		10 28		
Plumstead	d	09 06			09 16			09 31			09 36		09 46		10 01				10 06		10 16		10 31		
Woolwich Arsenal	d	09 09			09 19			09 34			09 39		09 49		10 04				10 09		10 19		10 34		
Woolwich Dockyard	d	09 12			09 22						09 42		09 52						10 12		10 22				
Charlton	d	09 15			09 25			09 40			09 45		09 55		10 10				10 15		10 25		10 40		
Westcombe Park	d				09 27			09 42					09 57		10 12						10 27		10 42		
Maze Hill	d				09 29			09 44					09 59		10 14						10 29		10 44		
Greenwich	d			09 11	09 33	09 41		09 47					10 03	10 11	10 17						10 33	10 41	10 47		
Deptford	a				09 35			09 49					10 05		10 19						10 35		10 49		
London Victoria	d								←							←								←	
London Bridge	d	09 35	09 41	10 30	09 43	11 00		09 58	10 00		10 05	10 11	10 13	11 30	10 28	10 30			10 35	10 41	10 43	12 00	10 58	11 00	
London Cannon Street	d			→	09a47	→			10a04				10a17	→		10a34					10a47	→		11a04	
Waterloo East	d	09 40	09 46								10 10	10 16							10 40	10 46					
London Charing Cross	a	09 43	09 49								10 13	10 19							10 43	10 49					
London Blackfriars	d							10 05							10 35								11 05		
City Thameslink	d																								
Farringdon	d							10 09							10 39								11 09		
St Pancras International	d							10a13		11a54					10a43			10a06					11a13		12a54
West Hampstead Thameslink	d																								
St Albans	d																								
Luton Airport Parkway	d																								
Luton	a																								

Please note, Network Rail have stated that further updates to this timetable are possible during the validity period.

Sundays

20 May to 2 December

Medway - Woolwich - Greenwich - London Thameslink

		SE		SE	SE	SE	TL	SE	SE	SE	SE	SE		SE	TL	SE	SE	SE	SE	SE	SE	TL		SE	SE
									◇								◇								◇
Rainham	d						10 00		10 16						10 30							11 00			11 16
Gillingham	d						10 06		10 21						10 36							11 06			11 21
Chatham	d						10 10		10 25						10 40							11 10			11 25
Rochester	d						10 14		10 29						10 44							11 14			11 29
Strood	d						10 17		10 32						10 47		10 59					11 17			11 32
Higham	d						10 22								10 52							11 22			
Gravesend	d			10 18			10 29		10 42		10 48				10 59				11 18			11 29			11 42
Northfleet	d			10 21			10 33				10 51				11 03				11 21			11 33			
Swanscombe	d			10 23			10 35				10 53				11 05				11 23			11 35			
Greenhithe	d			10 27			10 38				10 57				11 08				11 27			11 38			
Stone Crossing	d			10 29			10 40				10 59				11 10				11 29			11 40			
Dartford	d	10 20		10 34			10 46			10 50	11 04				11 15			11 20	11 34			11 45			
Slade Green	d	10 25			10 35		10 51			10 55		11 05			11 21			11 25		11 35		11 51			
Erith	d	10 27			10 37					10 57		11 07						11 27		11 37					
Belvedere	d	10 30			10 40					11 00		11 10						11 30		11 40					
Abbey Wood	d	10 33			10 43		10 58			11 03		11 13			11 28			11 33		11 43		11 58			
Plumstead	d	10 36			10 46		11 01			11 06		11 16			11 31			11 36		11 46		12 01			
Woolwich Arsenal	d	10 39			10 49		11 04			11 09		11 19			11 34			11 39		11 49		12 04			
Woolwich Dockyard	d	10 42			10 52					11 12		11 22						11 42		11 52					
Charlton	d	10 45			10 55		11 10			11 15		11 25			11 40			11 45		11 55		12 10			
Westcombe Park	d				10 57		11 12					11 27			11 42					11 57		12 12			
Maze Hill	d				10 59		11 14					11 29			11 44					11 59		12 14			
Greenwich	d				11 03	11 11	11 17					11 33		11 41	11 47					12 03	12 11	12 17			
Deptford	a				11 05		11 19					11 35			11 49					12 05		12 19			
London Victoria	d							←								←								←	
London Bridge	d	11 05		11 11	11 13	12 30	11 28	11 30		11 35	11 41	11 43		13 00	11 58	12 00		12 05	12 11	12 13	13 30	12 28		12 30	
London Cannon Street	d				11a17	→		11a34				11a47		→		12a04				12a17	→			12a34	
Waterloo East	d	11 10		11 16						11 40	11 46							12 10	12 16						
London Charing Cross	a	11 13		11 19						11 43	11 49							12 13	12 19						
London Blackfriars	d						11 35								12 05							12 35			
City Thameslink	d																								
Farringdon	d						11 39								12 09							12 39			
St Pancras International	d						11a43		11a06						12a13		13a54					12a43			12a05
West Hampstead Thameslink	d																								
St Albans	d																								
Luton Airport Parkway	d																								
Luton	a																								

		SE	SE	SE	SE	TL	SE	SE		SE	SE	SE	SE	SE	TL	SE	SE	SE		SE	SE	SE	TL	SE	SE
								◇		◇							◇								◇
Rainham	d					11 30				11 46					12 00		12 16						12 30		
Gillingham	d					11 36				11 51					12 06		12 21						12 36		
Chatham	d					11 40				11 55					12 10		12 25						12 40		
Rochester	d					11 44				11 59					12 14		12 29						12 44		
Strood	d					11 47		11 59		12 02					12 17		12 32						12 47		12 59
Higham	d					11 52									12 22								12 52		
Gravesend	d		11 48			11 59				12 12		12 18			12 29		12 42			12 48			12 59		
Northfleet	d		11 51			12 03						12 21			12 33					12 51			13 03		
Swanscombe	d		11 53			12 05						12 23			12 35					12 53			13 05		
Greenhithe	d		11 57			12 08						12 27			12 38					12 57			13 08		
Stone Crossing	d		11 59			12 10						12 29			12 40					12 59			13 10		
Dartford	d	11 50	12 04			12 15					12 20	12 34			12 45			12 50		13 04			13 15		
Slade Green	d	11 55		12 05		12 21					12 25		12 35		12 51			12 55			13 05		13 21		
Erith	d	11 57		12 07							12 27		12 37					12 57			13 07				
Belvedere	d	12 00		12 10							12 30		12 40					13 00			13 10				
Abbey Wood	d	12 03		12 13		12 28					12 33		12 43		12 58			13 03			13 13		13 28		
Plumstead	d	12 06		12 16		12 31					12 36		12 46		13 01			13 06			13 16		13 31		
Woolwich Arsenal	d	12 09		12 19		12 34					12 39		12 49		13 04			13 09			13 19		13 34		
Woolwich Dockyard	d	12 12		12 22							12 42		12 52					13 12			13 22				
Charlton	d	12 15		12 25		12 40					12 45		12 55		13 10			13 15			13 25		13 40		
Westcombe Park	d			12 27		12 42							12 57		13 12						13 27		13 42		
Maze Hill	d			12 29		12 44							12 59		13 14						13 29		13 44		
Greenwich	d			12 33	12 41	12 47							13 03	13 11	13 17						13 33	13 41	13 47		
Deptford	a			12 35		12 49							13 05		13 19						13 35		13 49		
London Victoria	d						←									←								←	
London Bridge	d	12 35	12 41	12 43	14 00	12 58	13 00				13 05	13 11	13 13	14 30	13 28	13 30		13 35		13 41	13 43	15 00	13 58	14 00	
London Cannon Street	d			12a47	→		13a04						13a17	→		13a34					13a47	→		14a04	
Waterloo East	d	12 40	12 46								13 10	13 16						13 40		13 46					
London Charing Cross	a	12 43	12 49								13 13	13 19						13 43		13 49					
London Blackfriars	d					13 05									13 35								14 05		
City Thameslink	d																								
Farringdon	d					13 09									13 39								14 09		
St Pancras International	d					13a13		14a54		12a36					13a43		13a06						14a13		15a54
West Hampstead Thameslink	d																								
St Albans	d																								
Luton Airport Parkway	d																								
Luton	a																								

Table T201-R

Sundays

20 May to 2 December

Medway - Woolwich - Greenwich - London Thameslink

		SE	SE	SE		SE	SE	TL	SE	SE	SE	SE	SE	SE		TL	SE	SE	SE	SE	SE	SE	SE	TL	
		◇								◇								◇	◇						
Rainham	d	12 46						13 00		13 16						13 30			13 46					14 00	
Gillingham	d	12 51						13 06		13 21						13 36			13 51					14 06	
Chatham	d	12 55						13 10		13 25						13 40			13 55					14 10	
Rochester	d	12 59						13 14		13 29						13 44			13 59					14 14	
Strood	d	13 02						13 17		13 32						13 47		13 59	14 02					14 17	
Higham	d							13 22								13 52								14 22	
Gravesend	d	13 12		13 18				13 29		13 42		13 48				13 59			14 12		14 18			14 29	
Northfleet	d			13 21				13 33				13 51				14 03					14 21			14 33	
Swanscombe	d			13 23				13 35				13 53				14 05					14 23			14 35	
Greenhithe	d			13 27				13 38				13 57				14 08					14 27			14 38	
Stone Crossing	d			13 29				13 40				13 59				14 10					14 29			14 40	
Dartford	d		13 20	13 34				13 45			13 50	14 04				14 15				14 20	14 34			14 45	
Slade Green	d		13 25			13 35		13 51			13 55		14 05			14 21				14 25		14 35		14 51	
Erith	d		13 27			13 37					13 57		14 07							14 27		14 37			
Belvedere	d		13 30			13 40					14 00		14 10							14 30		14 40			
Abbey Wood	d		13 33			13 43		13 58			14 03		14 13			14 28				14 33		14 43		14 58	
Plumstead	d		13 36			13 46		14 01			14 06		14 16			14 31				14 36		14 46		15 01	
Woolwich Arsenal	d		13 39			13 49		14 04			14 09		14 19			14 34				14 39		14 49		15 04	
Woolwich Dockyard	d		13 42			13 52					14 12		14 22							14 42		14 52			
Charlton	d		13 45			13 55		14 10			14 15		14 25			14 40				14 45		14 55		15 10	
Westcombe Park	d					13 57		14 12					14 27			14 42						14 57		15 12	
Maze Hill	d					13 59		14 14					14 29			14 44						14 59		15 14	
Greenwich	d					14 03	14 11	14 17					14 33	14 41		14 47						15 03	15 11	15 17	
Deptford	a					14 05		14 19					14 35			14 49						15 05		15 19	
London Victoria	d								←								←								
London Bridge	d		14 05	14 11		14 13	15 30	14 28	14 30		14 35	14 41	14 43	16 00		14 58	15 00			15 05	15 11	15 13	16 30	15 28	
London Cannon Street	d					14a17	→		14a34				14a47	→			15a04					15a17	→		
Waterloo East	d		14 10	14 16							14 40	14 46								15 10	15 16				
London Charing Cross	a		14 13	14 19							14 43	14 49								15 13	15 19				
London Blackfriars	d							14 35								15 05								15 35	
City Thameslink	d																								
Farringdon	d							14 39								15 09								15 39	
St Pancras International	d	13a37						14a43		14a06						15a13		16a54	14a36					15a43	
West Hampstead Thameslink	d																								
St Albans	d																								
Luton Airport Parkway	d																								
Luton	a																								

		SE	SE	SE	SE	SE	SE	TL	SE	SE		SE	SE	SE	SE	SE	TL	SE	SE	SE		SE	SE	SE	TL
			◇							◇		◇							◇						
Rainham	d		14 16					14 30				14 46					15 00		15 16						15 30
Gillingham	d		14 21					14 36				14 51					15 06		15 21						15 36
Chatham	d		14 25					14 40				14 55					15 10		15 25						15 40
Rochester	d		14 29					14 44				14 59					15 14		15 29						15 44
Strood	d		14 32					14 47		14 59		15 02					15 17		15 32						15 47
Higham	d							14 52									15 22								15 52
Gravesend	d		14 42		14 48			14 59				15 12		15 18			15 29		15 42			15 48			15 59
Northfleet	d				14 51			15 03						15 21			15 33					15 51			16 03
Swanscombe	d				14 53			15 05						15 23			15 35					15 53			16 05
Greenhithe	d				14 57			15 08						15 27			15 38					15 57			16 08
Stone Crossing	d				14 59			15 10						15 29			15 40					15 59			16 10
Dartford	d			14 50	15 04			15 15					15 20	15 34			15 45			15 50		16 04			16 15
Slade Green	d			14 55		15 05		15 21					15 25		15 35		15 51			15 55			16 05		16 21
Erith	d			14 57		15 07							15 27		15 37					15 57			16 07		
Belvedere	d			15 00		15 10							15 30		15 40					16 00			16 10		
Abbey Wood	d			15 03		15 13		15 28					15 33		15 43		15 58			16 03			16 13		16 28
Plumstead	d			15 06		15 16		15 31					15 36		15 46		16 01			16 06			16 16		16 31
Woolwich Arsenal	d			15 09		15 19		15 34					15 39		15 49		16 04			16 09			16 19		16 34
Woolwich Dockyard	d			15 12		15 22							15 42		15 52					16 12			16 22		
Charlton	d			15 15		15 25		15 40					15 45		15 55		16 10			16 15			16 25		16 40
Westcombe Park	d					15 27		15 42							15 57		16 12						16 27		16 42
Maze Hill	d					15 29		15 44							15 59		16 14						16 29		16 44
Greenwich	d					15 33	15 41	15 47							16 03	16 11	16 17						16 33	16 41	16 47
Deptford	a					15 35		15 49							16 05		16 19						16 35		16 49
London Victoria	d	←							←									←							
London Bridge	d	15 30		15 35	15 41	15 43	17 00	15 58	16 00				16 05	16 11	16 13	17 30	16 28	16 30		16 35		16 41	16 43	18 00	16 58
London Cannon Street	d	15a34				15a47	→		16a04						16a17	→		16a34					16a47	→	
Waterloo East	d			15 40	15 46								16 10	16 16						16 40		16 46			
London Charing Cross	a			15 43	15 49								16 13	16 19						16 43		16 49			
London Blackfriars	d							16 05									16 35								17 05
City Thameslink	d																								
Farringdon	d							16 09									16 39								17 09
St Pancras International	d		15a06					16a13		17a55		15a40					16a43		16a10						17a13
West Hampstead Thameslink	d																								
St Albans	d																								
Luton Airport Parkway	d																								
Luton	a																								

Table T201-R

Sundays
20 May to 2 December

Medway - Woolwich - Greenwich - London Thameslink

		SE	SE	SE	SE	SE		SE	SE	TL	SE	SE	SE	SE	SE	SE		TL	SE	SE	SE	SE	SE	SE	SE
			◇	◇								◇								◇	◇				
Rainham	d			15 46						16 00		16 16						16 30			16 46				
Gillingham	d			15 51						16 06		16 21						16 36			16 51				
Chatham	d			15 55						16 10		16 25						16 40			16 55				
Rochester	d			15 59						16 14		16 29						16 44			16 59				
Strood	d		15 59	16 02						16 17		16 32						16 47		16 59	17 02				
Higham	d									16 22								16 52							
Gravesend	d			16 12		16 18				16 29		16 42		16 48				16 59			17 12		17 18		
Northfleet	d					16 21				16 33				16 51				17 03					17 21		
Swanscombe	d					16 23				16 35				16 53				17 05					17 23		
Greenhithe	d					16 27				16 38				16 57				17 08					17 27		
Stone Crossing	d					16 29				16 40				16 59				17 10					17 29		
Dartford	d				16 20	16 34				16 45			16 50	17 04				17 15				17 20	17 34		
Slade Green	d				16 25			16 35		16 51			16 55		17 05			17 21				17 25		17 35	
Erith	d				16 27			16 37					16 57		17 07							17 27		17 37	
Belvedere	d				16 30			16 40					17 00		17 10							17 30		17 40	
Abbey Wood	d				16 33			16 43		16 58			17 03		17 13			17 28				17 33		17 43	
Plumstead	d				16 36			16 46		17 01			17 06		17 16			17 31				17 36		17 46	
Woolwich Arsenal	d				16 39			16 49		17 04			17 09		17 19			17 34				17 39		17 49	
Woolwich Dockyard	d				16 42			16 52					17 12		17 22							17 42		17 52	
Charlton	d				16 45			16 55		17 10			17 15		17 25			17 40				17 45		17 55	
Westcombe Park	d							16 57		17 12					17 27			17 42						17 57	
Maze Hill	d							16 59		17 14					17 29			17 44						17 59	
Greenwich	d							17 03	17 11	17 17					17 33	17 41		17 47						18 03	18 11
Deptford	a							17 05		17 19					17 35			17 49						18 05	
London Victoria	d	←									←								←						
London Bridge	d	17 00			17 05	17 11		17 13	18 30	17 28	17 30		17 35	17 41	17 43	19 00		17 58	18 00			18 05	18 11	18 13	19 30
London Cannon Street	d	17a04						17a17	→		17a34				17a47	→			18a04					18a17	→
Waterloo East	d				17 10	17 16							17 40	17 46								18 10	18 16		
London Charing Cross	a				17 13	17 19							17 43	17 49								18 13	18 19		
London Blackfriars	d									17 35								18 05							
City Thameslink	d																								
Farringdon	d									17 39								18 09							
St Pancras International	d		18a54	16a36						17a43		17a06						18a13		19a54	17a36				
West Hampstead Thameslink	d																								
St Albans	d																								
Luton Airport Parkway	d																								
Luton	a																								

		TL		SE	SE	SE	SE	SE	SE	TL	SE	SE		SE	SE	SE	SE	SE	TL	SE	SE	SE		SE	SE
					◇							◇		◇							◇				
Rainham	d	17 00			17 16					17 30				17 46					18 00		18 16				
Gillingham	d	17 06			17 21					17 36				17 51					18 06		18 21				
Chatham	d	17 10			17 25					17 40				17 55					18 10		18 25				
Rochester	d	17 14			17 29					17 44				17 59					18 14		18 29				
Strood	d	17 17			17 32					17 47		17 59		18 02					18 17		18 32				
Higham	d	17 22								17 52									18 22						
Gravesend	d	17 29			17 42		17 48			17 59				18 12		18 18			18 29		18 42			18 48	
Northfleet	d	17 33					17 51			18 03						18 21			18 33					18 51	
Swanscombe	d	17 35					17 53			18 05						18 23			18 35					18 53	
Greenhithe	d	17 38					17 57			18 08						18 27			18 38					18 57	
Stone Crossing	d	17 40					17 59			18 10						18 29			18 40					18 59	
Dartford	d	17 45				17 50	18 04			18 15					18 20	18 34			18 45			18 50		19 04	
Slade Green	d	17 51				17 55		18 05		18 21					18 25		18 35		18 51			18 55			19 05
Erith	d					17 57		18 07							18 27		18 37					18 57			19 07
Belvedere	d					18 00		18 10							18 30		18 40					19 00			19 10
Abbey Wood	d	17 58				18 03		18 13		18 28					18 33		18 43		18 58			19 03			19 13
Plumstead	d	18 01				18 06		18 16		18 31					18 36		18 46		19 01			19 06			19 16
Woolwich Arsenal	d	18 04				18 09		18 19		18 34					18 39		18 49		19 04			19 09			19 19
Woolwich Dockyard	d					18 12		18 22							18 42		18 52					19 12			19 22
Charlton	d	18 10				18 15		18 25		18 40					18 45		18 55		19 10			19 15			19 25
Westcombe Park	d	18 12						18 27		18 42							18 57		19 12						19 27
Maze Hill	d	18 14						18 29		18 44							18 59		19 14						19 29
Greenwich	d	18 17						18 33	18 41	18 47							19 03	19 11	19 17						19 33
Deptford	a	18 19						18 35		18 49							19 05		19 19						19 35
London Victoria	d			←							←									←					
London Bridge	d	18 28		18 30		18 35	18 41	18 43	20 00	18 58	19 00				19 05	19 11	19 13	20 30	19 28	19 30		19 35		19 41	19 43
London Cannon Street	d			18a34				18a47	→		19a04						19a17	→		19a34					19a47
Waterloo East	d					18 40	18 46								19 10	19 16						19 40		19 46	
London Charing Cross	a					18 43	18 49								19 13	19 19						19 43		19 49	
London Blackfriars	d	18 35								19 05									19 35						
City Thameslink	d																								
Farringdon	d	18 39								19 09									19 39						
St Pancras International	d	18a43			18a11					19a13		20a54		18a37					19a43		19a10				
West Hampstead Thameslink	d																								
St Albans	d																								
Luton Airport Parkway	d																								
Luton	a																								

Table T201-R

Sundays
20 May to 2 December

Medway - Woolwich - Greenwich - London Thameslink

		SE	TL	SE	SE	SE	SE	SE		SE	SE	TL	SE	SE	SE	SE	SE	SE		TL	SE	SE	SE	SE	SE
					◇	◇								◇								◇	◇		
Rainham	d		18 30			18 46						19 00		19 16						19 30			19 46		
Gillingham	d		18 36			18 51						19 06		19 21						19 36			19 51		
Chatham	d		18 40			18 55						19 10		19 25						19 40			19 55		
Rochester	d		18 44			18 59						19 14		19 29						19 44			19 59		
Strood	d		18 47		18 59	19 02						19 17		19 32						19 47		19 59	20 02		
Higham	d		18 52									19 22								19 52					
Gravesend	d		18 59			19 12		19 18				19 29		19 42		19 48				19 59			20 12		20 18
Northfleet	d		19 03					19 21				19 33				19 51				20 03					20 21
Swanscombe	d		19 05					19 23				19 35				19 53				20 05					20 23
Greenhithe	d		19 08					19 27				19 38				19 57				20 08					20 27
Stone Crossing	d		19 10					19 29				19 40				19 59				20 10					20 29
Dartford	d		19 15				19 20	19 34				19 45			19 50	20 04				20 15				20 20	20 34
Slade Green	d		19 21				19 25			19 35		19 51			19 55		20 05			20 21				20 25	
Erith	d						19 27			19 37					19 57		20 07							20 27	
Belvedere	d						19 30			19 40					20 00		20 10							20 30	
Abbey Wood	d		19 28				19 33			19 43		19 58			20 03		20 13			20 28				20 33	
Plumstead	d		19 31				19 36			19 46		20 01			20 06		20 16			20 31				20 36	
Woolwich Arsenal	d		19 34				19 39			19 49		20 04			20 09		20 19			20 34				20 39	
Woolwich Dockyard	d						19 42			19 52					20 12		20 22							20 42	
Charlton	d		19 40				19 45			19 55		20 10			20 15		20 25			20 40				20 45	
Westcombe Park	d		19 42							19 57		20 12					20 27			20 42					
Maze Hill	d		19 44							19 59		20 14					20 29			20 44					
Greenwich	d	19 41	19 47							20 03	20 11	20 17					20 33	20 41		20 47					
Deptford	a		19 49							20 05		20 19					20 35			20 49					
London Victoria	d			←									←								←				
London Bridge	d	21 00	19 58	20 00			20 05	20 11		20 13	21 30	20 28	20 30		20 35	20 41	20 43	22 00		20 58	21 00			21 05	21 11
London Cannon Street	d	→		20a04						20a17	→		20a34				20a47	→			21a04				
Waterloo East	d						20 10	20 16							20 40	20 46								21 10	21 16
London Charing Cross	a						20 13	20 19							20 43	20 49								21 13	21 19
London Blackfriars	d		20 05									20 35								21 05					
City Thameslink	d																								
Farringdon	d		20 09									20 39								21 09					
St Pancras International	d		20a13		21a54	19a36						20a43		20a09						21a13		22a54	20a36		
West Hampstead Thameslink	d																								
St Albans	d																								
Luton Airport Parkway	d																								
Luton	a																								

		SE	SE	TL		SE	SE	SE	SE	SE	SE	TL	SE	SE		SE	SE	SE	SE	TL	SE	SE	SE	SE	
							◇							◇								◇			
Rainham	d			20 00			20 16					20 30		20 46						21 00		21 16			
Gillingham	d			20 06			20 21					20 36		20 51						21 06		21 21			
Chatham	d			20 10			20 25					20 40		20 55						21 10		21 25			
Rochester	d			20 14			20 29					20 44		20 59						21 14		21 29			
Strood	d			20 17			20 32					20 47		21 02						21 17		21 32			
Higham	d			20 22								20 52								21 22					
Gravesend	d			20 29			20 42		20 48			20 59		21 12			21 18			21 29		21 42		21 48	
Northfleet	d			20 33					20 51			21 03					21 21			21 33				21 51	
Swanscombe	d			20 35					20 53			21 05					21 23			21 35				21 53	
Greenhithe	d			20 38					20 57			21 08					21 27			21 38				21 57	
Stone Crossing	d			20 40					20 59			21 10					21 29			21 40				21 59	
Dartford	d			20 45				20 50	21 04			21 15				21 20	21 34			21 45			21 50	22 04	
Slade Green	d	20 35		20 51				20 55		21 05		21 21				21 25		21 35		21 51			21 55		
Erith	d	20 37						20 57		21 07						21 27		21 37					21 57		
Belvedere	d	20 40						21 00		21 10						21 30		21 40					22 00		
Abbey Wood	d	20 43		20 58				21 03		21 13		21 28				21 33		21 43		21 58			22 03		
Plumstead	d	20 46		21 01				21 06		21 16		21 31				21 36		21 46		22 01			22 06		
Woolwich Arsenal	d	20 49		21 04				21 09		21 19		21 34				21 39		21 49		22 04			22 09		
Woolwich Dockyard	d	20 52						21 12		21 22						21 42		21 52					22 12		
Charlton	d	20 55		21 10				21 15		21 25		21 40				21 45		21 55		22 10			22 15		
Westcombe Park	d	20 57		21 12						21 27		21 42						21 57		22 12					
Maze Hill	d	20 59		21 14						21 29		21 44						21 59		22 14					
Greenwich	d	21 03	21 11	21 17						21 33	21 41	21 47						22 03	22 11	22 17					
Deptford	a	21 05		21 19						21 35		21 49						22 05		22 19					
London Victoria	d					←							←								←				
London Bridge	d	21 13	22 30	21 28		21 30		21 35	21 41	21 43	23 00	21 58	22 00			22 05	22 11	22 13	23 30	22 28	22 30		22 35	22 41	
London Cannon Street	d	21a17	→			21a34				21a47	→		22a04					22a17	→		22a34				
Waterloo East	d							21 40	21 46							22 10	22 16						22 40	22 46	
London Charing Cross	a							21 43	21 49							22 13	22 19						22 43	22 49	
London Blackfriars	d			21 35								22 05								22 35					
City Thameslink	d																								
Farringdon	d			21 39								22 09								22 39					
St Pancras International	d			21a43			21a05					22a13		21a36						22a43		22a07			
West Hampstead Thameslink	d																								
St Albans	d																								
Luton Airport Parkway	d																								
Luton	a																								

Table T201-R

Sundays

20 May to 2 December

Medway - Woolwich - Greenwich - London Thameslink

		SE	SE	TL	SE	SE ◇	SE	SE	SE	TL	SE	SE ◇	SE	SE	TL	SE	SE	SE	SE	TL	TL
Rainham	d			21 30		21 46				22 00		22 16			22 30					23 00	23 30
Gillingham	d			21 36		21 51				22 06		22 21			22 36					23 06	23 36
Chatham	d			21 40		21 55				22 10		22 25			22 40					23 10	23 40
Rochester	d			21 44		21 59				22 14		22 29			22 44					23 14	23 44
Strood	d			21 47		22 02				22 17		22 32			22 47					23 17	23 47
Higham	d			21 52						22 22					22 52					23 22	23 52
Gravesend	d			21 59		22 12		22 18		22 29		22 42		22 48	22 59				23 18	23 29	23 59
Northfleet	d			22 03				22 21		22 33				22 51	23 03				23 21	23 33	00 03
Swanscombe	d			22 05				22 23		22 35				22 53	23 05				23 23	23 35	00 05
Greenhithe	d			22 08				22 27		22 38				22 57	23 08				23 27	23 38	00 08
Stone Crossing	d			22 10				22 29		22 40				22 59	23 10				23 29	23 40	00 10
Dartford	d			22 15			22 20	22 34		22 45			22 50	23 04	23a15			23 20	23 34	23a45	00a15
Slade Green	d	22 05		22 21			22 25		22 35	22 51			22 55			23 05		23 25			
Erith	d	22 07					22 27		22 37				22 57			23 07		23 27			
Belvedere	d	22 10					22 30		22 40				23 00			23 10		23 30			
Abbey Wood	d	22 13		22 28			22 33		22 43	22 58			23 03			23 13		23 33			
Plumstead	d	22 16		22 31			22 36		22 46	23 01			23 06			23 16		23 36			
Woolwich Arsenal	d	22 19		22 34			22 39		22 49	23 04			23 09			23 19		23 39			
Woolwich Dockyard	d	22 22					22 42		22 52				23 12			23 22		23 42			
Charlton	d	22 25		22 40			22 45		22 55	23 10			23 15			23 25		23 45			
Westcombe Park	d	22 27		22 42					22 57	23 12						23 27					
Maze Hill	d	22 29		22 44					22 59	23 14						23 29					
Greenwich	d	22 33	22 41	22 47					23 03	23 17						23 33					
Deptford	a	22 35		22 49					23 05	23 19						23 35					
London Victoria	d				←						←						←				
London Bridge	d	22 43	23 59	22 58	23 00		23 05	23 11	23 13	23 28	23 30		23 35	23 41		23 43	23 59	00 05	00 11		
London Cannon Street	d	22a47	→		23a04				23a17		23a34					23a47	00a04				
Waterloo East	d						23 10	23 16					23 40	23 46				00 10	00 16		
London Charing Cross	a						23 13	23 19					23 43	23 49				00 13	00 19		
London Blackfriars	d			23 05						23 37											
City Thameslink	d																				
Farringdon	d			23 09						23 41											
St Pancras International	d			23 14		22a36				23 46		23a06									
West Hampstead Thameslink	d			23a22						23 54											
St Albans	d									00 21											
Luton Airport Parkway	d									00 32											
Luton	a									00 36											

Table T203-F

Mondays to Fridays

21 May to 7 December

London - Hayes via Catford Bridge

Miles	Miles			SE MX	SE MO	SE MX	SE ThFO	SE TWO	SE	SE	SE	SE	SE	SE	SE	SE	SE	SE	SE	SE	SE	SE
0	—	**London Charing Cross** ⊖	d				00 07		05 48	06 17		06 47			07 31	07 43	08 00	08 04		08 36		09 07
0¾	—	**London Waterloo (East)** ⊖	d				00 10		05 51	06 20		06 50			07 34	07 46	08 03	08 07		08 39		09 10
—	0	**London Cannon Street** ⊖	d					00 27			06 28		07 00	07 19					08 22		08 58	
1¾	0¾	**London Bridge** ⊖	d				00 16	00 32	05 57	06 26	06 32	06 56	07 04	07 23	07 40	07 52	08 09	08 13		08 45	09 02	09 17
4¾	—	New Cross ⊖	d					00 38			06 38		07 10	07 29					08 34		09 08	
5½	—	St Johns	d					00 40			06 40		07 12	07 31					08 36		09 10	
6	—	**Lewisham**	d				00 25	00 43	06 08		06 43		07 18	07 36					08 39		09 13	
6¾	—	Ladywell	d				00 28	00 46	06 11	06 36	06 46	07 05	07 21	07 39	07 51	08 02	08 18	08 25	08 42	08 55	09 16	09 26
7½	—	**Catford Bridge**	d				00 30	00 48	06 13	06 39	06 48	07 08	07 23	07 42	07 54	08 05	08 21	08 27	08 44	08 58	09 18	09 29
9	—	Lower Sydenham	d			00 01	00 33	00 51	06 16	06 42	06 51	07 11	07 26	07 45	07 57	08 08	08 24	08 30	08 47	09 01	09 21	09 32
9½	—	New Beckenham	d			00 03	00 35	00 53	06 18	06 44	06 53	07 13	07 28	07 47	07 59	08 10	08 26	08 32	08 49	09 03	09 23	09 34
10¼	—	Clock House	d		00 01	00 05	00 38	00 56	06 21	06 46	06 56	07 15	07 31	07 49	08 01	08 12	08 28	08 35	08 52	09 05	09 26	09 36
11	—	Elmers End	d		00 04	00 08	00 41	00 59	06 24	06 49	06 59	07 18	07 34	07 52	08 04	08 15	08 31	08 38	08 55	09 08	09 29	09 39
12½	—	Eden Park	d	00 02	00 07	00 12	00 44	01 02	06 27	06 53	07 02	07 22	07 37	07 56		08 19		08 41	08 58	09 12	09 32	09 43
13¼	—	West Wickham	d	00 05	00 10	00 14	00 47	01 05	06 30	06 55	07 05	07 24	07 40	07 58		08 21		08 44	09 01	09 14	09 35	09 45
14½	—	**Hayes**	a	00 08	00 14	00 18	00 53	01 10	06 35	07 01	07 11	07 30	07 46	08 06	08 13	08 28	08 40	08 50	09 07	09 21	09 40	09 49

		SE	SE	SE	SE		SE	SE	SE	SE	SE	SE	SE	SE	SE	SE	SE	SE	SE	SE	SE	SE
London Charing Cross ⊖	d		09 37		10 07			14 37		15 07		15 37		16 07		16 35		16 58		17 21		17 43
London Waterloo (East) ⊖	d		09 40		10 10			14 40		15 10		15 40		16 10		16 38		17 01		17 24		17 46
London Cannon Street ⊖	d	09 27		09 57			14 27		14 57		15 27		15 57		16 25		16 50		17 11		17 32	
London Bridge ⊖	d	09 31	09 46	10 01	10 16	and at the same minutes past each hour until	14 31	14 46	15 01	15 16	15 31	15 46	16 01	16 16	16 30	16 44	16 55	17 07	17 16	17 30	17 37	17 52
New Cross ⊖	d	09 37		10 07			14 37		15 07		15 37		16 07		16 36		17 01		17 22		17 43	
St Johns	d	09 39		10 09			14 39		15 09		15 39		16 09		16 38		17 03		17 24		17 45	
Lewisham	d	09 43		10 13			14 43		15 13		15 43		16 13		16 42		17 07		17 29		17 49	
Ladywell	d	09 46	09 55	10 16	10 25		14 46	14 55	15 16	15 25	15 46	15 55	16 16	16 26	16 45	16 55	17 10	17 18	17 32	17 42	17 52	18 02
Catford Bridge	d	09 48	09 58	10 18	10 28		14 48	14 58	15 18	15 28	15 48	15 58	16 18	16 28	16 48	16 57	17 13	17 20	17 35	17 44	17 55	18 04
Lower Sydenham	d	09 51	10 01	10 21	10 31		14 51	15 01	15 21	15 31	15 51	16 01	16 21	16 31	16 51	17 00	17 16	17 23	17 38	17 47	17 58	18 08
New Beckenham	d	09 53	10 03	10 23	10 33		14 53	15 03	15 23	15 33	15 53	16 03	16 23	16 34	16 53	17 03	17 18	17 26	17 40	17 50	18 00	18 10
Clock House	d	09 56	10 05	10 26	10 35		14 56	15 05	15 26	15 35	15 56	16 05	16 26	16 36	16 56	17 06	17 21	17 28	17 43	17 52	18 03	18 13
Elmers End	d	09 59	10 08	10 29	10 38		14 59	15 08	15 29	15 38	15 59	16 08	16 29	16 39	16 59	17 09	17 24	17 31	17 46	17 55	18 06	18 16
Eden Park	d	10 02	10 12	10 32	10 42		15 02	15 12	15 32	15 42	16 02	16 12	16 32	16 43	17 02	17 12	17 27	17 35	17 49	17 59	18 09	18 20
West Wickham	d	10 05	10 14	10 35	10 44		15 05	15 14	15 35	15 44	16 05	16 14	16 35	16 45	17 05	17 15	17 30	17 37	17 52	18 01	18 12	18 22
Hayes	a	10 08	10 18	10 38	10 48		15 08	15 18	15 38	15 48	16 08	16 18	16 38	16 51	17 11	17 21	17 36	17 44	17 57	18 08	18 18	18 28

		SE	SE	SE	SE	SE	SE	SE	SE	SE	SE	SE	SE		SE	SE	SE	SE	SE	SE	SE FO
London Charing Cross ⊖	d		18 04		18 27		18 52		19 07		19 37		20 07			22 37		23 07		23 37	
London Waterloo (East) ⊖	d		18 07		18 30		18 55		19 10		19 40		20 10			22 40		23 10		23 40	
London Cannon Street ⊖	d	17 55		18 15		18 38		18 57		19 27		19 57			22 27		22 57		23 27		23 57
London Bridge ⊖	d	18 00	18 13	18 20	18 36	18 43	19 01	19 02	19 16	19 31	19 46	20 01	20 16	and at the same minutes past each hour until	22 31	22 46	23 01	23 16	23 31	23 46	00 01
New Cross ⊖	d	18 06		18 26		18 49		19 08		19 37		20 07			22 37		23 07		23 37		00 07
St Johns	d	18 08		18 28		18 51		19 10		19 39		20 09			22 39		23 09		23 39		00 09
Lewisham	d	18 13		18 32		18 55		19 14		19 43		20 13			22 43		23 13		23 43		00 13
Ladywell	d	18 16	18 23	18 35	18 46	18 58	19 11	19 17	19 26	19 46	19 55	20 16	20 25		22 46	22 55	23 16	23 25	23 46	23 55	00 16
Catford Bridge	d	18 19	18 26	18 38	18 48	19 01	19 13	19 20	19 28	19 48	19 58	20 18	20 28		22 48	22 58	23 18	23 28	23 48	23 58	00 18
Lower Sydenham	d	18 22	18 29	18 41	18 52	19 04	19 17	19 23	19 31	19 51	20 01	20 21	20 31		22 51	23 01	23 21	23 31	23 51	00 01	00 21
New Beckenham	d	18 24	18 32	18 43	18 54	19 06	19 19	19 25	19 34	19 53	20 03	20 23	20 33		22 53	23 03	23 23	23 33	23 53	00 03	00 23
Clock House	d	18 27	18 35	18 46	18 57	19 09	19 22	19 28	19 36	19 56	20 05	20 26	20 35		22 56	23 05	23 26	23 35	23 56	00 05	00 26
Elmers End	d	18 30	18 38	18 49	19 00	19 12	19 25	19 31	19 39	19 59	20 08	20 29	20 38		22 59	23 08	23 29	23 38	23 59	00 08	00 29
Eden Park	d	18 33	18 41	18 52	19 04	19 15	19 29	19 34	19 43	20 02	20 12	20 32	20 42		23 02	23 12	23 32	23 42	00 02	00 12	00 32
West Wickham	d	18 36	18 44	18 55	19 06	19 18	19 31	19 37	19 45	20 05	20 14	20 35	20 44		23 05	23 14	23 35	23 44	00 05	00 14	00 35
Hayes	a	18 42	18 50	19 01	19 13	19 24	19 37	19 43	19 51	20 08	20 18	20 38	20 48		23 08	23 18	23 38	23 48	00 08	00 18	00 40

Saturdays

26 May to 8 December

		SE	SE	SE	SE	SE	SE	SE	SE	SE	SE	SE		SE	SE	SE	SE	SE	SE	SE	SE	SE
London Charing Cross ⊖	d				00 07	05 37	06 07	06 37		07 07		07 37			22 07		22 37		23 07		23 37	
London Waterloo (East) ⊖	d				00 10	05 40	06 10	06 40		07 10		07 40			22 10		22 40		23 10		23 40	
London Cannon Street ⊖	d								06 57		07 27			21 57		22 27		22 57		23 27		23 57
London Bridge ⊖	d			00 01	00 16	05 46	06 16	06 46	07 01	07 16	07 31	07 46	and at the same minutes past each hour until	22 01	22 16	22 31	22 46	23 01	23 16	23 31	23 46	00 01
New Cross ⊖	d			00 07					07 07		07 37			22 07		22 37		23 07		23 37		00 07
St Johns	d			00 09					07 09		07 39			22 09		22 39		23 10		23 40		00 09
Lewisham	d			00 13		05 57	06 27	06 57	07 13		07 43			22 13		22 43		23 13		23 43		00 13
Ladywell	d			00 16	00 25	06 00	06 30	07 00	07 16	07 25	07 46	07 55		22 16	22 25	22 46	22 55	23 16	23 25	23 46	23 55	00 16
Catford Bridge	d			00 18	00 28	06 02	06 32	07 02	07 18	07 28	07 48	07 58		22 18	22 28	22 48	22 58	23 18	23 28	23 48	23 58	00 18
Lower Sydenham	d		00 01	00 21	00 31	06 05	06 35	07 05	07 21	07 31	07 51	08 01		22 21	22 31	22 51	23 01	23 21	23 31	23 51	00 01	00 21
New Beckenham	d		00 03	00 23	00 33	06 07	06 37	07 07	07 23	07 33	07 53	08 03		22 23	22 33	22 53	23 03	23 23	23 33	23 53	00 03	00 23
Clock House	d		00 05	00 26	00 35	06 10	06 40	07 10	07 26	07 35	07 56	08 05		22 26	22 35	22 56	23 05	23 26	23 35	23 56	00 05	00 26
Elmers End	d		00 08	00 29	00 38	06 13	06 43	07 13	07 29	07 38	07 59	08 08		22 29	22 38	22 59	23 08	23 29	23 38	23 59	00 08	00 29
Eden Park	d	00 02	00 12	00 32	00 42	06 16	06 46	07 16	07 32	07 42	08 02	08 12		22 32	22 42	23 02	23 12	23 32	23 42	00 02	00 12	00 32
West Wickham	d	00 05	00 14	00 35	00 44	06 19	06 49	07 19	07 35	07 44	08 05	08 14		22 35	22 44	23 05	23 14	23 35	23 44	00 05	00 14	00 35
Hayes	a	00 08	00 18	00 40	00 48	06 22	06 52	07 22	07 38	07 48	08 08	08 18		22 38	22 48	23 08	23 18	23 38	23 48	00 08	00 18	00 38

Table T203-F

Sundays

20 May to 2 December

London - Hayes via Catford Bridge

		SE A	SE A	SE A	SE	SE		SE
London Charing Cross ⊖	d				00 07			
London Waterloo (East) ⊖	d				00 10			
London Cannon Street ⊖	d					07 33	and every 30 minutes until	23 33
London Bridge ⊖	d			00 01	00 16	07 37		23 37
New Cross ⊖	d			00 07		07 43		23 43
St Johns	d			00 09		07 45		23 45
Lewisham	d			00 13		07 48		23 48
Ladywell	d			00 16	00 25	07 51		23 51
Catford Bridge	d			00 18	00 28	07 53		23 53
Lower Sydenham	d		00 01	00 21	00 31	07 56		23 56
New Beckenham	d		00 03	00 23	00 33	07 58		23 58
Clock House	d		00 05	00 26	00 35	08 01		00 01
Elmers End	d		00 08	00 29	00 38	08 04		00 04
Eden Park	d	00 02	00 12	00 32	00 42	08 07		00 07
West Wickham	d	00 05	00 14	00 35	00 44	08 10		00 10
Hayes	a	00 08	00 18	00 38	00 48	08 14		00 14

A not 20 May

Table T203-R

Sundays

20 May to 2 December

Hayes - London via Catford Bridge

		SE		SE	SE
Hayes	d	07 32	and every 30 minutes until	23 02	23 32
West Wickham	d	07 35		23 05	23 35
Eden Park	d	07 37		23 07	23 37
Elmers End	d	07 41		23 11	23 41
Clock House	d	07 43		23 13	23 43
New Beckenham	d	07 46		23 16	23 46
Lower Sydenham	d	07 48		23 18	23 48
Catford Bridge	d	07 51		23 21	23 51
Ladywell	d	07 53		23 23	23 53
Lewisham	d	07 58		23 28	23 58
St Johns	a	08 00		23 30	23 59
New Cross ⊖	a	08 02		23 32	00 02
London Bridge ⊖	a	08 07		23 37	00 07
London Cannon Street ⊖	a	08 13		23 43	00 13
London Waterloo (East) ⊖	a				
London Charing Cross ⊖	a				

Table T203-R

Mondays to Fridays

21 May to 7 December

Hayes - London via Catford Bridge

Miles	Miles			SE	SE	SE	SE	SE	SE	SE	SE	SE	SE	SE	SE	SE	SE	SE	SE	SE	SE
0	—	Hayes	d	05 10	05 44	06 11	06 23	06 38	06 54	07 11	07 21	07 31	07 45	07 51	08 01	08 11	08 21	08 34	08 50	09 02	09 13
1¼	—	West Wickham	d	05 13	05 47	06 14	06 26	06 41	06 57	07 14	07 24	07 34	07 48	07 54	08 04	08 14	08 24	08 37	08 53	09 05	09 16
2	—	Eden Park	d	05 15	05 49	06 16	06 28	06 43	06 59	07 16	07 26	07 36	07 50	07 56	08 06	08 16	08 26	08 39	08 55	09 07	09 18
3½	—	Elmers End	d	05 19	05 53	06 20	06 32	06 47	07 03	07 20	07 30	07 40	07 54	08 00	08 10	08 20	08 30	08 43	08 59	09 11	09 22
4¼	—	Clock House	d	05 21	05 55	06 22	06 34	06 50	07 06	07 23	07 33	07 43	07 57	08 03	08 13	08 23	08 33	08 46	09 02	09 13	09 24
5	—	New Beckenham	d	05 24	05 58	06 25	06 37	06 53	07 09	07 26	07 36	07 46	08 00	08 06	08 16	08 26	08 36	08 49	09 05	09 16	09 27
5½	—	Lower Sydenham	d	05 26	06 00	06 27	06 39	06 55	07 11	07 28	07 38	07 48	08 02	08 08	08 18	08 28	08 38	08 51	09 07	09 18	09 30
7	—	Catford Bridge	d	05 29	06 03	06 31	06 42	06 59	07 15	07 32	07 42	07 52	08 06	08 12	08 22	08 32	08 42	08 55	09 11	09 21	09 33
7¾	—	Ladywell	d	05 31	06 05	06 33	06 44	07 01	07 17	07 34	07 44	07 54	08 09	08 14	08 24	08 34	08 44	08 57	09 13	09 23	09 36
8½	—	Lewisham	d	05 35	06 09	06 38	06 48		07 21		07 48		08 13		08 29		08 48	09 01	09 17		09 39
9	—	St Johns	a		06 11		06 50				07 50		08 15		08 31		08 50		09 19		09 41
9¾	—	New Cross ⊖	a		06 13		06 52		07 24		07 52		08 17		08 33		08 52		09 22		09 43
12¾	0	London Bridge ⊖	a	05 43	06 19	06 46	06 58	07 10	07 30	07 43	07 58	08 03	08 23	08 23	08 39	08 43	08 58	09 09	09 28	09 32	09 49
—	0¾	London Cannon Street ⊖	a		06 26		07 06		07 38		08 06		08 31		08 47		09 07		09 36		09 57
13¾	—	London Waterloo (East) ⊖	a	05 49		06 52		07 16		07 49		08 09		08 29		08 49		09 15		09 38	
14½	—	London Charing Cross ⊖	a	05 57		06 58		07 23		07 56		08 16		08 36		08 56		09 22		09 45	

		SE	SE	SE	SE		SE	SE	SE	SE	SE	SE	SE	SE	SE	SE	SE	SE	SE	SE	SE	SE
Hayes	d	09 30	09 45	10 00	10 15	and at the same minutes past each hour until	12 30	12 45	13 00	13 15	13 30	13 45	14 00	14 15	14 30	14 45	15 00	15 15	15 30	15 45	16 00	16 17
West Wickham	d	09 33	09 48	10 03	10 18		12 33	12 48	13 03	13 18	13 33	13 48	14 03	14 18	14 33	14 48	15 03	15 18	15 33	15 48	16 03	16 20
Eden Park	d	09 35	09 50	10 05	10 20		12 35	12 50	13 05	13 20	13 35	13 50	14 05	14 20	14 35	14 50	15 05	15 20	15 35	15 50	16 05	16 22
Elmers End	d	09 39	09 54	10 09	10 24		12 39	12 54	13 09	13 24	13 39	13 54	14 09	14 24	14 39	14 54	15 09	15 24	15 39	15 54	16 09	16 26
Clock House	d	09 41	09 56	10 11	10 26		12 41	12 56	13 11	13 26	13 41	13 56	14 11	14 26	14 41	14 56	15 11	15 26	15 41	15 56	16 11	16 28
New Beckenham	d	09 44	09 59	10 14	10 29		12 44	12 59	13 14	13 29	13 44	13 59	14 14	14 29	14 44	14 59	15 14	15 29	15 44	15 59	16 14	16 31
Lower Sydenham	d	09 46	10 01	10 16	10 31		12 46	13 01	13 16	13 31	13 46	14 01	14 16	14 31	14 46	15 01	15 16	15 31	15 46	16 01	16 16	16 33
Catford Bridge	d	09 49	10 04	10 19	10 34		12 49	13 04	13 19	13 34	13 49	14 04	14 19	14 34	14 49	15 04	15 19	15 34	15 49	16 04	16 19	16 36
Ladywell	d	09 51	10 06	10 21	10 36		12 51	13 06	13 21	13 36	13 51	14 06	14 21	14 36	14 51	15 06	15 21	15 36	15 51	16 06	16 21	16 38
Lewisham	d		10 09		10 39			13 09		13 39		14 09		14 39		15 09		15 39		16 09		16 42
St Johns	a		10 11		10 41			13 11		13 41		14 11		14 41		15 11		15 41		16 11		16 45
New Cross ⊖	a		10 13		10 43			13 13		13 43		14 13		14 43		15 13		15 43		16 13		16 48
London Bridge ⊖	a	10 00	10 19	10 30	10 49		13 00	13 19	13 30	13 49	14 00	14 19	14 30	14 49	15 00	15 19	15 30	15 49	16 00	16 19	16 30	16 54
London Cannon Street ⊖	a		10 24		10 54			13 24		13 54		14 24		14 55		15 24		15 54		16 24		17 02
London Waterloo (East) ⊖	a	10 06		10 36			13 06		13 36		14 06		14 36		15 06		15 36		16 06		16 37	
London Charing Cross ⊖	a	10 10		10 40			13 10		13 40		14 10		14 40		15 10		15 40		16 10		16 42	

		SE	SE	SE	SE	SE	SE	SE	SE	SE	SE	SE	SE	SE	SE	SE	SE	SE	SE	SE	SE	SE	SE
Hayes	d	16 29	16 47	16 59	17 17	17 29	17 52	18 03	18 25	18 35	18 50	19 00	19 15	19 30	19 45	20 00	20 15	20 30	20 45	21 00	21 15	21 30	21 45
West Wickham	d	16 32	16 50	17 02	17 20	17 32	17 55	18 06	18 28	18 38	18 53	19 03	19 18	19 33	19 48	20 03	20 18	20 33	20 48	21 03	21 18	21 33	21 48
Eden Park	d	16 34	16 52	17 04	17 22	17 34	17 57	18 08	18 30	18 40	18 55	19 05	19 20	19 35	19 50	20 05	20 20	20 35	20 50	21 05	21 20	21 35	21 50
Elmers End	d	16 38	16 56	17 08	17 26	17 38	18 01	18 12	18 34	18 44	18 59	19 09	19 24	19 39	19 54	20 09	20 24	20 39	20 54	21 09	21 24	21 39	21 54
Clock House	d	16 40	16 58	17 10	17 28	17 40	18 03	18 14	18 36	18 46	19 01	19 11	19 26	19 41	19 56	20 11	20 26	20 41	20 56	21 11	21 26	21 41	21 56
New Beckenham	d	16 43	17 01	17 13	17 31	17 43	18 06	18 17	18 39	18 49	19 04	19 14	19 29	19 44	19 59	20 14	20 29	20 44	20 59	21 14	21 29	21 44	21 59
Lower Sydenham	d	16 45	17 03	17 15	17 33	17 45	18 08	18 19	18 41	18 51	19 06	19 16	19 31	19 46	20 01	20 16	20 31	20 46	21 01	21 16	21 31	21 46	22 01
Catford Bridge	d	16 48	17 07	17 18	17 36	17 48	18 12	18 22	18 44	18 54	19 09	19 19	19 34	19 49	20 04	20 19	20 34	20 49	21 04	21 19	21 34	21 49	22 04
Ladywell	d	16 50	17 09	17 20	17 38	17 50	18 14	18 24	18 46	18 56	19 11	19 21	19 36	19 51	20 06	20 21	20 36	20 51	21 06	21 21	21 36	21 51	22 06
Lewisham	d		17 13		17 42		18 19		18 50		19 16		19 39		20 09		20 39		21 09		21 39		22 09
St Johns	a		17 16		17 44		18 21		18 52		19 19		19 41		20 11		20 41		21 11		21 41		22 11
New Cross ⊖	a		17 18		17 46		18 24		18 54		19 21		19 43		20 13		20 43		21 13		21 43		22 13
London Bridge ⊖	a	16 59	17 25	17 29	17 52	18 01	18 33	18 34	19 00	19 06	19 28	19 30	19 49	20 00	20 19	20 30	20 49	21 00	21 19	21 30	21 49	22 00	22 19
London Cannon Street ⊖	a		17 32		18 00		18 40		19 05		19 33		19 54		20 24		20 54		21 25		21 54		22 24
London Waterloo (East) ⊖	a	17 05		17 35		18 06		18 40		19 11		19 36		20 06		20 36		21 06		21 36		22 06	
London Charing Cross ⊖	a	17 11		17 44		18 12		18 46		19 15		19 43		20 10		20 40		21 10		21 40		22 10	

		SE	SE	SE	SE	SE	SE FO	SE W ThO	SE FO	SE MTO	SE WTh FO	SE MTO
Hayes	d	22 00	22 15	22 30	22 45	23 00	23 15	23 15		23 18	23 30	23 35
West Wickham	d	22 03	22 18	22 33	22 48	23 03	23 18	23 18		23 21	23 33	23 38
Eden Park	d	22 05	22 20	22 35	22 50	23 05	23 20	23 20		23 23	23 35	23 40
Elmers End	d	22 09	22 24	22 39	22 54	23 09	23 24	23 24		23 27	23 39	23 44
Clock House	d	22 11	22 26	22 41	22 56	23 11	23 26	23 26		23 29	23 41	23 46
New Beckenham	d	22 14	22 29	22 44	22 59	23 14	23 29	23 29		23 32	23 44	23 49
Lower Sydenham	d	22 16	22 31	22 46	23 01	23 16	23 31	23 31		23 34	23 46	23 51
Catford Bridge	d	22 19	22 34	22 49	23 04	23 19	23 34	23 34		23 37	23 49	23 54
Ladywell	d	22 21	22 36	22 51	23 06	23 21	23 36	23 36		23 40	23 51	23 56
Lewisham	d		22 39		23 09		23 39	23 40	←	23a43		23 59
St Johns	a		22 41		23 11		23 41		23 41			00 02
New Cross ⊖	a		22 43		23 13		→		23 43			00 04
London Bridge ⊖	a	22 30	22 49	23 00	23 19	23 30		23 48	23 49		00 01	00 10
London Cannon Street ⊖	a		22 54		23 24				23 54			00 18
London Waterloo (East) ⊖	a	22 36		23 06		23 36		23 54			00 06	
London Charing Cross ⊖	a	22 40		23 10		23 40		00 01			00 10	

Saturdays

26 May to 8 December

		SE	SE	SE	SE	SE	SE	SE		SE	SE	SE	SE	SE	SE
Hayes	d	05 54	06 24	06 54	07 15	07 30	07 45	08 00	and at the same minutes past each hour until	22 15	22 30	22 45	23 00	23 15	23 30
West Wickham	d	05 57	06 27	06 57	07 18	07 33	07 48	08 03		22 18	22 33	22 48	23 03	23 18	23 33
Eden Park	d	05 59	06 29	06 59	07 20	07 35	07 50	08 05		22 20	22 35	22 50	23 05	23 20	23 35
Elmers End	d	06 03	06 33	07 03	07 24	07 39	07 54	08 09		22 24	22 39	22 54	23 09	23 24	23 39
Clock House	d	06 05	06 35	07 05	07 26	07 41	07 56	08 11		22 26	22 41	22 56	23 11	23 26	23 41
New Beckenham	d	06 08	06 38	07 08	07 29	07 44	07 59	08 14		22 29	22 44	22 59	23 14	23 29	23 44
Lower Sydenham	d	06 10	06 40	07 10	07 31	07 46	08 01	08 16		22 31	22 46	23 01	23 16	23 31	23 46
Catford Bridge	d	06 13	06 43	07 13	07 34	07 49	08 04	08 19		22 34	22 49	23 04	23 19	23 34	23 49
Ladywell	d	06 15	06 45	07 15	07 36	07 51	08 06	08 21		22 36	22 51	23 06	23 21	23 36	23 51
Lewisham	d	06 20	06 50	07 20	07 39		08 09			22 39		23 09		23 39	
St Johns	a				07 41		08 11			22 41		23 11		23 41	
New Cross ⊖	a				07 43		08 13			22 43		23 13		23 43	
London Bridge ⊖	a	06 28	06 58	07 28	07 49	08 00	08 19	08 30		22 49	23 00	23 19	23 30	23 49	00 01
London Cannon Street ⊖	a				07 54		08 24			22 54		23 24		23 54	
London Waterloo (East) ⊖	a	06 34	07 04	07 34		08 06		08 36			23 06		23 36		00 07
London Charing Cross ⊖	a	06 39	07 09	07 39		08 10		08 40			23 10		23 40		00 11

London Charing Cross/Cannon Street - Grove Park, Orpington, Sevenoaks and Tonbridge, Grove Park - Bromley North

Miles	Miles			SE MO ◇1	SE MX ◇1	SE MO	SE MX ◇1	SE MO ◇1	SE MX ◇1	SE MX	SE TWO	SE ThFO		SE MO	SE MX	SE ThFO	SE MX	SE ThFO	SE MO	SE TWO	SE ThFO	SE MX		SE MO A	SE ThFO
0	—	London Charing Cross ⊖	d													00 05		00 15	00 16		00 18			00 46	00 50
0¾	—	London Waterloo (East) ⊖	d													00 08		00 18	00 19		00 21			00 49	00 53
—	—	London Cannon Street ⊖	d																	00 20					
1¾	—	London Bridge ⊖	d													00 14		00 24	00 25	00 24	00 28			00 55	00 59
4¾	—	New Cross ⊖	d																	00 30					
5½	—	St Johns	d								00 02									00 32					
6	—	Lewisham	d								00 05	00 05		00 05					00 35	00 35	00 37			01 05	01 08
7¼	—	Hither Green	d								00 09	00 09		00 09		00 23			00 39	00 39	00 41			01 09	01 13
9	0	Grove Park	d								00 13	00 13		00 13	00 15	00 28	00 35		00 43	00 43	00 45	00 55		01 13	01 17
—	1¼	Sundridge Park	d												00 18		00 38					00 58			
—	1¾	Bromley North	a												00 20		00 40					01 00			
10¼	—	Elmstead Woods	d							00 01	00 16	00 16		00 16		00 31			00 46	00 46	00 48			01 16	01 20
11¼	—	Chislehurst	d							00 03	00 19	00 19		00 18		00 33			00 48	00 49	00 51			01 18	01 22
12¾	—	Petts Wood	d							00 06	00 22	00 22		00 22		00 36			00 52	00 52	00 54			01 22	01 25
13¾	—	Orpington	a							00 12	00 25	00 25		00 27		00 42		00 50	00 55	00 57	01 00			01 27	01 32
—	—		d					00 06	00 10	00 13				00 28				00 51							
15¼	—	Chelsfield	d			00 01				00 16				00 31				00 54							
16½	—	Knockholt	d			00 04				00 19				00 34											
20½	—	Dunton Green	d			00 09				00 24				00 39				01 00							
22	—	Sevenoaks	a			00 12		00 15	00 19	00 27				00 42				01 03							
—	—		d		00 06		00 13	00 16	00 20									01 04							
27	—	Hildenborough	d	00 06	00 12													01s10							
29½	—	Tonbridge	a	00 10	00 16		00 21	00 24	00 28									01 14							

		SE	SE ◇1	SE	SE	SE	SE ◇1	SE		SE	SE ◇1	SE	SE	SE ◇1	SE	SE	SE	SE		SE ◇1	SE	SE	SE ◇1	SE ◇1	SE
London Charing Cross ⊖	d		05 30		05 32		05 56	06 05			06 28				06 35					07 00		07 06	07 09	07 15	
London Waterloo (East) ⊖	d		05 33		05 35		05 59	06 08			06 31				06 38					07 03		07 09	07 12	07 18	
London Cannon Street ⊖	d											06 16		06 32			06 49								
London Bridge ⊖	d		05 39		05 41		06 05	06 14			06 37	06 20		06 36	06 44		06 53			07 09		07 15	07 18	07 24	
New Cross ⊖	d											06 26					06 59								
St Johns	d											06 28					07 01								
Lewisham	d				05 50							06 32					07 04								
Hither Green	d				05 54			06 23				06 36			06 53		07 08					07 26			
Grove Park	d	05 24		05 44	05 58	06 04		06 28		06 28		06 40	06 45		06 58	06 59	07 12	07 12			07 26	07 30			
Sundridge Park	d	05 27		05 47		06 07				06 31			06 48					07 15							
Bromley North	a	05 29		05 49		06 09				06 33			06 50			07 03		07 17			07 30				
Elmstead Woods	d				06 01			06 31				06 43			07 01		07 15					07 33			
Chislehurst	d				06 03			06 33				06 45			07 03		07 17					07 35			←
Petts Wood	d				06 06			06 37				06 48			07 06		07 20					07 38			07 38
Orpington	a		05 55		06 11		06 22	06 40			06 53	06 54			07 09		07 25			07 25		→		07 40	07 41
	d		05 55		06 13		06 22	06 43			06 53				07 11					07 26				07 40	07 44
Chelsfield	d		05 58		06 16			06 46							07 14										07 47
Knockholt	d				06 19			06 49							07 17										07 50
Dunton Green	d				06 24			06 54							07 22										07 55
Sevenoaks	a		06 06		06 27		06 31	06 59			07 02			07 06	07 25					07 35			07 41	07 49	08 02
	d		06 06				06 32				07 03			07 06						07 36			07 42	07 50	
Hildenborough	d		06 12				06 38							07 12						07 42					
Tonbridge	a		06 16				06 42				07 11			07 16						07 46			07 50	07 58	

		SE	SE	SE ◇1		SE ◇1	SE	SE	SE	SE ◇1	SE	SE ◇1	SE ◇1	SE		SE	SE	SE	SE ◇1	SE ◇1	SE	SE	SE	SE ◇1	
London Charing Cross ⊖	d			07 27				07 33		07 37	07 47	07 57	08 00				08 06	08 10	08 16	08 18		08 20	08 24	08 28	
London Waterloo (East) ⊖	d			07 30				07 36		07 40	07 50	08 01	08 05				08 09	08 13	08 19	08 21		08 23	08 27	08 31	
London Cannon Street ⊖	d	07 15				07 42								07 53											
London Bridge ⊖	d	07 19		07 36		07 46		07 42		07 46	07 56	08 07	08 11	07 57			08 15	08 19	08 25	08 27		08 29	08 33	08 37	
New Cross ⊖	d	07 26												08 03											
St Johns	d													08 05											
Lewisham	d													08 10											
Hither Green	d	07 31						07 53						08 15			08 27								
Grove Park	d	07 35	07 39				07 53	07 58	08 08					08 19		08 23	08 31								
Sundridge Park	d		07 42				07 56									08 26									
Bromley North	a		07 44				07 58		08 12							08 28									
Elmstead Woods	d	07 38						08 01						08 22			08 34								
Chislehurst	d	07 41						08 03						08 24			08 37				←				
Petts Wood	d	07 44						08 06						08 27			08 40				08 40				
Orpington	a	07 48		07 55		08 07		08 10			08 17		08 29	08 33			→	08 42		08 43	08 45	08 52	08 55	08 56	
	d			07 55		08 08		08 12					08 32							08 43	08 46			08 56	
Chelsfield	d			07 58				08 15																08 59	
Knockholt	d							08 18													08 50				
Dunton Green	d							08 23													08 55				
Sevenoaks	a			08 06		08 17		08 28		08 12			08 41						08 48	08 52	09 01			09 07	
	d			08 06		08 18				08 13			08 41						08 49	08 53				09 07	
Hildenborough	d			08 12									08 47											09 13	
Tonbridge	a			08 16		08 26				08 21		08 36	08 51						08 57	09 01				09 17	

A from 4 June, not 25 June

Table T204-F

Mondays to Fridays

21 May to 7 December

London Charing Cross/Cannon Street - Grove Park, Orpington, Sevenoaks and Tonbridge, Grove Park - Bromley North

		SE	SE	SE ◇1	SE	SE		SE ◇1	SE	SE ◇1	SE ◇1	SE	SE	SE ◇1	SE	SE		SE ◇1	SE ◇1	SE	SE	SE	SE	SE	SE ◇1
London Charing Cross ⊖	d				08 32			08 34	08 44	08 58	09 02				09 06			09 22	09 24				09 34		09 40
London Waterloo (East) ⊖	d				08 35			08 37	08 47	09 01	09 05				09 09			09 25	09 27				09 37		09 43
London Cannon Street ⊖	d	08 17		08 40									08 52	09 14							09 20				
London Bridge ⊖	d	08 21		08 44	08 41			08 43	08 53	09 07	09 11		08 56	09 18	09 15			09 31	09 33		09 24		09 43		09 49
New Cross ⊖	d	08 28											09 02								09 31				
St Johns	d	08 30											09 04								09 33				
Lewisham	d	08 34											09 07								09 37				
Hither Green	d	08 38			08 54								09 13		09 24						09 41		09 53		
Grove Park	d	08 42	08 46		08 58	09 00						09 14	09 17		09 28	09 29				09 43	09 45	09 58	09 58	10 12	
Sundridge Park	d		08 49			09 03						09 17				09 32				09 46		10 01		10 15	
Bromley North	a		08 51			09 05						09 19				09 34				09 48		10 03		10 17	
Elmstead Woods	d	08 45			09 01								09 20		09 31						09 48		10 01		
Chislehurst	d	08 48			09 03								09 22		09 33						09 51		10 03		
Petts Wood	d	08 51			09 06								09 25		09 36						09 54		10 06		
Orpington	a	08 58		09 05	09 09				09 16	09 24	09 30		09 31	09 38	09 40			09 48	09 53		09 59		→		
	d			09 07	09 13					09 26	09 31			09 40	09 43			09 50	09 56						
Chelsfield	d				09 16										09 46										
Knockholt	d				09 19										09 49										
Dunton Green	d				09 24										09 54										
Sevenoaks	a			09 17	09 29			09 10		09 35	09 40			09 49	09 59			10 01	10 05						10 12
	d			09 20				09 13		09 36	09 41			09 50				10 02	10 06						10 13
Hildenborough	d									09 42									10 12						
Tonbridge	a			09 28				09 21		09 46	09 50			09 58				10 10	10 16						10 21

		SE ◇1		SE	SE ◇1	SE	SE	SE	SE ◇1	SE ◇1	SE	SE		SE	SE ◇1	SE	SE ◇1	SE ◇1	SE	SE	SE	SE ◇1		SE	SE
London Charing Cross ⊖	d	09 45			10 00			10 05	10 10	10 15					10 30	10 35	10 40	10 45				11 00		11 05	
London Waterloo (East) ⊖	d	09 48			10 03			10 08	10 13	10 18					10 33	10 38	10 43	10 48				11 03		11 08	
London Cannon Street ⊖	d					09 50						10 20								10 50					
London Bridge ⊖	d	09 54			10 09	09 54		10 14	10 19	10 24		10 24			10 39	10 44	10 49	10 54		10 54		11 09		11 14	
New Cross ⊖	d					10 00						10 30								11 00					
St Johns	d					10 02						10 32								11 02					
Lewisham	d					10 05						10 35								11 05					
Hither Green	d					10 10		10 23				10 39				10 53				11 09				11 23	
Grove Park	d					10 14	10 28	10 28				10 43		10 50		10 58				11 13	11 15			11 28	11 35
Sundridge Park	d						10 31							10 53							11 18				11 38
Bromley North	a						10 33							10 55							11 20				11 40
Elmstead Woods	d					10 17		10 31				10 46				11 01				11 16				11 31	
Chislehurst	d			←		10 19		10 33			←	10 49				11 03			←	11 19				11 33	
Petts Wood	d			10 06		10 22		10 36			10 36	10 52				11 06			11 06	11 22				11 36	
Orpington	a	10 09		10 09	10 25	10 28		→		10 39	10 39	10 55			10 55	→		11 09	11 09	11 25		11 25		→	
	d	10 10		10 13	10 26					10 39	10 43				10 56			11 10	11 13			11 26			
Chelsfield	d			10 16							10 46								11 16						
Knockholt	d			10 19							10 49								11 19						
Dunton Green	d			10 24							10 54								11 24						
Sevenoaks	a	10 19		10 29	10 35				10 42	10 49	10 57				11 05		11 12	11 19	11 27			11 35			
	d	10 20			10 36				10 43	10 50					11 06		11 13	11 20				11 36			
Hildenborough	d				10 42										11 12							11 42			
Tonbridge	a	10 28			10 46				10 51	10 58					11 16		11 21	11 28				11 46			

		SE ◇1	SE ◇1	SE	SE ◇1	SE	SE	SE		SE ◇1	SE ◇1	SE	SE	SE	SE ◇1	SE	SE	SE ◇1		SE ◇1	SE	SE	SE	SE ◇1	SE
London Charing Cross ⊖	d	11 10	11 15		11 30			11 35		11 40	11 45				12 00	12 05		12 10		12 15				12 30	12 35
London Waterloo (East) ⊖	d	11 13	11 18		11 33			11 38		11 43	11 48				12 03	12 08		12 13		12 18				12 33	12 38
London Cannon Street ⊖	d					11 20							11 50									12 20			
London Bridge ⊖	d	11 19	11 24		11 39	11 24		11 44		11 49	11 54		11 54		12 09	12 14		12 19		12 24		12 24		12 39	12 44
New Cross ⊖	d					11 30							12 00									12 30			
St Johns	d					11 32							12 02									12 32			
Lewisham	d					11 35							12 05									12 35			
Hither Green	d					11 39		11 53					12 09			12 23						12 39			12 53
Grove Park	d					11 43	11 55	11 58					12 13	12 15		12 28	12 35					12 43	12 55		12 58
Sundridge Park	d						11 58							12 18			12 38						12 58		
Bromley North	a						12 00							12 20			12 40						13 00		
Elmstead Woods	d					11 46		12 01					12 16			12 31						12 46			13 01
Chislehurst	d			←		11 49		12 03				←	12 19			12 33					←	12 49			13 03
Petts Wood	d			11 36		11 52		12 06				12 06	12 22			12 36					12 36	12 52			13 06
Orpington	a		11 39	11 40	11 55	11 57		→			12 09	12 09	12 25		12 25	→				12 39	12 39	12 55		12 55	→
	d		11 39	11 43	11 56						12 10	12 13			12 26					12 39	12 43			12 56	
Chelsfield	d			11 46								12 16									12 46				
Knockholt	d			11 49								12 19									12 49				
Dunton Green	d			11 54								12 24									12 54				
Sevenoaks	a	11 42	11 49	11 57	12 05					12 12	12 19	12 27			12 35			12 42		12 49	12 57			13 05	
	d	11 43	11 50		12 06					12 13	12 20				12 36			12 43		12 50				13 06	
Hildenborough	d				12 12										12 42									13 12	
Tonbridge	a	11 51	11 58		12 16					12 21	12 28				12 46			12 51		12 58				13 16	

London Charing Cross/Cannon Street - Grove Park, Orpington, Sevenoaks and Tonbridge, Grove Park - Bromley North

		SE ◇1	SE ◇1	SE	SE	SE	SE ◇1	SE	SE	SE ◇1		SE ◇1	SE	SE	SE	SE ◇1	SE	SE ◇1	SE ◇1	SE		SE	SE	SE ◇1	SE
London Charing Cross ⊖	d	12 40	12 45				13 00	13 05		13 10		13 15				13 30	13 35	13 40	13 45					14 00	14 05
London Waterloo (East) ⊖	d	12 43	12 48				13 03	13 08		13 13		13 18				13 33	13 38	13 43	13 48					14 03	14 08
London Cannon Street ⊖	d				12 50									13 20								13 50			
London Bridge ⊖	d	12 49	12 54		12 54		13 09	13 14		13 19		13 24		13 24		13 39	13 44	13 49	13 54			13 54		14 09	14 14
New Cross ⊖	d				13 00									13 30								14 00			
St Johns	d				13 02									13 32								14 02			
Lewisham	d				13 05									13 35								14 05			
Hither Green	d				13 09			13 23						13 39			13 53					14 09			14 23
Grove Park	d				13 13	13 15		13 28	13 35					13 43	13 55		13 58					14 13	14 15		14 28
Sundridge Park	d					13 18			13 38						13 58								14 18		
Bromley North	a					13 20			13 40						14 00								14 20		
Elmstead Woods	d				13 16			13 31						13 46			14 01					14 16			14 31
Chislehurst	d			←	13 19			13 33					←	13 49			14 03			←		14 19			14 33
Petts Wood	d			13 06	13 22			13 36					13 36	13 52			14 06			14 06		14 22			14 36
Orpington	a		13 09	13 09	13 25		13 25	→				13 39	13 39	13 55		13 55	→		14 09	14 09		14 25		14 25	→
	d		13 10	13 13			13 26					13 39	13 43			13 56			14 10	14 13				14 26	
Chelsfield	d			13 16									13 46							14 16					
Knockholt	d			13 19									13 49							14 19					
Dunton Green	d			13 24									13 54							14 24					
Sevenoaks	a	13 12	13 19	13 27			13 35			13 42		13 49	13 57			14 05		14 12	14 19	14 27				14 35	
	d	13 13	13 20				13 36			13 43		13 50				14 06		14 13	14 20					14 36	
Hildenborough	d						13 42									14 12								14 42	
Tonbridge	a	13 21	13 28				13 46			13 51		13 58				14 16		14 21	14 28					14 46	

		SE	SE ◇1	SE ◇1	SE	SE		SE	SE ◇1	SE	SE ◇1	SE ◇1	SE	SE ◇1	SE	SE		SE	SE	SE ◇1	SE ◇1	SE	SE	SE	SE ◇1
London Charing Cross ⊖	d		14 10	14 15					14 30	14 35	14 40	14 45		15 00				15 05		15 10	15 15				15 30
London Waterloo (East) ⊖	d		14 13	14 18					14 33	14 38	14 43	14 48		15 03				15 08		15 13	15 18				15 33
London Cannon Street ⊖	d					14 20									14 50								15 20		
London Bridge ⊖	d		14 19	14 24		14 24			14 39	14 44	14 49	14 54		15 09	14 54			15 14		15 19	15 24		15 24		15 39
New Cross ⊖	d					14 30									15 00								15 30		
St Johns	d					14 32									15 02								15 32		
Lewisham	d					14 35									15 05								15 35		
Hither Green	d					14 39				14 53					15 09			15 23					15 39		
Grove Park	d	14 35				14 43		14 55		14 58					15 13	15 15		15 28	15 35				15 43	15 55	
Sundridge Park	d	14 38						14 58								15 18			15 38					15 58	
Bromley North	a	14 40						15 00								15 20			15 40					16 00	
Elmstead Woods	d					14 46				15 01					15 16			15 31					15 46		
Chislehurst	d				←	14 49				15 03			←		15 19			15 33				←	15 49		
Petts Wood	d				14 36	14 52				15 06			15 06		15 22			15 36				15 36	15 52		
Orpington	a			14 39	14 39	14 55			14 55	→		15 09	15 09	15 25	15 27			→			15 39	15 39	15 55		15 55
	d			14 39	14 43				14 56			15 10	15 13	15 26							15 39	15 43			15 56
Chelsfield	d				14 46								15 16									15 46			
Knockholt	d				14 49								15 19									15 49			
Dunton Green	d				14 54								15 24									15 54			
Sevenoaks	a		14 42	14 49	14 57				15 05		15 12	15 19	15 27	15 35						15 42	15 49	15 57			16 05
	d		14 43	14 50					15 06		15 13	15 20		15 36						15 43	15 50				16 06
Hildenborough	d								15 12					15 42											16 12
Tonbridge	a		14 51	14 58					15 16		15 21	15 28		15 46						15 51	15 58				16 16

		SE		SE ◇1	SE ◇1	SE	SE ◇1	SE	SE	SE	SE	SE ◇1		SE ◇1	SE	SE ◇1	SE	SE	SE	SE	SE ◇1	SE		SE ◇1	SE ◇1
London Charing Cross ⊖	d	15 35		15 40	15 45		16 00			16 05		16 10		16 14		16 28			16 30		16 39	16 41		16 43	16 51
London Waterloo (East) ⊖	d	15 38		15 43	15 48		16 03			16 08		16 13		16 17		16 31			16 33		16 42	16 44		16 46	16 54
London Cannon Street ⊖	d							15 50									16 18								
London Bridge ⊖	d	15 44		15 49	15 54		16 09	15 54		16 14		16 19		16 23		16 37	16 23		16 39		16 48	16 50		16 52	17 00
New Cross ⊖	d							16 01									16 29								
St Johns	d							16 03									16 31								
Lewisham	d							16 06									16 36					17 00			
Hither Green	d	15 53						16 10		16 23							16 42		16 49			17 05			
Grove Park	d	15 58						16 14	16 18	16 28	16 34						16 46	16 49	16 53	17 02		17 09			
Sundridge Park	d								16 21		16 37							16 52		17 05					
Bromley North	a								16 23		16 39							16 54		17 07					
Elmstead Woods	d	16 01						16 17		16 31							16 49		16 56			17 12			
Chislehurst	d	16 03						16 20		16 33					←		16 51		16 59			17 15			
Petts Wood	d	16 06				←		16 23		16 36					16 36		16 54		17 02			17 18			
Orpington	a	16 09			16 10	16 09	16 25	16 29		→				16 39	16 40	16 54	17 00		17 06			17 24			17 17
	d	16 13			16 10	16 13	16 26							16 39	16 44	16 55			17 10						17 18
Chelsfield	d	→				16 16									16 47				17 13						
Knockholt	d					16 19									16 50				17 16						
Dunton Green	d					16 24									16 55				17 21						
Sevenoaks	a			16 12	16 19	16 27	16 35					16 42		16 48	17 00	17 04			17 26		17 11			17 15	17 27
	d			16 13	16 20		16 36					16 43		16 49		17 05					17 12			17 16	17 28
Hildenborough	d						16 42									17 11									
Tonbridge	a			16 22	16 28		16 46					16 51		16 58		17 15					17 20			17 24	17 36

Table T204-F

Mondays to Fridays
21 May to 7 December

London Charing Cross/Cannon Street - Grove Park, Orpington, Sevenoaks and Tonbridge, Grove Park - Bromley North

		SE	SE	SE ◇1		SE ◇1	SE	SE ◇1	SE	SE	SE ◇1	SE ◇1	SE	SE		SE	SE	SE ◇1	SE ◇1	SE ◇1	SE	SE	SE	SE ◇1	
London Charing Cross ⊖	d					17 01	17 03	17 11				17 24	17 26					17 39		17 44	17 47			18 01	
London Waterloo (East) ⊖	d					17 04	17 06	17 14				17 27	17 29					17 42		17 48	17 50			18 04	
London Cannon Street ⊖	d	16 52		17 01					17 16		17 23					17 39			17 45			17 58			
London Bridge ⊖	d	16 57		17 06		17 10	17 12	17 20	17 21		17 28	17 33	17 35			17 44		17 48	17 50	17 54	17 56	18 03		18 10	
New Cross ⊖	d	17 04														17 50						18 09			
St Johns	d																								
Lewisham	d						17 21						17 45								18 05				
Hither Green	d	17 10					17 26		17 32				17 50			17 55						18 14			
Grove Park	d	17 14	17 19				17 30		17 36	17 40			17 54	17 56		18 00	18 09				18 12	18 18	18 23		
Sundridge Park	d		17 22							17 43				17 59			18 12						18 26		
Bromley North	a		17 24							17 45				18 01			18 14						18 28		
Elmstead Woods	d	17 17					17 33		17 39				17 57			18 03					18 15	18 21			
Chislehurst	d	17 20					17 35		17 42				18 00			18 06					18 18	18 24			
Petts Wood	d	17 24					17 39		17 46				18 03			18 09					18 22	18 28			
Orpington	a	17 27					17 45		17 49				18 09			18 12					18 28	18 32			
	d	17 28							17 51							18 13						18 34			
Chelsfield	d	17 31				17 28			17 54			17 51				18 16				18 12		18 37			
Knockholt	d	17 34							17 57							18 19						18 40			
Dunton Green	d	17 39							18 02							18 24						18 45			
Sevenoaks	a	17 44		17 31		17 35		17 45	18 07		17 53	17 59				18 29		18 11	18 15	18 20		18 50		18 33	
	d			17 32		17 36		17 46			17 54	18 00						18 12	18 16	18 21				18 34	
Hildenborough	d					17 42					18 01	18 06								18 27					
Tonbridge	a			17 40		17 46		17 54			18 05	18 10						18 20	18 24	18 31				18 42	

		SE ◇1	SE ◇1	SE	SE	SE	SE ◇1	SE ◇1	SE	SE		SE ◇1	SE	SE ◇1	SE ◇1	SE	SE	SE ◇1	SE	SE ◇1		SE	SE	SE ◇1	SE ◇1
London Charing Cross ⊖	d		18 07	18 09			18 19		18 29			18 31		18 41	18 45	18 48		19 00				19 05		19 10	19 15
London Waterloo (East) ⊖	d		18 10	18 12			18 22		18 32			18 34		18 44	18 49	18 51		19 03				19 08		19 13	19 18
London Cannon Street ⊖	d	18 07				18 20		18 31											18 48	19 02					
London Bridge ⊖	d	18 12	18 16	18 18		18 25	18 28	18 36	18 38			18 40		18 50	18 55	18 57		19 09	18 53	19 07		19 14		19 19	19 24
New Cross ⊖	d					18 31													18 59						
St Johns	d																		19 01						
Lewisham	d					18 37													19 05						
Hither Green	d					18 41			18 49							19 07			19 11			19 23			
Grove Park	d			18 31	18 38	18 46			18 53	18 57						19 11	19 15		19 15			19 28	19 33		
Sundridge Park	d				18 41					19 00							19 18						19 36		
Bromley North	a				18 43					19 02							19 20						19 38		
Elmstead Woods	d			18 34		18 49			18 56							19 14			19 18			19 31			
Chislehurst	d			18 37		18 52			18 59							19 17			19 21			19 33			
Petts Wood	d			18 41		18 56			19 03				←			19 20			19 24			19 36			
Orpington	a			18 47		18 59			19 08			18 56	18 59		19 11	19 26		19 26	19 30			→			19 39
	d					19 00						18 57	19 00		19 12			19 26							19 40
Chelsfield	d		18 34			→							19 03	19 08				19 29							
Knockholt	d												19 06												
Dunton Green	d												19 11												
Sevenoaks	a	18 37	18 42				18 52	18 59				19 06	19 16	19 17	19 21			19 37		19 30				19 41	19 49
	d	18 38	18 43				18 53	19 00				19 07		19 18	19 22			19 38		19 31				19 42	19 50
Hildenborough	d	18 44	18 49									19 13						19 44		19 37					
Tonbridge	a	18 48	18 53				19 01	19 08				19 17		19 26	19 30			19 48		19 41				19 51	19 58

		SE	SE ◇1	SE	SE	SE		SE	SE ◇1	SE ◇1	SE	SE	SE	SE ◇1	SE	SE		SE ◇1	SE ◇1	SE	SE	SE	SE ◇1	SE	SE
London Charing Cross ⊖	d		19 30			19 35			19 40	19 45				20 00	20 05			20 10	20 15				20 30	20 35	
London Waterloo (East) ⊖	d		19 33			19 38			19 43	19 48				20 03	20 08			20 13	20 18				20 33	20 38	
London Cannon Street ⊖	d			19 22								19 50									20 20				
London Bridge ⊖	d		19 39	19 26		19 44			19 49	19 54		19 54		20 09	20 14			20 19	20 24		20 24		20 39	20 44	
New Cross ⊖	d			19 32								20 00									20 30				
St Johns	d			19 34								20 02									20 32				
Lewisham	d			19 37								20 05									20 35				
Hither Green	d			19 41		19 53						20 09			20 23						20 39			20 53	
Grove Park	d			19 45	19 49	19 58		20 03				20 13	20 17		20 28	20 33					20 43	20 47		20 58	21 05
Sundridge Park	d				19 52			20 06					20 20			20 36						20 50			21 08
Bromley North	a				19 54			20 08					20 22			20 38						20 52			21 10
Elmstead Woods	d			19 48		20 01						20 16			20 31						20 46			21 01	
Chislehurst	d	←		19 51		20 03					←	20 19			20 33					←	20 49			21 03	
Petts Wood	d	19 36		19 54		20 06					20 06	20 22			20 36					20 36	20 52			21 06	
Orpington	a	19 39	19 55	19 59		→				20 09	20 09	20 25		20 25	→				20 39	20 39	20 55		20 55	→	
	d	19 43	19 56							20 10	20 13			20 26					20 40	20 43			20 56		
Chelsfield	d	19 46									20 16									20 46					
Knockholt	d	19 49									20 19									20 49					
Dunton Green	d	19 54									20 24									20 54					
Sevenoaks	a	19 59	20 05						20 12	20 19	20 27			20 35				20 42	20 49	20 57			21 05		
	d		20 06						20 13	20 20				20 36				20 43	20 50				21 06		
Hildenborough	d		20 12											20 42									21 12		
Tonbridge	a		20 16						20 21	20 28				20 46				20 51	20 58				21 16		

Table T204-F

Mondays to Fridays

21 May to 7 December

London Charing Cross/Cannon Street - Grove Park, Orpington, Sevenoaks and Tonbridge, Grove Park - Bromley North

		SE	SE	SE	SE	SE	SE	SE		SE	SE	SE	SE	SE	SE	SE	SE	SE		SE	SE	SE	SE	SE	SE
		◇1	◇1			◇1				◇1				◇1		◇1	◇1					◇1			◇1
London Charing Cross ⊖	d	20 40	20 45			21 00	21 05			21 10				21 30	21 35	21 40	21 45					22 00	22 05		22 10
London Waterloo (East) ⊖	d	20 43	20 48			21 03	21 08			21 13				21 33	21 38	21 43	21 48					22 03	22 08		22 13
London Cannon Street ⊖	d				20 50							21 20								21 50					
London Bridge ⊖	d	20 49	20 54		20 54	21 09	21 14			21 19		21 24		21 39	21 44	21 49	21 54			21 54		22 09	22 14		22 19
New Cross ⊖	d				21 00							21 30								22 00					
St Johns	d				21 02							21 32								22 02					
Lewisham	d				21 05							21 35								22 05					
Hither Green	d				21 09		21 23					21 39			21 53					22 09			22 23		
Grove Park	d				21 13		21 28	21 35				21 43	21 55		21 58					22 13	22 15		22 28	22 35	
Sundridge Park	d							21 38					21 58								22 18			22 38	
Bromley North	a							21 40					22 00								22 20			22 40	
Elmstead Woods	d				21 16		21 31					21 46			22 01					22 16			22 31		
Chislehurst	d			←	21 19		21 33				←	21 49			22 03			←		22 19			22 33		
Petts Wood	d			21 06	21 22		21 36				21 36	21 52			22 06			22 06		22 22			22 36		
Orpington	a		21 09	21 09	21 25	21 25	→			21 34	21 39	21 55		21 55	→		22 09	22 09		22 25		22 25	→		22 34
	d		21 10	21 13		21 26				21 35	21 43			21 56			22 10	22 13				22 26			22 35
Chelsfield	d			21 16							21 46							22 16							
Knockholt	d			21 19							21 49							22 19							
Dunton Green	d			21 24							21 54							22 24							
Sevenoaks	a	21 12	21 19	21 27		21 35				21 44	21 57			22 05		22 12	22 19	22 27				22 35			22 44
	d	21 13	21 20			21 36				21 45				22 06		22 13	22 20					22 36			22 45
Hildenborough	d					21 42								22 12								22 42			
Tonbridge	a	21 21	21 28			21 46				21 53				22 16		22 21	22 28					22 46			22 53

		SE	SE	SE		SE	SE	SE	SE	SE	SE MT FO	SE	SE W ThO	SE		SE	SE	SE	SE	SE	SE	SE	SE	SE	
						◇1		◇1	◇1			◇1								◇1		◇1	◇1		
London Charing Cross ⊖	d					22 30	22 35	22 40	22 45			23 00				23 05				23 30	23 35	23 40	23 45		
London Waterloo (East) ⊖	d					22 33	22 38	22 43	22 48			23 03				23 08				23 33	23 38	23 43	23 48		
London Cannon Street ⊖	d		22 20								22 50		22 50					23 20							
London Bridge ⊖	d		22 24			22 39	22 44	22 49	22 54		22 54	23 09	22 54			23 14		23 24		23 39	23 44	23 49	23 54		
New Cross ⊖	d		22 30								23 00		23 00					23 30							
St Johns	d		22 32								23 02		23 02					23 32							
Lewisham	d		22 35								23 05		23 05					23 35							
Hither Green	d		22 39				22 53				23 09		23 09			23 23		23 39			23 53				
Grove Park	d		22 43	22 55			22 58				23 13		23 13	23 15		23 28	23 35	23 43	23 55		23 58				
Sundridge Park	d			22 58										23 18			23 38		23 58						
Bromley North	a			23 00										23 20			23 40		00 01						
Elmstead Woods	d		22 46				23 01				23 16		23 16			23 31		23 46			00 01				
Chislehurst	d	←	22 49				23 03			←	23 19		23 19			23 33		23 49			00 03			←	
Petts Wood	d	22 36	22 52				23 06			23 06	23 22		23 22			23 36		23 52			00 06			00 06	
Orpington	a	22 39	22 55			22 55	→		23 09	23 09	23 25	23 25	23 27			23 39		23 55		23 55	→		00 09	00 12	
	d	22 43				22 56			23 10	23 13		23 26				23 43				23 56			00 10	00 13	
Chelsfield	d	22 46								23 16						23 46								00 16	
Knockholt	d	22 49								23 19						23 49								00 19	
Dunton Green	d	22 54								23 24						23 54								00 24	
Sevenoaks	a	22 57				23 05		23 12	23 19	23 27		23 35				23 57				00 05		00 12	00 19	00 27	
	d					23 06		23 13	23 20			23 36								00 06		00 13	00 20		
Hildenborough	d					23 12						23 42								00 12					
Tonbridge	a					23 16		23 21	23 28			23 46								00 16		00 21	00 28		

		SE W ThO	SE MT FO
London Charing Cross ⊖	d		
London Waterloo (East) ⊖	d		
London Cannon Street ⊖	d	23 45	23 50
London Bridge ⊖	d	23 49	23 54
New Cross ⊖	d	23 54	23 59
St Johns	d	23 57	00 02
Lewisham	d	00 05	00 05
Hither Green	d	00 09	00 09
Grove Park	d	00 13	00 13
Sundridge Park	d		
Bromley North	a		
Elmstead Woods	d	00 16	00 16
Chislehurst	d	00 19	00 19
Petts Wood	d	00 22	00 22
Orpington	a	00 25	00 25
	d		
Chelsfield	d		
Knockholt	d		
Dunton Green	d		
Sevenoaks	a		
	d		
Hildenborough	d		
Tonbridge	a		

Table T204-F

Saturdays

26 May to 8 December

London Charing Cross/Cannon Street - Grove Park, Orpington, Sevenoaks and Tonbridge, Grove Park - Bromley North

		SE	SE	SE	SE	SE		SE	SE	SE	SE	SE	SE	SE	SE	SE		SE	SE	SE	SE	SE	SE	SE	SE
		◇1	◇1	◇1														◇1							
London Charing Cross ⊖	d										00 50			05 35				06 00	06 05				06 35		
London Waterloo (East) ⊖	d										00 53			05 38				06 03	06 08				06 38		
London Cannon Street ⊖	d														05 50						06 20			06 50	
London Bridge ⊖	d										00 59			05 44	05 54			06 09	06 14		06 24		06 44	06 54	
New Cross ⊖	d														06 00						06 30			07 00	
St Johns	d					00 02									06 02						06 32			07 02	
Lewisham	d					00 05					01 08				06 05						06 35			07 05	
Hither Green	d					00 09					01 13			05 53	06 09				06 23		06 39		06 53	07 09	
Grove Park	d					00 13		00 15	00 35	00 55	01 17	05 35	05 55	05 58	06 13	06 15			06 28	06 35	06 43	06 55	06 58	07 13	07 15
Sundridge Park	d							00 18	00 38	00 58		05 38	05 58			06 18				06 38		06 58			07 18
Bromley North	a							00 20	00 40	01 00		05 40	06 00			06 20				06 40		07 00			07 20
Elmstead Woods	d				00 01	00 16					01 20			06 01	06 16				06 31		06 46		07 01	07 16	
Chislehurst	d				00 03	00 19					01 22			06 03	06 19				06 33		06 49		07 03	07 19	
Petts Wood	d				00 06	00 22					01 25			06 06	06 22				06 36		06 52		07 06	07 22	
Orpington	a				00 12	00 25					01 32			06 09	06 25			06 25	06 39		06 55		07 09	07 25	
	d			00 10	00 13									06 13				06 26	06 43				07 13		
Chelsfield	d				00 16									06 16					06 46				07 16		
Knockholt	d				00 19									06 19					06 49				07 19		
Dunton Green	d				00 24									06 24					06 54				07 24		
Sevenoaks	a			00 19	00 27									06 27				06 35	06 57				07 27		
	d	00 06	00 13	00 20														06 36							
Hildenborough	d	00 12																06 42							
Tonbridge	a	00 16	00 21	00 28														06 46							

		SE		SE	SE	SE	SE	SE	SE	SE	SE	SE		SE	SE	SE	SE	SE	SE	SE	SE	SE		SE	SE
					◇1	◇1					◇1	◇1							◇1	◇1					◇1
London Charing Cross ⊖	d	07 05			07 10	07 15				07 35	07 40	07 45					08 05		08 10	08 15					08 30
London Waterloo (East) ⊖	d	07 08			07 13	07 18				07 38	07 43	07 48					08 08		08 13	08 18					08 33
London Cannon Street ⊖	d							07 20							07 50							08 20			
London Bridge ⊖	d	07 14			07 19	07 24		07 24		07 44	07 49	07 54			07 54		08 14		08 19	08 24		08 24			08 39
New Cross ⊖	d							07 30							08 00							08 30			
St Johns	d							07 32							08 02							08 32			
Lewisham	d							07 35							08 05							08 35			
Hither Green	d	07 23						07 39		07 53					08 09		08 23					08 39			
Grove Park	d	07 28		07 35				07 43	07 55	07 58					08 13	08 15	08 28	08 35				08 43		08 55	
Sundridge Park	d			07 38					07 58							08 18		08 38						08 58	
Bromley North	a			07 40					08 00							08 20		08 40						09 00	
Elmstead Woods	d	07 31						07 46		08 01					08 16		08 31					08 46			
Chislehurst	d	07 33					←	07 49		08 03				←	08 19		08 33				←	08 49			
Petts Wood	d	07 36					07 36	07 52		08 06				08 06	08 22		08 36				08 36	08 52			
Orpington	a	→				07 39	07 39	07 55		→		08 09		08 09	08 25		→			08 39	08 39	08 55			08 55
	d					07 40	07 43					08 10		08 13						08 40	08 43				08 56
Chelsfield	d						07 46							08 16							08 46				
Knockholt	d						07 49							08 19							08 49				
Dunton Green	d						07 54							08 24							08 54				
Sevenoaks	a				07 42	07 49	07 57				08 12	08 19		08 27					08 42	08 49	08 57				09 05
	d				07 43	07 49					08 13	08 19							08 43	08 50					09 06
Hildenborough	d					07 55						08 25													09 12
Tonbridge	a				07 51	07 59					08 21	08 29							08 51	08 58					09 16

		SE	SE	SE	SE	SE	SE	SE		SE	SE	SE	SE	SE	SE	SE	SE	SE		SE	SE	SE	SE	SE	SE
			◇1	◇1				◇1				◇1	◇1				◇1			◇1	◇1				◇1
London Charing Cross ⊖	d	08 35	08 40	08 45				09 00		09 05		09 10	09 15				09 30	09 35		09 40	09 45				10 00
London Waterloo (East) ⊖	d	08 38	08 43	08 48				09 03		09 08		09 13	09 18				09 33	09 38		09 43	09 48				10 03
London Cannon Street ⊖	d					08 50									09 20								09 50		
London Bridge ⊖	d	08 44	08 49	08 54		08 54		09 09		09 14		09 19	09 24		09 24		09 39	09 44		09 49	09 54		09 54		10 09
New Cross ⊖	d					09 00									09 30								10 00		
St Johns	d					09 02									09 32								10 02		
Lewisham	d					09 05									09 35								10 05		
Hither Green	d	08 53				09 09				09 23					09 39			09 53					10 09		
Grove Park	d	08 58				09 13	09 15			09 28	09 35				09 43	09 55		09 58					10 13	10 15	
Sundridge Park	d						09 18				09 38					09 58								10 18	
Bromley North	a						09 20				09 40					10 00								10 20	
Elmstead Woods	d	09 01				09 16				09 31					09 46			10 01					10 16		
Chislehurst	d	09 03			←	09 19				09 33				←	09 49			10 03				←	10 19		
Petts Wood	d	09 06			09 06	09 22				09 36				09 36	09 52			10 06				10 06	10 22		
Orpington	a	→		09 09	09 09	09 25		09 25		→			09 39	09 39	09 55		09 55	→			10 09	10 09	10 25		10 25
	d			09 10	09 13			09 26					09 40	09 43			09 56				10 10	10 13			10 26
Chelsfield	d				09 16									09 46								10 16			
Knockholt	d				09 19									09 49								10 19			
Dunton Green	d				09 24									09 54								10 24			
Sevenoaks	a		09 12	09 19	09 27			09 35				09 42	09 49	09 57			10 05			10 12	10 19	10 27			10 35
	d		09 13	09 20				09 36				09 43	09 50				10 06			10 13	10 20				10 36
Hildenborough	d							09 42									10 12								10 42
Tonbridge	a		09 21	09 28				09 46				09 51	09 58				10 16			10 21	10 28				10 46

Table T204-F

Saturdays

26 May to 8 December

London Charing Cross/Cannon Street - Grove Park, Orpington, Sevenoaks and Tonbridge, Grove Park - Bromley North

Station		SE	SE	SE ◇1	SE ◇1	SE	SE	SE	SE ◇1	SE		SE ◇1	SE ◇1	SE	SE	SE	SE ◇1	SE	SE	SE ◇1		SE ◇1	SE	SE	SE
London Charing Cross	d	10 05		10 10	10 15				10 30	10 35		10 40	10 45				11 00	11 05		11 10		11 15			
London Waterloo (East)	d	10 08		10 13	10 18				10 33	10 38		10 43	10 48				11 03	11 08		11 13		11 18			
London Cannon Street	d						10 20								10 50									11 20	
London Bridge	d	10 14		10 19	10 24		10 24		10 39	10 44		10 49	10 54		10 54		11 09	11 14		11 19		11 24		11 24	
New Cross	d						10 30								11 00									11 30	
St Johns	d						10 32								11 02									11 32	
Lewisham	d						10 35								11 05									11 35	
Hither Green	d	10 23					10 39			10 53					11 09			11 23						11 39	
Grove Park	d	10 28	10 35				10 43	10 55		10 58					11 13	11 15		11 28	11 35					11 43	11 55
Sundridge Park	d		10 38					10 58								11 18			11 38						11 58
Bromley North	a		10 40					11 00								11 20			11 40						12 00
Elmstead Woods	d	10 31					10 46			11 01					11 16			11 31						11 46	
Chislehurst	d	10 33				←	10 49			11 03				←	11 19			11 33					←	11 49	
Petts Wood	d	10 36				10 36	10 52			11 06				11 06	11 22			11 36					11 36	11 52	
Orpington	a	→			10 39	10 39	10 55		10 55	→			11 09	11 09	11 25		11 25	→				11 39	11 39	11 55	
	d				10 40	10 43			10 56				11 10	11 13			11 26					11 40	11 43		
Chelsfield	d					10 46								11 16									11 46		
Knockholt	d					10 49								11 19									11 49		
Dunton Green	d					10 54								11 24									11 54		
Sevenoaks	a			10 42	10 49	10 57			11 05			11 12	11 19	11 27			11 35			11 42		11 49	11 57		
	d			10 43	10 50				11 06			11 13	11 20				11 36			11 43		11 50			
Hildenborough	d								11 12								11 42								
Tonbridge	a			10 51	10 58				11 16			11 21	11 28				11 46			11 51		11 58			

Station		SE ◇1	SE	SE ◇1	SE ◇1	SE		SE	SE	SE ◇1	SE	SE	SE ◇1	SE ◇1	SE	SE		SE	SE ◇1	SE	SE ◇1	SE ◇1	SE	SE	SE
London Charing Cross	d	11 30	11 35	11 40	11 45					12 00	12 05		12 10	12 15					12 30	12 35	12 40	12 45			
London Waterloo (East)	d	11 33	11 38	11 43	11 48					12 03	12 08		12 13	12 18					12 33	12 38	12 43	12 48			
London Cannon Street	d							11 50								12 20								12 50	
London Bridge	d	11 39	11 44	11 49	11 54			11 54		12 09	12 14		12 19	12 24		12 24			12 39	12 44	12 49	12 54		12 54	
New Cross	d							12 00								12 30								13 00	
St Johns	d							12 02								12 32								13 02	
Lewisham	d							12 05								12 35								13 05	
Hither Green	d		11 53					12 09			12 23					12 39				12 53				13 09	
Grove Park	d		11 58					12 13	12 15		12 28	12 35				12 43		12 55		12 58				13 13	13 15
Sundridge Park	d								12 18			12 38						12 58							13 18
Bromley North	a								12 20			12 40						13 00							13 20
Elmstead Woods	d		12 01					12 16			12 31					12 46				13 01				13 16	
Chislehurst	d		12 03			←		12 19			12 33				←	12 49				13 03			←	13 19	
Petts Wood	d		12 06			12 06		12 22			12 36				12 36	12 52				13 06			13 06	13 22	
Orpington	a	11 55	→		12 09	12 09		12 25		12 25	→			12 39	12 39	12 55			12 55	→		13 09	13 09	13 25	
	d	11 56			12 10	12 13				12 26				12 40	12 43				12 56			13 10	13 13		
Chelsfield	d					12 16									12 46								13 16		
Knockholt	d					12 19									12 49								13 19		
Dunton Green	d					12 24									12 54								13 24		
Sevenoaks	a	12 05		12 12	12 19	12 27				12 35			12 42	12 49	12 57				13 05		13 12	13 19	13 27		
	d	12 06		12 13	12 20					12 36			12 43	12 50					13 06		13 13	13 20			
Hildenborough	d	12 12								12 42									13 12						
Tonbridge	a	12 16		12 21	12 28					12 46			12 51	12 58					13 16		13 21	13 28			

Station		SE ◇1		SE	SE	SE ◇1	SE ◇1	SE	SE	SE	SE ◇1	SE		SE ◇1	SE ◇1	SE	SE	SE	SE ◇1	SE	SE	SE ◇1		SE ◇1	SE
London Charing Cross	d	13 00		13 05		13 10	13 15				13 30	13 35		13 40	13 45				14 00	14 05		14 10		14 15	
London Waterloo (East)	d	13 03		13 08		13 13	13 18				13 33	13 38		13 43	13 48				14 03	14 08		14 13		14 18	
London Cannon Street	d								13 20								13 50								
London Bridge	d	13 09		13 14		13 19	13 24		13 24		13 39	13 44		13 49	13 54		13 54		14 09	14 14		14 19		14 24	
New Cross	d								13 30								14 00								
St Johns	d								13 32								14 02								
Lewisham	d								13 35								14 05								
Hither Green	d			13 23					13 39			13 53					14 09			14 23					
Grove Park	d			13 28	13 35				13 43	13 55		13 58					14 13	14 15		14 28	14 35				
Sundridge Park	d				13 38					13 58								14 18			14 38				
Bromley North	a				13 40					14 00								14 20			14 40				
Elmstead Woods	d			13 31					13 46			14 01					14 16			14 31					
Chislehurst	d			13 33				←	13 49			14 03				←	14 19			14 33					←
Petts Wood	d			13 36				13 36	13 52			14 06				14 06	14 22			14 36					14 36
Orpington	a	13 25		→			13 39	13 39	13 55		13 55	→			14 09	14 09	14 25		14 25	→				14 39	14 39
	d	13 26					13 40	13 43			13 56				14 10	14 13			14 26					14 40	14 43
Chelsfield	d							13 46								14 16									14 46
Knockholt	d							13 49								14 19									14 49
Dunton Green	d							13 54								14 24									14 54
Sevenoaks	a	13 35				13 42	13 49	13 57			14 05			14 12	14 19	14 27			14 35			14 42		14 49	14 57
	d	13 36				13 43	13 50				14 06			14 13	14 20				14 36			14 43		14 50	
Hildenborough	d	13 42									14 12								14 42						
Tonbridge	a	13 46				13 51	13 58				14 16			14 21	14 28				14 46			14 51		14 58	

Table T204-F

Saturdays

26 May to 8 December

London Charing Cross/Cannon Street - Grove Park, Orpington, Sevenoaks and Tonbridge, Grove Park - Bromley North

Station		SE	SE	SE ◇1		SE	SE ◇1	SE ◇1	SE	SE	SE	SE ◇1	SE	SE		SE ◇1	SE ◇1	SE	SE	SE	SE ◇1	SE	SE ◇1	SE ◇1	
London Charing Cross	d			14 30		14 35	14 40	14 45				15 00	15 05			15 10	15 15				15 30	15 35	15 40	15 45	
London Waterloo (East)	d			14 33		14 38	14 43	14 48				15 03	15 08			15 13	15 18				15 33	15 38	15 43	15 48	
London Cannon Street	d	14 20								14 50									15 20						
London Bridge	d	14 24		14 39		14 44	14 49	14 54		14 54		15 09	15 14			15 19	15 24		15 24		15 39	15 44	15 49	15 54	
New Cross	d	14 30								15 00									15 30						
St Johns	d	14 32								15 02									15 32						
Lewisham	d	14 35								15 05									15 35						
Hither Green	d	14 39				14 53				15 09			15 23						15 39			15 53			
Grove Park	d	14 43	14 55			14 58				15 13	15 15		15 28	15 35					15 43	15 55		15 58			
Sundridge Park	d		14 58								15 18			15 38						15 58					
Bromley North	a		15 00								15 20			15 40						16 00					
Elmstead Woods	d	14 46				15 01				15 16			15 31						15 46			16 01			
Chislehurst	d	14 49				15 03			←	15 19			15 33					←	15 49			16 03			
Petts Wood	d	14 52				15 06			15 06	15 22			15 36					15 36	15 52			16 06			
Orpington	a	14 55		14 55		→		15 09	15 09	15 25		15 25	→				15 39	15 39	15 55		15 55	→		16 09	
	d			14 56				15 10	15 13			15 26					15 40	15 43			15 56			16 10	
Chelsfield	d								15 16									15 46							
Knockholt	d								15 19									15 49							
Dunton Green	d								15 24									15 54							
Sevenoaks	a			15 05			15 12	15 19	15 27			15 35				15 42	15 49	15 57			16 05		16 12	16 19	
	d			15 06			15 13	15 20				15 36				15 43	15 50				16 06		16 13	16 20	
Hildenborough	d			15 12								15 42									16 12				
Tonbridge	a			15 16			15 21	15 28				15 46				15 51	15 58				16 16		16 21	16 28	

Station		SE	SE	SE	SE ◇1	SE	SE	SE ◇1	SE ◇1	SE		SE	SE	SE ◇1	SE	SE ◇1	SE ◇1	SE	SE	SE		SE ◇1	SE	SE	SE ◇1
London Charing Cross	d				16 00	16 05		16 10	16 15					16 30	16 35	16 40	16 45					17 00	17 05		17 10
London Waterloo (East)	d				16 03	16 08		16 13	16 18					16 33	16 38	16 43	16 48					17 03	17 08		17 13
London Cannon Street	d		15 50									16 20							16 50						
London Bridge	d		15 54		16 09	16 14		16 19	16 24			16 24		16 39	16 44	16 49	16 54		16 54			17 09	17 14		17 19
New Cross	d		16 00									16 30							17 00						
St Johns	d		16 02									16 32							17 02						
Lewisham	d		16 05									16 35							17 05						
Hither Green	d		16 09			16 23						16 39			16 53				17 09				17 23		
Grove Park	d		16 13	16 15		16 28	16 35					16 43	16 55		16 58				17 13	17 15			17 28	17 35	
Sundridge Park	d			16 18			16 38						16 58							17 18				17 38	
Bromley North	a			16 20			16 40						17 00							17 20				17 40	
Elmstead Woods	d		16 16			16 31						16 46			17 01				17 16				17 31		
Chislehurst	d	←	16 19			16 33				←		16 49			17 03			←	17 19				17 33		
Petts Wood	d	16 06	16 22			16 36				16 36		16 52			17 06			17 06	17 22				17 36		
Orpington	a	16 09	16 25		16 25	→			16 39	16 39		16 55		16 55	→		17 09	17 09	17 25			17 25	→		
	d	16 13			16 26				16 40	16 43				16 56			17 10	17 13				17 26			
Chelsfield	d	16 16								16 46								17 16							
Knockholt	d	16 19								16 49								17 19							
Dunton Green	d	16 24								16 54								17 24							
Sevenoaks	a	16 27			16 35			16 42	16 49	16 57				17 05		17 12	17 19	17 27				17 35			17 42
	d				16 36			16 43	16 50					17 06		17 13	17 20					17 36			17 43
Hildenborough	d				16 42									17 12								17 42			
Tonbridge	a				16 46			16 51	16 58					17 16		17 21	17 28					17 46			17 51

Station		SE ◇1	SE	SE	SE	SE ◇1		SE	SE ◇1	SE ◇1	SE	SE	SE	SE ◇1	SE	SE		SE ◇1	SE ◇1	SE	SE	SE	SE ◇1	SE	SE ◇1
London Charing Cross	d	17 15				17 30		17 35	17 40	17 45				18 00	18 05			18 10	18 15				18 30	18 35	18 40
London Waterloo (East)	d	17 18				17 33		17 38	17 43	17 48				18 03	18 08			18 13	18 18				18 33	18 38	18 43
London Cannon Street	d			17 20								17 50									18 20				
London Bridge	d	17 24		17 24		17 39		17 44	17 49	17 54		17 54		18 09	18 14			18 19	18 24		18 24		18 39	18 44	18 49
New Cross	d			17 30								18 00									18 30				
St Johns	d			17 32								18 02									18 32				
Lewisham	d			17 35								18 05									18 35				
Hither Green	d			17 39				17 53				18 09			18 23						18 39			18 53	
Grove Park	d			17 43	17 55			17 58				18 13	18 15		18 28	18 35					18 43	18 55		18 58	
Sundridge Park	d				17 58								18 18			18 38						18 58			
Bromley North	a				18 00								18 20			18 40						19 00			
Elmstead Woods	d			17 46				18 01				18 16			18 31						18 46			19 01	
Chislehurst	d		←	17 49				18 03			←	18 19			18 33					←	18 49			19 03	
Petts Wood	d		17 36	17 52				18 06			18 06	18 22			18 36					18 36	18 52			19 06	
Orpington	a	17 39	17 39	17 55		17 55		→		18 09	18 09	18 25		18 25	→				18 39	18 39	18 55		18 55	→	
	d	17 40	17 43			17 56				18 10	18 13			18 26					18 40	18 43			18 56		
Chelsfield	d		17 46								18 16									18 46					
Knockholt	d		17 49								18 19									18 49					
Dunton Green	d		17 54								18 24									18 54					
Sevenoaks	a	17 49	17 57			18 05			18 12	18 19	18 27			18 35				18 42	18 49	18 57			19 05		19 12
	d	17 50				18 06			18 13	18 20				18 36				18 43	18 50				19 06		19 13
Hildenborough	d					18 12								18 42									19 12		
Tonbridge	a	17 58				18 16			18 21	18 28				18 46				18 51	18 58				19 16		19 21

London Charing Cross/Cannon Street - Grove Park, Orpington, Sevenoaks and Tonbridge, Grove Park - Bromley North

		SE ◇1	SE	SE	SE	SE ◇1	SE	SE		SE ◇1	SE ◇1	SE	SE	SE	SE ◇1	SE	SE ◇1	SE ◇1		SE	SE	SE	SE ◇1	SE	SE
London Charing Cross 4 ⊖	d	18 45				19 00	19 05			19 10	19 15				19 30	19 35	19 40	19 45					20 00	20 05	
London Waterloo (East) 4 ⊖	d	18 48				19 03	19 08			19 13	19 18				19 33	19 38	19 43	19 48					20 03	20 08	
London Cannon Street 4 ⊖	d			18 50									19 20								19 50				
London Bridge 4 ⊖	d	18 54		18 54		19 09	19 14			19 19	19 24		19 24		19 39	19 44	19 49	19 54			19 54		20 09	20 14	
New Cross 4 ⊖	d			19 00									19 30								20 00				
St Johns	d			19 02									19 32								20 02				
Lewisham 4	d			19 05									19 35								20 05				
Hither Green 4	d			19 09			19 23						19 39			19 53					20 09			20 23	
Grove Park 4	d			19 13	19 15		19 28	19 35					19 43	19 55		19 58					20 13	20 15		20 28	20 35
Sundridge Park	d				19 18			19 38						19 58								20 18			20 38
Bromley North	a				19 20			19 40						20 00								20 20			20 40
Elmstead Woods	d			19 16			19 31						19 46			20 01					20 16			20 31	
Chislehurst	d		←	19 19			19 33					←	19 49			20 03				←	20 19			20 33	
Petts Wood 4	d		19 06	19 22			19 36					19 36	19 52			20 06				20 06	20 22			20 36	
Orpington 4	a	19 09	19 09	19 25		19 25	→				19 39	19 39	19 55		19 55	→		20 09		20 09	20 25		20 25	→	
	d	19 10	19 13			19 26					19 40	19 43			19 56			20 10		20 13			20 26		
Chelsfield 3	d		19 16									19 46								20 16					
Knockholt	d		19 19									19 49								20 19					
Dunton Green	d		19 24									19 54								20 24					
Sevenoaks 4	a	19 19	19 27			19 35				19 42	19 49	19 57			20 05		20 12	20 19		20 27			20 35		
	d	19 20				19 36				19 43	19 50				20 06		20 13	20 20					20 36		
Hildenborough	d					19 42									20 12								20 42		
Tonbridge 4	a	19 28				19 46				19 51	19 58				20 16		20 21	20 28					20 46		

		SE ◇1	SE ◇1	SE		SE	SE	SE ◇1	SE	SE ◇1	SE ◇1	SE	SE	SE		SE ◇1	SE	SE	SE ◇1	SE	SE	SE	SE ◇1	SE	
London Charing Cross 4 ⊖	d	20 10	20 15					20 30	20 35	20 40	20 45					21 00	21 05		21 10				21 30	21 35	
London Waterloo (East) 4 ⊖	d	20 13	20 18					20 33	20 38	20 43	20 48					21 03	21 08		21 13				21 33	21 38	
London Cannon Street 4 ⊖	d					20 20							20 50								21 20				
London Bridge 4 ⊖	d	20 19	20 24			20 24		20 39	20 44	20 49	20 54		20 54			21 09	21 14		21 19		21 24		21 39	21 44	
New Cross 4 ⊖	d					20 30							21 00								21 30				
St Johns	d					20 32							21 02								21 32				
Lewisham 4	d					20 35							21 05								21 35				
Hither Green 4	d					20 39			20 53				21 09				21 23				21 39			21 53	
Grove Park 4	d					20 43	20 55		20 58				21 13	21 15			21 28	21 35			21 43	21 55		21 58	
Sundridge Park	d						20 58							21 18				21 38				21 58			
Bromley North	a						21 00							21 20				21 40				22 00			
Elmstead Woods	d					20 46			21 01				21 16				21 31				21 46			22 01	
Chislehurst	d			←		20 49			21 03			←	21 19				21 33			←	21 49			22 03	
Petts Wood 4	d			20 36		20 52			21 06			21 06	21 22				21 36			21 36	21 52			22 06	
Orpington 4	a		20 39	20 39		20 55		20 55	→		21 09	21 09	21 25			21 25	→		21 34	21 39	21 55		21 55	→	
	d		20 40	20 43				20 56			21 10	21 13				21 26			21 35	21 43			21 56		
Chelsfield 3	d			20 46								21 16								21 46					
Knockholt	d			20 49								21 19								21 49					
Dunton Green	d			20 54								21 24								21 54					
Sevenoaks 4	a	20 42	20 49	20 57				21 05		21 12	21 19	21 27				21 35			21 44	21 57			22 05		
	d	20 43	20 50					21 06		21 13	21 20					21 36			21 45				22 06		
Hildenborough	d							21 12								21 42							22 12		
Tonbridge 4	a	20 51	20 58					21 16		21 21	21 28					21 46			21 53				22 16		

		SE ◇1	SE ◇1	SE	SE	SE	SE ◇1	SE	SE	SE ◇1		SE	SE	SE	SE ◇1	SE	SE ◇1	SE ◇1	SE	SE		SE	SE ◇1	SE	SE
London Charing Cross 4 ⊖	d	21 40	21 45				22 00	22 05		22 10					22 30	22 35	22 40	22 45					23 00	23 05	
London Waterloo (East) 4 ⊖	d	21 43	21 48				22 03	22 08		22 13					22 33	22 38	22 43	22 48					23 03	23 08	
London Cannon Street 4 ⊖	d				21 50								22 20							22 50					
London Bridge 4 ⊖	d	21 49	21 54		21 54		22 09	22 14		22 19			22 24		22 39	22 44	22 49	22 54		22 54			23 09	23 14	
New Cross 4 ⊖	d				22 00								22 30							23 00					
St Johns	d				22 02								22 32							23 02					
Lewisham 4	d				22 05								22 35							23 05					
Hither Green 4	d				22 09			22 23					22 39			22 53				23 09				23 23	
Grove Park 4	d				22 13	22 15		22 28	22 35				22 43	22 55		22 58				23 13		23 15		23 28	23 35
Sundridge Park	d					22 18			22 38					22 58								23 18			23 38
Bromley North	a					22 20			22 40					23 00								23 20			23 40
Elmstead Woods	d				22 16			22 31					22 46			23 01				23 16				23 31	
Chislehurst	d			←	22 19			22 33				←	22 49			23 03			←	23 19				23 33	
Petts Wood 4	d			22 06	22 22			22 36				22 36	22 52			23 06			23 06	23 22				23 36	
Orpington 4	a		22 09	22 09	22 25		22 25	→		22 34		22 39	22 55		22 55	→		23 09	23 09	23 25			23 25	→	
	d		22 10	22 13			22 26			22 35		22 43			22 56			23 10	23 13				23 26		
Chelsfield 3	d			22 16								22 46							23 16						
Knockholt	d			22 19								22 49							23 19						
Dunton Green	d			22 24								22 54							23 24						
Sevenoaks 4	a	22 12	22 19	22 27			22 35			22 44		22 57			23 05		23 12	23 19	23 27				23 35		
	d	22 13	22 20				22 36			22 45					23 06		23 13	23 20					23 36		
Hildenborough	d						22 42								23 12								23 42		
Tonbridge 4	a	22 21	22 28				22 46			22 53					23 16		23 21	23 28					23 46		

		SE ◇1	SE	SE	SE		SE ◇1	SE	SE ◇1	SE ◇1	SE	SE
London Charing Cross 4 ⊖	d	23 10					23 30	23 35	23 40	23 45		
London Waterloo (East) 4 ⊖	d	23 13					23 33	23 38	23 43	23 48		
London Cannon Street 4 ⊖	d			23 20								23 50
London Bridge 4 ⊖	d	23 19		23 24			23 39	23 44	23 49	23 54		23 54
New Cross 4 ⊖	d			23 30								23 59
St Johns	d			23 32								00 02
Lewisham 4	d			23 35								00 05
Hither Green 4	d			23 39				23 53				00 09
Grove Park 4	d			23 43	23 55			23 58				00 13
Sundridge Park	d				23 58							
Bromley North	a				00 01							
Elmstead Woods	d			23 46				00 01				00 16
Chislehurst	d		←	23 49				00 03			←	00 19
Petts Wood 4	d		23 36	23 52				00 06			00 06	00 22
Orpington 4	a	23 34	23 39	23 55			23 55	→		00 09	00 09	00 25
	d	23 35	23 43				23 56			00 10	00 13	
Chelsfield 3	d		23 46								00 16	
Knockholt	d		23 49								00 19	
Dunton Green	d		23 54								00 24	
Sevenoaks 4	a	23 45	23 57				00 05		00 12	00 19	00 27	
	d	23 46					00 06		00 13	00 20		
Hildenborough	d						00 12					
Tonbridge 4	a	23 54					00 16		00 21	00 28		

Sundays

20 May to 2 December

		SE ◇1 A	SE ◇1 A	SE ◇1 A	SE A	SE A	SE	SE	SE	SE		SE	SE	SE	SE ◇1	SE	SE ◇1	SE	SE ◇1	SE	SE ◇1	SE	
London Charing Cross 4 ⊖	d							00 05					00 50	07 46	08 10	08 16	08 25		08 40	08 46	08 55		and at the same minutes past each hour until
London Waterloo (East) 4 ⊖	d							00 08					00 53	07 49	08 13	08 19	08 28		08 43	08 49	08 58		
London Cannon Street 4 ⊖	d									00 20													
London Bridge 4 ⊖	d							00 14		00 24			00 58	07 55	08 19	08 25	08 34		08 49	08 55	09 04		
New Cross 4 ⊖	d									00 30													
St Johns	d					00 02				00 32													
Lewisham 4	d					00 05				00 35			01 08	08 05		08 35				09 05			
Hither Green 4	d					00 09		00 23		00 39			01 12	08 09		08 39				09 09			
Grove Park 4	d					00 13	00 15	00 28	00 35	00 43		00 55	01 16	08 13		08 43				09 13			
Sundridge Park	d						00 18		00 38			00 58											
Bromley North	a						00 20		00 40			01 00											
Elmstead Woods	d				00 01	00 16		00 31		00 46			01 19	08 16		08 46				09 16			
Chislehurst	d				00 03	00 19		00 33		00 49			01 22	08 18		08 48		←		09 18		←	
Petts Wood 4	d				00 06	00 22		00 37		00 52			01 25	08 22		08 52		08 52		09 22		09 22	
Orpington 4	a				00 09	00 25		00 42		00 55			01 29	08 27	08 36	→	08 50	08 57	09 06	→	09 20	09 27	
	d			00 10	00 13									08 28	08 36		08 50	08 58	09 06		09 20	09 28	
Chelsfield 3	d				00 16									08 31				09 01				09 31	
Knockholt	d				00 19									08 34				09 04				09 34	
Dunton Green	d				00 24									08 39				09 09				09 39	
Sevenoaks 4	a			00 19	00 27									08 42	08 45		08 59	09 12	09 15		09 29	09 42	
	d	00 06	00 13	00 20											08 46		09 00		09 16		09 30		
Hildenborough	d	00 12																			09 36		
Tonbridge 4	a	00 16	00 21	00 28											08 54		09 08		09 24		09 40		

		SE ◇1	SE	SE ◇1	SE	SE ◇1	SE	SE ◇1	SE		SE ◇1	SE	SE ◇1	SE	SE ◇1	SE	SE ◇1	SE	SE ◇1		SE	SE ◇1	SE	SE ◇1	SE
London Charing Cross 4 ⊖	d	19 10	19 16	19 25		19 40	19 46	19 55			20 10	20 16	20 25		20 40	20 46	21 10	21 16	21 25			21 40	21 46	22 10	22 16
London Waterloo (East) 4 ⊖	d	19 13	19 19	19 28		19 43	19 49	19 58			20 13	20 19	20 28		20 43	20 49	21 13	21 19	21 28			21 43	21 49	22 13	22 19
London Cannon Street 4 ⊖	d																								
London Bridge 4 ⊖	d	19 19	19 25	19 34		19 49	19 55	20 04			20 19	20 25	20 34		20 49	20 55	21 19	21 25	21 34			21 49	21 55	22 19	22 25
New Cross 4 ⊖	d																								
St Johns	d																								
Lewisham 4	d		19 35				20 05					20 35				21 05		21 35					22 05		22 35
Hither Green 4	d		19 39				20 09					20 39				21 09		21 39					22 09		22 39
Grove Park 4	d		19 43				20 13					20 43				21 13		21 43					22 13		22 43
Sundridge Park	d																								
Bromley North	a																								
Elmstead Woods	d		19 46				20 16					20 46				21 16		21 46					22 16		22 46
Chislehurst	d		19 48		←		20 18		←			20 48		←		21 18		21 48			←		22 18		22 48
Petts Wood 4	d		19 52		19 52		20 22		20 22			20 52		20 52		21 22		21 52			21 52		22 22		22 52
Orpington 4	a	19 36	→	19 50	19 57	20 06	→	20 20	20 27		20 36	→	20 50	20 57	21 06	21 27	21 36	→	21 50		21 57	22 06	22 27	22 36	→
	d	19 36		19 50	19 58	20 06		20 20	20 28		20 36		20 50	20 58	21 06	21 28	21 36		21 50		21 58	22 06	22 28	22 36	
Chelsfield 3	d				20 01				20 31					21 01		21 31					22 01		22 31		
Knockholt	d				20 04				20 34					21 04		21 34					22 04		22 34		
Dunton Green	d				20 09				20 39					21 09		21 39					22 09		22 39		
Sevenoaks 4	a	19 45		19 59	20 12	20 15		20 29	20 42		20 45		20 59	21 12	21 15	21 42	21 45		21 59		22 12	22 15	22 42	22 45	
	d	19 46		20 00		20 16		20 30			20 46		21 00		21 16		21 46		22 00			22 16		22 46	
Hildenborough	d							20 36					21 06						22 06						
Tonbridge 4	a	19 54		20 08		20 24		20 40			20 54		21 10		21 24		21 54		22 10			22 24		22 54	

A not 20 May

Table T204-F

Sundays
20 May to 2 December

London Charing Cross/Cannon Street - Grove Park, Orpington, Sevenoaks and Tonbridge, Grove Park - Bromley North

		SE ◇■	SE	SE ◇■	SE	SE ◇■	SE	SE ◇■	SE	SE ◇■	SE
London Charing Cross ⊖	d	22 25		22 40	22 46	23 10	23 16	23 25		23 40	23 46
London Waterloo (East) ⊖	d	22 28		22 43	22 49	23 13	23 19	23 28		23 43	23 49
London Cannon Street ⊖	d										
London Bridge ⊖	d	22 34		22 49	22 55	23 19	23 25	23 34		23 49	23 55
New Cross ⊖	d										
St Johns	d										
Lewisham	d				23 05		23 35				00 05
Hither Green	d				23 09		23 39				00 09
Grove Park	d				23 13		23 43				00 13
Sundridge Park	d										
Bromley North	a										
Elmstead Woods	d				23 16		23 46				00 16
Chislehurst	d		←		23 18		23 48		←		00 18
Petts Wood	d		22 52		23 22		23 52		23 52		00 22
Orpington	a	22 50	22 57	23 06	23 27	23 36	→	23 50	23 57	00 06	00 27
	d	22 50	22 58	23 06	23 28	23 36		23 50	23 58	00 06	00 28
Chelsfield	d		23 01		23 31				00 01		00 31
Knockholt	d		23 04		23 34				00 04		00 34
Dunton Green	d		23 09		23 39				00 09		00 39
Sevenoaks	a	23 00	23 12	23 15	23 42	23 45		23 59	00 12	00 15	00 42
	d	23 00		23 16		23 46		23 59		00 16	
Hildenborough	d	23 06						00 06			
Tonbridge	a	23 10		23 24		23 54		00 10		00 24	

Table T204-R

Mondays to Fridays
21 May to 7 December

Bromley North to Grove Park, Tonbridge, Sevenoaks, Orpington and Grove Park - London Cannon Street/Charing Cross

Miles	Miles			SE MO	SE ThFO	SE TWO	SE MX	SE MX	SE MX	SE	SE ■	SE	SE	SE ◇■	SE	SE	SE ◇■	SE	SE	SE	SE ◇■	SE ◇■	SE
0	—	**Tonbridge**	d								04 50			05 28			05 40				05 58	06 07	
2½	—	Hildenborough	d								04 54			05 32							06 02		
7½	—	**Sevenoaks**	a								05 01			05 39			05 49				06 09	06 16	
—	—		d								05 02		05 17	05 40			05 50			06 01	06 09	06 17	
1½	—	Dunton Green	d										05 20							06 04			
5½	—	Knockholt	d										05 25							06 09			
6¾	—	Chelsfield	d								05 09		05 28	05 47						06 12	06 17		
8¼	—	**Orpington**	a								05 12		05 31	05 50			05 58			06 15	06 20	06 25	
—	—		d							05 00	05 13		05 33	05 51		05 55	05 59	06 00		06 18	06 21	06 27	
9¼	—	Petts Wood	d							05 03			05 36			05 58		06 03		06 21			
10¾	—	Chislehurst	d							05 06			05 39			06 01		06 06		06 25			
11¾	—	Elmstead Woods	d							05 08			05 41			06 03		06 08		06 28			
—	0	**Bromley North**	d				00 04	00 24	00 44			05 34			05 54				06 19				06 35
—	0½	Sundridge Park	d				00 06	00 26	00 46			05 36			05 56				06 21				06 37
13	1¾	**Grove Park**	d	00 02	00 02	00 02	00a09	00a29	00a49	05 12		05a39	05 45		05a59	06 07		06 12	06a24	06 31			06a40
14¾	—	Hither Green	d	00 05	00 06	00 06				05 16			05 49			06 11		06 16		06 36			
16	—	**Lewisham**	d	00 11	00 11	00 13				05 21			05 54					06 21		06 41			
16½	—	St Johns	a															06 23					
17¼	—	New Cross ⊖	a															06 25			06 32		
20¼	—	**London Bridge** ⊖	a	00 19	00 19	00 20				05 29	05 35		06 02	06 06		06 20	06 16	06 31		06 50	06 38	06 43	
—	—	**London Cannon Street** ⊖	a			00 27											06 24	06 39			06 46		
21¼	—	**London Waterloo (East)** ⊖	a	00 25	00 25					05 35	05 41		06 07	06 12		06 26				06 56		06 49	
22	—	**London Charing Cross** ⊖	a	00 29	00 31					05 41	05 48		06 14	06 19		06 33				07 03		06 56	

		SE	SE ◇■	SE	SE	SE	SE ◇■	SE ◇■	SE	SE	SE ◇■	SE	SE ◇■	SE ◇■	SE ◇■	SE	SE	SE	SE	SE ◇■	SE ◇■	SE ◇■	SE ◇■
Tonbridge	d		06 19				06 29	06 39			06 44		06 51	07 03	07 10					07 15	07 23	07 31	07 35
Hildenborough	d		06 23				06 33						06 56		07 14					07 20		07 36	07 39
Sevenoaks	a		06 30				06 40	06 48			06 53		07 02	07 11	07 22					07 27	07 31	07 43	07 46
	d		06 31			06 34	06 41	06 49			06 54	06 56	07 03	07 12	07 23				07 17	07 28	07 32	07 43	07 47
Dunton Green	d					06 37						06 59							07 20				
Knockholt	d					06 42						07 04							07 25				
Chelsfield	d					06 45	06 49					07 07	07 11		07 31				07 28			07 52	
Orpington	a		06 39			06 48	06 52				07 02	07 10	07 14						07 31				
	d	06 33	06 40	06 41		06 49	06 53			07 02	07 04	07 11	07 15				07 20		07 33				
Petts Wood	d	06 36		06 44		06 52				07 05		07 14					07 23		07 36				
Chislehurst	d	06 39		06 48		06 56				07 08		07 17					07 27		07 40				
Elmstead Woods	d	06 42		06 51		06 58				07 11		07 20					07 30		07 43				
Bromley North	d				06 52				07 05							07 19		07 32					
Sundridge Park	d				06 54				07 07							07 21		07 34					
Grove Park	d	06 45		06 54	06a57	07 02			07a10	07 14		07 24				07a24	07 34	07a37	07 46				
Hither Green	d	06 50		06 58		07 06				07 19		07 29					07 38		07 50				
Lewisham	d			07 04						07 25							07 44						
St Johns	a																						
New Cross ⊖	a	06 55				07 11						07 34							07 55				
London Bridge ⊖	a	07 01	06 55	07 12		07 17	07 08	07 14		07 33	07 23	07 40	07 30	07 35	07 49		07 53		08 01	07 52	07 55	08 09	08 13
London Cannon Street ⊖	a	07 09				07 25					07 31	07 48							08 09	08 00			08 21
London Waterloo (East) ⊖	a		07 01	07 18			07 14	07 21		07 39			07 36	07 42	07 55		07 59				08 01	08 15	
London Charing Cross ⊖	a		07 08	07 25			07 21	07 27		07 46			07 44	07 49	08 02		08 06				08 09	08 22	

		SE ◇■	SE	SE	SE	SE	SE	SE ◇■	SE	SE	SE	SE ◇■	SE ◇■	SE ◇■	SE	SE	SE	SE ◇■	SE ◇■	SE	SE ◇	SE ◇■
Tonbridge	d	07 42						07 50				07 58	08 02	08 10				08 14	08 21			08 36
Hildenborough	d							07 55						08 15				08 19				08 40
Sevenoaks	a	07 50						08 02				08 07	08 11	08 22				08 26	08 30			08 46
	d	07 51			07 37			08 03			07 57	08 08	08 12	08 23			08 17	08 27	08 31			08 47
Dunton Green	d				07 40						08 00						08 20					
Knockholt	d				07 45						08 05						08 25					
Chelsfield	d				07 48			08 11			08 08			08 32			08 28					08 55
Orpington	a				07 51						08 11						08 31					
	d			07 42	07 51		07 57		08 03		08 12				08 21		08 34			08 42	08 46	
Petts Wood	d			07 46	07 54		08 00		08 06		08 15				08 24		08 37			08 45		
Chislehurst	d			07 49	07 58		08 03		08 09		08 19				08 27		08 41			08 49		
Elmstead Woods	d			07 52	08 00		08 06		08 11		08 22				08 30		08 44			08 51		
Bromley North	d		07 46			08 01				08 14						08 35						
Sundridge Park	d		07 48			08 03				08 16						08 37						
Grove Park	d		07a51	07 56	08 04	08a06	08 10		08 15	08a19	08 25				08 33	08a40	08 48			08 55		
Hither Green	d			08 00					08 19		08 30				08 38		08 52			08 59		
Lewisham	d			08 08					08 24						08 44					09 05		
St Johns	a																					
New Cross ⊖	a				08 11						08 36						08 58					
London Bridge ⊖	a	08 15		08 17	08 17		08 21	08 29	08 33		08 42	08 34	08 35	08 50	08 52		09 04	08 54	08 56	09 13	09 02	09 11
London Cannon Street ⊖	a				08 25						08 50	08 42					09 12	09 02				
London Waterloo (East) ⊖	a	08 21		08 23			08 27	08 35	08 39				08 41	08 56	08 59				09 03	09 19	09 08	09 17
London Charing Cross ⊖	a	08 28		08 30			08 34	08 42	08 46				08 48	09 03	09 05				09 10	09 27	09 15	09 26

Bromley North to Grove Park, Tonbridge, Sevenoaks, Orpington and Grove Park - London Cannon Street/Charing Cross

	SE ◇1	SE	SE		SE ◇1	SE	SE	SE	SE	SE ◇1	SE ◇1	SE ◇1	SE		SE	SE	SE	SE ◇1	SE ◇1	SE ◇1	SE	SE	SE	
Tonbridge d	08 40				08 46					09 01	09 09	09 19						09 31	09 39	09 49				
Hildenborough d										09 05								09 35						
Sevenoaks a	08 50				08 55					09 12	09 18	09 28						09 42	09 48	09 58				
Sevenoaks d	08 51		08 37		08 56				09 06	09 13	09 19	09 29					09 35	09 43	09 49	09 59				
Dunton Green d			08 40						09 09								09 38							
Knockholt d			08 45						09 14								09 43							
Chelsfield d			08 48						09 17								09 46							
Orpington a			08 51		09 04				09 20	09 23		09 37					09 49	09 51		10 07				
Orpington d			08 52		09 05		09 11		09 21	09 24		09 38			09 41		09 50	09 52		10 08		10 11		
Petts Wood d			08 55				09 14		09 24						09 44		09 53					10 14		
Chislehurst d			08 58				09 17		09 27						09 47		09 56					10 17		
Elmstead Woods d			09 01				09 19		09 29						09 49		09 58					10 19		
Bromley North d		08 53				09 07		09 22					09 36			09 50					10 05		10 20	
Sundridge Park d		08 55				09 09		09 24					09 38			09 52					10 07		10 22	
Grove Park d		08a58	09 05			09a12	09 23	09a27	09 33				09a41		09 53	09a55	10 02				10a10	10 23	10a25	
Hither Green d			09 09				09 27		09 37						09 57		10 06					10 27		
Lewisham d							09 34								10 04							10 34		
St Johns a							09 36								10 06							10 36		
New Cross a							09 38								10 08							10 38		
London Bridge a	09 15		09 18		09 20		09 43		09 46	09 39	09 41	09 53			10 13		10 15	10 07	10 11	10 23		10 43		
London Cannon Street a							09 51								10 18							10 48		
London Waterloo (East) a	09 21		09 24		09 26				09 52	09 45	09 49	09 59					10 21	10 13	10 17	10 29				
London Charing Cross a	09 29		09 31		09 33				09 59	09 52	09 56	10 06					10 27	10 20	10 24	10 36				

	SE	SE ◇1	SE ◇1	SE ◇1	SE	SE	SE	SE ◇1	SE ◇1		SE ◇1	SE	SE	SE	SE	SE ◇1	SE ◇1	SE ◇1	SE		SE	SE	SE ◇1	SE ◇1
Tonbridge d		10 01	10 09	10 19				10 31	10 39		10 49					11 01	11 09	11 19					11 31	11 39
Hildenborough d		10 05						10 35								11 05							11 35	
Sevenoaks a		10 12	10 18	10 28				10 42	10 48		10 58					11 12	11 18	11 28					11 42	11 48
Sevenoaks d	10 05	10 13	10 19	10 29			10 35	10 43	10 49		10 59				11 05	11 13	11 19	11 29				11 35	11 43	11 49
Dunton Green d	10 08						10 38								11 08							11 38		
Knockholt d	10 13						10 43								11 13							11 43		
Chelsfield d	10 16						10 46								11 16							11 46		
Orpington a	10 19	10 21		10 37			10 49	10 51			11 07				11 19	11 21		11 37				11 49	11 51	
Orpington d	10 20	10 22		10 38		10 41	10 50	10 52			11 08		11 11		11 20	11 22		11 38			11 41	11 50	11 52	
Petts Wood d	10 23					10 44	10 53						11 14		11 23						11 44	11 53		
Chislehurst d	10 26					10 47	10 56						11 17		11 26						11 47	11 56		
Elmstead Woods d	10 28					10 49	10 58						11 19		11 28						11 49	11 58		
Bromley North d					10 40							11 05		11 24					11 44					
Sundridge Park d					10 42							11 07		11 26					11 46					
Grove Park d	10 32				10a45	10 53	11 02					11a10	11 23	11a29	11 32				11a49		11 53	12 02		
Hither Green d	10 36					10 57	11 06						11 27		11 36						11 57	12 06		
Lewisham d						11 04							11 34								12 04			
St Johns a						11 06							11 36								12 06			
New Cross a						11 08							11 38								12 08			
London Bridge a	10 45	10 37	10 41	10 53		11 13	11 15	11 07	11 11		11 23		11 43		11 45	11 37	11 41	11 53			12 13	12 15	12 07	12 11
London Cannon Street a						11 18							11 48								12 18			
London Waterloo (East) a	10 51	10 43	10 47	10 59			11 21	11 13	11 17		11 29				11 51	11 43	11 47	11 59				12 21	12 13	12 17
London Charing Cross a	10 57	10 48	10 52	11 04			11 27	11 18	11 22		11 34				11 57	11 48	11 52	12 04				12 27	12 18	12 22

	SE ◇1	SE	SE	SE	SE		SE ◇1	SE ◇1	SE ◇1	SE	SE	SE	SE ◇1	SE ◇1	SE ◇1		SE	SE	SE	SE	SE ◇1	SE ◇1	SE ◇1	SE
Tonbridge d	11 49						12 01	12 09	12 19				12 31	12 39	12 49						13 01	13 09	13 19	
Hildenborough d							12 05						12 35								13 05			
Sevenoaks a	11 58						12 12	12 18	12 28				12 42	12 48	12 58						13 12	13 18	13 28	
Sevenoaks d	11 59				12 05		12 13	12 19	12 29			12 35	12 43	12 49	12 59					13 05	13 13	13 19	13 29	
Dunton Green d					12 08							12 38								13 08				
Knockholt d					12 13							12 43								13 13				
Chelsfield d					12 16							12 46								13 16				
Orpington a	12 07				12 19		12 21		12 37			12 49	12 51		13 07					13 19	13 21		13 37	
Orpington d	12 08		12 11		12 20		12 22		12 38		12 41	12 50	12 52		13 08			13 11		13 20	13 22		13 38	
Petts Wood d			12 14		12 23						12 44	12 53						13 14		13 23				
Chislehurst d			12 17		12 26						12 47	12 56						13 17		13 26				
Elmstead Woods d			12 19		12 28						12 49	12 58						13 19		13 28				
Bromley North d		12 04		12 24						12 44							13 04		13 24					13 44
Sundridge Park d		12 06		12 26						12 46							13 06		13 26					13 46
Grove Park d		12a09	12 23	12a29	12 32					12a49	12 53	13 02					13a09	13 23	13a29	13 32				13a49
Hither Green d			12 27		12 36						12 57	13 06						13 27		13 36				
Lewisham d			12 34								13 04							13 34						
St Johns a			12 36								13 06							13 36						
New Cross a			12 38								13 08							13 38						
London Bridge a	12 23		12 43		12 45		12 37	12 41	12 53		13 13	13 15	13 07	13 11	13 23			13 43		13 45	13 37	13 41	13 53	
London Cannon Street a			12 48								13 18							13 48						
London Waterloo (East) a	12 29				12 51		12 43	12 47	12 59			13 21	13 13	13 17	13 29					13 51	13 43	13 47	13 59	
London Charing Cross a	12 34				12 57		12 48	12 52	13 04			13 27	13 18	13 22	13 34					13 57	13 48	13 52	14 04	

Bromley North to Grove Park, Tonbridge, Sevenoaks, Orpington and Grove Park - London Cannon Street/Charing Cross

	SE	SE	SE ◇1	SE ◇1	SE ◇1	SE	SE		SE	SE	SE ◇1	SE ◇1	SE ◇1	SE	SE	SE	SE ◇1		SE ◇1	SE ◇1	SE	SE	SE	SE
Tonbridge d			13 31	13 39	13 49						14 01	14 09	14 19				14 31		14 39	14 49				
Hildenborough d			13 35								14 05						14 35							
Sevenoaks a			13 42	13 48	13 58						14 12	14 18	14 28				14 42		14 48	14 58				
Sevenoaks d		13 35	13 43	13 49	13 59					14 05	14 13	14 19	14 29			14 35	14 43		14 49	14 59				15 05
Dunton Green d		13 38								14 08						14 38								15 08
Knockholt d		13 43								14 13						14 43								15 13
Chelsfield d		13 46								14 16						14 46								15 16
Orpington a		13 49	13 51		14 07					14 19	14 21		14 37			14 49	14 51			15 07				15 19
Orpington d	13 41	13 50	13 52		14 08		14 11			14 20	14 22		14 38		14 41	14 50	14 52			15 08		15 11		15 20
Petts Wood d	13 44	13 53					14 14			14 23					14 44	14 53						15 14		15 23
Chislehurst d	13 47	13 56					14 17			14 26					14 47	14 56						15 17		15 26
Elmstead Woods d	13 49	13 58					14 19			14 28					14 49	14 58						15 19		15 28
Bromley North d						14 04			14 24					14 44							15 04		15 24	
Sundridge Park d						14 06			14 26					14 46							15 06		15 26	
Grove Park d	13 53	14 02				14a09	14 23		14a29	14 32				14a49	14 53	15 02					15a09	15 23	15a29	15 32
Hither Green d	13 57	14 06					14 27			14 36					14 57	15 06						15 27		15 36
Lewisham d	14 04						14 34								15 04							15 34		
St Johns a	14 06						14 36								15 06							15 36		
New Cross a	14 08						14 38								15 08							15 38		
London Bridge a	14 13	14 15	14 07	14 11	14 23		14 43			14 45	14 37	14 41	14 53		15 13	15 15	15 07		15 11	15 23		15 43		15 45
London Cannon Street a	14 18						14 48								15 18							15 48		
London Waterloo (East) a		14 21	14 13	14 17	14 29					14 51	14 43	14 47	14 59			15 21	15 13		15 17	15 29				15 51
London Charing Cross a		14 27	14 18	14 22	14 34					14 57	14 48	14 52	15 04			15 27	15 18		15 22	15 34				15 57

	SE ◇1	SE ◇1	SE ◇1		SE	SE	SE	SE ◇1	SE ◇1	SE ◇1	SE	SE 1	SE		SE	SE ◇1	SE ◇1	SE ◇1	SE	SE	SE	SE	SE	
Tonbridge d	15 01	15 09	15 19					15 31	15 39	15 49						16 01	16 09	16 19						
Hildenborough d	15 05							15 35								16 05								
Sevenoaks a	15 12	15 18	15 28					15 42	15 48	15 58						16 12	16 18	16 28						
Sevenoaks d	15 13	15 19	15 29				15 35	15 43	15 49	15 59					16 05	16 13	16 19	16 29					16 35	
Dunton Green d							15 38								16 08								16 38	
Knockholt d							15 43								16 13								16 43	
Chelsfield d							15 46								16 16	16 20							16 46	
Orpington a	15 21		15 37				15 49	15 51		16 07					16 19	16 23		16 37					16 49	
Orpington d	15 22		15 38			15 41	15 50	15 52		16 08		16 11	16 11		16 20	16 24		16 38			16 41		16 50	
Petts Wood d						15 44	15 53						16 14		16 23						16 44		16 53	
Chislehurst d						15 47	15 56						16 17		16 26						16 47		16 56	
Elmstead Woods d						15 49	15 58						16 19		16 28						16 49		16 58	
Bromley North d					15 44						16 04								16 27	16 41		16 56		
Sundridge Park d					15 46						16 06								16 29	16 43				
Grove Park d					15a49	15 53	16 02				16a09		16 23		16 32				16a32	16a46	16 54	17a00	17 05	
Hither Green d						15 57	16 06						16 27		16 36						16 58		17 09	
Lewisham d						16 04							16 34								17 05			
St Johns a						16 06							16 36											
New Cross a						16 08							16 38								17 10			
London Bridge a	15 37	15 41	15 53			16 13	16 15	16 07	16 11	16 23		16 27	16 43		16 45	16 39	16 41	16 53			17 15		17 18	
London Cannon Street a						16 19							16 50								17 23			
London Waterloo (East) a	15 43	15 47	15 59				16 21	16 13	16 17	16 29		16 33			16 52	16 45	16 48	16 59					17 27	
London Charing Cross a	15 48	15 52	16 04				16 27	16 18	16 22	16 34		16 38			16 58	16 51	16 54	17 07					17 31	

	SE ◇1	SE ◇1	SE ◇1	SE	SE	SE	SE	SE	SE ◇1		SE ◇1	SE	SE	SE	SE ◇1	SE ◇1	SE	SE ◇1	SE ◇1		SE	SE ◇1	SE	SE
Tonbridge d	16 31	16 39	16 49						17 00		17 09				17 23	17 33		17 41	17 49			18 09		
Hildenborough d	16 35								17 04															
Sevenoaks a	16 42	16 48	16 58						17 10		17 17				17 31	17 41		17 49	17 58			18 18		
Sevenoaks d	16 43	16 49	16 59					17 05	17 11		17 18				17 32	17 42	17 34	17 50	17 59			18 19		
Dunton Green d								17 08									17 37							
Knockholt d									17 17								17 42							
Chelsfield d								17 14									17 45							
Orpington a	16 51	16 57	17 07					17 17	17 22						17 40		17 48	17 58	18 07					
Orpington d	16 52	16 59	17 09		17 11	17 15		17 18	17 23			17 28		17 40	17 41		17 48	18 00	18 09					18 09
Petts Wood d					17 14			17 24						17 44			17 52							18 14
Chislehurst d					17 17			17 27						17 47			17 55							18 17
Elmstead Woods d					17 19			17 29						17 49			17 57							18 19
Bromley North d				17 10			17 25						17 47								18 03		18 16	
Sundridge Park d				17 12			17 27						17 49										18 18	
Grove Park d				17a15	17 23		17a30	17 35					17a52	17 53			18 01				18a07		18a21	18 23
Hither Green d					17 29			17 40						17 57			18 05							18 27
Lewisham d					17 34									18 02										18 35
St Johns a					17 37									18 07										18 40
New Cross a					17 39									18 09										18 43
London Bridge a	17 09	17 16	17 30		17 44	17 36		17 49	17 38		17 42	17 44			17 59	18 06	18 15	18 19	18 24			18 42		18 51
London Cannon Street a			17 37		17 51									18 20										18 56
London Waterloo (East) a	17 15	17 24				17 41		17 54	17 44		17 48	17 50			18 05	18 12	18 21	18 26	18 30			18 48		
London Charing Cross a	17 21	17 30				17 48		18 00	17 50		17 54	17 54			18 12	18 20	18 27	18 33	18 37			18 57		

Table T204-R

Mondays to Fridays
21 May to 7 December

Bromley North to Grove Park, Tonbridge, Sevenoaks, Orpington and Grove Park - London Cannon Street/Charing Cross

		SE		SE	SE	SE	SE	SE	SE	SE	SE	SE		SE	SE	SE	SE	SE	SE	SE	SE	SE		SE	SE
				◇1		◇1					◇1	◇1		◇1					◇1	◇1	◇1				
Tonbridge	d			18 01		18 22					18 31	18 42		18 52					19 02	19 09	19 19				
Hildenborough	d			18 05							18 35								19 06						
Sevenoaks	a			18 12		18 30					18 42	18 50		19 00					19 13	19 18	19 28				
	d	18 02		18 13		18 31				18 35	18 43	18 51		19 00				19 05	19 14	19 19	19 29				
Dunton Green	d	18 05								18 38								19 08							
Knockholt	d	18 10								18 43								19 13							
Chelsfield	d	18 13								18 46								19 16							
Orpington	a	18 16		18 21		18 39				18 49	18 51			19 08				19 19	19 22		19 37				
	d	18 20		18 22	18 29	18 40			18 41	18 50	18 52			19 09		19 11		19 20	19 23		19 38			19 41	
Petts Wood	d	18 23							18 44	18 53						19 14		19 23						19 44	
Chislehurst	d	18 26							18 47	18 56						19 17		19 26						19 47	
Elmstead Woods	d	18 28							18 49	18 58						19 19		19 28						19 49	
Bromley North	d						18 31	18 46							19 06		19 22					19 40			19 56
Sundridge Park	d						18 33	18 48							19 08		19 24					19 42			19 58
Grove Park	d	18 34					18a36	18a51	18 53	19 02					19a11	19 23	19a27	19 32				19a45		19 53	20a01
Hither Green	d	18 39							18 57	19 06						19 27		19 36						19 57	
Lewisham	d								19 03							19 34								20 04	
St Johns	a								19 05							19 36								20 06	
New Cross	a								19 08							19 38								20 08	
London Bridge	a	18 48		18 40	18 46	18 55			19 13	19 17	19 08	19 13		19 24		19 43		19 45	19 38	19 41	19 53			20 13	
London Cannon Street	a			18 47					19 19							19 48								20 18	
London Waterloo (East)	a	18 54			18 53	19 00				19 23	19 14	19 19		19 30				19 51	19 44	19 47	19 59				
London Charing Cross	a	19 02			18 57	19 05				19 28	19 19	19 23		19 35				19 57	19 49	19 52	20 04				

		SE	SE	SE	SE	SE	SE	SE		SE	SE	SE	SE	SE	SE	SE	SE	SE		SE	SE	SE	SE	SE	SE
			◇1	◇1	◇1						◇1	◇1					◇1	◇1		◇1				◇1	◇1
Tonbridge	d		19 31	19 39	19 49						20 01	20 09					20 31	20 39		20 50				21 01	21 09
Hildenborough	d		19 35								20 05						20 35							21 05	
Sevenoaks	a		19 42	19 48	19 58						20 12	20 18					20 42	20 48		20 58				21 12	21 18
	d	19 35	19 43	19 49	19 59					20 05	20 13	20 19				20 35	20 43	20 49		20 59			21 05	21 13	21 19
Dunton Green	d	19 38								20 08						20 38							21 08		
Knockholt	d	19 43								20 13						20 43							21 13		
Chelsfield	d	19 46								20 16						20 46							21 16		
Orpington	a	19 49	19 51		20 07					20 19	20 21					20 49	20 51			21 07			21 19	21 21	
	d	19 50	19 52		20 08		20 11			20 20	20 22			20 41		20 50	20 52			21 08	21 11		21 20	21 22	
Petts Wood	d	19 53					20 14			20 23				20 44		20 53					21 14		21 23		
Chislehurst	d	19 56					20 17			20 26				20 47		20 56					21 17		21 26		
Elmstead Woods	d	19 58					20 19			20 28				20 49		20 58					21 19		21 28		
Bromley North	d					20 10		20 24					20 40		20 54							21 20			
Sundridge Park	d					20 12		20 26					20 42		20 56							21 22			
Grove Park	d	20 02				20a15	20 23	20a29		20 32			20a45	20 53	20a59	21 02					21 23	21a25	21 32		
Hither Green	d	20 06					20 27			20 36				20 57		21 06					21 27		21 36		
Lewisham	d						20 34							21 04							21 34				
St Johns	a						20 36							21 06							21 36				
New Cross	a						20 38							21 08							21 38				
London Bridge	a	20 15	20 07	20 11	20 23		20 43			20 45	20 37	20 41		21 13		21 15	21 07	21 11		21 23	21 44		21 45	21 37	21 41
London Cannon Street	a						20 48							21 18							21 48				
London Waterloo (East)	a	20 21	20 13	20 17	20 29					20 51	20 43	20 47				21 21	21 13	21 17		21 29			21 51	21 43	21 47
London Charing Cross	a	20 27	20 18	20 22	20 34					20 57	20 48	20 52				21 27	21 18	21 22		21 34			21 57	21 48	21 52

		SE	SE	SE		SE	SE	SE	SE	SE	SE	SE	SE	SE		SE	SE	SE	SE	SE	SE	SE	SE MT FO	SE	
						◇1	◇1	◇1					◇1	◇1					◇1	◇1	◇1				
Tonbridge	d					21 31	21 39	21 49					22 01	22 09					22 31	22 39	22 49				
Hildenborough	d					21 35							22 05						22 35						
Sevenoaks	a					21 42	21 48	21 58					22 12	22 18					22 42	22 48	22 58				
	d			21 35		21 43	21 49	21 59				22 05	22 13	22 19				22 35	22 43	22 49	22 59				
Dunton Green	d			21 38								22 08						22 38							
Knockholt	d			21 43								22 13						22 43							
Chelsfield	d			21 46								22 16						22 46							
Orpington	a			21 49		21 51		22 07				22 19	22 21					22 49	22 51		23 07				
	d		21 41	21 50		21 52		22 08		22 11		22 20	22 22				22 41	22 50	22 52		23 08		23 11		
Petts Wood	d		21 44	21 53						22 14		22 23					22 44	22 53					23 14		
Chislehurst	d		21 47	21 56						22 17		22 26					22 47	22 56					23 17		
Elmstead Woods	d		21 49	21 58						22 19		22 28					22 49	22 58					23 19		
Bromley North	d	21 44							22 04		22 24					22 44						23 04		23 24	
Sundridge Park	d	21 46							22 06		22 26					22 46						23 06		23 26	
Grove Park	d	21a49	21 53	22 02					22a09	22 23	22a29	22 32				22a49	22 53	23 02				23a09	23 23	23a29	
Hither Green	d		21 57	22 06						22 27		22 36					22 57	23 06					23 27		
Lewisham	d		22 04							22 34							23 04						23 34		
St Johns	a		22 06							22 36							23 06						23 36		
New Cross	a		22 08							22 38							23 08						23 38		
London Bridge	a		22 13	22 15		22 07	22 11	22 23		22 43		22 45	22 37	22 41			23 13	23 15	23 07	23 11	23 23		23 43		
London Cannon Street	a		22 18							22 48							23 18						23 48		
London Waterloo (East)	a			22 21		22 13	22 17	22 29				22 51	22 43	22 47				23 21	23 13	23 17	23 29				
London Charing Cross	a			22 27		22 18	22 22	22 34				22 57	22 48	22 52				23 27	23 18	23 22	23 34				

Table T204-R

Mondays to Fridays
21 May to 7 December

Bromley North to Grove Park, Tonbridge, Sevenoaks, Orpington and Grove Park - London Cannon Street/Charing Cross

		SE WTh FO	SE MTO		SE WTh FO	SE MTO	SE	SE WTh FO	SE MTO
					◇1	◇1			
Tonbridge	d				23 15	23 15			
Hildenborough	d				23 19	23 19			
Sevenoaks	a				23 26	23 26			
	d	23 05	23 05		23 27	23 27		23 35	23 35
Dunton Green	d	23 08	23 08					23 38	23 38
Knockholt	d	23 13	23 13					23 43	23 43
Chelsfield	d	23 16	23 16					23 46	23 46
Orpington	a	23 19	23 19		23 35	23 35		23 49	23 49
	d	23 20	23 20		23 36	23 36		23 50	23 50
Petts Wood	d	23 23	23 23					23 53	23 53
Chislehurst	d	23 26	23 26					23 56	23 56
Elmstead Woods	d	23 28	23 28					23 58	23 58
Bromley North	d						23 44		
Sundridge Park	d						23 46		
Grove Park	d	23 32	23 32				23a49	00 02	00 02
Hither Green	d	23 36	23 36					00 06	00 06
Lewisham	d		23 41					00 11	00 13
St Johns	a		23 43						
New Cross	a		23 45						
London Bridge	a	23 45	23 51		23 52	23 54		00 19	00 20
London Cannon Street	a		23 58			00 03			00 27
London Waterloo (East)	a	23 51			23 58			00 25	
London Charing Cross	a	23 57			00 03			00 31	

Saturdays
26 May to 8 December

		SE	SE	SE	SE	SE	SE	SE	SE	SE		SE	SE	SE	SE	SE	SE	SE	SE	SE		SE	SE	SE	SE
																◇1	◇1	◇1					◇1		◇1
Tonbridge	d															06 01	06 09	06 39					06 47		07 09
Hildenborough	d															06 05							06 51		
Sevenoaks	a															06 12	06 18	06 48					06 58		07 18
	d									05 35					06 05	06 13	06 19	06 49				06 35	06 59		07 19
Dunton Green	d									05 38					06 08							06 38			
Knockholt	d									05 43					06 13							06 43			
Chelsfield	d									05 46					06 16							06 46			
Orpington	a									05 49					06 19	06 21						06 49	07 07		
	d						05 20		05 41	05 50			06 11		06 20	06 22				06 41		06 50	07 08		
Petts Wood	d						05 23		05 44	05 53			06 14		06 23					06 44		06 53			
Chislehurst	d						05 26		05 47	05 56			06 17		06 26					06 47		06 56			
Elmstead Woods	d						05 28		05 49	05 58			06 19		06 28					06 49		06 58			
Bromley North	d		00 04	00 24	00 44	05 22		05 44				06 04		06 24					06 44					07 04	
Sundridge Park	d		00 06	00 26	00 46	05 24		05 46				06 06		06 26					06 46					07 06	
Grove Park	d	00 02	00a09	00a29	00a49	05a27	05 32	05a49	05 53	06 02		06a09	06 23	06a29	06 32				06a49	06 53		07 02		07a09	
Hither Green	d	00 06					05 36		05 57	06 06			06 27		06 36					06 57		07 06			
Lewisham	d	00 11							06 04				06 34							07 04					
St Johns	a								06 06				06 36							07 06					
New Cross	a								06 08				06 38							07 08					
London Bridge	a	00 19					05 45		06 13	06 15			06 43		06 45	06 37	06 41	07 11		07 13		07 15	07 23		07 41
London Cannon Street	a								06 18				06 48							07 18					
London Waterloo (East)	a	00 25					05 52			06 21					06 51	06 43	06 47	07 17				07 21	07 29		07 47
London Charing Cross	a	00 31					05 57			06 27					06 57	06 48	06 52	07 22				07 27	07 34		07 52

		SE	SE	SE	SE	SE		SE	SE	SE	SE	SE	SE	SE	SE	SE		SE	SE	SE	SE	SE	SE	SE	SE
					◇1					◇1	◇1	◇1						◇1	◇1	◇1				◇1	◇1
Tonbridge	d				07 19					07 31	07 39	07 49						08 01	08 09	08 19				08 31	08 39
Hildenborough	d									07 35								08 05						08 35	
Sevenoaks	a				07 28					07 42	07 48	07 58						08 12	08 18	08 28				08 42	08 48
	d			07 05	07 29				07 35	07 43	07 49	07 59				08 05		08 13	08 19	08 29			08 35	08 43	08 49
Dunton Green	d			07 08					07 38							08 08							08 38		
Knockholt	d			07 13					07 43							08 13							08 43		
Chelsfield	d			07 16					07 46							08 16							08 46		
Orpington	a			07 19	07 37				07 49	07 51		08 07				08 19		08 21		08 37			08 49	08 51	
	d	07 11		07 20	07 38			07 41	07 50	07 52		08 08		08 11		08 20		08 22		08 38		08 41	08 50	08 52	
Petts Wood	d	07 14		07 23				07 44	07 53					08 14		08 23						08 44	08 53		
Chislehurst	d	07 17		07 26				07 47	07 56					08 17		08 26						08 47	08 56		
Elmstead Woods	d	07 19		07 28				07 49	07 58					08 19		08 28						08 49	08 58		
Bromley North	d		07 24			07 44							08 04		08 24						08 44				
Sundridge Park	d		07 26			07 46							08 06		08 26						08 46				
Grove Park	d	07 23	07a29	07 32		07a49		07 53	08 02				08a09	08 23	08a29	08 32					08a49	08 53	09 02		
Hither Green	d	07 27		07 36				07 57	08 06					08 27		08 36						08 57	09 06		
Lewisham	d	07 34						08 04						08 34								09 04			
St Johns	a	07 36						08 06						08 36								09 06			
New Cross	a	07 38						08 08						08 38								09 08			
London Bridge	a	07 43		07 45	07 53			08 13	08 15	08 07	08 11	08 23		08 43		08 45		08 37	08 41	08 53		09 13	09 15	09 07	09 11
London Cannon Street	a	07 48						08 18						08 48								09 18			
London Waterloo (East)	a			07 51	07 59				08 21	08 13	08 17	08 29				08 51		08 43	08 47	08 59			09 21	09 13	09 17
London Charing Cross	a			07 57	08 04				08 27	08 18	08 22	08 34				08 57		08 48	08 52	09 04			09 27	09 18	09 22

Table T204-R

Saturdays

26 May to 8 December

Bromley North to Grove Park, Tonbridge, Sevenoaks, Orpington and Grove Park - London Cannon Street/Charing Cross

		SE ◇1	SE	SE	SE	SE	SE ◇1	SE ◇1		SE ◇1	SE	SE	SE	SE ◇1	SE ◇1	SE ◇1	SE	SE		SE	SE	SE ◇1	SE ◇1	SE ◇1	SE
Tonbridge	d	08 49					09 01	09 09		09 19				09 31	09 39	09 49						10 01	10 09	10 19	
Hildenborough	d						09 05							09 35								10 05			
Sevenoaks	a	08 58					09 12	09 18		09 28				09 42	09 48	09 58						10 12	10 18	10 28	
	d	08 59				09 05	09 13	09 19		09 29			09 35	09 43	09 49	09 59					10 05	10 13	10 19	10 29	
Dunton Green	d					09 08							09 38								10 08				
Knockholt	d					09 13							09 43								10 13				
Chelsfield	d					09 16							09 46								10 16				
Orpington	a	09 07				09 19	09 21			09 37			09 49	09 51		10 07					10 19	10 21		10 37	
	d	09 08		09 11		09 20	09 22			09 38		09 41	09 50	09 52		10 08		10 11			10 20	10 22		10 38	
Petts Wood	d			09 14		09 23						09 44	09 53					10 14			10 23				
Chislehurst	d			09 17		09 26						09 47	09 56					10 17			10 26				
Elmstead Woods	d			09 19		09 28						09 49	09 58					10 19			10 28				
Bromley North	d		09 04		09 24						09 44						10 04			10 24					10 44
Sundridge Park	d		09 06		09 26						09 46						10 06			10 26					10 46
Grove Park	d		09a09	09 23	09a29	09 32					09a49	09 53	10 02				10a09	10 23		10a29	10 32				10a49
Hither Green	d			09 27		09 36						09 57	10 06					10 27			10 36				
Lewisham	d			09 34								10 04						10 34							
St Johns	a			09 36								10 06						10 36							
New Cross ⊖	a			09 38								10 08						10 38							
London Bridge ⊖	a	09 23		09 43		09 45	09 37	09 41		09 53		10 13	10 15	10 07	10 11	10 23		10 43			10 45	10 37	10 41	10 53	
London Cannon Street ⊖	a			09 48								10 18						10 48							
London Waterloo (East) ⊖	a	09 29				09 51	09 43	09 47		09 59			10 21	10 13	10 17	10 29					10 51	10 43	10 47	10 59	
London Charing Cross ⊖	a	09 34				09 57	09 48	09 52		10 04			10 27	10 18	10 22	10 34					10 57	10 48	10 52	11 04	

		SE	SE	SE ◇1		SE ◇1	SE ◇1	SE	SE	SE	SE	SE ◇1	SE ◇1	SE ◇1		SE	SE	SE	SE ◇1	SE ◇1	SE ◇1	SE	SE	SE	
Tonbridge	d			10 31		10 39	10 49					11 01	11 09	11 19					11 31	11 39	11 49				
Hildenborough	d			10 35								11 05							11 35						
Sevenoaks	a			10 42		10 48	10 58					11 12	11 18	11 28					11 42	11 48	11 58				
	d		10 35	10 43		10 49	10 59				11 05	11 13	11 19	11 29				11 35	11 43	11 49	11 59				
Dunton Green	d		10 38								11 08							11 38							
Knockholt	d		10 43								11 13							11 43							
Chelsfield	d		10 46								11 16							11 46							
Orpington	a		10 49	10 51			11 07				11 19	11 21		11 37				11 49	11 51		12 07				
	d	10 41	10 50	10 52			11 08		11 11		11 20	11 22		11 38			11 41	11 50	11 52		12 08		12 11		
Petts Wood	d	10 44	10 53						11 14		11 23						11 44	11 53					12 14		
Chislehurst	d	10 47	10 56						11 17		11 26						11 47	11 56					12 17		
Elmstead Woods	d	10 49	10 58						11 19		11 28						11 49	11 58					12 19		
Bromley North	d							11 04		11 24						11 44						12 04		12 24	
Sundridge Park	d							11 06		11 26						11 46						12 06		12 26	
Grove Park	d	10 53	11 02					11a09	11 23	11a29	11 32					11a49	11 53	12 02				12a09	12 23	12a29	
Hither Green	d	10 57	11 06						11 27		11 36						11 57	12 06					12 27		
Lewisham	d	11 04							11 34								12 04						12 34		
St Johns	a	11 06							11 36								12 06						12 36		
New Cross ⊖	a	11 08							11 38								12 08						12 38		
London Bridge ⊖	a	11 13	11 15	11 07		11 11	11 23		11 43		11 45	11 37	11 41	11 53			12 13	12 15	12 07	12 11	12 23		12 43		
London Cannon Street ⊖	a	11 18							11 48								12 18						12 48		
London Waterloo (East) ⊖	a		11 21	11 13		11 17	11 29				11 51	11 43	11 47	11 59				12 21	12 13	12 17	12 29				
London Charing Cross ⊖	a		11 27	11 18		11 22	11 34				11 57	11 48	11 52	12 04				12 27	12 18	12 22	12 34				

		SE	SE ◇1	SE ◇1	SE ◇1	SE	SE	SE	SE ◇1	SE ◇1		SE ◇1	SE	SE	SE	SE	SE ◇1	SE ◇1	SE ◇1	SE		SE	SE	SE ◇1	SE ◇1
Tonbridge	d		12 01	12 09	12 19				12 31	12 39		12 49					13 01	13 09	13 19					13 31	13 39
Hildenborough	d		12 05						12 35								13 05							13 35	
Sevenoaks	a		12 12	12 18	12 28				12 42	12 48		12 58					13 12	13 18	13 28					13 42	13 48
	d	12 05	12 13	12 19	12 29			12 35	12 43	12 49		12 59				13 05	13 13	13 19	13 29				13 35	13 43	13 49
Dunton Green	d	12 08						12 38								13 08							13 38		
Knockholt	d	12 13						12 43								13 13							13 43		
Chelsfield	d	12 16						12 46								13 16							13 46		
Orpington	a	12 19	12 21		12 37			12 49	12 51			13 07				13 19	13 21		13 37				13 49	13 51	
	d	12 20	12 22		12 38		12 41	12 50	12 52			13 08		13 11		13 20	13 22		13 38			13 41	13 50	13 52	
Petts Wood	d	12 23					12 44	12 53						13 14		13 23						13 44	13 53		
Chislehurst	d	12 26					12 47	12 56						13 17		13 26						13 47	13 56		
Elmstead Woods	d	12 28					12 49	12 58						13 19		13 28						13 49	13 58		
Bromley North	d					12 44							13 04		13 24					13 44					
Sundridge Park	d					12 46							13 06		13 26					13 46					
Grove Park	d	12 32				12a49	12 53	13 02					13a09	13 23	13a29	13 32				13a49		13 53	14 02		
Hither Green	d	12 36					12 57	13 06						13 27		13 36						13 57	14 06		
Lewisham	d						13 04							13 34								14 04			
St Johns	a						13 06							13 36								14 06			
New Cross ⊖	a						13 08							13 38								14 08			
London Bridge ⊖	a	12 45	12 37	12 41	12 53		13 13	13 15	13 07	13 11		13 23		13 43		13 45	13 37	13 41	13 53			14 13	14 15	14 07	14 11
London Cannon Street ⊖	a						13 18							13 48								14 18			
London Waterloo (East) ⊖	a	12 51	12 43	12 47	12 59			13 21	13 13	13 17		13 29				13 51	13 43	13 47	13 59				14 21	14 13	14 17
London Charing Cross ⊖	a	12 57	12 48	12 52	13 04			13 27	13 18	13 22		13 34				13 57	13 48	13 52	14 04				14 27	14 18	14 22

Table T204-R

Saturdays

26 May to 8 December

Bromley North to Grove Park, Tonbridge, Sevenoaks, Orpington and Grove Park - London Cannon Street/Charing Cross

		SE ◇1		SE	SE	SE	SE	SE ◇1	SE ◇1	SE ◇1	SE	SE		SE	SE ◇1	SE ◇1	SE ◇1	SE	SE	SE	SE	SE ◇1		SE ◇1	SE ◇1
Tonbridge	d	13 49						14 01	14 09	14 19					14 31	14 39	14 49					15 01		15 09	15 19
Hildenborough	d							14 05							14 35							15 05			
Sevenoaks	a	13 58						14 12	14 18	14 28					14 42	14 48	14 58					15 12		15 18	15 28
	d	13 59					14 05	14 13	14 19	14 29				14 35	14 43	14 49	14 59				15 05	15 13		15 19	15 29
Dunton Green	d						14 08							14 38							15 08				
Knockholt	d						14 13							14 43							15 13				
Chelsfield	d						14 16							14 46							15 16				
Orpington	a	14 07					14 19	14 21		14 37				14 49	14 51		15 07				15 19	15 21			15 37
	d	14 08			14 11		14 20	14 22		14 38		14 41		14 50	14 52		15 08		15 11		15 20	15 22			15 38
Petts Wood	d				14 14		14 23					14 44		14 53					15 14		15 23				
Chislehurst	d				14 17		14 26					14 47		14 56					15 17		15 26				
Elmstead Woods	d				14 19		14 28					14 49		14 58					15 19		15 28				
Bromley North	d			14 04		14 24					14 44							15 04		15 24					
Sundridge Park	d			14 06		14 26					14 46							15 06		15 26					
Grove Park	d			14a09	14 23	14a29	14 32				14a49	14 53		15 02				15a09	15 23	15a29	15 32				
Hither Green	d				14 27		14 36					14 57		15 06					15 27		15 36				
Lewisham	d				14 34							15 04							15 34						
St Johns	a				14 36							15 06							15 36						
New Cross ⊖	a				14 38							15 08							15 38						
London Bridge ⊖	a	14 23			14 43		14 45	14 37	14 41	14 53		15 13		15 15	15 07	15 11	15 23		15 43		15 45	15 37		15 41	15 53
London Cannon Street ⊖	a				14 48							15 18							15 48						
London Waterloo (East) ⊖	a	14 29					14 51	14 43	14 47	14 59				15 21	15 13	15 17	15 29				15 51	15 43		15 47	15 59
London Charing Cross ⊖	a	14 34					14 57	14 48	14 52	15 04				15 27	15 18	15 22	15 34				15 57	15 48		15 52	16 04

		SE	SE	SE	SE ◇1	SE ◇1	SE ◇1	SE		SE	SE	SE	SE ◇1	SE ◇1	SE ◇1	SE	SE	SE		SE ◇1	SE ◇1	SE ◇1	SE	SE	SE
Tonbridge	d				15 31	15 39	15 49						16 01	16 09	16 19					16 31	16 39	16 49			
Hildenborough	d				15 35								16 05							16 35					
Sevenoaks	a				15 42	15 48	15 58						16 12	16 18	16 28					16 42	16 48	16 58			
	d			15 35	15 43	15 49	15 59					16 05	16 13	16 19	16 29			16 35		16 43	16 49	16 59			
Dunton Green	d			15 38								16 08						16 38							
Knockholt	d			15 43								16 13						16 43							
Chelsfield	d			15 46								16 16						16 46							
Orpington	a			15 49	15 51		16 07					16 19	16 21		16 37			16 49		16 51		17 07			
	d		15 41	15 50	15 52		16 08			16 11		16 20	16 22		16 38		16 41	16 50		16 52		17 08		17 11	
Petts Wood	d		15 44	15 53						16 14		16 23					16 44	16 53						17 14	
Chislehurst	d		15 47	15 56						16 17		16 26					16 47	16 56						17 17	
Elmstead Woods	d		15 49	15 58						16 19		16 28					16 49	16 58						17 19	
Bromley North	d	15 44						16 04			16 24					16 44							17 04		17 24
Sundridge Park	d	15 46						16 06			16 26					16 46							17 06		17 26
Grove Park	d	15a49	15 53	16 02				16a09		16 23	16a29	16 32				16a49	16 53	17 02					17a09	17 23	17a29
Hither Green	d		15 57	16 06						16 27		16 36					16 57	17 06						17 27	
Lewisham	d		16 04							16 34							17 04							17 34	
St Johns	a		16 06							16 36							17 06							17 36	
New Cross ⊖	a		16 08							16 38							17 08							17 38	
London Bridge ⊖	a		16 13	16 15	16 07	16 11	16 23			16 43		16 45	16 37	16 41	16 53		17 13	17 15		17 07	17 11	17 23		17 43	
London Cannon Street ⊖	a		16 18							16 48							17 18							17 48	
London Waterloo (East) ⊖	a			16 21	16 13	16 17	16 29					16 51	16 43	16 47	16 59			17 21		17 13	17 17	17 29			
London Charing Cross ⊖	a			16 27	16 18	16 22	16 34					16 57	16 48	16 52	17 04			17 27		17 18	17 22	17 34			

		SE	SE ◇1	SE ◇1		SE ◇1	SE	SE	SE	SE ◇1	SE ◇1	SE ◇1	SE	SE		SE	SE	SE ◇1	SE ◇1	SE ◇1	SE	SE	SE	SE ◇1	
Tonbridge	d		17 01	17 09		17 19				17 31	17 39	17 49						18 01	18 09	18 19				18 31	
Hildenborough	d		17 05							17 35								18 05						18 35	
Sevenoaks	a		17 12	17 18		17 28				17 42	17 48	17 58						18 12	18 18	18 28				18 42	
	d	17 05	17 13	17 19		17 29			17 35	17 43	17 49	17 59					18 05	18 13	18 19	18 29			18 35	18 43	
Dunton Green	d	17 08							17 38								18 08						18 38		
Knockholt	d	17 13							17 43								18 13						18 43		
Chelsfield	d	17 16							17 46								18 16						18 46		
Orpington	a	17 19	17 21			17 37			17 49	17 51		18 07					18 19	18 21		18 37			18 49	18 51	
	d	17 20	17 22			17 38		17 41	17 50	17 52		18 08		18 11			18 20	18 22		18 38		18 41	18 50	18 52	
Petts Wood	d	17 23						17 44	17 53					18 14			18 23					18 44	18 53		
Chislehurst	d	17 26						17 47	17 56					18 17			18 26					18 47	18 56		
Elmstead Woods	d	17 28						17 49	17 58					18 19			18 28					18 49	18 58		
Bromley North	d						17 44						18 04			18 24					18 44				
Sundridge Park	d						17 46						18 06			18 26					18 46				
Grove Park	d	17 32					17a49	17 53	18 02				18a09	18 23		18a29	18 32				18a49	18 53	19 02		
Hither Green	d	17 36						17 57	18 06					18 27			18 36					18 57	19 06		
Lewisham	d							18 04						18 34								19 04			
St Johns	a							18 06						18 36								19 06			
New Cross ⊖	a							18 08						18 38								19 08			
London Bridge ⊖	a	17 45	17 37	17 41		17 53		18 13	18 15	18 07	18 11	18 23		18 43			18 45	18 37	18 41	18 53		19 13	19 15	19 07	
London Cannon Street ⊖	a							18 18						18 48								19 18			
London Waterloo (East) ⊖	a	17 51	17 43	17 47		17 59			18 21	18 13	18 17	18 29					18 51	18 43	18 47	18 59			19 21	19 13	
London Charing Cross ⊖	a	17 57	17 48	17 52		18 04			18 27	18 18	18 22	18 34					18 57	18 48	18 52	19 04			19 27	19 18	

Table T204-R

Saturdays

26 May to 8 December

Bromley North to Grove Park, Tonbridge, Sevenoaks, Orpington and Grove Park - London Cannon Street/Charing Cross

		SE ◇1	SE ◇1	SE	SE	SE	SE	SE ◇1	SE ◇1	SE ◇1	SE	SE	SE	SE ◇1	SE ◇1	SE ◇1	SE	SE	SE	SE	SE ◇1	SE ◇1	SE
Tonbridge	d	18 39	18 49					19 01	19 09	19 19				19 31	19 39	19 49					20 01	20 09	
Hildenborough	d							19 05						19 35							20 05		
Sevenoaks	a	18 48	18 58					19 12	19 18	19 28				19 42	19 48	19 58					20 12	20 18	
	d	18 49	18 59				19 05	19 13	19 19	19 29			19 35	19 43	19 49	19 59				20 05	20 13	20 19	
Dunton Green	d						19 08						19 38							20 08			
Knockholt	d						19 13						19 43							20 13			
Chelsfield	d						19 16						19 46							20 16			
Orpington	a		19 07				19 19	19 21		19 37			19 49	19 51		20 07				20 19	20 21		
	d		19 08		19 11		19 20	19 22		19 38		19 41	19 50	19 52		20 08		20 11		20 20	20 22		
Petts Wood	d				19 14		19 23					19 44	19 53					20 14		20 23			
Chislehurst	d				19 17		19 26					19 47	19 56					20 17		20 26			
Elmstead Woods	d				19 19		19 28					19 49	19 58					20 19		20 28			
Bromley North	d			19 04		19 24					19 44						20 04		20 24				20 44
Sundridge Park	d			19 06		19 26					19 46						20 06		20 26				20 46
Grove Park	d			19a09	19 23	19a29	19 32				19a49	19 53	20 02				20a09	20 23	20a29	20 32			20a49
Hither Green	d				19 27		19 36					19 57	20 06					20 27		20 36			
Lewisham	d				19 34							20 04						20 34					
St Johns	a				19 36							20 06						20 36					
New Cross	a				19 38							20 08						20 38					
London Bridge	a	19 11	19 23		19 43		19 45	19 37	19 41	19 53		20 13	20 15	20 07	20 11	20 23		20 43		20 45	20 37	20 41	
London Cannon Street	a				19 48							20 18						20 48					
London Waterloo (East)	a	19 17	19 29				19 51	19 43	19 47	19 59			20 21	20 13	20 17	20 29				20 51	20 43	20 47	
London Charing Cross	a	19 22	19 34				19 57	19 48	19 52	20 04			20 27	20 18	20 22	20 34				20 57	20 48	20 52	

		SE	SE	SE ◇1	SE ◇1	SE ◇1	SE	SE	SE	SE	SE ◇1	SE ◇1	SE	SE	SE	SE ◇1	SE ◇1	SE ◇1	SE	SE	SE	SE
Tonbridge	d			20 31	20 39	20 49					21 01	21 09				21 31	21 39	21 49				
Hildenborough	d			20 35							21 05					21 35						
Sevenoaks	a			20 42	20 48	20 58					21 12	21 18				21 42	21 48	21 58				
	d		20 35	20 43	20 49	20 59				21 05	21 13	21 19			21 35	21 43	21 49	21 59				22 05
Dunton Green	d		20 38							21 08					21 38							22 08
Knockholt	d		20 43							21 13					21 43							22 13
Chelsfield	d		20 46							21 16					21 46							22 16
Orpington	a		20 49	20 51		21 07				21 19	21 21				21 49	21 51		22 07				22 19
	d	20 41	20 50	20 52		21 08		21 11		21 20	21 22			21 41	21 50	21 52		22 08		22 11		22 20
Petts Wood	d	20 44	20 53					21 14		21 23				21 44	21 53					22 14		22 23
Chislehurst	d	20 47	20 56					21 17		21 26				21 47	21 56					22 17		22 26
Elmstead Woods	d	20 49	20 58					21 19		21 28				21 49	21 58					22 19		22 28
Bromley North	d						21 04		21 24				21 44						22 04		22 24	
Sundridge Park	d						21 06		21 26				21 46						22 06		22 26	
Grove Park	d	20 53	21 02				21a09	21 23	21a29	21 32			21a49	21 53	22 02				22a09	22 23	22a29	22 32
Hither Green	d	20 57	21 06					21 27		21 36				21 57	22 06					22 27		22 36
Lewisham	d	21 04						21 34						22 04						22 34		
St Johns	a	21 06						21 36						22 06						22 36		
New Cross	a	21 08						21 38						22 08						22 38		
London Bridge	a	21 13	21 15	21 07	21 11	21 23		21 43		21 45	21 37	21 41		22 13	22 15	22 07	22 11	22 23		22 43		22 45
London Cannon Street	a	21 18						21 48						22 18						22 48		
London Waterloo (East)	a		21 21	21 13	21 17	21 29				21 51	21 43	21 47			22 21	22 13	22 17	22 29				22 51
London Charing Cross	a		21 27	21 18	21 22	21 34				21 57	21 48	21 52			22 27	22 18	22 22	22 34				22 57

		SE ◇1	SE ◇1	SE	SE	SE	SE ◇1	SE ◇1	SE ◇1	SE	SE	SE	SE	SE ◇1	SE	SE
Tonbridge	d	22 01	22 09				22 31	22 39	22 49					23 15		
Hildenborough	d	22 05					22 35							23 19		
Sevenoaks	a	22 12	22 18				22 42	22 48	22 58					23 26		
	d	22 13	22 19			22 35	22 43	22 49	22 59				23 05	23 27		23 35
Dunton Green	d					22 38							23 08			23 38
Knockholt	d					22 43							23 13			23 43
Chelsfield	d					22 46							23 16			23 46
Orpington	a	22 22				22 49	22 51		23 07				23 19	23 35		23 49
	d	22 22			22 41	22 50	22 52		23 08		23 11		23 20	23 36		23 50
Petts Wood	d				22 44	22 53					23 14		23 23			23 53
Chislehurst	d				22 47	22 56					23 17		23 26			23 56
Elmstead Woods	d				22 49	22 58					23 19		23 28			23 58
Bromley North	d			22 44						23 04		23 24			23 44	
Sundridge Park	d			22 46						23 06		23 26			23 46	
Grove Park	d			22a49	22 53	23 02				23a09	23 23	23a29	23 32		23a49	00 02
Hither Green	d				22 57	23 06					23 27		23 36			00 06
Lewisham	d				23 04						23 34					00 12
St Johns	a				23 06						23 36					
New Cross	a				23 08						23 38					
London Bridge	a	22 38	22 41		23 13	23 15	23 07	23 11	23 23		23 43		23 45	23 52		00 20
London Cannon Street	a				23 18						23 48					
London Waterloo (East)	a	22 44	22 47			23 21	23 13	23 17	23 29				23 51	23 58		00 26
London Charing Cross	a	22 48	22 52			23 27	23 18	23 22	23 34				23 57	00 03		00 30

Table T204-R

Sundays

20 May to 2 December

Bromley North to Grove Park, Tonbridge, Sevenoaks, Orpington and Grove Park - London Cannon Street/Charing Cross

		SE A	SE	SE	SE	SE	SE	SE ◇1	SE ◇1	SE	SE ◇1	SE	SE ◇1	SE ◇1	SE	SE ◇1	SE ◇1		SE	SE ◇1	SE ◇1	SE
Tonbridge	d							07 07	07 21		07 37		08 07	08 21		08 37	08 49			12 07	12 21	
Hildenborough	d																08 53					
Sevenoaks	a							07 16	07 30		07 46		08 16	08 30		08 46	09 00			12 16	12 30	
	d						07 04	07 17	07 31	07 34	07 47	08 04	08 17	08 31	08 34	08 47	09 01		12 04	12 17	12 31	12 34
Dunton Green	d						07 07			07 37		08 07			08 37				12 07			12 37
Knockholt	d						07 12			07 42		08 12			08 42				12 12			12 42
Chelsfield	d						07 15			07 45		08 15			08 45				12 15			12 45
Orpington	a						07 18	07 25	07 39	07 48	07 55	08 18	08 25	08 39	08 48	08 55	09 09	and at the same minutes past each hour until	12 18	12 25	12 39	12 48
	d					06 49	07 19	07 26	07 40	07 49	07 56	08 19	08 26	08 40	08 49	08 56	09 10		12 19	12 26	12 40	12 49
Petts Wood	d					06 52	07 22			07 52		08 22			08 52				12 22			12 52
Chislehurst	d					06 55	07 25			07 55		08 25			08 55				12 25			12 55
Elmstead Woods	d					06 57	07 27			07 57		08 27			08 57				12 27			12 57
Bromley North	d		00 04	00 24	00 44																	
Sundridge Park	d		00 06	00 26	00 46																	
Grove Park	d	00 02	00a09	00a29	00a49	07 01	07 31			08 01		08 31			09 01				12 31			13 01
Hither Green	d	00 06				07 05	07 35			08 05		08 35			09 05				12 35			13 05
Lewisham	d	00 12				07 11	07 41			08 11		08 41			09 11				12 41			13 11
St Johns	a																					
New Cross	a																					
London Bridge	a	00 20				07 19	07 49	07 41	07 55	08 19	08 11	08 49	08 41	08 55	09 19	09 11	09 25		12 49	12 41	12 55	13 19
London Cannon Street	a																					
London Waterloo (East)	a	00 26				07 25	07 55	07 47	08 01	08 25	08 17	08 55	08 47	09 01	09 25	09 17	09 31		12 55	12 47	13 01	13 25
London Charing Cross	a	00 30				07 29	07 59	07 52	08 05	08 29	08 22	08 59	08 52	09 05	09 29	09 22	09 35		12 59	12 52	13 05	13 29

		SE ◇1	SE ◇1	SE	SE ◇1	SE ◇1	SE	SE ◇1	SE ◇1	SE	SE ◇1	SE ◇1	SE	SE ◇1	SE ◇1		SE	SE ◇1	SE ◇1	SE	SE ◇1	SE ◇1
Tonbridge	d	12 37	12 49		13 07	13 21		13 37	13 50		14 07	14 21		14 37	14 49			19 07	19 21		19 37	19 49
Hildenborough	d		12 53						13 54						14 53							19 53
Sevenoaks	a	12 46	13 00		13 16	13 30		13 46	14 00		14 16	14 30		14 46	15 00			19 16	19 30		19 46	20 00
	d	12 47	13 01	13 04	13 17	13 31	13 34	13 47	14 01	14 04	14 17	14 31	14 34	14 47	15 01		19 04	19 17	19 31	19 34	19 47	20 01
Dunton Green	d			13 07			13 37			14 07			14 37				19 07			19 37		
Knockholt	d			13 12			13 42			14 12			14 42				19 12			19 42		
Chelsfield	d			13 15			13 45			14 15			14 45				19 15			19 45		
Orpington	a	12 55	13 09	13 18	13 25	13 39	13 48	13 55	14 09	14 18	14 25	14 39	14 48	14 55	15 09	and at the same minutes past each hour until	19 18	19 25	19 39	19 48	19 55	20 09
	d	12 56	13 10	13 19	13 26	13 40	13 49	13 56	14 10	14 19	14 26	14 40	14 49	14 56	15 10		19 19	19 26	19 40	19 49	19 56	20 10
Petts Wood	d			13 22			13 52			14 22			14 52				19 22			19 52		
Chislehurst	d			13 25			13 55			14 25			14 55				19 25			19 55		
Elmstead Woods	d			13 27			13 57			14 27			14 57				19 27			19 57		
Bromley North	d																					
Sundridge Park	d																					
Grove Park	d			13 31			14 01			14 31			15 01				19 31			20 01		
Hither Green	d			13 35			14 05			14 35			15 05				19 35			20 05		
Lewisham	d			13 41			14 11			14 41			15 11				19 41			20 11		
St Johns	a																					
New Cross	a																					
London Bridge	a	13 11	13 25	13 49	13 41	13 55	14 19	14 11	14 25	14 49	14 41	14 55	15 19	15 11	15 25		19 49	19 41	19 55	20 19	20 11	20 25
London Cannon Street	a																					
London Waterloo (East)	a	13 17	13 31	13 55	13 47	14 01	14 25	14 17	14 31	14 55	14 47	15 01	15 25	15 17	15 31		19 55	19 47	20 01	20 25	20 17	20 31
London Charing Cross	a	13 22	13 35	13 59	13 52	14 05	14 29	14 22	14 35	14 59	14 52	15 05	15 29	15 22	15 35		19 59	19 52	20 05	20 29	20 22	20 35

		SE	SE ◇1	SE	SE ◇1	SE ◇1	SE	SE ◇1	SE	SE ◇1	SE ◇1	SE	SE ◇1	SE	SE ◇1	SE	SE
Tonbridge	d		20 07		20 37	20 49		21 07		21 37	21 49		22 07		22 37		
Hildenborough	d					20 53					21 53						
Sevenoaks	a		20 16		20 46	21 00		21 16		21 46	22 00		22 16		22 46		
	d	20 04	20 17	20 34	20 47	21 01	21 04	21 17	21 34	21 47	22 01	22 04	22 17	22 34	22 47	23 04	23 34
Dunton Green	d	20 07		20 37			21 07		21 37			22 07		22 37		23 07	23 37
Knockholt	d	20 12		20 42			21 12		21 42			22 12		22 42		23 12	23 42
Chelsfield	d	20 15		20 45			21 15		21 45			22 15		22 45		23 15	23 45
Orpington	a	20 18	20 25	20 48	20 55	21 09	21 18	21 25	21 48	21 55	22 09	22 18	22 25	22 48	22 55	23 18	23 48
	d	20 19	20 26	20 49	20 56	21 10	21 19	21 26	21 49	21 56	22 10	22 19	22 26	22 49	22 56	23 19	23 49
Petts Wood	d	20 22		20 52			21 22		21 52			22 22		22 52		23 22	23 52
Chislehurst	d	20 25		20 55			21 25		21 55			22 25		22 55		23 25	23 55
Elmstead Woods	d	20 27		20 57			21 27		21 57			22 27		22 57		23 27	23 57
Bromley North	d																
Sundridge Park	d																
Grove Park	d	20 31		21 01			21 31		22 01			22 31		23 01		23 31	00 02
Hither Green	d	20 35		21 05			21 35		22 05			22 35		23 05		23 35	00 05
Lewisham	d	20 41		21 11			21 41		22 11			22 41		23 11		23 41	00 11
St Johns	a																
New Cross	a																
London Bridge	a	20 49	20 41	21 19	21 11	21 25	21 49	21 41	22 19	22 11	22 25	22 49	22 41	23 19	23 11	23 49	00 19
London Cannon Street	a																
London Waterloo (East)	a	20 55	20 47	21 25	21 17	21 31	21 55	21 47	22 25	22 17	22 31	22 55	22 47	23 25	23 17	23 55	00 25
London Charing Cross	a	20 59	20 52	21 29	21 22	21 35	21 59	21 52	22 29	22 22	22 35	22 59	22 52	23 29	23 22	23 59	00 29

A not 20 May

Table T206-F

Mondays to Fridays
21 May to 7 December

London and Tonbridge - Tunbridge Wells and Hastings

Miles			SE MO ◇■	SE MX ◇■	SE MO ◇■	SE MX ◇■	SE MX ◇■	SE ThFO	SE ■	SE ■	SE ◇■	SE ■	SE ◇■	SE ◇■	SE ■	SE ◇■	SE ◇■	SE ◇■	SE ◇■	SE ◇■	SE ◇■	SE ◇■	SE ◇■
0	London Charing Cross ■ ⊖	d						00 15						05 56		06 28	07 00	07 15	07 27		08 00	08 18	08 28
0¾	London Waterloo (East) ■ ⊖	d						00 18						05 59		06 31	07 03	07 18	07 30		08 05	08 21	08 31
—	London Cannon Street ■ ⊖	d																		07 42			
1¾	London Bridge ■ ⊖	d						00 24						06 05		06 37	07 09	07 24	07 36	07 46	08 11	08 27	08 37
13¾	Orpington ■	d					00 10	00 51						06 22		06 53	07 26	07 40	07 55	08 08	08 32	08 43	08 56
15¼	Chelsfield	d						00 54											07 58				08 59
22	Sevenoaks ■	d				00 06	00 20	01 04						06 32		07 03	07 36	07 50	08 06	08 18	08 41	08 53	09 07
27	Hildenborough	d			00 06	00 12		01s10						06 38			07 42		08 12		08 47		09 13
29½	Tonbridge ■	a			00 10	00 16	00 28	01 14						06 42		07 11	07 46	07 58	08 16	08 26	08 51	09 01	09 17
—		d			00 11	00 17	00 29	01 15	05 00	05 30	06 08	06 20	06 35	06 42	06 56	07 12	07 47	07 59	08 17	08 27	08 52	09 02	09 18
33	High Brooms	d			00 16	00 24	00 35	01s20	05 06	05 36	06 13	06 26	06 40	06 48	07 02	07 17	07 55	08 05	08 24	08 33	08 57	09 07	09 24
34½	Tunbridge Wells ■	a			00 20	00 28	00 40	01 27	05 10	05 40	06 17	06 30	06 45	06 54	07 06	07 21	08 03	08 09	08 33	08 40	09 01	09 11	09 30
—		d			00 21		00 41				06 18		06 45			07 22		08 15		08 49		09 20	
36¾	Frant	d			00s25		00s45				06 22		06 51			07 27		08 19				09 24	
39¼	Wadhurst	d			00s30		00s50				06 27		06 57			07 32		08 24		08 56		09 29	
43¼	Stonegate	d			00s36		00s56				06 33		07 03			07 38		08 30				09 35	
47½	Etchingham	d			00s41		01s01				06 38		07 08			07 43		08 35		09 05		09 40	
49¼	Robertsbridge	d		00 03	00s44		01s05				06 42		07 12			07 47		08 39		09 09		09 45	
55½	Battle	d		00 11	00s52		01s13				06 50		07 20			07 55		08 47		09 17		09 57	
57½	Crowhurst	d		00s15	00s56		01s17				06 53		07 24			07 58		08 50		09 21			
60¾	West St Leonards	d	00 02	00 20	01s02		01s22				06 59		07 30			08 04		08 56		09 27			
—	St Leonards Warrior Sq ■	d	00 05	00 24	01s05		01s26				07 03		07 33			08 08		09 00		09 30		10 08	
62½	Hastings ■	a	00 09	00 28	01 09		01 33				07 07		07 36			08 11		09 06		09 37		10 13	
63½	Ore	a																					

		SE ◇■	SE ◇■	SE ◇■	SE ◇■	SE ◇■	SE ◇■	SE ◇■	SE ◇■	SE ◇■	SE ◇■	SE ◇■	SE ◇■	SE ◇■	SE ◇■	SE ◇■	SE ◇■	SE ◇■	SE ◇■	SE ◇■	SE ◇■	SE ◇■	SE ◇■
London Charing Cross ■ ⊖	d		08 58		09 24	09 45	10 00	10 15	10 30	10 45	11 00	11 15	11 30	11 45	12 00	12 15	12 30	12 45	13 00	13 15	13 30	13 45	14 00
London Waterloo (East) ■ ⊖	d		09 01		09 27	09 48	10 03	10 18	10 33	10 48	11 03	11 18	11 33	11 48	12 03	12 18	12 33	12 48	13 03	13 18	13 33	13 48	14 03
London Cannon Street ■ ⊖	d	08 40		09 14																			
London Bridge ■ ⊖	d	08 44	09 07	09 18	09 33	09 54	10 09	10 24	10 39	10 54	11 09	11 24	11 39	11 54	12 09	12 24	12 39	12 54	13 09	13 24	13 39	13 54	14 09
Orpington ■	d	09 07	09 26	09 40	09 56	10 10	10 26	10 39	10 56	11 10	11 26	11 39	11 56	12 10	12 26	12 39	12 56	13 10	13 26	13 39	13 56	14 10	14 26
Chelsfield	d																						
Sevenoaks ■	d	09 20	09 36	09 50	10 06	10 20	10 36	10 50	11 06	11 20	11 36	11 50	12 06	12 20	12 36	12 50	13 06	13 20	13 36	13 50	14 06	14 20	14 36
Hildenborough	d		09 42		10 12		10 42		11 12		11 42		12 12		12 42		13 12		13 42		14 12		14 42
Tonbridge ■	a	09 28	09 46	09 58	10 16	10 28	10 46	10 58	11 16	11 28	11 46	11 58	12 16	12 28	12 46	12 58	13 16	13 28	13 46	13 58	14 16	14 28	14 46
	d	09 29	09 47	09 59	10 17	10 29	10 47	10 59	11 17	11 29	11 47	11 59	12 17	12 29	12 47	12 59	13 17	13 29	13 47	13 59	14 17	14 29	14 47
High Brooms	d	09 35	09 54	10 05	10 23	10 35	10 54	11 05	11 24	11 35	11 54	12 05	12 24	12 35	12 54	13 05	13 24	13 35	13 54	14 05	14 24	14 35	14 54
Tunbridge Wells ■	a	09 38	09 58	10 08	10 28	10 38	10 58	11 08	11 28	11 38	11 58	12 08	12 28	12 38	12 58	13 08	13 28	13 38	13 58	14 08	14 28	14 38	14 58
	d	09 43		10 10		10 40		11 10		11 40		12 10		12 40		13 10		13 40		14 10		14 40	
Frant	d			10 14				11 14				12 14				13 14				14 14			
Wadhurst	d	09 51		10 19		10 47		11 19		11 47		12 19		12 47		13 19		13 47		14 19		14 47	
Stonegate	d			10 25				11 25				12 25				13 25				14 25			
Etchingham	d			10 30				11 30				12 30				13 30				14 30			
Robertsbridge	d			10 33				11 33				12 33				13 33				14 33			
Battle	d	10 08		10 41		11 02		11 41		12 02		12 41		13 02		13 41		14 02		14 41		15 02	
Crowhurst	d	10 12		10 45				11 45				12 45				13 45				14 45			
West St Leonards	d	10 22		10 52				11 52				12 52				13 52				14 52			
St Leonards Warrior Sq ■	d	10 27		10 55		11 13		11 55		12 13		12 55		13 14		13 55		14 13		14 55		15 13	
Hastings ■	a	10 32		11 02		11 17		12 00		12 17		13 00		13 17		14 00		14 17		15 00		15 17	
Ore	a																						

		SE ◇■	SE ◇■	SE ◇■	SE ◇■	SE ◇■	SE ◇■	SE ◇■	SE ◇■	SE ◇■	SE ◇■	SE ◇■	SE ◇■	SE ◇■	SE ◇■	SE ◇■	SE ◇■	SE ◇■		SE ◇■	SE ◇■	SE ◇■
London Charing Cross ■ ⊖	d	14 15	14 30	14 45	15 00	15 15	15 30	15 45	16 00		16 14	16 28	16 43		17 01	17 15	17 24			17 44	17 57	18 07
London Waterloo (East) ■ ⊖	d	14 18	14 33	14 48	15 03	15 18	15 33	15 48	16 03		16 17	16 31	16 46		17 04	17 18	17 27			17 48	18 00	18 10
London Cannon Street ■ ⊖	d									16 22				17 01				17 36				
London Bridge ■ ⊖	d	14 24	14 39	14 54	15 09	15 24	15 39	15 54	16 09	16 27	16 23	16 37	16 52	17 06	17 10	17 24	17 33	17 41		17 54	18 06	18 16
Orpington ■	d	14 39	14 56	15 10	15 26	15 39	15 56	16 10	16 26		16 39	16 55										
Chelsfield	d														17 28		17 51			18 12		18 34
Sevenoaks ■	d	14 50	15 06	15 20	15 36	15 50	16 06	16 20	16 36		16 49	17 05	17 16	17 32	17 36		18 00			18 21		18 43
Hildenborough	d		15 12		15 42		16 12		16 42			17 11			17 42		18 06			18 27		18 49
Tonbridge ■	a	14 58	15 16	15 28	15 46	15 58	16 16	16 28	16 46		16 58	17 15	17 24	17 40	17 46		18 10			18 31		18 53
	d	14 59	15 17	15 29	15 47	15 59	16 17	16 29	16 47		17 04	17 16	17 25	17 40	17 48		18 11			18 32		18 53
High Brooms	d	15 05	15 24	15 35	15 54	16 05	16 24	16 35	16 53	17 06	17 10	17 22	17 31	17 46	17 54	18 04	18 17	18 23		18 38	18 43	19 00
Tunbridge Wells ■	a	15 08	15 28	15 38	15 58	16 09	16 28	16 38	16 58	17 10	17 14	17 28	17 35	17 50	18 01	18 07	18 24	18 26		18 44	18 47	19 06
	d	15 10		15 40		16 13		16 40		17 11	17 15		17 40	17 51		18 08		18 30	18 34		18 49	
Frant	d	15 14				16 18		16 44			17 20			17 56		18 13			18 38		18 54	
Wadhurst	d	15 19		15 47		16 24		16 49			17 25		17 47	18 01		18 18		18 37	18 43		18 59	
Stonegate	d	15 25				16 30		16 55			17 31			18 07		18 24			18 49		19 05	
Etchingham	d	15 30				16 35		17 00			17 36		17 56	18 12		18 28		18 46	18 54		19 10	
Robertsbridge	d	15 33				16 39		17 04			17 40		18 00	18 15		18 32			18 58		19 14	
Battle	d	15 41		16 02		16 47		17 14		17 33	17 51		18 08	18 23		18 40		18 56	19 06		19 22	
Crowhurst	d	15 45				16 51		17 17			17 54			18 27		18 44			19 10		19 25	
West St Leonards	d	15 52		16 12		16 56		17 23			18 00			18 33		18 52			19 17		19 31	
St Leonards Warrior Sq ■	d	15 55		16 16		16 59		17 28		17 44	18 03		18 20	18 36		18 55		19 08	19 20		19 35	
Hastings ■	a	16 00		16 21		17 05		17 33		17 50	18 08		18 25	18 42		19 01		19 13	19 23		19 41	
Ore	a																					

Table T206-F

Mondays to Fridays
21 May to 7 December

London and Tonbridge - Tunbridge Wells and Hastings

		SE ◇■	SE ◇■	SE ◇■	SE ◇■	SE ◇■	SE ◇■	SE ◇■	SE ◇■	SE ◇■	SE ◇■	SE ◇■	SE ◇■	SE ◇■	SE ◇■	SE ◇■	SE ◇■	SE ◇■	SE ◇■	SE ◇■	SE ◇■	SE ◇■
London Charing Cross ■ ⊖	d		18 31	18 45		19 00	19 15	19 30	19 45	20 00	20 15	20 30	20 45	21 00	21 30	21 45	22 00	22 30	22 45	23 00	23 30	23 45
London Waterloo (East) ■ ⊖	d		18 34	18 49		19 03	19 18	19 33	19 48	20 03	20 18	20 33	20 48	21 03	21 33	21 48	22 03	22 33	22 48	23 03	23 33	23 48
London Cannon Street ■ ⊖	d	18 26			19 02																	
London Bridge ■ ⊖	d	18 31	18 40	18 55	19 07	19 09	19 24	19 39	19 54	20 09	20 24	20 39	20 54	21 09	21 39	21 54	22 09	22 39	22 54	23 09	23 39	23 54
Orpington ■	d		18 57	19 12		19 26	19 40	19 56	20 10	20 26	20 40	20 56	21 10	21 26	21 56	22 10	22 26	22 56	23 10	23 26	23 56	00 10
Chelsfield	d					19 29																
Sevenoaks ■	d		19 07	19 22	19 31	19 38	19 50	20 06	20 20	20 36	20 50	21 06	21 20	21 36	22 06	22 20	22 36	23 06	23 20	23 36	00 06	00 20
Hildenborough	d		19 13		19 37	19 44		20 12		20 42		21 12		21 42	22 12		22 42	23 12		23 42	00 12	
Tonbridge ■	a		19 17	19 30	19 41	19 48	19 58	20 16	20 28	20 46	20 58	21 16	21 28	21 46	22 16	22 28	22 46	23 16	23 28	23 46	00 16	00 28
	d		19 18	19 31	19 42	19 49	19 59	20 17	20 29	20 47	20 59	21 17	21 29	21 47	22 17	22 29	22 47	23 17	23 29	23 47	00 17	00 29
High Brooms	d	19 09	19 24	19 37	19 48	19 55	20 05	20 24	20 35	20 54	21 05	21 24	21 35	21 54	22 24	22 35	22 54	23 24	23 35	23 54	00 24	00 35
Tunbridge Wells ■	a	19 13	19 32	19 40	19 51	20 02	20 08	20 28	20 38	20 58	21 08	21 28	21 38	21 58	22 28	22 38	22 58	23 28	23 38	23 58	00 28	00 40
	d	19 18		19 42	19 53		20 10		20 40		21 10		21 40			22 40			23 40			00 41
Frant	d	19 22		19 46	19 57		20 14		20 44		21 14		21 44			22 44			23 44			00s45
Wadhurst	d	19 27		19 51	20 02		20 19		20 49		21 19		21 49			22 49			23 49			00s50
Stonegate	d	19 33		19 57	20 08		20 25		20 55		21 25		21 55			22 55			23 55			00s56
Etchingham	d	19 38		20 02	20 13		20 30		21 00		21 30		22 00			23 00			23 59			01s01
Robertsbridge	d	19 42		20 06	20 17		20 34		21 03		21 33		22 03			23 03			00 03			01s05
Battle	d	19 50		20 14	20 25		20 42		21 11		21 41		22 11			23 11			00 11			01s13
Crowhurst	d	19 53			20 29		20 46		21 15		21 45		22 15			23 15			00s15			01s17
West St Leonards	d	19 59		20 23	20 38		20 53		21 22		21 51		22 22			23 21			00 20			01s22
St Leonards Warrior Sq ■	d	20 02		20 26	20 42		20 57		21 26		21 54		22 25			23 24			00 24			01s26
Hastings ■	a	20 05		20 32	20 47		21 02		21 29		21 58		22 29			23 27			00 28			01 33
Ore	a	20 13																				

Saturdays
26 May to 8 December

		SE ◇■	SE ◇■	SE ◇■	SE ■	SE ■	SE ◇■	SE ■	SE ■	SE ◇■	SE ■	SE ◇■	SE ◇■	SE ◇■	SE ◇■	SE ◇■	SE ◇■	and at the same minutes past each hour until	SE ◇■	SE ◇■	SE ◇■	SE ◇■
London Charing Cross ■ ⊖	d									07 15		07 45		08 15	08 30	08 45	09 00		13 15	13 30	13 45	14 00
London Waterloo (East) ■ ⊖	d									07 18		07 48		08 18	08 33	08 48	09 03		13 18	13 33	13 48	14 03
London Cannon Street ■ ⊖	d																					
London Bridge ■ ⊖	d									07 24		07 54		08 24	08 39	08 54	09 09		13 24	13 39	13 54	14 09
Orpington ■	d			00 10						07 40		08 10		08 40	08 56	09 10	09 26		13 40	13 56	14 10	14 26
Chelsfield	d																					
Sevenoaks ■	d		00 06	00 20						07 49		08 19		08 50	09 06	09 20	09 36		13 50	14 06	14 20	14 36
Hildenborough	d		00 12							07 55		08 25			09 12		09 42			14 12		14 42
Tonbridge ■	a		00 16	00 28						07 59		08 29		08 58	09 16	09 28	09 46		13 58	14 16	14 28	14 46
	d		00 17	00 29	05 29	06 29	06 59	07 29	07 47	08 00	08 15	08 30	08 50	08 59	09 17	09 29	09 47		13 59	14 17	14 29	14 47
High Brooms	d		00 24	00 35	05 35	06 35	07 05	07 35	07 54	08 06	08 24	08 36	08 56	09 05	09 24	09 35	09 54		14 05	14 24	14 35	14 54
Tunbridge Wells ■	a		00 28	00 40	05 39	06 39	07 09	07 39	07 58	08 10	08 28	08 40	09 00	09 09	09 28	09 39	09 58		14 09	14 28	14 39	14 58
	d			00 41			07 10			08 10		08 40		09 10		09 40			14 10		14 40	
Frant	d			00s45			07 15			08 15				09 15					14 15			
Wadhurst	d			00s50			07 20			08 20		08 48		09 20		09 48			14 20		14 48	
Stonegate	d			00s56			07 26			08 26				09 26					14 26			
Etchingham	d			01s01			07 30			08 30				09 30					14 30			
Robertsbridge	d	00 03		01s05			07 34			08 34				09 34					14 34			
Battle	d	00 11		01s13			07 42			08 42		09 04		09 42		10 04			14 42		15 04	
Crowhurst	d	00s15		01s17			07 46			08 46				09 46					14 46			
West St Leonards	d	00 20		01s22			07 52			08 52				09 52					14 52			
St Leonards Warrior Sq ■	d	00 24		01s26			07 55			08 55		09 16		09 55		10 15			14 55		15 15	
Hastings ■	a	00 28		01 33			07 59			08 59		09 19		09 59		10 19			14 59		15 19	
Ore	a																					

		SE ◇■	SE ◇■	SE ◇■	SE ◇■	and at the same minutes past each hour until	SE ◇■	SE ◇■	SE ◇■	SE ◇■	SE ◇■	SE ◇■	SE ◇■	SE ◇■	SE ◇■	SE ◇■	SE ◇■	SE ◇■	SE ◇■	SE ◇■	SE ◇■
London Charing Cross ■ ⊖	d	14 15	14 30	14 45	15 00		17 15	17 30	17 45	18 00	18 15	18 30	18 45	19 00	19 15	19 30	19 45	20 00	20 15	20 30	20 45
London Waterloo (East) ■ ⊖	d	14 18	14 33	14 48	15 03		17 18	17 33	17 48	18 03	18 18	18 33	18 48	19 03	19 18	19 33	19 48	20 03	20 18	20 33	20 48
London Cannon Street ■ ⊖	d																				
London Bridge ■ ⊖	d	14 24	14 39	14 54	15 09		17 24	17 39	17 54	18 09	18 24	18 39	18 54	19 09	19 24	19 39	19 54	20 09	20 24	20 39	20 54
Orpington ■	d	14 40	14 56	15 10	15 26		17 40	17 56	18 10	18 26	18 40	18 56	19 10	19 26	19 40	19 56	20 10	20 26	20 40	20 56	21 10
Chelsfield	d																				
Sevenoaks ■	d	14 50	15 06	15 20	15 36		17 50	18 06	18 20	18 36	18 50	19 06	19 20	19 36	19 50	20 06	20 20	20 36	20 50	21 06	21 20
Hildenborough	d		15 12		15 42			18 12		18 42		19 12		19 42		20 12		20 42		21 12	
Tonbridge ■	a	14 58	15 16	15 28	15 46		17 58	18 16	18 28	18 46	18 58	19 16	19 28	19 46	19 58	20 16	20 28	20 46	20 58	21 16	21 28
	d	14 59	15 17	15 29	15 47		17 59	18 17	18 29	18 47	18 59	19 17	19 29	19 47	19 59	20 17	20 29	20 47	20 59	21 17	21 29
High Brooms	d	15 05	15 24	15 35	15 54		18 05	18 24	18 35	18 54	19 05	19 24	19 35	19 54	20 05	20 24	20 35	20 54	21 05	21 24	21 35
Tunbridge Wells ■	a	15 09	15 28	15 39	15 58		18 09	18 28	18 39	18 58	19 09	19 28	19 39	19 58	20 09	20 28	20 39	20 58	21 09	21 28	21 39
	d	15 10		15 40			18 10		18 40		19 10		19 40		20 10		20 40		21 10		21 40
Frant	d	15 15					18 15				19 15				20 15				21 15		21 45
Wadhurst	d	15 20		15 48			18 20		18 48		19 20		19 48		20 20		20 48		21 20		21 50
Stonegate	d	15 26					18 26				19 26				20 26				21 26		21 56
Etchingham	d	15 30					18 30				19 30				20 30				21 30		22 00
Robertsbridge	d	15 34					18 34				19 34				20 34				21 34		22 04
Battle	d	15 42		16 04			18 42		19 04		19 42		20 04		20 42		21 04		21 42		22 12
Crowhurst	d	15 46					18 46				19 46				20 46				21 46		22 16
West St Leonards	d	15 52					18 52				19 52				20 52				21 52		22 21
St Leonards Warrior Sq ■	d	15 55		16 16			18 55		19 16		19 55		20 15		20 55		21 15		21 55		22 25
Hastings ■	a	15 59		16 19			18 59		19 19		19 59		20 19		20 59		21 19		21 59		22 29
Ore	a																				

Table T206-F

Saturdays

26 May to 8 December

London and Tonbridge - Tunbridge Wells and Hastings

		SE ◇1	SE ◇1	SE ◇1	SE ◇1	SE ◇1	SE ◇1	SE ◇1	SE ◇1	SE ◇1
London Charing Cross ■ ⊖	d	21 00	21 30	21 45	22 00	22 30	22 45	23 00	23 30	23 45
London Waterloo (East) ■ ⊖	d	21 03	21 33	21 48	22 03	22 33	22 48	23 03	23 33	23 48
London Cannon Street ■ ⊖	d									
London Bridge ■ ⊖	d	21 09	21 39	21 54	22 09	22 39	22 54	23 09	23 39	23 54
Orpington ■	d	21 26	21 56	22 10	22 26	22 56	23 10	23 26	23 56	00 10
Chelsfield	d									
Sevenoaks ■	d	21 36	22 06	22 20	22 36	23 06	23 20	23 36	00 06	00 20
Hildenborough	d	21 42	22 12		22 42	23 12		23 42	00 12	
Tonbridge ■	a	21 46	22 16	22 28	22 46	23 16	23 28	23 46	00 16	00 28
	d	21 47	22 17	22 29	22 47	23 17	23 29	23 47	00 17	00 29
High Brooms	d	21 54	22 24	22 35	22 54	23 24	23 35	23 54	00 24	00 35
Tunbridge Wells ■	a	21 58	22 28	22 39	22 58	23 28	23 39	23 58	00 28	00 40
	d			22 40			23 40			00 41
Frant	d			22 45			23 45			00s46
Wadhurst	d			22 50			23 50			00s50
Stonegate	d			22 56			23 56			00s57
Etchingham	d			23 00			23 59			01s01
Robertsbridge	d			23 04			00 04			01s05
Battle	d			23 12			00 12			01s13
Crowhurst	d			23 16			00s16			01s17
West St Leonards	d			23 21			00 21			01s22
St Leonards Warrior Sq ■	d			23 25			00 25			01s25
Hastings ■	a			23 29			00 29			01 33
Ore	a									

Sundays

20 May to 2 December

		SE ◇1 A	SE ◇1 A	SE ◇1 A	SE ◇1	SN	SE ◇1	SN	SE ◇1	SE ◇1	and at the same minutes past each hour until	SE ◇1	SE ◇1	SE ◇1	SE ◇1	SE ◇1	SE ◇1
London Charing Cross ■ ⊖	d								08 25	08 55		19 25	19 55	20 25	21 25	22 25	23 25
London Waterloo (East) ■ ⊖	d								08 28	08 58		19 28	19 58	20 28	21 28	22 28	23 28
London Cannon Street ■ ⊖	d																
London Bridge ■ ⊖	d								08 34	09 04		19 34	20 04	20 34	21 34	22 34	23 34
Orpington ■	d			00 10					08 50	09 20		19 50	20 20	20 50	21 50	22 50	23 50
Chelsfield	d																
Sevenoaks ■	d		00 06	00 20					09 00	09 30		20 00	20 30	21 00	22 00	23 00	23 59
Hildenborough	d		00 12							09 36			20 36	21 06	22 06	23 06	00 06
Tonbridge ■	a		00 16	00 28					09 08	09 40		20 08	20 40	21 10	22 10	23 10	00 10
	d		00 17	00 29	07 41		08 41		09 11	09 41		20 11	20 41	21 11	22 11	23 11	00 11
High Brooms	d		00 24	00 35	07 46		08 46		09 16	09 46		20 16	20 46	21 16	22 16	23 17	00 16
Tunbridge Wells ■	a		00 28	00 40	07 50		08 50		09 20	09 50		20 20	20 50	21 20	22 20	23 20	00 20
	d			00 41	07 51		08 51		09 21	09 51		20 21	20 51	21 21	22 21	23 21	00 21
Frant	d			00s46	07 55		08 55			09 55			20 55	21 25	22 25	23 25	00s25
Wadhurst	d			00s50	08 00		09 00		09 29	10 00		20 29	21 00	21 30	22 30	23 30	00s30
Stonegate	d			00s57	08 06		09 06			10 06			21 06	21 36	22 36	23 36	00s36
Etchingham	d			01s01	08 11		09 11			10 11			21 11	21 41	22 41	23 41	00s41
Robertsbridge	d	00 04		01s05	08 15		09 15			10 15			21 15	21 45	22 45	23 45	00s44
Battle	d	00 12		01s13	08 23		09 23		09 45	10 23		20 45	21 23	21 53	22 53	23 53	00s52
Crowhurst	d	00s16		01s17	08 26		09 26			10 26			21 26	21 56	22 56	23s56	00s56
West St Leonards	d	00 21		01s22	08 32		09 32			10 32			21 32	22 02	23 02	00 02	01s02
St Leonards Warrior Sq ■	d	00 25		01s25	08 35	08 55	09 35	09 55	09 55	10 35		20 55	21 35	22 05	23 05	00 05	01s05
Hastings ■	a	00 29		01 33	08 39	08 58	09 39	09 58	09 59	10 39		20 59	21 39	22 09	23 09	00 09	01 09
Ore	a					09 02		10 02									

A not 20 May

Table T206-R

Mondays to Fridays

21 May to 7 December

Hastings and Tunbridge Wells - Tonbridge and London

Miles			SE MX ◇1	SE MX ◇1	SE ◇1	SE ◇1	SE ◇1	SE ◇1	SE ◇1	SE ◇1	SE ◇1	SE ◇1	SE ◇1	SE ◇1	SE ◇1	SE ◇1	SE ◇1	SE ◇1	SE ◇1	SE ◇1	SE ◇1	SE ◇1	SE ◇1
0	Ore	d												06 16			06 40						
1	**Hastings** ■	d					05 18		05 38	05 48		06 05		06 20	06 27		06 44		07 03		07 26		07 44
1¾	St Leonards Warrior Sq ■	d					05 21		05 41	05 51		06 08		06 24	06 30		06 47		07 06		07 29		07 47
2¾	West St Leonards	d					05 25		05 44			06 12			06 35		06 51		07 10		07 33		07 51
6	Crowhurst	d					05 31		05 50			06 18			06 41		06 57		07 16		07 39		07 57
8	Battle	d					05 35		05 54	06 02		06 22		06 35	06 45		07 01		07 20		07 43		08 01
14¼	Robertsbridge	d					05 42		06 01			06 29		06 42			07 08		07 27		07 50		08 08
16	Etchingham	d					05 46		06 05	06 11		06 33		06 46	06 54		07 12		07 31		07 54		08 12
19¾	Stonegate	d					05 51		06 10			06 38		06 51			07 18		07 37		07 59		08 17
24¼	Wadhurst	d					05 58		06 16	06 22		06 45		06 57	07 04		07 25		07 44		08 06		08 23
26¾	Frant	d					06 02		06 20			06 49		07 01			07 29		07 48		08 10		08 27
29	**Tunbridge Wells** ■	a					06 06		06 25	06 29		06 53		07 06	07 12		07 33		07 52		08 14		08 32
—		d	00 05	00 35	05 17	05 48	06 08	06 18	06 34		06 39	06 55	06 59	07 16		07 20	07 35	07 39	07 55	07 59	08 16	08 24	08 36
30½	High Brooms	d	00 08	00 38	05 20	05 51	06 11	06 22	06 37		06 43	06 59	07 03	07 20		07 24	07 39	07 43	07 59	08 04	08 20	08 28	08 39
34	**Tonbridge** ■	a	00 15	00 45	05 26	05 57	06 17	06 28	06 43		06 50		07 09			07 30		07 49		08 10	08 26	08 35	08 45
36½	Hildenborough	d			05 32	06 02	06 23	06 33			06 56		07 14			07 36		07 55		08 15		08 40	
41½	Sevenoaks ■	a			05 39	06 09	06 30	06 40	06 53		07 02		07 22			07 43		08 02		08 22		08 46	08 55
48¼	Chelsfield	d			05 47	06 17		06 49			07 11		07 31			07 52		08 11		08 32		08 55	
49¾	Orpington ■	a			05 50	06 20	06 39	06 52	07 02		07 14												09 04
61¼	**London Bridge** ■ ⊖	a			06 06	06 38	06 55	07 08	07 23		07 30	07 37	07 49	07 58		08 09	08 19	08 29	08 39	08 50	09 00	09 11	09 20
—	**London Cannon Street** ■ ⊖	a				06 46			07 31								08 27				09 09		
62¾	**London Waterloo (East)** ■ ⊖	a			06 12		07 01	07 14			07 36	07 44	07 55	08 04		08 15		08 35	08 45	08 56		09 17	09 26
63½	**London Charing Cross** ■ ⊖	a			06 19		07 08	07 21			07 44	07 51	08 02	08 11		08 22		08 42	08 52	09 03		09 26	09 33

		SE ◇1	SE ◇1	SE ◇1	SE ◇1	SE ◇1	SE ◇1	SE ◇1	SE ◇1	SE ◇1	SE ◇1	SE ◇1	SE ◇1	SE ◇1	and at the same minutes past each hour until	SE ◇1	SE ◇1	SE ◇1	SE ◇1	SE ◇1	SE ◇1	SE ◇1
Ore	d																					
Hastings ■	d	08 04		08 17		08 47		09 29		09 47		10 31		10 50			14 31		14 50		15 31	
St Leonards Warrior Sq ■	d	08 07		08 20		08 50		09 32		09 50		10 34		10 53			14 34		14 53		15 34	
West St Leonards	d			08 24		08 53				09 54				10 57					14 57			
Crowhurst	d			08 30		08 59				10 00				11 03					15 03			
Battle	d	08 18		08 34		09 03		09 42		10 04		10 44		11 07			14 44		15 07		15 44	
Robertsbridge	d			08 41		09 10				10 11				11 14					15 14			
Etchingham	d			08 45		09 13				10 15				11 18					15 18			
Stonegate	d			08 50		09 18				10 20				11 23					15 23			
Wadhurst	d			08 56		09 24		09 58		10 26		11 00		11 29			15 00		15 29		16 00	
Frant	d			09 00		09 28				10 30				11 33					15 33			
Tunbridge Wells ■	a	08 41		09 05		09 34		10 06		10 35		11 08		11 38			15 08		15 38		16 08	
	d	08 43	08 51	09 09	09 21	09 39	09 51	10 09	10 21	10 39	10 51	11 09	11 21	11 39		14 51	15 09	15 21	15 39	15 51	16 09	16 21
High Brooms	d	08 47	08 54	09 12	09 24	09 42	09 54	10 13	10 24	10 42	10 54	11 12	11 24	11 42		14 54	15 12	15 24	15 42	15 54	16 12	16 24
Tonbridge ■	a		09 00	09 18	09 30	09 48	10 00	10 19	10 30	10 48	11 00	11 18	11 30	11 48		15 00	15 18	15 30	15 48	16 00	16 18	16 30
Hildenborough	d		09 05		09 35		10 05		10 35		11 05		11 35			15 05		15 35		16 05		16 35
Sevenoaks ■	a		09 12	09 28	09 42	09 58	10 12	10 28	10 42	10 58	11 12	11 28	11 42	11 58		15 12	15 28	15 42	15 58	16 12	16 28	16 42
Chelsfield	d																			16 20		
Orpington ■	a		09 23	09 37	09 51	10 07	10 21	10 37	10 51	11 07	11 21	11 37	11 51	12 07		15 21	15 37	15 51	16 07	16 23	16 37	16 51
London Bridge ■ ⊖	a	09 23	09 39	09 53	10 07	10 23	10 37	10 53	11 07	11 23	11 37	11 53	12 07	12 23		15 37	15 53	16 07	16 23	16 39	16 53	17 09
London Cannon Street ■ ⊖	a	09 32																				
London Waterloo (East) ■ ⊖	a		09 45	09 59	10 13	10 29	10 43	10 59	11 13	11 29	11 43	11 59	12 13	12 29		15 43	15 59	16 13	16 29	16 45	16 59	17 15
London Charing Cross ■ ⊖	a		09 52	10 06	10 20	10 36	10 48	11 04	11 18	11 34	11 48	12 04	12 18	12 34		15 48	16 04	16 18	16 34	16 51	17 07	17 21

		SE ◇1	SE ◇1	SE ◇1	SE ◇1	SE ◇1	SE ◇1	SE ◇1	SE ◇1	SE ◇1	SE ◇1	SE ◇1	SE ◇1	SE ◇1	SE ◇1	SE 1	SE ◇1	SE ◇1	SE ◇1	SE ◇1	SE ◇1	SE ◇1	SE ◇1
Ore	d																						
Hastings ■	d	15 45		16 20		16 45		17 21		17 50		18 20		18 46		19 30		19 50			20 50		
St Leonards Warrior Sq ■	d	15 48		16 23		16 48		17 24		17 53		18 23		18 49		19 33		19 53			20 53		
West St Leonards	d	15 52		16 26		16 51		17 28		17 57		18 27		18 53		19 36		19 57			20 57		
Crowhurst	d	15 58		16 32		16 57		17 34		18 03		18 33		18 59				20 03			21 03		
Battle	d	16 02		16 36		17 01		17 38		18 07		18 37		19 03		19 44		20 07			21 07		
Robertsbridge	d	16 09		16 43		17 08		17 45		18 14		18 44		19 10				20 16			21 14		
Etchingham	d	16 13		16 47		17 12		17 48		18 18		18 47		19 13				20 20			21 18		
Stonegate	d	16 18		16 52		17 17		17 53		18 23		18 52		19 18				20 25			21 23		
Wadhurst	d	16 24		16 59		17 24		18 00		18 29		18 59		19 25		20 00		20 31			21 29		
Frant	d	16 28		17 03		17 28		18 04		18 33		19 03		19 29				20 35			21 33		
Tunbridge Wells ■	a	16 33		17 08		17 33		18 08		18 41		19 07		19 34		20 08		20 39			21 38		
	d	16 39	16 49	17 12	17 21	17 38	17 49	18 12	18 18	18 42	18 51	19 08	19 21	19 39	19 51	20 09	20 21	20 40	20 51	21 21	21 39	21 51	22 21
High Brooms	d	16 42	16 52	17 16	17 25	17 41	17 53	18 16	18 24	18 45	18 54	19 11	19 24	19 42	19 54	20 12	20 24	20 43	20 54	21 24	21 42	21 54	22 24
Tonbridge ■	a	16 48	16 58	17 23	17 33	17 48	17 59	18 22	18 30	18 51	19 01	19 17	19 30	19 49	20 00	20 19	20 30	20 49	21 00	21 30	21 48	22 00	22 30
Hildenborough	d		17 04				18 05		18 35		19 06		19 35		20 05		20 35		21 05	21 35		22 05	22 35
Sevenoaks ■	a	16 58	17 10	17 31	17 41	17 58	18 12	18 30	18 42	19 00	19 13	19 28	19 42	19 58	20 12		20 42	20 58	21 12	21 42	21 58	22 12	22 42
Chelsfield	d																						
Orpington ■	a	17 07	17 22	17 40		18 07	18 21	18 39	18 51	19 08	19 22	19 37	19 51	20 07	20 21		20 51	21 07	21 21	21 51	22 07	22 21	22 51
London Bridge ■ ⊖	a	17 30	17 38	17 59	18 06	18 24	18 40	18 55	19 08	19 24	19 38	19 53	20 07	20 23	20 37		21 07	21 23	21 37	22 07	22 23	22 37	23 07
London Cannon Street ■ ⊖	a	17 37					18 47																
London Waterloo (East) ■ ⊖	a		17 44	18 05	18 12	18 30		19 00	19 14	19 30	19 44	19 59	20 13	20 29	20 43		21 13	21 29	21 43	22 13	22 29	22 43	23 13
London Charing Cross ■ ⊖	a		17 50	18 12	18 20	18 37		19 05	19 19	19 35	19 49	20 04	20 18	20 34	20 48		21 18	21 34	21 48	22 18	22 34	22 48	23 18

Table T206-R

Mondays to Fridays
21 May to 7 December

Hastings and Tunbridge Wells - Tonbridge and London

		SE	SE WTh FO		SE MTO	SE
		◇1	◇1		◇1	1
Ore	d					
Hastings	d	21 50				22 50
St Leonards Warrior Sq	d	21 53				22 53
West St Leonards	d	21 57				22 57
Crowhurst	d	22 03				23 03
Battle	d	22 07				23 07
Robertsbridge	d	22 14				23 14
Etchingham	d	22 18				23 18
Stonegate	d	22 23				23 23
Wadhurst	d	22 29				23 29
Frant	d	22 33				23 33
Tunbridge Wells	a	22 38				23 37
	d	22 39	23 05		23 05	23 38
High Brooms	d	22 42	23 08		23 08	23 41
Tonbridge	a	22 48	23 14		23 14	23 49
Hildenborough	d		23 19		23 19	
Sevenoaks	a	22 58	23 26		23 26	
Chelsfield	d					
Orpington	a	23 07	23 35		23 35	
London Bridge ⊖	a	23 23	23 52		23 54	
London Cannon Street ⊖	a				00 03	
London Waterloo (East) ⊖	a	23 29	23 58			
London Charing Cross ⊖	a	23 34	00 03			

Saturdays
26 May to 8 December

		SE	SE	SE	SE	SE	SE	SE	SE	SE		SE	SE	SE	SE	SE	SE	SE	SE		SE	SE	SE	SE
		◇1	◇1	◇1	◇1	◇1	◇1	◇1	◇1	◇1		◇1	◇1	◇1	◇1	◇1	◇1	◇1	◇1		◇1	◇1	◇1	◇1
Ore	d																							
Hastings	d				05 48	06 19		06 50		07 19			07 50		08 19		08 50		09 31			15 50		16 31
St Leonards Warrior Sq	d				05 51	06 22		06 53		07 22			07 53		08 22		08 53		09 34			15 53		16 34
West St Leonards	d				05 55	06 26		06 57		07 26			07 57		08 26		08 57					15 57		
Crowhurst	d				06 01	06 33		07 03		07 33			08 03		08 33		09 03					16 03		
Battle	d				06 05	06 37		07 07		07 37			08 07		08 37		09 07		09 44			16 07		16 44
Robertsbridge	d				06 12	06 44		07 14		07 44			08 14		08 44		09 14			and at the same minutes past each hour until		16 14		
Etchingham	d				06 16	06 48		07 18		07 48			08 18		08 48		09 18					16 18		
Stonegate	d				06 21	06 53		07 23		07 53			08 23		08 53		09 23					16 23		
Wadhurst	d				06 27	06 59		07 29		07 59			08 29		08 59		09 29		10 00			16 29		17 00
Frant	d				06 31	07 03		07 33		08 03			08 33		09 03		09 33					16 33		
Tunbridge Wells	a				06 35	07 08		07 38		08 08			08 38		09 08		09 38		10 08			16 38		17 08
	d	00 05	00 35	05 51	06 37	07 09	07 21	07 39	07 51	08 09		08 21	08 39	08 51	09 09	09 21	09 39	09 51	10 09		16 21	16 39	16 51	17 09
High Brooms	d	00 08	00 38	05 54	06 40	07 12	07 24	07 42	07 54	08 12		08 24	08 42	08 54	09 12	09 24	09 42	09 54	10 12		16 24	16 42	16 54	17 12
Tonbridge	a	00 15	00 45	06 00	06 46	07 18	07 30	07 48	08 00	08 18		08 30	08 48	09 00	09 18	09 30	09 48	10 00	10 18		16 30	16 48	17 00	17 18
Hildenborough	d			06 05	06 51		07 35		08 05			08 35		09 05		09 35		10 05			16 35		17 05	
Sevenoaks	a			06 12	06 58	07 28	07 42	07 58	08 12	08 28		08 42	08 58	09 12	09 28	09 42	09 58	10 12	10 28		16 42	16 58	17 12	17 28
Chelsfield	d																							
Orpington	a			06 21	07 07	07 37	07 51	08 07	08 21	08 37		08 51	09 07	09 21	09 37	09 51	10 07	10 21	10 37		16 51	17 07	17 21	17 37
London Bridge ⊖	a			06 37	07 23	07 53	08 07	08 23	08 37	08 53		09 07	09 23	09 37	09 53	10 07	10 23	10 37	10 53		17 07	17 23	17 37	17 53
London Cannon Street ⊖	a																							
London Waterloo (East) ⊖	a			06 43	07 29	07 59	08 13	08 29	08 43	08 59		09 13	09 29	09 43	09 59	10 13	10 29	10 43	10 59		17 13	17 29	17 43	17 59
London Charing Cross ⊖	a			06 48	07 34	08 04	08 18	08 34	08 48	09 04		09 18	09 34	09 48	10 04	10 18	10 34	10 48	11 04		17 18	17 34	17 48	18 04

			SE	SE	SE	SE	SE	SE	SE	SE	SE		SE	SE	SE	SE	SE	SE	SE	SE	SE		SE	SE	SE
			◇1	◇1	◇1	◇1	◇1	◇1	◇1	◇1	◇1		◇1	◇1	◇1	◇1	◇1	◇1	◇1	◇1	◇1		◇1	◇1	◇1
Ore	d																								
Hastings	d			16 50		17 19		17 50		18 19			18 50			19 50			20 50				21 50		22 50
St Leonards Warrior Sq	d			16 53		17 22		17 53		18 22			18 53			19 53			20 53				21 53		22 53
West St Leonards	d			16 57		17 26		17 57		18 26			18 57			19 57			20 57				21 57		22 57
Crowhurst	d			17 03		17 33		18 03		18 33			19 03			20 03			21 03				22 03		23 03
Battle	d			17 07		17 37		18 07		18 37			19 07			20 07			21 07				22 07		23 07
Robertsbridge	d			17 14		17 44		18 14		18 44			19 14			20 14			21 14				22 14		23 14
Etchingham	d			17 18		17 48		18 18		18 48			19 18			20 18			21 18				22 18		23 18
Stonegate	d			17 23		17 53		18 23		18 53			19 23			20 23			21 23				22 23		23 23
Wadhurst	d			17 29		17 59		18 29		18 59			19 29			20 29			21 29				22 29		23 29
Frant	d			17 33		18 03		18 33		19 03			19 33			20 33			21 33				22 33		23 33
Tunbridge Wells	a			17 38		18 08		18 38		19 08			19 38			20 38			21 38				22 38		23 38
	d		17 21	17 39	17 51	18 09	18 21	18 39	18 51	19 09	19 21		19 39	19 51	20 21	20 39	20 51	21 21	21 39	21 51	22 21		22 39	23 05	23 39
High Brooms	d		17 24	17 42	17 54	18 12	18 24	18 42	18 54	19 12	19 24		19 42	19 54	20 24	20 42	20 54	21 24	21 42	21 54	22 24		22 42	23 08	23 42
Tonbridge	a		17 30	17 48	18 00	18 18	18 30	18 48	19 00	19 18	19 30		19 48	20 00	20 30	20 48	21 00	21 30	21 48	22 00	22 30		22 48	23 14	23 49
Hildenborough	d		17 35		18 05		18 35		19 05		19 35			20 05	20 35		21 05	21 35		22 05	22 35			23 19	
Sevenoaks	a		17 42	17 58	18 12	18 28	18 42	18 58	19 12	19 28	19 42		19 58	20 12	20 42	20 58	21 12	21 42	21 58	22 12	22 42		22 58	23 26	
Chelsfield	d																								
Orpington	a		17 51	18 07	18 21	18 37	18 51	19 07	19 21	19 37	19 51		20 07	20 21	20 51	21 07	21 21	21 51	22 07	22 22	22 51		23 07	23 35	
London Bridge ⊖	a		18 07	18 23	18 37	18 53	19 07	19 23	19 37	19 53	20 07		20 23	20 37	21 07	21 23	21 37	22 07	22 23	22 38	23 07		23 23	23 52	
London Cannon Street ⊖	a																								
London Waterloo (East) ⊖	a		18 13	18 29	18 43	18 59	19 13	19 29	19 43	19 59	20 13		20 29	20 43	21 13	21 29	21 43	22 13	22 29	22 44	23 13		23 29	23 58	
London Charing Cross ⊖	a		18 18	18 34	18 48	19 04	19 18	19 34	19 48	20 04	20 18		20 34	20 48	21 18	21 34	21 48	22 18	22 34	22 48	23 18		23 34	00 03	

Table T206-R

Sundays
20 May to 2 December

Hastings and Tunbridge Wells - Tonbridge and London

		SE	SE	SE	SE		SE	SE		SE	SE	SE	SE		SE	SE	SE	SE		SE
		◇1	◇1	◇1	◇1		◇1	◇1		◇1	◇1	◇1	◇1		◇1	◇1	◇1	◇1		◇1
Ore	d																			
Hastings	d			07 31	07 50		11 31	11 50		12 31	12 50	13 31	13 50		18 31	18 50	19 50	20 50		22 50
St Leonards Warrior Sq	d			07 34	07 53		11 34	11 53		12 34	12 53	13 34	13 53		18 34	18 53	19 53	20 53		22 53
West St Leonards	d				07 57			11 57			12 57		13 57			18 57	19 57	20 57		22 57
Crowhurst	d				08 03			12 03			13 03		14 03			19 03	20 03	21 03		23 03
Battle	d			07 44	08 07		11 44	12 07		12 44	13 07	13 44	14 07		18 44	19 07	20 07	21 07		23 07
Robertsbridge	d				08 14	and at the same minutes past each hour until		12 14			13 14		14 14	and at the same minutes past each hour until		19 14	20 14	21 14		23 14
Etchingham	d				08 18			12 18			13 18		14 18			19 18	20 18	21 18		23 18
Stonegate	d				08 23			12 23			13 23		14 23			19 23	20 23	21 23		23 23
Wadhurst	d			08 00	08 29		12 00	12 29		13 00	13 29	14 00	14 29		19 00	19 29	20 29	21 29		23 29
Frant	d				08 33			12 33			13 33		14 33			19 33	20 33	21 33		23 33
Tunbridge Wells	a			08 08	08 38		12 08	12 38		13 08	13 38	14 08	14 38		19 08	19 38	20 38	21 38		23 38
	d	00 05	00 35	08 09	08 39		12 09	12 39		13 09	13 39	14 09	14 39		19 09	19 39	20 39	21 39		23 38
High Brooms	d	00 08	00 38	08 12	08 42		12 12	12 42		13 12	13 42	14 12	14 42		19 12	19 42	20 42	21 42		23 42
Tonbridge	a	00 15	00 45	08 19	08 49		12 19	12 49		13 19	13 49	14 19	14 49		19 19	19 49	20 49	21 49		23 49
Hildenborough	d				08 53			12 53			13 54		14 53			19 53	20 53	21 53		
Sevenoaks	a			08 30	09 00		12 30	13 00		13 30	14 00	14 30	15 00		19 30	20 00	21 00	22 00		
Chelsfield	d																			
Orpington	a			08 39	09 09		12 39	13 09		13 39	14 09	14 39	15 09		19 39	20 09	21 09	22 09		
London Bridge ⊖	a			08 55	09 25		12 55	13 25		13 55	14 25	14 55	15 25		19 55	20 25	21 25	22 25		
London Cannon Street ⊖	a																			
London Waterloo (East) ⊖	a			09 01	09 31		13 01	13 31		14 01	14 31	15 01	15 31		20 01	20 31	21 31	22 31		
London Charing Cross ⊖	a			09 05	09 35		13 05	13 35		14 05	14 35	15 05	15 35		20 05	20 35	21 35	22 35		

Table T207-F

Mondays to Fridays

21 May to 7 December

London and Tonbridge - Ashford International, Folkestone, Dover, Canterbury West, Ramsgate and Margate

Miles	Miles	Miles	Miles		SE MX ◇■	SE MO ◇■	SE MO ◇■	SE MO ◇	SE WThFO ◇■	SE MX ◇	SE MO ◇	SE WO ◇	SE ThFO ◇	SE MX ◇	SE MO ◇■	SE MX ◇	SE MX ◇■	SE WThFO ◇■ A	SE MO ◇■	SE ■	SE	SE ■
—	—	—	0	St Pancras Intl. ⊖ d												00 12						
—	—	—	6	Stratford International ⊖ d												00 19						
—	—	—	22¼	Ebbsfleet International d												00 30						
0	—	—	—	London Charing Cross ⊖ d																		
0¾	—	—	—	London Waterloo (East) ⊖ d																		
—	—	—	—	London Cannon Street ⊖ d																		
1¾	—	—	—	London Bridge ⊖ d																		
13¾	—	—	—	Orpington d															00 06			
22	—	—	—	Sevenoaks d													00 13	00 13	00 16			
27	—	—	—	Hildenborough d																		
29½	—	—	—	Tonbridge a													00 21	00 21	00 24			
—	—	—	—	d													00 22	00 22	00 26			05 22
34¾	—	—	—	Paddock Wood d											00 03		00 29	00 29	00 33		05 28	05 29
—	—	—	—	Maidstone West 208 a																	05 49	
39½	—	—	—	Marden d											00 08		00 34	00 34	00 38			05 34
41¾	—	—	—	Staplehurst d											00 12		00 38	00 38	00 42			05 38
45¼	—	—	—	Headcorn d											00 18		00 44	00 44	00 48			05 44
50½	—	—	—	Pluckley d													00s50	00s50	00s54			05 50
56	0	—	56	Ashford International a											00 30	00 50	01 00	01 00	01 04			06 00
—	—	—	—	d	00 04	00 05								00 15			01 05	01 07		05 25		06 05
—	4¼	—	—	Wye d														01s13				06 11
—	9	—	—	Chilham d														01s19				06 17
—	11	—	—	Chartham d														01s23				06 21
—	14¼	—	—	Canterbury West d							00 09	00 09	00 09					01a30				06 27
—	16½	—	—	Sturry d																		06 31
64¼	—	—	—	Westenhanger d	00 12	00 13											01s13			05 33		
65¾	—	—	—	Sandling d	00 15	00 16											01s16			05 36		
69¼	—	—	—	Folkestone West d	00 21	00 21								00 28			01s22			05 42		
70	—	—	—	Folkestone Central d	00 24	00 24								00 30			01s24			05 45		
77¼	—	—	—	Dover Priory a	00 35	00 35								00 41			01 38			05 56		
—	—	—	—	d										00 42						06 05		
82¼	—	—	—	Martin Mill d										00s51						06 14		
85	—	—	—	Walmer d										00s55						06 18		
86½	—	—	—	Deal d						00 01				00s59						06 22		
90¼	—	—	—	Sandwich d				00 06		00 08				01s06						06 29		
—	25½	4¾	—	Minster d			00 09		00 12													06 43
99	29½	—	—	Ramsgate a			00 15	00 18	00 18	00 21	00 27	00 30	00 31	01 23						06 43		06 51
101¼	31¾	—	—	Broadstairs a							00s33		00s36									
104½	35	—	—	Margate a							00 39		00 42									

	SE	SE ■	SE	SE ◇■	SE	SE	SE ◇	SE ◇	SE ◇	SE ◇■	SE	SE ◇	SE ◇■	SE ◇	SE ◇	SE ◇■	SE ◇■	SE	SE ◇	SE ◇■	SE ◇■	SE ◇
St Pancras Intl. ⊖ d							06 25	06 40	07 04			07 22		07 25	07 37				08 12			08 25
Stratford International ⊖ d							06 32	06 47	07 11			07 29		07 32	07 44				08 19			08 32
Ebbsfleet International d							06 43	06 59	07 22			07 40		07 46	07 55				08 30			08 43
London Charing Cross ⊖ d				05 30												07 09				07 37		
London Waterloo (East) ⊖ d				05 33												07 12				07 40		
London Cannon Street ⊖ d										06 32												
London Bridge ⊖ d				05 39						06 36						07 18				07 46		
Orpington d				05 55																		
Sevenoaks d				06 06						07 06						07 42				08 13		
Hildenborough d				06 12						07 12												
Tonbridge a				06 16						07 16						07 50				08 21		
d				06 22						07 17						07 51				08 22		
Paddock Wood d	06 18			06 29		06 49				07 24	07 41					07 57		08 11		08 29		
Maidstone West 208 a	06 39					07 10	07 16				08 02							08 32				
Marden d				06 34						07 29						08 03				08 34		
Staplehurst d				06 38						07 33						08 07				08 38		
Headcorn d				06 44						07 39						08 13				08 44		
Pluckley d				06 50						07 45						08 19				08 50		
Ashford International a				06 59				07 19	07 41	07 54				08 05	08 15	08 28			08 50	09 00		
d		06 28	06 30	07 00	07 05				07 42	07 58			08 05	08 09	08 16	08 33	08 38		08 52	09 05	09 08	
Wye d			06 36		07 11					08 04			08 12			08 39					09 14	
Chilham d			06 42		07 17								08 18			08 45					09 20	
Chartham d			06 46		07 21								08 21			08 49					09 24	
Canterbury West d			06 52		07a27				07 59	08 17			08a29			08 55			09 09		09a30	
Sturry d			06 56						08 04	08 21						08 59						
Westenhanger d		06 36		07 08										08 17			08 46			09 13		
Sandling d		06 39		07 11										08 20			08 49			09 16		
Folkestone West d		06 45		07 17										08 25	08 29		08 55			09 21		
Folkestone Central d		06 48		07 20										08 28	08 31		08 58			09 24		
Dover Priory a		06 58		07 33										08 39	08 42		09 10			09 38		
d		07 10		07 36											08 44							
Martin Mill d		07 19		07 45											08 53							
Walmer d		07 23		07 50											08 57							
Deal d		07 27		07 55											09 01							
Sandwich d		07 34		08 04											09 08							
Minster d			07 08						08 18	08 33						09 11						
Ramsgate a		07 46	07 13	08 20					08 24	08 41					09 19	09 18			09 27			
Broadstairs a			07 19						08 30						09 25				09 36			
Margate a			07 26						08 36			08 58			09 29				09 42			09 59

A ■ ◇ to Ashford International

Table T207-F

Mondays to Fridays

21 May to 7 December

London and Tonbridge - Ashford International, Folkestone, Dover, Canterbury West, Ramsgate and Margate

	SE ◇	SE ◇■	SE ◇■	SE	SE ◇	SE ◇■	SE ◇■	SE ◇	SE ◇	SE ◇■	SE	SE ◇■	SE ◇	SE ◇■	SE ◇■	SE ◇	SE ◇	SE ◇■	SE	SE ◇	SE ◇■	SE ◇■
St Pancras Intl. ⊖ d	08 37				09 09			09 25	09 37				10 08			10 27	10 37			11 12		
Stratford International ⊖ d	08 44				09 16			09 32	09 44				10 15			10 34	10 44			11 19		
Ebbsfleet International d	08 55				09 27			09 44	09 55				10 26			10 45	10 55			11 30		
London Charing Cross ⊖ d		07 57	08 16				08 34			09 02		09 22		09 40				10 10			10 40	
London Waterloo (East) ⊖ d		08 01	08 19				08 37			09 05		09 25		09 43				10 13			10 43	
London Cannon Street ⊖ d																						
London Bridge ⊖ d		08 07	08 25				08 43			09 11		09 31		09 49				10 19			10 49	
Orpington d										09 31		09 50										
Sevenoaks d			08 49				09 13			09 41		10 02		10 13				10 43			11 13	
Hildenborough d																						
Tonbridge a		08 36	08 57				09 21			09 50		10 10		10 21				10 51			11 21	
d		08 38	08 58	09 05			09 22			09 52	10 04	10 11		10 22				10 52	11 04		11 22	
Paddock Wood d		08 45	09 05	09 12			09 29			09 59	10 11			10 29				10 59	11 11		11 29	
Maidstone West 208 a				09 32							10 31								11 31			
Marden d		08 51	09 11				09 34			10 04				10 34				11 04			11 34	
Staplehurst d		08 55	09 15				09 38			10 08				10 38				11 08			11 38	
Headcorn d		09 01	09 21				09 44			10 14				10 44				11 14			11 44	
Pluckley d		09 07					09 50			10 20				10 50				11 20			11 50	
Ashford International a	09 14	09 19	09 33		09 47		10 00		10 14	10 30		10 41	10 46	11 00			11 14	11 30		11 50	12 00	
d	09 15		09 35		09 52	10 05	10 05		10 15	10 35			10 52	11 02	11 05		11 15	11 35		11 52	12 02	12 05
Wye d			09 41			10 11				10 41					11 11			11 41				12 11
Chilham d						10 17									11 17							12 17
Chartham d						10 21									11 21							12 21
Canterbury West d			09 54		10 09	10a27				10 54			11 09		11a27			11 54		12 09		12a27
Sturry d			09 59							10 59								11 58				
Westenhanger d							10 13							11 10							12 10	
Sandling d							10 16							11 13							12 13	
Folkestone West d	09 28						10 22		10 28					11 19			11 28				12 19	
Folkestone Central d	09 30						10 25		10 30					11 22			11 30				12 22	
Dover Priory a	09 41						10 38		10 41					11 33			11 41				12 33	
d	09 43								10 42								11 42					
Martin Mill d	09 52								10 51								11 51					
Walmer d	09 56								10 55								11 55					
Deal d	10 00								11 00								12 00					
Sandwich d	10 07								11 06								12 06					
Minster d			10 10							11 10								12 10				
Ramsgate a	10 19		10 18		10 27				11 19	11 19			11 27				12 19	12 16		12 27		
Broadstairs a	10 25				10 33				11 25				11 33				12 25			12 33		
Margate a	10 29				10 39			10 59	11 29				11 39			11 59	12 29			12 39		

	SE ◇	SE ◇	SE ◇■	SE	SE ◇	SE ◇■	SE ◇■	SE ◇	SE ◇	SE ◇■	SE	SE ◇	SE ◇■	SE ◇■	SE ◇	SE ◇	SE ◇■	SE ◇■	SE	SE ◇	SE ◇■
St Pancras Intl. ⊖ d	11 25	11 37			12 12			12 27	12 37			13 12			13 25	13 37				14 09	
Stratford International ⊖ d	11 32	11 44			12 19			12 34	12 44			13 19			13 32	13 44				14 16	
Ebbsfleet International d	11 43	11 55			12 30			12 45	12 55			13 30			13 43	13 55				14 27	
London Charing Cross ⊖ d			11 10			11 40				12 10			12 40				13 10				13 40
London Waterloo (East) ⊖ d			11 13			11 43				12 13			12 43				13 13				13 43
London Cannon Street ⊖ d																					
London Bridge ⊖ d			11 19			11 49				12 19			12 49				13 19				13 49
Orpington d																					
Sevenoaks d			11 43			12 13				12 43			13 13				13 43				14 13
Hildenborough d																					
Tonbridge a			11 51			12 21				12 51			13 21				13 51				14 21
d			11 52	12 04		12 22				12 52	13 04		13 22				13 52		14 04		14 22
Paddock Wood d			11 59	12 11		12 29				12 59	13 11		13 29				13 59		14 11		14 29
Maidstone West 208 a				12 31							13 31								14 31		
Marden d			12 04			12 34				13 04			13 34				14 04				14 34
Staplehurst d			12 08			12 38				13 08			13 38				14 08				14 38
Headcorn d			12 14			12 44				13 14			13 44				14 14				14 44
Pluckley d			12 20			12 50				13 20			13 50				14 20				14 50
Ashford International a		12 14	12 30		12 50	13 00			13 14	13 30		13 50	14 00			14 14	14 29			14 47	15 00
d		12 15	12 35		12 52	13 02	13 05		13 15	13 35		13 52	14 02	14 05		14 15	14 35	14 38		14 52	15 02
Wye d			12 41				13 11			13 41				14 11			14 41				
Chilham d							13 17							14 17							
Chartham d							13 21							14 21							
Canterbury West d			12 54		13 09		13a27			13 54		14 09		14a27			14 54			15 09	
Sturry d			12 59							13 58							14 58				
Westenhanger d						13 10							14 10					14 46			15 10
Sandling d						13 13							14 13					14 49			15 13
Folkestone West d		12 28				13 19			13 28				14 19			14 28		14 55			15 19
Folkestone Central d		12 30				13 22			13 30				14 22			14 30		14 58			15 22
Dover Priory a		12 41				13 33			13 41				14 33			14 41		15 09			15 33
d		12 42							13 42							14 42		15 25			
Martin Mill d		12 51							13 51							14 51		15 34			
Walmer d		12 55							13 55							14 55		15 38			
Deal d		13 00							14 00							15 00		15 42			
Sandwich d		13 06							14 06							15 06		15 50			
Minster d			13 10							14 10							15 10	16 02			
Ramsgate a		13 19	13 16		13 27				14 19	14 16		14 27				15 19	15 16	16 11		15 27	
Broadstairs a		13 25			13 33				14 25			14 33				15 25				15 33	
Margate a	12 59	13 29			13 39			13 59	14 29			14 39			14 59	15 29				15 39	

Table T207-F

Mondays to Fridays
21 May to 7 December

London and Tonbridge - Ashford International, Folkestone, Dover, Canterbury West, Ramsgate and Margate

		SE ◇■	SE ◇	SE ◇	SE ◇■		SE	SE ◇	SE ◇■	SE ◇■	SE ◇	SE ◇	SE ◇■		SE	SE ◇	SE ◇■	SE ◇■	SE ◇	SE ◇	SE ◇■		SE
St Pancras Intl. ⊖	d		14 25	14 37				15 12			15 25	15 37				16 12			16 37	16 50			
Stratford International ⊖	d		14 32	14 44				15 19			15 32	15 44				16 19			16 44	16 57			
Ebbsfleet International	d		14 43	14 55				15 30			15 43	15 55				16 30			16 55				
London Charing Cross ⊖	d				14 10				14 40				15 10				15 40				16 10		
London Waterloo (East) ⊖	d				14 13				14 43				15 13				15 43				16 13		
London Cannon Street ⊖	d																						
London Bridge ⊖	d				14 19				14 49				15 19				15 49				16 19		
Orpington	d																						
Sevenoaks	d				14 43				15 13				15 43				16 13				16 43		
Hildenborough	d																						
Tonbridge	a				14 51				15 21				15 51				16 22				16 51		
	d				14 52		15 04		15 22				15 52		16 04		16 23				16 52		
Paddock Wood	d				14 59		15 11		15 29				15 59		16 11		16 30				16 59		17 04
Maidstone West 208	a						15 31								16 31								17 25
Marden	d				15 04				15 34				16 04				16 36				17 04		
Staplehurst	d				15 08				15 38				16 08				16 40				17 08		
Headcorn	d				15 14				15 44				16 14				16 46				17 14		
Pluckley	d				15 20				15 50				16 20				16 52				17 20		
Ashford International	a			15 14	15 30			15 50	16 00			16 14	16 30			16 50	17 01		17 14	17 24	17 30		
	d	15 05		15 15	15 35	15 38		15 52	16 02	16 05		16 15	16 35	16 38		16 52	17 03	17 05	17 18	17 26	17 35	17 38	
Wye	d	15 11			15 41					16 11			16 41					17 11			17 41		
Chilham	d	15 17								16 17			16 47					17 17			17 47		
Chartham	d	15 21								16 21			16 51					17 21			17 51		
Canterbury West	d	15a27			15 54			16 09		16a27			16 57			17 09		17a27		17 42	17 57		
Sturry	d				15 58								17 01								18 01		
Westenhanger	d					15 46			16 10					16 46			17 11					17 46	
Sandling	d					15 49			16 13					16 49			17 14					17 49	
Folkestone West	d			15 28		15 55			16 19			16 28		16 55			17 20		17 30			17 55	
Folkestone Central	d			15 30		15 58			16 22			16 30		16 58			17 23		17 33			17 58	
Dover Priory	a			15 41		16 09			16 33			16 41		17 09			17 34		17 44			18 09	
	d			15 42		16 10						16 42		17 11					17 45			18 12	
Martin Mill	d			15 51		16 19						16 51		17 20					17 54			18 21	
Walmer	d			15 55		16 23						16 55		17 24					17 58			18 25	
Deal	d			16 00		16 28						17 00		17 28					18 02			18 30	
Sandwich	d			16 06		16 36						17 06		17 35					18 09			18 37	
Minster	d				16 10	16 48							17 16								18 13		
Ramsgate	a			16 19	16 16	16 54		16 27				17 18	17 24	17 49		17 31			18 23	18 01	18 21	18 53	
Broadstairs	a			16 25				16 33				17 25				17 37			18 32	18 07			
Margate	a		16 01	16 29				16 39			17 01	17 29				17 42			18 37	18 15			

		SE ◇	SE ◇■	SE ◇	SE ◇	SE ◇■		SE	SE ◇	SE ◇	SE ◇■	SE	SE ◇■	SE ◇	SE ◇	SE ◇■	SE ◇	SE ◇	SE ◇■	SE ◇■	SE ◇	SE ◇
St Pancras Intl. ⊖	d	17 07		17 16	17 20				17 25	17 37				17 46	17 50		17 55	18 07			18 16	18 20
Stratford International ⊖	d	17 14		17 23	17 27				17 32	17 44				17 53	17 57		18 02	18 14			18 23	18 27
Ebbsfleet International	d	17 26		17 35					17 43	17 56				18 05			18 13	18 26			18 35	
London Charing Cross ⊖	d					16 39					16 51					17 11						
London Waterloo (East) ⊖	d					16 42					16 54					17 14						
London Cannon Street ⊖	d		16 30										17 09						17 23	17 30		
London Bridge ⊖	d		16 35			16 48					17 00		17 14			17 20			17 28	17 35		
Orpington	d										17 18											
Sevenoaks	d					17 12					17 28					17 46			17 54			
Hildenborough	d																		18 01			
Tonbridge	a					17 20					17 36					17 54			18 05			
	d					17 21					17 37					17 55			18 06			
Paddock Wood	d					17 28		17 34			17 44	17 52				18 03			18 13			
Maidstone West 208	a			18 08				17 55				18 15		18 38							19 09	
Marden	d					17 34					17 50					18 09			18 19			
Staplehurst	d					17 38					17 54					18 13			18 23			
Headcorn	d					17 44					18 00					18 19			18 29			
Pluckley	d					17 50					18 06								18 35			
Ashford International	a	17 45			17 54	17 59				18 15	18 15				18 24	18 31		18 45	18 45			18 54
	d	17 47			17 56	18 03	18 05			18 17	18 20				18 26	18 33		18 47	18 51			18 56
Wye	d					18 09										18 39						
Chilham	d					18 15										18 46						
Chartham	d					18 19										18 50						
Canterbury West	d				18 12	18 25									18 42	18 56						19 12
Sturry	d					18 29										19 01						
Westenhanger	d						18 13				18 29								19 00			
Sandling	d						18 16				18 32								19 03			
Folkestone West	d	18 00					18 22			18 30	18 38							19 00	19 09			
Folkestone Central	d	18 03					18 25			18 35	18a43							19 03	19 12			
Dover Priory	a	18 15	18 43				18 39			18 45								19 15	19 23	19 42		
	d									18 46									19 25			
Martin Mill	d									18 55									19 34			
Walmer	d									19 00									19 39			
Deal	d									19 04									19 44			
Sandwich	d									19 11									19 52			
Minster	d					18 41										19 12						
Ramsgate	a				18 31	18 49				19 25					19 01	19 21			20 08			19 31
Broadstairs	a				18 37										19 07							19 37
Margate	a				18 45				18 57				18 56		19 15		19 35					19 45

Table T207-F

Mondays to Fridays
21 May to 7 December

London and Tonbridge - Ashford International, Folkestone, Dover, Canterbury West, Ramsgate and Margate

		SE ◇■	SE ◇■	SE	SE ◇■	SE ◇	SE ◇	SE ◇■	SE ◇	SE ◇■	SE ◇■	SE ◇■	SE	SE ◇	SE ◇■	SE ◇■	SE ◇	SE ◇■	SE	SE ◇	SE ◇	SE ◇■	
St Pancras Intl. ⊖	d					18 25	18 37		18 50					19 07			19 20			19 25	19 37		
Stratford International ⊖	d					18 32	18 45		18 57					19 14			19 27			19 32	19 44		
Ebbsfleet International	d					18 43	18 56							19 26						19 43	19 55		
London Charing Cross ⊖	d	17 39						18 01				18 19						18 41				19 10	
London Waterloo (East) ⊖	d	17 42						18 04				18 22						18 44				19 13	
London Cannon Street ⊖	d		17 45		17 52					18 07	18 11				18 31	18 45							
London Bridge ⊖	d	17 48	17 50		17 57			18 10		18 12	18 16	18 28			18 36	18 50		18 50				19 19	
Orpington	d																						
Sevenoaks	d	18 12	18 16					18 34		18 38		18 53			19 00			19 18				19 42	
Hildenborough	d									18 44													
Tonbridge	a	18 20	18 24					18 42		18 48		19 01			19 08			19 26				19 51	
	d	18 21	18 25					18 44		18 49		19 02			19 10			19 27				19 53	
Paddock Wood	d	18 28	18 32	18 43				18 51		18 56		19 10	19 13		19 17			19 34	19 42			19 59	
Maidstone West 208	a			19 04									19 34						20 03				
Marden	d		18 38					18 57		19 02		19 16			19 23			19 40				20 05	
Staplehurst	d	18 36	18 42					19 01		19 06		19 20			19 27			19 44				20 09	
Headcorn	d	18 42	18 48					19 07		19 12		19 26			19 33			19 50				20 15	
Pluckley	d	18 48	18 54							19 18		19 32			19 39			19 56				20 21	
Ashford International	a	18 58	19 04				19 15	19 20	19 25	19 30		19 45		19 45	19 50		19 54	20 05			20 14	20 31	
	d	19 02	19 06				19 17	19 22	19 27	19 32				19 47	19 52		19 56	20 07			20 15	20 35	20 38
Wye	d	19 08								19 38								20 13				20 41	
Chilham	d	19 15								19 45								20 20				20 47	
Chartham	d	19 19								19 49								20 24				20 51	
Canterbury West	d	19 25							19 43	19 55							20 12	20 30				20 57	
Sturry	d	19 30								20 00								20 35				21 01	
Westenhanger	d		19 15					19 31							20 01								20 46
Sandling	d		19 18					19 34							20 04								20 49
Folkestone West	d		19 23				19 31	19 40						20 00	20 09						20 28		20 55
Folkestone Central	d		19a28				19 34	19 43						20 03	20 12						20 30		20 58
Dover Priory	a						19 45	19 53			20 14			20 14	20 27						20 41		21 09
	d						19 46	19 55													20 42		21 10
Martin Mill	d						19 55	20 05													20 51		21 19
Walmer	d						20 00	20 10													20 55		21 23
Deal	d						20 04	20 15													21 00		21 27
Sandwich	d						20a13	20 23													21 06		21 34
Minster	d	19 42								20 11								20 46				21 15	
Ramsgate	a	19 52						20 38	20 02	20 21							20 31	20 57			21 18	21 23	21 50
Broadstairs	a								20 08								20 37				21 25		
Margate	a				19 30	20 02			20 16							20 32	20 45			21 03	21 29		

		SE ◇	SE ◇■	SE ◇■	SE ◇	SE	SE ◇	SE ◇■	SE ◇	SE ◇■	SE ◇	SE	SE ◇	SE ◇■	SE TX ◇	SE TO ◇	SE ◇■	SE TX ◇	SE TO ◇	SE	SE ◇	SE MX ◇■	SE MO ◇■
St Pancras Intl. ⊖	d	20 12			20 25		20 37		21 12		21 25		21 37		22 12	22 12		22 25	22 25		22 37		
Stratford International ⊖	d	20 19			20 32		20 44		21 19		21 32		21 44		22 19	22 19		22 32	22 32		22 44		
Ebbsfleet International	d	20 30			20 43		20 55		21 30		21 43		21 55		22 30	22 30		22 43	22 43		22 55		
London Charing Cross ⊖	d			19 40				20 10		20 40				21 10			21 40					22 10	22 10
London Waterloo (East) ⊖	d			19 43				20 13		20 43				21 13			21 43					22 13	22 13
London Cannon Street ⊖	d																						
London Bridge ⊖	d			19 49				20 19		20 49				21 19			21 49					22 19	22 19
Orpington	d													21 35								22 35	22 35
Sevenoaks	d			20 13				20 43		21 13				21 45			22 13					22 45	22 45
Hildenborough	d																						
Tonbridge	a			20 21				20 51		21 21				21 53			22 21					22 53	22 53
	d			20 22		20 34		20 52		21 22		21 34		21 54			22 22			22 34		22 54	22 54
Paddock Wood	d			20 29		20 41		20 59		21 29		21 41		22 01			22 29			22 41		23 01	23 01
Maidstone West 208	a					21 01						22 01								23 01			
Marden	d			20 34				21 04		21 34				22 06			22 34					23 06	23 06
Staplehurst	d			20 38				21 08		21 38				22 10			22 38					23 10	23 10
Headcorn	d			20 44				21 14		21 44				22 16			22 44					23 16	23 16
Pluckley	d			20 50				21 20		21 50				22 22			22 50					23 22	23 22
Ashford International	a	20 50		20 59			21 14	21 30	21 50	22 00			22 14	22 32	22 50	22 50	23 00				23 14	23 32	23 32
	d	20 52	21 05	21 05			21 15	21 32	21 52	22 04			22 15	22 34	22 52	22 52	23 04				23 15	23 34	23 34
Wye	d		21 11					21 38						22 40								23 40	
Chilham	d		21 17					21 44						22 46								23 46	
Chartham	d		21 21					21 48						22 50								23 50	
Canterbury West	d	21 10	21a27					21 53	22 09					22 56	23 09	23 09						23 56	
Sturry	d							21 58						23 00								23 59	
Westenhanger	d			21 13						22 12							23 12						
Sandling	d			21 16						22 15							23 15						
Folkestone West	d			21 21			21 28			22 21			22 28				23 21				23 28		
Folkestone Central	d			21 24			21 30			22 24			22 30				23 24				23 30		
Dover Priory	a			21 37			21 41			22 35			22 41				23 35				23 43		
	d						21 42						22 42								23 44		
Martin Mill	d						21 51						22 51								23 53		
Walmer	d						21 55						22 55								23 57		
Deal	d						22 00						23 00								00 01		
Sandwich	d						22 06						23 06								00 08		
Minster	d							22 09						23 12								00 12	
Ramsgate	a	21 32					22 19	22 17	22 27				23 22	23 18	23 29	23 30			00 39		00 21	00 18	00 29
Broadstairs	a	21 37							22 33						23 35								
Margate	a	21 43			22 03				22 39		23 03				23 40			00 03					

Table T207-F

Mondays to Fridays

21 May to 7 December

London and Tonbridge - Ashford International, Folkestone, Dover, Canterbury West, Ramsgate and Margate

		SE TO ◇	SE WTh FO ◇	SE MO ◇	SE ◇■	SE ◇	SE ◇■	SE TW ThO ◇■ A
St Pancras Intl. ■ ⊖	d	23 12	23 12	23 12		23 37		
Stratford International ⊖	d	23 19	23 19	23 19		23 44		
Ebbsfleet International	d	23 30	23 30	23 30		23 55		
London Charing Cross ■ ⊖	d				22 40		23 40	23 40
London Waterloo (East) ■ ⊖	d				22 43		23 43	23 43
London Cannon Street ■ ⊖	d							
London Bridge ■ ⊖	d				22 49		23 49	23 49
Orpington ■	d							
Sevenoaks ■	d				23 13		00 13	00 13
Hildenborough	d							
Tonbridge ■	a				23 21		00 21	00 21
	d				23 22		00 22	00 22
Paddock Wood ■	d				23 29		00 29	00 29
Maidstone West ■ 208	a							
Marden	d				23 34		00 34	00 34
Staplehurst	d				23 38		00 38	00 38
Headcorn	d				23 44		00 44	00 44
Pluckley	d				23 50		00s50	00s50
Ashford International	a	23 50	23 50	23 50	23 59	00 14	01 00	01 00
	d	23 52	23 52	23 52	00 04	00 15	01 05	01 07
Wye	d							01s13
Chilham	d							01s19
Chartham	d							01s23
Canterbury West ■	d	00 09	00 09					01a30
Sturry	d							
Westenhanger	d				00 12		01s13	
Sandling	d				00 15		01s16	
Folkestone West	d				00 21	00 28	01s22	
Folkestone Central	d				00 24	00 30	01s24	
Dover Priory ■	a				00 35	00 41	01 38	
	d					00 42		
Martin Mill	d					00s51		
Walmer	d					00s55		
Deal	d					00s59		
Sandwich	d					01s06		
Minster ■	d							
Ramsgate ■	a	00 30	00 31	00 43		01 23		
Broadstairs	a		00s36	00s49				
Margate ■	a		00 42	00 58				

Saturdays

26 May to 8 December

		SE ◇■	SE ◇■	SE ◇	SE ◇	SE ◇	SE ◇	SE ◇■	SE	SE ◇	SE	SE ■	SE ■	SE ◇	SE ◇■	SE	SE ◇	SE ■	SE ◇■	SE ◇	SE ◇	SE ◇■	SE
St Pancras Intl. ■ ⊖	d						00 12							06 37			07 08			07 25	07 37		
Stratford International ⊖	d						00 19							06 44			07 15			07 32	07 44		
Ebbsfleet International	d						00 30							06 55			07 26			07 43	07 55		
London Charing Cross ■ ⊖	d														06 00							07 10	
London Waterloo (East) ■ ⊖	d														06 03							07 13	
London Cannon Street ■ ⊖	d																						
London Bridge ■ ⊖	d														06 09							07 19	
Orpington ■	d														06 26								
Sevenoaks ■	d							00 13							06 36							07 43	
Hildenborough	d														06 42								
Tonbridge ■	a							00 21							06 46							07 51	
	d							00 22	06 04			06 22			06 52	07 04		07 22				07 52	08 04
Paddock Wood ■	d							00 29	06 11			06 29			06 59	07 11		07 29				07 59	08 11
Maidstone West ■ 208	a								06 31							07 31							08 31
Marden	d							00 34				06 34			07 04			07 34				08 04	
Staplehurst	d							00 38				06 38			07 08			07 38				08 08	
Headcorn	d							00 44				06 44			07 14			07 44				08 14	
Pluckley	d							00s50				06 50			07 20			07 50				08 20	
Ashford International	a						00 50	01 00				07 00		07 14	07 30		07 46	08 00			08 14	08 30	
	d	00 04				00 15		01 05		06 15	06 35	07 02	07 05	07 15	07 35		07 52	08 02	08 05		08 15	08 35	
Wye	d										06 41		07 11		07 41				08 11			08 41	
Chilham	d												07 17						08 17				
Chartham	d												07 21						08 21				
Canterbury West ■	d				00 09						06 54		07a27		07 54		08 09		08a27			08 54	
Sturry	d										06 58				07 58							08 58	
Westenhanger	d	00 12						01s13				07 10						08 10					
Sandling	d	00 15						01s16				07 13						08 13					
Folkestone West	d	00 21				00 28		01s22		06 28		07 19		07 28				08 19			08 28		
Folkestone Central	d	00 24				00 30		01s24		06 30		07 22		07 30				08 22			08 30		
Dover Priory ■	a	00 35				00 41		01 38		06 41		07 33		07 41				08 33			08 41		
	d					00 42				06 42				07 42							08 42		
Martin Mill	d					00s51				06 51				07 51							08 51		
Walmer	d					00s55				06 55				07 55							08 55		
Deal	d			00 01		00s59				07 00				08 00							09 00		
Sandwich	d			00 08		01s06				07 06				08 06							09 06		
Minster ■	d		00 12								07 10				08 10							09 10	
Ramsgate ■	a		00 18	00 21	00 31	01 23				07 19	07 15			08 19	08 16		08 27				09 19	09 16	
Broadstairs	a				00s36					07 25	07 21			08 25			08 33				09 25		
Margate ■	a				00 42					07 29	07 26			08 29			08 39			08 59	09 29		

A ■ ◇ to Ashford International

Table T207-F

Saturdays

26 May to 8 December

London and Tonbridge - Ashford International, Folkestone, Dover, Canterbury West, Ramsgate and Margate

		SE ◇	SE ◇■	SE ◇■	SE ◇	SE ◇	SE ◇■	SE	SE ◇	SE ◇■	SE ◇■	SE ◇	SE ◇	SE ◇■	SE	SE ◇	SE ◇■	SE ◇■	SE ◇	SE ◇	SE ◇■	SE	SE ◇
St Pancras Intl. ■ ⊖	d	08 12			08 25	08 37			09 09			09 25	09 34			10 08			10 22	10 37			11 12
Stratford International ⊖	d	08 19			08 32	08 44			09 16			09 32	09 41			10 15			10 32	10 44			11 19
Ebbsfleet International	d	08 30			08 43	08 55			09 27			09 44	09 52			10 26			10 44	10 55			11 30
London Charing Cross ■ ⊖	d		07 40				08 10			08 40				09 10			09 40				10 10		
London Waterloo (East) ■ ⊖	d		07 43				08 13			08 43				09 13			09 43				10 13		
London Cannon Street ■ ⊖	d																						
London Bridge ■ ⊖	d		07 49				08 19			08 49				09 19			09 49				10 19		
Orpington ■	d																						
Sevenoaks ■	d		08 13				08 43			09 13				09 43			10 13				10 43		
Hildenborough	d																						
Tonbridge ■	a		08 21				08 51			09 21				09 51			10 21				10 51		
	d		08 22				08 52	09 04		09 22				09 52	10 04		10 22				10 52	11 04	
Paddock Wood ■	d		08 29				08 59	09 11		09 29				09 59	10 11		10 29				10 59	11 11	
Maidstone West ■ 208	a							09 31							10 31							11 31	
Marden	d		08 34				09 04			09 34				10 04			10 34				11 04		
Staplehurst	d		08 38				09 08			09 38				10 08			10 38				11 08		
Headcorn	d		08 44				09 14			09 44				10 14			10 44				11 14		
Pluckley	d		08 50				09 20			09 50				10 20			10 50				11 20		
Ashford International	a	08 50	09 00			09 14	09 30		09 47	10 00			10 11	10 30		10 46	11 00			11 14	11 30		11 50
	d	08 52	09 02	09 05		09 15	09 35		09 52	10 02	10 05		10 15	10 35		10 52	11 02	11 05		11 15	11 35		11 52
Wye	d			09 11			09 41				10 11			10 41				11 11			11 41		
Chilham	d			09 17							10 17							11 17					
Chartham	d			09 21							10 21							11 21					
Canterbury West ■	d	09 09		09a27			09 54		10 09		10a27			10 54		11 09		11a27			11 54		12 09
Sturry	d						09 58							10 58							11 58		
Westenhanger	d		09 10							10 10							11 10						
Sandling	d		09 13							10 13							11 13						
Folkestone West	d		09 19			09 28				10 19			10 28				11 19			11 28			
Folkestone Central	d		09 22			09 30				10 22			10 30				11 22			11 30			
Dover Priory ■	a		09 33			09 41				10 33			10 41				11 33			11 41			
	d					09 42							10 42							11 42			
Martin Mill	d					09 51							10 51							11 51			
Walmer	d					09 55							10 55							11 55			
Deal	d					10 00							11 00							12 00			
Sandwich	d					10 06							11 06							12 06			
Minster ■	d						10 10							11 10							12 10		
Ramsgate ■	a	09 27				10 19	10 16		10 27				11 19	11 16		11 27				12 19	12 16		12 27
Broadstairs	a	09 33				10 25			10 33				11 25			11 33				12 25			12 33
Margate ■	a	09 39			09 59	10 29			10 39			10 59	11 29			11 39			11 59	12 29			12 39

		SE ◇■	SE ◇■	SE ◇	SE ◇	SE ◇■	SE	SE ◇	SE ◇■	SE ◇■	SE ◇	SE ◇	SE ◇■	SE	SE ◇	SE ◇■	SE ◇■	SE ◇	SE ◇	SE ◇■	SE	SE ◇
St Pancras Intl. ■ ⊖	d			11 25	11 37			12 12			12 27	12 37			13 12			13 25	13 37			14 09
Stratford International ⊖	d			11 32	11 44			12 19			12 34	12 44			13 19			13 32	13 44			14 16
Ebbsfleet International	d			11 43	11 55			12 30			12 45	12 55			13 30			13 43	13 55			14 27
London Charing Cross ■ ⊖	d	10 40				11 10			11 40				12 10			12 40				13 10		
London Waterloo (East) ■ ⊖	d	10 43				11 13			11 43				12 13			12 43				13 13		
London Cannon Street ■ ⊖	d																					
London Bridge ■ ⊖	d	10 49				11 19			11 49				12 19			12 49				13 19		
Orpington ■	d																					
Sevenoaks ■	d	11 13				11 43			12 13				12 43			13 13				13 43		
Hildenborough	d																					
Tonbridge ■	a	11 21				11 51			12 21				12 51			13 21				13 51		
	d	11 22				11 52	12 04		12 22				12 52	13 04		13 22				13 52	14 04	
Paddock Wood ■	d	11 29				11 59	12 11		12 29				12 59	13 11		13 29				13 59	14 11	
Maidstone West ■ 208	a						12 31							13 31							14 31	
Marden	d	11 34				12 04			12 34				13 04			13 34				14 04		
Staplehurst	d	11 38				12 08			12 38				13 08			13 38				14 08		
Headcorn	d	11 44				12 14			12 44				13 14			13 44				14 14		
Pluckley	d	11 50				12 20			12 50				13 20			13 50				14 20		
Ashford International	a	12 00			12 14	12 30		12 50	13 00			13 14	13 30		13 50	14 00			14 14	14 30		14 47
	d	12 02	12 05		12 15	12 35		12 52	13 02	13 05		13 15	13 35		13 52	14 02	14 05		14 15	14 35		14 52
Wye	d		12 11			12 41				13 11			13 41				14 11			14 41		
Chilham	d		12 17							13 17							14 17					
Chartham	d		12 21							13 21							14 21					
Canterbury West ■	d		12a27			12 54		13 09		13a27			13 54		14 09		14a27			14 54		15 09
Sturry	d					12 58							13 58							14 58		
Westenhanger	d	12 10							13 10							14 10						
Sandling	d	12 13							13 13							14 13						
Folkestone West	d	12 19			12 28				13 19			13 28				14 19			14 28			
Folkestone Central	d	12 22			12 30				13 22			13 30				14 22			14 30			
Dover Priory ■	a	12 33			12 41				13 33			13 41				14 33			14 41			
	d				12 42							13 42							14 42			
Martin Mill	d				12 51							13 51							14 51			
Walmer	d				12 55							13 55							14 55			
Deal	d				13 00							14 00							15 00			
Sandwich	d				13 06							14 06							15 06			
Minster ■	d					13 10							14 10							15 10		
Ramsgate ■	a				13 19	13 16		13 27				14 19	14 16		14 27				15 19	15 16		15 27
Broadstairs	a				13 25			13 33				14 25			14 33				15 25			15 33
Margate ■	a			12 59	13 29			13 39			13 59	14 29			14 39			14 59	15 29			15 39

Table T207-F

Saturdays

26 May to 8 December

London and Tonbridge - Ashford International, Folkestone, Dover, Canterbury West, Ramsgate and Margate

		SE	SE	SE	SE	SE	SE	SE		SE	SE	SE	SE	SE	SE	SE	SE	SE	SE	SE	SE	SE	SE
		◇■	◇■	◇	◇	◇■		◇		◇■	◇■	◇	◇	◇■		◇	◇■	◇■	◇	◇	◇■		◇
St Pancras Intl. ⊖	d			14 25	14 37			15 12				18 25	18 37			19 12			19 25	19 37			20 12
Stratford International ⊖	d			14 32	14 44			15 19				18 32	18 44			19 19			19 32	19 44			20 19
Ebbsfleet International	d			14 43	14 55			15 30				18 43	18 55			19 30			19 43	19 55			20 30
London Charing Cross ⊖	d	13 40				14 10				17 40				18 10			18 40				19 10		
London Waterloo (East) ⊖	d	13 43				14 13				17 43				18 13			18 43				19 13		
London Cannon Street ⊖	d																						
London Bridge ⊖	d	13 49				14 19				17 49				18 19			18 49				19 19		
Orpington	d																						
Sevenoaks	d	14 13				14 43				18 13				18 43			19 13				19 43		
Hildenborough	d																						
Tonbridge	a	14 21				14 51				18 21				18 51			19 21				19 51		
	d	14 22				14 52	15 04			18 22				18 52	19 04		19 22				19 52	20 04	
Paddock Wood	d	14 29				14 59	15 11			18 29				18 59	19 11		19 29				19 59	20 11	
Maidstone West 208	a						15 31								19 31							20 31	
Marden	d	14 34				15 04			and at the same minutes past each hour until	18 34				19 04			19 34				20 04		
Staplehurst	d	14 38				15 08				18 38				19 08			19 38				20 08		
Headcorn	d	14 44				15 14				18 44				19 14			19 44				20 14		
Pluckley	d	14 50				15 20				18 50				19 20			19 50				20 20		
Ashford International	a	15 00			15 14	15 30		15 50		19 00			19 14	19 30		19 50	20 00			20 14	20 30		20 50
	d	15 02	15 05		15 15	15 35		15 52		19 02	19 05		19 15	19 35		19 52	20 02	20 05		20 15	20 32		20 52
Wye	d		15 11			15 41					19 11			19 41				20 11			20 38		
Chilham	d		15 17								19 17							20 17			20 44		
Chartham	d		15 21								19 21							20 21			20 48		
Canterbury West	d		15a27			15 54		16 09			19a27			19 54		20 09		20a27			20 54		21 09
Sturry	d					15 58								19 58							20 58		
Westenhanger	d	15 10								19 10							20 10						
Sandling	d	15 13								19 13							20 13						
Folkestone West	d	15 19			15 28					19 19			19 28				20 19			20 28			
Folkestone Central	d	15 22			15 30					19 22			19 30				20 22			20 30			
Dover Priory	a	15 33			15 41					19 33			19 41				20 33			20 41			
	d				15 42								19 42							20 42			
Martin Mill	d				15 51								19 51							20 51			
Walmer	d				15 55								19 55							20 55			
Deal	d				16 00								20 00							21 00			
Sandwich	d				16 06								20 06							21 06			
Minster	d					16 10								20 10							21 10		
Ramsgate	a				16 19	16 16		16 27					20 19	20 16		20 27				21 19	21 16		21 27
Broadstairs	a				16 25			16 33					20 25			20 33				21 25			21 33
Margate	a			15 59	16 29			16 39				19 59	20 29			20 39			20 59	21 29			21 39

		SE	SE	SE	SE	SE	SE	SE	SE	SE	SE	SE	SE	SE	SE	SE	SE	SE	SE	SE	SE	SE
		◇■	◇	◇	◇■		◇	◇■	◇	◇	◇■		◇	◇■	◇	◇	◇■	◇	◇■	◇	◇■	◇■
St Pancras Intl. ⊖	d		20 25	20 37			21 12		21 25	21 37			22 12		22 25	22 37		23 12		23 37		
Stratford International ⊖	d		20 32	20 44			21 19		21 32	21 44			22 19		22 32	22 44		23 19		23 44		
Ebbsfleet International	d		20 43	20 55			21 30		21 43	21 55			22 30		22 43	22 55		23 30		23 55		
London Charing Cross ⊖	d	19 40			20 10			20 40			21 10			21 40			22 10		22 40		23 10	23 40
London Waterloo (East) ⊖	d	19 43			20 13			20 43			21 13			21 43			22 13		22 43		23 13	23 43
London Cannon Street ⊖	d																					
London Bridge ⊖	d	19 49			20 19			20 49			21 19			21 49			22 19		22 49		23 19	23 49
Orpington	d										21 35						22 35				23 35	
Sevenoaks	d	20 13			20 43			21 13			21 45			22 13			22 45		23 13		23 46	00 13
Hildenborough	d																					
Tonbridge	a	20 21			20 51			21 21			21 53			22 21			22 53		23 21		23 54	00 21
	d	20 22			20 52	21 04		21 22			21 54	22 04		22 22			22 54		23 22		23 55	00 22
Paddock Wood	d	20 29			20 59	21 11		21 29			22 01	22 11		22 29			23 01		23 29		00 02	00 29
Maidstone West 208	a					21 31						22 31										
Marden	d	20 34			21 04			21 34			22 06			22 34			23 06		23 34		00 07	00 34
Staplehurst	d	20 38			21 08			21 38			22 10			22 38			23 10		23 38		00 11	00 38
Headcorn	d	20 44			21 14			21 44			22 16			22 44			23 16		23 44		00 17	00 44
Pluckley	d	20 50			21 20			21 50			22 22			22 50			23 22		23 50		00 23	00s50
Ashford International	a	21 00		21 14	21 30		21 50	22 00		22 14	22 32		22 50	23 00		23 14	23 32	23 50	23 59	00 14	00 33	01 00
	d	21 02		21 15	21 32		21 52	22 02		22 15	22 34		22 52	23 04		23 15	23 34	23 52	00 04	00 15	00 34	01 05
Wye	d				21 38						22 40						23 40				00s40	
Chilham	d				21 44						22 46						23 46				00s46	
Chartham	d				21 48						22 50						23 50				00s50	
Canterbury West	d				21 54		22 09				22 56		23 09				23 56	00 09			00 56	
Sturry	d				21 58						23 00						23 59				01s00	
Westenhanger	d	21 10						22 10						23 12					00 12			01s13
Sandling	d	21 13						22 13						23 15					00 15			01s16
Folkestone West	d	21 19		21 28				22 19		22 28				23 21		23 28			00 21	00 28		01s22
Folkestone Central	d	21 22		21 30				22 22		22 30				23 24		23 30			00 24	00 30		01s24
Dover Priory	a	21 33		21 41				22 33		22 41				23 35		23 41			00 35	00 41		01 38
	d			21 42						22 42						23 42				00 42		
Martin Mill	d			21 51						22 51						23 51				00s51		
Walmer	d			21 55						22 55						23 55				00s55		
Deal	d			22 00						23 00						23 59				00s59		
Sandwich	d			22 06						23 06						00 06				01s06		
Minster	d				22 10						23 12						00 12				01s11	
Ramsgate	a			22 19	22 16		22 27			23 21	23 18		23 29			00 21	00 18	00 27		01 23	01 20	
Broadstairs	a						22 33						23 34					00s33				
Margate	a		21 59				22 39		22 59				23 40		23 59			00 39				

Table T207-F

Sundays

20 May to 2 December

London and Tonbridge - Ashford International, Folkestone, Dover, Canterbury West, Ramsgate and Margate

		SE	SE	SE	SE	SE	SE	SE	SE	SE	SE	SE	SE	SE	SE	SE	SE	SE	SE	SE	SE	SE	SE
		◇■	◇■	◇	◇	◇	◇■	◇	◇■	■			◇	◇	■	■	◇■		◇	◇■	◇	◇■	◇■
		A	A	A	A	A	A		A														
St Pancras Intl. ⊖	d							00 12						08 25					08 37		09 09		
Stratford International ⊖	d							00 19						08 32					08 44		09 16		
Ebbsfleet International	d							00 30						08 43					08 55		09 27		
London Charing Cross ⊖	d																			08 10		08 40	
London Waterloo (East) ⊖	d																			08 13		08 43	
London Cannon Street ⊖	d																						
London Bridge ⊖	d																			08 19		08 49	
Orpington	d																			08 36		09 06	
Sevenoaks	d								00 13											08 46		09 16	
Hildenborough	d																						
Tonbridge	a								00 21											08 54		09 24	
	d								00 22		06 33	07 33				08 26		08 33		08 56		09 26	
Paddock Wood	d						00 02		00 29		06 40	07 40				08 33		08 40		09 03		09 33	
Maidstone West 208	a										07 00	08 00						09 00					
Marden	d						00 07		00 34							08 38				09 08		09 38	
Staplehurst	d						00 11		00 38							08 42				09 12		09 42	
Headcorn	d						00 17		00 44							08 48				09 18		09 48	
Pluckley	d						00 23		00s50							08 54						09 54	
Ashford International	a						00 33	00 50	01 00							09 03			09 14	09 30	09 47	10 03	
	d	00 04				00 15	00 34		01 05	08 08			08 15		08 32	09 05	09 08		09 15	09 32	09 52	10 05	10 08
Wye	d						00s40			08 14					08 38		09 14			09 38			10 14
Chilham	d						00s46			08 20							09 20						10 20
Chartham	d						00s50			08 24							09 24						10 24
Canterbury West	d				00 09		00 56			08a30					08 51		09a30			09 51	10 09		10a30
Sturry	d						01s00								08 55					09 55			
Westenhanger	d	00 12							01s13							09 13						10 13	
Sandling	d	00 15							01s16							09 16						10 16	
Folkestone West	d	00 21				00 28			01s22				08 28			09 21			09 28			10 21	
Folkestone Central	d	00 24				00 30			01s24				08 30			09 24			09 30			10 24	
Dover Priory	a	00 35				00 41			01 38				08 41			09 35			09 41			10 35	
	d					00 42							08 42						09 42				
Martin Mill	d					00s51							08 51						09 51				
Walmer	d					00s55							08 55						09 55				
Deal	d					00s59							09 00						10 00				
Sandwich	d			00 06		01s06							09 06						10 06				
Minster	d		00 12				01s11								09 07					10 07			
Ramsgate	a		00 18	00 21	00 27	01 23	01 20						09 19		09 15				10 19	10 15	10 27		
Broadstairs	a				00s33								09 25						10 25		10 33		
Margate	a				00 39								09 29	09 59					10 29		10 39		

		SE	SE	SE	SE	SE	SE	SE	SE	SE	SE	SE	SE	SE	SE	SE	SE	SE	SE	SE	SE	SE	SE
		◇		◇	◇■	◇	◇■	◇■	◇		◇	◇■	◇	◇■	◇■	◇		◇	◇■	◇	◇■	◇■	◇
St Pancras Intl. ⊖	d	09 25		09 37		10 08			10 27		10 37		11 12			11 25		11 37		12 12			12 27
Stratford International ⊖	d	09 32		09 44		10 15			10 34		10 44		11 19			11 32		11 44		12 19			12 34
Ebbsfleet International	d	09 44		09 55		10 26			10 45		10 55		11 30			11 43		11 55		12 30			12 45
London Charing Cross ⊖	d				09 10		09 40					10 10		10 40					11 10		11 40		
London Waterloo (East) ⊖	d				09 13		09 43					10 13		10 43					11 13		11 43		
London Cannon Street ⊖	d																						
London Bridge ⊖	d				09 19		09 49					10 19		10 49					11 19		11 49		
Orpington	d				09 36		10 06					10 36		11 06					11 36		12 06		
Sevenoaks	d				09 46		10 16					10 46		11 16					11 46		12 16		
Hildenborough	d																						
Tonbridge	a				09 54		10 24					10 54		11 24					11 54		12 24		
	d		09 33		09 56		10 26			10 33		10 56		11 26			11 33		11 56		12 26		
Paddock Wood	d		09 40		10 03		10 33			10 40		11 03		11 33			11 40		12 03		12 33		
Maidstone West 208	a		10 00							11 00							12 00						
Marden	d				10 08		10 38					11 08		11 38					12 08		12 38		
Staplehurst	d				10 12		10 42					11 12		11 42					12 12		12 42		
Headcorn	d				10 18		10 48					11 18		11 48					12 18		12 48		
Pluckley	d						10 54							11 54							12 54		
Ashford International	a			10 14	10 30	10 46	11 03				11 14	11 30	11 50	12 03				12 14	12 30	12 50	13 03		
	d			10 15	10 32	10 52	11 05	11 08			11 15	11 32	11 52	12 05	12 08			12 15	12 32	12 52	13 05	13 08	
Wye	d				10 38			11 14				11 38			12 14				12 38			13 14	
Chilham	d							11 20							12 20							13 20	
Chartham	d							11 24							12 24							13 24	
Canterbury West	d				10 51	11 09		11a30				11 51	12 09		12a30				12 51	13 09		13a30	
Sturry	d				10 55							11 55							12 55				
Westenhanger	d						11 13							12 13							13 13		
Sandling	d						11 16							12 16							13 16		
Folkestone West	d			10 28			11 21				11 28			12 21				12 28			13 21		
Folkestone Central	d			10 30			11 24				11 30			12 24				12 30			13 24		
Dover Priory	a			10 41			11 35				11 41			12 35				12 41			13 35		
	d			10 42							11 42							12 42					
Martin Mill	d			10 51							11 51							12 51					
Walmer	d			10 55							11 55							12 55					
Deal	d			11 00							12 00							13 00					
Sandwich	d			11 06							12 06							13 06					
Minster	d				11 07							12 07							13 07				
Ramsgate	a			11 19	11 15	11 27					12 19	12 15	12 27					13 19	13 15	13 27			
Broadstairs	a			11 25		11 33					12 25		12 33					13 25		13 33			
Margate	a	10 59		11 29		11 39			11 59		12 29		12 39			12 59		13 29		13 39			13 59

A not 20 May

Table T207-F

Sundays
20 May to 2 December

London and Tonbridge - Ashford International, Folkestone, Dover, Canterbury West, Ramsgate and Margate

		SE		SE	SE	SE	SE	SE	SE	SE	SE	SE		SE	SE	SE	SE	SE	SE	SE	SE	SE		SE	SE
				◇	◇■	◇	◇■	◇■	◇		◇	◇■		◇	◇■	◇■	◇		◇	◇■	◇	◇■		◇■	◇
St Pancras Intl. ⊖	d			12 37		13 12			13 25		13 37			14 09			14 25		14 37		15 12				15 25
Stratford International ⊖	d			12 44		13 19			13 32		13 44			14 16			14 32		14 44		15 19				15 32
Ebbsfleet International	d			12 55		13 30			13 43		13 55			14 27			14 43		14 55		15 30				15 43
London Charing Cross ⊖	d				12 10		12 40					13 10			13 40					14 10		14 40			
London Waterloo (East) ⊖	d				12 13		12 43					13 13			13 43					14 13		14 43			
London Cannon Street ⊖	d																								
London Bridge ⊖	d				12 19		12 49					13 19			13 49					14 19		14 49			
Orpington	d				12 36		13 06					13 36			14 06					14 36		15 06			
Sevenoaks	d				12 46		13 16					13 46			14 16					14 46		15 16			
Hildenborough	d																								
Tonbridge	a				12 54		13 24					13 54			14 24					14 54		15 24			
	d	12 33			12 56		13 26			13 33		13 56			14 26			14 33		14 56		15 26			
Paddock Wood	d	12 40			13 03		13 33			13 40		14 03			14 33			14 40		15 03		15 33			
Maidstone West 208	a	13 00								14 00								15 00							
Marden	d				13 08		13 38					14 08			14 38					15 08		15 38			
Staplehurst	d				13 12		13 42					14 12			14 42					15 12		15 42			
Headcorn	d				13 18		13 48					14 18			14 48					15 18		15 48			
Pluckley	d						13 54								14 54							15 54			
Ashford International	a			13 14	13 30	13 50	14 03				14 14	14 30		14 47	15 05				15 14	15 30	15 50	16 03			
	d			13 15	13 32	13 52	14 05	14 08			14 15	14 32		14 52	15 07	15 08			15 15	15 32	15 52	16 05		16 08	
Wye	d				13 38			14 14				14 38				15 14				15 38				16 14	
Chilham	d							14 20								15 20								16 20	
Chartham	d							14 24								15 24								16 24	
Canterbury West	d				13 51	14 09		14a30				14 51		15 09		15a30				15 51	16 09			16a30	
Sturry	d				13 55							14 55								15 55					
Westenhanger	d						14 13								15 15							16 13			
Sandling	d						14 16								15 18							16 16			
Folkestone West	d			13 28			14 21				14 28				15 23				15 28			16 21			
Folkestone Central	d			13 30			14 24				14 30				15 26				15 30			16 24			
Dover Priory	a			13 41			14 35				14 41				15 37				15 41			16 35			
	d			13 42							14 42								15 42						
Martin Mill	d			13 51							14 51								15 51						
Walmer	d			13 55							14 55								15 55						
Deal	d			14 00							15 00								16 00						
Sandwich	d			14 06							15 06								16 06						
Minster	d				14 07							15 07								16 07					
Ramsgate	a			14 19	14 15	14 27					15 19	15 15		15 27					16 19	16 15	16 27				
Broadstairs	a			14 25		14 33					15 25			15 33					16 25		16 33				
Margate	a			14 29		14 39			14 59		15 29			15 39			15 59		16 29		16 39				16 59

		SE	SE	SE	SE	SE	SE	SE		SE	SE	SE	SE	SE	SE	SE	SE	SE		SE	SE	SE	SE	SE	SE
			◇	◇■	◇	◇■	◇■	◇			◇	◇■	◇	◇■	◇■	◇		◇		◇■	◇	◇■	◇		◇
St Pancras Intl. ⊖	d		15 37		16 12			16 25			16 37		17 12			17 25		17 37			18 12		18 25		18 37
Stratford International ⊖	d		15 44		16 19			16 32			16 44		17 19			17 32		17 44			18 19		18 32		18 44
Ebbsfleet International	d		15 55		16 31			16 43			16 55		17 30			17 43		17 55			18 30		18 43		18 55
London Charing Cross ⊖	d			15 10		15 40						16 10		16 40						17 10		17 40			
London Waterloo (East) ⊖	d			15 13		15 43						16 13		16 43						17 13		17 43			
London Cannon Street ⊖	d																								
London Bridge ⊖	d			15 19		15 49						16 19		16 49						17 19		17 49			
Orpington	d			15 36		16 06						16 36		17 06						17 36		18 06			
Sevenoaks	d			15 46		16 16						16 46		17 16						17 46		18 16			
Hildenborough	d																								
Tonbridge	a			15 54		16 24						16 54		17 24						17 54		18 24			
	d	15 33		15 56		16 26				16 33		16 56		17 26			17 33			17 56		18 26		18 33	
Paddock Wood	d	15 40		16 03		16 33				16 40		17 03		17 33			17 40			18 03		18 33		18 40	
Maidstone West 208	a	16 00								17 00							18 00							19 00	
Marden	d			16 08		16 38						17 08		17 38						18 08		18 38			
Staplehurst	d			16 12		16 42						17 12		17 42						18 12		18 42			
Headcorn	d			16 18		16 48						17 18		17 48						18 18		18 48			
Pluckley	d					16 54								17 54								18 54			
Ashford International	a		16 14	16 30	16 50	17 03					17 14	17 30	17 50	18 03				18 14		18 30	18 50	19 03			19 14
	d		16 15	16 32	16 52	17 05	17 08				17 15	17 32	17 52	18 05	18 08			18 15		18 32	18 52	19 05			19 15
Wye	d			16 38			17 14					17 38			18 14					18 38					
Chilham	d						17 20								18 20					18 44					
Chartham	d						17 24								18 24					18 48					
Canterbury West	d			16 51	17 09		17a30					17 51	18 09		18a30					18 54	19 09				
Sturry	d			16 55								17 55								18 58					
Westenhanger	d					17 13								18 13								19 13			
Sandling	d					17 16								18 16								19 16			
Folkestone West	d		16 28			17 21					17 28			18 21				18 28				19 21			19 28
Folkestone Central	d		16 30			17 24					17 30			18 24				18 30				19 24			19 30
Dover Priory	a		16 41			17 35					17 41			18 35				18 41				19 35			19 41
	d		16 42								17 42							18 42							19 42
Martin Mill	d		16 51								17 51							18 51							19 51
Walmer	d		16 55								17 55							18 55							19 55
Deal	d		17 00								18 00							19 00							20 00
Sandwich	d		17 06								18 06							19 06							20 06
Minster	d			17 07								18 07								19 09					
Ramsgate	a		17 19	17 15	17 27						18 19	18 15	18 27					19 19		19 15	19 27				20 19
Broadstairs	a		17 25		17 33						18 25		18 33					19 25			19 33				20 25
Margate	a		17 29		17 39			17 59			18 29		18 39			18 59		19 29			19 39		19 59		20 29

Table T207-F

Sundays
20 May to 2 December

London and Tonbridge - Ashford International, Folkestone, Dover, Canterbury West, Ramsgate and Margate

		SE	SE	SE		SE	SE	SE	SE	SE	SE	SE	SE	SE		SE	SE	SE	SE	SE	SE	SE	SE	SE
		◇■	◇	◇■		◇		◇	◇■	◇	◇■	◇		◇		◇■	◇	◇■	◇		◇	◇■	◇	◇■
St Pancras Intl. ⊖	d		19 12			19 25		19 37		20 12		20 25		20 37			21 12		21 25		21 37		22 12	
Stratford International ⊖	d		19 19			19 32		19 44		20 19		20 32		20 44			21 19		21 32		21 44		22 19	
Ebbsfleet International	d		19 30			19 43		19 55		20 30		20 43		20 55			21 30		21 43		21 55		22 30	
London Charing Cross ⊖	d	18 10		18 40					19 10		19 40					20 10		20 40				21 10		21 40
London Waterloo (East) ⊖	d	18 13		18 43					19 13		19 43					20 13		20 43				21 13		21 43
London Cannon Street ⊖	d																							
London Bridge ⊖	d	18 19		18 49					19 19		19 49					20 19		20 49				21 19		21 49
Orpington	d	18 36		19 06					19 36		20 06					20 36		21 06				21 36		22 06
Sevenoaks	d	18 46		19 16					19 46		20 16					20 46		21 16				21 46		22 16
Hildenborough	d																							
Tonbridge	a	18 54		19 24					19 54		20 24					20 54		21 24				21 54		22 24
	d	18 56		19 26			19 33		19 56		20 26		20 33			20 56		21 26		21 33		21 56		22 26
Paddock Wood	d	19 03		19 33			19 40		20 03		20 33		20 40			21 03		21 33		21 40		22 03		22 33
Maidstone West 208	a						20 00						21 00							22 00				
Marden	d	19 08		19 38					20 08		20 38					21 08		21 38				22 08		22 38
Staplehurst	d	19 12		19 42					20 12		20 42					21 12		21 42				22 12		22 42
Headcorn	d	19 18		19 48					20 18		20 48					21 18		21 48				22 18		22 48
Pluckley	d			19 54							20 54							21 54						22 54
Ashford International	a	19 30	19 50	20 03				20 14	20 30	20 50	21 03			21 14		21 30	21 50	22 03			22 14	22 30	22 50	23 03
	d	19 32	19 52	20 05				20 15	20 32	20 52	21 05			21 15		21 32	21 52	22 05			22 15	22 32	22 52	23 05
Wye	d	19 38							20 38							21 38						22 38		
Chilham	d	19 44							20 44							21 44						22 44		
Chartham	d	19 48							20 48							21 48						22 48		
Canterbury West	d	19 54	20 09						20 54	21 09						21 54	22 09					22 54	23 09	
Sturry	d	19 58							20 58							21 58						22 58		
Westenhanger	d			20 13							21 13							22 13						23 13
Sandling	d			20 16							21 16							22 16						23 16
Folkestone West	d			20 21				20 28			21 21			21 28				22 21			22 28			23 21
Folkestone Central	d			20 24				20 30			21 24			21 30				22 24			22 30			23 24
Dover Priory	a			20 35				20 41			21 35			21 41				22 35			22 41			23 35
	d							20 42						21 42							22 42			
Martin Mill	d							20 51						21 51							22 51			
Walmer	d							20 55						21 55							22 55			
Deal	d							21 00						22 00							23 00			
Sandwich	d							21 06						22 06							23 06			
Minster	d	20 09							21 09							22 09						23 09		
Ramsgate	a	20 15	20 27					21 19	21 15	21 27				22 18		22 15	22 27				23 18	23 15	23 27	
Broadstairs	a		20 33					21 25		21 33							22 33						23 33	
Margate	a		20 39			20 59		21 29		21 39		21 59					22 39		22 59				23 39	

		SE	SE	SE	SE	SE	SE	SE	SE	SE
		◇		◇	◇■	◇	◇■	◇	◇■	◇■
St Pancras Intl. ⊖	d	22 25		22 37		23 12		23 37		
Stratford International ⊖	d	22 32		22 44		23 19		23 44		
Ebbsfleet International	d	22 43		22 55		23 30		23 55		
London Charing Cross ⊖	d				22 10		22 40		23 10	23 40
London Waterloo (East) ⊖	d				22 13		22 43		23 13	23 43
London Cannon Street ⊖	d									
London Bridge ⊖	d				22 19		22 49		23 19	23 49
Orpington	d				22 36		23 06		23 36	00 06
Sevenoaks	d				22 46		23 16		23 46	00 16
Hildenborough	d									
Tonbridge	a				22 54		23 24		23 54	00 24
	d		22 33		22 56		23 26		23 56	00 26
Paddock Wood	d		22 40		23 03		23 33		00 03	00 33
Maidstone West 208	a		23 00							
Marden	d				23 08		23 38		00 08	00 38
Staplehurst	d				23 12		23 42		00 12	00 42
Headcorn	d				23 18		23 48		00 18	00 48
Pluckley	d						23 54			00s54
Ashford International	a			23 14	23 30	23 50	00 03	00 15	00 30	01 04
	d			23 15	23 32	23 52	00 05			
Wye	d				23 38					
Chilham	d				23 44					
Chartham	d				23 48					
Canterbury West	d				23 54	00 09				
Sturry	d				23 58					
Westenhanger	d						00 13			
Sandling	d						00 16			
Folkestone West	d			23 28			00 21			
Folkestone Central	d			23 30			00 24			
Dover Priory	a			23 41			00 35			
	d			23 42						
Martin Mill	d			23 51						
Walmer	d			23 55						
Deal	d			23 59						
Sandwich	d			00 06						
Minster	d				00 09					
Ramsgate	a			00 18	00 15	00 27				
Broadstairs	a					00s33				
Margate	a	23 58				00 39				

Table T207-R

Mondays to Fridays

21 May to 7 December

Margate, Ramsgate, Canterbury West, Dover, Folkestone, Ashford International - Tonbridge and London

Miles	Miles	Miles	Miles			SE MX ■	SE	SE ◇■	SE ◇	SE ◇■	SE ◇	SE	SE ◇■	SE ◇		SE ◇	SE	SE ◇■	SE ◇■	SE ◇	SE ◇■	SE ◇■	SE ◇	SE ◇
0	0	—	—	Margate ■	d															05 46				
3¼	3¼	—	—	Broadstairs	d															05 52				
5½	5½	—	—	Ramsgate ■	d						04 55		04 51			05 12		05 38	05 20	05 58				
—	9½	0	—	Minster ■	d						05 01							05 44						
13¾	—	4¾	—	Sandwich	d								05 06						05 34				05 54	
18	—	—	—	Deal	d								05 12						05 40				06 00	
19½	—	—	—	Walmer	d								05 15						05 43				06 03	
22¼	—	—	—	Martin Mill	d								05 20						05 48				06 08	
27¼	—	—	—	Dover Priory ■	a								05 29						05 57				06 17	
—	—	—	—		d			04 30					05 29	05 45					05 59				06 18	
34½	—	—	—	Folkestone Central	d			04 42					05 41	05 56					06 10				06 29	
35¼	—	—	—	Folkestone West	d	00 02		04 44					05 43	05 58					06 12				06 31	
39	—	—	—	Sandling	d	00 07		04 49					05 48						06 18					
40¼	—	—	—	Westenhanger	d	00 10		04 52					05 51						06 21					
—	18½	—	—	Sturry	d						05 13							05 56						
—	20¾	—	—	Canterbury West ■	d						05 18							06 01		06 18				
—	24	—	—	Chartham	d						05 24							06 06						
—	26	—	—	Chilham	d						05 28							06 10						
—	30¾	—	—	Wye	d						05 34							06 17			←			
48½	35	—	0	Ashford International	a	00 20		05 01			05 41		06 01	06 11				06 23	06 30	06 34	06 30		06 44	
—	—	—	—		d			05 03	05 13	05 29	05 43		06 02	06 13				06 25	06 37	06 36	06 37	06 45	06 46	
54	—	—	—	Pluckley	d			05 09		05 36			06 09					06 32	→		06 44	06 52		
59¼	—	—	—	Headcorn	d			05 16		05 43			06 16					06 39			06 51	06 59		
62¾	—	—	—	Staplehurst	d			05 21		05 48			06 21					06 44			06 56	07 04		
65	—	—	—	Marden	d			05 25		05 52			06 25					06 48			07 00	07 08		
—	—	—	—	Maidstone West ■ 208	d		05 00					05 54					06 24							06 53
69¾	—	—	—	Paddock Wood ■	d		05a20	05 31		05 58		06a13	06 31				06a43	06 54			07 06	07 14		
75	—	—	—	Tonbridge ■	a			05 39		06 05			06 38					07 02			07 14	07 22		
—	—	—	—		d			05 40		06 07			06 39					07 03			07 15	07 23		
77½	—	—	—	Hildenborough	a																07 19			
82¼	—	—	—	Sevenoaks ■	a			05 49		06 16			06 48					07 11			07 27	07 31		
90¾	—	—	—	Orpington ■	a			05 58		06 25														
102¾	—	—	—	London Bridge ■ ⊖	a			06 16		06 43			07 14					07 35			07 52	07 55		
—	—	—	—	London Cannon Street ■ ⊖	a			06 24													08 00			
103¾	—	—	—	London Waterloo (East) ■ ⊖	a					06 49			07 21					07 42				08 01		
104½	—	—	—	London Charing Cross ■ ⊖	a					06 56			07 27					07 49				08 09		
—	—	—	33¼	Ebbsfleet International	a				05 32		06 02			06 32		06 42				06 55			07 05	07 25
—	—	—	50	Stratford International ⊖	a				05 44		06 14			06 44		06 55				07 07			07 17	07 39
—	—	—	56	St Pancras Intl. ■ ⊖	a				05 51		06 21			06 51		07 02				07 14			07 25	07 46

		SE	SE ◇■	SE ◇■	SE ◇	SE ◇	SE ◇■	SE ◇■	SE ◇	SE		SE ◇■	SE ◇	SE ◇■	SE ◇	SE ◇■	SE ◇■	SE ◇■	SE ◇	SE ◇		SE ◇	SE ◇■	SE ◇■	SE
Margate ■	d				06 16								06 46						07 16			06 54			
Broadstairs	d				06 22								06 52						07 22			07 00			
Ramsgate ■	d		06 10		06 28	06 14							06 58			06 55	06 50	07 05	07 28			07 10	07 19		
Minster ■	d		06 16					06 45										07 14							
Sandwich	d			06 05		06 26									06 50		07 02					07 22			
Deal	d			06 11		06 32									06 56		07 08					07 28			
Walmer	d			06 14											06 59		07 11					07 32			
Martin Mill	d			06 19											07 04		07 16					07 37			
Dover Priory ■	a			06 28		06 47									07 12		07 24					07 45			
	d			06 30		06 48									07 13		07 25					07 46			
Folkestone Central	d			06 42		06 59						07 11			07 24		07 36					07 57			
Folkestone West	d			06 44		07 01						07 14			07 27		07 38					07 59			
Sandling	d			06 49								07 19					07 43								
Westenhanger	d			06 52								07 22					07 46								
Sturry	d		06 28					06 57										07 26							
Canterbury West ■	d		06 34		06 48			07 03					07 18					07 36	07 48					08 04	
Chartham	d		06 39					07 08										07 41						08 09	
Chilham	d		06 42					07 12										07 44						08 12	
Wye	d		06 49					07 19										07 51						08 19	
Ashford International	a		06 55	07 01	07 04	07 14		07 25				07 31	07 34		07 40		07 55	07 57	08 04			08 12		08 26	
	d		06 57	07 03	07 06	07 16	07 19	07 27				07 36	07 36	07 43	07 44		08 03		08 06			08 16			
Pluckley	d		07 04	07 09			07 26					07 43		07 50			08 09								
Headcorn	d		07 11	07 16			07 33	07 38				07 50		07 57			08 16								
Staplehurst	d		07 16	07 22			07 38	07 43				07 55		08 02			08 21								
Marden	d		07 20	07 26			07 42	07 48				07 59		08 06			08 25								
Maidstone West ■ 208	d	07 00							07 25	07 36										07 53					08 16
Paddock Wood ■	d	07a19	07 26	07 33			07 48	07 54		07a56		08 05		08 12			08 31								08 35
Tonbridge ■	a		07 34	07 40			07 56	08 01				08 13		08 20			08 39								08 43
	d		07 35	07 42			07 58	08 02				08 14		08 21			08 40								
Hildenborough	a		07 39									08 18													
Sevenoaks ■	a		07 46	07 50			08 07	08 11				08 26		08 30			08 50								
Orpington ■	a																								
London Bridge ■ ⊖	a		08 13	08 15			08 34	08 35				08 54		08 56		08 51	09 15						09 10		
London Cannon Street ■ ⊖	a		08 21				08 42					09 02				08 59							09 18		
London Waterloo (East) ■ ⊖	a			08 21				08 41						09 03			09 21								
London Charing Cross ■ ⊖	a			08 28				08 48						09 10			09 29								
Ebbsfleet International	a					07 35			07 56											08 25		08 35			
Stratford International ⊖	a				07 34	07 47			08 09				08 04		08 12				08 34	08 39		08 47			
St Pancras Intl. ■ ⊖	a				07 42	07 54			08 16				08 12		08 20				08 42	08 46		08 54			

Table T207-R

Mondays to Fridays

21 May to 7 December

Margate, Ramsgate, Canterbury West, Dover, Folkestone, Ashford International - Tonbridge and London

		SE ◇■	SE ◇	SE ◇■	SE ◇■	SE ◇		SE ◇■	SE	SE ◇■	SE ◇	SE ◇■	SE ◇■	SE ◇	SE ◇	SE ◇		SE ◇■	SE	SE ◇■	SE ◇	SE ◇■	SE ◇	SE ◇	SE ◇■
Margate ■	d		07 48								08 51				08 59						09 53		09 59		
Broadstairs	d		07 54								08 57				09 05						09 59		10 05		
Ramsgate ■	d		08 01	07 42	08 14					08 05	09 03		09 15	09 35	09 12	09 20					10 05	10 19	10 12	10 20	
Minster ■	d		08 07	07 54	08 20					08 16			09 22									10 25			
Sandwich	d			08 02						08 30					09 25								10 25		
Deal	d			08 08						08 36					09 31								10 31		
Walmer	d			08 11						08 39					09 34								10 34		
Martin Mill	d			08 16						08 43					09 38								10 38		
Dover Priory ■	a			08 24						08 52					09 47								10 47		
	d	07 58		08 25		08 49				08 58		09 25			09 49					09 58			10 49		
Folkestone Central	d	08 09		08 36		09 00				09 09		09 36			10 00					10 09			11 00		
Folkestone West	d	08 11		08 38		09 02				09 11		09 38			10 02					10 11			11 02		
Sandling	d	08 16		08 43						09 16		09 43								10 16					
Westenhanger	d	08 19		08 46						09 19		09 46								10 19					
Sturry	d		08 19		08 31								09 33									10 37			
Canterbury West ■	d		08 25		08 36			09 05			09 23		09 38	09 54				10 05			10 25	10 42			11 05
Chartham	d				08 41			09 10					09 43					10 10							11 10
Chilham	d				08 44			09 13					09 46					10 13							11 13
Wye	d				08 51			09 20					09 52					10 20				10 54			11 20
Ashford International	a	08 28	08 41	08 55	08 58	09 15		09 27		09 28	09 39	09 55	09 58	10 10	10 15			10 27		10 28	10 41	11 00	11 15		11 27
	d	08 32	08 43	09 02		09 16				09 32	09 43	10 02		10 11	10 16					10 32	10 43	11 02	11 16		
Pluckley	d	08 38		09 08						09 38		10 08								10 38		11 08			
Headcorn	d	08 45		09 15						09 45		10 15								10 45		11 15			
Staplehurst	d	08 50		09 20						09 50		10 20								10 50		11 20			
Marden	d	08 54		09 24						09 54		10 24								10 54		11 24			
Maidstone West ■ 208	d								09 28										10 28						
Paddock Wood ■	d	09 00		09 30					09 47	10 00		10 30							10 47	11 00		11 30			
Tonbridge ■	a	09 08		09 37					09 55	10 07		10 38							10 55	11 08		11 38			
	d	09 09		09 39						10 09		10 39								11 09		11 39			
Hildenborough	a																								
Sevenoaks ■	a	09 18		09 48						10 18		10 48								11 18		11 48			
Orpington ■	a																								
London Bridge ■ ⊖	a	09 41		10 11						10 41		11 11								11 41		12 11			
London Cannon Street ■ ⊖	a																								
London Waterloo (East) ■ ⊖	a	09 49		10 17						10 47		11 17								11 47		12 17			
London Charing Cross ■ ⊖	a	09 56		10 24						10 52		11 22								11 52		12 22			
Ebbsfleet International	a		09 02			09 35					10 02				10 35	10 46					11 02		11 35	11 46	
Stratford International ⊖	a		09 14			09 47					10 14			10 39	10 47	10 59					11 14		11 47	11 58	
St Pancras Intl. ■ ⊖	a		09 21			09 54					10 21			10 47	10 55	11 07					11 21		11 54	12 05	

		SE		SE ◇■	SE ◇	SE ◇■	SE ◇	SE ◇	SE ◇■	SE	SE ◇■	SE ◇		SE ◇■	SE ◇	SE ◇	SE ◇■	SE	SE ◇■	SE ◇	SE ◇■	SE ◇		SE ◇	SE ◇■
Margate ■	d				10 53		10 59					11 53			11 59					12 53		12 59			
Broadstairs	d				10 59		11 05					11 59			12 05					12 59		13 05			
Ramsgate ■	d				11 05	11 19	11 12	11 20				12 05		12 19	12 12	12 20				13 05	13 19	13 12		13 20	
Minster ■	d					11 25								12 25							13 25				
Sandwich	d						11 25								12 25							13 25			
Deal	d						11 31								12 31							13 31			
Walmer	d						11 34								12 34							13 34			
Martin Mill	d						11 38								12 38							13 38			
Dover Priory ■	a						11 47								12 47							13 47			
	d			10 58			11 49				11 58				12 49				12 58			13 49			
Folkestone Central	d			11 09			12 00				12 09				13 00				13 09			14 00			
Folkestone West	d			11 11			12 02				12 11				13 02				13 11			14 02			
Sandling	d			11 16							12 16								13 16						
Westenhanger	d			11 19							12 19								13 19						
Sturry	d					11 37								12 37							13 37				
Canterbury West ■	d				11 25	11 42			12 05			12 25		12 42			13 05			13 25	13 42				14 05
Chartham	d								12 10								13 10								14 10
Chilham	d								12 13								13 13								14 13
Wye	d					11 54			12 20					12 54			13 20				13 54				14 20
Ashford International	a			11 28	11 41	12 00	12 15		12 27		12 28	12 41		13 00	13 15		13 27		13 28	13 41	14 00	14 15			14 27
	d			11 32	11 43	12 02	12 16				12 32	12 43		13 02	13 16				13 32	13 43	14 02	14 16			
Pluckley	d			11 38		12 08					12 38			13 08					13 38		14 08				
Headcorn	d			11 45		12 15					12 45			13 15					13 45		14 15				
Staplehurst	d			11 50		12 20					12 50			13 20					13 50		14 20				
Marden	d			11 54		12 24					12 54			13 24					13 54		14 24				
Maidstone West ■ 208	d	11 28								12 28								13 28							
Paddock Wood ■	d	11 47		12 00		12 30				12 47	13 00			13 30				13 47	14 00		14 30				
Tonbridge ■	a	11 55		12 08		12 38				12 58	13 08			13 38				13 55	14 08		14 38				
	d			12 09		12 39					13 09			13 39					14 09		14 39				
Hildenborough	a																								
Sevenoaks ■	a			12 18		12 48					13 18			13 48					14 18		14 48				
Orpington ■	a																								
London Bridge ■ ⊖	a			12 41		13 11					13 41			14 11					14 41		15 11				
London Cannon Street ■ ⊖	a																								
London Waterloo (East) ■ ⊖	a			12 47		13 17					13 47			14 17					14 47		15 17				
London Charing Cross ■ ⊖	a			12 52		13 22					13 52			14 22					14 52		15 22				
Ebbsfleet International	a				12 02		12 35	12 46				13 02			13 35	13 46				14 02		14 35		14 46	
Stratford International ⊖	a				12 14		12 47	12 58				13 14			13 47	14 02				14 14		14 47		14 58	
St Pancras Intl. ■ ⊖	a				12 21		12 55	13 06				13 21			13 54	14 10				14 21		14 54		15 06	

Table T207-R

Mondays to Fridays

21 May to 7 December

Margate, Ramsgate, Canterbury West, Dover, Folkestone, Ashford International - Tonbridge and London

		SE	SE	SE	SE	SE	SE	SE		SE	SE	SE	SE	SE	SE	SE	SE	SE		SE	SE	SE	SE	SE	SE
			◇■	◇	◇■	◇	◇	◇■			◇■	◇	◇■	◇	◇	◇■		◇■		◇		◇■	◇■	◇	◇
Margate ■	d			13 53		13 59						14 53		14 59						15 53				16 02	
Broadstairs	d			13 59		14 05						14 59		15 05						15 59				16 08	
Ramsgate ■	d			14 05	14 19	14 12	14 20					15 05	15 17	15 12	15 20			15 21		16 05		15 50	16 18	16 13	16 20
Minster ■	d				14 25								15 23										16 24		
Sandwich	d					14 25								15 25				15 34				16 02		16 26	
Deal	d					14 31								15 31				15 41				16 08		16 32	
Walmer	d					14 34								15 34				15 44				16 11		16 35	
Martin Mill	d					14 38								15 38				15 49				16 16		16 39	
Dover Priory ■	a					14 47								15 47				15 57				16 24		16 48	
	d		13 58			14 49					14 58			15 49				15 58				16 25		16 49	
Folkestone Central	d		14 09			15 00					15 09			16 00				16 09				16 36		17 00	
Folkestone West	d		14 11			15 02					15 11			16 02				16 11				16 38		17 02	
Sandling	d		14 16								15 16							16 16				16 43			
Westenhanger	d		14 19								15 19							16 19				16 46			
Sturry	d				14 37								15 35										16 36		
Canterbury West ■	d			14 25	14 42			15 05				15 25	15 42			16 05				16 25			16 41		
Chartham	d							15 10								16 10									
Chilham	d							15 13								16 13									
Wye	d				14 54			15 20					15 54			16 20							16 53		
Ashford International	a		14 28	14 41	15 00	15 15		15 27			15 28	15 41	16 00	16 15		16 27		16 28		16 41		16 55	16 59	17 15	
	d		14 32	14 43	15 02	15 16					15 32	15 43	16 02	16 16				16 32		16 45		17 05		17 16	
Pluckley	d		14 38		15 08						15 38		16 08					16 38				17 11			
Headcorn	d		14 45		15 15						15 45		16 15					16 45				17 18			
Staplehurst	d		14 50		15 20						15 50		16 20					16 50				17 23			
Marden	d		14 54		15 24						15 54		16 24					16 54				17 27			
Maidstone West ■ 208	d	14 28								15 28							16 28				16 58				
Paddock Wood ■	d	14 47	15 00		15 30					15 47	16 00		16 30				16a47	17 00			17a17	17 32			
Tonbridge ■	a	14 55	15 08		15 38					15 55	16 08		16 38					17 07				17 40			
	d		15 09		15 39						16 09		16 39					17 09				17 41			
Hildenborough	a																								
Sevenoaks ■	a		15 18		15 48						16 18		16 48					17 17				17 49			
Orpington ■	a												16 57									17 58			
London Bridge ■ ⊖	a		15 41		16 11						16 41		17 16					17 42				18 19			
London Cannon Street ■ ⊖	a																								
London Waterloo (East) ■ ⊖	a		15 47		16 17						16 48		17 24					17 48				18 26			
London Charing Cross ■ ⊖	a		15 52		16 22						16 54		17 30					17 54				18 33			
Ebbsfleet International	a			15 02		15 35	15 46					16 02		16 35	16 46					17 04				17 35	17 46
Stratford International ⊖	a			15 14		15 47	16 02					16 14		16 47	17 00					17 16				17 47	17 58
St Pancras Intl. ■ ⊖	a			15 21		15 54	16 10					16 21		16 54	17 10					17 23				17 54	18 10

		SE	SE	SE		SE	SE	SE	SE	SE	SE	SE	SE	SE		SE	SE	SE	SE	SE	SE	SE	SE	SE	
		◇■		◇■		◇	◇■	◇■	◇	◇	◇■		◇■	◇		◇		◇■	◇■	◇		◇■	◇		
Margate ■	d					16 53			17 02					17 53									18 53		
Broadstairs	d					16 59			17 08					17 59									18 59		
Ramsgate ■	d					17 05	16 50	17 18	17 13	17 20				18 05				17 50	18 10			18 23	19 05		
Minster ■	d							17 24											18 20						
Sandwich	d						17 02		17 26									18 02				18 35			
Deal	d						17 08		17 32									18 08				18 41			
Walmer	d						17 11		17 35									18 11				18 44			
Martin Mill	d						17 16		17 39									18 16				18 49			
Dover Priory ■	a						17 24		17 48									18 24				18 57			
	d			16 58			17 25		17 49				17 58					18 25		18 49		18 58			
Folkestone Central	d			17 09			17 36		18 00				18 09					18 36		19 00		19 09			
Folkestone West	d			17 11			17 38		18 02				18 11					18 38		19 02		19 11			
Sandling	d			17 16			17 43						18 16					18 43				19 16			
Westenhanger	d			17 19			17 46						18 19					18 46				19 19			
Sturry	d							17 35											18 31						
Canterbury West ■	d	17 05				17 25		17 40			18 05			18 25					18 36				19 25		
Chartham	d	17 10									18 10								18 41						
Chilham	d	17 13									18 13								18 44						
Wye	d	17 20						17 52			18 20								18 51						
Ashford International	a	17 28		17 28		17 41	17 55	17 58	18 15		18 27		18 28	18 41				18 55	18 58	19 15		19 28	19 41		
	d			17 32		17 43	18 02		18 16				18 32	18 43				19 02		19 16		19 32	19 43		
Pluckley	d			17 38			18 08						18 38					19 08				19 38			
Headcorn	d			17 45			18 15						18 45					19 15				19 45			
Staplehurst	d			17 50			18 20						18 50					19 20				19 50			
Marden	d			17 54			18 24						18 54					19 24				19 54			
Maidstone West ■ 208	d		17 28									18 19				18 42	18 48				19 18			19 58	
Paddock Wood ■	d		17a47	18 00			18 30					18a38	19 00				19a07	19 30			19a37	20 00		20 17	
Tonbridge ■	a			18 08			18 40						19 08					19 38				20 08		20 25	
	d			18 09			18 42						19 09					19 39				20 09			
Hildenborough	a																								
Sevenoaks ■	a			18 18			18 50						19 18					19 48				20 18			
Orpington ■	a																								
London Bridge ■ ⊖	a			18 42			19 13						19 41					20 11				20 41			
London Cannon Street ■ ⊖	a																								
London Waterloo (East) ■ ⊖	a			18 48			19 19						19 47					20 17				20 47			
London Charing Cross ■ ⊖	a			18 57			19 23						19 52					20 22				20 52			
Ebbsfleet International	a					18 02			18 35	18 49				19 02		19 12				19 35			20 02		
Stratford International ⊖	a					18 14			18 47	19 02				19 14		19 24				19 47			20 14		
St Pancras Intl. ■ ⊖	a					18 23			18 54	19 10				19 21		19 31				19 54			20 21		

Table T207-R

Mondays to Fridays

21 May to 7 December

Margate, Ramsgate, Canterbury West, Dover, Folkestone, Ashford International - Tonbridge and London

		SE	SE	SE	SE	SE	SE	SE	SE	SE		SE	SE	SE	SE	SE	SE	SE	SE	SE		SE	SE	SE	SE
		◇■	◇	◇	◇■	◇		◇■	◇	◇		◇■	◇		◇■	◇	◇	◇■	◇			■	◇		■
Margate ■	d					19 53							20 53			21 00			21 53					22 53	
Broadstairs	d					19 59							20 59			21 06			21 59					22 59	
Ramsgate ■	d	19 16		19 20	19 23	20 05		20 16		20 20		20 23	21 05		21 16	21 12	21 20		22 05			22 16	22 12	23 05	23 12
Minster ■	d	19 22						20 22							21 22							22 22			
Sandwich	d				19 35							20 35				21 25							22 25		23 25
Deal	d				19 41							20 41				21 31							22 31		23 31
Walmer	d				19 44							20 44				21 34							22 34		23 34
Martin Mill	d				19 49							20 49				21 38							22 38		23 38
Dover Priory ■	a				19 57							20 57				21 47							22 47		23 47
	d		19 49		19 58				20 49			20 58				21 49		21 58					22 49		23 49
Folkestone Central	d		20 00		20 09				21 00			21 09				22 00		22 09					23 00		23 59
Folkestone West	d		20 02		20 11				21 02			21 11				22 02		22 11					23 02		00 02
Sandling	d				20 16							21 16						22 16							00 07
Westenhanger	d				20 19							21 19						22 19							00 10
Sturry	d	19 34						20 34							21 34							22 34			
Canterbury West ■	d	19 39				20 25		20 39					21 25		21 39				22 25			22 39		23 25	
Chartham	d	19 44						20 44							21 44							22 44			
Chilham	d	19 47						20 47							21 47							22 47			
Wye	d	19 54						20 54							21 54							22 54			
Ashford International	a	20 00	20 15		20 28	20 41		21 00	21 15			21 28	21 41		22 00	22 15		22 28	22 41			23 00	23 15	23 41	00 20
	d	20 02	20 16		20 32	20 43		21 02	21 16			21 32	21 43		22 02	22 16		22 32	22 43			23 02	23 16		
Pluckley	d	20 08			20 38			21 08				21 38			22 08			22 38				23 08			
Headcorn	d	20 15			20 45			21 15				21 45			22 15			22 45				23 15			
Staplehurst	d	20 20			20 50			21 20				21 50			22 20			22 50				23 20			
Marden	d	20 24			20 54			21 24				21 54			22 24			22 54				23 24			
Maidstone West ■ 208	d						20 58							21 58						22 58					
Paddock Wood ■	d	20 30			21 00		21 17	21 30				22 00		22 17	22 30			23 00		23 17		23 30			
Tonbridge ■	a	20 38			21 08		21 25	21 38				22 08		22 25	22 38			23 08		23 25		23 39			
	d	20 39			21 09			21 39				22 09			22 39										
Hildenborough	a																								
Sevenoaks ■	a	20 48			21 18			21 48				22 18			22 48										
Orpington ■	a																								
London Bridge ■ ⊖	a	21 11			21 41			22 11				22 41			23 11										
London Cannon Street ■ ⊖	a																								
London Waterloo (East) ■ ⊖	a	21 17			21 47			22 17				22 47			23 17										
London Charing Cross ■ ⊖	a	21 22			21 52			22 22				22 52			23 22										
Ebbsfleet International	a		20 35	20 46		21 02			21 35	21 46			22 02			22 35	22 46		23 02				23 35		
Stratford International ⊖	a		20 47	21 02		21 14			21 47	21 58			22 14			22 47	22 58		23 14				23 47		
St Pancras Intl. ■ ⊖	a		20 54	21 10		21 21			21 54	22 06			22 21			22 54	23 06		23 21				23 54		

Saturdays

26 May to 8 December

		SE	SE	SE	SE	SE	SE	SE	SE	SE		SE	SE	SE	SE	SE	SE	SE	SE	SE		SE	SE	SE	SE
		■	◇■	◇	◇■	◇		◇■	◇	◇■		◇	◇		◇■	◇	◇■	◇	◇	◇■			◇■	◇	◇■
Margate ■	d								05 53							06 53		06 57						07 53	
Broadstairs	d								05 59							06 59		07 03						07 59	
Ramsgate ■	d			05 05	05 15				06 05	06 15		06 12	06 20			07 05	07 15	07 12	07 20					08 05	08 17
Minster ■	d				05 21					06 21							07 21								08 23
Sandwich	d											06 25						07 25							
Deal	d											06 31						07 31							
Walmer	d											06 34						07 34							
Martin Mill	d											06 38						07 38							
Dover Priory ■	a											06 47						07 47							
	d		04 58			05 49		05 58				06 49			06 58			07 49					07 58		
Folkestone Central	d		05 09			06 00		06 09				07 00			07 09			08 00					08 09		
Folkestone West	d	00 02	05 11			06 02		06 11				07 02			07 11			08 02					08 11		
Sandling	d	00 07	05 16					06 16							07 16								08 16		
Westenhanger	d	00 10	05 19					06 19							07 19								08 19		
Sturry	d				05 32					06 32							07 32								08 35
Canterbury West ■	d			05 25	05 37				06 25	06 37						07 25	07 37			08 05				08 25	08 40
Chartham	d				05 42					06 42							07 42			08 10					
Chilham	d				05 45					06 45							07 45			08 13					
Wye	d				05 52					06 52							07 52			08 20					08 52
Ashford International	a	00 20	05 28	05 41	05 58	06 15		06 28	06 41	06 58		07 15			07 28	07 41	07 58	08 15		08 27			08 30	08 41	08 58
	d		05 32	05 43	06 02	06 16		06 32	06 43	07 02		07 16			07 32	07 43	08 02	08 16					08 32	08 43	09 02
Pluckley	d		05 38		06 08			06 38		07 08					07 38		08 08						08 38		09 08
Headcorn	d		05 45		06 15			06 45		07 15					07 45		08 15						08 45		09 15
Staplehurst	d		05 50		06 20			06 50		07 20					07 50		08 20						08 50		09 20
Marden	d		05 54		06 24			06 54		07 24					07 54		08 24						08 54		09 24
Maidstone West ■ 208	d						06 28							07 28								08 28			
Paddock Wood ■	d		06 00		06 30		06 47	07 00		07 30				07 47	08 00		08 30					08 47	09 00		09 30
Tonbridge ■	a		06 08		06 38		06 55	07 08		07 38				07 55	08 08		08 38					08 55	09 08		09 38
	d		06 09		06 39			07 09		07 39					08 09		08 39						09 09		09 39
Hildenborough	a																								
Sevenoaks ■	a		06 18		06 48			07 18		07 48					08 18		08 48						09 18		09 48
Orpington ■	a																								
London Bridge ■ ⊖	a		06 41		07 11			07 41		08 11					08 41		09 11						09 41		10 11
London Cannon Street ■ ⊖	a																								
London Waterloo (East) ■ ⊖	a		06 47		07 17			07 47		08 17					08 47		09 17						09 47		10 17
London Charing Cross ■ ⊖	a		06 52		07 22			07 52		08 22					08 52		09 22						09 52		10 22
Ebbsfleet International	a			06 02		06 35			07 02			07 35	07 46			08 02		08 35	08 46					09 02	
Stratford International ⊖	a			06 14		06 47			07 14			07 47	07 58			08 14		08 47	08 58					09 14	
St Pancras Intl. ■ ⊖	a			06 21		06 54			07 21			07 54	08 06			08 21		08 55	09 06					09 21	

Table T207-R

Saturdays

26 May to 8 December

Margate, Ramsgate, Canterbury West, Dover, Folkestone, Ashford International - Tonbridge and London

	SE ◇	SE ◇	SE ◇■	SE	SE ◇■	SE ◇	SE ◇■	SE ◇	SE ◇	SE ◇■	SE	SE ◇■	SE ◇	SE ◇■	SE ◇	SE ◇	SE ◇■	SE	SE ◇■	SE ◇	SE ◇■	SE ◇
Margate ■ d						08 53		08 59					09 53		09 59					10 53		10 59
Broadstairs d						08 59		09 05					09 59		10 05					10 59		11 05
Ramsgate ■ d	08 12	08 20				09 05	09 17	09 12	09 20				10 05	10 19	10 12	10 20				11 05	11 19	11 12
Minster ■ d							09 23							10 25							11 25	
Sandwich d	08 25							09 25							10 25							11 25
Deal d	08 31							09 31							10 31							11 31
Walmer d	08 34							09 34							10 34							11 34
Martin Mill d	08 38							09 38							10 38							11 38
Dover Priory ■ a	08 47							09 47							10 47							11 47
d	08 49				08 58			09 49				09 58			10 49				10 58			11 49
Folkestone Central d	09 00				09 09			10 00				10 09			11 00				11 09			12 00
Folkestone West d	09 02				09 11			10 02				10 11			11 02				11 11			12 02
Sandling d					09 16							10 16							11 16			
Westenhanger d					09 19							10 19							11 19			
Sturry d							09 35							10 37							11 37	
Canterbury West ■ d			09 05			09 25	09 40			10 05			10 25	10 42			11 05			11 25	11 42	
Chartham d			09 10							10 10							11 10					
Chilham d			09 13							10 13							11 13					
Wye d			09 20				09 52			10 20				10 54			11 20				11 54	
Ashford International a	09 15		09 27		09 30	09 41	09 58	10 15		10 27		10 30	10 41	11 00	11 15		11 27		11 28	11 41	12 00	12 15
d	09 16				09 32	09 43	10 02	10 16				10 32	10 43	11 02	11 16				11 32	11 43	12 02	12 16
Pluckley d					09 38		10 08					10 38		11 08					11 38		12 08	
Headcorn d					09 45		10 15					10 45		11 15					11 45		12 15	
Staplehurst d					09 50		10 20					10 50		11 20					11 50		12 20	
Marden d					09 54		10 24					10 54		11 24					11 54		12 24	
Maidstone West ■ 208 d				09 28							10 28							11 28				
Paddock Wood ■ d				09 47	10 00		10 30				10 47	11 00		11 30				11 47	12 00		12 30	
Tonbridge ■ a				09 55	10 08		10 38				10 55	11 08		11 38				11 55	12 08		12 38	
d					10 09		10 39					11 09		11 39					12 09		12 39	
Hildenborough a																						
Sevenoaks ■ a					10 18		10 48					11 18		11 48					12 18		12 48	
Orpington ■ a																						
London Bridge ■ ⊖ a					10 41		11 11					11 41		12 11					12 41		13 11	
London Cannon Street ■ ⊖ a																						
London Waterloo (East) ■ ⊖ a					10 47		11 17					11 47		12 17					12 47		13 17	
London Charing Cross ■ ⊖ a					10 52		11 22					11 52		12 22					12 52		13 22	
Ebbsfleet International a	09 35	09 46				10 02		10 35	10 46				11 02		11 35	11 46				12 02		12 35
Stratford International ⊖ a	09 47	09 58				10 14		10 47	10 59				11 14		11 47	11 58				12 14		12 47
St Pancras Intl. ■ ⊖ a	09 54	10 06				10 21		10 55	11 06				11 21		11 54	12 06				12 21		12 55

	SE ◇	SE ◇■	SE	SE ◇■	SE ◇	SE ◇■	SE ◇	SE ◇	SE ◇■	SE	SE ◇■	SE ◇	SE ◇■	SE ◇	SE ◇	SE ◇■	SE	SE ◇■	SE ◇	SE ◇■	SE ◇
Margate ■ d					11 53		11 59					12 53		12 59					13 53		13 59
Broadstairs d					11 59		12 05					12 59		13 05					13 59		14 05
Ramsgate ■ d	11 20				12 05	12 19	12 12	12 20				13 05	13 19	13 12	13 20				14 05	14 19	14 12
Minster ■ d						12 25							13 25							14 25	
Sandwich d							12 25							13 25							14 25
Deal d							12 31							13 31							14 31
Walmer d							12 34							13 34							14 34
Martin Mill d							12 38							13 38							14 38
Dover Priory ■ a							12 47							13 47							14 47
d				11 58			12 49				12 58			13 49				13 58			14 49
Folkestone Central d				12 09			13 00				13 09			14 00				14 09			15 00
Folkestone West d				12 11			13 02				13 11			14 02				14 11			15 02
Sandling d				12 16							13 16							14 16			
Westenhanger d				12 19							13 19							14 19			
Sturry d						12 37							13 37							14 37	
Canterbury West ■ d		12 05			12 25	12 42			13 05			13 25	13 42			14 05			14 25	14 42	
Chartham d		12 10							13 10							14 10					
Chilham d		12 13							13 13							14 13					
Wye d		12 20				12 54			13 20				13 54			14 20				14 54	
Ashford International a		12 27		12 29	12 41	13 00	13 15		13 27		13 28	13 41	14 00	14 15		14 27		14 28	14 41	15 00	15 15
d				12 32	12 43	13 02	13 16				13 32	13 43	14 02	14 16				14 32	14 43	15 02	15 16
Pluckley d				12 38		13 08					13 38		14 08					14 38		15 08	
Headcorn d				12 45		13 15					13 45		14 15					14 45		15 15	
Staplehurst d				12 50		13 20					13 50		14 20					14 50		15 20	
Marden d				12 54		13 24					13 54		14 24					14 54		15 24	
Maidstone West ■ 208 d			12 28							13 28							14 28				
Paddock Wood ■ d			12 47	13 00		13 30				13 47	14 00		14 30				14 47	15 00		15 30	
Tonbridge ■ a			12 55	13 08		13 38				13 55	14 08		14 38				14 55	15 08		15 38	
d				13 09		13 39					14 09		14 39					15 09		15 39	
Hildenborough a																					
Sevenoaks ■ a				13 18		13 48					14 18		14 48					15 18		15 48	
Orpington ■ a																					
London Bridge ■ ⊖ a				13 41		14 11					14 41		15 11					15 41		16 11	
London Cannon Street ■ ⊖ a																					
London Waterloo (East) ■ ⊖ a				13 47		14 17					14 47		15 17					15 47		16 17	
London Charing Cross ■ ⊖ a				13 52		14 22					14 52		15 22					15 52		16 22	
Ebbsfleet International a	12 46				13 02		13 35	13 46				14 02		14 35	14 46				15 02		15 35
Stratford International ⊖ a	12 58				13 14		13 47	14 02				14 14		14 47	14 59				15 14		15 47
St Pancras Intl. ■ ⊖ a	13 06				13 21		13 54	14 09				14 21		14 54	15 07				15 21		15 54

Table T207-R

Saturdays

26 May to 8 December

Margate, Ramsgate, Canterbury West, Dover, Folkestone, Ashford International - Tonbridge and London

	SE ◇	SE ◇■	SE	SE ◇■	SE ◇	SE ◇■	SE ◇	SE ◇	SE ◇■	SE	SE ◇■	SE ◇	SE ◇■	SE ◇	SE ◇	SE ◇■	SE	SE ◇■	SE ◇	SE ◇■	SE ◇	SE ◇
Margate ■ d					14 53		14 59					15 53		15 59					16 53		16 59	
Broadstairs d					14 59		15 05					15 59		16 05					16 59		17 05	
Ramsgate ■ d	14 20				15 05	15 19	15 12	15 20				16 05	16 19	16 12	16 20				17 05	17 19	17 12	17 20
Minster ■ d						15 25							16 25							17 25		
Sandwich d							15 25							16 25							17 25	
Deal d							15 31							16 31							17 31	
Walmer d							15 34							16 34							17 34	
Martin Mill d							15 38							16 38							17 38	
Dover Priory ■ a							15 47							16 47							17 47	
d				14 58			15 49				15 58			16 49				16 58			17 49	
Folkestone Central d				15 09			16 00				16 09			17 00				17 09			18 00	
Folkestone West d				15 11			16 02				16 11			17 02				17 11			18 02	
Sandling d				15 16							16 16							17 16				
Westenhanger d				15 19							16 19							17 19				
Sturry d						15 37							16 37							17 37		
Canterbury West ■ d		15 05			15 25	15 42			16 05			16 25	16 42			17 05			17 25	17 42		
Chartham d		15 10							16 10							17 10						
Chilham d		15 13							16 13							17 13						
Wye d		15 20				15 54			16 20				16 54			17 20				17 54		
Ashford International a		15 27		15 28	15 41	16 00	16 15		16 27		16 28	16 41	17 00	17 15		17 27		17 28	17 41	18 00	18 15	
d				15 32	15 46	16 02	16 16				16 32	16 43	17 02	17 16				17 32	17 43	18 02	18 16	
Pluckley d				15 38		16 08					16 38		17 08					17 38		18 08		
Headcorn d				15 45		16 15					16 45		17 15					17 45		18 15		
Staplehurst d				15 50		16 20					16 50		17 20					17 50		18 20		
Marden d				15 54		16 24					16 54		17 24					17 54		18 24		
Maidstone West ■ 208 d			15 28							16 28							17 28					
Paddock Wood ■ d			15 47	16 00		16 30				16 47	17 00		17 30				17 47	18 00		18 30		
Tonbridge ■ a			15 55	16 08		16 38				16 55	17 08		17 38				17 55	18 08		18 38		
d				16 09		16 39					17 09		17 39					18 09		18 39		
Hildenborough a																						
Sevenoaks ■ a				16 18		16 48					17 18		17 48					18 18		18 48		
Orpington ■ a																						
London Bridge ■ ⊖ a				16 41		17 11					17 41		18 11					18 41		19 11		
London Cannon Street ■ ⊖ a																						
London Waterloo (East) ■ ⊖ a				16 47		17 17					17 47		18 17					18 47		19 17		
London Charing Cross ■ ⊖ a				16 52		17 22					17 52		18 22					18 52		19 22		
Ebbsfleet International a	15 46				16 05		16 35	16 46				17 02		17 35	17 46				18 02		18 35	18 46
Stratford International ⊖ a	16 02				16 17		16 47	16 58				17 14		17 47	17 58				18 14		18 47	18 58
St Pancras Intl. ■ ⊖ a	16 09				16 24		16 54	17 06				17 21		17 54	18 09				18 21		18 54	19 06

	SE ◇■	SE	SE ◇■	SE ◇	SE ◇■	SE ◇	SE ◇	SE ◇■	SE	SE ◇■	SE ◇	SE ◇■	SE ◇	SE ◇	SE ◇■	SE	SE ◇■	SE ◇	SE ◇■	SE ◇	SE ◇
Margate ■ d				17 53		17 59					18 53		18 59					19 53		19 59	
Broadstairs d				17 59		18 05					18 59		19 05					19 59		20 05	
Ramsgate ■ d				18 05	18 19	18 12	18 20				19 05	19 19	19 12	19 20				20 05	20 19	20 12	20 20
Minster ■ d					18 25							19 25							20 25		
Sandwich d						18 25							19 25							20 25	
Deal d						18 31							19 31							20 31	
Walmer d						18 34							19 34							20 34	
Martin Mill d						18 38							19 38							20 38	
Dover Priory ■ a						18 47							19 47							20 47	
d			17 58			18 49				18 58			19 49				19 58			20 49	
Folkestone Central d			18 09			19 00				19 09			20 00				20 09			21 00	
Folkestone West d			18 11			19 02				19 11			20 02				20 11			21 02	
Sandling d			18 16							19 16							20 16				
Westenhanger d			18 19							19 19							20 19				
Sturry d					18 37							19 37							20 37		
Canterbury West ■ d	18 05			18 25	18 42			19 05			19 25	19 42			20 05			20 25	20 42		
Chartham d	18 10							19 10							20 10						
Chilham d	18 13							19 13							20 13						
Wye d	18 20				18 54			19 20				19 54			20 20				20 54		
Ashford International a	18 27		18 28	18 41	19 00	19 15		19 27		19 28	19 41	20 00	20 15		20 27		20 28	20 41	21 00	21 15	
d			18 32	18 43	19 02	19 16				19 32	19 43	20 02	20 16				20 32	20 43	21 02	21 16	
Pluckley d			18 38		19 08					19 38		20 08					20 38		21 08		
Headcorn d			18 45		19 15					19 45		20 15					20 45		21 15		
Staplehurst d			18 50		19 20					19 50		20 20					20 50		21 20		
Marden d			18 54		19 24					19 54		20 24					20 54		21 24		
Maidstone West ■ 208 d		18 28							19 28							20 28					
Paddock Wood ■ d		18 47	19 00		19 30				19 47	20 00		20 30				20 47	21 00		21 30		
Tonbridge ■ a		18 55	19 08		19 38				19 55	20 08		20 38				20 55	21 08		21 38		
d			19 09		19 39					20 09		20 39					21 09		21 39		
Hildenborough a																					
Sevenoaks ■ a			19 18		19 48					20 18		20 48					21 18		21 48		
Orpington ■ a																					
London Bridge ■ ⊖ a			19 41		20 11					20 41		21 11					21 41		22 11		
London Cannon Street ■ ⊖ a																					
London Waterloo (East) ■ ⊖ a			19 47		20 17					20 47		21 17					21 47		22 17		
London Charing Cross ■ ⊖ a			19 52		20 22					20 52		21 22					21 52		22 22		
Ebbsfleet International a				19 02		19 35	19 46				20 02		20 35	20 46				21 02		21 35	21 46
Stratford International ⊖ a				19 14		19 47	19 58				20 14		20 47	21 02				21 14		21 47	21 58
St Pancras Intl. ■ ⊖ a				19 21		19 54	20 06				20 21		20 54	21 09				21 21		21 54	22 06

Table T207-R

Saturdays
26 May to 8 December

Margate, Ramsgate, Canterbury West, Dover, Folkestone, Ashford International - Tonbridge and London

		SE ◇1	SE	SE ◇1	SE ◇	SE ◇1	SE ◇	SE ◇	SE	SE ◇1	SE ◇	SE 1	SE ◇	SE	SE	SE 1
Margate 4	d				20 53		20 59				21 53		21 59		22 53	
Broadstairs	d				20 59		21 05				21 59		22 05		22 59	
Ramsgate 4	d				21 05	21 16	21 12	21 20			22 05	22 16	22 12		23 05	23 12
Minster 4	d					21 22						22 22				
Sandwich	d						21 25						22 25			23 25
Deal	d						21 31						22 31			23 31
Walmer	d						21 34						22 34			23 34
Martin Mill	d						21 38						22 38			23 38
Dover Priory 4	a						21 47						22 47			23 47
	d			20 58			21 49			21 58			22 49	22 58		23 49
Folkestone Central	d			21 09			22 00			22 09			23 00	23 09		23 59
Folkestone West	d			21 11			22 02			22 11			23 02	23 11		00 02
Sandling	d			21 16						22 16				23 16		00 07
Westenhanger	d			21 19						22 19				23 19		00 10
Sturry	d					21 34						22 34				
Canterbury West 4	d	21 05			21 25	21 39					22 25	22 39			23 25	
Chartham	d	21 10				21 44						22 44				
Chilham	d	21 13				21 47						22 47				
Wye	d	21 20				21 54						22 54				
Ashford International	a	21 27		21 28	21 41	22 00	22 15			22 28	22 41	23 00	23 15	23 29	23 41	00 20
	d			21 32	21 43	22 02	22 16			22 32	22 43	23 02	23 16			
Pluckley	d			21 38		22 08				22 38		23 08				
Headcorn	d			21 45		22 15				22 45		23 15				
Staplehurst	d			21 50		22 20				22 50		23 20				
Marden	d			21 54		22 24				22 54		23 24				
Maidstone West 4 208	d		21 28						22 28							
Paddock Wood 4	d		21 47	22 00		22 30			22 47	23 00		23 30				
Tonbridge 4	a		21 55	22 08		22 38			22 55	23 08		23 39				
	d			22 09		22 39										
Hildenborough	a															
Sevenoaks 4	a			22 18		22 48										
Orpington 4	a															
London Bridge 4 ⊖	a			22 41		23 11										
London Cannon Street 4 ⊖	a															
London Waterloo (East) 4 ⊖	a			22 47		23 17										
London Charing Cross 4 ⊖	a			22 52		23 22										
Ebbsfleet International	a				22 02		22 35	22 46			23 02		23 35			
Stratford International ⊖	a				22 14		22 47	22 58			23 14		23 47			
St Pancras Intl. 15 ⊖	a				22 21		22 54	23 06			23 21		23 54			

Sundays
20 May to 2 December

		SE 1 A	SE ◇1	SE	SE ◇1	SE ◇1	SE ◇	SE	SE ◇1	SE ◇	SE ◇1	SE ◇	SE	SE ◇1	SE ◇	SE ◇	SE ◇1	SE ◇1	SE ◇	SE	SE ◇1	SE ◇	SE ◇
Margate 4	d											07 53							08 53				
Broadstairs	d											07 59							08 59				
Ramsgate 4	d								07 16	07 12		08 05		08 16	08 12	08 20			09 05		09 20	09 12	09 20
Minster 4	d								07 22					08 22							09 26		
Sandwich	d									07 25					08 25							09 25	
Deal	d									07 31					08 31							09 31	
Walmer	d									07 34					08 34							09 34	
Martin Mill	d									07 38					08 38							09 38	
Dover Priory 4	a									07 47					08 47							09 47	
	d									07 49	07 58				08 49			08 58				09 49	
Folkestone Central	d									08 00	08 09				09 00			09 09				10 00	
Folkestone West	d	00 02								08 02	08 11				09 02			09 11				10 02	
Sandling	d	00 07									08 16							09 16					
Westenhanger	d	00 10									08 19							09 19					
Sturry	d								07 34					08 34							09 38		
Canterbury West 4	d								07 39			08 25		08 39			09 04		09 25		09 43		
Chartham	d								07 44					08 44			09 09						
Chilham	d								07 47					08 47			09 12						
Wye	d								07 55					08 55			09 19				09 55		
Ashford International	a	00 20							08 01	08 15	08 28	08 41		09 01	09 15		09 26	09 28	09 41		10 01	10 15	
	d		06 31		07 03	07 31	07 43		08 03	08 16	08 31	08 43		09 03	09 16			09 31	09 43		10 03	10 16	
Pluckley	d		06 37			07 37					08 37							09 37					
Headcorn	d		06 44		07 14	07 44			08 14		08 44			09 14				09 44			10 14		
Staplehurst	d		06 48		07 18	07 48			08 18		08 48			09 18				09 48			10 18		
Marden	d		06 52		07 22	07 52			08 22		08 52			09 22				09 52			10 22		
Maidstone West 4 208	d			07 00				08 00					09 00							10 00			
Paddock Wood 4	d		06 58	07 19	07 28	07 58		08 19	08 28		08 58		09 19	09 28				09 58		10 19	10 28		
Tonbridge 4	a		07 06	07 27	07 36	08 06		08 27	08 36		09 06		09 27	09 36				10 06		10 27	10 36		
	d		07 07		07 37	08 07			08 37		09 07			09 37				10 07			10 37		
Hildenborough	a																						
Sevenoaks 4	a		07 16		07 46	08 16			08 46		09 16			09 46				10 16			10 46		
Orpington 4	a		07 25		07 55	08 25			08 55		09 25			09 55				10 25			10 55		
London Bridge 4 ⊖	a		07 41		08 11	08 41			09 11		09 41			10 11				10 41			11 11		
London Cannon Street 4 ⊖	a																						
London Waterloo (East) 4 ⊖	a		07 47		08 17	08 47			09 17		09 47			10 17				10 47			11 17		
London Charing Cross 4 ⊖	a		07 52		08 22	08 52			09 22		09 52			10 22				10 52			11 22		
Ebbsfleet International	a						08 02			08 35		09 02			09 35	09 46			10 02			10 35	10 46
Stratford International ⊖	a						08 14			08 47		09 14			09 47	09 58			10 14			10 47	10 58
St Pancras Intl. 15 ⊖	a						08 21			08 54		09 21			09 54	10 06			10 21			10 54	11 06

A not 20 May

Table T207-R

Sundays
20 May to 2 December

Margate, Ramsgate, Canterbury West, Dover, Folkestone, Ashford International - Tonbridge and London

		SE ◇1	SE ◇1	SE ◇	SE	SE ◇1	SE ◇	SE ◇	SE ◇1	SE ◇1	SE ◇	SE	SE ◇1	SE ◇	SE ◇	SE ◇1	SE ◇1	SE ◇	SE	SE ◇1	SE ◇	SE ◇	SE ◇1
Margate 4	d			09 53			09 59				10 53			10 59				11 53			11 59		
Broadstairs	d			09 59			10 05				10 59			11 05				11 59			12 05		
Ramsgate 4	d			10 05		10 20	10 12	10 20			11 05		11 20	11 12	11 20			12 05		12 20	12 12	12 20	
Minster 4	d					10 26							11 26							12 26			
Sandwich	d						10 25							11 25							12 25		
Deal	d						10 31							11 31							12 31		
Walmer	d						10 34							11 34							12 34		
Martin Mill	d						10 38							11 38							12 38		
Dover Priory 4	a						10 47							11 47							12 47		
	d		09 58				10 49			10 58				11 49			11 58				12 49		
Folkestone Central	d		10 09				11 00			11 09				12 00			12 09				13 00		
Folkestone West	d		10 11				11 02			11 11				12 02			12 11				13 02		
Sandling	d		10 16							11 16							12 16						
Westenhanger	d		10 19							11 19							12 19						
Sturry	d					10 38							11 38							12 38			
Canterbury West 4	d	10 04		10 25		10 43			11 04		11 25		11 43			12 04		12 25		12 43			13 04
Chartham	d	10 09							11 09							12 09							13 09
Chilham	d	10 12							11 12							12 12							13 12
Wye	d	10 19				10 55			11 19				11 55			12 19				12 55			13 19
Ashford International	a	10 26	10 28	10 41		11 01	11 15		11 26	11 29	11 41		12 01	12 15		12 26	12 28	12 41		13 01	13 15		13 26
	d		10 31	10 43		11 03	11 16			11 31	11 43		12 03	12 16			12 31	12 43		13 03	13 16		
Pluckley	d		10 37							11 37							12 37						
Headcorn	d		10 44			11 14				11 44			12 14				12 44			13 14			
Staplehurst	d		10 48			11 18				11 48			12 18				12 48			13 18			
Marden	d		10 52			11 22				11 52			12 22				12 52			13 22			
Maidstone West 4 208	d				11 00							12 00							13 00				
Paddock Wood 4	d		10 58		11 19	11 28				11 58		12 19	12 28				12 58		13 19	13 28			
Tonbridge 4	a		11 06		11 27	11 36				12 06		12 27	12 36				13 06		13 27	13 36			
	d		11 07			11 37				12 07			12 37				13 07			13 37			
Hildenborough	a																						
Sevenoaks 4	a		11 16			11 46				12 16			12 46				13 16			13 46			
Orpington 4	a		11 25			11 55				12 25			12 55				13 25			13 55			
London Bridge 4 ⊖	a		11 41			12 11				12 41			13 11				13 41			14 11			
London Cannon Street 4 ⊖	a																						
London Waterloo (East) 4 ⊖	a		11 47			12 17				12 47			13 17				13 47			14 17			
London Charing Cross 4 ⊖	a		11 52			12 22				12 52			13 22				13 52			14 22			
Ebbsfleet International	a			11 02			11 35	11 46			12 02			12 35	12 46			13 02			13 35	13 46	
Stratford International ⊖	a			11 14			11 47	11 58			12 14			12 47	12 58			13 14			13 47	13 58	
St Pancras Intl. 15 ⊖	a			11 21			11 54	12 05			12 21			12 54	13 06			13 21			13 54	14 06	

		SE ◇1	SE ◇	SE	SE ◇1	SE ◇	SE ◇	SE ◇1	SE ◇1	SE ◇	SE	SE ◇1	SE ◇	SE ◇	SE ◇1	SE ◇1	SE ◇	SE	SE ◇1	SE ◇	SE ◇	SE ◇1
Margate 4	d		12 53			12 59				13 53			13 59				14 53			14 59		
Broadstairs	d		12 59			13 05				13 59			14 05				14 59			15 05		
Ramsgate 4	d		13 05		13 20	13 12	13 20			14 05		14 20	14 12	14 20			15 05		15 20	15 12	15 20	
Minster 4	d				13 26							14 26							15 26			
Sandwich	d					13 25							14 25							15 25		
Deal	d					13 31							14 31							15 31		
Walmer	d					13 34							14 34							15 34		
Martin Mill	d					13 38							14 38							15 38		
Dover Priory 4	a					13 47							14 47							15 47		
	d	12 58				13 49			13 58				14 49			14 58				15 49		
Folkestone Central	d	13 09				14 00			14 09				15 00			15 09				16 00		
Folkestone West	d	13 11				14 02			14 11				15 02			15 11				16 02		
Sandling	d	13 16							14 16							15 16						
Westenhanger	d	13 19							14 19							15 19						
Sturry	d				13 38							14 38							15 38			
Canterbury West 4	d		13 25		13 43			14 04		14 25		14 43			15 04		15 25		15 43			16 04
Chartham	d							14 09							15 09							16 09
Chilham	d							14 12							15 12							16 12
Wye	d				13 55			14 19				14 55			15 19				15 55			16 19
Ashford International	a	13 28	13 41		14 01	14 15		14 26	14 28	14 41		15 01	15 15		15 26	15 28	15 41		16 01	16 15		16 26
	d	13 31	13 43		14 03	14 16			14 31	14 43		15 03	15 16			15 31	15 43		16 03	16 16		
Pluckley	d	13 37							14 37							15 37						
Headcorn	d	13 44			14 14				14 44			15 14				15 44			16 14			
Staplehurst	d	13 48			14 18				14 48			15 18				15 48			16 18			
Marden	d	13 52			14 22				14 52			15 22				15 52			16 22			
Maidstone West 4 208	d			14 00							15 00							16 00				
Paddock Wood 4	d	13 58		14 19	14 28				14 58		15 19	15 28				15 58		16 19	16 28			
Tonbridge 4	a	14 06		14 27	14 36				15 06		15 27	15 36				16 06		16 27	16 36			
	d	14 07			14 37				15 07			15 37				16 07			16 37			
Hildenborough	a																					
Sevenoaks 4	a	14 16			14 46				15 16			15 46				16 16			16 46			
Orpington 4	a	14 25			14 55				15 25			15 55				16 25			16 55			
London Bridge 4 ⊖	a	14 41			15 11				15 41			16 11				16 41			17 11			
London Cannon Street 4 ⊖	a																					
London Waterloo (East) 4 ⊖	a	14 47			15 17				15 47			16 17				16 47			17 17			
London Charing Cross 4 ⊖	a	14 52			15 22				15 52			16 22				16 52			17 22			
Ebbsfleet International	a		14 02			14 35	14 46			15 02			15 35	15 46			16 02			16 35	16 46	
Stratford International ⊖	a		14 14			14 47	14 59			15 14			15 47	16 02			16 14			16 47	16 58	
St Pancras Intl. 15 ⊖	a		14 21			14 54	15 06			15 21			15 54	16 10			16 21			16 54	17 06	

Table T207-R

Sundays
20 May to 2 December

Margate, Ramsgate, Canterbury West, Dover, Folkestone, Ashford International - Tonbridge and London

Station		SE ◇■	SE ◇	SE	SE ◇■	SE ◇	SE ◇	SE ◇■	SE ◇■	SE ◇	SE	SE ◇■
Margate	d		15 53			15 59				16 53		
Broadstairs	d		15 59			16 05				16 59		
Ramsgate	d		16 05		16 20	16 12	16 20			17 05		17 20
Minster	d				16 26							17 26
Sandwich	d					16 25						
Deal	d					16 31						
Walmer	d					16 34						
Martin Mill	d					16 38						
Dover Priory	a					16 47						
	d	15 58				16 49			16 58			
Folkestone Central	d	16 09				17 00			17 09			
Folkestone West	d	16 11				17 02			17 11			
Sandling	d	16 16							17 16			
Westenhanger	d	16 19							17 19			
Sturry	d				16 38							17 38
Canterbury West	d		16 25		16 43			17 04		17 25		17 43
Chartham	d							17 09				
Chilham	d							17 12				
Wye	d				16 55			17 19				17 55
Ashford International	a	16 28	16 41		17 01	17 15		17 26	17 28	17 41		18 01
	d	16 31	16 43		17 03	17 16			17 31	17 43		18 03
Pluckley	d	16 37							17 37			
Headcorn	d	16 44			17 14				17 44			18 14
Staplehurst	d	16 48			17 18				17 48			18 18
Marden	d	16 52			17 22				17 52			18 22
Maidstone West 208	d			17 00							18 00	
Paddock Wood	d	16 58		17 19	17 28				17 58		18 19	18 28
Tonbridge	a	17 06		17 27	17 36				18 06		18 27	18 36
	d	17 07			17 37				18 07			18 37
Hildenborough	a											
Sevenoaks	a	17 16			17 46				18 16			18 46
Orpington	a	17 25			17 55				18 25			18 55
London Bridge ⊖	a	17 41			18 11				18 41			19 11
London Cannon Street ⊖	a											
London Waterloo (East) ⊖	a	17 47			18 17				18 47			19 17
London Charing Cross ⊖	a	17 52			18 22				18 52			19 22
Ebbsfleet International	a		17 02			17 35	17 46			18 02		
Stratford International ⊖	a		17 14			17 47	18 04			18 14		
St Pancras Intl. ⊖	a		17 21			17 55	18 11			18 21		

Station		SE ◇	SE ◇	SE ◇■	SE ◇■	SE ◇	SE	SE ◇■	SE ◇	SE ◇	SE ◇■	SE ◇■
Margate	d	16 59				17 53			17 59			
Broadstairs	d	17 05				17 59			18 05			
Ramsgate	d	17 12	17 20			18 05		18 20	18 12	18 20		
Minster	d							18 26				
Sandwich	d	17 25							18 25			
Deal	d	17 31							18 31			
Walmer	d	17 34							18 34			
Martin Mill	d	17 38							18 38			
Dover Priory	a	17 47							18 47			
	d	17 49			17 58				18 49			18 58
Folkestone Central	d	18 00			18 09				19 00			19 09
Folkestone West	d	18 02			18 11				19 02			19 11
Sandling	d				18 16							19 16
Westenhanger	d				18 19							19 19
Sturry	d							18 38				
Canterbury West	d			18 04		18 25		18 43			19 04	
Chartham	d			18 09							19 09	
Chilham	d			18 12							19 12	
Wye	d			18 19				18 55			19 19	
Ashford International	a	18 15		18 26	18 28	18 41		19 01	19 15		19 26	19 28
	d	18 16			18 31	18 43		19 03	19 16			19 31
Pluckley	d				18 37							19 37
Headcorn	d				18 44			19 14				19 44
Staplehurst	d				18 48			19 18				19 48
Marden	d				18 52			19 22				19 52
Maidstone West 208	d						19 00					
Paddock Wood	d				18 58		19 19	19 28				19 58
Tonbridge	a				19 06		19 27	19 36				20 06
	d				19 07			19 37				20 07
Hildenborough	a											
Sevenoaks	a				19 16			19 46				20 16
Orpington	a				19 25			19 55				20 25
London Bridge ⊖	a				19 41			20 11				20 41
London Cannon Street ⊖	a											
London Waterloo (East) ⊖	a				19 47			20 17				20 47
London Charing Cross ⊖	a				19 52			20 22				20 52
Ebbsfleet International	a	18 35	18 46			19 02			19 35	19 46		
Stratford International ⊖	a	18 47	19 02			19 14			19 47	20 02		
St Pancras Intl. ⊖	a	18 54	19 10			19 21			19 54	20 09		

Station		SE ◇	SE	SE ◇■	SE ◇	SE ◇	SE ◇■	SE ◇	SE	SE ◇■	SE ◇
Margate	d	18 53			18 59			19 53			19 59
Broadstairs	d	18 59			19 05			19 59			20 05
Ramsgate	d	19 05		19 16	19 12	19 20		20 05		20 16	20 12
Minster	d			19 22						20 22	
Sandwich	d				19 25						20 25
Deal	d				19 31						20 31
Walmer	d				19 34						20 34
Martin Mill	d				19 38						20 38
Dover Priory	a				19 47						20 47
	d				19 49		19 58				20 49
Folkestone Central	d				20 00		20 09				21 00
Folkestone West	d				20 02		20 11				21 02
Sandling	d						20 16				
Westenhanger	d						20 19				
Sturry	d			19 34						20 34	
Canterbury West	d	19 25		19 39				20 25		20 39	
Chartham	d			19 44						20 44	
Chilham	d			19 47						20 47	
Wye	d			19 55						20 55	
Ashford International	a	19 41		20 01	20 15		20 28	20 41		21 01	21 15
	d	19 43		20 03	20 16		20 31	20 43		21 03	21 16
Pluckley	d						20 37				
Headcorn	d			20 14			20 44			21 14	
Staplehurst	d			20 18			20 48			21 18	
Marden	d			20 22			20 52			21 22	
Maidstone West 208	d		20 00						21 00		
Paddock Wood	d		20 19	20 28			20 58		21 19	21 28	
Tonbridge	a		20 27	20 36			21 06		21 27	21 36	
	d			20 37			21 07			21 37	
Hildenborough	a										
Sevenoaks	a			20 46			21 16			21 46	
Orpington	a			20 55			21 25			21 55	
London Bridge ⊖	a			21 11			21 41			22 11	
London Cannon Street ⊖	a										
London Waterloo (East) ⊖	a			21 17			21 47			22 17	
London Charing Cross ⊖	a			21 22			21 52			22 22	
Ebbsfleet International	a	20 02			20 35	20 46		21 02			21 35
Stratford International ⊖	a	20 14			20 47	20 58		21 14			21 47
St Pancras Intl. ⊖	a	20 21			20 54	21 05		21 21			21 54

Station		SE ◇	SE ◇■	SE ◇	SE	SE ◇■	SE ◇	SE ◇	SE ■	SE ◇	SE	SE ■
Margate	d			20 53			20 59			21 53		
Broadstairs	d			20 59			21 05			21 59		
Ramsgate	d	20 20		21 05		21 16	21 12	21 20		22 05		22 16
Minster	d					21 22						22 22
Sandwich	d						21 25					
Deal	d						21 31					
Walmer	d						21 34					
Martin Mill	d						21 38					
Dover Priory	a						21 47					
	d		20 58				21 49		21 58			
Folkestone Central	d		21 09				22 00		22 09			
Folkestone West	d		21 11				22 02		22 11			
Sandling	d		21 16						22 16			
Westenhanger	d		21 19						22 19			
Sturry	d					21 34						22 34
Canterbury West	d			21 25		21 39				22 25		22 39
Chartham	d					21 44						22 44
Chilham	d					21 47						22 47
Wye	d					21 55						22 55
Ashford International	a		21 28	21 41		22 01	22 15		22 28	22 41		23 01
	d		21 31	21 43		22 03	22 16			22 43		23 03
Pluckley	d		21 37									23 09
Headcorn	d		21 44			22 14						23 16
Staplehurst	d		21 48			22 18						23 21
Marden	d		21 52			22 22						23 25
Maidstone West 208	d				22 00						23 00	
Paddock Wood	d		21 58		22 19	22 28					23 19	23 30
Tonbridge	a		22 06		22 27	22 36					23 27	23 39
	d		22 07			22 37						
Hildenborough	a											
Sevenoaks	a		22 16			22 46						
Orpington	a		22 25			22 55						
London Bridge ⊖	a		22 41			23 11						
London Cannon Street ⊖	a											
London Waterloo (East) ⊖	a		22 47			23 17						
London Charing Cross ⊖	a		22 52			23 22						
Ebbsfleet International	a	21 46		22 02			22 35	22 46		23 02		
Stratford International ⊖	a	21 59		22 14			22 47	22 58		23 14		
St Pancras Intl. ⊖	a	22 07		22 21			22 54	23 06		23 21		

Table T207-R

Sundays
20 May to 2 December

Margate, Ramsgate, Canterbury West, Dover, Folkestone, Ashford International - Tonbridge and London

Station		SE ◇	SE
Margate	d	21 59	22 53
Broadstairs	d	22 05	22 59
Ramsgate	d	22 12	23 05
Minster	d		
Sandwich	d	22 25	
Deal	d	22 31	
Walmer	d	22 34	
Martin Mill	d	22 38	
Dover Priory	a	22 47	
	d	22 49	
Folkestone Central	d	23 00	
Folkestone West	d	23 02	
Sandling	d		
Westenhanger	d		
Sturry	d		
Canterbury West	d		23 25
Chartham	d		
Chilham	d		
Wye	d		
Ashford International	a	23 15	23 41
	d		
Pluckley	d		
Headcorn	d		
Staplehurst	d		
Marden	d		
Maidstone West 208	d		
Paddock Wood	d		
Tonbridge	a		
	d		
Hildenborough	a		
Sevenoaks	a		
Orpington	a		
London Bridge ⊖	a		
London Cannon Street ⊖	a		
London Waterloo (East) ⊖	a		
London Charing Cross ⊖	a		
Ebbsfleet International	a		
Stratford International ⊖	a		
St Pancras Intl. ⊖	a		

Table T208-F

Strood - Maidstone West and Paddock Wood

Mondays to Fridays
21 May to 7 December

Miles	Station		SE	SE	SE	SE	SE ◇	SE	SE	SE	SE	SE	SE	SE	SE	SE	SE	SE	SE	SE	SE	SE	SE
0	St Pancras International	d					06 25																
5¼	Stratford International	d					06 32																
22	Ebbsfleet International	d					06 43																
25	Gravesend	d					06 48																
33	**Strood**	d	04 35	05 25	06 00	06 35	07 01	07 10	07 52	08 34	09 04	09 34	10 04	10 34	11 04	11 34	12 04	12 34	13 04	13 34	14 04	14 34	15 04
35¼	Cuxton	d	04 39	05 29	06 04	06 39		07 14	07 56	08 38	09 08	09 38	10 08	10 38	11 08	11 38	12 08	12 38	13 08	13 38	14 08	14 38	15 08
37	Halling	d	04 43	05 33	06 08	06 43		07 18	08 00	08 42	09 12	09 42	10 12	10 42	11 12	11 42	12 12	12 42	13 12	13 42	14 12	14 42	15 12
38½	Snodland	d	04 46	05 36	06 11	06 46		07 21	08 03	08 45	09 15	09 45	10 15	10 45	11 15	11 45	12 15	12 45	13 15	13 45	14 15	14 45	15 15
39¾	New Hythe	d	04 48	05 38	06 13	06 48		07 23	08 05	08 47	09 17	09 47	10 17	10 47	11 17	11 47	12 17	12 47	13 17	13 47	14 17	14 47	15 17
40¾	Aylesford	d	04 51	05 41	06 16	06 51		07 26	08 08	08 50	09 20	09 50	10 20	10 50	11 20	11 50	12 20	12 50	13 20	13 50	14 20	14 50	15 20
43¾	Maidstone Barracks	d	04 56	05 46	06 21	06 56		07 31	08 13	08 55	09 25	09 55	10 25	10 55	11 25	11 55	12 25	12 55	13 25	13 55	14 25	14 55	15 25
44¼	**Maidstone West** 208	a	04 58	05 48	06 23	06 58	07 16	07 33	08 15	08 57	09 27	09 57	10 27	10 57	11 27	11 57	12 27	12 57	13 27	13 57	14 27	14 57	15 27
—		d	05 00	05 54	06 24	07 00		07 36	08 16		09 28		10 28		11 28		12 28		13 28		14 28		15 28
46	East Farleigh	d	05 03	05 57	06 27	07 03		07 39	08 19		09 31		10 31		11 31		12 31		13 31		14 31		15 31
49	Wateringbury	d	05 08	06 02	06 32	07 08		07 44	08 24		09 36		10 36		11 36		12 36		13 36		14 36		15 36
50¾	Yalding	d	05 12	06 06	06 36	07 12		07 48	08 28		09 40		10 40		11 40		12 40		13 40		14 40		15 40
52¼	Beltring	d	05 15	06 09	06 39	07 15		07 51	08 31		09 43		10 43		11 43		12 43		13 43		14 43		15 43
54¼	**Paddock Wood**	a	05 20	06 13	06 43	07 19		07 56	08 35		09 47		10 47		11 47		12 47		13 47		14 47		15 47
59½	Tonbridge	a							08 43		09 55		10 55		11 55		12 58		13 55		14 55		15 55

Station		SE	SE	SE	SE	SE ◇	SE	SE ◇	SE	SE ◇	SE	SE	SE	SE	SE	SE	SE	SE
St Pancras International	d					17 16		17 46		18 16								
Stratford International	d					17 23		17 53		18 23								
Ebbsfleet International	d					17 35		18 05		18 35								
Gravesend	d					17 39		18 09		18 39								
Strood	d	15 34	16 04	16 34	17 04	17 50	17 55	18 20	18 24	18 51	18 54	19 34	20 04	20 34	21 04	21 34	22 04	22 34
Cuxton	d	15 38	16 08	16 38	17 08		17 59		18 28		18 58	19 38	20 08	20 38	21 08	21 38	22 08	22 38
Halling	d	15 42	16 12	16 42	17 12		18 03		18 32		19 02	19 42	20 12	20 42	21 12	21 42	22 12	22 42
Snodland	d	15 45	16 15	16 45	17 15	17 58	18 06	18 28	18 35	18 59	19 05	19 45	20 15	20 45	21 15	21 45	22 15	22 45
New Hythe	d	15 47	16 17	16 47	17 17		18 08		18 37		19 07	19 47	20 17	20 47	21 17	21 47	22 17	22 47
Aylesford	d	15 50	16 20	16 50	17 20		18 11		18 40		19 10	19 50	20 20	20 50	21 20	21 50	22 20	22 50
Maidstone Barracks	d	15 55	16 25	16 55	17 25		18 16		18 45		19 15	19 55	20 25	20 55	21 25	21 55	22 25	22 55
Maidstone West 208	a	15 57	16 27	16 57	17 27	18 08	18 18	18 38	18 47	19 09	19 17	19 57	20 29	20 57	21 27	21 57	22 27	22 57
	d		16 28	16 58	17 28		18 19		18 48		19 18	19 58		20 58		21 58		22 58
East Farleigh	d		16 31	17 01	17 31		18 22		18 51		19 21	20 01		21 01		22 01		23 01
Wateringbury	d		16 36	17 06	17 36		18 27		18 56		19 26	20 06		21 06		22 06		23 06
Yalding	d		16 40	17 10	17 40		18 31		19 00		19 30	20 10		21 10		22 10		23 10
Beltring	d		16 43	17 13	17 43		18 34		19 03		19 33	20 13		21 13		22 13		23 13
Paddock Wood	a		16 47	17 17	17 47		18 38		19 07		19 37	20 17		21 17		22 17		23 17
Tonbridge	a											20 25		21 25		22 25		23 25

Saturdays
26 May to 8 December

Station		SE	SE		SE	SE
St Pancras International	d					
Stratford International	d					
Ebbsfleet International	d					
Gravesend	d					
Strood	d	06 04	06 34		22 04	22 34
Cuxton	d	06 08	06 38	and at	22 08	22 38
Halling	d	06 12	06 42	the same	22 12	22 42
Snodland	d	06 15	06 45	minutes	22 15	22 45
New Hythe	d	06 17	06 47	past	22 17	22 47
Aylesford	d	06 20	06 50	each	22 20	22 50
Maidstone Barracks	d	06 25	06 55	hour until	22 25	22 55
Maidstone West 208	a	06 27	06 57		22 27	22 57
	d	06 28			22 28	
East Farleigh	d	06 31			22 31	
Wateringbury	d	06 36			22 36	
Yalding	d	06 40			22 40	
Beltring	d	06 43			22 43	
Paddock Wood	a	06 47			22 47	
Tonbridge	a	06 55			22 55	

Sundays
20 May to 2 December

Station		SE		SE
St Pancras International	d			
Stratford International	d			
Ebbsfleet International	d			
Gravesend	d			
Strood	d	06 35		22 35
Cuxton	d	06 39		22 39
Halling	d	06 43	and	22 43
Snodland	d	06 46	hourly	22 46
New Hythe	d	06 48	until	22 48
Aylesford	d	06 51		22 51
Maidstone Barracks	d	06 56		22 56
Maidstone West 208	a	06 58		22 58
	d	07 00		23 00
East Farleigh	d	07 03		23 03
Wateringbury	d	07 08		23 08
Yalding	d	07 12		23 12
Beltring	d	07 15		23 15
Paddock Wood	a	07 19		23 19
Tonbridge	a	07 27		23 27

Table T208-R

Paddock Wood and Maidstone West - Strood

Mondays to Fridays
21 May to 7 December

Miles	Station		SE	SE	SE	SE ◇	SE	SE ◇	SE ◇	SE	SE	SE	SE	SE	SE		SE	SE	SE	SE	SE	SE ◇
0	Tonbridge	d											09 05		10 04			16 04				
5¼	**Paddock Wood**	d		05 28	06 18		06 49			07 41	08 11		09 12		10 11			16 11	17 04	17 34	17 52	
7	Beltring	d		05 32	06 22		06 53			07 45	08 15		09 16		10 15			16 15	17 08	17 38	17 56	
8¾	Yalding	d		05 36	06 26		06 57			07 49	08 19		09 19		10 18			16 18	17 12	17 42	18 00	
10½	Wateringbury	d		05 39	06 29		07 00			07 52	08 22		09 23		10 22	and at		16 22	17 15	17 45	18 03	
13½	East Farleigh	d		05 44	06 34		07 05			07 57	08 27		09 28		10 27	the same		16 27	17 20	17 50	18 08	
15¼	**Maidstone West** 208	a		05 49	06 39		07 10			08 02	08 32		09 32		10 31	minutes		16 31	17 25	17 55	18 15	
—		d	05 38	05 50	06 40	06 53	07 11	07 25	07 53	08 03	08 33	09 03	09 33	10 03	10 33	past	16 03	16 33	17 26	17 56	18 16	18 42
15½	Maidstone Barracks	d	05 40	05 52	06 42		07 13			08 05	08 35	09 05	09 35	10 05	10 35	each	16 05	16 35	17 28	17 58	18 18	
18¾	Aylesford	d		05 57	06 47		07 18			08 10	08 40	09 10	09 40	10 10	10 40	hour until	16 10	16 40	17 33	18 03	18 23	
19½	New Hythe	d		05 59	06 49		07 20			08 12	08 42	09 12	09 43	10 12	10 42		16 12	16 42	17 35	18 05	18 25	
21	Snodland	d		06 02	06 52	07 01	07 23	07 33	08 01	08 15	08 45	09 15	09 46	10 15	10 45		16 15	16 45	17 38	18 08	18 28	
22½	Halling	d		06 05	06 55		07 26			08 18	08 48	09 18	09 49	10 18	10 48		16 18	16 48	17 41	18 11	18 31	
24¼	Cuxton	d		06 09	06 59		07 30			08 22	08 52	09 22	09 52	10 22	10 52		16 22	16 52	17 45	18 15	18 35	
26½	**Strood**	a	05 55	06 13	07 03	07 09	07 34	07 42	08 10	08 26	08 56	09 26	09 57	10 26	10 56		16 26	16 56	17 49	18 19	18 39	18 57
34½	Gravesend	d				07 21		07 53	08 21													19 08
37½	Ebbsfleet International	d				07 26		07 57	08 26													19 13
54¼	Stratford International	d				07 39		08 09	08 39													19 24
59½	St Pancras International	a				07 46		08 16	08 46													19 31

Station		SE	SE	SE	SE	SE	SE	SE	SE	SE
Tonbridge	d					20 34		21 34		22 34
Paddock Wood	d	18 43	19 13	19 42		20 41		21 41		22 41
Beltring	d	18 47	19 17	19 46		20 45		21 45		22 45
Yalding	d	18 51	19 21	19 50		20 48		21 48		22 48
Wateringbury	d	18 54	19 24	19 53		20 52		21 52		22 52
East Farleigh	d	18 59	19 29	19 58		20 57		21 57		22 57
Maidstone West 208	a	19 04	19 34	20 03		21 01		22 01		23 01
	d	19 05	19 35	20 04	20 33	21 03	21 33	22 03	22 33	23 03
Maidstone Barracks	d	19 07	19 37	20 06	20 35	21 05	21 35	22 05	22 35	23 05
Aylesford	d	19 12	19 42	20 11	20 40	21 10	21 40	22 10	22 40	23 10
New Hythe	d	19 14	19 44	20 13	20 42	21 12	21 42	22 12	22 42	23 12
Snodland	d	19 17	19 47	20 16	20 45	21 15	21 45	22 15	22 45	23 15
Halling	d	19 20	19 50	20 19	20 48	21 18	21 48	22 18	22 48	23 18
Cuxton	d	19 24	19 54	20 23	20 52	21 22	21 52	22 22	22 52	23 22
Strood	a	19 29	19 58	20 27	20 56	21 26	21 56	22 26	22 56	23 26
Gravesend	d									
Ebbsfleet International	d									
Stratford International	d									
St Pancras International	a									

Saturdays
26 May to 8 December

Station		SE	SE		SE	SE
Tonbridge	d	06 04			22 04	
Paddock Wood	d	06 11			22 11	
Beltring	d	06 15			22 15	
Yalding	d	06 18			22 18	
Wateringbury	d	06 22			22 22	
East Farleigh	d	06 27		and at	22 27	
Maidstone West 208	a	06 31		the same	22 31	
	d	06 33	07 03	minutes	22 33	23 03
Maidstone Barracks	d	06 35	07 05	past	22 35	23 05
Aylesford	d	06 40	07 10	each	22 40	23 10
New Hythe	d	06 42	07 12	hour until	22 42	23 12
Snodland	d	06 45	07 15		22 45	23 15
Halling	d	06 48	07 18		22 48	23 18
Cuxton	d	06 52	07 22		22 52	23 22
Strood	a	06 56	07 26		22 56	23 26
Gravesend	d					
Ebbsfleet International	d					
Stratford International	d					
St Pancras International	a					

Sundays
20 May to 2 December

Station		SE		SE
Tonbridge	d	06 33		22 33
Paddock Wood	d	06 40		22 40
Beltring	d	06 44		22 44
Yalding	d	06 47		22 47
Wateringbury	d	06 51		22 51
East Farleigh	d	06 56		22 56
Maidstone West 208	a	07 00		23 00
	d	07 01	and	23 01
Maidstone Barracks	d	07 03	hourly	23 03
Aylesford	d	07 08	until	23 08
New Hythe	d	07 11		23 11
Snodland	d	07 14		23 14
Halling	d	07 17		23 17
Cuxton	d	07 20		23 20
Strood	a	07 25		23 25
Gravesend	d			
Ebbsfleet International	d			
Stratford International	d			
St Pancras International	a			

Table T212-F

Mondays to Fridays

21 May to 7 December

London - Medway, Sheerness-on-Sea, Dover and Ramsgate

Miles	Miles	Miles	Miles	Miles	Station		SE MO ◇ A	SE TTh FO ◇ A	SE TTh FO ◇■ B	SE MO ◇■ B	SE WO ◇■ B	SE TTh FO ◇■ B	SE MX ◇ A	SE MO ◇ A	SE MO ◇■ B	SE MX ◇ A	SE MO ◇■ B	SE MX B	SE WO ■	SE ■	SE MX ◇ C	SE	SE	SE ◇ D
—	—	—	—	0	**St Pancras Intl.** ⊖	d															00 12			
—	—	—	—	6	Stratford International ⊖	d										00 02					00 19			
—	—	—	—	22¾	Ebbsfleet International	d										00 13					00a30			
—	—	—	—	—	**London Blackfriars** ⊖	d																		
—	—	—	—	—	Elephant & Castle ⊖	d																		
0	0	—	—	—	**London Victoria** ⊖	d													00 10					
11	11	—	—	—	Bromley South	d												00 05	00s33					
14¾	14¾	—	—	—	St Mary Cray	d											00 03	00 11						
17½	17½	—	—	—	Swanley	d											00 07	00 15						
20½	20½	—	—	—	Farningham Road	d											00s12	00 20						
23½	23½	—	—	—	Longfield	d											00s16	00 25						
26	26	—	—	—	Meopham	d											00s21	00 29						
27	27	—	—	—	Sole Street	d											00s23	00s31						
—	—	—	0	—	**London Charing Cross** ⊖	d																		
—	—	—	0¾	—	**London Waterloo (East)** ⊖	d																		
—	—	—	—	—	**London Cannon Street** ⊖	d																		
—	—	—	1¾	—	**London Bridge** ⊖	d																		
—	—	—	18¾	—	Dartford	d																		
—	—	—	21½	—	Greenhithe for Bluewater	d																		
—	—	—	25½	24¾	Gravesend	d										00 18								
—	—	—	32¾	32	Strood	d										00 29								
33¾	33¾	—	33¾	33	Rochester	d							00 02	00 02	00 08	00 32	00 32	00 40	00 56					
34¾	34¾	—	34¾	33½	**Chatham**	d							00 06	00 06	00 12	00 36	00 36	00 44	00 59					
36	36	—	36	35¼	**Gillingham (Kent)**	d					00 01	00 01	00 10	00 10	00a17	00 40	00 41	00a49	01 04			04 56		
39	39	—	—	38¼	Rainham (Kent)	d					00 06	00 06	00 15	00 15		00 45	00 46		01 09			05 01		
41½	41½	—	—	40¾	Newington	d					00 10	00 10					00s50		01s13			05 05		
44¾	44¾	0	—	44	**Sittingbourne**	a					00 15	00 15	00 22	00 22		00 52	00 54		01 18					
—	—	—	—	—		d					00 15	00 15	00 23	00 23		00 53	00 55		01 18				05 22	
—	—	2	—	—	Kemsley	d																05 12	05 27	
—	—	4	—	—	Swale	d																05 16	05 30	
—	—	6	—	—	Queenborough	d																05 20	05 38	
—	—	8	—	—	**Sheerness-on-Sea**	a																05 26	05 43	
47½	47½	—	—	46¾	Teynham	d					00 20	00 20					00s59		01s23					
52	52	—	—	51¼	**Faversham**	a					00 26	00 26	00 31	00 32		01 03	01 06		01 28					
—	—	—	—	—		d					00 28	00 36							01 29	05 26				
—	55¼	—	—	—	Selling	d														05 30				
—	61¾	—	—	—	**Canterbury East**	d														05 40				
—	64¾	—	—	—	Bekesbourne	d														05 44				
—	67¾	—	—	—	Adisham	d														05 48				
—	68¾	—	—	—	Aylesham	d														05 51				
—	69¾	—	—	—	Snowdown	d														05 54				
—	71¾	—	—	—	Shepherds Well	d														05 58				
—	75	—	—	—	Kearsney	d														06 02				
—	77¼	—	—	—	**Dover Priory**	a														06 08				
59	—	—	—	—	Whitstable	d			00 02	00 04		00 44												
60½	—	—	—	—	Chestfield & Swalecliffe	d			00 05	00 07		00 47												
62¾	—	—	—	—	**Herne Bay**	d			00 09	00 11		00 51												
70¾	—	—	—	—	Birchington-on-Sea	d			00 18	00 20		01 00												
72½	—	—	—	—	Westgate-on-Sea	d			00 21	00 23		01 04												
73¾	—	—	—	—	**Margate**	d		00 04	00 25	00 27		01 08												05 46
77	—	—	—	—	Broadstairs	d	00 05	00 10	00 31	00 33		01 14												05 52
78¼	—	—	—	—	Dumpton Park	d		00 13	00 34	00 36		01 17												
79¼	—	—	—	—	**Ramsgate**	a	00 11	00 17	00 38	00 40	01 35	01 21							02 33					05 57

A From St Pancras International
B From London Victoria
C To Ashford International
D To St Pancras International

For further services between St Pancras International, London Blackfriars and Elephant & Castle and Bromley South, St Mary Cray and Swanley refer to table T52

Table T212-F

Mondays to Fridays

21 May to 7 December

London - Medway, Sheerness-on-Sea, Dover and Ramsgate

Station		SE	SE ◇ A	SE ◇ B	SE ◇ C	SE ◇ A	SE ◇ A	SE ■	SE	SE ◇■	SE	SE ◇ A	SE ■	SE ◇■	SE	SE ◇ A	SE ■	SE ◇■	SE	SE ■	SE ◇	SE ◇■
St Pancras Intl. ⊖	d			06 25	06 40																06 55	
Stratford International ⊖	d			06 32	06 47																07 02	
Ebbsfleet International	d			06 43	06a58																07 13	
London Blackfriars ⊖	d																					
Elephant & Castle ⊖	d																					
London Victoria ⊖	d									05 12				05 42				06 12				06 40
Bromley South	d									05 35				06 05				06 36				06 58
St Mary Cray	d									05 40				06 10				06 41				07 04
Swanley	d									05 45				06 15				06 45				07 08
Farningham Road	d									05 50				06 20				06 50				07 13
Longfield	d									05 54				06 24				06 54				07 17
Meopham	d									05 58				06 28				06 58				07 21
Sole Street	d									06 01				06 31				07 01				07 24
London Charing Cross ⊖	d																					
London Waterloo (East) ⊖	d																					
London Cannon Street ⊖	d																					
London Bridge ⊖	d																					
Dartford	d																					
Greenhithe for Bluewater	d																					
Gravesend	d			06 48																	07 19	
Strood	d			06a58																	07 31	
Rochester	d									06 10				06 40				07 10			07 34	07 38
Chatham	d									06 13				06 43				07 13			07 38	07 42
Gillingham (Kent)	d							05 50		06 20				06 50				07 20			07 43	07 50
Rainham (Kent)	d							05 55		06 25				06 55				07 25			07 47	07 55
Newington	d							05 59		06 29				06 59				07 29				07 59
Sittingbourne	a							06 03		06 33				07 05				07 33			07 54	08 03
	d	05 56						06 04	06 22	06 34	07 00			07 06	07 14			07 34	07 55		07 55	08 04
Kemsley	d	06 02							06 32		07 08				07 19				08 00			
Swale	d	06 07							06 36		07 12				07 22				08 03			
Queenborough	d	06 12							06 42		07 16				07 32				08 08			
Sheerness-on-Sea	a	06 17							06 47		07 21				07 37				08 13			
Teynham	d							06 08		06 38				07 10				07 38				08 08
Faversham	a							06 14		06 44				07 16				07 44			08 03	08 14
	d						06 22	06 26		06 48			06 52	07 18			07 23	07 48		07 52		08 18
Selling	d							06 30		06 52				07 22				07 52				08 22
Canterbury East	d							06 40		07 02				07 32				08 03				08 33
Bekesbourne	d							06 44		07 06				07 36				08 07				08 37
Adisham	d							06 48		07 10				07 40				08 11				08 41
Aylesham	d							06 51		07 13				07 43				08 14				08 44
Snowdown	d							06 54		07 16				07 46				08 17				08 47
Shepherds Well	d							06 58		07 20				07 50				08 21				08 51
Kearsney	d							07 02		07 24				07 54				08 25				08 55
Dover Priory	a							07 08		07 30				08 02				08 33				09 00
Whitstable	d						06 31						07 01				07 32			08 01		
Chestfield & Swalecliffe	d						06 34						07 04				07 35			08 04		
Herne Bay	d						06 38						07 08				07 39			08 08		
Birchington-on-Sea	d						06 46						07 16				07 47			08 16		
Westgate-on-Sea	d						06 50						07 20				07 51			08 20		
Margate	d		06 16			06 46	06 54					07 16	07 24			07 48	07 55			08 24		
Broadstairs	d		06 22			06 52	07 00					07 22	07 30			07 54	08 01			08 30		
Dumpton Park	d						07 03						07 33				08 04			08 33		
Ramsgate	a		06 27			06 57	07 07					07 27	07 36			07 59	08 07			08 36		

A To St Pancras International
B To Maidstone West
C To Ashford International

For further services between St Pancras International, London Blackfriars and Elephant & Castle and Bromley South, St Mary Cray and Swanley refer to table T52

Table T212-F

Mondays to Fridays

21 May to 7 December

London - Medway, Sheerness-on-Sea, Dover and Ramsgate

		SE ◇ A	SE ◇ A	SE	SE ◇1	SE ◇1	SE	SE ◇1	SE ◇	SE ◇1	SE ◇ A	SE ◇ A	SE	SE ◇1	SE ◇	SE	SE ◇1	SE ◇1	SE ◇ A	SE ◇ A	SE	SE ◇1	SE ◇
St Pancras Intl. ⊖	d		07 22						08 07			08 25			08 58					09 25			09 55
Stratford International ⊖	d		07 29						08 14			08 32			09 05					09 32			10 02
Ebbsfleet International	d		07 40						08 26			08 43			09 16					09 44			10 13
London Blackfriars ⊖	d																						
Elephant & Castle ⊖	d																						
London Victoria ⊖	d				07 10	07 40		07 42		08 10				08 40			08 42	09 10				09 37	
Bromley South	d				07 33	07 59		08 05		08 27				08 57			09 05	09 27				09 57	
St Mary Cray	d				07 39			08 10									09 10						
Swanley	d				07 43			08 15									09 15						
Farningham Road	d				07 48			08 20									09 20						
Longfield	d				07 53	08 11		08 24		08 39				09 09			09 24	09 39				10 09	
Meopham	d				07 57	08 16		08 28		08 43				09 13			09 28	09 43				10 13	
Sole Street	d				07 59			08 31									09 31						
London Charing Cross ⊖	d																						
London Waterloo (East) ⊖	d																						
London Cannon Street ⊖	d																						
London Bridge ⊖	d																						
Dartford	d																						
Greenhithe for Bluewater	d																						
Gravesend	d		07 44						08 30			08 48			09 20					09 48			10 18
Strood	d		07 54						08 40			08 59			09 30					09 59			10 29
Rochester	d		07 58		08 08	08 28		08 40	08 44	08 53		09 02		09 23	09 34		09 40	09 53		10 02		10 23	10 32
Chatham	d		08 02		08 12	08 31		08 43	08 47	08 57		09 06		09 27	09 37		09 43	09 57		10 06		10 27	10 36
Gillingham (Kent)	d		08 06		08a18	08 36		08 48	08 53	09 01		09 10		09 31	09 42		09 48	10 01		10 10		10 31	10 40
Rainham (Kent)	d		08 11			08 40		08 53	08 58	09 06		09 15		09 36	09 47		09 53	10 06		10 15		10 36	10 45
Newington	d					08 44				09 10								10 10					
Sittingbourne	a		08 18			08 49		09 00	09 05	09 15		09 22		09 43	09 54		10 00	10 15		10 22		10 43	10 52
	d		08 18	08 25		08 49	08 55	09 01	09 05	09 15		09 23	09 25	09 44	09 54	09 55	10 01	10 15		10 23	10 25	10 44	10 54
Kemsley	d			08 30			09 00						09 30			10 00					10 30		
Swale	d			08 33			09 03						09 33			10 03					10 33		
Queenborough	d			08 38			09 08						09 38			10 08					10 38		
Sheerness-on-Sea	a			08 43			09 13						09 43			10 13					10 43		
Teynham	d					08 54				09 20								10 20					
Faversham	a		08 26			08 59		09 09	09 14	09 25		09 31		09 52	10 05		10 09	10 25		10 31		10 52	11 05
	d		08 27			09 01		09 10		09 26		09 31		09 53			10 10	10 26		10 31		10 53	
Selling	d									09 31								10 31					
Canterbury East	d							09 22		09 40							10 22	10 40					
Bekesbourne	d									09 45								10 45					
Adisham	d									09 49								10 49					
Aylesham	d									09 52								10 52					
Snowdown	d									09 54								10 54					
Shepherds Well	d							09 32		09 58								10 58					
Kearsney	d							09 37		10 03								11 03					
Dover Priory	a							09 42		10 08							10 39	11 08					
Whitstable	d		08 35			09 09						09 40		10 02						10 40		11 02	
Chestfield & Swalecliffe	d		08 38			09 12								10 05								11 05	
Herne Bay	d		08 42			09 16						09 45		10 09						10 45		11 09	
Birchington-on-Sea	d		08 51			09 25						09 54		10 18						10 54		11 18	
Westgate-on-Sea	d		08 55			09 29								10 21								11 21	
Margate	d	08 51	08 59			09 33					09 53	09 59		10 25					10 53	10 59		11 25	
Broadstairs	d	08 57	09 05			09 39					09 59	10 05		10 31					10 59	11 05		11 31	
Dumpton Park	d		09 08			09 42								10 34								11 34	
Ramsgate	a	09 02	09 11			09 45					10 04	10 11		10 38					11 04	11 11		11 38	

A To St Pancras International

For further services between St Pancras International, London Blackfriars and Elephant & Castle and Bromley South, St Mary Cray and Swanley refer to table T52

Table T212-F

Mondays to Fridays

21 May to 7 December

London - Medway, Sheerness-on-Sea, Dover and Ramsgate

		SE	SE ◇1	SE ◇1	SE ◇ A	SE ◇ A	SE	SE ◇1	SE ◇	SE	SE ◇1	SE ◇1	SE ◇ A	SE ◇ A	SE	SE ◇1	SE ◇	SE	SE ◇1	SE ◇1	SE ◇ A	SE ◇ A
St Pancras Intl. ⊖	d					10 27			10 52					11 25			11 55					12 27
Stratford International ⊖	d					10 34			10 59					11 32			12 02					12 34
Ebbsfleet International	d					10 45			11 13					11 43			12 13					12 45
London Blackfriars ⊖	d																					
Elephant & Castle ⊖	d																					
London Victoria ⊖	d		09 42	10 10				10 40			10 42	11 10				11 40			11 42	12 10		
Bromley South	d		10 05	10 27				10 57			11 05	11 27				11 57			12 05	12 27		
St Mary Cray	d		10 10								11 10								12 10			
Swanley	d		10 15								11 15								12 15			
Farningham Road	d		10 20								11 20								12 20			
Longfield	d		10 24	10 39				11 09			11 24	11 39				12 09			12 24	12 39		
Meopham	d		10 28	10 43				11 13			11 28	11 43				12 13			12 28	12 43		
Sole Street	d		10 31								11 31								12 31			
London Charing Cross ⊖	d																					
London Waterloo (East) ⊖	d																					
London Cannon Street ⊖	d																					
London Bridge ⊖	d																					
Dartford	d																					
Greenhithe for Bluewater	d																					
Gravesend	d					10 49			11 18					11 48			12 18					12 49
Strood	d					10 59			11 29					11 59			12 29					12 59
Rochester	d		10 40	10 53		11 02		11 23	11 32		11 40	11 53		12 02		12 23	12 32		12 40	12 53		13 02
Chatham	d		10 43	10 57		11 06		11 27	11 36		11 43	11 57		12 06		12 27	12 36		12 43	12 57		13 06
Gillingham (Kent)	d		10 48	11 01		11 10		11 31	11 40		11 48	12 01		12 10		12 31	12 40		12 48	13 01		13 10
Rainham (Kent)	d		10 53	11 06		11 15		11 36	11 45		11 53	12 06		12 15		12 36	12 45		12 53	13 06		13 15
Newington	d			11 10								12 10								13 10		
Sittingbourne	a		11 00	11 15		11 22		11 43	11 52		12 00	12 15		12 22		12 43	12 52		13 00	13 15		13 22
	d	10 55	11 01	11 15		11 23	11 25	11 44	11 54	11 55	12 01	12 15		12 23	12 25	12 44	12 54	12 55	13 01	13 15		13 23
Kemsley	d	11 00					11 30			12 00					12 30			13 00				
Swale	d	11 03					11 33			12 03					12 33			13 03				
Queenborough	d	11 08					11 38			12 08					12 38			13 08				
Sheerness-on-Sea	a	11 13					11 43			12 13					12 43			13 13				
Teynham	d			11 20								12 20								13 20		
Faversham	a		11 09	11 25		11 31		11 52	12 05		12 09	12 25		12 31		12 52	13 05		13 09	13 25		13 31
	d		11 10	11 26		11 31		11 53			12 10	12 26		12 31		12 53			13 10	13 26		13 31
Selling	d			11 31								12 31								13 31		
Canterbury East	d		11 22	11 40							12 22	12 40							13 22	13 40		
Bekesbourne	d			11 45								12 45								13 45		
Adisham	d			11 49								12 49								13 49		
Aylesham	d			11 52								12 52								13 52		
Snowdown	d			11 54								12 54								13 54		
Shepherds Well	d			11 58								12 58								13 58		
Kearsney	d			12 03								13 03								14 03		
Dover Priory	a		11 39	12 08							12 39	13 08							13 39	14 08		
Whitstable	d					11 40		12 02						12 40		13 02						13 40
Chestfield & Swalecliffe	d							12 05								13 05						
Herne Bay	d					11 45		12 09						12 45		13 09						13 45
Birchington-on-Sea	d					11 54		12 18						12 54		13 18						13 54
Westgate-on-Sea	d							12 21								13 21						
Margate	d				11 53	11 59		12 25					12 53	12 59		13 25					13 53	13 59
Broadstairs	d				11 59	12 05		12 31					12 59	13 05		13 31					13 59	14 05
Dumpton Park	d							12 34								13 34						
Ramsgate	a				12 04	12 11		12 38					13 04	13 11		13 38					14 04	14 11

A To St Pancras International

For further services between St Pancras International, London Blackfriars and Elephant & Castle and Bromley South, St Mary Cray and Swanley refer to table T52

Table T212-F

Mondays to Fridays

21 May to 7 December

London - Medway, Sheerness-on-Sea, Dover and Ramsgate

		SE	SE ◇1	SE ◇	SE	SE ◇1	SE ◇1	SE ◇ A	SE ◇ A	SE	SE ◇1	SE ◇	SE	SE ◇1	SE ◇1	SE ◇ A	SE ◇ A	SE	SE ◇1		SE ◇	SE	SE ◇1
St Pancras Intl. ⊖	d			12 52					13 25			13 55					14 25				14 55		
Stratford International ⊖	d			12 59					13 32			14 02					14 32				15 02		
Ebbsfleet International	d			13 13					13 43			14 13					14 43				15 13		
London Blackfriars ⊖	d																						
Elephant & Castle ⊖	d																						
London Victoria ⊖	d		12 40			12 42	13 10				13 40			13 42	14 10				14 40				14 42
Bromley South	d		12 57			13 05	13 27				13 57			14 05	14 27				14 57				15 05
St Mary Cray	d					13 10								14 10									15 10
Swanley	d					13 15								14 15									15 15
Farningham Road	d					13 20								14 20									15 20
Longfield	d		13 09			13 24	13 39				14 09			14 24	14 39				15 09				15 24
Meopham	d		13 13			13 28	13 43				14 13			14 28	14 43				15 13				15 28
Sole Street	d					13 31								14 31									15 31
London Charing Cross ⊖	d																						
London Waterloo (East) ⊖	d																						
London Cannon Street ⊖	d																						
London Bridge ⊖	d																						
Dartford	d																						
Greenhithe for Bluewater	d																						
Gravesend	d			13 18					13 48			14 18					14 48				15 18		
Strood	d			13 29					13 59			14 29					14 59				15 29		
Rochester	d		13 23	13 32		13 40	13 53		14 02		14 23	14 32		14 40	14 53		15 02		15 23		15 32		15 40
Chatham	d		13 27	13 36		13 43	13 57		14 06		14 27	14 36		14 43	14 57		15 05		15 27		15 36		15 43
Gillingham (Kent)	d		13 31	13 40		13 48	14 01		14 10		14 31	14 40		14 48	15 01		15 10		15 31		15 40		15a48
Rainham (Kent)	d		13 36	13 45		13 53	14 06		14 15		14 36	14 45		14 53	15 06		15 14		15 36		15 45		
Newington	d						14 10								15 10								
Sittingbourne	a		13 43	13 52		14 00	14 15		14 22		14 43	14 52		15 00	15 15		15 21		15 43		15 52		
	d	13 25	13 44	13 54	13 55	14 01	14 15		14 23	14 25	14 44	14 54	14 55	15 01	15 15		15 22	15 25	15 44		15 54	15 55	
Kemsley	d	13 30			14 00					14 30			15 00					15 30				16 00	
Swale	d	13 33			14 03					14 33			15 03					15 33				16 03	
Queenborough	d	13 38			14 08					14 38			15 08					15 38				16 08	
Sheerness-on-Sea	a	13 43			14 13					14 43			15 13					15 43				16 13	
Teynham	d						14 20								15 20								
Faversham	a		13 52	14 05		14 09	14 25		14 31		14 52	15 05		15 09	15 25		15 30		15 52		16 05		
	d		13 53			14 10	14 26		14 31		14 53			15 10	15 26		15 30		15 56	15 58			
Selling	d						14 31								15 31					16 02			
Canterbury East	d					14 22	14 40							15 22	15 40					16 12			
Bekesbourne	d						14 45								15 45					16 16			
Adisham	d						14 49								15 49					16 20			
Aylesham	d						14 52								15 52					16 23			
Snowdown	d						14 54								15 54					16 26			
Shepherds Well	d						14 58								15 58					16 30			
Kearsney	d						15 03								16 03					16 34			
Dover Priory	a					14 39	15 08							15 39	16 08					16 42			
Whitstable	d		14 02						14 40		15 02						15 39		16 04				
Chestfield & Swalecliffe	d		14 05								15 05						15 42		16 07				
Herne Bay	d		14 09						14 45		15 09						15 46		16 11				
Birchington-on-Sea	d		14 18						14 54		15 18						15 54		16 20				
Westgate-on-Sea	d		14 21								15 21						15 58		16 24				
Margate	d		14 25					14 53	14 59		15 25					15 53	16 02		16 28				
Broadstairs	d		14 31					14 59	15 05		15 31					15 59	16 08		16 34				
Dumpton Park	d		14 34								15 34								16 37				
Ramsgate	a		14 38					15 04	15 11		15 38					16 04	16 13		16 40				

A To St Pancras International

For further services between St Pancras International, London Blackfriars and Elephant & Castle and Bromley South, St Mary Cray and Swanley refer to table T52

Table T212-F

Mondays to Fridays

21 May to 7 December

London - Medway, Sheerness-on-Sea, Dover and Ramsgate

		SE ◇1	SE ◇ A	SE ◇ A	SE	SE ◇1		SE ◇	SE ◇1	SE	SE ◇ A	SE ◇1		SE ◇	SE 1	SE	SE ◇1 B	SE ◇1	SE ◇1 C	SE ◇	SE	SE ◇ D	SE ◇ A
St Pancras Intl. ⊖	d			15 25				15 55						16 25						16 55		17 16	
Stratford International ⊖	d			15 32				16 02						16 32						17 02		17 23	
Ebbsfleet International	d			15 43				16 13						16 43						17 13		17 35	
London Blackfriars ⊖	d																						
Elephant & Castle ⊖	d																						
London Victoria ⊖	d	15 10				15 40			15 42			16 10			16 12			16 40					
Bromley South	d	15 27				15 57			16 05			16 27			16 35			16 57					
St Mary Cray	d								16 10						16 40								
Swanley	d								16 15						16 45								
Farningham Road	d								16 20						16 50								
Longfield	d	15 39				16 09			16 24			16 39			16 54								
Meopham	d	15 43				16 13			16 28			16 43			16 58								
Sole Street	d								16 31						17 01								
London Charing Cross ⊖	d																						
London Waterloo (East) ⊖	d																						
London Cannon Street ⊖	d																16 30						
London Bridge ⊖	d																16 35						
Dartford	d																						
Greenhithe for Bluewater	d																						
Gravesend	d			15 48				16 18						16 48						17 18		17 39	
Strood	d			15 59				16 29						16 59						17 28		17a49	
Rochester	d	15 53		16 02		16 23		16 32	16 40			16 53		17 02	17 10		17 15	17 19		17 31			
Chatham	d	15 57		16 05		16 27		16 36	16 43			16 57		17 06	17 13		17 18	17 23		17 35			
Gillingham (Kent)	d	16 01		16 10		16 31		16 40	16a50			17 02		17 10	17a20		17 23	17 28		17 41			
Rainham (Kent)	d	16 06		16 14		16 36		16 45				17 07		17 15			17 28	17 33		17 46			
Newington	d	16 10				16 40						17 11						17 37					
Sittingbourne	a	16 15		16 21		16 45		16 52				17 15		17 22			17 35	17 41		17 53			
	d	16 15		16 22	16 25	16 45		16 53		16 55		17 16		17 23		17 25	17 36	17 42		17 54	17 55		
Kemsley	d				16 30					17 00						17 30					18 00		
Swale	d				16 33					17 03						17 33					18 03		
Queenborough	d				16 38					17 08						17 38					18 08		
Sheerness-on-Sea	a				16 43					17 13						17 43					18 15		
Teynham	d	16 20				16 50						17 20						17 46	←				
Faversham	a	16 25		16 30		16 56		17 01				17 26		17 31			17 44	17 52	17 44	18 02			
	d	16 29		16 30		17 00	17 02					17 30	17 36				17 58	17 54	17 58				
Selling	d	16 33					17 06					17 34					→		18 02				
Canterbury East	d	16 43					17 16					17 43							18 12				
Bekesbourne	d	16 47					17 20					17 48							18 16				
Adisham	d	16 51					17 24					17 52							18 21				
Aylesham	d	16 54					17 27					17 54							18 24				
Snowdown	d	16 57					17 30					17 57							18 26				
Shepherds Well	d	17 01					17 34					18 01							18 30				
Kearsney	d	17 05					17 38					18 05							18 35				
Dover Priory	a	17 12					17 45					18 13							18 43				
Whitstable	d			16 39		17 08							17 44					18 02					
Chestfield & Swalecliffe	d			16 42		17 11							17 47					18 05					
Herne Bay	d			16 46		17 15							17 51					18 09					
Birchington-on-Sea	d			16 54		17 24							18 00					18 18					
Westgate-on-Sea	d			16 58		17 28							18 04					18 22					
Margate	d		16 53	17 02		17 32					17 53		18 08					18 26					18 53
Broadstairs	d		16 59	17 08		17 38					17 59		18 14					18 32					18 59
Dumpton Park	d					17 41							18 17					18 35					
Ramsgate	a		17 04	17 13		17 46					18 04		18 22					18 41					19 04

A To St Pancras International
B To Dover Priory
C From London Cannon Street
D To Maidstone West

For further services between St Pancras International, London Blackfriars and Elephant & Castle and Bromley South, St Mary Cray and Swanley refer to table T52

21 May to 7 December

London - Medway, Sheerness-on-Sea, Dover and Ramsgate

		SE ◇■	SE ◇■	SE ◇	SE	SE ◇	SE ◇ A	SE	SE ◇■ B	SE ◇■	SE ◇■ C	SE ◇■	SE ◇	SE	SE ◇ A	SE	SE ◇ D	SE ◇■	SE ◇■	SE	SE	SE ◇
St Pancras Intl. ■ ⊖	d			17 25			17 46						17 55		18 16							18 25
Stratford International ⊖	d			17 32			17 53						18 02		18 23							18 32
Ebbsfleet International	d			17 43			18 05						18 13		18 35							18 43
London Blackfriars ■ ⊖	d																					
Elephant & Castle ⊖	d																					
London Victoria ■ ⊖	d		17 10			17 12				17 40								18 10				
Bromley South ■	d		17 30			17 37				17 57								18 29				
St Mary Cray	d					17 43																
Swanley ■	d					17 48																
Farningham Road	d					17 53																
Longfield	d					17 57																
Meopham	d					18 01																
Sole Street	d					18 04																
London Charing Cross ■ ⊖	d							17 17								17 59						
London Waterloo (East) ■ ⊖	d							17 20								18 02						
London Cannon Street ■ ⊖	d	17 09							17 30			17 52							18 11		18 24	
London Bridge ■ ⊖	d	17 14						17 26	17 35			17 57				18 08			18 16		18 29	
Dartford ■	d							18 03								18 46					19 10	
Greenhithe for Bluewater	d							18 09								18 51					19 16	
Gravesend ■	d						18 09	18 22					18 18		18 39	19 00					19 26	
Strood ■	d						18a19	18a36					18 31		18a49	19a14					19a40	
Rochester ■	d	17 48	17 53	17 58		18 13			18 17	18 21		18 31	18 36					18 52	18 56			19 01
Chatham ■	d	17 52	17 57	18 02		18 16			18 21	18 25		18 35	18 40					18 56	19 00			19 05
Gillingham (Kent) ■	d	17 57	18 02	18 07		18 21			18 26	18 30		18 41	18 45					19 01	19 05			19 10
Rainham (Kent)	d	18 02	18 07	18 12		18 26			18 31	18 35		18 46	18 50					19 06	19 10			19 15
Newington	d	18 06	18 11							18 39									19 14			
Sittingbourne ■	a	18 10	18 15	18 19					18 38	18 44		18 53	18 57					19 13	19 18			19 24
	d	18 11	18 16	18 19	18 22				18 38	18 44		18 53	18 58	19 00				19 13	19 19	19 25		19 25
Kemsley	d				18 27	18 37								19 05						19 30		
Swale	d				18 31									19 08						19 34		
Queenborough	d				18 35	18 44								19 13						19 38		
Sheerness-on-Sea	a				18 42	18 52								19 19						19 43		
Teynham	d	18 15							18 43		←							19 18				
Faversham ■	a	18 21	18 24	18 27					18 49	18 53	18 49	19 01	19 06					19 24	19 27			19 33
	d	18 22	18 26	18 28					18 58	18 54	18 58	19 02	19 07					19 25	19 28			19 34
Selling	d		18 30						→		19 02								19 33			
Canterbury East ■	d		18 40								19 12								19 42			
Bekesbourne	d		18 44								19 16								19 47			
Adisham	d		18 48								19 21								19 51			
Aylesham	d		18 51								19 24								19 54			
Snowdown	d		18 54								19 26								19 57			
Shepherds Well	d		18 58								19 30								20 01			
Kearsney	d		19 03								19 35								20 06			
Dover Priory ■	a		19 11								19 42								20 14			
Whitstable	d	18 31		18 37						19 02		19 10	19 15					19 33				19 42
Chestfield & Swalecliffe	d	18 34								19 05								19 36				
Herne Bay	d	18 38		18 43						19 09		19 16	19 21					19 40				19 48
Birchington-on-Sea	d	18 46		18 52						19 18		19 25	19 30					19 49				19 57
Westgate-on-Sea	d	18 50								19 22								19 53				
Margate ■	d	18a56		18 58						19 26		19 30	19 36				19 53	19 57				20 02
Broadstairs	d			19 04						19 32		19a39	19a45				19 59	20 03				20a10
Dumpton Park	d			19 07						19 35								20 06				
Ramsgate ■	a			19 13						19 39							20 04	20 12				

A To Maidstone West
B To Dover Priory
C From London Cannon Street
D To St Pancras International

For further services between St Pancras International, London Blackfriars and Elephant & Castle and Bromley South, St Mary Cray and Swanley refer to table T52

21 May to 7 December

London - Medway, Sheerness-on-Sea, Dover and Ramsgate

		SE ◇■	SE ◇■	SE ◇■	SE	SE ◇	SE ◇■	SE	SE ◇ A	SE ◇ A	SE ◇	SE ◇■	SE ■	SE ◇■		SE ◇	SE	SE ◇	SE ◇■	SE ◇ A	SE ◇	SE	SE ◇
St Pancras Intl. ■ ⊖	d					18 55					19 25					19 55					20 25		
Stratford International ⊖	d					19 02					19 32					20 02					20 32		
Ebbsfleet International	d					19 13					19 43					20 13					20 43		
London Blackfriars ■ ⊖	d																						
Elephant & Castle ⊖	d																						
London Victoria ■ ⊖	d	18 12	18 40				19 10						19 12	19 40				19 42	20 10				20 12
Bromley South ■	d	18 37	18 57				19 30						19 35	19 57				20 05	20 27				20 37
St Mary Cray	d	18 43											19 41					20 10					20 42
Swanley ■	d	18 47											19 47					20 15					20 47
Farningham Road	d	18 52											19 52					20 20					20 52
Longfield	d	18 57											19 56	20 09				20 24	20 39				20 56
Meopham	d	19 01											20 01	20 13				20 28	20 43				21 00
Sole Street	d	19 04											20 03					20 31					21 03
London Charing Cross ■ ⊖	d																						
London Waterloo (East) ■ ⊖	d																						
London Cannon Street ■ ⊖	d			18 45								19 20											
London Bridge ■ ⊖	d			18 50								19 25											
Dartford ■	d																						
Greenhithe for Bluewater	d																						
Gravesend ■	d					19 18					19 48					20 18					20 48		
Strood ■	d					19 30					19 59					20 29					20 59		
Rochester ■	d	19 13	19 21	19 26		19 35	19 52				20 02	20 06	20 12	20 23		20 32		20 40	20 53		21 02		21 12
Chatham ■	d	19 17	19 25	19 30		19 39	19 56				20 06	20 10	20 16	20 27		20 36		20 43	20 57		21 06		21 16
Gillingham (Kent) ■	d	19 22	19 30	19 35		19 44	20 00				20 11	20 15	20a25	20 31		20 40		20a48	21 01		21 10		21a23
Rainham (Kent)	d	19 27	19 35	19 40		19 49	20 05				20 16	20 20		20 36		20 45			21 06		21 15		
Newington	d		19 39	19 44			20 09					20 24							21 10				
Sittingbourne ■	a		19 44	19 49		19 56	20 14				20 23	20 29		20 43		20 52			21 15		21 22		
	d		19 44	19 49	19 53	19 56	20 14	20 19			20 23	20 29		20 44		20 54	20 55		21 15		21 23	21 25	
Kemsley	d	19 38			20 02			20 29									21 00					21 30	
Swale	d				20 06			20 32									21 03					21 33	
Queenborough	d	19 45			20 10			20 37									21 08					21 38	
Sheerness-on-Sea	a	19 53			20 15			20 42									21 13					21 43	
Teynham	d		19 49	19 54			20 19					20 34							21 20				
Faversham ■	a		19 55	20 00		20 05	20 24				20 31	20 43		20 52		21 05			21 25		21 31		
	d		19 58	20 01			20 25				20 32			20 56	20 58				21 26		21 32		
Selling	d		20 03				20 30								21 02				21 31				
Canterbury East ■	d		20 12				20 39								21 12				21 40				
Bekesbourne	d		20 17				20 44								21 16				21 45				
Adisham	d		20 21				20 48								21 20				21 49				
Aylesham	d		20 24				20 51								21 23				21 52				
Snowdown	d		20 27				20 53								21 26				21 54				
Shepherds Well	d		20 31				20 57								21 30				21 58				
Kearsney	d		20 36				21 02								21 34				22 03				
Dover Priory ■	a		20 44				21 10								21 40				22 08				
Whitstable	d			20 09							20 40			21 04							21 40		
Chestfield & Swalecliffe	d			20 12							20 43			21 07							21 43		
Herne Bay	d			20 16							20 47			21 11							21 47		
Birchington-on-Sea	d			20 25							20 56			21 20							21 56		
Westgate-on-Sea	d			20 29							21 00			21 24							22 00		
Margate ■	d			20 33					20 53	21 00	21 04			21 28						21 53	22 04		
Broadstairs	d			20 39					20 59	21 06	21 10			21 34						21 59	22 10		
Dumpton Park	d			20 42							21 13			21 37							22 13		
Ramsgate ■	a			20 48					21 04	21 11	21 17			21 42						22 04	22 17		

A To St Pancras International

For further services between St Pancras International, London Blackfriars and Elephant & Castle and Bromley South, St Mary Cray and Swanley refer to table T52

Table T212-F

London - Medway, Sheerness-on-Sea, Dover and Ramsgate

		SE	SE	SE	SE	SE	SE	SE	SE	SE	SE	SE	SE	SE	SE	SE	SE	SE	SE	SE	SE	SE
													TX	TO	TX	TO	TX	TO		TX	TO	
		◇1	◇		◇	◇1		◇		◇1	◇	◇	◇1	◇1	◇	◇	◇1	◇1		◇1	◇1	◇
							A						B	B			C	C				
St Pancras Intl. 15 ⊖	d		20 55					21 25			21 55				22 25	22 25						22 55
Stratford International ⊖	d		21 02					21 32			22 02				22 32	22 32						23 02
Ebbsfleet International	d		21 13					21 43			22 13				22 43	22 43						23 13
London Blackfriars 3 ⊖	d																					
Elephant & Castle ⊖	d																					
London Victoria 15 ⊖	d	20 40			20 42	21 10				21 40		21 42	22 10	22 10						22 40	22 40	
Bromley South 4	d	20 57			21 05	21 27				21 57		22 05	22 27	22 27						22 57	22 57	
St Mary Cray	d				21 10							22 10										
Swanley 4	d				21 15							22 15										
Farningham Road	d				21 20							22 20										
Longfield	d	21 09			21 24	21 39				22 09		22 24	22 39	22 39						23 09	23 09	
Meopham	d	21 13			21 28	21 43				22 13		22 28	22 43	22 43						23 13	23 13	
Sole Street	d				21 31							22 31										
London Charing Cross 4 ⊖	d																					
London Waterloo (East) 4 ⊖	d																					
London Cannon Street 4 ⊖	d																					
London Bridge 4 ⊖	d																					
Dartford 4	d																					
Greenhithe for Bluewater	d																					
Gravesend 4	d		21 18					21 48			22 18				22 48	22 48						23 18
Strood 4	d		21 29					21 59			22 29				22 59	22 59						23 29
Rochester 4	d	21 23	21 32		21 40	21 53		22 02		22 23	22 32	22 40	22 53	22 53	23 02	23 02				23 23	23 23	23 32
Chatham 4	d	21 27	21 36		21 43	21 57		22 06		22 27	22 36	22 43	22 57	22 57	23 06	23 06				23 27	23 27	23 36
Gillingham (Kent) 4	d	21 31	21 40		21 48	22 01		22 10		22 31	22 40	22 48	23 01	23 01	23 10	23 10				23 31	23 31	23 40
Rainham (Kent)	d	21 36	21 45		21 53	22 06		22 15		22 36	22 45	22 53	23 06	23 06	23 15	23 15				23 36	23 36	23 45
Newington	d					22 10							23 10	23 10								
Sittingbourne 4	a	21 43	21 52		22 00	22 15		22 22		22 43	22 52	23 00	23 15	23 15	23 22	23 22				23 43	23 43	23 52
	d	21 44	21 53	21 55	22 01	22 15		22 23	22 25	22 44	22 53	23 01	23 15	23 15	23 23	23 23			23 25	23 44	23 44	23 53
Kemsley	d			22 00					22 30										23 30			
Swale	d			22 03					22 33										23 33			
Queenborough	d			22 08					22 38										23 38			
Sheerness-on-Sea	a			22 13					22 43										23 43			
Teynham	d					22 20							23 20	23 20			←	←				
Faversham 2	a	21 52	22 01		22 09	22 25		22 31		22 52	23 01	23 09	23 25	23 25	23 31	23 31	23 25	23 25		23 52	23 52	00 05
	d	21 53			22 10	22 26		22 32		22 53		23 10	23 34	23 40	23 32	23 32	23 34	23 40		23 53	23 56	
Selling	d					22 31							→	→			23s38	23s44				
Canterbury East 4	d				22a23	22 40						23a23					23 48	23 54				
Bekesbourne	d					22 45											23s52	23s58				
Adisham	d					22 49											23s56	00s02				
Aylesham	d					22 52											23s59	00s05				
Snowdown	d					22 54											00s01	00s07				
Shepherds Well	d					22 58											00s05	00s11				
Kearsney	d					23 03											00s10	00s16				
Dover Priory 4	a					23 08											00 16	00 23				
Whitstable	d	22 02						22 40		23 02					23 40					00 02		
Chestfield & Swalecliffe	d	22 05						22 43		23 05					23 43					00 05		
Herne Bay	d	22 09						22 47		23 09					23 47					00 09		
Birchington-on-Sea	d	22 18						22 56		23 18					23 56					00 18		
Westgate-on-Sea	d	22 21						23 00		23 21					23 59					00 21		
Margate 4	d	22 25					22 53	23 04		23 25					00 04					00 25		
Broadstairs	d	22 31					22 59	23 10		23 31					00 10					00 31		
Dumpton Park	d	22 34						23 13		23 34					00 13					00 34		
Ramsgate 4	a	22 38					23 04	23 17		23 38					00 17	00 39				00 38	01 10	

A To Ashford International B To Dover Priory C From London Victoria

For further services between St Pancras International, London Blackfriars and Elephant & Castle and Bromley South, St Mary Cray and Swanley refer to table T52

Table T212-F

Mondays to Fridays

21 May to 7 December

London - Medway, Sheerness-on-Sea, Dover and Ramsgate

		SE	SE	SE	SE	SE	SE
			TO	TX			
		◇	◇1	◇1	◇	◇	
St Pancras Intl. 15 ⊖	d				23 25	23 55	
Stratford International ⊖	d				23 32	00 02	
Ebbsfleet International	d				23 43	00 13	
London Blackfriars 3 ⊖	d						
Elephant & Castle ⊖	d						
London Victoria 15 ⊖	d	22 42	23 10	23 10			23 42
Bromley South 4	d	23 05	23 27	23 27			00 05
St Mary Cray	d	23 10					00 11
Swanley 4	d	23 15					00 15
Farningham Road	d	23 20					00 20
Longfield	d	23 24	23 39	23 39			00 25
Meopham	d	23 28	23 43	23 43			00 29
Sole Street	d	23 31					00s31
London Charing Cross 4 ⊖	d						
London Waterloo (East) 4 ⊖	d						
London Cannon Street 4 ⊖	d						
London Bridge 4 ⊖	d						
Dartford 4	d						
Greenhithe for Bluewater	d						
Gravesend 4	d				23 48	00 18	
Strood 4	d				23 59	00 29	
Rochester 4	d	23 40	23 53	23 53	00 02	00 32	00 40
Chatham 4	d	23 43	23 57	23 57	00 06	00 36	00 44
Gillingham (Kent) 4	d	23a48	00 01	00 01	00 10	00 40	00a49
Rainham (Kent)	d		00 06	00 06	00 15	00 45	
Newington	d		00 10	00 10			
Sittingbourne 4	a		00 15	00 15	00 22	00 52	
	d		00 15	00 15	00 23	00 53	
Kemsley	d						
Swale	d						
Queenborough	d						
Sheerness-on-Sea	a						
Teynham	d		00 20	00 20			
Faversham 2	a		00 26	00 26	00 31	01 03	
	d		00 28	00 36			
Selling	d						
Canterbury East 4	d						
Bekesbourne	d						
Adisham	d						
Aylesham	d						
Snowdown	d						
Shepherds Well	d						
Kearsney	d						
Dover Priory 4	a						
Whitstable	d			00 44			
Chestfield & Swalecliffe	d			00 47			
Herne Bay	d			00 51			
Birchington-on-Sea	d			01 00			
Westgate-on-Sea	d			01 04			
Margate 4	d			01 08			
Broadstairs	d			01 14			
Dumpton Park	d			01 17			
Ramsgate 4	a		01 35	01 21			

For further services between St Pancras International, London Blackfriars and Elephant & Castle and Bromley South, St Mary Cray and Swanley refer to table T52

Table T212-F

London - Medway, Sheerness-on-Sea, Dover and Ramsgate

Saturdays
26 May to 8 December

		SE ◇ A	SE ◇■ B	SE ◇■ B	SE ◇ A	SE ◇ A	SE B	SE ◇ C	SE ◇ D	SE ◇ D	SE ◇ D	SE ■	SE	SE	SE ◇■	SE	SE ◇ D	SE ■	SE ■	SE ■	SE	SE ◇■	SE ◇■
St Pancras Intl. ⊖	d							00 12															
Stratford International ⊖	d					00 02		00 19															
Ebbsfleet International	d					00 13		00a30															
London Blackfriars ⊖	d																						
Elephant & Castle ⊖	d																						
London Victoria ⊖	d														05 42							06 42	07 10
Bromley South	d						00 05								06 05							07 05	07 27
St Mary Cray	d						00 11								06 10							07 10	
Swanley	d						00 15								06 15							07 15	
Farningham Road	d						00 20								06 20							07 20	
Longfield	d						00 25								06 24							07 24	07 39
Meopham	d						00 29								06 28							07 28	07 43
Sole Street	d						00s31								06 31							07 31	
London Charing Cross ⊖	d																						
London Waterloo (East) ⊖	d																						
London Cannon Street ⊖	d																						
London Bridge ⊖	d																						
Dartford	d																						
Greenhithe for Bluewater	d																						
Gravesend	d					00 18																	
Strood	d					00 29																	
Rochester	d				00 02	00 32	00 40								06 40							07 40	07 53
Chatham	d				00 06	00 36	00 44								06 43							07 43	07 57
Gillingham (Kent)	d			00 01	00 10	00 40	00a49					05 53			06 48					07 28		07 48	08 01
Rainham (Kent)	d			00 06	00 15	00 45						05 58			06 53					07 33		07 53	08 06
Newington	d			00 10								06 02			06 57					07 37			08 10
Sittingbourne	a			00 15	00 22	00 52						06 06			07 01					07 41		08 00	08 15
	d			00 15	00 23	00 53						06 07	06 25	06 55	07 02	07 25				07 42	07 55	08 01	08 15
Kemsley	d												06 30	07 00		07 30					08 00		
Swale	d												06 33	07 03		07 33					08 03		
Queenborough	d												06 38	07 08		07 38					08 08		
Sheerness-on-Sea	a												06 43	07 13		07 43					08 13		
Teynham	d			00 20								06 11			07 06					07 46			08 20
Faversham	a			00 26	00 31	01 03						06 17			07 12					07 52		08 09	08 25
	d			00 36							06 24	06 26			07 13			07 24	07 26	07 53		08 10	08 26
Selling	d											06 31							07 31				08 31
Canterbury East	d											06 40			07 25				07 40			08 22	08 40
Bekesbourne	d											06 45							07 45				08 45
Adisham	d											06 49							07 49				08 49
Aylesham	d											06 52							07 52				08 52
Snowdown	d											06 54							07 54				08 54
Shepherds Well	d											06 58							07 58				08 58
Kearsney	d											07 03							08 03				09 03
Dover Priory	a											07 08			07 41				08 08			08 39	09 08
Whitstable	d		00 02	00 44							06 32							07 32		08 02			
Chestfield & Swalecliffe	d		00 05	00 47							06 35							07 35		08 05			
Herne Bay	d		00 09	00 51							06 39							07 39		08 09			
Birchington-on-Sea	d		00 18	01 00							06 48							07 48		08 18			
Westgate-on-Sea	d		00 21	01 04							06 52							07 52		08 21			
Margate	d	00 04	00 25	01 08					05 53	06 53	06 57						07 53	07 57		08 25			
Broadstairs	d	00 10	00 31	01 14					05 59	06 59	07 03						07 59	08 03		08 31			
Dumpton Park	d	00 13	00 34	01 17							07 06							08 06		08 34			
Ramsgate	a	00 17	00 38	01 21					06 04	07 04	07 09						08 04	08 09		08 38			

A From St Pancras International
B From London Victoria
C To Ashford International
D To St Pancras International

For further services between St Pancras International, London Blackfriars and Elephant & Castle and Bromley South, St Mary Cray and Swanley refer to table T52

Table T212-F

London - Medway, Sheerness-on-Sea, Dover and Ramsgate

Saturdays
26 May to 8 December

		SE ◇ A	SE ◇ A	SE	SE ◇■	SE ◇	SE	SE ◇■	SE ◇■	SE ◇ A	SE ◇ A	SE	SE ◇■	SE ◇	SE	SE ◇■	SE ◇■	SE ◇ A	SE ◇ A	SE	SE ◇■	SE ◇	SE
St Pancras Intl. ⊖	d		07 25			07 55					08 25			08 52					09 25			09 55	
Stratford International ⊖	d		07 32			08 02					08 32			08 59					09 32			10 02	
Ebbsfleet International	d		07 43			08 13					08 43			09 13					09 44			10 13	
London Blackfriars ⊖	d																						
Elephant & Castle ⊖	d																						
London Victoria ⊖	d				07 40			07 42	08 10				08 40			08 42	09 10				09 40		
Bromley South	d				07 57			08 05	08 27				08 57			09 05	09 27				09 57		
St Mary Cray	d							08 10								09 10							
Swanley	d							08 15								09 15							
Farningham Road	d							08 20								09 20							
Longfield	d				08 09			08 24	08 39				09 09			09 24	09 39				10 09		
Meopham	d				08 13			08 28	08 43				09 13			09 28	09 43				10 13		
Sole Street	d							08 31								09 31							
London Charing Cross ⊖	d																						
London Waterloo (East) ⊖	d																						
London Cannon Street ⊖	d																						
London Bridge ⊖	d																						
Dartford	d																						
Greenhithe for Bluewater	d																						
Gravesend	d		07 48			08 18					08 48			09 18					09 48			10 18	
Strood	d		07 59			08 29					08 59			09 29					09 59			10 29	
Rochester	d		08 02		08 23	08 32		08 40	08 53		09 02		09 23	09 32		09 40	09 53		10 02		10 23	10 32	
Chatham	d		08 06		08 27	08 36		08 43	08 57		09 06		09 27	09 36		09 43	09 57		10 06		10 27	10 36	
Gillingham (Kent)	d		08 10		08 31	08 40		08 48	09 01		09 10		09 31	09 40		09 48	10 01		10 10		10 31	10 40	
Rainham (Kent)	d		08 15		08 36	08 45		08 53	09 06		09 15		09 36	09 45		09 53	10 06		10 15		10 36	10 45	
Newington	d								09 10								10 10						
Sittingbourne	a		08 22		08 43	08 52		09 00	09 15		09 22		09 43	09 52		10 00	10 15		10 22		10 43	10 52	
	d		08 23	08 25	08 44	08 54	08 55	09 01	09 15		09 23	09 25	09 44	09 54	09 55	10 01	10 15		10 23	10 25	10 44	10 54	10 55
Kemsley	d			08 30			09 00					09 30			10 00					10 30			11 00
Swale	d			08 33			09 03					09 33			10 03					10 33			11 03
Queenborough	d			08 38			09 08					09 38			10 08					10 38			11 08
Sheerness-on-Sea	a			08 43			09 13					09 43			10 13					10 43			11 13
Teynham	d								09 20								10 20						
Faversham	a		08 31		08 52	09 05		09 09	09 25		09 31		09 52	10 05		10 09	10 25		10 31		10 52	11 05	
	d		08 31		08 53			09 10	09 26		09 31		09 53			10 10	10 26		10 31		10 53		
Selling	d								09 31								10 31						
Canterbury East	d							09 22	09 40							10 22	10 40						
Bekesbourne	d								09 45								10 45						
Adisham	d								09 49								10 49						
Aylesham	d								09 52								10 52						
Snowdown	d								09 54								10 54						
Shepherds Well	d								09 58								10 58						
Kearsney	d								10 03								11 03						
Dover Priory	a							09 39	10 08							10 39	11 08						
Whitstable	d		08 40		09 02						09 40		10 02						10 40		11 02		
Chestfield & Swalecliffe	d				09 05								10 05								11 05		
Herne Bay	d		08 45		09 09						09 45		10 09						10 45		11 09		
Birchington-on-Sea	d		08 54		09 18						09 54		10 18						10 54		11 18		
Westgate-on-Sea	d				09 21								10 21								11 21		
Margate	d	08 53	08 59		09 25					09 53	09 59		10 25					10 53	10 59		11 25		
Broadstairs	d	08 59	09 05		09 31					09 59	10 05		10 31					10 59	11 05		11 31		
Dumpton Park	d				09 34								10 34								11 34		
Ramsgate	a	09 04	09 11		09 38					10 04	10 11		10 38					11 04	11 11		11 38		

A To St Pancras International

For further services between St Pancras International, London Blackfriars and Elephant & Castle and Bromley South, St Mary Cray and Swanley refer to table T52

Table T212-F

Saturdays

26 May to 8 December

London - Medway, Sheerness-on-Sea, Dover and Ramsgate

		SE ◇■	SE ◇■	SE ◇ A	SE ◇ A	SE	SE ◇■	SE ◇	SE	SE ◇■	SE ◇■	SE ◇ A	SE ◇ A	SE	SE ◇■	SE ◇	SE	SE ◇■	SE ◇■	SE ◇ A	SE ◇ A	SE
St Pancras Intl. ⊖	d				10 22			10 52					11 25			11 55					12 27	
Stratford International ⊖	d				10 32			10 59					11 32			12 02					12 34	
Ebbsfleet International	d				10 44			11 13					11 43			12 13					12 45	
London Blackfriars ⊖	d																					
Elephant & Castle ⊖	d																					
London Victoria ⊖	d	09 42	10 10				10 40			10 42	11 10				11 40			11 42	12 10			
Bromley South	d	10 05	10 27				10 57			11 05	11 27				11 57			12 05	12 27			
St Mary Cray	d	10 10								11 10								12 10				
Swanley	d	10 15								11 15								12 15				
Farningham Road	d	10 20								11 20								12 20				
Longfield	d	10 24	10 39				11 09			11 24	11 39				12 09			12 24	12 39			
Meopham	d	10 28	10 43				11 13			11 28	11 43				12 13			12 28	12 43			
Sole Street	d	10 31								11 31								12 31				
London Charing Cross ⊖	d																					
London Waterloo (East) ⊖	d																					
London Cannon Street ⊖	d																					
London Bridge ⊖	d																					
Dartford	d																					
Greenhithe for Bluewater	d																					
Gravesend	d				10 48			11 18					11 48			12 18					12 49	
Strood	d				10 59			11 29					11 59			12 29					12 59	
Rochester	d	10 40	10 53		11 02		11 23	11 32		11 40	11 53		12 02		12 23	12 32		12 40	12 53		13 02	
Chatham	d	10 43	10 57		11 06		11 27	11 36		11 43	11 57		12 06		12 27	12 36		12 43	12 57		13 06	
Gillingham (Kent)	d	10 48	11 01		11 10		11 31	11 40		11 48	12 01		12 10		12 31	12 40		12 48	13 01		13 10	
Rainham (Kent)	d	10 53	11 06		11 15		11 36	11 45		11 53	12 06		12 15		12 36	12 45		12 53	13 06		13 15	
Newington	d		11 10								12 10								13 10			
Sittingbourne	a	11 00	11 15		11 22		11 43	11 52		12 00	12 15		12 22		12 43	12 52		13 00	13 15		13 22	
	d	11 01	11 15		11 23	11 25	11 44	11 54	11 55	12 01	12 15		12 23	12 25	12 44	12 54	12 55	13 01	13 15		13 23	13 25
Kemsley	d					11 30			12 00					12 30			13 00					13 30
Swale	d					11 33			12 03					12 33			13 03					13 33
Queenborough	d					11 38			12 08					12 38			13 08					13 38
Sheerness-on-Sea	a					11 43			12 13					12 43			13 13					13 43
Teynham	d		11 20								12 20								13 20			
Faversham	a	11 09	11 25		11 31		11 52	12 05		12 09	12 25		12 31		12 52	13 05		13 09	13 25		13 31	
	d	11 10	11 26		11 31		11 53			12 10	12 26		12 31		12 53			13 10	13 26		13 31	
Selling	d		11 31								12 31								13 31			
Canterbury East	d	11 22	11 40							12 22	12 40							13 22	13 40			
Bekesbourne	d		11 45								12 45								13 45			
Adisham	d		11 49								12 49								13 49			
Aylesham	d		11 52								12 52								13 52			
Snowdown	d		11 54								12 54								13 54			
Shepherds Well	d		11 58								12 58								13 58			
Kearsney	d		12 03								13 03								14 03			
Dover Priory	a	11 39	12 08							12 39	13 08							13 39	14 08			
Whitstable	d				11 40		12 02						12 40		13 02						13 40	
Chestfield & Swalecliffe	d						12 05								13 05							
Herne Bay	d				11 45		12 09						12 45		13 09						13 45	
Birchington-on-Sea	d				11 54		12 18						12 54		13 18						13 54	
Westgate-on-Sea	d						12 21								13 21							
Margate	d			11 53	11 59		12 25					12 53	12 59		13 25					13 53	13 59	
Broadstairs	d			11 59	12 05		12 31					12 59	13 05		13 31					13 59	14 05	
Dumpton Park	d						12 34								13 34							
Ramsgate	a			12 04	12 11		12 38					13 04	13 11		13 38					14 04	14 11	

A To St Pancras International

For further services between St Pancras International, London Blackfriars and Elephant & Castle and Bromley South, St Mary Cray and Swanley refer to table T52

Table T212-F

Saturdays

26 May to 8 December

London - Medway, Sheerness-on-Sea, Dover and Ramsgate

		SE ◇■	SE ◇	SE	SE ◇■	SE ◇■	SE ◇ A	SE ◇ A	SE	SE ◇■	SE ◇		SE	SE ◇■	SE ◇■	SE ◇ A	SE ◇ A	SE	SE ◇■	SE ◇	SE	SE ◇■	SE ◇■
St Pancras Intl. ⊖	d		12 52					13 25			13 55						19 25			19 55			
Stratford International ⊖	d		12 59					13 32			14 02						19 32			20 02			
Ebbsfleet International	d		13 13					13 43			14 13						19 43			20 13			
London Blackfriars ⊖	d																						
Elephant & Castle ⊖	d																						
London Victoria ⊖	d	12 40			12 42	13 10				13 40				18 42	19 10				19 40			19 42	20 10
Bromley South	d	12 57			13 05	13 27				13 57				19 05	19 27				19 57			20 05	20 27
St Mary Cray	d				13 10									19 10								20 10	
Swanley	d				13 15									19 15								20 15	
Farningham Road	d				13 20									19 20								20 20	
Longfield	d	13 09			13 24	13 39				14 09				19 24	19 39				20 09			20 24	20 39
Meopham	d	13 13			13 28	13 43				14 13				19 28	19 43				20 13			20 28	20 43
Sole Street	d				13 31									19 31								20 31	
London Charing Cross ⊖	d																						
London Waterloo (East) ⊖	d																						
London Cannon Street ⊖	d																						
London Bridge ⊖	d																						
Dartford	d																						
Greenhithe for Bluewater	d																						
Gravesend	d		13 18					13 48			14 18						19 48			20 18			
Strood	d		13 29					13 59			14 29						19 59			20 29			
Rochester	d	13 23	13 32		13 40	13 53		14 02		14 23	14 32	and at		19 40	19 53		20 02		20 23	20 32		20 40	20 53
Chatham	d	13 27	13 36		13 43	13 57		14 06		14 27	14 36	the same		19 43	19 57		20 06		20 27	20 36		20 43	20 57
Gillingham (Kent)	d	13 31	13 40		13 48	14 01		14 10		14 31	14 40	minutes		19 48	20 01		20 10		20 31	20 40		20 48	21 01
Rainham (Kent)	d	13 36	13 45		13 53	14 06		14 15		14 36	14 45	past		19 53	20 06		20 15		20 36	20 45		20 53	21 06
Newington	d					14 10						each			20 10								21 10
Sittingbourne	a	13 43	13 52		14 00	14 15		14 22		14 43	14 52	hour until		20 00	20 15		20 22		20 43	20 52		21 00	21 15
	d	13 44	13 54	13 55	14 01	14 15		14 23	14 25	14 44	14 54		19 55	20 01	20 15		20 23	20 25	20 44	20 54	20 55	21 01	21 15
Kemsley	d			14 00					14 30				20 00					20 30			21 00		
Swale	d			14 03					14 33				20 03					20 33			21 03		
Queenborough	d			14 08					14 38				20 08					20 38			21 08		
Sheerness-on-Sea	a			14 13					14 43				20 13					20 43			21 13		
Teynham	d					14 20									20 20								21 20
Faversham	a	13 52	14 05		14 09	14 25		14 31		14 52	15 05			20 09	20 25		20 31		20 52	21 05		21 09	21 25
	d	13 53			14 10	14 26		14 31		14 53				20 10	20 26		20 31		20 53			21 10	21 26
Selling	d					14 31									20 31								21 31
Canterbury East	d				14 22	14 40								20 22	20 40							21 22	21 40
Bekesbourne	d					14 45									20 45								21 45
Adisham	d					14 49									20 49								21 49
Aylesham	d					14 52									20 52								21 52
Snowdown	d					14 54									20 54								21 54
Shepherds Well	d					14 58									20 58								21 58
Kearsney	d					15 03									21 03								22 03
Dover Priory	a				14 39	15 08								20 39	21 08							21 39	22 08
Whitstable	d	14 02						14 40		15 02							20 40		21 02				
Chestfield & Swalecliffe	d	14 05								15 05									21 05				
Herne Bay	d	14 09						14 45		15 09							20 45		21 09				
Birchington-on-Sea	d	14 18						14 54		15 18							20 54		21 18				
Westgate-on-Sea	d	14 21								15 21									21 21				
Margate	d	14 25					14 53	14 59		15 25						20 53	20 59		21 25				
Broadstairs	d	14 31					14 59	15 05		15 31						20 59	21 05		21 31				
Dumpton Park	d	14 34								15 34									21 34				
Ramsgate	a	14 38					15 04	15 11		15 38						21 04	21 11		21 38				

A To St Pancras International

For further services between St Pancras International, London Blackfriars and Elephant & Castle and Bromley South, St Mary Cray and Swanley refer to table T52

Table T212-F

Saturdays

26 May to 8 December

London - Medway, Sheerness-on-Sea, Dover and Ramsgate

		SE	SE	SE	SE	SE	SE	SE	SE	SE	SE	SE	SE	SE	SE	SE	SE	SE	SE	SE	SE	SE	SE
		◇	◇		◇1	◇		◇1	◇1		◇		◇1	◇	◇1	◇1	◇	◇1		◇1	◇	◇1	◇1
		A	A							B						C		D					
St Pancras Intl. ⊖	d		20 25			20 55					21 25			21 55			22 25				22 55		
Stratford International ⊖	d		20 32			21 02					21 32			22 02			22 32				23 02		
Ebbsfleet International	d		20 43			21 13					21 43			22 13			22 43				23 13		
London Blackfriars ⊖	d																						
Elephant & Castle ⊖	d																						
London Victoria ⊖	d				20 40			20 42	21 10				21 40		21 42	22 10				22 40		22 42	23 10
Bromley South	d				20 57			21 05	21 27				21 57		22 05	22 27				22 57		23 05	23 27
St Mary Cray	d							21 10							22 10							23 10	
Swanley	d							21 15							22 15							23 15	
Farningham Road	d							21 20							22 20							23 20	
Longfield	d				21 09			21 24	21 39				22 09		22 24	22 39				23 09		23 24	23 39
Meopham	d				21 13			21 28	21 43				22 13		22 28	22 43				23 13		23 28	23 43
Sole Street	d							21 31							22 31							23 31	
London Charing Cross ⊖	d																						
London Waterloo (East) ⊖	d																						
London Cannon Street ⊖	d																						
London Bridge ⊖	d																						
Dartford	d																						
Greenhithe for Bluewater	d																						
Gravesend	d		20 48			21 18					21 48			22 18			22 48				23 18		
Strood	d		20 59			21 29					21 59			22 29			22 59				23 29		
Rochester	d		21 02		21 23	21 32		21 40	21 53		22 02		22 23	22 32	22 40	22 53	23 02			23 23	23 32	23 40	23 53
Chatham	d		21 06		21 27	21 36		21 43	21 57		22 06		22 27	22 36	22 43	22 57	23 06			23 27	23 36	23 43	23 57
Gillingham (Kent)	d		21 10		21 31	21 40		21 48	22 01		22 10		22 31	22 40	22 48	23 01	23 10			23 31	23 40	23a48	00 01
Rainham (Kent)	d		21 15		21 36	21 45		21 53	22 06		22 15		22 36	22 45	22 53	23 06	23 15			23 36	23 45		00 06
Newington	d								22 10							23 10							00 10
Sittingbourne	a		21 22		21 43	21 52		22 00	22 15		22 22		22 43	22 52	23 00	23 15	23 22			23 43	23 52		00 15
	d		21 23	21 25	21 44	21 53	21 55	22 01	22 15		22 23	22 25	22 44	22 53	23 01	23 15	23 23		23 25	23 44	23 53		00 15
Kemsley	d			21 30			22 00					22 30							23 30				
Swale	d			21 33			22 03					22 33							23 33				
Queenborough	d			21 38			22 08					22 38							23 38				
Sheerness-on-Sea	a			21 43			22 13					22 43							23 43				
Teynham	d								22 20							23 20		←					00 20
Faversham	a		21 31		21 52	22 01		22 09	22 25		22 31		22 52	23 01	23 09	23 26	23 31	23 26		23 52	00 01		00 26
	d		21 31		21 53			22 10	22 26		22 31		22 54		23 10	23 34	23 31	23 34		23 54			00 35
Selling	d								22 31							→		23s38					
Canterbury East	d							22a23	22 40						23a23			23 48					
Bekesbourne	d								22 45									23s52					
Adisham	d								22 49									23s56					
Aylesham	d								22 52									23s59					
Snowdown	d								22 54									00s02					
Shepherds Well	d								22 58									00s05					
Kearsney	d								23 03									00s10					
Dover Priory	a								23 08									00 15					
Whitstable	d		21 40		22 02						22 40		23 02				23 40			00 02			00 43
Chestfield & Swalecliffe	d				22 05								23 05							00 05			00 46
Herne Bay	d		21 45		22 09						22 45		23 09				23 45			00 09			00 50
Birchington-on-Sea	d		21 54		22 18						22 54		23 18				23 54			00 18			00 59
Westgate-on-Sea	d				22 21								23 21							00 21			01 03
Margate	d	21 53	21 59		22 25					22 53	22 59		23 25				23 59			00 25			01 07
Broadstairs	d	21 59	22 05		22 31					22 59	23 05		23 31				00 05			00 31			01 13
Dumpton Park	d				22 34								23 34							00 34			01 16
Ramsgate	a	22 04	22 11		22 38					23 04	23 11		23 38				00 11			00 38			01 20

A To St Pancras International
B To Ashford International
C To Dover Priory
D From London Victoria

For further services between St Pancras International, London Blackfriars and Elephant & Castle and Bromley South, St Mary Cray and Swanley refer to table T52

Table T212-F

Saturdays

26 May to 8 December

London - Medway, Sheerness-on-Sea, Dover and Ramsgate

		SE	SE	SE
		◇	◇	◇1
St Pancras Intl. ⊖	d	23 25	23 55	
Stratford International ⊖	d	23 32	00 02	
Ebbsfleet International	d	23 43	00 13	
London Blackfriars ⊖	d			
Elephant & Castle ⊖	d			
London Victoria ⊖	d			23 42
Bromley South	d			00 05
St Mary Cray	d			00 10
Swanley	d			00 15
Farningham Road	d			00 20
Longfield	d			00 24
Meopham	d			00 28
Sole Street	d			00s31
London Charing Cross ⊖	d			
London Waterloo (East) ⊖	d			
London Cannon Street ⊖	d			
London Bridge ⊖	d			
Dartford	d			
Greenhithe for Bluewater	d			
Gravesend	d	23 48	00 18	
Strood	d	23 59	00 29	
Rochester	d	00 02	00 32	00 40
Chatham	d	00 06	00 36	00 43
Gillingham (Kent)	d	00 10	00 40	00a48
Rainham (Kent)	d	00 15	00 45	
Newington	d			
Sittingbourne	a	00 22	00 52	
	d	00 23	00 53	
Kemsley	d			
Swale	d			
Queenborough	d			
Sheerness-on-Sea	a			
Teynham	d			
Faversham	a	00 31	01 01	
	d			
Selling	d			
Canterbury East	d			
Bekesbourne	d			
Adisham	d			
Aylesham	d			
Snowdown	d			
Shepherds Well	d			
Kearsney	d			
Dover Priory	a			
Whitstable	d			
Chestfield & Swalecliffe	d			
Herne Bay	d			
Birchington-on-Sea	d			
Westgate-on-Sea	d			
Margate	d			
Broadstairs	d			
Dumpton Park	d			
Ramsgate	a			

For further services between St Pancras International, London Blackfriars and Elephant & Castle and Bromley South, St Mary Cray and Swanley refer to table T52

Table T212-F

Sundays

20 May to 2 December

London - Medway, Sheerness-on-Sea, Dover and Ramsgate

		SE	SE	SE	SE	SE	SE	SE	SE	SE		SE	SE	SE	SE		SE	SE	SE	SE		SE		SE	SE
		◇	◇■	◇■	◇		◇	◇■				◇	◇	◇	◇■		◇	◇	◇■			◇■		◇	◇
		A	B	B	A		A	B				C	D	D			D	D						D	D
St Pancras Intl. ⊖	d											00 12						08 25							09 25
Stratford International ⊖	d						00 02					00 19						08 32							09 32
Ebbsfleet International	d						00 13					00a30						08 43							09 44
London Blackfriars ⊖	d																								
Elephant & Castle ⊖	d																								
London Victoria ⊖	d														07 40				08 10			08 40			
Bromley South	d							00 05							07 57				08 34			08 57			
St Mary Cray	d							00 10											08 39						
Swanley	d							00 15											08 44						
Farningham Road	d							00 20											08 49						
Longfield	d							00 24											08 53						
Meopham	d							00 28											08 57						
Sole Street	d							00s31											08 59						
London Charing Cross ⊖	d																								
London Waterloo (East) ⊖	d																								
London Cannon Street ⊖	d																								
London Bridge ⊖	d																								
Dartford	d																								
Greenhithe for Bluewater	d																								
Gravesend	d						00 18											08 48							09 48
Strood	d						00 29											08 59							09 59
Rochester	d				00 02		00 32	00 40							08 20			09 02	09 08			09 20			10 02
Chatham	d				00 06		00 36	00 43							08 24			09 06	09 12			09 24			10 06
Gillingham (Kent)	d			00 01	00 10		00 40	00a48	08 17						08 28			09 10	09 17			09 28			10 10
Rainham (Kent)	d			00 06	00 15		00 45		08 21						08 33			09 15	09 21			09 33			10 15
Newington	d			00 10					08 25										09 25						
Sittingbourne	a			00 15	00 22		00 52		08 30						08 40			09 22	09 30			09 40			10 22
	d			00 15	00 23	00 25	00 53		08 30	08 34					08 41			09 23	09 30	09 34		09 41			10 23
Kemsley	d					00s29				08 39										09 39					
Swale	d					00s33				08 42										09 42					
Queenborough	d					00s37				08 46										09 46					
Sheerness-on-Sea	a					00 43				08 51										09 51					
Teynham	d			00 20					08 35										09 35						
Faversham	a			00 26	00 31		01 01		08 40						08 49			09 31	09 40			09 49			10 31
	d			00 35					08 41						08 52	08 55		09 31	09 41			09 52	09 55		10 31
Selling	d															08 59							09 59		
Canterbury East	d								08a53							09 09			09a53				10 09		
Bekesbourne	d															09 13							10 13		
Adisham	d															09 17							10 17		
Aylesham	d															09 20							10 20		
Snowdown	d															09 22							10 22		
Shepherds Well	d															09 26							10 26		
Kearsney	d															09 31							10 31		
Dover Priory	a															09 36							10 36		
Whitstable	d		00 02	00 43											09 01			09 40				10 01			10 40
Chestfield & Swalecliffe	d		00 05	00 46											09 04							10 04			
Herne Bay	d		00 09	00 50											09 08			09 45				10 08			10 45
Birchington-on-Sea	d		00 18	00 59											09 17			09 54				10 17			10 54
Westgate-on-Sea	d		00 21	01 03											09 20							10 20			
Margate	d		00 25	01 07									07 53	08 53	09 24		09 53	09 59				10 24		10 53	10 59
Broadstairs	d	00 05	00 31	01 13									07 59	08 59	09 30		09 59	10 05				10 30		10 59	11 05
Dumpton Park	d		00 34	01 16											09 33							10 33			
Ramsgate	a	00 11	00 38	01 20									08 04	09 04	09 37		10 04	10 11				10 37		11 04	11 11

A not 20 May. From St Pancras International

B not 20 May. From London Victoria

C To Ashford International

D To St Pancras International

For further services between St Pancras International, London Blackfriars and Elephant & Castle and Bromley South, St Mary Cray and Swanley refer to table T52

Table T212-F

Sundays

20 May to 2 December

London - Medway, Sheerness-on-Sea, Dover and Ramsgate

		SE	SE	SE		SE		SE	SE	SE	SE		SE	SE	SE	SE		SE		SE	SE	SE	SE	SE	
		◇■		◇■		◇		◇	◇■		◇■		◇	◇	◇■			◇■		◇	◇	◇■		◇■	
						A		A					A	A						A	A				
St Pancras Intl. ⊖	d							10 27						11 25							12 27				
Stratford International ⊖	d							10 34						11 32							12 34				
Ebbsfleet International	d							10 45						11 43							12 45				
London Blackfriars ⊖	d																								
Elephant & Castle ⊖	d																								
London Victoria ⊖	d	09 10		09 40					10 10		10 40				11 10			11 40				12 10		12 40	
Bromley South	d	09 34		09 57					10 34		10 57				11 34			11 57				12 34		12 57	
St Mary Cray	d	09 39							10 39						11 39							12 39			
Swanley	d	09 44							10 44						11 44							12 44			
Farningham Road	d	09 49							10 49						11 49							12 49			
Longfield	d	09 53							10 53						11 53							12 53			
Meopham	d	09 57							10 57						11 57							12 57			
Sole Street	d	09 59							10 59						11 59							12 59			
London Charing Cross ⊖	d																								
London Waterloo (East) ⊖	d																								
London Cannon Street ⊖	d																								
London Bridge ⊖	d																								
Dartford	d																								
Greenhithe for Bluewater	d																								
Gravesend	d							10 49						11 48							12 49				
Strood	d							10 59						11 59							12 59				
Rochester	d	10 08		10 20				11 03	11 08		11 20			12 02	12 08			12 20			13 03	13 08		13 20	
Chatham	d	10 12		10 24				11 06	11 12		11 24			12 06	12 12			12 24			13 06	13 12		13 24	
Gillingham (Kent)	d	10 17		10 28				11 11	11 17		11 28			12 10	12 17			12 28			13 11	13 17		13 28	
Rainham (Kent)	d	10 21		10 33				11 15	11 21		11 33			12 15	12 21			12 33			13 15	13 21		13 33	
Newington	d	10 25							11 25						12 25							13 25			
Sittingbourne	a	10 30		10 40				11 22	11 30		11 40			12 22	12 30			12 40			13 22	13 30		13 40	
	d	10 30	10 34	10 41				11 23	11 30	11 34	11 41			12 23	12 30	12 34		12 41			13 23	13 30	13 34	13 41	
Kemsley	d		10 39							11 39						12 39							13 39		
Swale	d		10 42							11 42						12 42							13 42		
Queenborough	d		10 46							11 46						12 46							13 46		
Sheerness-on-Sea	a		10 51							11 51						12 51							13 51		
Teynham	d	10 35							11 35						12 35							13 35			
Faversham	a	10 40		10 49				11 31	11 40		11 49			12 31	12 40			12 49			13 31	13 40		13 49	
	d	10 41		10 52	10 55			11 31	11 41		11 52	11 55		12 31	12 41			12 52	12 55		13 31	13 41		13 52	13 55
Selling	d				10 59							11 59							12 59						13 59
Canterbury East	d	10a53			11 09				11a53			12 09			12a53				13 09			13a53			14 09
Bekesbourne	d				11 13							12 13							13 13						14 13
Adisham	d				11 17							12 17							13 17						14 17
Aylesham	d				11 20							12 20							13 20						14 20
Snowdown	d				11 22							12 22							13 22						14 22
Shepherds Well	d				11 26							12 26							13 26						14 26
Kearsney	d				11 31							12 31							13 31						14 31
Dover Priory	a				11 36							12 36							13 36						14 36
Whitstable	d			11 01				11 40			12 01			12 40				13 01			13 40			14 01	
Chestfield & Swalecliffe	d			11 04							12 04							13 04						14 04	
Herne Bay	d			11 08				11 45			12 08			12 45				13 08			13 45			14 08	
Birchington-on-Sea	d			11 17				11 54			12 17			12 54				13 17			13 54			14 17	
Westgate-on-Sea	d			11 20							12 20							13 20						14 20	
Margate	d			11 24		11 53		11 59			12 24		12 53	12 59				13 24		13 53	13 59			14 24	
Broadstairs	d			11 30		11 59		12 05			12 30		12 59	13 05				13 30		13 59	14 05			14 30	
Dumpton Park	d			11 33							12 33							13 33						14 33	
Ramsgate	a			11 37		12 04		12 11			12 37		13 04	13 11				13 37		14 04	14 11			14 37	

A To St Pancras International

For further services between St Pancras International, London Blackfriars and Elephant & Castle and Bromley South, St Mary Cray and Swanley refer to table T52

Table T212-F

20 May to 2 December

London - Medway, Sheerness-on-Sea, Dover and Ramsgate

Station		SE ◇ A	SE ◇ A	SE ◇ A	SE ◇1	SE	SE ◇1		SE ◇ A		SE ◇ A	SE ◇ A	SE ◇1	SE	SE ◇1		SE ◇ A	SE ◇ A	SE ◇ A	SE ◇1	SE	SE ◇1	
St Pancras Intl. ⊖	d	12 52		13 25					13 55			16 25					16 55		17 25				
Stratford International ⊖	d	12 59		13 32					14 02			16 32					17 02		17 32				
Ebbsfleet International	d	13 13		13 43					14 13			16 43					17 13		17 43				
London Blackfriars ⊖	d																						
Elephant & Castle ⊖	d																						
London Victoria ⊖	d				13 10		13 40						16 10		16 40					17 10		17 40	
Bromley South	d				13 34		13 57						16 34		16 57					17 34		17 57	
St Mary Cray	d				13 39								16 39							17 39			
Swanley	d				13 44								16 44							17 44			
Farningham Road	d				13 49								16 49							17 49			
Longfield	d				13 53								16 53							17 53			
Meopham	d				13 57								16 57							17 57			
Sole Street	d				13 59								16 59							17 59			
London Charing Cross ⊖	d																						
London Waterloo (East) ⊖	d																						
London Cannon Street ⊖	d																						
London Bridge ⊖	d																						
Dartford	d																						
Greenhithe for Bluewater	d																						
Gravesend	d	13 18		13 48					14 18			16 48					17 18		17 48				
Strood	d	13 29		13 59					14 29			16 59					17 29		17 59				
Rochester	d	13 32		14 02	14 08		14 20		14 32	and at		17 02	17 08		17 20		17 32		18 02	18 08		18 20	
Chatham	d	13 36		14 06	14 12		14 24		14 36	the same		17 06	17 12		17 24		17 36		18 06	18 12		18 24	
Gillingham (Kent)	d	13 40		14 10	14 17		14 28		14 40	minutes		17 10	17 17		17 28		17 40		18 10	18 17		18 28	
Rainham (Kent)	d	13 45		14 15	14 21		14 33		14 45	past		17 15	17 21		17 33		17 45		18 15	18 21		18 33	
Newington	d				14 25					each			17 25							18 25			
Sittingbourne	a	13 52		14 22	14 30		14 40		14 52	hour until		17 22	17 30		17 40		17 52		18 22	18 30		18 40	
	d	13 53		14 23	14 30	14 34	14 41		14 53			17 23	17 30	17 34	17 41		17 53		18 23	18 30	18 34	18 41	
Kemsley	d					14 39								17 39							18 39		
Swale	d					14 42								17 42							18 42		
Queenborough	d					14 46								17 46							18 46		
Sheerness-on-Sea	a					14 51								17 51							18 51		
Teynham	d				14 35								17 35							18 35			
Faversham	a	14 02		14 31	14 40		14 49		15 02			17 31	17 40		17 49		18 02		18 31	18 40		18 49	
	d			14 31	14 41		14 52	14 55				17 31	17 41		17 52	17 55			18 31	18 41		18 52	18 55
Selling	d							14 59								17 59							18 59
Canterbury East	d				14a53			15 09					17a53			18 09				18a53			19 09
Bekesbourne	d							15 13								18 13							19 13
Adisham	d							15 17								18 17							19 17
Aylesham	d							15 20								18 20							19 20
Snowdown	d							15 22								18 22							19 22
Shepherds Well	d							15 26								18 26							19 26
Kearsney	d							15 31								18 31							19 31
Dover Priory	a							15 36								18 36							19 36
Whitstable	d			14 40			15 01					17 40			18 01				18 40			19 01	
Chestfield & Swalecliffe	d						15 04								18 04							19 04	
Herne Bay	d			14 45			15 08					17 45			18 08				18 45			19 08	
Birchington-on-Sea	d			14 54			15 17					17 54			18 17				18 54			19 17	
Westgate-on-Sea	d						15 20								18 20							19 20	
Margate	d		14 53	14 59			15 24				17 53	17 59			18 24			18 53	18 59			19 24	
Broadstairs	d		14 59	15 05			15 30				17 59	18 05			18 30			18 59	19 05			19 30	
Dumpton Park	d						15 33								18 33							19 33	
Ramsgate	a		15 04	15 11			15 37				18 04	18 11			18 37			19 04	19 11			19 37	

A To St Pancras International

For further services between St Pancras International, London Blackfriars and Elephant & Castle and Bromley South, St Mary Cray and Swanley refer to table T52

Table T212-F

20 May to 2 December

London - Medway, Sheerness-on-Sea, Dover and Ramsgate

Station		SE ◇ A	SE ◇ A	SE ◇ A	SE ◇1	SE	SE ◇1		SE ◇	SE ◇ A	SE ◇ A	SE ◇1	SE	SE ◇1		SE ◇ A	SE ◇ A	SE ◇ B	SE ◇1	SE	SE ◇1	
St Pancras Intl. ⊖	d	17 52		18 25					18 55		19 25					19 55		20 25				
Stratford International ⊖	d	18 02		18 32					19 02		19 32					20 02		20 32				
Ebbsfleet International	d	18 13		18 43					19 13		19 43					20 13		20 43				
London Blackfriars ⊖	d																					
Elephant & Castle ⊖	d																					
London Victoria ⊖	d				18 10		18 40					19 10		19 40					20 10		20 40	
Bromley South	d				18 34		18 57					19 34		19 57					20 34		20 57	
St Mary Cray	d				18 39							19 39							20 39			
Swanley	d				18 44							19 44							20 44			
Farningham Road	d				18 49							19 49							20 49			
Longfield	d				18 53							19 53							20 53			
Meopham	d				18 57							19 57							20 57			
Sole Street	d				18 59							19 59							20 59			
London Charing Cross ⊖	d																					
London Waterloo (East) ⊖	d																					
London Cannon Street ⊖	d																					
London Bridge ⊖	d																					
Dartford	d																					
Greenhithe for Bluewater	d																					
Gravesend	d	18 18		18 48					19 18		19 48					20 18		20 48				
Strood	d	18 29		18 59					19 29		19 59					20 29		20 59				
Rochester	d	18 32		19 02	19 08		19 20		19 32		20 02	20 08		20 20		20 32		21 02	21 08		21 20	
Chatham	d	18 36		19 06	19 12		19 24		19 36		20 06	20 12		20 24		20 36		21 06	21 12		21 24	
Gillingham (Kent)	d	18 40		19 10	19 17		19 28		19 40		20 10	20 17		20 28		20 40		21 10	21 17		21 28	
Rainham (Kent)	d	18 45		19 15	19 21		19 33		19 45		20 15	20 21		20 33		20 45		21 15	21 21		21 33	
Newington	d				19 25							20 25							21 25			
Sittingbourne	a	18 52		19 22	19 30		19 40		19 52		20 22	20 30		20 40		20 52		21 22	21 30		21 40	
	d	18 53		19 23	19 30	19 34	19 41		19 53		20 23	20 30	20 34	20 41		20 53		21 23	21 30	21 34	21 41	
Kemsley	d					19 39							20 39							21 39		
Swale	d					19 42							20 42							21 42		
Queenborough	d					19 46							20 46							21 46		
Sheerness-on-Sea	a					19 51							20 51							21 51		
Teynham	d				19 35							20 35							21 35			
Faversham	a	19 02		19 31	19 40		19 49		20 02		20 31	20 40		20 49		21 02		21 31	21 40		21 49	
	d			19 31	19 41		19 52	19 55			20 31	20 41		20 52	20 55			21 31	21 41		21 52	21 55
Selling	d							19 59							20 59							21 59
Canterbury East	d				19a53			20 09				20a53			21 09				21a53			22 09
Bekesbourne	d							20 13							21 13							22 13
Adisham	d							20 17							21 17							22 17
Aylesham	d							20 20							21 20							22 20
Snowdown	d							20 22							21 22							22 22
Shepherds Well	d							20 26							21 26							22 26
Kearsney	d							20 31							21 31							22 31
Dover Priory	a							20 36							21 36							22 36
Whitstable	d			19 40			20 01				20 40			21 01				21 40			22 01	
Chestfield & Swalecliffe	d						20 04							21 04							22 04	
Herne Bay	d			19 45			20 08				20 45			21 08				21 45			22 08	
Birchington-on-Sea	d			19 54			20 17				20 54			21 17				21 54			22 17	
Westgate-on-Sea	d						20 20							21 20							22 20	
Margate	d		19 53	19 59			20 24			20 53	20 59			21 24			21 53	21 59			22 24	
Broadstairs	d		19 59	20 05			20 30			20 59	21 05			21 30			21 59	22 05			22 30	
Dumpton Park	d						20 33							21 33							22 33	
Ramsgate	a		20 04	20 11			20 37			21 04	21 11			21 37			22 04	22 11			22 37	

A To St Pancras International

B To Ashford International

For further services between St Pancras International, London Blackfriars and Elephant & Castle and Bromley South, St Mary Cray and Swanley refer to table T52

Table T212-F

Sundays
20 May to 2 December

London - Medway, Sheerness-on-Sea, Dover and Ramsgate

		SE ◇	SE A	SE ◇	SE	SE ◇■		SE ◇	SE ◇	SE	SE ◇■	SE ◇	SE ◇	SE ◇■	SE ◇ A
St Pancras Intl. ⊖	d	20 55		21 25				21 55	22 25			22 55	23 25		23 37
Stratford International ⊖	d	21 02		21 32				22 02	22 32			23 02	23 32		23 44
Ebbsfleet International	d	21 13		21 43				22 13	22 43			23 13	23 43		23a54
London Blackfriars ⊖	d														
Elephant & Castle ⊖	d														
London Victoria ⊖	d					21 40					22 40			23 10	
Bromley South	d					21 57					22 57			23 34	
St Mary Cray	d													23 39	
Swanley	d													23 44	
Farningham Road	d													23 49	
Longfield	d													23 53	
Meopham	d													23 57	
Sole Street	d													23s59	
London Charing Cross ⊖	d														
London Waterloo (East) ⊖	d														
London Cannon Street ⊖	d														
London Bridge ⊖	d														
Dartford	d														
Greenhithe for Bluewater	d														
Gravesend	d	21 18		21 48				22 18	22 48			23 18	23 48		
Strood	d	21 29		21 59				22 29	22 59			23 29	23 59		
Rochester	d	21 32		22 02		22 20		22 32	23 02		23 20	23 32	00 02	00 08	
Chatham	d	21 36		22 06		22 24		22 36	23 06		23 24	23 36	00 06	00 12	
Gillingham (Kent)	d	21 40		22 10		22 28		22 40	23 10		23 28	23 40	00 10	00a17	
Rainham (Kent)	d	21 45		22 15		22 33		22 45	23 15		23 33	23 45	00 15		
Newington	d										23 37				
Sittingbourne	a	21 52		22 22		22 40		22 52	23 22		23 42	23 52	00 22		
	d	21 53		22 23	22 34	22 41		22 53	23 23	23 36	23 42	23 53	00 23		
Kemsley	d				22 39					23 41					
Swale	d				22 42					23 44					
Queenborough	d				22 46					23 48					
Sheerness-on-Sea	a				22 51					23 53					
Teynham	d										23 47				
Faversham	a	22 02		22 31		22 49		23 02	23 31		23 52	00 02	00 32		
	d			22 31		22 52	22 55		23 31		23 56				
Selling	d						22 59								
Canterbury East	d						23 09								
Bekesbourne	d						23 13								
Adisham	d						23 17								
Aylesham	d						23 20								
Snowdown	d						23 22								
Shepherds Well	d						23 26								
Kearsney	d						23 31								
Dover Priory	a						23 36								
Whitstable	d			22 40		23 01			23 40		00 04				
Chestfield & Swalecliffe	d					23 04					00 07				
Herne Bay	d			22 45		23 08			23 45		00 11				
Birchington-on-Sea	d			22 54		23 17			23 54		00 20				
Westgate-on-Sea	d					23 20					00 23				
Margate	d		22 53	22 59		23 24			23 59		00 27				
Broadstairs	d		22 59	23 05		23 30			00 05		00 33				
Dumpton Park	d					23 33					00 36				
Ramsgate	a		23 04	23 11		23 37			00 11		00 40				

A To Ashford International

For further services between St Pancras International, London Blackfriars and Elephant & Castle and Bromley South, St Mary Cray and Swanley refer to table T52

Table T212-R

Mondays to Fridays
21 May to 7 December

Ramsgate, Dover, Sheerness-on-Sea and Medway - London

Miles	Miles	Miles	Miles	Miles			SE MX ■ A	SE ■	SE MO ◇ B	SE ThFO ◇ B	SE TO ◇ B	SE ◇	SE ◇■	SE ◇■	SE	SE ◇	SE ◇■	SE	SE ◇	SE	SE ■	SE ◇■	SE ◇■	SE ◇■
0	—	—	—	—	**Ramsgate**	d			00 28	00 31	00 44		04 25						05 12					
1	—	—	—	—	Dumpton Park	d							04 28						05 15					
2¼	—	—	—	—	Broadstairs	d			00s33	00s36	00s49		04 31						05 18					05 46
5½	—	—	—	—	**Margate**	d			00a39	00a42	00a58		04 36						05 23					05 51
6¾	—	—	—	—	Westgate-on-Sea	d							04 40						05 27					05 54
8½	—	—	—	—	Birchington-on-Sea	d							04 43						05 31					05 58
16¼	—	—	—	—	**Herne Bay**	d							04 52						05 40					06 07
18½	—	—	—	—	Chestfield & Swalecliffe	d							04 56						05 43					06 10
20½	—	—	—	—	Whitstable	d							04 59						05 47					06 14
—	0	—	—	—	**Dover Priory**	d											04 48						05 32	
—	2¼	—	—	—	Kearsney	d											04 53						05 36	
—	5½	—	—	—	Shepherds Well	d											04 58						05 42	
—	7½	—	—	—	Snowdown	d											05 02						05 45	
—	8½	—	—	—	Aylesham	d											05 05						05 48	
—	9½	—	—	—	Adisham	d											05 07						05 51	
—	12½	—	—	—	Bekesbourne	d											05 12						05 55	
—	15½	—	—	—	**Canterbury East**	d											05 17						06 02	
—	22	—	—	—	Selling	d											05 27						06 11	
27¼	25¼	—	—	0	**Faversham**	a							05 07				05 31		05 55				06 16	06 22
—	—	—	—	—		d	00 02					04 58	05 09			05 28	05 33		05 56			06 07	06 18	06 23
31¾	29¾	—	—	4½	Teynham	d	00 08										05 39					06 13		
—	—	0	—	—	**Sheerness-on-Sea**	d												05 32		05 55				
—	—	2	—	—	Queenborough	d												05 37		06 00				
—	—	4	—	—	Swale	d												05 41		06 04				
—	—	6	—	—	Kemsley	d												05 45		06 08				
34½	32½	8	—	7¼	**Sittingbourne**	a	00 12					05 06	05 16			05 36	05 44	05 50	06 03	06 13		06 17	06 25	06 30
—	—	—	—	—		d	00 13					05 07	05 17			05 37	05 44		06 04			06 18	06 26	06 31
37¾	35¾	—	—	10½	Newington	d	00 18										05 50					06 23		
40¼	38¼	—	—	13	Rainham (Kent)	d	00 22					05 15	05 24			05 45	05 54		06 11			06 28	06 34	06 38
43¼	41¼	—	0	16	**Gillingham (Kent)**	d	00a29	05 14				05 20	05 30	05 40	05 45	05 50	06 00		06 17		06 21	06 33	06 39	06 44
45	43	—	1¾	17¾	**Chatham**	d		05 18				05 24	05 34	05 44	05 49	05 54	06 04		06 21		06 25	06 37	06 43	06 48
45½	43½	—	2¼	18¼	Rochester	d		05 22				05 28	05 38	05 48	05 53	05 58	06 08		06 25		06 29	06 41	06 47	06 52
—	—	—	3¼	19¼	Strood	a						05 31				06 01			06 28					
—	—	—	10½	26½	Gravesend	a						05 41				06 11			06 38					
—	—	—	14½	—	Greenhithe for Bluewater	a																		
—	—	—	17¼	—	Dartford	a																		
—	—	—	34¼	—	**London Bridge** ⊖	a								06 25								07 19		
—	—	—	—	—	**London Cannon Street** ⊖	a								06 33								07 27		
—	—	—	35¼	—	**London Waterloo (East)** ⊖	a																		
—	—	—	36	—	**London Charing Cross** ⊖	a																		
52¼	50¼	—	—	—	Sole Street	d		05 31							06 02						06 38			
53¼	51¼	—	—	—	Meopham	d		05 34							06 05						06 41			
55¾	53¾	—	—	—	Longfield	d		05 38							06 10						06 46			
58¾	56¾	—	—	—	Farningham Road	d		05 42							06 14						06 50			
61¾	59¾	—	—	—	Swanley	a		05 47							06 18						06 55			
64½	62½	—	—	—	St Mary Cray	a		05 51							06 23						07 00			
68¼	66¼	—	—	—	Bromley South	a		05 58					06 01		06 29		06 32				07 06		07 10	07 15
79¼	77¼	—	—	—	**London Victoria** ⊖	a		06 20					06 23		06 51		06 54				07 34		07 38	
—	—	—	—	—	Elephant & Castle ⊖	a																		07 38
—	—	—	—	—	**London Blackfriars** ⊖	a																		07 45
—	—	—	—	28½	Ebbsfleet International	a						05 45				06 15			06 42					
—	—	—	—	45¼	Stratford International ⊖	a						05 57				06 27			06 55					
—	—	—	—	51¾	**St Pancras International**	a						06 05				06 35			07 02					

A From Dover Priory
B From St Pancras International

For further services between St Pancras International, London Blackfriars and Elephant & Castle and Bromley South, St Mary Cray and Swanley refer to table T52

Table T212-R

21 May to 7 December

Ramsgate, Dover, Sheerness-on-Sea and Medway - London

		SE ◇	SE	SE ◇■	SE ■	SE ■	SE	SE ◇■	SE ◇	SE	SE ■	SE ◇■	SE ■	SE ◇■	SE ■	SE ◇	SE	SE ◇■	SE ◇■	SE A	SE	SE ◇
Ramsgate	d			05 56								06 30						06 55		07 14		
Dumpton Park	d			05 59								06 33		06 43				06 58				
Broadstairs	d			06 02				06 23	06 29			06 36		06 46		06 58		07 02		07 20		
Margate	d			06 07				06 28	06 34			06 41		06 51		07 03		07 07		07a26		
Westgate-on-Sea	d			06 11								06 44		06 55				07 10				
Birchington-on-Sea	d			06 14				06 33	06 39			06 48		06 58		07 08		07 14				
Herne Bay	d			06 23				06 42	06 48			06 57		07 07		07 17		07 23				
Chestfield & Swalecliffe	d			06 27								07 00		07 11				07 26				
Whitstable	d			06 30				06 48	06 53			07 04		07 14		07 23		07 30				
Dover Priory	d					06 02							06 32						07 04			
Kearsney	d					06 06							06 36						07 08			
Shepherds Well	d					06 12							06 42						07 14			
Snowdown	d					06 15							06 45						07 17			
Aylesham	d					06 18							06 48						07 20			
Adisham	d					06 21							06 51						07 23			
Bekesbourne	d					06 25							06 55						07 27			
Canterbury East	d					06 31							07 01						07 33			
Selling	d					06 40							07 10						07 42			
Faversham	a			06 38		06 46		06 56	07 01			07 12	07 15	07 22		07 31		07 38	07 46			
	d	06 28		06 39				06 57	07 02			07 13		07 23		07 31		07 39	07 47			07 59
Teynham	d			06 46								07 19							07 53			
Sheerness-on-Sea	d		06 24				06 36			06 52	07 00						07 26				07 42	
Queenborough	d		06 29				06 42			06 56	07 05						07 30				07 47	
Swale	d						06 46			07 00							07 34				07 51	
Kemsley	d		06 37				06 50			07 04	07 12						07 38				07 55	
Sittingbourne	a	06 36		06 50			06 55	07 04	07 09	07 09		07 23		07 31		07 39	07 42	07 46	07 58		07 59	08 06
	d	06 36		06 51				07 05	07 10			07 24		07 31		07 39		07 47	07 58			08 07
Newington	d			06 56								07 29						07 52	08 03			
Rainham (Kent)	d	06 44	06 48	07 01				07 12	07 17		07 22	07 34		07 39		07 47		07 57	08 08			08 14
Gillingham (Kent)	d	06 49	06 53	07 06				07 17	07 22		07 27	07 39		07 44		07 52		08 03	08 13			08 19
Chatham	d	06 53	06 58	07 10				07 22	07 27		07 32	07 44		07 49		07 56		08 07	08 17			08 24
Rochester	d	06 57	07 01	07 14	07 17			07 26	07 30		07 35	07 48		07 52	07 56	08 00		08 11	08 21			08 27
Strood	a								07 33							08 03						08 31
Gravesend	a								07 43							08 13						08 41
Greenhithe for Bluewater	a																					
Dartford	a																					
London Bridge ⊖	a							08 07						08 32				08 51				
London Cannon Street ⊖	a							08 15						08 40				08 59				
London Waterloo (East) ⊖	a																					
London Charing Cross ⊖	a																					
Sole Street	d		07 11		07 27										08 06							
Meopham	d		07 13		07 30						07 46				08 09				08 32			
Longfield	d		07 18	07 27							07 51				08 13				08 36			
Farningham Road	d		07 22		07 36										08 18							
Swanley	a		07 27		07 40						07 57				08 22							
St Mary Cray	a		07 31		07 45						08 02				08 27							
Bromley South	a		07 38	07 44	07 52						08 08	08 12			08 33				08 48			
London Victoria ⊖	a		08 07	08 09	08 25						08 36	08 39			09 03				09 13			
Elephant & Castle ⊖	a																					
London Blackfriars ⊖	a																					
Ebbsfleet International	a	07 11							07 48							08 17						08 46
Stratford International ⊖	a	07 24							08 00							08 30						08 59
St Pancras International	a	07 31							08 08							08 38						09 07

A From Ashford International

For further services between St Pancras International, London Blackfriars and Elephant & Castle and Bromley South, St Mary Cray and Swanley refer to table T52

Table T212-R

Mondays to Fridays

21 May to 7 December

Ramsgate, Dover, Sheerness-on-Sea and Medway - London

		SE ◇■	SE	SE ■	SE ◇	SE ◇■	SE ◇■	SE ■	SE ◇	SE	SE ◇■	SE ◇■	SE ◇ A	SE ◇■	SE	SE ◇	SE ◇■	SE ◇ A	SE ◇ A	SE	SE ◇■	SE ◇■	SE
Ramsgate	d	07 19				07 40					08 10		08 25				08 53	09 20	09 31				
Dumpton Park	d	07 22				07 43					08 13						08 56						
Broadstairs	d	07 25				07 46					08 16		08 30				08 59	09 25	09 36				
Margate	d	07 30				07 52					08 21		08a36				09 04	09 30	09a42				
Westgate-on-Sea	d	07 34				07 55					08 25						09 08						
Birchington-on-Sea	d	07 37				07 59					08 28						09 11	09 35					
Herne Bay	d	07 46				08 08					08 37						09 20	09 44					
Chestfield & Swalecliffe	d	07 50				08 11					08 41						09 24						
Whitstable	d	07 53				08 15					08 44						09 27	09 49					
Dover Priory	d						07 40					08 15		08 52							09 18	09 52	
Kearsney	d						07 44					08 19									09 22		
Shepherds Well	d						07 50					08 25									09 28		
Snowdown	d						07 53					08 28									09 31		
Aylesham	d						07 56					08 31									09 34		
Adisham	d						07 59					08 34									09 37		
Bekesbourne	d						08 03					08 38									09 41		
Canterbury East	d						08 11					08 44		09 09							09 47	10 09	
Selling	d						08 20					08 53									09 56		
Faversham	a	08 01				08 23	08 25				08 53	08 58		09 20			09 35	09 57			10 01	10 20	
	d	08 03			08 28	08 32			08 59		09 02			09 22		09 30	09 37	09 58			10 02	10 22	
Teynham	d					08 38					09 08										10 08		
Sheerness-on-Sea	d		08 18							08 50					09 18					09 48			10 18
Queenborough	d		08 23							08 55					09 23					09 53			10 23
Swale	d		08 27							08 59					09 27					09 57			10 27
Kemsley	d		08 31							09 03					09 31					10 01			10 31
Sittingbourne	a	08 10	08 35		08 36	08 42			09 07	09 08	09 12			09 29	09 36	09 38	09 44	10 05		10 06	10 12	10 29	10 36
	d	08 11			08 38	08 43			09 08		09 13			09 30		09 38	09 45	10 08			10 13	10 30	
Newington	d					08 48					09 18										10 18		
Rainham (Kent)	d	08 18			08 46	08 52			09 16		09 22			09 37		09 46	09 52	10 16			10 22	10 37	
Gillingham (Kent)	d	08 24		08 28	08 51	08 57			09 21		09 27			09 44		09 51	09 57	10 21			10 27	10 44	
Chatham	d	08 28		08 32	08 55	09 02			09 25		09 32			09 48		09 55	10 02	10 25			10 32	10 48	
Rochester	d	08 32		08 36	08 59	09 05		09 20	09 29		09 35			09 52		09 59	10 05	10 29			10 35	10 52	
Strood	a				09 02				09 32							10 02		10 32					
Gravesend	a				09 12				09 42							10 12		10 42					
Greenhithe for Bluewater	a																						
Dartford	a																						
London Bridge ⊖	a	09 10																					
London Cannon Street ⊖	a	09 18																					
London Waterloo (East) ⊖	a																						
London Charing Cross ⊖	a																						
Sole Street	d			08 45				09 31						10 01								11 01	
Meopham	d			08 48		09 16		09 34			09 46			10 04			10 16				10 46	11 04	
Longfield	d			08 52		09 20		09 38			09 50			10 08			10 20				10 50	11 08	
Farningham Road	d			08 56				09 42						10 12								11 12	
Swanley	a			09 01				09 47						10 17								11 17	
St Mary Cray	a			09 05				09 51						10 21								11 21	
Bromley South	a			09 12		09 32		09 59			10 02			10 29			10 32				11 02	11 29	
London Victoria ⊖	a			09 41		09 56		10 32			10 25			11 00			10 53				11 25	12 00	
Elephant & Castle ⊖	a																						
London Blackfriars ⊖	a																						
Ebbsfleet International	a				09 16				09 46							10 16		10 46					
Stratford International ⊖	a				09 28				09 59							10 28		10 59					
St Pancras International	a				09 36				10 06							10 35		11 07					

A From St Pancras International

For further services between St Pancras International, London Blackfriars and Elephant & Castle and Bromley South, St Mary Cray and Swanley refer to table T52

21 May to 7 December

Ramsgate, Dover, Sheerness-on-Sea and Medway - London

		SE	SE	SE	SE	SE	SE	SE	SE	SE	SE	SE	SE	SE	SE	SE	SE	SE	SE	SE	SE	SE
		◇	■	◇	◇		◇■	◇■		◇	◇■	◇	◇		◇■	◇■		◇	◇■	◇	◇	
				A	A							A	A							A	A	
Ramsgate	d		09 53	10 20	10 28						10 53	11 20	11 28						11 53	12 20	12 28	
Dumpton Park	d		09 56								10 56								11 56			
Broadstairs	d		09 59	10 25	10 33						10 59	11 25	11 33						11 59	12 25	12 33	
Margate	d		10 04	10 30	10a39						11 04	11 30	11a39						12 04	12 30	12a39	
Westgate-on-Sea	d		10 08								11 08								12 08			
Birchington-on-Sea	d		10 11	10 35							11 11	11 35							12 11	12 35		
Herne Bay	d		10 20	10 44							11 20	11 44							12 20	12 44		
Chestfield & Swalecliffe	d		10 24								11 24								12 24			
Whitstable	d		10 27	10 49							11 27	11 49							12 27	12 49		
Dover Priory	d						10 18	10 52							11 18	11 52						
Kearsney	d						10 22								11 22							
Shepherds Well	d						10 28								11 28							
Snowdown	d						10 31								11 31							
Aylesham	d						10 34								11 34							
Adisham	d						10 37								11 37							
Bekesbourne	d						10 41								11 41							
Canterbury East	d						10 47	11 09							11 47	12 09						
Selling	d						10 56								11 56							
Faversham	a		10 35	10 57			11 01	11 20			11 35	11 57			12 01	12 20			12 35	12 57		
	d	10 30	10 37	10 58			11 02	11 22		11 30	11 37	11 58			12 02	12 22		12 30	12 37	12 58		
Teynham	d						11 08								12 08							
Sheerness-on-Sea	d					10 48			11 18					11 48			12 18					12 48
Queenborough	d					10 53			11 23					11 53			12 23					12 53
Swale	d					10 57			11 27					11 57			12 27					12 57
Kemsley	d					11 01			11 31					12 01			12 31					13 01
Sittingbourne	a	10 38	10 44	11 05		11 06	11 12	11 29	11 36	11 38	11 44	12 05		12 06	12 12	12 29	12 36	12 38	12 44	13 05		13 06
	d	10 38	10 45	11 08			11 13	11 30		11 38	11 45	12 08			12 13	12 30		12 38	12 45	13 08		
Newington	d						11 18								12 18							
Rainham (Kent)	d	10 46	10 52	11 16			11 22	11 37		11 46	11 52	12 16			12 22	12 37		12 46	12 52	13 16		
Gillingham (Kent)	d	10 51	10 57	11 21			11 27	11 44		11 51	11 57	12 21			12 27	12 44		12 51	12 57	13 21		
Chatham	d	10 55	11 02	11 25			11 32	11 48		11 55	12 02	12 25			12 32	12 48		12 55	13 02	13 25		
Rochester	d	10 59	11 05	11 29			11 35	11 52		11 59	12 05	12 29			12 35	12 52		12 59	13 05	13 29		
Strood	a	11 02		11 32						12 02		12 32						13 02		13 32		
Gravesend	a	11 12		11 42						12 12		12 42						13 12		13 42		
Greenhithe for Bluewater	a																					
Dartford	a																					
London Bridge ⊖	a																					
London Cannon Street ⊖	a																					
London Waterloo (East) ⊖	a																					
London Charing Cross ⊖	a																					
Sole Street	d							12 01								13 01						
Meopham	d		11 16				11 46	12 04			12 16				12 46	13 04			13 16			
Longfield	d		11 20				11 50	12 08			12 20				12 50	13 08			13 20			
Farningham Road	d							12 12								13 12						
Swanley	a							12 17								13 17						
St Mary Cray	a							12 21								13 21						
Bromley South	a		11 32				12 02	12 29			12 32				13 02	13 29			13 32			
London Victoria ⊖	a		11 53				12 25	13 00			12 53				13 26	14 01			13 53			
Elephant & Castle ⊖	a																					
London Blackfriars ⊖	a																					
Ebbsfleet International	a	11 16		11 46						12 16		12 46						13 16		13 46		
Stratford International ⊖	a	11 29		11 58						12 28		12 58						13 29		14 02		
St Pancras International	a	11 40		12 05						12 36		13 06						13 37		14 10		

A From St Pancras International

For further services between St Pancras International, London Blackfriars and Elephant & Castle and Bromley South, St Mary Cray and Swanley refer to table T52

21 May to 7 December

Ramsgate, Dover, Sheerness-on-Sea and Medway - London

		SE	SE	SE	SE	SE	SE	SE	SE	SE	SE	SE	SE	SE	SE	SE	SE	SE	SE	SE	SE	SE	SE
		◇■	◇■		◇	◇■	◇	◇		◇■	◇■		◇	◇■	◇	◇		◇■	◇		◇	◇■	◇
							A	A							A	A							A
Ramsgate	d					12 53	13 20	13 28						13 53	14 20	14 28						14 49	15 20
Dumpton Park	d					12 56								13 56								14 52	
Broadstairs	d					12 59	13 25	13 33						13 59	14 25	14 33						14 55	15 25
Margate	d					13 04	13 30	13a39						14 04	14 30	14a39						15 00	15 30
Westgate-on-Sea	d					13 08								14 08								15 03	
Birchington-on-Sea	d					13 11	13 35							14 11	14 35							15 07	15 35
Herne Bay	d					13 20	13 44							14 20	14 44							15 16	15 44
Chestfield & Swalecliffe	d					13 24								14 24								15 19	
Whitstable	d					13 27	13 49							14 27	14 49							15 23	15 49
Dover Priory	d	12 18	12 52							13 18	13 52							14 18	14 52				
Kearsney	d	12 22								13 22								14 22					
Shepherds Well	d	12 28								13 28								14 28					
Snowdown	d	12 31								13 31								14 31					
Aylesham	d	12 34								13 34								14 34					
Adisham	d	12 37								13 37								14 37					
Bekesbourne	d	12 41								13 41								14 41					
Canterbury East	d	12 47	13 09							13 47	14 09							14 47	15 09				
Selling	d	12 56								13 56								14 56					
Faversham	a	13 01	13 20			13 35	13 57			14 01	14 20			14 35	14 57			15 01	15 20			15 31	15 57
	d	13 02	13 22		13 30	13 37	13 58			14 02	14 22		14 30	14 37	14 58			15 02	15 22		15 28	15 32	15 58
Teynham	d	13 08								14 08								15 08				15 38	
Sheerness-on-Sea	d			13 18					13 48			14 18					14 48			15 18			
Queenborough	d			13 23					13 53			14 23					14 53			15 23			
Swale	d			13 27					13 57			14 27					14 57			15 27			
Kemsley	d			13 31					14 01			14 31					15 01			15 31			
Sittingbourne	a	13 12	13 29	13 36	13 38	13 44	14 05		14 06	14 12	14 29	14 36	14 38	14 44	15 05		15 06	15 12	15 29	15 36	15 36	15 42	16 05
	d	13 13	13 30		13 38	13 45	14 08			14 13	14 30		14 38	14 45	15 08			15 13	15 30		15 38	15 43	16 08
Newington	d	13 18								14 18								15 18				15 48	
Rainham (Kent)	d	13 22	13 37		13 46	13 52	14 16			14 22	14 37		14 46	14 52	15 16			15 22	15 37		15 46	15 52	16 16
Gillingham (Kent)	d	13 27	13 44		13 51	13 57	14 21			14 27	14 44		14 51	14 57	15 21			15 27	15 44		15 51	15 57	16 21
Chatham	d	13 32	13 48		13 55	14 02	14 25			14 32	14 48		14 55	15 02	15 25			15 32	15 48		15 55	16 02	16 25
Rochester	d	13 35	13 52		13 59	14 05	14 29			14 35	14 52		14 59	15 05	15 29			15 35	15 52		15 59	16 05	16 29
Strood	a				14 02		14 32						15 02		15 32						16 02		16 32
Gravesend	a				14 12		14 42						15 12		15 42						16 12		16 42
Greenhithe for Bluewater	a																						
Dartford	a																						
London Bridge ⊖	a																						
London Cannon Street ⊖	a																						
London Waterloo (East) ⊖	a																						
London Charing Cross ⊖	a																						
Sole Street	d		14 01								15 01								16 01				
Meopham	d	13 46	14 04			14 16				14 46	15 04			15 16				15 46	16 04			16 16	
Longfield	d	13 50	14 08			14 20				14 50	15 08			15 20				15 50	16 08			16 20	
Farningham Road	d		14 12								15 12								16 12				
Swanley	a		14 17								15 17								16 17				
St Mary Cray	a		14 21								15 21								16 21				
Bromley South	a	14 02	14 29			14 32				15 02	15 29			15 32				16 02	16 29			16 32	
London Victoria ⊖	a	14 25	15 00			14 53				15 25	16 01			15 53				16 25	17 01			16 54	
Elephant & Castle ⊖	a																						
London Blackfriars ⊖	a																						
Ebbsfleet International	a				14 16		14 46						15 16		15 46						16 16		16 46
Stratford International ⊖	a				14 28		14 58						15 28		16 02						16 28		17 00
St Pancras International	a				14 36		15 06						15 36		16 10						16 36		17 10

A From St Pancras International

For further services between St Pancras International, London Blackfriars and Elephant & Castle and Bromley South, St Mary Cray and Swanley refer to table T52

Table T212-R

Mondays to Fridays

21 May to 7 December

Ramsgate, Dover, Sheerness-on-Sea and Medway - London

		SE	SE	SE	SE	SE	SE	SE	SE	SE	SE	SE	SE	SE	SE	SE	SE	SE	SE	SE	SE	SE	SE
		◇ A		◇■	■	◇		◇■	◇■	■	■	◇ A	◇ A		◇■	■	◇		◇■	◇■	■	◇ A	◇ A
Ramsgate	d	15 28						15 44		16 05		16 20	16 28						16 52		17 05	17 20	17 32
Dumpton Park	d							15 47		16 08									16 55		17 08		
Broadstairs	d	15 33						15 50		16 11		16 25	16 33						16 58		17 11	17 25	17 37
Margate	d	15a39						15 55		16 16		16 30	16a39						17 03		17 16	17 30	17a42
Westgate-on-Sea	d							15 58		16 20									17 07		17 20		
Birchington-on-Sea	d							16 02		16 23		16 35							17 10		17 23	17 35	
Herne Bay	d							16 11		16 32		16 44							17 19		17 32	17 44	
Chestfield & Swalecliffe	d							16 14		16 36									17 23		17 36		
Whitstable	d							16 18		16 39		16 49							17 26		17 39	17 49	
Dover Priory	d			15 18					15 48						16 20					16 55			
Kearsney	d			15 22					15 52						16 24					16 59			
Shepherds Well	d			15 28					15 57						16 29					17 05			
Snowdown	d			15 31					16 01											17 08			
Aylesham	d			15 34					16 03						16 34					17 11			
Adisham	d			15 37											16 36								
Bekesbourne	d			15 41					16 09											17 17			
Canterbury East	d			15 47					16 14						16 44					17 23			
Selling	d			15 56					16 23						16 53					17 32			
Faversham	a			16 01				16 26	16 28	16 48		16 57			16 58				17 35	17 37	17 48	17 57	
	d			16 02		16 25		16 32				16 58			17 02		17 28		17 41			17 58	
Teynham	d			16 08				16 38							17 08								
Sheerness-on-Sea	d		15 51				16 18							16 48				17 21					
Queenborough	d		15 56				16 23							16 53				17 25					
Swale	d		16 00				16 27							16 57				17 29					
Kemsley	d		16 04				16 31							17 01				17 33					
Sittingbourne	a		16 09	16 12		16 33	16 36	16 42				17 05		17 06	17 12		17 36	17 38	17 48			18 05	
	d			16 13		16 37		16 43				17 08			17 13		17 38		17 49			18 08	
Newington	d			16 18				16 48							17 18								
Rainham (Kent)	d			16 22		16 46		16 52				17 16			17 22		17 46		17 56			18 16	
Gillingham (Kent)	d			16 27	16 44	16 51		16 57			17 14	17 21			17 27	17 44	17 51		18 01			18 21	
Chatham	d			16 32	16 48	16 55		17 02			17 18	17 25			17 32	17 48	17 55		18 06			18 25	
Rochester	d			16 35	16 52	16 59		17 05			17 22	17 29			17 35	17 52	17 59		18 09			18 29	
Strood	a					17 02						17 32					18 02					18 34	
Gravesend	a					17 12						17 42					18 13					18 44	
Greenhithe for Bluewater	a																						
Dartford	a																						
London Bridge ⊖	a																						
London Cannon Street ⊖	a																						
London Waterloo (East) ⊖	a																						
London Charing Cross ⊖	a																						
Sole Street	d				17 01						17 31					18 01							
Meopham	d			16 46	17 04			17 16			17 34				17 46	18 04							
Longfield	d			16 50	17 08			17 20			17 38				17 50	18 08							
Farningham Road	d				17 12						17 42					18 12							
Swanley	a				17 17						17 47					18 17							
St Mary Cray	a				17 21						17 51					18 21							
Bromley South	a			17 02	17 29			17 32			17 59				18 02	18 29			18 33				
London Victoria ⊖	a			17 24	18 00			17 53			18 30				18 25	19 00			18 55				
Elephant & Castle ⊖	a																						
London Blackfriars ⊖	a																						
Ebbsfleet International	a					17 16						17 46					18 17					18 49	
Stratford International ⊖	a					17 28						17 58					18 29					19 02	
St Pancras International	a					17 36						18 10					18 37					19 10	

A From St Pancras International

For further services between St Pancras International, London Blackfriars and Elephant & Castle and Bromley South, St Mary Cray and Swanley refer to table T52

Table T212-R

Mondays to Fridays

21 May to 7 December

Ramsgate, Dover, Sheerness-on-Sea and Medway - London

		SE	SE	SE	SE	SE	SE	SE	SE	SE	SE	SE	SE	SE	SE	SE	SE	SE	SE	SE	SE	SE
			◇■			◇	◇■	◇■	◇ A	◇		◇■	■	◇ A	◇	◇ A		◇■	◇■	◇ A	◇	◇ A
Ramsgate	d						17 48		18 02					18 26		18 32		18 48		19 02	19 20	19 32
Dumpton Park	d						17 51							18 29				18 51				
Broadstairs	d						17 54		18 07					18 32		18 37		18 54		19 07	19 25	19 37
Margate	d						17 59		18a15	18 25				18 38		18a45		18 59		19a15	19 30	19a45
Westgate-on-Sea	d						18 03			18 29				18 41				19 03				
Birchington-on-Sea	d						18 06			18 33				18 45				19 06			19 35	
Herne Bay	d						18 15			18 42				18 54				19 15			19 44	
Chestfield & Swalecliffe	d						18 19			18 45				18 58				19 19				
Whitstable	d						18 22			18 49				19 01				19 22			19 49	
Dover Priory	d		17 20					17 52				18 20							18 52			
Kearsney	d		17 24					17 56				18 24							18 56			
Shepherds Well	d		17 29					18 02				18 29							19 02			
Snowdown	d							18 05											19 05			
Aylesham	d		17 34					18 08				18 34							19 08			
Adisham	d		17 36									18 36										
Bekesbourne	d							18 14											19 14			
Canterbury East	d		17 44					18 19				18 44							19 19			
Selling	d		17 53					18 28				18 53							19 28			
Faversham	a		17 58				18 31	18 33		18 57		18 58		19 10				19 31	19 33		19 57	
	d		18 02			18 28	18 37			18 58		19 02			19 30			19 37			19 58	
Teynham	d		18 08									19 08										
Sheerness-on-Sea	d	17 51			18 18						18 52						19 22					
Queenborough	d	17 55			18 23						18 56						19 26					
Swale	d	17 59			18 27						19 00						19 30					
Kemsley	d	18 03			18 30						19 04						19 34					
Sittingbourne	a	18 08	18 12		18 35	18 36	18 44			19 05	19 08	19 12			19 38		19 38	19 44			20 05	
	d		18 13			18 38	18 45			19 08		19 13			19 38			19 45			20 08	
Newington	d		18 18									19 18										
Rainham (Kent)	d		18 22			18 46	18 52			19 16		19 22			19 46			19 52			20 16	
Gillingham (Kent)	d		18 27			18 51	18 57			19 21		19 27			19 51			19 57			20 21	
Chatham	d		18 32			18 55	19 02			19 25		19 32			19 55			20 02			20 25	
Rochester	d		18 35	18 53		18 59	19 05			19 29		19 35	19 53		19 59			20 05			20 29	
Strood	a					19 02				19 32					20 02						20 32	
Gravesend	a					19 12				19 42					20 12						20 42	
Greenhithe for Bluewater	a																					
Dartford	a																					
London Bridge ⊖	a																					
London Cannon Street ⊖	a																					
London Waterloo (East) ⊖	a																					
London Charing Cross ⊖	a																					
Sole Street	d			19 02									20 02									
Meopham	d		18 46	19 05			19 16					19 46	20 05					20 16				
Longfield	d		18 50	19 09			19 20					19 50	20 09					20 20				
Farningham Road	d			19 13									20 13									
Swanley	a			19 18									20 18									
St Mary Cray	a			19 22									20 22									
Bromley South	a		19 02	19 29			19 32					20 02	20 29					20 32				
London Victoria ⊖	a		19 24	20 00			19 54					20 23	21 00					20 53				
Elephant & Castle ⊖	a																					
London Blackfriars ⊖	a																					
Ebbsfleet International	a					19 16				19 46					20 16						20 46	
Stratford International ⊖	a					19 28				19 59					20 28						21 02	
St Pancras International	a					19 36				20 07					20 36						21 10	

A From St Pancras International

For further services between St Pancras International, London Blackfriars and Elephant & Castle and Bromley South, St Mary Cray and Swanley refer to table T52

Table T212-R

Mondays to Fridays
21 May to 7 December

Ramsgate, Dover, Sheerness-on-Sea and Medway - London

		SE	SE ◇■	SE	SE ■	SE ◇	SE ■	SE ◇■	SE ◇ A	SE ◇	SE ◇ A	SE	SE ◇■	SE	SE ◇■	SE ◇	SE ◇■	SE ◇■	SE ◇ A	SE ◇ A	SE	SE	SE ◇■
Ramsgate ■	d							19 53	20 03	20 20	20 32						20 53		21 20	21 32			
Dumpton Park	d							19 56									20 56						
Broadstairs	d							19 59	20 08	20 25	20 37						20 59		21 25	21 38			
Margate ■	d							20 04	20a16	20 30	20a45						21 04		21 30	21a43			
Westgate-on-Sea	d							20 08									21 08						
Birchington-on-Sea	d							20 11		20 35							21 11		21 35				
Herne Bay	d							20 20		20 44							21 20		21 44				
Chestfield & Swalecliffe	d							20 24									21 24						
Whitstable	d							20 27		20 49							21 27		21 49				
Dover Priory ■	d		19 22				19 50						20 22					21 05					22 05
Kearsney	d		19 26				19 54						20 26					21 09					22 09
Shepherds Well	d		19 32				20 00						20 32					21 15					22 15
Snowdown	d						20 03											21 18					22 18
Aylesham	d		19 36				20 06						20 36					21 21					22 21
Adisham	d		19 39										20 39					21 24					22 24
Bekesbourne	d						20 12											21 28					22 28
Canterbury East ■	d		19 47				20 19						20 47					21 33					22 39
Selling	d		19 56				20 28						20 56					21 42					22 48
Faversham ■	a		20 01				20 33	20 35		20 57			21 01				21 35	21 47	21 57				22 53
	d		20 02			20 30		20 37		20 58			21 02			21 30	21 37	21 47	21 58				22 54
Teynham	d		20 08										21 08					21 53					23 00
Sheerness-on-Sea	d	19 52		20 20								20 48		21 18							21 48	22 18	
Queenborough	d	19 56		20 25								20 53		21 23							21 53	22 23	
Swale	d	20 00		20 29								20 57		21 27							21 57	22 27	
Kemsley	d	20 04		20 33								21 01		21 31							22 01	22 31	
Sittingbourne ■	a	20 09	20 12	20 37		20 38		20 44		21 05		21 06	21 12	21 36		21 38	21 44	21 58	22 05		22 06	22 36	23 04
	d		20 13			20 38		20 45		21 08			21 13			21 38	21 45	21 58	22 08				23 05
Newington	d		20 18										21 18					22 03					23 10
Rainham (Kent)	d		20 22			20 46		20 52		21 16			21 22			21 46	21 52	22 08	22 16				23 14
Gillingham (Kent) ■	d		20 27		20 44	20 51		20 57		21 21			21 27		21 44	21 51	21 57	22 14	22 21				23 20
Chatham ■	d		20 32		20 48	20 55		21 02		21 25			21 32		21 48	21 55	22 02	22 18	22 25				23 24
Rochester ■	d		20 35		20 52	20 59		21 05		21 29			21 35		21 52	21 59	22 05	22 22	22 29				23 28
Strood ■	a					21 02				21 32						22 02			22 32				
Gravesend ■	a					21 12				21 42						22 12			22 42				
Greenhithe for Bluewater	a																						
Dartford ■	a																						
London Bridge ■ ⊖	a																						
London Cannon Street ■ ⊖	a																						
London Waterloo (East) ■ ⊖	a																						
London Charing Cross ■ ⊖	a																						
Sole Street	d				21 01										22 01			22 31					23 37
Meopham	d		20 46		21 04			21 16					21 46		22 04		22 16	22 34					23 40
Longfield	d		20 50		21 08			21 20					21 50		22 08		22 20	22 38					23 44
Farningham Road	d				21 12										22 12			22 42					23 48
Swanley ■	a				21 17										22 17			22 47					23 53
St Mary Cray	a				21 21										22 21			22 51					23 57
Bromley South ■	a		21 02		21 29			21 32					22 02		22 29		22 32	22 59					00 03
London Victoria ■ ⊖	a		21 25		22 00			21 53					22 23		23 00		22 53	23 31					00 24
Elephant & Castle ⊖	a																						
London Blackfriars ■ ⊖	a																						
Ebbsfleet International	a					21 16				21 46						22 16			22 46				
Stratford International ⊖	a					21 32				21 58						22 28			22 58				
St Pancras International	a					21 39				22 06						22 36			23 06				

A From St Pancras International

For further services between St Pancras International, London Blackfriars and Elephant & Castle and Bromley South, St Mary Cray and Swanley refer to table T52

Table T212-R

Mondays to Fridays
21 May to 7 December

Ramsgate, Dover, Sheerness-on-Sea and Medway - London

		SE ◇ A	SE	SE TO ■	SE	SE TO ■	SE TX ■	SE TX ■	SE TX ◇ A
Ramsgate ■	d	22 28		22 50				23 15	23 30
Dumpton Park	d			22 53				23 18	
Broadstairs	d	22 33		22 56				23 21	23 35
Margate ■	d	22a39		23 01				23 26	23a40
Westgate-on-Sea	d			23 05				23 30	
Birchington-on-Sea	d			23 08				23 33	
Herne Bay	d			23 17				23 42	
Chestfield & Swalecliffe	d			23 21				23 46	
Whitstable	d			23 24				23 49	
Dover Priory ■	d					23 10	23 10		
Kearsney	d					23 14	23 14		
Shepherds Well	d					23 20	23 20		
Snowdown	d					23 23	23 23		
Aylesham	d					23 26	23 26		
Adisham	d					23 29	23 29		
Bekesbourne	d					23 33	23 33		
Canterbury East ■	d					23 39	23 39		
Selling	d					23 48	23 48		
Faversham ■	a			23 33		23 53	23 54	23 58	
	d					00 02		00 02	
Teynham	d					00 08		00 08	
Sheerness-on-Sea	d		22 48		23 48				
Queenborough	d		22 53		23 53				
Swale	d		22 57		23 57				
Kemsley	d		23 01		23 59				
Sittingbourne ■	a		23 06		00 06	00 12		00 12	
	d					00 13		00 13	
Newington	d					00 18		00 18	
Rainham (Kent)	d					00 22		00 22	
Gillingham (Kent) ■	d					00a29		00a29	
Chatham ■	d								
Rochester ■	d								
Strood ■	a								
Gravesend ■	a								
Greenhithe for Bluewater	a								
Dartford ■	a								
London Bridge ■ ⊖	a								
London Cannon Street ■ ⊖	a								
London Waterloo (East) ■ ⊖	a								
London Charing Cross ■ ⊖	a								
Sole Street	d								
Meopham	d								
Longfield	d								
Farningham Road	d								
Swanley ■	a								
St Mary Cray	a								
Bromley South ■	a								
London Victoria ■ ⊖	a								
Elephant & Castle ⊖	a								
London Blackfriars ■ ⊖	a								
Ebbsfleet International	a								
Stratford International ⊖	a								
St Pancras International	a								

A From St Pancras International

For further services between St Pancras International, London Blackfriars and Elephant & Castle and Bromley South, St Mary Cray and Swanley refer to table T52

Ramsgate, Dover, Sheerness-on-Sea and Medway - London

		SE ■ A	SE ◇ B	SE ◇■	SE ◇	SE	SE ◇■	SE ◇	SE ◇■	SE ◇		SE	SE ◇■	SE ◇■	SE	SE ◇	SE ◇■	SE C	SE ◇ C	SE		SE ◇■	SE ◇■	SE	SE ◇
Ramsgate	d		00 31	04 30					05 53	06 20							06 53	07 16	07 20						
Dumpton Park	d								05 56								06 56								
Broadstairs	d		00s36	04 35					05 59	06 25							06 59	07 21	07 25						
Margate	d		00a42	04 40					06 04	06 30							07 04	07a26	07 30						
Westgate-on-Sea	d								06 08								07 08								
Birchington-on-Sea	d			04 45					06 11	06 35							07 11		07 35						
Herne Bay	d			04 54					06 20	06 44							07 20		07 44						
Chestfield & Swalecliffe	d								06 24								07 24								
Whitstable	d			05 00					06 27	06 49							07 27		07 49						
Dover Priory	d												06 18	06 52								07 18	07 52		
Kearsney	d												06 22									07 22			
Shepherds Well	d												06 28									07 28			
Snowdown	d												06 31									07 31			
Aylesham	d												06 34									07 34			
Adisham	d												06 37									07 37			
Bekesbourne	d												06 41									07 41			
Canterbury East	d												06 47	07 09								07 47	08 09		
Selling	d												06 56									07 56			
Faversham	a			05 08					06 35	06 57			07 01	07 20			07 35		07 57			08 01	08 20		
	d	00 02		05 09	05 30			06 30	06 37	06 58			07 02	07 22		07 30	07 37		07 58			08 02	08 22		08 30
Teynham	d	00 08											07 08									08 08			
Sheerness-on-Sea	d					06 18						06 48			07 18					07 48				08 18	
Queenborough	d					06 23						06 53			07 23					07 53				08 23	
Swale	d					06 27						06 57			07 27					07 57				08 27	
Kemsley	d					06 31						07 01			07 31					08 01				08 31	
Sittingbourne	a	00 12		05 16	05 38	06 36		06 38	06 44	07 05		07 06	07 12	07 29	07 36	07 38	07 44		08 05	08 06		08 12	08 29	08 36	08 38
	d	00 13		05 17	05 38			06 38	06 45	07 08			07 13	07 30		07 38	07 45		08 08			08 13	08 30		08 38
Newington	d	00 18											07 18									08 18			
Rainham (Kent)	d	00 22		05 24	05 46			06 46	06 52	07 16			07 22	07 37		07 46	07 52		08 16			08 22	08 37		08 46
Gillingham (Kent)	d	00a29		05 29	05 51		06 44	06 51	06 57	07 21			07 27	07 44		07 51	07 57		08 21			08 27	08 44		08 51
Chatham	d			05 34	05 55		06 48	06 55	07 02	07 25			07 32	07 48		07 55	08 02		08 25			08 32	08 48		08 55
Rochester	d			05 37	05 59		06 52	06 59	07 05	07 29			07 35	07 52		07 59	08 05		08 29			08 35	08 52		08 59
Strood	a				06 02			07 02		07 32						08 02			08 32						09 02
Gravesend	a				06 12			07 12		07 42						08 12			08 42						09 12
Greenhithe for Bluewater	a																								
Dartford	a																								
London Bridge ⊖	a																								
London Cannon Street ⊖	a																								
London Waterloo (East) ⊖	a																								
London Charing Cross ⊖	a																								
Sole Street	d			05 46			07 01							08 01									09 01		
Meopham	d			05 49			07 04		07 16				07 46	08 04			08 16					08 46	09 04		
Longfield	d			05 53			07 08		07 20				07 50	08 08			08 20					08 50	09 08		
Farningham Road	d			05 57			07 12							08 12									09 12		
Swanley	a			06 01			07 17							08 17									09 17		
St Mary Cray	a			06 06			07 21							08 21									09 21		
Bromley South	a			06 13			07 29		07 32				08 02	08 29			08 32					09 02	09 29		
London Victoria ⊖	a			06 38			08 00		07 53				08 23	09 00			08 53					09 23	10 00		
Elephant & Castle ⊖	a																								
London Blackfriars ⊖	a																								
Ebbsfleet International	a				06 16			07 16		07 46						08 16			08 46						09 16
Stratford International ⊖	a				06 28			07 28		07 58						08 29			08 58						09 29
St Pancras International	a				06 36			07 36		08 06						08 36			09 06						09 36

A From Ramsgate B From St Pancras International C From Ashford International

For further services between St Pancras International, London Blackfriars and Elephant & Castle and Bromley South, St Mary Cray and Swanley refer to table T52

Table T212-R

Saturdays

26 May to 8 December

Ramsgate, Dover, Sheerness-on-Sea and Medway - London

		SE ◇■	SE ◇ A	SE ◇ A	SE	SE ◇■		SE ◇■	SE	SE ◇	SE ◇■	SE ◇ A	SE ◇ A	SE	SE ◇■	SE ◇■		SE	SE ◇	SE ◇■	SE ◇ A	SE ◇ A	SE	SE ◇■	SE ◇■
Ramsgate	d	07 53	08 20	08 28							08 53	09 20	09 28							09 53	10 20	10 28			
Dumpton Park	d	07 56									08 56									09 56					
Broadstairs	d	07 59	08 25	08 33							08 59	09 25	09 33							09 59	10 25	10 33			
Margate	d	08 04	08 30	08a39							09 04	09 30	09a39							10 04	10 30	10a39			
Westgate-on-Sea	d	08 08									09 08									10 08					
Birchington-on-Sea	d	08 11	08 35								09 11	09 35								10 11	10 35				
Herne Bay	d	08 20	08 44								09 20	09 44								10 20	10 44				
Chestfield & Swalecliffe	d	08 24									09 24									10 24					
Whitstable	d	08 27	08 49								09 27	09 49								10 27	10 49				
Dover Priory	d					08 18		08 52							09 18	09 52								10 18	10 52
Kearsney	d					08 22									09 22									10 22	
Shepherds Well	d					08 28									09 28									10 28	
Snowdown	d					08 31									09 31									10 31	
Aylesham	d					08 34									09 34									10 34	
Adisham	d					08 37									09 37									10 37	
Bekesbourne	d					08 41									09 41									10 41	
Canterbury East	d					08 47		09 09							09 47	10 09								10 47	11 09
Selling	d					08 56									09 56									10 56	
Faversham	a	08 35	08 57			09 01		09 20			09 35	09 57			10 01	10 20				10 35	10 57			11 01	11 20
	d	08 37	08 58			09 02		09 22		09 30	09 37	09 58			10 02	10 22			10 30	10 37	10 58			11 02	11 22
Teynham	d					09 08									10 08									11 08	
Sheerness-on-Sea	d				08 48				09 18					09 48				10 18					10 48		
Queenborough	d				08 53				09 23					09 53				10 23					10 53		
Swale	d				08 57				09 27					09 57				10 27					10 57		
Kemsley	d				09 01				09 31					10 01				10 31					11 01		
Sittingbourne	a	08 44	09 05		09 06	09 12		09 29	09 36	09 38	09 44	10 05		10 06	10 12	10 29		10 36	10 38	10 44	11 05		11 06	11 12	11 29
	d	08 45	09 08			09 13		09 30		09 38	09 45	10 08			10 13	10 30			10 38	10 45	11 08			11 13	11 30
Newington	d					09 18									10 18									11 18	
Rainham (Kent)	d	08 52	09 16			09 22		09 37		09 46	09 52	10 16			10 22	10 37			10 46	10 52	11 16			11 22	11 37
Gillingham (Kent)	d	08 57	09 21			09 27		09 44		09 51	09 57	10 21			10 27	10 44			10 51	10 57	11 21			11 27	11 44
Chatham	d	09 02	09 25			09 32		09 48		09 55	10 02	10 25			10 32	10 48			10 55	11 02	11 25			11 32	11 48
Rochester	d	09 05	09 29			09 35		09 52		09 59	10 05	10 29			10 35	10 52			10 59	11 05	11 29			11 35	11 52
Strood	a		09 32							10 02		10 32							11 02		11 32				
Gravesend	a		09 42							10 12		10 42							11 12		11 42				
Greenhithe for Bluewater	a																								
Dartford	a																								
London Bridge ⊖	a																								
London Cannon Street ⊖	a																								
London Waterloo (East) ⊖	a																								
London Charing Cross ⊖	a																								
Sole Street	d							10 01								11 01									12 01
Meopham	d	09 16				09 46		10 04			10 16				10 46	11 04				11 16				11 46	12 04
Longfield	d	09 20				09 50		10 08			10 20				10 50	11 08				11 20				11 50	12 08
Farningham Road	d							10 12								11 12									12 12
Swanley	a							10 17								11 17									12 17
St Mary Cray	a							10 21								11 21									12 21
Bromley South	a	09 32				10 02		10 29			10 32				11 02	11 29				11 32				12 02	12 29
London Victoria ⊖	a	09 53				10 23		11 00			10 53				11 23	12 00				11 53				12 23	13 00
Elephant & Castle ⊖	a																								
London Blackfriars ⊖	a																								
Ebbsfleet International	a		09 46							10 16		10 46							11 16		11 46				
Stratford International ⊖	a		09 58							10 28		10 59							11 29		11 58				
St Pancras International	a		10 06							10 35		11 06							11 37		12 06				

A From St Pancras International

For further services between St Pancras International, London Blackfriars and Elephant & Castle and Bromley South, St Mary Cray and Swanley refer to table T52

Table T212-R

Saturdays

26 May to 8 December

Ramsgate, Dover, Sheerness-on-Sea and Medway - London

		SE		SE	SE	SE	SE	SE	SE	SE	SE	SE		SE	SE	SE	SE	SE	SE	SE	SE	SE		SE	SE
				◇	◇■	◇	◇		◇■	◇■		◇		◇■	◇	◇		◇■	◇■		◇	◇■		◇	◇
						A	A								A	A								A	A
Ramsgate	d				10 53	11 20	11 28							11 53	12 20	12 28						12 53		13 20	13 28
Dumpton Park	d				10 56									11 56								12 56			
Broadstairs	d				10 59	11 25	11 33							11 59	12 25	12 33						12 59		13 25	13 33
Margate	d				11 04	11 30	11a39							12 04	12 30	12a39						13 04		13 30	13a39
Westgate-on-Sea	d				11 08									12 08								13 08			
Birchington-on-Sea	d				11 11	11 35								12 11	12 35							13 11		13 35	
Herne Bay	d				11 20	11 44								12 20	12 44							13 20		13 44	
Chestfield & Swalecliffe	d				11 24									12 24								13 24			
Whitstable	d				11 27	11 49								12 27	12 49							13 27		13 49	
Dover Priory	d								11 18	11 52								12 18	12 52						
Kearsney	d								11 22									12 22							
Shepherds Well	d								11 28									12 28							
Snowdown	d								11 31									12 31							
Aylesham	d								11 34									12 34							
Adisham	d								11 37									12 37							
Bekesbourne	d								11 41									12 41							
Canterbury East	d								11 47	12 09								12 47	13 09						
Selling	d								11 56									12 56							
Faversham	a				11 35	11 57			12 01	12 20				12 35	12 57			13 01	13 20			13 35		13 57	
	d			11 30	11 37	11 58			12 02	12 22		12 30		12 37	12 58			13 02	13 22		13 30	13 37		13 58	
Teynham	d								12 08									13 08							
Sheerness-on-Sea	d	11 18						11 48			12 18						12 48			13 18					
Queenborough	d	11 23						11 53			12 23						12 53			13 23					
Swale	d	11 27						11 57			12 27						12 57			13 27					
Kemsley	d	11 31						12 01			12 31						13 01			13 31					
Sittingbourne	a	11 36		11 38	11 44	12 05		12 06	12 12	12 29	12 36	12 38		12 44	13 05		13 06	13 12	13 29	13 36	13 38	13 44		14 05	
	d			11 38	11 45	12 08			12 13	12 30		12 38		12 45	13 08			13 13	13 30		13 38	13 45		14 08	
Newington	d								12 18									13 18							
Rainham (Kent)	d			11 46	11 52	12 16			12 22	12 37		12 46		12 52	13 16			13 22	13 37		13 46	13 52		14 16	
Gillingham (Kent)	d			11 51	11 57	12 21			12 27	12 44		12 51		12 57	13 21			13 27	13 44		13 51	13 57		14 21	
Chatham	d			11 55	12 02	12 25			12 32	12 48		12 55		13 02	13 25			13 32	13 48		13 55	14 02		14 25	
Rochester	d			11 59	12 05	12 29			12 35	12 52		12 59		13 05	13 29			13 35	13 52		13 59	14 05		14 29	
Strood	a			12 02		12 32						13 02			13 32						14 02			14 32	
Gravesend	a			12 12		12 42						13 12			13 42						14 12			14 42	
Greenhithe for Bluewater	a																								
Dartford	a																								
London Bridge ⊖	a																								
London Cannon Street ⊖	a																								
London Waterloo (East) ⊖	a																								
London Charing Cross ⊖	a																								
Sole Street	d									13 01									14 01						
Meopham	d				12 16				12 46	13 04				13 16				13 46	14 04			14 16			
Longfield	d				12 20				12 50	13 08				13 20				13 50	14 08			14 20			
Farningham Road	d									13 12									14 12						
Swanley	a									13 17									14 17						
St Mary Cray	a									13 21									14 21						
Bromley South	a				12 32				13 02	13 29				13 32				14 02	14 29			14 32			
London Victoria ⊖	a				12 53				13 23	14 00				13 53				14 23	15 00			14 53			
Elephant & Castle ⊖	a																								
London Blackfriars ⊖	a																								
Ebbsfleet International	a			12 16		12 46						13 16			13 46						14 16			14 46	
Stratford International ⊖	a			12 28		12 58						13 29			14 02						14 28			14 59	
St Pancras International	a			12 36		13 06						13 37			14 09						14 36			15 07	

A From St Pancras International

For further services between St Pancras International, London Blackfriars and Elephant & Castle and Bromley South, St Mary Cray and Swanley refer to table T52

Table T212-R

Saturdays

26 May to 8 December

Ramsgate, Dover, Sheerness-on-Sea and Medway - London

		SE	SE	SE	SE	SE	SE	SE		SE	SE	SE	SE	SE	SE	SE	SE	SE		SE	SE	SE	SE	SE	SE
			◇■	◇■		◇	◇■	◇		◇		◇■	◇■		◇	◇■	◇	◇			◇■	◇■		◇	◇■
								A		A							A	A							
Ramsgate	d						13 53	14 20		14 28						14 53	15 20	15 28							15 53
Dumpton Park	d						13 56									14 56									15 56
Broadstairs	d						13 59	14 25		14 33						14 59	15 25	15 33							15 59
Margate	d						14 04	14 30		14a39						15 04	15 30	15a39							16 04
Westgate-on-Sea	d						14 08									15 08									16 08
Birchington-on-Sea	d						14 11	14 35								15 11	15 35								16 11
Herne Bay	d						14 20	14 44								15 20	15 44								16 20
Chestfield & Swalecliffe	d						14 24									15 24									16 24
Whitstable	d						14 27	14 49								15 27	15 49								16 27
Dover Priory	d		13 18	13 52								14 18	14 52								15 18	15 52			
Kearsney	d		13 22									14 22									15 22				
Shepherds Well	d		13 28									14 28									15 28				
Snowdown	d		13 31									14 31									15 31				
Aylesham	d		13 34									14 34									15 34				
Adisham	d		13 37									14 37									15 37				
Bekesbourne	d		13 41									14 41									15 41				
Canterbury East	d		13 47	14 09								14 47	15 09								15 47	16 09			
Selling	d		13 56									14 56									15 56				
Faversham	a		14 01	14 20			14 35	14 57				15 01	15 20			15 35	15 57				16 01	16 20			16 35
	d		14 02	14 22		14 30	14 37	14 58				15 02	15 22		15 30	15 37	15 58				16 02	16 22		16 30	16 37
Teynham	d		14 08									15 08									16 08				
Sheerness-on-Sea	d	13 48			14 18						14 48			15 18						15 48			16 18		
Queenborough	d	13 53			14 23						14 53			15 23						15 53			16 23		
Swale	d	13 57			14 27						14 57			15 27						15 57			16 27		
Kemsley	d	14 01			14 31						15 01			15 31						16 01			16 31		
Sittingbourne	a	14 06	14 12	14 29	14 36	14 38	14 44	15 05			15 06	15 12	15 29	15 36	15 38	15 44	16 05			16 06	16 12	16 29	16 36	16 38	16 44
	d		14 13	14 30		14 38	14 45	15 08				15 13	15 30		15 38	15 45	16 08				16 13	16 30		16 38	16 45
Newington	d		14 18									15 18									16 18				
Rainham (Kent)	d		14 22	14 37		14 46	14 52	15 16				15 22	15 37		15 46	15 52	16 16				16 22	16 37		16 46	16 52
Gillingham (Kent)	d		14 27	14 44		14 51	14 57	15 21				15 27	15 44		15 51	15 57	16 21				16 27	16 44		16 51	16 57
Chatham	d		14 32	14 48		14 55	15 02	15 25				15 32	15 48		15 55	16 02	16 25				16 32	16 48		16 55	17 02
Rochester	d		14 35	14 52		14 59	15 05	15 29				15 35	15 52		15 59	16 05	16 29				16 35	16 52		16 59	17 05
Strood	a					15 02		15 32							16 02		16 32							17 02	
Gravesend	a					15 12		15 42							16 12		16 42							17 12	
Greenhithe for Bluewater	a																								
Dartford	a																								
London Bridge ⊖	a																								
London Cannon Street ⊖	a																								
London Waterloo (East) ⊖	a																								
London Charing Cross ⊖	a																								
Sole Street	d			15 01									16 01									17 01			
Meopham	d		14 46	15 04			15 16					15 46	16 04			16 16					16 46	17 04			17 16
Longfield	d		14 50	15 08			15 20					15 50	16 08			16 20					16 50	17 08			17 20
Farningham Road	d			15 12									16 12									17 12			
Swanley	a			15 17									16 17									17 17			
St Mary Cray	a			15 21									16 21									17 21			
Bromley South	a		15 02	15 29			15 32					16 02	16 29			16 32					17 02	17 29			17 32
London Victoria ⊖	a		15 23	16 00			15 53					16 23	17 00			16 53					17 23	18 00			17 53
Elephant & Castle ⊖	a																								
London Blackfriars ⊖	a																								
Ebbsfleet International	a					15 16		15 46							16 16		16 46							17 16	
Stratford International ⊖	a					15 29		16 02							16 28		16 58							17 28	
St Pancras International	a					15 40		16 09							16 36		17 06							17 36	

A From St Pancras International

For further services between St Pancras International, London Blackfriars and Elephant & Castle and Bromley South, St Mary Cray and Swanley refer to table T52

Table T212-R

Ramsgate, Dover, Sheerness-on-Sea and Medway - London

		SE ◇ A	SE ◇ A	SE	SE ◇1	SE ◇1	SE	SE ◇	SE ◇1	SE ◇ A	SE ◇ A	SE	SE ◇1	SE ◇1	SE	SE ◇	SE ◇1	SE ◇ A	SE ◇ A	SE	SE ◇1	SE ◇1
Ramsgate	d	16 20	16 28						16 53	17 20	17 28						17 53	18 20	18 28			
Dumpton Park	d								16 56								17 56					
Broadstairs	d	16 25	16 33						16 59	17 25	17 33						17 59	18 25	18 33			
Margate	d	16 30	16a39						17 04	17 30	17a39						18 04	18 30	18a39			
Westgate-on-Sea	d								17 08								18 08					
Birchington-on-Sea	d	16 35							17 11	17 35							18 11	18 35				
Herne Bay	d	16 44							17 20	17 44							18 20	18 44				
Chestfield & Swalecliffe	d								17 24								18 24					
Whitstable	d	16 49							17 27	17 49							18 27	18 49				
Dover Priory	d				16 18	16 52							17 18	17 52							18 18	18 52
Kearsney	d				16 22								17 22								18 22	
Shepherds Well	d				16 28								17 28								18 28	
Snowdown	d				16 31								17 31								18 31	
Aylesham	d				16 34								17 34								18 34	
Adisham	d				16 37								17 37								18 37	
Bekesbourne	d				16 41								17 41								18 41	
Canterbury East	d				16 47	17 09							17 47	18 09							18 47	19 09
Selling	d				16 56								17 56								18 56	
Faversham	a	16 57			17 01	17 20			17 35	17 57			18 01	18 20			18 35	18 57			19 01	19 20
	d	16 58			17 02	17 22		17 30	17 37	17 58			18 02	18 22		18 30	18 37	18 58			19 02	19 22
Teynham	d				17 08								18 08								19 08	
Sheerness-on-Sea	d			16 48			17 18					17 48			18 18					18 48		
Queenborough	d			16 53			17 23					17 53			18 23					18 53		
Swale	d			16 57			17 27					17 57			18 27					18 57		
Kemsley	d			17 01			17 31					18 01			18 31					19 01		
Sittingbourne	a	17 05		17 06	17 12	17 29	17 36	17 38	17 44	18 05		18 06	18 12	18 29	18 36	18 38	18 44	19 05		19 06	19 12	19 29
	d	17 08			17 13	17 30		17 38	17 45	18 08			18 13	18 30		18 38	18 45	19 08			19 13	19 30
Newington	d				17 18								18 18								19 18	
Rainham (Kent)	d	17 16			17 22	17 37		17 46	17 52	18 16			18 22	18 37		18 46	18 52	19 16			19 22	19 37
Gillingham (Kent)	d	17 21			17 27	17 44		17 51	17 57	18 21			18 27	18 44		18 51	18 57	19 21			19 27	19 44
Chatham	d	17 25			17 32	17 48		17 55	18 02	18 25			18 32	18 48		18 55	19 02	19 25			19 32	19 48
Rochester	d	17 29			17 35	17 52		17 59	18 05	18 29			18 35	18 52		18 59	19 05	19 29			19 35	19 52
Strood	a	17 32						18 02		18 32						19 02		19 32				
Gravesend	a	17 42						18 12		18 42						19 12		19 42				
Greenhithe for Bluewater	a																					
Dartford	a																					
London Bridge ⊖	a																					
London Cannon Street ⊖	a																					
London Waterloo (East) ⊖	a																					
London Charing Cross ⊖	a																					
Sole Street	d					18 01								19 01								20 01
Meopham	d				17 46	18 04			18 16				18 46	19 04			19 16				19 46	20 04
Longfield	d				17 50	18 08			18 20				18 50	19 08			19 20				19 50	20 08
Farningham Road	d					18 12								19 12								20 12
Swanley	a					18 17								19 17								20 17
St Mary Cray	a					18 21								19 21								20 21
Bromley South	a				18 02	18 29			18 32				19 02	19 29			19 32				20 02	20 29
London Victoria ⊖	a				18 23	19 00			18 53				19 23	20 00			19 53				20 23	21 00
Elephant & Castle ⊖	a																					
London Blackfriars ⊖	a																					
Ebbsfleet International	a	17 46						18 16		8 46						19 16		19 46				
Stratford International ⊖	a	17 58						18 29		8 58						19 28		19 58				
St Pancras International	a	18 09						18 36		19 06						19 36		20 06				

A From St Pancras International

For further services between St Pancras International, London Blackfriars and Elephant & Castle and Bromley South, St Mary Cray and Swanley refer to table T52

Table T212-R

Ramsgate, Dover, Sheerness-on-Sea and Medway - London

		SE	SE ◇	SE ◇1	SE ◇ A	SE ◇ A	SE	SE ◇1	SE ◇1	SE	SE ◇	SE ◇1	SE ◇ A	SE ◇ A	SE	SE ◇1	SE	SE ◇	SE ◇1	SE ◇1	SE ◇ A	SE ◇ A	SE
Ramsgate	d			18 53	19 20	19 28						19 53	20 20	20 28					20 53		21 20	21 28	
Dumpton Park	d			18 56								19 56							20 56				
Broadstairs	d			18 59	19 25	19 33						19 59	20 25	20 33					20 59		21 25	21 33	
Margate	d			19 04	19 30	19a39						20 04	20 30	20a39					21 04		21 30	21a39	
Westgate-on-Sea	d			19 08								20 08							21 08				
Birchington-on-Sea	d			19 11	19 35							20 11	20 35						21 11		21 35		
Herne Bay	d			19 20	19 44							20 20	20 44						21 20		21 44		
Chestfield & Swalecliffe	d			19 24								20 24							21 24				
Whitstable	d			19 27	19 49							20 27	20 49						21 27		21 49		
Dover Priory	d							19 18	19 52							20 18				21 05			
Kearsney	d							19 22								20 22				21 09			
Shepherds Well	d							19 28								20 28				21 15			
Snowdown	d							19 31								20 31				21 18			
Aylesham	d							19 34								20 34				21 21			
Adisham	d							19 37								20 37				21 24			
Bekesbourne	d							19 41								20 41				21 28			
Canterbury East	d							19 47	20 09							20 47				21 33			
Selling	d							19 56								20 56				21 42			
Faversham	a			19 35	19 57			20 01	20 20			20 35	20 57			21 01			21 35	21 47	21 57		
	d		19 30	19 37	19 58			20 02	20 22		20 30	20 37	20 58			21 02		21 30	21 37	21 47	21 58		
Teynham	d							20 08								21 08				21 53			
Sheerness-on-Sea	d	19 18					19 48			20 18					20 48		21 18						21 48
Queenborough	d	19 23					19 53			20 23					20 53		21 23						21 53
Swale	d	19 27					19 57			20 27					20 57		21 27						21 57
Kemsley	d	19 31					20 01			20 31					21 01		21 31						22 01
Sittingbourne	a	19 36	19 38	19 44	20 05		20 06	20 12	20 29	20 36	20 38	20 44	21 05		21 06	21 12	21 36	21 38	21 44	21 58	22 05		22 06
	d		19 38	19 45	20 08			20 13	20 30		20 38	20 45	21 08			21 13		21 38	21 45	21 58	22 08		
Newington	d							20 18								21 18				22 03			
Rainham (Kent)	d		19 46	19 52	20 16			20 22	20 37		20 46	20 52	21 16			21 22		21 46	21 52	22 08	22 16		
Gillingham (Kent)	d		19 51	19 57	20 21			20 27	20 44		20 51	20 57	21 21			21 27		21 51	21 57	22 14	22 21		
Chatham	d		19 55	20 02	20 25			20 32	20 48		20 55	21 02	21 25			21 32		21 55	22 02	22 18	22 25		
Rochester	d		19 59	20 05	20 29			20 35	20 52		20 59	21 05	21 29			21 35		21 59	22 05	22 22	22 29		
Strood	a		20 02		20 32						21 02		21 32					22 02			22 32		
Gravesend	a		20 12		20 42						21 12		21 42					22 12			22 42		
Greenhithe for Bluewater	a																						
Dartford	a																						
London Bridge ⊖	a																						
London Cannon Street ⊖	a																						
London Waterloo (East) ⊖	a																						
London Charing Cross ⊖	a																						
Sole Street	d								21 01											22 31			
Meopham	d			20 16				20 46	21 04			21 16				21 46			22 16	22 34			
Longfield	d			20 20				20 50	21 08			21 20				21 50			22 20	22 38			
Farningham Road	d								21 12											22 42			
Swanley	a								21 17											22 47			
St Mary Cray	a								21 21											22 51			
Bromley South	a			20 32				21 02	21 29			21 32				22 02			22 32	22 59			
London Victoria ⊖	a			20 53				21 23	22 00			21 53				22 23			22 52	23 30			
Elephant & Castle ⊖	a																						
London Blackfriars ⊖	a																						
Ebbsfleet International	a		20 16		20 46						21 16		21 46					22 16			22 46		
Stratford International ⊖	a		20 28		21 02						21 28		21 58					22 28			22 58		
St Pancras International	a		20 36		21 09						21 36		22 06					22 36			23 06		

A From St Pancras International

For further services between St Pancras International, London Blackfriars and Elephant & Castle and Bromley South, St Mary Cray and Swanley refer to table T52

Table T212-R

Saturdays
26 May to 8 December

Ramsgate, Dover, Sheerness-on-Sea and Medway - London

		SE	SE	SE	SE	SE	SE	SE	SE	SE
			◇■	◇■	◇		■		■	◇
					A					A
Ramsgate	d		21 53		22 28				23 15	23 29
Dumpton Park	d		21 56						23 18	
Broadstairs	d		21 59		22 33				23 21	23 35
Margate	d		22 04		22a39				23 26	23a40
Westgate-on-Sea	d		22 08						23 30	
Birchington-on-Sea	d		22 11						23 33	
Herne Bay	d		22 20						23 42	
Chestfield & Swalecliffe	d		22 24						23 46	
Whitstable	d		22 27						23 49	
Dover Priory	d			22 05			23 10			
Kearsney	d			22 09			23 14			
Shepherds Well	d			22 15			23 20			
Snowdown	d			22 18			23 23			
Aylesham	d			22 21			23 26			
Adisham	d			22 24			23 29			
Bekesbourne	d			22 28			23 33			
Canterbury East	d			22 39			23 39			
Selling	d			22 48			23 48			
Faversham	a		22 35	22 53			23 54		23 58	
	d		22 37	22 54					00 02	
Teynham	d			23 00					00 08	
Sheerness-on-Sea	d	22 18				22 48		23 48		
Queenborough	d	22 23				22 53		23 53		
Swale	d	22 27				22 57		23 57		
Kemsley	d	22 31				23 01		23 59		
Sittingbourne	a	22 36	22 44	23 04		23 06		00 06	00 12	
	d		22 45	23 05					00 13	
Newington	d			23 10					00 18	
Rainham (Kent)	d		22 52	23 14					00 22	
Gillingham (Kent)	d		22 57	23 20					00a27	
Chatham	d		23 02	23 24						
Rochester	d		23 05	23 28						
Strood	a									
Gravesend	a									
Greenhithe for Bluewater	a									
Dartford	a									
London Bridge ⊖	a									
London Cannon Street ⊖	a									
London Waterloo (East) ⊖	a									
London Charing Cross ⊖	a									
Sole Street	d			23 37						
Meopham	d		23 16	23 40						
Longfield	d		23 20	23 44						
Farningham Road	d			23 48						
Swanley	a			23 53						
St Mary Cray	a			23 57						
Bromley South	a		23 32	00 03						
London Victoria ⊖	a		23 52	00 24						
Elephant & Castle ⊖	a									
London Blackfriars ⊖	a									
Ebbsfleet International	a									
Stratford International ⊖	a									
St Pancras International	a									

A From St Pancras International

For further services between St Pancras International, London Blackfriars and Elephant & Castle and Bromley South, St Mary Cray and Swanley refer to table T52

Table T212-R

Sundays
20 May to 2 December

Ramsgate, Dover, Sheerness-on-Sea and Medway - London

		SE	SE	SE	SE	SE	SE	SE	SE	SE	SE	SE
		■	◇■	◇	◇	◇■	◇■	◇		◇■	◇■	◇
		A		B								
Ramsgate	d			00 28			07 05				08 05	08 20
Dumpton Park	d						07 08				08 08	
Broadstairs	d			00s33			07 11				08 11	08 25
Margate	d			00a39			07 16				08 16	08 30
Westgate-on-Sea	d						07 20				08 20	
Birchington-on-Sea	d						07 24				08 24	08 35
Herne Bay	d						07 33				08 33	08 44
Chestfield & Swalecliffe	d						07 36				08 36	
Whitstable	d						07 39				08 39	08 49
Dover Priory	d					07 03				08 03		
Kearsney	d					07 07				08 07		
Shepherds Well	d					07 13				08 13		
Snowdown	d					07 16				08 16		
Aylesham	d					07 19				08 19		
Adisham	d					07 22				08 22		
Bekesbourne	d					07 26				08 26		
Canterbury East	d					07 32				08 32		
Selling	d					07 41				08 41		
Faversham	a					07 46	07 48			08 46	08 48	08 57
	d	00 02			07 00		07 52	08 00			08 52	08 58
Teynham	d	00 08										
Sheerness-on-Sea	d								08 00			
Queenborough	d								08 04			
Swale	d								08 08			
Kemsley	d								08 12			
Sittingbourne	a	00 12			07 08		07 59	08 08	08 17		08 59	09 05
	d	00 13			07 08		08 00	08 08			09 00	09 08
Newington	d	00 18										
Rainham (Kent)	d	00 22			07 16		08 07	08 16			09 07	09 16
Gillingham (Kent)	d	00a27	06 40		07 21		08 13	08 21			09 13	09 21
Chatham	d		06 44		07 25		08 18	08 25			09 18	09 25
Rochester	d		06 48		07 29		08 21	08 29			09 21	09 29
Strood	a				07 32			08 32				09 32
Gravesend	a				07 42			08 42				09 42
Greenhithe for Bluewater	a											
Dartford	a											
London Bridge ⊖	a											
London Cannon Street ⊖	a											
London Waterloo (East) ⊖	a											
London Charing Cross ⊖	a											
Sole Street	d		06 57									
Meopham	d		07 00									
Longfield	d		07 04									
Farningham Road	d		07 08									
Swanley	a		07 13									
St Mary Cray	a		07 17									
Bromley South	a		07 25				08 46				09 46	
London Victoria ⊖	a		07 48				09 09				10 05	
Elephant & Castle ⊖	a											
London Blackfriars ⊖	a											
Ebbsfleet International	a				07 46			08 46				09 46
Stratford International ⊖	a				07 58			08 58				09 58
St Pancras International	a				08 06			09 06				10 06

		SE	SE	SE	SE	SE	SE	SE	SE	SE	SE	SE
			◇■	◇■	◇■	◇		◇■	◇■	◇■	◇	◇
						C					D	D
Ramsgate	d				09 05	09 20				10 05	10 20	10 28
Dumpton Park	d				09 08					10 08		
Broadstairs	d				09 11	09 25				10 11	10 25	10 33
Margate	d				09 16	09 30				10 16	10 30	10a39
Westgate-on-Sea	d				09 20					10 20		
Birchington-on-Sea	d				09 24	09 35				10 24	10 35	
Herne Bay	d				09 33	09 44				10 33	10 44	
Chestfield & Swalecliffe	d				09 36					10 36		
Whitstable	d				09 39	09 49				10 39	10 49	
Dover Priory	d			09 03					10 03			
Kearsney	d			09 07					10 07			
Shepherds Well	d			09 13					10 13			
Snowdown	d			09 16					10 16			
Aylesham	d			09 19					10 19			
Adisham	d			09 22					10 22			
Bekesbourne	d			09 26					10 26			
Canterbury East	d		09 02	09 32				10 02	10 32			
Selling	d			09 41					10 41			
Faversham	a		09 13	09 46	09 48	09 57		10 13	10 46	10 48	10 57	
	d		09 14		09 52	09 58		10 14		10 52	10 58	
Teynham	d		09 20					10 20				
Sheerness-on-Sea	d	09 00					10 00					
Queenborough	d	09 04					10 04					
Swale	d	09 08					10 08					
Kemsley	d	09 12					10 12					
Sittingbourne	a	09 17	09 24		09 59	10 05	10 17	10 24		10 59	11 05	
	d		09 25		10 00	10 08		10 25		11 00	11 08	
Newington	d		09 30					10 30				
Rainham (Kent)	d		09 34		10 07	10 16		10 34		11 07	11 16	
Gillingham (Kent)	d		09 40		10 13	10 21		10 40		11 13	11 21	
Chatham	d		09 44		10 18	10 25		10 44		11 18	11 25	
Rochester	d		09 48		10 21	10 29		10 48		11 21	11 29	
Strood	a					10 32					11 32	
Gravesend	a					10 42					11 42	
Greenhithe for Bluewater	a											
Dartford	a											
London Bridge ⊖	a											
London Cannon Street ⊖	a											
London Waterloo (East) ⊖	a											
London Charing Cross ⊖	a											
Sole Street	d		09 57					10 57				
Meopham	d		10 00					11 00				
Longfield	d		10 04					11 04				
Farningham Road	d		10 08					11 08				
Swanley	a		10 13					11 13				
St Mary Cray	a		10 17					11 17				
Bromley South	a		10 25		10 46			11 25		11 46		
London Victoria ⊖	a		10 48		11 05			11 48		12 05		
Elephant & Castle ⊖	a											
London Blackfriars ⊖	a											
Ebbsfleet International	a					10 46					11 46	
Stratford International ⊖	a					10 58					11 58	
St Pancras International	a					11 06					12 05	

A not 20 May. From Ramsgate
B not 20 May. From St Pancras International
C From Ashford International
D From St Pancras International

For further services between St Pancras International, London Blackfriars and Elephant & Castle and Bromley South, St Mary Cray and Swanley refer to table T52

Sundays

20 May to 2 December

Ramsgate, Dover, Sheerness-on-Sea and Medway - London

		SE	SE	SE	SE	SE	SE	SE	SE	SE	SE	SE	SE	SE	SE	SE	SE	SE	SE	SE	SE	SE	SE
			◇1	◇	◇1	◇1	◇	◇		◇1	◇	◇1	◇1	◇	◇		◇1	◇	◇1	◇1	◇	◇	
							A	A			B			A	A			C			A	A	
Ramsgate	d					11 05	11 20	11 28					12 05	12 20	12 28					13 05	13 20	13 28	
Dumpton Park	d					11 08							12 08							13 08			
Broadstairs	d					11 11	11 25	11 33					12 11	12 25	12 33					13 11	13 25	13 33	
Margate	d					11 16	11 30	11a39					12 16	12 30	12a39					13 16	13 30	13a39	
Westgate-on-Sea	d					11 20							12 20							13 20			
Birchington-on-Sea	d					11 24	11 35						12 24	12 35						13 24	13 35		
Herne Bay	d					11 33	11 44						12 33	12 44						13 33	13 44		
Chestfield & Swalecliffe	d					11 36							12 36							13 36			
Whitstable	d					11 39	11 49						12 39	12 49						13 39	13 49		
Dover Priory	d				11 03							12 03							13 03				
Kearsney	d				11 07							12 07							13 07				
Shepherds Well	d				11 13							12 13							13 13				
Snowdown	d				11 16							12 16							13 16				
Aylesham	d				11 19							12 19							13 19				
Adisham	d				11 22							12 22							13 22				
Bekesbourne	d				11 26							12 26							13 26				
Canterbury East	d		11 02		11 32					12 02		12 32					13 02		13 32				
Selling	d				11 41							12 41							13 41				
Faversham	a		11 13		11 46	11 48	11 57			12 13		12 46	12 48	12 57			13 13		13 46	13 48	13 57		
	d		11 14	11 30	11 52		11 58			12 14	12 30	12 52		12 58			13 14	13 30	13 52		13 58		
Teynham	d		11 20							12 20							13 20						
Sheerness-on-Sea	d	11 00							12 00							13 00							14 00
Queenborough	d	11 04							12 04							13 04							14 04
Swale	d	11 08							12 08							13 08							14 08
Kemsley	d	11 12							12 12							13 12							14 12
Sittingbourne	a	11 17	11 24	11 38	11 59		12 05		12 17	12 24	12 38	12 59		13 05		13 17	13 24	13 38	13 59		14 05		14 17
	d		11 25	11 38	12 00		12 08			12 25	12 38	13 00		13 08			13 25	13 38	14 00		14 08		
Newington	d		11 30							12 30							13 30						
Rainham (Kent)	d		11 34	11 46	12 07		12 16			12 34	12 46	13 07		13 16			13 34	13 46	14 07		14 16		
Gillingham (Kent)	d		11 40	11 51	12 13		12 21			12 40	12 51	13 13		13 21			13 40	13 51	14 13		14 21		
Chatham	d		11 44	11 55	12 18		12 25			12 44	12 55	13 18		13 25			13 44	13 55	14 18		14 25		
Rochester	d		11 48	11 59	12 21		12 29			12 48	12 59	13 21		13 29			13 48	13 59	14 21		14 29		
Strood	a			12 02			12 32				13 02			13 32				14 02			14 32		
Gravesend	a			12 12			12 42				13 12			13 42				14 12			14 42		
Greenhithe for Bluewater	a																						
Dartford	a																						
London Bridge ⊖	a																						
London Cannon Street ⊖	a																						
London Waterloo (East) ⊖	a																						
London Charing Cross ⊖	a																						
Sole Street	d		11 57							12 57							13 57						
Meopham	d		12 00							13 00							14 00						
Longfield	d		12 04							13 04							14 04						
Farningham Road	d		12 08							13 08							14 08						
Swanley	a		12 13							13 13							14 13						
St Mary Cray	a		12 17							13 17							14 17						
Bromley South	a		12 25		12 46					13 25		13 46					14 25		14 46				
London Victoria ⊖	a		12 48		13 05					13 48		14 05					14 48		15 05				
Elephant & Castle ⊖	a																						
London Blackfriars ⊖	a																						
Ebbsfleet International	a			12 16			12 46				13 16			13 46				14 16			14 46		
Stratford International ⊖	a			12 28			12 58				13 29			13 58				14 28			14 59		
St Pancras International	a			12 36			13 06				13 37			14 06				14 36			15 06		

A From St Pancras International B From Faversham Up Sidings C From Ramsgate E.M.U.D.

For further services between St Pancras International, London Blackfriars and Elephant & Castle and Bromley South, St Mary Cray and Swanley refer to table T52

Table T212-R

Sundays

20 May to 2 December

Ramsgate, Dover, Sheerness-on-Sea and Medway - London

		SE	SE	SE	SE	SE	SE	SE	SE	SE	SE	SE	SE	SE	SE	SE	SE	SE	SE	SE	SE	SE	SE
		◇1	◇	◇1	◇1	◇	◇		◇1	◇	◇1	◇1	◇	◇		◇1	◇	◇1	◇1	◇	◇		◇1
			A			A	A			A			A	A			A			A	A		
Ramsgate	d				14 05	14 20	14 28					15 05	15 20	15 28					16 05	16 20	16 28		
Dumpton Park	d				14 08							15 08							16 08				
Broadstairs	d				14 11	14 25	14 33					15 11	15 25	15 33					16 11	16 25	16 33		
Margate	d				14 16	14 30	14a39					15 16	15 30	15a39					16 16	16 30	16a39		
Westgate-on-Sea	d				14 20							15 20							16 20				
Birchington-on-Sea	d				14 24	14 35						15 24	15 35						16 24	16 35			
Herne Bay	d				14 33	14 44						15 33	15 44						16 33	16 44			
Chestfield & Swalecliffe	d				14 36							15 36							16 36				
Whitstable	d				14 39	14 49						15 39	15 49						16 39	16 49			
Dover Priory	d			14 03							15 03							16 03					
Kearsney	d			14 07							15 07							16 07					
Shepherds Well	d			14 13							15 13							16 13					
Snowdown	d			14 16							15 16							16 16					
Aylesham	d			14 19							15 19							16 19					
Adisham	d			14 22							15 22							16 22					
Bekesbourne	d			14 26							15 26							16 26					
Canterbury East	d	14 02		14 32					15 02		15 32					16 02		16 32					17 02
Selling	d			14 41							15 41							16 41					
Faversham	a	14 13		14 46	14 48	14 57			15 13		15 46	15 48	15 57			16 13		16 46	16 48	16 57			17 13
	d	14 14	14 30	14 52		14 58			15 14	15 30	15 52		15 58			16 14	16 30	16 52		16 58			17 14
Teynham	d	14 20							15 20							16 20							17 20
Sheerness-on-Sea	d							15 00							16 00							17 00	
Queenborough	d							15 04							16 04							17 04	
Swale	d							15 08							16 08							17 08	
Kemsley	d							15 12							16 12							17 12	
Sittingbourne	a	14 24	14 38	14 59		15 05		15 17	15 24	15 38	15 59		16 05		16 17	16 24	16 38	16 59		17 05		17 17	17 24
	d	14 25	14 38	15 00		15 08			15 25	15 38	16 00		16 08			16 25	16 38	17 00		17 08			17 25
Newington	d	14 30							15 30							16 30							17 30
Rainham (Kent)	d	14 34	14 46	15 07		15 16			15 34	15 46	16 07		16 16			16 34	16 46	17 07		17 16			17 34
Gillingham (Kent)	d	14 40	14 51	15 13		15 21			15 40	15 51	16 13		16 21			16 40	16 51	17 13		17 21			17 40
Chatham	d	14 44	14 55	15 18		15 25			15 44	15 55	16 18		16 25			16 44	16 55	17 18		17 25			17 44
Rochester	d	14 48	14 59	15 21		15 29			15 48	15 59	16 21		16 29			16 48	16 59	17 21		17 29			17 48
Strood	a		15 02			15 32				16 02			16 32				17 02			17 32			
Gravesend	a		15 12			15 42				16 12			16 42				17 12			17 42			
Greenhithe for Bluewater	a																						
Dartford	a																						
London Bridge ⊖	a																						
London Cannon Street ⊖	a																						
London Waterloo (East) ⊖	a																						
London Charing Cross ⊖	a																						
Sole Street	d	14 57							15 57							16 57							17 57
Meopham	d	15 00							16 00							17 00							18 00
Longfield	d	15 04							16 04							17 04							18 04
Farningham Road	d	15 08							16 08							17 08							18 08
Swanley	a	15 13							16 13							17 13							18 13
St Mary Cray	a	15 17							16 17							17 17							18 17
Bromley South	a	15 25		15 46					16 25		16 46					17 25		17 46					18 25
London Victoria ⊖	a	15 48		16 05					16 48		17 05					17 48		18 05					18 48
Elephant & Castle ⊖	a																						
London Blackfriars ⊖	a																						
Ebbsfleet International	a		15 16			15 46				16 16			16 46				17 16			17 46			
Stratford International ⊖	a		15 29			16 02				16 28			16 58				17 28			18 04			
St Pancras International	a		15 40			16 10				16 36			17 06				17 36			18 11			

A From St Pancras International

For further services between St Pancras International, London Blackfriars and Elephant & Castle and Bromley South, St Mary Cray and Swanley refer to table T52

Table T212-R

Sundays
20 May to 2 December

Ramsgate, Dover, Sheerness-on-Sea and Medway - London

		SE	SE	SE	SE	SE	SE	SE	SE	SE	SE	SE	SE	SE	SE	SE	SE	SE	SE	SE	SE	SE
		◇	◇■	◇■	◇	◇		◇■	◇	◇■	◇■	◇	◇		◇■	◇	◇■	◇■	◇	◇		◇■
					A	A			A			A	A			A			A	A		
Ramsgate ■	d			17 05	17 20	17 28					18 05	18 20	18 28					19 05	19 20	19 28		
Dumpton Park	d			17 08							18 08							19 08				
Broadstairs	d			17 11	17 25	17 33					18 11	18 25	18 33					19 11	19 25	19 33		
Margate ■	d			17 16	17 30	17a39					18 16	18 30	18a39					19 16	19 30	19a39		
Westgate-on-Sea	d			17 20							18 20							19 20				
Birchington-on-Sea	d			17 24	17 35						18 24	18 35						19 24	19 35			
Herne Bay	d			17 33	17 44						18 33	18 44						19 33	19 44			
Chestfield & Swalecliffe	d			17 36							18 36							19 36				
Whitstable	d			17 39	17 49						18 39	18 49						19 39	19 49			
Dover Priory ■	d		17 03							18 03							19 03					
Kearsney	d		17 07							18 07							19 07					
Shepherds Well	d		17 13							18 13							19 13					
Snowdown	d		17 16							18 16							19 16					
Aylesham	d		17 19							18 19							19 19					
Adisham	d		17 22							18 22							19 22					
Bekesbourne	d		17 26							18 26							19 26					
Canterbury East ■	d		17 32					18 02		18 32					19 02		19 32					20 02
Selling	d		17 41							18 41							19 41					
Faversham ■	a		17 46	17 48	17 57			18 13		18 46	18 48	18 57			19 13		19 46	19 48	19 57			20 13
	d	17 30	17 52		17 58			18 14	18 30	18 52		18 58			19 14	19 30	19 52		19 58			20 14
Teynham	d							18 20							19 20							20 20
Sheerness-on-Sea	d						18 00							19 00							20 00	
Queenborough	d						18 04							19 04							20 04	
Swale	d						18 08							19 08							20 08	
Kemsley	d						18 12							19 12							20 12	
Sittingbourne ■	a	17 38	17 59		18 05		18 17	18 24	18 38	18 59		19 05		19 17	19 24	19 38	19 59		20 05		20 17	20 24
	d	17 38	18 00		18 08			18 25	18 38	19 00		19 08			19 25	19 38	20 00		20 08			20 25
Newington	d							18 30							19 30							20 30
Rainham (Kent)	d	17 46	18 07		18 16			18 34	18 46	19 07		19 16			19 34	19 46	20 07		20 16			20 34
Gillingham (Kent) ■	d	17 51	18 13		18 21			18 40	18 51	19 13		19 21			19 40	19 51	20 13		20 21			20 40
Chatham ■	d	17 55	18 18		18 25			18 44	18 55	19 18		19 25			19 44	19 55	20 18		20 25			20 44
Rochester ■	d	17 59	18 21		18 29			18 48	18 59	19 21		19 29			19 48	19 59	20 21		20 29			20 48
Strood ■	a	18 02			18 32				19 02			19 32				20 02			20 32			
Gravesend ■	a	18 12			18 42				19 12			19 42				20 12			20 42			
Greenhithe for Bluewater	a																					
Dartford ■	a																					
London Bridge ■ ⊖	a																					
London Cannon Street ■ ⊖	a																					
London Waterloo (East) ■ ⊖	a																					
London Charing Cross ■ ⊖	a																					
Sole Street	d							18 57							19 57							20 57
Meopham	d							19 00							20 00							21 00
Longfield	d							19 04							20 04							21 04
Farningham Road	d							19 08							20 08							21 08
Swanley ■	a							19 13							20 13							21 13
St Mary Cray	a							19 17							20 17							21 17
Bromley South ■	a		18 46					19 25		19 46					20 25		20 46					21 25
London Victoria ■ ⊖	a		19 05					19 48		20 05					20 48		21 05					21 48
Elephant & Castle ⊖	a																					
London Blackfriars ■ ⊖	a																					
Ebbsfleet International	a	18 16			18 46				19 16			19 46				20 16			20 46			
Stratford International ⊖	a	18 29			19 02				19 28			20 02				20 28			20 58			
St Pancras International	a	18 37			19 10				19 36			20 09				20 36			21 05			

A From St Pancras International

For further services between St Pancras International, London Blackfriars and Elephant & Castle and Bromley South, St Mary Cray and Swanley refer to table T52

Table T212-R

Sundays
20 May to 2 December

Ramsgate, Dover, Sheerness-on-Sea and Medway - London

		SE	SE	SE	SE	SE	SE	SE	SE	SE	SE	SE	SE	SE	SE	SE	SE	SE	SE	SE
		◇	◇■	◇■	◇	◇		◇■	◇	◇■	◇■	◇	◇		◇■	◇	◇■		◇■	◇
					A	A			A			A	A			A				A
Ramsgate ■	d			20 05	20 20	20 28					21 05	21 20	21 28			22 28			22 35	23 28
Dumpton Park	d			20 08							21 08								22 38	
Broadstairs	d			20 11	20 25	20 33					21 11	21 25	21 33			22 33			22 41	23 33
Margate ■	d			20 16	20 30	20a39					21 16	21 30	21a39			22a39			22 46	23a39
Westgate-on-Sea	d			20 20							21 20								22 50	
Birchington-on-Sea	d			20 24	20 35						21 24	21 35							22 54	
Herne Bay	d			20 33	20 44						21 33	21 44							23 03	
Chestfield & Swalecliffe	d			20 36							21 36								23 06	
Whitstable	d			20 39	20 49						21 39	21 49							23 09	
Dover Priory ■	d		20 03							21 03							22 33			
Kearsney	d		20 07							21 07							22 37			
Shepherds Well	d		20 13							21 13							22 43			
Snowdown	d		20 16							21 16							22 46			
Aylesham	d		20 19							21 19							22 49			
Adisham	d		20 22							21 22							22 52			
Bekesbourne	d		20 26							21 26							22 56			
Canterbury East ■	d		20 32					21 02		21 32					22 02		23 02			
Selling	d		20 41							21 41							23 11			
Faversham ■	a		20 46	20 48	20 57			21 13		21 46	21 48	21 57			22 13		23 16		23 18	
	d	20 30	20 52		20 58			21 14	21 30	21 52		21 58			22 14				23 22	
Teynham	d							21 20							22 20				23 28	
Sheerness-on-Sea	d						21 00							22 00				23 00		
Queenborough	d						21 04							22 04				23 04		
Swale	d						21 08							22 08				23 08		
Kemsley	d						21 12							22 12				23 12		
Sittingbourne ■	a	20 38	20 59		21 05		21 17	21 24	21 38	21 59		22 05		22 17	22 24			23 17	23 32	
	d	20 38	21 00		21 08			21 25	21 38	22 00		22 08			22 25				23 33	
Newington	d							21 30							22 30				23 38	
Rainham (Kent)	d	20 46	21 07		21 16			21 34	21 46	22 07		22 16			22 34				23 42	
Gillingham (Kent) ■	d	20 51	21 13		21 21			21 40	21 51	22 13		22 21			22 40				23 47	
Chatham ■	d	20 55	21 18		21 25			21 44	21 55	22 18		22 25			22 44				23 52	
Rochester ■	d	20 59	21 21		21 29			21 48	21 59	22 21		22 29			22 48				23 55	
Strood ■	a	21 02			21 32				22 02			22 32								
Gravesend ■	a	21 12			21 42				22 12			22 42								
Greenhithe for Bluewater	a																			
Dartford ■	a																			
London Bridge ■ ⊖	a																			
London Cannon Street ■ ⊖	a																			
London Waterloo (East) ■ ⊖	a																			
London Charing Cross ■ ⊖	a																			
Sole Street	d							21 57							22 57					
Meopham	d							22 00							23 00					
Longfield	d							22 04							23 04					
Farningham Road	d							22 08							23 08					
Swanley ■	a							22 13							23 13					
St Mary Cray	a							22 17							23 17					
Bromley South ■	a		21 46					22 25		22 46					23 25				00 19	
London Victoria ■ ⊖	a		22 05					22 48		23 05					23 48				00 36	
Elephant & Castle ⊖	a																			
London Blackfriars ■ ⊖	a																			
Ebbsfleet International	a	21 16			21 46				22 16			22 46								
Stratford International ⊖	a	21 28			21 59				22 28			22 58								
St Pancras International	a	21 36			22 07				22 36			23 06								

A From St Pancras International

For further services between St Pancras International, London Blackfriars and Elephant & Castle and Bromley South, St Mary Cray and Swanley refer to table T52

Table T216-F

Mondays to Fridays

21 May to 7 December

Carlisle and Dumfries - Kilmarnock and Glasgow Central

Miles			SR	SR	SR	SR 🛒	NT	SR	SR 🛒	SR	SR 🛒	SR	SR 🛒	SR	SR	SR 🛒	SR 🛒	SR	SR 🛒	SR
—	Newcastle 8	48 d					06 30													
0	**Carlisle 8**	65 d			05 31	06 08	08 16	09 58	11 12	12 20	13 10	14 30	15 05	16 17	17 30	17 57	19 10	20 20	21 12	23 10
9¾	Gretna Green	d			05 42	06 19	08 27	10 09	11 23	12 32	13 23	14 41	15 17	16 28	17 41	18 08	19 21	20 31	21 24	23 21
17½	Annan	d			05 53	06 27	08 35	10 17	11 31	12 40	13 32	14 49	15 26	16 36	17 51	18 17	19 29	20 39	21 32	23 29
33	**Dumfries**	d	05 13	05 45	06a10	06 46	08 54	10a35	11 53	12a58	13 51	15a07	15 45	16a54	18a08	18 35	19 48	20a57	21 51	23a47
59¾	Sanquhar	d	05 39	06 12		07 12	09 20		12 19		14 17		16 12			19 01	20 14		22 17	
62½	Kirkconnel	d	05 44	06 17		07 17	09 25		12 24		14 22		16 18			19 06	20 19		22 22	
69¾	New Cumnock	d	05 53	06 26		07 26	09 34		12 33		14 31		16 28			19 15	20 28		22 31	
77¼	Auchinleck	d	06 01	06 34		07 34	09 42		12 41		14 39		16 37			19 24	20 36		22 39	
91	**Kilmarnock 3**	218,222 a	06 18	06 51		07 52	09 59		12 58		14 57		16 55			19 41	20 53		22 56	
—		d	06 20	06 52		07 55	10 00		12 59		14 59		16 57			19 57	20 59		22 57	
107¾	Barrhead	222 d	06 44	07 17		08 22	10 24						17 22			20 21	21 23		23 22	
115¾	**Glasgow Central 15**	65,222 a	07 07	07 31		08 38	10 37		13 35		15 38		17 37			20 37	21 39		23 36	

Saturdays

26 May to 8 December

		SR	SR	SR	SR 🛒	NT	SR	SR 🛒	SR	SR 🛒	SR	SR 🛒	SR	SR	SR 🛒	SR 🛒	SR	SR 🛒	SR
Newcastle 8	48 d					06 30													
Carlisle 8	65 d			05 25	06 08	08 05	09 55	11 11	12 20	13 12	14 22	15 05	16 17	17 21	17 56	19 10	20 22	21 08	23 10
Gretna Green	d			05 36	06 19	08 16	10 06	11 23	12 32	13 24	14 33	15 17	16 28	17 32	18 08	19 21	20 33	21 21	23 21
Annan	d			05 45	06 27	08 24	10 14	11 31	12 40	13 32	14 41	15 26	16 36	17 40	18 17	19 29	20 41	21 31	23 29
Dumfries	d	05 13	05 46	06a02	06 46	08 43	10a32	11 54	12a58	13 51	14a59	15 45	16a54	17a58	18 35	19 48	20a59	21 51	23a47
Sanquhar	d	05 39	06 12		07 12	09 09		12 20		14 17		16 12			19 01	20 14		22 17	
Kirkconnel	d	05 44	06 17		07 17	09 14		12 25		14 22		16 18			19 06	20 19		22 22	
New Cumnock	d	05 53	06 26		07 26	09 23		12 34		14 31		16 28			19 15	20 28		22 31	
Auchinleck	d	06 01	06 34		07 34	09 31		12 42		14 39		16 37			19 24	20 36		22 39	
Kilmarnock 3	218,222 a	06 18	06 51		07 52	09 49		12 59		14 56		16 55			19 41	20 53		22 57	
	d	06 20	06 52		07 55	09 50		13 00		14 58		16 57			19 57	20 59		22 58	
Barrhead	222 d	06 44	07 18		08 21	10 16						17 22			20 21	21 23		23 22	
Glasgow Central 15	65,222 a	07 11	07 32		08 34	10 31		13 36		15 38		17 36			20 35	21 40		23 36	

Sundays

20 May to 2 December

		SR	SR	SR	SR	SR
Newcastle 8	48 d					
Carlisle 8	65 d	13 12	15 12	17 12	19 12	21 26
Gretna Green	d	13 24	15 23	17 23	19 23	21 37
Annan	d	13 32	15 31	17 31	19 31	21 45
Dumfries	d	13 51	15a49	17a49	19 50	22a03
Sanquhar	d	14 17			20 16	
Kirkconnel	d	14 22			20 21	
New Cumnock	d	14 31			20 30	
Auchinleck	d	14 39			20 38	
Kilmarnock 3	218,222 a	14 56			20 55	
	d	14 57			20 57	
Barrhead	222 d	15 22			21 21	
Glasgow Central 15	65,222 a	15 42			21 35	

For connections from London Euston please refer to Table T65

Some through services between Glasgow Central and Newcastle and vice versa are jointly operated with Northern Rail.

Table T216-R

Mondays to Fridays

21 May to 7 December

Glasgow Central and Kilmarnock - Dumfries and Carlisle

Miles			SR MX	SR MO	SR	SR	SR	SR	SR 🛒	SR 🛒	SR	SR 🛒	SR	SR 🛒	SR 🛒	SR	SR	SR A 🛒	SR	SR 🛒	SR 🛒	SR	SR
0	**Glasgow Central 15**	65,222 d							07 09	08 37		10 13		12 13	13 13			16 13		17 42	19 13	20 13	21 13
7½	Barrhead	222 d							07 22	08 51								16 25		17 55	19 25	20 25	21 26
24¼	**Kilmarnock 3**	218,222 a							07 49	09 18		10 51		12 50	13 50			16 52		18 22	19 52	20 52	21 53
—		d	00 02						07 54	09 18		10 51		12 50	13 50			16 52		18 25	19 52	20 58	21 53
38	Auchinleck	d	00 20						08 11	09 35		11 08		13 07	14 07			17 09		18 42	20 09	21 25	22 10
45½	New Cumnock	d	00 30						08 19	09 43		11 16		13 15	14 15			17 17		18 51	20 17	21 41	22 18
52¾	Kirkconnel	d	00 44						08 28	09 52		11 25		13 24	14 24			17 26		18 59	20 26	21 50	22 27
56	Sanquhar	d	00 49						08 33	09 57		11 30		13 29	14 29			17 31		19 04	20 31	21 55	22 32
82¼	**Dumfries**	d	01a15		04 58	06 18	07 13	07 43	09 01	10 25	11 02	11 58	13 04	13 57	14 57	16 02	17 07	17 59	18 41	19 33	21 00	22a22	23 00
97¾	Annan	d		00 11	05 13	06 33	07 28	07 58	09 16	10 40	11 17	12 13	13 19	14 13	15 12	16 17	17 22	18 14	18 56	19 48	21 15		23 15
105½	Gretna Green	d		00 20	05 22	06 42	07 37	08 07	09 25	10 49	11 26	12 22	13 28	14 21	15 21	16 26	17 31	18 23	19 05	19 57	21 24		23 24
115½	**Carlisle 8**	65 a		00 33	05 35	06 55	07 53	08 20	09 42	11 03	11 39	12 35	13 42	14 36	15 34	16 40	17 45	18 36	19 18	20 11	21 43		23 38
—	Newcastle 8	48 a				08 38		09 48										20 13					

		SR
Glasgow Central 15	65,222 d	23 13
Barrhead	222 d	23 35
Kilmarnock 3	218,222 a	00 01
	d	00 02
Auchinleck	d	00 20
New Cumnock	d	00 30
Kirkconnel	d	00 44
Sanquhar	d	00 49
Dumfries	d	01a15
Annan	d	
Gretna Green	d	
Carlisle 8	65 a	
Newcastle 8	48 a	

Saturdays

26 May to 8 December

		SR	SR	SR	SR	SR 🛒	SR 🛒	SR	SR 🛒	SR	SR 🛒	SR 🛒	SR	SR	SR A 🛒	SR	SR 🛒	SR 🛒	SR	SR	SR
Glasgow Central 15	65,222 d					07 07	08 37		10 13		12 13	13 13			16 13		17 43	19 13	20 13		22 13
Barrhead	222 d					07 22	08 51								16 25		17 55	19 25	20 25		22 25
Kilmarnock 3	218,222 a					07 49	09 18		10 51		12 50	13 50			16 52		18 22	19 52	20 52		22 52
	d	00 02				07 54	09 18		10 51		12 50	13 50			16 52		18 25	19 52	20 58		22 53
Auchinleck	d	00 20				08 11	09 35		11 08		13 07	14 07			17 09		18 42	20 09	21 14		23 09
New Cumnock	d	00 30				08 19	09 43		11 16		13 15	14 15			17 17		18 51	20 17	21 38		23 18
Kirkconnel	d	00 44				08 28	09 52		11 25		13 24	14 24			17 26		18 59	20 26	21 46		23 26
Sanquhar	d	00 49				08 33	09 57		11 30		13 29	14 29			17 31		19 04	20 31	21 51		23 31
Dumfries	d	01a15	04 58	06 18	07 42	09 01	10 25	11 02	11 58	13 14	13 57	14 57	16 02	17 07	17 59	18 41	19 33	21 00	22a18	22 20	23 59
Annan	d		05 13	06 33	07 57	09 16	10 40	11 17	12 13	13 29	14 13	15 12	16 17	17 22	18 14	18 56	19 48	21 15		22 35	00 14
Gretna Green	d		05 22	06 42	08 06	09 25	10 49	11 26	12 22	13 38	14 21	15 21	16 26	17 31	18 25	19 05	19 57	21 24		22 44	00 23
Carlisle 8	65 a		05 35	06 55	08 19	09 41	11 03	11 39	12 35	13 54	14 36	15 35	16 39	17 45	18 44	19 18	20 11	21 43		22 57	00 36
Newcastle 8	48 a			08 42											20 19						

Sundays

20 May to 2 December

		SR B	SR	SR	SR	SR	SR
Glasgow Central 15	65,222 d				15 03		22 12
Barrhead	222 d				15 24		22 24
Kilmarnock 3	218,222 a				15 50		22 48
	d				15 51		22 49
Auchinleck	d				16 08		23 06
New Cumnock	d				16 16		23 14
Kirkconnel	d				16 25		23 23
Sanquhar	d				16 30		23 28
Dumfries	d		13 00	15 01	17 00	19 01	23 56
Annan	d	00 14	13 15	15 16	17 15	19 16	00 11
Gretna Green	d	00 23	13 24	15 25	17 24	19 25	00 20
Carlisle 8	65 a	00 36	13 38	15 38	17 38	19 38	00 33
Newcastle 8	48 a						

A 🛒 to Carlisle

B not 20 May

For connections to London Euston refer to Table T65

Some through services between Glasgow Central and Newcastle and vice versa are jointly operated with Northern Rail.

Table T217-F

Mondays to Saturdays
21 May to 8 December

Glasgow Central - Paisley Canal

Miles			SR SO	SR		SR
0	**Glasgow Central** 15	d	00 12	06 12	and every 30 minutes until	23 12
1¾	Dumbreck	d	00 17	06 17		23 17
3¼	Corkerhill	d	00 20	06 20		23 20
3¾	Mosspark	d	00 22	06 22		23 22
4½	Crookston	d	00 24	06 24		23 24
6½	Hawkhead	d	00 27	06 27		23 27
7	**Paisley Canal**	a	00 30	06 30		23 30

Sundays
20 May to 2 December

		SR		SR
Glasgow Central 15	d	09 12	and hourly until	18 12
Dumbreck	d	09 17		18 17
Corkerhill	d	09 20		18 20
Mosspark	d	09 22		18 22
Crookston	d	09 24		18 24
Hawkhead	d	09 27		18 27
Paisley Canal	a	09 30		18 30

Table T217-R

Mondays to Saturdays
21 May to 8 December

Paisley Canal - Glasgow Central

Miles			SR	SR	SR	SR SO	SR SX	SR		SR	SR	SR SX	SR SO	SR	SR	SR	SR FX	SR FO	SR SO	SR SX	SR	SR SO
0	**Paisley Canal**	d	06 35	07 05	07 35	08 05	08 05	08 35	and every 30 minutes until	18 35	19 05	19 35	19 35	20 05	20 35	21 05	21 35	21 35	22 05	22 05	22 35	23 05
0½	Hawkhead	d	06 37	07 07	07 37	08 07	08 07	08 37		18 37	19 07	19 37	19 37	20 07	20 37	21 07	21 37	21 37	22 07	22 07	22 37	23 07
2½	Crookston	d	06 40	07 10	07 40	08 10	08 10	08 40		18 40	19 10	19 40	19 40	20 10	20 40	21 10	21 40	21 40	22 10	22 10	22 40	23 10
3¼	Mosspark	d	06 43	07 13	07 43	08 13	08 13	08 43		18 43	19 13	19 43	19 43	20 13	20 43	21 13	21 43	21 43	22 13	22 13	22 43	23 13
3¾	Corkerhill	d	06 45	07 15	07 45	08 15	08 15	08 45		18 45	19 15	19 45	19 45	20 15	20 45	21 15	21 45	21 45	22 15	22 15	22 45	23 15
5¼	Dumbreck	d	06 48	07 18	07 48	08 18	08 18	08 48		18 48	19 18	19 48	19 48	20 18	20 48	21 18	21 48	21 48	22 18	22 18	22 48	23 18
7	**Glasgow Central** 15	a	06 55	07 25	07 56	08 24	08 26	08 54		18 54	19 27	19 55	19 56	20 24	20 56	21 26	21 56	21 58	22 25	22 26	22 56	23 25

		SR SX
Paisley Canal	d	23 05
Hawkhead	d	23 07
Crookston	d	23 10
Mosspark	d	23 13
Corkerhill	d	23 15
Dumbreck	d	23 20
Glasgow Central 15	a	23 27

Sundays
20 May to 2 December

		SR		SR
Paisley Canal	d	09 35	and hourly until	18 35
Hawkhead	d	09 37		18 37
Crookston	d	09 40		18 40
Mosspark	d	09 43		18 43
Corkerhill	d	09 45		18 45
Dumbreck	d	09 48		18 48
Glasgow Central 15	a	09 54		18 54

Table T218-F

Mondays to Saturdays
21 May to 8 December

Glasgow Central and Kilmarnock - Girvan, Stranraer

Miles	Miles			SR MX ◇	SR	SR	SR	SR	SR SO ◇	SR SX ◇	SR	SR	SR
0	—	**Glasgow Cen.** 15 219,221,222	d						08 07	08 08			
7¼	—	Paisley Gilmour St. 219,221 ✈	d										
26¾	—	Kilwinning 4 221	d										
—	0	**Kilmarnock** 3 222	a						08 49	08 49			
—	—		d					08 01	09 00	09 00		11 04	
35	10¾	Troon 221	d					08 14	09 12	09 12		11 16	
37¾	11¾	Prestwick Int. Airport 221 ✈	d										
38¼	12½	Prestwick Town 221	d					08 20				11 21	
41½	15½	**Ayr** 221	a					08 27	09 23	09 23		11 29	
—	—		d		05 25	06 21	07 16	08 28	09 23	09 23	10 26	11 31	12 26
50½	24½	Maybole	d		05 36	06 32	07 28	08 39	09 35	09 35	10 39	11 42	12 37
62¾	36½	**Girvan**	d	00 01	05a52	06a48	07 56	08a55	09 54	09 54	10a55	12 01	12a53
75	51¼	Barrhill	d	00 20			08 16		10 13	10 13		12 20	
101	77¼	**Stranraer**	a	00 56			08 52		10 49	10 49		12 56	

Miles	Miles			SR	SR	SR ◇	SR	SR	SR	SR ◇	SR	SR	SR
0	—	**Glasgow Cen.** 15 219,221,222	d			14 13			17 13	18 13			
7¼	—	Paisley Gilmour St. 219,221 ✈	d										
26¾	—	Kilwinning 4 221	d										
—	0	**Kilmarnock** 3 222	a			14 50			17 52	18 52			
—	—		d	13 03		14 58		17 00	18 04	19 04		21 04	
35	10¾	Troon 221	d	13 15		15 10		17 12	18 18	19 16		21 16	
37¾	11¾	Prestwick Int. Airport 221 ✈	d										
38¼	12½	Prestwick Town 221	d	13 21		15 16							
41½	15½	**Ayr** 221	a	13 28		15 24		17 23	18 28	19 27		21 27	
—	—		d	13 29	14 24	15 25	16 25	17 23	18 29	19 27	20 32	21 28	22 30
50½	24½	Maybole	d	13 40	14 37	15 36	16 36	17 35	18 40	19 39	20 43	21 39	22 41
62¾	36½	**Girvan**	d	13 59	14a53	15 55	16a52	17 54	18a56	19 58	20a59	21a53	22a57
75	51¼	Barrhill	d	14 18		16 14		18 13		20 17			
101	77¼	**Stranraer**	a	14 54		16 50		18 49		20 53			

		SR SX ◇	SR SO
Glasgow Cen. 15 219,221,222	d	22 13	
Paisley Gilmour St. 219,221 ✈	d		
Kilwinning 4 221	d		
Kilmarnock 3 222	a	22 52	
	d	23 05	23 05
Troon 221	d	23 17	23 17
Prestwick Int. Airport 221 ✈	d		
Prestwick Town 221	d	23 23	23 23
Ayr 221	a	23 30	23 30
	d	23 31	23 31
Maybole	d	23 42	23 42
Girvan	d	00 01	00 01
Barrhill	d	00 20	00 20
Stranraer	a	00 56	00 56

Sundays
20 May to 2 December

		SR A	SR	SR	SR	SR	SR
Glasgow Cen. 15 219,221,222	d						
Paisley Gilmour St. 219,221 ✈	d						
Kilwinning 4 221	d						
Kilmarnock 3 222	a						
	d						
Troon 221	d						
Prestwick Int. Airport 221 ✈	d						
Prestwick Town 221	d						
Ayr 221	a						
	d		11 06	12 27	15 05	18 05	19 27
Maybole	d		11 17	12 38	15 16	18 16	19 38
Girvan	d	00 01	11 36	12 53	15 35	18 35	19 53
Barrhill	d	00 20	11 55	13 18	15 54	18 54	20 17
Stranraer	a	00 56	12 31	13 54	16 30	19 30	20 53

A not 20 May

Table T218-R

Mondays to Saturdays

21 May to 8 December

Stranraer and Girvan - Kilmarnock and Glasgow Central

Miles	Miles			SR	SR	SR	SR	SR	SR	SR	SR	SR	SR	SR	SR	SR	SR	SR	SR	SR SO	SR SX	SR	SR
						◇										◇							
0	—	**Stranraer**	d			07 02		08 58		11 06		13 04		15 00		16 59		19 03		21 03	21 03		
26	—	Barrhill	d			07 36		09 32		11 40		13 38		15 34		17 33		19 37		21 37	21 37		
38¼	—	**Girvan**	d	05 57	06 53	07 54	09 00	09 52	11 00	11 59	13 00	13 57	15 00	15 53	16 59	17 51	19 01	19 56	21 04	21 57	21 57	22 30	23 02
50½	—	Maybole	d	06 13	07 09	08 10	09 16	10 08	11 16	12 16	13 16	14 13	15 16	16 09	17 15	18 07	19 17	20 12	21 20	22 13	22 13	22 57	23 18
59¼	—	**Ayr** 221	a	06 27	07 21	08 23	09 28	10 20	11 28	12 29	13 28	14 29	15 28	16 26	17 28	18 20	19 29	20 26	21 32	22 25	22 25	23 09	23 30
—	—		d		07 22	08 24		10 21		12 29		14 30		16 27	17 28	18 21		20 27		22 26	22 26		
62½	—	Prestwick Town 221	a		07 27							14 35		16 32	17 34			20 32		22 31	22 31		
63	—	Prestwick Int. Airport 221 ✈	a																	22 34	22 34		
63½	0	Troon 221	a		07 32	08 33		10 29		12 38		14 41		16 38	17 39	18 29		20 38		22 39	22 39		
—	10¾	**Kilmarnock**	a		07 49	08 52		10 44		12 54		14 56		16 53	17 56	18 44		20 55		22 56	23 03		
—	—		d			08 57										18 57							
74¼	—	Kilwinning 221	a																				
93¾	—	Paisley Gilmour St. 219,221 ✈	a																				
101	—	**Glasgow Cen.** 219,221,222	a			09 37										19 37							

Sundays

20 May to 2 December

		SR	SR	SR	SR	SR
Stranraer	d	10 41	12 41	14 40	17 40	19 40
Barrhill	d	11 16	13 16	15 14	18 14	20 15
Girvan	d	11 34	13 34	15 33	18 33	20 33
Maybole	d	11 50	13 50	15 49	18 49	20 49
Ayr 221	a	12 02	14 02	16 01	19 01	21 01
	d					
Prestwick Town 221	a					
Prestwick Int. Airport 221 ✈	a					
Troon 221	a					
Kilmarnock	a					
	d					
Kilwinning 221	a					
Paisley Gilmour St. 219,221 ✈	a					
Glasgow Cen. 219,221,222	a					

Table T219-F

Mondays to Saturdays

21 May to 8 December

Glasgow Central - Wemyss Bay and Gourock

Miles	Miles			SR MO	SR MX	SR MX	SR	SR	SR	SR	SR	SR SO	SR SX	SR	SR	SR	SR SX	SR SO	SR SO	SR SX	SR SO	SR SX	SR
0	0	**Glasgow Central** 221	d				05 55	06 05	06 25	06 32	06 54	07 06	07 07	07 22	07 40	07 50	08 04	08 05	08 25	08 28	08 40	08 40	08 55
3¾	3¾	Cardonald	d							06 39		07 13	07 14	07 29	07 47		08 11	08 12			08 47	08 47	
4½	4½	Hillington East	d					06 12		06 41		07 15	07 16	07 31	07 49		08 13	08 14			08 49	08 49	
5	5	Hillington West	d			00 01	06 03	06 14		06 43	07 02	07 17	07 18	07 33	07 51	07 59	08 15	08 16			08 51	08 51	
7¼	7¼	Paisley Gilmour Street 221 ✈	a			00 05	06 08	06 18	06 36	06 47	07 06	07 22	07 22	07 38	07 55	08 03	08 20	08 20	08 35	08 38	08 55	08 56	09 06
—	—		d			00 05	06 08	06 19	06 36	06 47	07 06	07 22	07 22	07 38	07 55	08 04	08 21	08 20	08 35	08 38	08 56	08 56	09 06
8	8	Paisley St James	d			00 07			06 38			07 24	07 24		07 57		08 23	08 22			08 58	08 58	
12¼	12¼	Bishopton	d			00 12	06 14	06 24	06 43	06 53	07 13	07 29	07 29	07 44	08 02	08 10	08 28	08 27	08 41	08 44	09 03	09 03	09 13
16½	16½	Langbank	d			00 18			06 48			07 35	07 35		08 08		08 33	08 33			09 09	09 09	
19	19	Woodhall	d			00 22		06 32	06 52	07 00		07 39	07 39	07 51	08 12		08 37	08 37			09 13	09 13	
20¼	20¼	Port Glasgow	d			00 25	06 23	06 35	06 55	07 05	07 22	07 42	07 42	07 54	08 15	08 19	08 40	08 40	08 50	08 53	09 17	09 17	09 22
—	22½	Whinhill	d					06 39		07 09						08 23							09 26
—	23	Drumfrochar	d					06 41		07 11						08 26							09 28
—	24¾	Branchton	d					06 44		07 14						08 29							09 31
—	25½	I.B.M.	d					06 47		07 17						08 31							09 34
—	28¾	Inverkip	d					06 52		07 27						08 36							09 39
—	31	**Wemyss Bay**	a					06 57		07 32						08 41							09 43
21¼	—	Bogston	d			00 27			06 57		07 24	07 44	07 44	07 56	08 17		08 42	08 42			09 19	09 19	
22	—	Cartsdyke	d			00 29	06 26		07 00		07 26	07 46	07 46	07 59	08 19		08 45	08 44			09 22	09 22	
23	—	Greenock Central	d	00 01	00 02	00 31	06 28		07 02		07 28	07 48	07 48	08 01	08 21		08 47	08 46	08 54	08 57	09 24	09 24	
23¾	—	Greenock West	d	00 03	00 04	00 33	06 30		07 04		07 30	07 50	07 50	08 03	08 23		08 49	08 48	08 56	08 59	09 26	09 26	
25	—	Fort Matilda	d	00 06	00 07	00 36			07 07		07 33	07 53	07 53	08 06	08 26		08 52	08 51	08 59	09 02	09 29	09 29	
26¼	—	**Gourock**	a	00 11	00 11	00 40	06 36		07 11		07 37	07 58	07 58	08 10	08 31		08 55	08 55	09 03	09 06	09 32	09 32	

		SR	SR SX	SR SO	SR	SR	SR	SR	SR	SR	SR	SR	SR	SR	SR	SR	SR	SR	SR	SR	SR	SR	SR
Glasgow Central 221	d	09 06	09 08	09 09	09 25	09 36	09 55	09 57	10 06	10 25	10 36	10 55	10 57	11 06	11 25	11 36	11 55	11 57	12 06	12 25	12 36	12 55	12 57
Cardonald	d		09 16	09 16		09 43			10 13		10 43			11 13		11 43			12 14		12 43		
Hillington East	d		09 18	09 18		09 45			10 15		10 45			11 15		11 45			12 16		12 45		
Hillington West	d		09 20	09 20		09 47			10 17		10 47			11 17		11 47			12 18		12 47		
Paisley Gilmour Street 221 ✈	a	09 17	09 24	09 24	09 35	09 53	10 05	10 08	10 21	10 35	10 51	11 05	11 08	11 24	11 36	11 51	12 05	12 08	12 22	12 37	12 51	13 05	13 08
	d	09 18	09 24	09 24	09 36	09 53	10 06	10 10	10 22	10 36	10 51	11 06	11 10	11 24	11 37	11 51	12 06	12 10	12 22	12 37	12 52	13 06	13 10
Paisley St James	d		09 26	09 26		09 55			10 24		10 53			11 26		11 53			12 24		12 54		
Bishopton	d	09 23	09 31	09 31	09 41	10 00	10 11	10 16	10 29	10 41	10 58	11 11	11 16	11 31	11 42	11 58	12 11	12 16	12 29	12 43	12 59	13 11	13 16
Langbank	d		09 37	09 37		10 06			10 34		11 04			11 37		12 04			12 35		13 04		
Woodhall	d		09 41	09 41		10 10			10 39		11 08			11 41		12 08			12 39		13 08		
Port Glasgow	d	09 32	09 44	09 44	09 50	10 13	10 20	10 25	10 42	10 50	11 11	11 20	11 25	11 44	11 51	12 11	12 20	12 25	12 42	12 52	13 11	13 20	13 25
Whinhill	d							10 29					11 29					12 29					13 29
Drumfrochar	d							10 31					11 31					12 31					13 31
Branchton	d							10 34					11 34					12 34					13 34
I.B.M.	d							10 37					11 37					12 37					13 37
Inverkip	d							10 42					11 42					12 42					13 42
Wemyss Bay	a							10 47					11 47					12 47					13 47
Bogston	d		09 46	09 46		10 15			10 44		11 13			11 46		12 13			12 44		13 13		
Cartsdyke	d		09 48	09 48		10 17			10 46		11 15			11 48		12 15			12 46		13 16		
Greenock Central	d	09 37	09 50	09 50	09 55	10 19	10 25		10 48	10 55	11 17	11 25		11 50	11 56	12 17	12 25		12 48	12 56	13 18	13 25	
Greenock West	d	09 39	09 52	09 52	09 57	10 21	10 27		10 50	10 57	11 19	11 27		11 52	11 58	12 19	12 27		12 50	12 58	13 20	13 27	
Fort Matilda	d	09 42	09 55	09 55	10 00	10 24	10 30		10 53	11 00	11 22	11 30		11 55	12 01	12 22	12 30		12 53	13 01	13 23	13 30	
Gourock	a	09 46	09 59	09 59	10 04	10 28	10 34		10 58	11 04	11 27	11 34		11 59	12 04	12 27	12 34		12 57	13 05	13 27	13 34	

		SR	SR	SR	SR	SR	SR	SR	SR	SR	SR	SR	SR	SR	SR	SR SO	SR	SR	SR	SR	SR	SR SO
Glasgow Central 221	d	13 06	13 25	13 36	13 55	13 57	14 07	14 25	14 36	14 55	14 57	15 06	15 25	15 36	15 50	15 55	16 06	16 18	16 35	16 55	17 07	17 16
Cardonald	d	13 14		13 43			14 14		14 43			15 13		15 44			16 13	16 25	16 42		17 14	17 25
Hillington East	d	13 16		13 45			14 16		14 45			15 15		15 46			16 15	16 27	16 44		17 16	17 27
Hillington West	d	13 18		13 47			14 18		14 47			15 17		15 48	15 58		16 17	16 29	16 46	17 03	17 18	
Paisley Gilmour Street 221 ✈	a	13 24	13 36	13 51	14 06	14 09	14 23	14 35	14 51	15 05	15 08	15 24	15 36	15 52	16 03	16 07	16 22	16 33	16 50	17 07	17 22	17 32
	d	13 25	13 37	13 51	14 07	14 11	14 23	14 36	14 52	15 06	15 10	15 24	15 37	15 52	16 03	16 08	16 22	16 34	16 50	17 08	17 22	17 33
Paisley St James	d	13 27		13 53			14 25		14 54			15 26		15 54			16 24	16 36			17 24	
Bishopton	d	13 32	13 42	13 58	14 12	14 17	14 30	14 41	14 59	15 11	15 16	15 31	15 42	15 59	16 09	16 13	16 29	16 41	16 56	17 13	17 29	17 38
Langbank	d	13 37		14 04			14 36		15 05			15 37		16 05			16 35	16 46			17 35	
Woodhall	d	13 41		14 08			14 40		15 09			15 41		16 09			16 39	16 50			17 39	
Port Glasgow	d	13 44	13 51	14 11	14 21	14 26	14 43	14 50	15 12	15 20	15 25	15 44	15 51	16 12	16 18	16 22	16 42	16 53	17 06	17 22	17 42	17 47
Whinhill	d					14 30					15 29				16 22				17 10			17 51
Drumfrochar	d					14 32					15 31				16 24				17 12			17 54
Branchton	d					14 35					15 34				16 27				17 15			17 57
I.B.M.	d					14 38					15 37				16 30							17 59
Inverkip	d					14 43					15 42				16 35				17 21			18 05
Wemyss Bay	a					14 48					15 47				16 39				17 25			18 09
Bogston	d	13 46		14 13			14 45		15 14			15 46		16 14			16 44	16 55		17 24	17 44	
Cartsdyke	d	13 49		14 15			14 47		15 16			15 48		16 16			16 46	16 58		17 27	17 46	
Greenock Central	d	13 51	13 56	14 17	14 26		14 49	14 55	15 18	15 25		15 50	15 56	16 18		16 27	16 48	17 00		17 29	17 48	
Greenock West	d	13 53	13 58	14 19	14 28		14 51	14 57	15 20	15 27		15 52	15 58	16 20		16 29	16 50	17 02		17 31	17 50	
Fort Matilda	d	13 56	14 01	14 22	14 31		14 54	15 00	15 23	15 30		15 55	16 01	16 23		16 32	16 53	17 05		17 34	17 53	
Gourock	a	13 59	14 04	14 27	14 35		14 58	15 04	15 27	15 34		15 59	16 05	16 27		16 35	16 58	17 09		17 38	17 57	

Table T219-F

Mondays to Saturdays

21 May to 8 December

Glasgow Central - Wemyss Bay and Gourock

		SR SX	SR SO	SR SX	SR SO	SR SX	SR SO	SR SX	SR	SR	SR SO	SR SX	SR	SR	SR	SR	SR	SR	SR	SR	SR	SR	SR
Glasgow Central 221	d	17 18	17 25	17 26	17 37	17 38	17 55	17 56	18 06	18 26	18 38	18 40	18 55	19 06	19 25	19 36	19 50	20 06	20 36	20 50	21 06	21 36	21 50
Cardonald	d	17 26			17 44	17 45			18 13		18 45	18 47		19 13		19 43		20 13	20 43		21 13	21 43	
Hillington East	d	17 28			17 46	17 47			18 15		18 47	18 49		19 15		19 45		20 15	20 45		21 15	21 45	
Hillington West	d				17 48	17 49			18 17		18 49	18 51		19 17		19 47		20 17	20 47		21 17	21 47	
Paisley Gilmour Street 221 ✈	a	17 32	17 36	17 36	17 52	17 53	18 05	18 06	18 21	18 37	18 53	18 55	19 05	19 22	19 35	19 52	20 01	20 22	20 51	21 00	21 22	21 51	22 00
	d	17 33	17 37	17 37	17 52	17 53	18 05	18 06	18 21	18 38	18 55	18 55	19 05	19 23	19 36	19 52	20 01	20 22	20 51	21 01	21 22	21 51	22 01
Paisley St James	d				17 54	17 55			18 23		18 57	18 57		19 25		19 54		20 24	20 53		21 24	21 53	
Bishopton	d	17 38			17 59	18 00	18 11	18 12	18 28	18 43	19 02	19 02	19 11	19 30	19 41	19 59	20 07	20 29	20 58	21 06	21 29	21 58	22 06
Langbank	d				18 05	18 06			18 34		19 08	19 08		19 35		20 05		20 35	21 04		21 35	22 04	
Woodhall	d				18 09	18 10			18 38		19 12	19 12		19 39		20 09		20 39	21 08		21 39	22 08	
Port Glasgow	d	17 47	17 52	17 52	18 12	18 13	18 20	18 21	18 41	18 52	19 15	19 15	19 20	19 42	19 50	20 12	20 17	20 42	21 11	21 16	21 42	22 12	22 16
Whinhill	d	17 51					18 24	18 25			19 19	19 19				20 16			21 15			22 16	
Drumfrochar	d	17 54					18 26	18 27			19 22	19 22				20 18			21 17			22 18	
Branchton	d	17 57					18 29	18 30			19 25	19 25				20 21			21 20			22 21	
I.B.M.	d	17 59					18 32	18 33			19 27	19 27				20 24			21 23			22 24	
Inverkip	d	18 05					18 37	18 38			19 32	19 32				20 29			21 28			22 29	
Wemyss Bay	a	18 09					18 42	18 43			19 38	19 38				20 34			21 33			22 33	
Bogston	d				18 14	18 15			18 43				19 22	19 44				20 44			21 44		
Cartsdyke	d				18 16	18 17			18 45				19 24	19 47			20 20	20 47		21 19	21 46		22 19
Greenock Central	d		17 56	17 56	18 18	18 19			18 47	18 57			19 26	19 49	19 55		20 22	20 49		21 21	21 48		22 21
Greenock West	d		17 58	17 58	18 20	18 21			18 49	18 59			19 28	19 51	19 57		20 24	20 51		21 23	21 50		22 23
Fort Matilda	d		18 01	18 01	18 23	18 24			18 52	19 02			19 31	19 54	20 00		20 27	20 54		21 26	21 53		22 26
Gourock	a		18 05	18 05	18 28	18 29			18 57	19 05			19 36	19 57	20 04		20 30	20 57		21 30	21 57		22 30

		SR	SR	SR	SR	SR
Glasgow Central 221	d	22 06	22 36	22 52	23 21	23 50
Cardonald	d	22 13	22 43		23 28	23 57
Hillington East	d	22 15	22 45		23 30	23 59
Hillington West	d	22 17	22 47		23 32	00 01
Paisley Gilmour Street 221 ✈	a	22 21	22 51	23 02	23 36	00 05
	d	22 22	22 51	23 03	23 36	00 05
Paisley St James	d	22 24	22 53		23 38	00 07
Bishopton	d	22 29	22 58	23 08	23 43	00 12
Langbank	d	22 34	23 04		23 49	00 18
Woodhall	d	22 38	23 08		23 53	00 22
Port Glasgow	d	22 41	23 11	23 17	23 56	00 25
Whinhill	d		23 15			
Drumfrochar	d		23 17			
Branchton	d		23 20			
I.B.M.	d		23 23			
Inverkip	d		23 28			
Wemyss Bay	a		23 33			
Bogston	d	22 43			23 58	00 27
Cartsdyke	d	22 46		23 20	23 59	00 29
Greenock Central	d	22 48		23 22	00 02	00 31
Greenock West	d	22 50		23 24	00 04	00 33
Fort Matilda	d	22 53		23 27	00 07	00 36
Gourock	a	22 57		23 31	00 11	00 40

Sundays

20 May to 2 December

		SR A	SR A	SR	SR	SR		SR	SR	SR	SR	SR	SR	SR	SR	SR	SR	SR	SR	SR	SR	SR
Glasgow Central 221	d			07 20	07 50	08 20	and at the same minutes past each hour until	11 50	12 20	12 50	13 20	13 50	14 20	14 50	15 20	15 50	16 20	16 50	17 20	17 50	18 20	18 50
Cardonald	d			07 27		08 27			12 27		13 27		14 27		15 27		16 27		17 27		18 27	
Hillington East	d			07 29	07 57	08 29		11 57	12 29	12 57	13 29	13 57	14 29	14 57	15 29	15 57	16 29	16 57	17 29	17 57	18 29	18 57
Hillington West	d		00 01	07 31		08 31			12 31	12 59	13 31		14 31		15 31		16 31		17 31		18 31	
Paisley Gilmour Street 221 ✈	a		00 05	07 35	08 02	08 35		12 02	12 35	13 03	13 35	14 02	14 35	15 03	15 35	16 02	16 35	17 02	17 35	18 02	18 35	19 02
	d		00 05	07 35	08 02	08 35		12 02	12 35	13 04	13 35	14 02	14 35	15 03	15 35	16 02	16 35	17 02	17 35	18 02	18 36	19 02
Paisley St James	d		00 07			08 37			12 37		13 37		14 37		15 37		16 37		17 37		18 38	
Bishopton	d		00 12	07 41	08 08	08 42		12 08	12 42	13 09	13 42	14 08	14 42	15 09	15 42	16 08	16 42	17 08	17 42	18 08	18 43	19 08
Langbank	d		00 18			08 48			12 48		13 48		14 48		15 48		16 48		17 48		18 48	
Woodhall	d		00 22	07 48		08 52			12 52		13 52		14 52		15 52		16 52		17 52		18 52	
Port Glasgow	d		00 25	07 51	08 17	08 55		12 17	12 55	13 18	13 55	14 17	14 55	15 18	15 55	16 17	16 55	17 17	17 55	18 17	18 55	19 17
Whinhill	d				08 21			12 21		13 22		14 21		15 22		16 21		17 21		18 21		19 21
Drumfrochar	d				08 23			12 23		13 25		14 23		15 24		16 23		17 23		18 23		19 23
Branchton	d				08 26			12 26		13 28		14 26		15 27		16 26		17 26		18 26		19 26
I.B.M.	d				08 29			12 29		13 30		14 29		15 30		16 29		17 29		18 29		19 29
Inverkip	d				08 34			12 34		13 35		14 34		15 35		16 34		17 34		18 38		19 34
Wemyss Bay	a				08 39			12 39		13 40		14 39		15 39		16 39		17 39		18 43		19 39
Bogston	d		00 27	07 53		08 57			12 57		13 57		14 57		15 57		16 57		17 57		18 57	
Cartsdyke	d		00 29	07 56		08 59			12 59		13 59		14 59		15 59		16 59		17 59		19 00	
Greenock Central	d	00 02	00 31	07 58		09 01			13 01		14 01		15 01		16 01		17 01		18 01		19 02	
Greenock West	d	00 04	00 33	08 00		09 03			13 03		14 03		15 03		16 03		17 03		18 03		19 04	
Fort Matilda	d	00 07	00 36			09 06			13 06		14 06		15 06		16 06		17 06		18 06		19 07	
Gourock	a	00 11	00 40	08 06		09 11			13 11		14 11		15 11		16 11		17 11		18 11		19 11	

A not 20 May

Table T219-F

Sundays

20 May to 2 December

Glasgow Central - Wemyss Bay and Gourock

		SR	SR	SR	SR	SR	SR	SR
Glasgow Central 221	d	19 20	19 50	20 20	20 50	21 21	22 20	23 20
Cardonald	d	19 27		20 27		21 28	22 27	23 27
Hillington East	d	19 29	19 57	20 29	20 57	21 30	22 29	23 29
Hillington West	d	19 31		20 31		21 32	22 31	23 31
Paisley Gilmour Street 221 ✈	a	19 35	20 02	20 35	21 02	21 36	22 35	23 35
	d	19 35	20 02	20 35	21 02	21 36	22 35	23 35
Paisley St James	d	19 37		20 37		21 38	22 37	23 37
Bishopton	d	19 42	20 08	20 42	21 08	21 43	22 42	23 42
Langbank	d	19 48		20 48		21 49	22 48	23 48
Woodhall	d	19 52		20 52		21 53	22 52	23 52
Port Glasgow	d	19 55	20 17	20 55	21 17	21 56	22 55	23 55
Whinhill	d		20 21		21 21			
Drumfrochar	d		20 23		21 23			
Branchton	d		20 26		21 26			
I.B.M.	d		20 29		21 29			
Inverkip	d		20 34		21 34			
Wemyss Bay	a		20 39		21 39			
Bogston	d	19 57		20 57		21 58	22 57	23 57
Cartsdyke	d	19 59		20 59		22 00	22 59	23 59
Greenock Central	d	20 01		21 01		22 02	23 01	00 01
Greenock West	d	20 03		21 03		22 04	23 03	00 03
Fort Matilda	d	20 06		21 06		22 07	23 06	00 06
Gourock	a	20 11		21 11		22 11	23 11	00 11

Table T219-R

Sundays

20 May to 2 December

Gourock and Wemyss Bay - Glasgow Central

		SR A	SR A	SR	SR	SR	SR	SR	SR	SR	SR		SR	SR	SR	SR	SR	SR	SR	SR	SR	SR	SR
Gourock	d			08 23		09 23		10 23		11 23		and at the same minutes past each hour until	14 23		15 23		16 23		17 23		18 23		19 23
Fort Matilda	d			08 26		09 26		10 26		11 26			14 26		15 26		16 26		17 26		18 26		19 26
Greenock West	d			08 29		09 29		10 29		11 29			14 29		15 29		16 29		17 29		18 29		19 29
Greenock Central	d			08 31		09 31		10 31		11 31			14 31		15 31		16 31		17 31		18 31		19 31
Cartsdyke	d			08 34		09 34		10 34		11 34			14 34		15 34		16 34		17 34		18 34		19 34
Bogston	d			08 36		09 36		10 36		11 36			14 36		15 36		16 36		17 36		18 36		19 36
Wemyss Bay	d				08 50		09 50		10 55		11 50			14 50		15 55		16 50		17 50		18 55	
Inverkip	d				08 54		09 54		10 59		11 54			14 54		15 59		16 54		17 54		18 59	
I.B.M.	d				08 59		09 59		11 04		11 59			14 59		16 04		16 59		17 59		19 04	
Branchton	d				09 01		10 01		11 06		12 01			15 01		16 06		17 01		18 01		19 06	
Drumfrochar	d				09 04		10 04		11 09		12 04			15 04		16 09		17 04		18 04		19 09	
Whinhill	d				09 06		10 06		11 11		12 06			15 06		16 11		17 06		18 06		19 11	
Port Glasgow	d		00 02	08 38	09 11	09 38	10 11	10 38	11 16	11 38	12 11		14 38	15 11	15 38	16 16	16 38	17 11	17 38	18 11	18 38	19 16	19 38
Woodhall	d			08 41		09 41		10 41		11 41			14 41		15 41		16 41		17 41		18 41		19 41
Langbank	d			08 45		09 45		10 45		11 45			14 45		15 45		16 45		17 45		18 45		19 45
Bishopton	d		00 10	08 50	09 20	09 50	10 20	10 50	11 25	11 50	12 20		14 50	15 20	15 50	16 25	16 50	17 20	17 50	18 20	18 50	19 25	19 50
Paisley St James	d			08 55		09 55		10 55		11 55			14 55		15 55		16 55		17 55		18 55		19 55
Paisley Gilmour Street 221 ✈	a		00 16	08 58	09 26	09 58	10 26	10 58	11 31	11 58	12 26		14 58	15 26	15 58	16 31	16 58	17 26	17 58	18 26	18 58	19 31	19 58
	d		00 17	08 58	09 26	09 58	10 26	10 58	11 31	11 58	12 26		14 58	15 26	15 58	16 31	16 58	17 26	17 58	18 26	18 58	19 31	19 58
Hillington West	d	00 03		09 02		10 02		11 02		12 02			15 02		16 02		17 02		18 02		19 02		20 02
Hillington East	d	00 05		09 04	09 30	10 04	10 30	11 04	11 35	12 04	12 30		15 04	15 30	16 04	16 35	17 04	17 30	18 04	18 30	19 04	19 35	20 04
Cardonald	d	00 07		09 06		10 06		11 06		12 06			15 06		16 06		17 06		18 06		19 06		20 06
Glasgow Central 221	a	00 14	00 27	09 13	09 39	10 13	10 39	11 13	11 43	12 13	12 39		15 13	15 39	16 13	16 43	17 13	17 39	18 13	18 39	19 14	19 44	20 13

A not 20 May

		SR	SR	SR	SR	SR
Gourock	d		20 23		21 23	22 23
Fort Matilda	d		20 26		21 26	22 26
Greenock West	d		20 29		21 29	22 29
Greenock Central	d		20 31		21 31	22 31
Cartsdyke	d		20 34		21 34	22 34
Bogston	d		20 36		21 36	22 36
Wemyss Bay	d	19 50		20 50		
Inverkip	d	19 54		20 54		
I.B.M.	d	19 59		20 59		
Branchton	d	20 01		21 01		
Drumfrochar	d	20 04		21 04		
Whinhill	d	20 06		21 06		
Port Glasgow	d	20 11	20 38	21 11	21 38	22 38
Woodhall	d		20 41		21 41	22 41
Langbank	d		20 45		21 45	22 45
Bishopton	d	20 20	20 50	21 20	21 50	22 50
Paisley St James	d		20 55		21 55	22 55
Paisley Gilmour Street 221 ✈	a	20 26	20 58	21 26	21 58	22 58
	d	20 26	20 58	21 26	21 58	22 58
Hillington West	d		21 02		22 02	23 02
Hillington East	d	20 30	21 04	21 30	22 04	23 04
Cardonald	d		21 06		22 06	23 06
Glasgow Central 221	a	20 39	21 15	21 39	22 13	23 13

Table T219-R

Mondays to Saturdays

21 May to 8 December

Gourock and Wemyss Bay - Glasgow Central

Miles	Miles			SR MX	SR	SR	SR SX	SR SX	SR SO	SR SX	SR SX	SR SO	SR	SR SX	SR SO	SR SX	SR	SR	SR SX	SR	SR	SR	SR
0	—	**Gourock**	d		05 20	06 05		06 25	06 38	06 47	07 07	07 07		07 28	07 38	07 46	07 50		08 11	08 23	08 38		09 08
1¼	—	Fort Matilda	d		05 23	06 08		06 28	06 41	06 50	07 10	07 10		07 31	07 41		07 53		08 14	08 26	08 41		09 11
2½	—	Greenock West	d		05 26	06 11		06 31	06 44	06 53	07 13	07 13		07 34	07 44	07 51	07 56		08 17	08 29	08 44		09 14
3¼	—	Greenock Central	d		05 28	06 13		06 33	06 46	06 55	07 15	07 15		07 36	07 46	07 53	07 58		08 19	08 31	08 46		09 16
4¼	—	Cartsdyke	d		05 31	06 16		06 36	06 49	06 58	07 18	07 18		07 39	07 49		08 01			08 34	08 49		09 19
5	—	Bogston	d		05 33			06 38	06 51	07 00	07 20	07 20		07 41	07 51		08 03			08 36	08 51		09 21
—	0	**Wemyss Bay**	d				06 12						07 15					07 54				08 57	
—	2¼	Inverkip	d				06 16						07 19					07 58				09 01	
—	4¼	I.B.M.	d				06 21						07 24					08 03				09 06	
—	6¼	Branchton	d				06 23						07 27					08 05				09 08	
—	8	Drumfrochar	d				06 26						07 29					08 08				09 11	
—	8½	Whinhill	d				06 28						07 32					08 10				09 13	
6	10¾	Port Glasgow	d		05 35	06 19	06 33	06 40	06 53	07 02	07 22	07 22	07 36	07 43	07 53	07 58	08 05	08 15	08 24	08 38	08 53	09 18	09 23
7¼	12	Woodhall	d		05 38			06 43	06 56	07 05		07 25	07 39	07 46	07 56		08 08	08 17		08 41	08 56		09 26
10	14¾	Langbank	d		05 42			06 47	07 00	07 09		07 29		07 50	08 00			08 21		08 45	09 00		09 30
14	18¾	Bishopton	d		05 47	06 28	06 42	06 52	07 05	07 14	07 31	07 34	07 46	07 55	08 05	08 07	08 15	08 27	08 33	08 50	09 05	09 27	09 35
18¼	23	Paisley St James	d		05 52	06 33		06 57	07 10	07 19		07 39		08 00	08 10			08 32		08 55	09 10		09 40
19	23¾	Paisley Gilmour Street 221	a		05 55	06 36	06 48	07 00	07 13	07 22	07 37	07 43	07 52	08 03	08 13	08 14	08 21	08 34	08 39	08 58	09 13	09 33	09 43
—	—		d		05 55	06 36	06 48	07 00	07 13	07 22	07 38	07 43	07 53	08 04	08 14	08 14	08 22	08 35	08 39	08 58	09 13	09 33	09 43
21¼	26	Hillington West	d	00 03	05 59	06 40		07 04	07 17	07 26	07 41	07 47	07 56	08 07	08 18	08 18	08 25			09 02	09 17		09 47
21¾	26½	Hillington East	d	00 05	06 01	06 42		07 06	07 19	07 28	07 43	07 49	07 58	08 09	08 20	08 20	08 27			09 04	09 19		09 49
22½	27¼	Cardonald	d	00 07	06 03	06 44		07 08	07 21	07 30	07 45	07 51	08 00	08 11	08 22	08 22	08 29			09 06	09 21		09 51
26½	31	**Glasgow Central** 15 221	a	00 14	06 11	06 52	07 02	07 16	07 29	07 38	07 54	07 58	08 08	08 18	08 29	08 30	08 37	08 46	08 50	09 14	09 29	09 44	09 59

		SR	SR	SR	SR	SR	SR	SR	SR	SR	SR	SR	SR	SR	SR	SR	SR	SR	SR	SR	SR	SR	SR
Gourock	d	09 24	09 39	09 54		10 08	10 24	10 38	10 54		11 08	11 24	11 38	11 54		12 08	12 24	12 38	12 54		13 08	13 24	13 38
Fort Matilda	d	09 27	09 42	09 57		10 11	10 27	10 41	10 57		11 11	11 27	11 41	11 57		12 11	12 27	12 41	12 57		13 11	13 27	13 41
Greenock West	d	09 30	09 45	10 00		10 14	10 30	10 44	11 00		11 14	11 30	11 44	12 00		12 14	12 30	12 44	13 00		13 14	13 30	13 44
Greenock Central	d	09 32	09 47	10 02		10 16	10 32	10 46	11 02		11 16	11 32	11 46	12 02		12 16	12 32	12 46	13 02		13 16	13 32	13 46
Cartsdyke	d		09 50			10 19		10 49			11 19		11 49			12 19		12 49			13 19		13 49
Bogston	d		09 52			10 21		10 51			11 21		11 51			12 21		12 51			13 21		13 51
Wemyss Bay	d				09 57					10 57					11 57					12 57			
Inverkip	d				10 01					11 01					12 01					13 01			
I.B.M.	d				10 06					11 06					12 06					13 06			
Branchton	d				10 08					11 08					12 08					13 08			
Drumfrochar	d				10 11					11 11					12 11					13 11			
Whinhill	d				10 13					11 13					12 13					13 13			
Port Glasgow	d	09 37	09 54	10 07	10 18	10 23	10 37	10 53	11 07	11 18	11 23	11 37	11 53	12 07	12 18	12 23	12 37	12 53	13 07	13 18	13 23	13 37	13 53
Woodhall	d		09 57			10 26		10 56			11 26		11 56			12 26		12 56			13 26		13 56
Langbank	d		10 01			10 30		11 00			11 30		12 00			12 30		13 00			13 30		14 00
Bishopton	d	09 46	10 06	10 16	10 27	10 35	10 46	11 05	11 16	11 27	11 35	11 46	12 05	12 16	12 27	12 35	12 46	13 05	13 16	13 27	13 35	13 46	14 05
Paisley St James	d		10 11			10 40		11 10			11 40		12 10			12 40		13 10			13 40		14 10
Paisley Gilmour Street 221	a	09 52	10 14	10 22	10 33	10 43	10 52	11 13	11 22	11 33	11 43	11 52	12 13	12 22	12 33	12 43	12 52	13 13	13 22	13 33	13 43	13 52	14 13
	d	09 52	10 14	10 22	10 34	10 43	10 52	11 13	11 22	11 33	11 43	11 52	12 13	12 22	12 33	12 43	12 52	13 13	13 25	13 33	13 43	13 52	14 13
Hillington West	d		10 18			10 47		11 17			11 47		12 17			12 47		13 17			13 47		14 17
Hillington East	d		10 20			10 49		11 19			11 49		12 19			12 49		13 19			13 49		14 19
Cardonald	d		10 22			10 51		11 21			11 51		12 21			12 51		13 21			13 51		14 21
Glasgow Central 15 221	a	10 03	10 29	10 32	10 44	10 59	11 03	11 29	11 33	11 44	11 59	12 03	12 29	12 33	12 44	12 59	13 03	13 29	13 35	13 44	13 59	14 03	14 29

		SR	SR	SR	SR	SR	SR	SR SX	SR SO	SR	SR SO	SR SX	SR	SR	SR	SR	SR	SR SX	SR SO	SR	SR SO	SR
Gourock	d	13 54		14 08	14 24	14 38	14 54			15 08	15 24	15 24	15 38	15 50		16 08	16 27	16 38	16 38		16 54	17 08
Fort Matilda	d	13 57		14 11	14 27	14 41	14 57			15 11	15 27	15 27	15 41	15 53		16 11	16 30	16 41	16 41		16 57	17 11
Greenock West	d	14 00		14 14	14 30	14 44	15 00			15 14	15 30	15 30	15 44	15 56		16 14	16 33	16 44	16 44		17 00	17 14
Greenock Central	d	14 02		14 16	14 32	14 46	15 02			15 16	15 32	15 32	15 46	15 58		16 16	16 35	16 46	16 46		17 02	17 16
Cartsdyke	d			14 19		14 49				15 19			15 49			16 19		16 49	16 49		17 05	17 19
Bogston	d			14 21		14 51				15 21			15 51			16 21		16 51	16 51		17 07	17 21
Wemyss Bay	d		13 57					14 57	14 57						15 57					16 45		
Inverkip	d		14 01					15 01	15 01						16 01					16 49		
I.B.M.	d		14 06					15 06	15 06						16 06					16 54		
Branchton	d		14 08					15 08	15 08						16 08					16 56		
Drumfrochar	d		14 11					15 11	15 11						16 11					16 59		
Whinhill	d		14 13					15 13	15 13						16 13					17 01		
Port Glasgow	d	14 07	14 18	14 23	14 37	14 53	15 07	15 18	15 18	15 23	15 37	15 37	15 53	16 03	16 18	16 23	16 40	16 53	16 53	17 06	17 10	17 23
Woodhall	d			14 26		14 56				15 26			15 56			16 26		16 56	16 56			17 26
Langbank	d			14 30		15 00				15 30			16 00			16 30		17 00	17 00			17 30
Bishopton	d	14 16	14 27	14 35	14 46	15 05	15 16	15 27	15 27	15 35	15 46	15 46	16 05	16 12	16 27	16 35	16 49	17 05	17 05	17 15	17 20	17 35
Paisley St James	d			14 40		15 10				15 40			16 10			16 40		17 11	17 11			17 40
Paisley Gilmour Street 221	a	14 22	14 33	14 43	14 52	15 13	15 22	15 33	15 33	15 43	15 52	15 52	16 13	16 18	16 33	16 43	16 55	17 14	17 14	17 21	17 26	17 43
	d	14 22	14 33	14 43	14 52	15 13	15 22	15 33	15 33	15 43	15 52	15 52	16 13	16 18	16 33	16 43	16 55	17 14	17 14	17 21	17 26	17 43
Hillington West	d			14 47		15 17				15 47	15 56	15 56	16 17			16 47	16 59	17 18	17 18			17 47
Hillington East	d			14 49		15 19				15 49			16 19			16 49		17 20	17 20			17 49
Cardonald	d			14 51		15 21				15 51			16 21			16 51		17 22	17 22			17 51
Glasgow Central 15 221	a	14 33	14 44	14 59	15 03	15 29	15 33	15 44	15 45	15 59	16 06	16 07	16 30	16 28	16 46	16 59	17 08	17 30	17 31	17 33	17 36	17 59

Table T219-R

Mondays to Saturdays

21 May to 8 December

Gourock and Wemyss Bay - Glasgow Central

		SR SO	SR SX	SR	SR	SR	SR	SR	SR	SR SX	SR SO	SR	SR SO	SR SX	SR	SR	SR	SR	SR	SR	SR	SR SX
Gourock	d	17 24	17 24	17 43		18 08	18 24		18 39			19 08	19 24	19 24	19 48		20 24	20 48		21 24	21 48	
Fort Matilda	d	17 27	17 27	17 46		18 11	18 27		18 42			19 11	19 27	19 27	19 51		20 27	20 51		21 27	21 51	
Greenock West	d	17 30	17 30	17 49		18 14	18 30		18 45			19 14	19 30	19 30	19 54		20 30	20 54		21 30	21 54	
Greenock Central	d	17 32	17 32	17 51		18 16	18 32		18 47			19 16	19 32	19 32	19 56		20 32	20 56		21 32	21 56	
Cartsdyke	d			17 54		18 19			18 50			19 19	19 35	19 35	19 59		20 35	20 59		21 35	21 59	
Bogston	d			17 56		18 21			18 52			19 21	19 37	19 37			20 37			21 37		
Wemyss Bay	d				17 51			18 24		18 55	18 56					19 47			20 47			21 47
Inverkip	d				17 55			18 28		18 59	19 00					19 51			20 51			21 51
I.B.M.	d				18 05			18 39		19 04	19 05					19 56			20 56			21 56
Branchton	d				18 08			18 41		19 06	19 07					19 58			20 58			21 58
Drumfrochar	d				18 10			18 44		19 09	19 10					20 01			21 01			22 01
Whinhill	d				18 13			18 46		19 11	19 12					20 03			21 03			22 03
Port Glasgow	d	17 37	17 37	17 58	18 18	18 23	18 37	18 51	18 55	19 16	19 17	19 23	19 39	19 39	20 02	20 08	20 39	21 02	21 08	21 39	22 02	22 08
Woodhall	d			18 01		18 26			18 57			19 26	19 42	19 42		20 10	20 42		21 10	21 42		22 10
Langbank	d			18 05		18 30			19 01			19 30	19 46	19 46		20 14	20 46		21 14	21 46		22 14
Bishopton	d	17 46	17 46	18 10	18 27	18 35	18 46	19 00	19 07	19 25	19 26	19 35	19 51	19 51	20 11	20 20	20 51	21 11	21 20	21 51	22 11	22 20
Paisley St James	d			18 15		18 40			19 12			19 40	19 56	19 56		20 25	20 56		21 25	21 56		22 25
Paisley Gilmour Street 221	a	17 52	17 52	18 18	18 33	18 43	18 52	19 06	19 14	19 31	19 32	19 43	19 59	19 59	20 17	20 27	20 59	21 17	21 27	21 59	22 17	22 27
	d	17 52	17 52	18 18	18 34	18 43	18 52	19 07	19 15	19 31	19 32	19 43	19 59	19 59	20 18	20 28	20 59	21 18	21 28	21 59	22 18	22 28
Hillington West	d			18 22		18 47			19 18			19 47	20 03	20 03		20 31	21 03		21 31	22 03		22 31
Hillington East	d			18 24		18 49			19 20			19 49	20 05	20 05		20 33	21 05		21 33	22 05		22 33
Cardonald	d			18 26		18 51			19 22			19 51	20 07	20 07		20 35	21 07		21 35	22 07		22 35
Glasgow Central 15 221	a	18 03	18 04	18 33	18 44	18 59	19 03	19 17	19 29	19 42	19 42	19 59	20 14	20 15	20 29	20 43	21 16	21 28	21 44	22 15	22 29	22 43

		SR SO	SR	SR	SR	SR SO
Gourock	d		22 24		23 24	
Fort Matilda	d		22 27		23 27	
Greenock West	d		22 30		23 30	
Greenock Central	d		22 32		23 32	
Cartsdyke	d		22 35		23 35	
Bogston	d		22 37		23 37	
Wemyss Bay	d	21 52		22 47		23 39
Inverkip	d	21 56		22 51		23 43
I.B.M.	d	22 01		22 56		23 48
Branchton	d	22 03		22 58		23 50
Drumfrochar	d	22 06		23 01		23 53
Whinhill	d	22 08		23 03		23 55
Port Glasgow	d	22 13	22 39	23 08	23 39	00 02
Woodhall	d	22 15	22 42	23 10	23 42	
Langbank	d	22 19	22 46	23 14	23 46	
Bishopton	d	22 25	22 51	23 20	23 51	00 10
Paisley St James	d	22 30	22 56	23 25	23 56	
Paisley Gilmour Street 221	a	22 32	22 59	23 27	23 59	00 16
	d	22 33	22 59	23 28	23 59	00 17
Hillington West	d	22 36	23 03	23 31	00 03	
Hillington East	d	22 38	23 05	23 33	00 05	
Cardonald	d	22 40	23 07	23 35	00 07	
Glasgow Central 15 221	a	22 49	23 14	23 43	00 14	00 27

See previous page for Sunday return journeys

See previous page for Sunday return journeys

Table T221-F

Mondays to Fridays

21 May to 7 December

Glasgow Central - Ardrossan, Largs and Ayr

Miles	Miles	Miles	Station		SR MX A	SR MX A	SR MX A	SR MX	SR	SR	SR	SR	SR	SR	SR	SR B	SR	SR	SR ◇ C	SR	SR	SR ◇ D	SR
0	0	0	**Glasgow Central** 15 219	d				00 15	06 00	06 15	06 30	06 45	07 00	07 15	07 30		07 46	08 00	08 08	08 15	08 30		08 33
7¼	7¼	7¼	Paisley Gilmour Street 219	a				00 25	06 12	06 24	06 39	06 54	07 09	07 24	07 40		07 58	08 10		08 25			08 43
—	—	—		d				00 25	06 12	06 25	06 40	06 55	07 10	07 25	07 41		07 58	08 11		08 26			08 44
10¾	10¾	10¾	Johnstone	d				00 29	06 16	06 29	06 44	06 59	07 14	07 29	07 45		08 02	08 15		08 30			08 48
11½	11½	11½	Milliken Park	d			00 02			06 32		07 02		07 32			08 05			08 33			
13	13	13	Howwood	d			00 04			06 34		07 04		07 34			08 08			08 35			
16½	16½	16½	Lochwinnoch	d			00 08			06 38		07 08		07 38			08 12			08 39			
20½	20½	20½	Glengarnock	d			00 13			06 43		07 13		07 43			08 16	08 23					
23¼	23¼	23¼	Dalry	d			00 17			06 47		07 17		07 47			08 20	08 27					
26¾	26¾	26¾	Kilwinning 4	d			00 21	00 45	06 30	06 51	06 57	07 21	07 27	07 51	07 58		08 24	08 31		08 48	08 54		09 03
—	29	29	Stevenston	d			00 25			06 55		07 25		07 55						08 52			09 07
—	30¼	30¼	Saltcoats	d			00 28			07 01		07 28		08 01						08 55			09 12
—	31¼	31¼	Ardrossan South Beach	d		00 02	00a31			07 03		07 30		08 03						08 57			09 14
—	—	31¾	Ardrossan Town	d								07 33								09a00			09 17
—	—	32¼	**Ardrossan Harbour**	a								07 35											09 20
—	35¾	—	West Kilbride	d		00 07				07 09				08 09									
—	39¾	—	Fairlie	d		00 12				07 14				08 14									
—	42¾	—	**Largs**	a		00 17				07 19				08 19									
30	—	—	Irvine	d	00 01			00 49	06 34		07 01		07 31		08 02		08 28	08 35			08 58		
33¾	—	—	Barassie	d	00 06			00 54	06 38		07 06		07 38		08 07			08 42				←	
35	—	—	Troon	d	00 09			00 57	06 41		07 09		07 41		08 10	08 14	08 35	08 45	09 12		09 05	09 12	
37¾	—	—	Prestwick Int. Airport ✈	d	00 13			01 01	06 45		07 13		07 45		08 14		08 39	08 49	→		09 09		
38¼	—	—	Prestwick Town	d	00 14			01 02	06 47		07 14		07 47		08 15	08 20	08 40	08 50			09 10		
40¼	—	—	Newton-on-Ayr	d	00 18			01 06	06 50		07 18		07 50		08 19			08 56					
41½	—	—	**Ayr**	a	00 21			01 09	06 55		07 21		07 55		08 22	08 27	08 46	08 59			09 16	09 23	

Station		SR	SR	SR	SR	SR	SR	SR	SR	SR	SR	SR	SR	SR E	SR	SR	SR	SR	SR	SR	SR	SR	SR
Glasgow Central 15 219	d	08 38	08 48	09 00	09 04	09 18	09 31	09 34	09 48	10 00	10 04	10 18	10 30		10 34	10 48	11 00	11 04	11 18	11 30	11 34	11 48	12 00
Paisley Gilmour Street 219	a	08 47	08 58		09 13	09 27		09 44	09 57		10 13	10 29			10 43	10 57		11 13	11 27		11 43	11 57	
	d	08 48	08 59		09 14	09 28		09 45	09 58		10 14	10 29			10 44	10 58		11 14	11 28		11 44	11 58	
Johnstone	d	08 52	09 03		09 18	09 32		09 49	10 02		10 18	10 33			10 48	11 02		11 18	11 32		11 48	12 02	
Milliken Park	d	08 55			09 21			09 52			10 21				10 51			11 21			11 51		
Howwood	d	08 57			09 23			09 54			10 23				10 53			11 23			11 53		
Lochwinnoch	d	09 01			09 27			09 58			10 27				10 57			11 27			11 57		
Glengarnock	d	09 06	09 11		09 32			10 03	10 10		10 32				11 02	11 10		11 32			12 02	12 10	
Dalry	d	09 10			09 36	09 43		10 07			10 36	10 46			11 06			11 36	11 46		12 06		
Kilwinning 4	d	09 14	09 18	09 26	09 40	09 48	09 56	10 11	10 17	10 26	10 40	10 50	10 55		11 10	11 17	11 25	11 40	11 51	11 55	12 10	12 18	12 25
Stevenston	d		09 22			09 52			10 21			10 54				11 21			11 55			12 22	
Saltcoats	d		09 25			09 55			10 24			10 57				11 24			11 58			12 25	
Ardrossan South Beach	d		09 27			09 57			10 26			10 59				11 26			12 00			12 27	
Ardrossan Town	d					10 00						11 02							12 03				
Ardrossan Harbour	a					10 03						11 04							12 05				
West Kilbride	d		09 33						10 32							11 33						12 33	
Fairlie	d		09 38						10 37							11 38						12 38	
Largs	a		09 43						10 42							11 43						12 43	
Irvine	d	09 18		09 30	09 44		10 00	10 15		10 30	10 44		10 59		11 14		11 29	11 44		11 59	12 14		12 29
Barassie	d	09 22		09 35	09 48			10 20		10 35	10 48				11 18		11 35	11 48			12 18		12 33
Troon	d	09 25		09 38	09 51		10 07	10 23		10 38	10 51		11 06	11 16	11 21		11 38	11 51		12 07	12 21		12 36
Prestwick Int. Airport ✈	d	09 29		09 42	09 55		10 11	10 27		10 42	10 55		11 10		11 25		11 42	11 55		12 11	12 25		12 40
Prestwick Town	d	09 31		09 43	09 57		10 12	10 28		10 43	10 57		11 11	11 21	11 27		11 43	11 57		12 12	12 27		12 42
Newton-on-Ayr	d	09 34		09 47	10 01			10 32		10 47	11 00				11 30		11 47	12 00			12 30		12 48
Ayr	a	09 39		09 50	10 06		10 18	10 35		10 52	11 05		11 17	11 29	11 35		11 51	12 05		12 20	12 35		12 53

Station		SR	SR	SR	SR E	SR	SR	SR	SR	SR	SR	SR F	SR	SR	SR	SR ◇ C	SR	SR	SR ◇ D	SR	SR	SR	SR
Glasgow Central 15 219	d	12 04	12 18	12 30		12 34	12 48	13 00	13 04	13 18	13 30	13 34	13 49	14 00	14 04	14 13	14 18	14 30		14 34	14 48	15 00	15 04
Paisley Gilmour Street 219	a	12 15	12 27			12 43	12 57		13 13	13 27		13 43	13 59		14 13		14 27			14 43	14 58		15 13
	d	12 16	12 28			12 44	12 58		13 14	13 28		13 44	13 59		14 14		14 28			14 44	14 59		15 14
Johnstone	d	12 20	12 32			12 48	13 02		13 18	13 32		13 48	14 03		14 18		14 32			14 48	15 03		15 18
Milliken Park	d	12 23				12 51			13 21			13 51			14 21					14 51			15 21
Howwood	d	12 26				12 53			13 23			13 53			14 23					14 53			15 23
Lochwinnoch	d	12 30				12 57			13 27			13 57			14 27					14 57			15 27
Glengarnock	d	12 34				13 02	13 10		13 32			14 02	14 12		14 32					15 02	15 11		15 32
Dalry	d	12 38	12 45			13 06			13 36	13 44		14 06			14 36		14 43			15 06			15 36
Kilwinning 4	d	12 42	12 50	12 55		13 10	13 17	13 25	13 40	13 49	13 55	14 10	14 18	14 28	14 40		14 49	14 55		15 10	15 18	15 26	15 40
Stevenston	d		12 54				13 21			13 53			14 22				14 53				15 22		
Saltcoats	d		12 57				13 24			13 56			14 25				14 56				15 25		
Ardrossan South Beach	d		12 59				13 26			13 59			14 27				14 58				15 27		
Ardrossan Town	d		13 02							14 02							15 01						
Ardrossan Harbour	a		13 04							14 04							15 04						
West Kilbride	d						13 33						14 33								15 33		
Fairlie	d						13 38						14 38								15 38		
Largs	a						13 44						14 44								15 43		
Irvine	d	12 46		12 59		13 14		13 29	13 44		13 59	14 14		14 32	14 44			14 59		15 14		15 30	15 44
Barassie	d	12 51				13 18		13 35	13 48			14 18		14 37	14 48				←	15 18		15 34	15 48
Troon	d	12 54		13 06	13 15	13 21		13 39	13 51		14 06	14 21		14 40	14 51	15 10		15 05	15 10	15 21		15 37	15 51
Prestwick Int. Airport ✈	d	12 58		13 10		13 25		13 43	13 55		14 10	14 25		14 44	14 55	→		15 09		15 25		15 41	15 55
Prestwick Town	d	12 59		13 11	13 21	13 27		13 44	13 57		14 11	14 27		14 45	14 57			15 11	15 16	15 27		15 43	15 57
Newton-on-Ayr	d	13 03				13 30		13 48	14 00			14 30		14 49	15 00					15 30		15 46	16 00
Ayr	a	13 09		13 19	13 28	13 34		13 53	14 05		14 19	14 34		14 54	15 05			15 18	15 24	15 35		15 51	16 05

A From Glasgow Central
B From Kilmarnock to Girvan
C To Stranraer
D From Glasgow Central to Stranraer
E From Kilmarnock to Stranraer
F From Edinburgh

Table T221-F

Mondays to Fridays

21 May to 7 December

Glasgow Central - Ardrossan, Largs and Ayr

Station		SR	SR A	SR	SR	SR	SR	SR	SR	SR	SR B	SR	SR	SR	SR	SR C	SR	SR	SR	SR D	SR	SR
Glasgow Central 15 219	d	15 18	15 30	15 34	15 48	16 00	16 04	16 14	16 28	16 31		16 40	16 49	17 01	17 05	17 13	17 16	17 23	17 28		17 36	17 47
Paisley Gilmour Street 219	a	15 27		15 47	15 57		16 13	16 24		16 40		16 52	16 58		17 14		17 26	17 34			17 46	17 56
	d	15 28		15 48	15 58		16 14	16 24		16 41		16 52	16 59		17 15		17 27	17 35			17 47	17 57
Johnstone	d	15 32		15 52	16 02		16 18	16 28		16 45		16 56	17 03		17 19		17 31	17 39			17 51	
Milliken Park	d			15 55			16 21					16 59			17 22			17 42			17 54	
Howwood	d			15 57			16 23					17 02			17 24		17 35				17 56	
Lochwinnoch	d			16 01			16 27					17 06			17 28						18 00	
Glengarnock	d			16 06	16 10		16 32	16 37				17 10	17 14		17 33		17 41				18 05	
Dalry	d	15 43		16 10			16 36	16 41				17 14	17 18		17 37		17 46				18 09	
Kilwinning 4	d	15 48	15 56	16 14	16 17	16 26	16 40	16 46	16 52	16 58		17 18	17 22	17 26	17 41		17 50	17 54	17 57		18 13	
Stevenston	d	15 52			16 21			16 50		17 02			17 26					17 58			18 17	
Saltcoats	d	15 55			16 24			16 53		17 07			17 29					18 01			18 20	
Ardrossan South Beach	d	15 57			16 26			16 55		17 09			17 31					18 03			18 22	
Ardrossan Town	d	16 00						16 58					17 34								18 25	
Ardrossan Harbour	a	16 03						17 01					17 36								18 27	
West Kilbride	d				16 32					17 15								18 09				
Fairlie	d				16 37					17 20								18 14				
Largs	a				16 42					17 25								18 20				
Irvine	d		16 00	16 18		16 30	16a44		16 56			17 22		17 30	17 45		17 54		18 02			18 18
Barassie	d			16 22		16 35			17 01					17 36			17 59		18 06	←		18 23
Troon	d		16 07	16 25		16 38			17 04		17 12	17 29		17 39	17 51	18 18	18 02		18 10	18 18		18 26
Prestwick Int. Airport ✈	d		16 11	16 29		16 42			17 08			17 33		17 43	17 55	→	18 06		18 14			18 30
Prestwick Town	d		16 12	16 31		16 43			17 09			17 34		17 44	17 57		18 07		18 16			18 31
Newton-on-Ayr	d			16 34		16 47			17 13					17 48			18 11		18 19			18 35
Ayr	a		16 20	16 39		16 50			17 17		17 23	17 42		17 51	18 04		18 14		18 24	18 28		18 38

Station		SR	SR	SR	SR ◇ E	SR	SR	SR ◇ F	SR	SR	SR A	SR	SR	SR	SR G	SR	SR	SR	SR H	SR	SR	SR	SR
Glasgow Central 15 219	d	17 49	18 00	18 04	18 13	18 18	18 30		18 34	18 50	19 01	19 15	19 30	19 45	20 00	20 15	20 30	20 45		20 59	21 15	21 30	21 45
Paisley Gilmour Street 219	a	17 59		18 13		18 27			18 43	18 59	19 10	19 24	19 39	19 55	20 10	20 26	20 39	20 54		21 10	21 24	21 39	21 54
	d	18 00		18 14		18 28			18 44	19 00	19 11	19 25	19 40	19 55	20 10	20 27	20 40	20 55		21 10	21 25	21 40	21 55
Johnstone	d	18 04		18 18		18 32			18 48	19 04	19 15	19 29	19 44	19 59	20 14	20 31	20 44	20 59		21 14	21 29	21 44	21 59
Milliken Park	d			18 21					18 51			19 32		20 02		20 34		21 02			21 32		22 02
Howwood	d			18 23					18 53			19 34				20 36					21 34		
Lochwinnoch	d			18 27					18 57			19 38				20 40					21 38		
Glengarnock	d	18 12		18 32					19 02	19 12		19 43		20 10		20 45		21 09			21 43		22 09
Dalry	d			18 36		18 43			19 06			19 47		20 14		20 49		21 13			21 47		22 13
Kilwinning 4	d	18 19	18 26	18 40		18 48	18 59		19 10	19 19	19 28	19 51	19 58	20 18	20 28	20 54	20 57	21 17		21 28	21 51	21 57	22 17
Stevenston	d	18 23				18 52				19 23		19 55		20 22		20 58		21 21			21 55		22 21
Saltcoats	d	18 26				18 55				19 26		19 58		20 25		21 01		21 24			21 58		22 24
Ardrossan South Beach	d	18 28				18 57				19 28		20 00		20 27		21 03		21 26			22 00		22 26
Ardrossan Town	d					19 00						20 03				21 06					22 03		
Ardrossan Harbour	a					19 03						20 06				21 08					22 05		
West Kilbride	d	18 34								19 34				20 33				21 32					22 33
Fairlie	d	18 39								19 39				20 38				21 37					22 38
Largs	a	18 44								19 45				20 43				21 43					22 44
Irvine	d		18 30	18 44			19 03		19 14		19 32		20 02		20 32		21 01			21 32		22 01	
Barassie	d		18 36	18 48				←	19 18		19 37				20 37					21 36			
Troon	d		18 39	18 51	19 16		19 09	19 16	19 21		19 40		20 08		20 40		21 08		21 16	21 39		22 08	
Prestwick Int. Airport ✈	d		18 43	18 55	→		19 13		19 25		19 44		20 12		20 44		21 12			21 43		22 12	
Prestwick Town	d		18 44	18 57			19 15		19 27		19 45		20 14		20 45		21 13			21 45		22 13	
Newton-on-Ayr	d		18 48	19 00					19 30		19 49				20 49					21 48			
Ayr	a		18 53	19 05			19 22	19 27	19 35		19 52		20 21		20 54		21 21		21 27	21 53		22 21	

Station		SR	SR ◇ E	SR	SR	SR ◇ F	SR	SR	SR FO	SR FX	SR	SR FO	SR FX
Glasgow Central 15 219	d	22 00	22 13	22 16	22 30		22 45	23 00	23 15	23 15	23 30	23 45	23 45
Paisley Gilmour Street 219	a	22 09		22 25	22 39		22 54	23 09	23 24	23 24	23 39	23 54	23 54
	d	22 10		22 26	22 40		22 55	23 10	23 25	23 25	23 40	23 55	23 55
Johnstone	d	22 14		22 30	22 44		22 59	23 14	23 29	23 29	23 44	23 59	23 59
Milliken Park	d			22 33			23 02		23 32	23 32		00 02	00 02
Howwood	d			22 35					23 34	23 34		00 04	00 04
Lochwinnoch	d			22 39					23 38	23 38		00 08	00 08
Glengarnock	d			22 44			23 09		23 43	23 43		00 13	00 13
Dalry	d			22 48			23 13		23 47	23 47		00 17	00 17
Kilwinning 4	d	22 27		22 52	22 57		23 17	23 27	23 51	23 51	23 57	00 21	00 21
Stevenston	d			22 56			23 21		23 55	23 55		00 25	00 25
Saltcoats	d			22 59			23 24		23 58	23 58		00 28	00 28
Ardrossan South Beach	d			23 02			23 26		00 02	00 02		00 30	00a31
Ardrossan Town	d			23a04					00a04				
Ardrossan Harbour	a												
West Kilbride	d						23 35			00 07		00 36	
Fairlie	d						23 40			00 12		00 41	
Largs	a						23 45			00 17		00 48	
Irvine	d	22 31			23 01			23 31			00 01		
Barassie	d	22 36				←		23 36			00 06		
Troon	d	22 39	23 17		23 10	23 17		23 39			00 09		
Prestwick Int. Airport ✈	d	22 43	→		23 14			23 43			00 13		
Prestwick Town	d	22 45			23 15	23 23		23 44			00 14		
Newton-on-Ayr	d	22 48						23 48			00 18		
Ayr	a	22 53			23 21	23 30		23 51			00 21		

A From Edinburgh
B From Kilmarnock to Stranraer
C To Girvan
D From Glasgow Central to Girvan
E To Stranraer
F From Glasgow Central to Stranraer
G From North Berwick
H From Kilmarnock to Girvan

Glasgow Central - Ardrossan, Largs and Ayr

		SR	SR	SR	SR	SR	SR	SR	SR	SR		SR	SR	SR	SR	SR	SR	SR	SR	SR		SR	SR	SR	SR
		A	A	A										B			◇ C		◇ D						
Glasgow Central 219	d				00 15	06 00	06 15	06 30	06 45	07 00		07 15	07 30		07 46	08 00	08 07	08 30		08 34		08 38	08 49	09 00	09 04
Paisley Gilmour Street 219	a				00 25	06 12	06 24	06 39	06 54	07 09		07 24	07 40		07 58	08 10				08 43		08 47	08 58		09 13
	d				00 25	06 12	06 25	06 40	06 55	07 10		07 25	07 41		07 58	08 11				08 44		08 48	08 59		09 14
Johnstone	d				00 29	06 16	06 29	06 44	06 59	07 14		07 29	07 45		08 02	08 15				08 48		08 52	09 03		09 18
Milliken Park	d			00 02			06 32		07 02			07 32			08 05							08 55			09 21
Howwood	d			00 04			06 34		07 04			07 34			08 08							08 57			09 23
Lochwinnoch	d			00 08			06 38		07 08			07 38			08 12							09 01			09 27
Glengarnock	d			00 13			06 43		07 13			07 43			08 16	08 23						09 06	09 11		09 32
Dalry	d			00 17			06 47		07 17			07 47			08 20	08 27						09 10			09 36
Kilwinning	d			00 21	00 45	06 30	06 51	06 57	07 21	C7 27		07 51	07 58		08 24	08 31		08 54		09 03		09 14	09 18	09 26	09 40
Stevenston	d			00 25			06 55		07 25			07 55								09 07			09 22		
Saltcoats	d			00 28			07 01		07 28			08 01								09 12			09 25		
Ardrossan South Beach	d		00 02	00 30			07 03		07 30			08 03								09 14			09 27		
Ardrossan Town	d		00a04						07 33											09 17					
Ardrossan Harbour	a								07 35											09 20					
West Kilbride	d			00 36			07 09					08 10											09 34		
Fairlie	d			00 41			07 14					08 15											09 39		
Largs	a			00 48			07 19					08 20											09 44		
Irvine	d	00 01			00 49	06 34		07 01		07 31			08 02		08 28	08 35		08 58				09 18		09 30	09 44
Barassie	d	00 06			00 54	06 38		07 06		07 38			08 07			08 42			←			09 22		09 35	09 48
Troon	d	00 09			00 57	06 41		07 09		07 41			08 10	08 14	08 35	08 45	09 12	09 05	09 12			09 25		09 38	09 51
Prestwick Int. Airport ✈	d	00 13			01 01	06 45		07 13		07 45			08 14		08 39	08 49	→	09 09				09 29		09 42	09 55
Prestwick Town	d	00 14			01 02	06 47		07 14		07 47			08 15	08 20	08 40	08 50		09 10				09 31		09 43	09 57
Newton-on-Ayr	d	00 18			01 06	06 50		07 18		07 50			08 19			08 54						09 34		09 47	10 01
Ayr	a	00 21			01 09	06 55		07 21		07 55			08 22	08 27	08 46	08 59		09 16	09 23			09 39		09 50	10 06

		SR	SR	SR	SR	SR		SR	SR	SR	SR	SR	SR	SR	SR	SR		SR	SR	SR	SR	SR	SR	SR	SR
			E								F														F
Glasgow Central 219	d	09 18	09 32	09 34	09 48	10 00		10 04	10 18	10 30		10 34	10 48	11 00	11 04	11 18		11 30	11 34	11 48	12 00	12 04	12 18	12 30	
Paisley Gilmour Street 219	a	09 27		09 44	09 57			10 13	10 29			10 43	10 57		11 13	11 27			11 43	11 57		12 15	12 27		
	d	09 28		09 45	09 58			10 14	10 29			10 44	10 58		11 14	11 28			11 44	11 58		12 16	12 28		
Johnstone	d	09 32		09 49	10 02			10 18	10 33			10 48	11 02		11 18	11 32			11 48	12 02		12 20	12 32		
Milliken Park	d			09 52				10 21				10 51			11 21				11 51			12 23			
Howwood	d			09 54				10 23				10 53			11 23				11 53			12 26			
Lochwinnoch	d			09 58				10 27				10 57			11 27				11 57			12 30			
Glengarnock	d			10 03	10 10			10 32				11 02	11 10		11 32				12 02	12 10		12 34			
Dalry	d	09 43		10 07				10 36	10 46			11 06			11 36	11 46			12 06			12 38	12 45		
Kilwinning	d	09 48	09 56	10 11	10 17	10 26		10 40	10 50	10 55		11 10	11 17	11 25	11 40	11 51		11 55	12 10	12 18	12 25	12 42	12 50	12 55	
Stevenston	d	09 52			10 21				10 54				11 21			11 55				12 22			12 54		
Saltcoats	d	09 55			10 24				10 57				11 24			11 58				12 25			12 57		
Ardrossan South Beach	d	09 57			10 26				10 59				11 26			12 00				12 27			12 59		
Ardrossan Town	d	10 00							11 02							12 03							13 02		
Ardrossan Harbour	a	10 03							11 04							12 05							13 04		
West Kilbride	d				10 33								11 33							12 33					
Fairlie	d				10 38								11 38							12 38					
Largs	a				10 43								11 43							12 43					
Irvine	d		10 00	10 15		10 30		10 44		10 59		11 14		11 29	11 44			11 59	12 14		12 29	12 46		12 59	
Barassie	d			10 20		10 35		10 48				11 18		11 35	11 48				12 18		12 33	12 51			
Troon	d		10 07	10 23		10 38		10 51		11 06	11 16	11 21		11 38	11 51			12 07	12 21		12 36	12 54		13 06	13 15
Prestwick Int. Airport ✈	d		10 11	10 27		10 42		10 55		11 10		11 25		11 42	11 55			12 11	12 25		12 40	12 58		13 10	
Prestwick Town	d		10 12	10 28		10 43		10 57		11 11	11 21	11 27		11 43	11 57			12 12	12 27		12 42	12 59		13 11	13 21
Newton-on-Ayr	d			10 32		10 47		11 00				11 30		11 47	12 00				12 30		12 48	13 03			
Ayr	a		10 18	10 35		10 52		11 05		11 17	11 29	11 35		11 51	12 05			12 18	12 35		12 53	13 09		13 18	13 28

		SR		SR	SR	SR	SR	SR	SR	SR	SR	SR		SR	SR	SR	SR	SR	SR	SR	SR	SR		SR	SR
									G					◇ C			◇ D							G	
Glasgow Central 219	d	12 34		12 48	13 00	13 04	13 18	13 30	13 34	13 49	4 00	14 04		14 13	14 18	14 30		14 34	14 48	15 00	15 04	15 18		15 30	15 34
Paisley Gilmour Street 219	a	12 43		12 57		13 13	13 27		13 43	13 59		14 13			14 27			14 43	14 58		15 13	15 27			15 47
	d	12 44		12 58		13 14	13 28		13 44	13 59		14 14			14 28			14 44	14 59		15 14	15 28			15 48
Johnstone	d	12 48		13 02		13 18	13 32		13 48	14 03		14 18			14 32			14 48	15 03		15 18	15 32			15 52
Milliken Park	d	12 51				13 21			13 51			14 21						14 51			15 21				15 55
Howwood	d	12 53				13 23			13 53			14 23						14 53			15 23				15 57
Lochwinnoch	d	12 57				13 27			13 57			14 27						14 57			15 27				16 01
Glengarnock	d	13 02		13 10		13 32			14 02	14 12		14 32						15 02	15 11		15 32				16 06
Dalry	d	13 06				13 36	13 44		14 06			14 36			14 43			15 06			15 36	15 43			16 10
Kilwinning	d	13 10		13 17	13 25	13 40	13 49	13 55	14 10	14 18	14 28	14 40			14 49	14 55		15 10	15 18	15 26	15 40	15 48		15 56	16 14
Stevenston	d			13 21			13 53			14 22					14 53				15 22			15 52			
Saltcoats	d			13 24			13 56			14 25					14 56				15 25			15 55			
Ardrossan South Beach	d			13 26			13 59			14 27					14 58				15 27			15 57			
Ardrossan Town	d						14 02								15 01							16 00			
Ardrossan Harbour	a						14 04								15 04							16 03			
West Kilbride	d			13 33						14 33									15 33						
Fairlie	d			13 38						14 38									15 38						
Largs	a			13 44						14 44									15 43						
Irvine	d	13 14			13 29	13 44		13 59	14 14		14 32	14 44				14 59		15 14		15 30	15 44			16 00	16 18
Barassie	d	13 18			13 35	13 48			14 18		14 37	14 48					←	15 18		15 34	15 48				16 22
Troon	d	13 21			13 39	13 51		14 06	14 21		14 40	14 51		15 10		15 05	15 10	15 21		15 37	15 51			16 07	16 25
Prestwick Int. Airport ✈	d	13 25			13 43	13 55		14 10	14 25		14 44	14 55		→		15 09		15 25		15 41	15 55			16 11	16 29
Prestwick Town	d	13 27			13 44	13 57		14 11	14 27		14 45	14 57				15 11	15 16	15 27		15 43	15 57			16 12	16 31
Newton-on-Ayr	d	13 30			13 48	14 00			14 30		14 49	15 00						15 30		15 46	16 00				16 34
Ayr	a	13 34			13 53	14 05		14 19	14 34		14 54	15 05				15 18	15 24	15 35		15 51	16 05			16 20	16 39

A From Glasgow Central
B From Kilmarnock to Girvan
C To Stranraer
D From Glasgow Central to Stranraer
E From North Berwick
F From Kilmarnock to Stranraer
G From Edinburgh

Table T221-F

Saturdays
26 May to 8 December

Glasgow Central - Ardrossan, Largs and Ayr

		SR	SR	SR	SR	SR	SR	SR		SR	SR	SR	SR	SR	SR	SR	SR	SR		SR	SR	SR	SR	SR	SR
								A						B		C	D						◇ E		
Glasgow Central 219	d	15 48	16 00	16 04	16 14	16 28	16 31			16 40	16 50	17 01	17 05	17 13	17 14	17 30		17 34		17 49	18 00	18 04	18 13	18 18	18 30
Paisley Gilmour Street 219	a	15 57		16 13	16 24		16 40			16 52	16 59		17 14		17 25	17 39		17 44		17 59		18 13		18 27	
	d	15 58		16 14	16 24		16 41			16 52	17 00		17 15		17 25	17 40		17 45		18 00		18 14		18 28	
Johnstone	d	16 02		16 18	16 28		16 45			16 56	17 04		17 19		17 29			17 49		18 04		18 18		18 32	
Milliken Park	d			16 21						16 59			17 22		17 32			17 52				18 21			
Howwood	d			16 23						17 02			17 24		17 35			17 55				18 23			
Lochwinnoch	d			16 27						17 06			17 28					17 59				18 27			
Glengarnock	d	16 10		16 32	16 37					17 10	17 14		17 33		17 41			18 03		18 12		18 32			
Dalry	d			16 36	16 41					17 14	17 18		17 37		17 45			18 07				18 36		18 43	
Kilwinning	d	16 17	16 26	16 40	16 46	16 52	16 58			17 18	17 22	17 26	17 41		17 52	17 57		18 11		18 19	18 26	18 40		18 48	18 59
Stevenston	d	16 21			16 50		17 02				17 26				17 56			18 15		18 23				18 52	
Saltcoats	d	16 24			16 53		17 07				17 29				17 59			18 18		18 26				18 55	
Ardrossan South Beach	d	16 26			16 55		17 09				17 31				18 01			18 20		18 28				18 57	
Ardrossan Town	d				16 58						17 34							18 23						19 00	
Ardrossan Harbour	a				17 01						17 36							18 26						19 03	
West Kilbride	d	16 32					17 15								18 07					18 34					
Fairlie	d	16 37					17 20								18 12					18 39					
Largs	a	16 42					17 25								18 17					18 44					
Irvine	d		16 30	16 44		16 56				17 22		17 30	17 45			18 02					18 30	18 44			19 03
Barassie	d		16 35	16 48		17 01						17 36				18 06	←				18 36	18 48			
Troon	d		16 38	16 51		17 04		17 12		17 29		17 39	17 51	18 18		18 10	18 18				18 39	18 51	19 16		19 09
Prestwick Int. Airport ✈	d		16 42	16 55		17 08				17 33		17 43	17 55	→		18 14					18 43	18 55	→		19 13
Prestwick Town	d		16 43	16 57		17 09				17 34		17 44	17 57			18 16					18 44	18 57			19 15
Newton-on-Ayr	d		16 47	17 00		17 13						17 48				18 19					18 48	19 00			
Ayr	a		16 50	17 05		17 17		17 23		17 42		17 51	18 04			18 24	18 28				18 53	19 05			19 22

		SR	SR	SR		SR	SR	SR	SR	SR	SR	SR	SR	SR		SR	SR	SR	SR	SR	SR	SR	SR	SR	
		◇ F				C				G				H										A	
Glasgow Central 219	d		18 34	18 50		19 01	19 15	19 30	19 45	20 00	20 17	20 30	20 45			20 59	21 15	21 30	21 45	22 00	22 16	22 30	22 45		
Paisley Gilmour Street 219	a		18 43	18 59		19 10	19 24	19 39	19 55	20 10	20 26	20 39	20 54			21 10	21 24	21 39	21 54	22 09	22 25	22 39	22 54		
	d		18 44	19 00		19 11	19 25	19 40	19 55	20 10	20 27	20 40	20 55			21 10	21 25	21 40	21 55	22 10	22 26	22 40	22 55		
Johnstone	d		18 48	19 04		19 15	19 29	19 44	19 59	20 14	20 31	20 44	20 59			21 14	21 29	21 44	21 59	22 14	22 30	22 44	22 59		
Milliken Park	d		18 51				19 32		20 02		20 34		21 02				21 32		22 02		22 33		23 02		
Howwood	d		18 53				19 34				20 36						21 34				22 35				
Lochwinnoch	d		18 57				19 38				20 40						21 38				22 39				
Glengarnock	d		19 02	19 12			19 43		20 10		20 45		21 09				21 43		22 09		22 44		23 09		
Dalry	d		19 06				19 47		20 14		20 49		21 13				21 47		22 13		22 48		23 13		
Kilwinning	d		19 10	19 19		19 28	19 51	19 58	20 18	20 28	20 54	20 57	21 17			21 28	21 51	21 57	22 17	22 27	22 52	22 57	23 17		
Stevenston	d			19 23			19 55		20 22		20 58		21 21				21 55		22 21		22 56		23 21		
Saltcoats	d			19 26			19 58		20 25		21 01		21 24				21 58		22 24		22 59		23 24		
Ardrossan South Beach	d			19 28			20 00		20 27		21 03		21 26				22 00		22 26		23 02		23 26		
Ardrossan Town	d						20 03				21 06						22 03				23a04				
Ardrossan Harbour	a						20 06				21 08						22 05								
West Kilbride	d			19 34					20 33				21 32						22 33				23 35		
Fairlie	d			19 39					20 38				21 37						22 38				23 40		
Largs	a			19 45					20 43				21 43						22 44				23 45		
Irvine	d		19 14			19 32		20 02		20 32		21 01				21 32		22 01		22 31		23 01			
Barassie	d	←	19 18			19 37				20 37						21 36				22 36					
Troon	d	19 16	19 21			19 40		20 08		20 40		21 08		21 16		21 39		22 08		22 39		23 10		23 17	
Prestwick Int. Airport ✈	d		19 25			19 44		20 12		20 44		21 12				21 43		22 12		22 43		23 14			
Prestwick Town	d		19 27			19 45		20 14		20 45		21 13				21 45		22 13		22 45		23 15		23 23	
Newton-on-Ayr	d		19 30			19 49				20 49						21 48				22 48					
Ayr	a	19 27	19 35			19 52		20 21		20 54		21 21		21 27		21 53		22 21		22 53		23 21		23 30	

		SR	SR	SR
Glasgow Central 219	d	23 00	23 15	23 30
Paisley Gilmour Street 219	a	23 09	23 24	23 39
	d	23 10	23 25	23 40
Johnstone	d	23 14	23 29	23 44
Milliken Park	d		23 32	
Howwood	d		23 34	
Lochwinnoch	d		23 38	
Glengarnock	d		23 43	
Dalry	d		23 47	
Kilwinning	d	23 27	23 51	23 57
Stevenston	d		23 55	
Saltcoats	d		23 58	
Ardrossan South Beach	d		00 02	
Ardrossan Town	d			
Ardrossan Harbour	a			
West Kilbride	d		00 07	
Fairlie	d		00 12	
Largs	a		00 17	
Irvine	d	23 31		00 01
Barassie	d	23 36		00 06
Troon	d	23 39		00 09
Prestwick Int. Airport ✈	d	23 43		00 13
Prestwick Town	d	23 44		00 14
Newton-on-Ayr	d	23 48		00 18
Ayr	a	23 51		00 21

A From Kilmarnock to Stranraer
B To Girvan
C From Edinburgh
D From Glasgow Central to Girvan
E To Stranraer
F From Glasgow Central to Stranraer
G From North Berwick
H From Kilmarnock to Girvan

Table T221-F

Glasgow Central - Ardrossan, Largs and Ayr

Sundays
20 May to 2 December

	SR A	SR A	SR	SR	SR	SR	SR	SR	SR	SR	SR	SR	SR	SR	SR	SR	SR	SR	SR	SR	SR	SR
Glasgow Central 15 219 d			08 40	09 30	09 40	10 00	10 30	10 40	11 00	11 15	11 30	11 40	12 00	12 30	12 33	12 40	13 00	13 30	13 40	14 00	14 05	14 30
Paisley Gilmour Street 219 a			08 49	09 39	09 49	10 09	10 39	10 49	11 09	11 24	11 39	11 49	12 09	12 39	12 42	12 49	13 09	13 39	13 49	14 09	14 14	14 39
d			08 50	09 40	09 50	10 10	10 40	10 50	11 10	11 25	11 40	11 50	12 10	12 40	12 43	12 50	13 10	13 40	13 50	14 10	14 15	14 40
Johnstone d			08 54	09 44	09 54	10 14	10 44	10 54	11 14	11 29	11 44	11 54	12 14	12 44	12 47	12 54	13 14	13 44	13 54	14 14	14 19	14 44
Milliken Park d			08 57		09 57			10 57		11 32		11 57			12 50	12 57			13 57		14 22	
Howwood d					09 59			10 59				11 59				12 59			13 59			
Lochwinnoch d					10 03			11 03				12 03				13 03			14 03			
Glengarnock d			09 04		10 08			11 08				12 08				13 08			14 08			
Dalry d			09 08		10 12			11 12				12 12				13 12			14 12			
Kilwinning 4 d			09 13	09 58	10 16	10 28	10 58	11 16	11 28	11 45	11 58	12 16	12 28	12 58	13 03	13 16	13 28	13 58	14 16	14 28	14 35	14 58
Stevenston d			09 17		10 20			11 20		11 49		12 20			13 08	13 20			14 20		14 39	
Saltcoats d			09 20		10 23			11 23		11 52		12 23			13 13	13 23			14 23		14 42	
Ardrossan South Beach d		00 02	09 22		10 25			11 25		11 54		12 25			13 15	13 25			14 25		14 44	
Ardrossan Town d			09 25							11 57					13 18						14 47	
Ardrossan Harbour a			09 28							12 00					13 20						14 50	
West Kilbride d		00 07			10 31			11 31				12 31				13 31			14 31			
Fairlie d		00 12			10 37			11 37				12 37				13 37			14 37			
Largs a		00 17			10 43			11 43				12 43				13 43			14 43			
Irvine d	00 01			10 02		10 32	11 02		11 32		12 02		12 32	13 02			13 32	14 02		14 32		15 02
Barassie d	00 06					10 36			11 36				12 36				13 36			14 36		
Troon d	00 09			10 08		10 39	11 08		11 39		12 08		12 39	13 08			13 39	14 08		14 39		15 08
Prestwick Int. Airport ✈ d	00 13			10 12		10 43	11 12		11 43		12 12		12 43	13 12			13 43	14 12		14 43		15 12
Prestwick Town d	00 14			10 14		10 45	11 14		11 45		12 14		12 45	13 14			13 45	14 14		14 45		15 14
Newton-on-Ayr d	00 18					10 48			11 48				12 48				13 48			14 48		
Ayr a	00 21			10 21		10 53	11 21		11 53		12 21		12 53	13 21			13 53	14 21		14 53		15 21

	SR	SR	SR	SR	SR	SR	SR	SR	SR	SR	SR	SR	SR	SR	SR	SR	SR	SR	SR	SR	SR	SR
Glasgow Central 15 219 d	14 40	15 00	15 30	15 40	16 00	16 30	16 40	16 55	17 00	17 30	17 40	18 00	18 30	18 40	19 00	19 40	20 00	20 40	21 00	21 40	22 00	22 42
Paisley Gilmour Street 219 a	14 49	15 09	15 39	15 49	16 09	16 39	16 49	17 04	17 09	17 39	17 49	18 09	18 39	18 49	19 09	19 49	20 09	20 49	21 09	21 49	22 09	22 51
d	14 50	15 10	15 40	15 50	16 10	16 40	16 50	17 05	17 10	17 40	17 50	18 10	18 40	18 50	19 10	19 50	20 10	20 50	21 10	21 50	22 10	22 52
Johnstone d	14 54	15 14	15 44	15 54	16 14	16 44	16 54	17 09	17 14	17 44	17 54	18 14	18 44	18 54	19 14	19 54	20 14	20 54	21 14	21 54	22 14	22 56
Milliken Park d	14 57			15 57			16 57	17 12			17 57			18 57		19 57		20 57		21 57		22 59
Howwood d	14 59			15 59			16 59				17 59			18 59		19 59		20 59		21 59		23 01
Lochwinnoch d	15 03			16 03			17 03				18 03			19 03		20 03		21 03		22 03		23 05
Glengarnock d	15 08			16 08			17 08				18 08			19 08		20 08		21 08		22 08		23 10
Dalry d	15 12			16 12			17 12				18 12			19 12		20 12		21 12		22 12		23 14
Kilwinning 4 d	15 16	15 28	15 58	16 16	16 28	16 58	17 16	17 25	17 29	17 58	18 16	18 28	18 58	19 16	19 28	20 16	20 28	21 16	21 28	22 16	22 28	23 26
Stevenston d	15 20			16 20			17 20	17 29			18 20			19 20		20 20		21 20		22 20		23 30
Saltcoats d	15 23			16 23			17 23	17 32			18 23			19 23		20 23		21 23		22 23		23 33
Ardrossan South Beach d	15 25			16 25			17 25	17 34			18 25			19 25		20 25		21 25		22 25		23 35
Ardrossan Town d								17 37														
Ardrossan Harbour a								17 40														
West Kilbride d	15 31			16 31			17 31				18 31			19 31		20 31		21 31		22 31		23 41
Fairlie d	15 37			16 37			17 37				18 37			19 37		20 37		21 37		22 37		23 46
Largs a	15 43			16 43			17 43				18 43			19 43		20 43		21 43		22 43		23 51
Irvine d		15 32	16 02		16 32	17 02			17 33	18 02		18 32	19 02		19 32		20 32		21 32		22 32	
Barassie d		15 36			16 36				17 37			18 36			19 36		20 36		21 36		22 36	
Troon d		15 39	16 08		16 39	17 08			17 40	18 08		18 39	19 08		19 39		20 39		21 39		22 39	
Prestwick Int. Airport ✈ d		15 43	16 12		16 43	17 12			17 44	18 12		18 43	19 12		19 43		20 43		21 43		22 43	
Prestwick Town d		15 45	16 14		16 45	17 14			17 46	18 14		18 45	19 14		19 45		20 45		21 45		22 45	
Newton-on-Ayr d		15 48			16 48				17 49			18 48			19 48		20 48		21 48		22 48	
Ayr a		15 53	16 21		16 53	17 21			17 54	18 21		18 53	19 21		19 53		20 53		21 53		22 53	

	SR
Glasgow Central 15 219 d	23 00
Paisley Gilmour Street 219 a	23 09
d	23 10
Johnstone d	23 14
Milliken Park d	
Howwood d	
Lochwinnoch d	
Glengarnock d	
Dalry d	
Kilwinning 4 d	23 30
Stevenston d	
Saltcoats d	
Ardrossan South Beach d	
Ardrossan Town d	
Ardrossan Harbour a	
West Kilbride d	
Fairlie d	
Largs a	
Irvine d	23 34
Barassie d	23 38
Troon d	23 41
Prestwick Int. Airport ✈ d	23 45
Prestwick Town d	23 47
Newton-on-Ayr d	23 50
Ayr a	23 54

A not 20 May. From Glasgow Central

Table T221-R

Ayr, Largs and Ardrossan - Glasgow Central

Mondays to Fridays
21 May to 7 December

Miles	Miles	Miles		SR	SR	SR	SR	SR	SR	SR	SR	SR	SR	SR A	SR	SR	SR	SR	SR	SR	SR	SR ◇ B
0	—	—	**Ayr** d	05 13	05 40	06 02	06 20		06 33		06 50	07 05	07 17	07 22		07 34	07 40			08 05		08 24
1¼	—	—	Newton-on-Ayr d	05 15	05 42	06 04			06 35		06 52	07 07	07 19				07 42			08 07		
3¼	—	—	Prestwick Town d	05 18	05 45	06 07	06 25		06 38		06 55	07 10	07 22	07 27		07 39	07 46			08 10		
3¾	—	—	Prestwick Int. Airport ✈ d	05 20	05 47	06 09	06 26		06 40		06 57	07 12	07 24			07 41	07 47			08 12		
6½	—	—	Troon d	05 24	05 51	06 13	06 30		06 44		07 01	07 16	07 28	07a32		07 45	07 52			08 16		08 36
7¾	—	—	Barassie d	05 26	05 54	06 15			06 49		07 03	07 18	07 30				07 54			08 18		
11½	—	—	Irvine d	05 31	05 58	06 20	06 36		06 53		07 08	07 23	07 37			07 51	07 59			08 23		
—	0	—	**Largs** d							06 42					07 22			07 42				
—	3	—	Fairlie d							06 47					07 27			07 47				
—	7	—	West Kilbride d							06 52					07 32			07 52				
—	—	0	**Ardrossan Harbour** d					06 34													08 19	
—	—	0½	Ardrossan Town d					06 36													08 21	
—	11½	1	Ardrossan South Beach d					06 38		06 59					07 39			07 59			08 24	
—	12½	2	Saltcoats d					06 40		07 01					07 41			08 01			08 26	
—	13¾	3¼	Stevenston d					06 43		07 03					07 43			08 03			08 28	
14¾	16	5½	Kilwinning 4 d	05 35	06 02	06 24	06 40	06 46	06 57	07 07	07 12	07 27	07 41		07 49	07 55	08 03	08 07	08 14	08 27	08 32	
18½	19¾	9¼	Dalry d	05 39	06 07	06 28		06 51	07 02	07 11		07 31	07 46						08 18		08 37	
21	22¼	11¾	Glengarnock d	05 43	06 11	06 32			07 06	07 15		07 35	07 50		07 55				08 22		08 41	
25	26¼	15¾	Lochwinnoch d	05 48	06 15	06 37			07 10			07 40				08 04			08 27		08 45	
28½	29¾	19¼	Howwood d	05 52	06 19	06 41			07 14			07 44				08 08			08 31		08 49	
30	31¼	20¾	Milliken Park d	05 54	06 22	06 43			07 17		07 26	07 46				08 11			08 33		08 52	
30¾	32	21½	Johnstone d	05 57	06 25	06 46		07 01	07 20	07 24	07 29	07 49	07 59		08 04		08 17	08 20	08 36	08 41	08 55	
34¼	35½	25	Paisley Gilmour Street 219 a	06 02	06 29	06 51	06 55	07 05	07 24	07 28	07 33	07 54	08 03		08 08	08 16	08 21	08 24	08 41	08 45	08 59	
—	—	—	d	06 02	06 29	06 52	06 56	07 06	07 24	07 28	07 33	07 54	08 03		08 10	08 16	08 21	08 25	08 41	08 46	08 59	
41½	42¾	32¼	**Glasgow Central** 15 219 a	06 13	06 39	07 03	07 08	07 18	07 36	07 40	07 44	08 04	08 13		08 21	08 28	08 32	08 35	08 52	08 58	09 11	09 37

	SR C	SR	SR	SR	SR	SR	SR	SR	SR	SR	SR	SR D	SR	SR	SR	SR C	SR	SR	SR	SR	SR	SR
Ayr d	08 29		08 51		09 06	09 24		09 36	09 50		10 07	10 21	10 25		10 36	10 50		11 08	11 24		11 36	11 52
Newton-on-Ayr d	08 31		08 54		09 08			09 38	09 52		10 09				10 38	10 52		11 10			11 38	11 54
Prestwick Town d	08 34		08 57		09 11	09 29		09 41	09 55		10 12		10 30		10 41	10 55		11 13	11 29		11 41	11 57
Prestwick Int. Airport ✈ d	08 36		08 58		09 13	09 30		09 43	09 57		10 14		10 31		10 43	10 57		11 15	11 30		11 43	11 59
Troon d	08 40		09 02		09 17	09 34		09 47	10 01		10 18	10a29	10 35		10 47	11 01		11 19	11 34		11 47	12 03
Barassie d	08 43		09 05		09 19			09 49	10 03		10 20				10 49	11 03		11 21			11 49	12 05
Irvine d	08 48		09 09		09 24	09 40		09 54	10 08		10 25		10 41		10 54	11 08		11 26	11 40		11 54	12 10
Largs d		08 33								09 53							10 53					
Fairlie d		08 38								09 58							10 58					
West Kilbride d		08 43								10 03							11 03					
Ardrossan Harbour d							09 36							10 36						11 36		
Ardrossan Town d				09 07			09 39							10 38						11 38		
Ardrossan South Beach d		08 50		09 10			09 42			10 10				10 41			11 10			11 41		
Saltcoats d		08 52		09 13			09 44			10 13				10 43			11 13			11 43		
Stevenston d		08 54		09 15			09 46			10 15				10 45			11 15			11 45		
Kilwinning 4 d	08 52	08 58	09 13	09 19	09 28	09 44	09 50	09 58	10 12	10 19	10 29		10 45	10 49	10 58	11 12	11 19	11 30	11 45	11 51	11 58	12 14
Dalry d		09 02			09 32		09 54	10 03			10 33			10 53	11 02			11 34		11 56	12 02	
Glengarnock d		09 06		09 25	09 36			10 07		10 25	10 37				11 06		11 25	11 38			12 06	
Lochwinnoch d		09 11			09 41			10 12			10 42				11 11			11 43			12 11	
Howwood d		09 15			09 45			10 16			10 46				11 15			11 47			12 15	
Milliken Park d		09 17			09 47			10 19			10 48				11 18			11 49			12 17	
Johnstone d	09 07	09 20		09 34	09 50		10 05	10 22		10 34	10 51			11 05	11 21		11 34	11 52		12 06	12 20	
Paisley Gilmour Street 219 a	09 11	09 24		09 38	09 55		10 09	10 26		10 39	10 55			11 12	11 25		11 39	11 56		12 10	12 24	
d	09 12	09 25		09 39	09 55		10 10	10 26		10 39	10 56			11 12	11 25		11 40	11 57		12 11	12 25	
Glasgow Central 15 219 a	09 24	09 36	09 40	09 51	10 06	10 09	10 20	10 36	10 38	10 50	11 06		11 10	11 22	11 35	11 40	11 50	12 07	12 11	12 22	12 35	12 40

	SR	SR	SR	SR D	SR	SR C	SR	SR	SR	SR	SR	SR	SR	SR	SR	SR	SR D	SR	SR	SR E	SR	SR
Ayr d		12 06	12 23	12 29		12 37	12 50		13 06	13 25		13 36	13 50		14 06	14 26	14 30		14 36	14 50		15 06
Newton-on-Ayr d		12 08				12 39	12 52		13 08			13 38	13 52		14 08				14 38	14 52		15 08
Prestwick Town d		12 11	12 28			12 42	12 55		13 11	13 30		13 41	13 55		14 11	14 31	14 36		14 41	14 55		15 11
Prestwick Int. Airport ✈ d		12 13	12 29			12 44	12 57		13 13	13 31		13 43	13 57		14 13	14 32			14 43	14 57		15 13
Troon d		12 17	12 33	12a38		12 48	13 01		13 17	13 35		13 47	14 01		14 17	14 36	14a41		14 47	15 01		15 17
Barassie d		12 19				12 50	13 04		13 19			13 49	14 03		14 19				14 49	15 03		15 19
Irvine d		12 24	12 39			12 55	13 09		13 24	13 42		13 54	14 08		14 24	14 42			14 54	15 08		15 24
Largs d	11 53							12 53						13 53							14 53	
Fairlie d	11 58							12 58						13 58							14 58	
West Kilbride d	12 03							13 03						14 03							15 03	
Ardrossan Harbour d					12 36						13 36							14 36				
Ardrossan Town d					12 38						13 38							14 38				
Ardrossan South Beach d	12 10				12 41			13 10			13 40			14 10				14 41			15 10	
Saltcoats d	12 13				12 43			13 13			13 43			14 13				14 43			15 13	
Stevenston d	12 15				12 45			13 15			13 45			14 15				14 45			15 15	
Kilwinning 4 d	12 19	12 28	12 43		12 49	12 59	13 13	13 19	13 28	13 46	13 49	13 58	14 12	14 19	14 28	14 46		14 49	14 58	15 12	15 19	15 28
Dalry d		12 32			12 54	13 03			13 33		13 53	14 02			14 33			14 53	15 03			15 33
Glengarnock d	12 25	12 36				13 07		13 25	13 37			14 06		14 26	14 37				15 07		15 25	15 37
Lochwinnoch d		12 41				13 12			13 41			14 11			14 41				15 12			15 41
Howwood d		12 45				13 16			13 45			14 15			14 45				15 16			15 45
Milliken Park d		12 47				13 19			13 48			14 17			14 48				15 19			15 48
Johnstone d	12 34	12 50			13 04	13 22		13 34	13 51		14 04	14 20		14 37	14 51			15 04	15 22		15 34	15 51
Paisley Gilmour Street 219 a	12 38	12 55			13 10	13 26		13 38	13 55		14 08	14 24		14 41	14 55			15 08	15 26		15 38	15 55
d	12 39	12 55			13 11	13 26		13 39	13 55		14 09	14 25		14 42	14 56			15 09	15 26		15 38	15 55
Glasgow Central 15 219 a	12 50	13 05	13 09		13 21	13 39	13 42	13 50	14 05	14 10	14 19	14 35	14 40	14 52	15 07	15 11		15 22	15 39	15 42	15 52	16 08

A From Girvan to Kilmarnock
B From Stranraer
C To Edinburgh
D From Stranraer to Kilmarnock
E To North Berwick

Table T221-R

Ayr, Largs and Ardrossan - Glasgow Central

Mondays to Fridays

21 May to 7 December

		SR	SR	SR	SR	SR	SR	SR	SR	SR	SR	SR	SR	SR	SR	SR	SR	SR	SR	SR	SR	SR
									A								B					◇ C
Ayr	d	15 25		15 37	15 48		16 00	16 23	16 27				16 54	17 06		17 24	17 28		17 53		18 05	18 21
Newton-on-Ayr	d			15 39	15 50		16 02						16 56	17 08		17 26			17 55		18 07	
Prestwick Town	d	15 30		15 42	15 53		16 06	16 28	16 33				16 59	17 11		17 29	17 34		17 58		18 10	
Prestwick Int. Airport ✈	d	15 31		15 44	15 55		16 08	16 29					17 01	17 13		17 31			18 00		18 12	
Troon	d	15 35		15 48	15 59		16 13	16 33	16a38				17 05	17 17		17 35	17a39		18 04		18 16	18 29
Barassie	d			15 50	16 01		16 15						17 07	17 19		17 37			18 06		18 18	
Irvine	d	15 41		15 55	16 06		16 20	16 39			16 58		17 12	17 24		17 42			18 11		18 23	
Largs	d					15 53						16 48						17 33				
Fairlie	d					15 58						16 53						17 38				
West Kilbride	d					16 03						16 58						17 43				
Ardrossan Harbour	d		15 36							16 36					17 21					18 07		
Ardrossan Town	d		15 38							16 38					17 23					18 09		
Ardrossan South Beach	d		15 41			16 10				16 41		17 05			17 26			17 50		18 12		
Saltcoats	d		15 43			16 13				16 43		17 07			17 30			17 52		18 14		
Stevenston	d		15 45			16 15				16 45		17 09			17 32			17 54		18 16		
Kilwinning	d	15 45	15 49	15 59	16 10	16 19	16 25	16 43		16 49	17 02	17 13	17 17	17 28	17 41	17 46		17 58	18 15	18 20	18 27	
Dalry	d		15 53	16 04			16 29			16 53	17 06		17 21	17 32		17 51		18 02			18 31	
Glengarnock	d			16 08		16 25	16 33				17 10		17 25	17 36	17 48			18 06		18 26	18 35	
Lochwinnoch	d			16 12			16 38				17 15			17 41				18 11			18 40	
Howwood	d			16 16			16 42				17 19			17 45				18 15			18 44	
Milliken Park	d			16 19			16 44				17 21			17 47				18 17			18 46	
Johnstone	d		16 04	16 22		16 34	16 47			17 04	17 24		17 36	17 50		18 01		18 20		18 35	18 49	
Paisley Gilmour Street 219	a		16 08	16 26		16 39	16 51			17 11	17 28	17 32	17 40	17 54	17 58	18 05		18 24	18 30	18 39	18 54	
	d		16 09	16 26		16 40	16 52			17 11	17 29	17 33	17 41	17 55	17 59	18 06		18 25	18 31	18 40	18 55	
Glasgow Central 219	a	16 11	16 21	16 37	16 39	16 52	17 05	17 10		17 22	17 41	17 43	17 52	18 06	18 10	18 17		18 36	18 41	18 51	19 05	19 37

		SR	SR	SR	SR	SR	SR	SR	SR	SR	SR	SR	SR	SR	SR	SR	SR	SR	SR	SR	SR	SR	SR
				D								A									A		
Ayr	d	18 25		18 39	18 50		19 15		19 45		20 15	20 27		20 45		21 15		21 45		22 15	22 26		23 00
Newton-on-Ayr	d			18 41	18 52				19 47					20 47				21 47		22 17			23 02
Prestwick Town	d	18 30		18 44	18 55		19 20		19 50		20 20	20 32		20 50		21 20		21 50		22 20	22 31		23 05
Prestwick Int. Airport ✈	d	18 31		18 46	18 57		19 21		19 52		20 21			20 52		21 21		21 52		22 22	22 34		23 07
Troon	d	18 35		18 50	19 01		19 25		19 56		20 25	20a38		20 56		21 26		21 56		22 26	22a39		23 11
Barassie	d			18 52	19 03				19 59					20 58				21 58		22 28			23 13
Irvine	d	18 41		18 57	19 09		19 31		20 04		20 31			21 03		21 32		22 03		22 33			23 18
Largs	d					18 52				19 52					20 52				21 52			22 52	
Fairlie	d					18 57				19 57					20 57				21 57			22 57	
West Kilbride	d					19 02				20 02					21 02				22 02			23 02	
Ardrossan Harbour	d		18 36					19 31					20 31				21 31						
Ardrossan Town	d		18 38					19 33					20 34				21 33						
Ardrossan South Beach	d		18 41			19 09		19 36		20 09			20 36		21 09		21 36		22 09			23 09	
Saltcoats	d		18 43			19 11		19 38		20 11			20 38		21 11		21 38		22 11			23 11	
Stevenston	d		18 45			19 13		19 40		20 13			20 41		21 13		21 40		22 13			23 13	
Kilwinning	d	18 45	18 49	19 01	19 13	19 17	19 35	19 44	20 08	20 17	20 35		20 44	21 07	21 17	21 36	21 44	22 08	22 17	22 37		23 17	23 22
Dalry	d		18 53	19 05		19 21		19 48		20 21			20 52		21 22		21 48		22 21				23 26
Glengarnock	d			19 09		19 25		19 52		20 25			20 56		21 26		21 52		22 25				23 30
Lochwinnoch	d			19 14				19 57					21 00				21 57						23 35
Howwood	d			19 18				20 01					21 04				22 01						23 39
Milliken Park	d			19 20		19 33		20 03		20 33			21 07		21 35		22 03		22 33				23 41
Johnstone	d		19 04	19 23		19 36	19 48	20 06	20 22	20 36	20 48		21 10	21 21	21 38	21 49	22 06	22 21	22 36	22 50		23 30	23 44
Paisley Gilmour Street 219	a	19 00	19 08	19 27	19 32	19 40	19 52	20 10	20 26	20 40	20 52		21 14	21 25	21 42	21 53	22 10	22 25	22 41	22 55		23 35	23 49
	d	19 01	19 09	19 28	19 35	19 40	19 53	20 11	20 27	20 40	20 53		21 14	21 25	21 42	21 54	22 11	22 26	22 42	22 55		23 36	23 49
Glasgow Central 219	a	19 12	19 19	19 39	19 46	19 51	20 04	20 21	20 37	20 53	21 04		21 24	21 35	21 54	22 04	22 22	22 36	22 54	23 06		23 46	00 01

Saturdays

26 May to 8 December

		SR	SR	SR	SR	SR	SR	SR	SR	SR	SR	SR	SR	SR	SR	SR	SR	SR	SR	SR	SR	SR	SR
											B				◇ C	D							
Ayr	d	05 13	05 40	06 02		06 33		06 50	07 05	07 17	07 22	07 40		08 05	08 24	08 29		08 51		09 06	09 24		09 36
Newton-on-Ayr	d	05 15	05 42	06 04		06 35		06 52	07 07	07 19		07 42		08 07		08 31		08 54		09 08			09 38
Prestwick Town	d	05 18	05 45	06 07		06 38		06 55	07 10	07 22	07 27	07 46		08 10		08 34		08 57		09 11	09 29		09 41
Prestwick Int. Airport ✈	d	05 20	05 47	06 09		06 40		06 57	07 12	07 24		07 47		08 12		08 36		08 58		09 13	09 30		09 43
Troon	d	05 24	05 51	06 13		06 44		07 01	07 16	07 28	07a32	07 52		08 16	08 36	08 40		09 02		09 17	09 34		09 47
Barassie	d	05 26	05 54	06 15		06 49		07 03	07 18	07 30		07 54		08 18		08 43		09 05		09 19			09 49
Irvine	d	05 31	05 58	06 20		06 53		07 08	07 23	07 37		07 59		08 23		08 48		09 09		09 24	09 40		09 54
Largs	d						06 42						07 42						08 53				
Fairlie	d						06 47						07 47						08 58				
West Kilbride	d						06 52						07 52						09 03				
Ardrossan Harbour	d				06 34												08 45					09 36	
Ardrossan Town	d				06 36												08 47					09 39	
Ardrossan South Beach	d				06 38		06 59						07 59				08 50		09 10			09 42	
Saltcoats	d				06 40		07 01						08 01				08 52		09 13			09 44	
Stevenston	d				06 43		07 03						08 03				08 54		09 15			09 46	
Kilwinning	d	05 35	06 02	06 24	06 46	06 57	07 07	07 12	07 27	07 41		08 03	08 07	08 27		08 52	08 58	09 13	09 19	09 28	09 44	09 50	09 58
Dalry	d	05 39	06 07	06 28	06 51	07 02	07 11		07 31	07 46			08 11	08 31			09 02			09 32		09 54	10 03
Glengarnock	d	05 43	06 11	06 32		07 06	07 15		07 35	07 50			08 15	08 35			09 06		09 25	09 36			10 07
Lochwinnoch	d	05 48	06 15	06 37		07 10			07 40				08 20	08 40			09 11			09 41			10 12
Howwood	d	05 52	06 19	06 41		07 14			07 44				08 24	08 44			09 15			09 45			10 16
Milliken Park	d	05 54	06 22	06 43		07 17		07 26	07 46				08 26	08 46			09 17			09 47			10 19
Johnstone	d	05 57	06 25	06 46	07 01	07 20	07 24	07 29	07 49	07 59		08 17	08 29	08 49		09 07	09 20		09 34	09 50		10 05	10 22
Paisley Gilmour Street 219	a	06 02	06 29	06 51	07 05	07 24	07 28	07 33	07 54	08 03		08 21	08 33	08 53		09 11	09 24		09 38	09 55		10 09	10 26
	d	06 02	06 29	06 52	07 06	07 24	07 28	07 33	07 54	08 03		08 21	08 35	08 55		09 12	09 25		09 39	09 55		10 10	10 26
Glasgow Central 219	a	06 13	06 39	07 03	07 18	07 34	07 40	07 44	08 04	08 13		08 33	08 48	09 05	09 37	09 22	09 35	09 40	09 52	10 06	10 09	10 20	10 36

A From Stranraer to Kilmarnock
B From Girvan to Kilmarnock
C From Stranraer
D To Edinburgh

Table T221-R

Ayr, Largs and Ardrossan - Glasgow Central

Saturdays

26 May to 8 December

		SR	SR	SR	SR	SR	SR	SR	SR	SR	SR	SR	SR	SR	SR	SR	SR	SR	SR	SR	SR	SR	SR
					A				B										A		B		
Ayr	d	09 50		10 07	10 21	10 25		10 36	10 50		11 08	11 24		11 36	11 52		12 06	12 23	12 29		12 37	12 50	
Newton-on-Ayr	d	09 52		10 09				10 38	10 52		11 10			11 38	11 54		12 08				12 39	12 52	
Prestwick Town	d	09 55		10 12		10 30		10 41	10 55		11 13	11 29		11 41	11 57		12 11	12 28			12 42	12 55	
Prestwick Int. Airport ✈	d	09 57		10 14		10 31		10 43	10 57		11 15	11 30		11 43	11 59		12 13	12 29			12 44	12 57	
Troon	d	10 01		10 18	10a29	10 35		10 47	11 01		11 19	11 34		11 47	12 03		12 17	12 33	12a38		12 48	13 01	
Barassie	d	10 03		10 20				10 49	11 03		11 21			11 49	12 05		12 19				12 50	13 04	
Irvine	d	10 08		10 25		10 41		10 54	11 08		11 26	11 40		11 54	12 10		12 24	12 39			12 55	13 09	
Largs	d		09 53							10 53						11 53							12 53
Fairlie	d		09 58							10 58						11 58							12 58
West Kilbride	d		10 03							11 03						12 03							13 03
Ardrossan Harbour	d						10 36						11 36							12 36			
Ardrossan Town	d						10 38						11 38							12 38			
Ardrossan South Beach	d		10 10				10 41			11 10			11 41			12 10				12 41			13 10
Saltcoats	d		10 13				10 43			11 13			11 43			12 13				12 43			13 13
Stevenston	d		10 15				10 45			11 15			11 45			12 15				12 45			13 15
Kilwinning	d	10 12	10 19	10 29		10 45	10 49	10 58	11 12	11 19	11 30	11 45	11 51	11 58	12 14	12 19	12 28	12 43		12 49	12 59	13 13	13 19
Dalry	d			10 33			10 53	11 02			11 34		11 56	12 02			12 32			12 54	13 03		
Glengarnock	d		10 25	10 37				11 06		11 25	11 38			12 06		12 25	12 36				13 07		13 25
Lochwinnoch	d			10 42				11 11			11 43			12 11			12 41				13 12		
Howwood	d			10 46				11 15			11 47			12 15			12 45				13 16		
Milliken Park	d			10 48				11 18			11 49			12 17			12 47				13 19		
Johnstone	d		10 34	10 51			11 05	11 21		11 34	11 52		12 06	12 20		12 34	12 50			13 04	13 22		13 34
Paisley Gilmour Street 219	a		10 39	10 55			11 12	11 25		11 39	11 56		12 10	12 24		12 38	12 55			13 10	13 26		13 38
	d		10 39	10 56			11 12	11 25		11 40	11 57		12 11	12 25		12 39	12 55			13 11	13 26		13 39
Glasgow Central 219	a	10 38	10 52	11 06		11 10	11 22	11 35	11 40	11 50	12 07	12 11	12 22	12 35	12 40	12 50	13 05	13 09		13 21	13 39	13 42	13 50

		SR	SR	SR	SR	SR	SR	SR	SR	SR	SR	SR	SR	SR	SR	SR	SR	SR	SR	SR	SR	SR
										A			C									
Ayr	d	13 06	13 25		13 36	13 50		14 06	14 26	14 30		14 36	14 50		15 06	15 25		15 37	15 48		16 00	16 23
Newton-on-Ayr	d	13 08			13 38	13 52		14 08				14 38	14 52		15 08			15 39	15 50		16 02	
Prestwick Town	d	13 11	13 30		13 41	13 55		14 11	14 31	14 36		14 41	14 55		15 11	15 30		15 42	15 53		16 06	16 28
Prestwick Int. Airport ✈	d	13 13	13 31		13 43	13 57		14 13	14 32			14 43	14 57		15 13	15 31		15 44	15 55		16 08	16 29
Troon	d	13 17	13 35		13 47	14 01		14 17	14 36	14a41		14 47	15 01		15 17	15 35		15 48	15 59		16 13	16 33
Barassie	d	13 19			13 49	14 03		14 19				14 49	15 03		15 19			15 50	16 01		16 15	
Irvine	d	13 24	13 42		13 54	14 08		14 24	14 42			14 54	15 08		15 24	15 41		15 55	16 06		16 20	16 39
Largs	d						13 53							14 53						15 53		
Fairlie	d						13 58							14 58						15 58		
West Kilbride	d						14 03							15 03						16 03		
Ardrossan Harbour	d			13 36							14 36						15 36					
Ardrossan Town	d			13 38							14 38						15 38					
Ardrossan South Beach	d			13 40			14 10				14 41			15 10			15 41			16 10		
Saltcoats	d			13 43			14 13				14 43			15 13			15 43			16 13		
Stevenston	d			13 45			14 15				14 45			15 15			15 45			16 15		
Kilwinning	d	13 28	13 46	13 49	13 58	14 12	14 19	14 28	14 46		14 49	14 58	15 12	15 19	15 28	15 45	15 49	15 59	16 10	16 19	16 25	16 43
Dalry	d	13 33		13 53	14 02			14 33			14 53	15 03			15 33		15 53	16 04			16 29	
Glengarnock	d	13 37			14 06		14 26	14 37				15 07		15 25	15 37			16 08		16 25	16 33	
Lochwinnoch	d	13 41			14 11			14 41				15 12			15 41			16 12			16 38	
Howwood	d	13 45			14 15			14 45				15 16			15 45			16 16			16 42	
Milliken Park	d	13 48			14 17			14 48				15 19			15 48			16 19			16 44	
Johnstone	d	13 51		14 04	14 20		14 37	14 51			15 04	15 22		15 34	15 51		16 04	16 22		16 34	16 47	
Paisley Gilmour Street 219	a	13 55		14 08	14 24		14 41	14 55			15 08	15 26		15 38	15 55		16 08	16 26		16 39	16 51	
	d	13 55		14 09	14 25		14 42	14 56			15 09	15 26		15 38	15 55		16 09	16 26		16 40	16 52	
Glasgow Central 219	a	14 05	14 10	14 19	14 35	14 38	14 52	15 07	15 11		15 22	15 37	15 40	15 52	16 08	16 12	16 19	16 37	16 39	16 51	17 04	17 11

		SR	SR	SR	SR	SR	SR	SR	SR	SR	SR	SR	SR	SR	SR	SR	SR	SR	SR	SR	SR	SR	SR
		A								D					◇ E			B					
Ayr	d	16 27		16 40		16 54	17 06		17 24	17 28		17 53		18 05	18 21	18 25		18 39	18 50		19 15		19 34
Newton-on-Ayr	d			16 42		16 56	17 08		17 26			17 55		18 07				18 41	18 52				19 36
Prestwick Town	d	16 33		16 45		16 59	17 11		17 29	17 34		17 58		18 10		18 30		18 44	18 55		19 20		19 39
Prestwick Int. Airport ✈	d			16 47		17 01	17 13		17 31			18 00		18 12		18 31		18 46	18 57		19 21		19 41
Troon	d	16a38		16 51		17 05	17 17		17 35	17a39		18 04		18 16	18 29	18 35		18 50	19 01		19 25		19 45
Barassie	d			16 53		17 07	17 19		17 37			18 06		18 18				18 52	19 03				19 47
Irvine	d			16 58		17 12	17 24		17 42			18 11		18 23		18 41		18 57	19 09		19 31		19 52
Largs	d				16 48						17 33									18 52			
Fairlie	d				16 53						17 38									18 57			
West Kilbride	d				16 58						17 43									19 02			
Ardrossan Harbour	d		16 36					17 21					18 07				18 36					19 31	
Ardrossan Town	d		16 38					17 23					18 09				18 38					19 33	
Ardrossan South Beach	d		16 41		17 05			17 26			17 50		18 12				18 41			19 09		19 36	
Saltcoats	d		16 43		17 07			17 30			17 52		18 14				18 43			19 11		19 38	
Stevenston	d		16 45		17 09			17 32			17 54		18 16				18 45			19 13		19 40	
Kilwinning	d		16 49	17 02	17 13	17 17	17 28	17 41	17 46		17 58	18 15	18 20	18 27		18 45	18 49	19 01	19 13	19 17	19 35	19 44	19 56
Dalry	d		16 53	17 06		17 21	17 32		17 51		18 02			18 31			18 53	19 05		19 21		19 48	20 00
Glengarnock	d			17 10		17 25	17 36	17 48			18 06		18 26	18 35				19 09		19 25		19 52	20 04
Lochwinnoch	d			17 15			17 41				18 11			18 40				19 14				19 57	20 09
Howwood	d			17 19			17 45				18 15			18 44				19 18				20 01	20 13
Milliken Park	d			17 21			17 47				18 17			18 46				19 20		19 33		20 03	20 15
Johnstone	d		17 04	17 24		17 36	17 50		18 01		18 20		18 35	18 49			19 04	19 23		19 36	19 48	20 06	20 18
Paisley Gilmour Street 219	a		17 10	17 28	17 32	17 41	17 54	17 58	18 05		18 24	18 30	18 39	18 54		19 00	19 08	19 27	19 32	19 40	19 52	20 10	20 22
	d		17 10	17 29	17 33	17 42	17 55	18 00	18 06		18 25	18 31	18 39	18 55		19 01	19 09	19 28	19 35	19 40	19 53	20 11	20 23
Glasgow Central 219	a		17 21	17 39	17 45	17 52	18 06	18 10	18 17		18 36	18 41	18 49	19 05	19 37	19 12	19 20	19 39	19 46	19 52	20 04	20 21	20 33

A From Stranraer to Kilmarnock
B To Edinburgh
C To North Berwick
D From Girvan to Kilmarnock
E From Stranraer

Ayr, Largs and Ardrossan - Glasgow Central

Saturdays
26 May to 8 December

		SR	SR	SR		SR A	SR	SR	SR	SR	SR	SR	SR	SR		SR A	SR	SR
Ayr	d	19 45		20 15		20 27		20 45		21 15		21 45		22 15		22 26		23 00
Newton-on-Ayr	d	19 47						20 47				21 47		22 17				23 02
Prestwick Town	d	19 50		20 20		20 32		20 50		21 20		21 50		22 20		22 31		23 05
Prestwick Int. Airport ✈	d	19 52		20 21				20 52		21 21		21 52		22 22		22 34		23 07
Troon	d	19 56		20 25		20a38		20 56		21 26		21 56		22 26		22a39		23 11
Barassie	d	19 59						20 58				21 58		22 28				23 13
Irvine	d	20 04		20 31				21 03		21 32		22 03		22 33				23 18
Largs	d		19 52						20 52				21 52				22 52	
Fairlie	d		19 57						20 57				21 57				22 57	
West Kilbride	d		20 02						21 02				22 02				23 02	
Ardrossan Harbour	d						20 31				21 31							
Ardrossan Town	d						20 34				21 33							
Ardrossan South Beach	d		20 09				20 36		21 09		21 36		22 09				23 09	
Saltcoats	d		20 11				20 38		21 11		21 38		22 11				23 11	
Stevenston	d		20 13				20 41		21 13		21 40		22 13				23 13	
Kilwinning 4	d	20 08	20 17	20 35			20 44	21 07	21 17	21 36	21 44	22 08	22 17	22 37			23 17	23 22
Dalry	d		20 21				20 52		21 22		21 48		22 21					23 26
Glengarnock	d		20 25				20 56		21 26		21 52		22 25					23 30
Lochwinnoch	d						21 00				21 57							23 35
Howwood	d						21 04				22 01							23 39
Milliken Park	d		20 33				21 07		21 35		22 03		22 33					23 41
Johnstone	d	20 22	20 36	20 48			21 10	21 21	21 38	21 49	22 06	22 21	22 36	22 50			23 30	23 44
Paisley Gilmour Street 219	a	20 26	20 40	20 52			21 14	21 25	21 42	21 53	22 10	22 25	22 41	22 55			23 35	23 49
	d	20 27	20 40	20 53			21 14	21 25	21 42	21 54	22 11	22 26	22 42	22 55			23 36	23 49
Glasgow Central 15 219	a	20 37	20 54	21 04			21 24	21 35	21 54	22 04	22 22	22 36	22 54	23 06			23 46	00 01

Sundays
20 May to 2 December

		SR	SR	SR	SR	SR	SR	SR	SR	SR		SR	SR
Ayr	d	08 45		09 15		09 45		10 15	10 45			11 15	11 45
Newton-on-Ayr	d	08 47				09 47			10 47				11 47
Prestwick Town	d	08 50		09 20		09 50		10 20	10 50			11 20	11 50
Prestwick Int. Airport ✈	d	08 52		09 21		09 52		10 21	10 52			11 21	11 52
Troon	d	08 56		09 25		09 56		10 25	10 56			11 25	11 56
Barassie	d	08 58				09 58			10 58				11 58
Irvine	d	09 03		09 31		10 03		10 31	11 03			11 31	12 03
Largs	d		08 54				09 54			10 54			
Fairlie	d		08 59				09 59			10 59			
West Kilbride	d		09 04				10 04			11 04			
Ardrossan Harbour	d				09 35								
Ardrossan Town	d				09 37								
Ardrossan South Beach	d		09 11		09 39		10 11			11 11			
Saltcoats	d		09 13		09 41		10 13			11 13			
Stevenston	d		09 15		09 44		10 15			11 15			
Kilwinning 4	d	09 07	09 19	09 35	09 48	10 07	10 19	10 35	11 07	11 19		11 35	12 07
Dalry	d		09 24				10 24			11 24			
Glengarnock	d		09 28				10 28			11 28			
Lochwinnoch	d		09 32				10 32			11 32			
Howwood	d		09 36				10 36			11 36			
Milliken Park	d		09 39				10 39			11 39			
Johnstone	d	09 21	09 42	09 49	10 01	10 21	10 42	10 49	11 21	11 42		11 49	12 21
Paisley Gilmour Street 219	a	09 25	09 46	09 53	10 05	10 25	10 46	10 53	11 25	11 46		11 53	12 25
	d	09 25	09 46	09 53	10 06	10 25	10 46	10 53	11 25	11 46		11 53	12 25
Glasgow Central 15 219	a	09 36	09 57	10 04	10 17	10 36	10 57	11 04	11 36	11 57		12 04	12 36

		SR	SR	SR	SR	SR	SR	SR		SR	SR	SR	SR
Ayr	d		12 15		12 45		13 15	13 45			14 15	14 45	
Newton-on-Ayr	d				12 47			13 47				14 47	
Prestwick Town	d		12 20		12 50		13 20	13 50			14 20	14 50	
Prestwick Int. Airport ✈	d		12 21		12 52		13 21	13 52			14 21	14 52	
Troon	d		12 25		12 56		13 25	13 56			14 25	14 56	
Barassie	d				12 58			13 58				14 58	
Irvine	d		12 31		13 03		13 31	14 03			14 31	15 03	
Largs	d	11 54				12 54				13 54			
Fairlie	d	11 59				12 59				13 59			
West Kilbride	d	12 04				13 04				14 04			
Ardrossan Harbour	d			12 35									15 02
Ardrossan Town	d			12 37									15 04
Ardrossan South Beach	d	12 11		12 39		13 11				14 11			15 06
Saltcoats	d	12 13		12 41		13 13				14 13			15 08
Stevenston	d	12 15		12 44		13 15				14 15			15 11
Kilwinning 4	d	12 19	12 35	12 47	13 07	13 19	13 35	14 07		14 19	14 38	15 07	15 14
Dalry	d	12 24				13 24				14 24			
Glengarnock	d	12 28				13 28				14 28			
Lochwinnoch	d	12 32				13 32				14 32			
Howwood	d	12 36				13 36				14 36			
Milliken Park	d	12 39		13 00		13 39				14 39			15 27
Johnstone	d	12 42	12 49	13 03	13 21	13 42	13 49	14 21		14 42	14 52	15 21	15 30
Paisley Gilmour Street 219	a	12 46	12 53	13 07	13 25	13 46	13 54	14 25		14 46	14 56	15 25	15 34
	d	12 46	12 53	13 07	13 25	13 46	13 54	14 25		14 46	14 56	15 25	15 35
Glasgow Central 15 219	a	12 57	13 04	13 18	13 36	13 57	14 05	14 36		14 57	15 06	15 36	15 45

		SR	SR	SR	SR	SR		SR	SR	SR	SR	SR	SR
Ayr	d		15 15	15 45		16 15		16 45		17 15	17 45		
Newton-on-Ayr	d			15 47				16 47			17 47		
Prestwick Town	d		15 20	15 50		16 20		16 50		17 20	17 50		
Prestwick Int. Airport ✈	d		15 21	15 52		16 21		16 52		17 21	17 52		
Troon	d		15 25	15 56		16 25		16 56		17 25	17 56		
Barassie	d			15 58				16 58			17 58		
Irvine	d		15 31	16 03		16 31		17 03		17 31	18 03		
Largs	d	14 54			15 54				16 54				17 54
Fairlie	d	14 59			15 59				16 59				17 59
West Kilbride	d	15 04			16 04				17 04				18 04
Ardrossan Harbour	d											18 00	
Ardrossan Town	d											18 02	
Ardrossan South Beach	d	15 11			16 11				17 11			18 04	18 11
Saltcoats	d	15 13			16 13				17 13			18 06	18 13
Stevenston	d	15 15			16 15				17 15			18 09	18 15
Kilwinning 4	d	15 19	15 35	16 07	16 19	16 35		17 07	17 19	17 35	18 07	18 12	18 19
Dalry	d	15 24			16 24				17 24				18 24
Glengarnock	d	15 28			16 28				17 28				18 28
Lochwinnoch	d	15 32			16 32				17 32				18 32
Howwood	d	15 36			16 36				17 36				18 36
Milliken Park	d	15 39			16 39				17 39			18 25	18 39
Johnstone	d	15 42	15 49	16 21	16 42	16 49		17 21	17 42	17 49	18 21	18 28	18 42
Paisley Gilmour Street 219	a	15 46	15 53	16 25	16 46	16 53		17 25	17 46	17 53	18 25	18 32	18 46
	d	15 46	15 53	16 25	16 46	16 53		17 25	17 46	17 53	18 25	18 32	18 46
Glasgow Central 15 219	a	15 57	16 04	16 36	16 57	17 04		17 36	17 58	18 04	18 36	18 44	18 57

		SR	SR	SR		SR	SR	SR	SR	SR	SR	SR	SR
Ayr	d	18 15	18 45			19 15	19 45			20 45		21 45	
Newton-on-Ayr	d		18 47				19 47			20 47		21 47	
Prestwick Town	d	18 20	18 50			19 20	19 50			20 50		21 50	
Prestwick Int. Airport ✈	d	18 21	18 52			19 21	19 52			20 52		21 52	
Troon	d	18 25	18 56			19 25	19 56			20 56		21 56	
Barassie	d		18 58				19 58			20 58		21 58	
Irvine	d	18 31	19 03			19 31	20 03			21 03		22 03	
Largs	d			18 54				19 54			20 54		21 54
Fairlie	d			18 59				19 59			20 59		21 59
West Kilbride	d			19 04				20 04			21 04		22 04
Ardrossan Harbour	d								20 30				
Ardrossan Town	d								20 32				
Ardrossan South Beach	d			19 11				20 11	20 34		21 11		22 11
Saltcoats	d			19 13				20 13	20 36		21 13		22 13
Stevenston	d			19 15				20 15	20 39		21 15		22 15
Kilwinning 4	d	18 35	19 07	19 19		19 35	20 07	20 19	20 42	21 07	21 19	22 07	22 19
Dalry	d			19 24				20 24			21 24		22 24
Glengarnock	d			19 28				20 28			21 28		22 28
Lochwinnoch	d			19 32				20 32			21 32		22 32
Howwood	d			19 36				20 36			21 36		22 36
Milliken Park	d			19 39				20 39	20 55		21 39		22 39
Johnstone	d	18 49	19 21	19 42		19 49	20 21	20 42	20 58	21 21	21 42	22 21	22 42
Paisley Gilmour Street 219	a	18 53	19 25	19 46		19 53	20 25	20 46	21 02	21 25	21 46	22 25	22 46
	d	18 53	19 25	19 46		19 53	20 25	20 46	21 02	21 25	21 46	22 25	22 46
Glasgow Central 15 219	a	19 04	19 36	19 57		20 04	20 36	20 56	21 13	21 36	21 57	22 36	22 57

A From Stranraer to Kilmarnock

Ayr, Largs and Ardrossan - Glasgow Central

Sundays
20 May to 2 December

		SR		SR
Ayr	d	23 00		
Newton-on-Ayr	d	23 02		
Prestwick Town	d	23 05		
Prestwick Int. Airport ✈	d	23 07		
Troon	d	23 11		
Barassie	d	23 13		
Irvine	d	23 18		
Largs	d			23 00
Fairlie	d			23 05
West Kilbride	d			23 10
Ardrossan Harbour	d			
Ardrossan Town	d			
Ardrossan South Beach	d			23 17
Saltcoats	d			23 19
Stevenston	d			23 21
Kilwinning 4	d	23 22		23 26
Dalry	d			23 30
Glengarnock	d			23 34
Lochwinnoch	d			23 39
Howwood	d			23 43
Milliken Park	d			23 45
Johnstone	d	23 36		23 48
Paisley Gilmour Street 219	a	23 40		23 52
	d	23 40		23 53
Glasgow Central 15 219	a	23 51		00 04

Kilmarnock, Barrhead and East Kilbride - Glasgow Central

21 May to 7 December

Miles	Miles			SR MX A	SR MO A	SR	SR	SR B	SR	SR B	SR	SR		SR	SR	SR	SR	SR C ✠	SR	SR	SR	SR		SR	SR
0	—	**Kilmarnock 3**	d			05 22		06 20		06 52				07 20				07 55				08 23			
2¼	—	Kilmaurs	d			05 26		06 24		06 56				07 24				07 59				08 27			
5½	—	Stewarton	d			05 31		06 29		07 02				07 31				08 05				08 32			
7¾	—	Dunlop	d			05 36		06 34		07 06				07 36				08 10				08 37			
16¾	—	**Barrhead**	d			05 46		06 44		07 17	07 26			07 49		07 56		08 22		08 30		08 50		08 57	
18½	—	Nitshill	d			05 49		06 47			07 29					07 59				08 33				09 00	
19½	—	Priesthill & Darnley	d			05 52		06 50			07 31					08 01				08 35				09 02	
20	—	Kennishead	d			05 54		06 52			07 33					08 03				08 37				09 04	
—	0	**East Kilbride**	d				06 18		06 51			07 25			07 43		07 59		08 11		08 26				08 57
—	1½	Hairmyres	d	00 02	00 03		06 22		06 55			07 29			07 47		08 03		08 19		08 30				09 01
—	3	Thorntonhall	d	00 06	00 06		06 25		06 58			07 32					08 06				08 33				09 04
—	4¼	Busby	d	00 09	00 09		06 28		07 01			07 36					08 10		08 24		08 36				09 07
—	5	Clarkston	d	00 12	00 12		06 31		07 04			07 39			07 54		08 13		08 27		08 39				09 10
—	6¼	Giffnock	d	00 15	00 16		06 35		07 08			07 42					08 16		08 30		08 43				09 14
—	7¼	Thornliebank	d	00 18	00 18		06 37		07 10			07 46					08 19		08 34		08 46				09 16
21¼	8¾	Pollokshaws West	d	00 21	00 21	05 57	06 40	06 55	07 13		07 37	07 49				08 07	08 22		08 37	08 41	08 49			09 08	09 19
22¼	9¾	Crossmyloof	d	00 24	00 24	06 00	06 43	06 58	07 16		07 40	07 52				08 10	08 24		08 40	08 44	08 51			09 11	09 22
24¼	11½	**Glasgow Central 15**	a	00 30	00 30	06 08	06 49	07 07	07 23	07 31	07 46	07 58		08 01	08 09	08 16	08 31	08 38	08 46	08 50	08 58	09 01		09 17	09 28

		SR ◇ D	SR	SR	SR	SR	SR	NT E		SR	SR	SR	SR	SR	SR F	SR	SR	SR		SR	SR	SR	SR	SR	SR
Kilmarnock 3	d	08 57			09 27			10 00				10 28			11 00			11 27				11 58			12 27
Kilmaurs	d	09 01			09 31			10 04				10 32			11 04			11 31				12 02			12 31
Stewarton	d	09 06			09 36			10 09				10 37			11 09			11 36				12 07			12 36
Dunlop	d	09 11			09 41			10 14				10 42			11 14			11 41				12 12			12 41
Barrhead	d	09 22	09 27		09 53	09 57		10 24		10 27		10 52	10 57			11 27		11 52		11 57			12 27		12 52
Nitshill	d		09 30			10 00				10 30			11 00			11 30				12 00			12 30		
Priesthill & Darnley	d		09 32			10 02				10 33			11 02			11 32				12 02			12 32		
Kennishead	d		09 34			10 04				10 35			11 04			11 34				12 04			12 34		
East Kilbride	d			09 28			09 57				10 28			10 57			11 28				11 57			12 28	
Hairmyres	d			09 32			10 01				10 32			11 01			11 32				12 01			12 32	
Thorntonhall	d						10 04							11 04							12 04				
Busby	d			09 37			10 07				10 37			11 07			11 37				12 07			12 37	
Clarkston	d			09 40			10 10				10 40			11 10			11 40				12 10			12 40	
Giffnock	d			09 43			10 14				10 43			11 14			11 43				12 14			12 43	
Thornliebank	d			09 46			10 16				10 46			11 16			11 46				12 16			12 46	
Pollokshaws West	d		09 38	09 49		10 08	10 20			10 38	10 49		11 08	11 20		11 38	11 49			12 08	12 20		12 38	12 49	
Crossmyloof	d		09 41	09 52		10 11	10 23			10 41	10 52		11 11	11 23		11 41	11 52			12 11	12 23		12 41	12 52	
Glasgow Central 15	a	09 37	09 47	09 59	10 06	10 17	10 29	10 37		10 47	10 59	11 06	11 17	11 29	11 37	11 47	11 59	12 06		12 17	12 29	12 34	12 47	12 59	13 05

		SR	SR	SR C ✠		SR	SR	SR	SR	SR	SR	SR	SR	SR		SR	SR	SR C ✠	SR	SR	SR	SR	SR	SR	
Kilmarnock 3	d			12 59				13 28			13 58			14 28				14 59			15 27			16 00	
Kilmaurs	d			13 03				13 32			14 02			14 32				15 03			15 31			16 04	
Stewarton	d			13 08				13 37			14 07			14 37				15 08			15 36			16 10	
Dunlop	d			13 13				13 42			14 12			14 42				15 13			15 41			16 14	
Barrhead	d	12 57				13 27		13 52	13 57			14 27		14 52		14 57			15 27		15 53	15 57			
Nitshill	d	13 00				13 30			14 00			14 30				15 00			15 30			16 00			
Priesthill & Darnley	d	13 02				13 32			14 03			14 32				15 02			15 32			16 02			
Kennishead	d	13 04				13 34			14 05			14 34				15 04			15 34			16 04			
East Kilbride	d		12 57				13 28			13 57			14 28				14 57			15 28			15 57		
Hairmyres	d		13 01				13 32			14 01			14 32				15 01			15 32			16 01		
Thorntonhall	d		13 04							14 04							15 04						16 04		
Busby	d		13 07				13 37			14 07			14 37				15 07			15 37			16 07		
Clarkston	d		13 10				13 40			14 10			14 40				15 10			15 40			16 10		
Giffnock	d		13 14				13 43			14 14			14 43				15 14			15 43			16 14		
Thornliebank	d		13 16				13 46			14 16			14 46				15 16			15 46			16 16		
Pollokshaws West	d	13 08	13 20			13 38	13 49		14 08	14 20		14 38	14 49			15 08	15 20		15 38	15 49		16 08	16 20		
Crossmyloof	d	13 11	13 23			13 41	13 52		14 11	14 23		14 41	14 52			15 11	15 23		15 41	15 52		16 11	16 23		
Glasgow Central 15	a	13 17	13 29	13 35		13 47	13 59	14 07	14 17	14 29	14 34	14 47	14 59	15 06		15 17	15 29	15 38	15 47	15 59	16 09	16 19	16 29	16 36	

		SR	SR	SR	SR	SR	SR C ✠	SR	SR	SR		SR	SR	SR	SR	SR	SR	SR	SR	SR ◇ D		SR	SR	SR	SR
Kilmarnock 3	d			16 28			16 57			17 27				17 59			18 29			18 57				19 27	
Kilmaurs	d			16 32			17 01			17 31				18 03			18 33			19 01				19 31	
Stewarton	d			16 37			17 06			17 36				18 09			18 39			19 06				19 36	
Dunlop	d			16 42			17 11			17 41				18 13			18 43			19 11				19 41	
Barrhead	d	16 28		16 52	16 59		17 22	17 27		17 52		17 57		18 24	18 28		18 54	18 58		19 22		19 27		19 51	
Nitshill	d	16 31			17 02			17 30				18 00			18 31			19 01				19 30		19 54	
Priesthill & Darnley	d	16 33			17 04			17 32				18 02			18 33			19 04				19 32		19 57	
Kennishead	d	16 35			17 06			17 34				18 04			18 35			19 06				19 34		19 59	
East Kilbride	d		16 28			16 57			17 25				17 57			18 29			18 57				19 28		19 57
Hairmyres	d		16 32			17 01			17 32				18 05			18 37			19 01				19 32		20 01
Thorntonhall	d					17 04							18 09						19 04						20 04
Busby	d		16 37			17 07			17 37				18 12			18 43			19 07				19 37		20 07
Clarkston	d		16 40			17 10			17 40				18 15			18 46			19 10				19 40		20 10
Giffnock	d		16 43			17 14			17 44				18 18			18 50			19 14				19 43		20 14
Thornliebank	d		16 46			17 16			17 46				18 21			18 52			19 16				19 46		20 16
Pollokshaws West	d	16 39	16 49		17 10	17 20		17 38	17 49			18 08	18 24		18 39	18 55		19 09	19 20			19 38	19 49	20 02	20 20
Crossmyloof	d	16 41	16 52		17 13	17 23		17 40	17 52			18 11	18 26		18 41	18 58		19 12	19 23			19 41	19 52	20 05	20 23
Glasgow Central 15	a	16 48	16 59	17 07	17 19	17 29	17 37	17 47	17 58	18 05		18 17	18 33	18 37	18 48	19 04	19 07	19 19	19 29	19 37		19 48	19 59	20 14	20 29

A From East Kilbride
B From Dumfries
C From Carlisle
D From Stranraer
E From Newcastle
F From Auchinleck

Kilmarnock, Barrhead and East Kilbride - Glasgow Central

21 May to 7 December

		SR A ✠	SR	SR	SR	SR A ✠	SR	SR	SR		SR	SR	SR	SR	SR A ✠	SR	SR
Kilmarnock 3	d	19 57		20 27		20 59		21 28			21 57		22 27		22 57		
Kilmaurs	d	20 01		20 31		21 03		21 32			22 01		22 31		23 01		
Stewarton	d	20 06		20 36		21 08		21 38			22 07		22 36		23 06		
Dunlop	d	20 11		20 41		21 13		21 42			22 11		22 41		23 11		
Barrhead	d	20 21		20 51		21 23		21 53			22 22		22 51		23 22		
Nitshill	d			20 54				21 56					22 54				
Priesthill & Darnley	d			20 57				21 58					22 57				
Kennishead	d			20 59				22 00					22 59				
East Kilbride	d		20 28		20 57		21 28		21 57			22 28		22 57		23 28	23 58
Hairmyres	d		20 32		21 01		21 32		22 01			22 32		23 01		23 32	00 02
Thorntonhall	d				21 04				22 04					23 04			00 06
Busby	d		20 37		21 07		21 37		22 07			22 37		23 07		23 37	00 09
Clarkston	d		20 40		21 10		21 40		22 10			22 40		23 10		23 40	00 12
Giffnock	d		20 43		21 14		21 43		22 14			22 43		23 14		23 43	00 15
Thornliebank	d		20 46		21 16		21 46		22 16			22 46		23 16		23 46	00 18
Pollokshaws West	d		20 49	21 02	21 20		21 49	22 04	22 20			22 49	23 02	23 20		23 49	00 21
Crossmyloof	d		20 52	21 05	21 23		21 52	22 06	22 23			22 52	23 05	23 23		23 52	00 24
Glasgow Central 15	a	20 37	20 59	21 13	21 29	21 39	21 59	22 15	22 29		22 37	22 59	23 13	23 29	23 36	23 59	00 30

Saturdays

26 May to 8 December

		SR B	SR	SR C	SR	SR C	SR	SR	SR	SR		SR A ✠	SR	SR	SR	SR	SR	SR ◇ D	SR	SR		SR	SR	SR	NT E
Kilmarnock 3	d		05 22	06 20		06 52			07 22			07 55			08 23			08 57				09 27			09 50
Kilmaurs	d		05 26	06 24		06 56			07 26			07 59			08 27			09 01				09 31			09 55
Stewarton	d		05 31	06 29		07 02			07 31			08 05			08 32			09 06				09 36			10 01
Dunlop	d		05 36	06 34		07 06			07 36			08 10			08 37			09 11				09 41			10 06
Barrhead	d		05 46	06 44		07 18	07 26		07 47			08 21	08 27		08 50	08 57		09 22	09 27			09 53	09 57		10 16
Nitshill	d		05 49	06 47			07 29		07 50				08 30			09 00			09 30				10 00		
Priesthill & Darnley	d		05 52	06 50			07 31		07 53				08 32			09 02			09 32				10 02		
Kennishead	d		05 54	06 52			07 33		07 55				08 34			09 04			09 34				10 04		
East Kilbride	d				06 54			07 27		07 57				08 27			08 57			09 28				09 57	
Hairmyres	d	00 02			06 58			07 31		08 01				08 31			09 01			09 32				10 01	
Thorntonhall	d	00 06			07 01			07 34		08 04				08 34			09 04							10 04	
Busby	d	00 09			07 04			07 37		08 07				08 37			09 07			09 37				10 07	
Clarkston	d	00 12			07 07			07 40		08 10				08 40			09 10			09 40				10 10	
Giffnock	d	00 15			07 11			07 44		08 14				08 44			09 14			09 43				10 14	
Thornliebank	d	00 18			07 13			07 47		08 16				08 46			09 16			09 46				10 16	
Pollokshaws West	d	00 21	05 57	06 55	07 17		07 37	07 50	07 58	08 20			08 38	08 50		09 08	09 20		09 38	09 49			10 08	10 20	
Crossmyloof	d	00 24	06 00	06 58	07 19		07 40	07 53	08 01	08 23			08 41	08 53		09 11	09 23		09 41	09 52			10 11	10 23	
Glasgow Central 15	a	00 30	06 09	07 11	07 26	07 32	07 46	07 59	08 09	08 29		08 34	08 47	08 59	09 03	09 17	09 29	09 37	09 47	09 59		10 06	10 17	10 29	10 31

		SR	SR	SR	SR	SR		SR F	SR	SR	SR	SR	SR	SR	SR	SR		SR	SR	SR	SR A ✠	SR	SR	SR	SR
Kilmarnock 3	d			10 28				11 00			11 27			11 58				12 27			13 00			13 28	
Kilmaurs	d			10 32				11 04			11 31			12 02				12 31			13 04			13 32	
Stewarton	d			10 37				11 09			11 36			12 07				12 36			13 09			13 37	
Dunlop	d			10 42				11 14			11 41			12 12				12 41			13 14			13 42	
Barrhead	d	10 27		10 52	10 57				11 27		11 52	11 57			12 27			12 52	12 57			13 27		13 52	13 57
Nitshill	d	10 30			11 00				11 30			12 00			12 30				13 00			13 30			14 00
Priesthill & Darnley	d	10 33			11 02				11 32			12 02			12 32				13 02			13 32			14 03
Kennishead	d	10 35			11 04				11 34			12 04			12 34				13 04			13 34			14 05
East Kilbride	d		10 28			10 57				11 28			11 57			12 28				12 57			13 28		
Hairmyres	d		10 32			11 01				11 32			12 01			12 32				13 01			13 32		
Thorntonhall	d					11 04							12 04							13 04					
Busby	d		10 37			11 07				11 37			12 07			12 37				13 07			13 37		
Clarkston	d		10 40			11 10				11 40			12 10			12 40				13 10			13 40		
Giffnock	d		10 43			11 14				11 43			12 14			12 43				13 14			13 43		
Thornliebank	d		10 46			11 16				11 46			12 16			12 46				13 16			13 46		
Pollokshaws West	d	10 38	10 49		11 08	11 20			11 38	11 49		12 08	12 20		12 38	12 49			13 08	13 20		13 38	13 49		14 08
Crossmyloof	d	10 41	10 52		11 11	11 23			11 41	11 52		12 11	12 23		12 41	12 52			13 11	13 23		13 41	13 52		14 11
Glasgow Central 15	a	10 47	10 59	11 06	11 17	11 29		11 36	11 47	11 59	12 05	12 17	12 29	12 34	12 47	12 59		13 05	13 17	13 29	13 36	13 47	13 59	14 06	14 17

		SR		SR	SR	SR	SR	SR	SR	SR A ✠	SR	SR		SR	SR	SR	SR	SR	SR	SR	SR	SR		SR A ✠	SR
Kilmarnock 3	d			13 58			14 28			14 58				15 27			16 00			16 28				16 57	
Kilmaurs	d			14 02			14 32			15 02				15 31			16 04			16 32				17 01	
Stewarton	d			14 07			14 37			15 07				15 36			16 10			16 37				17 06	
Dunlop	d			14 12			14 42			15 12				15 41			16 14			16 42				17 11	
Barrhead	d				14 27		14 52	14 57			15 27			15 53	15 57			16 28		16 52	16 59			17 22	17 27
Nitshill	d				14 30			15 00			15 30				16 00			16 31			17 02				17 30
Priesthill & Darnley	d				14 32			15 02			15 32				16 02			16 33			17 04				17 32
Kennishead	d				14 34			15 04			15 34				16 04			16 35			17 06				17 34
East Kilbride	d	13 57				14 28			14 57			15 28				15 57			16 29			16 57			
Hairmyres	d	14 01				14 32			15 01			15 32				16 01			16 33			17 01			
Thorntonhall	d	14 04							15 04							16 04						17 04			
Busby	d	14 07				14 37			15 07			15 37				16 07			16 38			17 07			
Clarkston	d	14 10				14 40			15 10			15 40				16 10			16 41			17 10			
Giffnock	d	14 14				14 43			15 14			15 43				16 14			16 44			17 14			
Thornliebank	d	14 16				14 46			15 16			15 46				16 16			16 47			17 16			
Pollokshaws West	d	14 20			14 38	14 49		15 08	15 20		15 38	15 49			16 08	16 20		16 39	16 50		17 10	17 20			17 38
Crossmyloof	d	14 23			14 41	14 52		15 11	15 23		15 41	15 52			16 11	16 23		16 41	16 53		17 12	17 23			17 41
Glasgow Central 15	a	14 31		14 34	14 47	14 59	15 06	15 17	15 29	15 38	15 47	15 59		16 06	16 17	16 31	16 36	16 48	17 00	17 05	17 20	17 29		17 36	17 47

A From Carlisle
B From East Kilbride
C From Dumfries
D From Stranraer
E From Newcastle
F From Auchinleck

Table T222-F

Saturdays

26 May to 8 December

Kilmarnock, Barrhead and East Kilbride - Glasgow Central

		SR	SR	SR	SR	SR	SR	SR	SR	SR	SR	SR	SR	SR	SR	SR	SR	SR	SR	SR	SR	SR
												◇ A					B				B	
Kilmarnock	d		17 27			17 59			18 29			18 57			19 27		19 57		20 27		20 59	
Kilmaurs	d		17 31			18 03			18 33			19 01			19 31		20 01		20 31		21 03	
Stewarton	d		17 36			18 09			18 39			19 06			19 36		20 06		20 36		21 08	
Dunlop	d		17 41			18 13			18 43			19 11			19 41		20 11		20 41		21 13	
Barrhead	d		17 52	17 57		18 24	18 28		18 54	18 58		19 22	19 27		19 51		20 21		20 51		21 23	
Nitshill	d			18 00			18 31			19 01			19 30		19 54				20 54			
Priesthill & Darnley	d			18 02			18 33			19 04			19 32		19 57				20 57			
Kennishead	d			18 04			18 35			19 06			19 34		19 59				20 59			
East Kilbride	d	17 28			17 57			18 28			18 57			19 28		19 57		20 28		20 57		21 28
Hairmyres	d	17 32			18 01			18 32			19 01			19 32		20 01		20 32		21 01		21 32
Thorntonhall	d				18 04						19 04					20 04				21 04		
Busby	d	17 37			18 07			18 37			19 07			19 37		20 07		20 37		21 07		21 37
Clarkston	d	17 40			18 10			18 40			19 10			19 40		20 10		20 40		21 10		21 40
Giffnock	d	17 43			18 14			18 43			19 14			19 43		20 14		20 43		21 14		21 43
Thornliebank	d	17 46			18 16			18 46			19 16			19 46		20 16		20 46		21 16		21 46
Pollokshaws West	d	17 49		18 08	18 20		18 39	18 49		19 09	19 20		19 38	19 49	20 02	20 20		20 49	21 02	21 20		21 49
Crossmyloof	d	17 52		18 11	18 23		18 41	18 52		19 12	19 23		19 41	19 52	20 05	20 23		20 52	21 05	21 23		21 52
Glasgow Central	a	18 01	18 06	18 17	18 29	18 37	18 48	18 59	19 07	19 18	19 29	19 37	19 47	19 59	20 13	20 29	20 35	20 59	21 13	21 29	21 40	21 59

		SR	SR	SR	SR	SR	SR	SR	SR	SR
								B		
Kilmarnock	d	21 31		21 57		22 29		22 58		
Kilmaurs	d	21 35		22 01		22 33		23 02		
Stewarton	d	21 41		22 07		22 38		23 07		
Dunlop	d	21 45		22 11		22 43		23 12		
Barrhead	d	21 56		22 22		22 53		23 22		
Nitshill	d	21 59				22 56				
Priesthill & Darnley	d	22 01				22 59				
Kennishead	d	22 03				23 01				
East Kilbride	d		21 57		22 28		22 57		23 28	23 58
Hairmyres	d		22 01		22 32		23 01		23 32	00 02
Thorntonhall	d		22 04				23 04			00 06
Busby	d		22 07		22 37		23 07		23 37	00 09
Clarkston	d		22 10		22 40		23 10		23 40	00 12
Giffnock	d		22 14		22 43		23 14		23 43	00 15
Thornliebank	d		22 16		22 46		23 16		23 46	00 18
Pollokshaws West	d	22 07	22 20		22 49	23 04	23 20		23 49	00 21
Crossmyloof	d	22 09	22 23		22 52	23 07	23 23		23 52	00 24
Glasgow Central	a	22 21	22 29	22 37	22 59	23 15	23 29	23 36	23 59	00 30

Sundays

20 May to 2 December

		SR	SR	SR	SR	SR	SR	SR	SR		SR	SR	SR	SR	SR	SR	SR	SR	SR	SR	SR	SR
		C													B							
Kilmarnock	d				08 55			09 55		and at the same minutes past each hour until		13 55			14 57			15 55			16 55	
Kilmaurs	d				08 59			09 59				13 59			15 01			15 59			16 59	
Stewarton	d				09 04			10 04				14 04			15 06			16 04			17 04	
Dunlop	d				09 09			10 09				14 09			15 11			16 09			17 09	
Barrhead	d				09 20			10 20				14 20			15 22			16 20			17 19	
Nitshill	d				09 23			10 23				14 23			15 25			16 23			17 23	
Priesthill & Darnley	d				09 25			10 25				14 25			15 27			16 25			17 25	
Kennishead	d				09 27			10 27				14 27			15 29			16 27			17 27	
East Kilbride	d		08 26	08 55		09 26	09 55		10 26		13 55		14 26	14 55		15 26	15 55		16 26	16 55		17 26
Hairmyres	d	00 02	08 30	08 59		09 30	09 59		10 30		13 59		14 30	14 59		15 30	15 59		16 30	16 59		17 30
Thorntonhall	d	00 06		09 02			10 02				14 02			15 02			16 02			17 02		
Busby	d	00 09	08 35	09 05		09 35	10 05		10 35		14 05		14 35	15 05		15 35	16 05		16 35	17 05		17 35
Clarkston	d	00 12	08 38	09 08		09 38	10 08		10 38		14 08		14 38	15 08		15 38	16 08		16 38	17 08		17 38
Giffnock	d	00 15	08 42	09 12		09 42	10 12		10 42		14 12		14 42	15 12		15 42	16 12		16 42	17 12		17 42
Thornliebank	d	00 18	08 44	09 14		09 44	10 14		10 44		14 14		14 44	15 14		15 44	16 14		16 44	17 14		17 44
Pollokshaws West	d	00 21	08 47	09 17	09 31	09 48	10 17	10 31	10 47		14 17	14 31	14 47	15 17	15 33	15 47	16 17	16 31	16 47	17 17	17 31	17 47
Crossmyloof	d	00 24	08 50	09 20		09 51	10 20		10 50		14 20		14 50	15 20		15 50	16 20		16 50	17 20		17 50
Glasgow Central	a	00 30	08 56	09 26	09 40	09 57	10 26	10 40	10 56		14 26	14 40	14 56	15 26	15 42	15 56	16 26	16 41	16 56	17 26	17 40	17 56

		SR	SR	SR	SR	SR	SR	SR	SR	SR	SR	SR	SR	SR	SR	SR	SR	SR	SR
						D	E						B						
Kilmarnock	d		17 55			18 55	18 55			19 55			20 57						
Kilmaurs	d		17 59			18 59	18 59			19 59			21 01						
Stewarton	d		18 04			19 04	19 04			20 04			21 06						
Dunlop	d		18 09			19 09	19 09			20 09			21 11						
Barrhead	d		18 19			19 19	19 19			20 20			21 21						
Nitshill	d		18 23			19 23	19 23			20 23									
Priesthill & Darnley	d		18 25			19 25	19 25			20 25									
Kennishead	d		18 27			19 27	19 27			20 27									
East Kilbride	d	17 55		18 26	18 55			19 26	19 55		20 26	20 55		21 26	21 55	22 26	22 55	23 26	23 58
Hairmyres	d	17 59		18 30	18 59			19 30	19 59		20 30	20 59		21 30	21 59	22 30	22 59	23 30	00 03
Thorntonhall	d	18 02			19 02				20 02			21 02			22 02		23 02		00 06
Busby	d	18 05		18 35	19 05			19 35	20 05		20 35	21 05		21 35	22 05	22 35	23 05	23 35	00 09
Clarkston	d	18 08		18 38	19 08			19 38	20 08		20 38	21 08		21 38	22 08	22 38	23 08	23 38	00 12
Giffnock	d	18 12		18 42	19 12			19 42	20 12		20 42	21 12		21 42	22 12	22 42	23 12	23 42	00 16
Thornliebank	d	18 14		18 44	19 14			19 44	20 14		20 44	21 14		21 44	22 14	22 44	23 14	23 44	00 18
Pollokshaws West	d	18 17	18 31	18 47	19 17	19 31	19 31	19 47	20 17	20 31	20 47	21 17		21 47	22 17	22 47	23 17	23 47	00 21
Crossmyloof	d	18 20		18 50	19 20			19 50	20 20		20 50	21 20		21 50	22 20	22 50	23 20	23 50	00 24
Glasgow Central	a	18 26	18 40	18 56	19 26	19 40	19 41	19 56	20 26	20 40	20 56	21 26	21 35	21 56	22 26	22 56	23 26	23 57	00 30

A From Stranraer
B From Carlisle
C not 20 May. From East Kilbride
D from 16 September
E until 9 September

Table T222-R

Mondays to Fridays

21 May to 7 December

Glasgow Central - East Kilbride, Barrhead and Kilmarnock

Miles	Miles			SR	SR	SR	SR	SR	SR	SR	SR	SR	SR	SR	SR	SR	SR	SR	SR	SR	SR	SR	SR
								A						◇ B			A			C			
0	0	**Glasgow Central**	d	06 12	06 26	06 47	06 54	07 09	07 13	07 24	07 37	07 42	07 52	08 08	08 15	08 22	08 37	08 48	08 57	09 13	09 18	09 27	09 43
2¼	2¼	Crossmyloof	d	06 18	06 32	06 53	07 00		07 19	07 30		07 50	08 00		08 22	08 29		08 56	09 03		09 25	09 34	
3¼	3¼	Pollokshaws West	d	06 21	06 35	06 56	07 03		07 22	07 33		07 52	08 02		08 24	08 32		08 59	09 06		09 27	09 37	
—	4½	Thornliebank	d	06 24		06 59			07 25			07 55			08 27			09 02			09 30		
—	5¼	Giffnock	d	06 27		07 02			07 28			07 59			08 31			09 05			09 34		
—	6½	Clarkston	d	06 31		07 06			07 32			08 03			08 35			09 09			09 38		
—	7¼	Busby	d	06 34		07 09			07 36			08 10			08 38			09 12			09 41		
—	8½	Thorntonhall	d	06 37											08 41			09 15					
—	10	Hairmyres	d	06 41		07 15			07 42			08 16			08 45			09 19			09 47		
—	11½	**East Kilbride**	a	06 45		07 18			07 49			08 19			08 48			09 23			09 50		
4½	—	Kennishead	d		06 38		07 06			07 36			08 05			08 35			09 09			09 40	
5	—	Priesthill & Darnley	d		06 40		07 08			07 38			08 08			08 37			09 11			09 42	
5¾	—	Nitshill	d		06 43		07 11			07 41			08 11			08 40			09 14			09 45	
7½	—	**Barrhead**	d		06 48		07a15	07 22		07a46	07 51		08a15	08 22		08a45	08 51		09a19			09a50	09 55
16½	—	Dunlop	d		07 00			07 34			08 03			08 34			09 03			09 35			10 07
18¾	—	Stewarton	d		07 04			07 38			08 07			08 38			09 07			09 39			10 11
22	—	Kilmaurs	d		07 08			07 43			08 11			08 43			09 12			09 44			10 15
24¾	—	**Kilmarnock**	a		07 14			07 49			08 17			08 49			09 18			09 50			10 21

		SR	SR	SR	SR	SR	SR	SR	SR	SR	SR	SR	SR	SR	SR	SR	SR	SR	SR	SR	SR	SR	SR
				A												A						A	
Glasgow Central	d	09 47	09 57	10 13	10 17	10 27	10 43	10 47	10 57	11 13	11 17	11 27	11 43	11 47	11 57	12 13	12 17	12 27	12 43	12 47	12 57	13 13	13 17
Crossmyloof	d	09 54	10 03		10 24	10 33		10 54	11 03		11 24	11 33		11 54	12 03		12 24	12 33		12 54	13 03		13 24
Pollokshaws West	d	09 56	10 06		10 26	10 36		10 56	11 06		11 26	11 36		11 56	12 06		12 26	12 36		12 56	13 06		13 26
Thornliebank	d	09 59			10 29			10 59			11 29			11 59			12 29			12 59			13 29
Giffnock	d	10 03			10 33			11 03			11 33			12 03			12 33			13 03			13 33
Clarkston	d	10 07			10 37			11 07			11 37			12 07			12 37			13 07			13 37
Busby	d	10 10			10 40			11 10			11 40			12 10			12 40			13 10			13 40
Thorntonhall	d	10 13						11 13						12 13						13 13			
Hairmyres	d	10 17			10 46			11 17			11 46			12 17			12 46			13 17			13 46
East Kilbride	a	10 20			10 49			11 20			11 49			12 20			12 49			13 20			13 49
Kennishead	d		10 09			10 39			11 09			11 39			12 09			12 39			13 09		
Priesthill & Darnley	d		10 11			10 41			11 11			11 41			12 11			12 41			13 11		
Nitshill	d		10 14			10 44			11 14			11 44			12 14			12 44			13 14		
Barrhead	d		10a19			10a49	10 55		11a19			11a49	11 55		12a19			12a49	12 55		13a19		
Dunlop	d			10 36			11 07			11 36			12 07			12 35			13 07			13 35	
Stewarton	d			10 40			11 11			11 40			12 11			12 39			13 11			13 39	
Kilmaurs	d			10 45			11 15			11 45			12 15			12 44			13 15			13 44	
Kilmarnock	a			10 51			11 21			11 51			12 21			12 50			13 21			13 50	

		SR	SR	SR	SR	SR	SR	SR	SR	SR	SR	SR	SR	SR	SR	SR	SR	SR	SR	SR	SR	SR
						◇ B												D				
Glasgow Central	d	13 27	13 43	13 47	13 58	14 13	14 17	14 27	14 43	14 47	14 57	15 13	15 17	15 28	15 43	15 47	15 57	16 13	16 17	16 27	16 43	16 47
Crossmyloof	d	13 33		13 54	14 04		14 24	14 33		14 54	15 03		15 24	15 34		15 54	16 03		16 24	16 33		16 54
Pollokshaws West	d	13 36		13 56	14 07		14 26	14 36		14 56	15 06		15 26	15 37		15 56	16 06		16 26	16 36		16 56
Thornliebank	d			13 59			14 29			14 59			15 29			15 59			16 29			16 59
Giffnock	d			14 03			14 33			15 03			15 33			16 03			16 33			17 03
Clarkston	d			14 07			14 37			15 07			15 37			16 07			16 37			17 07
Busby	d			14 10			14 40			15 10			15 40			16 10			16 40			17 10
Thorntonhall	d			14 13						15 13						16 13			16 43			17 13
Hairmyres	d			14 17			14 46			15 17			15 46			16 17			16 47			17 17
East Kilbride	a			14 20			14 49			15 20			15 49			16 20			16 50			17 20
Kennishead	d	13 39			14 10			14 39			15 09			15 40			16 09			16 39		
Priesthill & Darnley	d	13 41			14 12			14 41			15 11			15 42			16 11			16 41		
Nitshill	d	13 44			14 15			14 44			15 14			15 45			16 14			16 44		
Barrhead	d	13a49	13 55		14a20			14a49	14 55		15a19			15a50	15 56		16a19	16 25		16a49	16 55	
Dunlop	d		14 07			14 36			15 07			15 35			16 08			16 37			17 07	
Stewarton	d		14 11			14 40			15 11			15 39			16 12			16 41			17 11	
Kilmaurs	d		14 15			14 44			15 15			15 44			16 16			16 46			17 15	
Kilmarnock	a		14 21			14 50			15 21			15 50			16 22			16 52			17 21	

		SR	SR	SR	SR	SR	SR	SR	SR	SR	SR	SR	SR	SR	SR	SR	SR	SR	SR	SR	SR	SR	SR
				E				A				◇ B						A				F	
Glasgow Central	d	16 57	17 01	17 13	17 21	17 27	17 33	17 42	17 48	17 58	18 04	18 13	18 19	18 27	18 43	18 47	18 57	19 13	19 17	19 33	19 47	20 13	20 17
Crossmyloof	d	17 03	17 07			17 33	17 39		17 56	18 04	18 11		18 26	18 35		18 54	19 03		19 24	19 39	19 54		20 24
Pollokshaws West	d	17 06	17 10			17 36	17 42		17 58	18 07	18 13		18 28	18 38		18 56	19 06		19 26	19 42	19 56		20 26
Thornliebank	d		17 13				17 45		18 01		18 16		18 31			18 59			19 29		19 59		20 29
Giffnock	d		17 16				17 48		18 05		18 20		18 35			19 03			19 33		20 03		20 33
Clarkston	d		17 20		17 33		17 52		18 09		18 24		18 39			19 07			19 37		20 07		20 37
Busby	d		17 23				17 55		18 12		18 27		18 43			19 10			19 40		20 10		20 40
Thorntonhall	d						17 58				18 30					19 13					20 13		
Hairmyres	d		17 29		17 44		18 02		18 18		18 34		18 49			19 17			19 46		20 17		20 46
East Kilbride	a		17 34		17 47		18 06		18 22		18 37		18 52			19 20			19 49		20 20		20 49
Kennishead	d	17 09				17 39				18 10				18 41			19 09			19 45			
Priesthill & Darnley	d	17 11				17 41				18 12				18 43			19 11			19 47			
Nitshill	d	17 14				17 44				18 15				18 46			19 14			19 50			
Barrhead	d	17a19		17 25		17a49		17 55		18a20		18 26		18a51	18 56		19a19	19 25		19 54		20 25	
Dunlop	d			17 37				18 07				18 38			19 08			19 37		20 06		20 37	
Stewarton	d			17 41				18 11				18 42			19 12			19 41		20 10		20 41	
Kilmaurs	d			17 46				18 16				18 46			19 16			19 46		20 14		20 46	
Kilmarnock	a			17 52				18 22				18 52			19 22			19 52		20 20		20 52	

A To Carlisle
B To Stranraer
C To New Cumnock
D To Newcastle
E To Girvan
F To Dumfries

Table T222-R

Mondays to Fridays
21 May to 7 December

Glasgow Central - East Kilbride, Barrhead and Kilmarnock

		SR	SR	SR	SR	SR	SR	SR	SR	SR	SR	SR	SR
				A				◇ B				C	
Glasgow Central 15	d	20 33	20 47	21 13	21 17	21 33	21 47	22 13	22 17	22 33	22 47	23 13	23 17
Crossmyloof	d	20 39	20 54		21 24	21 39	21 54		22 24	22 39	22 54	23 19	23 24
Pollokshaws West	d	20 42	20 56		21 26	21 42	21 56		22 26	22 42	22 56	23 22	23 26
Thornliebank	d		20 59		21 29		21 59		22 29		22 59		23 29
Giffnock	d		21 03		21 33		22 03		22 33		23 03		23 33
Clarkston	d		21 07		21 37		22 07		22 37		23 07		23 37
Busby	d		21 10		21 40		22 10		22 40		23 10		23 40
Thorntonhall	d		21 13				22 13				23 13		23 43
Hairmyres	d		21 17		21 46		22 17		22 46		23 17		23 47
East Kilbride	a		21 20		21 49		22 20		22 49		23 20		23 50
Kennishead	d	20 45				21 45				22 45		23 25	
Priesthill & Darnley	d	20 47				21 47				22 47		23 27	
Nitshill	d	20 50				21 50				22 50		23 30	
Barrhead	d	20 54		21 26		21 54		22 25		22 54		23 35	
Dunlop	d	21 06		21 38		22 06		22 37		23 06		23 47	
Stewarton	d	21 10		21 42		22 10		22 41		23 10		23 51	
Kilmaurs	d	21 15		21 47		22 14		22 46		23 14		23 55	
Kilmarnock 3	a	21 21		21 53		22 20		22 52		23 20		00 01	

Saturdays
26 May to 8 December

		SR	SR	SR	SR	SR	SR	SR	SR	SR	SR	SR	SR	SR	SR	SR	SR	SR	SR	SR	SR	SR	SR
								A 🍴					◇ B			A 🍴			D				
Glasgow Central 15	d	00 12	00 18	06 12	06 28	06 47	06 54	07 07	07 20	07 37	07 47	07 53	08 07	08 17	08 23	08 37	08 47	08 57	09 13	09 17	09 27	09 43	09 47
Crossmyloof	d	00 18	00 24	06 18	06 34	06 55	07 00		07 26		07 54	08 00		08 24	08 29		08 54	09 04		09 24	09 34		09 54
Pollokshaws West	d	00 21	00 27	06 21	06 37	06 57	07 03		07 29		07 56	08 02		08 26	08 32		08 56	09 07		09 26	09 37		09 56
Thornliebank	d		00 30	06 24		07 00			07 32		07 59			08 29			08 59			09 29			09 59
Giffnock	d		00 33	06 27		07 04			07 35		08 03			08 33			09 03			09 33			10 03
Clarkston	d		00 37	06 31		07 08			07 39		08 07			08 37			09 07			09 37			10 07
Busby	d		00 40	06 34		07 11			07 42		08 10			08 40			09 10			09 40			10 10
Thorntonhall	d		00 43	06 37							08 13						09 13						10 13
Hairmyres	d		00 47	06 41		07 17			07 48		08 17			08 46			09 17			09 46			10 17
East Kilbride	a		00 51	06 45		07 20			07 52		08 20			08 49			09 20			09 49			10 20
Kennishead	d	00 24			06 40		07 06					08 05			08 35			09 10			09 40		
Priesthill & Darnley	d	00 26			06 42		07 08					08 08			08 37			09 12			09 42		
Nitshill	d	00 29			06 45		07 11					08 11			08 40			09 15			09 45		
Barrhead	d	00 33			06 50		07a15	07 22		07 51		08a15	08 22		08a45	08 51		09a20			09a50	09 55	
Dunlop	d	00 45			07 02			07 34		08 03			08 34			09 03			09 35			10 07	
Stewarton	d	00 49			07 06			07 38		08 07			08 38			09 07			09 39			10 11	
Kilmaurs	d	00 53			07 10			07 43		08 11			08 43			09 12			09 44			10 15	
Kilmarnock 3	a	00 59			07 16			07 49		08 17			08 49			09 18			09 50			10 21	

		SR	SR	SR	SR	SR	SR	SR	SR	SR	SR	SR	SR	SR	SR	SR	SR	SR	SR	SR	SR	SR	SR
			A 🍴												A 🍴						A 🍴		
Glasgow Central 15	d	09 57	10 13	10 17	10 27	10 43	10 47	10 57	11 13	11 17	11 27	11 43	11 47	11 57	12 13	12 17	12 27	12 43	12 47	12 57	13 13	13 17	13 27
Crossmyloof	d	10 03		10 24	10 33		10 54	11 03		11 24	11 33		11 54	12 03		12 24	12 33		12 54	13 03		13 24	13 33
Pollokshaws West	d	10 06		10 26	10 36		10 56	11 06		11 26	11 36		11 56	12 06		12 26	12 36		12 56	13 06		13 26	13 36
Thornliebank	d			10 29			10 59			11 29			11 59			12 29			12 59			13 29	
Giffnock	d			10 33			11 03			11 33			12 03			12 33			13 03			13 33	
Clarkston	d			10 37			11 07			11 37			12 07			12 37			13 07			13 37	
Busby	d			10 40			11 10			11 40			12 10			12 40			13 10			13 40	
Thorntonhall	d						11 13						12 13						13 13				
Hairmyres	d			10 46			11 17			11 46			12 17			12 46			13 17			13 46	
East Kilbride	a			10 49			11 20			11 49			12 20			12 49			13 20			13 49	
Kennishead	d	10 09			10 39			11 09			11 39			12 09			12 39			13 09			13 39
Priesthill & Darnley	d	10 11			10 41			11 11			11 41			12 11			12 41			13 11			13 41
Nitshill	d	10 14			10 44			11 14			11 44			12 14			12 44			13 14			13 44
Barrhead	d	10a19			10a49	10 55		11a19			11a49	11 55		12a19			12a49	12 55		13a19			13a49
Dunlop	d		10 36			11 07			11 36			12 07			12 35			13 07			13 35		
Stewarton	d		10 40			11 11			11 40			12 11			12 39			13 11			13 39		
Kilmaurs	d		10 45			11 15			11 45			12 15			12 44			13 15			13 44		
Kilmarnock 3	a		10 51			11 21			11 51			12 21			12 50			13 21			13 50		

		SR	SR	SR	SR	SR	SR	SR	SR	SR	SR	SR	SR	SR	SR	SR	SR	SR	SR	SR	SR	SR
					◇ B												E 🍴					
Glasgow Central 15	d	13 43	13 47	13 58	14 13	14 17	14 27	14 43	14 47	14 57	15 13	15 17	15 27	15 43	15 47	15 57	16 13	16 17	16 27	16 44	16 48	16 57
Crossmyloof	d		13 54	14 04		14 24	14 33		14 54	15 03		15 24	15 33		15 54	16 03		16 24	16 33		16 55	17 03
Pollokshaws West	d		13 56	14 07		14 26	14 36		14 56	15 06		15 26	15 36		15 56	16 06		16 26	16 36		16 57	17 06
Thornliebank	d		13 59			14 29			14 59			15 29			15 59			16 29			17 00	
Giffnock	d		14 03			14 33			15 03			15 33			16 03			16 33			17 04	
Clarkston	d		14 07			14 37			15 07			15 37			16 07			16 37			17 08	
Busby	d		14 10			14 40			15 10			15 40			16 10			16 40			17 11	
Thorntonhall	d		14 13						15 13						16 13			16 43			17 14	
Hairmyres	d		14 17			14 46			15 17			15 46			16 17			16 47			17 18	
East Kilbride	a		14 20			14 49			15 20			15 49			16 20			16 50			17 21	
Kennishead	d			14 10			14 39			15 09			15 39			16 09			16 39			17 09
Priesthill & Darnley	d			14 12			14 41			15 11			15 41			16 11			16 41			17 11
Nitshill	d			14 15			14 44			15 14			15 44			16 14			16 44			17 14
Barrhead	d	13 55		14a20			14a49	14 55		15a19			15a49	15 56		16a19	16 25		16a49	16 56		17a19
Dunlop	d	14 07			14 36			15 07			15 35			16 08			16 37			17 08		
Stewarton	d	14 11			14 40			15 11			15 39			16 12			16 41			17 12		
Kilmaurs	d	14 15			14 44			15 15			15 44			16 16			16 46			17 16		
Kilmarnock 3	a	14 21			14 50			15 21			15 50			16 22			16 52			17 22		

A To Carlisle
B To Stranraer
C To Dumfries
D To New Cumnock
E To Newcastle

Table T222-R

Saturdays
26 May to 8 December

Glasgow Central - East Kilbride, Barrhead and Kilmarnock

		SR	SR	SR	SR	SR	SR	SR	SR	SR	SR	SR	SR	SR	SR	SR	SR	SR	SR	SR	SR	SR
		A			B 🍴			◇ C						B 🍴				D				
Glasgow Central 15	d	17 13	17 17	17 27	17 43	17 47	17 57	18 13	18 17	18 27	18 43	18 47	18 57	19 13	19 17	19 31	19 47	20 13	20 17	20 33	20 47	21 13
Crossmyloof	d		17 24	17 33		17 54	18 03		18 24	18 35		18 54	19 03		19 24	19 39	19 54		20 24	20 39	20 54	
Pollokshaws West	d		17 26	17 36		17 56	18 06		18 26	18 38		18 56	19 06		19 26	19 42	19 56		20 26	20 42	20 56	
Thornliebank	d		17 29			17 59			18 29			18 59			19 29		19 59		20 29		20 59	
Giffnock	d		17 33			18 03			18 33			19 03			19 33		20 03		20 33		21 03	
Clarkston	d		17 37			18 07			18 37			19 07			19 37		20 07		20 37		21 07	
Busby	d		17 40			18 10			18 40			19 10			19 40		20 10		20 40		21 10	
Thorntonhall	d		17 43			18 13						19 13					20 13				21 13	
Hairmyres	d		17 47			18 17			18 46			19 17			19 46		20 17		20 46		21 17	
East Kilbride	a		17 50			18 20			18 49			19 20			19 49		20 20		20 49		21 20	
Kennishead	d			17 39			18 09			18 41			19 09			19 45				20 45		
Priesthill & Darnley	d			17 41			18 11			18 43			19 11			19 47				20 47		
Nitshill	d			17 44			18 14			18 46			19 14			19 50				20 50		
Barrhead	d	17 25		17a49	17 55		18a19	18 26		18a51	18 56		19a19	19 25		19 54		20 25		20 54		21 26
Dunlop	d	17 37			18 07			18 38			19 08			19 37		20 06		20 37		21 06		21 38
Stewarton	d	17 41			18 11			18 42			19 12			19 41		20 10		20 41		21 10		21 42
Kilmaurs	d	17 46			18 16			18 46			19 16			19 46		20 14		20 46		21 15		21 47
Kilmarnock 3	a	17 52			18 22			18 52			19 22			19 52		20 20		20 52		21 21		21 53

		SR	SR	SR	SR	SR	SR	SR	SR	SR
					B					
Glasgow Central 15	d	21 17	21 34	21 47	22 13	22 17	22 33	22 47	23 13	23 17
Crossmyloof	d	21 24	21 40	21 54		22 24	22 39	22 54	23 19	23 24
Pollokshaws West	d	21 26	21 43	21 56		22 26	22 42	22 56	23 22	23 26
Thornliebank	d	21 29		21 59		22 29		22 59		23 29
Giffnock	d	21 33		22 03		22 33		23 03		23 33
Clarkston	d	21 37		22 07		22 37		23 07		23 37
Busby	d	21 40		22 10		22 40		23 10		23 40
Thorntonhall	d			22 13				23 13		23 43
Hairmyres	d	21 46		22 17		22 46		23 17		23 47
East Kilbride	a	21 49		22 20		22 49		23 20		23 50
Kennishead	d		21 46				22 45		23 25	
Priesthill & Darnley	d		21 48				22 47		23 27	
Nitshill	d		21 51				22 50		23 30	
Barrhead	d		21 58		22 25		22 54		23 35	
Dunlop	d		22 10		22 37		23 06		23 47	
Stewarton	d		22 14		22 41		23 10		23 51	
Kilmaurs	d		22 18		22 46		23 14		23 55	
Kilmarnock 3	a		22 24		22 52		23 20		00 01	

Sundays
20 May to 2 December

		SR	SR	SR		SR	SR	SR	SR	SR	SR	SR		SR	SR	SR	SR	SR	SR	SR	SR	SR
									B													
Glasgow Central 15	d	08 03	08 18	08 48	and at the same minutes past each hour until	14 03	14 18	14 48	15 03	15 18	15 48	16 03	and at the same minutes past each hour until	18 18	18 48	19 03	19 18	19 48	20 18	20 48	21 18	21 48
Crossmyloof	d		08 24	08 54			14 24	14 54		15 24	15 54			18 24	18 54		19 24	19 54	20 24	20 54	21 24	21 54
Pollokshaws West	d	08 11	08 27	08 57		14 11	14 27	14 57	15 11	15 27	15 57	16 11		18 27	18 57	19 11	19 27	19 57	20 27	20 57	21 27	21 57
Thornliebank	d		08 30	09 00			14 30	15 00		15 30	16 00			18 30	19 00		19 30	20 00	20 30	21 00	21 30	22 00
Giffnock	d		08 33	09 03			14 33	15 03		15 33	16 03			18 33	19 03		19 33	20 03	20 33	21 03	21 33	22 03
Clarkston	d		08 37	09 07			14 37	15 07		15 37	16 07			18 37	19 07		19 37	20 07	20 37	21 07	21 37	22 07
Busby	d		08 40	09 10			14 40	15 10		15 40	16 10			18 40	19 10		19 40	20 10	20 40	21 10	21 40	22 10
Thorntonhall	d			09 13				15 13			16 13				19 13			20 13		21 13		22 13
Hairmyres	d		08 46	09 17			14 46	15 17		15 46	16 17			18 46	19 17		19 46	20 17	20 46	21 17	21 46	22 17
East Kilbride	a		08 50	09 21			14 50	15 21		15 50	16 21			18 50	19 21		19 50	20 21	20 50	21 21	21 50	22 21
Kennishead	d	08 14				14 14			15 14			16 14				19 14						
Priesthill & Darnley	d	08 16				14 16			15 16			16 16				19 16						
Nitshill	d	08 19				14 19			15 19			16 19				19 19						
Barrhead	d	08 23				14 23			15 24			16 23				19 23						
Dunlop	d	08 35				14 35			15 36			16 35				19 35						
Stewarton	d	08 39				14 39			15 40			16 39				19 39						
Kilmaurs	d	08 43				14 43			15 44			16 43				19 43						
Kilmarnock 3	a	08 49				14 49			15 50			16 49				19 49						

		SR	SR	SR	SR
		B			
Glasgow Central 15	d	22 12	22 18	22 48	23 18
Crossmyloof	d		22 24	22 54	23 24
Pollokshaws West	d		22 27	22 57	23 27
Thornliebank	d		22 30	23 00	23 30
Giffnock	d		22 33	23 03	23 33
Clarkston	d		22 37	23 07	23 37
Busby	d		22 40	23 10	23 40
Thorntonhall	d			23 13	23 43
Hairmyres	d		22 46	23 17	23 47
East Kilbride	a		22 50	23 21	23 51
Kennishead	d				
Priesthill & Darnley	d				
Nitshill	d				
Barrhead	d	22 24			
Dunlop	d	22 36			
Stewarton	d	22 40			
Kilmaurs	d	22 44			
Kilmarnock 3	a	22 48			

A To Girvan
B To Carlisle
C To Stranraer
D To Dumfries

Table T223-F

Mondays to Fridays

21 May to 7 December

Newton, Neilston, Cathcart Circle and Glasgow Central

Miles	Miles	Miles		SR MO A	SR B	SR	SR	SR	SR B	SR	SR	SR B		SR	SR B	SR	SR	SR	SR B	SR	SR	SR B		SR B
0	0	—	**Newton** 226 d			06 24		06 49			07 15					07 41		07 50						
1½	1½	—	Kirkhill d	00 01		06 27		06 52			07 18					07 44		07 53						
2¾	2¾	—	Burnside d	00 04		06 30		06 55			07 21					07 47		07 56						
3¾	3¾	—	Croftfoot d	00 07		06 32		06 57			07 23					07 49		07 58						
4¼	4¼	—	Kings Park d	00 09		06 34		06 59			07 25					07 51		08 02						
—	—	0	**Neilston** d				06 29			06 58				07 26			07 41			07 55	08 07			
—	—	3¾	Patterton d				06 35			07 04				07 32			07 47			08 01	08 13			
—	—	4¾	Whitecraigs d				06 37			07 06				07 34			07 49			08 04	08 15			
—	—	5½	Williamwood d				06 39			07 08				07 36			07 51			08 07	08 17			
—	—	7	Muirend d				06 42			07 12				07 39			07 54			08 10	08 20			
4¾	—	7¾	Cathcart d		06 31		06 45		07 02	07 15		07 34		07 42	07 47		07 58		08 11	08 15		08 27		08 25
—	5½	8½	Mount Florida d		06 33		06 47	07 03		07 17		07 36		07 44		07 55	08 00		08 14	08 17		08 29		
—	6	9	Crosshill d		06 35		06 49	07 05		07 19		07 38		07 46		07 57	08 02		08 16	08 19		08 31		
—	6½	9½	Queens Park d		06 37		06 51	07 07		07 21		07 40		07 48		07 59	08 05		08 18	08 22		08 33		
—	6¾	9¾	Pollokshields East d		06 38		06 53	07 08		07 23		07 43		07 51		08 01	08 07		08 20	08 23		08 34		
5¾	—	—	Langside d	00 13		06 38			07 05		07 29				07 49			08 06						08 28
6¼	—	—	Pollokshaws East d	00 15		06 40			07 07		07 31				07 51			08 08						08 30
6¾	—	—	Shawlands d	00 17		06 42			07 09		07 33				07 53			08 10						08 32
7½	—	—	Maxwell Park d	00 19		06 44			07 11		07 35				07 55			08 12						08 34
8	—	—	Pollokshields West d	00 21		06 48			07 13		07 37				07 57			08 14						08 36
10	8¾	11¾	**Glasgow Central** 15 226 a	00 27	06 43	06 56	06 58	07 14	07 19	07 28	07 44	07 49		07 56	08 03	08 06	08 12	08 20	08 25	08 28	08 33	08 39		08 43

	SR	SR B	SR	SR B	SR	SR	SR B	SR		SR	SR B	SR	SR	SR	SR B	SR	SR B	SR		SR	SR	SR B	SR	SR B
Newton 226 d	08 20				08 31			09 02				09 19		09 49				10 19			10 49			
Kirkhill d	08 23				08 36			09 09				09 22		09 52				10 22			10 52			
Burnside d	08 26				08 39			09 12				09 25		09 55				10 25			10 55			
Croftfoot d	08 28				08 42			09 14				09 27		09 57				10 27			10 57			
Kings Park d	08 30				08 44			09 16				09 29		09 59				10 29			10 59			
Neilston d			08 24			08 43				09 05			09 28			09 58				10 28			10 58	
Patterton d			08 30			08 49				09 11			09 34			10 04				10 34			11 04	
Whitecraigs d			08 33			08 51				09 13			09 36			10 06				10 36			11 06	
Williamwood d			08 35			08 53				09 15			09 38			10 08				10 38			11 08	
Muirend d			08 38			08 56				09 18			09 41			10 11				10 41			11 11	
Cathcart d		08 33	08 42	08 50		09 00	09 04			09 21	09 32		09 44		10 04	10 14	10 31			10 44		11 04	11 14	11 31
Mount Florida d	08 34		08 44	08 52		09 02		09 20		09 23	09 34		09 46	10 03		10 16	10 33			10 46	11 03		11 16	11 33
Crosshill d	08 36		08 46	08 54		09 04		09 22		09 25	09 36		09 48	10 05		10 18	10 35			10 48	11 05		11 18	11 35
Queens Park d	08 39		08 49	08 56		09 06		09 24		09 27	09 38		09 50	10 07		10 20	10 37			10 50	11 07		11 20	11 37
Pollokshields East d	08 42		08 51	08 58		09 07		09 25		09 29	09 39		09 52	10 08		10 22	10 39			10 52	11 08		11 22	11 39
Langside d		08 36			08 49		09 07					09 34			10 06			10 34				11 06		
Pollokshaws East d		08 38			08 51		09 09					09 36			10 08			10 36				11 08		
Shawlands d		08 40			08 54		09 11					09 38			10 10			10 38				11 10		
Maxwell Park d		08 42			08 56		09 13					09 40			10 12			10 40				11 12		
Pollokshields West d		08 46			09 00		09 15					09 43			10 14			10 42				11 14		
Glasgow Central 15 226 a	08 48	08 52	08 56	09 03	09 06	09 12	09 22	09 30		09 34	09 44	09 49	09 57	10 13	10 21	10 27	10 44	10 51		10 57	11 13	11 21	11 27	11 44

	SR	SR	SR	SR B		SR	SR B	SR	SR	SR	SR B	SR	SR B	SR		SR	SR	SR B	SR	SR B	SR	SR	SR	SR B
Newton 226 d	11 19		11 49					12 19		12 49				13 19			13 49				14 19		14 49	
Kirkhill d	11 22		11 52					12 22		12 52				13 22			13 52				14 22		14 52	
Burnside d	11 25		11 55					12 25		12 55				13 25			13 55				14 25		14 55	
Croftfoot d	11 27		11 57					12 27		12 57				13 27			13 57				14 27		14 57	
Kings Park d	11 29		11 59					12 29		12 59				13 29			13 59				14 29		14 59	
Neilston d		11 28				11 58			12 28			12 58				13 28			13 58			14 28		
Patterton d		11 34				12 04			12 34			13 04				13 34			14 04			14 34		
Whitecraigs d		11 36				12 06			12 36			13 06				13 36			14 06			14 36		
Williamwood d		11 38				12 08			12 38			13 08				13 38			14 08			14 38		
Muirend d		11 41				12 11			12 41			13 11				13 41			14 11			14 41		
Cathcart d		11 44		12 04		12 14	12 31		12 44		13 04	13 14	13 31			13 44		14 04	14 14	14 31		14 44		15 04
Mount Florida d		11 46	12 03			12 16	12 33		12 46	13 03		13 16	13 33			13 46	14 03		14 16	14 33		14 46	15 03	
Crosshill d		11 48	12 05			12 18	12 35		12 48	13 05		13 18	13 35			13 48	14 05		14 18	14 35		14 48	15 05	
Queens Park d		11 50	12 07			12 20	12 37		12 50	13 07		13 20	13 37			13 50	14 07		14 20	14 37		14 50	15 07	
Pollokshields East d		11 52	12 08			12 22	12 39		12 52	13 08		13 22	13 39			13 52	14 08		14 22	14 39		14 52	15 08	
Langside d	11 34			12 06				12 34			13 06			13 34				14 06			14 34			15 06
Pollokshaws East d	11 36			12 08				12 36			13 08			13 36				14 08			14 36			15 08
Shawlands d	11 38			12 10				12 38			13 10			13 38				14 10			14 38			15 10
Maxwell Park d	11 40			12 12				12 40			13 12			13 40				14 12			14 40			15 12
Pollokshields West d	11 42			12 14				12 42			13 14			13 42				14 14			14 42			15 14
Glasgow Central 15 226 a	11 49	11 57	12 13	12 21		12 27	12 44	12 50	12 57	13 13	13 21	13 27	13 44	13 49		13 57	14 13	14 21	14 27	14 44	14 51	14 57	15 13	15 24

		SR	SR B	SR	SR	SR	SR B	SR	SR B	SR		SR	SR	SR B	SR	SR B	SR	SR	SR B	SR		SR	SR B	SR
Newton 226 d				15 19		15 49				16 19			16 49					17 19				17 49		
Kirkhill d				15 22		15 52				16 22			16 52					17 22				17 52		
Burnside d				15 25		15 55				16 25			16 55					17 25				17 55		
Croftfoot d				15 27		15 57				16 27			16 57					17 27				17 57		
Kings Park d				15 29		15 59				16 29			16 59					17 31				17 59		
Neilston d		14 58			15 28			15 58				16 28			16 55		17 14			17 41				17 56
Patterton d		15 04			15 34			16 04				16 34			17 01		17 20			17 47				18 02
Whitecraigs d		15 06			15 36			16 06				16 36			17 03		17 22			17 50				18 04
Williamwood d		15 08			15 38			16 08				16 38			17 05		17 24			17 52				18 06
Muirend d		15 11			15 41			16 11				16 41			17 08		17 27			17 55				18 09
Cathcart d		15 14	15 31		15 44		16 07	16 14	16 31			16 44		17 04	17 12	17 23	17 30		17 41	17 58			18 04	18 12
Mount Florida d		15 16	15 33		15 46	16 03		16 16	16 33			16 46	17 03		17 14	17 25	17 32		17 43	18 00		18 03		18 14
Crosshill d		15 18	15 35		15 48	16 05		16 18	16 35			16 48	17 05		17 16	17 27	17 34		17 45	18 02		18 05		18 16
Queens Park d		15 20	15 37		15 50	16 07		16 20	16 37			16 50	17 07		17 18	17 29	17 36		17 47	18 04		18 07		18 18
Pollokshields East d		15 22	15 39		15 52	16 08		16 22	16 39			16 52	17 08		17 19	17 33	17 38		17 50	18 05		18 09		18 20
Langside d				15 34			16 10			16 34				17 06				17 35					18 06	
Pollokshaws East d				15 36			16 12			16 36				17 08				17 37					18 08	
Shawlands d				15 38			16 14			16 38				17 10				17 39					18 10	
Maxwell Park d				15 40			16 16			16 40				17 12				17 41					18 12	
Pollokshields West d				15 43			16 18			16 43				17 14				17 43					18 14	
Glasgow Central 15 226 a		15 27	15 44	15 49	15 57	16 13	16 24	16 27	16 44	16 53		16 57	17 17	17 22	17 24	17 39	17 43	17 49	17 56	18 10		18 14	18 20	18 25

A until 10 September. From Larkhall

B From Glasgow Central

	SR	SR A	SR	SR	SR	SR A		SR	SR A	SR	SR	SR	SR A	SR	SR A	SR		SR	SR	SR A	SR	SR A	SR	SR
Newton 226 d			18 19		18 49					19 19		19 49				20 19			20 49				21 19	
Kirkhill d			18 22		18 52					19 22		19 52				20 22			20 52				21 23	
Burnside d			18 25		18 55					19 25		19 55				20 25			20 55				21 26	
Croftfoot d			18 27		18 58					19 27		19 57				20 27			20 57				21 28	
Kings Park d			18 29		19 00					19 29		19 59				20 29			20 59				21 30	
Neilston d	18 06			18 28				18 58			19 28			19 58				20 28			20 58			21 28
Patterton d	18 12			18 34				19 04			19 34			20 04				20 34			21 04			21 34
Whitecraigs d	18 14			18 36				19 06			19 36			20 06				20 36			21 06			21 36
Williamwood d	18 16			18 38				19 08			19 38			20 08				20 38			21 08			21 38
Muirend d	18 19			18 41				19 11			19 41			20 11				20 41			21 11			21 41
Cathcart d	18 22	18 31		18 44		19 05		19 14	19 31		19 44		20 04	20 14	20 31			20 44		21 04	21 14	21 31		21 44
Mount Florida d	18 24	18 33		18 46	19 03			19 16	19 33		19 46	20 03		20 16	20 33			20 46	21 03		21 16	21 33		21 46
Crosshill d	18 26	18 35		18 48	19 05			19 18	19 35		19 48	20 05		20 18	20 35			20 48	21 05		21 18	21 35		21 48
Queens Park d	18 28	18 37		18 50	19 07			19 20	19 37		19 50	20 07		20 20	20 37			20 50	21 07		21 20	21 37		21 50
Pollokshields East d	18 30	18 39		18 52	19 09			19 22	19 39		19 52	20 10		20 22	20 39			20 52	21 10		21 22	21 38		21 52
Langside d			18 34			19 07				19 34			20 07			20 34				21 06			21 35	
Pollokshaws East d			18 36			19 09				19 36			20 09			20 36				21 08			21 37	
Shawlands d			18 38			19 11				19 38			20 11			20 38				21 10			21 39	
Maxwell Park d			18 40			19 13				19 40			20 13			20 40				21 12			21 41	
Pollokshields West d			18 43			19 15				19 43			20 15			20 43				21 14			21 44	
Glasgow Central 15 226 a	18 35	18 44	18 50	18 58	19 14	19 21		19 27	19 44	19 51	19 57	20 15	20 21	20 27	20 45	20 51		20 57	21 15	21 21	21 27	21 43	21 51	21 57

	SR	SR A		SR	SR A	SR	SR	SR	SR A	SR	SR A	SR		SR
Newton 226 d	21 49					22 19		22 49				23 19		
Kirkhill d	21 52					22 22		22 52				23 22		
Burnside d	21 55					22 25		22 55				23 25		
Croftfoot d	21 57					22 27		22 57				23 27		
Kings Park d	21 59					22 29		22 59				23 29		
Neilston d				21 58			22 28			22 58				23 28
Patterton d				22 04			22 34			23 04				23 34
Whitecraigs d				22 06			22 36			23 06				23 36
Williamwood d				22 08			22 38			23 08				23 38
Muirend d				22 11			22 41			23 11				23 41
Cathcart d		22 04		22 14	22 31		22 44		23 04	23 14	23 31			23 44
Mount Florida d	22 03			22 16	22 33		22 46	23 03		23 16	23 33			23 46
Crosshill d	22 05			22 18	22 35		22 48	23 05		23 18	23 35			23 48
Queens Park d	22 07			22 20	22 37		22 50	23 07		23 20	23 37			23 50
Pollokshields East d	22 08			22 22	22 39		22 52	23 09		23 22	23 39			23 52
Langside d		22 06				22 34			23 06			23 34		
Pollokshaws East d		22 08				22 36			23 08			23 36		
Shawlands d		22 10				22 38			23 10			23 38		
Maxwell Park d		22 12				22 40			23 12			23 40		
Pollokshields West d		22 14				22 43			23 14			23 43		
Glasgow Central 15 226 a	22 13	22 20		22 27	22 44	22 49	22 57	23 15	23 20	23 27	23 44	23 50		23 57

Saturdays

26 May to 8 December

	SR A	SR A	SR	SR	SR	SR	SR	SR	SR		SR	SR	SR	SR	SR A	SR	SR A	SR	SR		SR	SR A	SR	SR A
Newton 226 d			06 24		06 49		07 20		07 49			08 20		08 48				09 19			09 49			
Kirkhill d			06 27		06 52		07 23		07 52			08 23		08 52				09 22			09 52			
Burnside d			06 30		06 55		07 26		07 55			08 26		08 55				09 25			09 55			
Croftfoot d			06 32		06 57		07 28		07 57			08 28		08 57				09 27			09 57			
Kings Park d			06 34		06 59		07 30		07 59			08 30		08 59				09 29			09 59			
Neilston d				06 29		07 01		07 28			07 58		08 28			08 58			09 28				09 58	
Patterton d				06 35		07 07		07 34			08 04		08 34			09 04			09 34				10 04	
Whitecraigs d				06 37		07 09		07 36			08 06		08 36			09 06			09 36				10 06	
Williamwood d				06 39		07 11		07 38			08 08		08 38			09 08			09 38				10 08	
Muirend d				06 42		07 14		07 41			08 11		08 41			09 11			09 41				10 11	
Cathcart d	00 37	06 31		06 45		07 17		07 44			08 14		08 44		09 04	09 14	09 32		09 44			10 03	10 14	10 31
Mount Florida d	00 39	06 33		06 47	07 03	07 19		07 46	08 03		08 16		08 46	09 03		09 16	09 34		09 46		10 03		10 16	10 33
Crosshill d	00 41	06 35		06 49	07 05	07 21		07 48	08 05		08 18		08 48	09 05		09 18	09 36		09 48		10 05		10 18	10 35
Queens Park d	00 43	06 37		06 51	07 07	07 23		07 50	08 07		08 20		08 50	09 07		09 20	09 38		09 50		10 07		10 20	10 37
Pollokshields East d	00 44	06 38		06 53	07 08	07 25		07 52	08 08		08 22		08 52	09 08		09 22	09 39		09 52		10 08		10 22	10 39
Langside d			06 38				07 35					08 34			09 06			09 34				10 06		
Pollokshaws East d			06 40				07 37					08 36			09 08			09 36				10 08		
Shawlands d			06 42				07 39					08 38			09 10			09 38				10 10		
Maxwell Park d			06 44				07 41					08 40			09 12			09 40				10 12		
Pollokshields West d			06 48				07 43					08 43			09 14			09 43				10 14		
Glasgow Central 15 226 a	00 49	06 43	06 54	06 58	07 13	07 30	07 49	07 57	08 13		08 27	08 49	08 57	09 13	09 21	09 27	09 44	09 49	09 57		10 13	10 21	10 27	10 44

A From Glasgow Central

Table T223-F

Saturdays

26 May to 8 December

Newton, Neilston, Cathcart Circle and Glasgow Central

	SR	SR	SR	SR A	SR	SR A	SR	SR	SR	SR A	SR	SR A	SR	SR	SR	SR A	SR	SR A	SR	SR	SR
Newton 226 d	10 19		10 49				11 19		11 49				12 19		12 49				13 19		13 49
Kirkhill d	10 22		10 52				11 22		11 52				12 22		12 52				13 22		13 52
Burnside d	10 25		10 55				11 25		11 55				12 25		12 55				13 25		13 55
Croftfoot d	10 27		10 57				11 27		11 57				12 27		12 57				13 27		13 57
Kings Park d	10 29		10 59				11 29		11 59				12 29		12 59				13 29		13 59
Neilston d		10 28			10 58			11 28			11 58			12 28			12 58			13 28	
Patterton d		10 34			11 04			11 34			12 04			12 34			13 04			13 34	
Whitecraigs d		10 36			11 06			11 36			12 06			12 36			13 06			13 36	
Williamwood d		10 38			11 08			11 38			12 08			12 38			13 08			13 38	
Muirend d		10 41			11 11			11 41			12 11			12 41			13 11			13 41	
Cathcart d		10 44		11 03	11 14	11 31		11 44		12 04	12 14	12 31		12 44		13 04	13 14	13 31		13 44	
Mount Florida d		10 46	11 03		11 16	11 33		11 46	12 03		12 16	12 33		12 46	13 03		13 16	13 33		13 46	14 03
Crosshill d		10 48	11 05		11 18	11 35		11 48	12 05		12 18	12 35		12 48	13 05		13 18	13 35		13 48	14 05
Queens Park d		10 50	11 07		11 20	11 37		11 50	12 07		12 20	12 37		12 50	13 07		13 20	13 37		13 50	14 07
Pollokshields East d		10 52	11 08		11 22	11 39		11 52	12 08		12 22	12 39		12 52	13 08		13 22	13 39		13 52	14 08
Langside d	10 34			11 06			11 34			12 06			12 34			13 06			13 34		
Pollokshaws East d	10 36			11 08			11 36			12 08			12 36			13 08			13 36		
Shawlands d	10 38			11 10			11 38			12 10			12 38			13 10			13 38		
Maxwell Park d	10 40			11 12			11 40			12 12			12 40			13 12			13 40		
Pollokshields West d	10 42			11 14			11 42			12 14			12 42			13 14			13 42		
Glasgow Central 226 a	10 51	10 57	11 13	11 21	11 27	11 44	11 49	11 57	12 13	12 21	12 27	12 44	12 50	12 57	13 13	13 21	13 27	13 44	13 49	13 57	14 13

	SR A	SR	SR A	SR	SR	SR	SR A	SR	SR A	SR	SR	SR	SR A	SR	SR A	SR	SR	SR	SR A	SR	SR A	SR
Newton 226 d				14 19		14 49				15 19		15 49				16 19		16 49				17 19
Kirkhill d				14 22		14 52				15 22		15 52				16 22		16 52				17 22
Burnside d				14 25		14 55				15 25		15 55				16 25		16 55				17 25
Croftfoot d				14 27		14 57				15 27		15 57				16 27		16 57				17 27
Kings Park d				14 29		14 59				15 29		15 59				16 29		16 59				17 31
Neilston d		13 58			14 28			14 58			15 28			15 58			16 29			16 58		
Patterton d		14 04			14 34			15 04			15 34			16 04			16 35			17 04		
Whitecraigs d		14 06			14 36			15 06			15 36			16 06			16 37			17 06		
Williamwood d		14 08			14 38			15 08			15 38			16 08			16 39			17 08		
Muirend d		14 11			14 41			15 11			15 41			16 11			16 42			17 11		
Cathcart d	14 04	14 14	14 31		14 44		15 04	15 14	15 31		15 44		16 03	16 14	16 31		16 45		17 04	17 14	17 31	
Mount Florida d		14 16	14 33		14 46	15 03		15 16	15 33		15 46	16 03		16 16	16 33		16 47	17 03		17 16	17 33	
Crosshill d		14 18	14 35		14 48	15 05		15 18	15 35		15 48	16 05		16 18	16 35		16 49	17 05		17 18	17 35	
Queens Park d		14 20	14 37		14 50	15 07		15 20	15 37		15 50	16 07		16 20	16 37		16 51	17 07		17 20	17 37	
Pollokshields East d		14 22	14 39		14 52	15 08		15 22	15 39		15 52	16 08		16 22	16 39		16 53	17 08		17 22	17 39	
Langside d	14 06			14 34			15 06			15 34			16 06			16 34			17 06			17 35
Pollokshaws East d	14 08			14 36			15 08			15 36			16 08			16 36			17 08			17 37
Shawlands d	14 10			14 38			15 10			15 38			16 10			16 38			17 10			17 39
Maxwell Park d	14 12			14 40			15 12			15 40			16 12			16 40			17 12			17 41
Pollokshields West d	14 14			14 42			15 14			15 43			16 14			16 43			17 15			17 43
Glasgow Central 226 a	14 21	14 27	14 44	14 51	14 58	15 14	15 20	15 27	5 44	15 49	15 57	16 13	16 21	16 27	16 44	16 50	16 58	17 14	17 22	17 27	17 44	17 49

	SR	SR	SR A	SR	SR A	SR	SR	SR	SR A	SR	SR A	SR	SR	SR	SR A	SR	SR A	SR	SR	SR	SR A
Newton 226 d		17 49				18 19		18 49				19 19		19 49				20 19		20 49	
Kirkhill d		17 52				18 22		18 52				19 22		19 52				20 22		20 52	
Burnside d		17 55				18 25		18 55				19 25		19 55				20 25		20 55	
Croftfoot d		17 57				18 27		18 58				19 27		19 57				20 27		20 57	
Kings Park d		17 59				18 29		19 00				19 29		19 59				20 29		20 59	
Neilston d	17 28			17 58			18 28			18 58			19 28			19 58			20 28		
Patterton d	17 34			18 04			18 34			19 04			19 34			20 04			20 34		
Whitecraigs d	17 36			18 06			18 36			19 06			19 36			20 06			20 36		
Williamwood d	17 38			18 08			18 38			19 08			19 38			20 08			20 38		
Muirend d	17 41			18 11			18 41			19 11			19 41			20 11			20 41		
Cathcart d	17 44		18 04	18 14	18 31		18 44		19 05	19 14	19 31		19 44		20 04	20 14	20 31		20 44		21 04
Mount Florida d	17 46	18 03		18 16	18 33		18 46	19 03		19 16	19 33		19 46	20 03		20 16	20 33		20 46	21 03	
Crosshill d	17 48	18 05		18 18	18 35		18 48	19 05		19 18	19 35		19 48	20 05		20 18	20 35		20 48	21 05	
Queens Park d	17 50	18 07		18 20	18 37		18 50	19 07		19 20	19 37		19 50	20 07		20 20	20 37		20 50	21 07	
Pollokshields East d	17 52	18 08		18 22	18 39		18 52	19 09		19 22	19 39		19 52	20 10		20 22	20 39		20 52	21 09	
Langside d			18 06			18 34			19 07			19 34			20 06			20 34			21 06
Pollokshaws East d			18 08			18 36			19 09			19 36			20 08			20 36			21 08
Shawlands d			18 10			18 38			19 11			19 38			20 10			20 38			21 10
Maxwell Park d			18 12			18 40			19 13			19 40			20 12			20 40			21 12
Pollokshields West d			18 14			18 43			19 15			19 43			20 14			20 43			21 14
Glasgow Central 226 a	17 57	18 13	18 21	18 27	18 44	18 50	18 57	19 15	19 22	19 27	19 44	19 50	19 57	20 15	20 20	20 27	20 44	20 49	20 57	21 15	21 20

	SR	SR A	SR	SR	SR	SR A	SR	SR A	SR	SR	SR	SR A	SR	SR A	SR	SR
Newton 226 d			21 19		21 49				22 19		22 49				23 19	
Kirkhill d			21 23		21 52				22 22		22 52				23 22	
Burnside d			21 26		21 55				22 25		22 55				23 25	
Croftfoot d			21 28		21 57				22 27		22 57				23 27	
Kings Park d			21 30		21 59				22 29		22 59				23 29	
Neilston d	20 58			21 28			21 58			22 28			22 58			23 28
Patterton d	21 04			21 34			22 04			22 34			23 04			23 34
Whitecraigs d	21 06			21 36			22 06			22 36			23 06			23 36
Williamwood d	21 08			21 38			22 08			22 38			23 08			23 38
Muirend d	21 11			21 41			22 11			22 41			23 11			23 41
Cathcart d	21 14	21 31		21 44		22 04	22 14	22 31		22 44		23 04	23 14	23 31		23 44
Mount Florida d	21 16	21 33		21 46	22 03		22 16	22 33		22 46	23 03		23 16	23 33		23 46
Crosshill d	21 18	21 35		21 48	22 05		22 18	22 35		22 48	23 05		23 18	23 35		23 48
Queens Park d	21 20	21 37		21 50	22 07		22 20	22 37		22 50	23 07		23 20	23 37		23 50
Pollokshields East d	21 22	21 39		21 52	22 08		22 22	22 39		22 52	23 08		23 22	23 39		23 52
Langside d			21 35			22 06			22 34			23 06			23 34	
Pollokshaws East d			21 37			22 08			22 36			23 08			23 36	
Shawlands d			21 39			22 10			22 38			23 10			23 38	
Maxwell Park d			21 41			22 12			22 40			23 12			23 40	
Pollokshields West d			21 44			22 14			22 43			23 14			23 43	
Glasgow Central 226 a	21 27	21 44	21 50	21 57	22 13	22 25	22 27	22 44	22 49	22 57	23 13	23 20	23 27	23 44	23 50	23 57

A From Glasgow Central

Table T223-F

Sundays

20 May to 9 September

Newton, Neilston, Cathcart Circle and Glasgow Central

	SR A	SR	SR A	SR	SR A	SR	SR A	SR B	SR	SR A	SR	SR C	SR	SR B	SR A	SR	SR C	SR	SR B	SR A	SR	SR C
Newton 226 d	08 48		09 19		09 39		10 13	10 16		10 39		11 14		11 19	11 39		12 19		12 30	12 41		13 15
Kirkhill d					09 42			10 19		10 42				11 22	11 42				12 33	12 44		
Burnside d					09 45			10 22		10 45				11 25	11 45				12 36	12 47		
Croftfoot d					09 47			10 24		10 47				11 28	11 47				12 39	12 49		
Kings Park d					09 49			10 26		10 49				11 30	11 49				12 41	12 51		
Neilston d		08 48		09 19		09 48			10 19		10 48		11 19			11 48		12 19			12 48	
Patterton d		08 54		09 25		09 54			10 25		10 54		11 25			11 54		12 25			12 54	
Whitecraigs d		08 56		09 27		09 56			10 27		10 56		11 27			11 56		12 27			12 56	
Williamwood d		08 58		09 29		09 58			10 29		10 58		11 29			11 58		12 29			12 58	
Muirend d		09 01		09 32		10 01			10 32		11 01		11 32			12 01		12 32			13 01	
Cathcart d		09 05		09 36		10 05			10 36		11 05		11 36			12 05		12 36			13 05	
Mount Florida d		09 07		09 38	09 53	10 07			10 38	10 53	11 07		11 38		11 53	12 07		12 38		12 55	13 07	
Crosshill d		09 09		09 40	09 55	10 09			10 40	10 55	11 09		11 40		11 55	12 09		12 40		12 57	13 09	
Queens Park d		09 11		09 42	09 57	10 11			10 42	10 57	11 11		11 42		11 57	12 11		12 42		12 59	13 11	
Pollokshields East d		09 12		09 43	09 58	10 12			10 43	10 58	11 12		11 43		11 58	12 12		12 43		13 00	13 12	
Langside d								10 30						11 34					12 45			
Pollokshaws East d								10 32						11 36					12 47			
Shawlands d								10 34						11 39					12 49			
Maxwell Park d								10 36						11 42					12 51			
Pollokshields West d								10 39						11 44					12 53			
Glasgow Central 226 a	09 05	09 17	09 36	09 48	10 03	10 17	10 28	10 45	10 49	11 03	11 17	11 30	11 48	11 50	12 03	12 17	12 36	12 48	12 59	13 05	13 17	13 31

	SR	SR B	SR A	SR	SR C	SR B	SR	SR A	SR	SR C	SR	SR B	SR A	SR	SR C	SR	SR A	SR B	SR	SR C	SR	SR B
Newton 226 d		13 19	13 39		14 23	14 14		14 39		15 18		15 24	15 39		16 23		16 39	16 35		17 21		17 25
Kirkhill d		13 22	13 42			14 17		14 42				15 28	15 42				16 42	16 38				17 29
Burnside d		13 25	13 45			14 20		14 45				15 31	15 45				16 45	16 41				17 32
Croftfoot d		13 28	13 47			14 23		14 47				15 34	15 47				16 47	16 43				17 35
Kings Park d		13 30	13 49			14 25		14 49				15 37	15 49				16 49	16 45				17 38
Neilston d	13 19			13 48			14 19		14 48		15 19			15 48		16 19			16 48		17 19	
Patterton d	13 25			13 54			14 25		14 54		15 25			15 54		16 25			16 54		17 25	
Whitecraigs d	13 27			13 56			14 27		14 56		15 27			15 56		16 27			16 56		17 27	
Williamwood d	13 29			13 58			14 29		14 58		15 29			15 58		16 29			16 58		17 29	
Muirend d	13 32			14 01			14 32		15 01		15 32			16 01		16 32			17 01		17 32	
Cathcart d	13 36			14 05			14 36		15 05		15 36			16 05		16 36			17 04		17 36	
Mount Florida d	13 38		13 53	14 07			14 38	14 53	15 07		15 38		15 53	16 07		16 38	16 53		17 06		17 38	
Crosshill d	13 40		13 55	14 09			14 40	14 55	15 09		15 40		15 55	16 09		16 40	16 55		17 08		17 40	
Queens Park d	13 42		13 57	14 11			14 42	14 57	15 11		15 42		15 57	16 11		16 42	16 57		17 10		17 42	
Pollokshields East d	13 43		13 58	14 12			14 43	14 58	15 12		15 43		15 58	16 12		16 43	16 58		17 12		17 43	
Langside d		13 34				14 29						15 42						16 49				17 43
Pollokshaws East d		13 36				14 31						15 44						16 51				17 45
Shawlands d		13 39				14 33						15 47						16 53				17 48
Maxwell Park d		13 42				14 35						15 50						16 55				17 51
Pollokshields West d		13 44				14 38						15 53						16 59				17 54
Glasgow Central 226 a	13 48	13 50	14 03	14 17	14 37	14 44	14 48	15 03	15 17	15 38	15 48	15 59	16 03	16 17	16 38	16 48	17 03	17 05	17 17	17 35	17 48	18 00

	SR A	SR	SR C	SR	SR B	SR A	SR	SR C	SR B	SR	SR A	SR	SR B	SR	SR C	SR A	SR	SR C	SR	SR B	SR A
Newton 226 d	17 39		18 22		18 31	18 39		19 25	19 13		19 39		20 13		20 36	20 39		21 19		21 29	21 39
Kirkhill d	17 42				18 34	18 42			19 16		19 42		20 16			20 42				21 32	21 42
Burnside d	17 45				18 37	18 45			19 19		19 45		20 19			20 45				21 35	21 45
Croftfoot d	17 47				18 40	18 47			19 22		19 47		20 22			20 48				21 38	21 47
Kings Park d	17 49				18 42	18 49			19 24		19 49		20 24			20 50				21 40	21 49
Neilston d		17 48		18 19			18 48			19 19		19 48		20 19			20 48		21 19		
Patterton d		17 54		18 25			18 54			19 25		19 54		20 25			20 54		21 25		
Whitecraigs d		17 56		18 27			18 56			19 27		19 56		20 27			20 56		21 27		
Williamwood d		17 58		18 29			18 58			19 29		19 58		20 29			20 58		21 29		
Muirend d		18 01		18 32			19 01			19 32		20 01		20 32			21 01		21 32		
Cathcart d		18 05		18 36			19 05			19 36		20 05		20 36			21 05		21 36		
Mount Florida d	17 53	18 07		18 38		18 53	19 07			19 38	19 53	20 07		20 38		20 53	21 07		21 38		21 53
Crosshill d	17 55	18 09		18 40		18 55	19 09			19 40	19 55	20 09		20 40		20 55	21 09		21 40		21 55
Queens Park d	17 57	18 11		18 42		18 57	19 11			19 42	19 57	20 11		20 42		20 57	21 11		21 42		21 57
Pollokshields East d	17 58	18 12		18 43		18 58	19 12			19 43	19 58	20 12		20 43		20 59	21 12		21 43		21 58
Langside d					18 46				19 28				20 28							21 44	
Pollokshaws East d					18 48				19 30				20 30							21 46	
Shawlands d					18 50				19 32				20 32							21 48	
Maxwell Park d					18 53				19 34				20 34							21 51	
Pollokshields West d					18 55				19 36				20 36							21 53	
Glasgow Central 226 a	18 03	18 17	18 36	18 48	19 01	19 03	19 17	19 39	19 43	19 48	20 03	20 17	20 42	20 48	20 52	21 04	21 17	21 33	21 48	21 59	22 03

	SR	SR B	SR	SR C	SR A	SR	SR C	SR	SR A	SR B	SR B
Newton 226 d		22 12		22 36	22 40		23 25		23 39	23 28	23 58
Kirkhill d		22 15			22 43					23 31	00 01
Burnside d		22 18			22 46					23 34	00 04
Croftfoot d		22 21			22 48					23 36	00 07
Kings Park d		22 23			22 50					23 38	00 09
Neilston d	21 48		22 19			22 48		23 19			
Patterton d	21 54		22 25			22 54		23 25			
Whitecraigs d	21 56		22 27			22 57		23 27			
Williamwood d	21 58		22 29			23 00		23 29			
Muirend d	22 01		22 32			23 03		23 32			
Cathcart d	22 05		22 36			23 07		23 36			
Mount Florida d	22 07		22 38		22 54	23 11		23 38			
Crosshill d	22 09		22 40		22 56	23 13		23 40			
Queens Park d	22 11		22 42		22 58	23 15		23 42			
Pollokshields East d	22 12		22 43		22 59	23 16		23 43			
Langside d		22 27								23 42	00 13
Pollokshaws East d		22 29								23 44	00 15
Shawlands d		22 31								23 46	00 17
Maxwell Park d		22 33								23 48	00 19
Pollokshields West d		22 35								23 53	00 21
Glasgow Central 226 a	22 18	22 41	22 50	22 52	23 04	23 21	23 39	23 48	23 55	23 59	00 27

A From Motherwell B From Larkhall C From Lanark

Table T223-F

Sundays

16 September to 2 December

Newton, Neilston, Cathcart Circle and Glasgow Central

	SR	SR	SR	SR	SR	SR	SR	SR	SR	SR	SR		SR	SR	SR	SR	SR	SR	SR	SR	SR	SR
Newton 226 d		09 09		09 39		10 09		10 39		11 09			19 39		20 09		20 39		21 09		21 39	
Kirkhill d		09 12		09 42		10 12		10 42		11 12			19 42		20 12		20 42		21 12		21 42	
Burnside d		09 15		09 45		10 15		10 45		11 15			19 45		20 15		20 45		21 15		21 45	
Croftfoot d		09 17		09 47		10 17		10 47		11 17			19 47		20 17		20 47		21 17		21 47	
Kings Park d		09 19		09 49		10 19		10 49		11 19			19 49		20 19		20 49		21 19		21 49	
Neilston d	08 48		09 19		09 48		10 19		10 48		11 19			19 48		20 19		20 48		21 19		21 48
Patterton d	08 54		09 25		09 54		10 25		10 54		11 25			19 54		20 25		20 54		21 25		21 54
Whitecraigs d	08 56		09 27		09 56		10 27		10 56		11 27	and at the same minutes past each hour until		19 56		20 27		20 56		21 27		21 56
Williamwood d	08 58		09 29		09 58		10 29		10 58		11 29			19 58		20 29		20 58		21 29		21 58
Muirend d	09 01		09 32		10 01		10 32		11 01		11 32			20 01		20 32		21 01		21 32		22 01
Cathcart d	09 05		09 36		10 05		10 36		11 05		11 36			20 05		20 36		21 05		21 36		22 05
Mount Florida d	09 07		09 38	09 53	10 07		10 38	10 53	11 07		11 38		19 53	20 07		20 38	20 53	21 07		21 38	21 53	22 07
Crosshill d	09 09		09 40	09 55	10 09		10 40	10 55	11 09		11 40		19 55	20 09		20 40	20 55	21 09		21 40	21 55	22 09
Queens Park d	09 11		09 42	09 57	10 11		10 42	10 57	11 11		11 42		19 57	20 11		20 42	20 57	21 11		21 42	21 57	22 11
Pollokshields East d	09 12		09 43	09 58	10 12		10 43	10 58	11 12		11 43		19 58	20 12		20 43	20 58	21 12		21 43	21 58	22 12
Langside d		09 23				10 23				11 23					20 23				21 23			
Pollokshaws East d		09 25				10 25				11 25					20 25				21 25			
Shawlands d		09 27				10 27				11 27					20 27				21 27			
Maxwell Park d		09 29				10 29				11 29					20 29				21 29			
Pollokshields West d		09 32				10 32				11 32					20 32				21 31			
Glasgow Central 226 a	09 17	09 38	09 48	10 03	10 17	10 38	10 49	11 03	11 17	11 38	11 48		20 03	20 17	20 38	20 48	21 03	21 17	21 37	21 48	22 03	22 18

	SR	SR	SR	SR	SR	SR
Newton 226 d	22 09		22 39		23 09	
Kirkhill d	22 12		22 42		23 12	
Burnside d	22 15		22 45		23 15	
Croftfoot d	22 17		22 47		23 17	
Kings Park d	22 19		22 49		23 19	
Neilston d		22 19		22 48		23 19
Patterton d		22 25		22 54		23 25
Whitecraigs d		22 27		22 56		23 27
Williamwood d		22 29		22 58		23 29
Muirend d		22 32		23 01		23 32
Cathcart d		22 36		23 05		23 36
Mount Florida d		22 38	22 53	23 07		23 38
Crosshill d		22 40	22 55	23 09		23 40
Queens Park d		22 42	22 57	23 11		23 42
Pollokshields East d		22 43	22 58	23 12		23 43
Langside d	22 23				23 23	
Pollokshaws East d	22 25				23 25	
Shawlands d	22 27				23 27	
Maxwell Park d	22 29				23 29	
Pollokshields West d	22 31				23 31	
Glasgow Central 226 a	22 37	22 50	23 03	23 17	23 37	23 48

Table T223-R

Mondays to Fridays

21 May to 7 December

Glasgow Central, Cathcart Circle, Neilston and Newton

Miles	Miles	Miles		SR A	SR	SR	SR	SR	SR A	SR	SR	SR	SR A	SR	SR	SR A	SR	SR	SR A	SR	SR	SR A
0	0	0	**Glasgow Central** 226 d	06 14	06 17	06 20	06 34	06 36	06 50	06 58	07 03	07 06	07 17	07 21	07 28	07 34	07 45	07 50	07 54	07 57	08 02	08 11
2¼	—	—	Pollokshields West d	06 21				06 42			07 09		07 23				07 51		08 00			08 17
2¾	—	—	Maxwell Park d	06 23				06 44			07 11		07 25				07 53		08 02			08 19
3½	—	—	Shawlands d	06 25				06 46			07 13		07 27				07 55		08 04			08 21
3¾	—	—	Pollokshaws East d	06 26				06 48			07 14		07 29				07 57		08 05			08 22
4¼	—	—	Langside d	06 28				06 50			07 16		07 31				07 59		08 07			08 24
—	1¾	1¾	Pollokshields East d		06 22	06 25	06 39		06 55	07 03		07 11		07 26	07 33	07 39				08 02	08 07	
—	2¼	2¼	Queens Park d		06 23	06 27	06 40		06 56	07 04		07 12		07 27	07 35	07 41				08 03	08 08	
—	2½	2½	Crosshill d		06 25	06 29	06 42		06 58	07 06		07 14		07 29	07 37	07 43				08 05	08 10	
—	3¼	3¼	Mount Florida d		06 27	06 31	06 44		07 00	07 08		07 16		07 31	07 39	07 45				08 07	08 12	
5¼	—	4	Cathcart d	06a31	06 29		06 46		07a02	07 10		07 20	07a34		07 41	07a47			08a11		08 14	08a27
—	—	4¾	Muirend d		06 32		06 49			07 13		07 23			07 43			08 00			08 17	
—	—	6	Williamwood d		06 35		06 52			07 16		07 26			07 46			08 03			08 20	
—	—	6¾	Whitecraigs d		06 37		06 54			07 18		07 28			07 49			08 05			08 22	
—	—	7¾	Patterton d		06 40		06 57			07 21		07 31			07 51			08 08			08 25	
—	—	11¾	**Neilston** a		06 46		07 03			07 27		07 38			07 58			08 14			08 31	
5¾	4½	—	Kings Park d			06 34		06 54			07 20			07 34			08 05			08 10		
6	4¾	—	Croftfoot d			06 36		06 57			07 22			07 36			08 07			08 12		
7	5¾	—	Burnside d			06 38		07 00			07 25			07 39			08 09			08 15		
8½	7¼	—	Kirkhill a			06 41		07 03			07 28			07 42			08 12			08 18		
10	8¾	—	**Newton** 226 a			06 44		07 06			07 31			07 45			08 15			08 21		

	SR A	SR A	SR	SR	SR A	SR	SR	SR A	SR	SR A	SR	SR	SR	SR A	SR	SR A	SR	SR	SR	SR A	SR	
Glasgow Central 226 d	08 13	08 18	08 20	08 26	08 34	08 42	08 46	08 51	09 05	09 16	09 20	09 35	09 45	09 51	10 06	10 15	10 20	10 35	10 45	10 51	11 05	
Pollokshields West d					08 40		08 52			09 22			09 51			10 21			10 51			
Maxwell Park d					08 42		08 54			09 24			09 53			10 23			10 53			
Shawlands d					08 44		08 56			09 26			09 55			10 25			10 55			
Pollokshaws East d					08 45		08 57			09 27			09 56			10 26			10 56			
Langside d					08 47		09 00			09 29			09 58			10 28			10 58			
Pollokshields East d	08 18	08 23	08 26	08 31		08 47		08 57	09 10		09 25	09 40		09 56	10 11		10 25	10 40		10 56	11 10	and at the same minutes past each hour until
Queens Park d	08 19	08 24	08 28	08 32		08 48		08 58	09 11		09 26	09 41		09 57	10 12		10 26	10 41		10 57	11 11	
Crosshill d	08 21	08 26	08 30	08 34		08 50		09 00	09 13		09 28	09 43		09 59	10 14		10 28	10 43		10 59	11 13	
Mount Florida d	08 23	08 28	08 32	08 36		08 52		09 02	09 15		09 30	09 45		10 01	10 16		10 30	10 45		11 01	11 15	
Cathcart d	08a25	08a30		08 38	08a50	08 54		09a04	09 17	09a32		09 47		10a04	10 18	10a31		10 47		11a04	11 17	
Muirend d				08 41		08 57			09 20			09 50			10 21			10 50			11 20	
Williamwood d				08 44		09 00			09 23			09 53			10 24			10 53			11 23	
Whitecraigs d				08 46		09 02			09 25			09 55			10 26			10 55			11 25	
Patterton d				08 49		09 05			09 28			09 58			10 29			10 58			11 28	
Neilston a				08 55		09 11			09 34			10 04			10 35			11 04			11 34	
Kings Park d			08 35				09 04				09 34		10 04				10 34		11 04			
Croftfoot d			08 37				09 06				09 36		10 06				10 36		11 06			
Burnside d			08 39				09 08				09 38		10 08				10 38		11 08			
Kirkhill a			08 42				09 11				09 41		10 11				10 41		11 11			
Newton 226 a			08 45				09 14				09 44		10 14				10 44		11 14			

	SR A	SR	SR	SR	SR A	SR	SR A	SR	SR	SR	SR A	SR	SR A	SR	SR	SR	SR A	SR	SR A	SR	SR	SR
Glasgow Central 226 d	13 15	13 20	13 35	13 45	13 51	14 05	14 15	14 20	14 35	14 45	14 51	15 06	15 15	15 20	15 35	15 45	15 51	16 08	16 15	16 20	16 35	16 45
Pollokshields West d	13 21			13 51			14 21			14 51			15 21			15 51			16 21			16 51
Maxwell Park d	13 23			13 53			14 23			14 53			15 23			15 53			16 23			16 53
Shawlands d	13 25			13 55			14 25			14 55			15 25			15 55			16 25			16 55
Pollokshaws East d	13 26			13 56			14 26			14 56			15 26			15 56			16 26			16 56
Langside d	13 28			13 58			14 28			14 58			15 28			15 58			16 28			16 58
Pollokshields East d		13 25	13 40		13 56	14 10		14 25	14 40		14 56	15 11		15 25	15 40		15 56	16 13		16 25	16 40	
Queens Park d		13 26	13 41		13 57	14 11		14 26	14 41		14 57	15 12		15 26	15 41		15 57	16 14		16 27	16 41	
Crosshill d		13 28	13 43		13 59	14 13		14 28	14 43		14 59	15 14		15 28	15 43		16 03	16 16		16 29	16 43	
Mount Florida d		13 30	13 45		14 01	14 15		14 30	14 45		15 01	15 16		15 30	15 45		16 05	16 18		16 31	16 45	
Cathcart d	13a31		13 47		14a04	14 17	14a31		14 47		15a04	15 18	15a31		15 47		16a07	16 20	16a31		16 47	
Muirend d			13 50			14 20			14 50			15 21			15 50			16 23			16 50	
Williamwood d			13 53			14 23			14 53			15 24			15 53			16 26			16 53	
Whitecraigs d			13 55			14 25			14 55			15 26			15 55			16 28			16 55	
Patterton d			13 58			14 28			14 58			15 29			15 58			16 31			16 58	
Neilston a			14 04			14 34			15 04			15 35			16 04			16 37			17 04	
Kings Park d		13 34		14 04				14 34		15 04				15 34		16 04				16 34		17 04
Croftfoot d		13 36		14 06				14 36		15 06				15 36		16 06				16 36		17 06
Burnside d		13 38		14 08				14 38		15 08				15 38		16 08				16 38		17 08
Kirkhill a		13 41		14 11				14 41		15 11				15 41		16 11				16 41		17 11
Newton 226 a		13 44		14 14				14 44		15 14				15 44		16 14				16 44		17 14

	SR A	SR	SR A	SR	SR	SR A	SR	SR	SR	SR	SR A	SR	SR A	SR	SR	SR	SR A	SR	SR A	SR	SR
Glasgow Central 226 d	16 51	17 03	17 06	17 11	17 18	17 23	17 25	17 31	17 37	17 45	17 51	18 06	18 15	18 21	18 35	18 45	18 50	19 05	19 15	19 20	19 35
Pollokshields West d			17 13			17 30				17 51			18 21			18 51			19 21		
Maxwell Park d			17 15			17 32				17 53			18 23			18 53			19 23		
Shawlands d			17 17			17 34				17 55			18 25			18 55			19 25		
Pollokshaws East d			17 19			17 35				17 56			18 26			18 56			19 26		
Langside d			17 21			17 37				17 58			18 28			18 59			19 28		
Pollokshields East d	16 56	17 08		17 16			17 30	17 36	17 42		17 56	18 12		18 26	18 40		18 57	19 10		19 25	19 40
Queens Park d	16 57	17 09		17 18			17 31	17 37	17 43		17 58	18 13		18 27	18 41		18 58	19 11		19 26	19 41
Crosshill d	16 59	17 11		17 20			17 33	17 39	17 45		18 00	18 15		18 29	18 43		19 00	19 13		19 28	19 43
Mount Florida d	17 01	17 13		17 22			17 35	17 41	17 47		18 02	18 17		18 31	18 45		19 02	19 15		19 30	19 45
Cathcart d	17a04	17 15	17a23			17a40	17 37		17 49		18a04	18 19	18a31		18 47		19a05	19 17	19a31		19 47
Muirend d		17 18			17 28		17 40		17 52			18 22			18 50			19 20			19 50
Williamwood d		17 21			17 31		17 44		17 55			18 25			18 53			19 23			19 53
Whitecraigs d		17 23			17 33		17 46		17 57			18 27			18 55			19 25			19 55
Patterton d		17 26			17 36		17 49		18 00			18 30			18 58			19 28			19 58
Neilston a		17 32			17 44		17 55		18 06			18 36			19 04			19 34			20 04
Kings Park d				17 25				17 44		18 04				18 34		19 04				19 34	
Croftfoot d				17 28				17 46		18 06				18 36		19 06				19 36	
Burnside d				17 31				17 49		18 08				18 39		19 08				19 38	
Kirkhill a				17 34				17 52		18 11				18 42		19 11				19 41	
Newton 226 a				17 40				17 57		18 14				18 45		19 14				19 44	

A To Glasgow Central

Glasgow Central, Cathcart Circle, Neilston and Newton

Mondays to Fridays

21 May to 7 December

		SR	SR A	SR	SR A	SR	SR	SR	SR A	SR	SR A	SR	SR	SR	SR A	SR	SR A	SR	SR	SR	SR A	SR	SR A
Glasgow Central 15	226 d	19 45	19 52	20 05	20 15	20 20	20 35	20 45	20 50	21 05	21 15	21 20	21 35	21 45	21 50	22 05	22 15	22 20	22 35	22 45	22 50	23 05	23 15
Pollokshields West	d	19 51			20 21			20 51			21 21			21 51			22 21			22 51			23 21
Maxwell Park	d	19 53			20 23			20 53			21 23			21 53			22 23			22 53			23 23
Shawlands	d	19 55			20 25			20 55			21 25			21 55			22 25			22 55			23 25
Pollokshaws East	d	19 56			20 26			20 56			21 26			21 56			22 26			22 56			23 26
Langside	d	19 58			20 28			20 58			21 28			21 58			22 28			22 58			23 28
Pollokshields East	d		19 57	20 10		20 25	20 40		20 55	21 10		21 25	21 40		21 55	22 10		22 25	22 40		22 55	23 10	
Queens Park	d		19 58	20 11		20 26	20 41		20 56	21 11		21 26	21 41		21 56	22 11		22 26	22 41		22 56	23 11	
Crosshill	d		20 00	20 13		20 28	20 43		20 58	21 13		21 28	21 43		21 58	22 13		22 28	22 43		22 58	23 13	
Mount Florida	d		20 02	20 15		20 30	20 45		21 00	21 15		21 30	21 45		22 00	22 15		22 30	22 45		23 00	23 15	
Cathcart	d		20a04	20 17	20a31		20 47		21a04	21 17	21a31		21 47		22a04	22 17	22a31		22 47		23a04	23 17	23a31
Muirend	d			20 20			20 50			21 20			21 50			22 20			22 50			23 20	
Williamwood	d			20 23			20 53			21 23			21 53			22 23			22 53			23 23	
Whitecraigs	d			20 25			20 55			21 25			21 55			22 25			22 55			23 25	
Patterton	d			20 28			20 58			21 28			21 58			22 28			22 58			23 28	
Neilston	a			20 34			21 04			21 34			22 04			22 34			23 04			23 34	
Kings Park	d	20 04				20 34		21 04				21 34		22 04				22 34		23 04			
Croftfoot	d	20 06				20 36		21 06				21 36		22 06				22 36		23 06			
Burnside	d	20 08				20 38		21 08				21 38		22 08				22 38		23 08			
Kirkhill	a	20 11				20 41		21 11				21 41		22 11				22 41		23 11			
Newton	226 a	20 14				20 44		21 14				21 44		22 14				22 44		23 14			

		SR	SR FO
Glasgow Central 15	226 d	23 20	23 50
Pollokshields West	d		
Maxwell Park	d		
Shawlands	d		
Pollokshaws East	d		
Langside	d		
Pollokshields East	d	23 25	23 55
Queens Park	d	23 26	23 56
Crosshill	d	23 28	23 58
Mount Florida	d	23 30	23 59
Cathcart	d		
Muirend	d		
Williamwood	d		
Whitecraigs	d		
Patterton	d		
Neilston	a		
Kings Park	d	23 34	00 04
Croftfoot	d	23 36	00 06
Burnside	d	23 38	00 08
Kirkhill	a	23 41	00 11
Newton	226 a	23 44	00 14

Saturdays

26 May to 8 December

		SR B	SR	SR A	SR A	SR	SR	SR	SR	SR	SR	SR	SR	SR	SR	SR	SR	SR A	SR	SR A	SR	SR	SR
Glasgow Central 15	226 d		00 05	00 20	06 15	06 17	06 20	06 34	06 45	07 05	07 18	07 35	07 45	08 05	08 20	08 35	08 45	08 51	09 05	09 15	09 20	09 35	09 45
Pollokshields West	d			00 27	06 21				06 51				07 51				08 51			09 22			09 51
Maxwell Park	d			00 29	06 23				06 53				07 53				08 53			09 24			09 53
Shawlands	d			00 31	06 25				06 55				07 55				08 55			09 26			09 55
Pollokshaws East	d			00 32	06 26				06 56				07 56				08 56			09 27			09 56
Langside	d			00 34	06 28				06 59				07 58				08 58			09 29			09 58
Pollokshields East	d		00 10			06 22	06 25	06 39		07 10	07 23	07 40		08 10	08 25	08 40		08 56	09 10		09 25	09 40	
Queens Park	d		00 11			06 23	06 27	06 40		07 11	07 24	07 41		08 11	08 26	08 41		08 58	09 11		09 26	09 41	
Crosshill	d		00 13			06 25	06 29	06 42		07 13	07 26	07 43		08 13	08 28	08 43		09 00	09 13		09 28	09 43	
Mount Florida	d		00 15			06 27	06 31	06 44		07 15	07 28	07 45		08 15	08 30	08 45		09 02	09 15		09 30	09 45	
Cathcart	d		00 17	00a37	06a31	06 29		06 46		07 17		07 47		08 17		08 47		09a04	09 17	09a32		09 47	
Muirend	d		00 20			06 32		06 49		07 20		07 50		08 20		08 50			09 20			09 50	
Williamwood	d		00 23			06 35		06 52		07 23		07 53		08 23		08 53			09 23			09 53	
Whitecraigs	d		00 25			06 37		06 54		07 25		07 55		08 25		08 55			09 25			09 55	
Patterton	d		00 28			06 40		06 57		07 28		07 58		08 28		08 58			09 28			09 58	
Neilston	a		00 34			06 46		07 03		07 34		08 04		08 34		09 04			09 34			10 04	
Kings Park	d	00 04					06 34		07 05		07 31		08 05		08 33		09 04				09 34		10 04
Croftfoot	d	00 06					06 36		07 07		07 33		08 07		08 35		09 06				09 36		10 06
Burnside	d	00 08					06 38		07 09		07 36		08 09		08 38		09 08				09 38		10 08
Kirkhill	a	00 11					06 41		07 12		07 39		08 12		08 41		09 11				09 41		10 11
Newton	226 a	00 14					06 44		07 15		07 42		08 15		08 44		09 14				09 44		10 14

A To Glasgow Central

B From Glasgow Central

Glasgow Central, Cathcart Circle, Neilston and Newton

Saturdays

26 May to 8 December

		SR A	SR	SR A	SR	SR	SR	SR A	SR	SR A	SR	SR	SR	SR A		SR	SR A	SR	SR	SR	SR A	SR	SR A
Glasgow Central 15	226 d	09 51	10 06	10 15	10 20	10 35	10 45	10 51	11 05	11 15	11 20	11 35	11 45	11 51		14 05	14 15	14 20	14 35	14 45	14 51	15 05	15 15
Pollokshields West	d			10 21			10 51			11 21			11 51				14 21			14 51			15 21
Maxwell Park	d			10 23			10 53			11 23			11 53				14 23			14 53			15 23
Shawlands	d			10 25			10 55			11 25			11 55				14 25			14 55			15 25
Pollokshaws East	d			10 26			10 56			11 26			11 56				14 26			14 56			15 26
Langside	d			10 28			10 58			11 28			11 58				14 28			14 58			15 28
Pollokshields East	d	09 56	10 11		10 25	10 40		10 56	11 10		11 25	11 40		11 56	and at	14 10		14 25	14 40		14 56	15 11	
Queens Park	d	09 57	10 12		10 26	10 41		10 57	11 11		11 26	11 41		11 57	the same	14 11		14 26	14 41		14 57	15 12	
Crosshill	d	09 59	10 14		10 28	10 43		10 59	11 13		11 28	11 43		11 59	minutes	14 13		14 28	14 43		14 59	15 14	
Mount Florida	d	10 01	10 16		10 30	10 45		11 01	11 15		11 30	11 45		12 01	past	14 15		14 30	14 45		15 01	15 16	
Cathcart	d	10a03	10 18	10a31		10 47		11a03	11 17	11a31		11 47		12a04	each	14 17	14a31		14 47		15a04	15 18	15a31
Muirend	d		10 21			10 50			11 20			11 50			hour until	14 20			14 50			15 21	
Williamwood	d		10 24			10 53			11 23			11 53				14 23			14 53			15 24	
Whitecraigs	d		10 26			10 55			11 25			11 55				14 25			14 55			15 26	
Patterton	d		10 29			10 58			11 28			11 58				14 28			14 58			15 29	
Neilston	a		10 35			11 04			11 34			12 04				14 34			15 04			15 35	
Kings Park	d				10 34		11 04				11 34		12 04					14 34		15 04			
Croftfoot	d				10 36		11 06				11 36		12 06					14 36		15 06			
Burnside	d				10 38		11 08				11 38		12 08					14 38		15 08			
Kirkhill	a				10 41		11 11				11 41		12 11					14 41		15 11			
Newton	226 a				10 44		11 14				11 44		12 14					14 44		15 14			

		SR	SR	SR	SR A	SR	SR A	SR	SR	SR	SR A	SR	SR A	SR	SR	SR	SR A	SR	SR A	SR	SR	SR	SR A
Glasgow Central 15	226 d	15 20	15 35	15 45	15 51	16 08	16 15	16 20	16 35	16 46	16 50	17 07	17 15	17 20	17 35	17 45	17 51	18 07	18 15	18 20	18 35	18 45	18 51
Pollokshields West	d			15 51			16 21			16 52			17 21			17 51			18 21			18 51	
Maxwell Park	d			15 53			16 23			16 54			17 23			17 53			18 23			18 53	
Shawlands	d			15 55			16 25			16 56			17 25			17 55			18 25			18 55	
Pollokshaws East	d			15 56			16 26			16 57			17 26			17 56			18 26			18 56	
Langside	d			15 58			16 28			16 59			17 28			17 58			18 28			18 59	
Pollokshields East	d	15 25	15 40		15 56	16 13		16 25	16 40		16 55	17 12		17 25	17 40		17 56	18 12		18 26	18 40		18 57
Queens Park	d	15 26	15 41		15 57	16 14		16 27	16 41		16 56	17 13		17 26	17 41		17 58	18 13		18 27	18 41		18 58
Crosshill	d	15 28	15 43		15 59	16 16		16 29	16 43		16 58	17 15		17 28	17 43		18 00	18 15		18 29	18 43		19 00
Mount Florida	d	15 30	15 45		16 01	16 18		16 31	16 45		17 00	17 17		17 30	17 45		18 02	18 17		18 31	18 45		19 02
Cathcart	d		15 47		16a03	16 20	16a31		16 47		17a04	17 19	17a31		17 47		18a04	18 19	18a31		18 47		19a05
Muirend	d		15 50			16 23			16 50			17 22			17 50			18 22			18 50		
Williamwood	d		15 53			16 26			16 53			17 25			17 53			18 25			18 53		
Whitecraigs	d		15 55			16 28			16 55			17 27			17 55			18 27			18 55		
Patterton	d		15 58			16 31			16 58			17 30			17 58			18 30			18 58		
Neilston	a		16 04			16 37			17 04			17 36			18 04			18 36			19 04		
Kings Park	d	15 34		16 04				16 34		17 04				17 34		18 04				18 34		19 04	
Croftfoot	d	15 36		16 06				16 36		17 06				17 36		18 06				18 36		19 06	
Burnside	d	15 38		16 08				16 38		17 08				17 38		18 08				18 39		19 08	
Kirkhill	a	15 41		16 11				16 41		17 11				17 41		18 11				18 42		19 11	
Newton	226 a	15 44		16 14				16 44		17 14				17 44		18 14				18 45		19 14	

		SR	SR A	SR	SR	SR	SR A	SR	SR A	SR	SR	SR	SR A	SR	SR A	SR	SR	SR	SR A	SR	SR A	SR
Glasgow Central 15	226 d	19 05	19 15	19 20	19 35	19 45	19 50	20 05	20 15	20 20	20 35	20 45	20 50	21 05	21 15	21 20	21 36	21 45	21 51	22 05	22 15	22 20
Pollokshields West	d		19 21			19 51			20 21			20 51			21 21			21 51			22 21	
Maxwell Park	d		19 23			19 53			20 23			20 53			21 23			21 53			22 23	
Shawlands	d		19 25			19 55			20 25			20 55			21 25			21 55			22 25	
Pollokshaws East	d		19 26			19 56			20 26			20 56			21 26			21 56			22 26	
Langside	d		19 28			19 58			20 28			20 58			21 28			21 58			22 28	
Pollokshields East	d	19 10		19 25	19 40		19 55	20 10		20 25	20 40		20 55	21 10		21 25	21 41		21 56	22 10		22 25
Queens Park	d	19 11		19 26	19 41		19 56	20 11		20 26	20 41		20 56	21 11		21 26	21 42		21 57	22 11		22 26
Crosshill	d	19 13		19 28	19 43		19 58	20 13		20 28	20 43		20 58	21 13		21 28	21 44		21 59	22 13		22 28
Mount Florida	d	19 15		19 30	19 45		20 00	20 15		20 30	20 45		21 00	21 15		21 30	21 46		22 02	22 15		22 30
Cathcart	d	19 17	19a31		19 47		20a04	20 17	20a31		20 47		21a04	21 17	21a31		21 48		22a04	22 17	22a31	
Muirend	d	19 20			19 50			20 20			20 50			21 20			21 51			22 20		
Williamwood	d	19 23			19 53			20 23			20 53			21 23			21 54			22 23		
Whitecraigs	d	19 25			19 55			20 25			20 55			21 25			21 56			22 25		
Patterton	d	19 28			19 58			20 28			20 58			21 28			21 59			22 28		
Neilston	a	19 34			20 04			20 34			21 04			21 34			22 05			22 34		
Kings Park	d			19 34		20 04				20 34		21 04				21 34		22 04				22 34
Croftfoot	d			19 36		20 06				20 36		21 06				21 36		22 06				22 36
Burnside	d			19 38		20 08				20 38		21 08				21 38		22 08				22 38
Kirkhill	a			19 41		20 11				20 41		21 11				21 41		22 11				22 41
Newton	226 a			19 44		20 14				20 44		21 14				21 44		22 14				22 44

		SR	SR	SR A	SR	SR A	SR
Glasgow Central 15	226 d	22 35	22 45	22 50	23 05	23 15	23 20
Pollokshields West	d		22 51			23 21	
Maxwell Park	d		22 53			23 23	
Shawlands	d		22 55			23 25	
Pollokshaws East	d		22 56			23 26	
Langside	d		22 58			23 28	
Pollokshields East	d	22 40		22 55	23 10		23 25
Queens Park	d	22 41		22 56	23 11		23 26
Crosshill	d	22 43		22 58	23 13		23 28
Mount Florida	d	22 45		23 00	23 15		23 30
Cathcart	d	22 47		23a04	23 17	23a31	
Muirend	d	22 50			23 20		
Williamwood	d	22 53			23 23		
Whitecraigs	d	22 55			23 25		
Patterton	d	22 58			23 28		
Neilston	a	23 04			23 34		
Kings Park	d		23 04				23 34
Croftfoot	d		23 06				23 36
Burnside	d		23 08				23 38
Kirkhill	a		23 11				23 41
Newton	226 a		23 14				23 44

A To Glasgow Central

Table T223-R

Sundays

20 May to 9 September

Glasgow Central, Cathcart Circle, Neilston and Newton

		SR	SR A	SR B	SR	SR A	SR	SR C	SR B	SR A		SR	SR A	SR C	SR	SR B	SR	SR A	SR	SR C		SR B	SR	SR A	SR
Glasgow Central 15	226 d	08 23	08 34	08 36	08 53	09 08	09 22	09 28	09 35	09 50		09 53	10 07	10 20	10 23	10 36	10 53	11 08	11 23	11 28		11 38	11 53	12 08	12 22
Pollokshields West	d			08 42					09 41							10 42						11 44			
Maxwell Park	d			08 44					09 43							10 44						11 46			
Shawlands	d			08 46					09 45							10 46						11 48			
Pollokshaws East	d			08 47					09 46							10 47						11 49			
Langside	d			08 49					09 48							10 49						11 51			
Pollokshields East	d	08 28			08 58	09 13	09 27					09 58	10 12		10 28		10 58	11 13	11 28				11 58	12 13	12 27
Queens Park	d	08 29			08 59	09 14	09 28					09 59	10 13		10 29		10 59	11 14	11 29				11 59	12 14	12 28
Crosshill	d	08 31			09 01	09 16	09 30					10 01	10 15		10 31		11 01	11 16	11 31				12 01	12 16	12 30
Mount Florida	d	08 33			09 03	09 18	09 32					10 03	10 17		10 33		11 03	11 18	11 33				12 03	12 18	12 32
Cathcart	d	08 35			09 05		09 35					10 05			10 35		11 05		11 35				12 05		12 34
Muirend	d	08 38			09 08		09 38					10 08			10 38		11 08		11 38				12 08		12 38
Williamwood	d	08 41			09 11		09 41					10 11			10 41		11 11		11 41				12 11		12 41
Whitecraigs	d	08 43			09 13		09 43					10 13			10 43		11 13		11 43				12 13		12 43
Patterton	d	08 46			09 16		09 46					10 16			10 46		11 16		11 46				12 16		12 46
Neilston	a	08 52			09 22		09 52					10 22			10 52		11 22		11 52				12 22		12 52
Kings Park	d			08 54		09 21			09 53				10 20			10 54		11 21				11 56		12 21	
Croftfoot	d			08 56		09 23			09 55				10 22			10 56		11 23				11 58		12 23	
Burnside	d			08 58		09 26			09 57				10 25			10 58		11 26				12 00		12 26	
Kirkhill	a			09 01		09 29			10 00				10 28			11 01		11 29				12 03		12 29	
Newton	226 a		08 51	09 04		09 32		09 42	10 03	10 06			10 31	10 34		11 04		11 32		11 42		12 06		12 32	

		SR C	SR B	SR	SR A	SR		SR C	SR B	SR	SR A	SR	SR C	SR B	SR	SR A		SR	SR C	SR B	SR	SR A	SR	SR C	SR B
Glasgow Central 15	226 d	12 31	12 36	12 59	13 10	13 23		13 35	13 37	13 53	14 08	14 21	14 27	14 36	14 53	15 08		15 23	15 28	15 36	15 53	16 08	16 21	16 27	16 36
Pollokshields West	d		12 42						13 43					14 42						15 42					16 42
Maxwell Park	d		12 44						13 45					14 44						15 44					16 44
Shawlands	d		12 46						13 47					14 46						15 46					16 46
Pollokshaws East	d		12 47						13 48					14 48						15 47					16 48
Langside	d		12 49						13 50					14 50						15 49					16 50
Pollokshields East	d			13 04	13 15	13 28				13 58	14 13	14 26			14 58	15 13		15 28			15 58	16 13	16 26		
Queens Park	d			13 05	13 16	13 29				13 59	14 14	14 27			14 59	15 14		15 29			15 59	16 14	16 27		
Crosshill	d			13 07	13 18	13 31				14 01	14 16	14 29			15 01	15 16		15 31			16 01	16 16	16 29		
Mount Florida	d			13 09	13 20	13 33				14 03	14 18	14 31			15 03	15 18		15 33			16 03	16 18	16 31		
Cathcart	d			13 11		13 35				14 05		14 34			15 05			15 35			16 05		16 35		
Muirend	d			13 14		13 38				14 08		14 38			15 08			15 38			16 08		16 38		
Williamwood	d			13 17		13 41				14 11		14 41			15 11			15 41			16 11		16 41		
Whitecraigs	d			13 19		13 43				14 13		14 43			15 13			15 43			16 13		16 43		
Patterton	d			13 22		13 46				14 16		14 46			15 16			15 46			16 16		16 46		
Neilston	a			13 28		13 52				14 22		14 52			15 22			15 52			16 22		16 52		
Kings Park	d		12 55		13 23				13 55		14 21			14 54		15 21				15 54		16 21			16 54
Croftfoot	d		12 57		13 25				13 57		14 23			14 56		15 23				15 56		16 23			16 56
Burnside	d		12 59		13 28				13 59		14 26			14 58		15 26				15 58		16 26			16 58
Kirkhill	a		13 02		13 31				14 02		14 29			15 01		15 29				16 01		16 29			17 01
Newton	226 a	12 47	13 05		13 34			13 50	14 05		14 32		14 41	15 04		15 32			15 43	16 04		16 32		16 41	17 07

		SR		SR A	SR	SR C	SR B	SR	SR A	SR	SR C	SR B		SR	SR A	SR C	SR	SR B	SR	SR A	SR C	SR		SR B	SR
Glasgow Central 15	226 d	16 53		17 08	17 21	17 27	17 36	17 53	18 08	18 20	18 26	18 36		18 53	19 08	19 20	19 23	19 36	19 53	20 08	20 20	20 23		20 36	20 53
Pollokshields West	d						17 42					18 42						19 42						20 42	
Maxwell Park	d						17 44					18 44						19 44						20 44	
Shawlands	d						17 46					18 46						19 46						20 46	
Pollokshaws East	d						17 47					18 48						19 47						20 47	
Langside	d						17 49					18 50						19 49						20 49	
Pollokshields East	d	16 58		17 13	17 26			17 58	18 13	18 25				18 58	19 13		19 28		19 58	20 13		20 28			20 58
Queens Park	d	16 59		17 14	17 27			17 59	18 14	18 26				18 59	19 14		19 29		19 59	20 14		20 29			20 59
Crosshill	d	17 01		17 16	17 29			18 01	18 16	18 28				19 01	19 16		19 31		20 01	20 16		20 31			21 01
Mount Florida	d	17 03		17 18	17 31			18 03	18 18	18 30				19 03	19 18		19 33		20 03	20 18		20 33			21 03
Cathcart	d	17 05			17 33			18 05		18 32				19 05			19 35		20 05			20 35			21 05
Muirend	d	17 08			17 38			18 08		18 37				19 08			19 38		20 08			20 38			21 08
Williamwood	d	17 11			17 41			18 11		18 41				19 11			19 41		20 11			20 41			21 11
Whitecraigs	d	17 13			17 43			18 13		18 43				19 13			19 43		20 13			20 43			21 13
Patterton	d	17 16			17 46			18 16		18 46				19 16			19 46		20 16			20 46			21 16
Neilston	a	17 22			17 52			18 22		18 52				19 22			19 52		20 22			20 52			21 22
Kings Park	d			17 21			17 54		18 21			18 54			19 21			19 54		20 21				20 54	
Croftfoot	d			17 23			17 56		18 23			18 56			19 23			19 56		20 23				20 56	
Burnside	d			17 26			17 58		18 26			18 58			19 26			19 58		20 26				20 58	
Kirkhill	a			17 29			18 01		18 29			19 01			19 29			20 01		20 29				21 01	
Newton	226 a			17 32		17 41	18 04		18 32		18 40	19 06			19 32	19 36		20 04		20 32	20 39			21 04	

		SR A	SR C	SR	SR B	SR	SR A	SR C		SR	SR B	SR	SR A	SR A
Glasgow Central 15	226 d	21 08	21 20	21 23	21 38	21 53	22 08	22 20		22 23	22 36	22 53	23 08	23 22
Pollokshields West	d				21 44						22 44			
Maxwell Park	d				21 46						22 46			
Shawlands	d				21 48						22 48			
Pollokshaws East	d				21 49						22 49			
Langside	d				21 51						22 51			
Pollokshields East	d	21 13		21 28		21 58	22 13			22 28		22 58	23 13	
Queens Park	d	21 14		21 29		21 59	22 14			22 29		22 59	23 14	
Crosshill	d	21 16		21 31		22 01	22 16			22 31		23 01	23 16	
Mount Florida	d	21 18		21 33		22 03	22 18			22 33		23 03	23 18	
Cathcart	d			21 35		22 05				22 35		23 05		
Muirend	d			21 38		22 08				22 38		23 08		
Williamwood	d			21 41		22 11				22 41		23 11		
Whitecraigs	d			21 43		22 13				22 43		23 13		
Patterton	d			21 46		22 16				22 46		23 16		
Neilston	a			21 52		22 22				22 52		23 22		
Kings Park	d	21 21			21 56		22 21				22 55		23 21	
Croftfoot	d	21 23			21 58		22 23				22 57		23 23	
Burnside	d	21 26			22 00		22 26				23 00		23 26	
Kirkhill	a	21 29			22 03		22 29				23 03		23 29	
Newton	226 a	21 32	21 36		22 06		22 32	22 38			23 06		23 32	23 37

A To Motherwell
B To Larkhall
C To Lanark

Table T223-R

Sundays

16 September to 2 December

Glasgow Central, Cathcart Circle, Neilston and Newton

		SR	SR	SR	SR		SR	SR	SR	SR		SR	SR	SR	SR	SR	SR	SR		SR	SR	SR	SR
Glasgow Central 15	226 d	08 23	08 36	08 53	09 08		11 23	11 36	11 53	12 08		12 22	12 36	12 59	13 08	13 23	13 36	13 53		22 08	22 23	22 36	22 53
Pollokshields West	d		08 42					11 42					12 42				13 42					22 42	
Maxwell Park	d		08 44					11 44					12 44				13 44					22 44	
Shawlands	d		08 46					11 46					12 46				13 46					22 46	
Pollokshaws East	d		08 47					11 47					12 47				13 47					22 47	
Langside	d		08 49					11 49					12 49				13 49					22 49	
Pollokshields East	d	08 28		08 58	09 13	and at the same minutes past each hour until	11 28		11 58	12 13		12 27		13 04	13 13	13 28		13 58	and at the same minutes past each hour until	22 13	22 28		22 58
Queens Park	d	08 29		08 59	09 14		11 29		11 59	12 14		12 28		13 05	13 14	13 29		13 59		22 14	22 29		22 59
Crosshill	d	08 31		09 01	09 16		11 31		12 01	12 16		12 30		13 07	13 16	13 31		14 01		22 16	22 31		23 01
Mount Florida	d	08 33		09 03	09 18		11 33		12 03	12 18		12 32		13 09	13 18	13 33		14 03		22 18	22 33		23 03
Cathcart	d	08 35		09 05			11 35		12 05			12 34		13 11		13 35		14 05			22 35		23 05
Muirend	d	08 38		09 08			11 38		12 08			12 38		13 14		13 38		14 08			22 38		23 08
Williamwood	d	08 41		09 11			11 41		12 11			12 41		13 17		13 41		14 11			22 41		23 11
Whitecraigs	d	08 43		09 13			11 43		12 13			12 43		13 19		13 43		14 13			22 43		23 13
Patterton	d	08 46		09 16			11 46		12 16			12 46		13 22		13 46		14 16			22 46		23 16
Neilston	a	08 52		09 22			11 52		12 22			12 52		13 28		13 52		14 22			22 52		23 22
Kings Park	d		08 54		09 21			11 54		12 21			12 54		13 21		13 54			22 21		22 54	
Croftfoot	d		08 56		09 23			11 56		12 23			12 56		13 23		13 56			22 23		22 56	
Burnside	d		08 58		09 26			11 58		12 26			12 58		13 26		13 58			22 26		22 58	
Kirkhill	a		09 01		09 29			12 01		12 29			13 01		13 29		14 01			22 29		23 01	
Newton	226 a		09 04		09 32			12 04		12 32			13 04		13 32		14 04			22 32		23 04	

		SR
Glasgow Central 15	226 d	23 08
Pollokshields West	d	
Maxwell Park	d	
Shawlands	d	
Pollokshaws East	d	
Langside	d	
Pollokshields East	d	23 13
Queens Park	d	23 14
Crosshill	d	23 16
Mount Florida	d	23 18
Cathcart	d	
Muirend	d	
Williamwood	d	
Whitecraigs	d	
Patterton	d	
Neilston	a	
Kings Park	d	23 21
Croftfoot	d	23 23
Burnside	d	23 26
Kirkhill	a	23 29
Newton	226 a	23 32

Table T224-F

Mondays to Fridays

21 May to 7 December

Edinburgh - Shotts, Carstairs, Motherwell and Glasgow Central

Miles	Miles			SR MX	SR MX	SR MX	SR MX	SR	SR	XC	SR	TP		SR	XC	SR	SR	SR	SR	XC	TP	SR		SR	SR
				A	A	A	A			◇1		◇1 B			◇1 C	D				◇1 E	◇1 F				
0	0	**Edinburgh** 10 230,238,242	d						05 52	06 24	06 36			06 55	07 27	07 42	07 57	08 27	08 58	09 12		09 25		09 56	10 19
1¼	1¼	Haymarket 230,238,242	d						05 56		06 42			07 00	07 31	07 46	08 01	08 31	09 02	09 16		09 30		10 01	10 24
3	3	Slateford	d						06 00					07 04				08 35				09 35			
3¾	3¾	Kingsknowe	d						06 04					07 08				08 39				09 39			
4¾	4¾	Wester Hailes	d						06 06					07 10				08 41				09 41			
7½	7½	Curriehill	d						06 10					07 14				08 45				09 45			
11	11	Kirknewton	d				00 01		06 17					07 21				08 52				09 52			
14	—	Livingston South	d				00 16		06 22		06 56			07 26			08 19	08 57	09 17			09 57		10 16	
16¾	—	West Calder	d			00 09	00 32		06 28		07 01			07 31			08 24	09 02	09 22			10 02		10 21	
18¾	—	Addiewell	d				00 39		06 32					07 34				09 06				10 06			
21	—	Breich	d																						
23¾	—	Fauldhouse	d				00 54		06 39					07 41				09 13				10 13			
26¾	—	**Shotts**	d			00s34	01s03		06 44		07 14			07 46			08 37	09 18	09 35			10 18		10 35	
28¾	—	Hartwood	d				01s11		06 48					07 49				09 21				10 21			
31½	—	Cleland	d				01s19		06 53					07 54				09 26				10 26			
33¾	—	Carfin	d				01s25		06 56					07 58				09 30				10 30			
34¾	—	Holytown	d	00 04			01s33		06 58					08 04				09 32				10 32			
—	28½	Carstairs	d					05 48				07 46				08 10									11 10
—	—	Carluke 225	d		00 07			05 56								08 18									11 20
—	—	Wishaw 225	d		00 14			06 06								08 27									11 28
—	44½	**Motherwell** 225	a		00 19			06 14		07 04		07 59			08 14	08 33				09 54					11 34
—	—		d					06 15		07 05		08 01			08 15	08 34				09 55	10 14				11 34
36	—	Bellshill 225	d	00 15		01s05	01s44	06 22	07 06		07 27			08 09			08 49	09 37	09 48			10 37		10 50	
38¾	—	Uddingston 225	d	00 31			02s00	06 26	07 13					08 13		08 39		09 41				10 41			
42	—	Cambuslang 225	d				02s16	06 30	07 18																
47¾	57¾	**Glasgow Central** 15 225	a	00 55		01 36	02 32	06 39	07 29	07 21	07 52	08 20		08 28	08 31	08 55	09 10	09 56	10 10	10 15	10 33	10 56		11 10	11 53

		SR	SR	XC	TP	SR	SR	SR		SR	SR	XC	TP	SR	SR	SR	SR	SR		XC	TP	SR	SR	SR	SR
				◇1 G	◇1 F		H					◇1 I	◇1 F		H					◇1 J	◇1 F				
Edinburgh 10 230,238,242	d	10 27	10 56	11 11		11 26	11 53	11 57		12 27	12 58	13 13		13 28	13 52	13 56	14 26	14 57		15 12		15 26	15 49	15 55	16 26
Haymarket 230,238,242	d	10 31	11 01	11 16		11 30	11 58	12 01		12 31	13 02	13 17		13 32	13 57	14 01	14 31	15 01		15 17		15 30	15 54	16 01	16 30
Slateford	d	10 35				11 35				12 35				13 36			14 35					15 35			16 35
Kingsknowe	d	10 39				11 39				12 39				13 39			14 39					15 39			16 39
Wester Hailes	d	10 41				11 41				12 41				13 42			14 41					15 41			16 41
Curriehill	d	10 45				11 45				12 45				13 45			14 45					15 45			16 45
Kirknewton	d	10 52				11 52				12 52				13 53			14 52					15 52			16 53
Livingston South	d	10 57	11 16			11 57		12 17		12 57	13 18			13 57		14 16	14 57	15 17				15 57		16 15	16 57
West Calder	d	11 02	11 21			12 02		12 22		13 02	13 23			14 02		14 21	15 02	15 22				16 02		16 20	17 02
Addiewell	d	11 06				12 06				13 06				14 06			15 06					16 06			17 06
Breich	d																								
Fauldhouse	d	11 13				12 13				13 13				14 13			15 13					16 13			17 13
Shotts	d	11 18	11 33			12 18		12 35		13 18	13 36			14 18		14 34	15 18	15 35				16 18		16 33	17 18
Hartwood	d	11 21				12 21				13 21				14 21			15 21					16 21			17 21
Cleland	d	11 26				12 26				13 26				14 26			15 26					16 26			17 26
Carfin	d	11 30				12 30				13 30				14 30			15 30					16 30			17 29
Holytown	d	11 32				12 32				13 32				14 32			15 32					16 32			17 31
Carstairs	d						12 47								14 32								16 17		
Carluke 225	d						12 56								14 41								16 25		
Wishaw 225	d						13 03								14 53										
Motherwell 225	a			11 54			13 09					13 54			15 03					15 54			16 32		
	d			11 55	12 22		13 09					13 55	14 22		15 06					15 55	16 22		16 33		
Bellshill 225	d	11 37	11 47			12 37		12 48		13 37	13 50			14 37		14 47	15 37	15 47				16 36		16 46	17 35
Uddingston 225	d	11 42				12 41				13 41				14 41			15 41					16 40			17 39
Cambuslang 225	d																								17 44
Glasgow Central 15 225	a	11 57	12 09	12 12	12 39	12 56	13 24	13 10		13 56	14 10	14 12	14 40	14 56	15 24	15 09	15 56	16 10		16 12	16 41	16 55	16 51	17 10	17 56

A From Edinburgh
B From Manchester Piccadilly
C From Dunbar
D From North Berwick
E From York
F From Manchester Airport
G From Derby
H To Ayr
I From Bath Spa
J From Plymouth

Table T224-F

Mondays to Fridays

21 May to 7 December

Edinburgh - Shotts, Carstairs, Motherwell and Glasgow Central

		SR	XC	XC	TP	SR	SR	SR	SR	SR		SR	SR	XC	XC	TP	SR	GR	XC	TP		SR FO	SR FX	SR FX	SR FX
			◇1 A	◇1 B	◇1 C		D					E		◇1 A	1 B	◇1 C		1 F	◇1 G	◇1 C					H
Edinburgh 10 230,238,242	d	16 57	17 12	17 12		17 23	17 40	17 49	17 58			18 26	18 57	19 11	19 11		19 27	20 17	21 14			21 25	21 26	21 26	22 56
Haymarket 230,238,242	d	17 01	17 16	17 16		17 28	17 46	17 53	18 03			18 31	19 01	19 16	19 16		19 31	20 22	21 19			21 31	21 47	21 47	23 17
Slateford	d					17 33			18 06			18 34					19 35					21 35		21 53	→
Kingsknowe	d					17 37			18 10			18 37					19 39					21 39		21 58	
Wester Hailes	d					17 40		17 59	18 13			18 40					19 41					21 41		22 06	
Curriehill	d					17 44		18 02				18 43					19 45					21 45		22 16	
Kirknewton	d					17 51		18 10				18 50					19 52					21 52		22 30	
Livingston South	d	17 16				17 56		18 15	18 25				19 17				19 57					21 57	22 23	22 46	
West Calder	d	17 21				18 02		18 20	18 30				19 22				20 02					22 02	22 39	23 02	
Addiewell	d					18 06			18 33								20 06					22 06		23 09	
Breich	d								18 38																
Fauldhouse	d					18 13			18 42								20 13					22 13		23 24	
Shotts	d	17 34				18 18		18 32	18 47				19 35				20 18					22 18	23 05	23 34	
Hartwood	d					18 21			18 50								20 21					22 21		23 42	
Cleland	d					18 26			18 55								20 26					22 26		23 50	
Carfin	d					18 30			18 58								20 30					22 30		23 56	
Holytown	d					18 32			19 00								20 32					22 32		00 04	
Carstairs	d						18 10			18 39		19 13													
Carluke 225	d						18 18			18 47		19 22													
Wishaw 225	d						18 25			19 00		19 27													
Motherwell 225	a		17 55	17 55			18 31			19 08		19 33		19 54	19 54			21 03	22 04						
	d		17 56	17 56	18 22		18 32					19 34		19 55	19 55	20 22		21 04	22 05	22 22					
Bellshill 225	d	17 47				18 37		18 44	19 04				19 47				20 37					22 36	23 36	00 15	
Uddingston 225	d					18 41			19 08								20 41					22 40		00 31	
Cambuslang 225	d							18 51	19 15																
Glasgow Central 15 225	a	18 09	18 11	18 11	18 41	18 56	18 54	19 03	19 27			19 54	20 10	20 15	20 15	20 42	20 56	21 25	22 21	22 38		22 55	00 06	00 55	

		SR FX	SR FO	SR FX	SR FX	SR
		H		I	I	
Edinburgh 10 230,238,242	d	22 56	22 57	←	←	23 14
Haymarket 230,238,242	d	23 17	23 01	23 17	23 17	23 18
Slateford	d	→	23 05		23 23	23 22
Kingsknowe	d		23 09		23 28	23 25
Wester Hailes	d		23 11		23 36	23 27
Curriehill	d		23 15		23 46	23 31
Kirknewton	d		23 22		00 01	23 37
Livingston South	d		23 27	23 53	00 16	
West Calder	d		23 32	00 09	00 32	
Addiewell	d		23 35		00 39	
Breich	d					
Fauldhouse	d		23 42		00 54	
Shotts	d		23 47	00s34	01s03	
Hartwood	d		23 50		01s11	
Cleland	d		23 55		01s19	
Carfin	d		23 59		01s25	
Holytown	d		00 01		01s33	
Carstairs	d					23 57
Carluke 225	d					00 07
Wishaw 225	d					00 14
Motherwell 225	a					00 19
	d					
Bellshill 225	d		00 05	01s05	01s44	
Uddingston 225	d		00 09		02s00	
Cambuslang 225	d		00 14		02s16	
Glasgow Central 15 225	a		00 26	01 36	02 32	

A until 20 July, from 8 October. From Penzance
B from 23 July until 5 October. From Reading
C From Manchester Airport
D To Ayr
E From North Berwick to Ayr
F From London Kings Cross
G From Plymouth
H To Glasgow Central
I From Edinburgh

Table T224-F

Saturdays
26 May to 8 December

Edinburgh - Shotts, Carstairs, Motherwell and Glasgow Central

Station		SR	SR	SR	SR	XC	SR	TP	SR	XC	SR	SR	SR	SR	XC	TP	SR	SR	SR	SR	SR	XC	TP
		A	A			◇1		◇1 B 🍴		◇1	C				◇1 D 🍴	◇1 E 🍴						◇1 F	◇1 E 🍴
Edinburgh	230,238,242 d				05 52	06 27	06 42		06 55	07 27	07 54	07 57	08 26	08 57	09 14		09 25	09 56	10 20	10 26	10 56	11 13	
Haymarket	230,238,242 d				05 56		06 47		07 00	07 31	07 58	08 01	08 31	09 01	09 18		09 32	10 01	10 24	10 31	11 00	11 17	
Slateford	d				06 00				07 04				08 35				09 36			10 36			
Kingsknowe	d				06 04				07 08				08 39				09 40			10 39			
Wester Hailes	d				06 06				07 10				08 41				09 42			10 42			
Curriehill	d				06 10				07 14				08 45				09 46			10 45			
Kirknewton	d				06 17				07 21				08 52				09 53			10 53			
Livingston South	d				06 22		07 01		07 26			08 19	08 57	09 17			09 58	10 16		10 57	11 17		
West Calder	d				06 28		07 06		07 31			08 24	09 02	09 22			10 03	10 21		11 02	11 22		
Addiewell	d				06 32				07 34				09 06				10 07			11 06			
Breich	d																						
Fauldhouse	d				06 39				07 41				09 13				10 14			11 13			
Shotts	d				06 44		07 19		07 46			08 37	09 18	09 35			10 19	10 35		11 18	11 35		
Hartwood	d				06 48				07 49				09 21				10 22			11 21			
Cleland	d				06 53				07 54				09 26				10 27			11 26			
Carfin	d				06 56				07 58				09 30				10 31			11 30			
Holytown	d	00 01			06 58				08 04				09 32				10 33			11 32			
Carstairs	d			05 48				07 45			08 32								11 10				
Carluke	225 d		00 07	05 57							08 41								11 20				
Wishaw	225 d		00 14	06 08							08 55								11 28				
Motherwell	225 a		00 19	06 14		07 05		07 59		08 13	09 00				09 54				11 34			11 53	
	d			06 16		07 06		08 01		08 14	09 01				09 57	10 21			11 34			11 54	12 23
Bellshill	225 d	00 05		06 23	07 06		07 30		08 09			08 49	09 37	09 48			10 37	10 50		11 37	11 49		
Uddingston	225 d	00 09		06 27	07 13				08 13				09 41				10 41			11 42			
Cambuslang	225 d	00 14		06 31	07 18																		
Glasgow Central	225 a	00 26		06 40	07 29	07 22	07 52	08 20	08 28	08 30	09 23	09 10	09 56	10 10	10 14	10 39	10 56	11 10	11 53	11 57	12 09	12 12	12 42

Station		SR	SR	SR	SR	SR	XC	TP	SR	SR	SR	SR	SR	XC	XC	TP	SR	SR	SR	SR	SR	XC
			G				◇1 H	◇1 E 🍴		G				◇1 I	◇1 J	◇1 E 🍴		G				◇1 K
Edinburgh	230,238,242 d	11 26	11 53	11 56	12 26	12 57	13 13		13 27	13 52	13 55	14 26	14 57	15 11	15 12		15 26	15 49	15 55	16 26	16 56	17 13
Haymarket	230,238,242 d	11 31	11 58	12 01	12 30	13 02	13 17		13 31	13 57	14 01	14 31	15 01	15 16	15 16		15 30	15 54	16 00	16 30	17 01	17 18
Slateford	d	11 35			12 35				13 35			14 35					15 35			16 35		
Kingsknowe	d	11 39			12 39				13 39			14 39					15 39			16 39		
Wester Hailes	d	11 41			12 41				13 41			14 41					15 41			16 41		
Curriehill	d	11 45			12 45				13 45			14 45					15 45			16 45		
Kirknewton	d	11 52			12 52				13 52			14 52					15 52			16 53		
Livingston South	d	11 57		12 17	12 57	13 18			13 57		14 16	14 57	15 17				15 57		16 15	16 57	17 17	
West Calder	d	12 02		12 22	13 02	13 23			14 02		14 21	15 02	15 22				16 02		16 20	17 02	17 22	
Addiewell	d	12 06			13 06				14 06			15 06					16 06			17 06		
Breich	d																					
Fauldhouse	d	12 13			13 13				14 13			15 13					16 13			17 13		
Shotts	d	12 18		12 35	13 18	13 36			14 18		14 34	15 18	15 35				16 18		16 33	17 18	17 34	
Hartwood	d	12 21			13 21				14 21			15 21					16 21			17 21		
Cleland	d	12 26			13 26				14 26			15 26					16 26			17 26		
Carfin	d	12 30			13 30				14 30			15 30					16 30			17 29		
Holytown	d	12 32			13 32				14 32			15 32					16 32			17 31		
Carstairs	d		12 47							14 32								16 32				
Carluke	225 d		12 56							14 41								16 41				
Wishaw	225 d		13 03							14 53								16 57				
Motherwell	225 a		13 09				13 54			15 03				15 54	15 54			17 04				17 54
	d		13 09				13 55	14 22		15 06				15 55	15 55	16 22		17 06				17 55
Bellshill	225 d	12 37		12 48	13 37	13 50			14 36		14 47	15 37	15 46				16 36		16 46	17 35	17 47	
Uddingston	225 d	12 41			13 41				14 40			15 41					16 40			17 39		
Cambuslang	225 d																			17 44		
Glasgow Central	225 a	12 56	13 24	13 10	13 56	14 10	14 12	14 40	14 55	15 25	15 09	15 56	16 10	16 12	16 12	16 40	16 55	17 23	17 10	17 56	18 09	18 11

Station		SR	SR	SR	SR	SR	SR	XC	TP	SR	XC	SR	SR	SR
			G			C		◇1 K	◇1 E 🍴		◇1 L			
Edinburgh	230,238,242 d	17 24	17 41	17 49	17 58	18 27	18 56	19 12		19 26	21 14	21 26	22 56	23 13
Haymarket	230,238,242 d	17 28	17 47	17 54	18 02	18 32	19 01	19 17		19 30	21 19	21 30	23 00	23 18
Slateford	d	17 33			18 06	18 35				19 35		21 35	23 04	23 22
Kingsknowe	d	17 37			18 10	18 38				19 39		21 39	23 08	23 25
Wester Hailes	d	17 40		18 00	18 13	18 41				19 41		21 41	23 10	23 27
Curriehill	d	17 44		18 04		18 44				19 45		21 45	23 14	23 31
Kirknewton	d	17 51		18 12		18 51				19 52		21 52	23 21	23 37
Livingston South	d	17 56		18 16	18 25		19 17			19 57		21 57	23 26	
West Calder	d	18 02		18 21	18 30		19 22			20 02		22 02	23 31	
Addiewell	d	18 06			18 33					20 06		22 06	23 34	
Breich	d				18 38									
Fauldhouse	d	18 13			18 42					20 13		22 13	23 41	
Shotts	d	18 18		18 34	18 47		19 35			20 18		22 18	23 46	
Hartwood	d	18 21			18 50					20 21		22 21	23 49	
Cleland	d	18 26			18 55					20 26		22 26	23 54	
Carfin	d	18 30			18 59					20 30		22 30	23 58	
Holytown	d	18 32			19 01					20 32		22 32	00 01	
Carstairs	d		18 10			19 13								23 57
Carluke	225 d		18 20			19 22								00 07
Wishaw	225 d		18 26			19 27								00 15
Motherwell	225 a		18 32			19 33		19 53			21 56			00 20
	d		18 32			19 34		19 54	20 22		21 58			
Bellshill	225 d	18 37		18 46	19 05		19 47			20 37		22 36	00 05	
Uddingston	225 d	18 41			19 09					20 41		22 40	00 09	
Cambuslang	225 d			18 59	19 15								00 14	
Glasgow Central	225 a	18 56	18 54	19 11	19 27	19 54	20 10	20 15	20 42	20 57	22 19	22 55	00 26	

A From Edinburgh
B From Manchester Piccadilly
C From North Berwick to Ayr
D From Newcastle
E From Manchester Airport
F From Birmingham New Street
G To Ayr
H From Bristol Temple Meads
I from 28 July until 6 October. From Bournemouth
J until 21 July, from 13 October. From Plymouth
K From Penzance
L From Plymouth

Table T224-F

Sundays
20 May to 2 December

Edinburgh - Shotts, Carstairs, Motherwell and Glasgow Central

Station		SR	SR	SR	SR	SR	SR	SR	SR	SR	SR	SR	SR	XC	XC	SR	SR	SR	TP	TP	SR	SR	XC
		A	A	B	C	C	B	B	C	B	C	B	🚌	◇1 C 🍴	B 🚌	C	B	B	◇1 D 🍴	◇1 E 🍴	C	🚌	◇1 F 🍴
Edinburgh	230,238,242 d												08 39	10 23								10 49	12 17
Haymarket	230,238,242 d												09 00									11 10	12 21
Slateford	d																						
Kingsknowe	d																						
Wester Hailes	d																						
Curriehill	d																						
Kirknewton	d																						
Livingston South	d												09 36									11 46	
West Calder	d												09 52									12 02	
Addiewell	d												09 59									12 09	
Breich	d																						
Fauldhouse	d												10 14									12 24	
Shotts	d												10 24									12 34	
Hartwood	d												10 32									12 42	
Cleland	d												10 40									12 50	
Carfin	d												10 46									12 56	
Holytown	d	00 01											10 54									13 04	
Carstairs	d																						
Carluke	225 d		00 07																				
Wishaw	225 d		00 15																				
Motherwell	225 a		00 20											11 03									12 59
	d			08 34	08 35	09 05	09 05	09 20	09 54	09 54	10 19	10 20		11 04	11 10	11 20	11 20	12 20	12 21	12 23	12 24		13 00
Bellshill	225 d	00 05		08 40	08 41	09 11	09 11		10 00	10 00	10 26		11s04			11 26					12 31	13s14	
Uddingston	225 d	00 09		08 44	08 45	09 15	09 15		10 04	10 07	10 30		11s20			11 32					12 35	13s30	
Cambuslang	225 d	00 14			08 50	09 20			10 09		10 34					11 37					12 39		
Glasgow Central	225 a	00 26		09 05	09 01	09 31	09 36	10 03	10 19	10 28	10 45	11 03	11 45	11 28	11 40	11 48	12 03	13 05	12 44	12 46	12 50	13 55	13 19

Station		XC	SR	SR	SR	XC	XC	SR	SR	TP	TP	SR	SR	SR	XC	XC	SR	SR	TP	TP	SR	SR	SR
		B 🚌	C	B	🚌	◇1 G	B 🚌	C	B	◇1 E 🍴	◇1 H 🍴	C	B	🚌	◇1 I	B 🚌	C	B	◇1 E 🍴	◇1 H 🍴	C	B	🚌
Edinburgh	230,238,242 d				12 49	13 13								14 49	15 10								16 49
Haymarket	230,238,242 d				13 10	13 18								15 10	15 14								17 10
Slateford	d																						
Kingsknowe	d																						
Wester Hailes	d																						
Curriehill	d																						
Kirknewton	d																						
Livingston South	d				13 46									15 46									17 46
West Calder	d				14 02									16 02									18 02
Addiewell	d				14 09									16 09									18 09
Breich	d																						
Fauldhouse	d				14 24									16 24									18 24
Shotts	d				14 34									16 34									18 34
Hartwood	d				14 42									16 42									18 42
Cleland	d				14 50									16 50									18 50
Carfin	d				14 56									16 56									18 56
Holytown	d				15 04									17 04									19 04
Carstairs	d																						
Carluke	225 d																						
Wishaw	225 d																						
Motherwell	225 a					13 54									15 55								
	d	13 10	13 20	13 20		13 55	14 05	14 20	14 20	14 22	14 22	15 20	15 20		15 56	16 05	16 20	16 20	16 22	16 22	17 20	17 20	
Bellshill	225 d		13 26		15s14			14 27				15 27		17s14			16 27				17 27		19s14
Uddingston	225 d		13 32		15s30			14 31				15 32		17s30			16 31				17 31		19s30
Cambuslang	225 d		13 37					14 35				15 36					16 35				17 35		
Glasgow Central	225 a	13 40	13 48	14 03	15 55	14 14	14 35	14 46	15 03	14 42	14 44	15 47	16 03	17 55	16 12	16 35	16 44	17 03	16 42	16 45	17 44	18 03	19 55

A not 20 May. From Edinburgh
B until 9 September
C from 16 September
D from 24 June until 9 September. From Manchester Airport
E from 16 September. From Manchester Airport
F from 16 September. From Leeds
G from 16 September. From Sheffield
H until 9 September. From Manchester Airport
I from 16 September. From Birmingham New Street

Table T224-F

Sundays
20 May to 2 December

Edinburgh - Shotts, Carstairs, Motherwell and Glasgow Central

	XC	XC	SR	SR	TP	SR	SR	SR	XC	XC	SR	TP	TP	SR	SR	SR	SR	XC	GR	XC	SR	SR
	◇1 A ⊼	B 🚌	C	B	◇1 D ⊼	B	C	🚌	◇1 E	B 🚌	B	◇1 F ⊼	◇1 G ⊼	C	C	B	🚌	◇1 H	1 I	B 🚌	C	B
Edinburgh 10 230,238,242 d	17 11							18 49	19 18								20 49	21 12	21 22			
Haymarket 230,238,242 d	17 15							19 10	19 23								21 10	21 17	21 26			
Slateford d																						
Kingsknowe d																						
Wester Hailes d																						
Curriehill d																						
Kirknewton d																						
Livingston South d								19 46									21 46					
West Calder d								20 02									22 02					
Addiewell d								20 09									22 09					
Breich d																						
Fauldhouse d								20 24									22 24					
Shotts d								20 34									22 34					
Hartwood d								20 42									22 42					
Cleland d								20 50									22 50					
Carfin d								20 56									22 56					
Holytown d								21 04									23 04					
Carstairs d																						
Carluke 225 d																						
Wishaw 225 d																						
Motherwell 225 a	17 52								19 59									21 55	22 04			
d	17 53	18 05	18 20	18 20	18 22	19 20	19 22		20 02	20 10	20 20	20 22	20 22	20 24	21 20	21 20		21 56	22 05	22 05	22 20	22 20
Bellshill 225 d			18 26				19 28	21s14						20 30	21 26		23s14				22 27	
Uddingston 225 d			18 30				19 32	21s30						20 34	21 30		23s30				22 31	
Cambuslang 225 d			18 35				19 37							20 39	21 35						22 35	
Glasgow Central 15 225 a	18 13	18 35	18 44	19 03	18 44	20 03	19 46	21 55	20 19	20 40	21 04	20 40	20 48	20 48	21 44	22 03	23 55	22 12	22 24	22 35	22 44	23 04

	TP	TP	SR	SR
	◇1 F ⊼	◇1 G ⊼	C	B
Edinburgh 10 230,238,242 d				
Haymarket 230,238,242 d				
Slateford d				
Kingsknowe d				
Wester Hailes d				
Curriehill d				
Kirknewton d				
Livingston South d				
West Calder d				
Addiewell d				
Breich d				
Fauldhouse d				
Shotts d				
Hartwood d				
Cleland d				
Carfin d				
Holytown d				
Carstairs d				
Carluke 225 d				
Wishaw 225 d				
Motherwell 225 a				
d	22 22	22 23	23 20	23 20
Bellshill 225 d			23 26	23 26
Uddingston 225 d			23 30	23 30
Cambuslang 225 d			23 35	
Glasgow Central 15 225 a	22 42	22 46	23 44	23 55

A from 16 September. From Bristol Temple Meads
B until 9 September
C from 16 September
D From Manchester Airport
E from 16 September. From Plymouth
F from 16 September. From Manchester Airport
G until 9 September. From Manchester Airport
H from 16 September. From Penzance
I from 16 September. From London Kings Cross

G... Shotts

Mondays to Fridays
21 May to 7 December

Miles	Miles															SR	SR	XC	XC	SR	SR	SR
			A 🚌	A 🚌		◇1 B ⊼	◇1 C			1 D		E		B ⊼	C			⊼				
0	0	**Glasgow Central** 15 225 d				06 01	06 01		06 16	06 48	07 00	07 05	07 13	07 48	07 48	08 03	08 17	09 00	09 00	09 03	09 17	09 33
5¼	—	Cambuslang 225 d							06 25				07 24									
8½	—	Uddingston 225 d							06 30				07 30				08 29				09 29	
11¼	—	Bellshill 225 d							06 36		07 16		07 35			08 20	08 34			09 19	09 34	
—	12¾	**Motherwell** 225 a				06 16	06 16			07 03		07 21		08 03	08 03			09 14	09 14			09 56
—	—	d			06 00	06 17	06 17	07 00		07 05		07 22		08 08	08 08			09 15	09 15			09 57
—	—	Wishaw 225 d						07 07				07 33										10 03
—	—	Carluke 225 d						07 17				07 40										10 09
—	28½	Carstairs d						07a25				07 50										10 18
13¼	—	Holytown d		00 01	06 07				06 40				07 40				08 40				09 39	
14	—	Carfin d		00 09	06 10				06 42				07 42				08 43				09 41	
15¾	—	Cleland d		00 17	06 14				06 46				07 46				08 47				09 45	
19	—	Hartwood d		00 27	06 19				06 52				07 52				08 53				09 51	
20½	—	**Shotts** d		00s34	06 23				06 56		07 28		07 56			08 33	08 57			09 32	09 57	
24	—	Fauldhouse d		00s44	06 29				07 02				08 02				09 03				10 03	
26¼	—	Breich d											08 05									
28¾	—	Addiewell d		00s59	06 35				07 08				08 09				09 09				10 09	
30½	—	West Calder d		01s06	06 39				07 11		07 40		08 13			08 45	09 12			09 44	10 12	
33¼	—	Livingston South d		01s22	06 45				07 16		07 45		08 18			08 49	09 17			09 49	10 17	
36¼	46¼	Kirknewton d		01s38	06 50				07 22		07 50	08 07	08 23				09 22				10 22	
40¼	49¾	Curriehill d	00 01	01s52	06 56				07 28		07 56	08 12	08 29				09 28				10 28	
42½	52½	Wester Hailes d	00 10	02s02	07 00				07 32			08 15	08 32				09 32				10 31	
43½	53½	Kingsknowe d	00 18	02s10	07 02				07 34			08 17	08 35				09 34				10 34	
44¼	54¼	Slateford d	00 23	02s15	07 06				07 39			08 20	08 40				09 39				10 38	
46	56	Haymarket 230,238,242 d	00 29	02s21	07 12	06 57	06 57		07 43	07 48	08 05	08 28	08 44	08 51	08 51	09 07	09 44	09 54	09 54	10 05	10 42	10 49
47¼	57¼	**Edinburgh** 10 230,238,242 a	00 49	02 42	07 16	07 01	07 01		07 47	07 52	08 10	08 34	08 49	08 56	08 56	09 12	09 49	09 58	09 58	10 10	10 48	10 54

	SR	SR	XC	XC	SR	SR	SR	SR	SR	XC	XC	SR	SR	SR	SR	SR	XC	SR	SR	SR	SR	SR
			◇1 F ⊼	◇1 G			H			◇1 F ⊼	◇1 C				H		◇1 I ⊼			J		
Glasgow Central 15 225 d	10 03	10 16	11 00	11 00	11 03	11 16	11 46	12 03	12 16	13 00	13 00	13 03	13 16	14 03	14 06	14 16	15 00	15 03	15 16	15 47	16 03	16 16
Cambuslang 225 d																						
Uddingston 225 d		10 28				11 28			12 29				13 28			14 28			15 28			16 29
Bellshill 225 d	10 18	10 34			11 19	11 34		12 19	12 35			13 19	13 34	14 19		14 34		15 19	15 34		16 21	16 35
Motherwell 225 a			11 14	11 14			12 02			13 15	13 15				14 25		15 15			16 03		
d			11 15	11 15			12 02			13 16	13 16				14 25		15 16			16 04		
Wishaw 225 d							12 08								14 31					16 22		
Carluke 225 d							12 14								14 38					16 28		
Carstairs d							12 23								14 52					16 37		
Holytown d		10 39				11 39			12 39				13 39			14 38			15 40			16 39
Carfin d		10 42				11 42			12 42				13 41			14 41			15 42			16 42
Cleland d		10 46				11 46			12 46				13 45			14 46			15 47			16 46
Hartwood d		10 51				11 52			12 52				13 51			14 52			15 52			16 52
Shotts d	10 31	10 55			11 32	11 56		12 32	12 56			13 32	13 55	14 32		14 56		15 32	15 56		16 34	16 56
Fauldhouse d		11 01				12 02			13 02				14 01			15 02			16 02			17 02
Breich d																						
Addiewell d		11 07				12 08			13 08				14 07			15 08			16 08			17 08
West Calder d	10 44	11 10			11 44	12 11		12 44	13 11			13 44	14 11	14 44		15 12		15 44	16 12		16 47	17 11
Livingston South d	10 49	11 15			11 49	12 16		12 49	13 16			13 48	14 16	14 48		15 16		15 49	16 17		16 52	17 16
Kirknewton d		11 21				12 21			13 22				14 21			15 22			16 24			17 23
Curriehill d		11 27				12 27			13 28				14 27			15 28			16 30			17 29
Wester Hailes d		11 30				12 31			13 31				14 30			15 31			16 33			17 32
Kingsknowe d		11 33				12 33			13 34				14 33			15 34			16 36			17 35
Slateford d		11 38				12 38			13 39				14 38			15 39			16 41			17 39
Haymarket 230,238,242 d	11 05	11 43	11 54	11 54	12 05	12 42	12 49	13 05	13 44	13 55	13 55	14 05	14 48	15 04	15 18	15 43	15 56	16 05	16 47	17 05	17 09	17 43
Edinburgh 10 230,238,242 a	11 09	11 48	11 58	11 58	12 10	12 47	12 54	13 11	13 48	13 59	13 59	14 10	14 52	15 10	15 24	15 48	16 01	16 09	16 51	17 11	17 14	17 48

A From Glasgow Central
B from 23 July until 5 October. To Southampton Central
C until 20 July, from 8 October. To Plymouth
D To London Kings Cross
E To North Berwick
F from 23 July until 5 October. To Reading
G until 20 July, from 8 October. To Penzance
H From Ayr
I To Birmingham New Street
J From Ayr to North Berwick

Table T225-F

Mondays to Fridays

21 May to 7 December

Edinburgh, Lanark, Coatbridge, Motherwell, Whifflet, Larkhall and Hamilton - Glasgow

	SR A	SR B	SR C	SR D	SR	SR	SR D	SR A	SR E	SR	SR	SR	SR A	SR A	SR E	SR C	SR A	SR	SR D	SR A	SR E	TP ◇1 F ⚹
Edinburgh d		07 42			07 57						08 27	08 58										
Haymarket d		07 46			08 01						08 31	09 02										
Lanark d						08 23				08 53								09 23				
Carstairs d		08 10																				
Carluke d		08 18				08 33				09 03								09 33				
Wishaw d		08 27				08 39				09 09								09 39				
Holytown d											09 32											
Shieldmuir d						08 42				09 12								09 42				
Cumbernauld 226 d	08 12																09 22					
Greenfaulds 226 d	08 14																09 24					
Coatbridge Central d	08 21																09 31					
Whifflet d	08 24			←													09 34					
Motherwell a	08 32	08 33		08 32		08 46				09 15							09 41	09 46				
Motherwell d	08 46	08 34	08 43	08 46		08 47				09 16			09 16	09 22		09 43	09 45	09 47				10 14
Whifflet d	→		08a50					08 58						09 29		09a50				09 58		
Kirkwood d								09 01						09 32						10 01		
Bargeddie d								09 04						09 35						10 04		
Baillieston d								09 07						09 39						10 07		
Mount Vernon d								09 09						09 41						10 09		
Carmyle d								09 12						09 43						10 12		
Bellshill d					08 49	08 55				09 23	09 37	09 48						09 53				
Uddingston d		08 39				08 59	←			09 27	09 41							09 57	←			
Airbles d				08 48			08 48						09 18				09 48		09 48			
Larkhall d				→					09 03						09 33		→				10 03	
Merryton d									09 05						09 35						10 05	
Chatelherault d									09 08						09 38						10 08	
Hamilton Central d							08 54		09 12				09 24		09 42				09 53		10 12	
Hamilton West d							08 56		09 15				09 26		09 45				09 56		10 15	
Blantyre d							09 00		09 18				09 30		09 48				09 59		10 18	
Newton d							09 05		09 22				09 34		09 52				10 04		10 22	
Cambuslang d						09 03	09 09		09 26	09 31			09 37		09 56			10 03	10 09		10 26	
Rutherglen d							09 13	09 17	09 30				09 42	09 48	10 00				10 13	10 17	10 30	
Dalmarnock d							09 15	09 19	09 32				09 44	09 51	10 03				10 15	10 19	10 32	
Bridgeton d							09 17	09 21	09 34				09 46	09 53	10 05				10 17	10 21	10 34	
Argyle Street d							09 20	09 25	09 37				09 49	09 56	10 08				10 20	10 25	10 37	
Glasgow Central H. Level a		08 55			09 10	09 12				09 40	09 56	10 10						10 12				10 33
Glasgow Central L. Level a							09 22	09 26	09 39				09 51	09 58	10 09				10 22	10 26	10 39	
Anderston a							09 24	09 29	09 40				09 53	10 00	10 11				10 23	10 29	10 41	
Exhibition Centre a							09 26	09 31	09 42				09 55	10 02	10 13				10 25	10 31	10 43	
Partick 226 a							09 29	09 35	09 46				09 58	10 05	10 16				10 29	10 35	10 46	
Hyndland 226 a							09 31	09 37	09 48				10 00	10 07	10 18				10 31	10 37	10 48	

	SR A	SR	SR G	SR	SR	SR A	SR E	SR C	SR A	SR	SR D	SR A	SR E	SR A	SR	SR G	SR A	SR	SR C	SR	SR
Edinburgh d				09 25	09 56													10 19		10 27	10 56
Haymarket d				09 30	10 01													10 24		10 31	11 01
Lanark d		09 53								10 23					10 53						
Carstairs d																		11 10			
Carluke d		10 03								10 33					11 03			11 20			
Wishaw d		10 09								10 39					11 09			11 28			
Holytown d				10 32																11 32	
Shieldmuir d		10 14								10 45					11 13						
Cumbernauld 226 d									10 21												
Greenfaulds 226 d									10 23												
Coatbridge Central d									10 30												
Whifflet d									10 33												
Motherwell a		10 18							10 40	10 48					11 16			11 34			
Motherwell d	10 16	10 18				10 23		10 45	10 46	10 48				11 16	11 17		11 20	11 34	11 45		
Whifflet d						10 30		10a52				11 00					11 28		11a52		
Kirkwood d						10 33						11 03					11 31				
Bargeddie d						10 36						11 06					11 34				
Baillieston d						10 40						11 09					11 38				
Mount Vernon d						10 42						11 11					11 40				
Carmyle d						10 44						11 14					11 42				
Bellshill d		10 26		10 37	10 50					10 55					11 23					11 37	11 47
Uddingston d		10 30	←	10 41						10 59	←				11 27	←				11 42	
Airbles d	10 18		10 18						10 48		10 48			11 18		11 18					
Larkhall d	→						10 33		→				11 03	→							
Merryton d							10 35						11 05								
Chatelherault d							10 38						11 08								
Hamilton Central d			10 24				10 42				10 54		11 12			11 24					
Hamilton West d			10 26				10 45				10 56		11 15			11 26					
Blantyre d			10 30				10 48				11 00		11 18			11 30					
Newton d			10 34				10 52				11 05		11 23			11 34					
Cambuslang d		10 34	10 38				10 56			11 03	11 09		11 26		11 32	11 37					
Rutherglen d			10 42			10 49	11 00				11 13	11 19	11 30			11 41	11 48				
Dalmarnock d			10 44			10 51	11 02				11 15	11 21				11 44	11 50				
Bridgeton d			10 46			10 53	11 04				11 17	11 23				11 46	11 52				
Argyle Street d			10 49			10 57	11 07				11 20	11 27	11 36			11 49	11 56				
Glasgow Central H. Level a		10 45		10 56	11 10					11 12					11 41			11 53		11 57	12 09
Glasgow Central L. Level a			10 51			10 58	11 09				11 22	11 28	11 38			11 51	11 57				
Anderston a			10 53			11 00	11 11				11 23	11 30	11 40			11 53	11 59				
Exhibition Centre a			10 55			11 02	11 13				11 25	11 32	11 42			11 55	12 01				
Partick 226 a			10 58			11 06	11 16				11 29	11 36	11 45			11 58	12 05				
Hyndland 226 a			11 00			11 08	11 18				11 31	11 38	11 47			12 00	12 07				

A To Dalmuir
B From North Berwick
C From Milngavie to Cumbernauld
D From Cumbernauld to Dalmuir
E To Milngavie
F From Manchester Airport
G From Motherwell to Dalmuir

Table T225-F

Mondays to Fridays

21 May to 7 December

Edinburgh, Lanark, Coatbridge, Motherwell, Whifflet, Larkhall and Hamilton - Glasgow

	SR A	SR B	SR	SR C	SR B	SR A	SR B	SR	SR D	SR B	TP ◇1 E ⚹	SR	SR A	SR F	SR B	SR G	SR H	SR	SR I	SR C	SR B	SR A
Edinburgh d												11 26					11 53	11 57				
Haymarket d												11 30					11 58	12 01				
Lanark d			11 23					11 53								12 23						
Carstairs d																	12 47					
Carluke d			11 33					12 03								12 33	12 56					
Wishaw d			11 39					12 10								12 39	13 03					
Holytown d												12 32										
Shieldmuir d			11 45					12 13								12 44						
Cumbernauld 226 d		11 21													12 21							
Greenfaulds 226 d		11 23													12 23							
Coatbridge Central d		11 30													12 30							
Whifflet d		11 33													12 33							
Motherwell a		11 40	11 48					12 16							12 40	12 48	13 09					
Motherwell d		11 46	11 48				12 16	12 17		12 20	12 22			12 45	12 46	12 48	13 09					
Whifflet d					11 58					12 30				12a52							12 58	
Kirkwood d					12 01					12 33											13 01	
Bargeddie d					12 04					12 36											13 04	
Baillieston d					12 07					12 40											13 07	
Mount Vernon d					12 09					12 42											13 09	
Carmyle d					12 12					12 44									←		13 12	
Bellshill d			11 55					12 23				12 37				12 55		12 48	12 55			
Uddingston d			12 02	←				12 29	←			12 41				→			12 59	←		
Airbles d		11 48		11 48			12 18		12 18						12 48					12 48		
Larkhall d	11 33	→				12 03	→						12 33		→							13 03
Merryton d	11 35					12 05							12 35									13 05
Chatelherault d	11 38					12 08							12 38									13 08
Hamilton Central d	11 42			11 54		12 13			12 24				12 42							12 54		13 13
Hamilton West d	11 45			11 56		12 15			12 26				12 45							12 56		13 15
Blantyre d	11 48			12 00		12 19			12 30				12 48							13 00		13 19
Newton d	11 52			12 05		12 23			12 34				12 52							13 05		13 23
Cambuslang d	11 56		12 06	12 09		12 26		12 34	12 37				12 56						13 03	13 09		13 26
Rutherglen d	12 00			12 13	12 17	12 30			12 41	12 48			13 00							13 13	13 17	13 30
Dalmarnock d	12 02			12 16	12 20	12 33			12 44	12 51										13 15	13 20	13 33
Bridgeton d	12 04			12 18	12 22	12 35			12 46	12 53										13 17	13 22	13 35
Argyle Street d	12 07			12 21	12 25	12 38			12 49	12 56			13 06							13 20	13 25	13 38
Glasgow Central H. Level a			12 15					12 43			12 39	12 56					13 24	13 10	13 12			
Glasgow Central L. Level a	12 09			12 22	12 27	12 39			12 51	12 58			13 07							13 22	13 27	13 39
Anderston a	12 10			12 24	12 29	12 41			12 53	13 00			13 09							13 23	13 29	13 41
Exhibition Centre a	12 12			12 26	12 31	12 43			12 55	13 02			13 11							13 25	13 31	13 43
Partick 226 a	12 16			12 29	12 35	12 46			12 58	13 05			13 15							13 29	13 35	13 46
Hyndland 226 a	12 18			12 31	12 37	12 48			13 00	13 07			13 17							13 31	13 37	13 48

	SR	SR	SR	SR B	SR B	SR A	SR F	SR B	SR	SR C	SR B	SR A	SR B	SR	SR D	SR B	TP ◇1 E ⚹	SR	SR A	SR F	SR B	SR G
Edinburgh d		12 27	12 58															13 28				
Haymarket d		12 31	13 02															13 32				
Lanark d	12 53								13 23					13 53								14 23
Carstairs d																						
Carluke d	13 03								13 33					14 03								14 33
Wishaw d	13 09								13 41					14 09								14 39
Holytown d		13 32																14 32				
Shieldmuir d	13 12								13 45					14 13								14 44
Cumbernauld 226 d								13 20													14 21	
Greenfaulds 226 d								13 22													14 23	
Coatbridge Central d								13 29													14 30	
Whifflet d								13 33													14 33	
Motherwell a	13 15							13 40	13 48					14 16							14 40	14 48
Motherwell d	13 16			13 16	13 21		13 45	13 46	13 48				14 16	14 17		14 20	14 22			14 45	14 46	14 48
Whifflet d					13 28		13a52				13 58					14 28				14a52		
Kirkwood d					13 31						14 01					14 31						
Bargeddie d					13 34						14 04					14 34						
Baillieston d					13 38						14 07					14 38						
Mount Vernon d					13 40						14 09					14 40						
Carmyle d					13 42						14 12					14 42						
Bellshill d	13 22	13 37	13 50						13 55					14 23				14 37				14 55
Uddingston d	13 26	13 41							14 02	←				14 29	←			14 41				→
Airbles d				13 18				13 48		13 48			14 18		14 18						14 48	
Larkhall d						13 33		→				14 03	→						14 33		→	
Merryton d						13 35						14 05							14 35			
Chatelherault d						13 38						14 08							14 38			
Hamilton Central d				13 24		13 42				13 54		14 12			14 24				14 42			
Hamilton West d				13 26		13 45				13 56		14 15			14 26				14 45			
Blantyre d				13 30		13 48				14 00		14 18			14 30				14 48			
Newton d				13 34		13 52				14 05		14 22			14 34				14 52			
Cambuslang d	13 31			13 37		13 56			14 06	14 09		14 26		14 33	14 37				14 56			
Rutherglen d				13 41	13 48	14 00				14 13	14 17	14 30			14 41	14 46			15 00			
Dalmarnock d				13 44	13 50	14 02				14 16	14 20	14 32			14 44	14 49			15 02			
Bridgeton d				13 46	13 52	14 04				14 18	14 22	14 34			14 46	14 51			15 04			
Argyle Street d				13 49	13 56	14 08				14 21	14 25	14 37			14 49	14 54			15 08			
Glasgow Central H. Level a	13 40	13 56	14 10						14 15					14 42			14 40	14 56				
Glasgow Central L. Level a				13 51	13 57	14 09				14 22	14 27	14 39			14 51	14 56			15 09			
Anderston a				13 53	14 00	14 11				14 24	14 29	14 40			14 53	14 59			15 11			
Exhibition Centre a				13 55	14 02	14 13				14 26	14 31	14 42			14 55	15 01			15 13			
Partick 226 a				13 58	14 05	14 16				14 29	14 35	14 46			14 58	15 05			15 16			
Hyndland 226 a				14 00	14 07	14 18				14 31	14 37	14 48			15 00	15 07			15 18			

A To Milngavie
B To Dalmuir
C From Cumbernauld to Dalmuir
D From Motherwell to Dalmuir
E From Manchester Airport
F From Milngavie to Cumbernauld
G To Glasgow Central
H To Ayr
I From Lanark

21 May to 7 December

Edinburgh, Lanark, Coatbridge, Motherwell, Whifflet, Larkhall and Hamilton - Glasgow

	VT	SR	SR	SR	SR	SR	SR	SR	SR	SR	SR	SR	SR	SR	SR	SR	SR	SR	SR	SR	SR
	◇1 A ⊠	B		C	D	E	F				E	E	F	G	E		D	E	F	E	
Edinburgh d		13 52	13 56						14 26	14 57											
Haymarket d		13 57	14 01						14 31	15 01											
Lanark d								14 53								15 23					15 53
Carstairs d		14 32																			
Carluke d		14 41						15 03								15 33					16 03
Wishaw d		14 53						15 09								15 39					16 10
Holytown d									15 32												
Shieldmuir d								15 12								15 45					16 13
Cumbernauld 226 d															15 21						
Greenfaulds 226 d															15 23						
Coatbridge Central d															15 30						
Whifflet d															15 33						
Motherwell a		15 03						15 15							15 40	15 48					16 16
Motherwell d	14 59	15 06						15 16			15 16	15 20		15 45	15 46	15 48				16 15	16 17
Whifflet d						14 58						15 28		15a52				15 58			
Kirkwood d						15 01						15 31						16 01			
Bargeddie d						15 04						15 34						16 04			
Baillieston d						15 07						15 38						16 07			
Mount Vernon d						15 09						15 40						16 09			
Carmyle d				←		15 12						15 42						16 12			
Bellshill d			14 47	14 55				15 22	15 37	15 47						15 55					16 23
Uddingston d				14 59	←			15 26	15 41							16 02	←				16 29
Airbles d					14 48						15 18				15 48		15 48			16 17	
Larkhall d							15 03						15 33		→				16 03	→	
Merryton d							15 05						15 35						16 05		
Chatelherault d							15 08						15 38						16 08		
Hamilton Central d					14 54		15 13				15 24		15 42				15 54		16 12		
Hamilton West d					14 56		15 15				15 26		15 45				15 56		16 15		
Blantyre d					15 00		15 19				15 30		15 48				16 00		16 18		
Newton d					15 05		15 23				15 34		15 52				16 05		16 22		
Cambuslang d				15 03	15 09		15 26	15 31			15 37		15 56			16 06	16 09		16 26		16 33
Rutherglen d					15 13	15 18	15 30				15 41	15 47	16 01				16 13	16 18	16 30		
Dalmarnock d					15 15	15 20	15 33				15 44	15 50					16 16	16 20	16 32		
Bridgeton d					15 17	15 22	15 35				15 46	15 52					16 18	16 22	16 34		
Argyle Street d					15 20	15 26	15 38				15 49	15 55	16 07				16 21	16 26	16 37		
Glasgow Central H. Level a	15 15	15 24	15 09	15 12				15 40	15 56	16 10						16 15					16 42
Glasgow Central L. Level a					15 22	15 27	15 39				15 51	15 57	16 09				16 22	16 27	16 39		
Anderston a					15 23	15 29	15 41				15 53	15 59	16 11				16 24	16 29	16 41		
Exhibition Centre a					15 25	15 31	15 43				15 55	16 01	16 13				16 26	16 31	16 43		
Partick 226 a					15 29	15 35	15 46				15 58	16 05	16 16				16 30	16 35	16 46		
Hyndland 226 a					15 31	15 37	15 48				16 00	16 07	16 18				16 32	16 37	16 48		

	SR	SR	TP	SR	SR	SR	SR	SR	SR	SR	SR	SR	SR	SR	SR	SR	SR	SR	SR	SR	SR	SR
	H	E	◇1 I ✠			G		F	E		D	E	F	E		H			E	F	G	E
Edinburgh d				15 26	15 49		15 55										16 26	16 57				
Haymarket d				15 30	15 54		16 01										16 30	17 01				
Lanark d										16 23					16 53							
Carstairs d					16 17																	
Carluke d					16 25					16 33					17 03							
Wishaw d										16 39					17 09							
Holytown d				16 32													17 31					
Shieldmuir d										16 45					17 12							
Cumbernauld 226 d									16 20													17 21
Greenfaulds 226 d									16 22													17 23
Coatbridge Central d									16 30													17 30
Whifflet d									16 33													17 33
Motherwell a					16 32				16 41	16 48					17 15							17 40
Motherwell d		16 20	16 22		16 33	16 45			16 46	16 48				17 15	17 16				17 20		17 45	17 46
Whifflet d		16 28				16a52						16 58							17 29		17a52	
Kirkwood d		16 31										17 01							17 32			
Bargeddie d		16 34										17 04							17 35			
Baillieston d		16 38										17 08							17 39			
Mount Vernon d		16 40										17 10							17 41			
Carmyle d		16 42										17 12							17 43			
Bellshill d				16 36			16 46			16 55					17 22		17 35	17 47				
Uddingston d	←			16 40						16 59	←				17 26	←	17 39					
Airbles d	16 17								16 48		16 48			17 17		17 17						17 49
Larkhall d								16 33	→				17 03	→						17 33		→
Merryton d								16 35					17 05							17 35		
Chatelherault d								16 38					17 08							17 38		
Hamilton Central d	16 23							16 42			16 54		17 12			17 23				17 42		
Hamilton West d	16 26							16 45			16 56		17 15			17 26				17 45		
Blantyre d	16 29							16 48			17 00		17 18			17 29				17 48		
Newton d	16 34							16 52			17 05		17 22			17 34				17 52		
Cambuslang d	16 37							16 56		17 03	17 09		17 26		17 31	17 37	17 44			17 56		
Rutherglen d	16 41	16 47						17 00			17 13	17 16	17 30			17 41			17 47	18 00		
Dalmarnock d	16 44	16 49						17 02				17 19	17 32			17 44			17 50	18 02		
Bridgeton d	16 46	16 51						17 04				17 21	17 34			17 46			17 52	18 04		
Argyle Street d	16 49	16 55						17 07			17 19	17 24	17 37			17 49			17 55	18 07		
Glasgow Central H. Level a			16 41	16 55	16 51		17 10			17 12					17 41		17 56	18 09				
Glasgow Central L. Level a	16 51	16 56						17 09			17 20	17 25	17 39			17 51			17 57	18 09		
Anderston a	16 53	16 59						17 11			17 22	17 27	17 41			17 53			17 59	18 11		
Exhibition Centre a	16 55	17 01						17 13			17 24	17 30	17 43			17 55			18 01	18 13		
Partick 226 a	16 59	17 05						17 16			17 28	17 35	17 46			17 58			18 05	18 16		
Hyndland 226 a	17 01	17 07						17 18			17 31	17 37	17 48			18 00			18 07	18 18		

A From London Euston
B To Ayr
C From Lanark
D From Cumbernauld to Dalmuir
E To Dalmuir
F To Milngavie
G From Milngavie to Cumbernauld
H From Motherwell to Dalmuir
I From Manchester Airport

Table T225-F

Mondays to Fridays

21 May to 7 December

Edinburgh, Lanark, Coatbridge, Motherwell, Whifflet, Larkhall and Hamilton - Glasgow

	SR	SR	SR	SR	SR	SR	TP	SR	SR	SR	SR	SR	SR	SR	SR	SR	SR	SR	SR	SR	SR
		A	B	C		B	◇1 D ✠		B	E	F		C	B		A			B	C	
Edinburgh d								17 23		17 40		17 49					17 58				
Haymarket d								17 28		17 46		17 53					18 03				
Lanark d	17 23				17 53										18 25						18 53
Carstairs d										18 10								18 39			
Carluke d	17 33				18 03					18 18					18 35			18 47			19 03
Wishaw d	17 39				18 09					18 25					18 41			19 00			19 09
Holytown d								18 32									19 00				
Shieldmuir d	17 44				18 12										18 45			19 04			19 12
Cumbernauld 226 d														18 18							
Greenfaulds 226 d														18 20							
Coatbridge Central d														18 31							
Whifflet d														18 34							
Motherwell a	17 49				18 15					18 31				18 41	18 48			19 08			19 15
Motherwell d	17 49				18 16	18 17	18 22		18 24	18 32	18 45			18 48	18 49						19 16
Whifflet d			17 58						18 31		18a51								18 58		
Kirkwood d			18 01						18 34										19 01		
Bargeddie d			18 04						18 37										19 04		
Baillieston d			18 07						18 40										19 07		
Mount Vernon d			18 09						18 42										19 09		
Carmyle d			18 12						18 45										19 12		
Bellshill d	17 56				18 22			18 37				18 44			18 55		19 04				19 22
Uddingston d	18 02	←			18 29			18 41							18 59	←	19 08				19 26
Airbles d		17 49				18 19								18 50		18 50					
Larkhall d				18 03									18 33	→						19 03	
Merryton d				18 05									18 35							19 05	
Chatelherault d				18 08									18 38							19 08	
Hamilton Central d		17 54		18 13		18 25							18 42			18 56				19 12	
Hamilton West d		17 57		18 15		18 28							18 45			18 58				19 15	
Blantyre d		18 00		18 19		18 31							18 48			19 02				19 18	
Newton d		18 06		18 23		18 35							18 52			19 06				19 22	
Cambuslang d	18 06	18 09		18 27	18 33	18 39						18 51	18 56		19 04	19 09	19 15			19 26	19 31
Rutherglen d		18 13	18 17	18 31		18 43			18 49				19 01			19 13			19 18	19 30	
Dalmarnock d		18 16	18 20			18 45			18 51				19 04			19 16			19 21	19 32	
Bridgeton d		18 18	18 22			18 47			18 53				19 06			19 18			19 23	19 34	
Argyle Street d		18 21	18 26	18 37		18 50			18 56				19 09			19 22			19 26	19 38	
Glasgow Central H. Level a	18 15				18 42		18 41	18 56		18 54		19 03			19 13		19 27				19 40
Glasgow Central L. Level a		18 22	18 27	18 39		18 52			18 58				19 10			19 23			19 27	19 39	
Anderston a		18 24	18 29	18 41		18 54			19 00				19 12			19 26			19 29	19 41	
Exhibition Centre a		18 26	18 32	18 43		18 56			19 02				19 14			19 28			19 31	19 43	
Partick 226 a		18 30	18 35	18 47		18 59			19 06				19 18			19 32			19 35	19 47	
Hyndland 226 a		18 32	18 37	18 49		19 01			19 08				19 20			19 34			19 37	19 49	

	SR	SR	SR	SR	SR	SR	SR	SR	SR	SR	SR	SR	SR	SR	TP	SR	SR	SR	SR	SR	SR	SR
	B	B	G	F		C	B		A	B	C	B		H	◇1 D ✠		B	C	F	B		A
Edinburgh d			18 26		18 57											19 27						
Haymarket d			18 31		19 01											19 31						
Lanark d								19 23					19 53								20 23	
Carstairs d			19 13																			
Carluke d			19 22					19 33					20 03								20 33	
Wishaw d			19 27					19 39					20 11								20 39	
Holytown d																20 32						
Shieldmuir d								19 45					20 14								20 45	
Cumbernauld 226 d							19 21													20 21		
Greenfaulds 226 d							19 23													20 23		
Coatbridge Central d							19 30													20 30		
Whifflet d							19 33		←											20 33		
Motherwell a			19 33				19 40	19 48	19 40				20 17							20 40	20 48	
Motherwell d	19 16	19 21	19 34	19 45			19 48	19 48	19 48			20 16	20 18		20 22		20 26		20 45	20 46	20 48	
Whifflet d		19 28		19a52			→			19 59							20 33		20a52			
Kirkwood d		19 31								20 02							20 36					
Bargeddie d		19 34								20 05							20 39					
Baillieston d		19 38								20 08							20 43					
Mount Vernon d		19 40								20 10							20 45					
Carmyle d		19 42								20 13							20 47					
Bellshill d					19 47			19 55					20 24			20 37					20 55	
Uddingston d								19 59					20 29	←		20 41					20 59	←
Airbles d	19 18								19 50			20 18		20 18						20 48		20 48
Larkhall d						19 33					20 03	→						20 33		→		
Merryton d						19 35					20 05							20 35				
Chatelherault d						19 38					20 08							20 38				
Hamilton Central d	19 25					19 42			19 56		20 12			20 25				20 44				20 55
Hamilton West d	19 27					19 45			19 58		20 15			20 28				20 46				20 58
Blantyre d	19 31					19 49			20 02		20 19			20 31				20 50				21 01
Newton d	19 35					19 53			20 06		20 24			20 37				20 54				21 05
Cambuslang d	19 38					19 56		20 03	20 10		20 28		20 33	20 40				20 57			21 03	21 09
Rutherglen d	19 42	19 47				20 00			20 14	20 17	20 32			20 44			20 51	21 01				21 13
Dalmarnock d	19 45	19 49				20 03			20 16	20 20	20 34			20 47			20 54	21 04				21 15
Bridgeton d	19 47	19 51				20 05			20 18	20 22	20 36			20 49			20 56	21 06				21 17
Argyle Street d	19 50	19 55				20 08			20 21	20 25	20 39			20 52			20 59	21 09				21 21
Glasgow Central H. Level a			19 54		20 10			20 12					20 44		20 42	20 56					21 12	
Glasgow Central L. Level a	19 51	19 56				20 09			20 23	20 27	20 41			20 54			21 00	21 10				21 22
Anderston a	19 53	19 59				20 11			20 25	20 30	20 43			20 56			21 02	21 12				21 24
Exhibition Centre a	19 55	20 01				20 13			20 27	20 32	20 45			20 58			21 04	21 14				21 26
Partick 226 a	19 59	20 05				20 17			20 30	20 35	20 48			21 01			21 08	21 18				21 30
Hyndland 226 a	20 01	20 07				20 19			20 32	20 37	20 50			21 03			21 10	21 20				21 32

A From Cumbernauld to Dalmuir
B To Dalmuir
C To Milngavie
D From Manchester Airport
E To Ayr
F From Milngavie to Cumbernauld
G From North Berwick to Ayr
H From Motherwell to Dalmuir

Mondays to Fridays

21 May to 7 December

Edinburgh, Lanark, Coatbridge, Motherwell, Whifflet, Larkhall and Hamilton - Glasgow

		SR A	SR B	SR	SR A	SR A	VT ◇1 C ⊠	SR B	VT ◇1 C ⊠	SR D	SR A	SR	SR E	SR A	SR B	SR	SR A	SR A	TP ◇1 F	SR FO	SR B	SR D	SR G
Edinburgh	d																			21 25			
Haymarket	d																			21 31			
Lanark	d			20 51								21 23				21 53							
Carstairs	d																						
Carluke	d			21 02								21 33				22 03							
Wishaw	d			21 08								21 39				22 09							
Holytown	d																			22 32			
Shieldmuir	d			21 12								21 44				22 12							
Cumbernauld 226	d										21 21												22 21
Greenfaulds 226	d										21 23												22 23
Coatbridge Central	d										21 30												22 30
Whifflet	d										21 33												22 33
Motherwell	a			21 15							21 40	21 49				22 16							22 40
	d			21 16	21 16	21 23	21 28		21 45	21 46	21 46	21 49				22 16	22 16	22 20	22 22			22 45	22 46
Whifflet	d	20 59				21 30				21a53				21 59				22 29				22a52	
Kirkwood	d	21 02				21 33								22 02				22 32					
Bargeddie	d	21 05				21 36								22 05				22 35					
Baillieston	d	21 08				21 40								22 08				22 38					
Mount Vernon	d	21 10				21 42								22 10				22 40					
Carmyle	d	21 13				21 44								22 13				22 43					
Bellshill	d			21 22								21 56				22 23				22 36			
Uddingston	d			21 26								22 00	←			22 29				22 40			
Airbles	d				21 18						21 48		21 48				22 18						22 48
Larkhall	d		21 03					21 33			→				22 03						22 33		→
Merryton	d		21 05					21 35							22 05						22 35		
Chatelherault	d		21 08					21 38							22 08						22 38		
Hamilton Central	d		21 12		21 24			21 42					21 54		22 12		22 24				22 42		
Hamilton West	d		21 15		21 27			21 45					21 56		22 15		22 26				22 45		
Blantyre	d		21 18		21 30			21 48					22 00		22 18		22 30				22 48		
Newton	d		21 22		21 34			21 52					22 04		22 22		22 34				22 53		
Cambuslang	d		21 26	21 31	21 38			21 56				22 04	22 08		22 26	22 33	22 37				22 56		
Rutherglen	d	21 17	21 30		21 42	21 48		22 00					22 13	22 18	22 30		22 41	22 47			23 01		
Dalmarnock	d	21 20	21 32		21 44	21 51		22 02					22 15	22 20	22 32		22 44	22 49					
Bridgeton	d	21 22	21 34		21 46	21 53		22 04					22 17	22 22	22 34		22 46	22 51					
Argyle Street	d	21 25	21 37		21 50	21 56		22 07					22 20	22 26	22 37		22 49	22 55			23 07		
Glasgow Central H. Level 15	a			21 41			21 44		22 02			22 13				22 43			22 38	22 55			
Glasgow Central L. Level 15	a	21 27	21 39		21 51	21 58		22 09					22 22	22 27	22 39		22 51	22 56			23 08		
Anderston	a	21 29	21 41		21 53	22 00		22 11					22 24	22 29	22 41		22 53	22 58			23 10		
Exhibition Centre	a	21 31	21 43		21 55	22 02		22 13					22 26	22 31	22 43		22 55	23 00			23 12		
Partick 226 ⛴	a	21 35	21 46		21 59	22 05		22 16					22 29	22 35	22 46		22 58	23 04			23 16		
Hyndland 3 226	a	21 37	21 48		22 01	22 07		22 18					22 31	22 37	22 48		23 00	23 06			23 18		

		SR	SR H	VT ◇1 C ⊠	SR A	SR B	SR	SR FO A	SR FX 🚌	SR	SR FO B	SR FO	SR	SR
Edinburgh	d								21 26			22 57		23 14
Haymarket	d								21 47			23 01		23 18
Lanark	d	22 23					22 51			23 23			23 51	
Carstairs	d													23 57
Carluke	d	22 33					23 01			23 33			00 01	00 07
Wishaw	d	22 40					23 07			23 39			00 07	00 14
Holytown	d											00 01		
Shieldmuir	d	22 44					23 10			23 42			00 10	
Cumbernauld 226	d													
Greenfaulds 226	d													
Coatbridge Central	d													
Whifflet	d													
Motherwell	a	22 47					23 14			23 45			00 15	00 19
	d	22 48		22 53			23 14	23 22						
Whifflet	d				22 58			23 29						
Kirkwood	d				23 01			23 32						
Bargeddie	d				23 04			23 35						
Baillieston	d				23 07			23 39						
Mount Vernon	d				23 09			23 41						
Carmyle	d				23 12			23 43						
Bellshill	d	22 55					23 21		23 36			00 05		
Uddingston	d	23 00	←				23 25					00 09		
Airbles	d		22 48											
Larkhall	d					23 03					23 33			
Merryton	d					23 05					23 35			
Chatelherault	d					23 08					23 38			
Hamilton Central	d		22 54			23 12					23 42			
Hamilton West	d		22 57			23 15					23 45			
Blantyre	d		23 00			23 18					23 48			
Newton	d		23 07			23 23					23 55			
Cambuslang	d	23 05	23 11			23 26	23 29				23 58	00 14		
Rutherglen	d		23 15		23 18	23 30		23 47			00 03			
Dalmarnock	d		23 17		23 20	23 33		23 50			00 06			
Bridgeton	d		23 19		23 22	23 35		23 52			00 08			
Argyle Street	d		23 22		23 26	23 38		23 55			00 11			
Glasgow Central H. Level 15	a	23 14		23 09			23 38		00 06			00 26		
Glasgow Central L. Level 15	a		23 24		23 27	23 39		23 57			00 12			
Anderston	a		23 25		23 29	23 41		23 59			00 14			
Exhibition Centre	a		23 27		23 31	23 43		00 02			00 16			
Partick 226 ⛴	a		23 31		23 35	23 47		00 05			00 20			
Hyndland 3 226	a		23 33		23 37	23 49		00 07			00 22			

A To Dalmuir
B To Milngavie
C From London Euston
D From Milngavie to Cumbernauld
E From Cumbernauld to Dalmuir
F From Manchester Airport
G To Garscadden
H From Cumbernauld to Garscadden

Saturdays

26 May to 8 December

Edinburgh, Lanark, Coatbridge, Motherwell, Whifflet, Larkhall and Hamilton - Glasgow

		SR A	SR B	SR C	SR A	SR D	SR E	SR E	SR F	SR E	SR	SR G	SR E	SR F	SR D	SR E	SR	SR H	SR	SR E	SR F	SR E	SR
Edinburgh	d																		05 52				
Haymarket	d																		05 56				
Lanark	d																06 22						06 53
Carstairs	d										05 48												
Carluke	d		00 01		00 07						05 57						06 32						07 03
Wishaw	d		00 07		00 14						06 08						06 38						07 09
Holytown	d	00 01																	06 58				
Shieldmuir	d		00 10								06 11						06 41						07 13
Cumbernauld 226	d															06 12							
Greenfaulds 226	d															06 14							
Coatbridge Central	d															06 22							
Whifflet	d															06 25							
Motherwell	a		00 15		00 19						06 14					06 37	06 45						07 16
	d					05 42	05 45	05 56		06 15	06 16		06 24		06 40	06 44	06 46					07 15	07 16
Whifflet	d					05a49		06 03					06 32		06a47					06 59			
Kirkwood	d							06 06					06 35							07 02			
Bargeddie	d							06 09					06 38							07 05			
Baillieston	d							06 13					06 42							07 08			
Mount Vernon	d							06 15					06 44							07 10			
Carmyle	d							06 17					06 46							07 13			
Bellshill	d	00 05									06 23						06 52		07 06				07 23
Uddingston	d	00 09									06 27	←					06 56	←	07 13				07 27
Airbles	d						05 47			06 17		06 17				06 47		06 47				07 18	
Larkhall	d								06 00	→				06 33		→					07 03	→	
Merryton	d								06 02					06 35							07 05		
Chatelherault	d								06 05					06 38							07 08		
Hamilton Central	d						05 53		06 09			06 23		06 42				06 52			07 12		
Hamilton West	d						05 55		06 12			06 25		06 45				06 55			07 15		
Blantyre	d						05 59		06 15			06 29		06 48				06 58			07 19		
Newton	d						06 03		06 19			06 33		06 53				07 02			07 23		
Cambuslang	d	00 14					06 06		06 23		06 31	06 36		06 56			07 01	07 06	07 18		07 27		07 31
Rutherglen	d			00 03			06 10	06 21	06 27			06 40	06 50	07 02				07 10		07 18	07 31		
Dalmarnock	d			00 06			06 13	06 24	06 29			06 43	06 53					07 13		07 21			
Bridgeton	d			00 08			06 15	06 26	06 31			06 45	06 55					07 15		07 23			
Argyle Street	d			00 11			06 18	06 29	06 35			06 48	06 58	07 07				07 18		07 26	07 37		
Glasgow Central H. Level 15	a	00 26									06 40						07 13		07 29				07 40
Glasgow Central L. Level 15	a			00 12			06 20	06 30	06 36			06 50	06 59	07 09				07 20		07 28	07 39		
Anderston	a			00 14			06 22	06 32	06 39			06 52	07 01	07 11				07 22		07 30	07 41		
Exhibition Centre	a			00 16			06 24	06 34	06 41			06 54	07 03	07 13				07 24		07 32	07 43		
Partick 226 ⛴	a			00 20			06 27	06 37	06 45			06 58	07 07	07 16				07 28		07 35	07 46		
Hyndland 3 226	a			00 22			06 29	06 39	06 47			07 00	07 09	07 18				07 30		07 37	07 48		

		SR G	SR	SR E	SR F	SR I	SR E	SR	SR H	TP ◇1 J	SR	SR E	SR F	SR E	SR	SR G	SR E	SR F	SR I	SR E	SR K	SR L	SR
Edinburgh	d		06 42								06 55											07 54	07 57
Haymarket	d		06 47								07 00											07 58	08 01
Lanark	d							07 23							07 52						08 23		
Carstairs	d									07 45												08 32	
Carluke	d							07 33							08 02						08 33	08 41	
Wishaw	d							07 39							08 08						08 39	08 55	
Holytown	d										08 04												
Shieldmuir	d							07 42							08 14						08 42		
Cumbernauld 226	d						07 13													08 12			
Greenfaulds 226	d						07 15													08 14			
Coatbridge Central	d						07 22													08 21			
Whifflet	d						07 25													08 24			
Motherwell	a						07 32	07 45		07 59					08 18					08 32	08 46	09 00	
	d			07 22		07 43	07 45	07 46		08 01				08 16	08 18		08 22		08 43	08 46	08 47	09 01	
Whifflet	d			07 29		07a49						08 02					08 30		08a50				
Kirkwood	d			07 32								08 05					08 33						
Bargeddie	d			07 35								08 08					08 36						
Baillieston	d			07 39								08 12					08 39						
Mount Vernon	d			07 41								08 14					08 41						
Carmyle	d			07 43								08 17					08 44						
Bellshill	d		07 30					07 52			08 09				08 25						08 56		08 49
Uddingston	d	←						07 56	←		08 13				08 29	←					→		
Airbles	d	07 18					07 48		07 48					08 18		08 18				08 48			
Larkhall	d				07 33		→						08 03	→				08 33		→			
Merryton	d				07 35								08 05					08 35					
Chatelherault	d				07 38								08 08					08 38					
Hamilton Central	d	07 24			07 43				07 53				08 12			08 24		08 42					
Hamilton West	d	07 26			07 45				07 56				08 15			08 27		08 45					
Blantyre	d	07 30			07 49				07 59				08 19			08 30		08 48					
Newton	d	07 34			07 53				08 03				08 23			08 34		08 52					
Cambuslang	d	07 37			07 57			08 01	08 07				08 27		08 33	08 38		08 56					
Rutherglen	d	07 41		07 47	08 01				08 11			08 21	08 31			08 42	08 48	09 00					
Dalmarnock	d	07 44		07 50	08 03				08 13			08 24	08 33			08 44	08 50	09 02					
Bridgeton	d	07 46		07 52	08 05				08 15			08 26	08 35			08 46	08 52	09 04					
Argyle Street	d	07 49		07 55	08 08				08 18			08 29	08 38			08 50	08 56	09 07					
Glasgow Central H. Level 15	a		07 52					08 10		08 20	08 28				08 42							09 23	09 10
Glasgow Central L. Level 15	a	07 50		07 57	08 10				08 20			08 31	08 40			08 51	08 57	09 09					
Anderston	a	07 52		07 59	08 12				08 22			08 33	08 42			08 53	08 59	09 10					
Exhibition Centre	a	07 54		08 01	08 14				08 24			08 35	08 44			08 55	09 01	09 12					
Partick 226 ⛴	a	07 58		08 04	08 17				08 27			08 39	08 47			08 59	09 05	09 16					
Hyndland 3 226	a	08 00		08 06	08 19				08 29			08 42	08 49			09 01	09 07	09 18					

A From Edinburgh
B From Lanark
C From Larkhall to Milngavie
D To Cumbernauld
E To Dalmuir
F To Milngavie
G From Motherwell to Dalmuir
H From Cumbernauld to Dalmuir
I From Milngavie to Cumbernauld
J From Manchester Piccadilly
K To Glasgow Central
L From North Berwick to Ayr

Table T225-F

Saturdays

26 May to 8 December

Edinburgh, Lanark, Coatbridge, Motherwell, Whifflet, Larkhall and Hamilton - Glasgow

Station	SR A	SR B	SR C	SR D	SR	SR	SR	SR C	SR C	SR D	SR E	SR C	SR	SR B	SR C	SR D	SR C	SR	SR F	TP ◇1 G	SR
Edinburgh d						08 26	08 57														09 25
Haymarket d						08 31	09 01														09 32
Lanark d					08 53								09 23					09 52			
Carstairs d																					
Carluke d					09 03								09 33					10 02			
Wishaw d					09 09								09 39					10 08			
Holytown d						09 32															10 33
Shieldmuir d					09 12								09 42					10 12			
Cumbernauld 226 d												09 22									
Greenfaulds 226 d												09 24									
Coatbridge Central d												09 31									
Whifflet d												09 34									
Motherwell a					09 15							09 41	09 46					10 16			
d					09 16			09 16	09 22		09 43	09 45	09 47				10 16	10 17		10 21	
Whifflet d			08 58						09 29		09a50				09 58						
Kirkwood d			09 01						09 32						10 01						
Bargeddie d			09 04						09 35						10 04						
Baillieston d			09 07						09 39						10 07						
Mount Vernon d			09 09						09 41						10 09						
Carmyle d	←		09 12						09 43						10 12						
Bellshill d	08 56				09 23	09 37	09 48						09 53					10 23			10 37
Uddingston d	09 01	←			09 27	09 41							09 57	←				10 28	←		10 41
Airbles d		08 48						09 18				09 48		09 48			10 18		10 18		
Larkhall d				09 03						09 33		→				10 03	→				
Merryton d				09 05						09 35						10 05					
Chatelherault d				09 08						09 38						10 08					
Hamilton Central d		08 54		09 12				09 24		09 42				09 53		10 12			10 24		
Hamilton West d		08 56		09 15				09 26		09 45				09 56		10 15			10 26		
Blantyre d		09 00		09 18				09 30		09 48				09 59		10 18			10 30		
Newton d		09 05		09 22				09 34		09 52				10 04		10 22			10 34		
Cambuslang d	09 06	09 09		09 26	09 31			09 37		09 56			10 03	10 09		10 26		10 33	10 38		
Rutherglen d		09 13	09 17	09 30				09 42	09 48	10 00				10 13	10 17	10 30			10 42		
Dalmarnock d		09 15	09 19	09 32				09 44	09 51	10 03				10 15	10 19	10 32			10 44		
Bridgeton d		09 17	09 21	09 34				09 46	09 53	10 05				10 17	10 21	10 34			10 46		
Argyle Street d		09 20	09 25	09 37				09 49	09 56	10 08				10 20	10 25	10 37			10 49		
Glasgow Central H. Level a	09 16				09 42	09 56	10 10						10 12					10 42		10 39	10 56
Glasgow Central L. Level a		09 22	09 26	09 39				09 51	09 58	10 09				10 22	10 26	10 39			10 51		
Anderston a		09 24	09 29	09 40				09 53	10 00	10 11				10 23	10 29	10 41			10 53		
Exhibition Centre a		09 26	09 31	09 42				09 55	10 02	10 13				10 25	10 31	10 43			10 55		
Partick 226 a		09 29	09 35	09 46				09 58	10 05	10 16				10 29	10 35	10 46			10 58		
Hyndland 226 a		09 31	09 37	09 48				10 00	10 07	10 18				10 31	10 37	10 48			11 00		

Station	SR	SR C	SR D	SR E	SR C	SR	SR B	SR C	SR D	SR C	SR	SR F	SR C	SR	SR E	SR	SR	SR D	SR C	SR	SR B	SR C
Edinburgh d	09 56													10 20		10 26	10 56					
Haymarket d	10 01													10 24		10 31	11 00					
Lanark d						10 23					10 53									11 23		
Carstairs d														11 10								
Carluke d						10 33					11 03			11 20						11 33		
Wishaw d						10 39					11 09			11 28						11 39		
Holytown d																11 32						
Shieldmuir d						10 45					11 14									11 45		
Cumbernauld 226 d					10 21														11 21			
Greenfaulds 226 d					10 23														11 23			
Coatbridge Central d					10 30														11 30			
Whifflet d					10 33														11 33			
Motherwell a					10 40	10 48					11 17			11 34					11 40	11 48		
d		10 23		10 45	10 46	10 48				11 16	11 17		11 20	11 34	11 45				11 46	11 48		
Whifflet d		10 30		10a52				11 00					11 28		11a52							11 58
Kirkwood d		10 33						11 03					11 31									12 01
Bargeddie d		10 36						11 06					11 34									12 04
Baillieston d		10 40						11 09					11 38									12 07
Mount Vernon d		10 42						11 11					11 40									12 09
Carmyle d		10 44						11 14					11 42									12 12
Bellshill d	10 50					10 55					11 24					11 37	11 49			11 55		
Uddingston d						10 59	←				11 28	←				11 42				12 02	←	
Airbles d					10 48		10 48			11 18		11 18							11 48		11 48	
Larkhall d			10 33		→				11 03	→								11 33	→			
Merryton d			10 35						11 05									11 35				
Chatelherault d			10 38						11 08									11 38				
Hamilton Central d			10 42				10 54		11 12			11 24						11 42			11 54	
Hamilton West d			10 45				10 56		11 15			11 26						11 45			11 56	
Blantyre d			10 48				11 00		11 18			11 30						11 48			12 00	
Newton d			10 52				11 05		11 23			11 34						11 52			12 05	
Cambuslang d			10 56			11 03	11 09		11 26		11 32	11 37						11 56		12 06	12 09	
Rutherglen d		10 49	11 00				11 13	11 19	11 30			11 41	11 48					12 00			12 13	12 17
Dalmarnock d		10 51	11 02				11 15	11 21				11 44	11 50					12 02			12 16	12 20
Bridgeton d		10 53	11 04				11 17	11 23				11 46	11 52					12 04			12 18	12 22
Argyle Street d		10 57	11 07				11 20	11 27	11 36			11 49	11 56					12 07			12 21	12 25
Glasgow Central H. Level a	11 10					11 12					11 42			11 53		11 57	12 09			12 15		
Glasgow Central L. Level a		10 58	11 09				11 22	11 28	11 38			11 51	11 57					12 09			12 22	12 27
Anderston a		11 00	11 11				11 23	11 30	11 40			11 53	11 59					12 10			12 24	12 29
Exhibition Centre a		11 02	11 13				11 25	11 32	11 42			11 55	12 01					12 12			12 26	12 31
Partick 226 a		11 06	11 16				11 29	11 36	11 45			11 58	12 05					12 16			12 29	12 35
Hyndland 226 a		11 08	11 18				11 31	11 38	11 47			12 00	12 07					12 18			12 31	12 37

A From Lanark
B From Cumbernauld to Dalmuir
C To Dalmuir
D To Milngavie
E From Milngavie to Cumbernauld
F From Motherwell to Dalmuir
G From Manchester Airport

Table T225-F

Saturdays

26 May to 8 December

Edinburgh, Lanark, Coatbridge, Motherwell, Whifflet, Larkhall and Hamilton - Glasgow

Station	SR A	SR B	SR	SR C	SR B	TP ◇1 D	SR	SR A	SR E	SR B	SR F	SR G	SR	SR H	SR I	SR B	SR A	SR	SR	SR	SR B
Edinburgh d							11 26					11 53	11 56						12 26	12 57	
Haymarket d							11 31					11 58	12 01						12 30	13 02	
Lanark d			11 53								12 23							12 53			
Carstairs d												12 47									
Carluke d			12 03								12 33	12 56						13 03			
Wishaw d			12 10								12 39	13 03						13 09			
Holytown d							12 32												13 32		
Shieldmuir d			12 13								12 44							13 12			
Cumbernauld 226 d										12 21											
Greenfaulds 226 d										12 23											
Coatbridge Central d										12 30											
Whifflet d										12 33											
Motherwell a			12 16							12 40	12 48	13 09						13 15			
d		12 16	12 17		12 20	12 23			12 45	12 46	12 48	13 09						13 16			13 16
Whifflet d					12 30				12a52							12 58					
Kirkwood d					12 33											13 01					
Bargeddie d					12 36											13 04					
Baillieston d					12 40											13 07					
Mount Vernon d					12 42											13 09					
Carmyle d					12 44									←		13 12					
Bellshill d			12 23				12 37				12 55		12 48	12 55				13 22	13 37	13 50	
Uddingston d			12 30	←			12 41				→			12 59	←			13 26	13 41		
Airbles d		12 18		12 18						12 48					12 48						13 18
Larkhall d	12 03	→						12 33		→							13 03				
Merryton d	12 05							12 35									13 05				
Chatelherault d	12 08							12 38									13 08				
Hamilton Central d	12 13			12 24				12 42							12 54		13 13				13 24
Hamilton West d	12 15			12 26				12 45							12 56		13 15				13 26
Blantyre d	12 19			12 30				12 48							13 00		13 19				13 30
Newton d	12 23			12 35				12 52							13 05		13 23				13 34
Cambuslang d	12 26		12 34	12 39				12 56						13 03	13 09		13 26	13 31			13 37
Rutherglen d	12 30			12 43	12 48			13 00							13 13	13 17	13 30				13 41
Dalmarnock d	12 33			12 45	12 51										13 15	13 20	13 33				13 44
Bridgeton d	12 35			12 47	12 53										13 17	13 22	13 35				13 46
Argyle Street d	12 38			12 50	12 56			13 06							13 20	13 25	13 38				13 49
Glasgow Central H. Level a			12 45			12 42	12 56					13 24	13 10	13 12				13 40	13 56	14 10	
Glasgow Central L. Level a	12 39			12 52	12 58			13 07							13 22	13 27	13 39				13 51
Anderston a	12 41			12 53	13 00			13 09							13 23	13 29	13 41				13 53
Exhibition Centre a	12 43			12 55	13 02			13 11							13 25	13 31	13 43				13 55
Partick 226 a	12 46			12 59	13 05			13 15							13 29	13 35	13 46				13 58
Hyndland 226 a	12 48			13 01	13 07			13 17							13 31	13 37	13 48				14 00

Station	SR B	SR A	SR E	SR B	SR	SR I	SR B	SR A	SR B	SR	SR C	SR B	TP ◇1 D	SR	SR A	SR E	SR B	SR F	VT ◇1 J	SR G	SR	SR H
Edinburgh d														13 27						13 52	13 55	
Haymarket d														13 31						13 57	14 01	
Lanark d					13 23					13 53								14 23				
Carstairs d																				14 32		
Carluke d					13 33					14 03								14 33		14 41		
Wishaw d					13 41					14 09								14 39		14 53		
Holytown d														14 32								
Shieldmuir d					13 45					14 13								14 44				
Cumbernauld 226 d				13 20													14 21					
Greenfaulds 226 d				13 22													14 23					
Coatbridge Central d				13 29													14 30					
Whifflet d				13 33													14 33					
Motherwell a				13 40	13 48					14 16							14 40	14 48		15 03		
d	13 21		13 45	13 46	13 48				14 16	14 17		14 20	14 22			14 45	14 46	14 48	14 59	15 06		
Whifflet d	13 28		13a52				13 58					14 28				14a52						
Kirkwood d	13 31						14 01					14 31										
Bargeddie d	13 34						14 04					14 34										
Baillieston d	13 38						14 07					14 38										
Mount Vernon d	13 40						14 09					14 40										
Carmyle d	13 42						14 12					14 42										←
Bellshill d					13 55					14 23				14 36				14 55			14 47	14 55
Uddingston d					14 02	←				14 28	←			14 40				→				14 59
Airbles d				13 48		13 48			14 18		14 18						14 48					
Larkhall d		13 33		→				14 03	→						14 33		→					
Merryton d		13 35						14 05							14 35							
Chatelherault d		13 38						14 08							14 38							
Hamilton Central d		13 42				13 54		14 12			14 24				14 42							
Hamilton West d		13 45				13 56		14 15			14 26				14 45							
Blantyre d		13 48				14 00		14 18			14 30				14 48							
Newton d		13 52				14 05		14 22			14 34				14 52							
Cambuslang d		13 56			14 06	14 09		14 26		14 33	14 37				14 56							15 03
Rutherglen d	13 48	14 00				14 13	14 17	14 30			14 41	14 46			15 00							
Dalmarnock d	13 50	14 02				14 16	14 20	14 32			14 44	14 49			15 02							
Bridgeton d	13 52	14 04				14 18	14 22	14 34			14 46	14 51			15 04							
Argyle Street d	13 56	14 08				14 21	14 25	14 37			14 49	14 54			15 08							
Glasgow Central H. Level a					14 15					14 42			14 40	14 55					15 15	15 25	15 09	15 12
Glasgow Central L. Level a	13 57	14 09				14 22	14 27	14 39			14 51	14 56			15 09							
Anderston a	14 00	14 11				14 24	14 29	14 40			14 53	14 59			15 11							
Exhibition Centre a	14 02	14 13				14 26	14 31	14 42			14 55	15 01			15 13							
Partick 226 a	14 05	14 16				14 29	14 35	14 46			14 58	15 05			15 16							
Hyndland 226 a	14 07	14 18				14 31	14 37	14 48			15 00	15 07			15 18							

A To Milngavie
B To Dalmuir
C From Motherwell to Dalmuir
D From Manchester Airport
E From Milngavie to Cumbernauld
F To Glasgow Central
G To Ayr
H From Lanark
I From Cumbernauld to Dalmuir
J From London Euston

26 May to 8 December

Edinburgh, Lanark, Coatbridge, Motherwell, Whifflet, Larkhall and Hamilton - Glasgow

	SR A	SR B	SR C	SR	SR	SR	SR B	SR B	SR C	SR D	SR B	SR	SR A	SR B	SR C	SR B	SR	SR E	SR B	TP ◇1 F ⚒	SR	SR C
Edinburgh d					14 26	14 57															15 26	
Haymarket d					14 31	15 01															15 30	
Lanark d				14 53								15 23					15 53					
Carstairs d																						
Carluke d				15 03								15 33					16 03					
Wishaw d				15 09								15 39					16 10					
Holytown d					15 32																16 32	
Shieldmuir d				15 12								15 45					16 13					
Cumbernauld 226 d											15 21											
Greenfaulds 226 d											15 23											
Coatbridge Central d											15 30											
Whifflet d											15 33											
Motherwell a				15 15							15 40	15 48					16 16					
d				15 16			15 16	15 20		15 45	15 46	15 48				16 15	16 17		16 20	16 22		
Whifflet d		14 58						15 28		15a52				15 58					16 28			
Kirkwood d		15 01						15 31						16 01					16 31			
Bargeddie d		15 04						15 34						16 04					16 34			
Baillieston d		15 07						15 38						16 07					16 38			
Mount Vernon d		15 09						15 40						16 09					16 40			
Carmyle d		15 12						15 42						16 12					16 42			
Bellshill d				15 22	15 37	15 46						15 55					16 23				16 36	
Uddingston d	←			15 26	15 41							16 02	←				16 29	←			16 40	
Airbles d	14 48						15 18				15 48		15 48			16 17		16 17				
Larkhall d			15 03						15 33		→				16 03	→						16 33
Merryton d			15 05						15 35						16 05							16 35
Chatelherault d			15 08						15 38						16 08							16 38
Hamilton Central d	14 54		15 13				15 24		15 42				15 54		16 12			16 23				16 42
Hamilton West d	14 56		15 15				15 26		15 45				15 56		16 15			16 26				16 45
Blantyre d	15 00		15 19				15 30		15 48				16 00		16 18			16 29				16 48
Newton d	15 05		15 23				15 34		15 52				16 05		16 22			16 34				16 52
Cambuslang d	15 09		15 26	15 31			15 37		15 56			16 06	16 09		16 26		16 33	16 37				16 56
Rutherglen d	15 13	15 18	15 30				15 41	15 47	16 01				16 13	16 18	16 30			16 41	16 47			17 00
Dalmarnock d	15 15	15 20	15 33				15 44	15 50					16 16	16 20	16 32			16 44	16 49			17 02
Bridgeton d	15 17	15 22	15 35				15 46	15 52					16 18	16 22	16 34			16 46	16 51			17 04
Argyle Street d	15 20	15 26	15 38				15 49	15 55	16 07				16 21	16 26	16 37			16 49	16 55			17 07
Glasgow Central H. Level 15 a				15 40	15 56	16 10						16 15					16 42			16 40	16 55	
Glasgow Central L. Level 15 a	15 22	15 27	15 39				15 51	15 57	16 09				16 22	16 27	16 39			16 51	16 56			17 09
Anderston a	15 23	15 29	15 41				15 53	15 59	16 11				16 24	16 29	16 41			16 53	16 59			17 11
Exhibition Centre a	15 25	15 31	15 43				15 55	16 01	16 13				16 26	16 31	16 43			16 55	17 01			17 13
Partick 226 a	15 29	15 35	15 46				15 58	16 05	16 16				16 30	16 35	16 46			16 59	17 05			17 16
Hyndland 3 226 a	15 31	15 37	15 48				16 00	16 07	16 18				16 32	16 37	16 48			17 01	17 07			17 18

	SR D	SR B	SR G	SR H	SR	SR I	SR A	SR B	SR C	SR B	SR	SR E	SR	SR	SR B	SR C	SR D	SR B	SR	SR A	SR B
Edinburgh d				15 49	15 55								16 26	16 56							
Haymarket d				15 54	16 00								16 30	17 01							
Lanark d			16 23								16 53								17 23		
Carstairs d				16 32																	
Carluke d			16 33	16 41							17 03								17 33		
Wishaw d			16 39	16 57							17 09								17 39		
Holytown d													17 31								
Shieldmuir d			16 45								17 12								17 45		
Cumbernauld 226 d		16 20																17 21			
Greenfaulds 226 d		16 22																17 23			
Coatbridge Central d		16 30																17 30			
Whifflet d		16 33																17 33			
Motherwell a		16 41	16 48	17 04							17 16							17 40	17 49		
d	16 45	16 46	16 48	17 06						17 15	17 16				17 20		17 45	17 46	17 49		
Whifflet d	16a52							16 58							17 29		17a52				17 58
Kirkwood d								17 01							17 32						18 01
Bargeddie d								17 04							17 35						18 04
Baillieston d								17 08							17 39						18 07
Mount Vernon d								17 10							17 41						18 09
Carmyle d						←		17 12							17 43						18 12
Bellshill d			16 55		16 46	16 55					17 23		17 35	17 47					17 56		
Uddingston d			→			16 59	←				17 27	←	17 39						18 02	←	
Airbles d		16 48					16 48			17 17		17 17						17 49		17 49	
Larkhall d		→							17 03	→						17 33		→			
Merryton d									17 05							17 35					
Chatelherault d									17 08							17 38					
Hamilton Central d							16 54		17 12			17 23				17 42				17 54	
Hamilton West d							16 56		17 15			17 26				17 45				17 57	
Blantyre d							17 00		17 18			17 29				17 48				18 00	
Newton d							17 05		17 22			17 34				17 52				18 06	
Cambuslang d						17 03	17 09		17 26		17 31	17 37	17 44			17 56			18 06	18 09	
Rutherglen d							17 13	17 16	17 30			17 41			17 47	18 00				18 13	18 17
Dalmarnock d								17 19	17 32			17 44			17 50	18 02				18 16	18 20
Bridgeton d								17 21	17 34			17 46			17 52	18 04				18 18	18 22
Argyle Street d							17 19	17 24	17 37			17 49			17 55	18 07				18 21	18 26
Glasgow Central H. Level 15 a				17 23	17 10	17 12					17 40		17 56	18 09					18 15		
Glasgow Central L. Level 15 a							17 20	17 25	17 39			17 51			17 57	18 09				18 22	18 27
Anderston a							17 22	17 27	17 41			17 53			17 59	18 11				18 24	18 29
Exhibition Centre a							17 24	17 30	17 43			17 55			18 01	18 13				18 26	18 32
Partick 226 a							17 28	17 35	17 46			17 58			18 05	18 16				18 30	18 35
Hyndland 3 226 a							17 31	17 37	17 48			18 00			18 07	18 18				18 32	18 37

A From Cumbernauld to Dalmuir
B To Dalmuir
C To Milngavie
D From Milngavie to Cumbernauld
E From Motherwell to Dalmuir
F From Manchester Airport
G To Glasgow Central
H To Ayr
I From Lanark

26 May to 8 December

Edinburgh, Lanark, Coatbridge, Motherwell, Whifflet, Larkhall and Hamilton - Glasgow

	SR A	SR B	SR	SR C	SR	SR B	SR D	SR E	SR A	SR	SR B	SR	SR F	SR	SR B	SR A	SR	SR B	SR B	SR G	SR E	SR
Edinburgh d					17 24		17 41			17 49				17 58						18 27		18 56
Haymarket d					17 28		17 47			17 54				18 02						18 32		19 01
Lanark d			17 53									18 23					18 53					
Carstairs d							18 10													19 13		
Carluke d			18 03				18 20					18 33					19 03			19 22		
Wishaw d			18 09				18 26					18 39					19 09			19 27		
Holytown d					18 32									19 01								
Shieldmuir d			18 15									18 45					19 12					
Cumbernauld 226 d											18 18											
Greenfaulds 226 d											18 20											
Coatbridge Central d											18 31											
Whifflet d											18 34											
Motherwell a			18 18				18 32				18 41	18 48					19 15			19 33		
d		18 17	18 18			18 20	18 32	18 45			18 48	18 49					19 16	19 16	19 21	19 34	19 45	
Whifflet d						18 29		18a51							18 58				19 28		19a52	
Kirkwood d						18 32									19 01				19 31			
Bargeddie d						18 35									19 04				19 34			
Baillieston d						18 39									19 07				19 38			
Mount Vernon d						18 41									19 09				19 40			
Carmyle d						18 43									19 12				19 42			
Bellshill d			18 25		18 37					18 46		18 55		19 05			19 22					19 47
Uddingston d			18 29	←	18 41							18 59	←	19 09			19 26					
Airbles d		18 19		18 19							18 50		18 50					19 18				
Larkhall d	18 03	→							18 33		→					19 03						
Merryton d	18 05								18 35							19 05						
Chatelherault d	18 08								18 38							19 08						
Hamilton Central d	18 13			18 25					18 42				18 56			19 12		19 25				
Hamilton West d	18 15			18 28					18 45				18 58			19 15		19 27				
Blantyre d	18 19			18 31					18 48				19 02			19 18		19 31				
Newton d	18 23			18 35					18 52				19 06			19 22		19 35				
Cambuslang d	18 27		18 33	18 39					18 56	18 59		19 04	19 09	19 15		19 26	19 31	19 38				
Rutherglen d	18 31			18 43		18 47			19 01				19 13		19 18	19 30		19 42	19 47			
Dalmarnock d				18 45		18 50			19 04				19 16		19 21	19 32		19 45	19 49			
Bridgeton d				18 47		18 52			19 06				19 18		19 23	19 34		19 47	19 51			
Argyle Street d	18 37			18 50		18 55			19 09				19 22		19 26	19 38		19 50	19 55			
Glasgow Central H. Level 15 a			18 42		18 56		18 54			19 11		19 13		19 27			19 40			19 54		20 10
Glasgow Central L. Level 15 a	18 39			18 52		18 57			19 10				19 23		19 27	19 39		19 51	19 56			
Anderston a	18 41			18 54		18 59			19 12				19 26		19 29	19 41		19 53	19 59			
Exhibition Centre a	18 43			18 56		19 01			19 14				19 28		19 31	19 43		19 55	20 01			
Partick 226 a	18 47			18 59		19 05			19 18				19 32		19 35	19 47		19 59	20 05			
Hyndland 3 226 a	18 49			19 01		19 07			19 20				19 34		19 37	19 49		20 01	20 07			

	SR A	SR B	SR	SR F	SR B	SR A	SR B	SR	SR C	TP ◇1 H ⚒	SR	SR B	SR A	SR B	SR	SR F	SR E	SR B	SR A	SR	SR B
Edinburgh d											19 26										
Haymarket d											19 30										
Lanark d			19 23					19 55							20 20					20 51	
Carstairs d																					
Carluke d			19 33					20 05							20 30					21 01	
Wishaw d			19 39					20 11							20 36					21 07	
Holytown d											20 32										
Shieldmuir d			19 45					20 14							20 39					21 11	
Cumbernauld 226 d		19 21												20 21							
Greenfaulds 226 d		19 23												20 23							
Coatbridge Central d		19 30												20 30							
Whifflet d		19 33		←										20 33		←					
Motherwell a		19 40	19 48	19 40				20 17						20 40	20 42	20 40				21 14	
d		19 48	19 48	19 48			20 16	20 18		20 22		20 26		20 46	20 43	20 46	20 48			21 14	21 16
Whifflet d		→			19 59							20 33		→			20a54	21 00			
Kirkwood d					20 02							20 36						21 03			
Bargeddie d					20 05							20 39						21 06			
Baillieston d					20 08							20 43						21 09			
Mount Vernon d					20 10							20 45						21 11			
Carmyle d					20 13							20 47						21 14			
Bellshill d			19 55					20 24			20 37				20 49					21 21	
Uddingston d			19 59					20 29	←		20 41				20 53					21 25	
Airbles d				19 50			20 18		20 18							20 48					21 18
Larkhall d	19 33					20 03	→						20 33						21 03		
Merryton d	19 35					20 05							20 35						21 05		
Chatelherault d	19 38					20 08							20 38						21 08		
Hamilton Central d	19 42			19 56		20 12			20 25				20 44			20 55			21 12		21 24
Hamilton West d	19 45			19 58		20 15			20 28				20 46			20 58			21 15		21 27
Blantyre d	19 49			20 02		20 19			20 31				20 50			21 01			21 18		21 30
Newton d	19 53			20 06		20 24			20 37				20 54			21 06			21 22		21 34
Cambuslang d	19 56		20 03	20 10		20 28		20 34	20 40				20 57		21 00	21 10			21 26	21 29	21 38
Rutherglen d	20 00			20 14	20 17	20 32			20 44			20 51	21 01			21 14		21 18	21 30		21 42
Dalmarnock d	20 03			20 16	20 20	20 34			20 47			20 54	21 04			21 16		21 21	21 32		21 44
Bridgeton d	20 05			20 18	20 22	20 36			20 49			20 56	21 06			21 18		21 23	21 34		21 46
Argyle Street d	20 08			20 21	20 25	20 39			20 52			20 59	21 09			21 21		21 26	21 37		21 50
Glasgow Central H. Level 15 a			20 12					20 45		20 42	20 57				21 10					21 38	
Glasgow Central L. Level 15 a	20 09			20 23	20 27	20 41			20 54			21 00	21 10			21 23		21 27	21 39		21 51
Anderston a	20 11			20 25	20 30	20 43			20 56			21 02	21 12			21 24		21 29	21 41		21 53
Exhibition Centre a	20 13			20 27	20 32	20 45			20 58			21 04	21 14			21 26		21 31	21 43		21 55
Partick 226 a	20 17			20 30	20 35	20 48			21 01			21 08	21 18			21 30		21 35	21 46		21 59
Hyndland 3 226 a	20 19			20 32	20 37	20 50			21 03			21 10	21 20			21 32		21 37	21 48		22 01

A To Milngavie
B To Dalmuir
C From Motherwell to Dalmuir
D To Ayr
E From Milngavie to Cumbernauld
F From Cumbernauld to Dalmuir
G From North Berwick to Ayr
H From Manchester Airport

Table T225-F

Saturdays
26 May to 8 December

Edinburgh, Lanark, Coatbridge, Motherwell, Whifflet, Larkhall and Hamilton - Glasgow

		SR A	SR B	SR C	SR A	SR	SR D	SR A	SR B	SR	SR	SR A	SR A	SR B	SR C	SR E	SR	SR F	VT ◇ G	SR A	SR B	SR	SR
Edinburgh	d										21 26												22 56
Haymarket	d										21 30												23 00
Lanark	d					21 23				21 53							22 23					22 51	
Carstairs	d																						
Carluke	d					21 33				22 03							22 33					23 01	
Wishaw	d					21 39				22 09							22 40					23 07	
Holytown	d										22 32												00 01
Shieldmuir	d					21 46				22 12							22 44					23 10	
Cumbernauld 226	d				21 21											22 21							
Greenfaulds 226	d				21 23											22 23							
Coatbridge Central	d				21 30											22 30							
Whifflet	d				21 33											22 33							
Motherwell	a				21 40	21 49				22 16						22 40	22 48					23 13	
	d	21 23		21 46	21 46	21 50				22 16		22 16	22 20		22 45	22 46	22 48		22 53			23 14	
Whifflet	d	21 30		21a52				21 59					22 29		22a52					22 58			
Kirkwood	d	21 33						22 02					22 32							23 01			
Bargeddie	d	21 36						22 05					22 35							23 04			
Baillieston	d	21 40						22 08					22 38							23 07			
Mount Vernon	d	21 42						22 10					22 40							23 09			
Carmyle	d	21 44						22 13					22 43							23 12			
Bellshill	d					21 56				22 23	22 36						22 55					23 20	00 05
Uddingston	d					22 00	←			22 29	22 40						23 00	←				23 24	00 09
Airbles	d				21 48		21 48					22 18				22 48		22 48					
Larkhall	d		21 33		→				22 03					22 33		→					23 03		
Merryton	d		21 35						22 05					22 35							23 05		
Chatelherault	d		21 38						22 08					22 38							23 08		
Hamilton Central	d		21 42				21 54		22 12			22 24		22 42				22 54			23 12		
Hamilton West	d		21 45				21 56		22 15			22 26		22 45				22 57			23 15		
Blantyre	d		21 48				22 00		22 18			22 30		22 48				23 00			23 18		
Newton	d		21 52				22 04		22 22			22 34		22 53				23 07			23 23		
Cambuslang	d		21 56			22 05	22 08		22 26	22 35		22 37		22 56			23 05	23 11			23 26	23 29	00 14
Rutherglen	d	21 48	22 00				22 13	22 18	22 30			22 41	22 47	23 01				23 15		23 18	23 30		
Dalmarnock	d	21 51	22 02				22 15	22 20	22 32			22 44	22 49					23 17		23 20	23 33		
Bridgeton	d	21 53	22 04				22 17	22 22	22 34			22 46	22 51					23 19		23 22	23 35		
Argyle Street	d	21 56	22 07				22 20	22 26	22 37			22 49	22 55	23 07				23 22		23 26	23 38		
Glasgow Central H. Level 15	a					22 14				22 44	22 55						23 14		23 09			23 38	00 26
Glasgow Central L. Level 15	a	21 58	22 09				22 22	22 27	22 39			22 51	22 56	23 08				23 24		23 27	23 39		
Anderston	a	22 00	22 11				22 24	22 29	22 41			22 53	22 58	23 10				23 25		23 29	23 41		
Exhibition Centre	a	22 02	22 13				22 26	22 31	22 43			22 55	23 00	23 12				23 27		23 31	23 43		
Partick 226	a	22 05	22 16				22 29	22 35	22 46			22 58	23 04	23 16				23 31		23 35	23 47		
Hyndland 3 226	a	22 07	22 18				22 31	22 37	22 48			23 00	23 06	23 18				23 33		23 37	23 49		

		SR	SR	SR
Edinburgh	d			23 13
Haymarket	d			23 18
Lanark	d	23 23	23 51	
Carstairs	d			23 57
Carluke	d	23 33	00 01	00 07
Wishaw	d	23 39	00 07	00 15
Holytown	d			
Shieldmuir	d	23 42	00 10	
Cumbernauld 226	d			
Greenfaulds 226	d			
Coatbridge Central	d			
Whifflet	d			
Motherwell	a	23 45	00 13	00 20
	d			
Whifflet	d			
Kirkwood	d			
Bargeddie	d			
Baillieston	d			
Mount Vernon	d			
Carmyle	d			
Bellshill	d			
Uddingston	d			
Airbles	d			
Larkhall	d			
Merryton	d			
Chatelherault	d			
Hamilton Central	d			
Hamilton West	d			
Blantyre	d			
Newton	d			
Cambuslang	d			
Rutherglen	d			
Dalmarnock	d			
Bridgeton	d			
Argyle Street	d			
Glasgow Central H. Level 15	a			
Glasgow Central L. Level 15	a			
Anderston	a			
Exhibition Centre	a			
Partick 226	a			
Hyndland 3 226	a			

A To Dalmuir
B To Milngavie
C From Milngavie to Cumbernauld
D From Cumbernauld to Dalmuir
E To Garscadden
F From Cumbernauld to Garscadden
G From London Euston

Table T225-F

Sundays
20 May to 2 December

Edinburgh, Lanark, Coatbridge, Motherwell, Whifflet, Larkhall and Hamilton - Glasgow

		SR A	SR B	SR A	SR C	SR D	SR E	SR F	SR C	SR E	SR D	SR G	SR D	SR C	SR F	SR C	SR E	SR H	SR D	SR I	SR E	SR D	SR C
Edinburgh	d																						
Haymarket	d																						
Lanark	d																						
Carstairs	d																						
Carluke	d		00 01	00 07																			
Wishaw	d		00 07	00 15																			
Holytown	d	00 01																					
Shieldmuir	d		00 10																				
Cumbernauld 226	d																						
Greenfaulds 226	d																						
Coatbridge Central	d																						
Whifflet	d																						
Motherwell	a		00 13	00 20																			
	d				08 24	08 34	08 35	08 41	08 53	09 05	09 05		09 20	09 21	09 41	09 53	09 54		09 54		10 19	10 20	10 21
Whifflet	d							08 48							09 49								
Kirkwood	d							08 51							09 52								
Bargeddie	d							08 54							09 55								
Baillieston	d							08 58							09 58								
Mount Vernon	d							09 00							10 00								
Carmyle	d							09 02							10 03								
Bellshill	d	00 05				08 40	08 41			09 11	09 11						10 00		10 00		10 26		
Uddingston	d	00 09				08 44	08 45			09 15	09 15						10 04	←	10 07		10 30		
Airbles	d				08 26				08 55				09 22	09 23		09 55		09 55				10 22	10 23
Larkhall	d											09 08				→				10 08			
Merryton	d											09 10								10 10			
Chatelherault	d											09 13								10 13			
Hamilton Central	d				08 32				09 02			09 17	09 28	09 32				10 02		10 17		10 28	10 32
Hamilton West	d				08 35				09 05			09 20	09 31	09 35				10 05		10 20		10 31	10 35
Blantyre	d				08 38				09 08			09 23	09 34	09 38				10 08		10 23		10 34	10 38
Newton	d				08 42	08 48			09 12		09 19	09 27	09 39	09 42				10 12	10 13	10 27		10 39	10 42
Cambuslang	d	00 14			08 46		08 50		09 16	09 20		09 31		09 46			10 09	10 16		10 31	10 34		10 46
Rutherglen	d				08 50			09 06	09 20			09 35		09 50	10 07			10 20		10 35			10 50
Dalmarnock	d													09 52	10 09			10 22		10 37			10 52
Bridgeton	d				08 54			09 10	09 24			09 39		09 54	10 11			10 24		10 39			10 54
Argyle Street	d													09 58	10 14			10 28		10 43			10 58
Glasgow Central H. Level 15	a	00 26				09 05	09 01			09 31	09 36		10 03				10 19		10 28		10 45	11 03	
Glasgow Central L. Level 15	a				08 57			09 13	09 27			09 42		09 59	10 16			10 29		10 44			10 59
Anderston	a													10 05	10 18			10 35		10 46			11 06
Exhibition Centre	a				09 07			09 17	09 37			09 47		10 07	10 20			10 37		10 48			11 08
Partick 226	a				09 11			09 22	09 41			09 52		10 11	10 23			10 41		10 52			11 11
Hyndland 3 226	a				09 14			09 24	09 44			09 54		10 14	10 25			10 44		10 54			11 14

		SR F	SR E	SR C	SR D	SR J	SR E	SR D	SR C	SR F	SR E	SR C	SR D	SR K	SR D	TP ◇1 L	TP ◇1 M	SR C	SR E	SR H	SR F	SR E	SR C
Edinburgh	d																						
Haymarket	d																						
Lanark	d		10 19		10 33						11 21		11 41									12 19	
Carstairs	d																						
Carluke	d		10 29		10 43						11 31		11 51									12 29	
Wishaw	d		10 35		10 49						11 37		11 57									12 35	
Holytown	d																						
Shieldmuir	d		10 38		10 55						11 40		12 00									12 40	
Cumbernauld 226	d																						
Greenfaulds 226	d																						
Coatbridge Central	d																						
Whifflet	d																						
Motherwell	a		10 41		10 58						11 44		12 04									12 43	
	d	10 41	10 44	10 53	10 58		11 20	11 20	11 21	11 42	11 45	11 53	12 05		12 20	12 21	12 23	12 23	12 24		12 41	12 44	12 53
Whifflet	d	10 48								11 49											12 49		
Kirkwood	d	10 51								11 52											12 52		
Bargeddie	d	10 54								11 55											12 55		
Baillieston	d	10 58								11 59											12 58		
Mount Vernon	d	11 00								12 01											13 00		
Carmyle	d	11 02								12 03											13 03		
Bellshill	d		10 51		11 06		11 26				11 51		12 11						12 31			12 51	
Uddingston	d		10 55		11 10		11 32				11 55		12 15						12 35	←		12 55	
Airbles	d			10 55				11 22	11 23			11 55			12 22			12 25		12 25			12 55
Larkhall	d					11 08								12 08				→					
Merryton	d					11 10								12 10									
Chatelherault	d					11 13								12 13									
Hamilton Central	d			11 02		11 17		11 28	11 32			12 02		12 17	12 28					12 32			13 02
Hamilton West	d			11 05		11 20		11 31	11 35			12 05		12 20	12 31					12 35			13 05
Blantyre	d			11 08		11 23		11 34	11 38			12 08		12 23	12 34					12 38			13 08
Newton	d			11 13	11 14	11 27		11 39	11 42			12 12	12 19	12 27	12 41					12 42			13 15
Cambuslang	d		10 59	11 18		11 31	11 37		11 46		12 00	12 16		12 31					12 39	12 46		12 59	13 18
Rutherglen	d	11 06		11 22		11 35			11 50	12 07		12 20		12 35						12 50	13 07		13 22
Dalmarnock	d	11 09		11 24		11 38			11 53	12 10		12 22		12 37						12 53	13 09		13 25
Bridgeton	d	11 11		11 26		11 40			11 55	12 12		12 24		12 39						12 55	13 11		13 27
Argyle Street	d	11 14		11 30		11 43			11 58	12 15		12 28		12 43						12 58	13 14		13 30
Glasgow Central H. Level 15	a		11 10		11 30		11 48	12 03			12 12		12 36		13 05	12 44	12 46		12 50			13 10	
Glasgow Central L. Level 15	a	11 15		11 31		11 44			12 00	12 16		12 29		12 44						13 00	13 16		13 32
Anderston	a	11 17		11 35		11 46			12 05	12 18		12 35		12 46						13 05	13 18		13 35
Exhibition Centre	a	11 19		11 37		11 48			12 07	12 20		12 37		12 48						13 07	13 20		13 37
Partick 226	a	11 23		11 41		11 52			12 11	12 23		12 41		12 52						13 11	13 23		13 41
Hyndland 3 226	a	11 25		11 44		11 54			12 14	12 25		12 44		12 54						13 14	13 25		13 44

A not 20 May. From Edinburgh
B not 20 May. From Lanark
C from 16 September. To Milngavie
D until 9 September
E from 16 September
F from 16 September. To Balloch
G from 16 September. To Balloch. Forms tight booked connection out of 2C26.
H from 16 September. From Motherwell to Milngavie
I from 16 September. To Balloch. Forms tight booked connection out of 2C54.
J from 16 September. To Balloch. Forms tight booked connection out of 2C56.
K from 16 September. To Balloch. Forms tight booked connection out of 2C58.
L from 24 June until 9 September. From Manchester Airport
M from 16 September. From Manchester Airport

Table T225-F

Sundays

20 May to 2 December

Edinburgh, Lanark, Coatbridge, Motherwell, Whifflet, Larkhall and Hamilton - Glasgow

		SR	SR	SR	SR	SR	SR	SR	SR	SR	SR	SR	SR	TP	TP	SR	SR	SR	SR	SR	SR	SR
		A	B	C	A	D	E	C	D	A	F	C	A	◇1 G ✠	◇1 H ✠	D	E	C	D	A	I	C
Edinburgh	d																					
Haymarket	d																					
Lanark	d	12 33						13 19		13 44								14 19		14 37		
Carstairs	d																					
Carluke	d	12 43						13 29		13 54								14 29		14 47		
Wishaw	d	12 49						13 35		14 00								14 35		14 54		
Holytown	d																					
Shieldmuir	d	12 52						13 38		14 03								14 38		14 58		
Cumbernauld 226	d																					
Greenfaulds 226	d																					
Coatbridge Central	d																					
Whifflet	d																					
Motherwell	a	12 55						13 42		14 07								14 42		15 02		
	d	12 56		13 20	13 20	13 23	13 41	13 43	13 53	14 08		14 20	14 20	14 22	14 22	14 23	14 41	14 43	14 53	15 04		15 20
Whifflet	d						13 49										14 49					
Kirkwood	d						13 52										14 52					
Bargeddie	d						13 55										14 55					
Baillieston	d						13 58										14 58					
Mount Vernon	d						14 00										15 00					
Carmyle	d						14 03										15 03					
Bellshill	d	13 02		13 26				13 51		14 14		14 27						14 51		15 10		15 27
Uddingston	d	13 06		13 32				13 55		14 18		14 31						14 55		15 14		15 32
Airbles	d				13 22	13 25			13 55				14 22			14 25			14 55			
Larkhall	d		13 08								14 08										15 08	
Merryton	d		13 10								14 10										15 10	
Chatelherault	d		13 13								14 13										15 13	
Hamilton Central	d		13 17		13 28	13 32			14 02		14 17		14 28			14 32			15 02		15 17	
Hamilton West	d		13 20		13 31	13 35			14 05		14 20		14 31			14 35			15 05		15 20	
Blantyre	d		13 23		13 34	13 38			14 08		14 23		14 34			14 38			15 08		15 23	
Newton	d	13 15	13 27		13 39	13 42			14 16	14 23	14 27		14 39			14 42			15 12	15 18	15 27	
Cambuslang	d		13 31	13 37		13 46		13 59	14 19		14 31	14 35				14 46		14 59	15 16		15 31	15 36
Rutherglen	d		13 35			13 50	14 09		14 23		14 35					14 50	15 07		15 20		15 35	
Dalmarnock	d		13 37			13 52	14 11		14 26		14 37					14 52	15 09		15 22		15 37	
Bridgeton	d		13 39			13 54	14 13		14 28		14 39					14 54	15 11		15 24		15 39	
Argyle Street	d		13 43			13 58	14 16		14 31		14 43					14 58	15 14		15 28		15 43	
Glasgow Central H. Level 15	a	13 31		13 48	14 03			14 10		14 37		14 46	15 03	14 42	14 44			15 10		15 38		15 47
Glasgow Central L. Level 15	a		13 44			13 59	14 18		14 33		14 44					14 59	15 16		15 29		15 44	
Anderston	a		13 46			14 06	14 19		14 36		14 46					15 05	15 18		15 35		15 46	
Exhibition Centre	a		13 48			14 08	14 21		14 38		14 48					15 07	15 20		15 37		15 48	
Partick 226	a		13 52			14 11	14 25		14 41		14 52					15 11	15 23		15 41		15 52	
Hyndland 3 226	a		13 54			14 14	14 27		14 44		14 54					15 14	15 25		15 44		15 54	

		SR	SR	SR	SR	SR	SR	SR	SR	SR	SR	TP	TP	SR	SR	SR	SR	SR	SR	SR	SR	SR	SR
		A	D	E	C	D	A	J	C	A	D	◇1 G ✠	◇1 H ✠	E	C	D	A	K	C	A	D	E	C
Edinburgh	d																						
Haymarket	d																						
Lanark	d				15 19		15 46								16 19		16 39						17 20
Carstairs	d																						
Carluke	d				15 29		15 56								16 29		16 49						17 30
Wishaw	d				15 35		16 02								16 35		16 57						17 36
Holytown	d																						
Shieldmuir	d				15 40		16 05								16 39		17 01						17 39
Cumbernauld 226	d																						
Greenfaulds 226	d																						
Coatbridge Central	d																						
Whifflet	d																						
Motherwell	a				15 43		16 08								16 43		17 05						17 42
	d	15 20	15 21	15 41	15 44	15 53	16 09		16 20	16 20	16 21	16 22	16 22	16 40	16 43	16 53	17 06		17 20	17 20	17 21	17 41	17 43
Whifflet	d			15 49										16 48								17 48	
Kirkwood	d			15 52										16 51								17 51	
Bargeddie	d			15 55										16 54								17 54	
Baillieston	d			15 58										16 58								17 58	
Mount Vernon	d			16 00										17 00								18 00	
Carmyle	d			16 03										17 02								18 02	
Bellshill	d				15 51		16 15		16 27						16 51		17 12		17 27				17 49
Uddingston	d				15 55		16 19		16 31						16 55		17 16		17 31				17 53
Airbles	d	15 22	15 23			15 55				16 22	16 23					16 55				17 22	17 23		
Larkhall	d							16 08										17 08					
Merryton	d							16 10										17 10					
Chatelherault	d							16 13										17 13					
Hamilton Central	d	15 28	15 32			16 02		16 17		16 28	16 32					17 02		17 17		17 28	17 32		
Hamilton West	d	15 31	15 35			16 05		16 20		16 31	16 35					17 05		17 20		17 31	17 35		
Blantyre	d	15 34	15 38			16 08		16 23		16 34	16 38					17 08		17 23		17 34	17 38		
Newton	d	15 39	15 42			16 16	16 23	16 27		16 39	16 42					17 12	17 21	17 27		17 39	17 42		
Cambuslang	d		15 46		15 59	16 20		16 31	16 35		16 46				16 59	17 16		17 31	17 35		17 46		17 58
Rutherglen	d		15 50	16 08		16 24		16 35			16 50			17 06		17 20		17 35			17 50	18 06	
Dalmarnock	d		15 53	16 11		16 27		16 37			16 52			17 09		17 22		17 37			17 52	18 09	
Bridgeton	d		15 55	16 13		16 29		16 39			16 54			17 11		17 24		17 39			17 54	18 11	
Argyle Street	d		15 58	16 16		16 32		16 43			16 58			17 14		17 28		17 43			17 58	18 14	
Glasgow Central H. Level 15	a	16 03			16 10		16 38		16 44	17 03		16 42	16 45		17 08		17 35		17 44	18 03			18 07
Glasgow Central L. Level 15	a		16 00	16 17		16 34		16 44			16 59			17 15		17 29		17 44			17 59	18 15	
Anderston	a		16 05	16 19		16 36		16 46			17 06			17 17		17 35		17 46			18 05	18 17	
Exhibition Centre	a		16 07	16 21		16 38		16 48			17 08			17 19		17 37		17 48			18 07	18 19	
Partick 226	a		16 11	16 24		16 41		16 52			17 12			17 23		17 41		17 52			18 11	18 23	
Hyndland 3 226	a		16 14	16 26		16 44		16 54			17 14			17 25		17 44		17 54			18 14	18 25	

A until 9 September
B from 16 September. To Balloch. Forms tight booked connection out of 2C48.
C from 16 September
D from 16 September. To Milngavie
E from 16 September. To Balloch
F from 16 September. To Balloch. Forms tight booked connection out of 2C50.
G from 16 September. From Manchester Airport
H until 9 September. From Manchester Airport
I from 16 September. To Balloch. Forms tight booked connection out of 2C52.
J from 16 September. To Balloch. Forms tight booked connection out of 2C54.
K from 16 September. To Balloch. Forms tight booked connection out of 2C56.

Table T225-F

Sundays

20 May to 2 December

Edinburgh, Lanark, Coatbridge, Motherwell, Whifflet, Larkhall and Hamilton - Glasgow

		SR	SR	SR	SR	SR	SR	TP	SR	SR	SR	SR	SR	SR	SR	SR	SR	SR	SR	SR	SR	SR
		A	B	C	D	B	A	◇1 E ✠	F	D	A	B	G	B	A	D	H	F	D	A	I	B
Edinburgh	d																					
Haymarket	d																					
Lanark	d		17 41							18 19		18 46							19 19			19 54
Carstairs	d																					
Carluke	d		17 51							18 29		18 56							19 29			20 04
Wishaw	d		17 57							18 35		19 02							19 35			20 10
Holytown	d																					
Shieldmuir	d		18 02							18 38		19 06							19 38			20 13
Cumbernauld 226	d																					
Greenfaulds 226	d																					
Coatbridge Central	d																					
Whifflet	d																					
Motherwell	a		18 07							18 42		19 10							19 42			20 17
	d	17 53	18 08		18 20	18 20	18 21	18 22	18 41	18 43	18 53	19 10		19 20	19 21	19 22		19 41	19 43	19 53		20 18
Whifflet	d								18 49									19 48				
Kirkwood	d								18 52									19 51				
Bargeddie	d								18 55									19 54				
Baillieston	d								18 58									19 58				
Mount Vernon	d								19 00									20 00				
Carmyle	d								19 03									20 02				
Bellshill	d		18 14		18 26					18 50		19 17				19 28			19 50			20 24
Uddingston	d		18 18		18 30					18 54		19 21				19 32	←		19 54			20 32
Airbles	d	17 55				18 22	18 23				18 55			19 22	19 23		19 23			19 55		
Larkhall	d			18 08									19 08		→						20 08	
Merryton	d			18 10									19 10								20 10	
Chatelherault	d			18 13									19 13								20 13	
Hamilton Central	d	18 02		18 17		18 28	18 32				19 02		19 17	19 28			19 32			20 02	20 17	
Hamilton West	d	18 05		18 20		18 31	18 35				19 05		19 20	19 31			19 35			20 05	20 20	
Blantyre	d	18 08		18 23		18 34	18 38				19 08		19 23	19 34			19 38			20 08	20 23	
Newton	d	18 16	18 22	18 27		18 39	18 42				19 12	19 25	19 27	19 39			19 42			20 12	20 28	20 36
Cambuslang	d	18 20		18 31	18 35		18 46			18 59	19 16		19 31			19 37	19 46		20 00	20 16	20 32	
Rutherglen	d	18 24		18 35			18 50		19 07		19 22		19 35				19 50	20 06		20 20	20 36	
Dalmarnock	d																					
Bridgeton	d	18 27		18 39			18 54		19 10		19 26		19 39				19 54	20 10		20 24	20 40	
Argyle Street	d																					
Glasgow Central H. Level 15	a		18 36		18 44	19 03		18 44		19 08		19 39		20 03		19 46			20 09			20 52
Glasgow Central L. Level 15	a	18 32		18 42			18 57		19 14		19 30		19 42				19 57	20 14		20 28	20 43	
Anderston	a																					
Exhibition Centre	a	18 38		18 47			19 07		19 18		19 37		19 47				20 07	20 18		20 37	20 48	
Partick 226	a	18 41		18 52			19 11		19 22		19 41		19 52				20 11	20 22		20 41	20 53	
Hyndland 3 226	a	18 44		18 54			19 14		19 24		19 44		19 54				20 14	20 24		20 44	20 55	

		SR	SR	TP	TP	SR	SR	SR	SR	SR	SR	SR	SR	SR	SR	SR	SR	SR	SR	SR	SR	SR	SR
		B	A	◇1 J ✠	◇1 K ✠	D	H	F	D	A	B	L	D	B	A	F	D	A	M	N	D	O	B
Edinburgh	d																						
Haymarket	d																						
Lanark	d								20 19		20 36						21 19			21 44			
Carstairs	d																						
Carluke	d								20 29		20 46						21 29			21 54			
Wishaw	d								20 35		20 54						21 35			22 01			
Holytown	d																						
Shieldmuir	d								20 38		20 58						21 38			22 06			
Cumbernauld 226	d																						
Greenfaulds 226	d																						
Coatbridge Central	d																						
Whifflet	d																						
Motherwell	a								20 42		21 02						21 42			22 12			
	d	20 20	20 21	20 22	20 22	20 24		20 41	20 44	20 53	21 03		21 20	21 20	21 21	21 41	21 44	21 53		22 13	22 20		22 20
Whifflet	d							20 48								21 49							
Kirkwood	d							20 51								21 52							
Bargeddie	d							20 54								21 55							
Baillieston	d							20 58								21 58							
Mount Vernon	d							21 00								22 00							
Carmyle	d							21 02								22 03							
Bellshill	d					20 30			20 50		21 09		21 26				21 51			22 24	22 27	←	
Uddingston	d					20 34	←		20 55		21 13		21 30				21 55			22 32	22 31	22 32	
Airbles	d	20 22	20 23				20 23			20 55				21 22	21 23			21 55		→			22 22
Larkhall	d		→									21 08							22 08				
Merryton	d											21 10							22 10				
Chatelherault	d											21 13							22 13				
Hamilton Central	d	20 28					20 32			21 02		21 17		21 28	21 32			22 02	22 18				22 28
Hamilton West	d	20 31					20 35			21 05		21 20		21 31	21 35			22 05	22 20				22 31
Blantyre	d	20 34					20 38			21 08		21 23		21 34	21 38			22 08	22 24				22 34
Newton	d	20 39					20 42			21 12	21 19	21 27		21 39	21 42			22 12	22 28			22 36	22 40
Cambuslang	d					20 39	20 46		20 59	21 16		21 31	21 35		21 46		21 59	22 16	22 31		22 35		
Rutherglen	d						20 50	21 06		21 20		21 35			21 50	22 07		22 20	22 35				
Dalmarnock	d																						
Bridgeton	d						20 54	21 10		21 24		21 39			21 54	22 10		22 24	22 39				
Argyle Street	d																						
Glasgow Central H. Level 15	a	21 04		20 40	20 48	20 48			21 08		21 33		21 44	22 03			22 08				22 44	22 52	23 04
Glasgow Central L. Level 15	a						20 57	21 14		21 27		21 42			21 57	22 14		22 27	22 42				
Anderston	a																						
Exhibition Centre	a						21 07	21 18		21 37		21 47			22 07	22 18		22 37	22 47				
Partick 226	a						21 12	21 22		21 41		21 52			22 11	22 22		22 41	22 52				
Hyndland 3 226	a						21 14	21 24		21 44		21 54			22 14	22 24		22 44	22 54				

A from 16 September. To Milngavie
B until 9 September
C from 16 September. To Balloch. Forms tight booked connection out of 2C58.
D from 16 September
E From Manchester Airport
F from 16 September. To Balloch
G from 16 September. To Balloch. Forms tight booked connection out of 2C48.
H from 16 September. From Motherwell to Milngavie
I from 16 September. To Balloch. Forms tight booked connection out of 2C50.
J from 16 September. From Manchester Airport
K until 9 September. From Manchester Airport
L from 16 September. To Balloch. Forms tight booked connection out of 2C52.
M from 16 September. To Balloch. Forms tight booked connection out of 2C54.
N until 9 September. To Glasgow Central
O until 9 September. From Lanark

Table T225-F

Sundays

20 May to 2 December

Edinburgh, Lanark, Coatbridge, Motherwell, Whifflet, Larkhall and Hamilton - Glasgow

		SR A	TP B	TP C	SR D	SR E	VT F	VT G	SR H	VT F	VT G	SR I	SR J	SR E	SR I	SR
Edinburgh	d															
Haymarket	d															
Lanark	d					22 19						22 43				23 36
Carstairs	d															
Carluke	d					22 29						22 53				23 46
Wishaw	d					22 35						23 01				23 52
Holytown	d															
Shieldmuir	d					22 38						23 04				23 55
Cumbernauld 226	d															
Greenfaulds 226	d															
Coatbridge Central	d															
Whifflet	d															
Motherwell	a					22 42						23 08				23 59
	d	22 21	22 22	22 23	22 41	22 45	22 50	22 53	22 53	23 05	23 05	23 09		23 20	23 20	
Whifflet	d				22 48											
Kirkwood	d				22 51											
Bargeddie	d				22 54											
Baillieston	d				22 58											
Mount Vernon	d				23 00											
Carmyle	d				23 02											
Bellshill	d					22 51						23 15		23 26	23 26	
Uddingston	d					22 57						23 21		23 30	23 30	
Airbles	d	22 23							22 55							
Larkhall	d												23 08			
Merryton	d												23 10			
Chatelherault	d												23 13			
Hamilton Central	d	22 32							23 02				23 17			
Hamilton West	d	22 35							23 05				23 20			
Blantyre	d	22 38							23 08				23 23			
Newton	d	22 42							23 12			23 25	23 27		23 39	
Cambuslang	d	22 46				23 02			23 16				23 31	23 35		
Rutherglen	d	22 50			23 06				23 20				23 35			
Dalmarnock	d															
Bridgeton	d	22 54			23 10				23 24				23 39			
Argyle Street	d															
Glasgow Central H. Level 15	a		22 42	22 46		23 11	23 07	23 15		23 21	23 24	23 39		23 44	23 55	
Glasgow Central L. Level 15	a	22 57			23 14				23 27				23 42			
Anderston	a															
Exhibition Centre	a	23 07			23 18				23 37				23 50			
Partick 226	a	23 11			23 22				23 41				23 53			
Hyndland 3 226	a	23 14			23 24				23 44				23 56			

A from 16 September. To Milngavie
B from 16 September. From Manchester Airport
C until 9 September. From Manchester Airport
D from 16 September. To Balloch
E from 16 September
F from 16 September. From London Euston
G until 9 September. From London Euston
H from 16 September. To Garscadden
I until 9 September
J from 16 September. To Garscadden. Forms tight booked connection out of 2C56.

Table T225-R

Mondays to Fridays

21 May to 7 December

Glasgow - Hamilton, Larkhall, Whifflet, Motherwell, Coatbridge, Lanark and Edinburgh

Miles	Miles	Miles	Miles	Miles			SR MX A	SR MX A	SR MX A	SR	SR	SR B	SR	SR	SR C	SR	SR B	SR D	SR	SR	SR	SR C	SR
0	0	—	0	—	Hyndland 3 226	d									06 07							06 17	06 22
0¾	0¾	—	0¾	—	**Partick** 226	d									06 10							06 19	06 24
2	2	—	2	—	Exhibition Centre	d									06 13							06 22	06 28
2½	2½	—	2¼	—	Anderston	d									06 15							06 24	06 30
3	3	—	3	—	**Glasgow Central L. Level** 15	a									06 17							06 25	06 31
—	—	—	—	—		d									06 18							06 27	06 34
—	—	0	—	0	**Glasgow Central H. Level** 15	d								06 16									
3½	3½	—	3½	—	Argyle Street	d									06 20							06 29	06 36
—	4¾	—	4¾	—	Bridgeton	d									06 23							06 32	06 39
—	5¼	—	5¼	—	Dalmarnock	d									06 25							06 34	06 41
5	6	—	6	—	Rutherglen	d									06 27							06 36	06 44
7	8	—	—	4¼	Cambuslang	d								06 25	06 31								06 47
8½	9½	—	—	—	Newton	d									06 34								06 50
11	12	—	—	—	Blantyre	d									06 38								06 54
12¾	13¾	—	—	—	Hamilton West	d									06 41								06 57
13¾	14¾	—	—	—	**Hamilton Central**	d									06 44								07 00
15½	—	—	—	—	Chatelherault	d									06 49								
17	—	—	—	—	Merryton	d									06 52								
17¾	—	—	—	—	**Larkhall**	a									06 55								
—	17	—	—	—	Airbles	d																	07 06
—	—	—	—	8¾	Uddingston	d			00 03					06 30									
—	—	—	—	11	Bellshill	d			00 08					06 36									
—	—	—	8½	—	Carmyle	d																06 40	
—	—	—	10	—	Mount Vernon	d																06 43	
—	—	—	10¾	—	Baillieston	d																06 45	
—	—	—	12¾	—	Bargeddie	d																06 48	
—	—	—	13¼	—	Kirkwood	d																06 52	
—	—	—	14½	—	**Whifflet**	d												06 25				06 56	
—	17¾	12½	18½	13¾	**Motherwell**	a			00 14									06 37				07 09	07 08
—	—	—	—	—		d				05 42	05 48	05 56	06 00			06 21	06 24		06 40	06 50	07 00		
—	21¾	—	—	—	Whifflet	d				05 49		06a03					06a32		06 47				
—	22¾	—	—	—	Coatbridge Central	d				05 52									06 50				
—	28¼	—	—	—	Greenfaulds 226	d				05 59									06 59				
—	29¼	—	—	—	**Cumbernauld** 226	a				06 01									07 01				
—	—	—	—	15½	Shieldmuir	d					05 51					06 24				06 54	07 03		
—	—	—	—	—	Holytown	d	00 01						06 07	06 40									
—	—	15¾	—	17	Wishaw	d					05 55					06 28				06 57	07 07		
—	—	20¼	—	21½	Carluke	d		00 01			06 02					06 34				07 03	07 17		
—	—	28½	—	—	Carstairs	a															07 25		
—	—	—	—	30	**Lanark**	a		00 12			06 13					06 45				07 15			
—	—	56	—	—	Haymarket	a	02s21						07 11	07 42									
—	—	57¼	—	—	**Edinburgh**	a	02 42						07 16	07 47									

		SR C	SR	SR B	SR E	SR D	SR C	SR F	SR	SR	SR C	SR C	SR F	SR	SR B	SR C	SR	SR D	SR C	SR F	SR	SR C
Hyndland 3 226	d	06 32					06 48	06 52			07 03	07 17	07 23			07 34			07 48	07 53		08 04
Partick 226	d	06 34					06 50	06 54			07 06	07 19	07 25			07 37			07 50	07 55		08 07
Exhibition Centre	d	06 37					06 53	06 57			07 09	07 22	07 28			07 40			07 53	07 58		08 10
Anderston	d	06 39					06 55	07 00			07 11	07 24	07 31			07 42			07 55	08 00		08 12
Glasgow Central L. Level 15	a	06 41					06 57	07 02			07 12	07 26	07 32			07 43			07 57	08 02		08 14
	d	06 43					06 58	07 04			07 16	07 26	07 36			07 47			07 58	08 04		08 16
Glasgow Central H. Level 15	d		06 52		07 05				07 13	07 20				07 51			08 17				08 20	
Argyle Street	d	06 46					07 00	07 08			07 19	07 28	07 38			07 50			08 00	08 07		08 19
Bridgeton	d	06 49					07 03	07 11			07 22	07 31	07 41			07 53			08 03	08 10		08 22
Dalmarnock	d	06 52					07 05	07 13			07 25	07 33	07 43			07 55			08 05	08 12		08 24
Rutherglen	d	06 55					07 07	07 17			07 29	07 35	07 47			07 59			08 07	08 17		08 29
Cambuslang	d	06 59	07 02					07 21	07 24	07 28	07 33		07 51	07 59		08 03				08 21	08 29	08 32
Newton	d	07 03						07 24			07 36		07 54			08 06				08 24		08 35
Blantyre	d	07 07						07 28			07 40		07 58			08 10				08 28		08 39
Hamilton West	d	07 11						07 31			07 43		08 01			08 13				08 31		08 42
Hamilton Central	d	07 13						07 34			07 45		08 04			08 16				08 34		08 45
Chatelherault	d	07 18									07 50					08 20						08 49
Merryton	d	07 21									07 53					08 23						08 52
Larkhall	a	07 24									07 56					08 26						08 55
Airbles	d							07 39					08 09							08 39		
Uddingston	d		07 06						07 30	07 34				08 04			08 29				08 34	
Bellshill	d		07 11						07 35	07 39				08 09			08 34				08 39	
Carmyle	d						07 11					07 40							08 12			
Mount Vernon	d						07 14					07 42							08 14			
Baillieston	d						07 16					07 45							08 17			
Bargeddie	d						07 19					07 48							08 20			
Kirkwood	d						07 23					07 52							08 24			
Whifflet	d					07 25	07a28					07 56						08 24	08a28			
Motherwell	a		07 17		07 21	07 32		07 42		07 46		08 07	08 12	08 16				08 32		08 42	08 45	
	d		07 18	07 22	07 22			07 43		07 47				08 17	08 22					08 43	08 47	
Whifflet	d			07a29				07 49							08a30					08 50		
Coatbridge Central	d							07 52												08 53		
Greenfaulds 226	d							08 00												09 00		
Cumbernauld 226	a							08 02												09 02		
Shieldmuir	d		07 21							07 51				08 23							08 51	
Holytown	d								07 40								08 40					
Wishaw	d		07 25		07 33					07 54				08 28							08 54	
Carluke	d		07 35		07 40					08 04				08 35							09 02	
Carstairs	a				07 50																	
Lanark	a		07 46							08 15				08 48							09 13	
Haymarket	a				08 27				08 43								09 43					
Edinburgh	a				08 34				08 49								09 49					

A From Glasgow Central
B To Dalmuir
C From Dalmuir
D From Cumbernauld to Dalmuir
E To North Berwick
F From Milngavie

Table T225-R

Mondays to Fridays

21 May to 7 December

Glasgow - Hamilton, Larkhall, Whifflet, Motherwell, Coatbridge, Lanark and Edinburgh

		SR A	SR B	SR A	SR A	SR	SR C	SR	SR D	SR B	SR	SR A	SR E	SR A	SR B	SR A	SR A	SR	SR C	SR	SR D	SR B	SR
Hyndland ■ 226	d	08 17	08 23	08 35	08 48					08 53		09 06		09 17	09 23	09 34	09 47					09 53	
Partick 226 ⇌	d	08 20	08 25	08 37	08 51					08 56		09 08		09 19	09 25	09 37	09 49					09 55	
Exhibition Centre	d	08 23	08 29	08 40	08 54					08 59		09 11		09 22	09 28	09 40	09 52					09 58	
Anderston	d	08 25	08 31	08 42	08 56					09 01		09 13		09 24	09 30	09 42	09 54					10 00	
Glasgow Central L. Level 15	a	08 26	08 33	08 44	08 57					09 02		09 15		09 26	09 32	09 43	09 56					10 02	
	d	08 27	08 35	08 44	08 58					09 04		09 16		09 27	09 34	09 44	09 57					10 04	
Glasgow Central H. Level 15	d					08 50		09 17			09 21		09 33					09 50		10 16			10 20
Argyle Street	d	08 29	08 38	08 46	09 00					09 07		09 19		09 28	09 37	09 46	09 59					10 07	
Bridgeton	d	08 32	08 41	08 49	09 03					09 10		09 22		09 31	09 40	09 49	10 02					10 10	
Dalmarnock	d	08 34	08 43	08 51	09 05					09 12		09 24		09 33	09 42	09 51	10 04					10 12	
Rutherglen	d	08 37	08 47	08 53	09 07					09 17		09 29		09 35	09 47	09 53	10 07					10 17	
Cambuslang	d		08 51	08 56		09 00				09 21	09 29	09 33			09 51	09 57		10 00				10 21	10 28
Newton	d		08 54	09 00						09 24		09 36			09 54	10 01						10 24	
Blantyre	d		08 58	09 04						09 28		09 40			09 58	10 05						10 28	
Hamilton West	d		09 01	09 07						09 31		09 43			10 01	10 08						10 31	
Hamilton Central	d		09 04	09 14						09 34		09 45			10 04	10 13						10 34	
Chatelherault	d			09 18								09 50				10 18							
Merryton	d			09 21								09 53				10 21							
Larkhall	a			09 24								09 56				10 24							
Airbles	d		09 09							09 39					10 09							10 39	
Uddingston	d					09 05		09 29			09 34							10 06		10 28			10 33
Bellshill	d					09 10		09 34			09 41							10 11		10 34			10 38
Carmyle	d	08 41			09 11									09 40			10 12						
Mount Vernon	d	08 44			09 14									09 42			10 14						
Baillieston	d	08 46			09 16									09 45			10 17						
Bargeddie	d	08 49			09 19									09 48			10 20						
Kirkwood	d	08 53			09 23									09 52			10 24						
Whifflet	d	08 57			09a27				09 34					09 55			10a27				10 33		
Motherwell	a	09 04	09 12			09 18			09 41	09 42	09 47		09 56	10 07	10 12			10 17			10 40	10 42	10 45
	d					09 19	09 22			09 43	09 48		09 57					10 17	10 23			10 45	10 48
Whifflet	d						09a29			09 50									10a30			10 52	
Coatbridge Central	d									09 52												10 54	
Greenfaulds 226	d									10 01												11 02	
Cumbernauld 226	a									10 03												11 04	
Shieldmuir	d					09 22					09 51							10 21					10 51
Holytown	d							09 39												10 39			
Wishaw	d					09 26					09 55		10 03					10 26					10 55
Carluke	d					09 33					10 03		10 09					10 32					11 03
Carstairs	a												10 18										
Lanark	a					09 44					10 15							10 43					11 14
Haymarket ⇌	a							10 42					10 49							11 43			
Edinburgh	a							10 48					10 54							11 48			

		SR A	SR A	SR B	SR A	SR A	SR	SR C	SR	SR D	SR B	SR	SR A	SR E	SR A	SR B	SR A	SR A	SR	SR C	SR	SR D
Hyndland ■ 226	d	10 04	10 17	10 23	10 34	10 47					10 53		11 05		11 17	11 23	11 35	11 47				
Partick 226 ⇌	d	10 07	10 19	10 25	10 36	10 49					10 55		11 08		11 19	11 25	11 37	11 49				
Exhibition Centre	d	10 10	10 22	10 28	10 39	10 52					10 58		11 11		11 22	11 28	11 40	11 52				
Anderston	d	10 12	10 24	10 30	10 41	10 54					11 00		11 13		11 24	11 30	11 42	11 54				
Glasgow Central L. Level 15	a	10 13	10 26	10 31	10 43	10 56					11 02		11 14		11 26	11 32	11 44	11 56				
	d	10 16	10 27	10 35	10 44	10 56					11 04		11 18		11 27	11 34	11 44	11 57				
Glasgow Central H. Level 15	d						10 50		11 16			11 20		11 46					11 50		12 16	
Argyle Street	d	10 19	10 29	10 38	10 46	10 58					11 07		11 20		11 29	11 37	11 46	11 59				
Bridgeton	d	10 22	10 32	10 41	10 49	11 01					11 10		11 23		11 32	11 40	11 49	12 02				
Dalmarnock	d	10 24	10 34	10 43	10 51	11 03					11 12		11 25		11 34	11 42	11 51	12 04				
Rutherglen	d	10 29	10 37	10 47	10 53	11 05					11 17		11 28		11 37	11 47	11 53	12 07				
Cambuslang	d	10 32		10 51	10 56		11 00				11 21	11 28	11 32			11 51	11 57		12 00			
Newton	d	10 36		10 54	11 01						11 24		11 35			11 54	12 01					
Blantyre	d	10 40		10 58	11 05						11 28		11 39			11 58	12 05					
Hamilton West	d	10 43		11 01	11 08						11 31		11 42			12 01	12 08					
Hamilton Central	d	10 46		11 04	11 13						11 34		11 45			12 03	12 13					
Chatelherault	d	10 50			11 18								11 49				12 18					
Merryton	d	10 53			11 21								11 52				12 21					
Larkhall	a	10 56			11 24								11 55				12 24					
Airbles	d			11 09							11 39					12 09						
Uddingston	d						11 05		11 28			11 33							12 05		12 29	
Bellshill	d						11 10		11 34			11 38							12 10		12 35	
Carmyle	d		10 41			11 10									11 42			12 11				
Mount Vernon	d		10 44			11 12									11 44			12 14				
Baillieston	d		10 46			11 15									11 47			12 16				
Bargeddie	d		10 49			11 18									11 50			12 19				
Kirkwood	d		10 53			11 22									11 54			12 23				
Whifflet	d		10 57			11a25				11 33					11 58			12a27				12 33
Motherwell	a		11 07	11 12			11 18			11 40	11 42	11 44		12 02	12 07	12 11			12 17			12 40
	d						11 19	11 20			11 45	11 47		12 02					12 17	12 20		
Whifflet	d							11a27			11 52									12a30		
Coatbridge Central	d										11 54											
Greenfaulds 226	d										12 02											
Cumbernauld 226	a										12 04											
Shieldmuir	d						11 22					11 51							12 21			
Holytown	d								11 39												12 39	
Wishaw	d						11 26					11 54		12 08					12 24			
Carluke	d						11 34					12 02		12 14					12 32			
Carstairs	a													12 23								
Lanark	a						11 45					12 13							12 43			
Haymarket ⇌	a								12 42					12 49							13 43	
Edinburgh	a								12 47					12 54							13 48	

A From Dalmuir
B From Milngavie
C To Dalmuir
D From Cumbernauld to Dalmuir
E From Ayr

Table T225-R

Mondays to Fridays

21 May to 7 December

Glasgow - Hamilton, Larkhall, Whifflet, Motherwell, Coatbridge, Lanark and Edinburgh

		SR A	SR	SR B	SR B	SR A	SR B	SR B	SR	SR C	SR	SR D	SR A	SR	SR B	SR B	SR A	SR B	SR B	SR	SR C	SR E	SR
Hyndland ■ 226	d	11 53		12 04	12 17	12 24	12 34	12 47					12 53		13 05	13 17	13 25	13 34	13 47				
Partick 226 ⇌	d	11 55		12 07	12 20	12 26	12 37	12 49					12 55		13 08	13 19	13 27	13 37	13 49				
Exhibition Centre	d	11 58		12 10	12 23	12 29	12 40	12 52					12 58		13 11	13 22	13 30	13 40	13 52				
Anderston	d	12 00		12 12	12 25	12 31	12 42	12 54					13 00		13 13	13 24	13 32	13 42	13 54				
Glasgow Central L. Level 15	a	12 02		12 13	12 26	12 32	12 43	12 56					13 02		13 14	13 26	13 33	13 43	13 56				
	d	12 04		12 16	12 27	12 36	12 44	12 57					13 04		13 16	13 27	13 36	13 44	13 57				
Glasgow Central H. Level 15	d		12 20						12 50		13 16			13 20						13 50		14 06	14 16
Argyle Street	d	12 07		12 19	12 29	12 38	12 46	12 59					13 07		13 19	13 29	13 39	13 46	13 59				
Bridgeton	d	12 10		12 22	12 32	12 41	12 49	13 02					13 10		13 22	13 32	13 42	13 49	14 02				
Dalmarnock	d	12 12		12 24	12 34	12 43	12 51	13 04					13 12		13 24	13 34	13 44	13 51	14 04				
Rutherglen	d	12 17		12 29	12 37	12 47	12 53	13 07					13 17		13 28	13 36	13 47	13 53	14 07				
Cambuslang	d	12 21	12 28	12 32		12 51	12 56		13 00				13 21	13 28	13 32		13 51	13 56		14 00			
Newton	d	12 24		12 35		12 54	13 00						13 24		13 35		13 54	14 01					
Blantyre	d	12 28		12 39		12 58	13 04						13 28		13 39		13 58	14 05					
Hamilton West	d	12 31		12 42		13 01	13 07						13 31		13 42		14 01	14 08					
Hamilton Central	d	12 34		12 45		13 04	13 13						13 34		13 45		14 04	14 13					
Chatelherault	d			12 49			13 18								13 49			14 18					
Merryton	d			12 52			13 21								13 52			14 21					
Larkhall	a			12 55			13 24								13 55			14 24					
Airbles	d	12 39				13 09							13 39				14 09						
Uddingston	d		12 33						13 05		13 28			13 33						14 05			14 28
Bellshill	d		12 38						13 10		13 34			13 39						14 10			14 34
Carmyle	d				12 41			13 11								13 41			14 11				
Mount Vernon	d				12 44			13 14								13 43			14 14				
Baillieston	d				12 46			13 16								13 46			14 16				
Bargeddie	d				12 49			13 19								13 49			14 19				
Kirkwood	d				12 53			13 23								13 53			14 23				
Whifflet	d				12 57			13a27				13 33				13 56			14a27				
Motherwell	a	12 42	12 44		13 04	13 12			13 19			13 40	13 42	13 45		14 04	14 12			14 18		14 25	
	d	12 45	12 47						13 19	13 21			13 45	13 48						14 18	14 20	14 25	
Whifflet	d	12 52								13a28			13 52								14a27		
Coatbridge Central	d	12 54											13 54										
Greenfaulds 226	d	13 02											14 02										
Cumbernauld 226	a	13 04											14 04										
Shieldmuir	d		12 51						13 23					13 51						14 22			
Holytown	d										13 39												14 38
Wishaw	d		12 56						13 26					13 55						14 25		14 31	
Carluke	d		13 02						13 34					14 03						14 32		14 38	
Carstairs	a																					14 49	
Lanark	a		13 13						13 45					14 14						14 43			
Haymarket ⇌	a										14 47											15 17	15 42
Edinburgh	a										14 52											15 24	15 48

		SR D	SR A	SR	SR B	SR B	SR A	SR B	SR B	SR	SR C	SR	SR D	SR A	SR	SR B	SR F	SR B	SR A	SR B	SR B	SR	SR C
Hyndland ■ 226	d		13 54		14 04	14 18	14 23	14 34	14 47					14 53		15 04		15 17	15 23	15 34	15 47		
Partick 226 ⇌	d		13 56		14 07	14 21	14 25	14 37	14 49					14 55		15 07		15 20	15 25	15 37	15 49		
Exhibition Centre	d		13 59		14 10	14 24	14 28	14 40	14 52					14 58		15 10		15 23	15 28	15 40	15 52		
Anderston	d		14 01		14 12	14 26	14 30	14 42	14 54					15 00		15 12		15 25	15 30	15 42	15 54		
Glasgow Central L. Level 15	a		14 02		14 13	14 27	14 32	14 43	14 56					15 01		15 13		15 26	15 31	15 43	15 56		
	d		14 04		14 16	14 28	14 34	14 44	14 57					15 04		15 16		15 27	15 34	15 45	15 57		
Glasgow Central H. Level 15	d			14 20						14 50		15 16			15 20		15 47					15 50	
Argyle Street	d		14 07		14 19	14 30	14 37	14 46	14 59					15 07		15 19		15 29	15 37	15 47	15 59		
Bridgeton	d		14 10		14 22	14 33	14 40	14 49	15 02					15 10		15 22		15 32	15 40	15 50	16 02		
Dalmarnock	d		14 12		14 24	14 35	14 42	14 51	15 04					15 12		15 24		15 34	15 42	15 52	16 04		
Rutherglen	d		14 17		14 28	14 37	14 47	14 53	15 07					15 17		15 28		15 37	15 47	15 54	16 07		
Cambuslang	d		14 21	14 28	14 32		14 51	14 56		15 00				15 21	15 28	15 32			15 51	15 58		16 01	
Newton	d		14 24		14 35		14 54	15 00						15 24		15 35			15 54	16 01			
Blantyre	d		14 28		14 39		14 58	15 04						15 28		15 39			15 58	16 05			
Hamilton West	d		14 31		14 42		15 01	15 07						15 31		15 42			16 01	16 08			
Hamilton Central	d		14 34		14 45		15 04	15 13						15 34		15 45			16 04	16 13			
Chatelherault	d				14 49			15 18								15 49				16 18			
Merryton	d				14 52			15 21								15 52				16 21			
Larkhall	a				14 55			15 24								15 55				16 24			
Airbles	d		14 39				15 09							15 39					16 09				
Uddingston	d			14 33						15 05		15 28			15 33							16 05	
Bellshill	d			14 38						15 10		15 34			15 39							16 10	
Carmyle	d					14 41			15 11									15 41			16 11		
Mount Vernon	d					14 44			15 14									15 44			16 14		
Baillieston	d					14 46			15 16									15 46			16 16		
Bargeddie	d					14 49			15 19									15 49			16 19		
Kirkwood	d					14 53			15 23									15 53			16 23		
Whifflet	d	14 33				14 57			15a27				15 33					15 57			16a27		
Motherwell	a	14 40	14 42	14 44		15 05	15 12			15 19			15 40	15 42	15 45		16 03	16 06	16 12			16 16	
	d		14 45	14 45						15 19	15 20			15 45	15 48		16 04					16 17	16 20
Whifflet	d		14 52								15a27			15 52									16a27
Coatbridge Central	d		14 54											15 54									
Greenfaulds 226	d		15 02											16 02									
Cumbernauld 226	a		15 04											16 04									
Shieldmuir	d			14 49						15 23					15 51							16 20	
Holytown	d											15 40											
Wishaw	d			14 52						15 27					15 55		16 22					16 26	
Carluke	d			15 02						15 34					16 02		16 28					16 33	
Carstairs	a																16 37						
Lanark	a			15 13						15 45					16 13							16 45	
Haymarket ⇌	a											16 46					17 05						
Edinburgh	a											16 51					17 11						

A From Milngavie
B From Dalmuir
C To Dalmuir
D From Cumbernauld to Dalmuir
E From Ayr
F From Ayr to North Berwick

Table T225-R

Mondays to Fridays

21 May to 7 December

Glasgow - Hamilton, Larkhall, Whifflet, Motherwell, Coatbridge, Lanark and Edinburgh

		SR		SR A	SR B	SR	SR C	SR C	SR B	SR D	SR C	SR C		SR	SR	SR	SR A	SR B	SR	SR C	SR C	SR B		SR	SR
Hyndland ■ 226	d				15 53		16 04	16 17	16 23		16 34	16 47						16 53		17 05	17 17	17 23			
Partick 226	d				15 55		16 07	16 19	16 25		16 37	16 49						16 55		17 07	17 20	17 25			
Exhibition Centre	d				15 58		16 10	16 22	16 28		16 40	16 52						17 01		17 11	17 23	17 28			
Anderston	d				16 00		16 12	16 24	16 30		16 42	16 54			17 00			17 04		17 13	17 25	17 30		17 42	
Glasgow Central L. Level	a				16 01		16 13	16 26	16 31		16 43	16 56			17 01			17 05		17 14	17 26	17 31		17 43	
	d				16 04		16 16	16 27	16 34		16 44	16 56			17 02			17 06		17 17	17 27	17 34		17 44	
Glasgow Central H. Level	d	16 16				16 21								16 50		17 18			17 20						17 50
Argyle Street	d				16 07		16 19	16 29	16 37		16 45	16 58			17 04			17 08		17 20	17 29	17 37		17 46	
Bridgeton	d				16 10		16 22	16 32	16 40		16 48	17 01						17 11		17 23	17 32	17 40			
Dalmarnock	d				16 12		16 24	16 34	16 42		16 50	17 03						17 13		17 25	17 34	17 42			
Rutherglen	d				16 17		16 29	16 37	16 47		16 53	17 05			17 10			17 17		17 30	17 37	17 47		17 51	
Cambuslang	d				16 21	16 29	16 33		16 51		16 56			17 00				17 21	17 31	17 34		17 51			17 58
Newton	d				16 24		16 36		16 54		17 01							17 24		17 37		17 54			
Blantyre	d				16 28		16 40		16 58		17 05							17 28		17 41		17 58			
Hamilton West	d				16 31		16 43		17 01		17 08							17 31		17 44		18 01			
Hamilton Central	d				16 34		16 45		17 04		17 13							17 34		17 46		18 04			
Chatelherault	d						16 50				17 18									17 51					
Merryton	d						16 53				17 21									17 54					
Larkhall	a						16 56				17 24									17 57					
Airbles	d				16 39				17 09									17 39				18 09			
Uddingston	d	16 29				16 34								17 06		17u30			17 35					17 59	18 04
Bellshill	d	16 35				16 39								17 11	17 22	17 36			17 40					18 05	18 10
Carmyle	d							16 41				17 10									17 41				
Mount Vernon	d							16 44				17 12									17 44				
Baillieston	d							16 46				17 15									17 46				
Bargeddie	d							16 49				17 18									17 49				
Kirkwood	d							16 53				17 22									17 53				
Whifflet	d			16 33				16 57				17a25					17 33				17 58				
Motherwell	a			16 41	16 42	16 45		17 04	17 12					17 19			17 40	17 42	17 48		18 05	18 12		18 11	18 16
	d				16 45	16 45				17 20				17 20				17 45	17 49					18 12	18 17
Whifflet	d				16 52					17a29								17 52							
Coatbridge Central	d				16 54													17 54							
Greenfaulds 226	d				17 02													18 02							
Cumbernauld 226	a				17 04													18 04							
Shieldmuir	d					16 49								17 23					17 52					18 16	18 21
Holytown	d	16 39													17 26	17 41									
Wishaw	d					16 55								17 27	17 33				18 00					18 19	18 24
Carluke	d					17 06								17 35	17 39				18 08					18 25	18 30
Carstairs	a														17 50									18 34	
Lanark	a					17 17								17 46					18 20						18 41
Haymarket	a	17 43														18 44									
Edinburgh	a	17 48														18 49									

		SR D	SR C	SR C	SR A	SR B	SR	SR		SR C	SR C	SR B	SR C	SR C	SR	SR D	SR	SR A		SR B	SR	SR C	SR E	SR C	SR B
Hyndland ■ 226	d		17 35	17 47		17 53				18 04	18 17	18 23	18 34	18 47						18 53		19 04		19 17	19 23
Partick 226	d		17 37	17 49		17 55				18 07	18 19	18 25	18 37	18 49						18 55		19 07		19 20	19 25
Exhibition Centre	d		17 43	17 52		17 58				18 10	18 22	18 28	18 40	18 52						18 58		19 10		19 23	19 28
Anderston	d		17 46	17 54		18 00				18 13	18 24	18 30	18 42	18 54						19 00		19 12		19 25	19 30
Glasgow Central L. Level	a		17 47	17 56		18 02				18 14	18 26	18 32	18 43	18 56						19 01		19 13		19 26	19 32
	d		17 51	17 56		18 04				18 18	18 27	18 34	18 44	18 57						19 04		19 16		19 27	19 34
Glasgow Central H. Level	d						18 17	18 22							18 50		19 16				19 21		19 46		
Argyle Street	d		17 53	17 58		18 07				18 21	18 29	18 37	18 46	18 59						19 07		19 19		19 29	19 37
Bridgeton	d		17 56	18 01		18 10				18 24	18 32	18 40	18 49	19 02						19 10		19 22		19 32	19 40
Dalmarnock	d		17 58	18 03		18 12				18 26	18 34	18 42	18 51	19 04						19 12		19 24		19 34	19 42
Rutherglen	d		18 01	18 05		18 17				18 30	18 37	18 47	18 54	19 07						19 17		19 28		19 37	19 47
Cambuslang	d		18 05			18 21		18 30		18 34		18 51	18 58		19 01					19 21	19 29	19 32			19 51
Newton	d		18 08			18 24				18 37		18 54	19 01							19 24		19 35			19 54
Blantyre	d		18 12			18 28				18 41		18 58	19 05							19 28		19 39			19 58
Hamilton West	d		18 15			18 31				18 44		19 01	19 08							19 31		19 42			20 01
Hamilton Central	d		18 17			18 34				18 46		19 04	19 13							19 34		19 45			20 04
Chatelherault	d		18 22							18 51			19 18									19 49			
Merryton	d		18 25							18 54			19 21									19 52			
Larkhall	a		18 28							18 57			19 24									19 55			
Airbles	d					18 39						19 09								19 39					20 09
Uddingston	d						18 29	18 35							19 06		19 28				19 34				
Bellshill	d						18 33	18 40							19 11		19 34				19 39				
Carmyle	d			18 10							18 41			19 11										19 41	
Mount Vernon	d			18 12							18 44			19 14										19 44	
Baillieston	d			18 15							18 46			19 16										19 46	
Bargeddie	d			18 18							18 49			19 19										19 49	
Kirkwood	d			18 22							18 53			19 23										19 53	
Whifflet	d			18a25	18 34						18 57			19a27				19 33						19 57	
Motherwell	a				18 41	18 42		18 47			19 04	19 12			19 19			19 40		19 42	19 45		20 03	20 07	20 12
	d	18 24				18 45		18 48							19 19	19 21				19 45	19 49		20 04		
Whifflet	d	18a31				18 51										19a28				19 52					
Coatbridge Central	d					18 54														19 54					
Greenfaulds 226	d					19 01														20 02					
Cumbernauld 226	a					19 03														20 04					
Shieldmuir	d							18 51							19 23						19 53				
Holytown	d						18 38										19 41								
Wishaw	d							18 55							19 26						19 56		20 10		
Carluke	d							19 02							19 34						20 02		20 16		
Carstairs	a																						20 25		
Lanark	a							19 13							19 45						20 13				
Haymarket	a						19 47										20 44						20 54		
Edinburgh	a						19 52										20 49						21 00		

A From Cumbernauld to Dalmuir
B From Milngavie
C From Dalmuir
D To Dalmuir
E From Ayr

Table T225-R

Mondays to Fridays

21 May to 7 December

Glasgow - Hamilton, Larkhall, Whifflet, Motherwell, Coatbridge, Lanark and Edinburgh

		SR	SR A	SR B		SR B	SR C	SR D	SR	SR B	SR B	SR D	SR B	SR B		SR	SR A	SR FO	SR FX	SR C	SR D	SR B	SR	SR B
Hyndland ■ 226	d			19 35		19 47		19 53		20 06	20 17	20 23	20 34	20 47							20 53	21 06		21 17
Partick 226	d			19 38		19 50		19 55		20 08	20 19	20 25	20 37	20 50							20 55	21 08		21 20
Exhibition Centre	d			19 41		19 53		19 58		20 11	20 22	20 29	20 40	20 53							20 58	21 11		21 23
Anderston	d			19 43		19 55		20 00		20 13	20 26	20 33	20 42	20 55							21 00	21 13		21 25
Glasgow Central L. Level	a			19 45		19 56		20 01		20 15	20 27	20 34	20 43	20 56							21 02	21 15		21 26
	d			19 48		19 57		20 02		20 18	20 28	20 36	20 44	20 57							21 04	21 15		21 27
Glasgow Central H. Level	d	19 50							20 21							20 51		21 16	21 17				21 22	
Argyle Street	d			19 51		19 59		20 03		20 20	20 30	20 38	20 46	20 59							21 07	21 17		21 29
Bridgeton	d			19 54		20 02		20 06		20 23	20 33	20 41	20 49	21 02							21 10	21 20		21 32
Dalmarnock	d			19 56		20 04		20 08		20 25	20 35	20 43	20 51	21 04							21 12	21 22		21 34
Rutherglen	d			19 59		20 07		20 17		20 28	20 37	20 47	20 54	21 07							21 17	21 25		21 37
Cambuslang	d	19 58		20 02				20 21	20 29	20 33		20 51	20 57			21 01					21 21	21 28	21 32	
Newton	d			20 08				20 26		20 38		20 54	21 02								21 24	21 32		
Blantyre	d			20 12				20 30		20 42		20 58	21 06								21 28	21 36		
Hamilton West	d			20 15				20 33		20 45		21 01	21 09								21 31	21 39		
Hamilton Central	d			20 17				20 36		20 47		21 04	21 14								21 34	21 43		
Chatelherault	d			20 22						20 52			21 18									21 48		
Merryton	d			20 25						20 55			21 21									21 51		
Larkhall	a			20 28						20 58			21 24									21 54		
Airbles	d							20 41				21 09									21 39			
Uddingston	d	20 03							20 34							21 06		21 29	21 42				21 37	
Bellshill	d	20 08							20 39							21 11		21 34	21 57				21 42	
Carmyle	d					20 11					20 41			21 11										21 41
Mount Vernon	d					20 14					20 44			21 14										21 44
Baillieston	d					20 16					20 46			21 16										21 46
Bargeddie	d					20 19					20 49			21 19										21 49
Kirkwood	d					20 23					20 53			21 23										21 53
Whifflet	d					20a27	20 33				20 58			21a27						21 33				21 57
Motherwell	a	20 14					20 40	20 44	20 46		21 07	21 12				21 17				21 40	21 42		21 49	22 05
	d	20 18	20 26					20 45	20 47							21 17	21 23				21 46		21 49	
Whifflet	d		20a33					20 52									21a30				21 53			
Coatbridge Central	d							20 54													21 55			
Greenfaulds 226	d							21 02													22 03			
Cumbernauld 226	a							21 04													22 05			
Shieldmuir	d	20 22							20 50							21 21							21 53	
Holytown	d																	21 40	22 08					
Wishaw	d	20 25							20 54							21 25							21 56	
Carluke	d	20 33							21 02							21 34							22 02	
Carstairs	a																							
Lanark	a	20 44							21 13							21 45							22 13	
Haymarket	a																	22 42	00 28					
Edinburgh	a																	22 47	00 49					

		SR D	SR B	SR B	SR	SR A	SR E	SR D	SR	SR B		SR B	SR D	SR B	SR	SR FO A	SR B	SR FO	SR FX	SR D		SR	SR B	SR B	SR D
Hyndland ■ 226	d	21 23	21 35	21 47				21 53		22 06		22 18	22 24	22 34			22 47			22 53			23 05	23 17	23 23
Partick 226	d	21 25	21 37	21 50				21 55		22 08		22 20	22 26	22 37			22 50			22 55			23 08	23 20	23 25
Exhibition Centre	d	21 28	21 40	21 53				21 58		22 11		22 23	22 29	22 40			22 53			22 59			23 12	23 23	23 29
Anderston	d	21 30	21 42	21 55				22 00		22 13		22 25	22 31	22 42			22 55			23 01			23 14	23 25	23 31
Glasgow Central L. Level	a	21 32	21 44	21 56				22 02		22 15		22 27	22 33	22 44			22 57			23 02			23 15	23 27	23 32
	d	21 34	21 44	21 57				22 04		22 17		22 27	22 34	22 44			22 57			23 06			23 17	23 27	23 36
Glasgow Central H. Level	d				21 50				22 20						22 50			23 03	23 03			23 20			
Argyle Street	d	21 37	21 46	21 59				22 07		22 20		22 29	22 37	22 46			22 59			23 08			23 19	23 29	23 38
Bridgeton	d	21 40	21 49	22 02				22 10		22 23		22 32	22 40	22 49			23 02			23 11			23 22	23 32	23 41
Dalmarnock	d	21 42	21 51	22 04				22 12		22 25		22 34	22 42	22 51			23 04			23 13			23 24	23 34	23 43
Rutherglen	d	21 47	21 53	22 07				22 17		22 29		22 37	22 47	22 54			23 07			23 17			23 28	23 37	23 48
Cambuslang	d	21 50	21 57		22 00			22 21	22 28	22 32			22 51	22 57	23 01			23 12	23 19	23 21		23 28	23 32		23 51
Newton	d	21 54	22 01					22 24		22 35			22 54	23 03						23 24			23 35		
Blantyre	d	21 58	22 06					22 28		22 39			22 58	23 08						23 28			23 39		
Hamilton West	d	22 01	22 09					22 31		22 42			23 01	23 11						23 31			23 42		
Hamilton Central	d	22 04	22 13					22 34		22 45			23 04	23 14						23 33			23 46		
Chatelherault	d		22 18							22 50				23 18									23 50		
Merryton	d		22 21							22 53				23 21									23 53		
Larkhall	a		22 24							22 56				23 24									23 56		
Airbles	d	22 09						22 39					23 09							23 39					
Uddingston	d				22 05				22 33						23 06			23 17	23 35			23 33			
Bellshill	d				22 10				22 38						23 11			23 23	23 50			23 38			
Carmyle	d			22 11								22 41					23 11							23 41	
Mount Vernon	d			22 14								22 44					23 14							23 44	
Baillieston	d			22 16								22 46					23 16							23 46	
Bargeddie	d			22 19								22 49					23 19							23 49	
Kirkwood	d			22 23								22 53					23 23							23 53	
Whifflet	d			22a27			22 33					22 57					23 27							23 57	
Motherwell	a	22 12			22 16		22 40	22 42	22 46			23 04	23 12		23 17		23 34			23 41		23 44		00 04	00 01
	d				22 18	22 20		22 45	22 47						23 19	23 22	23 39					23 48			
Whifflet	d					22a27		22 52								23a29									
Coatbridge Central	d							22 54																	
Greenfaulds 226	d							23 02																	
Cumbernauld 226	a							23 04																	
Shieldmuir	d				22 22				22 51						23 22		23 42					23 52			
Holytown	d																	23 27	00 01						
Wishaw	d				22 25				22 55						23 26		23 48					23 55			
Carluke	d				22 31				23 03						23 32		23 55					00 01			
Carstairs	a																00 05								
Lanark	a				22 42				23 14						23 43							00 12			
Haymarket	a																	00 27	02s21						
Edinburgh	a																	00 32	02 42						

A To Dalmuir
B From Dalmuir
C From Cumbernauld to Dalmuir
D From Milngavie
E From Cumbernauld to Garscadden

Table T225-R

Mondays to Fridays

21 May to 7 December

Glasgow - Hamilton, Larkhall, Whifflet, Motherwell, Coatbridge, Lanark and Edinburgh

		SR FX	SR FO	SR FO A	SR FO A	SR FO B
Hyndland 226	d			23 34	23 48	23 53
Partick 226	d			23 37	23 50	23 55
Exhibition Centre	d			23 41	23 54	23 59
Anderston	d			23 43	23 56	00 01
Glasgow Central L. Level	a			23 44	23 58	00 03
	d			23 46	23 59	00 06
Glasgow Central H. Level	d	23 50	23 50			
Argyle Street	d			23 49	00 03	00 09
Bridgeton	d			23 52	00 06	00 12
Dalmarnock	d			23 54	00 08	00 14
Rutherglen	d			23 58	00 12	00 18
Cambuslang	d	23 58	23 58	00 01		00 21
Newton	d			00 05		00 24
Blantyre	d			00 09		00 28
Hamilton West	d			00 12		00 31
Hamilton Central	d			00 15		00 34
Chatelherault	d			00 19		
Merryton	d			00 22		
Larkhall	a			00 25		
Airbles	d					00 39
Uddingston	d	00 03	00 03			
Bellshill	d	00 08	00 08			
Carmyle	d				00 17	
Mount Vernon	d				00 20	
Baillieston	d				00 23	
Bargeddie	d				00 26	
Kirkwood	d				00 32	
Whifflet	d				00 36	
Motherwell	a	00 14	00 16		00 48	00 42
	d		00 18			
Whifflet	d					
Coatbridge Central	d					
Greenfaulds 226	d					
Cumbernauld 226	a					
Shieldmuir	d		00 21			
Holytown	d					
Wishaw	d		00 25			
Carluke	d		00 31			
Carstairs	a					
Lanark	a		00 42			
Haymarket	a					
Edinburgh	a					

Saturdays

26 May to 8 December

		SR A	SR C	SR C	SR A	SR	SR B	SR	SR	SR D	SR	SR	SR A	SR	SR D	SR E	SR	SR	SR A	SR	SR A	SR	SR D
Hyndland 226	d												06 07						06 17	06 22	06 32		
Partick 226	d												06 10						06 19	06 24	06 34		
Exhibition Centre	d												06 13						06 22	06 28	06 37		
Anderston	d						00 01						06 15						06 24	06 30	06 39		
Glasgow Central L. Level	a						00 03						06 17						06 25	06 31	06 41		
	d						00 06						06 18						06 27	06 34	06 43		
Glasgow Central H. Level	d					00 05						06 16										06 50	
Argyle Street	d				00 03		00 09						06 20						06 29	06 36	06 46		
Bridgeton	d				00 06		00 12						06 23						06 32	06 39	06 49		
Dalmarnock	d				00 08		00 14						06 25						06 34	06 41	06 52		
Rutherglen	d				00 12		00 18						06 27						06 36	06 44	06 55		
Cambuslang	d	00 01				00 14	00 21					06 25	06 31							06 47	06 59	07 02	
Newton	d	00 05					00 24						06 34							06 50	07 03		
Blantyre	d	00 09					00 28						06 38							06 54	07 07		
Hamilton West	d	00 12					00 31						06 41							06 57	07 11		
Hamilton Central	d	00 15					00 34						06 44							07 00	07 13		
Chatelherault	d	00 19											06 49								07 18		
Merryton	d	00 22											06 52								07 21		
Larkhall	a	00 25											06 55								07 24		
Airbles	d						00 39													07 06			
Uddingston	d			00 03		00 19						06 30										07 06	
Bellshill	d			00 08		00 25						06 36										07 11	
Carmyle	d				00 17														06 40				
Mount Vernon	d				00 20														06 43				
Baillieston	d				00 23														06 45				
Bargeddie	d				00 26														06 48				
Kirkwood	d				00 32														06 52				
Whifflet	d				00 36											06 25			06 56				
Motherwell	a			00 16	00 48		00 42									06 37			07 09	07 08		07 17	
	d			00 18				05 42	05 48	05 56	06 00			06 21	06 24		06 40	06 50				07 18	07 22
Whifflet	d							05 49		06a03					06a32		06 47						07a29
Coatbridge Central	d							05 52									06 50						
Greenfaulds 226	d							05 59									06 59						
Cumbernauld 226	a							06 01									07 01						
Shieldmuir	d			00 21					05 51					06 24				06 54				07 21	
Holytown	d					00 29					06 07	06 40											
Wishaw	d			00 25					05 55					06 28				06 57				07 25	
Carluke	d		00 01	00 31					06 02					06 34				07 03				07 35	
Carstairs	a																						
Lanark	a		00 12	00 42					06 13					06 45				07 14				07 47	
Haymarket	a					01 20					07 11	07 42											
Edinburgh	a					01 26					07 16	07 48											

A From Dalmuir
B From Milngavie
C From Glasgow Central
D To Dalmuir
E From Cumbernauld to Dalmuir

Table T225-R

Saturdays

26 May to 8 December

Glasgow - Hamilton, Larkhall, Whifflet, Motherwell, Coatbridge, Lanark and Edinburgh

		SR A	SR B	SR C	SR D	SR	SR	SR C	SR C	SR D	SR	SR E	SR C	SR	SR B	SR C	SR D	SR	SR C	SR C	SR D	SR C	SR C
Hyndland 226	d			06 48	06 52			07 03	07 17	07 23			07 34			07 48	07 53		08 04	08 17	08 23	08 35	08 48
Partick 226	d			06 50	06 54			07 06	07 19	07 25			07 37			07 50	07 55		08 07	08 20	08 25	08 37	08 51
Exhibition Centre	d			06 53	06 57			07 09	07 22	07 28			07 40			07 53	07 58		08 10	08 23	08 29	08 40	08 54
Anderston	d			06 55	07 00			07 11	07 24	07 31			07 42			07 55	08 00		08 12	08 25	08 31	08 42	08 56
Glasgow Central L. Level	a			06 57	07 02			07 12	07 26	07 32			07 43			07 57	08 02		08 14	08 26	08 33	08 44	08 57
	d			06 58	07 04			07 16	07 26	07 36			07 47			07 58	08 04		08 16	08 27	08 35	08 44	08 58
Glasgow Central H. Level	d	07 03				07 13	07 20				07 51			08 17				08 20					
Argyle Street	d			07 00	07 08			07 19	07 28	07 38			07 50			08 00	08 07		08 19	08 29	08 38	08 46	09 00
Bridgeton	d			07 03	07 11			07 22	07 31	07 41			07 53			08 03	08 10		08 22	08 32	08 41	08 49	09 03
Dalmarnock	d			07 05	07 13			07 25	07 33	07 43			07 55			08 05	08 12		08 24	08 34	08 43	08 51	09 05
Rutherglen	d			07 07	07 17			07 29	07 35	07 47			07 59			08 07	08 17		08 29	08 37	08 47	08 53	09 07
Cambuslang	d				07 21	07 24	07 28	07 33		07 51	07 59		08 03				08 21	08 29	08 32		08 51	08 56	
Newton	d				07 24			07 36		07 54			08 06				08 24		08 35		08 54	09 00	
Blantyre	d				07 28			07 40		07 58			08 10				08 28		08 39		08 58	09 04	
Hamilton West	d				07 31			07 43		08 01			08 13				08 31		08 42		09 01	09 07	
Hamilton Central	d				07 34			07 45		08 04			08 16				08 34		08 45		09 04	09 14	
Chatelherault	d							07 50					08 20						08 49			09 18	
Merryton	d							07 53					08 23						08 52			09 21	
Larkhall	a							07 56					08 26						08 55			09 24	
Airbles	d				07 39					08 09							08 39				09 09		
Uddingston	d					07 30	07 33				08 04			08 29				08 34					
Bellshill	d					07 35	07 39				08 09			08 34				08 39					
Carmyle	d			07 11					07 40							08 12				08 41			09 11
Mount Vernon	d			07 14					07 42							08 14				08 44			09 14
Baillieston	d			07 16					07 45							08 17				08 46			09 16
Bargeddie	d			07 19					07 48							08 20				08 49			09 19
Kirkwood	d			07 23					07 52							08 24				08 53			09 23
Whifflet	d		07 25	07a28					07 56						08 24	08a28				08 57			09a27
Motherwell	a	07 21	07 32		07 42		07 46		08 07	08 12	08 17				08 32		08 42	08 45		09 04	09 12		
	d	07 22			07 43		07 47				08 17	08 22					08 43	08 47					
Whifflet	d				07 49							08a30					08 50						
Coatbridge Central	d				07 52												08 53						
Greenfaulds 226	d				08 00												09 00						
Cumbernauld 226	a				08 02												09 02						
Shieldmuir	d						07 51				08 21							08 51					
Holytown	d					07 40								08 40									
Wishaw	d	07 32					07 54				08 24							08 54					
Carluke	d	07 39					08 03				08 30							09 02					
Carstairs	a	07 48																					
Lanark	a						08 14				08 43							09 13					
Haymarket	a	08 22				08 43								09 43									
Edinburgh	a	08 29				08 48								09 49									

		SR	SR E	SR	SR B	SR D	SR	SR C	SR F	SR C	SR D	SR C	SR C	SR	SR E	SR	SR B	SR D	SR	SR C	SR C	SR D
Hyndland 226	d					08 53		09 06		09 17	09 23	09 34	09 47					09 53		10 04	10 17	10 23
Partick 226	d					08 56		09 08		09 19	09 25	09 37	09 49					09 55		10 07	10 19	10 25
Exhibition Centre	d					08 59		09 11		09 22	09 28	09 40	09 52					09 58		10 10	10 22	10 28
Anderston	d					09 01		09 13		09 24	09 30	09 42	09 54					10 00		10 12	10 24	10 30
Glasgow Central L. Level	a					09 02		09 15		09 26	09 32	09 43	09 56					10 02		10 13	10 26	10 31
	d					09 04		09 16		09 27	09 34	09 44	09 57					10 04		10 16	10 27	10 35
Glasgow Central H. Level	d	08 50		09 17			09 21		09 30					09 50		10 16			10 20			
Argyle Street	d					09 07		09 19		09 28	09 37	09 46	09 59					10 07		10 19	10 29	10 38
Bridgeton	d					09 10		09 22		09 31	09 40	09 49	10 02					10 10		10 22	10 32	10 41
Dalmarnock	d					09 12		09 24		09 33	09 42	09 51	10 04					10 12		10 24	10 34	10 43
Rutherglen	d					09 17		09 29		09 35	09 47	09 53	10 07					10 17		10 29	10 37	10 47
Cambuslang	d	09 00				09 21	09 29	09 33			09 51	09 57		10 00				10 21	10 28	10 32		10 51
Newton	d					09 24		09 36			09 54	10 01						10 24		10 36		10 54
Blantyre	d					09 28		09 40			09 58	10 05						10 28		10 40		10 58
Hamilton West	d					09 31		09 43			10 01	10 08						10 31		10 43		11 01
Hamilton Central	d					09 34		09 45			10 04	10 13						10 34		10 46		11 04
Chatelherault	d							09 50				10 18								10 50		
Merryton	d							09 53				10 21								10 53		
Larkhall	a							09 56				10 24								10 56		
Airbles	d					09 39					10 09							10 39				11 09
Uddingston	d	09 05		09 29			09 34							10 06		10 28			10 33			
Bellshill	d	09 10		09 34			09 41							10 11		10 34			10 38			
Carmyle	d									09 40			10 12								10 41	
Mount Vernon	d									09 42			10 14								10 44	
Baillieston	d									09 45			10 17								10 46	
Bargeddie	d									09 48			10 20								10 49	
Kirkwood	d									09 52			10 24								10 53	
Whifflet	d				09 34					09 55			10a27				10 33				10 57	
Motherwell	a	09 18			09 41	09 42	09 47		09 56	10 07	10 12			10 17			10 40	10 42	10 45		11 07	11 12
	d	09 19	09 22			09 43	09 48		09 57					10 17	10 23			10 45	10 48			
Whifflet	d		09a29			09 50									10a30			10 52				
Coatbridge Central	d					09 52												10 54				
Greenfaulds 226	d					10 01												11 02				
Cumbernauld 226	a					10 03												11 04				
Shieldmuir	d	09 22					09 51							10 21					10 51			
Holytown	d			09 39												10 39						
Wishaw	d	09 26					09 55		10 03					10 26					10 55			
Carluke	d	09 33					10 03		10 09					10 32					11 03			
Carstairs	a								10 18													
Lanark	a	09 44					10 15							10 43					11 14			
Haymarket	a			10 42					10 49							11 39						
Edinburgh	a			10 47					10 54							11 44						

A To North Berwick
B From Cumbernauld to Dalmuir
C From Dalmuir
D From Milngavie
E To Dalmuir
F From Ayr

26 May to 8 December

Glasgow - Hamilton, Larkhall, Whifflet, Motherwell, Coatbridge, Lanark and Edinburgh

		SR A	SR A	SR	SR B	SR	SR C	SR D		SR	SR A	SR E	SR A	SR D	SR A	SR A	SR	SR B		SR	SR C	SR D	SR	SR A	SR A
Hyndland 226	d	10 34	10 47					10 53			11 05		11 17	11 23	11 35	11 47						11 53		12 04	12 17
Partick 226	d	10 36	10 49					10 55			11 08		11 19	11 25	11 37	11 49						11 55		12 07	12 20
Exhibition Centre	d	10 39	10 52					10 58			11 11		11 22	11 28	11 40	11 52						11 58		12 10	12 23
Anderston	d	10 41	10 54					11 00			11 13		11 24	11 30	11 42	11 54						12 00		12 12	12 25
Glasgow Central L. Level	a	10 43	10 56					11 02			11 14		11 26	11 32	11 44	11 56						12 02		12 13	12 26
	d	10 44	10 56					11 04			11 18		11 27	11 34	11 44	11 57						12 04		12 16	12 27
Glasgow Central H. Level	d			10 50		11 16				11 20		11 46					11 50			12 16			12 20		
Argyle Street	d	10 46	10 58					11 07			11 20		11 29	11 37	11 46	11 59						12 07		12 19	12 29
Bridgeton	d	10 49	11 01					11 10			11 23		11 32	11 40	11 49	12 02						12 10		12 22	12 32
Dalmarnock	d	10 51	11 03					11 12			11 25		11 34	11 42	11 51	12 04						12 12		12 24	12 34
Rutherglen	d	10 53	11 05					11 17			11 28		11 37	11 47	11 53	12 07						12 17		12 29	12 37
Cambuslang	d	10 56		11 00				11 21		11 28	11 32			11 51	11 57		12 00					12 21	12 28	12 32	
Newton	d	11 01						11 24			11 35			11 54	12 01							12 24		12 35	
Blantyre	d	11 05						11 28			11 39			11 58	12 05							12 28		12 39	
Hamilton West	d	11 08						11 31			11 42			12 01	12 08							12 31		12 42	
Hamilton Central	d	11 13						11 34			11 45			12 03	12 13							12 34		12 45	
Chatelherault	d	11 18									11 49				12 18									12 49	
Merryton	d	11 21									11 52				12 21									12 52	
Larkhall	a	11 24									11 55				12 24									12 55	
Airbles	d							11 39						12 09								12 39			
Uddingston	d			11 05		11 28				11 33							12 05			12 28			12 33		
Bellshill	d			11 10		11 34				11 38							12 10			12 34			12 38		
Carmyle	d		11 10										11 42			12 11									12 41
Mount Vernon	d		11 12										11 44			12 14									12 44
Baillieston	d		11 15										11 47			12 16									12 46
Bargeddie	d		11 18										11 50			12 19									12 49
Kirkwood	d		11 22										11 54			12 23									12 53
Whifflet	d		11a25				11 33						11 58			12a27					12 33				12 57
Motherwell	a			11 18			11 40	11 42		11 44		12 03	12 07	12 11			12 17				12 40	12 42	12 44		13 04
	d			11 19	11 20			11 45		11 47		12 04					12 17	12 20				12 45	12 47		
Whifflet	d				11a27			11 52										12a30				12 52			
Coatbridge Central	d							11 54														12 54			
Greenfaulds 226	d							12 02														13 02			
Cumbernauld 226	a							12 04														13 04			
Shieldmuir	d			11 22						11 51							12 21						12 51		
Holytown	d					11 39														12 39					
Wishaw	d			11 26						11 54		12 09					12 24						12 56		
Carluke	d			11 34						12 02		12 15					12 32						13 02		
Carstairs	a											12 24													
Lanark	a			11 45						12 13							12 43						13 13		
Haymarket	a					12 46						12 50								13 42					
Edinburgh	a					12 52						12 55								13 47					

		SR D	SR A	SR A		SR	SR B	SR	SR C	SR D	SR	SR A	SR A	SR D		SR A	SR A	SR	SR B	SR E	SR	SR C	SR D	SR	
Hyndland 226	d	12 24	12 34	12 47						12 53		13 05	13 17	13 25		13 34	13 47						13 54		
Partick 226	d	12 26	12 37	12 49						12 55		13 08	13 19	13 27		13 37	13 49						13 56		
Exhibition Centre	d	12 29	12 40	12 52						12 58		13 11	13 22	13 30		13 40	13 52						13 59		
Anderston	d	12 31	12 42	12 54						13 00		13 13	13 24	13 32		13 42	13 54						14 01		
Glasgow Central L. Level	a	12 32	12 43	12 56						13 02		13 14	13 26	13 33		13 43	13 56						14 02		
	d	12 36	12 44	12 57						13 04		13 16	13 27	13 36		13 44	13 57						14 04		
Glasgow Central H. Level	d					12 50		13 16			13 20							13 50		14 06	14 16			14 20	
Argyle Street	d	12 38	12 46	12 59						13 07		13 19	13 29	13 39		13 46	13 59						14 07		
Bridgeton	d	12 41	12 49	13 02						13 10		13 22	13 32	13 42		13 49	14 02						14 10		
Dalmarnock	d	12 43	12 51	13 04						13 12		13 24	13 34	13 44		13 51	14 04						14 12		
Rutherglen	d	12 47	12 53	13 07						13 17		13 28	13 36	13 47		13 53	14 07						14 17		
Cambuslang	d	12 51	12 56			13 00				13 21	13 28	13 32		13 51		13 56		14 00					14 21	14 28	
Newton	d	12 54	13 00							13 24		13 35		13 54		14 01							14 24		
Blantyre	d	12 58	13 04							13 28		13 39		13 58		14 05							14 28		
Hamilton West	d	13 01	13 07							13 31		13 42		14 01		14 08							14 31		
Hamilton Central	d	13 04	13 13							13 34		13 45		14 04		14 13							14 34		
Chatelherault	d		13 18									13 49				14 18									
Merryton	d		13 21									13 52				14 21									
Larkhall	a		13 24									13 55				14 24									
Airbles	d	13 09								13 39				14 09									14 39		
Uddingston	d					13 05		13 28			13 33							14 05			14 28			14 33	
Bellshill	d					13 10		13 34			13 39							14 10			14 34			14 38	
Carmyle	d			13 11									13 41				14 11								
Mount Vernon	d			13 14									13 43				14 14								
Baillieston	d			13 16									13 46				14 16								
Bargeddie	d			13 19									13 49				14 19								
Kirkwood	d			13 23									13 53				14 23								
Whifflet	d			13a27					13 33				13 56				14a27					14 33			
Motherwell	a	13 12				13 19			13 40	13 42	13 45		14 04	14 12				14 18		14 25		14 40	14 42	14 44	
	d					13 19	13 21			13 45	13 48							14 18	14 20	14 25			14 45	14 45	
Whifflet	d						13a28			13 52									14a27				14 52		
Coatbridge Central	d									13 54													14 54		
Greenfaulds 226	d									14 02													15 02		
Cumbernauld 226	a									14 04													15 04		
Shieldmuir	d					13 23					13 51							14 22						14 49	
Holytown	d							13 39													14 38				
Wishaw	d					13 26					13 55							14 25		14 31				14 52	
Carluke	d					13 34					14 02							14 32		14 38				15 02	
Carstairs	a																			14 49					
Lanark	a					13 45					14 13							14 43						15 13	
Haymarket	a							14 43												15 18	15 43				
Edinburgh	a							14 48												15 24	15 50				

A From Dalmuir
B To Dalmuir
C From Cumbernauld to Dalmuir
D From Milngavie
E From Ayr

26 May to 8 December

Glasgow - Hamilton, Larkhall, Whifflet, Motherwell, Coatbridge, Lanark and Edinburgh

		SR A	SR A	SR B	SR A	SR A	SR	SR C	SR	SR D		SR B	SR	SR A	SR E	SR A	SR B	SR A	SR A	SR		SR C	SR	SR D	SR B
Hyndland 226	d	14 04	14 18	14 23	14 34	14 47						14 53		15 04		15 17	15 23	15 34	15 47						15 53
Partick 226	d	14 07	14 21	14 25	14 37	14 49						14 55		15 07		15 20	15 25	15 37	15 49						15 55
Exhibition Centre	d	14 10	14 24	14 28	14 40	14 52						14 58		15 10		15 23	15 28	15 40	15 52						15 58
Anderston	d	14 12	14 26	14 30	14 42	14 54						15 00		15 12		15 25	15 30	15 42	15 54						16 00
Glasgow Central L. Level	a	14 13	14 27	14 32	14 43	14 56						15 01		15 13		15 26	15 31	15 43	15 56						16 01
	d	14 16	14 28	14 34	14 44	14 57						15 04		15 16		15 27	15 34	15 45	15 57						16 04
Glasgow Central H. Level	d						14 50		15 16				15 20		15 46					15 50			16 16		
Argyle Street	d	14 19	14 30	14 37	14 46	14 59						15 07		15 19		15 29	15 37	15 47	15 59						16 07
Bridgeton	d	14 22	14 33	14 40	14 49	15 02						15 10		15 22		15 32	15 40	15 50	16 02						16 10
Dalmarnock	d	14 24	14 35	14 42	14 51	15 04						15 12		15 24		15 34	15 42	15 52	16 04						16 12
Rutherglen	d	14 28	14 37	14 47	14 53	15 07						15 17		15 28		15 37	15 47	15 54	16 07						16 17
Cambuslang	d	14 32		14 51	14 56		15 00					15 21	15 28	15 32			15 51	15 58		16 01					16 21
Newton	d	14 35		14 54	15 00							15 24		15 35			15 54	16 01							16 24
Blantyre	d	14 39		14 58	15 04							15 28		15 39			15 58	16 05							16 28
Hamilton West	d	14 42		15 01	15 07							15 31		15 42			16 01	16 08							16 31
Hamilton Central	d	14 45		15 04	15 13							15 34		15 45			16 04	16 13							16 34
Chatelherault	d	14 49			15 18									15 49				16 18							
Merryton	d	14 52			15 21									15 52				16 21							
Larkhall	a	14 55			15 24									15 55				16 24							
Airbles	d			15 09								15 39					16 09								16 39
Uddingston	d						15 05		15 28				15 33							16 05			16 29		
Bellshill	d						15 10		15 34				15 39							16 10			16 35		
Carmyle	d		14 41			15 11										15 41			16 11						
Mount Vernon	d		14 44			15 14										15 44			16 14						
Baillieston	d		14 46			15 16										15 46			16 16						
Bargeddie	d		14 49			15 19										15 49			16 19						
Kirkwood	d		14 53			15 23										15 53			16 23						
Whifflet	d		14 57			15a27				15 33						15 57			16a27					16 33	
Motherwell	a		15 05	15 12			15 19			15 40		15 42	15 45		16 02	16 06	16 12			16 17				16 41	16 42
	d						15 19	15 20				15 45	15 48		16 03					16 18		16 20			16 45
Whifflet	d							15a27				15 52										16a27			16 52
Coatbridge Central	d											15 54													16 54
Greenfaulds 226	d											16 02													17 02
Cumbernauld 226	a											16 04													17 04
Shieldmuir	d						15 23						15 51							16 21					
Holytown	d								15 39														16 39		
Wishaw	d						15 27						15 55		16 09					16 25					
Carluke	d						15 34						16 02		16 24					16 32					
Carstairs	a														16 33										
Lanark	a						15 45						16 13							16 43					
Haymarket	a								16 46						17 04								17 43		
Edinburgh	a								16 51						17 11								17 48		

		SR	SR A	SR A	SR B	SR C		SR A	SR A	SR	SR	SR D	SR B	SR	SR A	SR A		SR B	SR	SR C	SR A	SR A	SR D	SR B	SR
Hyndland 226	d		16 04	16 17	16 23			16 34	16 47				16 53		17 05	17 17		17 23			17 35	17 47		17 53	
Partick 226	d		16 07	16 19	16 25			16 37	16 49				16 55		17 07	17 20		17 25			17 37	17 49		17 55	
Exhibition Centre	d		16 10	16 22	16 28			16 40	16 52				17 01		17 11	17 23		17 28			17 43	17 52		17 58	
Anderston	d		16 12	16 24	16 30			16 42	16 54				17 04		17 13	17 25		17 30			17 46	17 54		18 00	
Glasgow Central L. Level	a		16 13	16 26	16 31			16 43	16 56				17 05		17 14	17 26		17 31			17 47	17 56		18 02	
	d		16 16	16 27	16 34			16 44	16 56				17 06		17 17	17 27		17 34			17 49	17 56		18 04	
Glasgow Central H. Level	d	16 20								16 50	17 18			17 20					17 50						18 16
Argyle Street	d		16 19	16 29	16 37			16 45	16 58				17 08		17 20	17 29		17 37			17 51	17 58		18 07	
Bridgeton	d		16 22	16 32	16 40			16 48	17 01				17 11		17 23	17 32		17 40			17 54	18 01		18 10	
Dalmarnock	d		16 24	16 34	16 42			16 50	17 03				17 13		17 25	17 34		17 42			17 56	18 03		18 12	
Rutherglen	d		16 29	16 37	16 47			16 53	17 05				17 17		17 30	17 37		17 47			18 01	18 05		18 17	
Cambuslang	d	16 29	16 33		16 51			16 56		17 00			17 21	17 31	17 34			17 51	17 58		18 05			18 21	
Newton	d		16 36		16 54			17 01					17 24		17 37			17 54			18 08			18 24	
Blantyre	d		16 40		16 58			17 05					17 28		17 41			17 58			18 12			18 28	
Hamilton West	d		16 43		17 01			17 08					17 31		17 44			18 01			18 15			18 31	
Hamilton Central	d		16 45		17 04			17 13					17 34		17 46			18 04			18 17			18 34	
Chatelherault	d		16 50					17 18							17 51						18 22				
Merryton	d		16 53					17 21							17 54						18 25				
Larkhall	a		16 56					17 24							17 57						18 28				
Airbles	d				17 09								17 39					18 09						18 39	
Uddingston	d	16 34								17 06	17u30			17 35					18 04						18 28
Bellshill	d	16 39								17 11	17 36			17 40					18 10						18 33
Carmyle	d			16 41					17 10							17 41						18 10			
Mount Vernon	d			16 44					17 12							17 44						18 12			
Baillieston	d			16 46					17 15							17 46						18 15			
Bargeddie	d			16 49					17 18							17 49						18 18			
Kirkwood	d			16 53					17 22							17 53						18 22			
Whifflet	d			16 57					17a25			17 33				17 58						18a25	18 34		
Motherwell	a	16 45		17 04	17 12					17 19		17 40	17 42	17 47		18 05		18 12	18 17				18 41	18 42	
	d	16 45				17 20				17 20			17 45	17 48					18 17	18 20				18 45	
Whifflet	d					17a29							17 52							18a29				18 51	
Coatbridge Central	d												17 54											18 54	
Greenfaulds 226	d												18 02											19 01	
Cumbernauld 226	a												18 04											19 03	
Shieldmuir	d	16 49								17 23				17 51					18 21						
Holytown	d										17 41														18 39
Wishaw	d	16 55								17 27				17 56					18 24						
Carluke	d	17 06								17 34				18 04					18 30						
Carstairs	a																								
Lanark	a	17 17								17 45				18 15					18 41						
Haymarket	a										18 48														19 43
Edinburgh	a										18 54														19 48

A From Dalmuir
B From Milngavie
C To Dalmuir
D From Cumbernauld to Dalmuir
E From Ayr to North Berwick

Table T225-R

Saturdays

26 May to 8 December

Glasgow - Hamilton, Larkhall, Whifflet, Motherwell, Coatbridge, Lanark and Edinburgh

	SR	SR A	SR A	SR B	SR A	SR A	SR	SR C	SR	SR D	SR B	SR	SR A	SR E	SR A	SR B	SR	SR C	SR A	SR A	SR D
Hyndland 226 d		18 04	18 17	18 23	18 34	18 47					18 53		19 04		19 17	19 23			19 35	19 47	
Partick 226 ⇌ d		18 07	18 19	18 25	18 37	18 49					18 55		19 07		19 20	19 25			19 38	19 50	
Exhibition Centre d		18 10	18 22	18 28	18 40	18 52					18 58		19 10		19 23	19 28			19 41	19 53	
Anderston d		18 13	18 24	18 30	18 42	18 54					19 00		19 12		19 25	19 30			19 43	19 55	
Glasgow Central L. Level 15 a		18 14	18 26	18 32	18 43	18 56					19 01		19 13		19 26	19 32			19 45	19 56	
d		18 18	18 27	18 34	18 44	18 57					19 04		19 16		19 27	19 34			19 48	19 57	
Glasgow Central H. Level 15 d	18 20						18 50		19 16			19 21		19 46			19 50				
Argyle Street d		18 21	18 29	18 37	18 46	18 59					19 07		19 19		19 29	19 37			19 51	19 59	
Bridgeton d		18 24	18 32	18 40	18 49	19 02					19 10		19 22		19 32	19 40			19 54	20 02	
Dalmarnock d		18 26	18 34	18 42	18 51	19 04					19 12		19 24		19 34	19 42			19 56	20 04	
Rutherglen d		18 30	18 37	18 47	18 54	19 07					19 17		19 28		19 37	19 47			19 59	20 07	
Cambuslang d	18 30	18 34		18 51	18 58		19 01				19 21	19 29	19 32			19 51	19 58		20 02		
Newton d		18 37		18 54	19 01						19 24		19 35			19 54			20 08		
Blantyre d		18 41		18 58	19 05						19 28		19 39			19 58			20 12		
Hamilton West d		18 44		19 01	19 08						19 31		19 42			20 01			20 15		
Hamilton Central d		18 46		19 04	19 13						19 34		19 45			20 04			20 17		
Chatelherault d		18 51			19 18								19 49						20 22		
Merryton d		18 54			19 21								19 52						20 25		
Larkhall a		18 57			19 24								19 55						20 28		
Airbles d				19 09							19 39					20 09					
Uddingston d	18 35						19 06		19 28			19 34					20 03				
Bellshill d	18 40						19 11		19 34			19 39					20 08				
Carmyle d			18 41			19 11									19 41					20 11	
Mount Vernon d			18 44			19 14									19 44					20 14	
Baillieston d			18 46			19 16									19 46					20 16	
Bargeddie d			18 49			19 19									19 49					20 19	
Kirkwood d			18 53			19 23									19 53					20 23	
Whifflet d			18 57			19a27				19 33					19 57					20a27	20 33
Motherwell a	18 47		19 04	19 12			19 19			19 40	19 42	19 45		20 03	20 07	20 12	20 14				20 40
d	18 48						19 19	19 21			19 45	19 49		20 04			20 19	20 26			
Whifflet d								19a28			19 52							20a33			
Coatbridge Central d											19 54										
Greenfaulds 226 d											20 02										
Cumbernauld 226 a											20 04										
Shieldmuir d	18 51						19 23					19 53					20 23				
Holytown d									19 41												
Wishaw d	18 55						19 26					19 56		20 10			20 26				
Carluke d	19 02						19 32					20 02		20 16			20 34				
Carstairs a														20 25							
Lanark a	19 13						19 43					20 13					20 45				
Haymarket ⇌ a									20 43					20 52							
Edinburgh a									20 48					20 58							

	SR B	SR	SR A	SR A	SR B	SR A	SR A	SR	SR C	SR	SR D	SR B	SR A	SR	SR A	SR B	SR A	SR A	SR	SR C	SR F	SR B
Hyndland 226 d	19 53		20 06	20 17	20 23	20 34	20 47					20 53	21 06		21 17	21 23	21 35	21 47				21 53
Partick 226 ⇌ d	19 55		20 08	20 19	20 25	20 37	20 50					20 55	21 08		21 20	21 25	21 37	21 50				21 55
Exhibition Centre d	19 58		20 11	20 22	20 29	20 40	20 53					20 58	21 11		21 23	21 28	21 40	21 53				21 58
Anderston d	20 00		20 13	20 26	20 33	20 42	20 55					21 00	21 13		21 25	21 30	21 42	21 55				22 00
Glasgow Central L. Level 15 a	20 01		20 15	20 27	20 34	20 43	20 56					21 02	21 15		21 26	21 32	21 44	21 56				22 02
d	20 02		20 18	20 28	20 36	20 44	20 57					21 04	21 15		21 27	21 34	21 44	21 57				22 04
Glasgow Central H. Level 15 d		20 21						20 52		21 16				21 20					21 50			
Argyle Street d	20 03		20 20	20 30	20 38	20 46	20 59					21 07	21 17		21 29	21 37	21 46	21 59				22 07
Bridgeton d	20 06		20 23	20 33	20 41	20 49	21 02					21 10	21 20		21 32	21 40	21 49	22 02				22 10
Dalmarnock d	20 08		20 25	20 35	20 43	20 51	21 04					21 12	21 22		21 34	21 42	21 51	22 04				22 12
Rutherglen d	20 17		20 28	20 37	20 45	20 54	21 07					21 17	21 25		21 37	21 47	21 53	22 07				22 17
Cambuslang d	20 21	20 29	20 33		20 49	20 57		21 01				21 21	21 28	21 33		21 50	21 57		22 00			22 21
Newton d	20 26		20 38		20 55	21 02						21 24	21 32			21 54	22 01					22 24
Blantyre d	20 30		20 42		20 59	21 06						21 28	21 36			21 58	22 06					22 28
Hamilton West d	20 33		20 45		21 02	21 09						21 31	21 39			22 01	22 09					22 31
Hamilton Central d	20 36		20 47		21 04	21 14						21 34	21 43			22 04	22 13					22 34
Chatelherault d			20 52			21 18							21 48				22 18					
Merryton d			20 55			21 21							21 51				22 21					
Larkhall a			20 58			21 24							21 54				22 24					
Airbles d	20 41				21 10							21 39				22 09						22 39
Uddingston d		20 34						21 06		21 29				21 37					22 04			
Bellshill d		20 39						21 11		21 34				21 42					22 09			
Carmyle d				20 41			21 11								21 41			22 11				
Mount Vernon d				20 44			21 14								21 44			22 14				
Baillieston d				20 46			21 16								21 46			22 16				
Bargeddie d				20 49			21 19								21 49			22 19				
Kirkwood d				20 53			21 23								21 53			22 23				
Whifflet d				20 58			21a27				21 33				21 57			22a27			22 33	
Motherwell a	20 44	20 46		21 07	21 12			21 17			21 40	21 42		21 48	22 05	22 12			22 15		22 40	22 42
d	20 48	20 47						21 18	21 23			21 46		21 49					22 17	22 20		22 45
Whifflet d	20 54								21a30			21 52								22a27		22 52
Coatbridge Central d	20 57											21 55										22 54
Greenfaulds 226 d	21 04											22 02										23 02
Cumbernauld 226 a	21 06											22 04										23 04
Shieldmuir d		20 50						21 21						21 52					22 21			
Holytown d										21 40												
Wishaw d		20 54						21 25						21 56					22 24			
Carluke d		21 02						21 33						22 02					22 30			
Carstairs a																						
Lanark a		21 13						21 44						22 13					22 41			
Haymarket ⇌ a										22 42												
Edinburgh a										22 47												

A From Dalmuir
B From Milngavie
C To Dalmuir
D From Cumbernauld to Dalmuir
E From Ayr
F From Cumbernauld to Garscadden

Table T225-R

Saturdays

26 May to 8 December

Glasgow - Hamilton, Larkhall, Whifflet, Motherwell, Coatbridge, Lanark and Edinburgh

	SR	SR A	SR A	SR B	SR A	SR	SR A	SR	SR B	SR	SR A	SR A	SR B	SR
Hyndland 226 d		22 06	22 18	22 24	22 34		22 47		22 53		23 05	23 17	23 23	
Partick 226 ⇌ d		22 08	22 20	22 26	22 37		22 50		22 55		23 08	23 20	23 25	
Exhibition Centre d		22 11	22 23	22 29	22 40		22 53		22 59		23 12	23 23	23 29	
Anderston d		22 13	22 25	22 31	22 42		22 55		23 01		23 14	23 25	23 31	
Glasgow Central L. Level 15 a		22 15	22 27	22 33	22 44		22 57		23 02		23 15	23 27	23 32	
d		22 17	22 27	22 34	22 44		22 57		23 06		23 17	23 27	23 36	
Glasgow Central H. Level 15 d	22 20					22 50		23 03		23 20				23 50
Argyle Street d		22 20	22 29	22 37	22 46		22 59		23 08		23 19	23 29	23 38	
Bridgeton d		22 23	22 32	22 40	22 49		23 02		23 11		23 22	23 32	23 41	
Dalmarnock d		22 25	22 34	22 42	22 51		23 04		23 13		23 24	23 34	23 43	
Rutherglen d		22 29	22 37	22 47	22 54		23 07		23 17		23 28	23 37	23 48	
Cambuslang d	22 28	22 32		22 51	22 57	23 01		23 12	23 21	23 28	23 32		23 51	23 58
Newton d		22 35		22 54	23 03				23 24		23 35			
Blantyre d		22 39		22 58	23 08				23 28		23 39			
Hamilton West d		22 42		23 01	23 11				23 31		23 42			
Hamilton Central d		22 45		23 04	23 14				23 33		23 46			
Chatelherault d		22 50			23 18						23 50			
Merryton d		22 53			23 21						23 53			
Larkhall a		22 56			23 24						23 56			
Airbles d				23 09					23 39					
Uddingston d	22 33					23 06		23 17		23 33				00 03
Bellshill d	22 38					23 11		23 23		23 38				00 08
Carmyle d			22 41				23 11					23 41		
Mount Vernon d			22 44				23 14					23 44		
Baillieston d			22 46				23 16					23 46		
Bargeddie d			22 49				23 19					23 49		
Kirkwood d			22 53				23 23					23 53		
Whifflet d			22 57				23 27					23 57		
Motherwell a	22 46		23 04	23 12		23 17	23 34		23 41	23 44		00 04	00 01	00 14
d	22 47					23 18								
Whifflet d														
Coatbridge Central d														
Greenfaulds 226 d														
Cumbernauld 226 a														
Shieldmuir d	22 51					23 22								
Holytown d								23 27						
Wishaw d	22 55					23 25								
Carluke d	23 01					23 31								
Carstairs a														
Lanark a	23 12					23 42								
Haymarket ⇌ a								00 30						
Edinburgh a								00 35						

Sundays

20 May to 2 December

	SR C	SR D	SR E	SR 🚌	SR F	SR G	SR G	SR H	SR F	SR D	SR G	SR F	SR H	SR G	SR I	SR G	SR F	SR G	SR H	SR I	SR D	SR G
Hyndland 226 d			08 15					08 45	08 55				09 15		09 25				09 45	09 55		
Partick 226 ⇌ d			08 18					08 48	08 57				09 18		09 27				09 48	09 57		
Exhibition Centre d			08 21					08 51	09 00				09 21		09 30				09 51	10 00		
Anderston d																			09 53	10 02		
Glasgow Central L. Level 15 a			08 23					08 53	09 03				09 23		09 33				09 54	10 04		
d			08 25					08 56	09 06				09 25		09 37				09 56	10 05		
Glasgow Central H. Level 15 d				08 16	08 33	08 34	08 36				09 08	09 20		09 28		09 35	09 50	09 50				10 07
Argyle Street d																			09 58	10 07		
Bridgeton d			08 29					09 00	09 11				09 29		09 42				10 01	10 10		
Dalmarnock d																			10 03	10 12		
Rutherglen d			08 34					09 05	09 15				09 34		09 47				10 05	10 14		
Cambuslang d			08 37		08 42				09 19			09 29	09 37		09 50		09 59			10 19		
Newton d			08 41			08 52	09 05		09 22		09 32		09 41	09 42	09 54	10 03		10 06		10 22		10 31
Blantyre d			08 45				09 09		09 26		09 36		09 45		09 58	10 08				10 26		10 35
Hamilton West d			08 48				09 12		09 29		09 39		09 48		10 01	10 12				10 29		10 38
Hamilton Central d			08 51				09 15		09 31		09 42		09 50		10 03	10 15				10 31		10 41
Chatelherault d			08 55				09 18						09 55			10 18						
Merryton d			08 58				09 21						09 58			10 21						
Larkhall a			09 01				09 24						10 01			10 24						
Airbles d									09 37		09 48				10 09					10 37		10 47
Uddingston d	00 03			08 41	08 47	08 55						09 34		09 45			10 04	10 11				
Bellshill d	00 08			08 56	08 52	09 00						09 39		09 51			10 09	10 17				
Carmyle d								09 10											10 09			
Mount Vernon d								09 13											10 12			
Baillieston d								09 16											10 14			
Bargeddie d								09 19											10 17			
Kirkwood d								09 23											10 21			
Whifflet d								09 27											10 25			
Motherwell a	00 14				08 59	09 06		09 35	09 39		09 50	09 45		09 58	10 11		10 15	10 23	10 33	10 39		10 49
d		08 41								09 41		09 46		09 58							10 41	
Whifflet d		08a48								09a49											10a48	
Coatbridge Central d																						
Greenfaulds 226 d																						
Cumbernauld 226 a																						
Shieldmuir d												09 49		10 02								
Holytown d				09 07																		
Wishaw d												09 53		10 05								
Carluke d												10 02		10 11								
Carstairs a																						
Lanark a												10 13		10 22								
Haymarket ⇌ a				11s04																		
Edinburgh a				11 25																		

A From Dalmuir
B From Milngavie
C not 20 May. From Glasgow Central
D from 16 September. To Balloch
E from 16 September. From Dalmuir
F from 16 September
G until 9 September
H from 16 September. From Balloch
I from 16 September. From Milngavie

20 May to 2 December

Glasgow - Hamilton, Larkhall, Whifflet, Motherwell, Coatbridge, Lanark and Edinburgh

		SR	SR A	SR B	SR C	SR D	SR B	SR A	SR C	SR D	SR E	SR B	SR A	SR C	SR B	SR D	SR B	SR A	SR C	SR D	SR E	SR B	SR
Hyndland 226	d				10 15	10 25			10 45	10 55				11 15		11 25			11 45	11 55			
Partick 226	d				10 18	10 27			10 48	10 57				11 18		11 27			11 48	11 57			
Exhibition Centre	d				10 21	10 30			10 51	11 00				11 21		11 30			11 51	12 00			
Anderston	d				10 23	10 32			10 53	11 02				11 23		11 32			11 53	12 02			
Glasgow Central L. Level	a				10 24	10 34			10 54	11 04				11 24		11 34			11 54	12 04			
	d				10 25	10 37			10 56	11 06				11 25		11 37			11 56	12 06			
Glasgow Central H. Level	d	10 16	10 20	10 20			10 36	10 50				11 08	11 20		11 28		11 38	11 50				12 08	12 16
Argyle Street	d				10 26	10 39			10 57	11 08				11 26		11 39			11 57	12 08			
Bridgeton	d				10 29	10 42			11 00	11 11				11 29		11 42			12 00	12 11			
Dalmarnock	d				10 31	10 44			11 02	11 13				11 31		11 44			12 02	12 13			
Rutherglen	d				10 33	10 46			11 05	11 15				11 33		11 46			12 05	12 15			
Cambuslang	d		10 29		10 37	10 50		10 59		11 19			11 29	11 37		11 50		11 59		12 18			
Newton	d			10 34	10 40	10 53	11 08			11 22		11 32		11 40	11 42	11 53	12 09			12 21		12 32	
Blantyre	d				10 44	10 57	11 12			11 26		11 36		11 44		11 57	12 13			12 25		12 36	
Hamilton West	d				10 47	11 00	11 15			11 29		11 39		11 47		12 00	12 16			12 28		12 39	
Hamilton Central	d				10 50	11 03	11 18			11 32		11 42		11 50		12 03	12 19			12 32		12 42	
Chatelherault	d				10 54		11 21							11 54			12 22						
Merryton	d				10 57		11 24							11 57			12 25						
Larkhall	a				11 00		11 27							12 00			12 28						
Airbles	d					11 08				11 37		11 48				12 08				12 38		12 48	
Uddingston	d	10 41	10 34	10 38				11 04					11 34		11 46			12 04					12 41
Bellshill	d	10 56	10 39	10 43				11 09					11 39		11 51			12 09					12 56
Carmyle	d								11 09										12 09				
Mount Vernon	d								11 12										12 12				
Baillieston	d								11 14										12 14				
Bargeddie	d								11 17										12 17				
Kirkwood	d								11 21										12 21				
Whifflet	d								11 25										12 25				
Motherwell	a		10 45	10 49		11 11		11 15	11 34	11 40		11 50	11 47		11 57	12 11		12 20	12 33	12 40		12 50	
	d		10 46	10 49							11 42		11 48		11 57						12 41		
Whifflet	d										11a49										12a49		
Coatbridge Central	d																						
Greenfaulds 226	d																						
Cumbernauld 226	a																						
Shieldmuir	d		10 49	10 56									11 51		12 04								
Holytown	d	11 07																					13 07
Wishaw	d		10 53	10 59									11 55		12 07								
Carluke	d		11 05	11 05									12 02		12 13								
Carstairs	a																						
Lanark	a		11 16	11 16									12 13		12 24								
Haymarket	a	13s04																					15s04
Edinburgh	a	13 25																					15 25

		SR A	SR C	SR B	SR D	SR B	SR A	SR C	SR D	SR E	SR B	SR A	SR C	SR B	SR D	SR B	SR A	SR C	SR D	SR E	SR B	SR
Hyndland 226	d		12 15		12 25			12 45	12 55				13 15		13 25			13 45	13 55			
Partick 226	d		12 18		12 27			12 48	12 57				13 18		13 27			13 48	13 57			
Exhibition Centre	d		12 21		12 30			12 51	13 00				13 21		13 30			13 51	14 00			
Anderston	d		12 23		12 32			12 53	13 02				13 23		13 32			13 53	14 02			
Glasgow Central L. Level	a		12 24		12 34			12 54	13 04				13 24		13 34			13 54	14 04			
	d		12 25		12 35			12 56	13 06				13 25		13 37			13 56	14 06			
Glasgow Central H. Level	d	12 20		12 31		12 36	12 50				13 10	13 20		13 35		13 37	13 51				14 08	14 16
Argyle Street	d		12 26		12 37			12 57	13 08				13 26		13 39			13 57	14 08			
Bridgeton	d		12 29		12 40			13 00	13 11				13 29		13 42			14 00	14 11			
Dalmarnock	d		12 31		12 42			13 02	13 13				13 31		13 44			14 02	14 13			
Rutherglen	d		12 33		12 46			13 05	13 15				13 33		13 46			14 05	14 15			
Cambuslang	d	12 29	12 37		12 50		12 59		13 18			13 29	13 37		13 50		14 00		14 18			
Newton	d		12 41	12 47	12 53	13 09			13 21		13 34		13 40	13 52	13 53	14 09			14 21		14 32	
Blantyre	d		12 45		12 57	13 13			13 25		13 38		13 44		13 57	14 13			14 25		14 36	
Hamilton West	d		12 48		13 00	13 16			13 28		13 41		13 47		14 00	14 16			14 28		14 39	
Hamilton Central	d		12 51		13 03	13 19			13 32		13 44		13 50		14 03	14 19			14 32		14 42	
Chatelherault	d		12 55			13 22							13 54			14 22						
Merryton	d		12 58			13 25							13 57			14 25						
Larkhall	a		13 01			13 28							14 00			14 28						
Airbles	d				13 08				13 37		13 50				14 08				14 37		14 48	
Uddingston	d	12 34		12 51			13 04					13 34		13 55			14 05					14 41
Bellshill	d	12 39		12 56			13 09					13 39		14 01			14 10					14 56
Carmyle	d							13 09										14 09				
Mount Vernon	d							13 12										14 12				
Baillieston	d							13 14										14 14				
Bargeddie	d							13 17										14 17				
Kirkwood	d							13 21										14 21				
Whifflet	d							13 25										14 25				
Motherwell	a	12 45		13 02	13 11		13 15	13 34	13 40		13 52	13 45		14 07	14 11		14 16	14 33	14 40		14 50	
	d	12 46		13 02						13 41		13 46		14 08						14 41		
Whifflet	d									13a49										14a49		
Coatbridge Central	d																					
Greenfaulds 226	d																					
Cumbernauld 226	a																					
Shieldmuir	d	12 49		13 06								13 49		14 11								
Holytown	d																					15 07
Wishaw	d	12 53		13 11								13 53		14 15								
Carluke	d	13 02		13 18								14 02		14 21								
Carstairs	a																					
Lanark	a	13 13		13 29								14 13		14 32								
Haymarket	a																					17s04
Edinburgh	a																					17 25

A from 16 September
B until 9 September
C from 16 September. From Balloch
D from 16 September. From Milngavie
E from 16 September. To Balloch

Table T225-R

Sundays

20 May to 2 December

Glasgow - Hamilton, Larkhall, Whifflet, Motherwell, Coatbridge, Lanark and Edinburgh

		SR A	SR B	SR C	SR D	SR B	SR A	SR C	SR D	SR E	SR B	SR A	SR C	SR B	SR D	SR B	SR A	SR C	SR D	SR E	SR B	SR	SR A
Hyndland 226	d			14 15	14 25			14 45	14 55				15 15		15 25			15 45	15 55				
Partick 226	d			14 18	14 27			14 48	14 57				15 18		15 28			15 48	15 57				
Exhibition Centre	d			14 21	14 30			14 51	15 00				15 21		15 31			15 51	16 00				
Anderston	d			14 23	14 32			14 53	15 02				15 23		15 33			15 53	16 02				
Glasgow Central L. Level	a			14 24	14 34			14 54	15 04				15 24		15 34			15 54	16 04				
	d			14 25	14 37			14 56	15 06				15 25		15 37			15 57	16 06				
Glasgow Central H. Level	d	14 20	14 27			14 36	14 50				15 08	15 20		15 28		15 36	15 50				16 08	16 16	16 20
Argyle Street	d			14 26	14 39			14 57	15 08				15 26		15 39			15 59	16 08				
Bridgeton	d			14 29	14 42			15 00	15 11				15 29		15 42			16 02	16 11				
Dalmarnock	d			14 31	14 44			15 02	15 13				15 31		15 44			16 04	16 13				
Rutherglen	d			14 33	14 46			15 05	15 15				15 33		15 46			16 06	16 15				
Cambuslang	d	14 29		14 37	14 50		14 59		15 18			15 29	15 37		15 50		15 59		16 18				16 29
Newton	d		14 41	14 43	14 54	15 09			15 21		15 32		15 40	15 43	15 55	16 09			16 21		16 32		
Blantyre	d			14 47	14 58	15 13			15 25		15 36		15 44		15 59	16 13			16 25		16 36		
Hamilton West	d			14 50	15 01	15 16			15 28		15 39		15 47		16 02	16 16			16 28		16 39		
Hamilton Central	d			14 52	15 04	15 19			15 31		15 42		15 50		16 05	16 19			16 31		16 42		
Chatelherault	d			14 57		15 22							15 54			16 22							
Merryton	d			15 00		15 25							15 57			16 25							
Larkhall	a			15 03		15 28							16 00			16 28							
Airbles	d				15 09				15 36		15 48				16 10				16 36		16 48		
Uddingston	d	14 34	14 45				15 04					15 34		15 46			16 03					16 41	16 33
Bellshill	d	14 39	14 50				15 09					15 39		15 51			16 08					16 56	16 38
Carmyle	d							15 09										16 10					
Mount Vernon	d							15 12										16 13					
Baillieston	d							15 14										16 15					
Bargeddie	d							15 17										16 18					
Kirkwood	d							15 21										16 22					
Whifflet	d							15 25										16 26					
Motherwell	a	14 45	14 56		15 12		15 16	15 35	15 39		15 50	15 45		15 57	16 12		16 16	16 33	16 39		16 50		16 47
	d	14 46	14 56							15 41		15 47		15 58						16 40			16 47
Whifflet	d									15a49										16a48			
Coatbridge Central	d																						
Greenfaulds 226	d																						
Cumbernauld 226	a																						
Shieldmuir	d	14 49	15 02									15 51		16 06									16 51
Holytown	d																					17 07	
Wishaw	d	14 53	15 09									15 54		16 09									16 54
Carluke	d	15 03	15 15									16 03		16 15									17 04
Carstairs	a																						
Lanark	a	15 14	15 26									16 14		16 26									17 15
Haymarket	a																					19s04	
Edinburgh	a																					19 25	

		SR C	SR B	SR D	SR B	SR A	SR C	SR D	SR E	SR B	SR A	SR C	SR B	SR D	SR B	SR A	SR C	SR D	SR E	SR B	SR	SR A
Hyndland 226	d	16 15		16 25			16 45	16 55				17 15		17 25			17 45	17 55				
Partick 226	d	16 18		16 27			16 48	16 57				17 18		17 27			17 48	17 57				
Exhibition Centre	d	16 21		16 30			16 51	17 00				17 21		17 30			17 51	18 00				
Anderston	d	16 23		16 32			16 53	17 02				17 23		17 32			17 53	18 02				
Glasgow Central L. Level	a	16 24		16 34			16 54	17 04				17 24		17 34			17 54	18 04				
	d	16 25		16 37			16 56	17 06				17 25		17 37			17 56	18 06				
Glasgow Central H. Level	d		16 27		16 36	16 50				17 08	17 20		17 27		17 36	17 50				18 08	18 16	18 20
Argyle Street	d	16 26		16 39			16 57	17 08				17 26		17 39			17 57	18 08				
Bridgeton	d	16 29		16 42			17 00	17 11				17 29		17 42			18 00	18 11				
Dalmarnock	d	16 31		16 44			17 02	17 13				17 31		17 44			18 02	18 13				
Rutherglen	d	16 33		16 46			17 05	17 15				17 33		17 46			18 05	18 15				
Cambuslang	d	16 37		16 50		16 58		17 18			17 29	17 37		17 51		17 58		18 18				18 28
Newton	d	16 40	16 41	16 54	17 09			17 21		17 32		17 40	17 41	17 54	18 09			18 21		18 32		
Blantyre	d	16 44		16 58	17 13			17 25		17 36		17 44		17 58	18 13			18 25		18 36		
Hamilton West	d	16 47		17 01	17 16			17 28		17 39		17 47		18 01	18 16			18 28		18 39		
Hamilton Central	d	16 50		17 04	17 19			17 31		17 42		17 50		18 04	18 19			18 31		18 42		
Chatelherault	d	16 54			17 22							17 54			18 22							
Merryton	d	16 57			17 25							17 57			18 25							
Larkhall	a	17 00			17 28							18 00			18 28							
Airbles	d			17 09				17 36		17 48				18 10				18 36		18 48		
Uddingston	d		16 44			17 03					17 33		17 45			18 03					18 41	18 33
Bellshill	d		16 51			17 08					17 38		17 50			18 08					18 56	18 38
Carmyle	d						17 09										18 09					
Mount Vernon	d						17 12										18 12					
Baillieston	d						17 14										18 14					
Bargeddie	d						17 17										18 17					
Kirkwood	d						17 21										18 21					
Whifflet	d						17 25										18 25					
Motherwell	a		16 57	17 12		17 15	17 33	17 39		17 50	17 45		17 56	18 12		18 15	18 33	18 39		18 50		18 44
	d		16 57						17 41		17 46		17 58						18 41			18 45
Whifflet	d								17a48										18a49			
Coatbridge Central	d																					
Greenfaulds 226	d																					
Cumbernauld 226	a																					
Shieldmuir	d		17 04								17 49		18 04									18 48
Holytown	d																				19 07	
Wishaw	d		17 07								17 53		18 07									18 52
Carluke	d		17 13								18 02		18 13									19 01
Carstairs	a																					
Lanark	a		17 24								18 13		18 24									19 12
Haymarket	a																				21s04	
Edinburgh	a																				21 25	

A from 16 September
B until 9 September
C from 16 September. From Balloch
D from 16 September. From Milngavie
E from 16 September. To Balloch

Glasgow - Hamilton, Larkhall, Whifflet, Motherwell, Coatbridge, Lanark and Edinburgh

	SR A	SR B	SR C	SR A	SR D	SR B	SR C	SR E	SR A		SR D	SR A	SR B	SR C	SR A	SR D	SR B	SR C	SR E		SR A	SR	SR D	SR A
Hyndland 226 d		18 15	18 25			18 45	18 55						19 17	19 25			19 45	19 55						
Partick 226 d		18 18	18 27			18 48	18 57						19 19	19 27			19 48	19 57						
Exhibition Centre d		18 21	18 30			18 51	19 00						19 22	19 30			19 51	20 00						
Anderston d																								
Glasgow Central L. Level a		18 23	18 34			18 54	19 03						19 25	19 33			19 54	20 03						
d		18 25	18 37			18 57	19 06						19 26	19 37			19 56	20 06						
Glasgow Central H. Level d	18 26			18 36	18 50				19 08		19 20	19 20			19 36	19 50					20 08	20 16	20 20	20 20
Argyle Street d																								
Bridgeton d		18 29	18 42			19 01	19 11						19 30	19 42			20 00	20 11						
Dalmarnock d																								
Rutherglen d		18 34	18 46			19 05	19 15						19 34	19 47			20 05	20 15						
Cambuslang d		18 37	18 49		19 00		19 19				19 29		19 37	19 50		19 59		20 19					20 29	
Newton d	18 40	18 41	18 54	19 07			19 22		19 32			19 36	19 41	19 55	20 07			20 22			20 32			20 39
Blantyre d		18 45	18 58	19 11			19 26		19 36				19 45	19 59	20 11			20 26			20 36			
Hamilton West d		18 48	19 01	19 14			19 29		19 39				19 48	20 02	20 14			20 29			20 39			
Hamilton Central d		18 50	19 04	19 17			19 31		19 42				19 50	20 05	20 17			20 31			20 42			
Chatelherault d		18 55		19 20									19 55		20 20									
Merryton d		18 58		19 23									19 58		20 23									
Larkhall a		19 01		19 26									20 01		20 26									
Airbles d			19 09				19 37		19 48					20 10				20 37			20 48			
Uddingston d	18 43				19 05						19 33	19 40				20 03						20 41	20 33	20 43
Bellshill d	18 49				19 10						19 38	19 45				20 08						20 56	20 38	20 49
Carmyle d						19 09											20 09							
Mount Vernon d						19 12											20 12							
Baillieston d						19 15											20 15							
Bargeddie d						19 18											20 18							
Kirkwood d						19 22											20 22							
Whifflet d						19 26											20 26							
Motherwell a	18 55		19 12		19 17	19 33	19 39		19 50		19 44	19 51		20 13		20 16	20 33	20 39			20 50		20 44	20 56
d	18 55							19 41			19 46	19 51							20 41				20 46	20 56
Whifflet d								19a48											20a48					
Coatbridge Central d																								
Greenfaulds 226 d																								
Cumbernauld 226 a																								
Shieldmuir d	18 59										19 49	19 55											20 49	21 02
Holytown d																						21 07		
Wishaw d	19 02										19 53	19 58											20 53	21 05
Carluke d	19 08										20 00	20 04											20 59	21 11
Carstairs a																								
Lanark a	19 19										20 12	20 15											21 12	21 23
Haymarket a																						23s04		
Edinburgh a																						23 25		

	SR B	SR C	SR A	SR D	SR B		SR C	SR E	SR A	SR D	SR A	SR B	SR C	SR A	SR D		SR B	SR C	SR E	SR A	SR D	SR A	SR B	SR C
Hyndland 226 d	20 15	20 25			20 45		20 55					21 15	21 25				21 45	21 55					22 15	22 25
Partick 226 d	20 18	20 27			20 48		20 57					21 18	21 27				21 48	21 57					22 18	22 27
Exhibition Centre d	20 21	20 30			20 51		21 00					21 21	21 30				21 51	22 00					22 21	22 30
Anderston d																								
Glasgow Central L. Level a	20 23	20 33			20 53		21 03					21 23	21 33				21 53	22 03					22 23	22 33
d	20 25	20 37			20 56		21 06					21 25	21 35				21 56	22 06					22 25	22 37
Glasgow Central H. Level d			20 36	20 50					21 08	21 20	21 20			21 38	21 50					22 08	22 20	22 20		
Argyle Street d																								
Bridgeton d	20 29	20 42			21 00		21 11					21 29	21 40				22 00	22 11					22 29	22 42
Dalmarnock d																								
Rutherglen d	20 34	20 46			21 05		21 15					21 34	21 45				22 05	22 15					22 34	22 47
Cambuslang d	20 37	20 49		20 58			21 19			21 29		21 37	21 48		21 58			22 19			22 28		22 37	22 50
Newton d	20 41	20 52	21 07				21 22		21 32		21 36	21 41	21 52	22 07				22 22		22 32		22 38	22 41	22 54
Blantyre d	20 45	20 56	21 11				21 26		21 36			21 45	21 56	22 11				22 26		22 36			22 45	22 58
Hamilton West d	20 48	20 59	21 14				21 29		21 39			21 48	22 00	22 14				22 29		22 39			22 48	23 01
Hamilton Central d	20 50	21 03	21 17				21 31		21 42			21 50	22 03	22 17				22 31		22 42			22 50	23 03
Chatelherault d	20 55		21 20									21 55		22 20									22 55	
Merryton d	20 58		21 23									21 58		22 23									22 58	
Larkhall a	21 01		21 26									22 01		22 26									23 01	
Airbles d		21 08					21 37		21 48				22 09					22 37		22 48				23 09
Uddingston d				21 03						21 34	21 40				22 03						22 33	22 42		
Bellshill d				21 08						21 39	21 45				22 08						22 38	22 47		
Carmyle d					21 09												22 09							
Mount Vernon d					21 12												22 12							
Baillieston d					21 15												22 15							
Bargeddie d					21 18												22 18							
Kirkwood d					21 22												22 22							
Whifflet d					21 26												22 26							
Motherwell a		21 11		21 14	21 33		21 39		21 50	21 45	21 51		22 11		22 14		22 33	22 39		22 50	22 44	22 53		23 11
d								21 41		21 48	21 51								22 41		22 44	22 53		
Whifflet d								21a49											22a48					
Coatbridge Central d																								
Greenfaulds 226 d																								
Cumbernauld 226 a																								
Shieldmuir d										21 52	21 55										22 48	22 57		
Holytown d																								
Wishaw d										21 55	21 58										22 51	23 00		
Carluke d										22 01	22 04										22 58	23 06		
Carstairs a																								
Lanark a										22 13	22 15										23 09	23 17		
Haymarket a																								
Edinburgh a																								

A until 9 September
B from 16 September. From Balloch
C from 16 September. From Milngavie
D from 16 September
E from 16 September. To Balloch

Glasgow - Hamilton, Larkhall, Whifflet, Motherwell, Coatbridge, Lanark and Edinburgh

	SR A		SR B	SR C	SR D	SR A	SR B	SR A	SR D
Hyndland 226 d				22 45	22 55				23 25
Partick 226 d				22 48	22 57				23 27
Exhibition Centre d				22 51	23 00				23 30
Anderston d									
Glasgow Central L. Level a				22 53	23 03				23 33
d				22 56	23 06				23 37
Glasgow Central H. Level d	22 36		22 50			23 08	23 22	23 22	
Argyle Street d									
Bridgeton d				23 00	23 11				23 42
Dalmarnock d									
Rutherglen d				23 05	23 15				23 47
Cambuslang d			22 58		23 19		23 30		23 50
Newton d	23 06				23 22	23 32		23 38	
Blantyre d	23 10				23 26	23 36			
Hamilton West d	23 13				23 29	23 39			
Hamilton Central d	23 16				23 31	23 42			
Chatelherault d	23 19								
Merryton d	23 22								
Larkhall a	23 25								
Airbles d					23 37	23 48			
Uddingston d			23 03				23 35	23 41	
Bellshill d			23 08				23 40	23 46	
Carmyle d				23 09					
Mount Vernon d				23 12					
Baillieston d				23 15					
Bargeddie d				23 18					
Kirkwood d				23 22					
Whifflet d				23 26					
Motherwell a			23 15	23 33	23 39	23 50	23 46	23 52	00 01
d									
Whifflet d									
Coatbridge Central d									
Greenfaulds 226 d									
Cumbernauld 226 a									
Shieldmuir d									
Holytown d									
Wishaw d									
Carluke d									
Carstairs a									
Lanark a									
Haymarket a									
Edinburgh a									

A until 9 September
B from 16 September
C from 16 September. From Balloch
D from 16 September. From Milngavie

Table T226-F

Mondays to Fridays

21 May to 7 December

Edinburgh, Bathgate, Airdrie, Cumbernauld and Springburn - Glasgow - Milngavie, Dalmuir, Balloch and Helensburgh

Miles	Miles	Miles	Miles			SR MX A	SR MO B	SR MO C	SR MX C	SR MO D	SR MX C	SR MX C	SR MX E	SR MX C	SR MX C	SR MX E	SR F	CS G	CS H	SR	SR	SR	SR
—	—	—	0	**Edinburgh** 228,230	d													04 50					
—	—	—	1¼	Haymarket 228,230	d							00 01											
—	—	—	4¾	Edinburgh Park 230	d							00 05											
—	—	—	12¾	Uphall	d							00 13											
—	—	—	14¾	Livingston North	d						00 02	00 17											
—	—	—	18¾	**Bathgate**	a						00 05	00 21											
—	—	—	—		d																		
—	—	—	21	Armadale	d																		
—	—	—	23¾	Blackridge	d																		
—	—	—	28¾	Caldercruix	d																		
—	—	—	31¾	Drumgelloch	d																		
—	—	0	33¼	**Airdrie**	d																05 32		
—	—	1	34¼	Coatdyke	d																05 34		
—	—	2	35¼	Coatbridge Sunnyside	d																05 36		
—	—	2¾	35¾	Blairhill	d																05 42		
—	—	5¼	38½	Easterhouse	d																05 46		
—	—	6¼	39½	Garrowhill	d																05 48		
—	—	7¼	40½	Shettleston	d																05 51		
—	—	8	41½	Carntyne	d																05 53		
—	0	—	—	**Cumbernauld**	d																		
—	1	—	—	Greenfaulds	d																		
—	12¾	—	—	**Springburn**	d																		
—	13¼	—	—	Barnhill	d																		
—	14¼	—	—	Alexandra Parade	d																		
—	14¾	—	—	Duke Street	d											00 03							
—	15¼	10	43¼	Bellgrove	d										00 01	00 05					05 56		
—	15¾	10½	43¾	High Street	d										00 02	00 07					05 59		
—	16¼	11	44¼	**Glasgow Queen St LL**	a										00 04	00 09					06 01		
—	—	—	—		d										00 05	00 10		05u48	05u48		06 01		
—	17	11¾	45	Charing Cross	d										00 07	00 12					06 04		
0	—	—	—	Argyle Street 225	d																		
0½	—	—	—	**Glasgow Central LL** 225	a																		
—	—	—	—		d																		
1	—	—	—	Anderston 225	d																		
1½	—	—	—	Exhibition Centre 225	d																		
2¾	18¾	13½	47	**Partick** 225	d			00 01						00 02	00 11	00 16					06 08		
3½	19½	15¼	47½	Hyndland	d			00 03						00 03	00 13	00 18					06 10		
—	20	—	—	Jordanhill	d			00 05								00 22							
—	21	—	—	Scotstounhill	d		00 01	00 08								00 24							
—	21½	—	—	Garscadden	d		00a02	00 10							00a17	00a26							
—	22½	—	—	Yoker	d			00 12															
—	23¼	—	—	Clydebank	d			00 14															
4½	—	15¼	48½	Anniesland	d									00 06									
5	—	16¾	49¾	Westerton	d									00 09									
6¼	—	—	—	Bearsden	d																		
6¾	—	—	—	Hillfoot	d	00 01																	
7½	—	—	—	**Milngavie**	a	00 03																	
—	—	18	51	Drumchapel	d									00 12									
—	—	18¾	51¾	Drumry	d									00 14									
—	—	19¾	52¾	Singer	d									00 16									
—	24½	20½	53½	**Dalmuir** 227	a			00 18						00 19				06 03	06 03		06 19		
—	—	—	—		d									00 20			05 39	06 04	06 04	06 11	06 20	06 29	06 38
—	—	21¾	54¾	Kilpatrick	d								00 03									06 31	
—	—	23½	56½	Bowling	d								00 06									06 35	
—	—	26	59¼	Dumbarton East	d								00 11	00 28						06 18	06 28	06 39	06 46
—	—	26½	60	Dumbarton Central 227	d								00 13	00 31			05 48	06 15	06 15	06 21	06 30	06a42	06 49
—	—	26¾	60¼	Dalreoch	d					00 01			00 15	00 32						06 22	06 31		06 50
—	—	28½	—	Renton	d								00 18							06 25			06 53
—	—	29½	—	Alexandria	d								00 20							06 28			06 56
—	—	31¼	—	**Balloch**	a								00 25							06 32			07 00
—	—	—	63½	Cardross	d				00 02	00 06				00 37							06 36		
—	—	—	67¼	Craigendoran	d				00 06	00 11				00 42							06 41		
—	—	—	68¼	**Helensburgh Central**	a				00 13	00 15				00 46							06 45		
—	—	—	—	Helensburgh Upper 227	a												06 00	06 29	06 29				

A From Larkhall
B From Larkhall. Forms tight booked connection out of 2C56.
C From Edinburgh
D From Airdrie
E From Cumbernauld
F From Glasgow Queen Street to Oban
G To Fort William
H From London Euston to Fort William

Table T226-F

Mondays to Fridays

21 May to 7 December

Edinburgh, Bathgate, Airdrie, Cumbernauld and Springburn - Glasgow - Milngavie, Dalmuir, Balloch and Helensburgh

		SR A	SR	SR	SR A	SR	SR B	SR	SR A	SR	SR A	SR	SR	SR B	SR	SR	SR	SR C	SR	SR	SR B	SR	SR A
Edinburgh 228,230	d																06 08		06 20				
Haymarket 228,230	d																06 13		06 24				
Edinburgh Park 230	d																06 17		06 29				
Uphall	d																06 25		06 37				
Livingston North	d																06 29		06 41				
Bathgate	a																06 33		06 46				
	d									06 05		06 19					06 34		06 49				
Armadale	d									06 10							06 38						
Blackridge	d									06 13							06 42						
Caldercruix	d									06 20							06 48						
Drumgelloch	d									06 23		06 32					06 52		07 02				
Airdrie	d			05 57				06 16		06 28		06 35			06 46		06 57		07 05			07 16	
Coatdyke	d							06 18				06 37			06 48				07 07			07 18	
Coatbridge Sunnyside	d			06 01				06 21		06 31		06 40			06 51		07 01		07 10			07 21	
Blairhill	d							06 23				06 42			06 53				07 12			07 23	
Easterhouse	d							06 27				06 46			06 57				07 16			07 27	
Garrowhill	d							06 30				06 49			07 00				07 19			07 30	
Shettleston	d			06 12				06 32		06 43					07 02		07 12					07 32	
Carntyne	d			06 14				06 34		06 45					07 04		07 14					07 34	
Cumbernauld	d					05 56							06 29			06 12				06 58			
Greenfaulds	d					05 58							06 31			06 14				07 00			
Springburn	d					06 19							06 52							07 21			
Barnhill	d					06 23							06 53							07 23			
Alexandra Parade	d					06 26							06 56							07 26			
Duke Street	d					06 28							06 58							07 28			
Bellgrove	d			06 18		06 30		06 38		06 48			07 00		07 08		07 18			07 30		07 38	
High Street	d			06 20		06 32		06 40		06 50		06 56	07 02		07 10		07 20		07 26	07 32		07 40	
Glasgow Queen St LL	a			06 22		06 34		06 42		06 52		06 58	07 04		07 12		07 22		07 28	07 34		07 42	
	d			06 25		06 35		06 42		06 55		07 02	07 06		07 12		07 25		07 31	07 36		07 42	
Charing Cross	d			06 27		06 38		06 44		06 58		07 05	07 09		07 15		07 28		07 35	07 39		07 45	
Argyle Street 225	d	06 18			06 29		06 35		06 48		06 58			07 07		07 18		07 26			07 37		07 49
Glasgow Central LL 225	a	06 20			06 30		06 36		06 50		06 59			07 09		07 20		07 28			07 39		07 50
	d	06 20			06 30		06 37		06 51		07 00			07 09		07 21		07 28			07 39		07 51
Anderston 225	d	06 22			06 32		06 39		06 52		07 01			07 11		07 22		07 30			07 41		07 52
Exhibition Centre 225	d	06 24			06 34		06 41		06 54		07 03			07 13		07 24		07 32			07 43		07 54
Partick 225	d	06 27		06 31	06 37	06 42	06 45	06 48	06 58	07 02	07 07	07 10	07 13	07 16	07 19	07 28	07 32	07 35	07 39	07 43	07 46	07 49	07 58
Hyndland	d	06 30		06 34	06 40	06 44	06 47	06 51	07 00	07 04	07 09	07 12	07 15	07 19	07 22	07 30	07 34	07 38	07 42	07 45	07 49	07 52	08 00
Jordanhill	d	06 32				06 47			07 02				07 17			07 32				07 47			08 02
Scotstounhill	d	06 35				06 49			07 05				07 20			07 35				07 50			08 05
Garscadden	d	06 38				06 52			07 07				07 22			07 37				07 52			08 07
Yoker	d	06 40				06 54			07 09				07 25			07 39				07 55			08 09
Clydebank	d	06 42				06 56			07 11				07 27			07 41				07 57			08 11
Anniesland	d			06 37	06 43		06 50	06 54		07 07	07 12			07 22	07 25		07 37	07 41			07 52	07 55	
Westerton	d			06 40	06 46		06 53	06 57		07 10	07 15			07 25	07 28		07 40	07 44			07 55	07 58	
Bearsden	d			06 42			06 56			07 13				07 28			07 43				07 57		
Hillfoot	d			06 44			06 58			07 15				07 30			07 45				07 59		
Milngavie	a			06 48			07 02			07 18				07 33			07 48				08 03		
Drumchapel	d				06 48			07 00			07 18				07 30			07 46				08 00	
Drumry	d				06 50			07 02			07 20				07 32			07 48				08 02	
Singer	d				06 53			07 04			07 22				07 35			07 51				08 05	
Dalmuir 227	a	06 46			06 55	06 59		07 07	07 15		07 25	07 19	07 30		07 37	07 45		07 53	07 49	08 00		08 07	08 15
	d		06 51			07 00		07 08				07 21	07 30		07 38				07 51	08 00		08 08	
Kilpatrick	d					07 02							07 33							08 03			
Bowling	d					07 05							07 36							08 06			
Dumbarton East	d		06 58			07 10		07 16				07 28	07 40		07 46				07 58	08 10		08 16	
Dumbarton Central 227	d		07 00			07a13		07 19				07 30	07a43		07 49				08 00	08a13		08 19	
Dalreoch	d		07 02					07 20				07 32			07 50				08 02			08 20	
Renton	d							07 23							07 53							08 23	
Alexandria	d							07 26							07 56							08 26	
Balloch	a							07 30							08 00							08 30	
Cardross	d		07 07									07 37							08 07				
Craigendoran	d		07 12									07 42							08 12				
Helensburgh Central	a		07 16									07 46							08 16				
Helensburgh Upper 227	a																						

A From Motherwell
B From Larkhall
C From Whifflet

Edinburgh, Bathgate, Airdrie, Cumbernauld and Springburn - Glasgow - Milngavie, Dalmuir, Balloch and Helensburgh

		SR	SR	SR	SR	SR	SR	SR	SR	SR	SR	SR	SR	SR	SR	SR	SR	SR	SR	SR	SR	SR	SR
			A		B		C		◇ D ✠			B		E		C		A		A			C
Edinburgh 228,230	d	06 39		06 51							07 07		07 21						07 37		07 52		
Haymarket 228,230 ⛴	d	06 45		06 55							07 11		07 25						07 42		07 56		
Edinburgh Park 230	d	06 50		07 01							07 18		07 30						07 48		08 03		
Uphall	d	06 58		07 09							07 26		07 38						07 56		08 12		
Livingston North	d	07 01		07 13							07 29		07 42						07 59		08 15		
Bathgate	a	07 06		07 17							07 34		07 46						08 04		08 20		
	d	07 06		07 19							07 35		07 49						08 05		08 20		
Armadale	d	07 10									07 39								08 09				
Blackridge	d	07 14									07 42								08 12				
Caldercruix	d	07 20									07 49								08 19				
Drumgelloch	d	07 24		07 32							07 52		08 01						08 22		08 33		
Airdrie	d	07 28		07 35				07 46			07 57		08 05				08 16		08 27		08 36		
Coatdyke	d	07 30		07 37				07 48			07 59		08 07				08 18		08 29		08 38		
Coatbridge Sunnyside	d	07 33		07 40				07 51			08 02		08 09				08 21		08 32		08 41		
Blairhill	d	07 35		07 42				07 53			08 04		08 12				08 23		08 34		08 43		
Easterhouse	d			07 46				07 57					08 16				08 27				08 47		
Garrowhill	d			07 49				08 00					08 18				08 30				08 50		
Shettleston	d	07 43						08 02			08 10						08 32		08 42				
Carntyne	d	07 45						08 04			08 12						08 34		08 44				
Cumbernauld	d					07 26				07 13					07 59							08 27	
Greenfaulds	d					07 28				07 15					08 01							08 29	
Springburn	d					07 49									08 22							08 50	
Barnhill	d					07 50									08 23							08 51	
Alexandra Parade	d					07 53									08 26							08 54	
Duke Street	d					07 55									08 28							08 58	
Bellgrove	d	07 48				07 59		08 08			08 16				08 30		08 38		08 48			09 00	
High Street	d	07 50		07 56		08 02		08 10			08 18		08 26		08 32		08 40		08 50		08 57	09 02	
Glasgow Queen St LL 10 ⛴	a	07 52		07 58		08 04		08 12			08 20		08 28		08 34		08 42		08 52		08 59	09 04	
	d	07 55		08 01		08 07		08 12			08 25		08 31		08 36		08 42		08 55		09 02	09 06	
Charing Cross	d	07 57		08 03		08 09		08 16			08 27		08 33		08 39		08 46		08 58		09 05	09 09	
Argyle Street 225	d		07 55		08 00		08 08			08 18		08 23		08 29		08 38		08 50		08 56			09 07
Glasgow Central LL 15 225	a		07 57		08 01		08 10			08 20		08 25		08 31		08 40		08 51		08 57			09 09
	d		07 57		08 03		08 10			08 20		08 26		08 31		08 40		08 52		08 58			09 09
Anderston 225	d		07 59		08 05		08 12			08 22		08 28		08 33		08 42		08 53		08 59			09 10
Exhibition Centre 225	d		08 01		08 07		08 14			08 24		08 30		08 36		08 44		08 55		09 01			09 12
Partick 225 ⛴	d	08 01	08 04	08 07	08 10	08 13	08 17	08 20		08 27	08 31	08 34	08 37	08 40	08 43	08 47	08 50	08 59	09 02	09 05	09 10	09 13	09 16
Hyndland 3	d	08 04	08 07	08 10	08 13	08 16	08 20	08 22		08 30	08 33	08 36	08 39	08 42	08 45	08 50	08 53	09 01	09 04	09 07	09 12	09 15	09 18
Jordanhill	d					08 18				08 32					08 47			09 03				09 17	
Scotstounhill	d					08 21				08 34					08 50			09 06				09 20	
Garscadden	d				08a17	08 23				08 36		08a41			08 52			09 08				09 22	
Yoker	d					08 26				08 39					08 55			09 10				09 25	
Clydebank	d					08 28				08 41					08 57			09 12				09 27	
Anniesland	d	08 07	08 11				08 23	08 26			08 37			08 45		08 53	08 56		09 07	09 11			09 21
Westerton	d	08 10	08 14				08 26	08 29			08 40			08 48		08 56	08 59		09 10	09 14			09 24
Bearsden	d	08 13					08 28				08 42					08 58			09 13				09 27
Hillfoot	d	08 15					08 30				08 44					09 00			09 15				09 29
Milngavie	a	08 18					08 34				08 48					09 04			09 18				09 32
Drumchapel	d		08 16					08 31						08 51			09 01			09 16			
Drumry	d		08 18					08 33						08 53			09 03			09 18			
Singer	d		08 21					08 36						08 55			09 06			09 21			
Dalmuir 227	a		08 23	08 21		08 31		08 38		08 45			08 49	08 58	09 00		09 08	09 16		09 23	09 20	09 30	
	d			08 21		08 31		08 38	08 42				08 50		09 00		09 09				09 21	09 30	
Kilpatrick	d					08 34									09 03							09 33	
Bowling	d					08 37									09 06							09 36	
Dumbarton East	d			08 29		08 41		08 46					08 58		09 10		09 16				09 29	09 40	
Dumbarton Central 227	d			08 31		08a44		08 48	08 52				09 00		09a13		09 19				09 31	09a43	
Dalreoch	d			08 32				08 49					09 01				09 20				09 32		
Renton	d							08 52									09 23						
Alexandria	d							08 55									09 26						
Balloch	a							08 59									09 30						
Cardross	d			08 37									09 06								09 37		
Craigendoran	d			08 43									09 11								09 44		
Helensburgh Central	a			08 46									09 14								09 47		
Helensburgh Upper 227	a								09 05														

A From Motherwell
B From Carstairs
C From Larkhall
D From Glasgow Queen Street to Oban
E From Whifflet

Edinburgh, Bathgate, Airdrie, Cumbernauld and Springburn - Glasgow - Milngavie, Dalmuir, Balloch and Helensburgh

		SR	SR	SR	SR	SR	SR	SR	SR	SR	SR	SR	SR	SR	SR	SR	SR	SR	SR	SR	SR	SR
					A			B		C		C			B				A		◇ D ✠	
Edinburgh 228,230	d			08 07		08 21					08 39		08 49					09 13		09 21		
Haymarket 228,230 ⛴	d			08 12		08 27					08 46		08 54					09 17		09 27		
Edinburgh Park 230	d			08 18		08 32					08 50		09 00					09 22		09 32		
Uphall	d			08 27		08 40					08 58		09 08					09 30		09 40		
Livingston North	d			08 30		08 44					09 02		09 12					09 33		09 43		
Bathgate	a			08 35		08 48					09 06		09 16					09 38		09 48		
	d			08 35		08 49					09 07		09 20					09 38		09 50		
Armadale	d			08 39							09 11							09 42				
Blackridge	d			08 43							09 15							09 46				
Caldercruix	d			08 49							09 21							09 52				
Drumgelloch	d			08 53		09 02					09 25		09 33					09 56		10 02		
Airdrie	d	08 46		08 57		09 05			09 16		09 29		09 36			09 46		10 00		10 06		
Coatdyke	d	08 48				09 07			09 18				09 38			09 48				10 08		
Coatbridge Sunnyside	d	08 51		09 01		09 10			09 21		09 33		09 41			09 51		10 03		10 10		
Blairhill	d	08 53				09 12			09 23				09 43			09 53				10 13		
Easterhouse	d	08 57				09 16			09 27				09 47			09 57				10 17		
Garrowhill	d	09 00				09 19			09 30				09 50			10 00				10 19		
Shettleston	d	09 02		09 12					09 32		09 44					10 02		10 15				
Carntyne	d	09 04		09 14					09 34		09 46					10 04		10 17				
Cumbernauld	d		08 12				08 59							09 29			09 22					09 59
Greenfaulds	d		08 14				09 01							09 31			09 24					10 01
Springburn	d						09 22							09 52								10 22
Barnhill	d						09 23							09 53								10 23
Alexandra Parade	d						09 26							09 56								10 26
Duke Street	d						09 28							09 58								10 28
Bellgrove	d	09 08		09 18			09 30		09 38		09 50			10 00		10 08		10 20				10 30
High Street	d	09 10		09 20		09 26	09 33		09 40		09 52		09 57	10 02		10 10		10 22		10 27		10 32
Glasgow Queen St LL 10 ⛴	a	09 12		09 22		09 28	09 35		09 42		09 54		09 59	10 04		10 12		10 24		10 29		10 34
	d	09 12		09 25		09 32	09 36		09 42		09 55		10 02	10 06		10 13		10 25		10 31		10 36
Charing Cross	d	09 15		09 28		09 34	09 38		09 45		09 57		10 05	10 09		10 15		10 27		10 35		10 39
Argyle Street 225	d		09 20		09 25			09 37		09 49		09 56			10 08		10 20		10 25			
Glasgow Central LL 15 225	a		09 22		09 26			09 39		09 51		09 58			10 09		10 22		10 26			
	d		09 22		09 28			09 39		09 51		09 58			10 09		10 22		10 27			
Anderston 225	d		09 24		09 29			09 40		09 53		10 00			10 11		10 23		10 29			
Exhibition Centre 225	d		09 26		09 32			09 42		09 55		10 02			10 13		10 25		10 31			
Partick 225 ⛴	d	09 19	09 29	09 32	09 35	09 39	09 42	09 46	09 50	09 58	10 01	10 05	10 10	10 13	10 16	10 19	10 29	10 32	10 35	10 39		10 43
Hyndland 3	d	09 22	09 32	09 35	09 38	09 41	09 45	09 48	09 52	10 01	10 04	10 08	10 12	10 15	10 19	10 22	10 31	10 34	10 37	10 42		10 45
Jordanhill	d		09 34				09 47			10 03				10 17			10 33					10 47
Scotstounhill	d		09 36				09 49			10 05				10 20			10 36					10 50
Garscadden	d		09 38				09 52			10 08				10 22			10 38					10 52
Yoker	d		09 41				09 54			10 10				10 25			10 41					10 55
Clydebank	d		09 43				09 56			10 12				10 27			10 43					10 57
Anniesland	d	09 25		09 38	09 41			09 51	09 55		10 07	10 11			10 22	10 25		10 37	10 40			
Westerton	d	09 28		09 41	09 44			09 54	09 58		10 10	10 14			10 25	10 28		10 40	10 43			
Bearsden	d			09 44				09 57			10 12				10 27			10 43				
Hillfoot	d			09 46				09 59			10 14				10 29			10 45				
Milngavie	a			09 49				10 02			10 18				10 33			10 48				
Drumchapel	d	09 30			09 46				10 00			10 16				10 30			10 46			
Drumry	d	09 32			09 48				10 02			10 18				10 32			10 48			
Singer	d	09 35			09 51				10 05			10 21				10 35			10 50			
Dalmuir 227	a	09 37	09 47		09 53	09 50	09 59		10 07	10 16		10 23	10 21	10 30		10 37	10 47		10 53	10 50		11 01
	d	09 38				09 51	10 00		10 08				10 21	10 30		10 38				10 50	10 57	11 01
Kilpatrick	d						10 03							10 33								11 04
Bowling	d						10 06							10 36								11 07
Dumbarton East	d	09 46				09 59	10 10		10 16				10 29	10 40		10 46				10 58		11 11
Dumbarton Central 227	d	09 49				10 01	10a13		10 19				10 31	10a43		10 49				11 00	11 06	11a14
Dalreoch	d	09 50				10 03			10 20				10 33			10 50				11 01		
Renton	d	09 53							10 23							10 53						
Alexandria	d	09 56							10 26							10 56						
Balloch	a	10 00							10 30							11 00						
Cardross	d					10 08							10 38							11 06		
Craigendoran	d					10 13							10 43							11 11		
Helensburgh Central	a					10 16							10 46							11 14		
Helensburgh Upper 227	a																				11 24	

A From Whifflet
B From Larkhall
C From Motherwell
D From Glasgow Queen Street to Oban

Table T226-F

Mondays to Fridays
21 May to 7 December

Edinburgh, Bathgate, Airdrie, Cumbernauld and Springburn - Glasgow - Milngavie, Dalmuir, Balloch and Helensburgh

		SR A	SR	SR B	SR	SR B	SR	SR	SR A	SR	SR	SR	SR C	SR	SR	SR A	SR	SR B	SR	SR B	SR	SR	SR A
Edinburgh	228,230 d				09 38		09 51					10 07		10 23					10 38		10 49		
Haymarket	228,230 ⇌ d				09 43		09 56					10 13		10 28					10 42		10 53		
Edinburgh Park	230 d				09 48		10 01					10 19		10 33					10 48		10 59		
Uphall	d				09 56		10 09					10 27		10 41					10 56		11 07		
Livingston North	d				10 00		10 12					10 30		10 45					10 59		11 10		
Bathgate	a				10 04		10 17					10 35		10 49					11 04		11 15		
	d				10 05		10 19					10 36		10 50					11 05		11 19		
Armadale	d				10 09							10 40							11 09				
Blackridge	d				10 12							10 44							11 12				
Caldercruix	d				10 19							10 50							11 19				
Drumgelloch	d				10 22		10 32					10 54		11 02					11 22		11 32		
Airdrie	d		10 16		10 27		10 35			10 46		10 58		11 06			11 16		11 27		11 35		
Coatdyke	d		10 18				10 37			10 48				11 08			11 18				11 37		
Coatbridge Sunnyside	d		10 21		10 31		10 40			10 51		11 02		11 10			11 21		11 31		11 40		
Blairhill	d		10 23				10 42			10 53				11 13			11 23				11 42		
Easterhouse	d		10 27				10 46			10 57				11 17			11 27				11 46		
Garrowhill	d		10 30				10 49			11 00				11 19			11 30				11 49		
Shettleston	d		10 32		10 42					11 02		11 13					11 32		11 42				
Carntyne	d		10 34		10 44					11 04		11 15					11 34		11 44				
Cumbernauld	d							10 27			10 21				10 59							11 29	
Greenfaulds	d							10 29			10 23				11 01							11 31	
Springburn	d							10 52							11 22							11 52	
Barnhill	d							10 53							11 23							11 53	
Alexandra Parade	d							10 56							11 26							11 56	
Duke Street	d							10 58							11 28							11 58	
Bellgrove	d		10 38		10 48			11 00		11 08		11 19			11 30		11 38		11 48			12 00	
High Street	d		10 40		10 50		10 56	11 03		11 10		11 21		11 27	11 32		11 40		11 50		11 56	12 02	
Glasgow Queen St LL 13	⇌ a		10 42		10 52		10 58	11 05		11 12		11 23		11 29	11 34		11 42		11 52		11 58	12 04	
	d		10 42		10 55		11 02	11 07		11 12		11 25		11 32	11 36		11 42		11 55		12 02	12 06	
Charing Cross	d		10 45		10 58		11 05	11 09		11 15		11 28		11 35	11 38		11 45		11 58		12 06	12 09	
Argyle Street	225 d	10 37		10 49		10 57			11 07		11 20		11 27			11 36		11 49		11 56			12 07
Glasgow Central LL 15	225 a	10 39		10 51		10 58			11 09		11 22		11 28			11 38		11 51		11 57			12 09
	d	10 39		10 51		10 59			11 09		11 22		11 29			11 38		11 51		11 58			12 09
Anderston	225 d	10 41		10 53		11 00			11 11		11 23		11 30			11 40		11 53		11 59			12 10
Exhibition Centre	225 d	10 43		10 55		11 02			11 13		11 25		11 32			11 42		11 55		12 02			12 12
Partick	225 ⇌ d	10 46	10 49	10 58	11 02	11 06	11 10	11 13	11 16	11 20	11 29	11 32	11 36	11 39	11 42	11 45	11 49	11 58	12 02	12 05	12 10	12 13	12 16
Hyndland 3	d	10 49	10 52	11 01	11 04	11 08	11 12	11 15	11 19	11 22	11 31	11 34	11 38	11 41	11 45	11 48	11 52	12 01	12 04	12 08	12 12	12 15	12 18
Jordanhill	d			11 03				11 17			11 33				11 47			12 03				12 17	
Scotstounhill	d			11 05				11 20			11 36				11 50			12 05				12 20	
Garscadden	d			11 07				11 22			11 38				11 52			12 07				12 22	
Yoker	d			11 10				11 25			11 41				11 55			12 10				12 25	
Clydebank	d			11 12				11 27			11 43				11 57			12 12				12 27	
Anniesland	d	10 52	10 55		11 07	11 11			11 22	11 25		11 37	11 45			11 51	11 55		12 07	12 11			12 21
Westerton	d	10 55	10 58		11 10	11 14			11 25	11 28		11 40	11 48			11 54	11 58		12 10	12 14			12 24
Bearsden	d	10 57			11 13				11 27			11 43				11 57			12 13				12 27
Hillfoot	d	10 59			11 15				11 29			11 45				11 59			12 15				12 29
Milngavie	a	11 03			11 18				11 33			11 48				12 03			12 18				12 33
Drumchapel	d		11 00			11 17				11 30			11 50				12 00			12 16			
Drumry	d		11 02			11 19				11 32			11 52				12 02			12 18			
Singer	d		11 05			11 21				11 35			11 55				12 05			12 21			
Dalmuir	227 a		11 07	11 16		11 24	11 20	11 30		11 37	11 47		11 57	11 50	12 00		12 07	12 16		12 23	12 20	12 30	
	d		11 08				11 21	11 30		11 38				11 51	12 00		12 08				12 21	12 30	
Kilpatrick	d							11 33							12 03							12 33	
Bowling	d							11 36							12 06							12 36	
Dumbarton East	d		11 16				11 29	11 40		11 46				11 59	12 10		12 16				12 29	12 40	
Dumbarton Central	227 d		11 19				11 31	11a43		11 49				12 01	12a13		12 19				12 31	12a43	
Dalreoch	d		11 20				11 32			11 50				12 02			12 20				12 32		
Renton	d		11 23							11 53							12 23						
Alexandria	d		11 26							11 56							12 26						
Balloch	a		11 30							12 00							12 30						
Cardross	d						11 37							12 07							12 37		
Craigendoran	d						11 43							12 12							12 43		
Helensburgh Central	a						11 46							12 16							12 46		
Helensburgh Upper	227 a																						

A From Larkhall
B From Motherwell
C From Whifflet

Table T226-F

Mondays to Fridays
21 May to 7 December

Edinburgh, Bathgate, Airdrie, Cumbernauld and Springburn - Glasgow - Milngavie, Dalmuir, Balloch and Helensburgh

		SR	SR ◇ A	SR	SR	SR B	SR	SR	SR C	SR	SR D	SR	SR D	SR	SR	SR C	SR	SR	SR	SR B	SR	SR
Edinburgh	228,230 d				11 07		11 20					11 37		11 50					12 08		12 21	
Haymarket	228,230 ⇌ d				11 11		11 24					11 44		11 54					12 12		12 26	
Edinburgh Park	230 d				11 17		11 30					11 49		11 59					12 18		12 31	
Uphall	d				11 26		11 38					11 57		12 07					12 26		12 39	
Livingston North	d				11 30		11 42					12 01		12 11					12 30		12 43	
Bathgate	a				11 34		11 46					12 05		12 15					12 34		12 47	
	d				11 35		11 49					12 06		12 20					12 35		12 49	
Armadale	d				11 39							12 10							12 39			
Blackridge	d				11 42							12 13							12 43			
Caldercruix	d				11 49							12 20							12 49			
Drumgelloch	d				11 52		12 02					12 23		12 32					12 53		13 02	
Airdrie	d	11 46			11 57		12 07			12 16		12 28		12 36			12 46		12 57		13 05	
Coatdyke	d	11 48					12 09			12 18				12 38			12 48				13 07	
Coatbridge Sunnyside	d	11 51			12 01		12 11			12 21		12 32		12 40			12 51		13 01		13 10	
Blairhill	d	11 53					12 14			12 23				12 43			12 53				13 12	
Easterhouse	d	11 57					12 18			12 27				12 47			12 57				13 16	
Garrowhill	d	12 00					12 20			12 30				12 49			13 00				13 19	
Shettleston	d	12 02			12 12					12 32		12 43					13 02		13 12			
Carntyne	d	12 04			12 14					12 34		12 45					13 04		13 14			
Cumbernauld	d			11 21				11 56							12 29			12 21				12 59
Greenfaulds	d			11 23				11 58							12 31			12 23				13 01
Springburn	d							12 21							12 52							13 24
Barnhill	d							12 23							12 53							13 25
Alexandra Parade	d							12 26							12 56							13 28
Duke Street	d							12 27							12 58							13 30
Bellgrove	d	12 08			12 18			12 29		12 38		12 49			13 00		13 08		13 18			13 32
High Street	d	12 10			12 20		12 27	12 32		12 40		12 51		12 59	13 02		13 10		13 20		13 26	13 34
Glasgow Queen St LL 13	⇌ a	12 12			12 22		12 29	12 34		12 42		12 53		13 01	13 04		13 12		13 22		13 28	13 36
	d	12 12			12 25		12 31	12 36		12 44		12 55		13 02	13 06		13 13		13 25		13 33	13 37
Charing Cross	d	12 15			12 28		12 34	12 38		12 46		12 58		13 04	13 08		13 15		13 28		13 36	13 39
Argyle Street	225 d			12 21		12 25			12 38		12 49		12 56			13 06		13 20		13 25		
Glasgow Central LL 15	225 a			12 22		12 27			12 39		12 51		12 58			13 07		13 22		13 27		
	d			12 22		12 28			12 39		12 51		12 58			13 08		13 22		13 28		
Anderston	225 d			12 24		12 29			12 41		12 53		13 00			13 09		13 23		13 29		
Exhibition Centre	225 d			12 26		12 32			12 43		12 55		13 02			13 11		13 25		13 32		
Partick	225 ⇌ d	12 19		12 29	12 32	12 35	12 38	12 42	12 46	12 50	12 58	13 02	13 05	13 08	13 12	13 15	13 19	13 29	13 32	13 35	13 40	13 43
Hyndland 3	d	12 21		12 32	12 35	12 38	12 41	12 45	12 49	12 52	13 01	13 04	13 08	13 11	13 14	13 17	13 22	13 31	13 34	13 38	13 42	13 45
Jordanhill	d			12 34				12 47			13 03				13 17			13 33				13 47
Scotstounhill	d			12 36				12 49			13 05				13 20			13 36				13 50
Garscadden	d			12 38				12 52			13 07				13 22			13 38				13 52
Yoker	d			12 41				12 54			13 10				13 25			13 40				13 55
Clydebank	d			12 43				12 56			13 12				13 27			13 42				13 57
Anniesland	d	12 24			12 38	12 41			12 52	12 56		13 07	13 11			13 20	13 25		13 37	13 41		
Westerton	d	12 27			12 41	12 44			12 55	12 59		13 10	13 14			13 23	13 28		13 40	13 44		
Bearsden	d				12 43				12 57			13 13				13 26			13 43			
Hillfoot	d				12 45				12 59			13 15				13 28			13 45			
Milngavie	a				12 49				13 03			13 18				13 32			13 48			
Drumchapel	d	12 30				12 46				13 01			13 16				13 30			13 46		
Drumry	d	12 32				12 48				13 03			13 18				13 32			13 48		
Singer	d	12 34				12 51				13 06			13 21				13 35			13 51		
Dalmuir	227 a	12 37		12 47		12 53	12 50	12 59		13 08	13 16		13 23	13 22	13 30		13 37	13 46		13 53	13 50	14 00
	d	12 37	12 42				12 51	13 00		13 08				13 23	13 30		13 38				13 51	14 00
Kilpatrick	d							13 02							13 33							14 03
Bowling	d							13 05							13 36							14 06
Dumbarton East	d	12 45					12 59	13 10		13 16				13 30	13 40		13 46				13 59	14 10
Dumbarton Central	227 d	12 47	12 51				13 01	13a13		13 19				13 32	13a43		13 49				14 01	14a13
Dalreoch	d	12 48					13 02			13 20				13 34			13 50				14 02	
Renton	d	12 51								13 23							13 53					
Alexandria	d	12 54								13 26							13 56					
Balloch	a	12 58								13 30							14 00					
Cardross	d						13 07							13 39							14 07	
Craigendoran	d						13 13							13 44							14 13	
Helensburgh Central	a						13 16							13 47							14 16	
Helensburgh Upper	227 a		13 03																			

A From Glasgow Queen Street to Oban
B From Whifflet
C From Larkhall
D From Motherwell

Table T226-F

Mondays to Fridays

21 May to 7 December

Edinburgh, Bathgate, Airdrie, Cumbernauld and Springburn - Glasgow - Milngavie, Dalmuir, Balloch and Helensburgh

		SR A	SR	SR B	SR	SR B	SR	SR	SR A	SR	SR	SR	SR C	SR	SR	SR A	SR	SR B	SR	SR B	SR	SR	SR A
Edinburgh 228,230	d				12 37		12 53					13 08		13 19					13 38		13 49		
Haymarket 228,230	d				12 42		13 00					13 12		13 25					13 43		13 54		
Edinburgh Park 230	d				12 47		13 05					13 18		13 31					13 48		14 01		
Uphall	d				12 55		13 13					13 26		13 39					13 56		14 09		
Livingston North	d				12 59		13 17					13 30		13 43					13 59		14 13		
Bathgate	a				13 03		13 21					13 34		13 47					14 04		14 17		
	d				13 04		13 22					13 36		13 49					14 04		14 19		
Armadale	d				13 08							13 40							14 08				
Blackridge	d				13 12							13 43							14 12				
Caldercruix	d				13 18							13 50							14 18				
Drumgelloch	d				13 22		13 34					13 53		14 02					14 22		14 32		
Airdrie	d		13 16		13 27		13 38			13 46		13 58		14 05			14 16		14 27		14 35		
Coatdyke	d		13 18				13 40			13 48				14 07			14 18				14 37		
Coatbridge Sunnyside	d		13 21		13 31		13 42			13 51		14 01		14 10			14 21		14 31		14 40		
Blairhill	d		13 23				13 45			13 53				14 12			14 23				14 42		
Easterhouse	d		13 27				13 49			13 57				14 16			14 27				14 46		
Garrowhill	d		13 30				13 51			14 00				14 19			14 30				14 49		
Shettleston	d		13 32		13 42					14 02		14 13					14 32		14 42				
Carntyne	d		13 34		13 44					14 04		14 15					14 34		14 44				
Cumbernauld	d							13 29			13 20				13 59							14 29	
Greenfaulds	d							13 31			13 22				14 01							14 31	
Springburn	d							13 52							14 24							14 52	
Barnhill	d							13 53							14 25							14 53	
Alexandra Parade	d							13 56							14 28							14 56	
Duke Street	d							13 58							14 30							14 58	
Bellgrove	d		13 38		13 48			14 00		14 08		14 18			14 32		14 38		14 48			15 00	
High Street	d		13 40		13 50		13 58	14 03		14 10		14 20		14 26	14 34		14 40		14 50		14 56	15 02	
Glasgow Queen St LL	a		13 42		13 52		14 00	14 05		14 12		14 22		14 28	14 36		14 42		14 52		14 58	15 04	
	d		13 42		13 55		14 01	14 06		14 12		14 25		14 32	14 37		14 42		14 55		15 02	15 06	
Charing Cross	d		13 45		13 58		14 05	14 09		14 15		14 28		14 35	14 39		14 45		14 58		15 06	15 09	
Argyle Street 225	d	13 38		13 49		13 56			14 08		14 21		14 25			14 37		14 49		14 54			15 08
Glasgow Central LL 225	a	13 39		13 51		13 57			14 09		14 22		14 27			14 39		14 51		14 56			15 09
	d	13 39		13 51		13 58			14 09		14 22		14 28			14 39		14 51		14 58			15 09
Anderston 225	d	13 41		13 53		14 00			14 11		14 24		14 29			14 40		14 53		14 59			15 11
Exhibition Centre 225	d	13 43		13 55		14 02			14 13		14 26		14 32			14 42		14 55		15 02			15 13
Partick 225	d	13 46	13 49	13 58	14 02	14 05	14 09	14 13	14 16	14 19	14 29	14 32	14 35	14 39	14 43	14 46	14 49	14 58	15 02	15 05	15 10	15 13	15 16
Hyndland	d	13 49	13 52	14 01	14 04	14 08	14 12	14 15	14 19	14 22	14 32	14 35	14 38	14 41	14 45	14 48	14 52	15 01	15 04	15 08	15 12	15 15	15 19
Jordanhill	d			14 03				14 17			14 34				14 47			15 03				15 17	
Scotstounhill	d			14 05				14 20			14 36				14 50			15 05				15 20	
Garscadden	d			14 07				14 22			14 38				14 52			15 07				15 22	
Yoker	d			14 10				14 25			14 41				14 55			15 10				15 25	
Clydebank	d			14 12				14 27			14 43				14 57			15 12				15 27	
Anniesland	d	13 52	13 55		14 08	14 12			14 22	14 25		14 38	14 41			14 51	14 55		15 07	15 11			15 22
Westerton	d	13 55	13 58		14 11	14 15			14 25	14 28		14 41	14 44			14 54	14 58		15 10	15 14			15 25
Bearsden	d	13 57			14 14				14 27			14 43				14 57			15 13				15 27
Hillfoot	d	13 59			14 16				14 29			14 45				14 59			15 15				15 29
Milngavie	a	14 03			14 19				14 33			14 49				15 03			15 18				15 33
Drumchapel	d		14 00			14 17				14 30			14 46				15 00			15 16			
Drumry	d		14 02			14 19				14 32			14 48				15 02			15 18			
Singer	d		14 05			14 22				14 35			14 51				15 05			15 21			
Dalmuir 227	a		14 07	14 16		14 24	14 20	14 30		14 37	14 47		14 53	14 51	15 00		15 07	15 16		15 23	15 20	15 30	
	d		14 08				14 21	14 30		14 38				14 52	15 00		15 08				15 21	15 30	
Kilpatrick	d							14 33							15 03							15 33	
Bowling	d							14 36							15 06							15 36	
Dumbarton East	d		14 16				14 29	14 40		14 46				14 59	15 10		15 16				15 29	15 40	
Dumbarton Central 227	d		14 19				14 31	14a43		14 49				15 01	15a13		15 19				15 31	15a43	
Dalreoch	d		14 20				14 32			14 50				15 03			15 20				15 32		
Renton	d		14 23							14 53							15 23						
Alexandria	d		14 26							14 56							15 26						
Balloch	a		14 30							15 00							15 30						
Cardross	d						14 37							15 08							15 37		
Craigendoran	d						14 43							15 13							15 43		
Helensburgh Central	a						14 46							15 16							15 46		
Helensburgh Upper 227	a																						

A From Larkhall
B From Motherwell
C From Whifflet

Table T226-F

Mondays to Fridays

21 May to 7 December

Edinburgh, Bathgate, Airdrie, Cumbernauld and Springburn - Glasgow - Milngavie, Dalmuir, Balloch and Helensburgh

		SR	SR	SR	SR A	SR	SR	SR B	SR	SR C	SR	SR C	SR	SR	SR B	SR	SR	SR	SR A	SR	SR ◇ D	SR	SR B
Edinburgh 228,230	d			14 07		14 21					14 38		14 49					15 08		15 20			
Haymarket 228,230	d			14 13		14 27					14 43		14 54					15 13		15 25			
Edinburgh Park 230	d			14 19		14 33					14 48		14 59					15 17		15 30			
Uphall	d			14 27		14 42					14 56		15 08					15 25		15 38			
Livingston North	d			14 30		14 45					15 00		15 11					15 29		15 42			
Bathgate	a			14 35		14 50					15 04		15 16					15 33		15 46			
	d			14 38		14 50					15 05		15 19					15 35		15 51			
Armadale	d			14 42							15 09							15 39					
Blackridge	d			14 45							15 12							15 42					
Caldercruix	d			14 52							15 19							15 49					
Drumgelloch	d			14 55		15 03					15 22		15 31					15 52		16 03			
Airdrie	d	14 46		15 00		15 06			15 16		15 27		15 35			15 46		15 57		16 07			
Coatdyke	d	14 48				15 08			15 18				15 37			15 48				16 09			
Coatbridge Sunnyside	d	14 51		15 03		15 13			15 21		15 31		15 40			15 51		16 01		16 12			
Blairhill	d	14 53				15 15			15 23				15 42			15 53				16 14			
Easterhouse	d	14 57				15 19			15 27				15 46			15 57				16 18			
Garrowhill	d	15 00				15 22			15 30				15 49			16 00				16 21			
Shettleston	d	15 02		15 15					15 32		15 42					16 02		16 12					
Carntyne	d	15 04		15 17					15 34		15 44					16 04		16 15					
Cumbernauld	d		14 21				14 56							15 29			15 21					15 59	
Greenfaulds	d		14 23				14 58							15 31			15 23					16 01	
Springburn	d						15 21							15 52								16 24	
Barnhill	d						15 23							15 53								16 25	
Alexandra Parade	d						15 26							15 56								16 28	
Duke Street	d						15 28							15 58								16 30	
Bellgrove	d	15 08		15 20			15 30		15 38		15 48			16 00		16 08		16 18				16 32	
High Street	d	15 10		15 23		15 29	15 33		15 40		15 50		15 56	16 03		16 10		16 20		16 28		16 34	
Glasgow Queen St LL	a	15 12		15 25		15 31	15 35		15 42		15 52		15 58	16 05		16 12		16 22		16 30		16 36	
	d	15 12		15 26		15 31	15 36		15 42		15 55		16 02	16 06		16 12		16 25		16 32		16 37	
Charing Cross	d	15 15		15 28		15 35	15 39		15 45		15 58		16 05	16 09		16 15		16 28		16 35		16 39	
Argyle Street 225	d		15 20		15 26			15 38		15 49		15 55			16 07		16 21		16 26				16 37
Glasgow Central LL 225	a		15 22		15 27			15 39		15 51		15 57			16 09		16 22		16 27				16 39
	d		15 22		15 28			15 39		15 51		15 58			16 09		16 23		16 28				16 39
Anderston 225	d		15 23		15 29			15 41		15 53		15 59			16 11		16 24		16 29				16 41
Exhibition Centre 225	d		15 25		15 32			15 43		15 55		16 02			16 13		16 26		16 32				16 43
Partick 225	d	15 19	15 29	15 32	15 35	15 39	15 43	15 46	15 49	15 58	16 02	16 05	16 10	16 13	16 16	16 19	16 30	16 32	16 35	16 40		16 43	16 46
Hyndland	d	15 22	15 31	15 34	15 38	15 41	15 45	15 49	15 52	16 01	16 04	16 08	16 12	16 15	16 19	16 22	16 32	16 34	16 38	16 42		16 45	16 49
Jordanhill	d		15 33				15 47			16 03				16 17			16 34					16 47	
Scotstounhill	d		15 36				15 50			16 05				16 20			16 36					16 50	
Garscadden	d		15 38				15 52			16 08				16 22			16 38					16 52	
Yoker	d		15 40				15 55			16 10				16 25			16 41					16 55	
Clydebank	d		15 42				15 57			16 12				16 27			16 43					16 57	
Anniesland	d	15 25		15 37	15 41			15 52	15 55		16 07	16 11			16 22	16 25		16 37	16 41				16 52
Westerton	d	15 28		15 40	15 44			15 55	15 58		16 10	16 14			16 25	16 28		16 40	16 44				16 55
Bearsden	d			15 43				15 57			16 13				16 27			16 43					16 57
Hillfoot	d			15 45				15 59			16 15				16 29			16 45					16 59
Milngavie	a			15 48				16 03			16 18				16 33			16 48					17 03
Drumchapel	d	15 30			15 46				16 00			16 16				16 30			16 46				
Drumry	d	15 32			15 48				16 02			16 18				16 32			16 48				
Singer	d	15 35			15 51				16 05			16 21				16 35			16 51				
Dalmuir 227	a	15 37	15 46		15 53	15 50	16 01		16 07	16 16		16 23	16 20	16 30		16 37	16 47		16 53	16 51		17 00	
	d	15 38				15 51	16 02		16 07				16 21	16 30		16 38				16 52	16 57	17 01	
Kilpatrick	d						16 04							16 33								17 03	
Bowling	d						16 07							16 36								17 06	
Dumbarton East	d	15 46				15 59	16 12		16 16				16 29	16 40		16 46				16 59		17 11	
Dumbarton Central 227	d	15 49				16 01	16a15		16 18				16 31	16a43		16 49				17 01	17 07	17a14	
Dalreoch	d	15 50				16 02			16 20				16 32			16 50				17 03			
Renton	d	15 53							16 23							16 53							
Alexandria	d	15 56							16 25							16 56							
Balloch	a	16 00							16 29							17 00							
Cardross	d					16 07							16 37							17 08			
Craigendoran	d					16 12							16 43							17 13			
Helensburgh Central	a					16 16							16 46							17 16			
Helensburgh Upper 227	a																				17 20		

A From Whifflet
B From Larkhall
C From Motherwell
D From Glasgow Queen Street to Oban

Table T226-F

Mondays to Fridays
21 May to 7 December

Edinburgh, Bathgate, Airdrie, Cumbernauld and Springburn - Glasgow - Milngavie, Dalmuir, Balloch and Helensburgh

	SR	SR	SR	SR	SR	SR	SR	SR	SR	SR	SR	SR	SR	SR	SR	SR	SR	SR	SR	SR	SR
		A		A			B				C			B		A		A			B
Edinburgh 228,230 d			15 41		15 52					16 08		16 23					16 40		16 49		
Haymarket 228,230 ⇌ d			15 46		15 57					16 12		16 27					16 46		16 53		
Edinburgh Park 230 d			15 50		16 02					16 18		16 32					16 51		17 01		
Uphall d			15 58		16 10					16 26		16 40					16 59		17 10		
Livingston North d			16 02		16 14					16 30		16 44					17 02		17 14		
Bathgate a			16 06		16 18					16 34		16 49					17 07		17 18		
d			16 07		16 20					16 35		16 49					17 08		17 19		
Armadale d			16 11							16 39							17 12				
Blackridge d			16 15							16 43							17 15				
Caldercruix d			16 21							16 49							17 22				
Drumgelloch d			16 25		16 33					16 53		17 02					17 25		17 32		
Airdrie d	16 16		16 29		16 36			16 46		16 57		17 05			17 16		17 29		17 35		
Coatdyke d	16 18				16 38			16 48				17 07			17 18				17 37		
Coatbridge Sunnyside d	16 21		16 33		16 41			16 51		17 01		17 10			17 21		17 33		17 40		
Blairhill d	16 23				16 43			16 53				17 12			17 23				17 42		
Easterhouse d	16 27				16 47			16 57				17 16			17 27				17 46		
Garrowhill d	16 30				16 50			17 00				17 19			17 30				17 49		
Shettleston d	16 32		16 44					17 02		17 12					17 32		17 44				
Carntyne d	16 34		16 46					17 04		17 14					17 34		17 46				
Cumbernauld d						16 29			16 20				16 59							17 26	
Greenfaulds d						16 31			16 22				17 01							17 28	
Springburn d						16 52							17 22							17 49	
Barnhill d						16 53							17 23							17 50	
Alexandra Parade d						16 56							17 26							17 53	
Duke Street d						16 58							17 28							17 56	
Bellgrove d	16 38		16 50			17 00		17 08		17 18			17 30		17 38		17 50			18 00	
High Street d	16 40		16 52		16 57	17 02		17 10		17 20		17 26	17 32		17 40		17 52		17 56	18 02	
Glasgow Queen St LL 15 ⇌ a	16 42		16 54		16 59	17 04		17 12		17 22		17 28	17 34		17 42		17 54		17 58	18 04	
d	16 42		16 55		17 01	17 06		17 12		17 25		17 32	17 36		17 42		17 55		18 02	18 06	
Charing Cross d	16 45		16 58		17 04	17 09		17 15		17 28		17 35	17 39		17 45		17 58		18 05	18 09	
Argyle Street 225 d		16 49		16 55			17 07		17 19		17 24			17 37		17 49		17 55			18 07
Glasgow Central LL 15 225 a		16 51		16 56			17 09		17 20		17 25			17 39		17 51		17 57			18 09
d		16 52		16 57			17 09		17 21		17 26			17 39		17 51		17 57			18 09
Anderston 225 d		16 53		16 59			17 11		17 22		17 28			17 41		17 53		17 59			18 11
Exhibition Centre 225 d		16 55		17 01			17 13		17 25		17 32			17 43		17 55		18 01			18 13
Partick 225 ⇌ d	16 49	16 59	17 02	17 05	17 09	17 13	17 16	17 20	17 29	17 32	17 35	17 39	17 43	17 46	17 49	17 58	18 02	18 05	18 10	18 13	18 16
Hyndland 3 d	16 52	17 01	17 04	17 07	17 11	17 15	17 19	17 22	17 31	17 34	17 38	17 42	17 45	17 49	17 52	18 01	18 04	18 07	18 12	18 15	18 19
Jordanhill d		17 03				17 17			17 33				17 47			18 03				18 17	
Scotstounhill d		17 05				17 20			17 36				17 50			18 05				18 20	
Garscadden d		17 08				17 22			17 38				17 52			18 07				18 22	
Yoker d		17 10				17 25			17 40				17 55			18 10				18 25	
Clydebank d		17 12				17 27			17 42				17 57			18 12				18 27	
Anniesland d	16 55		17 07	17 11			17 22	17 25		17 37	17 41			17 52	17 55		18 07	18 11			18 22
Westerton d	16 58		17 10	17 14			17 25	17 28		17 40	17 44			17 55	17 58		18 10	18 14			18 25
Bearsden d			17 13				17 27			17 43				17 57			18 13				18 27
Hillfoot d			17 15				17 29			17 45				17 59			18 15				18 29
Milngavie a			17 18				17 33			17 48				18 03			18 18				18 33
Drumchapel d	17 00			17 16				17 30			17 46				18 00			18 16			
Drumry d	17 02			17 18				17 32			17 48				18 02			18 18			
Singer d	17 05			17 21				17 35			17 51				18 05			18 21			
Dalmuir 227 a	17 07	17 16		17 23	17 19	17 30		17 37	17 46		17 53	17 50	18 00		18 07	18 16		18 23	18 20	18 30	
d	17 08				17 19	17 30		17 38				17 51	18 00		18 08				18 21	18 30	
Kilpatrick d						17 33							18 03							18 33	
Bowling d						17 36							18 06							18 36	
Dumbarton East d	17 16				17 27	17 40		17 46				17 59	18 10		18 16				18 29	18 40	
Dumbarton Central 227 d	17 19				17 29	17a43		17 49				18 01	18a13		18 19				18 31	18a43	
Dalreoch d	17 20				17 31			17 50				18 02			18 20				18 32		
Renton d	17 23							17 53							18 23						
Alexandria d	17 26							17 56							18 26						
Balloch a	17 30							18 00							18 30						
Cardross d					17 36							18 07							18 37		
Craigendoran d					17 41							18 13							18 43		
Helensburgh Central a					17 44							18 16							18 46		
Helensburgh Upper 227 a																					

A From Motherwell
B From Larkhall
C From Whifflet

Table T226-F

Mondays to Fridays
21 May to 7 December

Edinburgh, Bathgate, Airdrie, Cumbernauld and Springburn - Glasgow - Milngavie, Dalmuir, Balloch and Helensburgh

	SR	SR	SR	SR	SR	SR	SR	SR	SR	SR	SR	SR	SR	SR	SR	SR	SR	SR	SR	SR	SR	SR
		◇ A		B				C		D		D			C				B			C
Edinburgh 228,230 d				17 08		17 20					17 37		17 53				18 06			18 23		
Haymarket 228,230 ⇌ d				17 13		17 24					17 43		17 58				18 10			18 27		
Edinburgh Park 230 d				17 18		17 30					17 48		18 03				18 18			18 33		
Uphall d				17 26		17 38					17 56		18 11				18 26			18 41		
Livingston North d				17 30		17 43					18 00		18 14				18 30			18 44		
Bathgate a				17 34		17 47					18 04		18 19				18 34			18 49		
d				17 35		17 50					18 05		18 20				18 36			18 49		
Armadale d				17 39							18 09						18 40					
Blackridge d				17 43							18 13						18 43					
Caldercruix d				17 49							18 19						18 50					
Drumgelloch d				17 53		18 02					18 23		18 32				18 53			19 02		
Airdrie d	17 46			17 57		18 06			18 16		18 28		18 36			18 46	18 58			19 05		
Coatdyke d	17 48					18 08			18 18				18 38			18 48				19 07		
Coatbridge Sunnyside d	17 51			18 01		18 10			18 21		18 31		18 40			18 51	19 02			19 10		
Blairhill d	17 53					18 13			18 23				18 43			18 53				19 12		
Easterhouse d	17 57					18 17			18 27				18 47			18 57				19 16		
Garrowhill d	18 00					18 19			18 30				18 49			19 00				19 19		
Shettleston d	18 02			18 12					18 32		18 43					19 02	19 13					
Carntyne d	18 04			18 14					18 34		18 45					19 04	19 15					
Cumbernauld d			17 21				17 59							18 26				18 18			19 01	
Greenfaulds d			17 23				18 01							18 28				18 20			19 03	
Springburn d							18 22							18 52							19 25	
Barnhill d							18 23							18 53							19 26	
Alexandra Parade d							18 26							18 56							19 29	
Duke Street d							18 28							18 59							19 31	
Bellgrove d	18 08			18 18			18 30		18 38		18 48			19 01		19 08	19 19				19 33	
High Street d	18 10			18 20		18 26	18 32		18 40		18 51		18 57	19 03		19 10	19 21			19 26	19 35	
Glasgow Queen St LL 15 ⇌ a	18 12			18 22		18 28	18 34		18 42		18 53		18 59	19 05		19 12	19 23			19 28	19 37	
d	18 12			18 25		18 32	18 37		18 42		18 55		19 02	19 06		19 13	19 23			19 33	19 37	
Charing Cross d	18 15			18 28		18 35	18 39		18 45		18 58		19 06	19 09		19 16	19 25			19 36	19 39	
Argyle Street 225 d			18 21		18 26			18 37		18 50		18 56			19 09			19 22	19 26			19 38
Glasgow Central LL 15 225 a			18 22		18 27			18 39		18 52		18 58			19 10			19 23	19 27			19 39
d			18 23		18 28			18 39		18 52		18 58			19 11			19 24	19 28			19 40
Anderston 225 d			18 24		18 30			18 41		18 54		19 00			19 12			19 26	19 29			19 41
Exhibition Centre 225 d			18 26		18 32			18 43		18 56		19 02			19 14			19 28	19 32			19 43
Partick 225 ⇌ d	18 19		18 30	18 32	18 35	18 40	18 43	18 47	18 50	18 59	19 02	19 06	19 10	19 13	19 18	19 20	19 29	19 32	19 35	19 40	19 43	19 47
Hyndland 3 d	18 22		18 32	18 35	18 38	18 42	18 45	18 49	18 52	19 01	19 04	19 08	19 13	19 15	19 20	19 23	19 31	19 34	19 38	19 42	19 46	19 49
Jordanhill d			18 34				18 47			19 03				19 17				19 36			19 48	
Scotstounhill d			18 36				18 50			19 06				19 20				19 39			19 50	
Garscadden d			18 38				18 52			19 08				19 22				19 41			19 52	
Yoker d			18 41				18 55			19 10				19 25				19 43			19 55	
Clydebank d			18 43				18 57			19 12				19 27				19 45			19 57	
Anniesland d	18 25			18 38	18 41			18 52	18 55		19 08	19 11			19 23	19 26	19 34		19 41			19 52
Westerton d	18 28			18 41	18 44			18 55	18 58		19 11	19 14			19 26	19 29	19 40		19 44			19 55
Bearsden d				18 43				18 57			19 14				19 28		19 42					19 57
Hillfoot d				18 45				18 59			19 16				19 30		19 44					19 59
Milngavie a				18 49				19 03			19 19				19 34		19 48					20 03
Drumchapel d	18 30				18 46				19 00			19 17				19 31			19 46			
Drumry d	18 32				18 48				19 02			19 19				19 33			19 48			
Singer d	18 35				18 51				19 05			19 21				19 36			19 51			
Dalmuir 227 a	18 38		18 47		18 53	18 50	19 01		19 08	19 16		19 24	19 21	19 30		19 38		19 49	19 53	19 52	20 00	
d	18 38	18 41				18 50	19 01		19 08				19 22	19 30		19 39				19 53	20 00	
Kilpatrick d							19 04							19 33							20 03	
Bowling d							19 07							19 36							20 06	
Dumbarton East d	18 45					18 59	19 11		19 16				19 29	19 40		19 46				20 00	20 10	
Dumbarton Central 227 d	18 47	18 50				19 01	19a14		19 18				19 31	19a43		19 49				20 02	20a13	
Dalreoch d	18 49					19 02			19 20				19 33			19 52				20 04		
Renton d	18 52								19 23							19 55						
Alexandria d	18 54								19 25							19 57						
Balloch a	18 58								19 30							20 02						
Cardross d						19 07							19 38							20 09		
Craigendoran d						19 13							19 43							20 14		
Helensburgh Central a						19 16							19 46							20 17		
Helensburgh Upper 227 a		19 04																				

A From Glasgow Queen Street to Oban
B From Whifflet
C From Larkhall
D From Motherwell

Edinburgh, Bathgate, Airdrie, Cumbernauld and Springburn - Glasgow - Milngavie, Dalmuir, Balloch and Helensburgh

		SR	SR A	SR	SR A	SR	SR	SR	SR B	SR	SR	SR C	SR B	SR	SR	SR	SR A	SR A	SR B	SR	SR	SR
Edinburgh 228,230	d			18 38		18 48	19 07								19 22	19 38					19 51	20 07
Haymarket 228,230	d			18 44		18 53	19 12								19 26	19 43					19 55	20 12
Edinburgh Park 230	d			18 49		18 59	19 19								19 31	19 48					20 00	20 18
Uphall	d			18 57		19 07	19 27								19 40	19 56					20 09	20 26
Livingston North	d			19 00		19 11	19 30								19 43	20 00					20 12	20 29
Bathgate	a			19 05		19 15	19 35								19 48	20 04					20 17	20 34
	d			19 07		19 19									19 50						20 18	
Armadale	d			19 11		19 23									19 54						20 22	
Blackridge	d			19 14		19 27									19 57						20 25	
Caldercruix	d			19 21		19 33									20 04						20 32	
Drumgelloch	d			19 24		19 37									20 07						20 35	
Airdrie	d	19 16		19 29		19 40				19 46					20 17						20 48	
Coatdyke	d	19 18								19 48					20 19						20 50	
Coatbridge Sunnyside	d	19 21		19 32		19 44				19 51					20 21						20 52	
Blairhill	d	19 23								19 53					20 24						20 55	
Easterhouse	d	19 27								19 57					20 28						20 59	
Garrowhill	d	19 30								20 00					20 30						21 01	
Shettleston	d	19 32		19 44						20 02					20 33						21 04	
Carntyne	d	19 34		19 46						20 04					20 35						21 06	
Cumbernauld	d							19 27			19 21			19 59						20 27		
Greenfaulds	d							19 29			19 23			20 01						20 29		
Springburn	d							19 51						20 22						20 51		
Barnhill	d							19 53						20 24						20 53		
Alexandra Parade	d							19 56						20 27						20 56		
Duke Street	d							19 58						20 29						20 58		
Bellgrove	d	19 38		19 49				20 00		20 08				20 31	20 39					21 00	21 09	
High Street	d	19 40		19 51		19 59		20 03		20 10				20 33	20 41					21 03	21 12	
Glasgow Queen St LL	a	19 42		19 53		20 01		20 05		20 12				20 35	20 43					21 05	21 14	
	d	19 42		19 55		20 01		20 06		20 12				20 40	20 48					21 09	21 19	
Charing Cross	d	19 45		19 58		20 05		20 08		20 15				20 45	20 50					21 15	21 21	
Argyle Street 225	d		19 50		19 55				20 08		20 21	20 25	20 39				20 52	20 59	21 09			
Glasgow Central LL 225	a		19 51		19 56				20 09		20 23	20 27	20 41				20 54	21 00	21 10			
	d		19 52		19 57				20 10		20 23	20 28	20 41				20 54	21 01	21 11			
Anderston 225	d		19 53		19 59				20 11		20 25	20 30	20 43				20 56	21 02	21 12			
Exhibition Centre 225	d		19 55		20 01				20 13		20 27	20 32	20 45				20 58	21 04	21 14			
Partick 225	d	19 50	19 59	20 02	20 05	20 09		20 12	20 17	20 19	20 30	20 35	20 48	20 51	20 55		21 01	21 08	21 18	21 21	21 25	
Hyndland	d	19 52	20 01	20 04	20 07	20 12		20 15	20 19	20 22	20 32	20 38	20 50	20 53	20 57		21 03	21 10	21 20	21 23	21 28	
Jordanhill	d		20 03					20 17			20 34			20 55			21 05			21 25		
Scotstounhill	d		20 05					20 19			20 37			20 58			21 08			21 28		
Garscadden	d		20 07					20 22			20 39			21 00			21 10			21 30		
Yoker	d		20 10					20 24			20 41			21 03			21 12			21 33		
Clydebank	d		20 12					20 26			20 43			21 05			21 14			21 35		
Anniesland	d	19 55		20 07	20 11				20 22	20 25		20 41	20 53		21 00			21 13	21 23		21 31	
Westerton	d	19 58		20 10	20 14				20 25	20 28		20 44	20 56		21 03			21 16	21 26		21 34	
Bearsden	d			20 13					20 27				20 59						21 28			
Hillfoot	d			20 15					20 29				21 01						21 30			
Milngavie	a			20 18					20 33				21 04						21 34			
Drumchapel	d	20 00			20 16					20 30		20 46			21 06			21 18			21 36	
Drumry	d	20 02			20 18					20 32		20 48			21 08			21 20			21 38	
Singer	d	20 05			20 21					20 35		20 51			21 10			21 23			21 41	
Dalmuir 227	a	20 07	20 16		20 23	20 22		20 30		20 37	20 47	20 53		21 08	21 13		21 18	21 25		21 38	21 43	
	d	20 08				20 23		20 30		20 38				21 08	21 14					21 39	21 44	
Kilpatrick	d							20 33						21 11						21 41		
Bowling	d							20 36						21 14						21 44		
Dumbarton East	d	20 16				20 30		20 40		20 46				21 18	21 23					21 49	21 54	
Dumbarton Central 227	d	20 19				20 33		20a43		20 51				21 21	21 26					21 51	21 56	
Dalreoch	d	20 22				20 35				20 53				21 23	21 28					21 53	21 58	
Renton	d	20 25								20 56				21 26						21 56		
Alexandria	d	20 27								20 58				21 28						21 58		
Balloch	a	20 32								21 03				21 33						22 03		
Cardross	d					20 40									21 33						22 03	
Craigendoran	d					20 46									21 40						22 09	
Helensburgh Central	a					20 49									21 44						22 12	
Helensburgh Upper 227	a																					

A From Motherwell
B From Larkhall
C From Whifflet

Table T226-F

Mondays to Fridays

21 May to 7 December

Edinburgh, Bathgate, Airdrie, Cumbernauld and Springburn - Glasgow - Milngavie, Dalmuir, Balloch and Helensburgh

		SR	SR A	SR B	SR	SR	SR C	SR C	SR B	SR	SR	SR	SR A	SR B	SR	SR	SR C	SR C	SR B	SR	SR	SR	SR A
Edinburgh 228,230	d					20 24					20 54					21 22					21 50		
Haymarket 228,230	d					20 28					20 58					21 27					21 54		
Edinburgh Park 230	d					20 33					21 03					21 32					21 59		
Uphall	d					20 41					21 11					21 40					22 07		
Livingston North	d					20 44					21 14					21 44					22 10		
Bathgate	a					20 49					21 19					21 48					22 15		
	d					20 49					21 19					21 49					22 19		
Armadale	d					20 53					21 23					21 53					22 23		
Blackridge	d					20 57					21 27					21 57					22 27		
Caldercruix	d					21 03					21 33					22 03					22 33		
Drumgelloch	d					21 07					21 37					22 07					22 37		
Airdrie	d					21 16					21 46					22 16					22 46		
Coatdyke	d					21 18					21 48					22 18					22 48		
Coatbridge Sunnyside	d					21 21					21 51					22 21					22 51		
Blairhill	d					21 23					21 53					22 23					22 53		
Easterhouse	d					21 27					21 57					22 27					22 57		
Garrowhill	d					21 30					22 00					22 30					23 00		
Shettleston	d					21 32					22 02					22 32					23 02		
Carntyne	d					21 34					22 04					22 34					23 04		
Cumbernauld	d	20 21			20 59					21 27		21 21			21 59					22 26		22 21	
Greenfaulds	d	20 23			21 01					21 29		21 23			22 01					22 28		22 23	
Springburn	d				21 22					21 50					22 24					22 49			
Barnhill	d				21 23					21 51					22 25					22 55			
Alexandra Parade	d				21 26					21 54					22 28					22 58			
Duke Street	d				21 28					21 58					22 30					23 00			
Bellgrove	d				21 30	21 38				22 00	22 08				22 32	22 38				23 02	23 08		
High Street	d				21 33	21 41				22 03	22 11				22 34	22 41				23 04	23 11		
Glasgow Queen St LL	a				21 35	21 43				22 05	22 13				22 36	22 43				23 06	23 13		
	d				21 39	21 47				22 09	22 17				22 39	22 47				23 09	23 17		
Charing Cross	d				21 45	21 50				22 15	22 20				22 46	22 50				23 15	23 20		
Argyle Street 225	d	21 21	21 25	21 37			21 50	21 56	22 07			22 20	22 26	22 37			22 49	22 55	23 07			23 22	23 26
Glasgow Central LL 225	a	21 22	21 27	21 39			21 51	21 58	22 09			22 22	22 27	22 39			22 51	22 56	23 08			23 24	23 27
	d	21 23	21 28	21 39			21 52	21 58	22 09			22 22	22 28	22 39			22 51	22 57	23 09			23 24	23 28
Anderston 225	d	21 24	21 29	21 41			21 53	22 00	22 11			22 24	22 29	22 41			22 53	22 58	23 10			23 25	23 29
Exhibition Centre 225	d	21 26	21 32	21 43			21 55	22 02	22 13			22 26	22 32	22 43			22 55	23 01	23 12			23 27	23 32
Partick 225	d	21 30	21 35	21 46	21 49	21 54	21 59	22 05	22 16	22 19	22 24	22 29	22 35	22 46	22 50	22 54	22 58	23 04	23 16	23 19	23 24	23 31	23 35
Hyndland	d	21 32	21 38	21 49	21 52	21 56	22 01	22 08	22 19	22 22	22 26	22 32	22 38	22 49	22 52	22 56	23 01	23 07	23 18	23 22	23 26	23 33	23 38
Jordanhill	d	21 34			21 54		22 03			22 24		22 34			22 54		23 03			23 24		23 35	
Scotstounhill	d	21 37			21 56		22 05			22 26		22 36			22 57		23 05			23 26		23 37	
Garscadden	d	21 39			21 59		22 08			22 29		22 38			22 59		23 08			23 29		23a39	
Yoker	d	21 41			22 01		22 10			22 31		22 41			23 01		23 10			23 31			
Clydebank	d	21 43			22 03		22 12			22 33		22 43			23 03		23 12			23 34			
Anniesland	d		21 41	21 52		21 59		22 11	22 22		22 29		22 41	22 52		22 59		23 10	23 21		23 29		23 41
Westerton	d		21 44	21 55		22 02		22 14	22 25		22 32		22 44	22 55		23 02		23 13	23 24		23 32		23 44
Bearsden	d			21 57					22 27					22 57					23 27				
Hillfoot	d			21 59					22 29					22 59					23 29				
Milngavie	a			22 03					22 33					23 03					23 33				
Drumchapel	d		21 46			22 04		22 16			22 35		22 46			23 05		23 15			23 35		23 46
Drumry	d		21 48			22 06		22 18			22 37		22 48			23 07		23 17			23 37		23 48
Singer	d		21 51			22 09		22 21			22 39		22 51			23 09		23 20			23 39		23 51
Dalmuir 227	a	21 47	21 53		22 06	22 11	22 16	22 23		22 36	22 42	22 47	22 53		23 06	23 12	23 16	23 22		23 37	23 42		23 53
	d				22 07	22 13				22 37	22 43				23 07	23 13				23 37	23 43		
Kilpatrick	d				22 09					22 39					23 10					23 39			
Bowling	d				22 12					22 42					23 13					23 42			
Dumbarton East	d				22 17	22 21				22 47	22 52				23 17	23 22				23 47	23 52		
Dumbarton Central 227	d				22 19	22 24				22 49	22 54				23 20	23 24				23 49	23 54		
Dalreoch	d				22 22	22 26				22 52	22 56				23 22	23 26				23 52	23 56		
Renton	d				22 25					22 55					23 25					23 55			
Alexandria	d				22 27					22 57					23 27					23 57			
Balloch	a				22 32					23 02					23 32					00 02			
Cardross	d					22 31					23 01					23 31					00 02		
Craigendoran	d					22 38					23 08					23 38					00 06		
Helensburgh Central	a					22 42					23 12					23 42					00 13		
Helensburgh Upper 227	a																						

A From Whifflet
B From Larkhall
C From Motherwell

Table T226-F

Mondays to Fridays
21 May to 7 December

Edinburgh, Bathgate, Airdrie, Cumbernauld and Springburn - Glasgow - Milngavie, Dalmuir, Balloch and Helensburgh

	SR	SR A	SR	SR FO B	SR	SR	SR	SR	SR
Edinburgh 228,230 d			22 23		22 52	23 09		23 39	23 56
Haymarket 228,230 ⇌ d			22 27		22 56	23 13		23 44	00 01
Edinburgh Park 230 d			22 32		23 01	23 18		23 50	00 05
Uphall d			22 40		23 09	23 26		23 58	00 13
Livingston North d			22 44		23 12	23 29		00 02	00 17
Bathgate a			22 48		23 17	23 34		00 05	00 21
d			22 49		23 17	23 35			
Armadale d			22 53		23 21	23 39			
Blackridge d			22 57		23 25	23 42			
Caldercruix d			23 03		23 31	23 49			
Drumgelloch d			23 07		23 35	23 52			
Airdrie d			23 22		23 39	23a55			
Coatdyke d			23 25		23 41				
Coatbridge Sunnyside d			23 28		23 43				
Blairhill d			23 31		23 46				
Easterhouse d			23 35		23 50				
Garrowhill d			23 38		23 52				
Shettleston d			23 41		23 55				
Carntyne d			23 44		23 57				
Cumbernauld d	22 59						23 29		
Greenfaulds d	23 01						23 31		
Springburn d	23 22						23 54		
Barnhill d	23 23						23 55		
Alexandra Parade d	23 26						23 58		
Duke Street d	23 29						00 03		
Bellgrove d	23 31		23 48		00 01		00 05		
High Street d	23 33		23 51		00 02		00 07		
Glasgow Queen St LL 10 ⇌ a	23 35		23 53		00 04		00 09		
d	23 37		23 54		00 05		00 10		
Charing Cross d	23 39		23 57		00 07		00 12		
Argyle Street 225 d		23 38		23 55					
Glasgow Central LL 15 225 a		23 39		23 57					
d		23 40		23 57					
Anderston 225 d		23 41		23 59					
Exhibition Centre 225 d		23 43		00 02					
Partick 225 ⇌ d	23 43	23 47	00 02	00 05	00 11		00 16		
Hyndland 8 d	23 46	23 49	00 03	00 07	00 13		00 18		
Jordanhill d	23 48						00 22		
Scotstounhill d	23 50						00 24		
Garscadden d	23 53				00a17		00a26		
Yoker d	23 55								
Clydebank d	23 57								
Anniesland d		23 52	00 06	00 11					
Westerton d		23 55	00 09	00 14					
Bearsden d		23 58							
Hillfoot d		00 01							
Milngavie a		00 03							
Drumchapel d			00 12	00 16					
Drumry d			00 14	00 18					
Singer d			00 16	00 21					
Dalmuir 227 a	23 58		00 19	00 23					
d	23 59		00 20						
Kilpatrick d	00 03								
Bowling d	00 06								
Dumbarton East d	00 11		00 28						
Dumbarton Central 227 d	00 13		00 31						
Dalreoch d	00 15		00 32						
Renton d	00 18								
Alexandria d	00 20								
Balloch a	00 25								
Cardross d			00 37						
Craigendoran d			00 42						
Helensburgh Central a			00 46						
Helensburgh Upper 227 a									

A From Larkhall
B From Motherwell

Table T226-F

Saturdays
26 May to 8 December

Edinburgh, Bathgate, Airdrie, Cumbernauld and Springburn - Glasgow - Milngavie, Dalmuir, Balloch and Helensburgh

	SR A	SR B	SR B	SR B	SR C	SR B	SR D	SR E	SR B	SR C	SR A	CS F ✕	CS G ✕	SR	SR	SR	SR	SR D	SR	SR	SR D	SR
Edinburgh 228,230 d												04 50										
Haymarket 228,230 ⇌ d				00 01																		
Edinburgh Park 230 d				00 05																		
Uphall d				00 13																		
Livingston North d			00 02	00 17																		
Bathgate a			00 05	00 21																		
d																						
Armadale d																						
Blackridge d																						
Caldercruix d																						
Drumgelloch d																						
Airdrie d															05 32					05 57		
Coatdyke d															05 34							
Coatbridge Sunnyside d															05 36					06 01		
Blairhill d															05 42							
Easterhouse d															05 46							
Garrowhill d															05 48							
Shettleston d															05 51					06 12		
Carntyne d															05 53					06 14		
Cumbernauld d																						05 56
Greenfaulds d																						05 58
Springburn d																						06 19
Barnhill d																						06 23
Alexandra Parade d																						06 26
Duke Street d										00 03												06 28
Bellgrove d									00 01	00 05					05 56					06 18		06 30
High Street d									00 02	00 07					05 59					06 20		06 32
Glasgow Queen St LL 10 ⇌ a									00 04	00 09					06 01					06 22		06 34
d									00 05	00 10		05u48	05u48		06 01					06 25		06 35
Charing Cross d									00 07	00 12					06 04					06 27		06 38
Argyle Street 225 d											00 11							06 18			06 29	
Glasgow Central LL 15 225 a											00 12							06 20			06 30	
d											00 13							06 20			06 30	
Anderston 225 d											00 14							06 22			06 32	
Exhibition Centre 225 d							00 02				00 16							06 24			06 34	
Partick 225 ⇌ d						00 02	00 05		00 11	00 16	00 20				06 08			06 27		06 31	06 37	06 42
Hyndland 8 d						00 03	00 07		00 13	00 18	00 22				06 10			06 30		06 34	06 40	06 44
Jordanhill d										00 22								06 32				06 47
Scotstounhill d										00 24								06 35				06 49
Garscadden d									00a17	00a26								06 38				06 52
Yoker d																		06 40				06 54
Clydebank d																		06 42				06 56
Anniesland d						00 06	00 11				00 25									06 37	06 43	
Westerton d						00 09	00 14				00 28									06 40	06 46	
Bearsden d											00 30									06 42		
Hillfoot d	00 01										00 32									06 44		
Milngavie a	00 03										00 36									06 48		
Drumchapel d						00 12	00 16														06 48	
Drumry d						00 14	00 18														06 50	
Singer d						00 16	00 21														06 53	
Dalmuir 227 a						00 19	00 23					06 03	06 03		06 19			06 46			06 55	06 59
d						00 20		05 39				06 04	06 04	06 11	06 20	06 29	06 38		06 51			07 00
Kilpatrick d					00 03											06 31						07 02
Bowling d					00 06											06 35						07 05
Dumbarton East d					00 11	00 28								06 18	06 28	06 39	06 46		06 58			07 10
Dumbarton Central 227 d					00 13	00 31		05 48				06 15	06 15	06 21	06 30	06a42	06 49		07 00			07a13
Dalreoch d					00 15	00 32								06 22	06 31		06 50		07 02			
Renton d					00 18									06 25			06 53					
Alexandria d					00 20									06 28			06 56					
Balloch a					00 25									06 32			07 00					
Cardross d		00 02				00 37									06 36				07 07			
Craigendoran d		00 06				00 42									06 41				07 12			
Helensburgh Central a		00 13				00 46									06 45				07 16			
Helensburgh Upper 227 a								06 00				06 29	06 29									

A From Larkhall
B From Edinburgh
C From Cumbernauld
D From Motherwell
E From Glasgow Queen Street to Oban
F To Fort William
G From London Euston to Fort William

Table T226-F

Saturdays

26 May to 8 December

Edinburgh, Bathgate, Airdrie, Cumbernauld and Springburn - Glasgow - Milngavie, Dalmuir, Balloch and Helensburgh

		SR A	SR	SR B	SR	SR B	SR	SR	SR A	SR	SR	SR	SR C	SR	SR	SR A	SR	SR B	SR	SR B	SR	SR	SR A
Edinburgh 228,230	d											06 08		06 20					06 39		06 51		
Haymarket 228,230 ⛴	d											06 13		06 24					06 43		06 55		
Edinburgh Park 230	d											06 17		06 29					06 48		07 01		
Uphall	d											06 25		06 37					06 57		07 09		
Livingston North	d											06 29		06 41					07 01		07 13		
Bathgate	a											06 33		06 46					07 05		07 17		
	d				06 05		06 19					06 34		06 49					07 06		07 19		
Armadale	d				06 10							06 38							07 10				
Blackridge	d				06 13							06 42							07 13				
Caldercruix	d				06 20							06 48							07 20				
Drumgelloch	d				06 23		06 32					06 52		07 02					07 23		07 32		
Airdrie	d		06 16		06 28		06 35			06 46		06 57		07 05			07 16		07 28		07 35		
Coatdyke	d		06 18				06 37			06 48				07 07			07 18		07 30		07 37		
Coatbridge Sunnyside	d		06 21		06 31		06 40			06 51		07 01		07 10			07 21		07 32		07 40		
Blairhill	d		06 23				06 42			06 53				07 12			07 23		07 35		07 42		
Easterhouse	d		06 27				06 46			06 57				07 16			07 27				07 46		
Garrowhill	d		06 30				06 49			07 00				07 19			07 30				07 49		
Shettleston	d		06 32		06 43					07 02		07 12					07 32		07 43				
Carntyne	d		06 34		06 45					07 04		07 14					07 34		07 45				
Cumbernauld	d							06 29			06 12				06 58							07 26	
Greenfaulds	d							06 31			06 14				07 00							07 28	
Springburn	d							06 52							07 21							07 49	
Barnhill	d							06 53							07 23							07 50	
Alexandra Parade	d							06 56							07 26							07 53	
Duke Street	d							06 58							07 28							07 55	
Bellgrove	d		06 38		06 48			07 00		07 08		07 18			07 30		07 38		07 48			07 59	
High Street	d		06 40		06 50		06 56	07 02		07 10		07 20		07 26	07 32		07 40		07 50		07 56	08 02	
Glasgow Queen St LL **10** ⛴	a		06 42		06 52		06 58	07 04		07 12		07 22		07 28	07 34		07 42		07 52		07 58	08 04	
	d		06 42		06 55		07 02	07 06		07 12		07 25		07 31	07 36		07 42		07 55		08 01	08 07	
Charing Cross	d		06 44		06 58		07 05	07 09		07 15		07 28		07 35	07 39		07 45		07 57		08 03	08 09	
Argyle Street 225	d	06 35		06 48		06 58			07 07		07 18		07 26			07 37		07 49		07 55			08 08
Glasgow Central LL **15** 225	a	06 36		06 50		06 59			07 09		07 20		07 28			07 39		07 50		07 57			08 10
	d	06 37		06 51		07 00			07 09		07 21		07 28			07 39		07 51		07 57			08 10
Anderston 225	d	06 39		06 52		07 01			07 11		07 22		07 30			07 41		07 52		07 59			08 12
Exhibition Centre 225	d	06 41		06 54		07 03			07 13		07 24		07 32			07 43		07 54		08 01			08 14
Partick 225 ⛴	d	06 45	06 48	06 58	07 02	07 07	07 10	07 13	07 16	07 19	07 28	07 32	07 35	07 39	07 43	07 46	07 49	07 58	08 01	08 04	08 07	08 13	08 17
Hyndland **3**	d	06 47	06 51	07 00	07 04	07 09	07 12	07 15	07 19	07 22	07 30	07 34	07 38	07 42	07 45	07 49	07 52	08 00	08 04	08 07	08 10	08 16	08 20
Jordanhill	d			07 02				07 17			07 32				07 47			08 02				08 18	
Scotstounhill	d			07 05				07 20			07 35				07 50			08 05				08 21	
Garscadden	d			07 07				07 22			07 37				07 52			08 07				08 23	
Yoker	d			07 09				07 25			07 39				07 55			08 09				08 26	
Clydebank	d			07 11				07 27			07 41				07 57			08 11				08 28	
Anniesland	d	06 50	06 54		07 07	07 12			07 22	07 25		07 37	07 41			07 52	07 55		08 07	08 11			08 23
Westerton	d	06 53	06 57		07 10	07 15			07 25	07 28		07 40	07 44			07 55	07 58		08 10	08 14			08 26
Bearsden	d	06 56			07 13				07 28			07 43				07 57			08 13				08 28
Hillfoot	d	06 58			07 15				07 30			07 45				07 59			08 15				08 30
Milngavie	a	07 02			07 18				07 33			07 48				08 03			08 18				08 34
Drumchapel	d		07 00			07 18				07 30			07 46				08 00			08 16			
Drumry	d		07 02			07 20				07 32			07 48				08 02			08 18			
Singer	d		07 04			07 22				07 35			07 51				08 05			08 21			
Dalmuir 227	a		07 07	07 15		07 25	07 19	07 30		07 37	07 45		07 53	07 49	08 00		08 07	08 15		08 23	08 21	08 31	
	d		07 08				07 21	07 30		07 38				07 51	08 00		08 08				08 21	08 31	
Kilpatrick	d							07 33							08 03							08 34	
Bowling	d							07 36							08 06							08 37	
Dumbarton East	d		07 16				07 28	07 40		07 46				07 58	08 10		08 16				08 29	08 41	
Dumbarton Central 227	d		07 19				07 30	07a43		07 49				08 00	08a13		08 19				08 31	08a44	
Dalreoch	d		07 20				07 32			07 50				08 02			08 20				08 32		
Renton	d		07 23							07 53							08 23						
Alexandria	d		07 26							07 56							08 26						
Balloch	a		07 30							08 00							08 30						
Cardross	d						07 37							08 07							08 37		
Craigendoran	d						07 42							08 12							08 43		
Helensburgh Central	a						07 46							08 16							08 46		
Helensburgh Upper 227	a																						

A From Larkhall
B From Motherwell
C From Whifflet

Table T226-F

Saturdays

26 May to 8 December

Edinburgh, Bathgate, Airdrie, Cumbernauld and Springburn - Glasgow - Milngavie, Dalmuir, Balloch and Helensburgh

		SR	SR ◇ A	SR	SR	SR	SR B	SR	SR C	SR	SR D	SR	SR D	SR	SR	SR C	SR	SR	SR	SR B	SR	SR
Edinburgh 228,230	d				07 07	07 21						07 37		07 49					08 08		08 21	
Haymarket 228,230 ⛴	d				07 11	07 25						07 42		07 54					08 12		08 27	
Edinburgh Park 230	d				07 18	07 30						07 48		08 03					08 18		08 32	
Uphall	d				07 26	07 38						07 56		08 12					08 27		08 40	
Livingston North	d				07 29	07 42						07 59		08 15					08 30		08 44	
Bathgate	a				07 34	07 46						08 04		08 20					08 35		08 48	
	d				07 35	07 49						08 05		08 20					08 35		08 49	
Armadale	d				07 39							08 09							08 39			
Blackridge	d				07 42							08 12							08 43			
Caldercruix	d				07 49							08 19							08 49			
Drumgelloch	d				07 52	08 01						08 22		08 33					08 53		09 02	
Airdrie	d	07 46			07 57	08 05				08 16		08 27		08 36			08 46		08 57		09 05	
Coatdyke	d	07 48			07 59	08 07				08 18		08 29		08 38			08 48				09 07	
Coatbridge Sunnyside	d	07 51			08 02	08 09				08 21		08 32		08 41			08 51		09 01		09 10	
Blairhill	d	07 53			08 04	08 12				08 23		08 34		08 43			08 53				09 12	
Easterhouse	d	07 57				08 16				08 27				08 47			08 57				09 16	
Garrowhill	d	08 00				08 18				08 30				08 50			09 00				09 19	
Shettleston	d	08 02			08 10					08 32		08 42					09 02		09 12			
Carntyne	d	08 04			08 12					08 34		08 44					09 04		09 14			
Cumbernauld	d			07 13				07 59							08 27			08 12				08 59
Greenfaulds	d			07 15				08 01							08 29			08 14				09 01
Springburn	d							08 22							08 50							09 22
Barnhill	d							08 23							08 51							09 23
Alexandra Parade	d							08 26							08 54							09 26
Duke Street	d							08 28							08 58							09 28
Bellgrove	d	08 08			08 16			08 30		08 38		08 48			09 00		09 08		09 18			09 30
High Street	d	08 10			08 18	08 26		08 32		08 40		08 50		08 57	09 02		09 10		09 20		09 26	09 33
Glasgow Queen St LL **10** ⛴	a	08 12			08 20	08 28		08 34		08 42		08 52		08 59	09 04		09 12		09 22		09 28	09 35
	d	08 12			08 25	08 31		08 36		08 42		08 55		09 02	09 06		09 12		09 25		09 32	09 36
Charing Cross	d	08 16			08 27	08 33		08 39		08 46		08 58		09 05	09 09		09 15		09 28		09 34	09 38
Argyle Street 225	d			08 18			08 29		08 38		08 50		08 56			09 07		09 20		09 25		
Glasgow Central LL **15** 225	a			08 20			08 31		08 40		08 51		08 57			09 09		09 22		09 26		
	d			08 20			08 31		08 40		08 52		08 58			09 09		09 22		09 28		
Anderston 225	d			08 22			08 33		08 42		08 53		08 59			09 10		09 24		09 29		
Exhibition Centre 225	d			08 24			08 36		08 44		08 55		09 01			09 12		09 26		09 32		
Partick 225 ⛴	d	08 20		08 27	08 31	08 37	08 40	08 43	08 47	08 50	08 59	09 02	09 05	09 10	09 13	09 16	09 19	09 29	09 32	09 35	09 39	09 42
Hyndland **3**	d	08 22		08 30	08 33	08 39	08 42	08 45	08 50	08 53	09 01	09 04	09 07	09 12	09 15	09 18	09 22	09 32	09 35	09 38	09 41	09 45
Jordanhill	d			08 32				08 47			09 03				09 17			09 34				09 47
Scotstounhill	d			08 34				08 50			09 06				09 20			09 36				09 49
Garscadden	d			08 36				08 52			09 08				09 22			09 38				09 52
Yoker	d			08 39				08 55			09 10				09 25			09 41				09 54
Clydebank	d			08 41				08 57			09 12				09 27			09 43				09 56
Anniesland	d	08 26			08 37		08 45		08 53	08 56		09 07	09 11			09 21	09 25		09 38	09 41		
Westerton	d	08 29			08 40		08 48		08 56	08 59		09 10	09 14			09 24	09 28		09 41	09 44		
Bearsden	d				08 42				08 58			09 13				09 27			09 44			
Hillfoot	d				08 44				09 00			09 15				09 29			09 46			
Milngavie	a				08 48				09 04			09 18				09 32			09 49			
Drumchapel	d	08 31					08 51			09 01			09 16				09 30			09 46		
Drumry	d	08 33					08 53			09 03			09 18				09 32			09 48		
Singer	d	08 36					08 55			09 06			09 21				09 35			09 51		
Dalmuir 227	a	08 38		08 45		08 49	08 58	09 00		09 08	09 16		09 23	09 20	09 30		09 37	09 47		09 53	09 50	09 59
	d	08 38	08 42			08 50		09 00		09 09				09 21	09 30		09 38				09 51	10 00
Kilpatrick	d							09 03							09 33							10 03
Bowling	d							09 06							09 36							10 06
Dumbarton East	d	08 46				08 57		09 10		09 16				09 29	09 40		09 46				09 59	10 10
Dumbarton Central 227	d	08 48	08 52			08 59		09a13		09 19				09 31	09a43		09 49				10 01	10a13
Dalreoch	d	08 49				09 01				09 20				09 32			09 50				10 03	
Renton	d	08 52								09 23							09 53					
Alexandria	d	08 55								09 26							09 56					
Balloch	a	08 59								09 30							10 00					
Cardross	d					09 06								09 37							10 08	
Craigendoran	d					09 11								09 44							10 13	
Helensburgh Central	a					09 14								09 47							10 16	
Helensburgh Upper 227	a		09 05																			

A From Glasgow Queen Street to Oban
B From Whifflet
C From Larkhall
D From Motherwell

Table T226-F

Saturdays
26 May to 8 December

Edinburgh, Bathgate, Airdrie, Cumbernauld and Springburn - Glasgow - Milngavie, Dalmuir, Balloch and Helensburgh

		SR A	SR	SR B	SR	SR B	SR	SR	SR A	SR	SR	SR	SR C	SR	SR ◇ D	SR	SR A	SR	SR B	SR	SR B	SR	SR
Edinburgh 228,230	d				08 39		08 52					09 11		09 21						09 38		09 51	
Haymarket 228,230	d				08 45		08 56					09 15		09 27						09 43		09 56	
Edinburgh Park 230	d				08 50		09 03					09 20		09 32						09 48		10 01	
Uphall	d				08 58		09 11					09 28		09 40						09 56		10 09	
Livingston North	d				09 01		09 15					09 31		09 44						10 00		10 12	
Bathgate	a				09 06		09 19					09 36		09 48						10 04		10 17	
	d				09 07		09 20					09 37		09 50						10 05		10 19	
Armadale	d				09 11							09 41								10 09			
Blackridge	d				09 15							09 45								10 12			
Caldercruix	d				09 21							09 51								10 19			
Drumgelloch	d				09 25		09 33					09 55		10 03						10 22		10 32	
Airdrie	d		09 16		09 29		09 36			09 46		09 59		10 06				10 16		10 27		10 35	
Coatdyke	d		09 18				09 38			09 48				10 08				10 18				10 37	
Coatbridge Sunnyside	d		09 21		09 33		09 41			09 51		10 03		10 11				10 21		10 31		10 40	
Blairhill	d		09 23				09 43			09 53				10 13				10 23				10 42	
Easterhouse	d		09 27				09 47			09 57				10 17				10 27				10 46	
Garrowhill	d		09 30				09 50			10 00				10 20				10 30				10 49	
Shettleston	d		09 32		09 44					10 02		10 14						10 32		10 42			
Carntyne	d		09 34		09 46					10 04		10 16						10 34		10 44			
Cumbernauld	d							09 29			09 22					09 55							10 27
Greenfaulds	d							09 31			09 24					09 57							10 29
Springburn	d							09 52								10 22							10 52
Barnhill	d							09 53								10 23							10 53
Alexandra Parade	d							09 56								10 26							10 56
Duke Street	d							09 58								10 28							10 58
Bellgrove	d		09 38		09 50			10 00		10 08		10 20				10 30		10 38		10 48			11 00
High Street	d		09 40		09 52		09 57	10 02		10 10		10 22		10 27		10 32		10 40		10 50		10 56	11 03
Glasgow Queen St LL 10	a		09 42		09 54		09 59	10 04		10 12		10 24		10 29		10 34		10 42		10 52		10 58	11 05
	d		09 42		09 55		10 02	10 06		10 13		10 25		10 32		10 36		10 42		10 55		11 02	11 07
Charing Cross	d		09 45		09 57		10 05	10 09		10 15		10 27		10 35		10 39		10 45		10 58		11 06	11 09
Argyle Street 225	d	09 37		09 49		09 56			10 08		10 20		10 25				10 37		10 49		10 57		
Glasgow Central LL 15 225	a	09 39		09 51		09 58			10 09		10 22		10 26				10 39		10 51		10 58		
	d	09 39		09 51		09 58			10 09		10 22		10 27				10 39		10 51		10 59		
Anderston 225	d	09 40		09 53		10 00			10 11		10 23		10 29				10 41		10 53		11 00		
Exhibition Centre 225	d	09 42		09 55		10 02			10 13		10 25		10 31				10 43		10 55		11 02		
Partick 225	d	09 46	09 50	09 58	10 01	10 05	10 10	10 13	10 16	10 19	10 29	10 32	10 35	10 40		10 43	10 46	10 49	10 58	11 02	11 06	11 10	11 13
Hyndland 8	d	09 48	09 52	10 01	10 04	10 08	10 12	10 15	10 19	10 22	10 31	10 34	10 37	10 42		10 45	10 49	10 52	11 01	11 04	11 08	11 12	11 15
Jordanhill	d			10 03				10 17			10 33					10 47			11 03				11 17
Scotstounhill	d			10 05				10 20			10 36					10 50			11 05				11 20
Garscadden	d			10 08				10 22			10 38					10 52			11 07				11 22
Yoker	d			10 10				10 25			10 41					10 55			11 10				11 25
Clydebank	d			10 12				10 27			10 43					10 57			11 12				11 27
Anniesland	d	09 51	09 55		10 07	10 11			10 22	10 25		10 37	10 40				10 52	10 55		11 07	11 11		
Westerton	d	09 54	09 58		10 10	10 14			10 25	10 28		10 40	10 43				10 55	10 58		11 10	11 14		
Bearsden	d	09 57			10 12				10 27			10 43					10 57			11 13			
Hillfoot	d	09 59			10 14				10 29			10 45					10 59			11 15			
Milngavie	a	10 02			10 18				10 33			10 48					11 03			11 18			
Drumchapel	d		10 00			10 16				10 30			10 46					11 00			11 17		
Drumry	d		10 02			10 18				10 32			10 48					11 02			11 19		
Singer	d		10 05			10 21				10 35			10 50					11 05			11 21		
Dalmuir 227	a		10 07	10 16		10 23	10 21	10 30		10 37	10 47		10 53	10 50		11 01		11 07	11 16		11 24	11 20	11 30
	d		10 08				10 22	10 30		10 38				10 50	10 57	11 01		11 08				11 21	11 30
Kilpatrick	d							10 33								11 04							11 33
Bowling	d							10 36								11 07							11 36
Dumbarton East	d		10 16				10 29	10 40		10 46				10 58		11 11		11 16				11 29	11 40
Dumbarton Central 227	d		10 19				10 31	10a43		10 49				11 00	11 06	11a14		11 19				11 31	11a43
Dalreoch	d		10 20				10 33			10 50				11 01				11 20				11 32	
Renton	d		10 23							10 53								11 23					
Alexandria	d		10 26							10 56								11 26					
Balloch	a		10 30							11 00								11 30					
Cardross	d						10 38							11 06								11 37	
Craigendoran	d						10 43							11 11								11 43	
Helensburgh Central	a						10 46							11 14								11 46	
Helensburgh Upper 227	a														11 24								

A From Larkhall
B From Motherwell
C From Whifflet
D From Glasgow Queen Street to Oban

Table T226-F

Saturdays
26 May to 8 December

Edinburgh, Bathgate, Airdrie, Cumbernauld and Springburn - Glasgow - Milngavie, Dalmuir, Balloch and Helensburgh

		SR A	SR	SR	SR	SR B	SR	SR	SR A	SR	SR C	SR	SR C	SR	SR	SR A	SR	SR ◇ D	SR	SR	SR B	SR
Edinburgh 228,230	d				10 08		10 23					10 39		10 48						11 08		11 20
Haymarket 228,230	d				10 12		10 28					10 43		10 53						11 13		11 24
Edinburgh Park 230	d				10 18		10 33					10 48		10 59						11 18		11 29
Uphall	d				10 26		10 41					10 56		11 07						11 26		11 37
Livingston North	d				10 29		10 45					10 59		11 10						11 29		11 41
Bathgate	a				10 34		10 49					11 04		11 15						11 34		11 45
	d				10 36		10 50					11 05		11 19						11 35		11 49
Armadale	d				10 40							11 09								11 39		
Blackridge	d				10 44							11 12								11 42		
Caldercruix	d				10 50							11 19								11 49		
Drumgelloch	d				10 54		11 02					11 22		11 32						11 52		12 02
Airdrie	d		10 46		10 58		11 06			11 16		11 27		11 35			11 46			11 57		12 07
Coatdyke	d		10 48				11 08			11 18				11 37			11 48					12 09
Coatbridge Sunnyside	d		10 51		11 02		11 10			11 21		11 31		11 40			11 51			12 01		12 11
Blairhill	d		10 53				11 13			11 23				11 42			11 53					12 14
Easterhouse	d		10 57				11 17			11 27				11 46			11 57					12 18
Garrowhill	d		11 00				11 19			11 30				11 49			12 00					12 20
Shettleston	d		11 02		11 13					11 32		11 42					12 02			12 12		
Carntyne	d		11 04		11 15					11 34		11 44					12 04			12 14		
Cumbernauld	d			10 21				10 59							11 29				11 21			
Greenfaulds	d			10 23				11 01							11 31				11 23			
Springburn	d							11 22							11 52							
Barnhill	d							11 23							11 53							
Alexandra Parade	d							11 26							11 56							
Duke Street	d							11 28							11 58							
Bellgrove	d		11 08		11 19			11 30		11 38		11 48			12 00		12 08			12 18		
High Street	d		11 10		11 21		11 27	11 32		11 40		11 50		11 56	12 02		12 10			12 20		12 27
Glasgow Queen St LL 10	a		11 12		11 23		11 29	11 34		11 42		11 52		11 58	12 04		12 12			12 22		12 29
	d		11 12		11 25		11 32	11 36		11 42		11 55		12 02	12 06		12 12			12 25		12 31
Charing Cross	d		11 15		11 28		11 35	11 38		11 45		11 58		12 06	12 09		12 15			12 28		12 34
Argyle Street 225	d	11 07		11 20		11 27			11 36		11 49		11 56			12 07			12 21		12 25	
Glasgow Central LL 15 225	a	11 09		11 22		11 28			11 38		11 51		11 57			12 09			12 22		12 27	
	d	11 09		11 22		11 29			11 38		11 51		11 58			12 09			12 22		12 28	
Anderston 225	d	11 11		11 23		11 30			11 40		11 53		11 59			12 10			12 24		12 29	
Exhibition Centre 225	d	11 13		11 25		11 32			11 42		11 55		12 02			12 12			12 26		12 32	
Partick 225	d	11 16	11 20	11 29	11 32	11 36	11 39	11 42	11 45	11 49	11 58	12 02	12 05	12 10	12 13	12 16	12 19		12 29	12 32	12 35	12 38
Hyndland 8	d	11 19	11 22	11 31	11 34	11 38	11 41	11 45	11 48	11 52	12 01	12 04	12 08	12 12	12 15	12 18	12 21		12 32	12 35	12 38	12 41
Jordanhill	d			11 33				11 47			12 03				12 17				12 34			
Scotstounhill	d			11 36				11 50			12 05				12 20				12 36			
Garscadden	d			11 38				11 52			12 07				12 22				12 38			
Yoker	d			11 41				11 55			12 10				12 25				12 41			
Clydebank	d			11 43				11 57			12 12				12 27				12 43			
Anniesland	d	11 22	11 25		11 37	11 45			11 51	11 55		12 07	12 11			12 21	12 24			12 38	12 41	
Westerton	d	11 25	11 28		11 40	11 48			11 54	11 58		12 10	12 14			12 24	12 27			12 41	12 44	
Bearsden	d	11 27			11 43				11 57			12 13				12 27				12 43		
Hillfoot	d	11 29			11 45				11 59			12 15				12 29				12 45		
Milngavie	a	11 33			11 48				12 03			12 18				12 33				12 49		
Drumchapel	d		11 30			11 50				12 00			12 16				12 30				12 46	
Drumry	d		11 32			11 52				12 02			12 18				12 32				12 48	
Singer	d		11 35			11 55				12 05			12 21				12 34				12 51	
Dalmuir 227	a		11 37	11 47		11 57	11 50	12 00		12 07	12 16		12 23	12 20	12 30		12 37		12 47		12 53	12 50
	d		11 38				11 51	12 00		12 08				12 21	12 30		12 37	12 42				12 51
Kilpatrick	d							12 03							12 33							
Bowling	d							12 06							12 36							
Dumbarton East	d		11 46				11 59	12 10		12 16				12 29	12 40		12 45					12 59
Dumbarton Central 227	d		11 49				12 01	12a13		12 19				12 31	12a43		12 47	12 51				13 01
Dalreoch	d		11 50				12 02			12 20				12 32			12 48					13 02
Renton	d		11 53							12 23							12 51					
Alexandria	d		11 56							12 26							12 54					
Balloch	a		12 00							12 30							12 58					
Cardross	d						12 07							12 37								13 07
Craigendoran	d						12 12							12 43								13 13
Helensburgh Central	a						12 16							12 46								13 16
Helensburgh Upper 227	a																	13 03				

A From Larkhall
B From Whifflet
C From Motherwell
D From Glasgow Queen Street to Oban

Table T226-F

Saturdays
26 May to 8 December

Edinburgh, Bathgate, Airdrie, Cumbernauld and Springburn - Glasgow - Milngavie, Dalmuir, Balloch and Helensburgh

		SR	SR A	SR	SR B	SR	SR B	SR	SR	SR A	SR	SR	SR	SR C	SR	SR	SR A	SR	SR B	SR	SR B	SR	SR
Edinburgh 228,230	d					11 38		11 50					12 08		12 22					12 37		12 53	
Haymarket 228,230	d					11 43		11 54					12 13		12 26					12 41		12 59	
Edinburgh Park 230	d					11 49		11 59					12 18		12 31					12 47		13 05	
Uphall	d					11 57		12 07					12 26		12 39					12 55		13 13	
Livingston North	d					12 00		12 11					12 30		12 43					12 59		13 16	
Bathgate	a					12 05		12 15					12 34		12 47					13 03		13 21	
	d					12 06		12 20					12 35		12 49					13 04		13 22	
Armadale	d					12 10							12 39							13 08			
Blackridge	d					12 13							12 43							13 12			
Caldercruix	d					12 20							12 49							13 18			
Drumgelloch	d					12 23		12 32					12 53		13 02					13 22		13 34	
Airdrie	d			12 16		12 28		12 36			12 46		12 57		13 05			13 16		13 27		13 38	
Coatdyke	d			12 18				12 38			12 48				13 07			13 18				13 40	
Coatbridge Sunnyside	d			12 21		12 32		12 40			12 51		13 01		13 10			13 21		13 31		13 42	
Blairhill	d			12 23				12 43			12 53				13 12			13 23				13 45	
Easterhouse	d			12 27				12 47			12 57				13 16			13 27				13 49	
Garrowhill	d			12 30				12 49			13 00				13 19			13 30				13 51	
Shettleston	d			12 32		12 43					13 02		13 12					13 32		13 42			
Carntyne	d			12 34		12 45					13 04		13 14					13 34		13 44			
Cumbernauld	d	11 56							12 29			12 21				12 59							13 29
Greenfaulds	d	11 58							12 31			12 23				13 01							13 31
Springburn	d	12 21							12 52							13 24							13 52
Barnhill	d	12 23							12 53							13 25							13 53
Alexandra Parade	d	12 26							12 56							13 28							13 56
Duke Street	d	12 27							12 58							13 30							13 58
Bellgrove	d	12 29		12 38		12 49			13 00		13 08		13 18			13 32		13 38		13 48			14 00
High Street	d	12 32		12 40		12 51		12 59	13 02		13 10		13 20		13 26	13 34		13 40		13 50		13 58	14 03
Glasgow Queen St LL	a	12 34		12 42		12 53		13 01	13 04		13 12		13 22		13 28	13 36		13 42		13 52		14 00	14 05
	d	12 36		12 44		12 55		13 02	13 06		13 13		13 25		13 33	13 37		13 42		13 55		14 02	14 06
Charing Cross	d	12 38		12 46		12 58		13 04	13 08		13 15		13 28		13 36	13 39		13 45		13 58		14 05	14 09
Argyle Street 225	d		12 38		12 50		12 56			13 06		13 20		13 25			13 38		13 49		13 56		
Glasgow Central LL 225	a		12 39		12 52		12 58			13 07		13 22		13 27			13 39		13 51		13 57		
	d		12 39		12 52		12 58			13 08		13 22		13 28			13 39		13 51		13 58		
Anderston 225	d		12 41		12 53		13 00			13 09		13 23		13 29			13 41		13 53		14 00		
Exhibition Centre 225	d		12 43		12 55		13 02			13 11		13 25		13 32			13 43		13 55		14 02		
Partick 225	d	12 42	12 46	12 50	12 59	13 02	13 05	13 08	13 12	13 15	13 19	13 29	13 32	13 35	13 40	13 43	13 46	13 49	13 58	14 02	14 05	14 09	14 13
Hyndland	d	12 45	12 49	12 52	13 01	13 04	13 08	13 11	13 14	13 17	13 22	13 31	13 34	13 38	13 42	13 45	13 49	13 52	14 01	14 04	14 08	14 12	14 15
Jordanhill	d	12 47			13 03				13 17			13 33				13 47			14 03				14 17
Scotstounhill	d	12 49			13 06				13 20			13 36				13 50			14 05				14 20
Garscadden	d	12 52			13 08				13 22			13 38				13 52			14 07				14 22
Yoker	d	12 54			13 10				13 25			13 40				13 55			14 10				14 25
Clydebank	d	12 56			13 12				13 27			13 42				13 57			14 12				14 27
Anniesland	d		12 52	12 56		13 07	13 11			13 20	13 25		13 37	13 41			13 52	13 55		14 08	14 12		
Westerton	d		12 55	12 59		13 10	13 14			13 23	13 28		13 40	13 44			13 55	13 58		14 11	14 15		
Bearsden	d		12 57			13 13				13 26			13 43				13 57			14 14			
Hillfoot	d		12 59			13 15				13 28			13 45				13 59			14 16			
Milngavie	a		13 03			13 18				13 32			13 48				14 03			14 19			
Drumchapel	d			13 01			13 16				13 30			13 46				14 00			14 17		
Drumry	d			13 03			13 18				13 32			13 48				14 02			14 19		
Singer	d			13 06			13 21				13 35			13 51				14 05			14 22		
Dalmuir 227	a	12 59		13 08	13 17		13 23	13 22	13 30		13 37	13 46		13 53	13 50	14 00		14 07	14 16		14 24	14 20	14 30
	d	13 00		13 08				13 23	13 30		13 38				13 51	14 00		14 08				14 21	14 30
Kilpatrick	d	13 02							13 33							14 03							14 33
Bowling	d	13 05							13 36							14 06							14 36
Dumbarton East	d	13 10		13 16				13 30	13 40		13 46				13 59	14 10		14 16				14 29	14 40
Dumbarton Central 227	d	13a13		13 19				13 32	13a43		13 49				14 01	14a13		14 19				14 31	14a43
Dalreoch	d			13 20				13 34			13 50				14 02			14 20				14 32	
Renton	d			13 23							13 53							14 23					
Alexandria	d			13 26							13 56							14 26					
Balloch	a			13 30							14 00							14 30					
Cardross	d							13 39							14 07							14 37	
Craigendoran	d							13 44							14 13							14 43	
Helensburgh Central	a							13 47							14 16							14 46	
Helensburgh Upper 227	a																						

A From Larkhall B From Motherwell C From Whifflet

Table T226-F

Saturdays
26 May to 8 December

Edinburgh, Bathgate, Airdrie, Cumbernauld and Springburn - Glasgow - Milngavie, Dalmuir, Balloch and Helensburgh

		SR A	SR	SR	SR	SR B	SR	SR	SR A	SR	SR C	SR	SR C	SR	SR	SR A	SR	SR	SR	SR B	SR	SR	SR A
Edinburgh 228,230	d				13 09		13 22					13 38		13 49					14 11		14 22		
Haymarket 228,230	d				13 13		13 26					13 43		13 54					14 16		14 27		
Edinburgh Park 230	d				13 18		13 31					13 47		14 01					14 21		14 33		
Uphall	d				13 26		13 39					13 55		14 09					14 29		14 42		
Livingston North	d				13 30		13 43					13 59		14 13					14 33		14 45		
Bathgate	a				13 34		13 47					14 03		14 17					14 37		14 50		
	d				13 36		13 49					14 04		14 19					14 38		14 50		
Armadale	d				13 40							14 08							14 42				
Blackridge	d				13 43							14 12							14 45				
Caldercruix	d				13 50							14 18							14 52				
Drumgelloch	d				13 53		14 02					14 22		14 32					14 55		15 03		
Airdrie	d		13 46		13 58		14 05			14 16		14 27		14 35			14 46		15 00		15 06		
Coatdyke	d		13 48				14 07			14 18				14 37			14 48				15 08		
Coatbridge Sunnyside	d		13 51		14 01		14 10			14 21		14 31		14 40			14 51		15 03		15 13		
Blairhill	d		13 53				14 12			14 23				14 42			14 53				15 15		
Easterhouse	d		13 57				14 16			14 27				14 46			14 57				15 19		
Garrowhill	d		14 00				14 19			14 30				14 49			15 00				15 22		
Shettleston	d		14 02		14 13					14 32		14 42					15 02		15 15				
Carntyne	d		14 04		14 15					14 34		14 44					15 04		15 17				
Cumbernauld	d			13 20				13 59							14 29			14 21				14 56	
Greenfaulds	d			13 22				14 01							14 31			14 23				14 58	
Springburn	d							14 24							14 52							15 21	
Barnhill	d							14 25							14 53							15 23	
Alexandra Parade	d							14 28							14 56							15 26	
Duke Street	d							14 30							14 58							15 28	
Bellgrove	d		14 08		14 18			14 32		14 38		14 48			15 00		15 08		15 20			15 30	
High Street	d		14 10		14 20		14 26	14 34		14 40		14 50		14 56	15 02		15 10		15 23		15 29	15 33	
Glasgow Queen St LL	a		14 12		14 22		14 28	14 36		14 42		14 52		14 58	15 04		15 12		15 25		15 31	15 35	
	d		14 12		14 25		14 32	14 37		14 42		14 55		15 02	15 06		15 12		15 26		15 32	15 36	
Charing Cross	d		14 15		14 28		14 35	14 39		14 45		14 58		15 06	15 09		15 15		15 28		15 35	15 39	
Argyle Street 225	d	14 08		14 21		14 25			14 37		14 49		14 54			15 08		15 20		15 26			15 38
Glasgow Central LL 225	a	14 09		14 22		14 27			14 39		14 51		14 56			15 09		15 22		15 27			15 39
	d	14 09		14 22		14 28			14 39		14 51		14 58			15 09		15 22		15 28			15 39
Anderston 225	d	14 11		14 24		14 29			14 40		14 53		14 59			15 11		15 23		15 29			15 41
Exhibition Centre 225	d	14 13		14 26		14 32			14 42		14 55		15 02			15 13		15 25		15 32			15 43
Partick 225	d	14 16	14 19	14 29	14 32	14 35	14 39	14 43	14 46	14 49	14 58	15 02	15 05	15 10	15 13	15 16	15 19	15 29	15 32	15 35	15 39	15 43	15 46
Hyndland	d	14 19	14 22	14 32	14 35	14 38	14 41	14 45	14 48	14 52	15 01	15 04	15 08	15 12	15 15	15 19	15 22	15 31	15 34	15 38	15 41	15 45	15 49
Jordanhill	d			14 34				14 47			15 03				15 17			15 33				15 47	
Scotstounhill	d			14 36				14 50			15 05				15 20			15 36				15 50	
Garscadden	d			14 38				14 52			15 07				15 22			15 38				15 52	
Yoker	d			14 41				14 55			15 10				15 25			15 40				15 55	
Clydebank	d			14 43				14 57			15 12				15 27			15 42				15 57	
Anniesland	d	14 22	14 25		14 38	14 41			14 51	14 55		15 07	15 11			15 22	15 25		15 37	15 41			15 52
Westerton	d	14 25	14 28		14 41	14 44			14 54	14 58		15 10	15 14			15 25	15 28		15 40	15 44			15 55
Bearsden	d	14 27			14 43				14 57			15 13				15 27			15 43				15 57
Hillfoot	d	14 29			14 45				14 59			15 15				15 29			15 45				15 59
Milngavie	a	14 33			14 49				15 03			15 18				15 33			15 48				16 03
Drumchapel	d		14 30			14 46				15 00			15 16				15 30			15 46			
Drumry	d		14 32			14 48				15 02			15 18				15 32			15 48			
Singer	d		14 35			14 51				15 05			15 21				15 35			15 51			
Dalmuir 227	a		14 37	14 47		14 53	14 51	15 00		15 07	15 16		15 23	15 20	15 30		15 37	15 46		15 53	15 50	16 01	
	d		14 38				14 52	15 00		15 08				15 21	15 30		15 38				15 51	16 02	
Kilpatrick	d							15 03							15 33							16 04	
Bowling	d							15 06							15 36							16 07	
Dumbarton East	d		14 46				14 59	15 10		15 16				15 29	15 40		15 46				15 59	16 12	
Dumbarton Central 227	d		14 49				15 01	15a13		15 19				15 31	15a43		15 49				16 01	16a15	
Dalreoch	d		14 50				15 03			15 20				15 32			15 50				16 02		
Renton	d		14 53							15 23							15 53						
Alexandria	d		14 56							15 26							15 56						
Balloch	a		15 00							15 30							16 00						
Cardross	d						15 08							15 37							16 07		
Craigendoran	d						15 13							15 43							16 12		
Helensburgh Central	a						15 16							15 46							16 16		
Helensburgh Upper 227	a																						

A From Larkhall B From Whifflet C From Motherwell

Table T226-F

Saturdays

26 May to 8 December

Edinburgh, Bathgate, Airdrie, Cumbernauld and Springburn - Glasgow - Milngavie, Dalmuir, Balloch and Helensburgh

		SR	SR	SR	SR	SR	SR	SR	SR	SR	SR	SR	SR	SR	SR	SR	SR	SR	SR	SR	SR	SR
			A		A			B				C		◇ D		B		A		A		
Edinburgh 228,230	d			14 37		14 49					15 08		15 21						15 41		15 52	
Haymarket 228,230 ⇌	d			14 42		14 54					15 12		15 26						15 46		15 57	
Edinburgh Park 230	d			14 48		14 59					15 17		15 32						15 50		16 02	
Uphall	d			14 56		15 08					15 25		15 40						15 58		16 10	
Livingston North	d			14 59		15 11					15 29		15 44						16 02		16 14	
Bathgate	a			15 04		15 16					15 33		15 48						16 06		16 18	
	d			15 05		15 19					15 35		15 51						16 07		16 20	
Armadale	d			15 09							15 39								16 11			
Blackridge	d			15 12							15 42								16 15			
Caldercruix	d			15 19							15 49								16 21			
Drumgelloch	d			15 22		15 31					15 52		16 03						16 25		16 33	
Airdrie	d	15 16		15 27		15 35			15 46		15 57		16 07				16 16		16 29		16 36	
Coatdyke	d	15 18				15 37			15 48				16 09				16 18				16 38	
Coatbridge Sunnyside	d	15 21		15 31		15 40			15 51		16 01		16 12				16 21		16 33		16 41	
Blairhill	d	15 23				15 42			15 53				16 14				16 23				16 43	
Easterhouse	d	15 27				15 46			15 57				16 18				16 27				16 47	
Garrowhill	d	15 30				15 49			16 00				16 21				16 30				16 50	
Shettleston	d	15 32		15 42					16 02		16 12						16 32		16 44			
Carntyne	d	15 34		15 44					16 04		16 15						16 34		16 46			
Cumbernauld	d						15 29			15 21					15 59							16 29
Greenfaulds	d						15 31			15 23					16 01							16 31
Springburn	d						15 52								16 24							16 52
Barnhill	d						15 53								16 25							16 53
Alexandra Parade	d						15 56								16 28							16 56
Duke Street	d						15 58								16 30							16 58
Bellgrove	d	15 38		15 48			16 00		16 08		16 18				16 32		16 38		16 50			17 00
High Street	d	15 40		15 50		15 56	16 03		16 10		16 20		16 28		16 34		16 40		16 52		16 57	17 02
Glasgow Queen St LL 10 ⇌	a	15 42		15 52		15 58	16 05		16 12		16 22		16 30		16 36		16 42		16 54		16 59	17 04
	d	15 42		15 55		16 02	16 06		16 12		16 25		16 32		16 37		16 42		16 55		17 01	17 06
Charing Cross	d	15 45		15 58		16 05	16 09		16 15		16 28		16 35		16 39		16 45		16 58		17 04	17 09
Argyle Street 225	d		15 49		15 55			16 07		16 21		16 26				16 37		16 49		16 55		
Glasgow Central LL 15 225	a		15 51		15 57			16 09		16 22		16 27				16 39		16 51		16 56		
	d		15 51		15 58			16 09		16 23		16 28				16 39		16 52		16 57		
Anderston 225	d		15 53		15 59			16 11		16 24		16 29				16 41		16 53		16 59		
Exhibition Centre 225	d		15 55		16 02			16 13		16 26		16 32				16 43		16 55		17 01		
Partick 225 ⇌	d	15 49	15 58	16 02	16 05	16 10	16 13	16 16	16 19	16 30	16 32	16 35	16 40		16 43	16 46	16 49	16 59	17 02	17 05	17 09	17 13
Hyndland 8	d	15 52	16 01	16 04	16 08	16 12	16 15	16 19	16 22	16 32	16 34	16 38	16 42		16 45	16 49	16 52	17 01	17 04	17 07	17 11	17 15
Jordanhill	d		16 03				16 17			16 34					16 47			17 03				17 17
Scotstounhill	d		16 05				16 20			16 36					16 50			17 05				17 20
Garscadden	d		16 08				16 22			16 38					16 52			17 08				17 22
Yoker	d		16 10				16 25			16 41					16 55			17 10				17 25
Clydebank	d		16 12				16 27			16 43					16 57			17 12				17 27
Anniesland	d	15 55		16 07	16 11			16 22	16 25		16 37	16 41				16 52	16 55		17 07	17 11		
Westerton	d	15 58		16 10	16 14			16 25	16 28		16 40	16 44				16 55	16 58		17 10	17 14		
Bearsden	d			16 13				16 27			16 43					16 57			17 13			
Hillfoot	d			16 15				16 29			16 45					16 59			17 15			
Milngavie	a			16 18				16 33			16 48					17 03			17 18			
Drumchapel	d	16 00			16 16				16 30			16 46					17 00			17 16		
Drumry	d	16 02			16 18				16 32			16 48					17 02			17 18		
Singer	d	16 05			16 21				16 35			16 51					17 05			17 21		
Dalmuir 227	a	16 07	16 16		16 23	16 20	16 30		16 37	16 47		16 53	16 51		17 00		17 07	17 16		17 23	17 19	17 30
	d	16 07				16 21	16 30		16 38				16 52	16 57	17 01		17 08				17 19	17 30
Kilpatrick	d						16 33								17 03							17 33
Bowling	d						16 36								17 06							17 36
Dumbarton East	d	16 16				16 29	16 40		16 46				16 59		17 11		17 16				17 27	17 40
Dumbarton Central 227	d	16 18				16 31	16a43		16 49				17 01	17 06	17a14		17 19				17 29	17a43
Dalreoch	d	16 20				16 32			16 50				17 03				17 20				17 31	
Renton	d	16 23							16 53								17 23					
Alexandria	d	16 25							16 56								17 26					
Balloch	a	16 29							17 00								17 30					
Cardross	d					16 37							17 08								17 36	
Craigendoran	d					16 43							17 13								17 41	
Helensburgh Central	a					16 46							17 16								17 44	
Helensburgh Upper 227	a													17 20								

A From Motherwell
B From Larkhall
C From Whifflet
D From Glasgow Queen Street to Oban

Table T226-F

Saturdays

26 May to 8 December

Edinburgh, Bathgate, Airdrie, Cumbernauld and Springburn - Glasgow - Milngavie, Dalmuir, Balloch and Helensburgh

		SR	SR	SR	SR	SR	SR	SR	SR	SR	SR	SR	SR	SR	SR	SR	SR	SR	SR	SR	SR	SR	SR
		A				B			A		C		C			A		◇ D			B		
Edinburgh 228,230	d				16 07		16 21					16 42		16 48						17 08		17 19	
Haymarket 228,230 ⇌	d				16 11		16 25					16 46		16 53						17 13		17 24	
Edinburgh Park 230	d				16 19		16 30					16 51		17 01						17 18		17 30	
Uphall	d				16 27		16 38					16 59		17 10						17 26		17 38	
Livingston North	d				16 30		16 42					17 03		17 14						17 30		17 43	
Bathgate	a				16 35		16 47					17 07		17 18						17 34		17 47	
	d				16 35		16 49					17 08		17 19						17 35		17 50	
Armadale	d				16 39							17 12								17 39			
Blackridge	d				16 43							17 15								17 43			
Caldercruix	d				16 49							17 22								17 49			
Drumgelloch	d				16 53		17 02					17 25		17 32						17 53		18 02	
Airdrie	d		16 46		16 57		17 05			17 16		17 29		17 35			17 46			17 57		18 06	
Coatdyke	d		16 48				17 07			17 18				17 37			17 48					18 08	
Coatbridge Sunnyside	d		16 51		17 01		17 10			17 21		17 33		17 40			17 51			18 01		18 10	
Blairhill	d		16 53				17 12			17 23				17 42			17 53					18 13	
Easterhouse	d		16 57				17 16			17 27				17 46			17 57					18 17	
Garrowhill	d		17 00				17 19			17 30				17 49			18 00					18 19	
Shettleston	d		17 02		17 12					17 32		17 44					18 02			18 12			
Carntyne	d		17 04		17 14					17 34		17 46					18 04			18 14			
Cumbernauld	d			16 20				16 59							17 26				17 21				17 59
Greenfaulds	d			16 22				17 01							17 28				17 23				18 01
Springburn	d							17 22							17 49								18 22
Barnhill	d							17 23							17 50								18 23
Alexandra Parade	d							17 26							17 53								18 26
Duke Street	d							17 28							17 56								18 28
Bellgrove	d		17 08		17 18			17 30		17 38		17 50			18 00		18 08			18 18			18 30
High Street	d		17 10		17 20		17 26	17 32		17 40		17 52		17 56	18 02		18 10			18 20		18 26	18 32
Glasgow Queen St LL 10 ⇌	a		17 12		17 22		17 28	17 34		17 42		17 54		17 58	18 04		18 12			18 22		18 28	18 34
	d		17 12		17 25		17 32	17 36		17 42		17 55		18 02	18 06		18 12			18 25		18 32	18 37
Charing Cross	d		17 15		17 28		17 35	17 39		17 45		17 58		18 05	18 09		18 15			18 28		18 35	18 39
Argyle Street 225	d	17 07		17 19		17 24			17 37		17 49		17 55			18 07			18 21		18 26		
Glasgow Central LL 15 225	a	17 09		17 20		17 25			17 39		17 51		17 57			18 09			18 22		18 27		
	d	17 09		17 21		17 26			17 39		17 51		17 57			18 09			18 23		18 28		
Anderston 225	d	17 11		17 22		17 28			17 41		17 53		17 59			18 11			18 24		18 30		
Exhibition Centre 225	d	17 13		17 25		17 32			17 43		17 55		18 01			18 13			18 26		18 32		
Partick 225 ⇌	d	17 16	17 20	17 29	17 32	17 35	17 39	17 43	17 46	17 49	17 58	18 02	18 05	18 10	18 13	18 16	18 19		18 30	18 32	18 35	18 40	18 43
Hyndland 8	d	17 19	17 22	17 31	17 34	17 38	17 42	17 45	17 49	17 52	18 01	18 04	18 07	18 12	18 15	18 19	18 22		18 32	18 35	18 38	18 42	18 45
Jordanhill	d			17 33				17 47			18 03				18 17				18 34				18 47
Scotstounhill	d			17 36				17 50			18 05				18 20				18 36				18 50
Garscadden	d			17 38				17 52			18 07				18 22				18 38				18 52
Yoker	d			17 40				17 55			18 10				18 25				18 41				18 55
Clydebank	d			17 42				17 57			18 12				18 27				18 43				18 57
Anniesland	d	17 22	17 25		17 37	17 41			17 52	17 55		18 07	18 11			18 22	18 25			18 38	18 41		
Westerton	d	17 25	17 28		17 40	17 44			17 55	17 58		18 10	18 14			18 25	18 28			18 41	18 44		
Bearsden	d	17 27			17 43				17 57			18 13				18 27				18 43			
Hillfoot	d	17 29			17 45				17 59			18 15				18 29				18 45			
Milngavie	a	17 33			17 48				18 03			18 18				18 33				18 49			
Drumchapel	d		17 30			17 46				18 00			18 16				18 30				18 46		
Drumry	d		17 32			17 48				18 02			18 18				18 32				18 48		
Singer	d		17 35			17 51				18 05			18 21				18 35				18 51		
Dalmuir 227	a		17 37	17 46		17 53	17 50	18 00		18 07	18 16		18 23	18 20	18 30		18 38		18 47		18 53	18 50	19 01
	d		17 38				17 51	18 00		18 08				18 21	18 30		18 38	18 41				18 50	19 01
Kilpatrick	d							18 03							18 33								19 04
Bowling	d							18 06							18 36								19 07
Dumbarton East	d		17 46				17 59	18 10		18 16				18 29	18 40		18 45					18 59	19 11
Dumbarton Central 227	d		17 49				18 01	18a13		18 19				18 31	18a43		18 47	18 50				19 01	19a14
Dalreoch	d		17 50				18 02			18 20				18 32			18 49					19 02	
Renton	d		17 53							18 23							18 52						
Alexandria	d		17 56							18 26							18 54						
Balloch	a		18 00							18 30							18 58						
Cardross	d						18 07							18 37								19 07	
Craigendoran	d						18 13							18 43								19 13	
Helensburgh Central	a						18 16							18 46								19 16	
Helensburgh Upper 227	a																	19 04					

A From Larkhall
B From Whifflet
C From Motherwell
D From Glasgow Queen Street to Oban

Table T226-F

Saturdays

26 May to 8 December

Edinburgh, Bathgate, Airdrie, Cumbernauld and Springburn - Glasgow - Milngavie, Dalmuir, Balloch and Helensburgh

		SR A	SR	SR B	SR	SR B	SR	SR	SR A	SR	SR	SR	SR C	SR	SR	SR A	SR	SR B	SR	SR B	SR	SR
Edinburgh	228,230 d				17 38		17 53				18 07			18 24					18 40		18 48	19 08
Haymarket	228,230 ⇌ d				17 43		17 57				18 11			18 28					18 45		18 53	19 13
Edinburgh Park	230 d				17 48		18 03				18 19			18 33					18 50		18 59	19 20
Uphall	d				17 56		18 11				18 27			18 41					18 58		19 07	19 28
Livingston North	d				18 00		18 14				18 31			18 44					19 02		19 11	19 31
Bathgate	a				18 04		18 19				18 35			18 49					19 06		19 15	19 36
	d				18 05		18 20				18 36			18 49					19 07		19 19	
Armadale	d				18 09						18 40								19 11		19 23	
Blackridge	d				18 13						18 43								19 14		19 27	
Caldercruix	d				18 19						18 50								19 21		19 33	
Drumgelloch	d				18 23		18 32				18 53			19 02					19 24		19 37	
Airdrie	d		18 16		18 28		18 36			18 46	18 58			19 05			19 16		19 29		19 40	
Coatdyke	d		18 18				18 38			18 48				19 07			19 18					
Coatbridge Sunnyside	d		18 21		18 31		18 40			18 51	19 02			19 10			19 21		19 32		19 44	
Blairhill	d		18 23				18 43			18 53				19 12			19 23					
Easterhouse	d		18 27				18 47			18 57				19 16			19 27					
Garrowhill	d		18 30				18 49			19 00				19 19			19 30					
Shettleston	d		18 32		18 43					19 02	19 13						19 32		19 44			
Carntyne	d		18 34		18 45					19 04	19 15						19 34		19 46			
Cumbernauld	d							18 26				18 18			19 01							
Greenfaulds	d							18 28				18 20			19 03							
Springburn	d							18 52							19 25							
Barnhill	d							18 53							19 26							
Alexandra Parade	d							18 56							19 29							
Duke Street	d							18 59							19 31							
Bellgrove	d		18 38		18 48			19 01		19 08	19 19				19 33		19 38		19 49			
High Street	d		18 40		18 51		18 57	19 03		19 10	19 21			19 26	19 35		19 40		19 51		19 59	
Glasgow Queen St LL 10	⇌ a		18 42		18 53		18 59	19 05		19 12	19 23			19 28	19 37		19 42		19 53		20 01	
	d		18 42		18 55		19 02	19 06		19 13	19 23			19 33	19 37		19 42		19 55		20 01	
Charing Cross	d		18 45		18 58		19 06	19 09		19 16	19 25			19 35	19 39		19 45		19 58		20 05	
Argyle Street	225 d	18 37		18 50		18 55			19 09			19 22	19 26			19 38		19 50		19 55		
Glasgow Central LL 15	225 a	18 39		18 52		18 57			19 10			19 23	19 27			19 39		19 51		19 56		
	d	18 39		18 52		18 57			19 11			19 24	19 28			19 40		19 52		19 57		
Anderston	225 d	18 41		18 54		18 59			19 12			19 26	19 29			19 41		19 53		19 59		
Exhibition Centre	225 d	18 43		18 56		19 01			19 14			19 28	19 32			19 43		19 55		20 01		
Partick	225 ⇌ d	18 47	18 50	18 59	19 02	19 05	19 10	19 13	19 18	19 20	19 29	19 32	19 35	19 40	19 43	19 47	19 50	19 59	20 02	20 05	20 09	
Hyndland 3	d	18 49	18 52	19 01	19 04	19 07	19 13	19 15	19 20	19 23	19 31	19 34	19 38	19 42	19 46	19 49	19 52	20 01	20 04	20 07	20 12	
Jordanhill	d			19 03				19 17				19 36			19 48			20 03				
Scotstounhill	d			19 06				19 20				19 39			19 50			20 05				
Garscadden	d			19 08				19 22				19 41			19 52			20 07				
Yoker	d			19 10				19 25				19 43			19 55			20 10				
Clydebank	d			19 12				19 27				19 45			19 57			20 12				
Anniesland	d	18 52	18 55		19 08	19 11			19 23	19 26	19 34		19 41			19 52	19 55		20 07	20 11		
Westerton	d	18 55	18 58		19 11	19 14			19 26	19 29	19 40		19 44			19 55	19 58		20 10	20 14		
Bearsden	d	18 57			19 14				19 28		19 42					19 57			20 13			
Hillfoot	d	18 59			19 16				19 30		19 44					19 59			20 15			
Milngavie	a	19 03			19 19				19 34		19 48					20 03			20 18			
Drumchapel	d		19 00			19 16				19 31			19 46				20 00			20 16		
Drumry	d		19 02			19 18				19 33			19 48				20 02			20 18		
Singer	d		19 05			19 21				19 36			19 51				20 05			20 21		
Dalmuir	227 a		19 08	19 16		19 23	19 21	19 30		19 38		19 49	19 53	19 52	20 00		20 07	20 16		20 23	20 22	
	d		19 08				19 22	19 30		19 39				19 53	20 00		20 08				20 23	
Kilpatrick	d							19 33							20 03							
Bowling	d							19 36							20 06							
Dumbarton East	d		19 16				19 29	19 40		19 46				20 00	20 10		20 16				20 30	
Dumbarton Central	227 d		19 18				19 31	19a43		19 49				20 02	20a13		20 19				20 33	
Dalreoch	d		19 20				19 33			19 52				20 04			20 22				20 35	
Renton	d		19 23							19 55							20 25					
Alexandria	d		19 25							19 57							20 27					
Balloch	a		19 30							20 02							20 32					
Cardross	d						19 38							20 09							20 40	
Craigendoran	d						19 43							20 14							20 45	
Helensburgh Central	a						19 46							20 17							20 49	
Helensburgh Upper	227 a																					

A From Larkhall B From Motherwell C From Whifflet

Table T226-F

Saturdays

26 May to 8 December

Edinburgh, Bathgate, Airdrie, Cumbernauld and Springburn - Glasgow - Milngavie, Dalmuir, Balloch and Helensburgh

		SR	SR A	SR	SR	SR B	SR A	SR	SR	SR	SR C	SR C	SR A	SR	SR	SR	SR	SR B	SR A	SR	SR	SR C	SR C
Edinburgh	228,230 d								19 19	19 41					19 49	20 09					20 22		
Haymarket	228,230 ⇌ d								19 26	19 45					19 53	20 14					20 26		
Edinburgh Park	230 d								19 31	19 50					19 58	20 19					20 32		
Uphall	d								19 40	19 58					20 06	20 27					20 40		
Livingston North	d								19 44	20 02					20 09	20 30					20 43		
Bathgate	a								19 48	20 06					20 14	20 35					20 48		
	d								19 50						20 18						20 49		
Armadale	d								19 54						20 22						20 53		
Blackridge	d								19 57						20 25						20 57		
Caldercruix	d								20 04						20 32						21 03		
Drumgelloch	d								20 07						20 35						21 07		
Airdrie	d			19 46					20 17						20 48						21 16		
Coatdyke	d			19 48					20 19						20 50						21 18		
Coatbridge Sunnyside	d			19 51					20 21						20 52						21 21		
Blairhill	d			19 53					20 24						20 55						21 23		
Easterhouse	d			19 57					20 28						20 59						21 27		
Garrowhill	d			20 00					20 30						21 01						21 30		
Shettleston	d			20 02					20 33						21 04						21 32		
Carntyne	d			20 04					20 35						21 06						21 34		
Cumbernauld	d	19 27			19 21			19 59						20 27			20 21			20 59			
Greenfaulds	d	19 29			19 23			20 01						20 29			20 23			21 01			
Springburn	d	19 51						20 22						20 51						21 22			
Barnhill	d	19 53						20 24						20 53						21 23			
Alexandra Parade	d	19 56						20 27						20 56						21 26			
Duke Street	d	19 58						20 29						20 58						21 28			
Bellgrove	d	20 00		20 08				20 31	20 39					21 00	21 09					21 30	21 38		
High Street	d	20 03		20 10				20 33	20 41					21 03	21 12					21 33	21 41		
Glasgow Queen St LL 10	⇌ a	20 05		20 12				20 35	20 43					21 05	21 14					21 35	21 43		
	d	20 06		20 12				20 40	20 48					21 09	21 19					21 39	21 47		
Charing Cross	d	20 08		20 15				20 45	20 50					21 15	21 21					21 45	21 50		
Argyle Street	225 d		20 08		20 21	20 25	20 39				20 52	20 59	21 09				21 21	21 26	21 37			21 50	21 56
Glasgow Central LL 15	225 a		20 09		20 23	20 27	20 41				20 54	21 00	21 10				21 23	21 27	21 39			21 51	21 58
	d		20 10		20 23	20 28	20 41				20 54	21 01	21 11				21 23	21 28	21 39			21 52	21 58
Anderston	225 d		20 11		20 25	20 30	20 43				20 56	21 02	21 12				21 24	21 29	21 41			21 53	22 00
Exhibition Centre	225 d		20 13		20 27	20 32	20 45				20 58	21 04	21 14				21 26	21 32	21 43			21 55	22 02
Partick	225 ⇌ d	20 12	20 17	20 19	20 30	20 35	20 48	20 51	20 55		21 01	21 08	21 18	21 21	21 25		21 30	21 35	21 46	21 49	21 54	21 59	22 05
Hyndland 3	d	20 15	20 19	20 22	20 32	20 38	20 50	20 53	20 57		21 03	21 10	21 20	21 23	21 28		21 32	21 38	21 49	21 52	21 56	22 01	22 08
Jordanhill	d	20 17			20 34			20 55			21 05			21 25			21 34			21 54		22 03	
Scotstounhill	d	20 19			20 37			20 58			21 08			21 28			21 37			21 56		22 05	
Garscadden	d	20 22			20 39			21 00			21 10			21 30			21 39			21 59		22 08	
Yoker	d	20 24			20 41			21 03			21 12			21 33			21 41			22 01		22 10	
Clydebank	d	20 26			20 43			21 05			21 14			21 35			21 43			22 03		22 12	
Anniesland	d		20 22	20 25		20 41	20 53		21 00			21 13	21 23		21 31			21 41	21 52		21 59		22 11
Westerton	d		20 25	20 28		20 44	20 56		21 03			21 16	21 26		21 34			21 44	21 55		22 02		22 14
Bearsden	d		20 27				20 59						21 28						21 57				
Hillfoot	d		20 29				21 01						21 30						21 59				
Milngavie	a		20 33				21 04						21 34						22 03				
Drumchapel	d			20 30		20 46			21 06			21 18			21 36			21 46			22 04		22 16
Drumry	d			20 32		20 48			21 08			21 20			21 38			21 48			22 06		22 18
Singer	d			20 35		20 51			21 10			21 23			21 41			21 51			22 09		22 21
Dalmuir	227 a	20 30		20 37	20 47	20 53		21 08	21 13		21 18	21 25		21 38	21 43		21 47	21 53		22 06	22 11	22 16	22 23
	d	20 30		20 38				21 08	21 14					21 39	21 44					22 07	22 13		
Kilpatrick	d	20 33						21 11						21 41						22 09			
Bowling	d	20 36						21 14						21 44						22 12			
Dumbarton East	d	20 40		20 46				21 18	21 23					21 49	21 54					22 17	22 21		
Dumbarton Central	227 d	20a43		20 51				21 21	21 26					21 51	21 56					22 19	22 24		
Dalreoch	d			20 53				21 23	21 28					21 53	21 58					22 22	22 26		
Renton	d			20 56				21 26						21 56						22 25			
Alexandria	d			20 58				21 28						21 58						22 27			
Balloch	a			21 03				21 33						22 03						22 32			
Cardross	d								21 33						22 03						22 31		
Craigendoran	d								21 40						22 09						22 38		
Helensburgh Central	a								21 44						22 13						22 42		
Helensburgh Upper	227 a																						

A From Larkhall B From Whifflet C From Motherwell

Table T226-F

Saturdays
26 May to 8 December

Edinburgh, Bathgate, Airdrie, Cumbernauld and Springburn - Glasgow - Milngavie, Dalmuir, Balloch and Helensburgh

	SR A	SR	SR	SR	SR B		SR A	SR	SR	SR C	SR C	SR A	SR	SR	SR		SR B	SR	SR A	SR	SR	SR	SR	SR
Edinburgh 228,230 d			20 54						21 21					21 50						22 22	22 51	23 09		23 40
Haymarket 228,230 ⇌ d			20 58						21 26					21 55						22 26	22 55	23 13		23 44
Edinburgh Park 230 d			21 03						21 32					21 59						22 31	23 00	23 18		23 49
Uphall d			21 11						21 40					22 07						22 39	23 08	23 26		23 57
Livingston North d			21 14						21 44					22 11						22 43	23 11	23 29		00 01
Bathgate a			21 19						21 48					22 15						22 47	23 16	23 34		00 05
d			21 19						21 49					22 19						22 49	23 17	23 35		
Armadale d			21 23						21 53					22 23						22 53	23 21	23 39		
Blackridge d			21 27						21 57					22 27						22 57	23 25	23 42		
Caldercruix d			21 33						22 03					22 33						23 03	23 31	23 49		
Drumgelloch d			21 37						22 07					22 37						23 07	23 35	23 52		
Airdrie d			21 46						22 16					22 46						23 22	23 39	23a55		
Coatdyke d			21 48						22 18					22 48						23 25	23 41			
Coatbridge Sunnyside d			21 51						22 21					22 51						23 28	23 43			
Blairhill d			21 53						22 23					22 53						23 31	23 46			
Easterhouse d			21 57						22 27					22 57						23 35	23 50			
Garrowhill d			22 00						22 30					23 00						23 38	23 52			
Shettleston d			22 02						22 32					23 02						23 41	23 55			
Carntyne d			22 04						22 34					23 04						23 44	23 57			
Cumbernauld d		21 27		21 21				21 59					22 26		22 21			22 59					23 29	
Greenfaulds d		21 29		21 23				22 01					22 28		22 23			23 01					23 31	
Springburn d		21 50						22 24					22 49					23 22					23 54	
Barnhill d		21 51						22 25					22 55					23 23					23 55	
Alexandra Parade d		21 54						22 28					22 58					23 26					23 58	
Duke Street d		21 58						22 30					23 00					23 29					00 03	
Bellgrove d		22 00	22 08					22 32	22 38				23 02	23 08				23 31		23 48	00 01		00 05	
High Street d		22 03	22 11					22 34	22 41				23 04	23 11				23 33		23 51	00 02		00 07	
Glasgow Queen St LL ⇌ a		22 05	22 13					22 36	22 43				23 06	23 13				23 35		23 53	00 04		00 09	
d		22 09	22 17					22 39	22 47				23 09	23 17				23 37		23 54	00 05		00 10	
Charing Cross d		22 15	22 20					22 46	22 50				23 15	23 20				23 39		23 57	00 07		00 12	
Argyle Street 225 d	22 07			22 20	22 26		22 37			22 49	22 55	23 07			23 22		23 26		23 38					
Glasgow Central LL 225 a	22 09			22 22	22 27		22 39			22 51	22 56	23 08			23 24		23 27		23 39					
d	22 09			22 22	22 28		22 39			22 51	22 57	23 09			23 24		23 28		23 40					
Anderston 225 d	22 11			22 24	22 29		22 41			22 53	22 58	23 10			23 25		23 29		23 41					
Exhibition Centre 225 d	22 13			22 26	22 32		22 43			22 55	23 01	23 12			23 27		23 32		23 43					
Partick 225 ⇌ d	22 16	22 19	22 24	22 29	22 35		22 46	22 50	22 54	22 58	23 04	23 16	23 19	23 24	23 31		23 35	23 43	23 47	00 02	00 11		00 16	
Hyndland d	22 19	22 22	22 26	22 32	22 38		22 49	22 52	22 56	23 01	23 07	23 18	23 22	23 26	23 33		23 38	23 46	23 49	00 03	00 13		00 18	
Jordanhill d		22 24		22 34				22 54		23 03			23 24		23 35			23 48					00 22	
Scotstounhill d		22 26		22 36				22 57		23 05			23 26		23 37			23 50					00 24	
Garscadden d		22 29		22 38				22 59		23 08			23 29		23a39			23 53			00a17		00a26	
Yoker d		22 31		22 41				23 01		23 10			23 31					23 55						
Clydebank d		22 33		22 43				23 03		23 12			23 34					23 57						
Anniesland d	22 22		22 29		22 41		22 52		22 59		23 10	23 21		23 29			23 41		23 52	00 06				
Westerton d	22 25		22 32		22 44		22 55		23 02		23 13	23 24		23 32			23 44		23 55	00 09				
Bearsden d	22 27						22 57					23 27							23 58					
Hillfoot d	22 29						22 59					23 29							00 01					
Milngavie a	22 33						23 03					23 33							00 03					
Drumchapel d			22 35		22 46				23 05		23 15			23 35			23 46			00 12				
Drumry d			22 37		22 48				23 07		23 17			23 37			23 48			00 14				
Singer d			22 39		22 51				23 09		23 20			23 39			23 51			00 16				
Dalmuir 227 a		22 36	22 42	22 47	22 53			23 06	23 12	23 16	23 22		23 37	23 42			23 53	23 58		00 19				
d		22 37	22 43					23 07	23 13				23 37	23 43				23 59		00 20				
Kilpatrick d		22 39						23 10					23 39					00 03						
Bowling d		22 42						23 13					23 42					00 06						
Dumbarton East d		22 47	22 52					23 17	23 22				23 47	23 52				00 11		00 28				
Dumbarton Central 227 d		22 49	22 54					23 20	23 24				23 49	23 54				00 13		00 31				
Dalreoch d		22 52	22 56					23 22	23 26				23 52	23 56				00 15		00 32				
Renton d		22 55						23 25					23 55					00 18						
Alexandria d		22 57						23 27					23 57					00 20						
Balloch a		23 02						23 32					00 02					00 25						
Cardross d			23 01						23 31					00 01						00 37				
Craigendoran d			23 08						23 38					00 07						00 42				
Helensburgh Central a			23 12						23 42					00 10						00 46				
Helensburgh Upper 227 a																								

A From Larkhall
B From Whifflet
C From Motherwell

Table T226-F

Saturdays
26 May to 8 December

Edinburgh, Bathgate, Airdrie, Cumbernauld and Springburn - Glasgow - Milngavie, Dalmuir, Balloch and Helensburgh

	SR
Edinburgh 228,230 d	23 52
Haymarket 228,230 ⇌ d	23 57
Edinburgh Park 230 d	00 02
Uphall d	00 10
Livingston North d	00 14
Bathgate a	00 18
d	
Armadale d	
Blackridge d	
Caldercruix d	
Drumgelloch d	
Airdrie d	
Coatdyke d	
Coatbridge Sunnyside d	
Blairhill d	
Easterhouse d	
Garrowhill d	
Shettleston d	
Carntyne d	
Cumbernauld d	
Greenfaulds d	
Springburn d	
Barnhill d	
Alexandra Parade d	
Duke Street d	
Bellgrove d	
High Street d	
Glasgow Queen St LL ⇌ a	
d	
Charing Cross d	
Argyle Street 225 d	
Glasgow Central LL 225 a	
d	
Anderston 225 d	
Exhibition Centre 225 d	
Partick 225 ⇌ d	
Hyndland d	
Jordanhill d	
Scotstounhill d	
Garscadden d	
Yoker d	
Clydebank d	
Anniesland d	
Westerton d	
Bearsden d	
Hillfoot d	
Milngavie a	
Drumchapel d	
Drumry d	
Singer d	
Dalmuir 227 a	
d	
Kilpatrick d	
Bowling d	
Dumbarton East d	
Dumbarton Central 227 d	
Dalreoch d	
Renton d	
Alexandria d	
Balloch a	
Cardross d	
Craigendoran d	
Helensburgh Central a	
Helensburgh Upper 227 a	

Table T226-F

Sundays
20 May to 2 December

Edinburgh, Bathgate, Airdrie, Cumbernauld and Springburn - Glasgow - Milngavie, Dalmuir, Balloch and Helensburgh

	SR	SR	SR	SR	SR	SR	SR	SR	SR	SR	SR	SR	SR	SR	SR	SR	SR	SR	SR	SR	SR	SR
	A	B	A	A	C	A	A	C					◇ D	E	E		E	F	◇ G		H	I
Edinburgh 228,230 d													08 08							08 38		
Haymarket 228,230 d													08u12							08 42		
Edinburgh Park 230 d				00 02																08 48		
Uphall d				00 10																09 01		
Livingston North d			00 01	00 14																09 04		
Bathgate a			00 05	00 18																09 09		
d												08 06								09 09		
Armadale d												08 10								09 13		
Blackridge d												08 14								09 17		
Caldercruix d												08 20								09 23		
Drumgelloch d												08 24								09 27		
Airdrie d										07 57		08 27				08 57				09 30		
Coatdyke d										07 59		08 29				08 59				09 32		
Coatbridge Sunnyside d										08 02		08 32				09 02				09 35		
Blairhill d										08 05		08 35				09 05				09 37		
Easterhouse d										08 09		08 39				09 09				09 41		
Garrowhill d										08 11		08 41				09 11				09 44		
Shettleston d										08 14		08 44				09 14				09 46		
Carntyne d										08 16		08 46				09 16				09 48		
Cumbernauld d																						
Greenfaulds d																						
Springburn d																						
Barnhill d																						
Alexandra Parade d																						
Duke Street d								00 03														
Bellgrove d							00 01	00 05		08 19		08 49				09 19				09 52		
High Street d							00 02	00 07		08 21		08 51				09 21				09 54		
Glasgow Queen St LL a							00 04	00 09		08 23		08 53				09 23				09 56		
d							00 05	00 10		08 24		08 54				09 24				09 56		
Charing Cross d							00 07	00 12		08 27		08 57				09 27				09 58		
Argyle Street 225 d																					09 58	09 59
Glasgow Central LL 225 a																					09 59	10 00
d														09 04	09 15		09 34	09 45			10 04	10 04
Anderston 225 d																					10 05	10 05
Exhibition Centre 225 d														09 08	09 18		09 38	09 48			10 07	10 07
Partick 225 d						00 02	00 11	00 16		08 31		09 01		09 12	09 22	09 31	09 42	09 52		10 02	10 12	10 12
Hyndland d						00 03	00 13	00 18		08 34		09 04		09 16	09 24	09 34	09 45	09 54		10 05	10 15	10 15
Jordanhill d								00 22							09 26			09 56				
Scotstounhill d								00 24							09 29			09 59				
Garscadden d							00a17	00a26							09 31			10 01				
Yoker d									08 34		09 04				09 34			10 04				
Clydebank d									08 36		09 06				09 36			10 06				
Anniesland d						00 06				08 37		09 07		09 19		09 37	09 48			10 08	10 18	10 18
Westerton d						00 09				08 40		09 10		09 22		09 40	09 51			10 11	10 21	10 21
Bearsden d														09 25			09 55				10 25	10 25
Hillfoot d		00 01												09 27			09 57				10 27	10 27
Milngavie a		00 03												09 30			10 00				10 30	10 30
Drumchapel d						00 12				08 42		09 12				09 42				10 13		
Drumry d						00 14				08 44		09 14				09 44				10 15		
Singer d						00 16				08 47		09 17				09 47				10 18		
Dalmuir 227 a						00 19			08 39	08 49	09 09	09 19			09 39	09 49		10 09		10 20		
d						00 20			08 40	08 50	09 10	09 20	09u27		09 40	09 50		10 10	10 16	10 21		
Kilpatrick d					00 03				08 42		09 12				09 42			10 12				
Bowling d					00 06				08 45		09 15				09 45			10 15				
Dumbarton East d					00 11	00 28			08 50	08 58	09 20	09 28			09 50	09 58		10 20		10 28		
Dumbarton Central 227 d					00 13	00 31			08 52	09 00	09 22	09 30			09 52	10 00		10 22	10 26	10 30		
Dalreoch d					00 15	00 32			08 53	09 01	09 23	09 31			09 53	10 01		10 23		10 32		
Renton d					00 18				08 56		09 26				09 56			10 26				
Alexandria d					00 20				08 59		09 29				09 59			10 29				
Balloch a					00 25				09 03		09 33				10 03			10 33				
Cardross d	00 01					00 37				09 06		09 36				10 06				10 37		
Craigendoran d	00 07					00 42				09 11		09 41				10 11				10 42		
Helensburgh Central a	00 10					00 46				09 15		09 45				10 15				10 46		
Helensburgh Upper 227 a													09 49						10 38			

A not 20 May. From Edinburgh
B not 20 May. From Larkhall
C not 20 May. From Cumbernauld
D from 24 June until 26 August. To Oban
E From Motherwell
F From Larkhall. Forms tight booked connection out of 2C26.
G From Glasgow Queen Street to Oban
H from 16 September. From Motherwell
I until 9 September. From Rutherglen

Table T226-F

Sundays
20 May to 2 December

Edinburgh, Bathgate, Airdrie, Cumbernauld and Springburn - Glasgow - Milngavie, Dalmuir, Balloch and Helensburgh

	SR	SR	SR	SR	SR	SR	SR	SR	SR	SR	SR	SR	SR	SR	SR	SR	SR	SR	SR	SR	SR	SR
	A		B	C	D		B	C	A		C	B	E		B	C	◇ F	C	B		B	C
Edinburgh 228,230 d		09 06				09 38				10 06				10 40						11 10		
Haymarket 228,230 d		09 10				09 42				10 10				10 44						11 14		
Edinburgh Park 230 d		09 16				09 47				10 15				10 49						11 19		
Uphall d		09 29				10 00				10 28				10 57						11 27		
Livingston North d		09 32				10 03				10 31				11 00						11 30		
Bathgate a		09 37				10 08				10 36				11 05						11 35		
d		09 37				10 08				10 36				11 06						11 36		
Armadale d		09 41				10 12				10 40				11 10						11 40		
Blackridge d		09 45				10 16				10 44				11 14						11 44		
Caldercruix d		09 51				10 22				10 50				11 20						11 50		
Drumgelloch d		09 55				10 26				10 54				11 24						11 54		
Airdrie d		09 58				10 29				10 57				11 27						11 57		
Coatdyke d		10 00				10 31				10 59				11 29						11 59		
Coatbridge Sunnyside d		10 03				10 34				11 02				11 32						12 02		
Blairhill d		10 06				10 36				11 05				11 35						12 05		
Easterhouse d		10 10				10 40				11 09				11 39						12 09		
Garrowhill d		10 12				10 43				11 11				11 41						12 11		
Shettleston d		10 15				10 45				11 14				11 44						12 14		
Carntyne d		10 17				10 47				11 16				11 46						12 16		
Cumbernauld d																						
Greenfaulds d																						
Springburn d																						
Barnhill d																						
Alexandra Parade d																						
Duke Street d																						
Bellgrove d		10 20				10 51				11 19				11 49						12 19		
High Street d		10 22				10 53				11 21				11 51						12 21		
Glasgow Queen St LL a		10 24				10 55				11 23				11 53						12 23		
d		10 25				10 55				11 24				11 54						12 24		
Charing Cross d		10 27				10 57				11 27				11 57						12 27		
Argyle Street 225 d	10 14		10 28	10 29	10 43		10 58	10 59	11 14		11 29	11 30	11 43		11 58	11 59		12 14	12 15		12 28	12 29
Glasgow Central LL 225 a	10 16		10 29	10 30	10 44		10 59	11 00	11 15		11 30	11 31	11 44		12 00	12 00		12 16	12 16		12 29	12 30
d	10 16		10 34	10 34	10 45		11 04	11 04	11 16		11 34	11 34	11 45		12 04	12 04		12 16	12 16		12 34	12 34
Anderston 225 d	10 18		10 35	10 35	10 46		11 06	11 06	11 17		11 35	11 35	11 46		12 05	12 05		12 18	12 18		12 35	12 35
Exhibition Centre 225 d	10 20		10 37	10 37	10 48		11 08	11 08	11 19		11 37	11 37	11 48		12 07	12 07		12 20	12 20		12 37	12 37
Partick 225 d	10 23	10 31	10 42	10 42	10 52	11 01	11 12	11 12	11 23	11 32	11 42	11 42	11 52	12 01	12 12	12 12		12 23	12 23	12 31	12 42	12 42
Hyndland d	10 25	10 34	10 45	10 45	10 54	11 04	11 15	11 15	11 25	11 34	11 45	11 45	11 54	12 04	12 15	12 15		12 25	12 25	12 34	12 45	12 45
Jordanhill d	10 27				10 56				11 27				11 56					12 27	12 27			
Scotstounhill d	10 30				10 59				11 29				11 59					12 30	12 30			
Garscadden d	10 32				11 01				11 31				12 01					12 32	12 32			
Yoker d	10 34				11 04				11 34				12 04					12 34	12 34			
Clydebank d	10 36				11 06				11 36				12 06					12 36	12 36			
Anniesland d		10 37	10 48	10 48		11 07	11 18	11 18		11 37	11 48	11 48		12 07	12 18	12 18				12 37	12 48	12 48
Westerton d		10 40	10 51	10 51		11 10	11 21	11 21		11 40	11 51	11 51		12 10	12 21	12 21				12 40	12 51	12 51
Bearsden d			10 55	10 55			11 25	11 25			11 55	11 55			12 25	12 25					12 55	12 55
Hillfoot d			10 57	10 57			11 27	11 27			11 57	11 57			12 27	12 27					12 57	12 57
Milngavie a			11 00	11 00			11 30	11 30			12 00	12 00			12 30	12 30					13 00	13 00
Drumchapel d		10 42				11 12				11 42				12 12						12 42		
Drumry d		10 44				11 14				11 44				12 14						12 44		
Singer d		10 47				11 17				11 47				12 17						12 47		
Dalmuir 227 a	10 39	10 49			11 09	11 19			11 39	11 49			12 09	12 19				12 39	12 39	12 49		
d	10 40	10 50			11 10	11 20			11 40	11 50			12 10	12 20			12 34	12 40	12 40	12 50		
Kilpatrick d	10 43				11 12				11 42				12 12					12 43	12 43			
Bowling d	10 46				11 15				11 45				12 15					12 46	12 46			
Dumbarton East d	10 50	10 58			11 20	11 28			11 50	11 58			12 20	12 28				12 50	12 50	12 58		
Dumbarton Central 227 d	10 52	11 00			11 22	11 30			11 52	12 00			12 22	12 30			12 47	12 52	12 52	13 00		
Dalreoch d	10 54	11 01			11 23	11 31			11 53	12 01			12 23	12 31				12 54	12 54	13 01		
Renton d	10 57				11 26				11 56				12 26					12 57	12 57			
Alexandria d	10 59				11 29				11 59				12 29					12 59	12 59			
Balloch a	11 03				11 33				12 03				12 33					13 03	13 03			
Cardross d		11 06				11 36				12 06				12 36						13 06		
Craigendoran d		11 11				11 41				12 11				12 41						13 11		
Helensburgh Central a		11 15				11 45				12 15				12 45						13 15		
Helensburgh Upper 227 a																	12 59					

A From Motherwell
B from 16 September. From Motherwell
C until 9 September. From Rutherglen
D From Larkhall. Forms tight booked connection out of 2C54.
E From Larkhall. Forms tight booked connection out of 2C56.
F From Glasgow Queen Street to Oban

Table T226-F

Sundays

20 May to 2 December

Edinburgh, Bathgate, Airdrie, Cumbernauld and Springburn - Glasgow - Milngavie, Dalmuir, Balloch and Helensburgh

	SR A	SR	SR B	SR C	SR D	SR	SR C	SR B	SR E	SR	SR B	SR C	SR C	SR B	SR	SR C	SR B	SR F	SR	SR B	SR C
Edinburgh 228,230 d		11 40				12 10				12 40					13 09				13 40		
Haymarket 228,230 d		11 44				12 15				12 45					13 14				13 46		
Edinburgh Park 230 d		11 49				12 21				12 50					13 19				13 50		
Uphall d		11 57				12 29				12 58					13 28				13 58		
Livingston North d		12 00				12 32				13 01					13 31				14 02		
Bathgate a		12 05				12 37				13 06					13 36				14 06		
d		12 06				12 37				13 06					13 36				14 06		
Armadale d		12 10				12 41				13 10					13 40				14 10		
Blackridge d		12 14				12 44				13 14					13 44				14 14		
Caldercruix d		12 20				12 51				13 20					13 50				14 20		
Drumgelloch d		12 24				12 54				13 24					13 54				14 24		
Airdrie d		12 27				12 58				13 27					13 57				14 27		
Coatdyke d		12 29				13 00				13 29					13 59				14 29		
Coatbridge Sunnyside d		12 32				13 03				13 32					14 02				14 32		
Blairhill d		12 35				13 05				13 35					14 05				14 35		
Easterhouse d		12 39				13 09				13 39					14 09				14 39		
Garrowhill d		12 41				13 12				13 41					14 11				14 41		
Shettleston d		12 44				13 14				13 44					14 14				14 44		
Carntyne d		12 46				13 16				13 46					14 16				14 46		
Cumbernauld d																					
Greenfaulds d																					
Springburn d																					
Barnhill d																					
Alexandra Parade d																					
Duke Street d																					
Bellgrove d		12 49				13 20				13 49					14 19				14 49		
High Street d		12 51				13 22				13 51					14 21				14 51		
Glasgow Queen St LL 10 a		12 53				13 24				13 53					14 23				14 53		
d		12 54				13 24				13 54					14 24				14 54		
Charing Cross d		12 57				13 27				13 57					14 27				14 57		
Argyle Street 225 d	12 43		12 58	12 59	13 14		13 29	13 30	13 43		13 58	13 59	14 15	14 16		14 29	14 31	14 43		14 58	14 59
Glasgow Central LL 15 225 a	12 44		13 00	13 00	13 16		13 30	13 32	13 44		13 59	14 00	14 16	14 18		14 31	14 33	14 44		14 59	15 00
d	12 45		13 04	13 04	13 16		13 34	13 34	13 45		14 04	14 04	14 18	14 18		14 34	14 34	14 45		15 04	15 04
Anderston 225 d	12 46		13 05	13 05	13 18		13 35	13 35	13 46		14 06	14 06	14 19	14 19		14 36	14 36	14 46		15 05	15 05
Exhibition Centre 225 d	12 48		13 07	13 07	13 20		13 37	13 37	13 48		14 08	14 08	14 21	14 21		14 38	14 38	14 48		15 07	15 07
Partick 225 d	12 52	13 01	13 12	13 12	13 23	13 31	13 42	13 42	13 52	14 01	14 12	14 12	14 25	14 25	14 31	14 42	14 42	14 52	15 01	15 12	15 12
Hyndland 8 d	12 54	13 04	13 15	13 15	13 25	13 34	13 45	13 45	13 54	14 04	14 15	14 15	14 27	14 27	14 34	14 45	14 45	14 54	15 04	15 15	15 15
Jordanhill d	12 56				13 27				13 56				14 29	14 29				14 56			
Scotstounhill d	12 59				13 30				13 59				14 31	14 31				14 59			
Garscadden d	13 01				13 32				14 01				14 33	14 33				15 01			
Yoker d	13 04				13 34				14 04				14 36	14 36				15 04			
Clydebank d	13 06				13 36				14 06				14 38	14 38				15 06			
Anniesland d		13 07	13 18	13 18		13 37	13 48	13 48		14 07	14 18	14 18			14 37	14 48	14 48		15 07	15 18	15 18
Westerton d		13 10	13 21	13 21		13 40	13 51	13 51		14 10	14 21	14 21			14 40	14 51	14 51		15 10	15 21	15 21
Bearsden d			13 25	13 25			13 55	13 55			14 25	14 25				14 55	14 55			15 25	15 25
Hillfoot d			13 27	13 27			13 57	13 57			14 27	14 27				14 57	14 57			15 27	15 27
Milngavie a			13 30	13 30			14 00	14 00			14 30	14 30				15 00	15 00			15 30	15 30
Drumchapel d		13 12				13 42				14 12					14 42				15 12		
Drumry d		13 14				13 44				14 14					14 44				15 14		
Singer d		13 17				13 47				14 17					14 47				15 17		
Dalmuir 227 a	13 09	13 19			13 39	13 49			14 09	14 19			14 41	14 41	14 49			15 09	15 19		
d	13 10	13 20			13 40	13 50			14 10	14 20			14 41	14 41	14 50			15 10	15 20		
Kilpatrick d	13 12				13 43				14 12				14 43	14 43				15 12			
Bowling d	13 15				13 46				14 15				14 46	14 46				15 15			
Dumbarton East d	13 20	13 28			13 50	13 58			14 20	14 28			14 51	14 51	14 58			15 20	15 28		
Dumbarton Central 227 d	13 22	13 30			13 52	14 00			14 22	14 30			14 53	14 53	15 00			15 22	15 30		
Dalreoch d	13 23	13 31			13 54	14 01			14 23	14 31			14 54	14 54	15 01			15 23	15 31		
Renton d	13 26				13 57				14 26				14 57	14 57				15 26			
Alexandria d	13 29				13 59				14 29				15 00	15 00				15 29			
Balloch a	13 33				14 03				14 33				15 03	15 03				15 33			
Cardross d		13 36				14 06				14 36					15 06				15 36		
Craigendoran d		13 41				14 11				14 41					15 11				15 41		
Helensburgh Central a		13 45				14 15				14 45					15 15				15 45		
Helensburgh Upper 227 a																					

A From Larkhall. Forms tight booked connection out of 2C58.
B from 16 September. From Motherwell
C until 9 September. From Rutherglen
D From Motherwell
E From Larkhall. Forms tight booked connection out of 2C48.
F From Larkhall. Forms tight booked connection out of 2C50.

Table T226-F

Sundays

20 May to 2 December

Edinburgh, Bathgate, Airdrie, Cumbernauld and Springburn - Glasgow - Milngavie, Dalmuir, Balloch and Helensburgh

	SR A	SR	SR B	SR C	SR D	SR	SR B	SR C	SR C	SR B	SR	SR C	SR B	SR E	SR	SR B	SR C	SR A	SR	SR B	SR C	SR F
Edinburgh 228,230 d		14 09				14 41					15 10				15 40				16 09			
Haymarket 228,230 d		14 13				14 45					15 15				15 44				16 13			
Edinburgh Park 230 d		14 20				14 50					15 21				15 49				16 19			
Uphall d		14 28				14 58					15 29				15 57				16 27			
Livingston North d		14 32				15 01					15 32				16 00				16 31			
Bathgate a		14 36				15 06					15 37				16 05				16 35			
d		14 37				15 06					15 37				16 06				16 38			
Armadale d		14 41				15 10					15 41				16 10				16 42			
Blackridge d		14 45				15 14					15 44				16 14				16 45			
Caldercruix d		14 51				15 20					15 51				16 20				16 52			
Drumgelloch d		14 55				15 24					15 54				16 24				16 55			
Airdrie d		14 58				15 27					15 58				16 27				16 59			
Coatdyke d		15 00				15 29					16 00				16 29				17 01			
Coatbridge Sunnyside d		15 03				15 32					16 03				16 32				17 03			
Blairhill d		15 05				15 35					16 05				16 35				17 06			
Easterhouse d		15 09				15 39					16 09				16 39				17 10			
Garrowhill d		15 12				15 41					16 12				16 41				17 12			
Shettleston d		15 14				15 44					16 14				16 44				17 15			
Carntyne d		15 16				15 46					16 16				16 46				17 17			
Cumbernauld d																						
Greenfaulds d																						
Springburn d																						
Barnhill d																						
Alexandra Parade d																						
Duke Street d																						
Bellgrove d		15 20				15 49					16 20				16 49				17 20			
High Street d		15 22				15 51					16 22				16 51				17 22			
Glasgow Queen St LL 10 a		15 24				15 53					16 24				16 53				17 24			
d		15 24				15 54					16 24				16 54				17 25			
Charing Cross d		15 27				15 57					16 27				16 57				17 27			
Argyle Street 225 d	15 14		15 28	15 29	15 43		15 58	15 59	16 15	16 16		16 29	16 32	16 43		16 58	16 59	17 14		17 28	17 29	17 43
Glasgow Central LL 15 225 a	15 16		15 29	15 30	15 44		16 00	16 00	16 16	16 17		16 30	16 34	16 44		16 59	17 00	17 15		17 29	17 30	17 44
d	15 16		15 34	15 34	15 45		16 04	16 04	16 17	16 17		16 34	16 34	16 45		17 04	17 04	17 16		17 34	17 34	17 45
Anderston 225 d	15 18		15 35	15 35	15 46		16 05	16 05	16 19	16 19		16 36	16 36	16 46		17 06	17 06	17 17		17 35	17 35	17 46
Exhibition Centre 225 d	15 20		15 37	15 37	15 48		16 07	16 07	16 21	16 21		16 38	16 38	16 48		17 08	17 08	17 19		17 37	17 37	17 48
Partick 225 d	15 23	15 31	15 42	15 42	15 52	16 01	16 12	16 12	16 24	16 24	16 31	16 42	16 42	16 52	17 01	17 12	17 12	17 23	17 31	17 42	17 42	17 52
Hyndland 8 d	15 25	15 34	15 45	15 45	15 54	16 04	16 15	16 15	16 26	16 26	16 34	16 45	16 45	16 54	17 04	17 15	17 15	17 25	17 34	17 45	17 45	17 54
Jordanhill d	15 27				15 56				16 28	16 28				16 56				17 27				17 56
Scotstounhill d	15 30				15 59				16 31	16 31				16 59				17 29				17 59
Garscadden d	15 32				16 01				16 33	16 33				17 01				17 31				18 01
Yoker d	15 35				16 04				16 35	16 35				17 04				17 34				18 04
Clydebank d	15 37				16 06				16 37	16 37				17 06				17 36				18 06
Anniesland d		15 37	15 48	15 48		16 07	16 18	16 18			16 37	16 48	16 48		17 07	17 18	17 18		17 37	17 48	17 48	
Westerton d		15 40	15 51	15 51		16 10	16 21	16 21			16 40	16 51	16 51		17 10	17 21	17 21		17 40	17 51	17 51	
Bearsden d			15 55	15 55			16 25	16 25				16 55	16 55			17 25	17 25			17 55	17 55	
Hillfoot d			15 57	15 57			16 27	16 27				16 57	16 57			17 27	17 27			17 57	17 57	
Milngavie a			16 00	16 00			16 30	16 30				17 00	17 00			17 30	17 30			18 00	18 00	
Drumchapel d		15 42				16 12					16 42				17 12				17 42			
Drumry d		15 44				16 14					16 44				17 14				17 44			
Singer d		15 47				16 17					16 47				17 17				17 47			
Dalmuir 227 a	15 40	15 49			16 09	16 19			16 40	16 40	16 49			17 09	17 19			17 39	17 49			18 09
d	15 41	15 50			16 10	16 20			16 40	16 40	16 50			17 10	17 20			17 40	17 50			18 10
Kilpatrick d	15 43				16 12				16 43	16 43				17 12				17 42				18 12
Bowling d	15 46				16 15				16 46	16 46				17 15				17 45				18 15
Dumbarton East d	15 51	15 58			16 20	16 28			16 50	16 50	16 58			17 20	17 28			17 50	17 58			18 20
Dumbarton Central 227 d	15 53	16 00			16 22	16 30			16 52	16 52	17 00			17 22	17 30			17 52	18 00			18 22
Dalreoch d	15 54	16 01			16 23	16 31			16 54	16 54	17 01			17 23	17 31			17 53	18 01			18 23
Renton d	15 57				16 26				16 57	16 57				17 26				17 56				18 26
Alexandria d	16 00				16 29				16 59	16 59				17 29				17 59				18 29
Balloch a	16 03				16 33				17 03	17 03				17 33				18 03				18 33
Cardross d		16 06				16 36					17 06				17 36				18 06			
Craigendoran d		16 11				16 41					17 11				17 41				18 11			
Helensburgh Central a		16 15				16 45					17 15				17 45				18 15			
Helensburgh Upper 227 a																						

A From Motherwell
B from 16 September. From Motherwell
C until 9 September. From Rutherglen
D From Larkhall. Forms tight booked connection out of 2C52.
E From Larkhall. Forms tight booked connection out of 2C54.
F From Larkhall. Forms tight booked connection out of 2C56.

Table T226-F

Sundays

20 May to 2 December

Edinburgh, Bathgate, Airdrie, Cumbernauld and Springburn - Glasgow - Milngavie, Dalmuir, Balloch and Helensburgh

		SR	SR	SR	SR	SR	SR	SR	SR	SR	SR	SR	SR	SR	SR	SR	SR	SR	SR	SR	SR	SR
			A	B	◇ C	D		D	E		D	D		D	F			D	D		D	G
Edinburgh 228,230	d	16 40					17 10			17 40			18 09			18 40	19 10					
Haymarket 228,230 ⛴	d	16 44					17 14			17 44			18 13			18 44	19 14					
Edinburgh Park 230	d	16 49					17 20			17 49			18 20			18 49	19 19					
Uphall	d	16 58					17 28			17 57			18 28			18 57	19 27					
Livingston North	d	17 01					17 31			18 00			18 31			19 00	19 30					
Bathgate	a	17 06					17 36			18 05			18 36			19 05	19 35					
	d	17 06					17 36			18 06			18 36			19 06						
Armadale	d	17 10					17 40			18 10			18 40			19 10						
Blackridge	d	17 14					17 44			18 14			18 44			19 14						
Caldercruix	d	17 20					17 50			18 20			18 50			19 20						
Drumgelloch	d	17 24					17 54			18 24			18 54			19 24						
Airdrie	d	17 27					17 57			18 27			18 57			19 27				19 57		
Coatdyke	d	17 29					17 59			18 29			18 59			19 29				19 59		
Coatbridge Sunnyside	d	17 32					18 02			18 32			19 02			19 32				20 02		
Blairhill	d	17 35					18 05			18 35			19 05			19 35				20 05		
Easterhouse	d	17 39					18 09			18 39			19 09			19 39				20 09		
Garrowhill	d	17 41					18 11			18 41			19 11			19 41				20 11		
Shettleston	d	17 44					18 14			18 44			19 14			19 44				20 14		
Carntyne	d	17 46					18 16			18 46			19 16			19 46				20 16		
Cumbernauld	d																					
Greenfaulds	d																					
Springburn	d																					
Barnhill	d																					
Alexandra Parade	d																					
Duke Street	d																					
Bellgrove	d	17 49					18 19			18 49			19 19			19 49				20 19		
High Street	d	17 51					18 21			18 51			19 21			19 51				20 21		
Glasgow Queen St LL 10 ⛴	a	17 53					18 23			18 53			19 23			19 53				20 23		
	d	17 54					18 24			18 54			19 24			19 54				20 24		
Charing Cross	d	17 57					18 27			18 57			19 27			19 57				20 27		
Argyle Street 225	d		17 58	17 59		18 14																
Glasgow Central LL 15 225	a		17 59	18 00		18 15																
	d		18 04	18 04		18 16		18 34	18 45		19 04	19 15		19 34	19 45			20 04	20 15		20 34	20 46
Anderston 225	d		18 05	18 05		18 17																
Exhibition Centre 225	d		18 07	18 07		18 19		18 38	18 48		19 08	19 18		19 38	19 48			20 08	20 18		20 38	20 49
Partick 225 ⛴	d	18 01	18 12	18 12		18 23	18 31	18 42	18 52	19 01	19 12	19 22	19 31	19 42	19 52	20 01		20 12	20 22	20 31	20 42	20 53
Hyndland 3	d	18 04	18 15	18 15		18 25	18 34	18 45	18 54	19 04	19 17	19 24	19 34	19 45	19 54	20 04		20 15	20 24	20 34	20 45	20 55
Jordanhill	d					18 27			18 56			19 26			19 56				20 26			20 57
Scotstounhill	d					18 29			18 59			19 29			19 59				20 29			20 59
Garscadden	d					18 31			19 01			19 31			20 01				20 31			21 01
Yoker	d					18 34			19 04			19 34			20 04				20 34			21 04
Clydebank	d					18 36			19 06			19 36			20 06				20 36			21 06
Anniesland	d	18 07	18 18	18 18			18 37	18 48		19 07	19 20		19 37	19 48		20 07		20 18		20 37	20 48	
Westerton	d	18 10	18 21	18 21			18 40	18 51		19 10	19 23		19 40	19 51		20 10		20 21		20 40	20 51	
Bearsden	d		18 25	18 25				18 55			19 25			19 55				20 25			20 55	
Hillfoot	d		18 27	18 27				18 57			19 27			19 57				20 27			20 57	
Milngavie	a		18 30	18 30				19 00			19 31			20 00				20 30			21 00	
Drumchapel	d	18 12					18 42			19 12			19 42			20 12				20 42		
Drumry	d	18 14					18 44			19 14			19 44			20 14				20 44		
Singer	d	18 17					18 47			19 17			19 47			20 17				20 47		
Dalmuir 227	a	18 19				18 39	18 49		19 09	19 19		19 39	19 49		20 09	20 19			20 39	20 49		21 09
	d	18 20			18 36	18 40	18 50		19 10	19 20		19 40	19 50		20 10	20 20			20 40	20 50		21 10
Kilpatrick	d					18 42			19 12			19 42			20 12				20 42			21 12
Bowling	d					18 45			19 15			19 45			20 15				20 45			21 15
Dumbarton East	d	18 28				18 50	18 58		19 20	19 28		19 50	19 58		20 20	20 28			20 50	20 58		21 20
Dumbarton Central 227	d	18 30			18 47	18 52	19 00		19 22	19 30		19 52	20 00		20 22	20 30			20 52	21 00		21 22
Dalreoch	d	18 31				18 53	19 01		19 23	19 31		19 53	20 01		20 23	20 31			20 53	21 01		21 23
Renton	d					18 56			19 26			19 56			20 26				20 56			21 26
Alexandria	d					18 59			19 29			19 59			20 29				20 59			21 29
Balloch	a					19 03			19 33			20 03			20 33				21 03			21 33
Cardross	d	18 36					19 06			19 36			20 06			20 36				21 06		
Craigendoran	d	18 41					19 11			19 41			20 11			20 41				21 11		
Helensburgh Central	a	18 45					19 15			19 45			20 15			20 45				21 15		
Helensburgh Upper 227	a				18 59																	

A from 16 September. From Motherwell
B until 9 September. From Rutherglen
C From Glasgow Queen Street to Oban
D From Motherwell
E From Larkhall. Forms tight booked connection out of 2C58.
F From Larkhall. Forms tight booked connection out of 2C48.
G From Larkhall. Forms tight booked connection out of 2C50.

Table T226-F

Sundays

20 May to 2 December

Edinburgh, Bathgate, Airdrie, Cumbernauld and Springburn - Glasgow - Milngavie, Dalmuir, Balloch and Helensburgh

		SR	SR	SR	SR	SR	SR	SR	SR	SR	SR	SR	SR	SR	SR	SR	SR	SR	SR	SR	SR	SR
				A	A		A	B		A	A		A	C		A	A		A	D		
Edinburgh 228,230	d	19 40	20 10						20 40						21 40						22 40	23 18
Haymarket 228,230 ⛴	d	19 44	20 14						20 44						21 44						22 44	23 22
Edinburgh Park 230	d	19 49	20 19						20 49						21 49						22 49	23 27
Uphall	d	19 57	20 27						20 57						21 57						22 57	23 35
Livingston North	d	20 00	20 30						21 01						22 00						23 00	23 38
Bathgate	a	20 05	20 35						21 05						22 05						23 05	23 43
	d	20 06							21 06						22 06						23 06	
Armadale	d	20 10							21 10						22 10						23 10	
Blackridge	d	20 14							21 14						22 14						23 14	
Caldercruix	d	20 20							21 20						22 20						23 20	
Drumgelloch	d	20 24							21 24						22 24						23 24	
Airdrie	d	20 27				20 57			21 27			21 57			22 27			22 57			23 27	
Coatdyke	d	20 29				20 59			21 29			21 59			22 29			22 59			23 29	
Coatbridge Sunnyside	d	20 32				21 02			21 32			22 02			22 32			23 02			23 32	
Blairhill	d	20 35				21 05			21 35			22 05			22 35			23 05			23 35	
Easterhouse	d	20 39				21 09			21 39			22 09			22 39			23 09			23 39	
Garrowhill	d	20 41				21 11			21 41			22 11			22 41			23 11			23 41	
Shettleston	d	20 44				21 14			21 44			22 14			22 44			23 14			23 44	
Carntyne	d	20 46				21 16			21 46			22 16			22 46			23 16			23 46	
Cumbernauld	d																					
Greenfaulds	d																					
Springburn	d																					
Barnhill	d																					
Alexandra Parade	d																					
Duke Street	d																					
Bellgrove	d	20 49				21 19			21 49			22 19			22 49			23 19			23 49	
High Street	d	20 51				21 21			21 51			22 21			22 51			23 21			23 51	
Glasgow Queen St LL 10 ⛴	a	20 53				21 23			21 53			22 23			22 53			23 23			23 53	
	d	20 54				21 24			21 54			22 24			22 54			23 24			23 54	
Charing Cross	d	20 57				21 27			21 57			22 27			22 57			23 27			23 57	
Argyle Street 225	d																					
Glasgow Central LL 15 225	a																					
	d			21 04	21 15		21 34	21 45		22 04	22 15		22 34	22 45		23 04	23 15		23 34	23 47		
Anderston 225	d																					
Exhibition Centre 225	d			21 08	21 18		21 38	21 48		22 08	22 18		22 38	22 48		23 08	23 18		23 38	23 50		
Partick 225 ⛴	d	21 01		21 12	21 22	21 31	21 42	21 52	22 01	22 12	22 22	22 31	22 42	22 52	23 01	23 12	23 22	23 31	23 42	23 54	00 01	
Hyndland 3	d	21 04		21 15	21 24	21 34	21 45	21 54	22 04	22 15	22 24	22 34	22 45	22 54	23 04	23 15	23 24	23 34	23 45	23 56	00 03	
Jordanhill	d				21 26			21 56			22 26			22 56			23 26		23 47	23 58	00 05	
Scotstounhill	d				21 29			21 59			22 29			22 59			23 29		23 49	00 01	00 08	
Garscadden	d				21 31			22 01			22 31			23 01			23 31		23a51	00a02	00 10	
Yoker	d				21 34			22 04			22 34			23 04			23 34				00 12	
Clydebank	d				21 36			22 06			22 36			23 06			23 36				00 14	
Anniesland	d	21 11		21 18		21 37	21 48		22 07	22 18		22 37	22 48		23 07	23 18		23 37				
Westerton	d	21 14		21 21		21 40	21 51		22 10	22 21		22 40	22 51		23 10	23 21		23 40				
Bearsden	d			21 25			21 55			22 25			22 55			23 25						
Hillfoot	d			21 27			21 57			22 27			22 57			23 27						
Milngavie	a			21 30			22 00			22 30			23 01			23 30						
Drumchapel	d	21 16				21 42			22 12			22 42			23 12			23 42				
Drumry	d	21 18				21 44			22 14			22 44			23 14			23 44				
Singer	d	21 21				21 47			22 17			22 47			23 17			23 47				
Dalmuir 227	a	21 23			21 39	21 49		22 09	22 19		22 39	22 49		23 09	23 19		23 39	23 49			00 18	
	d	21 23			21 40	21 50		22 10	22 20		22 40	22 50		23 10	23 20		23 40	23 50				
Kilpatrick	d				21 42			22 12			22 42			23 12			23 42					
Bowling	d				21 45			22 15			22 45			23 15			23 45					
Dumbarton East	d	21 31			21 50	21 58		22 20	22 28		22 50	22 58		23 20	23 28		23 50	23 58				
Dumbarton Central 227	d	21 33			21 52	22 00		22 22	22 30		22 52	23 00		23 22	23 30		23 52	23 59				
Dalreoch	d	21 34			21 53	22 01		22 23	22 31		22 53	23 01		23 23	23 31		23 53	00 01				
Renton	d				21 56			22 26			22 56			23 26			23 56					
Alexandria	d				21 59			22 29			22 59			23 29			23 59					
Balloch	a				22 03			22 33			23 03			23 33			00 03					
Cardross	d	21 39				22 06			22 36			23 06			23 36			00 06				
Craigendoran	d	21 44				22 11			22 41			23 11			23 41			00 11				
Helensburgh Central	a	21 48				22 15			22 45			23 15			23 46			00 15				
Helensburgh Upper 227	a																					

A From Motherwell
B From Larkhall. Forms tight booked connection out of 2C52.
C From Larkhall. Forms tight booked connection out of 2C54.
D From Larkhall. Forms tight booked connection out of 2C56.

Table T226-R

Mondays to Fridays
21 May to 7 December

Helensburgh, Balloch, Dalmuir and Milngavie - Glasgow - Springburn, Cumbernauld, Airdrie, Bathgate and Edinburgh

Miles	Miles	Miles	Miles	Station		SR MX A	SR MX A	SR	SR MX A	SR	SR	SR	SR	SR	SR B	SR	SR C	SR C	SR	SR	SR B	SR	SR
—	—	—	—	**Helensburgh Upper** 227	d																		
0	—	—	—	**Helensburgh Central**	d															05 56			
1¼	—	—	—	Craigendoran	d															05 59			
4¼	—	—	—	Cardross	d															06 04			
—	0	—	—	**Balloch**	d																		06 07
—	1	—	—	Alexandria	d																		06 09
—	2¼	—	—	Renton	d																		06 12
8	3¾	—	—	Dalreoch	d															06 09			06 15
8¾	4	—	—	Dumbarton Central 227	d															06 11			06 17
9	4¾	—	—	Dumbarton East	d															06 13			06 19
11¾	7½	—	—	Bowling	d																		
13½	9¼	—	—	Kilpatrick	d																		
14¾	10½	0	0	**Dalmuir** 227	a															06 20			06 27
—	—	—	—		d									05 47	05 51	05 58	06 00		06 12	06 21	06 16		06 28
15½	11¼	—	0¾	Singer	d				00 01						05 53	06 00					06 18		06 30
16½	12¼	—	1¾	Drumry	d				00 03						05 56	06 03					06 21		06 33
17¼	13	—	2½	Drumchapel	d				00 06						05 58	06 05					06 23		06 35
—	—	—	—	**Milngavie**	d																		
—	—	—	—	Hillfoot	d																		
—	—	—	—	Bearsden	d																		
18½	14¼	—	3¾	Westerton	d				00 08						06 01	06 08					06 26		06 38
19¾	15½	—	5	Anniesland	d				00 11						06 04	06 11					06 29		06 41
—	—	1¼	—	Clydebank	d									05 49			06 02		06 14				
—	—	2¼	—	Yoker	d									05 51			06 04		06 16				
—	—	3¼	—	Garscadden	d							05 45	05 49	05 54			06 07		06 19				
—	—	3¾	—	Scotstounhill	d							05 47	05 51	05 57			06 09		06 21				
—	—	4¾	—	Jordanhill	d							05 49	05 53	05 59			06 14		06 23				
20¾	16½	5¼	6	Hyndland	d				00 14		05 37	05 52	05 56	06 01	06 07	06 14	06 17	06 22	06 25	06 28	06 32	06 37	06 44
21¼	17	6	6½	**Partick** 225	d				00 17		05 39	05 54	05 58	06 04	06 10	06 16	06 19	06 24	06 27	06 31	06 34	06 39	06 46
—	—	—	8¼	Exhibition Centre 225	a										06 13		06 22	06 27			06 37		
—	—	—	8¼	Anderston 225	a										06 15		06 24	06 30			06 39		
—	—	—	8¾	**Glasgow Central LL** 225	a										06 17		06 25	06 31			06 41		
—	—	—	9¼	Argyle Street 225	a										06 19		06 28	06 35			06 44		
23¼	19	7¾	—	Charing Cross	d				00 21		05 43	05 59	06 03	06 08		06 21			06 32	06 35		06 43	06 51
24	19¾	8½	—	**Glasgow Queen St LL**	a				00 23		05 45	06 01	06 05	06 10		06 23			06 34	06 37		06 45	06 53
—	—	—	—		d				00 23		05 45	06 01	06 05	06 16		06 26			06 34	06 38		06 47	06 56
24½	20¼	9	—	High Street	d				00 25		05 47	06 03	06 07	06 18		06 29			06 36	06 40		06 49	06 59
25	20¾	9½	—	Bellgrove	d				00 27		05 49		06 09	06 20		06 32			06 38			06 51	07 02
—	21¼	10	—	Duke Street	d								06 11						06 41				
—	21½	10¼	—	Alexandra Parade	d								06 13						06 42				
—	22¾	11¼	—	Barnhill	d								06 16						06 45				
—	23	11¾	—	Springburn	a								06 18						06 47				
—	—	23½	—	Greenfaulds	d														07 14				
—	—	24½	—	Cumbernauld	a														07 16				
26¾	—	—	—	Carntyne	d		00 02		00 31		05 53			06 24		06 36						06 54	07 05
27½	—	—	—	Shettleston	d		00 03		00 33		05 55			06 27		06 38						06 57	07 08
28¾	—	—	—	Garrowhill	d		00 06		00 36			06 11				06 41				06 47			07 10
29¼	—	—	—	Easterhouse	d		00 08		00 38			06 13				06 43				06 50			07 13
32½	—	—	—	Blairhill	d		00 12		00 42			06 17				06 47				06 54			07 17
33	—	—	—	Coatbridge Sunnyside	d		00 15		00 45		06 04	06 20		06 35		06 50				06 56		07 05	07 19
34	—	—	—	Coatdyke	d		00 17		00 47			06 22				06 52				06 59			07 22
35	—	—	—	**Airdrie**	d		00 20		00a51		06 09	06 29		06 40		06a56				07 02		07 10	07a26
36½	—	—	—	Drumgelloch	d		00 23				06 12	06 32		06 43						07 05		07 13	
39½	—	—	—	Caldercruix	d		00 27				06 16			06 47								07 17	
45	—	—	—	Blackridge	d	00 03	00 33				06 22			06 53								07 23	
47¼	—	—	—	Armadale	d	00 07	00 36				06 25			06 57								07 27	
49¾	—	—	—	**Bathgate**	a	00 11	00 40				06 29	06 44		07 01						07 17		07 31	
—	—	—	—		d			05 46		06 20	06 30	06 45		07 02						07 18		07 32	
52¾	—	—	—	Livingston North	d			05 50		06 24	06 34	06 50		07 07						07 22		07 37	
55¾	—	—	—	Uphall	d			05 53		06 27	06 37	06 53		07 10						07 25		07 40	
64½	—	—	—	Edinburgh Park 230	d			06 02		06 35	06 47	07 03		07 18						07 34		07 49	
67	—	—	—	Haymarket 228,230	a			06 06		06 40	06 51	07 07		07 23						07 38		07 53	
68¼	—	—	—	**Edinburgh** 228,230	a			06 11		06 45	06 56	07 13		07 29						07 43		07 58	

A From Helensburgh Central
B To Larkhall
C To Motherwell

Table T226-R

Mondays to Fridays
21 May to 7 December

Helensburgh, Balloch, Dalmuir and Milngavie - Glasgow - Springburn, Cumbernauld, Airdrie, Bathgate and Edinburgh

Station		SR A	SR	SR	SR	SR B	SR	SR	SR C	SR C	SR	SR	SR B	SR	SR	SR A	SR	SR	SR	SR B	SR	SR	SR C
Helensburgh Upper 227	d																						
Helensburgh Central	d				06 26							06 56							07 26				
Craigendoran	d				06 29							06 59							07 29				
Cardross	d				06 34							07 04							07 34				
Balloch	d							06 37							07 07							07 37	
Alexandria	d							06 39							07 09							07 39	
Renton	d							06 42							07 12							07 42	
Dalreoch	d				06 39			06 45				07 09			07 15				07 39			07 45	
Dumbarton Central 227	d			06 26	06 41			06 47			06 56	07 11			07 17			07 26	07 41			07 47	
Dumbarton East	d			06 28	06 43			06 49			06 58	07 13			07 19			07 28	07 43			07 49	
Bowling	d			06 33							07 03							07 33					
Kilpatrick	d			06 36							07 07							07 36					
Dalmuir 227	a			06 39	06 50			06 56			07 10	07 20			07 26			07 39	07 50			07 56	
	d	06 33		06 41	06 51	06 46		06 58	07 02		07 11	07 21	07 18		07 28	07 33		07 41	07 51	07 48		07 58	08 02
Singer	d					06 48		07 00					07 20		07 30					07 50		08 00	
Drumry	d					06 51		07 03					07 23		07 33					07 53		08 03	
Drumchapel	d					06 53		07 05					07 25		07 35					07 56		08 05	
Milngavie	d		06 38				06 54			07 09				07 24			07 39				07 54		
Hillfoot	d		06 41				06 57			07 12				07 27			07 42				07 57		
Bearsden	d		06 43				06 59			07 14				07 29			07 44				07 59		
Westerton	d		06 46			06 57	07 02	07 08		07 17			07 28	07 32	07 38		07 47			07 58	08 02	08 08	
Anniesland	d		06 49			07 00	07 05	07 11		07 20			07 31	07 35	07 41		07 50			08 01	08 05	08 11	
Clydebank	d	06 35		06 43					07 04		07 13					07 35		07 43					08 04
Yoker	d	06 37		06 45					07 06		07 15					07 37		07 45					08 06
Garscadden	d	06 40		06 48					07 10		07 19					07 40		07 49					08 10
Scotstounhill	d	06 42		06 50					07 12		07 21					07 42		07 51					08 12
Jordanhill	d	06 45		06 53					07 14		07 24					07 45		07 54					08 15
Hyndland	d	06 48	06 52	06 55	06 58	07 03	07 08	07 14	07 17	07 23	07 26	07 29	07 34	07 38	07 44	07 48	07 53	07 56	07 59	08 04	08 08	08 14	08 17
Partick 225	d	06 50	06 54	06 57	07 00	07 06	07 10	07 16	07 19	07 25	07 28	07 31	07 37	07 40	07 46	07 50	07 55	07 58	08 01	08 07	08 11	08 16	08 20
Exhibition Centre 225	a	06 53	06 57			07 09			07 22	07 28			07 40			07 53	07 58			08 10			08 23
Anderston 225	a	06 55	06 59			07 11			07 24	07 30			07 42			07 55	08 00			08 12			08 25
Glasgow Central LL 225	a	06 57	07 02			07 12			07 26	07 32			07 43			07 57	08 02			08 14			08 26
Argyle Street 225	a	06 59	07 06			07 17			07 28	07 37			07 48			07 59	08 06			08 17			08 29
Charing Cross	d			07 01	07 04		07 14	07 21			07 32	07 36		07 45	07 51			08 02	08 06		08 15	08 21	
Glasgow Queen St LL	a			07 03	07 06		07 16	07 23			07 34	07 38		07 47	07 53			08 04	08 08		08 17	08 23	
	d			07 03	07 07		07 17	07 26			07 35	07 38		07 47	07 56			08 05	08 08		08 18	08 26	
High Street	d			07 05	07 09		07 19	07 29			07 37	07 40		07 49	07 59			08 07	08 10		08 20	08 29	
Bellgrove	d			07 07			07 21	07 32			07 39			07 51	08 02			08 09			08 22	08 32	
Duke Street	d			07 11							07 41							08 11					
Alexandra Parade	d			07 13							07 42							08 12					
Barnhill	d			07 22							07 45							08 15					
Springburn	a			07 24							07 47							08 17					
Greenfaulds	d		08 00	07 46							08 14						09 00	08 41					
Cumbernauld	a		08 02	07 49							08 17						09 02	08 44					
Carntyne	d						07 24	07 35						07 55	08 05						08 25	08 35	
Shettleston	d						07 27	07 38						07 57	08 08						08 28	08 38	
Garrowhill	d				07 16			07 40				07 48			08 10				08 18			08 40	
Easterhouse	d				07 19			07 43				07 50			08 13				08 20			08 43	
Blairhill	d				07 23			07 47				07 54			08 17				08 24			08 47	
Coatbridge Sunnyside	d				07 25		07 35	07 49				07 57		08 06	08 19				08 27		08 36	08 49	
Coatdyke	d				07 28			07 52				07 59			08 22				08 29			08 52	
Airdrie	d				07 31		07 40	07a56				08 02		08 10	08a26				08 32		08 41	08a56	
Drumgelloch	d				07 34		07 43					08 05		08 13					08 35		08 44		
Caldercruix	d						07 47							08 17							08 48		
Blackridge	d						07 53							08 23							08 54		
Armadale	d						07 57							08 27							08 57		
Bathgate	a				07 46		08 01					08 18		08 31					08 48		09 01		
	d				07 47		08 02					08 19		08 31					08 49		09 02		
Livingston North	d				07 52		08 07					08 24		08 36					08 53		09 06		
Uphall	d				07 55		08 10					08 28		08 39					08 56		09 09		
Edinburgh Park 230	d				08 03		08 19					08 38		08 49					09 05		09 19		
Haymarket 228,230	a				08 08		08 23					08 44		08 54					09 10		09 26		
Edinburgh 228,230	a				08 14		08 31					08 49		09 01					09 18		09 31		

A To Whifflet
B To Larkhall
C To Motherwell

Table T226-R

Mondays to Fridays

21 May to 7 December

Helensburgh, Balloch, Dalmuir and Milngavie - Glasgow - Springburn, Cumbernauld, Airdrie, Bathgate and Edinburgh

	SR A	SR	SR ◇ B	SR	SR C	SR	SR	SR	SR D	SR	SR	SR	SR C	SR	SR	SR A	SR A	SR	SR	SR C	SR	SR
Helensburgh Upper 227 d			07 42																			
Helensburgh Central d				07 56			08 05					08 26							08 54			
Craigendoran d				07 59			08 08					08 29							08 57			
Cardross d			07 50	08 04			08 14					08 34							09 04			
Balloch d								08 07							08 37							09 07
Alexandria d								08 09							08 39							09 09
Renton d								08 12							08 42							09 12
Dalreoch d				08 09			08 19	08 15				08 39			08 45				09 09			09 15
Dumbarton Central 227 d		07 51	07 59	08 11			08 22	08 17			08 27	08 41			08 47			08 56	09 11			09 17
Dumbarton East d		07 53		08 13			08 24	08 19			08 30	08 43			08 49			08 58	09 13			09 19
Bowling d		07 58									08 34							09 03				
Kilpatrick d		08 01									08 37							09 06				
Dalmuir 227 a		08 05		08 20				08 26			08 40	08 50			08 56			09 09	09 20			09 26
d		08 11		08 21	08 18			08 28	08 35		08 41	08 51	08 50		08 58	09 03		09 11	09 21	09 18		09 28
Singer d			08a11		08 20			08 30					08 52		09 00					09 20		09 30
Drumry d					08 22			08 33					08 54		09 03					09 23		09 33
Drumchapel d					08 26			08 35					08 57		09 05					09 25		09 35
Milngavie d	08 09					08 24				08 39				08 54			09 09				09 24	
Hillfoot d	08 12					08 27				08 42				08 57			09 12				09 27	
Bearsden d	08 14					08 29				08 44				08 59			09 14				09 29	
Westerton d	08 17				08 29	08 33		08 38		08 47			08 59	09 03	09 08		09 17			09 28	09 32	09 38
Anniesland d	08 20				08 32	08 36		08 42		08 50			09 02	09 06	09 11		09 20			09 31	09 35	09 41
Clydebank d		08 13							08 37		08 43					09 05		09 13				
Yoker d		08 15							08 39		08 45					09 07		09 15				
Garscadden d		08 19							08 42		08 49					09 10		09 19				
Scotstounhill d		08 21							08 44		08 51					09 12		09 21				
Jordanhill d		08 24							08 46		08 55					09 15		09 24				
Hyndland 3 d	08 23	08 26		08 29	08 35	08 39		08 45	08 48	08 53	08 57	09 00	09 06	09 09	09 14	09 17	09 23	09 26	09 28	09 34	09 38	09 44
Partick 225 ⛴ d	08 25	08 28		08 31	08 37	08 42	08 45	08 48	08 51	08 56	08 59	09 02	09 08	09 11	09 17	09 19	09 25	09 28	09 31	09 37	09 40	09 46
Exhibition Centre 225 a	08 28				08 40				08 54	08 59			09 11			09 22	09 28			09 40		
Anderston 225 a	08 31				08 42				08 56	09 01			09 13			09 24	09 30			09 42		
Glasgow Central LL 15 225 a	08 33				08 44				08 57	09 02			09 15			09 26	09 32			09 43		
Argyle Street 225 a	08 36				08 46				08 59	09 05			09 18			09 28	09 36			09 45		
Charing Cross d		08 32		08 36		08 46	08 49	08 53			09 03	09 06		09 15	09 22			09 32	09 35		09 44	09 51
Glasgow Queen St LL 10 ⛴ a		08 34		08 38		08 48	08 51	08 55			09 05	09 08		09 17	09 24			09 34	09 37		09 46	09 53
d		08 35		08 38		08 48	08 52	08 56			09 05	09 09		09 17	09 27			09 34	09 38		09 47	09 56
High Street d		08 37		08 40		08 50	08 54	08 59			09 07	09 11		09 19	09 30			09 36	09 40		09 49	09 59
Bellgrove d		08 39				08 52		09 02			09 09			09 21	09 32			09 38			09 51	10 02
Duke Street d		08 41									09 11							09 41				
Alexandra Parade d		08 42									09 13							09 42				
Barnhill d		08 45									09 16							09 45				
Springburn a		08 47					09 03				09 18							09 47				
Greenfaulds d		09 11								10 01	09 41							10 11				
Cumbernauld a		09 14								10 03	09 44							10 14				
Carntyne d						08 56		09 06						09 25	09 36						09 54	10 05
Shettleston d						08 58		09 08						09 27	09 38						09 57	10 08
Garrowhill d				08 48				09 11				09 18			09 41				09 47			10 10
Easterhouse d				08 50				09 13				09 21			09 43				09 50			10 13
Blairhill d				08 54				09 17				09 25			09 47				09 54			10 17
Coatbridge Sunnyside d				08 57		09 07		09 20				09 27		09 36	09 50				09 56		10 05	10 19
Coatdyke d				08 59				09 22				09 30			09 52				09 59			10 22
Airdrie d				09 02		09 11		09a26				09 32		09 40	09a56				10 02		10 10	10a26
Drumgelloch d				09 05		09 14						09 35		09 43					10 05		10 13	
Caldercruix d						09 18								09 47							10 17	
Blackridge d						09 24								09 53							10 23	
Armadale d						09 28								09 57							10 27	
Bathgate a				09 18		09 32						09 48		10 01					10 17		10 31	
d				09 18		09 32						09 48		10 01					10 18		10 31	
Livingston North d				09 23		09 37						09 53		10 06					10 22		10 36	
Uphall d				09 26		09 40						09 56		10 09					10 25		10 39	
Edinburgh Park 230 d				09 35		09 48						10 04		10 18					10 33		10 48	
Haymarket 228,230 ⛴ a				09 40		09 52						10 08		10 23					10 38		10 52	
Edinburgh 228,230 a				09 45		09 57						10 14		10 28					10 44		10 57	

A To Motherwell
B From Oban to Glasgow Queen Street
C To Larkhall
D To Whifflet

Table T226-R

Mondays to Fridays

21 May to 7 December

Helensburgh, Balloch, Dalmuir and Milngavie - Glasgow - Springburn, Cumbernauld, Airdrie, Bathgate and Edinburgh

	SR A	SR	SR	SR	SR B	SR	SR	SR C	SR C	SR	SR	SR B	SR	SR	SR A	SR	SR	SR	SR B	SR	SR
Helensburgh Upper 227 d																					
Helensburgh Central d				09 26							09 56							10 26			
Craigendoran d				09 29							09 59							10 29			
Cardross d				09 34							10 04							10 34			
Balloch d							09 37							10 07							10 37
Alexandria d							09 39							10 09							10 39
Renton d							09 42							10 12							10 42
Dalreoch d				09 39			09 45				10 09			10 15				10 39			10 45
Dumbarton Central 227 d			09 22	09 41			09 46			09 57	10 11			10 16			10 26	10 41			10 47
Dumbarton East d			09 24	09 43			09 48			09 59	10 13			10 18			10 28	10 43			10 49
Bowling d			09 29							10 03							10 33				
Kilpatrick d			09 33							10 06							10 36				
Dalmuir 227 a			09 36	09 50			09 56			10 10	10 20			10 26			10 39	10 50			10 56
d	09 33		09 41	09 51	09 48		09 58	10 03		10 11	10 21	10 18		10 27	10 33		10 41	10 51	10 48		10 58
Singer d					09 50		10 00					10 20		10 29					10 51		11 00
Drumry d					09 53		10 02					10 23		10 32					10 53		11 03
Drumchapel d					09 55		10 05					10 26		10 34					10 56		11 05
Milngavie d		09 39				09 54			10 09				10 24			10 39				10 53	
Hillfoot d		09 42				09 57			10 12				10 27			10 42				10 56	
Bearsden d		09 44				09 59			10 14				10 29			10 44				10 58	
Westerton d		09 47			09 58	10 02	10 07		10 17			10 28	10 32	10 37		10 47			10 58	11 02	11 08
Anniesland d		09 50			10 01	10 05	10 11		10 20			10 31	10 35	10 41		10 50			11 02	11 06	11 11
Clydebank d	09 35		09 43					10 05		10 13					10 35		10 43				
Yoker d	09 37		09 45					10 07		10 15					10 37		10 45				
Garscadden d	09 40		09 49					10 10		10 19					10 40		10 49				
Scotstounhill d	09 42		09 51					10 12		10 21					10 42		10 51				
Jordanhill d	09 45		09 54					10 15		10 24					10 45		10 54				
Hyndland 3 d	09 47	09 53	09 56	09 58	10 04	10 08	10 14	10 17	10 23	10 26	10 29	10 34	10 38	10 44	10 47	10 53	10 56	10 59	11 05	11 09	11 14
Partick 225 ⛴ d	09 49	09 55	09 58	10 01	10 07	10 10	10 16	10 19	10 25	10 28	10 31	10 36	10 40	10 46	10 49	10 55	10 58	11 01	11 08	11 11	11 16
Exhibition Centre 225 a	09 52	09 58			10 10			10 22	10 28			10 39			10 52	10 58			11 11		
Anderston 225 a	09 54	10 00			10 12			10 24	10 30			10 41			10 54	11 00			11 13		
Glasgow Central LL 15 225 a	09 56	10 02			10 13			10 26	10 31			10 43			10 56	11 02			11 14		
Argyle Street 225 a	09 58	10 05			10 17			10 28	10 36			10 46			10 58	11 05			11 19		
Charing Cross d			10 02	10 05		10 14	10 22			10 32	10 35		10 44	10 51			11 02	11 05		11 15	11 21
Glasgow Queen St LL 10 ⛴ a			10 04	10 07		10 16	10 24			10 34	10 37		10 46	10 53			11 04	11 07		11 17	11 23
d			10 04	10 07		10 16	10 26			10 35	10 38		10 47	10 56			11 04	11 08		11 17	11 26
High Street d			10 06	10 10		10 18	10 29			10 37	10 40		10 49	10 59			11 06	11 10		11 19	11 29
Bellgrove d			10 08			10 20	10 32			10 39			10 51	11 02			11 08			11 21	11 32
Duke Street d			10 11							10 41							11 11				
Alexandra Parade d			10 12							10 42							11 12				
Barnhill d			10 15							10 45							11 16				
Springburn a			10 17							10 47							11 18				
Greenfaulds d		11 02	10 41							11 11						12 02	11 41				
Cumbernauld a		11 04	10 44							11 14						12 04	11 44				
Carntyne d						10 24	10 35						10 54	11 05						11 25	11 35
Shettleston d						10 26	10 38						10 57	11 08						11 27	11 38
Garrowhill d				10 17			10 40				10 47			11 10				11 17			11 40
Easterhouse d				10 20			10 43				10 50			11 13				11 20			11 43
Blairhill d				10 24			10 47				10 54			11 17				11 24			11 47
Coatbridge Sunnyside d				10 26		10 35	10 49				10 56		11 05	11 19				11 26		11 36	11 49
Coatdyke d				10 29			10 52				10 59			11 22				11 29			11 52
Airdrie d				10 32		10 40	10a56				11 02		11 10	11a26				11 32		11 40	11a56
Drumgelloch d				10 35		10 43					11 05		11 13					11 35		11 43	
Caldercruix d						10 47							11 17							11 47	
Blackridge d						10 53							11 23							11 53	
Armadale d						10 56							11 26							11 57	
Bathgate a				10 47		11 00					11 18		11 30					11 47		12 01	
d				10 47		11 01					11 19		11 31					11 48		12 02	
Livingston North d				10 52		11 06					11 24		11 35					11 52		12 06	
Uphall d				10 55		11 09					11 27		11 38					11 55		12 09	
Edinburgh Park 230 d				11 03		11 17					11 35		11 48					12 03		12 18	
Haymarket 228,230 ⛴ a				11 08		11 22					11 39		11 57					12 09		12 23	
Edinburgh 228,230 a				11 13		11 27					11 44		12 02					12 14		12 28	

A To Whifflet
B To Larkhall
C To Motherwell

Table T226-R

Mondays to Fridays
21 May to 7 December

Helensburgh, Balloch, Dalmuir and Milngavie - Glasgow - Springburn, Cumbernauld, Airdrie, Bathgate and Edinburgh

	SR	SR	SR	SR	SR	SR	SR	SR	SR	SR	SR	SR	SR	SR	SR	SR	SR	SR	SR	SR	SR	SR
	A	A		◇ B		C			D			◇ E		C			A	A			C	
Helensburgh Upper 227 d				10 44								11 16										
Helensburgh Central d					10 56								11 26							11 51		
Craigendoran d					10 59								11 29							11 54		
Cardross d					11 04								11 34							11 59		
Balloch d								11 07								11 37						
Alexandria d								11 09								11 39						
Renton d								11 12								11 42						
Dalreoch d					11 09			11 15					11 39			11 45				12 04		
Dumbarton Central 227 d			10 54	11 01	11 11			11 17			11 22	11 29	11 41			11 47			11 56	12 06		
Dumbarton East d			10 56		11 13			11 19			11 24		11 43			11 49			11 58	12 08		
Bowling d			11 00								11 29								12 03			
Kilpatrick d			11 03								11 32								12 06			
Dalmuir 227 a			11 06	11 12	11 20			11 26			11 35	11 38	11 50			11 56			12 09	12 19		
d	11 03		11 11		11 21	11 18		11 28	11 33		11 41		11 51	11 48		11 58	12 03		12 11	12 21	12 18	
Singer d						11 20		11 30						11 50		12 00					12 20	
Drumry d						11 23		11 33						11 53		12 03					12 23	
Drumchapel d						11 25		11 35						11 55		12 05					12 25	
Milngavie d		11 08					11 24			11 39					11 54			12 10				12 24
Hillfoot d		11 11					11 27			11 42					11 57			12 13				12 27
Bearsden d		11 13					11 29			11 44					11 59			12 15				12 29
Westerton d		11 16				11 29	11 32	11 38		11 47				11 58	12 02	12 08		12 18			12 28	12 32
Anniesland d		11 20				11 32	11 35	11 41		11 50				12 01	12 05	12 11		12 21			12 31	12 35
Clydebank d	11 05		11 13						11 35		11 43						12 05		12 13			
Yoker d	11 07		11 15						11 37		11 45						12 07		12 15			
Garscadden d	11 10		11 19						11 40		11 49						12 10		12 19			
Scotstounhill d	11 12		11 21						11 42		11 51						12 12		12 21			
Jordanhill d	11 15		11 24						11 45		11 54						12 15		12 24			
Hyndland d	11 17	11 23	11 26		11 28	11 35	11 38	11 44	11 47	11 53	11 56		11 59	12 04	12 08	12 14	12 17	12 24	12 26	12 29	12 34	12 38
Partick 225 d	11 19	11 25	11 28		11 31	11 37	11 41	11 46	11 49	11 55	11 58		12 01	12 07	12 10	12 17	12 20	12 26	12 28	12 32	12 37	12 40
Exhibition Centre 225 a	11 22	11 28				11 40			11 52	11 58				12 10			12 23	12 29			12 40	
Anderston 225 a	11 24	11 30				11 42			11 54	12 00				12 12			12 25	12 31			12 42	
Glasgow Central LL [15] 225 a	11 26	11 32				11 44			11 56	12 02				12 13			12 26	12 32			12 43	
Argyle Street 225 a	11 28	11 35				11 46			11 58	12 05				12 17			12 29	12 37			12 45	
Charing Cross d			11 32		11 35		11 45	11 51			12 02		12 05		12 14	12 22			12 32	12 36		12 44
Glasgow Queen St LL [10] a			11 34		11 37		11 47	11 53			12 04		12 07		12 16	12 24			12 34	12 38		12 46
d			11 34		11 38		11 47	11 56			12 04		12 08		12 17	12 26			12 35	12 38		12 47
High Street d			11 36		11 40		11 49	11 59			12 06		12 10		12 19	12 29			12 37	12 40		12 49
Bellgrove d			11 38				11 51	12 02			12 08				12 21	12 32			12 39			12 51
Duke Street d			11 41								12 11								12 41			
Alexandra Parade d			11 42								12 12								12 42			
Barnhill d			11 45								12 15								12 45			
Springburn a			11 47								12 17								12 47			
Greenfaulds d			12 11							13 02	12 41								13 11			
Cumbernauld a			12 13							13 04	12 44								13 13			
Carntyne d							11 55	12 05							12 24	12 35						12 54
Shettleston d							11 57	12 08							12 27	12 38						12 57
Garrowhill d					11 47			12 10					12 17			12 40				12 48		
Easterhouse d					11 50			12 13					12 20			12 43				12 50		
Blairhill d					11 54			12 17					12 24			12 47				12 54		
Coatbridge Sunnyside d					11 56		12 06	12 19					12 26		12 35	12 49				12 57		13 05
Coatdyke d					11 59			12 22					12 29			12 52				12 59		
Airdrie d					12 02		12 10	12a26					12 32		12 40	12a56				13 03		13 10
Drumgelloch d					12 05		12 13						12 35		12 43					13 06		13 13
Caldercruix d							12 17								12 47							13 17
Blackridge d							12 23								12 53							13 23
Armadale d							12 27								12 57							13 27
Bathgate a					12 17		12 31						12 48		13 01					13 18		13 31
d					12 18		12 32						12 49		13 01					13 19		13 32
Livingston North d					12 22		12 36						12 53		13 06					13 23		13 36
Uphall d					12 25		12 39						12 56		13 09					13 26		13 39
Edinburgh Park 230 d					12 33		12 47						13 04		13 19					13 34		13 49
Haymarket 228,230 a					12 38		12 52						13 09		13 24					13 39		13 58
Edinburgh 228,230 a					12 43		12 59						13 15		13 29					13 44		14 03

A To Motherwell
B From Mallaig to Glasgow Queen Street
C To Larkhall
D To Whifflet
E From Oban to Glasgow Queen Street

Table T226-R

Mondays to Fridays
21 May to 7 December

Helensburgh, Balloch, Dalmuir and Milngavie - Glasgow - Springburn, Cumbernauld, Airdrie, Bathgate and Edinburgh

	SR	SR	SR	SR	SR	SR	SR	SR	SR	SR	SR	SR	SR	SR	SR	SR	SR	SR	SR	SR	SR
		A				B			C	C			B			A				B	
Helensburgh Upper 227 d																					
Helensburgh Central d					12 26							12 53							13 26		
Craigendoran d					12 29							12 56							13 29		
Cardross d					12 34							13 06							13 34		
Balloch d	12 07							12 37							13 07						
Alexandria d	12 09							12 39							13 09						
Renton d	12 12							12 42							13 12						
Dalreoch d	12 15				12 39			12 45				13 11			13 15				13 39		
Dumbarton Central 227 d	12 17			12 26	12 41			12 47			12 56	13 13			13 17			13 26	13 41		
Dumbarton East d	12 19			12 28	12 43			12 49			12 58	13 15			13 19			13 28	13 43		
Bowling d				12 33							13 03							13 33			
Kilpatrick d				12 36							13 06							13 36			
Dalmuir 227 a	12 27			12 39	12 50			12 56			13 09	13 23			13 26			13 39	13 50		
d	12 28	12 33		12 41	12 51	12 49		12 58	13 03		13 11	13 23	13 18		13 27	13 33		13 41	13 51	13 48	
Singer d	12 30					12 51		13 00					13 20		13 29					13 50	
Drumry d	12 32					12 54		13 03					13 22		13 32					13 53	
Drumchapel d	12 35					12 56		13 05					13 25		13 34					13 56	
Milngavie d			12 39				12 54			13 11				13 23			13 40				13 54
Hillfoot d			12 42				12 57			13 14				13 26			13 43				13 57
Bearsden d			12 44				12 59			13 16				13 28			13 45				13 59
Westerton d	12 37		12 47			12 59	13 03	13 08		13 19			13 27	13 31	13 37		13 48			13 58	14 02
Anniesland d	12 41		12 50			13 02	13 06	13 11		13 22			13 30	13 34	13 40		13 51			14 01	14 05
Clydebank d		12 35		12 43					13 05		13 13					13 35		13 43			
Yoker d		12 37		12 45					13 07		13 15					13 37		13 45			
Garscadden d		12 40		12 49					13 10		13 19					13 40		13 49			
Scotstounhill d		12 42		12 51					13 12		13 21					13 42		13 51			
Jordanhill d		12 45		12 54					13 15		13 25					13 45		13 54			
Hyndland d	12 44	12 47	12 53	12 56	12 59	13 05	13 09	13 14	13 17	13 25	13 27	13 30	13 34	13 37	13 43	13 47	13 54	13 56	13 59	14 04	14 08
Partick 225 d	12 46	12 49	12 55	12 58	13 01	13 08	13 11	13 16	13 19	13 27	13 29	13 32	13 37	13 40	13 45	13 49	13 56	13 58	14 02	14 07	14 10
Exhibition Centre 225 a		12 52	12 58			13 11			13 22	13 30			13 40			13 52	13 59			14 10	
Anderston 225 a		12 54	13 00			13 13			13 24	13 32			13 42			13 54	14 01			14 12	
Glasgow Central LL [15] 225 a		12 56	13 02			13 14			13 26	13 33			13 43			13 56	14 02			14 13	
Argyle Street 225 a		12 58	13 06			13 17			13 28	13 37			13 45			13 58	14 05			14 17	
Charing Cross d	12 51			13 02	13 05		13 15	13 21			13 33	13 37		13 44	13 50			14 02	14 06		14 14
Glasgow Queen St LL [10] a	12 53			13 04	13 07		13 17	13 23			13 35	13 39		13 46	13 52			14 04	14 08		14 16
d	12 56			13 05	13 08		13 18	13 25			13 36	13 39		13 46	13 55			14 05	14 09		14 17
High Street d	12 59			13 07	13 10		13 20	13 27			13 38	13 41		13 48	13 59			14 07	14 11		14 19
Bellgrove d	13 02			13 09			13 22	13 29			13 40			13 50	14 02			14 09			14 21
Duke Street d				13 11							13 42							14 11			
Alexandra Parade d				13 12							13 43							14 12			
Barnhill d				13 15							13 46							14 15			
Springburn a				13 17							13 48							14 17			
Greenfaulds d			14 02	13 39							14 13						15 02	14 39			
Cumbernauld a			14 04	13 42							14 15						15 04	14 42			
Carntyne d	13 05						13 25	13 33						13 54	14 05						14 24
Shettleston d	13 08						13 28	13 35						13 56	14 08						14 27
Garrowhill d	13 10				13 18			13 38				13 49			14 10				14 19		
Easterhouse d	13 13				13 20			13 40				13 51			14 13				14 21		
Blairhill d	13 17				13 24			13 44				13 55			14 17				14 25		
Coatbridge Sunnyside d	13 19				13 27		13 36	13 47				13 58		14 05	14 19				14 28		14 35
Coatdyke d	13 22				13 29			13 49				14 00			14 22				14 30		
Airdrie d	13a26				13 32		13 41	13a53				14 03		14 09	14a26				14 33		14 40
Drumgelloch d					13 35		13 44					14 06		14 12					14 36		14 43
Caldercruix d							13 48							14 16							14 47
Blackridge d							13 54							14 22							14 53
Armadale d							13 57							14 26							14 56
Bathgate a					13 48		14 01					14 19		14 30					14 49		15 00
d					13 48		14 02					14 19		14 30					14 49		15 01
Livingston North d					13 52		14 06					14 24		14 35					14 54		15 05
Uphall d					13 55		14 09					14 27		14 38					14 57		15 08
Edinburgh Park 230 d					14 03		14 18					14 36		14 47					15 05		15 18
Haymarket 228,230 a					14 08		14 22					14 40		14 52					15 10		15 22
Edinburgh 228,230 a					14 13		14 27					14 45		15 00					15 16		15 29

A To Whifflet
B To Larkhall
C To Motherwell

Table T226-R

Mondays to Fridays

21 May to 7 December

Helensburgh, Balloch, Dalmuir and Milngavie - Glasgow - Springburn, Cumbernauld, Airdrie, Bathgate and Edinburgh

		SR	SR	SR	SR	SR	SR	SR	SR	SR	SR	SR	SR	SR	SR	SR	SR	SR	SR	SR	SR	SR	SR
			A	A			B			C				B			A	A		◇ D		B	
Helensburgh Upper 227	d																			14 43			
Helensburgh Central	d					13 56							14 26								14 56		
Craigendoran	d					13 59							14 29								14 59		
Cardross	d					14 04							14 34								15 04		
Balloch	d	13 37							14 07							14 37							
Alexandria	d	13 39							14 09							14 39							
Renton	d	13 42							14 12							14 42							
Dalreoch	d	13 47				14 09			14 15				14 39			14 45					15 09		
Dumbarton Central 227	d	13 49			13 56	14 11			14 17			14 26	14 41			14 47			14 54	15 02	15 11		
Dumbarton East	d	13 51			13 58	14 13			14 19			14 28	14 43			14 49			14 56		15 13		
Bowling	d				14 03							14 33							15 00				
Kilpatrick	d				14 06							14 36							15 03				
Dalmuir 227	a	14 00			14 09	14 20			14 26			14 39	14 50			14 56			15 06	15 13	15 20		
	d	14 00	14 03		14 11	14 21	14 18		14 27	14 32		14 41	14 51	14 48		14 58	15 03		15 11		15 21	15 18	
Singer	d	14 02					14 20		14 29					14 50		15 00						15 20	
Drumry	d	14 05					14 23		14 32					14 53		15 03						15 23	
Drumchapel	d	14 07					14 26		14 34					14 55		15 05						15 26	
Milngavie	d			14 09				14 24			14 39				14 54			15 08					15 24
Hillfoot	d			14 12				14 27			14 42				14 57			15 11					15 27
Bearsden	d			14 14				14 29			14 44				14 59			15 13					15 29
Westerton	d	14 10		14 17			14 28	14 32	14 37		14 47			14 58	15 02	15 08		15 17				15 28	15 32
Anniesland	d	14 13		14 20			14 31	14 35	14 40		14 50			15 01	15 05	15 11		15 20				15 31	15 35
Clydebank	d		14 05		14 13					14 34		14 43					15 05		15 13				
Yoker	d		14 07		14 15					14 36		14 45					15 07		15 15				
Garscadden	d		14 10		14 19					14 40		14 49					15 10		15 19				
Scotstounhill	d		14 12		14 21					14 42		14 51					15 12		15 21				
Jordanhill	d		14 16		14 24					14 44		14 54					15 15		15 24				
Hyndland [3]	d	14 16	14 18	14 23	14 26	14 28	14 34	14 38	14 43	14 47	14 53	14 56	14 58	15 04	15 08	15 14	15 17	15 23	15 26		15 28	15 34	15 38
Partick 225	d	14 18	14 21	14 25	14 28	14 31	14 37	14 40	14 45	14 49	14 55	14 58	15 01	15 07	15 10	15 17	15 20	15 25	15 28		15 31	15 37	15 40
Exhibition Centre 225	a		14 24	14 28			14 40			14 52	14 58			15 10			15 23	15 28				15 40	
Anderston 225	a		14 26	14 30			14 42			14 54	15 00			15 12			15 25	15 30				15 42	
Glasgow Central LL [15] 225	a		14 27	14 32			14 43			14 56	15 01			15 13			15 26	15 31				15 43	
Argyle Street 225	a		14 29	14 36			14 45			14 58	15 05			15 17			15 29	15 35				15 46	
Charing Cross	d	14 22			14 32	14 35		14 44	14 50			15 02	15 05		15 14	15 22			15 32		15 35		15 44
Glasgow Queen St LL [10]	a	14 24			14 34	14 37		14 46	14 52			15 04	15 07		15 16	15 24			15 34		15 37		15 46
	d	14 25			14 34	14 38		14 47	14 55			15 04	15 08		15 17	15 26			15 34		15 38		15 47
High Street	d	14 27			14 36	14 40		14 49	14 59			15 06	15 10		15 19	15 29			15 36		15 40		15 49
Bellgrove	d	14 29			14 38			14 51	15 02			15 08			15 21	15 32			15 38				15 51
Duke Street	d				14 41							15 11							15 41				
Alexandra Parade	d				14 42							15 12							15 42				
Barnhill	d				14 45							15 15							15 45				
Springburn	a				14 47							15 17							15 47				
Greenfaulds	d				15 11						16 02	15 40							16 11				
Cumbernauld	a				15 13						16 04	15 43							16 13				
Carntyne	d	14 35						14 54	15 05						15 24	15 35							15 54
Shettleston	d	14 38						14 57	15 08						15 27	15 38							15 57
Garrowhill	d	14 40				14 47			15 10				15 17			15 40					15 47		
Easterhouse	d	14 43				14 50			15 13				15 20			15 43					15 50		
Blairhill	d	14 47				14 54			15 17				15 24			15 47					15 54		
Coatbridge Sunnyside	d	14 49				14 56		15 05	15 19				15 26		15 35	15 50					15 56		16 05
Coatdyke	d	14 52				14 59			15 22				15 29			15 52					15 59		
Airdrie	d	14a56				15 02		15 10	15a26				15 32		15 40	15a56					16 02		16 10
Drumgelloch	d					15 05		15 13					15 35		15 43						16 05		16 13
Caldercruix	d							15 17							15 47								16 17
Blackridge	d							15 23							15 53								16 23
Armadale	d							15 27							15 56								16 27
Bathgate	a					15 17		15 31					15 48		16 00						16 18		16 31
	d					15 18		15 32					15 48		16 01						16 19		16 31
Livingston North	d					15 22		15 36					15 53		16 05						16 24		16 36
Uphall	d					15 25		15 39					15 56		16 08						16 27		16 39
Edinburgh Park 230	d					15 33		15 47					16 04		16 18						16 35		16 48
Haymarket 228,230	a					15 38		15 52					16 09		16 22						16 39		16 52
Edinburgh 228,230	a					15 45		15 59					16 14		16 29						16 44		16 57

A To Motherwell
B To Larkhall
C To Whifflet
D From Mallaig to Glasgow Queen Street

Table T226-R

Mondays to Fridays

21 May to 7 December

Helensburgh, Balloch, Dalmuir and Milngavie - Glasgow - Springburn, Cumbernauld, Airdrie, Bathgate and Edinburgh

		SR	SR	SR	SR	SR	SR	SR	SR	SR	SR	SR	SR	SR	SR	SR	SR	SR	SR	SR	SR	SR	SR
			A				B			C	C			B			A				B		
Helensburgh Upper 227	d																						
Helensburgh Central	d					15 26							15 56							16 26			
Craigendoran	d					15 29							15 59							16 29			
Cardross	d					15 34							16 04							16 34			
Balloch	d	15 07							15 37							16 07							16 37
Alexandria	d	15 09							15 39							16 09							16 39
Renton	d	15 12							15 42							16 12							16 42
Dalreoch	d	15 15				15 39			15 45				16 09			16 15				16 39			16 45
Dumbarton Central 227	d	15 17			15 26	15 41			15 47			15 56	16 11			16 17			16 26	16 41			16 47
Dumbarton East	d	15 19			15 28	15 43			15 49			15 58	16 13			16 19			16 28	16 43			16 49
Bowling	d				15 33							16 03							16 33				
Kilpatrick	d				15 36							16 06							16 36				
Dalmuir 227	a	15 26			15 39	15 50			15 57			16 09	16 20			16 26			16 39	16 50			16 56
	d	15 28	15 33		15 41	15 51	15 48		15 58	16 03		16 11	16 21	16 18		16 28	16 33		16 41	16 51	16 48		16 58
Singer	d	15 30					15 50		16 00					16 20		16 30					16 50		17 00
Drumry	d	15 33					15 53		16 03					16 23		16 33					16 53		17 03
Drumchapel	d	15 35					15 56		16 05					16 26		16 35					16 55		17 05
Milngavie	d			15 39				15 54			16 09				16 24			16 39				16 54	
Hillfoot	d			15 42				15 57			16 12				16 27			16 42				16 57	
Bearsden	d			15 44				15 59			16 14				16 29			16 44				16 59	
Westerton	d	15 38		15 47			15 58	16 02	16 08		16 17			16 28	16 32	16 38		16 47			16 58	17 02	17 08
Anniesland	d	15 41		15 50			16 01	16 05	16 11		16 20			16 31	16 35	16 41		16 50			17 01	17 05	17 11
Clydebank	d		15 35		15 43					16 05		16 13					16 35		16 43				
Yoker	d		15 37		15 45					16 07		16 15					16 37		16 45				
Garscadden	d		15 40		15 49					16 10		16 19					16 40		16 49				
Scotstounhill	d		15 42		15 51					16 12		16 21					16 42		16 51				
Jordanhill	d		15 45		15 54					16 15		16 24					16 44		16 54				
Hyndland [3]	d	15 44	15 47	15 53	15 56	15 58	16 04	16 08	16 14	16 17	16 23	16 26	16 29	16 34	16 38	16 44	16 47	16 53	16 56	16 58	17 05	17 08	17 14
Partick 225	d	15 46	15 49	15 55	15 58	16 01	16 07	16 10	16 16	16 19	16 25	16 28	16 32	16 37	16 40	16 46	16 49	16 55	16 58	17 01	17 07	17 11	17 16
Exhibition Centre 225	a		15 52	15 58			16 10			16 22	16 28			16 40			16 52	16 58			17 10		
Anderston 225	a		15 54	16 00			16 12			16 24	16 30			16 42			16 54	17 03			17 13		
Glasgow Central LL [15] 225	a		15 56	16 01			16 13			16 26	16 31			16 43			16 56	17 05			17 14		
Argyle Street 225	a		15 58	16 05			16 17			16 28	16 35			16 45			16 58	17 07			17 18		
Charing Cross	d	15 51			16 02	16 05		16 14	16 21			16 32	16 36		16 44	16 51			17 02	17 05		17 15	17 21
Glasgow Queen St LL [10]	a	15 53			16 04	16 07		16 16	16 23			16 34	16 38		16 46	16 53			17 04	17 07		17 17	17 23
	d	15 56			16 04	16 08		16 17	16 24			16 34	16 38		16 47	16 56			17 04	17 08		17 18	17 26
High Street	d	15 59			16 06	16 10		16 19	16 27			16 36	16 40		16 49	16 59			17 06	17 10		17 20	17 29
Bellgrove	d	16 02			16 08			16 21	16 29			16 38			16 51	17 02			17 08			17 22	17 32
Duke Street	d				16 11							16 41							17 11				
Alexandra Parade	d				16 12							16 42							17 12				
Barnhill	d				16 15							16 45							17 15				
Springburn	a				16 17							16 47							17 17				
Greenfaulds	d			17 02	16 39							17 11						18 02	17 41				
Cumbernauld	a			17 04	16 43							17 13						18 04	17 44				
Carntyne	d	16 05						16 24	16 33						16 54	17 05						17 25	17 35
Shettleston	d	16 08						16 27	16 35						16 57	17 08						17 28	17 38
Garrowhill	d	16 10				16 17			16 38				16 48			17 10				17 17			17 40
Easterhouse	d	16 13				16 20			16 40				16 50			17 13				17 20			17 43
Blairhill	d	16 17				16 24		16 33	16 44				16 54		17 03	17 17				17 24		17 34	17 47
Coatbridge Sunnyside	d	16 19				16 26		16 36	16 47				16 57		17 06	17 19				17 26		17 37	17 49
Coatdyke	d	16 22				16 29		16 38	16 49				16 59		17 08	17 22				17 29		17 39	17 52
Airdrie	d	16a26				16 32		16 41	16a53				17 02		17 11	17a26				17 32		17 42	17a56
Drumgelloch	d					16 35		16 44					17 05		17 14					17 35		17 45	
Caldercruix	d							16 48							17 18							17 49	
Blackridge	d							16 54							17 24							17 55	
Armadale	d							16 58							17 28							17 59	
Bathgate	a					16 48		17 02					17 18		17 32					17 47		18 03	
	d					16 50		17 02					17 18		17 32					17 48		18 03	
Livingston North	d					16 55		17 07					17 23		17 37					17 52		18 08	
Uphall	d					16 58		17 10					17 26		17 40					17 55		18 11	
Edinburgh Park 230	d					17 07		17 18					17 34		17 49					18 04		18 19	
Haymarket 228,230	a					17 12		17 22					17 39		17 58					18 09		18 24	
Edinburgh 228,230	a					17 19		17 27					17 45		18 04					18 16		18 29	

A To Whifflet
B To Larkhall
C To Motherwell

Helensburgh, Balloch, Dalmuir and Milngavie - Glasgow - Springburn, Cumbernauld, Airdrie, Bathgate and Edinburgh

	SR A	SR A	SR	SR	SR B	SR ◇ C	SR	SR	SR D	SR	SR	SR	SR B	SR	SR	SR A	SR A	SR	SR	SR B	SR
Helensburgh Upper 227 d						17 00															
Helensburgh Central d				16 54								17 26							17 56		
Craigendoran d				16 57								17 29							17 59		
Cardross d				17 02								17 34							18 04		
Balloch d								17 07							17 37						
Alexandria d								17 09							17 39						
Renton d								17 12							17 42						
Dalreoch d				17 07				17 15				17 39			17 45				18 09		
Dumbarton Central 227 d			16 56	17 09		17 13		17 17			17 26	17 41			17 47			17 56	18 11		
Dumbarton East d			16 58	17 11				17 19			17 28	17 43			17 49			17 58	18 13		
Bowling d			17 03								17 33							18 03			
Kilpatrick d			17 06								17 36							18 06			
Dalmuir 227 a			17 09	17 18		17 23		17 27			17 39	17 50			17 56			18 09	18 20		
d	17 03		17 11	17 21	17 18			17 28	17 33		17 41	17 51	17 48		17 58	18 03		18 11	18 21	18 18	
Singer d					17 20			17 30					17 50		18 00					18 20	
Drumry d					17 23			17 33					17 53		18 03					18 23	
Drumchapel d					17 25			17 35					17 56		18 05					18 26	
Milngavie d		17 09					17 24			17 39				17 54			18 09				18 24
Hillfoot d		17 12					17 27			17 42				17 57			18 12				18 27
Bearsden d		17 14					17 29			17 44				17 59			18 14				18 29
Westerton d		17 17			17 28		17 32	17 38		17 47			17 58	18 02	18 08		18 17			18 28	18 32
Anniesland d		17 20			17 31		17 35	17 41		17 50			18 01	18 05	18 11		18 20			18 31	18 35
Clydebank d	17 05		17 13						17 35		17 43					18 05		18 13			
Yoker d	17 07		17 15						17 37		17 45					18 07		18 15			
Garscadden d	17 10		17 19						17 40		17 49					18 10		18 19			
Scotstounhill d	17 12		17 21						17 42		17 51					18 12		18 21			
Jordanhill d	17 15		17 24						17 45		17 54					18 15		18 24			
Hyndland d	17 17	17 23	17 26	17 28	17 35		17 38	17 44	17 47	17 53	17 56	18 00	18 04	18 08	18 14	18 17	18 23	18 26	18 28	18 34	18 38
Partick 225 ⛴ d	17 20	17 25	17 28	17 31	17 37		17 41	17 46	17 49	17 55	17 58	18 02	18 07	18 10	18 16	18 19	18 25	18 28	18 31	18 37	18 40
Exhibition Centre 225 a	17 23	17 28			17 41				17 52	17 58			18 10			18 22	18 28			18 40	
Anderston 225 a	17 25	17 30			17 45				17 54	18 00			18 12			18 24	18 30			18 42	
Glasgow Central LL 225 a	17 26	17 31			17 47				17 56	18 02			18 14			18 26	18 32			18 43	
Argyle Street 225 a	17 29	17 35			17 52				17 58	18 05			18 19			18 28	18 35			18 45	
Charing Cross d			17 32	17 35			17 45	17 51			18 02	18 06		18 14	18 22			18 32	18 35		18 44
Glasgow Queen St LL ⛴ a			17 34	17 37			17 47	17 53			18 04	18 08		18 16	18 24			18 34	18 37		18 46
d			17 34	17 38			17 48	17 56			18 04	18 08		18 17	18 26			18 34	18 38		18 47
High Street d			17 36	17 40			17 50	17 59			18 06	18 10		18 19	18 29			18 36	18 40		18 49
Bellgrove d			17 38				17 52	18 02			18 08			18 21	18 32			18 38			18 51
Duke Street d			17 41								18 11							18 41			
Alexandra Parade d			17 42								18 12							18 42			
Barnhill d			17 45								18 15							18 45			
Springburn a			17 47								18 17							18 47			
Greenfaulds d			18 11							19 01	18 41							19 14			
Cumbernauld a			18 13							19 03	18 44							19 16			
Carntyne d							17 55	18 05						18 24	18 35						18 54
Shettleston d							17 58	18 08						18 27	18 38						18 57
Garrowhill d				17 47				18 10				18 18			18 40				18 47		
Easterhouse d				17 50				18 13				18 20			18 43				18 50		
Blairhill d				17 54				18 17				18 24			18 47				18 54		
Coatbridge Sunnyside d				17 56			18 06	18 19				18 27		18 35	18 49				18 56		19 05
Coatdyke d				17 59				18 22				18 29			18 52				18 59		
Airdrie d				18 02			18 11	18a26				18 32		18 40	18a56				19 02		19 10
Drumgelloch d				18 05			18 14					18 35		18 43					19 05		19 13
Caldercruix d							18 18							18 47							19 17
Blackridge d							18 24							18 53							19 23
Armadale d							18 27							18 57							19 27
Bathgate a				18 17			18 31					18 48		19 01					19 17		19 31
d				18 18			18 32					18 48		19 02					19 18		19 31
Livingston North d				18 23			18 37					18 53		19 06					19 22		19 36
Uphall d				18 26			18 40					18 56		19 09					19 25		19 39
Edinburgh Park 230 d				18 34			18 49					19 04		19 18					19 33		19 56
Haymarket 228,230 ⛴ a				18 39			18 53					19 08		19 22					19 39		20 01
Edinburgh 228,230 a				18 44			18 58					19 13		19 27					19 44		20 06

A To Motherwell
B To Larkhall
C From Oban to Glasgow Queen Street
D To Whifflet

Helensburgh, Balloch, Dalmuir and Milngavie - Glasgow - Springburn, Cumbernauld, Airdrie, Bathgate and Edinburgh

	SR	SR A	SR	SR	SR	SR B	SR	SR C	SR C	SR	SR	SR B	SR	SR A	SR	SR	SR B	SR	SR	SR C	SR C	SR
Helensburgh Upper 227 d																						
Helensburgh Central d					18 25						18 54								19 32			
Craigendoran d					18 28						18 57								19 35			
Cardross d					18 33						19 02								19 40			
Balloch d	18 07						18 38						19 07									19 44
Alexandria d	18 09						18 40						19 09									19 46
Renton d	18 12						18 43						19 12									19 49
Dalreoch d	18 15				18 38		18 46				19 07		19 15						19 45			19 52
Dumbarton Central 227 d	18 17			18 26	18 40		18 48			18 54	19 11		19 17			19 26			19 47			19 57
Dumbarton East d	18 19			18 28	18 42		18 50			18 56	19 13		19 19			19 28			19 49			19 59
Bowling d				18 33						19 01						19 33						20 04
Kilpatrick d				18 36						19 04						19 36						20 07
Dalmuir 227 a	18 26			18 39	18 49		18 59			19 07	19 22		19 26			19 39			19 56			20 10
d	18 27	18 33		18 41	18 51	18 48	18 59	19 03		19 11	19 22	19 15	19 28	19 33		19 41	19 48		19 59	20 02		20 11
Singer d	18 29					18 50	19 01					19 17	19 30				19 50		20 01			
Drumry d	18 32					18 53	19 04					19 20	19 33				19 53		20 03			
Drumchapel d	18 34					18 55	19 06					19 23	19 35				19 56		20 06			
Milngavie d			18 39						19 09						19 39						20 09	
Hillfoot d			18 42						19 12						19 42						20 12	
Bearsden d			18 44						19 14						19 44						20 14	
Westerton d	18 37		18 47			18 58	19 09		19 17			19 29	19 38		19 47		19 58		20 08		20 17	
Anniesland d	18 40		18 50			19 01	19 12		19 20			19 32	19 41		19 50		20 03		20 11		20 20	
Clydebank d		18 35		18 43				19 05		19 13				19 35		19 43				20 04		20 13
Yoker d		18 37		18 45				19 07		19 15				19 37		19 45				20 06		20 16
Garscadden d		18 40		18 49				19 10		19 19				19 41		19 49				20 10		20 19
Scotstounhill d		18 42		18 51				19 12		19 21				19 43		19 51				20 12		20 21
Jordanhill d		18 45		18 54				19 15		19 25				19 45		19 54				20 15		20 24
Hyndland d	18 43	18 47	18 53	18 56	18 58	19 04	19 15	19 17	19 23	19 27	19 29	19 35	19 44	19 47	19 53	19 56	20 06		20 14	20 17	20 23	20 26
Partick 225 ⛴ d	18 45	18 49	18 55	18 58	19 01	19 07	19 17	19 20	19 25	19 29	19 32	19 38	19 46	19 50	19 55	19 58	20 08		20 17	20 19	20 25	20 28
Exhibition Centre 225 a		18 52	18 58			19 10		19 23	19 28			19 41		19 53	19 58		20 11			20 22	20 29	
Anderston 225 a		18 54	19 00			19 12		19 25	19 30			19 43		19 55	20 00		20 13			20 26	20 33	
Glasgow Central LL 225 a		18 56	19 01			19 13		19 26	19 32			19 45		19 56	20 01		20 15			20 27	20 34	
Argyle Street 225 a		18 58	19 05			19 17		19 29	19 35			19 50		19 59	20 03		20 19			20 29	20 37	
Charing Cross d	18 50			19 02	19 05		19 21			19 33	19 36		19 50			20 02			20 21			20 32
Glasgow Queen St LL ⛴ a	18 52			19 04	19 07		19 23			19 35	19 38		19 52			20 04			20 23			20 34
d	18 52			19 04	19 08		19 23			19 35	19 38		19 52			20 04			20 23			20 34
High Street d	18 55			19 06	19 10		19 25			19 37	19 40		19 54			20 06			20 25			20 36
Bellgrove d	18 57			19 08			19 27			19 39			19 56			20 08			20 27			20 38
Duke Street d				19 11						19 43						20 10						20 40
Alexandra Parade d				19 12						19 47						20 17						20 42
Barnhill d				19 15						19 53						20 24						20 45
Springburn a				19 17						19 55						20 26						20 47
Greenfaulds d			20 02	19 39						20 17					21 02	20 47						21 16
Cumbernauld a			20 04	19 42						20 19					21 04	20 50						21 18
Carntyne d	19 01						19 31						20 00						20 31			
Shettleston d	19 03						19 33						20 02						20 33			
Garrowhill d	19 06						19 36						20 05						20 36			
Easterhouse d	19 08						19 38						20 07						20 38			
Blairhill d	19 12						19 42						20 11						20 42			
Coatbridge Sunnyside d	19 15				19 22		19 45				19 53		20 14						20 45			
Coatdyke d	19 17						19 47						20 16						20 47			
Airdrie d	19a21				19 27		19a50				19 58		20a20						20 50			
Drumgelloch d					19 30						20 01								20 53			
Caldercruix d					19 34						20 05								20 57			
Blackridge d					19 40						20 11								21 03			
Armadale d					19 43						20 14								21 07			
Bathgate a					19 47						20 18								21 11			
d					19 49						20 18							20 47	21 11			
Livingston North d					19 53						20 23							20 51	21 16			
Uphall d					19 56						20 26							20 54	21 19			
Edinburgh Park 230 d					20 04						20 34							21 02	21 27			
Haymarket 228,230 ⛴ a					20 12						20 38							21 07	21 36			
Edinburgh 228,230 a					20 20						20 43							21 12	21 42			

A To Whifflet
B To Larkhall
C To Motherwell

Table T226-R

Mondays to Fridays
21 May to 7 December

Helensburgh, Balloch, Dalmuir and Milngavie - Glasgow - Springburn, Cumbernauld, Airdrie, Bathgate and Edinburgh

Station		SR	SR	SR	SR	SR	SR	SR	SR	SR	SR	SR	SR	SR	SR	SR	SR	SR	SR	SR	SR	SR
		A		B			A		◇ C	D	D		A		B			A		D	D	
Helensburgh Upper 227	d								20 37													
Helensburgh Central	d		20 02					20 32						21 02					21 32			
Craigendoran	d		20 05					20 35						21 05					21 35			
Cardross	d		20 10					20 40						21 10					21 40			
Balloch	d					20 14						20 45					21 14					21 44
Alexandria	d					20 16						20 47					21 16					21 46
Renton	d					20 19						20 50					21 19					21 49
Dalreoch	d		20 15			20 22		20 45				20 53		21 15			21 24		21 45			21 52
Dumbarton Central 227	d		20 17			20 26		20 47	20 51			20 56		21 17			21 26		21 47			21 56
Dumbarton East	d		20 19			20 28		20 49				20 58		21 19			21 28		21 49			21 58
Bowling	d					20 33						21 03					21 33					22 03
Kilpatrick	d					20 36						21 06					21 36					22 06
Dalmuir 227	a		20 26			20 39		20 57	21 03			21 09		21 26			21 39		21 57			22 09
	d	20 18	20 28	20 33		20 41	20 48	20 59		21 03		21 11	21 18	21 29	21 33		21 41	21 49	21 59	22 03		22 11
Singer	d	20 20	20 30				20 50	21 01					21 20	21 31				21 51	22 01			
Drumry	d	20 23	20 32				20 53	21 03					21 23	21 33				21 54	22 04			
Drumchapel	d	20 26	20 35				20 55	21 06					21 25	21 36				21 56	22 06			
Milngavie	d				20 38						21 09					21 39					22 10	
Hillfoot	d				20 41						21 12					21 42					22 13	
Bearsden	d				20 43						21 14					21 44					22 15	
Westerton	d	20 28	20 37		20 46		21 00	21 08			21 17		21 29	21 38		21 47		21 59	22 09		22 18	
Anniesland	d	20 31	20 40		20 50		21 03	21 11			21 20		21 32	21 41		21 50		22 03	22 12		22 21	
Clydebank	d			20 35		20 43				21 05		21 13			21 35		21 43			22 05		22 13
Yoker	d			20 37		20 45				21 07		21 15			21 37		21 45			22 07		22 15
Garscadden	d			20 40		20 49				21 10		21 19			21 40		21 49			22 10		22 19
Scotstounhill	d			20 42		20 51				21 12		21 21			21 42		21 51			22 12		22 21
Jordanhill	d			20 45		20 55				21 15		21 24			21 45		21 54			22 15		22 25
Hyndland 3	d	20 34	20 43	20 47	20 53	20 57	21 06	21 14		21 17	21 23	21 26	21 35	21 44	21 47	21 53	21 56	22 06	22 15	22 18	22 24	22 27
Partick 225 ⛴	d	20 37	20 46	20 50	20 55	20 59	21 08	21 17		21 20	21 25	21 28	21 37	21 47	21 50	21 55	21 58	22 08	22 17	22 20	22 26	22 29
Exhibition Centre 225	a	20 40		20 53	20 58		21 11			21 23	21 28		21 40		21 53	21 58		22 11		22 23	22 29	
Anderston 225	a	20 42		20 55	21 00		21 13			21 25	21 30		21 42		21 55	22 00		22 13		22 25	22 31	
Glasgow Central LL 15 225	a	20 43		20 56	21 02		21 15			21 26	21 32		21 44		21 56	22 02		22 15		22 27	22 33	
Argyle Street 225	a	20 46		20 59	21 05		21 17			21 29	21 36		21 46		21 59	22 05		22 18		22 29	22 35	
Charing Cross	d		20 50			21 03		21 21				21 32		21 51			22 02		22 21			22 33
Glasgow Queen St LL 10 ⛴	a		20 52			21 05		21 23				21 34		21 53			22 04		22 23			22 35
	d		20 53			21 06		21 23				21 34		21 53			22 04		22 24			22 35
High Street	d		20 55			21 08		21 25				21 36		21 55			22 06		22 26			22 37
Bellgrove	d		20 57			21 10		21 27				21 38		21 57			22 08		22 28			22 39
Duke Street	d					21 12						21 40					22 10					22 41
Alexandra Parade	d					21 18						21 42					22 12					22 43
Barnhill	d					21 23						21 45					22 15					22 46
Springburn	a					21 25						21 47					22 17					22 48
Greenfaulds	d				22 03	21 47						22 11				23 02	22 38					23 09
Cumbernauld	a				22 05	21 49						22 13				23 04	22 41					23 12
Carntyne	d		21 01					21 31						22 01					22 31			
Shettleston	d		21 03					21 33						22 03					22 34			
Garrowhill	d		21 06					21 36						22 06					22 36			
Easterhouse	d		21 08					21 38						22 08					22 39			
Blairhill	d		21 12					21 42						22 12					22 43			
Coatbridge Sunnyside	d		21 15					21 45						22 15					22 45			
Coatdyke	d		21 17					21 47						22 17					22 48			
Airdrie	d		21 20					21 50						22 20					22 51			
Drumgelloch	d		21 23					21 53						22 23					22 54			
Caldercruix	d		21 27					21 57						22 27					22 58			
Blackridge	d		21 33					22 03						22 33					23 04			
Armadale	d		21 37					22 07						22 37					23 07			
Bathgate	a		21 41					22 11						22 41					23 11			
	d		21 41					22 11						22 41					23 12			
Livingston North	d		21 46					22 16						22 46					23 16			
Uphall	d		21 49					22 19						22 49					23 19			
Edinburgh Park 230	d		21 57					22 27						23 03					23 27			
Haymarket 228,230 ⛴	a		22 01					22 31						23 08					23 35			
Edinburgh 228,230	a		22 06					22 36						23 13					23 40			

A To Larkhall
B To Whifflet
C From Mallaig to Glasgow Queen Street
D To Motherwell

Table T226-R

Mondays to Fridays
21 May to 7 December

Helensburgh, Balloch, Dalmuir and Milngavie - Glasgow - Springburn, Cumbernauld, Airdrie, Bathgate and Edinburgh

Station		SR	SR	SR	SR	SR	SR	SR	SR	SR	SR	SR	SR FO	SR	SR FO	SR	CS	SR FO	SR	SR
		A		B	C		A		C	C		◇ D	A		C		🛏 E ✕	C		
Helensburgh Upper 227	d											22 49					23 25			
Helensburgh Central	d		22 02					22 31						23 02					23 32	
Craigendoran	d		22 05					22 34						23 05					23 35	
Cardross	d		22 10					22 40						23 10					23 40	
Balloch	d					22 14					22 44					23 14				23 44
Alexandria	d					22 16					22 46					23 16				23 46
Renton	d					22 19					22 49					23 19				23 49
Dalreoch	d		22 15			22 22		22 45			22 52			23 15		23 22			23 45	23 52
Dumbarton Central 227	d		22 17			22 26		22 47			22 54	23 02		23 17		23 24	23 40		23 47	23 55
Dumbarton East	d		22 19			22 28		22 49			22 56			23 19		23 26			23 49	23 57
Bowling	d					22 33					23 00					23 31				
Kilpatrick	d					22 36					23 03					23 34				
Dalmuir 227	a		22 26			22 39		22 56			23 06	23 11		23 26		23 37	23 51		23 56	00 05
	d	22 18	22 29	22 33		22 41	22 48	22 59	23 03		23 11		23 18	23 29	23 33		23 52		23 59	
Singer	d	22 20	22 31				22 50	23 01					23 20	23 31					00 01	
Drumry	d	22 23	22 33				22 53	23 03					23 23	23 33					00 03	
Drumchapel	d	22 26	22 36				22 55	23 06					23 25	23 36					00 06	
Milngavie	d				22 38					23 09								23 39		
Hillfoot	d				22 41					23 12								23 42		
Bearsden	d				22 43					23 14								23 44		
Westerton	d	22 28	22 38		22 46		22 59	23 08		23 17			23 28	23 38				23 47	00 08	
Anniesland	d	22 31	22 41		22 50		23 02	23 11		23 20			23 31	23 41				23 50	00 11	
Clydebank	d			22 35		22 43			23 05		23 13				23 35					
Yoker	d			22 37		22 45			23 07		23 15				23 37					
Garscadden	d			22 40		22 49			23 10		23 19				23 40					
Scotstounhill	d			22 42		22 51			23 12		23 21				23 42					
Jordanhill	d			22 45		22 55			23 15		23 24				23 45					
Hyndland 3	d	22 34	22 44	22 47	22 53	22 57	23 05	23 14	23 17	23 23	23 26		23 34	23 44	23 48			23 53	00 14	
Partick 225 ⛴	d	22 37	22 47	22 50	22 55	22 59	23 08	23 17	23 20	23 25	23 28		23 37	23 47	23 50			23 55	00 17	
Exhibition Centre 225	a	22 40		22 53	22 58		23 11		23 23	23 28			23 40		23 53			23 59		
Anderston 225	a	22 42		22 55	23 01		23 14		23 25	23 31			23 43		23 56			00 01		
Glasgow Central LL 15 225	a	22 44		22 57	23 02		23 15		23 27	23 32			23 44		23 58			00 03		
Argyle Street 225	a	22 46		22 59	23 07		23 18		23 29	23 37			23 47		00 02			00 07		
Charing Cross	d		22 51			23 03		23 21			23 32			23 51					00 21	
Glasgow Queen St LL 10 ⛴	a		22 53			23 05		23 23			23 34			23 53			00s14		00 23	
	d		22 53			23 05		23 23			23 34			23 53					00 23	
High Street	d		22 55			23 07		23 25			23 36			23 55					00 25	
Bellgrove	d		22 57			23 09		23 27			23 38			23 57					00 27	
Duke Street	d					23 11					23 40									
Alexandra Parade	d					23 13					23 42									
Barnhill	d					23 16					23 45									
Springburn	a					23 18					23 47									
Greenfaulds	d					23 41														
Cumbernauld	a					23 44														
Carntyne	d		23 01					23 31						00 02					00 31	
Shettleston	d		23 03					23 33						00 03					00 33	
Garrowhill	d		23 06					23 36						00 06					00 36	
Easterhouse	d		23 08					23 38						00 08					00 38	
Blairhill	d		23 12					23 42						00 12					00 42	
Coatbridge Sunnyside	d		23 15					23 45						00 15					00 45	
Coatdyke	d		23 17					23 47						00 17					00 47	
Airdrie	d		23 20					23 50						00 20					00a51	
Drumgelloch	d		23 23					23 53						00 23						
Caldercruix	d		23 27					23 57						00 27						
Blackridge	d		23 33					00 03						00 33						
Armadale	d		23 37					00 07						00 36						
Bathgate	a		23 41					00 11						00 40						
	d																			
Livingston North	d																			
Uphall	d																			
Edinburgh Park 230	d																			
Haymarket 228,230 ⛴	a																			
Edinburgh 228,230	a																			

A To Larkhall
B To Carstairs
C To Motherwell
D From Oban to Glasgow Queen Street
E From Fort William to London Euston

Table T226-R

Saturdays

26 May to 8 December

Helensburgh, Balloch, Dalmuir and Milngavie - Glasgow - Springburn, Cumbernauld, Airdrie, Bathgate and Edinburgh

	SR A	SR A	SR	SR A	SR	SR	SR	SR	SR	SR B	SR	SR C	SR C	SR	SR	SR B	SR	SR	SR D	SR	SR	SR
Helensburgh Upper 227 d																						
Helensburgh Central d															05 56							06 26
Craigendoran d															05 59							06 29
Cardross d															06 04							06 34
Balloch d																		06 07				
Alexandria d																		06 09				
Renton d																		06 12				
Dalreoch d															06 09			06 15				06 39
Dumbarton Central 227 d															06 11			06 17			06 26	06 41
Dumbarton East d															06 13			06 19			06 28	06 43
Bowling d																					06 33	
Kilpatrick d																					06 36	
Dalmuir 227 a															06 20			06 27			06 39	06 50
d									05 47	05 51	05 58	06 00		06 12	06 21	06 16		06 28	06 33		06 41	06 51
Singer d				00 01						05 53	06 00					06 18		06 30				
Drumry d				00 03						05 56	06 03					06 21		06 33				
Drumchapel d				00 06						05 58	06 05					06 23		06 35				
Milngavie d																				06 38		
Hillfoot d																				06 41		
Bearsden d																				06 43		
Westerton d				00 08						06 01	06 08					06 26		06 38		06 46		
Anniesland d				00 11						06 04	06 11					06 29		06 41		06 49		
Clydebank d									05 49			06 02		06 14					06 35		06 43	
Yoker d									05 51			06 04		06 16					06 37		06 45	
Garscadden d							05 45	05 49	05 54			06 07		06 19					06 40		06 48	
Scotstounhill d							05 47	05 51	05 57			06 09		06 21					06 42		06 50	
Jordanhill d							05 49	05 53	05 59			06 14		06 23					06 45		06 53	
Hyndland ■ d				00 14		05 37	05 52	05 56	06 01	06 07	06 14	06 17	06 22	06 25	06 28	06 32	06 37	06 44	06 48	06 52	06 55	06 58
Partick 225 ⇌ d				00 17		05 39	05 54	05 58	06 04	06 10	06 16	06 19	06 24	06 27	06 31	06 34	06 39	06 46	06 50	06 54	06 57	07 00
Exhibition Centre 225 a										06 13		06 22	06 27			06 37			06 53	06 57		
Anderston 225 a										06 15		06 24	06 30			06 39			06 55	06 59		
Glasgow Central LL ■ 225 a										06 17		06 25	06 31			06 41			06 57	07 02		
Argyle Street 225 a										06 19		06 28	06 35			06 44			06 59	07 06		
Charing Cross d				00 21		05 43	05 59	06 03	06 08		06 21			06 32	06 35		06 43	06 51			07 01	07 04
Glasgow Queen St LL ■ ⇌ a				00 23		05 45	06 01	06 05	06 10		06 23			06 34	06 37		06 45	06 53			07 03	07 06
d				00 23		05 45	06 01	06 05	06 16		06 26			06 34	06 38		06 47	06 56			07 03	07 07
High Street d				00 25		05 47	06 03	06 07	06 18		06 29			06 36	06 40		06 49	06 59			07 05	07 09
Bellgrove d				00 27		05 49		06 09	06 20		06 32			06 38			06 51	07 02			07 07	
Duke Street d								06 11						06 41							07 11	
Alexandra Parade d								06 13						06 42							07 13	
Barnhill d								06 16						06 45							07 22	
Springburn a								06 18						06 47							07 24	
Greenfaulds d														07 14						08 00	07 46	
Cumbernauld a														07 16						08 02	07 49	
Carntyne d		00 02		00 31		05 53			06 24		06 36						06 54	07 05				
Shettleston d		00 03		00 33		05 55			06 27		06 38						06 57	07 08				
Garrowhill d		00 06		00 36			06 11				06 41				06 47			07 10				07 16
Easterhouse d		00 08		00 38			06 13				06 43				06 50			07 13				07 19
Blairhill d		00 12		00 42			06 17				06 47				06 54			07 17				07 23
Coatbridge Sunnyside d		00 15		00 45		06 04	06 20		06 35		06 50				06 56		07 05	07 19				07 25
Coatdyke d		00 17		00 47			06 22				06 52				06 59			07 22				07 28
Airdrie d		00 20		00a51		06 09	06 29		06 40		06a56				07 02		07 10	07a26				07 31
Drumgelloch d		00 23				06 12	06 32		06 43						07 05		07 13					07 34
Caldercruix d		00 27				06 16			06 47								07 17					
Blackridge d	00 03	00 33				06 22			06 53								07 23					
Armadale d	00 07	00 36				06 25			06 57								07 27					
Bathgate a	00 11	00 40				06 29	06 44		07 01						07 17		07 31					07 46
d			05 47		06 20	06 30	06 47		07 04						07 18		07 32					07 47
Livingston North d			05 51		06 24	06 34	06 52		07 09						07 22		07 37					07 51
Uphall d			05 54		06 27	06 39	06 55		07 12						07 25		07 40					07 54
Edinburgh Park 230 d			06 03		06 35	06 49	07 03		07 26						07 34		07 50					08 02
Haymarket 228,230 ⇌ a			06 07		06 40	06 53	07 08		07 32						07 38		07 54					08 07
Edinburgh 228,230 a			06 14		06 47	06 58	07 13		07 38						07 43		07 59					08 12

A From Helensburgh Central
B To Larkhall
C To Motherwell
D To Whifflet

Table T226-R

Saturdays

26 May to 8 December

Helensburgh, Balloch, Dalmuir and Milngavie - Glasgow - Springburn, Cumbernauld, Airdrie, Bathgate and Edinburgh

	SR A	SR	SR	SR B	SR B	SR	SR	SR A	SR	SR	SR C	SR	SR	SR	SR A	SR	SR	SR B	SR B	SR	SR ◇ D ✠	SR
Helensburgh Upper 227 d																					07 42	
Helensburgh Central d							06 56							07 26								07 56
Craigendoran d							06 59							07 29								07 59
Cardross d							07 04							07 34							07 50	08 04
Balloch d			06 37							07 07							07 37					
Alexandria d			06 39							07 09							07 39					
Renton d			06 42							07 12							07 42					
Dalreoch d			06 45				07 09			07 15				07 39			07 45					08 09
Dumbarton Central 227 d			06 47			06 56	07 11			07 17			07 26	07 41			07 47			07 51	07 59	08 11
Dumbarton East d			06 49			06 58	07 13			07 19			07 28	07 43			07 49			07 53		08 13
Bowling d						07 03							07 33							07 58		
Kilpatrick d						07 07							07 36							08 01		
Dalmuir 227 a			06 56			07 10	07 20			07 26			07 39	07 50			07 56			08 05		08 20
d	06 46		06 58	07 02		07 11	07 21	07 18		07 28	07 33		07 41	07 51	07 48		07 58	08 02		08 11		08 21
Singer d	06 48		07 00					07 20		07 30					07 50		08 00				08a11	
Drumry d	06 51		07 03					07 23		07 33					07 53		08 03					
Drumchapel d	06 53		07 05					07 25		07 35					07 56		08 05					
Milngavie d		06 54			07 09				07 24			07 39				07 54			08 09			
Hillfoot d		06 57			07 12				07 27			07 42				07 57			08 12			
Bearsden d		06 59			07 14				07 29			07 44				07 59			08 14			
Westerton d	06 57	07 02	07 08		07 17			07 28	07 32	07 38		07 47			07 58	08 02	08 08		08 17			
Anniesland d	07 00	07 05	07 11		07 20			07 31	07 35	07 41		07 50			08 01	08 05	08 11		08 20			
Clydebank d				07 04		07 13					07 35		07 43					08 04		08 13		
Yoker d				07 06		07 15					07 37		07 45					08 06		08 15		
Garscadden d				07 10		07 19					07 40		07 49					08 10		08 19		
Scotstounhill d				07 12		07 21					07 42		07 51					08 12		08 21		
Jordanhill d				07 14		07 24					07 45		07 54					08 15		08 24		
Hyndland ■ d	07 03	07 08	07 14	07 17	07 23	07 26	07 29	07 34	07 38	07 44	07 48	07 53	07 56	07 59	08 04	08 08	08 14	08 17	08 23	08 26		08 29
Partick 225 ⇌ d	07 06	07 10	07 16	07 19	07 25	07 28	07 31	07 37	07 40	07 46	07 50	07 55	07 58	08 01	08 07	08 11	08 16	08 20	08 25	08 28		08 31
Exhibition Centre 225 a	07 09			07 22	07 28			07 40			07 53	07 58			08 10			08 23	08 28			
Anderston 225 a	07 11			07 24	07 30			07 42			07 55	08 00			08 12			08 25	08 31			
Glasgow Central LL ■ 225 a	07 12			07 26	07 32			07 43			07 57	08 02			08 14			08 26	08 33			
Argyle Street 225 a	07 17			07 28	07 37			07 48			07 59	08 06			08 17			08 29	08 36			
Charing Cross d		07 14	07 21			07 32	07 36		07 45	07 51			08 02	08 06		08 15	08 21			08 32		08 36
Glasgow Queen St LL ■ ⇌ a		07 16	07 23			07 34	07 38		07 47	07 53			08 04	08 08		08 17	08 23			08 34		08 38
d		07 17	07 26			07 35	07 38		07 47	07 56			08 05	08 08		08 18	08 26			08 35		08 38
High Street d		07 19	07 29			07 37	07 40		07 49	07 59			08 07	08 10		08 20	08 29			08 37		08 40
Bellgrove d		07 21	07 32			07 39			07 51	08 02			08 09			08 22	08 32			08 39		
Duke Street d						07 41							08 11							08 41		
Alexandra Parade d						07 42							08 12							08 42		
Barnhill d						07 45							08 15							08 45		
Springburn a						07 47							08 17							08 47		
Greenfaulds d						08 14						09 00	08 41							09 11		
Cumbernauld a						08 17						09 02	08 44							09 14		
Carntyne d		07 24	07 35						07 55	08 05						08 25	08 35					
Shettleston d		07 27	07 38						07 57	08 08						08 28	08 38					
Garrowhill d			07 40				07 48			08 10				08 18			08 40					08 48
Easterhouse d			07 43				07 50			08 13				08 20			08 43					08 50
Blairhill d			07 47				07 54			08 17				08 24			08 47					08 54
Coatbridge Sunnyside d		07 35	07 49				07 57		08 06	08 19				08 27		08 36	08 49					08 57
Coatdyke d			07 52				07 59			08 22				08 29			08 52					08 59
Airdrie d		07 40	07a56				08 02		08 10	08a26				08 32		08 41	08a56					09 02
Drumgelloch d		07 43					08 05		08 13					08 35		08 44						09 05
Caldercruix d		07 47							08 17							08 48						
Blackridge d		07 53							08 23							08 54						
Armadale d		07 57							08 27							08 57						
Bathgate a		08 01					08 18		08 31					08 48		09 01						09 18
d		08 02					08 19		08 31					08 49		09 02						09 18
Livingston North d		08 07					08 23		08 36					08 53		09 06						09 23
Uphall d		08 10					08 26		08 39					08 56		09 09						09 26
Edinburgh Park 230 d		08 19					08 34		08 49					09 05		09 19						09 35
Haymarket 228,230 ⇌ a		08 28					08 39		08 54					09 09		09 25						09 39
Edinburgh 228,230 a		08 34					08 44		09 00					09 14		09 31						09 44

A To Larkhall
B To Motherwell
C To Whifflet
D From Oban to Glasgow Queen Street

Table T226-R

Saturdays
26 May to 8 December

Helensburgh, Balloch, Dalmuir and Milngavie - Glasgow - Springburn, Cumbernauld, Airdrie, Bathgate and Edinburgh

	SR A	SR	SR	SR B	SR	SR	SR	SR A	SR	SR	SR C	SR C	SR	SR	SR A	SR	SR	SR B	SR	SR	SR
Helensburgh Upper 227 d																					
Helensburgh Central d							08 26							08 54							09 26
Craigendoran d							08 29							08 57							09 29
Cardross d							08 34							09 04							09 34
Balloch d			08 07							08 37							09 07				
Alexandria d			08 09							08 39							09 09				
Renton d			08 12							08 42							09 12				
Dalreoch d			08 15				08 39			08 45				09 09			09 15				09 39
Dumbarton Central 227 d			08 17			08 27	08 41			08 47			08 56	09 11			09 17			09 22	09 41
Dumbarton East d			08 19			08 30	08 43			08 49			08 58	09 13			09 19			09 24	09 43
Bowling d						08 34							09 03							09 29	
Kilpatrick d						08 37							09 06							09 33	
Dalmuir 227 a			08 26			08 40	08 50			08 56			09 09	09 20			09 26			09 36	09 50
d	08 18		08 28	08 35		08 41	08 51	08 50		08 58	09 03		09 11	09 21	09 18		09 28	09 33		09 41	09 51
Singer d	08 20		08 30					08 52		09 00					09 20		09 30				
Drumry d	08 22		08 33					08 54		09 03					09 23		09 33				
Drumchapel d	08 26		08 35					08 57		09 05					09 25		09 35				
Milngavie d		08 24			08 39				08 54			09 09				09 24			09 39		
Hillfoot d		08 27			08 42				08 57			09 12				09 27			09 42		
Bearsden d		08 29			08 44				08 59			09 14				09 29			09 44		
Westerton d	08 29	08 33	08 38		08 47			08 59	09 03	09 08		09 17			09 28	09 32	09 38		09 47		
Anniesland d	08 32	08 36	08 42		08 50			09 02	09 06	09 11		09 20			09 31	09 35	09 41		09 50		
Clydebank d				08 37		08 43					09 05		09 13					09 35		09 43	
Yoker d				08 39		08 45					09 07		09 15					09 37		09 45	
Garscadden d				08 42		08 49					09 10		09 19					09 40		09 49	
Scotstounhill d				08 44		08 51					09 12		09 21					09 42		09 51	
Jordanhill d				08 46		08 55					09 15		09 24					09 45		09 54	
Hyndland ■ d	08 35	08 39	08 45	08 48	08 53	08 57	09 00	09 06	09 09	09 14	09 17	09 23	09 26	09 28	09 34	09 38	09 44	09 47	09 53	09 56	09 58
Partick 225 ⛴ d	08 37	08 42	08 48	08 51	08 56	08 59	09 02	09 08	09 11	09 17	09 19	09 25	09 28	09 31	09 37	09 40	09 46	09 49	09 55	09 58	10 01
Exhibition Centre 225 a	08 40			08 54	08 59			09 11			09 22	09 28			09 40			09 52	09 58		
Anderston 225 a	08 42			08 56	09 01			09 13			09 24	09 30			09 42			09 54	10 00		
Glasgow Central LL 15 225 a	08 44			08 57	09 02			09 15			09 26	09 32			09 43			09 56	10 02		
Argyle Street 225 a	08 46			08 59	09 05			09 18			09 28	09 36			09 45			09 58	10 05		
Charing Cross d		08 46	08 53			09 03	09 06		09 15	09 22			09 32	09 35		09 44	09 51			10 02	10 05
Glasgow Queen St LL 10 ⛴ a		08 48	08 55			09 05	09 08		09 17	09 24			09 34	09 37		09 46	09 53			10 04	10 07
d		08 48	08 56			09 05	09 09		09 17	09 27			09 34	09 38		09 47	09 56			10 04	10 07
High Street d		08 50	08 59			09 07	09 11		09 19	09 30			09 36	09 40		09 49	09 59			10 06	10 10
Bellgrove d		08 52	09 02			09 09			09 21	09 32			09 38			09 51	10 02			10 08	
Duke Street d						09 11							09 41							10 11	
Alexandra Parade d						09 13							09 42							10 12	
Barnhill d						09 16							09 45							10 15	
Springburn a						09 18							09 47							10 17	
Greenfaulds d					10 01	09 41							10 11						11 02	10 41	
Cumbernauld a					10 03	09 44							10 14						11 04	10 44	
Carntyne d		08 56	09 06						09 25	09 36						09 54	10 05				
Shettleston d		08 58	09 08						09 27	09 38						09 57	10 08				
Garrowhill d			09 11				09 18			09 41				09 47			10 10				10 17
Easterhouse d			09 13				09 21			09 43				09 50			10 13				10 20
Blairhill d			09 17				09 25			09 47				09 54			10 17				10 24
Coatbridge Sunnyside d		09 07	09 20				09 27		09 36	09 50				09 56		10 05	10 19				10 26
Coatdyke d			09 22				09 30			09 52				09 59			10 22				10 29
Airdrie d		09 11	09a26				09 32		09 40	09a56				10 02		10 10	10a26				10 32
Drumgelloch d		09 14					09 35		09 43					10 05		10 13					10 35
Caldercruix d		09 18							09 47							10 17					
Blackridge d		09 24							09 53							10 23					
Armadale d		09 28							09 57							10 27					
Bathgate a		09 32					09 48		10 01					10 17		10 31					10 47
d		09 32					09 48		10 01					10 18		10 31					10 47
Livingston North d		09 37					09 53		10 06					10 22		10 36					10 52
Uphall d		09 40					09 56		10 09					10 25		10 39					10 55
Edinburgh Park 230 d		09 48					10 04		10 19					10 33		10 48					11 03
Haymarket 228,230 ⛴ a		09 52					10 08		10 25					10 38		10 53					11 08
Edinburgh 228,230 a		09 57					10 14		10 30					10 43		10 58					11 14

A To Larkhall
B To Whifflet
C To Motherwell

Table T226-R

Saturdays
26 May to 8 December

Helensburgh, Balloch, Dalmuir and Milngavie - Glasgow - Springburn, Cumbernauld, Airdrie, Bathgate and Edinburgh

	SR A	SR	SR	SR B	SR B	SR	SR	SR A	SR	SR	SR C	SR	SR	SR	SR A	SR	SR	SR B	SR B	SR	SR ◇ D	SR
Helensburgh Upper 227 d																					10 44	
Helensburgh Central d							09 56							10 26								10 56
Craigendoran d							09 59							10 29								10 59
Cardross d							10 04							10 34								11 04
Balloch d			09 37							10 07							10 37					
Alexandria d			09 39							10 09							10 39					
Renton d			09 42							10 12							10 42					
Dalreoch d			09 45				10 09			10 15				10 39			10 45					11 09
Dumbarton Central 227 d			09 46			09 57	10 11			10 16			10 26	10 41			10 47			10 54	11 01	11 11
Dumbarton East d			09 48			09 59	10 13			10 18			10 28	10 43			10 49			10 56		11 13
Bowling d						10 03							10 33							11 00		
Kilpatrick d						10 06							10 36							11 03		
Dalmuir 227 a			09 56			10 10	10 20			10 26			10 39	10 50			10 56			11 06	11 12	11 20
d	09 48		09 58	10 03		10 11	10 21	10 18		10 27	10 33		10 41	10 51	10 48		10 58	11 03		11 11		11 21
Singer d	09 50		10 00					10 20		10 29					10 51		11 00					
Drumry d	09 53		10 02					10 23		10 32					10 53		11 03					
Drumchapel d	09 55		10 05					10 26		10 34					10 56		11 05					
Milngavie d		09 54			10 09				10 24			10 39				10 53			11 08			
Hillfoot d		09 57			10 12				10 27			10 42				10 56			11 11			
Bearsden d		09 59			10 14				10 29			10 44				10 58			11 13			
Westerton d	09 58	10 02	10 07		10 17			10 28	10 32	10 37		10 47			10 58	11 02	11 08		11 16			
Anniesland d	10 01	10 05	10 11		10 20			10 31	10 35	10 41		10 50			11 02	11 06	11 11		11 20			
Clydebank d				10 05		10 13					10 35		10 43					11 05		11 13		
Yoker d				10 07		10 15					10 37		10 45					11 07		11 15		
Garscadden d				10 10		10 19					10 40		10 49					11 10		11 19		
Scotstounhill d				10 12		10 21					10 42		10 51					11 12		11 21		
Jordanhill d				10 15		10 24					10 45		10 54					11 15		11 24		
Hyndland ■ d	10 04	10 08	10 14	10 17	10 23	10 26	10 29	10 34	10 38	10 44	10 47	10 53	10 56	10 59	11 05	11 09	11 14	11 17	11 23	11 26		11 28
Partick 225 ⛴ d	10 07	10 10	10 16	10 19	10 25	10 28	10 31	10 36	10 40	10 46	10 49	10 55	10 58	11 01	11 08	11 11	11 16	11 19	11 25	11 28		11 31
Exhibition Centre 225 a	10 10			10 22	10 28			10 39			10 52	10 58			11 11			11 22	11 28			
Anderston 225 a	10 12			10 24	10 30			10 41			10 54	11 00			11 13			11 24	11 30			
Glasgow Central LL 15 225 a	10 13			10 26	10 31			10 43			10 56	11 02			11 14			11 26	11 32			
Argyle Street 225 a	10 17			10 28	10 36			10 46			10 58	11 05			11 19			11 28	11 35			
Charing Cross d		10 14	10 22			10 32	10 35		10 44	10 51			11 02	11 05		11 15	11 21			11 32		11 35
Glasgow Queen St LL 10 ⛴ a		10 16	10 24			10 34	10 37		10 46	10 53			11 04	11 07		11 17	11 23			11 34		11 37
d		10 16	10 26			10 35	10 38		10 47	10 56			11 04	11 08		11 17	11 26			11 34		11 38
High Street d		10 18	10 29			10 37	10 40		10 49	10 59			11 06	11 10		11 19	11 29			11 36		11 40
Bellgrove d		10 20	10 32			10 39			10 51	11 02			11 08			11 21	11 32			11 38		
Duke Street d						10 41							11 11							11 41		
Alexandra Parade d						10 42							11 12							11 42		
Barnhill d						10 45							11 16							11 45		
Springburn a						10 47							11 18							11 47		
Greenfaulds d						11 11						12 02	11 41							12 11		
Cumbernauld a						11 14						12 04	11 44							12 13		
Carntyne d		10 24	10 35						10 54	11 05						11 25	11 35					
Shettleston d		10 26	10 38						10 57	11 08						11 27	11 38					
Garrowhill d			10 40				10 47			11 10				11 17			11 40					11 47
Easterhouse d			10 43				10 50			11 13				11 20			11 43					11 50
Blairhill d			10 47				10 54			11 17				11 24			11 47					11 54
Coatbridge Sunnyside d		10 35	10 49				10 56		11 05	11 19				11 26		11 36	11 49					11 56
Coatdyke d			10 52				10 59			11 22				11 29			11 52					11 59
Airdrie d		10 40	10a56				11 02		11 10	11a26				11 32		11 40	11a56					12 02
Drumgelloch d		10 43					11 05		11 13					11 35		11 43						12 05
Caldercruix d		10 47							11 17							11 47						
Blackridge d		10 53							11 23							11 53						
Armadale d		10 56							11 26							11 57						
Bathgate a		11 00					11 18		11 30					11 47		12 01						12 17
d		11 01					11 20		11 31					11 48		12 02						12 18
Livingston North d		11 06					11 25		11 35					11 52		12 06						12 22
Uphall d		11 09					11 31		11 38					11 55		12 09						12 25
Edinburgh Park 230 d		11 18					11 43		11 48					12 03		12 18						12 33
Haymarket 228,230 ⛴ a		11 22					11 48		11 54					12 08		12 23						12 38
Edinburgh 228,230 a		11 27					11 54		11 59					12 16		12 29						12 43

A To Larkhall
B To Motherwell
C To Whifflet
D From Mallaig to Glasgow Queen Street

Table T226-R

Saturdays

26 May to 8 December

Helensburgh, Balloch, Dalmuir and Milngavie - Glasgow - Springburn, Cumbernauld, Airdrie, Bathgate and Edinburgh

	SR	SR	SR	SR	SR	SR	SR	SR	SR	SR	SR	SR	SR	SR	SR	SR	SR	SR	SR	SR	SR
	A			B			◇ C		A			D	D			A			B		
Helensburgh Upper 227 d							11 16														
Helensburgh Central d								11 26							11 51						
Craigendoran d								11 29							11 54						
Cardross d								11 34							11 59						
Balloch d			11 07								11 37							12 07			
Alexandria d			11 09								11 39							12 09			
Renton d			11 12								11 42							12 12			
Dalreoch d			11 15					11 39			11 45				12 04			12 15			
Dumbarton Central 227 d			11 17			11 22	11 29	11 41			11 47			11 56	12 06			12 17			12 26
Dumbarton East d			11 19			11 24		11 43			11 49			11 58	12 08			12 19			12 28
Bowling d						11 29								12 03							12 33
Kilpatrick d						11 32								12 06							12 36
Dalmuir 227 a			11 26			11 35	11 38	11 50			11 56			12 09	12 19			12 27			12 39
d	11 18		11 28	11 33		11 41		11 51	11 48		11 58	12 03		12 11	12 21	12 18		12 28	12 33		12 41
Singer d	11 20		11 30						11 50		12 00					12 20		12 30			
Drumry d	11 23		11 33						11 53		12 03					12 23		12 32			
Drumchapel d	11 25		11 35						11 55		12 05					12 25		12 35			
Milngavie d		11 24			11 39					11 54			12 10				12 24			12 39	
Hillfoot d		11 27			11 42					11 57			12 13				12 27			12 42	
Bearsden d		11 29			11 44					11 59			12 15				12 29			12 44	
Westerton d	11 29	11 32	11 38		11 47				11 58	12 02	12 08		12 18			12 28	12 32	12 37		12 47	
Anniesland d	11 32	11 35	11 41		11 50				12 01	12 05	12 11		12 21			12 31	12 35	12 41		12 50	
Clydebank d				11 35		11 43						12 05		12 13					12 35		12 43
Yoker d				11 37		11 45						12 07		12 15					12 37		12 45
Garscadden d				11 40		11 49						12 10		12 19					12 40		12 49
Scotstounhill d				11 42		11 51						12 12		12 21					12 42		12 51
Jordanhill d				11 45		11 54						12 15		12 24					12 45		12 54
Hyndland 8 d	11 35	11 38	11 44	11 47	11 53	11 56		11 59	12 04	12 08	12 14	12 17	12 24	12 26	12 29	12 34	12 38	12 44	12 47	12 53	12 56
Partick 225 ⇌ d	11 37	11 41	11 46	11 49	11 55	11 58		12 01	12 07	12 10	12 17	12 20	12 26	12 28	12 32	12 37	12 40	12 46	12 49	12 55	12 58
Exhibition Centre 225 a	11 40			11 52	11 58				12 10			12 23	12 29			12 40			12 52	12 58	
Anderston 225 a	11 42			11 54	12 00				12 12			12 25	12 31			12 42			12 54	13 00	
Glasgow Central LL 15 225 a	11 44			11 56	12 02				12 13			12 26	12 32			12 43			12 56	13 02	
Argyle Street 225 a	11 46			11 58	12 05				12 17			12 29	12 37			12 45			12 58	13 06	
Charing Cross d		11 45	11 51			12 02		12 05		12 14	12 22			12 32	12 36		12 44	12 51			13 02
Glasgow Queen St LL 15 ⇌ a		11 47	11 53			12 04		12 07		12 16	12 24			12 34	12 38		12 46	12 53			13 04
d		11 47	11 56			12 04		12 08		12 17	12 26			12 35	12 38		12 47	12 56			13 05
High Street d		11 49	11 59			12 06		12 10		12 19	12 29			12 37	12 40		12 49	12 59			13 07
Bellgrove d		11 51	12 02			12 08				12 21	12 32			12 39			12 51	13 02			13 09
Duke Street d						12 11								12 41							13 11
Alexandra Parade d						12 12								12 42							13 12
Barnhill d						12 15								12 45							13 15
Springburn a						12 17								12 47							13 17
Greenfaulds d					13 02	12 41								13 11						14 02	13 39
Cumbernauld a					13 04	12 44								13 13						14 04	13 42
Carntyne d		11 55	12 05							12 24	12 35						12 54	13 05			
Shettleston d		11 57	12 08							12 27	12 38						12 57	13 08			
Garrowhill d			12 10					12 17			12 40				12 48			13 10			
Easterhouse d			12 13					12 20			12 43				12 50			13 13			
Blairhill d			12 17					12 24			12 47				12 54			13 17			
Coatbridge Sunnyside d		12 06	12 19					12 26		12 35	12 49				12 57		13 05	13 19			
Coatdyke d			12 22					12 29			12 52				12 59			13 22			
Airdrie d		12 10	12a26					12 32		12 40	12a56				13 03		13 10	13a26			
Drumgelloch d		12 13						12 35		12 43					13 06		13 13				
Caldercruix d		12 17								12 47							13 17				
Blackridge d		12 23								12 53							13 23				
Armadale d		12 27								12 57							13 27				
Bathgate a		12 31						12 48		13 01					13 18		13 31				
d		12 32						12 49		13 01					13 20		13 32				
Livingston North d		12 36						12 53		13 06					13 24		13 36				
Uphall d		12 39						12 56		13 09					13 27		13 39				
Edinburgh Park 230 d		12 48						13 04		13 19					13 35		13 48				
Haymarket 228,230 ⇌ a		12 53						13 09		13 24					13 40		13 55				
Edinburgh 228,230 a		12 58						13 14		13 29					13 47		14 01				

A To Larkhall
B To Whifflet
C From Oban to Glasgow Queen Street
D To Motherwell

Table T226-R

Saturdays

26 May to 8 December

Helensburgh, Balloch, Dalmuir and Milngavie - Glasgow - Springburn, Cumbernauld, Airdrie, Bathgate and Edinburgh

	SR	SR	SR	SR	SR	SR	SR	SR	SR	SR	SR	SR	SR	SR	SR	SR	SR	SR	SR	SR	SR	SR
		A			B	B			A			C				A			B	B		
Helensburgh Upper 227 d																						
Helensburgh Central d	12 26							12 53							13 26							13 56
Craigendoran d	12 29							12 56							13 29							13 59
Cardross d	12 34							13 06							13 34							14 04
Balloch d				12 37							13 07							13 37				
Alexandria d				12 39							13 09							13 39				
Renton d				12 42							13 12							13 42				
Dalreoch d	12 39			12 45				13 11			13 15				13 39			13 47				14 09
Dumbarton Central 227 d	12 41			12 47			12 56	13 13			13 17			13 26	13 41			13 49			13 56	14 11
Dumbarton East d	12 43			12 49			12 58	13 15			13 19			13 28	13 43			13 51			13 58	14 13
Bowling d							13 03							13 33							14 03	
Kilpatrick d							13 06							13 36							14 06	
Dalmuir 227 a	12 50			12 56			13 09	13 23			13 26			13 39	13 50			14 00			14 09	14 20
d	12 51	12 49		12 58	13 03		13 11	13 23	13 18		13 27	13 33		13 41	13 51	13 48		14 00	14 03		14 11	14 21
Singer d		12 51		13 00					13 20		13 29					13 50		14 02				
Drumry d		12 54		13 03					13 22		13 32					13 53		14 05				
Drumchapel d		12 56		13 05					13 25		13 34					13 56		14 07				
Milngavie d			12 54			13 11				13 23			13 40				13 54			14 09		
Hillfoot d			12 57			13 14				13 26			13 43				13 57			14 12		
Bearsden d			12 59			13 16				13 28			13 45				13 59			14 14		
Westerton d		12 59	13 03	13 08		13 19			13 27	13 31	13 37		13 48			13 58	14 02	14 10		14 17		
Anniesland d		13 02	13 06	13 11		13 22			13 30	13 34	13 40		13 51			14 01	14 05	14 13		14 20		
Clydebank d					13 05		13 13					13 35		13 43					14 05		14 13	
Yoker d					13 07		13 15					13 37		13 45					14 07		14 15	
Garscadden d					13 10		13 19					13 40		13 49					14 10		14 19	
Scotstounhill d					13 12		13 21					13 42		13 51					14 12		14 21	
Jordanhill d					13 15		13 25					13 45		13 54					14 16		14 24	
Hyndland 8 d	12 59	13 05	13 09	13 14	13 17	13 25	13 27	13 30	13 34	13 37	13 43	13 47	13 54	13 56	13 59	14 04	14 08	14 16	14 18	14 23	14 26	14 28
Partick 225 ⇌ d	13 01	13 08	13 11	13 16	13 19	13 27	13 29	13 32	13 37	13 40	13 45	13 49	13 56	13 58	14 02	14 07	14 10	14 18	14 21	14 25	14 28	14 31
Exhibition Centre 225 a		13 11			13 22	13 30			13 40			13 52	13 59			14 10			14 24	14 28		
Anderston 225 a		13 13			13 24	13 32			13 42			13 54	14 01			14 12			14 26	14 30		
Glasgow Central LL 15 225 a		13 14			13 26	13 33			13 43			13 56	14 02			14 13			14 27	14 32		
Argyle Street 225 a		13 17			13 28	13 37			13 45			13 58	14 05			14 17			14 29	14 36		
Charing Cross d	13 05		13 15	13 21			13 33	13 37		13 44	13 50			14 02	14 06		14 14	14 22			14 32	14 35
Glasgow Queen St LL 15 ⇌ a	13 07		13 17	13 23			13 35	13 39		13 46	13 52			14 04	14 08		14 16	14 24			14 34	14 37
d	13 08		13 18	13 25			13 36	13 39		13 46	13 55			14 05	14 09		14 17	14 25			14 34	14 38
High Street d	13 10		13 20	13 27			13 38	13 41		13 48	13 59			14 07	14 11		14 19	14 27			14 36	14 40
Bellgrove d			13 22	13 29			13 40			13 50	14 02			14 09			14 21	14 29			14 38	
Duke Street d							13 42							14 11							14 41	
Alexandra Parade d							13 43							14 12							14 42	
Barnhill d							13 46							14 15							14 45	
Springburn a							13 48							14 17							14 47	
Greenfaulds d							14 13						15 02	14 39							15 11	
Cumbernauld a							14 15						15 04	14 42							15 13	
Carntyne d			13 25	13 33						13 54	14 05						14 24	14 35				
Shettleston d			13 28	13 35						13 56	14 08						14 27	14 38				
Garrowhill d	13 18			13 38				13 49			14 10				14 19			14 40				14 47
Easterhouse d	13 20			13 40				13 51			14 13				14 21			14 43				14 50
Blairhill d	13 24			13 44				13 55			14 17				14 25			14 47				14 54
Coatbridge Sunnyside d	13 27		13 36	13 47				13 58		14 05	14 19				14 28		14 35	14 49				14 56
Coatdyke d	13 29			13 49				14 00			14 22				14 30			14 52				14 59
Airdrie d	13 32		13 41	13a53				14 03		14 09	14a26				14 33		14 40	14a56				15 02
Drumgelloch d	13 35		13 44					14 06		14 12					14 36		14 43					15 05
Caldercruix d			13 48							14 16							14 47					
Blackridge d			13 54							14 22							14 53					
Armadale d			13 57							14 26							14 56					
Bathgate a	13 48		14 01					14 19		14 30					14 49		15 00					15 17
d	13 48		14 02					14 19		14 31					14 49		15 01					15 18
Livingston North d	13 52		14 06					14 24		14 35					14 54		15 05					15 22
Uphall d	13 55		14 09					14 27		14 38					14 57		15 08					15 25
Edinburgh Park 230 d	14 03		14 18					14 35		14 49					15 05		15 18					15 33
Haymarket 228,230 ⇌ a	14 09		14 22					14 40		14 54					15 09		15 23					15 39
Edinburgh 228,230 a	14 14		14 27					14 45		14 59					15 14		15 28					15 45

A To Larkhall
B To Motherwell
C To Whifflet

Table T226-R

Saturdays
26 May to 8 December

Helensburgh, Balloch, Dalmuir and Milngavie - Glasgow - Springburn, Cumbernauld, Airdrie, Bathgate and Edinburgh

	SR A	SR	SR	SR B	SR	SR	SR	SR A	SR	SR	SR C	SR C	SR	SR ◇ D	SR	SR A	SR	SR	SR B	SR	SR	SR
Helensburgh Upper 227 d														14 43								
Helensburgh Central d							14 26								14 56							15 26
Craigendoran d							14 29								14 59							15 29
Cardross d							14 34								15 04							15 34
Balloch d			14 07							14 37								15 07				
Alexandria d			14 09							14 39								15 09				
Renton d			14 12							14 42								15 12				
Dalreoch d			14 15				14 39			14 45					15 09			15 15				15 39
Dumbarton Central 227 d			14 17			14 26	14 41			14 47			14 54	15 04	15 11			15 17			15 26	15 41
Dumbarton East d			14 19			14 28	14 43			14 49			14 56		15 13			15 19			15 28	15 43
Bowling d						14 33							15 00								15 33	
Kilpatrick d						14 36							15 03								15 36	
Dalmuir 227 a			14 26			14 39	14 50			14 56			15 06	15 13	15 20			15 26			15 39	15 50
d	14 18		14 27	14 32		14 41	14 51	14 48		14 58	15 03		15 11		15 21	15 18		15 28	15 33		15 41	15 51
Singer d	14 20		14 29					14 50		15 00						15 20		15 30				
Drumry d	14 23		14 32					14 53		15 03						15 23		15 33				
Drumchapel d	14 26		14 34					14 55		15 05						15 26		15 35				
Milngavie d		14 24			14 39				14 54			15 08					15 24			15 39		
Hillfoot d		14 27			14 42				14 57			15 11					15 27			15 42		
Bearsden d		14 29			14 44				14 59			15 13					15 29			15 44		
Westerton d	14 28	14 32	14 37		14 47			14 58	15 02	15 08		15 17				15 28	15 32	15 38		15 47		
Anniesland d	14 31	14 35	14 40		14 50			15 01	15 05	15 11		15 20				15 31	15 35	15 41		15 50		
Clydebank d				14 34		14 43					15 05		15 13						15 35		15 43	
Yoker d				14 36		14 45					15 07		15 15						15 37		15 45	
Garscadden d				14 40		14 49					15 10		15 19						15 40		15 49	
Scotstounhill d				14 42		14 51					15 12		15 21						15 42		15 51	
Jordanhill d				14 44		14 54					15 15		15 24						15 45		15 54	
Hyndland d	14 34	14 38	14 43	14 47	14 53	14 56	14 58	15 04	15 08	15 14	15 17	15 23	15 26		15 28	15 34	15 38	15 44	15 47	15 53	15 56	15 58
Partick 225 d	14 37	14 40	14 45	14 49	14 55	14 58	15 01	15 07	15 10	15 17	15 20	15 25	15 28		15 31	15 37	15 40	15 46	15 49	15 55	15 58	16 01
Exhibition Centre 225 a	14 40			14 52	14 58			15 10			15 23	15 28				15 40			15 52	15 58		
Anderston 225 a	14 42			14 54	15 00			15 12			15 25	15 30				15 42			15 54	16 00		
Glasgow Central LL 225 a	14 43			14 56	15 01			15 13			15 26	15 31				15 43			15 56	16 01		
Argyle Street 225 a	14 45			14 58	15 05			15 17			15 29	15 35				15 46			15 58	16 05		
Charing Cross d		14 44	14 50			15 02	15 05		15 14	15 22			15 32		15 35		15 44	15 51			16 02	16 05
Glasgow Queen St LL a		14 46	14 52			15 04	15 07		15 16	15 24			15 34		15 37		15 46	15 53			16 04	16 07
d		14 47	14 55			15 04	15 08		15 17	15 26			15 34		15 38		15 47	15 56			16 04	16 08
High Street d		14 49	14 59			15 06	15 10		15 19	15 29			15 36		15 40		15 49	15 59			16 06	16 10
Bellgrove d		14 51	15 02			15 08			15 21	15 32			15 38				15 51	16 02			16 08	
Duke Street d						15 11							15 41								16 11	
Alexandra Parade d						15 12							15 42								16 12	
Barnhill d						15 15							15 45								16 15	
Springburn a						15 17							15 47								16 17	
Greenfaulds d					16 02	15 40							16 11							17 02	16 39	
Cumbernauld a					16 04	15 43							16 13							17 04	16 43	
Carntyne d		14 54	15 05						15 24	15 35							15 54	16 05				
Shettleston d		14 57	15 08						15 27	15 38							15 57	16 08				
Garrowhill d			15 10				15 17			15 40					15 47			16 10				16 17
Easterhouse d			15 13				15 20			15 43					15 50			16 13				16 20
Blairhill d			15 17				15 24			15 47					15 54			16 17				16 24
Coatbridge Sunnyside d		15 05	15 19				15 26		15 35	15 50					15 56		16 05	16 19				16 26
Coatdyke d			15 22				15 29			15 52					15 59			16 22				16 29
Airdrie d		15 10	15a26				15 32		15 40	15a56					16 02		16 10	16a26				16 32
Drumgelloch d		15 13					15 35		15 43						16 05		16 13					16 35
Caldercruix d		15 17							15 47								16 17					
Blackridge d		15 23							15 53								16 23					
Armadale d		15 27							15 56								16 27					
Bathgate a		15 31					15 48		16 00						16 18		16 31					16 48
d		15 32					15 48		16 01						16 18		16 31					16 50
Livingston North d		15 36					15 53		16 05						16 23		16 36					16 55
Uphall d		15 39					15 56		16 08						16 26		16 39					16 58
Edinburgh Park 230 d		15 48					16 05		16 18						16 34		16 48					17 07
Haymarket 228,230 a		15 53					16 09		16 23						16 38		16 52					17 12
Edinburgh 228,230 a		15 58					16 14		16 28						16 43		16 59					17 18

A To Larkhall
B To Whifflet
C To Motherwell
D From Mallaig to Glasgow Queen Street

Table T226-R

Saturdays
26 May to 8 December

Helensburgh, Balloch, Dalmuir and Milngavie - Glasgow - Springburn, Cumbernauld, Airdrie, Bathgate and Edinburgh

	SR A	SR	SR	SR B	SR B	SR	SR	SR A	SR	SR	SR C	SR	SR	SR	SR A	SR	SR	SR B	SR B	SR	SR
Helensburgh Upper 227 d																					
Helensburgh Central d							15 56							16 26							16 54
Craigendoran d							15 59							16 29							16 57
Cardross d							16 04							16 34							17 02
Balloch d			15 37							16 07							16 37				
Alexandria d			15 39							16 09							16 39				
Renton d			15 42							16 12							16 42				
Dalreoch d			15 45				16 09			16 15				16 39			16 45				17 07
Dumbarton Central 227 d			15 47			15 56	16 11			16 17			16 26	16 41			16 47			16 56	17 09
Dumbarton East d			15 49			15 58	16 13			16 19			16 28	16 43			16 49			16 58	17 11
Bowling d						16 03							16 33							17 03	
Kilpatrick d						16 06							16 36							17 06	
Dalmuir 227 a			15 57			16 09	16 20			16 26			16 39	16 50			16 56			17 09	17 19
d	15 48		15 58	16 03		16 11	16 21	16 18		16 28	16 33		16 41	16 51	16 48		16 58	17 03		17 11	17 21
Singer d	15 50		16 00					16 20		16 30					16 50		17 00				
Drumry d	15 53		16 03					16 23		16 33					16 53		17 03				
Drumchapel d	15 56		16 05					16 26		16 35					16 55		17 05				
Milngavie d		15 54			16 09				16 24			16 39				16 54			17 09		
Hillfoot d		15 57			16 12				16 27			16 42				16 57			17 12		
Bearsden d		15 59			16 14				16 29			16 44				16 59			17 14		
Westerton d	15 58	16 02	16 08		16 17			16 28	16 32	16 38		16 47			16 58	17 02	17 08		17 17		
Anniesland d	16 01	16 05	16 11		16 20			16 31	16 35	16 41		16 50			17 01	17 05	17 11		17 20		
Clydebank d				16 05		16 13					16 35		16 43					17 05		17 13	
Yoker d				16 07		16 15					16 37		16 45					17 07		17 15	
Garscadden d				16 10		16 19					16 40		16 49					17 10		17 19	
Scotstounhill d				16 12		16 21					16 42		16 51					17 12		17 21	
Jordanhill d				16 15		16 24					16 44		16 54					17 15		17 24	
Hyndland d	16 04	16 08	16 14	16 17	16 23	16 26	16 29	16 34	16 38	16 44	16 47	16 53	16 56	16 58	17 05	17 08	17 14	17 17	17 23	17 26	17 28
Partick 225 d	16 07	16 10	16 16	16 19	16 25	16 28	16 32	16 37	16 40	16 46	16 49	16 55	16 58	17 01	17 07	17 11	17 16	17 20	17 25	17 28	17 31
Exhibition Centre 225 a	16 10			16 22	16 28			16 40			16 52	16 58			17 10			17 23	17 28		
Anderston 225 a	16 12			16 24	16 30			16 42			16 54	17 03			17 13			17 25	17 30		
Glasgow Central LL 225 a	16 13			16 26	16 31			16 43			16 56	17 05			17 14			17 26	17 31		
Argyle Street 225 a	16 17			16 28	16 35			16 45			16 58	17 07			17 18			17 29	17 35		
Charing Cross d		16 14	16 21			16 32	16 36		16 44	16 51			17 02	17 05		17 15	17 21			17 32	17 35
Glasgow Queen St LL a		16 16	16 23			16 34	16 38		16 46	16 53			17 04	17 07		17 17	17 23			17 34	17 37
d		16 17	16 24			16 34	16 38		16 47	16 56			17 04	17 08		17 18	17 26			17 34	17 38
High Street d		16 19	16 27			16 36	16 40		16 49	16 59			17 06	17 10		17 20	17 29			17 36	17 40
Bellgrove d		16 21	16 29			16 38			16 51	17 02			17 08			17 22	17 32			17 38	
Duke Street d						16 41							17 11							17 41	
Alexandra Parade d						16 42							17 12							17 42	
Barnhill d						16 45							17 15							17 45	
Springburn a						16 47							17 17							17 47	
Greenfaulds d						17 11						18 02	17 41							18 11	
Cumbernauld a						17 13						18 04	17 44							18 13	
Carntyne d		16 24	16 33						16 54	17 05						17 25	17 35				
Shettleston d		16 27	16 35						16 57	17 08						17 28	17 38				
Garrowhill d			16 38				16 48			17 10				17 17			17 40				17 47
Easterhouse d			16 40				16 50			17 13				17 20			17 43				17 50
Blairhill d		16 33	16 44				16 54		17 03	17 17				17 24		17 34	17 47				17 54
Coatbridge Sunnyside d		16 36	16 47				16 57		17 06	17 19				17 26		17 37	17 49				17 56
Coatdyke d		16 38	16 49				16 59		17 08	17 22				17 29		17 39	17 52				17 59
Airdrie d		16 41	16a53				17 02		17 11	17a26				17 32		17 42	17a56				18 02
Drumgelloch d		16 44					17 05		17 14					17 35		17 45					18 05
Caldercruix d		16 48							17 18							17 49					
Blackridge d		16 54							17 24							17 55					
Armadale d		16 58							17 28							17 59					
Bathgate a		17 02					17 18		17 32					17 47		18 03					18 17
d		17 02					17 18		17 32					17 48		18 03					18 18
Livingston North d		17 07					17 23		17 37					17 52		18 08					18 23
Uphall d		17 10					17 26		17 40					17 55		18 11					18 26
Edinburgh Park 230 d		17 19					17 34		17 49					18 03		18 20					18 34
Haymarket 228,230 a		17 23					17 39		17 58					18 08		18 24					18 39
Edinburgh 228,230 a		17 28					17 44		18 04					18 13		18 30					18 44

A To Larkhall
B To Motherwell
C To Whifflet

Table T226-R

Saturdays
26 May to 8 December

Helensburgh, Balloch, Dalmuir and Milngavie - Glasgow - Springburn, Cumbernauld, Airdrie, Bathgate and Edinburgh

Station	SR A	SR	SR	SR B	SR	SR	SR	SR A	SR	SR	SR C	SR C	SR	SR	SR A	SR	SR	SR B	SR	SR	SR	SR A
Helensburgh Upper 227 d																						
Helensburgh Central d							17 26							17 56							18 25	
Craigendoran d							17 29							17 59							18 28	
Cardross d							17 34							18 04							18 33	
Balloch d			17 07							17 37							18 07					
Alexandria d			17 09							17 39							18 09					
Renton d			17 12							17 42							18 12					
Dalreoch d			17 15				17 39			17 45				18 09			18 15				18 38	
Dumbarton Central 227 d			17 17			17 26	17 41			17 47			17 56	18 11			18 17			18 26	18 40	
Dumbarton East d			17 19			17 28	17 43			17 49			17 58	18 13			18 19			18 28	18 42	
Bowling d						17 33							18 03							18 33		
Kilpatrick d						17 36							18 06							18 36		
Dalmuir 227 a			17 27			17 39	17 50			17 56			18 09	18 20			18 26			18 39	18 49	
d	17 18		17 28	17 33		17 41	17 51	17 48		17 58	18 03		18 11	18 21	18 18		18 27	18 33		18 41	18 51	18 48
Singer d	17 20		17 30					17 50		18 00					18 20		18 29					18 50
Drumry d	17 23		17 33					17 53		18 03					18 23		18 32					18 53
Drumchapel d	17 25		17 35					17 56		18 05					18 26		18 34					18 55
Milngavie d		17 24			17 39				17 54			18 09				18 24			18 39			
Hillfoot d		17 27			17 42				17 57			18 12				18 27			18 42			
Bearsden d		17 29			17 44				17 59			18 14				18 29			18 44			
Westerton d	17 28	17 32	17 38		17 47			17 58	18 02	18 08		18 17			18 28	18 32	18 37		18 47			18 58
Anniesland d	17 31	17 35	17 41		17 50			18 01	18 05	18 11		18 20			18 31	18 35	18 40		18 50			19 01
Clydebank d				17 35		17 43					18 05		18 13					18 35		18 43		
Yoker d				17 37		17 45					18 07		18 15					18 37		18 45		
Garscadden d				17 40		17 49					18 10		18 19					18 40		18 49		
Scotstounhill d				17 42		17 51					18 12		18 21					18 42		18 51		
Jordanhill d				17 45		17 54					18 15		18 24					18 45		18 54		
Hyndland ■ d	17 35	17 38	17 44	17 47	17 53	17 56	18 00	18 04	18 08	18 14	18 17	18 23	18 26	18 28	18 34	18 38	18 43	18 47	18 53	18 56	18 58	19 04
Partick 225 ⛴ d	17 37	17 41	17 46	17 49	17 55	17 58	18 02	18 07	18 10	18 16	18 19	18 25	18 28	18 31	18 37	18 40	18 45	18 49	18 55	18 58	19 01	19 07
Exhibition Centre 225 a	17 41			17 52	17 58			18 10			18 22	18 28			18 40			18 52	18 58			19 10
Anderston 225 a	17 45			17 54	18 00			18 12			18 24	18 30			18 42			18 54	19 00			19 12
Glasgow Central LL ■ 225 a	17 47			17 56	18 02			18 14			18 26	18 32			18 43			18 56	19 01			19 13
Argyle Street 225 a	17 50			17 58	18 05			18 19			18 28	18 35			18 45			18 58	19 05			19 17
Charing Cross d		17 45	17 51			18 02	18 06		18 14	18 22			18 32	18 35		18 44	18 50			19 02	19 05	
Glasgow Queen St LL ■ ⛴ a		17 47	17 53			18 04	18 08		18 16	18 24			18 34	18 37		18 46	18 52			19 04	19 07	
d		17 48	17 56			18 04	18 08		18 17	18 26			18 34	18 38		18 47	18 52			19 04	19 08	
High Street d		17 50	17 59			18 06	18 10		18 19	18 29			18 36	18 40		18 49	18 55			19 06	19 10	
Bellgrove d		17 52	18 02			18 08			18 21	18 32			18 38			18 51	18 57			19 08		
Duke Street d						18 11							18 41							19 11		
Alexandra Parade d						18 12							18 42							19 12		
Barnhill d						18 15							18 45							19 15		
Springburn a						18 17							18 47							19 17		
Greenfaulds d					19 01	18 41							19 14						20 02	19 39		
Cumbernauld a					19 03	18 44							19 16						20 04	19 42		
Carntyne d		17 55	18 05						18 24	18 35						18 54	19 01					
Shettleston d		17 58	18 08						18 27	18 38						18 57	19 03					
Garrowhill d			18 10				18 18			18 40				18 47			19 06					
Easterhouse d			18 13				18 20			18 43				18 50			19 08					
Blairhill d			18 17				18 24			18 47				18 54			19 12					
Coatbridge Sunnyside d		18 06	18 19				18 27		18 35	18 49				18 56		19 05	19 15				19 22	
Coatdyke d			18 22				18 29			18 52				18 59			19 17					
Airdrie d		18 11	18a26				18 32		18 40	18a56				19 02		19 10	19a21				19 27	
Drumgelloch d		18 14					18 35		18 43					19 05		19 13					19 30	
Caldercruix d		18 18							18 47							19 17					19 34	
Blackridge d		18 24							18 53							19 23					19 40	
Armadale d		18 27							18 57							19 27					19 43	
Bathgate a		18 31					18 48		19 01					19 17		19 31					19 47	
d		18 32					18 51		19 02					19 18		19 31					19 48	
Livingston North d		18 37					18 56		19 07					19 22		19 36					19 52	
Uphall d		18 40					18 59		19 10					19 25		19 39					19 55	
Edinburgh Park 230 d		18 49					19 13		19 19					19 33		19 47					20 03	
Haymarket 228,230 ⛴ a		18 54					19 17		19 23					19 38		19 53					20 10	
Edinburgh 228,230 a		19 00					19 22		19 28					19 43		19 58					20 15	

A To Larkhall
B To Whifflet
C To Motherwell

Table T226-R

Saturdays
26 May to 8 December

Helensburgh, Balloch, Dalmuir and Milngavie - Glasgow - Springburn, Cumbernauld, Airdrie, Bathgate and Edinburgh

Station	SR ◇ A ⛴	SR	SR B	SR B	SR	SR	SR C	SR	SR D	SR	SR	SR C	SR	SR	SR B	SR B	SR	SR C	SR	SR D	SR
Helensburgh Upper 227 d	18 31																				
Helensburgh Central d						18 54								19 32					20 02		
Craigendoran d						18 57								19 35					20 05		
Cardross d						19 02								19 40					20 10		
Balloch d		18 38						19 07									19 44				
Alexandria d		18 40						19 09									19 46				
Renton d		18 43						19 12									19 49				
Dalreoch d		18 46				19 07		19 15						19 45			19 52		20 15		
Dumbarton Central 227 d	18 44	18 48			18 54	19 11		19 17			19 26			19 47			19 57		20 17		
Dumbarton East d		18 50			18 56	19 13		19 19			19 28			19 49			19 59		20 19		
Bowling d					19 01						19 33						20 04				
Kilpatrick d					19 04						19 36						20 07				
Dalmuir 227 a	18 54	18 59			19 07	19 22		19 26			19 39			19 56			20 10		20 26		
d		18 59	19 03		19 11	19 22	19 15	19 28	19 33		19 41	19 48		19 59	20 02		20 11	20 18	20 28	20 33	
Singer d		19 01					19 17	19 30				19 50		20 01				20 20	20 30		
Drumry d		19 04					19 20	19 33				19 53		20 03				20 23	20 32		
Drumchapel d		19 06					19 23	19 35				19 56		20 06				20 26	20 35		
Milngavie d				19 09						19 39						20 09					20 38
Hillfoot d				19 12						19 42						20 12					20 41
Bearsden d				19 14						19 44						20 14					20 43
Westerton d		19 09		19 17			19 29	19 38		19 47		19 58		20 08		20 17		20 28	20 37		20 46
Anniesland d		19 12		19 20			19 32	19 41		19 50		20 03		20 11		20 20		20 31	20 40		20 50
Clydebank d			19 05		19 13				19 35		19 43				20 04		20 13			20 35	
Yoker d			19 07		19 15				19 37		19 45				20 06		20 16			20 37	
Garscadden d			19 10		19 19				19 41		19 49				20 10		20 19			20 40	
Scotstounhill d			19 12		19 21				19 43		19 51				20 12		20 21			20 42	
Jordanhill d			19 15		19 25				19 45		19 54				20 15		20 24			20 45	
Hyndland ■ d		19 15	19 17	19 23	19 27	19 29	19 35	19 44	19 47	19 53	19 56	20 06		20 14	20 17	20 23	20 26	20 34	20 43	20 47	20 53
Partick 225 ⛴ d		19 17	19 20	19 25	19 29	19 32	19 38	19 46	19 50	19 55	19 58	20 08		20 17	20 19	20 25	20 28	20 37	20 46	20 50	20 55
Exhibition Centre 225 a			19 23	19 28			19 41		19 53	19 58		20 11			20 22	20 29		20 40		20 53	20 58
Anderston 225 a			19 25	19 30			19 43		19 55	20 00		20 13			20 26	20 33		20 42		20 55	21 00
Glasgow Central LL ■ 225 a			19 26	19 32			19 45		19 56	20 01		20 15			20 27	20 34		20 43		20 56	21 02
Argyle Street 225 a			19 29	19 35			19 50		19 59	20 03		20 19			20 29	20 37		20 46		20 59	21 05
Charing Cross d		19 21			19 33	19 36		19 50			20 02			20 21			20 32		20 50		
Glasgow Queen St LL ■ ⛴ a		19 23			19 35	19 38		19 52			20 04			20 23			20 34		20 52		
d		19 23			19 35	19 38		19 52			20 04			20 23			20 34		20 53		
High Street d		19 25			19 37	19 40		19 54			20 06			20 25			20 36		20 55		
Bellgrove d		19 27			19 39			19 56			20 08			20 27			20 38		20 57		
Duke Street d					19 43						20 10						20 40				
Alexandra Parade d					19 47						20 17						20 42				
Barnhill d					19 53						20 24						20 45				
Springburn a					19 55						20 26						20 47				
Greenfaulds d					20 17					21 04	20 47						21 16				22 02
Cumbernauld a					20 19					21 06	20 50						21 18				22 04
Carntyne d		19 31						20 00						20 31					21 01		
Shettleston d		19 33						20 02						20 33					21 03		
Garrowhill d		19 36						20 05						20 36					21 06		
Easterhouse d		19 38						20 07						20 38					21 08		
Blairhill d		19 42						20 11						20 42					21 12		
Coatbridge Sunnyside d		19 45				19 53		20 14						20 45					21 15		
Coatdyke d		19 47						20 16						20 47					21 17		
Airdrie d		19a50				19 58		20a20						20 50					21 20		
Drumgelloch d						20 01								20 53					21 23		
Caldercruix d						20 05								20 57					21 27		
Blackridge d						20 11								21 03					21 33		
Armadale d						20 14								21 07					21 37		
Bathgate a						20 18								21 11					21 41		
d						20 18							20 48	21 11					21 41		
Livingston North d						20 23							20 52	21 16					21 46		
Uphall d						20 26							20 55	21 19					21 49		
Edinburgh Park 230 d						20 38							21 03	21 27					21 57		
Haymarket 228,230 ⛴ a						20 42							21 08	21 33					22 01		
Edinburgh 228,230 a						20 47							21 13	21 38					22 06		

A From Oban to Glasgow Queen Street
B To Motherwell
C To Larkhall
D To Whifflet

Table T226-R

Saturdays
26 May to 8 December

Helensburgh, Balloch, Dalmuir and Milngavie - Glasgow - Springburn, Cumbernauld, Airdrie, Bathgate and Edinburgh

		SR	SR	SR	SR	SR	SR	SR	SR	SR	SR	SR	SR	SR	SR	SR	SR	SR	SR	SR	SR	SR	SR
			A		◇ B	C	C		A		D			A		C	C		A		C	C	
Helensburgh Upper 227	d				20 37																		
Helensburgh Central	d			20 32						21 02					21 32					22 02			
Craigendoran	d			20 35						21 05					21 35					22 05			
Cardross	d			20 40						21 10					21 40					22 10			
Balloch	d	20 14						20 45					21 14					21 44					22 14
Alexandria	d	20 16						20 47					21 16					21 46					22 16
Renton	d	20 19						20 50					21 19					21 49					22 19
Dalreoch	d	20 22		20 45				20 53		21 15			21 24		21 45			21 52		22 15			22 22
Dumbarton Central 227	d	20 26		20 47	20 51			20 56		21 17			21 26		21 47			21 56		22 17			22 26
Dumbarton East	d	20 28		20 49				20 58		21 19			21 28		21 49			21 58		22 19			22 28
Bowling	d	20 33						21 03					21 33					22 03					22 33
Kilpatrick	d	20 36						21 06					21 36					22 06					22 36
Dalmuir 227	a	20 39		20 57	21 03			21 09		21 26			21 39		21 57			22 09		22 26			22 39
	d	20 41	20 48	20 59		21 03		21 11	21 18	21 29	21 33		21 41	21 49	21 59	22 03		22 11	22 18	22 29	22 33		22 41
Singer	d		20 50	21 01					21 20	21 31				21 51	22 01				22 20	22 31			
Drumry	d		20 53	21 03					21 23	21 33				21 54	22 04				22 23	22 33			
Drumchapel	d		20 55	21 06					21 25	21 36				21 56	22 06				22 26	22 36			
Milngavie	d						21 09					21 39					22 10					22 38	
Hillfoot	d						21 12					21 42					22 13					22 41	
Bearsden	d						21 14					21 44					22 15					22 43	
Westerton	d		21 00	21 08			21 17		21 29	21 38		21 47		21 59	22 09		22 18		22 28	22 38		22 46	
Anniesland	d		21 03	21 11			21 20		21 32	21 41		21 50		22 03	22 12		22 21		22 31	22 41		22 50	
Clydebank	d	20 43				21 05		21 13			21 35		21 43			22 05		22 13			22 35		22 43
Yoker	d	20 45				21 07		21 15			21 37		21 45			22 07		22 15			22 37		22 45
Garscadden	d	20 49				21 10		21 19			21 40		21 49			22 10		22 19			22 40		22 49
Scotstounhill	d	20 51				21 12		21 21			21 42		21 51			22 12		22 21			22 42		22 51
Jordanhill	d	20 55				21 15		21 24			21 45		21 54			22 15		22 25			22 45		22 55
Hyndland	d	20 57	21 06	21 14		21 17	21 23	21 26	21 35	21 44	21 47	21 53	21 56	22 06	22 15	22 18	22 24	22 27	22 34	22 44	22 47	22 53	22 57
Partick 225	d	20 59	21 08	21 17		21 20	21 25	21 28	21 37	21 47	21 50	21 55	21 58	22 08	22 17	22 20	22 26	22 29	22 37	22 47	22 50	22 55	22 59
Exhibition Centre 225	a		21 11			21 23	21 28		21 40		21 53	21 58		22 11		22 23	22 29		22 40		22 53	22 58	
Anderston 225	a		21 13			21 25	21 30		21 42		21 55	22 00		22 13		22 25	22 31		22 42		22 55	23 01	
Glasgow Central LL 225	a		21 15			21 26	21 32		21 44		21 56	22 02		22 15		22 27	22 33		22 44		22 57	23 02	
Argyle Street 225	a		21 17			21 29	21 36		21 46		21 59	22 05		22 18		22 29	22 35		22 46		22 59	23 07	
Charing Cross	d	21 03		21 21				21 32		21 51			22 02		22 21			22 33		22 51			23 03
Glasgow Queen St LL	a	21 05		21 23				21 34		21 53			22 04		22 23			22 35		22 53			23 05
	d	21 06		21 23				21 34		21 53			22 04		22 24			22 35		22 53			23 05
High Street	d	21 08		21 25				21 36		21 55			22 06		22 26			22 37		22 55			23 07
Bellgrove	d	21 10		21 27				21 38		21 57			22 08		22 28			22 39		22 57			23 09
Duke Street	d	21 12						21 40					22 10					22 41					23 11
Alexandra Parade	d	21 18						21 42					22 12					22 43					23 13
Barnhill	d	21 23						21 45					22 15					22 46					23 16
Springburn	a	21 25						21 47					22 17					22 48					23 18
Greenfaulds	d	21 47						22 11				23 02	22 38					23 09					23 41
Cumbernauld	a	21 49						22 13				23 04	22 41					23 12					23 44
Carntyne	d			21 31						22 01					22 31					23 01			
Shettleston	d			21 33						22 03					22 34					23 03			
Garrowhill	d			21 36						22 06					22 36					23 06			
Easterhouse	d			21 38						22 08					22 39					23 08			
Blairhill	d			21 42						22 12					22 43					23 12			
Coatbridge Sunnyside	d			21 45						22 15					22 45					23 15			
Coatdyke	d			21 47						22 17					22 48					23 17			
Airdrie	d			21 50						22 20					22 51					23 20			
Drumgelloch	d			21 53						22 23					22 54					23 23			
Caldercruix	d			21 57						22 27					22 58					23 27			
Blackridge	d			22 03						22 33					23 04					23 33			
Armadale	d			22 07						22 37					23 07					23 37			
Bathgate	a			22 11						22 41					23 11					23 41			
	d			22 11						22 41					23 11								
Livingston North	d			22 16						22 46					23 16								
Uphall	d			22 19						22 49					23 19								
Edinburgh Park 230	d			22 27						22 57					23 27								
Haymarket 228,230	a			22 33						23 03					23 31								
Edinburgh 228,230	a			22 39						23 08					23 39								

A To Larkhall
B From Mallaig to Glasgow Queen Street
C To Motherwell
D To Whifflet

Table T226-R

Saturdays
26 May to 8 December

Helensburgh, Balloch, Dalmuir and Milngavie - Glasgow - Springburn, Cumbernauld, Airdrie, Bathgate and Edinburgh

		SR	SR	SR	SR	SR	SR	SR	SR	SR	SR
		A		B	B		◇ C				
Helensburgh Upper 227	d						22 49				
Helensburgh Central	d		22 31					23 02		23 32	
Craigendoran	d		22 34					23 05		23 35	
Cardross	d		22 40					23 10		23 40	
Balloch	d					22 44			23 14		23 44
Alexandria	d					22 46			23 16		23 46
Renton	d					22 49			23 19		23 49
Dalreoch	d		22 45			22 52		23 15	23 22	23 45	23 52
Dumbarton Central 227	d		22 47			22 54	23 02	23 17	23 24	23 47	23 55
Dumbarton East	d		22 49			22 56		23 19	23 26	23 49	23 57
Bowling	d					23 00			23 31		
Kilpatrick	d					23 03			23 34		
Dalmuir 227	a		22 56			23 06	23 11	23 26	23 37	23 56	00 05
	d	22 48	22 59	23 03		23 11		23 29		23 59	
Singer	d	22 50	23 01					23 31		00 01	
Drumry	d	22 53	23 03					23 33		00 03	
Drumchapel	d	22 55	23 06					23 36		00 06	
Milngavie	d				23 09						
Hillfoot	d				23 12						
Bearsden	d				23 14						
Westerton	d	22 59	23 08		23 17			23 38		00 08	
Anniesland	d	23 02	23 11		23 20			23 41		00 11	
Clydebank	d			23 05		23 13					
Yoker	d			23 07		23 15					
Garscadden	d			23 10		23 19					
Scotstounhill	d			23 12		23 21					
Jordanhill	d			23 15		23 24					
Hyndland	d	23 05	23 14	23 17	23 23	23 26		23 44		00 14	
Partick 225	d	23 08	23 17	23 20	23 25	23 28		23 47		00 17	
Exhibition Centre 225	a	23 11		23 23	23 28						
Anderston 225	a	23 14		23 25	23 31						
Glasgow Central LL 225	a	23 15		23 27	23 32						
Argyle Street 225	a	23 18		23 29	23 37						
Charing Cross	d		23 21			23 32		23 51		00 21	
Glasgow Queen St LL	a		23 23			23 34		23 53		00 23	
	d		23 23			23 34		23 53		00 23	
High Street	d		23 25			23 36		23 55		00 25	
Bellgrove	d		23 27			23 38		23 57		00 27	
Duke Street	d					23 40					
Alexandra Parade	d					23 42					
Barnhill	d					23 45					
Springburn	a					23 47					
Greenfaulds	d										
Cumbernauld	a										
Carntyne	d		23 31					00 02		00 31	
Shettleston	d		23 33					00 03		00 33	
Garrowhill	d		23 36					00 06		00 36	
Easterhouse	d		23 38					00 08		00 38	
Blairhill	d		23 42					00 12		00 42	
Coatbridge Sunnyside	d		23 45					00 15		00 45	
Coatdyke	d		23 47					00 17		00 47	
Airdrie	d		23 50					00 20		00a51	
Drumgelloch	d		23 53					00 23			
Caldercruix	d		23 57					00 27			
Blackridge	d		00 03					00 33			
Armadale	d		00 07					00 36			
Bathgate	a		00 11					00 40			
	d										
Livingston North	d										
Uphall	d										
Edinburgh Park 230	d										
Haymarket 228,230	a										
Edinburgh 228,230	a										

A To Larkhall
B To Motherwell
C From Oban to Glasgow Queen Street

Table T226-R

Sundays
20 May to 2 December

Helensburgh, Balloch, Dalmuir and Milngavie - Glasgow - Springburn, Cumbernauld, Airdrie, Bathgate and Edinburgh

		SR A	SR A	SR	SR A	SR	SR	SR B	SR C	SR	SR D	SR C	SR D	SR C	SR	SR	SR B	SR C	SR D	SR C	SR	SR D	SR C
Helensburgh Upper 227	d																						
Helensburgh Central	d									07 55						08 25					08 55		
Craigendoran	d									07 58						08 28					08 58		
Cardross	d									08 03						08 33					09 03		
Balloch	d										08 09	08 09					08 39	08 39				09 09	09 09
Alexandria	d										08 11	08 11					08 41	08 41				09 11	09 11
Renton	d										08 14	08 14					08 44	08 44				09 14	09 14
Dalreoch	d									08 08	08 17	08 17				08 38	08 47	08 47			09 08	09 17	09 17
Dumbarton Central 227	d									08 10	08 18	08 18				08 40	08 48	08 48			09 10	09 18	09 18
Dumbarton East	d									08 12	08 20	08 20				08 42	08 50	08 50			09 12	09 20	09 20
Bowling	d										08 25	08 25					08 55	08 55				09 25	09 25
Kilpatrick	d										08 28	08 28					08 58	08 58				09 28	09 28
Dalmuir 227	a									08 19	08 31	08 31				08 49	09 01	09 01			09 19	09 31	09 31
	d						07 46	08 01	08 01	08 20	08 32	08 32				08 50	09 02	09 02			09 20	09 32	09 32
Singer	d				00 01		07 48			08 22						08 52					09 22		
Drumry	d				00 03		07 50			08 25						08 55					09 25		
Drumchapel	d				00 06		07 53			08 27						08 57					09 27		
Milngavie	d																		09 11	09 11			
Hillfoot	d																		09 14	09 14			
Bearsden	d																		09 16	09 16			
Westerton	d				00 08		07 55			08 30						09 00			09 19	09 19	09 30		
Anniesland	d				00 11		07 59			08 33						09 03			09 22	09 22	09 33		
Clydebank	d							08 04	08 04		08 34	08 34					09 04	09 04				09 34	09 34
Yoker	d							08 06	08 06		08 36	08 36					09 06	09 06				09 36	09 36
Garscadden	d							08 09	08 09		08 39	08 39					09 09	09 09				09 39	09 39
Scotstounhill	d							08 11	08 11		08 41	08 41					09 11	09 11				09 41	09 41
Jordanhill	d							08 13	08 13		08 43	08 43					09 13	09 13				09 43	09 43
Hyndland [8]	d				00 14		08 02	08 15	08 15	08 36	08 45	08 45	08 55	08 55		09 06	09 15	09 15	09 25	09 25	09 36	09 45	09 45
Partick 225	d				00 17	08 01	08 05	08 18	08 18	08 38	08 48	08 48	08 57	08 57	09 01	09 08	09 18	09 18	09 27	09 27	09 38	09 48	09 48
Exhibition Centre 225	a							08 21	08 21		08 51	08 51	09 00	09 00			09 21	09 21	09 30	09 30		09 51	09 51
Anderston 225	a																					09 53	09 53
Glasgow Central LL [15] 225	a							08 23	08 24		08 53	08 54	09 03	09 04			09 23	09 24	09 33	09 34		09 54	09 54
Argyle Street 225	a																					09 57	10 00
Charing Cross	d				00 21	08 05	08 09			08 43					09 05	09 13					09 43		
Glasgow Queen St LL [10]	a				00 23	08 07	08 11			08 45					09 07	09 15					09 45		
	d				00 23	08 07	08 11			08 45					09 07	09 15					09 45		
High Street	d				00 25	08 09	08 13			08 47					09 09	09 17					09 47		
Bellgrove	d				00 27	08 11	08 15			08 49					09 11	09 19					09 49		
Duke Street	d														09 13								
Alexandra Parade	d														09 15								
Barnhill	d														09 18								
Springburn	a					08 20									09 20								
Greenfaulds	d					08 41									09 41								
Cumbernauld	a					08 44									09 44								
Carntyne	d		00 02		00 31		08 19			08 53						09 23					09 53		
Shettleston	d		00 03		00 33		08 21			08 55						09 25					09 55		
Garrowhill	d		00 06		00 36		08 24			08 58						09 28					09 58		
Easterhouse	d		00 08		00 38		08 26			09 00						09 30					10 00		
Blairhill	d		00 12		00 42		08 30			09 04						09 34					10 04		
Coatbridge Sunnyside	d		00 15		00 45		08 33			09 07						09 37					10 07		
Coatdyke	d		00 17		00 47		08 35			09 09						09 39					10 09		
Airdrie	d		00 20		00a51		08 38			09 12						09 42					10 12		
Drumgelloch	d		00 23				08 41			09 15						09 45					10 15		
Caldercruix	d		00 27				08 45			09 19						09 49					10 19		
Blackridge	d	00 03	00 33				08 51			09 25						09 55					10 25		
Armadale	d	00 07	00 36				08 55			09 29						09 59					10 29		
Bathgate	a	00 11	00 40				08 59			09 33						10 03					10 33		
	d			07 55			08 59			09 34						10 04					10 34		
Livingston North	d			07 59			09 04			09 39						10 09					10 38		
Uphall	d			08 02			09 07			09 42						10 12					10 41		
Edinburgh Park 230	d			08 10			09 16			09 53						10 23					10 49		
Haymarket 228,230	a			08 21			09 27			10 03						10 33					10 54		
Edinburgh 228,230	a			08 26			09 32			10 08						10 40					10 59		

A not 20 May. From Helensburgh Central
B from 16 September. To Larkhall
C until 9 September. To Rutherglen
D from 16 September. To Motherwell

Table T226-R

Sundays
20 May to 2 December

Helensburgh, Balloch, Dalmuir and Milngavie - Glasgow - Springburn, Cumbernauld, Airdrie, Bathgate and Edinburgh

		SR A	SR B	SR	SR	SR C	SR B	SR A	SR B	SR	SR A	SR B	SR A	SR B	SR	SR	SR C	SR B	SR A	SR B	SR	SR A	SR B
Helensburgh Upper 227	d																						
Helensburgh Central	d				09 25					09 55						10 25					10 55		
Craigendoran	d				09 28					09 58						10 28					10 58		
Cardross	d				09 33					10 03						10 33					11 03		
Balloch	d					09 39	09 39				10 09	10 09					10 39	10 39				11 09	11 09
Alexandria	d					09 41	09 41				10 11	10 11					10 41	10 41				11 11	11 11
Renton	d					09 44	09 44				10 14	10 14					10 44	10 44				11 14	11 14
Dalreoch	d				09 38	09 47	09 47			10 08	10 17	10 17				10 38	10 47	10 47			11 08	11 17	11 17
Dumbarton Central 227	d				09 40	09 48	09 48			10 10	10 18	10 18				10 40	10 48	10 48			11 10	11 18	11 18
Dumbarton East	d				09 42	09 50	09 50			10 12	10 20	10 20				10 42	10 50	10 50			11 12	11 20	11 20
Bowling	d					09 55	09 55				10 25	10 25					10 55	10 55				11 25	11 25
Kilpatrick	d					09 58	09 58				10 28	10 28					10 58	10 58				11 28	11 28
Dalmuir 227	a				09 49	10 01	10 01			10 19	10 31	10 31				10 49	11 01	11 01			11 19	11 31	11 31
	d				09 50	10 02	10 02			10 20	10 32	10 32				10 50	11 02	11 02			11 20	11 32	11 32
Singer	d				09 52					10 22						10 52					11 22		
Drumry	d				09 55					10 25						10 55					11 25		
Drumchapel	d				09 57					10 27						10 57					11 27		
Milngavie	d	09 41	09 41					10 11	10 11				10 41	10 41					11 11	11 11			
Hillfoot	d	09 44	09 44					10 14	10 14				10 44	10 44					11 14	11 14			
Bearsden	d	09 46	09 46					10 16	10 16				10 46	10 46					11 16	11 16			
Westerton	d	09 49	09 49		10 00			10 19	10 19	10 30			10 49	10 49		11 00			11 19	11 19	11 30		
Anniesland	d	09 52	09 52		10 03			10 22	10 22	10 33			10 52	10 52		11 03			11 22	11 22	11 33		
Clydebank	d					10 04	10 04				10 34	10 34					11 04	11 04				11 34	11 34
Yoker	d					10 06	10 06				10 36	10 36					11 06	11 06				11 36	11 36
Garscadden	d					10 09	10 09				10 39	10 39					11 09	11 09				11 39	11 39
Scotstounhill	d					10 11	10 11				10 41	10 41					11 11	11 11				11 41	11 41
Jordanhill	d					10 13	10 13				10 43	10 43					11 13	11 13				11 43	11 43
Hyndland [8]	d	09 55	09 55		10 06	10 15	10 15	10 25	10 25	10 36	10 45	10 45	10 55	10 55		11 06	11 15	11 15	11 25	11 25	11 36	11 45	11 45
Partick 225	d	09 57	09 57	10 01	10 08	10 18	10 18	10 27	10 27	10 38	10 48	10 48	10 57	10 57	11 01	11 08	11 18	11 18	11 27	11 27	11 38	11 48	11 48
Exhibition Centre 225	a	10 00	10 00			10 21	10 21	10 30	10 30		10 51	10 51	11 00	11 00			11 21	11 21	11 30	11 30		11 51	11 51
Anderston 225	a	10 02	10 02			10 23	10 23	10 32	10 32		10 53	10 53	11 02	11 02			11 23	11 23	11 32	11 32		11 53	11 53
Glasgow Central LL [15] 225	a	10 04	10 04			10 24	10 24	10 34	10 34		10 54	10 54	11 04	11 04			11 24	11 24	11 34	11 34		11 54	11 54
Argyle Street 225	a	10 07	10 13			10 26	10 30	10 39	10 43		10 57	11 00	11 07	11 13			11 26	11 30	11 39	11 43		11 57	12 00
Charing Cross	d			10 05	10 13					10 43					11 05	11 13					11 43		
Glasgow Queen St LL [10]	a			10 07	10 15					10 45					11 07	11 15					11 45		
	d			10 07	10 15					10 45					11 07	11 15					11 45		
High Street	d			10 09	10 17					10 47					11 09	11 17					11 47		
Bellgrove	d			10 11	10 19					10 49					11 11	11 19					11 49		
Duke Street	d			10 13											11 13								
Alexandra Parade	d			10 15											11 15								
Barnhill	d			10 18											11 18								
Springburn	a			10 20											11 20								
Greenfaulds	d			10 41											11 41								
Cumbernauld	a			10 44											11 44								
Carntyne	d				10 23					10 53						11 23					11 53		
Shettleston	d				10 25					10 55						11 25					11 55		
Garrowhill	d				10 28					10 58						11 28					11 58		
Easterhouse	d				10 30					11 00						11 30					12 00		
Blairhill	d				10 34					11 04						11 34					12 04		
Coatbridge Sunnyside	d				10 37					11 07						11 37					12 07		
Coatdyke	d				10 39					11 09						11 39					12 09		
Airdrie	d				10 42					11 12						11 42					12 12		
Drumgelloch	d				10 45					11 15						11 45					12 15		
Caldercruix	d				10 49					11 19						11 49					12 19		
Blackridge	d				10 55					11 25						11 55					12 25		
Armadale	d				10 59					11 29						11 59					12 29		
Bathgate	a				11 03					11 33						12 03					12 33		
	d				11 04					11 34						12 04					12 34		
Livingston North	d				11 08					11 38						12 08					12 38		
Uphall	d				11 11					11 41						12 11					12 41		
Edinburgh Park 230	d				11 19					11 49						12 19					12 49		
Haymarket 228,230	a				11 24					11 59						12 24					12 55		
Edinburgh 228,230	a				11 29					12 04						12 29					13 00		

A from 16 September. To Motherwell
B until 9 September. To Rutherglen
C from 16 September. To Larkhall

Table T226-R

Sundays

20 May to 2 December

Helensburgh, Balloch, Dalmuir and Milngavie - Glasgow - Springburn, Cumbernauld, Airdrie, Bathgate and Edinburgh

		SR A		SR B	SR	SR	SR C	SR B	SR A	SR B	SR	SR A		SR B	SR A	SR B	SR	SR	SR C	SR B	SR A	SR B		SR	SR A
Helensburgh Upper 227	d																								
Helensburgh Central	d					11 25					11 55							12 25						12 55	
Craigendoran	d					11 28					11 58							12 28						12 58	
Cardross	d					11 33					12 03							12 33						13 04	
Balloch	d						11 39	11 39				12 09		12 09					12 39	12 39					13 09
Alexandria	d						11 41	11 41				12 11		12 11					12 41	12 41					13 11
Renton	d						11 44	11 44				12 14		12 14					12 44	12 44					13 14
Dalreoch	d					11 38	11 47	11 47			12 08	12 17		12 17				12 38	12 47	12 47				13 09	13 17
Dumbarton Central 227	d					11 40	11 48	11 48			12 10	12 18		12 18				12 40	12 48	12 48				13 10	13 18
Dumbarton East	d					11 42	11 50	11 50			12 12	12 20		12 20				12 42	12 50	12 50				13 12	13 20
Bowling	d						11 55	11 55				12 25		12 25					12 55	12 55					13 25
Kilpatrick	d						11 58	11 58				12 28		12 28					12 58	12 58					13 28
Dalmuir 227	a					11 49	12 01	12 01			12 19	12 31		12 31				12 49	13 01	13 01				13 20	13 31
	d					11 50	12 02	12 02			12 20	12 32		12 32				12 50	13 02	13 02				13 21	13 32
Singer	d					11 52					12 22							12 52						13 23	
Drumry	d					11 55					12 25							12 55						13 25	
Drumchapel	d					11 57					12 27							12 57						13 28	
Milngavie	d	11 41		11 41					12 11	12 11					12 41	12 41					13 11	13 11			
Hillfoot	d	11 44		11 44					12 14	12 14					12 44	12 44					13 14	13 14			
Bearsden	d	11 46		11 46					12 16	12 16					12 46	12 46					13 16	13 16			
Westerton	d	11 49		11 49		12 00			12 19	12 19	12 30				12 49	12 49		13 00			13 19	13 19		13 30	
Anniesland	d	11 52		11 52		12 03			12 22	12 22	12 33				12 52	12 52		13 03			13 22	13 22		13 33	
Clydebank	d						12 04	12 04				12 34		12 34					13 04	13 04					13 34
Yoker	d						12 06	12 06				12 36		12 36					13 06	13 06					13 36
Garscadden	d						12 09	12 09				12 39		12 39					13 09	13 09					13 39
Scotstounhill	d						12 11	12 11				12 41		12 41					13 11	13 11					13 41
Jordanhill	d						12 13	12 13				12 43		12 43					13 13	13 13					13 43
Hyndland 3	d	11 55		11 55		12 06	12 15	12 15	12 25	12 25	12 36	12 45		12 45	12 55	12 55		13 06	13 15	13 15	13 25	13 25		13 36	13 45
Partick 225 ⛴	d	11 57		11 57	12 01	12 08	12 18	12 18	12 27	12 27	12 38	12 48		12 48	12 57	12 57	13 01	13 08	13 18	13 18	13 27	13 27		13 38	13 48
Exhibition Centre 225	a	12 00		12 00			12 21	12 21	12 30	12 30		12 51		12 51	13 00	13 00			13 21	13 21	13 30	13 30			13 51
Anderston 225	a	12 02		12 02			12 23	12 23	12 32	12 32		12 53		12 53	13 02	13 02			13 23	13 23	13 32	13 32			13 53
Glasgow Central LL 15 225	a	12 04		12 04			12 24	12 24	12 34	12 34		12 54		12 54	13 04	13 04			13 24	13 24	13 34	13 34			13 54
Argyle Street 225	a	12 07		12 13			12 26	12 30	12 37	12 43		12 57		13 00	13 07	13 13			13 26	13 30	13 39	13 43			13 57
Charing Cross	d				12 05	12 13					12 43						13 05	13 13						13 43	
Glasgow Queen St LL 10 ⛴	a				12 07	12 15					12 45						13 07	13 15						13 45	
	d				12 07	12 15					12 45						13 07	13 15						13 45	
High Street	d				12 09	12 17					12 47						13 09	13 17						13 47	
Bellgrove	d				12 11	12 19					12 49						13 11	13 19						13 49	
Duke Street	d				12 13												13 13								
Alexandra Parade	d				12 15												13 15								
Barnhill	d				12 18												13 18								
Springburn	a				12 20												13 20								
Greenfaulds	d				12 41												13 41								
Cumbernauld	a				12 44												13 44								
Carntyne	d					12 23					12 53							13 23						13 53	
Shettleston	d					12 25					12 55							13 25						13 55	
Garrowhill	d					12 28					12 58							13 28						13 58	
Easterhouse	d					12 30					13 00							13 30						14 00	
Blairhill	d					12 34					13 04							13 34						14 04	
Coatbridge Sunnyside	d					12 37					13 07							13 37						14 07	
Coatdyke	d					12 39					13 09							13 39						14 09	
Airdrie	d					12 42					13 12							13 42						14 12	
Drumgelloch	d					12 45					13 15							13 45						14 15	
Caldercruix	d					12 49					13 19							13 49						14 19	
Blackridge	d					12 55					13 25							13 55						14 25	
Armadale	d					12 59					13 29							13 59						14 29	
Bathgate	a					13 03					13 33							14 03						14 33	
	d					13 04					13 34							14 04						14 34	
Livingston North	d					13 08					13 38							14 08						14 38	
Uphall	d					13 11					13 41							14 11						14 41	
Edinburgh Park 230	d					13 21					13 49							14 19						14 49	
Haymarket 228,230 ⛴	a					13 26					13 54							14 24						14 54	
Edinburgh 228,230	a					13 31					13 59							14 29						14 59	

A from 16 September. To Motherwell B until 9 September. To Rutherglen C from 16 September. To Larkhall

Table T226-R

Sundays

20 May to 2 December

Helensburgh, Balloch, Dalmuir and Milngavie - Glasgow - Springburn, Cumbernauld, Airdrie, Bathgate and Edinburgh

		SR A	SR B	SR A	SR	SR	SR C	SR A		SR B	SR A	SR	SR B	SR A	SR B	SR A	SR	SR		SR C	SR A	SR ◇ D 🚲	SR B	SR A	SR
Helensburgh Upper 227	d																					14 40			
Helensburgh Central	d					13 25						13 55						14 25							14 55
Craigendoran	d					13 28						13 58						14 28							14 58
Cardross	d					13 33						14 03						14 33							15 03
Balloch	d	13 09					13 39	13 39					14 09	14 09						14 39	14 39				
Alexandria	d	13 11					13 41	13 41					14 11	14 11						14 41	14 41				
Renton	d	13 14					13 44	13 44					14 14	14 14						14 44	14 44				
Dalreoch	d	13 17				13 38	13 47	13 47				14 08	14 17	14 17				14 38		14 47	14 47				15 08
Dumbarton Central 227	d	13 18				13 40	13 48	13 48				14 10	14 18	14 18				14 40		14 48	14 48	14 56			15 10
Dumbarton East	d	13 20				13 42	13 50	13 50				14 12	14 20	14 20				14 42		14 50	14 50				15 12
Bowling	d	13 25					13 55	13 55					14 25	14 25						14 55	14 55				
Kilpatrick	d	13 28					13 58	13 58					14 28	14 28						14 58	14 58				
Dalmuir 227	a	13 31				13 49	14 01	14 01				14 19	14 31	14 31				14 49		15 01	15 01	15 05			15 19
	d	13 32				13 50	14 02	14 02				14 20	14 32	14 32				14 50		15 02	15 02				15 20
Singer	d					13 52						14 22						14 52							15 22
Drumry	d					13 55						14 25						14 55							15 25
Drumchapel	d					13 57						14 27						14 57							15 27
Milngavie	d		13 41	13 41						14 11	14 11				14 41	14 41							15 11	15 11	
Hillfoot	d		13 44	13 44						14 14	14 14				14 44	14 44							15 14	15 14	
Bearsden	d		13 46	13 46						14 16	14 16				14 46	14 46							15 16	15 16	
Westerton	d		13 49	13 49		14 00				14 19	14 19	14 30			14 49	14 49		15 00					15 19	15 19	15 30
Anniesland	d		13 52	13 52		14 03				14 22	14 22	14 33			14 52	14 52		15 03					15 22	15 22	15 33
Clydebank	d	13 34					14 04	14 04					14 34	14 34						15 04	15 04				
Yoker	d	13 36					14 06	14 06					14 36	14 36						15 06	15 06				
Garscadden	d	13 39					14 09	14 09					14 39	14 39						15 09	15 09				
Scotstounhill	d	13 41					14 11	14 11					14 41	14 41						15 11	15 11				
Jordanhill	d	13 43					14 13	14 13					14 43	14 43						15 13	15 13				
Hyndland 3	d	13 45	13 55	13 55		14 06	14 15	14 15		14 25	14 25	14 36	14 45	14 45	14 55	14 55		15 06		15 15	15 15		15 25	15 25	15 36
Partick 225 ⛴	d	13 48	13 57	13 57	14 01	14 08	14 18	14 18		14 27	14 27	14 38	14 48	14 48	14 57	14 57	15 01	15 08		15 18	15 18		15 28	15 28	15 38
Exhibition Centre 225	a	13 51	14 00	14 00			14 21	14 21		14 30	14 30		14 51	14 51	15 00	15 00				15 21	15 21		15 31	15 31	
Anderston 225	a	13 53	14 02	14 02			14 23	14 23		14 32	14 32		14 53	14 53	15 02	15 02				15 23	15 23		15 33	15 33	
Glasgow Central LL 15 225	a	13 54	14 04	14 04			14 24	14 24		14 34	14 34		14 54	14 54	15 04	15 04				15 24	15 24		15 34	15 34	
Argyle Street 225	a	14 00	14 07	14 13			14 26	14 30		14 39	14 43		14 57	15 00	15 07	15 13				15 26	15 30		15 39	15 43	
Charing Cross	d				14 05	14 13						14 43					15 05	15 13							15 43
Glasgow Queen St LL 10 ⛴	a				14 07	14 15						14 45					15 07	15 15							15 45
	d				14 07	14 15						14 45					15 07	15 15							15 45
High Street	d				14 09	14 17						14 47					15 09	15 17							15 47
Bellgrove	d				14 11	14 19						14 49					15 11	15 19							15 49
Duke Street	d				14 13												15 13								
Alexandra Parade	d				14 15												15 15								
Barnhill	d				14 18												15 18								
Springburn	a				14 20												15 20								
Greenfaulds	d				14 41												15 41								
Cumbernauld	a				14 44												15 44								
Carntyne	d					14 23						14 53						15 23							15 53
Shettleston	d					14 25						14 55						15 25							15 55
Garrowhill	d					14 28						14 58						15 28							15 58
Easterhouse	d					14 30						15 00						15 30							16 00
Blairhill	d					14 34						15 04						15 34							16 04
Coatbridge Sunnyside	d					14 37						15 07						15 37							16 07
Coatdyke	d					14 39						15 09						15 39							16 09
Airdrie	d					14 42						15 12						15 42							16 12
Drumgelloch	d					14 45						15 15						15 45							16 15
Caldercruix	d					14 49						15 19						15 49							16 19
Blackridge	d					14 55						15 25						15 55							16 25
Armadale	d					14 59						15 29						15 59							16 29
Bathgate	a					15 03						15 33						16 03							16 33
	d					15 04						15 34						16 04							16 34
Livingston North	d					15 08						15 38						16 08							16 38
Uphall	d					15 11						15 41						16 11							16 41
Edinburgh Park 230	d					15 19						15 49						16 19							16 51
Haymarket 228,230 ⛴	a					15 24						15 55						16 24							16 56
Edinburgh 228,230	a					15 29						16 00						16 31							17 01

A until 9 September. To Rutherglen
B from 16 September. To Motherwell
C from 16 September. To Larkhall
D From Mallaig to Glasgow Queen Street

Table T226-R

Sundays

20 May to 2 December

Helensburgh, Balloch, Dalmuir and Milngavie - Glasgow - Springburn, Cumbernauld, Airdrie, Bathgate and Edinburgh

		SR A	SR B	SR A	SR B	SR	SR	SR C	SR B	SR A	SR B	SR	SR A	SR B	SR A	SR B	SR	SR	SR C	SR B	SR A	SR B
Helensburgh Upper	227 d																					
Helensburgh Central	d						15 25					15 55						16 25				
Craigendoran	d						15 28					15 58						16 28				
Cardross	d						15 33					16 03						16 33				
Balloch	d	15 09	15 09					15 39	15 39				16 09	16 09					16 39	16 39		
Alexandria	d	15 11	15 11					15 41	15 41				16 11	16 11					16 41	16 41		
Renton	d	15 14	15 14					15 44	15 44				16 14	16 14					16 44	16 44		
Dalreoch	d	15 17	15 17				15 38	15 47	15 47			16 08	16 17	16 17				16 38	16 47	16 47		
Dumbarton Central	227 d	15 18	15 18				15 40	15 48	15 48			16 10	16 18	16 18				16 40	16 48	16 48		
Dumbarton East	d	15 20	15 20				15 42	15 50	15 50			16 12	16 20	16 20				16 42	16 50	16 50		
Bowling	d	15 25	15 25					15 55	15 55				16 25	16 25					16 55	16 55		
Kilpatrick	d	15 28	15 28					15 58	15 58				16 28	16 28					16 58	16 58		
Dalmuir	227 a	15 31	15 31				15 49	16 01	16 01			16 19	16 31	16 31				16 49	17 01	17 01		
	d	15 32	15 32				15 50	16 02	16 02			16 20	16 32	16 32				16 50	17 02	17 02		
Singer	d						15 52					16 22						16 52				
Drumry	d						15 55					16 25						16 55				
Drumchapel	d						15 57					16 27						16 57				
Milngavie	d			15 41	15 41					16 11	16 11				16 41	16 41					17 11	17 11
Hillfoot	d			15 44	15 44					16 14	16 14				16 44	16 44					17 14	17 14
Bearsden	d			15 46	15 46					16 16	16 16				16 46	16 46					17 16	17 16
Westerton	d			15 49	15 49		16 00			16 19	16 19	16 30			16 49	16 49		17 00			17 19	17 19
Anniesland	d			15 52	15 52		16 03			16 22	16 22	16 33			16 52	16 52		17 03			17 22	17 22
Clydebank	d	15 34	15 34					16 04	16 04				16 34	16 34					17 04	17 04		
Yoker	d	15 36	15 36					16 06	16 06				16 36	16 36					17 06	17 06		
Garscadden	d	15 39	15 39					16 09	16 09				16 39	16 39					17 09	17 09		
Scotstounhill	d	15 41	15 41					16 11	16 11				16 41	16 41					17 11	17 11		
Jordanhill	d	15 43	15 43					16 13	16 13				16 43	16 43					17 13	17 13		
Hyndland ■	d	15 45	15 45	15 55	15 55		16 06	16 15	16 15	16 25	16 25	16 36	16 45	16 45	16 55	16 55		17 06	17 15	17 15	17 25	17 25
Partick	225 ⇌ d	15 48	15 48	15 57	15 57	16 01	16 08	16 18	16 18	16 27	16 27	16 38	16 48	16 48	16 57	16 57	17 01	17 08	17 18	17 18	17 27	17 27
Exhibition Centre	225 a	15 51	15 51	16 00	16 00			16 21	16 21	16 30	16 30		16 51	16 51	17 00	17 00			17 21	17 21	17 30	17 30
Anderston	225 a	15 53	15 53	16 02	16 02			16 23	16 23	16 32	16 32		16 53	16 53	17 02	17 02			17 23	17 23	17 32	17 32
Glasgow Central LL 15	225 a	15 54	15 54	16 04	16 04			16 24	16 24	16 34	16 34		16 54	16 54	17 04	17 04			17 24	17 24	17 34	17 34
Argyle Street	225 a	15 58	16 00	16 07	16 13			16 26	16 30	16 39	16 43		16 57	17 00	17 07	17 13			17 26	17 30	17 39	17 43
Charing Cross	d					16 05	16 13					16 43					17 05	17 13				
Glasgow Queen St LL 10	⇌ a					16 07	16 15					16 45					17 07	17 15				
	d					16 07	16 15					16 45					17 07	17 15				
High Street	d					16 09	16 17					16 47					17 09	17 17				
Bellgrove	d					16 11	16 19					16 49					17 11	17 19				
Duke Street	d					16 13											17 13					
Alexandra Parade	d					16 15											17 15					
Barnhill	d					16 18											17 18					
Springburn	a					16 20											17 20					
Greenfaulds	d					16 41											17 41					
Cumbernauld	a					16 44											17 44					
Carntyne	d						16 23					16 53						17 23				
Shettleston	d						16 25					16 55						17 25				
Garrowhill	d						16 28					16 58						17 28				
Easterhouse	d						16 30					17 00						17 30				
Blairhill	d						16 34					17 04						17 34				
Coatbridge Sunnyside	d						16 37					17 07						17 37				
Coatdyke	d						16 39					17 09						17 39				
Airdrie	d						16 42					17 12						17 42				
Drumgelloch	d						16 45					17 15						17 45				
Caldercruix	d						16 49					17 19						17 49				
Blackridge	d						16 55					17 25						17 55				
Armadale	d						16 59					17 29						17 59				
Bathgate	a						17 03					17 33						18 03				
	d						17 04					17 34						18 04				
Livingston North	d						17 08					17 38						18 08				
Uphall	d						17 11					17 41						18 11				
Edinburgh Park	230 d						17 19					17 49						18 19				
Haymarket	228,230 ⇌ a						17 24					17 54						18 24				
Edinburgh	228,230 a						17 29					17 59						18 32				

A from 16 September. To Motherwell
B until 9 September. To Rutherglen
C from 16 September. To Larkhall

Table T226-R

Sundays

20 May to 2 December

Helensburgh, Balloch, Dalmuir and Milngavie - Glasgow - Springburn, Cumbernauld, Airdrie, Bathgate and Edinburgh

		SR	SR A	SR B	SR A	SR B	SR	SR	SR C	SR B	SR D	SR	SR D	SR A	SR B	SR	SR	SR ◇ E	SR D	SR A	SR B	SR	SR D
Helensburgh Upper	227 d																	18 31					
Helensburgh Central	d	16 55						17 25				17 55					18 25					18 55	
Craigendoran	d	16 58						17 28				17 58					18 28					18 58	
Cardross	d	17 03						17 33				18 03					18 33					19 04	
Balloch	d		17 09	17 09					17 39	17 39			18 09						18 39				19 09
Alexandria	d		17 11	17 11					17 41	17 41			18 11						18 41				19 11
Renton	d		17 14	17 14					17 44	17 44			18 14						18 44				19 14
Dalreoch	d	17 08	17 17	17 17				17 38	17 47	17 47		18 08	18 17				18 38		18 50			19 09	19 17
Dumbarton Central	227 d	17 10	17 18	17 18				17 40	17 48	17 48		18 10	18 18				18 40	18 47	18 51			19 10	19 18
Dumbarton East	d	17 12	17 20	17 20				17 42	17 50	17 50		18 12	18 20				18 42		18 53			19 12	19 20
Bowling	d		17 25	17 25					17 55	17 55			18 25						18 58				19 25
Kilpatrick	d		17 28	17 28					17 58	17 58			18 28						19 01				19 28
Dalmuir	227 a	17 19	17 31	17 31				17 49	18 01	18 01		18 19	18 31				18 49	18 58	19 04			19 20	19 31
	d	17 20	17 32	17 32				17 50	18 02	18 02		18 20	18 32				18 50		19 04			19 21	19 32
Singer	d	17 22						17 52				18 22					18 52					19 23	
Drumry	d	17 25						17 55				18 25					18 55					19 25	
Drumchapel	d	17 27						17 57				18 27					18 57					19 28	
Milngavie	d				17 41	17 41					18 11			18 41	18 41					19 11	19 11		
Hillfoot	d				17 44	17 44					18 14			18 44	18 44					19 14	19 14		
Bearsden	d				17 46	17 46					18 16			18 46	18 46					19 16	19 16		
Westerton	d	17 30			17 49	17 49		18 00			18 19	18 30		18 49	18 49		19 00			19 19	19 19	19 30	
Anniesland	d	17 33			17 52	17 52		18 03			18 22	18 33		18 52	18 52		19 03			19 22	19 22	19 33	
Clydebank	d		17 34	17 34					18 04	18 04			18 34						19 06				19 34
Yoker	d		17 36	17 36					18 06	18 06			18 36						19 08				19 36
Garscadden	d		17 39	17 39					18 09	18 09			18 39						19 11				19 39
Scotstounhill	d		17 41	17 41					18 11	18 11			18 41						19 13				19 41
Jordanhill	d		17 43	17 43					18 13	18 13			18 43						19 15				19 43
Hyndland ■	d	17 36	17 45	17 45	17 55	17 55		18 06	18 15	18 15	18 25	18 36	18 45	18 55	18 55		19 06		19 17	19 25	19 25	19 36	19 45
Partick	225 ⇌ d	17 38	17 48	17 48	17 57	17 57	18 01	18 08	18 18	18 18	18 27	18 38	18 48	18 57	18 57	19 01	19 08		19 19	19 27	19 27	19 38	19 48
Exhibition Centre	225 a		17 51	17 51	18 00	18 00			18 21	18 21	18 30		18 51	19 00	19 00				19 22	19 30	19 30		19 51
Anderston	225 a		17 53	17 53	18 02	18 02																	
Glasgow Central LL 15	225 a		17 54	17 54	18 04	18 04			18 23	18 24	18 34		18 54	19 03	19 04				19 25	19 33	19 34		19 54
Argyle Street	225 a		17 57	18 00	18 07	18 13																	
Charing Cross	d	17 43					18 05	18 13				18 43				19 05	19 13					19 43	
Glasgow Queen St LL 10	⇌ a	17 45					18 07	18 15				18 45				19 07	19 15					19 45	
	d	17 45					18 07	18 15				18 45				19 07	19 15					19 45	
High Street	d	17 47					18 09	18 17				18 47				19 09	19 17					19 47	
Bellgrove	d	17 49					18 11	18 19				18 49				19 11	19 19					19 49	
Duke Street	d						18 13									19 13							
Alexandra Parade	d						18 15									19 15							
Barnhill	d						18 18									19 18							
Springburn	a						18 20									19 20							
Greenfaulds	d						18 41									19 41							
Cumbernauld	a						18 44									19 44							
Carntyne	d	17 53						18 23				18 53					19 23					19 53	
Shettleston	d	17 55						18 25				18 55					19 25					19 55	
Garrowhill	d	17 58						18 28				18 58					19 28					19 58	
Easterhouse	d	18 00						18 30				19 00					19 30					20 00	
Blairhill	d	18 04						18 34				19 04					19 34					20 04	
Coatbridge Sunnyside	d	18 07						18 37				19 07					19 37					20 07	
Coatdyke	d	18 09						18 39				19 09					19 39					20 09	
Airdrie	d	18 12						18 42				19 12					19a43					20 12	
Drumgelloch	d	18 15						18 45				19 15										20 15	
Caldercruix	d	18 19						18 49				19 19										20 19	
Blackridge	d	18 25						18 55				19 25										20 25	
Armadale	d	18 29						18 59				19 29										20 29	
Bathgate	a	18 33						19 03				19 33										20 33	
	d	18 34						19 04				19 34										20 34	
Livingston North	d	18 38						19 08				19 38										20 38	
Uphall	d	18 41						19 11				19 41										20 41	
Edinburgh Park	230 d	18 49						19 19				19 49										20 49	
Haymarket	228,230 ⇌ a	18 54						19 24				19 54										20 54	
Edinburgh	228,230 a	18 59						19 29				19 59										20 59	

A from 16 September. To Motherwell
B until 9 September. To Rutherglen
C from 16 September. To Larkhall
D To Rutherglen
E From Oban to Glasgow Queen Street

Table T226-R

Sundays
20 May to 2 December

Helensburgh, Balloch, Dalmuir and Milngavie - Glasgow - Springburn, Cumbernauld, Airdrie, Bathgate and Edinburgh

	SR A	SR B	SR	SR	SR ◇ C	SR D	SR B	SR A	SR B	SR	SR A	SR B	SR A	SR B	SR	SR	SR D	SR B	SR ◇ E	SR A	SR B	SR
Helensburgh Upper 227 d					19 29														20 40			
Helensburgh Central d				19 25						19 55						20 25						20 55
Craigendoran d				19 28						19 58						20 28						20 58
Cardross d				19 33						20 03						20 33						21 03
Balloch d						19 39	19 39				20 09	20 09					20 39	20 39				
Alexandria d						19 41	19 41				20 11	20 11					20 41	20 41				
Renton d						19 44	19 44				20 14	20 14					20 44	20 44				
Dalreoch d				19 38		19 47	19 47			20 08	20 17	20 17				20 38	20 47	20 47				21 08
Dumbarton Central 227 d				19 40		19 48	19 48			20 10	20 18	20 18				20 40	20 48	20 48	20 53			21 10
Dumbarton East d				19 42		19 50	19 50			20 12	20 20	20 20				20 42	20 50	20 50				21 12
Bowling d						19 55	19 55				20 25	20 25					20 55	20 55				
Kilpatrick d						19 58	19 58				20 28	20 28					20 58	20 58				
Dalmuir 227 a				19 49	19s55	20 01	20 01			20 19	20 31	20 31				20 49	21 01	21 01	21 04			21 19
d				19 50		20 02	20 02			20 20	20 32	20 32				20 50	21 02	21 02				21 20
Singer d				19 52						20 22						20 52						21 22
Drumry d				19 55						20 25						20 55						21 25
Drumchapel d				19 57						20 27						20 57						21 27
Milngavie d	19 41	19 41						20 11	20 11				20 41	20 41						21 11	21 11	
Hillfoot d	19 44	19 44						20 14	20 14				20 44	20 44						21 14	21 14	
Bearsden d	19 46	19 46						20 16	20 16				20 46	20 46						21 16	21 16	
Westerton d	19 49	19 49		20 00				20 19	20 19	20 30			20 49	20 49		21 00				21 19	21 19	21 30
Anniesland d	19 52	19 52		20 03				20 22	20 22	20 33			20 52	20 52		21 03				21 22	21 22	21 33
Clydebank d						20 04	20 04				20 34	20 34					21 04	21 04				
Yoker d						20 06	20 06				20 36	20 36					21 06	21 06				
Garscadden d						20 09	20 09				20 39	20 39					21 09	21 09				
Scotstounhill d						20 11	20 11				20 41	20 41					21 11	21 11				
Jordanhill d						20 13	20 13				20 43	20 43					21 13	21 13				
Hyndland 3 d	19 55	19 55		20 06		20 15	20 15	20 25	20 25	20 36	20 45	20 45	20 55	20 55		21 06	21 15	21 15		21 25	21 25	21 36
Partick 225 ⛴ d	19 57	19 57	20 01	20 08		20 18	20 18	20 27	20 27	20 38	20 48	20 48	20 57	20 57	21 01	21 08	21 18	21 18		21 27	21 27	21 38
Exhibition Centre 225 a	20 00	20 00				20 21	20 21	20 30	20 30		20 51	20 51	21 00	21 00			21 21	21 21		21 30	21 30	
Anderston 225 a																						
Glasgow Central LL 15 225 a	20 03	20 04				20 23	20 24	20 33	20 34		20 53	20 54	21 03	21 04			21 23	21 24		21 33	21 34	
Argyle Street 225 a																						
Charing Cross d			20 05	20 13						20 43					21 05	21 13						21 43
Glasgow Queen St LL 10 ⛴ a			20 07	20 15						20 45					21 07	21 15						21 45
d			20 07	20 15						20 45					21 07	21 15						21 45
High Street d			20 09	20 17						20 47					21 09	21 17						21 47
Bellgrove d			20 11	20 19						20 49					21 11	21 19						21 49
Duke Street d																						
Alexandra Parade d																						
Barnhill d																						
Springburn a			20 20												21 20							
Greenfaulds d			20 41												21 41							
Cumbernauld a			20 44												21 44							
Carntyne d				20 23						20 53						21 23						21 53
Shettleston d				20 25						20 55						21 25						21 55
Garrowhill d				20 28						20 58						21 28						21 58
Easterhouse d				20 30						21 00						21 30						22 00
Blairhill d				20 34						21 04						21 34						22 04
Coatbridge Sunnyside d				20 37						21 07						21 37						22 07
Coatdyke d				20 39						21 09						21 39						22 09
Airdrie d				20a43						21 12						21a43						22 12
Drumgelloch d										21 15												22 15
Caldercruix d										21 19												22 19
Blackridge d										21 25												22 25
Armadale d										21 29												22 29
Bathgate a										21 33												22 33
d										21 34												22 34
Livingston North d										21 38												22 38
Uphall d										21 41												22 41
Edinburgh Park 230 d										21 49												22 49
Haymarket 228,230 ⛴ a					21s04					21 54												22 55
Edinburgh 228,230 a					21 09					21 59												23 00

A from 16 September. To Motherwell
B until 9 September. To Rutherglen
C from 24 June until 26 August. From Oban
D from 16 September. To Larkhall
E From Mallaig to Glasgow Queen Street

Table T226-R

Sundays
20 May to 2 December

Helensburgh, Balloch, Dalmuir and Milngavie - Glasgow - Springburn, Cumbernauld, Airdrie, Bathgate and Edinburgh

	SR A	SR B	SR A	SR B	SR	SR	SR C	SR B	SR A	SR B	SR	SR A	SR B	SR A	SR B	SR	SR	SR	CS D	SR	SR
Helensburgh Upper 227 d																			22 38		
Helensburgh Central d						21 25					21 55						22 25			22 55	
Craigendoran d						21 28					21 58						22 28			22 58	
Cardross d						21 33					22 03						22 33			23 03	
Balloch d	21 09	21 09					21 39	21 39				22 09	22 09					22 39			23 09
Alexandria d	21 11	21 11					21 41	21 41				22 11	22 11					22 41			23 11
Renton d	21 14	21 14					21 44	21 44				22 14	22 14					22 44			23 14
Dalreoch d	21 17	21 17				21 38	21 47	21 47			22 08	22 17	22 17				22 38	22 47		23 08	23 17
Dumbarton Central 227 d	21 18	21 18				21 40	21 48	21 48			22 10	22 18	22 18				22 40	22 48	22 53	23 10	23 18
Dumbarton East d	21 20	21 20				21 42	21 50	21 50			22 12	22 20	22 20				22 42	22 50		23 12	23 20
Bowling d	21 25	21 25					21 55	21 55				22 25	22 25					22 55			23 25
Kilpatrick d	21 28	21 28					21 58	21 58				22 28	22 28					22 58			23 28
Dalmuir 227 a	21 31	21 31				21 49	22 01	22 01			22 19	22 31	22 31				22 49	23 01	23 06	23 19	23 31
d	21 32	21 32				21 50	22 02	22 02			22 20	22 32	22 32				22 50	23 01	23 07		23 31
Singer d						21 52					22 22						22 52				
Drumry d						21 55					22 25						22 55				
Drumchapel d						21 57					22 27						22 57				
Milngavie d			21 41	21 41					22 11	22 11				22 41	22 41						
Hillfoot d			21 44	21 44					22 14	22 14				22 44	22 44						
Bearsden d			21 46	21 46					22 16	22 16				22 46	22 46						
Westerton d			21 49	21 49		22 00			22 19	22 19	22 30			22 49	22 49		23 00				
Anniesland d			21 52	21 52		22 03			22 22	22 22	22 33			22 52	22 52		23 03				
Clydebank d	21 34	21 34					22 04	22 04				22 34	22 34					23 03			23 33
Yoker d	21 36	21 36					22 06	22 06				22 36	22 36					23a05			23a35
Garscadden d	21 39	21 39					22 09	22 09				22 39	22 39								
Scotstounhill d	21 41	21 41					22 11	22 11				22 41	22 41								
Jordanhill d	21 43	21 43					22 13	22 13				22 43	22 43								
Hyndland 3 d	21 45	21 45	21 55	21 55		22 06	22 15	22 15	22 25	22 25	22 36	22 45	22 45	22 55	22 55		23 06				
Partick 225 ⛴ d	21 48	21 48	21 57	21 57	22 01	22 08	22 18	22 18	22 27	22 27	22 38	22 48	22 48	22 57	22 57	23 01	23 08				
Exhibition Centre 225 a	21 51	21 51	22 00	22 00			22 21	22 21	22 30	22 30		22 51	22 51	23 00	23 00						
Anderston 225 a																					
Glasgow Central LL 15 225 a	21 53	21 54	22 03	22 04			22 23	22 24	22 33	22 34		22 53	22 54	23 03	23 04						
Argyle Street 225 a																					
Charing Cross d					22 05	22 13					22 43					23 05	23 13				
Glasgow Queen St LL 10 ⛴ a					22 07	22 15					22 45					23 07	23 15		23s29		
d					22 07	22 15					22 45					23 07	23 15				
High Street d					22 09	22 17					22 47					23 09	23 17				
Bellgrove d					22 11	22 19					22 49					23 11	23 19				
Duke Street d																					
Alexandra Parade d																					
Barnhill d																					
Springburn a					22 20											23 20					
Greenfaulds d					22 41											23 41					
Cumbernauld a					22 44											23 44					
Carntyne d						22 23					22 53						23 23				
Shettleston d						22 25					22 55						23 25				
Garrowhill d						22 28					22 58						23 28				
Easterhouse d						22 30					23 00						23 30				
Blairhill d						22 34					23 04						23 34				
Coatbridge Sunnyside d						22 37					23 07						23 37				
Coatdyke d						22 39					23 09						23 39				
Airdrie d						22a43					23 12						23a43				
Drumgelloch d											23 15										
Caldercruix d											23 19										
Blackridge d											23 25										
Armadale d											23 29										
Bathgate a											23 33										
d																					
Livingston North d																					
Uphall d																					
Edinburgh Park 230 d																					
Haymarket 228,230 ⛴ a																					
Edinburgh 228,230 a																					

A from 16 September. To Motherwell
B until 9 September. To Rutherglen
C from 16 September. To Larkhall
D From Fort William to London Euston

	SR A	SR B
Helensburgh Upper 227 d		
Helensburgh Central d		
Craigendoran d		
Cardross d		
Balloch d		
Alexandria d		
Renton d		
Dalreoch d		
Dumbarton Central 227 d		
Dumbarton East d		
Bowling d		
Kilpatrick d		
Dalmuir 227 a		
d		
Singer d		
Drumry d		
Drumchapel d		
Milngavie d	23 11	23 11
Hillfoot d	23 14	23 14
Bearsden d	23 16	23 16
Westerton d	23 19	23 19
Anniesland d	23 22	23 22
Clydebank d		
Yoker d		
Garscadden d		
Scotstounhill d		
Jordanhill d		
Hyndland 3 d	23 25	23 25
Partick 225 ⛴ d	23 27	23 27
Exhibition Centre 225 a	23 30	23 30
Anderston 225 a		
Glasgow Central LL 15 225 a	23 33	23 34
Argyle Street 225 a		
Charing Cross d		
Glasgow Queen St LL 10 ⛴ a		
d		
High Street d		
Bellgrove d		
Duke Street d		
Alexandra Parade d		
Barnhill d		
Springburn a		
Greenfaulds d		
Cumbernauld a		
Carntyne d		
Shettleston d		
Garrowhill d		
Easterhouse d		
Blairhill d		
Coatbridge Sunnyside d		
Coatdyke d		
Airdrie d		
Drumgelloch d		
Caldercruix d		
Blackridge d		
Armadale d		
Bathgate a		
d		
Livingston North d		
Uphall d		
Edinburgh Park 230 d		
Haymarket 228,230 ⛴ a		
Edinburgh 228,230 a		

A from 16 September. To Motherwell

Table T227-F

Glasgow Queen Street - Oban, Fort William and Mallaig

Mondays to Fridays

21 May to 26 October

Miles	Miles		SR	SR	CS	CS	WR	SR		SR	WR		SR		SR	SR	SR	SR FX	SR FO
					▣	▣													
				◇				◇		◇			◇			◇	◇	◇	◇
											A							B	B
					✕	⇌ ✕		⌶		⌶			⌶			⌶	⌶	⌶	⌶
—	—	Edinburgh 228 d			04 50														
0	0	**GlasgowQueenSt** 10 226 ⇌ d	05 20					08 21		10 37			12 21			16 37	18 21		18 21
10	10	Dalmuir 226 d	05 39		06 04	06 04		08 42		10 57			12 42			16 57	18 41		18 41
16½	16½	Dumbarton Central 226 d	05 48		06 15	06 15		08 52		11 06			12 51			17 07	18 50		18 50
25½	25½	Helensburgh Upper a	06 00		06 29	06 29		09 05		11 24			13 03			17 20	19 04		19 04
—	—	d	06 03		06 32	06 32		09 07		11 27			13 06			17 22	19 06		19 06
32¼	32¼	Garelochhead d	06 14		06 45	06 45		09 18		11 40			13 18			17 33	19 17		19 17
43	43	Arrochar & Tarbet d	06 34		07 09	07 09		09 38		12 00			13 38			17 57	19 37		19 37
51	51	Ardlui d	06 52		07x24	07x24		09 51		12 14			13 56			18 10	19 51		19 51
59¾	59¾	**Crianlarich** a	07 08		07 45	07 45		10 07		12 30			14 12			18 26	20 07		20 07
—	—	d	07 18		07 47	07 47		10 15	10 21	12 33			14 18	14 24		18 29	20 14	20 20	20 20
64¾	—	Tyndrum Lower d	07 27					10 24		12 41			14 26			18 37	20 22		
76¾	—	Dalmally d	07 51					10 42		12 59			14 44		17 05	18 55	20 40		
79½	—	Loch Awe d	07 56					10 47		13 04			14 49		17 10	19 04	20 45		
83½	—	Falls of Cruachan § d						10 52		13 09			14 54			19 09	20 50		
88½	—	Taynuilt d	08 11					11 03		13 20			15 05		17 24	19 20	21 00		
95¼	—	Connel Ferry d	08 22					11 14		13 30			15 15		17 34	19 30	21 11		
101½	—	**Oban** a	08 35					11 27		13 43			15 28		17 47	19 43	21 24		
—	64¾	Upper Tyndrum d			08 00	08 00			10 32					14 35				20 31	20 31
—	72¼	Bridge of Orchy d			08 18	08 18			10 48					14 49				20 45	20 45
—	87¾	Rannoch d			08 46	08 46			11 09					15 12				21 08	21 08
—	95	Corrour d			08x59	08x59			11 21					15 24				21 20	21 20
—	105	Tulloch d			09 21	09 21			11 38					15 40				21 36	21 36
—	110¾	Roy Bridge d			09x31	09x31			11 48					15 50				21 46	21 46
—	114	Spean Bridge d			09 39	09 39			11 56					15 56				21 53	21 56
—	122¾	**Fort William** a			09 57	09 57			12 09					16 09				22 06	22 09
—	—	d		08 30			10 15		12 13		14 40			16 19				22 14	22 17
—	125	Banavie d		08 36					12 20					16 25				22 20	22 23
—	126	Corpach d		08 42					12 24					16 30				22 25	22 28
—	129	Loch Eil Outward Bound d		08 49					12 31					16 36				22 31	22 34
—	132¾	Locheilside d		08x53					12x35					16x40				22x35	22x38
—	139¼	Glenfinnan d		09 05					12 47					16 55				22 47	22 50
—	148½	Lochailort d		09x19					13x02					17x09				23x02	23x05
—	153¼	Beasdale d		09x28					13x11					17x18				23x11	23x14
—	156¾	Arisaig d		09 38					13 20					17 27				23 20	23 23
—	161¼	Morar d		09 46					13 28					17 36				23 28	23 31
—	164¼	**Mallaig** a		09 53			12 26		13 35		16 42			17 43				23 35	23 38

Mondays to Fridays

29 October to 7 December

	SR	SR	CS	CS	SR		SR	SR	SR		SR	SR	SR	SR FX	SR FO
			▣	▣											
		◇			◇		◇	◇	◇			◇	◇	◇	◇
									B					B	B
			✕	⇌ ✕	⌶		⌶	⌶	⌶			⌶	⌶	⌶	⌶
Edinburgh 228 d			04 50												
GlasgowQueenSt 10 226 ⇌ d	05 20				08 21		10 37	12 21				16 37	18 21		18 21
Dalmuir 226 d	05 39		06 04	06 04	08 42		10 57	12 42				16 57	18 41		18 41
Dumbarton Central 226 d	05 48		06 15	06 15	08 52		11 06	12 51				17 07	18 50		18 50
Helensburgh Upper a	06 00		06 29	06 29	09 05		11 24	13 03				17 20	19 04		19 04
d	06 03		06 32	06 32	09 07		11 27	13 06				17 22	19 06		19 06
Garelochhead d	06 14		06 45	06 45	09 18		11 40	13 18				17 33	19 17		19 17
Arrochar & Tarbet d	06 34		07 09	07 09	09 38		12 00	13 38				17 57	19 37		19 37
Ardlui d	06 52		07x24	07x24	09 51		12 14	13 56				18 10	19 51		19 51
Crianlarich a	07 08		07 45	07 45	10 07		12 30	14 12				18 26	20 07		20 07
d	07 18		07 47	07 47	10 15	10 21	12 33	14 18	14 24			18 29	20 14	20 20	20 20
Tyndrum Lower d	07 27				10 24		12 41	14 26				18 37	20 22		
Dalmally d	07 51				10 42		12 59	14 44			17 05	18 55	20 40		
Loch Awe d	07 56				10 47		13 04	14 49			17 10	19 04	20 45		
Falls of Cruachan § d															
Taynuilt d	08 11				11 03		13 20	15 05			17 24	19 20	21 00		
Connel Ferry d	08 22				11 14		13 30	15 15			17 34	19 30	21 11		
Oban a	08 35				11 27		13 43	15 28			17 47	19 43	21 24		
Upper Tyndrum d			08 00	08 00		10 32			14 35					20 31	20 31
Bridge of Orchy d			08 18	08 18		10 48			14 49					20 45	20 45
Rannoch d			08 46	08 46		11 09			15 12					21 08	21 08
Corrour d			08x59	08x59		11 21			15 24					21 20	21 20
Tulloch d			09 21	09 21		11 38			15 40					21 36	21 36
Roy Bridge d			09x31	09x31		11 48			15 50					21 46	21 46
Spean Bridge d			09 39	09 39		11 56			15 56					21 53	21 56
Fort William a			09 57	09 57		12 09			16 09					22 06	22 09
d		08 30				12 13			16 19					22 14	22 17
Banavie d		08 36				12 20			16 25					22 20	22 23
Corpach d		08 42				12 24			16 30					22 25	22 28
Loch Eil Outward Bound d		08 49				12 31			16 36					22 31	22 34
Locheilside d		08x53				12x35			16x40					22x35	22x38
Glenfinnan d		09 05				12 47			16 55					22 47	22 50
Lochailort d		09x19				13x02			17x09					23x02	23x05
Beasdale d		09x28				13x11			17x18					23x11	23x14
Arisaig d		09 38				13 20			17 27					23 20	23 23
Morar d		09 46				13 28			17 36					23 28	23 31
Mallaig a		09 53				13 35			17 43					23 35	23 38

§ Summer station only
A until 14 September
B ⌶ to Fort William

Table T227-F

Glasgow Queen Street - Oban, Fort William and Mallaig

Saturdays

26 May to 27 October

	SR	SR	CS	CS	WR	SR		SR	WR		SR		SR	SR	
			▣	▣											
		◇				◇		◇			◇		◇	◇	
					A				B						
			✕	⇌ ✕		⌶		⌶			⌶		⌶	⌶	
Edinburgh 228 d			04 50												
GlasgowQueenSt 10 226 ⇌ d	05 20					08 21		10 37			12 21		16 37	18 21	
Dalmuir 226 d	05 39		06 04	06 04		08 42		10 57			12 42		16 57	18 41	
Dumbarton Central 226 d	05 48		06 15	06 15		08 52		11 06			12 51		17 06	18 50	
Helensburgh Upper a	06 00		06 29	06 29		09 05		11 24			13 03		17 20	19 04	
d	06 03		06 32	06 32		09 07		11 27			13 06		17 22	19 06	
Garelochhead d	06 14		06 45	06 45		09 18		11 40			13 18		17 33	19 17	
Arrochar & Tarbet d	06 34		07 09	07 09		09 38		12 01			13 38		17 57	19 37	
Ardlui d	06 52		07x24	07x24		09 51		12 14			13 56		18 10	19 51	
Crianlarich a	07 08		07 45	07 45		10 07		12 30			14 12		18 26	20 07	
d	07 18		07 47	07 47		10 15	10 21	12 33			14 18	14 24	18 29	20 14	20 20
Tyndrum Lower d	07 27					10 24		12 41			14 26		18 37	20 22	
Dalmally d	07 51					10 42		12 59			14 44		18 55	20 40	
Loch Awe d	07 56					10 47		13 04			14 49		19 04	20 45	
Falls of Cruachan § d						10 52		13 09			14 54		19 09	20 50	
Taynuilt d	08 11					11 03		13 20			15 05		19 20	21 00	
Connel Ferry d	08 22					11 14		13 30			15 15		19 30	21 11	
Oban a	08 35					11 27		13 43			15 28		19 43	21 24	
Upper Tyndrum d			08 00	08 00			10 32					14 35			20 31
Bridge of Orchy d			08 18	08 18			10 48					14 49			20 45
Rannoch d			08 46	08 46			11 09					15 12			21 08
Corrour d			08x59	08x59			11 21					15 24			21 20
Tulloch d			09 21	09 21			11 38					15 40			21 36
Roy Bridge d			09x31	09x31			11 48					15 50			21 46
Spean Bridge d			09 39	09 39			11 56					15 56			21 53
Fort William a			09 57	09 57			12 09					16 09			22 06
d		08 30			10 15		12 13		14 40			16 19			22 14
Banavie d		08 36					12 20					16 25			22 20
Corpach d		08 42					12 24					16 30			22 25
Loch Eil Outward Bound d		08 49					12 31					16 36			22 31
Locheilside d		08x53					12x35					16x40			22x35
Glenfinnan d		09 05					12 47					16 55			22 47
Lochailort d		09x19					13x02					17x09			23x02
Beasdale d		09x28					13x11					17x18			23x11
Arisaig d		09 38					13 20					17 27			23 20
Morar d		09 46					13 28					17 36			23 28
Mallaig a		09 53			12 26		13 35		16 42			17 43			23 35

Saturdays

3 November to 8 December

	SR	SR	CS	CS	SR		SR	SR	SR		SR	SR	
			▣	▣									
		◇			◇		◇	◇	◇		◇	◇	
									C				
			✕	⇌ ✕	⌶		⌶	⌶	⌶		⌶	⌶	
Edinburgh 228 d			04 50										
GlasgowQueenSt 10 226 ⇌ d	05 20				08 21		10 37	12 21			16 37	18 21	
Dalmuir 226 d	05 39		06 04	06 04	08 42		10 57	12 42			16 57	18 41	
Dumbarton Central 226 d	05 48		06 15	06 15	08 52		11 06	12 51			17 06	18 50	
Helensburgh Upper a	06 00		06 29	06 29	09 05		11 24	13 03			17 20	19 04	
d	06 03		06 32	06 32	09 07		11 27	13 06			17 22	19 06	
Garelochhead d	06 14		06 45	06 45	09 18		11 40	13 18			17 33	19 17	
Arrochar & Tarbet d	06 34		07 09	07 09	09 38		12 01	13 38			17 57	19 37	
Ardlui d	06 52		07x24	07x24	09 51		12 14	13 56			18 10	19 51	
Crianlarich a	07 08		07 45	07 45	10 07		12 30	14 12			18 26	20 07	
d	07 18		07 47	07 47	10 15	10 21	12 33	14 18	14 24		18 29	20 14	20 20
Tyndrum Lower d	07 27				10 24		12 41	14 26			18 37	20 22	
Dalmally d	07 51				10 42		12 59	14 44			18 55	20 40	
Loch Awe d	07 56				10 47		13 04	14 49			19 04	20 45	
Falls of Cruachan § d													
Taynuilt d	08 11				11 03		13 20	15 05			19 20	21 00	
Connel Ferry d	08 22				11 14		13 30	15 15			19 30	21 11	
Oban a	08 35				11 27		13 43	15 28			19 43	21 24	
Upper Tyndrum d			08 00	08 00		10 32			14 35				20 31
Bridge of Orchy d			08 18	08 18		10 48			14 49				20 45
Rannoch d			08 46	08 46		11 09			15 12				21 08
Corrour d			08x59	08x59		11 21			15 24				21 20
Tulloch d			09 21	09 21		11 38			15 40				21 36
Roy Bridge d			09x31	09x31		11 48			15 50				21 46
Spean Bridge d			09 39	09 39		11 56			15 56				21 53
Fort William a			09 57	09 57		12 09			16 09				22 06
d		08 30				12 13			16 19				22 14
Banavie d		08 36				12 20			16 25				22 20
Corpach d		08 42				12 24			16 30				22 25
Loch Eil Outward Bound d		08 49				12 31			16 36				22 31
Locheilside d		08x53				12x35			16x40				22x35
Glenfinnan d		09 05				12 47			16 55				22 47
Lochailort d		09x19				13x02			17x09				23x02
Beasdale d		09x28				13x11			17x18				23x11
Arisaig d		09 38				13 20			17 27				23 20
Morar d		09 46				13 28			17 36				23 28
Mallaig a		09 53				13 35			17 43				23 35

§ Summer station only
A from 2 June until 29 September
B from 16 June until 1 September
C ⌶ to Fort William

Table T227-F

Sundays
20 May to 28 October

Glasgow Queen Street - Oban, Fort William and Mallaig

		SR ◇ A 🛒	SR ◇ 🛒	WR B	SR ◇	WR C	SR ◇ 🛒		SR ◇ 🛒	
Edinburgh 228	d	08 08								
GlasgowQueenSt 10 226 ⛴	d		09 56				12 20		18 21	
Dalmuir 226	d	09u27	10 16				12 34		18 36	
Dumbarton Central 226	d		10 26				12 47		18 47	
Helensburgh Upper	a	09 49	10 38				12 59		18 59	
	d	09 52	10 41				13 06		19 05	
Garelochhead	d	10 03	10 52				13 18		19 16	
Arrochar & Tarbet	d	10 23	11 12				13 38		19 36	
Ardlui	d	10 37	11 28				13 56		19 51	
Crianlarich	a	10 53	11 45				14 12		20 07	
	d	10 56	11 47				14 18	14 24	20 14	20 20
Tyndrum Lower	d	11 04	11 56				14 26		20 22	
Dalmally	d	11 22	12 15				14 44		20 40	
Loch Awe	d	11 27	12 20				14 49		20 45	
Falls of Cruachan §	d	11 32	12 25				14 54		20 50	
Taynuilt	d	11 42	12 40				15 04		21 00	
Connel Ferry	d	11 53	12 51				15 14		21 11	
Oban	a	12 06	13 04				15 27		21 24	
Upper Tyndrum	d							14 35		20 31
Bridge of Orchy	d							14 49		20 45
Rannoch	d							15 12		21 08
Corrour	d							15 24		21 20
Tulloch	d							15 40		21 36
Roy Bridge	d							15 50		21 46
Spean Bridge	d							15 56		21 53
Fort William	a							16 09		22 06
	d			10 15	12 12	14 40		16 19		22 14
Banavie	d				12 19			16 25		22 20
Corpach	d				12 23			16 30		22 25
Loch Eil Outward Bound	d				12 30			16 36		22 31
Locheilside	d				12x34			16x40		22x35
Glenfinnan	d				12 46			16 55		22 47
Lochailort	d				13x01			17x09		23x02
Beasdale	d				13x10			17x18		23x11
Arisaig	d				13 19			17 27		23 20
Morar	d				13 27			17 36		23 28
Mallaig	a			12 26	13 34	16 42		17 43		23 35

Sundays
4 November to 2 December

		SR ◇ 🛒	SR ◇ 🛒	SR ◇ 🛒	SR ◇ D 🛒
Edinburgh 228	d				
GlasgowQueenSt 10 226 ⛴	d	09 56	12 20	18 21	
Dalmuir 226	d	10 16	12 34	18 36	
Dumbarton Central 226	d	10 26	12 47	18 47	
Helensburgh Upper	a	10 38	12 59	18 59	
	d	10 41	13 06	19 05	
Garelochhead	d	10 52	13 18	19 16	
Arrochar & Tarbet	d	11 12	13 38	19 36	
Ardlui	d	11 28	13 56	19 51	
Crianlarich	a	11 45	14 12	20 07	
	d	11 47	14 18	20 14	20 20
Tyndrum Lower	d	11 56	14 26	20 22	
Dalmally	d	12 15	14 44	20 40	
Loch Awe	d	12 20	14 49	20 45	
Falls of Cruachan §	d				
Taynuilt	d	12 40	15 04	21 00	
Connel Ferry	d	12 51	15 14	21 11	
Oban	a	13 04	15 27	21 24	
Upper Tyndrum	d				20 31
Bridge of Orchy	d				20 45
Rannoch	d				21 08
Corrour	d				21 20
Tulloch	d				21 36
Roy Bridge	d				21 46
Spean Bridge	d				21 53
Fort William	a				22 06
	d				22 14
Banavie	d				22 20
Corpach	d				22 25
Loch Eil Outward Bound	d				22 31
Locheilside	d				22x35
Glenfinnan	d				22 47
Lochailort	d				23x02
Beasdale	d				23x11
Arisaig	d				23 20
Morar	d				23 28
Mallaig	a				23 35

§ Summer station only
A from 24 June until 26 August
B from 3 June until 30 September
C from 17 June until 2 September
D 🛒 to Fort William

NRT MAY 2018 EDITION

Table T227-R

Mondays to Fridays
21 May to 26 October

Mallaig, Fort William and Oban - Glasgow Queen Street

Miles	Miles			SR ◇ 🛒	SR ◇ A 🛒	SR ◇ 🛒	SR ◇ 🛒	SR ◇ B 🛒	SR ◇ 🛒	SR ◇ A 🛒	SR	SR ◇ 🛒		SR ◇ 🛒	CS R 🛏 ✕
—	0	**Mallaig**	d		06 03		10 10			16 05					
—	3	Morar	d		06 09		10 17			16 12					
—	7½	Arisaig	d		06 19		10 27			16 21					
—	11	Beasdale	d		06x24		10x32			16x27					
—	15¾	Lochailort	d		06x33		10x41			16x36					
—	25	Glenfinnan	d		06 51		11 01			16 54					
—	31½	Locheilside	d		07x00		11x09			17x02					
—	35¼	Loch Eil Outward Bound	d		07 07		11 17			17 10					
—	38¼	Corpach	d		07 13		11 23			17 16					
—	39¼	Banavie	d		07 17		11 27			17 20					
—	41½	**Fort William**	a		07 25		11 34			17 28					
—	—		d		07 44		11 41			17 37					19 50
—	50¼	Spean Bridge	d		07 57		11 56			17 51					20 10
—	53½	Roy Bridge	d		08 04		12 02			17 57					20x16
—	59¼	Tulloch	d		08 15		12 14			18 08					20 31
—	69¼	Corrour	d		08 32		12 30			18 25					20x51
—	76½	Rannoch	d		08 47		12 42			18 38					21 07
—	92	Bridge of Orchy	d		09 07		13 03			18 58					21 35
—	99¾	Upper Tyndrum	d		09 23		13 19			19 14					21 53
0	—	**Oban**	d	05 21		08 57		12 11	14 41		16 11	18 11		20 36	
6¼	—	Connel Ferry	d	05 32		09 08		12 23	14 52		16 22	18 22		20 47	
13	—	Taynuilt	d	05 44		09 20		12 35	15 06		16 34	18 33		21 01	
18½	—	Falls of Cruachan §	d			09 28		12 43	15 14			18 42			
22	—	Loch Awe	d	05 57		09 35		12 50	15 21		16 49	18 48		21 14	
24¾	—	Dalmally	d	06 03		09 40		13 00	15 26		16a54	18 56		21 20	
36¾	—	Tyndrum Lower	d	06 22		09 59		13 20	15 45			19 15		21 38	
42	104½	**Crianlarich**	a	06 31	09 31	10 08	13 27	13 32	15 54	19 22		19 27		21 47	22 05
—	—		d	06 33	09 33	10 14	13 37		15 56	19 32				21 48	22 06
50¾	113¼	Ardlui	d	06 51	09 52	10 29	13 55		16 11	19 52				22 04	22x26
58¾	121¼	Arrochar & Tarbet	d	07 10	10 06	10 43	14 09		16 27	20 06				22 18	22 45
69½	132	Garelochhead	d	07 30	10 32	11 04	14 31		16 49	20 26				22 38	23 11
76¼	138¾	Helensburgh Upper	a	07 40	10 42	11 15	14 41		16 59	20 37				22 48	23 24
—	—		d	07 42	10 44	11 16	14 43		17 00	20 37				22 49	23 25
85¼	147¾	Dumbarton Central 226	a	07 56	10 59	11 29	15 01		17 13	20 51				23 02	23 39
92½	154¼	Dalmuir 226	a		11 12	11 38	15 13		17 23	21 03				23 11	23 51
101½	164¼	**GlasgowQueenStreet** 10 226 ⛴	a	08 37	11 30	11 56	15 29		17 47	21 21				23 33	
—	—	Edinburgh 228	a												

Mondays to Fridays
29 October to 7 December

		SR ◇ 🛒	SR ◇ A 🛒	SR ◇ 🛒	SR ◇ 🛒	SR ◇ 🛒	SR ◇ 🛒	SR ◇ A 🛒	SR	SR FO ◇ 🛒		SR FX ◇ 🛒	SR ◇ 🛒	CS R 🛏 ✕
Mallaig	d		06 03		10 10			16 05						
Morar	d		06 09		10 17			16 12						
Arisaig	d		06 19		10 27			16 21						
Beasdale	d		06x24		10x32			16x27						
Lochailort	d		06x33		10x41			16x36						
Glenfinnan	d		06 51		11 01			16 54						
Locheilside	d		07x00		11x09			17x02						
Loch Eil Outward Bound	d		07 07		11 17			17 10						
Corpach	d		07 13		11 23			17 16						
Banavie	d		07 17		11 27			17 20						
Fort William	a		07 25		11 34			17 28						
	d		07 44		11 41			17 37						19 50
Spean Bridge	d		07 57		11 56			17 51						20 10
Roy Bridge	d		08 04		12 02			17 57						20x16
Tulloch	d		08 15		12 14			18 08						20 31
Corrour	d		08 32		12 30			18 25						20x51
Rannoch	d		08 47		12 42			18 38						21 07
Bridge of Orchy	d		09 07		13 03			18 58						21 35
Upper Tyndrum	d		09 23		13 19			19 14						21 53
Oban	d	05 21		08 57		12 11	14 41		16 11	18 11		18 11	20 36	
Connel Ferry	d	05 32		09 08		12 23	14 52		16 22	18 22		18 22	20 47	
Taynuilt	d	05 44		09 20		12 35	15 06		16 34	18 33		18 33	21 01	
Falls of Cruachan §	d													
Loch Awe	d	05 57		09 35		12 50	15 21		16 49	18 48		18 48	21 14	
Dalmally	d	06 03		09 40		13 00	15 26		16a54	18 56		18 56	21 20	
Tyndrum Lower	d	06 22		09 59		13 20	15 45			19 15		19 15	21 38	
Crianlarich	a	06 31	09 31	10 08	13 27	13 32	15 54	19 22		19 27		19 27	21 47	22 05
	d	06 33	09 33	10 14	13 37		15 56	19 32				19 32	21 48	22 06
Ardlui	d	06 51	09 52	10 29	13 55		16 11	19 52				19 52	22 04	22x26
Arrochar & Tarbet	d	07 10	10 06	10 43	14 09		16 27	20 06				20 06	22 18	22 45
Garelochhead	d	07 30	10 32	11 04	14 31		16 49	20 26				20 26	22 38	23 11
Helensburgh Upper	a	07 40	10 42	11 15	14 41		16 59	20 37				20 37	22 48	23 24
	d	07 42	10 44	11 16	14 43		17 00	20 37				20 37	22 49	23 25
Dumbarton Central 226	a	07 56	10 59	11 29	15 01		17 13	20 51				20 51	23 02	23 39
Dalmuir 226	a		11 12	11 38	15 13		17 23	21 03				21 03	23 11	23 51
GlasgowQueenStreet 10 226 ⛴	a	08 37	11 30	11 56	15 29		17 47	21 21				21 21	23 33	
Edinburgh 228	a													

§ Summer station only
A 🛒 from Fort William
B 🛒 from Crianlarich

Table T227-R

Saturdays
26 May to 27 October

Mallaig, Fort William and Oban - Glasgow Queen Street

		SR	SR	SR	SR	SR	SR	SR	SR	SR
		◇	◇	◇	◇	◇	◇	◇	◇	◇
			A			B		A		
		🛒	🛒	🛒	🛒	🛒	🛒	🛒	🛒	🛒
Mallaig	d		06 03		10 10			16 05		
Morar	d		06 09		10 17			16 12		
Arisaig	d		06 19		10 27			16 21		
Beasdale	d		06x24		10x32			16x27		
Lochailort	d		06x33		10x41			16x36		
Glenfinnan	d		06 51		11 01			16 54		
Locheilside	d		07x00		11x09			17x02		
Loch Eil Outward Bound	d		07 07		11 17			17 10		
Corpach	d		07 13		11 23			17 16		
Banavie	d		07 17		11 27			17 20		
Fort William	a		07 25		11 34			17 28		
	d		07 44		11 41			17 37		
Spean Bridge	d		07 57		11 56			17 51		
Roy Bridge	d		08 04		12 02			17 57		
Tulloch	d		08 15		12 14			18 08		
Corrour	d		08 32		12 30			18 25		
Rannoch	d		08 47		12 42			18 38		
Bridge of Orchy	d		09 07		13 03			18 58		
Upper Tyndrum	d		09 23		13 19			19 14		
Oban	d	05 21		08 57		12 11	16 11		18 11	20 36
Connel Ferry	d	05 32		09 08		12 23	16 22		18 22	20 47
Taynuilt	d	05 44		09 20		12 35	16 34		18 33	21 01
Falls of Cruachan §	d			09 28		12 43	16 42		18 42	
Loch Awe	d	05 57		09 35		12 50	16 49		18 48	21 14
Dalmally	d	06 03		09 40		13 00	16 54		18 56	21 20
Tyndrum Lower	d	06 22		09 59		13 20	17 13		19 15	21 38
Crianlarich	a	06 31	09 31	10 08	13 27	13 32	17 22	19 22	19 27	21 47
	d	06 33	09 33	10 14	13 37		17 24	19 32		21 48
Ardlui	d	06 51	09 52	10 29	13 55		17 42	19 52		22 04
Arrochar & Tarbet	d	07 10	10 06	10 43	14 09		17 56	20 06		22 18
Garelochhead	d	07 30	10 32	11 04	14 31		18 19	20 26		22 38
Helensburgh Upper	a	07 40	10 42	11 15	14 41		18 29	20 37		22 48
	d	07 42	10 44	11 16	14 43		18 31	20 37		22 49
Dumbarton Central 226	a	07 56	10 59	11 29	15 01		18 44	20 51		23 02
Dalmuir 226	a		11 12	11 38	15 13		18 54	21 03		23 11
GlasgowQueenStreet ■10 226 ⛴	a	08 37	11 30	11 56	15 29		19 20	21 21		23 33
Edinburgh 228	a									

Saturdays
3 November to 8 December

		SR	SR	SR	SR	SR	SR	SR	SR	SR
		◇	◇	◇	◇	◇	◇	◇	◇	◇
			A					A		
		🛒	🛒	🛒	🛒	🛒	🛒	🛒	🛒	🛒
Mallaig	d		06 03		10 10			16 05		
Morar	d		06 09		10 17			16 12		
Arisaig	d		06 19		10 27			16 21		
Beasdale	d		06x24		10x32			16x27		
Lochailort	d		06x33		10x41			16x36		
Glenfinnan	d		06 51		11 01			16 54		
Locheilside	d		07x00		11x09			17x02		
Loch Eil Outward Bound	d		07 07		11 17			17 10		
Corpach	d		07 13		11 23			17 16		
Banavie	d		07 17		11 27			17 20		
Fort William	a		07 25		11 34			17 28		
	d		07 44		11 41			17 37		
Spean Bridge	d		07 57		11 56			17 51		
Roy Bridge	d		08 04		12 02			17 57		
Tulloch	d		08 15		12 14			18 08		
Corrour	d		08 32		12 30			18 25		
Rannoch	d		08 47		12 42			18 38		
Bridge of Orchy	d		09 07		13 03			18 58		
Upper Tyndrum	d		09 23		13 19			19 14		
Oban	d	05 21		08 57		12 11	16 11		18 11	20 36
Connel Ferry	d	05 32		09 08		12 23	16 22		18 22	20 47
Taynuilt	d	05 44		09 20		12 35	16 34		18 33	21 01
Falls of Cruachan §	d									
Loch Awe	d	05 57		09 35		12 50	16 49		18 48	21 14
Dalmally	d	06 03		09 40		13 00	16 54		18 56	21 20
Tyndrum Lower	d	06 22		09 59		13 20	17 13		19 15	21 38
Crianlarich	a	06 31	09 31	10 08	13 27	13 32	17 22	19 22	19 27	21 47
	d	06 33	09 33	10 14	13 37		17 24	19 32		21 48
Ardlui	d	06 51	09 52	10 29	13 55		17 42	19 52		22 04
Arrochar & Tarbet	d	07 10	10 06	10 43	14 09		17 56	20 06		22 18
Garelochhead	d	07 30	10 32	11 04	14 31		18 19	20 26		22 38
Helensburgh Upper	a	07 40	10 42	11 15	14 41		18 29	20 37		22 48
	d	07 42	10 44	11 16	14 43		18 31	20 37		22 49
Dumbarton Central 226	a	07 56	10 59	11 29	15 01		18 44	20 51		23 02
Dalmuir 226	a		11 12	11 38	15 13		18 54	21 03		23 11
GlasgowQueenStreet ■10 226 ⛴	a	08 37	11 30	11 56	15 29		19 20	21 21		23 33
Edinburgh 228	a									

§ Summer station only
A 🛒 from Fort William
B 🛒 from Crianlarich

Table T227-R

Sundays
20 May to 28 October

Mallaig, Fort William and Oban - Glasgow Queen Street

		SR	SR	SR	SR	SR	SR	CS
								[R]
		◇	◇	◇	◇	◇	◇	
			A		B			
		🛒	🛒	🛒	🛒	🛒	🛒	🛏 ✕
Mallaig	d		10 10			16 05		
Morar	d		10 17			16 12		
Arisaig	d		10 26			16 21		
Beasdale	d		10x32			16x27		
Lochailort	d		10x41			16x36		
Glenfinnan	d		10 59			16 54		
Locheilside	d		11x08			17x02		
Loch Eil Outward Bound	d		11 15			17 10		
Corpach	d		11 21			17 16		
Banavie	d		11 25			17 20		
Fort William	a		11 32			17 28		
	d		11 40			17 37		19 00
Spean Bridge	d		11 56			17 51		19 20
Roy Bridge	d		12 02			17 57		19x26
Tulloch	d		12 14			18 08		19 40
Corrour	d		12 30			18 25		20 00
Rannoch	d		12 42			18 38		20 15
Bridge of Orchy	d		13 03			18 58		20 48
Upper Tyndrum	d		13 19			19 14		21 06
Oban	d	12 11		16 11	17 11		18 11	
Connel Ferry	d	12 27		16 26	17 26		18 22	
Taynuilt	d	12 38		16 38	17 37		18 33	
Falls of Cruachan §	d	12 46		16 46	17 46		18 42	
Loch Awe	d	12 53		16 53	17 52		18 48	
Dalmally	d	12 59		16 58	17 58		18 56	
Tyndrum Lower	d	13 17		17 17	18 16		19 15	
Crianlarich	a	13 26	13 32	17 26	18 25	19 22	19 27	21 17
	d	13 37		17 27	18 26	19 32		21 19
Ardlui	d	13 55		17 43	18 41	19 52		21x39
Arrochar & Tarbet	d	14 09		17 57	18 55	20 06		21 58
Garelochhead	d	14 29		18 19	19 17	20 26		22 24
Helensburgh Upper	a	14 40		18 29	19 28	20 37		22 37
	d	14 40		18 31	19 29	20 40		22 38
Dumbarton Central 226	a	14 53		18 47		20 53		22 53
Dalmuir 226	a	15 05		18 58	19s55	21 04		23 06
GlasgowQueenStreet ■10 226 ⛴	a	15 26		19 18		21 19		
Edinburgh 228	a				21 09			

Sundays
4 November to 2 December

		SR	SR	SR	SR	CS
						[R]
		◇	◇	◇	◇	
		🛒	🛒	🛒	🛒	🛏 ✕
Mallaig	d			16 05		
Morar	d			16 12		
Arisaig	d			16 21		
Beasdale	d			16x27		
Lochailort	d			16x36		
Glenfinnan	d			16 54		
Locheilside	d			17x02		
Loch Eil Outward Bound	d			17 10		
Corpach	d			17 16		
Banavie	d			17 20		
Fort William	a			17 28		
	d			17 37		19 00
Spean Bridge	d			17 51		19 20
Roy Bridge	d			17 57		19x26
Tulloch	d			18 08		19 40
Corrour	d			18 25		20 00
Rannoch	d			18 38		20 15
Bridge of Orchy	d			18 58		20 48
Upper Tyndrum	d			19 14		21 06
Oban	d	12 11	16 11		18 11	
Connel Ferry	d	12 27	16 26		18 22	
Taynuilt	d	12 38	16 38		18 33	
Falls of Cruachan §	d					
Loch Awe	d	12 53	16 53		18 48	
Dalmally	d	12 59	16 58		18 56	
Tyndrum Lower	d	13 17	17 17		19 15	
Crianlarich	a	13 26	17 26	19 22	19 27	21 17
	d	13 37	17 27	19 32		21 19
Ardlui	d	13 55	17 43	19 52		21x39
Arrochar & Tarbet	d	14 09	17 57	20 06		21 58
Garelochhead	d	14 29	18 19	20 26		22 24
Helensburgh Upper	a	14 40	18 29	20 37		22 37
	d	14 40	18 31	20 40		22 38
Dumbarton Central 226	a	14 53	18 47	20 53		22 53
Dalmuir 226	a	15 05	18 58	21 04		23 06
GlasgowQueenStreet ■10 226 ⛴	a	15 26	19 18	21 19		
Edinburgh 228	a					

§ Summer station only
A 🛒 from Crianlarich
B from 24 June until 26 August

Table T228-F

Mondays to Fridays
21 May to 7 December

Edinburgh - Falkirk High - Glasgow Queen Street

Miles			SR	SR	SR	SR	SR	SR	SR	SR	SR	SR	SR	SR	SR	SR	SR	SR	SR	SR	SR	SR	SR
			MO	MX																			
			1	1	1	1	1	1	1	1		1		1	1	1	1	1	1	1	1	1	1
								🛒	🛒	🛒		🛒		🛒	🛒	🛒	🛒	🛒	🛒	🛒	🛒	🛒	🛒
0	Edinburgh [10]	225,230,242 d			05 55	06 30	06 45	07 00	07 15	07 30		07 45		08 00	08 15	08 30	08 45	09 00	09 15	09 30	09 45	10 00	10 15
1¼	Haymarket	225,230,242 d			06 00	06 35	06 50	07 05	07 20	07 34		07 49		08 05	08 19	08 35	08 51	09 07	09 20	09 35	09 50	10 06	10 20
17½	Linlithgow	230 d			06 15	06 50	07 06		07 35	07 49	08 00	08 05			08 34		09 06		09 38		10 05		10 35
22¼	Polmont [3]	230 d			06 21	06 56		07 23		07 56				08 23	08 41		09 13		09 44		10 11		10 41
25½	**Falkirk High [3]**	d	00 02	00 03	06 26	07 01	07 14	07 28	07 44	08 01	08b12	08 14		08 28	08 46	08 56	09 18	09 26	09 49	09 56	10 16	10 27	10 46
35¾	Croy [3]	230 a	00 11	00 10	06 35	07 11	07 24		07 53	08 10			←	08 38		09 06		09 35		10 05		10 36	
41	Lenzie [3]	230 a		00 16							08 32	08 26	08 32										
44	Bishopbriggs	230 a									→		08 37										
47¼	**Glasgow Queen Street [10]**	230 a	00 26	00 27	06 49	07 25	07 38	07 52	08 08	08 25		08 40	08 47	08 55	09 06	09 20	09 38	09 48	10 09	10 20	10 37	10 48	11 07

		SR	SR	SR	SR	SR	SR	SR	SR	SR	SR	SR	SR	SR	SR	SR	SR	SR	SR	SR	SR	SR	SR
		1	1	1	1	1	1	1	1	1	1	1	1	1	1	1	1	1	1	1	1	1	1
		🛒	🛒	🛒	🛒	🛒	🛒	🛒	🛒	🛒	🛒	🛒	🛒	🛒	🛒	🛒	🛒	🛒	🛒	🛒	🛒	🛒	🛒
Edinburgh [10]	225,230,242 d	10 30	10 45	11 00	11 15	11 30	11 45	12 00	12 15	12 30	12 45	13 00	13 15	13 30	13 45	14 00	14 15	14 30	14 45	15 00	15 15	15 30	15 45
Haymarket	225,230,242 d	10 35	10 50	11 04	11 21	11 34	11 49	12 05	12 20	12 34	12 49	13 06	13 21	13 36	13 49	14 05	14 22	14 35	14 50	15 05	15 20	15 34	15 50
Linlithgow	230 d		11 04		11 35		12 04		12 36		13 06		13 36		14 05		14 38		15 05		15 35		16 06
Polmont [3]	230 d		11 10		11 41		12 10		12 42		13 12		13 42		14 11		14 44		15 11		15 41		16 13
Falkirk High [3]	d	10 56	11 15	11 25	11 46	11 56	12 15	12 24	12 47	12 56	13 17	13 27	13 47	13 56	14 16	14 25	14 49	14 56	15 16	15 26	15 46	15 56	16 18
Croy [3]	230 a	11 05		11 34		12 06		12 32		13 05		13 36		14 06		14 35		15 06		15 34		16 06	
Lenzie [3]	230 a																						
Bishopbriggs	230 a																						
Glasgow Queen Street [10]	230 a	11 19	11 37	11 48	12 06	12 22	12 36	12 44	13 07	13 19	13 37	13 50	14 07	14 20	14 36	14 52	15 09	15 21	15 37	15 48	16 07	16 20	16 38

		SR	SR	SR	SR	SR	SR	SR	SR	SR	SR	SR	SR	SR	SR	SR	SR	SR	SR	SR	SR	SR
		1	1	1	1	1	1	1	1	1	1	1	1	1	1	1	1	1	1	1	1	1
		🛒	🛒	🛒	🛒	🛒	🛒	🛒	🛒	🛒	🛒	🛒	🛒									
Edinburgh [10]	225,230,242 d	16 00	16 15	16 30	16 45	17 00	17 15	17 30	17 45	18 00	18 15	18 30	18 45	19 00	19 15	19 30	20 00	20 30	21 00	21 30	22 00	22 30
Haymarket	225,230,242 d	16 05	16 19	16 34	16 50	17 05	17 20	17 35	17 50	18 06	18 21	18 35	18 49	19 05	19 20	19 35	20 04	20 35	21 05	21 34	22 04	22 35
Linlithgow	230 d		16 34		17 06		17 35		18 05		18 36		19 05		19 35	19 52	20 17	20 53	21 20	21 49	22 17	22 50
Polmont [3]	230 d		16 41		17 12		17 42		18 11		18 43		19 11		19 41		20 22		21 26		22 22	
Falkirk High [3]	d	16 27	16 46	16 55	17 17	17 25	17 47	17 56	18 16	18 27	18 48	18 56	19 16	19 24	19 46	20 00	20 27	21 01	21 31	21 58	22 26	22 58
Croy [3]	230 a	16 39		17 06		17 35		18 06		18 36		19 07		19 32		20 10		21 11		22 07		23 08
Lenzie [3]	230 a							18 12														
Bishopbriggs	230 a																					
Glasgow Queen Street [10]	230 a	16 55	17 07	17 21	17 38	17 50	18 07	18 24	18 37	18 50	19 09	19 21	19 36	19 44	20 08	20 25	20 49	21 25	21 52	22 21	22 44	23 22

		SR	SR
		1	1
Edinburgh [10]	225,230,242 d	23 00	23 30
Haymarket	225,230,242 d	23 05	23 34
Linlithgow	230 d	23 20	23 50
Polmont [3]	230 d	23 27	23 56
Falkirk High [3]	d	23 31	00 03
Croy [3]	230 a	23 41	00 10
Lenzie [3]	230 a	23 47	00 16
Bishopbriggs	230 a	23 51	
Glasgow Queen Street [10]	230 a	23 59	00 27

Saturdays
26 May to 8 December

		SR	SR	SR	SR	SR	SR	SR	SR	SR	SR	SR	SR	SR	SR	SR	SR	SR	SR	SR	SR	SR	SR
		1	1	1	1	1	1	1	1	1	1	1	1	1	1	1	1	1	1	1	1	1	1
																		A	B				
					🛒	🛒	🛒	🛒	🛒	🛒	🛒	🛒	🛒	🛒	🛒	🛒	🛒	🛒	🛒	🛒	🛒	🛒	🛒
Edinburgh [10]	225,230,242 d		05 55	06 30	07 00	07 15	07 30	07 45	08 00	08 15	08 30	08 45	09 00	09 15	09 30	09 45	10 00	10 14	10 15	10 30	10 45	11 00	11 15
Haymarket	225,230,242 d		06 00	06 35	07 04	07 20	07 34	07 49	08 05	08 19	08 35	08 51	09 05	09 19	09 35	09 50	10 05	10 19	10 19	10 35	10 50	11 04	11 21
Linlithgow	230 d		06 15	06 50		07 35	07 49	08 05		08 34		09 06		09 37		10 05		10 35	10 35		11 04		11 35
Polmont [3]	230 d		06 21	06 56	07 20		07 56		08 23	08 41		09 13		09 43		10 11		10 41	10 41		11 10		11 41
Falkirk High [3]	d	00 03	06 26	07 01	07 24	07 44	08 01	08 14	08 28	08 46	08 56	09 18	09 24	09 48	09 56	10 16	10 27	10 46	10 46	10 56	11 15	11 23	11 46
Croy [3]	230 a	00 10	06 35	07 11		07 53	08 10		08 38		09 06		09 35		10 05		10 35			11 05		11 32	
Lenzie [3]	230 a	00 16						08 26															
Bishopbriggs	230 a							08 31															
Glasgow Queen Street [10]	230 a	00 27	06 49	07 25	07 44	08 08	08 25	08 40	08 55	09 06	09 20	09 38	09 48	10 08	10 20	10 37	10 47	11 07	11 07	11 19	11 37	11 47	12 06

		SR	SR	SR	SR	SR	SR	SR	SR	SR	SR	SR	SR	SR	SR	SR	SR	SR	SR	SR	SR	SR	SR
		1	1	1	1	1	1	1	1	1	1	1	1	1	1	1	1	1	1	1	1	1	1
		🛒	🛒	🛒	🛒	🛒	🛒	🛒	🛒	🛒	🛒	🛒	🛒	🛒	🛒	🛒	🛒	🛒	🛒	🛒	🛒	🛒	🛒
Edinburgh [10]	225,230,242 d	11 30	11 45	12 00	12 15	12 30	12 45	13 00	13 15	13 30	13 45	14 00	14 15	14 30	14 45	15 00	15 15	15 30	15 45	16 00	16 15	16 30	16 45
Haymarket	225,230,242 d	11 34	11 49	12 05	12 20	12 35	12 50	13 05	13 21	13 35	13 49	14 05	14 19	14 35	14 50	15 05	15 20	15 35	15 50	16 05	16 19	16 34	16 49
Linlithgow	230 d		12 04		12 36		13 06		13 36		14 05		14 37		15 05		15 35		16 06		16 34		17 06
Polmont [3]	230 d		12 10		12 42		13 12		13 42		14 11		14 43		15 11		15 41		16 13		16 41		17 13
Falkirk High [3]	d	11 56	12 15	12 24	12 47	12 56	13 17	13 27	13 47	13 56	14 16	14 24	14 48	14 56	15 16	15 25	15 46	15 57	16 18	16 27	16 46	16 55	17 18
Croy [3]	230 a	12 06		12 32		13 05		13 36		14 05		14 32		15 06		15 34		16 06		16 37		17 06	
Lenzie [3]	230 a																						
Bishopbriggs	230 a																						
Glasgow Queen Street [10]	230 a	12 22	12 36	12 44	13 07	13 19	13 37	13 50	14 07	14 19	14 36	14 44	15 09	15 21	15 37	15 47	16 07	16 20	16 38	16 52	17 07	17 20	17 38

A from 25 August   B until 18 August   b Falkirk Grahamston

Table T228-F

Saturdays
26 May to 8 December

Edinburgh - Falkirk High - Glasgow Queen Street

		SR	SR	SR	SR	SR	SR	SR	SR	SR	SR	SR	SR	SR	SR	SR	SR	SR	SR	SR
		1	1	1	1	1	1	1	1	1	1	1	1	1	1	1	1	1	1	1
		🛒	🛒	🛒	🛒	🛒	🛒	🛒	🛒	🛒										
Edinburgh [10]	225,230,242 d	17 00	17 15	17 30	17 45	18 00	18 15	18 30	18 45	19 00	19 15	19 30	20 00	20 30	21 00	21 30	22 00	22 30	23 00	23 30
Haymarket	225,230,242 d	17 05	17 20	17 34	17 50	18 06	18 21	18 35	18 49	19 05	19 20	19 34	20 07	20 35	21 05	21 34	22 05	22 35	23 05	23 34
Linlithgow	230 d		17 35		18 05		18 36		19 06		19 35	19 52	20 21	20 52	21 20	21 49	22 18	22 50	23 20	23 50
Polmont [3]	230 d		17 42		18 12		18 42		19 12		19 41		20 27		21 26		22 23		23 27	23 56
Falkirk High [3]	d	17 24	17 47	17 55	18 17	18 25	18 47	18 56	19 17	19 26	19 46	20 00	20 32	21 00	21 31	21 58	22 28	22 58	23 31	00 03
Croy [3]	230 a	17 32		18 04		18 34		19 07		19 35		20 10		21 10		22 07		23 08	23 41	00 10
Lenzie [3]	230 a			18 10															23 47	00 16
Bishopbriggs	230 a																		23 51	
Glasgow Queen Street [10]	230 a	17 47	18 07	18 21	18 37	18 46	19 09	19 23	19 37	19 49	20 08	20 24	20 52	21 24	21 52	22 21	22 47	23 22	23 59	00 27

Sundays
20 May to 2 December

		SR	SR	SR	SR	SR	SR	SR	SR	SR	SR	SR	SR	SR	SR	SR	SR	SR	SR	SR	SR	SR	SR
		1	1	1	1	1	1	1	1	1	1	1	1	1	1	1	1	1	1	1	1	1	1
		A	B	C		C	B	B	C	B	C	B	C	B	C	B	C	B	C	B	C	B	C
					🛒					🛒	🛒	🛒	🛒	🛒	🛒	🛒	🛒	🛒	🛒	🛒	🛒	🛒	🛒
Edinburgh [10]	225,230,242 d		08 00		08 30		09 00	09 30		10 00		10 30		11 00		11 30		12 00		12 30		13 02	
Haymarket	225,230,242 d		08 04		08 34		09 04	09 34		10 04		10 34		11 04		11 34		12 05		12 34		13 06	
Linlithgow	230 d		08 25	08 25	08 55	09 25	09 25	09 54	09 54	10 24	10 24	10 49	10 50	11 19	11 20	11 49	11 50	12 20	12 20	12 49	12 50	13 19	13 20
Polmont [3]	230 d		08 31	08 31		09 30	09 31			10 30	10 30			11 25	11 26			12 26	12 27			13 25	13 26
Falkirk High [3]	d	00 03	08 36	08 36	09 04	09 35	09 36	10 03	10 03	10 35	10 35	10 58	10 58	11 30	11 31	11 58	11 58	12 31	12 32	12 58	12 58	13 30	13 31
Croy [3]	230 a	00 10	08 45	08 45	09 13			10 12	10 12			11 07	11 08			12 08	12 08			13 07	13 08		
Lenzie [3]	230 a	00 16																					
Bishopbriggs	230 a																						
Glasgow Queen Street [10]	230 a	00 27	09 00	09 00	09 28	09 56	09 57	10 26	10 26	10 55	10 55	11 22	11 23	11 51	11 52	12 23	12 24	12 52	12 53	13 22	13 23	13 51	13 52

		SR	SR	SR	SR	SR	SR	SR	SR	SR	SR	SR	SR	SR	SR	SR	SR	SR	SR	SR	SR	SR	SR
		1	1	1	1	1	1	1	1	1	1	1	1	1	1	1	1	1	1	1	1	1	1
		B	C	B	C	B	C	B	C	B	C		B	C	B	C	B	C	C	B	B	C	B
		🛒	🛒	🛒	🛒			🛒	🛒	🛒	🛒	🛒	🛒	🛒	🛒	🛒			🛒	🛒	🛒	🛒	🛒
Edinburgh [10]	225,230,242 d	13 30		14 00		14 30		15 00		15 30		16 00	16 30		17 00		17 30			18 00	18 30		19 00
Haymarket	225,230,242 d	13 35		14 04		14 34		15 04		15 34		16 05	16 34		17 04		17 34			18 04	18 34		19 04
Linlithgow	230 d	13 50	13 50	14 19	14 20	14 49	14 50	15 19	15 20	15 49	15 50	16 20	16 49	16 50	17 19	17 20	17 49	17 50	18 20	18 19	18 49	18 50	19 19
Polmont [3]	230 d			14 25	14 26			15 25	15 26			16 26			17 25	17 26			18 25	18 25			19 25
Falkirk High [3]	d	13 59	13 59	14 30	14 31	14 58	14 58	15 30	15 31	15 58	15 58	16 31	16 58	16 58	17 30	17 31	17 58	17 58	18 30	18 30	18 58	18 58	19 30
Croy [3]	230 a	14 08	14 08			15 07	15 08			16 07	16 08		17 07	17 08			18 07	18 08			19 07	19 08	
Lenzie [3]	230 a																						
Bishopbriggs	230 a																						
Glasgow Queen Street [10]	230 a	14 22	14 22	14 51	14 52	15 22	15 22	15 51	15 51	16 22	16 22	16 52	17 22	17 22	17 51	17 51	18 24	18 24	18 50	18 51	19 22	19 22	19 51

		SR	SR	SR	SR	SR	SR	SR	SR	SR	SR	SR	SR	SR	SR	SR	SR	SR	SR
		1	1	1	1	1	1	1	1	1	1	1	1	1	1	1	1	1	1
		C	B	C	B	C	C	B	B	C	B	C	B	C		C	B	B	C
		🛒																	
Edinburgh [10]	225,230,242 d		19 30		20 00			20 30	21 00		21 30		22 00		22 30		23 00	23 30	
Haymarket	225,230,242 d		19 34		20 05			20 34	21 04		21 36		22 04		22 34		23 04	23 34	
Linlithgow	230 d	19 20	19 49	19 50	20 20	20 20	20 50	20 49	21 19	21 20	21 51	21 52	22 19	22 20	22 49	23 19	23 19	23 49	23 49
Polmont [3]	230 d	19 26			20 26	20 26			21 25	21 26			22 25	22 26		23 25	23 25	23 55	23 55
Falkirk High [3]	d	19 31	19 58	19 58	20 31	20 31	20 58	20 58	21 30	21 31	22 00	22 00	22 30	22 31	22 58	23 30	23 30	00 02	00 02
Croy [3]	230 a		20 07	20 08			21 08	21 07			22 09	22 10			23 07	23 39	23 39	00 11	00 11
Lenzie [3]	230 a																		
Bishopbriggs	230 a																		
Glasgow Queen Street [10]	230 a	19 51	20 22	20 22	20 51	20 51	21 22	21 23	21 51	21 51	22 24	22 24	22 51	22 51	23 22	23 54	23 54	00 26	00 26

A not 20 May   B until 17 June, from 15 July   C 24 June, 1 July, 8 July

Table T228-R

Glasgow Queen Street - Falkirk High - Edinburgh

Mondays to Fridays

21 May to 7 December

Miles		SR	SR	SR	SR	SR	SR	SR	SR	SR	SR	SR	SR	SR	SR	SR	SR	SR	SR	SR	SR	SR
																				FX	FO	
		1	1	1	1	1	1	1	1	1	1	1	1	1	1	1	1	1	1	1	1	1
					🍴	🍴	🍴		🍴	🍴	🍴	🍴	🍴	🍴	🍴	🍴	🍴	🍴	🍴	🍴	🍴	🍴
0	**Glasgow Queen Street** 10 230 d	06 00	06 30	06 45	07 00	07 15	07 30	07 45	08 00	08 15	08 30	08 45	09 00	09 15	09 30	09 45	10 00	10 15	10 30	10 45	10 45	11 00
3¼	Bishopbriggs 230 d																					
6¼	Lenzie 3 230 d		06 39		07 08																	
11½	Croy 3 230 d			06 57			07 43		08 12		08 43		09 13		09 42		10 12		10 42			11 12
21¼	**Falkirk High** 3 d	06 19	06 51	07 07	07 21	07 34	07 53	08 05	08 22	08 35	08 53	09 04	09 23	09 35	09 52	10 05	10 22	10 35	10 52	11 04	11 04	11 22
25	Polmont 3 230 a	06 23	06 56		07 26	07 38		08 09	08 27			09 09		09 39		10 09		10 39		11 09	11 09	
29¾	Linlithgow 230 a	06 29	07 02	07 15	07 32	07 45	08 00	08 16		08 44		09 15		09 45		10 15		10 45		11 15	11 15	
46	Haymarket 225,230,242 a	06s45	07s18	07s31	07s50	08s01	08s19	08s32	08s47	09s03	09s17	09s34	09s48	10s01	10s17	10s32	10s45	11s01	11s16	11s31	11s32	11s46
47¼	**Edinburgh** 10 225,230,242 a	06 50	07 23	07 36	07 55	08 06	08 24	08 37	08 52	09 08	09 22	09 39	09 53	10 07	10 23	10 37	10 51	11 06	11 21	11 36	11 37	11 51

	SR	SR	SR	SR	SR	SR	SR	SR	SR	SR	SR	SR	SR	SR	SR	SR	SR	SR	SR	SR	SR
	1	1	1	1	1	1	1	1	1	1	1	1	1	1	1	1	1	1	1	1	1
	🍴	🍴	🍴	🍴	🍴	🍴	🍴	🍴	🍴	🍴	🍴	🍴	🍴	🍴	🍴	🍴	🍴	🍴	🍴	🍴	🍴
Glasgow Queen Street 10 230 d	11 15	11 30	11 45	12 00	12 15	12 30	12 45	13 00	13 15	13 30	13 45	14 00	14 15	14 30	14 45	15 00	15 15	15 30	15 45	16 00	16 15
Bishopbriggs 230 d																					
Lenzie 3 230 d																					
Croy 3 230 d		11 42		12 12		12 42		13 12		13 42		14 12		14 42		15 12		15 42		16 12	
Falkirk High 3 d	11 34	11 52	12 04	12 22	12 34	12 52	13 04	13 22	13 34	13 53	14 04	14 22	14 34	14 52	15 04	15 22	15 33	15 52	16 04	16 22	16 34
Polmont 3 230 a	11 38		12 09		12 38		13 09		13 39		14 09		14 38		15 08		15 38		16 09		16 38
Linlithgow 230 a	11 44		12 15		12 44		13 15		13 45		14 15		14 44		15 14		15 44		16 15		16 45
Haymarket 225,230,242 a	12s01	12s13	12s31	12s45	13s00	13s15	13s32	13s48	14s02	14s17	14s32	14s43	15s00	15s14	15s31	15s46	16s01	16s13	16s32	16s43	17s01
Edinburgh 10 225,230,242 a	12 07	12 19	12 36	12 50	13 07	13 21	13 37	13 53	14 07	14 23	14 37	14 48	15 07	15 20	15 36	15 51	16 06	16 18	16 38	16 48	17 06

	SR	SR	SR	SR	SR	SR	SR	SR	SR	SR	SR	SR	SR	SR	SR	SR	SR	SR	SR	SR	SR	SR
										FX	FO											
	1	1	1	1	1	1	1	1	1	1	1	1	1	1	1	1		1	1	1	1	1
	🍴	🍴	🍴	🍴	🍴	🍴	🍴	🍴	🍴	🍴	🍴	🍴										
Glasgow Queen Street 10 230 d	16 30	16 45	17 00	17 15	17 30	17 45	18 00	18 15	18 30	18 45	18 45	19 00	19 15	19 30	20 00	20 30	21 00	21 30	22 00	22 30	23 00	23 30
Bishopbriggs 230 d																						
Lenzie 3 230 d																						
Croy 3 230 d	16 44		17 12		17 42		18 14		18 43			19 11			20 13		21 13		22 12		23 12	23 43
Falkirk High 3 d	16 54	17 07	17 22	17 37	17 52	18 04	18 24	18 34	18 53	19 04	19 04	19 20	19 34	19 50	20 22	20 50	21 22	21 50	22 22	22 50	23 23	23 53
Polmont 3 230 a		17 12	17 27		17 57	18 09		18 39		19 08	19 08		19 38	19 54		20 55		21 55		22 54	23 27	23 57
Linlithgow 230 a		17 18		17 44	18 03	18 15		18 45		19 14	19 14		19 44	20 00	20 30	21 01	21 29	22 01	22 29	23 00	23 34	00 04
Haymarket 225,230,242 a	17s16	17s35	17s47	18s02	18s19	18s31	18s48	19s01	19s13	19s31	19s31	19s42	20s05	20s21	20s47	21s17	21s42	22s18	22s45	23s16	23s50	00s21
Edinburgh 10 225,230,242 a	17 22	17 40	17 52	18 07	18 25	18 36	18 53	19 07	19 18	19 36	19 37	19 47	20 10	20 28	20 52	21 23	21 47	22 24	22 50	23 21	23 55	00 26

Saturdays

26 May to 8 December

	SR	SR	SR	SR	SR	SR	SR	SR	SR	SR	SR	SR	SR	SR	SR	SR	SR	SR	SR	SR	SR	SR
	1	1	1	1	1	1	1	1	1	1	1	1	1	1	1	1	1	1	1	1	1	1
			🍴	🍴	🍴		🍴	🍴	🍴	🍴	🍴	🍴	🍴		🍴	🍴	🍴	🍴	🍴	🍴	🍴	🍴
Glasgow Queen Street 10 230 d	06 00	06 30	07 00	07 15	07 30	07 45	08 00	08 15	08 30	08 45	09 00	09 15	09 30	09 45	10 00	10 15	10 30	10 45	11 00	11 15	11 30	11 45
Bishopbriggs 230 d																						
Lenzie 3 230 d		06 38	07 08																			
Croy 3 230 d		06 44			07 43		08 12		08 43		09 13		09 42		10 12		10 42		11 12		11 42	
Falkirk High 3 d	06 19	06 54	07 21	07 34	07 53	08 04	08 22	08 35	08 53	09 04	09 23	09 35	09 52	10 05	10 22	10 35	10 52	11 04	11 22	11 34	11 52	12 04
Polmont 3 230 a	06 23	06 58	07 26	07 38		08 10	08 27			09 09		09 39		10 09		10 39		11 09		11 38		12 09
Linlithgow 230 a	06 30	07 05	07 32	07 45	08 00	08 16		08 44		09 15		09 45		10 15		10 45		11 15		11 44		12 15
Haymarket 225,230,242 a	06s46	07s22	07s50	08s01	08s18	08s33	08s47	09s03	09s13	09s35	09s47	10s01	10s17	10s32	10s46	11s01	11s16	11s31	11s43	12s00	12s13	12s32
Edinburgh 10 225,230,242 a	06 51	07 27	07 55	08 06	08 23	08 38	08 52	09 08	09 18	09 40	09 53	10 06	10 22	10 37	10 51	11 06	11 21	11 36	11 48	12 06	12 19	12 37

	SR	SR	SR	SR	SR	SR	SR	SR	SR	SR	SR	SR	SR	SR	SR	SR	SR	SR	SR	SR	SR	SR
	1	1	1	1	1	1	1	1	1	1	1	1	1	1	1	1	1	1	1	1	1	1
	🍴	🍴	🍴	🍴	🍴	🍴	🍴	🍴	🍴	🍴	🍴	🍴	🍴	🍴	🍴	🍴	🍴	🍴	🍴		🍴	🍴
Glasgow Queen Street 10 230 d	12 00	12 15	12 30	12 45	13 00	13 15	13 30	13 45	14 00	14 15	14 30	14 45	15 00	15 15	15 30	15 45	16 00	16 15	16 30	16 45	17 00	17 15
Bishopbriggs 230 d																						
Lenzie 3 230 d																						
Croy 3 230 d	12 12		12 42		13 12		13 42		14 12		14 42		15 12		15 43		16 12		16 44		17 12	
Falkirk High 3 d	12 22	12 34	12 52	13 04	13 22	13 34	13 53	14 04	14 22	14 34	14 52	15 04	15 22	15 34	15 53	16 04	16 22	16 34	16 54	17 08	17 22	17 37
Polmont 3 230 a		12 38		13 09		13 39		14 09		14 38		15 09		15 38		16 09		16 38		17 12	17 27	
Linlithgow 230 a		12 44		13 15		13 45		14 15		14 44		15 15		15 44		16 15		16 45		17 18		17 44
Haymarket 225,230,242 a	12s43	13s01	13s12	13s32	13s46	14s01	14s15	14s31	14s48	15s01	15s14	15s32	15s47	16s02	16s13	16s31	16s43	17s01	17s16	17s33	17s46	18s02
Edinburgh 10 225,230,242 a	12 48	13 06	13 18	13 39	13 51	14 06	14 22	14 36	14 53	15 06	15 19	15 37	15 53	16 07	16 18	16 38	16 48	17 06	17 22	17 38	17 51	18 07

	SR	SR	SR	SR	SR	SR	SR	SR	SR	SR	SR	SR	SR	SR	SR	SR	SR
	1	1	1	1	1	1	1	1	1	1	1	1	1	1	1	1	1
	🍴	🍴	🍴	🍴	🍴	🍴	🍴										
Glasgow Queen Street 10 230 d	17 30	17 45	18 00	18 15	18 30	18 45	19 00	19 15	19 30	20 00	20 30	21 00	21 30	22 00	22 30	23 00	23 30
Bishopbriggs 230 d																	
Lenzie 3 230 d																	
Croy 3 230 d	17 43		18 14		18 43		19 12			20 13		21 12		22 12		23 12	23 43
Falkirk High 3 d	17 53	18 05	18 24	18 34	18 52	19 05	19 22	19 34	19 50	20 22	20 50	21 21	21 50	22 22	22 49	23 23	23 53
Polmont 3 230 a	17 57	18 09		18 39		19 10		19 38	19 54		20 55		21 55		22 54	23 27	23 57
Linlithgow 230 a	18 04	18 16		18 45		19 16		19 44	20 00	20 30	21 01	21 28	22 01	22 29	23 00	23 34	00 04
Haymarket 225,230,242 a	18s20	18s32	18s44	19s01	19s13	19s34	19s46	20s01	20s18	20s47	21s17	21s43	22s17	22s45	23s16	23s49	00s20
Edinburgh 10 225,230,242 a	18 25	18 37	18 51	19 06	19 18	19 40	19 51	20 08	20 26	20 52	21 23	21 48	22 25	22 50	23 22	23 56	00 26

Table T228-R

Glasgow Queen Street - Falkirk High - Edinburgh

Sundays

20 May to 2 December

	SR	SR	SR	SR	SR	SR	SR	SR	SR	SR	SR	SR	SR	SR	SR	SR	SR	SR	SR	SR	SR	SR
	1	1	1	1	1	1	1	1	1	1	1	1	1	1	1	1	1	1	1	1	1	1
		🍴	🍴	🍴	🍴	🍴	🍴	🍴	🍴	🍴	🍴		🍴				🍴	🍴	🍴	🍴	🍴	🍴
Glasgow Queen Street 10 230 d	07 50	08 30	09 00	09 30	10 00	10 30	11 00	11 30	12 00	12 31	13 00	13 30	14 00	14 30	15 00	15 30	16 00	16 30	17 00	17 30	18 00	18 30
Bishopbriggs 230 d																						
Lenzie 3 230 d																						
Croy 3 230 d	08 02		09 12		10 13		11 12		12 12		13 12		14 12		15 12		16 12		17 12		18 12	
Falkirk High 3 d	08 12	08 48	09 22	09 49	10 22	10 50	11 22	11 49	12 22	12 52	13 22	13 49	14 22	14 49	15 22	15 49	16 22	16 50	17 22	17 49	18 22	18 49
Polmont 3 230 a	08 16	08 53		09 53		10 55		11 54		12 59		13 54		14 54		15 53		16 55		17 54		18 54
Linlithgow 230 a	08 22	08 59	09 29	09 59	10 30	11 01	11 29	12 00	12 29	13 05	13 29	14 00	14 29	15 00	15 29	15 59	16 29	17 01	17 29	18 00	18 29	19 00
Haymarket 225,230,242 a	08 49	09s20	09s49	10s20	10s46	11s17	11s48	12s16	12s45	13s21	13s50	14s19	14s45	15s16	15s47	16s19	16s45	17s20	17s46	18s20	18s45	19s16
Edinburgh 10 225,230,242 a	08 54	09 25	09 54	10 25	10 51	11 22	11 53	12 21	12 50	13 26	13 55	14 24	14 50	15 22	15 52	16 24	16 50	17 25	17 51	18 25	18 50	19 21

	SR	SR	SR	SR	SR	SR	SR	SR	SR	SR
	1	1	1	1	1	1	1	1	1	1
	🍴									
Glasgow Queen Street 10 230 d	19 00	19 30	20 00	20 30	21 00	21 30	22 00	22 30	23 00	23 30
Bishopbriggs 230 d										
Lenzie 3 230 d										
Croy 3 230 d	19 12		20 12		21 12		22 12		23 12	23 42
Falkirk High 3 d	19 22	19 49	20 22	20 49	21 22	21 49	22 22	22 49	23 22	23 52
Polmont 3 230 a		19 53		20 53		21 53		22 53		23 56
Linlithgow 230 a	19 29	19 59	20 29	20 59	21 29	21 59	22 29	22 59	23 29	00 03
Haymarket 225,230,242 a	19s48	20s20	20s45	21s15	21s45	22s18	22s45	23s15	23s45	00s18
Edinburgh 10 225,230,242 a	19 53	20 25	20 50	21 20	21 50	22 23	22 50	23 21	23 52	00 23

Table T229-F

Mondays to Fridays

21 May to 7 December

Edinburgh and Glasgow Queen Street - Perth, Inverness, Dundee, Aberdeen, Dyce and Inverurie

Miles	Miles	Miles	Miles	Miles			SR MX	SR MO	SR MX	SR MX	SR	SR	CS	SR	SR	SR	XC	SR	SR	SR	SR	SR	SR	SR
							◇■ A	◇■ A [trolley]	◇ A	◇ B	◇ C		D	◇ E	■ C	■ E	◇■	◇■	◇■ C [trolley]	◇■ F [trolley]	◇	◇	◇■ [trolley]	◇■ C [trolley]
—	0	—	0	0	**Edinburgh ■** 242	d												05 30			06 30	07 00		07 31
—	1¼	—	1¼	1¼	Haymarket 242	d												05 34			06 34	07 04		07 35
—	5½	—	5½	—	Edinburgh Gateway	d															06 40	07 10		
—	13¼	—	13¼	—	Inverkeithing 242	d												05 47			06 50	07 20		
—	26	—	26	—	Kirkcaldy 242	d												06 03			07 06	07 36		08 03
—	33¼	—	33¼	—	Markinch	d				00 05								06 12			07 15	07 45		
—	39¼	—	39¼	—	Ladybank	d				00 12								06 20			07 22	07 53		
—	42¼	—	—	—	Springfield	d																		
—	44½	—	—	—	Cupar	d				00 18								06 26				07 59		
—	51	—	—	—	Leuchars ■	a				00 25								06 33				08 06		08 26
—	—	—	—	—	St Andrews Bus Station	a																		
—	—	—	—	—	St Andrews Bus Station	d																		
—	—	—	—	—	Leuchars ■	d				00 25								06 33				08 06		08 26
0	—	0	—	—	**Glasgow Queen St. ■** 230	d													05 56	05 56			07 10	
21	—	21	—	28¼	Larbert 230	d													06 16	06 16				
29	—	29	—	36½	Stirling 230	d													06 25	06 25			07 36	
32½	—	32½	—	40	Bridge of Allan 230	d																		
34½	—	34½	—	42	Dunblane 230	d													06 32	06 32			07 43	
46¾	—	46¾	—	54¼	Gleneagles	d													06 43	06 43				
62½	—	62½	57	70¾	**Perth**	a													06 59	06 59	07 45		08 09	
—	—	—	—	—		d			00 13			05 08			06 00	06 00			07 00	07 00	07 46		08 10	
79¾	—	—	—	88	Invergowrie	d															08 03			
83¾	59¼	—	—	—	**Dundee**	a			00 36	00 41					06 24	06 24		06 46	07 22	07 22	08 12	08 22		08 42
—	—	—	—	—		d					05 39			05 39	06 25	06 25	06 42	06 52	07 23	07 23				08 43
87¼	63¼	—	—	—	Broughty Ferry	d					05 46			05 46	06 32	06 32								
89	65	—	—	—	Balmossie	d																		
89¾	65¾	—	—	—	Monifieth	d					05 50			05 50										
92¾	68¾	—	—	—	Barry Links	d																		
93½	69½	—	—	—	Golf Street	d																		
94	70	—	—	—	Carnoustie	d					05 59			05 59	06 40	06 40		07 04	07 35	07 35				
100¼	76¼	—	—	—	Arbroath	a					06 05			06 05	06 46	06 46	06 57	07 10	07 41	07 41				08 59
—	—	—	—	—		d					06 06			06 06	06 48	06 48	06 59	07 12	07 42	07 42				08 59
114	90	—	—	—	Montrose	a					06 21			06 21	07 03	07 03	07 13	07 26	07 56	07 56				09 13
—	—	—	—	—		d					06 26			06 26	07 04	07 04	07 15	07 26	07 57	07 57				09 14
124	100	—	—	—	Laurencekirk	d					06 37			06 37				07 37	08 08	08 08				
138¼	114¼	—	—	—	Stonehaven	d	00 05	00 05			06 51			06 51	07 26	07 26	07 37	07 51	08 21	08 21				09 35
146½	122½	—	—	—	Portlethen	d					07 00			07 00	07 35	07 35		07 59	08 30	08 30				
154½	130½	—	—	—	**Aberdeen**	a	00 25	00 25			07 14			07 14	07 49	07 49	07 58	08 13	08 47	08 47				09 55
—	—	—	—	—		d								07 15		07 50				08 49				
160¾	136¾	—	—	—	Dyce 240	a								07 25		07 58				08 57				
171½	147½	—	—	—	**Inverurie** 240	a								07 40		08 13								
—	—	78	72½	86¼	Dunkeld & Birnam	d						05 25											08 30	
—	—	91	85½	99¼	Pitlochry	d						05 38											08 43	
—	—	97¾	92¼	106	Blair Atholl	d						05 47											08 52	
—	—	121	116¼	130¼	Dalwhinnie	d						06 13											09 17	
—	—	131¼	126¾	140½	Newtonmore	d																	09 27	
—	—	134	129½	143¼	Kingussie	d						06 43	07 20										09 36	
—	—	145¾	141¼	155	Aviemore	d						07 04	07 43										09 50	
—	—	152¾	148¼	162	Carrbridge	d						07 19	07 56										09 59	
—	—	180	175	188¾	**Inverness**	a						07 49	08 41	09 35									10 28	

A From Glasgow Queen Street
B From Edinburgh
C until 17 August
D From London Euston
E from 20 August
F from 20 August. [trolley] to Aberdeen

Table T229-F

Mondays to Fridays

21 May to 7 December

Edinburgh and Glasgow Queen Street - Perth, Inverness, Dundee, Aberdeen, Dyce and Inverurie

		SR	SR	SR	SR	SR	SR	SR	SR	SR	SR	SR	SR	SR	SR	SR	SR	GR	SR	SR	SR	SR
		◇■ A [trolley]	◇■ [trolley]	◇	◇	◇■ B [trolley]	◇■ A [trolley]	◇	◇■ [trolley]	◇■ [trolley]	◇	◇■ [trolley]	◇	◇■ [trolley]	◇	◇	◇■ [trolley]	■ C	◇■ [trolley]	◇■ [trolley]	◇	◇■ [trolley]
Edinburgh ■ 242	d	07 31		07 34	08 01	08 31	08 31			08 34	09 00	09 30			09 36	10 00		10 28		10 36	11 00	11 31
Haymarket 242	d	07 35		07 39	08 07	08 35	08 35			08 39	09 04	09 34			09 40	10 04		10 33		10u41	11 04	11 35
Edinburgh Gateway	d			07 44	08 12					08 44	09 10				09 46	10 10				10 46	11 10	
Inverkeithing 242	d			07 56	08 23						09 20				09 56	10 20		10 48		10u57	11 20	
Kirkcaldy 242	d	08 03		08 12	08 39					09 10	09 36				10 12	10 36		11 05		11u13	11 36	
Markinch	d			08 22	08 48					09 19	09 45				10 22	10 45				11 22	11 45	
Ladybank	d			08 29	08 55						09 52				10 29	10 52				11 29	11 52	
Springfield	d				09 00																	
Cupar	d				09 04						09 58					10 58					11 58	
Leuchars ■	a	08 26			09 11	09 24	09 24				10 05					11 05		11 28			12 05	12 24
St Andrews Bus Station	a																					
St Andrews Bus Station	d																					
Leuchars ■	d	08 26			09 11	09 25	09 25				10 05					11 05		11 30			12 05	12 24
Glasgow Queen St. ■ 230	d		07 42					08 08	08 41				09 08	09 41			10 11		10 41			
Larbert 230	d																					
Stirling 230	d		08u09					08 36	09 08				09 35	10 08			10 37		11 09			
Bridge of Allan 230	d							08 40									10 41					
Dunblane 230	d		08 15					08 44					09 41				10 46					
Gleneagles	d							08 56					09 53				10 58					
Perth	a		08 41	08 57				09 10	09 41	09 49			10 10	10 39	10 54		11 15		11 38	11 54		
	d		08 42					09 15	09 42	09 50			10 15	10 40			11 16		11 39	11 55		
Invergowrie	d							09 32					10 33									
Dundee	a	08 42	09 03		09 27	09 38	09 38	09 43	10 04		10 21	10 33	10 41	11 01		11 21		11 43	12 01		12 21	12 37
	d	08 43	09 04			09 40	09 40		10 05			10 34		11 02				11 44	12 02			12 38
Broughty Ferry	d					09 47	09 47							11 09								
Balmossie	d																					
Monifieth	d																					
Barry Links	d																					
Golf Street	d																					
Carnoustie	d		09 16											11 17								
Arbroath	a	08 59	09 23			09 59	09 59		10 21			10 50		11 23				12 00	12 18			12 54
	d	08 59	09 23			09 59	09 59		10 21			10 51		11 24				12 02	12 18			12 55
Montrose	a	09 13	09 37						10 41			11 05		11 38				12 16	12 32			
	d	09 14	09 38						10 41			11 05		11 44				12 18	12 33			
Laurencekirk	d					10 22	10 22							11 58								
Stonehaven	d	09 35				10 36	10 36		11 02			11 26		12 12				12 41				13 28
Portlethen	d								11 11													
Aberdeen	a	09 55	10 17			10 55	10 55		11 25			11 46		12 36				13 03	13 13			13 51
	d	09 58					11 03															
Dyce 240	a	10 06					11 11															
Inverurie 240	a	10 20					11 27															
Dunkeld & Birnam	d																11 37					
Pitlochry	d									10 22							11 50			12 24		
Blair Atholl	d									10 31										12 33		
Dalwhinnie	d									10 56										12 59		
Newtonmore	d																			13 09		
Kingussie	d									11 09							12 35			13 15		
Aviemore	d									11 23							12 47			13 33		
Carrbridge	d																			13 42		
Inverness	a									11 58							13 29			14 17		

A from 20 August. [trolley] to Aberdeen
B until 17 August
C From Leeds

Table T229-F

Mondays to Fridays
21 May to 7 December

Edinburgh and Glasgow Queen Street - Perth, Inverness, Dundee, Aberdeen, Dyce and Inverurie

	SR	SR	SR	SR	SR	SR	SR	SR	SR	SR	SR	SR	SR	GR	SR	SR	SR	SR	SR	SR	SR	SR
	◇1	◇	◇	◇1	◇1	◇1	◇1	◇	◇	◇1	◇1	◇1	◇	R 1	◇1	◇1	◇	◇	◇1	◇	◇1	◇1
					A	B								C	A	D				A	B	
	🛒			🛒	🛒	🛒	🛒			🛒	🛒	🛒		🍴	🛒	🛒			🛒	🛒	🛒	🛒
Edinburgh 10 242 d		11 39	12 03		12 30	12 30		12 37	13 00	13 30		13 36	14 00	14 28			14 37	15 01		15 31	15 31	
Haymarket 242 d		11 43	12 07		12 34	12 34		12 41	13 04	13 34		13u40	14 04	14 33			14 41	15 05		15 35	15 35	
Edinburgh Gateway d		11 49	12 13					12 47	13 10			13 46	14 10				14 47	15 11				
Inverkeithing 242 d		11 59	12 23					12 57	13 20				14 20	14 49			14 57	15 21				
Kirkcaldy 242 d		12 15	12 39					13 13	13 36			14u12	14 36	15 06			15 13	15 37				
Markinch d		12 25	12 48					13 23	13 45			14 20	14 45				15 23	15 46				
Ladybank d		12 32	12 55					13 30	13 52				14 52				15 30	15 53				
Springfield d																						
Cupar d			13 01						13 58				14 58					15 59				
Leuchars 5 a			13 08		13 24	13 24			14 05	14 24			15 05	15 29				16 06		16 24	16 24	
St Andrews Bus Station a																						
St Andrews Bus Station d																						
Leuchars 5 d			13 08		13 24	13 24			14 05	14 24			15 05	15 31				16 06		16 24	16 24	
Glasgow Queen St. 10 230 d	11 41			12 09			12 41				13 41				14 41	14 41			15 09			15 41
Larbert 230 d																						
Stirling 230 d	12 07			12 37			13 07				14 08				15 07	15 07			15 37			
Bridge of Allan 230 d				12 41															15 41			
Dunblane 230 d				12 46															15 46			
Gleneagles d							13 22															
Perth a	12 36	12 57		13 12			13 38	13 55			14 37	14 50			15 39	15 39	15 55		16 12			16 34
d	12 37			13 13			13 39				14 38	14 51			15 40	15 40			16 16			16 36
Invergowrie d																						
Dundee a	12 59		13 24		13 37	13 37	14 01		14 21	14 37	15 01		15 21	15 46	16 01	16 01		16 22		16 37	16 37	16 57
d	13 00				13 39	13 39	14 02			14 38	15 02			15 48	16 02	16 02				16 39	16 39	16 58
Broughty Ferry d											15 09											
Balmossie d																						
Monifieth d																						
Barry Links d																						
Golf Street d																						
Carnoustie d	13 12										15 17				16 14	16 14						17 10
Arbroath a	13 18				13 55	13 55	14 18			14 54	15 23			16 04	16 21	16 21				16 55	16 55	17 17
d	13 19				13 55	13 55	14 18			14 55	15 24			16 05	16 21	16 21				16 55	16 55	17 17
Montrose a	13 33				14 09	14 09	14 32				15 41			16 20	16 35	16 35				17 09	17 09	17 31
d	13 33				14 10	14 10	14 33				15 41			16 21	16 36	16 36				17 09	17 09	17 32
Laurencekirk d	13 44										15 53									17 20	17 20	
Stonehaven d					14 31	14 31	14 54			15 29				16 44						17 33	17 33	17 53
Portlethen d											16 13											
Aberdeen a	14 15				14 50	14 50	15 14			15 49	16 27			17 04	17 15	17 15				17 53	17 53	18 13
d						14 57										17 26					17 55	
Dyce 240 a						15 05										17 34					18 03	
Inverurie 240 a						15 19										17 48					18 17	
Dunkeld & Birnam d				13 30								15 08							16 33			
Pitlochry d				13 43								15 21							16 46			
Blair Atholl d				13 52								15 30							16 55			
Dalwhinnie d												15 55										
Newtonmore d																			17 28			
Kingussie d				14 28								16 08							17 33			
Aviemore d				14 40								16 19							17 44			
Carrbridge d																			17 52			
Inverness a				15 23								16 54				19 38			18 21			

A until 17 August
B from 20 August. 🛒 to Aberdeen
C From London Kings Cross
D from 20 August

Table T229-F

Mondays to Fridays
21 May to 7 December

Edinburgh and Glasgow Queen Street - Perth, Inverness, Dundee, Aberdeen, Dyce and Inverurie

	SR	SR	SR	SR	SR	SR	SR	GR	SR	SR	SR	SR	SR	SR	SR	XC	SR	GR	SR	SR	SR
	◇	◇	◇1	◇1		◇1		R 1			◇1	◇	◇1	◇1	◇	◇1	◇1	R 1	◇1	◇	◇
			A	B				C								D		C			
			🛒	🛒		🛒		🍴			🛒		🛒	🛒			🛒	🍴	🛒		
Edinburgh 10 242 d	15 35	16 00	16 30	16 30			16 34	16 34	17 02	17 27	17 36			17 41	18 00	18 10		18 33		18 41	19 00
Haymarket 242 d	15 39	16 04	16u34	16u34			16 39	16 39	17 06	17 31	17 41			17u46	18 05	18 15		18 38		18 45	19 04
Edinburgh Gateway d	15 47	16 10					16 46		17 12					17 51	18 11					18 51	19 10
Inverkeithing 242 d	15 57	16 20					16 57		17 22						18 23	18 29		18 55		19 01	19 20
Kirkcaldy 242 d	16 13	16 36					17 13		17 38					18 17	18 42	18 47		19 13		19 19	19 36
Markinch d	16 23	16 45					17 22		17 48					18 27	18 51	18 57				19 29	19 45
Ladybank d	16 30	16 52					17 29		17 55					18 34	18 58	19 05				19 36	19 52
Springfield d									18 00												
Cupar d		16 58	17 19	17 19					18 04		18 27				19 04	19 16					19 59
Leuchars 5 a		17 05	17 25	17 25					18 11		18 33				19 11	19 22		19 39			20 05
St Andrews Bus Station a																					
St Andrews Bus Station d																					
Leuchars 5 d		17 05	17 26	17 26					18 11		18 34				19 11	19 23		19 40			20 06
Glasgow Queen St. 10 230 d					16 11	16 41						17 11	17 40				18 11		18 41		
Larbert 230 d										17 57		17 35					18 31				
Stirling 230 d					16 39			17 23		18 06		17 46	18 16				18 42		19 07		
Bridge of Allan 230 d					16 44					18 10		17 51					18 46				
Dunblane 230 d					16 50					18a16		17 56	18 23				18 50		19 14		
Gleneagles d					17 02			17 41				18 09	18 36				19 02		19 26		
Perth a	16 55				17 18	17 40	17 54	17 58				18 23	18 52	18 58			19 19		19 42	20 01	
d					17 19	17 41		18 02				18 25	18 55	19 00			19 23		19 43		
Invergowrie d					17 37							18 43									
Dundee a		17 21	17 39	17 39	17 45	18 03			18 27		18 47	18 52	19 17		19 27	19 35		19 53	20 04		20 22
d			17 40	17 40	17 46	18 04					18 48	18 55	19 18			19 36		19 55	20 05		
Broughty Ferry d					17 53							19 01							20 12		
Balmossie d												19 05									
Monifieth d					17 57							19 07									
Barry Links d												19 12									
Golf Street d												19 14									
Carnoustie d					18 03	18 17						19a18	19 30						20 19		
Arbroath a			17 56	17 56	18 12	18 23					19 04		19 37			19 51		20 11	20 26		
d			17 56	17 56		18 24					19 05		19 37			19 52		20 12	20 26		
Montrose a			18 10	18 10							19 22		19 51			20 05		20 27	20 40		
d			18 12	18 12							19 22		19 51			20 06		20 28	20 41		
Laurencekirk d			18 23	18 23									20 02								
Stonehaven d			18 37	18 37		18 59					19 44		20 15			20 27		20 51			
Portlethen d			18 47	18 47							19 53										
Aberdeen a			19 01	19 01		19 19					20 07		20 35			20 48		21 11	21 22		
d				19 18																	
Dyce 240 a				19 27																	
Inverurie 240 a				19 41																	
Dunkeld & Birnam d														19 20			19 40				
Pitlochry d								18 31						19 33			19 53				
Blair Atholl d																	20 02				
Dalwhinnie d																	20 26				
Newtonmore d																	20 36				
Kingussie d								19 16						20 16			20 41				
Aviemore d								19 29						20 27			20 53				
Carrbridge d																					
Inverness a								20 04						21 02			21 27				

A until 17 August
B from 20 August. 🛒 to Aberdeen
C From London Kings Cross
D From Plymouth

Table T229-F

Mondays to Fridays
21 May to 7 December

Edinburgh and Glasgow Queen Street - Perth, Inverness, Dundee, Aberdeen, Dyce and Inverurie

	SR	GR	SR	SR	SR	SR	SR	XC	GR	SR	SR	SR	SR	SR	SR	SR	SR	SR	SR
	◇	■	◇■	◇■	◇■	◇■	◇	◇■	■	◇■	◇	◇	◇■	◇■	◇	◇	◇	◇	
		A	B	C		D		E	A										F
		☕	🛒	🛒	🛒	🛒			☕										
Edinburgh 242 d		19 25	19 34	19 35		19 42	20 00	20 14	20 32		20 40	21 05	21 43		22 10	22 37		23 09	23 14
Haymarket 242 d		19 30	19 38	19 39		19 46	20 04	20 17	20 37		20 44	21 09	21 47		22 14	22 41		23 13	23a18
Edinburgh Gateway d						19 52	20 11				20 50	21 16			22 21	22 48		23 21	
Inverkeithing 242 d						20 03	20 25	20 31	20 53		21 00	21 30			22 35	23 02		23 34	
Kirkcaldy 242 d						20 19	20 47		21 11		21 16	21 51	22 15		22 57	23 24		23 56	
Markinch d						20 28	20 56	21 02			21 26	22 00			23 06	23 33		00 05	
Ladybank d						20 36	21 03	21 10			21 33	22 08			23 13	23 40		00 12	
Springfield d															23 18				
Cupar d			20 22	20 22			21 09	21 20				22 14			23 21			00 18	
Leuchars a			20 29	20 29			21 16	21 26	21 37			22 21	22 39		23 28			00 25	
St Andrews Bus Station a																			
St Andrews Bus Station d																			
Leuchars d			20 29	20 29			21 16	21 28	21 39			22 22	22 39		23 28			00 25	
Glasgow Queen St. 230 d	19 09				19 41					20 41				21 42			22 48		
Larbert 230 d																	23 20		
Stirling 230 d	19 37	20a15			20 08					21 08				22 08			23 33		
Bridge of Allan 230 d	19 41																23 37		
Dunblane 230 d	19 46									21 15							23 42		
Gleneagles d	19 57									21 26							23 53		
Perth a	20 11				20 37	21 00				21 42	21 58			22 37		00 05	00 09		
d	20 12				20 38	21 01				21 43				22 41			00 13		
Invergowrie d	20 29									22 00									
Dundee a	20 38		20 43	20 43	20 59		21 32	21 43	21 52	22 07		22 38	22 52	23 02	23 44		00 36	00 41	
d			20 44	20 44	21 00				21 53	22 09			22 53	23 03					
Broughty Ferry d														23 10					
Balmossie d																			
Monifieth d														23 14					
Barry Links d																			
Golf Street d																			
Carnoustie d										22 20				23 20					
Arbroath a			21 00	21 00	21 16				22 09	22 27			23 09	23 26					
d			21 00	21 00	21 17				22 11	22 27			23 09	23 27					
Montrose a			21 14	21 14	21 31				22 25	22 41			23 23	23 41					
d			21 15	21 15	21 31				22 27	22 41			23 24	23 41					
Laurencekirk d					21 42									23 52					
Stonehaven d			21 36	21 36	21 55				22 50	23 02			23 45	00 05					
Portlethen d													23 54						
Aberdeen a			21 56	21 56	22 15				23 10	23 22			00 08	00 25					
d			22 00																
Dyce 240 a			22 08																
Inverurie 240 a			22 21																
Dunkeld & Birnam d						21 18													
Pitlochry d						21 35													
Blair Atholl d						21 44													
Dalwhinnie d						22 13													
Newtonmore d						22 23													
Kingussie d						22 28													
Aviemore d						22 39													
Carrbridge d						22 48													
Inverness a			00 08			23 16													

A From London Kings Cross
B from 20 August. 🛒 to Aberdeen
C until 17 August
D 🛒 from Perth
E From Plymouth
F To Motherwell

Table T229-F

Saturdays
26 May to 8 December

Edinburgh and Glasgow Queen Street - Perth, Inverness, Dundee, Aberdeen, Dyce and Inverurie

	SR	SR	SR	SR	SR	CS	SR	SR	SR	XC	SR	SR	SR	SR	SR	SR	SR	SR	SR	SR	SR	SR
	◇■	◇	◇		◇	R	◇	■	■	◇■	◇■	◇■	◇■	◇	◇	◇■	◇■	◇■	◇■	◇	◇	◇■
	A	A	B		C	D	E	C	E			C	F				C	F				C
						🛏 ✕						🛒	🛒			🛒	🛒	🛒	🛒			🛒
Edinburgh 242 d											05 30			06 30	07 00		07 30	07 30		07 36	08 00	08 28
Haymarket 242 d											05 34			06 34	07 04		07 34	07 34		07 41	08 04	08 33
Edinburgh Gateway d														06 40	07 10					07 47	08 10	
Inverkeithing 242 d											05 47			06 50	07 20					07 57	08 20	
Kirkcaldy 242 d											06 03			07 06	07 36		08 02	08 02		08 13	08 36	
Markinch d			00 05								06 12			07 15	07 45					08 23	08 45	
Ladybank d			00 12								06 20			07 22	07 53					08 30	08 53	
Springfield d																					08 57	
Cupar d			00 18								06 26				07 59						09 01	
Leuchars a			00 25								06 33				08 06		08 25	08 25			09 08	09 24
St Andrews Bus Station a																						
St Andrews Bus Station d																						
Leuchars d			00 25								06 33				08 06		08 25	08 25			09 09	09 25
Glasgow Queen St. 230 d												05 56	05 56			07 10			07 42			
Larbert 230 d												06 16	06 16									
Stirling 230 d												06 25	06 25			07 36			08u09			
Bridge of Allan 230 d																						
Dunblane 230 d												06 32	06 32			07 43			08 15			
Gleneagles d												06 43	06 43									
Perth a												06 59	06 59	07 45		08 09			08 41	08 55		
d		00 13		05 08				06 00	06 00			07 00	07 00	07 46		08 10			08 42			
Invergowrie d														08 03								
Dundee a		00 36	00 41					06 24	06 24		06 46	07 22	07 22	08 12	08 22		08 42	08 42	09 03		09 25	09 38
d								06 25	06 25	06 42	06 52	07 23	07 23				08 43	08 43	09 04			09 40
Broughty Ferry d								06 32	06 32													09 47
Balmossie d																						
Monifieth d																						
Barry Links d																						
Golf Street d																						
Carnoustie d								06 40	06 40		07 04	07 35	07 35						09 16			
Arbroath a								06 46	06 46	06 57	07 10	07 41	07 41				08 59	08 59	09 23			09 59
d								06 48	06 48	06 59	07 12	07 42	07 42				08 59	08 59	09 23			09 59
Montrose a								07 03	07 03	07 13	07 26	07 56	07 56				09 13	09 13	09 37			
d					06 26		06 26	07 04	07 04	07 15	07 26	07 57	07 57				09 14	09 14	09 38			
Laurencekirk d					06 37		06 37				07 37	08 08	08 08									10 22
Stonehaven d	00 05				06 51		06 51	07 26	07 26	07 37	07 51	08 21	08 21				09 35	09 35				10 36
Portlethen d					07 00		07 00	07 35	07 35		07 59	08 30	08 30									
Aberdeen a	00 25				07 14		07 14	07 49	07 49	07 58	08 13	08 47	08 47				09 55	09 55	10 17			10 55
d							07 15		07 50				08 49					09 58				
Dyce 240 a							07 25		07 58				08 57					10 06				
Inverurie 240 a							07 40		08 12									10 20				
Dunkeld & Birnam d				05 25												08 30						
Pitlochry d				05 38												08 43						
Blair Atholl d				05 47												08 52						
Dalwhinnie d				06 13												09 17						
Newtonmore d																09 27						
Kingussie d				06 43		07 20										09 36						
Aviemore d				07 04		07 43										09 50						
Carrbridge d				07 19		07 56										09 59						
Inverness a				07 49		08 41	09 35									10 28						

A From Glasgow Queen Street
B From Edinburgh
C until 18 August
D From London Euston
E from 25 August
F from 25 August. 🛒 to Aberdeen

Table T229-F

Saturdays
26 May to 8 December

Edinburgh and Glasgow Queen Street - Perth, Inverness, Dundee, Aberdeen, Dyce and Inverurie

		SR	SR	SR	SR	SR	SR	SR	SR	SR	SR	SR	GR	SR	SR	SR	SR	SR	SR	SR	SR	SR	SR
		◇1 A ⚲	◇	◇1 ⚲	◇1 ⚲	◇	◇1 ⚲	◇	◇1 ⚲	◇	◇	◇1 ⚲	1 B ⊡	◇1 ⚲	◇1 ⚲	◇	◇1 ⚲	◇1 ⚲	◇	◇	◇1 ⚲	◇1 C ⚲	◇1 A ⚲
Edinburgh 10 242	d	08 28			08 31	09 01	09 30			09 36	10 00		10 28		10 36	11 00	11 30		11 35	12 00		12 30	12 30
Haymarket 242	d	08 33			08 36	09 05	09 34			09 43	10 05		10 33		10u41	11 04	11 34		11 41	12 04		12 34	12 34
Edinburgh Gateway	d				08 42	09 11				09 48	10 11				10 46	11 10			11 46	12 10			
Inverkeithing 242	d					09 21				09 59	10 21		10 48		10u57	11 20			11 57	12 20			
Kirkcaldy 242	d				09 07	09 37				10 15	10 37		11 05		11u13	11 36			12 13	12 36			
Markinch	d				09 16	09 46				10 24	10 46				11 22	11 45			12 22	12 45			
Ladybank	d					09 53				10 31	10 53				11 29	11 52			12 29	12 52			
Springfield	d																						
Cupar	d					09 59					10 59					11 58				12 58			
Leuchars 5	a	09 24				10 06	10 23				11 06		11 28			12 05	12 23			13 05		13 23	13 23
St Andrews Bus Station	a																						
St Andrews Bus Station	d																						
Leuchars 5	d	09 25				10 06	10 23				11 06		11 30			12 05	12 23			13 05		13 23	13 23
Glasgow Queen St. 10 230	d		08 08	08 41				09 08	09 41			10 11		10 41				11 41			12 09		
Larbert 230	d																						
Stirling 230	d		08 36	09 08				09 35	10 08			10 37		11 09				12 07			12 37		
Bridge of Allan 230	d		08 40									10 41									12 41		
Dunblane 230	d		08 44					09 41				10 46									12 46		
Gleneagles	d		08 56					09 53				10 58											
Perth	a		09 10	09 41	09 46			10 07	10 39	10 56		11 15		11 38	11 54			12 36	12 54		13 12		
	d		09 15	09 42	09 50			10 15	10 40			11 16		11 39	11 55			12 37			13 13		
Invergowrie	d		09 32					10 33															
Dundee	a	09 38	09 43	10 04		10 22	10 36	10 41	11 01		11 22		11 43	12 01		12 21	12 36	12 59		13 21		13 36	13 36
	d	09 40		10 05			10 37		11 02				11 44	12 02			12 40	13 00				13 39	13 39
Broughty Ferry	d	09 47							11 09														
Balmossie	d																						
Monifieth	d																						
Barry Links	d																						
Golf Street	d																						
Carnoustie	d								11 17									13 12					
Arbroath	a	09 59		10 21			10 53		11 23				12 00	12 18			12 56	13 18				13 55	13 55
	d	09 59		10 21			10 54		11 24				12 02	12 18			12 56	13 19				13 55	13 55
Montrose	a			10 41			11 08		11 38				12 16	12 32				13 33				14 09	14 09
	d			10 41			11 08		11 38				12 18	12 33				13 33				14 10	14 10
Laurencekirk	d	10 22							11 49									13 44					
Stonehaven	d	10 36		11 02			11 29		12 03				12 41				13 30					14 31	14 31
Portlethen	d			11 11																			
Aberdeen	a	10 55		11 25			11 49		12 23				13 01	13 13			13 50	14 15				14 50	14 50
	d	11 03																					14 57
Dyce 240	a	11 11																					15 05
Inverurie 240	a	11 27																					15 19
Dunkeld & Birnam	d											11 37									13 30		
Pitlochry	d				10 22							11 50			12 24						13 43		
Blair Atholl	d				10 31										12 33						13 52		
Dalwhinnie	d				10 56										12 59								
Newtonmore	d														13 09								
Kingussie	d				11 09							12 35			13 15						14 28		
Aviemore	d				11 23							12 47			13 33						14 40		
Carrbridge	d														13 42								
Inverness	a				11 58							13 29			14 17						15 23		

A from 25 August. ⚲ to Aberdeen
B From Leeds
C until 18 August

Table T229-F

Saturdays
26 May to 8 December

Edinburgh and Glasgow Queen Street - Perth, Inverness, Dundee, Aberdeen, Dyce and Inverurie

		SR	SR	SR	SR	SR	SR	SR	SR	GR	SR	SR	SR	SR	SR	SR	SR	SR	SR	SR	SR	SR
		◇1 ⚲	◇	◇	◇1 A ⚲	◇1 B ⚲	◇1 ⚲	◇1 ⚲	◇	1 C ⊡	◇1 ⚲	◇	◇	◇1 ⚲	◇1 A ⚲	◇1 B ⚲	◇1 ⚲	◇	◇	◇1 A ⚲	◇1 B ⚲	
Edinburgh 10 242	d		12 35	13 00	13 30	13 30		13 36	14 00	14 29		14 34	15 00		15 30	15 30		15 37	16 00	16 30	16 30	
Haymarket 242	d		12 41	13 04	13 34	13 34		13u41	14 04	14 34		14 38	15 04		15 34	15 34		15 41	16 04	16u34	16u34	
Edinburgh Gateway	d		12 46	13 10				13 46	14 10			14 47	15 10					15 47	16 10			
Inverkeithing 242	d		12 57	13 20					14 20	14 50		14 58	15 20					15 57	16 20			
Kirkcaldy 242	d		13 13	13 36				14u12	14 36	15 07		15 14	15 36					16 13	16 36			
Markinch	d		13 22	13 45				14 20	14 45			15 23	15 45					16 23	16 45			
Ladybank	d		13 29	13 52					14 52			15 30	15 52					16 30	16 53			
Springfield	d																					
Cupar	d			13 58					14 58				15 58						16 59	17 19	17 19	
Leuchars 5	a			14 05	14 23	14 23			15 05	15 30			16 05		16 24	16 24			17 06	17 25	17 25	
St Andrews Bus Station	a																					
St Andrews Bus Station	d																					
Leuchars 5	d			14 05	14 23	14 23			15 05	15 32			16 05		16 24	16 24			17 06	17 26	17 26	
Glasgow Queen St. 10 230	d	12 41					13 41				14 41			15 09			15 41					16 11
Larbert 230	d																					
Stirling 230	d	13 07					14 08				15 07			15 37								16 39
Bridge of Allan 230	d													15 41								16 44
Dunblane 230	d													15 46								16 50
Gleneagles	d	13 22																				17 02
Perth	a	13 38	13 54				14 37	14 50			15 39	15 55		16 12			16 34	16 55				17 18
	d	13 39					14 38	14 51			15 40			16 16			16 36					17 19
Invergowrie	d																					17 37
Dundee	a	14 01		14 21	14 36	14 36	15 01		15 21	15 46	16 01		16 21		16 37	16 37	16 57		17 22	17 39	17 39	17 45
	d	14 02			14 37	14 37	15 02			15 48	16 02				16 39	16 39	16 58			17 40	17 40	17 48
Broughty Ferry	d						15 09															17 54
Balmossie	d																					
Monifieth	d																					17 59
Barry Links	d																					
Golf Street	d																					
Carnoustie	d						15 17				16 14						17 10					18 05
Arbroath	a	14 18			14 53	14 53	15 23			16 04	16 21				16 55	16 55	17 17			17 56	17 56	18 13
	d	14 18			14 54	14 54	15 24			16 05	16 21				16 55	16 55	17 17			17 56	17 56	
Montrose	a	14 32					15 41			16 20	16 35				17 09	17 09	17 31			18 10	18 10	
	d	14 33					15 41			16 21	16 36				17 09	17 09	17 32			18 12	18 12	
Laurencekirk	d						15 52								17 20	17 20				18 23	18 23	
Stonehaven	d	14 54			15 27	15 27				16 44					17 33	17 33	17 53			18 37	18 37	
Portlethen	d						16 12													18 47	18 47	
Aberdeen	a	15 14			15 47	15 47	16 26			17 04	17 15				17 53	17 53	18 13			19 01	19 01	
	d					15 52										17 55					19 18	
Dyce 240	a					16 00										18 03					19 27	
Inverurie 240	a					16 14										18 19					19 41	
Dunkeld & Birnam	d							15 08						16 33								
Pitlochry	d							15 21						16 46								
Blair Atholl	d							15 30						16 55								
Dalwhinnie	d							15 55														
Newtonmore	d													17 28								
Kingussie	d							16 08						17 33								
Aviemore	d							16 19						17 44								
Carrbridge	d													17 52								
Inverness	a							16 54						18 21								

A until 18 August
B from 25 August. ⚲ to Aberdeen
C From London Kings Cross

Table T229-F

Saturdays
26 May to 8 December

Edinburgh and Glasgow Queen Street - Perth, Inverness, Dundee, Aberdeen, Dyce and Inverurie

	SR	GR	SR	SR	SR	SR	SR	SR	XC	XC	SR	GR	SR	SR	SR	SR	SR	SR	SR	SR	SR	XC
	◇1	1			◇1	◇	◇1	◇1	◇1	◇1	◇1	1	◇1	◇	◇		◇1	◇1	◇1	◇1	◇	◇1
		A							B	C		A					D	E		F		G
Edinburgh 10 242 d		16 34	16 36	17 00	17 38			17 41	18 11	18 11		18 33		18 37	19 01		19 30	19 30		19 41	20 00	20 14
Haymarket 242 d		16 39	16 41	17 05	17 42			17u46	18 15	18 15		18 38		18 41	19 05		19 34	19 34		19 45	20 04	20 18
Edinburgh Gateway d			16 46	17 10				17 51						18 51	19 11					19 51	20 11	
Inverkeithing 242 d			16 57	17 21					18 29	18 29		18 55		19 01	19 21					20 01	20 25	20 35
Kirkcaldy 242 d			17 13	17 37				18 17	18 44	18 44		19 13		19 19	19 37					20 17	20 47	20 52
Markinch d			17 22	17 46				18 27	18 53	18 53				19 29	19 46					20 26	20 56	21 02
Ladybank d			17 29	17 53				18 34	19 00	19 00				19 36	19 53					20 34	21 03	21 10
Springfield d				17 58																		
Cupar d				18 02	18 27				19 07	19 07					20 00		20 22	20 22			21 09	21 20
Leuchars 8 a				18 09	18 33				19 13	19 13		19 39			20 06		20 29	20 29			21 16	21 26
St Andrews Bus Station a																						
St Andrews Bus Station d																						
Leuchars 8 d				18 09	18 34				19 14	19 14		19 40			20 07		20 29	20 29			21 16	21 28
Glasgow Queen St. 10 230 d	16 41					17 04	17 41				18 11		18 41			19 09			19 41			
Larbert 230 d						17 35					18 31											
Stirling 230 d	17 13	17 22				17 46	18 16				18 42		19 07			19 37			20 08			
Bridge of Allan 230 d						17 51					18 46					19 41						
Dunblane 230 d						17 56	18 23				18 50		19 14			19 46						
Gleneagles d		17 40				18 09	18 36				19 02		19 26			19 57						
Perth a	17 42	17 58	17 54			18 23	18 52	18 58			19 19		19 42	20 01		20 11			20 37	20 58		
d	17 43	18 01				18 25	18 55	19 00			19 23		19 43			20 12			20 38	21 01		
Invergowrie d						18 43										20 29						
Dundee a	18 05			18 25	18 47	18 52	19 17		19 29	19 29		19 53	20 04		20 23	20 38	20 42	20 42	20 59		21 32	21 43
d	18 06				18 48	18 55	19 18		19 30	19 30		19 55	20 05				20 43	20 43	21 00			
Broughty Ferry d						19 01							20 12									
Balmossie d						19 05																
Monifieth d						19 07																
Barry Links d						19 12																
Golf Street d						19 14																
Carnoustie d	18 18					19a18	19 30						20 19									
Arbroath a	18 24				19 04		19 37		19 45	19 45		20 11	20 26				20 59	20 59	21 16			
d	18 25				19 05		19 37		19 48	19 48		20 12	20 26				20 59	20 59	21 17			
Montrose a					19 22		19 51		20 01	20 03		20 27	20 40				21 13	21 13	21 31			
d					19 22		19 51		20 02	20 04		20 28	20 41				21 14	21 14	21 31			
Laurencekirk d							20 02												21 42			
Stonehaven d	18 58				19 44		20 15		20 23	20 25		20 51					21 35	21 35	21 55			
Portlethen d					19 53																	
Aberdeen a	19 18				20 07		20 35		20 42	20 44		21 11	21 22				21 55	21 55	22 15			
d																	21 56					
Dyce 240 a																	22 04					
Inverurie 240 a																	22 17					
Dunkeld & Birnam d								19 20			19 40									21 18		
Pitlochry d		18 30						19 33			19 53									21 33		
Blair Atholl d											20 02									21 42		
Dalwhinnie d											20 26									22 07		
Newtonmore d											20 36									22 17		
Kingussie d		19 15						20 16			20 41									22 22		
Aviemore d		19 28						20 27			20 53									22 34		
Carrbridge d																				22 43		
Inverness a		20 03						21 02			21 27						00 08			23 11		

A From London Kings Cross
B until 21 July, from 13 October. From Plymouth
C from 28 July until 6 October. From Southampton Central
D from 25 August. to Aberdeen
E until 18 August
F from Perth
G From Newquay

Table T229-F

Saturdays
26 May to 8 December

Edinburgh and Glasgow Queen Street - Perth, Inverness, Dundee, Aberdeen, Dyce and Inverurie

	SR	SR	SR	SR	SR	SR	SR	SR	SR
	◇1	◇	◇	◇1	◇1	◇	◇	◇	
									A
Edinburgh 10 242 d		20 37	21 05	21 43		22 10	22 37	23 09	23 13
Haymarket 242 d		20 41	21 09	21 47		22 14	22 42	23 13	23a18
Edinburgh Gateway d		20 47	21 16			22 21	22 49	23 21	
Inverkeithing 242 d		20 58	21 30			22 35	23 02	23 34	
Kirkcaldy 242 d		21 15	21 51	22 15		22 57	23 24	23 56	
Markinch d		21 24	22 00			23 06	23 33	00 05	
Ladybank d		21 31	22 08			23 13	23 40	00 12	
Springfield d						23 18			
Cupar d			22 14			23 21		00 18	
Leuchars 8 a			22 21	22 39		23 28		00 25	
St Andrews Bus Station a									
St Andrews Bus Station d									
Leuchars 8 d			22 22	22 39		23 28		00 25	
Glasgow Queen St. 10 230 d	20 41				21 42				
Larbert 230 d									
Stirling 230 d	21 08				22 08				
Bridge of Allan 230 d									
Dunblane 230 d	21 15								
Gleneagles d	21 26								
Perth a	21 42	21 56			22 37		00 05		
d	21 43				22 41				
Invergowrie d	22 00								
Dundee a	22 07		22 38	22 52	23 02	23 44		00 41	
d	22 09			22 53	23 03				
Broughty Ferry d					23 10				
Balmossie d									
Monifieth d					23 14				
Barry Links d									
Golf Street d									
Carnoustie d	22 20				23 20				
Arbroath a	22 27			23 09	23 26				
d	22 27			23 09	23 27				
Montrose a	22 41			23 23	23 41				
d	22 41			23 24	23 41				
Laurencekirk d					23 52				
Stonehaven d	23 02			23 45	00 05				
Portlethen d				23 54					
Aberdeen a	23 22			00 08	00 25				
d									
Dyce 240 a									
Inverurie 240 a									
Dunkeld & Birnam d									
Pitlochry d									
Blair Atholl d									
Dalwhinnie d									
Newtonmore d									
Kingussie d									
Aviemore d									
Carrbridge d									
Inverness a									

A To Motherwell

Table T229-F

Sundays
20 May to 2 December

Edinburgh and Glasgow Queen Street - Perth, Inverness, Dundee, Aberdeen, Dyce and Inverurie

	SR	SR	XC	SR	GR	SR	SR	SR	SR	SR	SR	SR	SR	SR	XC	SR	SR	SR	XC	SR	SR	SR
	◇■ A	◇ B	◇■	C 🚌	■	◇■	◇■	◇■	C 🚌	◇■	◇■	◇■	◇	◇■	◇■ D	C 🚌	◇■	◇■	◇■ E	◇	◇■	◇■
Edinburgh 242 d			08 04	08 11	09 10	09 15		09 33	10 21	10 50			11 32		12 17	12 21	12 41		13 13	13 34		13 56
Haymarket 242 d			08 08	08a31	09 15	09 21		09 37	10a41	10 54			11 36		12a20	12a41	12 45		13a17	13 38		14 00
Edinburgh Gateway d						09 28		09 43					11 42							13 44		14 06
Inverkeithing 242 d			08 25		09 33	09 45		09 56		11 07			11 52				12 58			13 54		14 16
Kirkcaldy 242 d			08 40		09 50	10 07		10 12		11 23			12 08				13 14			14 10		14 32
Markinch d		00 05				10 16		10 22					12 17							14 19		
Ladybank d		00 12				10 23		10 29					12 25							14 27		
Springfield d																						
Cupar d		00 18	08 58			10 30							12 31							14 33		
Leuchars ■ a		00 25	09 06		10 13	10 37				11 46			12 38				13 37			14 40		
St Andrews Bus Station 🚌 a																						
St Andrews Bus Station 🚌 d																						
Leuchars ■ d		00 25	09 07		10 14	10 37				11 47			12 39				13 38			14 41		
Glasgow Queen St. ■ 230 d							09 37				10 45	11 11		11 45				12 45			13 45	
Larbert 230 d							10 01					11 31										
Stirling 230 d							10 10				11 11	11 41		12 11				13 11			14 13	
Bridge of Allan 230 d																						
Dunblane 230 d							10 17				11 18	11 47		12 18				13 18			14 20	
Gleneagles d							10 30					11 59		12 29							14 33	
Perth a							10 46	10 54			11 41	12 16		12 45				13 41			14 49	15 09
d							10 47	10 55			11 42	12 17		12 46				13 42			14 50	15 14
Invergowrie d																						
Dundee a		00 41	09 19		10 27	10 51	11 10			12 00	12 05		12 55	13 08			13 51	14 04		14 57	15 12	
d			09 20		10 29	10 52	11 11			12 10				13 10			13 52	14 07			15 13	
Broughty Ferry d							11 18															
Balmossie d																						
Monifieth d																						
Barry Links d																						
Golf Street d																						
Carnoustie d							11 26														15 25	
Arbroath a			09 35		10 45	11 09	11 32			12 26				13 26			14 08	14 23			15 32	
d			09 36		10 46	11 09	11 32			12 27				13 26			14 08	14 23			15 32	
Montrose a			09 49		11 01	11 24	11 47			12 41				13 40			14 22	14 37			15 47	
d			09 50		11 02	11 24	11 48			12 41				13 41			14 22	14 39			15 48	
Laurencekirk d							11 59										14 33					
Stonehaven d	00 05		10 11		11 25	11 46	12 13			13 03				14 02			14 46	15 00			16 10	
Portlethen d						11 56	12 23														16 20	
Aberdeen a	00 25		10 29		11 45	12 10	12 37			13 23				14 22			15 06	15 20			16 33	
d																						
Dyce 240 a																						
Inverurie 240 a																						
Dunkeld & Birnam d								11 11				12 35										15 31
Pitlochry d								11 24				12 48										15 44
Blair Atholl d								11 34														15 53
Dalwhinnie d								11 58														16 22
Newtonmore d								12 08														16 32
Kingussie d								12 13				13 36										16 37
Aviemore d								12 25				13 48										16 49
Carrbridge d								12 33				14 01										16 58
Inverness a								13 02				14 29										17 27

A not 20 May. From Glasgow Queen Street
B not 20 May. From Edinburgh
C To Livingston South
D until 9 September. From Leeds to Motherwell
E until 9 September. From Sheffield to Motherwell

Table T229-F

Sundays
20 May to 2 December

Edinburgh and Glasgow Queen Street - Perth, Inverness, Dundee, Aberdeen, Dyce and Inverurie

	SR	GR	SR	SR	XC	SR	SR	SR	SR	SR	SR	GR	SR	XC	SR	SR	SR	SR	XC	SR	GR	SR
	A 🚌	■ B	◇■ C	◇■	◇■ D		◇■	◇■	◇■	A 🚌	◇■	■ E	◇■	◇■ F		◇■ G	◇	◇■ C	◇■ H	A 🚌	■ I	◇
Edinburgh 242 d	14 21	14 33			15 10	15 34		15 50	16 05	16 21		16 32	17 05	17 11	17 34		17 50		18 13	18 21	18 36	19 15
Haymarket 242 d	14a41	14 39			15a13	15 38		15 54	16 09	16a41		16 37	17 09	17a14	17 38		17 54		18 16	18a41	18 41	19 19
Edinburgh Gateway d						15 44		16 00							17 44		18 00					19 26
Inverkeithing 242 d		14 54				15 54		16 10	16 24				17 23		17 54		18 10		18 30		18 56	19 40
Kirkcaldy 242 d		15 11				16 10		16 26	16 40				17 39		18 10		18 26		18 45		19 13	20 02
Markinch d						16 21		16 35	16 49						18 19		18 36		18 54			20 11
Ladybank d						16 28		16 43							18 27				19 02			20 18
Springfield d																						
Cupar d						16 35			17 02						18 33				19 08			20 25
Leuchars ■ a		15 34				16 42			17 09				18 03		18 40				19 14		19 36	20 32
St Andrews Bus Station 🚌 a																						
St Andrews Bus Station 🚌 d																						
Leuchars ■ d		15 36				16 42			17 09				18 04		18 41				19 15		19 37	20 32
Glasgow Queen St. ■ 230 d			14 38	14 49			15 45				16 45					17 45		18 11				
Larbert 230 d			14 58															18 31				
Stirling 230 d			15 07	15 18			16 12				17 11	17 25				18 13		18 41				
Bridge of Allan 230 d																						
Dunblane 230 d			15 14	15 28			16 18											18 47				
Gleneagles d			15 26				16 30					17 42						18 59				
Perth a			15 43	15 51			16 46	17 07			17 38	17 59				18 44	19 06	19 16				
d			15 46	15 52			16 47	17 08			17 40	18 04				18 45		19 17				
Invergowrie d																						
Dundee a		15 51		16 14		16 58	17 09		17 22		18 01		18 17		18 57	19 08			19 29		19 50	20 48
d		15 52		16 15			17 10		17 23		18 02		18 18			19 09			19 31		19 52	
Broughty Ferry d									17 30													
Balmossie d																						
Monifieth d																						
Barry Links d																						
Golf Street d																						
Carnoustie d									17 38													
Arbroath a		16 08		16 31			17 26		17 44		18 18		18 34			19 26			19 46		20 08	
d		16 10		16 31			17 26		17 44		18 19		18 35			19 26			19 47		20 09	
Montrose a		16 24		16 45			17 40		17 59		18 36		18 50			19 41			20 00		20 24	
d		16 26		16 45			17 41		18 00		18 37		18 50			19 42			20 01		20 25	
Laurencekirk d							17 52									19 53						
Stonehaven d		16 49		17 07			18 05		18 22		18 58		19 12			20 07			20 23		20 48	
Portlethen d													19 21									
Aberdeen a		17 06		17 26			18 25		18 42		19 18		19 35			20 27			20 42		21 08	
d																						
Dyce 240 a																						
Inverurie 240 a																						
Dunkeld & Birnam d								17 25										19 33				
Pitlochry d			16 13					17 38				18 35						19 46				
Blair Atholl d																		19 56				
Dalwhinnie d																		20 20				
Newtonmore d																		20 31				
Kingussie d			16 57					18 22				19 20						20 36				
Aviemore d			17 10					18 33				19 34						20 47				
Carrbridge d																		20 56				
Inverness a			17 45					19 08				20 09						21 25				

A To Livingston South
B From London Kings Cross. The Northern Lights
C To Elgin
D until 9 September. From Birmingham New Street to Motherwell
E From London Kings Cross. The Highland Chieftain
F until 9 September. From Bristol Temple Meads to Motherwell
G to Dundee
H From Plymouth
I From London Kings Cross

Table T229-F

Sundays

20 May to 2 December

Edinburgh and Glasgow Queen Street - Perth, Inverness, Dundee, Aberdeen, Dyce and Inverurie

		XC		SR	SR	SR	XC	SR	SR	SR
		◇■		◇■		◇■	◇■	◇■	◇	
		A		B	C		D			
				✠	🚌			✠		
Edinburgh ■ 242	d	19 18			20 21	21 00	21 12		22 26	23 34
Haymarket 242	d	19a22			20a41	21 05	21a16		22 30	23 38
Edinburgh Gateway	d								22 37	23 45
Inverkeithing 242	d					21 19			22 51	23a58
Kirkcaldy 242	d					21 35			23 13	
Markinch	d					21 44			23 22	
Ladybank	d					21 51			23 29	
Springfield	d									
Cupar	d					21 58			23 36	
Leuchars ■	a					22 05			23 43	
St Andrews Bus Station 🚌	a									
St Andrews Bus Station 🚌	d									
Leuchars ■	d					22 05			23 43	
Glasgow Queen St. ■ 230	d			19 45				21 45		
Larbert 230	d									
Stirling 230	d			20 12				22 12		
Bridge of Allan 230	d									
Dunblane 230	d			20 18				22 18		
Gleneagles	d			20 30				22 30		
Perth	a			20 46				22 46		
	d			20 47				22 47		
Invergowrie	d									
Dundee	a			21 09				23 09	23 59	
	d			21 10				23 10		
Broughty Ferry	d					22 28				
Balmossie	d									
Monifieth	d									
Barry Links	d									
Golf Street	d									
Carnoustie	d							23 22		
Arbroath	a			21 26		22 40		23 29		
	d			21 26		22 40		23 29		
Montrose	a			21 40		22 54		23 43		
	d			21 41		22 55		23 44		
Laurencekirk	d			21 52						
Stonehaven	d			22 05		23 16		00 05		
Portlethen	d					23 25				
Aberdeen	a			22 25		23 39		00 25		
	d									
Dyce 240 ✈	a									
Inverurie 240	a									
Dunkeld & Birnam	d									
Pitlochry	d									
Blair Atholl	d									
Dalwhinnie	d									
Newtonmore	d									
Kingussie	d									
Aviemore	d									
Carrbridge	d									
Inverness	a									

A until 9 September. From Plymouth to Motherwell
B ✠ from Dundee
C To Livingston South
D until 9 September. From Penzance to Motherwell

Table T229-R

Mondays to Fridays

21 May to 7 December

Inverurie, Dyce, Aberdeen, Dundee, Inverness and Perth - Glasgow Queen Street and Edinburgh

Miles	Miles	Miles	Miles	Miles			GR	SR	SR	SR	SR	SR	XC	XC	SR		SR	SR	SR	SR	SR	SR	SR	SR	SR
							■	◇	◇	◇	◇		◇■	◇■					◇■	◇■	◇		◇	◇■	◇
							A						B	C											
							🍴						✠											✠	
—	—	0	0	0	**Inverness**	d																	05 36		
—	—	28	28	28	Carrbridge	d																			
—	—	34¾	34¾	34¾	Aviemore	d																	06 12		
—	—	46½	46½	46½	Kingussie	d																	06 27		
—	—	49¼	49¼	49¼	Newtonmore	d																			
—	—	59½	59½	59½	Dalwhinnie	d																	06 40		
—	—	82¾	82¾	82¾	Blair Atholl	d																	07 12		
—	—	89½	89½	89½	Pitlochry	d																	07 26		
—	—	102½	102½	102½	Dunkeld & Birnam	d																	07 39		
0	0	—	—	—	**Inverurie** 240	d																			
10¾	10¾	—	—	—	Dyce 240 ✈	d																			
17	17	—	—	—	**Aberdeen** 240	a																			
—	—	—	—	—		d													05 26	05 46				06 34	
27	27	—	—	—	Portlethen	d													05 37					06 44	
33	33	—	—	—	Stonehaven	d													05 46	06 03				06 53	
47½	47½	—	—	—	Laurencekirk	d													06 00						
57½	57½	—	—	—	Montrose	a													06 10	06 24				07 14	
—	—	—	—	—		d													06 11	06 24				07 15	
71¼	71¼	—	—	—	Arbroath	a													06 25	06 38				07 28	
—	—	—	—	—		d													06 26	06 38				07 28	
77½	77½	—	—	—	Carnoustie	d						06 03								06 45				07 35	
78	78	—	—	—	Golf Street	d						06 05													
79	79	—	—	—	Barry Links	d						06 08													
82	82	—	—	—	Monifieth	d						06 12													
82¾	82¾	—	—	—	Balmossie	d						06 15													
84½	84½	—	—	—	Broughty Ferry	d						06 18												07 42	
88¼	88¼	—	—	—	**Dundee**	a						06 26							06 46	06 57				07 52	
—	—	—	—	—		d				05 53	06 05		06 32	06 32					06 50	06 58	07 09	07 38		07 53	08 17
92¼	—	—	—	100¾	Invergowrie	d				05 58															08 22
109½	—	118	118	118	**Perth**	a				06 17									07 12				07 57	08 13	08 40
—	—	—	—	—		d		05 13	05 18	06 20					06 39		06 56	07 01	07 15				08 01	08 14	08 41
125	—	133¾	—	133¾	Gleneagles	d			05 33	06 35					06 54			07 17	07 30					08 29	08 56
136½	—	146	—	146	Dunblane 230	d			05 46	06 47					07 08			07 31	07 44						09 07
139	—	148	—	148	Bridge of Allan 230	d			05 49	06 50					07 11			07 34	07 48						09 10
142½	—	151½	—	151½	Stirling 230	d	05 26		05 54	06 55					07 17			07 39	07 53					08 45	09 15
150½	—	159½	—	159½	Larbert 230	d			06 03	07 04					07 26			07 47	08 03						
172	—	180½	—	—	**Glasgow Queen St.** ■ 230	a			06 35	07 34								08 19	08 34					09 15	09 45
—	96½	—	—	—	Leuchars ■	a					06 17		06 44	06 44						07 11	07 22	07 50			
—	—	—	—	—	St Andrews Bus Station 🚌	a																			
—	—	—	—	—	St Andrews Bus Station 🚌	d																			
—	—	—	—	—	Leuchars ■	d					06 18		06 46	06 46						07 11	07 23	07 51			
—	102¾	—	—	—	Cupar	d					06 25		06 54	06 54						07 19	07 30	07 59			
—	105	—	—	—	Springfield	d															07 35				
—	108½	—	135¾	—	Ladybank	d		05 38			06 33		07 03	07 03			07 30				07 39		08 22		
—	114¼	—	141	—	Markinch	d		05 46			06 40		07 11	07 11			07 37				07 47	08 12	08 30		
—	121½	—	149	—	Kirkcaldy 242	d		05 55			06 50		07 21	07 21			07 46			07 41	07 57	08 21	08 40		
—	134½	—	161¾	—	Inverkeithing 242	d		06 18			07 12		07 40	07 40			08 02				08 19	08 37	08 56		
—	142	—	169½	—	Edinburgh Gateway	d		06 32			07 25						08 13				08 31	08 48	09 08		
—	146¼	—	173¾	186½	Haymarket 242	a	06 11	06 42			07 34		07 57	07 57	08 12		08 25			08 18	08 39	08 57	09 19		
—	147½	—	175	187¾	**Edinburgh** ■ 242	a	06 17	06 47			07 39		08 04	08 04	08 17		08 30			08 23	08 44	09 03	09 24		

A To London Kings Cross
B from 23 July until 5 October. To Reading
C until 20 July, from 8 October. To Plymouth

Table T229-R

Inverurie, Dyce, Aberdeen, Dundee, Inverness and Perth - Glasgow Queen Street and Edinburgh

	SR	SR	SR	SR	SR	SR	GR	XC	XC	SR	GR
	◇1	◇1	◇	◇1	◇1	◇1	■ 1	◇1	■ 1	◇	■ 1
	A	B			C	D	E	F	G		H
	🛒	🛒		🛒	🛒	🛒	🍽	🛒			🍽
Inverness d	04 53			06 50							07 55
Carrbridge d											
Aviemore d				07 25							08 31
Kingussie d				07 37							08 43
Newtonmore d											
Dalwhinnie d											
Blair Atholl d											
Pitlochry d				08 18							09 25
Dunkeld & Birnam d				08 30							
Inverurie 240 d	06 37				07 13						
Dyce 240 ✈ d	06 51				07 26						
Aberdeen 240 a	07 02				07 36						
d	07 03	07 03			07 39	07 39	07 52	08 20	08 20		
Portlethen d											
Stonehaven d	07 20	07 20			07 56	07 56	08 10	08 38	08 38		
Laurencekirk d	07 33	07 33									
Montrose a	07 43	07 43			08 17	08 17	08 31	08 57	08 57		
d	07 44	07 44			08 17	08 17	08 33	08 59	08 59		
Arbroath a	07 57	07 57			08 31	08 31	08 48	09 14	09 14		
d	07 58	07 58			08 31	08 31	08 49	09 15	09 15		
Carnoustie d	08 05	08 05			08 38	08 38					
Golf Street d											
Barry Links d											
Monifieth d	08 10	08 10									
Balmossie d											
Broughty Ferry d											
Dundee a	08 19	08 19			08 53	08 53	09 05	09 31	09 31		
d	08 20	08 20	08 29		08 54	08 54	09 07	09 35	09 35	09 44	
Invergowrie d											
Perth a				08 49	09 14	09 14					09 55
d				08 50	09 15	09 15					09 57
Gleneagles d											10 13
Dunblane 230 d											
Bridge of Allan 230 d											
Stirling 230 d					09 43	09 43					10 32
Larbert 230 d											
Glasgow Queen St. 10 230 ⛴ a					10 17	10 17					
Leuchars 5 a			08 41				09 19	09 47	09 47	09 57	
St Andrews Bus Station 🚌 a											
St Andrews Bus Station 🚌 d											
Leuchars 5 d			08 42				09 21	09 48	09 48	09 57	
Cupar d			08 49					09 55	09 55	10 05	
Springfield d											
Ladybank d			08 57					10 02	10 02	10 12	
Markinch d			09 04					10 09	10 09	10 20	
Kirkcaldy 242 d			09 13	09 26			09 45	10 18	10 18	10 29	
Inverkeithing 242 d			09 35				10 01	10 33	10 33	10 46	
Edinburgh Gateway ⛴✈ d			09 46	09 51						10 57	
Haymarket 242 ⛴ a	09 24	09 24	09 54	10 03			10 19	10 49	10 49	11 07	11 11
Edinburgh 10 242 a	09 29	09 29	09 59	10 11			10 25	10 55	10 55	11 13	11 17

	SR	SR	SR	SR	SR	SR	SR	SR	GR	SR
	◇	◇1	◇1	◇1	◇	◇	◇1	◇1	■ 1	◇
							A	B	E	
		🛒	🛒	🛒			🛒	🛒	🍽	
Inverness d			08 45							
Carrbridge d			09 16							
Aviemore d			09 24							
Kingussie d			09 36							
Newtonmore d			09 40							
Dalwhinnie d										
Blair Atholl d										
Pitlochry d			10 22							
Dunkeld & Birnam d			10 33							
Inverurie 240 d										
Dyce 240 ✈ d							09 07			
Aberdeen 240 a							09 17			
d		08 42		09 07			09 35	09 35	09 52	
Portlethen d							09 45	09 45		
Stonehaven d							09 54	09 54	10 10	
Laurencekirk d				09 35						
Montrose a		09 17		09 45			10 15	10 15	10 31	
d		09 18		09 46			10 16	10 16	10 33	
Arbroath a		09 31		09 59			10 29	10 29	10 48	
d		09 32		10 00			10 30	10 30	10 49	
Carnoustie d		09 39					10 36	10 36		
Golf Street d										
Barry Links d										
Monifieth d										
Balmossie d										
Broughty Ferry d							10 44	10 44		
Dundee a		09 53		10 15			10 53	10 53	11 05	
d		09 54		10 17	10 30		10 54	10 54	11 07	11 29
Invergowrie d										
Perth a		10 15	10 54				11 15	11 15		
d	10 03	10 16	10 56			11 02	11 16	11 16		
Gleneagles d			11 10							
Dunblane 230 d			11 22							
Bridge of Allan 230 d			11 25							
Stirling 230 d		10 44	11 29				11 44	11 44		
Larbert 230 d										
Glasgow Queen St. 10 230 ⛴ a		11 16	12 13				12 16	12 16		
Leuchars 5 a				10 29	10 42				11 20	11 41
St Andrews Bus Station 🚌 a										
St Andrews Bus Station 🚌 d										
Leuchars 5 d				10 30	10 43				11 23	11 42
Cupar d					10 50					11 49
Springfield d										
Ladybank d	10 24				10 57	11 24				11 56
Markinch d	10 32				11 04	11 32				12 03
Kirkcaldy 242 d	10 42				11 14	11 41			11 47	12 13
Inverkeithing 242 d	11 03				11 30	11 57			12 03	12 29
Edinburgh Gateway ⛴✈ d	11 15				11 41	12 08				12 40
Haymarket 242 ⛴ a	11 23			11 30	11 49	12 17			12 20	12 48
Edinburgh 10 242 a	11 29			11 35	11 54	12 22			12 26	12 53

A from 20 August. 🛒 from Aberdeen
B until 17 August
C from 20 August. Forms booked connection out of 1B08.. 🛒 from Aberdeen
D until 17 August. Forms booked connection out of 1B08.
E To London Kings Cross
F from 23 July until 5 October. To Guildford
G until 20 July, from 8 October. To Penzance
H To London Kings Cross. The Highland Chieftain

Table T229-R

Inverurie, Dyce, Aberdeen, Dundee, Inverness and Perth - Glasgow Queen Street and Edinburgh

	SR	SR	SR	SR	SR	SR	SR	SR	SR	SR	SR
	◇1	◇1	◇	◇1	◇1	◇	◇1	◇1	◇1	◇	◇
				A	B				A	B	
	🛒	🛒		🛒	🛒		🛒	🛒	🛒	🛒	
Inverness d	09 41						10 45				
Carrbridge d											
Aviemore d	10 27						11 23				
Kingussie d	10 39						11 36				
Newtonmore d											
Dalwhinnie d	10 53										
Blair Atholl d	11 15										
Pitlochry d	11 25						12 24				
Dunkeld & Birnam d	11 37						12 37				
Inverurie 240 d				10 38					11 34		
Dyce 240 ✈ d				10 50					11 46		
Aberdeen 240 a				11 00					11 56		
d		10 38		11 03	11 03			11 42	12 05	12 05	
Portlethen d									12 15	12 15	
Stonehaven d				11 20	11 20				12 24	12 24	
Laurencekirk d				11 34	11 34						
Montrose a		11 13		11 44	11 44			12 17			
d		11 14		11 44	11 44			12 18			
Arbroath a		11 27		11 58	11 58			12 31	12 58	12 58	
d		11 28		11 58	11 58			12 32	12 58	12 58	
Carnoustie d		11 35						12 39			
Golf Street d											
Barry Links d											
Monifieth d											
Balmossie d											
Broughty Ferry d											
Dundee a		11 49		12 15	12 15			12 53	13 14	13 14	
d		11 50	12 13	12 17	12 17	12 36		12 54	13 20	13 20	13 33
Invergowrie d			12 18								
Perth a	11 56	12 11	12 36				12 57	13 15			
d	12 02	12 12	12 38				13 02	13 16			
Gleneagles d			12 53								
Dunblane 230 d			13 05								
Bridge of Allan 230 d			13 08								
Stirling 230 d		12 43	13 13					13 44			
Larbert 230 d											
Glasgow Queen St. 10 230 ⛴ a		13 16	13 47					14 16			
Leuchars 5 a				12 29	12 29	12 48			13 32	13 32	13 45
St Andrews Bus Station 🚌 a											
St Andrews Bus Station 🚌 d											
Leuchars 5 d				12 30	12 30	12 49			13 33	13 33	13 46
Cupar d						12 56					13 53
Springfield d											
Ladybank d	12 23					13 03					14 00
Markinch d	12 31					13 10	13 31				14 07
Kirkcaldy 242 d	12 41					13 20	13 41				14 17
Inverkeithing 242 d	13 00					13 36					14 33
Edinburgh Gateway ⛴✈ d	13 11					13 46	14 09				14 43
Haymarket 242 ⛴ a	13 19			13 23	13 23	13 57	14 19		14 26	14 26	14 52
Edinburgh 10 242 a	13 24			13 28	13 28	14 04	14 25		14 33	14 33	14 57

	SR	SR	SR	SR	SR	SR	SR	SR	SR	SR	SR
	◇	◇1	◇1	◇	◇1	◇1	◇	◇1	◇	◇	◇1
		🛒	🛒		🛒	🛒		🛒			🛒
Inverness d					12 53						
Carrbridge d					13 25						
Aviemore d					13 33						
Kingussie d					13 45						
Newtonmore d					13 49						
Dalwhinnie d											
Blair Atholl d					14 21						
Pitlochry d					14 32						
Dunkeld & Birnam d					14 44						
Inverurie 240 d											
Dyce 240 ✈ d											
Aberdeen 240 a											
d		12 40	13 08			13 37		14 04			14 39
Portlethen d						13 47					
Stonehaven d		12 56	13 25			13 56		14 21			
Laurencekirk d		13 10						14 35			
Montrose a		13 20	13 46			14 17					15 14
d		13 20	13 46			14 18					15 15
Arbroath a		13 34	14 00			14 31		14 57			15 28
d		13 34	14 00			14 32		14 58			15 29
Carnoustie d						14 39					15 36
Golf Street d											
Barry Links d											
Monifieth d											
Balmossie d											
Broughty Ferry d								15 09			
Dundee a		13 53	14 16			14 53		15 15			15 50
d		13 54	14 17	14 34		14 54	15 13	15 17	15 33		15 51
Invergowrie d							15 18				
Perth a		14 14			15 03	15 15	15 36				16 12
d	14 02	14 15			15 04	15 16	15 37			16 00	16 13
Gleneagles d							15 52				
Dunblane 230 d							16 06				
Bridge of Allan 230 d							16 09				
Stirling 230 d		14 44				15 44	16 14				16s41
Larbert 230 d											
Glasgow Queen St. 10 230 ⛴ a		15 18				16 17	16 52				17 17
Leuchars 5 a			14 30	14 46				15 29	15 46		
St Andrews Bus Station 🚌 a											
St Andrews Bus Station 🚌 d											
Leuchars 5 d			14 30	14 47				15 30	15 47		
Cupar d				14 54					15 54		
Springfield d											
Ladybank d	14 23			15 01					16 01	16 21	
Markinch d	14 31			15 08	15 31				16 08	16 29	
Kirkcaldy 242 d	14 41			15 18	15 41				16 18	16 39	
Inverkeithing 242 d	14 57			15 34	15 58				16 34	16 55	
Edinburgh Gateway ⛴✈ d	15 10			15 44	16 09				16 44	17 06	
Haymarket 242 ⛴ a	15 18		15 25	15 53	16 17			16 23	16 53	17 14	
Edinburgh 10 242 a	15 24		15 30	15 58	16 22			16 28	17 00	17 19	

A from 20 August. 🛒 from Aberdeen
B until 17 August

Table T229-R

Mondays to Fridays
21 May to 7 December

Inverurie, Dyce, Aberdeen, Dundee, Inverness and Perth - Glasgow Queen Street and Edinburgh

		SR	GR	SR	SR	SR	SR	SR	SR	SR	SR	SR	SR	SR	SR	SR	SR	SR	SR	SR	GR	SR
		◇1	B 1	◇	◇1	◇	◇	◇1	◇1	◇	◇1	◇1	1	◇1	◇1	◇	◇	◇1	◇	◇1	B 1	◇
			A	B			C	D	E					D	E				F		G	
		🛒	🍴		🛒			🛒	🛒		🛒	🛒		🛒	🛒			🛒	🛒	🛒	🍴	
Inverness	d	14 47									15 51								15 29	17 30		
Carrbridge	d										16 27									18 07		
Aviemore	d	15 23									16 35									18 14		
Kingussie	d	15 35									16 47									18 26		
Newtonmore	d										16 51											
Dalwhinnie	d	15 48																				
Blair Atholl	d										17 23											
Pitlochry	d	16 18									17 33									19 07		
Dunkeld & Birnam	d	16 33									17 45									19 20		
Inverurie 240	d							15 24											17 19			
Dyce 240 ✈	d							15 38						16 39					17 35			
Aberdeen 240	a							15 48						16 50					17 46			
	d		14 52		15 33			16 02	16 02			16 27	16 36	17 09	17 09			17 36	17 47		18 18	
Portlethen	d												16 47						17 59			
Stonehaven	d		15 10		15 49			16 19	16 19			16u45	16a58					17 53	18a07		18 36	
Laurencekirk	d							16 32	16 32					17 39	17 39			18 07				
Montrose	a		15 31		16 10							17 08		17 51	17 51			18 17			18 57	
	d		15 33		16 10							17 10		17 51	17 51			18 17			18 59	
Arbroath	a		15 48		16 24			16 55	16 55			17 24		18 05	18 05			18 31			19 14	
	d		15 49		16 24			16 55	16 55			17 26		18 05	18 05	18 20		18 32			19 15	
Carnoustie	d							17 02	17 02							18 27		18 39				
Golf Street	d																					
Barry Links	d																					
Monifieth	d															18 33						
Balmossie	d																					
Broughty Ferry	d				16 36											18 37						
Dundee	a		16 05		16 45			17 16	17 16			17 45		18 20	18 20	18 43		18 53			19 31	
	d		16 07		16 46	16 51		17 17	17 17	17 34		17 48		18 23	18 23	18 44		18 54			19 33	
Invergowrie	d				16 52																	
Perth	a	16 53			17 11						18 04	18 11						19 15		19 39		
	d	16 54		17 03	17 12						18 06	18 14					19 10	19 16		19 42		20 02
Gleneagles	d	17 09			17 26															19 57		
Dunblane 230	d	17 21			17 38							18 38								20 08		
Bridge of Allan 230	d	17 24																		20 11		
Stirling 230	d	17 29			17 44							18 44						19 45		20 16		
Larbert 230	d																					
Glasgow Queen St. 10 230 ⛴	a	18 10			18 21							19 17						20 15		20 46		
Leuchars 5	a		16 19			17 03		17 30	17 30	17 47				18 35	18 35	18 57					19 45	
St Andrews Bus Station 🚌	a																					
St Andrews Bus Station 🚌	d																					
Leuchars 5	d		16 22			17 04		17 31	17 31	17 47				18 36	18 36	18 57					19 47	
Cupar	d					17 11				17 54						19 04						
Springfield	d						←			17 59												
Ladybank	d			17 24		17 19	17 24			18 03	18 27					19 12	19 32					20 24
Markinch	d			→		17 26	17 32			18 11	18 35					19 19	19 40					20 32
Kirkcaldy 242	d		16 46			17 36	17 47			18 20	18 44					19 28	19 50				20 11	20 41
Inverkeithing 242	d		17 03			17 58	18 05			18 36	19 00					19 44	20 06				20 27	20 57
Edinburgh Gateway ⛴✈	d					18 12	18 17			18 47	19 11					19 55	20 17					21 08
Haymarket 242 ⛴	a		17 20			18 21	18 26	18 29	18 29	18 55	19 19			19 29	19 29	20 03	20 28				20 44	21 17
Edinburgh 10 242	a		17 26			18 28	18 31	18 34	18 34	19 03	19 24			19 34	19 34	20 09	20 33				20 50	21 22

A To London Kings Cross
B To Edinburgh
C From Perth
D from 20 August. 🛒 from Aberdeen
E until 17 August
F from 20 August
G To Leeds

Table T229-R

Mondays to Fridays
21 May to 7 December

Inverurie, Dyce, Aberdeen, Dundee, Inverness and Perth - Glasgow Queen Street and Edinburgh

		SR	SR	SR	SR	SR	SR	SR	SR	SR	SR	SR	SR	XC	SR	SR
											FO	FX			FX	FO
		◇1	◇1	◇1	◇	◇1	◇1	◇1	◇1	◇1	◇	◇1	◇1	◇1	1	1
			A	B				A	B							
		🛒	🛒	🛒		🛒	🛒	🛒	🛒							
Inverness	d					18 45					20 15	20 15				
Carrbridge	d					19 16					21 00	21 00				
Aviemore	d					19 28					21 08	21 08				
Kingussie	d					19 40					21 20	21 20				
Newtonmore	d					19 45					21 24	21 24				
Dalwhinnie	d					19 57					21 36	21 36				
Blair Atholl	d					20 19					21 57	21 57				
Pitlochry	d					20 29					22 07	22 07				
Dunkeld & Birnam	d					20 42					22 19	22 19				
Inverurie 240	d		18 45					19 46								
Dyce 240 ✈	d		18 58					19 57								
Aberdeen 240	a		19 08					20 08								
	d	18 28	19 11	19 11			19 46	20 09	20 09	20 42			21 04	21 31	22 26	23 23
Portlethen	d	18 39					19 56								22 37	23 34
Stonehaven	d	18 49	19 28	19 28			20 05	20 25	20 25	20 59			21 21	21 49	22 46	23 43
Laurencekirk	d		19 42	19 42									21 34		22 59	23 56
Montrose	a	19 10	19 52	19 52			20 26	20 46	20 46	21 20			21 44	22 11	23 09	00 06
	d	19 12	19 52	19 52			20 27	20 46	20 46	21 20			21 45	22 12	23 10	00 07
Arbroath	a	19 26	20 06	20 06			20 41	21 00	21 00	21 34			21 58	22 27	23 24	00 21
	d	19 26	20 06	20 06			20 41	21 00	21 00	21 34			21 59	22 28	23 24	00 21
Carnoustie	d	19 33						21 07	21 07						23 31	00 28
Golf Street	d															
Barry Links	d															
Monifieth	d															
Balmossie	d															
Broughty Ferry	d														23 38	00 35
Dundee	a	19 48	20 22	20 22			21 00	21 18	21 18	21 55			22 14	22 44	23 48	00 45
	d	19 49	20 23	20 23	20 42		21 01	21 19	21 19	21 56			22 16	22 48	23 49	00 46
Invergowrie	d														23 54	00 51
Perth	a	20 09				21 00	21 21			22 16	22 37	22 37			00 12	01 10
	d	20 11				21 06	21 22			22 17	22 38	22 38				
Gleneagles	d	20 26								22 32						
Dunblane 230	d										23 02	23 02				
Bridge of Allan 230	d										23 05	23 05				
Stirling 230	d	20 42					21 50			22 48	23 10	23 10				
Larbert 230	d															
Glasgow Queen St. 10 230 ⛴	a	21 15					22 25			23 18	23 43	23 43				
Leuchars 5	a		20 36	20 36	20 54			21 32	21 32				22 29	23 00		
St Andrews Bus Station 🚌	a															
St Andrews Bus Station 🚌	d															
Leuchars 5	d		20 36	20 36	20 55			21 32	21 32				22 29	23 01		
Cupar	d				21 02			21 39	21 39				22 36	23 08		
Springfield	d															
Ladybank	d				21 09			21 47	21 47				22 44	23 15		
Markinch	d				21 16	21 33		21 54	21 54				22 51	23 22		
Kirkcaldy 242	d				21 26	21 43		22 03	22 03				23 00	23 31		
Inverkeithing 242	d				21 48			22 25	22 25				23 22	23 46		
Edinburgh Gateway ⛴✈	d				22 02	22 08		22 39	22 39				23 36			
Haymarket 242 ⛴	a		21 29	21 29	22 10	22 18		22 48	22 48				23 46	00 02		
Edinburgh 10 242	a		21 34	21 34	22 15	22 23		22 53	22 53				23 52	00 08		

A from 20 August. 🛒 from Aberdeen
B until 17 August

Table T229-R

Saturdays
26 May to 8 December

Inverurie, Dyce, Aberdeen, Dundee, Inverness and Perth - Glasgow Queen Street and Edinburgh

	SR	SR	SR	SR	SR	SR	XC	XC	SR		SR	SR	SR	SR	SR	SR	SR	SR	SR		SR	SR	SR	SR
	■	◇		◇	◇		◇■	◇■				◇■	◇■	◇		◇	◇■	◇	◇■		◇■	◇	◇■	◇■
	A						B 🛒	C				🛒					🛒		D 🛒		E 🛒		🛒	D 🛒
Inverness d																05 36			04 53				06 50	
Carrbridge d																								
Aviemore d																06 12							07 25	
Kingussie d																06 27							07 37	
Newtonmore d																								
Dalwhinnie d																06 40								
Blair Atholl d																07 12								
Pitlochry d																07 26							08 18	
Dunkeld & Birnam d																07 39							08 30	
Inverurie 240 d																			06 37					07 13
Dyce 240 ✈ d																			06 51					07 26
Aberdeen 240 a																			07 02					07 36
d												05 26	05 46				06 34		07 03		07 03			07 39
Portlethen d												05 37					06 44							
Stonehaven d												05 46	06 03				06 53		07 20		07 20			07 56
Laurencekirk d												06 00							07 33		07 33			
Montrose a												06 10	06 24				07 14		07 43		07 43			08 17
d	00 07											06 11	06 24				07 15		07 44		07 44			08 17
Arbroath a	00 21											06 25	06 38				07 28		07 57		07 57			08 31
d	00 21											06 26	06 38				07 28		07 58		07 58			08 31
Carnoustie d	00 28					06 03							06 45				07 35		08 05		08 05			08 38
Golf Street d						06 05																		
Barry Links d						06 08																		
Monifieth d						06 12													08 10		08 10			
Balmossie d						06 15																		
Broughty Ferry d	00 35					06 18											07 42							
Dundee a	00 45					06 26						06 46	06 57				07 52		08 19		08 19			08 53
d	00 46			05 53	06 05		06 32	06 32				06 50	06 58	07 09	07 38		07 53	08 17	08 20		08 20	08 28		08 54
Invergowrie d	00 51			05 58														08 22						
Perth a	01 10			06 17								07 12				07 57	08 13	08 40					08 49	09 14
d		05 18	05 35	06 19					06 39		06 56	07 15				08 01	08 14	08 41					08 50	09 15
Gleneagles d		05 33		06 34					06 54			07 30					08 29	08 56						
Dunblane 230 d		05 46		06 47					07 08			07 44						09 07						
Bridge of Allan 230 d		05 49		06 50					07 11			07 48						09 10						
Stirling 230 d		05 54		06 55					07 17			07 53					08 45	09 15						09 43
Larbert 230 d		06 03		07 04					07 26			08 03												
Glasgow Queen St. ■ 230 a		06 35		07 34								08 34					09 15	09 45						10 17
Leuchars ■ a					06 17		06 44	06 44					07 11	07 22	07 50							08 40		
St Andrews Bus Station a																								
St Andrews Bus Station d																								
Leuchars ■ d					06 18		06 46	06 46					07 11	07 23	07 51							08 41		
Cupar d					06 25		06 54	06 54					07 19	07 30	07 59							08 48		
Springfield d														07 35										
Ladybank d			05 57		06 33		07 03	07 03			07 30			07 39		08 22						08 56		
Markinch d			06 05		06 40		07 11	07 11			07 37			07 47	08 12	08 30						09 03		
Kirkcaldy 242 d			06 14		06 50		07 21	07 21			07 46		07 41	07 57	08 21	08 40						09 12	09 25	
Inverkeithing 242 d			06 37		07 12		07 38	07 38			08 02			08 19	08 37	08 56						09 35		
Edinburgh Gateway d			06 51		07 25						08 13			08 31	08 48	09 10						09 45	09 50	
Haymarket 242 a			07 01		07 33		07 55	07 55	08 11		08 21		08 16	08 39	08 57	09 18			09 25		09 25	09 54	10 02	
Edinburgh ■ 242 a			07 06		07 39		08 01	08 01	08 16		08 26		08 21	08 45	09 02	09 24			09 30		09 30	09 59	10 10	

A From Aberdeen
B from 28 July until 6 October. To Reading
C until 21 July, from 13 October. To Plymouth
D from 25 August. 🛒 from Aberdeen
E until 18 August

Table T229-R

Saturdays
26 May to 8 December

Inverurie, Dyce, Aberdeen, Dundee, Inverness and Perth - Glasgow Queen Street and Edinburgh

	SR	GR	XC	XC	SR		GR	SR	SR	SR	SR	SR	SR	SR	SR		GR	SR	SR	SR	SR	SR	SR	SR
	◇■	■ ■	◇■	◇■	◇		■ ■	◇	◇■	◇■	◇■	◇	◇	◇■	◇■		■ ■	◇	◇■	◇■	◇	◇■	◇■	◇
	A 🛒	B 🍴	C 🛒	D			E 🍴		🛒	🛒	🛒			F 🛒	A 🛒		B 🍴		🛒	🛒		F 🛒	A 🛒	
Inverness d							07 55			08 45									09 41					
Carrbridge d										09 16														
Aviemore d							08 30			09 24									10 27					
Kingussie d							08 43			09 36									10 39					
Newtonmore d										09 40														
Dalwhinnie d																			10 53					
Blair Atholl d																			11 15					
Pitlochry d							09 25			10 22									11 25					
Dunkeld & Birnam d										10 33									11 37					
Inverurie 240 d																						10 38		
Dyce 240 ✈ d														09 07								10 50		
Aberdeen 240 a														09 17								11 00		
d	07 39	07 52	08 20	08 20					08 42		09 07			09 35	09 35		09 52			10 38		11 03	11 03	
Portlethen d														09 45	09 45									
Stonehaven d	07 56	08 10	08 38	08 38										09 54	09 54		10 10					11 20	11 20	
Laurencekirk d											09 35											11 34	11 34	
Montrose a	08 17	08 31	08 57	08 57					09 17		09 45			10 15	10 15		10 31			11 13		11 44	11 44	
d	08 17	08 33	08 59	08 59					09 18		09 46			10 16	10 16		10 33			11 14		11 44	11 44	
Arbroath a	08 31	08 48	09 14	09 14					09 31		09 59			10 29	10 29		10 48			11 27		11 58	11 58	
d	08 31	08 49	09 15	09 15					09 32		10 00			10 30	10 30		10 49			11 28		11 58	11 58	
Carnoustie d	08 38								09 39					10 36	10 36					11 35				
Golf Street d																								
Barry Links d																								
Monifieth d																								
Balmossie d																								
Broughty Ferry d														10 44	10 44									
Dundee a	08 53	09 05	09 31	09 31					09 53		10 15			10 53	10 53		11 05			11 49		12 15	12 15	
d	08 54	09 07	09 35	09 35	09 43				09 54		10 18	10 34		10 54	10 54		11 07	11 28		11 50	12 13	12 17	12 17	12 33
Invergowrie d																					12 18			
Perth a	09 14						09 54		10 15	10 54				11 15	11 15				11 56	12 11	12 36			
d	09 15						09 57	10 03	10 16	10 56			11 02	11 16	11 16				12 02	12 12	12 38			
Gleneagles d							10 13			11 10											12 53			
Dunblane 230 d										11 22											13 05			
Bridge of Allan 230 d										11 25											13 08			
Stirling 230 d	09 43						10 32		10 44	11 29				11 44	11 44					12 43	13 13			
Larbert 230 d																								
Glasgow Queen St. ■ 230 a	10 17								11 16	12 13				12 16	12 16					13 16	13 47			
Leuchars ■ a		09 19	09 47	09 47	09 56						10 30	10 46					11 20	11 40				12 29	12 29	12 45
St Andrews Bus Station a																								
St Andrews Bus Station d																								
Leuchars ■ d		09 21	09 48	09 48	09 56						10 31	10 47					11 23	11 41				12 30	12 30	12 46
Cupar d			09 55	09 55	10 03							10 54						11 48						12 53
Springfield d																								
Ladybank d			10 02	10 02	10 11			10 24				11 01	11 24					11 56	12 23					13 00
Markinch d			10 09	10 09	10 18			10 32				11 08	11 32					12 03	12 31					13 07
Kirkcaldy 242 d		09 45	10 18	10 18	10 27			10 42				11 18	11 41				11 47	12 12	12 41					13 17
Inverkeithing 242 d		10 01	10 33	10 33	10 47			11 02				11 34	11 57				12 03	12 30	12 58					13 33
Edinburgh Gateway d					10 57			11 13				11 44	12 08					12 40	13 09					13 43
Haymarket 242 a		10 19	10 49	10 49	11 08		11 11	11 21			11 24	11 58	12 17				12 20	12 48	13 17			13 23	13 23	13 52
Edinburgh ■ 242 a		10 25	10 55	10 55	11 15		11 17	11 26			11 29	12 03	12 22				12 26	12 53	13 22			13 28	13 28	13 57

A until 18 August
B To London Kings Cross
C from 28 July until 6 October. To Guildford
D until 21 July, from 13 October. To Penzance
E To London Kings Cross. The Highland Chieftain
F from 25 August. 🛒 from Aberdeen

Table T229-R

Saturdays
26 May to 8 December

Inverurie, Dyce, Aberdeen, Dundee, Inverness and Perth - Glasgow Queen Street and Edinburgh

		SR	SR	SR	SR	SR	SR	SR	SR	SR	SR	SR	SR	SR	SR	SR	SR	SR	GR	SR	SR	SR
		◇1	◇1	◇1	◇1	◇	◇	◇1	◇1	◇	◇1	◇1	◇	◇1	◇	◇	◇1	◇1	■ 1	◇	◇1	◇
				A	B														C	D		
		🚲	🚲	🚲	🚲			🚲	🚲		🚲	🚲		🚲			🚲	🚲	⊡		🚲	
Inverness	d	10 45									12 53							14 47				
Carrbridge	d										13 25											
Aviemore	d	11 23									13 33							15 23				
Kingussie	d	11 36									13 45							15 35				
Newtonmore	d										13 49											
Dalwhinnie	d																	15 48				
Blair Atholl	d										14 21											
Pitlochry	d	12 24									14 32							16 18				
Dunkeld & Birnam	d	12 37									14 44							16 33				
Inverurie 240	d			11 34																		
Dyce 240 ✈	d			11 46																		
Aberdeen 240	a			11 56																		
	d		11 42	12 05	12 05			12 40	13 08			13 37		14 04			14 39		14 52		15 33	
Portlethen	d			12 15	12 15							13 47										
Stonehaven	d			12 24	12 24			12 56	13 25			13 56		14 21					15 10		15 49	
Laurencekirk	d							13 10						14 35								
Montrose	a		12 17					13 20	13 46			14 17					15 14		15 31		16 10	
	d		12 18					13 20	13 46			14 18					15 15		15 33		16 10	
Arbroath	a		12 31	12 58	12 58			13 34	14 00			14 31		14 57			15 28		15 48		16 24	
	d		12 32	12 58	12 58			13 34	14 00			14 32		14 58			15 29		15 49		16 24	
Carnoustie	d		12 39									14 39					15 36					
Golf Street	d																					
Barry Links	d																					
Monifieth	d																					
Balmossie	d																					
Broughty Ferry	d													15 09							16 36	
Dundee	a		12 53	13 14	13 14			13 53	14 16			14 53		15 15			15 50		16 05		16 45	
	d		12 54	13 17	13 17	13 34		13 54	14 17	14 34		14 54	15 13	15 17	15 34		15 51		16 07		16 46	16 50
Invergowrie	d												15 18								16 52	
Perth	a	12 57	13 15					14 14			15 03	15 15	15 36				16 12	16 53			17 11	
	d	13 02	13 16				14 02	14 15			15 04	15 16	15 37			16 00	16 13	16 54		17 03	17 12	
Gleneagles	d												15 52					17 09			17 26	
Dunblane 230	d												16 06					17 21			17 38	
Bridge of Allan 230	d												16 09					17 24				
Stirling 230	d		13 44					14 44				15 44	16 14				16s41	17 29			17 44	
Larbert 230	d																					
Glasgow Queen St. 10 230 ⛴	a		14 16					15 18				16 17	16 48				17 17	18 10			18 17	
Leuchars 5	a			13 29	13 29	13 46			14 30	14 46				15 29	15 46				16 19			17 02
St Andrews Bus Station 🚌	a																					
St Andrews Bus Station 🚌	d																					
Leuchars 5	d			13 30	13 30	13 47			14 30	14 47				15 30	15 47				16 22			17 03
Cupar	d					13 54				14 54					15 54							17 10
Springfield	d																					
Ladybank	d					14 01	14 23			15 01					16 01	16 21				17 24		17 18
Markinch	d	13 31				14 08	14 31			15 08	15 31				16 08	16 29				↪		17 25
Kirkcaldy 242	d	13 41				14 18	14 41			15 18	15 41				16 18	16 39			16 46			17 35
Inverkeithing 242	d					14 34	14 58			15 34	15 59				16 34	16 55			17 03			17 57
Edinburgh Gateway ⛴✈	d	14 09				14 44	15 10			15 44	16 10				16 44	17 06						18 11
Haymarket 242 ⛴	a	14 17		14 23	14 23	14 53	15 18		15 23	15 53	16 18			16 23	16 53	17 14			17 20			18 20
Edinburgh 10 242	a	14 24		14 28	14 28	14 58	15 23		15 29	15 58	16 23			16 28	16 58	17 20			17 26			18 25

A from 25 August. 🚲 from Aberdeen
B until 18 August
C To London Kings Cross
D To Edinburgh

Table T229-R

Saturdays
26 May to 8 December

Inverurie, Dyce, Aberdeen, Dundee, Inverness and Perth - Glasgow Queen Street and Edinburgh

		SR	SR	SR	SR	SR	SR	SR	SR	SR	SR	SR	SR	SR	SR	SR	SR	SR	SR	SR	SR	SR	SR
		◇	◇1	◇1	◇	◇1	◇1	◇1	◇1	◇		◇	◇1	◇1	◇1	◇	◇1	◇1	◇1	◇	◇1	◇1	◇1
		A	B	C				B	C									B	C				B
			🚲	🚲		🚲	🚲	🚲	🚲				🚲	🚲	🚲		🚲	🚲	🚲		🚲	🚲	🚲
Inverness	d					15 51								17 30							18 45		
Carrbridge	d					16 27								18 07							19 16		
Aviemore	d					16 35								18 14							19 28		
Kingussie	d					16 47								18 26							19 40		
Newtonmore	d					16 51															19 45		
Dalwhinnie	d																				19 57		
Blair Atholl	d					17 23															20 19		
Pitlochry	d					17 33								19 07							20 29		
Dunkeld & Birnam	d					17 45								19 20							20 42		
Inverurie 240	d		15 24					16 38										18 45					19 46
Dyce 240 ✈	d		15 38					16 53										18 58					19 57
Aberdeen 240	a		15 48					17 03										19 08					20 08
	d		16 02	16 02			16 36	17 09	17 09				17 36		18 18		18 28	19 11	19 11			19 46	20 09
Portlethen	d						16 46										18 39					19 56	
Stonehaven	d		16 19	16 19			16 55						17 53		18 36		18 49	19 28	19 28			20 05	20 25
Laurencekirk	d		16 32	16 32				17 39	17 39				18 07					19 42	19 42				
Montrose	a						17 16	17 51	17 51				18 17		18 57		19 10	19 52	19 52			20 26	20 46
	d						17 17	17 51	17 51				18 17		18 59		19 12	19 52	19 52			20 27	20 46
Arbroath	a		16 55	16 55			17 30	18 05	18 05				18 31		19 14		19 26	20 06	20 06			20 41	21 00
	d		16 55	16 55			17 31	18 05	18 05	18 22			18 32		19 15		19 26	20 06	20 06			20 41	21 00
Carnoustie	d		17 02	17 02						18 28			18 39				19 33						21 07
Golf Street	d																						
Barry Links	d																						
Monifieth	d									18 34													
Balmossie	d																						
Broughty Ferry	d									18 38													
Dundee	a		17 16	17 16			17 49	18 20	18 20	18 45			18 53		19 31		19 48	20 22	20 22			21 00	21 18
	d		17 18	17 18	17 34		17 50	18 22	18 22	18 46			18 54		19 32		19 49	20 23	20 23	20 43		21 01	21 19
Invergowrie	d																						
Perth	a					18 04	18 13						19 15	19 39			20 09				21 00	21 21	
	d					18 06	18 14				18 28	19 10	19 16	19 42		20 02	20 11				21 06	21 22	
Gleneagles	d													19 57			20 26						
Dunblane 230	d						18 38				18 52			20 08									
Bridge of Allan 230	d										18 55			20 11									
Stirling 230	d						18 44				18a59		19 45	20 16			20 42					21 50	
Larbert 230	d																						
Glasgow Queen St. 10 230 ⛴	a						19 17						20 15	20 46			21 15					22 26	
Leuchars 5	a		17 30	17 30	17 47			18 34	18 34	18 58					19 44			20 36	20 36	20 55			21 32
St Andrews Bus Station 🚌	a																						
St Andrews Bus Station 🚌	d																						
Leuchars 5	d		17 31	17 31	17 47			18 35	18 35	18 59					19 46			20 36	20 36	20 56			21 32
Cupar	d				17 54					19 06										21 03			21 39
Springfield	d	←			17 59																		
Ladybank	d	17 24			18 03	18 27				19 13		19 32				20 24				21 10			21 47
Markinch	d	17 32			18 11	18 35				19 20		19 40				20 32				21 17	21 33		21 54
Kirkcaldy 242	d	17 47			18 20	18 44				19 30		19 50			20 11	20 41				21 27	21 43		22 03
Inverkeithing 242	d	18 03			18 36	19 00				19 46		20 06			20 27	20 57				21 49			22 25
Edinburgh Gateway ⛴✈	d	18 15			18 47	19 11				19 57		20 17				21 08				22 03	22 08		22 39
Haymarket 242 ⛴	a	18 24	18 27	18 27	18 55	19 20		19 28	19 28	20 05		20 26			20 43	21 17		21 30	21 30	22 12	22 16		22 49
Edinburgh 10 242	a	18 29	18 32	18 32	19 00	19 27		19 36	19 36	20 11		20 31			20 48	21 22		21 37	21 37	22 17	22 22		22 54

A From Perth
B from 25 August. 🚲 from Aberdeen
C until 18 August

Table T229-R

Saturdays
26 May to 8 December

Inverurie, Dyce, Aberdeen, Dundee, Inverness and Perth - Glasgow Queen Street and Edinburgh

	SR	SR	SR	SR	XC	SR
	◇1 A 🍴	◇1	◇1	◇1	◇1	1
Inverness d			20 15			
Carrbridge d			21 00			
Aviemore d			21 08			
Kingussie d			21 20			
Newtonmore d			21 24			
Dalwhinnie d			21 36			
Blair Atholl d			21 57			
Pitlochry d			22 07			
Dunkeld & Birnam d			22 19			
Inverurie 240 d						
Dyce 240 ✈ d						
Aberdeen 240 a						
d	20 09	20 42		21 04	21 31	22 26
Portlethen d						22 37
Stonehaven d	20 25	20 59		21 21	21 49	22 46
Laurencekirk d				21 34		22 59
Montrose a	20 46	21 20		21 44	22 11	23 09
d	20 46	21 20		21 45	22 12	23 10
Arbroath a	21 00	21 34		21 58	22 27	23 24
d	21 00	21 34		21 59	22 28	23 24
Carnoustie d	21 07					23 31
Golf Street d						
Barry Links d						
Monifieth d						
Balmossie d						
Broughty Ferry d						23 38
Dundee a	21 18	21 55		22 14	22 44	23 48
d	21 19	21 56		22 16	22 48	
Invergowrie d						
Perth a		22 16	22 37			
d		22 17	22 38			
Gleneagles d		22 32				
Dunblane 230 d			23 02			
Bridge of Allan 230 d			23 05			
Stirling 230 d		22 48	23 10			
Larbert 230 d						
Glasgow Queen St. 10 230 ⛴ a		23 18	23 43			
Leuchars 5 a	21 32			22 29	23 01	
St Andrews Bus Station 🚌 a						
St Andrews Bus Station 🚌 d						
Leuchars 5 d	21 32			22 29	23 02	
Cupar d	21 39			22 36	23 09	
Springfield d						
Ladybank d	21 47			22 44	23 16	
Markinch d	21 54			22 51	23 23	
Kirkcaldy 242 d	22 03			23 00	23 32	
Inverkeithing 242 d	22 25			23 22	23 47	
Edinburgh Gateway ⛴✈ d	22 39			23 36		
Haymarket 242 ⛴ a	22 49			23 46	00 02	
Edinburgh 10 242 a	22 54			23 51	00 08	

A until 18 August

Table T229-R

Sundays
20 May to 2 December

Inverurie, Dyce, Aberdeen, Dundee, Inverness and Perth - Glasgow Queen Street and Edinburgh

	SR	SR	SR	SR	SR	SR	SR	SR	GR	SR	SR	GR	SR	SR	XC	SR	SR	SR	GR	SR	SR	SR
	◇		◇	◇	◇			◇1 🍴	1 A 🍽		◇	1 B 🍽	◇1 🍴		◇1 C	◇1 🍴	◇1 D 🍴	◇1 E 🍴	1 F 🍽		◇	◇1 🍴
Inverness d												09 40				10 50						
Carrbridge d												10 11										
Aviemore d												10 19				11 25						
Kingussie d												10 32				11 37						
Newtonmore d												10 37										
Dalwhinnie d																11 51						
Blair Atholl d												11 09										
Pitlochry d												11 23				12 20						
Dunkeld & Birnam d												11 37				12 35						
Inverurie 240 d																	11 02					
Dyce 240 ✈ d																	11 13					
Aberdeen 240 a																	11 25					
d								09 24	09 47				10 30		11 10		11 29	11 29	11 47			12 29
Portlethen d																						
Stonehaven d								09 41	10 05				10 47		11 27		11 45	11 45	12 05			12 46
Laurencekirk d								09 55														
Montrose a								10 05	10 26				11 08		11 47		12 06	12 06	12 26			13 07
d								10 06	10 28				11 08		11 48		12 08	12 08	12 28			13 07
Arbroath a								10 20	10 43				11 22		12 03		12 21	12 21	12 43			13 21
d								10 20	10 44				11 23		12 04		12 22	12 22	12 44			13 22
Carnoustie d								10 27														
Golf Street d																						
Barry Links d																						
Monifieth d																						
Balmossie d																						
Broughty Ferry d								10 35														
Dundee a								10 45	11 00				11 42		12 22		12 40	12 40	13 00			13 41
d	07 24			08 45		09 24		10 46	11 03		11 20		11 44		12 24		12 43	12 43	13 02		13 20	13 43
Invergowrie d																						
Perth a				09 05				11 07				11 56	12 05			12 54	13 03	13 03				14 04
d			08 50	09 06	09 16		10 10	11 08				11 59	12 09			12 55	13 05	13 05				14 06
Gleneagles d				09 21	09 31		10 25	11 24				12 15					13 20	13 20				
Dunblane 230 d				09 33	09 43		10 38	11 36				12 28	12 36				13 31	13 31				14 32
Bridge of Allan 230 d					09 47		10 41															
Stirling 230 d		09 05		09 39	09 51		10 46	11 43		11 48		12 35	12 43	12 47			13 38	13 38		13 46		14 38
Larbert 230 d		09 13		09 47	10 00		10 55			11 57				12 56						13 55		
Glasgow Queen St. 10 230 ⛴ a				10 14				12 14					13 14				14 09	14 09				15 09
Leuchars 5 a	07 36					09 36			11 15		11 32				12 36				13 14		13 32	
St Andrews Bus Station 🚌 a																						
St Andrews Bus Station 🚌 d																						
Leuchars 5 d	07 37					09 37			11 17		11 33				12 37				13 17		13 33	
Cupar d	07 44					09 44					11 40				12 44						13 40	
Springfield d																						
Ladybank d	07 52		09 11			09 52					11 48				12 51						13 48	
Markinch d	07 59		09 19			09 59					11 55				12 58	13 23					13 55	
Kirkcaldy 242 d	08 09		09 29			10 09			11 41		12 05				13 07	13 32			13 42		14 05	
Inverkeithing 242 d	08 31		09 51			10 31			11 57		12 21				13 22	13 48			14 03		14 21	
Edinburgh Gateway ⛴✈ d	08 48		10 08			10 45					12 32					13 59					14 32	
Haymarket 242 ⛴ a	08 58	09 59	10 18		10 40	10 55	11 35		12 16	12 37	12 40	13 15		13 36	13 37	14 07			14 20	14 35	14 40	
Edinburgh 10 242 a	09 03	10 04	10 23		10 46	11 01	11 41		12 22	12 42	12 45	13 21		13 41	13 43	14 12			14 26	14 42	14 45	

A To London Kings Cross. The Northern Lights
B To London Kings Cross. The Highland Chieftain
C To Plymouth
D from 26 August. 🍴 from Aberdeen
E until 19 August
F To London Kings Cross

Table T229-R

Sundays
20 May to 2 December

Inverurie, Dyce, Aberdeen, Dundee, Inverness and Perth - Glasgow Queen Street and Edinburgh

		SR	SR	SR	SR	GR	SR	SR	SR	SR	SR	SR	SR	SR	SR	SR	SR	SR	SR	SR	SR	SR	SR
		◇1		◇1	◇1	1	◇		◇1	◇1	◇1		◇1	◇1	◇	◇1	◇1	◇1	◇1	◇1	◇	◇1	◇1
						A													B	C		D	
				🛒	🛒	🍽			🛒	🛒	🛒		🛒	🛒		🛒	🛒	🛒	🛒	🛒		🛒	🛒
Inverness	d			12 44					13 30					15 22			16 23		15 29				18 50
Carrbridge	d			13 17													16 58						19 23
Aviemore	d			13 25					14 07					15 57			17 10						19 31
Kingussie	d			13 37					14 19					16 09			17 22						19 43
Newtonmore	d			13 41																			19 47
Dalwhinnie	d																						19 59
Blair Atholl	d			14 13													17 55						20 21
Pitlochry	d			14 23					15 00					16 50			18 05						20 31
Dunkeld & Birnam	d			14 34										17 02			18 18						20 42
Inverurie 240	d																		17 14				
Dyce 240 ✈	d																		17 28				
Aberdeen 240	a																		17 39				
	d	12 45			13 31	13 47				14 31	15 09		15 28			16 28		17 09	17 47	17 47		19 07	
Portlethen	d	12 56									15 20												
Stonehaven	d	13 05			13 48	14 05				14 48	15 29		15 44			16 45		17 26	18 04	18 04		19 24	
Laurencekirk	d	13 19											15 58						18 18	18 18			
Montrose	a	13 29			14 09	14 26				15 09	15 50		16 08			17 06		17 47	18 28	18 28		19 45	
	d	13 30			14 09	14 28				15 09	15 50		16 09			17 06		17 47	18 28	18 28		19 46	
Arbroath	a	13 44			14 23	14 43				15 23	16 03		16 22			17 20		18 01	18 42	18 42		20 00	
	d	13 44			14 24	14 44				15 24	16 04		16 23			17 21		18 01	18 43	18 43		20 00	
Carnoustie	d	13 51									16 10											20 07	
Golf Street	d																						
Barry Links	d																						
Monifieth	d																						
Balmossie	d																						
Broughty Ferry	d	13 58																				20 14	
Dundee	a	14 05			14 43	15 00				15 43	16 22		16 42			17 40		18 16	19 02	19 02		20 21	
	d	14 07			14 45	15 02	15 15			15 45	16 24		16 43		17 21	17 42		18 18	19 03	19 03	19 16	20 22	
Invergowrie	d																						
Perth	a			14 53	15 06				15 29	16 06			17 04	17 20		18 03	18 38		19 25	19 25			21 01
	d			14 54	15 08				15 32	16 08			17 05	17 22		18 05	18 39		19 26	19 26			21 06
Gleneagles	d				15 23								17 20						19 42	19 42			
Dunblane 230	d			15 18	15 36					16 34			17 31			18 31	19 03						
Bridge of Allan 230	d																						
Stirling 230	d		14 46	15 24	15 42			15 47		16 40		16 46	17 38			18 37	19 09		19 58	19 58			
Larbert 230	d		14 55	15 33				15 56				16 55					19 17						
Glasgow Queen St. 10 230 ⛴	a			15 58	16 17					17 13			18 13			19 08	19 41		20 29	20 29			
Leuchars 5	a	14 19				15 14	15 27				16 36				17 33			18 30			19 28	20 35	
St Andrews Bus Station 🚌	a																						
St Andrews Bus Station 🚌	d																						
Leuchars 5	d	14 20				15 16	15 28				16 37				17 34			18 31			19 29	20 35	
Cupar	d						15 35								17 41						19 36		
Springfield	d																						
Ladybank	d						15 43		15 53					17 43	17 49						19 44		
Markinch	d						15 50		16 00					17 50	17 56						19 51		21 33
Kirkcaldy 242	d	14 46				15 41	16 00		16 10		17 02			18 00	18 06			18 56			20 01	21 01	21 43
Inverkeithing 242	d	15 02				15 58	16 16		16 26		17 18			18 16	18 22			19 12			20 23	21 17	21 59
Edinburgh Gateway ⛴✈	d						16 27		16 36					18 26	18 33						20 37		22 09
Haymarket 242 ⛴	a	15 18	15 35			16 18	16 35	16 36	16 45		17 34	17 35		18 35	18 41			19 28			20 47	21 33	22 20
Edinburgh 10 242	a	15 23	15 41			16 26	16 40	16 41	16 50		17 40	17 43		18 42	18 46			19 33			20 52	21 38	22 25

A To London Kings Cross
B from 26 August. 🛒 from Aberdeen
C until 19 August
D 🛒 to Dundee

		SR	SR	XC	SR
		◇1	◇1	◇1	
		A			
		🛒	🛒		
Inverness	d				
Carrbridge	d				
Aviemore	d				
Kingussie	d				
Newtonmore	d				
Dalwhinnie	d				
Blair Atholl	d				
Pitlochry	d				
Dunkeld & Birnam	d				
Inverurie 240	d				
Dyce 240 ✈	d				
Aberdeen 240	a				
	d	19 36	20 06	21 29	22 26
Portlethen	d		20 17		22 37
Stonehaven	d	19 52	20 26	21 46	22 46
Laurencekirk	d		20 40		23 00
Montrose	a	20 13	20 50	22 06	23 10
	d	20 14	20 50	22 07	23 10
Arbroath	a	20 27	21 04	22 22	23 24
	d	20 28	21 04	22 23	23 24
Carnoustie	d				23 31
Golf Street	d				
Barry Links	d				
Monifieth	d				
Balmossie	d				
Broughty Ferry	d				23 38
Dundee	a	20 46	21 21	22 39	23 48
	d	20 50	21 22	22 41	23 49
Invergowrie	d				
Perth	a	21 10			00 13
	d	21 11			
Gleneagles	d	21 26			
Dunblane 230	d	21 38			
Bridge of Allan 230	d				
Stirling 230	d	21 44			
Larbert 230	d	21 52			
Glasgow Queen St. 10 230 ⛴	a	22 18			
Leuchars 5	a		21 34	22 53	
St Andrews Bus Station 🚌	a				
St Andrews Bus Station 🚌	d				
Leuchars 5	d		21 35	22 54	
Cupar	d		21 42	23 01	
Springfield	d				
Ladybank	d		21 50	23 08	
Markinch	d		21 57	23 16	
Kirkcaldy 242	d		22 07	23 24	
Inverkeithing 242	d		22 23	23 40	
Edinburgh Gateway ⛴✈	d				
Haymarket 242 ⛴	a		22 39	23 57	
Edinburgh 10 242	a		22 44	00 02	

A 🛒 from Dundee

Table T230-F

Mondays to Fridays
21 May to 7 December

Edinburgh, Glasgow Queen Street and Falkirk Grahamston - Stirling, Alloa and Dunblane

Miles	Miles	Miles			SR	SR	SR	SR	SR	SR	SR	SR	SR	SR	SR	SR	SR	SR	SR	SR	SR	SR	SR
					MX	MX	MO	MX	MX														
						◇	◇				◇1		1	1	1	1			1	1	◇1		
					A	B	B	C	A		D		E	F	F	E			E	F	G		
											🛒									🛒	🛒		
0	—	—	**Edinburgh** 10	d						05 18			05 55			06 30	06 33		06 45			07 03	
1¼	—	—	Haymarket ⛴	d						05 22			06 00			06 35	06 38		06 50			07 08	
3¾	—	—	Edinburgh Park ⛴	d						05 27							06 43					07 14	
17½	—	—	Linlithgow	d						05 39			06 15			06 50	06 55		07 06			07 26	
22¼	—	—	Polmont 3	d				00 01		05 45			06 21			06 56	07 01					07 32	
—	0	0	**Glasgow Queen Street** 10 ⛴	d							05 56	06 14		06 30	06 45			06 50		07 00	07 10		07 18
—	3¼	3¼	Bishopbriggs	d								06 21						06 56					07 24
—	6¼	6¼	Lenzie 3	d					00 01			06 26		06a38				07 01		07a08			07 30
—	11½	11½	Croy 3	d					00 06			06 32	06a35		06a57	07a11		07 08	07a24				07 36
25½	—	—	**Falkirk Grahamston** 3	d				00 08		05 52							07 08					07 39	
27	—	—	Camelon 4	d				00 11		05 55							07 11					07 42	
28¼	21	21	Larbert	d			00 11	00 16	00 21	06 00	06 16	06 43					07 16	07 21				07 47	07 51
36½	29	29	**Stirling**	a			00 19	00 25	00 32	06 08	06 24	06 52					07 25	07 30			07 36	07 56	08 00
—	—	—		d	00 01	00 05	00 20	00 26		06 09	06 25	06 53					07 25	07 41			07 36	07 56	08 07
—	—	35¾	**Alloa**	a	00 13							07 05											08 19
40	32½	—	Bridge of Allan	d		00 10	00 24	00 30		06 13							07 30	07 45				08 01	
42	34½	—	**Dunblane**	a		00 14	00 28	00 37		06 19	06 31						07 37	07 52			07 42	08 08	

		SR	SR	SR	SR	SR	SR	SR	SR	SR	SR	SR	SR	SR	SR	SR	SR	SR	SR	SR	SR	SR	SR
		1	1	◇1		1			1	1	◇		1		1	◇1			1	◇			1
		F	E	D		E		H	E	F	I		E		F	D			F	I			F
		🛒	🛒	🛒		🛒			🛒	🛒			🛒		🛒	🛒			🛒				🛒
Edinburgh 10	d		07 15			07 30	07 34		07 45				08 00	08 04			08 33				09 03		
Haymarket ⛴	d		07 20			07 34	07 38		07 49				08 05	08 09			08 39				09 10		
Edinburgh Park ⛴	d						07 44							08 14			08 44				09 15		
Linlithgow	d		07 35			07 49	07 55	08 00	08 05					08 26			08 55				09 27		
Polmont 3	d					07 56	08 01						08 23	08 32			09 02				09 33		
Glasgow Queen Street 10 ⛴	d	07 30		07 42	07 49					08 00	08 08	08 18			08 30	08 41		08 49	09 00	09 08		09 20	09 30
Bishopbriggs	d				07 55							08 24						08 55				09 26	
Lenzie 3	d				08 01				08a26			08 30						09 01				09 31	
Croy 3	d	07a42	07a53		08 07	08a10				08a12		08 36	08a38		08a42			09 07	09a12			09 38	09a42
Falkirk Grahamston 3	d						08 08	08 12						08 39			09 08				09 39		
Camelon 4	d						08 11	08a15						08 42			09 11				09 42		
Larbert	d				08 21		08 16					08 52		08 48			09 17	09 21			09 48	09 52	
Stirling	a				08 31		08 24				08 35	09 01		08 56		09 07	09 25	09 30		09 34	09 56	10 01	
	d			08u09			08 25				08 36	09 01		08 57			09 25	09 46		09 35	09 56	10 02	
Alloa	a											09 14										10 14	
Bridge of Allan	d						08 29				08 40			09 01			09 29	09 51			10 01		
Dunblane	a			08 15			08 36				08 44			09 08			09 36	09 58		09 41	10 08		

		SR	SR	SR	SR	SR	SR	SR	SR	SR	SR	SR	SR	SR	SR	SR	SR	SR	SR	SR	SR	SR	SR
		◇1			1	◇1			1	◇1			1			1	◇1			1	◇1		
		D			F	G			F	D			F			F	D			F	G		
		🛒			🛒	🛒			🛒	🛒			🛒			🛒	🛒			🛒	🛒		
Edinburgh 10	d		09 34				10 05				10 33			11 03				11 36				12 04	
Haymarket ⛴	d		09 38				10 09				10 37			11 08				11 40				12 09	
Edinburgh Park ⛴	d		09 44				10 15				10 43			11 13				11 46				12 14	
Linlithgow	d		09 56				10 26				10 55			11 25				11 57				12 27	
Polmont 3	d		10 02				10 32				11 01			11 31				12 03				12 32	
Glasgow Queen Street 10 ⛴	d	09 41		09 49	10 00	10 11		10 20	10 30	10 41		10 48	11 00		11 19	11 30	11 41		11 48	12 00	12 09		12 18
Bishopbriggs	d			09 55				10 26				10 54			11 25				11 57				12 24
Lenzie 3	d			10 01				10 32				11 00			11 31				12 02				12 30
Croy 3	d			10 07	10a12			10 38	10a42			11 06	11a12		11 37	11a42			12 09	12a12			12 36
Falkirk Grahamston 3	d		10 09				10 39				11 08			11 38				12 10				12 38	
Camelon 4	d		10 12				10 42				11 11			11 41				12 13				12 41	
Larbert	d		10 17	10 20			10 47	10 51			11 16	11 21		11 46	11 51			12 18	12 22			12 48	12 52
Stirling	a	10 08	10 25	10 31		10 37	10 56	11 00		11 09	11 25	11 31		11 55	12 00		12 07	12 26	12 33		12 37	12 56	13 01
	d		10 26			10 37	10 56	11 01			11 25	11 32		11 55	12 01			12 27			12 37	12 57	13 02
Alloa	a							11 13							12 13								13 14
Bridge of Allan	d		10 30			10 41	11 01				11 30	11 37		12 00				12 31			12 41	13 01	
Dunblane	a		10 37			10 45	11 08				11 37	11 43		12 07				12 37			12 45	13 08	

		SR	SR	SR	SR	SR	SR	SR	SR	SR	SR	SR	SR	SR	SR	SR	SR	SR	SR	SR	SR	SR
		1	◇1			1			1	◇1			1			1	◇1			1	◇1	
		F	D			F			F	D			F			F	D			F	G	
		🛒	🛒			🛒			🛒	🛒			🛒			🛒	🛒			🛒	🛒	
Edinburgh 10	d			12 33			13 03				13 34			14 03				14 34				15 04
Haymarket ⛴	d			12 38			13 09				13 39			14 08				14 39				15 08
Edinburgh Park ⛴	d			12 43			13 15				13 44			14 14				14 44				15 13
Linlithgow	d			12 55			13 26				13 56			14 26				14 56				15 26
Polmont 3	d			13 01			13 32				14 02			14 31				15 02				15 32
Glasgow Queen Street 10 ⛴	d	12 30	12 41		12 48	13 00		13 19	13 30	13 41		13 48	14 00		14 19	14 30	14 41		14 49	15 00	15 09	
Bishopbriggs	d				12 54			13 25				13 54			14 25				14 55			
Lenzie 3	d				13 00			13 31				14 00			14 30				15 01			
Croy 3	d	12a42			13 06	13a12		13 37	13a42			14 06	14a12		14 37	14a42			15 07	15a12		
Falkirk Grahamston 3	d			13 08			13 38				14 08			14 38				15 09				15 38
Camelon 4	d			13 11			13 41				14 11			14 41				15 12				15 41
Larbert	d			13 17	13 21		13 47	13 51			14 17	14 21		14 47	14 51			15 17	15 21			15 47
Stirling	a		13 07	13 25	13 31		13 55	14 00		14 07	14 25	14 31		14 55	15 00		15 07	15 26	15 32		15 36	15 55
	d			13 26	13 33		13 57	14 01			14 26	14 33		14 56	15 01			15 26			15 37	15 55
Alloa	a							14 13							15 13							
Bridge of Allan	d			13 30	13 37		14 01				14 30	14 37		15 00				15 31			15 41	15 59
Dunblane	a			13 37	13 43		14 08				14 37	14 43		15 07				15 38			15 45	16 06

A From Glasgow Queen Street
B From Glasgow Queen Street to Perth
C From Edinburgh
D To Aberdeen
E To Glasgow Queen Street
F To Edinburgh
G To Inverness
H From Kirkcaldy to Glasgow Queen Street
I To Dundee

Table T230-F

Mondays to Fridays

21 May to 7 December

Edinburgh, Glasgow Queen Street and Falkirk Grahamston - Stirling, Alloa and Dunblane

		SR	SR 1 A ✠		SR	SR	SR 1 A ✠	SR B	SR	SR	SR 1 A ✠	SR	GR ■ 1 C ▭		SR	SR	SR 1 A ✠	SR	SR ◇ D	SR	SR	SR	SR 1 A ✠		SR E
Edinburgh	d				15 33				16 03				16 34		16 37					17 05		17 27			
Haymarket	d				15 38				16 09				16 39		16 42					17 09		17 31			
Edinburgh Park	d				15 43				16 14						16 47					17 14					
Linlithgow	d				15 54				16 26						16 59					17 26					
Polmont	d				16 01				16 32						17 05					17 32					
Glasgow Queen Street	d	15 18	15 30			15 48	16 00	16 11		16 18	16 30	16 33				16 49	17 00	17 04	17 11		17 18		17 30		17 33
Bishopbriggs	d	15 24				15 54				16 25		16 39				16 56		17 11			17 25				17 39
Lenzie	d	15 30				16 00				16 30		16a44				17 01		17 16			17 31				17 44
Croy	d	15 36	15a42			16 06	16a12			16 37	16a43					17 08	17a12				17 38		17a42		
Falkirk Grahamston	d				16 08				16 39				17 05		17 12			17a35		17 39					18a03
Camelon	d				16 11				16 42						17 15					17 42					
Larbert	d	15 51			16 17	16 22			16 47	16 51					17 20	17 25			17 35	17 48	17 52	17 57			
Stirling	a	16 02			16 25	16 33		16 39	16 56	17 00			17 19		17 29	17 35			17 44	17 56	18 01	18 05			
	d	16 03			16 26			16 39	16 56	17 08					17 29	17 36			17 46	17 57	18 02	18 06			
Alloa	a	16 15								17 20											18 14				
Bridge of Allan	d				16 30			16 44	17 01						17 34	17 41			17 51	18 01		18 10			
Dunblane	a				16 37			16 50	17 08						17 41	17 47			17 55	18 08		18 16			

		SR ◇1 F ✠	SR	SR	SR 1 A ✠	SR ◇1 G ✠	SR	SR	SR 1 A ✠		SR ◇1 F ✠	SR	SR	SR 1 A ✠	SR ◇ H	SR	SR	SR ◇1 F ✠	GR ■ 1 I ▭		SR	SR 1 J	SR	SR 1 A	SR
Edinburgh	d		17 34				18 05					18 35				19 04			19 25			19 30	19 43		
Haymarket	d		17 39				18 09					18 39				19 08			19 30			19 35	19 47		
Edinburgh Park	d		17 44				18 14					18 45				19 15							19 52		
Linlithgow	d		17 56				18 27					18 57				19 27						19 52	20 04		
Polmont	d		18 02				18 32					19 02				19 32							20 09		
Glasgow Queen Street	d	17 40		17 52	18 00	18 11		18 18	18 30		18 41		18 48	19 00	19 09		19 18	19 41			19 46			20 00	20 18
Bishopbriggs	d			17 58				18 25					18 54				19 24				19 53				20 24
Lenzie	d			18 03				18 30					19 00				19 29				19 58				20 29
Croy	d			18 10	18a14			18 37	18a43				19 06	19a11			19 35				20 05	20a10		20a12	20 36
Falkirk Grahamston	d		18 09				18 39					19 09				19 39			19 57				20 16		
Camelon	d		18 12				18 42					19 12				19 42							20 19		
Larbert	d		18 17	18 21		18 31	18 48	18 53				19 18	19 22			19 48	19 53				20 17		20 26		20 50
Stirling	a	18 12	18 29	18 33		18 39	18 56	19 02			19 07	19 26	19 33		19 37	19 56	20 01	20 07	20 15		20 28		20 34		20 59
	d	18 16	18 30	18 34		18 42	18 57	19 02			19 07	19 27			19 37	19 57	20 02				20 29		20 35		21 00
Alloa	a		18 42					19 15									20 14								21 13
Bridge of Allan	d			18 38		18 46	19 01					19 31			19 41	20 01					20 33		20 39		
Dunblane	a	18 22		18 44		18 50	19 08				19 13	19 38			19 45	20 08					20 39		20 46		

		SR ◇1 F	SR	SR 1 J	SR		SR A	SR	SR 1 J	SR ◇1 F	SR FX K	SR FO ◇ K	SR	SR 1 A	SR		SR 1 J	SR	SR ◇ H	SR 1 A	SR	SR 1 J	SR	SR 1 A	SR ◇ K
Edinburgh	d			20 30	20 34				21 30		21 35	21 35					22 30	22 33				23 00	23 04		
Haymarket	d			20 35	20 39				21 34		21 39	21 39					22 35	22 37				23 05	23 08		
Edinburgh Park	d				20 43						21 44	21 44						22 43					23 13		
Linlithgow	d			20 53	20 58				21 49		21 56	21 56					22 50	22 55				23 20	23 25		
Polmont	d				21 03						22 01	22 01						23 01				23 27	23 31		
Glasgow Queen Street	d	20 41	20 48				21 00	21 18		21 42			21 48	22 00	22 18				22 48	23 00	23 19			23 30	23 37
Bishopbriggs	d		20 55					21 25					21 54		22 24				22 54		23 25				
Lenzie	d		21 01					21 30					22 00		22 29				22 59		23 30				
Croy	d		21 07	21a11			21a12	21 37	22a07				22 06	22a12	22 36		23a08		23 06	23a12	23 37	23a41		23a42	
Falkirk Grahamston	d				21 10						22 08	22 08						23 08					23 37		
Camelon	d				21 13						22 11	22 11						23 11					23 40		
Larbert	d		21 23		21 19			21 50			22 16	22 16	22 21		22 50			23 16	23 20		23 50		23 46		
Stirling	a	21 07	21 34		21 27			21 59		22 08	22 25	22 25	22 31		22 59			23 25	23 30		23 59		23 56		00 04
	d	21 08			21 28			22 01			22 25	22 25	22 33		23 01			23 25	23 33		00 01				00 05
Alloa	a							22 13							23 13						00 13				
Bridge of Allan	d				21 32						22 30	22 30	22 38					23 30	23 37						00 10
Dunblane	a	21 14			21 39						22 34	22 34	22 44					23 37	23 41						00 14

			SR	SR 1 J	SR
Edinburgh	d			23 30	23 33
Haymarket	d			23 34	23 37
Edinburgh Park	d				23 44
Linlithgow	d			23 50	23 56
Polmont	d			23 56	00 01
Glasgow Queen Street	d		23 48		
Bishopbriggs	d		23 55		
Lenzie	d		00 01		
Croy	d		00 06	00a10	
Falkirk Grahamston	d				00 08
Camelon	d				00 11
Larbert	d		00 21		00 16
Stirling	a		00 32		00 25
	d				00 26
Alloa	a				
Bridge of Allan	d				00 30
Dunblane	a				00 37

A To Edinburgh
B To Arbroath
C From London Kings Cross to Inverness
D To Carnoustie
E To Markinch
F To Aberdeen
G To Inverness
H To Dundee
I From London Kings Cross
J To Glasgow Queen Street
K To Perth

Please check the 'Additional Notes to Individual Tables' section for any other general notes that apply to this Table

Table T230-F

Saturdays

26 May to 8 December

Edinburgh, Glasgow Queen Street and Falkirk Grahamston - Stirling, Alloa and Dunblane

		SR A	SR ◇ B	SR C	SR A	SR		SR ◇1 D ✠	SR	SR 1 E	SR 1 F	SR 1 E	SR	SR	SR	SR 1 F ✠		SR ◇1 G ✠	SR	SR	SR 1 F ✠	SR 1 E ✠	SR ◇1 D ✠	SR	SR 1 E ✠
Edinburgh	d					05 18				05 55		06 30		06 33					07 03			07 15			07 30
Haymarket	d					05 22				06 00		06 35		06 38					07 07			07 20			07 34
Edinburgh Park	d					05 27								06 43					07 14						
Linlithgow	d					05 39				06 15		06 50		06 55					07 26			07 35			07 49
Polmont	d			00 01		05 45				06 21		06 56		07 01					07 32						07 56
Glasgow Queen Street	d							05 56	06 14		06 30				06 50	07 00		07 10		07 18	07 30		07 42	07 49	
Bishopbriggs	d								06 21						06 56					07 24				07 55	
Lenzie	d				00 01				06 26		06 38				07 01	07a08				07 30				08 01	
Croy	d				00 06				06 32	06a35	06a44	07a11			07 08					07 36	07a42	07a53		08 07	08a10
Falkirk Grahamston	d			00 08		05 52								07 08					07 39						
Camelon	d			00 11		05 55								07 11					07 42						
Larbert	d			00 16	00 21	06 00		06 16	06 43					07 16	07 21				07 47	07 51				08 21	
Stirling	a			00 25	00 32	06 08		06 24	06 52					07 25	07 30			07 36	07 56	08 00				08 31	
	d	00 01	00 05	00 26		06 09		06 25	06 53				07 01	07 25	07 41			07 36	07 56	08 07			08u09		
Alloa	a	00 13							07 05											08 19					
Bridge of Allan	d		00 10	00 30		06 13							07 05	07 30	07 45				08 01						
Dunblane	a		00 14	00 37		06 19		06 31					07 12	07 37	07 52			07 42	08 08				08 15		

		SR		SR 1 E ✠	SR 1 F ✠	SR ◇ H	SR	SR 1 E ✠	SR	SR 1 F ✠	SR ◇1 D ✠	SR		SR	SR 1 F ✠	SR ◇ H	SR	SR	SR 1 F ✠	SR ◇1 D ✠	SR	SR		SR 1 F ✠	SR ◇1 G ✠
Edinburgh	d	07 33		07 45				08 00	08 03			08 35					09 04				09 33				
Haymarket	d	07 38		07 49				08 05	08 08			08 40					09 10				09 38				
Edinburgh Park	d	07 44							08 14			08 44					09 15				09 44				
Linlithgow	d	07 56		08 05					08 26			08 55					09 27				09 56				
Polmont	d	08 02						08 23	08 32			09 02					09 32				10 02				
Glasgow Queen Street	d				08 00	08 08	08 18			08 30	08 41			08 49	09 00	09 08		09 20	09 30	09 41		09 49		10 00	10 11
Bishopbriggs	d						08 24							08 55				09 26				09 55			
Lenzie	d			08a26			08 30							09 01				09 31				10 01			
Croy	d				08a12		08 36	08a38		08a42				09 07	09a12			09 38	09a42			10 07		10a12	
Falkirk Grahamston	d	08 09							08 39			09 08					09 39				10 09				
Camelon	d	08 12							08 42			09 11					09 42				10 12				
Larbert	d	08 17					08 52		08 48			09 17		09 21			09 48	09 51			10 17	10 21			
Stirling	a	08 25				08 35	09 01		08 56		09 07	09 25		09 30		09 34	09 57	10 00		10 08	10 25	10 31			10 37
	d	08 26				08 36	09 01		08 57			09 25		09 46		09 35	09 57	10 01			10 26				10 37
Alloa	a						09 14											10 13							
Bridge of Allan	d	08 30				08 40			09 01			09 29		09 51			10 02				10 30				10 41
Dunblane	a	08 37				08 44			09 08			09 36		09 58		09 41	10 09				10 37				10 45

		SR	SR	SR 1 F ✠	SR ◇1 D ✠	SR	SR	SR 1 F ✠		SR	SR	SR 1 F ✠	SR ◇1 D ✠	SR	SR	SR 1 F ✠	SR ◇1 G ✠	SR		SR	SR 1 F ✠	SR ◇1 D ✠	SR	SR	SR 1 F ✠
Edinburgh	d	10 04				10 33				11 05				11 35				12 04					12 33		
Haymarket	d	10 09				10 37				11 09				11 39				12 09					12 38		
Edinburgh Park	d	10 14				10 43				11 14				11 45				12 14					12 43		
Linlithgow	d	10 26				10 56				11 25				11 57				12 27					12 56		
Polmont	d	10 32				11 02				11 31				12 03				12 32					13 01		
Glasgow Queen Street	d		10 20	10 30	10 41		10 48	11 00			11 19	11 30	11 41		11 48	12 00	12 09			12 18	12 30	12 41		12 48	13 00
Bishopbriggs	d		10 26				10 54				11 25				11 57					12 24				12 54	
Lenzie	d		10 32				11 00				11 31				12 02					12 30				13 00	
Croy	d		10 38	10a42			11 06	11a12			11 37	11a42			12 09	12a12				12 36	12a42			13 06	13a12
Falkirk Grahamston	d	10 39				11 09				11 38				12 10				12 38					13 08		
Camelon	d	10 42				11 12				11 41				12 13				12 41					13 11		
Larbert	d	10 47	10 51			11 17	11 22			11 46	11 51			12 18	12 22			12 48		12 52			13 17	13 21	
Stirling	a	10 55	11 00		11 09	11 26	11 32			11 55	12 00		12 07	12 27	12 33		12 37	12 56		13 01		13 07	13 25	13 31	
	d	10 56	11 01			11 26	11 33			11 55	12 01			12 27			12 37	12 57		13 02			13 26	13 33	
Alloa	a		11 13								12 13									13 14					
Bridge of Allan	d	11 00				11 31	11 38			12 00				12 32			12 41	13 01					13 30	13 37	
Dunblane	a	11 07				11 38	11 44			12 07				12 39			12 45	13 08					13 37	13 43	

		SR	SR	SR 1 F ✠		SR ◇1 D ✠	SR	SR	SR 1 F ✠	SR	SR	SR 1 F ✠	SR ◇1 D ✠	SR		SR	SR 1 F ✠	SR ◇1 G ✠	SR	SR	SR 1 F ✠	SR	SR	SR 1 F ✠
Edinburgh	d	13 03					13 33			14 03				14 35					15 05			15 33		
Haymarket	d	13 09					13 38			14 08				14 39					15 09			15 38		
Edinburgh Park	d	13 15					13 43			14 14				14 44					15 14			15 44		
Linlithgow	d	13 26					13 55			14 26				14 56					15 26			15 56		
Polmont	d	13 32					14 01			14 31				15 02					15 32			16 01		
Glasgow Queen Street	d		13 20	13 30		13 41		13 48	14 00		14 19	14 30	14 41			14 49	15 00	15 09		15 18	15 30		15 48	16 00
Bishopbriggs	d		13 26					13 54			14 25					14 55				15 24			15 54	
Lenzie	d		13 32					14 00			14 30					15 01				15 30			16 00	
Croy	d		13 38	13a42				14 06	14a12		14 37	14a42				15 07	15a12			15 36	15a43		16 06	16a12
Falkirk Grahamston	d	13 38					14 08			14 38				15 09					15 38			16 08		
Camelon	d	13 41					14 11			14 41				15 12					15 41			16 11		
Larbert	d	13 47	13 51				14 16	14 20		14 47	14 51			15 17		15 21			15 47	15 51		16 17	16 22	
Stirling	a	13 55	14 00			14 07	14 25	14 30		14 55	15 00		15 07	15 26		15 32		15 36	15 55	16 02		16 25	16 33	
	d	13 57	14 01				14 26	14 33		14 56	15 01			15 26				15 37	15 55	16 03		16 26		
Alloa	a		14 13								15 13									16 15				
Bridge of Allan	d	14 01					14 30	14 37		15 00				15 31				15 41	15 59			16 30		
Dunblane	a	14 08					14 37	14 43		15 07				15 38				15 45	16 06			16 37		

A From Glasgow Queen Street
B From Glasgow Queen Street to Perth
C From Edinburgh
D To Aberdeen
E To Glasgow Queen Street
F To Edinburgh
G To Inverness
H To Dundee

Table T230-F

Saturdays
26 May to 8 December

Edinburgh, Glasgow Queen Street and Falkirk Grahamston - Stirling, Alloa and Dunblane

		SR A	SR	SR	SR B	SR ◇ C		GR D	SR	SR	SR B	SR ◇ E	SR	SR	SR B	SR ◇ C		SR	SR	SR B	SR ◇ F	SR	SR	SR B	SR ◇ C
Edinburgh	d		16 04					16 34	16 38				17 05					17 33				18 03			
Haymarket	d		16 08					16 39	16 43				17 09					17 38				18 08			
Edinburgh Park	d		16 14						16 47				17 14					17 44				18 14			
Linlithgow	d		16 26						16 59				17 26					17 56				18 27			
Polmont	d		16 32						17 05				17 32					18 02				18 32			
Glasgow Queen Street	d	16 11		16 18	16 30	16 41				16 49	17 00	17 04		17 18	17 30	17 41			17 52	18 00	18 11		18 18	18 30	18 41
Bishopbriggs	d			16 25						16 56		17 11		17 25					17 58				18 25		
Lenzie	d			16 30						17 01		17 15		17 31					18 03				18 30		
Croy	d			16 37	16a43					17 08	17a12	17 22		17 38	17a42				18 10	18a14			18 37	18a42	
Falkirk Grahamston	d		16 39					17 04	17 11				17 39					18 09				18 39			
Camelon	d		16 42						17 14				17 42					18 12				18 42			
Larbert	d		16 47	16 51					17 20	17 27		17 35	17 48	17 52				18 17	18 21		18 31	18 48	18 53		
Stirling	a	16 39	16 56	17 00		17 11		17 18	17 28	17 37		17 44	17 56	18 01		18 12		18 29	18 33		18 39	18 56	19 02		19 07
	d	16 39	16 56	17 08					17 28	17 38		17 46	17 57	18 02		18 16		18 30	18 34		18 42	18 57	19 02		19 07
Alloa	a			17 20										18 14				18 42					19 15		
Bridge of Allan	d	16 44	17 01						17 32	17 42		17 51	18 01						18 38		18 46	19 01			
Dunblane	a	16 50	17 08						17 39	17 48		17 55	18 08			18 22			18 44		18 50	19 08			19 13

		SR		SR	SR B	SR G	SR	SR	SR H	SR ◇ C	SR	SR		SR B	SR	SR ◇ C	SR	SR H	SR	SR B	SR	SR H		SR ◇ C	SR ◇ I
Edinburgh	d	18 36					19 05		19 30		19 33							20 30	20 33			21 30			21 34
Haymarket	d	18 40					19 09		19 34		19 38							20 35	20 38			21 34			21 39
Edinburgh Park	d	18 45					19 15				19 45								20 43						21 44
Linlithgow	d	18 57					19 27		19 52		19 57							20 52	20 57			21 49			21 56
Polmont	d	19 02					19 32				20 02								21 03						22 01
Glasgow Queen Street	d			18 48	19 00	19 09		19 18		19 41		19 48		20 00	20 18	20 41	20 48			21 00	21 18			21 42	
Bishopbriggs	d			18 54				19 24				19 55			20 24		20 55				21 25				
Lenzie	d			19 00				19 29				20 00			20 29		21 01				21 30				
Croy	d			19 06	19a12			19 36	20a10			20 07		20a12	20 36		21 07	21a10		21a11	21 37	22a07			
Falkirk Grahamston	d	19 09					19 39				20 08								21 10						22 08
Camelon	d	19 12					19 42				20 11								21 13						22 11
Larbert	d	19 18		19 22			19 48	19 53			20 18	20 23			20 50		21 23		21 19		21 50				22 16
Stirling	a	19 26		19 33		19 37	19 56	20 01		20 07	20 26	20 33			20 59	21 07	21 34		21 27		21 59			22 08	22 25
	d	19 27				19 37	19 57	20 02			20 27	20 33			21 00	21 08			21 28		22 01				22 25
Alloa	a							20 14							21 13						22 13				
Bridge of Allan	d	19 31				19 41	20 01				20 31	20 38							21 32						22 30
Dunblane	a	19 38				19 45	20 08				20 38	20 44				21 14			21 39						22 34

		SR	SR B	SR	SR H	SR	SR ◇ I	SR B		SR	SR H	SR	SR B	SR ◇ I	SR	SR H	SR
Edinburgh	d				22 30	22 33					23 00	23 03				23 30	23 33
Haymarket	d				22 35	22 37					23 05	23 08				23 34	23 38
Edinburgh Park	d					22 43						23 13					23 44
Linlithgow	d				22 50	22 55					23 20	23 25				23 50	23 56
Polmont	d					23 01					23 27	23 31				23 56	00 01
Glasgow Queen Street	d	21 48	22 00	22 18			22 52	23 00		23 19			23 30	23 37	23 48		
Bishopbriggs	d	21 54		22 24			22 58			23 25					23 55		
Lenzie	d	22 00		22 29			23 02			23 30					00 01		
Croy	d	22 06	22a12	22 36	23a08		23 08	23a12		23 37	23a41		23a42		00 06	00a10	
Falkirk Grahamston	d					23 08						23 37					00 08
Camelon	d					23 11						23 40					00 11
Larbert	d	22 21		22 50		23 16	23 20			23 50		23 46			00 21		00 16
Stirling	a	22 31		22 59		23 25	23 30			23 59		23 56		00 04	00 32		00 25
	d	22 33		23 01		23 25	23 33			00 01				00 05			00 26
Alloa	a			23 13						00 13							
Bridge of Allan	d	22 38				23 30	23 37							00 10			00 30
Dunblane	a	22 44				23 37	23 41							00 14			00 37

A To Arbroath
B To Edinburgh
C To Aberdeen
D From London Kings Cross to Inverness
E To Carnoustie
F To Inverness
G To Dundee
H To Glasgow Queen Street
I To Perth

Table T230-F

Sundays
20 May to 2 December

Edinburgh, Glasgow Queen Street and Falkirk Grahamston - Stirling, Alloa and Dunblane

		SR A	SR ◇ B	SR C	SR A	SR D		SR E	SR F	SR D	SR G	SR ◇ H	SR I	SR D	SR E	SR F		SR	SR	SR ◇ H	SR I	SR E	SR F	SR	SR D
Edinburgh	d							08 00			08 30				09 30			09 34				10 30		10 35	
Haymarket	d							08 04			08 34				09 34			09 38				10 34		10 39	
Edinburgh Park	d																	09 43						10 44	
Linlithgow	d							08 25	08 25		08 55		09 25		09 54	09 54		10 01			10 24	10 49	10 50	10 57	
Polmont	d			00 01				08 31	08 31				09 30					10 06			10 30			11 02	
Glasgow Queen Street	d					07 50				09 00		09 37	09a56	10 00					10 15	10 45	10a55				11 00
Bishopbriggs	d																		10 21						
Lenzie	d				00 01							09 46							10 27						
Croy	d				00 06	08a02		08a45	08a45	09a12	09a13			10a12	10a12	10a12			10 33			11a07	11a08		11a12
Falkirk Grahamston	d			00 08														10 13						11 09	
Camelon	d			00 11														10 16						11 12	
Larbert	d			00 16	00 21							10 01						10 22	10 45					11 18	
Stirling	a			00 25	00 32							10 10						10 30	10 54	11 11				11 26	
	d	00 01	00 05	00 26								10 10						10 31	10 55	11 11				11 27	
Alloa	a	00 13																	11 07						
Bridge of Allan	d		00 10	00 30														10 35						11 31	
Dunblane	a		00 14	00 37								10 17						10 42		11 17				11 38	

		SR ◇ J		SR	SR ◇ H	SR I	SR	SR E	SR F	SR	SR D	SR		SR ◇ H	SR I	SR	SR E	SR F	SR	SR D	SR	SR ◇ H		SR I	SR
Edinburgh	d						11 06	11 30		11 35						12 06	12 30		12 36						13 06
Haymarket	d						11 10	11 34		11 40						12 10	12 34		12 40						13 10
Edinburgh Park	d						11 15			11 45						12 15			12 45						13 15
Linlithgow	d					11 20	11 27	11 49	11 50	11 57					12 20	12 27	12 49	12 50	12 57					13 20	13 28
Polmont	d					11 26	11 32			12 02					12 27	12 32			13 02					13 26	13 34
Glasgow Queen Street	d	11 11		11 15	11 45	11a52					12 00	12 15		12 45	12a53					13 00	13 15	13 45		13a52	
Bishopbriggs	d			11 21								12 21									13 21				
Lenzie	d			11 27								12 27									13 27				
Croy	d			11 33				12a08	12a08		12a12	12 33					13a07	13a08		13a12	13 33				
Falkirk Grahamston	d						11 39			12 09						12 39			13 09						13 41
Camelon	d						11 42			12 12						12 42			13 12						13 44
Larbert	d	11 31		11 45			11 50			12 18		12 45				12 50			13 18		13 45				13 51
Stirling	a	11 40		11 54	12 11		11 59			12 26		12 54		13 11		12 59			13 26		13 54	14 12			14 00
	d	11 41		11 55	12 11					12 27		12 55		13 11					13 27		13 55	14 13			
Alloa	a			12 07								13 07									14 07				
Bridge of Allan	d									12 31									13 31						
Dunblane	a	11 47			12 17					12 38				13 17					13 38			14 19			

		SR E	SR F	SR	SR D	SR	SR ◇ K	SR ◇ H		SR I	SR	SR E	SR F	SR	SR D	SR	SR ◇ H	SR I		SR	SR E	SR F	SR	SR D	SR
Edinburgh	d	13 30		13 37							14 06	14 30		14 36						15 06	15 30		15 35		
Haymarket	d	13 35		13 42							14 10	14 34		14 41						15 10	15 34		15 39		
Edinburgh Park	d			13 46							14 15			14 45						15 15			15 44		
Linlithgow	d	13 50	13 50	13 58						14 20	14 27	14 49	14 50	14 57				15 20		15 27	15 49	15 50	15 57		
Polmont	d			14 04						14 26	14 32			15 03				15 26		15 32			16 02		
Glasgow Queen Street	d				14 00	14 15	14 38	14 49		14a52					15 00	15 15	15 45	15a51						16 00	16 15
Bishopbriggs	d					14 21										15 21									16 21
Lenzie	d					14 27										15 27									16 27
Croy	d	14a08	14a08		14a12	14 33						15a07	15a08		15a12	15 33					16a07	16a08		16a12	16 33
Falkirk Grahamston	d			14 11							14 39			15 10						15 39			16 09		
Camelon	d			14 14							14 42			15 13						15 42			16 12		
Larbert	d			14 19		14 45	14 58				14 51			15 18		15 45				15 50			16 18		16 45
Stirling	a			14 28		14 54	15 06	15 17			14 59			15 31		15 54	16 11			15 59			16 26		16 54
	d			14 28		14 55	15 07	15 18						15 32		15 55	16 12						16 27		16 55
Alloa	a					15 07										16 07									17 07
Bridge of Allan	d			14 33										15 36									16 31		
Dunblane	a			14 40			15 13	15 24						15 43			16 18						16 38		

		SR	SR E	SR ◇ H		GR L	SR F	SR	SR D	SR	SR ◇ H	SR I	SR	SR E		SR F	SR	SR D	SR ◇ K	SR	SR I	SR M	SR E	SR F
Edinburgh	d	16 06	16 30			16 32		16 36					17 07	17 30			17 35					18 06	18 30	
Haymarket	d	16 10	16 34			16 37		16 40					17 11	17 34			17 39					18 11	18 34	
Edinburgh Park	d	16 15						16 46					17 16				17 44					18 16		
Linlithgow	d	16 27	16 49				16 50	16 58				17 20	17 28	17 49		17 50	17 57				18 20	18 28	18 49	18 50
Polmont	d	16 32						17 04				17 26	17 33				18 02				18 25	18 33		
Glasgow Queen Street	d			16 45					17 00	17 15	17 45	17a51						18 00	18 11	18 16	18a50			
Bishopbriggs	d									17 21										18 22				
Lenzie	d									17 27										18 27				
Croy	d		17a07				17a08		17a12	17 33				18a07		18a08		18a12		18 34			19a07	19a08
Falkirk Grahamston	d	16 39				17 08		17 13					17 40				18 09					18 40		
Camelon	d	16 42						17 16					17 43				18 12					18 43		
Larbert	d	16 50						17 21		17 45			17 49				18 18		18 31	18 45		18 50		
Stirling	a	16 58		17 11		17 22		17 34		17 54	18 12		17 59				18 26		18 40	18 54		18 59		
	d							17 35		17 55							18 27		18 41	18 55		19 00		
Alloa	a									18 07										19 07				
Bridge of Allan	d							17 39									18 31					19 04		
Dunblane	a							17 46									18 38		18 47			19 09		

A not 20 May. From Glasgow Queen Street
B not 20 May. From Glasgow Queen Street to Perth
C not 20 May. From Edinburgh
D To Edinburgh
E until 17 June, from 15 July. To Glasgow Queen Street
F 24 June, 1 July, 8 July. To Glasgow Queen Street
G To Glasgow Queen Street
H To Aberdeen
I 24 June, 1 July, 8 July
J To Inverness
K To Elgin
L From London Kings Cross to Inverness. The Highland Chieftain
M To Perth

Table T230-F

Sundays
20 May to 2 December

Edinburgh, Glasgow Queen Street and Falkirk Grahamston - Stirling, Alloa and Dunblane

		SR	SR	SR	SR	SR		SR	SR	SR	SR	SR	SR	SR	SR	SR		SR	SR	SR	SR	SR	SR	SR	SR
			■		◇■	■		■	■		■		■	■	■			■		◇■	■	■	■		■
			A ⊼		B	C ⊼		D	E		A		C	D	E			A		B ⊼	C	D	E		A
Edinburgh [10]	d	18 35						19 30		19 35				20 30		20 35						21 30		21 35	
Haymarket	d	18 39						19 34		19 39				20 34		20 39						21 36		21 40	
Edinburgh Park	d	18 44								19 44						20 44								21 45	
Linlithgow	d	18 57				19 20		19 49	19 50	19 57			20 20	20 49	20 50	20 57					21 20	21 51	21 52	21 58	
Polmont [3]	d	19 02				19 26				20 02			20 26			21 02					21 26			22 03	
Glasgow Queen Street [10]	d		19 00	19 15	19 45	19a51					20 00	20 15	20a51					21 00	21 15	21 45	21a51				22 00
Bishopbriggs	d			19 21								20 21							21 22						
Lenzie [3]	d			19 27								20 27							21 27						
Croy [3]	d		19a12	19 33				20a07	20a08		20a12	20 33		21a07	21a08			21a12	21 34			22a09	22a10		22a12
Falkirk Grahamston [3]	d	19 09								20 09						21 09								22 10	
Camelon [4]	d	19 12								20 12						21 12								22 13	
Larbert	d	19 18		19 45						20 18		20 45				21 18			21 45					22 18	
Stirling	a	19 26		19 54	20 11					20 26		20 54				21 26			21 54	22 11				22 26	
	d	19 27		19 55	20 12					20 27		20 55				21 27			21 55	22 12				22 27	
Alloa	a			20 07								21 07							22 07						
Bridge of Allan	d	19 31								20 31						21 31								22 31	
Dunblane	a	19 38			20 18					20 38						21 38				22 18				22 38	

		SR		SR	SR	SR	SR	SR	SR	SR	SR	SR		SR
				■	■	◇	■	■	■	■	◇	■		■
				C	F	G	A	D	E	A	G	D		E
Edinburgh [10]	d				22 30	22 36		23 00				23 30		
Haymarket	d				22 34	22 41		23 04				23 34		
Edinburgh Park	d					22 45								
Linlithgow	d			22 20	22 49	22 58		23 19	23 19			23 49		23 49
Polmont [3]	d			22 26		23 03		23 25	23 25			23 55		23 55
Glasgow Queen Street [10]	d	22 15		22a51			23 00			23 30	23 45			
Bishopbriggs	d	22 21									23 50			
Lenzie [3]	d	22 27									23 55			
Croy [3]	d	22 33			23a07		23a12	23a39	23a39	23a42	23 59	00a11		00a11
Falkirk Grahamston [3]	d					23 10								
Camelon [4]	d					23 14								
Larbert	d	22 45				23 19					00 11			
Stirling	a	22 54				23 28					00 19			
	d	22 55				23 28					00 20			
Alloa	a	23 07												
Bridge of Allan	d					23 33					00 24			
Dunblane	a					23 37					00 28			

A To Edinburgh
B To Aberdeen
C 24 June, 1 July, 8 July
D until 17 June, from 15 July. To Glasgow Queen Street
E 24 June, 1 July, 8 July. To Glasgow Queen Street
F To Glasgow Queen Street
G To Perth

Table T230-R

Mondays to Fridays
21 May to 7 December

Dunblane, Alloa and Stirling - Falkirk Grahamston, Glasgow Queen Street and Edinburgh

Miles	Miles	Miles			SR MO	SR MX	SR MO	SR MX	GR	SR	SR	SR		SR	SR	SR	SR	SR	SR	SR	SR	SR		SR	SR
					■	■	■	■	■		◇	■		■	■			■	■	■	◇	■			■
					A	A	B	B	C		D	A		B	A			A	A ⊼	B	E	B			A ⊼
0	0	—	**Dunblane**	d						05 13	05 46						06 29				06 47				
2	2	—	Bridge of Allan	d						05 16	05 49						06 32				06 50				
—	—	0	**Alloa**	d												06 11									
5½	5½	6¾	**Stirling**	a						05 20	05 53					06 20	06 36				06 54				
—	—	—		d					05 26	05 30	05 54					06 23	06 37				06 55				
13½	13½	14¾	Larbert	d						05 39	06 03					06 32	06 45				07 04				
—	15	—	Camelon [4]	d						05 44							06 51								
—	16½	—	**Falkirk Grahamston** [3]	d					05 42	05 47							06 56								
24	—	25¼	Croy [3]	d			00 12	00 10			06 16			06 35		06 43		06 57		07 11	07 15	07 24			
29¼	—	30½	Lenzie [3]	d				00 16			06 22				06 39	06 50			07 08		07 21			07 34	
32¼	—	33½	Bishopbriggs	d							06 27					06 54					07 26			07 38	
34½	—	35¾	**Glasgow Queen Street** [10]	a			00 26	00 27			06 35			06 49		07 03				07 25	07 34	07 38		07 48	
—	19½	—	Polmont [3]	d						05 53		06 23			06 56		07 01		07 26						07 39
—	24¼	—	Linlithgow	d	00 03	00 04				06 00		06 30			07 03		07 08	07 15	07 33						07 45
—	38	—	Edinburgh Park	d						06 14							07 22								
—	40½	—	Haymarket	d	00s18	00s21			06 13	06 20		06s45			07s18		07 28	07s31	07s50						08s01
—	41¾	—	**Edinburgh** [10] 225,242	a	00 23	00 26			06 17	06 26		06 50			07 23		07 32	07 36	07 55						08 06

		SR	SR	SR	SR	SR	SR	SR		SR	SR	SR	SR	SR	SR	SR	SR	SR		SR	SR	SR	SR	SR	SR
					■	■		■			■	◇■	■	■				■		■	■			◇■	■
		D			A ⊼	B ⊼	D	A			B ⊼	F	A ⊼	B ⊼	G			B ⊼		A ⊼	A ⊼			F ⊼	B ⊼
Dunblane	d	07 08		07 23			07 31					07 44				07 58						08 13	08 28		
Bridge of Allan	d	07 11		07 26			07 34					07 48				08 01						08 16	08 31		
Alloa	d		07 12							07 39							07 57								
Stirling	a	07 15	07 21	07 30			07 38			07 48		07 52				08 05	08 06					08 20	08 35		
	d	07 17	07 23	07 31			07 39			07 49		07 53				08 07	08 11					08 23	08 37	08 45	
Larbert	d	07 26	07 32	07 40			07 47			07 58		08 03				08 16	08 20					08 32	08 46		
Camelon [4]	d	07 32								08 03						08 21							08 51		
Falkirk Grahamston [3]	d	07 36								08 07					08 12	08 24							08 54		
Croy [3]	d		07 43		07 43	07 54	07 59				08 11		08 12				08 33	08 38			08 43	08 44			09 06
Lenzie [3]	d		07 50				08 06					08 20		08 27	08 32		08 39					08 50			
Bishopbriggs	d		07 55				08 10								08 38		08 44					08 55			
Glasgow Queen Street [10]	a		08 04			08 08	08 19				08 25	08 34		08 40	08 47		08 52	08 55				09 03		09 15	09 20
Polmont [3]	d	07 44						08 10		08 14			08 27			08 32							09 01		
Linlithgow	d	07 51			08 01			08 16		08 21						08 39				08 45			09 08		
Edinburgh Park	d	08 06								08 34						08 53							09 23		
Haymarket	d	08 12		08 16	08s19			08s32		08 40			08s47			09 00				09s03	09s17		09 31		
Edinburgh [10] 225,242	a	08 17		08 20	08 24			08 37		08 45			08 52			09 05				09 08	09 22		09 36		

		SR	SR	SR		SR	SR	SR	SR	SR	SR	SR	SR	SR		SR	SR	SR	SR	SR	SR	SR	GR	SR
		■	■				◇	■	■	■			◇■	■		■	■			■		■	■	■
		A ⊼	A ⊼				E	B ⊼	A ⊼	A ⊼			H ⊼	B ⊼		A ⊼	A ⊼			B ⊼		A ⊼	I	A ⊼
Dunblane	d					09 03	09 07					09 28							09 58		10 13			
Bridge of Allan	d						09 10					09 31							10 01		10 16			
Alloa	d			08 41														09 42						
Stirling	a			08 50		09 08	09 14					09 35						09 52	10 05		10 20			
	d			08 53		09 09	09 15				09 23	09 37	09 43					09 53	10 07		10 23		10 32	
Larbert	d			09 02		09 17					09 32	09 46						10 02	10 16		10 32			
Camelon [4]	d					09 23						09 51							10 21					
Falkirk Grahamston [3]	d					09 26						09 54							10 24				10 47	
Croy [3]	d		09 13	09 15				09 36		09 42	09 43			10 05			10 12	10 14		10 36	10 43			10 42
Lenzie [3]	d			09 21							09 50							10 20			10 50			
Bishopbriggs	d			09 26							09 54							10 25			10 54			
Glasgow Queen Street [10]	a			09 34			09 45	09 48			10 03		10 17	10 20				10 33		10 48	11 03			
Polmont [3]	d	09 09				09 31			09 39			10 00				10 09			10 30			10 39		
Linlithgow	d	09 16				09 37			09 46			10 07				10 16			10 37			10 46		
Edinburgh Park	d					09 51						10 23							10 51					
Haymarket	d	09s34	09s48			10 00			10s01	10s17		10 29				10s32	10s45		10 59			11s01	11 13	11s16
Edinburgh [10] 225,242	a	09 39	09 53			10 06			10 07	10 23		10 34				10 37	10 51		11 06			11 06	11 17	11 21

A From Glasgow Queen Street
B From Edinburgh
C To London Kings Cross
D From Perth
E From Dundee
F From Aberdeen
G From Kirkcaldy
H From Inverurie. Forms booked connection out of IB08.
I From Inverness to London Kings Cross. The Highland Chieftain

Table T230-R

Mondays to Fridays
21 May to 7 December

Dunblane, Alloa and Stirling - Falkirk Grahamston, Glasgow Queen Street and Edinburgh

		SR	SR ◇1 A ✠	SR 1 B ✠	SR FX 1 C ✠	SR FO 1 C ✠		SR 1 C ✠	SR	SR	SR 1 B ✠	SR 1 C ✠	SR 1 C ✠	SR	SR ◇1 D ✠	SR		SR ◇1 E ✠	SR 1 B ✠	SR 1 C ✠	SR 1 C ✠	SR	SR	SR 1 B ✠	SR 1 C ✠
Dunblane	d	10 30								10 58					11 22	11 29							11 58		
Bridge of Allan	d	10 33								11 01					11 25	11 32							12 01		
Alloa	d								10 41													11 42			
Stirling	a	10 37							10 50	11 05					11 29	11 36						11 52	12 05		
	d	10 38	10 44						10 53	11 07				11 23	11 29	11 37		11 44				11 53	12 07		
Larbert	d	10 47							11 02	11 16				11 32		11 46						12 02	12 16		
Camelon 4	d	10 52								11 21						11 51							12 21		
Falkirk Grahamston 3	d	10 55								11 24						11 54							12 24		
Croy 3	d			11 05				11 12	11 14		11 34		11 42	11 43					12 06		12 12	12 14		12 32	
Lenzie 3	d								11 20					11 50								12 20			
Bishopbriggs	d								11 25					11 54								12 25			
Glasgow Queen Street 10	a		11 16	11 19					11 34		11 48			12 03	12 13			12 16	12 22			12 33		12 44	
Polmont 3	d	11 01			11 09	11 09				11 30		11 38				12 00				12 09			12 30		12 38
Linlithgow	d	11 07			11 15	11 15				11 37		11 45				12 07				12 15			12 37		12 45
Edinburgh Park	d	11 21								11 51						12 21							12 51		
Haymarket	d	11 27			11s31	11s32		11s46		11 58		12s01	12s13			12 29				12s31	12s45		12 57		13s00
Edinburgh 10 225,242	a	11 32			11 36	11 37		11 51		12 04		12 07	12 19			12 36				12 36	12 50		13 04		13 07

		SR 1 C ✠		SR	SR	SR ◇1 A ✠	SR 1 B ✠	SR 1 C ✠	SR 1 C ✠	SR	SR	SR ◇ F		SR 1 B ✠	SR 1 C ✠	SR 1 C ✠	SR	SR	SR ◇1 A ✠	SR 1 B ✠	SR 1 C ✠	SR 1 C ✠		SR	SR
Dunblane	d			12 13	12 28						12 58	13 05						13 28							13 58
Bridge of Allan	d			12 16	12 31						13 01	13 08						13 31							14 01
Alloa	d									12 41														13 41	
Stirling	a			12 20	12 35					12 50	13 05	13 12						13 35						13 50	14 05
	d			12 23	12 37	12 43				12 53	13 07	13 13					13 23	13 37	13 44					13 53	14 07
Larbert	d			12 32	12 46					13 02	13 16						13 32	13 46						14 02	14 16
Camelon 4	d				12 51						13 21							13 51							14 21
Falkirk Grahamston 3	d				12 54						13 24							13 54							14 24
Croy 3	d	12 42		12 43			13 05		13 12	13 13				13 36		13 42	13 43			14 06		14 12		14 13	
Lenzie 3	d			12 50						13 20							13 50							14 20	
Bishopbriggs	d			12 54						13 24							13 54							14 24	
Glasgow Queen Street 10	a			13 03		13 16	13 19			13 33		13 47		13 50			14 03		14 16	14 20				14 33	
Polmont 3	d				13 00			13 09			13 30				13 39			14 00			14 09				14 30
Linlithgow	d				13 07			13 15			13 37				13 45			14 07			14 15				14 37
Edinburgh Park	d				13 23						13 52							14 21							14 51
Haymarket	d	13s15			13 29			13s32	13s48		14 02				14s02	14s17		14 32			14s32	14s43			14 57
Edinburgh 10 225,242	a	13 21			13 34			13 37	13 53		14 06				14 07	14 23		14 37			14 37	14 48			15 03

		SR 1 B ✠	SR 1 C ✠	SR 1 C ✠	SR	SR	SR ◇1 A ✠	SR 1 B ✠		SR 1 C ✠	SR 1 C ✠	SR	SR	SR 1 B ✠	SR 1 C ✠	SR 1 C ✠	SR	SR		SR ◇1 A ✠	SR 1 B ✠	SR 1 C ✠	SR 1 C ✠	SR	SR
Dunblane	d				14 13	14 29							14 58				15 13	15 28							15 58
Bridge of Allan	d				14 16	14 32							15 01				15 16	15 31							16 01
Alloa	d											14 41												15 41	
Stirling	a				14 20	14 36						14 50	15 05				15 20	15 35						15 50	16 05
	d				14 23	14 37	14 44					14 53	15 07				15 23	15 37		15 44				15 53	16 07
Larbert	d				14 32	14 46						15 02	15 16				15 32	15 46						16 02	16 16
Camelon 4	d					14 51							15 21					15 51							16 21
Falkirk Grahamston 3	d					14 54							15 24					15 54							16 24
Croy 3	d	14 35		14 42	14 43			15 06			15 12	15 13		15 34		15 42	15 44				16 06		16 12	16 14	
Lenzie 3	d				14 50							15 20					15 50							16 20	
Bishopbriggs	d				14 54							15 24					15 55							16 25	
Glasgow Queen Street 10	a	14 52			15 03		15 18	15 21				15 33		15 48			16 03			16 17	16 20			16 33	
Polmont 3	d		14 38			15 00				15 08			15 30		15 38			16 00				16 09			16 30
Linlithgow	d		14 45			15 07				15 15			15 37		15 44			16 07				16 15			16 37
Edinburgh Park	d					15 21							15 51					16 22							16 52
Haymarket	d		15s00	15s14		15 29				15s31	15s46		15 59		16s01	16s13		16 28				16s32	16s43		16 58
Edinburgh 10 225,242	a		15 07	15 20		15 36				15 36	15 51		16 06		16 06	16 18		16 34				16 38	16 48		17 03

		SR ◇ F	SR 1 B ✠	SR		SR 1 C ✠	SR 1 C ✠	SR	SR 1 B ✠	SR 1 C ✠	SR 1 C ✠	SR	SR	SR 1 B ✠		SR	SR ◇1 D ✠	SR 1 C ✠	SR 1 C ✠	SR	SR ◇1 A ✠	SR 1 B ✠	SR	SR 1 C ✠	
Dunblane	d	16 06						16 28					16 58				17 21			17 29	17 38				
Bridge of Allan	d	16 09						16 31					17 01				17 24			17 32					
Alloa	d											16 41											17 41		
Stirling	a	16 13						16 35				16 50	17 05				17 28			17 36	17 43		17 50		
	d	16 14		16 23				16 37				16 53	17 07			17 19	17 29			17 38	17 44		17 51		
Larbert	d			16 32				16 46				17 02	17 16			17 29				17 47			18 00		
Camelon 4	d							16 52					17 21							17 52					
Falkirk Grahamston 3	d							16 56					17 24							17 55					
Croy 3	d		16 39	16 43			16 44		17 06		17 12	17 15		17 35		17 42			17 42			18 06	18 14		
Lenzie 3	d			16 50								17 21				17 48						18 12	18 20		
Bishopbriggs	d			16 54								17 26				17 53							18 25		
Glasgow Queen Street 10	a	16 52	16 55	17 03					17 21			17 34		17 50		18 03	18 10				18 21	18 24	18 34		
Polmont 3	d					16 39		17 06		17 12	17 27		17 31						17 57	18 02				18 09	
Linlithgow	d					16 45		17 12		17 19			17 38					17 45	18 04	18 09				18 16	
Edinburgh Park	d							17 25					17 52							18 23					
Haymarket	d					17s01	17s16	17 32		17s35	17s47		18 00					18s02	18s19	18 29				18s31	
Edinburgh 10 225,242	a					17 06	17 22	17 37		17 40	17 52		18 04					18 07	18 25	18 33				18 36	

A From Aberdeen
B From Edinburgh
C From Glasgow Queen Street
D From Inverness
E From Dyce
F From Dundee

Table T230-R

Mondays to Fridays
21 May to 7 December

Dunblane, Alloa and Stirling - Falkirk Grahamston, Glasgow Queen Street and Edinburgh

		SR 1 A ✠	SR	SR 1 B ✠	SR	SR 1 A ✠		SR 1 A ✠	SR	SR ◇1 C ✠	SR 1 B ✠	SR FX 1 A ✠	SR FO 1 A ✠	SR 1 A ✠	SR	SR		SR 1 B	SR	SR 1 A	SR 1 A	SR	SR ◇1 C ✠	SR 1 B	SR 1 A
Dunblane	d		17 58		18 11				18 29	18 38									19 14			19 28			
Bridge of Allan	d		18 01		18 14				18 32										19 17			19 31			
Alloa	d														18 28	18 53									
Stirling	a		18 05		18 18				18 36	18 43					18 43				19 21			19 35			
	d		18 07		18 19				18 37	18 44					18 53				19 23			19 37	19 45		
Larbert	d		18 16		18 28				18 47						19 02	19 16			19 32			19 46			
Camelon 4	d		18 21						18 53							19 22						19 51			
Falkirk Grahamston 3	d		18 24						18 56							19 25						19 54			
Croy 3	d	18 14		18 36	18 43			18 43			19 07			19 11	19 14			19 32	19 44					20 10	20 13
Lenzie 3	d				18 50										19 20				19 50						
Bishopbriggs	d				18 54										19 25				19 55						
Glasgow Queen Street 10	a			18 50	19 03					19 17	19 21				19 33			19 44	20 05				20 15	20 25	
Polmont 3	d		18 32			18 39			19 01			19 08	19 08			19 30				19 38	19 54	20 01			
Linlithgow	d		18 39			18 46			19 08			19 15	19 15			19 37				19 45	20 01	20 08			20 30
Edinburgh Park	d		18 52						19 22							19 51						20 22			
Haymarket	d	18s48	18 58			19s01		19s13	19 28			19s31	19s31	19s42		19 58				20s05	20s21	20 28			20s47
Edinburgh 10 225,242	a	18 53	19 03			19 07		19 18	19 33			19 36	19 37	19 47		20 03				20 10	20 28	20 32			20 52

		SR		SR	SR ◇1 D ✠	SR	SR 1 A	SR	SR ◇1 C ✠	SR 1 B	SR A	SR		SR	SR	SR 1 A	SR 1 B	SR ◇1 C ✠	SR 1 A	SR	SR	SR		SR ◇1 C	SR 1 A
Dunblane	d			19 58	20 08			20 28						20 58	21 14						21 58				
Bridge of Allan	d			20 01	20 11			20 31						21 01	21 17						22 01				
Alloa	d	19 41										20 41								21 42					
Stirling	a	19 50		20 05	20 15			20 35				20 50		21 05	21 21					21 51	22 05				
	d	19 53		20 07	20 16	20 21		20 37	20 42			20 53		21 07	21 23			21 50		21 54	22 07	22 23		22 48	
Larbert	d	20 02		20 16		20 30		20 46				21 02		21 16	21 32					22 03	22 16	22 32			
Camelon 4	d			20 21				20 51						21 21							22 21				
Falkirk Grahamston 3	d			20 24				20 54						21 24							22 24				
Croy 3	d	20 14				20 45				21 11	21 13	21 15			21 45		22 07		22 12	22 14		22 44			
Lenzie 3	d	20 21				20 52						21 21			21 51					22 21		22 51			
Bishopbriggs	d	20 25				20 56						21 26			21 56					22 25		22 55			
Glasgow Queen Street 10	a	20 34			20 46	21 07			21 15	21 25		21 34			22 04		22 21	22 25		22 34		23 04		23 18	
Polmont 3	d			20 30			20 55	21 00						21 30		21 55					22 30				22 54
Linlithgow	d			20 37			21 01	21 06			21 29			21 37		22 01			22 30		22 37				23 01
Edinburgh Park	d			20 51				21 19						21 51							22 51				
Haymarket	d			20 58			21s17	21 25			21s42			21 58		22s18			22s45		22 57				23s16
Edinburgh 10 225,242	a			21 03			21 23	21 31			21 47			22 03		22 24			22 50		23 04				23 21

		SR 1 B	SR 1 A	SR	SR FO ◇ D	SR FX ◇1 D	SR	SR		SR 1 B	SR 1 A
Dunblane	d				23 02	23 02	23 09				
Bridge of Allan	d				23 05	23 05	23 13				
Alloa	d			22 41				23 18			
Stirling	a			22 50	23 09	23 09	23 17	23 27			
	d			22 53	23 10	23 10	23 17				
Larbert	d			23 02			23 26				
Camelon 4	d						23 29				
Falkirk Grahamston 3	d						23 32				
Croy 3	d	23 08	23 12	23 13						23 41	23 43
Lenzie 3	d			23 20						23 47	
Bishopbriggs	d			23 24						23 52	
Glasgow Queen Street 10	a	23 22		23 36	23 43	23 43				23 59	
Polmont 3	d		23 28				23 40				23 58
Linlithgow	d		23 34				23 47				00 04
Edinburgh Park	d						00 02				
Haymarket	d		23s50				00 11				00s21
Edinburgh 10 225,242	a		23 55				00 15				00 26

Saturdays
26 May to 8 December

		SR 1 A	SR 1 B	SR	SR ◇ E	SR 1 A	SR 1 B	SR	SR 1 A	SR		SR 1 A ✠	SR 1 B	SR ◇ F	SR 1 A ✠	SR E	SR	SR 1 A ✠	SR 1 B ✠	SR		SR 1 A	SR 1 B ✠	SR ◇1 C ✠	SR 1 B ✠
Dunblane	d			05 21	05 46					06 29				06 47		07 08				07 31				07 44	
Bridge of Allan	d			05 24	05 49					06 32				06 50		07 11				07 34				07 48	
Alloa	d							06 11									07 12								
Stirling	a			05 28	05 53			06 20		06 36				06 54		07 15	07 21			07 38				07 52	
	d			05 30	05 54			06 23		06 37				06 55		07 17	07 23			07 39				07 53	
Larbert	d			05 39	06 03			06 32		06 45				07 04		07 26	07 32			07 47				08 03	
Camelon 4	d			05 44						06 51						07 32									
Falkirk Grahamston 3	d			05 47						06 56						07 36									
Croy 3	d		00 10		06 16		06 35	06 43	06 44				07 11	07 15			07 43	07 43	07 54	07 59			08 11		
Lenzie 3	d		00 16		06 22			06 50				07 08		07 21			07 50			08 06				08 20	08 27
Bishopbriggs	d				06 27			06 54						07 26			07 55			08 10					08 31
Glasgow Queen Street 10	a		00 27		06 35		06 49	07 03					07 25	07 34			08 04		08 08	08 19			08 25	08 34	08 40
Polmont 3	d			05 53		06 24			06 59	07 03		07 26			07 39	07 44						08 10			
Linlithgow	d	00 04		06 00		06 30			07 05	07 10		07 33			07 45	07 51		08 01				08 17			
Edinburgh Park	d			06 14						07 22						08 06									
Haymarket	d	00s21		06 20		06s46			07s22	07 30		07s50			08s01	08 12		08s18				08s33			
Edinburgh 10 225,242	a	00 26		06 25		06 51			07 27	07 34		07 55			08 06	08 16		08 23				08 38			

A From Glasgow Queen Street
B From Edinburgh
C From Aberdeen
D From Inverness
E From Perth
F From Dundee

Dunblane, Alloa and Stirling - Falkirk Grahamston, Glasgow Queen Street and Edinburgh

		SR 1 A 🍴		SR	SR	SR 1 B 🍴	SR 1 A 🍴	SR 1 A 🍴	SR	SR	SR ◇1 C 🍴	SR 1 B 🍴		SR 1 A 🍴	SR 1 A 🍴	SR	SR	SR ◇ D	SR 1 B 🍴	SR 1 A 🍴	SR 1 A 🍴	SR		SR	SR ◇1 E 🍴
Dunblane	d			07 58					08 13	08 28							09 03	09 07						09 28	
Bridge of Allan	d			08 01					08 16	08 31								09 10						09 31	
Alloa	d				07 57											08 41									
Stirling	a			08 05	08 06				08 20	08 35						08 50	09 08	09 14						09 35	
	d			08 07	08 11				08 23	08 37	08 45					08 53	09 09	09 15				09 23		09 37	09 43
Larbert	d			08 16	08 20				08 32	08 46						09 02	09 17					09 32		09 46	
Camelon	d			08 21						08 51							09 23							09 51	
Falkirk Grahamston	d			08 24						08 54							09 26							09 54	
Croy	d	08 12			08 33	08 38		08 43	08 44			09 06			09 13	09 15			09 35		09 42	09 43			
Lenzie	d				08 39				08 50							09 21						09 50			
Bishopbriggs	d				08 44				08 55							09 26						09 54			
Glasgow Queen Street	a				08 52	08 55			09 03		09 15	09 20				09 34		09 45	09 48			10 03			10 17
Polmont	d	08 27		08 32						09 01				09 09			09 31			09 39				10 00	
Linlithgow	d			08 39			08 45			09 08				09 16			09 37			09 46				10 07	
Edinburgh Park	d			08 52						09 22							09 51							10 23	
Haymarket	d	08s47		09 00			09s03	09s13		09 30				09s35	09s47		09 59			10s01	10s17			10 29	
Edinburgh 225,242	a	08 52		09 07			09 08	09 18		09 36				09 40	09 53		10 03			10 06	10 22			10 34	

		SR 1 B 🍴	SR 1 A	SR 1 A 🍴	SR	SR	SR 1 B 🍴	SR		SR 1 A 🍴	GR 1 F	SR 1 A 🍴	SR	SR ◇1 C 🍴	SR 1 B 🍴	SR 1 A 🍴	SR 1 A 🍴	SR		SR	SR 1 B 🍴	SR 1 A 🍴	SR 1 A 🍴	SR	SR ◇1 G 🍴
Dunblane	d					09 58		10 13					10 30							10 58					11 22
Bridge of Allan	d					10 01		10 16					10 33							11 01					11 25
Alloa	d				09 42													10 41							
Stirling	a				09 52	10 05		10 20					10 37					10 50		11 05					11 29
	d				09 53	10 07		10 23			10 32		10 38	10 44				10 53		11 07				11 23	11 29
Larbert	d				10 02	10 16		10 32					10 47					11 02		11 16				11 32	
Camelon	d					10 21							10 52							11 21					
Falkirk Grahamston	d					10 24					10 47		10 55							11 24					
Croy	d	10 05		10 12	10 14		10 35	10 43				10 42			11 05		11 12	11 14			11 32		11 42	11 43	
Lenzie	d				10 20			10 50										11 20						11 50	
Bishopbriggs	d				10 25			10 54										11 25						11 54	
Glasgow Queen Street	a	10 20			10 33		10 47	11 03						11 16	11 19			11 34			11 47			12 03	12 13
Polmont	d		10 09			10 30				10 39			11 01			11 09				11 30		11 38			
Linlithgow	d		10 16			10 37				10 46			11 08			11 15				11 37		11 45			
Edinburgh Park	d					10 52							11 22							11 51					
Haymarket	d		10s32	10s46		10 59				11s01	11 13	11s16	11 28			11s31	11s43			11 57		12s00	12s13		
Edinburgh 225,242	a		10 37	10 51		11 03				11 06	11 17	11 21	11 32			11 36	11 48			12 03		12 06	12 19		

		SR	SR ◇1 H 🍴	SR 1 B 🍴		SR 1 A 🍴	SR 1 A 🍴	SR	SR	SR 1 B 🍴	SR 1 A 🍴	SR 1 A 🍴	SR	SR		SR ◇1 C 🍴	SR 1 B 🍴	SR 1 A 🍴	SR 1 A 🍴	SR	SR	SR ◇ D	SR 1 B 🍴	SR 1 A 🍴	
Dunblane	d	11 29							11 58				12 13	12 28							12 58	13 05			
Bridge of Allan	d	11 32							12 01				12 16	12 31							13 01	13 08			
Alloa	d							11 42												12 41					
Stirling	a	11 36						11 52	12 05				12 20	12 35						12 50	13 05	13 12			
	d	11 37	11 44					11 53	12 07				12 23	12 37		12 43				12 53	13 07	13 13			
Larbert	d	11 46						12 02	12 16				12 32	12 46						13 02	13 16				
Camelon	d	11 51							12 21					12 51							13 21				
Falkirk Grahamston	d	11 54							12 24					12 54							13 24				
Croy	d			12 06			12 12	12 14		12 32		12 42	12 43				13 05		13 12	13 13			13 36		
Lenzie	d							12 20					12 50							13 20					
Bishopbriggs	d							12 25					12 54							13 24					
Glasgow Queen Street	a		12 16	12 22				12 33		12 44			13 03			13 16	13 19			13 33		13 47	13 50		
Polmont	d	12 00				12 09			12 30		12 38			13 00				13 09			13 30			13 39	
Linlithgow	d	12 07				12 15			12 37		12 45			13 07				13 15			13 37			13 45	
Edinburgh Park	d	12 21							12 52					13 23							13 52				
Haymarket	d	12 28				12s32	12s43		12 58		13s01	13s12		13 29				13s32	13s46		14 00			14s01	
Edinburgh 225,242	a	12 34				12 37	12 48		13 02		13 06	13 18		13 33				13 39	13 51		14 06			14 06	

		SR 1 A 🍴	SR	SR	SR ◇1 C 🍴	SR 1 B 🍴	SR 1 A 🍴	SR 1 A 🍴	SR	SR		SR 1 B 🍴	SR 1 A 🍴	SR 1 A 🍴	SR	SR	SR ◇1 C 🍴	SR 1 B 🍴	SR 1 A 🍴	SR 1 A 🍴		SR	SR	SR 1 B 🍴	SR 1 A 🍴
Dunblane	d			13 28						13 58					14 13	14 29							14 58		
Bridge of Allan	d			13 31						14 01					14 16	14 32							15 01		
Alloa	d								13 41													14 41			
Stirling	a			13 35					13 50	14 05					14 20	14 36						14 50	15 05		
	d		13 23	13 37	13 44				13 53	14 07					14 23	14 37	14 44					14 53	15 07		
Larbert	d		13 32	13 46					14 02	14 16					14 32	14 46						15 02	15 16		
Camelon	d			13 51						14 21						14 51							15 21		
Falkirk Grahamston	d			13 54						14 24						14 54							15 24		
Croy	d	13 42	13 43			14 05		14 12	14 13			14 32		14 42	14 43			15 06		15 12		15 13		15 34	
Lenzie	d		13 50						14 20						14 50							15 20			
Bishopbriggs	d		13 54						14 24						14 54							15 25			
Glasgow Queen Street	a		14 03		14 16	14 19			14 33			14 44			15 03		15 18	15 21				15 33		15 47	
Polmont	d			14 00			14 09			14 30			14 38			15 00			15 09				15 30		15 38
Linlithgow	d			14 07			14 15			14 37			14 45			15 07			15 15				15 37		15 45
Edinburgh Park	d			14 21						14 52						15 23							15 52		
Haymarket	d	14s15		14 27			14s31	14s48		14 58			15s01	15s14		15 30			15s32	15s47			16 00		16s02
Edinburgh 225,242	a	14 22		14 33			14 36	14 53		15 03			15 06	15 19		15 36			15 37	15 53			16 07		16 07

A From Glasgow Queen Street
B From Edinburgh
C From Aberdeen
D From Dundee
E From Inverurie
F From Inverness to London Kings Cross. The Highland Chieftain
G From Inverness
H From Dyce

Please check the 'Additional Notes to Individual Tables' section for any other general notes that apply to this Table

Table T230-R

Saturdays

26 May to 8 December

Dunblane, Alloa and Stirling - Falkirk Grahamston, Glasgow Queen Street and Edinburgh

		SR 1 A 🍴		SR	SR	SR ◇1 B 🍴	SR 1 C 🍴	SR 1 A 🍴	SR 1 A 🍴	SR	SR	SR ◇ D		SR 1 C 🍴	SR	SR 1 A 🍴	SR 1 A 🍴	SR	SR 1 C 🍴	SR 1 A	SR 1 A 🍴	SR		SR	SR 1 C 🍴
Dunblane	d			15 13	15 28						15 58	16 06						16 28						16 58	
Bridge of Allan	d			15 16	15 31						16 01	16 09						16 31						17 01	
Alloa	d									15 41												16 41			
Stirling	a			15 20	15 35					15 50	16 05	16 13						16 35				16 50		17 05	
	d			15 23	15 37	15 44				15 53	16 07	16 14			16 23			16 37				16 53		17 07	
Larbert	d			15 32	15 46					16 02	16 16				16 32			16 46				17 02		17 16	
Camelon	d				15 51						16 21							16 52						17 21	
Falkirk Grahamston	d				15 54						16 24							16 55						17 24	
Croy	d	15 43		15 44			16 06		16 12	16 14				16 37	16 43		16 44		17 06		17 12	17 15			17 33
Lenzie	d			15 50						16 20					16 50							17 21			
Bishopbriggs	d			15 55						16 25					16 54							17 26			
Glasgow Queen Street	a			16 03		16 17	16 20			16 33		16 48		16 52	17 03				17 20			17 34			17 47
Polmont	d				16 00			16 09			16 30					16 39		17 01		17 12	17 27			17 31	
Linlithgow	d				16 07			16 15			16 37					16 45		17 08		17 19				17 38	
Edinburgh Park	d				16 22						16 52							17 22						17 52	
Haymarket	d	16s13			16 28			16s31	16s43		16 58					17s01	17s16	17 31		17s33	17s46			18 00	
Edinburgh 225,242	a	16 18			16 33			16 38	16 48		17 04					17 06	17 22	17 35		17 38	17 51			18 04	

		SR	SR ◇1 E 🍴	SR 1 A 🍴	SR 1 A 🍴	SR	SR ◇1 B 🍴	SR 1 C 🍴		SR	SR 1 A 🍴	SR 1 A 🍴	SR	SR 1 C 🍴	SR	SR 1 A 🍴	SR 1 A 🍴	SR		SR ◇1 B 🍴	SR 1 C 🍴	SR 1 A 🍴	SR 1 A 🍴	SR	SR
Dunblane	d		17 21			17 29	17 38						17 58		18 11			18 29		18 38					
Bridge of Allan	d		17 24			17 32							18 01		18 14			18 32							
Alloa	d									17 41														18 28	18 53
Stirling	a		17 28			17 36	17 43			17 50			18 05		18 18			18 36		18 43				18 43	
	d	17 23	17 29			17 38	17 44			17 51			18 07		18 19			18 37		18 44				18 53	
Larbert	d	17 32				17 47				18 00			18 16		18 28			18 47						19 02	19 16
Camelon	d					17 52							18 21					18 53							19 22
Falkirk Grahamston	d					17 55							18 24					18 56							19 25
Croy	d	17 43			17 43			18 04		18 14		18 14		18 34	18 43		18 43				19 07		19 12	19 14	
Lenzie	d	17 50						18 10		18 20					18 50									19 20	
Bishopbriggs	d	17 54								18 25					18 54									19 25	
Glasgow Queen Street	a	18 03	18 10				18 17	18 21		18 33				18 46	19 03					19 17	19 23			19 33	
Polmont	d				17 58	18 03					18 10		18 32			18 39		19 01				19 10			19 30
Linlithgow	d			17 45	18 04	18 10					18 16		18 39			18 46		19 08				19 16			19 37
Edinburgh Park	d					18 23							18 52					19 23							19 51
Haymarket	d			18s02	18s20	18 29					18s32	18s44	18 58			19s01	19s13	19 29				19s34	19s46		19 57
Edinburgh 225,242	a			18 07	18 25	18 34					18 37	18 51	19 03			19 06	19 18	19 33				19 40	19 51		20 03

		SR 1 C 🍴	SR	SR 1 A		SR 1 A	SR	SR ◇1 B 🍴	SR 1 C	SR 1 A	SR	SR	SR ◇1 E 🍴	SR		SR 1 A	SR	SR ◇1 B 🍴	SR 1 C	SR 1 A	SR	SR	SR	SR 1 A	
Dunblane	d		19 14				19 28					19 58	20 08				20 28					20 58	21 14		
Bridge of Allan	d		19 17				19 31					20 01	20 11				20 31					21 01	21 17		
Alloa	d										19 41										20 41				
Stirling	a		19 21				19 35				19 50	20 05	20 15				20 35				20 50	21 05	21 21		
	d		19 23				19 37	19 45			19 53	20 07	20 16	20 21			20 37	20 42			20 53	21 07	21 23		
Larbert	d		19 32				19 46				20 02	20 16		20 30			20 46				21 02	21 16	21 32		
Camelon	d						19 51					20 21					20 51					21 21			
Falkirk Grahamston	d						19 54					20 24					20 54					21 24			
Croy	d	19 35	19 44						20 10	20 13	20 14			20 45					21 10	21 12	21 14		21 45		
Lenzie	d		19 50								20 21			20 52							21 20		21 51		
Bishopbriggs	d		19 55								20 25			20 56							21 25		21 56		
Glasgow Queen Street	a	19 49	20 05					20 15	20 24		20 34		20 46	21 06				21 15	21 24		21 33		22 04		
Polmont	d			19 38		19 54	20 01					20 30				20 55	21 00					21 30		21 55	
Linlithgow	d			19 45		20 01	20 08			20 30		20 37				21 01	21 07			21 28		21 37		22 01	
Edinburgh Park	d						20 22					20 51					21 20					21 51			
Haymarket	d			20s01		20s18	20 28			20s47		20 57				21s17	21 27			21s43		21 59		22s17	
Edinburgh 225,242	a			20 08		20 26	20 33			20 52		21 01				21 23	21 31			21 48		22 03		22 25	

		SR 1 C	SR ◇1 B 🍴	SR 1 A	SR	SR	SR	SR ◇1 B	SR 1 A	SR 1 C		SR 1 A	SR	SR ◇1 E	SR	SR	SR 1 C	SR 1 A
Dunblane	d					21 58								23 02	23 09			
Bridge of Allan	d					22 01								23 05	23 13			
Alloa	d				21 42								22 41			23 18		
Stirling	a				21 51	22 05							22 50	23 09	23 17	23 27		
	d		21 50		21 54	22 07	22 23	22 48					22 53	23 10	23 17			
Larbert	d				22 03	22 16	22 32						23 02		23 26			
Camelon	d					22 21									23 29			
Falkirk Grahamston	d					22 24									23 32			
Croy	d	22 07		22 12	22 14		22 44			23 08		23 12	23 13				23 41	23 43
Lenzie	d				22 21		22 51						23 20				23 47	
Bishopbriggs	d				22 25		22 55						23 24				23 52	
Glasgow Queen Street	a	22 21	22 26		22 35		23 04	23 18		23 22			23 36	23 43			23 59	
Polmont	d					22 30			22 54			23 28			23 40			23 58
Linlithgow	d			22 30		22 37			23 00			23 34			23 47			00 04
Edinburgh Park	d					22 51									00 02			
Haymarket	d			22s45		22 57			23s16			23s49			00 08			00s20
Edinburgh 225,242	a			22 50		23 03			23 22			23 56			00 12			00 26

A From Glasgow Queen Street
B From Aberdeen
C From Edinburgh
D From Dundee
E From Inverness

Dunblane, Alloa and Stirling - Falkirk Grahamston, Glasgow Queen Street and Edinburgh

		SR	SR	SR	SR	SR		SR	SR	SR	SR	SR	SR	SR	SR	SR		SR	SR	SR	SR	SR	SR	SR	SR
		■	■	■	■	■		■		■		◇	■	◇	■	■			■		■	■	■		
		A	B	C	D	C		C		D		E	C	F	D	C			C	F	G	H	C		
						🛒		🛒		🛒			🛒			🛒			🛒		🛒	🛒	🛒		
Dunblane	d											09 33		09 43						10 38				11 01	
Bridge of Allan	d													09 47						10 41				11 04	
Alloa	d										09 14							10 14							11 14
Stirling	a										09 23	09 38		09 51				10 23		10 45				11 08	11 23
	d								09 05		09 26	09 39		09 51				10 26		10 46				11 10	11 25
Larbert	d								09 13		09 36	09 47		10 00				10 36		10 55				11 19	11 34
Camelon ■	d								09 19					10 05						11 00				11 24	
Falkirk Grahamston ■	d								09 22					10 08						11 03				11 27	
Croy ■	d		00 10	08 02	08 46			09 12		09 14	09 52				10 12	10 13		10 48			11 08	11 08	11 12		11 45
Lenzie ■	d		00 16								09 57	10 01						10 55							11 52
Bishopbriggs	d										10 02							10 59							11 56
Glasgow Queen Street ■	a		00 27		09 00					09 28	10 10	10 14			10 26			11 08			11 22	11 23			12 05
Polmont ■	d			08 16		08 53			09 29				09 53	10 14					10 55	11 09				11 33	
Linlithgow	d	00 04		08 23		08 59		09 30	09 36				10 00	10 21		10 30			11 01	11 16			11 30	11 40	
Edinburgh Park	d								09 50					10 34						11 30				11 54	
Haymarket	d	00s20		08 50		09s20		09s49	10 00				10s20	10 40		10s46			11s17	11 36			11s48	12 03	
Edinburgh ■ 225,242	a	00 26		08 54		09 25		09 54	10 04				10 25	10 46		10 51			11 22	11 41			11 53	12 10	

		SR		SR	SR	SR	SR	SR	SR	SR	GR	SR		SR	SR	SR	SR	SR	SR	SR	SR	SR		SR	SR
		◇■		■		■	■	■			■ ■	◇■		■		■	■	■			◇■	■			■
		I		C		G	H	C			J	I		C		G	H	C			K	C			D
		🛒		🛒		🛒	🛒	🛒			🍴	🛒		🛒		🛒	🛒	🛒			🛒				🛒
Dunblane	d	11 36							12 01		12 28	12 36							13 01		13 31				
Bridge of Allan	d								12 04										13 04						
Alloa	d									12 14										13 14					
Stirling	a	11 42							12 08	12 23	12 34	12 42							13 08	13 23	13 37				
	d	11 43			11 48				12 10	12 25	12 35	12 43			12 47				13 10	13 25	13 38			13 46	
Larbert	d				11 57				12 19	12 34					12 56				13 19	13 34				13 55	
Camelon ■	d				12 02				12 24						13 01				13 24					14 00	
Falkirk Grahamston ■	d				12 05				12 27		12 51				13 04				13 27					14 03	
Croy ■	d					12 08	12 09	12 12		12 45						13 08	13 08	13 12		13 45					14 08
Lenzie ■	d									12 52										13 52					
Bishopbriggs	d									12 56										13 56					
Glasgow Queen Street ■	a	12 14				12 23	12 24			13 05		13 14				13 22	13 23			14 05	14 09				14 22
Polmont ■	d			11 54	12 11				12 33					12 59	13 10				13 33			13 54		14 09	
Linlithgow	d			12 00	12 18			12 30	12 40					13 05	13 17			13 30	13 40			14 00		14 16	
Edinburgh Park	d				12 32				12 54						13 30				13 54					14 30	
Haymarket	d			12s16	12 38			12s45	13 00		13 17			13s21	13 36			13s50	14 00			14s19		14 36	
Edinburgh ■ 225,242	a			12 21	12 42			12 50	13 06		13 21			13 26	13 41			13 55	14 04			14 24		14 42	

		SR	SR	SR	SR	SR	SR	SR		SR	SR	SR	SR	SR	SR	SR	SR	SR		SR	SR	SR	SR	SR	SR
		■			◇■	■		■		■		◇■		◇■	■		■	■				◇■	■		■
		C			I	C		D		C		L		I	C		D	C				I	C		D
		🛒			🛒							🛒		🛒			🛒	🛒				🛒	🛒		🛒
Dunblane	d		14 01		14 32						15 01	15 18		15 36						16 01		16 34			
Bridge of Allan	d		14 04								15 04									16 04					
Alloa	d			14 14									15 14								16 14				
Stirling	a		14 08	14 23	14 38						15 08	15 24	15 23	15 42						16 08	16 23	16 40			
	d		14 10	14 25	14 38		14 46				15 10	15 24	15 28	15 42		15 47				16 10	16 25	16 40		16 46	
Larbert	d		14 19	14 34			14 55				15 19	15 33	15 37			15 56				16 19	16 34			16 55	
Camelon ■	d		14 24				15 00				15 24					16 01				16 24				17 00	
Falkirk Grahamston ■	d		14 27				15 03				15 27					16 04				16 27				17 03	
Croy ■	d	14 12		14 45				15 08		15 12			15 52				16 08	16 12			16 45				17 08
Lenzie ■	d			14 52									15 58								16 52				
Bishopbriggs	d			14 56									16 03								16 56				
Glasgow Queen Street ■	a			15 05	15 09			15 22				15 58	16 11	16 17			16 22				17 05	17 13			17 22
Polmont ■	d		14 33			14 54	15 09				15 33				15 53	16 10				16 33			16 55	17 09	
Linlithgow	d	14 30	14 40			15 00	15 16			15 30	15 40				16 00	16 17		16 30		16 40			17 01	17 16	
Edinburgh Park	d		14 54				15 30				15 53					16 31				16 55				17 30	
Haymarket	d	14s45	15 00			15s16	15 36			15s47	16 00				16s19	16 37		16s45		17 01			17s20	17 36	
Edinburgh ■ 225,242	a	14 50	15 06			15 22	15 41			15 52	16 05				16 24	16 41		16 50		17 06			17 25	17 43	

		SR	SR	SR		SR	SR	SR	SR	SR	SR	SR	SR	SR		SR	SR	XC	SR	SR	SR	SR	SR	SR	
		■				◇■	■	■	■			◇■	■	■		◇■	■	◇■			■	■	◇■	■	
		C				I	C	D	C			I	C	D		L	C	M			C	D	L	C	
		🛒				🛒	🛒		🛒			🛒	🛒	🛒		🛒	🛒						🛒		
Dunblane	d		17 01			17 31				18 01		18 31				19 03			19 11						
Bridge of Allan	d		17 04							18 04									19 14						
Alloa	d			17 14							18 14									19 14					
Stirling	a		17 08	17 23		17 37				18 08	18 23	18 37				19 08			19 18	19 23					
	d		17 10	17 25		17 38				18 10	18 25	18 37				19 09			19 19	19 25			19 58		
Larbert	d		17 19	17 34						18 19	18 34					19 17			19 28	19 34					
Camelon ■	d		17 24							18 24									19 33						
Falkirk Grahamston ■	d		17 27							18 27									19 36						
Croy ■	d	17 12		17 45				18 08	18 12		18 45			19 08			19 12			19 45		20 08		20 12	
Lenzie ■	d			17 52							18 52									19 52					
Bishopbriggs	d			17 56							18 56									19 56					
Glasgow Queen Street ■	a			18 05		18 13		18 24			19 05	19 08		19 22		19 41				20 05		20 22	20 29		
Polmont ■	d		17 33				17 54			18 33			18 54						19 42		19 53				
Linlithgow	d	17 30	17 40				18 00		18 30	18 40			19 00				19 30		19 49		20 00			20 30	
Edinburgh Park	d		17 54							18 54									20 02						
Haymarket	d	17s46	18 00				18s20		18s45	19 01			19s16				19s48	19 59	20 08		20s20			20s45	
Edinburgh ■ 225,242	a	17 51	18 04				18 25		18 50	19 06			19 21				19 53	20 03	20 13		20 25			20 50	

A not 20 May. From Glasgow Queen Street
B not 20 May. From Edinburgh
C From Glasgow Queen Street
D From Edinburgh
E From Dundee
F From Perth
G until 17 June, from 15 July. From Edinburgh
H 24 June, 1 July, 8 July. From Linlithgow
I From Aberdeen
J From Inverness to London Kings Cross. The Highland Chieftain
K From Inverurie
L From Inverness
M until 9 September. From Motherwell to Newcastle

Dunblane, Alloa and Stirling - Falkirk Grahamston, Glasgow Queen Street and Edinburgh

		SR	SR	SR	SR	SR	SR	SR	SR		SR	XC	SR	SR	SR	SR	SR	SR	SR		SR	SR			
				■	■	■	■				◇■	◇■	■	■	■		■	■	■		■	■			
				A	B	C	A				D	E	A	F	A		A	F	A		F	A			
											🛒														
Dunblane	d	20 01						21 01			21 38					22 01									
Bridge of Allan	d	20 04						21 04								22 04									
Alloa	d		20 14						21 14																
Stirling	a	20 08	20 23					21 08	21 23		21 43					22 08									
	d	20 10	20 25					21 10	21 25		21 44					22 10									
Larbert	d	20 19	20 34					21 19	21 34		21 52					22 19									
Camelon ■	d	20 24						21 24								22 24									
Falkirk Grahamston ■	d	20 27						21 27								22 27									
Croy ■	d		20 45		21 08	21 08	21 12		21 45					22 10	22 12			23 08	23 12		23 40	23 42			
Lenzie ■	d		20 52						21 52		22 05														
Bishopbriggs	d		20 56						21 56																
Glasgow Queen Street ■	a		21 05		21 22	21 23			22 05		22 18			22 24				23 22			23 54				
Polmont ■	d	20 33		20 53				21 33					21 53			22 33	22 53					23 57			
Linlithgow	d	20 40		21 00			21 30	21 40					22 00		22 30	22 40	23 00		23 30			00 03			
Edinburgh Park	d	20 53						21 54								22 54									
Haymarket	d	21 02		21s15			21s45	22 00				22 04	22s18		22s45	23 01	23s15		23s45			00s18			
Edinburgh ■ 225,242	a	21 06		21 20			21 50	22 04				22 08	22 23		22 50	23 07	23 21		23 52			00 23			

A From Glasgow Queen Street
B 24 June, 1 July, 8 July. From Linlithgow
C until 17 June, from 15 July. From Edinburgh
D From Aberdeen
E until 9 September. From Motherwell
F From Edinburgh

Table T231-F

Mondays to Fridays

21 May to 7 December

Motherwell, Glasgow Queen Street - Falkirk Grahamston

		SR	SR	SR	SR	SR	SR	SR	SR	SR		SR	SR	SR	SR	SR	SR	SR	SR	SR		SR	SR	SR	SR
Motherwell	d	05 42		06 40				07 43					08 43				09 43					10 45			
Whifflet	d	05 49		06 47				07 49					08 50				09 50					10 52			
Coatbridge Central	d	05 52		06 50				07 52					08 53				09 52					10 54			
Glasgow Queen Street	d		06 17			07 07						08 24				09 23				10 23					11 22
Springburn	d		06 23		06 55	07 13	07 29		07 55	08 24		08 31		08 54	09 24	09 31		09 54	10 24	10 31			10 54	11 24	11 31
Stepps	d		06 30		07 01	07 20	07 35		08 01	08 30		08 38		09 00	09 30	09 38		10 00	10 30	10 38			11 00	11 30	11 38
Gartcosh	d		06 33		07 05	07 23	07 39		08 05	08 34		08 41		09 04	09 34	09 41		10 04	10 34	10 41			11 04	11 34	11 41
Greenfaulds	d	05 59	06 41	06 59	07 14	07 31	07 46	08 00	08 14	08 41		08 49	09 00	09 11	09 41	09 49	10 01	10 11	10 41	10 49		11 02	11 11	11 41	11 49
Cumbernauld	d	06a01	06 43	07a01	07a16	07 33	07a49	08a02	08a17	08a44		08 51	09a02	09a14	09a44	09 51	10a03	10a14	10a44	10 51		11a04	11a14	11a44	11 51
Camelon	d		07 01			07 48						09 04				10 04				11 04					12 04
Falkirk Grahamston	a		07 05			07 51						09 07				10 07				11 07					12 07

		SR	SR	SR	SR	SR		SR	SR	SR	SR	SR	SR	SR	SR	SR		SR	SR	SR	SR	SR	SR	SR	SR
Motherwell	d	11 45				12 45					13 45				14 45					15 45				16 45	
Whifflet	d	11 52				12 52					13 52				14 52					15 52				16 52	
Coatbridge Central	d	11 54				12 54					13 54				14 54					15 54				16 54	
Glasgow Queen Street	d				12 24					13 23				14 22					15 22				16 23		
Springburn	d		11 54	12 23	12 30			12 54	13 22	13 30		13 54	14 22	14 30		14 54		15 23	15 30		15 54	16 22	16 29		16 54
Stepps	d		12 00	12 30	12 37			13 00	13 28	13 37		14 00	14 28	14 37		15 00		15 30	15 37		16 00	16 28	16 36		17 00
Gartcosh	d		12 04	12 33	12 41			13 04	13 32	13 41		14 04	14 32	14 41		15 04		15 33	15 41		16 04	16 32	16 40		17 04
Greenfaulds	d	12 02	12 11	12 41	12 48	13 02		13 11	13 39	13 48	14 02	14 13	14 39	14 48	15 02	15 11		15 40	15 48	16 02	16 11	16 39	16 47	17 02	17 11
Cumbernauld	d	12a04	12a13	12a44	12 51	13a04		13a13	13a42	13 51	14a04	14a15	14a42	14 51	15a04	15a13		15a43	15 51	16a04	16a13	16a43	16 50	17a04	17a13
Camelon	d				13 04					14 04				15 04					16 04				17 03		
Falkirk Grahamston	a				13 07					14 07				15 07					16 07				17 06		

		SR		SR	SR	SR	SR	SR	SR	SR	SR	SR		SR	SR	SR	SR	SR	SR	SR	SR	SR		SR	SR
Motherwell	d				17 45				18 45					19 45				20 45				21 46			
Whifflet	d				17 52				18 51					19 52				20 52				21 53			
Coatbridge Central	d				17 54				18 54					19 54				20 54				21 55			
Glasgow Queen Street	d			17 23				18 24				19 23				20 12				21 11					
Springburn	d	17 24		17 32		17 54	18 24	18 31		18 54	19 22	19 31			20 00	20 20	20 30		20 59	21 21	21 30			21 52	22 21
Stepps	d	17 30		17 39		18 00	18 30	18 38		19 00	19 28	19 38			20 06	20 27	20 37		21 05	21 28	21 36			21 58	22 28
Gartcosh	d	17 34		17 43		18 04	18 34	18 41		19 04	19 32	19 41			20 10	20 31	20 40		21 09	21 31	21 40			22 02	22 31
Greenfaulds	d	17 41		17 51	18 02	18 11	18 41	18 49	19 01	19 14	19 39	19 49		20 02	20 17	20 38	20 47	21 02	21 16	21 39	21 47	22 03		22 11	22 38
Cumbernauld	d	17a44		17 54	18a04	18a13	18a44	18 51	19a03	19a16	19a42	19 51		20a04	20a19	20 41	20a50	21a04	21a18	21 41	21a49	22a05		22a13	22a41
Camelon	d			18 08				19 04				20 04				20 56				21 54					
Falkirk Grahamston	a			18 11				19 07				20 07				20 59				21 57					

		SR	SR	SR	SR	SR	SR
Motherwell	d		22 45				
Whifflet	d		22 52				
Coatbridge Central	d		22 54				
Glasgow Queen Street	d	22 22				23 23	23 52
Springburn	d	22 29		22 52	23 24	23 31	23 59
Stepps	d	22 36		22 59	23 30	23 38	00 07
Gartcosh	d	22 40		23 02	23 34	23 41	00 10
Greenfaulds	d	22 47	23 02	23 09	23 41	23 49	00 18
Cumbernauld	d	22 50	23a04	23a12	23a44	23 51	00a21
Camelon	d	23 03				00 04	
Falkirk Grahamston	a	23 06				00 07	

Saturdays

26 May to 8 December

		SR	SR	SR	SR	SR	SR	SR	SR	SR		SR	SR	SR	SR	SR	SR	SR	SR	SR		SR	SR	SR	SR
Motherwell	d		05 42		06 40				07 43					08 43				09 43					10 45		
Whifflet	d		05 49		06 47				07 49					08 50				09 50					10 52		
Coatbridge Central	d		05 52		06 50				07 52					08 53				09 52					10 54		
Glasgow Queen Street	d	05 15		06 17			07 07						08 24				09 23					10 23			
Springburn	d	05 21		06 23		06 55	07 13	07 29		07 55		08 24	08 31		08 54	09 24	09 31		09 54	10 24		10 31		10 54	11 24
Stepps	d	05 28		06 30		07 01	07 20	07 35		08 01		08 30	08 38		09 00	09 30	09 38		10 00	10 30		10 38		11 00	11 30
Gartcosh	d	05 31		06 33		07 05	07 23	07 39		08 05		08 34	08 41		09 04	09 34	09 41		10 04	10 34		10 41		11 04	11 34
Greenfaulds	d	05 39	05 59	06 41	06 59	07 14	07 31	07 46	08 00	08 14		08 41	08 49	09 00	09 11	09 41	09 49	10 01	10 11	10 41		10 49	11 02	11 11	11 41
Cumbernauld	d	05 41	06a01	06 43	07a01	07a16	07 33	07a49	08a02	08a17		08a44	08 51	09a02	09a14	09a44	09 51	10a03	10a14	10a44		10 51	11a04	11a14	11a44
Camelon	d	05 54		06 59			07 48						09 04				10 04					11 04			
Falkirk Grahamston	a	05 57		07 02			07 51						09 07				10 07					11 07			

		SR	SR	SR	SR	SR		SR	SR	SR	SR	SR	SR	SR	SR	SR		SR	SR	SR	SR	SR	SR	SR	SR
Motherwell	d		11 45					12 45				13 45				14 45					15 45				16 45
Whifflet	d		11 52					12 52				13 52				14 52					15 52				16 52
Coatbridge Central	d		11 54					12 54				13 54				14 54					15 54				16 54
Glasgow Queen Street	d	11 22				12 24					13 23				14 22					15 22				16 23	
Springburn	d	11 31		11 54	12 23	12 30			12 54	13 22	13 30		13 54	14 22	14 30			14 54	15 23	15 30		15 54	16 22	16 29	
Stepps	d	11 38		12 00	12 30	12 37			13 00	13 28	13 37		14 00	14 28	14 37			15 00	15 30	15 37		16 00	16 28	16 36	
Gartcosh	d	11 41		12 04	12 33	12 41			13 04	13 32	13 41		14 04	14 32	14 41			15 04	15 33	15 41		16 04	16 32	16 39	
Greenfaulds	d	11 49	12 02	12 11	12 41	12 48		13 02	13 11	13 39	13 48	14 02	14 13	14 39	14 48	15 02		15 11	15 40	15 48	16 02	16 11	16 39	16 47	17 02
Cumbernauld	d	11 51	12a04	12a13	12a44	12 51		13a04	13a13	13a42	13 51	14a04	14a15	14a42	14 51	15a04		15a13	15a43	15 51	16a04	16a13	16a43	16 49	17a04
Camelon	d	12 04				13 04					14 04				15 04					16 04				17 02	
Falkirk Grahamston	a	12 07				13 07					14 07				15 07					16 07				17 05	

		SR		SR	SR	SR	SR	SR	SR	SR	SR	SR		SR	SR	SR	SR	SR	SR	SR	SR	SR		SR	SR
Motherwell	d					17 45				18 45					19 45				20 48					21 46	
Whifflet	d					17 52				18 51					19 52				20 54					21 52	
Coatbridge Central	d					17 54				18 54					19 54				20 57					21 55	
Glasgow Queen Street	d				17 23				18 24					19 23			20 12				21 12				
Springburn	d	16 54		17 24	17 32		17 54	18 24	18 31		18 54	19 22		19 31		20 00	20 20	20 30		20 59	21 21	21 30			21 52
Stepps	d	17 00		17 30	17 39		18 00	18 30	18 38		19 00	19 28		19 38		20 06	20 27	20 37		21 05	21 28	21 36			21 58
Gartcosh	d	17 04		17 34	17 43		18 04	18 34	18 41		19 04	19 32		19 41		20 10	20 31	20 40		21 09	21 31	21 40			22 02
Greenfaulds	d	17 11		17 41	17 51	18 02	18 11	18 41	18 49	19 01	19 14	19 39		19 49	20 02	20 17	20 38	20 47	21 04	21 16	21 39	21 47		22 02	22 11
Cumbernauld	d	17a13		17a44	17 54	18a04	18a13	18a44	18 51	19a03	19a16	19a42		19 51	20a04	20a19	20 41	20a50	21a06	21a18	21 41	21a49		22a04	22a13
Camelon	d				18 08				19 04					20 04			20 56				21 57				
Falkirk Grahamston	a				18 11				19 07					20 07			20 59				22 00				

Please check the 'Additional Notes to Individual Tables' section for any other general notes that apply to this Table

Table T231-F

Saturdays

26 May to 8 December

Motherwell, Glasgow Queen Street - Falkirk Grahamston

		SR	SR	SR	SR	SR	SR	SR
Motherwell	d			22 45				
Whifflet	d			22 52				
Coatbridge Central	d			22 54				
Glasgow Queen Street	d		22 22				23 23	23 52
Springburn	d	22 21	22 29		22 52	23 24	23 31	23 59
Stepps	d	22 28	22 36		22 59	23 30	23 38	00 07
Gartcosh	d	22 31	22 40		23 02	23 34	23 41	00 10
Greenfaulds	d	22 38	22 47	23 02	23 09	23 41	23 49	00 18
Cumbernauld	d	22a41	22 50	23a04	23a12	23a44	23 51	00a21
Camelon	d		23 03				00 04	
Falkirk Grahamston	a		23 06				00 07	

Sundays

20 May to 2 December

		SR		SR
Motherwell	d			
Whifflet	d			
Coatbridge Central	d			
Glasgow Queen Street	d		and hourly until	
Springburn	d	08 24		23 24
Stepps	d	08 31		23 31
Gartcosh	d	08 34		23 34
Greenfaulds	d	08 41		23 41
Cumbernauld	d	08a44		23a44
Camelon	d			
Falkirk Grahamston	a			

Table T231-R

Saturdays

26 May to 8 December

Falkirk Grahamston - Glasgow Queen Street, Motherwell

		SR	SR	SR	SR	SR	SR	SR
Falkirk Grahamston	d				22 17			23 23
Camelon	d				22 20			23 26
Cumbernauld	d	21 59	22 21	22 26	22 31	22 59	23 29	23 39
Greenfaulds	d	22 01	22 23	22 28	22 34	23 01	23 31	23 41
Gartcosh	d	22 07		22 34	22 41	23 07	23 39	23 48
Stepps	d	22 11		22 38	22 45	23 11	23 43	23 53
Springburn	d	22a17		22a44	22 53	23a17	23a49	00 02
Glasgow Queen Street	a				22 59			00 08
Coatbridge Central	d		22 30					
Whifflet	d		22 33					
Motherwell	a		22 40					

Sundays

20 May to 2 December

		SR		SR
Falkirk Grahamston	d			
Camelon	d			
Cumbernauld	d	09 04		23 04
Greenfaulds	d	09 06	and hourly until	23 06
Gartcosh	d	09 12		23 12
Stepps	d	09 16		23 16
Springburn	d	09a22		23a22
Glasgow Queen Street	a			
Coatbridge Central	d			
Whifflet	d			
Motherwell	a			

Table T231-R

Mondays to Fridays

21 May to 7 December

Falkirk Grahamston - Glasgow Queen Street, Motherwell

		SR	SR	SR	SR	SR		SR	SR	SR	SR	SR	SR	SR	SR	SR		SR	SR	SR	SR	SR	SR	SR	SR
Falkirk Grahamston	d	05 24								07 14				08 03					09 23				10 24		
Camelon	d	05 27								07 17				08 06					09 27				10 27		
Cumbernauld	d	05 39	05 56	06 12	06 29	06 58		07 13	07 26	07 30	07 59	08 12	08 27	08 31	08 59	09 22		09 29	09 38	09 59	10 21	10 27	10 39	10 59	11 21
Greenfaulds	d	05 41	05 58	06 14	06 31	07 00		07 15	07 28	07 33	08 01	08 14	08 29	08 33	09 01	09 24		09 31	09 41	10 01	10 23	10 29	10 42	11 01	11 23
Gartcosh	d	05 48	06 05		06 37	07 06			07 34	07 40	08 07		08 35	08 41	09 07			09 37	09 48	10 07		10 37	10 50	11 07	
Stepps	d	05 53	06 09		06 41	07 10			07 38	07 45	08 11		08 39	08 45	09 11			09 41	09 52	10 11		10 41	10 54	11 11	
Springburn	d	06 01	06a15		06a47	07a16			07a44	07 53	08a17		08a45	08 53	09a17			09a47	10 00	10a17		10a47	11 03	11a17	
Glasgow Queen Street	a	06 07								07 59				08 59					10 06				11 10		
Coatbridge Central	d			06 22				07 22				08 21				09 31					10 30				11 30
Whifflet	d			06 25				07 25				08 24				09 34					10 33				11 33
Motherwell	a			06 37				07 32				08 32				09 41					10 40				11 40

		SR		SR	SR	SR	SR	SR	SR	SR	SR	SR		SR	SR	SR	SR	SR	SR	SR	SR	SR		SR	SR
Falkirk Grahamston	d			11 20				12 24				13 20					14 20				15 25				
Camelon	d			11 23				12 28				13 24					14 23				15 28				
Cumbernauld	d	11 29		11 40	11 56	12 21	12 29	12 41	12 59	13 20	13 29	13 37		13 59	14 21	14 29	14 35	14 56	15 21	15 29	15 40	15 59		16 20	16 29
Greenfaulds	d	11 31		11 42	11 58	12 23	12 31	12 44	13 01	13 22	13 31	13 39		14 01	14 23	14 31	14 37	14 58	15 23	15 31	15 43	16 01		16 22	16 31
Gartcosh	d	11 37		11 50	12 07		12 37	12 51	13 07		13 37	13 51		14 07		14 37	14 50	15 07		15 37	15 51	16 07			16 37
Stepps	d	11 41		11 55	12 11		12 41	12 55	13 11		13 41	13 55		14 11		14 41	14 55	15 11		15 41	15 55	16 11			16 41
Springburn	d	11a47		12 03	12a17		12a47	13 03	13a17		13a47	14 03		14a17		14a47	15 03	15a17		15a47	16 04	16a17			16a47
Glasgow Queen Street	a			12 09				13 10				14 10					15 12				16 10				
Coatbridge Central	d					12 30				13 29					14 30				15 30					16 30	
Whifflet	d					12 33				13 33					14 33				15 33					16 33	
Motherwell	a					12 40				13 40					14 40				15 40					16 41	

		SR	SR	SR	SR	SR	SR	SR		SR	SR	SR	SR	SR	SR	SR	SR	SR		SR	SR	SR	SR	SR	SR
Falkirk Grahamston	d	16 25				17 17					18 22				19 19					20 21				21 15	
Camelon	d	16 28				17 20					18 25				19 22					20 24				21 18	
Cumbernauld	d	16 42	16 59	17 21	17 26	17 32	17 59	18 18		18 26	18 37	19 01	19 21	19 27	19 35	19 59	20 21	20 27		20 37	20 59	21 21	21 27	21 31	21 59
Greenfaulds	d	16 44	17 01	17 23	17 28	17 34	18 01	18 20		18 28	18 39	19 03	19 23	19 29	19 37	20 01	20 23	20 29		20 39	21 01	21 23	21 29	21 34	22 01
Gartcosh	d	16 51	17 07		17 34	17 41	18 07			18 37	18 46	19 09		19 37	19 44	20 07		20 37		20 46	21 07		21 35	21 41	22 07
Stepps	d	16 55	17 11		17 38	17 45	18 11			18 41	18 50	19 13		19 41	19 48	20 11		20 41		20 50	21 11		21 39	21 45	22 11
Springburn	d	17 02	17a17		17a44	17 53	18a17			18a47	18 58	19a20		19a47	19 56	20a17		20a47		20 58	21a17		21a45	21 53	22a17
Glasgow Queen Street	a	17 10				18 00					19 06				20 02					21 04				21 59	
Coatbridge Central	d			17 30				18 31					19 30				20 30					21 30			
Whifflet	d			17 33				18 34					19 33				20 33					21 33			
Motherwell	a			17 40				18 41					19 40				20 40					21 40			

		SR	SR	SR		SR	SR	SR
Falkirk Grahamston	d			22 17				23 23
Camelon	d			22 20				23 26
Cumbernauld	d	22 21	22 26	22 31		22 59	23 29	23 39
Greenfaulds	d	22 23	22 28	22 34		23 01	23 31	23 41
Gartcosh	d		22 34	22 41		23 07	23 39	23 48
Stepps	d		22 38	22 45		23 11	23 43	23 53
Springburn	d		22a44	22 53		23a17	23a49	00 02
Glasgow Queen Street	a			22 59				00 08
Coatbridge Central	d	22 30						
Whifflet	d	22 33						
Motherwell	a	22 40						

Saturdays

26 May to 8 December

		SR	SR	SR	SR	SR	SR	SR	SR	SR		SR	SR	SR	SR	SR	SR	SR	SR	SR		SR	SR	SR	SR
Falkirk Grahamston	d	05 24			06 08					07 14					08 03				09 23					10 24	
Camelon	d	05 27			06 11					07 17					08 06				09 27					10 27	
Cumbernauld	d	05 39	05 56	06 12	06 22	06 29	06 58	07 13	07 26	07 30		07 59	08 12	08 27	08 31	08 59	09 22	09 29	09 38	09 55		10 21	10 27	10 39	10 59
Greenfaulds	d	05 41	05 58	06 14	06 24	06 31	07 00	07 15	07 28	07 33		08 01	08 14	08 29	08 33	09 01	09 24	09 31	09 41	09 57		10 23	10 29	10 42	11 01
Gartcosh	d	05 48	06 05		06 31	06 37	07 06		07 34	07 40		08 07		08 35	08 41	09 07		09 37	09 48	10 03			10 37	10 50	11 07
Stepps	d	05 53	06 09		06 35	06 41	07 10		07 38	07 45		08 11		08 39	08 45	09 11		09 41	09 52	10 07			10 41	10 54	11 11
Springburn	d	06 01	06a15		06 42	06a47	07a16		07a44	07 53		08a17		08a45	08 53	09a17		09a47	10 03	10a13			10a47	11 03	11a17
Glasgow Queen Street	a	06 07			06 52					07 59					08 59				10 11					11 10	
Coatbridge Central	d			06 22				07 22					08 21				09 31					10 30			
Whifflet	d			06 25				07 25					08 24				09 34					10 33			
Motherwell	a			06 37				07 32					08 32				09 41					10 40			

		SR	SR	SR	SR	SR		SR	SR	SR	SR	SR	SR	SR	SR	SR		SR	SR	SR	SR	SR	SR	SR	SR
Falkirk Grahamston	d			11 20					12 24				13 20					14 20				15 25			
Camelon	d			11 23					12 28				13 24					14 23				15 28			
Cumbernauld	d	11 21	11 29	11 40	11 56	12 21		12 29	12 41	12 59	13 20	13 29	13 37	13 59	14 21	14 29		14 35	14 56	15 21	15 29	15 40	15 59	16 20	16 29
Greenfaulds	d	11 23	11 31	11 42	11 58	12 23		12 31	12 44	13 01	13 22	13 31	13 39	14 01	14 23	14 31		14 37	14 58	15 23	15 31	15 43	16 01	16 22	16 31
Gartcosh	d		11 37	11 50	12 07			12 37	12 51	13 07		13 37	13 51	14 07		14 37		14 50	15 07		15 37	15 51	16 07		16 37
Stepps	d		11 41	11 55	12 11			12 41	12 55	13 11		13 41	13 55	14 11		14 41		14 55	15 11		15 41	15 55	16 11		16 41
Springburn	d		11a47	12 03	12a17			12a47	13 03	13a17		13a47	14 03	14a17		14a47		15 03	15a17		15a47	16 04	16a17		16a47
Glasgow Queen Street	a			12 10					13 10				14 10					15 12				16 10			
Coatbridge Central	d	11 30				12 30					13 29				14 30					15 30				16 30	
Whifflet	d	11 33				12 33					13 33				14 33					15 33				16 33	
Motherwell	a	11 40				12 40					13 40				14 40					15 40				16 41	

		SR		SR	SR	SR	SR	SR	SR	SR	SR	SR		SR	SR	SR	SR	SR	SR	SR	SR	SR		SR	SR
Falkirk Grahamston	d	16 25					17 17				18 22					19 19				20 21					21 15
Camelon	d	16 28					17 20				18 25					19 22				20 24					21 18
Cumbernauld	d	16 42		16 59	17 21	17 26	17 32	17 59	18 18	18 26	18 37	19 01		19 21	19 27	19 35	19 59	20 21	20 27	20 36	20 59	21 21		21 27	21 31
Greenfaulds	d	16 44		17 01	17 23	17 28	17 34	18 01	18 20	18 28	18 39	19 03		19 23	19 29	19 37	20 01	20 23	20 29	20 38	21 01	21 23		21 29	21 34
Gartcosh	d	16 51		17 07		17 34	17 41	18 07		18 37	18 46	19 09			19 37	19 44	20 07		20 37	20 45	21 07			21 35	21 41
Stepps	d	16 55		17 11		17 38	17 45	18 11		18 41	18 50	19 13			19 41	19 48	20 11		20 41	20 49	21 11			21 39	21 45
Springburn	d	17 03		17a17		17a44	17 53	18a17		18a47	18 58	19a20			19a47	19 56	20a17		20a47	20 57	21a17			21a45	21 53
Glasgow Queen Street	a	17 10					17 59				19 06					20 02				21 03					21 59
Coatbridge Central	d				17 30				18 31					19 30				20 30				21 30			
Whifflet	d				17 33				18 34					19 33				20 33				21 33			
Motherwell	a				17 40				18 41					19 40				20 40				21 40			

Table T232-F

Mondays to Fridays

21 May to 7 December

Glasgow Queen Street - Maryhill and Annisland

Miles			SR		SR	SR	SR	SR		SR	SR		SR	SR	SR		SR	SR	SR		SR
0	**Glasgow Queen Street**	d	06 26	and every 30 minutes until	07 56	08 27	08 56	09 26	and every 30 minutes until	10 56	11 27		11 57	12 27	12 56	and every 30 minutes until	14 56	15 26	15 56	and every 30 minutes until	17 26
2¼	Ashfield	d	06 31		08 01	08 32	09 01	09 31		11 01	11 33		12 02	12 32	13 01		15 01	15 32	16 01		17 31
3	Possilpark & Parkhouse	d	06 34		08 04	08 35	09 03	09 34		11 04	11 35		12 05	12 35	13 04		15 04	15 35	16 04		17 34
3¼	Gilshochill	d	06 36		08 06	08 37	09 05	09 36		11 06	11 37		12 07	12 37	13 06		15 06	15 37	16 06		17 36
4¼	Summerston	d	06 38		08 08	08 39	09 07	09 38		11 08	11 40		12 09	12 39	13 08		15 08	15 39	16 08		17 38
4¾	**Maryhill**	d	06 40		08 10	08 41	09 09	09 40		11 10	11 41		12 11	12 41	13 10		15 10	15 41	16 10		17 40
5½	Kelvindale	d	06 42		08 12	08 43	09 11	09 42		11 12	11 44		12 13	12 43	13 12		15 12	15 43	16 12		17 42
6¼	**Anniesland** 226	a	06 45		08 15	08 46	09 14	09 45		11 15	11 47		12 16	12 46	13 15		15 15	15 46	16 15		17 45

			SR	SR	SR	SR A	SR	SR	SR	SR		SR		SR FO
Glasgow Queen Street	d		17 57	18 27	18 56	19 26	19 56	20 26	20 56	21 26	and every 30 minutes until	23 26		23 56
Ashfield	d		18 02	18 32	19 01	19 31	20 01	20 31	21 02	21 31		23 31		00 02
Possilpark & Parkhouse	d		18 05	18 35	19 04	19 34	20 04	20 34	21 04	21 34		23 34		00 04
Gilshochill	d		18 07	18 37	19 06	19 36	20 06	20 36	21 06	21 36		23 36		00 06
Summerston	d		18 09	18 39	19 08	19 38	20 08	20 38	21 09	21 38		23 38		00 09
Maryhill	d		18 11	18 41	19 10	19 40	20 10	20 40	21 10	21 40		23 40		00 10
Kelvindale	d		18 13	18 43	19 12	19 42	20 12	20 42	21 13	21 42		23 42		00 12
Anniesland 226	a		18 16	18 46	19 15	19 45	20 15	20 45	21 16	21 45		23 45		00 15

Saturdays

26 May to 8 December

		SR	SR		SR	SR	SR	SR		SR		SR	SR	SR	SR		SR	SR	SR		SR
Glasgow Queen Street	d		06 26	and every 30 minutes until	07 56	08 27	08 56	09 26	and every 30 minutes until	10 56		11 27	11 57	12 27	12 56	and every 30 minutes until	14 56	15 26	15 56	and every 30 minutes until	17 56
Ashfield	d	00 02	06 31		08 01	08 32	09 01	09 31		11 01		11 33	12 02	12 32	13 01		15 01	15 32	16 01		18 01
Possilpark & Parkhouse	d	00 04	06 34		08 04	08 35	09 03	09 34		11 04		11 35	12 05	12 35	13 04		15 04	15 35	16 04		18 04
Gilshochill	d	00 06	06 36		08 06	08 37	09 05	09 36		11 06		11 37	12 07	12 37	13 06		15 06	15 37	16 06		18 06
Summerston	d	00 09	06 38		08 08	08 39	09 07	09 38		11 08		11 40	12 09	12 39	13 08		15 08	15 39	16 08		18 08
Maryhill	d	00 10	06 40		08 10	08 41	09 09	09 40		11 10		11 41	12 11	12 41	13 10		15 10	15 41	16 10		18 10
Kelvindale	d	00 12	06 42		08 12	08 43	09 11	09 42		11 12		11 44	12 13	12 43	13 12		15 12	15 43	16 12		18 12
Anniesland 226	a	00 15	06 45		08 15	08 46	09 14	09 45		11 15		11 47	12 16	12 46	13 15		15 15	15 46	16 15		18 15

			SR	SR		SR	SR	SR		SR
Glasgow Queen Street	d		18 27	18 56	and every 30 minutes until	20 26	20 56	21 26	and every 30 minutes until	23 26
Ashfield	d		18 32	19 01		20 31	21 02	21 31		23 31
Possilpark & Parkhouse	d		18 35	19 04		20 34	21 04	21 34		23 34
Gilshochill	d		18 37	19 06		20 36	21 06	21 36		23 36
Summerston	d		18 39	19 08		20 38	21 09	21 38		23 38
Maryhill	d		18 41	19 10		20 40	21 10	21 40		23 40
Kelvindale	d		18 43	19 12		20 42	21 13	21 42		23 42
Anniesland 226	a		18 46	19 15		20 45	21 16	21 45		23 45

Sundays

20 May to 2 December

		SR	SR	SR	SR	SR		SR
Glasgow Queen Street	d	09 33	10 27	11 26	12 25	13 26	and hourly until	18 26
Ashfield	d	09 38	10 32	11 31	12 31	13 31		18 31
Possilpark & Parkhouse	d	09 41	10 35	11 34	12 34	13 34		18 34
Gilshochill	d	09 43	10 37	11 36	12 36	13 36		18 36
Summerston	d	09 45	10 39	11 38	12 38	13 38		18 38
Maryhill	d	09 47	10 41	11 40	12 40	13 40		18 40
Kelvindale	d	09 49	10 43	11 42	12 42	13 42		18 42
Anniesland 226	a	09 52	10 46	11 45	12 45	13 45		18 45

A from 29 October

Table T232-R

Mondays to Fridays

21 May to 7 December

Annlesland and Maryhill - Glasgow Queen Street

Miles			SR	SR	SR	SR	SR	SR	SR	SR	SR	SR	SR	SR	SR	SR	SR	SR	SR	SR	SR	SR	SR
							◇ ✕																
0	Anniesland 226	d	06 21	06 51	07 21	07 52		08 25	08 51	09 21	09 53	10 21	10 53	11 21	11 56	12 21	12 53	13 21	13 53	14 21	14 53	15 21	15 53
0¾	Kelvindale	d	06 23	06 53	07 23	07 54		08 27	08 53	09 23	09 55	10 23	10 55	11 23	11 58	12 23	12 55	13 23	13 55	14 23	14 55	15 23	15 55
1½	Maryhill	d	06 25	06 55	07 25	07 56	08 24	08 30	08 55	09 25	09 57	10 25	10 57	11 25	12 00	12 25	12 57	13 25	13 57	14 25	14 57	15 25	15 57
2	Summerston	d	06 27	06 57	07 27	07 58		08 31	08 57	09 27	09 59	10 27	10 59	11 27	12 02	12 27	12 59	13 27	13 59	14 27	14 59	15 27	15 59
3	Gilshochill	d	06 29	06 59	07 29	08 00		08 33	08 59	09 29	10 01	10 29	11 01	11 29	12 04	12 29	13 01	13 29	14 01	14 29	15 01	15 29	16 01
3¼	Possilpark & Parkhouse	d	06 31	07 01	07 31	08 02	08 28	08 35	09 01	09 31	10 03	10 31	11 03	11 31	12 06	12 31	13 03	13 31	14 03	14 31	15 03	15 31	16 03
4	Ashfield	d	06 34	07 04	07 36	08 05		08 38	09 04	09 34	10 06	10 34	11 06	11 34	12 09	12 34	13 06	13 34	14 06	14 34	15 06	15 34	16 06
6¼	Glasgow Queen Street [10] ⛴	a	06 41	07 10	07 45	08 12	08 37	08 44	09 11	09 41	10 14	10 40	11 13	11 44	12 19	12 41	13 13	13 40	14 13	14 40	15 15	15 40	16 14

		SR	SR	SR	SR	SR	SR	SR	SR	SR		SR	SR	SR	SR
									A						
Anniesland 226	d	16 21	16 55	17 21	17 51	18 21	18 52	19 21	19 51	20 21	and every 30 minutes until	21 51	22 21	22 51	23 21
Kelvindale	d	16 23	16 57	17 23	17 53	18 23	18 54	19 23	19 53	20 23		21 53	22 23	22 53	23 23
Maryhill	d	16 25	16 59	17 25	17 55	18 25	18 56	19 25	19 55	20 25		21 55	22 25	22 55	23 25
Summerston	d	16 27	17 01	17 27	17 57	18 27	18 58	19 27	19 57	20 27		21 57	22 27	22 57	23 27
Gilshochill	d	16 29	17 03	17 29	17 59	18 29	19 00	19 29	19 59	20 29		21 59	22 29	22 59	23 29
Possilpark & Parkhouse	d	16 31	17 05	17 31	18 01	18 31	19 02	19 31	20 01	20 31		22 01	22 31	23 01	23 31
Ashfield	d	16 34	17 08	17 34	18 04	18 34	19 05	19 34	20 04	20 34		22 04	22 34	23 04	23 34
Glasgow Queen Street [10] ⛴	a	16 45	17 14	17 44	18 13	18 41	19 12	19 40	20 11	20 40		22 10	22 41	23 10	23 40

Saturdays

26 May to 8 December

		SR	SR	SR	SR	SR	SR	SR	SR	SR	SR	SR	SR	SR	SR	SR	SR	SR	SR	SR	SR	SR	SR
						◇ ✕																	
Anniesland 226	d	06 21	06 51	07 21	07 52		08 25	08 51	09 21	09 53	10 21	10 53	11 21	11 56	12 21	12 53	13 21	13 53	14 21	14 53	15 21	15 53	16 21
Kelvindale	d	06 23	06 53	07 23	07 54		08 27	08 53	09 23	09 55	10 23	10 55	11 23	11 58	12 23	12 55	13 23	13 55	14 23	14 55	15 23	15 55	16 23
Maryhill	d	06 25	06 55	07 25	07 56	08 24	08 30	08 55	09 25	09 57	10 25	10 57	11 25	12 00	12 25	12 57	13 25	13 57	14 25	14 57	15 25	15 57	16 25
Summerston	d	06 27	06 57	07 27	07 58		08 31	08 57	09 27	09 59	10 27	10 59	11 27	12 02	12 27	12 59	13 27	13 59	14 27	14 59	15 27	15 59	16 27
Gilshochill	d	06 29	06 59	07 29	08 00		08 33	08 59	09 29	10 01	10 29	11 01	11 29	12 04	12 29	13 01	13 29	14 01	14 29	15 01	15 29	16 01	16 29
Possilpark & Parkhouse	d	06 31	07 01	07 31	08 02	08 28	08 35	09 01	09 31	10 03	10 31	11 03	11 31	12 06	12 31	13 03	13 31	14 03	14 31	15 03	15 31	16 03	16 31
Ashfield	d	06 34	07 04	07 34	08 05		08 38	09 04	09 34	10 06	10 34	11 06	11 34	12 09	12 34	13 06	13 34	14 06	14 34	15 06	15 34	16 06	16 34
Glasgow Queen Street [10] ⛴	a	06 41	07 10	07 41	08 12	08 37	08 44	09 11	09 41	10 14	10 40	11 13	11 44	12 19	12 41	13 13	13 40	14 13	14 40	15 15	15 40	16 14	16 41

		SR	SR	SR	SR	SR	SR	SR	SR		SR	SR	SR	SR
Anniesland 226	d	16 55	17 21	17 51	18 21	18 52	19 21	19 51	20 21	and every 30 minutes until	21 51	22 21	22 51	23 21
Kelvindale	d	16 57	17 23	17 53	18 23	18 54	19 23	19 53	20 23		21 53	22 23	22 53	23 23
Maryhill	d	16 59	17 25	17 55	18 25	18 56	19 25	19 55	20 25		21 55	22 25	22 55	23 25
Summerston	d	17 01	17 27	17 57	18 27	18 58	19 27	19 57	20 27		21 57	22 27	22 57	23 27
Gilshochill	d	17 03	17 29	17 59	18 29	19 00	19 29	19 59	20 29		21 59	22 29	22 59	23 29
Possilpark & Parkhouse	d	17 05	17 31	18 01	18 31	19 02	19 31	20 01	20 31		22 01	22 31	23 01	23 31
Ashfield	d	17 08	17 34	18 04	18 34	19 05	19 34	20 04	20 34		22 04	22 34	23 04	23 34
Glasgow Queen Street [10] ⛴	a	17 14	17 44	18 14	18 41	19 12	19 40	20 11	20 40		22 10	22 41	23 10	23 40

Sundays

20 May to 2 December

		SR	SR	SR	SR	SR	SR	SR	SR	SR	SR
Anniesland 226	d	09 57	10 51	11 51	12 51	13 53	14 51	15 51	16 51	17 51	18 51
Kelvindale	d	09 59	10 53	11 53	12 53	13 55	14 53	15 53	16 53	17 53	18 53
Maryhill	d	10 01	10 55	11 55	12 55	13 57	14 55	15 55	16 55	17 55	18 55
Summerston	d	10 03	10 57	11 57	12 57	13 59	14 57	15 57	16 57	17 57	18 57
Gilshochill	d	10 05	10 59	11 59	12 59	14 01	14 59	15 59	16 59	17 59	18 59
Possilpark & Parkhouse	d	10 07	11 01	12 01	13 01	14 03	15 01	16 01	17 01	18 01	19 01
Ashfield	d	10 10	11 04	12 04	13 04	14 06	15 04	16 04	17 04	18 04	19 04
Glasgow Queen Street [10] ⛴	a	10 17	11 11	12 11	13 10	14 12	15 12	16 14	17 10	18 10	19 11

A from 29 October

Table T238-F

Mondays to Fridays

21 May to 7 December

Dunbar and North Berwick - Edinburgh and Haymarket

Miles	Miles			SR	SR	XC	SR	GR	SR	SR	SR	GR	SR	GR	SR	SR	SR	XC	SR	SR	SR	XC	SR
						◇1		■ 1 ☕				■ 1 ☕		■ 1 ☕				◇1 ✕				◇1 ✕	
0	—	North Berwick	d	06 07	06 47		07 17			07 55	08 45		09 27		10 27		11 27		12 25		13 26		14 29
—	0	Dunbar	d			07 00		07 42				08 56		09 55		11 02		11 39		13 00		13 42	
4½	10¼	Drem	d	06 14	06 54		07 25			08 03	08 53		09 34		10 35		11 34		12 33		13 33		14 36
9	14¾	Longniddry	d	06 20	07 00		07 31			08 09	08 58		09 40		10 41		11 40		12 39		13 39		14 42
12½	18¼	Prestonpans	d	06 25	07 05		07 36		08 07	08 14	09 03		09 45		10 46		11 45		12 44		13 44		14 47
14¾	20½	Wallyford	d	06 28	07 08		07 40		08 10	08 18	09 06		09 48		10 49		11 48		12 47		13 47		14 50
17	22¾	Musselburgh	d	06 32	07 12		07 44		08 16	08 22	09 10		09 52		10 53	11 21	11 52		12 51	13 18	13 51		14 54
22¼	28	Edinburgh [10] 225,230,242	a	06 39	07 19	07 22	07 51	08 07	08 24	08 29	09 16	09 22	10 00	10 20	11 00	11 29	12 00	12 03	12 59	13 27	14 00	14 07	15 01
—	—		d		07 42	07 27	07 54			08 36				10 28									
23½	29¼	Haymarket 225,230,242 ⛴	a		07 45	07 30	07 57			08 42				10 31									

		SR	SR	XC	SR	SR	SR	XC	SR	SR	SR	SR	XC	SR	SR	GR	XC	SR
				◇1 ✕				◇1 A ✕					◇1 A ✕			■ 1 ☕	◇1 ✕	
North Berwick	d		15 23		16 26		17 28		17 56	18 27	19 04	19 29		20 25	21 27			22 27
Dunbar	d	15 12		15 42		17 05		17 45					19 46			21 43	21 50	
Drem	d		15 33		16 33		17 35			18 35	19 11	19 36		20 32	21 34			22 34
Longniddry	d		15 39		16 39		17 41			18 41	19 17	19 42		20 38	21 40			22 40
Prestonpans	d		15 44		16 44		17 46			18 47	19 22	19 47		20 43	21 45			22 45
Wallyford	d		15 47		16 47		17 49			18 50	19 25	19 51		20 46	21 48			22 48
Musselburgh	d	15 30	15 51		16 51	17 23	17 54		18 13	18 54	19 31	19 55		20 50	21 52			22 52
Edinburgh [10] 225,230,242	a	15 36	15 59	16 06	16 59	17 29	18 01	18 07	18 19	19 01	19 40	20 02	20 08	20 59	21 59	22 10	22 13	23 00
	d							18 10	18 26				20 14					
Haymarket 225,230,242 ⛴	a							18 13	18 30				20 16					

Saturdays

26 May to 8 December

		SR	SR	GR	SR	GR	SR	SR	GR	SR	SR	SR	SR	XC	SR	SR	SR	SR	SR	XC	SR	SR	SR
				■ 1 ☕		■ 1 ☕			■ 1 ☕					◇1 ✕						◇1 ✕			
North Berwick	d	06 07	07 17		08 19		09 19	09 49		10 21	10 50		11 21		11 50	12 22	12 50		13 20		13 50	14 21	14 50
Dunbar	d			07 41		08 56			09 56			11 06		11 40				13 08		13 40			
Drem	d	06 16	07 25		08 27		09 26	09 57		10 29	10 59		11 28		11 57	12 29	12 57		13 28		13 59	14 29	14 58
Longniddry	d	06 22	07 31		08 32		09 32	10 02		10 34	11 04		11 34		12 03	12 35	13 03		13 33		14 04	14 34	15 03
Prestonpans	d	06 27	07 36		08 37		09 37	10 07		10 39	11 09		11 39		12 08	12 40	13 08		13 38		14 09	14 39	15 08
Wallyford	d	06 30	07 40		08 40		09 40	10 10		10 42	11 12		11 42		12 11	12 43	13 11		13 41		14 12	14 42	15 11
Musselburgh	d	06 34	07 44		08 44		09 44	10 14		10 46	11 16	11 28	11 46		12 15	12 47	13 15	13 30	13 45		14 16	14 46	15 15
Edinburgh [10] 225,230,242	a	06 41	07 51	08 03	08 50	09 18	09 50	10 20	10 24	10 53	11 22	11 37	11 52	12 05	12 21	12 53	13 21	13 37	13 51	14 05	14 23	14 55	15 22
	d		07 54						10 28														
Haymarket 225,230,242 ⛴	a		07 57						10 31														

		SR	SR	XC	SR	SR	SR	SR	SR	XC	SR	SR	SR	SR	XC	SR	SR	XC	GR	SR
				◇1 ✕						◇1 A ✕					◇1 A ✕			◇1	■ 1 ☕	
North Berwick	d		15 21		15 50	16 22	16 51		17 21		17 51	18 21	18 50	19 21		20 21	21 21			22 22
Dunbar	d	15 05		15 40				17 08		17 41					19 42			21 47	22 11	
Drem	d		15 28		15 57	16 30	16 59		17 28		17 59	18 28	18 58	19 28		20 28	21 28			22 29
Longniddry	d		15 34		16 03	16 35	17 04		17 34		18 04	18 34	19 04	19 34		20 34	21 34			22 35
Prestonpans	d		15 39		16 08	16 40	17 09		17 39		18 09	18 39	19 09	19 39		20 39	21 39			22 40
Wallyford	d		15 42		16 11	16 43	17 12		17 42		18 12	18 42	19 12	19 42		20 42	21 42			22 43
Musselburgh	d	15 27	15 46		16 15	16 47	17 16	17 30	17 46		18 16	18 46	19 16	19 46		20 46	21 46			22 47
Edinburgh [10] 225,230,242	a	15 36	15 52	16 02	16 21	16 53	17 22	17 42	17 52	18 03	18 22	18 52	19 23	19 53	20 04	20 53	21 54	22 09	22 36	22 54
	d									18 11	18 27				20 14					
Haymarket 225,230,242 ⛴	a									18 14	18 31				20 17					

Sundays

20 May to 9 September

		GR	SR	SR	GR	SR	SR	XC	GR	SR	SR	XC	SR	SR	XC	SR	SR	XC	XC	SR	GR	SR	XC
		■ 1 ☕			■ 1 ☕			◇1 ✕	■ 1 ☕			◇1 ✕			◇1 A ✕			◇1 B ✕	◇1 C ✕		■ 1 ☕		◇1 D ✕
North Berwick	d		10 24	11 20		12 20	13 20			14 20	15 20		16 20	17 20		18 20	19 20			20 20		21 20	
Dunbar	d	10 04			11 33			13 37	13 51			15 40			17 36			19 34	19 38		20 50		21 44
Drem	d		10 31	11 27		12 27	13 27			14 27	15 27		16 27	17 27		18 27	19 27			20 27		21 27	
Longniddry	d		10 37	11 33		12 33	13 33			14 33	15 33		16 33	17 33		18 33	19 33			20 33		21 33	
Prestonpans	d		10 42	11 38		12 38	13 38			14 38	15 38		16 38	17 38		18 38	19 38			20 38		21 38	
Wallyford	d		10 45	11 41		12 41	13 41			14 41	15 41		16 41	17 41		18 41	19 41			20 41		21 41	
Musselburgh	d		10 49	11 45		12 45	13 45			14 45	15 45		16 45	17 45		18 45	19 45			20 45		21 45	
Edinburgh [10] 225,230,242	a	10 26	10 59	11 53	11 56	12 53	13 53	14 01	14 16	14 54	15 53	16 03	16 53	17 53	17 58	18 55	19 53	19 57	20 00	20 53	21 12	21 52	22 06
	d														18 13								
Haymarket 225,230,242 ⛴	a														18 16								

A ✕ to Edinburgh
B until 15 July
C from 22 July
D 9 September

Table T238-F

Dunbar and North Berwick - Edinburgh and Haymarket

Sundays
20 May to 9 September

		XC A	SR	GR
North Berwick	d		22 20	
Dunbar	d	21 46		23 13
Drem	d		22 27	
Longniddry	d		22 33	
Prestonpans	d		22 38	
Wallyford	d		22 41	
Musselburgh	d		22 45	
Edinburgh 10 225,230,242	a	22 07	22 52	23 36
	d			
Haymarket 225,230,242	a			

Sundays
16 September to 2 December

		GR	SR	SR	GR	SR	SR	XC	GR	SR	SR	XC	SR	SR	XC B	SR	SR	XC C	XC D	SR	GR	SR	XC D
North Berwick	d		10 24	11 20		12 20	13 20			14 20	15 20		16 20	17 20		18 20	19 20			20 20		21 20	
Dunbar	d	10 04			11 33			13 37	13 51			15 40			17 36			19 34	19 38		20 50		21 44
Drem	d		10 31	11 27		12 27	13 27			14 27	15 27		16 27	17 27		18 27	19 27			20 27		21 27	
Longniddry	d		10 37	11 33		12 33	13 33			14 33	15 33		16 33	17 33		18 33	19 33			20 33		21 33	
Prestonpans	d		10 42	11 38		12 38	13 38			14 33	15 38		16 38	17 38		18 38	19 38			20 38		21 38	
Wallyford	d		10 45	11 41		12 41	13 41			14 41	15 41		16 41	17 41		18 41	19 41			20 41		21 41	
Musselburgh	d		10 49	11 45		12 45	13 45			14 45	15 45		16 45	17 45		18 45	19 45			20 45		21 45	
Edinburgh 10 225,230,242	a	10 26	10 59	11 53	11 56	12 53	13 53	14 01	14 16	14 54	15 53	16 03	16 53	17 53	17 58	18 55	19 53	19 57	20 00	20 53	21 12	21 52	22 06
	d														18 13						21 22		
Haymarket 225,230,242	a														18 16						21 25		

		XC C	SR	GR
North Berwick	d		22 20	
Dunbar	d	21 46		23 13
Drem	d		22 27	
Longniddry	d		22 33	
Prestonpans	d		22 38	
Wallyford	d		22 41	
Musselburgh	d		22 45	
Edinburgh 10 225,230,242	a	22 07	22 52	23 36
	d			
Haymarket 225,230,242	a			

A not 9 September
B to Edinburgh
C from 14 October
D until 7 October

Table T238-R

Haymarket and Edinburgh - North Berwick and Dunbar

Mondays to Fridays
21 May to 20 July

Miles	Miles			GR	XC A	SR	SR	SR	XC A	SR	SR	SR	XC B	SR	SR	SR	XC	SR	SR	SR	XC	SR	SR
0	0	Haymarket 225,230,242	d		06 57			08 28	08 51				10 51										
1¼	1¼	Edinburgh 10 225,230,242	a		07 01			08 34	08 56				10 55										
—	—		d	05 48	07 10	07 13	08 15	08 42	09 08	09 43	10 14	10 43	11 06	11 42	12 12	12 43	13 07	13 43	14 14	14 43	15 08	15 43	16 33
6½	6½	Musselburgh	d			07 19	08 21	08 48		09 49	10 20	10 49		11 49	12 18	12 49		13 49	14 20	14 49		15 49	16 39
8¾	8¾	Wallyford	d			07 23		08 52		09 53		10 53		11 53		12 53		13 53		14 53		15 53	
11	11	Prestonpans	d			07 26		08 55		09 56		10 56		11 56		12 56		13 56		14 56		15 56	
14½	14½	Longniddry	d			07 31		09 00		10 01		11 01		12 01		13 01		14 01		15 01		16 01	
19	19	Drem	d			07 37		09 06		10 07		11 07		12 08		13 07		14 07		15 07		16 07	
—	29¼	Dunbar	a	06 09	07 31				09 28		10 39		11 26		12 37		13 30		14 39		15 28		16 59
23½	—	North Berwick	a			07 46	08 40	09 15		10 16		11 16		12 16		13 16		14 16		15 16		16 16	

		SR	XC	SR	GR	SR	XC A	SR	GR	SR	SR	XC	SR	GR	SR	GR FO	SR FX	SR FO	SR
Haymarket 225,230,242	d			17 05	17 21	17 41	17 55			18 36		19 55		20 46					
Edinburgh 10 225,230,242	a			17 11	17 26	17 45	18 00			18 40		19 59		20 50					
	d	16 42	17 07	17 15	17 31	17 48	18 08	18 14	18 30	18 47	19 45	20 03	20 43	21 00	21 43	22 00	22 07	23 01	23 13
Musselburgh	d	16 49		17 21		17 55		18 20		18 54	19 52		20 49		21 49		22 13	23 09	23 19
Wallyford	d	16 53		17 25		17 59		18 24		18 59	19 56		20 53		21 53				23 23
Prestonpans	d	16 56		17 29		18 02		18 27		19 02	19 59		20 56		21 56				23 26
Longniddry	d	17 01		17 34		18 07		18 32		19 08	20 04		21 01		22 01				23 31
Drem	d	17 07		17 40		18 13		18 38		19 15	20 11		21 07		22 07				23 37
Dunbar	a		17 27		17 52		18 28		18 51			20 23		21 21		22 21	22 41	23 34	
North Berwick	a	17 16		17 49		18 22		18 47		19 24	20 19		21 16		22 16				23 56

Mondays to Fridays
23 July to 5 October

		GR	XC	SR	SR	SR	XC	SR	SR	SR	XC	SR	SR	SR	XC	SR	SR	SR	XC	SR	SR	SR	XC
Haymarket 225,230,242	d		06 57			08 28	08 51				10 51												
Edinburgh 10 225,230,242	a		07 01			08 34	08 56				10 55												
	d	05 48	07 10	07 13	08 15	08 42	09 08	09 43	10 14	10 43	11 06	11 42	12 12	12 43	13 07	13 43	14 14	14 43	15 08	15 43	16 33	16 42	17 07
Musselburgh	d			07 19	08 21	08 48		09 49	10 20	10 49		11 49	12 18	12 49		13 49	14 20	14 49		15 49	16 39	16 49	
Wallyford	d			07 23		08 52		09 53		10 53		11 53		12 53		13 53		14 53		15 53		16 53	
Prestonpans	d			07 26		08 55		09 56		10 56		11 56		12 56		13 56		14 56		15 56		16 56	
Longniddry	d			07 31		09 00		10 01		11 01		12 01		13 01		14 01		15 01		16 01		17 01	
Drem	d			07 37		09 06		10 07		11 07		12 08		13 07		14 07		15 07		16 07		17 07	
Dunbar	a	06 09	07 31				09 28		10 39		11 26		12 37		13 30		14 39		15 28		16 59		17 27
North Berwick	a			07 46	08 40	09 15		10 16		11 16		12 16		13 16		14 16		15 16		16 16		17 16	

		SR	GR	SR	XC A	SR	GR	SR	SR	XC	SR	GR	SR	GR FO	SR FX	SR FO	SR
Haymarket 225,230,242	d	17 05	17 21	17 41	17 55			18 36		19 55		20 46					
Edinburgh 10 225,230,242	a	17 11	17 26	17 45	18 00			18 40		19 59		20 50					
	d	17 15	17 31	17 48	18 08	18 14	18 30	18 47	19 45	20 03	20 43	21 00	21 43	22 00	22 07	23 01	23 13
Musselburgh	d	17 21		17 55		18 20		18 54	19 52		20 49		21 49		22 13	23 09	23 19
Wallyford	d	17 25		17 59		18 24		18 59	19 56		20 53		21 53				23 23
Prestonpans	d	17 29		18 02		18 27		19 02	19 59		20 56		21 56				23 26
Longniddry	d	17 34		18 07		18 32		19 08	20 04		21 01		22 01				23 31
Drem	d	17 40		18 13		18 38		19 15	20 11		21 07		22 07				23 37
Dunbar	a		17 52		18 28		18 51			20 23		21 21		22 21	22 41	23 34	
North Berwick	a	17 49		18 22		18 47		19 24	20 19		21 16		22 16				23 56

Mondays to Fridays
8 October to 7 December

		GR	XC A	SR	SR	SR	XC A	SR	SR	SR	XC B	SR	SR	SR	XC FX	SR	SR	SR	XC	SR	SR	SR	XC
Haymarket 225,230,242	d		06 57			08 28	08 51				10 51												
Edinburgh 10 225,230,242	a		07 01			08 34	08 56				10 55												
	d	05 48	07 10	07 13	08 15	08 42	09 08	09 43	10 14	10 43	11 06	11 42	12 12	12 43	13 07	13 43	14 14	14 43	15 08	15 43	16 33	16 42	17 07
Musselburgh	d			07 19	08 21	08 48		09 49	10 20	10 49		11 49	12 18	12 49		13 49	14 20	14 49		15 49	16 39	16 49	
Wallyford	d			07 23		08 52		09 53		10 53		11 53		12 53		13 53		14 53		15 53		16 53	
Prestonpans	d			07 26		08 55		09 56		10 56		11 56		12 56		13 56		14 56		15 56		16 56	
Longniddry	d			07 31		09 00		10 01		11 01		12 01		13 01		14 01		15 01		16 01		17 01	
Drem	d			07 37		09 06		10 07		11 07		12 08		13 07		14 07		15 07		16 07		17 07	
Dunbar	a	06 09	07 31				09 28		10 39		11 26		12 37		13 30		14 39		15 28		16 59		17 27
North Berwick	a			07 46	08 40	09 15		10 16		11 16		12 16		13 16		14 16		15 16		16 16		17 16	

A from Edinburgh
B ◇ from Edinburgh to Edinburgh

Table T238-R

Mondays to Fridays
8 October to 7 December

Haymarket and Edinburgh - North Berwick and Dunbar

	SR	GR	SR	XC	SR	GR	SR	SR	XC	SR	GR	SR	GR FO	SR FX	SR FO	SR
		1 ⊡		◇1 A ✕		1 ⊡			◇1 ✕		1 ⊡		1 ⊡			
Haymarket 225,230,242 ⇌ d	17 05	17 21	17 41	17 55			18 36		19 55		20 46					
Edinburgh 10 225,230,242 a	17 11	17 26	17 45	18 00			18 40		19 59		20 50					
d	17 15	17 31	17 48	18 08	18 14	18 30	18 47	19 45	20 03	20 43	21 00	21 43	22 00	22 07	23 01	23 13
Musselburgh d	17 21		17 55		18 20		18 54	19 52		20 49		21 49		22 13	23 09	23 19
Wallyford d	17 25		17 59		18 24		18 59	19 56		20 53		21 53				23 23
Prestonpans d	17 29		18 02		18 27		19 02	19 59		20 56		21 56				23 26
Longniddry d	17 34		18 07		18 32		19 08	20 04		21 01		22 01				23 31
Drem d	17 40		18 13		18 38		19 15	20 11		21 07		22 07				23 37
Dunbar a		17 52		18 28		18 51			20 23		21 21		22 21	22 41	23 34	
North Berwick a	17 49		18 22		18 47		19 24	20 19		21 16		22 16				23 56

Saturdays
26 May to 21 July

	GR	XC	SR	SR	XC	SR	SR	SR	SR	SR	XC	SR	SR	SR	SR	SR	XC	SR	SR	SR	SR	SR
	1 ⊡	◇1 A ✕			◇1 A ✕						◇1 A ✕						◇1 ✕					
Haymarket 225,230,242 ⇌ d		06 57		08 22	08 52						10 50											
Edinburgh 10 225,230,242 a		07 01		08 29	08 57						10 55											
d	05 48	07 07	07 42	08 41	09 08	09 12	09 43	10 08	10 12	10 43	11 08	11 12	11 43	12 08	12 12	12 43	13 09	13 12	13 43	14 08	14 12	14 43
Musselburgh d			07 48	08 47		09 18	09 49	10 14	10 18	10 49		11 18	11 49	12 14	12 18	12 49		13 18	13 49	14 14	14 19	14 49
Wallyford d			07 52	08 51		09 22	09 53		10 22	10 53		11 22	11 53		12 22	12 53		13 22	13 53		14 23	14 53
Prestonpans d			07 55	08 54		09 25	09 56		10 25	10 56		11 25	11 56		12 25	12 56		13 25	13 56		14 26	14 56
Longniddry d			08 00	08 59		09 30	10 01		10 30	11 01		11 30	12 01		12 30	13 01		13 30	14 01		14 31	15 01
Drem d			08 06	09 05		09 36	10 07		10 37	11 07		11 36	12 07		12 36	13 07		13 36	14 07		14 37	15 07
Dunbar a	06 09	07 28			09 28			10 41			11 28			12 36			13 29			14 42		
North Berwick a			08 15	09 14		09 45	10 16		10 45	11 16		11 45	12 16		12 45	13 16		13 45	14 16		14 46	15 16

	XC	SR	SR	SR	SR	SR	XC	SR	GR	SR	XC	SR	SR	GR	SR	GR	SR	SR	SR	SR
	◇1 ✕						◇1 ✕		1 ⊡		◇1 A ✕			1 ⊡		1 ⊡				
Haymarket 225,230,242 ⇌ d								17 05	17 21		17 55									
Edinburgh 10 225,230,242 a								17 11	17 26		18 00									
d	15 08	15 12	15 43	16 08	16 12	16 43	17 08	17 14	17 31	17 43	18 08	18 12	18 43	19 00	19 43	20 00	20 43	21 43	22 06	23 11
Musselburgh d		15 18	15 49	16 14	16 19	16 49		17 20		17 49		18 18	18 49		19 49		20 49	21 49	22 12	23 17
Wallyford d		15 22	15 53		16 23	16 53		17 24		17 53		18 23	18 53		19 53		20 53	21 53		23 21
Prestonpans d		15 25	15 56		16 26	16 56		17 27		17 56		18 26	18 56		19 56		20 56	21 56		23 24
Longniddry d		15 30	16 01		16 31	17 01		17 32		18 01		18 31	19 01		20 01		21 01	22 01		23 29
Drem d		15 36	16 07		16 37	17 07		17 38		18 07		18 38	19 07		20 07		21 07	22 07		23 35
Dunbar a	15 28			16 36			17 30		17 52		18 28			19 20		20 21			22 31	
North Berwick a		15 45	16 16		16 46	17 16		17 47		18 16		18 46	19 16		20 16		21 16	22 16		23 54

Saturdays
28 July to 6 October

	GR	XC	SR	SR	XC	SR	SR	SR	SR	SR	XC	SR	SR	SR	SR	SR	XC	SR	SR	SR	SR	SR
	1 ⊡	◇1 ✕			◇1 ✕						◇1 ✕						◇1 ✕					
Haymarket 225,230,242 ⇌ d		06 57		08 22	08 52						10 50											
Edinburgh 10 225,230,242 a		07 01		08 29	08 57						10 55											
d	05 48	07 07	07 42	08 41	09 08	09 12	09 43	10 08	10 12	10 43	11 08	11 12	11 43	12 08	12 12	12 43	13 09	13 12	13 43	14 08	14 12	14 43
Musselburgh d			07 48	08 47		09 18	09 49	10 14	10 18	10 49		11 18	11 49	12 14	12 18	12 49		13 18	13 49	14 14	14 19	14 49
Wallyford d			07 52	08 51		09 22	09 53		10 22	10 53		11 22	11 53		12 22	12 53		13 22	13 53		14 23	14 53
Prestonpans d			07 55	08 54		09 25	09 56		10 25	10 56		11 25	11 56		12 25	12 56		13 25	13 56		14 26	14 56
Longniddry d			08 00	08 59		09 30	10 01		10 30	11 01		11 30	12 01		12 30	13 01		13 30	14 01		14 31	15 01
Drem d			08 06	09 05		09 36	10 07		10 37	11 07		11 36	12 07		12 36	13 07		13 36	14 07		14 37	15 07
Dunbar a	06 09	07 28			09 28			10 41			11 28			12 36			13 29			14 42		
North Berwick a			08 15	09 14		09 45	10 16		10 45	11 16		11 45	12 16		12 45	13 16		13 45	14 16		14 46	15 16

	XC	SR	SR	SR	SR	SR	XC	SR	GR	SR	XC	SR	SR	GR	SR	GR	SR	SR	SR	SR
	◇1 ✕						◇1		1 ⊡		◇1 A ✕			1 ⊡		1 ⊡				
Haymarket 225,230,242 ⇌ d								17 05	17 21		17 55									
Edinburgh 10 225,230,242 a								17 11	17 26		18 00									
d	15 08	15 12	15 43	16 08	16 12	16 43	17 08	17 14	17 31	17 43	18 08	18 12	18 43	19 00	19 43	20 00	20 43	21 43	22 06	23 11
Musselburgh d		15 18	15 49	16 14	16 19	16 49		17 20		17 49		18 18	18 49		19 49		20 49	21 49	22 12	23 17
Wallyford d		15 22	15 53		16 23	16 53		17 24		17 53		18 23	18 53		19 53		20 53	21 53		23 21
Prestonpans d		15 25	15 56		16 26	16 56		17 27		17 56		18 26	18 56		19 56		20 56	21 56		23 24
Longniddry d		15 30	16 01		16 31	17 01		17 32		18 01		18 31	19 01		20 01		21 01	22 01		23 29
Drem d		15 36	16 07		16 37	17 07		17 38		18 07		18 38	19 07		20 07		21 07	22 07		23 35
Dunbar a	15 28			16 36			17 30		17 52		18 28			19 20		20 21			22 31	
North Berwick a		15 45	16 16		16 46	17 16		17 47		18 16		18 46	19 16		20 16		21 16	22 16		23 54

A ✕ from Edinburgh

Table T238-R

Saturdays
13 October to 8 December

Haymarket and Edinburgh - North Berwick and Dunbar

	GR	XC	SR	SR	XC	SR	SR	SR	SR	SR	XC	SR	SR	SR	SR	SR	XC	SR	SR	SR	SR	SR
	1 ⊡	◇1 A ✕			◇1 A ✕						◇1 A ✕						◇1 ✕					
Haymarket 225,230,242 ⇌ d		06 57		08 22	08 52						10 50											
Edinburgh 10 225,230,242 a		07 01		08 29	08 57						10 55											
d	05 48	07 07	07 42	08 41	09 08	09 12	09 43	10 08	10 12	10 43	11 08	11 12	11 43	12 08	12 12	12 43	13 09	13 12	13 43	14 08	14 12	14 43
Musselburgh d			07 48	08 47		09 18	09 49	10 14	10 18	10 49		11 18	11 49	12 14	12 18	12 49		13 18	13 49	14 14	14 19	14 49
Wallyford d			07 52	08 51		09 22	09 53		10 22	10 53		11 22	11 53		12 22	12 53		13 22	13 53		14 23	14 53
Prestonpans d			07 55	08 54		09 25	09 56		10 25	10 56		11 25	11 56		12 25	12 56		13 25	13 56		14 26	14 56
Longniddry d			08 00	08 59		09 30	10 01		10 30	11 01		11 30	12 01		12 30	13 01		13 30	14 01		14 31	15 01
Drem d			08 06	09 05		09 36	10 07		10 37	11 07		11 36	12 07		12 36	13 07		13 36	14 07		14 37	15 07
Dunbar a	06 09	07 28			09 28			10 41			11 28			12 36			13 29			14 42		
North Berwick a			08 15	09 14		09 45	10 16		10 45	11 16		11 45	12 16		12 45	13 16		13 45	14 16		14 46	15 16

	XC	SR	SR	SR	SR	SR	XC	SR	GR	SR	XC	SR	SR	GR	SR	GR	SR	SR	SR	SR
	◇1 ✕						◇1 ✕		1 ⊡		◇1 A ✕			1 ⊡		1 ⊡				
Haymarket 225,230,242 ⇌ d								17 05	17 21		17 55									
Edinburgh 10 225,230,242 a								17 11	17 26		18 00									
d	15 08	15 12	15 43	16 08	16 12	16 43	17 08	17 14	17 31	17 43	18 08	18 12	18 43	19 00	19 43	20 00	20 43	21 43	22 06	23 11
Musselburgh d		15 18	15 49	16 14	16 19	16 49		17 20		17 49		18 18	18 49		19 49		20 49	21 49	22 12	23 17
Wallyford d		15 22	15 53		16 23	16 53		17 24		17 53		18 23	18 53		19 53		20 53	21 53		23 21
Prestonpans d		15 25	15 56		16 26	16 56		17 27		17 56		18 26	18 56		19 56		20 56	21 56		23 24
Longniddry d		15 30	16 01		16 31	17 01		17 32		18 01		18 31	19 01		20 01		21 01	22 01		23 29
Drem d		15 36	16 07		16 37	17 07		17 38		18 07		18 38	19 07		20 07		21 07	22 07		23 35
Dunbar a	15 28			16 36			17 30		17 52		18 28			19 20		20 21			22 31	
North Berwick a		15 45	16 16		16 46	17 16		17 47		18 16		18 46	19 16		20 16		21 16	22 16		23 54

Sundays
20 May to 15 July

	SR	SR	XC	SR	SR	XC	SR	SR	XC	SR	SR	XC	GR	SR	XC	SR	GR	SR	GR	XC	SR	GR
			◇1 ✕			◇1 ✕			◇1 A ✕			◇1 ✕	1 ⊡		◇1 A ✕		1 ⊡		1 ⊡	◇1		1 ⊡
Haymarket 225,230,242 ⇌ d						12 56			14 42						17 51					19 59		
Edinburgh 10 225,230,242 a						13 01			14 47						17 55					20 03		
d	09 33	10 33	11 05	11 33	12 33	13 08	13 33	14 33	15 08	15 33	16 33	17 08	17 30	17 33	18 06	18 33	19 00	19 33	20 00	20 18	20 33	21 00
Musselburgh d	09 39	10 39		11 39	12 39		13 39	14 39		15 39	16 39			17 39		18 39		19 39			20 39	
Wallyford d	09 43	10 43		11 43	12 43		13 43	14 43		15 43	16 43			17 43		18 43		19 43			20 43	
Prestonpans d	09 46	10 46		11 46	12 46		13 46	14 46		15 46	16 46			17 46		18 46		19 46			20 46	
Longniddry d	09 51	10 51		11 51	12 51		13 51	14 51		15 51	16 51			17 51		18 51		19 51			20 51	
Drem d	09 58	10 58		11 58	12 58		13 58	14 58		15 58	16 58			17 58		18 58		19 58			20 58	
Dunbar a			11 25			13 28			15 28			17 28	17 51		18 27		19 21		20 21	20 39		21 20
North Berwick a	10 06	11 06		12 06	13 06		14 06	15 06		16 06	17 06			18 06		19 06		20 06			21 06	

	SR
Haymarket 225,230,242 ⇌ d	
Edinburgh 10 225,230,242 a	
d	21 33
Musselburgh d	21 39
Wallyford d	21 43
Prestonpans d	21 46
Longniddry d	21 51
Drem d	21 58
Dunbar a	
North Berwick a	22 06

Sundays
22 July to 7 October

	SR	SR	XC	SR	SR	XC	SR	SR	XC	SR	SR	XC	GR	SR	XC	SR	GR	SR	GR	XC	SR	GR
			◇1 ✕			◇1			◇1 A ✕			◇1	1 ⊡		◇1 A ✕		1 ⊡		1 ⊡	◇1		1 ⊡
Haymarket 225,230,242 ⇌ d						12 56			14 42						17 51					19 59		
Edinburgh 10 225,230,242 a						13 01			14 47						17 55					20 03		
d	09 33	10 33	11 05	11 33	12 33	13 08	13 33	14 33	15 08	15 33	16 33	17 08	17 30	17 33	18 06	18 33	19 00	19 33	20 00	20 18	20 33	21 00
Musselburgh d	09 39	10 39		11 39	12 39		13 39	14 39		15 39	16 39			17 39		18 39		19 39			20 39	
Wallyford d	09 43	10 43		11 43	12 43		13 43	14 43		15 43	16 43			17 43		18 43		19 43			20 43	
Prestonpans d	09 46	10 46		11 46	12 46		13 46	14 46		15 46	16 46			17 46		18 46		19 46			20 46	
Longniddry d	09 51	10 51		11 51	12 51		13 51	14 51		15 51	16 51			17 51		18 51		19 51			20 51	
Drem d	09 58	10 58		11 58	12 58		13 58	14 58		15 58	16 58			17 58		18 58		19 58			20 58	
Dunbar a			11 25			13 28			15 28			17 28	17 51		18 27		19 21		20 21	20 39		21 20
North Berwick a	10 06	11 06		12 06	13 06		14 06	15 06		16 06	17 06			18 06		19 06		20 06			21 06	

A ✕ from Edinburgh

Table T238-R

Haymarket and Edinburgh - North Berwick and Dunbar

Sundays

22 July to 7 October

		SR
Haymarket 225,230,242 ⇌	d	
Edinburgh ■ 225,230,242	a	
	d	21 33
Musselburgh	d	21 39
Wallyford	d	21 43
Prestonpans	d	21 46
Longniddry	d	21 51
Drem	d	21 58
Dunbar	a	
North Berwick	a	22 06

Sundays

14 October to 2 December

		SR	SR	XC	SR	SR	XC	SR	SR	XC	SR	SR	XC	GR	SR	XC	SR	GR	SR	GR	XC	SR	GR
				◇1			◇1			◇1			◇1	■ 1		◇1		■ 1		■ 1	◇1		■ 1
										A						A							
				🛒			🛒			🛒			🛒	🍽		🛒		🍽		🍽			🍽
Haymarket 225,230,242 ⇌	d						12 56			14 42						17 51					19 59		
Edinburgh ■ 225,230,242	a						13 01			14 47						17 55					20 03		
	d	09 33	10 33	11 05	11 33	12 33	13 08	13 33	14 33	15 08	15 33	16 33	17 08	17 30	17 33	18 06	18 33	19 00	19 33	20 00	20 18	20 33	21 00
Musselburgh	d	09 39	10 39		11 39	12 39		13 39	14 39		15 39	16 39			17 39		18 39		19 39			20 39	
Wallyford	d	09 43	10 43		11 43	12 43		13 43	14 43		15 43	16 43			17 43		18 43		19 43			20 43	
Prestonpans	d	09 46	10 46		11 46	12 46		13 46	14 46		15 46	16 46			17 46		18 46		19 46			20 46	
Longniddry	d	09 51	10 51		11 51	12 51		13 51	14 51		15 51	16 51			17 51		18 51		19 51			20 51	
Drem	d	09 58	10 58		11 58	12 58		13 58	14 58		15 58	16 58			17 58		18 58		19 58			20 58	
Dunbar	a			11 25			13 28			15 28			17 28	17 51		18 27		19 21		20 21	20 39		21 20
North Berwick	a	10 06	11 06		12 06	13 06		14 06	15 06		16 06	17 06			18 06		19 06		20 06			21 06	

		SR
Haymarket 225,230,242 ⇌	d	
Edinburgh ■ 225,230,242	a	
	d	21 33
Musselburgh	d	21 39
Wallyford	d	21 43
Prestonpans	d	21 46
Longniddry	d	21 51
Drem	d	21 58
Dunbar	a	
North Berwick	a	22 06

A 🛒 from Edinburgh

Table T239-F

Inverness - Kyle of Lochalsh, Thurso and Wick

Mondays to Fridays

21 May to 26 October

Miles	Miles			SR	SR	SR	SR	SR	SR	SR	SR	SR	SR	SR	SR	SR
																FO
				◇	◇	◇	◇		◇	◇			◇	◇		
						🛒				🛒				🛒		
0	0	**Inverness**	d	07 00	08 55	10 41	10 56	11 42	13 35	14 00	14 50	17 12	17 54	18 30	21 07	23 33
10	10	Beauly	d	07 15	09 10		11 13	11 57	13 50	14 15	15 05	17 27	18 09	18 45	21 22	23 48
13	13	Muir of Ord	d	07 23	09 16	11 01	11 19	12 07	13 56	14 23	15 11	17 33	18 15	18 51	21 28	23 54
16	16	Conon Bridge	d	07 31	09 23		11 26	12 14	14 03	14 31	15 18	17 41	18 23	18 58	21 35	00 01
18¾	18¾	Dingwall	d	07 39	09 29	11 12	11 32	12a19	14 11	14 37	15 24	17 47	18 29	19 06	21 41	00 07
—	30½	Garve	d		09 52		11 55		14 33				18 53			
—	36	Lochluichart	d		09x59		12x02		14x41				19x01			
—	40¼	Achanalt	d		10x06		12x09		14x47				19x07			
—	46½	Achnasheen	d		10 18		12 21		15 00				19 20			
—	59¼	Achnashellach	d		10x36		12x39		15x17				19x37			
—	64½	Strathcarron	d		10 48		12 53		15 30				19 49			
—	67	Attadale	d		10x51		12x56		15x33				19x52			
—	72	Stromeferry	d		11 05		13 10		15 47				20 06			
—	75¾	Duncraig	d		11x12		13x17		15x54				20x13			
—	77	Plockton	d		11 17		13 22		15 59				20 18			
—	78½	Duirinish	d		11x20		13x25		16x02				20x21			
—	82¼	**Kyle of Lochalsh**	a		11 30		13 35		16 12				20 31			
28½	—	Alness	d	07 51		11 24				14 49	15 36	17 59		19 18	21 53	00 19
31½	—	Invergordon	d	07 58		11 30				14 54	15a41	18 04		19 26	21 58	00 24
40¾	—	Fearn	d	08 11		11 42				15 07		18 17		19 39	22 11	00 37
44¼	—	Tain	d	08 17		11 49				15 13		18 24		19 45	22a17	00a43
57¾	—	Ardgay	d	08 33		12 05				15 29		18a39		20 01		
61	—	Culrain	d	08x37		12x09				15x33				20x05		
61½	—	Invershin	d	08x38		12x10				15x34				20x06		
67	—	Lairg	d	08 53		12 21				15 45				20 17		
77	—	Rogart	d	09x06		12x34				15x58				20x30		
84½	—	Golspie	d	09 18		12 46				16 10				20 42		
87	—	Dunrobin Castle §	d	09x20		12x48				16x12						
90½	—	Brora	d	09 29		12 57				16 21				20 52		
101½	—	Helmsdale	d	09 47		13 12				16 36				21 08		
111	—	Kildonan	d	09x59		13x24				16x48				21x19		
118¼	—	Kinbrace	d	10x09		13x34				16x58				21x29		
125¾	—	Forsinard	d	10 21		13 46				17 12				21 42		
134	—	Altnabreac	d	10x29		13x54				17x20				21x50		
143	—	Scotscalder	d	10x38		14x03				17x29				21x59		
147¼	—	Georgemas Junction	a	10 45		14 10				17 36				22 06		
—	—		d	10 49		14 14				17 40				22 10		
154	—	**Thurso**	a	10 59		14 24				17 50				22 20		
—	—		d	11 02		14 27				17 53				22 23		
160¾	—	Georgemas Junction	d	11 14		14 39				18 05				22 35		
175	—	**Wick**	a	11 31		14 56				18 22				22 52		

Mondays to Fridays

29 October to 7 December

		SR	SR	SR	SR	SR	SR	SR	SR	SR	SR	SR	SR	SR
														FO
		◇	◇	◇	◇		◇	◇			◇	◇		
		A		B										
		🛒		🛒				🛒				🛒		
Inverness	d	07 00	08 55	10 41	10 56	11 42	13 35	14 00	14 50	17 12	17 54	18 30	21 07	23 33
Beauly	d	07 15	09 10		11 13	11 57	13 50	14 15	15 05	17 27	18 09	18 45	21 22	23 48
Muir of Ord	d	07 23	09 16	11 01	11 19	12 07	13 56	14 23	15 11	17 33	18 15	18 51	21 28	23 54
Conon Bridge	d	07 31	09 23		11 26	12 14	14 03	14 31	15 18	17 41	18 23	18 58	21 35	00 01
Dingwall	d	07 39	09 29	11 12	11 32	12a19	14 11	14 37	15 24	17 47	18 29	19 06	21 41	00 07
Garve	d		09 52		11 55		14 33				18 53			
Lochluichart	d		09x59		12x02		14x41				19x01			
Achanalt	d		10x06		12x09		14x47				19x07			
Achnasheen	d		10 18		12 21		15 00				19 20			
Achnashellach	d		10x36		12x39		15x17				19x37			
Strathcarron	d		10 48		12 53		15 30				19 49			
Attadale	d		10x51		12x56		15x33				19x52			
Stromeferry	d		11 05		13 10		15 47				20 06			
Duncraig	d		11x12		13x17		15x54				20x13			
Plockton	d		11 17		13 22		15 59				20 18			
Duirinish	d		11x20		13x25		16x02				20x21			
Kyle of Lochalsh	a		11 30		13 35		16 12				20 31			
Alness	d	07 51		11 24				14 49	15 36	17 59		19 18	21 53	00 19
Invergordon	d	07 58		11 30				14 54	15a41	18 04		19 26	21 58	00 24
Fearn	d	08 11		11 42				15 07		18 17		19 39	22 11	00 37
Tain	d	08 17		11 49				15 13		18 24		19 45	22a17	00a43
Ardgay	d	08 33		12 05				15 29		18a39		20 01		
Culrain	d	08x37		12x09				15x33				20x05		
Invershin	d	08x38		12x10				15x34				20x06		
Lairg	d	08 53		12 21				15 45				20 17		
Rogart	d	09x06		12x34				15x58				20x30		
Golspie	d	09 18		12 46				16 10				20 42		
Dunrobin Castle §	d													
Brora	d	09 29		12 57				16 21				20 52		
Helmsdale	d	09 47		13 12				16 36				21 08		
Kildonan	d	09x59		13x24				16x48				21x19		
Kinbrace	d	10x09		13x34				16x58				21x29		
Forsinard	d	10 21		13 46				17 12				21 42		
Altnabreac	d	10x29		13x54				17x20				21x50		
Scotscalder	d	10x38		14x03				17x29				21x59		
Georgemas Junction	a	10 45		14 10				17 36				22 06		
	d	10 49		14 14				17 40				22 10		
Thurso	a	10 59		14 24				17 50				22 20		
	d	11 02		14 27				17 53				22 23		
Georgemas Junction	d	11 14		14 39				18 05				22 35		
Wick	a	11 31		14 56				18 22				22 52		

§ Open 29 March until 27 October - Dec 14 Timetable

A 🛒 from Lairg

B Forms booked connection into 1A58 and 1T62.

Inverness - Kyle of Lochalsh, Thurso and Wick

Saturdays
26 May to 27 October

		SR	SR	SR	SR	SR	SR	SR	SR	SR	SR	SR	SR	SR	SR
			◇ A 🛒	◇	◇ 🛒	◇		◇	◇ 🛒			◇	◇ 🛒		
Inverness	d		07 00	08 55	10 41	10 56	11 42	13 35	14 00	14 50	17 12	17 54	18 30	21 07	23 33
Beauly	d		07 15	09 10		11 13	11 57	13 50	14 15	15 05	17 27	18 09	18 45	21 22	23 48
Muir of Ord	d		07 23	09 16	11 01	11 19	12 07	13 56	14 23	15 11	17 33	18 15	18 51	21 28	23 54
Conon Bridge	d	00 01	07 31	09 23		11 26	12 14	14 03	14 31	15 18	17 41	18 23	18 58	21 35	00 01
Dingwall	d	00 07	07 39	09 29	11 12	11 32	12a19	14 11	14 37	15 24	17 47	18 29	19 06	21 41	00 07
Garve	d			09 52		11 55		14 33				18 53			
Lochluichart	d			09x59		12x02		14x41				19x01			
Achanalt	d			10x06		12x09		14x47				19x07			
Achnasheen	d			10 18		12 21		15 00				19 20			
Achnashellach	d			10x36		12x39		15x17				19x37			
Strathcarron	d			10 48		12 53		15 30				19 49			
Attadale	d			10x51		12x56		15x33				19x52			
Stromeferry	d			11 05		13 10		15 47				20 06			
Duncraig	d			11x12		13x17		15x54				20x13			
Plockton	d			11 17		13 22		15 59				20 18			
Duirinish	d			11x20		13x25		16x02				20x21			
Kyle of Lochalsh	a			11 30		13 35		16 12				20 31			
Alness	d	00 19	07 51		11 24				14 49	15 36	17 59		19 18	21 53	00 19
Invergordon	d	00 24	07 58		11 30				14 54	15a41	18 04		19 26	21 58	00 24
Fearn	d	00 37	08 11		11 42				15 07		18 17		19 39	22 11	00 37
Tain	d	00a43	08 17		11 49				15 13		18 24		19 45	22a17	00a43
Ardgay	d		08 33		12 05				15 29		18a39		20 01		
Culrain	d		08x37		12x09				15x33				20x05		
Invershin	d		08x38		12x10				15x34				20x06		
Lairg	d		08 53		12 21				15 45				20 17		
Rogart	d		09x06		12x34				15x58				20x30		
Golspie	d		09 18		12 46				16 10				20 42		
Dunrobin Castle §	d		09x20		12x48				16x12						
Brora	d		09 29		12 57				16 21				20 52		
Helmsdale	d		09 47		13 12				16 36				21 08		
Kildonan	d		09x59		13x24				16x48				21x19		
Kinbrace	d		10x09		13x34				16x58				21x29		
Forsinard	d		10 21		13 46				17 12				21 42		
Altnabreac	d		10x29		13x54				17x20				21x50		
Scotscalder	d		10x38		14x03				17x29				21x59		
Georgemas Junction	a		10 45		14 10				17 36				22 06		
	d		10 49		14 14				17 40				22 10		
Thurso	a		10 59		14 24				17 50				22 20		
	d		11 02		14 27				17 53				22 23		
Georgemas Junction	d		11 14		14 39				18 05				22 35		
Wick	a		11 31		14 56				18 22				22 52		

Saturdays
3 November to 8 December

		SR	SR	SR	SR	SR	SR	SR	SR	SR	SR	SR	SR	SR	SR
			◇ A 🛒	◇	◇ B 🛒	◇		◇	◇ 🛒			◇	◇ 🛒		
Inverness	d		07 00	08 55	10 41	10 56	11 42	13 35	14 00	14 50	17 12	17 54	18 30	21 07	23 33
Beauly	d		07 15	09 10		11 13	11 57	13 50	14 15	15 05	17 27	18 09	18 45	21 22	23 48
Muir of Ord	d		07 23	09 16	11 01	11 19	12 07	13 56	14 23	15 11	17 33	18 15	18 51	21 28	23 54
Conon Bridge	d	00 01	07 31	09 23		11 26	12 14	14 03	14 31	15 18	17 41	18 23	18 58	21 35	00 01
Dingwall	d	00 07	07 39	09 29	11 12	11 32	12a19	14 11	14 37	15 24	17 47	18 29	19 06	21 41	00 07
Garve	d			09 52		11 55		14 33				18 53			
Lochluichart	d			09x59		12x02		14x41				19x01			
Achanalt	d			10x06		12x09		14x47				19x07			
Achnasheen	d			10 18		12 21		15 00				19 20			
Achnashellach	d			10x36		12x39		15x17				19x37			
Strathcarron	d			10 48		12 53		15 30				19 49			
Attadale	d			10x51		12x56		15x33				19x52			
Stromeferry	d			11 05		13 10		15 47				20 06			
Duncraig	d			11x12		13x17		15x54				20x13			
Plockton	d			11 17		13 22		15 59				20 18			
Duirinish	d			11x20		13x25		16x02				20x21			
Kyle of Lochalsh	a			11 30		13 35		16 12				20 31			
Alness	d	00 19	07 51		11 24				14 49	15 36	17 59		19 18	21 53	00 19
Invergordon	d	00 24	07 58		11 30				14 54	15a41	18 04		19 26	21 58	00 24
Fearn	d	00 37	08 11		11 42				15 07		18 17		19 39	22 11	00 37
Tain	d	00a43	08 17		11 49				15 13		18 24		19 45	22a17	00a43
Ardgay	d		08 33		12 05				15 29		18a39		20 01		
Culrain	d		08x37		12x09				15x33				20x05		
Invershin	d		08x38		12x10				15x34				20x06		
Lairg	d		08 53		12 21				15 45				20 17		
Rogart	d		09x06		12x34				15x58				20x30		
Golspie	d		09 18		12 46				16 10				20 42		
Dunrobin Castle §	d														
Brora	d		09 29		12 57				16 21				20 52		
Helmsdale	d		09 47		13 12				16 36				21 08		
Kildonan	d		09x59		13x24				16x48				21x19		
Kinbrace	d		10x09		13x34				16x58				21x29		
Forsinard	d		10 21		13 46				17 12				21 42		
Altnabreac	d		10x29		13x54				17x20				21x50		
Scotscalder	d		10x38		14x03				17x29				21x59		
Georgemas Junction	a		10 45		14 10				17 36				22 06		
	d		10 49		14 14				17 40				22 10		
Thurso	a		10 59		14 24				17 50				22 20		
	d		11 02		14 27				17 53				22 23		
Georgemas Junction	d		11 14		14 39				18 05				22 35		
Wick	a		11 31		14 56				18 22				22 52		

§ Open 29 March until 27 October - Dec 14 Timetable
A 🛒 from Lairg
B Forms booked connection into 1A58 and 1T62.

Table T239-F

Inverness - Kyle of Lochalsh, Thurso and Wick

Sundays
20 May to 30 September

		SR	SR	SR	SR	SR	SR		SR
		A		◇			◇ 🛒		
Inverness	d		09 40	10 59	12 53	15 33	17 54		21 08
Beauly	d		09 55	11 15	13 08	15 48	18 09		21 23
Muir of Ord	d		10 01	11 21	13 14	15 56	18 15		21 29
Conon Bridge	d	00 01	10 08	11 28	13 21	16 03	18 22		21 36
Dingwall	d	00 07	10 14	11 34	13 27	16 09	18 31	18 33	21 42
Garve	d			11 58				18 55	
Lochluichart	d			12x06				19x03	
Achanalt	d			12x12				19x09	
Achnasheen	d			12 25				19 22	
Achnashellach	d			12x43				19x39	
Strathcarron	d			12 55				19 51	
Attadale	d			12x58				19x54	
Stromeferry	d			13 12				20 08	
Duncraig	d			13x19				20x15	
Plockton	d			13 24				20 20	
Duirinish	d			13x27				20x22	
Kyle of Lochalsh	a			13 37				20 33	
Alness	d	00 19	10 26		13 39	16 21	18 43		21 54
Invergordon	d	00 24	10 32		13 45	16a26	18 48		22 00
Fearn	d	00 37	10 44		13 57		19 01		22 12
Tain	d	00a43	10a50		14a03		19 07		22a18
Ardgay	d						19 23		
Culrain	d						19x27		
Invershin	d						19x28		
Lairg	d						19 42		
Rogart	d						19x55		
Golspie	d						20 07		
Dunrobin Castle §	d								
Brora	d						20 18		
Helmsdale	d						20 33		
Kildonan	d						20x45		
Kinbrace	d						20x55		
Forsinard	d						21 07		
Altnabreac	d						21x15		
Scotscalder	d						21x24		
Georgemas Junction	a						21 31		
	d						21 35		
Thurso	a						21 45		
	d						21 48		
Georgemas Junction	d						22 00		
Wick	a						22 17		

Sundays
7 October to 2 December

		SR	SR	SR	SR	SR	SR	SR
				◇			◇ 🛒	
Inverness	d		09 40	10 59	12 53	15 33	17 54	21 08
Beauly	d		09 55	11 15	13 08	15 48	18 09	21 23
Muir of Ord	d		10 01	11 21	13 14	15 56	18 15	21 29
Conon Bridge	d	00 01	10 08	11 28	13 21	16 03	18 22	21 36
Dingwall	d	00 07	10 14	11 34	13 27	16 09	18 31	21 42
Garve	d			11 58				
Lochluichart	d			12x06				
Achanalt	d			12x12				
Achnasheen	d			12 25				
Achnashellach	d			12x43				
Strathcarron	d			12 55				
Attadale	d			12x58				
Stromeferry	d			13 12				
Duncraig	d			13x19				
Plockton	d			13 24				
Duirinish	d			13x27				
Kyle of Lochalsh	a			13 37				
Alness	d	00 19	10 26		13 39	16 21	18 43	21 54
Invergordon	d	00 24	10 32		13 45	16a26	18 48	22 00
Fearn	d	00 37	10 44		13 57		19 01	22 12
Tain	d	00a43	10a50		14a03		19 07	22a18
Ardgay	d						19 23	
Culrain	d						19x27	
Invershin	d						19x28	
Lairg	d						19 42	
Rogart	d						19x55	
Golspie	d						20 07	
Dunrobin Castle §	d							
Brora	d						20 18	
Helmsdale	d						20 33	
Kildonan	d						20x45	
Kinbrace	d						20x55	
Forsinard	d						21 07	
Altnabreac	d						21x15	
Scotscalder	d						21x24	
Georgemas Junction	a						21 31	
	d						21 35	
Thurso	a						21 45	
	d						21 48	
Georgemas Junction	d						22 00	
Wick	a						22 17	

§ Open 29 March until 27 October - Dec 14 Timetable
A not 20 May

Table T239-R

Wick, Thurso and Kyle of Lochalsh - Inverness

Mondays to Fridays
21 May to 26 October

Miles	Miles			SR	SR	SR ◇	SR ◇	SR ◇ A 🛒	SR	SR ◇	SR ◇	SR	SR ◇ B 🛒	SR ◇	SR ◇ C 🛒	SR	SR
0	—	**Wick**	d				06 18	08 02					12 34		16 00		
14¼	—	Georgemas Junction	d				06 36	08 20					12 52		16 18		
21	—	**Thurso**	a				06 46	08 30					13 02		16 28		
—	—		d				06 50	08 34					13 06		16 32		
27¾	—	Georgemas Junction	a				07 00	08 44					13 16		16 42		
—	—		d				07 03	08 47					13 19		16 45		
32	—	Scotscalder	d					08x52					13x24		16x50		
41	—	Altnabreac	d					09x02					13x34		17x00		
49¼	—	Forsinard	d				07 27	09 13					13 47		17 11		
56¾	—	Kinbrace	d					09x22					13x56		17x20		
64	—	Kildonan	d				07 47	09x32					14x06		17x30		
73½	—	Helmsdale	d				08 00	09 46					14 21		17 44		
84½	—	Brora	d				08 16	10 02					14 36		18 00		
88	—	Dunrobin Castle §	d					10x07					14x42		18x05		
90½	—	Golspie	d				08 25	10 12					14 47		18 10		
98	—	Rogart	d				08x34	10x21					14x56		18x19		
108	—	Lairg	d		06 26		08 52	10 38					15 12		18 36		
113½	—	Invershin	d		06x34			10x46					15x20		18x44		
114	—	Culrain	d		06x36			10x47					15x21		18x45		
117¼	—	Ardgay	d	06 14	06 43		09 07	10 54					15 30		18 52	19 28	
130¾	—	Tain	d	06 30	06 59		09 23	11 10					15 46		19 08	19 46	22 21
134¼	—	Fearn	d	06 36	07 05		09 29	11 16					15 53			19 52	22 27
143½	—	Invergordon	d	06 49	07 19		09 42	11 31				15 51	16 06		19 25	20 05	22 40
146½	—	Alness	d	06 55	07 25		09 48	11 36				15 56	16 11			20 11	22 46
—	0	**Kyle of Lochalsh**	d			06 11				12 08	13 46			17 13			
—	3¾	Duirinish	d			06x20				12x16	13x54			17x21			
—	5¼	Plockton	d			06 27				12 21	13 59			17 26			
—	6½	Duncraig	d			06x29				12x23	14x01			17x28			
—	10¼	Stromeferry	d			06 39				12 33	14 11			17 38			
—	15¼	Attadale	d			06x50				12x44	14x22			17x49			
—	17¾	Strathcarron	d			06 58				12 52	14 30			17 57			
—	23	Achnashellach	d			07x06				13x00	14x38			18x05			
—	35¾	Achnasheen	d			07 26				13 20	15 01			18 25			
—	42	Achanalt	d			07x35				13x29	15x10			18x34			
—	46¼	Lochluichart	d			07x42				13x36	15x16			18x41			
—	51¾	Garve	d			07 53				13 47	15 27			18 52			
156¼	63½	Dingwall	d	07 08	07 38	08 16	10 01	11 53	12 45	14 10	15 50	16 11	16 26	19 19	19 41	20 24	22 58
159¼	66¼	Conon Bridge	d	07 14	07 44	08 22	10 06	11 58	12 50	14 15	15 56	16 16	16 31	19 24		20 29	23 03
162	69¼	Muir of Ord	d	07 22	07 51	08 30	10 14	12 06	12 58	14 22	16 03	16 24	16 39	19 31	19 52	20 37	23 11
164¾	72¼	Beauly	d	07 28	07 57	08 35	10 20	12 11	13 04	14 27	16 09	16 29	16 45	19 36		20 42	23 16
175	82¼	**Inverness**	a	07 43	08 12	08 50	10 35	12 26	13 19	14 42	16 26	16 46	17 02	20 00	20 10	20 57	23 31

Mondays to Fridays
29 October to 7 December

		SR	SR	SR ◇	SR ◇	SR ◇ A 🛒	SR	SR ◇	SR ◇	SR	SR ◇ B 🛒	SR ◇	SR ◇ B 🛒	SR	SR
Wick	d				06 18	08 02					12 34		16 00		
Georgemas Junction	d				06 36	08 20					12 52		16 18		
Thurso	a				06 46	08 30					13 02		16 28		
	d				06 50	08 34					13 06		16 32		
Georgemas Junction	a				07 00	08 44					13 16		16 42		
	d				07 03	08 47					13 19		16 45		
Scotscalder	d					08x52					13x24		16x50		
Altnabreac	d					09x02					13x34		17x00		
Forsinard	d				07 27	09 13					13 47		17 11		
Kinbrace	d					09x22					13x56		17x20		
Kildonan	d				07 47	09x32					14x06		17x30		
Helmsdale	d				08 00	09 46					14 21		17 44		
Brora	d				08 16	10 02					14 36		18 00		
Dunrobin Castle §	d														
Golspie	d				08 25	10 12					14 47		18 10		
Rogart	d				08x34	10x21					14x56		18x19		
Lairg	d		06 26		08 52	10 38					15 12		18 36		
Invershin	d		06x34			10x46					15x20		18x44		
Culrain	d		06x36			10x47					15x21		18x45		
Ardgay	d	06 14	06 43		09 07	10 54					15 30		18 52	19 28	
Tain	d	06 30	06 59		09 23	11 10					15 46		19 08	19 46	22 21
Fearn	d	06 36	07 05		09 29	11 16					15 53			19 52	22 27
Invergordon	d	06 49	07 19		09 42	11 31				15 51	16 06		19 25	20 05	22 40
Alness	d	06 55	07 25		09 48	11 36				15 56	16 11			20 11	22 46
Kyle of Lochalsh	d			06 11				12 08	13 46			17 13			
Duirinish	d			06x20				12x16	13x54			17x21			
Plockton	d			06 27				12 21	13 59			17 26			
Duncraig	d			06x29				12x23	14x01			17x28			
Stromeferry	d			06 39				12 33	14 11			17 38			
Attadale	d			06x50				12x44	14x22			17x49			
Strathcarron	d			06 58				12 52	14 30			17 57			
Achnashellach	d			07x06				13x00	14x38			18x05			
Achnasheen	d			07 26				13 20	15 01			18 25			
Achanalt	d			07x35				13x29	15x10			18x34			
Lochluichart	d			07x42				13x36	15x16			18x41			
Garve	d			07 53				13 47	15 27			18 52			
Dingwall	d	07 08	07 38	08 16	10 01	11 53	12 45	14 10	15 50	16 11	16 26	19 19	19 41	20 24	22 58
Conon Bridge	d	07 14	07 44	08 22	10 06	11 58	12 50	14 15	15 56	16 16	16 31	19 24		20 29	23 03
Muir of Ord	d	07 22	07 51	08 30	10 14	12 06	12 58	14 22	16 03	16 24	16 39	19 31	19 52	20 37	23 11
Beauly	d	07 28	07 57	08 35	10 20	12 11	13 04	14 27	16 09	16 29	16 45	19 36		20 42	23 16
Inverness	a	07 43	08 12	08 50	10 35	12 26	13 19	14 42	16 26	16 46	17 02	20 00	20 10	20 57	23 31

§ Open 29 March until 27 October - Dec 14 Timetable
A Forms booked connection into 1A52 and 1B31.
B Forms booked connection into 1A58 and 1T62.
C Forms tight booked connection into 1T56.

Table T239-R

Wick, Thurso and Kyle of Lochalsh - Inverness

Saturdays
26 May to 27 October

		SR	SR	SR	SR ◇	SR ◇ A 🛒	SR ◇ B 🛒	SR	SR ◇	SR ◇	SR	SR ◇ C 🛒	SR ◇	SR ◇ D 🛒	SR	SR
Wick	d					06 18	08 02					12 34		16 00		
Georgemas Junction	d					06 36	08 20					12 52		16 18		
Thurso	a					06 46	08 30					13 02		16 28		
	d					06 50	08 34					13 06		16 32		
Georgemas Junction	a					07 00	08 44					13 16		16 42		
	d					07 03	08 47					13 19		16 45		
Scotscalder	d						08x52					13x24		16x50		
Altnabreac	d						09x02					13x34		17x00		
Forsinard	d					07 27	09 13					13 47		17 11		
Kinbrace	d						09x22					13x56		17x20		
Kildonan	d					07 47	09x32					14x06		17x30		
Helmsdale	d					08 00	09 46					14 21		17 44		
Brora	d					08 16	10 02					14 36		18 00		
Dunrobin Castle §	d						10x07					14x42		18x05		
Golspie	d					08 25	10 12					14 47		18 10		
Rogart	d					08x34	10x21					14x56		18x19		
Lairg	d			06 26		08 52	10 38					15 12		18 36		
Invershin	d			06x34			10x46					15x20		18x44		
Culrain	d			06x36			10x47					15x21		18x45		
Ardgay	d		06 14	06 43		09 07	10 54					15 30		18 52	19 28	
Tain	d	00 48	06 30	06 59		09 23	11 10					15 46		19 08	19 46	22 21
Fearn	d		06 36	07 05		09 29	11 16					15 53			19 52	22 27
Invergordon	d	01 05	06 49	07 19		09 42	11 31				15 51	16 06		19 25	20 05	22 40
Alness	d		06 55	07 25		09 48	11 36				15 56	16 11			20 11	22 46
Kyle of Lochalsh	d				06 11				12 08	13 46			17 13			
Duirinish	d				06x20				12x16	13x54			17x21			
Plockton	d				06 27				12 21	13 59			17 26			
Duncraig	d				06x29				12x23	14x01			17x28			
Stromeferry	d				06 39				12 33	14 11			17 38			
Attadale	d				06x50				12x44	14x22			17x49			
Strathcarron	d				06 58				12 52	14 30			17 57			
Achnashellach	d				07x06				13x00	14x38			18x05			
Achnasheen	d				07 26				13 20	15 01			18 25			
Achanalt	d				07x35				13x29	15x10			18x34			
Lochluichart	d				07x42				13x36	15x16			18x41			
Garve	d				07 53				13 47	15 27			18 52			
Dingwall	d	01 21	07 08	07 38	08 16	10 01	11 53	12 45	14 10	15 50	16 11	16 26	19 19	19 41	20 24	22 58
Conon Bridge	d		07 14	07 44	08 22	10 06	11 58	12 50	14 15	15 56	16 16	16 31	19 24		20 29	23 03
Muir of Ord	d	01a31	07 22	07 51	08 30	10 14	12 06	12 58	14 22	16 03	16 24	16 39	19 31	19 52	20 37	23 11
Beauly	d		07 28	07 57	08 35	10 20	12 11	13 04	14 27	16 09	16 29	16 45	19 36		20 42	23 16
Inverness	a		07 43	08 12	08 50	10 35	12 26	13 19	14 42	16 26	16 46	17 02	20 00	20 10	20 57	23 31

Saturdays
3 November to 8 December

		SR	SR	SR	SR ◇	SR ◇ A 🛒	SR ◇ B 🛒	SR	SR ◇	SR ◇	SR	SR ◇ C 🛒	SR ◇	SR ◇ C 🛒	SR	SR
Wick	d					06 18	08 02					12 34		16 00		
Georgemas Junction	d					06 36	08 20					12 52		16 18		
Thurso	a					06 46	08 30					13 02		16 28		
	d					06 50	08 34					13 06		16 32		
Georgemas Junction	a					07 00	08 44					13 16		16 42		
	d					07 03	08 47					13 19		16 45		
Scotscalder	d						08x52					13x24		16x50		
Altnabreac	d						09x02					13x34		17x00		
Forsinard	d					07 27	09 13					13 47		17 11		
Kinbrace	d						09x22					13x56		17x20		
Kildonan	d					07 47	09x32					14x06		17x30		
Helmsdale	d					08 00	09 46					14 21		17 44		
Brora	d					08 16	10 02					14 36		18 00		
Dunrobin Castle §	d															
Golspie	d					08 25	10 12					14 47		18 10		
Rogart	d					08x34	10x21					14x56		18x19		
Lairg	d			06 26		08 52	10 38					15 12		18 36		
Invershin	d			06x34			10x46					15x20		18x44		
Culrain	d			06x36			10x47					15x21		18x45		
Ardgay	d		06 14	06 43		09 07	10 54					15 30		18 52	19 28	
Tain	d	00 48	06 30	06 59		09 23	11 10					15 46		19 08	19 46	22 21
Fearn	d		06 36	07 05		09 29	11 16					15 53			19 52	22 27
Invergordon	d	01 05	06 49	07 19		09 42	11 31				15 51	16 06		19 25	20 05	22 40
Alness	d		06 55	07 25		09 48	11 36				15 56	16 11			20 11	22 46
Kyle of Lochalsh	d				06 11				12 08	13 46			17 13			
Duirinish	d				06x20				12x16	13x54			17x21			
Plockton	d				06 27				12 21	13 59			17 26			
Duncraig	d				06x29				12x23	14x01			17x28			
Stromeferry	d				06 39				12 33	14 11			17 38			
Attadale	d				06x50				12x44	14x22			17x49			
Strathcarron	d				06 58				12 52	14 30			17 57			
Achnashellach	d				07x06				13x00	14x38			18x05			
Achnasheen	d				07 26				13 20	15 01			18 25			
Achanalt	d				07x35				13x29	15x10			18x34			
Lochluichart	d				07x42				13x36	15x16			18x41			
Garve	d				07 53				13 47	15 27			18 52			
Dingwall	d	01 21	07 08	07 38	08 16	10 01	11 53	12 45	14 10	15 50	16 11	16 26	19 19	19 41	20 24	22 58
Conon Bridge	d		07 14	07 44	08 22	10 06	11 58	12 50	14 15	15 56	16 16	16 31	19 24		20 29	23 03
Muir of Ord	d	01a31	07 22	07 51	08 30	10 14	12 06	12 58	14 22	16 03	16 24	16 39	19 31	19 52	20 37	23 11
Beauly	d		07 28	07 57	08 35	10 20	12 11	13 04	14 27	16 09	16 29	16 45	19 36		20 42	23 16
Inverness	a		07 43	08 12	08 50	10 35	12 26	13 19	14 42	16 26	16 46	17 02	20 00	20 10	20 57	23 31

§ Open 29 March until 27 October - Dec 14 Timetable
A 🛒 to Lairg
B Forms booked connection into 1A52 and 1B31.
C Forms booked connection into 1A58 and 1T62.
D Forms tight booked connection into 1T56.

Table T239-R

Sundays
20 May to 28 October

Wick, Thurso and Kyle of Lochalsh - Inverness

		SR	SR	SR ◇ A	SR	SR ◇ ✠	SR	SR ◇	SR
Wick	d					11 58			
Georgemas Junction	d					12 16			
Thurso	a					12 26			
	d					12 30			
Georgemas Junction	a					12 40			
	d					12 43			
Scotscalder	d					12x48			
Altnabreac	d					12x58			
Forsinard	d					13 09			
Kinbrace	d					13x18			
Kildonan	d					13x28			
Helmsdale	d					13 42			
Brora	d					13 58			
Dunrobin Castle §	d					14x03			
Golspie	d					14 08			
Rogart	d					14x17			
Lairg	d					14 33			
Invershin	d					14x41			
Culrain	d					14x42			
Ardgay	d					14 49			
Tain	d	00 48	10 55		14 08	15 05			22 23
Fearn	d		11 01		14 14	15 11			22 29
Invergordon	d	01 05	11 14		14 27	15 24	16 31		22 42
Alness	d		11 19		14 32	15 30	16 36		22 47
Kyle of Lochalsh	d			10 20				15 12	
Duirinish	d			10x28				15x20	
Plockton	d			10 33				15 25	
Duncraig	d			10x35				15x27	
Stromeferry	d			10 45				15 37	
Attadale	d			10x56				15x48	
Strathcarron	d			11 03				15 56	
Achnashellach	d			11x11				16x04	
Achnasheen	d			11 31				16 24	
Achanalt	d			11x40				16x33	
Lochluichart	d			11x46				16x40	
Garve	d			11 57				16 51	
Dingwall	d	01 21	11 35	12 20	14 45	15 43	16 49	17 14	23 00
Conon Bridge	d		11 40	12 25	14 50	15 48	16 54	17 19	23 05
Muir of Ord	d	01a31	11 48	12 32	14 57	15 55	17 02	17 26	23 13
Beauly	d		11 53	12 37	15 02	16 01	17 07	17 32	23 18
Inverness	a		12 08	12 52	15 17	16 16	17 22	17 47	23 33

Sundays
4 November to 2 December

		SR	SR	SR	SR ◇ B ✠	SR	SR ◇	SR
Wick	d				11 58			
Georgemas Junction	d				12 16			
Thurso	a				12 26			
	d				12 30			
Georgemas Junction	a				12 40			
	d				12 43			
Scotscalder	d				12x48			
Altnabreac	d				12x58			
Forsinard	d				13 09			
Kinbrace	d				13x18			
Kildonan	d				13x28			
Helmsdale	d				13 42			
Brora	d				13 58			
Dunrobin Castle §	d							
Golspie	d				14 08			
Rogart	d				14x17			
Lairg	d				14 33			
Invershin	d				14x41			
Culrain	d				14x42			
Ardgay	d				14 49			
Tain	d	00 48	10 55	14 08	15 05			22 23
Fearn	d		11 01	14 14	15 11			22 29
Invergordon	d	01 05	11 14	14 27	15 24	16 31		22 42
Alness	d		11 19	14 32	15 30	16 36		22 47
Kyle of Lochalsh	d						15 12	
Duirinish	d						15x20	
Plockton	d						15 25	
Duncraig	d						15x27	
Stromeferry	d						15 37	
Attadale	d						15x48	
Strathcarron	d						15 56	
Achnashellach	d						16x04	
Achnasheen	d						16 24	
Achanalt	d						16x33	
Lochluichart	d						16x40	
Garve	d						16 51	
Dingwall	d	01 21	11 35	14 45	15 43	16 49	17 14	23 00
Conon Bridge	d		11 40	14 50	15 48	16 54	17 19	23 05
Muir of Ord	d	01a31	11 48	14 57	15 55	17 02	17 26	23 13
Beauly	d		11 53	15 02	16 01	17 07	17 32	23 18
Inverness	a		12 08	15 17	16 16	17 22	17 47	23 33

§ Open 29 March until 27 October - Dec 14 Timetable
A until 30 September
B Forms booked connection into 1A58 and 1T62.

Table T240-F

Mondays to Saturdays
21 May to 8 December

Aberdeen and Elgin - Inverness

Miles			SR ◇■	SR ◇	SR ◇■ A	SR SX ◇ B	SR SO ◇■ C	SR SO ◇ D	SR SX ◇ E	SR ◇ C	SR SO ■ F	SR SX ■ G	SR ◇ A	SR SX ◇■ B	SR SO ◇ C	SR ◇■ H	SR ◇■ I	SR SX ◇ A ✠	SR SO ◇■ J ✠	SR SX ◇■ B ✠	SR SO ◇ C ✠	SR ◇■ I	SR SO ◇■ J ✠
0	**Aberdeen**	d			06 14			07 15	07 15		07 50	07 50	08 19			08 49	09 58	10 13	10 13			11 03	12 00
6¼	Dyce ✈	d			06 23	06 23	06 23	07 27	07 27	07 31	07 59	07 59	08 30	08 40	08 40	08a57	10 07	10 22	10 22	10 22	10 22	11 14	12 09
17	**Inverurie**	a			06 35	06 35	06 35	07 40	07 40	07 43	08 12	08 13	08 42	08 52	08 52		10 20	10 34	10 34	10 34	10 34	11 27	12 21
—		d			06 39	06 39	06 39	07 43	07 43	07 46			08 43	08 52	08 52			10 34	10 34	10 34	10 34		12 21
27½	Insch	d			06 51	06 51	06 51	07 55	07 55	07 58			08 58	09 05	09 05			10 47	10 47	10 48	10 48		12 34
40¾	Huntly	d			07 13	07 13	07 13	08 12	08 12	08 15			09 14	09 21	09 21			11 03	11 03	11 05	11 05		12 50
53¼	Keith	d			07 27	07 27	07 27	08 26	08 26	08 29			09 28	09 35	09 35			11 18	11 18	11 19	11 19		13 05
71¼	**Elgin**	d	06 58	07 23	07 50	07 50	07 50	08 47	08 47	08 50			09 49	09 56	09 56			11 40	11 40	11 40	11 40		13 27
83½	Forres	d	07 11	07 36	08 03	08 03	08 03	09 00	09 01	09 04			10 02	10 09	10 09			11 53	11 53	11 53	11 53		13 40
93¼	Nairn	d	07 26	07 47	08 14	08 14	08 14	09 16	09 16	09 19			10 13	10 20	10 20			12 04	12 04	12 04	12 04		13 51
108¼	**Inverness**	a	07 45	08 05	08 32	08 32	08 32	09 35	09 35	09 38			10 32	10 39	10 39			12 22	12 22	12 24	12 24		14 09

		SR SX ◇ A ✠	SR SX ◇ B ✠	SR SO ◇■ C ✠	SR SX ■ A	SR SO J	SR ◇■ C ✠	SR ◇■ A ✠	SR ◇■ I	SR SX ◇ A ✠	SR SX ◇■ B ✠	SR SO ◇ C ✠	SR SO ◇ J ✠	SR SO ◇■ K	SR SX A	SR SX ■ A	SR SO ■ J	SR SX A	SR SO ◇■ J ✠	SR SX ◇■ H ✠	SR ◇ C	SR SX ◇■ I	SR SO ◇■ K
Aberdeen	d	12 00			12 50	12 50		13 38	14 57	15 27			15 27	15 52	15 52	16 19	16 44	16 52	17 22	17 26		17 55	17 55
Dyce ✈	d	12 09	12 09	12 09	13 01	13 01	13 47	13 47	15 05	15 37	15 37	15 37	15 37	16 01	16 01	16a29	16a52	17 01	17 32	17 35	17 54	18 04	18 05
Inverurie	a	12 21	12 21	12 21	13 14	13 14	13 59	13 59	15 19	15 49	15 49	15 49	15 49	16 14	16 14			17 14	17 44	17 48	18 06	18 17	18 19
	d	12 21	12 21	12 21			13 59	13 59		15 49	15 49	15 49	15 49						17 50	17 51	18 07		
Insch	d	12 34	12 34	12 34			14 12	14 12		16 02	16 02	16 02	16 02						18 03	18 03	18 19		
Huntly	d	12 50	12 50	12 50			14 28	14 28		16 18	16 18	16 18	16 18						18 20	18 20	18 42		
Keith	d	13 05	13 05	13 05			14 43	14 43		16 40	16 40	16 40	16 40						18 34	18 34	18 56		
Elgin	d	13 27	13 27	13 27			15 06	15 08		17 02	17 02	17 02	17 02						18 55	18 55	19 19		
Forres	d	13 40	13 40	13 40			15 19	15 21		17 15	17 15	17 15	17 15						19 08	19 08	19 31		
Nairn	d	13 51	13 51	13 51			15 45	15 46		17 30	17 30	17 30	17 31						19 19	19 19	19 42		
Inverness	a	14 09	14 09	14 09			16 04	16 04		17 49	17 49	17 49	17 49						19 38	19 38	20 00		

		SR SO ◇■ J ✠	SR SX ◇ A ✠	SR SX ◇ B ✠	SR SO ◇■ C ✠	SR ◇■ I	SR ◇ C ✠	SR ◇ A ✠	SR ■ A	SR SO ◇■ K	SR SX ◇■ I	SR SO ■ J	SR SX A
Aberdeen	d	18 22	18 22			19 18		20 14	20 57	21 56	22 00	22 50	22 50
Dyce ✈	d	18 31	18 31	18 34	18 34	19 28	20 12	20 24	21 06	22 05	22 09	22 59	22 59
Inverurie	a	18 44	18 44	18 46	18 46	19 41	20 24	20 36	21 19	22 17	22 21	23 12	23 12
	d	18 44	18 44	18 46	18 46		20 37	20 37		22 17	22 21		
Insch	d	18 57	18 57	18 59	18 59		20 49	20 49		22 29	22 33		
Huntly	d	19 13	19 13	19 15	19 15		21 07	21 07		22 50	22 50		
Keith	d	19 28	19 28	19 48	19 48		21 21	21 21		23 05	23 05		
Elgin	d	19 49	19 49	20 09	20 09		21 42	21 42		23 26	23 26		
Forres	d	20 01	20 01	20 31	20 31		21 59	21 59		23 39	23 39		
Nairn	d	20 21	20 21	20 42	20 42		22 10	22 10		23 50	23 50		
Inverness	a	20 39	20 39	21 00	21 00		22 28	22 28		00 08	00 08		

Sundays
20 May to 2 December

		SR ◇■ L ✠	SR ◇■ M ✠	SR ■ L	SR ■ L	SR ◇■ L ✠	SR ◇ M ✠	SR ■ L	SR ◇■ N ✠	SR ◇ L ✠	SR ■ L	SR ■ L	SR ◇■ L ✠	SR ◇ M ✠	SR ■ L	SR ◇ L ✠	SR ◇ M ✠
Aberdeen	d	10 00		10 35	12 25	13 00		14 26		15 22	15 50	16 48	18 01		20 35	21 27	
Dyce ✈	d	10 09	10 09	10 43	12 33	13 09	13 09	14 36	15 31	15 31	15 58	16 56	18 10	18 16	20 43	21 36	22 02
Inverurie	a	10 21	10 21	10 57	12 47	13 21	13 21	14 50	15 43	15 43	16 12	17 10	18 22	18 28	20 55	21 48	22 14
	d	10 21	10 21			13 21	13 21		15 43	15 43			18 22	18 28		21 48	22 14
Insch	d	10 34	10 34			13 34	13 34		15 56	15 56			18 35	18 41		22 01	22 27
Huntly	d	10 50	10 50			13 51	13 51		16 12	16 12			18 58	18 58		22 22	22 44
Keith	d	11 08	11 08			14 06	14 06		16 35	16 35			19 13	19 13		22 36	22 58
Elgin	d	11 29	11 29			14 27	14 27		16 56	16 56			19 35	19 35		22 57	23 19
Forres	d	11 42	11 42			14 40	14 40		17 09	17 09			19 48	19 48		23 10	23 32
Nairn	d	11 53	11 53			14 51	14 51		17 29	17 30			19 59	19 59		23 21	23 43
Inverness	a	12 11	12 11			15 09	15 09		17 49	17 49			20 18	20 18		23 40	00 02

A from 20 August
B until 17 August
C until 18 August
D from 25 August. From Montrose
E from 20 August. From Dundee
F from 25 August. From Perth
G from 20 August. From Perth
H from 20 August. From Glasgow Queen Street
I from 20 August. From Edinburgh
J from 25 August
K from 25 August. From Edinburgh
L from 26 August
M until 19 August
N until 19 August. ■ to Inverurie

Table T240-R

Mondays to Saturdays

21 May to 8 December

Inverness and Elgin - Aberdeen

Miles			SR SO ◇■ A	SR SX ■ B	SR ◇■ C	SR ◇ A	SR ◇■ D	SR SX ◇■ B 🍴	SR SO ◇ A 🍴	SR SO ◇ E 🍴	SR SX ◇■ F 🍴	SR SX F	SR SO ■ E	SR SX ■ B	SR SO A	SR SX ■ F	SR ◇■ G	SR SO ◇■ E	SR SX ◇ F	SR SX ◇■ B	SR SO ◇ A	SR ◇ A	SR ◇■ C
0	**Inverness**	d	04 53	04 53	04 53			05 54	05 54	05 54	05 54							07 09	07 09	07 09	07 09		
15	Nairn	d	05 09	05 09	05 09			06 10	06 10	06 10	06 10							07 25	07 25	07 25	07 25		
24¾	Forres	d	05 20	05 20	05 20			06 21	06 21	06 21	06 21							07 38	07 38	07 38	07 38		
37	**Elgin**	d	05 33	05 33	05 33			06 34	06 34	06 34	06 34							07 51	07 51	07 51	07 51		
55	Keith	d	05 54	05 54	05 54			06 55	06 55	06 55	06 55							08 13	08 13	08 22	08 22		
67½	Huntly	d	06 09	06 09	06 09			07 11	07 11	07 11	07 11	07 46						08 39	08 39	08 42	08 42		
80¾	Insch	d	06 24	06 24	06 24			07 29	07 29	07 29	07 29	08 02						08 57	08 57	09 05	09 05		
91¼	**Inverurie**	a	06 37	06 37	06 37			07 41	07 41	07 42	07 42	08 15						09 08	09 08	09 17	09 17		
—		d	06 37	06 37	06 37	07 13	07 13	07 43	07 43	07 43	07 43	08 16	08 17	08 21	08 21	08 46		09 09	09 09	09 17	09 17	10 03	10 38
102	Dyce	d	06a49	06a49	06 51	07a24	07 26	07a55	07a55	07 59	07 59	08 30	08 30	08a33	08a33	08 59	09 07	09 21	09 21	09a29	09a29	10a14	10 50
108¼	**Aberdeen**	a			07 02		07 36			08 11	08 11	08 41	08 40			09 09	09 17	09 33	09 33				11 00

		SR ◇ F 🍴	SR SX ◇ B 🍴	SR SO ◇■ A 🍴	SR ◇■ C	SR ◇ A	SR ◇■ F 🍴	SR ◇■ A 🍴	SR A	SR SO E	SR SX ■ F	SR SX ◇■ B 🍴	SR SO ◇ A 🍴	SR SO ◇■ E 🍴	SR SX ◇ F 🍴	SR ◇ A	SR ◇■ C	SR SX ◇ B 🍴	SR SO ◇■ A 🍴	SR SO ◇■ E 🍴	SR SX ◇ F 🍴	SR SX ◇■ C
Inverness	d	09 00	09 03	09 03			10 57	10 57				12 46	12 46	12 46	12 46			14 27	14 27	14 27	14 27	
Nairn	d	09 16	09 19	09 19			11 13	11 13				13 02	13 02	13 02	13 02			14 43	14 43	14 43	14 43	
Forres	d	09 27	09 30	09 30			11 24	11 24				13 13	13 13	13 13	13 13			14 54	14 54	14 54	14 54	
Elgin	d	09 48	09 55	09 55			11 40	11 40				13 28	13 28	13 28	13 28			15 07	15 07	15 07	15 07	
Keith	d	10 08	10 17	10 17			12 01	12 01				13 47	13 47	13 47	13 47			15 28	15 28	15 28	15 28	
Huntly	d	10 32	10 31	10 31			12 15	12 15				14 01	14 01	14 01	14 01			15 42	15 42	15 42	15 42	
Insch	d	10 48	10 48	10 48			12 35	12 37				14 17	14 17	14 17	14 17			16 03	16 03	16 03	16 03	
Inverurie	a	11 00	10 59	10 59			12 46	12 48				14 28	14 28	14 28	14 28			16 16	16 16	16 16	16 16	
	d	11 00	11 00	11 00	11 34	11 51	12 47	12 49	13 27	13 33	13 33	14 29	14 29	14 29	14 29	15 19	15 24	16 16	16 16	16 16	16 16	
Dyce	d	11 14	11a12	11a12	11 46	12a02	13 02	13a02	13a39	13 48	13 48	14a41	14a41	14 43	14 43	15a30	15 38	16a29	16a29	16 30	16 30	16 39
Aberdeen	a	11 25			11 56		13 13			13 58	13 58			14 55	14 55		15 48			16 41	16 41	16 50

		SR SO ◇■ H	SR SX F	SR SO ■ E	SR ◇ A	SR SO ◇■ E 🍴	SR SX ◇ I 🍴	SR SX ◇ B 🍴	SR SO ◇■ A 🍴	SR SX F	SR SO E	SR A	SR ◇■ C	SR ◇■ J 🍴	SR ◇■ F 🍴	SR ◇■ C	SR ◇ A	SR ◇ K	SR ◇■ J	SR ◇■ L	SR A	SR ■ F	SR SX ◇ B
Inverness	d					15 29	15 29	15 29	15 29					17 14	17 14			18 15	18 35	20 04			21 33
Nairn	d					15 45	15 45	15 45	15 45					17 30	17 30			18 31	18 51	20 21			21 49
Forres	d					15 56	15 56	15 56	15 56					17 41	17 41			18 42	19 02	20 32			21 59
Elgin	d					16 09	16 09	16 09	16 09					17 54	17 58			18 55	19 18	20a46			22 12
Keith	d					16 35	16 35	16 35	16 35					18 16	18 20			19 16	19 39				22 33
Huntly	d					16 50	16 50	16 50	16 50					18 36	18 47			19 42	19 54				22 50
Insch	d					17 06	17 06	17 07	17 07					18 59	19 02			19 58	20 09				23 06
Inverurie	a					17 19	17 19	17 18	17 18					19 12	19 15			20 10	20 24				23 19
	d	16 38	16 47		16 54	17 19	17 19	17 34	17 34	17 50	17 52	18 12	18 45	19 12	19 15	19 46	19 54	20 10	20 25		21 24	21 24	23 19
Dyce	d	16 53	17 05	17 05	17a05	17 35	17 35	17a47	17a47	18 04	18 06	18a24	18 58	19a25	19 29	19 57	20a05	20 24	20a38		21a36	21 37	23a31
Aberdeen	a	17 03	17 18	17 18		17 46	17 46			18 14	18 16		19 08		19 40	20 08		20 35				21 48	

		SR SO ◇■ A	SR ◇ F
Inverness	d	21 33	21 33
Nairn	d	21 49	21 49
Forres	d	21 59	21 59
Elgin	d	22 12	22 12
Keith	d	22 33	22 33
Huntly	d	22 50	22 51
Insch	d	23 06	23 06
Inverurie	a	23 19	23 19
	d	23 19	23 19
Dyce	d	23a31	23 32
Aberdeen	a		23 43

Sundays

20 May to 2 December

		SR ◇■ M	SR ◇ N 🍴	SR ◇■ O 🍴	SR ■ N	SR ■ O	SR ◇■ N 🍴	SR ◇ O 🍴	SR ■ O	SR ■ N	SR ■ O	SR ◇■ N	SR ◇■ M	SR ■ O	SR N	SR ◇ N 🍴	SR ◇ O 🍴	SR ◇■ P	SR ■ O	SR N	SR ◇ N 🍴	SR ◇ O 🍴	SR ◇■ P
Inverness	d		09 59	09 59			12 33	12 33				15 29	15 29			17 13	17 13	18 00			21 03	21 03	21 42
Nairn	d		10 15	10 15			12 49	12 49				15 45	15 45			17 30	17 30	18 16			21 19	21 19	21 57
Forres	d		10 26	10 26			13 00	13 00				15 56	15 56			17 41	17 41	18 27			21 30	21 30	22 07
Elgin	d		10 39	10 39			13 13	13 13				16 09	16 09			17 54	17 54	18a41			21 43	21 43	22a21
Keith	d		11 01	11 01			13 34	13 34				16 31	16 31			18 15	18 15				22 05	22 05	
Huntly	d		11 20	11 20			13 52	13 52				16 46	16 46			18 30	18 30				22 21	22 21	
Insch	d		11 36	11 36			14 08	14 08				17 02	17 02			18 46	18 46				22 37	22 37	
Inverurie	a		11 48	11 48			14 19	14 19				17 13	17 13			18 58	18 58				22 48	22 48	
	d	11 02	11 48	11 48	12 50	12 55	14 20	14 20	14 58	15 00	16 20	17 14	17 14	17 30	17 52	18 58	18 58		21 22	21 29	22 49	22 49	
Dyce	d	11 13	12a00	12 01	13a02	13 09	14a32	14 35	15 10	15a12	16 32	17a26	17 28	17 42	18a04	19a11	19 12		21 35	21a41	23a01	23 01	
Aberdeen	a	11 25		12 12		13 20		14 46	15 21		16 43		17 39	17 53			19 23		21 47			23 13	

A until 18 August
B until 17 August
C from 20 August. To Edinburgh
D from 20 August. To Glasgow Queen Street. Forms booked connection out of 1B08.
E from 25 August
F from 20 August
G from 20 August. To Glasgow Queen Street
H from 25 August. To Edinburgh
I from 20 August. To Stonehaven
J from 26 May until 18 August
K from 20 August until 7 December
L From Kyle of Lochalsh
M from 26 August. To Glasgow Queen Street
N until 19 August
O from 26 August
P From Glasgow Queen Street

Table T242-F

Mondays to Fridays

21 May to 7 December

Edinburgh - Dunfermline, Kirkcaldy and Glenrothes with Thornton

Miles	Miles			SR MX ◇ A	SR ◇■ B	SR	SR	SR ◇ C	SR	SR ◇ C	SR	SR	SR ◇■ B 🍴	SR ◇ D	SR E	SR ◇ C	SR E	SR	SR E	SR ◇■ F 🍴	SR	SR	SR E
0	0	**Edinburgh** ■	d		05 30	06 07	06 16	06 30	06 35	07 00	07 10	07 16	07 31	07 34	07 37	08 01	08 07	08 11	08 24	08 34	08 38	08 45	08 55
1¼	1¼	Haymarket	d		05 34	06 11	06 20	06 34	06 39	07 04	07 15	07 21	07 35	07 39	07 42	08 07	08 11	08 16	08 29	08 39	08 44	08 50	08 59
4½	4½	South Gyle	d			06 16	06 25		06 45		07 20				07 47			08 21	08a33		08 49		09a04
—	—	Edinburgh Gateway	d			06 18		06 40		07 10		07 26		07 44		08 12	08 17			08 44		08 59	
9½	9½	Dalmeny	d			06 24	06 31		06 52		07 26	07 32			07 54			08 28			08 56	09 05	
11¼	11¼	North Queensferry	d			06 28	06 35		06 56		07 30	07 36			07 57			08 31			08 59	09 08	
13¼	13¼	Inverkeithing	d		05 47	06 32	06 39	06 50	07 01	07 20	07 34	07 40		07 56	08 01	08 23	08 27	08 35			09 03	09 12	
—	14¾	Rosyth	d				06 42					07 43						08 39				09 16	
—	17	**Dunfermline Town**	d				06 47					07 48						08 44				09 21	
—	18¾	Dunfermline Queen Margaret	d				06 51					07 52						08 47				09 24	
—	22¾	Cowdenbeath	d	00 02			06 57					07 58						08 54				09 31	
—	25	Lochgelly	d	00 08			07 03					08 04						08 59				09 36	
—	27¼	Cardenden	d	00 12			07 07					08 08						09 03				09 40	
14¾	—	Dalgety Bay	d			06 35			07 05		07 37				08 04		08 30				09 06		
17½	—	Aberdour	d			06 40			07 11		07 42				08 09		08 35				09 11		
20¼	—	Burntisland	d			06 44			07 16		07 46				08 13		08 39				09 15		
22¾	—	Kinghorn	d			06 49			07 21		07 51				08 18		08 44				09 20		
25¾	—	Kirkcaldy	d		06a03	06a56		07a06	07 27	07a36	07 56		08a03	08a12	08 23	08a38	08 49			09a10	09 25		
30¾	30¾	Glenrothes With Thornton ■	a	00 18			07 16		07 40		08 06	08 17			08 34		09 01	09 13			09 36	09 50	

		SR ◇ C	SR	SR	SR ◇ D	SR	SR	SR ◇ C	SR	SR	GR ■ ■ G 🍽	SR ◇■ F 🍴	SR	SR	SR ◇ C	SR	SR	SR ◇ D	SR	SR	SR ◇ C	SR	SR
Edinburgh ■	d	09 00	09 07	09 20	09 36	09 41	09 50	10 00	10 08	10 19	10 28	10 36	10 40	10 47	11 00	11 10	11 18	11 39	11 43	11 48	12 03	12 10	12 20
Haymarket	d	09 04	09 13	09 24	09 40	09 46	09 54	10 04	10 13	10 23	10 33	10u41	10 44	10 52	11 04	11 14	11 22	11 43	11 47	11 52	12 07	12 14	12 25
South Gyle	d			09 29		09 50				10 28			10 49				11 27		11 52				12 29
Edinburgh Gateway	d	09 10	09 19		09 46		10 00	10 10	10 19			10a46		10 57	11 10	11 20		11 49		11 58	12 13	12 20	
Dalmeny	d		09 25	09 36		09 57	10 06		10 25	10 35			10 56	11 03		11 26	11 34		11 58	12 04		12 26	12 36
North Queensferry	d		09 28	09 39		10 00	10 09		10 28	10 38			10 59	11 07		11 29	11 37		12 02	12 07		12 29	12 39
Inverkeithing	d	09 20	09 32	09 43	09 56	10 04	10 13	10 20	10 32	10 42	10 48		11 03	11 11	11 20	11 33	11 41	11 59	12 06	12 11	12 23	12 33	12 43
Rosyth	d			09 47			10 17			10 46				11 14			11 45			12 15			12 47
Dunfermline Town	d			09 52			10 22			10 51				11 19			11 50			12 20			12 52
Dunfermline Queen Margaret	d			09 55			10 25			10 54				11 23			11 53			12 23			12 55
Cowdenbeath	d			10a04			10 32			11a03				11 29			12a02			12 30			13a04
Lochgelly	d						10 37							11 35						12 35			
Cardenden	d						10 41							11 39						12 39			
Dalgety Bay	d		09 35			10 07			10 35				11 06			11 36			12 09			12 36	
Aberdour	d		09 40			10 12			10 40				11 11			11 41			12 14			12 41	
Burntisland	d		09 44			10 16			10 44				11 15			11 45			12 18			12 45	
Kinghorn	d		09 49			10 21			10 49				11 20			11 50			12 23			12 50	
Kirkcaldy	d	09a36	09 54		10a12	10 26		10a36	10 54		11a04		11 25		11a36	11 55		12a15	12 28		12a39	12 55	
Glenrothes With Thornton ■	a		10 05			10 37	10 50		11 05				11 36	11 48		12 06			12 39	12 49		13 06	

		SR ◇ D	SR	SR	SR ◇ C	SR	SR	SR ◇■ F 🍴	SR	SR	SR ◇ C	SR	SR	GR ■ ■ H 🍽	SR ◇ D	SR	SR	SR ◇ C	SR	SR	SR ◇ D	SR
Edinburgh ■	d	12 37	12 40	12 48	13 00	13 08	13 18	13 36	13 41	13 49	14 00	14 09	14 19	14 28	14 37	14 41	14 48	15 01	15 08	15 17	15 35	15 42
Haymarket	d	12 41	12 45	12 53	13 04	13 13	13 23	13u40	13 45	13 54	14 04	14 13	14 25	14 33	14 41	14 45	14 52	15 05	15 12	15 22	15 39	15 46
South Gyle	d		12 50				13 28		13 50				14 30			14 50				15 27		15 51
Edinburgh Gateway	d	12 47		12 59	13 10	13 18		13a45		14 00	14 10	14 19			14 47		14 58	15 11	15 18		15 47	
Dalmeny	d		12 57	13 05		13 24	13 35		13 57	14 06		14 25	14 36			14 57	15 04		15 24	15 34		15 58
North Queensferry	d		13 00	13 08		13 28	13 38		14 00	14 09		14 28	14 40			15 00	15 08		15 27	15 37		16 01
Inverkeithing	d	12 57	13 04	13 12	13 20	13 32	13 42		14 04	14 13	14 20	14 32	14 44	14 49	14 57	15 04	15 12	15 21	15 31	15 41	15 57	16 05
Rosyth	d			13 16			13 46			14 17			14 47				15 15			15 45		
Dunfermline Town	d			13 21			13 51			14 22			14 52				15 20			15 50		
Dunfermline Queen Margaret	d			13 24			13 54			14 25			14 56				15 24			15 53		
Cowdenbeath	d			13 31			14a03			14 32			15a05				15 30			16a02		
Lochgelly	d			13 36						14 37							15 36					
Cardenden	d			13 40						14 41							15 40					
Dalgety Bay	d		13 07			13 35			14 07			14 35				15 07			15 34			16 08
Aberdour	d		13 12			13 40			14 12			14 40				15 12			15 39			16 13
Burntisland	d		13 16			13 44			14 16			14 44				15 16			15 43			16 17
Kinghorn	d		13 21			13 49			14 21			14 49				15 21			15 48			16 22
Kirkcaldy	d	13a13	13 26		13a36	13 54			14 26		14a36	14 54		15a04	15a13	15 26		15a37	15 53		16a13	16 27
Glenrothes With Thornton ■	a		13 37	13 50		14 06			14 37	14 50		15 05				15 37	15 49		16 04			16 38

A From Edinburgh to Perth
B To Aberdeen
C To Dundee
D To Perth
E From Tweedbank
F To Inverness
G From Leeds to Aberdeen
H From London Kings Cross to Aberdeen

Edinburgh - Dunfermline, Kirkcaldy and Glenrothes with Thornton

		SR	SR ◇ A	SR	SR	SR B	SR	SR	SR A	SR	SR	SR	SR ◇■ C	SR	SR	SR ◇ A	XC ◇■ D	SR	SR E	SR	GR ■ F	SR ◇ B	SR
Edinburgh	d	15 47	16 00	16 07	16 21	16 34	16 40	16 52	17 02	17 08	17 12	17 18	17 41	17 50	17 55	18 00	18 10	18 13		18 25	18 33	18 41	18 50
Haymarket	d	15 51	16 04	16 11	16 25	16 39	16 46	16 58	17 06	17 12	17 17	17 22	17u46	17 55	18 00	18 05	18 15	18 18		18 29	18 38	18 45	18 54
South Gyle	d				16 30		16 51			17 18		17 29		18 00				18 23					18 59
Edinburgh Gateway	d	15 57	16 10	16 18		16 46	16 53	17 04	17 12		17 24		17 51		18 05	18 11				18 35		18 51	
Dalmeny	d	16 03		16 24	16 37		16 59	17 09			17 30	17 36		18 07	18 11			18 30	18 36	18 41			19 05
North Queensferry	d	16 06		16 27	16 40		17 03	17 13			17 33	17 40		18 10	18 15			18 33		18 44			19 09
Inverkeithing	d	16 10	16 20	16 31	16 44	16 57	17 07	17 17	17 22	17 29	17 37	17 45		18 14	18 19	18 23	18 29	18 37	18 43	18 48	18 55	19 01	19 13
Rosyth	d	16 14			16 48			17 21		17 34		17 50			18 22					18 52			19 16
Dunfermline Town	d	16 19			16 53			17 26		17 40		17 55			18 27					18 57			19 21
Dunfermline Queen Margaret	d	16 22			16 56			17 29		17 45		18 01			18 31					19 00			19 25
Cowdenbeath	d	16 29			17a05			17a38		17 53		18 08			18 37					19 07			19 31
Lochgelly	d	16 34								17 59		18 15			18 43					19 12			19 37
Cardenden	d	16 38								18 04		18a22			18 47					19 16			19 41
Dalgety Bay	d			16 35			17 10				17 40			18 17				18 40	18 46				
Aberdour	d			16 39			17 15				17 45			18 22				18 45	18 51				
Burntisland	d			16 44			17 19				17 49			18 26				18 49	18 55				
Kinghorn	d			16 48			17 24				17 54			18 31				18 54	19 00				
Kirkcaldy	d		16a36	16 53		17a12	17 29		17a38		18a02		18a16	18 36		18a41	18a46	18 59	19a04		19a11	19a19	
Glenrothes With Thornton	a	16 48		17 04			17 40			18 14				18 47	18 56			19 10		19 26			19 50

		SR ◇ A	SR	SR	SR ◇■ C	SR	SR ◇ A	XC ◇■ G	GR ■ F	SR ◇ B	SR	SR ◇ A	SR ◇■ H	SR B	SR ◇ A	SR ◇ B	SR ◇ A	SR ◇ B
Edinburgh	d	19 00	19 12	19 19	19 42	19 49	20 00	20 14	20 32	20 40	20 51	21 05	21 43	21 53	22 10	22 37	23 09	23 19
Haymarket	d	19 04	19 16	19 24	19 46	19 54	20 04	20 17	20 37	20 44	20 55	21 09	21 47	21 57	22 14	22 41	23 13	23 23
South Gyle	d		19 21			19 59	20 09				21 00	21 14			22 19	22 46	23 18	23 28
Edinburgh Gateway	d	19 10		19 30	19 52		20 11			20 50	21 02	21 16		22 03	22 21	22 48	23 21	23 30
Dalmeny	d		19 27	19 36		20 05	20 17				21 08	21 22		22 09	22 27	22 54	23 27	23 36
North Queensferry	d		19 31	19 39		20 09	20 21				21 12	21 26		22 12	22 31	22 58	23 30	23 40
Inverkeithing	d	19 20	19 35	19 43	20 03	20 13	20 25	20a30	20 53	21 00	21 16	21 30		22 16	22 35	23 02	23 34	23 44
Rosyth	d			19 47		20 16					21 19			22 20				23 47
Dunfermline Town	d			19 52		20 21					21 24			22 25				23 52
Dunfermline Queen Margaret	d			19 55		20 25					21 28			22 28				23 56
Cowdenbeath	d			20 02		20 31					21 34			22 35				00 02
Lochgelly	d			20 07		20 37					21 40			22 40				00 08
Cardenden	d			20 11		20 41					21 44			22 44				00 12
Dalgety Bay	d		19 38				20 28					21 33			22 38	23 05	23 37	
Aberdour	d		19 43				20 33					21 38			22 43	23 10	23 42	
Burntisland	d		19 47				20 37					21 42			22 47	23 14	23 46	
Kinghorn	d		19 51				20 42					21 46			22 52	23 19	23 51	
Kirkcaldy	d	19a36	19a59		20a19		20a46		21a09	21a16		21a51	22a15		22a56	23a23	23a56	
Glenrothes With Thornton	a			20 21		20 50					21 53			22 51				00 18

Saturdays
26 May to 8 December

		SR ◇ I	SR ◇■ H	SR	SR ◇ A	SR	SR ◇ A	SR	SR	SR ◇■ H	SR ◇ B	SR	SR ◇ A	SR	SR	SR ◇■ C	SR	SR	SR ◇ A	SR	SR	SR ◇ B	SR
Edinburgh	d		05 30	06 14	06 30	06 38	07 00	07 10	07 18	07 30	07 36	07 40	08 00	08 10	08 14	08 31	08 39	08 48	09 01	09 09	09 18	09 36	09 41
Haymarket	d		05 34	06 18	06 34	06 42	07 04	07 15	07 22	07 34	07 41	07 45	08 04	08 14	08 18	08 36	08 45	08 53	09 05	09 13	09 23	09 43	09 46
South Gyle	d			06 23		06 47		07 20				07 50			08 23		08 49	08 57			09 28		09 51
Edinburgh Gateway	d			06 25	06 40	06 49	07 10		07 28		07 47		08 10	08 20		08 42		09 00	09 11	09 19		09 48	
Dalmeny	d			06 31		06 55		07 27	07 34			07 56			08 30		08 56	09 06		09 25	09 35		09 58
North Queensferry	d			06 35		06 59		07 30	07 37			08 00			08 33		08 59	09 09		09 28	09 38		10 01
Inverkeithing	d		05 47	06 39	06 50	07 03	07 20	07 34	07 41		07 57	08 04	08 20	08 30	08 37		09 03	09 13	09 21	09 32	09 42	09 59	10 05
Rosyth	d			06 42					07 45						08 41			09 17			09 46		
Dunfermline Town	d			06 47					07 50						08 46			09 22			09 51		
Dunfermline Queen Margaret	d			06 51					07 53						08 49			09 25			09 54		
Cowdenbeath	d	00 02		06 57					08 00						08 56			09 32			10a03		
Lochgelly	d	00 08		07 03					08 05						09 01			09 37					
Cardenden	d	00 12		07 07					08 09						09 05			09 41					
Dalgety Bay	d					07 06		07 37				08 07		08 33			09 06			09 35			10 08
Aberdour	d					07 11		07 42				08 12		08 38			09 11			09 40			10 13
Burntisland	d					07 15		07 46				08 16		08 42			09 15			09 44			10 17
Kinghorn	d					07 20		07 51				08 21		08 47			09 20			09 49			10 22
Kirkcaldy	d		06a03		07a06	07 25	07a36	07 56		08a02	08a13	08 26	08a36	08 52		09a07	09 25		09a37	09 54		10a14	10 27
Glenrothes With Thornton	a	00 18		07 16		07 36		08 07	08 19			08 37		09 03	09 15		09 36	09 51		10 05			10 38

A To Dundee
B To Perth
C To Inverness
D From Plymouth to Aberdeen
E From Glasgow Queen Street to Markinch
F From London Kings Cross to Aberdeen
G From Plymouth to Dundee
H To Aberdeen
I From Edinburgh to Perth

Edinburgh - Dunfermline, Kirkcaldy and Glenrothes with Thornton

		SR	SR ◇ A	SR	SR	GR ■ B	SR ◇■ C	SR	SR	SR ◇ A	SR	SR	SR ◇ D	SR	SR	SR ◇ A	SR	SR	SR ◇ D	SR	SR	SR ◇ A
Edinburgh	d	09 48	10 00	10 09	10 18	10 28	10 36	10 40	10 48	11 00	11 09	11 18	11 35	11 40	11 49	12 00	12 09	12 18	12 35	12 40	12 48	13 00
Haymarket	d	09 52	10 05	10 13	10 23	10 33	10u41	10 44	10 52	11 04	11 13	11 22	11 41	11 44	11 54	12 04	12 13	12 22	12 41	12 44	12 52	13 04
South Gyle	d				10 28			10 49				11 28		11 49				12 27		12 49		
Edinburgh Gateway	d	09 58	10 11	10 19			10a46		10 58	11 10	11 19		11 46		12 00	12 10	12 19		12 46		12 58	13 10
Dalmeny	d	10 04		10 25	10 35			10 56	11 04		11 25	11 35		11 56	12 06		12 25	12 34		12 56	13 04	
North Queensferry	d	10 07		10 28	10 38			10 59	11 07		11 28	11 38		11 59	12 09		12 28	12 37		12 59	13 07	
Inverkeithing	d	10 11	10 21	10 32	10 42	10 48		11 03	11 11	11 20	11 32	11 42	11 57	12 03	12 13	12 20	12 32	12 41	12 57	13 03	13 11	13 20
Rosyth	d	10 15			10 46				11 15			11 46			12 17			12 45			13 15	
Dunfermline Town	d	10 20			10 51				11 20			11 51			12 22			12 50			13 20	
Dunfermline Queen Margaret	d	10 23			10 54				11 23			11 54			12 25			12 53			13 23	
Cowdenbeath	d	10 30			11a03				11 30			12a03			12 32			13a02			13 30	
Lochgelly	d	10 35							11 35						12 37						13 35	
Cardenden	d	10 39							11 39						12 41						13 39	
Dalgety Bay	d			10 35				11 06			11 35			12 06			12 35			13 06		
Aberdour	d			10 40				11 11			11 40			12 11			12 40			13 11		
Burntisland	d			10 44				11 15			11 44			12 15			12 44			13 15		
Kinghorn	d			10 49				11 20			11 49			12 20			12 49			13 20		
Kirkcaldy	d		10a37	10 54		11a04		11 25		11a36	11 54		12a12	12 25		12a36	12 54		13a12	13 25		13a36
Glenrothes With Thornton	a	10 49		11 05				11 36	11 49		12 05			12 36	12 51		13 05			13 36	13 49	

		SR	SR	SR ◇■ C	SR	SR	SR ◇ A	SR	SR	GR ■ E	SR ◇ D	SR	SR	SR ◇ A	SR	SR	SR ◇ D	SR	SR	SR ◇ A	SR	SR	SR D
Edinburgh	d	13 09	13 18	13 36	13 41	13 48	14 00	14 08	14 18	14 29	14 34	14 41	14 48	15 00	15 08	15 18	15 37	15 41	15 47	16 00	16 08	16 19	16 36
Haymarket	d	13 13	13 22	13u41	13 45	13 55	14 04	14 12	14 24	14 34	14 38	14 46	14 53	15 04	15 12	15 22	15 41	15 45	15 51	16 04	16 13	16 24	16 41
South Gyle	d		13 27		13 50				14 29			14 51				15 27		15 50				16 28	
Edinburgh Gateway	d	13 19		13a46		14 00	14 10	14 18			14 47		14 58	15 10	15 18		15 47		15 57	16 10	16 19		16 46
Dalmeny	d	13 25	13 34		13 57	14 06		14 24	14 35			14 58	15 04		15 24	15 34		15 57	16 03		16 24	16 35	
North Queensferry	d	13 28	13 37		14 00	14 10		14 27	14 39			15 01	15 08		15 27	15 37		16 00	16 06		16 28	16 38	
Inverkeithing	d	13 32	13 41		14 04	14 14	14 20	14 31	14 43	14 50	14 58	15 05	15 12	15 20	15 31	15 41	15 57	16 04	16 10	16 20	16 32	16 42	16 57
Rosyth	d		13 45			14 17			14 46				15 15			15 45			16 14			16 46	
Dunfermline Town	d		13 50			14 22			14 51				15 20			15 50			16 19			16 51	
Dunfermline Queen Margaret	d		13 53			14 26			14 55				15 24			15 53			16 22			16 54	
Cowdenbeath	d		14a02			14 32			15a04				15 30			16a02			16 29			17a03	
Lochgelly	d					14 38							15 36						16 34				
Cardenden	d					14 42							15 40						16 38				
Dalgety Bay	d	13 35			14 07			14 34				15 08			15 34			16 07			16 35		
Aberdour	d	13 40			14 12			14 39				15 13			15 39			16 12			16 40		
Burntisland	d	13 44			14 16			14 43				15 17			15 43			16 16			16 44		
Kinghorn	d	13 49			14 21			14 48				15 22			15 48			16 21			16 49		
Kirkcaldy	d	13 54			14 26		14a36	14 53		15a05	15a13	15 27		15a36	15 53		16a13	16 26		16a36	16 54		17a12
Glenrothes With Thornton	a	14 05			14 37	14 50		15 04				15 38	15 49		16 04			16 37	16 48		17 05		

		SR	SR	SR A	SR	SR	SR	SR ◇■ C	SR	XC ◇■ F	SR	SR	GR ■ E	SR ◇ D	SR	SR ◇ A	SR	SR	SR ◇■ C	SR	SR ◇ A	XC ◇■ G
Edinburgh	d	16 40	16 48	17 00	17 08	17 12	17 19	17 41	17 46	18 11	18 14	18 25	18 33	18 37	18 50	19 01	19 13	19 18	19 41	19 52	20 00	20 14
Haymarket	d	16 44	16 53	17 05	17 12	17 17	17 24	17u46	17 50	18 15	18 19	18 29	18 38	18 41	18 54	19 05	19 18	19 23	19 45	19 56	20 04	20 18
South Gyle	d	16 49			17 18		17 29		17 55		18 23				18 59		19 22			20 01	20 09	
Edinburgh Gateway	d	16 51	16 59	17 10		17 23		17 51				18 35		18 51		19 11		19 29	19 51		20 11	
Dalmeny	d	16 57	17 04			17 29	17 36		18 02		18 30	18 41			19 05		19 28	19 35		20 07	20 17	
North Queensferry	d	17 01	17 08			17 33	17 40		18 05		18 33	18 44			19 09		19 32	19 38		20 11	20 21	
Inverkeithing	d	17 05	17 12	17 21	17 29	17 37	17 44		18 09	18 29	18 37	18 48	18 55	19 01	19 13	19 21	19 36	19 42	20 01	20 15	20 25	20 35
Rosyth	d		17 16		17 33		17 47					18 52			19 16			19 46		20 18		
Dunfermline Town	d		17 21		17 38		17 52					18 57			19 21			19 51		20 23		
Dunfermline Queen Margaret	d		17 24		17 42		17 56					19 00			19 25			19 54		20 27		
Cowdenbeath	d		17a33		17 49		18 02					19 07			19 31			20 01		20 33		
Lochgelly	d				17 55		18 08					19 12			19 37			20 06		20 39		
Cardenden	d				17 59		18 12					19 16			19 41			20 10		20 43		
Dalgety Bay	d	17 08				17 40			18 12		18 40						19 39				20 28	
Aberdour	d	17 13				17 45			18 17		18 45						19 43				20 33	
Burntisland	d	17 17				17 49			18 21		18 49						19 47				20 37	
Kinghorn	d	17 22				17 54			18 26		18 54						19 52				20 42	
Kirkcaldy	d	17 27		17a36		18a01		18a16	18 31	18a43	18 59		19a11	19a19		19a37	19a59		20a17		20a46	20a50
Glenrothes With Thornton	a	17 38			18 08		18 21		18 42		19 10	19 26			19 50			20 20		20 52		

A To Dundee
B From Leeds to Aberdeen
C To Inverness
D To Perth
E From London Kings Cross to Aberdeen
F From Plymouth to Aberdeen
G From Newquay to Dundee

Saturdays
26 May to 8 December

Edinburgh - Dunfermline, Kirkcaldy and Glenrothes with Thornton

		SR ◇ A	SR	SR ◇ B	SR ◇1 C	SR A	SR ◇ B	SR ◇ A	SR ◇ B	SR ◇ A
Edinburgh	d	20 37	20 50	21 05	21 43	21 50	22 10	22 37	23 09	23 19
Haymarket	d	20 41	20 54	21 09	21 47	21 55	22 14	22 42	23 13	23 23
South Gyle	d		21 00	21 14			22 19	22 46	23 18	23 28
Edinburgh Gateway	d	20 47	21 02	21 16		22 03	22 21	22 49	23 21	23 30
Dalmeny	d		21 08	21 22		22 09	22 27	22 55	23 27	23 36
North Queensferry	d		21 12	21 26		22 12	22 31	22 58	23 30	23 40
Inverkeithing	d	20 58	21 16	21 30		22 16	22 35	23 02	23 34	23 44
Rosyth	d		21 19			22 20				23 47
Dunfermline Town	d		21 24			22 25				23 52
Dunfermline Queen Margaret	d		21 28			22 28				23 56
Cowdenbeath	d		21 34			22 35				00 02
Lochgelly	d		21 40			22 40				00 08
Cardenden	d		21 44			22 44				00 12
Dalgety Bay	d			21 33			22 38	23 05	23 37	
Aberdour	d			21 38			22 43	23 10	23 42	
Burntisland	d			21 42			22 47	23 14	23 46	
Kinghorn	d			21 46			22 52	23 19	23 51	
Kirkcaldy	d	21a14		21a51	22a15		22a56	23a23	23a56	
Glenrothes With Thornton	a		21 53			22 51				00 18

Sundays
20 May to 2 December

		SR ◇ D	XC ◇1 C	GR 1 C	SR ◇1 C	SR ◇1 E	SR	SR	SR ◇1 C	SR		SR	SR ◇ B	SR	SR	XC ◇1 F	SR ◇1 C	SR	XC ◇1 G	SR		SR ◇ B	SR ◇1 E	SR	SR
Edinburgh	d		08 04	09 10	09 15	09 33	09 55	10 15	10 50	10 55		11 15	11 32	11 55	12 15	12 17	12 41	12 55	13 13	13 15		13 34	13 56	14 00	14 15
Haymarket	d		08 08	09 15	09 21	09 37	09 59	10 19	10 54	10 59		11 19	11 36	11 59	12 21	12a20	12 45	12 59	13a17	13 19		13 38	14 00	14 04	14 19
South Gyle	d				09 26		10 04	10 24		11 04		11 24		12 04	12 26			13 04		13 24				14 09	14 24
Edinburgh Gateway	d				09 28	09 43	10 06	10 26		11 06		11 26	11 42	12 06	12 28			13 06		13 26		13 44	14 06	14 11	14 26
Dalmeny	d				09 34		10 12	10 32		11 12		11 32		12 12	12 34			13 12		13 32				14 17	14 32
North Queensferry	d				09 41		10 19	10 36		11 16		11 36		12 16	12 38			13 16		13 36				14 21	14 36
Inverkeithing	d		08 25	09 33	09 45	09 56	10 23	10 40	11 07	11 20		11 40	11 52	12 20	12 42		12 58	13 20		13 40		13 54	14 16	14 25	14 40
Rosyth	d						10 26			11 23				12 23				13 23						14 28	
Dunfermline Town	d						10 31			11 28				12 28				13 28						14 33	
Dunfermline Queen Margaret	d						10 35			11 32				12 32				13 32						14 37	
Cowdenbeath	d	00 02					10 41			11 38				12 38				13 38						14 43	
Lochgelly	d	00 08					10 47			11 44				12 44				13 44						14 49	
Cardenden	d	00 12					10 51			11 48				12 48				13 48						14 53	
Dalgety Bay	d				09 48			10 43				11 43			12 45					13 43					14 43
Aberdour	d				09 53			10 48				11 48			12 50					13 48					14 48
Burntisland	d				09 57			10 52				11 52			12 54					13 52					14 52
Kinghorn	d				10 02			10 57				11 57			12 59					13 57					14 57
Kirkcaldy	d		08a39	09a48	10a06	10a12		11 02	11a23			12 02	12a08		13 04		13a14			14 02		14a10	14a32		15 02
Glenrothes With Thornton	a	00 18					11 00	11 13		11 57		12 13		12 57	13 15			13 57		14 13				15 02	15 15

		GR 1 H	SR	XC ◇1 I	SR	SR B		SR ◇1 E	SR	SR ◇1 C	SR	SR	SR ◇1 C	XC ◇1 J	SR	SR B		SR ◇ A	SR	XC ◇1 K	SR	GR 1 L	SR ◇ A	SR ◇ B	XC ◇1 M
Edinburgh	d	14 33	14 55	15 10	15 18	15 34		15 50	15 55	16 05	16 15	16 55	17 05	17 11	17 16	17 34		17 50	17 55	18 13	18 17	18 36	18 55	19 15	19 18
Haymarket	d	14 39	14 59	15a13	15 22	15 38		15 54	15 59	16 09	16 19	16 59	17 09	17a14	17 20	17 38		17 54	17 59	18 16	18 22	18 41	18 59	19 19	19a22
South Gyle	d		15 04		15 27				16 04		16 24	17 04			17 25				18 04		18 26		19 04	19 24	
Edinburgh Gateway	d		15 06		15 29	15 44		16 00	16 06		16 26	17 06			17 27	17 44		18 00	18 06		18 29		19 06	19 26	
Dalmeny	d		15 12		15 35				16 12		16 32	17 12			17 33				18 12		18 35		19 12	19 32	
North Queensferry	d		15 16		15 39				16 16		16 36	17 16			17 37				18 16		18 38		19 16	19 36	
Inverkeithing	d	14 54	15 20		15 43	15 54		16 10	16 20	16 24	16 40	17 20	17 23		17 41	17 54		18 10	18 20	18 30	18 42	18 56	19 20	19 40	
Rosyth	d		15 23						16 23			17 23							18 23				19 23		
Dunfermline Town	d		15 28						16 28			17 28							18 28				19 28		
Dunfermline Queen Margaret	d		15 32						16 32			17 32							18 32				19 32		
Cowdenbeath	d		15 38						16 38			17 38							18 38				19 38		
Lochgelly	d		15 44						16 44			17 44							18 44				19 44		
Cardenden	d		15 48						16 48			17 48							18 48				19 48		
Dalgety Bay	d				15 46						16 43				17 44						18 45			19 43	
Aberdour	d				15 51						16 48				17 49						18 50			19 48	
Burntisland	d				15 55						16 52				17 53						18 54			19 52	
Kinghorn	d				16 00						16 57				17 58						18 59			19 57	
Kirkcaldy	d	15a10			16 05	16a10		16a26		16a39	17 02		17a38		18 03	18a10		18a26		18a44	19 04	19a11		20a01	
Glenrothes With Thornton	a		15 57		16 18				16 57		17 13	17 57			18 14				18 57		19 15		19 57		

A To Perth
B To Dundee
C To Aberdeen
D not 20 May. From Edinburgh to Perth
E To Inverness
F until 9 September. From Leeds to Motherwell
G until 9 September. From Sheffield to Motherwell
H From London Kings Cross to Aberdeen. The Northern Lights
I until 9 September. From Birmingham New Street to Motherwell
J until 9 September. From Bristol Temple Meads to Motherwell
K From Plymouth to Aberdeen
L From London Kings Cross to Aberdeen
M until 9 September. From Plymouth to Motherwell

Sundays
20 May to 2 December

Edinburgh - Dunfermline, Kirkcaldy and Glenrothes with Thornton

		SR	SR		SR ◇1 A	XC ◇1 B	SR	SR	SR ◇ C	SR
Edinburgh	d	19 55	20 15		21 00	21 12	21 15	21 55	22 26	23 34
Haymarket	d	19 59	20 19		21 05	21a16	21 19	21 59	22 30	23 38
South Gyle	d	20 04	20 24				21 24	22 04	22 35	23 43
Edinburgh Gateway	d	20 06	20 26				21 26	22 06	22 37	23 45
Dalmeny	d	20 12	20 32				21 32	22 12	22 43	23 51
North Queensferry	d	20 16	20 36				21 36	22 16	22 47	23 55
Inverkeithing	d	20 20	20 40		21 19		21 40	22 20	22 51	23a58
Rosyth	d	20 23						22 23		
Dunfermline Town	d	20 28						22 28		
Dunfermline Queen Margaret	d	20 32						22 32		
Cowdenbeath	d	20 38						22 38		
Lochgelly	d	20 44						22 44		
Cardenden	d	20 48						22 48		
Dalgety Bay	d		20 43				21 43		22 54	
Aberdour	d		20 48				21 48		22 59	
Burntisland	d		20 52				21 52		23 03	
Kinghorn	d		20 57				21 57		23 08	
Kirkcaldy	d		21 02		21a34		22a04		23a12	
Glenrothes With Thornton	a	20 57	21 13					22 57		

A To Aberdeen
B until 9 September. From Penzance to Motherwell
C To Dundee

Table T242-R

Mondays to Fridays

21 May to 7 December

Glenrothes with Thornton, Kirkcaldy and Dunfermline - Edinburgh

Miles	Miles			XC MX	SR MX	GR	SR	SR	SR	SR	SR	SR	SR	SR	XC	XC	SR	SR	SR	SR	SR	SR	SR
				◇■ A	◇ B	■ C	◇ B	D		D	◇ E		B	F	◇■ G	◇■ H		◇■ A	B		◇ E		E
0	0	Glenrothes With Thornton ■	d					06 02		06 24			06 52				07 18					07 43	
5	—	**Kirkcaldy**	d				05 55		06 30		06 50			07 13	07 21	07 21	07 26	07 41	07 46		07 57		08 21
8	—	Kinghorn	d				06 00		06 35		06 54			07 18			07 31				08 01		
10½	—	Burntisland	d				06 05		06 39		06 59			07 22			07 36				08 06		
13¼	—	Aberdour	d				06 09		06 44		07 04			07 27			07 40				08 11		
16	—	Dalgety Bay	d				06 14		06 49		07 09			07 31			07 45				08 15		
—	3½	Cardenden	d					06 09		06 32			07 00							07 35		07 50	
—	5¾	Lochgelly	d					06 13		06 36			07 04							07 40		07 56	
—	8	Cowdenbeath	d					06 19		06 42			07 10							07 47		08 02	
—	12	Dunfermline Queen Margaret	d					06 25		06 47		07 06	07 15							07 53		08 08	
—	13¾	**Dunfermline Town**	d					06 29		06 51		07 09	07 19							07 57		08 13	
—	16	Rosyth	d					06 32		06 54		07 13	07 22							08 02		08 17	
17½	17½	Inverkeithing	d				06 18	06 36	06 52	06 58	07 12	07 17	07 26	07 35	07 40	07 40	07 49		08 02	08 06	08 19	08 22	08 37
19½	19½	North Queensferry	d				06 22	06 40	06 56	07 02		07 21	07 30				07 53					08 28	
21¼	21¼	Dalmeny	d		00 02		06 26	06 44	07 00	07 06	07 19		07 34	07a41			07 57			08 14	08 25		
—	—	Edinburgh Gateway	d		00 08		06 32	06 50		07 12	07 25		07 41				08 03		08 13		08 31		08 48
26¼	26¼	South Gyle	d		00 10		06 34	06 52	07 07			07 30	07 44				08 05			08 21		08 37	
29½	29½	Haymarket	d	00 03	00 18	06 13	06 43	07 01	07 15	07 21	07 35	07 39	07 54		08 00	08 00	08 15	08 19	08 25	08 31	08 40	08 47	08 58
30¾	30¾	**Edinburgh** ■	a	00 08	00 23	06 17	06 47	07 06	07 20	07 26	07 39	07 43	08 00		08 04	08 04	08 20	08 23	08 30	08 37	08 44	08 53	09 03

		SR	SR	SR	SR	SR	SR	SR	SR	GR	SR	SR	XC	XC	SR	SR	SR	SR	SR	SR	SR	SR	SR
				◇ I		◇ E	◇■ I			■ J			◇■ K	■ L		◇ E		◇ B			◇ E		
Glenrothes With Thornton ■	d	08 09	08 19		08 39			09 10	09 22		09 38	09 53					10 26		10 39	10 53			11 20
Kirkcaldy	d		08 27	08 40		09 13	09 26		09 30	09 45		10 01	10 18	10 18		10 29	10 34	10 42		11 01	11 14		11 28
Kinghorn	d		08 32			09 18			09 35			10 06					10 39			11 06			11 33
Burntisland	d		08 37			09 23			09 40			10 11					10 44			11 11			11 38
Aberdour	d		08 41			09 27			09 44			10 15					10 48			11 15			11 42
Dalgety Bay	d		08 46			09 32			09 49			10 20					10 53			11 20			11 47
Cardenden	d	08 16			08 46			09 17			09 45								10 46				
Lochgelly	d	08 20			08 50			09 21			09 49								10 50				
Cowdenbeath	d	08 26			08 56			09 27			09 55				10 23				10 56			11 23	
Dunfermline Queen Margaret	d	08 32			09 02			09 33			10 01				10 29				11 02			11 29	
Dunfermline Town	d	08 35			09 05			09 36			10 04				10 32				11 05			11 32	
Rosyth	d	08 39			09 09			09 40			10 08				10 36				11 09			11 36	
Inverkeithing	d	08 43	08 50	08 56	09 13	09 35		09 45	09 53	10 01	10 12	10 24	10 33	10 33	10 40	10 46	10 57	11 03	11 13	11 23	11 30	11 40	11 51
North Queensferry	d	08 47	08 54		09 17				09 57		10 16				10 44		11 01		11 17	11 27		11 44	
Dalmeny	d	08 51	08 58		09 21				10 01		10 20				10 48		11 05		11 21	11 31		11 48	
Edinburgh Gateway	d		09 04	09 08	09 27	09 46	09 51		10 07		10 26					10 57	11 11	11 15	11 27		11 41		12 02
South Gyle	d	09 00			09 29			09 57				10 37			10 54					11 37		11 54	
Haymarket	d	09 09	09 13	09 20	09 38	09 55	10 03	10 07	10 16	10 20	10 35	10 46	10 51	10 51	11 03	11 08	11 20	11 24	11 36	11 46	11 50	12 04	12 11
Edinburgh ■	a	09 14	09 19	09 24	09 42	09 59	10 11	10 14	10 20	10 25	10 39	10 50	10 55	10 55	11 09	11 13	11 24	11 29	11 40	11 51	11 54	12 09	12 16

		SR	GR	SR	SR	SR	SR	SR	SR	SR	SR	SR	SR	SR	SR	SR	SR	SR	SR	SR	SR	SR
		◇ B	■ J			◇ E			◇■ I			◇ E			◇■ I			◇ E			◇ B	
Glenrothes With Thornton ■	d			11 38	11 50			12 22		12 40	12 54			13 20		13 40	13 55			14 21		14 39
Kirkcaldy	d	11 41	11 47		11 58	12 13		12 30	12 41		13 02	13 20		13 28	13 41		14 03	14 17		14 29	14 41	
Kinghorn	d				12 03			12 35			13 07			13 33			14 08			14 34		
Burntisland	d				12 08			12 40			13 12			13 38			14 13			14 39		
Aberdour	d				12 12			12 44			13 16			13 42			14 17			14 43		
Dalgety Bay	d				12 17			12 49			13 21			13 47			14 22			14 48		
Cardenden	d			11 45						12 48						13 47						14 46
Lochgelly	d			11 49						12 52						13 51						14 50
Cowdenbeath	d			11 55			12 22			12 58			13 26			13 57			14 26			14 56
Dunfermline Queen Margaret	d			12 01			12 28			13 03			13 32			14 03			14 31			15 02
Dunfermline Town	d			12 04			12 31			13 07			13 35			14 06			14 35			15 05
Rosyth	d			12 08			12 35			13 10			13 39			14 10			14 38			15 09
Inverkeithing	d	11 57	12 03	12 12	12 21	12 29	12 39	12 53	13 00	13 14	13 25	13 36	13 43	13 51		14 14	14 25	14 33	14 42	14 52	14 57	15 13
North Queensferry	d			12 16	12 25		12 43	12 57		13 18	13 29		13 47	13 55		14 18	14 29		14 46	14 56		15 17
Dalmeny	d			12 20	12 29		12 47	13 01		13 22	13 33		13 51	13 59		14 22	14 33		14 50	15 00		15 21
Edinburgh Gateway	d	12 08		12 26		12 40		13 07	13 11	13 28		13 46		14 05	14 09	14 28		14 43		15 06	15 10	15 27
South Gyle	d				12 35		12 53				13 39		13 57				14 39		14 56			
Haymarket	d	12 17	12 22	12 35	12 44	12 49	13 01	13 16	13 20	13 37	13 47	13 58	14 06	14 14	14 20	14 37	14 48	14 52	15 05	15 15	15 19	15 36
Edinburgh ■	a	12 22	12 26	12 40	12 48	12 53	13 09	13 21	13 24	13 42	13 52	14 04	14 10	14 18	14 25	14 42	14 52	14 57	15 09	15 20	15 24	15 41

- **A** From Aberdeen
- **B** From Perth
- **C** From Stirling to London Kings Cross
- **D** From Markinch
- **E** From Dundee
- **F** To Glasgow Queen Street
- **G** from 23 July until 5 October. From Dundee to Reading
- **H** until 20 July, from 8 October. From Dundee to Plymouth
- **I** From Inverness
- **J** From Aberdeen to London Kings Cross
- **K** from 23 July until 5 October. From Aberdeen to Guildford
- **L** until 20 July, from 8 October. From Aberdeen to Penzance

Table T242-R

Mondays to Fridays

21 May to 7 December

Glenrothes with Thornton, Kirkcaldy and Dunfermline - Edinburgh

		SR	SR	SR	SR	SR	SR	SR	SR	SR	SR	SR	GR	SR	SR	SR	SR	SR	SR	SR	SR	SR
			◇ A		B	◇■ C		B	◇ A		B	◇ D	■ E		B		◇ A	◇ D		◇ A	F	◇■ C
Glenrothes With Thornton ■	d	14 52			15 20		15 39	15 52			16 19			16 40	16 50	17 07			17 44		18 16	
Kirkcaldy	d	15 01	15 18		15 28	15 41		16 00	16 18		16 27	16 39	16 46		16 59		17 36	17 47		18 20	18 25	18 44
Kinghorn	d	15 05			15 33			16 05			16 32				17 03		17 40				18 31	
Burntisland	d	15 10			15 38			16 10			16 37				17 08		17 45				18 36	
Aberdour	d	15 15			15 42			16 14			16 41				17 12		17 50				18 42	
Dalgety Bay	d	15 20			15 47			16 19			16 46				17 17		17 55				18 48	
Cardenden	d						15 46							16 47		17 14			17 51			
Lochgelly	d						15 50							16 51		17 18			17 55			
Cowdenbeath	d			15 28			15 56			16 25				16 57		17 24			18 01			
Dunfermline Queen Margaret	d			15 33			16 02			16 30				17 03		17 30			18 07			
Dunfermline Town	d			15 37			16 05			16 34				17 06		17 33			18 10			
Rosyth	d			15 40			16 09			16 37				17 10		17 37			18 14			
Inverkeithing	d	15 23	15 34	15 44	15 51	15 58	16 13	16 23	16 34	16 41	16 50	16 55	17 03	17 14	17 20	17 41	17 58	18 05	18 18	18 36	18 53	19 00
North Queensferry	d	15 27		15 48	15 55		16 17	16 27		16 45				17 18	17 24	17 45	18 02		18 22			
Dalmeny	d	15 31		15 52	15 59		16 21	16 31		16 49				17 22	17 28	17 49	18 06		18 26		19 01	
Edinburgh Gateway	d		15 44		16 05	16 09	16 27		16 44			17 06			17 34	17 55	18 12	18 17		18 47	→	19 11
South Gyle	d	15 37		15 58				16 37		16 55	17 01			17 28	17 37	17 58			18 32			
Haymarket	d	15 46	15 53	16 07	16 14	16 18	16 36	16 46	16 54	17 04	17 10	17 15	17 21	17 37	17 45	18 10	18 21	18 26	18 41	18 56		19 20
Edinburgh ■	a	15 52	15 58	16 13	16 18	16 22	16 43	16 50	17 00	17 08	17 15	17 19	17 26	17 42	17 50	18 16	18 28	18 31	18 45	19 03		19 24

		SR	SR	SR	SR	SR	SR	SR	GR	SR	SR	SR	SR	SR	SR	SR	SR	SR	XC	SR
		G			◇ H			◇ D	■ I			◇ D		◇ A	◇■ C	◇■ J		◇■ K	◇■ K	◇ D
Glenrothes With Thornton ■	d		18 50	18 59		19 14	19 28			20 05			21 07				22 05			23 19
Kirkcaldy	d			19 07	19 28		19 36	19 50	20 11		20 26	20 41		21 26	21 43	22 03		23 00	23 31	
Kinghorn	d			19 12			19 41				20 30			21 30		22 08		23 05		
Burntisland	d			19 17			19 46				20 35			21 35		22 13		23 10		
Aberdour	d			19 21			19 50				20 39			21 39		22 17		23 14		
Dalgety Bay	d			19 26			19 55				20 45			21 44		22 22		23 19		
Cardenden	d		18 57			19 21				20 12			21 14				22 12			23 27
Lochgelly	d		19 01			19 25				20 16			21 18				22 16			23 31
Cowdenbeath	d		19 07			19 31				20 22			21 24				22 22			23 37
Dunfermline Queen Margaret	d		19 13			19 37				20 28			21 30				22 28			23 42
Dunfermline Town	d		19 16			19 40				20 31			21 33				22 31			23 46
Rosyth	d		19 20			19 44				20 35			21 37				22 35			23 49
Inverkeithing	d		19 24	19 30	19 44	19 48	19 59	20 06	20 27	20 39	20 48	20 57	21 41	21 48		22 25	22 39	23 22	23 46	23 54
North Queensferry	d	←	19 28	19 34		19 52	20 03			20 43	20 52		21 45	21 52		22 29	22 43	23 26		23 58
Dalmeny	d	19 01	19 32	19 38		19 56	20 07			20 47	20 56		21 49	21 56		22 33	22 47	23 30		00 02
Edinburgh Gateway	d		19 38		19 55	20 02		20 17		20 53		21 08	21 55	22 02	22 08	22 39	22 53	23 36		00 08
South Gyle	d	19 16		19 44			20 13				21 02		21 57				22 55	23 38		00 10
Haymarket	d	19 25	19 47	19 54	20 04	20 14	20 21	20 29	20 46	21 02	21 11	21 17	22 06	22 11	22 19	22 48	23 04	23 47	00 03	00 18
Edinburgh ■	a	19 31	19 52	19 58	20 09	20 19	20 26	20 33	20 50	21 07	21 15	21 22	22 10	22 15	22 23	22 53	23 08	23 52	00 08	00 23

Saturdays

26 May to 8 December

		XC	SR	SR	SR	SR	XC	XC	SR	SR	SR	SR	SR	SR	SR	SR	SR	SR	SR	SR	SR	SR	GR
		◇■ K	◇ D	D	L	◇ A	◇■ M	◇■ N		◇■ K	D		◇ A	A			◇ C		◇ A	◇■ C			■ E
Glenrothes With Thornton ■	d				06 24				07 18			07 37			08 09	08 21		08 39			09 10	09 22	
Kirkcaldy	d			06 14		06 50	07 21	07 21	07 26	07 41	07 46		07 57	08 21		08 29	08 40		09 12	09 25		09 30	09 45
Kinghorn	d			06 19		06 54			07 31				08 01			08 34			09 17			09 35	
Burntisland	d			06 24		06 59			07 36				08 06			08 39			09 22			09 40	
Aberdour	d			06 28		07 04			07 40				08 11			08 43			09 26			09 44	
Dalgety Bay	d			06 33		07 09			07 45				08 15			08 48			09 31			09 49	
Cardenden	d				06 32							07 45			08 16			08 46			09 17		
Lochgelly	d				06 36							07 49			08 20			08 50			09 21		
Cowdenbeath	d				06 42							07 55			08 26			08 56			09 27		
Dunfermline Queen Margaret	d				06 47							08 00			08 32			09 02			09 33		
Dunfermline Town	d				06 51							08 04			08 35			09 05			09 36		
Rosyth	d				06 54							08 07			08 39			09 09			09 40		
Inverkeithing	d			06 37	06 58	07 12	07 38	07 38	07 49		08 02	08 11	08 19	08 37	08 43	08 52	08 56	09 13	09 35		09 44	09 53	10 01
North Queensferry	d			06 41	07 02				07 53			08 15			08 47	08 56		09 17				09 57	
Dalmeny	d		00 02	06 45	07 06	07 19			07 57			08 19	08 25		08 51	09 00		09 21				10 01	
Edinburgh Gateway	d		00 08	06 51	07 12	07 25			08 03		08 13		08 31	08 48		09 06	09 10	09 27	09 45	09 50		10 07	
South Gyle	d		00 10	06 53					08 05			08 25			08 57			09 29			09 57		
Haymarket	d	00 03	00 18	07 01	07 21	07 34	07 56	07 56	08 13	08 17	08 22	08 34	08 40	08 58	09 08	09 15	09 19	09 38	09 54	10 04	10 08	10 16	10 21
Edinburgh ■	a	00 08	00 23	07 06	07 25	07 39	08 01	08 01	08 18	08 21	08 26	08 38	08 45	09 02	09 14	09 21	09 24	09 45	09 59	10 10	10 15	10 21	10 25

- **A** From Dundee
- **B** To Tweedbank
- **C** From Inverness
- **D** From Perth
- **E** From Aberdeen to London Kings Cross
- **F** To Edinburgh
- **G** From Glenrothes With Thornton
- **H** From Arbroath
- **I** From Aberdeen to Leeds
- **J** until 17 August. From Aberdeen
- **K** From Aberdeen
- **L** From Markinch
- **M** from 28 July until 6 October. From Dundee to Reading
- **N** until 21 July, from 13 October. From Dundee to Plymouth

Table T242-R

Saturdays
26 May to 8 December

Glenrothes with Thornton, Kirkcaldy and Dunfermline - Edinburgh

		SR		SR	XC ◇■ A ✠	XC ◇■ B	SR	SR ◇ C	SR	SR ◇ D	SR	SR		SR ◇ C	SR	SR	SR ◇ D	GR ■ E	SR	SR	SR ◇ C	SR		SR	SR ◇■ F ✠
Glenrothes With Thornton	d	09 38		09 53					10 24		10 40	10 53				11 20			11 38	11 51				12 20	
Kirkcaldy	d			10 01	10 18	10 18		10 27	10 32	10 42		11 01		11 18		11 28	11 41	11 47		12 00	12 12			12 28	12 41
Kinghorn	d			10 06					10 37			11 06				11 33				12 05				12 33	
Burntisland	d			10 11					10 42			11 11				11 38				12 10				12 38	
Aberdour	d			10 15					10 46			11 15				11 42				12 14				12 42	
Dalgety Bay	d			10 20					10 51			11 20				11 47				12 19				12 47	
Cardenden	d	09 45									10 47								11 45						
Lochgelly	d	09 49									10 51								11 49						
Cowdenbeath	d	09 55					10 23				10 57				11 23				11 55			12 23			
Dunfermline Queen Margaret	d	10 01					10 29				11 03				11 29				12 01			12 29			
Dunfermline Town	d	10 04					10 32				11 06				11 32				12 04			12 32			
Rosyth	d	10 08					10 36				11 10				11 36				12 08			12 36			
Inverkeithing	d	10 12		10 24	10 33	10 33	10 40	10 47	10 55	11 02	11 14	11 24		11 34	11 40	11 51	11 57	12 03	12 12	12 23	12 30	12 40		12 51	12 58
North Queensferry	d	10 16					10 44		10 59		11 18	11 28			11 44				12 16	12 27		12 44		12 55	
Dalmeny	d	10 20					10 48		11 03		11 22	11 32			11 48				12 20	12 31		12 48		12 59	
Edinburgh Gateway	d	10 26						10 57	11 09	11 13	11 28			11 44		12 02	12 08		12 26		12 40			13 05	13 09
South Gyle	d			10 37			10 54					11 38			11 54					12 37		12 54			
Haymarket	d	10 35		10 46	10 50	10 50	11 03	11 09	11 18	11 22	11 37	11 46		11 58	12 03	12 11	12 17	12 22	12 35	12 45	12 49	13 03		13 14	13 18
Edinburgh	a	10 39		10 50	10 55	10 55	11 08	11 15	11 22	11 26	11 41	11 51		12 03	12 08	12 15	12 22	12 26	12 39	12 50	12 53	13 07		13 18	13 22

		SR	SR	SR ◇ C	SR	SR	SR ◇■ F ✠	SR		SR	SR ◇ C	SR	SR	SR ◇ D	SR	SR	SR ◇ C	SR		SR	SR ◇■ F ✠	SR	SR	SR ◇ C	SR
Glenrothes With Thornton	d	12 38	12 52			13 20		13 38		13 52			14 21		14 39	14 52				15 21		15 43	15 52		
Kirkcaldy	d		13 00	13 17		13 28	13 41			14 00	14 18		14 29	14 41		15 01	15 18			15 29	15 41		16 00	16 18	
Kinghorn	d		13 05			13 33				14 05			14 34			15 05				15 34			16 05		
Burntisland	d		13 10			13 38				14 10			14 39			15 10				15 39			16 10		
Aberdour	d		13 15			13 42				14 14			14 43			15 15				15 43			16 14		
Dalgety Bay	d		13 19			13 47				14 19			14 48			15 20				15 48			16 19		
Cardenden	d	12 45						13 45							14 46							15 50			
Lochgelly	d	12 49						13 49							14 50							15 54			
Cowdenbeath	d	12 55			13 23			13 55				14 24			14 56			15 26				16 00			16 24
Dunfermline Queen Margaret	d	13 01			13 29			14 01				14 29			15 02			15 31				16 06			16 29
Dunfermline Town	d	13 04			13 32			14 04				14 33			15 05			15 35				16 09			16 33
Rosyth	d	13 08			13 36			14 08				14 36			15 09			15 38				16 13			16 36
Inverkeithing	d	13 12	13 23	13 33	13 40	13 51		14 12		14 23	14 34	14 40	14 52	14 58	15 13	15 23	15 34	15 42		15 52	15 59	16 17	16 23	16 34	16 40
North Queensferry	d	13 16	13 27		13 44	13 55		14 16		14 27		14 44	14 56		15 17	15 27		15 46		15 56		16 21	16 27		16 44
Dalmeny	d	13 20	13 31		13 48	13 59		14 20		14 31		14 48	15 00		15 21	15 31		15 50		16 00		16 25	16 31		16 48
Edinburgh Gateway	d	13 26		13 43		14 05	14 09	14 26			14 44		15 06	15 10	15 27		15 44			16 06	16 10	16 31		16 44	
South Gyle	d		13 37		13 54					14 37		14 54				15 37		15 56					16 37		16 54
Haymarket	d	13 35	13 46	13 52	14 04	14 14	14 19	14 35		14 46	14 54	15 03	15 15	15 19	15 36	15 46	15 53	16 06		16 15	16 19	16 41	16 45	16 53	17 03
Edinburgh	a	13 40	13 50	13 57	14 09	14 21	14 24	14 41		14 51	14 58	15 07	15 19	15 23	15 40	15 50	15 58	16 11		16 19	16 23	16 47	16 50	16 58	17 07

		SR	SR ◇ D	GR ■ E		SR	SR	SR	SR ◇ C	SR ◇ D	SR	SR ◇ C	SR	SR ◇■ F ✠		SR	SR ◇ G	SR	SR	SR ◇ D	SR ◇■ H ✠	SR	SR	SR ◇ D	
Glenrothes With Thornton	d	16 19				16 38	16 52	17 07			17 43		18 16			18 48		19 15	19 28			20 05			
Kirkcaldy	d	16 27	16 39	16 46			17 00		17 35	17 47		18 20	18 25	18 44			19 30		19 36	19 50	20 11		20 27	20 41	
Kinghorn	d	16 32					17 05		17 39				18 30						19 41				20 32		
Burntisland	d	16 37					17 10		17 44				18 35						19 46				20 36		
Aberdour	d	16 41					17 14		17 49				18 39						19 50				20 41		
Dalgety Bay	d	16 46					17 19		17 54				18 44						19 55				20 46		
Cardenden	d					16 45		17 14			17 50					18 55		19 22				20 12			
Lochgelly	d					16 49		17 18			17 54					18 59		19 26				20 16			
Cowdenbeath	d					16 55		17 24			18 00					19 05		19 32				20 22			
Dunfermline Queen Margaret	d					17 01		17 30			18 06					19 11		19 38				20 28			
Dunfermline Town	d					17 04		17 33			18 09					19 14		19 41				20 31			
Rosyth	d					17 08		17 37			18 13					19 18		19 45				20 35			
Inverkeithing	d	16 50	16 55	17 03		17 12	17 23	17 41	17 57	18 03	18 17	18 36	18 48	19 00		19 22	19 46	19 50	19 59	20 06	20 27	20 39	20 50	20 57	
North Queensferry	d					17 16	17 27	17 45	18 01		18 21		18 52			19 26		19 54	20 03			20 43	20 54		
Dalmeny	d					17 20	17 31	17 49	18 05		18 25		18 56			19 30		19 58	20 07			20 47	20 58		
Edinburgh Gateway	d		17 06			17 26	17 37	17 55	18 11	18 15		18 47		19 11		19 36	19 57	20 04		20 17		20 53		21 08	
South Gyle	d	17 01					17 39	17 57			18 31		19 02						20 13				21 04		
Haymarket	d	17 10	17 15	17 21		17 35	17 48	18 06	18 20	18 24	18 39	18 56	19 10	19 20		19 46	20 06	20 13	20 21	20 27	20 44	21 02	21 13	21 17	
Edinburgh	a	17 17	17 20	17 26		17 39	17 52	18 10	18 25	18 29	18 44	19 00	19 15	19 27		19 51	20 11	20 18	20 27	20 31	20 48	21 06	21 17	21 22	

A from 28 July until 6 October. From Aberdeen to Guildford
B until 21 July, from 13 October. From Aberdeen to Penzance
C From Dundee
D From Perth
E From Aberdeen to London Kings Cross
F From Inverness
G From Arbroath
H From Aberdeen

Table T242-R

Saturdays
26 May to 8 December

Glenrothes with Thornton, Kirkcaldy and Dunfermline - Edinburgh

		SR		SR ◇ A	SR ◇■ B ✠	SR ◇■ C ✠	SR	SR ◇■ D	XC ◇■ D	SR ◇ E
Glenrothes With Thornton	d	21 05					22 05			23 19
Kirkcaldy	d			21 27	21 43	22 03		23 00	23 32	
Kinghorn	d			21 31		22 08		23 05		
Burntisland	d			21 36		22 13		23 10		
Aberdour	d			21 40		22 17		23 14		
Dalgety Bay	d			21 45		22 22		23 19		
Cardenden	d	21 12					22 12			23 27
Lochgelly	d	21 16					22 16			23 31
Cowdenbeath	d	21 22					22 22			23 37
Dunfermline Queen Margaret	d	21 28					22 28			23 42
Dunfermline Town	d	21 31					22 31			23 46
Rosyth	d	21 35					22 35			23 49
Inverkeithing	d	21 39		21 49		22 25	22 39	23 22	23 47	23 54
North Queensferry	d	21 43		21 53		22 29	22 43	23 26		23 58
Dalmeny	d	21 47		21 57		22 33	22 47	23 30		00 02
Edinburgh Gateway	d	21 53		22 03	22 08	22 39	22 53	23 36		00 08
South Gyle	d	21 55					22 55	23 38		00 10
Haymarket	d	22 04		22 13	22 17	22 50	23 06	23 47	00 03	00 19
Edinburgh	a	22 09		22 17	22 22	22 54	23 12	23 51	00 08	00 23

Sundays
20 May to 2 December

		XC ◇■ F	SR ◇ G	SR ◇ A	SR ◇ E	SR A	SR ◇ E	XC ◇■ H ✠	XC ◇■ I	SR		SR	GR ■ J	SR ◇ A	XC ◇■ K ✠	XC ◇■ H	SR	SR	XC ◇■ L	SR		SR ◇■ B ✠	SR	GR ■ M	SR ◇ A
Glenrothes With Thornton	d						10 13			11 02		11 15					12 02	12 15		13 04			13 18		
Kirkcaldy	d			08 09	09 29	10 09				11 11			11 41	12 05			12 11		13 07	13 13		13 32		13 42	14 05
Kinghorn	d			08 14	09 33	10 14				11 15							12 15			13 17					
Burntisland	d			08 18	09 38	10 18				11 20							12 20			13 22					
Aberdour	d			08 23	09 43	10 23				11 25							12 25			13 27					
Dalgety Bay	d			08 28	09 48	10 28				11 30							12 30			13 32					
Cardenden	d						10 20					11 22						12 22					13 25		
Lochgelly	d						10 24					11 26						12 26					13 29		
Cowdenbeath	d						10 30					11 32						12 32					13 35		
Dunfermline Queen Margaret	d						10 36					11 38						12 38					13 41		
Dunfermline Town	d						10 39					11 41						12 41					13 44		
Rosyth	d						10 43					11 45						12 45					13 48		
Inverkeithing	d			08 31	09 51	10 31	10 47			11 33		11 49	11 57	12 21			12 33	12 49	13 22	13 35		13 48	13 52	14 03	14 21
North Queensferry	d			08 35	09 55	10 35	10 51			11 37		11 53					12 37	12 53		13 39			13 56		
Dalmeny	d		00 02	08 42	10 02	10 39	10 55			11 41		11 57					12 41	12 57		13 43			14 00		
Edinburgh Gateway	d		00 08	08 48	10 08	10 45	11 01			11 47		12 03		12 32			12 47	13 03		13 49		13 59	14 06		14 32
South Gyle	d		00 10	08 50	10 10	10 47	11 03			11 49		12 05					12 49	13 05		13 51			14 08		
Haymarket	d	00 03	00 19	08 59	10 19	10 56	11 11	11 53	11 53	11 58		12 13	12 18	12 41	12 56	12 56	12 59	13 13	13 38	14 00		14 08	14 17	14 21	14 41
Edinburgh	a	00 08	00 23	09 03	10 23	11 01	11 16	11 57	11 57	12 02		12 19	12 22	12 45	13 01	13 01	13 04	13 18	13 43	14 06		14 12	14 21	14 26	14 45

		XC ◇■ N	SR	SR	SR ◇■ D	XC ◇■ O		XC ◇■ P ✠	SR	SR	GR ■ M	SR ◇ A	SR ◇■ B ✠	SR	SR	SR ◇■ D ✠		XC ◇■ Q	SR	SR	SR ◇■ B ✠	SR ◇ A	SR	SR	SR ◇■ D ✠
Glenrothes With Thornton	d		14 02	14 15					15 04	15 17				16 06	16 20				17 02	17 15			18 03	18 16	
Kirkcaldy	d		14 11		14 46				15 13		15 41	16 00	16 10	16 15		17 02			17 11		18 00	18 06	18 12		18 56
Kinghorn	d		14 15						15 17					16 19					17 15				18 16		
Burntisland	d		14 20						15 22					16 24					17 20				18 21		
Aberdour	d		14 25						15 27					16 29					17 25				18 26		
Dalgety Bay	d		14 30						15 32					16 34					17 30				18 31		
Cardenden	d			14 22						15 24					16 27					17 22				18 23	
Lochgelly	d			14 26						15 28					16 31					17 26				18 27	
Cowdenbeath	d			14 32						15 34					16 37					17 32				18 33	
Dunfermline Queen Margaret	d			14 38						15 40					16 43					17 38				18 39	
Dunfermline Town	d			14 41						15 43					16 46					17 41				18 42	
Rosyth	d			14 45						15 47					16 50					17 45				18 46	
Inverkeithing	d		14 33	14 49	15 02				15 35	15 51	15 58	16 16	16 26	16 37	16 54	17 18			17 33	17 49	18 16	18 22	18 34	18 50	19 12
North Queensferry	d		14 37	14 53					15 39	15 55				16 41	16 58				17 37	17 53			18 38	18 54	
Dalmeny	d		14 41	14 57					15 43	15 59				16 45	17 02				17 41	17 57			18 42	18 58	
Edinburgh Gateway	d		14 47	15 03					15 49	16 05		16 27	16 36	16 51	17 08				17 47	18 03	18 26	18 33	18 48	19 04	
South Gyle	d		14 49	15 05					15 51	16 07				16 53	17 10				17 49	18 05			18 50	19 06	
Haymarket	d	14 42	14 58	15 15	15 18	15 52		15 52	16 00	16 15	16 20	16 36	16 45	17 02	17 18	17 34		17 51	17 58	18 18	18 35	18 42	18 59	19 15	19 28
Edinburgh	a	14 47	15 02	15 19	15 23	15 57		15 57	16 04	16 21	16 26	16 40	16 50	17 06	17 23	17 40		17 55	18 02	18 22	18 42	18 46	19 03	19 21	19 33

A From Dundee
B From Inverness
C until 18 August. From Aberdeen
D From Aberdeen
E From Perth
F not 20 May. From Aberdeen
G not 20 May. From Perth
H from 22 July until 9 September. From Motherwell to Plymouth
I until 15 July. From Motherwell to Penzance
J From Aberdeen to London Kings Cross. The Northern Lights
K until 15 July. From Motherwell to Plymouth
L From Aberdeen to Plymouth
M From Aberdeen to London Kings Cross
N until 9 September. From Motherwell to Bristol Temple Meads
O until 15 July. From Motherwell to Bristol Temple Meads
P from 22 July until 9 September. From Motherwell to Bristol Temple Meads
Q until 9 September. From Motherwell to Birmingham New Street

Table T242-R

Sundays
20 May to 2 December

Glenrothes with Thornton, Kirkcaldy and Dunfermline - Edinburgh

		SR	XC ◇■ A	SR	SR ◇ B	SR ◇■ C	SR	XC ◇■ D	SR	SR ◇■ E ⚒	SR ◇■ C ⚒	SR	SR	XC ◇■ C
Glenrothes With Thornton ■	d	18 59		19 17			20 59		21 15				22 59	
Kirkcaldy	d	19 07			20 01	21 01	21 07			21 43	22 07	22 13	23 07	23 24
Kinghorn	d	19 12			20 06		21 12					22 17	23 12	
Burntisland	d	19 17			20 10		21 17					22 22	23 17	
Aberdour	d	19 21			20 15		21 21					22 27	23 21	
Dalgety Bay	d	19 26			20 20		21 26					22 32	23 26	
Cardenden	d			19 24					21 22					
Lochgelly	d			19 28					21 26					
Cowdenbeath	d			19 34					21 32					
Dunfermline Queen Margaret	d			19 40					21 38					
Dunfermline Town	d			19 43					21 41					
Rosyth	d			19 47					21 45					
Inverkeithing	d	19 30		19 51	20 23	21 17	21 30		21 49	21 59	22 23	22 35	23 30	23 40
North Queensferry	d	19 34		19 55	20 27		21 34		21 53			22 39	23 34	
Dalmeny	d	19 38		19 59	20 31		21 38		21 57			22 43	23 38	
Edinburgh Gateway	d	19 44		20 05	20 37		21 44		22 03	22 09		22 49	23 44	
South Gyle	d	19 46		20 07	20 39		21 46		22 05			22 51	23 46	
Haymarket 🚋	d	19 54	19 59	20 17	20 48	21 34	21 54	22 04	22 17	22 20	22 39	23 00	23 54	23 58
Edinburgh ■	a	20 01	20 03	20 21	20 52	21 38	22 01	22 08	22 21	22 25	22 44	23 04	23 59	00 02

A until 9 September. From Motherwell to Newcastle
B From Dundee
C From Aberdeen
D until 9 September. From Motherwell
E From Inverness

Table T243-F

Mondays to Fridays
21 May to 7 December

Edinburgh - Newcraighall - Tweedbank

Miles			SR MO A	SR MX A	SR	SR	SR	SR	SR	SR	SR	SR	SR	SR	SR	SR	SR	SR	SR	SR	SR	SR	SR
0	**Edinburgh** 226,230	d			05 44	06 22	06 50	07 23	07 53	08 24	08 55	09 24	09 55	10 24	10 54	11 24	11 54	12 24	12 54	13 24	13 55	14 25	14 55
4	Brunstane	d		00 01	05 51	06 29	06 58	07 30	08 00	08 31	09 03	09 31	10 02	10 31	11 01	11 31	12 02	12 31	13 01	13 31	14 03	14 32	15 02
4¾	**Newcraighall**	d		00 05	05 56	06 33	07 02	07 34	08 04	08 35	09 06	09 35	10 06	10 35	11 05	11 36	12 06	12 35	13 05	13 35	14 07	14 36	15 06
5¾	Shawfair	d		00 08	06 02	06 36	07 06	07 37	08 07	08 38	09 09	09 38	10 09	10 38	11 08	11 39	12 09	12 38	13 08	13 38	14 10	14 39	15 09
8¼	Eskbank	d		00 13	06 08	06 41	07 11	07 42	08 12	08 43	09 14	09 43	10 14	10 43	11 13	11 44	12 14	12 43	13 13	13 43	14 15	14 44	15 14
9¾	Newtongrange	d		00 16	06 12	06 44	07 14	07 45	08 15	08 46	09 17	09 46	10 17	10 46	11 16	11 47	12 17	12 46	13 16	13 46	14 18	14 47	15 17
12	Gorebridge	d		00 21	06 20	06 49	07 19	07 50	08 20	08 51	09 22	09 51	10 22	10 51	11 21	11 52	12 22	12 51	13 21	13 51	14 23	14 52	15 22
26¾	Stow	d		00 38		07 06	07 36	08 07	08 37	09 08		10 08		11 08		12 09		13 08		14 08		15 09	
36½	Galashiels	d	00 04	00 47	06 44	07 15	07 45	08 16	08 46	09 17	09 46	10 17	10 46	11 17	11 45	12 18	12 46	13 17	13 45	14 17	14 47	15 18	15 46
38½	**Tweedbank**	a	00 09	00 52	06 48	07 19	07 49	08 20	08 50	09 21	09 50	10 21	10 50	11 21	11 49	12 22	12 50	13 21	13 49	14 21	14 51	15 22	15 50

		SR	SR	SR B	SR B	SR B	SR B	SR	SR	SR	SR	SR	SR	SR	SR
Edinburgh 226,230	d	15 24	15 53	16 24	16 53	17 22	17 55	18 23	18 54	19 24	19 56	20 53	21 53	22 54	23 54
Brunstane	d	15 31	16 01	16 31	17 00	17 31	18 02	18 30	19 02	19 31	20 03	21 03	22 00	23 04	00 01
Newcraighall	d	15 35	16 05	16 35	17 04	17 35	18 06	18 34	19 06	19 35	20 07	21 07	22 04	23 08	00 05
Shawfair	d	15 38	16 08	16 38	17 08	17 38	18 09	18 37	19 09	19 38	20 10	21 10	22 07	23 11	00 08
Eskbank	d	15 43	16 13	16 43	17 13	17 43	18 14	18 42	19 14	19 43	20 15	21 15	22 12	23 15	00 13
Newtongrange	d	15 46	16 16	16 46	17 16	17 46	18 17	18 45	19 17	19 46	20 18	21 18	22 15	23 18	00 16
Gorebridge	d	15 51	16 21	16 51	17 21	17 51	18 22	18 50	19 22	19 51	20 23	21 23	22 20	23 23	00 21
Stow	d	16 08		17 08	17 38	18 08	18 39	19 07	19 39	20 08	20 40	21 40	22 37	23 41	00 38
Galashiels	d	16 17	16 46	17 17	17 47	18 17	18 48	19 16	19 48	20 17	20 49	21 49	22 46	23 49	00 47
Tweedbank	a	16 22	16 50	17 21	17 51	18 21	18 52	19 21	19 52	20 21	20 53	21 53	22 50	23 55	00 52

Saturdays
26 May to 8 December

		SR A	SR	SR	SR	SR	SR	SR	SR	SR	SR	SR	SR	SR	SR	SR	SR	SR	SR	SR	SR	SR	SR
Edinburgh 226,230	d		05 55	06 20	06 50	07 23	07 56	08 25	08 52	09 23	09 54	10 25	10 56	11 25	11 56	12 25	12 53	13 25	13 55	14 26	14 53	15 26	15 52
Brunstane	d	00 01	06 02	06 27	06 58	07 34	08 03	08 32	09 00	09 30	10 03	10 32	11 04	11 32	12 03	12 32	13 04	13 32	14 04	14 33	15 04	15 33	16 00
Newcraighall	d	00 05	06 06	06 31	07 01	07 37	08 07	08 36	09 04	09 34	10 07	10 36	11 08	11 36	12 07	12 36	13 08	13 36	14 08	14 37	15 08	15 37	16 04
Shawfair	d	00 08	06 09	06 36	07 07	07 41	08 10	08 39	09 10	09 37	10 10	10 39	11 11	11 39	12 10	12 39	13 11	13 39	14 11	14 40	15 11	15 40	16 09
Eskbank	d	00 13	06 14	06 41	07 12	07 45	08 15	08 44	09 14	09 42	10 15	10 44	11 16	11 44	12 15	12 44	13 16	13 44	14 16	14 45	15 15	15 45	16 14
Newtongrange	d	00 16	06 17	06 44	07 15	07 48	08 18	08 47	09 17	09 45	10 18	10 47	11 19	11 47	12 18	12 47	13 19	13 47	14 19	14 48	15 18	15 48	16 17
Gorebridge	d	00 21	06 22	06 49	07 20	07 53	08 23	08 52	09 22	09 50	10 23	10 52	11 24	11 52	12 23	12 52	13 24	13 52	14 24	14 53	15 23	15 53	16 22
Stow	d	00 38		07 06	07 37	08 11	08 40	09 09		10 08		11 09		12 09		13 09		14 09		15 10		16 10	
Galashiels	d	00 47	06 46	07 15	07 46	08 19	08 49	09 18	09 46	10 17	10 47	11 18	11 47	12 18	12 46	13 18	13 48	14 18	14 48	15 19	15 47	16 19	16 46
Tweedbank	a	00 52	06 50	07 19	07 50	08 24	08 53	09 22	09 50	10 21	10 51	11 22	11 52	12 22	12 51	13 22	13 52	14 22	14 52	15 23	15 51	16 23	16 50

		SR	SR	SR	SR	SR	SR	SR	SR	SR	SR	SR	SR
Edinburgh 226,230	d	16 25	16 54	17 23	17 54	18 26	18 55	19 25	19 54	20 56	21 56	22 55	23 54
Brunstane	d	16 32	17 04	17 31	18 04	18 33	19 04	19 33	20 01	21 03	22 03	23 02	00 01
Newcraighall	d	16 36	17 08	17 35	18 08	18 37	19 08	19 37	20 05	21 07	22 07	23 06	00 05
Shawfair	d	16 39	17 11	17 38	18 11	18 40	19 11	19 40	20 09	21 10	22 10	23 09	00 09
Eskbank	d	16 44	17 15	17 43	18 15	18 45	19 15	19 45	20 14	21 15	22 15	23 14	00 14
Newtongrange	d	16 47	17 18	17 46	18 18	18 48	19 18	19 48	20 17	21 18	22 18	23 17	00 17
Gorebridge	d	16 52	17 23	17 51	18 23	18 53	19 23	19 53	20 22	21 23	22 23	23 22	00 22
Stow	d	17 09	17 41	18 08	18 41	19 10		20 10	20 39	21 40	22 40	23 39	00 39
Galashiels	d	17 18	17 49	18 17	18 49	19 19	19 48	20 19	20 48	21 49	22 48	23 48	00 48
Tweedbank	a	17 22	17 54	18 21	18 53	19 23	19 52	20 24	20 52	21 53	22 53	23 52	00 53

Sundays
20 May to 2 December

		SR C	SR	SR	SR	SR	SR	SR	SR	SR	SR	SR	SR	SR	SR	SR	SR
Edinburgh 226,230	d		09 11	10 11	11 12	12 11	13 11	14 11	15 11	16 11	17 12	18 12	19 12	20 12	21 12	22 12	23 11
Brunstane	d	00 01	09 18	10 18	11 19	12 18	13 18	14 20	15 18	16 20	17 19	18 20	19 19	20 19	21 19	22 20	23 18
Newcraighall	d	00 05	09 22	10 22	11 23	12 22	13 22	14 24	15 22	16 24	17 23	18 24	19 23	20 23	21 23	22 24	23 22
Shawfair	d	00 09	09 25	10 25	11 26	12 25	13 25	14 27	15 25	16 27	17 26	18 27	19 26	20 26	21 26	22 27	23 25
Eskbank	d	00 14	09 30	10 30	11 31	12 30	13 30	14 32	15 30	16 32	17 31	18 32	19 31	20 31	21 31	22 32	23 30
Newtongrange	d	00 17	09 33	10 33	11 34	12 33	13 33	14 35	15 33	16 35	17 34	18 35	19 34	20 34	21 34	22 35	23 33
Gorebridge	d	00 22	09 38	10 38	11 39	12 38	13 38	14 40	15 38	16 40	17 39	18 40	19 39	20 39	21 39	22 40	23 38
Stow	d	00 39	09 55	10 55	11 56	12 55	13 55	14 57	15 55	16 57	17 56	18 57	19 56	20 56	21 56	22 57	23 55
Galashiels	d	00 48	10 04	11 04	12 05	13 04	14 04	15 06	16 04	17 06	18 05	19 06	20 05	21 05	22 05	23 06	00 04
Tweedbank	a	00 53	10 08	11 08	12 09	13 08	14 08	15 10	16 08	17 10	18 09	19 10	20 09	21 09	22 09	23 10	00 09

A From Edinburgh
B From Glenrothes With Thornton
C not 20 May. From Edinburgh

Table T243-R

Mondays to Fridays
21 May to 7 December

Tweedbank - Newcraighall - Edinburgh

Miles			SR MX A	SR	SR	SR B	SR B	SR C	SR C	SR	SR	SR	SR	SR	SR	SR	SR	SR	SR	SR	SR	SR	SR
0	**Tweedbank**	d	...	05 20	05 58	06 28	06 58	07 26	07 57	08 28	08 59	09 30	09 59	10 29	10 59	11 28	11 59	12 29	12 59	13 28	14 00	14 28	14 58
2	Galashiels	d		05 24	06 02	06 32	07 02	07 30	08 01	08 32	09 03	09 34	10 03	10 33	11 03	11 32	12 03	12 33	13 03	13 32	14 04	14 32	15 02
11¾	Stow	d	...	05 33	06 11	06 41	07 11	07 39	08 10	08 41	...	09 43	...	10 42	...	11 41	...	12 42	...	13 41	...	14 41	...
26½	Gorebridge	d		05 50	06 28	06 58	07 28	07 56	08 27	08 58	09 28	10 00	10 28	10 59	11 28	11 58	12 28	12 59	13 28	13 58	14 29	14 58	15 27
28¾	Newtongrange	d	00 01	05 53	06 31	07 01	07 31	08 00	08 30	09 01	09 31	10 03	10 31	11 02	11 31	12 01	12 31	13 02	13 31	14 01	14 32	15 01	15 31
30¼	Eskbank	d	00 04	05 56	06 34	07 04	07 34	08 03	08 33	09 04	09 34	10 06	10 34	11 05	11 34	12 04	12 34	13 05	13 34	14 04	14 35	15 04	15 34
32¾	Shawfair	d	00 08	06 00	06 40	07 08	07 38	08 07	08 37	09 08	09 38	10 10	10 38	11 09	11 38	12 08	12 38	13 09	13 38	14 09	14 39	15 08	15 38
33¾	**Newcraighall**	d	00 12	06 04	06 44	07 13	07 42	08 11	08 41	09 12	09 43	10 14	10 42	11 13	11 42	12 12	12 42	13 13	13 42	14 13	14 43	15 12	15 42
34½	Brunstane	d	00 16	06 08	06 47	07 19	07 47	08 14	08 45	09 16	09 47	10 18	10 46	11 17	11 46	12 16	12 46	13 17	13 46	14 17	14 47	15 16	15 45
38½	**Edinburgh** 226,230	a	00 23	06 15	06 56	07 28	07 59	08 21	08 52	09 23	09 54	10 26	10 53	11 24	11 54	12 23	12 53	13 24	13 54	14 24	14 53	15 23	15 52

		SR	SR	SR	SR	SR	SR	SR	SR	SR	SR	SR	SR	SR
Tweedbank	d	15 29	15 57	16 30	16 58	17 30	17 59	18 30	18 59	19 31	20 29	21 29	22 29	23 28
Galashiels	d	15 33	16 01	16 34	17 02	17 34	18 03	18 34	19 03	19 35	20 33	21 33	22 33	23 32
Stow	d	15 42	16 10	16 43	17 11	17 43	...	18 43	...	19 44	20 42	21 42	22 42	23 41
Gorebridge	d	15 59	16 27	17 00	17 28	18 00	18 28	19 00	19 28	20 01	20 59	21 59	22 59	23 58
Newtongrange	d	16 02	16 30	17 03	17 31	18 03	18 31	19 03	19 31	20 04	21 02	22 02	23 02	00 01
Eskbank	d	16 05	16 33	17 06	17 34	18 06	18 34	19 06	19 34	20 07	21 05	22 05	23 05	00 04
Shawfair	d	16 09	16 37	17 10	17 38	18 10	18 38	19 10	19 38	20 11	21 09	22 09	23 10	00 08
Newcraighall	d	16 16	16 41	17 14	17 42	18 14	18 42	19 15	19 43	20 15	21 13	22 13	23 14	00 12
Brunstane	d	16 20	16 45	17 18	17 46	18 20	18 46	19 18	19 48	20 19	21 17	22 17	23 17	00 16
Edinburgh 226,230	a	16 30	16 52	17 25	17 54	18 29	18 53	19 25	19 55	20 26	21 24	22 27	23 25	00 23

Saturdays
26 May to 8 December

		SR A	SR	SR	SR	SR	SR	SR	SR	SR	SR	SR	SR	SR	SR	SR	SR	SR	SR	SR	SR	SR	SR
Tweedbank	d	...	05 28	05 58	06 29	06 59	07 29	08 00	08 32	09 00	09 31	10 01	10 31	11 02	11 31	12 01	12 31	13 01	13 32	14 02	14 32	15 03	15 31
Galashiels	d		05 32	06 02	06 33	07 03	07 33	08 04	08 36	09 04	09 35	10 05	10 35	11 06	11 35	12 05	12 35	13 05	13 36	14 06	14 36	15 07	15 35
Stow	d	...	05 41	06 11	06 42	07 12	07 42	...	08 45	...	09 44	...	10 44	...	11 44	...	12 44	...	13 45	...	14 45	...	15 44
Gorebridge	d		05 58	06 28	06 59	07 29	07 59	08 29	09 01	09 29	10 00	10 30	11 01	11 31	12 01	12 30	13 01	13 30	14 02	14 31	15 02	15 32	16 01
Newtongrange	d	00 01	06 01	06 31	07 02	07 32	08 02	08 32	09 05	09 32	10 04	10 33	11 04	11 34	12 04	12 33	13 04	13 33	14 05	14 34	15 05	15 35	16 04
Eskbank	d	00 04	06 04	06 34	07 05	07 35	08 05	08 35	09 08	09 35	10 07	10 36	11 07	11 37	12 07	12 36	13 07	13 36	14 08	14 37	15 08	15 38	16 07
Shawfair	d	00 08	06 08	06 39	07 11	07 39	08 09	08 39	09 14	09 39	10 11	10 40	11 11	11 41	12 11	12 41	13 11	13 40	14 12	14 41	15 13	15 42	16 11
Newcraighall	d	00 12	06 12	06 43	07 15	07 43	08 13	08 43	09 18	09 43	10 15	10 44	11 15	11 45	12 15	12 45	13 17	13 44	14 16	14 45	15 17	15 46	16 15
Brunstane	d	00 16	06 16	06 46	07 19	07 47	08 17	08 47	09 21	09 47	10 21	10 49	11 21	11 49	12 21	12 50	13 21	13 48	14 22	14 49	15 20	15 50	16 20
Edinburgh 226,230	a	00 23	06 23	06 53	07 29	07 55	08 24	08 54	09 29	09 54	10 28	10 56	11 29	11 56	12 28	12 59	13 28	13 55	14 31	14 59	15 29	15 59	16 31

		SR	SR	SR	SR	SR	SR	SR	SR	SR	SR	SR	SR
Tweedbank	d	16 01	16 31	17 01	17 31	18 01	18 32	19 03	19 31	20 32	21 31	22 31	23 31
Galashiels	d	16 05	16 35	17 05	17 35	18 05	18 36	19 07	19 35	20 36	21 35	22 35	23 35
Stow	d	...	16 44	...	17 44	...	18 45	...	19 44	20 45	21 44	22 44	23 44
Gorebridge	d	16 30	17 00	17 30	18 01	18 30	19 02	19 32	20 01	21 02	22 01	23 01	00 02
Newtongrange	d	16 33	17 04	17 33	18 04	18 33	19 05	19 35	20 04	21 05	22 04	23 04	00 04
Eskbank	d	16 36	17 07	17 36	18 07	18 36	19 08	19 38	20 07	21 08	22 07	23 07	00 07
Shawfair	d	16 40	17 13	17 40	18 11	18 40	19 12	19 42	20 11	21 12	22 11	23 11	00 11
Newcraighall	d	16 44	17 17	17 44	18 15	18 44	19 16	19 46	20 15	21 16	22 15	23 15	00 15
Brunstane	d	16 50	17 22	17 49	18 19	18 49	19 20	19 50	20 19	21 20	22 19	23 19	00 19
Edinburgh 226,230	a	17 00	17 30	17 57	18 29	18 56	19 31	19 59	20 26	21 27	22 26	23 26	00 26

Sundays
20 May to 2 December

		SR D	SR		SR	SR	SR	SR	SR	SR	SR	SR	SR	SR	SR
Tweedbank	d	...	08 45	and hourly until	12 45	13 45	14 45	15 45	16 45	17 45	18 45	19 45	20 45	21 45	22 46
Galashiels	d		08 49		12 49	13 49	14 49	15 49	16 49	17 49	18 49	19 49	20 49	21 49	22 50
Stow	d	...	08 58		12 58	13 58	14 58	15 58	16 58	17 58	18 58	19 58	20 58	21 58	22 59
Gorebridge	d	00 02	09 15		13 15	14 15	15 15	16 15	17 15	18 15	19 15	20 15	21 15	22 15	23 16
Newtongrange	d	00 04	09 18		13 18	14 18	15 18	16 18	17 18	18 18	19 18	20 18	21 18	22 18	23 19
Eskbank	d	00 07	09 21		13 21	14 21	15 21	16 21	17 21	18 21	19 21	20 21	21 21	22 21	23 22
Shawfair	d	00 11	09 25		13 25	14 26	15 25	16 26	17 25	18 26	19 25	20 25	21 25	22 26	23 26
Newcraighall	d	00 15	09 29		13 29	14 30	15 29	16 30	17 29	18 30	19 29	20 29	21 29	22 30	23 30
Brunstane	d	00 19	09 33		13 33	14 34	15 33	16 34	17 33	18 34	19 33	20 33	21 33	22 34	23 34
Edinburgh 226,230	a	00 26	09 40		13 40	14 41	15 40	16 41	17 40	18 41	19 40	20 40	21 40	22 41	23 41

A From Tweedbank
B To Glenrothes With Thornton
C To South Gyle
D not 20 May. From Tweedbank

Table T400

Reproduced courtesy of *European Rail Timetable Ltd.*

Caledonian Sleeper — **Sleeper trains LONDON - SCOTLAND**

All trains in this table convey 1,2 cl., (2) (reservation compulsory) ✕ and 🍷. Only available for overnight journeys.

		⑦ a	⑦ a	⑦ a	①–⑤	①–⑤	①–⑤	⑦ ◐a	⑦ ◐a	Ⓐ ◐	Ⓐ ◐
London Euston **151/2/3**	d.	2100	2100	2100	2115	2115	2115	2328	2328	2350	2350
Watford Junction	d.	2120	2120	2120	2133	2133	2133	2349	2349	0010	0010
Crewe **151 152 153 154**	d.	2336	2336	2336	2350	2350	2350	|	|	|	|
Preston **154**	d.	0035	0035	0035	0058	0058	0058	|	|	|	|
Carlisle **154**	a.	|	|	|	|	|	|	0443	0443	0513	0513
Motherwell	a.	|	|	|	|	|	|	|	0655	|	0655
Glasgow Central **154** ◧	a.	|	|	|	|	|	|	|	0720	|	0720
Edinburgh Waverley **154** ◧	a.	|	|	|	|	|	|	0724	...	0724	...
Dundee **222**	a.	0608	|	|	0608	|	|	...	...	...	...
Aberdeen **222** ◧	a.	0737	|	|	0737	|	|	...	...	...	...
Perth **223**	a.	...	0541	|	...	0541	|	...	...	...	...
Inverness **223**	a.	...	0839	|	...	0839	|	...	...	...	...
Fort William **218**	a.	...	...	0955	...	...	0955	...	...	...	...

		⑦ a	⑦ a	①–⑤	①–⑤	①–⑤	①–⑤	①–⑤	⑦ a	⑦ a	⑦ a
Fort William **218**	d.	...	...	...	...	1950	...	...	1900	...	...
Inverness **223**	d.	...	...	...	...	|	2045	...	|	2026	...
Perth **223**	d.	...	...	...	...	|	2326	...	|	2306	...
Aberdeen **222**	d.	...	...	...	...	|	|	2143	|	|	2143
Dundee **222**	d.	...	...	...	...	|	|	2309	|	|	2307
Edinburgh Waverley **154**	d.	2315	...	2340	...	|	|	|	|	|	|
Glasgow Central **154**	d.	|	2305	|	2340	|	|	|	|	|	|
Motherwell	d.	|	2330	|	2359	|	|	|	|	|	|
Carlisle **154**	d.	0145	0145	0149	0149	|	|	|	|	|	|
Preston **154**	a.	|	|	|	|	0433	0433	0433	0432	0432	0432
Crewe **151 152 153 154**	a.	|	|	|	|	0536	0536	0536	0536	0536	0536
Watford Junction	a.	0642	0642	0643	0643	|	|	|	|	|	|
London Euston **151/2/3** ◧	a.	0707	0707	0707	0707	0747	0747	0747	0747	0747	0747

a – Service subject to alteration until June 17. Revised timings will be advised when reservations are made. Will not call at Watford Junction, Crewe, Preston or Carlisle.

◐ – Sleeping-car passengers may occupy their cabins from 2200.

◧ – Sleeping-car passengers may occupy their cabins until 0800 following arrival at these stations.

MP Middleton Press

EVOLVING THE ULTIMATE RAIL ENCYCLOPEDIA

Easebourne Midhurst GU29 9AZ. Tel:01730 813169

www.middletonpress.co.uk email:info@middletonpress.co.uk
A-978 0 906520 B- 978 1 873793 C- 978 1 901706 D-978 1 904474
E - 978 1 906008 F - 978 1 908174 G - 978 1 910356

Our RAILWAY titles are listed below. Please check availability by looking at our website *middletonpress.co.uk*, telephoning us or by requesting a Brochure which includes our *LATEST* RAILWAY TITLES also our TRAMWAY, TROLLEYBUS, MILITARY and COASTAL series

A
Abergavenny to Merthyr C 91 8
Abertillery & Ebbw Vale Lines D 84 5
Aberystwyth to Carmarthen E 90 1
Allhallows - Branch Line to A 62 8
Alton - Branch Lines to A 11 6
Andover to Southampton A 82 6
Ascot - Branch Lines around A 64 2
Ashburton - Branch Line to B 95 4
Ashford - Steam to Eurostar B 67 1
Ashford to Dover A 48 2
Austrian Narrow Gauge D 04 3
Avonmouth - BL around D 42 5
Aylesbury to Rugby D 91 3
B
Baker Street to Uxbridge D 90 6
Bala to Llandudno E 87 1
Banbury to Birmingham D 27 2
Banbury to Cheltenham E 63 5
Bangor to Holyhead F 01 7
Bangor to Portmadoc E 72 7
Barking to Southend C 80 2
Barmouth to Pwllheli E 53 6
Barry - Branch Lines around D 50 0
Bartlow - Branch Lines to F 27 7
Bath Green Park to Bristol C 36 9
Bath to Evercreech Junction A 60 4
Beamish 40 years on rails E94 9
Bedford to Wellingborough D 31 9
Berwick to Drem F 64 2
Berwick to St. Boswells F 75 8
B'ham to Tamworth & Nuneaton F 63 5
Birkenhead to West Kirby F 61 1
Birmingham to Wolverhampton E253
Blackburn to Hellifield F 95 6
Bletchley to Cambridge D 94 4
Bletchley to Rugby E 07 9
Bodmin - Branch Lines around B 83 1
Boston to Lincoln F 80 2
Bournemouth to Evercreech Jn A 46 8
Bournemouth to Weymouth A 57 4
Bradshaw's History F18 5
Bradshaw's Rail Times 1850 F 13 0
Branch Lines series - see town names
Brecon to Neath D 43 2
Brecon to Newport D 16 6
Brecon to Newtown E 06 2
Brighton to Eastbourne A 16 1
Brighton to Worthing A 03 1
Bristol to Taunton D 03 6
Bromley South to Rochester B 23 7
Bromsgrove to Birmingham D 87 6
Bromsgrove to Gloucester D 73 9
Broxbourne to Cambridge F16 1
Brunel - A railtour D 74 6
Bude - Branch Line to B 29 9
Burnham to Evercreech Jn B 68 0
C
Cambridge to Ely D 55 5
Canterbury - BLs around B 58 9
Cardiff to Dowlais (Cae Harris) E 47 5
Cardiff to Pontypridd E 95 6
Cardiff to Swansea E 42 0
Carlisle to Hawick E 85 7
Carmarthen to Fishguard E 66 6
Caterham & Tattenham Corner B251
Central & Southern Spain NG E 91 8
Chard and Yeovil - BLs a C 30 7
Charing Cross to Dartford A 75 8
Charing Cross to Orpington A 96 3
Cheddar - Branch Line to B 90 9
Cheltenham to Andover C 43 7
Cheltenham to Redditch D 81 4
Chesterfield to Lincoln G 21 0
Chester to Birkenhead F 21 5
Chester to Manchester F 51 2
Chester to Rhyl E 93 2
Chester to Warrington F 40 6
Chichester to Portsmouth A 14 7
Clacton and Walton - BLs to F 04 8
Clapham Jn to Beckenham Jn B 36 7
Cleobury Mortimer - BLs a E 18 5
Clevedon & Portishead - BLs to D180
Consett to South Shields E 57 4
Cornwall Narrow Gauge D 56 2
Corris and Vale of Rheidol E 65 9
Coventry to Leicester G 00 5
Craven Arms to Llandeilo E 35 2
Craven Arms to Wellington E 33 8
Crawley to Littlehampton A 34 5
Crewe to Manchester F 57 4
Crewe to Wigan G 12 8
Cromer - Branch Lines around C 26 0
Croydon to East Grinstead B 48 0
Crystal Palace & Catford Loop B 87 1
Cyprus Narrow Gauge E 13 0
D
Darjeeling Revisited F 09 3
Darlington Leamside Newcastle E 28 4
Darlington to Newcastle D 98 2
Dartford to Sittingbourne B 34 3
Denbigh - Branch Lines around F 32 1
Derby to Chesterfield G 11 1
Derby to Stoke-on-Trent F 93 2
Derwent Valley - BL to the D 06 7
Devon Narrow Gauge E 09 3
Didcot to Banbury D 02 9
Didcot to Swindon C 84 0
Didcot to Winchester C 13 0
Diss to Norwich G 22 7
Dorset & Somerset NG D 76 0
Douglas - Laxey - Ramsey E 75 8
Douglas to Peel C 88 8
Douglas to Port Erin C 55 0
Douglas to Ramsey D 39 5
Dover to Ramsgate A 78 9
Drem to Edinburgh G 06 7
Dublin Northwards in 1950s E 31 4
Dunstable - Branch Lines to E 27 7
E
Ealing to Slough C 42 0
Eastbourne to Hastings A 27 7
East Cornwall Mineral Railways D 22 7
East Croydon to Three Bridges A 53 6
Eastern Spain Narrow Gauge E 56 7
East Grinstead - BLs to A 07 9
East Kent Light Railway A 61 1
East London - Branch Lines of C 44 4
East London Line B 80 0
East of Norwich - Branch Lines E 69 7
Effingham Junction - BLs a A 74 1
Ely to Norwich C 90 1
Enfield Town & Palace Gates D 32 6
Epsom to Horsham A 30 7
Eritrean Narrow Gauge E 38 3
Euston to Harrow & Wealdstone C 89 5
Exeter to Barnstaple B 15 2
Exeter to Newton Abbot C 49 9
Exeter to Tavistock B 69 5
Exmouth - Branch Lines to B 00 8
F
Fairford - Branch Line to A 52 9
Falmouth, Helston & St. Ives C 74 1
Fareham to Salisbury A 67 3
Faversham to Dover B 05 3
Felixstowe & Aldeburgh - BL to D 20 3
Fenchurch Street to Barking C 20 8
Festiniog - 50 yrs of enterprise C 83 3
Festiniog 1946-55 E 01 7
Festiniog in the Fifties B 68 8
Festiniog in the Sixties B 91 6
Ffestiniog in Colour 1955-82 F 25 3
Finsbury Park to Alexandra Pal C 02 8
French Metre Gauge Survivors F 88 8
Frome to Bristol B 77 0
G
Gainsborough to Sheffield G 17 3
Galashiels to Edinburgh F 52 9
Gloucester to Bristol D 35 7
Gloucester to Cardiff D 66 1
Gosport - Branch Lines around A 36 9
Greece Narrow Gauge D 72 2
H
Hampshire Narrow Gauge D 36 4
Harrow to Watford D 14 2
Harwich & Hadleigh - BLs to F 02 4
Harz Revisited F 62 8
Hastings to Ashford A 37 6
Hawick to Galashiels F 36 9
Hawkhurst - Branch Line to A 66 6
Hayling - Branch Line to A 12 3
Hay-on-Wye - BL around D 92 0
Haywards Heath to Seaford A 28 4
Hemel Hempstead - BLs to D 88 3
Henley, Windsor & Marlow - BLa C77 2
Hereford to Newport D 54 8
Hertford & Hatfield - BLs a E 58 1
Hertford Loop E 71 0
Hexham to Carlisle D 75 3
Hexham to Hawick F 08 6
Hitchin to Peterborough D 07 4
Holborn Viaduct to Lewisham A 81 9
Horsham - Branch Lines to A 02 4
Huntingdon - Branch Line to A 93 2
I
Ilford to Shenfield C 97 0
Ilfracombe - Branch Line to B 21 3
Industrial Rlys of the South East A 09 3
Ipswich to Diss F 81 9
Ipswich to Saxmundham C 41 3
Isle of Man Railway Journey F 94 9
Isle of Wight Lines - 50 yrs C 12 3
Italy Narrow Gauge F 17 8
K
Kent Narrow Gauge C 45 1
Kettering to Nottingham F 82-6
Kidderminster to Shrewsbury E 10 9
Kingsbridge - Branch Line to C 98 7
Kings Cross to Potters Bar E 62 8
King's Lynn to Hunstanton F 58 1
Kingston & Hounslow Loops A 83 3
Kingswear - Branch Line to C 17 8
L
Lambourn - Branch Line to C 70 3
Launceston & Princetown - BLs C 19 2
Leek - Branch Line From G 01 2
Leicester to Burton F 85 7
Leicester to Nottingham G 15 9
Lewisham to Dartford A 92 5
Lincoln to Cleethorpes F 56 7
Lincoln to Doncaster G 03 6
Lines around Stamford F 98 7
Lines around Wimbledon B 75 6
Liverpool Street to Chingford D 01 2
Liverpool Street to Ilford C 34 5
Llandeilo to Swansea E 46 8
London Bridge to Addiscombe B 20 6
London Bridge to East Croydon A 58 1
Longmoor - Branch Lines to A 41 3
Looe - Branch Line to C 22 2
Loughborough to Nottingham F 68 0
Lowestoft - BLs around E 40 6
Ludlow to Hereford E 14 7
Lydney - Branch Lines around E 26 0
Lyme Regis - Branch Line to A 45 1
Lynton - Branch Line to B 04 6
M
Machynlleth to Barmouth E 54 3
Maesteg and Tondu Lines F 06 2
Majorca & Corsica Narrow Gauge F 41 3
March - Branch Lines around B 09 1
Market Drayton - BLs around F 67 3
Market Harborough to Newark F 86 4
Marylebone to Rickmansworth D 49 4
Melton Constable to Yarmouth Bch E031
Midhurst - Branch Lines of E 78 9
Midhurst - Branch Lines to F 00 0
Minehead - Branch Line to A 80 2
Mitcham Junction Lines B 01 5
Monmouth - Branch Lines to E 20 8
Monmouthshire Eastern Valleys D 71 5
Moretonhampstead - BL to C 27 7
Moreton-in-Marsh to Worcester D 26 5
Morpeth to Bellingham F 87 1
Mountain Ash to Neath D 80 7
N
Newark to Doncaster F 78 9
Newbury to Westbury C 66 6
Newcastle to Hexham D 69 2
Newport (IOW) - Branch Lines to A 26 0
Newquay - Branch Lines to C 71 0
Newton Abbot to Plymouth C 60 4
Newtown to Aberystwyth E 41 3
Northampton to Peterborough F 92 5
North East German NG D 44 9
Northern Alpine Narrow Gauge F 37 6
Northern France Narrow Gauge C 75 8
Northern Spain Narrow Gauge E 83 3
North London Line B 94 7
North of Birmingham F 55 0
North of Grimsby - Branch Lines G 09 8
North Woolwich - BLs around C 65 9
Nottingham to Boston F 70 3
Nottingham to Lincoln F 43 7
Nuneaton to Loughborough G 08 1
O
Ongar - Branch Line to E 05 5
Orpington to Tonbridge B 03 9
Oswestry - Branch Lines around E 60 4
Oswestry to Whitchurch E 81 9
Oxford to Bletchley D 57 9
Oxford to Moreton-in-Marsh D 15 9
P
Paddington to Ealing C 37 6
Paddington to Princes Risborough C819
Padstow - Branch Line to B 54 1
Peebles Loop G 19 7
Pembroke and Cardigan - BLs to F 29 1
Peterborough to Kings Lynn E 32 1
Peterborough to Lincoln F 89 5
Peterborough to Newark F 72 7
Plymouth - BLs around B 98 5
Plymouth to St. Austell C 63 5
Pontypool to Mountain Ash D 65 4
Pontypridd to Merthyr F 14 7
Pontypridd to Port Talbot E 86 4
Porthmadog 1954-94 - BLa B 31 2
Portmadoc 1923-46 - BLa B 13 8
Portsmouth to Southampton A 31 4
Portugal Narrow Gauge E 67 3
Potters Bar to Cambridge D 70 8
Preston to Blackpool G 16 6
Princes Risborough - BL to D 05 0
Princes Risborough to Banbury C 85 7
R
Railways to Victory C 16 1
Reading to Basingstoke B 27 5
Reading to Didcot C 79 6
Reading to Guildford A 47 5
Redhill to Ashford A 73 4
Return to Blaenau 1970-82 C 64 2
Rhyl to Bangor F 15 4
Rhymney & New Tredegar Lines E 48 2
Rickmansworth to Aylesbury D 61 6
Romania & Bulgaria NG E 23 9
Romneyrail C 32 1
Ross-on-Wye - BLs around E 30 7
Ruabon to Barmouth E 84 0
Rugby to Birmingham E 37 6
Rugby to Loughborough F 12 3
Rugby to Stafford F 07 9
Rugeley to Stoke-on-Trent F 90 1
Ryde to Ventnor A 19 2
S
Salisbury to Westbury B 39 8
Sardinia and Sicily Narrow Gauge F 50 5
Saxmundham to Yarmouth C 69 7
Saxony & Baltic Germany Revisited F 71 0
Saxony Narrow Gauge D 47 0
Seaton & Sidmouth - BLs to A 95 6
Selsey - Branch Line to A 04 8
Sheerness - Branch Line to B 16 2
Sheffield towards Manchester G 18 0
Shenfield to Ipswich E 96 3
Shrewsbury - Branch Line to A 86 4
Shrewsbury to Chester E 70 3
Shrewsbury to Crewe F 48 2
Shrewsbury to Ludlow E 21 5
Shrewsbury to Newtown E 29 1
Sierra Leone Narrow Gauge D 28 9
Sirhowy Valley Line E 12 3
Sittingbourne to Ramsgate A 90 1
Skegness & Mablethorpe - BL to F 84 0
Slough to Newbury C 56 7
South African Two-foot gauge E 51 2
Southampton to Bournemouth A 42 0
Southend & Southminster BLs E 76 5
Southern Alpine Narrow Gauge F 22 2
Southern France Narrow Gauge C 47 5
South London Line B 46 6
South Lynn to Norwich City F 03 1
Southwold - Branch Line to A 15 4
Spalding - Branch Lines around E 52 9
Spalding to Grimsby F 65 9 6
Stafford to Chester F 34 5
Stafford to Wellington F 59 8
St Albans to Bedford D 08 1
St. Austell to Penzance C 67 3
St. Boswell to Berwick F 44 4
Steaming Through Isle of Wight A 56 7
Steaming Through West Hants A 69 7
Stourbridge to Wolverhampton E 16 1
St. Pancras to Barking D 68 5
St. Pancras to Folkestone E 88 8
St. Pancras to St. Albans C 78 9
Stratford to Cheshunt F 53 6
Stratford-u-Avon to Birmingham D 77 7
Stratford-u-Avon to Cheltenham C 25 3
Sudbury - Branch Lines to F 19 2
Surrey Narrow Gauge C 87 1
Sussex Narrow Gauge C 68 0
Swaffham - Branch Lines around F 97 0
Swanage to 1999 - BL to A 33 8
Swanley to Ashford B 45 9
Swansea - Branch Lines around F 38 3
Swansea to Carmarthen E 59 8
Swindon to Bristol C 96 3
Swindon to Gloucester D 46 3
Swindon to Newport D 30 2
Swiss Narrow Gauge C 94 9
T
Talyllyn 60 E 98 7
Tamworth to Derby F 76 5
Taunton to Barnstaple B 60 2
Taunton to Exeter C 82 6
Taunton to Minehead F 39 0
Tavistock to Plymouth B 88 6
Tenterden - Branch Line to A 21 5
Three Bridges to Brighton A 35 2
Tilbury Loop C 86 4
Tiverton - BLs around C 62 8
Tivetshall to Beccles D 41 8
Tonbridge to Hastings A 44 4
Torrington - Branch Lines to B 37 4
Tourist Railways of France G 04 3
Towcester - BLs around E 39 0
Tunbridge Wells BLs A 32 1
U
Upwell - Branch Line to B 64 0
Uttoxeter to Macclesfield G 05 0
V
Victoria to Bromley South A 98 7
Victoria to East Croydon A 40 6
Vivarais Revisited E 08 6
W
Walsall Routes F 45 1
Wantage - Branch Line to D 25 8
Wareham to Swanage 50 yrs D 09 8
Waterloo to Windsor A 54 3
Waterloo to Woking A 38 3
Watford to Leighton Buzzard D 45 6
Wellingborough to Leicester F 73 4
Welshpool to Llanfair E 49 9
Wenford Bridge to Fowey C 09 3
Westbury to Bath B 55 8
Westbury to Taunton C 76 5
West Cornwall Mineral Rlys D 48 7
West Croydon to Epsom B 08 4
West German Narrow Gauge D 93 7
West London - BLs of C 50 5
West London Line B 84 8
West Wiltshire - BLs of D 12 8
Weymouth - BLs A 65 9
Willesden Jn to Richmond B 71 8
Wimbledon to Beckenham C 58 1
Wimbledon to Epsom B 62 6
Wimborne - BLs around A 97 0
Wirksworth - Branch Lines to G 10 4
Wisbech - BLs around C 01 7
Witham & Kelvedon - BLs a E 82 6
Woking to Alton A 59 8
Woking to Portsmouth A 25 3
Woking to Southampton A 55 0
Wolverhampton to Shrewsbury E 44 4
Wolverhampton to Stafford F 79 6
Worcester to Birmingham D 97 5
Worcester to Hereford D 38 8
Worthing to Chichester A 06 2
Wrexham to New Brighton F 47 5
Wroxham - BLs around F 31 4
Y
Yeovil - 50 yrs change C 38 3
Yeovil to Dorchester A 76 5
Yeovil to Exeter A 91 8
York to Scarborough F 23 9